RELIGIOUS BOOKS
1876-1982

This edition of RELIGIOUS BOOKS 1876-1982 was prepared
by the R.R. Bowker Company's Department of
Bibliography in collaboration with the
Publications Systems Department

Senior staff of the Department of Bibliography includes:
Peter Simon, Database Manager.
Dean Hollister, Senior Product Manager.
Andrew Grabois, Editorial Coordinator.

Michael B. Howell, Manager, Systems Development.

Andrew H. Uszak, Senior Vice President, Data Services/Systems.
Gertrude Jennings, Manager, Product Research and Development,
Data Services.
Debra K. Brown, Manager, Technical Development, Data Services.

RELIGIOUS BOOKS
1876-1982

SUBJECT INDEX

AUTHOR INDEX

TITLE INDEX

R. R. BOWKER COMPANY

New York & London

Published by the R.R. Bowker Company (a Xerox Publishing
Company)
1180 Avenue of the Americas, New York, N.Y. 10036
Copyright © 1983 by Xerox Corporation

International Standard Book Number (Set) 0-8352-1602-0
International Standard Book Number (Vol. 1) 0-8352-1739-6
International Standard Book Number (Vol. 2) 0-8352-1741-8
International Standard Book Number (Vol. 3) 0-8352-1742-6
International Standard Book Number (Vol. 4) 0-8352-1743-4

Printed and bound in the United States of America

Library of Congress Cataloging in Publication Data
Main entry under title:

Religious books, 1876-1982.

　　"Prepared by the R.R. Bowker Company's Department
of Bibliography in collaboration with the Publications
Systems Department"—T.p. verso.
Includes indexes.
1. Religion—Bibliography.　2. Theology—Bibliography.
3. Religions—Bibliography.　I. R.R. Bowker Company. Dept. of
Bibliography. II. R.R. Bowker Company. Publications Systems Dept.
Z7751.R385　1983　[BL48]　016.2　83-6028
ISBN 0-8352-1602-0 (set)

Contents

Contents

Foreword

Stephen Lee Peterson
Librarian, Yale Divinity School Library
New Haven, Connecticut

Religious Books 1876-1982 is a bibliographic instrument which will prove to be exceptionally useful in libraries, and to bibliographers and students of the humanities. This usefulness is due to the scope of the work, its format, its structure and its timely publication. More than being a useful bibliographic tool, however, *Religious Books 1876-1982* is a major contribution to the bibliography of religion and to the bibliography of the humanities generally.

Students of religion know, or soon learn, the substantial complexities presented by the literature of this field. Even to speak of religion as one field represents a simplification which most specialists would question. Religion has spawned an extensive and diverse literature. It is international in range and much of it ancient in origin. The diversity of this literature, of course, reflects the presence of religious practice in almost every society, ancient or modern. The literate religions have their own sacred writings and canonical interpretations or commentaries which sacred texts evoke. Each of these literary traditions is extensive, each has its own peculiarities of codification and access, and most often includes unusual languages.

Primal religions have their own texts and practices which are generally known through a body of technical literature produced in the main by social scientists. The fact that much of this literature is relatively recent does not reduce the complexity facing the bibliographer. Indeed, the diverse ways in which scholars have studied religion adds to the bibliographic complexity of the field. While the philosophy of religion and the psychology of religion have been well established disciplines for centuries,[1] the comparative study of religion and the phenomenological study of religion as well as the history of religion are somewhat newer approaches. Together, they have contributed a substantial body of literature to the traditional corpus of religious writing.

Beyond the traditional and the technical, i.e., scholarly, literature of religion, there is an even more voluminous body of writing given to the propagation of religion and the encouragement of religious practice. These popular or semi-popular publications now account for a large portion of the output of the American religious press.

Thus, the librarian, the bibliographer, the scholar, the student welcome the publication of *Religious Books 1876-1982.* The scope of this bibliographic work embraces the diversity and complexity of the field of religion. It does so without prejudice. It reflects the actual publication of religious writing to the extent this material has been reported in the book trade.

Not only does *Religious Books 1876-1982* bring a substantial measure of order to the bibliographic complexities of the field of religion, it also helps redress the rather uneven development of libraries in this field. In North America, there are few truly comprehensive library collections in religion. Some general educational institutions have collections covering most religions, but these libraries are not likely to have highly detailed literature pertaining to specific religions. The specifically religious institutions such as theological schools tend to have collections focused on the particular religious or intellectual traditions of the school. Thus, *Religious Books 1876-1982* brings together the description of a greater range of books important to the study of religion than the catalogues of all but the very largest and most comprehensive libraries in North America. Yet, *Religious Books 1876-1982* stands essentially as a bibliography rather than a library catalogue. In that even the Library of Congress does not keep for its collections all of the books it receives or catalogues, it is doubtful if any library holds all or most of the works cited in this tool.

Religious Books 1876-1982 is based on the large and old book publishing records of the Bowker Company. These files have been augmented by entries from the Library of Congress *National Union Catalog* and other sources. There is considerable coverage of British books. Cataloging-in-source records have been completed and the file has been read against MARC records. The result is simply the most comprehensive bibliography of books on religion for North American usage.

It is, of course, truly advantageous to have *Religious Books 1876-1982* organized primarily as a subject bibliography. Subject bibliography in religion is not well developed. The most comprehensive subject index to periodical literature began only in 1949.[2] Most of the other large continuing subject bibliographies are based in Europe and, while they include many English language materials, they necessarily concentrate on publications originating in Europe. The *Library of Congress Subject Catalog* began publication only in 1950. While bibliographers may use this work with benefit, students generally have not found it a convenient tool to use. The *Subject Index of Modern Books,* of the British Museum Library, begun in 1881, is an improvement in this regard, but its infrequent cumulations and its English and European orientation render it less helpful to North Amer-

---

[1]The modern discipline of the psychology of religion, however, may be said to have begun with the research of William Starbuck reported in his *The Psychology of Religion,* New York: Charles Scribner's Sons, 1901.

ican students. *Religious Books 1876-1982* then, occupies a place of singular importance in the constellation of subject bibliography in religion, particularly for North American scholars and institutions.

The author and title indexes, while not containing full bibliographic description, do not have diminished importance. Certainly there is no comparable bibliography listed by title in the field. In this regard as with the subject index, *Religious Books 1876-1982* makes a fresh and needed contribution to the bibliography of religion. Only the full *National Union Catalog* surpasses *Religious Books 1876-1982* as a comprehensive author file. Of course, cost alone makes the *NUC* inaccessible to many libraries. Furthermore, persons primarily interested in religion will find *Religious Books 1876-1982* the far easier and more efficient resource to consult.

In essence, this tool now makes it possible for the specialist and the non-specialist alike to make maximum use of the Library of Congress subject heading system as a source both of subject bibliography and of comprehensive bibliography.

A sound grasp of the structure of this bibliography will extend considerably its usefulness. The approximately 130,000 titles are organized under the first subject heading assigned by the Library of Congress. The result is that some 27,000 subject descriptors are used. These, of course, represent the historic practice of the Library of Congress so that some headings appear here which are not currently assigned. New headings appear as they have been introduced.

Bowker's decision to enter titles only under the first subject heading but to list all of the tracings for each entry must, in most cases, be considered prudential. It is a decision representing sound bibliographic theory. In a straightforward way, the user of this tool can extend his search to related or alternative topics simply by referring to the subject tracings. Indeed, the inexperienced bibliographer can construct a quite complex subject search in this manner. The tracings also will call the user's attention to uniform titles.

Uniform titles are used frequently to describe religious works, particularly works containing sacred texts. These uniform titles, indirectly, constitute an important aspect of subject searches. The more sophisticated bibliographer will use *Religious Books 1876-1982* in tandem with *Library of Congress Subject Headings*. The "see" and "see also" references in this aid will provide important clues for other useful headings in *Religious Books 1876-1982*. As a result, subject access to the literature of religion is greatly enhanced by this publication.

Who will use *Religious Books 1876-1982*? Certainly it may be anticipated that this tool will become the principal source of retrospective bibliography in religion in most libraries. Indeed, in many libraries it may supplant the card file for subjects as the source for first consultation in subject searches.

Synagogue and church libraries will find this work indispensable. Individual scholars will acquire and use this tool, and if not individuals, surely teaching groups and academic departments will want it in their offices. Libraries cooperating together will find that this work readily aids the work of resource sharing as well as providing a way of sharing bibliographic data effectively. At a time when many libraries are actively working on collection preservation, *Religious Books 1876-1982* will provide the foundation for this effort.

The R.R. Bowker Company is to be congratulated on bringing its considerable experience, its rich data base, modern technology, and its record of excellence in library service together to produce its series of large subject bibliographies. Specialists in religion should be grateful that their field is one of the early beneficiaries of this initiative. Subject access to information and literature must not be hindered by the conventions of local ownership of resources. *Religious Books 1876-1982* provides the broadest possible coverage to the field of religion and all persons interested in this field will find their interest and inquiry greatly assisted by this bibliography.

Stephen Lee Peterson, Ph.D
Librarian of the Yale University Divinity School

Dr. Peterson holds the following degrees: B.A. Bethel College, St. Paul, Minnesota; B.D. Colgate Rochester Divinity School, Rochester, New York; A.M.L.S. College and University Librarianship and A.M. New Eastern Languages and Literatures, University of Michigan, Ann Arbor, Michigan; Ph.D Religion, Vanderbilt University, Nashville, Tennessee. He has served in the library profession since 1968 at Vanderbilt University as Divinity Librarian and as Assistant Director for Bibliographic Services. Since 1972, Dr. Peterson has been Librarian of the Divinity School at Yale, serving also during 1978–1980 as Acting Librarian of the Beinecke Rare Book and Manuscript Library. These are a selection of Dr. Peterson's publications, lectures and projects: "The Theological Tasks of the Seminary Library," Lecture given at the Garrett-Evangelical Theological Seminary, Evanston, Illinois, March 1983. "Collection Development in Religion in the Library of Congress," *Proceedings of the American Theological Library Association 35:26-33 (1981)*. "Collection Development in Theological Libraries: A New Model—A New Hope," *in Essays on Theological Librarianship Presented to Calvin Henry Schmidt,* American Theological Library Association: Philadelphia, 1980. "The Subject Approach to Theology: An Alternative System for Libraries," *Proceedings of the American Theological Library Association 31:135-147 (1977)*. Director, Project 2000, sponsored by the Association of Theological Schools and the American Theological Library Association, 1981. This is a research project to develop planning strategies for theological libraries to the end of this century. It is funded by the Lilly Endowment.

---

[2]*Index to Religious Periodical Literature*, now *Religion Index One,* published by the American Theological Library Association.

Preface

As publishers of *Religious Books And Serials In Print,* the R.R. Bowker Company is especially pleased to be able to publish *Religious Books 1876-1982.* While *Religious Books And Serials In Print* provides current ordering and price information on in-print titles, *Religious Books 1876-1982* provides over one-hundred years of Library of Congress cataloging on religious titles published or distributed in the United States. This comprehensive bibliography of some 130,000 entries covers all aspects of the world's religions, including the religious implications of such topics as abortion, homosexuality, and business ethics. In addition, this collection provides broad coverage of areas related to religion such as philosophy, magic, astrology and occult sciences. Because of their extensive and complete coverage, these volumes offer a historical perspective of literature in religious and related fields and can serve as a basic resource for reference and research, collection assessment and development, and acquisitions and cataloging.

SURVEY OF PROFESSIONAL LIBRARIANS AND INFORMATION SPECIALISTS

It is an established routine at Bowker in designing new reference works to consult professional librarians and others involved in developing information before publishing. The surveys we made seek to establish a definite need for the reference work as well as to obtain practical direction from potential users as to content and format. This interaction has been most satisfying since it has resulted in direct hands on influence on the final design of *Religious Books 1876-1982* as well as enthusiastic acceptance of the concept by a great majority of those surveyed.

We mailed questionnaires to the users of *Religious Books And Serials In Print* and to others who use information in these subjects. Over 75 percent responded affirmatively to questions asking whether they would purchase *Religious Books 1876-1982,* and with comments such as these, confirmed the validity of our concept:

"...Religion is a major emphasis in our university and is one of the subjects for which we would need comprehensive retrospective coverage..."

"...This book would be a real asset to our collection because of its subject index and title index. Also having the author index in one alphabetical arrangement will save time in verfication...The price seems low for such a massive project."

DATA ACQUISITION

Entries were selected from the over 1.8 million titles in the *American Book Publishing Record* database, which represents all United States monographs in the National Union catalog, MARC tapes and titles cataloged at Bowker for the period covered. Titles were initially selected by Dewey Decimal and Library of Congress classification numbers for both core religious areas in these classification systems as well as all identifiable peripheral areas, ranging from astrology to philosophy. Each entry was then individually reviewed to determine its appropriateness for publication in *Religious Books 1876-1982.* The final book was produced from records stored on magnetic tape, edited by computer programs, and set in type by computer-controlled photocomposition.

ARRANGEMENT AND CONTENT OF ENTRIES

The user can access the information in *Religious Books 1876-1982* by subject, author and title. Complete entries appear in the subject index under Library of Congress subject headings and are arranged by main entry within the subject. Over 27,000 Library of Congress subject headings, including names when used as subjects, are listed. Each full entry represents cataloging prepared by the Library of Congress. Entry information includes: main entry, title (in italics), subtitle, author statement, publication place, publisher, publication date, collation, series statement, general note or contents note, LC classification number (in brackets), Dewey Decimal number, LC card number and tracings.

General Editorial Policies

In order to insure that the integrity of original Library of Congress cataloging is maintained in the subject index, and that entries are uniform and easy to find, the following editorial policies have been maintained:

Subject headings were made uniform whereas the entries listed within may contain variant forms of the tracing.

Dual listings are provided when an entry contains both subject and name tracings.

Entries without subject or name tracings in the original cataloging were assigned by editorial staff to appropriate subject headings. In this publication, over 20,000 titles without tracings were assigned subjects.

Subject Index

Entries are arranged alphabetically by main entry within subject.

Headings were derived from the primary subject and uniform name tracings in the original cataloging entries. Some of these headings were made uniform due to variances in the styling of tracings in these entries.

Subject headings are arranged alphabetically.

Abailard, Pierre, 1079-1142
Baptism
Convenants (Theology)

Many of the main headings are broken down still further:

Church
Church—Administration
Church—Authority
Church—Biblical Teachings

Headings, as used in Library of Congress cataloging practice, are explicit rather than general—thus books on God (Hinduism) are under God (Hinduism), not God.

Author and Title Indexes

The author and title indexes are alphabetically arranged by their authors and titles respectively. Page references are provided to the main entries in the subject index.

ACKNOWLEDGEMENTS

We extend special gratitude to Dr. Stephen L. Peterson, Librarian, Yale Divinity School Library for his support and encouragement and for preparation of the Foreword. Gertrude Jennings, Manager, Product Research and Development, Data Services Division, developed the concept of *Religious Books 1876-1982*. She, Peter Simon, Database Manager, and Dean Hollister, Senior Product Manager, were responsible for the design, planning, and production of this product. The book indexes were produced with the help of Andrew Grabois, Editorial Coordinator, Subject Guide Department, whom we thank for his conscientious and dedicated efforts. Data Processing support was received from Francis J. McWade, Data Processing Manager, John Murphy, Computer Operations Supervisor, and Joyce Edwards, Data Conversion Control Supervisor. Our thanks to all members of the Data Services/Systems Division who worked on this publication.

Peter Simon,
Database Manager

Gertrude Jennings,
Manager, Product Research
and Development,
Data Services Division

Dean Hollister,
Senior Product Manager,
Department of Bibliography

RELIGIOUS BOOKS
1876-1982

VOLUME 4

Author Index

Title Index

Author Index

A

Aaberg, Jens Christian. 1862
Aaberg, Theodore A. 1548
Aaen, Bernhard. 1, 2782
Aalders, G. Charles. 520
Aarflot, Andreas. 1790, 3655
Aaron, David. 561
Aaron, Richard Ithamar. 3755
Aaron, Samuel. 1290
Aaronic order. 1
Aaseng, Rolf E. 307, 899, 1604, 3161, 3660
Abailard, Pierre. 1, 2, 942, 3639
Abarbanel, Henry. 3025
Abata, Russell M. 3316, 3330
Abba, Raymond. 229, 3002
Abbadie, Jacques. 2002
Abbelen, Peter Matthias. 741
[Abbetmeyer, Charles Dietrich August Frederick] 1867. 2888
Abbetmeyer, Charles Dietrich August Frederick. 2297
Abbey, Charles John. 666, 1220
Abbey, Merrill R. 72, 298, 1263, 1316, 2434, 2896, 3743
Abbey, Richard. 76, 1116, 1240, 3074
Abbo, John A. 735
Abbot, Abiel. 3337
Abbot, Carolyn T. 1039, 3732
Abbot, Ezra. 418, 421, 1698
Abbot, Fanny Laroom. 1589
Abbot, Francis Ellingwood. 3097, 3607, 3097
Abbot, Gorham Dummer, 1807-1874. 1458
Abbot, Jacob. 954
Abbot, John Emery. 3725
Abbot, Lyman. 954
Abbott, Anne. 3494
Abbott, Anstice. 2529
Abbott, Benjamin. 3123
Abbott, Byrdine Akers. 1460
Abbott, David Phelps. 3494
Abbott, Edwin Abbott. 45, 381, 1460, 2475, 2702, 3458
Abbott, Edwin Milton. 3071
Abbott, Eric Symes. 2210
Abbott, Ernest Hamlin. 3743
Abbott, Freeland. 1925
Abbott, George Knapp. 3381, 3811
Abbott, Henry Pryor Almon. 1328, 2056, 2058
[Abbott, Jacob] 1803-1879. 902, 950, 954, 1606, 2589, 3883
Abbott, John. 1895
Abbott, John Stevens Cabot. 954, 1172, 2794
Abbott, Joshua Harris. 452
Abbott, Lyman. 2, 2061, 2, 183, 372, 498, 1047, 1055, 1093, 1333, 1589, 1719, 1785, 1886, 1959, 2028, 2794, 3347, 3440, 3637, 3670
Abbott, Martina. 1277
Abbott, Nabia. 20
Abbott, Orrin. 202
Abbott, R. L. 94
Abbott, Thomas Kingsmill. 341, 362
Abbott, Vera. 896

Abbott, Walter M. 3769
Abbott, Wilbur Cortez. 1758
Abboud, Michael Ben. 3390
'Abd ul-Baha ibn Baha Ullah, 1844-1921. 122, 125, 126, 129
Abdul Baha, 1844-1921. 129
'Abdul-Baha ibn Baha Ullah, 1844-1921. 126
Abdul-Haqq, Abdiyah Akbar, 1920. 2557
Abdul-Rauf, Muhammad, 1917. 1611, 1923, 3797
  Abd ul-Baha ibn Baha Ullah. 126
Abeel, David. 2
Abel, Aaron Ignatius. 1135
Abel, Barbara. 3877
Abel, Juan C. 2844
Abel, Juan Carlos. 2844
Abel, Russell William. 2, 2537
Abele, Jean. 3084
Abell, Aaron Ignatius. 1135, 1277, 3449
Abell, Aaron Igntius. 1135
Abell, William S. 2364
Abeloe, William N. 1300, 2736
Abelow, Samuel Philip. 2098
Abelson, Joshua. 1886, 2646
Abelson, Raziel. 1538
Aber, William W. 3494
Abercrombie, Alexander Vaughan. 1250
Abercrombie, James. 1348, 1349
Abercrombie, Nigel. 111, 1934, 2839
Aberle, David Friend. 2677, 2827
Aberly, John. 2491
[Abernathy, Elza Emmitt]. 3494
Abernethy, Alonzo. 3756
Abernethy, Arthur Talmage. 72, 1554, 3337
Abernethy, George L. 3097, 3204
Abernethy, Jean (Beaven) 2549, 3842, 3843
Abernethy, William Beaven. 3004, 3464
Abernethy, William Shattuck. 159
Abhedananda. 3052, 3774, 3849, 3867, 3052
Abhendananda. 3052
Abilene Christian College. 304
Abimbola, 'Wande. 1882
Abner, Maude M. 2261
Abney, Beth Mobley. 3, 2383
Aboth. 3, 573, 3
Aboth. 1962. 4
Aboth. 1964. 4, 2478
Aboth. 1967. 886
Aboth de-Rabbi Nathan. English. 1538
Aboth English. 4
Aboth. English. 1958. 4
Aboth. English. 1964. 3197
Aboth. 1969. 3197
Abouadaou, Said. 1365
Abraham bar Hiyya, 12th cent. 1538
Abraham ben Moses ben Malmon 1186-1237. 2075
Abraham ben Simeon. 2311
Abraham ben Simeon, 15th cent. 2311
Abraham, Gerald Ernest Heal. 2709
Abraham, Karl. 1479
Abraham, William Henry. 1146
Abraham, William J. 3223
Abrahams, Gerald. 2075
Abrahams, Israel. 2113, 387, 1732, 2081, 2109, 2121, 2828

Abrahams, Louis Barnett. 285, 597
Abrahams, Roger D. 2475
Abrahamsson, Hans. 1415
Abram, Victor P. 3300, 3318, 3524
Abramov, Shene'ur Zalman. 2097, 2151
Abrams, Julius H. 3143
Abrams, Richard I. 919, 1957
Abramson, Lillan S. 1614
Abramson, Lillian S. 1784
Abramtsov, David Feodor. 2751
Abravanel, Isaac. 2155, 2622, 2949
Abrecht, Paul. 1085
Abrerry, Arthur John. 1927
Abshire, Gary M. 1505
Abt, Emmanuel. 3525
Abu al-Fawaris Ahmad ibn Ya'qub, fl. 1000. 1884
Abu Shamah, 'Abd al-Rahman ibn Isma'il, 1203-1267. 1392, 3286
Abun-Nasr, Jamil M. 21
Academy of American Franciscan History. 834
Academy of California Church History. 726
Academy of Religion and Mental Health. Academy Symposium. 2410, 3056, 3069
Accola, Louis W. 1005
Accrediting Association of Bible Colleges. 219, 3613
Achenbach, Henry. 1375
Acheson, Edna Lucile. 3145, 3169
Achtemeier, Elizabeth Rice. 498, 510, 544, 2336, 2896, 3835
Achtemeier, Paul J. 304, 405, 431, 434, 598, 1689, 1737, 3030, 3070
Achutegui, Pedro S de. 18, 1882
Acken, Bernhard van. 1357, 2254
[Acker, Herman Joseph] 1871. 868
*Acker, Julius W. 3197
Acker, Julius William. 2347, 2383, 2867, 3322
Acker, William G. 871
Ackerman, Arthur Wilmot. 1343
Ackerman, Dorothy. 3863
Ackerman, George Everett. 2319, 3669
Ackerman, James Stokes. 210, 532
Ackerman, Nathan Ward. 53
Ackerman, Robert William. 596
Ackerman, Ross D. 2698
Ackermann, Carl. 299, 3399
Ackermann, Joseph. 855
Acklan, Jeannette (Tillotson) 1525
Ackland, Donald F. 155, 492, 2203
Ackland, Thomas Suter. 1379
Ackroyd, Peter R. 498, 532, 2149
Acland, Richard. 61
Acomb, Evelyn Martha. 1145
Aconcio, Giacomo. 3214
Acquaviva, Sabino S. 3085
Acta Alexandrinorum. 2330
Action, Alexander. 1986
Acton, Alexander Archibald. 2794
Acton, Henry. 2471
Acton, John Emerich Edward Dalberg Acton. 1140
Acyutananda Sarasvati. 2186
Adair, James R. 922, 1013, 1361, 1407, 2756, 3883
Adair, John Eric. 1038
Adair, Robert. 2794

Adair, Thelma. 3310
Adair, Thelma C. 3173, 3310
Adam, Adolf. 1261
[Adam, Alice Dana] 1864. 242
Adam de Perseigne, d. 1221. 6, 1276
Adam, George. 906
Adam, Isabel. 2760, 3828
Adam, James. 1765, 1766
Adam, John Douglas. 3056, 370, 954
Adam, Karl. 111, 783, 784, 861, 1047, 1950, 2035, 2272, 2954
Adam, Michael. 2844
Adam of Eynsham, 1196-1232. 1851
Adam, Robert. 3112
Adam, Yehudi. 2137
Adamnan. 1310
Adams, Ada E. 734
Adams, Agatha Boyd. 3470
Adams, Agnes Louise Logan. 1597, 1939, 1979
[Adams, Albert Augustus] 1871. 1047
Adams, Alice Dana. 1172, 643
Adams, Ambrose. 1959
Adams, Arthur Merrihew. 952, 1250
Adams, C. C. 157
Adams, Catherine Lyman. 1323
Adams, Charles. 2169, 2272, 3670, 3802, 3838
Adams, Charles Clarence. 1922, 2628
Adams, Charles Coffin. 3097
Adams, Charles Francis. 1858, 2371, 2929, 3582
Adams, Charles J. 3123
Adams, Charlotte. 1485
Adams, Charlotte H. 1589, 2413
Adams, Charlotte Hannah. 61, 423, 3838
Adams, Daniel J. 2412, 3710
Adams, David Ernest. 1959, 3756
Adams, Elizabeth Laura. 1363
Adams, Evangeline Smith. 94
Adams, F. W. 3618
Adams, Frank Durward. 3334, 1950
Adams, Frank O. 1826
Adams, Fred Baird. 3295
Adams, George Plimpton. 2416
Adams, Hampton. 3670, 1295, 1460, 1465, 3682, 3792
Adams, Hannah. 387, 3056, 3091, 1097
Adams, Harry Baker. 1201, 980
Adams, Henry Austin. 1918, 2702
Adams, Henry W. 2867
Adams, Henry Wright. 551
Adams, Herbert Baxter. 1128
Adams, James Clyde. 2434
Adams, James Donald. 2231
Adams, James Edward. 2481, 2549, 3828, 1300, 2938
Adams, James Lewis. 1149
Adams, James Luther. 3619, 3699
Adams, James McKee. 281, 307, 2544, 281, 514
Adams, Jane L. 2411
Adams, Jay E. 298, 669, 1839, 2779, 2785, 2804, 2896, 3523
Adams, Jay Edward. 1527
Adams, Jeremy duQuesnay. 116, 3451
Adams, Joey. 1520
Adams, John. 3670
Adams, John Coleman. 1323, 3751, 1732
Adams, John Colement. 3751

Adams, John Greenleaf. 922, 2589, 3751, 3754, 3814
[Adams, John] of Inverkeilor, Scotland. 600
Adams, John Quincy. 52, 635, 3299, 109, 457, 604
Adams, John Stowell. 3494
Adams, Joseph. 103, 635
Adams, Joseph Quincy. 2243
Adams, Juliette (Graves) "Mrs. Crosby Adams," 1207
Adams, Katherine (Smith) 3211
Adams, Kenneth Bernarr. 1037
Adams, L. La Mar. 543
Adams, Lane. 1010
Adams, Laura Merrihaw. 896
Adams, Laura Merrihew. 625, 633
Adams, Leonard P. 2055
Adams, Manette (Fishwick) 1201
Adams, Marjorie E. Cook. 3096
Adams, Mary. 3575
Adams, Michael. 3773, 3884
Adams, Miriam Annunciata. 29
Adams, Myron. 304, 1578
Adams, Nehemiah. 23, 133, 1339, 1349, 1357, 1839, 1905, 1994, 2006, 3639
Adams, Norman. 3591
Adams, Queenie Muriel. 3838
Adams, Rachel Swann. 3146
Adams, Revels A[loorn]. 2426

Adams, Robert Chamblet. 3022
Adams, Robert Hickman. 1269
Adams, Ruth (Holland) 2741
Adams, Seymour Webster. 2167
Adams, Theodore Floyd. 144, 954, 992, 2336
Adams, Walter Marsham. 1501
Adams, William. 337, 2061, 133, 25, 1705
Adams, William Cushing. 7, 1336
Adams, William Henry Davenport. 659, 1212, 1937, 2314, 3112, 3237
Adams, Williams. 3536
Adams, Zabdiel. 2633
Adamson, James B. 412
Adamson, William R. 719
Adamus Bremensis. 11th century. 1707
Adar, Zvi. 595
Adbhutananda. 7, 1816
Adcock, Adam Kennedy. 370, 2794, 327
Adcock, Elver F. 3523
Adcock, Mabel. 1385
Adcock, Roger. 494, 627, 632, 1979
Addams, James Lawrence. 3220
Adderley, James Granville. 3436
Addey, John Michael. 94
Addington, Jack Ensign. 229, 3573
Addis, William Edward. 778, 2113
Addison, Charles. 2888
Addison, Charles Greenstreet. 1665, 3598
Addison, Charles Morris. 2637, 2971
Addison, Daniel Dulany. 178, 1523
Addison, James Thayer. 2209, 899, 1694, 1925, 2027, 2059, 2210, 2525, 2540, 2966, 2967, 2970, 3792, 2525
Addison, Joseph. 1097, 2467
Addison, Josph. 58
Addison, William. 1690
Addison, William George. 1762, 2595, 3896
Additon, Lucia H. Faxon. 3833
Addleson, Abraham. 2087
Addy, Sidney Oldall. 2329
Adebonojo, Mary. 939
Adelberg, Roy P. 1013
Adelsperger, Charlotte. 2773
Adeney, Carol. 645
Adeney, David Howard. 1090, 2517
Adeney, Walter Frederic. 625, 307, 1486, 1719
Adi-Granth, English. 3408
Adickes, Erich. 2163
Adi-Granth. 3408
Adison, Jacob Myer. 300
Adkins, E. 1527
Adkins, Edward T. 3182
Adleman, Robert H. 2845
Adler, Bill. 2123, 2805
Adler, Charles S. 1418
Adler, Cyrus. 27, 1909, 2102, 3143
Adler, David A. 281, 1615, 2779, 3545
Adler, Denise Rinker. 2383
Adler, Elisabeth. 3368
Adler, Elkan Nathan. 2100, 2331
Adler, Felix. 3476, 2589, 2843, 3065, 3476
Adler, Frank J. 1332, 2100
Adler, Joshua. 2841
Adler, Margot. 3828
Adler, Morris. 2145, 3360, 3584
Adler, Mortimer Jerome. 41, 1719, 3680, 3696
Adler, Rudolph J. 3370
Adlerblum, Nima (Hirschensohn) 1623, 2219
Adolfs, Robert, 1922. 757, 1153
Adolph, Paul Ernest. 2507, 3299, 1597

Adomeit, Ruth E. 652, 657
Adoratskill, Vladimir Viktorovich. 2209, 3234
Adriel, Jean. 2400
Advance. 1239
Advent Christian association. 9
Advent Christian general conference of America. 9, 604
Aeby, Gervais. 1648
Aegidius, of Assisi. 1443
Aegidius of Assisi, d1962. 1443
Aelfric. 3362
Aelfric,abbot of Eynsham. 1843
Aethelwold. 2579
Affifi, Abul Ela. 1880, 2838
Affleck, Afton Grant. 3378
Aflaki, Shams al-Din Ahmad. 2460
Afnan, Ruhi. 126, 3112
Afnan, Ruhi Muhsen. 126, 1425, 3112
African Methodist Episcopal Church. 13, 14, 1860, 2442
African Methodist Episcopal Zion church. 13, 15
African Methodist Episcopal Zion Church. Christian Education Dept. 15
Agar, Frederick A. 1167
Agar, Frederick Alfred. 1116, 1167, 1239, 1250, 1408, 1422, 2202, 3528, 3670, 3836
Agar, William Macdonough. 3084
Agard, Walter Raymond. 2649
Agat'angeghos. 1773, 3639
Agate, Leonard D. 2272, 3033
Agate, Leonard Dendy. 2272, 3033
Agathocles. 695
Agee, James. 3056
Agehananda Bharati. 3585
Agehananda Bharati. 1923. 1813, 1815, 3585
Agerskov, Johanne. 2060, 3472
Aghajanian, Krikor Bedros. 806
Agines, Charles S. 1090
Aglionby, Francis Keyes Yates. 658
Agnellet, Michel. 2262, 2475
[Agnes de Jesus. 2261, 2335
Agnes de Jesus. 1861. 2335
Agnes Martha. 2717
Agnes Therese. 2369
[Agnes de Jesus. 2335
Agnew, Edith J. 75
Agnew, Marie. 938
Agnew, Milton S. 3187
Agnew, Patience. 737
Agnew, Theodore L. 3734
Agnon, Samuel Joseph. 1623
*Agnon, Samuel Joseph Samuel [Joseph Czaczkes]. 1623
Agora Inc. 1323
Agrimson, J. Elmo. 2814
Agrippa von Nettesheim, Heinrich Cornelius, 1486?-1535. 2731
[Agudath Israel Youth Council of America]. 2778
Agudo, Philomena. 2996
Aguilar, Grace. 492, 567, 3838
Aguilar, H. 3272, 3776
Agus, Irving Abraham. 2400, 3219
Agus, Jacob Bernard. 2107, 2113, 1538, 2094, 2097, 2107, 2146, 2148, 2153, 2183
Aharoni, Jochanan. 281
Aharoni, Yohanan. 283, 528, 2095
Ahedanada. 1562
Ahern, Barnabas M. 651
Ahern, Emily M. 39
Ahern, John. 179
Ahern, M. B. 1745
Ahimaaz ben Paltiel, 1017-ca. 1060. 20, 2087
Ahistrom, Louis John. 154
Ahlborn, Richard E. 1026, 3298
Ahlem, Lloyd H. 980
Ahlers, Lena C. 659
Ahlstrom, Louis John. 1497
Ahlstrom, Sydney E. 3659, 3743
Ahmad, Bashiruddin Mahmud. 20
Ahmad, Ghulam, hasrat mirza. 20
Ahmann, Matthew. 2681
Ahmed, Sami Said. 3863
Aho, Gerhard. 3372
Aho, James A. 3792
Ahrendt, Theodore G. 2290, 2302
Ahrendt, Vivian. 280, 2549, 2886, 3347
Ahrens, Herman C. 3882
*Ahresen, Bertha Fidjeland. 635
Aigrain, Rene. 450
Aikawa, Takaaki. 1101
Aiken, Alfred. 2693, 2767
Aiken, Charles Francis. 700
Aiken, Edwin J. 2688
Aiken, Janet (Rankin) 3141
Aiken, Lillian Woodworth. 3255
Aiken. Alfred. 2767
Aimee, Julie. 3419
Ainger, Alfred. 387
Ainger, Geoffrey. 1055, 2035, 3884
Ainslie, Edgar. 404, 452

Ainslie, Peter. 472, 635, 694, 2, 1039, 1109, 1290, 1460, 2867, 3869, 384, 1039, 1827, 2806, 3440
Ainsworth, Arthur Davis. 1145
Ainsworth, John. 1114
Ainsworth, Katherine. 3376
Ainsworth, Percy Clough. 584
Airhart, Arnold E. 327
Aitken, Dorothy Lockwood. 2501, 3386
Aitken, James J. 1013, 3386
Aitken, John. 812
Aitken, Robert. 3894
Aitleen, John. 812
Ajaya, 1940. 2379
Ajayi, J. F. Ade. 2542
Aked, Charles Frederic. 159, 549, 2246
Akeley, T. C. 138
Aken, Andreas Rudolphus Antonius van. 2658
Akens, David. 3090
Akerman, John Yonge. 481
Akerman, William. 1388
Akers, Charles W. 1368, 2375
Akers, Lewis Robeson. 2434
Akers, Peter. 218
Akhavi, Shahrough. 1923
Akhilananda. 20, 2024, 3491
Akhilananda, Swami. 2024
Akin, Button H. 604
Akin, Johnnye. 612
Akins, W. R. 2379
Akins, Wade. 20, 1562
Akron, O. St. Mary's church (Catholic) 855
Al-Bagilani, Muhammad ibn al-Tayyib, d. 1013. 2184
al-Bakillani, Muhammad ibn 'Abd al-Tayyib, d. 1013. 2184
al-Mutawakkil, caliph, 821-861. 2564
Alacoque, Marguerite Marie. 2217, 2383, 3279
Alamah, Saundra. 2722
Aland, Kurt. 139, 922, 2272, 3037
Alanus de Insulis. 2908
Albanese, Catherine L. 3742
Albany Forum, 2d, 1978. 793
Albaugh, Dana M. 30, 2502, 2529
al-Baydawi, 'Abd Allah ibn 'Umar. 2185
Alberic. 3709
Alberione, Giacomo Giuseppe. 767, 1417, 2032, 2353, 2358, 2360, 2569, 2867, 2896, 3449, 3484, 3566, 3843, 784, 995, 1827, 2569, 2804, 3475
Alberione, Giacomo Giussepe. 3449
Alberione, Giacomo Guiseppe. 995, 2015, 2353
Alberione. Giacomo Giuseppe. 2353
Albert, Alphaeus Homer. 1811
Albert, Hubert. 3176
Albert, Thomas. 442
Albertson, Augusta. 1793
Albertson, Charles Carroll. 1047, 2061, 2888, 3197, 3337
Albertson, Clinton. 3283
Albertson, Edward. 671, 721, 3494, 3683, 3863
Albertson, Garrett Vinton. 1562
Albertson, Sandra Hayward. 22, 1004
Albertus. 2311
Albertyn, Charles Murray. 2744
Albinski, Henry Stephen. 2190, 3525
Albiol Estape, Enrique. 2383
Albion, Gordon. 812, 862, 1189
Albrecht, Joseph H. 3337
Albrecht, Otto Edwin. 2707
Albrecht, Paul. 1133
Albrecht, Robert C. 2776
Albricus. 2657
Albright, Bliss. 1455
Albright, Isaac H. 3230
Albright, Leland Sanford. 532
[Albright, M. Catharine]. 1443
Albright, Raymond Wold. 2967
Albright, Raymond Wolf. 694, 1546
Albright, William Foxwell. 200, 487, 514, 537, 1583, 2095, 2150, 2585, 514, 2150, 2585
Albritton, Clarice. 3473
Albritton, Walter M. 1006, 1169
Albus, Harry James. 45, 910, 2709, 3580
Alcott, Amos Bronson. 384
Alcott, William Andrus. 38, 1506, 1979, 2018, 2203, 2271, 2336, 2795, 2824, 3258, 3701
al-Damanh uri, Ahmad ibn Abd al-Munim. 1270
Alden, Ebenezer. 1285
Alden, Hazel Gillmore. 617
Alden, Henry Mills. 1412, 1719
[Alden, Isabella (Macdonald)] 1841. 3551
Alden, Isabella (Macdonald) 1959, 1979
Alden, Joseph. 3550, 3572, 954, 2683, 2794, 2833, 3006
Alden, Joseph Pierce. 898
Alden, Robert. 574

Alder, George. 1719
Alder, Mortimer Jerome. 2834
Alder, Vera Stanley. 2722
Alderfer, Helen. 3528
Alderink, Larry J. 1459
Alderman, Clifford Lindsey. 35, 3826, 3827, 3828
Alderman, Joy. 2888
Alderman, Oliver P. 1589
Alderman, Paul R. 1950
Alderman, Paul Repton. 604
Alderman, Paul Repton, Jr. 604
Alderman, Rosalie Givens. 23, 171
Alderson, Charles M. 1886
Alderson, Jo Bartels. 2376
Aldhelm, 640?-709. 23
[Aldington, Hilda (Doolittle)] 1886. 3205
Aldrich, Bess Streeter. 3494
Aldrich, Clarence Knight. 2779
Aldrich, Donald Bradshaw. 2888
Aldrich, Doris (Coffin) 980, 2625
Aldrich, Ella Virginia, 1902. 3612
Aldrich, Guy V. 3278
Aldrich, Joe. 980
Aldrich, Joseph C. 1562
Aldrich, Louisa M. 3705
Aldrich, Richard. 1160
Aldrich, Thomas Bailey. 3197
Aldrich, Willard M. 1589
Aldrich, William Lloyd. 723
Aldridge, Alfred Owen. 1498
Aldridge, John William. 240, 1525
Aldwinckle, Russell Foster. 1078, 1412, 2035
Aleksandr Mikhailovich 1866-1933. 3141, 3521
Alekseev, Vasilii Ivanovich. 1149, 2750
Alessi, Vincie. 1562
Alessio, Luis. 784, 2346
Aleutian Islands and North America (Archdiooese) 2751
Alexander. 3141, 3460
Alexander, Anthony F. 762, 3264, 947, 3264, 3659
Alexander, Archibald. 59, 242, 275, 942, 1585, 2160, 2929, 2937, 3631, 906, 1067
Alexander, Archibald Browning Drysdale. 942
Alexander, Caleb. 2002
Alexander, Calvert. 869, 3770
Alexander, Cecil Frances (Humphreys) 1860
Alexander, Charles. 1261
Alexander, Charles McCallon. 24
Alexander, David. 381, 2764
Alexander, David S. 528, 2764
Alexander, Edward. 83, 2221
Alexander, Frances. 24
Alexander, George M. 217
Alexander, Gross. 1959
Alexander, Harley Burr. 1902
Alexander, Hartley Burr. 1047, 1902, 3097, 1902
Alexander, James Bradun. 3460
Alexander, James McKinney. 24
Alexander, James Waddel. 24, 281, 635, 1349, 2896
Alexander, James Waddell. 24
Alexander, John Bruce. 3757
Alexander, John I. 3551
Alexander, John Wesley. 954
Alexander, Joseph Addison. 327, 431, 439, 541, 542, 574
[Alexander, Juliette] 1865. 1047
Alexander, Lynn. 3879
Alexander, Maitland. 2259, 2929
Alexander, Martha G. 905
Alexander, Mary Anna. 3856
Alexander, Mithrapuram K. 3863
Alexander, Myrna. 589
Alexander, Neil. 368
Alexander, Olive J. 902
Alexander, Pat. 617
Alexander, Paul Julius. 1880, 2707, 3405
Alexander, Ralph. 517
Alexander, Samuel Davies. 2918
Alexander, Sidney Arthur. 3277
Alexander, Stella. 1152
Alexander Turnbull Library, Wellington, N.Z. 2469
Alexander, Wade. 254
Alexander, Walter Richardson. 146, 1377, 2761, 3465
Alexander, William. 577
Alexander, William Addison. 2919
Alexander, William Arnold. 2778
Alexander, William Hardy. 1308
Alexandra, 1908. 43
Alexandria, La. St. James Episcopal Church. 1523
Alexandria, Va. First Baptist Church. 1172
Alexandria, Va. Protestant Episcopal Theological Seminary in Virginia. 3331
al Faruqi, Isma'il Ragi A. 1921
Alfoldi, Andras. 1189, 1355

Alford, Delton L. 1209
Alford, Eugene Clair. 203
Alford, Neal B. 1133
Alfredson, James B. 1346
Algar, Hamid. 1918
Alger, Simeon. 2049, 2817
Alger, William Rounseville. 1694, 1698, 3460
Algermissen, Konrad. 3322
al-Ghazzali, Muhammad. 1924, 2169
Algisi, Leone. 2123
Alhadef, John J. 3627
Alho, Olli. 16
Ali, Ameer. 1924
Ali, Bader Salem. 3298
'Ali ibn Rabban Tabari, d. ca. 864. 2564
Ali ibn Sulaiman. 522
Ali, Zaki. 1921
Aligarh, India. Muslim University. Directorate of General Education Reading Material Project. 99, 2319
Alinari, Fratelli, Florence. 2760
Alington, Cyril Argentine. 1047, 1097, 1758, 1886
Ali Shah, Ikbal. 1321
Alison, Archibald. 2721
al-Kalabadhi, Muhammed ibn Ibrahim. 3544
al-Kisa'i, Muhammad ibn 'Abd Allah. 2207
All-Africa Church Conference, Ibadan, Nigeria, 1958. 1043
All Africa Church Conference, Salisbury, Southern Rhodesia, 1962-63. 1129
Allacci, Leone. 2240, 2746
Allaire, Edwin B. 2739
Allan, Alfred K. 764
Allan, Ann. 1011
Allan, Arthur. 2896
Allan, Ethan. 2956
Allan, John A. 362
Allan, John Robertson. 318, 3069
Allan, Tom. 1562
Allard, Daniel. 1959
All-Asia Consultation on Theological Education for Christian Ministry, Makati, Philippines, 1977. 2321
Allbeck, Willard Dow. 2282, 2283, 2291
Allchin, A. M. 1212, 2577, 3521, 3667, 3706
Alldredge, Eugene Perry. 553
Alldredge, Everett O. 1818
Alldredge, Margarete J. 2183
Allee, George Franklin. 1839, 2716, 2942
Allegheny, Pa. Western theological seminary of the Presbyterian church. 3331
Allegra, Gabriele Maria. 375, 2049
Allegro, John Marco. 316, 1090, 1409, 2091, 2632, 3013, 3400
Alleine, Joseph. 1357
Alleine, Theodosia. 25
Alleman, Herbert Christian. 954, 342, 474, 497, 597, 688
Alleman, Herbert Christian, 1868-1953. 687
Allemand, Edward. 1845
Allen, Alexander Vieta Griswold. 1172
Allen, Alexander Viets Griswold. 1498, 2964, 3615, 3667
Allen, Almira L. 1862
Allen, Anna H. 1029
Allen, Arthur Bruce. 635
Allen, Asa Alonso. 119
Allen, Beatrice Elizabeth. 1991
Allen, Belle Jane. 2538
Allen, Benjamin. 2272, 2855, 3038
Allen, Blaine. 980
Allen, Cady Hews. 458, 1740
Allen, Caroline Stetson. 910
Allen, Catherine B. 2485, 2588
Allen, Charles Livingston. 2244, 3330
Allen, Charles Livingstone. 26, 179, 588, 954, 1006, 1110, 1300, 1312, 1349, 1601, 1792, 1827, 1846, 1987, 2018, 2022, 2246, 2263, 2867, 3334, 3561, 3879
Allen, Charlotte Hale. 980
Allen, Chester L. 2896
Allen, Clifton J. 61, 471, 992
Allen County-Fort Wayne Historical Society. 817
Allen, Diogenes. 61, 1010, 1719, 2050
Allen, Don Cameron. 98, 1286, 2469, 2711, 3215
Allen, Donald R. 1244, 1787
Allen, Douglas. 1505, 3056
Allen, Edgar Leonard. 191, 1078
Allen, Edith (Hedden) 2526
Allen, Edward Jones. 2600
Allen, Elliott Douglass. 462
Allen, Emory Adams. 1349
Allen, Erastus D. 3334
Allen, Ethan. 3022
Allen, Eula. 525, 1383, 3460
Allen, Frank Emmett. 327, 547
Allen, Frank Gibbs. 3123
Allen, Frank James. 3705

Allen, Fred Hovey. 750, 3033
Allen, Geoffrey Francis. 954
[Allen, George]. 2845
Allen, George Francis. 700
Allen, George R. 248
Allen, Gordon E. 3318
Allen, Grant. 1742, 3093
Allen, Gwenfread Elaine. 3235, 3874
Allen, Harold. 1615
Allen, Harold W. G. 1385
Allen, Hattie Bell (McCracken) 1015, 1979, 3296
Allen, Horace T. 298, 1261
Allen, Hugh Anthony. 2715
Allen, Irene. 538
Allen, J. P. 159, 3852
Allen, J. S. 601
Allen, James. 1504, 954, 1436, 2693, 2808
Allen, James B. 2599
Allen, James Madison. 3494
Allen, John Harden. 45, 1928, 2087, 2118, 3072
Allen, Joseph. 384, 3847
Allen, Joseph Henry. 532, 1172, 2095, 3727, 3729, 3730, 3828, 1016
Allen, Leslie C. 558
Allen, Leslie Henri. 202, 698, 1578
Allen, Lorna Margaret. 1311, 2486
Allen, Marion Campbell. 1984
Allen, Mark. 3476
Allen, Martha (Meir) 23
Allen, Maurice. 3494
Allen-Michael. 3337
Allen, Michael. 3123
Allen, Nancy (Armistead) 2868, 2980
Allen Publishing Company, New York. 1668
Allen, R. Earl. 159, 181, 603, 1112, 1349, 1354, 1691, 1698, 1984, 2035, 2061, 2721, 2883, 3347
Allen, Ralph H. 26, 1256
Allen, Richard. 14
Allen, Richard Day. 2592
Allen, Richard Howe. 2830
Allen, Robert. 2217
Allen, Robert Cameron. 300
Allen, Roland. 1288, 2518, 1216, 2518, 2553, 2795
Allen, Ronald Barclay. 577, 2867, 3002
Allen, Stanton P. 3227
Allen, Stephen. 26, 2431
[Allen, Stephen Merrill] 1819-1894. 3074
Allen, Steve. 26, 1393
Allen, Sydney. 2538, 3380, 3386
Allen, Thomas. 2067
Allen, Timothy. 3751
Allen, Walser Haddon. 2594, 2595, 3247
Allen, Walter Smith. 3197
Allen, Ward. 368, 2194
Allen, William. 1305, 1339
Allen, William Charles. 1406
Allen, William Cox. 1311
Allen, William Osborne Bird. 3436
Allen, Yorke. 3680
[Allentree, Richard] 1619-1681. 954
Aller, Catherine. 1735, 3592, 3593
Alley, Frederick. 2321
Alley, Joe Kenneth. 1273
Alley, Robert S. 304, 2937
Alleyne, Cameron Chesterfield. 1744, 1837
Allford, Dorothy. 1379
Allgeier, Joseph L. 2908
Alliance of Reformed Churches throughout the World Holding the Presbyterian System. North American Area. 2285
Allibaco, W. A. 3097
[Allibone, Samuel Austin] 1816-1889. 1312, 3440
Allies, Mary Helen Agnes. 1181, 3779
Alling, Roger. 1369
Allinson, Anne Crosby (Emery) 2225
Allis, Oswald Thompson. 274, 355, 498, 543, 562, 563, 604
Allison, Alexander Henry. 458
Allison, Carol. 2489, 2491
Allison, Christopher Fitz Simmons. 3852
Allison, Christopher FitzSimons. 61, 3655, 3852
Allison, Edith Wolfe. 3831
Allison, Frances Harris. 1189
Allison, George William. 3337
Allison, Henry E. 2217
Allison, Karen J. 939
Allison, Lydia W. 2986
Allison, Thomas. 1758, 1760
Allison, Walter Leslie. 3272
Allison, William Henry. 147, 150, 3740
Allman, James. 1734
Allmen, Jean Jacques von. 242, 2250, 2896, 3852
Allnutt, Frank. 51, 604
Allport, Gordon Willard. 2996, 3096, 2383, 2996
Allred, Byron Harvey. 2610
Allred, G. Hugh. 2618
Allred, Gordon T. 1886

Allred, Hoyle T. 1703
Allshorn, Florence. 1443
Allstrom, Elizabeth C. 582, 2480, 2489, 2536, 2551, 3337
Allstrom. Elizabeth C. 2549
Allyn, Avery. 1668
[Allyn, Edmond Richmond]. 451
Alma College, Alma, Calif. Library. 764
Alma Marie. 1328, 1950
Almedingen, Martha Edith. 1508, 1639
Almedingen, Martha Edith von. 825
Almeras, Charles. 2767
Almond, David. 2086
Almond, David M. 2073, 2107
Almond, David Moses. 2073
Almquist, Arden. 2491
Alofsin, Dorothy. 2103
Alonso, Arthur. 753
Alonso, Joaquin Maria. 1618
Alonso Schokel, Luis, 1920. 200
Alonso Schokel, Luis. 200, 240, 537
Alpenfels, Ethel Josephine. 3182
Alper, Michael. 2106
Alpers, Kenneth P. 3187
[Alpi, Mrs. Fannie Francis]. 3494
Alston, Leonard. 3532
Alston, Wallace McPherson. 2929
Alston, William P. 2674
Alstruey Sanchez, Gregorio. 2362
Alt, Albrecht. 484, 2096
Altaner, Berthold. 1019
Alter, Karl Joseph. 780, 757
Alter, Robert. 556
Althaus, Paul. 1424, 2200, 1424, 2009, 2168, 2280
Altholz, Josef Lewis. 1181
Althouse, LaVonne. 2152
Althouse, Lawrence W. 1598
Alting von Geusau, Leo George Marie. 1042
Altizer, Thomas J. J. 1055, 1080, 1417, 1418, 1505, 1818, 2024, 3070
Altizer, Thomas J. J., comp. 1418
Altman, Addie (Richman) 627, 2093, 2949
Altmann, Alexander. 125, 484, 2141, 2147, 2403, 2646, 2842
[Altmeyer, Henry B.] d. 1930. 862
Alvarez de Paz, Diego 1560-1620. 1984
Alvarez Quintero Serafin, 1871-1938. 2855
Alvery, Robert. 28, 94, 1783
Alves, Colin. 474, 645, 3177
Alves, Rubem A. 1658
Alvey, Edward. 2915
Alward, Benjamin B. 280, 2600, 2610, 2618
Alway, Hester. 387
Alzog, Johannes Baptist. 1172
Amabel du Coeur de Jesus. 1712, 3690
Amandry, Pierre. 1421
Amann, Emile, 1880. 1189
Amar Jyoti. 3476
Amar Jyoti, Swami. 3476
Amariu, Constantin. 1135
Ambauen, Andrew Joseph. 1443, 3573
Amber, Lee. 2141
Amberley, John Russell. 3112
Amberson, Talmadge R. 1253
Ambler, R.P. 3494
Ambrose. 2319
Ambrose, W. Haydn. 3756
Ambrosius. 29, 1616, 1835, 2217, 2383, 3262, 3635
Ambrosius, Saint. 574, 3634
Ambrozic, Aloysius M. 434, 2176
Ambrust, Arthur. 2475
Ambruzzi, Aloysius. 1984, 3484
Amen, Carol. 2383
Amenian Missionary Association of America. 2162
Ament, James Elf. 2000
America. 1281
America (New York, 1909-) 757, 1281
American academy for Jewish research. 1713, 2076, 3259, 3456
American Academy of Political and Social Science, Philadelphia. 3742, 3743
American Academy of Political and Social Science, Philadelphia. Annals. 3743
American Academy of Political and Social Science, Philadelphia. Annals, v. 332. 3743
American Academy of Religion. Academic Study of Religion Section. 3112
American and foreign Sabbath union. 3546
American architect and Architecture. 1268
American association for the advancement of atheism. 101
American association for the advancement of atheism, inc. 101
American Association of School Administrators. Commission on Religion in the Public Schools. 3095, 3189

American Association of Theological Schools. 3590, 3612, 3680
American Association of Theological Schools. Task Force on Spiritual Development. 3331
American Baptist convention. Board of education. 3680
American Baptist Convention. Ministers and Missionaries Benefit Board. 30
American Baptist foreign mission society. 155
American Baptist historical society, Philadelphia. Library. 143
American Baptist Home Mission Societies. 1562
American Baptist home mission society. 155
American Baptist Publication Society. 3186
American Baptist publication society. Christian education dept. 3763
American Bible revision committee. 274
American Bible society. 30, 31, 225, 226, 248, 254, 272, 611, 612
American Bible society. Committee on versions. 254
American Bible society. Library. 212, 213, 655
American Bible union. 31
American Bible union. Library. 212
American board of commissioners for foreign missions. 31, 911, 1339, 2518, 2559
American board of commissioners for foreign missions. Prudential committee. 2524
American Board of Missions to the Jews. 1860
American Calvinistic Conference. 730
American Calvinistic conference. 2d, Grand Rapids, 1942. 730
American Catholic missionary congress. 1st, Chicago. 851
American Catholic missionary congress. 1st, Chicago, 1908. 851, 2514
American Catholic Missionary Congress. ed, Boston, 1913. 851
American Catholic Philosophical Association. 2649, 3694
American Catholic Psychological Association. 1777
American Church Union. 44, 3197
American Civil Liberties Union. 1140
American Committee of Jewish Writers, Artists and Scientists. 2111
American Congregational association, Boston. 1336, 1345
American congress of philologists. 1st, Philadelphia, 1894. 3814
American Council for Judaism. 2103, 2111, 3896
American Council of Learned Societies Devoted to Humanistic Studies. 200
American Council on Education. Committee on Religion and Education. 1129, 3189
American ecclesiastical review. 2354
American Evangelical Lutheran Church Board of Parish Education. 2287
American Federation of Astrologers. Committee on Public Relations. 95
American Federation of Jews from Central Europe. 2099
American Hebrew. 2076
American Herbrew. 2076
American Institute of Management. 807
American Institutes for Research in the Behavioral Sciences. 3436
American Jewish committee. 2099
American Jewish Committee. Institute of Human Relations. 3770
American Jewish committee. Research institute on peace and post-war problems. 3852
American Jewish Committee. Wilkes-Barre Chapter. 3882
American Jewish conference. 2099
American Library Association. Religious Books Committee. 3203
American Library Association. Religious Books Round Table. 3203
American Lutheran Church. 2302
American Lutheran Church (1930-1960) 32, 2302
The American Lutheran Church (1961-) 32, 1138
American Lutheran church. Commission on worship and church, art. 2294
American Lutheran conference. Committee representing the higher educational institutions. 2293
American Lutheran publication board. 1691
American McAll association. 2546
American medical association. 3690
American missionary association. 33, 2546

American philosophical association. Western division. 1787
American philosophical society, Philadelphia. 2833
American philosophical society, Philadelphia. Library. 745
American Scientific Affiliation. 3077
American seamen's friend society. 3317
American seating company. 1169
American secular union and freethought federation. 1657
American Society for Nocturnal Adoration. 2253
American society for prophetic study. 2952
American society for psychical research. (Founded 1884) 2993
American society for psychical research. (Founded 1906) 2993
American society for visiting Catholic prisoners. 2942
American society of church history. 1172, 1198
American Society of Missiology. 2501
American Sunday school union. 33, 301, 2181, 2594, 3146
American Theological Library Association. 2225, 3096, 3626
American theosophical society. 3682
American Tract Society. 33, 1862, 2250, 2688, 3705, 3706
American Tract Society, Boston. 3705, 3706
American tract society, New York. 34
American Unitarian Association. 34, 1862, 3706, 3723, 3725, 3741
American Unitarian association. Commission of appraisal. 3727
American Unitarian association. Dept. of social and public service. 3440
The American weekly (New York) 3077
American Zionist Council. 3897
Ames, Alfred H. 458
Ames, Charles Gordon. 657, 724
Ames, David C. 2383
Ames, Edward Remington. 1719, 1736
Ames, Edward Scribner. 1466, 2000, 2751, 2752, 2996, 3056, 3347, 3758
Ames, john quincy. 1620, 3434, 3870, 3875, 3877
Ames, Kenneth John. 1443, 3707
Ames, Mary (Clemmer) 743
Ames, Van Meter. 3894
Ames, William. 3615, 3640
Amherst college. 1911
Amick, Fred A. 3347
Amick, Lon Gilbert, 1920. 954, 3476
Amiel, Henri Frederic. 35
Amin, 'Uthman, 1905. 2628
Amiot, Francois. 374, 375, 1986, 2368, 3287
Amir 'Ali, Maulavi Saiyid. 2564
Amiranashvili, Shalva IAsonovich. 87
Amistad Research Center. 33, 2526
Ammerman, Leila Tremaine. 3144, 3528, 3856
A monk of the Eastern Church. 2015
[Amos, Mary Jane (Davies)]. 3534
Amoss, Pamela. 2713
Amram, David Werner. 1942
Amrtacandra, fl. 905. 1932
Amryc, C. 2767
Amson, Peter Frederick. 3316
Amundsen, Wesley. 103, 1827, 2504, 2559, 3386
Amy, William O. 2321
An, Yong-jun. 3458
Ana de San Bartolome. 741
Anabel du Coeur de Jesus. 1508, 2636
'Anan Isho', 7th cent. 54, 2578
Anand, Mulk Raj. 1621
Ananda Acharya. 1813
Ananda, Maitreya. 704
Anandamurti. 3476
Ananikian, Mardiros Harootioon. 2654
['Anan Isho. 54, 55, 2578
Anastos, Milton Vasil. 2035
Ancelet-Hustache, Jeanne. 1639
Anciaux, Paul. 1522, 2811
Ancient Arabic order of the nobles of the mystic shrine. Baltimore. Boumi temple. 39
Ancient Arabic order of the nobles of the mystic shrine. New York City. Mecca temple. 39
Ancona, Angelo Anthony. 1651
Ancreen riwle. 2579
Ancren riwie. 2575
Ancren riwle. 2580
*Andeen, G. Kenneth. 527
Andel, G. K. van. 1820, 3388
Andelson, Robert V. 1280
Ander, Oscar Fritiof. 1546, 1790, 2293
Anderl, Stephen. 1483
Anders, John Olson. 3569

Anders-Richards, Donald. 577
Andersen, Arlow William. 2438
Andersen, Francis I. 547, 1797
Andersen, Hans Jorgen. 332
Andersen, Johannes Carl. 2666, 2332
Andersen, Karen. 3178
Andersen, Niels Christian. 1694
Andersen, Richard. 1164, 1298, 1633, 1839, 2347, 3550
Andersen, Wilhelm. 2200
Andersen, William Niclaus. 3112
Anderson, Alexander Walter. 480
Anderson, Alfred B. 2028
Anderson, Alpha E. (Almquist) 2514, 2811
Anderson, Andrew Gustaf. 2888
Anderson, Andy. 39, 635, 1613, 3551
Anderson, Ardis Leroy. 3660
Anderson, Arlene May (Anderson) 3146
Anderson, Arnold Albert. 574
Anderson, Aron. 1357
Anderson, Arthur LeRoy. 1588
Anderson, August Magnus. 2499
Anderson, Benedict R O'G. 2664
Anderson, Bernard W. 1589
Anderson, Bernhard W. 229, 279, 308, 484, 522, 532, 544, 586, 598, 647, 2095, 2630, 3848
Anderson, C H C. 1399
Anderson, C. LeRoy. 1237, 2620
Anderson, C. Reuben. 589
Anderson, Carl Philip. 740, 2514
Anderson, Charles C. 1978
Anderson, Charles H. 2979
Anderson, Charles Palmerston. 954, 2176, 3197, 2173, 2966
Anderson, Charles S. 2283, 3033, 3667
Anderson, Chrysostom J. 3690
Anderson, Clifford V. 2191
Anderson, Colena M. 1349
Anderson, Courtney. 2157
Anderson, D. Carl. 1256, 2560
Anderson, David A. 480
Anderson, David D. 1907
Anderson, Dennis A. 2212
Anderson, Doris (Jones) 1606
Anderson, Douglas A. 1606
Anderson, Edward F. 2827
Anderson, Edward Henry. 72, 2600
Anderson, Edward M. 1562, 3123
Anderson, Edward W. 1320
Anderson, Edwin Raymond. 3852
Anderson, Einar. 2610, 2598, 2610
Anderson, Eliza N. 3722
Anderson, Elma K. 1873
Anderson, Elof. 39, 2512
Anderson, Emma Dean. 2529
Anderson, Erica. 3311
Anderson, Evelyn. 17
Anderson, Evelyn McCullough. 3842, 3845
Anderson, Florence Mary (Bennett) 28
Anderson, Floyd. 663
Anderson, Floyd [Edward]. 131, 2190
Anderson, Frederick Lincoln. 1527, 2016
Anderson, Galusha. 1285, 3619
Anderson, George Christian. 2996
Anderson, George M. 1950
Anderson, George Smith. 635, 1843, 2896, 3362, 3795
Anderson, George Wishart. 2148
Anderson, George Wood. 1443, 1543
Anderson, Gerald H. 1078, 1090, 2495, 2496, 2504, 2553, 2830
Anderson, Godfrey Tryggve. 1013, 2383
Anderson, Grace B. 635
*Anderson, H. George. 1172
Anderson, Harrison Ray. 2929
Anderson, Howard Elmer. 2529
Anderson, Hugh. 431, 1978, 2007, 2292
[Anderson, Issac]. 2217
Anderson, J A. 1744
Anderson, J Grant. 1533
Anderson, J. Keith. 954
Anderson, J. Kerby. 1412, 1705
Anderson, J. Max. 2858
Anderson, Jacob Grant. 1228, 1598
Anderson, James. 1375, 3869
Anderson, James A. 3112
Anderson, James Arthur. 1055, 2457
Anderson, James Burns. 2994
Anderson, James D. 1243
Anderson, James Desmond. 1199
Anderson, James Francis. 2672, 3699
Anderson, James Henry. 2607
Anderson, James Norman Dalrymple. 1078, 1534, 2050, 3112, 3619, 1892
Anderson, James W D. 2434
Anderson, Jean. 1710
Anderson, Jerome A. 1886, 2165
Anderson, John. 2984, 3094, 1705
Anderson, John Gray. 954
Anderson, John Mitchell. 1793
Anderson, John Piter. 41
Anderson, John Wesley. 3347
Anderson, Joseph. 1231
Anderson, Joseph Lyman. 1496

Anderson, Josephus. 1054
Anderson, Karl. 95
Anderson, Ken. 2208
Anderson, Kenneth. 39, 1426, 2507, 3675, 3678, 3828
Anderson, Leila W. 1335
Anderson, Leland E. 1013
Anderson, Leroy Dean. 1466
Anderson, Llewellyn Kennedy. 2506
Anderson, Louis Catherine Vallet. 2693
Anderson, Louis Francis. 1730, 2242, 2994, 3607, 3782
Anderson, Lulah (Ketcham) 899
Anderson, Lynn. 1273, 3347
*Anderson, Marbury E. 3188
Anderson, Margaret J. 902, 1604, 1733, 2983, 3203, 3660, 3882, 3884
Anderson, Margaret Jobe. 2736
Anderson, Marin. 1199
Anderson, Martin. 804, 1155, 1199, 1268, 1328
Anderson, Marvin Walter. 240
Anderson, Mary Desiree. 915, 1165, 2230
Anderson, Mary Eleanor (Roberts) 20
Anderson, Mary Gooch. 2649
Anderson, Maxwell. 2003
Anderson, Meta Louise. 895
Anderson, Nancy E. 95, 3399
Anderson, Neal Larkin. 2929
Anderson, Nels. 2615
Anderson, Nephi. 1233, 2600
Anderson, Norman G. 2298, 3347
Anderson, Palmer I. 1109
Anderson, Park Harris. 2507, 1295
Anderson, Paul B. 1148, 1149, 2750
Anderson, Paul Russell. 2596, 3097
Anderson, Philip A. 1200, 1848
Anderson, Phoebe M. 3146, 3173, 3660
Anderson, Rasmus Bjorn. 2665
Anderson, Ray Sherman. 1719, 2321
Anderson, Raymond. 9
Anderson, Reuben W. 635
Anderson, Richard Lloyd. 680, 3427
Anderson, Robert. 1748, 507, 3022, 229, 404, 508, 1054, 2087, 3287, 3318, 3720
Anderson, Robert Emory. 2383
Anderson, Robert Gordon. 2773
Anderson, Robert Grant. 3003
Anderson, Robert L. 2212
Anderson, Robert Mapes. 2816
Anderson, Robert Phillips. 1910, 1914, 1959, 3070, 3528, 3563
Anderson, Robert T. 3640
Anderson, Robin. 2850, 2851, 2861
Anderson, Roy Allan. 452, 508, 1012, 1401, 1562, 2035, 2907, 3318, 3381, 3494
[Anderson, Rufus] 1796-1880. 39, 2516, 2524, 2529, 2555
Anderson, Sir Robert. 2035
Anderson, Stanely Edwin. 275
Anderson, Stanley E. 2995
Anderson, Stanley Edwin. 83, 275, 560, 1163, 2250
Anderson, Stuart LeRoy. 2383
Anderson, Susan. 2542, 2820
Anderson, T M. 3372
Anderson, Ted. 39, 1357
Anderson, Thomas. 954
Anderson, Tony Marshall. 2896, 3640
Anderson, Uell Stanley. 2693, 3197
Anderson, Vernon E. 2287
Anderson, Vernon Ellsworth. 3169
Anderson, W. H. 2499
Anderson, Walt. 2193
Anderson, Wilhelm. 2200
Anderson, William Angor. 767
Anderson, William Francis Desnaux. 752
Anderson, William Franklin. 1839, 3347
Anderson, William Hamilton. 51
Anderson, William Ketcham. 1055, 2491, 2975, 2420, 2975
Anderson, William M. 1047
anderson, William Madison. 1067
Anderson, William Madison. 3347
Anderson, William P. 175
Anderson, William S. 2626
Anderson, Wing. 2946
[Andler, Ludwig] 1882. 3670
Andover Newton theological school. 40
Andover Newton Theological School, Newton Center, Mass. 3626
Andover theological seminary. 40, 3614
Andover theological seminary. Alumni association. 40, 3331
Andover theological seminary. Library. 40, 3626, 3627
Andra, Tor. 2628
Andrae, Tor. 2628
Andrae Tor, 1885-1947. 2628
Andre, Marie Joseph. 3484
Andrea, Raymund. 3249
Andreae, Christine. 3520
Andreae, Fritz. 899
Andreasen, Milian Lauritz. 48, 213, 402, 3260, 3381
Andreasen, Millian Lauritz. 2868

Andreasen, Niels-Erik A. 498, 3261, 3701
Andre-Delastre, Louise. 19
Andreen, Paul Harold. 3440, 3743
Andres, Stefan Paul. 617
Andrew. 992, 1073, 2517, 2246, 2868, 3476
Andrew, G. Findlay. 2567
Andrew, John A. 31, 1339
Andrew, Laurel B. 3600
Andrew, Marguerite [Sister M. Marguerite Andrew]. 2354
Andrewes, Lancelot. 1225, 1436, 2054
Andrews, A. H., & company, Chicago. 1169
Andrews, Charles Freer. 41, 2868, 3476, 3546, 3812, 3334, 3812
Andrews, Charles Richard. 425
Andrews, Charles Wesley. 2757
Andrews, Dean Timothy. 2745
Andrews, Dorothy Westlake. 902, 3164
Andrews, Edward Deming. 3394, 3397, 3398, 3394, 3398
Andrews, Elias. 375
Andrews, Emerson. 1576, 1554, 3094
Andrews, Ernest C. 1455
Andrews, George Arthur. 3056, 3065
Andrews, Gibson Callaway. 1379
Andrews, Gini. 123, 3415
Andrews, Herbert Tom. 488
Andrews, James F. 175, 2806, 3749
Andrews, John Nevins. 465, 3260
Andrews, Lancelot. 1113, 1436
Andrews, Lynn V. 41, 1309
Andrews, Marietta Minnigerode. 3494
Andrews, Mary Edith. 373
Andrews, Matthew T. 3146, 3347
Andrews, R L. 3372
Andrews, Robert Wells. 2533
Andrews, Samuel James. 1047, 41, 51, 1959, 3224
Andrews, Sheila. 3473
Andrews, Tailer. 292
Andrews, W P. 2817
Andrews, W. T. 2426
Andrews, William. 1631
Andrews, William Almon. 132
Andrews, William Eusebius. 2350
Andrews, William Loring. 1943
Andra, Tor. 2628
Andronis, Constantine. 2318
Andros, Elmer Ellsworth. 103
Andros, Thomas. 3410
Andross, Matilda (Erickson) 954, 1719, 3379, 3386
Andross, Matilda Ericson. 1719
Andrus, Bessie Edmond. 617
Andrus, Hyrum Leslie. 1152, 2600, 2610, 3427, 3428, 3430
Andrus, Paul F. 3539
Andruss, Bessie Edmond. 617
Andry, Carl Franklin. 350, 372, 2795
Ancelet-Hustache, Jeanne. 2707
Anesaki, Masaharu. 706, 2707, 85, 706, 1935, 2707
Angebert, Jean Michel. 1820, 2732
Angel, Marc. 1700, 3333
Angela. 1941. 902
Angela, of Foligno. 2646
Angeles, Peter Adam. 1719
Angelini-Larghetti, Ambrose, 1901. 41
Angell, C. Roy. 122, 160
Angell, Charles. 2794
Angell, Charles Roy. 160, 992, 2721
Angell, James W. 1010, 1277, 1349, 1619, 2383
Angell, Warren M. 917
Angelus, Gabriel. 695
Anger, Joseph. 1950
Anglican Church of Canada. Dept. of Religious Education. 1862
Anglican Congress, Toronto, 1963. 44
Anglican/Roman Catholic Joint Preparatory Commission. 1224
Anglin, Thomas Francis. 2254
Anglo-Catholic congress. 45
Anglo-Catholic congress, 5th, London and Oxford, 1933. 45
Angoff, Allan. 1702
Angoff, Charles. 1653
Angrisani, Giuseppe. 1263, 3331
Angus, Fay. 47, 930
Angus, Joseph. 308, 635, 1959
-Angus, Samuel, 188-1943. 1189
Angus, Samuel. 111, 407, 1047, 2636, 1189, 2636
Anirvan. 3301
Anjou, Lars Anton. 3042
Ankaum, Freeman. 1236
Anketell, John. 2968
Ankori, Zvi. 2164
Anler, Ludwig. 3670, 3676
[Anley, Charlotte]. 3716
Anna Louise, 1873. 292, 617, 855, 1825
Annan, Noel Gilroy Annan. 3535
[Annan, Robert] 1761-1819. 2921
[Annan, William]. 48
Annett, Edward Aldridge. 895

Annuity fund for Congregational ministers. 1338
Annunciacao Justiniano, Diogo da, 1854-1713. 1910
Anointed Music & Publishing Co. 445, 1987
Anonymous. 2383
Anrias, David. 95
Anscombe, Francis Charles. 1513, 1687
Anselm, 1033-1109. 775, 1739, 2835, 2888, 3636
Anshen, Ruth Nanda. 1426
Ansley, Delight. 3112
Ansley, Lula (Barnes) 3833
Ansley, Rufus. 1339
Anson, Elva. 1606
Anson, Harold. 118, 1589
Anson, Jay. 1423, 2303
Anson, Peter Frederick. 1169, 1791, 740, 825, 1155, 1169, 1269, 1806, 2761, 3316, 3322
Anspach, Frederick Rinehart. 1349, 1411
Anspacher, Louis Kaufman. 2986
Anstadt, Peter. 3197, 3309
Anstey, Martin. 635
Anstice, Henry. 1116, 3242, 2699
Anstruther, William. 3065
The ante-Nicene fathers. 1617
Antekeier, Charles. 1328
Antelman, Marvin S. 713, 3032
Anthon, Henry. 2699
Anthony, Alba (Riek) 922
Anthony, Alfred Williams. 1347, 1986, 3065, 3096
Anthony, Carol K. 1470, 1878
Anthony, Charles Volney. 2451, 3146
Anthony, Ole. 980
Anthony, Susan Brownell. 1361
Anthony, Susanna. 3143
Anti-Defamation League. 2076, 2103, 2111
Antimasonic state convention of Massachusetts, 3d, Boston, 1831. 52
Anti-Sabbath Convention, Boston. 3261
Antoine, Charles. 814, 1144
Anton, Hans Hubert. 2943, 3277
Anton, Rita. 54, 875
Antonellis, Costanzo J. 3690
Antonii, 1863-1936. 1327
Antony. 36
Antony, Judith. 55, 1365
Antrim, Eugene Marion. 954
Antrobus, Mary (Symonds) 2679
Anzar, Naosherwan. 2400
Anzia, Joan Meyer. 2342
Aoussat, Claude A. 1719
Ap, Richard. 2336
Apastamba. 2329
Apczynski, John V. 2180, 2857
Apel, Willi. 884
Apollodorus. 2660
Apophthegmata Patrum. English. 1019
Apostleship of prayer. 3269
Apostolic constitutions. English. 1239
Apostolic Faith Mission. 76
Apostolic Fathers. 76, 1018, 1019, 1617
Apostolic Fathers. English. 1018
Apostolical constitutions. 1488
Apostolic Fathers. 1019
Apostolie Fathers. 1019
Apostolon, Billy. 197, 1074, 1839, 2721, 3347, 3372
Appadurai, Arjun. 1897
Appasamy, Aiyadurai Jesudasen. 1082, 2061
Appel, Benjamin. 2311
Appel, Georg. 2887
Appel, Gersion. 1, 1312
Appel, Theodore. 3048, 2686
Appell, Ruby May. 954
Appelman, Hyman. 1554, 1836, 3232, 3372, 1554, 1555, 3372
Appelman, Hyman Jedidiah. 1555, 3372
Appere, Guy. 2868
Appert, Camille. 691, 2536
Applebaum, Edmond L. 2944
Applebaum, Morton M. 910, 3011
Applebury, T. R. 430
Applebury, Theodore Ralph. 322, 426
Appleby, David P. 1207
Appleby, Hazel F. 3052
Appleby, Rosalee Mills. 954, 1714
Appleby, Rosalee (Mills) 144, 954, 1443
Applegarth, Albert Clayton. 1687, 2813
Applegarth, Margaret Tyson. 739, 897, 1013, 1838, 2236, 2480, 2489, 2491, 2518, 2533, 2535, 2549, 3046, 3047, 3528, 3856
Applegate, Richard B. 1899
Applegate, Thomas. 2021
Appleman, Hyman Jedidiah. 1555
Appleman, Solomon. 3837
Appler, Augustus C. 1029
Appleton, Emily. 644
Appleton, Ernest Robert. 3094, 3140
Appleton, George. 423, 706, 1430, 1436
Appleton, LeRoy H. 922

Appleton, Nathaniel. 1741, 2742, 2868, 3347
Appleton, Wis. St. Joseph's church (Catholic) 835
Applewhite, Barry. 980
Applewhite, Harry. 2806
Appling, Phillip Holden. 3081
Appold, Mark L. 418, 2010
Apps, Jerold W. 1200, 3168
Apter, David Ernest. 3525
Aquinas Institute of Philosophy and Theology. Institute of Spiritual Theology. 3391
Aquinas Institute of Philosophy and Theology. School of Theology. Dubuque, Iowa. 219
Aradi, Zsolt. 2123, 2475, 2476, 2851, 2862, 3404
Arami, M M. 1750
Aranjo, Garcia Carlos. 2979
Arapura, John Geeverghese. 3017
Arasteh, A. Reza. 1933, 3542
Arbaugh, George Bartholomew. 954, 2600, 3428
Arbaugh, George E. 2169
Arber, Edward. 2336
Arberry, Arthur John. 1927, 2678, 3227
Arbois de Jubainville, Henry d', 1827-1910. 2655
Arcambeau, Edme. 752
Archambault, Alberic A. 2104
Archarya. 3863
Archbold, William Arthur Jobson. 3457
Archconfraternity of the Guard of honor of the Sacred heart of Jesus. 3269
Archconfraternity of the most holy cross and passion of Our Lord Jesus Christ. 855
Archer, Cathaline (Alford) 78
Archer, Gleason Leonard. 280, 405, 466, 538
Archer, John Clark. 2549, 2628, 2647, 3112, 3408, 2629, 3112, 3408
Archer, Norman. 1404
Archer, William. 3801
Archer, William George. 2187
Archibald, Andrew Webster. 1891, 2589, 275, 2675
Archibald, Arthur Crawley. 1555, 1562
Archibald, Ethel Jessie. 3551
Archibald, Francis A. 2422
Archibald, Frank E. 72, 1713, 2539, 3367, 3731
Archibald, G. D. 883
Archibald, George Hamilton. 3551
Archibald, Helen A. 333
Archibald, Warren Seymour. 3090
Architectural record. 1155
Archonfraternity of the Guard of honor of the Sacred heart of Jesus. 3269, 3270
Arden, Gothard Everett. 110, 2303, 3253
Arden House Conference on Family Living, 1962. 1604
Ardmore, Pa. St. Paul's Lutheran Church. 79
Ardsher Jamshedji Suravala. 3779
Are, Thomas L. 2633
Arendt, Hannah. 661
Arendzen, John Peter. 3006, 795, 1527, 1587, 1699, 1793, 1892, 3711
Arens, Eduardo. 387, 2069
Arenth, Mary Aurelia. 1540
Arentrout, James Sylvester. 3176
Ares, Richard. 1369, 3709
Aretin, Karl Otmar. 2768
Arfaud de Montor, Alexis Francois, 1772-1849. 2862
Argo, Fordyce Hubbard. 1959
Argow, Waldemar. 2221
Argow, Wendelin Waldemar Wieland. 3337
Arguelles, Jose. 2327
Arguelles, Miriam. 3838
Arguinzoni, Sonny. 1255
Argyle, Aubrey William. 1730, 1769
Argyle, Michael. 2996
Argyll, George Douglas Campbell. 3074
Arias, Juan. 995, 1456, 2383, 2888
Arichea, Daniel C. 325
Aridas, Chris. 849, 2346
Aries, Philippe. 1412, 1416
Arieti, Silvano. 4, 2995
Arintero, Juan Gonzalez. 2642, 2868
Arisian, Khoren. 2347
Aristeas' epistle. 528
Aristides, Marcianus. 68
Aristoteles. 80, 1534, 2416
Arjun. 3408
Arkus, Karen A. 2637
Armanet, Crescent. 2697
armaud d'Agnel, G. 771, 3779
Armbruster, Carl J., 1929. 3699
Armbruster, Wally. 980

Armenian Church. 82
Armenian church. Liturgy and ritual. 82, 884
Armenian Church Youth Organization of America. 82
Armenian Missionary Association of America. 82
Armentrout, James Sylvester. 3763
Armerding, Carl. 458, 514, 554, 584, 3220
Armerding, George D. 2734
Armerding, Hudson T. 952, 1074
Armes, Sybil (Leonard) 992, 1443
Armes, Woodson, 1912. 3852
Arminius, Jacobus. 3628, 3629
Armitage, John James Richard. 3452
Armitage, Merle. 2548
Armitage, Thomas. 151, 1326, 1691, 2896
Armitage, William James. 2883
Armor, Reginald Cavin. 2262
Armour, John M. 103, 3609
Armour, Rollin Stely. 137
Arms, Dorothy (Noyes) 1270
Arms, Goodsil Filley. 2547
Armstrong, Amzi. 462
Armstrong, Ann Seidel. 1509
Armstrong, April (Oursler) 617, 627, 757, 1363, 1618, 1639, 1979, 2024, 2803
Armstrong, April (Outsler) 757
Armstrong, Arthur Hilary. 111, 1081
Armstrong, Ben. 3018
Armstrong, Beulah. 3494
Armstrong, Brian G. 728, 730
Armstrong, Chloe. 210, 613
Armstrong, Christopher J. R. 3722
Armstrong, D. Wade. 3241
Armstrong, David Malet. 2473
Armstrong, Edward. 1639
Armstrong, Edward Allworthy. 47, 1639
Armstrong, Edyth Sage. 645
Armstrong, Edyth (Sage) 577
Armstrong, Fanny L. 897
Armstrong, Frieda. 3831
Armstrong, Garner Ted. 928, 1950, 1976
Armstrong, George Dodd. 3640
Armstrong, George Washington. 2077
Armstrong, H Parr. 954
Armstrong, Harry P. 1862
Armstrong, Herbert W. 45, 610
Armstrong, Housen Parr. 3347
Armstrong, Iscar Vance, 1876-   comp. 3209
Armstrong, James. 849, 1006, 1055, 1085, 1562, 2434, 2907
Armstrong, James Edward. 2446
Armstrong, James Francis. 2929, 3348
Armstrong, Joseph. 684
Armstrong, Karen. 83, 1582
Armstrong, Ken S. 1238
Armstrong, Lebbeus. 737, 3597
Armstrong, Maurice Whitman. 1757, 2924
Armstrong, O. K. 170, 1319
Armstrong, Orland Kay. 170
Armstrong, Oscar Vance. 1349, 1353
Armstrong, Ramsey Clarke. 1029
Armstrong, Richard Acland. 1518
Armstrong, Richard G. 1430, 1433, 2888
Armstrong, Richard Stoll. 1562
Armstrong, Robert Allen. 481, 635
Armstrong, Robert Cornell. 706, 1330
Armstrong, Robert G. 1821
Armstrong, Roger D. 3743
Armstrong, Terry A. 530, 1796
Armstrong, Walter W. 2433
Armstrong, William. 871
Armstrong, William Ayres. 1826
Armstrong, William Howard. 630, 1533
[Armstrong, William Park] 1874. 727
Arnaiz Baron, Rafael. 3484
Arnaud, Francois Thomas Marie de Baculard d. 3218
Arndt, Elmer J. F. 133, 1545, 3650
Arndt, Herman Theodore. 1613
Arndt, Johann. 1005, 1047, 2297
Arndt, Richard. 932
Arndt, William. 229, 406, 426, 2764, 2868, 229
*Arnellos, Gabriel J. 3203
Arnett, Benjamin William. 3761
Arnett, Ronald C. 2712
Arnett, Willard Eugene. 3097, 3108
Arnim, Bettina (Brentano) von. 1624
Arnobius. 68
Arnold, A. Stuart. 242
Arnold, Adelaide. 3494
Arnold, Albert Nicholas. 1458, 2250
Arnold, Alfreda. 2533
Arnold, Arthur Olof. 647, 954
Arnold, Benjamin William. 61
Arnold, Charles Edward. 1991
Arnold, Charles Harvey. 894
Arnold, Charlotte E. 613, 2549, 2489, 3560
Arnold, Don P. 83
Arnold, Dorothy Musgrave. 2168

Arnold, Eberhard. 8, 83, 431, 697, 698, 933, 938, 954, 1018, 1468, 1827, 2264, 2341, 2383, 3334, 3476, 3477, 3491, 3632
Arnold, Edward Vernon. 3532, 3776
Arnold, Edwin. 706, 1412
Arnold, Emmy. 698, 1430
Arnold, Frank Stutesman. 181, 3077
Arnold, Heini. 83, 980, 2336
Arnold, Helen. 43
Arnold, Helena. 3146
[Arnold, Henry Vernon] 1848. 1421
Arnold, James Oliver. 2986
Arnold, Jay. 3271
Arnold, Joan. 1320
Arnold, John Henry. 883, 2257
Arnold, John Motte. 3299
Arnold, Levi McKeen. 3494
Arnold, Louis Walker. 1555
Arnold, Matthew. 83, 229, 230
Arnold, Milo L. 1010, 2474
Arnold, Oren. 1289
Arnold, Robert Brandon. 2416
Arnold, Thomas. 3362
Arnold, Thomas Waker. 1283
Arnold, Thomas Walker. 2759, 726, 2564, 1283, 1924, 2759
Arnold, William Erastus. 2431
Arnold, William Rosenzweig. 2113
Arnold, William V. 2783
Arnold-Forster, Frances Egerton. 2985
Arnot, Frederick Stanley. 2513
Arnot, William. 330, 387, 572, 1195, 2024, 3362
Arnote, Thelma. 3173, 3534
Arnott, Anne. 1303, 1305
Arnoudt, Pierre. 3269
Arnsby-Jones, George. 3415, 3477
Arntzen, Araliot Mattias. 1790
Aron, Marguerite. 1475, 2131, 3761
Aron, Milton. 1789
Aron, Robert. 1732, 1977, 2003
Aronin, Ben. 898, 2097
Aronoff, Daisy Phillips. 627
Aronson, David. 1538
Aronson, Gregor. 2102
Aronson, Harvey B. 2263
Aronstam, Noah Ephraim. 2169
Arpee, Leon. 82, 2953
Arpita. 181
Arriaga, Pablo Jose de. 1904
Arrien, Rose Fe Narro. 84, 797
Arries, Crescenzia. 1037
Arrington, French L. 323, 325, 372, 1529
Arrington, Leonard J. 1232, 2609, 2615, 2619, 3235, 3762, 3847
Arrington, Mary Marie Koontz. 2626
Arrowsmith, John. 1043
Arrowsmith, Richard Staines. 1761
Arroyo, Stephen. 97
Arrupe, Pedro. 1950, 2572
Ars moriendi. English. 1416
Arscott, Albert John Loram, 1883. 3494
Arscott, Alexander. 1047, 3701
Arsen'ev, Nikolai Sergeevich. 1055, 2749
Arsen'ev, Nikolai Sergeevich, 1888. 1056
Ars moriendi. 1412
Arter, Rhetta Marie. 1133
Arthur, Donald Ramsay. c6. 3169
Arthur, Eric. 1349, 3464
Arthur, George Robert. 3874
Arthur, Joseph. 918, 1574
Arthur, Kay. 1430
Arthur, Luther A. 1719
Arthur, Timothy Shay. 1013
[Arthur, William]. 3494
[Arthur, William] 1819-1901. 712, 1827, 2434
Artis, William Wayne. 2441
Arts Council of Great Britain. 86
Artz, Thomas. 2370
Arundale, George Sydney. 2711, 3689, 89, 3683
Arundale, R. L. 3164
Arvine, Kazlitt. 41
Arvisenet, Claude. 2752
Arvon, Henri. 700
Arya, Usharbudh. 1412, 2379, 3774
Aryer, William Ward. 213
Arzt, Max. 3249
Asad, Muhammad. 1366
Asad, Muhammad [name orig.: Leopold Weiss]. 1366
Asanga. 3867
Asbhurn, Jesse Anderson. 2941
Asbury, Francis. 89, 954, 2444, 89
Asbury, Herbert. 89, 2420
Asbury Theological Seminary, Wilmore, Ky. 3299
Asch, Shalom. 627, 2113, 2117, 2803, 3394, 627
Ascham, John Bayne. 1172, 1928, 2113, 3088
Asgill, John. 3709

Ash, Anthony Lee. 427, 574, 980, 1466, 2868, 3348
*Ash, David. 905
Ash, James L. 1172, 3572
Ash, Lee. 2225
Ashbrook, James B. 337, 1028, 1323, 2319, 2795
Ashburn, Jesse Anderson. 2941
Ashby, La Verne. 313
Ashby, Leonard Beauclerc. 1225
Ashby, Philip H. 1815, 3112
Ashby, Robert H. 2986
Ashby, Thompson Eldridge. 698
Ashcraft, Frances B. 2047
Ashcraft, Morris. 1633, 1740
Ashcraft, Tom. 90, 2817
Ashcroft, Edgar A. 3027
Ashcroft, J Robert. 635
Ashcroft, Robert Leslie. 72
Ashe, Geoffrey. 2359, 3838
Ashenfelter, Ida Goodman. 3716
Ashenhurst, James Oliver. 3253
Asher, Hellen Drummond. 1733
Asher, Jeremiah. 3123
Asher, Percy Frank. 2806
Asheri, Michael. 2119
Ashford, Ray. 1016
Ashish, Madhava. 3683
Ashlag, Yehudah. 721
Ashley, Benedict M. 2377
Ashley, George Thomas. 3123
Ashley, R. K. 1103
Ashley, W. B. 10
Ashman, Chuck. 1754
Ashmore, Ann Lewis. 2220
Ashmore, Jerome. 3302
Ashmun, Jehudi. 124
Ashokananda. 3774
Ashton, John. 3097, 1110, 1426, 1427, 3826
Ashton, Joseph Nickerson. 1202
Ashton, Marvin J. 1008
Ashton, Sophia (Goodrich) 3838
Ashton, Wendell J. 2383, 2607, 2609
Ashwell, Arthur Rawson. 3815
Ashworth, Robert Archibald. 954, 1039
Asia Society. 85
Asimov, Isaac. 203, 292, 481, 525, 526, 565, 589, 1379, 1517
Asin Palacios, Miguel, 1871-1944. 1925, 2125
Askew, Mary W. 613, 1607
Askwith, Edward Harrison. 478
Asmussen, Hans. 2298
Asmussen, Jes Peter. 2328
Asmuth, Robert C. 1254
Asociacion General de la Iglesia Adventista del Septimo Dia. 3379
Asoka, fl. 259 B.C. 707
Aspen Interreligious Consultation, 1974. 1155
Asper, Wallace J. 3146
Aspinwall, Marguerite. 2829
Asplund, John. 142, 158
Asquith, Glenn H. 17, 955, 992, 1239, 1417, 2383, 2788, 2896
Assad'u'llah, mirza. 2949
Assemblies of God, General Council. 92
Assimakopoulos, Pat. 92, 930
Assmann, Hugo. 2222
Associate Reformed church in North America. 3044
Associate Reformed Church in North America. General Synod. 93
Associate Reformed synod of the South. 2915
Associated boards for Christian colleges in China. 3756
Associated Church Press. 3205
Associated Colleges of the St. Lawrence Valley. 89
Associated Jewish Philanthropies, Boston. 2098
Associated presbyteries. 2919
Association for research and enlightenment, inc., Virginia Beach, Va. 93
Association for Research and Enlightenment, Virginia Beach, Va. 93, 1539, 1741
Association for the relief of Jewish widows and orphans, New Orleans. 2081
Association of Disciples for Theological Discussion. 1462
Association of Methodist Historical Societies. 2432, 2433
Association of Spiritualists of Mantua. 3494
Association of the sacred hearts of Jesus and Mary. 1443
Association Press, New York. 3361
as-Sufi, 'Abd al-Qadir. 21, 3542
Asterius, ca. 375-405. 3337
Astley, Hugh John Dukinfield. 275
Aston, Frederick Alfred. 544, 3377
Aston, Hugh. 3271
Aston, Margaret. 89, 1761

Aston, Willard A. 2618
Aston, William George. 3403
Astro Numeric Service. 99
Asvaghosa. 700, 709, 1589, 3302
Asvaghosha. 700, 706, 709
Asvalayanagrhyasutra. English & Sanskrit. 1815
Atchison, Ray M. 143
Atchison, Robert Hall. 955
Atchley, Edward Godfrey Cuthbert Frederic. 1894, 2257, 3031
Ate National Multicultural Education Clinic, Ball State University, 1975. 2475
Athanasius. d. 55, 577
Athanasius. 55, 69, 80, 1835, 1894, 2046
Athavale, Pandurang Vaijnath. 2186, 3767
Athearn, Clarence Royalty. 732, 1169, 3146
Athearn, Laura (Armstrong) 3857
Athearn, Walter Scott. 1246, 2318, 3146, 3177, 3189
Athenagoras. 68, 69, 3634
-Athenagoras 2d cent. 1093
Atherton, Gertrude Franklin (Horn) 1750
Athill, Emmanuel. 849
Athy, Marion (Poppen) 3183
Atiya, Aziz Suryal. 1390, 1392, 1486
Atkins, Albert James. 3784
Atkins, Alma Newell. 3144
Atkins, Benedict M. 2377
[Atkins, Frederick Anthony] ed. 635
Atkins, Gaius Glenn. 169, 1047, 1338, 1339, 1719, 2056, 2209, 2702, 2896, 3112, 3141, 3334, 3362, 3460, 3743, 923
Atkins, James. 1253
Atkins, Mary (Sayles) 604
Atkins, Rebecca (Crittenden) 3124
[Atkins, Sarah]. 1497, 2720
Atkins, Susan. 102, 1363
Atkinson, Basil Ferris Campbell. 275
Atkinson, Benjamin Franklin. 464, 2464
Atkinson, Charles Harry. 1167, 3548
Atkinson, D. Watson. 700, 1678
Atkinson, David John. 1843, 2336
Atkinson, Edwin T. 1895
Atkinson, Frederick William. 1125
Atkinson, Gary. 663
Atkinson, George Wesley. 2434
Atkinson, Henry Avery. 2190
Atkinson, James. 2272, 3033, 3852
Atkinson, John. 2423, 643, 1285, 1349, 2423, 2432, 2433
Atkinson, Joseph Baines. 1822
Atkinson, Linda. 3055
Atkinson, Louise Warren. 2795
Atkinson, Mabel Sanford. 680
Atkinson, Nancy (Bates) 102
Atkinson, O'Brien. 762, 2896
Atkinson, Samuel. 1363
Atkinson, Sandy A. 102, 171
Atkinson, Tacy Wilkinson. 452
Atkinson, William Ezra. 3551
[Atkinson, William Walker]. 1895, 2693, 2722, 2737, 2839, 3052, 3138, 3863, 3867
Atkinson, William Walker. 2722
[Atkinson, William Walker]. 3863
Atlanta. Our Lady of Perpetual Help Free Cancer Home. 2245
Atlanta. Our lady of Perpetual Help Home. 2245
Atlanta theological seminary. 3681
Atling von Geusau, Leo George Marie. 841
Atmaprana, Pravrajika. 2712
Atreya, Bhikhan Lal. 2319
Attenborough, A Allen. 1172
Atterbury, Anson Phelps. 2564, 1923
Atthill, William Lombe. 1309
Attridge, Harold W. 2134, 2144
Attwater, Donald. 814, 851, 1115, 1487, 2169, 2236, 2350, 2359, 3279, 3283, 1025, 3283
Attwater, Rachel. 3306
Attwood, Frederick Spencer. 289
Atwater, George Parkin. 532, 1167, 1523, 2956
[Atwater, John Birdseye] 1855-1921. 1959
Atwater, John Milton. 1461
Atwater, W. D. 2004
[Atwell, Harriet Georgia]. 109
Atwood, Ann. 2228, 3312
Atwood, Anthony. 1378, 1822
Atwood, Edward Sumner. 1339
Atwood, Elijah Francis. 3077
Atwood, Isaac Morgan. 3224
Atwood, Jesse Howell. 3870
Atwood, John. 2847
[Atwter, J. B.]. 1950
Atzbaugh, William. 2693
Atzberger, Leonhard. 2010, 2242
Auberlen, Karl August. 477
Aubert. 3259
Aubert, Jean Marie. 3081
Aubert, Marcel. 1159
Aubert, Roger. 811
Aubin, Gideon. 797

Aubrey, Edwin Ewart. 2996, 3640, 3327, 3617
Auburn, N. Y. First Presbyterian church. 1791, 1911
Auburn theological seminary. 109, 3681
Auburn theological seminary, Auburn, N. Y. 109
Auchincloss, Louis. 3236
Auchincloss, William Stuart. 2946, 218, 496, 508, 2824, 496, 508
Auclair, Marcelle. 399, 1957, 1979, 3602
Audet, Jean Paul. 771, 877, 1093, 2035
Audin, Jean Marie Vincent. 2272
Audinet, Jacques. 3167
Audiovisual Council on Public Information, inc. 109
Auer, Alfons. 1065, 3484
Auerbach, Charles. 3582
Auerbach, Elias. 563, 2621
Auerbach, Joseph Smith. 200
Auerbach, Nina. 1517
Auge, Thomas E. 2755
Augrain, Charles. 370
Augsburg Publishing House. 1208
Augsburg Publishing House, Minneapolis. 1208
Augsburger, A. Don. 3167
Augsburger, David. 1006, 1633
Augsburger, David W. 1006, 2779, 3828
Augsburger, Myron S. 37, 61, 179, 287, 955, 1006, 1562, 1827, 2383, 2405
Augstein, Rudolf. 2035
August. 747
Augusta, Ga. First Presbyterian church. 2912
Augusta, Mary. 2717
Augustana college and theological seminary, Rock Island, Ill. Denkmann memorial library. 2282
Augustana Evangelical Lutheran Church. 110, 617, 2288, 3561
Augustana Evangelical Lutheran Church. Board of foreign missions. 2507
Augustana Evangelical Lutheran Church. Centennial Publication Committee. 110
Augustana Evangelical Lutheran Church. Columbia Conference. 110
Augustana Evangelical Lutheran Church. Iowa Conference. 110
Augustana Evangelical Lutheran Church. Kansas Conference. 110
Augustana Evangelical Lutheran church. Liturgy and ritual. 1546
Augustana Evangelical Lutheran Church. Luther League Council. 2272, 2297
Augustana Evangelical Lutheran Church. Minnesota Conference. 110, 1547
Augustana Evangelical Lutheran church. Nebraska conference. 2291
Augustana Evangelical Lutheran Church. Synodical Council. 110
Augustin, August F. 2284
Augustin, James M. 822
Augustin, Pius. 1142
Augustine. 111, 1024, 3669, 3670
Augustine, Father. 1027, 1639
Augustine, Irving Milton. 1886
Augustinian Educational Association. 833
Augustinus, Arelius. 112
Augustinus, Aurelius. 110, 111, 112, 113, 116, 117, 287, 387, 574, 586, 745, 955, 1024, 1265, 1476, 1486, 1601, 1657, 1785, 1804, 1885, 1886, 2173, 2217, 2336, 2583, 2980, 3334, 3413, 3422, 3460, 3461, 3477, 3634, 3635, 3667, 3714, 3790, 3796
Augustinus, Aurelius, Saint. 113, 116, 117, 422, 2173, 3714
Augustinus, Aurelius. 113, 1113, 2173, 2327, 3634
Augustinus, Aurelius, Saint,Bp. of Hippo. 3634
Augustinus Aurelius. 2327
Aukerman, Dale. 103
Aulaire, Ingri (Mortenson) d. 2249, 2662, 2665
Auld, William Muir. 1110, 2021
Aulen, Gustaf. 108
Aulen, Gustaf Emanuel Hildebrand. 108, 1116, 1719, 1783, 2009, 2010, 3033, 3640
Ault, Clare A. 1839
Aultman, Donald S. 2204, 3879
Aumann, Jordan. 3521
Aune, Kenneth E. 604
Aungerville, Richard. 1020
Auricchio, John. 3628
Auringer, Obadiah Cyrus. 2047
Aurora, W. Va. Saint Paul's Lutheran Church. 3122
Aus, George. 3183
Ausmus, Harry J. 3328
Austen, Wilfrid Abernethy Evers. 1167
Austgen, Robert J. 375, 2625
Austin, Arthur. 1862
Austin, Bill R. 1323, 2868
Austin, C Grey. 3056

Austin, Charles Marshall. 1242
[Austin, Dorothea]. 2693
Austin, Elva M. 2983
Austin, Emily M. 2600
Austin, Eugene Munger. 955
Austin, Frank Eugene. 1485
Austin, John D. 230
Austin, Lou. 902, 3538
Austin, Mary (Hunter) 1412, 1959, 2868
Austin, Mildred Chandler. 3832
Austin, Orval H. 2383
Austin, Richard Cartwright. 25, 1133
Austin, Robert A. 2942
Austin, Samuel. 3640
Austin, Telesphor. 851
Austin, William. 1994
Austin, William H. 3081, 3615
Austin, William R. 425, 3372
Australasian Association of Philosophy. 2474, 3259
Ausubel, Herman. 3050
Ausubel, Nathan. 2146, 1631, 2094
Auten, Edward. 736
Auth, Charles Robert. 3248
Auton, John G. 1204
Autrey, C E. 332, 532, 1562, 3230
Autry, Lola M. 899
Autton, Norman. 1258
Auzou, Georges. 289, 308
Avallone, Paul. 683, 937
Avalos, Beatrice. 804
Avancini, Nicolaus. 724, 1984
Ave Maria. 2859
Avebury, John Lubbock. 1323
Avedon, John F. 699
Aveling, Hugh. 872, 1946, 3868
Aven, Del. 2983
Averill, Edward Wilson. 2956, 2960
Averill, Lloyd James. 1056, 2221, 2953
Averill, William H. 1650
Averroes. 81
Avert, Margaret. 448
Avery, Adeline B E. 2383
-Avery, Ephraim K defendant. 1369
Avery, Giles Bushnell. 3394
Avery, Margaret. 450, 635
Avery, Myrtilla. 1884
Avery-Stuttle, Lilla Dale, 1855-1933. 2004
Avery, William S. 1434, 1436
Avesing, Frank B. 873
Avesta. English. 120
Avesta. English. 1972. 120
Avesta. Gathas. English. 121
Avesta Yashts. 2560
Avesta. Yasna. Gathas. English. 3898, 3899
Avesta. Yasna. Gathas. English & Avesta. 121, 3898
Avesta. Yasna. Gathas. Polyglot. 3899
Avey, Albert Edwin. 635, 3097
Avi-Yonah, Michael, 1904. 2764
Avicenna, 980-1037. 121, 1927, 3461
Avigdor, Isaac C. 3362
Avila P., Rafael. 836, 2254
Avis, Paul D. L. 1187
Avi-Yonah, Michael. 1944, 2765
Avril, A M. 1265
Avvakum, Protopope. 3022
Awe, Chulho. 2821
Awolalu, J. .Omosade. 3868
Axling, William. 2162, 2533, 2162
Axtell, Harold Lucius. 3245
Axtell, James Wickleff. 3550, 3551, 3564
Axtell, John Stockton. 133
Axup, Edward J. 1056, 1940
Ayandele, Emmanuel Ayankanmi. 2542
Aycock, Dell. 3337
Aycock, Don M. 1485
Aycock, Jarrette E. 1555
Aycock, Martha B. 3185
[Ayer, Joseph]. 121
Ayer, Joseph Cullen. 1198, 1197
Ayer, Lewis M. 1906
Ayer, William Ward. 160, 1357, 1513, 1562, 2024, 2067, 2562
Ayers, Anne. 2630
Ayers, Thomas W. 2538
Aylesworth, Thomas G. 95, 3826
Ayling, Stanley Edward. 1291, 3802
Aylsworth, Nicholas John. 133
Aylsworth, William Prince. 2948, 567
Aylward, Gladys. 121
Aylward, Stephen. 745
*Aymes, Maria de la Cruz. 1959
Ayre, G. B. 3146
Ayres, Anne. 2630
Ayres, Burt Wilmot. 670
Ayres, Clarence Edwin. 3314
Ayres, Francis O. 2191
Ayres, Lew. 91
Ayres, Rollin H. 955, 3884
Ayres, Samuel Gardiner. 1525, 2423
Ayres, Webb Wilford. 617
Ayres, William Adrian. 248
Ayrinhac, Henry Amans. 735, 807, 1166, 2341, 3264

Ayrton, Elizabeth. 3599
Aytoun, Robert Alexander. 1189, 1719
Azad, Abul Kalaam. 2184
Azad, Abul Kalam, maulana. 2184
Azamar, Linda (Prussing) 2225
Azariah, Vedanayakam Samuel. 951
Aziz, Ahmad. 1925
*Azrael. 1765
Azzam, Abdel Rahman. 2564, 2628

B

B Lewis 1906. 3302
B nai B rith Hillel Foundations. 2097
Ba a Ull ah, 1817-1892. 126
Baab, Otto J. 598
Baab, Otto Justice. 598, 2000, 2897, 3440, 3615
Baar, Marius. 1925
Baars, Conrad W. 771, 775
Baart, Peter A. 1241
Baba, 1877-1951. 122, 1790
[Babb, Clement Edwin]. 625, 942
Babb, Lawrence A. 1815
Babbage, Charles. 2672
Babbage, Stuart Barton. 337, 1067, 1754, 2232, 2322, 3230, 3392
Babbel, Frederick W. 1589
Babbel, June Andrew. 1008
Babbitt, Edmond Holt. 1258
Babbitt, Edwin Dwight. 3494
Babbitt, Marcy. 1037
Babbs, Arthur Vergil. 498
Babcock, Emma S. 1979
Babcock, Fern. 3537
Babcock, Maltbie Davenport. 1323, 2929
Babcock, Oliver Morell. 1578
Babcock, Winifred. 2018
Babin, David E. 2236, 2257, 2897, 2961
Babin, Pierre. 745, 939, 3146, 3167, 3169
Babington, John Albert. 3033
Babington, Thomas. 3146
Babis, Daniel George. 3741
[Babo, Bede]. 833
Babris, Peter J. 1097
Babson, Roger Ward. 955, 1056, 1116, 1182, 1250, 3440
Bacci, Antonio. 1433
Bach, Johann Sebastian. 736, 737, 917
Bach, Lester. 995, 1639
Bach, Marcus. 185, 595, 3324, 3777, 185, 881, 923, 1716, 1918, 2383, 2615, 2853, 3112, 3113, 3141, 3219, 3257, 3324, 3404, 3483, 3494, 3743, 3749, 3787
Bach, T J. 955, 1733, 1839, 2897
Bach, Thomas John. 2481
Bach, W H. 3494, 3601
Bache, Rene. 297, 1709
Bachelder, Horace Lyman. 2743
Bachelder, Louise. 3014
Bachhofer, Ludwig. 3316
Bachman, Albert John. 3347
Bachman, Calvin George. 2407
Bachman, John W. 3018
Bachman, Mae Graybill. 123
Bachmann, C. Charles. 2135, 2136
Bachmann, Ernest Theodore. 1809, 2290
[Bachofen, Charles Augustine]. 735, 775, 836, 2575, 2775
Bachofen, Johann Jakob. 3108, 3790
Bachrach, Bernard S. 1186
Bachrach, Jeanette (Wrottenberg) 3860
Bacigalupa, Andrea. 123, 875, 2359, 3283
Bacigalupo, Leonard. 1649, 1929
Bacik, James J. 61, 3018
Backes, James Adam. 1629, 1645
Backes, Magnus. 85
Backlund, Jonas Oscar. 61, 170
Backman, Eugene Louis. 1400
Backman, Milton Vaughn. 2615, 2619, 3324, 3428, 3782
Backus, Charles. 3050
Backus, Edwin Burdette. 2210
Backus, Irena Dorota. 196, 355
Backus, Isaac. 123, 146, 157, 1300, 2687, 3193
Backus, Issac. 157
Backus, William. 1329
Backus, William D. 980
[Bacle, Louis Lucien]. 1694
Bacon, Albion (Fellows) 1733
Bacon, Amos N. 2912
Bacon, Benjamin Wisner. 124, 442, 2795, 103, 124, 230, 387, 408, 418, 434, 516, 1169, 1978, 2006, 2007, 2631, 3334
Bacon, Bessie (Blanchard) 2507
[Bacon, David Francis]. 70, 3831
Bacon, Eliza Ann (Munroe) 124
Bacon, Ernest Wallace. 3523
Bacon, Eugenia (Jones) 1957, 2719
Bacon, Francis. 124, 2660
Bacon, George Blagden. 3566
Bacon, Henry Martyn. 2249
Bacon, Leonard. 91, 2223, 3009, 3596

[Bacon, Leonard Woolsey]. 124, 1343, 3546, 3737
Bacon, Margaret H. 1684
Bacon, Margaret Hope. 3835
Bacon, Mary Schell (Hoke) 1271, 1862
Bacon, Nathaniel. 3472
Bacon, Roger. 1645, 2314
Bacon, Thomas Scott. 80, 3742
Bacon, William. 1201, 3295
Bacote, Samuel William. 15, 157
Bacuez, Louis. 3124, 1288
Badarayana. 689, 3774
Badawy, Alexander. 85
*Badcock, D. I. 2157, 2529
Badcock, Francis John. 230, 372, 932, 1386
Bade, William Frederic. 3594, 498
Baden, Robert. 3884
Bader, Gershom. 2083
Bader, Golda Maude (Elam) 1303
Badger, Catharine Naomi. 3814
Badger, Colin Robert. 3536
Badger, George Henry. 1067
Badger, Joseph. 3808
Badham, Leslie Stephen Ronald. 2056
Badham, Paul. 1694
Badi, Joseph. 1928
Badia, Leonard F. 947, 2127, 3013
Badley, John Haden. 3056
Baecher, Charlotte Crawford. 2225
Baecher, Eharlotte Crawford. 2225
Baeck, Leo. 2113, 2828, 2087, 2137, 2151, 2828
Baelz, Peter. 3069
Baelz, Peter R. 1103, 2868
Baepler, Walter August. 1549
Baer, Dallas Clay. 570, 1265, 2027, 2034, 2212, 2298
Baer, Dorothea. 387
Baer, Yitzhak Fritz. 2085
Baerg, Harry J. 1379
Baerg, John. 2504, 3387
Baerwald, Reuben C. 1691
Baets, Maurice de. 3329
Baez, Camargo Gonzalo. 2461
Bagby, Daniel G. 43
Bagby, David Young. 2016, 2414
Bagby, James Thomas. 2427
Bagdoyan, Bagsar Manoog. 101, 1056
Bagg, Edward Parsons. 1838
Baggarly, Ioanne D. 38
Baggott, Louis John. 1443
Baggs, Ralph L. 3056, 3141
Baghdigian, Bagdasar Krekor. 1412
Bagley, Clarence Booth. 824
Baha Ullah, 1817-1892. 126, 127, 129, 130
Baha'i Committee on Music. 1860
Baha Allah. 127
Bahadur, Krishna Prakash. 3718
Baha Ullah. 125, 127, 130
Bahir. English & Hebrew. 721
Bahm, Archie J. 700, 1116, 2416, 3113
Bahmsen, Greg L. 1844
Bahr, Howard M. 1612
Bahr, Karl Christian Wilhelm Felix. 555
Bahr, Robert. 1576, 2310
Bahti, Tom. 1903
Baierl, Joseph John. 745, 747, 1385, 1419, 1750, 2370, 3139, 3224, 3264, 1142
Baikie, James. 289, 308
Bailes, Porter Marcellus. 160, 1555
Bailey, Alanson Q. 2210
Bailey, Albert Edward. 1114, 919, 1871, 1957, 2066, 2087, 2761, 2765, 399, 1957
Bailey, Alice A. 2722, 2067, 2379, 2722, 2994, 3683
Bailey, Alice Anne (La Trobe-Bateman) 2067, 2723, 3683, 2723, 3683
Bailey, Alice Anne Latiobe Bateman. 2723
Bailey, Alice Anne (LaTrobe-Bateman) 2067, 2379, 2723, 2994, 3683, 2067, 2723, 3318
Bailey, Ambrose M. 151
Bailey, Ambrose Moody. 1562, 2791, 2897
Bailey, Augustus Caesar. 1985, 2897, 3372
Bailey, Barry. 1737, 2434, 3348
Bailey, Carl W. 826
Bailey, Carolyn Sherwin. 3549
Bailey, Charles James Nice. 3668, 3855
Bailey, Charles R. 867
Bailey, Cyril. 3245
[Bailey, Daniel E]. 3494
Bailey, Derrick Sherwin. 182, 2336, 3038, 3389, 3522
Bailey, Edward L. 151
Bailey, Edwin Dunton. 2976
Bailey, Emma E. 3835
Bailey, Faith Coxe. 1357, 1857, 2157, 3784
Bailey, Foster. 1660, 2723
Bailey, George W. 3337
Bailey, Harold S. 1015
Bailey, Harold Walter. 711

Bailey, Helen L. 2487, 2529
Bailey, Henry Turner. 2760, 669
Bailey, Hugh C. 2631, 3468
Bailey, Jack S. 3539
Bailey, James H. 2018, 3348
Bailey, James Henry. 3237
Bailey, James Martin. 676, 3189, 3254, 3856
Bailey, John Amedee. 1056
Bailey, John Barton. 3337
Bailey, John William. 2803, 1047, 992
Bailey, Keith M. 2464
Bailey, Kenneth E. 428, 429, 431, 603, 1739, 2024
Bailey, Kenneth Kyle. 3468
Bailey, Lloyd R. 563, 1416
[Bailey, Melville Knox]. 659
Bailey, Ney. 130, 930
Bailey, Page. 1103
Bailey, Paul Dayton. 2600, 1782, 1902, 2600, 2616, 3860
Bailey, Pearle Provine. 1305
Bailey, Phillip James. 41
Bailey, Ralph. 1349
Bailey, Raymond. 2412, 2645, 3739
Bailey, Robert W. 159, 558, 1257, 1303, 1412, 3003
Bailey, Roscoe J. 955
Bailey, Rufus William. 1607
Bailey, Samuel. 185
Bailey, Thomas Melville. 2917
Bailey, Wilfred M. 2480, 3003
*Bailey, William Edwin. 955, 1013
Bailey, Wilson Gill. 2986, 3494
Bailie, Alfred J. 3494
Bailie, Victoria Worley. 130, 2507
Baillargeon, Anatole O. 2897
Baille, Donald Macpherson. 1234
Baillie, Alexander Stuart. 2056
Baillie, Donald Macpherson. 2035, 1234, 1892, 2035, 3262
Baillie, John. 1562, 1809, 61, 1281, 1436, 1739, 1740, 1886, 2035, 2888, 3056, 3224, 1010, 1436, 1740, 2888, 3051, 3056, 3097, 3362, 2705
Baillie, John Launcelot. 1263
Bailly, Auguste. 1639
Bain, Alexander. 2463
Bain, Foree. 2751
Bain, John Wallace. 2930
Bainbridge, Lucy (Seaman) 2518, 3833
Bainbridge, William Sims. 2866
Baines-Griffiths, David. 955, 1589
Bainton, Roland H. 3377
Bainton, Roland Herbert. 130, 1172, 1184, 1185, 1189, 1197, 1525, 1818, 1957, 2272, 2336, 2687, 3033, 3037, 3192, 3377, 3792, 3794, 3862
Bainton, Ronald Herbert. 3377
Bainum, George Washington. 1379
Bainvel, Jean Vincent. 1589, 3288, 3270
Bair, Bill. 130, 1254
Bair, Hazel. 3146
Baird, Alexander T. 3494
Baird, Alexander William Stewart. 2778
Baird, Andrew J. 1401
Baird, Annie L A. 2481
Baird, Annie Laurie (Adams) 2536
Baird, Charles Washington. 183, 1852, 2929, 3124
Baird, Doyle J. 141
Baird, Ernest Clay. 2225
Baird, George M P. 2491
Baird, Henry Martyn. 130, 196, 1497, 1803, 1852
Baird, James Oscar. 2233
Baird, Jesse H. 3348
Baird, Jesse Hays. 1010, 1315, 3298
Baird, John Edward. 2897
Baird, Joseph Armstrong. 1161
Baird, Joseph Arthur. 387, 1505, 2007, 2061
Baird, Lula Doyle. 3763
Baird, Mary Julian. 764, 2363
Baird, Mollie Elnora. 2529
Baird, P. J. 3337
Baird, Paul Jesse. 3337
Baird, Richard H. 130, 2536
Baird, Robert. 1181, 2231, 3301, 3737
Baird, Robert D. 1895
Baird, Samuel John. 2919, 2925
Baird, Thomas Dickson. 2984
Baird, William. 323, 345, 346, 375, 2007, 2795
Baird, William [Robb]. 375, 2795
Baird, William Robb. 1691
Baisnee, Jules Albert. 2674
Bajema, Clifford E. 3
Bakan, David. 2996
Baker, Abijah Richardson. 3334
Baker, Albert Edward. 720, 185
Baker, Aleta Blanche. 1607
Baker, Alonzo L. 3318
Baker, Alonzo Lafayette. 1379, 3257, 3379, 3448
Baker, Archibald Gillies. 2518, 1172
Baker, Arthur Mulford. 955, 3056

Baker, Augustine. 90
Baker, Betty. 1384, 2770
Baker, Bo. 160
Baker, C S. 421
Baker, Charles F. 327, 3640, 3660
Baker, Charles Richard. 2888
Baker City, Or. (Diocese) 3162
Baker, Clara Belle. 617, 3146
Baker, Clara Worth. 1598, 3494
Baker, Cosette. 3173
Baker, Cozy. 980
Baker, D. L. 450
Baker, David Walter. 2055
Baker, Delores. 3549, 3550
Baker, Dolores. 3169
Baker, Edna Dean. 1996, 2171, 3163, 3857
Baker, Edward Mayer. 3716
Baker, Elizabeth. 1607, 3830
Baker, Emilie Kip. 3197
Baker, Eric W. 179
Baker, Eugene. 896
Baker, Francis Aloysius. 862
Baker, Frank. 1516, 2428, 2438, 3802, 3806
Baker, George. 955
Baker, George Claude. 2431
Baker, Gilbert. 2559
Baker, Gladys. 1363
Baker, Gordon H. 2012
Baker, Gordon Pratt. 179, 571, 1006, 1562
Baker, H. A. 139
Baker, H H. 301
Baker, Harold Edwin. 3348
[Baker, Harriette Newell (Woods) 3405
[Baker, Harry Edgar]. 2061
Baker, Helen Elizabeth (Otte) 2549
Baker, Henry. 748
Baker, Herschel Clay. 2319
Baker, Isaac Newton. 1907
Baker, J. Wayne. 713, 1377
Baker, James Chamberlain. 3802
Baker, James Millard. 1895
Baker, James Thomas. 617, 2412
Baker, John Austin. 2383, 2949, 3660
Baker, John Clapp. 158, 171
Baker, Joseph Baer. 1443, 1555, 2624, 3113
Baker, Julius L. 3360
Baker, Leonard. 125, 3016
Baker, Liva. 3140
Baker, Martha. 980
Baker, Mary Ellen Penny. 876, 2379
Baker, Nelson Alloway. 2322, 3477
Baker, Nelson B. 651, 1527
Baker, Newton Diehl. 3743
Baker, Nina (Brown) 1809
Baker, Oren Huling. 145, 2996
Baker, Osmon Cleander. 2442
Baker, Pacificus, 1695-1774. 1263, 2210
Baker, Pat A. 992, 2383
Baker, Rannie Belle. 2649, 2822
Baker, Ray Stannard. 1056
Baker, Richard. 2984, 3605
*Baker, Richard C. 1015
Baker, Richard Terrill. 3440, 1281, 1935, 2491
Baker, Robert A. 3699
Baker, Robert Andrew. 30, 151, 152, 170, 171, 888, 1172, 3316, 3465, 3466, 3467, 3699
Baker, Robert J. 131, 2383
Baker, Roger. 1585
Baker, Sarah Schoonmaker (Tuthill) 1443
Baker, Septina. 1959
Baker, Sheridan. 1054, 1822
Baker, Smith. 2225
Baker, Thomas Eugene. 1690
Baker University, Baldwin, Kan. Library. 213
Baker, Wesley C. 522, 635, 658, 951, 1107, 2791
Baker, William Deal. 2830
Baker, William H. 3337
Baker, William M. 45, 3525
Baker, William Mumford. 131, 2414
Baketel, Oliver Sherman. 2425, 2458
Bakewell, Francis F. 3485
Bakhaila, Mikael. 1540
Bakhtiar, Laleh. 3542
Bakker, Jim. 131, 981, 1576, 3539
Bakst, James. 2634
Bakvis, Herman. 875, 2165
Balasubrahmanyam, S. R. 3599
Balasuriya, Tissa. 2254
Balbani, Niccolo. 1366, 3778
Balch, David L. 325, 1603
Balch, Stephen Bloomer. 2822, 3279
Balch, William Monroe. 3440
Balchin, John F. 230
Balcom, Mary Gilmore. 813
Balcomb, Raymond E. 613, 3528
Baldinger, Albert H. 458, 464
Baldridge, Samuel Coulter. 672
Balducci, Ernesto. 2123
Baldwin, Alfred Graham. 292

Baldwin, Charles Jacobs. 3737
[Baldwin, Charles N]. 661
Baldwin, Charles Sears. 1719
Baldwin, Edward Chauncey. 210, 571
Baldwin, Eugene F. 1653, 2129
Baldwin, George Colfax. 337, 1290, 3494, 3838
Baldwin, Gordon Cortis. 3110
Baldwin, Harmon Allen. 1444, 1822, 2156, 2636, 3138, 3299
Baldwin, Harry Anderson. 2061
Baldwin, Howard H. 1810
Baldwin, James Mark. 2242
Baldwin, Jesse Armon. 2420
Baldwin, Josephine L. 588, 3551, 3859
Baldwin, Joyce G. 505, 529
Baldwin, Judson D. 3238
Baldwin, Kenneth H. 32
Baldwin, Lindley J. 2620
Baldwin, Lizzie Thomas. 635
Baldwin, Louis. 928, 1959
Baldwin, Marshall Whithed. 24, 1143, 1186, 1197, 1198, 2768
Baldwin, Maud Junkin. 3146, 3169, 3528
Baldwin, Monica. 2580
Baldwin, P. C. 3029
Baldwin, R. Mae. 1525
Baldwin, Samuel Davies. 275, 2714
Baldwin, Stanley C. 2061
Baldwin, Stephen Livingstone. 2518
Baldwin, Summerfield. 1185
Bale, Christian Emil. 381
Bale, John, 1495-1563. 452, 2579, 2736, 3605
*Bales, James D. 1319
Bales, James D. 101, 681, 1319, 1598, 1716, 2061, 2633
Bales, Tipton C. 1304
Balfour, Alexander Hugh Bruce. 2915
Balfour, Arthur James Balfour. 185, 1853, 3607
Balfour, George William. 3494
Balfour, John Hutton. 480
Balfour, Robert C. 3697
Balfour, Walter. 1427, 1527, 1699, 1850, 3197, 3262, 3751
Balguy, John. 3782
Baliley, Faith Coxe. 1361
Balin, Peter. 1471
Balk, Alfred. 1242
Balke, Willem. 36, 727
Ball, Charles Ferguson. 1793, 2795
Ball, Charles Otis. 242, 1959
Ball, E. O. 1905
Ball, Elsie. 1979, 3146, 3763
[Ball, John]. 1652
Ball, Robert O. 2055
Ball, Robert R. 1010
Ball, Timothy Horton. 304, 427, 3071
[Ball, Timothy Horton] 1826-1913. 1240
Ball, Virginia. 1417
Ball, Wayland Dalrymple. 1578
Balla, Ignazia. 2569
Ballantine, Elisha. 2035
Ballantine, William Gay. 635, 230, 418, 659
Ballantyne, Murray. 1363
Ballard, Addison. 1047, 1444
Ballard, Adela J. 2526
Ballard, Dorothy. 694
Ballard, Frank. 3072, 61
Ballard, Frank Hewett. 2795
[Ballard, Guy W.]. 1444, 2311
[Ballard, Guy Warren]. 1444
Ballard, Jerry. 3817
Ballard, John Hudson. 674
Balleine, George Reginald. 1220, 1551, 1554
Balleine, R. W. 650
Ballenger, Albion Fox. 1067
[Ballentine, Frank Schell] 1859. 248, 301, 1732
Ballinger, J. F. 1653
Ballinger, James L. 1200
Ballou, Adin. 131, 1189, 1578, 3494, 3753
Ballou, Benedict. 847, 1826
Ballou, Earle Holt. 2507
Ballou, Hosea. 1699, 3751, 3752, 3753, 3754, 3755, 3752, 3754
Ballou, Maturin Murray. 131
Ballou, Moses. 183, 2322
Ballou, Robert Oleson. 1975, 600, 1732, 3056, 3197, 3268, 3403
Balm, Catherine Atkinson (Miller) 1247, 3884
Balmes, Jaime Luciano. 1542
Balmforth, Ramsden. 346, 2561
Balph, Florence. 2529
Balsiger, Dave. 2711
Balskus, Pat. 1288, 1379, 2203, 3279
Balswick, Jack O. 2264
Baltazar, Eulalio R. 2943, 3017, 3566, 3592
Balthasar, Hans Ure von. 3650

Balthasar, Hans Urs von. 175, 699, 775, 793, 995, 996, 1056, 1116, 1355, 1508, 1735, 1736, 1817, 1818, 2152, 3471, 3525, 3632, 3650
Baltimore. Beth Tfiloh congregation. 3577
Baltimore catechism. 766, 767, 768
Baltimore catechnism. 768
Baltimore. Church home and infirmary. 132
Baltimore. Church of the Redeemer. 2775
Baltimore. First Presbyterian church. 2917
Baltimore First Unitarian Church of Baltimore (Universalist and Unitarian) 132
Baltimore. St. James' church (Catholic) 755
Baltimore. St. John the Evangelist Church. 1273
Baltzer, Frederick. 3461
Baltzly, Oliver D. 745, 2279
Baly, Denis. 281, 1116, 2678, 3756
Balzac, Honore de. 100, 1375
Balzani, Ugo. 1822
Balzoflore, Filippo. 3580
Bamber, L. 3494
Bamberger, Bernard Jacob. 538, 557, 2080, 2137, 2146, 2952
Bamborough, Philip. 86
Bambrough, Renford. 3107
Ban, Arline J. 144, 155, 938, 3857
Ban, Joseph D. 1056, 1959, 3146
Banahan, John S. 2346
Bancroft, Aaron. 1337, 3724
Bancroft, Anne. 3113, 3124, 3891
Bancroft, Charles W. H. 3031
Bancroft, Emery H. 3640
Bancroft, Emery Herbert. 3640
Bancroft, George. 2820
Bancroft, John Raymond. 1316
Bancroft, Richard. 3008
Bancroft, Samuel Putnam. 1493
Bancroft, William Henry. 3348
Band, Benjamin. 2102
Bandas, Rudolph G. 745
Bandas, Rudolph George. 647, 745, 804, 1628, 2061, 3453, 3485
Bandel, Betty. 1321, 2597
Bandelier, Adolph Francis Alphonse. 3702
Bander, Peter. 2863, 3473
Bandey, David Wallis. 133
Bandtlow, Peter. 2737
Bane, Martin J. 813, 851, 2335, 2500, 2537, 3437
Banerjee, H. N. 3052
Banerjee, Hemendra Nath. 3055
Banerjee, P. 1897
Baney, Ralph E. 1409
Banez, Domingo. 3695
Banfield, Frank. 3802
Bang, Jacob Peter. 1116
Bangert, William V. 1587, 1945, 1946
Bangor, Me. Central Congregational church. 1332
Bangor theological seminary, Bangor, Me. 133, 3681
Bangs, Carl Oliver. 83, 1319
Bangs, Heman. 133
Bangs, Nathan. 83, 133, 1702, 2450, 2454, 2474, 2688, 3640, 3680, 3818
Banier, Antoine. 2649
Banigan, Sharon (Church) 898, 899
Banister, Corrilla. 2986
Banker, Floyd E. 3806
Banker, John C. 1292
Banker, Marie Sarrafian. 3768
Bankhead, Reid E. 678, 2610
Banki, Judith. 2152, 3770
Banks, Alfred John Gayner. 923, 3405
Banks, Charles Edward. 3006, 3820
Banks, Charles Eugene. 3582
Banks, Edgar James. 197, 552
Banks, Emily (Tiptaft) 2513
Banks, Florence (Aiken) 481, 647
Banks, Gabriel Conklyn. 1466
Banks, Helen Ward. 197, 1950
Banks, John Shaw. 3640
Banks, Joseph Ambrose. 1612
Banks, Louis Albert. 213, 304, 604, 651, 1357, 1361, 1444, 1506, 1524, 1555, 1950, 2024, 2886, 2897, 3232, 3337, 3348, 3596, 3869, 3884, 1555, 1562, 1839, 1874, 2425, 2434
Banks, Martha Burr. 2733
Banks, Natalie N. 2672
Banks, Robert J. 375, 1163, 1958, 2201
Banks, Theodore Howard. 2470
Banks, William L. 317, 552, 1430, 2129, 2681
Banna, Hasan. 1922, 1933
Banna, Joseph. 955
Banner of love. 2941
Banner, William Augustus. 1534
Bannerman, David Douglas. 1163

Bannerman, James. 1116
Bannerman-Phillips, E Ivy A, 1900. 95
Banning, Pierson Worrall. 2409
Bannister, Arthur Thomas. 1804
Bannister, Henry Marriott. 3333
Bannister, Paul. 2986
Banowsky, William Slater. 3, 1067, 1273
Banvard, Joseph. 3288
Banzer, Joseph, & co. 3333
Baptist-Catholic Regional Conference, Daytona Beach, Fla., 1971. 3467
Baptist Church Extension Society of Brooklyn and Queens. 155
Baptist congress. 140
Baptist General Conference of America. 140, 152
Baptist hour (Radio program) 160
Baptist Joint Committee on Public Affairs. 1140, 1149, 1269
Baptist training union. Southwide conference. 4th, Birmingham, Ala., Dec. 31, 1935-Jan. 3, 1936. 141
Baptist training union, Southwide conference. 5th, Memphis, Tenn., Dec. 31, 1940-Jan. 3, 1941. 3559
Baptist world alliance. 2d Congress, Philadelphia, 1911. 141
Baptist World Alliance. 8th Congress, Cleveland, 1950. 147
Baptist world alliance. 4th Congress, Toronto, 1928. 142
Baptist world alliance. 6th congress, Atlanta, 1939. 169
Baptist World Congress 11th, Miami Beach, 1965. 141
Baptist world alliance. 3d Congress, Stockholm, 1923. 141
Baptist young people's union of America. 142, 172, 1166, 1562, 3876, 3877
Baptist Youth World Conference, 5th, Toronto, 1958. 3881
Baptist Youth World Conference. 6th, Beirut, 1963. 147
Baptist Youth World Conference, 7th, Bern, 1968. 147
[Baptista. 3277
Baptists. 140
Baptists. Board of education. 155
Baptists. Georgia. Sarepta Baptist association. 1270
Baptists. Illinois. Salem Baptist association. 142
Baptists. Kentucky. General association of colored Baptists. 154
Baptists. Kentucky. Russell's Creek association. 154
Baptists. Maryland. Middle district association. 154
Baptists. Maryland. State association. 154
Baptists. Maryland. Western district association. 154
Baptists. Massachusetts. Berkshire association. 143
Baptists. Massachusetts. Framingham Baptist association. 143
Baptists. Mississippi. Convention. 156
Baptists. Missouri. Macon association. 156
Baptists. Missouri. Wyaconda Baptist association. 156
Baptists. New Hampshire. Association of Ministers on Piscataqua-River. 1604
Baptists. New York. Onondaga association. 142
Baptists. North Carolina. State convention. 152
Baptists. North Carolina. Union association (White) 158
Baptists. Oregon. Corvallis association. 159
Baptists. Pennsylvania. Pennsylvania Baptist convention. 159
Baptists. Pennsylvania. Philadelphia association. 145, 159
Baptists. South Carolina. Charleston Association. 150
Baptists. South Caroline. State convention. 169
Baptists. Texas. General convention. Executive board. 141, 170
Baptists. Washington (State) Washington Baptist convention. 142
Barack, Nathan A. 2116, 2137, 2141, 3261
Barackman, Paul F. 446
Baradi, Mauro. 955
Bar-Adon, Dorothy Ruth (Kahn) 3896
Barauna Guliherme. 836
Barbanell, Maurice. 3494
Barbar, Aghil M. 79, 657
Barbeau, Clayton C. 1615
Barber, Arthur. 1323
Barber, Charles Fitch. 3494
Barber, Cyril J. 552, 560, 955, 2204, 2346, 2683, 2773, 3089, 3612
Barber, Edward. 3270
Barber, Estelle Bianton. 3765
Barber, Estelle Blanton. 2047, 3857

Barber, John Warner. 219, 1013, 3113, 3197
Barber, Lora Ella. 1694
Barber, Lucie W. 939
Barber, Richard W. 2664
Barber, Walter Lanier. 3197
Barber, William Joseph. 1465
Barbet, Pierre. 1997
Barbieri, Albert. 2361
Barbieri, Louis A. 447
Barbieri, Sante Uberto. 2955
Barborka, Geoffrey A. 671, 2316, 2663, 3683
Barbotin, Edmond. 61, 1730, 2319
Barbould, Anna Letitia (Aikin) 1862
Barbour, Carence Augustus. 2402
Barbour, Clarence Augustus. 230
Barbour, Clifford Edward. 3410
Barbour, Dorothy Dickinson. 3146, 3185
Barbour, Hugh. 595, 1637, 1678, 1684
Barbour, Ian G. 3081
Barbour, James Murray. 659
Barbour, John. 1202
Barbour, Nelson H. 103
Barbour, Robert Stewart. 2480
Barbour, Russell. 919
Barbour, Russell B. 919, 1132
Barbre, Myrtle (Milford) 617
Barbusse, Henri. 1959
Barclay, George. 304, 1067
Barclay, Glen. 2723
Barclay, John. 1292, 1674
Barclay, Kate. 2855
Barclay, Oliver R. 61
Barclay, Robert. 1684, 58, 747, 1678, 1680, 1681, 1684, 1678
Barclay, Robert Anderson. 557
Barclay, Vera C. 3279
Barclay, Vera Charlesworth. 1578, 3284
Barclay, W. C. 103
Barclay, Wade Crawford. 8, 635, 1436, 1604, 2204, 2441, 2449, 2549, 3146, 3168, 3551
Barclay, Wilbur Fisk. 2456
Barclay, William. 70, 119, 173, 179, 180, 217, 317, 337, 341, 346, 375, 381, 397, 405, 408, 422, 429, 461, 577, 601, 647, 928, 942, 1067, 1195, 1265, 1312, 1357, 1430, 1562, 1577, 1768, 1959, 1979, 2010, 2017, 2024, 2250, 2383, 2795, 2888, 3406, 3856, 3882, 929, 1959, 2888
Barclay, William L. 1430
Barclay, William. 72, 1827, 2035
Barcus, Nancy B. 61
Bard, Andreas. 61, 1067, 3091
Bar-David, Molly (Lyons) 2765
Barden, William. 2364
Bardens, Dennis. 1709
Bardin, Shlomo. 2118
Bardis, Panos Demetrios. 1412
Bardo thodol. 707
Bardothodoe. 707, 3895
Bardsley, Cuthbert. 61
Bardsley, Cyril Charles Bowman. 1250, 1562
Barfer, Walter. 1768
Barfield, Janice. 173, 981
Barfield, Owen. 50
Barfoot, Earl F. 3530
Bargellini, Piero. 1404, 2852
Barger, R. Curtis. 939, 3385
Bargrave, John. 24, 738
Barham, Fisher. 3716
Barham, Marie. 2544
Baring, Margery Louise. 3330, 3477
Baringgould Sabine. 492
Baring-Gould, Sabine. 492, 3113, 3279
Barish, Louis. 2110, 2151, 3011
Barkatullah, Qazi Muhammad. 2007
Barker, Alfred Trevor. 3689
Barker, Anthony, full name: Eric Anthony Barker. 2540
Barker, Arthur Edward. 2471
Barker, C L. 3227
Barker, Charles Edward. 2996
Barker, Cicely Mary. 1862
Barker, Dorothy Oswald. 617
Barker, Elsa. 1979, 3495
Barker, Ernest. 1142, 1390
Barker, Esther T. 3404
Barker, Glenn W. 408
Barker, Harold P. 1444, 3318
Barker, Henry. 254
Barker, James Louis. 2610, 2615
Barker, John Dudley. 2156
Barker, John H J. 1822
Barker, John Marshall. 2452, 3440
Barker, Joseph. 1956
Barker, Joseph Edmund. 1458, 1513
Barker, Joseph G. 1802
Barker, Kenneth L. 492
Barker, Kenneth R. 940
Barker, Leo Vaughn. 2191
Barker, Rachel. 3851
Barker, Reginald J. 2173
Barker, Rosalind Allen. 1542

Barker, William Pierson. 70, 213, 217, 332, 337, 443, 492, 923, 1959, 2868, 2980, 3838
Barkley, H. E. 3807
Barkley, John Monteith. 2929
Barkman, Alma. 173, 930, 3843
Barkman, Paul Friesen. 2514, 2996
Barks, Herbert B. 2461
Barkway, Lumsden. 72, 2035
Barlaam and Joasaph. English & Ethiopic. 700
Barlag, Roy. 2212, 2298
Barlass, William. 3337
Barlett, Laile E. 3725
Barlow, Claude W. 1018
Barlow, Frank. 1483, 1516, 1761
Barlow, Fred. 213
Barlow, Fred S. 3551
Barlow, Richard Burgess. 3703
Barlow, Sanna Morrison. 1749, 2497, 2844, 3237
Barlow, T. Ed. 1169, 1848
Barlow, Walter. 2004, 1562
Barlow, Warren Sumner. 1472, 3206
Barlow, William. 1783
Barmann, Lawrence F. 1850, 2562
Barmby, James. 1773
Barnabas. 912
Barnard, Allison F. 3299
Barnard, David. 3838
Barnard, Floy Merwyn. 3828
Barnard, Henry E. 3495
Barnard, John. 955, 1504, 2016, 3295
Barnard, Laura Belle. 2553
Barnard, Leslie William. 76, 2161
Barnard, Mary. 2648
Barnard, Naomi Holt. 1113
Barnard, Percy Mordaunt. 1287
Barnard, Thomas. 3814
Barndollar, W. W. 1467, 2007
Barnes, A.M. 3890
Barnes, Albert. 59, 103, 174, 466, 1097, 1555, 2160, 2795, 2930, 3295, 3424, 3425
[Barnes, Annie Maria] 1857. 659, 3027
Barnes, Arthur Stapylton. 174
Barnes, Arthur Stapylton. 918, 2824, 3245
Barnes, Calvin Rankin. 3298, 3580
Barnes, Camilus Milo. 3458
Barnes, Charles Randall. 197, 213, 242
Barnes, Charles Wesley. 3440
Barnes, Claude Teancum. 174
Barnes, Donald L. 3146
Barnes, Earl. 1589
Barnes, Ernest William. 1189, 3077, 3495
Barnes, George Owen. 1555, 1750, 1928, 3338, 45
Barnes, Harry Elmer. 1047, 1090
Barnes, Hazel Estella. 1583, 2660
Barnes, Isaac A. 2459
Barnes, Kathleen H. 902, 1230, 2344, 2478, 2952
Barnes, Lavonia Jenkins. 1274
Barnes, Lemuel Call. 30, 2525, 2526
Barnes, Mary Stephenson. 3495
Barnes, Roswell Parkhurst. 1085, 1133
Barnes, William Emery. 1633, 2061
Barnes, William Goodman. 197
Barnes, William J. 2539
Barnes, William Wright. 3466
Barnes, Woodruff L. 3234
Barnes-Lawrence, Arthur Evelyn. 2250
Barnetson, Edwin. 2000
Barnetson, John. 1588
Barnett, Albert Edward. 333, 372, 375, 408, 432, 2024
Barnett, Eugene E. 2507
Barnett, Homer Garner. 1897, 1901
Barnett, James Monroe. 1408
Barnett, Joe R. 573, 584, 692
Barnett, Leon H. 2262
Barnett, Lionel David. 1895
Barnett, Minyard Merrell. 3884
Barnett, Richard David. 486
Barnett, Samuel Augustus. 174
Barnett, Stella Odell. 880
Barnett, Walter. 1959
Barnette, Henlee H. 942, 1139, 2676, 3656, 3784
Barnette, Jasper Newton. 952, 1562, 1574, 3551
Barney, Kenneth D. 330, 364, 458, 469, 981, 3348, 3660
Barnhart, Joe E. 1357, 1483, 1552, 1754, 3056, 3097
Barnhart, Nancy. 617
Barnhart, Nathaniel Gideon. 691
Barnhart, Phil. 1132, 1485
Barnhouse, Donald. 61
Barnhouse, Donald Grey. 471, 955, 1823, 1950, 2050, 2930, 3183, 332, 452, 471, 479, 524, 1010, 1065, 1427, 1839, 2930, 3348
Barnitz, Harry W. 2689
Barnitz, James Denning. 1323
Barnlund, A W. 375

Barns, Lucy. 3752
Barnum, Samuel Weed. 797
Barnwell, Robert Woodward. 1240
Barnwell, William Hazzard. 434
Baron, David. 543, 600, 2077, 2414
Barón, Joseph Louis. 3014, 3370
Baron, Salo Wittmayer. 2087, 2111, 2145, 2671
Baron, Samuel Halevi. 899
Baronti, Gerve. 1813
Baroody, Anees Tannus. 3124
Baroux, Louis. 849, 2865
Barr, Browne. 1244, 1339, 2785, 2787
Barr, Enoch Fitch. 3074
Barr, George. 217
Barr, James. 230, 238, 505, 1691, 1797, 3701, 200
Barr, John. 2259
Barr, Josiah Henry. 2440
Barr, Lillie E. 2847
Barr, Margaret. 3146
Barr, Mary Margaret Harrison. 3786
Barr, O. Sydney. 72, 3421
Barr, Pat. 2507
Barr, Robert R. 3658
Barr, Thomas E. 3607
Barr, Walter. 2309
Barrachina, Ignatius. 113, 3492
Barrack, Howard J. 2316, 3782
Barraclough, Geoffrey. 190, 807, 1282, 2768
Barragar, Pam. 1478
Barratt, Norris Stanley. 2829
Barreau, Jean Claude. 2553, 2868, 3056, 3660
Barreiro, Alvaro. 933
Barrell, Dilys. 2912
Barrell, Joseph. 2473
Barren Hill, Pa. St. Peter's Lutheran Church. 2282
Barrere, Dorothy B. 2207
Barres, Oliver. 1363, 2491
Barrett, Benjamin Fiske. 2690, 3569
Barrett, C K. 1827
Barrett, Charles D. 3660
Barrett, Charles Kingsley. 70, 298, 322, 375, 387, 407, 414, 418, 466, 1827, 2035, 2103, 2271
Barrett, David B. 1073
Barrett, Earl E. 2180
Barrett, Edward John Boyd. 755, 780, 826, 1944, 2264, 2939, 3197
Barrett, Ethel. 72, 174, 175, 337, 406, 492, 617, 631, 928, 955, 981, 991, 1300, 1323, 2824, 3801, 3822
Barrett, Florence Elizabeth (Perry). 175, 3495
Barrett, Francis. 2731
Barrett, George. 399
Barrett, George West. 181, 1288, 1527, 2210, 2211
Barrett, Harrison Delivan. 3237, 3495
Barrett, Ivan J. 1959, 1233
Barrett, J. Edward. 2322, 3660
Barrett, J O. 3495
Barrett, John. 117
Barrett, John Pressley. 1444
Barrett, Joseph O. 1349, 2810, 3495
Barrett, Joseph P. 3273
Barrett, Kate Waller. 1629
Barrett, Leonard Andrew. 1047
Barrett, Leonard E. 2681, 3022
Barrett, Patricia. 1149
Barrett, Roxanna Mae (Stephens) 3206
Barrett, Samuel. 3124
Barrett, Thomas van Braam. 175, 1607
Barrett, William. 1583
Barrett, William Alexander. 1321
Barrett, William Edmund. 1701, 2507, 2805
Barrett, William Fletcher. 1029, 3495
Barrickman, Van Ara. 3072
Barrington, Arthur H. 3495
Barrington, George. 981
Barrington, Leo. 2577
Barrington, Porter. 3828
Barritt, Denis P. 1139
Barrois, Georges Augustin. 315, 923, 2236, 3599
Barron, Howard H. 1859
Barron, J B. 1319
Barron, Mary Catherine. 217
Barron, Vance. 1265, 2930
Barrosse, Thomas. 1730, 2266, 2597
Barrow, Alfred Henry. 2524
Barrow, Andrew. 1221, 1516
Barrow, George Alexander. 3097
Barrow, George de Symons. 1404
[Barrow, Henry]. 697
Barrow, Isaac. 1216, 2767
Barrow, John Graves. 657
Barrows, Charles Henry. 2035
Barrows, Charles Mason. 2409
Barrows, Cliff. 1871
Barrows, Elijah Porter. 2761, 3124
Barrows, John Henry. 91, 394, 1047, 3852
Barrows, Mary Eleanor. 3124

Barrows, Samuel June. 1699
Barrows, William. 133, 3006
Barrows, William J. 3002
Barrus, Ben M. 1396
Barry, Clara (Reasoner) 2897
Barry, Colman James. 1198, 825, 826, 1198, 1309, 2627, 3275
Barry, David W. 1277, 2811
Barry, Frank Russell. 61, 108, 362, 364, 1056, 2322
Barry, Freedom. 3477
Barry, George Duncan. 3203
Barry, Henry Aloysius. 1827, 3288
Barry, James Patrick. 1589
Barry, Joseph Gayle Hurd. 74, 1827, 2246, 2383, 2774, 2868, 3056, 3224, 3415, 3124
Barry, Mack C. 3640
Barry, Mary Gerald. 2572
Barry, R. K. 124, 2753
Barry, Vincent E. 3433
Barry, William A. 3475
Barry, William Francis. 2702, 3077, 230, 755, 757, 2768, 3124, 3245
Bars, Henry. 185, 1589
Barsoum, Peter. 93
Barstad, Glenna. 923
Barstow, Robbins Wolcott. 1436, 1444
Bartak, Josef Pavel. 1857
Bartchy, S. Scott. 323, 3424
Bartek, Edward J. 1323
Bartel, Floyd G. 1170
Bartell, Ernest. 830
Bartell, Jan Bryant. 175, 1709
Bartelme, Elizabeth. 698
Bartels, Francis Lodowic. 2430
Bartels, Robert A. 386
Barth, Aquina. 1646
Barth, Christoph F. 584
Barth, Edna. 1397, 1486, 3277, 3279
Barth, Fritz. 418
Barth, J. Robert. 1307
Barth, Joseph. 3723
Barth, Karl. 3659, 49, 72, 73, 175, 324, 427, 448, 466, 472, 797, 955, 1047, 1067, 1110, 1116, 1145, 1457, 1707, 1739, 1801, 2783, 2868, 2897, 2942, 3049, 3124, 3611, 3618, 3640, 3650, 3651, 3655, 48, 175, 324, 673, 951, 1739, 1801, 2050, 2336, 2942, 3043, 3044, 3220, 3315, 3611, 3618, 3619, 3640, 3656, 3658, 3659
Barth, Lewis M. 2462
Barth, Markus. 308, 364, 375, 2050, 2073, 2152, 2161
Barthas, Casimir. 1618
Barthelemy, Dominique. 651
Barthelemy, Jean Jacques. 1765
Barthelemy-Madaule, Madeleine. 1578, 2193
[Barthelemy, Peter]. 3777
Barthelemy-Saint-Hilaire, Jules 1805-1895. 1850
Barthelemy-Saint-Hilaire, Jules. 700
Barthell, Edward E. 2660
Bartholomew, Edward Fry. 3146
Bartholomew, John Glass. 3560
Bartleman, Frank. 177, 2817
Bartlet, James Vernon. 1189
Bartlet, William Stoodley. 130
Bartlett, Alden Eugene. 955, 3477
Bartlett, Bob. 1261, 3592
Bartlett, Charles Norman. 466, 3711
Bartlett, Clarence. 2035
Bartlett, David. 615, 617
Bartlett, David Lyon. 377, 1248, 2051, 2476
Bartlett, Frederic Charles. 3056
Bartlett, Gene E. 160, 2785, 2897
Bartlett, Genus E. 3362
Bartlett, George C. 1635, 3495
Bartlett, Harriet (Tuttle) 2354, 3575
Bartlett, Josiah R. 3727
Bartlett, Laile E. 1288, 2986, 3725
Bartlett, Lester William. 1747, 3870
Bartlett, Lucy T. 2236
Bartlett, Margaret J. 3173
Bartlett, Robert Merrill. 955, 2210, 688, 2888, 3440
Bartlett, Samuel Colcord. 31, 48, 530, 564, 2491, 3752
Bartlett, W T. 3385
Bartlett, Willard. 3457
[Bartlett, Willard. 1653
Bartley, David. 3720
Bartley, Joseph Dana. 1862
Bartley, Robert F. 1090
Bartley, William Warren. 3022
Bartol, Cyrus Augustus. 177, 3727
Bartoli, Giorgio. 1379
Barton, Bruce. 1994, 230, 1047, 1950, 1959, 1994, 2795
Barton, Bruce Walter. 2506
Barton, Charles M. 2061
Barton, Frederick M. 230, 2886

Barton, George Aaron. 206, 346, 598, 1018, 1959, 3088, 3113, 3640, 3113
Barton, Harold Edwin. 604
Barton, James Levi. 2518, 2564, 2491, 2553
Barton, John. 486
Barton, John Mackintosh Tilney. 1827, 2811
Barton, Levi Elder. 1562, 1753, 3338, 3670
Barton, Lucy. 555
Barton, Peggy. 2128, 2952
Barton, Roy Franklin. 1882
Barton, William Eleazar. 1589, 400, 614, 1338, 1343, 3089, 577, 1333, 1335, 1349, 1886, 1960, 2005, 2680
Bartow, Charles L. 1509
Bartow, Donald W. 1243, 3476
Bartow, Harry Edwards. 3550
Bartsch, Hans Werner. 346
Bartz, Ulysses S. 1527
Baruch, Theodore H. 2092, 2103
Baruk, Henri. 1538
Basabe, Fernando M. 1936
Basansky, Bill. 177, 1367
Baschab, Charles Reinhard. 808
Bascio, Patrick. 1319
Bascom, Henry Bidleman. 1388, 3338
Bascom, John. 1054, 1579, 1719, 2672, 2835, 3097, 3338
Bascom, William Russell. 1882, 3400, 3868
Basetti-Sani, Giulio. 1912. 1082, 2184, 2372
Basen, Carol. 1132
Bash, Ewald. 526, 601, 2383
*Basham, Don. 2476
Basham, Don. 1717, 2730
Bashford, James Whitford. 911, 2481, 2454, 2518, 3338
Basile, Giacinta. 1027, 2270
Basilians. 812, 836
Basilius. 177, 1835, 2217, 3634, 177
Basilius, Harold A. 3065
Basilius, Saint. 525, 3634
Baskerville, Beatrice C. 2102
Baskin, Joseph R. 1093
Baskin, Wade. 2731
Bass, Altha Leah (Bierbower) 891, 3848
Bass, Archer Bryan. 2976
Bass, Clarence B. 342, 1467
Bass, E. Eulalia. 1996
Bass, George M. 527, 2212, 2213, 2298, 2897
Bass, John Letcher. 159
Bass, Reginald Howard. 3093
Bass, William A. 2751
Bassage, Harold Edwin. 1776
*Bassel, Bernard. 996
Bassert, Bernard. 996
Basset, Bernard. 401, 774, 996, 1326, 1947, 2524, 2706, 2788, 2868, 3769
Basset, Elizabeth. 1444
Bassett, Amos. 1503
Bassett, Henry Lawrence. 2618
Bassett, S. Denton. 3004
Bassett, Wallace. 160
Bassett, William W. 877
Bassham, Rodger C. 2555
Bassler, Jouette M. 375, 1733
[Basso, Carlo Andrea]. 2580
Basso, Keith H. 55
Bastaille, Edward Francis. 2701
Bastian, Ralph J. 2939
Bastide, Roger. 2645, 2647, 2681, 690
Bastien, Joseph William. 726
Bastion, N S. 1054
Bastnagel, Clement Vincent. 1290
Bataille, Georges. 1578
Batchelder, Calvin Redington. 1172
Batchelder, Lottie L. 3495
Batchelder, Robert C. 103
Batchelor, Arthur Douglas. 1950
Batchelor, Peter G. 19
Batdorf, Irvin W. 180
Bate, Herbert Newell. 374
Bateman, Josiah. 3818
Bates, Alisha. 1681
Bates, Arlo. 3279
Bates, Barbara S. 1614
Bates, Elisha. 168
Bates, Emily Katharine. 2986, 3495
Bates, Ernest Sutherland. 1493, 3740
Bates, Francis Van Ness How. 1065
Bates, Joseph. 178, 3379
Bates, Joshua. 3146
Bates, Lucille M. 2308
Bates, Lucy. 480
Bates, Maurice L. 3295
Bates, Miner Searle. 1056, 3192
Bates, Paul A. 1619
Bates, Paulina. 3394
Bates, Walter Gurney. 3334
Bates, William Henry. 230
Bates Riat. 1700
Batey, Irma Lee. 1202
Batey, Richard A. 334, 466, 981, 1153

Bath, Me. Winter street Congregational church. 1172
Bath, V. C. 2246
Batiffol, Pierre. 808, 841
Batist, Bessie Wittenberg. 1614
Batkin, Stanley I. 195, 2101
Batley, Ernest Lawson. 2897
Batman, Stephen. 2655
Batn, Alexander. 2463
Batsel, John D. 2434
Batsford, Harry. 751, 1158
Batson, Beatrice. 1021
Batson, C. Daniel. 1585
Batson, Charles Daniel. 1585
Batten, firm, advertising agents, New York. (1892. George Batten) 3205
Batten, firm advertising agents, New York. (1897. George Batten & co.) 3205
Batten, J. Rowena. 3838
Batten, John. 3495
Batten, Joseph Minton. 1045, 1484, 2978
Batten, Loring Woart. 497, 498, 519
Batten, Samuel Zane. 1055, 3440
Batten, Saumel Zane. 955
Battenfield, John Adam. 508
Battenhouse, Henry Martin. 230, 408, 1093, 1960, 3094
Battenhouse, Roy Wesley. 113
Battersby, Charles. 1349
Battersby, Henry Francis Prevost. 94
Battersby, William John. 695, 2189, 3457
Battis, Emery John. 53, 1858
Battiscombe, C F. 1397
Battiscombe, Georgina. 2166, 2754
Battista, O. A. 2262
Battle, Edith Kent. 3763
Battle, Edith Kent (Childs) 3763
Battle, Gerald N. 75
Battle, Jesse M. 871
Battle, William James. 117
Battles, Ford Lewis. 727, 3640
Batty, Beatrice (Stebbing) 1847, 1899
Baudier, Roger. 48, 822
Baudin, Noel. 1624
Baudot, Jules Leon. 841
Bauer, Arthur O. F. 2549
Bauer, Charles George. 230
Bauer, Clare. 178, 930
Bauer, Clemens. 818
Bauer, E. Charles. 906
Bauer, Evelyn (Showalter) 3124
Bauer, Harry Charles. 718, 1671
Bauer, Johannes Baptist. 242
Bauer, Paul. 1088, 3568
Bauer, Thomas J. 815
Bauer, Walter. 1768
Bauer, Walter. 1768, 1805
Bauer, Walter Emil. 2282
Bauerle, Richard. 586, 2213, 2298
Bauerle, Richard E. 570, 2298, 3362
Baugh, R P. 3495
Baughan, Raymond John. 1436
Baughen, Michael A. 492, 981, 2621
Baughey, Donald Robert. 1554
Baughman, Grace A. 3473
Baughman, Harold A. 3052
Baughman, Harry Fridley. 1942, 2897
Baughman, John Lee. 981
Baughman, Ray E. 635, 1960, 2173
[Bauhofer, Janos Gyorg]. 1856
Baum, Archie J. 3113
Baum, Daisy Mary (Davis) 1598
Baum, Gregory. 780, 784, 854, 859, 1039, 1042, 1046, 1082, 1110, 1456, 3436, 3440, 3447, 3628, 3640
Baum, Julius. 752
Bauman, Bert. 1589
Bauman, Edward W. 178, 409, 1006, 1056, 2062, 2868
Bauman, Louis Sylvester. 604, 611, 1513
Bauman, Mark K. 668, 734
Bauman, Mary Beata. 2305, 3417
Bauman, Richard. 1687
Bauman, William A. 1328
Baumann, Dan. 981, 1171
Baumann, Emile. 2795
Baumann, J. Daniel. 2897
Baumann, Margaret. 2162
Baumann, Richard. 2298
Baumeister, Edmund Joseph. 2334
Baumer, Franklin Le Van. 3422
Baumgaertner, John H. 70, 472, 2028, 2204, 2213, 2298, 2721
Baumgard, Herbert M. 2885
Baumgardt, David. 2637
Baumgarten, Paul Maria. 2203
Baumstark, Anton. 2236
[Baunard, Louis] 1826. 173
Baunard, Louis. 2246, 2735
Baur, Benedikt. 1327, 3485, 1263, 3485
Baur, Chrysostomus. 1115
Baur, Ferdinand Christian. 1184
Baur, Johannes. 2364
Baur, Paul Victor Christopher. 1509
[Baur, William] 1869. 2888
Baus, Karl. 1189, 1195

Bausch, William J. 808, 1172, 1245, 1326, 2788, 3264, 3628
Bauschatz, Paul C. 2660
Bauslin, David Henry. 3033
Bausman, Benjamin. 213, 955
Bavinck, Herman. 1317, 1706, 1719, 3224
Bavinck, Johan Herman. 1056, 1589, 2491, 2553, 1078
Bavink, Bernhard. 3077
Bax, Ernest Belfort. 2832, 36

Baxendale, Walter. 1839
Baxter, Batsell Barrett. 942, 61, 178, 283, 1272, 1349, 1928, 2897
Baxter, Betty Jean. 1598
Baxter, Clarice (Howard) 1749
Baxter, Daniel Minort. 26, 2420
Baxter, Dudley. 738
Baxter, Duncan. 1634
Baxter, Edna M. 473, 532, 3094, 3453, 3857
Baxter, Florence. 3495
Baxter, Francis K. 3495
Baxter, James Joseph. 862
Baxter, James Sidlow. 160, 213, 308, 647, 1430, 1444, 1550, 1598, 2035, 2980, 3286, 3288, 3299
Baxter, Kathleen Mary. 2059
[Baxter, Lucy E. (Barnes)] 1837-1902. 750, 753, 1312
Baxter, Michael Paget. 508
Baxter, Norman Allen. 1658
Baxter, Richard. 26, 34, 178, 955, 1297, 1357, 1358, 1436, 1444, 1764, 2790, 3630, 3670, 1444
[Baxter, Roger] 1792-1827. 780, 784
Baxter, Ronald E. 1717
Baxter, William. 3315, 3401
Baxter Richard. 1444
Bayard, Lewis Pintard. 1691
Bayard, Ralph Francis. 825, 3701
Bayard, Tania. 686, 3316
Bayat, Mangol. 3403
Baybrook, Gar. 2897
Bayer, Franz Joseph. 2860
Bayldon, Joan. 173
Bayle, Pierre. 1597
Bayles, George James. 1489
Bayless, C. Gordon. 1555
Bayless, O. L. 147
Bayless, Raymond. 1709, 2399, 2772
Bayley, Frank Tappan. 906
Bayley, James Roosevelt. 698, 823
Bayley, John. 1326
Bayley, Peter. 2908
Bayley, William. 1678
Baylis, Charles Augustus. 2420
Baylis, Harry James. 2475
Bayliss, Edward Ebenezer. 3431, 3589
Baylor, Byrd. 1899, 3546
Bayly, Joseph. 1550, 1562
Bayly, Joseph T. 1013, 1412, 1562, 2383, 3550
[Bayly, Lewis,] d. 1631. 955
Bayme, Steven. 2154
Bayne, Charles Gerwien. 860, 1763
Bayne, John Sloane. 3389
Bayne, Netta. 3473
Bayne, Peter. 955, 2059
*Bayne, Stephen F. 1047
Bayne, Stephen Fielding. 43, 44, 1015, 1056, 1065, 2211, 2259, 3852
Bayne H. Raymond. 2383
Baynes, Helton Godwin. 3308
Baynes, Norman Hepburn. 1195, 1355
[Bayonne, Emmanuel Ceslas], 1832-1885. 3051
Bays, Alice (Anderson) 3856, 3857, 3876
Bays, Bertie (Cole) 3670
Bazak, Jacob. 2144, 3219
Bazant, Jan. 1242
Bazin, Marie Rene. 1802, 3426
Bazin, Rene. 1332, 1636
Bazl, Frank M. 2723
Bea, Augustin. 397, 777, 1039, 1042, 1043, 3224, 3770, 3773, 1043, 1116, 3770
Beach, Alligood. 2854
Beach, Arthur Granville. 3211
Beach, Bert Beverly. 797, 1039, 3770
Beach, Charles Fisk. 1562
Beach, Curtis. 434
Beach, David N. 3197
Beach, David Nelson. 525, 1340, 1994
Beach, Emily J. 3495
Beach, Harlan Page. 1345, 2507, 2157, 2507, 2518, 2795
Beach, Harln Page. 1895
Beach, John. 1458, 1752, 1821
Beach, John G. 3837
Beach, Peter. 3705
Beach, Seth Curtis. 3328
Beach, Waldo. 741, 942, 950, 955, 3440
Beach, Walter Raymond. 73, 1012, 1435, 3381
Beachy, Alvin J. 3003
Beack, Leo. 2137

The Beacon (Washington D.C.) 3797
Beadle, John Hanson. 2600
Beahn, John Edward. 54, 1650
Beal, Alice Eunice (Barber) 1047
Beal, Samuel. 704
Beale, Arthur A. 3683
Beale, Harriet Stanwood (Blaine) 627
Beales, Arthur Charles Frederick. 818
Beall, B. B. 2633
Beall, Edgar Charles. 1653
Beall, James Lee. 981, 1613, 3294
Beall, Patricia. 1088
Beals, Charles Elmer. 2213
Beals, Ivan Anson. 2255
Beam, Maurice. 3324
Beaman, Edmund Addison. 3569
Beaman, Joyce Proctor. 981
Beamer, Charles. 899
Beamer, Jacob. 1719, 2979
Beamer, Mechack Franklin. 1999
Bean, Arthur Nicholas. 1444
Bean, George M. 3348
Bean, Willard, W. 2600
Bean, William Smith. 2062
Beane, John G. 2200
Bear, James E. 2504
Bear, Robert L. 1583, 3050
Beard, Augustus Field. 33, 2720
Beard, Charles. 3033
Beard, Charles Relly. 3582
Beard, Clarence M. 203, 1562
Beard, Frank. 617, 1810
Beard, Frank i.e. Thomas Francis. 1960
Beard, Frederica. 179, 595, 626, 899, 2549, 3146, 3564
Beard, Helen. 3835
Beard, Mattie Carson (Duncan) 3833
Beard, Paul. 1694, 3495
Beard, Rebecca. 1598
Beard, Richard. 1396, 3640, 3660
Bearden, George Steele. 2246
Beardslee, Clark Smith. 1991, 2061
Beardslee, John W. 3637
Beardslee, John Walter. 498, 653
Beardslee, William A. 346, 375, 2943, 3651
Beardsley, Eben Edwards. 3317
Beardsley, Frank Grenville. 3227, 3228, 34, 1172, 1574, 1625, 2017, 3230, 3232, 3737
Beardsley, Harry Markle. 2600, 3428
Beardsley, Isaac Haight. 2451
Beardsley, Lou. 2336
Beardsley, William Agur. 2688
Beardsmore, R. W. 2157
Beare, Francis Wright. 370, 385, 439, 448, 1950
Bearman, Jane. 1404, 2130
Beasley, A Roy. 2942
Beasley, Norman. 1037, 1493, 1976
Beasley, Walter J. 378, 2047
Beasley-Murray, G. R. 340
Beasley-Murray, George Raymond, 1916. 457
Beasley-Nurray, George Raymond. 133, 138, 339, 340, 438, 452, 458
Beaton, David. 3440
Beaton-Troker, Katherine. 2723
Beattie, Francis Robert. 1097, 61
Beattie, James. 1097, 1534, 3717
Beattie, Mallory. 308
Beattie, Nathaniel. 2377
Beattie, Robert Brewster. 3197
Beattie, William Gilbert. 2347
Beatty, Charles. 3021
Beatty, Frank M. 2915
Beatty, Hetty Burlingame. 1639
Beatty, James McGregor. 3495
Beattys, Harry Harvey. 1162
Beaty, Andrew. 462
Beaucamp, Evode. 1817, 2949, 3821
Beauchamp, Harvey. 645, 3551
Beauchamp, William. 1047, 1285, 1929, 2035
Beauchamp, William Martin. 1901, 2594
[Beaudenom, Leopold] 1840-1916. 1856
Beaudry, Louis Napoleon. 797
Beauduin, Lambert. 836
Beaven, Robert Haddow. 3660
Beaven, Thomas. 1681
Beaver, Gilbert A. 1116
Beaver, Robert Pierce. 1149, 1901, 1912, 2491, 2501, 2553, 2954, 3161, 3838
Beaverbrook, William Maxwell Aitken. 2062
Beazley, George G. 1460
Bebb, Evelyn Douglas. 1468
Bebbington, David. 1764, 1818
Bechanet, Jean Marie. 2379
Bechard, Henri. 876, 1849, 1949, 3269
Bechtel, John Hendricks. 301, 2659, 3026
Beck, Berenice. 1258
Beck, Brian E. 473
Beck,Dwight Marion. 387
Beck, Frances. 1412
Beck, Frank B. 3141
Beck, Frederick O. 862, 1265

Beck, Harrell Frederick. 647
Beck, Herbert F. 1393
Beck, Hubert F. 1004, 1914, 2067, 3592, 3600, 3667, 3884
Beck, Lewis White. 2835
Beck, Lily (Moresby) Adams. 700, 2839, 3864
Beck, Madeline H. 450
Beck, Mary Berenice. 1258
Beck, Stanley D. 3081
Beck, Victor Emanuel. 8, 1110, 1265, 2211, 2282
Beck, Vilhelm. 3124
Beck, Walter Herman. 2293
Beck, William F. 643, 1987
Beckelhymer, Hunter. 955, 1466, 3348
Becker, Antoinette. 905
Becker, Arthur H. 1777
Becker, August. 2383, 2888
Becker, C. 851, 2532
Becker, Carl Heinrich. 1082
Becker, Edwin L. 942
Becker, Ernest. 1412, 2169, 3894
Becker, Frederick W. 3206
Becker, Henry J. 1913, 3495
Becker, James A. 1579
Becker, Joachim. 498, 2414
Becker, Joyce. 229, 2073
Becker, Karl. 2246
Becker, Kurt. 2831
Becker, Leona Elizabeth. 2280
Becker, Mathias Birne. 1598
Becker, May (Lamberton) 617
Becker, Paula. 1748, 3470
Becker, Russell J. 1254
Becker, Siegbert W. 1077
Becker, Thomas Aloysius. 1977, 1986
*Becker, Vivian Bergsrud. 1074
Becker, Wilhard. 2264
Becker, Wilhelm. 804
Beckes, Isaac Kelley. 1247
Beckett, Helen. 647
Beckett, James Camlin. 1469, 2917
Beckett, Lemuel Morgan. 3197
Beckford, James A. 1939, 3085
Beckley, Timothy Green. 2730
Beckman, Peter. 3273
Beckmann, Beverly Ann. 2054
Beckmann, David M. 1497, 1894
Beckmeyer, Clement. 784
Beckwith, C. M. 3180
Beckwith, Charles Minnigerode. 2960, 1268
Beckwith, Clarence Augustine. 1732, 3640
Beckwith, George Derr. 604
Beckwith, Isbon Thaddeus. 2127, 452
Beckwith, John. 85
Beckwith, Martha Warren. 2663
Becon, Thomas. 1216, 1217, 3670
Becque, Maurice. 1694
Becquet, Thomas. 2883
Beda. 327, 1760, 1761
Beda Venerabilis, 673-735. 1397, 1760, 1761
Beddoe, Everett E. 1710
Bede, Elbert. 1663, 1666
Bedell, Edwin Augustus. 1199
Bedell, George C. 1108, 2169, 3743
Bedell, Gregory Thurston. 2785
Bedell, Gregory Townsend. 2621, 2795, 2972, 3236
Bedell, Kenneth B. 1200, 2236
[Bedell, William] d. 183
Bedenbaugh, J. Benjamin. 2056
Bedford, Arthur. 1225, 3605
Bedford, Eng. Bunyan Meeting. 183
Bedford, Sidney McHenry. 1694
Bedford, William Kirkpatrick Riland. 1755, 1804
Bedier, Mary Juliana. 74, 1315, 1607, 1733, 1979, 1996
Bedinger, Robert Dabney. 2513
Bedsole, Adolph. 1611, 2056, 2785, 2788, 3095
Bee, Fanna V. 663
Beebe, Catherine. 1627, 54, 617, 625, 1114, 1405, 1639, 1960, 1979, 2354, 2365, 2793, 3284
Beebe, George Monroe. 3596
Beebe, H. Keith. 538
Beebe, James Albert. 3670
Beebe, Ralph K. 1687
Beebe, Richard W. 1627, 1689
Beebe, Theodore Eaton. 1444
Beebe, Tom. 2696
Beebe, William Sully. 1898
Beecher, Catherine Ester. 3146
Beecher, Catherine Esther. 2589, 3097
Beecher, Charles. 103, 458, 526, 1977, 3495
Beecher, Edward. 133, 797, 1719, 2322
Beecher, George. 659
Beecher, George Allen. 664
[Beecher, Henry Ward] 1813-1887. 152, 183, 1332, 1340, 1579, 1960, 2021, 2888, 2897, 3006, 3066, 3348, 3361, 3362, 3869

Beecher, Lyman. 184, 797, 2922, 3228, 3348
Beecher, Margaret. 1029
Beecher, William Constantine. 659
Beecher, Willis Judson. 230, 496, 1694, 2922, 2949
Beechick, Allen. 3021
Beechick, Ruth. 938
Beeching, Jack. 2525
Beeck, Frans Jozef van. 2035, 3264
Beegle, Dewey M. 254, 304, 2621, 3224
Beehan, Martin Aloysius. 3247
Beek, Martinus Adrianus. 532, 2095
Beekman, John. 653
Beekman, John S. 1379
Beeler, Olando Gillman. 3141
Beem, Merrill A. 532
Beer, Sidney James. 2590
Beers, Eli. 2473
Beers, Forrest William. 3313
Beers, Gil. 247
Beers, Henry Augustin. 1322, 3247
Beers, Lorna Doone. 937
Beers, Richard G. 55, 2529
Beers, V. Gilbert. 292, 617
Beers, Victor Gilbert. 313, 400, 617, 618, 647, 1008, 2136, 2983, 3011
Beery, Mary. 686
Beesley, Charles Norbury. 1274
Beesley, Claude A. 1928
Beeson, Leola (Selman) 2463
Beeson, Trevor. 1108
Beet, Joseph Agar. 2059, 3477
Beetham, Thomas Allan. 1073
Beets, Henry. 1023, 1801
Beets, Nicolaas. 2766, 3049
Beevers, John. 179, 182, 1400, 1483, 1937, 2357, 3602, 3690
Beevers, John Leonard. 1937
Begbie, Harold. 1082, 1585, 1950, 3097, 618, 682, 1291, 1358, 1719, 2491, 2994, 3292
Begel, John Joseph. 1997
Begg, Alexander Clarke. 2409
Beggs, David W. 1128
Begley, Wayne E. 3316
Beglo, Joanne Nordley. 1274
*Beguesse, H. Hugh. 1579
Beguin, Olivier. 644
Beguiriztain, Justo. 2256, 2267
Beha, Ernest. 1663
Beha, Helen Marie. 2569, 2570
Behanan, Kovoor Thomas. 3864
Behanna, Gertrude Florence (Ingram) 1361
Beharrell, Thomas G. 213
Behler, G. M. 424
Behler, Gebhard Maria. 424
Behm, Bill. 2022
Behm, Ernst Gustav. 797, 798
Behney, J. Bruce. 1550
Behnke, Charles A. 17, 2213
Behnke, Daniel J. 906
Behnke, John. 930, 1979, 2205
Behnken, John William. 2284, 2298
Behr, Herman. 3313, 3495
Behrends, Adolphus Julius Frederick. 498, 1950, 2553, 2897
Behringer, William. 2363
Beidelman, T. O. 2556
Beidelman, Thomas O. 3088, 3432
Beiderbecke, Heinrich. 2497
Beighle, Nellie (Craib) 3495
Beilby, G.T. 156
Beiler, Edna. 2535, 2551
Beiler, Irwin Ross. 1960
Beiler, Samuel Lynch. 2443
Beilis, Mendel. 2102
Beillie, James Black. 1800, 2242
Beimfohr, Herman N. 2888, 3882
Bein, Alex. 1809
Beirne, Charles Joseph. 34, 824
Beirne, Francis F. 133
Beirne, Kilian. 1332
Beissel, Stephan. 2246
Beitel, Calvin Gustavus. 1490
Beit-Hallahmi, Benjamin. 3001
Beitzakhar, Michael Simonivitch. 2533
Beitzeil, Edwin Warfield. 3274
Beitzell, Edwin Warfield. 1949
Beker, Johan Christiaan. 375, 1529
Beker, Johan Christian. 367
Bekkers, W. M. 757
Bekkers, Willem Marinus. 757
Bel Geddes, Joan. 2888
Belanger, Merlyn. 3056
Belcastro, Joseph. 138
Belcher, Joseph. 3324, 3813
Belcher, Kate H. 3071
Belcher, Richard P. 279
Belden, Albert David. 955, 1719, 650, 1549, 2806, 2868, 3678, 3813
Belden, Franklin George. 3333
Belden, Henry Seymour. 1793
Belding, Warren S. 185
Belew, M. Wendell. 1170
Belew, Pascal P. 462, 2980

Belford, Lee Archer. 2146
Belfour, Algernon Okey. 3367
Belfour, Stanton. 2850
Belfrage, Henry. 1318
Belfrage, Sally. 2832, 3019
*Belgum, David. 1163, 2377
Belgum, David Rudolph. 1116, 1327, 1417, 2059, 2378, 2783, 2995, 3390
Belgum, Murrul J. 1606, 3766
Belk, Fred Richard. 2407
Belk, John Blanton. 2930
Belkin, Samuel. 2073, 2098, 2107, 2134, 2141, 2322, 2831, 3585
Belknap, George Nicholas. 1533
Belknap, Helen Olive. 1271
Belknap, Jeremy. 585, 1994, 2758, 3798
Belknap, Ralph L. 1167
Bell, Albert Dehner. 1407
Bell, Alvin E. 635, 1029
Bell, Alvin Eugene. 635, 1436, 1747
[Bell, Anne]. 1348
Bell, Arthur Donald. 2204, 3203, 3378, 3856
Bell, Aubrey Fitz Gerald. 80
Bell, Augustus Timothy. 186
Bell, Benjamin. 512, 1285
Bell, Bernard Iddings. 61, 1047, 1056, 1090, 1543, 1837, 2211, 2257, 3066, 3186, 3440, 3448
Bell, Carl Irving. 1114
Bell, Charles. 1783
Bell, Charles Alfred. 3699, 709
Bell, Charles Bailey. 1709
Bell, Charles Henry. 3810
Bell, Clark. 2993
Bell, Clinton C. 1172
Bell, D. Rayford. 2036
Bell, George Charles. 3146
Bell, George Kennedy Allen. 73, 186, 1039, 1056, 1210, 1406, 3849, 1492, 3849
Bell, Harold Idris. 100, 1501, 1502, 2099
Bell, Henry Hesketh Joudou. 3828
Bell, Hermon Fiske. 3056, 3066, 3197, 3615
Bell, James Ford. 1949
[Bell, James Pinkney Pleasant]. 1688
Bell, John. 2658
Bell, Joseph Norment. 2263
Bell, L. Nelson. 955, 2384
Bell, Lester C. 144
Bell, Louie M. 2649
Bell, Marion L. 3232
Bell, Mary I M (Ottley) 808, 2768
Bell, Ovid. 1690
Bell, R A Jack. 2303
Bell, Ralcy Husted. 3056
Bell, Ralph R. 2792
Bell, Ralph S. 981
Bell, Raymond Martin. 2447, 3735
Bell, Richard. 1082
Bell, Robert Bloomer Hare. 3197
Bell, Robert E. 2657
Bell, Robert Emmet. 160
Bell, Robert R. 1498
Bell, Roy E. 1436
Bell, Sadie. 942, 3190
Bell, Stephen. 2308, 2939
Bell, Walter Presley. 1372, 2783
Bell, Wilbur Cosby. 1047, 1067, 1719, 1886
Bell, William. 462
Bell, William Clarke. 2489
Bell, William M. 3822
[Bell, William Mara]. 2835
Bell, William Melvin. 3440
Bell, Winthrop Pickard. 2716
Bell, Wm. M. 1444
Bellafiore, Giuseppe. 2760
Bellah, Charles Greeley. 41, 1401, 3387
Bellah, Robert Neelly. 91, 1935, 3056, 3087
Bellah, Robert Neely. 3748
Bellamy, Joseph. 1333, 1334, 1376, 2373, 2952, 3338, 3348, 3609
Belland, John F. 203, 230, 643
Bellarmino, Roberto Francesco Romolo. 173, 187, 817, 1416, 2056, 2767, 2858
Bell. Clark. 2849, 3495
Bellegay, Michael M. 3495
Beller, Herbert N. 887
Bellet, Maurice. 3828
Bellhouse, Geoffrey Turner. 3363
Bellinger, Lucius. 2420
Belloc, Hilaire. 755, 758, 780, 784, 1281, 1542, 1639, 1804, 1937, 2077, 3033, 3037, 3236, 758, 1281, 1378, 1639, 1804, 3037, 3236
Belloc, Hilaire [Joseph Hilaire Pierre Belloc]. 3033
Bellord, James. 855
Bellot, Paul. 1161
Bellows, Russell Nevins. 881
Bellwald, Augustine Matthias. 1029
Belman, J. C. 3232
Belmont, Perry. 3703
Belo, Fernando. 432, 3439

Belo, Jane. 131, 1540
Beloit, Wis. First Congregational church. 1339
Belorgey, Godefroid. 2379
Belorgey, Jean Michel. 1356
Belser, Johannes Evangelist. 2028
Belsham, Thomas. 1097, 2217, 2939
Belt, Guy Chester. 187, 3495
Belter, Robert Rudolph. 230, 1691, 1996, 2211
Belton, Francis George. 942, 2811
Beltran, Orlando Alfredo. 88
Belvin, Agnes Lowry. 1376
Belz, Ella C. 1602
Beman, Lamar Taney. 3189
Bement, R B. 2655
Bemies, Charles Otis. 3253
Ben-Amos, Paula. 88
Ben-Horin, Meir, 1918. 2087, 3028
Ben-Jochannan, Yosef. 12, 230, 2681
Ben Zion, Raphael. 2646
Benade, Miriam McGaw. 2529
Benamozegh, Elijah. 942
Benard, Edmond Darvil. 2702, 3653
Benares, Camden. 2381
Benavides Alonso de, 1630. 2693
Bendall, Kent. 1589
Ben-David, Eliezer. 2853
Bender, Harold, Stauffer. 2403, 2404, 3224
Bender, Harold Stauffer. 1163, 36
Bender, Henry Richard. 307, 364, 418, 1429, 2447
Bender, John Alexander. 2270
Bender, Ross Thomas. 2404
Bender, Urie A. 1347, 2806, 3828
Bendit, Laurence John. 117, 1412, 3683
Bendit, Phoebe Daphne (Payne) 2986, 2987
Benedetto, Arnold J. 2672
Benedicite, omnia opera Domini. 1523
Benedict. 188
Benedict, Anna Louise. 3495
Benedict, David. 151, 170, 1476, 3113
Benedict, Don. 187, 1300
Benedict, George. 2085
Benedict, Ivan Howland. 3440
Benedict, Louise Cowles. 1029
Benedict, Marion Josephine. 1719
Benedict, Rex. 2159
Benedict, Robert P. 203
Benedict, Ruth (Fulton) 1902
Benedict, Samuel Durlin. 784
Benedict, Wayland Richardson. 180
Benedictines. American Cassinese congregation. 190
Benedictus. 187, 189, 190, 2583
Benes, Peter. 922
Benett, George Henry. 1802
Benett, W. 3859
Benett, William. 2223
Bengalee, Mutiur Rahman. 2628
Bengel, Johann Albrecht. 342
Bengis, Esther (Rosenberg) 3016
Ben-Gurion, David, 1886. 484
Benham, Asahel. 2632
Benham, Charles Orville. 276, 1513
Benham Club, Princeton, N. J. 3144
Benham, Hugh. 1206
Benham, William. 3637, 3819
Ben-Har, Bezalel. 283
Benjamin, Barbara. 1308, 1911
Benjamin, Charles Thomas. 3579
Benjamin, E Bedell. 562
Benjamin, Elsie. 3689
Benjamin, Frederick Albert. 2168, 2431
Benjamin, Mary Gladding (Wheeler) 1578
Benjamin, Mooshie Sargis. 2913
Benjamin, Paul. 1004, 1170
Benjamin, Philip S. 1138, 1687
Benjamins, Israel. 2080
Benko, Stephen. 1318, 2056, 2357, 2362
Benne, Robert. 1056, 3743
Benner, Hugh C. 1206, 1237
[Benner, Joseph Sieber]. 936, 2225
Bennet, Benjamin. 276
Bennet, James Arlington. 1653
Bennet, James E. 2824
Bennet, Moses P. 3640
Bennett, A H. 3415
Bennett, Abe F. 1555
Bennett, Adrian Arthur. 26, 2485
Bennett, Alfred Gordon. 2723
Bennett, Allan. 700
[Bennett, Ambrose Allen]. 2897
Bennett, Archibald F. 1704
*Bennett, Bishop George W. 1695
Bennett, Boyce M. 600
Bennett, Charles. 2833
Bennett, Charles Andrew Armstrong. 3056, 2637, 3056
Bennett, Charles T. 2833
Bennett, Charles Wesley. 918
Bennett, Clara Marion. 1747
Bennett, Clifford Alvin. 2634
Bennett, Curtis. 1743

Bennett, Daniel Miller. 2309, 3796
Bennett, De Robigne Mortimer. 659, 923, 1653
Bennett, Dennis J. 139, 981, 991
Bennett, Dink. 2384
Bennett, Edmund Hatch. 387
Bennett, Edward T. 2987
Bennett, Elbert Lansing. 906
Bennett, Ella Kellum. 1960
Bennett, Ernest Nathaniel. 2845, 2987, 77
Bennett, Frances Grant. 2600
Bennett, Fredna W. 544
Bennett, Gareth Vaughan. 109, 1146, 1762, 3573
Bennett, Georgann. 1747
Bennett, George. 1598, 2783
Bennett, George H. 3022
Bennett, George Henry. 1039, 3024
Bennett, J. A. W. 1519, 2012
Bennett, J Harry. 3424
Bennett, Joan Frankau. 1476, 1519
Bennett, John C. 2600, 3428
Bennett, John Coleman. 1085, 103, 942, 1056, 1085, 1103, 1140, 1913, 1914, 3440, 3447
Bennett, John Godolphin. 2643, 2996, 3139
Bennett, John Marshall. 1505
Bennett, John William. 1859
Bennett, Leo. 1960
Bennett, Lerone. 2172
Bennett, M R. 1056
Bennett, Margaret. 2427
Bennett, Margaret Elaine. 3536
Bennett, Marian. 3882
Bennett, Marjorie. 2544
[Bennett, Mela Isabel (Barrows) 155, 190
Bennett, Mrs. Anne R. (Gladstone) tr. 2253
Bennett, Ralph Francis. 1475
Bennett, Rita. 991
Bennett, Robert A. 230
Bennett, Robinson Potter Dunn. 2827, 3338
Bennett, Sarah R I. 1791
Bennett, T. Miles. 537, 558
Bennett, Thomas J. 1858
Bennett, Vincent. 955
Bennett, Wallace Foster. 2600
Bennett, Walter Leopold. 635
Bennett, William. 551
Bennett, William Harper. 873
Bennett, William Henry. 308, 618
Bennett, William L. 160
Bennett, William Wallace. 2453
Bennett, Willis G. 2813
Benneville, George de. 3819
Bennigsen, Alexandre. 1926
Bennink, Bernard John. 1188
Bennion, Adam S. 2600
Bennion, Adam Samuel. 2607
Bennion, Howard S. 1704
Bennion, Lowell L. 230, 2599
Bennion, Lowell Lindsay. 475, 950, 2061, 2600, 2610, 3056
Bennion, Milton. 3056
Bennion, Milton Lynn. 2614
Bennion, Samuel O. 2619
Benoit, Alphonse. 1773
Benoit, Hubert. 3894
Benoit, Pierre. 200, 304, 383, 2028, 2824
Benoliel, Evangeline. 3495
Benrath, Karl. 2734
Bension, Ariel. 3898
Benson, Alphonsus. 1730
Benson, Arthur Christopher. 27, 191, 1444, 2225
Benson, Bob. 191, 1010
Benson, Carmen. 191, 604, 1479, 1601
Benson, Clarence H. 1250, 3551
Benson, Clarence Herbert. 1250, 1485, 3077, 3178, 3551, 3561, 3670
Benson, Clarence Irving. 2753
Benson, Clement L. 1172
Benson, David V. 191, 341, 1574
Benson, Dennis C. 903, 981, 1261, 1323, 1701, 2384, 3003, 3018, 3679, 3884
Benson, Edward White. 327, 458, 1398
Benson, Erwin George. 3177
Benson, Ezra Taft. 1232, 1603, 2607
Benson, George. 1777
Benson, George Willard. 1388
Benson, Ginny. 2803
Benson, Hamar. 462
Benson, Jeanette. 1607
Benson, Joachim Vincent. 2156
Benson, John L. 51
Benson, Joseph. 955, 1629
Benson, Kathleen. 2280, 3037
Benson, Louis FitzGerald. 1871
Benson, Louis FitzGerald. 1871, 1874
Benson, Margaret H. 3843
Benson, Purnell Handy. 3056
Benson, Richard Meux. 991, 2217, 2577, 3438
Benson, Robert Hugh. 191, 758, 774, 780, 804, 862, 1363, 2019, 3197, 3324, 3362

Benson, Robert Louis. 666
Benson, Samuel Benney. 2847
Benson, William Newton. 1379
Bent, Charles N. 1417, 1473
Bent, James Appleton. 230
Bente, Josephine (Haserot) 659
Bentham, Jeremy. 1960
Bentley, Edmund Clerihew. 1478
Bentley, James. 3240
Bentley, Joseph. 3534
Bentley, Richard. 101, 862
[Bentley, William]. 1862, 3286
Bentley, William Preston. 1109
Bentley, William W. 3660
Benton, Angelo Ames. 2963, 3637, 2963
Benton, Harry. 3348
Benton, John. 1255
Benton, Joseph Augustine. 726
Benton, Josephine Moffett. 923, 1349, 1444, 3845, 3847
Benton, Patricia. 1114, 3206
Benton, Rita. 3146
Bentov, Itzhak. 1385
Bentwich Norman De Mattos. 1914
Bentwich, Norman De Mattos. 1802, 2315, 2831, 3306
Bentz van den Berg, John Cato. 3197
Benveniste, Meron. 1944
Beny, Roloff. 3245
Benz, Ernst. 708, 1582, 2744
Benz, Ernst Wilhelm. 2744
Benziger, Adelrich. 855
Benziger brothers. 869, 1169
Benziger brothers. New York. 1169
Benziger, Marieli G. 683, 2348
[Benziger brothers]. 1248
Ber, 1723-1805. 2098
Beranger, Clara. 567
Berberich, Wilhelm August. 2637
Bercovici, Myrna. 567
Bercovitch, Sacvan. 3721
Bercovitz, Moses. 2153
Berdiaev, Nikolai Aleksandrovich. 61, 1149, 1281, 1534, 2416, 3097, 3521
Berdoe, Edward. 697, 1047
Berechiah ben Natronai, 12th cent. 1538
Bereday, George Z.F. 1128
Berens, E M. 2655
Berenson, Mary. 2761
Berenson, Mary (Smith) 2761
Berenstain, Stanley. 903
Berg, Darrel E. 1006
Berg, David Eric. 916, 1202
Berg, Harold Edwin. 1312
Berg, Joseph Frederick. 276, 508, 1882, 3475
Berg Marina de 1926. 2384
Berg, Mary Kirkpatrick. 906, 1246, 3176, 3856
Berg, Orley. 610, 1927, 2791
Berg, Rebecka Carolina. 3141
Berg, Roger J. 2888
Berg, Sandra Beth. 514
Berge, Selmer Alonzo Eugene. 1562
Bergeaud, Jean. 2127
Bergen, John Tallmadge. 1047
Bergendoff, Conrad John Immanuel. 109, 110, 618, 1116, 1200, 1300, 2285, 2288, 2294, 2826, 3042
Berger, Alan L. 3581
Berger, Charles G. 2827
Berger, David. 2144
Berger, Elmer. 2077, 2137
Berger, Henry William. 378
Berger, Johann. 2685
Berger, Julius. 3370
Berger, Mannie. 484
Berger, Maxwell. 565
Berger, Melvin. 2993
Berger, Mike. 1418
Berger, Milton. 1348
Berger, Morroe. 1924
Berger, Peter L. 3085, 3566, 3617, 3743, 3749
Berger, Tom. 2937
Berger, William Francis. 2036, 3564
Bergere, Thea. 3768
Bergeron, Henri Paul. 1598
Bergevin, Paul Emile. 3168
Bergey, Alyce. 5, 430, 631, 634, 2711
Bergfelder, Otto. 2298
Bergh, Henry T. 1435
Bergherm, William H. 3456
Bergier, Jacques. 2723
Berglund, Ernest. 2348
Bergman, Shmuel Hugo, 1883. 2832
Bergmann, Mark. 1257
Bergmann, Samuel Hugo. 2832
Bergmenn, Gustar. 691, 2737
Bergounioux, Frederic Marie. 3108
Bergren, Richard Victor. 571, 2201
Bergson, Henri Louis. 1322, 193, 1534, 2416, 2834
Bergsten, Gote. 2995
Bergsten, Torsten. 37, 1850
Berguer, Georges. 2050
Berington, Joseph. 784

Berk, Stephen E. 730, 1484
Berkebile, Nora Elma (Flory) 2529
Berkeley, Calif. Free Church. 2236
Berkeley, George. 2179, 2838
Berkeley, James Percival. 414, 448, 499, 3178
*Berkemeyer, William C. 471, 1976
Berkenmeyer, Wilhelm Christoph. 2291
Berkery, Patrick J. 2575
Berkhof, H. 3475
Berkhof, Hendrikus. 375, 1529, 1818, 1833, 2866, 3475, 3640
Berkhof, Louis. 1473, 287, 1024, 1589, 3318, 3640, 3653
Berkhofer, Robert F. 1900
Berkobin, Henry J. 2295
Berkouwer, Gerrit Cornelis. 1504, 175, 230, 798, 861, 1200, 1589, 1750, 1950, 2036, 2160, 2326, 2822, 3044, 3224, 3262, 3318, 3410, 3656, 3769
Berkovits, Eliezer. 598, 1306, 1733, 1825, 2080, 2137, 2141, 2885
Berkowitz, David Sandler. 87, 601
Berkowitz, Henry. 192, 3147
Berkowitz, Max Edward. 192
Berkowitz, Morris I. 3089
Berkowitz, William. 2141
Berle, Adolf Augustus. 3440
Berlin, Charles. 1624, 2083
Berlin, Isaiah. 1520
Berling, Judith A. 1330, 2229
Berman, Edward H. 2500
Berman, Jeremiah J. 3423
Berman, Jeremiah Joseph. 3423
Berman, Louis Arthur. 3776
Berman, Morton Mayer. 893
Bermant, Chaim. 2080
Bernad de Clairvaux 1091?-1153. 587
Bernadot, Marie Vincent. 2354
Bernanos, Georges. 807, 1939
Bernard. 1862
Bernard, Alfred. 780
Bernard, David. 2597
Bernard de Clairvaux, 1091?-1153. 193, 595, 667, 862, 1026, 1657, 1741, 1742, 1855, 2318, 3368, 3369
Bernard de Clairvaux, 1901?-1153. 2767
Bernard, Jack F. 764
[Bernard, John Henry. 3367
Bernard, John Henry. 415, 492
Bernard, Mary. 3418
Bernard of Clairvaux. 193
Bernard of Clairvaux 1091?-1153. 595, 1265, 1855, 2217
Bernard, Paul P. 2134
Bernard, Pierre Rogatien. 1960
Bernard, Rogatien. 2362
Bernard, Theos. 3864, 2839, 3867
Bernard, Thomas Dehany. 424, 475
Bernardin, Joseph Buchanan. 1693, 1950, 2888, 2956
Bernardini statuary company, New York. 3525
Bernardino da Siena, 1380-1444. 2132
Berneking, William. 1444
Bernen, Satia. 2760
Berner, Carl W. 1349, 3528
Bernet Kempers, August Johan, 1906. 712
Bernfeld, Simon. 2113, 1538
Bernhard E. Olson Scholars' Conference on the Church Struggle and the Holocaust (1979) 1825
Bernhard, John T. 1366
Bernhardt, Charles E. 955
Bernhart, Joseph. 2768, 1027, 1640
Bernheim, Gotthardt Dellmann. 1549
Bernheim, Isaac Wolf. 2100
Bernicie, Lillian. 3495
Bernier, Paul. 795, 2254
Bernieres-Louvigny, Jean de. 996
Bernoville, Gaetan [Marie Joseph]. 2811
Bernstein, Herman. 2952, 659
Bernstein, Joanne E. 1416
Bernstein, Marcelle. 2717
Bernstein, Peretz. 53
Bernstein, Peretz Friedrich. 53
Bernstein, Philip Sidney. 2137, 2138, 2146
Beron, Richard. 618
Berquist, Millard J. 320
Berrett, LaMar C. 2616, 2678, 3846
Berrett, William Edwin. 678, 2600, 2615, 3430
Berrey, Lester V. 301
Berrian, William. 2701, 3406
Berrigan, Daniel. 194, 465, 558, 585, 758, 996, 1056, 1116, 1376, 1413, 2384, 3066, 3278
Berrigan, Philip. 195, 1131, 1139
Berrigan Daniel. 194
Berrill, Jacquelyn. 3311
Berry, Boyd M. 2467, 3008
Berry, Brewton. 3567
Berry, Carrie Adams. 1950
Berry, Elwood Sylvester. 451, 574, 780
Berry, George Keys. 1268
Berry, George Ricker. 499, 2760, 1768, 1771

Berry, Gerald L. 3113
Berry, Jo. 572, 981, 3830, 3845
Berry, Joan P. 1263, 1589
Berry, John Benton Nathaniel. 1886
Berry, John M. 1356
Berry, John Raymond. 3473
Berry, L Claude. 3269
Berry, Lawrence Frederick. 1477
Berry, Lloyd Eason. 1519
Berry, Lora Davis. 1991
Berry, Mabel Macena (Pennington) 1444
Berry, Mildred. 230
Berry, Robert Lee. 615, 1563, 2593, 1563, 1827
Berry, Ruth Muirhead. 3124
*Berry, S. Stanford. 955
Berry, Thomas Mary. 700, 707
Berry, William G. 3660
[Berryman, Elijah Josiah]. 1886
Bersell, Peter Olof Immanuel. 1114
Bersier, Eugene Arthur Francois. 3049
Berthe, Augustine. 1960
Berthier, Jean. 755
Berthier, Rene. 836, 955, 2888
Berthold, Fred. 1619, 3204
Bertocci, Peter Anthony. 1657, 1719, 1732, 3097
Berton, Pierre. 1065
Bertram, Martin H. 3183
Bertram, Robert W. 3619, 3679
Bertrams, Wilhelm. 877, 1522
Bertrand, Louis. 113, 3602
Bertrangs, A. 3541
Bertsche, Leopold. 2267, 2574
Berven, Ken. 195, 930, 981
Berwitt, Elaine. 955
Berzon, Bernard L. 565, 3361, 3370
Besant, Annie (Wood) 195, 2165, 3052, 3683, 3689, 1091, 1102, 1348, 2165, 3683, 3689, 3864
Beskin, Nathan Cohen. 604
Besly, Kathleen M H. 2228
Besnard, Albert Marie. 1589
Bespuda, Anastasia. 2751
Besse, Henry True. 1172, 3260
Besser, Wilhelm Friedrich. 2028, 2795
Bessiere, Gerard. 2384
Bessieres, Albert. 2329, 3580
Bessler, Helen. 3175
Bessley, Claude A. 2956
Best, Elsdon. 2332
Best, Ernest. 325, 405, 434, 447, 995, 2897
Best, Geoffrey Francis Andrew. 3011
Best, John Henry. 2017, 3072
Best, Johnston Valentine. 1376
Best, Mary Agnes. 1677
Best, Nolan Rice. 1127, 3197, 1910, 3197, 3414
Best, Thomas W. 2310
Best, W. E. 2036, 3051
Besterman, Theodore. 1392
Bestic, Alan. 3324
Beth, Karl. 2017
Beth, Loren P. 1149
Bethel Baptist Church, Washington Co., Ky. 195
Bethel College and Seminary, Saint Paul. 1065
Bethel College, North Newton, Va. 2403
Bethel, Jane. 923
Bether Consultation on Christian Literature, 1962. 3203
Bethge, Eberhard. 676, 1108
Bethlehem Evangelical Lutheran Church. 195
Bethlehem, Pa. Moravian church. 2594, 2595
Bethmann, Erich W. 1922
Bethune, George Washington. 196, 1349, 2384, 3206, 3218
Bethune-Baker, James Franklin. 73, 1354, 1960, 1986, 2000, 2007, 2561, 2684
Betjeman, John. 1270
Betowski, Edward Maximilian. 1358, 2370, 3372
Betsworth, Roger G. 3747
Bett, Henry. 2476, 2122, 2708
Bettan, Israel. 2113, 2910
Bettany, George Thomas. 3113, 1172, 1895, 3113
Betten, Francis Sales. 677
Betten, Neil. 1131
Bettenson, Henry Scowcraft. 1198
Bettenson, Henry Scowcroft. 1020, 1198
Bettestine, Della (Cabral) 1793
Bettex, Frederic. 3711, 230, 1379, 2000, 2476, 3074
Bettey, J. H. 2775
Bettis, Joseph Dabney. 3097
Bettner, George. 3206
Bettoni, Efrem. 675, 1645
Betts, Albert Deems. 2432
Betts, Anna (Freelove) 3147, 3551
Betts, Darby Wood. 1155
Betts, Frederick William. 1834, 3752
Betts, George Herbert. 1047, 3147, 3162

Betts, Gilbert Lee. 1739
Betts, Robert Brenton. 1109
Betz, Eva K. 1400, 1406, 1707
Betz, Eva (Kelly) 692, 742, 1311, 1406, 1484, 1713, 2348, 3329, 3420, 3778
Betz, Hans Dieter. 379
Betz, Margaret. 1077
Betz, Otto. 1327, 2007
Betzer, Dan. 3021
Beuckman, Frederick. 1172
Beutler, Harold Joseph. 3485
[Beuwens, J J]. 780
Beuyer, Louis. 836
Bevan, Edwyn Robert. 1172, 1766, 2084, 3532, 1081, 1189, 1766, 1882, 3405, 3573, 3574
Bevan, Gladys Mary. 919
Bevan, Philip. 3197
Bevan, William Latham. 3273
Bevan, Wilson Lloyd. 1185, 1187, 1140
Bevans, John. 1681
Bevenot, Hugh. 808
Bevenot, Maurice. 1398, 3709, 1398, 3709
Beveridge, Albert Jeremiah. 210
Beveridge, Thomas Hanna. 1784, 2930
Beveridge, William. 3003
Bevins, Andrew. 2067
Bewer, Julius August. 538
Bewes, Richard. 2868
Bewkes, Eugene Garrett. 2835
Bewley, Richard. 1653
Beyer, Bernhard. 1667
Beyer, Douglas. 3660
Beyer, Maximilian. 1777, 2018
Beyer, Stephan. 700, 3588
Beyerhaus, Peter. 1904, 2553, 3851
Beza, Marcu. 1632
Beze, Theodore de. 727
Bezou, Henry C. 1294
Bezzant, James Stanley. 1103
Bhadrabahu. 1932, 2317
Bhagat, M. G. 89
Bhaktivedanta, A. C., 1896. 2186
Bhaktivedanta, A.C., 1896. 2186, 2187, 3005, 3864, 3867
Bhaktivedanta Swami, A. C., 1896. 197
Bhaktivedanta Swami, A. C., 1896-1977. 2228, 3866
Bhaktivedanta A.c. 3867
Bhaktivedauta, A. C. 879
Bhaktivedenta, A.C., 1896. 2379
Bhaktivednta, A.C., 1896. 3864
Bhandarkar, Ramkrishna Gopal. 3766
Bharavi. 3206
Bhativedanta, A.C. 1896. 2663, 2867
Bhattacharji, Sukumari. 2664
Bhattacharya, Brindavan Chandra. 3316
Bhattacharyya, Krishnachandra. 197, 3774
Bhattacharyya, Narendra Nath. 3239, 3400, 2841, 3002
Bhave, Vinoba. 2316
Bhebe, Ngwabi. 3234
Bhikshu. 3864
Bhoothalingam, Mathuram. 3019
Bial, Morrison David. 1784, 2081, 2778, 3032
Biale, David. 2646, 3309, 3310
Bialek, Robert W. 1145
Bianchi, Eugene C. 861, 2480, 2954, 3085, 3389
Bianchi, Joseph Salvatore. 1371, 3081
Bias, Clifford. 2311
Biasiotto, Peter Regalatus. 1826
Bibbins, Ruthella Bernard (Mory) 2423
Bibeltheologisches Worterbuch. 242
Biberfeld, Philip Leon. 2087
Bibesco, Marthe Lucie (Lahovary) 2761
Bible. 197, 254, 368, 369, 395, 448, 510, 520, 525, 553, 562, 582, 603, 849, 1393, 1430, 2069, 2986
Bible abridged. 200, 292, 618
Bible. Anglo-Saxon. Selections. 1898. 612
Bible. Anglo-Saxon. Selections. 1903. 612
Bible. Anglo-Saxon. Selections. 1974. 612
Bible. Anglo-Saxon. Selections. 1976. 612
Bible. Apocryphal books. English. 1963. 335
Bible conference on the return of Our Lord, Philadelphia, 1918. 2055
Bible. Dakota, 1887. Williamson-Riggs. 197
Bible. English. 1560. Geneva version. 653
Bible. English. (1611) 1911. Authorized. 254
Bible. English. (1611) 1965. Authorized. 254
Bible. English. 1782. 254
Bible. English. 1782. Authorized. 255
Bible. English. 1783. 255
Bible. English. 1791. Authorized. 255
Bible. English. 1792. Authorized. 307
Bible. English. 1793. 255
Bible. English. 1794. Authorized. 358
Bible. English. 1796. Authorized. 255

Bible. English, 1798. Authorized. 255
Bible. English. 1801. Authorized. 255
Bible. English. 1802. Authorized. 255
Bible. English. 1803. 255
Bible. English. 1803. Authorized. 255, 358
Bible. English. 1804. Authorized. 219
Bible. English. 1806. Authorized. 255
Bible. English. 1806. Authorized. 307
Bible. English. 1808. Authorized. 256
Bible. English. 1812. 256
Bible. English. 1812. Authorized. 256
Bible. English. 1813. 230
Bible. English. 1816. 219
Bible. English. 1816. Authorized. 256, 358
Bible. English. 1817. Authorized. 256
Bible. English. 1818. Authorized. 219, 256
Bible. English. 1820. 256
Bible. English. 1822. Authorized. 219, 256
Bible. English. 1823. 256
Bible. English. 1826. Authorized. 256
Bible. English. 1827. Authorized. 219
Bible. English. 1828. Authorized. 256
Bible. English. 1829. Authorized. 219
Bible. English. 1830. Authorized. 220
Bible. English. 1831. Authorized. 256
Bible. English. 1832. Authorized. 220
Bible. English. 1833. Authorised. 220
Bible. English. 1833. Authorized. 256
Bible. English. 1833. Webster. 256
Bible. English. 1834. Authorized. 220, 256, 308
Bible. English. 1835. Authorised. 257
Bible. English. 1835. Authorized. 257
Bible. English. 1836. Authorized. 257, 585
Bible. English. 1837. Authorized. 257
Bible. English. 1839. Authorised. 257
Bible. English. 184. 257
Bible. English. 184-. Authorized. 257
Bible. English. 1840. 257
Bible. English. 1840. Authorized. 257
Bible. English. 1841. Authorized. 220
Bible. English. 1842. 257
Bible. English. 1844. Authorized. 220
Bible. English. 1845. Authorized. 257
Bible. English. 1845. Douai. 272
Bible. English. 1849. 257
Bible. English. 1852. Authorized. 1604
Bible. English. 1852. Douai. 272
Bible. English. 1853. Douai. 272
Bible. English. 1854. Authorized. 257
Bible. English. 1855. Authorized. 220
Bible. English. 1856. Authorized. 257
Bible. English. 1857. Authorzed. 257, 358
Bible. English. 1858. Authorized. 220
Bible. English. 1859. Authorized. 220, 257
Bible. English. 1863. Authorized. 257
Bible. English. 1866. Authorized. 257
Bible. English. 1867. Authorized. 258
Bible. English. 1869. Authorized. 220, 358
Bible. English. 187-. Authorized. 580
Bible. English. 1870. Authorized. 258
Bible. English. 1870. Douai. 272
Bible. English. 1876. Authorized. 258
Bible. English. 1877. 247, 258, 2755
Bible. English. 1881. Authorized. 242
Bible. English. 1883? Authorized. 258, 358
Bible. English. 1884. Authorized. 258
Bible. English. 1885. Revised. 258
Bible. English. 189-? Authorized. 258
Bible. English. 1892. 258
Bible. English. 1892. Authorized. 258, 358
Bible. English. 1893. Authorized. 258
Bible. English. 1894. Authorized. 258
Bible. English. 1895? Authorized. 258
Bible. English. 1896. 220, 258
Bible. English. 1897. Authorized. 249
Bible. English. 1898. 258, 271, 647
Bible. English. 1898. Revised. 258
Bible. English. 1899? Douai. 272
Bible. English. 19. 197, 226
Bible. English. 19--. Authorized. 258, 358
Bible. English. 190-? 258
Bible. English. 1900. 258
Bible. English. 1901. 242
Bible. English. 1901. American revised. 258, 259, 358
Bible. English. 1901. Authorized. 259, 271, 3591
Bible. English. 1902. 301, 653
Bible. English. 1902. Authorized. 301, 653
Bible. English. 1903. 259, 653
Bible. English. 1903. Authorized. 249, 259, 611
Bible. English. 1904. 259
Bible. English. 1904. Authorized. 259
Bible. English. 1905. 259
Bible. English. 1905. Authorized. 197, 220, 259, 301
Bible. English. 1906. Authorized. 225, 259
Bible. English. 1907. 259, 274, 301
Bible. English. 1908. 259, 271
Bible. English. 1908. Authorized. 308
Bible. English. 1909. 259, 271
Bible. English. 1909. Authorized. 259
Bible. English. 191-? Authorized. 259
Bible. English. 1910. 635, 3596

Bible. English. 1910. American revised. 1388
Bible. English. 1910. Authorized. 635
Bible. English. 1911. 289
Bible. English. 1911. Authorized. 259
Bible. English. 1913. 259
Bible. English. 1913. Westminster version. 259
Bible. English. 1914. Douai. 272
Bible. English. 1915. 394
Bible. English. 1915. Authorized. 259, 358
Bible. English. 1917. 259
Bible. English. 1921. 653
Bible. English. 1922. 259
Bible. English. 1923. 260
Bible. English. 1924. 260, 1660
Bible. English. 1924. Authorized. 260
Bible. English. 1925. 260, 1660
Bible. English. 1926. 271
Bible. English. 1926. Authorized. 271
Bible. English. 1926. Moffatt. 260, 358
Bible. English. 1927. 1660
Bible. English. 1928. 260, 271, 1660, 2740
Bible. English. 1929. 260, 635
Bible. English. 1929. American revised. 260, 358, 359
Bible, English. 1929. Authorized. 359
Bible, English. 193-? Authorised. 260
Bible. English. 193-? Authorized. 249, 260, 359
Bible. English. 1930. 242, 271
Bible. English. 1930. Authorised. 2741
Bible. English. 1930? Douci. 273
Bible. English. 1931. 260
Bible. English. 1931. Authorized. 260
Bible. English. 1932. Authorised. 260
Bible. English. 1932. Authorized. 260, 653, 1660
Bible. English. 1933. Fenton. 261
Bible. English. 1934. 635
Bible. English. 1934. Authorized. 261, 359
Bible. English. 1934 Revised. 230
Bible. English. 1935. 261
Bible. English. 1935. Authorized. 261
Bible. English. 1935. Moffat. 261
Bible. English. 1936. Authorized. 261, 1914
Bible. English. 1937? Authorized. 261, 271, 1660
Bible. English. 1937. Moffatt. 261
Bible. English. 1937. Revised. 261
Bible. English. 1938? Authorized. 261
Bible. English. 1938. Fenton. 261
Bible. English. 1939. Authorized. 261, 271, 359, 1665
Bible. English. 1939. Smith-Goodspeed. 653
Bible. English. 1940. Authorized. 229, 261, 262, 271, 1660
Bible. English. 1941. Authorized. 197, 262, 271, 635, 1660, 2755
Bible. English. 1941. Douai. 273
Bible. English. 1942. Authorized. 262
Bible, English. 1943? Authorized. 262
Bible. English. 1944. Authorized. 197, 198, 262
Bible. English. 1944. Douai. 273
Bible. English. 1944. Smith. 2599, 2600
Bible. English. 1945. Authorized. 262
Bible. English. 1946. Authorized. 198, 262, 1660
Bible. English. 1947. Authorized. 220, 262, 263, 359, 2197
Bible. English. 1948. Authorized. 247, 263, 271, 359
Bible. English. 1948. Catholic Biblical Association. 655
Bible. English. 1949. Authorized. 220, 263, 359, 1660
Bible. English. 1949. Douai. 263, 481
Bible. English. 1950. Moffatt. 263
Bible. English. 1951. Authorized. 359, 614
Bible. English. 1951. Douai. 273
Bible. English. 1952. Authorized. 263
Bible. English. 1952. Catholic Biblical Association. 655
Bible. English. 1952. Douai. 273
Bible. English. 1952. Revised standard. 263, 359
Bible. English. 1953. Authorized. 1808
Bible. English. 1953. Confraternity version. 655, 1329
Bible. English. 1953. Douai. 778
Bible. English. 1954. Authorized. 263, 636
Bible. English. 1954. Douai. 655
Bible. English. 1955. Authorized. 263, 614
Bible. English. 1955. Confraternity version. 273
Bible. English. 1955. Douai. 273
Bible. English. 1956. Authorized. 263, 264, 306
Bible. English. 1956. Confraternity version. 198, 273
Bible. English. 1956. Knox. 264
Bible. English. 1956. Revised standard. 264

Bible. English. 1957. American standard. 220
Bible. English. 1957. Authorized. 220, 264
Bible. English. 1957. Confraternity version. 264
Bible. English. 1957. Lamsa. 650
Bible. English. 1958. Authorized. 264, 359
Bible. English. 1958. Confraternity version. 273, 778
Bible. English. 1958. New Jerusalem Church. 2690
Bible. English. 1958. Westminster version. 247
Bible. English. 1959. 2600
Bible. English. 1959. American revised. 1388
Bible. English. 1959. Authorized. 264, 2601
Bible. English. 1959. Berkeley version. 273, 275
Bible. English. 1959. Confraternity version. 273
Bible. English. 1959. Revised standard. 264
Bible. English. 1959. Rotherham. 264
Bible. English. 196- ? 264
Bible. English. 1960? 264, 265
Bible. English. 1960. Authorized. 220, 265, 271
Bible. English. 1960. Confraternity version. 274
Bible. English. 1961. 265, 655, 2129
Bible. English. 1961. Confraternity version. 274, 655
Bible. English. 1961. New World. 265
Bible. English. 1961. Revised standard. 265
Bible. English. 1962. 265
Bible. English. 1962. Authorized. 30, 265
Bible. English. 1962. Children's version. 253
Bible. English. 1962. Revised standard. 265, 359
Bible. English. 1963. 265, 266, 614, 653, 655
Bible. English. 1963. Authorized. 266
Bible. English. 1963. Confraternity version. 266
Bible. English. 1963. Douai. 274
Bible. English. 1963. Holy Name version. 230, 266
Bible. English. 1964. 220, 226, 266, 274, 636, 1661
Bible. English. 1964. Authorized. 1661
Bible. English. 1964? Revised standard. 266, 274
Bible. English. 1965. 198, 247, 266, 275, 1329
Bible. English. 1965. Authorized. 1884
Bible. English. 1965. Revised Standard. 247, 249
Bible. English. 1966. 198, 266, 655
Bible. English. 1966. Jerusalem Bible. 266
Bible. English. 1966. Revised standard. 655
Bible. English. 1967. Authorized. 254, 266, 267
Bible. English. 1967. Confraternity version. 1330
Bible. English. 1967. Revised standard. 267
Bible. English. 1972. 267
Bible English Authorized, 1950. 267
Bible. English. Authorized. 1968. 267
Bible. English. Authorized. 1969. 267
Bible. English. Authorized. 1970. 267
Bible. English. Authorized. 1971. 267
Bible. English. Authorized. 1973. 267
Bible. English. Authorized. 1974. 267
Bible. English. Authorized. 1976. 267
Bible. English. Authorized. 1977. 220, 267
Bible. English. Authorized. Selections. 1952. 249
Bible. English. Authorized. Selections. 1964. 210
Bible. English. Authorized. Selections. 1968. 614
Bible. English. Authorized. Selections. 1969. 198, 249
Bible. English. Authorized. Selections. 1972. 210
Bible. English. Authorized. Selections. 1973. 200, 1737
Bible. English. Authorized. Selections. 1974. 249, 267, 612
Bible. English. Authorized. Selections. 1975. 249, 267
Bible. English. Authorized. Selections. 1976. 249, 653
Bible. English. Authorized. Selections. 1977. 249, 602
Bible. English. Authorized. Selections. 1980. 249, 301
Bible. English. Authorized version. 1798. 267
Bible. English (Basic English) 1949. 267
Bible. English. Beck. 1976. 275

Bible. English. Byington. 1972. 1940
Bible English Catholic Biblical Association, 1948. 655
Bible. English. Catholic Biblical Association of America. Selections. 1973. 3472
Bible. English. Confraternity version. 1961. 274
Bible. English. Jerusalem Bible. 1971. 268
Bible. English. Jerusalem Bible. 1975. 218
Bible. English. Jerusalem Bible. Selections. 1972. 1444
Bible. English. Lessons, Liturgical. 1850. 2960
Bible. English (Middle English) Selections. 1938. Wycliffe. 248
Bible. English. New American. 1970. 268
Bible. English. New American. 1971. 268
Bible. English. New American Standard. 1971. 268
Bible. English. New American Standard. 1973. 268
Bible. English. New American Standard. 1975. 268
Bible. English. New American standard. 1977. 2197
Bible. English. New Berkeley version. Selections. 1972. 1430
Bible. English. New English. 1971. 274
Bible. English. New English. 1976. 274
Bible. English. New international. 1978. 268
Bible. English. New international. Selections. 1979. 1430
Bible. English. Paraphrases. 1902. 1987
Bible. English. Paraphrases. 1934. 319
Bible. English. Paraphrases. 1943. 603
Bible. English. Revised standard. 1962. 268, 359
Bible. English. Revised standard. 1971. 268
Bible. English. Revised Standard. 1973. 268, 275
Bible. English. Revised standard. 1977. 275
Bible. English. Revised standard. Selections. 1959. 618
Bible. English. Revised standard. Selections. 1971. 275
Bible. English. Revised Standard. Selections. 1972. 1430
Bible. English. Revised standard. Selections. 1975. 696
Bible. English. Selection. 1936. Authorized. 210
Bible. English. Selection. 1962. 249
Bible. English. Selections. 1794. 1810
Bible. English. Selections. 1811. 618
Bible. English. Selections. 1815. 1810
Bible. English. Selections. 1819. 472, 590
Bible. English. Selections. 1825. 1810
Bible. English. Selections. 1829. 1810
Bible. English. Selections. 1836. 724, 1810
Bible. English. Selections. 1837. 1810
Bible. English. Selections. 1850. 603
Bible. English. Selections. 1853. 249
Bible. English. Selections. 1854. 618
Bible. English. Selections. 1858. 724
Bible. English. Selections. 1861. 724
Bible. English. Selections. 1865. 3219
Bible. English. Selections. 1868-70. Authorized. 254
Bible. English. Selections. 1869. 724
Bible. English. Selections. 1872. 724
Bible. English. Selections. 1873. 724
Bible. English. Selections. 1878. 249, 650
Bible. English. Selections. 1885. 102, 253
Bible. English. Selections. 1886. 249, 724
Bible. English. Selections. 1887. 249, 725
Bible. English. Selections. 1888. 268
Bible. English. Selections. 1891. 725
Bible. English. Selections. 1893. 725
Bible. English. Selections. 1894. 725
Bible. English. Selections. 1894. Revised. 249
Bible. English. Selections. 1896. 249
Bible. English. Selections. 1896. Authorized. 725
Bible. English. Selections. 1897. 249, 725
Bible. English. Selections. 1898. 618
Bible. English. Selections. 1900. 725
Bible. English. Selections. 1901. 292, 725
Bible. English. Selections. 1902. 249, 647
Bible. English. Selections. 1902. Authorized. 313
Bible. English. Selections. 1905. Authorized. 614, 3406
Bible. English. Selections. 1906. 213, 725
Bible. English. Selections. 1907. 249
Bible. English. Selections. 1907. Authorized. 249
Bible. English. Selections. 1908. 249
Bible. English. Selections. 1909. 632
Bible. English. Selections. 1909. American revised. 725
Bible. English. Selections. 1910. Authorized. 725

Bible. English. Selections. 1911. 200, 249
Bible. English. Selections. 1912. 213
Bible. English. Selections. 1913. 249
Bible. English. Selections. 1915. 249, 618, 2028
Bible. English. Selections. 1915. American revised. 249
Bible. English. Selections. 1916. 725
Bible. English. Selections. 1917. 249, 1230
Bible. English. Selections. 1917. Authorized. 725
Bible. English. Selections. 1918. 275
Bible. English. Selections. 1919. 249, 2476
Bible. English. Selections. 192-? 647
Bible. English. Selections. 1922. 200, 250, 301, 3220
Bible. English. Selections. 1923? 250
Bible. English. Selections. 1923. American revised. 210
Bible. English. Selections. 1923. Authorized. 250
Bible. English. Selections. 1924. 250, 618
Bible. English. Selections. 1924. American revised. 250
Bible. English. Selections. 1924. Authorized. 250
Bible. English. Selections. 1925. 250, 254
Bible. English. Selections. 1925. Authorized. 45, 250, 725
Bible. English. Selections. 1926. 725
Bible. English. Selections. 1928. 198, 250, 647
Bible. English. Selections. 1930. 198
Bible. English. Selections. 1931. 230, 250
Bible. English. Selections. 1932. 250, 725, 2023
Bible. English. Selections. 1933. 188, 250, 301, 590, 3318, 3848
Bible. English. Selections. 1934. 254, 590, 618, 725, 2069
Bible. English. Selections. 1935. 250
Bible. English. Selections. 1936. 725
Bible. English. Selections. 1936. Authorized. 210, 614, 618
Bible. English. Selections. 1936. Smith-Goodspeed. 250
Bible. English. Selections. 1937. Authorized. 480, 3560
Bible. English. Selections. 1938. American revised. 241
Bible. English. Selections. 1938. Authorized. 250, 499, 59 0
Bible. English. Selections. 1939. 250, 254, 292
Bible. English. Selections. 1939. American revised. 250
Bible. English. Selections. 1940. 292
Bible. English. Selections. 1940. Moffatt. 1436
Bible. English. Selections. 1941? 625
Bible. English. Selections. 1941. Authorized. 250
Bible. English. Selections. 1942. Authorized. 268, 602, 3220, 3376
Bible. English. Selections. 1943. 292
Bible. English. Selections. 1943. Authorized. 250, 618
Bible. English. Selections. 1943. Douai. 1349
Bible. English. Selections. 1944. 603
Bible. English. Selections. 1944. Authorized. 250, 555
Bible. English. Selections. 1945. Authorized. 313
Bible. English. Selections. 1946. 250
Bible. English. Selections. 1946. Authorised. 250
Bible. English. Selections. 1946. Authorized. 250
Bible. English. Selections. 1947. 198, 602, 618
Bible. English. Selections. 1947? Authorised. 618
Bible. English. Selections. 1947. Authorized. 251
Bible. English. Selections. 1949. 2023
Bible. English. Selections. 1949. Authorized. 251, 301
Bible. English. Selections. 1950. Authorized. 198, 268
Bible. English. Selections. 1951. 200
Bible. English. Selections. 1951. Authorized. 251, 268, 281, 317
Bible. English. Selections. 1952. Authorized. 251, 268, 301, 472
Bible. English. Selections. 1953. 251, 292
Bible. English. Selections. 1953. Authorized. 251, 313, 653, 1430
Bible. English. Selections. 1954. 251, 603
Bible. English. Selections. 1954. Authorized. 231, 251, 268, 618
Bible. English. Selections. 1954. Douai. 3247
Bible. English.Selections. 1955. Authorized. 653
Bible. English. Selections. 1955. Revised standard. 3220

Bible. English. Selections. 1956. 251
Bible. English. Selections. 1956. Authorized. 251
Bible. English. Selections. 1957. Authorized. 251, 1719
Bible. English. Selections. 1957. Revised standard. 1430
Bible. English. Selections. 1958. 618
Bible. English. Selections. 1958. Authorised. 317
Bible. English. Selections. 1959. Authorized. 602, 603, 2062
Bible. English. Selections. 196-? 481
Bible. English. Selections. 1961. Authorized. 198
Bible. English. Selections. 1962. 251, 292
Bible. English. Selections. 1962. Authorized. 654
Bible. English. Selections. 1963. 1430
Bible. English. Selections. 1963. Confraternity version. 251
Bible. English. Selections. 1964. 132, 210
Bible. English. Selections. 1965. 210, 527
Bible. English Selections. 1965 Authorized. 210, 251, 602
Bible. English. Selections. 1966. 251
Bible. English. Selections. 1966. Authorized. 251, 618
Bible. English. Selections. 1967. 251, 603
Bible. English. Selections. 1968. 198
Bible. English. Selections. 1969. 650
Bible. English. Selections. 1970. 587
Bible. English. Selections. 1970 Authorized. 210
Bible. English. Selections. 1973. 241, 251, 483, 3011
Bible. English. Selections. 1974. 251, 268
Bible. English. Selections. 1975. 180, 251
Bible. English. Selections. 1978. 251
Bible. English. Selections. 1979. 603
Bible. English. Selections. 1980. 1077
Bible. English. Selections. 1980. Authorized. 301
Bible. English. Selections. Authorized. 251
Bible. English. Selections. N. T. Gospels. 1901. 1979
Bible. English. Smith. 1970. 268
Bible. English. Smith. 1974. 2600
Bible. English. Today's English. 1976. 268
Bible. English. Today's English. Selections. 1972. 2266
Bible. English. Today's English. Selections. 1977. 614
Bible. Enlgish. Selections. 1963. 308
Bible extension society. 613
Bible. Manuscript, Hebrew. O. T. Psalms. Dead Sea Psalms scroll. 1409
Bible. Manuscripts, Greek. N. T. Rockefeller McCormick ms. 2330
Bible. Manuscripts, Greek. O. T. Ezekiel. Scheide papyrus. 518
Bible. Manuscripts, Hebrew. O.T. Psalms. Dead Sea Psalms scroll. 1409
Bible. Manuscripts. Latin. N. T. Revelation. 1884, 2331
Bible. Massachuset. 1663. 2370
Bible. N.T. 284, 415
Bible. N. T. 1 Corinthians. English. 1838. 322
Bible. N. T. 1 Corinthians. English. 1841. 322
Bible. N. T. 1 Corinthians. English. 1857. 322
Bible. N. T. 1 Corinthians. English. 1872. 322
Bible. N. T. 1 Corinthians. English. 1899. 322
Bible. N.T. 1 Corinthians. English. Orr-Walther. 1976. 322, 2795
Bible. N.T. 1 Corinthians. Greek. 1905. 345
Bible. N.T. 1 Corinthians XIII. English. New English. 1975. 2266
Bible. N. T. 1 Peter. English. 1851. Demarest. 325
Bible. N. T. 1881. 342
Bible. N. T. 192. 1769
Bible. N. T. 2 Corinthians. English. 1840. 325
Bible. N. T. 2 Corinthians. English. 1854. 325
Bible. N. T. 2 Corinthians. English. 1872. 325
Bible. N. T. 2 Corinthians. English. 1897. Authorized. 325
Bible. N. T. 2 Corinthians. English. 1903. Authorized. 325
Bible. N.T. 2 Timothy. English. 1977. 326
Bible. N. T. Acts and Epistles. English. Harmonies. 1895. 2795
Bible. N. T. Acts and Epistles. English. Harmonies. 1906. American revised. 2795
Bible. N.T. Acts and Epistles. English. Harmonies. 1964. 2795

Bible. N. T. Acts and Epistles. English Harmonies. 1964. Authorized. 2795
Bible. N. T. Acts. Cherokee. 1860? Worcester. 891
Bible. N. T. Acts. Coptic (Sahidic) 1932. 315
Bible. N. T. Acts. English. 1844. 327
Bible. N. T. Acts. English. 1848. 327
Bible. N. T. Acts. English. 1859. 327
Bible. N. T. Acts. English. 1860. 327
Bible. N. T. Acts. English. 1863. 327
Bible. N. T. Acts. English. 1866. 327
Bible. N. T. Acts. English. 1870. 327
Bible. N. T. Acts. English. 1876. 327
Bible. N. T. Acts. English. 1882. 327
Bible. N. T. Acts. English. 1882. Revised. 327
Bible. N. T. Acts. English. 1884. 333
Bible. N. T. Acts. English. 1891. 327
Bible. N. T. Acts. English. 1897. 327
Bible. N. T. Acts. English. 1901. 198
Bible. N. T. Acts. English. 1903. 327
Bible. N. T. Acts. English. 1906. 198
Bible. N. T. Acts. English. 1908. Revised. 327
Bible. N. T. Acts. English. 1915. 70
Bible. N. T. Acts. English. 1915. Sitterly. 328
Bible. N. T. Acts. English. 1919. Douai. 328
Bible. N. T. Acts. English. 1920. 328
Bible. N. T. Acts. English. 1922. 328
Bible. N. T. Acts. English. 1927. 330
Bible. N.T. Acts. English. 1941. American revised. 328
Bible. N. T. Acts. English. 1955. Phillips. 326
Bible. N. T. Acts. English. 1957. 328
Bible. N. T. Acts. English. 1957. Barclay. 328
Bible. N. T. Acts. English. 1958. Douai. 328
Bible. N.T. Acts. English. 1964. 328
Bible. N.T. Acts. English. 1965. 328
Bible. N.T. Acts. English. 1966. 328
Bible. N.T. Acts. English. 1966. New English. 328
Bible. N.T. Acts. English. 1967. Munck. 328
Bible. N.T. Acts. English. 1967. Revised standard. 328
Bible. N.T. Acts. English. 1976. 328
Bible. N.T. Acts. English. 1976. Barclay. 328
Bible. N. T. Acts, Epistles, and Revelation. English. 1895. Revised. 406
Bible. N. T. Acts. Greek. 1852. 328
Bible. N. T. Acts. Greek. 1878. 328
Bible. N. T. Acts. Greek. 1904. 328
Bible. N. T. Acts. Greek. 1933. 331
Bible. N. T. Acts. Greek. 1934. 326
Bible. N. T. Acts. Greek. 1966. 328
Bible. N.T. Acts i-xiv. English. 1881. 328
Bible. N. T. Apocryphal books. Coptic Gospel of Philip. English. 1962. 268
Bible. N. T. Apocryphal books. English. 1825. 335
Bible. N. T. Apocryphal books. English. 1832. Jones-Wake. 335
Bible. N. T. Apocryphal books. English. 1845? Jones-Wake. 336
Bible. N. T. Apocryphal books. English. 1849. Jones-Wake. 336
Bible. N. T. Apocryphal books. English. 1858. 2056
Bible. N. T. Apocryphal books. English. 1880. Jones-Wake. 336
Bible. N.T. Apocryphal books. English. 1889. Jones-Wake. 336
Bible. N. T. Apocryphal books. English. 1890. Jones-Wake. 336
Bible. N. T. Apocryphal books. English. 1908. 337
Bible. N. T. Apocryphal books. English. 1924. James. 336
Bible. N. T. Apocryphal books. English. 1925. 336
Bible. N. T. Apocryphal books. English. 1926. James. 336
Bible. N. T. Apocryphal books. English. 1926. Jones-Wake. 336
Bible. N.T. Apocryphal books. English. 1963. 336
Bible. N.T. Apocryphal books. English. Jones-Wake. 1979. 336
Bible. N. T. Apocryphal books. English. Selections. 1887. 1975
Bible. N. T. Apocryphal books. English. Selections. 1903. 1975
Bible. N. T. Apocryphal books. Epistle of Barnabas. Greek. (1642) 1883. 337
Bible. N. T. Apocryphal books. Gospels. Coptic. 1896. 337
Bible. N. T. Apocryphal books. Gospels. English. Selections. 1940. Walker. 336
Bible. N. T. Apocryphal books. Gospels. Latin. 1930. 381

Bible. N.T. Apocryphal books. Gospels of infancy. 336
Bible. N.T. Apocryphal books. Gospels. Syrian. 1899. 3093
Bible. N. T. Apocryphal books. Logia Iesou. Greek. 1920. 2755
Bible. N. T. Catholic epistles--Commentaries. 339, 340
Bible. N. T. Catholic epistles. English. 1848. 340
Bible. N. T. Catholic epistles. English. 1860. 340
Bible. N. T. Catholic epistles. English. 1875. 340
Bible. N.T. Catholic epistles. English. 1903. 340, 367
Bible. N.T. Catholic epistles. English. 1964. Reicke. 340
Bible. N. T. Catholic espistles. English. 1964. Reicke. 340
Bible. N. T. Colossians. English. 1898. 341
Bible. N. T. Colossians. English. 1910. American revised. 341
Bible. N. T. Colossians. English. 1977. 341
Bible. N.T. Colossians. English. Paraphrases. 1964. Neill. 341
Bible. N. T. Colossians. Greek. 1886. 341
Bible. N. T. Coptic. 1898. 315
Bible. N. T. Coptic (Sahidic) 1911. 229
Bible. N. T. Corinthians. English. 1902? 345
Bible. N. T. Corinthians. English. 1903. 345
Bible. N. T. Corinthians. English. 1909. 345
Bible. N. T. Corinthians. English. 1922. Revised. 345
Bible. N. T. Corinthians. English. 1930. Revised. 345
Bible. N. T. Corinthians. English. 1956. Barclay. 345
Bible. N. T. Corinthians. English. 1965. New English. 345
Bible. N.T. Corinthians. English. Barclay. 1975. 345
Bible. N.T. Dutch. 1963. New World. 320
Bible. N. T. English. 1789. Authorized. 360
Bible. N. T. English. 1790. 355
Bible. N. T. English. 1817. Rheims. 362
Bible. N. T. English. 1819. Authorised. 360
Bible. N. T. English. 1819. Authorized. 360
Bible. N. T. English. 1820. 320
Bible. N. T. English. 1823. 355
Bible. N. T. English. 1826. Authorized. 360
Bible. N.T. English. 1828. 352
Bible. N. T. English. 1833. 355
Bible. N. T. English. 1833. Dickinson. 352
Bible. N. T. English. 1834. Rheims. 362
Bible. N.T. English. 1837. Tyndale. 359
Bible. N.T. English. 1844. Authorized. 360
Bible. N. T. English. 1850. Authorized. 360
Bible. N. T. English. 1851. Murdock. 650
Bible. N. T. English. 1853. Authorized. 360
Bible. N. T. English. 1855. Murdock. 650
Bible. N. T. English. 1858. Sawyer. 355
Bible. N. T. English. 186-? Douai. 362
Bible. N. T. English. 1860. Authorized. 342
Bible. N. T. English. 1861. 206, 355
Bible. N. T. English. 1861. Authorized. 360
Bible. N. T. English. 1862. 355
Bible. N.T. English. 1862. Authorized. 360
Bible. N. T. English. 1864. Authorized. 342, 360
Bible. N. T. English. 1868. American Bible union. 355
Bible. N. T. English. 1869. Authorized. 360
Bible. N. T. English. 1879. Authorized. 360
Bible. N. T. English. 1880. Noyes. 356
Bible. N. T. English. 1881. Authorized. 360
Bible. N. T. English. 1881. Revised. 268, 355, 361
Bible. N. T. English. 1882. 361
Bible. N. T. English. 1885. Dillard. 2062
Bible. N. T. English. 1888. Authorized. 342
Bible. N. T. English. 1891. Sawyer. 352
Bible. N. T. English. 1892. Murdock. 650
Bible. N. T. English. 1898. 473
Bible. N. T. English. 1899. 360
Bible. N.T. English. 1899. Authorized. 360
Bible. N. T. English. 1900. 352, 654
Bible. N.T. English. 1900. Fenton. 352

Bible. N. T. English. 1900. Twentieth century. 352
Bible. N. T. English. 1901. American revised. 360
Bible. N. T. English. 1902. 352, 654
Bible. N. T. English. 1902. Authorized. 320, 360
Bible. N.T. English. 1903. Authorized. 479
Bible. N. T. English. 1903. Twentieth century. 352
Bible. N. T. English. 1904. 286, 352, 356, 359
Bible. N.T. English. 1904. American revised. 352
Bible. N. T. English. 1904. Rheims. 362
Bible. N. T. English. 1905. 352
Bible. N. T. English. 1905. Lloyd. 353
Bible. N. T. English. 1906. 356, 359, 3143
Bible. N.T. English. 1906. Authorized. 360
Bible. N. T. English. 1906. Revised. 342
Bible. N. T. English 1907. Authorized. 342, 1863
Bible. N. T. English. 1909. 353
Bible. N. T. English. 1909. Weymouth. 268, 353
Bible. N. T. English. 191-? Authorized. 360
Bible. N. T. English. 1910. 356
Bible. N. T. English. 1912. 353
Bible. N. T. English. 1913. 353
Bible. N.T. English. 1913. Authorized. 353
Bible. N.T. English. 1913. Westminster version. 353, 356
Bible. N. T. English. 1914. 353
Bible. N. T. English. 1915. 353
Bible. N. T. English. 1916. 353
Bible. N. T. English. 1917. 356
Bible. N. T. English. 1918. 268, 315, 353, 359
Bible. N. T. English. 1920. 269, 353
Bible. N. T. English. 1922. 353
Bible. N. T. English. 1922. Moffatt. 356
Bible. N. T. English. 1923. 353
Bible. N. T. English. 1923. Ballantine. 353
Bible. N. T. English. 1923. Goodspeed. 353, 356
Bible. N. T. English. 1924. 479
Bible. N. T. English. 1924. Montgomery. 353
Bible. N. T. English. 1925. 360
Bible. N. T. English. 1925. Goodspeed. 356
Bible. N. T. English. 1925. Overbury. 1. 353
Bible. N. T. English. 1929. 353
Bible. N. T. English. 1931. Rheims. 362
Bible. N. T. English. 1931. Westminster version. 356
Bible. N. T. English. 1932. 353
Bible. N. T. English. 1933. Authorized. 356
Bible. N. T. English. 1933. Revised. 361
Bible. N. T. English. 1934. 356
Bible. N. T. English. 1934. Rheims. 343
Bible. N. T. English. 1936. Weymouth. 353
Bible. N. T. English. 1937. 356
Bible. N. T. English. 1937. Spencer. 356
Bible. N. T. English. 1937. Williams. 356
Bible. N. T. English. 1938. Authorized. 360
Bible. N. T. English. 1938. Clementson. 356
Bible. N. T. English. 1938. Rheims. 343
Bible. N. T. English. 1938. Wesley. 356
Bible. N. T. English. 1940. Lamsa. 353
Bible. N. T. English. 1941. Authorized. 360
Bible. N. T. English. 1941. Rheims. 362
Bible. N.T. English. 1942. Authorized. 343
Bible. N.T. English. 1942. Rheims. 362
Bible. N.T. English. 1943. Authorized. 353
Bible. N.T. English. 1943. Rheims. 362
Bible. N.T. English. 1943. Weymouth. 353
Bible. N.T. English. 1944? Authorized. 360, 361
Bible. N.T. English. 1944. Concordant version. 356
Bible. N.T. English. 1944. Knox. 356
Bible. N.T. English. 1945. Authorized. 320, 361
Bible. N.T. English. 1945. Rheims. 362
Bible. N.T. English. 1945. Verkuyl. 479
Bible. N.T. English. 1946. Authorized. 353
Bible. N. T. English. 1946. Knox. 2182
Bible. N.T. English. 1946. Revised standard. 356
Bible. N.T. English. 1946. Rheims. 362
Bible. N.T. English. 1947. Swann. 356
Bible. N.T. English. 1948. Goodspeed. 356

Bible. N. T. English. 1948. Westminster version. 356
Bible. N. T. English. 1949. Smith. 361
Bible. N.T. English. 1950. Confraternity version. 361
Bible. N.T. English. 1950. Moffatt. 269
Bible. N.T. English. 1950. Rheims. 362
Bible. N.T. English. 1950. Sacred Name version. 356
Bible. N.T. English. 1950. Williams. 353
Bible. N.T. English. 1951. Authorized. 361
Bible. N.T. English. 1951. Brotherhood Authentic Bible Society. 359
Bible. N.T. English. 1952. Authorised. 343
Bible. N.T. English. 1952. Confraternity version. 359
Bible. N.T. English. 1953. Confraternity version. 361
Bible. N.T. English. 1953. Knox. 356
Bible. N.T. English. 1953. Wesley. 356
Bible. N.T. English. 1953. Weymouth. 269
Bible. N.T. English. 1954. 359
Bible. N.T. English. 1954. Kleist-Lilly. 356
Bible. N.T. English. 1954. Moore. 353
Bible. N.T. English. 1955. Authorized. 3640
Bible. N. T. English. 1956. Authorized. 269
Bible. N. T. English. 1956. Confraternity version. 361
Bible. N.T. English. 1956. Wuest. 356
Bible. N.T. English. 1958. 354, 359
Bible. N.T. English. 1958. Phillips. 359
Bible. N.T. English. 1958. Schonfield. 320
Bible. N.T. English. 1958. Siewert. 320
Bible. N. T. English. 1958. Tomanek. 356
Bible. N. T. English. 1959. 356
Bible. N. T. English. 1959. American revised. 343
Bible. N. T. English. 1959. Authorized. 354, 479
Bible. N. T. English. 1959. Rotherham. 357
Bible. N. T. English. 1960. Confraternity version. 343, 361
Bible. N. T. English. 1961. 354, 361
Bible. N.T. English. 1961. Authorized. 320, 354, 361
Bible. N.T. English. 1961. Noli. 357, 359
Bible. N. T. English. 1961. Norlie. 354
Bible. N. T. English. 1961. Wuest. 354, 357
Bible. N. T. English. 1962. 354, 357
Bible. N. T. English. 1962. Authorized. 343, 354, 3197
Bible. N. T. English. 1963. 357
Bible. N.T. English. 1963. Beck. 354
Bible. N.T. English. 1963. New American standard. 357
Bible. N.T. English. 1963. Norlie. 354
Bible. N.T. English. 1964. 343, 357, 362, 450
Bible. N. T. English. 1965. 251, 359, 362
Bible. N. T. English. 1965. Phillips. 360
Bible. N. T. English. 1965. Revised standard. 362
Bible. N. T. English. 354, 357, 479
Bible. N.T. English. 1966. Today's English. 354
Bible. N. T. English. 1967. 357, 360
Bible. N. T. English. 1967. Authorized. 361
Bible. N.T. English. 1967. Confraternity Version. 360
Bible. N.T. English. 1967. Craddock. 361
Bible. N. T. English. 1967. Jerusalem Bible. 3407
Bible. N.T. English. 1967. Revised standard. 362
Bible. N.T. English. 1974. 357
Bible. N. T. English. 1975. 357
Bible. N. T. English. Authorized. 1971. 361
Bible. N.T. English. Authorized. 1975. 401
Bible. N.T. English. Authorized. 1976. 361
Bible. N.T. English. Authorized. 1978. 361
Bible. N.T. English. Barclay. 1968. 357
Bible. N. T. English (Basic English) 1941. 177
Bible. N. T. English (Basic English) 1941. Hooke. 177
Bible. N.T. English. Catholic Biblical Association of America. Selections. 1972. 450
Bible. N.T. English. Concordant version. 1976. 357
Bible. N.T. English. Harmonies. 1840. Authorized. 346

Bible. N.T. English. Haugerud. Selections. 1977. 472
Bible. N.T. English. International. 1973. 582
*Bible. N.T. English. King James. 357
Bible. N.T. English. Klingensmith. 1972. 354
Bible. N.T. English. Klingensmith. 1974. 357
Bible. N.T. English. Klingensmith. Selections. 1969. 357
Bible. N.T. English. Layman's parallel. 1970. 357
Bible. N.T. English. Ledvard. 1969. 354
Bible. N. T. English (Middle English) 1879. 354
Bible. N.T. English (Middle English) Selections. 1902. 357
Bible. N.T. English (Middle English). Selections. 1974. 357
Bible. N.T. English. New American. 1970. 269
Bible. N.T. English. New American Standard. 1971. 582
Bible. N.T. English. New American Standard. 1975. 354
Bible. N.T. English. New Berkeley version. 1970. 357
Bible. N.T. English. New English. 1970. 274
Bible. N.T. English. New international. 1976. 582
Bible. N.T. English. New King James Bible. 1979. 269
Bible. N. T. English. Norlie. 1972. 354
Bible. N.T. English. Paraphrases. 1932. Ballentine. 354
Bible. N.T. English. Paraphrases. 1960. Roth. 354
Bible. N. T. English. Paraphrases. 1967. 357
Bible. N.T. English. Paraphrases. 1967. Taylor. 1430
Bible. N.T. English. Phillips. Selections. 1970. 472
Bible. N.T. English. Restoration of original name version. 1968. 357
Bible. N.T. English. Revised standard. 1955. 362
Bible. N.T. English. Revised standard. 1971. 358
Bible. N.T. English. Revised standard. Selections. 1970. 2069
Bible. N. T. English. Selections. 1899. 625, 3334
Bible. N.T. English. Selections. 1904. 2069
Bible. N.T. English. Selections. 1905. 2069
Bible. N.T. English. Selections. 1906. American revised. 1460
Bible. N.T. English. Selections. 1911. 2070
Bible. N.T. English. Selections. 1912. 198
Bible. N.T. English. Selections. 1922. 354
Bible. N.T. English. Selections. 1924. 355
Bible. N.T. English. Selections. 1927. Authorized. 2070
Bible. N.T. English. Selections. 1936. Authorized. 472
Bible. N.T. English. Selections. 1939. Authorized. 354
Bible. N.T. English. Selections. 1942. Authorized. 2070
Bible. N.T. English. Selections. 1942? Rheims. 725
Bible. N.T. English. Selections. 1947. Authorized. 626
Bible. N.T. English. Selections. 1953. Authorized. 472
Bible. N.T. English. Selections. 1955. 269
Bible. N.T. English. Selections. 1955. Authorized. 2070
Bible. N.T. English. Selections. 1963. Authorized. 1430
Bible. N.T. English. Selections. 1966. 354
Bible. N.T. English. Selections. 1967. Authorized. 320
Bible. N.T. English. Selections. 1967. Klingensmith. 251
Bible. N.T. English. Selections. 1969. 2072
Bible. N.T. English. Selections. 1974. 2062
Bible. N.T. English. Today's English. 1969. 354
Bible. N.T. English. Today's English. 1971. 354
Bible. N.T. English. Today's English. Selections. 1972. 354
Bible. N.T. English. Weymouth. 1978. 354
Bible. N.T. English. Worrell. 1980. 354
Bible. N. T. Enlgish. 1937. Weymouth. 354
Bible. N. T. Ephesians. English. 1899. Authorized. 362, 561

Bible. N. T. Ephesians. English. 1913. 363
Bible. N. T. Ephesians. English. Authorized. 1977. 363
Bible. N. T. Ephesians. English. Barth. 1974. 363
Bible. N. T. Ephesians. English. Caudill. 1979. 364
Bible. N. T. Ephesians. Greek. 1856. 363
Bible. N. T. Ephesians. Greek. 1906. 364
Bible. N. T. Ephesians. Greek. 1914. 363
Bible. N. T. Ephesians. Greek. Robinson. 1979. 363
Bible. N.T. Epislees and Gospels, Liturgical. English. 366
Bible. N. T. Epistles and Gospels. 654
Bible. N. T. Epistles and Gospels, Liturgical. 1922. 366
Bible. N. T. Epistles and Gospels, Liturgical. English. 1846. Rheims. 855
Bible. N. T. Epistles and Gospels, Liturgical. English. 1891. 366
Bible. N. T. Epistles and Gospels, Liturgical. English. 1905. 366
Bible. N. T. Epistles and Gospels, Liturgical. English. 1907. 366
Bible. N. T. Epistles and Gospels, Liturgical. English. 1931. 2205
Bible. N. T. Epistles and Gospels, Liturgical. English. 1941. 366
Bible. N. T. Epistles and Gospels, Liturgical. English. 1941. Rheims. 366
Bible. N. T. Epistles and Gospels, Liturgical. English. 1946. Knox. 366
Bible. N. T. Epistles and Gospels, Liturgical. English. 1951. Confraternity version. 366
Bible. N. T. Epistles and Gospels, Liturgical. English. 1959. Authorized. 366
Bible. N. T. Epistles and Gospels, Liturgical. Lithuanian (1579) 1966. Vilentas. 366
Bible. N. T. Epistles and Gospels, Lutirgical. English. 1942. 366
Bible. N. T. Epistles. English. 1850. Macknight. 367
Bible. N.T. Epistles. English. 1906. 366
Bible. N.T. Epistles. English. 1910. 367
Bible. N.T. Epistles. English. 1929. 269
Bible. N.T. Epistles. English. 1933. 367
Bible. N.T. Epistles. English. 1943. American revised. 367
Bible. N. T. Epistles. English. 1947. Phillips. 368
Bible. N. T. Epistles. English. 1956. Laubach. 354
Bible. N. T. Epistles. English. 1957. Phillips. 368
Bible. N. T. Epistles. English. Paraphrases. 1946. Wand. 374
Bible. N.T. Epistles. English. Paraphrases. 1956. Wand. 374
Bible. N.T. Epistles. English. Paraphrases. 1962. 358
Bible. N.T. Epistles. English. Paraphrases. 1967. 368, 1631
Bible. N.T. Epistles. English. Phillips. 1968. 368
Bible. N. T. Epistles of John. English. 1900. 368
Bible. N. T. Epistles of John. English. 1965. 368
Bible, N. T. Epistles of John. English. 1965. New English. 368
Bible. N. T. Epistles of John. English. Barclay. c1976. 368
Bible. N. T. Epistles of John. Greek. 1886. 368
Bible. N. T. Epistles of John. Greek. 1896. 369
Bible. N. T. Epistles of John. Greek. 1902. 369
Bible. N. T. Epistles of Paul. English. 1845. 370
Bible. N.T. Epistles of Paul. English. 1848. 370
Bible. N.T. Epistles of Paul. English. 1851. 370
Bible. N.T. Epistles of Paul. English. 1859. 370
Bible. N. T. Epistles of Paul. English. 1860. 370
Bible. N.T. Epistles of Paul. English. 1873. 370
Bible. N.T. Epistles of Paul. English. 1902? 370
Bible. N.T. Epistles of Paul. English. 1902. Ballentine. 369
Bible. N.T. Epistles of Paul. English. 1903. 370
Bible. N.T. Epistles of Paul. English. 1920. 363
Bible. N. T. Epistles of Paul. English. 1922. Douai. 370
Bible. N. T. Epistles of Paul. English. 1938. Cornish. 370

Bible. N. T. Epistles of Paul. English. 1958. Conybeare. 370
Bible. N. T. Epistles of Paul. English. 1959. Barclay. 370
Bible. N.T. Epistles of Paul. English. Barclay. 1975. 448
Bible. N.T. Epistles of Paul. English. Blackwelder. 1971. 370
Bible. N.T. Epistles of Paul. English. New American Bible. Selections. 1976. 370
Bible. N.T. Epistles of Paul. English. Paraphrases. 1900. Stevens. 374
Bible. N. T. Epistles of Paul English. Paraphrases. 1965. Bruce. 370
Bible. N. T. Epistles of Paul. English. Revised standard. 1975. 373
Bible. N.T. Epistles of Paul. English. Selections. 1911. 375, 2795
Bible. N.T. Epistles of Paul. English. Selections. 1941. 375, 2795
Bible. N. T. Epistles of Paul. Greek. 1876. 371
Bible. N. T. Epistles of Paul. Greek. 1887. 371
Bible. N. T. Epistles of Paul. Greek. 1890. 371
Bible. N. T. Epistles of Paul. Greek. 1918. 2330
Bible. N. T. Epistles of Paul. Greek. 1935. 2331
Bible. N. T. French. 1871. Osterwald. 269
Bible. N. T. French. 1908. 269
Bible. N.T. French. 1963. New World. 320
Bible. N. T. Galatians. English. 1863. Authorized. 379
Bible. N. T. Galatians. English. 1896. 379
Bible. N. T. Galatians. English. 1909. 379
Bible. N. T. Galatians. English. 1911. 379
Bible. N. T. Galatians. English. 1917. 379
Bible. N. T. Galatians. English. 1925. 379
Bible. N. T. Galatians. English. 1959. Barclay. 379
Bible. N.T. Galatians. English. 1967. New English. 379
Bible. N.T. Galatians. English. Barclay. 1976. 379
Bible. N. T. Galatians. English. Paraphrases. 1958. 381
Bible. N. T. Galatians. Greek. 1856. 379
Bible. N. T. Galatians. Greek. 1860. 379
Bible. N. T. Galatians. Greek. 1900. 379
Bible. N. T. Galatians. Greek. 1910. 379
Bible. N. T. German. 1916. 320
Bible. N.T. German. 1963. 3798
Bible. N.T. Gospel. English. Harmonies. 1894. American Bible union. 1987
Bible N.T. Gospel, English Selection 1966. revised standard. 1986
Bible. N.T. Gospels. 381
Bible. N. T. Gospels and Acts. Chamerre. 1908. 881
Bible. N. T. Gospels and Acts. English. 1959. Authorized. 450
Bible. N.T. Gospels and Acts. Paraphrases. English. 1966. Taylor. 383
Bible. N.T. Gospels. English. 1799. 381
Bible. N.T. Gospels. English. 1811. Campbell. 385
Bible. N. T. Gospels. English. 1837. Authorized. 385
Bible. N. T. Gospels. English. 1837. Campbell. 385
Bible. N. T. Gospels. English. 1846. 385
Bible. N. T. Gospels. English. 1848. 385
Bible. N. T. Gospels. English. 1849. Kenrick. 382
Bible. N. T. Gospels. English. 1855. 385
Bible. N. T. Gospels. English. 1856. Norton. 385
Bible. N. T. Gospels. English. 1857. 385
Bible. N. T. Gospels. English. 1860. 385
Bible. N. T. Gospels. English. 1867. 385
Bible. N. T. Gospels. English. 1868. 385
Bible. N. T. Gospels. English. 1869. 385
Bible. N. T. Gospels. English. 1869. Folsom. 385
Bible. N. T. Gospels. English. 1871. 385
Bible N.T. Gospels. English. 1871. Folsom. 385
Bible. N. T. Gospels. English. 1897. Ballentine. 269
Bible. N. T. Gospels. English. 1898. Campbell. 382
Bible. N. T. Gospels. English. 1898. Spencer. 382
Bible. N. T. Gospels. English. 1900. Revised. 354
Bible. N. T. Gospels. English. 1905. 382
Bible. N.T. Gospels. English. 1905. Authorized. 382
Bible. N. T. Gospels. English. 1906. Authorized. 385
Bible. N. T. Gospels. English. 1910. 382
Bible. N. T. Gospels. English. 1911. 284, 394

Bible. N. T. Gospels. English. 1913. 382
Bible. N. T. Gospels. English. 1914. Authorized. 385
Bible. N. T. Gospels. English. 1918. 385
Bible. N. T. Gospels. English. 1920. 382
Bible. N. T. Gospels. English. 1928. 385
Bible. N. T. Gospels. English. 1930. 382
Bible. N. T. Gospels. English. 1933. Lamsa. 382
Bible. N. T. Gospels. English. 1933. Torrey. 387
Bible. N. T. Gospels. English. 1935. 382
Bible. N. T. Gospels. English. 1940. Dakes. 382
Bible. N. T. Gospels. English. 1947. Torrey. 387
Bible. N. T. Gospels. English. 1948. Rheims. 382
Bible. N. T. Gospels. English. 1952. Confraternity version. 1960
Bible. N. T. Gospels. English. 1953. Rieu. 382
Bible. N. T. Gospels. English. 1954. Authorized. 382
Bible. N. T. Gospels. English. 1957. Heenan. 385
Bible. N.T. Gospels. English. 1962. 1960
Bible. N. T. Gospels. English. 1962. Confraternity version. 1960
Bible. N.T. Gospels. English. Alba House. 1970. 320
Bible. N.T. Gospels. English. Authorized. 1971. 284
Bible. N. T. Gospels. English. Authorized. 1973. 1987
Bible. N. T. Gospels. English. Authorized. Selections. 1968. 1987
Bible. N.T. Gospels. English. Authorized. Selections. 1976. 1987
Bible. N.T. Gospels. English. Coulter. 1974. 1987
Bible. N. T. Gospels. English. Harmonies. 1815. Thomson. 1987
Bible. N. T. Gospels. English. Harmonies. 1828. 382
Bible. N. T. Gospels. English. Harmonies. 1829. 395
Bible. N. T. Gospels. English. Harmonies. 1837. 1987
Bible. N. T. Gospels. English. Harmonies. 1845. 1987
Bible. N. T. Gospels. English. Harmonies. 1846. 2067
Bible. N. T. Gospels. English. Harmonies. 1846. Authorized. 395
Bible. N. T. Gospels. English. Harmonies. 1852. 382
Bible. N. T. Gospels. English. Harmonies. 1853. Authorized. 1987
Bible. N. T. Gospels. English. Harmonies. 1854. 1988
Bible. N. T. Gospels. English. Harmonies. 1867. 1985, 1988
Bible. N. T. Gospels. English. Harmonies. 1868. 2070
Bible. N. T. Gospels. English. Harmonies. 1869. 1988, 2035
Bible. N. T. Gospels. English. Harmonies. 1869. Authorized. 395
Bible. N. T. Gospels. English. Harmonies. 1870. 382
Bible. N. T. Gospels. English. Harmonies. 1871. 1988
Bible. N. T. Gospels. English. Harmonies. 1871. Authorized. 385, 395, 1988
Bible. N. T. Gospels. English. Harmonies. 1872. Authorized. 385
Bible. N. T. Gospels. English. Harmonies. 1874. 2035
Bible. N. T. Gospels English. Harmonies.(1874) 1965. 394
Bible. N. T. Gospels. English. Harmonies. 1874. Authorized. 394, 2068
Bible. N.T. Gospels. English. Harmonies. (1874) 1965. Authorized. 394
Bible. N.T. Gospels. English. Harmonies. 1875. Authorized. 1988
Bible. N. T. Gospels. English. Harmonies. 1877. 2035
Bible. N. T. Gospels. English. Harmonies. 1877. Authorized. 1988
Bible. N. T. Gospels. English. Harmonies. 1885. Hartpence. 1988
Bible. N. T. Gospels. English. Harmonies. 1885. Revised. 1988
Bible. N. T. Gospels. English. Harmonies. 1886. Authorized. 395
Bible. N. T. Gospels. English. Harmonies. 1886. Revised. 1988
Bible. N. T. Gospels. English. Harmonies. 1889. 382
Bible. N. T. Gospels. English. Harmonies. 1889. Authorized. 1988
Bible. N. T. Gospels. English. Harmonies. 1890. Authorized. 1988
Bible. N. T. Gospels. English. Harmonies. 1891. 382

Bible. N. T. Gospels. English. Harmonies. 1891. Revised. 399, 1988
Bible. N. T. Gospels. English. Harmonies. 1892. 382
Bible. N. T. Gospels. English. Harmonies. 1892. Revised. 1988
Bible. N. T. Gospels. English. Harmonies. 1893. 2035
Bible. N. T. Gospels. English. Harmonies. 1893. Authorized. 382
Bible. N. T. Gospels. English. Harmonies. 1893. Revised. 395
Bible. N. T. Gospels. English. Harmonies. 1894. 395, 1988
Bible. N. T. Gospels. English. Harmonies. 1895. Authorized. 399
Bible. N. T. Gospels. English. Harmonies. 1895. Revised. 395, 1988
Bible. N. T. Gospels. English. Harmonies. 1898. 383, 1988
Bible. N. T. Gospels. English. Harmonies. 1898. Authorized. 400
Bible. N. T. Gospels. English. Harmonies. 1898. Rheims. 396
Bible. N. T. Gospels. English. Harmonies. 1899. 1988
Bible. N. T. Gospels. English. Harmonies. 1900. Authorized. 1988
Bible. N. T. Gospels. English. Harmonies. 1901. Authorized. 396
Bible. N. T. Gospels. English. Harmonies. 1902. 385, 396
Bible. N. T. Gospels. English. Harmonies. 1903. American revised. 396
Bible. N. T. Gospels. English. Harmonies. 1903. Revised. 396
Bible. N. T. Gospels. English. Harmonies. 1904. 396
Bible. N. T. Gospels. English. Harmonies. 1905. 1960, 2035
Bible. N. T. Gospels. English. Harmonies. 1907. American revised. 394, 2028
Bible. N. T. Gospels. English. Harmonies. 1909. Rheims. 1988
Bible. N. T. Gospels. English. Harmonies. 1910. 383
Bible. N. T. Gospels. English. Harmonies. 1911. 2070
Bible. N. T. Gospels. English. Harmonies. 1911. American revised. 1988
Bible. N. T. Gospels. English. Harmonies. 1912. 1988, 1989
Bible. N. T. Gospels. English. Harmonies. 1913. 1989
Bible. N. T. Gospels. English. Harmonies. 1913. American revised. 1989
Bible. N. T. Gospels. English. Harmonies. 1913. Rheims. 1989
Bible. N. T. Gospels. English. Harmonies. 1916. 1989
Bible. N. T. Gospels. English. Harmonies. 1916. Bowen. 387, 1989
Bible. N. T. Gospels. English. Harmonies. 1917. American revised. 396
Bible. N. T. Gospels. English. Harmonies. 1917. Revised. 394
Bible. N. T. Gospels. English. Harmonies. 1917. Twentieth century. 1989
Bible. N. T. Gospels. English. Harmonies. 1919. American revised. 383
Bible. N. T. Gospels. English. Harmonies. 1922. 396
Bible. N. T. Gospels. English. Harmonies. 1923. Authorized. 383
Bible. N. T. Gospels. English. Harmonies. 1925. 1989
Bible. N. T. Gospels. English. Harmonies. 1925. Moffatt. 1989
Bible. N. T. Gospels. English. Harmonies. 1926. 396
Bible. N. T. Gospels. English. Harmonies. 1926. American revised. 1989
Bible. N. T. Gospels. English. Harmonies. 1926. Loux. 1989
Bible. N. T. Gospels. English. Harmonies. 1927. 248
Bible. N. T. Gospels. English. Harmonies. 1927. Authorized. 396
Bible. N. T. Gospels. English. Harmonies. 1927. Montgomery. 1989
Bible. N. T. Gospels. English. Harmonies. 1928. 396
Bible. N. T. Gospels. English. Harmonies. 1928. Osborn. 1989
Bible. N. T. Gospels. English. Harmonies. 1929. Authorized. 399, 1989
Bible. N T. Gospels. English. Harmonies. 1929. Towne. 1989
Bible. N. T. Gospels. English. Harmonies. 1932. 354, 355
Bible. N. T. Gospels. English. Harmonies. 1932. Osborn. 1989
Bible. N. T. Gospels. English. Harmonies. 1933. 1989
Bible. N. T. Gospels. English. Harmonies. 1934. 394, 1989

Bible. N. T. Gospels. English. Harmonies. 1935. 383, 1989
Bible. N. T. Gospels. English. Harmonies. 1936. 1989
Bible. N. T. Gospels. English. Harmonies. 1937. Authorized. 1989
Bible. N. T. Gospels. English. Harmonies. 1937. Ebersol. 1989
Bible. N. T. Gospels. English. Harmonies. 1937. Moffatt. 1989
Bible. N. T. Gospels. English. Harmonies. 1938. Authorized. 1989
Bible. N. T. Gospels. English. Harmonies. 1939. Douai. 396, 399, 1989, 1990
Bible. N. T. Gospels. English. Harmonies. 1940. Weymouth. 1436, 1990
Bible. N. T. Gospels. English. Harmonies. 1941. Authorized. 396, 1990, 1991
Bible. N. T. Gospels. English. Harmonies. 1941. Revised. 2054
Bible. N. T. Gospels. English. Harmonies. 1942. Authorized. 396
Bible. N. T. Gospels. English. Harmonies. 1942. Rheims. 387, 396
Bible. N.T. Gospels. English. Harmonies. 1943. American revised. 394
Bible. N. T. Gospels. English. Harmonies. 1943. Authorized. 1990
Bible. N. T. Gospels. English. Harmonies. 1943. Stringfellow. 401
Bible. N. T. Gospels. English. Harmonies. 1945. Rheims. 396
Bible. N. T. Gospels. English. Harmonies. 1946. 396, 1990
Bible. N. T. Gospels. English. Harmonies. 1946. Authorized. 1990
Bible. N. T. Gospels. English. Harmonies. 1947. 1990
Bible. N. T. Gospels. English. Harmonies. 1947. Revised standard. 387, 396
Bible. N. T. Gospels. English. Harmonies. 1948. Authorized. 1990
Bible. N. T. Gospels. English. Harmonies. 1949. 1990
Bible. N. T. Gospels. English. Harmonies. 1949. Revised standard. 3147
Bible. N. T. Gospels. English. Harmonies. 1950. Revised standard. 387
Bible. N. T. Gospels. English. Harmonies. 1951. Authorized. 1990
Bible. N. T. Gospels. English. Harmonies. 1951. Cary. 1990
Bible. N. T. Gospels. English. Harmonies. 1951. Peterson. 1990
Bible. N. T. Gospels. English. Harmonies. 1951. Revised standard. 1990
Bible. N. T. Gospels. English. Harmonies. 1953. 2060
Bible. N.T. Gospels. English. Harmonies. 1955. Confraternity version. 1434, 1985
Bible. N.T. Gospels. English. Harmonies. 1955. Revised standard. 1990
Bible. N. T. Gospels. English. Harmonies. 1956. Revised standard. 1990
Bible. N. T. Gospels. English. Harmonies. 1957. 396
Bible. N. T. Gospels. English. Harmonies. 1957. Authorized. 1990
Bible. N. T. Gospels. English. Harmonies. 1957. Revised standard. 387
Bible. N. T. Gospels. English. Harmonies. 1958. Knox. 1990
Bible. N. T. Gospels. English. Harmonies. 1958. Meissner. 1990
Bible, N. T. Gospels. English Harmonies. 1959. Beck. 1990
Bible. N. T. Gospels. English. Harmonies. 1960. Authorized. 1990
Bible. N. T. Gospels. English. Harmonies. 1961. American standard. 386
Bible. N. T. Gospels. English. Harmonies. 1961. Authorized. 1990
Bible. N.T. Gospels. English. Harmonies. 1962. 1990
Bible. N. T. Gospels. English. Harmonies. 1963. Knox. 396
Bible. N. T. Gospels. English. Harmonies. 1964. 1990
Bible. N. T. Gospels. English. Harmonies. 1967. 387
Bible. N. T. Gospels. English. Harmonies. 1973. Authorized. 1990
Bible. N.T. Gospels. English. Harmonies, 1979. Revised standard. 387
Bible. N. T. Gospels. English. Lattimore. 1979. 383
Bible. N. T. Gospels. English. Lessons, Liturgical. 1882. 2070, 3220
Bible. N. T. Gospels. English. (Middle English) Harmonies. 1922. 1517
Bible. N.T. Gospels. English. New English. Selections. 1973. 2062
Bible. N.T. Gospels. English. New International. Selections. 1976. 2062
Bible. N. T. Gospels. English. Paraphases. 1941. 383

Bible. N. T. Gospels. English. Paraphrases. 1879. Kimball. 397
Bible. N. T. Gospels. English. Paraphrases. 1915. 387
Bible. N. T. Gospels. English. Paraphrases. 1916. 387
Bible. N. T. Gospels. English. Revised. Harmonies. 1975. 1990
Bible. N. T. Gospels. English. Revised Standard. Selections. 1973. 2062
Bible. N. T. Gospels. English. Revised standard. Selections. 1980. 930, 1991
Bible. N. T. Gospels. English. Selection. 1890. 2070
Bible. N. T. Gospels. English Selection. 1967. Revised Standard. 2062
Bible. N. T. Gospels. English. Selections. 1847. 2070
Bible. N. T. Gospels. English. Selections. 1854. 1960
Bible. N. T. Gospels. English. Selections. 1882. 2070
Bible. N. T. Gospels. English. Selections. 1882. Revised. 2070
Bible. N. T. Gospels. English. Selections. 1894. 2070
Bible. N.T. Gospels. English. Selections. 1902. 400
Bible. N. T. Gospels. English. Selections. 1903. 2027
Bible. N. T. Gospels. English. Selections. 1905. 1979, 1990, 2070
Bible. N. T. Gospels. English. Selections. 1907. 2028
Bible. N. T. Gospels. English. Selections. 1908. 1990
Bible. N. T. Gospels. English. Selections. 1909. 1990
Bible. N. T. Gospels. English. Selections. 1911. 2070
Bible. N. T. Gospels. English. Selections. 1920. 725, 2070
Bible. N. T. Gospels. English. Selections. 1923. 1939
Bible. N. T. Gospels. English. Selections. 1923. Revised. 355
Bible. N. T. Gospels. English. Selections. 1926. 2070
Bible. N. T. Gospels. English. Selections. 1932. 2070
Bible. N. T. Gospels. English. Selections. 1936. Authorized. 626
Bible. N. T. Gospels. English. Selections. 1938. Easton. 2070
Bible. N. T. Gospels. English. Selections. 1939. Grant. 388
Bible. N. T. Gospels. English. Selections. 1940. 1990
Bible. N.T. Gospels. English. Selections. 1942. Authorized. 1979
Bible. N.T. Gospels. English. Selections. 1946. 1990
Bible. N. T. Gospels. English. Selections. 1948. 2070
Bible. N. T. Gospels. English. Selections. 1948. Authorized. 626
Bible. N. T. Gospels. English. Selections. 1949. Authorized. 2018
Bible. N. T. Gospels. English. Selections. 1950. Authorized. 1957, 1990
Bible. N. T. Gospels. English. Selections. 1951. Authorized. 1990
Bible. N. T. Gospels. English. Selections. 1952? Authorized. 2023
Bible. N. T. Gospels. English. Selections. 1956. Authorized. 1979
Bible. N. T. Gospels. English. Selections. 1956. Authorized. 1957, 1979
Bible. N. T. Gospels. English. Selections. 1956. Douai. 1957
Bible. N. T. Gospels. English. Selections. 1957. Authorised. 2070
Bible. N. T. Gospels. English. Selections. 1957. Authorized. 399, 1957
Bible. N. T. Gospels. English. Selections. 1960. Authorized. 2023, 2024
Bible. N.T. Gospels. English. Selections. 1960. Confraternity versiion. 626
Bible. N.T. Gospels. English. Selections. 1960. Confraternity version. 626
Bible. N.T. Gospels. English. Selections. 1963. 2036
Bible. N.T. Gospels. English. Selections. 1963. Knox. 2036
Bible. N.T. Gospels. English. Selections. 1966. 2024, 2028
Bible. N.T. Gospels. English. Selections. 1966. Revised standard version. 2028
Bible. N.T. Gospels. English. Selections. 1967. 1985, 2070
Bible. N.T. Gospels. English. Selections. 1967. Authorized. 2070
Bible. N.T. Gospels. English. Selections. 1967. Revised standard. 626, 1979
Bible. N.T. Gospels. English. Selections. 1975. Authorized. 2028

Bible. N.T Gospels. English. Today's English. Selections. 1970. 1991
Bible. N.T. Gospels. English. Today's English. Selections. 1973. 1991
Bible. N.T. Gospels. English. Today's English. Selections. 1979. 8, 2023
Bible. N. T. Gospels. Greek. 1825. 383
Bible. N.T. Gospels. Greek. 1899. 383
Bible. N. T. Gospels. Greek. 1902. 315
Bible. N. T. Gospels. Greek. 1932. 383
Bible. N. T. Gospels. Greek. 1976. 396
Bible. N. T. Gospels. Greek. 1978. 398
Bible. N. T. Gospels. Greek. Harmonies. 1834. 396
Bible. N. T. Gospels. Greek. Harmonies. 1845. 396
Bible. N. T. Gospels. Greek. Harmonies. 1847. 2017
Bible. N. T. Gospels. Greek. Harmonies. 1853. 396
Bible. N. T. Gospels. Greek. Harmonies. 1854. 396
Bible. N. T. Gospels. Greek. Harmonies. 1865. 396
Bible. N. T. Gospels. Greek. Harmonies. 1871. 396
Bible. N. T. Gospels. Greek. Harmonies. 1885. 396
Bible. N. T. Gospels. Greek. Harmonies. 1906. 388
Bible. N. T. Gospels. Greek. Harmonies. 1920. 397
Bible. N.T. Gospels. Greek. Nestle-Aland. 1969. 397
Bible. N. T. Gospels. Greek. Selections. 1951. 2070
Bible. N.T. Gospels. Greek. Selections. 1956. 393
Bible. N.T. Gospels. Harmonies. Delaware. 1821. 2007, 2008
Bible. N. T. Gospels, Harmonies English. 397
Bible. N. T. Gospels. Latin. 1886. Old Latin. 3718
Bible. N. T. Gospels. Latin. 1888. Old Latin. 2631
Bible. N. T. Gospels. Latin. 1907. Old Latin. 316
Bible. N. T. Gospels. Latin. 1911. Old Latin. 383
Bible. N. T. Gospels. Latin. 1931. Vulgate. 398
Bible. N. T. Gospels. Latin. 1934. Old Latin. 398
Bible. N. T. Gospels. Mpongwe. 1879. 2627
Bible. N.T. Gospels. Pennsylvania German dialect. Wood. 1968. 383
Bible. N. T. Gospels. Polyglot. Selection. (1904) 1964. 400
Bible. N.T. Gospels. Polyglot. Selections. 1904. 1991
Bible. N. T. Gospels. Polyglot. Selections. (1904) 1964. 400
Bible. N. T. Gospels. Selections. English. 1899. 400
Bible. N. T. Gospels. Selections. English. 1900. 400
Bible. N. T. Gospels. Selections. English. 1905. 400, 2070
Bible. N. T. Gospels. Selections. English. 1913. 400
Bible. N. T. Gospels. Selections. English. 1914. 394
Bible. N. T. Gospels. Selections. English. 1922. 400
Bible. N. T. Gospels. Selections. English. 1928. 400
Bible. N. T. Gospels. Selections. Polyglot. 1904. 400
Bible. N. T. Gospels. Seneca. 1874. Wright. 3332
Bible. N. T. Gospels. Shawnee. 1929. 3401
Bible. N. T. Gospels. Syriac. 1894. 383
Bible. N. T. Greek. 1837. 284
Bible. N. T. Greek. 1865. 320
Bible. N. T. Greek. 1877. 284
Bible. N. T. Greek. 1879. 284
Bible. N. T. Greek. 1881. 284, 343
Bible. N. T. Greek. 1882. 284
Bible. N. T. Greek. 1883. 284
Bible. N. T. Greek. 1886. 284
Bible. N. T. Greek. 1892. 284
Bible. N.T. Greek. 1897. 1768
Bible. N.T. Greek. (1897) 1961. 343
Bible. N.T. Greek. 1905? 284
Bible. N. T. Greek. 1908. 284, 1768
Bible. N. T. Greek. 1914. 343
Bible. N. T. Greek. 1925. 284
Bible. N.T. greek. 1926. 226
Bible. N. T. Greek. 1929. 284
Bible. N. T. Greek. 1931. 226
Bible. N. T. Greek. 1934. 3575
Bible. N. T. Greek. 1937. 284
Bible. N. T. Greek. 1958. 343, 479
Bible. N.t. Greek. 1961. 361

Bible. N.T. Greek. 1964. 285
Bible. N.T. Greek. 1966. 285
Bible. N.T. Greek. 1975. 307
Bible. N.T. Greek. 1976. 307
Bible. N. T. Greek. Scholz. 1975. 358
Bible. N. T. Greek. Selections. 1900. 1768
Bible. N. T. Greek. Selections. 1908. 1768
Bible. N.T. Hawaiian. 1860. 360
Bible. N. T. Hebrew. English. 1896. 402
Bible. N. T. Hebrews. English. 1843. 402
Bible. N. T. Hebrews. English. 1860. 402
Bible. N. T. Hebrews. English. 1867. Authorized. 402
Bible. N. T. Hebrews. English. 1868. Ripley. 402
Bible. N. T. Hebrews. English. 1873. 402
Bible. N. T. Hebrews. English. 1876. Authorized. 402
Bible. N. T. Hebrews. English. 1902? 402
Bible. N. T. Hebrews. English. 1919. American revised. 402
Bible. N. T. Hebrews. English. 1921. Revised. 402
Bible. N. T. Hebrews. English. 1930. 402
Bible. N. T. Hebrews. English. 1957. Barclay. 402
Bible. N.T. Hebrews. English. Barclay. 1976. 402
Bible. N. T. Hebrews. English. Paraphrases. 1933. 402
Bible. N. T. Hebrews. Greek. 1852. 402
Bible. N. T. Hebrews. Greek. 1906. 402
Bible. N. T. Hebrews. Greek. 1917. 402
Bible. N. T. Hebrews xi. Greek. 1896. 405
Bible. N.T. Italian. 1963. New World. 320
Bible. N. T. James. English. 1899. 412
Bible. N. T. James. English. 1911. 412
Bible. N. T. James. English. 1954. Johnstone. 412
Bible. N. T. James. English. 1961. Barclay. 412
Bible. N. T. James. English. Barclay. 1976. 412
Bible. N. T. James. Greek. 1899. 412
Bible. N. T. James. Polyglot. 1895. 411
Bible. N. T. Johannine literature. English. 1901. Ballentine. 413
Bible. N. T. Johannine literature. English. 1902. Ballentine. 355
Bible. N. T. John. Anglo-Saxon. 1904. 47
Bible. N. T. John. Anglo-Saxon. 1973. 47
Bible. N. T. John. Creek. 1871. 1386
Bible. N. T. John. Creek. 1875. 1386
Bible. N. T. John. English. 1860. 415
Bible. N. T. John. English. 1879. Authorized. 415
Bible. N. T. John. English. 1883. Revised. 415
Bible. N.T. John. English. 1885. Sawyer. 418
Bible. N. T. John. English. 1886. 415
Bible. N. T. John. English. 1894. 415
Bible. N. T. John. English. 1899. 415
Bible. N. T. John. English. 1902. 415
Bible. N. T. John. English. 1905. 418, 424
Bible. N. T. John. English. 1909. 414
Bible. N. T. John. English. 1912. 415
Bible. N. T. John. English. 1915. 414
Bible. N. T. John. English. 1917. 415
Bible. N. T. John. English. 1925. 414
Bible. N. T. John. English. 1930.? 414
Bible. N. T. John. English. 1937. Authorized. 1563
Bible. N.T. John. English. 1939. American revised. 415
Bible. N.T. John. English. 1952. Confraternity version. 418
Bible. N. T. John. English. 1956. 415, 418
Bible. N. T. John. English. 1956. Barclay. 415
Bible. N. T. John. English. 1956. Revised. 415
Bible. N. T. John. English. 1957. Douai. 415
Bible. N. T. John. English. 1958. Authorized. 415
Bible. N. T. John. English. 1960. Confraternity version. 415
Bible. N.T. John. English. 1961. 414
Bible. N.T. John. English. 1961. Vann. 418
Bible. N. T. John. English. 1965. 418
Bible. N. T. John. English. 1965. New English. 415
Bible. N.T. John. English. 1966. 415
Bible. N.T. John. English. 1966. Brown. 415
Bible. N.T. John. English. Authorized. 1976. 415
Bible. N.T. John. English. Barclay. 1975. 415
Bible. N.T. John. Grebo. 1852. 418
Bible. N. T. John. Greek. 1861. 307
Bible. N. T. John. Greek. 1889. 307
Bible. N. T. John. Greek. 1895. 418
Bible. N. T. John. Greek. 1900. 415, 418
Bible. N. T. John. Greek. 1962. 421

Bible. N.T. John. Greek. 1963. 421
Bible. N.T. John. Kcres. 1935. 320
Bible. N.T. John. Latin. Stonyhurst. 1969. 680
Bible. N. T. John. Mohawk. 1818. 2567
Bible. N. T. John. Shawnee. 1846. Barker. 414
Bible. N. T. John xvii. English. 1871. 424
Bible. N. T. John. Zapotec. 1912. 3891
Bible. N. T. Jude. Cherokee. 1860? 891
Bible. N. T. Jude. Greek. 1907. 269, 367
Bible. N. T. Jude. Greek. 1965. 425
Bible. N.T. Latin. Selections. 1923. Old Latin. 1919
Bible. N. T. Latin. Selections. 1935. Vulgate. 1960
Bible. N. T. Luke and Acts. English. 1898. 426
Bible. N. T. Luke and Acts. English. 1900. Revised. 426
Bible. N. T. Luke and Acts. English. 1902. Ballentine. 426
Bible. N. T. Luke. Anglo-Saxon. 1906. 654
Bible. N.T. Luke. Anglo-Saxon. Corpus Christi College Library. MSS. (140) 654
Bible. N. T. Luke. Cherokee. 1850. Worcester. 891
Bible. N. T. Luke. English. 1859. Authorized. 427
Bible. N. T. Luke. English. 1878. Authorized. 427
Bible. N. T. Luke. English. 1882. Revised. 427
Bible. N. T. Luke. English. 1899. 427
Bible. N. T. Luke. English. 1899. Ballentine. 426
Bible. N. T. Luke. English. 1902. 427
Bible. N. T. Luke. English. 1915. 429
Bible. N. T. Luke. English. 1916. 427
Bible. N. T. Luke. English. 1922. Revised. 427
Bible. N. T. Luke. English. 1923. Robertson. 320
Bible. N. T. Luke. English. 1924. 355, 429
Bible. N. T. Luke. English. 1930. 429
Bible. N. T. Luke. English. 1930. Revised. 427
Bible. N. T. Luke. English. 1931. 427
Bible. N. T. Luke. English. 1936. Revised. 427
Bible. N. T. Luke. English. 1940. American revised. 427
Bible. N. T. Luke. English. 1952. Confraternity version. 429
Bible. N T. Luke. English. 1956. Barclay. 427
Bible. N. T. Luke. English. 1957. Douai. 427
Bible. N. T. Luke. English. 1960. Authorized. 429
Bible. N.T. Luke. English. 1965. 427
Bible. N. T. Luke. English. 1965. New English. 427
Bible. N. T. Luke. English. Barclay. 1975. 427
Bible. N. T. Luke. English. Paraphrases. 1955. Taylor. 430
Bible. N.T. Luke. English. Revised standard. 1972. 427
Bible. N.T. Luke. English. Revised Standard. 1980. 427
Bible. N. T. Luke. Greek. 1878. 307
Bible. N. T. Luke. Greek. 1880. Robertson. 1386
Bible. N. T. Luke. Greek. 1900. 429
Bible. N. T. Luke. Greek. 1903. 427
Bible. N. T. Luke. Greek. 1933. 427
Bible. N.T. Luke. Greek. 1968. 1603
Bible. N. T. Luke I-IX. English. Fitzmyer. 1981. 427
Bible. N. T. Luke. Japanese. 1899. 320
Bible. N.T. Mark. Anglo-Saxon. 1905. 654
Bible. N. T. Mark. English. 1864. Sawyer. 432
Bible. N. T. Mark. English. 1873. Authorized. 432
Bible. N. T. Mark. English. 1878. 432
Bible. N. T. Mark. English. 1881. 432
Bible. N. T. Mark. English. 1881. Authorized. 432
Bible. N. T. Mark. English. 1881. Revised. 432
Bible. N. T. Mark. English. 1882. Authorized. 3471
Bible. N. T. Mark. English. 1897. 432
Bible. N. T. Mark. English. 1899. 437
Bible. N. T. Mark. English. 1902. Authorized. 432
Bible. N. T. Mark. English. 1902. Ballentine. 437
Bible. N. T. Mark. English. 1904. Revised. 437
Bible. N. T. Mark. English. 1905. 432
Bible. N. T. Mark. English. 1909. Revised. 432

Bible. N. T. Mark. English. 1911. American revised. 432
Bible. N. T. Mark. English. 1915. 432
Bible. N. T. Mark. English. 1917. 432
Bible. N. T. Mark. English. 1920. Moffatt. 437
Bible. N. T. Mark. English. 1922. 437
Bible. N. T. Mark. English. 1924. 435
Bible. N. T. Mark. English. 1926. Moffatt. 438
Bible. N. T. Mark. English. 1927. 437
Bible. N. T. Mark. English. 1929. Revised. 432
Bible. N. T. Mark. English. 1932. 432
Bible. N. T. Mark. English. 1938. American revised. 432
Bible. N. T. Mark. English. 1952. Vernon. 435
Bible. N. T. Mark. English. 1956. Douai. 432
Bible. N. T. Mark. English. 1957. 432
Bible. N.T. Mark. English. 1962. 437
Bible. N.T. Mark. English. 1963. 432
Bible. N.T. Mark, English, 1963. Revised standard. 432
Bible. N.T. Mark. English. 1965. 432
Bible. N.T. Mark. English. 1965. New English. 432
Bible. N.T. Mark. English. 1974. 432
Bible. N.T. Mark. English. 1976. 432
Bible. N.T. Mark. English. Barclay. 1975. 433
Bible. N. T. Mark. English. Paraphrases. 1930. 431
Bible. N.T. Mark. English. Price. 1976. 435
Bible. N.T. Mark. English. Selections. 1957. Revised standard. 438
Bible. N.T. Mark. English. Selections. 1963. 437
Bible. N. T. Mark. Greek. 1880. Robertson. 1771
Bible. N. T. Mark. Greek. 1898. 433
Bible. N. T. Mark. Greek. 1901. 433
Bible. N. T. Mark. Greek. 1904. 433
Bible. N. T. Mark. Greek. 1905. 433
Bible. N. T. Mark. Greek. 1914. 433
Bible. N. T. Mark. Greek. 1936. 433
Bible. N. T. Mark. Greek. 1941. 436
Bible. N.T. Mark. Greek. 1965. 436
Bible. N.T. Mark, Greek. 433
Bible. N.T. Mark. Greek. 1977. 433
Bible. N.T. Matthew. Anglo-Saxon. 1887. 46
Bible. N.T. Matthew. Anglo-Saxon. 1904. 654
Bible. N. T. Matthew. Cherokee. 1850. Worcester. 891
Bible. N. T. Matthew. Creek. 1855. 1386
Bible. N. T. Matthew. English. 1857. Authorized. 439
Bible. N. T. Matthew. English. 1862. 439
Bible. N. T. Matthew. English. 1870. Authorized. 439
Bible. N. T. Matthew. English. 1875. Authorized. 439
Bible. N. T. Matthew. English. 1876. 439
Bible. N. T. Matthew. English. 1876. Authorized. 439
Bible. N. T. Matthew. English. 1882. Revised. 439
Bible. N. T. Matthew. English. 1883. Guy. 438
Bible. N. T. Matthew. English. 1886. 439
Bible. N. T. Matthew. English. 1888. Guy. 438
Bible. N. T. Matthew. English. 1898. 439
Bible. N. T. Matthew. English. 1899. Authorized. 442
Bible. N. T. Matthew. English. 1902. 439
Bible. N. T. Matthew. English. 1902. Ballentine. 438
Bible. N. T. Matthew. English. 1911. 439
Bible. N. T. Matthew. English. 1920. 442
Bible. N. T. Matthew. English. 1921. 439
Bible. N. T. Matthew. English. 1922. Revised. 439
Bible. N. T. Matthew. English. 1936. American revised. 439
Bible. N. T. Matthew. English. 1936. Revised. 439
Bible. N. T. Matthew. English. 1937. Douai. 439
Bible. N. T. Matthew. English. 1957. Douai. 439
Bible. N. T. Matthew. English. 1958. Authorized. 588
Bible. N. T. Matthew. English. 1958. Barclay. 439
Bible. N.T. Matthew. English. 1962. 438
Bible. N.T. Matthew. English. 1963. 439
Bible. N. T. Matthew. English. 1963. New English. 439
Bible. N.T. Matthew. English. 1964. 442
Bible. N.T. Matthew. English. 1965. 439
Bible. N.T. Matthew. English. 1965. Revised standard. 439

Bible. N.T. Matthew. English. Albright-Mann. 1971. 440
Bible. N.T. Matthew. English. Authorized. 1972. 442
Bible. N.T. Matthew. English. Barclay. 1975. 440
Bible. N.T. Matthew. English. Einspruch. 1971? 442
Bible. N. T. Matthew. English. Paraphrases. 1900. Ellis. 438
Bible N. T. Matthew V-VII. English. 1957. Bowman-Tapp. 3334
Bible N. T. Matthew V-VII. English. Paraphrases. 1954. Scher. 3334
Bible. N. T. Matthew. Grebo. 1868. 442
Bible. N. T. Matthew. Greek. 1901. 440
Bible. N. T. Matthew. Greek. 1927. 440
Bible. N. T. Matthew. Greek. 1961. 440
Bible. N. T. Matthew. Greek. 1964. 438, 443
Bible. N. T. Matthew. Greek. 1966. 438
Bible. N. T. Matthew. Latin. 1883. Old Latin. 443
Bible. N. T. Matthew. Latin. 1934. Vulgate. 442
Bible. N. T. Matthew. Micmac. 1853. 2461
Bible. N. T. Matthew. Mohawk. 1831. Hill. 2056
Bible. N. T. Matthew. Mohawk. 1836. Hill. 2567
Bible. N. T. Matthew. v. English. 1926. 358
Bible. N. T. Matthew. v-vii. English. 1908. 3334
Bible. N. T. Pasoral epistles. English. 1897. 445
Bible. N, T. Pastoral epistles-- Commentaries. 445
Bible. N. T. Pastoral epistles. English. 446
Bible. N. T. Pastoral epistles. English. 1901? 367, 445
Bible. N. T. Pastoral epistles. English. 1963. 445
Bible. N. T. Pastoral epistles. English. 1966. 445
Bible. N. T. Pastoral epistles. English. 1966. New English. 445
Bible. N. T. Pastoral epistles. English. Barclay. 1975. 445
Bible. N. T. Pastoral epistles. Greek. 1906. 445
Bible. N. T. Pastoral epistles. Greek. 1954. 445
Bible. N. T. Peter. English. 1899. 447
Bible. N.T. Peter. English. 1910. 447
Bible. N.T. Peter. English. English. 1967. New English. 447
Bible. N. T. Philemon. English. 1860. American Bible union. 447
Bible. N. T. Philippians. English. 1899. 448
Bible. N. T. Philippians. English. 1917. 449
Bible. N.T. Philippians. English. 1977. 448
Bible. N.T. Philippians. Greek. 1897. 448
Bible N. T. Phillipians. English. 1955. Johnstone. 448
Bible. N.T. Polyglot. 1964. 473
Bible. N.T. Portuguese. 1909. 361
Bible. N.T. Portuguese. 1913. 361
Bible. N. T. Revelation. 1898. 452
Bible. N. T. Revelation. English. 1848. Authorized. 452, 462
Bible. N. T. Revelation. English. 1852. 452
Bible. N. T. Revelation. English. 1860. 452
Bible. N. T. Revelation. English. 1867. Authorized. 452
Bible. N. T. Revelation. English. 1883. Sawyer. 458
Bible. N. T. Revelation. English. 1903. 458
Bible. N. T. Revelation. English. 1903. Revised. 458
Bible. N. T. Revelation. English. 1910. 452
Bible. N. T. Revelation. English. 1911. 452
Bible. N. T. Revelation. English. 1914. 3226
Bible. N. T. Revelation. English. 1915. 452
Bible. N. T. Revelation. English. 1916. 461, 3224
Bible. N. T. Revelation. English. 1918. 461
Bible. N.T. Revelation. English. 1918. Whiting. 452
Bible. N. T. Revelation. English. 1925. 452
Bible. N. T. Revelation. English. 1928. 458
Bible. N. T. Revelation. English. 1936. Authorized. 452

Bible. N. T. Revelation. English. 1937. American revised. 452
Bible. N.T. Revelation, English. 1948. Carpenter. 452
Bible. N. T. Revelation. English. 1957. Phillips. 461
Bible. N.T. Revelation. English. 1958. Authorized. 452
Bible. N. T. Revelation. English. 1958. Torrey. 452
Bible. N. T. Revelation. English. 1961. Barclay. 452
Bible. N.T. Revelation. English. 1962. Confraternity version. 462
Bible. N.T. Revelation. English. 1962. Lattimore. 461
Bible. N. T. Revelation. English. 1964. Authorized. 452
Bible. N. T. Revelation. English. 1965. 452
Bible. N. T. Revelation. English. 1965. New English. 452
Bible. N. T. Revelation. English. 1966. 453
Bible. N. T. Revelation. English. Barclay. 1976. 453
Bible. N.T. Revelation. English. Durham. 1973. 461
Bible. N. T. Revelation. English. Ford. 1975. 453
Bible. N. T. Revelation. English. Paraphrases. 1862. 462
Bible. N. T. Revelation. English. Paraphrases. 1892. Briggs. 461
Bible. N. T. Revelation. English. Paraphrases. 1950. Rogers. 453
Bible. N. T. Revelation. English. Paraphrases. 1952. Scher. 462
Bible. N. T. Revelation. English. Paraphrases. 1955. Bowman. 453
Bible N. T. Revelation. Greek. 1893. 453
Bible. N. T. Revelation. Greek. 1907. 453
Bible. N. T. Revelation. Greek. 1923. 458
Bible. N. T. Revelation. Greek 1928. 458
Bible. N. T. Revelation. Greek. 1977. 453
Bible. N.T. Revelation. Latin. Cloisters Apocalypse. 602
Bible. N.T. Romans. 466
Bible. N.T. Romans. English. 1832. 466
Bible. N.T. Romans. English. 1839. 466
Bible. N.T. Romans. English. 1848. Whitwell. 466
Bible. N. T. Romans. English. 1851. 466
Bible. N. T. Romans. English. 1857. 466
Bible. N. T. Romans. English. 1859. 466
Bible. N. T. Romans. English. 1863. 466
Bible. N. T. Romans. English. 1871. 466
Bible. N. T. Romans. English. 1884. Revised. 466
Bible. N. T. Romans. English. 1888. 466
Bible. N. T. Romans. English. 1899. 466
Bible. N. T. Romans. English. 1901? 466
Bible. N. T. Romans. English. 1903. 466
Bible. N. T. Romans. English. 1914. 469
Bible. N. T. Romans. English. 1919. 466
Bible. N. T. Romans. English. 1919. Revised. 466
Bible. N. T. Romans. English. 1934. Boylan. 466
Bible. N. T. Romans. English. 1937. Revised. 467
Bible. N. T. Romans. English. 1957. Barclay. 467
Bible. N.T. Romans. English. 1961. Rhys. 467
Bible. N.T. Romans. English. 1962. Blackwelder. 320
Bible. N.T. Romans. English. 1964. 470
Bible. N.T. Romans. English. 1967. New English. 467
Bible. N.T. Romans. English. 1977. 467
Bible. N.T. Romans. English. Barclay. 1975. 467
Bible. N. T. Romans. Greek. 1879. 467
Bible. N. T. Romans. Greek. 1893. 467
Bible. N. T. Romans. Greek. 1912. 467
Bible N. T. 2 Corinthians English 1919. 346
Bible. N. T. Selections. English. 1899. 472
Bible. N. T. Selections. English. 1901. 473
Bible. N. T. Selections. English. 1902. 320
Bible. N. T. Selections. English. 1908. 2017
Bible. N. T. Selections. English. 1918. 473
Bible. N.T. Selections. English. 1923. 1950, 2771
Bible. N.T. Selections. English. 1924. 355
Bible. N. T. Selections. English. 1925. 473
Bible. N.T. Spanish. 1906. Valera. 320
Bible. N.T. Spanish. 1914. 320
Bible. N.T. Spanish. 1963. New World. 320
Bible. N.T. Swedish. 1865. 320
Bible. N. T. Thai. 1960. 320
Bible. N. T. Thessalonians. English. 1860. Lillie. 477
Bible. N. T. Thessalonians. English. 1898. 477

Bible. N. T. Thessalonians. English. 1902? 478
Bible. N. T. Thessalonians. English. 1911. 478
Bible. N. T. Thessalonians. English. 1965. Blackwelder. 478
Bible. N. T. Thessalonians. English. Revised standard. 1969. 478
Bible. N. T. Thessalonians. Greek. 1904. 478
Bible N. T. Thessalonians. Greek. 1940. 478
Bible. N.T. Thessalonians. Greek. 1957. 478
Bible. N.T. Tonga (Inhambane district) 1905. 479
Bible. N.T. Matthew 23-VIII 1. English. 1955. Authorized. 3334
Bible. N.T. Acts and Epistles. English. Knox. 1959. 286, 326, 2795
Bible. N. T. Acts. English. Phillips. 1955. 326
Bible. New Testament. English. 1873. 358
Bible. New Testament. English. 1899. 358
Bible. N. T. English. 1950. New World. 355
Bible. N. T. English. 1955. 450
Bible. N. T. English. 1963. 358
Bible. N. T. English. Authorized. 1954. 361
Bible. N.T. English. Phillips. 1962. 360
Bible. N. T. English. Phillips. 1965. 360
Siewert, Frances E. 320
Bible. N.T. English. Williams. 1963. 358
Bible. N. T. Epistles of Paul. English. Paraphrases. 1965. Bruce. 445
Bible. N. T. Gospels. Harmonies. English. Authorized. 1954. 286
Bible. New Testament. John. Hawaiian. 1854. 418
Bible. N. T. Pastoral epistles. English. 1960. Barclay. 445
Bible. N. T. Pastoral epistles. English. 1966. New English. 446
Bible. N. T. Philippians. Greek. 1913. 448
Bible. N.T. 1 Corinthians. Greek. 1916. 322
Bible. N.T. 1 Corinthians. Greek. 1905. 322
Bible, N.T. 1 Peter. Greek. 1914. 325
Bible. NT. Gospels. English. Selections. 1944. 1979
Bible. N.T. 2 Corinthians. Greek. 1903. 326
Bible. O. T. 1 Chronicles. English. 1965. Myers. 481
Bible. O.T. 1 Chronicles. English. 1965. Myers. 483
Bible. O.T. 1 Chronicles. English. New American. 1973. 496
Bible. O.T. 1 Kings. English. 1898. 483
Bible. O.T. 1 Kings. English. 1908. 483
Bible. O.T. 1 Kings. English. New American. 1973. 555
Bible. O.T. 1 Kings. English. New English. 1972. 483
Bible. O.T. 1 Samuel. English. 1899. 483
Bible. O. T. 1 Samuel. English. 1909. Revised. 483
Bible. O.T. 1 Samuel. English. 1919. Revised. 483
Bible. O.T. 1 Samuel. English. 1971. 589
Bible. O.T. 1 Samuel. English. McCarter. 1979. 483
Bible. O.T. 1 Samuel. English. New English. 1971. 483
Bible. O.T. 2 Chronicles. English. 1965. Myers. 481
Bible. O.T. 2 Chronicles. English. New American. 1973. 496
Bible. O. T. 2 Kings. English. 1897. 483
Bible. O. T. 2 Kings. English. 1908. Revised. 483
Bible. O.T. 2 Kings. English. New American. 1973. 556
Bible. O.T. 2 Kings. English. New English. 1976. 484
Bible. O.T. 2 Samuel. English. New American. 1971. 589
Bible. O.T. 2 Samuel. English. New English. 1977. 484
Bible. O. T. Amos. English. 1929. 485
Bible. O. T. Amos. Hebrew. 1923. 35
Bible. O. T. Apocrypha. 1-2 Maccabees. English. 1832. Cotton. 487
Bible. O.T. Apocrypha. 1-2 Maccabees. English. New English. 1973. 488
Bible. O. T. Apocrypha. 1 Maccabees Englaish 1948. 488
Bible. O. T. Apocrypha. 1 Maccabees. English. 1950. 487
Bible. O.T. Apocrypha. 1 Maccabees. English. Goldstein. 1976. 488

Bible. O.T. Apocrypha. 1 Maccabees. English. New American. 1973. 487
Bible. O. T. Apocrypha. 2 Maccabees. English. 1954- Tedesche. 487
Bible. O.T. Apocrypha. 2 Maccabees. English. New American. 1973. 488
Bible. O.T. Apocrypha and apocryphal books. English. 1913. 56
Bible. O.T. Apocrypha. Baruch. Polyglot. 1975. 488
Bible. O.T. Apocrypha. Ecclesiasticus. English. 1878. Authorized. 487
Bible.O.T.Apocrypha.Ecclesiasticus. English. 1896. 489
Bible. O.T Apocrypha. Ecclesiasticus. English. 1900. Revised. 489
Bible. O.T. Apocrypha. Ecclesiasticus. English. 1912. Revised. 489
Bible. O.T. Apocrypha. Ecclesiasticus. English. Revised Standard. Selections. 1973. 489
Bible. O. T. Apocrypha. Ecclesiasticus. Hebrew. 1899. 487
Bible. O. T. Apocrypha. Ecclesiasticus. xxxix.15--xiix.11. Hebrew. 1897. 487
Bible. O. T. Apocrypha. English. 1903. 487
Bible. O. T. Apocrypha. English. 1913. 487
Bible. O. T. Apocrypha. English. 1929. 56
Bible. O. T. Apocrypha. English. 1933. 487
Bible. O.T. Apocrypha. English. 1936. 490
Bible. O.T. Apocrypha. English. 1936. Authorized. 490
Bible. O.T. Apocrypha. English. 1938. Goodspeed. 490
Bible. O.T. Apocrypha. English. 1957. Revised standard. 490
Bible. O.T. Apocrypha. English. 1959. Goodspeed. 490
Bible. O.T. Apocrypha. English. 1962. Authorized. 490
Bible. O.T. Apocrypha. English. 1964. 491
Bible. O.T. Apocrypha. English. 1965. Revised standard. 487
Bible. O.T. Apocrypha. English. New English. 1970. 488
Bible. O. T. Apocrypha. English. Selections. 489
Bible. O. T. Apocrypha. English. Selections. 1878. Authorized. 488
Bible. O. T. Apocrypha. Selections. English. 1922. 488
Bible. O. T. Apocrypha. Tobit. English. 1958. Zimmermann. 490
Bible. O. T. Apocrypha. Tobit. Polyglot. 1878. 488
Bible. O. T. Apocrypha. Windom of Solomon. English. 1957. 490
Bible. O. T. Apocrypha. Wisdom of Solomon. English. 1909. Revised. 490
Bible. O. T. Apocrypha. Wisdom of Solomon. English. 1913. 490
Bible. O. T. Apocrypha. Wisdom of Solomon. English. 1914. 488
Bible. O. T. Apocrypha. Wisdom of Solomon. English, 1957. 490
Bible. O. T. Apocrypha. Wisdom of Solomon. English. Winston. 1979. 490
Bible. O.T. Apocrypha. Wisdom of Solomon. Polyglot. 1881. 490
Bible. O.T. Apocryphal books. 1 Enoch. English. 1882. Schodde. 491
Bible. O.T. Apocryphal books. 1 Enoch. English. Laurence. 1972. 567
Bible. O.T. Apocryphal books. 1 Enoch. Ethiopic. 1906. 1540
Bible. O.T. Apocryphal books. 1 Enoch. Rylands Ethiopic MSS. 23. 489
Bible. O. T. Apocryphal books. 2 Enoch. English. 1896. 490
Bible. O. T. Apocryphal books. 3-4 Maccabees. English. 1918. Emmet. 2305
Bible. O. T. Apocryphal books. 3-4 Maccabees. English. 1953. Hadas. 488
Bible. O.T. Apocryphal books. 3-4 Maccabees. Greek. 1976. 488
Bible. O.T. Apocryphal books. 3 Enoch. 1928. 1520
Bible. O.T. Apocryphal books. 3 Enoch. Hebrew. 1973. 491
Bible. O. T. Apocryphal books. 4 Ezra. Latin, 1895. 654
Bible. O. T. Apocryphal books. Apocalypse of Abraham. English. 1919. 491
Bible. O. T. Apocryphal books. Apocalypse of Baruch. English. 1918. 488
Bible. O. T. Apocryphal books. Apocalypse of Baruch. English. 1918. Charles. 488
Bible. O. T. Apocryphal books. Ascension of Isaiah. English 1919. 490
Bible. O. T. Apocryphal books. Book of Jubilees. English. 1917. 490
Bible. O. T. Apocryphal books. Book of Jubilees. Ethiopic, 1895. 1540

Bible. O. T. Apocryphal books. English. 1927. 491
Bible. O. T. Apocryphal books. Ezra. Latin. 1875. 490
Bible. O. T. Apocryphal books. Greek. 1893. 488
Bible. O. T. Apocryphal books. Joseph and Asenath. English. 1918. 488
Bible. O. T. Apocryphal books. Lives of the prophets. Greek. 1946. 568
Bible. O. T. Apocryphal books. Odes of Solomon. English. 1948. MarYosip. 492
Bible. O. T. Apocryphal Books. Odes of Solomon. Syriac. 1909. 490
Bible. O. T. Apocryphal books. Odes of Solomon. Syriac. 1916. 490
Bible. O. T. Apocryphal Books. Odes of Solomon. Syriac. 1973. 491
Bible. O.T. Apocryphal Books. Odes of Solomon. Syriac. 1977. 491
Bible. O. T. Apocryphal books. Testament of Abraham, English. 1927. Box. 491
Bible. O. T. Apocryphal books. Testament of Abraham. English. 1972. Stone. 491
Bible. O. T. Apocryphal books. Testament of Abraham. Greek. 1892. 491
Bible. O.T. Apocryphal books. Testaments of the twelve patriarchs. Joseph. Armenian. 1975. 2133
Bible. O. T. Apocrypphal books. 2 Esdras iii-xiv. Latin. 1875. 1532
Bible. O.T. Aramaic. Selections. 1971. 492
Bible. O. T. Chronicles. English. 1897. 590
Bible. O. T. Chronicles. English. 1899. 496
Bible. O. T. Chronicles. English. 1901. Revised. 590
Bible. O. T. Chronicles. English. 1906. Revised. 496
Bible. O. T. Chronicles. English. 1916. Revised. 496
Bible. O. T. Chronicles. English. New English. 1976. 496
Bible. O. T. Chronicles. Hebrew. 1895. 496
Bible. O. T. Daniel. English. 1853. 505
Bible. O. T. Daniel. English. 1902. 507
Bible. O. T. Daniel. English. 1913. Revised. 506
Bible. O. T. Daniel. English. 1915. 508
Bible. O.T. Daniel. English. 1948. Westminster version. 506
Bible. O. T. Daniel. English. 1959. Authorized. 506
Bible. O.T. Daniel. English. Authorized. 1975. 506
Bible. O.T. Daniel. English. Concordant version. 1968. 506
Bible. O.T. Daniel. English. Hartman. 1978. 506
Bible. O. T. Daniel. English. New English. 1976. 506
Bible. O. T. Delaware. Selections. 1838. 1420
Bible. O. T. Deuteronomy. English. 1896. 509
Bible. O. T. Deuteronomy. English. 1899. Revised. 509
Bible. O. T. Deuteronomy. English. 1902. 509
Bible. O. T. Deuteronomy. English. 1907. Revised. 510
Bible. O. T. Deuteronomy. English. 1911. 510
Bible. O. T. Deuteronomy. English. 1918. 510
Bible. O. T. Deuteronomy. English. 1937. 510
Bible. O. T. Deuteronomy. English. 1966, Revised standard. 510
Bible. O.T. Deuteronomy. English. Craigie. 1976. 510
Bible. O.T. Deuteronomy. English. New English. 1973. 510
Bible. O. T. Deuteronomy. Hebrew. 1935. 510
Bible. O.T. Ecclesiastes. English. 1895. 511
Bible. O. T. Ecclesiastes. English. 1896. 511
Bible. O. T. Ecclesiastes. English. 1900. Revised. 489
Bible. O. T. Ecclesiastes. English. 1904, Genung. 511
Bible. O. T. Ecclesiastes. English. 1919. 512
Bible. O. T. Ecclesiastes. English. 1940. Authorized. 512
Bible. O.T. Ecclesiastes. English. 1946. Authorized. 511
Bible. O. T. Ecclesiastes. English. 1952. Power. 511
Bible. O. T. Ecclesiastes. English. 1965. Authorized. 3394
Bible. O.T. Ecclesiastes. English. Authorized. 1971. 602

Bible. O.T. Ecclesiastes. English. Jastrow. 1972. 511
Bible. O.T. Ecclesiastes. English. Paraphrases. 1905. Haupt. 512
Bible. O.T. Ecclesiastes. English. Paraphrases. 1912. 513
Bible. O.T. Ecclesiastes. Hebrew. 1968. 512
Bible. O.T. Ecclesiastes III, 1-8. English. 1966. 512
Bible. O. T. Ecclesiatics. English, 1915. Gordis. 512
Bible. O.T. English. 481, 497
Bible. O. T. English. 1826. Authorized. 499
Bible. O. T. English. 1854. Lesser. 355
Bible. O. T. English. 1892. Revised. 522
Bible. O. T. English. 1898. 497
Bible. O. T. English. 1904. 497, 566
Bible. O. T. English. 1907. 481
Bible. O. T. English. 1920. Authorized. 482
Bible. O. T. English. 1924. 499
Bible. O. T. English. 1924. Moffatt. 513
Bible. O. T. English. 1927. 513
Bible. O. T. English. 1930. Douai. 654
Bible. O. T. English. 1931. Revised. 513
Bible. O. T. English. 1934. Westminster version. 513
Bible. O. T. English. 1936. Harkavy. 513
Bible. O. T. English. 1937. Jewish publication society. 530
Bible. O. T. English. 1941. Smith. 513
Bible. O. T. English. 1948. Know. 513
Bible. O.T. English. 1952. New American. 656
Bible. O. T. English. 1952. Revised standard. 482
Bible. O. T. English. 1953. New World. 482
Bible. O. T. English. 1954. Thomson. 528
Bible. O. T. English. 1955. Authorized. 497
Bible. O. T. English. 1957. Jewish Publication Society. 511
Bible. O. T. English. 1962. 482, 591
Bible. O. T. English. 1962. Children's version. 513, 528
Bible. O. T. English. 1962. Siewert. 482
Bible. O. T. English. 1963. 482
Bible. O. T. English. 1965. 513
Bible. O. T. English. 1965. Confraternity version. 513
Bible. O. T. English. Authorized. 1968. 482
Bible. O.T. English. Birnbaum. 1976. 3704
Bible. O.T. English. Jerusalem Bible. 1969. 513
Bible. O. T. English. Lessons, Liturgical. 1921. 2240
Bible. O. T. English. New English. 1970. 274
Bible. O. T. English. Selections. 1897. 591
Bible. O. T. English. Selections. 1899. 627
Bible. O. T. English. Selections. 1904. 532
Bible. O. T. English. Selections. 1905. 532
Bible. O. T. English. Selections. 1907. 2073, 2107
Bible. O. T. English. Selections. 1909. 532, 597
Bible. O. T. English. Selections. 1910. 532, 570, 591
Bible. O. T. English. Selections. 1910. American revised. 591
Bible. O. T. English. Selections. 1910. Sheffield. 591
Bible. O. T. English. Selections. 1911. 591
Bible. O. T. English. Selections. 1912. Authorized. 591
Bible. O. T. English. Selections. 1913. 591, 627
Bible. O. T. English. Selections. 1914. 1798
Bible. O. T. English. Selections. 1915. 591
Bible. O. T. English. Selections. 1916. 591, 618
Bible. O. T. English. Selections. 1919. 591
Bible. O. T. English. Selections. 1922. 251
Bible. O.T. English. Selections. 1924. Jewish publication society. 597
Bible. O.T. English. Selections. 1927. 591
Bible. O.T. English. Selections. 1928. 251
Bible. O.T. English. Selections. 1928. Authorized. 254, 591, 627
Bible. O.T. English. Selections. 1929. 591
Bible. O.T. English. Selections. 1929. Authorized. 251
Bible. O. T. English. Selections. 1930. 2095
Bible. O. T. English. Selections. 1930. Authorized. 482
Bible. O. T. English. Selections. 1931. 200, 592
Bible. O. T. English. Selections. 1935. 3144
Bible. O. T. English. Selections. 1936. 592
Bible. O.T. Ecglesish. Selections. 1937. 614

Bible. O.T. English. Selections. 1938. Authorised. 627
Bible. O. T. English. Selections. 1938. Douai. 591
Bible. O. T. English. Selections. 1941. 592
Bible. O.T. English. Selections. 1942. Jewish publication society. 81
Bible. O.T. English. Selections. 1943. American revised. 597
Bible. O.T. English. Selections. 1943. Jewish publication society. 81
Bible. O.T. English. Selections. 1944. Jewish publication society. 610
Bible. O.T. English. Selections. 1945. Authorized. 627
Bible. O.T. English. Selections. 1946. 251, 627
Bible. O. T. English. Selections. 1946. Authorized. 627
Bible. O. T. English. Selections. 1947. Authorized. 627
Bible. O. T. English. Selections. 1949. Authorized. 566
Bible. O. T. English. Selections. 1950. 592
Bible. O. T. English. Selections. 1950. Authorized. 482
Bible. O. T. English. Selections. 1950. Douai. 566
Bible. O. T. English. Selections. 1953. Revised standard. 597
Bible. O. T. English. Selections. 1956. Authorized. 592
Bible. O. T. English. Selections. 1957. 251
Bible. O.T. English. Selections. 1960. 251
Bible. O. T. English. Selections. 1960. Authorized. 602
Bible. O. T. English. Selections. 1960. Knox. 2414
Bible. O. T. English. Selections. 1962. 251
Bible. O. T. English. Selections. 1963. Confraternity version. 592
Bible. O.T. English. Selections. 1966. 497, 566, 582, 654
Bible. O.T. English. Selections. 1966. Authorized. 482, 566
Bible. O. T. English. Selections. 1967. 592
Bible. O.T. English. Selections. 1972. 527
Bible. O.T. English. Selections. 1976. 602
Bible. O. T. Esther. 1883. Sawyer. 514
Bible. O. T. Esther. English. 1885. 513
Bible. O.T. Esther. English. 1907. 513
Bible. O.T. Esther. English. Moore. 1971. 513
Bible. O.T. Esther. English. New American. 1973. 513
Bible. O. T. Exodus. English. 601
Bible. O. T. Exodus. English. 1843. 515
Bible. O. T. Exodus. English. 1867. 515
Bible. O. T. Exodus. English. 1874. 515
Bible. O. T. Exodus. English. 1896. 515
Bible. O. T. Exodus. English. 1900. Revised. 515
Bible. O. T. Exodus. English. 1908. 515
Bible. O. T. Exodus. English. 1911. Revised. 515
Bible. O. T. Exodus. English. 1914. 515
Bible. O.T. Exodus. English. 1924. 517
Bible. O.T. Exodus. English. New English. 1972. 515
Bible. O. T. Exodus xx, 1-17. Polyglot. 1893. 1312
Bible. O. T. Ezekiel. English. 1896. 517
Bible. O. T. Ezekiel. English. 1897. 269
Bible. O. T. Ezekiel. English. 1899. 517
Bible. O. T. Ezekiel. English. 1901. Authorized. 517
Bible. O. T. Ezekiel. English. 1901. Revised. 269
Bible. O. T. Ezekiel. English. 1904. 517
Bible. O. T. Ezekiel. English. 1907. Revised. 517
Bible. O. T. Ezekiel. English. 1939. Matthews. 517
Bible. O.T. Ezekiel. English. New English. 1974. 517
Bible. O.T. Ezekiel. Hebrew. 1899. 519
Bible. O.T. Ezra. English. 1897. 519
Bible. O.T. Ezra. English. 1916. 519
Bible. O.T. Ezra. English. 1965. Myers. 519
Bible. O.T. Ezra. English. New English. 1976. 519
Bible. O. T. Ezra. Hebrew. 1901. 519
Bible. O.T. I and II Chronicles. English. 1965. Myers. 496
Bible O.T. 1 Kings English 1910. 483
Bible. O. T. Five scrolls. English. 1896. 319
Bible. O. T. Five scrolls. English 1897. 319
Bible. O. T. Five scrolls. English. 1901. Revised. 319
Bible. O.T. Five Scrolls. English. New English. 1975. 519
Bible. O.T. Five scrolls. Hebrew. 1969. 519

Bible. O. T. Genesis. English. 1838. 520
Bible. O. T. Genesis. English. 1843. 520
Bible. O. T. Genesis. English. 1851. 521
Bible. O. T. Genesis. English. 1854. 521
Bible. O. T. Genesis. English. 1866. 521
Bible. O.T. Genesis. English. 1868. Conant. 520
Bible. O. T. Genesis. English. 1891. Revised. 522
Bible. O. T. Genesis. English. 1896. 524
Bible. O. T. Genesis. English. 1901. Revised. 524
Bible. O. T. Genesis. English. 1902. 522
Bible. O. T. Genesis. English. 1904. Revised. 521
Bible. O. T. Genesis. English. 1909. 521
Bible. O. T. Genesis. English. 1914. Revised. 521
Bible. O. T. Genesis. English. 1923. Revised. 521
Bible. O. T. Genesis. English. 1929. 524
Bible. O. T. Genesis. English. 1941. Martin. 520
Bible. O.T. Genesis. English. 1945. Smith. 520
Bible. O. T. Genesis. English. 1963. Watts. 527
Bible. O. T. Genesis. English. 1964. Speiser. 521
Bible. O. T. Genesis. English. 1965. 524
Bible. O. T. Genesis. English. 1966. Jewish Publication Society. 524
Bible. O. T. Genesis. English. Jerusalem. 1969. 527
Bible. O. T. Genesis. English. Selections. 1869. 2133
Bible. O. T. Genesis. English. Selections. 1922. Jewish publication society. 520
Bible. O.T. Genesis. English. Selections. 1947. Authorized. 2133
Bible. O. T. Genesis. Grebo. 1850. 520
Bible. O.T. Genesis. Hebrew. 1897. 538
Bible. O.T. Genesis. Hebrew. 1944. 520
Bible. O.T. Genesis. Hebrew. Baer-Delitzsch. 1970. 307
Bible. O.T. Genesis I. English. 1941. Authorized. 525
Bible. O.T. Genesis I-II, 4. English. Jerusalem Bible. 1970. 1379
Bible. O.T. Genesis I-II, 4a. English. 1975. 1379
Bible. O. T. Genesis I-XI. English. 1925. Fagnani. 2562
Bible. O.T. Genesis, I-XI. English. New English. 1973. 525
Bible. O. T. Genesis. Marshall. 1881. 198
Bible. O. T. Genesis. Massachuset. (1655) 1939. Eliot. 520
Bible. O. T. Genesis. Selections. English. 1907. 527
Bible. O. T. Genesis xii, 1-xxv, 11. English. 1884. Sawyer. 528
Bible. O.T. Genesis, XII-L. English. New English. 1979. 528
Bible. O.T. Genesis XLIX. English. Aberbach-Grossfeld. 1976. 528
Bible. O. T. Greek. 1906. Septuagint. 528
Bible. O. T. Greek. 1925. Septuagint. 528
Bible. O. T. Greek. 1930. Septuagint. 529
Bible. O.T. Greek. Septuagint. 1971. 284
Bible. O.T. Greek. Septuagint. 1972. 284
Bible. O. T. Haggai. English. 1897. 529
Bible. O. T. Haggai. English. 1920. 529
Bible. O.T. Haggai. English. New English. 1977. 529
Bible. O.T. Hagiographa. English. Selections. 1973. 591
Bible. O. T. Hebrew. 1815. 530
Bible. O. T. Hebrew. 1893. 505
Bible. O. T. Hebrew. 1916. 530
Bible. O.T. Hebrew. 1979. 538
Bible. O. T. Hebrew. Selections. 1960. 614
Bible. O. T. Hexateuch. English. 1900. Revised. 530
Bible. O. T. Hexateuch. English. 1918. 530
Bible. O. T. Historical books. Choctaw. 1871. 915
Bible. O. T. Historical books. Coptic (Sahidic) 1911. 531
Bible. O. T. Historical books. English. 1873. 531
Bible. O. T. Historical books. English. 1884. Conant. 591
Bible. O. T. Historical books. English. 1901. 531
Bible. O. T. Historical books. English. 1903. Authorized. 531
Bible. O. T. Historical books. English. 1909. Revised. 531
Bible. O. T. Historical books. English. 1918. 531
Bible. O. T. Historical books. English. Harmonies. 1897. Revised. 531
Bible. O. T. Historical books. English. Harmonies. 1939. Authorized. 2095

Bible. O. T. Historical Books. English. Harmonies. 1951. Revised. 3297
Bible. O.T. Historical books. English. Revised. Selections. 1973. 602
Bible. O.T. Historical books. English. Selections. 1957. Pfeiffer. 2096
Bible. O.T. Historical books. Hebrew. 1954. 1927
Bible. O.T. Historical books. Hebrew. 1973. 1927
Bible. O. T. Hosea. English. 1899. 537
Bible. O. T. Hosea. English. Andersen-Freedman. 1980. 537
Bible. O. T. Hosea. Hebrew. 1905. 538
Bible. O. T. Isaiah. Aramaic. 1949. 541
Bible. O. T. Isaiah. English. 1834. 542
Bible. O. T. Isaiah. English. 1840. 542
Bible. O. T. Isaiah. English. 1869. 542
Bible. O. T. Isaiah. English. 1875. 542
Bible. O. T. Isaiah. English. 1887. Sawyer. 543
Bible. O. T. Isaiah. English. 1897. 541, 542
Bible. O. T. Isaiah. English. 1898. 542
Bible. O. T. Isaiah. English. 1902. 541
Bible. O. T. Isaiah. English. 1903. 541
Bible. O. T. Isaiah. English. 1904. 542
Bible. O. T. Isaiah. English. 1905. 542
Bible. O. T. Isaiah. English. 1910. 542
Bible. O. T. Isaiah. English. 1914. 542
Bible. O. T. Isaiah. English. 1915. Revised. 542
Bible. O.T. Isaiah. English. 1925. 543
Bible. O.T. Isaiah. English. 1965. Young. 542
Bible. O.T. Isaiah. English. Jewish Publication Society. 1973. 541, 602
Bible. O.T. Isaiah. English. McKenzie. 1968. 545
Bible. O.T. Isaiah. English. New international. 1975. 541
Bible. O. T. Isaiah. English. Paraphrases. 1931. Popper. 541
Bible. O.T. Isaiah. Hebrew, 1899. 544
Bible. O.T. Isaiah I-XXXIX. English. New English. 1973. 544
Bible. O.T. Isaiah XL-LV. English. 1925. 545
Bible. O.T. Isaiah XL-LV. English. 1964. North. 545
Bible. O.T. Isaiah XL-LXVI. English. New English. 1975. 545
Bible. O.T. Isaiah. Yiddish, 1910. Blumgarten. 541
Bible. O. T. Jeremiah. English. 1897. 269
Bible. O. T. Jeremiah. English. 1899. 546
Bible. O. T. Jeremiah. English. 1901. Revised. 269
Bible. O. T. Jeremiah. English. 1906. 591
Bible. O. T. Jeremiah. English. 1907. 546
Bible. O. T. Jeremiah. English. 1910. 546
Bible. O. T. Jeremiah. English. 1952. Revised. 546
Bible. O. T. Jeremiah. English. 1964. Bright. 546
Bible. O. T. Jeremiah. Hebrew. 1895. 547
Bible. O.T. Jeremiah I-XXV. English. New English. 1973. 547
Bible. O.T. Jeremiah XXVI-LII. English. New English. 1975. 547
Bible. O.T. Job. English. 1838. 591
Bible. O.T. Job. English. 1844. 547
Bible. O.T. Job. English. 1845. 547
Bible. O.T. Job. English. 1858. 550
Bible. O.T. Job. English. 1858. Authorized. 551
Bible. O.T. Job. English. 1859. Douai. 547
Bible. O.T. Job. English. 1861. 591
Bible O.T. Job. English. 1866. 550
Bible. O.T. Job. English. 1872. 548
Bible. O.T. Job. English. 1894. 550
Bible. O.T. Job. English. 1896. 550
Bible. O.T. Job. English. 1899. 548
Bible. O.T. Job. English. 1900. Genung. 549
Bible. O.T. Job. English. 1900. Revised. 550
Bible. O.T. Job. English. 1904. 548
Bible. O.T. Job. English. 1905. Revised. 548
Bible. O.T. Job. English. 1906. 551
Bible. O.T. Job. English. 1906. Revised. 550
Bible. O.T. Job. English. 1907. 551
Bible. O.T. Job. English. 1911. 548
Bible. O.T. Job. English. 1912. 551
Bible. O.T. Job. English. 1914. 551
Bible. O.T. Job. English. 1918. 549
Bible. O.T. Job. English. 1918. Revised. 548
Bible. O.T. Job. English. 1920. 551
Bible. O.T. Job. English. 1922. Ball. 548
Bible. O.T. Job. English. 1929. 551
Bible. O.T. Job. English. 1935. Revised. 551
Bible. O.T. Job. English. 1938. O'Neill. 549

Bible. O.T. Job. English. 1944. Authorized. 551
Bible. O. T. Job. English. 1946. Authorized. 551
Bible. O. T. Job. English. 1947. Stevenson. 549
Bible. O. T. Job. English. 1951. Peterson. 549
Bible. O. T. Job. English. 1958. Jewish Publication Society. 548
Bible. O. T. Job. English. 1960. Revised. 548
Bible. O. T. Job. English. 1965. Pope. 548
Bible. O.T. Job. English. Authorized. 1976. 602
Bible. O. T. Job. English. Mitchell. 1979. 654
Bible. O. T. Job. English. New English. 1975. 548
Bible. O. T. Job. English. Paraphrases. 1913. 551
Bible. O. T. Job. English. Paraphrases. 1923. 551
Bible. O. T. Job. English. Paraphrases. 1934. 551
Bible. O. T. Job. English. Paraphrases. 1937. Dimnent. 551
Bible. O.T. Job. English. Pope. 1973. 548
Bible. O.T. Job. English. Selections. 1923. 2124
Bible. O. T. Job. English. Selections. 1947. Stevenson. 549
Bible. O. T. Job. Hebrew. 1822. 548
Bible. O. T. Job. Hebrew. 1893. 550
Bible. O. T. Job. Hebrew. 1980. 548
Bible. O. T. Job. xxxii-xxxvii. Hebrew. 1924. 549
Bible. O. T. Job. Yiddish. 1910. 482, 591
Bible. O. T. Joel. English. 1898. 552
Bible. O. T. Joel. English. 1919. 552
Bible. O.T. Jonah. English. 1938. Bird. 552
Bible. O.T. Jonah. English. Authorized. 1974. 552
Bible. O. T. Joshua. Choctaw. 1852. 915
Bible. O. T. Joshua. English. 1838. 553
Bible. O. T. Joshua. English. 1852. 553
Bible. O. t. Joshua. English. 1899. 553
Bible. O. T. Joshua. English. 1899. Authorized. 553
Bible. O. T. Joshua. English. 1904. 553
Bible. O. T. Joshua. English. 1911. 553
Bible. O. T. Joshua. English. 1931. 553
Bible. O.T. Joshua. English. New English. 1974. 553
Bible. O. T. Joshua. Hebrew. 1918. 553, 554
Bible. O. T. Judges. English. 1852. 554
Bible. O. T. Judges. English. 1896. 269, 554
Bible. O. T. Judges. English. 1898. 554
Bible. O. T. Judges. English. 1901. Revised. 274
Bible. O. T. Judges. English. 1904. 554
Bible. O. T. Judges. English. 1913. Revised. 554
Bible. O. T. Judges. English. 1915. 554
Bible. O. T. Judges. English. 1931. 554
Bible. O.T. Judges. English. 1968. 555
Bible. O.T. Judges. English. 1970. 554
Bible. O.T. Judges. English. Boling. 1975. 554
Bible. O.T. Judges. English. New English. 1975. 554
Bible. O. T. Judges. Hebrew. 1900. 555
Bible. O. T. Kings. English. 1896. 556
Bible. O. T. Kings. English. 1901. Revised. 556
Bible. O. T. Kings. English. 1904. Revised. 555
Bible. O. T. Kings. Hebrew. 1904. 556
Bible. O. T. Leviticus. English. 1843. 557
Bible. O. T. Leviticus. English. 1872. 557
Bible. O. T. Leviticus. English. 1898. 557
Bible. O. T. Leviticus. English. 1904. 557
Bible. O. T. Leviticus. English. 1906. 557
Bible. O. T. Leviticus. English. 1910. revised. 557
Bible. O. T. Leviticus. English. 1914. 557
Bible. O.T. Leviticus. English. 1965. Revised standard. 557
Bible. O.T. Leviticus. English. New English. 1976. 557
Bible. O.T. Leviticus. Wenham. 1979. 557
Bible. O. T. Micah. English. 1895. 558
Bible. O. T. Micah. English. 1908. 558
Bible. O. T. Minor prophets. English. 1864. 558
Bible. O. T. Minor prophets. English. 1885. 558
Bible. O. T. Minor prophets. English. 1899. 558
Bible. O. T. Minor prophets. English. 1904. 558
Bible. O. T. Minor prophets. English. 1907. Authorized. 559

Bible. O. T. Minor prophets. English. 1914. 559
Bible. O. T. Minor prophets. English. 1935. 559
Bible. O. T. Minor prophets. English. 1953. 559
Bible. O. T. Minor prophets, English. 1958. Deere. 559
Bible. O. T. Minor prophets. English. 1958. Deere. 559
Bible. O. T. Minor prophets. English. 1960. 559
Bible. O.T. Minor prophets. English. New English. 1971. 485
Bible. O.T. Minor prophets. English. New English. 1975. 559
Bible. O.T. Minor prophets. English. Paraphrases. 1965. Taylor. 570
Bible. O. T. Minor prophets. English. Paraphrases. 1965. Taylor. 570
Bible. O. T. Minor prophets. English. Paraphrases. 1967. Taylor. 570
Bible. O. T. Minor prophets. English. Paraphrases. 1967. Taylor. 570
Bible. O. T. Minor prophets. Greek. 1927. 316
Bible. O. T. Mpongwe. Selections. 1879. 2627
Bible. O. T, Nahum. Hebrew. 1907. 560
Bible. O. T. Numbers. English. 1858. 560
Bible. O. T. Numbers. English. 1906. 561
Bible. O. T. Numbers. English. 1911. 560
Bible. O. T. Numbers. English. 1939. 560
Bible. O. T. Numbers. English. 1939. Jewish publication society. 560
Bible. O.T. Numbers. English. New English. 1976. 560
Bible. O. T. Numbers. Hebrew. 1900. 561
Bible. O.T. Obadiah. English. 1898. 561
Bible. O.T. Pentateuch. Aramaic. Targum Yerushalmi. Selections. 1977. 562
Bible. O. T. Pentateuch. Choctaw. 1867. 915
Bible. O. T. Pentateuch. English. 1860. 562
Bible. O. T. Pentateuch. English. 1860. Douai. 566
Bible. O. T. Pentateuch. English. 1884. 566
Bible. O. T. Pentateuch. English. 1884. Tyndale. 564
Bible. O.T. Pentateuch. English. 1963. Kahane. 482
Bible. O.T. Pentateuch. English. 1963. Jewish Publication Society. 482
Bible. O.T. Pentateuch. English. 1967. Tyndale. 564
Bible. O.T. Pentateuch. English. Etheridge. 1968. 561
Bible. O. T. Pentateuch. English. Selections. 1801. Authorized. 1771
Bible. O. T. Pentateuch. English. Selections. 1906? 628
Bible. O. T. Pentateuch. English. Selections. 1944-Hershon. 482
Bible. O.T. Pentateuch. English. Selections. 1944. Scharfstein. 564
Bible. O.T. Pentateuch. Hebrew. 1915. 307
Bible. O. T. Pentateuch. Hebrew. 1916. 482
Bible. O.T. Pntateuch. English. 1967. Jewish Publication Society. 482
Bible. O.T. Poetical books. Englis. 1857. Kenrick. 567
Bible. O. T. Poetical books. English. 1846. Noyes. 591
Bible. O. T. Poetical books. English. 1867. Noyes. 591
Bible. O.T. Poetical books. English. 1880. Noyes. 591
Bible. O.T. Poetical books. English. 1903. Revised. 567
Bible. O.T. Poetical books. English. (Middle English) 1881. Purvey. 248
Bible. O.T. Polyglot. 1981. 591
Bible. O. T. Prophets. English. 1874. 567
Bible. O. T. Prophets. English. 1897. 633
Bible. O. T. Prophets. English. 1901. Revised. 633
Bible. O. T. Prophets. English. 1909. Revised. 567
Bible. O. T. Prophets. English. 1956. Authorized. 568
Bible. O.T. Prophets. English. 1963. Phillips. 654
Bible. O.T. Prophets. English. 1966. Revised standard. 497
Bible. O.T. Prophets (Nevi'im). English. Jewish Publication Society. 1978. 567
Bible. O. T. Proverbs. Coptic. 1931. 573
Bible. O. T. Proverbs. English. 1869. 573
Bible. O. T. Proverbs. English. 1895. 573
Bible. O. T. Proverbs. English. 1899. 572
Bible. O. T. Proverbs. English. 1901. Revised. 573

Bible. O. T. Proverbs. English. 1904. 254, 572
Bible. O. T. Proverbs. English. 1913. 572
Bible. O. T. Proverbs. English. 1918. 269
Bible. O. T. Proverbs. English. 1929. 3457
Bible. O. T. Proverbs. English. 1950. 572
Bible. O. T. Proverbs. English. 1961. Jewish Publication Society. 572
Bible. O.T. Proverbs. English. 1963. Authorized. 591
Bible. O.T. Proverbs. English. 1965. Scott. 572
Bible, O.T. Proverbs. English. 1966. Sperka. 572
Bible. O.T. Proverbs. English. New American Standard. Selections. 1973. 567
Bible. O.T. Proverbs. English. New English. 1972. 572
Bible. O. T. Proverbs. English. Paraphrases. 1912. 573
Bible. O.T. Proverbs. English. Selections. 1912. 482
Bible. O.T. Proverbs. English. Selections. 1968. 482
Bible. O.T. Proverbs. English. Today's English. 1974. 3821
Bible. O. T. Proverbs. Hebrew. 1901. 572
Bible. O. T. Psalms. Anglo-Saxon. Paraphrases. 1907. 585
Bible. O. T. Psalms. Anglo-Saxon. Paraphrases. 1932. 47
Bible. O. T. Psalms. Anglo-Saxon. Paraphrases. 1961. 573
Bible. O. T. Psalms. Coptic. Selections. 1916. 1369
Bible. O. T. Psalms cxx-cxxxiv. English. 1896. Stevens. 574
Bible. O. T. Psalms. English. 584
Bible. O. T. Psalms. English. (1535) 1935. Coverdale. 272
Bible. O. T. Psalms. English. 1784. 582
Bible. O. T. Psalms. English. 1792. 582
Bible. O. T. Psalms. English. 1794. 582
Bible. O. T. Psalms. English. 1808. 2985
Bible. O. T. Psalms. English. 1831. 573
Bible. O. T. Psalms. English. 1846. 573
Bible. O. T. Psalms. English. 1852. Authorized. 582
Bible. O. T. Psalms. English. 1862. 582
Bible. O. T. Psalms. English. 1864. Authorized. 29
Bible. O. T. Psalms. English. 1867. 591
Bible. O. T. Psalms. English. 1867. Authorized. 582
Bible. O. T. Psalms. English. 1868. 574
Bible. O.T. Psalms. English. 1871. Conant. 582
Bible. O. T. Psalms. English. 1880. 592
Bible. O. T. Psalms. English. 1881. 577
Bible. O. T. Psalms. English. 1892. 574
Bible. O. T. Psalms. English. 1895. 574
Bible. O. T. Psalms. English. 1897. Authorized. 574
Bible. O. T. Psalms. English. 1898. 574, 582
Bible. O. T. Psalms. English. 1899. 577
Bible. O. T. Psalms. English. 1901. 319
Bible. O. T. Psalms. English. 1901. Revised. 582
Bible. O. T. Psalms. English. 1902. 2985
Bible. O. T. Psalms. English. 1902. Coverdale. 2985
Bible. O. T. Psalms. English. 1903. 582
Bible. O. T. Psalms. English. 1904. 574
Bible. O. T. Psalms. English. 1904. Revised. 574
Bible. O. T. Psalms. English. 1909. 582
Bible. O.T. Psalms. English. 1911. 2986
Bible. O. T. Psalms. English. 1926. 582
Bible. O. T. Psalms. English. 1926. Smith. 582
Bible. O. T. Psalms. English. 1929. 577, 582
Bible. O. T. Psalms. English. 1929. Callan. 574
Bible. O. T. Psalms. English. 1934. 574, 586
Bible. O. T. Psalms. English. 1935. 574
Bible. O. T. Psalms. English. 1935. Wales. 582
Bible. O. T. Psalms. English. 1937. O'Neill. 577
Bible. O. T. Psalms. English. 1938. Jewish publication society. 574
Bible. O. T. Psalms. English. 1939. Lamsa. 582
Bible. O. T. Psalms. English. 1939. Lattey. 574
Bible. O. T. Psalms. English. 1940. Authorized. 883
Bible. O. T. Psalms. English. 1940. Martin. 582
Bible. O. T. Psalms. English. 1941. Authorized. 582
Bible. O.T. Psalms. English. 1944. Authorized. 582

Bible. O. T. Psalms. English. 1944. Callan. 574
Bible. O. T. Psalms. English. 1947. 2985
Bible. O. T. Psalms. English. 1947. Knox. 582
Bible. O. T. Psalms. English. 1948. Peterson. 573
Bible. O.T. Psalms. English. 1950. New American. 656
Bible. O. T. Psalms. English. 1952. Authorized. 582,
Bible. O. T. Psalms. English. 1955. Fides. 582
Bible. O. T. Psalms. English. 1960. Authorized. 582
Bible. O. T. Psalms. English. 1961. Authorized. 582
Bible. O. T. Psalms. English. 1961. Byington. 582
Bible. O. T. Psalms. English. 1963. 582
Bible. O.T. Psalms. English 1964. 583
Bible. O. T. Psalms. English. 1964. Hadas. 583
Bible. O. T. Psalms. English. 1966. Perowne. 575
Bible. O.T. Psalms. English. 1966. Dahood. 575
Bible. O. T. Psalms. English. 1967. Authorized. 583
Bible. O. T. Psalms. English. 1967. Authorized. 583
Bible. O. T. Psalms. English. Authorized. 1973. 575
Bible. O. T. Psalms. English. Authorized. Selections. 1968. 2985
Bible. O. T. Psalms. English. Coverdale. 1977. 583
Bible. O.T. Psalms. English. Hanson. 1968. 583
Bible. O.T. Psalms. English. Jerusalem Bible. 1977. 583
*Bible, O. T. Psalms. English. King James. 573
Bible. O. T. Psalms. English. New English. 1977. 575
Bible. O. T. Psalms. English. Parahrases. 1812. 1863
Bible. O. T. Psalms. English. Parahrases. 1817. 1863
Bible. O. T. Psalms. English. Paraphrases (1635) 1935. 580
Bible. O. T. Psalms. English. Paraphrases. 1729. Bay Psalm book. 580
Bible. O. T. Psalms. English. Paraphrases. 1742. Bay Psalm book. 580
Bible. O.T. Psalms. English. Paraphrases. 1758. Bay Psalm book. 1863
Bible. O. T. Psalms. English. Paraphrases. 1763. 585
Bible. O. T. Psalms. English. Paraphrases. 1765. 585
Bible. O. T. Psalms. English. Paraphrases. 1767. 585
Bible. O. T. Psalms. English. Paraphrases. 1768. 585
Bible. O.T. Psalms. English. Paraphrases. 1768. Watts. 580
Bible. O. T. Psalms. English. Paraphrases. 1771. 585, 2984
Bible. O. T. Psalms. English. Paraphrases. 1773. 585
Bible. O. T. Psalms. English. Paraphrases. 1773. Bay psalm book. 580
Bible. O. T. Psalms. English. Paraphrases. 1782. 586
Bible. O. T. Psalms. English. Paraphrases. 1791. 580, 2968
Bible. O. T. Psalms. English. Paraphrases. 1792. 1863
Bible. O. T. Psalms. English. Paraphrases. 1794. 580
Bible. O. T. Psalms. English. Paraphrases. 1795. 269, 580, 1863
Bible. O. T. Psalms. English. Paraphrases. 1797. 1863
Bible. O. T. Psalms. English. Paraphrases. 1798. 561
Bible. O. T. Psalms. English. Paraphrases. 1800? 561
Bible. O. T. Psalms. English. Paraphrases. 1801. 2968
Bible. O. T. Psalms. English. Paraphrases. 1803. 1863
Bible. O. T. Psalms. English. Paraphrases. 1804. 1863
Bible. O. T. Psalms. English. Paraphrases. 1807. Watts. 580
Bible. O.T. Psalms. English. Paraphrases. 1808. Watts. 580
Bible. O. T. Psalms. English. Paraphrases. 1809. 1863
Bible. O.T. Psalms. English. Paraphrases. 1809. Sternhold and Hopkins. 561
Bible. O. T. Psalms. English. Paraphrases. 1812. 580

Bible. O.T. Psalms English. Paraphrases. 1812. Watts. 1863
Bible. O.T. Psalms. English. Paraphrases. 1813. 561
Bible. O.T. Psalms. English. Paraphrases 1814. 580, 1863
Bible. O.T. Psalms. English. Paraphrases 1817. 1863
Bible. O.T. Psalms. English. Paraphrases. 1819. 2968
Bible. O. T. Psalms. English. Paraphrases. 1821. 1863
Bible. O. T. Psalms. English. Paraphrases. 1824. Watts. 1863
Bible. O. T. Psalms. English. Paraphrases. 1827. 1863
Bible. O. T. Psalms. English. Paraphrases. 1829. Sternhold and Hopkins. 561
Bible. O. T. Psalms. English. Paraphrases. 1830. 580
Bible. O. T. Psalms. English. Paraphrases. 1831. 580
Bible. O. T. Psalms. English. Paraphrases. 1833? 580
Bible. O. T. Psalms. English. Paraphrases. 1835. 1864
Bible. O. T. Psalms. English. Paraphrases. 1840. 2968
Bible. O. T. Psalms. English. Paraphrases. 1841. 1864
Bible. O. T. Psalms. English. Paraphrases. 1844. 581, 2968
Bible. O. T. Psalms. English. Paraphrases. 1845. 1864, 2968
Bible. O.T. Psalms. English. Paraphrases. 1846. 581
Bible. O. T. Psalms. English. Paraphrases. 1847. 1864
Bible. O. T. Psalms. English. Paraphrases. 1848? 1864
Bible. O. T. Psalms. English. Paraphrases. 1850. 1864
Bible. O. T. Psalms. English. Paraphrases. 1850. McClure. 581
Bible. O. T. Psalms. English. Paraphrases. 1853. 1864
Bible. O. T. Psalms. English. Paraphrases. 1854. 1864
Bible. O. T. Psalms. English. Paraphrases. 1857. 1864
Bible. O. T. Psalms. English. Paraphrases. 1858. 1864, 2969
Bible. O. T. Psalms. English. Paraphrases. 1862. Bay Psalm book. 581
Bible. O. T. Psalms. English. Paraphrases. 1863. 1864
Bible. O. T. Psalms. English. Paraphrases. 1869. 2968
Bible. O.T. Psalms. English. Paraphrases. 1872. 3736
Bible. O.T. Psalms. English. Paraphrases. 1887. 3736
Bible. O.T. Psalms. English. Paraphrases. 1888. 581
Bible. O.T. Psalms. English. Paraphrases. 1900. 2985
Bible. O.T. Psalms. English. Paraphrases. 1903. Bay Psalm Book. 581
Bible. O. T. Psalms. English. Paraphrases. 1906. 581
Bible. O. T. Psalms. English. Paraphrases. 1907. 190
Bible. O.T. Psalms. English. Paraphrases. 1912. Bay Psalm book. 581
Bible. O. T. Psalms. English. Paraphrases. 1915. 581
Bible. O. T. Psalms. English. Paraphrases. 1916. 581
Bible. O. T. Psalms. English. Paraphrases. 1923. 581
Bible. O. T. Psalms. English. Paraphrases. 1938. Pilgrim psalter. 2985
Bible. O. T. Psalms. English. Paraphrases. 1940. 2857
Bible. O. T. Psalms. English. Paraphrases. 1941. 581
Bible. O. T. Psalms. English. Paraphrases. 1941. Merritt. 581
Bible. O. T. Psalms. English. Paraphrases. 1948. Grimes. 581
Bible. O. T. Psalms. English. Paraphrases. 1954. Kleist-Lynam. 581
Bible. O. T. Psalms. English. Paraphrases. 1955. 583
Bible. O. T. Psalms. English. Paraphrases. 1960. Collins. 581
Bible. O. T. Psalms. English. Paraphrases. 1963. 581
Bible. O.T. Psalms. English. Paraphrases. 1967. Taylor. 581
Bible. O.T. Psalms. English. Paraphrases. 1967. Taylor. 570
Bible. O.T. Psalms. English. Paraphrases. Perowne, 1976. 577
Bible. O.T. Psalms. English. Selections. 18--. Authorized. 3220

Bible. O.T. Psalms. English. Selections. 1893. 583
Bible. O. T. Psalms. English. Selections. 1894. 2985
Bible. O. T. Psalms. English. Selections. 1898. 252
Bible. O. T. Psalms. English. Selections. 1901. 583
Bible. O. T. Psalms. English. Selections. 1911. 573
Bible. O. T. Psalms. English. Selections. 1934. 3220
Bible. O. T. Psalms. English. Selections. 1937. Laux. 583
Bible. O.T. Psalms. English. Selections. 1942 Authorized. 575
Bible. O.T. Psalms. English. Selections. 1946. 583
Bible. O.T. Psalms. English. Selections. 1952. Authorized. 583
Bible. O.T. Psalms. English. Selections. 1955. 583
Bible. O.T. Psalms. English. Selections. 1956. Authorized. 583
Bible. O.T. Psalms. English. Selections. 1956. Douai. 583
Bible. O.T. Psalms. English. Selections. 1960. 575
Bible. O.T. Psalms. English. Selections. 1960. Ward. 583
Bible. O.T. Psalms. English. Selections. 1962. 300
Bible. O.T. Psalms. English. Selections. 1965. Revised standard version. 583
Bible. O.T. Psalms. English. Selections. 1966. Authorized. 583
Bible. O.T. Psalms. English. Selections. 1966. Douai. 583
Bible. O.T. Psalms. English. Selections. 1967. Authorized. 583
Bible. O.T. Psalms. English. Selections. 1969. 575
Bible. O.T. Psalms. English. Selections. 1973. 575
Bible. O.T. Psalms. English. Selections. 1976. 583
Bible. O.T. Psalms. English. Selections. 1977. 581
Bible. O.T. Psalms. English. Taylor. Selections. 1973. 579
Bible. O.T. Psalms. English. Today's English. 1970. 583
Bible. O.T. Psalms. English. Today's English. Selections. 1974. 583
Bible. O.T. Psalms. English. Zerr. 1978. 583
Bible, O. T. Psalms. Enlish. Paraphrases. 1844. 1864
Bible. O. T. Psalms. German. 1658. 583
Bible. O. T. Psalms. Greek. 1917. 316
Bible. O.T. Psalms. Hebrew. 1895. 579
Bible. O. T. Psalms. Hebrew. 1916. 530
Bible. O. T. Psalms. Hebrew. 1934. 575
Bible. O. T. Psalms. Hebrew. 1961. 575
Bible. O.T. Psalms. Hebrew. 1973. 583
Bible. O.T. Psalms. Hebrew. Selections. 1899. 2985
Bible. O. T. Psalms. Hebrew. Selections. 1907. 573
Bible. O.T. Psalms I-XXXIV, XL-XLI. English. 1963. Kendon. 573
Bible. O. T. Psalms. Latin. 1884. 2985
Bible. O. T. Psalms. Latin. 1921. 1884
Bible. O. T. Psalms. Latin. 1929. 577
Bible. O. T. Psalms. Latin. Selections. 1930. 1876
Bible. O. T. Psalms. Paraphrases. 1817. 561
Bible. O. T. Psalms. Syriac. 1904. 573
Bible. O. T. Psalms. xxiii. English. 1866. 587
Bible. O. T. Psalms. xxiii. English. 1911. 587
Bible. O. T. Psalms. xxiii. English. 1933. 588
Bible. O. T. Psalms xxiii. English. 1939. Authorized. 587
Bible. O.T. Psalms XXIII. English 1965. Authorized. 586, 587
Bible. O.T. Psalms xxiii. English. 1965. Authorized. 586, 587
Bible. O.T. Psalms XXIII. English. Authorized. 1970. 587
Bible. O.T. Psalms XXIII. English. Paraphrases. 1911. 587
Bible. O.T. Pslams. English. 1911. 2986
Bible. O. T. Ruth. English. 1910. Authorized. 587
Bible. O. T. Ruth. English. 1913. 589
Bible. O. T. Ruth. English. 1930. 589
Bible. O. T. Ruth. English. 1935. Lattey. 589
Bible. O.T. Ruth. English. Campbell. 1975. 589

Bible. O.T. Ruth. English. New American. 1973. 592
Bible. O.T. Ruth. English. Sasson. 1979. 589
Bible. O. T. Ruth. Hebrew. 1928. 530
Bible. O. T. Ruth. Hebrew. 1937. 589
Bible. O.T. Samuel. English. 1903. Authorized. 590
Bible. O. T. Samuel. English. 1905. Revised. 589
Bible. O. T. Samuel. English. 1931. 589
Bible. O. T. Samuel. Hebrew. 1894. 590
Bible. O. T. Samuels. Choctaw. 1871. Wright. 915
Bible. O. T. Selections. Basque. 1894. 482
Bible. O. T. Selections. Cherokee. 1856. 891
Bible. O. T. Selections. English. 1907. 633
Bible. O. T. Selections. English. 1910. 592
Bible. O. T. Selections. English. 1912. 592
Bible. O. T. Selections. English. 1913. 592
Bible. O. T. Selections. English. 1915. 592
Bible. O. T. Selections. English. 1916. 592
Bible. O. T. Selections. English. 1922. 592, 618
Bible. O. T. Selections. English. 1924. 633
Bible. O. T. Selections. English. 1925. 592
Bible. O. T. Selections. English. 1926. 625
Bible. O. T. Selections. English. 1927. 592
Bible. O. T. Selections. English. 1928. 592
Bible. O. T. Selections. English. 1929. 592
Bible. O. T. Selections. English. 1930. 592, 614
Bible. O. T. Selections. Greek. 1905. 529
Bible. O. T. Selections. Mpongwe. 1859. 2627
Bible. O. T. Selections. Polyglot. 1913. 488
Bible. O.T. Song of Solomon. 593
Bible. O. T. Song of Solomon. English. 1803. 593
Bible. O. T. Song of Solomon. English. 1888. Daland. d. 1921. 593
Bible. O. T. Song of Solomon. English. 1893. Terry. 593
Bible. O. T. Song of Solomon. English. 1896. 593
Bible. O. T. Song of Solomon. English. 1902. 593
Bible. O. T. Song of Solomon. English. 1904. 593
Bible. O. T. Song of Solomon. English. 1911. Authorized. 593
Bible. O. T. Song of Solomon. English. 1927. 593
Bible. O. T. Song of Solomon. English. 1931. 593
Bible. O. T. Song of Solomon. English. 1935. 593
Bible. O.T. Song of Solomon. English. 1965. 593
Bible. O.T. Song of Solomon. English. 1966. 595
Bible. O.T. Song of Solomon. English. Falk. 1977. 593
Bible. O.T. Song of Solomon. English. Ginsburg. 1970. 593
Bible. O.T. Song of Solomon. English. Graves. 1973. 602
Bible. O. T. Song of Solomon. English. Paraphases. 1952. Wragg. 595
Bible. O. T. Song of Solomon. English. Paraphrases. 1932. 595
Bible. O. T. Song of Solomon. English. Paraphrases. 1948. Waterman. 595
Bible. O.T. Song of Solomon. English. Pope. 1977. 593
Bible. O.T. Song of Solomon. English. Revised standard. Selections. 1970. 593
Bible. O.T. Song of Solomon. English. Selections. 1975. 602
Bible. O. T. Apocrypha. English. Selections. 1957. 482
Bible. O. T. Minor prophets. English. Paraphrases. 1965. Taylor. 508
Bible. O.T. Psalms. English. Authorized. Selections. 1967. 583
Bible. O.T. Apocrypha. 1 Maccabees. English. 1897. 488
Bible. O.T. 1 Samuel. English. 1913. 483
Bible. O.T. 1 Samuel. Hebrew. 1884. 1797
Bible. O.T. 1 Chronicles XVI 8-36. English. 1953. Authorized in Bible O.T. Psalms. English 1952. 592
Bible. O.T 1 Kings. Jewish Publication Society. 483
Bible. OT. Psalms. English. Paraphrases. 1944. 2857
Bible. O.T. 2 Kings. English. 1917. 484
Bible. O.T. 2 Samuel. English. 1899. 484
Bible. O.T. Apocrypha. 1 Maccabees. English. 1948. 654
Bible. Polyglot. Selections. 1898. 725
Bible Sabbath Association. 3260
The Bible search and Gospel extension bureau. 285
Bible. Selections. 1902. 313
Bible. Selections. English. 1804. 473, 592
Bible. Selections. English. 1814. 231, 252
Bible. Selections. English. 1815. 231
Bible. Selections. English. 1816. 231
Bible. Selections. English. 1817. 231
Bible. Selections. English. 1836. 252
Bible. Selections. English. 1889. 2442
Bible. Selections. English. 1899. 650
Bible. Selections. English. 1900. 252
Bible. Selections. English. 1901. 252, 292
Bible. Selections. English. 1902. 304
Bible. Selections. English. 1903. 252
Bible. Selections. English. 1904. 252
Bible. Selections. English. 1905. 252, 636
Bible. Selections. English. 1906. 252
Bible. Selections. English. 1907. 252, 1740
Bible. Selections. English. 1908. 1444
Bible. Selections. English. 1910. 3596
Bible. Selections. English. 1912. 252
Bible. Selections. English. 1913. 614
Bible. Selections. English. 1914. 252, 3220
Bible. Selections. English. 1915. 252
Bible. Selections. English. 1917. 1230
Bible. Selections. English. 1919. 269
Bible. Selections. English. 1920. 252
Bible. Selections. English. 1921. 252, 650
Bible. Selections. English. 1922. 252
Bible. Selections. English. 1923. 252, 254
Bible. Selections. English. 1924. 252, 614
Bible. Selections. English. 1925. 252, 292, 603, 625, 636
Bible. Selections. English. 1926. 252, 614
Bible. Selections. English. 1927. 242, 252, 602, 1719
Bible. Selections. English. 1928. 636, 647
Bible. Selections. English. 1929. 252
Bible. Selections. English. 1930. 252
Bible. Selections. English. Jahsmann. 1977. 614
Bible. Selections. English. Pharaphrases. 1918. 618
Bible. Syriac (Palestinian) Selections. 1893. 2332
Bible. O. T. Apocrypha. 1 Esdras. English. Myers. 1974. 488
Bible. C. T. Minor prophets. English. 1960. 559
Bible. English. Selections. 301
Bible. English. Selections. 1933. 301
Bible. N. T. Apocryphal books. Coptic Gospel of Thomas. Coptic (Sahidic) 1959. 388
Bible. N. T. Apocryphal books. English. 1963. 336
Bible. N. T. Epistles of John. English. 1960. Barclay. 369
Bible. N. T. Greek. 269
Bible N. T. Matthew English. Revised standard, 1975. 440
Bible. N.T. Portuguese. 1963. New World. 320
Bible N. T. Prophets. Greek. 1920. 328
Bible. O. T. English. 1962. Siewert. 482
Bible. O. T. Exodus. English. 1962. Revised standard. 515
The Biblical archaeologist. 206
Biby, Mary Alice. 3181
Bicentennial Congress on Prophecy, Philadelphia, 1976. 610, 3748
Bichlmair, Georg. 2012
Bick, Abraham. 3896
Bick, Christopher. 1937
Bickel, Lothar. 2473
Bickel, Lucy V. 3763
Bickerman, Elias. 2091
Bickerman, Elias Joseph. 503, 552
Bickermann, Elias. 2305
Bickerstaff, George. 680, 896, 1230, 1233, 2886
Bickerstaffe-Drew, Francis Browning Drew, 1 58-1928. 758
[Bickerstaffe-Drew, Francis Browning Drew. 1750, 758
Bickersteth, Edward. 636, 658, 2250, 2868, 3124
Bickersteth, Edward Henry. 1827, 1013, 3406, 3713
Bicket, Zenas J. 92, 981, 1295
Bicknell, Edward John. 3679, 2868, 3410, 3679, 1212
Bicknell, Pearl Hunter. 319
Bicksler, Harry Edward. 2774
Bidder, Irmgard. 876
Biddle, Charles Wesley. 3753
Biddle, Conley J. 658
Biddle, Jacob Albert. 2817
Biddle, Maureen. 229
[Biddle, Moncure] 1882. 3822
[Biddle, Owen]. 1498
Biddle, Perry H. 1694, 2336
Biddle, William Earl. 2996
Biddulph, Thomas Tregenns. 1223
Biderwolf, William Edward. 1555
Bidez, Joseph. 1878, 3898
Bidlake, John. 58
Bidpa'i. Persian version. Anadr-i Suhaili. English. Harris 1784. 1587
Bidpa'i. Persian version. Anvcar-i Suhaili. English Harris 1784. 1587
Bidwell, Barnabas. 3197
Biebel, David B. 658, 1774
Bieber, Agnes Reiniger. 1056
Bieber, Edmund Ellis. 3714
Bieberman, Lisa. 1781
Biechler, James E. 735
Biedermann, Hermenegild Maria. 1957
Biederwolf, Wiliam Edward. 2930
Biederwolf, William Edward. 955, 2882, 276, 1555, 1598, 1695, 1827, 1839, 2868, 2930, 3228, 3318, 3338, 3477, 231, 1827, 2930, 3318, 3338
Biederwolf, William Eward, 1867. 1839
Biegeleisen, John. 1436
Biel, Gabriel. 2862
Biel, Gabriel, d. 2826
Bielak, Stanislawa Kostka. 2205, 3454
Bieler, Andre. 727, 1153, 1155
Bieler, Ludwig. 1918, 2793
Biemer, Gunter. 2702, 3707
Bien, David D. 724, 1852
Bierbaum, Athanasius. 1298, 2980
Bierbaum, Ewald. 3269
Bierbower, Austin. 2833, 2003
Bierer, Everard. 3113
Biernatzki, William E. 821
Biersack, Louis. 1649
Biersdorf, John E. 3144
Biersted, Sonja. 1102
Bietz, Arthur L. 2246
Bietz, Arthur Lee. 3387
Bietz, Arthur Leo. 337, 955, 1012, 2994, 3381, 3884
Bietz, Reinhold. 952, 2036
Biever, Bruce Francis. 819
Biezanek, Anne C. 663
Bifford, Miriam W. 1029
Bigane, John E. 444
Bigart, William. 1994
Bigelow, Abijah. 3546
Bigelow, Andrew. 1504
Bigelow, Herbert Seely. 3440
Bigelow, Jacob. 1286
Bigelow, John. 1067, 2568, 2589, 3569
Bigelow, William Sturgis. 700
Bigg, Charles. 378, 1172, 1182, 1189, 2683, 2743, 2831, 2854
Bigger, Jama Kehoe. 658, 930
Biggs, Charles Lewis. 2198
Biggs, Joseph. 2941
Biggs, Louise Ogan. 628
Biggs, Robert D. 1892
Biggs, Wilfred W. 1172
Bigg-Wither, Reginald Fitz Hugh. 3256
Bigham, Robert W. 3597
Bigham, Thomas James. 2250, 2253
Bigler, Margaret K. 3147
Bigler, Robert M. 2954
Bigler, Vernon. 3682
[Biglow, William]. 3197
Bigman, Stanley K. 2107
Bigo, Pierre. 1155
Bihlmeyer, Karl. 1173
Bikle, George B. 2162
Bilder, Jacob O. 2081
Bildersee, Adele. 2083
Bildstein, Walter J. 3242, 3328
Bile English Douai, 1950. 274
Bilezikian, Gilbert G. 435, 1768
Bilheimer, Robert S. 1116, 1125, 3737
Bilhorn, Peter Philip. 1862
Bill, Annie C. 185, 1029, 1038, 1496, 3081
Bill, Annie Cecilia (Bulmer) 1238, 1579, 2473
Bill, E.G.W. 3090
Bill, Ingram E. 1553
Billen, Albert Victor. 530
Billeter, Julius Caesar. 2618
Billheimer, Paul E. 981
Billikopf, Jacob. 2102
Billing, Gottfrid. 2735
Billings, Charles Towne. 1184
Billings, Peggy. 1090
Billings, Sherrard. 3175
Billings, William. 917
Billingsley, Amos Stevens. 2930, 3741, 3813
Billington, Dallas. 1719
Billington, Lina. 955
Billington, Ray Allen. 873, 1390, 873
Billion, Anna. 3330
Billon, B. M. 86
Bills, Paul. 659, 1532
Bills, Rex E. 98
Billups, Ann. 1259, 1467
Bilsen, Bertrand van. 758
Bilt, F. C. van de. 3406
Bimler, Richard. 1261, 2888
Bin Gorion, Micha Joseph, 1865-1921. 3581
Binchy, Daniel A. 1147
Binder, Abraham Wolf. 319
Binder, Leonard. 3088
Binder, Louis Richard. 3113
Binder, Pearl. 888
Binder, Rudolph Michael. 3056
Bindley, Thomas Herbert. 880, 2706
Binfield, Clyde. 1468
Bingham, Charles T. 1047
Bingham, Geoffrey C. 955
Bingham, Hiram. 2620
Bingham, June. 2708
[Bingham, Luther Goodyear[. 2306
Bingham, Robert E. 934, 1239
Bingham, Rowland V. 2552
Bingman, Margaret. 680
Bininger, Clem E. 2059, 3348
Binkley, Luther John. 2411
Binkley, Olin Trivette. 155, 636
Binney, Amos. 1047, 3640, 3641
Binney, Judith Mary Caroline Musgrove. 3144, 3252
Binney, Millard Fillmore. 1436
Binns, J. W. 2199
Binns, Walter Pope. 123, 3124
Binstock, Louis. 2138
Binyon, Gilbert Clives. 3435
Binyon, Laurence. 2855
Biondo, Giuseppe. 1021, 3305
Biot, Francois. 2583
Biot, Rene. 3531, 3785
Birch, Bruce C. 275, 483, 942, 2177, 3440
Birch, John Joseph. 2067, 2125, 3045, 3307
Birch, L. Charles. 3081
Birch, W Grayson. 1994, 3780
Birch, Walter de Gray. 1474
Birchmore, John W. 508
Bird, Annie Lake. 1445
Bird, Frederic Mayer. 1173
Bird, Herbert S. 3381
Bird, J. Malcolm. 3495
Bird, James Malcolm. 1378, 3496
Bird, John L. 413, 3348
Bird, Phyllis A. 276
[Bird, Robert]. 1960
Bird, Thomas Christopher. 461
Bird, Thomas E. 1979
Birdfeather, Barbara. 95
Birdsall, James Neville. 744, 3657
Birdsall, Ralph, 1871. 3338
Birdsong, Robert E. 663, 2723, 2993, 3251, 3473
Birge, John Kingsley. 185
Birkbeck, William John. 1768
Birkey, Verna. 317, 3845
Birkhaeuser, Jodocus Adolph. 1173
Birkitt, James N. 171, 740
Birkle, Suitbertus. 883
Birkle, Sultbertus. 883
Birks, Thomas Rawson. 304, 658, 1379
Birmingham, James. 2373, 3594
Birmingham, Stephen. 3333
Birmingham, William. 663
Birnbaum, Nathan. 2077, 2081
Birnbaum, Norman. 3088
Birnbaum, Philip. 2075, 2141, 2146, 2164
Birnbaum, Salomo. 1928
Birner, Herbert A. 2287, 2347
Birney, Hoffman. 2601
Birney, James Gillespie. 3423
Birrell, Verla Leone. 678
Birstein, Ann. 663, 3016
Birt, Henry Norbert. 188
Bisagno, John R. 160, 346, 422, 992, 1312, 1555, 1563, 2336, 2636, 2868
Bisbee, Frederick Adelbert. 2632, 3755
Bisceglia, John B. 2558
Bischoff, Louis V. 231
Bischoff, William Norbert. 2543
Bisek, Andrew C. 2068
Biser, Eugen. 2051
Bisgood, Marie Therese. 1346, 3438
Biship, Neal. 692, 3473
Bishop, Bette. 898, 1349, 2884
Bishop, Carl S. 2413
[Bishop, Carl Sidney] 1865. 3870
Bishop, Carlton Thomas. 3536
Bishop, Charles Cager. 3324
Bishop, Charles Cloophus. 1979, 2621
Bishop, Charles McTyeire. 886, 2003
Bishop, Claire Huchet. 941, 1114, 1638, 1996, 2348
Bishop, David S. 1316
Bishop, Edmund. 836
Bishop, Edna Earl. 955
Bishop, Edward. 682, 3292
Bishop, Eric Francis Fox. 388
Bishop, Garry. 3753
Bishop, George, George Sayles. 1750
Bishop, George Sayles. 381, 1753
Bishop, George Victor. 1598
Bishop, Hugh. 2029
Bishop, Isabella Lucy (Bird) 3743
Bishop, Ivyloy. 2549, 3466
Bishop, James Alonzo. 2888, 929, 1481, 1997, 2005, 2021, 2172, 2888
Bishop, James R. 1827
Bishop, Jesse Phelps. 7
Bishop, John. 1006, 1265, 1986, 2433, 2434, 3004, 3348

Bishop, John Love. 1950
Bishop, Jordan. 1147
Bishop, Joseph P. 664, 981, 1349
Bishop, Josiah Goodman. 650, 2480
Bishop, Mary. 1576, 1754
Bishop, Morris. 2777, 1640
Bishop, Patrick. 2365
Bishop, Richmond Leander. 3496
Bishop, Robert L. 647
Bishop, Selma Lewis. 1870, 3799
Bishop, Shelton Hale. 2868
Bishop, Tania Kroitor. 2693
Bishop, William Chatterley. 847
Bishop, William Henry. 1563
Bishop, William P. 133, 3214
Bishop, William Samuel. 1834, 2822, 3711
Bishop, William Warner. 3847
Biskupek, Aloysius. 771, 2231, 2363, 2741, 2029, 2365, 2570
Bispham, Clarence Wyatt. 1311
Bispham, Elizabeth Casey. 2246
Bissell, Edwin Cone. 206, 289, 489, 563
Bissell, Shelton. 3338
Bissieres, Rene. 2416
Bissonnette, Georges. 668, 1300, 774
Bissonnier, Henri. 939
Bithell, Richard. 19
Bitting, William Coleman. 1436, 3670
Bittinger, Desmond Wright. 2542
Bittinger, Emmert F. 1235
Bittinger, Foster Melvin. 1235
Bittinger, Lucy Forney. 2888, 3195
Bittle, Berchmans. 3282
Bittle, Celestine Nicholas Charles. 738, 2737
Bittlinger, Arnold. 323, 448, 1712
Bittner, Vernon. 643
Bittner, Vernon J. 3407
Bitton, Davis. 2608
Bivort de La Saudee, Jacques de. 762
Bixby, James Thompson. 1371, 3074, 3077
Bixler, Julius Seelye. 1056, 1886, 2220, 2221
Bixler, William Allen. 880, 1874
Bjalik, Hayyim Nahman. 1406
Bjerke, Svein. 3896
Bjerke, Ward. 613
Bjerregaard, Carl Henrick Andreas. 2637
Bjerregaard, Carl Henrik Andreas. 2637, 3838, 914
Bjorge, James R. 324, 1756, 2213, 2298, 2384, 3348
Bjorklund, Clifford W. 1549
Bjorklund, Gustaf. 1695
Bjornard, Reidar B. 544, 3031
Bjornstad, James. 1472, 2588, 2946, 3707
Black, Algernon David. 2346, 3238
Black, Antony. 1322
Black, Archibald. 906
Black, Campbell. 3197
Black, David. 94
Black, Don J. 1008
Black, Ernest Watson. 2434
Black, F. G. 3338
Black, George Fraser. 3828
Black, Harold Garnet. 1056, 1312, 1436, 2944
Black, Hubert. 3609
Black, Hugh. 1140, 1318, 1373, 2225, 2930, 3376, 3702
Black, Israel Putnam. 3551, 3564
Black, J. F. 1462
Black, James. 3197
Black, James A. 597
Black, James M. 3561
Black, James Macdougall. 213, 910, 1956, 2897
Black, Jane. 2659
Black, John. 39, 2984
Black, John Sutherland. 1103
Black, Linda Perlis. 3577
Black, Mattew. 221
Black, Matthew. 221, 383, 467, 3013
Black, Samuel Charles. 1047, 3211
Black, V. P. 3348
Black, Warren Columbus. 1887, 3338
Blackall, Christopher Rubey. 626, 1979, 1996
Blackburn, Emmeline Alethea. 3204
Blackburn, Joyce. 2867
Blackburn, Kate Eubank. 956, 1960
Blackburn, Laurence H. 1598
Blackburn, Margaret E. 3670
Blackburn, Mary Otis. 1719
Blackburn, Tom. 1905
Blackburn, William Maxwell. 5, 1612, 2178, 3348
Blackburne, Harry William, 1878. 3820
Blacker, Carmen. 3400
Blacker, Diane. 981
Blacker, Irwin R. 536
Blacker, Irwon R. 536
Blackham, Harold John. 1065, 1854
Blackhurst, James Herbert. 2584
Blackie, Bruce L. 1056
Blackie, John Stuart. 2319, 3206

Blackinton, Dora J. 3318
Blackman, Edwin Cyril. 287, 412, 2332
Blackman, George L. 731
Blackman, Murray. 32, 2087
Blackman, Nancy Dean. 1825
Blackmar, Mary K. 1005
Blackmer, Rollin Clinton. 1661
Blackmore, James H. 1298, 1393
Blackmore, Simon Augustine. 3496
Blackmun, Ora. 90
Blackstock, John W. 1455
Blackstone, W. E. 1427
[Blackstone, William E.]. 1427, 2464, 3318
Blackstone, William T. 2180
Blackwall, Anthony. 346
Blackwelder, Boyce W. 1769, 2795
Blackwell, Elizabeth. 3392
Blackwell, George Lincoln. 2945
Blackwell, Lois S. 1748
Blackwell, Muriel Fontenot. 72, 339, 2825
Blackwell, Thomas. 2912, 3641, 2649
Blackwood, Andrew W. 2897, 2949
Blackwood, Andrew Waltterson. 2949
Blackwood, Andrew Watterson. 548, 2785, 532, 570, 590, 1555, 1693, 2721, 2785, 2897, 3003, 3338, 3670, 3671, 381, 518, 546, 1247, 2056, 2888, 2930
Blackwood, Andrew Watterston. 590
Blackwood, Carolyn Philips. 1303, 3836
Blackwood, James Russell. 3241
Blagden, George Washington. 1911
Blaher, Damian J. 2593
Blaikie, Norman W. H. 2953
Blaikie, Robert J. 651, 3327
Blaikie, William Garden. 584, 289, 292, 880, 1652
Blaiklock, David A. 981
Blaiklock, E. M. 61, 62, 68, 308, 314, 324, 325, 328, 335, 343, 448, 471, 479, 575, 583, 584, 670, 981, 1277, 1774, 2246, 2868
Blain, Jacob. 48
Blaine, David Edwards. 670, 2460
Blair, Caroline Grant. 2625
Blair, Charles E. 670, 1290, 3348
Blair, Edward Payson. 444, 308, 333, 444, 613
Blair, Harold Arthur. 1386
Blair, Hugh. 2930, 3338, 3376
Blair, J Allen. 320, 323, 326, 415, 448, 449, 508, 548, 552, 587
[Blair, John] 1720-1771. 1786
Blair, John Livingston. 751
Blair, Lawrence. 24, 2723
Blair, Morris Myers. 62
Blair, Peter Hunter. 182, 1764
Blair, Robert. 1757
Blair, Samuel. 2250, 2911, 3011, 3813
Blair, William Newton. 2536, 670, 2486
Blair, William W. 678, 3428
Blair, Winfrey Dyer. 3763
Blaisdell, Ethel F. 3698
Blake, Buchanan. 549, 3539
Blake, Clinton Hamlin. 3056
Blake, Cornelia F. 3496

Blake, Edgar. 2434
Blake, Eugene Carson. 1085, 1153, 2059
Blake, James Vila. 1589
Blake, John Lauris. 647, 661, 662, 1328
Blake, Michael P. 1615
Blake, Morgan. 1361
Blake, Mortimer. 906, 1340, 2403
Blake, Nelson Morehouse. 3774, 3796
Blake, Reed. 3428
Blake, Silas Leroy. 3535
Blake, Thaddeus C. 1396, 3671
Blake, William. 2855, 670, 2384, 2855
Blake, Willson Wilberforce. 1388
Blakely, Fred Orville. 1462
Blakely, Hunter Bryson. 698, 2930, 3660
Blakely, Paul Lendrum. 367, 1263
Blakely, William Addison. 3548
Blakeman, Edward William. 3756
Blakeman, Wilbert C. 1719
Blakemore, William Barnett. 1465, 1466, 1492, 3228
Blakiston, Alban. 231
Blamires, Harry. 62, 956, 981, 1472, 1473, 2980, 3327
Blanchard, Birdsall Everard. 830
Blanchard, Calvin. 1653
Blanchard, Charles. 819
Blanchard, Charles Albert. 200, 320, 499, 2868
Blanchard, Edgar Franklin. 1116
[Blanchard, Edward Litt Laman] 1820-1889. 2649
Blanchard, Ferdinand Quincy. 1950, 1979
Blanchard, Jean. 1489
Blanchard, John. 62, 412
Blanchard, Jonathan. 1668
Blanchard, Kathleen (Barrett) 1874
Blanchard, Leora M. 3592
Blanchard, Raoul. 2761
Blanchard, Richard E. 690

Blanchard, Tim. 1712
Blanche. 2353
Blanchet, Augustine Magloire Alexander. 668, 670
Blanchet, Francis Norbert. 824
Blanchette, Alice (Bergin) 2590
Blanchette, Charles Alphonse. 777, 798
Bland, Oliver. 2733
Bland, Salem Goldworth. 3440
Bland, Thomas Augustus. 3496
Blandford, Benjamin W. 2104
Blandin, Isabella Margaret Elizabeth. 1173
Blandy, Gray M. 117
Blaney, John C. 3288
Blangee, James. 1674
Blank, Sheldon H. 503, 543, 1942, 2949, 3361
Blank, Stephanie B. 738
Blanke, Fritz. 37
Blankenbaker, Frances. 3563
Blankenship, Lois. 3169
Blankenship, Roberta. 670, 3822
Blankenship, William D. 3197
Blankinship, Carribel. 3173
Blanshard, Brand. 1534, 1597
Blanshard, Paul. 670, 798, 819, 1091, 1129, 1149, 1919, 3770
Blanshard, Paul [Bleecher]. 1149
Blanshard, Paul Bleecher. 798, 1129
Blanton, Margaret (Gray) 3460
Blanton, Smiley. 2995, 2996
Blanton, Wyndham Bolling. 3237
Blantz, Thomas E. 668, 1779
Blashfield, Clara (Beers) 3857
Blasi, Anthony. 1942
Blass, Friedrich Wilhelm. 393, 1769
Blassingame, Wyatt. 1300
Blatch, Mervyn. 750, 1160
Blau, Joel. 1455
Blau, Joseph Leon. 721, 2079, 2155, 2842, 3032, 3194
Blau, Yehoshua. 1797
Blauvelt, Augustus, 1832-1900. 1653
Blauvelt, Mary Taylor. 956
Blauw, Johannes. 2553
Blavatsky, Helen Petrovna (Hahn-Hahn). 671, 3683
Blavatsky Helene Petrovna (Hahn-Hahn) 1831-1891. 671, 1895, 2723, 3683, 3684, 3689
Blaydes, William C. 1445
Blayney, Ida Walz. 2272, 3215
Blazer, Dan G. 2783
Blazier, Kenneth D. 3551, 3561
Blazier, Kenneth L. 3147
Blechman, Nathan. 3859
Bledsoe, Albert Taylor. 1500, 1657, 1719, 3609
Bledsoe, W. C. 143
Blees, Robert A. 1259
Blegen, Allen Raymond. 2868
Bleich, J. David. 2074, 2377
Bleidorn, Eugene F. 2384, 3475
Bleiweiss, Robert M. 2172
Blekkink, Evert John. 1732
Blench, J. W. 2909
Blenkinsopp, Joseph. 510
Blenkinsopp, Joseph. 323, 495, 521, 526, 531, 652, 771, 877, 1404, 1711, 2795, 3389
Bles, Arthur de. 919
Blessing, William Lester. 1736, 3338
Blessitt, Arthur. 672, 1261, 1436, 1574, 1576, 3828
Blevins, James L. 436, 2415
Blevins, William L. 992
Blewett, George John. 1103
Blews, Richard R. 1652
Blick, Ida S. 3147
Blidstein, Gerald J. 1315
Blied, Benjamin J. 873
Blied, Benjamin Joseph. 668, 1801
Blieweis, Theodor. 774
Bligh, John. 342, 381, 407, 449, 511, 1601, 2023, 2067, 2741
Bliley, Nicholas Martin. 27
Blinn, Henry Clay. 2205, 3394, 3398
Blinzler, Josef. 2068
Blinzler, Joseph. 2068
Bliss, Douglas Percy. 1427
Bliss, Edwin Munsell. 82, 2481, 2516, 2518, 2525
Bliss, Frederick Jones. 3578
Bliss, Harry Augustus. 3333
Bliss, Kathleen. 2192, 3056
Bliss, Loretta Ann (Deering) 2384
Bliss, Philip Paul. 2633
[Bliss, Philip Paul] 1838-1876. 1864, 3230
Bliss, Sylvester. 2467
Bliss, William Root. 2688
Blitchington, Evelyn. 1604
Blitchington, W. Peter. 981, 1607, 3835
Blitz, Antonio. 1345
[Bliven, Ransom] 1898. 3288
Bloch, Abraham P. 1588, 1614, 2119
Bloch, Ernst. 1073, 3107
Bloch, Herbert. 2586

Bloch, Joshua. 56
Bloch-Hoell, Nils. 2814
Blochlinger, Alex. 2774
Block, Edward A. 3860
Block, Elizabeth. 3780
Block, Karl Morgan. 956, 1445
Block, Marguerite (Beck) 2689
Blocker, Hyacinth. 2580, 3279, 3485
Blocker, Simon. 956, 2868, 2897
Blodgett, Harvey Alvaro. 3232
Blodgett, May Nellie. 886
Blodgett, Ralph H. 1802, 3318
Bloede, Gustav August. 1546
Bloesch, Donald G. 62, 69, 175, 956, 1153, 1243, 1550, 1552, 2583, 2835, 2868, 3288, 3294, 3641
Blofeld, John. 2637
Blofeld, John Eaton Calthorpe. 704, 3586, 3810
Blofeld, John Eaton Calthrope. 2383
Blohm, Emily. 628
Blois, Louis de. 2642
Blom, Dorothea Johnson. 602
Blom, Mary Callixta. 804
Blomberg, Gustav. 289
Blome, Arnold. 1029
Blomfield, Sara Louisa (Ryan) Lady, d. 127
Blomgren, Carl August. 2285
Blondel, Jacques. 299, 2467
Blondel, Maurice. 2835
Blood, Benjamin Paul. 2854, 3097, 3609
Blood, William Morris. 3348
Blood, William W. 2186
Bloom, Alfred. 3403
Bloom, Anthony. 62, 2868, 3493
Bloom, Harold. 722, 1387
Bloom, Herbert Ivan. 2098
Bloom, James Harvey. 1237
Bloom, Marjorie. 437, 1604
Bloom, Naomi. 3138
Bloomfield, Arthur Edward. 51, 81, 462, 465, 508, 610, 647
Bloomfield, Bernard M. 2761
Bloomfield, Edward H. 1469
Bloomfield, Harold H. 3707
Bloomfield, Maurice. 3088, 689, 3776
Bloomfield, Morton Wilfred. 1411, 3413
Bloomfield theological seminary, Bloomfield, N.J. 1707
Bloomingdale, Teresa. 673, 875
Bloor, Robert Henry Underwood. 934, 3145
Bloore, John. 231, 2561
Blore, Eskell L. 625
*Blose, Elcy Marie. 3143
Bloss, Celestia Angenette. 1390
Blossom, Rose B. 292, 2610
Blossom, Willis W. 253
Blough, Jerome E. 1236
Blount, George Wood. 1950
[Blount, Melesina Mary]. 2943
Blount, Veronica. 941
Blowers, Russ. 1056
Bloy, Leon. 3286
Bloy, Myron B. 1065, 3854
Blue, Lionel. 2138
Blue, Rose. 3826
Bluem, A. William. 3594
Bluhm, Heinz Siegfried. 283
Blum, Neil Elliott. 1379
Blum, Owen J. 22, 1876
Blum, Virgil C. 1129
Blumberg, Rhoda. 3826
Blume, Friedrich. 1207
Blumenfeld, David. 2087
Blumenfeld, Gerry. 871
Blumenschein, Marian. 673, 2529
Blumenthal, Seymour M. 2084
Blumenthal, Walter Hart. 1429
Blumenthal, Warren B. 499, 1730, 1942
Blumhardt, Christoph. 2888
Blumhardt, Christoph Friedrich. 2298
Blumhorst, Roy. 1277, 1604, 3056
Blumit, Oswald A. 2319, 2979
Blund, Iohannes. 80, 3461
Blunsdon, Norman. 3520
Blunt, Alfred Alter Frank. 1730
Blunt, Alfred Walter Frank. 73, 388, 567, 2095
Blunt, Alfred Wlater Frank. 475
Blunt, Henry. 1225, 1960
Blunt, Hugh Francis. 180, 764, 845, 996, 1363, 1712, 2132, 2135, 2250, 2354, 2361, 2412, 2813, 3247, 3269, 3525, 3831
Blunt, John Henry. 1489, 3041, 3637
Blunt, John James. 276, 1293
Blunt, Ruth H. 2304, 2401
Blunt, Wilfrid. 86
Bluntach, John Alexander. 1029
Blustein, Jeffrey. 1604
Bluth, John V. 3430
Bly, Stephen A. 899, 1742, 3882
Blyden, Edward Wilmot. 2680
Blyth, John W. 2179, 3813
Blyth, John William. 2179, 3813

Blyth, Reginald Horace. 3891, 3892, 3894
Blyth, Robert Bayne. 956
Blythe, Le Gette. 2936
Blythe, LeGette. 1999
Blyton, Enid. 619
B'nai B'rith. Dept. of Adult Jewish Education. 2084, 2086
B'nai B'rith. District no. 1. Grand lodge. 673
B'nai B'rith. District no. 4. Grand lodge. 673
B'nai B'rith Hillel Foundations. 2151, 2154
B'nai B'rith, Independent order of. Constitution grand lodge. 673
B'nai B'rith, Independent order of. District grand lodge no. 1. 673
B'nai B'rith. Supreme lodge. 673
B'nai B'rith. Vocational Service. 2104, 2106, 2943
Boa, Kenneth. 3113, 3525, 3661
Board of missionary preparation (for North America) 2481
Boardman, Anne (Cawley) 2811, 3419, 3420, 3790
Boardman, George Dana. 673, 1116, 1312, 1380, 1956, 1960, 2051, 2173, 2246, 3334, 3461
Boardman, George Nye. 2688
Boardman, Henry Augustus. 719, 1358, 3299, 3413, 3426
Boardman, William Edwin. 673, 956, 1393
[Boarman, Marshall Ignatius] 1853. 747
Boas, Franz. 186, 2188
Boas, J. H. 2685
Boas, Maurits Ignatius. 1393
Boas, Maurits Ignatius, M.D. 1393
Boas, Ralph Philip. 2372
Boase, Leonard. 2868
Boase, Paul H. 3433
Boase, Thomas Sherrer Ross. 744, 848, 1640
Boat, Reverend William J. 3197
Boat, William J. 762
Boatman, Don Earl. 379
Boatman, James Austin. 1906
Boatman, Russell. 1529
Boatwright, Crichton Russ. 3751
Boaz, Charles. 3561
Boaz, Hiram Abiff. 3671
Bobango, Gerald J. 668, 3711
Bobb, Ruth (Hogue) 619
Bobbe, Dorothie (De Bear) 2737
Bobbitt, George G. 1067
Bobbitt, Paul. 915
Bobe, Louis Theodor Alfred. 1500
Bober, Harry. 848
Bobgan, Martin. 2779
Bobik, Joseph. 2737
Bobrow, Dorothy. 2151
Bochenski, Innocentius M. 1457, 3070
Bock, Janet. 1895, 1975
Bock, Lois. 1607
Bock, Paul. 1133, 3849
Bock, Valerie. 674, 2487
Bockelman, Eleanor. 27, 956, 3528
Bockelman, Wilfred. 1239, 1250, 1300, 1548, 1749, 2499, 3253
bocker, George Edward, 1872. 2426
Bocking, Eng. Saint Mary's church. 3051
Bocking, Hannah (Dakin) 3094
Bockle, Franz. 942, 947
Bockmuhl, Klaus. 1457, 2352
Bocock, John Holmes. 2231
Bocquet, Marcel. 1379
Boddie, Charles Emerson. 674, 2680
Boddy, William Henry. 2930
Bode, Frederick A. 2713
Bode, Henry. 1550, 1702
Bodein, Vernon Parker. 3025, 3440
Boden, Evan H. 2910
Bodensieck, Julius. 2285, 3324
Bodewitz, H. W. 19
Bodin, Edward. 2311
Bodin, Edward Longstreet. 3496
Bodin, Jean. 859, 3113
Bodine, Walter Ray. 555
Bodine, William Budd. 1874
Bodington, Charles. 3089
Bodington, Eric James. 1719
[Bodkin, D. G.]. 1622
Bodkin, Maud. 3097
Bodley, Homer S. 3237
Bodley, John Edward Courtenay. 1881, 2328
Bodley, Ronald Victor Courtenay. 1635, 2628
Bodman, Manoah. 1695
Bodo, John R. 338, 3243, 3737
Body, Charles William Edmund. 482
Boe, Viglelk Engebretson. 3561
Boecker, Hans Jochen. 499, 2201
Boedder, Bernard. 2672
[Boeddinghaus, Richard W.]. 1047
Boegner, Marc. 1719
Boegner, Mare. 2249
Boehlke, Frederick J 1926. 2826

Boehlke, Frederick J., Jr. 2826
Boehlke, Robert R. 3176
Boehm, Henry. 2474
Boehm, John Philip. 3048
Boehme, Jakob. 674, 2637
Boehmer, Francis W. 1377
Boehmer, Eduard. 656, 3470
Boehmer, Heinrich. 1944, 2267, 2272
Boehner, Philotheus, Father. 1645
Boelter, Francis W. 1377
Boer, Hans Alfred de. 3017
Boer, Harry R. 231, 388, 453, 1196, 2553
Boer, Tjitze J. De. 2840
Boerma, Conrad. 2866
Boers, Hendrikus. 475
Boesak, Allan Aubrey. 669, 1077
Boesch, Mark. 835
Boesch, Mark J. 835
Boese, Homer H. 2029
Boethius, d. 524. 2835
Boettcher, Henry John. 747, 2279
Boettner, Loraine. 305, 798, 1527, 2036, 2464, 2911, 3641, 3792
Boever, Richard A. 429
Boff, Leonardo. 1077, 1152, 1640, 1750, 1998, 2036
Bogard, Ben M. 142, 144
Bogard, David. 3477
Bogardus, Donald Fred. 2699
Bogardus, Harriet S.[teele]. 2003
Bogardus, LaDonna. 3173
[Bogatzky, Karl Heinrich von] 1690-1774. 956, 1430, 1436
Bogert, Cornelia H. 3496
Boggis, Robert James Edmund. 2960
Boggs, Annie Lee. 2812
Boggs, Evelyn (Bockley) 956
Boggs, Evelyn (Buckley) 956
Boggs, Norman Towar. 1173
Boggs, Wade H. 2377, 3784
Boggs, William Bambrick. 147
Bogigian, Hagop. 3124
Bogolepov, Aleksandr Aleksandrovich. 1373, 2747, 2750, 2751
Bogue, David. 378
Boguet, Henri. 3826
Bogusz, J. G. 560
Bohen, Marian. 1328
Bohl, Eduard. 2160
Bohlmann, Ralph A. 240, 2284
Bohme, Jakob. 956, 2637, 2641, 2643
Bohner, Olivine Nadeau. 1366, 1850
Bohnet, Martin Paul. 1056
Bohnstedt, John Wolfgang. 3718
Bohr, David. 76, 826
Bohren, Rudolf. 2897
Bohrs, Mary Ann. 1113
Boice, James Montgomery. 418, 3830, 4, 276, 369, 415, 448, 552, 604, 1010, 1602, 1719, 1818, 1827, 2036, 3334
Boice, Robert A. 1047
Boigelot, Rene. 2625
Boirac, Emile. 2987
Bois, John. 271, 674
Boise, James Robinson. 371
Boisen, Anton Theophilus. 1864, 2995, 2996, 3671
[Boisguillebert, Pierre Le Peasant, sieur de] 2353
Boismard, M E. 422
Boissarie, Prosper Gustau. 2262
Boissarie, Prosper Gustave. 2262
Bojorge, Horacio. 2358
Bok, Bart Jan. 98
Bokenkotter, Thomas S. 808, 1173
Boker, George Henry. 680
Bokser, Baruch M. 2479, 3297
Bokser, Ben Zion. 721, 1455, 1506, 2073, 2113, 2137, 2138, 2150, 2152, 2622, 2646, 3584
Boland, Peg. 764
Bolding, Amy. 1349, 1433, 1436, 1437, 1445, 1691, 1911
Boldrey, Richard. 375, 3832
Boldridge, John Henry. 778
Bolduan, Miriam F. 3070
Bolduc, Jean Baptiste Zacharie. 675, 1901
Bole, Simeon James. 3077
Bolek, Francis. 3422
Boler, James E. 2592
Boler, John Francis. 2810
Boles, Donald E. 300
Boles, Donald Edward. 300, 3095
Boles, Henry Leo. 280, 328, 440, 604, 1462, 1827
Boles, John B. 892, 2167, 3232
Bolich, Gregory G. 118, 175, 1550
*Bolick, James H. 3347, 3372
Boligham and Vaux, Henry Peter Brougham 1778-1868. 2672
Bolin, Gene. 3828
Bolin, William James. 160
Bolitho, Archie A. 1013, 2549
Bolitho, Hector. 2761
Bolitho, William. 659
Boll, Robert H. 1798
Boll, Robert Henry. 453

Bolle, Kees W. 2648
Bollen, John David. 2954
Bolles, James Aaron. 2966
Bollier, John A. 3626
Bollig, Richard Joseph. 820
Bolliger, Max. 633, 634, 1401, 1404, 2133, 2711
Bollinger, Hiel De Vere. 3537
*Bollinger, J. W. 3195
Bollman, Calvin Porter. 3318
Bolls, Kate (McChesney) 1368
Bologne, Charles Damian. 3333
Bolshakoff, Serge. 675, 1469, 2575, 2648, 2750
Bolster, Evelyn. 779
Bolt, David Langstone. 1093
Bolt, Peter. 324
Bolton, Barbara J. 3169
Bolton, Brett L. 2723
Bolton, Glorney. 2123
Bolton, Henrietta Irving. 2271, 2357
Bolton, Herbert Eugene. 2177
Bolton, Herbert Eugene, 1870-1953. 2177
Bolton, Horace Wilbert. 3338
Bolton, Ivy May. 3376
Bolton, James David Pennington. 1818
Bolton, Margaret. 1626, 3477
[Bolton, Rhoda]. 675
Bolton, Robert. 1225, 3295
Bolton, Robert J. 2552
Bolton, S. Charles. 1228, 3464
Bolton, Stacey. 675, 1259
Bolton, William Jay. 68
Boman, Thorleif. 2841
Bomar, Willie Melmoth. 2698
Bomberger, Henry Aymar. 1093
Bomberger, John Henry Augustus. 1906
Bomberger, John Huston. 3568
Bomhard, Emma Elise (Koch) 940
Bomhard, Emma Elsie (Koch) 940
[Bona, Giovanni] 1609-1674. 2642, 3477
Bonansea, Bernardino M. 1738
Bonar, Andrew Alexander. 577, 3720
Bonar, Horatius. 418, 521, 729, 1652, 2136, 2761, 3541, 3671
Bonar, James. 2319
Bonaventura. 775, 1985, 2819
Bonaventura, 1221-1274. 775, 862, 953, 1985, 2011, 2031, 2354, 2570, 2575, 2580, 2642, 2835, 2910, 3369, 3485, 3636, 3641
Bonaventura. 775
Boncompagni-Ludovisi, Maria Maddalena. 2250
Bond, Ahva John Clarence. 1543, 3261
Bond, Albert Richmond. 2049
Bond, Alvan. 1628, 2487
Bond, Beverly Waugh, 1843. 956
Bond, Beverly Waugh. 3802
Bond, Charles Lester. 903, 956, 3386, 3884
Bond, Elias. 3300
Bond, Francis. 919, 3316, 27, 79, 751, 753, 1160, 1632, 3808
Bond, Frederick Bligh. 3496
Bond, Frederick Clifton. 3249
Bond, Helen Merrick. 2723
Bond, Jesse Hickman. 1950
Bond, Kingsley G. 3828
Bond, Samson. 1681
Bond, Shelagh M. 3820
Bond, Thomas Emerson. 2376, 2422, 2450
Bonell, Harold C. 3372
Bones, Ben Roland. 3056
Bonet Correa, Antonio. 85
Bonewits, Philip Emmons Isaac. 2312
*Boney, Mary L. 1719
Boney, William Jerry. 764, 3610
Bonforte, John. 929, 1960
Bonham, Betty. 636, 1169
Bonham, John Milton. 3327
Bonham, Tal D. 3334
*Bonhoeffer, Dietrich. 1380
Bonhoeffer, Dietrich. 525, 584, 676, 942, 956, 1457, 1956, 2046, 2173, 2284, 3219, 3334, 3335, 3632
Bonhoffer, Dietrich. 1317
Bonifacius, 680-755. 677, 1026
Bonifacius, originally Winfried. 677
Bonifacius, originally Winifried. 677
Bonifazi, Conrad. 2843, 2844
Bonifazi, Flavian. 2766
Bonilla, Victor Daniel. 1903
Bonn, John Louis. 1860, 2942
Bonnar, William. 2987
Bonnard, Abel. 1640
Bonnechose, Francois Paul Emile Boisnormand de. 928, 1857
Bonnefoy, Jean Francois. 1886, 2049
Bonnell, John Sutherland. 2779, 1598, 1795, 1887, 2779, 2868, 2930, 2937, 2995, 3671
Bonner, Arthur. 2305
Bonner, Clint. 1874
Bonner, David Findley. 2984, 3288
Bonner, Gerald. 113, 1004
Bonner, J. William. 1285

Bonner, Stephen. 173, 2634
Bonner, William Jones. 1693
Bonnet, Charles. 1097
Bonnet, Leon. 2231
Bonnet, Louis. 424
Bonney, Thomas George. 751
Bonniwell, William Raymond. 843, 1999, 2332, 2365
Bonnot, Bernard R. 2123, 2861
Bonomelli, Geremia. 2636, 1265
Bononcini, Eugene 1835-1907. 1756
Bonsack, Charles Damian. 1237
Bonsall, Elizabeth Hubbard. 602, 1864
Bonser, Edna Madison (MacDonald) 1996, 2087, 3147, 3763
Bonsirven, Joseph. 475, 2149, 2150
Bonta, Robert Eugene. 3532
Bonthius, Robert Harold. 2996
Bontier, Pierre. 1358
Bontrager, G. Edwin. 1471
Bontrager, John Kenneth. 981, 3856
Bonwick, James. 1501, 1919
[Bonwicke, Ambrose] 1652-1722. 677
Bonzelet, Honoratus. 780
Boodin, John Elof. 1103, 1371, 2416
Booher, Dianna Daniels. 1416
Book, Morris Butler. 1466, 2633
Book of Mormon. 678, 680, 2019, 2598, 2600, 2601, 3428
Book of Mormon. Spanish. 3428
Book of opening the mouth. 1691
Book of the dead. 680
Book of two ways. English. 1501
Book, William Henry. 3338, 1466
Bookstaber, Philip David. 2113, 2138, 2841
Bookwalter, Lewis. 3218
Boome, Martha. 762
Boon, May Ellen (Watson) 3884
Boone, Abbott. 3088, 3089
Boone, Arthur Upshaw. 1437
Boone, Charles Eugene. 681, 1110, 1430, 2384, 2476, 2868, 3124
Boone, Clinton C. 2513
Boone, Edward. 589
Boone, Ilsley. 1999, 151
Boone, Jean Baptiste. 2580
Boone-Jones, Margaret. 2173
Boone, Joseph P. 141
Boone, Leslie A. 1380
Boone, Muriel. 681, 2507
Boone, Shirley. 681, 930, 931
Boone, Theodore Sylvester. 157, 681
Boone, William Cooke. 147, 2336
Boord, James A. 3792
Boorman, William Ryland. 686
Boose, Rose E. 647
Booth, Abraham. 1358, 1750, 2014, 3288
Booth, Alan R. 1076, 3792
Booth, Ballington. 3786
Booth, Charles Octavius. 3661
Booth, Edwin Prince. 2273, 346, 1056, 1960, 3083, 3141
Booth, Esma (Rideout) 2489
Booth, Evangeline Cory. 2264, 3338
Booth, Henry Kendall. 231, 407, 3440
Booth, Henry Matthias. 2930, 3671
Booth, Herbert. 1047, 1997, 3791, 3705
Booth, Howard J. 2996, 3525
Booth, James Scripps. 231
Booth, John Nicholls. 2897
Booth, Julianne. 318, 899
Booth, Lavaughn Venchael. 157
Booth, Maud Ballington (Charlesworth) 3292, 3461
Booth, Newell Snow. 2497
Booth, Osborne. 532
Booth, Sally Smith. 3828
Booth Tucker, Frederick St. George de Lautour, 1853-1929. 3293
Booth, William. 682
Booth-Clibborn, Arthur Sydney. 672
Boothe, Charles Octavius. 157, 3661
Booth Tucker, Frederick St. George de Lautour. 682, 3293
Booton, John Kaylor. 2941
Boots, Ra. 604
Booty, John. 956
Booty, John E. 1021, 1173, 1221
Booz, Gretchen. 682, 1349
Bopp, Linus. 836
Boraas, Roger S. 2217, 3172
Borchert, Gerald L. 1563
Bord, Janet. 2190
Bordeaux, Henry. 3526
Bordelon, Marvin. 2789
Borden, Eli Monroe. 3338
Borden, Lucille (Papin) 723, 1960, 2005
Borden, Mary G. 1792
Bordentown, N.J. St. Mary's church. 1173
Borders, M. Edward. 3475
Borders, William Holmes. 160, 3348
[Borduin, Meane] 1867. 134
Boreham, Frank William. 180, 3348
Boren, Carter E. 1467
Boren, James Basil. 1445

Borenius, Tancred. 3692
Borenmann, Robert E. 3184
Borer, Wilbur J. 929, 1960
Boresky, Theodosia. 1918
Borgia, Anthony V. 191, 3496
Borgmann, Henry. 871, 2365
Borgongini-Duca, Francesco. 367, 399, 508, 1263
Borgongini-Duca, Francesco, Cardinal. 367
Borgwardt, Robert G. 338
Bories, Marcel. 3525
Boring, M. Eugene. 388, 2070, 2949
Bork, Paul F. 517, 2621
Borland, James A. 499, 3682
Borleis, Harry F. 798
Borne, Etienne. 101
Borneman, Henry Stauffer. 1668
Bornemann, Friedrich Wilhelm Bernhard. 1960, 2036
Bornemann, Robert E. 3184
Bornkamm, Gunther. 375, 409, 444, 2036, 2795
Bornkamm, Heinrich. 504, 2273, 2281, 3617, 1143, 2273
Bornman, Ralph H. 990
Bornstein, Edward. 2113
Borochov, Ber. 2077
Borochow, Baer. 2077
Boros, Ladislaus. 41, 552, 682, 996, 1413, 1845, 1846, 1886, 2012, 2023, 2322, 2868, 3539, 3600, 3619, 3782
Borowitz, Eugene B. 879, 1583, 2010, 2080, 2138, 2141, 2154, 3032, 3392
Borren, Charles Jean Eugene van den. 2372
Borrow, George Henry. 3469
Borsch, Frederick Houk. 314, 601, 1719, 1950, 3458
Borsi, Giosue. 3456
Borthwick Institute of Historical Research. 682, 1243
[Borthwick, Jane Laurie] 1813-1897. 1874
Boruch, Behn. 4, 2133, 2793
Bos, Jacob. 1950
Bosanquet, Bernard. 1056
Bosanquet, Bernard Hugh. 346
Bosanquet, Mary. 676
Bosc, Jean. 794
Bosch, David Jacobus. 326, 2553, 3521
Bosch, F. W. Archibald. 333
Bosch, Henry Gerard. 1874, 1349
Bosch, Herbert A. 1167
Bosch, Hermann. 625
Bosch, Juan. 1404
Bosch, Paul. 2211, 2897
Bosco, Antoinette. 3329
Bosco, Giovanni. 1027, 3305
Boser, Fidelis. 2365
Bosher, J S. 171
Bosher, Robert S. 1220
Bosler, Raymond T. 2342
Bosley, Harold Augustus. 527, 586, 956, 1054, 1103, 1985, 1995, 2027, 2180, 2434, 2804, 3348, 3641, 3850
Bosley. Harold Augustus. 956
Boslooper, Thomas David. 3780
Bosma, Menno John. 3043
Bosniak, Jacob. 3370
Boso, d. 1178. 24
Boss, Judy. 120, 683, 3473
Boss, Nelson Riley. 2960
Bossaert, M. 3338
Bossard, James Herbert. 26
Bossart, Donald E. 1165
Bossenbroek, Edward. 595
Bossence, William Henry. 2188, 2431
Bostock, Allan Kenneth. 1214
Boston. Arlington street church. 1701
Boston. Assembly of pastors of churches in New England, 1743. 1757
Boston. Brattle Square church. 2985
Boston. Christ church. 1158
Boston. Church of the Advent. 1116
Boston. Church of the disciples. 34
Boston College, Boston, Mass. Theology Dept. 595
Boston. Essex street church. 7
Boston. First Baptist church. 154
Boston. First church. 1335, 1372
Boston. First church of Christ, Scientist. Board of directors. 1029, 1493
Boston. First church of Christ, Scientist. Committee on general welfare. 1038
Boston. First Universalist Church. 3754
Boston. General theological library. 3626
Boston. King's chapel. 1864, 2868
Boston. Museum of Fine Arts. 1387
Boston. Old South church. 684, 1748
Boston Psychotheological Symposium, 2d, Aquinas Junior College, 1976. 1374
Boston Psychotheological Symposium, 1st, Aquinas Junior College, 1975. 775, 2575
Boston. Public library. 745, 2687, 2847, 2884
Boston. South Congregational church. 3549

Boston. Special class teachers. 2590
Boston. Theological library. 3627
Boston, Thomas. 2322, 3288, 1234
Boston. Trinity church. 685, 1348
Boston. Twelfth Baptist church. 683
Boston university. School of theology. Conference on preaching, 1928. 2897
Boston university. School of theology. Conference on preaching, 1929. 2897
Boston university. School of theology. Conference on preaching, 1930. 2897
Boston university. School of theology. Conference on preaching, 1931. 2897
Boston. West church. 685, 1864
Bostrom, Christopher Jacob. 3097
Bostrom, Fred W. 1029
Bostrom, Otto Henry. 590
Bostwick, Catherine Finney. 995
Boswell, Fred. 2662
Boswell, Ira Matthews. 1466, 2633
Boswell, Jackson Campbell. 2470
Boswell, John Wesley. 2423
Boswell, Rolfe. 1820, 2946
Bosworth, Edward Increase, 1861. 3870
Bosworth, Edward Increase. 333, 475, 636, 956, 1960, 1991, 2062, 3619, 3870
Bosworth, Fred Francis. 1598, 1792
Bosworth, William Arthur. 817
Boteler, Mattie M. 956, 3362
Botfield, Beriah. 2677
Bothem, J. W. 3204
Bothwell, Mary de Angelis. 3181
Bothwell, Sister Mary de Angelis. 3186, 3189
Botsford, Edmund. 685
Bottel, Helen. 3879
Botterweck, G. Johannes. 511, 1796
Bottineau, Yves. 2773
Bottome, Francis. 3458
Bottome, Margaret (McDonald) 1437
Bottomley, Frank. 2321
Bottoms, Lawrence. 512
Botts, Eli Daniel. 2546
Botts, R A. 604
Botz, Paschal. 575
Bouchard, Constance Brittain. 666
Bouche-Leclercq, Auguste, 1842-1923. 1470, 2940
Boucher, Madeleine. 2024
Boucher, Sharon. 3124
Boucher, Theophiel. 2610
Boudet, Jacques. 1944
Boudinot, Elias. 276, 2758, 3124, 3318, 3601
Bouet, A. 2384
Bouffard, Alma. 3143
Bougaud, Emile. 21, 2000, 3269, 3779
Bougerol, J. Guy. 675
Boughton, Willis Arnold. 1960
Bougier, Marie. 2572
Bouillard, Henri. 62, 175, 1734
Bouilloc, Jean. 1845
Bouisson, Maurice. 2314
Boulden, James E. P. 2917
Boulding, Elise. 685
Bouley, Allan. 1541
Boulgaris, Nikolaos. 2745
Boulger, James D. 1519
Boult, Katherine F. 2665
Boulting, E. Frances. 1960
Boulting, William. 698
Boulton, Wayne G. 942
Boultwood, Alban. 1263, 2384
Bouma, Mary LaGrand. 1291
Bouman, Cornelius Adrianus. 845
Bouman, Herbert J. A. 1038
Bouman, Walter R. 3743
Bounds, Edward M. 2868
Bounds, Edward McKendnee. 2888
Bounds, Edward McKendree. 213, 1298, 1427, 1793, 2868, 2898, 3220
Bouquet, Alan Coates. 407, 1078, 1456, 1585, 1730, 1895, 2765, 3113, 3268
Bouquet, John Alexander. 2259, 3279
Bourdaloue, Louis. 3368
Bourdeau, Daniel T. 3299
Bourdeau, Francois. 947
Bourdeaux, Michael. 159, 2749, 2821, 3257, 3890
Bourgeois, Charles. 3256
Bourguignon, Erika. 2996, 3472, 3707
Bourgy, Paul. 2051
Bourke, John Gregory. 1846
Bourke, Ulick Joseph. 2308
Bourke, Vernon Joseph. 111, 113, 116, 1534, 3692
[Bourne, George] 1780-1845. 798, 1691, 3802
Bourne, Henry Eldridge. 1303
Bouscaren, Pierre. 1616
Bouscaren, Timothy Lincoln. 735, 775
Bousfield, Henry Brougham. 2557
Bousman, Emma. 3783
Bousman, Gary. 2788
Bousset, Wilhelm. 1056, 1950, 2010
Boussuet, Jacques Benigne. 399
Boutflower, Charles. 543, 507, 122, 507

Bouton, Alexander M. 636
Bouton, Nathaniel. 2307
Boutroux, Emile. 3080
Bouttier, Michel. 375
Bouwman, Gijs. 1659
Bouyer, Louis. 762, 2362, 2702, 2976, 118, 231, 415, 762, 811, 1156, 1187, 1245, 1276, 1363, 1625, 2036, 2235, 2240, 2256, 2362, 2384, 2570, 2702, 3485, 3637, 3773, 3848
Bouyer, Marie Dominique. 1749
Bovard, William Sherman, 1864. 3552
Bovet, Pierre. 2996
Bovet, Richard, ca. 3822
Bovet, Theodore. 1323, 2785
Boville, Robert G. 636
Bovis, Andre de. 1115
Bow, Russell. 1201
Bowan, Harold Leonard. 2757
Bowden, Charles Henry. 778
Bowden, Dina Moore. 2318, 3376
Bowden, Guy A G. 2868
Bowden, Henry Sebastian. 3279
Bowden, Henry Warner. 1184, 1901, 3124
Bowden, James. 1684
Bowden, Joan Chase. 1485, 2054
Bowden, John Edward. 1587, 2740
Bowden, John Stephen. 3651
Bowden, Robert J. 2014
Bowden, William Sheldon. 1110, 3321
Bowdish, T. M. 3561
Bowdoin, Herbert L. 2844
Bowdon, Boyce A. 2868
Bowen, Albert E. 2607
Bowen, Andrew Jackson. 1735
Bowen, Barbara (MacDonald) 206, 514, 614, 3143
Bowen, Cawthon Asbury. 2428, 2457, 3147, 3552
Bowen, Clayton Raymond. 231, 346, 3221
Bowen, David. 1158
Bowen, Eli. 1380
Bowen, Elias. 2428
Bowen, Emrys George. 3789
Bowen, Francis. 59
Bowen, Francis Joseph. 849, 1947, 2225
Bowen, George. 424, 2070, 2491
Bowen, Horace. 2833
Bowen, John W. E. 665
Bowen, Nathaniel. 3338
Bowen, Patrick Gillman. 2723
Bowen, V. S. 1239, 2966
Bowen, William Abraham. 2442
Bowen, William H. 1407
Bower, Alexander. 2273
Bower, Herbert Morris. 2377
Bower, Marian Bishop. 2529
Bower, Reuben Edward. 2523
Bower, Robert K. 3552
Bower, William. 2196
Bower, William Clayton. 653, 1463, 1912, 2220, 2590, 3057, 3124, 3147, 3189, 3678
Bowerman, George Franklin. 3739
Bowers, Alva Curtis. 2489
Bowers, Edwin Frederick. 3496
Bowers, Frederick A. 1266
Bowers, George K. 906, 956, 995
Bowers, Margaretta K. 1258, 1298
Bowes, Eric. 127
Bowes, George Seaton. 1839, 3338
Bowes, Pratima. 1813, 2416
Bowie, Mary Ella. 3777
Bowie, Theodore Robert. 86
Bowie, Walter Russell. 3714, 209, 213, 292, 533, 895, 923, 1116, 1734, 1956, 1961, 1980, 2021, 2384, 2888, 2898, 2972, 2978, 3197, 3348, 3369, 213, 406, 427, 619, 1189
Bowker, John. 3057, 3539
Bowker, John Westerdale. 492, 2068, 2828, 3057
Bowker, Margaret. 666, 1217, 1293
Bowker, Richard Rogers. 3057
Bowman, Allen. 274
Bowman, Alveretta (Warvel) 3763
Bowman, Archibald Allan. 1103
Bowman, Atha S. 1498
Bowman, Charles Victor. 3572
Bowman, Clarice M. 3169
Bowman, Clarice Marguerette. 3852
Bowman, Clarice Marguerette. 733, 2868, 3169, 3175, 3852
Bowman, David J. 2009
Bowman, Earl McKinley. 686, 1300
Bowman, Edward S. 1473
Bowman, Frank. 2723
Bowman, George M. 981
Bowman, George W. 906
Bowman, George William. 1326
Bowman, Harold Leonard. 1047
Bowman, Henry Adelbert. 2336
Bowman, Hezekiah J. 1823
Bowman, Jesse E. 1933
Bowman, John. 20, 418, 3297

Bowman, John Wick. 453, 636, 651, 1093, 2010, 2036
Bowman, Leonard. 3407
Bowman, Locke E. 934, 3175, 3179
Bowman, Louis A. 696
Bowman, Mary Ann. 2642
Bowman, Mary D. 2336, 2625
Bowman, Norman. 1308
Bowman, Paul Haynes. 1235
Bowman, Rufus David. 1236, 3792
Bowman, S Loren. 1237
Bowman, Shadrach Laycock. 1097
Bowman. John Wick. 2062
Bowne, Borden Parker. 103, 1047, 1886, 2163, 2416, 3057, 3224, 3607
Bowra, Cecil Maurice. 1505
Bowser, Sam E. 686, 1006
Bowyer, Jack. 1158
Bowyer, William A. 45
Box, George Herbert. 888, 2021, 2336, 529, 567, 1078
Box, Hubert Stanley. 1295, 1489, 1740, 2269, 2384, 2476, 3668
Boxer, Charles Ralph. 825, 1935
Boxer, James. 2667
Boxrud, Clara. 3147
Boyack, Kenneth. 836, 1563
Boyajian, Dickran H. 82
Boyarsky, Joseph. 2102
Boyce, Edward H. 3348
*Boyce, H. Spurgeon. 956
Boyce, James Petigru. 3641
Boyce, Mary. 2328, 3899
Boyd, Alvin. 292
[Boyd, Andrew Kennedy Hutchinson]. 1374, 2930, 3124, 3273
[Boyd, Andrew Kennedy Hutchison] 1825-1899. 2930
Boyd, Anne. 1483, 2570
Boyd, Beverly Mary. 2361
Boyd, Bob M. 3028
Boyd, Boston Napoleon Bonapart. 203, 3567
Boyd, Catherine Evangeline. 3237
Boyd, Charles Arthur. 577, 1250, 1871
Boyd, Charles Newell. 1202
Boyd, Doug. 3019, 3272
Boyd, E. 919
Boyd, Eleanor Herr. 3534
Boyd, Ellen Wright. 751
Boyd, Frank Mathews. 518, 542, 559
Boyd, George Adams. 2462
Boyd, George N. 1624
Boyd, Gwen. 990
Boyd, James Oscar. 289
Boyd, James Penny. 242, 292, 293
Boyd, James Shields. 2129, 2633
Boyd, Jesse Laney. 156, 171
Boyd, Malcolm. 1065, 1139, 1563, 2384, 2888, 686, 991, 1056, 1300, 1430, 2036, 2384, 2712, 2888
Boyd, Malcom. 1139
Boyd, Maurice. 3013
Boyd, Mildred. 2314
Boyd, Nelson. 3377
Boyd, Richard Henry. 152
Boyd, Robert. 1589, 2587, 3090, 896, 1999
Boyd, Robert T. 206, 207
Boyd, Robin H. S. 3659
Boyd, Thomas M. 1156
Boyd, Thomas Parker. 3477
Boyd, William Cowan. 1555
*Boyer, A. Leslie. 3318
Boyer, Charles. 1039
Boyer, Charles Emile George Augustin. 1039
Boyer, Edward Sterling. 3111
*Boyer, Frank J. 3348
Boyer, Harold W. 1228
Boyer, James L. 323
Boyer, Jonas William. 1318, 1563
Boyer, Laura F. 2806
Boyer, Leland. 1589, 1735
Boyer, Matthew Garner. 1056
Boyer, Merle William. 1116, 2976
Boyer, Onesimo Alfred. 1622, 3531
Boyer, Onesimus Alfred. 1622, 3531
Boyer, Reba Bayless. 102, 2347
*Boyer, Rev. Leland J. 1735
Boyer, Thomas. 2236
Boyet, John H. 1048
Boyet, Robert W. 8
Boyile, Zeolia J. 3575
Boylan, Anthony B. 2254
Boylan, Eugene. 1298, 2379
[Boylan, Grace (Duffie) 1861?-1935. 3496
Boylan, M Eugene. 1298, 3485
Boylan, Marguerite Theresa. 1135
Boylan, Patrick. 3698
Boyle, David John. 2346
Boyle, Francis. 3401
Boyle, George. 1429, 3704
Boyle, John. 21, 1284, 3690, 3779
Boyle, John P. 3527, 2723
Boyle, Joseph M. 1657

Boyle, Marjorie O'Rourke. 1525, 3071
Boyle, Mary Electa. 3378, 3416
[Boyle, Orrin Edwin] 1891. 2003
Boyle, William Hugh Wray. 2246
Boyle, William Joseph Vincent. 758
Boyln, M Eugene. 2019
Boylston, Ruth Harrington. 659
Boyna, Pearl Alexina. 3710
Boyne, Don. 2375
Boynton, George Mills. 1343, 2790
Boynton, Jeremy. 3299
Boynton, Nehemiah. 2907
Boynton, Richard Wilson. 3057
Boynton, Winifred Case. 130
Boys, Mary C. 241, 1820
Boyton, Neil. 683, 2308
Bozarth, Howard P. 1956
Bozarth, Howard Perry. 1340, 1956
Bozarth, Rene. 3438
Bozarth-Campbell, Alla, 1947. 1774, 688, 1300
Bozeman, Theodore Dwight. 124, 3085
Bozka, Honora. 3879
Braaten, Carl E. 287, 674, 1529, 1818, 2008, 2299, 2480, 3348, 3641, 3651
Brabaker, J. Omar. 1107
Brabant, Augustin J. 2558
Brabant, Frank Herbert. 1533, 1589, 3566
Brabazon, James. 2486, 3311
Brabham, Lewis F. 1754, 3230
Brabham, Mouzon William. 1156, 3552
Braby, Lois. 1013
Bracciolini, Poggio. 688, 3709
Brace, Beverly Waltmire. 1293, 3791
Brace, Charles Loring. 1048, 3113
Brace, Joab. 2702
Brace, John Pierce. 1427
Brace, Jonathan. 492
Brace, Josephine M. 3496
Brace, Josephine McHugh. 3496
Brace, Mary Margaret. 2558
Brace, Vern Edward. 3763
Bracewell, Joseph Searcy. 1167
Bracey, H. E. 1765
Bracher, Marjory Louise. 1604, 3406, 3564
Bracht, Tieleman Janseoon van. 2350
Brack, Harold Arthur. 2898
Brackberger, Raymond Leopold. 1961
Brackbill, William Thaddeus. 203
Bracken, Joseph A. 3714
Brackenridge, Henry Marie. 7, 2100
Brackenridge, R. Douglas. 670, 1300, 1396, 2557, 2919
Brackett, Edward Augustus. 3496
Brackett, Jeffrey Richardson. 3435
Brackett, Richard Newman. 1846
Brackney, Edwin Emerson. 2127
Bradbury, Ammi Ruhamah. 2018
Bradby, Godfrey Fox. 1048
Braddeson, Walter. 3314
Braddick, Muriel. 688, 3293
Braddock, William Locke. 1827
Braddon, Russell. 891, 3851
Braden, Charles H. 3751
Braden, Charles Samuel. 1029, 1078, 2461, 2696, 3113, 3267, 3293, 3325, 3792
Braden, Clark. 3074
Braden, Gayle Anderson. 2376
Braden, William. 1781
Bradfield, Irene. 1774, 3714
Bradford, Alden. 2375
Bradford, Amory Howe. 28, 1719, 2384, 3440, 3461, 3477
Bradford, Ann. 3169
Bradford, Charles E. 2898, 3381
Bradford, Columbus. 3052
Bradford, Ernle Dusgate Selby. 1390, 1391, 2179, 2795
Bradford, Gamaliel. 659, 2225, 2587
Bradford, George Franklin. 952
Bradford, Jesse F. 1929
Bradford, John. 1216
Bradford, Reed H. 1607, 3592
Bradlaugh, Charles. 1653, 3024
Bradlee, Ben. 2205
Bradlee, Caleb Davis. 3725
Bradley, Abraham. 1380
Bradley, Charles. 3338
Bradley, Cyprian. 675
Bradley, Dan Beach. 2546
Bradley, David G. 3113, 3141
Bradley, David Henry. 15
Bradley, Dwight. 3852, 3057
Bradley, Dwight Jacques. 1281
Bradley, Dwight Jaques. 956, 1589
Bradley, Edward Sculley. 2203
Bradley, Ernest. 2399
Bradley, Floyd N. 3143
Bradley, Floyd Norman. 1827
Bradley, Francis Herbert. 2416, 2839, 2416
Bradley, Francis James. 1602
Bradley, George Granville. 3525
Bradley, Henry Stiles. 2066
Bradley, Ian C. 1551

[Bradley, Joseph Henry]. 1555, 3029
Bradley, Joshua. 3228
Bradley, Paul John. 855
Bradley, Preston. 956, 1056, 2888
Bradley, Rolland. 3641
Bradley, Ruth Olive. 1607
Bradley, Samuel Carlyle. 1961
Bradley, Sidney Benjamin. 3810
Bradley, Walter Parke. 388
Bradley, William Lee. 950
Bradner, John. 919
Bradner, Lester. 3552
Bradner, Lester, jr. 933
Bradshaw, Brendan. 1803, 2582
Bradshaw, Emerson Otho. 2162, 3765
Bradshaw, Malcolm R. 1563
Bradshaw, Marion John. 1491, 1543, 2683, 3098
Bradshaw, William. 2865
Bradstreet, Anne. 2855
Bradt, Charles E[dwin]. 1765
Bradt, Charles Edwin. 1563, 3814
Brady, Donald. 3090
Brady, Frank. 3572
Brady, Gerard K. 1474
Brady, H. Edgar. 1950, 3124
Brady, James Boyd. 1300, 3348
Brady, Joseph Hugh. 1149
Brady, Nicholas. 1202
Brady, Rita G. 2166
Brady, Veronica. 1074
Braegelmann, Athanasius. 1883
Braemer, Alice. 689, 1363
Braga, James. 636, 2898
Bragdon, Claude Fayette. 3496
Bragers, Achille Pierre. 884, 1205
Bragg, George Freeman. 1524, 2219
Bragg, Juliana. 494, 2129, 2952
Bragg, Samuel Atherton. 418
Braham, Randolph L. 3851
Brahmanas. Aitareyabrahmana. English. 3775
Brahmopanisatsarasangraha. English & Sanskrit. 1816
Brailsford, Mabel Richmond. 2678
Brain, Belle Marvel. 2481, 2491, 3564, 3594
Brain, Belle, Marvel. 2481, 2518, 2524, 2533
Brain, Walter Russell Brain, 1895. 3081
Brainard, Addison. 1745
Brainard, John. 109
*Brainerd, David. 689
Brainerd, David. 689, 1900, 2888
Brainerd, Eveline Warner. 1877
Brainerd, Mary. 956
Braintree, Mass. St. Thomas More Church. 1261
Braisted, Ruth Evelyn (Wilder) 3815
Braiterman, Marvin. 3147
Braithwaite, Joseph Bevan. 1778
Braithwaite, William Charles. 3010, 1684
Braley, Edith Ross. 2091
Braley, Evelyn Foley. 3147
Braman, Milton Palmer. 1504, 3753
Bramblett, Agnes Cochran. 3197
[Brame, Charlotte Mary]. 54
Brame, Isaiah Jefferson. 160, 956, 2322
Bramer, John C. 1250, 1292
Bramly, Serge. 2333, 3722
Brams, Steven J. 499
Bramson, Ely. 1308
Bramwell, Enoch Ernest. 2601, 2610
Branagan, Leo. 636
Branagan, Thomas. 956
[Branagan, Thomas]. 1355, 2672, 3322
Branan, Donie Leone. 1482
Branch, Anna Hempstead. 1113
Branch, Harold Francis. 2930
Branch, James Orson. 3338
Branch, Robert. 690, 1717
Branch, William George. 1013
Brand, Eugene. 139, 3852
Brand, Mary Vivian. 1135
Brand, Paul Wilson. 1116
Brand, Ralph A. 1373
Brand, William Francis. 3814
Brande, William Thomas. 891
[Brandegee, S. K. 956
Brandeis, Donald. 450
Brandeis, Donald Asa. 3661
Brandeis University, Waltham, Mass. Poses Institute of Fine Arts. 88
Brandel-Syrier, Mia. 2499
Brandenburg, Hans. 3538
Brandenburg, Walter E. 1103
Brandes, Georg Morris Cohen. 2008
Brandon, David. 3197
Brandon, Joseph R. 2113
Brandon, Owen. 1361
Brandon, Samuel George Frederick. 84, 1384, 1819, 1933, 2068, 2157, 2326, 3066, 3293, 3294, 3891
Brandt, Catharine. 17, 2384, 3814
Brandt, Charles Michel Alexandre de. 1263
Brandt, Frans M. J. 2783

Brandt, Harry Alonzo. 575, 2188
Brandt, Henry R. 981, 1607, 2773, 2780, 2808
Brandt, John Lincoln. 614, 1950, 3338
Brandt, Kaspar. 83
Brandt, Leslie F. 399, 445, 551, 570, 583, 585, 586, 981, 1349, 1445, 1633, 1917, 2347, 2888
Brandt, Otto Sebastian. 2113
Brandt, Priscilla. 2869
Brandt, R. L. 2869
Brandt, Robert L. 3288

Brantord, Victor. 3439
Branley, Brendan R. 2533
Branley, Franklyn Mansfield. 3525
Brann, Henry Athanasius. 1851, 3098, 3245
Brannaka, Marjorie. 690, 1366
[Brannan, H K]. 3496
Brannen, Noah S. 3455
Branner, Robert. 686, 889
Brannon, Clarence Ham. 308
Brannon, T. Leo. 636, 1006
Branscomb, [Bennett] Harvie. 2062
Branscomb, Bennett Harvie. 2062
Bransiet, Philippe. 940, 3592
Bransiet, Philippe. 3270
Bransiet, Phillippe. 1347, 2032, 2384
Branson, Ann. 1674
Branson, Gene N. 1528
Branson, Levi. 2434
Branson, Mark Lau. 3626
Branson, Mary Kinney. 3843
Branson, William H. 736, 2497, 3288, 3381
Branson, William Henry. 1827, 2498, 3288, 3381
[Branstette, Otie G.]. 3801
Branston, Brian. 2659, 2665
Brantl, George. 784, 3204
Brantley, Allen Patterson. 1056
Brantley, Robert Augustus. 3701
Brasch, Rudolf. 2723
Brasch, Rudolph. 2138, 2723
Brasefield, Nell R. 3392
Brasher, John Lakin. 3211
*Brasington, Virginia H. 1631
Brasnett, Bertrand Rippington. 1719, 1733, 1741
Braso, Gabriel M. 836
Brassey, Thomas Brassey. 1589
Brasted, Alva Jennings. 2594, 3456
Brastow, Lewis Orsmond. 694, 1295, 2898, 2908, 3308
Braswell, Mary Flowers. 1518
Bratcher, Alfred Lewis. 2586
Bratcher, Lewis Malen. 2504, 2683, 3459
Bratcher, Robert G. 438
Bratcher, Samuel Robert. 3338
[Bratenahl, Florence (Brown) 3796
Bratenahl, George C F. 3796
Bratenahl, George Carl Fitch. 3796
Bratt, John H. 409, 727, 729, 730, 1169
Brattgard, Helge. 3528
Bratton, Fred Gladstone. 2220, 289, 1073, 2220, 2622, 2649
Bratton, Mary Elizabeth (Kinnier) 2304
Bratton, Theodore DuBose. 1481
Brauch, Manfred T. 469
Braude, Morris. 317, 1091
Brauer, George C. 2090
Brauer, Jerald C. 2955, 3739, 3743
Brauer, Theodor. 3450
Braun, Andrew Christian. 2434
Braun, Eunice. 130
Braun, Francois Marie. 414, 2358
Braun, Fred. 2541
Braun, Herbert. 2036
Braun, Jon E. 981, 1802
Braun, Leopold L S. 3257
Braun, Neil. 2554
Braun, Peter. 2723
Braun, Theodore A. 1153
Braunfels, Wolfgang. 2568
Braunstein, Baruch. 1909
Braunstein, Bruch. 1909
Braunthal, Alfred. 3293
Braure, Maurice. 808
Braus, Irene Samuelson. 3141
Brav, Stanley Rosenbaum. 2121, 3015, 3392
Braver, Hirsch. 2092
Braverman, Katherine. 3879
Bravo, Francisco. 3592
Brawley, Benjamin Griffith. 1871
Brawley, E M. 160
Brawley, Edward M. 160
Brawley, James P. 2440, 2681
Braxton, Bernard. 3392
Braxton, Edward K. 835, 1316
Bray, Allen F. 2790
Bray, Everett King. 1719
*Bray, Frank Chapin. 2658, 2659
Bray, Gerald Lewis. 3604
Bray, Henry Truro. 3027
Bray, Thomas. 2224, 2363

Bray, Thomas Wells. 462
Braybrooke, Marcus. 3111, 3849
Brayne, Frank Lugard. 2545
Brayshaw, Alfred Neave. 1674, 1683
Brazell, George. 3528
Brazer, John. 1827
Bready, Guy Pearre. 3048
Bready, John Wesley. 1762, 3802, 1762, 3802
Bready, Russell H. 3677
Breakstone, Raymond. 549
Bream, Gerry. 1112, 2287
Breasted, James Henry. 894, 1501, 1502, 1538
Breault, William. 2869, 2888
Breck, Allen duPont. 2963
Breck, Flora Elizabeth. 1204, 3169, 3173, 3552, 3560, 3857, 3876
Breck, James Lloyd. 956
Breckenridge, James F. 2816
Breckenridge, James Malcolm. 1671
Breckinridge, Robert Jefferson. 1289, 3641
Bredahl-Petersen, Frederik E. 1246
Brederveld, Jakob. 178
Bredesen, Harald. 2477
Breech, James. 388, 2024
Breed, David Riddle. 4, 2898, 1874, 3295
Breed, William Pratt. 2322, 2865
Breen, Andrew Edward. 386
Breen, Gertrude Iren. 956
Breen, Quirinus. 727, 1854
Breen, Stephen. 25, 2357, 2487
Breese, Dave W. 956, 3324
Breese, Frances. 3282
Bregman, Jay. 3578
Bregman, Lucy. 1585
Bregstone, Philip Pollack. 2098
Bregy, Katherine Marie Cornelia. 2353
Brehm, Mabel. 1184
Brehmer, Robert George, jr. 3450
Breig, James. 3799
Breig, Joseph A. 1263
Breig, Joseph Anthony. 996, 1263, 1618, 2123, 3525
Breisch, Francis. 597
Breit, Marquita. 2413
Breitfeld, Rose. 2987
Breithaupt, Gerald O. 1093
Breitigam, R. R. 2061, 3169
Breitman, George. 669, 2233
Brekke, Milo. 1297, 2293, 2303
Breland, Clyde Lamont. 415
*Brem, M. M. 553
*Brem M. M. 430
Bremond, Andre. 3024
Bremond, Henri. 817
Bremyer, Jayne Dickey. 3845
Brenan, Gerald. 2136
Brenan, John. 819
Brendan. 691
Brendle, Daniel F. 2944
Brengle, Elizabeth (Swift) 3292
Brennan, Gerald Thomas. 906, 43, 906, 1628, 1980, 2021, 2032, 906
Brennan, J. H. 2723
Brennan, James Henry. 2341
Brennan, James McClellan. 1290
Brennan, Martin Stanislaus. 203
Brennan, Niall. 117, 814, 2329
Brennan, Philip Vincent. 1652
Brennan, Richard. 2850, 3369
Brennan, Robert Edward. 1712, 2322, 3695
Brennan, S. J. 18
Brennan, Thomas Francis. 758
Brenneman, Charles Gage. 293
Brenneman, Helen Good. 1006, 1349, 2624, 2625, 3406
Brenner, Harry Lyon. 2242, 3027
Brenner, Henry. 399, 996, 1375, 1732, 1950, 2264
Brenner, Reeve Robert. 1825
Brenner, Scott Francis. 3003, 3004
Brenner, William. 1437
Brent, Charles Henry. 691, 2889, 3193, 3348, 1056, 1067, 1068, 1349, 1445, 2056, 2492, 2636, 2889, 2959, 3304, 3751
[Brent, Daniel] 1774-1841. 742
Brent, Peter Ludwig. 1778
Brentano, Joseph P. 2489
Brentano, Mary Bernarda. 2271, 2675
Brentano, Robert. 667, 1761
Brentford, William Joynson-Hicks. 1213
Brents, T. W. 3288
Brents, Thomas W. 3288
Bres, Guy de. 36
Bresee, Phineas Franklin. 1238
Breslin, Mary Thomas. 3761, 3861
Breslin, Thomas A. 849, 2507
Breslow, Marvin Arthur. 1763
Bresson, Bernard L. 1713
Bretall, Robert Walter, 1913. 3815
Brethren. 946
Breton, Valentin Marie. 1645, 2384, 2865
Bretscher, Paul G. 25, 180, 1823

Bretschneider, Karl Gottlieb. 1547
Brett, Gilbert James. 225, 2070
Brett, Jesse. 1833, 1999, 3147, 3477, 594
Brett, Laurence. 604
Brett, M. 816, 1516
Brett, R. L. 1518
[Brett, Robert]. 1224
Brett, William Henry. 2547
Brevick, Harald. 604
Brewbaker, Charles W. 1445, 3730
Brewbaker, Charles Warren. 1563, 3168, 3177, 3552, 3879
Brewer, Abraham Titus. 3552
Brewer, Charles Louis. 3292
Brewer, Charles Richard. 1349
Brewer, Clifton Hartwell. 747, 2965, 942, 2965
Brewer, Darius Richmond. 2972
Brewer, David Josiah. 3743
Brewer, Earl D. C. 2439
Brewer, Ebenezer Cobham. 1588, 2476, 2477, 2478
Brewer, Elizabeth Luella (Alexander) 3143
Brewer, Francis Alford. 1579
Brewer, George. 1437
Brewer, Grover Cleveland. 1116, 1272, 1273, 1462, 1999, 1272
Brewer, Jack A. 1166
Brewer, John Marks. 2590
Brewer, Willis. 1501
Brewer, Wilmon. 3206
Brewing, Willard E. 3367, 3731
Brewis, J S. 956
Brewsler, H. Pomeroy. 1388
Brewster, Ann Maria Hampton. 305
Brewster, Chauncey Bunce. 1747, 2056, 3224
Brewster, David Pearson. 21, 3543
Brewster, Dorothy D. 2538
Brewster, Earl H. 701
Brewster, Edward T. 3852
Brewster, Edward Thomson. 301, 3220
Brewster, Edwin Tenney. 3057, 1380
Brewster, H. Pomeroy. 1025, 3279
Brewster, Harold Sydney. 383
Brewster, John Monroe. 3749
Brewster, Mary B. 2231
Brewster, Mary M. 2425
Brewster, May M. 2757
Brewster, William Besbitt. 2420
Brewster, William Nesbitt. 956, 2507
Brewyn, William. 3245
Brey, Henriette. 1445
Breyfogle, William La Martine. 2843
Brezic, Marian Coe. 1881
Brezzi, Paolo. 2767
Brian, Denis. 1472, 2948
Brian, Dennis. 1472, 2948
Briancourt, Mathieu. 1318, 1636
Briault, Maurice. 3113
Brice. 2137, 2642, 3485, 3602
Brichto, Mira. 899
Brichto, Sidney. 633
Bricker, Garland Armor. 3253
Bricker, Luther Otterbein. 1466
Bricker, Victoria Reifler. 2375
Brickey, Janice. 3249
Brickley, Donald Paul. 691
Brickman, Clarence W. 3162
Brickman, William W. 1129
Brickner, Balfour. 571, 1538
Bridenbaugh, Carl. 1222, 1522
Bridge, Donald. 134, 1712
Bridgeport, Conn. First Presbyterian church. 2915
Bridger, Gordon Frederick. 1997
Bridges, Charles. 953, 572, 1297
Bridges, Earley Winfred. 1667
Bridges, Geoffrey G. 1881, 2826
Bridges, Horace James. 187, 1048, 1068, 1537, 1690, 2077
Bridges, James F. 3597
Bridges, Jerry. 1823
Bridges, John Henry. 2864
Bridges, Julian C. 2540
Bridges, Leonard Hal. 2648
Bridges, Ronald. 271
*Bridget, Lorraine. 2225
Bridget, Sister. 1412
Bridgett, Thomas Edward. 2250
Bridgman, Howard Allen. 3066, 956
Bridgman, Raymond Landon. 2980
Bridston, Keith R. 1085, 1491, 2549, 2554, 2938, 3680
Bridwell, Charles W. 2055
Bridwell, Charles William. 3318
Briegleb, Gustav A. 506
Brier, Bob. 876, 1700, 2314
Brierley, Jonathan. 1020, 1068
Briery Presbyterian church, Hampden district, Prince Edward co., Va. 2928
Briffault, Robert. 3388

Briggs, Charles Augustuc. 530

Briggs, Charles Augustus. 73, 118, 231, 276, 531, 563, 575, 636, 692, 942, 1039, 1386, 1892, 1961, 2016, 2413, 2414, 2922, 2936
Briggs, Charles Whitman. 2246, 2544
Briggs, Edward C. 160
Briggs, Everett Francis. 1935
[Briggs, G. C.]. 3496
Briggs, George Ware. 1354
Briggs, George Weston. 2163
Briggs, Henry Clay. 3227
Briggs, John. 1468
Briggs, Katharine Mary. 3826
Briggs, Robert Cook. 346, 388
Briggs, William A. 3894
Brigham, Amariah. 3238
Brigham, Charles Henry. 657
Brigham, Judith. 3466
Brigham Young University, Provo, Utah. Adult Education and Extension Services. 2607
Brigham Young University, Provo, Utah. University Archaeological Society. 679
Bright, Bill. 733, 1827, 3537, 3661
Bright, John. 530, 499, 530, 571, 2093, 2095, 2176, 2949
*Bright, Laurence. 322, 323, 1076
Bright, Vonette Z. 692, 3845
Bright, William. 1189, 1196
Brightman, Edgar Sheffield. 1068, 1719, 1720, 1887, 2417, 2822, 3098, 3477, 3098, 3492
Brihaddevata. 1816
[Brile] Tile. 1873. 3496
Briley, C. 1239
Brilioth, Yngve Torgny. 2908, 2256, 2754
Brilioth, Yngve Torgny, Abp. 2908
Brill, Earl H. 2955, 3743
Brillenburg Wurth, Gerrit. 2783
Brillet, Gaston. 558
Brillhart, Florence C. 3856
Brilliant, Nathan. 3166
Brim, Charles Jacob. 317
Brimm, Henry M. 2928
Brin, Herb. 2076
Brin, Ruth (Firestone) 562, 630, 658, 1533, 3260
Brinckerhoff, Isaac W. 658
Brinckerhoff, Theodore. 3044
Briney, John Benton. 134, 2067, 3338
Bring, Johan Christofer. 1318
Bring, Ragnar. 379, 3224
Bring, Sven Libert. 2885
Bringas de Manzaneda y Encinas, Diego Miguel. 1648, 1898
Bringgold, Diane. 45, 692
Bringhurst, Newell G. 1133, 2401
Bringle, Mary. 1472
*Bringman, Dale S. 2869
Bring Ragnar, [Anders Ebbe Ragner Bring] . 379
Brings, Erik. 3206
Brings, Lawrence Martin. 1113, 2869
Brink, Benjamin Deane. 647
Brink, Frederick Wright. 1437
*Brink, William P. 231
Brink, William P. 1023
Brinkel, B. G. F. 826
Brinkler, Alfred. 2864
Brinkmeyer, Henry. 854, 3223
Brinkworth, Edwin Robert Courtney. 1764,
Brinsmade, Horatio Nelson. 2261
Brinsmead, Bernard Hungerford. 381
Brinson, George W. 1427
[Brinson, Marion B]. 1463
Brinton, Anna (Cox) 723, 1577, 1676, 1677
Brinton, Clarence Crane. 2589, 2709
Brinton, Daniel Garrison. 698, 1902, 1904, 3098, 3139
Brinton, Howard Haines. 419, 674, 1636, 1674, 1676, 1681, 1683, 1684, 2242, 2637, 2644, 3453, 3493, 419, 1681
Brinton, Margaret Cooper. 1839
Brisbane, Albert. 1318, 1636
Brisbane, Arthur. 1493
Briscoe, D. Stuart. 518, 586, 636, 956, 981, 2869, 3335, 3348
Briscoe, Jill. 516, 692, 931, 981, 1588, 2869, 3839
Briscoe, John Fetherstonhaugh. 2754, 3021
Brisman, Shimeon. 657, 2083
Brist, Gladys Z. 2869
Brister, C. W. 62, 1634, 2191, 2780, 2785, 2788, 3879
Brister, Elaine H. 2488
Bristol, Frank Milton. 3348
Bristol, Goldie. 692, 931
Bristol, Lee Hastings. 1459
Bristol, Lyle O. 402, 478, 2047
Bristol, Sherlock. 2910
Bristol, V. Irene. 1627, 1809
Brite Divinity School. 3349
Brite, Mary. 3814

*British and Foreign Bible Society. Library. 212
British Broadcasting Corporation. 1864
British Council of Churches. Division of Community Affairs. 1321
British Council of Churches. Working Party on the Child in the Church. 938
British Library. Lending Division. 3678
Britt, Bertha Marie. 3206
Britt, Elizabeth T. 70
Britt, George L. 1513
Britt, Matthew. 189, 836, 848, 1876
Britt, Walter Daniel. 1445
Britt, William Morehead. 1048
Brittain, Alfred. 3836
Brittain, Grady. 149, 1004
Brittain, Harry Ernest. 2848
Brittain, Marion Luther. 102
Brittan, Samuel Bryon. 3496
Brittan, Samuel Byron. 183, 720, 3496
Britten, Emma (Hardinge) 3496, 3520, 3521
[Britten, William]. 3496
Britten Emma (Hardinge) 3496
Brittle, Gerald. 1424, 3796
Britton, Louisa. 619
Brix, Marie Louise. 185
Brizgys, Vincentas. 821, 2232
Bro, Bernard. 996, 1356, 2869, 3262
Bro, Harmon Hartzell. 876, 1479, 3072
Bro, Margueritte Harmon. 533, 1437, 1445, 2489, 2869
Broach, Claude U. 692, 2204
Broad, Charlie Dunbar. 2417, 2992
Broad, FitzGerald. 3057
Broadbent, John Barclay. 2467, 2470
Broaddus, Andrew. 2758, 293, 2758, 3338
Broadhurst, Allan R. 2809
Broadhurst, Cyrus Napoleon. 1048, 2869
Broadus, Eleanor (Hammond) 1996
Broadus, John Albert. 134, 160, 686, 2036, 2898, 2908, 2909, 3338
Brobst, Flavius J. 2059
Broches, Samuel. 2101
Brock, Charles. 1166
Brock, Earl E. 1871
Brock, Fred R. 206
Brock, Henry Irving. 1275
Brock, Horace. 2970
Brock, Jefferson Columbus. 3720
Brock, Peter. 1089, 1684, 2756
Brock, Raymond T. 1563
Brock, Thomas Sleeper. 2434
Brock, William. 508
Brockett, Clyde Waring. 847, 884
Brockett, Lorna. 138
Brockington, L. H. 530
Brockman, Fletcher Sims. 2508
Brockman, James R. 666, 3246
Brockman, Norbert. 867, 3088
Brockman, William Frasier. 3198
Brockmann, Charles Raven. 2927
Brockway, Allan R. 1056
Brockway, Charles Edward. 3267
Brockway, Esther. 3216, 3828
Brockway, K Nora. 3166
Brockway, Meme. 1253
[Brockway, Thomas, 1714-1807. 3206
Brod, Max. 3098
Brode, Anthony. 2788
Broder, Nathan. 123
Broderick, Francis L. 3258
Broderick, Robert C. 778, 952, 1167, 1274, 2240, 2774
Brodhead, Chloe Anna (Sanford) 1653
Brodie, Fawn (McKay) 3428
Brodie, James Fairbairn. 3338
Brodie, William Austin. 10
Brodrick, James. 186, 734, 1649, 1944, 1946, 2031, 2267, 2269, 2270, 3241, 3279
Brodsky, Alyn. 2305
Brody, Boruch A. 1534, 3107
Broeckaert, Joseph. 1947, 3472
Broecklin, Joseph von. 3496
Brogan, Frankie Fonde. 693, 1524
Broglie, Emmanuel. 3779
Broglie, Guy de. 1597
Broh, Robert A. 3010
Broholm, Richard R. 1065, 1199
Brokaw, George Lewis. 1466
Brokering, Herbert F. 1445, 2889
Brokhoff, John R. 636, 956, 1116
Brokke, Harold J. 1312, 1313
Broman, Oscar Francis. 3072
Bromiley, Geoffrey William. 175, 1039, 1295, 1905, 2336, 3262, 3641, 3653
Bromley, David G. 3329, 3747
Bromley, Dorothy (Dunbar) 663
Bronchain, Charles Louis Laurent. 2229
Bronder, Saul E. 667, 2270
Brong, Rosco. 3367
Brong, Rosco, 1908. 3349
Bronk, Mitchell. 956, 1349
Bronner, Edwin B. 1674
Bronner, Leah. 2079
Bronson, George Cathcart. 3461

Bronson, Oliver. 3522
Bronstein, Charlotte. 1614
Bronstein, Daniel J. 3098
Bronstein, David. 956
Bronstein, Esther. 693, 1366
Brook, Stella. 1213
Brook, Victor John Knight. 2775
Brooke, Alan England. 369
Brooke, Audrey. 1757
Brooke, Avery. 2379, 2384, 2889, 3882
Brooke, Christopher Nugent Lawrence. 1186, 2345, 2582
Brooke, Dorothy (Lamb) 1771
Brooke, Odo. 1777, 2572
Brooke, Robert Taliaferro. 1695
Brooke, Rosalind B. 1505, 1646
Brooke, Stopford A[ugustus]. 388
Brooke, Stopford Augustus. 980, 3057, 3338, 3363, 3725
Brooke, Zachary Nugent. 1146
Brookes, Edgar Harry. 113, 116, 1085
Brookes, George S. 1575
Brookes, James Hall. 2036, 2051, 3288, 3318
Brookfield, Charles Hallam Elton. 693
Brooklyn. Church of the Saviour. 890
Brooklyn city mission and tract society. 2505
Brooklyn diet dispensary. 1458
Brooklyn. Duryea Presbyterian Church. 693
Brooklyn. First Reformed Dutch church. Sunday-school library. 3549
Brooklyn Jewish center. 2098
Brooklyn. Lafayette avenue Presbyterian church. 1398
Brooklyn. Lutheran Church of the Good Shepherd. 693
Brooklyn. Plymouth Church of the Pilgrims. 693
Brooklyn. St. Ann's church (Protestant Episcopal) 2972
Brooklyn. St. John's Episcopal Church. 693
Brooklyn. St. Johns Methodist Episcopal church. 2452
Brooklyn. St. Mark's church (Protestant Episcopal) Brooklyn avenue. 1790
Brooklyn. Throop avenue Presbyterian church and mission. 1632
Brookman, Alice M. 922
Brooks, Annie Sills. 903
Brooks, Arthur Thomas. 1126
Brooks, Bart. 1634
Brooks, Charles Alvin. 155, 2488
Brooks, Charles H. 2829
Brooks, Charles L. 134, 2017
Brooks, Charles Mattoon. 3470
Brooks, Charles Timothy. 881
Brooks, Charles Wesley. 141
Brooks, Clara M. 903
Brooks, Cyrus Harry. 1107
Brooks, D. P. 636, 1413, 1658
Brooks, David Marshall. 100
Brooks, Elbridge Streeter. 694
Brooks, Erastus. 1242
Brooks, Eugene. 305
Brooks, Frank L. 2435
Brooks, Frank Lester. 2435, 3338
Brooks, Frederick Lewis. 453
Brooks, George. 3372
Brooks, George Alexander. 15
Brooks, Henry Chauncey. 3798
Brooks, Jesse Wendell. 1574
Brooks, John. 1392, 2453
Brooks, John Rives. 3299
Brooks, Julian. 1323
Brooks, Keith L. 198, 321, 363, 427
[Brooks, Keith Leroy] 1888. 321, 333, 368, 384, 444, 462, 474, 482, 509, 604, 645, 1437, 1513, 1839, 1950, 2118, 3457
Brooks, Lawrence E. 1167
Brooks, Lee Marshall. 3468
Brooks, Mary Wallace. 3198
Brooks, Melvin R. 601, 2610
Brooks Memorial Art Gallery. 1994
Brooks, Nathan Covington. 2032, 3147, 3720
Brooks, Neil Conwell. 1826
Brooks, Nona L. 2409
Brooks, Pat. 694, 981, 3742, 3845
Brooks, Peter Newman. 1378, 2256
Brooks, Phillips. 694, 1089, 1437, 1825, 2012, 2013, 2209, 2211, 2230, 2898, 2972, 3338, 3349, 3362, 3703
Brooks,Phillips. 3338
Brooks, R. T. 995
Brooks, Rachel Gleason. 3306
Brooks, Robert E. 990
Brooks, Seth R. 694, 3755
Brooks, Thomas. 3870, 3303
Brooks, Thomas Joseph. 62
Brooks, W. Hal. 1563
Brooks, William Erle. 2430
Brooks, William Henry. 694
Brooks, William Keith. 2270
Brookshire, Elijah Voorhees. 231

[Brooksmith, Clifford Edgar]. 3249
Brooks. Phillips. 2898
Broomall, Wick. 287, 1827
Broome, Connie. 3845
Broomfield, Gerald Webb. 419, 1039, 1913
*Broomhall, A. J. 956
Broomhall, Marshall. 289, 744, 881, 912, 1622, 2508, 3590, 2508, 2567, 2635
Brophy, Dennis P. 3206
Brophy, Donald. 1742, 3081
Brophy, Liam. 1640, 1645, 2271
Broschart, Charles B. 2359
Brose, Olive J. 1140, 2374
[Brosman, Aloysius A.] 2003
Brosman, Cornelius James. 2205, 2544
Brosman, William Joseph. 1720
Brosnahan, Timothy. 2384
Brosnan, Joseph Brodie. 2259
Brosnan, William J. 1720
Brosnan, William Joseph. 1730, 3607, 3608
Bross, William. 1673
Brostrom, Ernest O. 1156
The Brother, XII. 3684
Brothers, Joan. 3088
Brothers of Mary, Dayton, O. 3165
Brothers of the Christian schools. 695, 745, 768, 812, 934, 3025, 3310, 3592, 3786
Brothers of the Christian Schools, Australasian Province. 695
Brothers of the Christian Schools. Districts. San Francisco. 695, 747
Brothers, Richard. 1734, 2949
Brou, Alexandre. 173, 2267, 2269, 2310, 2379, 3475, 173
Broucker, Jose de. 731, 807, 1162
Brough, Franklin Keith. 658
Brough, Robert Clayton. 2896
Brougher, James Whitcomb. 143
Brougher, William Edward. 1016
Broughton, James Richard. 3208
Broughton, Leonard G[aston]. 2055
Broughton, Leonard Gaston. 444, 3198, 3294, 169, 1116, 2062, 3057, 3228, 3318, 1089
Broughton, Luke Dennis. 95
Broun, Heywood Campbell. 2077
Brousse, Jacques. 2136
Brouwer, Arie R. 3045
Brow, Robert. 1116, 3093
Brower, Bert. 2036
Brower, Floyd V. 1563
Brower, Frank E. 2319
Brown, Abbie Farwell. 47, 1028, 2665
Brown, Alan Willard. 2416
Brown, Alberta Z. 1323
Brown, Allan Reginald. 469
Brown, Alva Ross. 424, 2128
(Brown, Andrew F.) 2590
Brown, Annice Harris. 2889
Brown, Anton U. 3141
Brown, Archie E. 3465
Brown, Ario Ayres. 3177, 3147, 3552
Brown, Arthur Isaac. 101, 3077, 3318
Brown, Arthur Issac. 1513
Brown, Arthur Judson. 2492, 2508, 2518, 2544, 2546, 2913, 2921, 2926
Brown, Arthur W. 881
Brown, Azariah. 1116
[Brown, Batholomew]. 1864
Brown, Benjamin Warren. 2456, 2923
Brown, Bernard Joseph. 2077
Brown, Bertha B. 3363, 3868
Brown, Bessie Conner. 3718
Brown, Beverly Holladay. 10, 47, 92, 740, 1640, 2354, 3279
Brown, Beverly Holliday. 2359
Brown, Bob W. 1116, 2384
Brown, Brian. 701, 1330, 2084
Brown, Brian A. 733, 1258, 2714
Brown, Buford B. 473
Brown, Burdette Boardman. 1422, 3124
Brown, C H. 732
Brown, Carl Kelley. 2183
Brown, Carleton Fairchild. 1519, 3210
Brown, Carolyn C. 934
Brown, Charles. 1997, 103
Brown, Charles Ewing. 1029, 1039, 1117, 1173, 1228, 1589, 1823, 2464, 2869, 3011, 3288, 3318, 3325, 3477, 3796
Brown, Charles Kenneth Francis. 1215
Brown, Charles Reynolds. 70, 388, 533, 549, 615, 956, 1048, 1056, 1057, 1117, 1340, 1589, 1596, 1747, 1887, 1961, 2013, 2409, 2898, 3057, 3440, 3447, 3671, 3758
Brown, Charles William. 1579
Brown, Cheever Mackenzie. 3005
Brown, Clark. 2047
Brown, Clifford A. 2159, 2993
Brown, Clifton F. 20
Brown, Clinton C. 3198
Brown, Colin. 175, 2835
Brown, Cynthia. 1488, 3277
Brown, Dale W. 1153, 1834, 2846, 3233

Brown, David. 458
Brown, David Allan. 1082
Brown, David M. 3533
Brown, Deidamia (Covell) 1375, 2506
Brown, Delwin. 1658, 2944
Brown, Douglas Summers. 1686
Brown, Edgar S. 2294, 2295
Brown, Edmund Woodward. 1886
Brown, Elijah P. 1358, 1506, 2898, 2985, 3566
[Brown, Elizabeth W.]. 696
Brown, Elmore. 3394
Brown, Ernest Francis. 3025
Brown, Evelyn M. 2499, 3013
Brown, F. Eugene. 917
Brown, Ford K. 1551
Brown, Fortune Charles. 462
Brown,Francis. 1796
Brown, Francis F. 2671
Brown, Frank C. 3286
Brown, Frank Chilton. 1563
Brown, Frank Chouteau. 1158
Brown, Frank Llewellyn. 1553, 3550, 3552
Brown, Genevieve. 1464
Brown, George. 2994, 2427, 3031, 696, 2485
Brown, George Dobbin. 2472
Brown, George E. 293
Brown, George Kenneth. 3041
Brown, George Thompson. 2536
[Brown, George W.]. 1684
Brown, George Washington. 1653
Brown, Gerard Baldwin. 86
[Brown, Grace 3d Mann 4d] 1859. 2694
Brown, H E. 3124
Brown, Handel H. 1110, 2021
Brown, Harold O. J. 1108, 3433
*Brown, Harsh J. 1117, 1277
Brown, Helen Ada. 917, 3220
Brown, Helen (Benjamin) 1980
Brown, Henry. 2447
Brown, Henry Clay. 1093
Brown, Henry Clifton. 160, 1354, 1914, 2898, 2911, 3817
Brown, Henry E[dwin] Fitzgerald. 1720
Brown, Henry F. 138
Brown, Henry Harrison. 2246
Brown, Henry James. 923
Brown, Henry S. 3314
Brown, Hiram Chellis. 3108
Brown, Howard Miles. 1222, 1369
Brown, Howard Nicholson. 1980, 3349, 1980
Brown, Hubert L. 669, 696
Brown, Hubert William. 2547
Brown, Hugh. 2633
Brown, Hugh B. 2601, 2607, 2610
Brown, Hugh Stowell. 3349
Brown, Ina C. 2062
Brown, Ina Corinne. 2492, 2062, 3799
Brown, Ira Vernon. 2
Brown, Isaac Van Arsdale. 31, 1625, 2925
Brown, J. Paul. 1257
Brown, Jacob Tileston. 1408
Brown, James. 3615
Brown, James Baldwin. 3532
Brown, James Good. 2889
Brown, James Stephens. 696, 2601, 2609, 3807
Brown, Jean (Collier) 3877
Brown, Jeanette (Perkins) 3147, 3169, 3801, 3858
Brown, Jeff D. 422, 465, 2785, 3372
Brown, Jerry Wayne. 241, 2687
Brown, Joan Winmill. 928, 3600
Brown, John. 225, 226, 231, 314, 956, 2062, 119, 3497, 2601, 248, 269, 3006, 3008, 3856
Brown, John Daniel. 160
Brown, John Elward. 1029, 2601, 3256
Brown, John Newton. 3091, 3260
Brown, John Pairman. 1065
Brown, John Porter. 1425
Brown, John Richard. 1950
Brown, John Thomas. 1173
[Brown, John Walker] 1814-1849. 868, 1113
Brown, Jonathan M. 1822, 2751
Brown, Joseph. 3552
Brown, Joyce (Martin) 2541
Brown, Kenneth Irving. 134, 3147
Brown, L. B. 2996
Brown, L. David. 3528
Brown, L O. 880
Brown, Laurence Binet. 3002
Brown, Lawrence L. 2974
Brown, Leander. 231
Brown, Lenard E. 3278
Brown, Leo Kingsbury. 1625
Brown, LeRoy C. 923, 928, 1013
Brown, Leslie. 3278
Brown, Leslie Abp. 3854
Brown, Leslie Wilfred. 1720
Brown, Leslie Wilfrid. 1607, 3278, 3854
Brown, Leta May. 2489
Brown, Letitia J (Shaw) 3401

Brown, Lillian Brooks. 3797
Brown, Louise Fargo. 149
Brown, Lourie Ottis. 880
Brown, Lowell E. 3552
Brown, Margaret Winter. 1437
Brown, Marianna Catherine. 3179, 3552
Brown, Marshall. 2374
Brown, Marshall G. 1656
Brown, Mary Borromeo. 3419
Brown, Mary Florence. 1740, 3147, 3169
Brown, Milton Perry. 1882
Brown, Neal. 32, 2195
Brown, Norman Oliver. 2412
Brown, Opal Hartsell. 3113
Brown, Oswald Eugene. 1108, 1734
Brown, Parker B. 1961
Brown, Patricia O'Regan. 3877
Brown, Paul Frederick. 1396
Brown, Peter Robert Lamont. 113, 116, 3088
Brown, Philip L. 1305
[Brown, Philip Marshall] 1875. 62
Brown, Phyllis G. 3837
Brown, Pleasant David. 1838
Brown, Ramona Allen. 129, 696
Brown, Raphael. 92, 820
Brown, Ray F. 883
Brown, Raymond Bryan. 474
Brown, Raymond Edward. 221, 231, 334, 413, 443, 784, 1163, 1886, 2000, 2021, 2051, 2938
Brown, Raymond Kay. 1256
Brown, Raymond Lamont. 1709, 3822
Brown, Richmond O. 10
Brown, Robert. 2630, 2660
Brown, Robert Bruce. 1093
Brown, Robert Elliott. 747
Brown, Robert F. 2660, 3307
Brown, Robert McAfee, 1920. 175, 231, 696, 861, 1046, 1077, 1117, 1321, 1492, 1589, 1634, 1779, 2955, 2976, 3611, 3619, 3661, 3770, 3780
Brown, Robert McAffe. 1117
Brown, Robert R. 2056
Brown, Robert Raymond. 2056, 2944
Brown, Rosemary. 696, 3473, 3497
Brown, Roy Lish. 1555
Brown, Russell E. 2503
Brown, Ruth Mowry. 625
Brown, S. Spencer N. 3392, 3394
Brown, Samuel R. 1117
Brown, Samuel Windsor. 1129
Brown, Sanger. 2827
Brown, Slater. 2127, 2271, 3521
Brown, Stanley C. 330, 1169, 2337
Brown, Stephanie. 2031, 2759
Brown, Stephen James Meredith. 869, 3222
Brown, Stephen W. 62, 1010
Brown, Sterling N. 643
Brown, Sterling Nelson. 636
Brown, Sterling Wilson. 1015
Brown, Stuart C. 3098
Brown, Thelma Sharman. 3144
Brown, Theron. 1959
Brown, Thomas. 696, 3394, 3395
Brown, Thomas Dunlop. 1903
Brown, Thomas Elton. 824, 2735
Brown, Thurlow Weed. 3597
Brown, Ulysses Sherman. 3671
Brown University. Dept. of Art. 86
Brown, Velma Darbo. 636
Brown, Vinson. 1902
Brown, W. Herbert. 1834
Brown, Wendell. 533
Brown, Willard Dayton. 3044, 3045
Brown, William. 2522
Brown, William A. 2492
Brown, William Adams. 696, 1039, 1048, 1057, 1149, 1422, 1720, 1887, 2516, 2869, 2889, 2928, 2996, 3098, 3440, 3641, 3671, 3738, 1039, 2036, 3641

Brown, William Addison. 221
Brown, William Adrian. 1661, 1663
Brown, William Bryant. 1048, 3619
Brown, William E. 870
Brown, William Eric. 825
Brown, William Eugene. 458
[Brown, William Fiske] 1845. 2929
Brown, William Herbert. 3552
Brown, William James. 3590
Brown, William John. 636
Brown, William Leon. 1029
Brown, William Montgomery. 3427, 1319, 2956
Brown, William Moseley. 1664, 1671
Brown, William Norman. 2311, 2476
Brown, Willis M. 3124
Brown, James Buchan. 299, 3399
Browne. 696
Browne, Benjamin P. 144, 906, 1068, 1839, 2898
Browne, Earl Zollicoffer. 564
Browne, Edward Granville. 122
Browne, Frances. 1607

Browne, Frances Elizabeth. 3258
Browne, Frederic Zollicoffer. 1513
Browne, George Forrest. 1515, 3816, 182, 1515, 1761
Browne, Harris L. 231
Browne, Henry. 242, 1355
Browne, Henry Joseph. 1131, 2179, 2697, 2699
Browne, John. 1225
Browne, John R. 3335
Browne, Laurence Edward. 91, 2146, 91, 3077
Browne, Lewis. 281, 1173, 2077, 2087, 3113, 3268, 3472, 2075
Browne, Lewis Beeman. 1791
Browne, Lewis Crebasa. 3431, 3752
Browne, Lucy Lovina. 3497
Browne, Merry. 3052
Browne, Peter. 38
Browne, Pleasance Moore. 899
Browne, Robert Eric Charles. 2898
[Browne, Sara H.]. 1013
Browne, Thomas. 696, 3057
Brownell, Ada. 696, 2817
Brownell, Baker. 3098
Browning, Columbian. 2572
Browning, Don S. 103, 2787
Browning, Douglas. 881
Browning, Elizabeth (Barrett) 1772
Browning, Elva Ward. 1980
Browning, Louise Starkweather. 2637
Browning, Mary Carmel. 3704
Browning, Norma Lee. 3767
Browning, Robert. 803
Browning, Robert L. 3167
Browning, Webster E. 911, 2501, 2548
Browning, Wilfrid Robert Francis. 427
Browning, William Garritson. 1750
Brownlee, Frederick Leslie. 33, 231
Brownlee, William Hugh. 1409
Brownlie, John. 1873, 2747
Brownlow, Leroy. 1272, 956, 1319, 3372
Brownlow, William Gannaway. 1756, 2936
Brownrigg, Ronald. 70, 339
Brown-Serman, Stanley. 2062
Brownson, Henry Francis. 1103
Brownson, James Irvin. 1509
Brownson, Josephine Van Dyke. 615, 803, 910, 3181, 3184, 3192, 3262
Brownson, Orestes Augustus. 697, 784, 1363, 1365, 3124, 3283, 3422
Brownson, Sarah M. 1744
Brownson, William. 422, 3349
Brownson, William Clarence. 340, 366
Browntee, William Hugh. 1779
Brownville, Charles Gordon. 160, 573, 1445, 1836, 3318
Brox, Gertrude V. 1445
Brox, Norbert. 375
Broyer, John R. 1986
Brubacher, John Seiler. 2590
Brubaker, J. Lester. 3310
Bruce, Alexander Balmain. 59, 70, 338, 375, 1961, 2012, 2017, 2024, 2980, 3224
Bruce, Alma. 301
Bruce, Dickson D. 731
Bruce, F. F. 374, 379
Bruce, Frederick Fyvie. 69, 269, 271, 280, 289, 317, 328, 338, 343, 363, 369, 378, 402, 406, 409, 450, 451, 467, 475, 478, 504, 656, 697, 1028, 1102, 1189, 1409, 1986, 2095, 2795, 3011, 1197
Bruce, Gustav Marius. 956, 1163, 1198, 1547, 2715, 3552
Bruce, Helm. 406, 568
Bruce, Henry Addington Bayley. 2822, 2823, 2987
Bruce, Herbert. 3307
Bruce, Janet. 1644, 2360, 2804
Bruce, Mary Owen Campbell (Kelley) 628
Bruce, Michael. 73, 2742, 2869
Bruce, Robert. 2259, 2930
Bruce, Violet Rose. 1400
Bruce, William Franklin. 2062
Bruckbauer, Frederick. 2697
Bruckberger, Raymond Leopold. 780, 1003, 1085, 1961, 2353, 2869, 3124
Bruder, Ernest E. 1258
Bruder, Joseph Simon. 2362
Bruderhof Communities. 83, 3172
Brudno, Ezra Selig. 231
Brueckner, Herman H. 3884
Brueggeman, Ernst August. 2273
Brueggemann, Walter. 231, 495, 564, 647, 651, 934, 941, 2095, 2195, 2949, 3187, 3349, 3732, 3821
Bruehl, Charles Paul. 2851, 3450
Bruere, John. 3183, 1010
Bruggen, J. van. 269, 352
Bruggink, Donald J. 1156, 1801, 2240
Bruins, Elton J. 1824
Brumbach, John Clark. 918
Brumback, Carl. 1716, 1958, 92, 1864, 2817, 3711
Brumback, Robert H. 1173, 1961

Brumbaugh, Martin Grove. 1235, 698, 1236, 3147, 3179
Brumbaugh, Roy Talmage. 1589
Brumbaugh, Thoburn Taylor. 2178
Brumberg, Joan Jacobs. 171, 2158
Brumer, William T. 3413
Brumfield, Allaire Chandor. 1422
Brumfield, J C. 956
Brumley, Mary Cureton. 3765
Brumm, Ursula. 3721
Brummer, Heinrich Emil. 1117
Brummer, Vincent. 2832
Brummitt, Dan Brearley. 1437, 1525, 2492, 1525
Brummitt, Stella (Wyatt) 2481
Brundage, Burr Cartwright. 121
Brundage, James A. 1390, 1392
Brundage, William Milton. 3725, 1585
Bruneau, Joseph. 2938
Bruneau, Thomas C. 690, 765, 814, 1144
Brunello, Aristide. 2821
Bruner, B. H. 1445
Bruner, Benjamin Harrison. 1201, 1837, 2029, 2258, 2813, 2898, 3349
Bruner, Francis M. 1579
Bruner, Frederick Dale. 1834
Bruner, James W. 170
Bruner, William T. 3413
Brungs, Robert A. 996, 2939
Brunhes, Gabriel. 1589
Bruni, Gerardo. 3309
Brunini, John Gilland. 795, 3404
Brunk, Ada Zimmerman. 3167
Brunk, George Reuben. 2405, 2403, 2405
Brunk, Harry Anthony. 2408
Brunken, Juergen. 3412
Brunner, Edmund de Schweinitz. 1161, 1269, 1271, 1274, 1275, 1374, 3253, 3254, 3286
Brunner, Francis de Sales. 2940
Brunner, Heinrich Emil. 75, 103, 175, 470, 942, 1117, 1281, 1457, 1528, 1589, 2027, 2028, 2036, 2322, 2672, 3049, 3098, 3224, 3641, 3661, 3709, 1457, 1528, 3098, 3641
Brunner, Peter. 3852
Bruno de Jesus-Marie. 1427, 2136, 2642, 3690
Bruno, Giordano. 2417
Bruno de Jesus-Marie. 2136
Brunot, Amedee. 2795
[Bruns, Henry Arnold]. 3224
Bruns, J. Edgar. 308, 419, 706, 1717, 1975, 3833
Brunsmann, Johannes. 62
Brunson, Alfred. 462, 2228
Brunson, Grace Myra (Pitchford) 3461
Brunt, John. 275, 1418
Brunton, Paul. 2839, 3477, 3521, 3864, 2417, 3477, 3864
Brush, George Robert. 81, 1308
Brush, John W. 923, 2688
Brush, John Woolman. 154
Brusher, Joseph Stanislaus. 2860, 2861
Brushingham, John Patrick. 1563
Brusius, Ron. 1605
Brusselmans, Christiane. 938, 2369
Brustat, August W. 957
Bruteau, Beatrice. 1708, 3684
Bryan, Allene. 3552
Bryan, Christopher. 469
Bryan, Dawson Charles. 1563, 2898
Bryan, Ferrebee Catharine. 698, 2508, 3863
Bryan, G. McLeod. 137, 1300, 2004, 2676
Bryan, James A. 957
Bryan, Joseph Harris. 636, 3552
Bryan, Lawrence D. 3700
Bryan, Robert Thomas. 2508
Bryan, Tex. First Baptist Church. 1173
Bryan, William J. 3497
Bryan, William Jennings. 492, 699, 1068, 1579, 1950, 2007, 2562
Bryan, William Swan Plumer. 1750
Bryans, Edith Ama. 3540
Bryant, Al. 1445, 1839, 242, 1430, 1555, 1562, 1839, 1996, 3372, 3856, 3882
Bryant, Al [Thomas Alton Bryant]. 910, 1430, 3856
Bryant, Alfred. 2936
Bryant, Alice Franklin. 62
Bryant, Anita. 699, 981, 1607, 1844, 3828
Bryant, Bernice Morgan. 899
Bryant, Carvin C. 160
Bryant, Christopher Rex. 991
Bryant, Cyril E. 1816
Bryant, David. 2492
Bryant, Ernest Edward. 1385
*Bryant, Hilda. 1011
Bryant, Jacob. 2649
Bryant, James C. 3802
Bryant, John Delavan. 3029
Bryant, Lee. 305
Bryant, Lorinda (Munson) 922
Bryant, M. Darrol. 1139, 2860
Bryant, Marcus David. 3783
Bryant, Marion S. 3675

Bryant, Robert H. 118, 276
Bryant, Sophie (Willock) 613, 2590
Bryant, Stephen O. 1579
Bryant, T. A. 242
Bryant, Verda Evelyn (Bilger) 595, 678, 3217
Bryant, Wilbur Franklin. 2008
Bryant, William McKendree. 1534, 3098
Bryant, Willis Stanley. 45
Bryar, William. 1737, 3696
Bryce, Glendon E. 572, 3822
Bryce, James Bryce. 1826
Bryce, Lucy Winifred (Robinson) 2529
Bryce, Mary C,arles. 1626
Bryce, Mary Charles. 1626
Bryden, James Davenport. 3540, 3609
Bryden, John Rennie. 884
Brydon, George MacLaren. 736, 1223, 1511, 2956, 2974
Bryner, Mary Foster. 3552
Bryskett, Lodowick. 1326
Bryson, Bernarda. 2707
Bryson, Harold T. 1720, 1802, 2898
Bryson, Jeter Lawrence. 2706
Bryson, Mary Isabella. 2309
Bogholm, Niels. 2467
Borresen, Kari Elisabeth. 111, 113, 3834
Bstan-'dzin-rgya-mtsho, 1935. 707, 709, 710, 709
Bubba Free John. 699, 1407, 3477, 3491, 3859
Bube, Richard H. 3081, 3641
Bubeck, Mark I. 1427
Buber, Martin. 571, 1788, 2646, 3580, 571, 1745, 1788, 2082, 2138, 2141, 2152, 2834, 3098, 484, 699, 1457, 1747, 1788, 1789, 1928, 2118, 2141, 2173, 2225, 2621, 2646, 3098, 3896
Bubna, Donald L. 1620
Buchan, Alice. 1937
Buchan, James. 2487, 3425
Buchan-Sydserff, Rose Margaret. 2384
Buchanan, Alexander Cockburn. 2259
Buchanan, Charles Henry. 388
Buchanan, Claudius. 91, 1847
Buchanan, Colin Ogilvie. 1215, 1378, 2256, 2257
*Buchanan, Elizabeth. 617
Buchanan, Frances (Grant) 3052
Buchanan, Frederick S. 35
Buchanan, George Wesley. 402
Buchanan, Henry Donnelly. 3676
Buchanan, Howard. 2517
Buchanan, Isabelia (Reid) 3839
Buchanan, James. 2160
Buchanan, James Craig. 3338
Buchanan, James J. 1625
Buchanan, Joseph Rodes. 1048, 2590, 3002
Buchanan, Rosemary. 2197
Buchanan, Uriel. 3477
Bucher, Glenn Richard. 1065
Bucher, Hubert. 2364
Bucher, Janet Marie. 899
[Bucher, Victor G]. 1648
Buchheimer, Louis. 798
Buchheimer, Louis B. 2297, 2299
Buchler, Adolf. 2092, 2113, 2138, 491, 2150, 2846
Buchler, Ira R. 2648, 3376
Buchlor, Adolf. 2091
Buchman, Frank Nathan Daniel. 2593
Buchner, J. H. 2533, 2594
Buck, Adriaan de. 1502
Buck, Alan Michael. 2793
Buck, Carlton C. 2258, 3528
Buck, Charles. 1358, 3138, 3637, 3638, 3884
Buck, Charles Henry. 2795
Buck, Clifford. 2264
Buck, Daniel Dana. 2017, 2050
Buck, Dudley. 2634
Buck, Edward. 1489
Buck, Florence. 400, 401, 1961
Buck, Giddings Judson. 957
Buck, Harry Merwyn. 421, 533, 3491
Buck, Jacob Reverdy. 784
Buck, Jirah Dewey. 3684, 1671, 3463, 3684
Buck, Mary Merwyn. 538
Buck, Oscar MacMillan. 1082, 1950, 2502, 3057
Buck, Pearl (Sydenstricker) 619, 2508, 3198, 3572, 3573
Buck, Pearl Sydenstricker. 619
Buck, Peter Henry. 2859
Buck, William. 3139
Bucke, Emory Stevens. 2423
Buckham, John Wright. 1103, 1338, 1720, 1950, 2637, 2822, 3057
Buckingham, James. 1445
Buckingham, Jamie. 11, 700, 980, 981, 1575, 2159, 2187, 2384
Buckland, Raymond. 734, 2723, 2987, 3823, 3825
[Buckle, Elizabeth Braithwaite (Turner) 1309

Buckler, Francis William. 2174
Buckler, Henry Reginald. 2819, 3485
Bucklew, Henry. 1433
[Buckley, Annie L]. 2889
Buckley, Francis J. 903, 1633, 2811
Buckley, George Marcellus. 2417
Buckley, George Truett. 100, 101
Buckley, George Wright. 2070
Buckley, James Monroe. 1029, 1068, 2433, 2438, 2450
Buckley, Joseph. 2342, 3593
Buckley, Michael J. 2625
Buckley, Thomas E. 1152
Buckmaster, Henrietta. 2795
Buckminster, Harold Chase. 3349
Buckminster, Joseph Stevens. 3626
Buckner, George Walker. 1117
Buckner, Henry F. 1864
Buckner, Jack H. 2535
Buckner, James Dysart Monroe. 2898
Bucy, Wilma Geneva. 3468
Buczek, Daniel S. 675
Budd, C. A. 1057
Budd, Kenneth George. 1784
Budd, Nancy J. 2193
Budd, Susan. 3024
Budde, Karl Ferdinand Reinhardt. 2113
Budden, Charles William. 1158
Buddhadasa, Bhikkhu. 711
Buddhadatta. 711
Buddhaghosa. 3, 47, 701, 711, 3297, 3778, 3779
Buddhavamsa. 707
Buddhist Churches of America. 707
[Buddington, Thomas Cushman]. 689, 2158
Buddy, Charles Francis. 768, 775, 2721
Budenz, Louis Francis. 1363
Budge, Ernest Alfred Thompson Wallis. 2360, 1847, 35, 56, 656, 680, 1018, 1369, 1501, 1502, 1530, 1698, 2314, 2360, 2659, 2752, 3362, 3718
Budge, Frances Anne. 2777
Budington, Henry Aaron. 2688
Budvarson, Arthur. 678
Buechner, Frederick. 213, 712, 1300, 1957, 2384, 2898, 3349, 3638
Buege, William A. 2034, 2384, 2402
Buehne, Willis G. 3107
Buehner, Andrew J. 1065, 2206
Buehr, Walter. 1392
Buehrer, Edwin T. 1323, 3725
Buehrle, Marie Cecilia. 1802, 3426
Buehring, Paul Henry. 33
Buehrle, Marie Cecilia. 738, 2333, 2412, 3535
Buel, James William. 619
Buel, Samuel. 3641
Buell, Marcus Darius. 2795
Buell, Samuel. 1346, 3228, 3582
Buerger, Jane. 896, 2719
Buess, Lynn M. 3588
Buetow, Harold A. 830, 3186, 3525
Buettner, Daisy (Gibson) 3497
Buffalo, Central Presbyterian church. 2246
[Buffalo federation of German Caltholic societies]. 868
Buffalo Fine Arts Academy. 922
Buffet, Edward P. 2191
Buffum, Forest E. 293
[Bugbee, Glenn Wesley]. 957
Bugbee, Lucius Hatfield. 1015, 2204, 2433
Bugg, Lelia Hardin. 826
Bugge, John M. 3781
Bugge, Sophus. 1493, 2665
Bugnini, Annibale. 848
Buhler, Georg. 689
Buhlmaier, Marie. 3740
Buhlmann, Walbert. 810, 1057, 1078, 1125, 1155, 2499
Buhrig, Wanda Maria. 17
Buis, Harry. 1699, 2912
Buissink, P. J. 253, 2869, 3525, 3526
Buist, George. 2930
Buist, Werner. 854, 3224
Buitmann, Rudolf Karl. 388
Bujak, Adam. 1615
al-Bukhari, Muhammad ibn Isma'il. 1779
Buksbazen, John Daishin. 2383
Buksbazen, Lydia (Sitenhof) 3421
Buksbazen, Victor. 2354, 3720
Bulfinch, Stephen Greenleaf. 2384, 2764
Bulfinch, Thomas. 888, 2650, 2655, 2660
Bulgakov, Sergei Nikolaevich. 2750, 3632
Bulgakov, Sergei Nikolaevich. 2745
Bulgakov, Sergiel Nikolaevich. 1741
Bulger, James E. 3690
Bulka, Reuven P. 3582
Bull, Elias B. 888, 3051
Bull, G W. 423
Bull, Geoffrey T. 552, 2543, 713, 2487, 2543, 2555, 2820, 3698
Bull, George. 713, 3630
Bull, George Anthony. 3770
Bull, Henry. 2889

Bull, Henry De Saussure. 3788
Bull, Henry J. 3303
Bull, Norman J. 897
Bull, Paul Bertie. 2898, 3372, 3441
Bull, Robert J. 3653
Bulla, Clyde Robert. 633, 1640, 2130, 2133, 3279
[Bullard, Asa]. 3025, 3124, 3552
Bullard, Frank Dearborn. 1589
Bullard, John Vincent. 878, 1489, 2304
Bulle, Florence. 2409
Bullen, Frank Thomas. 957, 3317
Bullen, Leonard A. 3196
Bulletin de spiritualite monastique. 2577
Bullett, Gerald William. 3204, 2648, 3431
Bulliet, Clarence Joseph. 1957
*Bullinger, Ethelbert W. 307
Bullinger, Ethelbert William. 346, 2855, 99, 211, 314, 404, 405, 3575
Bullinger, Heinrich. 3049
Bullock, C. Hassell. 1798
Bullock, Charles. 299, 3399
Bullock, Frederick William Bagshawe. 1216
Bullock, James R. 3288
Bullock, Motier Acklin. 1337
Bullock, Randy. 713, 1358
Bullock, Robert H. 547
Bullock, Samuel Howard. 685
Bullough, Sebastian. 367, 755
Bullough, Vern L. 3390
Bulman, Raymond F. 1074, 3699
Bulmer, Agnes (Collinson) 2620, 3206
Bulst, Werner. 1826, 3224
Bultema, Harry. 542
Bulter, James Donald. 3147
Bultmann, Rudolf. 386, 1589
Bultmann, Rudolf Karl. 386, 369, 375, 386, 387, 415, 475, 651, 1078, 1424, 1457, 1817, 2062, 2299, 3619, 1078
Bump, Glen Hale. 3538
Bumpus, John Skelton. 3092
Bumpus, Thomas Francis. 751, 752, 753, 1160
Bumsted, J. M. 26, 1757
Bunce, Arthur. 911
Bunce, William K. 1935
Bunch, Josephine. 1605
Bunch, Taylor Grant. 180, 181, 321, 338, 461, 587, 957, 1313, 1997, 2029, 2068, 2246, 2869, 3381
Bundy, Edgar C. 2955, 3743
Bundy, Walter Ernest. 2029, 388, 2036, 2049, 2050, 2062, 2869
Bunge, Martin Ludwig Detloff. 3113
Bungener, Laurence Louis Felix. 897, 3710
Bunger, Fred S. 3227
Bunjes, Paul. 1917
Bunker, Alonzo. 2164
Bunkley, Josephine M. 3275
Bunnag, Jane. 2572
Bunnen, Lucinda. 1706
Bunnik, Ruud J. 771
Bunsen, Christian Karl Josias. 2273, 3113
Buntain, Ruth Jaeger. 3600
Bunting, Charles A. 2668
Bunting, Jabez. 713
Bunting, John Summerfield. 1598, 2889, 3477, 1437, 3792
Bunting, Robert H. 2633
Bunyan, Hohn. 942
*Bunyan, John. 51, 713, 1750
Bunyan, John. 1020, 51, 58, 174, 579, 713, 714, 715, 716, 717, 725, 933, 1018, 1022, 1354, 1456, 1470, 1619, 1699, 1720, 1750, 1752, 1753, 1823, 1846, 2036, 2049, 2160, 2919, 3198, 3294, 3457
Bunyon, Charles John. 2307
Buono, Anthony M. 836, 3485
Buoy, Charles Wesley. 2426
Burack, Irving. 1037
Burbach, Julius H. 871
Burbridge, Branse. 3391
Burch, Ernest Ward. 394
Burch, George Bosworth. 3098
Burch, Thomas. 1750
Burch, Thomas Kirby. 825
Burcham, Nancy A. 896
Burchard, Florence. 717, 2485
Burchard, Jedediah. 1555
Burchard, Samuel Dickinson. 3839
Burchett, Bessie Rebecca. 1935
Burchett, Harold Ewing. 2810
Burchett, Randall E. 957
Burckhard, Johann Christian. 2595
Burckhardt, Titus. 3542
Burd, Charlotte. 3198
Burdekin, Harold. 899
Burden, Billy. 1326
Burden, Dennis H. 2470
[Burden, Harold Nelson] 1860. 1222
Burden, Shirley. 1708, 2262
Burder, George. 910, 3363
Burder, Henry Forster. 3671
Burder, Samuel. 221, 3834

Burder, William. 3113
Burdette, Clara (Bradley) 2260
Burdette, Robert Jones. 1368
Burdick, Charles Rollin. 2768
Burdick, Donald W. 369, 1716
Burdick, Lewis Dayton. 20, 2650, 3238
Burdick, William Lewis. 3388
Buren, R. 2723
Burg, B. R. 2373, 3660
Burg, Barry Richard. 1333, 2373
Burgard, Charles. 845
Burgdorf, August. 2547
Burgdorf, Paul Herman. 1318
Burge, Hubert Murray. 3220
Burger, Douglas Clyde. 1115
Burger, Franklin. 301
Burger, William Harold. 3875
[Burges, Mary Anne] 1763-1813. 1518
Burgess, A. Parke. 2461
Burgess, Alan. 121, 3249, 3407
Burgess, Alexander. 717
Burgess, Andrew J. 1589, 2169
Burgess, Andrew Severance. 2195, 2295, 2499, 2508, 2518, 2538, 2812
Burgess, Cale Kight. 2264
Burgess, Charles A. 3497
*Burgess, E. T. 3839
Burgess, Ebenezer. 3717
Burgess, Ellis Beaver. 1548
Burgess, Francis. 883
Burgess, Francis Guild. 1266, 2960
Burgess, George. 429, 717, 1413, 2957, 3210
[Burgess, George, bp.] 1809-1866. 2687
Burgess, John H. 1091
Burgess, Nellie V. 3147, 3858
Burgess, Thomas. 2969, 2970
Burgess, Thornton Waldo. 657
Burgess, Tom. 319
Burgess, W. J. 151
Burgess-Olson, Vicky, 1945. 2609
Burgevin, Frederick Haviland. 2708
Burggraaff, Winfield. 191
Burggraff, Aloysius John. 770
Burghardt, Walter J. 755, 780, 862, 2358, 3279, 3349
Burghardt. Walter J. 755
[Burgon, John William] 1813-1888. 386, 1774
Burgoyne, Thomas H. 95, 2723
Burgwin, William Harry. 1553
Buri, Fritz. 1057, 1734, 2832, 3641
Burkard, Sisbert. 883
Burkart, Anna Driver. 2823
Burke, Ann Dempsey. 667, 1424
Burke, Anselm. 2354
[Burke, Bridget Ellen (Burke)] 1850. 919
Burke, Carl F. 213, 619, 2384, 3882
Burke, Clara (Baker) 1709, 1887
Burke, Edmund. 1700
Burke, Edmund M. 1169
Burke, Edward F. 744, 1107
Burke, Henry Robert. 2823
Burke, J. Bruce. 1173
Burke, James Cobb. 717
Burke, James Lee. 1686, 2626
Burke, Jane Revere. 3497
Burke, Jessie May. 2669
Burke, John. 231, 996, 2898
Burke, John James. 770, 771, 842, 1153, 1190, 2018, 2211, 3349, 3792
Burke, John Joseph. 856, 2015
Burke, Kenneth. 113, 526, 1538, 3070
Burke, Kenneth, [Kenneth Duva Burke]. 116, 3070
Burke, May Morse. 2723
Burke, Omar Michael. 3542
Burke, Thomas F. 3338
Burke, Thomas J M. 851, 1949, 2354
Burke, Thomas Nicolas. 758
Burke, Thomas Patrick. 1601, 3098, 3306, 3651
Burke, Thomas William. 2337
Burke, Verdia. 3552
Burkert, Walter. 2660
Burkett, Randall K. 16, 17, 1703, 3751
Burkhalter, Frank Elisha. 687, 3181, 3528, 3788
Burkhalter, L. Anna. 2036
Burkhard, Jacob. 2529
Burkhard, Leo Charles. 2189
Burkhardt, Edward C. 1330, 3179
Burkhardt, Godfrey F. 1168
Burkhart, Roy A. 3879, 3147, 3879, 3884
Burkhart, Roy Abram. 957, 1117, 1259, 3147, 3882, 3884
Burkhead, Jesse DeWitt. 3661
Burkholder, John David. 3778
Burkill, T. Alec. 435, 436, 2843, 3653
Burkitt, Francis Crawford. 314, 388, 401, 1521, 1717, 1987, 2328
Burkitt, Lemuel. 2166, 2941
Burkitt, William. 343, 957
Burkle, Howard R. 1733
Burks, Arthur J. 3684, 2408, 2631
Burks, John James. 3349
Burks, Thompson. 3142

Burland, Cottie Arthur. 121, 1898, 1902, 2650, 2732, 3566
Burleigh, John H. S. 3315
Burleson, Georgiana (Jenkins) 717, 3604
Burleson, Hugh Latimer. 2970, 3743
Burleson, Lolo Eaheart. 22
Burling, Donald Oscar. 2005
Burling, Nettie (Van Asselt) 3191
Burlingame, Eugene Watson. 2206
Burlingame, Hardin J. 1345, 1808
Burlington-Alamance County Chamber of Commerce. 144, 3732
Burlington, Vt. (Diocese) 717
Burman, Charles Augustus. 3381
Burn, Andrew. 957
Burn, Andrew Eubank. 99
Burn, John Henry. 3458
Burn-Murdoch, William Gordon, 1864-1927. 2706
Burnaby, John. 3081, 3682
Burnap, George Washington. 1098, 1173, 2322, 3711, 3727
Burnet, Adam Wilson. 453
Burnet, David Staats. 1465, 2535
Burnet, George B. 2255
Burnet, Gilbert. 1212, 3038
Burnet, Thomas. 1384
[Burnet, William]. 604
Burnett, Andrew Ian. 2930
Burnett, Charles Phillip Augustus. 3239
Burnett, Fred W. 444, 1531
Burnett, Irwin. 1804
Burnett, James Jehu. 170
Burnett, John Franklin. 1117
Burnett, Joseph D. 1168
Burnett, Mary Weeks. 2723
Burnett, Peter Hardeman. 784
Burnett, R. G. 2243
Burnett, Sibley Curtis. 3763
Burnett, Ulala Howard. 636
Burney, Charles Fox. 414, 556, 2070
Burney, Le Roy P. 2915
Burnham, Anna F. 1991
Burnham, Benjamin Franklin. 1978
Burnham, David. 586
Burnham, George. 1754, 3230, 3231
Burnham, Sarah Maria. 213, 1793
Burn-Murdoch, Hector. 1117, 2769
Burns, Betty. 1456
Burns, Dawson. 3594
Burns, Edward McNall. 1374
Burns, Elizabeth. 1361
Burns, Freeman M. 992
Burns, Islay. 718
Burns, J. H. 177
Burns, J. Patout. 2322
Burns, Jabez. 3372
Burns, James. 1839, 3230
Burns, James Aloysius. 830
Burns, John. 1054
Burns, John Francis. 2056, 2213
Burns, Katherine. 3420
Burns, Lytle. 3641
Burns, Marilyn. 1784
Burns, Norman T. 3464
Burns, Patrick J. 1125
Burns, Paul P. 1734
Burns, Robert. 718
Burns, Robert M. 1855, 2476
Burns, Thomas Joseph. 462
Burns, William Henry. 198, 2447
*Burnside, L. Brooks. 2804
Burnstein, Ira Jerry. 1164
Buroker, Leonard Peres. 604, 1515, 3031
Burow, Daniel R. 902
Burr, Aaron. 1511, 2002
Burr, Agnes Rush. 1368
Burr, Alexander George. 2795, 3244
Burr, Anna Robeson (Brown) 2996
Burr, Anna Robeson Brown. 2996
Burr, David. 1647, 2736
Burr, Enoch Fitch. 2980, 3057
Burr, George Lincoln. 3826
Burr, Hanford Montrose. 7
Burr, Harold Saxton. 2319
Burr, Henry. 3052
Burr, Leona L. 2508
Burr, Nelson Rollin. 1523, 1787, 1788, 2963, 2967, 2971, 3748, 3797
[Burr, William Henry] 1819. 3227
Burr, William Henry. 1091
Burr, William Hilton. 3497
Burrage, Champlin. 1376, 1468
Burrage, Henry Sweetser. 37, 154, 157
Burrell, David B. 1738, 3098, 3697
Burrell, David De Forest. 718
Burrell, David James. 718, 1589, 1730, 2062, 2199, 2796, 2803, 2944, 3220, 73, 200, 276, 328, 419, 533, 957, 1065, 1950, 2021, 2059, 2062, 2898, 2930, 3113, 3349
Burrell, Joseph Dunn. 1030, 104, 2029, 1030
Burrell, Maurice Claude. 3322
Burrell, Percy Jewett. 3238
Burrell, Sidney Alexander. 1187
Burres, Luther Rice. 473

Burrill, Donald R. 1737
Burris, Eli Edward. 3245
Burris, F. Holiday. 3711
Burritt, Carrie Turrell. 1653
Burritt, Elihu. 897
Burroughs, Charles. 2620, 3208
Burroughs, Edward Arthur. 2225
Burroughs, Henry. 683
Burroughs, James H. 3098
Burroughs, John. 3077
Burroughs, Prince Emanuel. 151, 597, 645, 952, 1156, 1239, 1250, 1563, 2669, 3467, 3552
Burrow, Barbara. 1688, 1720, 1733, 2625
Burrow, Reuben. 3641
Burrowes, George. 593
Burrows, Arthur Salter. 400
Burrows,George Sherman. 2975
Burrows, Lansing. 3182
Burrows, Millar. 207, 513, 651, 1409, 2345, 3124, 207
Burrows, Ruth. 2637
Burrows, William R. 1117
Burson, Bettie. 619
Burstall, Sara Annie. 499
Burstein, Abraham. 1506, 2622, 3371, 3456
Burt, Donald X. 3485
Burt, Jesse Clifton. 1748
Burt, Nathaniel Clark. 1961
Burt, Olive (Wooliey) 3868
Burt, Olive (Woolley) 899, 1980, 3868
Burt, Roy E. 3454
Burt, William. 2420
Burtchaell, James Tunstead. 306
Burtis, Mary Elizabeth. 1367
Burtness, James H. 1005, 1065
Burton, Alfred Henry. 462
Burton, Alma P. 1353, 2311, 2609, 2614, 2615, 2618
Burton, Charles Emerson. 957
Burton, Charles J. 211, 647, 3011
Burton, Doris. 764, 2577, 2581, 3284
Burton, Dorls. 764
Burton, Edward. 1805, 2000, 3714
Burton, Edwin Hubert. 848, 880
Burton, Ernest De Witt. 1770
Burton, Ernest DeWitt. 104, 379, 388, 397, 401, 425, 474, 1068, 1636, 1771, 1961, 1991, 2796, 3069, 3552
Burton, Eva. 3497
Burton, Irwin Huntington. 3767
Burton, Jack Robert. 719, 1291
Burton, Janet. 939, 1259, 3876
Burton, Jean. 1838
Burton, Joe. 3716
Burton, Joe Wright. 169, 1445, 1603, 1849, 145, 3466, 3468
Burton, John Wear. 2543
Burton, Juliette T. 3839
Burton, Katharine (Kurz) 1363
Burton, Katherine (Kruz) 194, 685, 1332, 1480, 3242
Burton, Katherine (Kurz) 3251, 40, 692, 720, 731, 740, 881, 892, 1363, 1392, 1403, 1475, 1480, 1481, 1799, 1936, 2134, 2198, 2205, 2216, 2233, 2309, 2319, 2334, 2364, 2481, 2699, 2766, 2820, 2851, 2852, 3378, 3407, 3416, 3417, 3418, 3419, 3421, 3437, 3533
Burton, Malcolm K. 1335
Burton, Margaret Ernestine. 659, 957, 1379, 2492, 3877
Burton, Marion Le Roy. 1745
Burton, Naomi. 119
Burton, Nathan Smith. 2017
Burton, Nathaniel Judson. 2898
Burton, Ormond Edward. 3139
Burton, Richard. 3206
Burton, Richard Francis. 3762
Burton, Spence. 2029
Burton, Theodore M. 1232, 1695
Burton, Warren. 2844, 3610
Burton, Wilma. 981
Burtsell, Richard Lalor. 719, 1290, 1294
Burtt, Edwin Arthur. 701, 707, 3077, 3098, 3113, 3114
Burtt, George. 2196
Bury, Herbert. 1653
Bury, John Bagnell. 1656, 2769 2793, 2850
Bury, Robert Gregg. 419
Busato, Daniel. 836
Busby, Horace W. 3338
Buscaglia, Leo F. 2262
Busch, Eberhard. 175, 3611
*Busch, Fred W. 3412, 3413
Busch, Joseph Francis. 1750
Busch, William. 2365
Busenbark, Ernest. 3114
Busenbender, Wilfrid. 1057
Bush, Bernard J. 3490
Bush, David Van. 2018
Bush, Douglas. 2470
Bush, George. 557, 1288, 2051, 2464, 2628, 2689, 2690, 3220, 3461

Bush, Gorge. 2628
Bush, Isidor. 673
Bush, L. Russ. 119, 306
Bush, Marian (Spore) 3497
Bush, Richard Clarence. 913
Bush, Roger. 2889
Bush, Sargent. 1845
Bushell, Gerard. 1961, 2761, 2764
Bushell, Thomas L. 1116
Bushey, Clinton Jay. 3114
Bushey, Franklin P. 231
Bushman, Richard L. 1757
[Bushnell, Eber]. 719
[Bushnell, Emma Helen] 1866. 719
Bushnell, Horace. 2000, 59, 104, 1068, 1333, 1340, 1633, 2000, 2036, 3147, 3148, 3271, 3338, 3349
Bushnell, John Edward. 2475, 3338
Bushnell, Katharine C. 594, 3848
Bushnell, Katharine Caroline. 3125
Businger, Lucas Caspar. 1961, 808, 1961
Busoni, Rafaello. 2489
Bussard, Paul C. 3785, 2365
Bussche, Henri van den. 415, 2246
Bussell, Frederick William. 3532, 1186
Busser, Samuel Edwin. 1579
Bussey, Abiah Whitmire. 1380
Bussierre, Marie Theodore Renouard. 3025
Bustanoby, Andre. 981
Busthoi, Ester Kerr. 957
Buswell, James Oliver. 3017, 104, 957, 1720, 2036, 2464, 2840, 2869, 3641
Buszin, Walter Edwin. 2939
Butcher, John M A. 780
Butin, Romain Francois. 1796, 2364
Butkovich, Anthony. 663
Butler, Alban. 3279
Butler, Alford Augustus. 647, 3166, 3564, 3859
Butler, Alfred Joshua. 1368, 919, 1368
[Butler, Arthur John] 1844-1910. 720
Butler, Basil Christopher. 442, 644, 762, 784, 1187, 1199, 2869, 3304
Butler, Bill. 3588, 720, 2485
Butler, Bion H. 3
Butler, Burris. 1562, 3347, 3372
Butler, C. E. 1797
Butler, Casper. 1467
[Butler, Charles] 1750-1832. 289, 1621, 2637
Butler, Clement Moore. 462, 1173, 2796, 2964
Butler, Clementina. 2454, 2518, 3020
*Butler, Dom Cuthbert. 2644
Butler, Edward Cuthbert. 3769, 113, 187, 2637, 3769
Butler, Eliza Marian. 2312, 2314
[Butler, Elizabeth F.] 1857. 685
Butler, Florence G. 2618
Butler, Frederick William James. 1098, 3098
Butler, George Ide. 3260
Butler, Hiram Erastus. 2723
Butler, Howard Crosby. 2, 1161
*Butler, Hugh McKay. 1429
Butler, James Glentworth. 2220, 301
Butler, John Jay. 3641
Butler, John Joseph. 2365
Butler, John V. 2962
Butler, John Wesley. 3734, 2452
Butler, Jon. 2953
Butler, Joseph. 38, 1225
Butler, Lionel Harry. 2179
Butler, Mary Joseph. 856
Butler, Paul T. 542, 560
Butler, Perry. 1715, 1764
Butler, Richard. 996, 3302, 3756, 3785
Butler, Ruth Gibson. 1848
Butler, Samuel. 720, 2036
Butler, Sarah Frances (Stringfield) 2457
Butler, William Archer. 1225, 1230
[Butler, William Frederick]. 253, 269, 2354
Butler, William Henry. 155
Butler, William Henry H. 1488
Butler, Willis Howard. 1340
Butman, Harry R. 1295
Butt, D. Gregory Claiborne. 2898
Butt, Edmund Dargan. 3253
Butt, Elsie Miller. 3763
Butt, Howard. 952
Butt, Israel La Fayette. 2433
Buttenwieser, Moses. 2949, 575
Butterfield, Erston M. 1277
Butterfield, Herbert. 1085, 1542, 1817, 1819
Butterfield, Jeanne A. 685, 1297
Butterfield, Kenyon Leech. 2516, 2529, 3253, 3254
Butterfield, Oliver. 388
Butterworth, Charles C. 248, 2941, 248, 2136, 2941
Butterworth, Eric. 1323, 2062, 2264, 3477, 3749, 3750
Butterworth, F. Edward. 1791, 2545, 3215, 3217

Butterworth, Frank E. 2435
Butterworth, George William. 1173, 3497
Butterworth, Hezekiah. 2476, 1874, 3560
Butterworth, John. 1393, 226
Butterworth, Mary Lynch Stuart. 253
Butterworth, Robert. 1380
Buttner, Heinrich. 1486, 3339
Buttrick, George A. 2024
Buttrick, George Arthur. 3148, 62, 181, 1093, 1818, 2024, 2869, 2898, 3540, 3641, 3758
Buttry, Lucas Wayne. 1250
Butts, Bryan J. 2409
Butts, R. Freeman. 1149
Butts, Robert Freeman. 1149
Butts, Thomas Lane. 1006
Butzer, Albert George. 2928
Butzer, Martin. 957
Buxbaum, Melvin H. 1651, 2937
Buxton, Charles Roden. 3777
Buxton, Clyne W. 604
Buxton, David Roden. 1159
Buxton, Jean Carlile. 2327
Buxton, Richard F. 2257
Buxton, William Richard. 660
Buxton, Wilson Riley. 1333
*Buys, J. 636
Buzzell, John. 3021
Byers, Andrew L. 3796
Byers, Carolyn. 3812
Byers, David M. 1574, 3255
Byers, Laurence P. 2785
Byers, Ralph E. 2005
Byers, Samuel Hawkins Marshall. 1976
Byfield, Barbara Ninde. 2731
Byfield, Richard. 952
Byfield, Ted. 1065
Byford-Jones, W. 2014, 2761
Bygott, Ursula M. L. 1947, 2503
Byington, Edwin Hallock. 2898, 3671, 3852
Byington, Ezra Hoyt. 3006, 3010
Byles, Marie Beuzeville. 701, 2381
Byne, Mildred Stapley. 2569
Byrd, Annie Ward. 3167
Byrd, Robert Lee. 721, 1301
Byrd, Robert Oakes. 1674
Byrd, Valois. 3192
Byrn, Marcus Lafayette. 1563
Byrne, Garreth. 851, 2498
Byrne, Herbert W. 934, 3148
Byrne, James E. 2814
Byrne, John F. 2697, 3031, 3252
[Byrne, Patrick James]. 2938
Byrnes, Lawrence. 3189
Byrnes, Robert Francis. 53, 1480
Byrns, Lois. 1518
Byrum, Bessie L. 660, 2792
Byrum, Enoch Edwin. 957, 1358, 1563, 1950, 2201, 2824, 2869, 3295
Byrum, Isabel C[oston]. 615
Byrum, Isabel Coston. 2624, 3198
Byrum, Isabel (Coston) 3047
Byrum, Russell R. 3641
Byrum, Russell Raymond. 284, 1117
Bywater, John C. 3497
Bywaters, B. 1445
Byzantine institute of America. 1354

C

Cabaniss, Allen. 1753
Cabaniss, James Allen. 19, 1753, 2240
Cabasilas, Nicolaus. 2636, 2745
Cabestrero, Teofilo. 665, 723
Cabl, John Henry. 388, 1961
Cable, Carole. 2303
Cable, John Henry. 363
Cable, Mildred. 612, 2373, 2503, 2508, 3457
Cable, William Arthur. 1236
Cabot, Ella (Lyman) 2590, 3148, 3166, 3453
Cabot, Philip. 1887
Cabot, Phillip. 1048
Cabot, Richard Clarke. 1258, 3392, 3848
Cabrera, Lydia. 2681
Cabrol, Fernand. 836
Cacella, Joseph. 1618, 2504
Cacopardo, J. Jerry. 3125
Cada, Joseph. 755
Cadbury, Henry Joel. 2271, 332, 387, 429, 1678, 1686, 1978, 1995, 2095
Caddell, Cecilia Mary. 2533
Cadden, John Paul. 833, 834
Caddy, Eileen. 723, 2384
Cade, James O. 1319
Cadet, J. M. 3605
Cadier, Jean. 727
Cadiou, Rene. 2743
Cadman, Samuel Parkes. 1110, 2422, 1140, 1884, 1956, 2024, 2806, 2898, 2949, 3860
Cadman, William Healey. 2016
Cadman, William Henry. 1230

Cadoux, Cecil John. 942, 957, 2062, 2176, 3661, 1089, 2756, 3791
Cadwallader, Edward Miles. 3385
Cadwallader, Mary E. 2162, 3497, 3768
Cadwell, Ernest Cadman. 367
Cady, Edwin Harrison. 3847
Cady, H Emilie. 1068, 1720, 3749
Cady, Harriett Emilie. 3749
Cady, Harriette Emilie. 1068, 3750, 3751
Cady, John Frank. 153
Cady, Marion Ernest. 2086
Caedmon. 2022
Caedmon, Father. 2022
Caemmerer, Richard Rudolph. 9, 1117, 1169, 1295, 1322, 2062, 2213, 2299, 2322, 2898
Caesar, C. Julius. 1703
Caesarius. 3369
Caffarel, Henri. 2342
Cagiati, Annie. 2809
Cahagnet, Louis Alphonse. 3473, 3497
Cahiers d'histoire mondiale. 3114
Cahn, Judah. 3361
Cahn, Steven M. 3108
Cahn, Walter. 3846
Cahn, Ziv. 2146
Cahn, Zvi. 2164
Caie, Norman Macleod. 231, 3410
Caiger, Stephen Langrish. 486, 514, 568
Caillard, Emma Marie. 1117
Cailliet, Emile. 62, 1103, 1394, 2777, 3025, 3456, 3477, 3593, 3869
Caillois, Roger. 3085, 2847, 3057
Cain, Arthur H. 3096
Cain, Benjamin H. 2722
Cain, John Buford. 2457
Caine, Hall. 1961
[Caine, Katherine B]. 3497
Caird, Edward. 2834
Caird, George B. 3661
Caird, George Bradford. 314, 363, 375, 427, 453, 1039, 3661, 3770
Caird, John. 3098, 3139
Cairns, Christopher. 667, 675
Cairns, David. 2323, 3707
Cairns, David Smith. 951, 1048, 1740
Cairns, Earle Edwin. 1138, 1173, 1497, 1818, 3738
Cairns, Frank. 2898
Cairns, Fred I. 2221
Cairns, John. 3024
Cairns, William Thomas. 2129, 3315
Calabrese, Alphonse. 724, 1107
Calam, John. 1222, 3736
Calaway, Bernie L. 3533
Caldecott, W Shaw. 3579
Calder, Frederick. 1525
Calderwood, Henry. 3074
Caldwell, Charles. 2585
Caldwell, Charles Turner. 2930, 3788
Caldwell, Erskine. 724, 2955, 3339, 3468
Caldwell, Frank H. 2898
Caldwell, Irene Catherine]Smith. 3552
Caldwell, Irene Catherine (Smith) 3168, 3169, 3179
Caldwell, John Cope. 911
Caldwell, John Walker. 1563, 3819
Caldwell, Louis O. 981, 1308, 2337
Caldwell, Louise. 339, 3701
Caldwell, Mack M. 3813
Caldwell, Marge. 1323, 3877
Caldwell, Martin. 2211
Caldwell, Merritt. 923, 2817
Caldwell, Otis William. 3567
Caldwell, Sallie (Bowman) 1493
[Caldwell, Samuel Lunt. 140, 152, 153, 1068

Caley, Llewellyn Neville. 636
Calfee, John Edward. 1323, 3175
Calhoon, Robert McCluer. 2713
Calhoun, Arthur Wallace. 1394
Calhoun, Dorothy Donnell. 897
Calhoun, George Albion. 124, 1346
Calhoun, Malcolm P. 1085
Calhoun, Mary. 938
Calhoun, Robert Lowry. 957, 2323, 3098, 3784
Calhoun, William Gunn. 1472
Cali, Francois. 2203
Calian, Carnegie Samuel. 191, 1010, 1046, 1057, 1075, 1530, 2746, 2785, 3789
Caliaro, Marco. 667, 3306
Calico, Forrest. 1270
California Committee for the Study of Education. Subcommittee on the Development of Moral and Spiritual Values in the Schools. 2590
California. Dept. of Education. 898
California. State Library, Sacramento. Sutro Branch, San Francisco. 2331
California. State normal school, San Jose. 3870
California. University. Library. 3626
California. University. Medical Center, San Francisco. 2473

California. University. University Extension. 3743
Caligan, James Henley. 480
Calisch, Edith Lindeman. 533
Calkin, Homer L. 3797
Calkin, Ruth Harms. 2337, 2346
[Calkins, Frances Manwaring] 1795-1869. 2940
Calkins, Gladys Gilkey. 3837
Calkins, Harold L. 2910
Calkins, Harvey Reeves. 2489, 3528, 1167, 2532
Calkins, Hugh. 2365
Calkins, Raymond. 453, 560, 731, 906, 1057, 1065, 1295, 1340, 1827, 1942, 2004, 2059, 2309, 2898
Calkins, Thomas M. 2499
Calkins, Wolcott. 2772, 3661
Call, Arthur Deerin. 2806
Callaghan, Adalbert John. 1648
Callaghan, James Frederic. 3125
Callaghan, Mary Lloyd. 2005
Callahan, Daniel J. 758, 828, 830, 1378, 2192, 2223, 2955, 3651, 3681
Callahan, Ethelbert. 231
Callahan, Gertrude E. 533
Callahan, Mary Geneosa. 3417
Callahan, Mary Generosa, 1901. 2627
Callahan, Mary T. 2575
Callahan, Nelson J. 2721
Callahan, Sidney Cornelia. 663, 2315, 3391
Callan, Charles Jerome. 370, 575, 784, 836, 854, 856, 1268, 1791, 1887, 2024, 3198, 3247, 3339
Callan, Louise. 1481
Callarman, Eva Avis. 3552
Callaway, Elvy E. 1496
Callaway, Godfrey. 13, 2162
Callaway, Morgan. 384
[Callaway, Timothy Walton]. 726, 798, 3372, 3720
Callaway, Tucker N. 726, 3893
Callcott, Wilfrid Hardy. 1147
Callen, Barry. 3168
Callender, John. 3234
Callender, S N. 3048
Callender, Willard D. 3783
Callens, L J. 3485
Calley, Malcolm J. C. 2814
Callies, Fritz A. 212, 481, 2249
Callimachus. 1873
Callinicos, Constantine. 1768, 2747
Callinicos, Constantine N. 2747
Callis, Charles A. 2607
Callow, Kathleen. 184, 654
Callus, Daniel Angelo Philip. 1775
Calman, Charles Jeffrey. 3287
Calmet, Augustin. 242
Calp, Nathaniel. 1340
Caltagirone, Carmen L. 748
Calthrop, Samuel Robert. 2417, 1987
Calvert, Albert Frederick. 1531
Calvert associates. 814
Calvert, Ian. 1784
Calvert, John Betts. 200, 1950, 3125
Calvert School, Baltimore. 814, 3164
Calvert school, Baltimore. Home instruction dept. 814, 3164
Calvet, Arthur. 1713
Calvet, Jean. 3779
Calvet, Jean [Antoine]. 2203
Calvez, Jean Yves. 853, 3449
Calvez, Jean Yves, 1947. 853
Calvin College, Grand Rapids. Curriculum Study Committee. 727
Calvin, Emily Ruth. 741
Calvin, Jean. 221, 328, 340, 345, 371, 379, 386, 402, 404, 415, 446, 467, 506, 518, 521, 542, 544, 546, 551, 553, 559, 562, 575, 727, 728, 729, 957, 1012, 1054, 1315, 1435, 2889, 2912, 3042, 3044, 3057, 3629, 3636, 3641, 3661, 2858
Calvin, John. 3049
Calvin, Ross. 1783
Calvinistic Action Committee. 729
Camaerts, Emile. 2806
[Caman, William Cooper]. 2601
Camara, Helder. 815, 1137, 2384, 3435
Camara y Castro, Tomas Jenaro, bp. 2743
Cambridge Lutheran Church. 2302
Cambridge Lutheran Church. Centennial Committee. 2290
Cambridge, Mass. Episcopal theological school. 2965
Cambridge, (Mass.) Synod, 1648. 1117, 1344
Cambridge. University. 2076
Cambridge. University. Fitzwilliam museum. Library. 2330
Cambridge. University. Library. 2047, 2331
Cambridge. University. St. John's college. 3756
Cambridge. University. Trinity college. Library. 2330, 2331

Cambron, Mark G. 3641
Cambron, Mark Gray. 474, 3641
Cameli, Louis John. 3485
Cameron, Ann. 43
Cameron, Edwin Ray. 2621
Cameron, James Munro. 118
Cameron, James Robertson. 2036
Cameron, Kenneth Walter. 1223, 1269, 1511, 1905, 1936, 2957, 2962, 2963, 2967, 3243, 3535, 3627
Cameron, Margaret. 3497
Cameron, Miriam. 981
Cameron, Regina May. 1117
Cameron, Richard Morgan. 1138, 1183
Cameron, Robert. 2051
Cameron, Ruth Hazelle. 3093
Cameron, William A. 957, 3339, 3671
Cameron, William John. 1315
Camfield, Frederick William. 175, 1457
Cammack, James C. 3181
Cammack, Phyllis. 2544
Cammaerts, Emile. 1961, 3716
Cammann, Henry J. 1215
Cammarerts, Emile. 62
Camp, Eugene Miner. 731, 2004
Camp, Norman H. 647
Camp, Norman Harvey. 3220
Campagnac, Ernest Trafford. 3165
Campanella, Tommaso. 1700, 1701, 3084
Campbell, Alastair V. 2785
Campbell, Alexander. 615, 1284, 1699, 732, 134, 563, 732, 1462, 1864, 1905, 1462
Campbell, Anna Zimdars. 3520
Campbell, Anthony. 2317, 2833, 3707
Campbell, Archibald. 2536
Campbell, Bruce F. 3689
Campbell, Carrie Lee. 2492
Campbell, Charles Arthur. 1537
Campbell, Charles Grimshaw. 3072
Campbell, Colin David. 992
Campbell, D. B. J. 386, 597, 1395
[Campbell, Daniel] 1665-1722. 2032
Campbell, Dennis M. 119
Campbell, Doak Sheridan. 3179, 3552
Campbell, Donald James. 3661
Campbell, Donald K. 506, 1401, 2952
Campbell, Dortch. 2869, 3716
Campbell, Douglas. 3022
Campbell, Edward Fay. 3852
Campbell, Elizabeth W. 3328
Campbell, Emma F. R. 1874
Campbell, Ernest Queener. 1290
Campbell, Ernest T. 1057, 2889, 2930, 3349
Campbell, Faith. 1689
Campbell, Frank G. 2869
Campbell, Frank R. 160, 547
Campbell, Frederick William Groves, d. 57
Campbell, Gay. 628, 631
Campbell, Gaye. 628, 631, 1538
Campbell, George. 2478, 3641, 1380
Campbell, George A. 3379, 3381
Campbell, George Alexander. 27, 1462, 952
Campbell, George Archibald. 3598
Campbell, George Gordon. 3422
Campbell, Henry D. 3832, 3838
Campbell, Henry Fraser. 1920
Campbell, Horace Wilbert. 1466
Campbell, James Ian. 3070
Campbell, James Mann. 733, 1030, 1793, 2869, 3011, 104, 1239, 1827, 2055, 2636, 2694, 3125
Campbell, James Marshall. 1616, 1617
Campbell, Jesse H. 150
Campbell, John. 1173
Campbell, John Bunyan. 3497
Campbell, John Lorne. 231
Campbell, John McLeod. 104
Campbell, Joseph. 2649, 2650, 2654, 3108, 3588
Campbell, Juliet H. (Lewis) 2047
Campbell, Katherine R. 298
Campbell, Keith. 2417
Campbell, Leslie Wayne. 2411
Campbell, Lewis. 1766
Campbell, Margaret. 899
Campbell, Mary J. 3594
Campbell, Mary Jane. 3594
Campbell, Myrtle. 127
[Campbell, N. W.]. 3671
Campbell, Ora Mae. 2942
Campbell, Oscar Pierce. 3552
Campbell, Paul. 2593
Campbell, Paul Edward. 804, 3310
Campbell, Paul Omar. 2260
Campbell, Ralph. 2384
Campbell, Raymond Kenneth. 1607
Campbell, Reginald John. 1048, 1110, 1340, 1961, 3339, 3441, 3641
Campbell, Richard James. 49, 1739
Campbell, Roberick. 1376
Campbell, Robert. 784, 3679, 3742
Campbell, Robert C. 323
Campbell, Robert Clifford. 36, 160, 1470, 3232

Campbell, Robert Edward. 2554, 3294
Campbell, Robert Fishburne. 1657
Campbell, Ross Turner. 73
Campbell, Roy G. 3203
Campbell, Samuel. 2304
Campbell, Samuel Arthur. 2136
Campbell, Samuel Miner. 1380, 2621
Campbell, Selina Huntington (Bakewell) 732
Campbell, Sidney S. 1206
Campbell, Stephanie. 187
Campbell, Strother Anderson. 160, 2337
Campbell, Thomas. 2855, 2856
Campbell, Thomas Charles. 1200, 3453
Campbell, Thomas H. 1392, 1396
Campbell, Thomas Joseph. 1946, 2849, 758
Campbell, Timothy James. 3743
Campbell, Will D. 145, 733, 1057, 1132, 3017
Campbell, William A. 1997, 2008, 3432
Campbell, William Edward. 1525, 3038, 883, 2830
[Campbell, William H. 2585
Campbell, William M. 1720, 2018, 2062
Campbell, Z. 3497
Campbell-Jones, Suzanne, 1941. 2581
Campenhausen, Hans. 217, 1162, 1617, 1618, 3781
Campenhausen, Hans, Freiherr von. 1182, 1241
Camphor, Alexander Priestley. 2489
Campion, Albert E. 3406
Campion, Nardi Reeder. 2205
Campion, Raymond J. 755, 2365
Campion, Raymond James. 804, 2590, 3186
Campion, Sidney Ronald. 3198
Campione, Michael J. 2312
Campolo, Anthony. 30, 3538
Camption, Raymond James. 804
Camus, Albert. 1745
[Camus, Jean Pierre, 1584-1652. 1445
CANA. Conference of Chicago. 2342
Canadian Catholic Press Convention, 2d, Sudbury, Ont., 1959. 2937
Canadian Opinicon Conference, Lake Opinion, Ont., 1960. 2994
Canale, Andrew. 3057
Canaris, Catharine. 1030
Candler, Warren Akin. 26, 73, 414, 734, 1110, 1306, 1563, 1701, 1950, 2051, 2508, 3806, 1098, 3089
Candlish, Robert Smith. 213, 324, 527, 3368, 324, 416
[Caner, Henry]. 2375, 3437
Canevin, Regis. 755
Canfield, Alyce. 1824
Canfield, Carolyn L. 2187, 2241
Canfield, John V. 3594
Canfield, Leon Hardy. 2821
Canice. 1856
Canion, W. G. 1734
Cann, Christian. 2468, 2470
Cann, Joseph C. 674, 3274
Cannan, Gilbert. 1765, 3461
Cannata, Sam. 734, 2485
Canney, Ella Mae. 604
Canney, Maurice Arthur. 3092
Canning, John. 2731
Cannon, Abraham H. 678
Cannon, Alexander. 2165, 2410
Cannon, Angus Munn. 2858
Cannon, Bryan Jay. 734, 1010
Cannon, D. James. 1008
Cannon, Elaine. 734, 1008, 2384, 2601
Cannon, Frank Jenne. 2601, 3868
Cannon, George Quayle. 678, 2601, 2609, 2858, 3234, 3428
Cannon, H. Brevoort. 1427
Cannon, James. 2457
Cannon, James Spencer. 3677
Cannon, John Quayle. 734
Cannon, Joseph L. 2492
Cannon, William Ragsdale. 2161, 3802
Cannon, William Ragsdale. 62, 1185, 430, 437, 1117, 1185, 1563, 2036
Cannon, William S. 3232
Canon Muratorianus. 339
[Canova, John L]. 2632
Canright, Dudley M. 276, 3379, 3461, 3811
Canright, Dudley Marvin. 3382
Cansdale, George Soper. 480, 3898
Canse, John Martin. 2205, 2544
Cant, Reginald. 2869
Cantelon, John E. 3538, 3757
Cantelon, Willard. 605, 2584
Canterbury, Eng. (Province) Archbishop, 1207-1228 (Stephen Langton) 1762
Canterbury, Eng. (Province) Archbishop, 1366-1368 (Simon Langham) 1762
Canterbury, Eng. (Province) archbishop, 1414-1443 (Henry Chichele) 1221
Canterbury, Eng. (Province) Archbishop, 1414-1443 (Henry Chickele) 1762

Canterbury, Eng. (Province) Convocation. 1220
Canterbury, Eng. (Provine) Archbishop, 1151-1186 (Thomas Bourchier) 1762
Cantinat, Jean. 371, 2354
Canton, Ohio. First Evangelical and Reformed Church. 1545
Canton, William. 308, 269, 308, 1508, 3279, 3284
(Cantoni, Louise. 1707
Cantoni, Louise Bellucci. 1707
Cantor, Alfred Joseph. 2377
Cantor, Aviva. 3842
Cantor, Norman F. 111, 1146
Cantrell, Edward Adams. 240
Cantwell, Edward Norton. 1358
Cantwell, Laurence. 3711
Cantwell, Mary. 3277
Canu, Jean. 2575
Capa, Cornell. 1928
Capaldi, Isaias G. 40
Capaldi, Nicholas. 1517
Capecelatro, Alfonso. 3619
Capel, Evelyn Francis. 50
Capell, Evone Wood. 3538
Capellmann, Carl Franz Nicolaus. 2378
Capen, Edward Warren. 2518
Capen, Elmer Hewitt. 122
Capen, Julia Frances. 3877
Capers, Walter Branham. 737
Capes, William Wolfe. 1761, 3533
Capey, Ernest F. H. 1525
Capitan, William H. 3098
Caplan, Harry. 2908
Caplan, Ruth B. 2783
Caplan, Samuel. 2145
Capley, M. J. 281
Caplice, Richard I. 93
Caplovitz, David. 1309
Capon, Robert Farrar. 1745, 3661
Caponigri, Aloysius Robert. 867, 868
Caporale, Rock. 3769
Caporaso, Anthony. 117
Caporn, Alice M. 1030
Capovilla, Loris. 2123
Capozzi, Francis Clement. 1039, 1640, 1887
Capper, Mary. 123
Capper, W. Melville. 2337
Capps, Donald. 231, 2780, 2783, 3001, 3002
Capps, Walter H. 737, 1845, 1846, 2568, 2575, 3091
Capron, Eliab Wilkinson. 3497
Capt, E. Raymond. 3599
Capuchin Educational Conference. 2260
Caputo, Mario Vincent. 1269
Carabel, Poleete. 738, 1598
Caracciolo, Enrichetta. 1357
Caraker, Andrew. 2694
Caraman, Philip. 41, 818, 1776, 1948, 2620, 2859
Caravaglios, Maria Genoino. 3423
Carayon, Jean. 2586, 3088
Carberry, John Joseph. 2357
Carbonel, J. 3690
Carboni, Romolo. 758
Carcich, Theodore. 3349, 3387
Carcopino, Jerome. 88
Card, Claudia F. 3090
Card, Orson Scott. 2598
Carden, Karen W. 3432
Carden, Maren Lockwood. 2737
[Carden, W Thomas]. 1301
Cardenal, Ernesto. 388, 2384
Cardey, Elmer L. 3318
Cardiff, Ira Detrich. 1653
Cardinal, Edward Victor. 733
Cardozo, Arlene. 2145
Cardwell, Edward. 1213, 1219
Cardwell Hill, Henry. 1961
Cardwell, Jerry Delmas. 3214
Cardwell, John Henry. 3273
Carew, Paul T. 2740
Carey, Eustace. 739
Carey, Floyd D. 3880, 3884
Carey, George. 2321, 1892, 2036
Carey, George L. 1892, 2036
Carey, George Washington. 1720, 3050
Carey, Howard Ray. 1023
Carey, James Aloysius. 366
Carey, John Jesse. 145, 2336
Carey, Marie Aimee. 868
Carey, Marine Aimee. 868
[Carey, Mathew]. 739, 1786, 2830
Carey, Samuel Pearce. 739, 2156
Carey, Walter Julius. 2174, 3097, 3029
Carey, William. 1702
Cargas, Harry J. 1415, 1825, 2384, 3884
Cargill, David. 739, 2487
Cargill, Oscar. 2636
Cargill, Robert L. 402, 2024
Carhart, Alfreda (Post) 2047, 2552
Carhart, John Wesley. 1503, 1799
Carington, Whately. 3497, 2473
Carison, Edgar Magnus. 2281

*Carl, Paul E. 1164
Carlberg, Gustav. 2508
Carlebach, Naphtali. 739
Carlen, Mary Claudia. 1512, 2771
Carleton, Arthur Patrick. 446, 1117

Carleton, James George. 362
Carleton, Will. 1113
Carleton, William Augustus. 333, 1197
[Carletti, Giuseppe]. 187
Carley, Keith W. 518
Carlin, John H D. 1702
Carling, Francis. 3536
Carlo da Sezze, Saint. 740
Carloy, Richard A. 2384
Carlsen, Clarence Johannes. 2302
Carlsen, Niels Christian. 1605
Carlson, Betty. 957, 1445, 1785, 2190, 2385
Carlson, Carl Emanuel. 3194
Carlson, Carole C. 740, 923, 981, 3600
[Carlson, Charles Emil] 1878. 1030, 1493
Carlson, Dwight L. 43, 982
Carlson, Edgar Magnus. 745, 1164, 2299, 3452
Carlson, Ellsworth C. 2517
Carlson, G. Raymond. 330, 419, 636, 995, 1827
Carlson, Gordon. 1311
Carlson, Jessie B. 3173
Carlson, John Alan. 231
Carlson, Leland Henry. 2336, 2860
Carlson, Lois. 2514
Carlson, Mary Callery. 896
Carlson, Morry. 3876
Carlson, Oscar W. 1563
Carlson, Sebastian. 1856
Carlston, Charles E. 388, 2024
Carlton, Ambrose B. 3762
Carlton, Anna Lee. 1607, 3179
Carlyle, Alexander. 740
Carlyle, Alexander James. 3192
Carlyle, H B. 218
Carlyle, Thomas. 740, 888, 3434
Carlyon, J T. 636
Carlyon, Richard. 1742
Carman, John B. 3020
Carman, John Spencer. 2529
Carmel, Abraham. 2952
Carmelite, Basra. 741
A Carmelite nun. 1445
Carmelites. 740, 3306, 3409
Carmelites, Boston. 740
Carmelites, New Orleans. 740
Carmen, Arlene. 3
Carmer, Carl Lamson. 1708, 2601
Carmichael, Alexander. 1873
Carmichael, Amy Willson. 1474
Carmichael, Calum M. 510, 2201, 3839
Carmichael, Carrie. 1346
Carmichael, Charles Theophilus. 3094
Carmichael, Joel. 1102, 2029
Carmichael, Montgomery. 2270, 3019
Carmichael, Patrick Henry. 409, 538
Carmichael, William Miller. 1616
Carmignac, Jean. 3591
Carmilly-Weinberger, Moshe. 879
Carmody, Denise Lardner. 3108, 3114, 3831, 3833
Carmody, James M. 1020, 2009, 2010, 2012
Carmody, John. 996, 3617, 3628
Carnapas, Anna Macdonald. 275
[Carne, John]. 2529
Carnegie, Amos Hubert. 3125
Carnegie, David. 1130
Carnegie, William Hartley. 1117, 1220
Carnell, Edward John. 62, 1093, 1103, 1457, 2169, 2708, 2709, 3632
Carnes, John Robb. 3668
Carnes, Paul Nathaniel. 3724
Carney, H. Stanton. 293
Carney, Thomas A. 2898
Carney, William Harrison Bruce. 1548, 3208
[Caro, Joseph]. 2073, 2074, 2086, 2377
Caro Baroja, Julio. 3823
Caroe, Alban D R. 78
Carol, Angela. 3299
Carol, Juniper B. 2334, 2354, 2362
Caronti, Emmanuele. 836
Carothers, J. Edward. 1152, 2672
Carothers, Merlin R. 742, 982, 2817
Carpathian Alliance. 766, 3722
Carpenter, Alton E. 588
Carpenter, Chaplin Howard. 2505
Carpenter, Charles Knapp. 3339
Carpenter, Charles Thomas. 2690
Carpenter, Delburn. 933
Carpenter, Edward. 3402, 3434, 2650
Carpenter, Edward Frederick. 942, 1321, 3402
Carpenter, Ellsworth. 3318
Carpenter, George Thomas. 3753
Carpenter, George Wayland. 1078

Carpenter, Gilbert Congdon. 1030
Carpenter, Grace (Van Wagenen) 2385
Carpenter, Hugh Smith. 3461
Carpenter, Humphrey. 2062
Carpenter, Joseph Estlin. 240, 413, 531, 1190, 1895, 1897, 3114
Carpenter, Lant. 381
Carpenter, Levy Leonidas. 3657
Carpenter, Mary. 689, 3020
Carpenter, Minnie Lindsay (Rowell) 2206, 3292
Carpenter, Nathanael. 484, 1225, 3363
Carpenter, Newton Cleveland. 3195
Carpenter, Sanford Ner. 3041
Carpenter, Spencer Cecil. 430, 1220, 1748, 2250, 3363
Carpenter, William. 480
Carpenter, William Benjamin. 2413
Carpenter, William Boyd. 1197, 2013, 2883, 59, 412, 1212, 1220, 2006, 3098
Carpentier, Rene. 3787
Carper, Eugene G. 1271
Carper, Frank S. 2766
Carr, Agnes. 47
Carr, Anne. 3019
Carr, Arthur. 1190
Carr, Burton W. 3114
Carr, Ceylon Spencer. 1057
Carr, Edwin Hamlin. 2889
Carr, Elizabeth Valentine (Durfee) 1602
Carr, Harry. 1664
Carr, Herbert Wildon. 2835, 1657
Carr, James B. 3641
Carr, James Bottorff. 1465
Carr, James McLeod. 1250, 2197, 2309, 3253, 3254
Carr, Jess. 742
Carr, Jo. 1605, 2889, 3842, 3858
Carr, John. 1706, 1476, 1706, 1785, 2537, 2570
Carr, John Foster. 3737
Carr, John J. 27
Carr, Michael W. 819
Carr, Sidney Eugene. 957
Carr, Warren. 134, 1117
Carr, Wesley. 375, 2866
Carr, Wesley Moore. 2955
Carr, William G. 440
Carr, William J. 741
Carr, William M. 2202
Carradine, Beverly. 957, 3228, 3299, 3410, 1555, 1823, 3299
Carrara, John. 36, 742, 798, 1513, 1553, 1555
Carrasco Pizana, Pedro 1921. 3588
Carrasco Y Garrorena, Pedro. 916
Carraway, Gertrude S. 2686
Carraway, Gertrude Sprague. 1667
Carraway, W. B. 3525
Carre, Ambrosius Maria. 771
Carre, Ambrosius Maris. 1845
Carre, Henry Beach. 375
Carrel, Alexis. 2262, 2869, 3057
Carrere, Jean. 2863
Carretto, Carlo. 317, 996, 1640, 2385, 3485
Carrico, James A. 2358
Carrier, Blanche. 1607, 2996, 3179
Carrier, Herve, 1921. 3085
Carriger, Sally A. 930, 1980
Carrillo de Albornoz, Angel Francisco. 3192
Carrillo, Emilia E. 2460
Carrillo de Albornoz, Angel Francisco. 3192, 3771
*Carrington, Hereward. 1709
Carrington, Hereward. 3497, 1709, 2766, 2845, 2987, 3497, 3864
Carrington, John W. 1078
Carrington, Patricia. 2379
Carrington, Philip. 388, 453, 1986, 43, 368, 433, 435, 1961
Carrington, Phillip. 1018
Carrington, Ulrich Steindorff. 3250
Carrington, William Langley. 2783
Carrington, William Orlando. 2425
Carrithers, Gale H. 1476, 2909
Carroll, Andrew. 2000, 3711
Carroll, Anne Kristin. 2346
Carroll, Benajah Harvey. 140, 520, 591, 1555, 1556, 160, 161, 221, 305, 328, 371, 386, 412, 446, 453, 458, 506, 515, 521, 527, 531, 1313, 1556, 1836, 2200, 2887, 2983, 3318, 3884, 467, 198, 367, 633
Carroll, Charles Borromeo. 3676
Carroll, Charles Eden. 3435
Carroll, Charles, of St Louis, Mo. 1577
Carroll, David. 2312, 2314
Carroll, Henry King. 2441, 3738
Carroll, Jackson W. 1300, 3748, 3835
Carroll, James. 742, 996, 1355, 1437, 2869, 2889
Carroll, James Elwood. 2459
Carroll, James F. 1828
Carroll, James Milton. 170, 742, 1173
Carroll, James P. 938

Carroll, John. 742, 784, 3809, 3810
Carroll, John Joseph. 1950
Carroll, John L. 1259
Carroll, Joseph. 1951
Carroll, Joseph Robert. 884, 1204, 1206
Carroll, Kenneth Lane. 1681, 1683, 2708
Carroll, Luke Michael. 3298
Carroll, Malachy Gerard. 2849
[Carroll, Mary Teresa Austin. 814, 826, 2305, 3418
Carroll, Patrick Joseph. 1992
Carroll, Peter N. 1294, 2129
Carroll, Phidellia Patton. 1563
Carroll, Ramon Leonard. 3528
Carroll, Richard Alexander. 15
Carroll, Robert P. 546, 568, 1470
Carroll, Robert Sproul. 3540
[Carroll, Rose Alma. 2004, 2132, 2354
[Carroll, Walter Nicholas]. 388
Carroll, Wesley Philemon. 3261
Carroll, William A. 856
Carron, Guy Toussaint Julien. 764
Carrouges, Michel. 1635, 1931
Carruth, Thomas A. 2869, 2883
Carruth, Thomas Albert. 2869
Carruthers, Donald Wallace. 3829
Carruthers, Samuel William. 3808
Carruthers, Thomas Neely. 1068
Carse, James. 1498
Carson, Alexander. 514, 134
Carson, D. A. 270, 423, 424, 2983, 3335
Carson, David M. 2385
Carson, Herbert M. 341, 758
Carson, Laura (Hardin) 2505
Carson, Norma (Bright) 632
Carson, Thomas G. 1745
Carstensen, Roger N. 549
Carswell, John. 1160
Carswell, Pamela. 3485
Carswell, Pamela Mary. 3485
Cart, Charles Leroy. 957
Cartari, Vincenzo. 2655
Carter, Anne. 631, 1383
Carter, Arthur H. 1596
Carter, C Sydney. 1221
Carter, Carlton. 3175
Carter, Carrol Joe. 3268
Carter, Charles Ernest Owen. 95
Carter, Charles Sydney. 3038, 2474, 3041
Carter, Charles Webb. 329, 1556, 1828
Carter, Cullen Tuller. 2432, 2438, 2439, 2453
Carter, Curtis L. 1534
Carter, Deane G. 2430
Carter, Del. 942, 982
Carter, Edward. 2385, 2869, 3485
Carter, Edward R. 157
Carter, Evelyn. 992
Carter, Frances (Tunnell) 156
Carter, Francis Edward. 2898
Carter, George William. 3898, 3899
Carter, Harold A. 1295, 2681
Carter, Harry Garlin. 3273
Carter, Hodding. 2957
Carter, Isabel Ray. 695
Carter, James David. 1671, 1672
Carter, James E. 1839, 992
Carter, James Everard. 1695, 2480
Carter, James R. 2050
[Carter, Jane Frances Mary]. 1622
Carter, Jesse Benedict. 2716, 3195, 3245
Carter, John. 643
Carter, John A. 3070
Carter, John Andrew. 957
Carter, John D. 1107
[Carter, John Franklin, 1897. 3050, 3125
Carter, John M. 1445
Carter, John Pim. 2985
Carter, John T. 2533, 3252
Carter, Kate B. 1881
Carter, Lawrence. 1244
Carter, Lee. 1091
Carter, Louise. 313
Carter, Mary Ellen. 2946, 2948, 3718
Carter, Melissa Booth. 119
Carter, Nathan Franklin. 2688
Carter, Paul Allen. 1139, 2945, 3747
Carter, Randall Albert. 2435, 2442
Carter, Ray Cecil. 2032, 2061
Carter, Robert F. 1810, 1903
Carter, Russell, 1881. 22
Carter, Russell Kelso. 3497
Carter, Samuel Thomson. 3615
Carter, Sarah Maud. 1961
Carter, Stephen J. 2337
Carter, Thomas. 338, 2796, 3033, 2817
Carter, Thomas William. 3527
Carter, W H. 2833
Carter, W. Leslie. 2245
Carthedge, Samuel Antoine. 308
Carthusians. 3269
Carthy, Mary Peter. 818, 2700
[Cartier, O]. 54
Cartland, Barbara. 1430
Cartledge, Groves Harrison. 2917
Cartledge, Samuel Antoine. 409, 538, 539, 1695, 1978

Cartledge, Samuel Jackson. 3029
Cartlidge, David R. 395
Cartwright, Charles. 1290
Cartwright, Colbert S. 2246
Cartwright, Frank Thomas. 891, 1845, 2504
Cartwright, John K. 3405
Cartwright, Lin Dorwin. 1563, 1589
Cartwright, Peter. 743
Cartwright, Thomas. 2650, 2665, 3198
Carty, James W. 10, 2885
Carty, Xavier. 3324
Carus, Paul. 1703, 2207, 2752, 3144, 3461, 98, 701, 705, 1190, 1330, 1368, 1427, 1457, 1703, 1720, 1961, 2165, 3074, 3297
Caruswilson, Mary Louisa Georgina] Petrie. 2536, 2826
Caruthers, J. Wade. 1689
Carver, Saxon Rowe. 739, 3235, 3240, 3466
Carver, Thomas Nixon. 1057
Carver, William Owen. 142, 347, 363, 409, 2062, 2492, 2503, 2525, 2549, 2554, 2869, 3211, 3546, 2062, 3125
Carvill, H. C. 697
Carville, Joseph. 1793, 3125
Carvosso, William. 743, 1999
Carwardine, Richard. 3233
Carwell, L'Ann. 1384
Cary, Alice. 743
Cary, George Lovell. 347
Cary, Lucius. 2577
Cary, Otis. 934, 2533
Cary, William Walter. 2669
Cary-Elwes, Columba. 755, 912
Cary-Elwes, Columbia. 2570
Casada, James A. 2241
Casaldaliga, Pedro. 665, 743
Casalis, Georges. 175
Casaubon, Meric. 58, 1520, 1521
Casavis, Jack Nicholas. 1664
Cascone, Gina. 870
Case, Adelaide Teague. 3092, 545, 584
Case, Brayton Clarke. 3010
Case, Carl D. 3877
Case, Carl Delos. 1048, 1068, 1057
Case, Elizabeth York. 3198
Case, Francis Higbee. 10
Case, Harold Claude. 1942
Case, Mabel (Hamm) 1303
Case, Mary Emily. 1445
Case, Oscar. 3218
Case, Paul F. 3588
Case, Paul Foster. 3250, 3588
Case, Shirley Jackson. 1190, 743, 1093, 1190, 1961, 2008, 2009, 2464, 3227, 3451, 3566, 3653, 1173, 1183, 1961, 3451, 3566
Casebolt, D. E. 3546
Casel, Odo [Secular name: Johannes Casel] . 2642
Casemore, Robert. 3528
Casey, Joseph H. 744, 1301
Casey, Lawrence B. 2385
Casey, Patrick H. 835, 1326
Casey, Robert Pierce. 3256
Casey, Thomas Francis. 2788
Casey, William Van Etten. 194
Cash, Grace. 957
Cash, William Wilson. 1084
Cashen, Richard Anthony. 2412, 3456
Cashin, Edward L. 695
Cashin, Helen. 1652
Cashman, Robert. 3671
Cashmore, Ernest. 3022
Caskey, Jefferson D. 1307
Caskey, Marie. 183, 3214
Cason, Mabel (Earp) 2536, 3387
Cason, Virginia. 3235
Caspary, Gerard E. 1088, 2743
Casper, Bernard Moses. 504, 2141
Casper, Henry Weber. 823
Cass, John Aloysius. 62
Cassandre. 1996, 2765
Cassara, Ernest. 131, 3752
Cassel, Daniel Kolb. 2405
Cassell, Charles Willis. 2302
Casselman, Arthur Vale. 2533, 2549, 3048
Casselman, Robert C. 744, 1590
Cassels, Louis. 62, 613, 1386, 1430, 1961, 2211, 2385, 3098, 3661, 3884
[Cassels, Walter Richard]. 347, 2229, 2476
Casserley, Julian Victor Langmead. 62, 1057, 1417, 1817, 2672, 3441
Cassidorus, Flavius Magnus Aurelius. 3668
Cassidy, Francis Patrick. 1128
Cassidy, James Francis. 1976
Cassidy, Joseph L. 2359
Cassidy, Laurence L. 1720
Cassidy, Massillon Alexander. 2590
Cassidy, Norma Cronin. 2716
[Cassidy, Patrick John] 1864. 795, 1181, 2224
Cassidy, Richard J. 429

Cassidy, Sheila. 744, 2869
Cassilly, Francis Bernard. 803, 3057, 3175, 773, 803
Cassin, Elena. 2952
Cassini, Francesco. 2032
Cassin-Scott, Jack. 3668
Cassiodores, Flavius Magnus, Aurelius. 2570
Cassiodorus Senator, Flavius Magnus Aurelius. 3668
Cassirer, Ernst. 1520, 3252
Cassler, G. Winston. 1486
Castagnola, Lawrence A. 940
Castaneda, Carlos. 744, 1782, 2137, 3862
Castanis, Christophoros Plato. 2655
Castberg, Leila Simon. 3148
Casteel, John Laurence. 1170, 2869, 3222, 3477
Castel, Eugene. 3791
Castelot, John J. 293, 308
Casteneda, Carlos. 744, 2137, 3862
Caster, Marcel van. 996, 3029, 3148
Castiglioni, Arturo. 2312
Castle, David. 1011
Castle, Edgar Bradshaw. 2592, 3441
Castle, Leon W. 906
Castle, Nicholas. 3339
[Castle, Robert Mason] 1873. 3594
Castle, Robert W. 1133
Castleberry, John Jackson. 3461
Castleman, William J. 1908
Casto, Earle Ray. 3010
Castor, George Dewitt. 442
Castro Albarren, A de. 3603
Castro Albarren, Aniceto de. 3603
Castro y Rossi, Adolfo de, 1823-1898. 2103
Caswall, Henry. 2967, 3740
Caswell, Edwin Whittier. 3477
Cate, Harold Webster. 3477
Cate, Robert L. 516
Cate, William B. 1039
Caterina Da Genova 1447-1510. 749, 3006
Caterina da Siena, 1347-1380. 749, 2646, 2647, 3284, 3415
Caterson, Robert. 3333
Cates, A B. 153
Cates, Wayne Edward. 2996
Catharine De Jesus Christ 1869. 2718
Catharine Frederic, 1902. 808
Catharine of Alexandria. 2476
Cathcart, William. 138, 147, 798, 1761
Cather, Katherine Dunlap. 3534
Cather, Willa Sibert. 1616
Catherine Frederic 1902. 2580
Catherine, Thomas of Divine Providence. 2717
[Catherine Frederic. 2353
Catherwood, Grace, Adele. 2005
Catherwood, Henry Frederick Ross. 1313
Catholic action conference. 1st, Milwaukee, 1937. 754
Catholic association for international peace. Inter-American committee. 822, 835
Catholic Biblical association of America. 343
Catholic Biblical association of America, Washington, D. C. 615
Catholic book merchandiser. 869
Catholic Central Union of America. 755
Catholic central verein of America. 771
Catholic Church. 741, 749, 768, 780, 836, 837, 842, 843, 844, 845, 846, 848, 849, 1265, 1693, 1848, 2237, 2342, 2369, 2574, 2741, 2806, 3247, 3715
Catholic Church 1939. 2256
Catholic Church. 1963. 755
Catholic Church. Archdiocese of Dubuque. Office of Religious Education. 1605
Catholic Church. Byzantine rite. Liturgy and ritual. Leitourgikon. English. 2239
Catholic Church. Byzantine rite (Ruthenian) Liturgy and ritual. English. 766
Catholic Church. Byzantine rite (Ruthenian) Liturgy and ritual. Leitourgikon. English. 766
Catholic Church. Byzantine rite (Ruthenian) Liturgy and ritual. Typikon. English. 2239
Catholic Church. Byzantine rite (Ukranian eparchate in the U.S.) 766
Catholic Church. Catechisms. 767
Catholic Church. Codex juris canonici. 735
Catholic Church. Codex juris canonici Orientalis. De matrimonium. 1490
Catholic Church. Congregatio de Propaganda Fide. 2684
Catholic Church. Congregatio pro Clericis. 934
Catholic Church. Congregatio pro Doctrina Fidei. 777, 3392

Catholic Church. Congregatio Sacrorum. Rituum. De musica sacra (3 Sept. 1958) English. 1204
Catholic Church. Diocese of Green Bay, Wis. Dept. of Education. 3162
Catholic Church. Ecumenical Commission for England and Wales. 866, 1044
Catholic Church in Gt. Brit. Bishops' Committee for Christian Unity. Conference. 1st, Heythrop College, 1962. 1039
Catholic church in the U. S. 814
Catholic church in the U. S. Bishops. 851, 852, 1153
Catholic Church in the U. S. Commission for Catholic Missionsamong the Colored People and the Indians. 2541
Catholic church. Liturgy and ritual. 808, 837, 1261
Catholic church. Liturgy and ritual. Augustinian. 3238
Catholic Church. Liturgy and ritual. Breuiary. English. 841
Catholic Church. Liturgy and ritual. Breviary. 841, 842, 843, 2239
Catholic Church. Liturgy and ritual. Breviary. English. 841, 842, 2239, 2885
Catholic church. Liturgy and ritual. Ceremonial. 814, 826, 843
Catholic church. Liturgy and ritual. Ceremonial of bishops. 842, 844, 3526
Catholic Church. Liturgy and ritual. Directory. Benedictine. 837
Catholic church. Liturgy and ritual. Dominican. 843
Catholic Church. Liturgy and ritual English. 27, 836, 2233, 2237
Catholic church. Liturgy and ritual. Franciscan. 845
Catholic Church. Liturgy and ritual. Holy Week offices. 844
Catholic Church. Liturgy and Ritual. Holy Week rite. 844, 1837
Catholic Church. Liturgy and ritual. Holy Week rite. English. 844
Catholic Church. Liturgy and ritual. Hymnary. 837, 1876
Catholic church. Liturgy and ritual. Hymnary. English. 1481, 1877
Catholic church. Liturgy and ritual. Kyriale. 837, 2239
Catholic Church. Liturgy and ritual. Lectionary. 2369
Catholic Church. Liturgy and ritual. Lectionary. English. 2369
Catholic church. Liturgy and ritual. Litanies. 837
Catholic church. Liturgy and ritual. Manual, Carmelite. 740, 844
Catholic Church. Liturgy and ritual. Manual for public devotions. English. 27, 843
Catholic Church. Liturgy and ritual. Martyrology. English. 2350
Catholic church. Liturgy and ritual. Memoriale rituum. English. 843
Catholic Church. Liturgy and ritual. Missal. 845, 846, 2237, 2365, 2883
Catholic church. Liturgy and ritual. Missal. English. 837, 843, 845, 846, 847, 856, 899, 905, 1714, 2210, 2237, 2239, 2370, 2883, 3262
Catholic church. Liturgy and ritual. Missal. Masses for the dead. 848
Catholic Church. Liturgy and ritual. Missal. Polyglot. 837
Catholic church. Liturgy and ritual. Missal. Salisbury. 845, 847
Catholic Church. Liturgy and ritual. Missel. English. 847
Catholic Church. Liturgy and ritual. Office of the Blessed Virgin Mary. 847
Catholic Church. Liturgy and ritual. Office of the Blessed Virgin Mary. English. 847
Catholic Church. Liturgy and ritual. Offices for the dead. English. 843
Catholic Church. Liturgy and ritual. Pontifical. Ritus ordinum. 848
Catholic church. Liturgy and ritual. Psalter. 575, 848
Catholic church. Liturgy and ritual. Psalter (Salisbury psalter) 848
Catholic church. Liturgy and ritual. Psalter (Vespasian psalter) 837
Catholic Church. Liturgy and ritual. Psalter (Vitellius psalter) 848
Catholic Church. Liturgy and ritual. Ritual. 837, 1258, 2239
Catholic Church. Liturgy Putie, Walter. 2883
Catholic Church. Maronite rite. Liturgy and ritual. English. 849
Catholic Church. National Conference of Catholic Bishops. 784, 2354, 3148
Catholic Church. National Conference of Catholic Bishops. Bishops' Committee on the Liturgy. 1205, 2912

CATHOLIC RELIGIOUS BOOKS 1876 - 1982

Catholic Church. National Conference of Catholic Bishops. Respect Life Committee. 3
Catholic Church. Opope (Joannes XXIII), 1958-1963. 1512
Catholic Church. Poenitentiaria Apostolica. 856
Catholic Church. Pope. 636, 753, 771, 784, 806, 848, 849, 1142, 1240, 1259, 1512, 2327, 2344, 2346, 2354, 2361, 2574, 2768, 2771, 2939, 3249, 3836
Catholic Church. Pope, 1198-1216 (Innocentius III) 812, 1826
Catholic Church. Pope. 1878-1903 (Leo XIII) 2768
Catholic Church. Pope, 1878-1903 (Leo XIII) 1135
Catholic Church. Pope, 1903-1914 (Pius x) 2851
Catholic church. Pope, 1903-1914 (Piusx) 745, 2851
Catholic Church. Pope, 1939-1958 (Pius XII) 754
Catholic Church. Pope, 1939-1958 (Pius XII) Sponsa Christi (21 Nov. 1950) English. 2581
Catholic Church. Pope, 1939- (Pius XII) 804, 2852
Catholic Church. Pope, 1939- (Pius XII) Christus Dominus (6 Jan. 1953) 2256
Catholic Church. Pope, 1939-(Pius xii) Mediator Dei (20 Nov. 1947) English. 837
Catholic Church. Pope, 1939- (Pius XII) Sedes sapientiae (31 May 1956) English. 2578
Catholic Church. Pope, 1958-1963. 2808
Catholic Church. Pope, 1958- (Joannes XXIII) Sacerdotii nostri primordia (1 Aug. 1959) English. 1298, 3778
Catholic Church. Pope, 1958-1963(Joannes xxiii)Pacem,in terris (11Apr. 1963)English. 2809
Catholic Church. Pope, 1963- (Paulus VI) 663, 853, 1137, 1563, 2570, 2771
Catholic Church Pope, (Gregorius VII), 1073-1085. 2860
Catholic Church. Pope (Joannes, XXII) 1958-1963 (Joannes XXIII) 1512
Catholic Church. Pope (Joannes XXIII), 1958-1963 (Joannes XXIII) Mater et magistra (15 May 1961) Spanish. 1135, 1137, 2809, 3453
Catholic Church. Pope (Joannes XXIII) 1958. 1137
Catholic Church. Pope (Joannes XXIII) 1958-1963 (Joannes XXIII) 1512
Catholic Church Pope (Pius x), 1903-1914. 2851
Catholic Church Pope (Pius Xi), 1922-1939. 1135
Catholic Church Pope (Pius Xii), 1922-1939. 852
Catholic Church. Pope (Pius XII), 1939. 771, 784, 837, 3077
Catholic Church. Pope (Pius XII), 1939-1958. (Pius XII) Munificentissimus Deus (1 Nov. 1950) English. 93, 1511, 2361, 3269, 3710
Catholic Church. Rota Romana. 2341
Catholic Church. Syrian rite. Liturgy and ritual. Kthobe Dkhourobo. English. 3578
Catholic club of the city of New York. 868
Catholic Commission on Intellectual and Cultural Affairs. 12
Catholic conference of the South. 826
The Catholic digest. 117, 758, 1503, 2462, 3286, 3405
Catholic encyclopedia. 735
Catholic foreign mission society of America. 2508, 2548, 2554
Catholic historical society of western Pennsylvania. 2849
Catholic Inter-American Cooperation Program. 1138
Catholic library association. 868
The Catholic mind. 758
The Catholic mirror, Springfield, Mass. 822
Catholic Press Association. Venezuela Study Committee. 2369
Catholic Renascence Society. 2702
Catholic Social Guild. 818
Catholic Students' Missionn Crusade, U. S. A. 2479, 2497
Catholic students' mission crusade. 834, 2530
Catholic students' mission crusade. Capuchin mission unit, Cumberland, Md. 2530
Catholic Students' Mission Crusade, U S A. 753, 762, 819, 825
Catholic Students' Mission Crusade, U.S.A. 814, 819, 825, 826, 2526
Catholic Students' Mission Crusade, U. S. A. 2530
Catholic Students' Mission Crusade, U. S. A. Africa Research Committee. 2497
Catholic Students' Mission Crusade, U. S. A. Capuchin Mission Unit, Cumberland, Md. 2530
Catholic Students' Mission Crusade, United States of America. 851
Catholic Students' Mission Crusade, United States of America Africa Research Committee. 12
Catholic Students' Mission Crusade, United States of America National Center. 1039
Catholic summer school of America. 870
Catholic Theological Society of America. 3611, 3619
Catholic Theological Society of America. Committee on the Renewal of the Sacrament of Penance. 2811
Catholic total abstinence union of America. 3598
Catholic union of the city of Albany. Circulating library. 868
Catholic unity league, New York. 869
Catholic University Conference of Clerics and religious of the Catholic Student's Mission Crusade, Washington, 1948. 2584
Catholic university of America. 830, 870, 1106, 2200
Catholic university of America. Commission on American citizenship. 1277, 3439
Catholic University of America. Committee on Affiliation and Extension. 870
Catholic University of America. Conference on the Curriculum of the Minor Seminary, 1951. 3613
Catholic University of America. Conference on the Curriculum of the Minor Seminary, 1952. 3613
Catholic University of America. Conference on the Curriculum of the Minor Seminary, 1954. 3612
Catholic University of America. Conference on the Curriculum of the Minor Seminary, 1955. 3611
Catholic University of America. Dept.of Education. 830, 1247
Catholic University of America. Institute of Ibero-American Studies. 754
Catholic University of America, Institute of Pastoral Counseling. 3002
Catholic university of America. Library. 658, 870
Catholic University of America. Library. Foster Stearns Collection. 2179
Catholic University of America. Music Education Workshop. 1205
Catholic University of America. O) 3435
Catholic University of America. Workshop in Catholic College Integration, 1949. 88
Catholic University of America. Workshop on Christian Philosophy and Religious Renewal, 1964. 1106, 2835
Catholic University of America. Workshop on Diciplin* and Integration in the Catholic College, 1950. 2409
Catholic University of America. Workshop on Integration in the Catholic Secondary School Curriculum, 1952. 830
Catholic University of America. Workshop on Integration in the Catholic Secondary School Curriculum, 1953. 830
Catholic University of America. Workshop on Philosophy and the Integration of Contemporary Catholic Education, 1961. 2835
Catholic University of America. Workshop on Philosophy of the Curriculum of the Catholic Elementary School, 1953. 830
Catholic University of America. Workshop on Religious Education through the Confraternity of Christian Doctrine, 1960. 804
Catholic University of America. Workshop on Spiritual Formation and Guidance-Counseling in the CCD Program, 1961. 3475
Catholic University of America. Workshop on the Catholic Curriculum and Basic Reading Instruction in Elementary Education, 1952. 830
Catholic University of America. Workshop on the Catholic Elementary School Program for Christian Family Living, 1954. 1607
Catholic University of America. Workshop on the Curriculum of the Catholic College, 1951. 3756
Catholic University of America. Workshop on the Philosophy of Catholic Higher Education, 1947. 830
Catholic University of America. Workshop on the Renewal in Scriptural and Liturgical Preaching, 1965. 2908
Catholic Youth Organization, Diocese of Galveston. Houston District. 1701
*Catholic Church, Pope (Paul VI) 2805
Catir, Norman Joseph. 2984
Catlin, George. 2327, 2719
Catlin, Jacob. 3641, 3642
Catlow, Richard. 3827
Cato, Nancy. 2373, 2484
Catoir, John T. 823, 1355, 2342, 2385, 3114
Caton, Dorothy Webber. 198, 3164, 3169
Caton-Thompson, Gertrude. 1857
Catta, Etienne. 1332, 2334, 2597
Catta, Tony. 1482
Cattan, Louise Armstrong. 156, 2586
Cattaui de Menasce, Giovanni. 947
Cattell, Ann. 3092
Cattell, Catherine (De Vol) 2505
Cattell, Everett Lewis. 1005
Cattell, Raymond Bernard. 2996
Cattermole, Richard. 3210
Catto, William T. 1717, 2829
Cauble, Sterling L. 1590
Cauble, Wesley. 1464
Caudhuri, Sukomal. 3, 3768
Caudill, Herbert. 147
Caudill, Marjorie Jacob. 2515
Caudill, Rodney C. 1229
Caudwell, Irene. 2778
Caughey, Andrew Hervey. 1487
Caughey, James. 1556, 3125, 3228, 3461
Cauley, Peter. 619, 1347
Caulfield, Sean. 996, 2869
Cauman, Samuel. 3822
Caussade, Jean Pierre de. 2642, 2869
Cauthen, Baker James. 992, 3466
Cauthen, Eloise Glass. 1715
Cauthen, Wilfred Kenneth. 1057, 1094, 2221, 3081, 3433
[Cavalero, George]. 2365
Cavallari, Alberto. 807
Cavalletti, Sofia. 3169
Cavallini, Giuliana. 2348
Cavally, Frederick Leopold. 301
Cavan, Ruth Shonle. 3832
Cavanagh, John R. 2780
Cavanagh, John W. 2715
Cavanagh, William Henry. 2976
Cavanah, Frances. 900
Cavanaugh, John. 758, 1332
Cavanaugh, Joseph Hubert. 62
Cavanaugh, William J. 132
Cavarnos, Constantine. 102, 1025, 1880, 2185, 2318, 2710, 2853
Cave, Charles John Philip. 683
Cave, Robert Catlett. 1293
Cave, Sydney. 108, 372, 1078, 1082, 1813, 2037
[Cave, William]. 70
Cavell, Jean (Moore) 898
[Cavender, Curtis H]. 2422
Cavendish, George. 3831
Cavendish, Richard. 1745, 1795, 2314, 2723, 3114, 3588
Cavengh, Francis A. 2853
Caverly, Robert Boodey. 1903
Caverno, Charles. 1313, 3608
Cavert, Inez M. 3836
Cavert, Samuel McCrea. 952, 1046, 1117, 1491, 1492, 2492
Cavert, Walter Dudley. 1435, 686, 906, 1435, 1437, 3882
[Caviness, Agnes Lewis. 1714
Caviness, Madeline Harrison. 737, 1715
Cavit, Marshal. 1824
Cawley, Robert Ralston. 2470
Cawood, John W. 308
Cayce, Edgar. 876, 930, 2060, 2225, 2382, 2987, 2993, 3052
Cayce, Edgar Evans. 102, 876
Cayce, Hugh Lynn. 876, 1619
Cayley, Cornelius. 957
Cayley, Edward Hamilton. 3475
Cayley, Murray Alexander. 1828
Caylor, John. 161, 3404, 3466
Cayre, Fulbert. 996, 2644
Cecil, Catharine. 1791
Cecil, Hugh Richard Heathcote. 2250
Cecil, Lord Martin. 3339
Cecil, Martin. 1511
Cecil, Richard. 1225, 1349, 2705
[Cecil, Ricjard]. 1349
Cecilia. 877, 2385, 3884
Cecilia, Sister. 585, 845, 2717
Cedar, Paul. 2264
Cedarbaum, David I. 2113
Cedarbaum, Sophia N. 1811, 3404, 3545
Cedarholm, A. 660
Cegielka, Francis A. 1117, 1620, 2037, 2186, 2499, 2570, 3420, 3485, 3716
Celaleddin, Rumi, Mevlana. 1455
Celestine. 1533
Cell, Charles W. 1961
Cell, Edward. 38, 1075
Cell, George Croft. 729, 3802
Cellerier, Jacob Elisee. 287
Celnik, Max. 2144
Centenary conference on the Protestant missions of the world, London, 1888. 2518
Centennial congress of liberals, Philadelphia, 1876. 1143
Center for Applied Research in the Apostolate, Washington, D.C. 3681
Center for Hermeneutical Studies in Hellenistic and Modern Culture. 24, 77, 241, 288, 326, 378, 393, 436, 490, 929, 1020, 1459, 1659, 1718, 1806, 1919, 1976, 2154, 2159, 2322, 2831, 3088, 3690, 3698, 3707
Center for Reformation Research. 879, 3626, 3628, 3668
Center for the Study of Democratic Institutions. 853, 1085, 3743
Center of Intercultural Formation. 862
Central Conference of American Rabbis. 196, 879, 2097, 2105, 2106, 2138, 2141, 2807, 2910, 3016, 3260
Central Conference of American Rabbis. Youth Committee. 3537
Central Kentucky Christian Ministers Association. 1043
Centre de pastorale liturgique, Strasbourg. 315
Centre, Michael. 3093
Centre national des vocations. 849, 2484
Centre de pastorale liturgigue, Strasbourg. 2742
Cepari, Virgilio. 2271
Ceresi, Vincenzo. 3485
Cerfaux, Lucien. 375, 398, 1163, 2024, 2503
Cerminara, Gina. 3052, 3098
Cernuschi, Alberto. 2737
Cerny, Jaroslav. 1501
Cerulli, Ernesta. 2207
Cerullo, Morris. 1427
Cerutti, Edwina. 3852
Cervantes, Lucius Ferdinand. 1135, 2019
Cerza, Alphonse. 1661, 1665
Cesaire de Tours. 1640, 1645
*Ceti, Tau. 3821
Cevetello, Joseph F X. 308, 2785
Ch'u silk manuscript. English. 98
Chabanel. 366
*Chabanel, Mother M. 2213
Chabannes, Jacques. 113
Chabot, Frederick C. 1903
Chabut, Elaine (Rice) 3235
Chace, Elizabeth (Buffum) 1677
Chace, George Ide. 2980
[Chadbourne, Carolyn Mirriam]. 2323
Chadbourne, Paul Ansel. 2672
Chadwick, Albert G. 3275
Chadwick, Enid M. 3284
Chadwick, Henry. 1021, 1190, 1196, 1287, 2161, 2942
Chadwick, John White. 308, 881, 2000, 2776, 3066, 3727
Chadwick, Mara Louise Pratt. 2650
Chadwick, Nora (Kershaw) 878, 1480, 2949
Chadwick, Norah (Kershaw) 1910
Chadwick, Owen. 89, 744, 817, 1473, 1760, 2172, 2309, 2543, 2575, 2578, 2754, 2769, 2770, 3033, 3328, 3768
Chadwick, Ronald P. 934
Chadwick, Samuel. 1828, 2818, 2869
Chadwick, William Edward. 3441
Chafe, Wallace L. 3332
Chafer, Lewis Sperry. 1427, 1553, 1751, 2174, 3288, 363, 1376, 3642, 1563, 1828, 3288, 3642, 3661, 3682
Chafer, Rollin Thomas. 287
Chaffee, Edmund Bigelow. 3441
Chaffee, John R. 1477
Chafin, Kenneth. 2191, 3829
Chagall, Marc. 566
Chagneau, Francois. 2889
Chai, Ch'u. 2839
Chai, Ch'u. 1331
Chaigne, Louis. 3779
Chaignon, Pierre. 2385, 3769
*Chaij, Fernando. 221, 1012, 1513, 1878, 3382
Chaikin, Miriam. 631, 1784
Chaine, Joseph. 568
Chainey, George. 2772, 3601, 521
Chakerian, Charles Garabed. 1255
Chakour, Charles M. 1693
Chalet, Francois. 586
Chalfant, Harry Malcolm. 3597
Chalfant, Paul H. 3747
Chalippe, Candide. 1640
Chalker, Kenneth W. 1006
Chalkley, Thomas. 1679
Challen, James. 59, 138
Challis, Gordon. 3206
Challoner, Richard. 768, 769, 770, 856, 1434, 2462
Chalmers, Allan Knigh. 957
Chalmers, Allan Knight. 957, 1094, 1340, 1590, 2007, 2869
Chalmers, Elden M. 1607

Chalmers, Mary (Maynard) 1247
Chalmers, Muriel J. 619
Chalmers, Randolph Carleton. 2228, 3661
Chalmers, Robert Scott. 1015, 1992, 333, 3264
Chalmers, Thomas. 732, 1465, 99, 467, 880, 887, 1098, 1234, 1277, 2593, 2672, 2913, 2914, 3074, 3227
Chalmers, William Everett. 3148, 3552, 1246, 3552
Chaman Lal, 1903. 3864
Chamberlain, Elsie. 1437
Chamberlain, Ernest Barrett. 2943
Chamberlain, Eugene. 930, 939, 1980, 3170
Chamberlain, Frances E. 1283
Chamberlain, George Summer. 595
Chamberlain, Georgia Louise. 571
Chamberlain, Jacob. 2530
Chamberlain, John. 3125
Chamberlain, L[eander] T. 1579
Chamberlain, Leander Trowbridge. 2869
Chamberlain, Mary Eleanor (Anable) 3047
Chamberlain, William Douglas. 2869, 3218
Chamberlayne, Israel. 1590
Chamberlin, Amory Nelson. 891
Chamberlin, Edwin Martin. 2189
Chamberlin, Eric Russell. 2464, 2860
Chamberlin, Georgia Louise. 532, 539, 571, 636, 894
Chamberlin, H B. 613
Chamberlin, John Gordon. 1259, 3148, 3170, 3757
Chamberlin, John S. 1476, 2909
[Chamberlin, Myron Holley]. 507, 508
Chamberlin, Richard. 2464
Chambers, Arthur. 3477, 1695, 3477
Chambers, Catherine. 881, 2817
Chambers, Christine (Coffee) 880
Chambers, Claire. 1854, 3390
Chambers, David Sanderson. 130
Chambers, Edmund Kerchever. 2231
Chambers, George W. 3273
Chambers, Howard K. 2731
Chambers, Isaiah Mench. 25, 1427
Chambers, Laurence T. 3579
Chambers, Mary Jane. 880, 982
Chambers, Moses Leonard. 3206, 3349
Chambers, Oswald. 601, 3335, 601, 1430, 1437, 1445, 2869, 3671
[Chambers, Robert]. 1579
Chambers, Roger R. 83
Chambers, Samuel David. 906, 1068, 3369
Chambers, Stanford. 134, 458
Chambliss, Alexander Wilds. 145
Chambre, A[lbert] St. John. 1747
Chambre, Albert St. John. 3339
Chamie, Joseph. 1622
Chaminade, Guillaume Joseph. 2354
Chaminade, Marie. 881
Champagnat, Joseph Benoit Marcellin. 2575
Champie, Sam H. 1091
Champion, John Benjamin. 104, 107, 305, 1951, 3617
Champion, L. G. 142
Champion, Richard G. 585, 982
Champion, Selwyn Gurney. 3114, 3268
Champlin, Joseph M. 755, 770, 807, 837, 900, 952, 2202, 2365, 2368, 2774, 3264, 3852
Champness, Ernest F. 3608
Champness, Thomas. 615
Champney, Elizabeth (Williams) 3560
Chan, Wing-tsit. 913, 2838
Chance, George Whitefield. 2477
Chance, Roger James Ferguson. 2047, 3414
Chandler, Albert Richard. 1533, 11
Chandler, Arthur. 1590, 2637, 3191
Chandler, Daniel Ross. 688, 3349
Chandler, E. Russell. 1573, 2167
Chandler, Edward Herrick. 3801
Chandler, Emma J. 253
Chandler, Frank Randolph. 300
Chandler, George. 3224
[Chandler, Peleg Whitman]. 394
Chandler, Russell. 923
Chandler, S C. 3642
Chandler, Samuel. 1404
Chandler, Thomas Bradbury. 1222
Chandler, Walter Marion. 2068
Chandler, Ward B. 3372
Chandler, William. 1674
Chandraprabhsagar, Muni. 1932, 2379, 3196
Chandras, Kananur V. 705
Chaney, Charles L. 1170, 2501
Chaney, Elmer V. 3743
Chaney, George Leonard. 684
Chaney, Robert Galen. 206, 2379, 2399, 2638, 3498
Chang, Ch'eng-chi. 3891
Chang, Ch'eng-chi, ed. 3586
Chang, Chia-sen. 1330, 2683

Chang, Chung-yuan. 3586
Chang, Lit-sen. 3893
Changey, Eugene. 1016, 3198
Chanler, Isaac. 1635, 1753
Chanler, Julie (Olin). 127, 3114, 3125
Channels, Lloyd V. 2869
Channels, Vera. 1607
Channing, William Ellery. 881, 882, 1701, 2471, 2742, 3470, 3718, 3724, 3725, 3727, 3729
Chanover, Hyman. 2106, 3172
Chantal, Jeanne Francoise (Fremiot) de Rabutin. 1650, 2885
Chantal, Jeanne Francoise (Fremiot) de Rabutin, Baronne de. 1650
Chantal, Jeanne Francoise (Fremiot) de Rabutin de. 882, 2385
Chantepie de la Saussaye, Pierre Daniel, 1848-1920. 2659, 3114
Chanter, William George. 571
Chantry, Walter J. 2814
Chao-chou, 778-897. 3893
Chapel Hill-Carrboro Ministerial Association. 885
Chapel, Paul. 837
Chapell, Frederic Leonard. 1757
Chapell, Frederick Leonard. 3642
Chapell, Harriet. 3762
Chapian, Marie. 995, 1576, 1713, 1835, 3768
[Chapin, Clara Christiana (Morgan)]. 3148
Chapin, Edwin Bubbell. 1323
Chapin, Edwin Hubbell. 180, 384, 2953, 3349, 3752, 3755
Chapin, Harry Lorenzo. 289
Chapin, James Henry. 3074
Chapin, John. 867, 869
Chapin, Lucy Stock. 1246, 3170
Chapin, Nathan. 1202
Chapin, Walter. 2525
Chaplain Ray, 1913. 1256
Chaplin, Annabel. 886, 3521
Chaplin, Dora P. 3011, 3170, 3177
Chaplin, James P. 2731
Chaplin, Jeremiah. 957
Chaplin, Leola Bowie. 1419
Chaplin, Maxwell. 2508
Chapman, Clifford Thomas. 3288
Chapman, Colin Gilbert. 62, 3661
Chapman, Edward Mortimer. 1057, 2561
Chapman, Eunice (Hawley) 3395
Chapman, Gary D. 2337
Chapman, George A. 1323
Chapman, George Thomas. 2964, 2972
Chapman, Gerard. 1758
Chapman, Harry. 584, 1798
Chapman, Herman L. 3498
Chapman, Ian M. 324, 2267
Chapman, J. Silbur. 1563
Chapman, J. Wilbur. 2385, 3125, 886, 2385, 3232, 3339, 1445, 1563, 3362, 3477
Chapman, James Archer. 1688, 2018, 2886, 3339
Chapman, James Blaine. 1238, 1445, 3372, 1237, 1445, 3021
Chapman, James L. 134
Chapman, John. 397, 414, 2126, 2127, 189, 388, 398, 808, 1190, 1196, 2575
Chapman, John Jay. 2217, 1068, 1397
Chapman, John Wilbur. 3671, 285, 957, 1437, 1556, 1563, 1780, 1828, 1839, 2587, 3552, 3671
Chapman, John Wilbur Chapman. 3228
Chapman, Joseph I. 2385
Chapman, June R. 3856
Chapman, Marie M. 229, 283, 940, 3005, 3565
Chapman, Mark Boatner. 207
Chapman, Michael Andrew. 837, 862, 2156, 3262, 3284, 3339, 3372, 3566
Chapman, Raymond. 2244
Chapman, Rex. 2015, 2889
Chapman, Rick. 1778
Chapman, Thomas Corwin. 1951
Chapman J. Wilbur. 2889
Chapoton, Joseph A. 856
Chappell, Ashley. 2012, 2425, 3339
Chappell, Clovis G. 1313, 1607, 1826, 2898, 3339,   1315
Chappell, Clovis Gilham. 2435, 1556, 2435
Chappell, Clovis Gillham. 217, 886, 2435, 3339, 213, 332, 338, 464, 492, 551, 577, 886, 1315, 2018, 2024, 2028, 2034, 2049, 2056, 2249, 2425, 2435, 2721, 2825, 2898, 2950, 3335, 3339, 3349, 3839, 213
Chappell, Edwin Barfield. 1563, 2456, 3148, 3802
Chappell, Wallace D. 886, 1301, 1837, 2054, 2435, 3349
Chappelle, E. E. 1735
Character education institution, Washington, D. C. 2590
Charbonneau, Joseph. 754
Chardon, Louis. 3485
Charity, Alan Clifford. 1402, 3720

Charland, Paul V[ictor]. 48
Charles City, Ia. Immaculate conception parish. 856
[Charles, Elizabeth (Rundle) 1013, 1874, 1875, 2240, 2280, 3040, 3125, 3839
Charles, Pierre. 2385
Charles, Robert Henry. 507, 3220, 458, 1530, 2149, 2150, 3114
Charles, Rodger. 3655
Charles-Edwards, Mervyn. 1225
[Charles Elizabeth (Rundle)]. 1875
Charleston, S. C. French Protestant church. 1852
Charleston, S.C. Second Presbyterian Church. 2919
Charleston, S. C. Unitarian church. 1165
Charlestown, Mass. Harvard church. 888
Charlesworth, Arthur R. 2471
Charlesworth, James H. 56, 2330, 3273
Charlesworth, Maxwell John. 3070, 3098
Charley, Julian. 243
Charlier, Celestin. 308, 313
Charlier, Jean Pierre. 332
Charlot, John. 475
*Charlton, David W. 1445, 2385
Charlton, Donald Geoffrey. 3324
Charlton, Emanuel Carlson. 3198, 3705
Charlton, John Edward. 906, 1318, 2454
Charmot, Francois. 659, 996, 2267, 2354, 2365, 3269, 3492
Charmot, Francois [Marie]. 2032
Charney, Leon. 2411
Charnwood, Godfrey Rathbone Benson. 419
Charpentier, Etienne. 347, 475, 539
Charpentier, Louis. 889
Charrat, Andre. 1980
Charroux, Robert. 3653
Charry, Dana. 1258
Charry, Elias. 2151
Charters, Jessie Blount (Allen) 3148
[Charters, Madeleine Searcy (Smith)] 1883. 888
Charters, Werrett Wallace. 1540, 2590
Chartier, Emile. 3098
Chartier, Myron Raymond. 2587, 2898, 3070
Charue, Antoine Marie. 771
Chase, Catherine. 2345, 2711
Chase, Daryl. 1173, 3428
[Chase, Francis]. 889
Chase, Frederic Henry. 330, 2246
Chase, Irah. 134
Chase, Jo Anne. 2723
Chase, Loriene. 2379
Chase, Loring D. 3187, 3732
Chase, Mary Ellen. 203, 210, 556, 577, 1628, 568
Chase, Philander. 889, 2137
Chase, Richard Volney. 2650, 2651
Chase, Simeon B. 1913
Chase, Thornton. 127
Chase, Warren. 2737, 3498
Chase, William Henry. 1456
Chassay, Frederic Edouard. 886
Chastain, James Garvin. 155, 1851
Chastel, Etienne Louis. 887
Chateaubriand, Francois August Rene. 1048
Chateaubriand, Francois Auguste Rene de. 1048
Chateaubriand, Francois Auguste Rene, vicomte de. 889
Chateillon, Sebastien. 1805, 2223
Chatfield, Mark. 1274
Chatham, Josiah George. 409, 1961
Chatham, N. J. Ogden memorial Presbyterian church. 890
Chattanooga. B'nai Zion congregation. 2098
Chattanooga. Centenary Methodist Church. 2432
Chattanooga. St. Jude's Church. 890
Chatterjee, Asim Kumar. 1933
Chatterji, Jagadish Chandra. 2839, 3775
Chatterji, Jagadish Chandre. 3775
Chatterton, Eyre. 1223
Chattopadhyaya, Kshetresh Chandra. 3776
Chaturvedi, Benarsidas. 41
Chatzeantoniou, Georgios A. 409, 461, 2261
Chatzedakes, Manoles. 1880
Chaucer, Geoffrey. 1519
Chaucer, Geoffrey, d. 3090
Chauchard, Paul. 3081
Chauchard, Paul Albert. 3081
Chaudet, Louis William. 1103
Chaudhuri, Haridas. 1708, 2225, 3864
Chaudhuri, Nirad C. 1813
Chaudhury, Haridas. 2379
Chauncey, George A. 942
Chauncey, Nathaniel. 1202, 1503
Chauncy, Charles. 1288, 686, 1582, 2567, 2687, 3743, 3752
Chautard, Jean Baptiste. 3485

Chautard, Jean Baptiste [Secular name: Auguste Philogene Gustave Chautard]. 3485
Chauvin, Constantin. 289
Chauvin, Remy. 3081
Chave, Ernest John. 3148, 895, 3148
Chavel, Charles Ber. 2623, 1614
[Chavez, Angelica]. 1263
Chavez, Angelica. 774, 1644, 1806, 2349, 2693, 3279, 3302
Chavez, Moises. 486, 2760
Cheam, Frederick. 750
Cheatham, Katharine Smiley. 3057
[Checkley, John]. 1522
Cheeseman, Lewis. 2567, 2914
Cheesman, Lulu Jordan. 957
Cheesman, Paul R. 678, 679, 1898
Cheetham, Henry H. 3730
[Cheetham, James]. 3846
Cheetham, Samuel. 1190
Cheever, George Barrell. 231, 300, 890, 2672, 3425, 3743
Cheever, Henry Theodore. 1528
Cheever, Samuel. 3339
Cheever, William Maxen. 1563
Chejne, Anwar G. 2598
Cheley, Frank Hobart. 3875, 1720
Cheley, John Austin. 1253
Chemnitz, Martin. 1295, 2256, 2283, 2326, 3710
Ch'en, Kenneth Kuan Sheng. 701, 704, 709
Ch'en, Ku-ying. 2196
Ch'en, Li-fu. 1330
Chen, Philip Stanley. 3081
Chen, Richard M. J. 3743
Chenault, Percy Baylor. 1556
Cheney, Christopher Robert. 1761, 1516, 1633, 1760, 1761, 1908
Cheney, Harry Morrison. 1667
Cheney, Johnston M. 1991
Cheney, Lois A. 2385
Cheney, Mary A. (Bushnell) 719
Cheney, Mary G. 1349
Cheney, Mary Gwendolen. 666, 3243
*Cheney, Ruth G. 3176
Cheney, Sheldon. 2643, 2645
Cheney, William Atwell. 1887
Chennakesavan, Sarasvati. 1813
Chenoweth, Carolina (Van Dusen) 2208
Chenoweth, Caroline (Van Dusen) 3284
Chenoweth, Oscar Buckman. 18
Chenu, Marie Dominique. 1590, 3449, 3615, 3659, 3692
Cherbonnier, Edmond La Beaume. 3410
Chereso, Cajetan. 3598, 3695
Chereso, James C. 3328
Cherington, Fletcher B. 3349
Cherniss, Harold Fredrik. 1773, 2853
Chernoff, Robert. 2119
Cherry, C. Conrad. 1152, 1498, 2676
Cherry, Clinton M. 1006
Cherry, Jeremiah Taylor. 3702
Chervin, Ronda. 891, 2264, 2360, 2816
Chery, Henri Charles. 2365
Chesebrough, Amos Sheffield. 1250
Chesen, Eli S. 2996
Chesham, Sallie. 1437, 3293
Cheshire, Conn. First Congregational church. 1336
Cheshire, Eng. Education Committee. 2411
Cheshire, Geoffrey Leonard. 1826, 3847
Cheshire, Joseph Blount. 2956
Chesley, Albert Meader. 3870
Chesley, Betsey Hotton. 2549
Cheslov, Esak. 1082, 1854
Chesnut, D Lee. 103
Chesnut, J. Stanley. 598, 1730
Chesnut, Roberta C. 2010, 2585
Chessman, Daniel. 131, 1691
Chessor, James E. 617
Chester, Allan Griffith. 666, 2198
Chester, Ann E. 2869
Chester, Arthur Herbert. 685
Chester, John. 1030
Chester, Samuel Hall. 2502, 2926, 3125
Chester, William. 1887
Chesterfield, Philip Dormer Stanhope. 892, 3870
Chesterton, Ada E.]Jones. 3603
Chesterton, G. K. 1358
Chesterton, Gilbert Keith. 1640, 62, 758, 762, 784, 892, 1057, 1100, 1358, 1640, 1913, 3057, 3692, 784
Chethimattam, John B. 2840
Chetverikov, Sergii. 2583, 2760
Chetwood, Thomas B. 784, 2702
Chetwood, Thomas Bradbury. 785
Chetwoood, Thomas Bradbury. 2702
Chevalier, Georges. 2312
Chevereuil, L. 2987
Cheverton, Cecil Frank. 293, 533, 3453, 533
Chevignard, Bernard Marie. 996, 3485

Cheville, Roy Arthur. 3884, 213, 678, 680, 798, 1008, 1015, 2609, 2610, 2614, 2616, 3069, 3215, 3216, 3428
Chevrot, Georges. 2365
Chew, Willa C. 2723
Cheyne, Thomas Kelly. 243, 600, 1942, 2113
Chiba, Reiko. 98, 3379
Chicago Area Theological Library Association. 3678
Chicago. Art Institute. 919
Chicago association for child study and parent education. 2590
Chicago. Assumption Church. 93
Chicago. Center for Research Libraries. 1202, 2499
Chicago Christian youth council. 3882
[Chicago. First Baptist church]. 145
Chicago. Good Shepherd Church. 1747
Chicago. Hebrew Theological College. 1308
Chicago Heights, Ill. First Presbyterian church. 1100, 2917
Chicago. Holy Cross Church Art Gallery. 87
Chicago. Holy Family church. Married men's sodality. Library. 934
Chicago Inter Student Catholic Action Organization. 852
Chicago. Our Redeemer Lutheran Church. 750
Chicago. Presbyterian theological seminary. 893, 2306, 3614
Chicago. Public library. 869, 2793, 2943
Chicago. Queen of All Saints. 3011
Chicago. Resurrection Church. 3221
Chicago. St. Alphonsus Church. 3272
Chicago. St. Charles Borromeo Church. 1269
Chicago. St. Felicitas Church. 3274
Chicago. St. Ferdinand Church. 734, 3274
Chicago. Saint Francis De Sales Parish. 3274
Chicago. St. Gall Church. 3274
Chicago Society for Biblical Research. 200
Chicago synod of the Evangelical Lutheran church. 1547
Chicago theological seminary. 893
Chicago Theological Seminary. Register. 1259
Chicago. Third Presbyterian church. Library association. 2927
Chicago. Third Unitarian church. 3852
Chicago. University. College. 1282
Chicago. University. Library. 431, 894, 1748
Chicago. University. New Testament club. 337
Chicago. University. Oriental institute. Epigraphic and architectural survey. 2378
Chicago. University. Press. 3165
Chicago. World's Columbian exposition, 1893. Catholic educational exhibit. 830
Chicargo theological seminary. 893
Chichester, James. 231
Chick, Jack T. 3293
[Chickering, John White] 1808-1888. 1396
Chicorel, Marietta. 2993
Chidley, Howard James. 906, 1340, 3369, 3534
Chidsey, Alan Lake. 3013
Chidsey, Donald Barr. 2231
Chiel, Arthur A. 562, 566, 2107
Chiel, Kinneret. 1784
Chiel, Samuel. 3361
Chiereghin, Franco. 113
Chifflot, Th. G. 613, 1818
[Chih-i] 531-597. 701
Chih-yu, Shih, 1185-1269. 2182
Chilcote, Thomas F. 74, 2427, 3183
Child, Asaph Bemis. 1745, 3498
Child, Charlotte Hoyt. 3144
Child, Frank Samuel. 1346, 2687, 1294
Child, George Chaplin. 187, 3074
Child, Gilbert William. 1146
Child, Heather. 919
Child, Henry T. 3498
Child, Lydia Maria (Francis) 3114
Child, Mark. 1158
Childe, Frederick W. 605
Childers, James Saxon. 151
Childers, Sylvester Earl. 313
Children of Mary. New York archdiocesan union. 3454
Childress, James F. 1089, 1749, 3327
Childress, William Glover. 406
Childs, Ann Taylor. 2024
Childs, Brevard S. 492, 516, 539, 651, 1424, 1920, 2401
Childs, James M. 2321
Childs, John Brown. 15
Childs, Marquis William. 1075
Childs, Stanley Herbert. 1217
Childs, Thomas Spencer. 2037
Chiles, Henry Clay. 1668

Chiles, John Russell. 1691
Chiles, Robert Eugene. 2423
Chiles(John Russell. 1691
Chill, Abraham. 562, 1312, 2119
Chillingworth, William. 1216, 2976, 3630
Chilson, Edna (Hill) 911, 2513
Chilson, Richard. 74, 138, 767, 794, 2869, 3475, 3628
Chilton, Charles George Eric. 422
Chilton, Harriett A. 77, 2736
Chilton, William Parish. 2249
China centenary missionary conference, Shanghai, 1907. 911
China centenary missionary conferences, Shanghai, 1907. 2508
China inland mission. 1109, 2508
Ching, Julia. 1330
Chiniquy, Charles Paschal Telesphore. 798, 1148, 1210, 1326
Chinmoy. 1416, 1815, 2316, 2385, 3477, 3864
Chinnici, Joseph P. 1520, 2230
Chipkin, Israel Solomon. 2106
Chipman, Charles. 3198
Chipman, Charles Phillips. 914
Chipman, Edward E. 2210
Chipman, Luzene. 1358
[Chipman, Richard Manning] 1806-1893. 3698
Chirainelli, Piero. 1838
Chirico, Peter. 2862
Chisholm, Archibald, 1889. 1016
Chisholm, William Hugh. 2536
Chisolm, J. Julian. 1627
Chittenden, Ezra Porter. 40, 695
Chitwood, Billy J. 413, 1243, 2037
Cho, Paul Yong-gi. 1169
Cho, Yong-gi. 915, 982, 1010
Chodorow, Stanley. 736, 1756
Chogyam Trungpa, 1939. 1537, 3698
Chogyam Trungpa, Trungpa Tulku, 1939. 915, 2194, 3484
Cholmeley, Katharine. 119, 2166
Chorley, Edward Clowes. 1173, 2699, 2701, 2971
Chorley, Edward Clowes, 1865-1949. 2971
Choron, Jacques. 1413
Chou, Po-chin. 3434
Choumnos, Georgios. 520
Chouraqui, Andre. 2084
Chouraqui, Andre Nathanael. 2146
Chow, Shu-kai. 1330
Chreitzberg, Abel McKee. 2432
Chrisman, Agnes G. 918
Chrisman, Lewis Herbert. 1843, 2425, 3255, 3367
Chrisman, Miriam Usher. 3041
Christ, Carol P. 3834
Christ Church Christiana Hundred, New Castle Co., Del. 1488
Christ, Frank L. 873
Christen, Robert J. 2585
Christensen, Anton M. 611
Christensen, Bernhard Marinus. 1021, 1065, 3477
Christensen, Carl C. 86
Christensen, Chuck. 333, 636, 2379
Christensen, Duane L. 568, 2671
Christensen, James L. 1162, 1693, 2780, 2790, 3800, 3853, 3856
Christensen, Leon N. 1232
Christensen, Michael J. 306, 2219
Christensen, Niels. 3215
Christensen, Otto H. 1720, 2541, 3387
Christensen, William E. 1311
Christensen, Winnie. 636, 1153
Christenson, Evelyn. 918, 982, 2869, 3540
Christenson, Larry. 3391
Christenson, Laurence. 982, 1005, 1607, 1716, 2337, 2814, 2816
Christenverfolgung in Sudamerika. 2821
Christesen, Barbara. 3787
Christiaens, Louis. 2385
Christian and missionary alliance. 918
Christian and missionary alliance. Foreign dept. 918
Christian beacon. 1754, 2562
Christian Board of Publication, St. Louis. 937, 1607
Christian brothers college, St. Louis, Mo. Library. 2224
Christian, C. W. 1417, 3308, 3661
Christian, Carol. 2506, 3425
The Christian century. 1065, 1274, 3211
Christian Century (The) 3211
Christian College Coalition (U.S.) 1164
Christian convention, Aurora, Ill., 1867. 3322
Christian, Dorothy E (White) 198, 619
Christian Education Movement. Primary Dept. 3142
Christian-evangelist. 1463
Christian-evangelist (Indexes) 1554
Christian hall library, Chestnut Hill, Philadelphia. 2224

Christian herald (New York, 1878-) 1156, 1445
Christian Information Bureau, Elkhorn, Wis. 1253
Christian, John Tyler. 134, 151, 154
Christian, Levi Hunt. 2160
Christian, Lewis Harrison. 519, 605, 3382, 3386, 3811
Christian life. 1013
Christian, Mary. 2536, 2558, 3467
Christian, Mary Blount. 494, 633, 903, 1384, 1401, 2130
Christian Methodist Episcopal Church. 1022
Christian Methodist Episcopal Church. Conferences. Tennessee. 1021
Christian Methodist Episcopal Church. Conferences. Washington and Philadelphia. 1021
Christian Methodist Episcopal Church. Conferences. West Tennessee. 1021
Christian publicity committee, Baltimore. 10
Christian reformed church. 1023
Christian Reformed Church. Centennial Committee. 1023
Christian Reformed church. Church order. 1023
Christian reformed church. Liturgy and ritual. 1023
Christian, S.L. 594
The Christian Science journal. 1493
Christian Science Publishing Society. 1030, 1037, 1210, 1493
Christian Science sentinel. 1496
Christian Service Brigade. 687
Christian Unity Conference, St. Pius x Seminary, 1964. 1523
Christian unity league. 1039
Christian, William A. 3331, 2417, 3114, 3813, 825, 2357, 2668, 3469, 3783
Christian Workers' Service Bureau Inc. 3876
Christian Writers and Editors' Conference. 2135
Christian Writers Institute. 3203
Christian youth conference of North America, Lakeside, O., 1936. 3884
Christianity and crisis. 1068, 3636
Christianity today. 1090, 3325, 3651
Christian Methodist Episcopal Church. 1127
Christiansen, Elmer E. 2887
Christianson, C.M. 625
Christianson, Christopher J. 1110
Christianson, Nora D. 293
Christianson, Paul. 1515
Christie, Anne. 3498
Christie, Christie. 2029
Christie, Francis Albert. 2376
Christie, John W. 686, 3424
Christie, Joseph William. 2484
Christie, Joseph William. 2484
Christie-Murray, David. 1805, 3052
Christ-Janer, Albert William. 1156
Christlich-Demokratische Union (Germany (Democratic Republic)) 1146
Christlieb, Theodor. 59, 2518
Christman, Duvillo Grant. 650, 1556
Christoff, Nicholas B. 1256
Christopher, 1950. 2385
Christopher, Beth. 1976
Christopher, Georgia B. 2471, 3041
Christopher, John B. 1921
Christopher, Milbourne. 2723, 2987
Christopher Study Week. 2d, New York, 1964. 3614

Christophil. 127
Christus (Paris) 2267, 3485
Christy, Arthur. 1510, 3708
Christy, David. 3425
Christy, George H. 3339
Christy, George Harvey. 1057
Christy, Wilbur A. 134
Chrosciechowski, Julian. 1736
[Chrysostom, John, 1863-1917. 780
Chrysostom John. 804
Chrysostomos, Archimandrite. 1250
Chrysostomus, Jeannes. 2939
Chrysostomus, Joannes. 1115, 1295, 2145, 3337
Chrysostomus, Joannes, Saint, Patriarch of Constaninople, d. 407. 138
Chrysostomus, Joannes, Saint, Patriarch of Constantinople, d. 407. 422, 2804, 3368
Chrystal, James. 1373, 1521, 2706
Chrystal, William G. 1301, 2708
Chu, Paul E. 50
Chuang-tzu. 914, 2188, 2641, 2838, 2856
Chuang-Tzu. 1731, 2188, 2412
Chuard, Henri. 734
Chubb, Thomas. 3022
Chudoba, Bohdan. 1281
Chumbley, Charles Melvin. 293
Chumbley, Joe W. 2167
[Ch'un, Yuan]. 3400

Chupp, Tommy. 213
Church, Alfred John. 1765
Church and Society Study Conference, Chicago, 1961. 2405, 3441
Church and Synagogue Library Association. 2224
Church, Brooke (Peters) 210, 499, 2950, 3743
Church club of New York. Library. 3627
Church Conference of Social Work. 1133, 3448
Church conference on African affairs, Otterbein college, 1942. 2497
Church Congress in the United States. 2957, 2963
Church, Daniel Webster. 2225
Church Directory Publications, Chicago. 893
Church Federation of Greater Chicago. Bureau of Research. 1133
[Church, Francis Pharcellus]. 2735, 3302
Church, Frederic Corss. 3041
Church historical society, Philadelphia. 2963
The Church in the Christian Roman Empire, by J. R. 1190
Church, Ivor F. 435
Church, John Edward. 301, 2162
Church, John Hubbard. 1376, 2014
Church, John Robert. 3299
The Church journal. 3228
Church League of America. 2670
Church League of America. Research Dept. 3850
Church, Leslie Frederic. 2423, 3716, 3802
Church Library Conference. 3d, Philadelphia, 1965. 2224
Church management. 1419
Church, Mary L. 1285
The Church militant, Boston. 2957
Church of Christ, Scientist. 1037
Church of Christ, Scientist. Hymnal. 1037
Church of England. 735, 1213, 1220, 1223, 1225, 1489, 2870, 3363, 3783
Church of England. Archbishop of Canterbury's committee on the ministry of women. 3837
Church of England. Archbishops' Commission on Christian Doctrine. 238, 3626
Church of England. Archbishops' Commission on Divine Healing. 1598
Church of England. Archbishops' Commission on Doctrine. 1212, 1217
Church of England. Book of common prayer. 1210, 1213, 2870, 2883, 2946, 3262
Church of England. Book of common prayer. Communion service. 2259
Church of England. Book of common prayer. Mohawk. 2567
Church of England. Book of common prayer. "Prayer-book of King Edward VII." 680
Church of England. Book of common prayer. Psalter. 1213, 1215, 2985
Church of England Constitutions and canons ecclesiastical, 1604. 1489
Church of England. Fulham conference, 1901-1902. 1326
Church of England. Homilies. 1225
Church of England in Australia. Missionary and Ecumenical Council. 2480
Church of England in Canada. Book of common praise. 1222
Church of England. Liturgy and ritual. 1223, 1837
Church of England. Liturgy and ritual. Coronation service. 1508
Church of England. Liturgy and ritual. Primer. 2889
Church of England. National assembly. Missionary council. 2497, 2516, 2530, 2540
Church of England. National Assembly. Prisons Commission. 2942
The Church of God. 1228, 1273
Church of God (Cleveland, Tenn.) 3177
Church of God evangel. 1229
Church of God in Christ. 1229
Church of God of Prophecy. Bible Training Camp. 1229
Church of Jesus Chirst of latter-day saints. 2616
Church of Jesus Christ (Bickertonites) 1230
[Church of Jesus Christ of latter-day saints]. 643, 1230, 1233, 1704, 2607, 2609, 2610, 2616
Church of Jesus Christ of latter-day saints. Church radio, publicity and missionary literature committee. 2601
Church of Jesus Christ of latter-day saints. Council of the twelve apostles. 2601

Church of Jesus Christ of latter-day saints. Deseret Sunday school union. 1992, 2614, 2615, 3188, 3552
Church of Jesus Christ of latter-day saints. General board of the Relief society. 2609
Church of Jesus Christ of Latter-day Saints. Primary Association. General Board. 2599
Church of Jesus Christ of Latter-Day Saints. Primary General Board Music Committee. 2599
Church of Jesus Christ of Latter-Day Saints. Southern Arizona Stake. San Manuel Ward. 1230
Church of St. Stephen and the Incarnation, Washington, D.C. 2237
Church of Scotland. 1234, 2936
Church of Scotland. General Assembly. Commission on Communism. 1128, 1137
Church of Scotland. General Assembly. Committee on Public Worship and Aids to Devotion. 1234, 2257
Church of Scotland. Liturgy and ritual. 1234
Church of Scotland. Presbytery of Glasgow. 1234
Church of South India. Liturgy and ritual. Book of common worship. 3853
Church of the brethen. Districts. Eastern Pennsylvania. 1236
Church of the brethen. Districts. Southern Ohio. 1236
Church of the Brethren. 1235, 1236
Church of the Brethren. Brethren Service Commission. 1235
Church of the Brethren. Districts. Eastern Pennsylvania. 1237
Church of the brethen. Districts. Southern Pennsylvania. 1237
Church of the Brethren. Districts. Western Pennsylvania. 1237
Church of the brethen. Eastern district of Pennsylvania. 1237
Church of the Brethren. General Brotherhood Board. 1236
Church of the Brethren. General Brotherhood Board. 1236
Church of the brethen. General ministerial board. 1236
Church of the brethen. General Sunday school board. 3551
Church of the Brethren. Ministry and Home Mission Commission. 1236, 1237
Church of the Brethren. Pastor's Association. 1237
Church of the brethen. Southern district of Ohio. 1236
Church of the Holy Trinity, Stratford-upon-Avon. 3535
Church of the Nazarene. 1237
Church of the Nazarene. Commission of the Mid-Century Crusade for Souls. 1563
Church of the Nazarene. General Assembly. 1237, 2814
Church of the United brethren in Christ 'New constitution) 3731
Church of the United brethren in Christ (New constitution) Foreign missionary society. 1238
Church Peace Mission. 2809
Church, Pharcellus. 1412, 3528
Church, Ralph W. 785
Church, Richard William. 1200, 1225, 1246, 1281, 2754, 3066, 3363
Church Service League of the Diocese of Massachusetts. 2889
Church surveys. 3848
Church, Virginia Woodson Frame. 62, 3882
Church, W. H. 6, 2322
Church, William Farr. 1639, 3236
Churchill, Clinton H. 388
Churchill, Irene Josephine. 1219
Churchill, John Wesley. 2669
Churchill, Lida Abbie. 1408
[Churchill, Matilda (Faulkner 54) 1840. 2530
Churchill, May Thirza. 957, 3498
Churchill, Rhona. 3329
/churchill, Winston, 1871. 2996
Churchill, Winston. 3473
Churchill, Winston Leonard Spencer. 1937
The Churchman. 739
Churchman, John. 1109, 3812
Church of England. Book of common prayer. 1213
Churchward, Albert. 1661, 3573
Churgin, Pinkhos. 570, 3588
Churton, Edward. 1758
Churton, Edward Townson. 2518
Churton, Ralph. 2716
Chute, Marchette Gaylord. 1730, 1731, 1980
Chwala, Adolf. 2213

Chysostomus, Joanne. 1115
Chytraeus, David. 3271
Chyzhevs'kyi, Dmytro. 3257, 2707
Ciampi, Luke M. 1648, 2385
Cianfarra, Camille Maximilian. 1319, 2852, 3852
Ciarlantini, Lino Aldo. 3189
Cicero, Marcus Tullius. 1742, 3244, 3245
Cicognani, Amleto Giovanni. 758, 771, 829, 1330
Cicognani, Anteto Giovanni. 758
Cicognani, Aruleto Giovanni. 758
Cihiar, Many. 2889
Cihlar, Many. 2889
Cincik, Joseph G. 843
Cincinnati diocesan commission on church music. 1204
Cincinnatus. 2104
Ciofalo, Andrew C. 2805
Cioni, Aaffaello. 3527
Cioran, Emile M. 1380
Circuit Riders. 145, 1300, 3724
Cirencester Abbey. 743
Cirlot, Felix Lossing. 2341
Cirne-Lima, Carlos. 1590
Ciruelo, Pedro. 2731
[Cist, Charles Morton] 1859. 2246
Cistercian Studies Conference, 2d, Kalamazoo, Mich., 1972. 1276
Cistercian Studies Conference, 7th-8th, Western Michigan University, 1977-1978. 194
Ciszek, Walter J. 1277, 2942, 3851
Citron, Bernhard. 3051
Citron, Samuel J. 2133, 2154, 3166
City missionary society, Boston. 683
Ciuba, Edward J. 388
Civardi, Luigi. 753, 1135
Civis romanus. 3244
Civrieux, Marc de. 3863
Clabaugh, Gary K. 1690
Clack, Henry P. 3552
Cladder, Hermann Johann. 440
Claessens, Pieter. 1780
Claflin, Sumner Franklin. 3206
Claggett, Ralph P. 957
Claggett, Ralph Palmer. 688, 2003
Claigh, Roberleigh H. 3575
Clampett, Frederick William. 717
Clampit, Vemon L. 1575
Clampit, Vernon L. 1564
Clancy, John G. 2805
Clancy, John Gregory. 2805
Clancy, Martha (Moore) 915
Clancy, Thomas H. 868, 1374, 1946, 2267, 3492
Clancy, Walter Burroughs. 2741
Clancy, William. 3057
Clap, Mathaniel. 3349
Clapham, Alfred William. 1158
Clapham, Sir Alfred William. 1158
Clapp, Charles. 1358
Clapp, Marie Wolcott (Welles) 2546, 3839
Clapp, Mary Constance. 3853
Clapp, Theodore. 2693
Clara. 3282
Clara, of Assisi, Saint, d. 1253. Legend. 1284
Clare, Austin. 1016
Claridge, Mary. 1304
Claridge, Richard. 276
Clarie, Thomas C. 2730
Clarison. 3421
Clark, Adrian V. 1371
Clark, Albert Curtis. 384
Clark, Alexander Griffin. 1667
Clark, Ann (Nolan) 40, 3005
Clark, Benjamin Franklin. 1504
Clark, Bill. 47, 480
Clark, Calvin Montague. 1336, 3614
Clark, Carol. 3415
Clark, Charles Allen. 2185, 2536, 2929
Clark, Chester A. 2694

Clark, Clare A. 1284, 3521
Clark, Clifford E. 184, 1333
*Clark, Cline. 1720
Clark, David L. 1173
Clark, Davis Wasgatt. 1800, 2425, 2435
Clark, Dennis E. 2492
Clark, Donna. 1284, 2817
Ciruelo, Dorothy. 939, 1258
Clark, Ecward Oliver. 3797
Clark, Edgar Frederick. 2715
Clark, Edith McGill. 1284, 2485
Clark, Edward Maurice. 2533
Clark, Elijah Columbus. 1828, 3676, 3711
Clark, Elizabeth. 3832
Clark, Ellery Harding. 1887
Clark, Elmer Talmage. 1117, 1553, 2457, 1250, 1437, 2425, 2426, 2457, 2492, 2526, 2527, 2693, 2996, 3254, 3325, 3470, 3802, 3803
Clark, Eugene Francis. 1284
Clark, Faye (Aldridge) 1303
Clark, Francis. 2259

Clark, Francis Edward. 937, 1288, 1958, 3736, 1914, 3148
*Clark, Frank H. 933
Clark, Fred. 3477
Clark, George B. 1672
Clark, George Edward. 3428
Clark, George L. 1288
Clark, George Luther. 231, 347, 1102
Clark, Georgia T. 1445
Clark, Glenn. 957, 1284, 1564, 1590, 1598, 1980, 2246, 2385, 2870, 3198, 3402
Clark, Gordon. 1030
Clark, Gordon Haddon. 62, 175, 325, 2911, 3084, 3098, 3668, 3809
Clark, Harold Ballard. 203
Clark, Harold Glen. 2615
Clark, Harold Willard. 202, 522, 523, 1380, 1579, 2743, 2938, 3470
Clark, Harriet Elizabeth (Abbott) 1850. 210, 896, 1914, 3055
Clark, Hattie Arnold. 1852
Clark, Hazel Davis. 1887
Clark, Henry. 1075, 1152, 1153, 2681
Clark, Henry William. 104, 416, 419, 957, 1100, 1468
Clark, Horace. 1961
Clark, Howard Gordon. 1239, 2964
Clark, Ira. 1518
Clark, Isaac Newton. 3125
Clark, Ivo MacNaughton. 1234
Clark, J O A. 1506
Clark, James A. 1865
Clark, James Alan. 826
Clark, James Albert. 3684
Clark, James Everett. 3148
Clark, James Midgley. 3274, 1491, 2644
Clark, James Osgood Andrew. 2420, 3803
Clark, James Ratcliffe. 2610, 3430
Clark, John Alonzo. 2826, 2964
Clark, John Brittan. 1695, 1951, 3368
Clark, John Guill. 1318
Clark, John Harriman. 2050
Clark, John Kenneth. 1284
Clark, John King. 2590
Clark, John P. 38, 1743
Clark, John Ruskin. 3081
Clark, John Thomas. 293
Clark, Joseph. 637, 3552
Clark, Joseph Bourne. 2527
Clark, Joseph Sylvester. 1343
Clark, Joshua Reuben. 271, 2610
Clark, Keith. 2870, 877, 1285
Clark, Kenneth Willis. 315, 316, 334
[Clark, L]. 1284, 1691
Clark, Leslie Savage. 1437
Clark, Lillian Rosaria. 3183
Clark, Linda. 3004
Clark, Lucius Charles. 3859
Clark, M. B. Sterling. 1961
Clark, M. Edward. 1250
Clark, Margaret Lasater. 1370
Clark, Margaret Logan. 3877
Clark, Marjorie A. 2537, 2740
Clark, Mary Ann. 829, 3737
Clark, Mary Craig. 313
Clark, Mary Latham. 1992, 3026
Clark, Mary Mead. 2503
Clark, Mary T. 113
Clark, Mavis Thorpe. 2503, 2708
Clark, Mayola Johns. 651
Clark, Miles Morton. 1284, 1323, 2385
Clark, Muriel. 2005
Clark, Myrtice (Neal) 1284
Clark, Neville. 2051, 2234, 3220
Clark, Peter. 3410, 1285, 3413, 3800
Clark, Raymond. 3318
Clark, Raymond Brooke. 2547
Clark, Rebecca. 3749
Clark, Robert Donald. 3410
Clark, Robert E. D. 1403
Clark, Robert Edward David. 1737, 3081, 3792
Clark Robert Lorenzo, 1849. 2927
Clark, Robert Thomas Rundle. 2659
Clark, Rufus Wheelwright. 300, 1510, 1961, 2587, 3230
Clark, Ruth. 1934, 2864
Clark, Ruth C. 1399
[Clark, Sam H.]. 1620
Clark, Samuel. 633
Clark, Samuel A. 1484
Clark, Samuel Adams. 1508
Clark, Samuel Delbert. 734
Clark, Sereno Dickenson. 3846
Clark, Stephen B. 1245, 2402
[Clark, Susie Champney] 1856. 3461
Clark, Sydney Aylmer. 752
Clark, Sydney Sylmer. 752
Clark, Thelma Wright. 891
Clark, Theodore R. 104
Clark, Thomas Arkle. 3536
Clark, Thomas Curtis. 2047, 3209, 1887
Clark, Thomas March. 1285, 2984
Clark, Tom. 2194, 3716
[Clark, Uriah]. 1284, 3498
Clark, Vivian Vreeland. 2889

Clark, Vynomma. 3843
Clark, Walter Eugene. 1895, 1743
Clark, Walter Houston. 1782, 2994
Clark, Wayne C. 2785
Clark, Will C. 1753
Clark, Wille Thorburn. 1875
Clark, William Crawford. 3642
Clark, William Edward. 1802
Clark, William H. 2830
Clark, William Loyd. 798
Clark, William Robinson. 3041, 3305
Clark, William S. 1156
Clark, William Samuel. 1156, 2240
Clark, Willie Thorburn. 1871, 1875, 3466
Clark Briscoe Baldwin. 1356
Clarke, Adam. 221, 285, 1109, 2250, 2427, 3642, 3802
Clarke, Andral Wellington. 3410
Clarke, Arthur G. 577
Clarke, ArthurG. 1163
Clarke, Basil Fulford Lowther. 1158
Clarke, Boden. 1487, 2792
Clarke, Catherine Goddard. 3288, 3294
Clarke, Charles. 1574
Clarke, Charles Philip Stewart. 923, 1198, 881, 1173, 1217, 3279, 1024
Clarke, E. P. ed. 2796
Clarke, Edith Goreham. 3579
Clarke, Edward Hammond. 1781
Clarke, Edwin Leavitt. 2060
Clarke, Eliza. 3806
Clarke, Elizabeth W. 1772
Clarke, Ernest George. 490
Clarke, Erskine. 16, 2130
Clarke, George Arthur. 213, 2213
Clarke, Helen Archibald. 2651
Clarke, Henry Lowther. 1219, 3041
Clarke, Henry William. 3702
Clarke, Howard W. 1839
Clarke, Ida Clyde (Gallagher) 1709
Clarke, James Everitt. 923, 957, 1189, 2926
Clarke, James Franklin. 612, 713
Clarke, James Freeman. 34, 375, 421, 933, 1048, 1091, 1173, 1633, 1634, 1962, 2751, 2796, 2870, 3114, 3125, 3615, 3725, 3727, 3729
Clarke, James W. 2899
Clarke, John. 1098, 3725
Clarke, John Bertrum. 2845
Clarke, John Caldwell Calhoun. 56, 605, 2835
Clarke, John Henry. 670, 2246
Clarke, John P. 3604
Clarke, John Patrick. 1622, 1700, 3690
Clarke, Kathleen M. 957, 958
Clarke, McDonald. 3594
Clarke, Martin Lowther. 2766
Clarke, Mary Patterson. 2202
Clarke, Maurice. 440, 3858, 3859, 586, 3560, 3858
Clarke, Oliver Fielding. 1094, 3242
Clarke, Philip G. 2974
Clarke, Richard Frederick. 2032, 2200, 2262, 2385, 2498, 3423, 3460
Clarke, Richard Henry. 667, 829, 833, 2216
Clarke, Samuel. 399, 1225, 3363, 301, 302, 1737
Clarke, Sarah Dunn) 1636
Clarke, Somers. 919
Clarke, Thomas. 3198
Clarke, Thomas E. 2570
Clarke, William B. 3141
Clarke, William Francis. 3703
[Clarke, William Horatio]. 2690
Clarke, William Kemp Lowther. 221, 243, 347, 533, 1213, 1214, 1225, 1266, 2012, 3283, 3437
Clarke, William Newton. 231, 1048, 1720, 2492, 3615, 3619, 3642
Clarke, William R. 3011
Clarke Samuel. 302
[Clarkson, David]. 2697
Clarkson, E. Margaret. 1998, 3542
Clarkson, Edith Margaret. 2249, 3540
Clarkson, Tom. 3690
Clary, Dexter. 1198
Clasen, Claus Peter. 37
Clasen, Sophonius. 54
Clason, Clyde B. 1429
Clasper, Paul D. 982, 1082, 2037
Claude, Jean. 2899, 2979
Claudel, Paul. 758, 2870, 75, 209, 758
Claudy, Carl Harry. 1661, 1671
Claus, Ted. 125, 127
Claus, Tom. 1286, 2567
*Clausen, Bernard C. 1318
Clausen, Bernard Chancellor. 70, 161, 717, 1997, 2056, 2250, 2757, 2899, 2950, 3362, 3671
Clausen, Henry C. 1671, 1672
Clausen, Robert Howard. 2299, 3349
Clausing, Ludwig. 1946
Claver, Francisco F. 852, 2830
Clawson, Bertha Fidelia. 660
Claxton, Ernest Edward. 900

Claxton, John W. 1340
Clay, Alber Tobias. 2113
Clay, Albert Tobias. 207, 526, 1384, 3706
Clay, Donice L. 2385
Clay, Lucretia Hart. 3198
Clay, Rotha Mary. 1807
Claydon, Graham. 3477
Claypool, John. 161, 1349, 2907
Clayton, Alfred Stafford. 1128
Clayton, Charles Lincoln. 3077
Clayton, Geoffrey Hare. 1238
Clayton, Henry James. 1218, 1291
Clayton, John Powell. 3669, 3699
Clayton, Joseph. 49, 1908, 2273, 3038
Clayton, Philip Thomas Byard. 3703
Clayton, William. 1287, 2601, 2617
Cleage, Albert B. 669, 2024, 2233, 2681
Clearwaters, Richard V. 3531
Cleary, William H. 773
Cleaveland, Elizabeth Whittlesey. 524, 3719
Cleaveland, George Julius. 3038
Cleaver, Solomon. 2870
Clebsch, William A. 1097, 1221, 2790, 3038, 3738, 3743, 3744
Clegg, Leland. 2432
Cleghorn, Sarah Norcliffe. 2172
Cleland, David M[artin]. 615
Cleland, George McKenzie. 231
Cleland, James T. 2059, 2258, 2899, 2907
Cleland, Thomas. 1463, 3727
Clem, Paul L. 2899
Clemen, Carl Christian. 3114
Clemens, Alphonse Henry. 2337
[Clemens, Augustine Ducas]. 1653
Clemens, Bryan T. 3884
Clemens, Clara. 1030
Clemens, E. Bryan. 3372
Clemens, Frances. 3028
Clemens, Karl. 2032
Clemens, Margaret Meyers. 900, 1240, 3764
Clemens Romanus. 1093, 1287
[Clemens, Samuel Langhorne] 1835-1910. 1030
Clemens, Titus Flavius, Alexandrinus. 68, 1004, 1287
Clemens Romanus. 1093
Clement, Ernest Wilson. 2533
Clement, George H. 605
Clement, Jecques. 2633
Clement, Lora Effle. 3884
Clement, Marcel. 3441
Clement, Mary. 1181
Clement, S. R. 2562
Clementine liturgy. 2239
Clements, Bernard. 1312, 3125, 1225
Clements, Colin Campbell. 688
Clements, George Robert. 107
Clements, Ronald Ernest. 504, 511, 528, 568, 598, 1377, 1944, 2950
Clements, William M. 1257
Clemes, Gene (Phillips) 2537
Clemmitt, Thomas. 3125
Clemmons, Robert S. 1259, 3168, 3169
Clemmons, William. 982, 1169
Clemo, Jack R. 1094
Clendenin, Angela (Aaron) 2370
Clendenin, Frank Montrose. 1373, 2706
Clendening, Corinne P. 1712
Clendinning, B. A. 1254
Cleobury, F. H. 5, 1288, 1291
Clerissac, Humbert. 1117, 2019
Clerk, N. W. 1349
Clerk, William. 1489
Cles-Reden, Sibylle Emilie (von Reden) Baronin von Cles. 3108
Cleveland, Catharine Caroline. 3738
Cleveland, Clyde C. 2533
Cleveland, Denton E. 3018
Cleveland (Diocese) Board of Catholic Education. 816, 3162, 3186
Cleveland, Earl E. 1435, 3017, 3350, 3382, 3387
Cleveland, Edmund Janes. 3369
Cleveland, Edward. 298
Cleveland, Edward Earl. 3350, 3382, 3387, 3670
Cleveland. Euclid avenue Congregational church. 1271
Cleveland, George Julius. 3038
Cleveland, Grace Elizabeth (Matthews) Harlan Cleveland. 1321, 1544
Cleveland, J.J. 1929
Cleveland, Philip Jerome. 1962, 1004, 2788
Cleveland, Theodore. 2174
Cliff, John. 2323, 3439
Cliffe, Albert B. 958
Cliffe, Albert E. 958
Clifford, Cornelius. 2237
Clifford, David Leonard. 610
Clifford, Joan. 3806
Clifford, John Joseph. 2262
Clifford, Paul Rowntree. 2785
Clifford, Philip Henry. 637
Clifford, Richard J. 507, 2626

Clifford, Richard L. 1304, 2487
Clifford, T. A. 2768, 2824
Clift, Jeannette. 930, 1304
Clifton-Taylor, Alec. 751
Climenhaga, Asa W. 691
Clinard, Turner Norman. 982, 2385, 3528
Clinchy, Everett Ross. 3194
Clinchy, Russell James. 1057, 1094, 2221
Cline, Colin Marion. 3642
Cline, Rodney. 3816
Clinebell, Charlotte H. 2780
Clinebell, Howard John. 2780, 2783
Clinefelter, William R. 1376
Clinton, Desmond Kenilworth. 2499
Clinton, Inez Funk. 2825
Clinton, Kenneth. 613, 1437, 1445
Clissold, Stephen. 1028, 3603
Clizbe, John A. 3722
Clodd, Edward. 3498, 2651, 3114
Clokey, Joseph Waddell. 1209
Clonmore, William Cecil James Phillop John Paul Howard. 860, 2851
Cloonan, John Joseph. 1403, 3485
Clopton, Abner W. 3596
Close, HenryT. 1737
Clothey, Fred W. 2632
[Clotilde Angela, 1895. 3761
Cloud, Fred. 2527, 2889, 2980, 3710
Cloud of unknowing. 2644, 2646, 2647
Clough, Charlotte Marvin. 1605
Clough, Fred M. 18
[Clough, Grace Evelyn] 1876. 3684
Clough, John Everett. 2530
Clough, William A. 1605
Clough, William Overton. 2069
Clouse, Joe V. 890, 2374, 3402
Clouse, Robert G. 1087, 1181, 1550
Clouser, George Brinton McClellan. 458, 1735, 2055
Clow, William Maccallum. 1951
Clow, William MacCallum. 104, 1986, 2034, 2930
Clower, Joseph B. 1169, 2062
Clowes, Amy. 3148
Clowes, John. 2250
Clowney, Edmund P. 1008, 2899
Cloyd, Betty Shannon. 1006
Cloyd, David Excelmons. 1951, 3148
Clubb, Merrel Dare. 2633
Cluett, Robert. 321, 592, 1605
Cluff, Charles E. 1088
Clump, Cyril C. 1135
Cluny, Roland. 3279, 3280
Cluny, Russell F. 2599
Clutton-Brock, Arthur. 1048, 3619
Clymer, Reuben Swinburne. 416, 440, 442, 654, 1048, 1501, 1887, 2312, 2638, 2724, 3021, 3241, 3250, 3458, 3461, 3498, 3821
Clymer, Wayne Kenton. 2435
Clynes, Raphael. 837
Coad, Frederick Roy. 2855
Coakley, Mary Lewis. 1305, 1774, 996, 1607, 3841
Coakley, Thomas Francis. 3498
Coan, Frederick Gaylord. 2544
Coan, Lydia (Bingham) 1305
Coan, Titus Munson. 1596
Coate, Samuel. 798
Coately, Mary Josephine. 3417
Coates, Edward Osborne. 3249
Coates, James. 2844
Coates, John Rider. 3792
Coates, Thomas. 573, 422, 570, 585, 1162, 2027, 3758
Coates, Thomas F. G. 682, 3292
Coats, George W. 516, 528, 2095, 2133
Coats, William R. 1085
Cobb, Alice. 1024, 3170
Cobb, Buell. 1871, 3268
Cobb, Cora Stanwood. 3148
Cobb, Eben. 2724
Cobb, Edwin Howard. 1598
Cobb, Eunice Hale (Wait) 1305
Cobb, George Thomas. 2562
Cobb, Gerald. 2243
Cobb, Henry Nitchie. 2502
Cobb, Howell. 3642
Cobb, James Harrel. 1748
Cobb, Jesse E. 30, 401, 30
Cobb, John. 1225
Cobb, John B. 1094, 2037, 2221, 2317, 2672, 2780, 2943, 2976, 3213, 3651, 3813
Cobb, John Ross. 992
Cobb, Margaret B. 2489
Cobb, Margaret Brown. 2489, 3181
[Cobb, Sanford. 1305
Cobb, Sanford Hoadley. 3194
Cobb, Stanwood. 127, 2638
Cobb, Sylvanus. 1305, 3752
Cobb, William Henry. 1046
Cobban, Alfred [Bert Carter]. 1520
Cobbe, Frances Power. 1048, 2776, 3022, 3066, 3198, 3608, 3619
Cobbet, Thomas. 1140
Cobbett, William. 3038

Cobbin, Ingram. 198, 644, 293, 619, 1962, 3534
Cobbins, Otho Beale. 1210
Cober, Alvin Alonzo. 3143
Cober, Kenneth Lorne. 937, 3148, 3175
Coberly, Zoral. 912
Cobern, Camden McCormack. 1887, 918, 919, 1887, 2435, 2760
Cobia, Daniel. 3339
Coble, Betty J. 1303
Coblentz, Flora. 3473
Coblentz, Stanton Arthur. 1695, 2987, 3206
Coburn, John B. 929, 1295, 1976, 2246, 2870, 2889, 2972, 3350, 3484
Cocagnac, A. M. 625, 628, 2369
Cochard, Thomas S. 2385
Cochin, Jacques Denis. 2365
Cochran, Alice Cowan. 2512
Cochran, Bess (White) 1460
Cochran, James Madison. 739
Cochran, Jean Carter. 3254
Cochran, Joseph Wilson. 1807
Cochran, Leonard Hill. 958
Cochran, Louis. 1464
Cochran, Samuel Davies. 104
Cochran, Sue Eleanor. 645
Cochran, Wesley. 3461
Cochrane, Arthur C. 174, 2254, 2737, 3043
Cochrane, Charles C. 2037
Cochrane, Charles Norris. 1281
Cochrane, Elvis E. 447
Cochrane, Glynn. 739
[Cochrane, Harriet B. 3498
[Cochrane, Warren Robert] 1835-1912. 55
Cockburn, Harold Andrew. 3372
Cockburn, James. 1687
Cockburn, James Hutchison. 670, 878, 1482, 3193
Cocke, A R. 134, 369
Cocke, Alonzo Rice. 134, 369
Cocke, Charles Francis. 2775, 2957, 2974
Cocker, Benjamin Franklin. 2834, 3608
Cockhran, Jean Carter. 2853
Cockin, Frederick Arthur. 1828
cocking, George. 3350
Cockrell, U C. 462
Cockshut, A. O. J. 3212
Cocroft, Ronald Edwin. 1525
Codd, Clara M. 3684
Coddington, Henry. 1590
Code, Joseph Bernard. 667, 771, 829, 2717, 3244, 3415, 3416
Codman, John. 3762
Cody, Alexander J. 862
Cody, Alexander John. 996
Cody, Hiram Alfred. 675
Cody, Zechariah Thornton. 732
Coe, Albert Buckner. 1340, 2889
Coe, Edward Benton. 881, 2698, 3477
Coe, Frances. 3477
Coe, George Albert. 1048, 2590, 2996, 3148, 3441, 934
Coe, Kenneth. 1731
Coen, Rena Neumann. 85, 567
Coester, Donald F. 958
Cofer, David Brooks. 740, 3436
Coffer, William E. 1902
Coffey, Cecil Reeves. 3381
Coffey, James Reginald. 1475
Coffey, John W. 81, 3350
Coffey, Peter. 2179, 2737, 2738
Coffey, Reginald Mary. 1475, 3692
Coffin, Frederick, F[rentress] B[edggood]. 1380
Coffin, Harold G. 204
Coffin, Henry Sloane. 62, 104, 943, 1094, 1305, 1313, 1445, 1951, 1997, 2701, 2899, 2930, 3003, 3214, 3441, 3758, 1065, 2031, 3003, 3214, 3666
Coffin, Joseph Herschel. 2225, 3461
Coffin, Robert Peter Tristram. 2199
Coffin, William Carey. 3077
Coffin, William H. 2464
Coffin, William Sloane. 1301, 1305, 3049, 3350
Coffman, Barbara Frances. 1305
Coffman, Casper, James. 318
Coffman, Harry E. 982
Coffman, James Burton. 1313
Coffman, Ralph A. 3532
[Coffman, Roxanna]. 958
Coffy, Robert. 101
Cogan, Mary de Paul. 1633
Cogan, Mary de Pual. 2363
Cogan, Morton. 2093, 2152
Cogan, William J. 748
Cogdell, Gaston D. 1247
Cogdill, Roy E. 1248
Coggan, Donald. 450
Coggan, Frederick Donald. 409, 450, 991, 1305, 2385, 3619
Coggeshall, William Turner. 3498
Coggins, James Caswell. 1463

Coggins, R. J. 213
Coggins, Ross. 1065, 2554
Coggins, Wade T. 2492
Coggle, Betrand J. 1133
Cogley, John. 826, 874, 3057, 3744
Cognet, Louis. 3492
Cogswell, Robert E. 3402
Cogswell, William. 958, 3661, 3671
Cohausz, Otto. 853, 2796, 3195
Cohen, Abraham. 2074, 3582, 3585
Cohen, Anne (Nathan) 1305
Cohen, Arthur A. 2080
Cohen, Arthur Allen. 1825, 2080, 2141, 2149, 2152
Cohen, Barbara. 494, 1920, 2134, 2792
Cohen, Bernard Lande. 499, 2087
Cohen, Beryl David. 3371
Cohen, Boaz. 1538, 2074, 2479, 2074
Cohen, Chapman. 1653, 3389
Cohen, Daniel. 672, 1427, 1470, 1709, 2731, 2987, 3052, 3233, 3823
Cohen, G. 1045
Cohen, Gary G. 453, 462
Cohen, H. Hirsch. 523, 2711
Cohen, Harry Alan. 2146
Cohen, Hermann. 2138, 2141
Cohen, Israel. 1809, 2081, 2090, 2103, 2107
Cohen, Jack Joseph. 2106, 3057
Cohen, Jacob Xenab. 2103
Cohen, Jeremy. 53
Cohen, Joan Lebold. 1703
Cohen, Joseph. 2013
Cohen, Kitty. 2471
Cohen, Lenore. 628, 631, 634, 1785
Cohen, Mark E. 3545
Cohen, Martin A. 743, 1909
Cohen, Morris Raphael. 2082
Cohen, Mortimer Joseph. 3703
Cohen, Richard. 3548
Cohen, S. I. 2113
Cohen, Sadie Alta. 1306
Cohen, Salomon Jacob. 2138
Cohen, Samuel Meir. 2086
Cohen, Seymour J. 1623, 3361
Cohen, Simon. 2699
Cohen, Solomon. 1720
Cohn. 1091
Cohn, Arthur. 1623
Cohn, Emil. 2087, 3831
Cohn, Haim Hermann. 2068, 2074
Cohn, Jacob. 2086
Cohn, Joseph. 1519, 1630
Cohn, Joseph Hoffman. 2535, 31
Cohn, Leopold. 231, 280
Cohn, Norman Rufus Colin. 1185, 1186
Cohn, Robert L. 528
Cohon, Beryl D. 1539, 2113, 2950
Cohon, Beryl David. 568, 1329, 2013, 2113, 2118, 2119, 2138, 2149, 2154, 3335, 3361, 3371, 3361
Cohon, Samuel Solomon. 673, 2113, 2138
Coil, Henry Wilson. 1661, 1664
Coit, Henry Augustus. 3310
Coit, Richard M. 1270, 2963
Coit, Stanton. 1149
Coit, Thomas Winthrop. 1761, 3006
Coke, Paul T. 3855
Coke, Tom S. 323, 982, 1828
Coker, Charles W. 1653
Coker, Marie. 3099
Colacci, Mario. 798, 2337
Colaianni, James F. 826, 877
Colaw, Emerson S. 1986, 3734
Colbaugh, Lloyd N. 1255
Colby, Albert. 289, 958
Colby, Benjamin N. 1930, 2182
Colby, James Adams. 1513
Colby, Jean (Poindexter) 1980
Colclasure, Chuck. 458
Colclough, Joseph C. 1713
*Cole, Alan. 473
Cole, Albert. 1306
Cole, Anna. 133
Cole, C. Donald. 4, 73, 492, 2792, 3661
Cole, Charles Chester, Jr. 1575
Cole, Charles Evans. 1259
Cole, Chlries Chester. 1576
Cole, Clifford A. 3179
Cole, Clifford Adair. 567, 3216
Cole, Clifford Alonson. 1462
Cole, David. 3587
Cole, Edmund Keith. 1202, 1238, 1484, 1775, 2503, 2523, 2543, 3247, 3527
Cole, Edward B. 147
Cole, Genos. 308
Cole, George Watson. 1851
Cole, Glenn Gates. 645, 1380
Cole, J Augustus. 3322
Cole, James. 1774
Cole, Jonathan. 3406
Cole, Lucy (Cole) 2927
Cole, Lucy (Cole) Charles F. Cole." 2927
Cole, Margaret Rice. 1306, 2488
Cole, Margie Austin. 206
Cole, Marley. 1939
Cole, Martin L. 958

Cole, Mary. 3125
Cole, Maurice F. 3252
[Cole, Myrl Meyer] 1909. 1823
Cole, Orma Jeanne. 3189
Cole, Otis. 2446
Cole, Robert Alan. 379, 433, 516, 2019
Cole, Robert Glenn. 1672
Cole, Robert John. 1653
Cole, Stephen, pseud. 3410
Cole, Stewart Grant. 1690, 2562, 3057, 3148
Cole, W. Douglas. 1603
Cole, Walton E. 958
Cole, William Graham. 1673, 3389
Cole, William Grahman. 1057
Cole, William Owen. 3408
Coleman, Albert John. 3757
Coleman, Arthur D. 207, 2733
Coleman, Benjamin. 1340, 1978
Coleman, Bernard. 713, 1900
Coleman, Caryl. 854
Coleman, Charles G. 982
Coleman, Christopher Bush. 1173
Coleman, Edward Davidson. 1517, 1809, 1517
Coleman, Eleanor. 3575
Coleman, Francis X. J. 2163
Coleman, Frank Guy. 1253
Coleman, George William. 2870
Coleman, Henry. 915
Coleman, Inabelle Graves. 3466, 3468
Coleman, J A. 2427
Coleman, James Melville. 3433
Coleman, John Aloysius. 826
Coleman, John E. 2379
Coleman, John Jerome. 1328
Coleman, John Winston. 1666
Coleman, L. H. 161, 992
Coleman, Lucien E. 637
Coleman, Lyman. 1455, 282, 1190, 1241
Coleman, Michael Edward. 3661
Coleman, Richard J. 2221, 2222, 2911
Coleman, Robert Emerson. 458, 1553, 1564, 1572, 2004, 2037
Coleman, Robert Henry. 3561
Coleman, Robert J. 2196
Coleman, Satis Narrona (Barton) 1113
Coleman, Sheila Schuller. 1301, 3311
Coleman, Thomas William. 2645
Coleman, William L. 281, 319, 338, 395, 900, 930, 982, 1605, 1958, 1980, 2050, 2828, 3882
Coleman, William L. Coleman. 3884
Coleman, William V. 982
Colen, B. D. 3013, 3604
Coler, Bird Sim. 1140
Coleridge, John Taylor. 1291, 2166
Coleridge, Samuel Taylor. 305, 1146, 1306
Coles, Abraham. 2047
Coles, George. 1290, 2422, 2423, 3125, 3226
Coles, Robert. 871
Coles, Samuel B. 2501
Coleson, Edward P. 3740
Colestock, Henry Thomas. 3619
Coletti, Mina S. 1611
Colgan, Harold V. 3206
Colgrave, Bertram. 952, 1397
Colhouer, Thomas H. 2459
Colin, Louis. 2264, 2578, 2716, 2819, 2870, 3485, 3566, 3787
*Colina, Tessa. 903, 905, 1980, 2517, 2549
Colish, Marcia L. 2180
Coliville, William Wilberforce Juvenal. 3498
Colla, Rienzo. 3449
Collcutt, Martin. 2584
Colle, Beau. 1277
Colledge, Edmund. 1025
Colledge, Eric. 2645
College Theology Society. 1585, 2046, 2222, 3620, 3748, 3757
Collegeville, Minn. St. John's abbey. 3450
Collet, Mathieu Benoit. 2545
Colleton, John. 771, 1291
Collett, Sidney. 308
Colley, Asa O. 645
Colliander, Tito [Fritiof Tito Colliander]. 89
Collier, Arthur. 2417
Collier, Francis James. 3595
Collier, Frank Wilbur. 3077, 3803
Collier, Jeremy. 1345, 1478, 3605, 3606
Collier, John. 1903
Collier, Joseph Avery. 214, 1793
Collier, Katharine Brownell. 1370
Collier, Richard. 682
Collier, Robert Gordon. 2946, 3864
Collier, Robert H. 1943
Collier, Sophia. 1309
Collier, William Miller. 25, 3469
Colligan, James A. 1876
Collin, Charles Augustus. 1579
Collin de Plancy, Jacques Albin Simon 1794-1881. 1424

[Collingridge, Ignatius,]. 1266
Collings, Lewis Edward. 3441
Collingwood, R. G. 84
Collingwood, Robin George. 2417, 3099
Collins, Adela Yarbro. 458, 1312
Collins, Almer M. 3288, 3596
Collins, Anna C. 2864
Collins, Anthony. 588, 1091, 1309, 1654, 3810
Collins, Camilla Holben. 1309
Collins, Clifton Wilbraham. 2853
Collins, David R. 930, 1980
Collins, Earl L. 1590
Collins, Elijah Thomas. 3461
Collins, Elizabeth (Ballinger) Mason. 3125
Collins, Gary R. 982, 1107, 1607, 2780, 2783, 2996, 3576, 3705
Collins, George W. 1748, 2557
Collins, Harold Edward. 1156
Collins, Helen (clark) 3148
Collins, J H. 3299
Collins, James Daniel. 1425, 1720, 1732, 2169, 3022, 3108
Collins, John. 2225
[Collins, John C]. 1048
Collins, John H. 47, 2258, 2365, 3296
Collins, John J. 3057
Collins, John Joseph. 507, 511, 2740
Collins, John P. 837, 2210
Collins, John Smiley. 89
Collins, Joseph Burns. 745, 2885, 3168, 3179
Collins, Judge Gould. 1022
Collins, Mahlon D. 3288
Collins, Marjorie A. 982, 2484, 2486
Collins, Mary Lucille. 1474
Collins, Maxie Carlton. 289
Collins, Robert O. 34
Collins, Sheila D. 3835
Collins, Stanley. 589
Collins, Thomas P. 1616, 2010
Collins, Willard. 1556
Collins, William Edward. 1184, 1291, 2199, 3038
Collins, William Lucas. 1839
Collins, Woodrow Wilson. 798
Collinson, John. 1617
Collinson, Patrick. 666, 1764, 1775
Collinsworth, James Ragan. 147
Collis, Maurice. 1330, 1331
Collison-Morley, Lacy, 1875. 1709
Colloms, Brenda. 1215, 1291
Colloms, Lester Hubert. 3699
Colloque, Orrok. 3593
Colloquium on Christian Medical Ethics. 2d, Concordia Senior College, 1964. 2377
Colloquium on Religious Studies, Auckland, N.Z., 1975. 3091
Colloquium on the Teaching of Judaica in American Universities, 1st, Brandeis University, 1969. 2154
[Colloway, H. G.]. 94
[Collyer, Mary (Mitchell)]. 723
Collyer, Robert. 1322, 3590, 1310
Collyer, William Bengo. 232
Colman, Benjamin. 525, 1340, 1504, 1720, 1817, 3303, 3350, 3601
Colman, Marion. 3148
Colodner, Solomon. 566, 1323, 2094
Colombiere, Claude de la. 3485
Colomer, Luis. 755
Colonel, Philip M. 812
Colonna, Egidio. 2738
Colonne, Guido delle. 3715
Colorado. University. Libraries. Western Historical Collections. 3833
Colored Methodist Episcopal church. 1310
Colquhoun, Archibald Ross. 1905
Colquhoun, Frank. 1094, 1871, 2899
Colquhoun, Ithell. 1806
Colson, Charles W. 171, 1310, 1367
Colson, Elizabeth. 1871
Colson, Howard P. 232, 412, 937, 3162
Colson, Percy. 1057
Colston, Lowell G. 1257, 2780
Colt, Elizabeth (Buhler) 1903
Coltart, J. S. 1161
Coltharp, Bruce R. 161, 2034
Coltman, William George. 471, 545
Colton, Aaron Merrick. 1310
Colton, Ann Ree. 567, 718, 903, 1413, 1479, 1962, 2187, 2724, 2740, 3052, 3461
Colton, Calvin. 3232
Colton, Charles Henry. 996
Colton, Clarence Eugene. 161, 458, 1977, 2785, 3671
Colton, Ethan Theodore. 3875
Colton, Harold Sellers. 2165
Colum, Padraic. 80, 1310, 2651
Columbia association of Baptist churches, Washington, D. C. 169
Columbia Broadcasting System, inc. CBS News. 2805

Columbia theological seminary, Columbia, S. C. 3332
Columbia theological seminary, Decatur, Ga. 1311
Columbia university. Library. 1469
Columbia university. Teachers college. 1311, 2590
[Colville, Samuel]. 720, 1375
Colville, William J. 2733, 3313
Colville, William Wilberforce Juvenal. 1313, 3566, 3684
Colvin, Howard Montagu. 2912
Colwell, Ernest Cadman. 308, 393, 419, 422, 308, 351, 352, 393, 419, 1718, 2008, 2062
Colwell, Stephen. 804, 1149, 3441
[Colwell, Stephen]. 1312
Coman, Peter. 872
Comay, Jean. 494
Comay, Joan. 494, 533, 2095
Comba, Emilio. 3788
Combaluzier, Charles. 1579
Combe, George. 3075
Comber, Leon. 2314
Comber, Thomas. 1211
Combes, Andre. 3690
Combes, Gustave. 2756
Comblin, Joseph. 422, 465, 2015, 2051, 2222, 2480, 3288
Comboni, Daniele. 1312, 2486
Combridge, B. J. 1272, 2503
Combrink, Charles E. 1951
Combs, Bob. 1255
Combs, George Hamilton. 2012, 3055, 3141, 1466
Combs, Louis K. 3456
Come, Arnold B. 175, 177, 1117, 3596
Comeau, Jean Ambroise. 48
Comenius, Johann Amos. 958, 1273, 1274
Comer, John. 159
Comerchero, Victor. 1016
[Comerford, Thomas J]. 1821, 3316
Comfort, Alexander. 3057
Comfort, Daniel. 1490
Comfort, Eugene Chambliss. 1951
Comfort, Silas. 1657
Comfort, William Wistar. 1674, 1684, 1687, 1774, 1674, 1687
Comin, John. 2918
The coming of Christ (Motion picture) 1957
Comings, S H. 1905
Comins, Harry Leon. 570, 571
Comly, John. 3125
Commager, Henry Steele. 2776
Commander, R. G. 3723
Commentary. 53, 2080
Commins, Marie C. 3280
Commission on Christian education in Japan. 3166
Commission on Christian higher education in India. 1127
Commission on Journals Academic and Professional. 852
Committee in the ear and the religious outlook. 3441
Committee of Old order Amish and Old order Mennonites for the purpose of advocating remission of depressive school acts. 2407
Committee on the war and the religious outlook. 1039, 2518, 3148, 3441
Committee on Undergraduate Teaching. 1309
Commons, John Rogers. 3441, 1133
The Commonweal. 826, 2192
Communaute de Saint Severin. 2365
Communaute de Taize. 2257, 2583
Communications Seminar Manhattan College, 1959. 3002
Community of the Resurrection. 3651
Como, John Freeman. 3642
Cameron, Richard Morgan. 2423
Compagnie des pasteurs et professeurs de Geneve. 3042
Compayre, Gabriel. 3252
Comper, Frances M M. 3209
Comprehensive index to the writings of Ellen G. White. 3812
Compston, Herbert Fuller Bright. 1798
Compton, Arthur Holly. 1657
Compton, W. H. 1321, 1691, 3296, 3347, 3372
Compton-Rickett, Joseph. 3028
Comstock, Cyrus. 1376
Comstock, Edna Elizabeth. 647
Comstock, Harriet Theresa (Smith) 628
Comstock, Harvey D. 1905
Comstock, Jim F. 1962
Comstock, John M. 1339
Comstock, John Moore. 1339
Comstock, W. Richard. 3057
Comstock, William Charles. 3498, 3198, 3498
Comte, Auguste. 656, 2864
Conable, Francis W. 2446
[Conant, Albert Francis] 1863. 1493

Conant, Albert Francis. 1493, 1494
Conant, Hannah (Chaplin) 270
Conant, Hannah O'Brien (Chaplin) 248
Conant, Judson E. 104, 1553, 1564, 1579, 3441
Conant, Kenneth John. 3303, 1159
Conant, Newton Cooper. 611
Conant, Robert Warren. 1951, 3125
Conant, Thomas Jefferson. 140
Conant, William C. 1358
Concannon, Helena. 2793
Concetta, 1916. 996, 2335, 3610
Conchita, 1862-1937. 875, 1322
Concord, N.H. First Congregational church. 1337, 1338
Concord school of philosophy. 1510, 3708
Concordant Publishing Concern. 344
Concordia Historical Institute, St. Louis. 2282
Concordia Publishing House. 2489
Concordia publishing house, St. Louis. 2282, 2297
Concordia Theological Seminary, St. Louis. Board of Control. 1322
Conde, Bertha. 958, 1553, 958
Conder, Francis Roubiliac. 207
Condit, Ira M. 2556
Condit, Jonathan Bailey. 3339
Condon, W. D. 1654
Condre, Bertha. 958
Cone, Cecil Wayne. 669
Cone, Erastus S. 458
Cone, James H. 669, 1131, 1326, 2222, 2680, 3522, 3642
Cone, Molly. 628, 1315, 1395, 2151, 3006, 3249, 3261
Cone, Orello. 367, 388, 2062, 3288, 3439, 3657
Conerly, Porter W. 3139
Conference for religious workers, Iowa City. 2492
Conference of Baptist theological seminaries. Boston and Newton &$ Center, Mass., 1918. 3681
Conference of Lutheran college faculties. 9th, Racine, Wis., 1944. 2293
Conference of Major Religious Superiors of Women's Institutes in the United States of America. 735
Conference of Major Religious Superiors of Women's Institutes of the United States of America. Research Committee. 2575
Conference of Practical Liturgy, Spode House, 1965. 2365
Conference on Administration on the Church-Related School, Green Lake, Wis., 1948. 1127
Conference on American-Jewish Dilemmas, New York, 1971. 2155
Conference on Business and the Social Order, Valparaiso University, 1965. 1076
Conference on Christian Humanism, Asheville, N.C. 829
Conference on Christian Political and Social Thought. 2d, Georgetown University, Washigton, D. C., 1961. 943
Conference on Christian politics, economics and citizenship. 3451
Conference on Christian politics, economics and citizenship. Commission on Christianity and war. 3792
Conference on Christian politics, economics and citizenship. Commission on international relations. 1913
Conference on Christian politics, economics and citizenship. Commission on leisure. 35
Conference on Christian politics, economics and citizenship. Commission on politics and citizenship. 2858
Conference on Christian politics, economics and citizenship. Commission on the home. 1838
Conference on Christian politics, economics and citizenship. Commission on the nature of God. 1720
Conference on Christian politics, economics and citizenship. Commission on the relation of the sexes. 3392
Conference on Christian politics, economics and citizenship. Commission on the social function of the church. 1048, 3441
Conference on Christian politics, economics and citizenship. Committee on leisure. 2209
Conference on Christian politics, economics and citizenship. Regional conference, Sheffield, 1924. 3451
Conference on Christianity and mental hygiene, Greenwich, Conn., 1938. 2996
Conference on Curriculum in General Education of the Church-Related School, Grenn Lake, Wis., 1949. 1127

Conference on Data Processing in Catholic Educational Administration, Marquette University, 1964. 830
Conference on Hope and the Future of Man, New York, 1971. 1846
Conference on Inner City Research Catholic University of America, 1965. 1278
Conference on Judaism and the Christian Seminary Curriculum, Chicago, 1965. 1084
Conference on Medieval and Renaissance Studies, 5th, Ohio State University, 1974. 1391
Conference on Metropolitan Planning, San Francisco, 1963. 1278
Conference on New Approaches in Social Anthropology, Jeses College, Cambridge, Eng., 1963. 3085
Conference on Philanthropy in Action, San Francisco, 1966. 1167
Conference on Religion and American Culture, Boston? 1965? 3069
Conference on religion and public education, Princeton, N.J., 1944. 1129
[Conference on religion as a factor in shaping conduct and character, Northwestern university, 1929]. 3057
Conference on Religion in South Asia, University of California, Berkeley, 1961. 3464
Conference on Scripture teaching in secondary schools. 1st, Cambridge, 192. 300
conference on Scripture teaching in secondary schools. 2d, Oxford, 1913. 300
Conference on Society, Development, and Peace, Beirut, 1968. 1155
Conference on the Christian approach to the Jews, Atlantic City, 1931. 2535
Conference on the Communication and Interpretation of the World Mission of the Church, New York, 1965. 1317
Conference on the Inspiration and Authority of Scripture, Ligonier, Pa., 1973. 279
Conference on the Layman as a Leader of Worship, Charleston, S.C., 1968. 3004
Conference on the Meaning of the First Amendment, Indianapolis, 1963. 1150
Conference on the ministry of the Holy Spirit, Brooklyn, N.Y., 1894. 1828
Conference on the Parish Communion, Swanwick, Eng., 1962. 2253
Conference on the past, present and future of Israel, Chicago, 1890. 2113
Conference on the Philosophy of Religion, University of Birmingham, 1970. 3108
Conference on the Spiritual Care of Puerto Rican Migrants, 1st, San Juan, P.R., 1955. 1255
Conference on Theology and Body, Emory University, 1973. 2326
Conference on Theravada Buddhism. University of Chicago 1962. 3110
Conference Towards a Global Congress of World Religions, 1st, San Francisco, 1977. 3091
Conference Towards a Global Congress of World Religions, 2d, Boston, 1978. 3091
Conference on Shared Time, University of Rhode Island, 1965. 3401
Conferences on Christian work in Latin America, Lima, Santiago, etc., 1916. 2548
Conforti, Joseph A. 1847, 3660
Confraternity of Christian Doctrine. 270, 274, 764, 853, 1330, 2851, 3165, 3762
Confraternity of Christian doctrine. National catechetical congress. 866
Confraternity of Christian doctrines. 1330
Confrey, Burton. 1262, 119, 753, 1129, 3175, 3333, 3453, 3537, 3884
Confucius. 1537, 2838
[Congar, Marie Joseph]. 807, 1731, 2009, 2191, 2192
Congar, Marie Joseph [secular name: Georges Yves Congar]. 1117, 2191
Congar, Marie Joseph, [Secular name: Georges Yves Congar]. 3294
Congar, Yves Marie Joseph. 776, 807, 817, 870, 1043, 1117, 2009, 2015, 2191, 2192, 3294, 3307, 3632, 3654, 3706
Congdon, Howard K. 1413
Congdon, Ruth. 2385
Conger, Arthur Bloomfield. 1098
Conger, George Perrigo. 2461, 2179, 3099
Conger, Margaret Guild. 671, 2317
Conger, Wilda Lowell. 1695

Congo Protestant council. 2513
Congregational board of publication. 3706
Congregational church building society. 1335
Congregational church extension boards. 1332

Congregational churches in Connecticut. General association. 1333, 1335, 1336, 1344, 1346
Congregational churches in Connecticut. General conference. 1336, 1339
Congregational churches in Connecticut. Saybrook synod, 1708. 1333, 1336
Congregational churches in Massachusetts. 1336, 1337
Congregational churches in Massachusetts. Boston synod, 1680. 1336
Congregational churches in Massachusetts. Cambridge synod, 1648. 1337, 1344
Congregational churches in Massachusetts. Ecclesiastical council, Groton. 1826. 1337
Congregational churches in Massachusetts. Mendon association. 58
Congregational churches in the U.S. Ecclesiastical council, Brooklyn, 1876. 184, 693
Congregational foundation for education. 1338
Congregational home missionary society. 1343
Congregational Methodist Church. 1343, 2439
Congregational Sunday school extension society. 1343
The Congregationalist and Advance, Boston. 1344
The Congregationalist and herald of gospel liberty. 1456
Congress of Colored Catholics of the United States. 15
Congress on Africa, Atlanta, 1895. 2497
Congress on Christian work in Latin America, Panama, 1916. 2548
Congress on Christian work in South America, Montevideo, 1925. 2547
Congress on prophecy, 1st, New York, 1942. 2464
Congress on prophecy. 2d, New York, 1943. 2465
Congress on Prophecy. 3d, Chicago, 1963. 610
Congress on Prophecy, 5th, New York, 1967. 605
Congress on Prophecy, 7th, New York, 1973. 610
Congress on Prophecy, 6th, New York, 1970. 610
Congress on the Church's Worldwide Mission, Wheaton, Ill., 1966. 2514
Congress on the Urban Church, Chicago, 1978. 1279
Congress on World Missions, Chicago. 1960. 2514
Congreve, George. 2735
Coniaris, Anthony M. 941, 2072, 2745, 2751, 3363
Conklin, Dorothy Whitney. 1828
Conklin, Edmund Smith. 2996
Conklin, George Newton. 240
Conklin, George W. 1521
Conklin, Robert. 3477
Conklin, Robert H. 134
Conkling, J. Christopher. 2617, 3430
Conkling, Wallace Edmonds. 2034, 2719, 3350, 958, 3675
Conley, Herbert N. 1413
Conley, John Wesley. 142, 232, 313, 1190, 1579
Conley, Kieran. 3693, 3821
Conley, Patrick T. 824, 3234
Conley, Thomas H. 1458, 2783
Conlon, Anastasia E. 3206
Conn, Charles Gerard. 2870
Conn, Charles Paul. 313, 744, 941, 1358, 2337, 3538
Conn, Charles W. 530, 533, 637, 958, 1229, 1427, 2814
Conn, Charless W. 1229
Conn, Grace L. 142
Conn, Harvie M. 3656
Conn, Howard James. 1757, 1845
Conn, Reuben R. 3413
Conn, Walter E. 1347
Connecticut congregational club, Hartford. 3549
Connell, Francis Jeremiah. 3011, 947, 1298, 3372, 3401, 3433
Connell, Francis Jermiah. 3011
[Connell, James MacLuckie] ed. 1223
Connell, James MacLuckie. 1445, 1455
Connell, James Maeluckie. 511
Connellan, Colm. 1745
Connelly, H. Walton. 3148
Conner, J.M. 3615
Conner, Miles Washington. 3148
Conner, Paul M. 877
Conner, Robert. 1347, 3425
Conner, Walter Thomas. 161, 369, 475, 1346, 1828, 3642, 107, 369
Conners, Kenneth Wray. 1006, 2385
Connery, John R. 3, 3166
Connick, C. Milo. 409, 637, 1962, 3335

Conniff, James C G. 1985, 2365, 2852, 3401
Conniff, Paul Raphael. 996
Conning, Gordon. 1010, 2930
Conning, John Stuart. 2082
Connole, Roger Joseph. 3184
Connolly, Donald. 2385
Connolly, Eileen. 3588
Connolly, Francis Xavier. 1090
Connolly, James M. 1817, 3617
Connolly, John Patrick. 1355
Connolly, John R. 1590
Connolly, Richard Hugh. 1816
Connolly, Sean. 836, 1293
Connor, Edward. 2357, 2946
Connor, Elizabeth. 1703
Connor, George Cooper. 1671
Connor, Helen N. 3498
Connors, Charles Paul. 18
Conover, Charles Eugene. 2590
Conover, Elbert Moore. 1156
Conovitz, Michael. 2101
Conquest, Robert. 3257
Conrad, Arcturus Z. 958, 1590, 1951, 1999, 3231
Conrad, Arcturus Zodiac. 1340, 2562
Conrad, Arcutus Z. 1048
Conrad, Donald Williams. 2889
Conrad, Jack Randolph. 713
Conrad, Paul. 1266
Conrad, Paul H. 3528
Conrad, Robert Taylor. 1445
[Conradi, Ludwig Richard] 1856-1939. 3382
Conrey, Helen Krystal. 318
Conroy, Joseph P. 338, 893, 1305, 1400, 3168, 3870
Considine, Daniel. 9
Considine, John J. 3245
Considine, John Joseph. 821, 849, 867, 1477, 2198, 2538, 3017, 3245
Considine, Michael J. 823
Considine, Robert Bernard. 867
Consortium Perfectae Caritatis. 2574
Constable, Giles. 2583, 3702
Constable, John W. 1198
Constant, Alphonse Louis. 2005, 2312, 2314, 3441, 3588
Constant, Gustave Leon Marie Joseph. 3038
Constantelos, Demetrios J. 2346, 2744
Constantino, Samuel August. 958
Constantinople (Patriarchate) 1354
Constas, Constantine J. 453
Consulta Latinoamericana de Iglesia y Sociedad. 2d, El Tabo, Chile, 1966. 3434
Consultation on Church Union. 1039, 1210, 1355, 2954
Consultation on Future Evangelical Concerns, Atlanta, 1977. 1553
Consultation on the Future of Philosophical Theology, McCormick Theological Seminary, 1970. 2832
Consultation on the Future of the Campus Ministry, 1st, Cambridge, Mass., 1969. 885
Consultation on the Lay Ministry, Charleston, S.C., 1967. 2192
Consultation on the Person and Work of the Holy Spirit, Eastern Mennonite College, 1972. 1833
Consultation on Theology and Mission, 2d, School of World Mission and Evangelism, Trinity Evangelical Divinity School, 1979. 2514
Consultation on Theology and Mission, School of World Mission and Evangelism, Trinity Evangelical Divinity School, 1976. 2481
Conte, Anthony E. 823
Contemporary Theology Institute, 2d, Loyola College, Montreal, 1965. 3654
Conti, Flavio. 750, 1156, 3142
Conti, Natale. 2655
Continuing Committee on Muslim-Christian Cooperation. 1925
Continuing Consultation on Future Evangelical Concerns, Overland Park, Kan., 1978. 1553
Contos, Leonidas. 2746
Convention of seceding masons. Le Roy, N.Y., 1828. 1668
Converse, Berthae Harris. 2549
[Converse, Chales Crozat] 1832. 2374
[Converse, Charles Crozat] 1832. 2374
[Converse, Charles Crozat] 1832-1918. 3561
Converse, Frederick Shepherd. 917
Converse, Gordon N. 2764
Converse, Hyla Stuntz. 2548
[Converse, Lizzie S.] 1835-1891. 1357
Convis, Lewis Albert. 1201
Convocation on Medicine and Theology, Mayo Clinic and Rochester Methodist Hospital, 1967. 2377

Convocation on Preaching in College and University Communities, 1st, Cincinnati, 1961. 3757
Conway, Bertrand Louis. 785, 3780, 785
Conway, Charles Abbott. 929, 2270
Conway, David. 2312
Conway, E. Carolyn. 3284
Conway, Flo. 1085
*Conway, J. D. 1117
Conway, James. 804
Conway, James D. 3011
Conway, James Franklin. 1057
Conway, Jim. 2462
Conway, John Donald. 795, 947, 1373
Conway, John Placid. 2899
Conway, John S. 1145
Conway, Joseph P. 874
Conway, Katherine Eleanor. 823, 870
Conway, Marion N. 3372
*Conway, Martin. 1048
Conway, Moncure Daniel. 1367, 1798, 2088, 3122, 3268, 3457, 3729
Conway, Robert Seymour. 3246
*Conway, Thomas D. 748
Conwell, Russell Herman. 3538, 958, 1368, 3350, 161, 958, 2870, 3339, 3523, 3538
Conybeare, Frederick Cornwallis. 351, 1083, 1469, 1770, 1978, 3324
Conybeare, John Josias. 287
Conybeare, William John. 2796
Conzad, Simeon Earl. 3369
Conze, Edward. 701, 704, 707, 709, 710
Conze, Edward [Name orig.: Eberhard Julius Dietrich Conze. 707
Conzelmann, Hans. 322, 431, 475, 1190, 2037
Coogan, Aloysius F. 8, 2211
Coogan, Jane. 3417
Cook, Abel Lincoln. 1371, 2225
Cook, Albert E. 1895
Cook, Albert Spaulding. 549, 2219, 2648
Cook, Albert Stanburrough. 210, 271, 1757
Cook, Alonzo Laker. 2610
Cook & Watkins. 3333
Cook, Arthur Bernard. 1395, 3895
Cook, Arthur Malcolm. 683
Cook, Charles Augustus. 190, 1741, 2518, 2870
Cook, Charles Cyrus. 1513, 1598, 1720
Cook, Charles Thomas. 1754
Cook, David C. 1111, 2385, 3552, 1368
Cook, David Caleb. 619, 1741, 1751, 1823, 1999, 2014, 2870
Cook, E.U. 298
Cook, E.W. 3410
Cook, E. Wake. 3330
Cook, Earleen H. 3238
Cook, Edmund Francis. 644, 2454
Cook, Elizabeth Blanchard. 300
Cook, Ellen A. Pennau. 3498
Cook, Ellen A. Peunau. 3498
Cook, Ezra Albert. 100, 951
Cook, Ezra Asher. 1665, 1894
Cook, Francis H. 120, 2166
Cook, Frederick. 3284
Cook, George Allan. 3822
Cook, George Henry. 751, 882, 1270, 2230, 2569
Cook, Georgiana (Hemingway) 2128
Cook, Harold E. 3398
Cook, Harold R. 1171, 2492, 2525, 2554
Cook, Harriet N. 480
Cook, Jerry. 2347, 3678
Cook, John Wesley. 637
Cook, Joseph. 662, 1068, 1368, 3620, 3708
Cook, Leland A. 2698
Cook, Mabel (Collins) 3684
Cook, Martha. 3461
Cook, Melvin Alonzo. 3082
Cook, Michael L. 2037
Cook, Olive. 2
Cook, Paul E. 2257
Cook, Peter. 1962
Cook, Richard Briscoe. 1962
Cook, Robert A. 982
Cook, Robert Dane. 1793
*Cook, Roselynn. 3766
Cook, Shirley. 1368, 2462
Cook, Silas Arthur. 1828, 3339, 3595
Cook, Stanley Arthur. 232, 309, 539, 1057, 3099, 309
Cook, Theodore Dwight. 1368
Cook, Thomas C. 1257
Cook, Virginia D. 3856
Cook, W. Robert. 414
Cook, Walter L. 1749, 1750, 1976, 2402, 3661, 3882, 3883
Cook, Warren F. 1199
Cook, Webster. 1538, 2163
Cook, William. 2856
Cook, William H. 992
Cooke, A. Ernest. 276
Cooke, Allan Worthington. 3238

Cooke, Bernard J. 62, 651, 996, 1602, 2254, 2791, 3264, 3711
Cooke, C. H. 605
Cooke, Frances E. 2776
Cooke, George Alfred. 2428
Cooke, George Willis. 33, 1457, 3086, 3727
Cooke, Gerald. 1078
Cooke, Greville. 1962
Cooke, Harriet B. 3090
Cooke, John Blair Deaver. 2899
Cooke, Joseph R. 1751
Cooke, Josiah Parsons. 3075
Cooke, Marjorie Benton. 1111
Cooke, Nicholas Francis. 3392
Cooke, Parsons. 952, 1775, 3498
Cooke, Patrick. 1287, 2111
Cooke, Richard Joseph. 1654, 2806, 1892, 2796, 3256, 3780
Cooke, Terence James. 856
Cooke, Walter Evans. 533
Cooking, George. 1445
Cookman, George Grimston. 1744, 2422
Cooksey, Joseph James. 2500
[Cooksey, Nicias B.]. 1427
[Cooksey, Nicias Ballard] 1846. 958, 1030, 1368, 1484, 3512
Cookson, Richard. 1962
Cookston, Roy. 24
Coole, Arthur Braddan. 1368, 2485
Cooledge, Daniel. 1674
*Cooley, Alva Edison. 2476
Cooley, Benjamin Franklin. 3498
Cooley, Charles Horton. 3198
Cooley, Donald Gray. 3539
Cooley, Frank L. 1101
Cooley, James H. 1117
Cooley, John K. 12
Cooley, Timothy Mather. 1792, 3807
Cooley, William Forbes. 1951
Coolidge, Herbert. 2624
Coolidge, John S. 3006
Coolidge, Olivia E. 2651
Coomaraswamy, Ananda Kentish. 701, 1813, 701, 1813
Coombe, Thomas. 2414
Coombs, J Vincent. 3114
Coombs, James Vincent. 1553, 1564, 3339
Coome, Hannah (Grier) 3125
Coon, Edwin C. 2865
Coon, Glenn A. 1012, 2337, 2385, 2887
Coon, J. M. 438
Coon, Reune Runyon. 1699
Coon, Zula Evelyn. 3856
Cooney, Barbara, 1917. 898, 1111
Cooney, Cyprian. 785, 3650
Cooney, Eugene J. 3182
Coonoor Conference on the Healing Ministry of the Church, 1967. 1601
Cooper, Aldrage B. 1668
Cooper, Allen B. 1250
Cooper, Cairbanu B. 1710
Cooper, Charles Champlin. 3057
Cooper, Charles S. 3381
Cooper, Claire (Hill) 3528
Cooper, Clay. 2554
Cooper, Clayton Sedgwick. 637, 1308
Cooper, Darien B. 2337
Cooper, David Lipscomb. 445, 458, 508, 605, 1731, 2000, 2016, 2414, 2760, 3288, 3661
Cooper, David Lipscomn. 519
Cooper, Donald B. 1224, 2537
Cooper, Douglas. 982, 2135, 2264
Cooper, Duff. 1404
*Cooper, Duff [Alfred Duff Cooper] 1st Viscount Norwich of Aldwick. 1404
Cooper, Harold E. 423
Cooper, Irving Steiger. 3052, 2987, 3052, 1785, 3052, 3053, 3684
Cooper, J. C. 3574
Cooper, James Alfred. 3552
Cooper, John Charles. 1553, 2462, 2733, 3409, 3656, 3884
Cooper, John Montgomery. 25, 780, 3057, 25
Cooper, Joseph. 232, 3803
Cooper, Luther L. 1167
Cooper, Mary (Hanson) 1285, 3125
Cooper, Michael. 3243
Cooper, Mildred. 3845
Cooper, Norman B. 825, 1149
Cooper-Oakley, Isabel. 3274
Cooper, Owen. 992, 3464
Cooper, Raymond Westervelt. 1564
Cooper, Robert. 232, 1887
Cooper, Rufus Thatcher. 1945
Cooper, Sara Kate. 2536
Cooper, Simon Wheeler. 1403
Cooper, Susan Fenimore. 3422
Cooper, Thomas. 2336, 2365, 204
Cooper, W. Norman. 2264, 2996
Cooper, William A. 3362
Cooper, William Barrett. 3719
Cooper, William Colby. 1887
Cooper, William Gustin. 1918
Cooper, William Wiseman. 1661

Cooperative Curriculum Development. 3162
Cooperative Curriculum Project. 3162
Coopersmith, Harry. 3577
Coosa River Baptist association. 143
Coote, Robert B. 35, 485
Copass, B A. 538
Copass, Benjamin Andrew. 35, 486, 542, 558
Cope, Gilbert Frederick. 1156, 3573
Cope, Henry Frederick. 3553, 940, 958, 1607, 1865, 3148, 3553, 3561, 3800
Cope, Jackson I. 58, 1715
Cope, O. Lamar. 442
Copeland, A Reilly. 253, 1030
Copenhaver, Laura Scherer. 2757, 3144
Copleston, Frederick Charles. 2737, 2835, 3695
Copleston, Reginald Stephen. 701
Copp, Zed Hopeful. 1605
Coppa, Frank J. 1101
Coppage, Lewellyn Jackson. 1030, 1057
Coppens, Charles. 1886, 785, 1945, 2365, 2385
Coppens, Joseph. 504
Copper, Arnold. 1368, 3519
Coppin, Ezra. 174, 928, 1368, 1573
Coptic Church. 1368
Coptic church. Liturgy and ritual. 1369
Coraopolis. Pa. First Presbyterian church. 2918
Coray, Henry W. 1301, 2308
Corbett, C T. 2620
Corbett, Charles H. 533
Corbett, Edwin A. 1574
Corbett, Jack Elliott. 568, 570, 1139, 2480, 2950
Corbett, James Arthur. 2769
Corbett, Janice M. 1253, 1261
Corbett, Pearson Harris. 1782, 2601, 3427
Corbin, Bruce. 453
Corbin, Henry. 3544
Corbishley, Thomas. 755, 758, 1065, 2049, 2060, 2182, 2870, 3475, 3521, 3592
Corbon, Jean. 241, 287, 996, 3224
Corcao, Gustavo. 1363
Corcoran, Jerome. 830
Corcoran, Mary Irma. 2470
Corcoran, Matthew J. 3238
Cord, Robert L. 3195
Corderoy, Edward. 3031
Cordes, Liane. 2385
Cordley, Richard. 3350
Cordovero, Moses. 1539
Corduan, Winfried. 3659
Core, Arthur C. 2752
Coreth, Emerich. 2417
Corey, Arthur. 1030, 1494
[Corey, George W]. 3527
Corey, Stephen J. 2540, 2547
Corey, Stephen Jared. 1464, 2513, 2518, 2519, 2549
Corey, Vickie Hyde. 1369, 2487
Corey, William A. 100
Corfe, Thomas Howell. 1763, 2517, 2793, 3692
Coriell, Ron. 109, 2719, 3782
Cork, Delores Freeman. 171, 1612
Corke, Helen. 2201
Corkey, Robert. 943
Corless, Roger. 2365, 3477
Corlett, William. 523, 707, 1094, 1813, 1921, 2138, 3057
Corley, Daniel B. 338
Corley, Francis J. 3280
Corley, Francis Joseph. 3280
Corliss, Carlton Jonathan. 894
Cormack, Alexander Allan. 3702
Cormack, Maribelle. 3819
Cormier, Henri. 2012
Cormier, Hyacinthe Marie. 3025
Cornelis, Humbert. 3221
Cornelison, Isaac Amada. 1150, 1358
Cornelius, Elias. 3848
Cornell, Clarence Ellsworth. 1564
Cornell College, Mount Vernon, Iowa. 3757
Cornell, George W. 338, 1044, 1094, 1962, 2805, 3620
Cornell, Jean Gay. 1930, 3414
[Cornell, John Henry]. 883
Cornell, Thomas Charles. 771, 1135
Cornell University. Libraries. 1369, 3825
Cornet, N E. 2870
Cornfeld, Gaalyahu. 207, 243, 3599
Cornford, Francis MacDonald. 1766, 2835
Cornford, Francis Macdonald. 1766
Cornil, Victor. 1817
Cornill, Carl Heinrich. 539, 2950, 2084
*Cornils, Stanley P. 1774
Corning, Amos Elwood. 673
Corning, James Leonard. 36, 3125
Corning, W H. 1406, 3498
Cornish, Frances Eliot(Foote) 1369
Cornish, G. P. 3096

Cornish, Louis Craig. 3725, 34, 1882, 3709
Cornwall Collective. 1300
Cornwall, E. Judson. 341, 517, 982, 1633, 1823, 2037, 2867, 3579
Cornwall, Judson. 584, 952, 1590
Cornwall, Nathanael Ellsworth. 1202
[Cornwallis, Caroline Frances]. 1038, 2835
Cornwell, Arthur Temple. 473
Corporation for the promoting and propagating the gospel of Jesus Christ in New England, London. 1507, 2541
Corporation for the relief of the widows and children of clergymen in the communion of the Church of England in America. 1222
Corporation Trust Company. 1369
Corpus, Severino F. 1625, 2556
Corrall, Alice Enid. 2948
Correa, Gustavo. 3145
Correctional research. 885
Correll, Charles Meclain. 1336
Correll, Marsha M. 1712
Corrigan, John E. 947
Corrigan, Patrick. 667
Corrigan, Raymond. 808
[Corry, Mary Alphonsa. 3767
Corsi, Cosimo. 746
Corson, Fred Pierce. 958, 1117, 2420, 3148
Corson, Hiram. 3498
Corstanje, Auspicius van. 1027, 1640, 1644, 1648
Corswant, Willy. 209
Corvin, R. O. 492, 1404
Corwin, Charles. 3086
Corwin, Charles Edward. 3045
Corwin, Edward Tanjore. 3044, 3045
Corwin, Virginia. 1882
Cory, Daniel. 3302
Cory, David Munroe. 3433
Cory, Herbert Ellsworth. 1363
Coryn, Sidney G P. 1590
Corzine, Jesse Lynn. 1259, 3148, 3179
Cosby, Eschol. 1022
Cosby, Gordon. 1169, 3797
[Cosgrove, Eugene Milne]. 2724, 3198, 3864
Cosgrove, Francis M. 1010
Cosgrove, John. 2860, 3278
Cosgrove, John J. 3469
Cosgrove, Joseph G. 1346
Cosin, John. 1224
Cosper, Wilbert Le Roy. 2675
Coss, Richard David. 1367, 1371
Coss, Thurman L. 1409
Cossitt, Franceway Ranna. 1396, 1582
Cossum, William Henry. 2626, 3339
Costa, Aloysius Maria. 104
Costa, Dennis. 56, 1402
Costa, Horacio de la. 1948
Costa, Isaac da. 397
Costa, Manuel Joseph. 982
Costanzo, Joseph F. 1128, 2188
Costas, Orlando E. 1117, 2555, 2954
Costas, Peter J. 3642
Coste, Pierre. 3779
Costello, Charles Joseph. 114, 305
Costello, Don. 2889
Costello, Gerald M. 2537
Costello, John Michael. 1474
Costello, Joseph A. 887
Costello, Mary Loretto. 3418
Costelloe, Laurence. 675
Costeloe, Michael P. 822, 1147
Cote, Richard G. 1751
Cotel, Pierre. 3787
Cotham, Perry C. 1085
Cothen, Grady C. 1564, 3464
Cothens, Joe. 2788
Cothern, Fayly H. 3884
Cothonay, Marie Bertrand. 2350, 2351
Cothran, J. Guy. 958, 1793, 1838
Cott, Elizabeth (Buhler) 1802, 2489, 3387
Cottam, Joseph Almond. 3339, 3661
Cotter, Anthony Charles. 62
Cotter, James Henry. 1112
Cotterell, Arthur. 2658
Cotterell, F. Peter. 2517
Cotto, Pablo. 1133
Cotton, Charles. 1647
Cotton, Edward Howe. 3084, 3081
Cotton, Henry. 212, 270, 274
Cotton, James Harry. 1068, 1740
Cotton, John. 324, 593, 1334, 1340, 2223, 3817, 134
Cotton, Paul. 3546
Cotton, Rowland. 723
Cottrell, Donald Peery. 3733, 3759
Cottrell, Georgia Wright. 3
Cottrell, Jack. 982, 1313, 3295
Cottrell, Ralph. 934, 3372
Cottrell, Roy Franklin. 1513, 207, 610, 645
Couasnon, Charles. 1943
Coube, Stephen. 2256
Couburn, John B. 2964

Couch, Helen F. 898, 3856, 3882
Couchman, Bob. 1169
Coudreau, Francois. 746, 3170
Cougar, Marie Joseph. 1951
Coughlan, Peter. 845, 856, 1265, 1838, 2257
Coughlin, Bernard J. 1139
Coughlin, Charles E. 3441
Coughlin, Charles Edward. 785, 862, 2862, 3450
Coughlin, D R. 221
Coughtry, Frank W. 232, 1091
Coulson, Charles Alfred. 3077, 3082, 3592
Coulson, John. 1188, 2702, 3681
Coult, Allan D. 3096
Coulton, George Gordon. 2582, 193, 798, 1185, 1908, 2583, 2862, 3274, 84, 193, 1185, 1186, 1908, 2582, 3286, 3287
Council against intolerance in America. 34
Council for Religion in Independent Schools. 2942
Council of church boards of education. 3191
Council of evangelism, East Northfield, Mass. 1564
Council on Christian Unity. 134, 1046
Council on Evangelism, St. Louis, 1968. 1573
Councillor, Homer, J. 1118
Countryman, L. William. 3799
Counts, Bill. 982, 1962
Coupland, William Chatterton. 3204
Courcy de Laroche-Heron, Henri de. 833
Courlander, Harold. 1780, 3582
Cournos, John. 2013, 2117, 2946
Coursey, Oscar William. 1962, 2127
[Courson, Barbara Frances Mary (Neave) de. 1946
Court, John Hugh. 2863
Court, John M. 458
Courtenay, Charles. 2735
Courtenay, Walter Rowe. 3661
Courtenay, William. 3783
Courtenay, William J. 599
Courtney, Lloyd McFarland. 2927
Courtney, Mary Prideaux. 1758
Courtney, Star L. 2625
Courtney, William Leonard. 2225
Courtois, Gaston. 1298, 2385, 2572, 3485
Courvoisier, Jaques. 3033, 3899
Couse, Adam. 2843
Cousins, Ewert H. 675, 2944, 3593
Cousins, Mary. 43, 2886, 3284
Cousins, Norman. 2225, 3311
Cousins, Oliver A. 1720
Cousins, Sidney Leslie. 461
Coutts, John James. 3293
Coutts, John William. 653
Couturier, Charles. 849
Couturier, Marie Alain. 2347
Cove, Mary K. 934
Covell, Jon Etta Hastings Carter. 1883, 2940
Covell, Ralph R. 2349, 2485, 3680
Coventry, John. 62, 1590, 2037, 2365
Coverdale, Miles. 1216
Covert, William Chalmers. 1048, 2925, 3057, 3441
Covey, Cyclone. 1413
Covina, Gina. 2752, 2753
Covington, Ava Marie. 3380
Covington, G. Edwin. 3537
Covington, Jim. 1377
Covington Ky. Western Baptist theological institute. 154
Cowan, Aldworth. 517, 2037, 3579
Cowan, Arthur Aitken. 1234, 2899
Cowan, George M. 652, 2230, 3545
Cowan, Henry. 2181, 1173, 2181
Cowan, Ian Borthwick. 1375, 2569, 3042
Cowan, John Franklin. 1152, 1564, 2886
Cowan, Paul. 1377, 2081
Cowan, Richard O. 2610, 3428
Cowan, St. Michael. 996, 1323, 3485
Cowan, Wayne H. 794
Cowan, William. 1199
Cowan, William Hardy. 1057
Cowan John Franklin. 2886
Coward, Parnell C. 453
Cowden, John Brandon. 413, 1039
Cowdrey, Herbert Edward John. 1304
Cowdrick, Ruth Elizabeth. 179
[Cowell, Harriet Hamilton. 742
Cowen, Clarence Eugene. 1229
Cowgill, Frank Brooks. 1962
Cowgill, George W. 3461
Cowherd, Raymond Gibson. 1765
Cowie, Ian. 1430
Cowie, Leonard W. 1173, 1262, 2273, 3033
Cowie, Vera. 121, 2744
Cowing, Cedric B. 3214
Cowing, Lawrence Albert. 1229
Cowles, Alton House. 1739
Cowles, Edward Spencer. 2378

Cowles, Henry. 367, 413, 426, 440, 453, 467, 402
Cowles, Justus A. B. 1078
Cowles, S. Macon. 1015, 2191
Cowley, Frederick George. 2584
Cowley, Matthew. 2607
Cowley, Matthias Foss. 2610, 3846
Cowley, Patrick. 8
[Cowley, Richard F]. 3259
Cowling, Ellis. 3528
Cowling, Maurice. 3452
Cowman, Lettie (Burd) 1350, 1377, 1430, 1437, 1445
Cowper, William. 2856
Cox, Alva I. 3149
Cox, Anna Grace. 1435
Cox, Christopher Christian. 1730
Cox, Claire. 3189, 3744
Cox, Clyde C. 463
Cox, David. 2159, 2160, 3661
Cox, Edward William. 3498
Cox, Edwin. 3164
Cox, Emmett D. 1238, 2546
Cox, Enos Kincheloe. 2870, 492
Cox, Ethlene (Boone) 958, 3468
Cox, Francis A. 2508
Cox, Francis Augustus. 170, 3839
Cox, Frank. 3339
Cox, Frank Lucius. 426, 3373
Cox, George William. 2651, 2654, 2660, 2664, 3244
Cox, Harvey. 1065
Cox, Harvey Gallagher. 1065, 1153, 1378, 1393, 1623, 1629, 3058, 3421, 3448
Cox, Hugh S. 546
Cox, James H. 3203
Cox, James Taylor. 1234
Cox, James William. 161, 298, 2899
Cox, Jeffrey. 1220, 3451
Cox, John Charles. 1159, 1169, 1270, 2827
Cox, John Dee. 1173
Cox, Joseph Godfrey. 3613
Cox, Mabel Crampton. 2757
Cox, Melville Babbage. 1378
Cox, Michael J. 3286
Cox, Norman Wade. 151, 2945, 3884
Cox, Richard H. 2996
Cox, Robert. 1629
Cox, Roger L. 1101, 3399
Cox, Samuel Hanson. 880, 1691, 2364, 3671
Cox, Thomas Edward. 769, 1118
Cox, William Edward. 2960, 1467, 1530, 2465
Coxe, Antony Hippisley. 1710
Coxe, Arthur Cleveland. 1173, 2889, 2960, 2969
Coxe, John Redman. 1654, 1999
Cox-Gedmark, Jan, 1950. 1783
Coy, Martin. 1839
Coyle, Henry. 3206, 755
Coyle, Neva. 931, 1378, 1430
Coyle, Robert Francis. 73
Coyle, Wallace. 3818
Coyne, Anne. 3778
Coyne, Jack. 2481
Coyne, William D. 2179
[Coyner, John McCutchen]. 2601
Cozad, Simeon Earl. 3533
Cozens, M L. 1804
Crabb, Cecil Van Meter. 2997
Crabb, Lawrence J. 1107
Crabbe, George. 3580
[Crabbe, J. K.]. 3094
Crabtree, Arthur Bamford. 2161
Crabtree, June. 934
Crabtree, T. T. 3373
Cracraft, James. 1148, 2824
Cracraft, John W. 3661
Cracroft, Richard H. 1231
Craddock, Fred B. 388, 2049, 2899
Crafts, Glenn Alty. 1531
Crafts, Sara J (Timanus) 3553
[Crafts, Wilbur Fisk]. 474, 3086, 3565
Crafts, Wilbur Fisk. 637, 906, 1202, 1980, 2720, 3075, 3441, 3539, 3546, 3547, 3559, 3595
[Crafts, William]. 2856
Cragg, G R. 1221
Cragg, Gerald Robertson. 119, 1181, 1221, 3006
Cragg, Herbert W. 341
Cragg, Kenneth. 1074, 1921, 2564, 2567, 2885
Craghan, John F. 563
Craghead, Robert. 2259
Cragin, Laura Ella. 625, 633, 3198, 3547
Cragin, Louisa T. 1962
Craig, Archibald C. 951, 2899
Craig, Archibald Gordon. 1133, 2062, 3441
Craig, Asa Hollister. 2820
Craig, Austin. 1705
Craig, Clarence Tucker. 3097, 406, 474, 658, 1057, 1394, 1491, 1951, 2258, 1395
Craig, David Irvin. 2688

Craig, Edward Marshall. 2928
Craig, Florence M. 3498
Craig, Floyd A. 3002
Craig, H. A. L. 658, 1925
Craig, Hazel Thompson. 3880
Craig, John Bradford. 637, 3553
Craig, Laura (Gerould) 302, 3816
Craig, Samuel G. 1094, 2037, 2059
Craig, Stephen Speers. 1528
Craig, William Lane. 1733, 1738, 2051
Craighead, James Geddes. 2915
Craighill, Marian G. 1378
[Craigie, Pearl Mary Teresa (Richards) 665
Craigie, Peter C. 499, 3794
Craigie, William Alexander. 2665
Craik, Dinah Maria (Mulock) 1113
Craik, Elmer Le Roy. 1236
Craik, James. 1220
Crain, C. 471
Crain, Clara (Moore) 3125
Crain, James Andrew. 1138, 1460
Crain, Orville E. 3780
Crain, Thomas Crowell Taylor. 3744
Cram, Ralph Adams. 2, 1156, 1159, 1162, 2575
Cram, Willard Gilden. 2457
Cramblet, Wilbur H. 1467
Cramer, Clarence H. 1907
Cramer, Fredrick Henry. 99
Cramer, George H. 447
Cramer, Lester Simon. 1521
Cramer, Malinda E. 1793
Cramer, Malinida E. 1471
Cramer, Raymond L. 1828, 2050
Cramer, Wilhelm. 78
Cramer, William Stuart. 2195
Crammer, Thomas. 1216
Cramp, John Mockett. 151, 798, 3033, 3710
Cranage, David Herbert Somerset. 1213, 1215, 2579
Cranch, Raymond Greenleaf. 1139
Crandall, A L. 463
Crandall, Edna M. 3149, 3858
Crandall, Lathan Augustus. 2597
Crane, Aaron Martin. 419, 1720, 2870
Crane, Arthur. 1745
Crane, Arthur Morton. 916
Crane, Dominic F. 2231
Crane, Frank. 1313, 3066, 1720
Crane, Jim. 1013
Crane, John de Murinelly Cirne. 3797
Crane, Jonathan Townley. 36, 1823, 2450
Crane, Louis Burton. 1828
Crane, Stephen. 2037
Crane, Thomas E. 413
Crane, Wendell K. 3099
Crane, William E. 2780
Cranfield, C. E. B. 433, 447
[Cranfield, Richard]. 1378
Cranfill, James Britton. 700
Cranford, Clarence William. 958, 3884, 958, 2061, 3777
Cranford, Mary Poole. 3406
Cranmer, Thomas. 1216
Crannell, Philip Wendell. 161, 596, 1128, 2323
Cranny, Titus. 1673, 2794
Cranny, Titus F. 388, 424, 2357, 2362
Cranor, Phoebe. 2886, 3615, 3831, 3884
Cranston, Earl. 2420
Cranston, Maurice William. 2241
Cranston, Ruth. 2262, 3114
Crapanzano, Vincent. 1782
Crapps, Robert W. 409
Crapsey, Algernon Sidney. 3114, 1140, 2008, 3654
Crapullo, George Anthony. 3559, 3879, 3884
Crashaw, William. 798, 3606
Craske, Frederick. 1778, 2400
Craven, Martha A. 1544
Craven, Rulon G. 1233, 1564
Craveri, Marcello. 1962
Cravner, William Charles. 1445, 1720, 2972, 3350, 3369
Crawford, Benjamin Franklin. 2451, 741, 1068, 2430, 2451
Crawford, Cecil Clement. 134, 326, 2034, 3347, 3373
Crawford, Daniel. 1068
Crawford, David Livingston. 2540, 3538
Crawford, Don. 1109, 2821, 3231
Crawford, Donald W. 2163
Crawford, Eugene Joseph. 2056, 3420
Crawford, Eula Wright. 1621
Crawford, Florence. 1590
Crawford, Florence Gloria. 1590, 2809
Crawford, George A. 2423
Crawford, George Williamson. 1667
Crawford, Harriet A. 551
Crawford, Isabel Alice Hartley. 2485
Crawford, Isaiah Wadsworth. 3373
Crawford, J. R. 3827
Crawford, Julius Earl. 1167, 3528, 3531
Crawford, Leonidas Wakefield. 1295

Crawford, Mary. 1980
Crawford, Mary Caroline. 2687
Crawford, Mattie. 2051, 2507
Crawford, Merwin Richard. 3053
Crawford, Nelson Antrim. 1860, 2047
Crawford, Percy B. 3350
Crawford, Percy Bartimus. 3350
Crawford, Quantz. 2724
Crawford, Richard. 2201
Crawford, Samuel John. 1185
Crawford, Tarleton Perry. 2519
Crawford, Thomas Jackson. 104
Crawford, William H. 1113
Crawford, William Henry. 1138
Crawford, William Jackson. 2987, 3498
Crawford, William Rex. 1749
Crawford-Frost, William Albert. 1103
Crawford-Frost, W[illiam] A[lbert]. 1473
Crawley, James Winston. 2516
Crawley, Peter. 2608
Crawley, Sadie Tiller. 3468
Crawley-Boevey, Mateo. 3269, 1826, 3269, 1298, 3269
Crawshaw, William Henry. 2062, 3461
Cray, Issac Charles. 282
Creager, Alfred L. 539
Creagh, John Thomas. 2346
Creake, Abbey. 1379
Creasman, Myrtle R. 2757
Crebs, Berry Stewart. 453
Credo. 1281
Creed, John Martin. 2000, 3211, 3659
Creedon, Lawrence P. 2979
Creegan, Charles Cole. 2481, 2482
Creel, George. 2047
Creel, Herrlee Glessner. 1331, 1330, 1331, 2838, 2839, 3587
Creel, James Cowherd. 1463, 3220
Creel, Richard E. 3058
Creelman, Harlan. 539
Creeth, Edmund. 2594, 3400
Crehan, Joseph. 414, 1020, 3698
Creigh, Dorothy (Weyer) 1790
Creighton, Charles Frisbie. 668, 1854, 3232
Creighton, David. 2651
Creighton, Frank Whittington. 958
[Creighton, Louise (von Glehn) 1386, 2525, 3331
Creighton, Mandell. 614, 808, 1140, 1226, 1817, 2769, 2862
Cremeans, Charles Davis. 730
Cremeans, Walter Rollo. 11
Cremer, Hermann. 1768, 1786
Crenshaw, James. 3498
Crenshaw, James L. 485, 568, 2867, 3017, 3821
Crenshaw, Rosa Dieu. 182
Crespy, Georges. 2337, 3592
Cressey, Frank Graves. 3869
Cresson, Charles Caleb. 1677
Cresson, Warder. 1091, 1387, 2952
Cressy, Earl Herbert. 2508
Creswell, John Baxter. 615
Creswell, Keppel Archibald Cameron. 79
Creten, J. 2764
Creusen, Joseph. 2577
Crew, Phyllis Mack. 1294
Crewdson, Jane (Fox) 632
Crews, Calloway S. 1652
Crews, Clyde F. 750
Cribb, C. C. 51, 605, 982, 1598, 3021, 3220, 3288, 3318
[Cribb, William Harris]. 1962
Cribbin, James J. 804
Crichlow, Cyril A. 3051
Crichton, Ian. 1413
Crichton, James D. 837, 2235, 3773
Cridge, Edward. 531, 2037
Crim, Keith R. 575
Crim, Mort. 1057
Crippen, J W. 302
Crippen, Layton W. 2225
Cripps, Jean Donaldson. 1790, 2539
Cripps, Richard Stafford. 958, 3441
Crisci, Elizabeth W. 3553
Criscoe, Arthur H. 72, 338, 2824
Crisler, Clarence Creager. 2508, 3386
Crismon, Leo T. 154
Crisp, Dorothy. 1057
Crisp, Stephen. 1585
Crispin, Thomas. 3414
Criss, Lillian M. 719
Criss, Mildred. 3284
Crist, Evamae Barton. 1256, 1387
Cristiani, Leon. 193, 1026, 1293, 1427, 1640, 1645, 1937, 1992, 2196, 2584, 3460
Cristiani, Leon [Augustin Louis Leon Pierre Cristiani]. 3033, 794, 2136
Cristy, Albert Barnes. 1304
Criswell, Jeron. 2715, 2946, 2948
Criswell, W. A. 161, 464, 565, 614, 1433, 3466

Criswell, Wallie A. 62, 139, 161, 202, 276, 330, 365, 413, 440, 447, 464, 509, 544, 565, 614, 992, 1836, 1837, 2788, 3077, 3318, 3350, 3363, 3466
[Critchfield, A]. 3333
Critchlow, Keith. 86
Critchlow, William J. 2619
Crite, Allan Rohan. 1957, 2680
Crites, Stephen. 1800
Croarkin, Walter Elias. 2361
Croatto, Jose Severino. 287, 1659
Croce, Benedetto. 2226
Crock, Clement. 1315, 3264
Crock, Clement Henry. 75, 862, 1312, 1315, 2034, 3264, 3784, 180, 862, 1150, 1268, 1691, 2031, 3540
Crocker, Henry. 151, 2209
Crocker, Lionel George. 184, 2899, 1635, 2909
Crocker, Zebulon. 2925
Crockett, Albert Stevens. 3498
Crockett, H. Dale. 3798
Crockett, Harriet Pritchard. 3597
Crockett, William David. 1243
Croegaert, August [Jan Marie Josef]. 845
Croft, aloysius. 2021
Croft, Aloysius, comp. 854
Croft, George. 1226
Crofton, Denis. 204
Crofts, Ambrose M. 753, 2254
Crofut, Doris. 3277, 3719
Croghan, Mary Edmund. 3418
Croil, James. 2482
Croke, John Joseph. 3405
Croly, George. 463
Crom, Scott. 1674, 2379
Crombie, Albert Harrison. 36
Cromer, Grace E. 958
Crompton, Arnold. 2173, 3727
Crompton, Rosamond. 1057
Cromwell, Richard S. 3535
Cronan, Edward Paul. 2319
Cronbach, Abraham. 2116, 2138, 2147, 2889, 3454, 3882
Crone, Patricia. 1924
Cronin, Charles. 771
Cronin, Charles John. 196
Cronin, Charles Patrick. 1886
Cronin, Gaynell Bordes. 1265, 1607
Cronin, John Francis. 1085, 1130, 1131, 1135, 1136, 1137, 2123
Cronin, Patrick. 3259
Cronin, Vincent. 2712, 3235, 3283
Cronk, Elwood F. 2474
Cronk, George. 309, 2745
Cronk, Katharine (Scherer) 2482
Cronk, Katherine (Scherer) 2482
Cronk, Walter. 2638, 3477
Crook, Isaac. 1499, 2181
Crook, Margaret Brackenbury. 210, 3835
*Crook, Roger H. 958, 1323, 1471, 1607
Crook, William H. 1133
Crookall, Robert. 94, 2987
Crooke, William. 1895
Crooker, Joseph Henry. 1118, 1951, 2414, 1118, 1173, 1987, 2012, 3192
Crookes, William. 3498
Crooks, Florence (Bingham) 2546
Crooks, George Richard. 3410
Crookston, Joseph Claude. 3267
Crookston, Minn. (Diocese) 735
Cropper, Margaret. 1212, 2889
Crosbie, Robert. 3684
[Crosby, Daniel]. 2037
Crosby, Ernest Howard. 601
Crosby, Ernest S. 3033
Crosby, Howard. 560, 958, 1962, 2113, 2899, 2930
Crosby, Jeremiah. 1645
Crosby, John F. 2159, 2160, 3829
[Crosby, Mary]. 1387
Crosby, Michael. 180, 2246, 3785
Crosby, Oscar Terry. 1496
Crosby, Rena L. 282
Crosby, Sumner McKnight. 3273
Crosland, Camilla Duflour (Toulmin) 3498
Cross and crown (St. Louis) 3485
Cross, Andrew Boyd. 3737
Cross, Arthur Lyon. 44, 1173, 1222
Cross, Christopher. 2889
Cross, Claire. 1515
Cross, Colin. 1196, 1962
Cross Currents. 3771
Cross, Earle Bennett. 577
Cross, Edward Markin. 958
Cross, Frank Leslie. 3077
Cross, Frank Moore. 499, 517, 733, 1409, 1798, 3613
Cross, George. 3296, 1057, 1094
Cross, Harold H U. 3498
Cross, Irvie Keil. 3464, 3465
Cross, James A. 1229
Cross, John A. 650
[Cross, Jonathan]. 34
Cross, Joseph. 2213, 3094
Cross, Kathryn Patricia. 1578
*Cross, Luther. 906

*Cross, Luther S. 3370
Cross, Marcus E. 3595
Cross, Robert Alan. 2457
Cross, Robert D. 34, 1279
Cross, Samuel Hazzard. 1274
[Cross, Thomas Joseph]. 102
Cross, Whitney R. 2700
Cross, Wilford Oakland. 104
Crossan, Dominic M. 366
Crossan, John Dominic. 414, 1810, 2024, 2027, 3815
Cross Creek, Ohio. Presbyterian Church. 2925
Crosse, Ernest Courtenay. 1543
Crosse, Gordon. 1748, 1220
Crosse, Sarah. 1810, 1992, 2593
Crossfield, R. C. 2611
Crossland, Weldon Frank. 1253, 1167, 1250, 1564, 3149
Crossley, Frederick Herbert. 2, 1159
Crossley, Robert. 1094
Crossley, Robert N. 2273, 2810
Crossley-Holland, Kevin. 2665
Crossman, Richard Howard Stafford. 2753
Crosthwaite, Charles. 1817
Croswell, Harry. 1389, 1605
Crothers, Louise (Bronson) 1389
Crothers, Samuel McChord. 1068, 2620, 2889
Crotty, Henrietta M. 3799
Crotty, Horace. 1057
Crotty, Matthew M. 1626
Crouch, Archibald Roy. 912
Crouch, Austin. 958, 1350, 3466
Crouch, Howard E. 1400
Crouch, Kate C. Maddry. 158, 3838
Crouch, Louisa J. 2714
Crouch, W Perry. 1607
Crouch, William. 1169
Crounse, Helen Louise. 3880
Crouse, John H. 463
Crouse, William H. 3717
Crow, Carl. 1331
Crow, Mark. 2385
Crow, Martha (Foote) 3095
Crow, Paul A. 1043, 1355, 1491, 1492
Crowder, Minnie M. 2427
Crowder, Richard. 3815
Crowe, Catherine (Stevens) 2987
Crowe, Charles M. 653, 958, 1085, 1435, 1986, 2028, 2399, 2721, 3337, 3363, 3531
Crowe, Frederick E. 1245, 2245, 3669, 3848
Crowe, Glen. 1272
Crowe, Jerome. 284
Crowe, Jimmy P. 952
Crowe, John H. 958
Crowe, W L. 2601, 3428
Crowe, Winfield Scott. 3744
Crowell, Eugene. 3498
Crowell, Frank. 2323
Crowell, Grace (Noll) 1437, 214, 900, 1437, 1985, 2386, 3843
Crowell, Katharine Roney. 2549, 3738
Crowell, Norton B. 696
Crowfoot, John Winter. 1273
Crowley, Aleister. 1389, 2312, 2314, 2724, 3473, 3588
Crowley, Dale. 280, 1513, 3097, 3350, 3744
Crowley, J. E. 1075
Crowley, Jeremiah J. 798, 829, 1247
Crowley, Mary C. 982, 1389, 2386, 3842
[Crowley, Timothy Leonard]. 2261
Crownfield, Frederic C. 347
Crownfield, Gertrude. 2021
Crowson, E H. 3498
Crowston, C C. 1361
Crowther, Arnold. 3823
Crowther, Clarence Edward. 1153
Crowther, Duane S. 570, 605, 678, 680, 1712, 2611, 2952, 3428, 3741
Crowther, Jean Decker. 3185
Crowther, Jonathan. 2420
Crowther, Patricia. 1389, 3823
Croxall, Thomas Henry. 2169
Croy, Eugene. 2732
Crozer theological seminary, Chester, Pa. 1389, 3042
Crozer theological seminary, (Upland), Chester, Pa. 1390
Crozer theological seminary (upland) Hester, Pa. 3332
Crozer theological seminary, Upland, Pa. 1390
Crozier, William Percival. 2847
Cruden, Alexander. 243, 226, 227
Cruickshank, Marjorie. 1129
[Crull, August]. 2289
Crum, John Macleod Campbell. 343
Crum, Mason. 3149
Crum, Milton. 2899
Crum, Rolfe Pomeroy. 1437, 2963
Crum, Walter Ewing. 2330
Crummell, Alexander. 2056
Crummey, Donald. 2517

Crummey, Robert O. 3022
Crump, Galbraith Miller. 2468
Crump, Spencer. 3470
Crumpler, Frank H. 104, 3406
Crumpton, Washington Bryan. 1605, 2401
Crunican, Paul. 1246
[Cruse, Mary Anne]. 1705, 2965
Crutchley, Brooke. 731, 1712
Cruttwell, Charles Thomas. 1616
Cruz, Nicky. 982, 1392, 1427, 2244, 3711, 3880
Cryer, Newman S. 2780
Cua, Antonio S. 2938
Cubitt, George. 2273
Cuddesdon College, Cuddesdon, Eng. 3756
Cuddihy, John Murray. 1038
Cuddihy, Robert Joseph. 2851
Cudney, Gerald E. 1199
[Cudney, Isaiah]. 3350
Cudworth, Angeline M. 1392
Cudworth, Ralph. 943
Cuenot, Joseph. 2537
Cuevas, Santos. 982
Cugno, Alain. 2125, 2648
Culavamsa. 3816
Culbertson, Paul T. 217, 958
[Culbertson, Rosamond] b. 1803. 798
Culbertson, William. 3350
Culbreth, James Marvin. 2226, 2423
Cullen, Franklin. 2349
Cullen, Margaret R. 1640
Cullen, Thomas Francis. 824, 1644, 2333, 2506, 3376
Culler, Arthur Dwight. 2702
Culler, Arthur Jerome. 299
Culler, David D. 1288
Culleton, Richard Gerald. 1513, 51
Culley, Iris V. 637, 3853
Culley, Paul G. 2549
Culley, Robert C. 531, 577, 2668
Culling, Louis T. 1470, 1765, 1878, 2724, 2733
Culliton, Joseph T. 2719, 3027, 3593
Cullmann, Oscar. 134, 137, 334, 409, 419, 475, 1142, 1197, 1818, 1951, 2010, 2037, 2125, 2824, 2955, 3260, 3642, 3771, 3855
Cullumber, Norman L. 2870
Cully, Iris V. 214, 637, 938, 3170, 3176, 3553, 3638
Cully, Kendig Brubaker. 9, 637, 936, 1279, 1328, 2889, 2965, 2966, 3149, 3160, 3163, 3182, 3262
Cully, Kendig Brubaknnr. 3162
Culmsee, Carlton Fordis. 1776
Culp, G. Richard. 1579
Culp, John. 3671
Culpepper, Burke. 3339
Culpepper, C. L. 3232
Culpepper, James. 1393
Culpepper, John B. 3412
Culpepper, R. Alan. 414, 2125
Culpepper, Robert H. 104, 1393, 2486, 2814
Culver, Douglas J. 293
Culver, Elsie Thomas. 1257
Culver, Newell. 2450
Culver, Raymond Benjamin. 2328, 1129, 2328
Culver, Robert D. 603, 2465
Culver, Robert Duncan. 508, 929, 1720, 1962, 2465
Culver, Samuel Wightman. 3304
Culverhouse, Cecil. 1751
Culverwel, Nathanael. 3099
Culwell, Kitty Jones. 637
Cumberland Presbyterian board of publication. 1396
Cumberland Presbyterian Church. 1396
Cumberland Presbyterian church in the U. S. 2919
Cumberland Presbyterian church in the U. S. General assembly. 1396
Cumberland, Richard. 958, 1997, 2047
Cumberland university, Lebanon, Tenn. Theological dept. 3681
Cumming, Alexander. 3288
Cumming, Charles Gordon. 578
Cumming, I A M. 2588
Cumming, James Elder. 923, 1828, 1834
Cumming, James T. 3670
Cumming, John. 451, 461, 508, 798, 1358, 1556, 1906, 2024, 2465, 3339, 2308
Cumming, Menzies. 45
Cumming, William James. 2919
Cumming, William Kenneth. 399, 2070
Cummings, Asa. 2806
Cummings, Charles. 3485
Cummings, Daniel Malachy. 762
Cummings, Ephraim Chamberlain. 3224
Cummings, Ephraim Chamberlain. 3224
Cummings, F D. 1654
Cummings, H. Wayland. 1316
Cummings, Lon. 1396, 2485
Cummings, M. Homer. 3561
Cummings, Marjorie. 2129, 2553

Cummings, Oliver De Wolf. 3149, 3175
Cummings, Oliver DeWolf. 3149, 3876
Cummings, Preston. 1344
Cummings, Samuel. 3204
Cummings, William L. 1661
Cummings Ebenezer Edson. 147
Cummins, Betty Jane. 232
Cummins, D. Duane. 932
Cummins, Damian Leander. 873
Cummins, Edmund Henry. 344
Cummins, George David. 1822, 2500, 3050
Cummins, Geraldine Dorothy. 24, 2335, 3473, 3498
Cummins, Horace Edson. 1358
Cummins, Robert. 3754
Cummins, Walter M. 2231
Cumminskey, John A. 747
Cumnock, Frances. 1208
Cumont, Franz. 3114
Cumont, Franz [Valery Marie]. 3246
Cumont, Franz Valery Marie. 2560, 3114, 3246, 2560, 3058, 3246
Cundall, Arthur Ernest. 554
Cundall, Frank. 2718
Cuneo, Bernard Henry. 138
Cuninggim, Jesse Lee. 958, 3553
Cuninggim, Merrimon. 3194, 3757
Cuninghame, William. 798
Cunliffe-Jones, Hubert. 276
Cunneen, Sally. 2386, 3835
Cunningham, Bessie Mothersill. 2761
*Cunningham, Charles B. 3339
Cunningham, Eleanor W. 1598, 3809
Cunningham, Francis L B. 2636, 3693
Cunningham, Gail Harano. 2889
Cunningham, George. 2172
Cunningham, J A. 3075
Cunningham, James F. 774
Cunningham, James Jefferson. 1668
Cunningham, James W. 1246, 3258
Cunningham, John William. 1226
Cunningham, Joseph Davey. 3408
Cunningham, Lawrence. 1024, 1640, 2354
Cunningham, Mabel E. 1720
Cunningham, Milton E. 3018
Cunningham, Richard B. 62, 2219, 3528
*Cunningham, Sam L. 3198
Cunningham, Terence P. 819
Cunningham, Thomas McHutchin. 3819
Cunningham, Thomas W. 764
Cunningham, W. J. 1133, 1930
Cunningham, Walter F. 2738
Cunningham, William. 3066, 1323, 2945, 3441, 3848
Cunningham, William Francis. 804
Cunnington, Susan. 809
Cunnyngham, William George Etler. 2488, 2519
Cupitt, Don. 62, 1855, 2180, 2832, 3082
Curcic, Slobodan. 1749
Cureton, Alfred N. 1323
Curl, James Stevens. 3333
Curley, Edmund F. 731
Curley, Mary Mildred. 677, 860
Curley, Michael Joseph. 3329
Curran, Charles Arthur. 1373, 2780, 2997
Curran, Charles E. 119, 783, 834, 947, 949, 1085, 2789, 3021, 3451
Curran, Charles F. 2250
Curran, Dolores. 938, 1607
Curran, Edward Lodge. 785, 811, 2851
Curran, Francis X. 3738
Curran, Francis Xavier. 834, 1949, 3738
Curran, James. 2233
Curran, Robert Emmett. 667, 1370
Currey, Cecil B. 1483, 2675
Currie, David M. 2783
Currie, Gilbert Eggleson. 694
Currie, Ian. 3498, 3499
Currie, Lauchlin Bernard. 615, 1375
Currie, Robert. 1171
Currie, Robert Ormiston. 3426
Currie, Thomas White. 117
Currie, William. 3791
Currier, Albert Henry. 923, 1747
Currier, Charles Warren. 2492, 741, 2575
Currier, Raymond Pillsbury. 2549
Currier, Richard. 2774
Currin, Beverly Madison. 104, 1094
Curry, Albert Bruce. 1976, 647, 3058, 3537
Curry, Daniel. 3860
Curry, James B. 916
Curry, James E. 1199
Curry, Lerond. 861, 2955
Curry, Louise H. 3144
Curry, Samuel Silas. 232, 1587
Curry, Walter Clyde. 2470
Curry, William Melville. 1839, 2785
Curtayne, Alice. 692, 749, 2854, 3283
Curtin, Jeremiah. 1632
Curtin, Leah. 1544
Curtis, Anna L. 1676
Curtis, Bardella Shipp. 2611
Curtis, Charles J. 1039, 2832, 3455, 3679

Curtis, Charles Minot. 3818
Curtis, Claude Hamilton. 1358, 2500
Curtis, Donald. 2386, 2694, 3749, 3750
Curtis, Edward Lewis. 496
[Curtis, Elizabeth Alden]. 3684
Curtis, Geoffrey William Seymour. 1044, 1375
Curtis, Georgina Pell. 1363
Curtis, Heber Doust. 3077
Curtis, Lewis Perry. 3212
Curtis, Lindsay R. 1008, 1013, 1607, 1839, 2386
Curtis, Lucius Q. 1887
Curtis, Muriel Anne (Streibert) 647, 2889
Curtis, Norah. 2718
Curtis, Olin Alfred. 3642
Curtis, Richard. 194
Curtis, Richard Kenneth. 2587
Curtis, T W. 2601
Curtis, Thomas Arnold. 3428
Curtis, Thomas Day. 1016
Curtis, Thomas Fenner. 147, 305, 1304, 1781
Curtis, William Alexander. 2062
Curtis, William Redmond. 1043, 2194
Curtis, Winterton Conway. 3084
[Curtiss, Alonzo Parker]. 2957
Curtiss, Anthony. 3280
Curtiss, Frank Homer. 2018, 2740, 1695
Curtiss, George Lewis. 3654
Curtiss, Harriette Augusta. 1921, 2638, 2641, 2740, 2724
Curtiss, Harriette Augusta (Brown) 1921, 2217, 2740, 3791
Curtiss, John Shelton. 1148, 1149
Curtiss, Lucy S. 691
Curtiss, Phebe A. 3553
Curtiss, Samuel Ives. 3332
Curts, Paul. 2273
Curwen, John. 3768
[Cusack, Mary Frances]. 3125
Cusack, William H. 1887
[Cusden, Richard A J]. 3701
Cushing, A. I. 3138
Cushing, Anthony J. 3485
Cushing, Frank Hamilton. 3899
Cushing, Josiah Nelson. 706
Cushing, Richard. 1826
Cushing, Richard Cardinal. 1397
Cushing, Richard J. 1803, 2537, 2543, 2546
Cushing, Richard James. 958, 1313, 1397, 1403, 2023, 2362, 2570, 2718, 2782, 3198, 3264, 754, 764, 806, 862, 1397, 2123, 2210, 2211, 2348, 2362, 2793, 3264, 3378, 3785
[Cushman, Emma (Crow)]. 3499
Cushman, Herbert Ernest. 1030
Cushman, Joseph D. 1630, 2966, 2974
Cushman, Ralph Spaulding. 1437, 1445, 2049, 2386, 2453, 2890, 2941, 3528, 3671
Cushman, Robert. 3350
Cushman, Robert Earl. 3620, 3653
Cushmeer, Bernard. 1506
Cuskelly, Eugene James. 996, 3485, 3661
Cussianovich, Alejandro. 2570
Custance, Arthur C. 238, 652, 1380, 1422, 1936, 2325, 2326, 2911, 3083, 3227, 3620
Custard, Harry Lewis. 3461
Custer, Chester E. 1006, 1564
Custer, Dan. 1445, 2694
Custer, Stewart. 306
Custis, W. Keith. 2930, 3350
Cuthbert. 780, 781, 1640, 1645, 2637
Cuthbert, 1866-1939. 737, 1374, 1640, 1645, 2332
Cuthbert, Arthur A. 1787
Cuthbert, Father. 1640
Cuthbert, James Hazzard. 1690
Cuthbert, Marion. 1425
Cuthbert, Marion Vera. 1425
Cuthers, John. 3125
Cutler, Ethel. 232, 388, 1987, 2950
Cutler, Helen R. 3125
Cutler, John Henry. 1397
Cutler, Samuel. 1835
Cutler, Timothy. 1503
Cutler, Uriel Waldo. 3847
Cutner, Herbert. 2008
Cuttat, Jacques Albert. 3114
Cuttaz, Francois Joseph. 137, 887, 1741, 1751
Cutten, George Barton. 1716, 2993, 2997
Cutting, George. 3288
Cutton, George Leon. 3175
Cutts, Edward Lewes. 1173, 1758, 1761, 1810
Cuyahoga Falls, Ohio. First United Methodist Church. History and Records Committee. 1398
Cuyler, John Potter, jr. 2697
Cuyler, Margery. 1614
Cuyler, Theodore Ledyard. 725, 958, 1111, 1350, 1398, 2899, 3671, 3884
Cygon, Joseph R. 3330

Cylwicki, Albert. 1263
Cynewulf. 1022, 1398
Cyprianus. 1166, 1398
Cyprianus, Saint. 2217
Cyprianus, Saint, Bp. of Carthage. 3635
Cyr, Narcisse. 159, 1372
Cyril, Robert. 2132, 2361
Cyrillus. 745, 3635
Czaja, Michael. 2827
Czarnowski, Stefan. 1807, 2793
Czerniejewski, Stanislaus. 2365
Czuba, Natalie Ann. 766, 3310

D

*D. 3164
Daane, James. 1505, 1751, 2899, 3017
Dabistan. 3114
Dabney, Elizabeth J. 2870
Dabney, Robert Lewis. 104, 2899, 2914, 3297, 3642
Dabney, Virginius. 735
[Dabney, Wendell Phillips] 1865. 1895, 3789
Dabovich, Sebastian. 2899, 3280
Dabovich, Sebastin. 2748
Da Costa, Leon. 804
Dada, 1917. 3477
Dadmun, Frances May. 3553
Dadmun, John H. 3499
Dadolle, Pierre. 2741
Daehlin, Marlene. 2890
Daehlin, Reidar A. 1005, 2791
*Daehling, Edythe. 3191
Dagg, John Leadley. 59, 147, 1240, 3642
[Daggett, William Wallace]. 1669
D'Agostino, Joseph D. 3588
Dague, Robert Addison. 3499
Daher, Paul. 2649
Dahinden, Justus. 1156
Dahl, Arthur. 127
Dahl, George. 1807
Dahl, Gerald L. 1399, 1917, 2337
Dahl, Gordon. 2209
Dahl, Murdoch E. 324, 346
Dahl, Nellie. 2538
Dahl, Nils Alstrup. 350, 378, 1997, 2011, 2481
Dahl, Paul E. 1287
Dahlberg, Edwin Theodore. 124, 146, 1068, 1399, 2337
Dahle, John. 1875
Dahlin, Therrin C. 1138
Dahlke, Paul. 701
Dahlstrom, Earl C. 943
Dahm, Charles W. 1305
Dahmus, Joseph Henry. 1375, 3860
Daiches, Belle Turner. 3499
Daiches, David. 271, 2098, 2621
alSaid, Labib. 2185
Daigle, Richard J. 243, 2658
Dailey, Abram Hoagland. 3499
Dailey, Edward Vincent. 2851, 2782
Dailey, William Nelson Potter. 3045
Daille, Jean. 1617
Daillie, Jean. 1617
Daily Bible readings. Inner City Parishes. 1434
Daily bread. 1839
Daily, Starr. 588, 696, 958, 1358, 1598, 2161, 2262, 2264, 3335
The Daily vacation church-school. 3149
Daim, Wilfried. 860, 1320, 3441
Dake, Dorothy Dobbins. 298
Dake, Finis Jennings. 453
Dake, Fins Jennings. 453
Dake, Vivian Adelbert. 1784
Dakers, Lionel. 1206
Dakin, Arthur. 729, 739
Dakin, Arthur Hazard, jr. 1850, 3099
Dakin, Edwin Franden. 1494
Dalaba, Oliver V. 1564
Dalby, Ezra Christiansen. 595
Dalcho, Frederick. 2000, 2974, 3464
Dalcourt, Gerald J. 3693
Dale, Abbey. 743
Dale, Alan T. 445, 533, 628
Dale, Godfrey. 2564, 3891
Dale, James Gary. 93, 1399
Dale, James Wilkinson. 134
Dale, Mary E. 3183
Dale, Mary Elizabeth. 2535
Dale, Robert William. 1313, 2899
Dale, Thomas Nelson. 3075
Daley, Charles Marie. 1475
Daley, Joseph Gordian. 28
Daley, Joseph John. 3690
Daley, Leo Charles. 114
Dal-Gal, Girolamo. 2851
Dalglish, Doris N. 1677, 3534
Dalglish, Garven. 1111
Dalglish, William A. 3161
Dall, Caroline Wells (Healey) 2660
Dallas, Harriet (Hughes) 2066, 3499

Dallas, Helen A. 2635, 2987
Dallas. Highland Park Presbyterian Church. 1250
Dallas, Mary (Kyle) 3499
Dallas Southern Methodist University Birdwell Library. 212
Dallen, James. 9, 2211, 2259
Dallimore, Arnold A. 1293, 3813
Dallmann, William. 276, 419, 1290, 1315, 1828, 2024, 2126, 2272, 2273, 2768, 2796, 2824, 3339
Dallmann, William i. e. Charles Frederick William. 400
Dalmais, Irenee Henri. 1487, 2235
Dalman, Gustaf Hermann. 388, 2761, 388, 2013, 2070, 3015
Dalpadado, J. Kingsley. 331, 388, 645
Dalphin, Marcia. 1112
Dalrymple, Gwynne. 1513, 3192, 3884
Dalton, Joseph Grinnell. 99
Dalton, L H. 3499
Dalton, Lee. 1399, 2619
Dalton, Len. 467, 578
Dalton, Luella Adams. 2618
Dalton, Tolbert Marion. 645
Dalton, William J. 1476
Daly, Cahal B. 3389, 3817
Daly, Emily Joseph. 2803
Daly, Gabriel. 2562
Daly, James Jeremiah. 191, 996, 1945
Daly, Lowrie John. 188, 1263, 3592
Daly, Marco. 3243
Daly, Mary. 3835, 3836
Daly, Myrtilla N. 1486
Daly, Robert J. 3271
Daly, Sheila John. 3880
Dalyell, John Graham. 3567
Dame, Clarence P. 1616
Dame, Lawrence. 2208
Dameron, James Palatin. 3058
*Dametz, Maurice Gordon. 1173
Damiani, G. 3499
Damm, John Silber. 3553
Dammers, A. H. 324
Damon, Ethel Moseley. 1791, 1400
Damon, William F. 3499
Damphoux, Edward. 2818
Damrell, Joseph D. 1394
Damrosch, Frank. 2056, 2964
Damsteegt, P. Gerard. 3379
[Dana, Daniel]. 1337
Dana, Ellis Huntington. 1039, 1127, 1137, 1319
Dana, Ethel Nathalie (Smith) 399, 1957
Dana, Harvey Eugene. 339, 343, 347, 371, 405, 406, 407, 413, 416, 419, 1118, 1834, 2796, 405
Dana, James. 1500, 1657
Dana, James Dwight. 204
Dana, John Monroe. 3204
Dana, Malcolm. 1962
[Dana, William Coombs]. 1400
Danagher, Edward F. 3331
Danagher, John Joseph. 777
Danby, Herbert. 1083, 1375
Dancy, John Christopher. 488
D'Andrade, Hugh. 1625
Dane, Charles W. 3299
Dane, Christopher. 2733
Dane, Susan Martha. 2632
Daneilou, Jean. 2240
Danelson, Effa E. 3499
Daner, Francine Jeanne. 1914, 2186
Daney, Isabel Stevenson. 2972
Danford, Samuel Alexander. 2482
Danforth, Florence Garrison. 3827
Danforth Foundation Saint Louis Mo Commission on Church Colleges and Universities. 1164
Danforth Foundations, St. Louis. Commission on Church Colleges and Universities. 1127
Danforth, Herbert M. 781
Danforth, John. 2157
Danforth, Joshua Noble. 1691, 3791, 3818
D'Angelo, Louise. 785, 3845
D'Angostino, Angelo A. 1254
Daniel, Anita. 3311
Daniel, Carey L. 232
Daniel, Charles. 1288, 1947
Daniel, David. 628
Daniel, Eleanor Ann. 934
Daniel, Emmett Randolph. 1648
Daniel, J C. 170
Daniel, John. 1131, 1480
Daniel, Lois. 2386
Daniel, Ralph T. 1209
Daniel, Robert Norman. 1772
Daniel, Robert T. 575
Daniel-Rops, Henry 1901. 2368
Daniel, William Andrew. 2681, 3612
Daniell, David. 155
Daniell, George William. 3815
Daniells, Arthur Grosvenor. 1602, 3379
Danielou, Alain. 1743

Danielou, Jean. 41, 43, 525, 785, 838, 860, 919, 1057, 1118, 1153, 1196, 1409, 1411, 1616, 1720, 1977, 2019, 2037, 2073, 2127, 2141, 2554, 2743, 3114, 3485, 3720
Danielou, Madeleine (Clamorgan) 2890
Danielou, Madeline (Clamorgan) 2890
Daniel-Rops, Henry. 293, 3280, 293, 309, 406, 533, 1181, 1185, 1187, 1190, 1284, 1962, 2262, 2368, 2765, 2796, 3033, 3637, 3779
Daniel-Rops, Henry, 1901-1965. 193, 809, 1185, 1186, 2482, 2978
Daniel-Rops, Henry [Henry Jules Charles Petiot]. 1190, 2266, 1185, 1284, 1374, 2482, 1190
Daniel-Rops, Henry [Name orig.: Henry Jules Charles Petiot]. 1185
Daniel-Rops, Henry [Real name: Henry Jules Charles Petiot]. 819, 2354, 2765, 1185, 1374, 2354, 3769
Daniels, Cora Linn (Morrison) 3499, 3567
Daniels, Earl. 1843
Daniels, Glenn. 1754
Daniels, Harold M. 2234
Daniels, J W. 3499
Daniels, Leverett Richmond. 1720
Daniels, Marilyn. 1401
Daniels, Morris S. 2733
[Daniels, Olive (Bell) 186
Daniels, Velma Seawell. 991, 992, 1401
Daniels, William Haven. 1790
Danielski, S E. 40
Danielson, Con. Westfieldd Congregational church. 1336
Danielson, Conn. Westfield Congregational church. 1336
Danielson, Dennis Richard. 1733, 2468
Danielson, Elmer R. 1401, 2487
Danielson, Frances Weld. 293, 1498, 1574, 2590, 2718, 2720, 3149
Daniken, Eric Von. 1917
Daniken, Erich von. 3783
Danish Baptist general conference of America. 142, 143
Dankenbring, William F. 605, 1384, 1513, 3082
Danker, Albert. 3839
Danker, Frederick W. 285, 402, 427, 429, 1125, 1386, 2297
Danker, William J. 2373, 2492, 2517, 2594
Danks, William. 388
Danmar, William. 3499
Dann, Bucky. 2911
Dannelly, Elizabeth Otis (Marshall) 2856
Dannemiller, Lawrence. 242, 647, 2027
Dannen, Kent. 2676
Dannenfeldt, Karl H. 3215
Danner, Thomas Jefferson. 1590
Danniel, Benjamin. 1083
Danniel, Francoise. 3836
Danskin, Washington A. 3499
Dante Alighieri, 1265-1321. 1140, 1402, 2858
Dante Alighieri. 3094, 1141, 1401, 1402, 3094
Dantec, Francois. 2342
Dantine, Wilhelm. 2160
Danto, Arthur Coleman. 1540
D'Antonio, William V. 2198
*Dantuma, Angelyn Grace. 1445,
Danville, Ky. Theological seminary of the Presbyterian church in the U. S. A. 3612
Danzas, IUllia Nikolaevna. 2749
Dapp, Charles Frederick. 3897
Daprato statuary company. 28
Dara. 1091
Daraul, Arkon. 3823
Darbishire, Helen. 2468
Darby, John Nelson. 645
D'Arch, Martin Cyril. 758
D'Arcy, Charles Frederick. 1049, 3642, 3077, 3099
D'Arcy, Eric. 1347
D'Arcy, Martin C. 3711
D'Arcy, Martin Cyril. 185, 755, 996, 1088, 1745, 1887, 1951, 2262, 2323, 2386, 2702, 2705, 3693
D'Arcy, Martin Cyrill. 755, 1319
D'Arcy, Mary Ryan. 1026
D'arcy, Paul F. 3613
D'Arcy, Paula. 1350, 1403
Darcy-Berube, Francoise. 1607, 2811
Dare, Marcus Paul. 2315
Dargan, Edwin Charles. 1248, 198, 3339, 3350, 140, 147, 1118, 2899, 2909
Dargitz, Robert E. 11, 1465
Darian, Mujana. 9, 2211
Daries, Frederick Reinhard. 1437
Dark, Harris Jeremiah. 1273
Dark, Sidney. 1307, 1319, 1764, 1781, 3008, 1307, 2702
Darley, Alexander M. 1806
Darley, George M. 3094

Darling, Charles David. 3211
Darling, Charles William. 212
Darling, Harold W. 1107
Darling, Harry F. 95
Darling, James Ralph. 1129, 1226
Darling, Nancy. 3752
Darlington, Charles Joseph. 3126
Darlington, Elliot Christopher Bearns. 3339
Darlington, Thomas. 130
Darlington, William. 2651
Darlow, Thomas Herbert. 232, 637
Darmesteter, Arsene. 3582
Darnell, Ermina Jett. 1634, 2167
Darnell, Theodore W. 1049
Darnton, Charles. 2633
[Darr, Vera (Campbell)]. 900
Darragh, John Thomas. 3220
Darras, Joseph Epiphane. 809
Darrow, Albert Lincoln. 1720
Darrow, Clarence Seward. 19
Darrow, Floyd Lavern. 2476, 3072
Darshan Singh, Maharaj. 3302
Darsie, Charles. 1573, 3149

Dart, John. 891
Dart, John Lovering Campbell. 3288
Darter, Francis M. 2601, 3010, 2611
Dartmouth college. 1403
Darton, Alice Weldon (Wasserbach) 2354
Darton, G C. 104
Darwin, Francis Darwin Swift. 1807
Das, Bhagavan. 3684, 3058, 3864
Das, Ranendra Kumar. 3053, 3539
Dasatir. English. 1918
Dasbach, Fernando L. 1282
Dasgupta, Shashibhusan. 1896, 3586
Dasgupta, Surendra Nath. 2645, 2791, 3864, 2638, 2839, 3864
Dashiell, Thomas Grayson. 1174, 2974
Daskam, Max F. 3350
Daskin, Washington A. 3499
D'Assigny, Fifield. 1665
Date, Henry. 3561
Dator, James Allen. 3455
Datta, Bimal Kumar. 3600
Datta, Dhirendra Mohan. 1701
Dau, William Herman Theodore. 2072
Daube, David. 99, 347, 499, 1584, 2074, 3015
Daubeny, Charles. 1211
D'Aubigne, J. H. Merle. 3033
Dauer, Dorothea W. 2838, 3311
Daughdrill, Jim. 720
Daugherty, Edgar Fay. 3090
Daugherty, Kathryn. 1513
Daugherty, Leonard. 3459
Daugherty, Mason. 2827
Daugherty, Myra (Mills) 1446
Daugherty, Silas Davis. 1564
Daughters of charity of St. Vincent de Paul, Emmitsburgh, Md. 2478
Daughters of Saint Mary of Providence. 1776, 3377
Daughters of St. Paul. 338, 409, 494, 573, 619, 625, 723, 769, 785, 809, 902, 923, 1024, 1027, 1029, 1153, 1290, 1313, 1400, 1403, 1404, 1430, 1564, 1644, 1650, 1793, 1937, 1980, 2066, 2194, 2349, 2412, 2567, 2570, 2717, 2719, 2804, 2825, 2913, 2943, 3011, 3264, 3283, 3284, 3460, 3484, 3592, 3670, 3693, 3771, 3778, 3785, 3839, 3841, 3884
Daughters of St. Paul, eds. 656
Daughters of St. Paul. 3317
Daughters of the American Revolution. Pennsylvania. Chester County Chapter, West Chester. 198
Daughters Of The American Revolution Pennsylvania Colonel William Wallace Chapter, Pittsburgh. 1243
Daughters Of The American Revolution, Pennsylvania Inddependence Hall Chapter. 198
Daughters of the Heart of Mary. 1275
Daughters of St. Paul. 656, 747, 1404, 2349, 2804, 3278
Daujat, Jean. 996, 2870
Dauphinee, Minnie E. 1437
Dausch, Michael. 2337
Davar, Ashok. 1720
Davenport, Frederick Morgan. 3228
Davenport, John. 134, 2217
Davenport, John Gaylord. 3126
Davenport, Reuben Briggs. 2162, 3499, 3520
Davenport, Salusbury Fynes. 1886
Davenport, Willard Goss. 1590
Davenport, William Edwards. 3362
Davenport, William Henry. 1201
Daves, Michael. 471, 906, 922, 1318, 1870, 2386
Davey, Cyril James. 923, 2433
Davey, James Ernest. 1049
David, Albert Augustus. 959

David, Ann Rosalie. 1501
David, Ira E. 3318
David, John Baptist Maria. 725, 3222
David-Noel, Alexandra, 1868-1969. 707
Davidheiser, Bolton. 202, 204
Davidman, Joy. 1313
David-Neel, Alexandra. 2993, 2193
Davids, Caroline Augusta (Foley) Rhys. 701
*Davids, David E. 3528
Davids, Peter H. 412
Davids, Richard C. 911, 2504
Davids, T. W. Rhys. 706
Davids, Thomas William Rhys. 701
Davidson, Alice Joyce. 3208
Davidson, Charles T. 2267
Davidson, Charles Theodore. 959, 1229, 1230, 3676
Davidson, Clarissa Start. 1292, 1350, 2709, 3843
Davidson, Donald. 338
Davidson, Edward Hutchins. 1499
Davidson, Elizabeth Huey. 1222
Davidson, Flora Marlon. 2543
Davidson, Francis. 221
Davidson, Gustav. 43
Davidson, Henry Martin Perkins. 1174
Davidson, Hilda Roderick (Ellis) 2659, 2665, 3306
Davidson, Hugh McCullough. 58, 2777
Davidson, J L. 798
Davidson, James Robert. 1209
Davidson, James West. 461, 2466
Davidson, John. 3149, 2824, 3149
Davidson, John A. 2246
Davidson, Norman James. 2482
Davidson, Peter. 2853
Davidson, Randall Thomas. 2194, 44, 1068
Davidson, Robert. 497, 651, 1507, 1905, 2037, 2917
Davidson, Robert Franklin. 2752
Davidson, Samuel. 241
Davidson, William. 2028
[Davidson, William B]. 174
Davidson, William Franklin. 1658
Davie, Donald. 1023, 1469
Davie, John. 1531
Davies, Alan T. 1083
Davies, Alfred Mervyn. 2915
Davies, Alfred T. 1131
Davies, Alfred Thomas. 727, 2976
Davies, Ann. 721
Davies, Archibald Donald. 1250
Davies, Arthur Powell. 232, 1102, 1313, 1409, 2796, 2890, 3725, 3744
Davies, Benjamin. 287
Davies, Blodwen. 2407
Davies, Caleb. 3318
Davies, Charles Maurice. 2243
Davies, D. R. 1817
Davies, David Richard. 1214, 1281, 1818, 2980, 62, 1133, 1214, 2323, 2709
Davies, Ebenezer Thomas. 1219, 1844, 3252, 3789
Davies, Edward. 1313, 1787, 1823, 2500, 3232, 3591, 3803
Davies, Elam. 1068
Davies, G. I. 517, 1584
Davies, George C. 2968
Davies, Henry Walford. 49, 2740, 1206
Davies, Horton. 13, 1022, 1468, 1762, 2909, 3141, 3853
Davies, James. 1809
Davies, John. 2552
Davies, John Dudley. 525
Davies, John Gordon. 1004, 1085, 1160, 1190, 1196, 1274, 1837, 2236, 2554, 3233, 3855
Davies, John Howard. 402
Davies, John Newton. 347
Davies, John Trevor. 1340
Davies, Joseph Kenneth. 1131, 1230
Davies, Margaret. 373
Davies, Michael. 843, 2236, 3771
Davies, Reginald Trevor. 3825
Davies, Richard. 1684
Davies, Richard N. 3711
Davies, Richard Newton. 2160
Davies, Rupert E. 2423
Davies, Rupert Eric. 119, 727, 1045, 2423
Davies, Russell P. 1190
Davies, Samuel. 1763, 2930, 3350, 3361
Davies, Stevan L. 337
Davies, Thomas Alfred. 202, 523, 1068, 1380, 2466
Davies, Thomas Frederick. 2945, 3884
Davies, Thomas Havren. 388
Davies, Thomas Witton. 2724
Davies, Trevor H. 70, 3094
Davies, William. 1667
Davies, William David. 334, 376, 409, 1083, 1190, 2765, 2828, 3335, 3758
Davies, William Watkin. 247
Davies-Rodgers, Ellen. 81, 2974
Davies-Rodgers, Ellen, 1903. 2401
Davis, Alice Pitman. 1030

Davis, Almond H. 2627
Davis, Alton Arthur. 151
Davis, Andrew Jackson. 719, 1406, 1654, 2226, 2833, 2980, 2987, 2988, 3499, 3500, 3566
Davis, Arthur Paul. 3799
Davis, Bert H. 1277, 1914
Davis, Bert Henry. 1914
Davis, Boothe Colwell. 1374
Davis, Calvin Olin. 48
Davis, Charles. 137, 1455, 2234, 3659, 3661, 781, 1078, 1087, 1107, 1153, 3058
Davis, Charles Edward. 2237
Davis, Charles Franklin. 302
Davis, Charles Gilbert. 2833
Davis, Charles Henry Stanley. 1521, 3533
Davis, Cos H. 938
Davis, Creath. 992, 2783
Davis, Denver Jackson. 3012
Davis, Dixon Louis. 3500
Davis, Douglas M. 85
Davis, Edith (Smith) 3595
Davis, Edward. 2829
Davis, Elisabeth Hamill. 2883, 2890
Davis, Elisabeth Logan. 2625
Davis, Elise Miller. 3243
Davis, Ella Dora. 602
Davis, Emerson. 664
Davis, Enid. 2107, 2151
Davis, Gary. 3695
Davis, George Thompson Brown. 605, 615, 1109, 1482, 1564, 1622, 1898, 2005, 2118, 2480, 2760, 2761, 3126, 3705
Davis, George Washington. 1583
Davis, George Wesley. 458
Davis, Grace Emeline (Tinker) 1344, 1407
Davis, Grace Weiser. 896, 3458
Davis, Helen Clarkson (Miller) 3194
Davis, Henry. 947
Davis, Henry Grady. 3853
Davis, Henry Stanton. 2462
Davis, Humphrey. 3615, 3711
-Davis, Inez (Smith) 1889. 1233, 2601
Davis, J Merle. 1406
Davis, James A. 1522
Davis, James Ernest. 3500, 603
Davis, James Hill. 1133, 1278, 2430
Davis, Jean Reynolds. 1446
Davis, Jerome. 719, 1133, 2806, 3143, 3441
Davis, Jerome Dean. 1406, 2679
Davis, John. 172
Davis, John D. 243, 523, 526, 2667
Davis, John F. 1301, 1407, 2126
Davis, John Henry. 2402
Davis, John James. 521, 553, 590, 2090, 2716
Davis, John Jefferson. 3638
Davis, John K. 3317
Davis, John Merle. 2519, 2953
Davis, Joseph Augustus. 453
Davis, Katherine Kennicott. 741
Davis, Kenneth Ronald. 36
Davis, Lawrence B. 170
Davis, Lenwood G. 2172, 2683
Davis, Lew A. 2492
Davis, Lewis. 1498
Davis, Lyman Edwyn. 2459
Davis, Margaret Alexander. 1859
Davis, Martin P. 1780, 2530
Davis, Martin Winfrid. 2717
Davis, Mary A. 1652
Davis, Mary Evelyn (Moore) 1113
Davis, Mona. 959
Davis, Morrison Meade. 1190, 1503, 3220, 3292
Davis, Moshe. 1348
Davis, Muriel Orlidge. 3282
Davis, Myrna. 1588
Davis, Nelson Wellington. 386
Davis, Noah. 1407, 3425
Davis, Noah Knowles. 1534, 578, 1962
Davis, O. B. 597
Davis, Ozora Stearns. 450, 1407, 1562, 3373, 637, 1118, 1338, 1407, 1951, 2899
Davis, Patricia Talbot. 195
Davis, Raymond J. 2517
Davis, Robert Clarence. 959
Davis, Robert Pickens. 1164
Davis, Roy Eugene. 102, 3301, 3477, 3864
Davis, S. J. S. 678
Davis, Sadie Holcombe. 627, 1980
Davis, Samuel Davis. 3388
Davis, Samuel Taylor. 1834
Davis, Staley Franklin. 1321
Davis, Stephen T. 276, 2180
Davis, Susan. 2596
Davis, Thomas A. 444, 467, 1012, 1435, 1446, 1602, 2012, 2541, 2740
Davis, Thomas Brabson. 1667
Davis, Thomas Kirby. 1107
Davis, Walter Bruce. 739
Davis, Warner Pendley. 2425
Davis, William Edward. 1315

[Davis, William Franklin] 1880. 3019
Davis, William Hatcher. 3099
Davis, William Henry. 214, 1850
Davis, William Hersey. 440, 2091
Davis, William Morton. 465, 637
Davis, William Thompson. 3237
Davis, William Watters. 3547
Davis, Winston Bradley. 1935, 3545
Davis, Woodbury. 2174
Davison, Alpheus. 650
Davison, Archibald Thompson. 1210, 49, 1202
Davison, Charles Wright. 3500
Davison, Ellen Scott. 1185, 2583
Davison, Frank Elon. 1460, 3012, 3671
Davison, Lucien Adelbert. 1118
Davison, Phineas. 3122
Davison, Ronald C. 95
Davy, Yvonne. 2489
Dawe, Donald G. 1892, 2037, 3679
Dawes, Bourbon A. 647
Dawes, Sarah Elizabeth. 619, 625, 2047
Dawkins, Albert. 610
Dawkins, Muriel (Bacheler) 2638
Dawley, Powel Mills. 1174, 1182, 2056, 2699, 3813
Dawley, William Wallace. 3339
Dawn Bible students association. 619
Daws, Gavan. 1400
Dawson, AEneas MacDonell. 2863
*Dawson, Christopher. 1394
Dawson, Christopher Henry. 3307, 91, 1074, 1085, 1281, 1282, 1394, 2754, 2945, 3058, 3066, 3307, 3436, 1074, 1281, 1282, 2754, 3114
Dawson, David Miles. 1564, 1828, 2887, 3671
Dawson, E Matthews. 615
Dawson, Edwin Collas. 1856, 2488, 1784
Dawson, Ernest Alured. 104
Dawson, Franklin Raymond. 1456
Dawson, George Ellsworth. 3149
Dawson, Grace Strickler. 982, 3492
Dawson, John B. 2870
Dawson, John Leard. 3029
Dawson, John William. 202, 204, 1421, 3075
Dawson, Joseph Martin. 170, 1150, 1556, 3441
Dawson, Lemuel Orah. 3671
Dawson, Louise Susie (Dewey) 1407
Dawson, Marshall. 2887, 1579, 2720
Dawson, Miles Menander. 3898
Dawson, Pa. Presbyterian Church. 2918
Dawson, Raymond Stanley. 1330
Dawson, Thomas Damon. 1661
[Dawson, William] 1773-1841. 3533
Dawson, William Bell. 1579
Dawson, William Edwy. 2062
Dawson, William Harrison. 3198
Dawson, William James. 3339, 1068, 1340, 1962, 2264, 2870
Day, Albert Edward. 3092, 1585, 1590, 1598, 2174, 2823, 2870, 3058
[Day, Benjamin Henry]. 1669
Day, Bertram. 605, 1962, 2133, 2870
Day, Clinton D. 138
Day, Dorothy. 1365, 1407, 2386, 959, 1363
Day, Edward. 809, 1174, 2121
[Day, Edward]. 3642
Day, Ernest Everett. 959
Day, Ernest Hermitage. 1270, 2719, 3333
Day, Gardiner Mumford. 73, 731, 1313, 2056, 2246
Day, George Tiffany. 891
Day, Gwynn McLendon. 276, 959, 1437
Day, Harvey. 3864
Day, Helen Caldwell. 672, 870, 1363
Day, Henry Noble. 1534, 2738
Day, James Wentworth. 1709
Day, Jeremiah. 1657
Day, John A. 3082
Day, Leroy J. 1621
Day, Marshall Mallory. 665
Day, Michael. 3690
Day, Owen T. 1407
Day, Peter. 1040, 2191
Day, Richard Ellisworth. 2587
Day, Richard Ellsworth. 3523, 689, 923, 1389, 1437, 1625, 1900, 1936
Day, Robert B. 2615
Day, Sebastian J. 3309
Dayan, Moshe. 533, 1407, 3525
Daynes, Robert W. 2618
Dayton, Charles Henry. 2919
Dayton, Donald W. 1552, 1824
Dayton, Edward R. 1199, 2492, 3701
Dayton, N. Y. St. Paul of the Cross Church. 2700
Dayton, O. First Presbyterian church. 2918
Dayton, O. University. 1407
Deacon, Samuel. 3288
Dead Sea scrolls. 1409
Dead Sea scrolls. English. 1409

Dead Sea scrolls. English & Aramaic. 1409
Deal, Haskell Robert. 2174
Deal, William S. 309, 959, 995, 1430, 1604, 2337, 3478
Deal, Williams. 2705
Dealey, James Quayle. 2857
[Deamude, Jesse Ross]. 2724
Dean, Aldhelm. 884
Dean, Bailey Sutton. 289, 327
Dean, Beryl. 1488, 2679
Dean, Elizabeth Rice. 92, 1856, 2482
Dean, George. 3205
Dean, George B. 1573, 2443
Dean, Herschel B. 317, 2386
Dean, Horace F. 1572, 3228
Dean, Ibzan Rice. 2465
Dean, James Elmer. 285
Dean, John Marvin. 161
Dean, John William. 935, 2250
Dean, Paul. 3220
Dean, Robert James. 62, 323, 448, 2228
Dean, Susie Kelly. 2985
Dean, Thomas. 2352, 3328
Dean, William D. 11
Deane, Anthony Charles. 232, 389, 1215, 1951, 1962
[Deane, Eleanor Sherburne (Reed)]. 2133
Deane, Elisabeth. 2890
Deane, Henry. 1401
Deane, Hazel. 694
Deane, Herbert Andrew. 116, 3441
*Deane, John. 3601
Deane, Samuel. 3350
Deane, William John. 4, 1404, 2134, 3297
Deanesly, Margaret. 248, 1761, 2243
De Anguerre, Charles Edgar. 3500
Deans, William Alexander. 2513
Deansley, Margaret. 1761
De Aragon, Ray John. 1294, 2349
Dearborn, Frances Ross. 2590
The Dearborn independent. 2104
Dearborn, Mich. First Presbyterian church. 2918
Dearden, Harold. 2988
Dearden, Robert R. 212
Dearden, Robert Rowland, jr. 289
Dearing, Trevor. 1291, 1412, 1598
Dearmer, Mabel (White) 1980
Dearmer, Percy. 28, 1049, 1214, 1223, 1828, 1223, 1224, 2409, 2960, 3003, 3459
Dearness, William. 595
Dearnley, Christopher. 1206
Deats, Richard L. 2671
De Bardeleben, Mary Christine. 545, 586, 2870
De Bary, Richard. 2037, 3853, 1645
De Bary, William Theodore. 705
De Beausobre, Iulia. 3334
De Benedictis, Matthew M. 675, 3449
De Benedittis, Suzanne M. 935
Debenham, Mary H. 2794
De Bethune, Adelaide. 3690
Debidour, Victor Henry. 3316
De Bit, Ralph M. 959
De Blacam, Aodh Sandrach. 692, 2793
De Blank, Joost. 1153, 1258
De Blank, Joost, Abp. 1250
De Blois, Austen Kennedy. 140, 144, 1250, 1564, 2829, 3149, 3642, 3671
De Boer, Annie M Long. 2833
De Boer, Cecil. 3043
DeBoer, John C. 1270
De Bona, Maurice. 100
DeBonville, Bob. 1256
DeBord, Samuel A. 2498
De Bower, Edward. 1057
DeBoy, James J. 938
[De Brahm, John Gerar William]. 218
De Breffny, Brian. 1160, 3576
Debroey, Steven. 1400
De Bunsen, Victoria. 1543
De Burgh, David J. 997, 2032
De Burgh, William George. 1534
Debuyst, Frederic. 2240
De Camp, Lyon Sprague. 2724
De Candole, Henry. 1211, 1214
Decarreaux, Jean. 2578
De Castille, Vernon. 997
De Castro, Adolphe Danziger. 2082
DeCenzo, John. 1367, 1418
Dechanet, Jean Marie. 674, 1777, 2379
DeChantal. 3420
De Charms, George. 458, 1187, 3579
De Charms, Richard. 2692
Decision. 1456
Decker, Beatrice. 1257, 1418
Decker, Florence Frazer (Boston) 3237
Decker, Florence Frazer (Roston) 3466
Decker, Frank Harmanest. 959, 2014
Decker, James A. 959
Decker, James Arthur. 2386
De Claremont, Lewis. 2312
De Corneille, Roland. 1083
De Courcy, Arthur George. 3434
DeCoursey, Mary Edwin. 3693

Decow, Stacy. 1674
De Craemer, Willy. 835, 1933
Dedek, John F. 744, 3392
Deden, D. 1163
Dederick, Colin. 1238
Dedham, Mass. First church. 179
Dedmon, Emmett. 3874
Dedrichs, Wilhelm. 3373
Deedy, John G. 194, 774, 836, 1066, 2717, 3768
Deedy, John G., Jr. 1066
Deegan, Arthur X. 771, 1199
Deegan, Paul J. 3275
Deeken, Alfons. 18, 3306
Deemer, Philip. 1164
Deems, Charles Force. 413, 416, 1692, 1962, 2458, 3405
Deems, Edward Mark. 1839
Deems, James Harry. 2124
Deen, Edith. 214, 1603, 1846, 3831, 3834, 3839
Deer Park, N.Y.St. Cyril and St. Methodius Church. 1269
Deere, George Henry. 2870
Deerforth, Daniel. 3567
*Deeter, Walter Wells. 3195
Deets, Lee Emerson. 1858
Deever, Philip O. 2024
DeFehr, J Jennings. 450
Defenders of the Christian Faith. 1419
De Fer, Hugo. 2145
Deferrari, Roy Joseph. 830, 831, 1020, 1616, 2984, 3258, 3695, 3696, 831
DeFerrari, Teresa Mary. 3330
Deffner, Donald L. 1005, 1250, 1308, 1737, 2899, 3537
De Fleury, Maria. 3208
[Defoe, Daniel]. 1427, 1607, 2337
De Forest, Charlotte Burgis. 1407
De Forest, Ernest Grant. 3189
De Forest, John Hyde. 2533, 2534
Defouri, James H. 823, 1647
De Frees, Madeline. 764
De Frees, Madeline [Name in religion: Mary Gilbert, Sister]. 3522
De Gaspar, Emmy. 2342
Degelman, William Creighton. 195
De George, Richard T. 2417
Degering, Etta B. 632
De Givry, Grillot. 2312
Degnan, Bertrand. 2305
De Goesbriand, Louis. 70, 1849, 2037
DeGolier, Florence. 2412
De Groot, Alfred Thomas. 1460
DeGroot, Alfred Thomas. 1460, 1462, 1463, 1465, 2503, 2753
*De Groot, Wilson. 3500
De Gruche, Kingston. 2508
De Gruchy, John W. 3464
DeHaan, Dan. 177, 931, 1720
Dehaan, Martin Ralph. 1513
De Haan, Martin Ralph. 4, 204, 280, 321, 330, 464, 509, 610, 1350, 1430, 1513, 2129, 3350, 3720, 1431, 3318
De Haan, Martin Ralph, M.D. 2201
DeHaan, Richard W. 325, 469, 512, 605, 610, 1427, 1720, 1785, 2870
Deharbe, Joseph. 746, 767, 769
DeHass, Frank S. 1419, 2761
Dehau, Pierre Thomas. 997
Dehejia, Vidya. 876, 3600
Dehey, Elinor Tong. 3205, 3416
Dehgani-Tafti, Hassan B. 1362
Dehnert, Amy Hales, comp. 2970
DeHoff, George Washington. 62, 232, 645
Dehon, Leon Gustave. 3269
Dehoney, Wayne. 161, 1246, 2500
Dehqani-Tafti, H. B. 44, 1419
De Hueck, Catherine. 753, 1136, 2541, 2580, 3331, 1407, 3485
DeHuff, Elizabeth (Willis) 3819
Deich, Max. 3141
Deikman, Arthur. 2647
Deiss, Lucien. 884, 2239, 2254, 3771
Deissman, Gustav Adolf. 2796
Deissmann, Gustav Adolf. 321, 347, 407, 2796
Deitering, Carolyn. 778, 1708
Deitrick, Bernard E. 3626
Deitz, Archibald Edwin. 3642
Deitz, Purd Eugene. 1992
Deitz, Reginald W. 240
DeJean, Edgar K. 3661
De Jong, Alexander C. 2337
DeJong, Benjamin R. 2386
De Jong, Gerald Francis. 3046
De Jong, Gerrit. 1008, 1232, 1756, 2601, 2611
De Jong, Jerome. 2847
De Jong, Meindert. 207, 533, 536, 634
DeJong, Peter. 3391
*De Jong, Peter Y. 1024
De Jong, Peter Ymen. 2688, 1023, 1239, 1477, 1564, 3677
De Jong, Ymen Peter. 1024
De Kadt, Emanuel Jehuda. 2627
De Kay, Charles. 47

De Kay, James T. 2173
Dekel, Ephraim. 192, 3050
De Knoop, Freda. 625, 637
De Kock, Gertrude. 959, 1446
De Korne, John C. 913
De Korne, John Cornelius. 913, 2542
DeKorte, Juliann. 3414, 3798
DeKoster, Lester. 613
De Koven, Anna (Farwell) 3500
De Koven, James. 45
DeKruyter, Arthur H. 1114
Delabays, Joseph. 1618
De La Bedoyere, Michael. 749, 758, 997, 1066, 1621, 1640, 1779, 1850, 2193, 3450
De La Bedoyere, Michael Anthony Maurice. 739, 1640, 1650, 3869
De La Camp, Otto A. 1371
De Laczay, Etti. 2244
Delafield, D. A. 1304, 3126, 3382
Delafield, D A. 959, 1013, 1437, 1446, 3811
Delage, Augustin. 3485
De La Mare, Edith. 2349
Delamare, Henriette Eugenie. 1354
De La Mare, Walter John. 628
Delamarter, Arthur R. 1962
DeLamotte, Roy Carroll. 929, 2062
De Lancey, William Heathcote. 2830
De Land, Charles Edmund. 2068
Delaney, John J. 765, 1025, 2357, 3703
Delaney, John P. 1266
Delaney, Walter. 2724
De Lange, Nicholas Robert Michael. 505, 2152, 2743, 56, 489
Delanghe, Jules A. 2264
Delanglez, Jean. 822, 1947
Delany, Francis Xavier. 820
Delany, Martin Robison. 2585
Delany, Selden Peabody. 959, 1326, 764, 781, 785, 1024, 2253, 3280
Delaporte, Ernest P. 1366, 1420
DeLapp, G. Leslie. 1420
DeLarme, Alonzo Alvin. 2713
Delarue, Jacques. 3779
Delarue-Mardrus, Lucie. 3690
Delatte, Paul. 190
Delaughter, Thomas J. 558
De Laune, Thomas. 1468
De Laurence, Lauron William. 1049, 1598, 1886, 2067, 2312, 2645, 2724
Delavignette, Robert Louis. 1310
Delbanco, Andrew. 882
Delderfield, Eric R. 1169
De Leeuw, Cateau. 3719
Delehanty, Frances W. 2365
Delehaye, Hippolyte. 191, 952, 1024, 1780
De Leon, Daniel. 794, 1703, 3436
Delespesse, Max. 1118
De Lew, Lewis. 2085
Delfeld, Paula. 915, 1748
Delfiner, Henry. 3095
Del Fiorentino, Dante. 602
Delforge, Thomas. 2335
[Delgado, Pablo L]. 2354
Delhaye, Philippe. 1347, 2842
Delimat, Casimir A. 180
De Liso, Oscar. 2849
Delitzsch, Franz Julius. 611, 637, 1951, 2016, 2117
Delitzsch, Friedrich. 207, 486
Delk, Edwin Heyl. 1621, 3615
Delke, James Almerius. 158
Dell, Edward Thomas. 3180, 3790, 3800
Dell, Jacob Albert. 62
Dell, William. 1288, 3630
Delling, Gerhard. 3855
Dellinger, Annetta E. 1605
Dell'Isola, Frank. 317, 592, 1991, 2413
Delloue. 62
Del Mar, Eugene. 2694
Del Mazza, Valentino. 1263, 2357
DeLoach, Charles F. 83, 611, 2073
De Long, Arthur Hamilton. 1693, 1956
DeLong, John Edmund. 2135
De Long, Ressell Victor. 1238
De Long, Russell Victor. 1238, 1556, 2783, 3782
Deloria, Vine. 1091, 3141
Delorme, Jean. 2254
DeLouise, Joseph. 2948
Delp, Alfred. 2399
Delp, Paul S. 982, 3478
Delpech, Jacques. 2979
Del Rey, Maria. 1633
Delsol, Paula. 98
[Deltwyn, Agnes Procter]. 3206
De Luca, Anthony J. 1673, 2993, 2994
De Luce, Robert. 98
Delumeau, Jean. 811
Delzell, Charles F. 2770
Demann, Paul. 2138
Demant, Vigo Auguste. 1075, 3389, 3442
Demaray, Donald E. 285, 333, 2871, 2899, 2909
De Marco, Angelus A. 2196, 2826, 3774

DeMarco, Ginilou. 931, 1422
Demaree, Doris Clore. 3170, 3764
Demarest, Bruce A. 404, 405, 2037, 3224
Demarest, David D. 3045, 3046
Demarest, Donald. 1776, 2342
Demarest, Gary W. 341, 2337
Demarest, John Terhune. 340
Demarest, Victoria Booth. 1353
Demarest, Victoria Booth-Clibborn. 1350, 1422, 1437, 1542, 1828, 1837, 3836
De Marquette, Jacques. 2643
Demarst, David D. 3677
De Mayer, Jenny E. 2540
Dembitz, Lewis Naphtali. 2107
Dembitz, Lewis Naphtall. 2107
Demby, Edward Thomas. 372
*De Mejo, Oscar. 2582
De Mello, Anthony. 3475
De Ment, Byron Hoover. 1962
Demerath, Nicholas Jay. 2979, 3086, 3115
Demerest, Ada Rose. 632, 1485, 2757, 3560
DeMerschman, Lucille. 1962, 3058
Demetrakopoulos, George H. 2745
Demetrio, Francisco M. 1103
Demetry Constas Hadzi. 2745
De Mill, Richard Mead. 1590
DeMille, George E. 45
De Mille, George Edmed. 45, 712, 2957, 2960, 2967
Deming, Wilbur Stone. 3214, 3796
De Monbrun, Sarah Ann. 3090
De Monco, Almo. 2988
De Montfort, Odile. 2262
De Montmorency, James Edward Geoffrey. 1884, 3692
DeMoss, Arthur. 3539
De Moss, James Andrew. 463, 508
De Moss, Lucy King. 3011
Demosthenes. 1771
DeMott, Barbara. 1473
Demouy, William. 1266
Dempsey, Elam Franklin. 1458, 1512, 1792
Dempsey, Martin. 695, 997, 1618, 2189, 2359
Dempsey, T. 1421
Dempster, Joseph S. 1823
Demurger. 785
Demus, Otto. 3777
Denbeaux, Fred J. 232, 1103, 2978
Denck, Johannes. 37
Dendy, Marshall C. 934, 3160
Dendy, Walter Cooper. 2731, 2988
Dengel, Anna. 2538
Dengler, Sandy. 637
Denham, Hardy R. 992
Denham, William Ernest. 474, 1828
Den Hartog, Egbert. 3598
De Nicolas, Antonio T. 2196, 2316, 2840, 3776
Denifle, Heinrich. 785, 2321
Denio, Francis Brigham. 1828
Denis, Henri. 3642
Denis, Leon. 2988
Denis-Boulet, Noele M. 1163
Denis-Boulet, Noele Maurice. 1163
Denison, Frederic. 158
Denison, George Anthony. 3126
Denison, John Henry. 1951
Denlinger, A. Martha. 2407
Denmark, L Polk. 1668
Dennen, Ernest Joseph. 2960, 3553
Dennen, Leon. 2102
Dennerle, George Mark. 746, 1627
Dennett, Herbert. 358
Dennett, Tyler. 2502
Denney, James. 3651, 104, 1425, 1951, 1997
Dennie, Joseph. 2899
Denning, Dennis. 1170
Denning, Melita. 2312
Dennis, Delmar. 2125
Dennis, Fred E. 3350
Dennis, James Shepard. 2519, 2522, 2554, 3434
Dennis, John. 1309, 3606
Dennis, Lane T. 982
Dennis, Lyman M. 2323
Dennis, Muriel. 1425
Dennis, Muriel (White) 1166
Dennison, Alfred Dudley. 982, 2051
Dennison, Walter. 919
Denniston, Denise. 3708
Denniston, Robin. 959
Dennistton, Denise. 2382
Denny, Don. 920, 2357
Denny, Edward. 1211
Denny, Robert. 696
Denny, Walter B. 959
Denny, Walter Bell. 1962
De Normandie, James. 3821
Denser, Albert. 2226
Denslow, Ray Vaugh. 1667
Denslow, Ray Vaughn. 1663, 1661, 1664, 2620

Denslow, William R. 1902
Densmore, Warren I., Rev. 482
Dent, Barbara. 2386
Dent, Phyllis. 3478
Dentan, Robert Claude. 309, 489, 555, 598, 651, 1735, 1837
Dentan, Robert Clause. 489
Dentler, Clara Louise. 2272
Dentler, Robert A. 879
Denton, J. A. 3198
Denton, James Elbert. 1293
Denton, Jeffrey Howard. 1145, 3819
Denton, Nellye H. 2386
Denton, Samuel Posey. 2264
Denton, Wallace. 1303, 2780
Denton, William. 2010, 202, 1654, 3002
Denver. Art Museum. 3303
Denver, Central Presbyterian Church. 1425
Denzer, George Anthony. 2024, 2176
Deoscher, Waldemar O. 1127
De Ovies, Raimundo. 3179
De Paola, Thomas Anthony. 1776, 2022
De Paola, Tomie. 1027, 1640
De Paor, Maire. 1919
De Pascale, Marc. 95
De Pauley, William Cecil. 731
De Pauw, Gommar Albert. 870
Depenning, George Alfred Guelph. 3206
De Pierrefeu, Elsa (tudor) 2871
De Pina, Albert. 2005
De Plata, William R. 144, 2698
DePree, Gladis. 1425, 2167, 2386
DePree, Gladys Lenore. 1425, 1435
DePree, Gordon. 2386
DePress, Gladis. 2386
De Pui, James. 463
De Puy, Irving N. 645
DePuy, Norman R. 2386, 3661
Dequer, John H. 3588
De Quincey, Thomas. 1937, 2638
Deratany, Edward. 3784
Derby, Marian. 2548
De Reeper, J. 2507
De Reeper, John. 3264
De Regniers, Beatrice Schenk. 1405
Deretz, Jacques. 3774
Derham, Arthur Morgan. 178, 637, 959
Derham, William. 2674
De Ridder, Richard. 1024
De Rios, Marlene Dobkin. 3108
Derk, Francis H. 2020
Derksen, Sandy. 192, 1425
Derleth, August William. 2267
Dermenghem, Emile. 1921, 2628
Dermott, Laurence. 1661
Der Nersessian, Sirarpie. 1237
De Robeck, Nesta. 1027, 1284, 1446, 1508, 1649
De Robeck, Nests. 1387
De Roo, Peter. 24
De Roover, Raymond Adrien. 194
De Ropp, Robert S. 3294
De Rosa, Peter. 991, 1835, 2037, 3295, 3413
Derr, Ezra Z. 2417
Derr, Thomas Sieger. 1853
Derrett, John Duncan Martin. 1812, 2121
Derrick, Christopher. 188, 189, 854, 1136, 1245, 1394
Derrick, June. 2475
Derstine, Clayton F. 3392
Derstine, Gerald. 1425, 1576
Derum, James Patrick. 744, 2755
De Rupert, A E D. 726
Derwacter, Frederick Milton. 2113
Des Plaines, Ill. First Congregational Church. 1425
Desai, Gandabhai Girijashanker. 3776
Desai, Ram. 1135
De Salvo, Raphael. 3264
De Santillana, Giorgio. 2648, 2844
De Santis, Zerlina. 1962, 2357
De Santo, Charles. 465, 2337, 3661
De Satge, John. 2354, 2788
Des Barres, Frederick W W. 248
Desbuquois, Gustave. 887, 1846
Desbuquoit, Achille M. 2379
Descartes, Rene. 1425, 1426
Deschamps, J[ohn] M[adison]. 650
Deschner, John. 2009, 3803
De Schweinitz, Edmund Alexander. 3891
De Selincourt, Beryl D. 1647
Deseret Sunday school union board. 1704
Deseret Sunday school union, Salt Lake City. 2614
Des Grange, Jane. 2245
Deshimaru, Taisen. 3460
Deshler, G Byron. 1976
Deshmukh, Panjabrao Shamran. 3108
Deshon, George. 959, 3877
De Siano, Frank. 762
De Silva, Lynn A. 38
De Silva, M. W. Padmasiri. 710
Desjardins, Lucile. 333, 3149, 3764, 3149, 3167, 3183
Des Marais, Louise M. 3173

Desmond, Cecelia. 3287
Desmond, Humphrey Joseph. 1289, 1490, 33, 758, 826, 1817, 3033
Desmond, Shaw. 1102, 2262
Desmonde, William Herbert. 2584
De Sola, J. Mendes. 2086
De Soyres, John. 2586
Desplanques, Francois. 2365
DesPortes, Elisa L. 1244, 2946
Desroche, Henri. 1845, 3086, 3395
Dessain, Charles Stephen. 2702
Dessauer, Philipp. 2379
De Tar, John Hensley. 753
Deter, Arthur B. 2504
Deterding, Paul E. 334
Dethlefsen, Thorwald. 3053
Detienne, Marcel. 7, 84, 1459
Detling, William Colbert. 3198
Detroit Archdiocese Tribunal. 2342
Detroit. Fort street Presbyterian church. 2918
Detroit. Jefferson Avenue Presbyterian Church. 1426
Detroit news. 1426
Detroit Ordination Conference, 1975. 2742
Dett, Robert Nathaniel. 2680
Detty, Victor Charles. 3245, 3861
Detweiler, Charles Samuel. 2559
Detweiler, Frederick German. 141
Detweiler, Herbert J. 3880
Detweiler, Richard C. 2405
Detweller, Charles Samuel. 1437
Detzler, Wayne A. 1542
Deursen, Arie van. 209
Deussen, Paul. 3760
Deutsch, Bernard Francis. 1521, 2360
Deutsch, Eliot. 2417, 3330, 3775
Deutsch, Emanuel Oscar Menahem. 3582
Deutsch, Gotthard. 2088, 2093
Deutsch, Helene. 1459
Deutsch, Henri. 2411
Deutsch, Karl Wolfgang. 1133
Deutsch, Solomon. 563
Deutscher Evangelischer Missionstag, Hermannsburg, Ger., 1974. 1573
Deutz, Verene (Lambert) 182
*Devadutt, Vinjamuri E. 206, 3115
Devamata. 1816, 2570, 2772, 3020
Devan, S Arthur. 3856
Devan, Samuel Arthur. 3853
Devanandam, Rajamma. 1426, 3476
Devanandan, Paul David. 1108
Devaraja, Nand Kishore. 1815
Devas, Charles Stanton. 755
Devas, Dominic. 2333
Devas, Francis. 3485
Devaux, Andre A. 3593, 3831
Deveny, Albert Lewis. 1288
Dever, Daniel Augustine. 2254
Dever, Joseph. 1397
Dever, William G. 207
Devereux, Christina Anne. 2269, 3475
DeVille, Jard. 3829
Devin, Robert. 1756
Devine, Arthur. 3269, 2365
Devine, Bob. 662, 1384, 2675, 2676, 3898
Devine, George. 826, 862, 1266, 2239, 3628
Devine, M. C. 1397
Devins, John Bancroft. 2508
De Visser, John. 3739
Devivier, Walter. 762, 785
Devlin, Christopher. 872
Devlin, Mary Ruth. 1277
Devlin, William Joseph. 2783
De Voil, Walter Harry. 2735
De Voist, Myron. 1652
Devol, Edmund. 3710
DeVos, Julius Emil. 1174
Devos, Karen Helder. 3845
De Vries, John. 6
De Vries, Simon John. 483, 2950, 3701
De Vries, Tiemen. 1654
Dew, Caroline, Wellborn. 1720
De Waal, Victor. 1118
De Waal Malefijt, Annemarie. 3108
Dewan, Wilfrid F. 785, 1044, 1720
Dewar, Donald L. 3011
Dewar, Lindsay. 1828, 2997, 378, 1585, 2995
Dewart, Edward Hartley. 3849
Dewart, Elizabeth Haven. 2226
Dewart, Leslie. 816, 1085, 1720, 3070, 3099
DeWaters. 1030
De Waters, Lillian (Stephenson) 5, 1030
Dewdney, Selwyn H. 915
DeWeerd, James Arthur. 959
Deweese, Charles W. 155, 1166, 1201, 1408
DeWeese, Henry Harrison. 3410
DeWeese, Paul Nathan. 1845
De Weese, Reuben Deaver. 2095
DeWelt, Don. 446, 467, 532, 557
De Wette, Wilheim Martin Leberecht. 539

De Wette, Wilhelm Martin Leberecht. 409, 539
De Wetter, Louise Hurlbutt. 3500
Dewey, Bradley R. 2004
Dewey, Daisy. 3500
[Dewey, Dellon Marcus]. 3500
Dewey, Joanna. 435, 995
Dewey, John. 3058, 1534, 2590, 3058
Dewey, John Hamlin. 2060, 2409, 2476, 2724, 3684
Dewey, Mark. 3473
Dewey, Melvil. 1286
Dewey, Orville. 1853, 2980, 3727
Dewey, Robert D. 1329, 1590, 3175, 3615, 3884
Dewhurst, Frederick Eli. 3339
Dewick, Edward Chisholm. 1078, 1528, 1886
De Wilde, James Copray. 1924
Dewing, Arthur Stone. 2226
DeWire, Harry A. 1316, 3829
De Witt, Charles N. 458
DeWitt, Cornelia. 3500
DeWitt, David A. 63
De Witt, Norman Wentworth. 376, 2796
[De Witt, Susan (Linn) 3208
DeWitt, Thomas. 2698
De Witt, William C. 1329
De Witt, William Converse. 3612
De Witt, William Radcliffe. 3459
De Wohl, Louis. 63, 116, 1937, 2853, 809
Dewolf, Daniel Fowler. 3678
De Wolf, Lotan Harold. 1057, 3656
DeWolf, Lotan Harold. 307, 381, 950, 1057, 1695, 3099, 3177, 3211, 3642, 3661
De Wolfe, James Pernette. 2346
Dexter, Elisabeth Williams (Anthony) 3671
Dexter, Henry Martyn. 1340, 1344, 1516, 1699, 3427
Dexter, Mary (Morton) 1692
[Dexter, Samuel]. 1931
Dexter, Thomas Francis George. 1388
[Deymann, Clementine. 3455
Deyneka, Anita. 2821, 3257
Deyneka, Peter. 1110
De Zoysa, Agampodi Paulus. 701
De Zulueta, Francis M. 785
DeZurko, Edward Robert. 1270
Dhalla, Maneckji Nusservanji. 3898
Dhamamjaya. 3301
Dhammamjaya. 701, 711
Dhammapada. 701, 711
Dhammapada English. 704, 711, 2193, 2638
Dhammapada. English. 701, 711
Dhanamjaya. 3301
Dhanapala, D. B. 2760
Dhavamony, Mariasusai. 197
Dheilly, Joseph. 571
Dhiegh, Khigh. 1878
Dhirananda, swami. 3339
Dhiravamsa. 704, 3780
Dhirendra Brahmachari. 3864
D'Humy, Fernand Emile. 1494
D'humy, Fernard Emile. 1494
Dialogus creaturarum. English. 1588
Diamond, Herbert Maynard. 3058
Diamond, Malcolm Luria. 3099
Diamond, Wilfrid Joseph. 843, 906, 1266
Diara, Agadem L. 2680
Diaz, Abby (Morton) 3149
Diaz, Tony. 1363, 1458
DiBacco, Thomas V. 2589
Dibble, Charles Lemuel. 63, 3093
Dibble, Ernest F. 2709
Dibble, Roy Floyd. 2628
Dibden, Jean T. 2386
Dibelius, Martin. 3335, 330, 387, 389, 409, 412, 446, 1019, 2037
Dibelius, Otto. 1458
DiBrandi, Herman A. 3661
Di Cesare, Mario A. 2951
Dick, Everett Newfon. 3380
Dick, Ignace. 1487
Dick, John. 305, 3642
Dick, Kenneth C. 3115
Dick, Opal Wheeler. 3528
Dick, Robert Paine. 1799
Dick, Russell Leslie. 2785
Dick, Samuel Medary. 2409
Dick, Thomas. 1695, 3075
Dick, Willis V. 3671
Dicken, E W Trueman. 2642, 3603
Dickens, Arthur Geoffrey. 1374, 1763, 3033, 3038, 3039
Dickens, Charles. 930, 1112, 1114, 1963, 1980, 2856, 3547
Dickens, John Lunsford. 2055, 3340
Dickerman, Benoni. 2047
Dickerson, Emma (Richardson) 1458
Dickerson, Roy Ernest. 959
Dickert, Thomas Wilson. 906, 1706, 3369
Dickey, Adam Herbert. 1494
Dickey, Christina Robinson. 45, 1818
Dickey, Douglas A. 3350
Dickey, Edgar Primrose. 3224

Dickey, James. 317, 318, 2952
Dickey, Rufus Needham. 1975
Dickey, Samuel. 3234
Dickhoff, Robert Ernst. 701
Dickie, Edgar Primrose. 906, 3288
Dickie, Mary Stevens. 3310
Dickinson, Alice. 3827
Dickinson, Charles Henry. 1057, 3442
Dickinson, Clarence Heber. 1985
Dickinson, Edward. 1207
Dickinson, Eleanor. 3230
Dickinson, Ellen E. 2611, 3470
Dickinson, George T. 492, 514, 1942
Dickinson, Goldsworthy Lowes. 1887, 3058
Dickinson, James Taylor. 3347
Dickinson, John Compton. 1516, 2579, 3790
Dickinson, Jonathan. 2914, 1098, 1218, 1458, 1651, 1751, 1753, 1905, 2914, 2936, 3340
Dickinson, Lydia Fuller. 2409
Dickinson, Mary Lowe. 3198
Dickinson, Mary (Lowe) 2047
Dickinson, Moses. 1503
Dickinson, Peard. 3126
Dickinson, Peter. 628, 2732
Dickinson, Richard C. 16, 2297
Dickinson, Richard D. N. 1127
Dickinson, Richard William. 2051, 293
Dickinson, Sarah (Truslow) 1621, 2890
Dickman, R. Thomas. 3478
Dicks, Lee E. 3744
Dicks, Russell Leslie. 2409, 1258, 1413, 2780, 3405, 3406, 3671, 3783
Dickson, Albert A. 2386
Dickson, Alexander. 1956
Dickson, Andrew Flinn. 2067, 2931, 3296
Dickson, Harley. 2037
Dickson, James A R. 1564
Dickson, James Jacobs. 2372, 3478
Dickson, James Milligan. 2586
Dickson, Kwesi A. 330
Dickson, Louis Klaer. 959, 2465, 2871
Dickson, Mathes Daniel. 3410
Dicus, A W. 467
Didier, Jean Charles. 3264
Didier, Ralph H. 2914
Didon, Henri. 1963
Di Donato, Pietro. 723, 2333
Diefenbach, Gabriel. 2379
Diefendorf, Dorr Frank. 1074
[Diefenthaler, George Theodore]. 1077
Dieffenbach, Albert Charles. 3744
Dieffenbach, Georg Christian. 2032
Dieffenbach, Ray J. 3052
Diehl, Calvin Wenner. 1040
Diehl, George West. 1849, 2736, 3242
Diehl, Katharine Smith. 1876, 3089
Diehl, Nona M. 3734
Diehl, Thomas. 3270
Diehl, William E. 2191, 2202
Diehm, Edgar G. 1235
Diehm, Floyd L. 1003
Diekmann, Godfrey. 2235, 2236, 2239
Diel, Paul. 2660
Diem, Hermann. 1583, 2169
Dienert, Ruth Graham. 615, 651
Dierenfield, Richard B. 3096
Dierick, Alfons. 1715
Dierks, Hartwig. 3439
Dierks, Theodore. 1661
Diertins, Joseph. 2269, 2386
*Dietel, Mary Holder. 1793
Dieter, Melvin Easterday. 1824
Diethelm, Walther. 2124, 2851
Diether, Lawrence C. 120
Dietrich, B. C. 1387
Dietrich, John Hassler. 3725
Dietrich, Suzanne de. 293, 369, 421, 448, 1658, 1659, 3661
Dietze, Charles E. 3528
Diez-Alegria, Jose Maria. 1911, 1091, 1459
Diffendorfer, Ralph Eugene. 2014, 2883, 894, 2549, 3442
Di Gangi, Mariano. 552
Digges, Mary Laurentia. 492, 838
Diggle, John William. 3115
Diggs, Bernard James. 3693
Diggs, Dorothy C. 27
Diggs, Margaret Agneta. 875
Digha-nikaya. 705
Dighton, Kan. First Christian Church. 1459
DiGiacomo, James. 1976, 3485, 3884
Dignam, Augustus. 3222
Dignam, F Philip. 2027
Dignan, Patrick Joseph. 826, 1242
Dilday, Russell H. 1350
Di Lella, Alexander A. 489
Diles, David L. 102
Dill, Jacob Smiser. 140, 144
[Dill, James Renwck]. 2231
Dill, James Renwick. 3547
Dillard, Annie. 2386
Dillard, Edward Banks. 1556, 1564

Dillard, J L. 3661
[Dillard, Lillian Leona (Madison) 1303
Dillard, Pauline (Hargis) 619, 1980
Dillenberger, Jane. 84, 920, 922
Dillenberger, John. 2978, 3084, 3617
Dillenschnedidr, Clement. 1828
Dillenschneider, Clement. 1298, 1828, 2049, 3264
Diller, William F. 2195
Dilley, Frank Brown. 2417
[Dilling, Elizabeth (Kirkpatrick)] 1894. 2104
Dillingham, Emma Louise (Smith) 2524
Dillingham, Fred Augustine. 1992
Dillingham, John. 3149
Dillistone, Frederick William. 104, 1828, 104, 200, 276, 1094, 1187, 2554, 2693, 3025, 3407
Dillman, Daisy Ellen. 1583
Dillon, Emile Joseph. 549
Dillon, John Joseph. 22
Dillon, Mary Earhart. 3816
Dillon, Valerie (Vance) 3390
Dillon, William. 2365
Dillon, William Simon. 1904
Dillow, Ida Souers. 3461
Dillow, Joseph. 1716
Dillow, Joseph C. 593, 3392
Dillow, Linda. 3831
Dilworth-Harrison, Talbot, 1886. 1220
Dilworth, Mark. 3301, 3314
Dilworth-Harrison, Talbot. 2754
Diman, Jeremiah Lewis. 3608
Dimier, Catherine. 491
Dimmick, Luther Fraseur. 1459, 3884
Dimock, Edward C. 3272
Dimock, Marshall Edward. 3066
Dimock, Nathaniel. 2049
Dimond, Sydney George. 3228
Dimont, Max I. 2088, 2155
Dinger, Jesse Eugene. 1840
Dingle, James Shannon. 204
Dingle, Theola (Atkinson) 3500
Dingwell, James Davidson. 3620
Dinin, Samuel. 2104, 3028
Dinkard. Books 6. English & Pahlavi. 2822
Dinneen, Joseph Francis. 2852
Dinsmore, Charles Allen. 210, 1049, 3077, 104, 3077
Dinsmore, Maret H. 1997
Dion, Philip E. 3486
Dione, R. L. 287
Dionysius, Areopagita. 1460
Dionysius Areopagita, Pseudo. 3635
Dionysius, of Alexandria, Saint. 3280
DiOrio, Ralph A. 1301, 1460, 3476
Dirks, John Edward. 2776
Dirks, Lee E. 1045, 3744, 3849
Dirks, Marvin J. 2899, 3692
Dirks, Walter. 2576
Dirksen, Cletus Francis. 3449
Dirkswager, Edward J. 1125
Dirscherl, Denis. 1729
Dirsztay, Patricia. 1165
Dirvin, Joseph I. 2190, 2261, 2478, 3275, 3378
Disciples of Christ. 1271, 1460
Disciples of Christ. Board of Ministerial Relief. 1462
Disciples of Christ. Commission on Church and Society. 1133
Disciples of Christ Historical Society. 6, 2683
Disciples of Christ. International convention. Columbus, O., 1937. 1461
Disciples of Christ. International convention. Denver, 1938. 1461
Disciples of Christ. International convention. Des Moines, 1934. 1461
Disciples of Christ. International convention. Kansas City, Mo., 1936. 1461
Disciples of Christ. International convention. Richmond, 1939. 1461
Disciples of Christ. International convention. San Antonio, 1935. 1461
Disciples of Christ. National Church Program Coordinating Council. 3149
Disciples of Christ. North Carolina. North Carolina Christian missionary convention. 1465
Disciples of Christ. Study Commission on Ministerial Education. 1462, 3681
Dishman, Pat. 1783
Disney, M G. 1118
Disney, Walter Reed. 198
Dispenza, Joseph. 1710
Distad, N. Merrill. 1291, 1786
Di Stasi, Anthony. 2915
DiStasi, Lawrence. 1578
Ditchfield, Peter Hampson. 752
Ditmanson, Harold H. 1127, 1752
Ditterich, Richard. 2976
Dittes, James E. 1131, 1165, 1295, 2785, 3612

Ditzen, Lowell Russell. 1012, 1200, 1247, 1250, 2244, 3716
Dives and pauper. 1315
Dix, Gregory. 104, 1190, 2056, 2386
Dix, Morgan. 2056, 2699, 2701, 2767, 2972, 3415
Dixon, William Frederick. 1720
Dixon, A[mzi] C[larence]. 3094
Dixon, Amzi Clarence. 161, 959, 1556, 1564, 1828
Dixon, Christa. 3522
Dixon, George Perry. 302
Dixon, Helen (Cadbury) Alexander. 2899
Dixon, Herbert Allen. 3685
Dixon, James Qallan. 2645
Dixon, Jeane. 2037, 2946, 2948, 3053
Dixon, John W. 84, 3642
Dixon, Joseph. 637
Dixon, Joseph Lawrence. 3461
Dixon, Madeline Cutler. 1397
Dixon, Richard Watson. 1220
Dixon, Robert L. 3350
Dixon, Roland Burrage. 2666
Dixon, William Caveness. 906
Dixon, William Hepworth. 1652
Djobadze, Wachtang Z. 53
Djwal Kul. 117
Doan, Eleanor Lloyd. 619, 3858
Doan, Frank Carleton. 1057, 3058, 2386
Doane, Clarence Eugene. 1057
Doane, Doris Chase. 95, 3588, 3701
Doane, George Hobart. 2217
Doane, George Washington. 1472, 1873, 2957
Doane, Pelagie. 313, 1644, 1733, 619, 897, 1996
Doane, Susan Heritage. 1721
Doane, Thomas William. 232, 2651
Doane, W[illiam] H[oward]. 3553
Doane, William Croswell. 2051
Dob Baer ben Samuel. 3580
Dobbert, John. 982, 3539, 3877
Dobbins, Austin C. 1472, 1498, 2468
Dobbins, Dunstan John. 2646
Dobbins, Frank Stockton. 3115
Dobbins, Fred E. 203
Dobbins, Gaines Stanley. 1250, 1253, 423, 959, 992, 1141, 1250, 1472, 3003, 3149, 3168, 3465, 3553, 3671, 3829
Dobbins, Richard O. 903
Dobbs, Ena H. 276
Dobbs, John Francis. 3058
Doberstein, John W. 900, 2297, 3406
Dobie, David. 287
Dobin, Joel C. 98
Dobler, Walter E. 3168
Dobraczynski, Jan. 1003, 2183
Dobree, Bonamy. 3803
[Dobs, Marcus]. 1892
Dobschutz, Ernst [Adolf Alfred Oskar Adalbert] von. 304
Dobschutz, Ernst von. 1190, 304, 1190
Dobson, Cyril Comyn. 1957
Dobson, Ed. 1690
Dobson, Eric John. 39, 2229, 2582
Dobson, John H. 516
Dobson, Richard Barrie. 1483
Dobson, Theodore Elliott. 1598, 3486
Dobyns, William Ray. 232
Dockery, John Berchmans. 1309
Docter, Kathryn. 3277
Dr. A. N. Upadhye Memorial Seminar on Jaina Philosophy, Literature and Culture, University of Mysore, 1976. 1932
Doctrinal tract and book society, Boston. 3706
Dodd, Alfred. 3400, 3500
Dodd, Charles Harold. 232, 276, 334, 369, 376, 389, 419, 467, 476, 588, 1530, 2024, 2031, 2037, 2176, 2200, 2024, 2176
Dodd, Edward Mills. 2538, 2539, 2540
Dodd, Ira Seymour. 2931
Dodd, John Theodore. 1219, 1472
*Dodd, Monroe E. 1840
Dodd, Monroe Elmon. 155, 1167, 1318, 1556, 1951, 2051, 2871, 3788
Dodd, Thomas J. 2017
Dodd, William. 1413
Dodder, G. Clyde. 3182
Doddridge, Philip. 58, 347, 959, 1472, 2258, 3050, 3051, 3671, 3884
Dodds, Elisabeth D. 1499
Dodds, Eric Robertson. 1587, 2683, 2732
Dodds, James E. 2694, 2724
Dodds, Lois. 3885
Dodds, Robert Clarence. 1506
Dodds, Samuel. 499, 1446
Dodewaard, J. A. E. van. 2363
Dodge, Arthur Pillsbury. 127
[Dodge, David Low]. 2217, 3792
Dodge, Ebenezer. 59
Dodge, James George. 2323
[Dodge, Mary Abigail] 1833-1896. 1068, 1118, 2037, 3471
Dodge, Ralph Edward. 2500, 2978

Do-Dinh, Pierre. 1330, 1854
Dods, John Bovee. 1098, 3500
Dods, Marcus. 232, 289, 2246, 2564
Dodshon, Joseph Henry. 3596
Dodson, George Rowland. 3115
Dodson, Kenneth. 1358, 3240
Dodson, Ralph H. 3340
Dodson, Samuel Kendrick. 2229
Dodwell, Charles Reginald. 317, 1883
Dodwell, William. 99
Doe, Paul. 3582
Doe, Walter P. 1556, 3126
Doebler, John. 920, 3399
Doederlein, Gertrude. 3170
Doege, Arthur John. 1318
Doell, E. W. 13
Doerffier, Alfred, jr. 3406
Doerffier, Alfred. 585, 2735, 3406, 3407
[Doerffler, Alfred]. 2890
Doering, Bertha Charlotte. 2497
Doerr, Edd. 1148
Doescher, Waldemar O. 1127
Doeswick, Peter J. 798
Doeswyck, Peter J. 798
Dogen, 1200-1253. 1472
Doggett, Laurence Locke. 2305, 3870, 3874
Doggett, Lawrence Locke. 3874
Doggett, Marshall Wellington. 3410
Dohanian, Diran Kavork. 2317
Dohen, Dorothy. 826, 997
Doheny, William Joseph. 1241, 2341, 3203
Doherty, Barbara. 3486
Doherty, Bessie L. 2492
Doherty, Catherine de Hueck. 771, 871, 997, 1013, 1322, 1473, 1602, 3478
Doherty, Dennis. 2342
Doherty, Edward Joseph. 683, 753, 1419, 1446, 3286, 3459, 3580, 2386
Doherty, Howard J. 893
Doherty, Joseph Francis. 2478
Doherty, Mary Michael. 804, 937, 939, 3175
Doherty, Reginald. 997
Doherty, Robert Remington. 2443
Doherty, Robert W. 1684
Dohrman, H. T. 186, 2328
Doig, Desmond. 2717, 3602
Doing, Robert B. 959
Doing, Robert Burns. 991
Dolaghan, Thomas. 2677
Dolak, George. 3426
Dolan, Albert H. 3690
Dolan, Albert Harold. 785, 1650, 3222, 3392, 3580, 3690
Dolan, Henry Thomas. 63
Dolan, Jay P. 833, 873, 2774
Dolan, John Patrick. 809, 3033
Dolan, Joseph M. 1258
Dolan, Rex Robert. 1243
Dolan, Thomas Stanislaus. 862, 1372, 1378, 2768
Dolan, William M. 2624
Dolbeer, William H. 189
Dolby, James R. 1107
Dolch, Edward William. 895
Dole, Charles Fletcher. 338, 628, 959, 1887, 2012, 3066, 3141
Dole, George Henry. 1166, 1380, 1963, 2689, 3608
Dole, Nathan Haskell. 2199
Doll, Louis William. 48
Dollar, George W. 1691
Dollar, Truman. 3528
Dollen, Charles. 1020, 1021, 1280, 1702, 2203, 2303, 2351, 2360, 3773, 3870
Dollinger, Johann Joseph Ignaz von. 1040, 2736, 2862, 3769
Dolloff, Eugene Dinsmore. 1210, 1250, 3003, 3671
Dolloff, Eugene Dinsmore. 3671
Dolman, Dirk Hermanis. 1828, 3579
Doloff, Eugene Dinsmore. 1239
Dolphin, Lambert. 3469
Dolson, Grace Neal. 2710
Dolto, Francoise Marette. 2050
Dolven, Oswald Earl. 2291
Domas, Anna Wirtz. 2359, 3738
Domaszewski, Alfred von. 3246
Domenach, Jean Marie. 817, 3449
Domenica, Angelo di. 799, 146, 871
Domesday commemoration, 1886. 1474
Domingos, Ann Maria. 3170
Dominian, Jack. 1162
Dominian, Jacob. 1003
Dominic. 3140
Dominican Sisters. Congregation of the Most Holy Rosary, Adrian, Mich. 1263
A Dominican tertiary. 3249
Dominicans. Third Order. 1476
Dominicis, Ercole H. 2213
Dominick, Mabel Axcy. 309
[Dominick, Maynard A.]. 1350
Doms, Herbert. 2337
Donaghy, Thomas J. 824, 867
Donaghy, William Andrew. 1266

Donahoe, Daniel Joseph. 1877, 1878
Donahoe, James. 887
Donahue, George Joseph. 771, 2702
Donahue, John R. 438, 2068
Donahue, Marilyn Cram. 180
Donald, Gertrude. 2702, 2754
Donald, Lea. 1801
Donaldson, Gordon. 3042, 3315
Donaldson, Margaret F. 1250
Donaldson, Mary Ethel Muir. 3315
Donaldson, O F. 221
Donaldson, Oscar Fielding. 3461
Donaldson, Stuart Alexander. 1183
Donaldson, Thomas. 1905
Donat, Josef. 3077
Donath, Dorothy C. 711
Don Carlos, Thomas Boone. 3126
Doncaster, L. Hugh. 1681
Donceel, Joseph F. 1721, 2672, 3461
Dondero, E Austin. 2570
Donders, Adolf. 1268
Donders, Joseph G. 398, 399, 430, 862, 1263, 2047, 3350, 3363
Dondeyne, Albert. 1058
Done, Willard. 3839
Donehoo, James De Quincey. 336
Donehoo, James Ramsey. 450
Doney, Carl Gregg. 885, 1118, 2425, 2442
Donfried, Karl P. 347
Doniach, Nakdimon Shabbethary. 3006
Donicht, Mark. 1476, 3747
Doniger, Simon. 2326, 2887
Donin, Hayim. 2079, 2081, 2107, 2119, 2885, 3361
Donkin, William. 2400
Donlan, Thomas C. 2342, 3757
Donle, Charles B. 3885
DonLeavy, Al. 2357
Donn, Thomas Mackenzie. 551
Donnan, Lizzie Glenn (Hunt) 1437
Donne, John. 872, 1016, 1226, 1418, 1934, 2268, 2386, 3363, 3406, 1226, 1228, 1946, 2268, 2386, 2871, 2890, 3642
Donnell, Robert. 1396
Donnellan, Michael. 935, 941
Donnelly, Dody. 1776
Donnelly, Doris. 1633
Donnelly, Dorothy (Boillotat) 3099
Donnelly, Eleanor Cecelia. 173
Donnelly, Eleanor Cecilla. 1750
Donnelly, Francis Patrick. 47, 1826, 1949, 2365, 2386, 2899, 3247, 3266, 3269
Donnelly, Gertrude Joseph. 2572
Donnelly, Harold I. 2919
Donnelly, Harold Irvin. 3553
Donnelly, Ignatius. 102
Donnelly, James S. 1276
Donnelly, John. 1347, 3609
Donnelly, John J. 2988
Donnelly, John Patrick. 2327, 3777, 3033
Donnelly, Joseph P. 1947
Donnelly, Joseph Peter. 691, 1857
Donnelly, Joseph W. 2988
Donnelly, Marian Card. 1271
Donnelly, Morwenna. 1708, 3864
Donner, Andreas Matthias. 1076
Donoghue, Richard Kingston. 4
Donohue, John. 997
Donohue, John W. 1946
Donohue, Thomas. 712
Donoso Cortes, Jaun, 1809-1853. 3436, 3449
Donoso Cortes, Juan. 3436
Donovan, C. F. 1590
Donovan, Cornelius Francis. 1590
Donovan, Frank Robert. 3826
Donovan, John D. 831
Donovan, John F. 1633, 2461, 2485, 2508
Donovan, John Thomas. 824, 1290
Donovan, Joseph Patrick. 1391, 1701
Donovan, Marcus. 2056
Donovan, Mary Annice. 2362
Donovan, Nelle Catherine (Donovan) 717
Donovan, Peter. 1585, 3070
Donovan, Robert O. 694
Donovan, Vincent J. 1094
Donze, Mary Terese. 1028, 3603
Doob, Leonard William. 1745
D'Ooge, Benjamin Leonard. 2657
Doolan, Leonard Weakley. 1840
Dooley, Anne Mary. 2997
Dooley, Bernard F J. 1114
Dooley, Catherine. 2360
Dooley, Kate. 1025
Dooley, Lester M. 1828, 1618, 1776, 1828, 1836, 3006, 3269
[Dooley, Patrick Joseph]. 2698
Dooley, Thomas A. 2539
Dooley, Thomas Anthony. 2539
-Dooley, William Joseph, 1917. 29, 2342
Doolittle, Nelson. 3752
Doolittle, Thomas. 2250
Dooman, Isaac. 2488
Door, Peter. 637

Doornik, Nicolaas Gerardus Maria van. 762, 795, 1027, 1640
Dooyeweerd, Herman. 2179
Dopfner, Julius, Cardinal. 758
Doppelt, Frederic Aubrey. 2119, 2871, 3032
Doran, Robert M. 1819, 2245
Dorcheff, George. 3250
Dorchester, Daniel. 831, 1174, 3642, 3738
Dorchester, Mass. Second church. 3350
Dorcy, Mary Jean. 2580, 22, 1475, 1613, 2359, 2580, 3284, 3404
Dore, Gustave. 84, 601, 602
Dore, Gustave [Louis Auguste Gustave Dore]. 601
[Doree, Nadage]. 1049, 1995, 2117, 3461
Doresse, Jean. 1717
Dorion, Eustache Charles Edouard. 2420
Dorman, Harry Gaylord. 1925, 2567
Dorman, Rushton M. 1904
Dorn, Jacob Henry. 1715
Dorn, John George. 2249
Dornblaser, Thomas Franklin. 3126
Dorner, Isaak August. 943, 1528, 2954, 3679
Dorney, Henry. 1446
Doronzo, Emmanuel. 1295, 3224
Dorotheus, 6th cent. 90
Dorough, C. Dwight. 3468
Dorr, Benjamin. 1695, 2414
Dorr, Donal. 139
Dorr, Julia Caroline (Ripley) 1516
Dorr, William Meriwether. 1750
Dorries, Hermann. 1355, 3194, 1196, 1355
Dorrill, Robert L. 3680
Dorris, Jonathan Truman. 3236
Dorsey, George Amos. 892
Dorsey, J. M. 1654
Dorsey, Noah Ernest. 25
Dorsey, Stephen Palmer. 1162
[Dorsey, Theodore Hooper] 1899. 1363
Dort, Synod of, 1618-1619. 2919
Dortch, David Elijah. 140, 1860
Dosker, Henry E[lias]. 1188
Dosker, Henry Elias. 1174, 1477
Doss, Helen (Grigsby) 615, 1721, 2130
Doss, Richard W. 1413
Dossetor, Roberts Francis. 1108
Dotan, Aron. 1, 2164
Doten, Elizabeth. 3500
Dotts, Maryann J. 632, 2022, 2224
Doty, Brant Lee. 2796, 2804
Doty, Harry L. 1477, 2785, 2886
Doty, James Edward. 2780
Doty, Thomas K. 1823, 1828
Doty, William G. 351, 368, 1019
Doty, William Lodewick. 771, 810, 826, 997, 1013, 1263, 1295, 1413, 1840, 2386, 2871, 3486, 3771
Doub, Peter. 1304
Douce, P. M. 1507, 3473
Douds, William S. 3442
[Dougall, Lily] 1858-1923. 1058, 1721, 2037, 3478
Dougherty, John Charles. 637
Dougherty, John J. 309
Dougherty, John M. 848
Dougherty, Kenneth Francis. 2738
Dougherty, Peter. 915
Dougherty, Raymond Philip. 3404
Dougherty, Robert Lee. 1963, 2018
Doughty, John. 526, 2690
Doughty, William Ellison. 2492
Doughty, William Lamplough. 3209
Douglas, Alfred. 1470, 1878, 3588
Douglas, Charles Edward. 458
Douglas, Charles Winfred. 1207
Douglas, Claude Cicero. 347
Douglas, Donald. 1851, 3227
Douglas, George. 2056
Douglas, George Cunninghame Monteath. 590, 3297
Douglas, George William. 479, 2972, 3350, 1822
Douglas, James Dixon. 243, 1043, 1356, 1375, 1575, 1715, 3638
Douglas, Kenneth. 1584
Douglas, Lloyd C. 2066
Douglas, Lloyd Cassel. 1250, 2476, 3671, 1825, 2825, 3350
Douglas, Mack R. 1564
Douglas, Mary Tew. 674, 3058
Douglas, Richard M. 3272
Douglas, Robert Kennaway. 913
Douglas, Robert W. 2126, 2861
Douglas, William G. T. 1303
Douglas, William Orville. 3096
Douglass, Aubrey Augustus. 895
Douglass, Earl Leroy. 73, 1431
Douglass, Harlan Paul. 1040, 1278, 1838, 2527, 2545, 2955, 3276, 3435, 3522, 2955, 3276
Douglass, Herbert E. 2037, 3318, 3350, 3385, 3387
Douglass, James W. 2712, 2809

Douglass, Paul Franklin. 1250, 1707, 2459, 3803
Douglass, R. 1905
Douglass, Robert. 1202
Douglass, Robert Sidney. 156
Douglass, Rufus Collins. 920
Douglass, Stephen B. 982
Douglass Sunday School Lessons. 1966 (The) 1915
Douglass, Truman B. 1201, 2558, 2899
Douglass, Truman Orville. 1336
Douglass, William. 1524, 2681
Douglass, William, of Philadelphia. 2973
Douie, Decima Langworthy. 2810
Douillet, Jacques Marie Joseph. 3280
Doukhan, Jacques. 2152
Doukhobor Research Committee. 1482
Doumato, Lamia. 78, 1161, 1237, 1929
Doumette, Hanna Jacob. 1446, 3053
Dourisboure, Pierre X. 849, 2559
Dournes, Jacques. 2559
Douthitt, Cecil B. 647
Doutney, Thomas N. 3595
Douty, Mary Alice. 3179
Douty, Norman Franklin. 324, 736, 1828, 3029, 3288, 3318, 3382
Dovey, J Whitsed. 2533
Dow, Daniel. 2688, 3402, 3403, 3711
Dow, Earle Wilbur. 2769
Dow, Edward French. 3395
Dow, James L. 3500
Dow, John. 1701, 1951
Dow, Lorenzo. 660, 1477, 1478, 2428, 2672, 3091, 3198
Dow, Peggy. 119
Dow, Robert Arthur. 1170, 1256
Dow, Sterling. 1505
Doward, Jan S. 3379, 3382, 3883
Dowd, Conell Martin. 1165
Dowd, Edward Francis. 2259
Dowd, F[reeman] B[enjamin]. 3050
[Dowd, Freeman Benjamin]. 3250
Dowd, John C. 2386
Dowd, Mary Amadeus. 7
Dowd, Matthew Hamilton. 3253
Dowd, Quincy Lamartine. 1951
Dowd, William Aloysius. 401
Dowdell, Victor Lyle. 1218
[Dowden, Hester]. 3500
Dowden, John. 1163, 2257, 2960
Dowding, Henry Wallace. 2976
Dowding, Hugh Caswall Tremenheere Dowding. 3500
Dowdy, Augustus W. 3594
Dowdy, Homer E. 1508, 2351, 2505, 2514, 2559
Dowdy, Rufus Edward. 1254
Dowell, Margaret Foulks. 2476
Dower, William H. 2724
Dowey, Edward A. 3735
Dowis, Solomon F. 1279
Dowkontt, George D. 2538
Dowkontt, George H. 276, 2871
Dowley, Tim. 1174
Dowling, Austin. 2721
Dowling, Enos E. 3220
Dowling, Enos Everett. 1464
Dowling, George Thomas. 3340
Dowling, Gerard Patrick. 1323
Dowling, John. 799, 1840
Dowling, John Goulter. 1019
[Dowling, Levi H.]. 2724
Dowling, Levi H. 1975, 2005, 1975
Dowling, Linda C. 1518
Dowling, Michael J. 2377
Dowling, Theodore Edward. 82, 1768, 82
Down, Goldie M. 1300, 1478, 2485, 3387, 3422, 3718
Downer, William Arthur. 3224
Downey, Anna. 1556
Downey, Columba. 854
Downey, David George. 2670
Downey, James. 2909
Downey, Murray W. 413, 1094
Downey, Richard. 758, 2980, 3711
Downey, William Scott. 2979, 2980
Downey, Winifred Truter. 1661
[Downie, Annie Hershey, 1852. 1478
Downie, David. 2502, 2530
Downie, Hugh Kerr. 450, 3373
Downie, Robert Mager. 3220
Downing, Barry H. 232
Downing, Christine. 1742
Downing, Francis Gerald. 1184, 1987, 2037, 3224
Downing, James. 3126
Downing, Jim. 2381
Downing, Joshua Wells. 2423
Downing, Mary Samuel. 3500
Downs, Barry. 1158
Downs, Francis Shunk. 3642
Downs, John Emmanuel. 1892
Downs, Mary Isabelle (Gary) J. W. Downs. 2457
Downs, Sarah Elizabeth (Forbush) 1590
Downs, Tom. 938
Downton, James V. 1361, 1471

Dowrick, Stephanie. 2660
Dowson, John. 2664
Dowson, Mary Emily. 1049, 1118, 3077
Dox, Henry L. 3815
Doxey, Roy Watkins. 1232, 2599, 2611, 3428, 3430, 3702, 3848
Doxiades, Konstantinos Apostolou. 1277
Doyen, Edward Grattan. 1427
Doyle, Arthur Conan. 3500, 3520
Doyle, Basil. 2370
Doyle, Cecil. 1721
Doyle, Charles Hugo. 1327, 2211, 2347, 2379, 2570, 2572, 2811, 2819, 2852, 3205
Doyle, Eric. 1640
Doyle, Francis X. 1838, 785, 1607, 1963, 3264
Doyle, John E. P. 184, 693
Doyle, John M. 1426
Doyle, Joseph Beatty. 1174
Doyle, P. 430
Doyle, Sherman Hoadley. 2926
Doyle, Stephen C. 478, 2570
Doyon, Bernard. 2721
Dozier, Edwin Burk. 2534
Dozier, Maude (Burke) 2489
Drabek, Jaroslav. 2596
Drach, George. 2279, 2295, 3143, 2482
Drachman, Bernard. 1478
Draffen, George. 1664
Dragan, Antin. 3425, 3722
Dragon, Antonio. 1421
Dragona-Monachou, Myrto. 1743
Drake, Alice Hutchins. 2890
Drake Conference, Drake University, 1944. 1085
Drake, Durant. 3140, 3058
Drake, E. R. 1828
Drake, Frederick William. 3478, 1835, 2029, 1836
Drake, James. 1309, 3606
Drake, Maud Eugenia (Barrock) Lord. 3500
Drake, Maurice. 1026
Drake, Samuel Adams. 2651
Drake, Samuel Gardner. 3827
Drake, Thomas Edward. 3423
Drake, Walter Raymond. 318, 533, 1917, 2018, 3069
Drakeford, John W. 572, 573, 637, 898, 1607, 1844, 2780, 2997, 3391
Drakeford, Paul. 3612
Drakeford, Robina. 573, 3832
*Drakos, Theodore Soter. 3778
Drane, Augusta Theodosia. 1474, 3126
Drane, Dora. 3500
Drane, James F. 779, 947, 1162, 2319, 2320, 3868
Drane, John William. 330, 372, 389, 929, 1029, 1196, 1963, 2796
Draper, Bourne Hall. 2760
Draper, Broune Hall. 619
Draper, Edgar. 2783
Draper, Edythe. 1431
Draper, George Otis. 1098
[Draper, George Otis] 1867. 1654
Draper, James T. 161, 402, 479, 552, 573, 651, 992
Draper, John William. 3072, 3084, 11
Draper, Maurice L. 1712, 2346
Draughon, Wallace R. 1233
Draun, Dorothy Jones. 2871
Dravid, Raja Ram. 3755
Drawbridge, C. L. 3149
Drawbridge, Cyprian Leycester. 3149, 57, 1406, 2899, 3078
Draycott, Gladys M. 2628
Dreany, E. Joseph. 628
Dreher, Diane Elizabeth. 1518
Drelincourt, Charles. 1413
Drennen, D. A. 2417
Drescher, John M. 1607, 2058, 2347, 2386, 2773, 2809, 2890
Drescher, Sandra. 3883, 3885
Dresdner, Leon. 2088
Dresner, Samuel H. 103, 1789, 1931, 2086, 2154, 2219, 3882
Dresselhaus, Richard L. 92, 1201, 1408, 3149
Dresser, Charlotte Elizabeth. 3500, 3501
Dresser, Horatio Willia. 2063
Dresser, Horatio Willis. 1800, 1835, 2326, 2409, 2694, 2988, 2997, 3099, 3141, 3478, 3792
Dressler, William. 812
[Dressman, Aloysius] 1898. 3276
*Dressman, Robert C. 1935
Dretke, James P. 1925
Dreves, Guido Maria. 812, 1876, 1877, 3210
Drew, Dwight C. 2204
Drew, Edward. 516
Drew, Harry. 1226
[Drew, Jacob Halls]. 1480
Drew, Louise C. 3170, 3173
Drew, Samuel. 1306, 1480, 2454, 3220

Drew university, Madision, N.J Theological seminary. 3331
Drew university, Madison, N.J. 1480
Drew university, Madison, N.J. Theological seminary. 3331
Drewelow, John Frederick. 2284
Drewery, Mary. 739, 2485
Drewes, Christopher F. 2295
Drewry, Patrick Henry. 2826
Drews, Arthur Christian Heinrich. 347, 2008
Drexel, Jeremias. 41, 785, 997, 1533, 3486
Dreyer, Edith G. 2508
*Dreze, A. 862
Driberg, Tom. 699, 2593
Dries, Angelyn. 586, 940
Driggs, Howard Roscoe. 2061, 3179
Drijvers, Pius. 578
Drillinger, Emma Ruder. 2724
Drimmer, Frederick. 3839
Drinan, Robert F. 1150, 3792
Drinker, Henry Sandwith. 916
Drinkhouse, Edward Jacob. 2423
Drinkwater, Anne T. 2864
Drinkwater, Francis Harold. 867, 664, 866, 1323, 1840
Driscoll, Annette Sophia (Hoogs) 754
Driscoll, John Thomas. 3099
Driscoll, Justin Albert. 819, 3310
Driver, Godfrey Rolles. 1409, 2331
Driver, John. 1118, 3335
Driver, Samuel Rolles. 232, 539, 543, 548, 590, 1921, 2985
Driver, Tom Faw. 943, 1107, 2038
Driver Samuel Rolles. 539
Drolet, Francis K. 1013
Drollinger, Emma Ruder. 3461
Dropsie College for Hebrew and Cognate Learning, Philadelphia. 2141, 2685
Dropsie College for Hebrew and Cognate Learning, Philadelphia. Alumni Association. 2333
Droste, Franz. 779
Drouet, Bessie (Clarke) 3501
Drouin, Edmond Gabriel. 1130
Drouin, Francis M. 2386
Drower, Ethel Stefana (Stevens) 2327
Drower, Ethel Stepana (Stevens) 3270
Drown, Edward Staples. 75, 1892
Drown, Frank. 2122
Drown, Harold J. 3539
Drown, Lessie Mae. 2796
Dru, Alexander. 818
Druck, David. 3259
Drucker, Aaron Phinias. 2068, 2084
Drucker, Malka. 1785, 1811, 2779
Drukker, Raymond B. 3455
Drumm, William Martin. 885
Drummond, Alvin A. 1371
Drummond, Andrew Landale. 2955, 3738
*Drummond, Henry. 959
Drummond, Henry. 59, 588, 637, 959, 1049, 1431, 1438, 1481, 2263, 2264, 2587, 2672, 3075, 3615, 3620, 3631, 1481
Drummond, James. 371, 2349
Drummond, Lewis A. 1243, 1564
Drummond, Margaret Mary. 686
Drummond, Norwell R. 1128
Drummond, Richard Henry. 1080, 1703, 2060, 2534
Drummond, William Francis. 1136, 2160
Drumwright, Huber L. 338, 1770, 2871
Drunx, Harry Anthony. 2408
Drury, Augustus Waldo. 1716, 2752, 3642, 3731, 3730
Drury, Clifford. 2929
Drury, Clifford M. 1900, 3789
Drury, Clifford Merrill. 31, 2488, 3096, 3315, 3875
Drury, Edwin. 785
Drury, John. 427, 429, 3099
Drury, John Benjamin. 1579
Drury, M[arion] R[ichardson]. 2790
Drury, Marion Richardson. 302
Drury, Nevill. 744, 2724, 3400
Drury, Ronan. 2907
Drury, Samuel Smith. 2253
Dryburgh, Bob. 593, 982
Dryer, George H. 1636
Dryer, George Herbert. 1190, 1239
D'Souza, Jerome. 1075
Duane, Richard Bache. 1387
Dubarle, A. M. 3414
Dubarle, Andre Marie. 3390, 3414
Dubarle, Dominique. 1854
Dubay, Thomas. 2572, 2871, 3223, 3331, 3781
DuBay, William H. 758
Dubb, Allie A. 197, 2814
Dubbs, Joseph Henry. 1857, 3037
Dubin, Reese P. 2724
Dubitsky, Cora Marie. 3149
Dublin. National Gallery of Ireland. 26, 1230, 1881
Dublin. St. Patrick's Cathedral. 1481

Dubnov, Semen Markovich. 2088, 2102, 2082, 2088
DuBois, Albert Julius. 2964
Dubois, Jean Antoine. 1897
Du Bois, John Harold. 1091
Dubois, Leo Louis. 1640
Dubois, Marcel. 3376
Du Bois, Patterson. 3288
Dubois, Pierre. 1390
Du Bois, Rachel (Davis) 2104
Du Bois, William Edward Burghardt. 2890
Du Bois, William Porcher. 2038
Dubor, Georges de. 2845
DuBose, Francis M. 1170
Du Bose, Hampden C. 913
DuBose, Henry Wade. 75
Du Bose, Horace Mellard. 232, 2423, 3126, 3464, 2038, 2420
Du Bose, William Porcher. 389, 401, 482, 1372, 2957
Dubouis, Alberic. 1022, 1640
Du Bourguet, Pierre. 85
Dubrouillet, Jane. 401, 938
Dubuisson, Odile. 1385
Du Buit, Michel. 207
Dubuque. 1205
Ducasse, Curt John. 1892, 2992, 3058
Du Castel, Francois. 3715
Ducat, William Methven Gordon. 3814
Duce, Ivy Oneita. 2400, 3715
Ducey, Michael H. 893
DuCharme, Jerome J. 314
Duchaussois, Pierre Jean Baptiste. 2721
Duchesne, Louis Marie Oliver. 2306
Duchesne, Louis Marie Olivier. 2770
Duchesne-Guillemin, Jacques. 3898
Du Choul, Guillaume. 3246
Duckat, Walter B. 207, 2733, 3015
Ducker, E. N. 2780, 2784
Duckert, Mary. 940, 3162, 3550, 3553
Duckett, Eleanor Shipley. 23, 1483, 2199
Duckworth, Marion. 931, 1481
*Dudde, John H. 3615
Dudden, Frederick Homes. 29, 1773, 3340, 1773
Duddle, John H. 3615
Duddy, Frank E. 3553
Dudine, M. Frederica. 1622
Dudko, Dmitrii. 2750, 3670
Dudley, Carl Hermon. 2796
Dudley, Carl S. 1201, 3426
Dudley, Carolyn. 3763, 3764
Dudley, Dean. 1355, 2706
Dudley, Goerge W. 3211
Dudley, Guilford. 1505, 3070, 3112
Dudley, Harold James. 2928
Dudley, Louise. 3461
Dudley, Marion. 1714
Dudley, Owen Francis. 762, 1854
Dudley, Roger L. 3885
Dudley, Walter Lee. 120
Dudon, Paul. 2268
Due, Lucille Stroud. 1446
Duemling, Enno. 1911
Duenser, Joseph V. 1298, 2402
Duesberg, Hilaire. 762
Duewel, W. Michael. 293
Duff, Alexander. 1772
Duff, Archibald. 1539, 504
Duff, Edward. 3849
Duff, Edward Macomb. 2017, 2476
Duff, Frank. 2208
Duff, Joseph M. 24, 2850
Duffey, Felix D. 90, 2570, 2576, 2716
Duffey, William Richard. 2899
Duff-Forbes, Lawrence W G. 527
Dufficy, Edward. 1605
Duffie, David. 2784
Duffie, Malcolm B. 3379
Duffield, George. 605, 3596
Duffield, Gervase E. 728
Duffield, Guy P. 282, 2678
Duffield, John Thomas. 2941, 3318
Duffield, Samuel Willoughby. 1871
Duffield, T Ewing. 3198
Duffill, James. 906
Duffin, Mary Gertrude. 1774
Duffy, Consuela Marie. 1480, 2532, 2533
Duffy, Joseph A. 644
Duffy, Patrick S. 2202
Duffy, Philip Gavan. 1792
Duffy, Regis A. 3853
Dufresne, Edward R. 2337
Dugan, Daniel O. 63
Dugan, Henry Francis. 1488
Dugan, LeRoy. 982
Dugdale, William Francis Stratford. 3796
Duggan, Alfred Leo. 1159, 3692, 1390, 3692
Duggan, Charles. 736
Duggan, G. H. 2188
Duggan, Lawrence G. 779
Duggan, Thomas Stephen. 816
Duggan, William J. 2648
Duggar, Elsie (Sampey) 3297
Duggar, John W. 144, 2474, 2543
Dugger, Andrew Nugent. 1228, 3260

Dugmore, Clifford William. 2239, 2250
Duguid, Julian. 2997
Duhamel, Pierre Albert. 828
Duhr, Joseph. 109, 2358
Duignan, Jim. 2712
Duin, Edgar Charles. 2292
Dujarier, Michel. 838
Du Jeu, Sabine. 903
Duke, John Alexander. 1311, 1918
Duke, Robert W. 2909
Dukehart, Claude Henry. 2819
Duker, Abraham Gordon. 2112
Dukes, Hubert N. 309
Dukes, Ona Brigham. 2386
Dukes, T. F. 56, 605
Dukker, Chrysostomus. 1640, 3218
Dulaure, Jacques-Antoine. 2827
Dulce, Berton. 2937
Du Leavy, Gareth W. 1761
Dulin, Alva. 1058
Duling, Dennis C. 2008
Dullea, Charles W. 1754
Dulles, Allen Macy. 1174
Dulles, Avery. 1118, 1363
Dulles, Avery Robert. 69, 276, 785, 866,
    1118, 1125, 1248, 1590, 2417, 3224,
    3227
Dulles, John Foster. 1076, 1077
Dumas, Alex[andre]. 2414
Dumas, Andre. 676, 1087
Du Maurier, Daphne. 2753
Dumbarton Oaks. 87, 721, 1482
Dumery, Henry. 1103, 1721, 3099
Dumezil, Georges. 731, 1807, 2664, 2665,
    2667, 3246
Dumham, Truman Richard. 605
Dumitriu, Petru. 1103, 1482
Dummelow, John Roberts. 221, 222
Dumond, Charles E. 3492
Dumont, Christophe Jean. 1491
Dumont, Henry. 3066
Dumoulin, Heinrich. 708, 1080, 1853,
    3893, 3895
Dumvill, William Solomon Joseph. 1358
Dumville, D. N. 56
Dun, Angus. 1040, 2057, 3288, 3853
Dunaway, Thomas Sanford. 2371, 3405
Dunbar, Charles. 3561
Dunbar, Helen Flanders. 3573
Dunbar, John W. 180
Dunbar, Newell. 694
Dunbar, Olivia Howard. 2588
Duncan, Alistair. 1943
Duncan, B. H. 161
Duncan, Benjamin H. 161
Duncan, Charles Lee. 3765
Duncan, Cleo. 2945, 3188
Duncan, David Douglas. 1926
Duncan, Denis. 2386
Duncan, Edward Joseph. 55, 138
Duncan, Elmer H. 2169
Duncan, Fannie Casseday. 2248
*Duncan, George. 959
Duncan, George B. 448, 1828
Duncan, George Simpson. 1995
Duncan, George Stewart. 207, 409
Duncan, Henry. 2672
Duncan, Herman Cope. 2970
Duncan, James. 2936
Duncan, James E. 993, 1751
Duncan, James Foulis. 2980
Duncan, John. 1652, 3368
Duncan, John Garrow. 514, 1501, 2097,
    2760
Duncan, John Mason. 2466, 2914, 2980
Duncan, John W. 1579
Duncan, John Wesley. 3702
Duncan, Joseph Ellis. 2468, 2772
Duncan, Malcolm C. 1669
[Duncan, Mary (Grey) Lundie]. 698
Duncan, Norman. 1811
Duncan, Norvin C. 2971
Duncan, Pope A. 1174, 2179
Duncan, Sylvia. 696, 3862
Duncan, Thomas. 307
Duncan, Victoria Helen (Macfarlane)
    3501
Duncan, Walter Wofford T. 2899, 3340
Duncan, Watson Boone. 1887, 2420
Duncan-Jones, Arthur Stuart. 1206
Duncan-Jones, Austin. 720
Duncan-Jones, Caroline Mary. 1640
Duncombe, David C. 959
[Dunford, Katherine]. 960
Dungan, David L. 372, 395, 2071
Dungan, David Roberts. 287, 2014, 2621,
    3126
Dunham, Arthur. 1674
Dunham, Chester Forrester. 3078
Dunham, Curtis. 878
Dunham, James Henry. 2127, 2832
Dunham, Montrew. 1930, 3414
Dunham, Samuel. 3126
Dunham, Truman Richard. 3318, 3885
Dunker, Marilee Pierce. 1575, 2845
[Dunklee, Corinne Smith]. 318
Dunkum, W B. 1887

Dunlap, Andrew. 670
Dunlap, Emma Wysor. 1438
Dunlap, Knight. 1951, 2638, 3058
Dunlap, Samuel Fales. 3108, 3115
Dunlap, W. C. 3818
Dunlap, William Cook. 1683
Dunlavy, Edward Flechter. 960
Dunlavy, John. 3395, 3533
Dunlevy, A H. 158
Dunlop, Colin. 1224
Dunlop, Ian. 752
Dunn, Branson E. 1612
Dunn, Charles W. 982
Dunn, David. 1545
Dunn, Dennis J. 860, 1149, 1542
Dunn, Edmond J. 2554
Dunn, Ellen Catherine. 1908
Dunn, Frank E. 3550
[Dunn, Henry]. 305
Dunn, James D. G. 139, 476, 1587, 1894,
    2060, 3658
Dunn, Joseph Bragg. 3671
Dunn, Lewis Romaine. 561, 1823, 1828,
    2627, 2818
Dunn, Loren C. 1233, 2484
Dunn, Louis Vincent. 822
Dunn, Mary Borromeo. 1773, 2199
Dunn, Mary Noreen. 2457, 2461, 2508
Dunn, Paul H. 952, 1008, 1009, 1413,
    3177, 3493, 3539, 3885
Dunn, Van Bogard. 637
Dunn, W[illiam] W. 1579
Dunnam, Maxie D. 1006, 2386, 2871,
    3330, 3492
Dunne, Edmund Michael. 785, 795
Dunne, George Harold. 670, 1155, 1947
Dunne, James Edward Craven. 2082
Dunne, John S. 1416, 1734, 1741, 3115,
    3456
Dunne, Peter M. 2334, 3438
Dunne, Peter Masten. 1948, 1949
Dunne, William. 838
Dunner, Josef. 2099
Dunnett, Walter M. 409
Dunney, Joseph Aloysius. 805, 809, 1174,
    1507, 2365
Dunning, Albert Elijah. 539
Dunning, Annie Ketchum. 2976
Dunning, James B. 3678
Dunning, John Wirt. 3758
Dunninger, Joseph. 3501
Dunnington, Lewis Le Roy. 960, 1598,
    3758
Dunnington, Lewis LeRoy. 960
Dunnington, Lewis Le Roy. 2435
Dunphy, Mary A. 2369
Dunphy, William. 947
Dunphy, William Henry. 1118
Dunraven, Windham Thomas Wyndham-
    Quin. 1838, 3501
Duns, Joannes. 2417, 2672, 3643
Duns, Joannes (Scotus) 2417, 3643
Dunstan. 3704
*Dunstan, J. Leslie. 1951
dunstan, John Leslie. 1279, 2976
Dunston, Alfred G. 2680
Dupee, Ethel Purdon. 539
Dupin, Andre Marie Jean Jacques. 2068
Dupler, Emmert Parker. 1235, 2178
Du Plessis, Johannes. 2499
Du Pont, Henry Algernon. 1851
Dupont, Jacques. 330
Dupont, Jean. 1159
Dupont-Sommer, Andre. 1410
Duportal, Marguerite. 3540
Dupre, Louis K. 664, 2169, 2320, 2641,
    3058, 3107
Dupree, L C. 1721
Du Preez, J. P. 3001
Du Prel, Karl Ludwig August Friedrich
    Maximilian Alfred. 2993
Dupuis, Charles Francois. 3093
Duquesne, Jacques. 771
Duquoc, Christian. 2871
Duran, Clement A. 3870
Duran, Diego. 121
Duran, Frederique. 2764
Durand, Alfred. 1996, 3780
Durand, Eugene F. 1301, 3432
Durand, Silas Horton. 3090
Durandeaux, Jacques. 1721
Durant, Gladys May. 1159
Durant, H. 1323
*Durant, Richard. 3501
Durant, William James. 2710
Durantis, Gulielmus. 920
Durasoff, Steve. 2814, 2955
Duratschek, Claudia. 825
Durbin, B. Paul. 1006
Durell, David. 499
Durell, Fletcher. 3149
Durell, John Carlyon Vavasor. 1174
Duren, Stephen. 3092
Duren, William Larkin. 89, 1701, 2206,
    2423, 2456
Durfee, Susan T. 2551
Durham, Betty. 931, 1483

Durham, Charles. 3600
Durham, Deanna. 931, 3722
Durham, Eng. (Diocese) Bishop, 1406-
    1437 (Thomas Langley) 1761
Durham, Eng. (Diocese) Bishop, 1530-
    1559 (Cuthbert Tunstall) 1762
Durham, Eng. University. Durham
    Colleges. Dept. of Palaeography and
    Diplomatic. 1212, 1412, 1483
Durham, Harriet Frorer. 1678
Durham, John Pinckney. 154
Durham, Reed C. 2615
Durieux, Pierre. 2251, 2341
Durka, Gloria. 935
Durkee, James Stanley. 1721, 3066, 3351
Durkheim, Emile. 3066, 3108, 3109
Durkin, Jim. 3719
Durkin, Joseph Thomas. 2374
Durkin, Mary Antonia. 805
Durkin, Mary G. 3837
Durland, William R. 3780
Durnbaugh, Donald F. 1235, 1236, 2976,
    3324
Durrant, Elizabeth. 1030
Durrant, George D. 1233, 1484, 2609,
    2617
Durrant, Michael. 1732
Durrett, John. 137
Durrell, F. X. 76, 776, 3029, 3486, 3633
Durward, John. 1745
Duryea, Joseph Tuthill. 3777
Dushaw, Amos Isaac. 2077, 3703
Dushaw, Amos Issac. 1963
Dushkin, Alexander Mordecai. 2086
Dushnyck, Walter. 3771
Duskie, John Aloysius. 851
Dussel, Enrique D. 949, 2198
Dusterdieck, Friedrich Hermann Christian.
    453
Dutch, Andrew K. 3058
Dutcher, Jacob Conkling. 2945
Duthie, Alexander. 2660
Duthie, Arthur Louis. 1165
Duthie, Charles S. 3662
Dutilliet, Henri Alexandre. 770
Dutt, K. Guru. 1583
Dutt, Meade E. 2014
Dutt, Meade Ervin. 1956
Dutt, Nalinaksha. 1704
Dutt, Sukumar. 705, 2577
Dutta, Rex. 3685
Dutton, Charles Judson. 1400, 2537,
    2556, 3143
Dutton, Dean Colfax. 960
Dutton, Joseph. 2568
Dutton, Walter. 1128
Duty, Guy. 1376, 1471, 3288, 3711
Duvall, C. H. 3126
Duvall, Evelyn Ruth (Millis) 3392
Duvall, Sylvanus Milne. 2449
Duveneck, Josephine Whitney. 1484
Duvoisin, Roger Antoine. 2711
Dux, Victor L. 2386
Duyckinck, Evert Augustus. 660, 1791
Duzy, Erminius Stanislaus. 1283, 3693
Dvornik, Francis. 861, 1372, 1373, 1398,
    2546, 2862
Dwelle, Jessie Merrill. 1114
Dwight, Benjamin Woodbridge. 3149
Dwight, Charles Abbott Schneider. 318
Dwight, Edwin Welles. 2721
Dwight, Henry Otis. 31
Dwight, Mary Ann. 2655, 2656
Dwight, Sereno Edwards. 896, 1340,
    1499, 1612
Dwight, Thomas. 3078
Dwight, Timothy. 122, 378, 1865, 3616,
    3643, 960
Dwight, Walter. 759
Dworaczyk, Edward J. 2857
Dwyer, Adrian I. 2341
Dwyer, John T. 666, 2734
Dwyer, Margaret Clifford. 2714
Dwyer, Richard E. 2189
Dwyer, Walter W. 1598, 2409
Dyal, William M. 993
[Dyar, Wallesca (Pollock) 127
Dybvig, Philip S. 2715
Dyck, Cornelius J. 37, 2186, 2404, 2406,
    3528
Dye, David L. 3082
Dye, Eva May. 3534, 2513
Dye, Harold Eldon. 161, 960, 1013, 2980
Dye, James W. 3198
Dye, Joseph M. 1897
Dye, William McEntyre. 1501
Dyer, Alvin R. 2618
Dyer, Alvin Rulon. 2601, 2611, 2617,
    3115
Dyer, Colin F. W. 1671
Dyer, Delbert. 960
Dyer, George J. 2229
Dyer, Helen S. 3020
Dyer, Heman. 3126
Dyer, Henry Page. 2971
Dyer, John Lewis. 2451
Dyer, Joseph. 2348, 3395

Dyer, Louis. 1766
Dyer, Ralph J. 2570
Dyer, Sidney. 1865
Dyer, Thomas Henry. 727
Dyer, William. 1742, 3363
Dyet, James T. 938
Dyggve, Ejnar. 1190
Dykshoorn, M. B. 1283
Dykstra, John Albert. 2721
Dymond, Jonathan. 1089, 3791, 3792
[Dympna, 1855. 741, 3310
Dyrness, William A. 598
Dziob, Michael Walter. 777

E

Eaches, O[wen] P[hilips]. 1485
Eade, Alfred Thompson. 1467
Eades, Ronald W. 1242, 3798
Eadie, John. 302
Eadie, John William. 1197, 1355
Eadmer, d. 1124? 49
Eadmer, d. 49
Eads, Buryl R. 202
Eads, H. L. 3397
Eads, Harvey L. 3395
Eagan, Frances W. 2724
Eager, John Howard. 799
Eaglesfield, Carrol Frederick. 2710
Eagleson, Hodge MacIlvain. 897
Eagleson, John. 1155
Eagleton, Terence. 1074
Eagon, Isaac Gregg. 605
Eakeley, Charles Wesley. 2174
Eakin, Bill. 3880
Eakin, Frank. 347, 3198, 527, 3744
Eakin, Frank E. 232, 533, 2148, 2150,
    3058
Eakin, Harvey Ellis. 1030
Eakin, Mildred Olivia (Moody) 910, 2121,
    2593, 3149, 3179, 3183, 3188, 3671,
    3764
Eales, Samuel John. 193
Ealy, Ruth Rea. 1485, 3899
Eames, Samuel Morris. 732
Eames, Wilberforce. 748
Earhart, H. Byron. 1935
Earhart, Mary. 3816
Earl Blue Associates. 1582
Earl, Sylvester. 3126
Earle, Absalom Backas. 1556, 1564, 3230,
    3351
Earle, Alice (Morse) 3547
Earle, Arthur. 496
Earle, Jabez. 2251
Earle, John. 3572
Earle, John R. 1138
Earle, Nick. 1211
Earle, Ralph. 289, 430, 433, 437, 471,
    474, 3318
Earle, William. 3461
Early, James Lawrence. 458
Early, Sarah J. W. 1485
Earnshaw, John R. 692
Earp, Edwin Lee. 309, 3254, 3442
Earshaw, George L. 1127
Eary, T. M. 3288
Eason, Joshua Lawrence. 309
Eason, R E. 2202, 2755
Eason, William. 567
East Boston. Maverick Congregational
    church. 3853
East Manchester, N.H. Woman's Christian
    temperance union mercy home for girls.
    3833
East Ohio synod of the Evangelical
    Lutheran church. 1547
East, Reginald. 1598
East Tennessee Historical Society,
    Knoxville. 2182
[East, Timothy]. 1013
Eastburg, Frederick. 1963
Eastburg, Frederick Emmanuel. 1963
Eastburn, Manton. 49, 449
Eastchester Historical Society, Eastchester,
    N. Y. 1485
Eastcott, Michal J. 3330
Eastep, Durward Belmont. 214, 3318
Easterby, William. 3702
Easterling, R. B. 1204
Easterly, Frederick John. 3249, 3276
Eastern Asia Christian Conference,
    Bangkok, 1949. 2516
Eastland, Elizabeth Wilson. 2471
Eastman, A. Theodore. 134
Eastman, Addison A. 413, 982, 2547
Eastman, Albert Theodore. 44, 2480,
    2549
Eastman, C. S. 2435
Eastman, Charles Alexander. 1902
Eastman, Dick. 1139, 2871
Eastman, Frances W. 619, 647, 935, 2489
Eastman, Fred. 2488, 1517, 2012, 2926,
    3144, 3442
Eastman, Mary Huse. 1589

Eastman, Mary Ruse. 1589
Eastman, Max. 3126
Eastman, Roger. 3138
Eastman, Theodore A. 2540
Easton, Burton Scott. 330, 366, 389, 429, 446, 1951, 2063, 2337, 3166
Easton, Mabel. 2513
[Easton, Peter Zaccheus] 1846-1915. 3413
Easton, Stewart Copinger. 50
Easton, William Burnet. 960, 3662
Eastvold, Seth C. 1887
Eastvold, Seth Clarence. 2796
Eastwood, Charles Cyril. 2939, 3093
Eastwood, Cyril. 2939
Eastwood, Edna. 3858, 3284
Eastwood, Laurie T. 2618
Easwaran, Eknath. 2316, 2329, 2379, 2387, 3483
Eatherly, Claude Robert. 103
Eaton, Arthur Wentworth Hamilton. 721, 1018, 1223, 721, 1018, 1054
Eaton, Charles Aubrey. 3228
[Eaton, Edward Byrom]. 2465
Eaton, Emma Florence. 637
Eaton, Ephraim Llewellyn. 3256, 3595
Eaton, Gai. 3099
Eaton, J. H. 559, 578, 2177
Eaton, James Demarest. 2540
Eaton, Jeanette. 749, 1937, 2240
Eaton, Jeffrey C. 1613, 3609
Eaton, Joseph W. 1858, 1859, 2823
Eaton, Kenneth Oxner. 450, 1004, 2871
Eaton, Samuel John Mills. 1458
Eaton, Thomas Ray. 299, 3399
Eaton, Thomas Treadwell. 1590
Eaton, William Dunseath. 3501
Eaton, William Harrison. 2370
Eavey, Charles Benton. 1438, 1840, 2721, 3165, 3179, 3565
Ebaugh, Helen Rose Fuchs. 2580
Ebbatson, Roger. 1403, 1517
Ebbert, George C. 3086
Ebbo. 2752
Ebbraunon, Christilina. 2724
Ebbutt, Maud Isabel. 3244
Ebeling, Gerhard. 239, 1165, 1590, 2249, 2280, 3198, 3368, 3616, 3620, 3651, 3668
Eberhard, Ernest. 2346
Eberhard, Kenneth D. 25
Eberhardt, Charles Richard. 2696, 3812
Eberhardt, Ernest Godlove. 302
Eberhardt, Newman C. 809, 814
Eberhart, Amedee Dilliner. 645
Eberhart, Elvin T. 2771
Eberle, Edith. 2309, 2508, 2544
Eberlein, Harold Donaldson. 3278
Eberlin, Barnard. 1663
Eberly, Daniel. 3731
Eberman, Clarence E. 2387
Eberschweiler, William. 3486
Ebersole, Eleanor. 3175
Ebersole, Luke Eugene. 1150
Ebersole, Mark C. 3662
Eberstadt (Edward) and Sons, New York. 2608, 3762
Ebersweiler, Friedrich. 2311
Ebinger, Warren R. 2387
Ebisawa, Arimichi. 1101
Ebizawa, Norimichi. 1110
Eblana, Sister. 48
Ebner, James H. 3628
Ebon, Martin. 1585, 2317, 2318, 2707, 2731, 2948, 2949, 3055, 3302, 3501, 3519, 3708
Ebstein, Wilhelm. 317
Ebsworth, Walter A. 835
Eby, Frederick. 3149, 1469, 2702
Eby, Kermit. 1137
Eby, Omar. 1776, 2547
Eby, Richard E. 931, 1488
Eccles, David McAdam Eccles, 1st viscount. 1058
Ecclesiastical History Society, London. 1183, 1184, 1373, 1805, 2526, 3620
Ecclesine, Margaret Wyvill. 1844
Ecclesiological society, Cambridge. 1270
Ecclestone, Alan. 2145, 2871
Echlin, Edward P. 771, 1408, 2253, 2909
Echols, Timothy B. 2428
Eck, Diana L. 1815
Eck, Herbert Vincent Shortgrave. 3410
Eck, Johann. 785, 2978
Eckardt, Arthur Roy. 1083, 1101, 2152, 3668
Eckardt, Frances Dyer. 3144
Eckel, Edward Henry. 1523
Eckel, Fred L. 3765
Eckel, Frederick L. 2963
Eckenstein, Lina. 1357, 3836
Ecker, Jakob. 619
Eckert, Fred J. 867
Eckhardt, Carl Conrad. 2769
Eckhardt, Henry P. 1549
Eckhardt, Thorvi. 1881
Eckhart, d. 1327. 862, 2644, 2646, 2647
Eckhart, George Boland. 1271

Eckhart, Meister. 2647
Eckhart, Meister, d. 1491, 264 7
Eckley, Joseph. 3362
Eckman, George Peck. 2004, 3220, 3340, 210, 416, 3319, 3340
Eckman, Lester Samuel. 2162, 2632
Eckstein, Emanuel. 1798
Eckstein, Stephen Daniel. 1273
Ecrement, Lloyd L. 2326
Ecumenical Dialogue of Third World Theologians, Dar es Salaam, 1976. 1155
Ecumenical methodist conference. 6th, atlanta, 1881. 2423
Ecumenical Methodist conference. 6th, atlanta, 1931. 2423
Ecumenical missions, new york 1900. 2519
Ecumenism Research Agency. 3327
Edberg, Rolf. 2320
Edda, Snaorra Sturlusonar. 2665
Edda Snorra. 2665
Edda, Snorra Sturlusonar. 2665
Edda Snorra Sturlusonar. Selections. 2665
Eddi. 1758, 3816
Eddington, Arthur Stanley. 3078, 1676, 3081
Eddins, James Frank. 637
Eddison, John. 63, 243
Eddleman, H Leo. 161, 2541, 3319, 3335
Eddy, Ansel Doane. 3885
Eddy, Benjamin Lee. 3149
Eddy, Daniel Clarke. 683, 1347, 1350, 2488
Eddy, David Brewer. 31
[Eddy, Fred J]. 1094
Eddy, George Sherwood. 389, 660, 886, 1090, 1497, 1734, 1740, 1896, 1963, 2508, 2525, 2980, 2988, 3086, 3198, 3442, 3870
Eddy, Howard Ranney. 2976
Eddy, Lois B. 2460, 3764
Eddy, Mary (Baker) 684, 1030, 1031, 1032, 1037, 1494, 1032
[Eddy, Mary (Baker)?Mrs.]. 1032
Eddy, Nary (Baker) 1032
Eddy, Richard. 3306, 3755
Eddy, Robert Leigh. 1840, 3671
Eddy, Zachary. 1963
Ede, William Moore. 3434
Edelbaum, Meyer. 2077
Edelblute, Lucius Aaron. 2697
Edelby, Neophytes. 735
Edelman, Daniel. 1674
Edelman, Lily. 2152, 3545
Edelson, Edward. 2948
Edelstein, Emma Jeannette Levy. 11, 1395
Edelweiss. 3501
Eden, George Rodney. 2229
Eden, Lynn. 1135, 1627
Edens, David. 1607, 1608
Eder, Karl. 771
Edersheim, Alfred. 289, 1963, 2092, 2414
Edershiem, Alfred. 1963
Edge, Findley B. 3179
Edge, Findley Bartow. 993, 1243
Edge, Henry T. 1579, 3685
Edgell, David P. 882
[Edgerly, Webster]. 2226, 2835, 2988, 2997
[Edgerly, Webster] 1852-1926. 2226, 2988
Edgerton, Franklin. 2316, 1816
Edgerton, James Arthur. 1951
Edgerton, Jedediah. 2692
Edgerton, Walter. 3880
Edgerton, Wealthy Rowena. 1860
Edghill, Ernest Arthur. 605
Edgren, John Alexis. 3643
Edidin, Ben. M. 1623, 2104, 2118, 2120
Ediger, Peter J. 570
Edington, Andrew. 601, 3662
Edkins, Joseph. 704, 913, 3115
Edland, Elisabeth. 2757, 3144, 3763
Edman, David. 214
Edman, Irwin. 2796, 2843
*Edman, V. Raymond. 1438, 1446, 1590
Edman, Victor Raymond. 1361, 241, 960, 1438, 1446, 1625, 2021, 2525, 241, 2197
Edmands, John. 1344
Edmiston, B[erry]. 304
Edmond, Amanda M. (Corey) 3206
Edmonds, Cyrus R. 2469
Edmonds, Franklin Spencer. 2830
Edmonds, Henry M. 2890
Edmonds, Henry Morris. 2890, 2931
Edmonds, I. G. 710, 1346, 1815, 1838, 1925, 1942, 2399, 2949, 3055, 3521
Edmonds, John Worth. 3501
Edmondson, Frank. 1748
Edmonson, George. 1170
Edmund, Ed. 3880
Edmund Rich, d. 1240. 3486
Edmunds, Albert Joseph. 1080
Edmunds, Charles Carroll. 315
Edmunds, Edward. 3589
[Edmunds, James]. 31
Edmunds, John K. 2601

Edmunds, Vincent. 1598
Edmunds, W. Hawksley. 892
Edmundson, George. 3245
Edmundson, William. 1497
Edna Mary. 2570
Edna Mary, Sister. 2871
Edson, Ambrose. 1782
Edson, Helen R. 3126
Educational Policies Commission. 2590
Educational Research Council of America. 2083
Educational Research Council of America. Social Science Staff. 3140
Edward. 2537
Edward, John Derek. 1590
Edwardes, Michael. 709, 2732
Edwardes, Stephen Meredyth. 730
Edwards, Andrew J. 313
Edwards, Anne. 628
Edwards, Annette. 2022
Edwards, Arthur. 218
Edwards, Bela Bates. 1369, 2523, 3620
Edwards, Ben F. 2719
Edwards, Boyd. 3310
Edwards, Brian H. 928, 3719
Edwards, Charles Eugene. 612, 2926, 3425
Edwards, Charles Thomas. 1721
Edwards, Charlotte Walrath. 2387, 3179
Edwards, Christopher. 1498
Edwards, Cliff. 2337
Edwards, Clifford Walter. 412
Edwards, Dan Luther. 3288
Edwards, David L. 1721
Edwards, David Lawrence. 499, 929, 1211, 1512, 1515, 1695, 1991, 3021, 3058, 3242
Edwards, David Miall. 3099
Edwards, Dixon. 284
Edwards, Douglas Allen. 1951
Edwards, E. J. 2544
Edwards, Edward J. 849, 2544
Edwards, Elizabeth. 3144
Edwards, Ethel. 2997, 3478
Edwards, F. Henry. 929, 1963
Edwards, Frances Rose. 3189
Edwards, Francis Henry. 1009, 1721, 1736, 1951, 2601, 2871, 2980, 3215, 3216, 3373, 3430, 3643
Edwards, Fred E. 2504
Edwards, Frederick. 1498, 3501
Edwards, Frederick George. 2402
Edwards, Gene. 1564
Edwards, George. 2918, 1498
Edwards, George Nelson. 888
Edwards, George R. 2038, 3780
Edwards, Gus Callaway. 3553
Edwards, Hal L. 1006, 1498
Edwards, Harry Elmo. 3386
Edwards, Helen. 3501
Edwards, Henry James. 3501, 3799
Edwards, J. W. 51
Edwards, Joan. 1165
Edwards, John Ellis. 911
Edwards, John Harrington. 2632
Edwards, Jonathan. 1512, 38, 453, 689, 691, 1201, 1333, 1334, 1340, 1343, 1499, 1512, 1564, 1657, 1751, 1757, 1835, 1900, 2162, 2688, 2838, 3008, 3029, 3030, 3058, 3231, 3351, 3410, 3413, 3522, 3711, 3714, 3782, 104, 890, 1658, 1695, 3807
Edwards, Josephine Cunnington. 1315, 1372, 2206, 2319, 2486, 2508, 3382, 3768
Edwards, Justin. 3595
Edwards, K. Morgan. 1058
Edwards, Kathleen. 886
Edwards, Loren M. 3058
Edwards, Loren McClain. 73, 1564
Edwards, Lyford Paterson. 1093, 3657
Edwards, Maldwyn Lloyd. 3803
Edwards, Mark U. 2273
Edwards, Martin Russ. 2482
Edwards, Mary Alice Douty. 952
Edwards, Maxwell D. 3038
Edwards, Mildred Speakes. 619
Edwards, Morgan. 2465
Edwards, O. C. 429, 2010
Edwards, Otis Carl. 298, 1102, 2899, 2973
Edwards, Paul M. 3149
Edwards, Peter. 1905
Edwards, Philip C. 1277, 1278
Edwards, Rem B. 3099
Edwards, Rex. 2939
Edwards, Richard Alan. 389, 3010, 3407
Edwards, Richard Henry. 3435, 36, 1369, 1574, 3537, 3671
Edwards, Robert. 2586, 2778
Edwards, Robert Dudley. 819, 1146, 1147
Edwards, Roselyn. 1431
Edwards, S. A. 2651
Edwards, Thomas Cynonfradd. 1500
Edwards, Tilden. 1301, 1500, 2379, 3400, 3475

Edwards, Tudor. 2569
Edwards, Vina Howland. 2927
Edwards, Viv. 2475
Edwards, Walter Oscar. 3382
Edwards, Walter Ross. 3288
Edwardson, Christian. 799
Edwin, B. 1347, 3223
Edyvean, Alfred R. 32
Eeles, Francis Carolus. 2237
[Eells, Edward]. 1049, 3340
Eells, Edward. 1400
Eells, Hastings. 720, 3040
Eells, Myron. 1332
Eells, Nathaniel. 2742
Effendi, Shoghi. 3115
Efird, James M. 232, 341, 409, 506, 539, 546, 2950
Efron, Benjamin. 172, 563, 2107
Efron, Marshall. 619
Efros, Israel Isaac. 2622, 2623, 2839, 2841, 3259, 3469
Egan, Eileen Mary, 1922. 2670
Egan, Harvey D. 1583, 2268
Egan, Joseph Burke. 886
Egan, Maurice Francis. 668, 1156, 1641, 2178
Egan, Patrick Kevin. 1920
Egar, John Hodson. 3711
Egbert, Donald Drew. 1883
Egbert, James. 732
Egbert, John Paul. 3468
Egbert, Maud Minkler. 619
Egelkraut, Helmuth L. 430
Egenter, Richard. 84
Egermeier, Elsie E. 615, 3803
Egermeier, Elsie Emilie. 615, 619, 620, 1980, 3026
Egermeler, Elsie Emilie. 620
Egge, Mandus A. 1878
Eggenschwiler, David. 1855, 2734
Eggerichs, Fred W. 3528
Eggers, Herman R. 681, 1626
Eggers, William T. 17
Eggleston, Edward. 2012
Eggleston, George Teeple. 3180
Eggleston, Margaret (While) 2489
Eggleston, Margaret (White). 910, 1014, 3066, 3149, 3179
Eggum, Tom. 1500, 1576
Egly, Alan. 3167
Egner, G. 664
Ehinger, Aline Noren. 2929
Ehl, Anton. 3416
Ehle, Charles Edwin. 3319
Ehle, John. 1778, 2697
Ehler, Sidney Z. 1143, 1144
Ehlert, Arnold D. 298, 1467, 2855
Ehlman, Dobbs Frederick. 3099
Ehrenborg, Ferdinand. 1305
Ehrenpreis, Andreas. 1859
Ehrensperger, Harold Adam. 3145
Ehrenstrom, Nils. 1141
Ehrenwald, Jan. 3698
Ehret, Walter. 3271
Ehrhardt, Arnold. 334
Ehrlich, Ernst Ludwig. 2095
Ehrlich, Jacob W. 203
Ehrlich, Rudolf J. 861
Eicher, HuBert Clark. 3874
Eichholz, Georg. 282, 2219
Eichhorn, David Max. 511, 2556, 2952
Eichrodt, Walther. 518, 598, 2326
Eickelman, Dale F. 2635
Eickenberg, Charles. 3616
Eickmann, Paul E. 3187
Eickmann, Walther. 217, 285, 2796
Eid, Joseph. 1602, 2318
Eide, Margaret (Wall) 1166, 3858, 3876
Eidenschink, John Albert. 666, 1773
Eidlitz, Walther. 1896
Eifert, William H. 2034
Eighmy, John Lee. 1135, 3465
Eikamp, Arthur R. 1963
Eikenberry, Ivan. 2543
Eilul, Jacques. 960
Eimer, Robert. 3280
Eims, LeRoy. 330, 533, 573, 953, 982, 3829
Einaudi, Mario. 933, 2777
[Einhard] 770 (ca.)-810. 2332
Einig, Peter. 3058
Einspahr, Bruce. 695
Einspruch, Henry. 2085, 1365, 2073
Einstein, Albert. 2118
Einstein, David G. 2113
Einstein, Morris. 3115
Eiselen, Frederick Carl. 482, 529, 565, 1069, 222, 309, 568, 571
Eiseley, Loren C. 2321
Eisen, Theophilus. 1545
Eisen, William. 721, 3575
Eisenach, George John. 1339, 2846
Eisenberg, Arlene. 1073
Eisenberg, Azriel Louis. 172, 207, 1329, 1410, 2081, 2094, 2106, 2145, 2207, 3306, 3577
Eisenberg, Rafael. 610

Eisenberg, William Edward. 3820
Eisenbise, Viola. 2535
Eisenbud, Jule. 1283
Eisendrath, Maurice Nathan. 2142
Eisenhofer, Ludwig. 838
Eisenring, Carl Jakob. 2209, 2211
Eisenstadt, Shmuel Noah. 943, 3800
Eisenstein-Barzilay, Isaac, 1915. 3022
Eisenstein, Ira. 2084, 2113, 2138, 2142, 2164, 3028, 3703
Eisenstein, Miriam. 2102
Eisentraut, Bernhard. 463
Eisler, Robert. 1987
Eissfeldt, Otto. 539
Eister, Allan W. 3111
Eitan, Israel. 505, 1797
Eiten, Robert B. 3540
Ekaku, 1686-1769. 3893
Ekechi, F. K. 2556
*Ekerholm, H. E. 3220
Ekholm, Augustus Conrad. 755, 1049
Ekvall, Robert Brainerd. 2193, 2555
El Paso, Tex. Christian Churches (Disciples of Christ) 932
Elazar, Daniel Judah. 1286
Elbee, Jean d. 3486
Elbert, John Aleysius. 2057, 2213, 2359
Elbert, John Aloysius. 1590, 2057, 2251, 2702, 2871
Elbin, Paul Newell. 3756
Elbin, Paul Nowell. 280, 1104, 3756, 3758
Elbogen, Ismar. 2081, 2092
Elbrecht, Paul G. 1085
Elbridgson, Edgar. 2320
Elchinger, Leon Arthur. 1066
Elder, Carl A. 3885
Elder, E. 344, 345
Elder, Frederick Stanton. 3091
Elder, John. 207
Elder, John Calvin. 2686
Elder, Michael. 2280
Elder, William. 3075
Elderkin, George D. 3561
Elderkin, George Wicker. 799, 1395
Eldersveld, Peter H. 1024, 1315, 2032, 3351
Eldon, Magdalen. 1996
Eldred, O. John. 3835
Eldredge, Anna Wayne. 660
Eldredge, Niles. 1579
Eldridge, Charles David. 1049
Eldridge, Gardner S. 307, 2055
Eldridge, J. L. 2015
Eldridge, Lawrence Allen. 393, 1522
Eldridge, Paul H. 1012
Eldridge, Richard B. 1836
Eleanore. 1714, 2354, 3280
Eleanore, Mary. 3280, 3284, 3420
[Eleazar ben Asher ha-Levi] 14th cent. 2207
Elefant, William L. 2622
Elefsiades, Juna (Carey) 1446
Elert, Werner. 934, 950, 1528, 2251, 2256, 2285, 2200, 2256, 2285
Elfenbein, Hiram. 3091
Elfenbein, Israel. 2145
Elford, Homer J. R. 1249, 3853
Elgin, Kathleen. 1472, 1674, 2581, 2618, 2657, 2957, 3725
Eliade, Mircea. 3058, 3140, 117, 1371, 1505, 1506, 1586, 1708, 1908, 2416, 2648, 2651, 2791, 3058, 3093, 3111, 3115, 3139, 3140, 3400, 3573, 3864
Elias, Arthuro M. 1147
Elias, John L. 1883, 3451
Elias, Joseph. 3454
Elick, Eva Marie. 3283
Elicker, Charles W. 3882
Elijoshius, Simonas. 285
Eliot, Alexander. 1507, 2660, 3493
Eliot, Charles Norton Edgecumbe. 706, 2707, 1813
Eliot, Charles William. 1046, 3141
Eliot, Charlotte Chauncy (Stearns) 1509
Eliot, Ethel (Cook) 1776
Eliot, Frederick May. 3723, 3187
Eliot, George. 1507, 3206
Eliot, John. 1507, 2370
Eliot, Samuel Atkins. 3727
Eliot, Thomas Stearns. 3442, 3448
Eliot, William Greenleaf. 1350, 3149, 3727, 3869
Elisabeth de la Trinite 1880-1906. 1508
Elison, George. 1101
Elizabeth. 2063, 2066, 3163
*Elizabeth, M. 960
Elizabeth, N.J. St. John's Church. 1268
Elizabeth de la Trinite. 2642
Elizabethtown, Pa. Christ Evangelical Lutheran Church. 1547
Elizondo, Vigil. 748
Elizondo, Virgil. 795
Elizondo, Virgilio P. 2557
Elkin, Benjamin. 3457
Elkins, Chris. 1834
Elkins, Dov Peretz. 2079, 2081, 2142, 3361, 3598

Elkins, Hervey. 3395
Elkins, W. F. 1933
Elkinton, Joseph. 212, 1482
Ellacuria, Ignacio. 821, 2480
Ellard, Gerald. 2741, 23, 844, 997, 2019, 2234, 2365, 3264, 3266, 3267, 838, 3267
Ellard, Virginia G. 3493
Elledge, Helen. 680
Ellens, J. Harold. 3018
Ellen Vincent. 3420
Ellenwood, James Lee. 3870
Eller, Ernest McNeill. 2595
Eller, Eugene R. 146
Eller, Meredith Freeman. 309
Eller, Paul Himmel. 1546, 1550
Eller, Vernard. 453, 943, 1118, 1313, 1721, 2063, 2169, 3262, 3409, 3620, 3682, 3795
Ellerton, John. 3198
Ellet, Elizabeth Fries (Lummis) 1603
Ellett, Frank Gates. 2047
Ellett, Oren D. 1078
Ellicott, Charles John. 1963, 3668
Ellicottville, N.Y. Holy Name of Mary Church. 2700
Elliff, Thomas D. 1509, 2871
Ellingboe, Betty. 3891
Ellingsen, Harald F J. 400
Ellingson, David R. 674
Ellinwood, Frank Field. 2519
Ellinwood, Leonard Webster. 1210
Elliot, Arthur Ralph Douglas. 1125
Elliot, Elisabeth. 931, 960, 983, 1509, 1943, 2340, 2402, 2515, 2516, 3535
Elliot, Harrison Sacket. 400
Elliot, James. 1509, 2485
Elliot, Leslie Robinson. 3612
Elliott, Andrew. 1963
Elliott, Ann. 1385
Elliott-Binns, Leonard Elliott, 1885. 531, 1760
Elliott, Charles. 799, 2456, 3241, 563, 2038
Elliott, Charles Wyllys. 214
Elliott, Charles Wyllys. 214
Elliott, Delber Harvey. 453, 1141, 1319
Elliott, Douglas A. 3829
Elliott, Edmund E. R. 2712
Elliott, Edward O. 1368, 2829
Elliott, Emory. 2910
Elliott, Ernest Eugene. 2202, 10, 1240
Elliott, Errol T. 1509, 1677, 1684, 2194
Elliott, George. 240, 2455
Elliott, George Roy. 1101, 3400, 1127, 1101, 3399
Elliott, Graeme Maurice. 2060
Elliott, Harrison Sacket. 960, 2997, 3149
Elliott, Harvey Edwin. 3115
Elliott, Hubert A. 1446
Elliott, James Habersham. 1700
Elliott, James Keith. 479
Elliott, John. 1503
Elliott, John G. 2226
Elliott, John Hall. 325, 3439
Elliott, John Henry. 637
Elliott, John Y. 1297
Elliott, Lawrence. 2123
Elliott, May. 1509
Elliott, Melvin E. 271, 1517
Elliott, Neil. 3604
Elliott, Norman K. 182, 588, 2246
Elliott, Paul Frederick. 1735
Elliott, Ralph H. 524, 527, 1170, 3028
Elliott, Stephen. 3351
Elliott, Wallace Harold. 960, 47, 960, 1226
Elliott, Walter. 3340, 1799, 1963, 2031, 3486
Elliott, William Anderson. 3671
Elliott, William Marion. 449, 960, 2931, 2944
Elliott, Willis Edwin. 446
Elliott-Binns, Leonard Elliott. 497, 1758, 1760, 1764, 1908, 2769, 3038, 2980, 2113
Ellis, Aaron. 48
Ellis, Arthur Blake. 1509
Ellis, Charles Calvert. 3885, 2213, 3001
Ellis, Clara Spalding (Brown) 1887
Ellis, Edith. 1695, 3053, 3501
Ellis, Edward Earle. 350, 374, 413, 429, 1530, 2952
Ellis, Edward Ellis. 2659
Ellis, Edward Sylvester. 2659
Ellis, Eric Kent. 104, 2051
Ellis, Florence Howard. 2590
Ellis, George Edward. 1509, 3713, 3727
Ellis, Hallett West. 1564
Ellis, Harold. 1328
Ellis, Henry Milton. 1471
Ellis, Howard W. 1574
Ellis, J. 2899, 3373
Ellis, James Benton. 1509
Ellis, James Fernando. 162
Ellis, James G. 1032
Ellis, James J. 2198
Ellis, Joe S. 983

Ellis, Joe Scott. 1564
Ellis, John. 1419, 1839, 3422, 3596, 2690, 2692
Ellis, John Tracy. 833, 834, 835, 860, 874, 1347, 1711, 3469, 3613, 3703, 3739
Ellis, John William. 3198
Ellis, Joseph J. 2129
Ellis, Keith. 2717
Ellis, Loudell O. 1168
Ellis, Maie Lenora. 389
Ellis, Marc H. 871, 875, 1509, 2374
Ellis, Mary Leith. 1174, 2287, 3478
Ellis, Matthew Elbridge. 214
Ellis, Peter F. 371, 539
Ellis, Samuel Moore. 300
Ellis, Samuel Robert. 2061
Ellis, Sumner. 886, 3755
Ellis, Thomas H. 1371
Ellis, William. 1509
Ellis, Edward Earle. 1530, 2796
Ellisen, Stanley A. 605, 1471
Ellison, Craig W. 1280, 2244
Ellison, Earl Jerome. 8
Ellison, Gerald [Alexander]. 43
Ellison, H. L. 516, 524
Ellison, Harry C. 1508
Ellison, Henry Leopold. 470, 539, 548, 570, 2091, 2149
Ellison, John Malcus. 960, 2899, 162, 960, 2899
Ellison, John William. 227
Elliston, Catherine. 747, 1721
Ellmore, Alfred. 3340
Ellspermann, Gerard Leo. 1020
Ellsworth, Donald Paul. 1207
Ellsworth, George. 3783
Ellsworth, Samuel George. 1287
Ellui, Jacques. 960
Ellul, Jacques. 458, 483, 943, 1153, 1277, 1509, 2130, 2223, 2871, 3327, 3611, 3620, 3780, 1845
Ellwood, Charles Abram. 3442
Ellwood, Robert S. 1936, 2072, 2643, 3058, 3115, 3747
Ellwood, Thomas. 293
Ellzey, William Clark. 2337
Elmen, Paul. 1934, 1935
Elmer, Irene. 2945
Elmer, Myrtie Louise. 1446
Elmore, Carl Hopkins. 3351, 3870
Elmore, Ellaine. 3501
Elmore, Robert Emmet. 2246
Elmore, Vernon O. 342, 993
Elmore, Wilber Theodore. 1813
Elmslie, William Alexander Leslie. 2113, 2138
Elphinstone, Andrew. 3610
Elphinstone-Fyffe, John M. 1747
Elrod, John W. 1104, 2170, 2171
Elsas, Christoph. 1717, 2854
Elsbree, Oliver Wendell. 2501
Elsdon, Ron. 1853
Else, Gerald Frank. 1839
Elsee, Charles. 2684
Elsey, Charles William. 2945
Elshemus, Louis Michael. 1427
Elsley, William James. 2000
Elsmere, Jane Shaffer. 184
Elsner, Paul J. 3526
Elson, Edward Lee Roy. 2006, 1438, 2931, 3744
Elson, Frances (Sandys) 1906-1933. 1303
Elson, James Hinsdale. 1781
Elspeth. 533
Elton, Charles. 1038
Elton, Godfrey Elton. 2824
Elton, Godfrey Elton, baron. 2824
Eltz, Louis Anthony. 6
Elvehjem Art Center. 1509, 1881
Elving, Set. 747
Elvy, Cora. 3051, 3199
Elwang, William Wilson. 3086
Elwell, Clarence Edward. 937, 3164
Elwin, Verrier. 2663, 2664
Elwood, Douglas J. 1499
Elwood, J. Murray. 399, 738, 1434, 2015, 2702
Elwood, Roger. 1427, 1695, 2724
Elworthy, Frederic Thomas. 1578
Ely, Ezra Stiles. 729, 1847, 1911, 3126, 3643, 3753
Ely, James E. 232
Ely, Richard George. 1144
Ely, Richard Theodore. 3058, 3434
Ely, Samuel. 3351
Ely, Simpson. 3347
Ely, Stephen Lee. 3813
Ely, Talfourd. 2656
Ely, Virginia. 1446, 1247, 1419, 1446, 1911, 1999, 3528
Ely, Virinia. 1431
Elzas, Barnett Abraham. 2226, 3050
el Zein, Abdul Hamid M. 1925
Elzholtz, Carl Frederik. 895
Emanuel, Cyprian William. 887, 3779
Embree, Ainslie Thomas. 1812

Embry, James Crawford. 3643
Embury, Aymar. 1162
Emch, Arnold Frederick. 687
Emch, William N. 3012
Emericus A Sancto Stephano, Father [Secular name: Bernard Josef Barrath]. 1906
Emerson, Charles Harris. 2724
Emerson, Dorothy. 55, 690
Emerson, Edward Randolph. 3596
Emerson, Edwin. 314
Emerson, Eleanor (Read) 1692
Emerson, Elizabeth (Holaday) 1636, 2242, 2757, 3031, 3847
Emerson, Ellen Russell. 1902
Emerson, Everett H. 1372, 3009, 3637
Emerson, George Homer. 1627, 2943
Emerson, James Christopher. 1957, 2759
Emerson, James Gordon. 526, 1422, 1471, 1633
Emerson, Joseph. 747, 748, 1550, 1551
Emerson, Laura B. Payne. 3227
Emerson, Laura S. 1446
Emerson, Nathaniel Bright. 2207
Emerson, Oliver Pomeroy. 1510, 2524
Emerson, Ralph. 1510
Emerson, Ralph Waldo. 1510, 1511, 3708, 3725
Emerson, Samuel Franklin. 1341
Emerson, Sara Anna. 232
Emerson, William A. 1963
Emerton, Ephraim. 3727, 1525
Emery, Allan C. 993, 1511
Emery, Joseph. 1276
Emery, Julia C. 2695, 2957
Emery, Philip Alfred. 1479, 2844
Emery, Pierre Yves. 1317, 2871
Emery, Richard Wilder. 1909, 22, 1673, 1909
Emery, Susan L. 822, 3461
Emhardt, William Chauncey. 1487, 2684, 2970, 3256
Eminyan, Maurice. 3294
Emley, Alban Maurice. 579
Emlyn, Thomas. 2002, 3727
Emma B. King Library. 3397
Emma, Ronald David. 2470
Emme, Earle Edward. 3149
Emmenegger, Joseph Eugene. 1811
Emmerich, Anna Katharina. 394, 2031, 2353, 2358
Emmerson, Elson Henry. 3382
Emmerson, Richard Kenneth. 52
Emmerson, W. L. 3382
Emmet, Dorothy Mary. 2417
Emminghaus, Johannes H. 2127, 2128, 2271, 2353, 2366, 2825
Emmison, Frederick George. 1489
Emmons, Charles Ashbury. 3206
Emmons, Helen Keith Boulware. 2387
Emmons, Henry. 1942
Emmons, Michael L. 92
Emmons, Nathanael. 134, 1341, 1803, 3262, 3643
Emmons, Samuel Bulfinch. 3501, 3567
Emmons, Viva. 3685
Emmott, Elizabeth (Braithwaite) 1684
Emmrich, Kurt. 1198
Emonts, Johannes. 2497
Emory, John. 2376, 2450, 1522, 2305, 2376, 2442, 2450, 2737
[Emory, Robert] 1814-1848. 1512, 2447
Empie, Paul C. 138, 2298, 3666
Empie, Paul E. 2929
Empson, William. 1732, 2471
Emrich, Richard Stanley. 2323, 2374
Emswiler, James P. 937, 1471
Emswiler, Sharon Neufer. 2237, 3839
Emswiler, Thomas Neufer. 3883
Emurian, Ernest K. 1860, 1871, 1875
Endersby, Victor A. 671
Endes, Jean. 3270
Endicott, Kirk Michael. 178, 2315
Endicott, Myles. 293
Endicott, Stephen Lyon. 1515, 2485
Endo, Shusaku. 929, 1963
Endore, S. Guy. 1937
Endy, Melvin B. 2813
Enelow, Hyman Gerson. 200, 2081, 2082, 2113, 2985, 3122, 3576, 2013, 2114, 3794
[Enete, William Walters] 1893. 2489
Engel, James F. 1316
Engelbert, E. F. 3351
[Engelder, Theodore Edward William] 1865. 305, 1386, 3024
Engelhardt, Zephyrin. 745, 2413, 3006, 3297, 3302, 1646, 1899, 2271, 2716, 3298, 3302
Engelkemier, Joe. 1012, 3382
Engelman, Uriah Zevi. 2099, 2106
Engelmann, Charles Pilling. 2289
Engelsma, David. 1751, 2337, 2975
Engelsman, Joan Chamberlain. 1621
Engeman, Jack. 775
Engemann, Antonellus. 3615
Engen, Sadie Owen. 900, 2487, 3589

Engineer, Asgharali. 1927
England, Herbert Kingsbury. 906
England, John. 776, 2415, 3424
England, Kathy. 139, 1230
England, Martha Winburn. 1875
England, Stephen Jackson. 138, 1190, 1464
Englar, George William. 2299
Engle, Caroline Kirkham (Dayton) 1477
Engle, Jon. 3408
Englebert, Omer. 764, 1641, 3283, 3376
Englehardt, Zephyrin. 1899
Engleman, James Ozro. 2590
Englert, Clement Cyril. 861
Englert, Donald M C. 482
Englewood, N.J., St. Cecilia's Catholic church. 823
English, E Lois. 603
English, Eugene Schulyer. 440
English, Eugene Schuyler. 232, 341, 433, 1920, 2824, 3524, 3662
English evangelical Lutheran church in New York Litergy and ritual. 1545
English Evangelical Lutheran synod of Missouri and other states. 2289, 2294
English Evangelical Lutheran synod of Ohio and adjacent states. 1548
English Evangelical Lutheran synod of the Northwest. 1547
[English, Francis M.]. 3596
[English, George Bethune] 1787-1826. 743, 3022
English, George Bethune. 1578, 3022
English, James W. 682, 2681
English, John J. 1517, 3486
English, John Mahan. 2474, 2899
English, Michael Ignatius. 3450
English, William F. 1579
Englizian, H. Crosby. 685
Engnell, Ivan. 499
Enquist, Richard. 990, 1014
Engstrom, Barbie. 2387
Engstrom, Theodore W. 3351, 3373
Engstrom, Theodore Wilhelm. 3856, 620, 952, 953, 983, 1840, 2492, 2886, 3340, 3351, 3373, 3856
Engstrom, W. A. 1253
Enlow, David R. 932, 1014, 1249, 2401, 3539
Ennemeser, Joseph. 2314
Ennery, Jonas. 2117
Enniss, Peyton Hervey. 207
Ennodius, Magnus Felix. 1522
Enns, Arno W. 2501
Enns, Paul P. 553, 554
[Eno, Joel Nelson] 1852. 2856
Enoch, H. 202
Enoch Pratt free library Baltimore. 869
Enrody, Ladislas J. 2826
Enroth, Ronald M. 1254, 1393, 2072, 3751
Ensign, Grayson. 983
Ensign, Samuel James Russell. 214
Ensley, Eddie. 1717
Ensley, Francis Gerald. 372, 1006, 2796, 2994
Enslin, Morton Scott. 409, 446, 1103, 1963, 2796
Ensrud, Paul. 1861
Enterline, Mildred Hahn. 3145
Entwisle, J. Howard. 1865
Entwistle, Basil. 2593
Entwistle, Mary. 897, 2489, 2549, 2621
Entz, Angeline J. 494, 633, 1507
Entzminger, Louis. 3553
Langdon, Stephen Herbert, 1876-1937, ed. 1380
Enz, Jacob J. 2809
Enziger rothers, New York. 1250
Ephros, Gershon. 3567
Episcopal Church in Scotland. 1524
Episcopal evangelical fellowship. 2960
The Episcopal series of the Protestant hour. 3351
Epistle to Diognetus. 2161
Epp, Eldon Jay. 316
Epp, Frank H. 2404, 2809
Epp, Theodore H. 3018
Epperson, Barbara. 121, 2542
Eppinga, Jacob D. 1277, 2251, 2387, 2796
Eppstein, John. 3233
Epperson, Benjamin. 2125
Epstein, Benjamin R. 2125
Epstein, Francis James. 1290
Epstein, Harry Hyman. 3371
Epstein, Isidore. 2146, 2103
Epstein, Louis M. 2345, 3392
Epstein, Morris. 565, 1614, 2121, 2152, 2886
Epstein, Mosheh. 204
Epstein, Perle S. 722, 1485, 1525, 1788, 3826
Epstein, Reuben. 3371
Erasmus, Desiderius. 343, 960, 1008, 1416, 1525, 1526, 1527, 1632, 1658, 1854, 2158, 2576, 3033, 3034, 3038, 3781, 3791

Erasmus, Desiderius, d. 1008, 1526, 1855
Erb, Alta Mae. 3170
Erb, Bessie Pehotsky. 3800
Erb, Fannie Stienbrecher. 3478
Erb, Frank Otis. 1247
Erb, J. Lawrence. 1875
Erb, Margaret. 1094
Erb, Paul. 611, 960, 1528, 1531, 2404, 2408, 2404
Erb, William Harvey. 2246
Erbacher, Sebastian Anthony. 1263
Erdahl, Lowell O. 1350, 1431, 2213, 2299, 2899
Erdman, Charles Rosenbury. 309, 322, 329, 340, 341, 346, 363, 380, 403, 416, 427, 433, 440, 446, 448, 453, 467, 478, 510, 516, 518, 521, 542, 546, 557, 560, 1295, 1317, 1828, 1835, 1976, 2051, 2263, 2587, 321, 322, 340, 341, 363, 380, 403, 416, 427, 433, 440, 446, 448, 453, 467, 478, 562
Erdman, F. E. 1693
Erdman, Mabel H. 2482
Erdman, Walter Collins. 923
Erdman, William Jacob. 1835, 459
Erdmann, Carl. 1390
Erdmann, Christian Friedrich David. 589
Erdozain, Placido. 666, 3247
[Erhard, Mary Alma, 1907. 3126
Ericksen, Ephraim Edward. 2601, 2602
Ericksen, Mabel Natalie. 3150
[Erickson, Elsa Forssell] 1885. 3501
Erickson, Judith B. 1308
Erickson, Lois Johnson. 2534
Erickson, Melvin E. 280, 1435
Erickson, Millard. 1534, 1552
Erickson, Millard J. 1729, 2465, 3288
Ericson, Carl George. 153, 892
Ericson, Elsa Forssell. 3501
Ericson, Eston Everett. 3257
Erie Co., N.Y. Buffalo and Erie County Public Library. 3397
Erikson, Erik Homburger. 2273
Erikson, Joan Mowat. 1641
Erikson, Kai T. 3009
Erikson, Martin. 1780
Erlanger, Philippe. 3236
Erlewine, Stephen. 1847
Erlich, J W. 203
Erman, Adolf. 1501
Ermarth, Margaret Sittler. 3836
Ernest. 1700, 19, 40, 41, 54, 133, 182, 191, 194, 686, 731, 740, 1115, 1284, 1474, 1618, 1641, 1649, 1700, 1706, 1776, 1778, 1906, 2132, 2190, 2194, 2216, 2260, 2262, 2270, 2271, 2319, 2348, 2358, 2478, 2584, 2793, 2850, 2851, 2859, 3025, 3286, 3305, 3409, 3460, 3580, 3690, 3761
Ernest, Brother. 1793
Ernest, Victor H. 3520
Ernle, Rowland Edmund Prothero. 586, 3525
Ernsberger, David J. 2480, 3168
Ernst, Alice (Henson) 3831
Ernst, Eldon G. 1109
Ernst, John. 3478
Ernst, Karl Julius. 447
Ernst, Morris Leopold. 2220
Erny, Edward. 2743
Erpestad, Emil. 2871
Errett, Isaac. 232, 1461, 1630, 3572
Erskine, Ebenezer. 1651
Erskine, John. 1963
Erskine, Marjory. 1481
Erskine, Noel Leo. 669
Erskine, Ralph. 2000
Erskine, Thomas. 1098, 1751
Ervin, Howard M. 1712, 2814
Ervin, Simon Billings. 1838
Ervin, Spencer. 43, 44, 1230, 1238, 2670, 2966
Ervine, St. John Greer. 682
[Erwin, Augusta]. 3501
Erwin, George B. M. 960, 1323
Erwin, John Robert. 885, 1527
Erwood, William Joseph. 1732, 2024, 2694, 3501
Esch, Ludwig. 997
Eschenburg, Johann Joachim. 1286
Escholier, Marc. 2864
Escobar, Samuel E. 2481
Escott, Harry. 1338
Escribano, Eugenio. 2387, 2940
Escriva de Balaguer, Jose Maria, 1902. 863, 3369
Escriva, Jose Maria. 1323, 2399, 3247, 3486
Escriva, Jose Maria [Jose Maria Escriva de Balaguer Albos]. 3486
Esgar, Mildred H. 3877
Eshbach, Warren M. 2735
Eshelman, Byron E. 885
Eshleman, Merle W. 2552, 3870
Eshleman, Paul. 1573, 1914
Eshliman, Nikolai. 2749
Esin, Emel (Tek) 2377

Esipov, Boris Petrovich. 2590
Eskew, Harry. 1875
Eskridge, James Burnette. 2474
Espeland, Pamela. 78, 178, 723, 2461, 2660, 3010, 3692
Espey, Clara Ewing. 1277
Espey, John Jenkins. 3126
Espie, John C. 3529
Espina, Noni. 3271
Espino, Jose. 2439
Espinosa, Isidro Felix de. 1647
Espinosa, Jose Edmundo. 3303
Espinosa Polit, Aurelio. 1289
Espinosa Polit, Manuel Maria. 2719
Esposito, John L. 3842
Espy, R H Edwin. 2670
Essad. 2628
Esselmont, John Ebenezer. 127, 1700
Esser, Franz Xaver. 2251
Esser, Gerard. 2738
Esser, Kajetan. 90, 1641, 1645, 3692
Esses, Michael. 492, 521, 1366, 1532
Essex, Eng. County Planning Dept. 1159
Essex, Eng. Record Office. 1270
Essex, Herbert James. 3150
Essex north association. 1532
Essien-Udom, Essien Udosen. 2567
Essig, Montgomery Ford. 302, 3167
Esslemont, John Ebenezer. 125, 127, 125, 127
Essrig, Issac David, 1893. 2120
Esswein, Anthony Albert. 2159
Estabrooks, George Hoben. 2473, 3501
Estaugh, John. 1651
Estborn, Sigfrid. 1897
Estcourt, Edgar Edmund. 1763
Esteb, Adlai Albert. 1435, 3883
Estella, Diego de. 2264
Estep, William. 3195, 3196, 3224
Estep, William Roscoe. 37, 1043, 2512
Esterer, Arnulf K. 2732, 3082
Estes, David Foster. 476
Estes, Hiram Cushman. 3461
Estes, L Frances. 3501
Esteve, Sirio. 2387
Estey, George F. 2713
Estey, Stephen Sewall. 2931
Esther. 77
[Esther-Carlotta. 2387
Estlake, Allan. 2737
Estornell, Camille. 2029
Estrada, David. 1411, 2721
Estrade, Jean Baptiste. 2262, 3460
*Esus, Hugam E. 1417
Eterovich, Adam S. 2751
Ethelred. 2264, 3493
Etheridge, Eugene W. 551
Etheridge, John Wesley. 1285
[Etheridge, Samuel]. 3026
Etherington, Charles L. 915
Ethiopic church. 1540
Ethiopic church. Liturgy and ritual. 2237
Ethridge, Willie (Snow) 3803
Etteldorf, Raymond. 2744
Ettelson, Harry William. 488
Etter, John W. 2899
Etter, Marie B. 1554
Ettinger, Cecil R. 943
Ettinger, Cecil Ray. 3218
Ettinger, Robert C W. 1887
Ettinghusen, Richard. 2759
Etzenhouser, Rudolph. 678, 2611, 3428
Etzweiler, Charles Cleveland. 232
Eucharistic Missionaries of St. Dominic. 3150
Eucken, Rudolf Christof. 1534, 2226, 1711, 1881, 2840, 3099
Eudes, Jean. 771, 997, 1541, 2354, 2387, 3269
Eugene. 647
Eugippius. 3388
Eugippus. 3388
Eulalia Teresa. 2335, 3420
Eusden, John Dykstra. 3893
Eusebius, Pamphili. 1090, 1190, 1191
Eusebius Pamphili. 1191
Eustace, Cecil John. 762, 1363, 1631, 2181, 2638, 3450
Eustace, Herbert Willoughby. 1032, 1037
Euster, William Tell. 1156
Euting, George L. 3182
Eva, Mary. 1321, 3199
Evagrius Ponticus, 345?-399? 90
Evangelical alliance Conference, New York, 1873. 1551
Evangelical alliance for the United States of America. 1544
Evangelical alliance for the United States of America. Conference, Washington, D.C., 1887. 1040, 1550
Evangelical Alliance for the United States of America, General Christian Conference. 1st, Washington, D.C., 1887. 1040

Evangelical Alliance for the United States of America, General Christian Conference, 2d, Boston, 1889. 1040
Evangelical and Reformed Church. 1545
Evangelical and Reformed Church. Board of Business Management. 1545
Evangelical and Reformed Church. Board of Christian Education and Publication. 1328, 1339
Evangelical and Reformed church. General synod. 1545
Evangelical and Reformed church. General synod. Committee on Book of worship. 1545
Evangelical and Reformed church. Synods. Lehigh. 1545
Evangelical and Reformed church. Synods. Northeast Ohio. 1545
Evangelical and Reformed Church. Synods. Southwest Ohio. 1550
Evangelical association of North America. 1546
Evangelical Church. Missionary Society. 1546
Evangelical church. Woman's missionary society. 1546
Evangelical congregational church. 1385, 1865
Evangelical education society of the Protestant Episcopal church. 1552, 2965
Evangelical Educational Society. 2960
Evangelical Lutheran Augustana synod of North America. 110, 620, 1547, 1865
Evangelical Lutheran Augustana synod of North America. Board of foreign missions. 2508, 2509
Evangelical Lutheran Augustana synod of North America. Liturgy and ritual. 1546, 1547
Evangelical Lutheran Augustana synod of North America. Luther League council. 2272, 2297
Evangelical Lutheran Augustana synod of North America. Nebraska conference. 2291
Evangelical Lutheran Church. 1547, 2289
Evangelical Lutheran Church. Board of Christian Education. Division of Higher Education. 2302
Evangelical Lutheran Church. Board of Foreign Missions. 2296
Evangelical Lutheran Church. Board of Parish Education. 3562
Evangelical Lutheran church. Centennial commission. 1547
Evangelical Lutheran joint synod of Ohio and other states. 1549
Evangelical Lutheran joint synod of Ohio and other states. Concordia English district. 1547
Evangelical Lutheran joint synod of Ohio and other states. English district. 1547
Evangelical Lutheran joint synod of Ohio and other states. Northern district. 3733
Evangelical Lutheran joint synod of Ohio and other states. Western district. 3733
Evangelical Lutheran Joint Synod of Wisconsin and Other States. 1548, 2297
Evangelical Lutheran ministerium of Pennsylvania and adjacent states. 1548, 2289
Evangelical Lutheran ministerium of Pennsylvania and adjacent states. Board of home missions. 2296
Evangelical Lutheran ministerium of Pennsylvania and adjacent states. Conferences. Lancaster. 2291
Evangelical Lutheran ministerium of Pennsylvania and adjacent states. Conferences. Norristown. 2291
Evangelical Lutheran ministerium of Pennsylvania and adjacent states. Conferences. Reading. 2291
Evangelical Lutheran ministerium of the state of New York and adjacent states and countries. 1547, 2289
Evangelical Lutheran Synod in the Midwest of the United Lutheran Church in America. 3733
Evangelical Lutheran synod of East Pennsylvania. 1548
Evangelical Lutheran synod of Maryland. 1548
Evangelical Lutheran synod of Miami. 1547
Evangelical Lutheran synod of Missouri, Ohio, and other states. 1549, 2289
Evangelical Lutheran synod of Missouri, Ohio, and other states. Board for parish education. 1549
Evangelical Lutheran synod of Missouri, Ohio, and other states. Dept. of missionary education. 2482, 2492, 2504, 2519
Evangelical Lutheran synod of Missouri, Ohio, and other states. Southeastern district. 1549

Evangelical Lutheran synod of Nebraska. 1548
Evangelical Lutheran Synod of South Carolina. 2292
Evangelical Lutheran synod of West Pennsylvania. 1548
Evangelical Methodist Church. 1549
Evangelical synod of North America. 620, 1550, 1865
Evangelical Theological Society. 484
Evangelical United Brethren Church. 1550
Evangelical United Brethren Church. Wisconsin Conference. 1550
Evangelical Wesleyan Church of North America. 1550
Evangelisch Luthersche Kerk. 2291
Evangelium veritatis. 3767
Evans, Adelaide Bee. 633, 637, 644, 896, 1532, 2177
Evans, Adelaide Bee (Cooper) 625, 628, 1980
Evans, Alec Richard. 3425
Evans, Alice (Pickford) 2489, 2761
Evans, Allan Stewart. 3115
Evans, Anna Laura. 1918
Evans, Arthur John. 2635
Evans, Arthur William. 3795
Evans, Austin Patterson. 2718
*Evans, B. Hoyt. 3885
Evans, Bergen. 2658
Evans, C. Stephen. 1426
Evans, Charles. 1684
Evans, Charles, b. 3711
Evans, Charles Worthington. 712
Evans, Christmas. 3369
Evans, Christopher Riche. 3322
Evans, Colleen Townsend. 180, 323, 424, 1010, 1577, 1633, 2266, 2337, 2871
Evans, Daniel Luther. 1104
Evans, David. 3710, 1994
Evans, David Beecher. 2217
Evans, David M. 1259
Evans, Donald D. 951, 1380, 1534
Evans, Edward Payson. 920
Evans, Edwin George. 1654
Evans, Elizabeth Cornelia. 3246
Evans, Elizabeth Edson Mrs. 2050
Evans, Elizabeth Edson (Gibson) 3115
Evans, Francis. 2366
[Evans, Frederick William]. 463, 1577, 2205, 3395, 3398, 3501
Evans, Garfield. 2549
Evans, George. 3853
Evans, Gillian. 49, 1733, 3659
Evans, Glenn. 1577, 2387
Evans, Gloria Jay. 983
Evans, Gwenllian Nesta (Jones) 43
Evans, Helen (Fiske) 2638
Evans, Henry Ridgely. 671, 723, 1345, 1411, 3240, 3501
Evans, Herbert Francis. 3548
Evans, Hiram Wesley. 827, 1150, 3244
Evans, Hugh Davey. 2337
Evans, Illtud. 755, 2019
Evans, Irwin Henry. 42, 2160, 2264, 2900
Evans, Ivor Hugh Norman. 1484
Evans, J. J. 3180
Evans, Joan. 86, 1304, 2569
Evans, John. 1687
Evans, John H. 1238
Evans, John Henry. 592, 678, 2602, 2615, 2618, 3111, 3235, 3428
Evans, John M. 153
Evans, John Whitney. 2702
Evans, Laura Margaret. 903
Evans, Lawton Bryan. 1807
Evans, Llewelyn John. 305, 2931
Evans, Louis Hadley. 412, 2000, 2176, 2337, 2871, 2931, 3885, 1170
Evans, Lucylle H. 3277, 3287
Evans, Madison. 1293
Evans, Mary Ellen. 2376
Evans, Melvin James. 2994
Evans, Mike. 1366
Evans, Milton G. 476, 2063
Evans, Morris Owen. 3058, 3602
Evans, Norm. 983, 1577
Evans, Owen E. 655
Evans, Paul. 849, 3715
Evans, Philip Saffery. 151
Evans-Pritchard, Edward Eban 1902. 3109
Evans, Richard L. 1577
Evans, Richard Louis. 1323, 2607, 2608, 2616
Evans, Robert A. 1094
Evans, Robert F. 1385, 2811
Evans, Robert Llewelyn. 425, 1350, 2118, 2465
Evans, Robert P. 660, 1542
Evans, Silas. 3529
Evans, Ted. 1049
Evans, Thomas. 1681, 3196
Evans, Walter LaFayette. 1058
Evans, Warren Felt. 2409, 2690, 3569
Evans-Wentz, W. Y. 1878-1965. 1902

Evans, William. 3126, 70, 232, 309, 321, 459, 520, 565, 588, 637, 645, 647, 960, 1695, 1956, 2029, 2031, 2055, 2882, 3347, 3643, 651, 2900, 3662
Evans, William Arthur. 1091
Evans, William Glyn. 1094, 1431, 1576
Evans, William Henry. 993, 1608
Evans, A. R. 2497
Evans-Pritchard, Edward Evan. 2716, 3109
Evans-Pritchard, Edward Evan, 1902-1973. 121
Evanston, Ill. St. Mary's church. 1269
Evarts, John Wesley. 1951
Evarts, Lewis L. 3501
Evdokimoff, Paul. 3493
Eveleth, Alice JTowne. 1578
Evely, Louis. 2343, 73, 389, 399, 863, 997, 1058, 1118, 1266, 1413, 2054, 2246, 2343, 2387, 2871, 3264, 3265, 3486, 3540
Evelyn, John. 2259, 3394
Evenhouse, Bill. 1393
Evening, Margaret. 3415
Evennett, Henry Outram. 2260, 3710, 1374
Evens, Tillie. 3126
Everard, George. 1608
Everding, H. Edward. 275, 1418
Everest, Elsie Eroica. 120
Everett, Caroline Kane (Mills) 3540
Everett, Charles Carroll. 376, 1049, 1624, 2179, 2997, 3115
Everett, Edward. 59, 1517
Everett, Harvey A. 1259
Everett, James. 1387, 1810
Everett, John Rutherford. 3115
Everett, Lawrence Patrick, 1917. 3265
Everett, Millard Spencer. 1534
Everett, Oliver P. 2871
Everett, Walter Goodnow. 3478
Everette, Oliver Page. 2871
Everitt, Alan Milner. 1468
Evers, Alf. 1384
Evers, Joseph Calvin. 2439
Everstine, Carl Nicholas. 1666
Eversull, Harry Kelso. 1485
Everts, William Wallace. 1118, 1308, 3267, 3677
Every, George. 134, 1281, 2207, 2368, 2747, 3307
Evjen, John Oluf. 2283, 3536
Evoy, John J. 2572
Evslin, Bernard. 628, 2660
Evslin, Bernard. 2661
Ewart, Andrew. 660
Ewart, Frank J. 1995
Ewbank, Walter F. 943
Ewell, John D. 2166
Ewen, Cecil Henry L'Estrange. 3823
Ewens, Mary. 2718
Ewer, Ferdinand Cartwright. 1828, 3501
Ewer, Mary Anita. 3573
Ewert, David. 347, 1530
Ewin, R. E. 1534
Ewing, Alfred Cyril. 1534, 1745, 2163, 2164
Ewing, Francis A. 480
Ewing, Harold. 3883
Ewing, James Caruthers Thea. 890, 2530
Ewing, Joseph Franklin. 298, 2679
Ewing, Juliana Horatia (Gatty) 935, 1016
Ewing, Ruth Grimes. 2503
Ewing, Upton Clary. 1963, 1978, 3591
Ewing, Walter Lee. 2423
Ewing, Ward B. 549, 2124
Ewing, William. 1343, 243
Ewton, Maynard Franklin. 162
Excell, Edwin Othello,221851-1921. 2884, 3562
Exel, Godfrey W. 2337
Exell, Joseph Samuel. 222
Exetastes. 1139, 2746
Exley, Richard. 1721
Exum, Jack. 1564
Eyer, Mary Sturlaugson. 1587, 2619
Eygun, Francios. 79
Eynon, Dana. 645, 650
Eyre, John. 887, 1587, 2731
Eyre, Linda. 938
Eyre, Richard M. 1009, 3362
Eyring, Henry. 3083
Ezekiel, Isaac A. 2162
Ezell, Douglas. 453
Ezell, Mancil. 645, 3175
Ezzell, S R. 3288

F

Faase, Thomas Philip. 1945
Faber, Andreas. 1976, 2165
Faber, Doris. 1858, 3399
Faber, Frederick William. 3289, 863, 1587, 1721, 1741, 2021, 2063, 2254, 3363, 3459, 3478, 3486

Faber, Geoffrey Cust. 2702, 2754
Faber, George Stanley. 57, 59, 60, 465, 508, 564, 567, 723, 799, 1828
Faber, Heije. 1258, 2780, 2994
Faber, Mathias. 1266
Faber, Richard. 1088
Faber, William Frederic. 1803
Fabian, Bela. 2474
Fabian, Johannes. 1933
Fabisch, Judith. 1587, 3814
Fabre, Lucien. 1937
Fabregues, Jean de. 1363, 2343, 3526
Fabricius, Urich. 1957
Fabrini, Placido. 2333
Fabro, Cornelio. 101
Facius, Johannes. 3880
Fackenheim, Emil L. 1800, 1825, 2080, 2138, 2144
Fackre, Gabriel J. 1016, 1153, 1259, 1491, 1564, 1573, 1603, 1845, 2709, 2785, 2791, 3183, 3538, 3617, 3643, 3666
Facter, Dolly. 701
Faddoul, Germain. 3703
Fadiman, Edwin. 1938, 3280
Fadner, Donald Edward. 2708
Faduma, Orishatukeh. 16
Faeber, Wilhelm i. e. Frederich Wilhelm. 747
Faensen, Hubert. 1161
Faerber, W[ilhelm], i. e. Friedrich Wilhelm. 748
Faerber, Whilhelm. 769
Faerber, Wilhelm. 746, 748, 769, 1588, 769, 1588
Faerber, Wilhelm i. e. Friedrich Wilhelm. 748
Fagal, William A. 1014, 3011, 3585
Fagan, Harry. 1136
Fagan, Sean. 3410
*Fagel, William A. 3382
Fagerberg, Holsten. 2280
Fagerburg, Frank Benjamin. 162, 1054, 3885
Fagerburg, Frank Bentamin. 3351
*Fagerlin, Elsie. 643, 2056, 2299
Fagerstjerna, P W P. 2018
Fages, Pierre Henri. 3247
Fages, Raymond. 1347
Fagg, John Gerardus. 3582
Fagley, Frederick L. 960, 1338, 1553
Fagley, Frederick Louis. 1118, 1188, 1338, 1339, 3115, 3671, 3677
Fa-Heen. 91
Faherty, William Barbey. 3836
Faherty, William Barnaby. 3276
Fahey, John F. 3025
Fahey, Michael Andrew. 3694, 3714
Fahey, Sheila Macmanus. 2814
Fahling, Adam. 3370, 2034, 2299
Fahling, Adams. 1963
Fahrner, Mary. 1367, 1588
Fahs, Charles Harvey. 1167, 2454, 2519
Fahs, Sophia Blanche (Lyon) 2229, 2664, 2667, 2005, 2229, 2308, 3170, 3185, 3289, 3858
Fair, Frank T. 16
Fair, Harold L. 1438, 1913, 3560
Fairbairn, Andrew Martin. 1049, 1963, 2038, 3099, 3340, 3643
Fairbairn, Charles V. 1823
Fairbairn, Charles Victor. 1564, 1823, 2435, 3299
Fairbairn, Henry Arnold. 1588
Fairbairn, Patrick. 243, 518
Fairbairn, Patrick. 243, 405, 605, 2130, 3720, 3721
Fairbairn, Robert Edis. 3027
Fairbairns, Arnold. 751
Fairbank, John King. 2509
Fairbanks, Alonzo Deming. 2055
Fairbanks, Arthur. 1766, 2656
Fairbanks, Edward Taylor. 3351
Fairbrother, Lafayette I. 3126
Fairchild, Hoxie Neale. 63
Fairchild, James Harris. 3643
Fairchild, Johnson E. 3115
Fairchild, Joy Hamlet. 685, 1406, 1612, 2943
Fairchild, Roy W. 7, 1608, 2782
Fairfax, Edward. 3823
Fairfield, Edmund Burke. 134
Fairfield, Francis Gerry. 3501
*Fairfield, James. 3126
Fairfield, James G. T. 983
Fairfield, Leslie P. 131
Fairfield, Oliver Jay. 625
Fairholme, George. 202
Fairhurst, Alfred. 1579
Fairlie, Henry. 1411, 1412
Fairman, Marion. 3736
Fairweather, Alan M. 3227, 3697
Fairweather, Eugene Rathbone. 1373, 2209, 3309, 3636
Fairweather, William. 2645, 2743
Faisal, Daoud Ahmed. 1921, 2564
Faith-Man-Nature Group. 1348

Faiz i, A.Q. 21, 3403
Fakhry, Majid. 2841
Falaquera, Shem-Tob ben Joseph, ca. 1225-ca. 1295. 1539
Falco, Giorgio. 1186, 1826
Falcon, Joseph. 3501
Falconer, John. 2354
Falconer, Robert Alexander. 446, 476, 1887
Falconer, Robert Crawford. 894
Falconer, Thomas. 394, 1577
Falconi, Carlo. 2123, 2770, 2852
Fales, William R. 3126
Faley, Roland James. 1747
Falk, Peter. 2497
Falk, Ze'ev Wilhelm. 2345
Falkson, Ferdinand. 698
Fallaw, Wesner. 1134, 2791, 3092, 3150
Fallding, Harold. 3058
Fallis, George Oliver. 3731
[Fallis, William J. 3237, 3373
Fallon, Patrick. 1980
Fallows, Alice Katharine. 1602
Fallows, Samuel. 243, 2409, 2602
Fallows, W.G. 1387
Fancher, Henry Wyley. 321
Fancher, Wilda. 2387, 3843, 3844
Fanchiotti, Margherita. 620
Fanfani, Amintore. 737, 3449
Fanfani, Lodovico Giuseppe. 2570, 2581
Fanning, Buckner. 993
Fannon, Patrick. 398, 795
Fanslow, Mrs. Robert H. 3252
Fant, Clyde E. 676, 2900, 2909, 3340
Fant, David Jones. 1598, 2696, 3643, 3705
Fanthorpe, P. A. 2732, 3304, 3305
Fantini, Mario D. 3761
Faraday, Lucy Winifred. 1493, 2665
Farago, Ladislas. 2761
Farah, Caesar E. 1921
Farah, Charles. 1608, 1590
Faramelli, Norman J. 3592
Faraon, Michael Joseph. 2262
Faraone, Joseph J. 330
Farb, Peter. 480
Farber, Marvin. 2738
Farber, Walter C. 1614
Farbridge, Maurice Harry. 2114, 3573
Fardan, Dorothy Blake. 668
Fargo, Gail B. 620, 2694
Fargues, Marie. 293, 746, 1418, 3170
Faricy, Robert L. 2570, 2871, 3476, 3492, 3593
Farid al-Din Attar 13th cent. 3542
Farid al-Din Attar. 3285
Faris, John Thomson. 270, 374, 923, 1375, 1590, 1612, 2884, 2980, 3096, 3553
Faris, Lillie Anne. 620, 625, 628, 2720, 3185
Faris, Paul Patton. 3762
[Faris, William Wallace]. 1734
[Faris, William Wallce]. 2871
Farish, Hunter Dickinson. 2456, 3468
Faristzaddi, Millard. 3022
Farjeon, Eleanor. 3284, 3280
Farkas, Jozsef. 1313
Farley, Claude J. 3175
Farley, Edward. 3707, 1010, 1104, 1858, 3668
Farley, Frederick Augustus. 3727
Farley, John Murphy. 2306, 2700
Farley, Leslie Howard. 1663
Farley, Luke A. 3285
Farley, William John. 567
Farlow, A M. 886
Farmer, Beulah Maude (Hollabaugh) 3534
Farmer, David Hugh. 1026
Farmer, David R. 315
Farmer, Florence Virginia. 2651
Farmer, Foy (Johnson) 2534, 158, 2489
Farmer, Harvey. 3478
Farmer, Herbert H. 1721
Farmer, Herbert Henry. 1590, 1094, 1721, 2038, 2900, 3058
Farmer, James Eugene. 3039
Farmer, James Leonard. 1963, 2127
Farmer, John. 319
Farmer, Penelope. 2821
Farmer, Silas. 923
Farmer, William Reuben. 389, 408, 438, 2010, 2090, 2134, 2150, 2671
Farmer, Wilmoth Alexander. 2485
Farnell, Lewis Richard. 1721, 1395, 1730, 1766, 1767, 3059
Farner, Oskar. 3899
Farnese, A. 3501
Farnsworth, Dewey. 678, 2598
Farnsworth, Edward Clarence. 1032, 1494, 2725, 3227, 3685
Farnsworth, H H. 453
Farnsworth, Kirk E. 1107
Farnum, George Rossiter. 1069
Farnum, Mabel Adelaide. 2189, 692, 723, 1284, 1286, 2189, 2851, 3243
Faron, Louis C. 78

Farques, Marie. 3170
Farquhar, John Nicol. 1813, 1896
al Faruqi, Isma'il Ragi A. 3115
Farr, Albert Melville. 960
Farr, Alfred Derek. 672
Farr, Edward. 1519
Farr, Eugene Ijams. 3236
Farr, Frederic William. 162
Farraher, Joseph J. 3017
Farrar, Adam Storey. 1654, 1656, 3075
Farrar, Francis Albert. 2661
Farrar, Frederic William. 232, 240, 347, 506, 751, 923, 960, 1191, 1528, 1612, 1616, 1699, 1721, 1793, 1963, 1964, 2760, 2796, 2797, 2950, 3340, 3363, 3457, 3808
Farrar, Frederick William. 3405
Farrar, James McNall. 906
Farrar, Reginald. 1613
Farrar, Stewart. 3823
Farrell, Allan Peter. 1946
Farrell, Ambrose. 2716
Farrell, Christopher. 941, 3265
Farrell, Edward P. 3785
Farrell, Eileen (Halligan) 664
Farrell, Martin. 748
Farrell, Mary Xavier. 3416
Farrell, Maureen. 146, 3810
Farrell, Melvin. 3331
Farrell, Melvin L. 1992, 3331
Farrell, Walter. 3696, 1427, 1712, 1964, 3410
Farrelly, Mark John. 2911
Farrelly, Natalena. 2399
Farren, David. 2312
Farrenc, Edmund. 1945
Farrer, Austin. 1446
Farrer, Austin Marsden. 435, 453, 459, 1226, 1590, 1613, 1721, 1907, 2067, 2832, 2980, 3099, 3363, 3620
Farrer, Carl. 995
Farrer, James Anson. 2756
Farrer, John. 2038
[Farrington, Elijah]. 3501, 3520
Farrington, Franklin Fillmore. 232, 1951
Farrington, Marie L. 3573
Farriss, N. M. 1147
Farrow, John. 1400, 2568, 2769, 2861, 1400
Farrow, Percy, E. 1528, 3216
Farrow, Stephen Septimus. 3868
Farsy, Fouad. 3304
Farthing, Geoffrey A. 3685
Farwell, Mary E. 739
Farwell, William. 1107
Farzan, Massud. 3542
Fasching, Darrell J. 1509
Fassett, O R. 1613
Fast, Howard Melvin. 2003, 2094, 2383
Fatemi, Nasrollah Saifpour. 3542
Faucett, Lawrence William. 707, 2063, 2316
Faucher, W. Thomas. 905
Faulhaber, Michael von. 9
Faulk, Lanette (O'Neal) 3236
Faulkner, Brooks R. 1298
Faulkner, Charles Draper. 1269
Faulkner, Georgene. 1114
Faulkner, Harold Underwood. 888
Faulkner, James. 3839
Faulkner, John Alfred. 1174, 2424, 1191, 1398, 1526, 2424, 2561, 3803
Faulkner, Joseph E. 3088
Faulkner, Robert Huntt. 142
Faulkner, Robert Kenneth. 1516, 1844
Faulstich, John. 3186
Faunce, Daniel Worcester. 280, 198, 233, 332, 340, 2021, 2980
Faunce, William Herbert Perry. 1058, 2519, 3671, 3792
Faupel, John Francis. 2351
Faure, Felix. 2489
Faus, William Arthur. 2950
Fauset, Arthur Huff. 2681, 2682, 3717
Fausset, Hugh I'Anson. 1476, 3775
Fausset, Hugh L'Anson. 3099
Faussett, Godfrey. 1212
[Faust, A. J.]. 2082
[Faust, Ambrose Jerome]. 3791
Faust, Arthur Huff. 2682
Faust, Bernhard Christoph. 1859
Faust, David. 3005
Faust, James E. 1009
Fauth, Robert T. 3003
Faville, John. 1341
Faw, Chalmer Ernest. 298, 1191
Fawcett, Edgar. 19
Fawcett, Thomas. 3070
Faxon, Alicia Craig. 1959, 3839
Fay, Bernard. 1664
Fay, Bertrand. 2254
Fay, Cyril Sigourney Webster. 1069
Fay, Don. 644
Fay, Fr. Rud. 553
Fay, Frederic Leighton. 243, 283
Fay, Thomas A. 445
Faye, Eugene de. 2743

Fealy, Lawrence A. 2007
Fealy, Lawrence Augustus. 2847
Fear, Leona K. 1653
Fearheiley, Don M. 2209
Fearnley, J. R. 3501
Fearon, John. 3265
Fearon, Nancy. 1027, 2229
Feather, R. Othal. 3829
Featherstone, Vaughn J. 1009, 1231, 1261, 3885
Featherstun, Henry Walter. 1624, 2005, 2047, 3289
Feaver, J. Clayton. 3107
Febvre, Lucien Paul Victor, 1878. 2273
Febvre, Lucien Paul Victor. 3017
Fechner, Gustav Theodor. 1887
Fechtenburg, Jorgen F H. 204
Feder, J. 2885
Feder, Jose. 1434
Federal council of the churches of Christ in America. 1040, 1046, 1210, 1249, 1253, 1271, 1272, 1543, 1619, 1875, 3253
Federal Government Accountants Association. 1625
Federn, Karl. 3236
Federspiel, Howard M. 2820
Fedorovich, Nicholas. 3722
Fee, Gordon D. 421, 637
Fee, William Ingram 1817-1900. 1564
Fee, Zephyrus Roy. 960, 1313, 1608, 2435, 3099
Feeley-Harnik, Gillian. 1940. 2256
Feely, Joseph Martin. 3501
Feely, Raymond T. 3094, 3096
Feely, Raymond Thomas. 1446
Feeman, Harlan Luther. 122, 2174, 3432
Feeney, Bernard. 2900, 3553
Feeney, Leonard. 119, 1620, 3289, 3378
Feeney, Thomas J. 2568
Feeney, Thomas John. 3220
Feeney, Thomas Joseph. 2366, 2538
Feer, Leon [Henri Leon Feer]. 1937
Feheruari, Geza. 87, 1407
Fehlauer, Adolph. 2280, 3040
Fehr, Wayne L. 1480, 3717
Fehren, Henry. 863, 1263, 1266
Feibelman, Julian Beck. 1620, 3016
Feibleman, James. 2738
Feibleman, James Kern. 2417, 2738, 2853
Feider, Paul A. 3540
Feidler, Clara (Smith) 1564, 2271
Feifel, Herman. 1413
Feige, Gregory. 2077
Feigon, Gershon J. 558
Feild, Reshad. 1620, 3542
Feilde, John. 3606
Feilding, Charles Rudolph. 2474
Feilding, Everard. 2766, 3501
Feilding, Everard [Francis Henry Everard Joseph Feilding]. 2766, 3501
[Feild-Palmer, Edith Marie (Sears)) 1879. 2063
Fein, H. Otto. 3768
Feinberg, Abraham L. 2138
Feinberg, Charles Lee. 506, 518, 559, 600, 610, 611, 2464, 2465
Feinberg, David B. 2082
Feinberg, Louis. 2142
Feine, Paul. 409
Feine, Paul i.e. Karl Eduard Paul. 2803
Feiner, Johannes. 3620, 3643
Feinsilver, Alexander. 2997, 2138
Feinsod, Ethan. 2817
Feinstein, Moses. 562
Felder, Aaron. 2627
Felder, Hilarin. 1641, 2038
Feldman, Abraham J. 3370
Feldman, Abraham Jehiel. 595, 1329, 1787, 2104, 2142, 3015, 3032, 3370, 3371, 3591
Feldman, Asher. 2462, 19, 2772
Feldman, Burton. 2664
Feldman, David Michael. 3389
Feldman, Emanuel. 1416
Feldman, Julian. 1243
Feldman, Louis H. 2134
Felici, Icilio. 3306
Felician Sisters of the Order of St. Francis. 1620
Felician Sisters of the Order of St. Francis. Province of Buffalo. 1620
Felicity, Sister. 1307
Felix, Joseph L. 2387
Fell, Doris Elaine. 1634, 2488
Feller, Richard T. 3796
Fellerer, Karl Gustav. 1205
Fellowes, Edmund Horace. 1206, 2311
Fellowes, Francis. 1421
[Fellows, John] 1759-1844. 3422
Fellows, Lawrence. 3293
Fellows, Stephen Norris. 2447

Fellows, Ward J. 3115
Fellowship of Catholic Scholars. 1820
Fellowship of Solanco Churches. 1273
Fellowship of the Kingdom. 923
Felsenthal, Emma. 1621
Felshin, Max. 2114, 2622
Felt, Marie Fox. 628
Felton, Herbert. 751
Felton, James Andrew. 3017
Felton, Ralph Almon. 3253, 1250, 1321, 1620, 1912, 2438, 2682, 2777, 3253, 3254, 3435, 3442
Feltus, George Haws. 1849
Female Society of Boston and Vicinity for Promoting Christianity among the Jews. 1083
Female society of Boston and vincinity for promoting Christianity among the Jews. 2085
Femiano, Samuel D. 2192, 2702
[Fendall, Philip Ricard] 1794-1868. 726
Fendrich, Joseph Lowrey. 1749, 2024, 3078
Fendt, Edward Charles. 2282
Fenelon, Francois de Salignac de La Mothe. 856, 960, 997, 1438, 1621, 2832, 3013, 3126, 3478, 3845
Fenelon, Francois de Salingnac de La Mothe. 997
Feng, Yu-lan. 2838
Fenhagen, James C. 2379, 2785
Fenichell, Stephen S. 1838
Fenimore, George. 233
Fenlon, Dermot. 1374, 2857
Fenn, Courtenay Hughes. 2519
Fenn, Dan Huntington. 906
Fenn, Don Frank. 3675
Fenn, Richard K. 3328
Fenn, William Wallace. 2063, 3608
Fennell, Desmond. 820
Fennell, Mark. 305
Fenner, Goodrich Robert. 2957
Fenner, Mabel B. 1721, 1980, 2007, 3173
Fenner, Mable B. 3150
Fennimore, Keith J. 179
Fensham, F. Charles. 519
Fensik, Eugene A. 1398
Fenton, Horace L. 2387
Fenton, John C. 416, 440
Fenton, John H. 874, 1397
Fenton, Joseph Clifford. 2871, 3659, 762, 771, 773
Fenwick, Charles Ghequiere. 2808
Fenwick, Malcolm C. 1418, 3199
Ferber, Adolph C. 1698, 3078, 3569
Feret, Henricus Maria. 2254
Ferguson, Amos J. 248
Ferguson, Beatrice. 2038
Ferguson, Ben. 4, 492, 983, 2792
Ferguson, Charles. 3059, 3442
Ferguson, Charles Wright. 1764, 2460, 3351, 3682, 3744, 3831
Ferguson, Clyde L. 202
Ferguson, Delseanure. 3191
Ferguson, Dowena. 1253
Ferguson, E.A. 1721
Ferguson, Everett. 1163, 1196
Ferguson, Franklin C. 2964
Ferguson, George Wells. 920
Ferguson, Helen. 3005
Ferguson, James. 2929
Ferguson, James P. 1285
Ferguson, Jesse Babcock. 3502
Ferguson, John. 1847, 347, 1287, 1766, 2644, 2712, 2811, 3246, 3540, 3792
Ferguson, John Calvin. 2655
Ferguson, John Lambuth. 2435
Ferguson, Richard. 3423, 960
Ferguson, Richard Saul. 1016
Ferguson, Robert Gracey. 122
Ferguson, Robert R. 2208
Ferguson, Rowena. 1259, 2492, 3885
Ferguson, Sinclair B. 1010, 3662
Ferguson, Thomas Stuart. 678
Ferguson, Walter. 481
Ferguson, Walter Dewey. 293
Ferguson, William Duncan. 321, 1771
Ferguson, William Martain. 2442
Fergusson, Edmund Morris. 3553, 3150, 3553, 3561
Fergusson, James. 371, 2560, 3599
Ferlin, Ignatius. 318
Ferlita, Ernest. 399
Ferm, Deane William. 3667
Ferm, Robert L. 1500, 2978, 3636
Ferm, Vergilius Ture Anselm. 3611, 2280, 2282, 2978, 2997, 3092, 3099, 3115, 3116, 3122, 3325, 3620, 3638, 3092, 3099
Fern, Vergilius Ture Anselm. 2294
Fernald, Woodbury M. 719, 2689, 2980
Fernan, John J. 409
Fernan, John Joseph. 409, 2049, 3643
Fernandez Arenas, Jose. 79
Fernandez, James W. 1612
Fernandez Nauarrete, Domingo 1689. 911
Fernie, Benjamin J. 3027

Fernie, E. C. 2715
Feroze, Muhammad Rashid. 6, 726
Ferranti, Philip. 3478
Ferrar, William John. 1020, 56, 459, 488
Ferrari, Erma Paul. 1714, 3784, 3876
Ferraro, John. 3249
Ferrater Mora, Jose 1912. 1413
Ferre, Frederick. 1387, 2242, 3099
Ferre, Gustave A. 3363
Ferre, Gustave Adolph. 1094
Ferre, Nels Frederick Solomon. 1040, 1094, 1590, 1597, 1721, 3662
Ferre, Nels Fredrick Solomon. 935, 960, 1040, 1058, 1094, 1104, 1127, 1590, 1591, 1597, 1721, 1745, 2871, 3099, 3351, 3442, 3478, 3643, 3659, 3699
Ferree, William. 753
Ferreira, M. Jamie. 2179, 2705
Ferrell, John Appley. 3621
Ferrell, Pauline Glover. 3601
Ferrell, William F. 1313
Ferretti, Paolo Maria. 838, 884
*Ferrier, Christine M. 2871
Ferrier, Francis. 1893
Ferrier, William Warren. 726, 3814
Ferrin, Clark Elam. 3596
Ferrin, Howard William. 73, 447, 1446, 960
Ferris, Anita Brockway. 2519, 1478, 2551, 2552, 2757
Ferris, Benjamin G. 2602
Ferris, Carrie Sivyer. 3560
Ferris, David. 3126
Ferris, Frank Halliday. 2931
Ferris, George Hooper. 3478, 339, 1887, 3461
Ferris, Helen. 1144
Ferris, Isaac. 2700
Ferris, Paul. 1211
Ferris, Theodore Parker. 1058, 1094, 1380, 1964, 1985, 2213, 2890, 2900, 2973, 3351
Ferriss, Walter. 3351
Ferriter, Mary C. 2694
Ferrucci, Piero. 3478
Ferry, John G. 3367
Fersen, Eugene. 1654
Ferwerda, Floris. 1058
Ferwerda, Vernon L. 1913
Fesch, Jacques. 2942
Feschotte, Jacques. 3311
Fesmire, W J. 2387
Fesquet, Henri. 759, 3771
Fessenden, Katharine. 628
Fessenden, Samuel Clement. 2474
Fessenden, Thomas. 3643
Festinger, Leon. 2948
Festugiere, Andre Marie Jean. 1766
Fetherling, Dale. 2130
Fetting, Otto. 1894
Fetty, Maurice A. 2213
Feucht, Oscar E. 285, 1254, 3177, 3678, 3837
Feuchtwanger, O. 3016
Feuer, Leon Israel. 2075, 2114, 3896
Feuerbach, Ludwig Andreas. 1507, 1591, 2273, 3059, 3099
Feuerlicht, Morris Marcus. 1624, 2100
*Feuerlicht, Robert Strauss. 2172
Feuerstein, Georg. 3864
Feuillet, Andre. 413, 460, 2049, 2938
Fevold, Eugene L. 2302
Fewkes, Jesse Walter. 1846, 3432
Fewler, Willis Hadley. 2900
*Fey, Harold E. 2251, 3211
Fey, Harold Edward. 1066, 1150, 2251, 2492, 2979
Fey, William R. 1597, 2702
Feyrer, Ernest Charles. 3698
Feys, Jan. 1708, 2316, 3492
Ffrench-Beytagh, Gonville Aubie. 1132, 1624
Fibiger, Johan Andreas Neergaard. 2031
Fichte, Johann Gottlieb. 3224
Fichter, Andrew. 1521, 3780
Fichter, Joseph Henry. 1398, 2191, 63, 828, 829, 831, 1278, 1279, 2378, 2814, 3662, 3785
Fichthorn, Claude Leslie. 736
Fichtner, Joseph. 492, 863, 1266, 2038, 2321, 2323
Fick, Henry H. 1400
Ficker, Victor B. 3636
Fickes, George Herman. 3150
Fickett, Harold L. 147, 214, 447, 657, 1626
Fides Forum, 1st, University of Notre Dame, 1966. 2192
Fidler, James E. 3177
Fidler, Marguerite. 2492
Fiedler, Ernest J. 3264
Fiedler, Fred J. 2530
Fiedler, Lois. 2890
Fiege, Marianus. 1101
Fiehler, Rudolph. 2736
Field, Benjamin. 3643
Field, Benjamin, d. 3643

Field, Benjamin Franklin. 206
Field, Claud Herbert Alwyn. 2207
Field, David. 1843, 3237
Field, Elliot. 2757
Field, Faye. 2007, 3841
Field, Filip. 1368
Field, Frank McCoy. 1964
Field, George. 1380, 2692
Field, Grenville O. 453
Field, Henry Martyn. 19
Field, Jay C. 2955
Field, John Edward. 663, 1224
Field, Laurence N. 17, 2211, 2284
Field, Margaret J. 1699
Field, Margaret Joyce. 43, 588, 1699
Field, Rachel. 898
Field, Rachel Lyman. 900
Field, Silas M. 1380
Field, Walter Taylor. 905
Fieldhouse, Marvin L. 386, 2976
Fielding, William John. 1654, 3567
Fielding-Hall, Harold. 701
*Fields, Harvey J. 3310
Fields, Rick. 710
Fields, W C. 1139
Fields, Wilbert J. 2258
Fields, Wilbur. 365, 450, 478
Fields, William. 1380
Fields, William H. 2890
Fields, William, jr. 3199
Fiering, Norman. 950, 1499
Fierman, Floyd S. 2106
Fierro Bardaji, Alfredo 1936. 1085
Fiers, Alan Dale. 1465, 2554
Fiester, Mark. 1301, 1484
Fife, Austin E. 2615, 2619
Fife, Clyde Lee. 3232
Fife, Earl Hanson. 3168
Fife, Eric S. 713, 1828, 2485, 2554, 2871
Fife, Robert Herndon. 2273
Fife, Robert O. 1045, 1132, 3758
Fife, Robert Oldham. 1045
Fifield, George Edward. 3502
Fifield, James W. 960
Fifield, Lawrence Wendell. 653
Fifield, James W. 960
Figart, Thomas O. 3017
Figgis, John Neville. 114, 116, 1069, 1141, 1211, 1226, 1764, 3199
Figueroa y Miranda, Miguel. 1532
Figuier, Louis. 1695
Fike, Earle W. 179
Filas, Francis Lad. 2004, 2132
Filbeck, David. 1273, 1465
Filbeck, James Orval. 69
Filby, Frederick Arthur. 204, 1421
Filhaut, Theodor. 1156
Filley, Dorothy M. 3399
Fillion, Louis Claude. 637, 1964
Fillmore, A. N. 1240
Fillmore, Charles. 416, 526, 1598, 1625, 2409, 3750, 3751, 1625, 3750
Fillmore, Cora G. (Dedrick) 2323
Fillmore, J. Henry. 3562
Fillmore, James Henry. 3026
*Fillmore, Lowell. 2960, 3324, 3750
Fillmore, Myrtle (Page) 1625
Filmer, Edmund. 1980
Filmer, Edward. 1309, 3606
Filson, Floyd Vivian. 217, 332, 389, 405, 406, 409, 418, 440, 476, 2009, 2824
Filthaut, Theodor. 838, 860, 1156
Finch, Josiah John. 162
Finck, Mary Helena. 3417
Finck, Susan J. 3502
Finck, William John. 2294
Finco, Gaetano. 397
Findlay, George Gillanders. 369
Findlay, James Alexander. 3335, 2824
Findlay, James Arthur. 3502
Findlay, James F. 2587
Findlay, Stephen William. 1290
[Findling, Joseph] 1892. 2946
Fine, Helen. 1539
*Fine, Herbert J. 3662
Fine, Jo Renee. 3578
Fine, William M. 2167, 3363
Fineberg, Solomon Andhil. 2086
Finegan, Jack. 3662, 56, 204, 218, 298, 335, 351, 516, 523, 960, 1058, 1817, 1964, 2008, 2038, 2399, 2808, 3012, 3139, 3224, 3537, 3662, 3885
Fineren, William Warrick. 1513
Finesinger, Sol Baruch. 2634
Fingarette, Herbert. 1330
Finger, Charles J. 2628
Finger, Charles Joseph. 2241
Fingesten, Peter. 1082, 3573
Fink, Leo Gregory. 1913, 1948, 1801, 2126, 2797
Fink, Louis Maria. 769
Fink, Peter E. 838, 2368
Fink, Reuben. 3896
*Fink, Russell E. 1164
Finkbeiner, John. 1446

Finkelstein, Louis. 20, 2088, 2095, 2108, 2112, 2138, 2146, 2148, 2828, 3126, 3744
Finlay, James. 1295
Finlay, M. H. 2124
Finlay, Terence J. 1313
Finlayson, John Livingstone. 1671
Finlayson, R. A. 3657
Finley, James. 771, 795, 947, 2047, 2346, 2412, 3492
Finley, James Bradley. 1689, 2450, 2453
Finn, Brendan A. 738
Finn, Edward E. 851, 2749
Finn, Elizabeth M. 3150
Finn, Francis James. 854, 1615
Finn, James. 103
[Finn, Mary Paulina] 1842. 3206
Finn, William Joseph. 1205
Finnegan, Edward G. 620
Finnell, R[euben] A[shford]. 451
Finnerty, Adam. 3409
Finnerty, Adam Daniel. 3409
Finney, Charles G. 1626
Finney, Charles Grandison. 3228, 471, 1333, 1556, 1625, 1626, 2886, 2887, 2941, 3228, 3229, 3351, 3414, 3621, 3643, 3651
Finney, Davida. 1501
Finney, John E. 1513
Finney, Lewis Erwin. 1804
Finney, Ross L. 3086
Finney, Thomas M. 2351
Finnis, H. P. 1308
Finucane, Ronald C. 1516
Fiolet, Hermanus Antonius Maria. 1044
Fiore, Amadeus P. 2468
Fiorenza, Elisabeth Schussler. 347, 453, 459, 1102
Fire, Esther. 1591
Fireman, Peter. 1654
Fireside, Harvey. 1149, 2749
Firey, Milton Jacob. 1906
Firmage, Edwin Brown. 2504, 2797
Firmicus Maternus, Julius. 69, 98
Firminger, Walter Kelly. 44
Firnhaber, R. Paul. 3885
First Baptist Church, Chamblee, Ga. 881, 1626
First Baptist Church, Miami, Fla. 1626, 2461
First United Methodist Church, Birmingham, Ala. 1627
Firth, Franklin Jones. 1079
Firth, Raymond William. 3573, 3699
Firth, Violet Mary. 2725
Fischbach, Julius. 906, 907
Fischer, Bela. 2833
Fischer, Carl John. 2661
Fischer, Clare Benedicks. 3834
Fischer, Della Reagan. 139
Fischer, Dorothy May. 1247
Fischer, Edward. 667, 1387, 1472, 1803, 2486, 2505, 2536, 3273
Fischer, Emil Eisenhardt. 3442
Fischer, Emily Lorena (Coleman) 3502
Fischer, George L. 3785
Fischer, Harold Arthur. 3230
Fischer, Helmut. 3003
Fischer, Henry. 2369
*Fischer, Howard A. 612, 637, 644
Fischer, Hubert. 755
Fischer, James A. 637, 2130, 3832
Fischer, M. Hadwin. 1964
Fischer, Michael M J. 3403
Fischer, Norma Bristol. 1014
Fischer, Robert Blanchard. 204
Fischer, Robert H. 1689, 2273, 3039
Fischer, William L. 3750
Fischman, Joyce. 1615, 3310
Fish, Edward B. 2056
Fish, Henry Clay. 960, 961, 1564, 3340
Fish, J. G. 233
Fish, John. 1131
Fish, Joseph. 1247, 1503, 2742, 3779, 2602
Fish, Roy J. 1554, 1564
[Fish, Samuel]. 3792
Fish, Simon. 2579
Fish, Stanley Eugene. 2470
Fishback, Elvin Holt. 2590
Fishbane, Michael A. 499
Fishburn, Janet Forsythe. 3025, 3433
Fisher, Aileen Lucia. 1384, 1486, 1939
Fisher, Allen Schanely. 2292
Fisher, Arabella Burton (Buckley) 3075
Fisher, Arthur Stanley Theodore. 3310
Fisher, C. William. 3540
Fisher, Clarence Stanley. 2400
Fisher, Clay C. 233, 1530
Fisher, Daniel Webster. 1249, 2372
Fisher, Desmond. 1245, 3771
Fisher, Ebenezer. 3753
Fisher, Edward, fl. 3294
Fisher, Ernest Arthur. 1159, 3705
Fisher, Eugene J. 2152

Fisher, Fred Bohn. 1240, 1628
Fisher, Fred C. 3351
Fisher, Fred L. 147, 345, 376, 389, 405, 2038, 2797, 2883, 3029, 3335
Fisher, Frederick Bohn. 961, 1446, 1628, 2059, 2425, 1250
Fisher, Galen Merriam. 3870, 2625
Fisher, Gary. 1556
Fisher, George D. 3237
Fisher, George Park. 60, 1098, 1174, 1191, 2672, 3034, 3224, 3621, 3643, 3654
Fisher, Harriet Irene, "Harry T. Fisher. 1401, 1980
Fisher, Herbert Albert Laurens. 1032
Fisher, Hiram Thomas. 3073
Fisher, Hugh. 1341, 3430
Fisher, Humphrey J. 2566
[Fisher, James] 1697-1775. 3809
Fisher, Joe. 2948
Fisher, Johanna. 2204
Fisher, John Douglas Close. 138, 665
Fisher, Jonathan. 134, 480, 536
Fisher, Judson. 1350
Fisher, Lee. 1627, 1638, 1755, 1803, 3885
Fisher, Lena Leonard. 2497
Fisher, Leonard Everett. 1384
Fisher, Lewis Beals. 3754, 3752
Fisher, Lillian Estelle. 1
Fisher, Lizette Andrews. 1402, 1755, 3709
Fisher, Lyman J. 2465
Fisher, Miles Mark. 743, 1627, 151
Fisher, Mitchell Salem. 2076
Fisher, Neal F. 3616
Fisher, Nevin Wishard. 1236
Fisher, Samuel W[are]. 2931
Fisher, Samuel Ware. 727, 2546
Fisher, Susanna G. 293
Fisher, Susanna Georgina. 2007
Fisher, Wallace E. 1058, 1153, 1243, 1313, 1565, 2195, 2299, 2900, 3351, 3529
Fisher, Welthy (Honsinger) 1628
Fisher, Wilfred. 3351
Fisher, William Arms. 3271
Fisher, William Logan. 1684, 3547
Fisher, Willis Williard. 543
Fisher-Hunter, William, 1899. 1471
Fishman, Isidore. 597
Fishman, Judah Loeb. 2560
Fishman, Samuel Z. 2122
Fishwick, Marshall William. 1427
Fisichella, Anthony J. 2725
Fisk, Alfred G. 63
Fisk, Elinor Williams. 726
Fisk, Elisha. 2741
Fisk, Franklin Woodbury. 2900
Fisk, Margaret (Palmer) 1400
Fisk, Marian. 3170
Fisk, Milton. 2738
Fisk, Pliny. 3340
Fisk, Samuel. 1598, 1658, 1504
Fisk, Stephen. 3240
Fisk University, Nashville. Social Science Institute. 2682
Fisk, Wilbur. 729
[Fiske, Albert Augustus] 1828. 1032
Fiske, Amos Kidder. 1798, 499, 526
Fiske, Asa Severance. 3023
Fiske, Charles. 101, 389, 961, 1049, 1591, 1893, 1951, 1964, 1999, 2474, 2973, 3059, 1069
Fiske, Daniel Taggart. 1628, 2541
Fiske, George Walter. 961, 1603, 1608, 2063, 3003, 3150, 3340, 3439, 3456
Fiske, John. 1628, 3802, 1628, 1721, 1887, 1888, 2651, 2672, 2835, 2836
Fiske, Martha Theresa. 645
Fiske, William O. 3377
Fison, J E. 533, 1528, 1828
Fitch, Albert Parker. 881, 2900
Fitch, Alger Morton. 732
Fitch, Charles. 3319
Fitch, Chauncey W. 76, 1933
Fitch, Eleazar Thompson. 3410
Fitch, Florence Mary. 91, 1395, 2564, 3853, 1996
Fitch, Lawrence. 2851, 2852
Fitch, Robert Elliot. 1104, 1394, 2264, 3071, 3399
[Fitch, T. 2602, 3428
Fitch, William. 180, 961, 1446, 1828, 3610
Fitchburg, Mass. Church of Christ. 1337
Fitchburg, Mass. Church of Christ. Ecclesiastical council. 1801. 1628
Fitchburg, Mass. Congregational church. 1628
Fitchen, John. 78
Fitchett, William Henry. 1387, 2474
Fite, Warner. 1995
FitGerald, Robert David. 3206
Fitt, Arthur Percy. 2587
Fitti, Charles J. 3391, 3716
Fittipaldi, Silvio. 2871
Fitton, James. 823

Fitts, James Hill. 734
Fitts, Leroy. 739, 2486
Fitts, Mary Pauline. 1774, 3890
Fitts, William Thrower. 90
Fitz, Asa. 1865, 3562
Fitzer, Joseph. 2568, 3656
Fitz-Gerald, Aaron Boylan. 2174
Fitzgerald, Anselm. 587
Fitzgerald, Byron John. 3502
Fitzgerald, Catherine Anita. 852
Fitzgerald, Ernest A. 63, 1006, 3337
Fitzgerald, George R. 2900
[Fitzgerald, Gerald Michael Joseph Cushing, 1894. 997, 1741, 2597
Fitzgerald, Gordon. 2167
FitzGerald, James Newbury. 3459
Fitzgerald, Lawrence P. 81, 993, 2387, 3012, 3456, 3885
Fitzgerald, Mary Innocentia. 2626, 3418
Fitzgerald, Maurice Henry. 692
Fitzgerald, Oscar Penn. 665, 24, 693, 1285, 1286, 1446, 2310, 2387, 2426, 3431
Fitzgerald, Penelope. 1515, 2182
Fitzgerald, Thomas Edward. 3116
Fitz-Gibbon, Ralph Edgerton. 3502
Fitzhugh, Josie (Millsaps) 1438
Fitzmyer, Joseph A. 334, 350, 376, 1411
Fitzpatrick, Benedict. 1857
Fitzpatrick, Daniel J. 2268, 3885
Fitzpatrick, Doyle C. 182, 3535
Fitzpatrick, Edmund J. 1602, 3693
Fitzpatrick, Edward Augustus. 767, 769, 803, 805, 1946, 2189, 2268, 2370, 3150, 3170
Fitzpatrick, Edwzrd Augustus. 805
Fitzpatrick, Florence Baillie. 625, 1980
Fitzpatrick, James Joseph. 997
Fitzpatrick, James K. 63, 2038
Fitzpatrick, Vincent de Paul. 831, 1397
Fitzroy, Anne. 2964
Fitzsimmons, James A. 3377
Fitz Simon, Vincent Alphonso. 2019
Fitzsimons, John. 738, 753, 2328
Fitzsimons, Matthew A. 817
Fitzwater, Perry Braxton. 473, 1134, 1893, 2038, 3643, 3836
Fix, Janet. 3415
Fjeldstad, Halvard O. 2283
Flaceliere, Robert. 2740
Flack, A. G. 2590
Flagg, Edward Octavus. 298
[Flagg, Samuel Benjamin] 1828-1900. 3856
Flagg, William Joseph. 3461
Flagstad, O A. 3502
Flahive, Robert F. 3284
Flake, Arthur. 141, 1167, 3553
Flake, Chad J. 2608
Flake, Lawrence R. 1231
Flamini, Roland. 860, 3741
Flamma, Thomas. 1490
Flammarion, Camille. 2988
Flammonde, Paris. 1601
Flanagan, Donal. 1245
Flanagan, James M. 1463
Flanagan, Neal M. 651
[Flanders, George Truesdell]. 3090
Flanders, Henry Jackson. 309, 533
Flanders, Robert Bruce. 2676
Flanery, E. B. 233, 1091
Flanigan, George Joseph. 825
Flanigan, James C. 1079
Flannery, Austin. 849, 1079
Flannery, Harry W. 1077
Flaque, Ferdinand Charles. 3150
Flaskerud, Ole E. 3260
[Flattery, Hugh]. 1706
Flavel, John. 961, 1350, 1358, 2931, 3126
Flavianus. 1191, 1521
Flavius. 1650, 692, 749, 753, 2685
Fleck, Alcyon Ruth. 3382
Fleck, G. Peter. 3725
Fleck, Raymond. 2132, 2348
Fleer, Gedaliah. 690, 2668
Fleetwood, John. 1964, 1977, 1978, 2088
Fleetwood, William. 3363
Fleg, Edmond. 2019, 2114, 2621, 2761, 2950, 3457, 3791, 1629, 2075, 2138
Fleharty, J. Q. A. 3230
Fleischer, Benjamin. 2082, 2094
Fleischner, Eva. 2152
Fleisher, David. 1743, 1748
Fleming, Archibald Lang. 1532
Fleming, Bruce C. E. 3668
Fleming, Daniel Johnson. 871, 920, 1015, 1079, 1156, 1321, 1371, 1394, 2492, 2519, 2530, 2890
Fleming, David L. 2268, 3475
Fleming, G. Granger. 2871
Fleming, John. 1556
Fleming, John R. 918
Fleming, John Robert. 1875
Fleming, John V. 186, 922
Fleming, Kenneth C. 202
Fleming, Mervin Robert. 1386
Fleming, Robert. 463

Fleming, Sandford. 145, 192, 937, 1999, 2014, 3167
[Fleming, Stanislaus, 1854-1932. 819, 2246
Fleming, William Sherman. 3189
Fleming-Mitchell, Leslie, 1953. 98
Flemington, N.J. Baptist church. 2688
Flender, Helmut. 431
Fletcher, Alexander. 2133, 2371
Fletcher, Alfred Johnston. 1629
Fletcher-Allen, Edgar. 198
Fletcher, Anna Louise (Paine) 3502
Fletcher, Annis. 1721
[Fletcher, Augusta W.]. 2725, 3502
Fletcher, Elaine J. 1612
Fletcher, Ella Adelia. 691
Fletcher, Grace (Nies) 961, 1629, 1820, 2684, 3850
Fletcher, Harris Francis. 299, 1798, 2469, 2470, 2471, 2470, 3015
Fletcher, Herbert Harvey. 1058
Fletcher, Howard A. 2156
Fletcher, James Henry. 3502
Fletcher, Jesse C. 3, 146, 876, 993, 1633, 1786, 2552, 3790
Fletcher, John Joseph Kilpin. 2538
Fletcher, John William. 59, 1629, 2038, 2217, 2427, 2797, 3410, 3413
[Fletcher, John William]. 3413
Fletcher, Joseph Francis. 943, 946, 1075, 3599
Fletcher, Joseph Smith. 1276, 3038
Fletcher, M. J. 28
Fletcher, M Scott. 611
Fletcher, Milton J. 961
Fletcher, R. A. 1459
Fletcher, Rupert J. 1230
Fletcher, Sarah. 620
Fletcher, Thomas P. 2320
Fletcher, William. 1749
Fletcher, William Aloysius. 289
Fletcher, William C. 214, 1149, 2710, 2749, 2750, 3257, 3611
Fletcher Herbert Harvey. 693
Flett, James. 1665
Flew, Antony Garrard Newton. 2672, 2832, 3621
Flew, Robert Newton. 2818
Flew, Robert Newton, 1886. 1163, 2819, 2976
Flew, Robert Newton. 2976
Flewelling, Ralph Tyler. 1591
Fliade, Mircea. 1908
Flick, Alexander Clarence. 1185, 1186
Flick, Ella Mary Elizabeth. 1482, 2307
Flickinger, Robert Elliott. 886
Flicoteaux, Emmanuel. 2813
Fliegel, Carl John. 2595
Flierl, Johann. 2541
Flight, John W. 293, 533
Flinders, Neil J. 2611
Flink, Eugene. 3260
Flinn, Avril. 1367, 1629
Flinn, Robert J. 3787
Flint, Bert C. 1210
Flint, Charles Wesley. 3802
Flint, Cort R. 1350, 2262
Flint, David. 1858
Flint, Edward. 786, 1040
Flint, Joseph Frederick. 3392
Flint, Robert. 19
Floethe, Louise Lee. 712, 2188
Flood, David Ethelbert. 2583
Flood, Edmund. 1721, 1964, 2025, 2051, 3029
Flood, Joseph Mary. 110, 114, 1026
Flood, Peter. 771, 937
Flood, Robert. 923, 3748
Flood, Theodore L. 2427
Floody, Robert John. 3260, 3547
Flora, Cornelia Butler. 2814
Flora, George R. 2537
Floreen, Harold. 961
Florer, Warren Washburn. 3307
Floridi, Ulisse Alessio. 1131
Florin, Hans W. 2292
Florio, Anthony. 2337
Floristan, Casiano. 2774
Florovskii, Georgii Vasel'evich. 2745, 3633
Florovskii, Georgii Vasil'evich. 1182, 2745, 3633, 1380
Flory, Ezra. 638
Flory, John Samuel. 549, 1236, 1485
Flory, Margaret. 1127
Flournoy, Parke Poindexter. 347
Flournoy, Theodore. 2988, 3427, 3502
Flower, Alice Reynolds. 1608
Flower, Benjamin Orange. 1033
Flower, Hattie C. 253
Flower, John Cyril. 1636, 2997
Floy, James. 492, 625, 628
Floyd, James Matthew. 1951
Floyd, John. 786
Floyd, L P. 1425
Floyd, Olive Beatrice. 1222
Floyd, Pat. 3763

Floyd, Silas Xavier. 162, 3789
Floyd, William. 233, 1654
Floyd, William A. 1295
Floyd, William Edward Gregory. 1287, 1745
Fluck, Jonathan Lewis. 3048
Flucke, John W. 1550
Fluckiger, Wilford Lynn. 953
Fluegel, Maurice. 2084, 3059, 2077, 2097, 2621, 2777, 2414
Flumiani, Carlo Maria. 1413
Flusser, David Gustav. 384, 1964
Fly, C. L. 995, 1630
Fly, Elijah M. 204
Flygt, Sten Gunnar. 130, 1520
Flyn, Edwin A. 2366
Flynn, Anthony J. 3181, 3186
Flynn, Clarence Edwin. 2387
Flynn, George Q. 875, 3247, 3740
Flynn, Jean Martin. 3591
Flynn, John Stephen. 3006, 3008
Flynn, Joseph Michael. 823, 873
Flynn, L. J. 764
Flynn, Leslie B. 72, 338, 492, 993, 1114, 1165, 1199, 1313, 1712, 1740, 1756, 2004, 2054, 2133, 2135, 2321, 2792, 2824, 3529, 3822, 3829
Flynn, Maureen. 1631, 2262
Flynn, Paul Vincent. 1187
Flynn, Thomas. 2354, 2370
Flynn, Thomas Edward. 3567
Flynn, Thomas J., & co., Boston, Mass. 869
Flynt, Faye DeBeck. 662, 3563
Floyd-Jones, Elbert. 1306
Foakes-Jackson, Frederick John. 329, 406, 533, 1185, 1191, 1220, 1758, 2134, 2797, 2824
Fodor, Nandor. 1709, 2845, 2993
Foelsch, Charles Berend. 1434, 2297
Foerster, Friedrich Wilhelm. 961, 3390
Foerster, Werner. 1717, 2148
[Fogal, Alonzo] 1877. 397, 2071
Fogarty, James Henry. 1288
Fogarty, John Patrick. 1272
Fogarty, Michael Patrick. 933
Fogarty, Robert S. 1849
Fogarty, Ronald. 814
Fogde, Myron Jean. 3739
Fogelklou, Emilia. 1684
*Fogelman, William J. 3166
Fogg, E S. 1860
Fogg, Mary Lape. 73
Fogle, Lerry W. 454
Foh, Susan T. 202
Fohrer, Georg. 598, 1796, 2150
Foisy, J Albert. 823
Foley, Albert Sidney. 191, 875, 1793, 3051
Foley, Barbara. 2349
Foley, George Cadwalader. 104
Foley, Gerald. 829
[Foley, John Thaddeus] 1858. 2254
Foley, Leonard. 1327, 3283, 1326, 3265
Foley, Louis. 2349
Foley, Rolla. 1110
Foley, Theodosius. 1641, 1645
Foliot, Gilbert. 1761
Foljambe, Samuel W. 3351
Folk, David Henry. 3221
Folk, Edgar Estes. 149, 2602
Folkman, Jerome D. 3363
Follansbee, Eleanor. 1793
Follen, Eliza Lee (Cabot) 1632
Follette, John Wright. 983
Folliet, Joseph. 811, 817, 2135
[Follin,Maynard Dauchy] 1864. 518, 521, 605
Following St. Francis. 3529
Folsom, John Dana. 961, 3150
Folsom, Nathaniel Smith. 3713
Folsom, Paul. 1853
Fonck, Leopold. 2025
Fonction symbolique. 3536
Foner, Philip Sheldon. 2104
Fontein, Jan. 2760
Fontenrose, Joseph Eddy. 1421, 1478, 1856, 2648, 3010
Fontinelli, Eugene. 1104
Foot, Joseph Ives. 3351
Foot, Stephen. 2753
Foote, Arthur. 1632, 2211, 2387
Foote, Elizabeth Louisa. 2224, 2225
Foote, Evelyn Carter. 3885
Foote, Gaston. 70, 961, 1318, 1446, 2057, 2246, 2435, 3879
Foote, George William. 233, 1656
Foote, Henry Wilder. 684, 1094, 1337, 1871, 3671
Foote, Mary Hastings. 384, 1992
Foote, Robert M. 1006
Foote, Theodore Clinton. 1521
Foote, Ulysses Grant. 3373
Footman, Henry. 1098
Foran, Donald J. 997

Forbes, Albert L. 3720
Forbes, Elmer Severance. 3442
Forbes, Forrest Dale. 3848, 3861
Forbes, Frances Alice Monica. 683, 809, 2412, 3286
Forbes, Harrie Rebecca Piper (Smith) 3470
Forbes, Harriette (Merrifield) 3333
Forbes, Henry Prentiss. 413
Forbes, John Van Gelder. 2974
Forbes, Robert. 3351
Forbes, S. Russell. 745
Forbes, Theodore Erwin. 1039
Forbes-Leith, William. 873
Forbush, Bliss. 586, 1992, 1677, 1810, 1992
Forbush, William Byron. 687, 1980, 1992, 2014, 2662
Force, Maynard Alfred. 553, 2299
Forcey, Clark Johnson. 162, 1354, 1556, 1557
Forchheimer, Paul. 4, 2144
Ford, Agnes Gibbs. 2890
Ford, Arthur A. 671, 1695, 3502
Ford, Charles Edward. 870
Ford, Charles William. 305, 638
Ford, Clay. 1261
Ford, David Barnes. 2687
Ford, David Everard. 1565
Ford, Desmond. 506, 605, 1012, 2038, 3385
Ford, Douglas William Cleverley. 428, 1094, 1226, 2900
Ford, Ernest Jennings. 1865
Ford, Francis xavier. 776, 1828
Ford, George L. 2476
Ford, George Lonnie. 1251
Ford, Gwen M. 961
Ford, Harold W. 1464
Ford, Harry Pringle. 2918
Ford, Jack. 1237
Ford, John Cuthbert. 947, 2343, 2575
*Ford, John H. 997
Ford, Josephine Massingberd. 877
Ford, Josephine Massyngberde. 645, 1828, 2211, 2815, 3406
Ford, Lauren [Julia Lauren Ford] 2357
Ford, Leighton. 1058, 1557, 1565
Ford, LeRoy. 954, 3161, 3179
Ford, Lewis S. 651, 2943
Ford, Lillian Gertrude (Shafer) 2516
Ford, Lillian Gertrude (Shafer) "Orley Ford," 2516
Ford, Marolyn. 171, 1633
Ford, Mary Hanford (Finney) 2, 127
Ford, Murray J. S. 3003, 3785
Ford, Patrick P. 2190, 2594
Ford, Sallie (Rochester) 1905
Ford, Samuel Howard. 147, 151
Ford, Stephen Van Rensselaer. 285, 638, 3310
Ford, T[homas] B[urgess]. 2450
Ford, Thomas Burgess. 2450
Ford, Wesley P. 961
Ford, William Herschel. 162, 332, 444, 592, 993, 1315, 1531, 1557, 1692, 2057, 2721, 2887, 3321
Forde, Gerhard O. 2201, 2280
Fordham, Forrest B. 1259
Fordham, Monroe. 2682
Fordham-Rural Life Socio-Economic Conference Maryknoll, N. Y., 1958. 1137
Fordham University Conference of Mission Specialists. 850
Fordham University Conference of Mission Specialists, 1953. 1363
Fordyce, James. 3363
Forehand, Mary Anne. 2263, 2490
Foreign Mission Conference of North America. 2523
Foreign missions conference of North America. 1608, 2523
Foreign missions conference of North America. Committee of reference and counsel. 2519
Foreign missions convention of the United States and Canada, Washington, D.C., 1925. 2519
Forell, Betty. 2022
Forell, George Walfgang. 2273, 3452
Forell, George Wolfgang. 109, 472, 950, 995, 1016, 1074, 1268, 2273, 2706, 2953, 2976, 3452
Forem, Jack. 3708
Foreman, Dennis Walden. 2017
Foreman, Kenneth Joseph. 1446, 2337, 2911, 3168
Foreman, Lawton Durant. 30, 674, 1376
Foresi, Pasquale M. 795
Forest Glen, Md. National park seminary for young women. 1633
Forest, Ilse. 3150
Forest, James H. 2412, 3710
Forestell, J. Terence. 492
Forestier, Peter. 657
Forey, Alan John. 3598

Forker, Cora. 2597
Forlines, Charles Edward. 3621
Forliti, John E. 1261
Forlong James George Roche. 3092
Forman, Charles W. 1090, 1094, 2492, 2533
Forman, Henry James. 2946, 3059, 3141
Forman, Max Leon. 1840, 2122
Forman, Raymond Lalor. 3340
Formby, Henry. 3246
Formoy, Beryl E. R. 1475
Fornell, Earl Wesley. 2162, 3502
Forner, Benjamin Nicholas. 809
Forney, Cinistian Henry. 1229
Forrer, Samuel Henry. 3191
Forrest, Earle Robert. 1846
Forrest, James Edward. 3256
Forrest, John K. 1534
Forrest, Katharine A. 620
Forrest, Michael D. 795, 2254, 2259, 2943
Forrest, William Mentzel. 593, 2530, 2562
Forrester, David. 2871
Forrester, William Roxburgh. 3784
Forrester-Brown, James S. 525, 1380
Forristal, Desmond. 809, 1174
Fors, Andrew Peter. 1534
Forsberg, Malcolm. 2552, 3539
Forse, Edward John George. 3238
Forsee, Aylesa. 628
Forst, Margaret. 1964
Forster, Ada L. 1464
Forster, Arnold. 53, 54
Forster, Arthur Haire. 3212
Forster, Margaret. 2337
Forster, Minnie Jane (Wyatt) 1446, 3143
Forster, Roger T. 1819, 3670
Forster, Thomas Gales. 3502
Forster, Walter Otto. 2297, 3527
Forstman, H. Jackson. 276, 729, 1118
Forsyth, Clarence Jane. 1049
Forsyth, David D. 2454
Forsyth, George H. 3414
Forsyth, John. 2979
Forsyth, Nathaniel Frederick. 1247, 2785, 3150
*Forsyth, P. T. 1634, 2900, 3461
Forsyth, Peter Taylor. 2337, 3616, 84, 118, 1049, 1591, 1951, 2038, 2492, 2871, 3038, 3610, 3633
Forsyth, Robert Coventry. 912
Forsythe, Sidney A. 2509
Fort, Adele Brooks. 2638
Fort Atkinson, Wis. St. Paul's Evangelical Lutheran Church. 1174
Fort Wayne (Diocese) Diocesan School Board. 1459
Fort Worth, Tex. Evans Avenue Baptist Church. 151
Fort Worth, Tex. Southwestern Baptist Theological Seminary. Fleming Library. 1469
Forte, Latmen F. 1033
Fortes, Meyer. 3580
Fortescue, Adrain. 838
Fortescue, Adrian. 1487, 2366, 2744, 3238, 765
Fortescue, Edward Francis Knottesford. 82
Fortini, Arnaldo. 1027, 1641
Fortman, Edmund J. 1695, 1732, 1750, 3714
Fortmann, Henricus Martinus Maria. 1485
Fortna, Robert Tomson. 419
Fortson, John L. 10
Fortunat, Father. 2361
Fortunato, Connie. 1208
Fortune, Alonzo Willard. 1460, 1118, 1464, 3432
Fortune, Charlton. 87
Fortune, Reo Franklin. 2329
Forward, Carnice E. 2806
Fosbroke, Hughell E W. 2057, 3621
Fosdick, Harry Emerson. 162, 233, 651, 961, 1049, 1069, 1431, 1438, 1591, 1635, 1888, 1964, 1995, 2761, 2804, 2871, 2978, 3059, 3351, 144, 929, 1058, 1069, 1964, 2273, 2871, 2978, 3059, 3351
Foshee, Howard B. 150, 1239, 1408
Foss, Cyrus David. 3116
Foss, Gerald D. 1667
Foss, Michael. 1946
Fossom, F. O. 1876
Foster, A. Durwood. 1739
Foster, Addison Pinneo. 1341, 3551
Foster, Alfred Edye Manning. 1218
Foster, Allyn Roge. 3078, 3228, 1090
Foster, Annie H. 660
Foster, Atwood. 293
Foster, Charles. 292, 293, 383, 625, 626, 1964, 1980, 1981
[Foster, Charles]. 293
Foster, Charles Henery. 3502
Foster, Charles I. 1551
Foster, Constance J. 3478
Foster, Dave. 1754, 3230
Foster, Elon. 1840

Foster, Ethel (Field) 3502
Foster, Eugene Clifford. 687, 3177, 3553, 638, 687
Foster, Finley Milligan. 1141
Foster, Frank Clifton. 3612
Foster, Frank Hugh. 961, 2060, 799, 2688, 2775, 2975, 3659
Foster, Frederick William. 614
Foster, Genevieve (Stump) 1282
Foster, George Burman. 1049, 1058, 2710, 3059
Foster, George Everett. 218, 891
Foster, George Sanford. 3078
Foster, Hazel Elora. 280
Foster, Henry. 3094
Foster, Iris. 3261
Foster, Isaac. 1635, 3524
Foster, Isaac J. 104
Foster, John. 912, 1040, 3059, 3363, 1187, 1189, 3280, 3676
Foster, John J. 2205, 3535
Foster, John McGaw. 73, 961
Foster, John Onesimus. 3767, 3834
Foster, John W. 1295
Foster, Judith Ellen (Horton) 3816, 3833
Foster, K. Neil. 961
Foster, K Neill. 1003, 1716
Foster, Kenneth E. 3300
Foster, L[orenzo] R. 3340
Foster, Lovelace Savidge. 156, 1379, 2509
Foster, Mary Jane (Chisholm) 3565
Foster, Michael Beresford. 2832
Foster, Myles Birket. 49
Foster, Neill. 983
Foster, Paul. 1143
Foster, Randolph Sinks. 60, 1380, 1730, 2438, 3410, 3608
Foster, Richard J. 3409, 3493
Foster, Robert Frederick. 2055
Foster, Robert Verrell. 3643
Foster, Rupert Clinton. 389, 405, 1964, 1987, 3340, 3351
Foster, Solomon. 2104
Foster, Stephen. 2208, 3008
Foster, Stephen Symonds. 3424
Foster, Steven. 3239
Foster, Timothy. 1732
Foster, Virgil E. 1251, 3150
Foster, Warren Dunham. 3831
Foster Randolph Sinks. 3659
Fothergill, Brian. 3822
Fothergill, John. 1674
Fothergill, Philip Gilbert. 1579
Fothergill, Samuel. 1211, 1635, 1688
Fotheringham, David Ross. 1163
Fotheringham, Ila Jean. 1704
Fotografia Industrial, S.A. 1369
Fouard, Constant Henri. 1964, 2797, 2824
Foucart, Paul Francois. 1505, 1766
Foucauld, Charles de. 2387
Foucauld, Charles Eugene. 1635, 3709
Foucault, Alphonse Gabriel. 2627, 3417
Foucher, Alfred Charles Auguste. 85, 1703
Foucher de Chartres, 1058?-ca. 1127. 1391
Foulds, Elfrida Vipont (Brown) 1613, 1677, 1685, 2794
Foulhouze, James. 737
Foulke, Frances Warder. 2409
Foulkes, Francis. 363, 409
Foulkes, William Hiram. 389, 961, 3199
Foulston, Pauline (Heckard) 961
Fountain, Rosanna B. 941, 3164
Fourard, Constant Henri. 2126
Foure, Helene (Selter) 752
Fournier, William. 1257
Fousek, Marianka S. 1196
Foushee, Clyde. 3376
Foushee, Clyde C. 2720
Foust, Leila Atwood. 2890
Foust, Paul J. 1565
Foust, Roscoe T. 3089
Fouyas, Mathodios. 1040, 2746
Fowle, James Luther. 2237, 2547
Fowle, John. 1739
Fowler, Alfred. 3071
Fowler, Charles Henry. 2496, 1306, 2492, 2496, 2519, 2422
Fowler, Charles J. 2813, 2818, 2887
Fowler, Clifton Lefevre. 1376, 3662
Fowler, Daniel Keener. 605, 1636
Fowler, David C. 299, 304, 645, 1811
Fowler, Ellen Thorneycroft. 1999
Fowler, Everett W. 351
Fowler, George Bingham. 1515
Fowler, George P. 309
Fowler, Grady. 3017
Fowler, Harold. 444
Fowler, Henry Thatcher. 600, 214, 409, 539, 571, 2114, 406, 1093
Fowler, Ira E. 3744
Fowler, James W. 1591, 2708, 3126
Fowler, Montague. 3437
Fowler, Nathaniel Clark. 3539
Fowler, Orson Squire. 2844

Fowler, Robert Booth. 1088
Fowler, Thomas. 1858, 2242
Fowler, William Chauncey. 1483
Fowler, William Stewart. 3819
Fowler, William Warde. 1395, 3246
Fowler, Wilton R. 1343
Fowlie, Wallace, 1908. 1638, 2810
Fox, Adam. 351, 2463
Fox, Adam, D. D. 1907
Fox, Arthur. 1557
Fox, Charles Elliot. 1540
Fox, Columba. 1404, 3416
Fox, Douglas A. 711, 2323, 3616
Fox, Edgar Alonzo. 3564, 3672
Fox, Edward Seccomb. 1721
Fox, Emmet. 233, 1313, 1323, 2246, 2410, 2411, 3335
Fox, Ethel. 2940
Fox, Frances Margaret. 1685, 1976, 3284
Fox, Frederic. 1865
Fox, George. 1636, 1637, 1677, 1679, 1681, 1684, 2476, 3010, 3630
Fox, George Townshend. 1637
Fox, Greeham George. 1083
Fox, Gresham George. 499, 2013, 2153, 2013, 2847
Fox, Henry J. 2438
Fox, Henry Watson. 628, 3150, 3165
Fox, Isadore (Hurlbut) 1637
Fox, James Joseph. 3059
Fox, John. 961
Fox, John Frederick. 1167
Fox, Kathryn Umstad. 603
Fox, Lorne F. 1601
Fox, Margaret (Askew) Fell. 1637
Fox, Margaret Mary. 177
Fox, Maria (Middleton) 3127
Fox, Mary Harrita. 1459
Fox, Mary Loyola. 3418
Fox, Matthew. 2872, 3486, 3521, 3701, 3744
Fox, Nettie Pease. 3502
Fox, Norman. 961
Fox, Paul. 2857, 3041
Fox, Robert J. 3150
Fox, Robert Joseph. 718, 786, 809, 854, 856, 875, 900, 1025, 1174, 2361, 3391
Fox, Selina Fitzherbert. 2890
Fox, Wilburn Mills. 1272
Fox, William Sherwood. 2656
Fox, Winifred Lowe (Baggett) 2761
Foxcroft, Elizabeth Howard. 1350
[Foxcroft, Thomas]. 890, 1326, 1344, 1637, 1692, 3351, 3761
Foxe, John. 1021, 1226, 1637, 2350, 2351, 3367, 2351
Foxell, William James. 2067
Fox Frederick. 741
Foy, Thomas. 1379
Fozdar, Jamshed. 130, 1703, 1721
Fracastoro, Girolamo. 3578
Fracchia, Charles A. 833, 3144, 3738
Fradenburgh, Jason Nelson. 91, 276, 1532, 1542, 3093, 3116, 3139
Fradenburgh, Oliver Perry. 1049
Frady, Marshall. 1576, 1754
Fraigneux, Maurice. 809
Fraine, Jean de. 492, 604, 2323, 2326, 3839
Frair, Wayne. 1380
Frakes, Margaret. 1544
Frame, James Everett. 478
Frame, John Davidson. 961
Frame, Nathan T. 1638
France, Dorothy D. 1262
France, Malcolm Norris. 1777
France, R. T. 1958
Frances de Chantal 1875. 659
Francesco d'Assisi. 1641, 2387
Francesco d'Assisi, 1182-1226. 2890, 3636
Francesco d'Assisi, Saint. 776
Francesco d'Assisi. 1641, 2159, 776, 1641, 3492
Francesco d'Assisi, Saint. 776, 3492
Francillon, Robert Edward. 2656
Francis. 1700
Francis, Anne. 1644, 2733
Francis, Anne F. 683
Francis, Connie. 3880
Francis, Connie [Constance Franconero]. 3880
Francis, Convers. 1507
Francis, Dale. 759
Francis d'assisi. 2856
Francis d'assisi 1881. 41, 3761
Francis de Sales, Brother, 1882. 831
Francis, Dorothy Brenner. 907, 2720
Francis, Fred O. 342
Francis, Geneieve Mae (Hilliard) 2694
Francis, Genevieve Mae (Hilliard) 3059
Francis, James Allan. 3340, 2246, 3340
Francis, Jerome. 2805
Francis, John Junkin. 2467, 3232
Francis, John Reynolds. 3502, 2988
Francis, Lon. 763
Francis, Mabel. 2534

*Francis, Mary Grace. 3163
Francis, T. M. 671, 3682
Franciscan Brothers of Brooklyn. 1649
Franciscan Education Conference. 866, 1646
Franciscan educational conference. 866, 1249, 1603, 1646
Franciscan sisters of Christian charity. 3150
Franciscan sisters of perpetual adoration, La Crosse, Wis. 812
Franciscan sisters of perpeutal adoration, La Crosse, Wis. 812
Franciscans. Custody of St. Mary of the Angels. 2945
Franciscans in California. 2778
Franciscans. Province of Saint Barbara. 1641, 1646
Franciscans. Province of the Assumption of the Blessed Virgin Mary. 2357
Franciscans, Province of the Saored Heart. 893
Franciscans, St. Michaels, Ariz. 2677
Franciscans. Thrid order. Province of the immaculate conception. 2d congress, Syracuse, N. Y., 1938. 1646
Francisco, Clyde T. 539
Franciscus. 2797
Franck, Adolphe. 721, 722
Franck, Frederick. 826, 1650, 2123, 3311, 3478, 3769, 3773
Franck, Ira Stoner. 3127
Franck, Sebastian. 2809
Franco, Fernando. 917
Francois de Sales. 2264, 2387, 3486
Francois de Sales 1567-1622. 1354, 2266, 2374, 2387, 2741, 3283, 3478, 3486
Francois desales 1567-1622. 2387, 2741
Francois Sales, 1567-1622. 2387
Francois de Sainte Marie. 3486
Francois de Sales. 1431, 2266, 2375, 2387, 2908, 3486
Francuch, Peter Daniel. 3478
Franfort, Henri. 1501
Frank, Edgar. 3261
Frank, Erich. 2836, 2837
Frank, Harry Thomas. 207, 289, 293
Frank, Henry. 1473, 1888, 2694, 2988, 347, 1964, 2694, 2988
Frank, Lawrence Kelso. 1199
Frank, Richard M. 2624
Frank, Robert John. 719
Frank, Robert Worth. 2931
Frank, Semen Liudvigovich. 1104
Frank, William P. 1851
Franke, Carl W. 961, 983
Franke, Carol W. 1004, 1591
Franke, Elmer E. 2756
Franke, Elmer Ellsworth. 1835, 305, 3380
Franke, Hermann. 2209
Franke, Merle G. 2890
[Franke, Willibald]. 3502
Frankel, Charles. 1520
Frankenberg, Ronald. 1765
Frankenberg, Theodore Thomas. 3566
Frankenstein, Ernst. 2077
Frankfort, Henri. 894, 1501, 2177, 3212, 1501, 2177
Frankforter, A. Daniel. 1174
Frankl, George. 3392
Frankl, Ludwig August. 1651, 2761
Frankl, Oscar Benjmin. 1809
Franklin, Benjamin. 1664, 1466, 1651, 60, 73, 1174
Franklin, Conn. Congregational church and society. 3051
Franklin, Denson N. 961, 1014
Franklin, Eric. 426, 1530, 2271
Franklin, Ind. First Presbyterian Church. 2912
Franklin, J. W. 753
Franklin, James Henry. 1543, 2482, 2519
Franklin, Jessie Merle. 1446
Franklin, Joseph. 1651
Franklin, Leo Morris. 3576
Franklin, Lottie M. 1259
Franklin, Marion Clyde. 3643
Franklin, Samuel. 2818
Franklyn, Julian. 3823
Franks, Robert Sleightholme. 104, 2009, 2038
Franks, Vincent Chesley. 2973
Fransen, Piet Frans. 1751
Frantz, Edward. 1235
Frantz, Ezra. 3099
Frantz, George Arthur. 1446
Franzblau, Abraham Norman. 2114, 3882
Franzen, August. 1174
Franzen, Lavern G. 430, 444, 907
Franziskus, Pius. 2624
Franzius, Enno. 92
Franzmann, Martin H. 342, 409, 440, 454, 467, 2299, 2399, 3351
Franzmann, Werner Herman. 533
Franzwa, Gregory M. 3276
Frappier, Jean. 918
Fraser, Abelk McIver. 3362

Fraser, Alexander Campbell. 1224, 192, 3608, 3609
[Fraser, Alexander N]. 3442
Fraser, Alexander (of Kirkhill) 605
Fraser, C M. 185
Fraser, Donald. 923, 2499, 2555, 2627
Fraser, Edith. 1981, 620, 633, 1981
Fraser, Gordon Holmes. 678, 1506, 1903, 2611
Fraser, Ian Watson. 409
Fraser, James. 309
Fraser, James Wallace. 961
Fraser, Jean M. 1058
Fraser, John Foster. 2112
Fraser, Neil McCormick. 2051, 3319
*Fraser, T. Layton. 482
Fraser, William. 204
Fraser, William P. 951
Frassinetti, Raphael. 907
Fraternity sons of Osiris. 3240
Fray, Harold R. 2706, 2785, 3538
Frayser, Anne Rebecca (Finch) 2559
Frayser, Nannie Lee. 3553
Frazee, Charles A. 1146, 2746
Frazee, Willmonte Doniphan. 3300, 3382
Frazer, George Stanley. 2326, 2421
Frazer, James George. 2651, 8, 1631, 2651, 2676, 8, 1408, 1409, 2312, 2651, 2676
Frazier, Allie M. 3090, 3108
Frazier, Claude Albee. 201, 241, 280, 1087, 1295, 1591, 1598, 3829
Frazier, Clifford. 934
Frazier, Edward Franklin. 2679, 2682
Frazier, Elizabeth P. 2957
Frazier, William Clark. 302
Fream, Donald. 412
Frear, Walter Francis. 2524
Freburger, William J. 900, 1327
Freda, Weston Harry. 305, 2226, 3373
Fredenburg, Charles Henry. 148
Frederic, Del W. 2694
Frederick, Anthony. 2334
Frederick, Arthur H. 1667
Frederick, Arthur L. 3435
Frederick, Arthur Lester. 1248, 3435
Frederick, James Mack Henry. 3502
Fredman, Joseph George. 2104
Fredman, Ruth Gruber. 2110, 3328
Fredrick, William. 1997, 3260, 3547
Fredrikson, Roger. 1626
Fredsell, Harold F. 2586
Free Baptist. General conference. 157
Free Baptists. General conference. 1652
Free Baptists. Rhode Island association. 1407, 1652
Free Europe Committee. 1542
Free, Jack. 2619
Free, Joseph P. 207
Free Lutheran Diet. 1st, Philadelphia, 1877. 2292
Free Lutheran Diet. 2d, Philadelphia, 1878. 2292
Free Methodist Church. 1652, 1653, 1865, 2429
Free Methodist church. General conference. 2429
Free Presbyterian Church of Scotland. Synod. 1653, 3042, 3315
Free religious association. 1865
Free religious association, Boston. 3066, 3193
Freece, Hans P. 2602
Freed, John B. 1708
Freed, Melvyn N. 1672
Freed, Paul E. 3018, 3707
Freedland, Nat. 2733
Freedman, David Noel. 209, 1799, 539
Freedman, Seymour E. 2086
Freehof, Lillian B (Simon) 1404, 1784, 2207, 3457
*Freehof, Solomon B. 2086
Freehof, Solomon Bennett. 3219, 518, 542, 1660, 2108, 2117, 2910, 3032, 3127, 3219, 3361
Freehold, N. J. First Presbyterian church. 2915
Freeland, John Maxwell. 1271
Freeman, Clifford Wade. 1557, 1572
Freeman, Daniel Roy. 3791
Freeman, David. 1531
Freeman, David Hugh. 2335, 3099
Freeman, Edward Anderson. 15, 2669
Freeman, Elmer Stone. 2251
Freeman, Enoch W. 1865
Freeman, Gary. 2788
Freeman, Grace R. 3032
Freeman, Hobart E. 560, 568
Freeman, James Dillet. 1625, 2387, 2872, 3750
Freeman, James Edward. 2900, 3340, 3362
Freeman, James Midwinter. 207
Freeman, Jean A. 253
Freeman, John Davis. 146, 2251, 3253, 3529
Freeman, John Dolliver. 587, 1951, 2985

Freeman, John Haskell. 2533
Freeman, Joseph. 1366, 1660
Freeman, Margaret N. 900, 1446
Freeman, Margery. 309
Freeman, Margery Fulton. 309
Freeman, New York (State) Scipio lodge, no. 110. 1668
Freeman, Olga Samuelson. 1273
Freeman, Robert. 70, 1438, 2931, 1438
Freeman, Ruth (St. John) 2756
Freeman, Thomas Franklin. 162
Freeman, Wendell K. 3018
Freeman, Winfield. 2944
Freeman, Z. 3614
Freemansons, New York (State) Grand lodge. 1666
Freemasons, Alabama. Grand lodge. 1661
Freemasons. Boston. Knights Templars. Boston Commandery. 1665
Freemasons. Boston. St. Andrews Royal arch chapter. 1670
Freemasons. California. Grand lodge. 1666
Freemasons Chicago. Ancient and accepted Scottish rite. Oriental consistory. 1671
Freemasons. Colorado. Grand Lodge. 1663
Freemasons. Conference of Grand Masters of Masons in North America, Washington, D. C., 1952. 1661
Freemasons. Connecticut. Royal Arch Masons. Grand Chapter. 1663
Freemasons. Constitutions. 1664
Freemasons. District of Columbia. Grand lodge (Colored) 1661
Freemasons. District of Columbia. Royal arch masons. Grand chapter. 1661
Freemasons. Illinois. Knights Templars. Grand Commandery. 3598
Freemasons. Illinois. Royal arch masons. Grand chapter. 1661
Freemasons. Kansas. Grand commandery, Knights templar. 1660
Freemasons. Louisiana. Grand lodge. 1669
Freemasons. Maine. Grand commandery of Knights templars. 1661
Freemasons. Maine. Grand council of royal and select masters. 1661
Freemasons. Maine. Grand lodge. 1661
Freemasons. Maryland. Ground royal arch chapter. 1666
Freemasons. Massachusetts and Rhode Island. Grand commandery of Knights templars. 3598
Freemasons. Massachusetts. Royal and Select masters. Grand Council. 1669
Freemasons. Massachusetts. Royal arch masons. Grand chapter. 1669
Freemasons. Michigan. Grand lodge. 1669
Freemasons. New York. Independent royal arch lodge, no. 2. 1664
Freemasons. New York (State) 1671
Freemasons. New York (State) Grand chapter of royal arch masons. 1670
Freemasons. New York (State) Grand chapter of royal arch masons. Committee on foreign correspondence. 1670
Freemasons. New York (State) Grand ladge. Committee on antiquities. 1667, 1668
Freemasons. New York (State) Grand lodge. 1666, 1668, 1669
Freemasons. News York (State) Grand lodge. 1666
Freemasons. North Carolina. Royal arch masons. Grand chapter. 1670
Freemasons. Ohio. Grand chapter of Royal arch masons. 1669
Freemasons. Ohio. Royal Arch Masons. Grand Chapter. Committee on History. 1670
Freemasons. Oklahoma. Grand lodge. 1669
Freemasons. Oregon. Grand Lodge. 1664
Freemasons. Scottish rite. 1671
Freemasons. South Carolina. Grand Lodge. 1669
Freemasons. Tennessee. Grand lodge (Colored) 1667
Freemasons. Texas. Grand Lodge. 1666
Freemasons. Texas. Grand lodge (Colored) 1669, 1671
Freemasons. Texas. Grand lodge. Committee on masonic education and service. 1661
Freemasons. Texas. Scottish Rite. Texas Scottish Rite History Committee. 1672
Freemasons. U. S. Conference of grand masters, Cedar Rapids. Ia., 1918. 2364
Freemasons. U.S. Knights templars. Grand encampment. Committee on templar history. 1665, 1672
Freemasons. U. S. Red cross of Constantine. Grand imperial conuncil. 1668

Freemasons. U. S. Red Cross of Constantine. Sovereign Grand Council. 1672
Freemasons. U. S. Royal and select masters. General grand council. 1670
Freemasons. U. S. Scottish Rite. National Supreme Council (Negro) 1669
Freemasons, U.S. Scottish Rite. Supreme Council for the Southern Jurisdiction. 1141, 1672
Freemasons. U. S. Scottish rite. Supreme council for the Southern jurisdiction. Library. Hanauer collection. 1667
Freemasons. Virginia. Grand lodge. 1661
Freemasons. Virginia. Grand Lodge (Negro) 1669
Freemasons. Wisconsin. Grand Lodge. 1672
Freemasons. Wisconsin. Grand lodge. Committee on masonic research. 1668
-Freer, Arthur Savile Beresford 1866. 933
Freer Gallery of Art, Washington, D.C. 86
Freer, Harold Freer. 2387
Freer, Harold Wiley. 1004, 1438, 1806, 2388, 2872
Freese, Doris A. 3858
Freese, J[acob] R. 1174
Freese, Jacob R. 2771
Freestone, William Herbert. 1541
Freethinkers' Convention, Watkins Glen, N.Y., 1878. 1656
Freeze, Gregory L. 1299, 2750
Frei, Hans W. 241, 2038
Freiberg, Walter Anthony. 1377
Freimann, Aron. 2099, 2331
*Frein, George H. 3769
Freitag, Anton. 2525
Freivogel, Esther. 1981, 3765
Freiwirth, Paul K. 3382
Freligh, Harold Meredith. 549, 3289
Frellick, Francis I. 1255
Fremantle, Anne (Jackson) 407, 1020, 1025, 1113, 1137, 1434, 1635, 2643, 2842, 3127, 3845
Fremantle, Anne (Jackson) [Anne Marie Huth (Jackson) Fremantle]. 1020
Fremantle, William Henry. 2672, 1118, 1226, 3127, 3442
Frenay, Adolph Dominic. 2366
French, Addie Marie. 1992, 3553, 3784, 3553
French, Curtis. 102
French, Daniel H. 3610
*French, Fannie. 1721
French, Hal W. 1896
French, Harold W. 3020
French, Holland. 309
French, Howard Dean. 3369
French, Joel. 42
French, Marion Flood. 1446, 2388
French, Mary Montague (Billings) 1456
French, Reginald Michael. 2747, 2847, 3891
French, W Maynard. 2433
Frend, W. H. C. 1191, 1196, 1197, 1476, 2585, 2821
Frere, Walter Howard. 838, 1487, 1758, 2334, 3006, 2238, 3009, 3239
Frere -Cook, Gervis. 1165
Frerichs, Albert C. 2541
Fresenborg, Bernard. 827, 2938
Fresno, Calif. Free Evangelical Lutheran Cross Church. 2303

Fretheim, Terence E. 553
Fretwell, John. 2129
Fretz, Joseph Winfield. 2405
Freud, Sigmund. 2585, 2621
*Freud, Sigmund. 1104, 1479, 2585, 2621, 2997
Freuder, Samuel. 2556
Freulich, Roman. 2864
Freund, Else. 2138, 3249
Freund, Ernest Hans. 1745
Freund, Miriam K. 2104
Freund, Philip. 1384
Freund, Ronald. 103
Frew, Duncan J. 3462
[Frew, George Smith]. 1118
Frey, Arthur. 1426, 1707
Frey, Edward Snively. 1156
Frey, Joseph Samuel Christian Frederick. 60, 2085, 3720
*Frey, Lash. 3376
Frey, Leibert Garland. 3253
Freyne, Sean. 433
Freytag, Gustav. 2273
Frick, Heinrich. 1058
Frick, Philip Louis. 3221
Frick, William Keller. 2629
Fridell, Elmer A. 170
Fridrichsen, Anton Johnson. 2017, 2476
Fridy, Wallace. 1438, 2890
Fried, Ralph. 2544
Friede, Juan. 3767
Friedel, Francis J. 2702

Friedemann, Lera-Biddena (Elliott) 147, 1673
Friedensrat der Deutschen Demokratischen Republik. 3
Friedenthal, Richard. 2273
Frieder, Emma. 309, 3066
Friederichs, Hulda. 3292
Friederichsen, Kathleen (Hockman) 1821
*Friederichsen, Mrs. Paul. 1721
Friedlaender, Israel. 2082, 1711, 2102, 2118
Friedlander, Albert H. 125
Friedlander, Gerald. 3335, 3581
Friedlander, Ira. 25, 1933, 2460, 3138
Friedlander, Michael. 2114
Friedlander, Saul. 860, 1708, 2852
Friedlander, Shems. 3544
Friedman, Bear Leib. 2375, 3015
Friedman, Bob. 270
Friedman, Daniel. 1818, 2164
Friedman, Edwin H. 108, 2696
Friedman, Elisha Michael. 2112
Friedman, Isidore. 2725
Friedman, Lee Max. 2104, 2106
Friedman, Maurice S. 699, 2756, 2832, 3066, 3099, 3116
Friedman, Richard E. 499
Friedman, Saul S. 672
Friedman, Terry. 1711
Friedman, Theodore. 2104, 3371, 3537
Friedmann, Robert. 36
Friedrich, Paul. 55
Friedrichsen, George Washington Salisbury. 368, 395
Frieling, Rudolf. 419, 2263
Frieman, Donald G. 2120
Friend, Edith Alice. 1015, 3764
Friend, J. B. B. 930, 1673
Friend, Nellie E. 2262, 3885
Friend of Youth. 786, 3885
Friends Council on Education. 3150
[Friends' historical association]. 2829
Friends, Society of. 1677, 1681, 1684, 1687, 2038
Friends, Society of, American Friends Service Committee. 1674, 1678, 2756
Friends, Society of. American Friends Service Committee. Fellowship Committee. 1679
Friends, Society of. Baltimore Yearly meeting. 1677
Friends, Society of. Five years meeting. 1681
Friends, Society of. Five years meeting. Board of Christian education. 1438
Friends, Society of (Hicksie) Philadelphia Yearly Meeting. 1679
Friends, Society of (Hicksite) Baltimore Yearly Meeting. 1679
Friends, Society of (Hicksite) General Conference. 1674, 1677
Friends, Society of (Hicksite). General Conference. Religious Education Committee. 1684
Friends, Society of (Hicksite) Genesee Yearly meeting. 1679
Friends, Society of (Hicksite) Philadelphia Yearly Meeting. 1680
Friends, Society of. Indiana Yearly Meeting. 1680
Friends, Society of. Literature Committee. 1637
Friends, Society of. London Yearly meeting. 1685
Friends, Society of. London Yearly Meeting. Meeting for Sufferings. Aborigines' Committee. 1686, 1901
Friends, Society of. Nebraska Yearly Meeting. 1674
Friends, Society of. New England Yearly Meeting. 1680
Friends, Society of. New York Yearly Meeting. 1680
Friends, Society of. New York Yearly Meeting. Meeting for Sufferings. 1677
Friends, Society of. North Carolina Yearly Meeting. 1687
Friends, Society of. Ohio Yearly Meeting. 1680
Friends, Society of. Philadelphia Yearly Meeting. 1591, 1680, 1681, 3475
Friends, Society of. Philadelphia. Yearly meeting. Book committee. 3127
Friends World Committee for Consultation. 1679
Friends world conference committee. 1674, 1679
Friends world conference. Swarthmore college and Haverford college, 1937. 1679
Fries, Adelaide Lisetta. 2594, 2595, 2594, 2595
Fries, Albert. 22, 2354
Fries, Heinrich. 118, 1591, 3224, 3628
Fries, Jakob Friedrich. 1534
Friese, Philip Christopher. 3608
Friesen, Duane K. 664

Friesen, Garry. 1740
Friesen, Gerhard. 3442
Friesen, Marie (Schmidt) 2388
Friess, Horace Leland. 7, 1533, 3116
Frigerio, Costanzo. 3196
Frikell, Samri. 3502
Frings, M J. 3248
Frings, Math Josef. 3248
Frink, Thomas. 1504
Frisbie, Granville Kimball. 1663
Frisbie, Richard P. 759
Frisch, Daniel. 3897
Frischauer, Willi. 1927, 2165
Frison, Basil M. 2578
Frist, Elizabeth (Ferran) 1303
Fritchman, Stephen Hole. 1259, 1688, 2890, 3723, 3724, 3728
Frith, Nigel. 2186
Fritsch, Charles Theodore. 50, 1410, 3013
Fritscher, John. 3823
Fritz, Dorothy B. 903, 935
Fritz, Dorothy Bertolet. 903, 922, 938, 3170, 3173, 3592, 3735
Fritz, Jean. 1027, 1311
Fritz, John Henry Charles. 2900, 3672
Fritz, William Grant. 3199
Fritzsche, Helga. 876
[Frizon, Nicolas]. 191
Frizzell, John Henry. 2890, 3756
Frodsham, Stanley H. 1689, 2815
Frodsham, Stanley Howard. 2813, 3815
Froget, Barthelemy. 1828
Frohlich, S H. 1905
Frohlich, Samuel Heinrich. 367, 369
Frohne, Marydel D. 3188, 3732
Frohne, Victor M. 3732
Froiseth, Jennie Anderson. 2602
Froman, Lewis Acrelius. 2320
Fromer, Margaret. 450, 3845
Fromm, Erich. 3894, 499, 1534, 1854, 3894
Fromm, Herbert. 917, 3577
Frommelt, Horace Aloysius. 1241
Frommer, Arthur. 3096
Frommer, Arthur, ed. 638, 3096
Fronmuller, G F C. 447
Froom, Le Roy Edwin. 1828, 1829, 1836, 10, 605, 1689
Froom, LeRoy Edwin. 48, 3502
Fror, Hans. 620
Frossard, Andre. 1358, 2576
Frost, Adelaide Gail. 2530
Frost, Bede. 991, 1295, 2125, 2209, 2210, 2264, 2323, 2379, 2872, 2939, 3335
Frost, Edwin Richardson. 70
Frost, Gavin. 3823, 3826
Frost, George Edwin. 3502
Frost, Gerhard E. 551, 1014, 1313, 2388, 3758
Frost, Henry Weston. 444, 595, 645, 1598, 1601, 1829, 2017, 2492, 2872, 3319, 3662
Frost, James Marion. 1553, 3467, 134, 142, 1357, 3553
Frost, Jerry William. 1674
Frost, John. 923
Frost, John Edward. 683
Frost, Marie. 18, 1689, 2624, 3830
Frost, Robert C. 983, 1732
Frost, S. E. 620, 923, 3267, 3268, 3340
Frost, S. S. 3340
Frost, Timothy Prescott. 2063
Frost, Wally. 1689, 2857
Frost, William P. 1730, 3069
Frothingham, Ebenezer. 1346, 3535
Frothingham, Ephraim Langdon. 3099, 3711
Frothingham, Nathaniel Langdon. 1911, 3013
Frothingham, Octavius Brooks. 882, 1509, 2027, 2776, 3199, 3352, 3708, 3724
Frothingham, Paul Revere. 660, 882, 1323
Frothingham, Richard. 2173
[Frothingham, Washington] b. 1822. 3024
Froude, James Anthony. 1526, 1654, 2273, 3075, 3710
Fruchtenbaum, Arnold G. 2038, 2073
Fruchter, Nandor. 1332, 2100
Fry, Benjamin St. James. 3241
Fry, C. George. 1921
Fry, Charles Luther. 1275, 3254, 1274, 1275
Fry, Christopher. 603
Fry, Evan. 3218, 3352
Fry, Evan Anselm. 3218
Fry, Jacob. 3672, 2900, 3027
Fry, John. 3206
Fry, John R. 943, 1058, 2912, 3168, 3735
Fry, Peter. 3895
Fry, Thomas A. 951, 1010, 1058
Fry, William Francis. 593
Frydman, Alexander Zusha. 565, 2073
Frye, Edwin Gibson. 2051
Frye, Northrop. 2468, 2472
Frye, Roland Mushat. 2470, 3071, 3094, 3399
Frye, Sally. 900

Fryer, Jane (Eayre) 625
Fryer, Ross B. 2552
Fryhling, Paul P. 2034, 2213
Fryling, Robert. 2345
Fuchs, Daniel. 2535
Fuchs, Emanuel. 368
Fuchs, Ernst. 2008
Fuchs, Harald. 114, 2806
Fuchs, Josef. 947
Fuchs, Lawrence H. 874, 2104, 2167
Fuchs, Stephen. 2672
Fuchs, William A. 1591
Fudge, Edward. 2051, 3221
Fuellenbach, John. 1248, 1287
Fuerbringer, Ludwig Ernest. 529
Fuerbringer, Ludwig Ernst. 366, 549, 3092
Fuerst, Anthony. 3248
Fuerst, Anthony Norman. 746, 3248
Fuerst, Bartholomew. 3626
*Fuerst, Wesley J. 614
Fuge, Fred T. 198
Fugette, J Preston. 2337
Fugette, James Preston. 2337
[Fuhlrott, Joseph]. 174
Fuhrmann, Joseph Paul. 2628
Fuhrmann, Paul Traugott. 727, 729, 1385, 3780
Fujimoto, Hogen. 3172
Fujimoto, Rindo. 2383
Fujimura, Bunyu. 3197
Fujisawa, Chikao. 2841
Fukurai, Tomokichi. 1283
Fukuyama, Toshio. 3006
Fukuyama, Yoshio. 3681, 3732
Fulbert, 960 (ca.)-1028. 666, 1689
Fulbright, Robert G. 628, 1505
Fulcher, Ernest A. 3846
Fulco, William J. 414, 3219
Fulda, Edeltraud. 1598, 2262
Fulk, Augustus Marion. 3053
Fulke, William. 270, 2348, 3525
Full declaration of the faith and ceremonies professed in the dominions of the most illustrious noble Prince Fredericke 5, Prince Elector Palatine. 3044
Full, William Lovell. 2088
Fullam, Everett L. 991, 1524, 2246, 3352
Fullam, Raymond B. 997, 3771
Fuller, Andrew. 729, 961, 1591, 1692, 2810, 3300, 3363, 3643
Fuller, Benjamin Apthorp Gould. 2840
Fuller, Benjamin Franklin. 170
Fuller, Charles Edward. 1438, 3579
Fuller, Daniel P. 644, 1690, 2051, 2200
Fuller, David Otis. 241, 271, 1551, 1552
Fuller, Dorothy Mason. 1353
Fuller, Edmund. 1016
Fuller, Edwin Wiley. 42
Fuller, Elizabeth. 1651, 3502
Fuller, Ellis Adams. 1557
Fuller, George Albion. 3502
Fuller, Grace (Payton) 1690, 2736
[Fuller, Ira C.] 3502
Fuller, James Henry. 2251
[Fuller, John]. 799
Fuller, Margaret Mary. 3378
Fuller, Mary Lucia Bierce. 3020
Fuller, Millard. 1690, 2559
Fuller, Morris Joseph. 1489
Fuller, Osgood Eaton. 889, 2048
Fuller, Raymond Tifft. 2719
Fuller, Reginald Horace. 299, 351, 431, 436, 1075, 2010, 2017, 2038, 2054, 2476, 2900, 3322
Fuller, Richard. 134, 162
[Fuller, Richard Frederick]. 3206
Fuller, Robert C. 2413
Fuller, Samuel. 454, 1690, 3215
Fuller, T. 3643
Fuller, Thomas. 1446, 1535, 1758
Fuller, Thomas Oscar. 157, 2681
Fuller, W. Harold. 2492, 2497
Fullerton, Arthur Grey. 3199
Fullerton, George Stuart. 2417, 3608
Fullerton, Georgiana Charlotte (Leveson-Gower) 1474, 1639
Fullerton, Kemper. 605, 3621, 2720, 3621
Fullerton, William Young. 961, 3523
*Fullington, James F. 592
Fullington, Walbridge B. 682
Fullman, Jeffrey L. 281
Fullmer, David Clarence. 3784
Fullwood, Anna (Mebane) 3588
Fulop-Miller, Rene. 55, 114, 1945, 3282, 2216, 2768
Fulton, Charles Darby. 2516, 2926
Fulton, John. 735, 736, 2706, 2761
Fulton, John Farquhar. 3377
Fulton, Justin Dewey. 799, 1713, 2940, 3741
Fulton, Lillian Britton. 2694
Fulton, Mary Beth. 2388, 2804, 3856
Fulton, Robert Lester. 1416, 2167, 3722, 1416
Fumet, Stanislas. 1937, 2348

Funck-Brentano, Frantz. 1937
Fund for Theological Education. 1497
Fundamental Baptist Congress of North America, Detroit, 1963. 147
*Fundamental Baptist Congress of North America, Grand Rapids, 1966. 140
Funk, E P. 3638
Funk, Franz Xaver von. 809, 1174
Funk, Isaac Kaufman. 1579, 3502
Funk, Issac Kaufman. 3502
Funk, John F. 2405, 2635
*Funk, Robert W. 3616
Funk, Robert Walter. 350, 2025, 2027, 3071, 3656
Funkhouser, Abram Paul. 3731
Funkhouser, G. A. 2000
Funkhouser, George Absalom. 2038
Funston, John Wesley. 3803
Furey, Francis Thomas. 2216
Furfey, Paul Hanley. 763, 1136
Furfey, Paul Hanly. 895, 947, 997, 1134, 1136, 2222, 2410, 3450
Furlan, William P. 2849
Furley, William D. 1626
Furlong, Monica. 1355, 2412, 3478, 3710
Furlonge, Geoffrey Warren. 21, 2765
Furman, Charles Edward. 3208
Furman, James Clement. 146, 1694
[Furman, Wood]. 660
Furneaux, Rupert. 1944, 2322
Furness, Charles Y. 1139
Furness, John Malcolm. 3662
Furness, John Marshall. 243, 3682
Furness, William Henry. 389, 1964, 1995, 2051, 2059
Furnish, Dorothy Jean. 638, 903
Furnish, Victor Paul. 373
Furniss, James J. 1380
Furniss, Norman F. 2562
Furniss, William. 1017
Furrow, (The) 201
Furse, Margaret Lewis. 2638
Furse, Michael Bolton. 1049
Furst, Jeffrey. 3055, 3816
Furst, Peter T. 1782
Fusco, Joseph P. 997
Fusco, Nicola. 2693
Fuss, Albertus G. 1661
Fuss, Peter Lawrence. 3252
Futch, Ladell J. 409
Futrell, John Carroll. 2268, 3566
Futterer, Antonia Fredrich. 1992, 2763
Future of the Missionary Enterprise Seminar/Workshop, Ventnor, N.J., 1974. 2514
Futuristic Conference, Ridgecrest, N.C., 1977. 3465, 3719
Fyffe, David. 1591
Fyvie, John. 1758
Fyzee, Asaf Ali Asghar. 1926, 2201, 2564, 2566

G

Gabbott, Mabel Jones. 679
Gabel, Leona Christine. 1291
Gabel, Richard James. 803
Gabert, Glen. 833
Gable, J. W. 3478
Gable, John Wesley. 961
Gable, Lee J. 1544, 3150
Gaboury, Placide Bernard. 961
Gabrele di Santa Maria Maddalena. 3603
Gabriel, Charles H. 1202, 2633, 3027
Gabriel, Charles Hutchinson. 1202
Gabriel, Henry Albert. 90, 3222
Gabriel, Ralph Henry. 1049, 3621
Gabriele di Santa Maria Maddalena. 771, 2136, 3475
Gabriele di Santa Maria Maddalene. 3783
Gabriele di Santa Marie Maddalena. 1263, 3602, 3603
Gabrieli, Francesco. 1390
Gabriels, Henry. 3275
Gabrielson, Catherine. 1700
Gabris, P. Paul. 2334
Gaby, Mary Isabel. 307
Gadamer, Hans Georg. 1801, 1855
Gaddis, Maxwell Pierson. 2452, 3352, 724, 1306, 2435, 2439, 2452, 2453, 3789, 131
Gaddy, C. Welton. 162, 993, 1085, 2054, 2213
Gade, John Allyne. 753, 2411
Gadla hawaryat English. 75
Gadla Hawaryat. English & Ethiopic. 75
Gaduel, Jean Pierre Laurent. 1347
Gaebelein, Arno Clemens. 42, 63, 332, 364, 419, 459, 463, 470, 508, 516, 518, 552, 567, 575, 605, 1513, 1598, 1700, 1951, 2015, 2063, 2077, 2200, 2427, 2621, 2797, 3059, 3319, 198, 329, 416, 518, 3227
Gaebelein, Frank E. 1431

Gaebelein, Frank Ely. 233, 248, 412, 561, 653, 1066, 1431, 1438, 3150
Gaebelien, Arno Clemens. 443
Gaell, Rene. 1543
Gaer, Joseph. 533, 1631, 1976, 2138, 3014, 3116, 3127, 3139, 3581, 3744
Gaertner, George W. 198
Gaetano Maria da Bergamo, 1660-1753. 2031
Gaffey, James P. 3238
Gaffield, Erastus Celley. 2725, 3502
Gaffin, Richard B. 425, 3221
Gaffney, Christopher. 769
Gaffney, James. 314, 943, 947, 3628
Gaffney, Thomas Clery. 638
Gafla hawaryat. 75
Gagarin, Jean Xavier. 1299
Gage, Albert Henry. 1162, 1565, 1621, 3553, 3763
Gage, Freddie. 1361
Gage, Joy P. 517, 1597, 2621, 3844
Gage, Matilda Joslyn. 3842
Gage, William Leonard. 2762, 3714
Gager, Charles Stuart. 3078
Gager, John G. 3451
Gagern, Friedrich Ernst. 2343
Gagern, Friedrich Ernst, Freiherr von. 997
Gagliostro, Vincenza. 756, 3885
Gahan, William. 1174
Gahl, Lois. 2273
Gaiani, Vito. 2570
Gail, Marzieh. 129, 3308
Gailey, James H. 559
Gaillard, Frye. 3468
Gaillard, Jean. 844
Gaillard, Thomas. 3034
Gailor, Thomas Frank. 1118, 1523, 3150
Gaines, David P. 148, 3849
Gaines, Elizabeth Venable. 1392
Gaines, John Wesley. 2226
Gaines, M. C. 626, 630
Gaines, Robert Edwin. 3150
Gaines, Stephen S. 1748
Gaines, Steven S. 1748
Gaines, Wesley John. 14
Gairdner, James. 1758, 1759, 2243
Gairdner, William Henry Temple. 3851
Gairns, David Smith. 2017
Gaither, Gloria. 1700, 1749, 2388
Gajard, Joseph. 884
Galamba de Oliveira, Joseph, 1903. 2349
Galarza, Ernest. 822
Galavaris, George. 690
Galbraith, John Albert. 2762
Galbraith, Robert Christy. 2919
Galdon, Joseph A. 3721
Gale, Elizabeth Wright. 3173
Gale, Herbert Morrison. 372
Gale, James Scarth. 2536
Gale, John Benjamin. 1472, 2347
Gale, Nahum. 2127
Gale, Richard Nelson. 558
Gale, Robert. 10, 2467
Galer, Roger Sherman. 1058, 2201
Gales, Louis A. 1733, 1981, 3284
Galgani, Gemma. 3531
Galilea, Segundo. 1003
Galinsky, Gotthard Karl. 11
Gall, Ernst. 1161
Gall, James. 344, 401
Gallagher, Augustine F. 2068
Gallagher, Charles F. 825, 1791
Gallagher, Charles Wesley. 1721
Gallagher, Chuck. 2343
Gallagher, Edward Joseph. 32
Gallagher, Edwin. 2872
Gallagher, Eugene V. 1742, 2046
Gallagher, John F. 3262, 3695
Gallagher, John Joseph. 1145
Gallagher, John P. 3316
Gallagher, Joseph. 997
Gallagher, Joseph Vincent. 769, 3182
Gallagher, Louis Joseph. 3790
Gallagher, Marie Patrice. 1247
Gallagher, Mason. 2957
Gallagher, Neil. 2501
Gallagher, Sharon. 85
Gallagher, Thomas Raphael. 2741
Gallaher, James. 615, 3066
Gallaher, Thomas. 1906
Gallahue, Alpheus Cornelius. 3610
Galland, Joseph Stanislaus. 1392
Gallant, Roy A. 95
Gallaudet, Thomas Hopkins. 4, 293, 555, 2130, 2133, 2135, 2672, 3218, 3462
Gallerani, Alessandro. 1964, 1999
Gallery, John Ireland. 2357
Gallery, Mary (Onahan) 872, 2737
Gallet, Paul. 690, 1701
Galli, Mario von. 1641, 3771
Galligan, Michael. 3610
Galliher, Daniel Michael. 1503
Gallik, George Aloysius. 2577
Gallois, Genevieve. 2853
Gallonio, Antonio. 1021

Galloway, Allan Douglas. 1074, 2767, 3029, 3636
Galloway, Charles Betts. 3738
Galloway, Dale E. 983, 1350, 1608, 1701, 2264
Galloway, George. 3099
Galloway, John T. 1010
Galloway, Thomas Walton. 3150
Gallup, George. 3747
Gallup, George Horace. 3002
Galot, Jean. 1845, 1893, 1999, 2038, 2358, 2360, 3566
Galpert, Maurice T. 2076
Galpin, C J. 3253
Galpin, Charles Josiah. 1268, 3254
Galpin, Francis William. 1446
Galpin, William Freeman. 1174, 3762
Galt, John. 3199
Galt, Sterling. 2209
Galter, Alberte. 2820
Galton, Arthur Howard. 816, 1145
Galus, Walter John. 2176
Galusha, Elinor G. 3853
*Galusha, Walter T. 3848
Galveston. Congregation B'nai Israel. 1305
Galvin, James J. 2685
Galy, A. 1951
Galyon, Carrie Barbour. 3313
Gambari, Elio. 2159, 2570, 2581, 3771
Gambhirananda, Swami. 3020
Gambino, Richard. 2631
Gamble, Eliza Burt. 3389
Gamble, Harry. 470
Gamble, Samuel Cooper. 1014
Gamble, Samuel Walter. 3547
Gamble, Thomas. 3803
Gambrell, James Bruton. 993, 2771
Gambrell, Mary Latimer. 3680, 3681
Gamertsfelder, S. J. 638
Gamertsfelder, Solomon J. 3643
Gamewell, Mary Louise (Ninde) 2509, 2711
Gamewell, Mary (Porter) 2509
Gamm, David B. 900
Gammack, Arthur James. 2057
Gammage, Smith P. 2231, 3232
Gammell, William. 155
Gammon, Roland. 1014, 1701, 3478
Gammon, Samuel R. 1546
Gamoran, Emanuel. 2086, 2114, 2087, 2103
Gamoran, Mamie (Goldsmith) 1614, 1615, 1623, 2088
Gamzey, Robert. 2104
Gandee, Lee R. 2988
Gandhi, Kishor. 1709
Gandhi, Mohads Karamchand. 2530
Gandhi, Mohandas Karamchand. 3405
Gandhi, Rajmohan. 2593
Gandhi, Ramchandra. 3100, 3107
Gandier, Alfred. 3458
Gangel, Kenneth O. 935, 953, 1608, 1843, 3179, 3551
Gangsei, Virginia. 1605
Gann, Joshua Arthur. 2435
Gannaway, Marian (Walter) 907
Gannett, Ezra Stiles. 1165, 1350
Gannett, William Channing. 1591, 900, 1701, 3317, 3340
Gannon, David. 1673, 2794
Gannon, John Mark. 2741
Gannon, Michael V. 817, 3273, 3777
Gannon, Patrick Joseph. 2337
Gannon, Robert Ignatius. 3471
Gannon, Thomas M. 3522
Ganoczy, Alexandre. 137
Ganser, Malcolm Hay. 2713
Gansfort, Johan Wessel. 3090
Ganss, George E. 1497, 2268
Ganss, H[enry] G. 289, 1174
Gant, Sophia. 2124
Gant, William John. 227, 2563
Ganta United Methodist Mission. 2433, 2537
Gantz, Charlotte Orr. 3714
Ganzfried, Solomon. 2074, 2107, 2114, 2138, 2155
Gara, Matthew. 997, 3537, 3885
Garabedian, John H. 3880
Garaudy, Roger. 1319
Garber, Richard von. 1081, 2839
Garber, Bernard J. 50
Garber, Mary Crumpacker. 1235, 1236
Garber, Paul Neff. 2421, 2430, 2433, 3803
Garber, William Allen. 2719
Garbett, Cyril Forster. 2775, 1137, 1281
Garcia Diego y Moreno, Francisco, 1785-1846. 666, 1702
Garcon, Maurice. 1427
Gard, Donald H. 551
Gard, Richard Abbott. 701
Gardavsky, Vitezslav. 3091
Gardeil, Ambroise. 1475
Gardeil, Henri Dominique. 3695
Gardell, Ambroise. 1712

Garden, Alexander. 1389
Garden, Charlotte Lockwood. 736, 737
Garden, Nancy. 1424, 3826
Gardener, Alice. 3437, 3578
Gardener, Harry J. 2725
Gardet, Louis. 2564
Gardiner, Erma Y. 2599
Gardiner, Ernest Alexander. 375
Gardiner, Frederic. 425, 557
Gardiner, George E. 492, 2816, 3258
Gardiner, Harold Charles. 733, 879
Gardiner, Harry Norman. 1499, 1500
Gardiner, John Hays. 210
Gardiner, M. James. 1199
Gardiner, Robert W. 103
Gardiner, Stephen. 781, 1141
Gardner, Adelaide. 2379
Gardner, Alice. 721, 3610
Gardner, Ann. 3170
Gardner, Arthur. 1159, 3333
Gardner, Augustus Kinsley. 3392
Gardner, Celia Emmeline. 305
Gardner, Charles. 3029
Gardner, Charles Spurgeon. 2003, 2900, 3442
Gardner, David Marshall. 162, 1557
Gardner, Edmund Garratt. 749, 1446
Gardner, Edward Clinton. 943, 1153
Gardner, Elizabeth. 3173
Gardner, Elva Babcock. 2490, 2530
Gardner, Ernest Arthur. 1766
Gardner, Eugene Clarence. 1156
Gardner, Eugene Norfleet. 1139, 1247
Gardner, Frank. 162
Gardner, George Lawrence Harter. 1202
Gardner, George North. 1785
Gardner, Helen Louise. 233, 1387, 1519, 3071
Gardner, Helena. 3823
Gardner, James. 3116
Gardner, Jeanne. 2948
Gardner, Johann von. 1209
Gardner, John. 1579, 1951, 3199, 3456
Gardner, John Edward. 89
Gardner, Lucile Blake. 3553, 3554
Gardner, Martin. 3575
Gardner, Mary Tracy. 1821, 2970
Gardner, Mass. First Congregational church. 1337
[Gardner, Milton Bliss] 1889. 2807, 3792
Gardner, Percy. 363, 419, 2797, 3651, 3654, 3333
Gardner, Preston Edwin. 605, 1625
Gardner, Robert Grosvenor. 3244
Gardner, Ruth Carver. 3465
Gardner, Ruth (Carver) 2549
Gardner, Thurman C. 142
Gardner, Vera C. 2962
Gardner, W W. 2251
Gardner, William Edward. 1100, 3554
Gardner-Smith, Percival. 3621, 419, 1174
Garelick, Herbert M. 2170
Garesche, Edward Francis. 772, 856, 961, 997, 1251, 1446, 1542, 1721, 2354, 2718, 2774, 2890, 3223, 3269, 3405, 3475, 3478, 3690
Garesche, Edward Franics. 1542
Garesche, Marie Louise. 1367
Garfield, Patricia L. 1479
Garfield, Rorke. 2988
Gargan, Edward T. 2216
Gargi, Balwant. 3302
[Gargilis, Stephen]. 1470
*Garhart, Marjorie. 1739, 3188
Gariepy, Henry. 2021
Gariepy, Robert J. 2272
Gariner, F. E. 2201
Garland, D. David. 486, 537, 544, 551
Garland, George Frederick. 302, 1793
Garland, Hamlin. 2988, 3502
Garland, Merwin A. 1652
Garlick, Bernard McKean. 1184
Garman, Wilford Ohlen Higget. 1964, 1965
Garmon, William Sewell. 1254
Garner, George B. 321
Garner, James Herbert. 1438
Garner, Kathryn F. 2872
Garner, Lloyd W. 140, 3340
Garner, Richard T. 1535
Garner, Roma Caleb. 1550
Garnett, Arthur Campbell. 1104, 3100
Garnett, Christine. 2515
Garnett, Emmeline. 2702, 3206, 3418
Garnett, Eve. 1500
Garnett, Lucy Mary Jane. 1425
Garofalo, Salvatore. 2358
Garr, A. G. 3340
Garraghan, Gilbert Joseph. 815, 873, 1630, 1948, 1900, 1949
Garrand, Victor. 2200, 3862
Garrard, Lancelot Austin. 2221
Garretson, Arthur Samuel. 1049
[Garretson, James Edmund] 1828-1895. 2738, 3462, 3502, 3503
Garrett, Adelaide Jefferys. 2388
Garrett, Alexander Charles. 1893

Garrett, Alfred Cope. 389, 1965, 3127, 1774
Garrett, Arthur. 1174
Garrett, Augusta Browne. 961
Garrett Biblical institute, Evanston, Ill. 1509, 3621
Garrett Biblical Institute. Evanston, Ill. Bureau of Social and Religious Research. 2426
Garrett, Christina Hallowell. 3007
Garrett, Clarke. 2464
Garrett, Constance. 2388, 2872, 3222
Garrett, Eileen Jeanette (Lyttle) 2988, 2725, 3503, 3698
Garrett, Eileen Jeanette Lyttle. 1702, 3503
Garrett, James Leo. 159, 1552, 3465
[Garrett, Julia E.] 3503
[Garrett, Julia H.] 3503
Garrett, Margueritte Bixler. 1871
Garrett, Paul D. 1028, 1908
Garrett, Randall. 2123, 3280
Garrett, Shirley S. 3874
Garrett, T. H. 169
Garrett, Thomas Samuel. 1235, 2236
Garrett, Willis Edward. 3296
Garrett, Willis Otis. 1239
Garrettson, Freeborn. 1702
Garrigan, Owen. 1541
Garrigou-Lagrange, Reginald, 1877. 1298, 1528, 1751, 2038, 3486, 3693, 3696
Garrigou-Lagrange, Reginald, 1877-1964. 1476
Garrigou-Lagrange, Reginald. 2819, 3486, 3615, 3693, 3695, 3696, 1740, 2911, 2980, 3693
Garrison, Arthur O. 1033
Garrison, Charles Eugene. 885
Garrison, Edwin William. 2849
Garrison, James Harvey. 1040, 1058, 1460, 1462, 1829, 732, 1464
Garrison, Karl Claudius. 3167
Garrison, Maxine. 3243
Garrison, Omar V. 2949, 3314
Garrison, Pinkney J. 2924
Garrison, R. Benjamin. 63, 1315, 2072, 2435, 2887, 2978, 3352
Garrison, Stephen Olin. 2454
Garrison, Webb B. 10, 318, 613, 1007, 1603, 2199, 2427, 2461, 2900, 3078, 3839
Garrison, Wilfred Ernest. 1464
Garrison, Winfred Ernest. 827, 732, 1045, 1464, 1491, 2820, 2976, 3059, 3529, 3621, 3744
Garrone, Gabriel Marie. 585, 786, 2572, 2872
Garrott, Dorothy Carver. 2534
Garrotto, Alfred J. 941
Garside, Bettis Alston. 2270
Garside, Charles. 728, 1089, 1165, 2633, 3899, 3900
Garsoian, Nina G. 2805
Garst, Laura (De Lany) 1703, 2534
Garstang, John. 553, 554, 2096, 2764
Garstein, Oskar. 1374
Garsva, Pranas. 2334
Gartenberg, Leo. 2142
Gartenhaus, Jacob. 1083, 1366, 1703, 2034, 2084, 2118, 2142
Garth, Helen Meredith. 2353
Garth, John Goodall. 2928, 3289
Garth, Sarah Lingle. 1320
Gartner, Bertil. 337, 3013, 3014
Gartner, Bertil Edgar. 2156
Garver, Isobel M. 3037
Garver, John J. 2088
Garver, Stuart P. 781, 1840, 2953
Garvey, Jane D. 2123, 2124
Garvey, John. 1025
[Garvey, Mary]. 1785
Garvey, Michael. 875, 1703
Garvey, Robert. 1615, 2778, 3006
Garvie, Alfred Ernest. 389, 1141, 1721, 2519, 2804, 2900, 3442
Garvin, Hugh Carson, 1842-1918. 651
Garvin, Mary H. 638
Garvin, Philip. 1789, 3749
Garvin, Richard M. 2725
Gary, A. L. 39
Gary, Ind. St. Sava Serbian Orthodox Church. 2750
Gary, Louis R. 2942
Gascoigne, Bamber. 1189
Gascoigne, Thomas. 1764
Gaskell, George Arthur. 3574
Gaskill, James T. 3702
Gaskin, Jesse Marvin. 148, 159, 2270
Gaskin, John Charles Addison. 1855
Gasnier, Henri Michel. 578, 2132
Gaspar, Geza. 3078
Gasparin, Agenor Etienne 1810-1871. 3521
Gasparri, Pietro. 767, 769
[Gaspey, Thomas] 1788-1871. 293
Gasque, W. Ward. 331, 3021
Gasquet, Frances Aidan. 872, 3814

Gasquet, Francis Aidan. 2570, 3036, 270, 860, 1497, 1516, 1761, 2579, 2582, 3245
Gass, Darwin Xavier. 1545
Gass, Sylvester Francis. 190
Gassner, Jerome. 842
Gasson, Raphael. 983, 2086
Gaster, Moses. 1583, 2168, 3296
Gaster, Theodor Herze. 499, 1631, 1652
Gaster, Theodor Herzl. 1614, 1631, 2121, 2219, 2654, 2678, 2778, 3006
Gaston, Grace Catherine (Dorwart) 579
[Gaston, Henry A.]. 3503
Gaston, Hugh. 227, 300, 302
Gaston, Lloyd. 389, 1771
Gatch, Hilip. 1703
Gatch, Milton McC. 11, 1413, 2909
Gates, A. Avery. 3363
Gates, Aaron Avery. 1888
Gates, Alan Frederick. 2509, 3580
Gates, Carl M. 1446
Gates, Charles W. 2953
Gates, Doris. 55, 57, 101, 1804, 2661, 3895
Gates, Edith Mildred. 3877
Gates, Errett. 1464
Gates, Granville. 2226
Gates, Helen (Dunn) 3127
Gates, Helen Litchfield (Kolb) 1694, 2815
Gates, Herbert Wright. 923, 1251, 1838, 2550
Gates, John Alexander. 2170, 2174, 3744
Gates, Sherwood. 905
Gates, Susa (Young) 2602, 3869
Gates, Theophilus Ransom. 463, 1703
Gatewood, Otis. 1565, 1721
Gatewood, Richard Duncan. 2500
Gatewood, Willard B. 2562, 3080
Gatewood, Willard B., Jr. 3080
Gathorne-Hardy, Robert, 1902. 3591
Gatje, Helmut. 2184
Gatlin, Dana. 2872, 3751
Gattell, Benoni Bernard. 3685
Gatterer, Michael. 746, 3393
Gatti, Enzo. 2480
Gatti, Lawrence P. 3798
Gaubert, Henri. 4, 2093, 3457
Gauch, Patricia Lee. 1028, 1715
Gaudefroy-Demombynes, Maurice. 2564
Gaudiose, Dorothy M. 2849
Gaudreau, Marie Agnes of Rome. 3434
Gaudreau, Marie M. 2136, 2645
Gaughan, J. Anthony. 2738
Gauker, Ralph H. 1664
Gauld, Alan. 2858
Gaulke, Earle H. 898
Gault, Clarence W. 2006
Gaume, Jean Joseph. 767, 1389
Gaumer, Irwin C. 1496
Gauquelin, Michel. 95
Gausdal, Johannes. 3302
Gause, R. H. 139
Gauss, Christian Frederick. 3189
Gaussen, Louis. 305
Gaustad, Edwin Scott. 1488, 1757, 3214, 3738, 3748
Gauthier, Jeffrey A. 3277
Gauthier, Paul. 1152
Gautier, Judith. 3094
Gautier, Leon. 849
Gautruche, Pierre. 2656
Gauvin, Marshall J. 1654, 3023
Gavan, Duffy Thomas. 850, 1263, 1845, 2498, 2501, 2507, 2519, 2530, 3206
Gavazzi, Alessandro. 781
Gaver, Jessyca Russell. 127
Gaverluk, Emil. 526, 2854
Gavin, Antonio. 756, 799
Gavin, Donald Phillip. 3417
Gavin, Frank Stanton Burns. 45, 104, 648, 1143, 2071, 3262, 55, 1143, 2110, 2153, 2746, 3262
Gavin, Tadhg. 2596
Gavin, Thomas F. 794, 2246
Gavitt, Loren N. 2969, 2971
Gaw, Lily (Storrs) 3554
Gawalewicz, Marjan. 1632, 2360
Gawler, John Cox. 45
Gawryn, Marvin. 3478
Gay, Charles Louis. 1546
Gay, Jessie Harper. 521
Gay, Jules. 860, 2860
Gay, Peter. 1420, 1520, 2270
Gay, Theressa. 2206, 2544
Gay, Volney Patrick. 1673, 3240
Gayatri Devi, 1906. 3491
Gaydos, Michael. 1704
Gayley, Charles Mills. 11, 2656
Gaylor, James Edward. 3138
Gaylord, Harding W. 1014
[Gaylord, Mary M (Welles)]. 1704
Gayman, Isaac. 1794
Gaynor, Frank. 3092
Gazvini, M.j. 125, 127
Gazzillo, Karen Weston. 72, 384, 2007

Geach, Peter Thomas. 3066, 3610, 3782
Geagea, Nilo. 2360
Gealy, Fred Daniel. 1266, 1318, 2430, 2435
Geanakoplos, Deno John. 1622, 3307
Geaney, Dennis J. 753, 759, 775, 997, 2192, 2789, 3880
Gear, Felix B. 2914, 3679
Gearhart, Robert Harris. 63, 73, 2063
Gearhart, Sally Miller. 1843
*Gearon, Patrick J. 741, 786, 905, 1886, 2354, 2360, 2363, 2882, 3223, 3248, 3273
Gearon, Patrick J. 48, 2352, 2363, 3223, 3248, 3223
Geary, Gerald Joseph. 815, 2506
Geary, Patrick J. 3056
Gebauer, Paul. 1470
Gebhard, Anna Laura. 1112
Gebhard, Anna Laura (Munro) 1608, 3094, 3254
Gebhardt, Gusti. 898
*Gebhardt. G. 896
Gedalius, Jeanette. 2085
Geddes, Charles L. 657, 1924
Geddes, Joseph A. 2617
Geddes, Joseph Arch. 2617
Geddes, Leonard. 1326
Geden, Alfred Shenington. 2560
Gee, Donald. 567, 1886, 2474, 2815
Gee, Henry. 2884, 1220, 1762
Gee, Howard James. 3554
Geer, Curtis Manning. 1788
Geer, Owen Meredith. 1166, 3885
Geer, Thelma. 2598
Geertz, Clifford. 1925, 2563
Geeson, W G. 1575
Geffcken, Johannes. 2756
Geffen, Elizabeth M. 3730
Geffen, Roger. 2783
Geffre, Claude. 3656
Gehman, Clayton H. 1297, 1704
Gehman, Henry E. 3410
Gehman, Henry Snyder. 243
Gehman, John Luke. 2931
Gehman, Richard. 2502, 2845, 3851
Gehring, Albert. 3100
Gehrke, Ralph David. 590
Geib, Richard W. 2388
Geier, Woodrow Augustus. 2388
Geiermann, Peter. 2049, 2251, 2490, 2712, 3340, 3373, 3478, 795, 3222
Geiger, Abraham. 1704, 1926, 2117, 2185, 3032
Geiger, C. Harve. 2923
Geiger, Horace and Miles, C Austin. 1860
Geiger, Joseph Roy. 2866
Geiger, Kenneth. 1823, 1824
Geiger, Maynard J. 1647, 3302
Geiger, Wilhelm. 3899
Geikie, John Cunningham. 492, 499, 532, 1965, 3039
Geil, William Edgar. 3127
Geis, Bernard. 1404
Geis, Rudolph. 3393
Geiselmann, Josef Rupert. 3706
Geiseman, Otto Albert. 1266, 2213, 2299
Geisler, Norman L. 63, 279, 287, 309, 539, 943, 1737, 1745
Geismar, Eduard Osvald. 2170
Geissinger, David H. 1992
Geissinger, James Allen. 1422
Geissler, Eugene S. 1591, 1616, 2259, 2343, 2773
Geistweit, William Henry. 198
Gelber, Sholome Michael. 3016
Geldenhuys, Johannes Norval. 118, 428
Gelder, Herman Arend Enno van. 3034
Geley, Gustave. 1283
Gelfand, Michael. 1474, 1948, 2364, 3109
Gelfand, Ravina. 3195
[Gelgud, Ella M]. 2226, 2401
Gelin, Albert. 578, 598, 2002, 2326, 2866, 3413
Gelineau, Joseph. 1206, 2235, 2984
Geller, Lawrence D. 658, 2847
Gellhorn, Walter. 1127
Gelling, Peter. 2665
Gelpi, Donald L. 1358, 1598, 2570, 2815, 3019, 3643
Gelsinger, Michael George Howard. 620, 2747
[Gelzer, Heinrich]. 2273, 3040
Gemelli, Agostino. 1641, 1645
Gemme, Mike. 595, 2346
Genealogical Society of the Church of Jesus Christ of Latter-Day Saints. 1704
General Assembly of Spiritualists. 3503
General church of the New Jerusalem. 2689, 3459
General Church of the New Jerusalem. Liturgy and ritual. 2689
General Conference Mennonite Church. 1705, 2406, 2408
General Conference Mennonite Church. India Mission. 2530

General conference of Friends' First-day schools. 1446
General conference of Unitarian and other Christian churches. 3723
General conference of Unitarian and other Christian churches. Commission on theological education. 3723
[General council of the Congregational and Christian churches of the United States]. 1251, 1333, 1335, 1338
General council of the Congregational and Christian churches of the United States. Board of home missions. 694, 1332, 1705
General council of the Congregational and Christian churches of the United States. Board of home missions. Division of Christian education. 3150
General council of the Congregational and Christian churches of the United States. Commission on church attendance. 1162
General Council of the Congregational and Christian Churches of the United States. Liturgy and ritual. 1339
General council of the Congregational and Christian churches of the United States. Missions council. 2517
General Council of the Congregational Christian Churches of the United States. 1249
[General council of the Evangelical Lutheran church in North America]. 2294, 3562
General Council of the Evangelical Lutheran church in North America. Liturgy and ritual. 916, 1705, 2289
General synod of the Evangelical Lutheran church in the United States of America. 2289, 2296, 3563
General synod of the Evangelical Lutheran church in the United States of America. Liturgy and ritual. 2289, 2294
Genesis Project, inc. 929, 1965
Genest, Emile. 2656
Genevieve de la Sainte Face. 2348
Gennaro, Camillus. 3615
Genne, Elizabeth. 1164, 1254, 3389
Genovese, Mary Rosalia. 3247
Genovese, Mary Rosalia, Sister. 3247
[Gensheimer, Dorothy Hildegard]. 2267
Gensichen, Hans Werner. 1804, 2280, 2554
Gentile, Ernest B. 748
Gentry, Curtis Gavin. 3026
Gentry, Gardiner. 2625
Gentry, Lelia Lindsay (Thornton) 1706
Gentz, William H. 1017, 1253, 2865
Genung, George Frederick. 398, 3335
Genung, John Franklin. 210, 600, 962
Genuyt, F. M. 1734
George. 3256
George, d. 303. 1706
George, Arapura Ghevarghese. 2323, 2468
George, Augustin. 309
George, Bill. 929, 1965
George, Carol V. R. 26, 2679
George, Carrie (Leigh) 962
George, Charles H. 3039
George, David C. 326
George, Denise. 3332
George, Edward Augustus. 70, 1781
*George, J.-M. 5
George, Lawrence W. 3585
George, Llewellyn. 95, 2409
George, Lyman Fairbanks. 1951
George, Marian M. 1638
George, Nathan Dow. 3754
[George, Robert Esmonde Gordon]. 2797
George, Timothy. 3241, 3653
George, Walter S. 1354
George Washington University, Washington, D.C. Office of the University Historian. 3235
George Williams College, Chicago. 3757
Georges, Norbert. 1458
Georgetown Presbyterian Church. Washington, D.C. 1706
Georgetown University Colloquium on the Church in the Modern World, 1966. 1153
Georgianna, Linda. 39
Gephart, Gertrude. 1591
Geraghty, Richard P. 950, 3695
Gerahrt, Emanuel Vogel. 3643
Gerando, Joseph Marie de. 2590
Gerard, Francois C. 1246, 3784
Gerard, Gilbert. 233
Gerard, John. 1945, 3682, 872, 786
Gerber, Israel Joshua. 551, 16, 527, 2743
Gerber, John A. 1091
Gerber, Vergil. 1565
Gerberding, George Henry. 2285, 2292, 2294, 747, 1361, 2285, 2286, 2299, 2778, 3677
Gerberding, Paul James. 1528
Gerbet, Olympe Philippe. 2354

Gerdener, G B A. 2499
Gerdes, Egon W. 2791
Geren, Paul Francis. 1110, 1319
Gergely, Tibor. 2711
[Gergeres, Jean Baptiste]. 111, 1363
Gerhard, Frederick. 3023
Gerhard, Heinz Paul. 2357
Gerhardt, Alfred C. P. 1399
Gerhardsson, Birger. 393, 1538
Gerhart, Emanuel Vogel. 3643, 3659
Gericke, Paul. 1576, 2206, 2587, 2909
Gerig, Donald. 953
Gerjol, Karl. 2576
Gerke, Leonard F. 2343
Gerken, John D. 2192
Gerkin, Charles V. 2780
Gerlinger, Lorena. 2022
Germain. 3693
Germane, Charles E. 2590
Germanus I, d. ca. 733. 2912
Germany, Charles Hugh. 1935
Germing, Matthew. 1860
Gernes, Sonia. 2856
Gerostergios, Asterios. 1028, 2844
Gerow, Richard Oliver. 822, 2669
Gerrard, Thomas John. 1446
Gerrish, B. A. 3036
Gerrish, Brian Albert. 1385, 2281, 3037, 3680
Gerrity, Benignus. 3693
Gersh, Harry. 1615, 2120, 3203
Gershator, Phillis. 1844, 3581, 3584
Gershenzon, Mikhail Osipovich. 598
Gerson, Joannes. 3636
Gerson, Noel Bertram. 1497
[Gerstein, D]. 2077
Gerstein, Israel. 3371
Gerstel, David U. 3578
Gerstenberger, Erhard. 2326, 3541
Gerster, Georg. 876
Gerstner, John H. 63, 276, 363, 1499, 2910, 2911, 3028, 3678
Gerthe, Julia Ethel. 95
Gertrude. 1708, 2647
Gertrude, Sister. 2872
Gervasius. 2254
Gervis, Pearce. 3864
Gerwick, Katherine. 1446
Gerwig, George William. 1965
Gesch, Dorothy K. 3842
Gesch, Roy G. 81, 899, 1308, 1446, 1858, 2890, 3830, 3883
Gese, Hartmut. 652
Gesenius, Friederich Heinrich Wilheim. 1796
Gesenius, Friedrich Heinrich Wilhelm. 1796
Geser, Fintan. 2577
Gesner, Herbert Mortimer. 3335
Gess, Wolfgang Fredrich. 2038
Gessler, Theodore A. 1888
Gessner, Robert. 2077
Gessner, Salomon. 723, 724
Gesta Francorum et aliorum Hierosolymitanorum. 1391
Gesta Romanorum. English. 3340, 3581
Gestefeld, Ursula Newell. 1417, 1033, 1323, 3053
Gestwicki, Ronald. 903
Gesu, Remo di. 748
Getlein, Frank. 759
Getman, Arthur Kendall. 3554
*Gettings, Fred. 1479, 3588
Getty, Alice. 702, 1701, 1743, 2317
Getty, Frank Dales. 3876
Getty, George Albert. 1266
Getty, Mary Ann. 365, 380
Gettys, Joseph M. 474
Gettys, Joseph Miller. 423, 321, 365, 374, 423, 431, 465, 531, 566, 571, 638, 2929
Getz, Gene A. 450, 479, 560, 983, 1118, 1253, 1565, 1608, 2402, 2587, 2683, 3763
Geus, C. H. J., de. 499, 2715, 3719
Gewehr, Wesley Marsh. 3233
Gewirtz, Leonard B. 2138
Geyer, Alan F. 103, 1085
Geyer, Nancy. 1170
Geyer, Robert Raine. 1413
Gfrindon, Leopold Hartley. 2226
Al-Ghazzali. 23, 1698, 1708, 1927, 3855
Al-Gazzali, Muhammad. 2566
Gheerbrant, Alain. 821
Gheon, Henri. 683, 1522, 3778, 3780, 3784, 2349, 2358
Gheon, Henri [Real name: Henri Leon Vangeon]. 3778
Gherandasamhita. English and Sanskrit. 3867
Gherit, van der Goude. 845
Gherwal, Rishi Singh. 3864
Ghilardi, Agostino. 1641
Gholson, Edward. 1905
Ghose, Aurobindo. 3864, 2417, 1579, 2316, 2417, 3305, 3864
Ghose, Sisirkumar. 2638, 2641
Ghouse, Mohammad. 3194

Ghunaim, Muhammad Zakariya. 3285, 3330
Ghurye, Govind Sadashiv. 1897
Ghysels, James Marinus. 2032
Giant oaks. 3239
Giaquinta, Guglielmo. 772
Giardini, Fabio. 1736
Gibb, Hamilton Alexander Rosskeen. 1922, 1924, 2564, 2566
Gibb, Robert E. 3183
Gibbard, Mark. 923, 997, 2872
Gibbes, Emily Oliver. 2797, 3075
Gibble, Kenneth L. 2388
Gibble, Phares Brubaker. 1238
Gibbon, Edward. 1191, 1196, 2628
Gibbon, Peter. 1919
Gibboney, Charles H. 2388
Gibbons, Alice. 918, 2557
Gibbons, Daniel. 1674
Gibbons, Francis M. 1756, 2617, 2619, 3428, 3869
Gibbons, Helen Bay. 1711, 1900
Gibbons, Hughes Oliphant. 2830
Gibbons, James. 772, 786, 863, 1049, 1266, 1591, 1711, 3127
Gibbons, John. 1711, 2762
Gibbons, John Presley. 1513
Gibbons, Joseph. 797
Gibbons, Phebe Earle. 35
Gibbons, William. 1687
Gibbons, William Cephus. 549
Gibbs, Alfred P. 600
Gibbs, Elsie. 1446, 2420, 2872
Gibbs, Jessie Wiseman. 1579
Gibbs, John C. 3433
Gibbs, Joseph C. 870
Gibbs, Josiah Francis. 2602
Gibbs, Margaret. 1026
Gibbs, Marion. 667
Gibbs, Mark. 2191
Gibbs, Paul T. 214, 493, 548, 1404, 2007, 2797
Gibbs, Willa. 1362
Gibier, Paul. 2988
Giblin, Charles Homer. 376
Giboney, Ezra P. 1240, 2373
Gibran, Kahlil. 2005, 3199
Gibson, Alan George Sumner. 1224, 2536
Gibson, Alexander Boyce. 943, 3100
Gibson, Arthur. 100, 314
Gibson, Axel Emil. 3053
Gibson, Bertha Askew. 305, 620
Gibson, Charles Knight. 424
Gibson, D B. 2251
Gibson, Edgar Charles Sumner. 1385
Gibson, Elsie. 2872, 3835
Gibson, George Miles. 1191, 1262, 2900
Gibson, H. S. 3209
Gibson, Henry Louis. 1308
Gibson, Isaac. 531
Gibson, John C. L. 521
Gibson, John Monro. 520
Gibson, John Paul. 1251
Gibson, Joseph Thompson. 1951
Gibson, Katharine. 620
Gibson, Litzka, R. 95
Gibson, Lucile L. (Foreman) 1711
Gibson, M Allan. 2538
Gibson, Margaret T. 666, 2195
Gibson, Maria Layng. 3306
Gibson, Marywebb. 3395
Gibson, Michael. 2661
Gibson, Raymond E. 3659
Gibson, Hamilton Edward Lee. 1397
Gibson, Roxie E. 900, 1112, 1734
Gibson, Ruth. 3843
Gibson, Van Rensselaer. 1591, 1660, 2017
Gibson, Walter Brown. 1470, 2725, 3823
Gibson, Walter Ernest. 162
Gibson, William E. 3409
Gichner, Lawrence Ernest. 1896
Gicovate, Bernard. 2136
Gidada Solon, 1901. 3127
Gideon, Virtus E. 430
Giehri, Emmy. 1388
Gielow, Frederick John. 1174
Gielow, Fredrick J. jr. 1174
Gieringer, Paul A. 850
Giertz, Bo Harald. 2005, 299, 1268
Giertz, Bo Harold. 2282
Giese, Frank S. 1426
Giese, Geneva. 1910
Giese, Vincent J. 753, 774, 1261, 1711
Gieseler, Carl Albert. 589
Gieseler, Johann Karl Ludwig. 1174, 1175
Gieselmann, Reinhard. 1156, 1158
Giesen, Heinrich. 3012
Giessler, Phillip B. 1308
Giesy, Samuel Hensel. 2038
Giffe, William T. 1202
Gifford, Frank Dean. 44, 2971, 2973, 3672
Gifford, George. 3823
Gifford, Miram Wentworth. 3059
Gifford, Orrin Philip. 3340
Gifford, Orrin Phillip. 3352
Gifford, William Alva. 1091, 1175, 2237

Gift, Foster U. 190, 934, 3150
*Gigliozzi, Giovanni. 1777, 2849, 3531
Gignac, Francis T. 1770
Gigot, Francis Ernest Charles. 533, 233, 309, 406, 539, 1965
Gihr, Nikolaus. 1458, 2366
Gil, Emma (Wiliams) 2765
Gilbert. 594
Gilbert, Alan D. 1516, 1765
Gilbert, Ariadne. 662
Gilbert, Arthur. 1614, 2152, 3771
Gilbert, Charles Kendall. 3442
Gilbert, Clark R. 3883
Gilbert, Dan. 1591, 1656, 2561, 3879, 3885, 2563
[Gilbert, Eliphalet Wheeler]. 1681
Gilbert, Fred Carnes. 1083, 1387, 1928, 2077, 2138, 3382
Gilbert, Fred V. 907
Gilbert, George Holley. 3073, 233, 347, 450, 476, 1191, 1965, 2063, 2797
Gilbert, George Holleyd. 233
Gilbert, Harold W. 1917
Gilbert, Harry. 1204
Gilbert, James Eleazer. 3191, 2421, 2454, 3662
Gilbert, James J. 1311
Gilbert, Janice Dee. 2693
Gilbert, Jesse Samuel. 180, 3662
Gilbert, John N[ewton]. 1049
Gilbert, Katherine (Everett) 672
Gilbert, Lela. 3835
Gilbert, Lem. 962
Gilbert, Levi. 1058, 3783, 1695, 1888
Gilbert, Miriam. 1921
Gilbert, Ralph Valentine. 10
Gilbert, Richard Henry. 3377
Gilbert, Thomas Walter. 962, 2126
Gilbert, W Kent. 3150, 3177, 3801
Gilbertson, Irvy. 3005
Gilbertson, Merrill T. 207, 282
Gilbreath, Joseph Earl. 2638, 3442
Gilby, Thomas. 1141, 1585, 3694
Gilchrist, Jack. 1289
Gildon, Charles. 1420
Gile, Louisa Boyd. 1446
Gilfillan, George. 1799
Gilfond, Henry. 3787
Gilhuis, C. 18
Gilkes, A. N. 1410
Gilkey, Charles Whitney. 1591, 2063, 3066, 3352
Gilkey, James Gordon. 962, 1058, 1098, 1104, 1591, 1721, 2061, 2980
Gilkey, Langdon Brown. 799, 1058, 1380, 1819, 2562, 3069, 3070, 3082, 3662
Gill, Charles Otis. 1374
Gill, Donald H. 983
Gill, Eric. 3442
Gill, Everett. 3241, 3466, 2548, 2504
Gill, Frederick Cyril. 63, 1549, 1550, 3802
Gill, Jerry H. 1586, 1734, 2170, 2181, 2837, 3021, 3643
Gill, John. 1285, 1722, 1906
Gill, Joseph. 1622
Gill, Mabel K., R. N. 2997, 3811
Gill, Richard Hooker Keller. 2994
Gill, Robert. 1345
Gill, Sam D. 1902, 2677
Gill, Theodore Alexander. 676
Gill, William Hugh. 514, 416
Gill, William Icrin. 3191
Gill, William Wyatt. 2666
Gillard, Georges. 3278
Gillard, John Thomas. 875, 2541, 2681, 2541
Gillchrest, Muriel Noyes. 2694
Gillelman, Gerard. 2264
Gillen, Jack. 2948
Gillenson, Lewis. W. 1361, 1362, 1754
Gillenwaters, William Phipps. 1049
Gillerman, Dorothy W. 2773, 2774
*Gillese, John Patrick. 8, 1645, 3540
Gillespie, Janet. 1713, 2937
Gillespie, Julia Berford (Wall) 2625
Gillespie, Virgil Bailey. 1361
Gillet, Edith Louise. 3170
Gillet, Lev. 2388
Gillet, Martin Stanislas. 3390, 749
Gillett, David. 1078
Gillett, Ezra Hall. 1857, 2672, 3038
Gillett, Henry Martin. 3394
Gillett, Henry Tregelles. 1085
[Gillette, Charles]. 1773
Gillette, Walter Bloomfield. 1713
Gillham, Helen L. 2590
Gilliam, E[dward] W[inslow]. 3127
Gilliam, Olive Kuntz. 3014

Gilliat-Smith, Ernest. 54
Gillies, Alexander. 1743, 2307
Gillies, Andrew. 2474, 3097
Gillies, John. 3813
Gillig, Ethel M. 3573
Gillilan, James David. 1883
Gilliland, Dolores Scott. 214, 3839
Gillin, John Lewis. 1236
Gillingham, E. Leonard. 2435, 3352
Gillingham, James. 3503
Gilliom, James O. 2480, 3187
Gillis, James Martin. 756, 759, 1069, 1313, 2805, 3486, 660
Gillispie, Charles Coulston. 3084
Gillman, Frederick John. 1871
Gillman, Neil. 2181, 2332
Gillon, Louis Bertrand. 947
Gillquist, Peter E. 983, 1712, 3662
Gillum, Perry. 1229
Gilly, William Stephen. 2679
Gilman, Arthur. 2564
Gilman, Bradley. 3127, 177
Gilman, Charlotte Perkins Stetson. 3846
Gilman, Daniel Coit. 132
Gilman, James Franklin. 1033, 1494
Gilman, Mary Rebecca (Foster) 3603
Gilman, Phillips Standish. 1438
Gilmer, Harry Wesley. 2075
Gilmore, Albert Field. 309, 1175, 1965
Gilmore, Alec. 137, 2900
Gilmore, Conal Gregory. 3524
Gilmore, Evelyn Langdon. 1702
Gilmore, G. Don. 42, 962, 1004, 1007, 1275, 3540
Gilmore, George William. 419
Gilmore, J. Herbert. 1132, 1626, 2388, 3352
Gilmore, Jan. 3744
Gilmore, Joseph Henry. 3026
Gilmore, Julia. 3251, 3416
Gilmour, George Peel. 389
Gilmour, Peter. 856
Gilmour, Richard. 293, 620
Gilmour, Samuel MacLean. 2063
Gilpin, Joshua. 1713
Gilpin, Richard O. 493, 2621
Gilpin, W. Clark. 2464, 3817
Gilpin, William]. 131
Gilruth, James H[enry]. 1740
Gilruth, James Henry. 302
Gilsenan, Michael. 21, 3544
Gilson, Etienne Henry. 3695, 116, 193, 675, 1535, 1740, 2646, 2836, 2840, 2842, 3592, 3693, 3695, 3696, 3697
Gilson. Etienne Henry. 1   2 6 4 7
Gimbel, Ann Matterand. 1515
Gimenez, John. 1713, 3798
Gimpel, Jean. 79
Ginder, Richard. 786, 3393
Ginever, Violet. 1313
*Ginger, Helen. 2890
Gingerich, Melvin. 2406, 1138, 3448
Gingrich, Raymond E. 324
Ginilou. 931, 1713
Ginn, D Perry. 482, 595
Ginsberg, Harold Louis. 507, 512
Ginsberg, Louis. 2101, 2426
Ginsberg, Mitchell. 185
Ginsberg, Morris. 1323
Ginsburg, Christian David. 530, 1532, 2364
Ginsburg, Leo. 2110
Ginsburgh, Irwin. 204, 526
Ginther, Rosamond D. 628
[Ginzberg, Asher]. 2112, 2622, 3027
Ginzberg, Eli. 247, 1713, 2084
Ginzberg, Louis. 2086, 2207, 1706, 2074, 2207, 3891
Ginzburg, Carlo. 1689, 3306
Giordani, Igino. 749, 1965, 2060, 2063, 2354, 2797, 2851, 3439, 3451
Giradey, Ferrol. 2360
Giraldi, Lilio Gregorio. 3215
Giran, Etienne. 1745
Girandola, Anthony. 781
Girard, Rafael. 2863, 3012
Girard, Rene. 3239
Girard, Robert C. 983, 1243, 1714
Girardeau, John Lafauette. 2633
Girardeau, John Lafayette. 729, 2931, 3643
Girardey, Ferrol. 1591, 2872, 2960, 3373, 1541, 3052, 3486
Giraud, S M. 2576
Giraud, Sylvain Marie. 2576
Girdlestone, Robert Baker. 556, 605
Girdwood, James. 547
Girgensohn, Herbert. 2279
Girod, Gordon H. 1557, 2034
Gisborne, Thomas. 1175
Gish, Arthur G. 933, 3233, 3409
Gisler, Otto. 770
Gispen, Willem Hendrik. 516
Gist, Margaret Adams. 2919
Gitelson-Kamaiko Foundation. 2847
Githens, Harry W. 616
Githens, Harry Wright. 2757

Gitlin, Murray. 2725
*Gittelsohn, Roland B. 2081
Gittelsohn, Roland Bertram. 2077, 2138, 2151, 2345, 3059, 3361
Giudice, Liliane. 17, 192
Giuliotti, Domencio. 2366
Giustiniani, L. 781
Giuzvlev, Vasil. 713
Givan, Timothy S. 1385
Givens, Nick K. 2939
Gjerlow, Lilli. 844, 2195
Gjurovich, Yovo. 1091
Gladden, Lee. 318, 1280
Gladden, John N. 163
Gladden, Washington. 1015, 104, 233, 660, 962, 1045, 1118, 1341, 1344, 1368, 1715, 2246, 2249, 3199, 3442, 3643, 3651, 3672
Gladstone, John N. 163
Gladstone, William Ewart. 201, 1380, 1715, 3199, 3621, 3769
Gladstone, William Louis. 3503
Gladwin, John W. 3442
Glaister, Robert. 2019
Glanvill, Joseph. 1226, 3100, 3363, 3823
Glanz, Rudolf. 2098, 2619
Glanzman, George S. 644
Glascock, James Luther. 3230, 3299
Glasenapp, Helmuth von. 710
Glasenapp, Helmuth von [Otto Max Helmuth von Glasenapp]. 1888, 3138
Glasfurd, Alexander Lamont. 190
Glasgow, George. 1913
Glasgow, Samuel McPheeters. 340, 1438, 2527, 3352
Glasgow, William Melancthon. 3050
Glasheen, P. 302
Glaskin, Gerald M. 3053
Glasner, Peter E. 3327
Glass, Bill. 1323
Glass, Daniel Grant. 3048
Glass, Esther Eby. 3185
Glass, Fides. 1744, 3378
Glass, Frederick Charles. 2504
Glass, Henry Alexander. 586, 2986
Glass, Kate Elizabeth (Perkins) 2988
Glass, Theodore. 3580
Glass, William. 1256
Glasse, James D. 1295, 2785, 3363, 3732
Glasser, Alan J. 1323
Glassman, Eugene H. 652
Glasson, Thomas Francis. 423, 2621
Glatzer, Nahum Norbert. 549, 1455, 1812, 2076, 2112, 2117, 2147, 2148, 2150, 2462, 3899
Glaze, R E. 404
Glazebrook, Michael George. 541
Glazer, Nathan. 2154
Glazer, Simon. 2146, 172, 2088, 2117, 3370
Glazier, Daniel Johnson. 3537
Glazier, Donna L. 2625
Gleadow, Rupert. 3897
Gleason, Gene. 2509, 3422
Gleason, George. 1248, 1257, 1259
Gleason, John J. 1527, 2038, 2997, 3059
Gleason, Judith Illsley. 1882, 2667
Gleason, Philip. 875, 1136
Gleason, Robert W. 786, 997, 1722, 1731, 1751, 1829, 2570, 3486, 3651
Gleason, Samuel Wight. 3503
Gleason, Sarell Everett. 179
Gleason, William Francis. 1253, 2307
Gledstone, James Paterson. 34, 3813
Gleeson, Richard A. 1710
Gleeson, William. 815
Glegg, Gordon Lindsay. 63
Gleig, George Robert. 289, 294
Glen, John Stanley. 1907. 322, 1058, 1288, 1689, 2025, 2976
Glen Moore, Pa. Fairview Presbyterian church. 2915
Glendining, Marion. 3879
Glenn, Ernest Neill. 1272
Glenn, Jacob B. 317, 3073
Glenn, Layona. 2504
Glenn, Leslie. 1118
Glenn, Mendel Gershon. 3581
Glenn, Paul Joseph. 63, 1371, 2738, 3450, 3610, 3696
Glenn, William Newton. 509
Glennie, Alexander. 3352
Glenville, N. Y. Second Reformed church. 3189
Glessner, Chloe Holt. 1822
Glicenstein, Henryk. 1623
Glick, Carl. 1538, 1668
Glick, Edward Bernard. 2764
Glick, Garland Wayne. 1786
Glick, Thomas F. 202
Glickman, S. Craig. 594, 930, 1985
Glicksberg, Charles Irving. 3071
Gliksman, Shlomo. 2077
Glitzenstein, Abraham Chanoch. 3404
Gloag, Paton James. 202
Globus, Alfred R. 2388
Glock, Charles Y. 1073, 3086, 3088, 3112, 3442

Glody, Robert. 3790
Gloege, Gerhard. 389
Glory in Him. 1438
Glover, Alfred Kingsley. 2121
Glover, Carl Archibald. 70, 1485, 2890, 3540
Glover, Christopher. 1249
Glover, Gloria (Diener) 1981, 3175
Glover, John Thomas. 134
Glover, Robert H. 2525
Glover, Robert Hall. 2525
Glover, Terrot Reaveley. 1191, 1040, 1058, 1069, 1093, 1951, 2063, 2797, 3116, 3862, 1058, 1196, 2008, 2038
Glovier, David Franklin. 1550
Gloyn, Cyril Kennard. 1146
Glubb, John Bagot. 983, 1926, 2628
Glubok, Shirley. 87
Gluck, Carl. 233, 1033, 1496
Glueck, Nelson. 282, 598, 1809, 2131
Glunz, Hans. 401
Glunz, Hans Hermann. 398
Glushkow, Abraham Dave. 2100
Glustrom, Simon. 7, 2146, 2154
*Glynn, Jeanne Davis. 3192
Glynn, Robert L. 1856
Gmeiner, John. 2038, 3075
Gnayalloor, Jacob. 114
Goad, Harold Elsdale. 1641
Goates, Lesley. 1009
Gobbel, A. Roger. 905
Goble, Phillip E. 2073
Goblet d'Alviella, Eugene Felicien Albert, 1846-1925. 1729, 3573
Goblet d'Alviella, Eugene Felicien Albert. 3141
Goblet d'Alviella, Eugene Feliclen Albert. 3573
Gobry, Ivan. 2866
Gockel, Herman William. 104, 1005, 1434, 1438, 1446, 2808
Godard, James McFate. 2337, 2338
Godber, Joyce. 183, 1677
Godbey, Allen Howard. 1929, 2114
Godbey, John Emory. 63, 2519
Godbey, Samuel Macginis. 2865
Godbey, William B. 70, 651, 1829, 1965, 343, 2762, 2818
Godbold, Albea. 1127
Goddard, Alice L. 2151
Goddard, Carolyn E. 3170
Goddard, Carrie Lou. 733, 930, 1384, 1981, 1996, 3150
Goddard, Charles. 60
Goddard, Donald. 676
Goddard, Dwight. 704, 707, 702, 707, 962, 1951, 2174
Goddard, Francis Wayland. 2509
Goddard, Harold Clarke. 3708
Goddard, John. 3503
Goddard, John Hunter. 1626
Goddard, Josiah. 1865
[Goddard, Neville Lancelot, 1905. 299, 2694, 2872
Goddard, Oscar Elmo. 1553, 2492
Goddijn, Walter. 826, 1245
Godet, Frederic. 322, 371, 416, 419, 428, 467
Godfrey, Frederick M. 1957
Godfrey, George. 3829
Godfrey, John. 1761
Godfrey, Richard Brown. 1049
Godfrey, Richmond Brown. 1049
Godfrey, William. 1731
Godin, Andre. 2780, 3001, 3176
Godman, Henry C. 1742, 2817
Godolphin, Francis Richard. 597
Godryez, John A. 807, 827, 2562
God's Bible school missionary prayer band. 2519
Godsey, John D. 676, 2174, 2708
Godwin, David. 762
Godwin, George Stanley. 2645
Godwin, John. 1849, 2733
Godwin, Johnnie C. 3051
Godwin, Joscelyn. 2636
Godwin, Polly. 805
Godwin, William. 2312, 2313, 3621
Goebel, Bernardin. 2742
Goebel, Edmund J. 3331
Goebel, Edmund Joseph. 3331, 3406
Goen, C. C. 1468, 1469
Goergen, Donald. 877, 2264
Goering, Gladys V. 1705, 3837
Goerner, Edward Alfred. 1143
Goerner, Henry Cornell. 2504, 2558
Goerss, Daniel Friedrich. 2213
Goetchius, Eugene Van Ness. 1770
Goethe, Johann Wolfgang von. 1618, 1619, 1743, 2771
[Goetten, Henry]. 2354, 2358
Goff, Charles Ray. 962, 2435
Goff, Eric Noel Porter. 991
Goff, John. 588
Goff, Walter Roy. 1530, 2051
Goff, William M. 3503

Goffart, Walter A. 2203
Goforth, Jonathan. 2509
Goforth, Rosalind (Bellsmith) 1744, 2509, 2872
Gogarten, Friedrich. 347, 1154, 1818, 2038
Gogarty, Oliver St. John. 1919, 2793
Goggins, Ralph Damian. 3676
Gogol', Nikolai Vasil'evich. 2748
Goguel, Maurice. 1965, 1191, 1951, 1965, 338, 1965
Gohdes, Clarence Louis Frank. 3709
Gohdes, Conrad Bruno. 2768
Goheen, John. 2738, 3695
Goitein, Solomon Dob Fritz. 2107
Gokak, Vinayak Krishna. 1709
Gokey, Francis X. 1429
Gokhale, Balkrishna Govind. 2839
Golann, Cecil Paige. 5, 633
Golay, Eugene E. 1565
Golbeck, Kay. 88, 1744
Gold, Don. 1294, 2734, 3877
Gold, Howard Reuben. 294
Gold, William Jason. 3853
Goldberg, Ben Zion. 3389
Goldberg, David. 1614, 2077, 2102, 2154, 2950
Goldberg, Henry. 3027
Goldberg, Hillel. 2632
Goldberg, Isaac. 3863
[Goldberg, Israel]. 2088, 3897
Goldberg, Israel. 2106
Goldberg, Louis. 557, 2138
Goldberg, Philip. 3708
Goldberg, Ruth L Polhemus. 2762
Goldblatt, David. 2082
Goldbrunner, Josef. 746, 997, 1529, 2784, 3150, 3267
Goldburg, Norman M. 3016
Golden Gate Baptist Theological Seminary. 3612
Golden, George Charles. 2409, 2694
Golden, Harry Lewis. 2104
Golden, Jerry. 1366, 1744
Golden, Mary Cortona. 3421
Golden, Meletios. 1358
Golden, Richard M. 772, 1292
Golden, Samuel A. 2203
Goldenberg, Naomi R. 3834
Golder, Christian. 1408
Golder, Frank Alfred. 1707, 2602
Goldfarb, Solomon David. 529, 3371
Goldhaber, Nat. 3708
Goldie, Frederick. 1524
Goldie, John. 887
Goldin, Hyman Elias. 294, 620, 1614, 1927, 2121, 2207, 2940, 3006, 3015, 3304, 3863
Goldin, Judah. 2400
Golding, Louis. 1501, 2621
Golding, Vautier. 2241
Goldingay, John. 119, 504, 587
Goldman, Alex J. 539, 2074, 3016, 3575
Goldman, Bernard Marvin. 1800
Goldman, Harvey S. 2145
Goldman, Irving. 2188
Goldman, Israel M. 1880, 2075, 2107
Goldman, Joseph. 2114
Goldman, June Parker. 2388
Goldman, Moses. 3370
Goldman, Moses B. 3371
Goldman, Peter Louis. 669, 2233
Goldman, Ronald. 903, 3170
Goldman, Solomon. 497, 2112, 2118, 2622, 2841, 3896, 517, 1313, 2623, 2841
Goldman, W. Darryl. 1301, 1744
Goldmann, Gereon Karl. 3851
Goldmann, Lucien. 1520, 2163
Goldschmidt, Lazarus. 530
Goldsmith, Elizabeth Edwards. 3573
Goldsmith, Joel S. 2694, 2872, 2264, 2694, 2695, 3478
Goldsmith, Martin. 2492
[Goldsmith, Milton]. 3567
Goldsmith, William Marion. 1579
Goldstein, David. 786, 755, 786, 2082, 2117
Goldstein, Doris S. 1088, 3703
Goldstein, Herbert Samuel. 497, 1312
Goldstein, Isaac. 2005
Goldstein, Israel. 2627, 2696, 2699
Goldstein-Jacobson, Ivy Martha-Marie, 1893. 95
Goldstein, Joseph. 2382
Goldstein, Marianne. 601, 2111, 2678
Goldstein, Morris. 2013, 2117
Goldstein, Sidney Emanuel. 2338, 2700
Goldston, Robert. 3303
Goldston, Robert C. 1429
Goldsworthy, Edwin Arthur. 3003
Goldwin, Robert A. 2681
[Goldzier, Julia]. 1037
Goldziher, Ignac. 1921, 1922, 2664
Goleman, Daniel. 2379
Golightly, Thomas Jefferson. 2590
Golisch, John. 2886
Golisyn, Dmitril Dmitrievich. 786

Golitsyn, Dmitril Dmitrievich. 786, 787
Golityn, Dmitril Dmitrievich. 787
Goll, George Philip. 1547
Golladay, Robert Emory. 3340, 1268, 1531, 1692, 2213, 2216
Gollancz, Samuel Marcus. 660
Gollancz, Victor. 103, 2231, 3199
Golland Trindade, Henrique Heitor 1897. 2388
Golland Trindade, Henrique Heitor. 3028, 3580
Goller, Edward D. 3880
Gollin, Gillian Lindt. 2596
Gollin, James. 807
Gollock, Georgina Anne. 2482, 2557
Gollwitzer, Helmet. 1737
Gollwitzer, Helmut. 595, 1085, 1088, 1319, 2032, 3392, 3850
Golomb, Morris. 1615, 2146
Golub, Jacob S. 2091, 2095, 2096
Golub, Jacob Solomin. 2096
Golub, Jacob Solomon. 2091, 2095
Golub, Rose W. 1623
Golz, L. 3299
Golz, Lud. 1431
Goma y Tomas, Isidro, 1869-1940. 2254
Gombosi, Marilyn. 1208
Gombrich, Richard Francis. 704
Gomez de Avellaneda y Arteaga, Gertrudis, 1814-1873. 28
Gompertz, Erich. 201
[Gongaware, George J.]. 1547
Gonsalves, Noel J. L. 1484
Gontard, Friedrich. 2769
[Gonzales, Ambrosio Jose]. 3503
Gonzales, Carmen. 3742
Gonzalez, Francisco Jose. 2057
Gonzalez, Garcia, Manuel. 2388
Gonzalez, James L. 2805
Gonzalez, Jose Luis. 2805
Gonzalez, Justo L. 233, 2559, 2900, 3654
Gonzalez, Nunez Angel. 4
Gonzalez Ruiz, Jose Maria, 1916. 1154
Gonzalez-Balado, Jose Luis. 2717, 3602
Gonzalez Ruiz, Jose Maria, 1916. 983
Gonzalez-Wippler, Migene. 721, 3302, 3303
Gonzalo de Jesus. 2568
Gooch, Betty. 2854
Gooch, George Peabody. 1638
Gooch, Stan. 2988
Good business. 2872
Good, Charles M. 2025
Good, Charles Martin. 2025
Good, Edwin Marshall. 499
Good, James. 1043
Good, James Isaac. 3034, 3043, 3047, 3048
Good, John Walter. 1952
Good, Merle. 35
Good, Nelson Manoah. 3848
Good, Phyllis Pellman. 1527, 2408
Goodall, Blake. 479, 1115
Goodall, J. L. 3100
Goodall, Norman. 1040, 1491, 2243, 3127, 3796
Goodavage, Joseph F. 95, 2725
Goodchild, Frank Marsden. 1098, 2251, 3073
Goodchild, Mary Antonine. 883
Goode, Francis. 3029
Goode, John Fleming. 150
Goode, M. M. 3093
Goode, Walter Everett. 962
Goode, William. 276, 2754, 3010
Goode, William J. 3086
Goode, William Josiah. 3086
Goodell, Charles Le Roy. 233, 1049, 1553, 1565, 1747, 2425, 2890, 3352, 1565, 1577
Goodell, Charles LeRoy. 2421, 3352
Goodell, Constans Liberty. 3672
Goodell, William. 2515
Goodenough & Woglom co. 3549
Goodenough, Arthur. 1288
Goodenough, Caroline Louisa Leonard. 1875
Goodenough, Erwin Ramsdell. 1094, 1102, 1191, 2118, 2831, 2997, 1196
Goodenow, Juliet S. 3503
Goodhart, Arthur Lehman. 3102
Goodier, Alban. 781, 1945, 539, 997, 1024, 1965, 2029, 2032, 2038, 3280, 3486
Goodier, Archbishop. 2388
Gooding, David Willoughby. 483
Gooding, Oliver Paul. 198, 3116
Goodland, Roger. 2828
Goodloe, Robert Wesley. 2450, 3267
Goodman, Abram Vossen. 2104
Goodman, Carlton T. 2625
Goodman, Felicitas D. 1585, 1716, 2461
Goodman, Florence Remington (Merriott) 3819
Goodman, Frederic Simeon. 372, 638, 2797
Goodman, George. 2038, 620

Goodman, Grace Ann. 1244
Goodman, Hannah Grad. 2950
Goodman, John. 3457
Goodman, Morris C. 3575
Goodman, Paul. 2088, 2114, 2088
Goodman, Philip. 1320, 2697, 2778, 3006, 3249, 3545, 3867
Goodman, William R. 1603
Goodnight, Cloyd. 3235
Goodpasture, John Ridley. 3090
Goodrich, Alfred Bailey. 3562
Goodrich, Asa Stanley. 597
Goodrich, Charles Augustus. 1175, 2032
Goodrich, Donna Clark. 900, 3843
Goodrich, Edward Payson. 48
Goodrich, Elizur. 1503
Goodrich, Frances C. 1094
Goodrich, Marcus. 482
Goodrich, Norma Lorre. 1807, 2206, 2232, 2651
Goodrich, Robert Edward. 2435
Goodrich, Robert Edward. 2435
Goodrich, Robert Eugene. 2435
Goodrich, Samuel Griswold. 662
[Goodrich, Samuel Griswold]. 282, 620, 632, 662, 2657
Goodrich, Wallace. 1209
Goodrich, William Lloyd. 2970
Goodrick, Edward W. 229
Goodsell, Buel. 3280
Goodsell, Daniel Ayres. 3651
Goodsell, Fred Field. 31, 241, 1621
Goodsell, Willystine. 3027
Goodspeed, Charles Ten Broeke. 2413, 3874
Goodspeed, Edgar Johnson. 1565, 1981, 2587, 70, 289, 309, 334, 337, 338, 339, 355, 358, 364, 383, 409, 489, 539, 612, 613, 894, 1020, 1965, 2797, 3100, 56, 120, 347, 364, 409, 442, 929, 1020, 1965, 1976, 2373, 2737, 2797
Goodspeed, Frank Lincoln. 2762
Goodspeed, George Stephen. 2415
Goodspeed, Thomas Wakefield. 893
Goodwill, Anna. 3503
Goodwin, Abb L. 2981
Goodwin, Benjamin Thelston. 3224
Goodwin, Bennie. 146, 2172
Goodwin, Conrad Harrison. 2872
Goodwin, Daniel Raynes. 104, 1846, 3425
Goodwin, Donald Watson. 505
Goodwin, Edward Lewis. 1223
Goodwin, Frank Judson. 2388, 2797
Goodwin, Henry Martyn. 2038, 3644
Goodwin, John. 600
Goodwin, Lavinia Stella (Tyler) 744
Goodwin, Mary Clare. 118, 2132
Goodwin, R Dean. 155, 3749
Goodwin, Thomas. 1344
Goodwin, Thomas A. 593
Goodwin, William Archer Rutherfoord. 24, 1118, 2774
Goodwin, William McAfee. 1033
Goody, John Rankine. 2658
Goodykoontz, Colin Brummitt. 2553, 1343, 2553
Goodykoontz, Harry G. 1295, 2323, 3177
Goose, Edmund William. 3590
Goosens, Mathias, 1916. 1263
Gopala, Chetti, D. 3422, 3569
Gopalan, Subramania. 1932
Gopi Krishna, 1903. 1579, 2187, 3059, 3865
Gopinatha Rao, T. A., 1872. 2663
Gopinatha Rao, T. A. 2663
Goppelt, Leonhard. 347, 2051
Gorainoff, Irina. 1363
Gorayeb, Joseph P. 1481
Gordh, George Rudolph. 1049
Gordin, Harry Mann. 2833
Gordis, Robert. 2082, 2364, 484, 505, 512, 548, 549, 556, 593, 1348, 1811, 2114, 2138, 2141, 2142, 2364, 3059, 3389
Gordon, Adoniram Jordan. 163
Gordon, Adoniram Judson. 1446, 1829, 2637, 3289
Gordon, Albert I. 2100
Gordon, Albert Isaac. 1361
Gordon, Alexander Reid. 515, 526, 568, 573
Gordon, Andrew. 1136, 2530
Gordon, Anna Adams. 3598, 3816
Gordon, Antoinette K. 88, 2193
Gordon, Arthur. 2388, 2809
Gordon, Buford Franklin. 3672, 3150
Gordon College of Theology and Missions. 3621
Gordon, Cyrus H. 210
Gordon, Cyrus Herzl. 537
Gordon, David. 745
Gordon, Elizabeth Putnam. 3833
Gordon, Ellen. 3503
Gordon, Emma K. 3027
Gordon, Ernest. 63, 983, 1256, 2931
Gordon, Ernest Barron. 343, 924, 1619, 1748, 3728

Gordon, Gary. 3742
Gordon, George Angier. 1855, 2476, 3651, 1049, 1438, 1591, 1722, 1888, 2038, 2476, 3097, 3225
Gordon, Helen. 1992
Gordon, Helen (Van Metre) Van-Anderson. 962
Gordon, Hirsch Loeb. 741
Gordon, James Logan. 3211
Gordon, John. 2005
Gordon, John M. 1486
Gordon, Johnson W. 185
Gordon, Julius. 2099
Gordon, Prentiss M. 3478
Gordon, Samuel Dickey. 233, 419, 459, 962, 1069, 1513, 1792, 1952, 2031, 2038, 2872, 2890, 3211, 3319, 3600, 3885, 1447, 2872
Gordon, Sarah Morgan (Groff) 1708
Gordon, Seth Reed. 233
Gordon, Solomon. 3361
Gordon, Thomas Crouther. 1942
Gordon, William. 2988
Gordon, William Robert. 2000, 2133, 2981, 3503
Gore, Charles. 9, 871, 943, 1118, 1218, 1748, 63, 76, 222, 276, 467, 799, 1049, 1098, 1214, 1722, 1737, 1893, 1952, 1965, 2038, 2039, 2872
Gore, Charles, bp. of Oxford. 2060, 3442
Gore, Russell Daniel. 962
Gore-Booth, Eva. 419, 1049
Goreham, Norman J. 29, 1469
Gorell, Ronald Gorell Barnes. 962
Gorham, B W. 731
Gorham, B. Weed. 1865, 3289
Gorham, Donald Rex. 3168, 3800
*Gorman, F. E. 2788
Gorman, George Humphrey. 1674
Gorman, J. T. 1380
Gorman, Michael J. 3
Gorman, Ralph. 1985, 2029
Gorman, Robert. 827, 869
Gorman, Thomas Kiely. 823
Gornall, Thomas. 3697
Gornitzka, A. Reuben. 1005, 2213
Gornitzka, Odd. 323, 1572
Gorodetzky, Nadejda. 1028, 3214, 3699
Gorree, Georges. 3602
Gorres, Ida Friederike (Coudenhove) 763, 877, 2217, 2580, 3127
Gorresio, Vittorio. 2123
Gorrie, Peter Douglass. 2427, 2446, 2450, 3325
*Gorrie, Ron. 3289
Gorrie, Ron. 3293
Gortner, J Narver. 506
Gortner, Stephen A. 620
Gorton, Benjamin. 730, 1305
Goshen college, Goshen Ind. 2406
Goslin, Martin Leland. 474
Gosling, David L. 3485
Gosling, Justin Cyril Bertrand. 2338
Gosnell, Frank Lemuel. 2071
Gospel of Barnabas (Mohammedan) 174
Gospel of the Egyptians. English & Coptic. 1717
Gospel on truth. English. 3767
Goss, Charles Frederic. 2931
Goss, Cornelia A. 3127
Goss, Edgar M. 1094
Goss, Michael. 2858
Gosse, Edmund William. 3590
Gosse, Philip Henry. 282
Gosselin, Jean Edme Auguste. 2863
Gosselink, Henrietta E. (Plasman) 3185
*Gosselink, Marion G. 895
Gosselink, Marion Gerard. 894, 895, 907, 3047, 3352
Gosselink, Sara Elizabeth. 2489, 2005, 2360
Gossens, Bruno. 3307, 3420
Gossett, Bob. 626
Gossip, Arthur John. 2872, 2931
Gosson, Stephen. 3606
Gosvami, Satsvarupa Dasa. 3776
Gotaas, Mary C. 683, 2910
Gother, John. 787
Gotshalk, Dilman Walter. 2417
Gott, John. 1212
Gott, John Kenneth. 2245
Gottcent, John H. 211
Gottemoller, Bartholomew. 2872
Gottfried, Paul. 814, 2464
Gottheil, Richard James Horatio. 2118, 2329
[Gotthell, Richard James Horatio]. 1749
Gottlieb, Nathan. 1276
Gottschalk, Alfred. 3016
Gottschalk, Max. 3028
Gottschalk, Stephen. 1210
Gottschall, Amos F. 1100
Gottschall, Amos H. 3783
Gottwald, Norman Karol. 567, 598, 1154, 2090, 3439
Gotwald, William Kurtz. 1583
Gotz, Ignacio L. 1782

Gotze, Albrecht. 93
Goucher, John Franklin. 1109, 2482, 1553, 2519
Goudeau, Henri. 1266
Goudey, Ray Freeman. 3053
Goudge, Elizabeth. 1431, 1965, 3206
Goudge, Henry Leighton. 45, 233, 364, 1040, 3373
Goudriaan, T. 2375
Gouge, Thomas. 3630
Gouge, William. 403
Gough, Henry. 1211
Gough, James. 3127
Gough, John Bartholomew. 3596
Gough, John Francis. 1943
Gough, Michael. 1093
Gouker, Loice. 217, 626
Goulburn, Edward Meyrick. 638, 962
Goulburn, Edward Meyriok. 3071
Gould, Alfred Ernest. 1362, 2039
Gould, E. M. Lawrence. 1093
Gould, Edwin Miner Lawrence. 962, 2690, 3569
Gould, Ezra Palmer. 433, 435, 476
Gould, Frederick James. 2591, 910
Gould, George H[enry]. 3340
Gould, George Milbry. 2417, 3075
Gould, Hannah Flagg. 905
Gould, Josephine. 3170
Gould, Nathaniel Duren. 1210
Gould, Robert Freke. 1664
Gould, William. 2845
Gould, William Blair. 676, 962
Gould, William L. 1305, 2242
Goulden, Colin. 3278
Goulet, Denis. 1155
Goullart, Peter. 2584
Goulooze, William. 2995, 3049, 3540, 3677, 924, 1350, 3376, 3540
Gouraud, Alcime. 2580
Gouwens, Teunis Earl. 73, 186, 2504, 2931, 3066, 3672
Gove, Floyd Sherman. 3801
Gover, Nora E. 1854
Govinda, Anagarika [Brahmacari]. 2193, 2382, 2383, 3538
Gow, Alexander Murdoch. 2591
Gowan, Donald E. 529, 537, 2091, 2149, 2326, 2931, 3352
Gowen, Herbert Henry. 9, 462, 1262, 3059, 3093
Gowen, Vincent Herbert. 2544
Goyau, Georges. 2411
Goyen, William. 1965
Graaf, Arnold H de. 1128
Grabar, Andre. 85
Grabar, Oleg. 86
Graber, Edith. 3592
Graber, Joseph Daniel. 2554
Graber, Linda H. 2675
Grabill, Joseph L. 3741
Grabmann, Martin. 3693, 3696, 3693
Grabner-Haider, Anton. 772
Grabo, Carl Henry. 2833
Grabo, Norman S. 3590
Grabowski, Stanislaus J. 114, 1188, 1737
Grace, John Patrick. 1740
Grace, Melania. 656
Grace, Richard William. 424, 2254
Grace, William Joseph. 795
Gracey, Annie Ryder. 2458, 2488
Gracey, Lilly Ryder. 2492
Gracey, Samuel Levis. 3026
Grade, Chaim. 3015
[Gradie, Barbara]. 2190
Graeber, Isacque. 2077
Graebner, Alan. 2193
Graebner, Martin. 2246
Graebner, Theodore Conrad. 7, 100, 109, 117, 243, 605, 719, 1040, 1239, 1322, 1447, 1661, 2279, 2291, 2292, 3503, 3672, 3237
Graef, Hilda C. 63, 998, 1363, 2359, 2360, 2642, 2645, 2685, 3526, 3531, 3662
Graef, Paul Hubert. 3289
Graef, Richard. 998, 1985, 2872
Graefe, John Edward. 324
Graeff, Grace M. 1324
Graef, Hilda C. 2702
Graf, Arthur E. 2299, 2721, 2791, 3187, 3352
Graf, Arturo. 1427
Graf, Ernest. 2366, 3786
Grafe, Loyola. 2071
Graff, John Franklin. 3662
Graff, Mab. 3830
Graff, Myrtle S. 685
Graft, Arthur E. 3352
Grafton, Charles Chapman. 3191, 2957, 2964, 2967, 3010
Grafton, Mary. 1447
Grafton, Thomas H. 3756
Grafton, Thomas W. 732
Grafton, Warren. 1461
Gragg, Alan. 1635, 1788

Graham, Aelred. 670, 763, 1081, 3059, 3478, 3894, 3895
Graham, Andrew J. 1591
Graham, Balus Joseph Winzer. 144, 3051, 3127
Graham, Billy. 1754, 3540
Graham, Bothwell. 1104, 1380
Graham, Catherine. 454
Graham, Clara. 1919
[Graham, Constantius]. 3592
Graham, Daniel McBride. 1652, 2844
Graham, David. 3053
Graham, Edward Arthur Pancras. 1935
Graham, Eleanor. 1965
Graham, Eric. 1985
Graham, Finlay M. 2557
Graham, Frances W. 3833
Graham, Gerald S. 2320
Graham, Henry. 2900, 3127
Graham, Henry Grey. 289
Graham, Isabella (Marshall) 1525, 1591, 1592, 1754
Graham, J. 2525
Graham, James. 1742
Graham, James John. 803
Graham, James McMahon. 1475
Graham, James R. 2509, 3029
Graham, James Robert. 2928, 1401
Graham, Jerry. 1363, 1754
Graham, John. 931, 1754, 84, 2931
Graham, John E. 787, 811, 1616, 2402
Graham, John H. 1930
Graham, John William. 1675
Graham, Jonathan. 3790
Graham, Lloyd. 233, 1091
Graham, Lorah Harris. 1069
Graham, Lorenz B. 632, 1422, 1584, 2022, 2945
Graham, Margaret Althea. 3554
Graham, Mary Jane. 1089
Graham, Morrow C. 158, 1754
Graham, Paul T. 1379
Graham, Phyllis Norton (Buckle) 2260
Graham, Robert Bontine Cunninghame. 2772
Graham, Ronald William. 1472
Graham, Roscoe. 1693
Graham, Rose. 2579
Graham, Ruth Bell. 1754, 2388
Graham, W. Fred. 63, 728
Graham, William. 1484, 1541, 1826, 2031, 3150, 3340, 3413, 3870
Graham, William Creighton. 568, 2765
Graham, William Franklin. 42, 180, 299, 1066, 1412, 1557, 1754, 1829, 3012, 3051, 3089, 3232, 3662, 3885
[Grahame, James]. 3260
Grahame, Nigel B M. 1784, 2157
Graham's Church, Pine Bush, N.Y. 1379
Grainge, Julia. 1447
Grainger, James Moses. 270
Gram, Moltke S. 2164
Gramelsbach, Helen W. 229
Gramling, Roger M. 668, 2589
Grammer, Carl Eckhardt. 33, 3066
Grams, Betty Jane. 3845
Granberg, Lars I. 2338
Granbery, John Cowper. 63, 476, 2039
Grand, Ben Zion. 3581
Grand Rapids. Public library. 868
Grand united order of Toussaint L'Ouverture. Samuel unity. 2576
Grandi, Domenico. 809
Grandmaison, Leonce de. 3486
Grandmaison, Leonce de [Septime Leonce de Grandmaison]. 1965, 3222
Grane, Leif. 1, 1104
Granet, Marcel. 913
Granfield, Patrick. 807, 2768, 3611
Granger, Lucy Nichols. 3458
Granger, Muriel. 620
Granger, William Alexander. 1251
Granger, William H. 198
Grannan, Charles P. 309
Grannan, Dick. 3222
Grannis, J. Christopher. 437, 2809
Granskou, David M. 2025
Grant, Alexander. 80
Grant, Arthur James. 1852
Grant, Asahel. 1929
Grant, Brian W. 1412
Grant, Campbell. 50
Grant, Carter Eldredge. 2615
Grant, Charles T. 907
Grant, Clara Odessa (Winkler) 3018
Grant, Daniel R. 1085
Grant, Dave. 983, 3885
Grant, Delbert A. Stewart. 2500
Grant, Dorothy (Fremont) 795, 1363, 1516
Grant, Edward Donald. 2519
Grant, Elihu. 1582
Grant, Fern (Babcock) 1257
Grant, Frances Ruth. 2839
Grant, Frederick Cliffon. 2063, 2176

Grant, Frederick Clifton. 222, 289, 321, 347, 389, 394, 435, 476, 613, 638, 962, 1049, 1081, 1191, 1747, 1837, 1888, 1992, 2057, 2769, 3116, 3246, 3662, 3801, 347, 1083
Grant, Frederick W. 454, 3075
Grant, Fredrick Clifton. 1058
Grant, Heber Jeddy. 2609
Grant, Helen Hardie. 743
Grant, James Ralph. 464, 2034, 2721
Grant, John Webster. 734, 1043, 3731
Grant, Kenneth. 2312
Grant, Melville Rosyn. 756, 1671
Grant, Michael. 338, 929, 1028, 1807, 1965, 2656, 2658, 2667, 2797
Grant, Miles. 3503
Grant, Myrna. 2568, 2821
Grant, Neil. 753
Grant, Percy Stickney. 3059
[Grant, Richard Southall]. 1038
Grant, Robert McQueen. 2671, 206, 240, 337, 339, 409, 1020, 1191, 1717, 1718, 1732, 2010, 3451
Grant, Terry. 3685
Grant, Vernon W. 3100
Grant Watson, Elliot Lovegood, 1885. 2621
Grant, William Daniel. 1182
Grant, William Milne. 499, 1952
Grant, Wilson W. 171, 1756
Grantham, Frederick William. 2226
Grantham,Rudolph E. 1258, 2377, 3406
Grashoff, Raphaei. 2851, 3248, 3535
Grasset, Joseph. 2725
Grassi, Joseph A. 937, 1029, 1093, 2061, 2526, 2797, 3165
Grassian, Victor. 1535
Grasso, Domenico. 1118, 2039, 2168, 2900
Grasty, John S. 2310
Grasty, Sue Watkins. 3252
Gratacap, Louis Pope. 1888, 3225, 3240
Gratry, Auguste Joseph Alphonse. 1732, 2360
Gratsch, Edward J. 795, 1187
Gratton, John. 134, 2127, 3127
Gratus, Jack. 2414
Gratz, Rebecca. 1756
Graubard, Mark Aaron. 98
Graubart, David. 2114
Grauer, Otto Christopher. 3306
Grauman, Helen G. 319
Graupe, Heinz Mosche. 2146
Gravel, Louis Peter. 73
Gravely, William. 1790, 3424
Gravengaard, Niels Peter. 1112
Graver, Jane. 3843
Graves, A P. 30
Graves, Alfred C. 2189
Graves, Alfred Perceval. 3209
Graves, Allen Willis. 150, 1242
Graves, Anson Rogers. 665
Graves, Charles B. 1350
Graves, Frank Pierrepont. 2063
Graves, Frederick David. 3588
Graves, Harold K. 150
Graves, Henry Clinton. 1843, 1849, 3644
Graves, James F. 3468
Graves, James Robinson. 1427
Graves, Kersey. 1427, 1091, 1321, 1654
Graves, Lucien Chase. 3503
Graves, Richard W. 1447
*Graves, Robert. 1743
Graves, Robert. 389, 523, 1102, 2005, 2661, 2662, 2664
Graves, William Whites. 1791, 2169, 3272, 3417
Gravis, Peter W. 2455
[Graw, Alexander C]. 1756, 2427
Gray, Albert Frederick. 1118, 2602, 3644
Gray, Andrew. 1761, 2962, 3678
Gray, Archie W. 1557
Gray, Arthur Herbert. 1049, 1952, 962, 2809, 3393, 3442
Gray, Arthur Romeyn. 912, 2548, 63
Gray, Asa. 3075
Gray, Charles Montgomery. 2198
Gray, Charlotte Elvira. 650
Gray, Donald P. 1722
Gray, Douglas. 1518
Gray, Eden. 3588
Gray, Edna. 3127
Gray, Edward Dundas McQueen. 499
Gray, Elma E. 1420, 2594
Gray, Ernest Alfred. 2014
Gray, Fannie Smith. 2489
Gray, Francine du Plessix. 764, 1468
Gray, Frederick Turell. 1712
Gray, Gary M. 1199, 1292
Gray, George. 398
Gray, George Buchanan. 539, 542, 560, 3271, 3272
[Gray, George Seaman]. 3260
[Gray, George Zabriskie. 1054, 2338
Gray, Harriett S (Flora) 1952
Gray, Henry David. 449, 1788, 3662

Gray, Horatio. 1397
Gray, James. 2039, 2049, 3720, 2129, 3367
Gray, James Comper. 222
Gray, James M. 276, 645, 1049, 1757, 1952, 3352, 3503
Gray, James Martin. 222, 309, 605, 638, 645, 1033, 1438, 1695, 1829, 3319, 3662
Gray, John. 486, 555
Gray, Joseph. 1824
Gray, Joseph Howard. 302, 588
Gray, Joseph M M. 1592
Gray, Joseph M. M. 1058, 1301, 1597, 2751, 2900
Gray, Jullian Thorburn. 218
Gray, Louis Herbert, 1875-1955, ed. 2651
Gray, Marcus Lemon. 1324, 2457
Gray, Marjorie V. 1258, 1757
Gray, Mary (Tudor) 2725, 3685
Gray, Patricia (Clark) 3591
Gray, Robert A. 2388
Gray, Robert M. 1257
Gray, Ronald F. 962
Gray, Terence James Stannus. 710, 3891
Gray, Thomas. 1757
Gray, W. Arthur. 325, 1007
[Gray, W D]. 330
Gray, Walter G. 2783
Gray, William. 2957
Gray, William Forbes. 1162
Gray, William G. 2312, 2725
Gray, William Powell. 459
Graybeal, David M. 1603
Graybill, Ben W. 1665
Graybill, Jacob Paul. 2308
Graybill, Ronald D. 1133, 2557, 3811, 3812
Gray-Cobb, Geof. 2725
Graydon, H. 243
*Grayson, H. D. 2226
Grayson, William S. 2323
Grayston, Kenneth. 448
Graystone, Geoffrey. 1102, 1410
Grayum, H. Frank. 648, 3182, 3830
*Grayzel, Solomon. 2146
Grayzel, Solomon. 2077, 2088
Gt. Brit. Army. 3007
Gt. Brit. Army Council. 3007
Gt. Brit. Commissioners on seizure of church goods, 1552-1553. 1242
Great Britain. General Register Office. 1275
Gt. Brit. India office. Library. 2331
Great Britain. Legation (Holy See) 860, 1763
Great Britain. Ministry of Public Building and Works. 2584
Great White Brotherhood, Los Angeles. 1765
*Greater Chicago Sunday School Association (The) 3177
Greater New York federation of churches. 1131
Greathouse, Josephine A. 1438, 3295
Greathouse, William M. 467
Greatorex, Henry Wellington. 2968
Greaves, Richard L. 716, 3667
Grebanier, Bernard D N. 2469
Grebel, Konrad. 37
Greber, Johannes. 3503
Grech, Prospero. 343
Greebie, Sydney. 743
Greeley, Andrew M. 51, 764, 772, 787, 795, 805, 810, 827, 829, 831, 833, 867, 870, 874, 998, 1058, 1118, 1300, 1313, 1491, 1621, 1624, 1695, 1722, 2039, 2126, 2362, 2789, 2862, 2938, 2993, 3086, 3449, 3487, 3538, 3662, 3744, 3748, 3759, 3844
Greeley, Dana McLean. 3724, 3725
Green, Alan Singer. 2110
Green, Alberto Ravinell Whitney. 3272
Green, Andrew. 998, 3222
Green, Arthur. 2668, 3016
Green, Arthur Jay. 2411
[Green, Ashbel]. 2919, 2926, 3740
Green, Beriah. 1341, 3621
Green, Bryan S W. 962, 1218, 1565
Green, Celia. 77
Green, Celia Elizabeth. 77, 94
Green, Charles Earl. 1663
Green, Charles Sylvester. 2542, 3472
Green, Clifford J. 676
Green, Constance (McLaughlin) 3797
Green, Doyle L. 1965, 2602, 2609
Green, Edmund Tyrrell. 1159, 1632, 1159
Green, Edward Michael Bankers. 1829
Green, Edward Michael Bankes. 326, 991, 1295, 1573, 1659, 2039, 2051, 3196, 3289
Green, Elisha Winfield. 154
Green, Emma Martha. 3196
Green, Ernest L. 1290, 3391
Green, Forace. 2611
Green, H. Benedict. 440
Green, Harold Frederic. 879
[Green, Harriet L. 3503

Green, Harrison. 3462
Green, Harry L. 3053
Green, Henry Gordon. 1772
Green, Hollis L. 962, 1170, 1573
Green, I. M. 1220
Green, Jacob. 1201
Green, James Benjamin. 1829
Green, James Frederick. 1758
Green, James Leo. 543
Green, John Edgar. 3127
Green, John L. 10
Green, Joseph Franklin. 3662, 993, 1202, 3184, 3662
Green, Landis Knight. 95
Green, Louisa Meigs. 1641
[Green, M. P. 3791
Green, Margaret Joan. 1275, 1783
Green, Max. 2118
Green, Michael. 1427, 2051
Green, Miranda J. 1764
Green, Nelson Winch. 2602, 3431
Green, Oscar Olin. 1565
Green, Paul. 32, 1722, 3273
Green, Paul D. 190
Green, Peter. 397, 424, 613, 962, 1328, 1565, 1722, 1829, 1952, 1965, 2057, 2212, 2259, 3610, 3672
Green, Rachel W. (Cope) 2973
Green, Richard. 2422, 2428, 3803, 3806
Green, Robert W. 737, 1076, 3800
Green, Roger Lancelyn. 2219, 2661, 2662, 2664, 2665
Green, Ronald. 294
Green, Ronald Michael. 2163, 3100
Green, Rufus Smith. 2130
Green, Samuel G[osnell]. 1175
Green, Sarah Elizabeth. 3763
Green, Thomas Henry. 2872
Green, Victor Gerard. 1647
Green, Vivian Hubert Howard. 924, 2273, 2274, 2810, 3034, 3803
Green, Will S. 3271
Green, William Henry. 495, 523, 563, 1306, 1798
Green, William Mercer. 2752
Green, William S. 2048
Greenacre, Roger. 1837
Greenall, Raphael. 3036
Greenaway, George William. 83, 928
Greenbaum, Joseph L. 1322
Greenbaum, Leon. 1037
Greenbaum, Marvin. 1845
Greenberg, Betty Davis. 1623
Greenberg, Blu. 3838
Greenberg, Hayim. 2142
Greenberg, Joseph. 1790
Greenberg, Joseph Harold. 1790
Greenberg, Louis. 2102
Greenberg, Louis Stanley. 2219
Greenberg, Moshe. 516
Greenberg, Sidney. 2076, 172, 1350, 1354, 1811, 3371
Greenberg, Simon. 1539, 2108, 2142, 3896
Greenbie, Marjorie Latta (Barstow) 2497
Greenbie, Sydney. 743
Greenblatt, Robert Benjamin. 317
Greenburg, Dan. 1772, 2725
Greencastle, Ind. Archives of DePauw University and Indiana Methodism. 2431
Greene, Barbara. 2890
Greene, Carla. 2621, 2624
Greene, Carol. 494, 633, 900, 902, 2667
Greene, Carroll. 2626
Greene, E. G. 3833
Greene, Eli B. 1091, 1722
Greene, Ellis. 2766
Greene, Emma Beatrice (Freeman) 605
Greene, Evarts Boutell. 1150, 1772, 2534, 1150
Greene, Genard. 723, 749, 877, 1286, 1700, 2127, 3455, 3777
Greene, George A. 2476
Greene, George Francis. 2797
Greene, Gerard. 2136
Greene, Glen Lee. 154, 158
Greene, Gwendolen Maud (Parry) 781, 2777, 3478
Greene, John C. 1582, 3084
Greene, John Priest. 3782
Greene, Joseph K. 2558
Greene, Joseph Nelson. 2824, 2944
Greene, Joshua. 879, 1816, 2187, 2663
Greene, Katherine (Glass) 1722
Greene, Laura. 2081
Greene, Lemuel Austin. 3225
Greene, Maria Louise. 1346
Greene, Mary. 1772
Greene, Nancy Lewis. 3395
Greene, Oliver B. 326, 341, 440, 446, 467, 471, 1557, 1795, 1802, 2039, 3225
Greene, Reuben. 1792
Greene, Reynolds W. 2388, 3199
Greene, Richard Arnold. 2824
Greene, Richard Gleason. 1141
Greene, Robert. 59

Greene, Robert W. 2509
Greene, Ruth Altman. 1772, 1850, 2488
Greene, Samuel Harrison. 3554
Greene, Sara L. 799
Greene, Shirley Edward. 3253
Greene, Theodore Ainsworth. 2807
Greene, Wade. 2872
Greene, Walter Kirkland. 1128
Greene, Walter Lackey. 285
Greene, Wilda. 405, 983
Greene, William Batchelder. 721, 1892, 3471
Greenfeld, Howard. 1784, 1811, 2779
Greenfield, John. 2595
Greenfield, John, 1865. 2594, 2595
Greenfield, Robert. 3744
Greenfield, William. 1768, 1769
Greenhouse, Herbert B. 94, 2946, 2948
Greenish, Arthur James. 2634
Greenleaf, Jonathan. 2698, 2872
[Greenleaf, Mary Coombs]. 1772
Greenleaf, Richard E. 821, 1909, 1910, 3899
Greenleaf, Simon. 1574
Greenlee, Jacob Harold. 315, 351, 1770
Greenley, Andrew M. 805
Greenough, Chester Noyes. 887
Greenough, Jeanie Ashley (Bates) 1438
Greenough, John James. 1654
Greenslade, Stanley Lawrence. 1020, 1144, 3307
Greenspun, William B. 1044
Greenstein, Howard R. 3033
Greenstein, Joseph. 2778
Greenstock, David L. 1413, 2210, 2211, 2819
Greenstone, Julius Hillel. 1614, 2118, 2414
Greenup, Albert William. 2108
Greenville Baptist church, Leicester, Mass. 1772
Greenwald, Emanuel. 134, 1605, 2033, 2286, 2296, 2872, 3034
Greenwalt, Emmett A. 2243, 3701
Greenway, Alfred L. 448, 4373
Greenway, Leonard. 648, 951, 3885
Greenway, Roger S. 1278, 2492, 2537
Greenway, Walter Burton. 2029, 2213
Greenway, William Norman. 1513, 2039, 2563
[Greenwell, Dora] 1821-1880. 1845
Greenwich, Conn. Second Congregational church. 1336
Greenwood, Annie Savilla (Rorke) 2063
Greenwood, David. 114
Greenwood, David Charles. 47
Greenwood, Elma L. 1153
Greenwood, Francis William Pitt. 70, 1354
Greenwood, Theresa. 1011
Greenwood, William Osborne. 3078
Greer, Art. 1016
Greer, David Hummell. 2013, 2900
Greer, Edward C. 1404
Greer, Genevieve. 2482
Greer, Hazel McElhany. 1773
Greer, Virginia. 734, 1261, 1773
Greet, Brian A. 2251
Greet, Kenneth G. 3389
Greever, Walton Harlowe. 1167, 1251, 3442, 3677
Greeves, Frederic, 1903. 2791
Greg, Walter Wilson, 1875. 2359
Greg, William Rathbone. 1654
Gregerson, Jon. 2647
Gregg, Abel Jones. 1253, 3870
Gregg, Albert Sidney. 1167
Gregg, Darrell L. 289, 292
Gregg, David. 1525, 531, 1888, 2000, 2091, 2872, 2931, 3352
Gregg, James Bartlett. 1341
[Gregg, Jarvis]. 2091
Gregg, John Chandler. 3741
Gregg, Lucy Corliss (Phinney) 3195
Gregg, Pauline. 2229
Gregg, Richard Bartlett. 2638, 2738, 3389
Gregg, Robert C. 80, 2010
Gregg, Samuel. 2446
Gregg, Thomas. 3428
Gregg, Wilson. 1773
Gregor, Arthur S. 35, 3823
Gregorich, Joseph. 172
Gregorius. 90, 493, 2247, 2621, 2644, 3635, 3644, 1651, 2478, 3635
Gregorius, Abu al-Faraj. 497
Gregorius I, 540 (ca.)-604. 189, 1027, 1028, 3284
Gregorius i, the Great. 3676
Gregorius I, the Great, Saint, Pope, 540 (ca.)-604. 3676
Gregorius I. 189, 190, 3284, 189
Gregorius Nazianzenus. 1542
Gregorius Thaumaturgus. 2743
Gregorovius, Ferdinand Adolf. 2102
Gregory, Caspar Rene. 339
Gregory, Daniel Seely. 398, 943, 3672
Gregory, Dick. 318

Gregory, George. 1100, 1175
Gregory, Harold Davis. 155
Gregory, Harry William. 983
Gregory, Horace. 3206
Gregory, Isabella Augusta (Persse) 764, 1026, 2003
Gregory, J. 3009
Gregory, John. 3299, 3596
Gregory, John E. 1531
Gregory, Olinthus Gilbert. 1049, 1098
Gregory, Timothy E. 1196
Gregory, William. 2487
Gregory, William Henry. 40
Greif, Edward L. 3002
Greifer, Julian L. 1320
Greiwe, Nicholas Henry. 672, 856
[Grellet, Stephen]. 648, 1774
Grelot, Pierre. 233, 294, 2341, 2779
Gremillion, Joseph B. 774, 1136, 3451
Grendler, Paul F. 1910, 2937
Grendon, Felix. 888
Grenell, Zelotes. 950, 1239
Grenelle, Levi Osborn. 163, 1774
Grenet, Paul Bernard. 3696
Grenfell, Wilfred Thomason. 40, 962, 1094, 1447, 1592, 1774
Grenier, Mildred B. 1112
Grennan, Stanislaus. 2900
Grenshaw, James L. 555, 3237, 3297
Grensted, Laurence William. 104, 108, 962, 2997
Grente, Georges. 3265
[greppo, Claude]. 2738
Gresham, James Wilmer. 1865
Gresham, Perry Epler. 732, 3672, 3759
Gresham, Walter J. 1592
Gresley, William. 2900
Gressmann, Hugo. 122
Gresty, L. Buxton. 46
Grether, Frank. 1438
Greven, Philip J. 2978
Grew, Henry. 2039
Grewal, Singh. 3865
Grewen, Robert F. 1447, 1977
Grey, George. 2666
Grey, J. D. 2785
Grey, Lisa Mae. 2695
Grey, Pamela Wyndham) Grey. 3503
Greyer, Bertha Anna. 3503
Griaule, Marcel. 1473
Gribbin, Raymond William. 73
Gribbin, William. 3747
Gribble, Florence Alma (Newberry) 1774, 2558, 3127
Gribble, Florence (Newberry) 1774, 2558
Gribble, Leonard R. 2048, 3209
Gribbon, R. T. 1257
Gribetz, Louis Judah. 2118
Grice, Ethel (Harrison) 3858
Grice, Homer Lamar. 3763, 3764
Grider, Edgar M. 1298
Gridley, Albert Leverett. 204, 962, 2039
[Gridley, Amos Delos]. 1350
Gridley, Josiah A. 3503
Gridley, Willis Timothy. 674, 2701
Grier, Albert C. 1049
Grier, Gladys C. 1471
Grier, James Alexander. 3612
Grierson, Francis. 2638
Grierson, Herbert John Clifford. 2012, 3204, 210, 248
Griese, Nicholas Orville. 1322, 2341
Griesinger, Theodor. 1947
Grieve, Christopher Murray. 2182
Griffen, Jonathan. 2872
Griffeth, Ross John. 474, 3150, 3454, 1541
Griffin, Benjamin. 2941
Griffin, Christopher P. 2208
Griffin, Dale E. 936, 1317, 3176, 3180
Griffin, David. 1952, 2943, 3610
Griffin, Edward Dorr. 1341, 1692, 2310
Griffin, Edward M. 890, 1333, 1499
Griffin, Emilie. 1361, 1775
Griffin, Emory A. 1316
Griffin, Eunice. 14
Griffin, Frederick Porter. 1370
Griffin, G. Edward. 2125
[Griffin, George]. 104
Griffin, Graeme Maxwell. 3393
Griffin, James A. 2211
Griffin, John. 3559, 3818
Griffin, John Howard. 875, 1132, 1775
Griffin, John Joseph Patrick. 2357
Griffin, Joseph Aloysius. 185, 823
Griffin, Kathryn. 940, 983, 1775
Griffin, Martin Ignatius Joseph. 1500
Griffin, Mary Annarose. 1775, 2572
Griffin, Nancy Hearn. 48, 799
Griffin, Nathaniel Edward. 1888
Griffin, Richard Andrew. 3728
Griffin, Robert. 1775, 2388
Griffin, William R. 1792
Griffin, Zebina Flavius. 1116
Griffing, C. S. S. 3596
Griffis, Sue Randolph. 3858

Griffis, William Elliot. 2067, 2775, 77, 594, 696, 880, 1804, 1935, 2534, 2536, 2775, 3777
Griffis, William Elliott. 1935
Griffiss, James E. 2067, 2872
Griffis. Sue (Randolph) 3858
Griffith, Arnnhur Leonard. 1266
Griffith, Arthur Leonard. 63, 105, 180, 365, 384, 424, 448, 470, 576, 1004, 1119, 1243, 2007, 2247, 3367, 3731
Griffith, Earle Gordon. 142, 2785
Griffith, Francis Llewelyn. 1503
Griffith, George W. 3029
Griffith, George William. 1438
Griffith, Gwilym Oswald. 1952, 2797
Griffith, Harrison Patillo. 163, 2195
Griffith, Harry C. 983
Griffith, Helen Stuart. 920
Griffith, Jeannette. 3877
Griffith, Jeannette, pseud. 3877
Griffith, Jim N. 993
Griffith, John. 1675
Griffith, John Thomas. 159, 3234
*Griffith, Leonard. 2017
Griffith, Michael Joseph. 2366, 463
Griffith, Roland Edward. 3319
Griffith, William. 920
Griffith, William H. 1413
Griffith-Jones, Ebenezer. 1695, 2981, 3029
Griffiths, Bede. 1082, 1363, 1364, 1815
Griffiths, Brian. 3448
Griffiths, Harry. 1775, 2484
Griffiths, Iris. 1775, 2617
Griffiths, Kitty Anna. 5, 495, 627, 631, 632, 1920, 1931, 1996, 2022, 2792, 3258
Griffiths, Louise Benckenstein. 3453
Griffiths, Louise (Benckenstein) 2550, 3167, 3765
Griffiths, Michael. 1712, 2496
Griffiths, Michael C. 962, 1119, 2484
Griffiths, Olive M. 2917
Griffiths, Thomas Sharp. 158
Griffiths, William Edward. 3096
Grigassy, Julius. 765, 766, 842
Grigg, David Henry. 1940
Griggs, Edward Howard. 660, 2226, 2591, 660
Griggs, Henry Septimus. 3141
Griggs, Nathan Kirk. 1443
Griggs, Patricia. 3534
Griggs, William Charles. 2492
Grignon, de Montfort, Louis Marie. 2359
Grignon de Montfort, Louis Marie, 1673-1716. 2354, 3248
Grignon de Montfort, Louis Marie. 2352
Grigson, Geoffrey. 55
Grihyasutras. 3239
Grill, Charles Franklin. 2713
Grillmeier, Alois. 2010, 2011
Grillo, Francesco. 732
Grillo, Scipione. 1506
Grillot de Givry, Emile Angelo, 1870-1929. 2725
Grillot de Givry, Emile Angelo. 2725
Grimal, Jules Leo. 2388
Grimal, Julius Leo. 854, 3487
Grimal, Pierre. 2651
Grimaud, Charles. 2019, 2366
Grime, William. 1992, 3554
Grimes, Hezekiah. 3059
Grimes, Howard. 1201, 2191, 3784
Grimes, James Stanley. 3503
Grimes, Lewis Howard. 1849
*Grimes. Howard. 3175
Grimke, Angelina Emily. 3424
Grimke, Francis James. 2914
Grimke, Sarah Stanley. 2725
Grimley, John B. 2542
Grimley, Mildred M. 2543
Grimm, Carl Ludwig Wilibald. 1769
Grimm, Carl ludwig Willibald. 1769
Grimm, George. 702
Grimm, Harold John. 2274, 3034, 3041, 3471
Grimm, Jakob Ludwig Karl. 2660
Grimm, Jakoh Ludwig Karl. 2660
Grimm, Robert. 3393
Grimme, Jeannette. 1248
Grimmer, C A. 2946
Grimsby, Henry Peterson. 2279, 2283
Grimshaw, William Henry. 1667
Grimshawe, Thomas Shuttleworth. 3236
Grimsley, R W. 1251
Grimsley, Ronald. 2170, 3252
Grindal, Edmund. 1216, 1622
Grindon, Leopold Hartley. 2226
Grindstaff, Wilmer E 1912. 150, 952, 1565
Grinnell, Charles Edward. 1612
Grinnell, Isabel Hoopes. 2698, 3599
Grinnell, John C. 3503
Grinstein, Hyman Bogomolny. 2101
Griolet, Pierre. 2890
Gripkey, Mary Vincentine. 2360
Grisar, Hartmann. 2274, 3040
Grisdale, D. M. 3367

Grisez, Germain Gabriel. 664, 3100
Grisez, Wanda R. 2388
Grisinger, George F. 2950
Grislis, Egil. 1844
Grispino, Joseph A. 3484
Grisso, Lillian. 1438
Grissom, Mary Allen. 2680
Grissom, William Lee. 2432
Grist, William Alexander. 1965
Griswold, Alexander Viets. 800, 1775, 2890, 2891
Griswold, Asa. 2973
Griswold, Bert Joseph. 880
Griswold, Clayton T. 3018
Griswold, Erwin Nathaniel. 3749
Griswold, Hervey De Witt. 1813, 2839, 3776
Griswold, J T. 2423
Griswold, Latta. 871, 1523, 2960, 2969, 1523
Griswold, Rufus Wilmot. 1350, 2048, 2224, 3209
Griswold, Stephen Morrell. 693
Griswold, W. C. 184
Gritsch, Eric W. 1361, 2631, 3667
Gritter, George. 2059, 3479
Gritti, Jules. 2900
*Gritton, George R. 1380
Gritzmacher, Victor J. 3289
Grob, Jean. 3900
Grobel, Kendrick. 3524
Grodecki, Louis. 78
Groell, Clara. 1775, 2509
Groenhoff, Edwin L. 578, 2197
Groenings, James. 769, 2029
Grof, Stanislav. 1695, 1698
Groff, Warren F. 1845, 2039, 3213, 3616
Grogg, Evelyn Leavitt. 3177
Grolimund, Raphael. 854
Grollenberg, Luc. H. 207
Grollenberg, Lucas Hendricus. 233, 240, 338, 1029, 2039, 2797
Grollenberg, Lucas Henricus. 310
Grollman, Earl A. 895, 1774, 2782
Gromacki, Robert Glenn. 326, 409, 605, 1716, 3289, 3319, 3780
Gromet, Robert Y. 628
Gronbech, Vilhelm Peter. 3059
Gronniosaw, James Albert Ukawsaw. 3127
Groom, Arthur William. 1406
*Groom, M.S. 2465
Groom, M S. 476
Groom, William M. 638
Groom, William Marion. 46, 644, 3720
Groome, Thomas H. 935
*Groomer, Vera MacKinnon. 3458
Groot, A. de. 2477, 3293
Groot, Adrianus Dingeman de. 2707
Groot, Jan Jakob Maria de. 913
Groppi, Ugo. 2123
Gros Louis, Kenneth R. R., 1936. 210
Grose, Christopher. 2468
Grose, George Richmond. 177, 2509, 3059, 3127
Grose, Howard Benjamin. 30, 2063, 2515, 2527
Grose, John Adams. 645
Grosheide, Frederik Willem. 322
Gross, Arthur William. 620, 627, 894, 2027
Gross, Dávid C. 2146
Gross, Don H. 2409
Gross, Fred W. 1775
Gross, Heinrich. 539
Gross, John Daniel. 1324
Gross, John Owen. 2433
Gross, Joseph. 2258, 2388
Gross, Joseph B. 1654, 3116, 3410
Gross, Josiah. 2638
Gross, Kathryn Patricia. 8
Gross, Leonard. 1673, 2997, 1398, 1858
Gross, Mark. 3100
Gross, Mary Viola. 638
Gross, Mynette. 3783
Gross, Shelley. 2263
Gross, William Joseph. 1807
Grosse, Pointe, Mich. Grosse Pointe Memorial Church. 1965 Centennial Committee. 2918
Grossman, Herbert. 2943
Grossman, Louis. 2114
Grossmann, Louis. 3199, 2086
Grossmann, Reinhardt. 1672, 2738
Grossmann, Walter. 1496, 3024
Grossouw, Willem Karel Maria. 347, 376, 416
Grossu, Sergiu. 2821
Grosvenor, Benjamin. 1350
Grote, Augustus Radcliffe. 525, 1380
Grote, John. 2833
Grotius, Hugo. 108
Groton, Mass. First Baptist church. Sunday school library. 2953
Groton, Mass. First parish church. Ecclastical council, 1826. 1335

Groton, William Mansfield. 2251, 3177
Grottke, Theodore L. 3542
Grou, Jean Nicholas. 1429
[Grou, Jean Nicolas]. 1429, 1741, 1966, 2872, 3479
[Grou, Jean Nicolas]5. 3462
Grou, Nicolas. 1429
Groues, Henri. 759, 863
Grounds, Vernon. 63
Grounds, Vernon C. 611, 1107, 3233, 3442
Group for the Advancement of Psychiatry. Committee on Psychiatry and Religion. 2638
Grousset, Rene. 705, 1390
[Grove, Harriet (McCrory)]. 3503
[Grove, Helen Harriet] 1917. 1996
Grove, Henry. 2251
*Grove, Nadina K. 1348
Grover, Delo Corydon. 2836
Grover, Edwin Osgood. 1621
Grover, Eulalie Osgood. 633, 628
Groves, Charles Pelham. 12
Groves, Ernest Rutherford. 1374, 1603
Groves, Reginald. 2512
Groves, Wayne. 1091, 2021
Grow, Stewart L. 3287
Grozovsky, Ruvin. 3584
Gronbech, Vilhelm Peter. 3059
Grubb, Edward. 105
Grubb, Kenneth G. 3464
Grubb, Kenneth George. 1491, 2507, 2548, 3464
Grubb, Norman P. 2513, 3536
Grubb, Norman Percy. 2513, 3536, 3777, 3852
Grubb, Wilfrid Barbrooke. 1904
Grubbs, I[saiah] B[oone]. 1184
Grubbs, Isaiah Boone. 378, 467
Grube, Ernst J. 86
Gruber, Jacob W. 2560, 3075
Gruber, L. Franklin. 358, 1380, 1695, 2282, 3714, 1380
Gruber, Otto. 1413
Gruber, Ruth. 1584, 2762
Grudem, Wayne A. 323, 2949
Gruden, John Capistran. 756, 2019
Gruen, Ferdinand Bernard. 1649
Gruenewald, Max. 2142
Grueningen, John Paul von. 1127
Gruenler, Royce Gordon. 2039, 2174
*Gruman, Lawrence L. 1040
Grumbine, J[esse] C[harles] F[remont]. 1283
Grumbine, Jesse Charles Freemont. 2695
Grumbine, Jesse Charles Fremont. 1579, 2401, 3503
Grundtvig, Nicolai Frederik Severin. 2284, 3631
Grundy, John M. 463
Grundy, Julia Margaret (Kunkle) 127
Grunenfelder, Josef. 750
Gruner, Mark. 3575
Grunlan, Stephen A. 1074
Grunwald, Constantin de. 3256, 3285
Grunwald, Max. 2107
Grunwald, Stefan. 2725
Gruppe, Otto. 1766
Grusa, Jiri. 2872
Grusd, Edward E. 673
Gruss, Edmond C. 1038
Gruss, Edmond G. 2753
Grussi, Alphonse Maria. 2668
Grutzmacher, Richard Heinrich. 3780
Gruver, Kate Ellen. 1139, 3466
Gryglak, Michael A. 998
Grymeston, Elizabeth. 2388
Grzynkowicz, Wineva Montooth. 2204
Gtsan-smyon He-ru-ka, 1452-1507. 2194, 2461
Guard, Samuel R. 1612
Guardini, Romana. 990
Guardini, Romano. 114, 585, 759, 763, 863, 1104, 1119, 1528, 1592, 1659, 1722, 1966, 2012, 2247, 2323, 2369, 2872, 2891, 3248, 3262, 3299, 3615, 3782, 1104, 1659, 3782
Guarducci, Margherita. 2825, 3768
[Guay, Marcellin]. 1308
Guazzo, Francesco Maria. 1423
Gubernatis, Angelo de. 47, 2654
Gudebrod, George Herrmann. 233
Guder, Eileen L. 181, 324, 983, 1688, 3844
Gudnason, Kay. 586, 1112, 2626, 3856
Gudorf, Christine E. 2222
Guelich, Robert A. 3335
Guellouz, Azzedine. 2635
Guelluy, Robert. 998
Guenee, Antoine]. 514, 2114, 3786
Guenon, Rene. 1388
Guenther, Bernard W. 1156
Guenther, Herbert V. 2193, 2667, 2838, 3586
Gueranger, Prosper Louis Paschal. 3116

Guerber, Helene Adeline. 628, 920, 1521, 2206, 2360, 2651, 2665
Guericke, Heinrich Ernst Ferdinand. 1191
Guerin, Louis Francis. 1707
Guerin, Theodore. 3419
Guerini, Edmund W. 1888
Guernsey, Alice Margaret. 2527, 2546, 2548
Guernsey, Dennis. 983, 2338
Guernsey, Lucy Ellen. 2211
Guerra, Almerico. 1327
Guerra, Cyvette. 2135
Guerra, Vincent. 1255
Guerrant, Edward Owings. 389, 1565
Guerrette, Richard H. 772, 2789
Guerricus, d. ca. 1157. 863, 1114, 1266
Guerry, Emile Maurice. 1130, 2388, 3449
Guerry, Herbert. 657
Guerry, William Alexander. 3621
Guest, Edgar Albert. 962, 1119
Guest, Francis F. 726, 2198
Guest, Gilbert. 805
Guest, William. 1774
Guettee, Rene Francois Wladimir. 795
Guffin, Gilbert Lee. 543, 1288, 2785, 2829, 3672
Guggenheimer, Samuel H. 2836
Gugle, Sara F. 1913
Guglielmi, Francesco. 3127
Guhse, Herman Paul. 2891
Guibbory, Moses. 2114
Guibert, Joseph de. 1945, 2268, 3521
Guideposts. 962, 1014, 2808, 2872
Guidry, Mary Gabriella. 1777
Guignebert, Charles Alfred Honore. 1175, 1966, 408, 1102, 1175, 1192, 2091, 2149
Guigo II, d. 1188. 3487
Guigues du Chastel, 1083-1137. 2570
Guild, Caroline Snowden (Whitmarsh) 2891
Guild, Clara T. 3551
Guild, Daniel R. 463, 2809
Guild, Everet Emmett. 1654
Guild, Reuben Aldridge. 3427
Guild, Roy Bergen. 1049, 1369, 1619, 3470
Guilday, Peter Keenan. 742, 811, 827, 829, 835, 1516, 2057, 3401, 742, 827, 829, 1516
Guilding, Aileen. 419
Guilelmus, ca. 1130-ca. 1190. 1390
Guilfoile, Elizabeth. 3279
Guillaume, Alfred. 1779, 2564
Guillaume de Saint-Thierry, 1085 (ca.)-1148? 468, 776, 1601, 1734, 1735, 2388, 3487, 3636
Guillaume de Saint Thierry 1085 (ca.)-1148? 2388
Guillemain, Bernard. 1185, 1186
Guillemin, Henri. 1938
[Guillerand, Agustin]. 742
Guillerand, Augustin. 2872, 3487
Guillet, Cephas. 1865, 2174, 3537
Guillet, Jacques. 450, 1586, 2004, 2039, 2060, 3848
Guillois, Ambroise. 2811
Guimond, Jean Claude. 846
Guinan, Edward. 2712
Guinan, Michael D. 1377
el Guindi, Fadwa. 3059
Guindon, Andre. 3393
Guiney, Louise Imogen. 660, 733, 1947
Guiniven, John Joseph. 1162
Guinn, B F. 2931
Guinness, Henry Grattan. 1514
Guinness, Howard. 962
Guinness, Os. 1592
Guinsburg, Elena Fried. 2101
Guiraud, Jean. 1909
Guirdham, Arthur. 1586, 1673, 2409, 3055
Guirey, William. 1522
Guiteau, Charles Julius. 1069
Guitton, Georges. 1310
Guitton, Jean. 63, 114, 763, 1043, 1182, 2039, 2192, 2354, 2358, 2702, 2805, 2865, 3690, 3769
Guitton, Jean Marie Pierre. 763
Guizot, Francois Pierre Guillaume. 1049
Gula, Richard M. 947
*Gulas, William. 638
Gulczynski, John Theophilus. 3272
Gulesserian, Papken. 82
Gulick, Edward Vose. 2509, 2776
Gulick, John Thomas. 2482
Gulick, Joseph Isaac. 2931
Gulick, Orramel Hickley. 2524
Gulick, Sidney Lewis. 1175, 2516, 2807
[Gulielmus. 217
Gulley, Norman R. 1528
Gulley, Samuel Samson. 3292
Gullixson, Thaddeus Frank. 962, 1313, 2299, 3352
Gulovich, Stephen C. 766
Gulston, Charles. 290, 493, 1404
Gumayon Parado, Cornelio. 3265
Gumbiner, Joseph Henry. 2084, 3822

Gumbley, Walter. 1024, 3280
Gummere, Amelia (Mott) 1675, 1685, 3823, 1372, 1675
Gummere, Ricahrd Mott. 2232, 3333
-Gummermann, Basil. 1649
Gumpertz, Sydney Gustave. 2083
Gunabhadra, 9th century. 1932
Gundersen, Valborg J. 1778
Gunderson, Carl M. 1389
Gundry, D. W. 3142
Gundry, Patricia. 573, 2338, 3832, 3845
Gundry, Robert Horton. 376, 440, 475, 2326
Gundry, Stanley N. 2587
Gunkel, Hermann. 499, 523, 577, 1834
Gunn, Alexander. 2241
Gunn, George Sinclair. 578
Gunn, Giles B. 3071
Gunn, Harriette Bronson. 30
Gunn, Jack Winton. 1774
Gunn, John R. 163, 2388, 3340, 3341, 3352
Gunn, Richard L. 1009, 1778
Gunn, William Thomas. 1843
Gunnemann, Jon P. 3233
Gunnemann, Louis H. 3732, 3853, 3859
Gunnison, John Williams. 2602
Gunneweg, Antonius H. J. 500, 2819
Gunsaulus, Frank Wakeley. 2274, 3215, 1341, 1966, 2067, 2891, 2900, 3352
Gunson, Niel. 2543
Gunstoee, John Thomas Arthur. 2885
Gunstone, John Thomas Arthur. 174, 2811, 2816
Gunther, Bernard. 2379, 3019, 3585
Gunther, John 2. 2797
Gunther, Peter F. 2527, 3364
Gunton, Colin E. 1733, 1788
Gupta, Hari Ram. 3408
Gupta, Marie. 3823
[Gupta, Mahendra Nath] 1855-1932. 3020
Gupta, Nolini Kanta. 1709, 1814
Gupta, Yogi. 3867
Guptill, Nathanael M. 1058, 1295, 2783
Guptill, Roger S. 1378
Gurian, Waldemar. 809, 1707
Gurley, Leonard B. 1919
Gurley, Ralph Randolph. 2197, 2931
Gurney, Edmund. 2993
Gurney, Eliza Paul (Kirkbride) 3127
Gurney, Joseph John. 1681, 1683
Gurney, Oliver Robert. 1820
Gurney, Priscilla. 1865, 3127
Gurney, Sarah Gamzu (Gerstang) 298
Gurney-Salter, Emma. 1647
Gurnhill, James. 2836, 3545, 1579, 2836
Guru Bawa, Shaikh Muhaiyaddeen. 1733, 3479, 3542
GuruBawa, Shaikh Muhaiyaddeen. 3479
Gustafson, Cloyd V. 2864
Gustafson, Gus. 1007, 1778
Gustafson, James M. 943, 946, 949, 950, 1119, 2059, 3443
Gustafson, Janie. 983
Gustavson, Eric J. 2388
Guterman, Simeon Leonard. 2671
Gutfreund, Ed. 1202
Guth, Christine. 88
Guth, William Wesley. 3225
Guth, William Westley. 3479
Gutheim, James Koppel. 3371
Guthrie, Donald. 70, 222, 310, 368, 372, 374, 380, 398, 406, 444, 476, 1966
Guthrie, Dwight Raymond. 2309
Guthrie, Ernest Graham. 2059
Guthrie, Harvey H. 500, 578
Guthrie, Harvey H., Jr. 578
[Guthrie, Kenneth Sylvan]. 2232, 3206, 3479
Guthrie, Kenneth Sylvan. 2560, 3050
Guthrie, Thomas. 493, 518, 2015, 2025, 2931
Guthrie, W. K. C. 3059
Guthrie, William. 1361, 1779, 3289
Guthrie, William Keith Chambers. 1766, 2744
Guthrie, William Norman. 2057, 2248, 2969, 3479

Gutierrez, Gustavo. 2222, 3443
Gutierrez, Juan. 1779, 2222
Gutkind, Eric. 2138, 2837
Gutkind, Erich. 2138
Gutman, Ernest M. 1966
Gutmann, Joseph. 602, 2073, 3576
Gutstein, Morris Aaron. 2101, 2705, 2779
Gutteridge, Don J. 63
Gutteridge, Richard Joseph Cooke. 54, 1073, 1426
Guttmacher, Adolf. 233, 601
Guttmann, Alexander. 2150, 3032, 3584, 3585
Guttmann, Julius. 2841
Gutzke, Manford G. 1829

Gutzke, Manford George. 242, 276, 329, 345, 363, 403, 412, 416, 428, 433, 435, 436, 443, 446, 447, 468, 478, 510, 511, 517, 523, 542, 557, 559, 638, 983, 1431, 1557, 1779, 2051, 2554, 2872, 3289, 341, 454
Gutzke, Manfred George. 369
Gutzwiller, Richard. 2025
Guy, Harold A. 352, 389, 398, 414, 433, 435, 1530
Guy, Norman M. 1602
Guyard, Jules. 3503
Guyau, Jean Marie, 1854-1888. 3059
Guynn, Henry M. 962
Guyon, Jeanne Marie. 1456, 1779, 3127
Guyon, Jeanne Marie Bouvier de La Motte. 872, 1779, 3013
Guyot, Arnold Henry. 204
Guyot, Gilmer Henry. 315
Guyot, Gilmore Henry. 132
Guzie, Tad W. 795, 2039, 2251, 2811, 3262
Guzzardo, Albert C. 2320
Gwaltney, Leslie Lee. 63, 143, 151, 163, 2981
Gwatkin, Henry Melvill. 80, 1146, 1192, 1196, 1198
Gwilym, David Vaughan. 1829, 3341
Gwinn, Ralph A. 412
Gwynn, Aubrey Osborn. 111, 3860, 81, 779, 820
Gwynn, Denis Rolleston. 816, 817, 818, 867, 1920
Gwynn, Dennis Rolleston. 1474, 3822
Gwynn, Price Henderson. 3178
Gwynne, John Harold. 620, 1114, 1318, 2054, 2063, 2213, 2388, 2931
Gwynne, Walker. 496, 748, 1413, 2338, 1262, 1912, 3855
Gyanee, Bhagwan Singh. 2165, 3865
Gyldenvand, Lily M. 73, 181, 1447, 2247, 2388, 3842
Gysi, Lydia. 1779, 2717
Gzi brjid. English. Selections. 3699

H

Haag, Herbert. 3413
Haake, Alfred Paul. 1075
Haakonson, Reidar Pareli. 1434, 1438
Haan, Sheri Dunham. 620, 621, 632
Haar, Franciscus ter. 2341
Haarhoff, Theodroe Johannes. 3245
Haas, Harold. 2338
Haas, Harry. 2502
Haas, Harry Forest. 1654
Haas, James E. 3858
Haas, John Augustus William. 240, 1098, 1141, 1592, 1931, 2223, 3211, 3341, 651, 3078, 3644
Haas, LaVerne. 1328
Haase, William F. 1251
Habakkuk commentary. English & Hebrew. 529, 1779
Habel, Bernhard H J. 1547
Habel, Norman C. 521, 546, 548, 563, 2765, 3186, 3219, 3883
Haber, Francis C. 3084
Haber, Julius. 3897
Haberl, Franz Xaver. 883
Haberman, Frederick. 606, 1514
Habermann, Johann. 2297, 2685
Habershon, Ada R. 638
Habershon, Ada Ruth. 601, 2476
Haberstroh, Ernest. 3503
Habgood, John Stapylton. 3082
Habig, Marion A. 1515, 2401, 2688
Habig, Marion Alphonse. 856, 1025, 1027, 1641, 1644, 1646, 1647, 1648, 1649, 2318, 2546, 2716, 3376
Habig, Marion Alphonse [secular name: Jchn Alphonse Habig]. 856
Habig, Marion Alphonse [Secular name: John Alphonse Habig]. 1645, 856
Haboush, Stephen A. 199
Habs, Hans. 1928
Hachard, Marie Madeleine. 1779, 2693
Hack, Mary Pryor. 924
Hack, Roy Kenneth. 2835
Hackensack, N. J. First Reformed church. 3247
Hackensack, N.J. Third Reformed Church. 2688
Hacker, John G. 812
Hacker, Paul. 2280
Hacker, Tina. 2152
Hackett, Allen. 2891, 3276
Hackett, Ann. 3053
Hackett, Horatio Balch. 329, 3741
Hackett, James Dominick. 668
Hackett, Jessie S. 1069
Hackett, Stuart Cornelius. 3608
Hackett, Willis J. 1012
Hacking, Ian. 1426, 1578
Hacking, W. 1575, 3815

Hackleman, William E M. 3458
Hackman, George Gottlob. 3059
Hackman, Jenny. 2891
Hackman, Ruth Y. 2388
Hackney, Vivian. 2872
Hackwood, Frederick William. 920
Hackworth, Dorothy South. 2608
Hadas, Moses. 1807
Hadassah, the Women's Zionist
  Organization of America. 3896
Hadd, John R. 1582
Haddad, Anis Charles. 2762
Haddad, Robert M. 1108
Haddad, Yvonne Y. 1922
Haddal, Ingvar. 3803
Haddam House, inc. 3537
Haddan, Arthur West. 76, 1762
Haddelsey, Stephen Andrew. 2719
Hadden, Jeffrey K. 1154, 1332, 1576,
  3088, 3433
Haddock, Frank Channing. 1014, 1779
Haddock, John A. 1779
Haddock, Laura. 2591
Haddon, Alfred Cort. 2312
Haden, Eric George. 3809
Haden, Lila Carpenter. 2602
Hadfield, John. 1111
Hadfield, Percival. 2177
Hadidian, Allen. 1565, 3415
Haditjaroko, Sunardjo. 1812
-Hadler, Mabel Lyles]Jacques: 1892.
  2302
Hadley, Hazel (Mason) 3883
Hadley, Helen L. 3503
Hadley, Henry Harrison. 3534
Hadley, Lucile F. 1688
Hadley, Martha E. 1686, 2500
Hadley, Mass. 1337
Hadley, Samuel Hopkins. 2305, 2699
Haeckel, Ernst Heinrich Philipp August.
  2584
Haecker, Theodor. 2170
Haenchen, Ernst. 329
Haendler, Gert. 2278, 2791
Haendschke, Martin A. 3561
Haentzschel, Adolph Theodore Esaias. 63
Haring, Bernhard. 1845
Haering, Otto. 838
Haes, Paul de. 998
Haessly, Jacqueline. 1608
Haessly, Mary Gonzaga. 845
Haeussler, Armin. 1545
Hafer, Harold Franklin. 3851
Hafer, W Keith. 2985
Haffert, John Mathias. 889, 953, 1618,
  2251, 2359
Haga, Koshiro. 2188
Hage, Hyacinth. 1700
Hagedorn, Eugene. 1647
Hagedorn, Hermann. 3311, 660
Hagedorn, Ivan Henry. 214, 2299
Hagee, John C. 611, 1423, 1503
Hageman, Alice L. 1392
Hageman, Gustav Ernest. 553
*Hageman, Howard G. 1175, 1266, 2057,
  2911, 3049
Hagemann, Gerard. 733, 1906
Hagen, John Francis. 3352
Hagen, John Milton. 1431
Hagen, Kristofer. 2378, 2530
Hagenbach, Karl Rudolf. 1181, 3654,
  3668
Hagendahl, Harald. 116
Hagenmeyer, Heinrich. 1391
Hager, Wesley H. 1007, 1604
Hager, William Frederick. 983
Hagerstrom, Axel Anders Theodor, 1868-
  1939. 2838
Hagerty, Cornelius. 787, 1745, 3711
[Hagerty, Josephine]. 1312
[Hagerty, Thomas Edwin]. 1704
Hagg, G Erik. 2213, 3352
Haggai, John Edmund. 983, 1565, 2244,
  2808
Haggai, Tom. 3880
Haggard, Henry Rider. 3292
Haggard, Mildreth. 3736
Haggeney, Francis J. 443
Haggerty, Brian A. 1313
Hagglund, Bengt. 2161, 2280, 3654
Hagin, Fred Eugene. 2534
Hagin, Kenneth E. 1956, 3783, 3832
Hagmaier, George. 2780
Hagood, Lewis Marshall. 2442, 2460
Hagspiel, Brund Martin. 2573
Hagspiel, Bruno. 2545, 850, 2573
Hagspiel, Bruno Martin. 2573
Hagstotz, Gideon David. 3050, 3386
Hague, Dyson. 1213
Hague, William. 422, 443, 1069, 2678
Hahn, Celia A. 1290, 2774
Hahn, Dietmar. 1085
Hahn, Emily. 42
Hahn, Ferdinand. 1004, 2020, 2504, 3855
Hahn, Hans R. 939
Hahn, Herbert Ferdinand. 504
Hahn, Herbert William. 962, 1058

Hahn, Herman J. 3443
Hahn, Julius. 2077
Hahn, Theophilus. 1848
Hahn, Wilhelm Traugott. 3853
Hai ben Sheira d. 1038. 2375
Haich, Elisabeth. 3391, 3865
Haich, Elizabeth. 3588
Haig, William F. 454
Haigh, Christopher. 3039
Haigh, Madelon. 2652
Haigh, Winifred. 962
Haight, Anne (Lyon) 1849
Haight, Elizabeth Hazelton. 3590
Haight, Roger. 1750
Hail, A. D. 2534
Haile, Berard. 2676, 2677
Haile, Harry Gerald. 2274, 3037
Haile, Martin. 26
Haile, Peter K. 983
Hailes, David Dalrymple. 1196, 1710
Hailey, Homer. 419, 454, 559, 1272
Hailey, Orren Luico. 2029
Hailperin, Herman. 2116, 3456
Haines, Aaron W. 2452
Haines, Charles Reginald. 1108
Haines, Elwood Lindsay. 2971
[Haines, F. E. H. 2172
Haines, Frederick Henry. 3503
Haines, Gardner. 1557
Haines, J. Harry. 1565, 2433
Haines, Joseph Harry. 1155, 1780
Haines, Marie. 1677
Haines, Perry F. 376, 2039
Haines, Perry Franklin. 63
Haining, Peter. 1709, 3823, 3825
Hains, Edmont. 3720
Haipt, Maria Carl. 3449
Hair, Mary Scott. 1857
Hair, Paul. 2734
Haislip, Barbara. 2732
Haithcox, Henry C. 3150
Haithcox, Henry Clay. 1049
Haitz, Linn. 2500
Haiz, Danah. 633, 2130
Haker, Milton Albert. 1202, 2295
Hakes, J Edward. 3151
Hakim, George. 1966
Halbfas, Hubertus. 935
Halbleib, Augustus J. 772
Halbwachs, Maurice. 1484, 3109
Halcyone, Ruth. 3503
Haldane, Alexander. 1780
Haldane, Richard Burdon Haldane. 2417
Haldeman, I. M. 3503
Haldeman, Isaac Massey. 1033, 141, 638,
  643, 1033, 1050, 1635, 1939, 2055, 2157,
  2174, 2374, 2561, 2907, 2938, 3199,
  3319, 3321, 3341, 3503, 592, 638, 1058,
  2000, 3321
Haldeman-Julius, Emmanuel, 1889. 3023
Haldeman-Julius, Emanuel. 19, 2226
Hale, Apollos. 10, 2467
Hale, Clarence Benjamin. 1770
Hale, Edward Everett. 660, 1014, 2891,
  3204
Hale, Frederick. 1546, 2846
Hale, Heber Quincy. 1781
Hale, James Russell. 2712
Hale, Joe. 1007, 1565
Hale, John. 3827
Hale, Lucretia Peabody. 1350, 1915
Hale, Philip Leslie. 2358
Hale, Robert. 2010
Hale, Swinburne. 1423
Hale, William Hale. 1756
[Hale, William Pillsbury]. 1050
Halecki, Oskar. 861, 2749, 2852
Hales, E. E. Y. 810
Hales, Edward Elton Young. 809, 810,
  2123, 2850, 2861
Hales, Edward J. 952
[Hales, Jacob Cecil] 1864. 3028, 3127
Hales, John. 3630
Halevy, Elie. 2424
Halevy, Zvi. 2103
Haley, Everett Guy. 1693
Haley, Jesse James. 732
Haley, John Wesley. 2541
Haley, Joseph Edmund. 889, 2580, 3327
Haley, Mary Jane. 638
Haley, Philip S. 2988
Haley, Philip Sheridan. 2988
Haley, Thomas Preston. 1465
Haley, William D'Arcy. 1603
Halford, Francis John. 2524
Halfyard, Samuel Follet. 3199, 3519
Halfyard, Samuel Follett. 1069
Haliburton, Gordon MacKay. 1787
Halifax, Charles Lindley Wood. 2216
Halifax, Edward Frederick Lindley Wood.
  2166
Halifax, Joan. 3400
Halkett, John G. 2345, 2470
Halkin, Abraham S. 2765
Hall, Abraham Oakey. 1781
Hall, Adelaide Susan. 3573

Hall, Alexander Wilford. 1888, 3462,
  3752, 3753
Hall, Alvin Willard. 2051
[Hall, Amanda H. (Ferry) 1781
Hall, Angelo. 199
Hall, Angus. 2948, 3322
Hall, Archibald. 1119
[Hall, Arethusa] 1802-1891. 943, 2156
Hall, Arlene Stevens. 621, 3179
Hall, Arthur Crawshay Alliston. 747,
  1633, 1781, 1829, 2239, 2474, 2872,
  2985, 3151, 3223, 963, 1952, 2033, 2067,
  2213, 2354, 2960, 3600, 3714, 3780,
  2033
Hall, Arthur Jackson. 3167
Hall, Asa Zadel. 338, 2797, 2891
*Hall, B. Frank. 1356
Hall, Barnes M. 1284
Hall, Basil. 603
Hall, Basil Douglas. 1781
Hall, Bennie Caroline. 1438
Hall, Bolton. 963, 3199
Hall, Brian P. 953, 3151
Hall, Burton Allen. 2814
Hall, Cameron P. 2191
Hall, Charles A. M. 729, 3668
Hall, Charles Cuthbert. 1875, 105, 907,
  1050, 1058, 1695, 1745, 2012, 2024,
  3672
Hall, Charles Henry. 2981, 1699, 1837
Hall, Charles Mercer. 2388
Hall, Clarence Wilbur. 691, 2198, 2463,
  2487, 2488, 2496, 2955, 3292
Hall, Colby Dixon. 1038, 1467, 1780
Hall, David. 1680
Hall, David D. 53, 1858, 2791
Hall, Donald E. 3856
Hall, Dorothy. 664
Hall, Douglas John. 1058, 1119, 1154
Hall, Douglas T. 829, 2733
Hall, Edgar Francis. 638
Hall, Edward Brooks. 3795
Hall, Edward Hagaman. 2197, 2697, 750,
  2697
Hall, Edward Henry. 648, 1192, 1805,
  2771, 2804, 3727
Hall, Edwin. 134, 3644
Hall, Elizabeth Boyd (White) 3303
Hall, Ennen Reaves. 18, 318, 1303
Hall, Enos T. 678
Hall, Ernest Eugene. 2388
Hall, Francis J[oseph]. 3660
Hall, Francis Joseph. 118, 1040, 1381,
  1579, 1893, 2561, 3644, 946, 1119, 1528,
  1722, 1893, 2029, 3262, 3644, 3711
Hall, Frank Oliver. 3341
Hall, Frederic Thomas. 1423
Hall, Frederick. 280
Hall, Frederick Fairchild. 280, 1871, 3012
Hall, George F. 3393
Hall, George Franklin. 1565
Hall, George Fridolph. 426, 1966, 2213
Hall, George Marion. 214, 638
Hall, Gordon. 1358
Hall, Grace. 3280
Hall, Granville Stanley. 1952,
  2050
[Hall, Isaac] 1852. 1033
Hall, Isaac Hollister. 337
Hall, J.A. 139, 3075
Hall, J. Lincoln. 2463
Hall, Jacob Henry. 1749
Hall, James. 3231, 3100
[Hall, James Eugene] 1867. 2388
[Hall, James Hamilton. 3341
Hall, Jesse T. 1385
Hall, John. 214, 276, 2349, 3468, 1054,
  2587, 2900
Hall, John Andrew. 1729, 2286
Hall, John G. 1730
Hall, John Vine. 34
Hall, Joseph. 1017, 1216, 3297, 3630
Hall, Kathryn Evangeline. 2766, 3698
Hall, Kenneth. 1228, 3175
Hall, Kenneth F. 1722, 3175
Hall, King S. 2460
Hall, Lawrence Kingsley. 3871
Hall, Lewis R. M. 3896
Hall, Manley Palmer. 3586
Hall, Manly Palmer. 702, 1579, 1661,
  1665, 2312, 2638, 2643, 2725, 2732,
  2733, 3053, 3127, 3503, 3573, 42, 95,
  98, 318, 319, 706, 1661, 1778, 2379,
  2638, 2725, 2732, 3053, 3089, 3588
Hall, Manly Plamer. 2677
Hall, Marcia B. 1160, 1630
Hall, Mary. 665, 731
Hall, Mary Penelope. 1215
Hall, Mary (Ross) 3871
Hall, Mildmay Francis. 1224
Hall, Newman. 1341, 1358, 1748, 3218,
  3596, 3597
Hall, Newton Marshall. 1518, 310
Hall, Noel. 3410
Hall, Ona. 3720
Hall, Ralph J. 2913
Hall, Richard Walter. 613

Hall, Robert. 963, 1447, 147, 1304, 3422
Hall, Robert Benjamin. 1712, 2949
Hall, Robert King. 3871, 3874
Hall, Robert William. 3100
Hall, Roland. 1855
Hall, Rufus. 3127, 3128
Hall, Samuel. 2754
Hall, Samuel H. 648, 1272
Hall, Samuel Read. 3151
Hall, Theodore. 947
Hall, Thomas Alton. 900
Hall, Thomas Bartlett. 3504
Hall, Thomas Cuming. 347, 1781, 3059,
  3443, 3738, 397, 1758, 3738
Hall, Thor. 314, 983, 1058, 2046, 2718,
  2900
Hall, Trevor H. 1345, 1369
Hall, Vivian Anderson. 1848
Hall, William Henry. 1381
Hall, William Phillips. 1736
Hall, William Preston. 163
Hall, Winfield Scott. 3303
Hallack, Cecily Rosemary. 2208, 1649
Hallam, Arthur F. 347, 1491
Hallam, Robert Alexander. 493, 2621
Halle, Marie. 26
Hallenbeck, Edwin Forrest. 1101
Hallenbeck, Wilbur Chapman. 79, 1278,
  2475
Haller, Frederick John. 3878
Haller, Herald T. 1089
Haller, John George. 2886
Haller, William. 1508, 1637, 3007, 3008,
  3009
*Hallesby, O. 1358, 1906
Hallesby, Ole Christian. 963, 1094, 1347,
  1605, 1906, 2872
Hallesche nachrichten. 2294
Hallet, Mary (Thomas) 3839
Hallett, Garth. 497, 3070, 3830
Hallett, Paul H. 724, 795
Halley, Ebenezer. 3024
Halley, Henry Hampton. 285, 638, 285
Halliday, James F. 3885
Halliday, Jerry. 3128
Halliday, Samuel Byram. 3462, 3738
Halliday, William Reginald. 1196, 1470
Halligan, Francis Nicholas. 137, 2742,
  2811, 3265, 3266
Hallimond, John G. 2872, 2542
[Hallinan, Joseph]. 654
Hallinan, Paul J. 776, 3633
Hallinan, Paul John, 1911. 1205
Halliwell, Leo B. 690, 2505
Hall-Lindquist, Arthur. 2509
Hallman, Ernest Clifton. 2439
Hallman, Lillian C. 3331
Hallmark, Erma Elder. 2388
Hallock, Charles. 2843
Hallock, Constance Magee. 2500, 2502,
  2503
Hallock, E. F. 3373
Hallock, Edgar Francis. 2873
Hallock, Frank Hudson. 3503
Hallock, Gerard Benjamin Fleet. 122, 907,
  963, 1050, 1565, 1692, 1840, 2251, 2347,
  2721, 2891, 2963, 3352, 3364, 3373
[Hallock, Mary Angeline (Ray) Lathrop b.
  1810. 1401, 2621, 3457
Hallock, Robert Crawford. 3352, 3369
Hallock, Robert T. 3504
Hallock, William Allen. 1500, 2757
Hallowell, Benjamin. 1678
Hallowell, Harold Atlee. 1668
Hallowell, Richard Price. 1685, 1686,
  2371
Hallworth, T. 280
Halpenny, Edmund Wesley. 805
Halper, Benzion. 2331
Halperin, Don A. 3577
Halperin, Samuel William. 1147
Halpern, Abraham E. 3370
Halpern, Ben. 2104
Halpern, Harry. 2142
Halpern, Herman. 2946
Halpern, Salomon Alter. 3581
Halpert, Stephen. 194
Halphide, A[lvan] C[avala]. 2988
Halpin, Patrick Albert. 805, 68, 805, 895,
  2591
Hals, Ronald M. 589, 598, 1752
Halsey, Abram Woodruff. 2928
Halsey, Don Peters. 1888
Halsey, Leroy Jones. 214, 1772, 1966,
  2307, 3667
Halsey, Lewis. 158
Halsey, William M. 833, 3739
Halstead, St. John. 1693, 3373
Halstead, William Riley. 963, 3059, 1134
Halsted, Carolyn Spencer. 3504
Haltner, Robert E. 2388
Halvarson, Carl M. 154
Halverson, Alton C. O. 1624, 2538
Halverson, Delia Touchton. 938

Halverson, Richard C. 470, 924, 983, 1010, 1058, 1119, 1439, 2039, 2402, 2931
Halvorson, Andt L. 2213
Halvorson, Arndt L. 1005, 2900
Halvorson, John V. 1819
Halvorson, Lawrence W. 1255
Halvorson, Loren E. 1058, 1066, 1134
Halyburton, Thomas. 3128, 3294
Ham, Edward Everett. 1782
Ham, John W. 1557, 3341
Ham, Richard. 1204
Ham, Wayne. 474, 1175, 1233, 3116, 3218, 3680
Hamann, Henry Paul. 276, 347, 1040
Hamar, Paul A. 322
Hamarneh, Sami Khalaf. 524
Hambidge, Jay. 102
Hamblen, Emily S. 548
Hamblin, Jacob. 1782, 2602, 1689
Hamblin, Robert Lee. 1829
Hambly, Wilfrid Dyson. 3376
Hambrick-Stowe, Charles E. 3492
Hambrick-Stowe, Elizabeth A. 1301, 1782
Hamburg, N.Y. Saints Peter and Paul's German Catholic church. 823
Hamburg, Staatsarchiv. 2291
Hamby, Warren C. 180, 547, 2435
Hamel, Johannes. 2282
Hamelin, Leonce. 2811
Hamell, Patrick J. 1616, 3367
Hameln 1646-1724. 2100
Hamelsdorf, Ora. 3842
Hamer, George Thomas. 480
Hamer, Jerome. 175, 1249
Hamerle, Andreas. 772, 1904
Hamersma, John E. 3563
Hamerton-Kelly, R. G. 2896, 3458
Hamerton-Kelly, Robert. 476, 1731, 2063
Hames, J. M. 1107
Hamid, Abdul. 20
Hamidullah, Muhammad. 1921
Hamill, E. J. 2450
Hamill, Howard Melancthon. 3565, 210, 3554
Hamill, Robert H. 3537
Hamilton, Albert. 824
Hamilton, Alfred P. 1930
Hamilton, Arthur. 1629
Hamilton, Bernard. 1908
Hamilton, Charles V. 2680
Hamilton, Clarence Herbert. 704, 707
*Hamilton, Darlene. 3056
Hamilton, Edith. 568, 1995, 2652, 567, 568, 569, 1995, 2652, 1995, 2652
[Hamilton, Edward John] 1834-1918. 2922
Hamilton, Eleanor Meyer. 2975
Hamilton, Elizabeth. 963, 1802, 2762, 3539, 3603
Hamilton, Ephraim Nelson. 480
Hamilton, Floyd E. 951
Hamilton, Floyd Eugene. 63, 68, 380, 468, 3319
Hamilton, Franklin. 1392
Hamilton, Franklin Elmer Ellsworth. 1069
Hamilton, Harold Francis. 1102, 1192
Hamilton, Herbert Alfred. 2891
Hamilton, Horace Ernest. 1782
Hamilton, James. 304, 512, 963, 2544, 3817
Hamilton, James D. 2780
Hamilton, James Wallace. 963, 1094, 1722, 3352
Hamilton, Jay Benson. 1251, 2435
Hamilton, John Arnott. 1156, 1158
Hamilton, John Taylor. 2594, 2595
Hamilton, John William. 2435
Hamilton, Kenneth. 233, 1104, 1417, 1882, 2170, 2976, 3070, 3390, 3617, 3656, 3699
Hamilton, Kenneth Gardiner. 2542, 2976
*Hamilton, Lawrie. 3164
Hamilton, Lulu (Snyder) 903
Hamilton, Mary Agnes (Adamson) 2661
Hamilton, Michael Pollock. 2816
Hamilton, Neill Quinn. 63, 2039
Hamilton, Peter Napier. 3644, 3813
Hamilton, William. 135, 1350, 2417
[Hamilton, William] b. 1811. 1876
Hamilton, William. 423, 437, 444, 2323, 3617
Hamilton, William [Hughes]. 401
Hamilton, William Hughes. 3617
Hamilton, William Thomas. 565
Hamilton, William Wistar. 500, 1553, 1557, 1565
Hamilton-Merritt, Jane. 1782, 2382
Hamiton, Kate Waterman. 1592
Hamlett, Earl Gregory. 1592
Hamlett, James Arthur. 135, 1310
Hamlett, William Alexander. 2226
[Hamlin, Alfred Dwight Foster] 1855. 1782
Hamlin, Benjamin Baird. 3066
Hamlin, Cyrus. 2489
Hamlin, E. John. 545

Hamlin, Fred. 723, 2519
Hamlin, George Scoville. 2226
Hamlin, Griffith A. 409, 539
Hamlin, Howard Harley. 1598
Hamlin, Richard E. 3874
Hamlin, Richard Eugene. 3871, 3874
Hamline, Melinda. 3317
Hamm, Jack. 1010
Hamma, B[enjamin]. 915
Hamma School of Theology. 1862, 3830
Hammack, Martin Vanburen. 2417
Hammack, Mary L. 3178
Hamman, Adalbert. 139, 2778, 2883
Hamman, Gauthier Adalbert. 838, 2891
Hammann, Louis J. 3059
Hammarberg, Melvin A. 2211, 2891
Hammarsten, Fredrik. 2399
Hammel, W. W. 3289
Hammer, Bonaventure. 781, 770, 787, 3222
Hammer, Frank L. 3053
Hammer, Louis. 500, 523, 3371, 172
Hammer, Paul L. 645, 995
Hammer, Raymond. 1935
Hammerich, Louis Leonor. 449, 1630
Hammershaimb, Erling. 485
Hammes, John A. 947, 1107, 3249, 3526
Hammett, John. 2633
Hammill, John Leo. 1474
Hammill, Martina. 824
Hammill, Richard. 963
Hammond, Charles. 3504
Hammond, Charles Edward. 347, 351, 2237
Hammond, Charles Lyman. 233
Hammond, Edmund Jordan. 2446
Hammond, Edward Payson. 903, 1783
*Hammond, Emily V. 253
Hammond, Fletcher B. 678
Hammond, Guyton B. 3699
Hammond Incorporated. 283
Hammond, Joseph Roe. 400
Hammond, Laurence. 924, 1783
Hammond, Lily (Hardy) 2482
Hammond, Muriel. 752
Hammond, Nicholas Geoffrey Lempriere. 3301
Hammond, Peter. 1156
Hammond, Phillip E. 885, 3454
Hammond, Phyllis. 1992
Hammond, Sally. 2988
Hammond, William. 3294
Hammond, William Alexander. 3504, 1533
Hammond, William E. 1661, 2976
[Hamon, Andre Jean Marie] 1795-1874. 892
Hamon, Louis. 2766, 3575
Hampe, Johann Christoph. 3670
Hampshire, Stuart. 1535, 2474, 3472
Hampton, Charles. 1413
Hampton, Mack W. 1350, 1783
Hampton, William Judson. 1313
Hamson, Robert L. 384, 2071
Han, Nathan E. 1771
Hanahoe, Edward Francis. 879, 2794
Hanayama, Shinsho. 704
Hance, Gertrude Rachel. 2499
Hance, Irma Watson. 3287
Hancher, John William. 1498
Hancock, Golman Bluford. 2611
Hancock, Harry N. 1263, 1528
Hancock, Henry Nicholas. 2957
Hancock, Laurice Hicks. 2873
Hancock, Maxine. 984, 1372, 3845
Hancock, Sibyl. 122, 2711
Hancock, Thomas. 1046, 1681, 1686
Hancock, Tyre. 3072
Hand, Geoffrey Joseph Philip. 820
Hand, Henry. 2994
Hand, James Edward. 3313, 3078
Hand, John Raymond. 63, 3662
Hand, Thomas A. 114, 2885
Handel, Georg Friedrich. 1783, 2979, 3072
Handelman, Susan A. 3015
*Handford, Elizabeth Rice. 241
Handford, Thomas W. 3523
Handler, Andrew. 672
Handlin, Oscar. 2106
Handrich, Theodore Lewis. 204, 3078
=Handy, Edward Smith Craighill, 1892. 2859
Handy, Francis Joshua. 2049
Handy, Robert T. 1119, 1839, 2713, 3433, 3738, 3746, 3748
Handy, Susan Clark. 290
Handy, William Christopher. 2680
Hanes, Elias. 2323
Hanes, James Oscar. 1565
Haney, David. 1243, 1244, 1433, 1806, 2191
Haney, Herbert M. 1742
Haney, John Dearling. 2217
Haney, John Louis. 1307
Haney, Thomas R. 2388, 2891
Hanff, Helene. 3195

Hanfmann, George Maxim Anossov. 3303
Hanford, James Holly. 2469
Hanft, Frank William. 63
Hanifi, Mohammed Jamil. 1922
Hanish, Otoman Zar-Adusht. 1966
Hanke, Howard A. 310, 450, 1163, 3780
Hankey, Cyril Patrick. 3484
Hankey, Donald William Alers. 1050, 1119, 1784, 1952
Hankins, Joe Henry. 1557
Hanko, Charles William. 1058, 1549
Hanks, Billie. 1565
Hanks, Marion D. 1009, 2611, 3885
Hanks, Mrs. Casset. 3298
[Hanley,]. 80
Hanley, Boniface. 1025, 1645
Hanley, Elizabeth. 1565
Hanley, George W. 225, 294, 400, 2063
Hanley, Katharine Rose. 2417
Hanley, Mary Laurence. 2334, 2556
Hanley, May Carr. 2189, 3379
Hanley, Philip L. 2020
Hanley, Thomas O'Brien. 1147, 2363
Hanlin, Katherine Hale. 1626, 3716
Hanly, Daniel Aloysius. 1945, 2846
Hanly, J Frank. 1739
Hanly, James Frank. 1956
Hanly, Joanna P. R. 1784
Hann, Dorothy (Owen) 1315
Hann, George R. 1880
Hanna, Emmanuel Elkouri. 3225
Hanna, Frederick Watson. 3554
Hanna, James Arthur MacClannahan. 1761
Hanna, Mark M. 68
[Hanna, William] 1808-1882. 880, 1952, 1966, 2015, 2029, 2051, 3221
Hanna, William Herbert. 733
Hannah, Ian Campbell. 2576
Hannah, John. 108
Hannam, Thomas. 3373
Hannam, Wilfrid Lawson. 429, 1966
Hannam, William Simpson. 123
Hannan, Frederick Watson. 1565
Hannan, James C. 787
Hannan, Jerome Daniel. 3534
Hannay, James Ballantyne. 3059
[Hannay, James Owen] 1865. 218
Hannay, James Owen. 1942
Hanne, John Anthony. 2873
Hannemann, Manfred. 3041
Hannon, Ruth. 628, 779, 2711
Hannover, Nathan Nata. 915, 2102
Hannum, Harold Byron. 1202
Hannum, John A. 3330
Hanny, Diane. 1835
Hanousek, Mary Eunice. 3421
Hanover College, Hanover, Ind. Insitute, 1960. 1282
[Hansbrough, Lucinda Victoria (Blair) 670
Hanscom, Beatrice. 3206
Hansel, Robert R. 116, 963
Hansel, Tim. 984
Hansell, George H. 158
Hansen, Andrew. 3369
Hansen, Chadwick. 3827
Hansen, Harold A. 3823
Hansen, Ian Victor. 1247
Hansen, Klaus J. 1232, 2176, 2602
Hansen-Krening, Nancy. 2475
Hansen, Leonhard. 3247
Hansen, Lillian E. 2539, 2712
Hansen, Louis A. 3387
Hansen, Matthew. 3100
Hansen, Theodore. 2286
Hanser, Adolf T. 616
Hanser, Richard. 1981
Hansjakob, Heinrich. 1751, 1753
Hanson, Anthony Tyrell. 3662
Hanson, Anthony Tyrrell. 351, 372, 548, 1295
Hanson, Carl F. 736
Hanson, Cscar Conrad. 3885
Hanson, E. F. 3504
Hanson, E. Kenneth. 2034
Hanson, E.R. 3754
Hanson, Eric O. 816, 1144
Hanson, Helen Patten. 3151, 3165
Hanson, Irene. 1784
Hanson, James H. 1164, 3600
Hanson, John Wesley. 3754, 2587, 3116, 3752
Hanson, Joseph John. 935, 3168
Hanson, Melvin B. 963
Hanson, Miles. 3128, 3341
Hanson, Muriel. 734, 1546, 2388
Hanson, Muriel R. 3237
Hanson, Olaf. 1966
Hanson, Oscar Conrad. 963, 1565, 2299
Hanson, Paul D. 56, 544, 651, 3644
Hanson, Paul M. 2602
Hanson, R. P. C. 1473
Hanson, Richard Patrick Crosland. 68, 240, 800, 2793, 3644, 3651, 3707
Hanson, Richard S. 526, 606, 2174
Hanson, Stig. 342
Hanson, Virginia. 1431, 2165, 2638

Hanssler, Bernhard. 1119
Hanu, Jose. 787
Hanulya, Joseph P. 1487
Hanus, Francis. 1148, 1673
Hanville, Merrill F. 100, 3023
Hanzsche, William Thomson. 569, 2063, 1301, 2915, 2920, 2929, 3735
Hapgood, Charles H. 122, 2988
Happe, Allen. 1127
Happel, Ralph. 3286
Happel, Robert A. 526
Happold, Frederick Crossfield. 1059, 2379, 2638, 2873
Harada, Tasuku. 1935
Haran, John P. 2359
Haran, Menahem. 1944, 3855
Harand, Irene. 2099
Haraszti, Zoltan. 580, 581
Harband, Beatrice M. 1896
Harbaugh, Henry. 480, 1119, 1795, 1628
Harbaugh, Linn. 1785
Harber, Francis. 3520
Harbin, Albert Leroy. 405
Harbin, Elvin Oscar. 1166
Harbison, Craig S. 2157
Harbison, Elmore Harris. 1818, 3034
Harbour, Brian L. 163, 214, 614, 2341, 3415
Harbrecht, John James. 1251
Harbuck, Don B. 1592
Harcourt, Melville. 924, 1287, 1474
Harcourt, Richard. 807
Harcourt-Smith, Simon. 22
Harde,. Frederick E J. 3382
Hardeman, N. B. 3352
Hardeman, Nicholas Brodie. 1273, 1829
Harden, John Mason. 1540, 425
Harden, John William. 3580
Harden, Margaret G. 2916
Harden, William Dearing. 1654
Hardenberg, Friedrich. 1074
Harder, Geraldine Gross. 2186, 2407
Harder, Helmut. 1705
Harder, Leland. 2854, 3452
Hardesty, H.H. 3204
Hardesty, Nancy. 3834
Hardick, Lothar. 678
Hardie, Alexander. 8, 1579
Hardie, Alexander, 1841. 91, 105, 459, 1952
Hardie, Katherine E (Hall) 1785, 2505
*Hardie, Katherine Johnson. 313, 918, 1005, 2896
Hardin, Daniel C. 2493
Hardin, H. Grady. 2237, 3003
Harding, Arthur Leon. 1535
Harding, Barbara. 3470
*Harding, Charles E. 2417
Harding, Denys Clement Wyatt. 1519
Harding, Douglas Edison. 1371
Harding, Frederic. 2556
Harding Lectures. 1066
Harding, Michael J. 2738
Harding, Ralph Conrad. 1239
Harding, Thomas. 787, 2072, 2368
Harding, Ulla Earl. 3128
Hardinge, Leslie. 878, 1506, 1997, 3225
Hardinge, Miriam. 1431
Hardison, O. B. 844, 1478
Hardman, Harvey. 3141
Hardman, Oscar. 89, 963, 1751, 2051, 3221, 3853
Hardon, John A. 769, 778, 787, 1059, 1308, 1386, 1949, 2155, 2269, 2570, 2873, 2976, 3116, 3325, 3490, 3628, 3638
Hardwick, Charles. 3093, 3116
Hardwick, John Charlton. 3073
Hardwicke, Henry. 3504
Hardwig, Oswald Guido. 1860
Hardy, Alister Clavering. 1582, 1586, 3082, 3192
Hardy, Arthur Sherburne. 2679
Hardy, Edward Rochie. 2350, 1175, 1501, 2009
Hardy, Edwin Noah. 1128, 1256, 3813
Hardy, Ernest George. 3245
[Hardy, Henry]. 3322
Hardy, Henry Bascom. 1447
Hardy, James M. 3871
Hardy, Mary (Earle) 1486
Hardy, Ray Morton. 2695
Hardy, Richard P. 1028, 2126
Hardy, Ruth (Bocock) 2873
Hardy, Thomas John. 2997
Hare, Douglas R. A. 442
Hare, Edward. 1776, 3438, 3439
Hare, Eric B. 897, 1431, 1690, 1786, 2505, 2517, 3885
Hare, Julius Charles. 1836, 1829
Hare, Richard Mervyn. 1535
Hare, Robert. 3504
Hare, Walter Ben. 3841
Hare, William Hobart. 3143
Harenberg, Werner. 2046, 3651
Harford, Charles Forbes. 2558, 2848
Harford, John Battersby. 518

Harger, Grace B. 938
Hargis, Billy James. 1786
Hargis, Pauline. 3173
Hargreaves, John Henry Monsarrat. 433, 2028
Hargreaves, William. 23
Hargrove, Barbara W. 3086, 3868
Hargrove, Hubbard Hoyt. 2029, 3337
Hargrove, Katharine T. 1083
Hari Dass, Baba. 1786
Haring, Bermhard. 947
Haring, Bernahrd, 1912. 3769
Haring, Bernard. 998
Haring, Bernhard. 181, 947, 948, 998, 1154, 1565, 1786, 2039, 2223, 2343, 2361, 2389, 2570, 2712, 2811, 2873, 3012, 3265, 3327, 3410, 3769, 3774, 3851
Haring, Norris Grover. 2411, 3592
Haring, Theodor von. 943
Harington, Joy. 2005, 2804
Harison, Francis. 2057
Haristein, Jacob I. 2107
Harkavy, Alexander. 3863
Harker, Ahimaaz. 3885
Harker, Ray Clarkson. 3565, 1033
Harker, Ronald. 209, 1583
Harkey, Mittie Jane (Farrester) 218, 307
Harkey, Simeon Walcher. 1565, 2160, 3672
Harkins, George F. 2290, 3733
Harkness, Georgia Elma. 1059, 2981, 3740, 118, 233, 727, 943, 963, 1007, 1059, 1439, 1447, 1829, 2174, 2191, 2323, 2638, 2873, 2981, 3028, 3100, 3206, 3328, 3452, 3662, 3836, 533, 2073, 3328
Harkness, Gustavus. 565
Harkness, Robert. 1861, 3705
Harkx, Peter. 878
Harlan, David. 1757
Harlan, Rolvix. 1478, 932, 1374, 1478, 3443
Harland, Gordon. 2709
Harle, James C. 894, 1778, 3316
Harle, Wilfried. 175, 2739
Harless, Christopher Mayhew. 1033
Harless, Dan. 305
Harley, Fanny Louise (Middleton) 2409
Harley, Willard F. 984
[Harley, William Nicholas]. 2274
Harlow, Henry Addison. 2920
Harlow, Jules. 2207
Harlow, Louis Kinney. 1860
Harlow, Robert Edward. 2497, 2548
*Harlow, Samuel Ralph. 2988
Harlow, Samuel Ralph. 943, 2558, 2891, 2988, 3885
Harlow, Sarah Grace (Steves) Bear. 3762
Harlow, Victor Emmanuel. 1807, 1952, 2016
Harman, Carl H. 3885
Harman, Dan. 963, 991
Harman, Henry Martyn. 310
Harman, John William. 3100
Harman, Nathaniel Bishop. 3078
Harmelink, Herman. 1046, 3046, 3047
[Harmer, Earl W.]. 2615
Harmer, Lewis J. 3227
Harmer, Mary Fabian. 656
[Harmon, Andre Jean Marie, 1795-1874. 892
Harmon, Francis Stuart. 2698
Harmon, Joseph. 3554
Harmon, Nolan Bailey. 1693, 2426, 2440, 2453, 3672, 3734
Harmon, Robert Bartlett. 1710
Harms, Abraham John. 163, 938
Harms, John Henry. 1439
Harms, John W. 2891
Harms, Paul W F. 1829, 2900
Harms, Ray. 443
Harms, Theodor. 1783
Harnack, Adolf von. 330, 1192, 330, 429, 613, 1050, 1089, 1094, 1192, 1196, 1251, 1786, 2271, 2563, 2576, 3654
Harnack, Adolf von [Carl Gustav Adolf von Harnack]. 1192
Harnack, Carl Gustav Adolf von. 1192
Harnan, J. W. 25, 2734
Harned, David Baily. 73, 1751, 2323, 3100, 3782
Harner, Michael J. 1782
Harner, Nevin Cowger. 1259, 2550, 3151, 3554, 3662, 3048, 3564
Harner, Philip B. 419, 650, 2247
Harnett, Cynthia. 2569
Harney, Martin Patrick. 809, 1175, 1918, 1947, 2374, 2793, 3280
Harney, William J. 2960
Harnish, J. Lester. 963
Harnly, Joseph W. 463
Harold, H J. 3141
Harold, Preston. 2039
Harper, Albert Foster. 1823, 3176, 3179
Harper & Row, inc. 2152

Harper, Anna Ellis. 3277
Harper, Earl Enyeart. 1202
Harper, Elsie Dorothy. 3878
Harper, Howard V. 1239, 1407, 2953, 2964
Harper, Irene (Mason) 2490, 2530
Harper, James. 3809
Harper, Joan. 931, 1786
Harper, John C. 1786
Harper, John Murdoch. 940
Harper, Marvin Henry. 3322
Harper, Michael. 1238, 1246, 3479, 2264
Harper, Norman E. 940
Harper, Ralph. 1583, 2262
Harper, Redd. 1362
Harper, Robert Henry. 2538
Harper, Samuel Alain. 3123
Harper, Steve. 421
Harper, Thomas Norton. 2417
Harper, Wilhelmina. 1485
Harper, William A. 1088
Harper, William Allen. 1059, 1165, 1243, 2191, 3151, 3886
Harper, William Rainey. 485, 500, 567, 600, 3758
Harpster, Mary Julia. 1705
Harr, Wilber Christian. 2199, 2525
Harrah, Allegra. 2873
Harrah, Barbara K. 3722
Harrah, Charles Clark. 2920
Harral, Stewart. 10, 1251, 1165
Harre, Romano. 2417
*Harrell, Costen J. 1447, 2891
Harrell, Costen Jordan. 290, 1069, 1439, 1447, 1722, 1794, 2428, 3352, 3414, 3529
Harrell, Costen Jordon. 569
Harrell, David Edwin. 1464, 3232, 3324
Harrell, Irene B. 2389
Harrell, Irene Burk. 924, 984, 1439, 1599, 1605, 2389, 2625
Harrell, John Grinnell. 3161
Harrell, Mack. 3271
Harrell, Pat Edwin. 448
Harrell, William Asa. 141, 1156, 1167
Harrelson, Walter J. 500, 547, 1313, 3855
Harribance, Sean. 1786
Harrington, Bob. 1565, 1574, 1575
Harrington, Charles Henry. 1406
Harrington, Charles Kendall. 658, 2534
Harrington, Daniel J. 450, 1163
Harrington, Donald Szantho. 1986, 3352
Harrington, Fern. 2545
Harrington, Gardner. 3199
Harrington, Henry. 2811
Harrington, Janette. 2490
Harrington, Janette T. 1257
Harrington, Jeremiah C. 756
Harrington, Jeremy. 2039
Harrington, John B. 3100
Harrington, Karl Pomeroy. 1203
Harrington, M. 2366
Harrington, Paul V. 3844
Harrington, Ty. 3796
Harrington, Vernon C[harles]. 3542
Harrington, Vernon Charles. 3540
Harrington, Virginia S. 2676
Harrington, Wilfrid J. 310, 398, 409, 428, 454, 539, 644, 998, 2025, 2063, 2341, 3222, 3225, 3248, 3771
Harrington, William Daniel. 454
Harris, Arthur Emerson. 645, 578, 1069
Harris, Ben. 3059
Harris, Benjamin. 803, 2940
Harris, Bertha. 1786
Harris, Carl Vernon. 2743
Harris, Carlton Danner. 3818
Harris, Charles. 57
Harris, Charles A[lbert] E[dwin]. 1623
Harris, Charles D. 2784
Harris, Charles Nelson. 1078
Harris, Charles William. 1786, 3785
Harris, Cyril. 3537
Harris, Edward George. 3756
Harris, Edward Norman. 2164
Harris, Elizabeth. 2550
Harris, Erdman. 1722
Harris, Errol E. 2417, 3078
Harris, F. Donald. 3711
Harris, Fletcher. 2436
Harris, Franklin Stewart. 2602
Harris, Frederick Brown. 1447, 2208
Harris, Frederick Morgan. 214, 355
Harris, George. 3151, 1182
Harris, Gordon L. 1301, 2377
Harris, Grace Gredys. 3580
Harris, Groege Emrick. 3548
Harris, Hannah. 2086
Harris, Harrison Llewellyn. 1667
Harris, Horton. 351, 3535, 3717
Harris, Hugh Henry. 3886
Harris, Irving D. 1301, 3404
Harris, J. Henry. 3019
Harris, James. 2900
Harris, James Coffee. 2820, 3073
Harris, James Rendel. 316, 744, 1083, 1743, 3895, 315

Harris, Jane Bowerman. 3170
Harris, John. 120, 1381, 1439, 2320, 2519, 3313
Harris, John Andrews. 1098
Harris, John William. 3143, 3289
Harris, Lancelot Minor. 1469
Harris, Margaret J. 3767
Harris, Maria. 937
Harris, Marilyn. 1470
Harris, Marquis Lafayette. 963
Harris, Martha Anstice. 47, 1785
Harris, Mary Kathleen. 1508, 1802
Harris, Maurice Henry. 2088, 2092
[Harris, Miriam (Coles)]. 2211
Harris, Obadiah Silas. 3479
Harris, Paul. 638
Harris, Philip. 805
Harris, Philip B. 953, 3151
Harris, Pierce. 3744
Harris, Ralph W. 233, 451, 1717, 3720
Harris, Ray Baker. 1672
Harris, Richie. 3707
Harris, Robert Laird. 305, 2326
Harris, Roy. 313
Harris, S. L. 141, 953
Harris, Samuel. 952, 1740, 3608
Harris, Samuel Smith. 3443
Harris, Sara. 131, 2574
Harris, Stephen L. 310
Harris, Styron. 2177
Harris, Thaddeus Mason. 480, 1865
Harris, Thaddeus William. 1966
Harris, Theodore. 3065
Harris, Thomas Allen. 1255
Harris, Thomas Lake. 73, 525, 694, 695, 1447, 1787, 1865, 3141, 3199, 3303, 3352
Harris, Thomas Leonard. 3003, 3257
Harris, Victor. 1514, 1747
Harris, W[illiam] S[huler]. 3199
[Harris, W] Prebyterian. 3373
Harris, Walter Stewart. 1038
Harris, Walter Stuart. 2517
Harris, William. 2603
Harris, William Coe. 1169
Harris, William G. 3292
Harris, William J. 3170, 3766
Harris, William Logan. 2449, 3423
Harris, William Richard. 2725
Harris, William Shuler. 963, 3341, 397, 2063
Harris, William Thomas. 2402
Harris, William Torrey. 1800, 2242
Harris, Zellig Sabbettai. 733
[Harrison, Alexina (Mackay) 2308, 2558
Harrison, Ann M. 1787, 2501
Harrison, Barbara Grizzuti. 1365, 1787, 1941
Harrison, Bob. 1132
Harrison, Charles George. 2706
Harrison, Charles H. 1290
Harrison, Deloris. 2172
Harrison, Edith (Ogden) 632
Harrison, Ernest Wilfrid. 1059, 1066
Harrison, Eugene Myers. 1565, 2482
Harrison, Eveleen. 621, 628, 897, 900, 1981, 3839
Harrison, Everett Falconer. 329, 343, 409, 419, 422, 1966
Harrison, Frank Mott. 716
Harrison, Frederic. 1385, 2864, 2865, 3255
Harrison, Frederick. 270
Harrison, G T. 3428
Harrison, George Bagshawe. 533, 716
Harrison, George Leib. 3089
Harrison, George W. 1168
Harrison, Grace Elizabeth (Simon) 3803
Harrison, Grant Von. 3719
Harrison, Hall. 1577, 2168
Harrison, Harrold D. 1301, 1658
Harrison, Helen (Bagby) 125
Harrison, Jane Ellen. 2661, 88, 1395, 1766, 2656, 2661
Harrison, John A. 1490, 3241
Harrison, John Fletcher Clews. 2464
Harrison, Jonathan. 1855, 2180
Harrison, Joshua H. 3225
Harrison, Leon. 3370
Harrison, McVeigh. 222, 2271, 2399, 57
Harrison, Margaret Wynne. 42
Harrison, Marie (Lemoine) 275, 963
Harrison, Martin. 795
Harrison, Max Hunter. 2584
Harrison, Norman B. 199, 419, 2055, 2125, 2873, 2937
Harrison, Norman Baldwin. 233, 365, 381, 454, 472, 648, 963, 1514
Harrison, Norvell. 3078
Harrison, Paul Mansfield. 30
Harrison, Paul Wilberforce. 2538
Harrison, Percy Neale. 446, 2858
Harrison, Robert. 697
Harrison, Roland Kenneth. 335, 486, 533, 539, 546, 557, 1410, 2678
Harrison, Ross. 2738
Harrison, Russell F. 2259

Harrison, Tank. 1007
Harrison, Traverce. 963, 1553, 1565
Harrison, William. 963
Harrison, William Henry. 2952, 3404
Harrison, William K. 3319
[Harrison, William Pope]. 135, 2039, 2541, 2557
Harrisonburg, Va. Baptist church. 1275
[Harrisse, Henry] 1829-1910. 3215
Harrisville, Roy A. 124, 287, 318, 435, 468, 2162, 2213, 2299, 2864, 3352
Harrity, Michael. 3540
Harrold, Charles Frederick. 2702, 2703
Harrold, Robert. 3520
Harrop, Clayton K. 412
Harrop, G. Gerald. 570, 1506
Harrow, Katharine. 2642
Harrowar, David. 3714
Harrsen, Meta Philippine. 18, 2331
Harry, Carolus P. 3041
Harry, Carolus Powel. 3034
Harsha, David Addison. 1472, 1956, 2028, 2039, 3813
Harsha, John W. 3295
Harsha, William Justin. 561
Harsha, William Willett. 3644
Harshaw, Ruth (Hetzel) 2662
Harshbarger, Luther H. 1083
Harshman, Charles William. 3702
Harshman, S[amuel] R[ufus]. 371
Harshman, Samuel Rufus. 963, 1557
Hart, Annie. 187, 1484
Hart, Arthur Tindal. 1291, 1765, 2806, 3255
Hart, Burdett. 2004
Hart, Edward LeRoy. 1787, 2609
Hart, Elizabeth Haven. 1836, 2315, 2355
Hart, Evanston Ives. 1787, 2509
Hart, Henry Martyn. 3199
Hart, Henry St. John. 539
Hart, Hornell Norris. 963, 3100
Hart, John Seely. 2247, 2656
Hart, Joseph. 1860
Hart, Joseph Coleman. 1158
Hart, Lee O. 1253
Hart, Lewis Alexander. 1083
Hart, Oliver James. 2310
Hart, Patrick. 2412
Hart, Ray L. 3225
Hart, Roderick P. 3747
Hart, Roger. 3823
Hart, Samuel. 1592, 2960
Hart, Samuel L. 1535
Hart, Thomas N. 2343, 2810
Hart, W Neill. 1608
Hart, Walter Osgood. 1047
Hart, William. 1787
[Hart, William] 1718-1784. 1334, 3810
Hart, William E. 2988
Hart, William J. 1840
Hart, William John. 1871, 1875
Hart-Davies, David Ephraim. 523
Harte, Thomas Joseph. 1136, 2768
Hartenberger, John Henry. 1692, 2299
Hartfeld, Hermann. 1110
Hartfield, Hermann. 169, 3455
Hartford, Asylum Hill Congregational Church. 1787
Hartford. Congregation Beth Israel. 1787
Hartford, Conn. First Baptist church. 1269
Hartford, Conn. Second church of Christ. 1210
Hartford, Ellis Ford. 2591
Hartford. First Baptist church. 1819
Hartford. First church of Christ. 1787
Hartford, Ione Pratt. 903
Hartford seminary foundation. 953, 1788
Hartford Seminary Foundation. Case Memorial Library. 1788
Hartford theological seminary, Hartford, Conn. 1182, 1788, 3332, 3612, 3614
Hartford theological seminary, Hartford, Conn. Alumni association. 1341, 2865
Hartford seminary foundation. 1788
Harth, John Phillip. 1481
Hartill, Percy. 105, 1722
Hartland, Edwin Sidney. 2652, 2822
Hartley, Al. 1367, 1788
Hartley, Catherine Gasquoine. 753
Hartley, Cecil B. 2157
Hartley, Elizabeth Lyman. 2856
Hartley, Fred. 1403, 3886
Hartley, Gertrude. 3179
Hartley, Issac S[mithson]. 3047
Hartley, Kenneth R. 1204
Hartley, William. 558
Hartley, William B. 182
Hartman, A Lincoln. 3295
Hartman, Charles. 2358
Hartman, David. 2623, 2841
Hartman, Doug. 984
Hartman, Gertrude. 621
Hartman, Joseph. 3504
Hartman, Levi Balmer. 1699, 3529
Hartman, Louis O. 2493, 3116
Hartman, Marvin J. 1439

Hartman, Olov. 9, 63, 2210
Hartman, Rachel. 1485
Hartman, William Emory. 2441
Hartmann, Arnaulf. 111
[Hartmann, Emil Clifford]. 963
Hartmann, Franz. 674, 2725, 674, 2312, 2725
Hartmann, Helen Louise. 3526
Hartmann, Marcus Kristian. 3289
Hartmann, Nicolai. 2738
Hartnagel, James Bruno. 787
[Hartnett, Mary Vincent. 2305
Harton, Frederic Percy. 89
*Harton, Sibyl. 2873
Harton, Sibyl. 18, 1413, 3280
Hartranft, Harry Carpenter. 459
Hartridge, Reginald Alfred Rupert. 1241
Harts, Harry Lawson. 49
Hartshorn, Chris B. 1050
Hartshorn, Chris Benson. 327, 678, 1196, 3216, 3217
Hartshorn, Leon R. 1009, 1231, 1232, 3428, 3831
Hartshorne, Charles. 49, 1722, 1739, 2673, 2832, 3608, 3609, 3813
Hartshorne, Hugh. 2411, 2591, 3151, 3189, 3560, 3562, 3853, 3858
Hartshorne, Marion Holmes. 2976, 3078
Hartsock, Donald E. 3212
Hartsoe, Colleen Ivey. 3839
Hartsough, Palmer. 3562
Hartsough, Palmer, and Fillmore, J[ames] H. 3554
Hartt, Frederick. 1629
Hartt, Julian Norris. 1074, 1565, 3621, 3668, 3757
[Hartt, Rollin Lynde] 1869. 1251, 1952
Hartwell, Herbert. 175
Hartwell, Ray. 2873
Hartwich, Ethelyn Miller. 3317
Hartwick seminary, Brooklyn. 3189
Hartwick seminary conference on the social mission of the Lutheran church, Princeton, N.J., 1944. 1138
Hartzel, Jonas Hazard. 60
Hartzell, Jacob Serenus. 2213
Hartzler, Arlene. 1865
Hartzler, Henry Burns. 894, 2587
Hartzler, Jacob. 3732
Hartzler, John Ellsworth. 2405, 3662
Hartzler, Jonas Smucker. 1543, 2502
Hartzog, William Benjamin. 2060
Harva, Uno. 2659
Harvard Colloquium, Harvard University, 1964. 3761
Harvard university. Class of 1863. 1812
Harvard University. Dept. of Church History. 1175
Harvard University. Divinity School. 555, 1584, 3614, 3621
Harvard University. Library. Houghton Library. 1788, 2331
Harvey, A. E. 2008
Harvey, Alexander. 1952
Harvey, Anthony Ernest. 343, 386, 409, 420, 2068
Harvey, Cyrus W. 1829
Harvey, Edwin Lawrence. 3341
Harvey, Hezekiah. 3672
Harvey, John Hooper. 751, 753
Harvey, Joseph. 184, 1658
Harvey, Lawrence F. 819
Harvey, Robert. 1871, 1945, 2268
Harvey, Rudolf John. 787, 2389
Harvey, Theodore Lee. 1288
Harvey, Van Austin. 241, 1819, 3617, 3638
Harvey, William Wirt. 1966
Harvey, Youngsook Kim. 3400
Harwell, Jack U. 952
Harwood, Anne. 1033
Harwood, Carl Clinton. 243
Harwood, Thomas. 2454
Hasbrouck, Kenneth Edward. 2165
Hasbrouck, Stephen. 1033
Hascall, Daniel. 3662
Haschek, Paul. 18
Hase, Karl Alfred von. 706
Hase, Karl August von. 1175, 1966
Hasegawa, Seikan. 2867
Hasel, Gerhard F. 500, 552, 598, 3214
Haselbarth, Hans. 943
Haselden, Kyle. 1059, 1131, 1853, 2548, 2900
Hasell, F. H Eva. 2506
Haselmayer, Louis August. 43
Haserodt, E V. 2302
Haserot, Francis Samuel. 2738
Hash, John A. 233, 1431
Hashagen, August. 2263
Hashim, Hassan A. 1924
Haskell, Arnold Lionel. 3284
Haskell, L. 1981
Haskell, Stephen N[elson]. 1401
Haskell, Stephen Nelson. 650, 1401, 3720
Haskell, Thomas Nelson. 2931, 3819
Haskew, Robert Jesse. 1838

Haskin, Dorothy C. 3462
Haskin, Dorothy (Clark) 1014, 924, 928, 1014, 1166, 1362, 1439, 1447, 1604, 1714, 2490, 2502, 2538, 2623, 2873, 3012
Haskin, Dorothy (Clarks) 3842
Haskin, Sara Estelle. 2457, 2543
Haskins, James. 2233, 2681, 3140, 3787, 3823
Haslehurst, Richard Stafford Tyndale. 1212, 2812
Hasler, August. 2850, 2862
Haslett, Samuel B. 3554
Hasley, Lucile. 1364
Hasluck, Frederick William. 1084, 1926
Hass, Lonnie, Headley. 2527
Hassakari, Gottlieb Christopher Henry. 2286
Hassall, Arthur. 1639, 2376
Hassam, Roswell H. 1913
Hassan, Bernard. 787
Hassan, Farooq. 1923
Hassard, John Rose Greene. 1851, 2850
Hasselblad, Marva. 2540
Hassell, Cushing Biggs. 1175
Hassell, Richard Burton. 3870
Hassenger, Robert. 831
Hasseveldt, Roger. 1119
Hasskarl, Gottlieb Christopher Henry. 943, 1381, 3178, 1421, 1487, 1580
Hassold, Ernest Christopher. 3311
[Hasted, Frederick] b. 1793. 3631
Hastings, Adrian. 426, 787, 813, 873, 1066, 1073, 1200, 1202, 2497, 2507
Hastings, Cecily. 613, 795, 2355, 3265
Hastings, Edward. 448
Hastings, George T. 3023
Hastings, H.L. 3292
Hastings, Horace Lorenzo. 3199, 201, 2981, 1981, 378, 2981
Hastings, Ila. 3573
Hastings, James. 214, 222, 243, 244, 615, 907, 2807, 2873
Hastings, Macdonald. 1945
Hastings, Mary Louise Cutter (Jones) 3165
Hastings, Maurice. 3808
Hastings, Robert J. 180, 1324, 1439, 1840, 2389, 3186, 3529
Hastings, Stella Flowers. 3865
Hastings, Thomas. 915, 1203, 1865
Hastings, Thomas Samuel. 3758
Hastings, William Thomson. 2829
Haswell, John Hirst Winn. 2762
Hatch, Alden. 40, 2123, 2805, 2852, 2853
Hatch, Arthur Elmer. 2174, 2948
Hatch, Benjamin Franklin. 3100, 3504
Hatch, Carl E. 692, 3711
Hatch, Charles E. 3868
Hatch, Clarence W. 3529
[Hatch, David Patterson]. 1059
Hatch, David Patterson. 2725
Hatch, Edward Wingate. 2068
Hatch, Edwin. 498, 529, 1192, 1240, 1241
Hatch, F. L. 1888
Hatch, Mildred M. 638
Hatch, Nathan O. 3213
*Hatch, P. C. 2174
Hatch, Susan L. 302
Hatch, Verena Ursenbach. 1206, 1231, 3853
Hatch, William Henry Paine. 315, 1592, 1884, 2330
Hatch, William Whitridge. 2618
Hatcher, Eldridge Burwell. 1790, 2900
Hatcher, William Eldridge. 1936, 2072, 2638, 3672
Hatchett, Marion J. 1204, 1213, 1523, 2210, 2234, 2957
Hater, Robert J. 805, 1257
Hatfield, Edwin Francis. 131, 1023, 1860, 1878, 2916
Hatfield, Louis Duane. 3145
Hatfield, Mark O. 1347
Hathaway, David. 612, 1790, 2942
Hathaway, [Evangeline] and Dunbar, [Mary Elizabeth]. 2766
Hathaway, Lulu. 2490, 3186
Hathaway, Michael. 662
Hathaway, Richard D. 2156, 3730
Hathcoat, Horace Carlton. 1127
Hatler, Grace. 2546
Hatley, Roy O. 3298
Hatt, Harold E. 3225, 3227
Hatton, Eleanor Beard. 621
Hatzfeld, Adolphe. 114
Hau Hoo. 3238
Hauben, Paul J. 1910
Hauck, Allan. 1262
Hauck, Gary L. 3678
Hauck, Paul A. 2780
Haudenschield, Charles Robert. 1033
Hauerwas, Stanley. 886, 943, 946
Haugaard, William P. 1220, 1759
Hauge, Hans-Egil. 2272
Haugg, Donatus. 3248
Haugh, Laura Esther. 638

Haugh, Richard. 2844, 3714
Haughey, John C. 1316, 1829
Haught, John F. 3100
Haughton, Edward. 3522
Haughton, Faith. 1014
Haughton, James. 1836
Haughton, Rosemary. 372, 628, 631, 811, 1094, 1282, 1358, 1502, 1586, 1592, 1735, 2323, 2335, 2338, 2621, 2797, 2997, 3170, 3280, 3389, 3690, 3845, 3145
Haughwout, Lefferd, Merle Alexander. 2482, 2957
Hauret, Charles. 310, 578, 1383
Haury, David A. 2406
Hausdorff, David Meyer. 565, 2145
Hause, Alvin George. 2163
Hauser, Conrad Augustine. 3043, 3189
Hauser, Raymond C. 3236
Hauser, Richard J. 3487
Hausherr, Irenee. 2020, 2873
Hausherr, Melchior. 3269
Hausherr, Walter M. 1243
Haushalter, Walter Milton. 105, 1040, 1494, 1747, 3792
Hausmann, Bernard Andrew. 842
Hausmann, William John. 175, 1505
Hausmann, Winifred Wilkinson. 1016
Havelock, Eric Alfred. 2835, 2853
[Haven, Alice (Bradley)] 1827-1863. 2211
[Haven, Charlotte Maria]. 963
Haven, Erastus Otis. 3128
Haven, Gilbert, bp. 3590
Haven, Gilbert. 1350
Haven, Jason. 694, 1504, 2742
Haven, Margaret J. Cushman. 645
Haven, Richard. 1307
Haven, Robert Marshall. 2891
[Haven, Samuel] 1771-1847. 1419, 2195
Havener, Ivan. 613
Havens, Joseph. 2997
Haverfield, William M. 155
Haverford College. 2131
Haverford College. Library. 1677
Havergal, Frances Ridley. 2873, 939, 963, 1439, 1447
Havergal, Maria Vernon Graham. 3401
Havergal, William Henry. 2736
Haverstick, Alexander Campbell. 2964, 3564
Haverstick, John. 2978
[Havey, Francis Patrick, 1864. 2029, 2033, 3222
Havighurst, Robert James. 3161
Haviland, Emma (Hillmon) 2499
Haviland, Frank Wood. 523
Haviland, Mae F. "Mrs. Foster L. Haviland." 1871
Havlik, John F. 233, 993, 1565
Havner, Vance. 1447, 146, 163, 214, 462, 984, 1350, 1431, 1439, 1447, 1557, 1791, 2389, 3128, 3225, 3352
Havner, Vance Houston. 1447
Havran, Martin J. 872
Hawaii. University, Honolulu. College of Education. 2942
Hawaiian evangelical association. 1551, 2524
Hawaiian mission centennial. 2524
Hawaiian mission children's society. 2524
Hawaiian Mission Children's Society, Honolulu. 2524
Hawaiian mission children's society, Honolulu. Library. 1791
Haweis, Hugh Reginald. 409, 2374
Haweis, Thomas. 2259
Hawes, Gordon K. 1488
Hawes, Joel. 91, 1337, 3431
[Hawes, Louisa. 1791
Hawes, Louisa (Fisher) 1692, 1791
Hawk, Charles Nathaniel. 163
Hawken, Paul. 2732
Hawker, Beatrice. 3128
Hawker, Robert. 963, 1439
Hawkes, Ernest William. 2735
Hawkes, Jacquetta (Hopkins) 3546
Hawkesworth, Alan Spencer. 1893
Hawkins, Ann Ballew. 3013
[Hawkins, Anthony Hope] 1863. 3128
Hawkins, Denis John Bernard. 948, 2418, 2833, 3608
Hawkins, Henry. 2362
Hawkins, Henry Gabriel. 2457
Hawkins, John Caesar. 3578
[Hawkins, John Dewey]. 2680
Hawkins, O. S. 993
Hawkins, Quail. 900
Hawkins, Robert Martyr. 372
Hawkins, William. 1218
Hawkins, William George. 1791
Hawkridge, Emma. 3116
Hawks, Edward. 45, 2307, 2830, 2976
Hawks, Francis Lister. 1222
Hawley, Bostwick. 2209
Hawley, Carrie Moss. 3128

Hawley, Charles Arthur. 489, 519, 533, 2736, 2950
Hawley, Emily Carrie. 2524
Hawley, Gloria Hope. 3835
Hawley, John Savage. 3116
Hawley, Thomas De Riemer. 2242, 3027
Hawley, Zerah Kent. 1344
Hawthorn, Horace Boies. 1888
Hawthorne, James Boardman. 1050
Hawthorne, Joseph M[atthew]. 2915
Hawthorne, Julian. 1326
Hawthorne, Marion Olive. 1100, 1246, 3151, 3179, 597, 3765
Hawthorne, Nathaniel. 2656, 2658, 2810, 2856, 2952
Hawthorne, Paul. 2617
Haxton, Jennie Norman. 3173
Hay, Charles Augustus. 1743
Hay, Charles E. 2274
Hay, Charles Ebert. 2274
Hay, Clyde Lemont. 894, 3189
Hay, David M. 579
Hay, Denys. 820, 1929
Hay, Edward G. 1547
Hay, Ella H. 1494
Hay, Florence E. 625
Hay, George. 1161, 2476
Hay, Kathleen. 1966
Hay, Malcolm Vivian. 2111, 3315
Hay, Marian Margaret. 2675
[Hay, William. 2231
Hayakawa, Sessue Kintaro. 3894
Hayburn, Robert F. 1205, 1206
Haycraft, Maud Adelaide. 2482
Hayden, Amos Sutton. 1465
Hayden, Dorothea (Hoaglin) 5
Hayden, Edwin V. 615, 3373
Hayden, Eric. 3373
Hayden, Eric W. 615, 1565, 2213, 3523
Hayden, Francis John. 907
Hayden, Frank. 63, 2226
Hayden, Horace Edwin. 29
Hayden, M. P. 3832
Hayden, Richard A. 2544
Hayden, Samuel Augustus. 140
Hayden, William Benjamin. 451, 3504
Haydn, Hiram Collins. 35, 2191, 2484
Haydon, Albert Eustace. 1283, 3059, 3116, 3122
Haydon, Mary F. 638
Hayes, Anthony. 1692
[Hayes, B. M. 2949
Hayes, Charles Harris. 1015, 73
Hayes, Charles Wells. 2975
Hayes, Christine. 2725
Hayes, Doremus Almy. 180, 367, 2051, 2247, 2264, 2797, 3335, 338, 383, 414, 429, 1040, 1768, 2126
Hayes, Edward J. 763, 795, 941, 948
Hayes, Edward L. 421, 1431
Hayes, Eva Fatima (Morris) 2509
Hayes, Everis Anson. 3341
Hayes, Florence (Sooy) 2500, 3838
Hayes, Francis D. 893
Hayes, G. H. 105
Hayes, Harold Vincent. 1033
Hayes, James M. 787, 2771, 3416, 787
Hayes, James T. 95
Hayes, Joel S. 1737
Hayes, John Alexander. 1313
Hayes, John Haralson. 310, 498, 504, 584, 2010
Hayes, Norvel. 1585
Hayes, Patrick Joseph. 3821
Hayes, W. M. 1792
*Hayes, Wanda. 616, 3128
Hayes, Zachary. 1381, 2011
Hayford, Jack W. 2873
Haygood, Atticus Greene. 2048
Hayley, John William. 1699
Haymaker, Edward McElwain. 756
Hayman, Carol Bessent. 1112
Hayman, Eric. 3853
Hayne, Coe. 2527
Hayne, Coe Smith. 155, 686, 2527, 2540, 2810
Haynes. 2055
Haynes, Carlyle Boynton. 233, 234, 606, 1428, 1514, 1528, 1565, 1601, 2051, 2054, 2055, 2133, 2465, 2900, 2981, 3260, 3319, 3504, 3756, 1288
Haynes, Carlyle Boyntou. 1514
Haynes, Dudley C. 142
Haynes, Edmund Sidney Pollock. 1888
Haynes, George Emerson. 1810
Haynes, James. 2432
Haynes, Leonard L. 2682
Haynes, Louise Marshall. 3206
Haynes, Marjorie. 3170
Haynes, Nathaniel Smith. 1464, 1966, 1464
Haynes, Robert Talmadge. 2033
Haynes, Willard Calvin. 2757
Haynes, Wilson Albinus. 222
Hays, Agnes Dubbs. 3833
Hays, Brooks. 142, 151
Hays, Calvin Cornwell. 2927

Hays, Edward M. 2389
Hays, Hoffman Reynolds. 3109
Hays, Marion Prather. 1792, 2389
Hays, Rhys W. 2
Hays, Wilma Pitchford. 2793
[Hayward, Aaron S.]. 3504
Hayward, Alan. 1737
Hayward, Charles E. 1251
Hayward, Edward Farwell. 184
Hayward, Fernand. 2862, 1908
Hayward, Helen (Harry) 3128
Hayward, J. K. 3504
Hayward, John. 3322
Hayward, John F. 2221
Hayward, Otis Madison. 454
Hayward, Percy R. 2896
Hayward, Percy Roy. 1202, 3012, 3151, 3883
Hayward, Robert. 562, 2402
Hayward, William Leete. 1332, 2307
Haywood, Garfield Thomas. 3227
Haywood, Harry Le Roy. 1661, 1662, 1672, 1662, 1666
Haywood, Harry LeRoy. 2643
Haywood, Kate Harper. 1253
Haywood, Marshall De Lancey. 667

Hazard, Caroline. 3777, 1685
Hazard, Christopher Grant. 1592
Hazard, Marshall Custiss. 290, 225, 1992, 3554
Hazard, Paul. 1503
Hazard, Rowland Gibson. 2418
Hazard, Thomas Benjamin. 3128
Hazard, Thomas Robinson. 672, 3504
Hazeltine, Katharine S. 1807
Hazelton, Anne. 912
Hazelton, Robert Morton. 1675
Hazelton, Roger. 1104, 225, 410, 963, 1104, 1734, 1737, 1741, 1952, 2873, 2981, 3707
Hazelwood, Lola. 2547, 3765
Hazen, Barbara Shook. 634, 1405, 1406
Hazen, Edward Adams. 3289
Hazlitt, Henry. 1535
Hazo, Samuel, John. 875
Hazzard, Lowell Brestel. 2428, 3188, 3764
Heacock, William Stockton. 1109
Head, David. 900, 2211, 2873, 2891
Head, Eldred Douglas. 163, 347, 2006
Head, Jean. 135
Head, Joseph. 3053
Head, Robert F. 1199
Headlam, Arthur Cayley. 376, 1040, 1220, 1966, 2798, 3644
Headland, Isaac Taylor. 2520
Headley, Joel Tyler. 294, 2351, 2626
Headley, John M. 1187, 2274
Headley, Phineas Camp. 1405, 1783, 2813, 3228, 3839
Heagle, David. 1416, 1582, 2591, 3319
Heagle, John. 998
Heagney, Harold J. 2131
Heagney, Harold Jerome. 21, 882, 2131
Heal, Felicity. 666
Healer, Carl T. 1673, 2389
Healey, Frances G. 3682
Healey, Francis G. 3621
Healey, John B. 2815
Healey, Joseph. 12, 816
Healey, Robert M. 1939, 3189
Healy, Christopher. 3128
Healy, Edwin F. 3265, 948
Healy, Emma Therese. 675, 3831
Healy, John. 2375
Healy, Kilian J. 1429
Healy, Martin J. 1175
Healy, Mary Lanigan. 1608
Healy, Patrick Joseph. 2820
Healy, Thomas C. B. 787
Heaney, John J. 1592, 1850, 2562, 3001
Heaps, Isabel (Warrington) 3839
Heard, Albert F. 2750, 3022, 3256
Heard, Gerald. 180, 1439, 1675, 2067, 2247, 2673, 2873, 3100
Heard, Richard Grenville. 410
Heard, Teddy Moody. 984
Heard, William Henry. 13
Hearing, Bernhard. 943
Hearley, John. 1147, 2635
Hearn, Charles Aubrey. 3595
Hearn, Florence. 1734
Hearn, Florence Conner. 939
Hearn, Janice W. 984, 1688
Hearn, Lafcadio. 1935
Hearn, Raymond. 687
Heath, Carl. 3322
Heath, Douglas H. 1683
Heath, Frank Stowe. 3464
Heath, Lilian M. 995
Heath, Lou Mishler. 1736
Heath, Robert George. 1304
Heath, Sidney Herbert. 920
Heath, Thomas Richard. 3610
Heathcote, Charles William. 2294, 3151
Heather. 3823

Heatn, Eric William. 2950
Heaton, Ada Beth. 3173
Heaton, Alma. 2720
Heaton, Charles Henry. 3662
Heaton, Charles Huddleston. 915, 1209
Heaton, Eric William. 497, 571, 2093, 2950
Heaton, EricWilliam. 486
Heaton, Kenneth Lewis. 2591
Heaton, Ronald E. 1672
Heatwole, Lewis James. 2404
Heazell, Francis Nicholson. 1389
Hebard, John J. 3066
Hebblethwaite, Brian. 943, 1745, 3616
Hebblethwaite, Peter. 762, 781, 866, 1119, 1319, 2126, 2770, 2805
Heber, Reginald. 1221, 1222, 1829, 1873, 3143
[Heberling], Alma, 1856. 2711
Hebert, Albert J. 772, 877
Hebert, Arthur Gabriel. 500, 1155, 1295, 2097, 2255
Hebert, Robert F. 1521
Hebly, J. A. 2955
Hebrew-Christian conference, Mountain Lake Park, Md., 1903. 2535
Hebrew education society of Philadelphia. 1796, 2086
Hebrew free school association of the city of New York. 2101
Hebrew gemilath chassodim association, New York. 2086
Hebrew Sabbath school union of America. 2086
Hebrew Sheltering and Immigrant Aid Society of America. 2086
Hebrew technical school for girls, New York. 2086
Hebrew union college, Cincinnati. 1799, 2082, 2183, 3166
Hebrew Union College-Jewish Institute of Religion. Library. 2110
Hechalutz Organization of America. 3897
Hechel, P. 3341
Hecht, Abraham B. 3353
Hecht, Emanuel. 533
Hecht, Michael. 2751
Heck, Fannie E. S. 3466
Heck, James Arthur. 3662
Heckart, Robert H. 3353
Heckel, Theodor. 3151
Hecker, Isaac Thomas. 756, 763, 787, 2805
Hecker, Julius Friedrich. 3257
Heckman, Jacob Hugh. 597
Heckman, John. 1236
Heckman, Shirley J. 935
Hedge, Frederic Henry. 101, 523, 3341, 3621, 3728
Hedges, Florence Edythe Blake. 745
Hedges, James A. 1293, 1800
Hedges, John W. 2443
Hedges, Sidney George. 2891
Hedges, Ursula M. 2541, 3247
Heding, Howard William. 3026
Hedley, George P. 1262
Hedley, George Percy. 73, 1920, 3003, 3084, 3325, 3672, 3714, 3744, 3758, 3853
Hedley, John Cuthbert. 2389
Hedman, Kathryn Pierpoint. 24, 3798
Hedrick, Basil Calvin. 2198
Hedrick, Charles W. 55
Hedstrom, Carl Bernhard. 1565
Heeg, Aloysius Joseph. 626, 627, 746
Heenan, Edward F. 3744
Heenan, John Carmel. 763, 2789, 2811, 3676
Heenan, John Carmen, 1905. 795
Heeney, William Brian Danford. 1291
Heeren, John J. 2546
Heering, Gerrit Jan. 3792
Heermance, Edgar Laing. 1240, 2320
Heermans, Josephine (Woodbury) 628
Hefele, Karl Joseph von. 1372
Heffern, Andrew Duff. 68
Heffernan, Arthur James. 816
Heffernan, Virginia Mary. 310
Heffey, Mary Winefride. 578
Heffner, Christine Fleming. 1447, 2389
Heffner, F. 863
Hefley, James C. 102, 155, 169, 184, 234, 652, 742, 943, 1021, 1085, 1362, 1393, 1552, 1807, 1840, 1898, 1904, 1915, 2197, 2389, 2503, 2539, 2540, 2559, 3005, 3314, 3390, 3404, 3705, 3744, 3860, 3803, 3881
Heflin, Cecil C. 692
Heflin, Jimmie H. 148, 248
Heflin, Nannie France. 3764
Hefling, Charles C. 1613
Hefner, Philip J. 3239, 3593, 3621, 3668
Hefner, Philip J.Ritschl, Albrecht Benjamin. 3669
Hege, Ruth. 2514
Hegedus, Lorant. 1110, 1999

Hegel, Georg Wilhelm Friedrich. 1800, 2242, 2473
Hegeman, James Winthrop. 1033
Hegener, Mark. 1641
Heggen, Franz J. 2811
[Heggie, Cora M. A.] 1861. 1364
Hegland, Martin. 310, 963, 1128, 1434, 1439, 1785, 2762
Hegre, Theodore A. 1592, 3295, 3299
Hegstad, Roland R. 2815
Hegy, Reginald. 3504
Heicher, Merlo Karl Wordsworth. 963, 1439
Heick, Otto William. 964
Heide, Florence Parry. 896, 1734, 2267, 2983, 3464
Heidegger, John James. 3606
Heidegger, Martin. 1707, 1881, 2163, 2418, 2738
Heidel, Alexander. 1370, 1713
Heidel, William Arthur. 2114
Heidelberg catechism. 3047
Heidelberg catechism. English. 1801, 3043
Heidelberg union church (Reformed and Lutheran) Heidelberg township, Lehigh co., Pa. 2813
Heidelberg catechism. English. 3043
Heideman, Eugene P. 1241
Heiden, Konrad. 2111
Heiderstadt, Dorothy. 290, 3138
Heidt, William George. 42
Heifner, Fred. 493, 1921, 2952
Heiges, Donald R. 964, 3784
Heighway, Osborn W. 2208
Heighway, Osborn W. Trenery. 2085, 2208
Heijke, John. 1316
Heikkinen, Jacob W. 638, 648
Heil, L E. 214
Heilbut, Tony. 1749, 2680
Heilig, Matthias R. 3066
Heilly, Alphonse. 2343, 2627
Heilman, Philip Alonzo. 1608
Heilman, Samuel C. 2751
Heilprin, Michael. 1799
Heim, Karl. 1059, 1958, 2039, 2299, 2976, 3078, 3082, 3651
*Heim, Ralph D. 1999
Heim, Ralph Daniel. 648, 3554
Heimarck, Theodore. 2299
Heimbeck, Raeburne Seeley. 3070
Heimert, Alan E. 1757, 3214
Heimsath, Charles Herman. 141, 163, 3003
Hein, Lucille E. 1604, 1605, 2886, 3191
Hein, Marvin. 1417
Heindel, Mas. 3250
Heindel, Max. 3250, 95, 672, 3250, 1111, 2636, 3250
Heinecken, Martin J. 1050, 1381, 1722, 2170, 2214, 2282, 2286, 3069, 3644
Heinecken, Martin J. J. 2286
Heineman, John L. 1347
Heinemann, Joseph. 2110, 2885
Heinemann, Thea. 1966, 1981
Heinerman, Joseph. 3600
Heinisch, Paul. 534, 598, 2415, 534, 598
Heins, Henry Hardy. 22
Heins, Lester F. 2031
Heinsohn, Edmund. 3436
Heintzen, Erich H. 2214, 2243
Heinz, Susanna Wilder. 1992
Heinze, Thomas F. 202
Heise, Bessie Eloise. 632
Heiser, Alta (Harvey) 2304
Heiser, Roy F. 3880
Heisey, Paul Harold. 2994, 2293, 3440
Heisig, James W. 2159, 3002
Heisler, Charles W. 1985
Heisler, Daniel Yost. 2944
Heisley, Charles Wesley. 2981
Heiss, Michael. 394
Heiss, Willard C. 1686
Heissenbuttel, Ernest G. 2850
Heissig, Walther. 2584
Heitland, William Emerton. 2199
Helbo, Florent. 2577
Held, John Adolf. 2553, 3168, 3604
Held, Ronald G. 935
Helder, Jacob. 1888
Helen, Louise. 2158
Helen, Madeleine. 2389
Helfaer, Philip M. 185
Helfenstein, Ernest. 1652
Helffenstein, Jacob. 105
Helffenstein, Samuel. 3644
Helfgott, Benjamin Wolf. 2087
Helfman, Elizabeth S. 3546
Heline, Corinne (Smith) Dunklee. 42, 234, 319, 526, 721, 1262, 1662, 2060, 2725
Heline, Theodore. 611, 1410
Heliopoulos, Demetrius. 2748
Hell, Vera. 2848
Helland, Andreas Andersen. 2493
Helldorfer, Martin C. 3848

Helleberg, Carl Gustaf. 3504
Helleberg, Marilyn M. 2379
Hellenbroek, Abraham. 1592, 3369
Heller, Abraham Mayer. 2118, 2139, 2154, 3371
Heller, Bernard. 2084
Heller, Herbert L. 2439
Heller, Imre. 3577
Heller, James Gutheim. 1275, 3822
Heller, Joseph. 3896
Heller, Maximilian. 2693
Heller, Melvin P. 3592
Heller, Nachman. 2118
Helleu, Arsene. 2158, 2233
Hellman, John. 872, 1532, 2626
Hellriegel, Martin B. 2366
Hellwig, Monika. 763, 1385, 1413, 2254, 3263, 3268, 3662
Hellyer, Henry Leon. 2117
Helm, James Isbell. 3401
Helm, Kathryn E. 964
Helm, MacKinley. 1192
Helman, Byron E. 1525
Helman, Patricia Kennedy. 1003, 1802
Helmarck, Theodore. 2214
Helmbold, Andrew K. 1718
Helmbold, F. Wilbur. 3297
Helmershausen, Adella. 1651
Helmreich, Ernst Christian. 820, 1143, 1146, 3164
Helmreich, William B. 1802, 2751, 3015
Helms, Edgar James. 2597
Helms, Elmer Ellsworth. 1447, 1732, 41, 214, 1318
Helser, Albert David. 2537, 2552
Helton, John. 173, 1681
Heltzel, Massey Mott. 2931
Helverson, Ralph N. 1439
Helwig, Aquinas. 852
Hembree, Charles R. 1439, 1712, 2389
Hembree, Maud. 276
Hembree, Ron. 713, 2485
Hemenway, Charles W. 2603
Hemenway, Francis Dana. 688
Hemenway, Frank F. 748
Hemesath, Caroline. 3704
[Heming, Harry Hooper]. 835
Heminger, Carl. 3412
Hemingway, Leslie. 664
Hemingway, Patricia Drake. 3708
Hemmenway, Moses. 135, 1125, 1504, 1847
Hemmer, H. 2319, 2864
Hempel, Arthur J. 984
Hempel, Charles Julius. 3569
Hemphill, Annie Mae Tooke. 3242
Hemphill, Basil. 3487
Hemphill, Elizabeth Anne. 26, 2534, 3255
Hemphill, La Breeska Rogers. 1749, 1803
Hemphill, Martha Locke. 1111, 3173
Henaghan, John. 2873, 1400
Hendee, Elizabeth Russell. 3878
Hendel, Charles William. 1281
Henderlite, Rachel. 1829, 2798, 3662
Henderson, Alice (Corbin) 1806
Henderson, Archibald. 885
Henderson, Arthur Weldon. 1506
Henderson, C. William. 3331
Henderson, Caroline D. 3178
Henderson, Charles Richmond. 378, 3443
Henderson, E Harold. 148
Henderson, Elisa Easter. 2766
Henderson, George. 878, 1134
Henderson, George David. 2916, 2936, 3315, 1584
Henderson, George David Smith. 889
Henderson, Glenna. 1422, 1803
Henderson, Henry F. 1402
Henderson, Howard. 1535
Henderson, Ian. 476, 1040, 1225
Henderson, J. A. 2436
Henderson, J. McLeod. 2332, 3022
Henderson, John. 1014
Henderson, John B. 3720
Henderson, John Clarence. 1059
Henderson, John L. H. 3535
Henderson, John Thompson. 1408
Henderson, Joseph L. 1416
Henderson, Joseph Luke. 163
Henderson, Martha Gray. 907
Henderson, Nancy. 1582
Henderson, Robert J. 207, 2765
Henderson, Robert T. 1566
Henderson, Robert W. 1248
Henderson, W. Guy. 2493
Henderson, Zelpha. 338
Hendley, George. 897
Hendren, Bob. 363
Hendrick, John R. 1566
Hendrick, William Jackson. 1803
Hendricks, Garland A. 1943, 2736
Hendricks, Geoff. 2389
Hendricks, Howard G. 1316, 1506, 2338
Hendricks, Jeanne W. 3830, 3845
Hendricks, Kenneth C. 2534, 3580
Hendricks, Rhoda A. 2656, 2658
Hendricks, Robert J. 3436

Hendricks, Virginia (Harris) 149
Hendricks, William C. 3151
Hendricks, William Cornelius. 281
Hendricks, William L. 369, 896
Hendrickson, Albert L. 3303
Hendrickson, Ford. 1326, 2351, 2558, 3423
Hendrickson, Frances. 3833
Hendrickson, Hubbard. 1665
Hendrickson, Raymond J. 2418
Hendrickson, William. 451
Hendriksen, William. 638, 1023, 3335, 310, 343, 478, 1528, 1695
Hendriks J A. 234
Hendrix, Eugene Russell. 1069, 1829, 1893, 2063, 3672
Hendrix, John. 935
Hendrix, Lela. 1608
Hendrix, Olan. 3142
Hendrix, Scott H. 2274, 3037
Hendry, George Stuart. 1740, 1829, 1893, 2676, 3809
Heneghan, John Joseph. 49, 3654
Hengel, Martin. 107, 330, 348, 444, 1197, 2004, 2039, 2154, 2866, 2946, 3233, 3458, 3780
Hengstenberg, Ernst Wilhelm. 512, 526, 2415
Hening, E. F. 2500, 2970
Henke, Frederick Goodrich. 3240
Henkel, David. 135, 2039, 2589, 3729
Henkel, Dieter. 1146
Henkel, Fred. 2988
Henkel, Paul. 2283
Henkle, Moses Montgomery. 177, 2421
Henle, Robert John. 2418
Henley, James Walton. 2055
Henley, Wallace. 993, 1086, 1552, 1803
Henn, Thomas Rice. 210
Hennacy, Ammon. 38
Hennelly, Alfred T. 2222, 3329
Hennesey, James J. 875, 3769
Hennessy, Augustine Paul. 3029, 3031
Hennessy, Nancy. 3181
Hennessy, Thomas C. 3222
Hennig, Kurt. 1313   *
[Henninges, E. C.]. 509, 1376
Henningsen, Gustav. 1909, 3825
Hennrich, Kilian J. 3390
Hennrich, Kilian Joseph. 998, 1260, 2015, 2361, 3222, 3692
Henrichs, Henry Frederick. 3402
Henrichsen, Margaret. 1301, 1803, 3128
Henrichsen, Walter A. 287, 403, 984
Henrie, Rodney Arden. 2740
Henriques, Henry Straus Quixano. 2099
Henriques, Ursula. 1762
Henry. 842
Henry, A. M. 781, 1829
Henry, Alfred Hylas. 3250
Henry, Antonin Marcel. 1829, 1966, 2554
Henry, Caleb Sprague. 1428, 1699
Henry, carl. 1599
Henry, Carl Ferdinand Howard. 63, 64, 201, 943, 1066, 1551, 1552, 1722, 1845, 2563, 2756, 3225, 3353, 3443, 3535, 3616, 3617, 3651, 3656, 3758, 3849
Henry, Caroline Vinton. 2703
Henry, Clifford Elmore Luke. 787
Henry, Desmond Paul. 49
Henry, Edwin Arthur. 3369
Henry, Francis Augustus. 1050, 3096
Henry, Freddie Elizabeth. 3554
Henry, G[eorge] W. 3199
Henry, George W. 1520, 3128
Henry, Helga Bender. 2260
Henry, Hugh Thomas. 812, 920, 2249, 2900
Henry, Iona. 1350
Henry, James A. 426
Henry, Jeanne Hand. 1667
Henry, Jerry Maurice. 1237
Henry, Jim. 163
Henry, Leroy. 1785, 1795
Henry, Lyman I. 2798
Henry, Mark. 1254
Henry, Mary (Davis) 1804
[Henry, Mary Gertrude, 1857. 3432
Henry, Matthew. 222, 615, 1431, 1447, 1803, 1856, 2251, 2258, 2873, 2887, 2891, 3373
Henry, Maureen. 1109
Henry, Patrick. 351, 984
Henry, Paul. 116, 2823
Henry, Paul B. 1086
Henry, Paul Emil. 727
Henry, Paul Emile. 1641
Henry, Philip. 2047, 3364
Henry, S[arepta] M. I[rish]. 1834
Henry, Sarepta Myrenda Irish. 1829
Henry, Sondra. 3842
Henry, Stuart Clark. 184, 3427, 3748, 3813
Henry VIII. 3263
Henry, Thomas Charlton. 36
Henry, Virgil. 3189
Henry, Waights Gibbs. 3151

Henry, William J. 1490
Hensel, Harry W. 1315
Henseler, Dorothy (Tanner) 621
Hensey, Andrew F. 1503, 2513
Hensey, Andrew Fitch. 1503, 2513
Hensey, James Andrew. 1470, 1929, 2191, 2865, 3702
Henshaw, John Prentiss Kewley. 2589
Henshaw, Paul W. 1605
Henshaw, Thomas. 410, 530
Hensley, John Clark. 3151, 3415
Hensley, Marie E. 337
Henslow, George. 3504
Henson, Herbert Hensley. 1040, 1211, 1212, 1226, 2753, 2900, 3128, 3008
Henson, John M. 3562
Henson, Llewellyn Lafayette. 1566
Henson, Poindexter Smith. 3341
Henthorne, Mary Evangein. 1920
Henthorne, Mary Evangela. 1920
Henze, Anton. 1156, 1373
[Henze, Clement] 1880. 2358
Hepburn, Daisy. 3835, 3837
Hepburn, Ronald W. 2836
Hephart, Cyrus Jeffries. 1966, 2168
Hepp, Valentin. 729
Heppenstall, Edward. 1435, 2039, 2049, 3289
Heppler, Richard Leo. 2355
Hepworth, George Hughes. 1324, 3341, 3353
Hequembourg, Charles Louis. 1381
Heracleon. 416
Heracleon, the Gnostic. 416
Herambourg, Peter. 1541
Herberg, Will. 652, 2139, 3100, 3747
Herberger, Charles F. 2665
Herbermann, Charles George. 3545
Herbert, A S. 3853
Herbert, Arthur Gabriel. 277, 1690
Herbert, Charles. 3820
Herbert, Christopher. 1478
Herbert, Edward. 2102
Herbert, Edward Herbert. 1419, 1804
Herbert, George. 1017, 1023, 1804, 3672
Herbert, Jean. 3403
[Herbert, Lewis Thomas] 1851. 934
Herbert, Mary Elizabeth (A'Court) Herbert. 2766
Herbert, Thomas. 1862
Herbert, Walter I. 2547
Herbine, Charlotte G. 3504
Herbrecht, O. G. 964
Herbst, Charles M. 863, 2211, 2214
Herbst, Eva. 534
Herbst, Winfred. 366
Herbst, Winfrid. 907, 935, 1952, 2251, 2389, 2591, 3284, 3533, 367, 688, 770, 795, 895, 998, 1014, 1905, 1977, 1999, 2366, 2573, 3785
Herbster, Ben M. 1722
Herbstreith, Ann. 2226
Herculano de Carvalho e Araujo, Alexandre, 1810-1877. 1910
Hercus, John. 1405, 1733
Herder correspondence. 2123
Herder, Johann Gottfired von. 1722
Herder, Johann Gottfried von. 1722, 1798, 1799, 2207
Herdia, Carlos Maria de. 2005
Heredia, Carlos Maria de. 1318, 3504
Herford, Brooke. 1008, 3479, 3723, 3725
Herford, Robert Travers. 2828, 514, 1101, 1539, 2828
Herge, Henry J. 1592
Hergenrother, Joseph Adam Gustav. 1474
Herget, John Francis. 1985
Herhold, Robert M. 1014, 1413, 2891, 3540
Hering, Jean. 1142
Heris, Ch V. 2039
Heris, Charles Vincent. 2039, 2264, 2819
Herkless, John. 1642, 1673, 731
Herklots, Hugh Gerard Gibson. 290, 410, 448, 1313, 2016, 2972, 3850
Herlong, T. L. 1245
Herman, Arthur L. 1745
Herman, Edward. 657, 2083
Herman, Emily. 1059, 2688, 2873
Herman, Nicolas. 998, 3479
Herman, Stewart Winfield. 1542, 1707, 1708
Hermance, William Ellsworth. 2738
Hermand, Pierre. 877
Hermann, Edward A G. 696, 697
Hermann, Ingo. 410, 1592
Hermann, Jacob Rudolph. 3504
Hermann, Placid. 1642, 1645, 1646
Hermann, Siegfried. 1819
Hermans, L. 1977
Hermanson, Renee. 2389
Hermansson, Magnus. 2077
Hermas. 1806, 2331
Hermes Trismegistus. 2638, 2661
Hermisson, Hans-Jurgen. 1597
Hernaez, Francisco Javier. 814

Hernaman, Claudia Frances. 3710
Herndon, Bob. 1786, 3230
Herndon, Booton. 3386
Herod, Frederic George. 390
Herod (Liturgical drama) 1807, 2233
Herodotus. 1807
Herold, Andre Ferdinand. 702
Herold, Duchesne. 2575
Herold, J. Christopher. 1938
Herold, Norbert. 2708, 3538
Heron, Alasdair. 3656
Heron, Frances (Dunlap) 1483, 3173, 3564
Heron, Henrietia. 3144
Heron, Henrietta. 645, 2757, 3554
Heron, Laurence Tunstall. 319, 3072
Herr, Dan. 759, 833, 867
Herr, Ethel L. 638, 1603, 3841
Herr, Horace Dumont. 3143
Herr, Johannes. 3335
Herr, Vincent V. 2997, 3331, 3785
Herrera, Barbara Hand. 1694
Herrera Oria, Angel 1886. 1268, 3722
Herrick, Cheesman Abiah. 3310
Herrick, Everett Carleton. 39
Herrick, George Frederick. 1084
Herrick, Henry Martyn. 2174
Herrick, Horace N. 2450, 2439
Herrick, Samuel Edward. 924
Herrick, Warren Crocker. 2683
Herrig, Hans. 2280
Herrigel, Eugen. 3891, 3892
Herring, Basil. 505, 744, 2841
Herring, Benjamin Oscar. 569
Herring, Clyde Lee. 3886
Herring, Daniel Boone. 1952, 2695, 2060, 2997
Herring, Hubert Clinton. 3453
Herring, Ralph A. 450, 1829, 2873
Herring, Reuben. 171, 1605, 1608, 2402, 3466
Herrington, J Wells and Pitney, J H. 3072
Herriott, Frank Wilbur. 3886
Herrlin, Olle. 3855
Herrmann, Alexander. 2312
Herrmann, Arthur R. 1666
Herrmann, J E. 2296
Herrmann, John Ewald. 1251
Herrmann, Nina. 893, 1806, 1808
Herrmann, Siegfried. 534, 2096
Herrmann, Wihelm. 2286
Herrmann, Wilhelm. 1592, 3239, 3650
Herron, George Davis. 1135, 1341, 2059, 3433, 3443
Herron, L. 1635
Herron, Mary Eulalia. 3418
Herron, Orley R. 984, 2389
Herrstrom, William Dewey. 201, 2156, 3792
Herrup, Steven J. 3112
Herschell, Ridley Haim. 2117
Hersey, April. 2177
Hersey, Harry G. 3716
Hersey, Harry Greenlief. 3225
Hersey, John. 465
Hersey, Norman L. 3856
Hershbell, Jackson P. 1416, 2853
Hershberger, Charles Edgar. 2039
Hershberger, Guy Franklin. 37, 187, 1134, 2403, 2807, 2809, 3792
Hershberger, Merlin. 964
Hershey, Robert D. 9, 2214, 2299
Hershman, Abraham Moses. 3371
Hershon, Jerome L. 1275
Herskovits, Melville Jean, 1895. 1399
Hertel, James R. 2341
Hertling, Ludwig. 809, 1196
Hertling, Ludwig, Freiherr von. 809
Hertsens, Marcel. 2389
Herttell, Thomas. 1654
Hertz, Emanuel. 1480, 2701
Hertz, Geraldine. 1608, 2355
Hertz, Jacky. 2625
Hertz, Joseph Herman. 2075, 2084, 2114, 2884
Hertz, Karl H. 1005, 1086, 2939
Hertz, Ricard C. 2142
Hertz, Richard. 2081
Hertz, Richard C. 1811, 2080, 2808, 3032, 3166
Hertz, Solange Strong. 201, 998, 2363, 3844, 3845
Hertzberg, Arthur. 2141, 2145, 3744, 3897
Hertzberg, Hans Wilhelm. 590
Hertzler, Arthur Emanuel. 3791
Hertzler, Daniel. 2407, 2408
Herve-Bazin, Marie Anne Henriette Lucie. 3128
Hervey, Arthur Charles. 496
Hervey, George Winfred. 155, 1566, 2901
Hervey, James. 1447, 1808, 1809, 2160, 2161, 2710
Hervey, James W. 1182, 3122
Hervey, Rev. James W. 1182
Hervey, Walter Lowrie. 3784
Hervieux, Jacques. 337

Herz, Stephanie M. 2389
Herzberg, Max John. 905, 2652, 2656
Herzberg, Wilhelm. 2114
Herzberger, Frederick William. 2209
Herzberger, Frederick William. 2274, 1605
Herzel, Catherine. 964, 1050, 1875, 3856
Herzel, Catherine B. 899, 903, 1112, 1408, 1605, 1875, 2891
Herzel, Frank Benton. 3253
Herzfeld, Ernst Emil. 3898
Herzl, Theodor. 3896
Herzog, Arthur. 3747
Herzog, Chaim. 558
Herzog, Charles G. 3151, 3263
Herzog, Eduard. 2735
Herzog, Frederick. 423, 1659, 3617, 3621, 3656
Hesburgh, Teodore Martin. 870
Hesburgh, Theodore M. 1528
Hesburgh, Theodore Martin. 787, 2049, 2191
Heschel, Abraham. 2075, 3259
Heschel, Abraham Joshua. 1907. 569, 1809, 2075, 2139, 2142, 2765, 2885, 2950, 3100, 3259, 3260
Heschel, Abraham Joshua. 2075, 2152, 2318, 2402, 2873, 3016, 3479
Heskes, Irene. 883
Heskyns, Thomas. 2254
Heslop, J. M. 3430
Heslop, William Greene. 371, 450, 454, 506, 516, 521, 557, 560, 568, 589, 1238, 1794, 1840, 3373
Hess, Bartlett L. 952
Hess, Geraldine. 1163
Hess, Hamilton. 3303
Hess, Isabella Rosa. 877
Hess, John Daniel. 1911
Hess, Margaret Johnston. 513, 589
Hess, Moses. 2099
Hess, Thomas. 3143
Hesse, Ferdinand. 3432
Hesse, Hermann, 1877-1962. 702
Hessel, Dieter T. 1139
Hesselgrave, David J. 425, 1166, 1316
Hessert, Paul. 1005, 1094
Hession, Brian. 1215
Hession, Edward I. 2048
Hession, Roy. 404, 1575, 1809
Hessler, Bertram. 204
Hester, Glenn M. 1367, 1809
Hester, Goldia. 212
Hester, Hubert Inm,an. 1128
Hester, Hubert Inman. 410, 534, 648, 2084
Hesterman, Lowell L. 32, 2482
Heston, Edward Louis. 772, 852, 1153, 1458, 1829, 3771
Heston, Newton. 3026
Heston, Watson. 319, 1654
Hetherington, John Aikman. 3778
Hetherington, William Maxwell. 1234
[Hetterich, Gustave J]. 870
Hettich, Blaise. 604
Hettinger, E D. 2873
Hettinger, Franz. 772
Hettinger, John. 3698
Hettrick, Ric. 2609
Hetzell, M. Carol. 3382, 3387
Heubach, Paul. 1350
Heubach, Paul C. 1012, 1435
Heubert, David Edmond, 1910. 479
Heuch, Johan Christian. 1258
Heufelder, Emmanuel Maria, 1898. 1043
[Heughan, Eleanor]. 670
Heuman, Fred S. 583, 1517
Heuser, Herman J. 2353
Heuser, Herman Joseph. 3273, 234, 842, 998, 1198, 2005, 2798, 3128, 3401
Heuss, John. 3662
Heusser, D-B. 1251
Heuvel, Albert H. van den. 964, 1059, 1260
Heuvel, Jules van den. 190
Heuver, Gerald Dirk. 2063
Hewat, Elizabeth Glendinning Kirkwood. 2520
Hewes, Philip. 3274
Hewett, Peter A. 2490
Hewins, James M. 1203
Hewit, Augustine Francis. 114, 131, 192, 414, 787, 3289
Hewitt, Arthur Wentworth. 1303, 1592, 1888, 2785, 3128, 3253, 3672
Hewitt, Charles Edward. 214
Hewitt, Clarence Horace. 9
Hewitt, Emily C. 2742, 3327
Hewitt, Frank E. 2180
Hewitt, Joe. 1809, 1940
Hewitt, John Haskell. 2493
[Hewitt, Joses]. 3672
Hewitt, Mary Elizabeth (Moore) 2752
Hewitt, Mildred. 2550, 3554
Hewitt, Paul Edward. 606, 1940
Hewitt, S C. 2632
Hewitt, Theodore Brown. 1706, 1707, 1871

Hewitt, Thomas. 403
Hewitt, William P H. 1175
Hewlett, Henry Charles. 2039, 3682
Hewlett, Maurice Henry. 1017
[Hewson, John]. 1952, 2019, 2051
Hexter, Jack H. 1910. 2139
Heyden, Thomas. 1744
Heydon, Joseph Kentigern. 787, 2673
Heydt, Henry J. 2139
Heyer, Robert. 2815, 3434, 3886
Heyer, Robert J. 984, 2742, 2873, 3186
Heyer, William Carl. 951
Heyl, Edgar G. 1345
Heyl, Paul Renno. 3078
Heymen, Ralph. 964, 2780
Heyne, William P. 3199
Heynen, Ralph. 964, 984, 1604, 3540
Heyrman, Jules. 1263
Heyser, Elwood Kenney. 736, 737
Heysham, Theodore. 307
Heyward, Carter. 1809, 2742
Heyward, Isabel Carter. 3670
Heywood, Ellis. 1785
Heywood, Hugh Christopher Lempriere. 1119
Heywood, John Healy. 1424, 3723
Heywood, Joseph Converse. 3287
Heywood, Sarah Louise. 964
Heywood, Thomas. 1809, 3606
Hezmall, Everett F. 2676, 2931
Hibbard, Billy. 1681
Hibbard, John Randolph. 2692
Hibbard, William D. 1654
Hibben, John Grier. 1800, 2242
Hibben, Paxton. 184
Hibben, W W. 1790, 2452, 2458
Hibbert, Eleanor. 1910
Hibbert-Ware, Samuel, 1782-1848. 77
Hibbs, Ben. 3353
Hibbs, Iverna. 121, 1687
Hibernians, Ancient order of. Ladies' auxiliary. 2576
Hibma, J. E. 1435
Hick, John. 49, 64, 175, 1079, 1100, 1695, 1696, 1737, 1738, 1739, 1853, 2181, 2836, 3002, 3100, 3107, 3108, 3610
Hickerson, Clyde Vernon. 163
Hickerson, May Josephine. 3529
Hickey, Edward John. 3437
Hickey, Isabel M. 95
Hickey, John Hosford. 2247
Hickey, Marilyn. 3391
Hickey, Raymond. 772, 1289
Hickie, William James. 1769
Hickle, Ruth. 281
Hickman, Franklin Simpson. 1059, 2997, 3191
Hickman, Josiah Edwin. 678
Hickman, Martha. 1303
Hickman, Martha Whitmore. 1810, 2460
Hickman, Wiliam A. 3762
Hickman, William A. 3762
Hickok, Laurens Perseus. 1371, 3029, 3100
Hicks, B R. 3720
Hicks, Betsey Belle. 3504
Hicks, Beulah Kay. 1447
Hicks, Bun E. 3373
Hicks, Darryl. 1749, 3816
Hicks, E. W. 290
Hicks, Elias. 1681, 1688, 1810
Hicks, Esther L. 3783
Hicks, H. Beecher. 16
Hicks, Harry Wade. 3249
Hicks, John Harden. 532
Hicks, John Solomon Soules. 610
Hicks, Joseph P. 1566
Hicks, Lewis Ezra. 2673
Hicks, Lewis Wilder. 3810
Hicks, Marcella DeCou. 3504
Hicks, Robert Drew. 3533
Hicks, William Watkin. 3859
Hicks, Williams. 157
Hickson, James Moore. 1599, 1792
Hiddleston, Barry. 6, 319
Hidebrandt, Franz. 2400
Hiebert, Clarence. 1229, 2408
Hiebert, D. Edmond. 479
Hiebert, David Edmond. 321, 368, 374, 398, 412, 433, 478, 2803
Hiebert, Erwin N. 103
Hiebert, Paul Gerhardt. 928, 1810
Hield, Charles R. 3216
Hieronymous. 1525
Hieronymus. 234, 506, 586, 1811, 2217, 2218, 2805, 3369, 3635
Hiers, Richard H. 310, 390, 950, 1530, 2003, 2063, 2176
Hiesberger, Jean Marie. 2389
Hifler, Joyce. 3702
Higbee E E. 2169
Higby, Chester Penn. 1144
Higdon, Barbara McFarlane. 2901
Higdon, David Andrew. 3663
Higdon, Elmer Kelso. 2484, 2545
Higgens, Elford. 2765

Higger, Michael. 2114
Higginbotham, Mary. 734
Higginbottom, David Baines. 1091
Higginbottom, Ethel (Cody) 2530
Higginbottom, Sam. 2530, 2920
Higgins, Albert Sidney. 1272
Higgins, Angus John Brockhurst. 390, 2254, 3458
[Higgins, David]. 1376
Higgins, Godfrey. 1480, 3093
Higgins, Herbert Ralph. 1135
Higgins, James. 662, 2066
Higgins, John J. 2412, 2885
Higgins, John Seville. 43, 2253, 2964
Higgins, Nicholas. 3487
Higgins, Paul Lambourne. 184, 1088, 2359, 2910, 3803
Higgins, Solomon. 2981
Higgins, Thomas J. 796
Higginson, Teresa Helena. 2218
Higginson, Vincent. 813, 883
High, Dallas M. 2196, 3071, 3830
High, Stanley. 660, 1150, 1754, 3443, 3744
Highbaugh, Irma. 1608
Highcliffe, William. 1324
Highet, John. 3315
Hightown, N. J. Baptist church. 1485
Hightower, Ted. 2063
Highwater, Jamake. 1902
Higley, Louis Allen. 204
Higman, Francis M. 69, 728
Hiker, Elmer Albert. 964
Hilarius. 3714
Hilbish, Benjamin F. 2427
Hilbun, Bruce S. 163
Hilburger, Mary Charitina. 1620
Hilburn, May Stafford. 2891
Hilde, Reuben. 572, 1012, 1316, 2061, 2798, 3385, 3457
Hildebidle, Ralph G. 3870
Hildebrand, Dietrich von. 838, 889
Hildebrand, E. T. and Vaughan, James D. 1203
Hildebrandt, Franz, 1909. 2366
Hilder, Enid. 3170
Hildner, George John. 3275
Hiles, John. 3271
[Hilf, G M]. 2389
Hilken, Glen A. 3823
[Hilkert, Robert C]. 772
Hill, Alice (Smith) 299
Hill, Benjamin, Dionysius. 2361
Hill, Bennett D. 1144, 1276
Hill, Brian Victor. 1497
Hill, Carl Richard. 681, 2323
Hill, Caroline (Miles) 3209, 3206
Hill, Christopher. 1219
Hill, Claude Eugene. 1466
Hill, Clifford S. 1132
Hill, Daniel Harvey. 1997, 3335
Hill, Dave. 280, 313, 422, 430, 554, 1966, 1981
Hill, David. 440, 450, 1769
Hill, David C. 338, 924
Hill, David Leslie. 3332
Hill, David R. 1104
Hill, Derek Ingram. 737
Hill, Donna. 2609, 3428
Hill, Dorothy Black. 4
Hill, Dorothy La Croix. 1734, 3167, 3170
Hill, Dorothy LaCroix. 3170
Hill, Douglas. 2725
Hill, Douglas Arthur. 2725
*Hill, Elmira D. 645
Hill, Frances M. 2550, 2552
Hill, Francis Constantine. 3228, 3800
Hill, George W. E. 1913
Hill, Harold. 931, 984, 995, 1381, 1811
Hill, Harry Granison. 3353
Hill, Henry Aaron. 1878, 2567
Hill, Ida Carleton Thallon. 6
Hill, Ira. 1381
Hill, James Langdon. 2237, 3287, 3309, 2157, 2182
Hill, Jeanne. 1811, 2389, 2873
Hill, John Arthur. 2988, 2989, 3504
Hill, John Boynton. 2927
Hill, John Edward Christopher. 52
Hill, John Godfrey. 569, 3196, 3663
Hill, John J. 748
Hill, John Leonard. 430, 433, 493, 3886
Hill, John Louis. 1461, 1463
Hill, John Wesley. 2475
Hill, Leonard. 1289
Hill, Luther Leonidas. 3353
Hill, Lysander. 1737, 3462
Hill, Mabel. 1324, 3078
Hill, Margaret Livingston. 625
Hill, Marie. 938
Hill, Marvin S. 2178, 2615, 2617
Hill, Mary V. 897, 1812
Hill, Michael. 3086
Hill, Michael Peter. 781
Hill, Norman Llewellyn. 1076
Hill, Owen Aloysius. 2267, 2997, 3566
Hill, Paul J. 2229

Hill, Percy William. 1616
Hill, Raymond Putnam. 2989
[Hill, Richard, 1732-1808. 36, 1447
Hill, Rowland. 964
Hill, Rowley. 2021
Hill, Ruth Livingston. 1004
Hill, Samuel S. 170, 1109, 2955, 3468
Hill, Stanley. 1575
Hill, Stephen. 1599
Hill, Thomas. 1263, 2673
Hill, William. 2925
Hill, William B. 3128
Hill, William Bancroft. 348, 381, 621, 1183, 1966, 2051
Hill, William J. 1735
Hill, William S. 1218
Hill, William Speed. 1844
Hillard, Frederick Hadaway. 3128
Hilldrup, Robert Leroy. 1775, 2534
Hiller, Carl E. 1270
Hiller, Francis L. L. 307
Hiller, George Irvine. 991
Hiller, Gustavus Emanuel. 234
[Hiller, Margaret]. 2690, 3569
Hiller, Margaret. 3435, 3878
Hiller, Oliver Prescott. 3208
Hillerbrand, Hans J. 3034
Hillerbrand, Hans Joachim. 37, 924, 2631, 3034, 3042
Hillerman, Abbie B. 3833
Hillern, Wilhelmine (Birch) von. 2778
Hillers, Delbert R. 556, 1376
[Hilles, David]. 1687
Hillesheim, James W. 3123
Hillgarth, J. N. 1187
Hillhouse, James. 1812
Hillhouse, John. 2361
[Hillhouse, Mary] d. 1874. 1878
Hilliard, David Lockhart. 1224, 2540
Hilliard, Dick. 905
Hilliard, Frances McAnally Blackburn. 2667
Hilliard, Frederick Hadaway. 1129, 3128, 3855
Hilliard, Marion Pharo. 1364
Hilling, Nikolaus. 778
Hillis, Aaron Merritt. 1626
Hillis, Dave. 1734
Hillis, Dick. 64, 1321, 1906, 2482, 2525
Hillis, Don W. 217, 552, 561, 621, 984, 1553, 1716, 2389, 2484, 2490, 3066, 3264, 3886
Hillis, Newell Dwight. 964, 3170, 660, 964, 1050, 1557, 1888, 2773, 2891
Hillman, Eugene. 1088, 2554
Hillman, Hugh H. 3504
Hillman, James. 2784
Hillman, James Noah. 1663
Hillman, Joseph. 2433
Hillman, Ruth Estelyn. 2389
Hillmann, Willibrord. 621
Hillock, Wilfred M. 1199
Hills, A[aron] M[erritt]. 1632, 2178
Hills, Aaron Merritt. 1253, 1992
Hills, Christopher B. 2063, 2379, 2725
Hills, Desmond B. 900
Hills, Dick. 1829
Hills, George Morgan. 717
Hills, Hannah Brummitt. 3173
Hills, L. Rust. 1324
Hills, Margaret Thorndike. 247
Hills, Oscar Armstrong. 70, 214, 3347, 2931
Hills, Tena G. 2263
Hillsdale, Paul. 374
Hillyer, Shaler Granby. 150
Hilpisch, Stephanus. 187, 188
Hilscher, Solomon S. 1553, 1696
Hilson, James Benjamin. 3807
Hiltebeitel, Alf. 2186, 2316
Hiltner, Seward. 1373, 2378, 2780, 2785, 2995, 3616
Hilton, Bruce. 1132, 1140, 1421
Hilton, Eugene. 2609
Hilton, Lynn M. 679, 2208, 3287, 3428, 3430
Hilton, Patricia A. 1739
Hilton, Walter. 1447
Himber, Charlotte. 687
Himes, Ellvern H. 1232, 2401
Himes, John Andrew. 2468
Himes, Paul. 1865
Himes, Roger. 64
Himmelfarb, Milton. 2107, 2141
Himmelheber, Diana (Martin) 3856
Hinchey, Roy W. 2788
Hinchman, Catharine Sellew. 628
Hinckley, Bryant S. 131, 943, 1756, 2609
Hinckley, Gordon Bitner. 1009, 1232, 2603, 2898
Hinckley, R. Wilbur. 298
Hinde, William. 698
Hinderlie, Mary. 1111
Hindman, Jane F. 1029, 2685, 3379
Hindmarsh, Robert. 2000, 2690
Hinds, John Thomas. 454

Hindson, Edward E. 534, 1608, 2831, 3228
Hine, Edward. 1929
Hine, Leland D. 121, 145, 2534
Hine, Sophia McDougall. 719
Hines, Harvey K. 1629, 2206, 2543
Hines, Herbert Waldo. 2493, 1304, 2530
Hines, John Elbridge. 1164, 2965, 2973, 3353
Hines, John M. 137, 2969
Hines, Robert Stephan. 916
Hines, Samuel Theophilus. 1615
Hingeley, Joseph Beaumont. 2444
Hinke, William John. 3048
Hinkle, Carl E. 964
Hinkle, Gerald H. 1855
Hinkle, J. Herbert. 1162
Hinkle, Joseph W. 1254
Hinkley, Frederic Allen. 3479
Hinkson, Katharine (Tynan) 1447, 2003
Hinman, Nelson. 64
Hinnant, Charles H. 1821
Hinnebusch, Paul. 400, 998, 1355, 1507, 1688, 2361, 2570, 2873, 3487, 3721
Hinnebusch, William A. 1474, 1475, 1476
Hinnebusch Paul. 3487
Hinnells, John R. 2664
Hinrichs, C F. 465
Hinsdale, Burke Aaron. 321, 394, 1952, 3706
Hinsdale, Grace Webster. 1439
Hinshaw, Cecil E. 1578
Hinshaw, David. 2131
Hinshaw, Joseph Howard. 3139
Hinshaw, Seth B. 1678
Hinshaw, William Wade. 1684
Hinson, E. Genn. 2039
Hinson, E. Glenn. 1119, 1554, 2873, 3484
Hinson, Walter Benwell. 3341, 1033
Hinterberger, Aloysius J. 893
Hinton, isaac Taylor. 138
Hinton, James. 3540
[Hinton, John Howard, 1791-1873. 1098, 1566
Hintz, Howard William. 3757
Hippolytus. 1239, 4805
Hipps, John Burder. 2509
Hire, Richard P. 3628
Hirn, Yrjo. 920
Hirsch, Arthur Henry. 1852
Hirsch, David Einhorn. 1816, 3361
Hirsch, Emil Gustav. 2034, 2080, 2142, 2114
Hirsch, Eric Donald. 1806
Hirsch, Mendel. 529
Hirsch, Rabbi Richard G. 2144
Hirsch, Richard G. 2144
Hirsch, Samson Raphael. 562, 572, 2114, 2155
Hirsch, Samuel Abraham. 2142
Hirsch, W. 3464
Hirschberg, Harris Hans. 2139
Hirschhorn, Harry J. 2110
Hirschmann, Maria Anne. 1362, 1817, 2501
Hirschowitz, Abraham Eber. 2118, 3116
Hirschy, Noah Calvin. 88, 2822
Hirsh, Marilyn. 122, 1785
Hirshburg, Leroy. 1794
Hirshler, Eric R. 2104
Hirshson, Stanley P. 3869
Hirst, Margaret E. 1685
Hirst, Margaret Esther. 1685, 2756
Hiscox, Edward Thurston. 135, 148, 150, 2766, 3672
Hiscox, Henry Orne. 1381, 1942
Hisey, Lehmann. 2725
Hislop, Alexander. 800
Hisperica famina. Verses 1-156. 3094
Historical Foundation of the Presbyterian and Reformed Churches. 2923, 3627
Historical records survey. Virginia. 171
Hitchcock, Albert Wellman. 638, 1952
Hitchcock, David. 3206
Hitchcock, Edward. 203, 1381, 2304, 3073, 3075, 3317
[Hitchcock, Ethan Allen] 1798-1870. 23, 2019, 3569
Hitchcock, Francis Ryan Montgomery. 1287
H itchcock, Helyn. 2726, 3575
Hitchcock, James. 811, 827, 2235
Hitchcock, Ripley. 2358
Hitchcock, Roswell Dwight. 108, 234, 302, 1345, 1865, 3241
Hitchcock, Ruth. 1820, 2509
[Hitchcock, Solomon G.]. 1406
Hitchen, Herbert. 2211
Hitchens, Edwin Lockhart. 2189
Hitchens, Kate. 3542
Hite, Jordan F. 735
Hite, Lewis Field. 3570
Hites, Laird Thomas. 1127
Hites, Robert W. 1251
Hitopadesa, English. 3302
Hitt, Russell T. 984, 2517, 2534, 2541, 3277, 3739, 3800, 3829, 3830

Hittell, John Shertzer. 1654, 2767
Hitti, Philip Khuri. 1481, 2566
Hitz, Paul. 2901
Hix, Hubert E. 313
Hixon, Lex. 3491
Hixson, Martha B. 2550
Ho lo li shu. 95, 1878
Hoade, Eugene. 2763
Hoadley, Burton James. 2051
Hoadley, Frank T. 144
Hoadly, Loammi Ives. 1592
Hoag, Amey R. 2401
Hoag, Frank Victor. 3179
Hoag, John D. 79
Hoag, Joseph. 3128
Hoare, Frederick Russell. 1616, 1617
Hoare, Mary Regis. 3378
Hoare, Rodney. 1827
Hobart, Alvah Sabin. 470, 473, 964, 1829, 3059, 447, 964, 3672
Hobart, Caleb. 2501
Hobart, Chauncey. 2452
Hobart, John Henry. 1912, 2589
[Hobart John Henry, bp.] 1775-1830. 612, 1613, 1912, 1937, 2130, 2209, 2589
Hobart, John Henry. 1681
Hobart, Margaret Jefferys. 2970
Hobart, Michael E. 2319
[Hobart, Nathaniel]. 2689, 3570
Hobart, Nehemiah. 3353
Hobart, Noah. 1503, 1787
Hobart, Richard. 2673
Hobart, William Kirk. 2271
Hobbes, Thomas. 1821, 2839
Hobbs, Albert Hoyt. 2321
Hobbs, Charles Albert. 3597
Hobbs, Charles R. 3170, 3179
Hobbs, Edward C. 484, 1920
Hobbs, Herschel H. 148, 163, 181, 342, 346, 363, 380, 403, 405, 416, 423, 428, 433, 440, 443, 454, 468, 493, 521, 1295, 1350, 1574, 1771, 1829, 1966, 2039, 2054, 2057, 2721, 3531, 3638, 3663
Hobbs, James. 1821
Hobbs, James Randolph. 3677
Hobby, Alvin. 643
Hobe, Laura. 1367, 3790
Hoben, Allan. 2069, 3151
Hobensack, Alice (Bartow) 3151
Hobhouse, Leonard Trelawney. 1580
Hobhouse, Stephen Henry. 2201
Hobson, Alphonzo Augustus. 2976, 3589
Hobson, Ina Jesperson. 1944
Hobson, John Atkinson. 3443
Hobson, Julius W. 3436
Hochberg, Gary M. 2163, 3816
Hochman, Baruch. 1517
Hock, Samuel Vanden. 209
Hocken, Peter. 2873
Hocker, Clarence. 1059, 3479
Hocker, Edward W. 2830
Hockin, Katharine. 1110
Hocking, David L. 953, 2346
Hocking, William Ernest. 1413, 3078, 3100, 1413, 3141, 3100, 3141
Hockman, William Smithson. 3784
Hodder, Alfred. 2843
Hodder-Williams, John Ernest. 3818
Hoddinott, Ralph F. 1160
Hodes, Aubrey. 699
Hodge, Archibald Alexander. 105, 1821, 2914, 3644, 3651
Hodge, Charles. 322, 326, 363, 466, 468, 1821, 2925, 2936, 3644
Hodge, Clarence. 3698
Hodge, Frederick Arthur. 1467
Hodge, John Aspinwall. 2915
Hodge, Richard Morse. 321
Hodge, Warren Sylvester. 1165
Hodgell, P. C. 1447
Hodges, Bert. 294
Hodges, Edward Lewis. 3151
Hodges, George. 285, 894, 1821, 3341, 397, 534, 629, 633, 638, 924, 1059, 1192, 1388, 1821, 1981, 2031, 2699, 2865, 2964, 2967, 2973, 3151, 3196, 3280, 3448
Hodges, Graham R. 907
Hodges, Henry Clay. 500
Hodges, Herbert Arthur. 1059, 1729, 2836
Hodges, Herman. 2641
Hodges, Isam B. 2048
Hodges, Jesse Wilson. 2174
Hodges, Julia Shelley. 1822
Hodges, Margaret. 2665, 2952
Hodges, Melvin L. 1119, 1566, 1904, 2493, 2550
Hodges, Norman E. 953
Hodges, Serena M. 92
Hodges, Tony. 1942
Hodges, Turner, ed. 621
Hodges, Zane Clark. 3289
Hodgetts, E. Brayley. 3570
Hodgin, Edwin Stanton. 1597
Hodgkin, Eliot. 399, 1957, 2760
Hodgkin, Henry Theodore. 2015, 3443, 1675, 3443

Hodgkin, Lucy Violet. 1675, 1782
Hodgkin, Thomas. 1637
Hodgkins, Louise Manning. 2525
Hodgkinson, Frank Cyril. 1698
Hodgman, Edwin Ruthven. 1811
Hodgman, Abraham Percival. 907
Hodgson, Francis. 2450, 2421, 2447, 3617
Hodgson, Geraldine Emma. 2638, 2645
Hodgson, Homera. 1997
Hodgson, James Thomas. 1822, 2857
Hodgson, Joan. 3897
Hodgson, Leonard. 105, 390, 1069, 1104, 1491, 1751, 1952, 1956, 2249, 3389, 3663, 3711
Hodgson, Marshall G. S. 92
Hodgson, Natalie. 3180, 3886
Hodgson, Peter Crafts. 178, 1659, 1819, 2039
Hodgson, Shadworth Hollway. 2418
Hodgson, William. 924, 1685
Hodous, Lewis. 702
Hodsdon, Nick. 2347
Hodshire, Edwin Brunnell. 1371
Hodson, Geoffrey. 390, 526, 2067, 3575, 3685, 3689
Hoeck, Louis George. 1119
Hoedemaker, Libertus Arend. 2708
Hoefler, Richard Carl. 1169, 2901
Hoeger, Frederick T. 1836, 2249, 2580
Hoeger, Fredreick T. 1836
Hoehn, Edward. 3382
Hoehn, Matthew. 754
Hoehner, Harold W. 1996
Hoek, Ann. 1012, 2773
Hoek, Samuel Vanden. 2016, 2415
Hoekema, Anthony A. 1716, 139, 1530, 2323, 3325
Hoekema, Hans. 1572
Hoekendijk, Johannes Christiaan. 1125
Hoekenga, P. J. 2380
Hoeksema, Gertrude. 903
Hoeksema, Herman. 108, 454, 470, 1751, 1801, 2022, 2031, 2214, 2249, 2975, 3289, 3353, 3644
Hoekstra, Harvey Thomas. 2554, 3850
Hoeller, Stephan A. 3588
Hoen, Reu Everett. 3382
Hoenig, Sidney B. 570
Hoenig, Sidney Benjamin. 570, 3223
Hoensbroech, Paul Kajus, graf von. 1945
Hoenshel, Elmer Ulysses. 4, 964, 3144
Hoernle, August Friedrich Rudolf. 711
Hoernle, Reinhold Friedrich Alfred. 2834
Hoes, Jack. 2389
Hoever, Hugo Henry. 193, 796, 900
Hoey, Robert F. 2368
Hofer, Ernst. 1952
Hofer, Johannes. 1713, 1822
Hoff, Benjamin. 2196
Hoff, Emanuel Buechley. 461
Hoff, Ernest Gockley. 1822
Hoffding, Harald. 3100
Hoffer, Frank William. 2919
Hoffer, Gertrude (Schafer) 1448
Hoffer, Paul. 2582
Hoffman, Bengt Runo. 2280
Hoffman, Charles F. 3504
Hoffman, Charles Fenno. 3206
Hoffman, Charles Frederick. 1996
Hoffman, Dominic M. 3487
Hoffman, Dona. 1822, 3540
Hoffman, Edward. 723
Hoffman, Edwin M. 937
Hoffman, Frank Sargent. 3060
Hoffman, Fred W. 3232
Hoffman, Gail. 2762
Hoffman, Harold Richard. 1897, 1898
Hoffman, Hazel. 2896
Hoffman, Hazel Ward. 964
Hoffman, Herman S. 3540
Hoffman, James W. 2558, 2713
Hoffman, John Charles. 2780
Hoffman, John Leslie. 762
Hoffman, Lawrence A. 2110, 2885
Hoffman, Levi Samuel. 1952
Hoffman, Mathias Martin. 2693
Hoffman, Murray. 1490, 2966
Hoffman, Reuben F. 1592
Hoffman, Ronan. 690, 2554
Hoffman, Ross John Swartz. 763
Hoffman, William Henry. 2997
Hoffmann, Alexius. 843
Hoffmann, Christoph. 3594
Hoffmann, Conrad. 2077
Hoffmann, Felix. 2022
Hoffmann, Friedrich. 606
Hoffmann, Gerhard. 1154
Hoffmann, Hans Peter. 1981
Hoffmann, Helmut. 2193
Hoffmann, Mathias Martin. 1481, 2246
Hoffmann, Oswald C. J. 1119, 1448, 2247, 2299
Hoffner, Joseph. 3449
Hofinger, Johannes. 746, 747, 838, 935, 1246, 1454, 1498, 1566, 3151
Hofman, David. 127
Hofmann, Hans. 2709, 2784, 3413

Hofmann, Hans F. 1923. 1258, 1297, 1324, 1659, 2709, 2784, 3413
Hofmann, Hans [Fritz]. 1258, 1297
Hofmann, Johann Christian Konrad von. 287
Hofmann, Julius. 133
Hofmann, Rudolf Hugo. 2249
Hofmans, Flor. 2039
Hofrenning, James B. 964
Hofrenning, Ralph W. 2503
Hogan, Benedict. 1793
Hogan, Bernice. 1199
Hogan, Bernice. 1286, 1418, 1439, 3843
Hogan, John Baptist. 3680, 856
Hogan, John Gerard. 764, 1024, 2389, 3280
Hogan, John Joseph. 822, 1294, 1822
Hogan, Joseph F. 3223
Hogan, Stanislaus M. 3780
Hogan, Thaddeus. 3341
Hogan, William. 869, 800, 2366
Hogan, William F. 2570, 3031, 3487
Hogan, William Francis. 2570
Hogarth, Charles Pinckney. 2432
Hogarth, Grace Allen. 3026
Hogbin, Herbert Ian. 1540
Hoge, Arista. 2912
Hoge, Dean R. 1309, 3679, 3735
Hoge, Moses Drury. 2819
Hoge, Peyton Harrison. 1822
Hoge, William James. 177
Hogg, Charles F. 380, 478
Hogg, Garry. 2569
Hogg, Rena L. 3128
Hogg, William B. 454
Hogg, William Richey. 2493, 1913, 2493
Hogins, James Burl. 2232
Hoglund, Gunnar. 3876
Hogue, C. Bill. 1170, 1566
Hogue, Harland E. 64
Hogue, Harland Edwin. 1100
Hogue, Richard. 984, 3829
Hogue, Richard Wallace. 964
Hogue, Roswell A. 2854
Hogue, Wilson Thomas. 19, 1835, 2408, 19, 1566, 1875, 2433
Hoh, Paul J. 2891
Hoh, Paul Jacob. 321, 431, 900, 2288
Hoh, Philip Richard. 3187
Hohensee, Donald. 3324
Hohenstein, Walter E. 2214, 2297
Hohmann, Harry E. 1599
Hohn, Hermann. 3784
Hoifjeld, Johannes. 2298
Hoiland, Richard. 3151
Holand, Hjalmar Rued. 2715
Holash, Lise M. 849
[Holbach, Paul Henri Thiry. 100, 1091, 1104, 1978, 2129, 3567, 3568
Holborn, Hajo. 1858, 3040, 1858, 3040
Holbrook, Clyde A. 1500, 1592, 3111, 3112
Holbrook, David. 1865
Holbrook, David Leverett. 638
Holbrook, Edwin A. 2949
Holbrook, Sabra. 3052
Holck, Frederick H. 1416
Holck, Manfred. 1168, 1292
Holcomb, Carlysle Henry. 964
Holcomb, Clifford A. 915, 1204
Holcomb, Harmon Robert. 201
Holcomb, Helen Harriet Howe. 2530
Holcomb, Hillman. 53
Holcomb, Jerry. 3179
Holcomb, Luther J. 3886
Holcomb, Walt. 1553, 2131
Holcombe, William Henry. 2689, 3199
Holdcraft, Paul Ellsworth. 880, 1168, 3730, 907, 1163, 1268, 1840, 3373
Holdcroft, L. Thomas. 1829
Holden, Douglas T. 1416
Holden, Elizabeth W. 900
Holden, John Stuart. 964, 3321
Holden, Vincent F. 1799
Holden, Warren. 298
Holder, Charles Frederick. 3093
Holder, J D. 2941
Holder, Naomi Dail. 3810
Holder, Ray. 1294, 3819
Holderness, Ginny Ward. 1253, 1260, 1261
Holdich, Joseph. 1628, 3128
Holdsworth, William West. 390
Hole, Charles. 662, 1184
Hole, Christina. 1485, 3285, 3825
Hole, Donald. 3505
Hole, Helen Griscom Bell. 1683
Hole, Samuel Reynolds. 2218
Holeman, Francis Rader. 1017
[Holgate, Jerome Bonaparte]. 463, 3644
Holifield, E. Brooks. 3266, 3666
Holisher, Desider. 2152, 3744
Holl, Adolf. 1027, 1413, 1642, 2039, 2040
Holl, Jack Monroe. 1663
Holl, Karl. 2280, 3034
Holladay, Carl R. 88, 2011
Holladay, James Minor. 1175

Holladay, William Lee. 543, 546, 547, 1796, 1943
Holland, Barron. 1815
Holland, Clifton L. 2460
Holland, Cornelius Joseph. 1981, 3676
Holland, Daniel W. 3594
Holland, David. 2063, 2409
Holland, Dewitte Talmage. 2910
Holland, Edith. 2628
Holland, Elihu Goodwin. 124
Holland, Frederic May. 3533
Holland, Frederick E. 2498
Holland, Henry. 1617
Holland, Henry Scott. 76, 1592, 3341
Holland, Isabelle. 1734
Holland, Jack H. 984, 3521
Holland, Jeanne. 1736
Holland, John. 3546
Holland, John W. 3353
Holland, John Wesley. 2425, 2436
Holland, Kenneth J. 1448
Holland, Mary Ildephonse. 3418
Holland, Richard. 3876
Holland, Robert E. 3051
Holland, Vivian. 734
Holland, William Webster. 1350
Hollander, Annette. 903
Hollander, P. Scott. 1802
Holland's, the magazine of the South. 1274
Hollaway, Ida Nelle. 984, 1824, 2245
Hollaway, Steve. 1308
Hollenbach, Blanche (Schwartz) 3151
Hollenbach, David. 1136
Hollenback, Roy L. 3299
Hollender, Betty Rosett. 629
Hollensen, Martin E. 2295
Hollenweger, Walter J. 2815
Holleran, Mary Patricia. 1146
Holley, Horace. 127, 129
Holley, Jasper Elza. 294, 646, 2764
Holley, Joseph Winthrop. 3319
Holley, Raymond. 3176
Holliday, Feranandez C. 2452
Holliday, Fernandez C. 303, 3815
Holliday, Robert Kelvin. 3432
Hollings, Michael. 1291, 1824, 2873, 2885, 2891
Hollingsworth, Thekla. 3782
Hollington, Richard Deming. 2997
Hollinson, Harry. 408
Hollis, Allen. 2584
Hollis, Christopher. 1526, 2268
Hollis, Christopher. 1075, 1098, 1947, 2703, 2769
Hollis, Daniel Walker. 1161
Hollis, Harry. 3391, 3780
Hollis, Marcia. 991
Hollis, Michael. 1235, 1895
Hollis, Michael [Arthur Michael Hollis]. 1895
Hollis, William Slater. 1995
Hollis. Christopher. 3771
Hollister, Alonzo Giles. 3395
Hollister, Horace Edward. 3319
Hollister, John Norman. 3403
Hollister, Mary Brewster. 2490, 2509
Holliwell, Raymond Neff. 46
Hollobough, Camillus J. 1700, 2057, 1700
Holloway, Alpheus H. 1413, 1966
Holloway, Fred Garrigus. 1566
Holloway, Henry. 3041
Holloway, J[ames] C[rawford]. 1830
Holloway, James Y. 1509, 3784
Holloway, Jerry Lloyd. 1630
Holloway, Leonard L. 3484
Holloway, Maurice R. 2673
Holloway, Pearl. 3026
Holloway, Richard. 991, 1722, 1998
Holloway, Vernon Howard. 1086
Holly, Alonzo Potter Burgess. 275
Holly, Henry Hudson. 1156
Holly, Israel. 440
Holly, Norman. 883
Holm, Dallas. 1749, 1824
Holm, Francis W. 1231
Holm, Frits. 2684
Holm, Jean L. 3111
Holm, Sarah E. 2167
Holman (A. J.) Company, Philadelphia. 227
Holman, Charles Thomas. 2997, 3672
Holman, Mary John. 114
Holmberg, Bengt. 1241, 2798
Holme, Benjamin. 1682
Holme, Leonard Ralph. 1183
Holmer, Paul L. 1592, 2219, 3060, 3622
Holmes, Abiel. 2742, 3810
Holmes, Almira E. 3186
Holmes, Arhtur. 2798
[Holmes, Arthur David] 1876. 2807
Holmes, Arthur Frank. 1104, 1127, 1597
Holmes, Brian. 2517
Holmes, C. Raymond. 1316, 1366, 1824
Holmes, Chauncey D. 3522
Holmes, David. 2421, 3753, 3803
Holmes, Deborah Aydt. 2625

[Holmes, Edmond Gore Alexander] 1850. 702, 1050, 3060, 3462
Holmes, Edmond Gore Alexander. 706, 1654, 1703, 2063
Holmes, Elkanah. 1376
Holmes, Ella Marie. 2503
Holmes, Ernest Edward. 1888
Holmes, Ernest Shurtleff. 2695
Holmes, Ethel Greenough. 2226
Holmes, Fenwicke Lindsay. 2695, 1825, 2005, 2695
Holmes, Frederick Lionel. 3709
Holmes, Gare Vincent Arthur. 2338
Holmes, George. 2040, 2901
Holmes, George S. 225
[Holmes, Georgiana (Klingle)]. 1388
Holmes, Harold. 3151
Holmes, Jerome Crane. 2695
Holmes, Jesse Herman. 3473
Holmes, John Andrew. 3821
Holmes, John Haynes. 1059, 1119, 1310, 1888, 2005, 2077, 2118, 3353, 1456, 1511, 3055
Holmes, John Mallory. 1069, 1992
Holmes, Kenneth A. 2561
Holmes, Mabel Dodge. 1938
Holmes, Marjorie. 984, 1714, 2267, 2389, 2625, 3842, 3843
Holmes, Nathaniel. 1881
Holmes, Nickels J. 2813
Holmes, Pauline. 684
Holmes, Peter. 872
Holmes, Phoebe Marie. 46, 887, 1277
Holmes, Prescott. 294, 1981
Holmes, Reed M. 294, 1928, 3216
Holmes, Samuel. 553
Holmes, Thomas. 2174
Holmes, Thomas, D.D. 3616
Holmes, Thomas Joseph. 1132, 2310
Holmes, Urban Tigner. 64, 1246, 1298, 1328, 1524, 2251, 2255, 2785, 2787, 3492, 3668
Holmes, Walter Herbert Greame. 2638, 2754, 2997
Holmes, William A. 1244
Holmes, Winnibel F. 1626
Holmgren, Charles John Augustus. 1059
Holmgren, Frederick. 2139
Holmgren, Virginia C. 480
Holmio, Armas Kustaa Ensio. 3034
Holms, A. Campbell. 3505
Holroyd, Stuart. 94
Holsinger, Henry R. 1235
Holsinger, Justus G. 2407
Holst, Lawrence E. 885
Holsworth, Dorris Campbell. 3820
Holt, Allan Eugene. 1966
Holt, Anne. 2939
Holt, Arthur Erastus. 1321, 3443, 1086, 3448
Holt, Basil. 3341
Holt, Basil Fenelon. 697, 1015, 1466, 2487, 2499, 3319, 3817
Holt, Benjamin M. 2291
Holt, David R. 1168
Holt, Edd. 800

Holt, Glenn. 3792
Holt, Harriet Maxson. 2550
Holt, Harry Quentin. 1270
Holt, Henry. 2989
Holt, Ivan Lee. 1040, 1803, 2425, 2436, 2950, 3851
Holt, John Agee. 1622, 2057
Holt, John Marshall. 523, 2792
Holt, John W. 1592
Holt, Peter. 1504
Holt, Simma. 1482
Holt, Turner Hamilton. 964
Holtby, Robert Tinsley. 1754
Holter, Don W. 2431
Holtermann, Carla. 964, 984, 2389
Holtmermann, Carla. 3492
Holtom, Daniel Clarence. 1935, 3403, 3404
Holtrop, Donald. 1132
Holtz, Avraham. 1944
Holtz, Gregory M. 825
Holum, John R. 3083
Holweck, Frederick George. 3280, 1025
The Holy Cross magazine. 2957
Holy name society. 856
Holy Order of MANS. 3588, 3811
Holy Spirit Association for Unification of World Christianity, Seoul, Korea. 3141
Holy Transfiguration Monastery. 3258
Holyoake, George Jacob. 3327
Holzer, Hans. 3053
Holzer, Hans W. 95, 1283, 1479, 1709, 2726, 2731, 2846, 2948, 2989, 3002, 3053, 3060, 3505, 3521, 3715, 3823
Holzer Hans W. 1111, 2021
Holzman, Donald. 1936
Holzner, Josef. 2798
Homan, Helen Mary (Walker) 70, 1642
Homan, Helen (Walker) 54, 70, 71, 1021, 1642, 2223, 2351, 2576

Homan, J A. 3595
Homan, Walter Joseph. 903, 1683
Homans, Peter. 1673, 2994
Home Altar (The) 1434
Home, Daniel Dunglas. 1838, 3520, 3505
Home, Georgina. 3285
Home life (Nashville) 1433
Home Missions Conference, Chicago, 1961. 1278
Homer, N.Y. Calvary Episcopal church. 1524
Homer, William Bradford. 1341
Homerus. 2860
Homrighausen, Elmer George. 3744, 1059, 1119, 1566
Hone, Joseph Maunsell. 192
Hone, Ralph E. 549, 550, 2124
Honeycutt, Roy Lee. 485, 537, 557, 558, 1313
Honeywell, Albert A. 1158
Honeywell, Betty. 3839
Hong, Christopher C. 234, 534, 2095, 2150, 2765
Hong, Edna (Hatlestad) 1448, 1751, 3540
Hong, Edna Hatlestead. 2321
Hong, Howard. 3328
Hong, Howard Vincent. 3328
Hong, Silas. 1090
Honline, Moses Alfred. 473, 3203, 473
Honness, Elizabeth Hoffman. 621, 631
Honor, Leo Lazarius. 2106
Honors, Mildred Olive. 280
Honour, Alan. 1410, 1411
Honourius. 2313
Hood, Alice Watkins. 3073
Hood, C Azella. 1448
Hood, David. 163
Hood, E. A. 964
Hood, Edmund Lyman. 2670, 2696
Hood, Edwin Paxton. 2901
Hood, Frances Arabella (Jones) 3505
Hood, Fred J. 2937, 3050
Hood, Frederic. 3663
Hood, George Ezekiel. 2322
Hood, Gwenyth. 3225
Hood, James Walker. 454
Hood, John. 1742
Hood, John Charles Fulton. 1880
Hood, John J. 3458
Hood, John O. 911
[Hood, Myer S. 2114
Hood, Robert. 1381
Hoogstra, Jacob Tunis. 727, 730
Hook, Diana ffarington. 1470, 1879
Hook, H. Phillip. 1730
Hook, Martha. 621
Hook, Milton Raymond. 28
Hook, Sidney. 1152
Hook, Walter Farquhar. 3638
Hooke, Samuel Henry. 2014, 94, 523, 1395, 2014, 2111, 2177, 2667, 201, 523
Hooker, Arlie J. 64
Hooker, Douglas. 175, 1107
Hooker, Edward William. 2552, 3431
Hooker, Elizabeth Robbins. 2547, 1040, 3253
Hooker, Horace. 294
Hooker, James. 2808
Hooker, Mary Ann (Brown) 1401, 1405, 1506
Hooker, Morna Dorothy. 372
Hooker, Richard. 1240, 1146, 1214, 1216, 1218, 1240, 1488, 1489, 3629
Hooker, Thomas. 964, 1240, 1361, 1845, 2637, 3029, 3030, 3630
Hooks, George W. 639
Hoole, Daryl Van Dam. 1233, 2614, 3188
Hooley, Thomas. 720, 3275
Hoon, Paul Waitman. 2235
Hooper, Carrie Thomas. 2695
Hooper, John. 1216, 1702
Hooper, John Stirling. 612
Hooper, John Stirling Morley. 1860, 612
Hooper, Joseph. 22
Hooper, Robert E. 1273, 2669
*Hooper, Roberta Anderson. 621
Hooper, William Lloyd. 1209
Hooper, William Loyd. 1209
Hoopes, Wilford Lawrence. 3601
Hoornaert, Rodolphe. 842
Hooton, Caradine R. 3595
Hooton, Walter Stewart. 2493
Hoover, Arlie J. 64
Hoover, David W. 1078
Hoover, Dorothy E. 14
Hoover, Mab Graff. 984, 1845, 3843
Hoover, Mario G. 92
Hoover, Oliver Perry. 435, 1952, 2056
Hoover, Thomas. 1935, 3893
Hoover, William I. T. 3116
Hooykaas, Christiaan. 131
Hooykaas, Reijer. 3084
Hope Evangeline. 2936, 3427
Hope, Ludvig. 1439, 3299, 3479
Hope, Marjorie. 1108
Hope, Mary. 18, 964
Hope, Norman Victor. 1491

Hope, William Henry St. John. 1310
Hope, Wingfield. 1608
Hopewell, William J. 1704
Hopfe, Lewis M. 3116
Hophan, Otto. 71, 2355
Hopkin, Charles Edward. 1424, 2786, 3693
Hopkins, Alfred. 1159
Hopkins, Archibald. 75
Hopkins, Charles Howard. 2625, 3433, 3452, 3871, 3874
Hopkins, Daniel C. 3413
Hopkins, Edward Washburn. 1521, 1812, 1896, 2316, 2663, 3109, 3116
[Hopkins, Emma Curtis]. 943, 1033, 2638
Hopkins, Erasius Whitford. 2695
Hopkins, Eva(Elliot) 1846
Hopkins, Eva (Elliott) 1846
Hopkins, Fred Washington. 2249
Hopkins, Garland Evans. 527
Hopkins, Granville Shelby. 3178
Hopkins, Harry Walter. 46
Hopkins, Hugh Alexander Evan. 1292, 3409
Hopkins, J G E. 1900, 3426
Hopkins, Jasper. 49
Hopkins, Jeannette. 3728
Hopkins, John Goddard. 3685
Hopkin's, John Henry. 52, 60, 73, 739, 800, 1189, 2467
Hopkins, John Henry. 1328, 1847, 2962
Hopkins, Joseph G E. 1901, 3426
Hopkins, Joseph Martin. 3852
Hopkins, Mark. 60, 122, 123, 1098, 1100, 1702, 2323
Hopkins, Martin K. 445, 561
Hopkins, Mary. 856, 1605
Hopkins, Paul A. 2480
Hopkins, Pryns. 92, 2997
Hopkins, Samuel. 3334, 3532, 729, 1334, 1823, 1847, 2375, 2465, 2752, 3353, 3644, 3007
Hopkins, Walter Sawyer. 290
Hopkins Josiah. 3663
Hopkinson, Alfred Stephan. 500
Hopkinson, Arthur Wells. 2638
Hopkinson, Henry Thomas. 2400
Hopler, Thom. 1074
Hopper, David. 676, 3699
Hopper, Myron Taggart. 475, 3856
Hopper, Stanley Romaine. 1104
[Hopper, Vincent Foster] 1906. 1373, 3575
Hoppin, James Mason. 2901, 3672
Hoppin, Ruth. 404, 2942, 3832
Hopson, Ella (Lord) 1465, 1847
Hopwood, Percy George Samuel. 907, 1586, 1592, 1888
Horace, J. Gentry. 442
Horace, Lillian B. 146, 3817
Horan, Ellamay. 887, 621, 746
Horatczuk, Michael. 998
Horatius Flaccus, Quintus. 2199
Horder, William Garrett. 1722
Hordern, William. 64, 314, 2160, 2683, 3654, 3682
Hordern, William Edward. 3654
Hore, Alexander Hugh. 1768, 1758
Horgan, Daniel F. 2415
Horgan, Paul. 2195
Horger, Jocob Travis. 234
Hori, Ichiro. 1935
Horine, John Winebrenner. 748, 2527, 3734
Horka-Follick, Lorayne Ann, 1940. 1806
Hormann, Karl. 948, 3792
Horn, Aloysius. 1111
Horn, Dorothy D. 1872
Horn, Edward Traill. 1262, 2237, 3341, 2237
Horn, Geoffrey. 621
[Horn, Henry]. 3505
Horn, Henry E. 1208, 2294, 2846
[Horn, Henry J.]. 3505
*Horn, James G. 1075
Horn, Robert Chisolm. 964
Horn, Robert Millen. 2160
Horn, S. G. 3505
Horn, Siegfried H. 207, 244, 1582
Horn, Susan G. 3505
Horn, Walter Williams. 182
*Horn, William M. 3056, 3184
Hornaday, William H. D. 1825
Hornback, Florence Mary. 3151
*Hornberger, J. C. 3373
[Hornbrooke, Orinda Althea (Dudley)]. 1847
Horne, Charles Francis. 310
Horne, Charles M. 479, 3289
Horne, Charles Silvester. 2901
Horne, Chavis F. 163
Horne, Chevis F. 2901
Horne, George. 3329
Horne, Herman Harrell. 639, 2004, 2061, 2063, 2592, 3151, 2061, 2592
Horne, Hugh R. 1351, 3353
Horne, John. 2873

Horne, Melville. 2520
Horne, Shirley. 2556
Horne, Thomas. 3039
Horne, Thomas Hartwell. 310
Hornef, Josef. 1408
Horner, Esther (Daniels) 2490
Horner, Isaline Blew. 3841
Horner, James M. 2860
*Horner, Jerry. 445
Horner, Joseph. 442, 1401
Horner, Norman A. 2513
Horner, Thomas Marland. 1844, 3390
Horner, Tom. 1844
Horner, William Wallace. 2873
Horning, Mary Eulogia. 3210
Hornshuh, Fred. 615
Hornus, Jean Michel. 3794
Hornyold, John Joseph. 1313, 3265
Horosz, William. 1801, 2320
Horowitz, Caroline. 629
Horowitz, David. 1777
Horowitz, George. 2074
Horr, George Edwin. 140, 534, 1888, 1966
*Horrell, B. C. 3373
Horrell, Benjamin. 3373
Horrell, Benjamin C. 3373
Horsch, John. 2221, 2403, 1175, 1859, 2563, 1578, 1859
Horsfield, L A E. 2253
Horsley, Albert E. 1363
Horsley, Samuel. 546, 1226, 2002, 2051
Horstmann, Ignatius Frederick. 274
Horstmann, J[ulius] H[ermann Edward] 1869. 1413
Horstmann, Julius Hermann Edward. 1545, 3886
Hort, Fenton John Anthony. 1192, 1616, 1617, 1848
Hort, William Jillard. 2656
Hortin, Paul. 1448
Horton, Adey. 1996
Horton, Dougals. 3784
Horton, Douglas. 964, 1040, 1044, 1343, 3732, 3769, 3770, 3771, 3853
Horton, Edward Augustus. 662
Horton, Fred L. 404, 2401
Horton, Gilmer Ayers. 3178
Horton, Isabelle. 894, 2461
Horton, James P. 3128
Horton, Jotham. 3819
Horton, M. B. 3393
Horton, Naomi. 631, 1533
Horton, Robert Forman. 440, 2014, 2531, 1335, 2901, 3602
Horton, Roy F. 1911, 2627
Horton, Stanley M. 329, 447, 478, 606, 1834
Horton, Thomas C. 964, 2020
Horton, Thomas Corvin. 2020
Horton, Thomas Corwin. 2020, 2873
Horton, Wade H. 1229, 1716, 3353
Horton, Walter M[arshall]. 1722
Horton, Walter Marshall. 1059, 1281, 1335, 1491, 1722, 2059, 2997, 3644, 3656, 3658, 3663
Horton-Billard, Peter H. 2749
Horvath, Tibor. 64, 348, 763, 2040, 3271
Horwitz, Elinor Lander. 1470
Hosain, Safdar. 2628
Hoschander, Jacob. 2114
Hoschouer, William Isaac. 3751
Hosford, Benjamin Franklin. 2798
Hosford, Dorothy G. 2660
Hoshor, John. 131
Hosie, Stanley W. 1308
Hosier, Helen Kooiman. 420, 924, 1471, 1576, 1633, 1735, 2011, 2187, 3846
Hoskier, Herman Charles. 1888, 317
Hoskins, Edgar. 1848
Hoskins, Frank W. 2813
Hoskins, Fred. 1344
Hoskins, Sarah Bartlett. 3221
Hoskyns, Edwyn. 348, 1226
Hosmer, Frederick Lucian. 1737
[Hosmer, Frederick Lucian] 1840-1929. 1456
Hosmer, James Kendall. 2088, 2089
Hosmer, John Wesley. 1351
Hosmer, Rachel. 3484
Hosmer, William. 3424
Hospers, John. 88
Hospital social service association of New York city. 887
Hospodar, Blaise. 3287
Hoss, Elijah Embree. 2442, 2308, 2620
Host, Mabel M (Browning) 621
Hoste, Charles Dixon. 1893
Hostetler, George. 2464
Hostetler, John Andrew. 1308, 1858, 1859, 2404, 2407, 2408, 3254
Hostetler, lester. 2406
Hostetler, Paul. 1301, 1848
*Hostetter, Charles. 3199
Hostie, Raymond. 2159, 2780, 2998, 3785
Hosty, Thomas J. 907, 3886
Hotchkin, Beriah Bishop. 1589, 2752

Hotchkin, Samuel Fitch. 1293, 2059, 2063
Hotchkiss, Samuel. 3505
Hotchkiss, Willis Ray. 2536
Hoth, Iva. 527, 629, 631, 1198, 1981
*Hotsinpiller, Stanley T. 2873
Hott, George P. 2063
Hottinger, Johann Jacob. 3900
Houck, Frederick Alfons. 42, 781, 998, 1100, 1448, 1733, 3078, 3798
Houck, George Francis. 824, 1304
Houdini, Harry. 1346, 3240, 3520, 3505
Houf, Horace Thomas. 3060, 3238
Hough, Charles Wesley. 940
Hough, H D. 2915
Hough, Joseph C. 1132
Hough, Lynn Harold. 493, 2901, 100, 214, 384, 964, 1050, 1055, 1059, 1094, 1119, 1281, 1448, 1551, 1566, 2226, 2232, 2425, 2436, 2784, 3034, 3341, 3353
Hough, Robert Ervin. 1696, 3682
Hough, Samuel Strickler. 3730
Houghton, Frank. 1592, 912, 964
Houghton, George Hendric. 2057
Houghton, Leighton. 752, 1938
Houghton, Louise (Seymour) 2241, 500, 616, 1439, 1966, 2954, 3534
Houghton, Ross C. 2127
Houghton, S. M. 1175
Houghton, Stanley. 912
Houghton, Walter Edwards. 2703, 2705
Houghton, Walter Raleigh. 1324
Houghton, Will H. 163
Houghton, Will Henry. 201, 2587
Houlbrooke, Ralph Anthony. 1488
Houlden, James Leslie. 348, 369, 371, 378, 446, 3644
Hoult, Thomas Ford. 3086
Houppert, Joseph W. 2703
Houpt, Charles Theodore. 2178
Hourani, George Fadlo. 21, 1926, 2840
House, Abigail (Clark) 3128
House, Agnes Augusta. 3505
House, Anne W. 1431, 1714, 2389
House, E C. 964
House, Elwin Lincoln. 964, 1050, 1599, 1793, 1952, 2726, 2994, 3199
House, Erwin. 3364, 1840
House, H. Wayne. 402
[House, Susan Deline (Beers) 1850. 1849, 3692
Houselander, Frances Caryll. 998, 1263, 1448, 1777, 2361, 3526, 3792
Houser, James Alfred. 3100
Houseworth, Henry. 463
Housman, Marzelius. 1575
[Houston, George]. 1083
Houston, Jack. 3829
Houston, James. A. 1532
Houston, James Macintosh. 1381
Houston, Rutherford Rowland. 500
Houston, Tex. University. 213
Houston, William. 1256
Houtart, Francois. 759, 1059, 1245, 2789
Houteff, Victor T. 3379
Houtepen, Anton W. J. 1155, 3771
Houtin, Albert. 3128
Houtryve, Idesbald van. 188
[Houts, Margaret J.]. 3520
Houts, Margaret Scott. 3505
Houtz, Alfred. 3043, 3377, 1321
Hovanesian, Archie. 1059
Hovda, Robert W. 2234, 2235, 3003
Hoven, Ard. 1466
Hoven, Victor Emanuel. 378, 454, 3720
Hovenkamp, Herbert. 3085
Hoversten, Chester E. 2214
Hovey, Alvah. 3616, 123, 476, 1141, 1699, 2706, 3616, 3644, 2040, 123
*Hovey, Bryon P. 3341
Hovey, Byron P. 3376, 1295
Hovey, George Rice. 1849, 2706
Hovey, Geroge Rice. 290
Hovey, Sallie. 2226
Hovis, William Forney. 3353, 1351
Hovre, Eugene de. 2685, 3531
How, John Charles Halland. 964
How, Samuel Blanchard. 3424
How, Thomas Yardley. 2466, 2964
Howard, Austin Marlow. 3505
Howard, Barbara. 1605, 3218
Howard, Burt Estes. 3199
Howard, Clifford. 1966, 2779, 2827, 2828, 3389
Howard, David M. 549, 1765, 1830, 1943, 2504, 2512, 2983
Howard, Dorothy. 984, 1849
Howard, Edith V. 1707, 2201
Howard, Ezra Lee. 3505
Howard, Frank E. 1159
Howard, Fred D. 363, 2251
Howard, George. 381
Howard, George Parkinson. 2955, 3194
Howard, Greenbery B. 3228
Howard, Harry Clay. 924
Howard, Harry F. 1514, 1696
Howard, Harry Frank. 606, 3792

Howard, Henry. 573, 587, 1577, 1592, 3341, 3353, 907, 2931
Howard, Irving E. 3436
Howard, J. Freeman. 3089
Howard, J. Grant. 1316, 1740
Howard, J. N. 3505
Howard, James Enos. 1383
Howard, James Keir. 485
Howard, John. 621
Howard, John Gordon. 2389, 3876
Howard, Joseph. 184
Howard, Leslie G. 1079
Howard, Linda. 931, 1849
Howard, Milford Wriarson. 3737
Howard, Minnie Frances. 2855
Howard Mission and Home for Little Wanderers, New York. 1865
Howard, Peter. 699, 2593, 2753
Howard, Philip Eugene. 964, 687, 964, 2503, 2891, 3179, 3564, 3600, 3716, 990, 3012
Howard, Randolph Levi. 2505
Howard, Richard E. 376, 2326
Howard, Richard P. 678, 3215
Howard, Roy J. 3222
Howard, Thomas. 64, 1473, 1608, 2420, 3327
Howard, Vernon Linwood. 281, 2482
Howard, Walden. 1244
Howard, Wayne. 883, 3776
Howard, Wilbert Francis. 414
Howard, Wilbur F. 964
Howard, William Lee. 3388
Howarth, Eleanor Katherine (Paget) 282
Howatt, J. Reid. 1888
Howe, Claude L. 171, 1285
Howe, Cora E. 3232
Howe, Daniel Wait. 3007
Howe, Daniel Walker. 3730
Howe, E. Margaret. 3835
Howe, Eber D. 2603, 2611
Howe, Ellic. 98, 2186
Howe, Frances R. 2198, 3531
Howe, Frederic R. 64
Howe, George. 2919, 3680, 2658, 2659
Howe, Henry. 1467, 3204
Howe, John. 3008, 3028
Howe, Laurence Henry. 3879
Howe, Lee Arthur. 2981
Howe, Leroy T. 2873
Howe, Mark Antony De Wolfe. 694
Howe, Mark Antony DeWolfe. 2865
Howe, Mark De Wolfe. 1150, 1152
Howe, Quincy. 3053
Howe, Reginald Heber. 2067, 2209
Howe, Reuel L. 1467, 2901, 1094, 1324, 1467, 2326, 3886
Howe, Solomon. 1865
Howell, Albert Thomas. 163, 2347, 3319
Howell, Alexander, Rutherford. 2891
Howell, Charles Boynton. 1490
Howell, Clifford. 848, 2366, 3265
Howell, Clifford Grant. 2482
Howell, Clinton Talmage. 1324
Howell, Elizabeth Dosher. 2777
Howell, Emma Elizabeth. 3379, 3385
Howell, Erle. 2432
Howell, John C. 2338
Howell, John Marion. 1849
Howell, Leslie Shackelford. 681, 2401
Howell, Mabel Katharine. 2457
Howell, Margaret. 2794
Howell, Ralph DeWitt. 880
Howell, Robert Boyte Crawford. 105, 171, 1239, 1376, 1906, 3289
Howell, Robert Lee. 1627, 1849
Howell, Roy Wilbur. 3529
Howell, Wallace S. 3505
Howells, Flora (Robinson) 2531
Howells, Rulon S. 3322
Howells, Rulon Stanley. 2619, 3322
Howells, Thomas Henry. 2321
Howells, William White. 3109
Howenstine, Lydia (Kimmel) 1460, 1849
Hower, Charles P. 3598
Howerth, Ira Woods. 204
Howerton, James Robert. 3443
Howes, Elizabeth Boyden. 2226, 2320
Howes, Jane. 796
Howes, Michael. 35
Howes, Robert G. 1136
Howes, Robert Gerard. 1136, 1278
Howey, M. Oldfield. 876, 3376
Howgate, George Washburne. 3302
Howgrave-Graham, Robert Pickersgill. 752
Howie, Carl Gordon. 534, 1410, 1722, 2150
Howington, Nolan P. 163
Howison, Robert Reid. 1722
Howitt, William. 2939, 3567
Howkins, Kenneth Gordon. 639
Howland, Arthur Hoag. 1654, 2220
Howland, Carl Leroy. 2493
Howland, Elihu S. 2998
Howland, Franklyn. 1818, 1819
Howland, Larry O. 1576, 1849

Howland, Louis. 750, 1448, 2013
Howlett, Duncan. 1119, 1532, 2181, 3031, 3744
Howlett, Thomas Rosling. 46
Howlett, Walter Main. 3151
Howlett, William Joseph. 2308, 3279
Howley, John F. Whittington. 2998
Howley, Michael Francis. 2366
Howorth, Henry Hoyle. 111, 1758
Howse, William Lewis. 150, 1251, 2550, 3175, 3179, 3554, 3856
Howson, George William Saul. 3364
Hoxie, Walter Palmer. 1448
Hoy, David. 3151, 3588
Hoye, Bjarne. 2714
Hoyer, George W. 1266, 3181, 3858
Hoyer, Harvey Conrad. 2480
Hoyer, Richard O. 2059
Hoyer, Robert. 941, 1005
Hoyer, Theodore. 1175, 1439
Hoyes, Herbert. 3538
Hoyland, Geoffrey. 1682
Hoyland, John. 294
Hoyland, John Somervell. 2064
Hoyland, John Somervill. 2891
Hoyle, Frances P. 3027, 3170
Hoyle, Fred. 1580
Hoyt, Alexander Stevenson. 132
Hoyt, Arthur Stephen. 1518, 2901, 2910, 2911, 3003
Hoyt, Charles Alva. 3823
Hoyt, Edyth Viola (Sage) Armstrong. 459, 578, 646
Hoyt, Eyth Viola (Sage) Armstrong. 459
Hoyt, Helen Brown. 1966
Hoyt, Herman Arthur. 1530, 2756, 3051
Hoyt, J. E. 2714
Hoyt, James S. 731
Hoyt, John William. 1620
Hoyt, Lucius W. 3205
Hoyt, Margaret. 3856, 3858
Hoyt, Marshall William. 2753
Hoyt, Olga. 1424, 1585, 3823
Hoyt, Ralph. 1022, 2401, 2697
Hoyt, Robert G. 664, 871, 2172
Hoyt, Wayland. 2061, 964, 3404
Hoyt, Wilbur Franklin. 3073
Hoyt, William C. 1791
Hoy W. E. 2509
Hromadka, Josef Lukl. 1181, 2364, 3212, 1817
Hrotsvit. 1849
Hrotsvit of Gandersheim. 1850
Hoffding, Harald. 3100
Hsu, Dorothy. 1850, 3814
Hsu, Sung-peng. 1783, 2940
Hsuan-hua, 1908. 3272, 3523, 3568
Hsueh, Kuang-ch'ien. 1364
Hsueh-tou, 980-1052. 2182
Hsu-yun, 1839-1959. 1850
Htin Aung, U. 709
Htin Aung. 702
Hu, Shih. 912
Hua, Ellen Kei. 2389
Huai-nan tzu, d. 122 B.C. 2196
Huang, Al Chung-liang. 3586
Huang-po, fl. 842-850. 3892
Hubartt, Paul. 313
Hubbard, Alice (Moore) 199
[Hubbard, Alice Philena]. 2648
Hubbard, Arthur John. 1069
Hubbard, Benjamin Jerome. 445
Hubbard, Celia T. 3161
Hubbard, David Allan. 163, 181, 279, 338, 342, 381, 412, 478, 493, 512, 537, 576, 585, 1551, 1619, 1836, 2028, 2341, 2873, 3742
Hubbard, Elbert. 3128, 660, 1355, 1966, 2621, 2856
Hubbard, Ethel Daniels. 1701, 2157, 2158, 2493, 2499, 2563
Hubbard, Geoffrey. 1675
Hubbard, George Henry. 2017, 2025, 3505
Hubbard, Henry Seward. 2989
Hubbard, Howard J. 1003
Hubbard, Ida Binger. 2550
Hubbard, Joseph. 1514
Hubbard, La Fayette Ronald. 1458, 1850, 3314
Hubbard, Margaret Ann. 1481, 2311, 3779
Hubbard, Sara Anderson. 3060
Hubbard, Thomas Franklin. 3595
Hubbard, Walter James. 1741
Hubbard, William. 1424
Hubbell, Gabriel G. 671, 3505
Hubbell, George Allen. 2591
Hubben, William. 1477, 1583, 2017, 2170, 2476
Hubbirt, John c. 3073
Hubbuck, Rodney. 1270
Huber, Evelyn. 935, 953
Huber, Georges. 2217
Huber, Harold E. 1772, 1773
Huber, Jack T. 2382
Huber, Leonard Victor. 2693

Huber, Mathias John. 2264, 2389
Huber, Paul. 1881
Huber, Raphael M. 1646, 2864
Huber, Roger. 1243
Huber, Samuel. 3730
Hubert. 2359, 2361, 3006
Hubert de Romans 1194?-1277. 2901
Hubert, Henri. 3271
Hubert, Marie Louise. 58, 2777
Hubert, Thomas S. 1566
Hubertus Albert. 746
Hubner, Charles William. 2274
Huby, Joseph. 390
Huby, Pamela M. 2853
Huc, Evariste Regis. 850
Hucal, Theodore P. 2938
Huck, Gabe. 1605, 2237
Huck, Gabriel. 838
Huckel, Oliver. 1347, 2409
Huckins, Sue Edwards. 1033, 1850
Huddle, William Peter. 1799
Huddleston, Trevor. 1066
Hudgings, William Franklyn. 2118
Hudgins, Frances E. 2553
Hudnut, Robert K. 64, 1010, 1011, 1059, 1199, 2786, 2931, 3353
Hudson, Charles Frederic. 1696, 3053, 3753
Hudson, Cyril Edward. 2993
Hudson, D F. 1770
Hudson, David. 3816
Hudson, Jay William. 1654, 2833
Hudson, John Allen. 1272
Hudson, Marshall Alonze. 3161, 3838
Hudson, Robert Lofton. 163, 964, 993, 1015, 1471, 1608, 2780
Hudson, Roland V. 474
Hudson, Roland Vernon. 474, 646
Hudson, Thomson Jay. 2989, 3075
Hudson, Virginia Cary. 621
Hudson, Winthrop Still. 148, 149, 800, 1119, 1150, 1189, 1274, 1765, 2671, 2955, 3744
Huebner, Charlotte K. 3313
Huebner, Louise. 1479, 2726, 3568, 3823
Huebsch, Adolph. 1850, 2077
Huebschmann, John Simon. 2873, 3702
Hueffer, Oliver Madox. 3823
*Huegel, F. J. 1388
Huegel, Frederick Julius. 3299, 105, 964, 1427, 2013, 2873
Huegle, Gregory. 883, 1205
Huegli, Albert George. 1150
Huelsman, Richard J. 2887
Huesman, Rose M. 3844
Huestis, Charles Herbert. 3547
Hueston, Ethel (Powelson) 2866
Huey, F. B. 516, 546, 569, 2950
Huey, Thomas E. 663
Huff, Archie Vernon. 3798
Huff, Harold S. 1239
Huff, Jane. 1850
Huff, Russell J. 821, 1776, 3880
Huffaker, Carolyn. 1303, 1850
Huffman, Charles Herbert. 3277
Huffman, Dan E. 218, 610
Huffman, Jasper Abraham. 1830, 1850, 2050, 2124, 3029, 207, 234, 348, 639, 964, 1608, 1830, 2016, 2040, 2156, 2406, 2414, 2415, 3644, 3886
Huffman, John. 1011, 1608
Huffman, John A. 470, 1313, 2247
Huffman, Lambert. 1850
Huffman, Robert W. 2726
Hufham, James Dunn. 2938
Hug, Fritz. 1981
Hugel, Friedrich. 749, 1722, 1850, 2016, 2873, 3100, 3101, 3487
Hugen, M D. 1256
Hugenberg, Joyce A. 2733
Huges De Ragnau, Edmond 1845. 3768
Hugg, George C. 3562
Huggenvik, Theodore. 71, 1188, 2000, 1188, 2057, 2274, 3663
Huggett, Joyce. 2346
Huggett, Renee. 1618
Hugh. 2253
Hughes, Albert. 332, 365, 366, 374, 420, 433, 1358, 1931, 2000, 2798
Hughes, Allison. 931, 1851
Hughes, Anselm. 45, 1206, 2633
Hughes, Archibald. 3319
Hughes, Catharine. 706, 1815, 3544, 3587
Hughes, Charles William. 32
Hughes, Daniel Lawrence. 2308, 2931
Hughes, David C. 438
Hughes, Edna Beougher. 214
Hughes, Edward James. 117, 2192
Hughes, Edwin Holt. 1722, 209, 1059, 1290, 1566, 2421, 3605
Hughes, Elizabeth Babbitt. 1033
*Hughes, Elmer R. 2624
Hughes, Elmer Ray. 2624
Hughes, Ernest Richard. 913
Hughes, Frank Charles. 1654
[Hughes, Frederic Stephen]. 2693
Hughes, George. 3767

[Hughes, George] 1828-1904. 1929
Hughes, Gerald. 310
Hughes, Gerard W. 1638, 1851, 1950
Hughes, Graham. 404
Hughes, Henry George. 756, 871, 2214
Hughes, Henry Maldwyn. 3644
Hughes, Henry Trevor. 2846, 3590
Hughes, Hugh Price. 1050, 3453
Hughes, Ingram. 2077
Hughes, Jasper Seaton. 454, 3225
Hughes, Jennie. 3236
Hughes, Jennie V. 2509
Hughes, John. 3752, 794, 873, 2168, 3192
Hughes, John A. 3101
Hughes, John Gilliam. 163, 174
Hughes, John Jay. 44, 853, 1295
Hughes, Kathleen. 1918, 1919
Hughes, Leonard. 919
Hughes, Mary Dawson. 318
Hughes, Matthew Simpson. 2442
Hughes, Meredith Jones. 2205
Hughes, Merritt Yerkes. 1101, 2471
Hughes, Nicholas Collin. 203
Hughes, Pennethorne. 3823
Hughes, Philip. 787, 809, 1175, 1373, 2851, 3034, 3039, 3450
Hughes, Philip Edgcumbe. 326, 403, 606, 1751, 1826, 3610, 3617, 3655
Hughes, Ray H. 606, 1229, 2813, 3554
Hughes, Riley. 698
Hughes, Robert. 1795
Hughes, Rupert. 1125
Hughes, Thomas. 1651, 1966, 1995
Hughes, Thomas Aloysius. 1948, 1945
Hughes, Thomas Hywel. 105, 2998
Hughes, Thomas Patrick. 1922, 1924
Hughes, Thomas Welburn. 2068
Hughes, W. 1331, 2550
Hughes, W. J. 1907
[Hughes, William H.]. 833
Hughes, William Jacoway. 898
Hughes, William James, bp. 1218
Hughey, Albert George. 463
Hughey, George Washington. 135, 800
Hughey, John David. 2517, 3194
Hughley, Judge Neal. 1095, 1134
Hughs, Milton A. 3109
Hughson, Shirley C[arter]. 2399
Hughson, Shirley Carter. 2029, 2476, 3600, 2873, 2985, 3265, 3484, 3479
Hughson, Walter. 2547
Hugo-Brunt, Michael. 187
Hugo, John. 3821
Hugo of Saint Victor. 3266, 3493
Hugo, Victor Marie, comte. 665
Huguenot society of America. 1497
Huguenot society of America. Library. 1851
Huguenot Society of New Jersey. 1852
Huguenot Society of the Founders of Manakin in the Colony of Virginia. Virginia Branch. 1275
Hugueny, Etienne. 787
Hui-neng, 638-713. 3893
Huidekoper, Frederic. 394, 1999
Huie, William Bradford. 2814, 3247
Huijbers, Bernard M. 1205
Hui-k'ai. 702
Hui-li. 1850
Hui Neng. 914, 3894
Huisjen, Albert. 2535, 2556
Huizenga, Lee S. 3524
Huizenga, Lee Sjoerds. 1853
Huizinga, A. v. C. P. 3097
Huizinga, Arnold van Couthen Piccardt. 118, 2867
Huizinga, Johan. 1526
Hujviri, 'Ali ibn 'Usman. 3544
Hulbert, Eri Baker. 1758
Hulbert, Henry Woodward. 1253
Hulbert, Terry C. 2550
Hulbert, Winifred. 2490, 2550
Hulbosh, Henricus. 1580
[Hulburt, D.]. 1654
Hulen, Amos Berry. 2863
Hull, Asa. 3562, 3563
Hull, Burling. 3520
Hull, Daniel. 1853, 3505
Hull, Eleanor Means. 30, 621, 1059, 2488, 3182, 3853
Hull, Ernest Reginald. 805
Hull, John Howarth Eric. 334, 1834
Hull, John M. 390, 2314
Hull, John Mervin. 2157
Hull, Judy Brown. 430, 896
Hull, Marion McHenry. 1915, 3575
Hull, Moses. 2695, 3505, 234, 3505
Hull, Robert Reuel. 853
Hull, Vida Joyce. 922, 2401
Hull, William E. 163, 422
Hull, William Isaac. 1685, 1686, 3388, 1688, 1694
Hulley, Lincoln. 578
Hullinger, Robert N. 678, 2614, 3428
Hullum, Everett. 2527, 3466
Hulme, Edward. 920
Hulme, Frank Howell. 2251

Hulme, Frederick Edward. 920
Hulme, Thomas Ferrier. 2424
Hulme, William Edward. 1373, 413, 548, 1005, 1298, 1324, 1418, 1592, 2244, 2347, 2380, 2780, 2995, 3299, 3388, 3678, 3886
Hulsbosch, A. 1361, 1381
Hulsbosch, Ansfridus. 1580
Hulse, Erroll. 984
Hulsebus, Gerhard. 461
Hulst, Alexander Reinard. 652
Hulst, Cornelia (Steketee) 2822
[Hulst, Maurice Lesage d'Hautecoeur d']. 691
Hult, Adolf. 410, 539, 2299
Hultgren, Arland J. 390, 1956
Hultkrantz, Ake. 1902, 1904
Hultstrand, Donald M. 2873
Human, Johnnie. 339, 632, 2128
Humbard, Martha Childers. 1576, 1855
Humbard, Rex. 1557, 1855
Humber, Thomas. 305
Humberd, Russell I. 454
Humberger, J. 300
Humberger, John. 2911
Humbert, Russell J. 990
Humble, Emil. 3101
Humboldt, Wilhelm, von. 3211
Hume, David. 1855, 2180, 2673, 2674, 2676, 2834, 3101, 3107
Hume, Edward Hicks. 2539
[Hume, Jean B.]. 3600
Hume, Paul. 915
Hume, Robert Allen. 1896, 2522
Hume, Robert Ernest. 3116, 3268, 3117
Hume, Ruth (Fox) 21, 1618
Hume, Theodore Carswell. 3875
Humensky, John Joseph. 1258
Hummel, Charles E. 1911, 2815
Hummel, Horace D. 540
Hummel, Margaret Gibson. 3837, 3876
Hummer, T. R. 42
Humphrey, Christopher Carter. 3588
Humphrey, Edward Frank. 3738
Humphrey, Edward Porter. 1287
Humphrey, Frances A. 907, 3525
Humphrey, Griffith Henry. 1050
Humphrey, Heman. 1566, 1701
Humphrey, Imogene. 3560
Humphrey, James Edward. 698
Humphrey, Jerry Miles. 935, 1362, 1553, 1794, 3094, 3341, 3373, 3479
Humphrey, Oscar W. 3505
Humphrey, Peggy. 1908
Humphrey, Zephine. 1722
Humphreys, Christmas. 702, 705, 708, 709, 710, 712, 1856, 2382, 3685, 3893, 3894
Humphreys, Christmas, [Travers Christmas Humphreys]. 3894
Humphreys, Christmas [Travers Christmas Humphreys]. 702, 705
Humphreys, Christmas [Travers Christmas Humphreys. 3894
[Humphreys, Daniel]. 234
Humphreys, David. 2543, 3437
Humphreys, E. W. 1705
Humphreys, Eliza M. J. (Gollan) 3505
Humphreys, Fisher. 1633, 1716, 2874, 3663
Humphreys, Francis Landon. 1207
Humphreys, George W. 2891, 3675
Humphreys, Otho Fairfield. 1952
*Humphreys, Robert Edward. 1592
Humphreys, W. Lee. 595
Humphries, Jackie. 3330
Humpstone, John. 2901
Humy, Fernand Emile d. 416, 1347
Hundley, William Thomas. 2373
Hunermann, Wilhelm. 1618, 2851
Hung Ying-ming, fl. 1596. 711
Hungate, Jesse A. 2742
[Hungerford, Edward]. 2884
[Hungtinton]. 1856
Hunke, Naomi Ruth. 143
Hunker, W. Carl. 2552
Hunkey, John. 800, 804, 1101, 1362, 1737
Hunkin, Joseph Wellington. 1192
Hunley, John Bunyan. 1290, 1439, 1830, 3402
Hunnex, Gloria G. 3590
Hunnicutt, Benjamin Harris. 2520
Hunolt, Franz. 863, 1531, 1986, 2811, 3410
Hunsberger, Herbert H. 544
Hunscher, Helen Alvina. 1703
Hunt, Alma. 3468
Hunt, Bernard Patteson Wathen Stather. 378
Hunt, Bernice Kohn. 3826
Hunt, Bruce H. 1662
Hunt, Cecil. 2891
Hunt, Charles Clyde. 1671
Hunt, Clark W. 493, 2436
Hunt, Darryl L. 867
Hunt, Dave. 1365, 1393, 1778, 1856
Hunt, Donald G. 234

Hunt, Douglas. 2726
Hunt, Duane Garrison. 173, 1241
Hunt, Earl G. 1833, 3663
Hunt, Elsie Denean. 3199
Hunt, Ernest. 702, 704, 706
Hunt, Ernest Edward. 1524, 2901
Hunt, Eva. 3721
Hunt, Everett Nichols. 2537
Hunt, F. Olen. 3663
Hunt, Geoffrey. 274
Hunt, George Laird. 1046, 1047, 1119, 1142, 3611, 3735
Hunt, Gladys M. 423, 454, 639, 924, 1413, 3832
Hunt, Ignatius. 234, 524
Hunt, Inez. 1310
Hunt, J[oseph] M[arion]. 2633
Hunt, Jerome. 855
Hunt, Joan. 2347
Hunt, Joel Ransom Eallis. 3183
Hunt, Joel Ransom Ellis. 1838, 2293
Hunt, Joel Ransom Ellis. 2296, 2527
Hunt, John. 1762, 2767
Hunt, Julian O. 1463
Hunt, June. 984, 1856
Hunt, Larry E. 2619, 3427
Hunt, Leavitt. 1575
Hunt, Lionel A. 896, 1253
Hunt, Marigold. 42, 626, 796, 1981, 2793
Hunt, Marion Palmer. 1557, 1939
Hunt, Mary A. 2672
Hunt, Mary Amelia. 290
Hunt, Noreen. 1304, 2582
Hunt, Patricia. 621
Hunt, Richard A. 3734
Hunt, Richard James. 1776, 2547
Hunt, Ruth. 214, 2230, 2244, 3851
Hunt, Sandford. 2451
Hunt, Sarah (Morey) 3129
Hunt, Thomas Poage. 3595
Hunt, Timothy Dwight. 1791
Hunt, William. 178, 1758
Hunt, William Remfry. 2509, 3403
Hunter, Allan Armstrong. 964, 1592, 2162, 2558, 2820, 3479
Hunter, Archibald Macbride. 334, 348, 350, 376, 410, 420, 433, 476, 1634, 1952, 2025, 2061, 3335, 3368, 3622, 3663
Hunter, Archibald Macbridge. 3368
Hunter, Armstrong. 1332
Hunter, Aylmer Douglas T. 2754
Hunter, Barton. 1164
Hunter, Carman St. John. 1084
Hunter, Charles. 1457, 2229, 2338, 3232
Hunter, David R. 1467
Hunter, Edith Fisher. 905, 3183
Hunter, Edward. 2240
Hunter, Edwin Alfred. 2427, 3254
Hunter, Elizabeth M. 3174, 3186
Hunter, Fannie McDowell. 3834
Hunter, Frances. 1324, 2064
Hunter, Frances Gardner. 2874
Hunter, George G. 1566, 1572
Hunter, George McPherson. 1448
Hunter, Gordon C. 984, 3028
Hunter, Graham Chambers. 2271
Hunter, Henry. 214, 1956, 1966
Hunter, Howard. 3089
Hunter, J. F. G. 1324
Hunter, Jack D. 3861
Hunter, James D. 2335
Hunter, James Hogg. 659, 918, 3539
Hunter, Johann Eduard. 340
Hunter, John. 1482
Hunter, John Edward. 367, 555, 559, 585, 964, 965, 993, 1439, 2981, 3479, 3483
Hunter, Joseph Boone. 2638
Hunter, Leslie Stannard. 1143, 2722, 3306
Hunter, Louise H. 705
Hunter, Marhta Angeline (Beck) 284
Hunter, Mary Moseley. 2482
Hunter, Milton Reed. 2603, 2611, 3869, 678, 2598, 2603, 2611, 3430, 3869
Hunter, Robert. 1109
Hunter, Robert Grams. 1101, 3400
Hunter, Rodello. 2603
Hunter, Stanley Armstrong. 1203, 1872, 3093
Hunter, Stephin Alexander. 451
Hunter, William. 1865, 1866
Hunter, William Bridges. 2471
Hunter, William C. 2633
Hunter, William M. 1095
Hunterberg, Max. 1997
Hunting, Gardner. 965
Hunting, Harold Bruce. 290, 639, 1966, 2121, 2482, 2527, 3443
Hunting, Henry Gardner. 965, 3750
Huntington, Arria Sargent. 1856
Huntington, De Witt Clinton. 965, 1823, 2436
Huntington, Joseph. 108
Huntington Park, Calif. St. Matthias' Parish. 1856
Huntley, Florence (Chance) 2874

Huntley, Frank Livingstone. 666, 1632, 1781, 3590
Huntley, Thomas Elliott. 1050, 1319
Huntress, Keith Gibson. 2615
Huot, Patricia W. 3014
Hurd, Edward Franklin. 1662
Hurd, Edward Payson. 1668
Hurd, John Coolidge. 323, 346, 657
Hurd, Mary Abby. 1341
Hurd, Mason Montraville. 1059
Hurd, Richard. 1857
[Hurd John R]. 454
Hurgronje, Christiaan Snouck. 3718, 1922, 2564
Huribut, Jesse Lyman. 621
Hurlbut, Gordon. 1840
Hurlbut, Mabel S. 1612
Hurlbut, Elisha P. 1141
Hurlbut, Jesse Lyman. 210, 247, 474, 616, 621, 633, 1100, 1512, 1981, 2421, 3364, 244, 282, 294, 401, 534, 597, 621, 1175, 1176, 2005, 3178, 3341, 3554
Hurlbut, Sidney S. 812
Hurlbut, Stephen Augustus. 1234, 1877, 1943, 2122, 2963
Hurlbutt, Gordon. 1840
Hurlbutt, Robert H. 2705, 3594
Hurley, Denis E. 772
Hurley, Doran. 1851
Hurley, Edmund Gregory. 883
Hurley, Helen Angela. 3419
Hurley, James B. 3839
Hurley, James Franklin. 2306, 3314
Hurley, John. 2323
Hurley, Karen. 984
Hurley, Timothy. 879
Hurley, W Maurice. 1347
Hurley, Wilfred Geoffrey. 73, 763, 3487
Hurlimann, Martin. 751, 752
Hurlin, William. 157
Hurll, Estelle May. 922, 2358, 1957, 2358, 2760
Hurm, Ken. 2033
Huron, Rod. 3883
Hurrell, Grace. 2370
Hurrey, Marjory. 75
Hurst, Duane v. 1566
Hurst, George Leopold. 406, 3267
Hurst, George Leopole. 3203
Hurst, Gloria. 931, 1857
Hurst, John Fletcher. 294, 1186, 1188, 1192, 2424, 3023, 3024, 3034, 3626, 29
Hurst, John Fletcher Hurst. 3626
Hurst, L R. 606
Hurst, Nellie. 626, 629
Hurst, Samuel Need. 2626
Hurst, William D. 2465
Hurstfield, Joel. 3036
[Hursts, John Fletcher]. 3803
Hurt, James. 11
Hurt, John Jeter. 146, 164, 1291
Hurt, Walter. 2077
[Hurtado, Evaristo]. 1069
Hurtado, Larry W. 436
[Hurter, Heinrich von]. 787
Hurter, Hugo. 2389, 3626
*Hurty, Kathleen. 3164
Hurwitz, Hyman. 1798, 3581
Hurwitz, Johanna. 1604
Hurwitz, Simon. 2074
*Hurwood, Bernhardt J. 1423, 2726, 3567
Hus, Alain. 1766
Hus, Jan. 1119
Hus, Jan. 1119
Husain, Ashfaque. 2185
Husain, Athar. 2628
Husain, Itrat. 1476
Husain, Muhammad Kamil. 2013
Husband, Richard Wellington. 2068
Huse, Dennis. 3537
Huse, Raymond Howard. 965, 3129, 3199, 3462, 3681
Huse, Sibyl Marvin. 500, 1033, 1037
Husenbeth, Frederick Charles. 3282
Huser, Roger John. 3
Hushower, Ida Alice. 2022
Husk, William Henry. 742
Huskey, Hyrum H. 2780
[Huskinson, Richard King]. 2226
Huson, Paul. 3588, 3823
[Huss, Bernard]. 2334
Huss, John Ervin. 164, 1199, 1439, 2886, 3672
Hussey, Arthur. 882
Husslein, Joseph Casper. 42, 753, 765, 853, 1952, 1977, 2189, 2251, 2369, 3690, 1429
[Huston, Martha Elizabeth]. 2891
Huston, Robert. 214
Huston, Rose A. 2509
Huston, Ruth. 3702
Hutchcroft, Vera. 3152
Hutchens, Paul. 11, 3353
Hutcheon, Robert James. 3070
Hutcheson, Francis. 1535
Hutcheson, George. 416
Hutcheson, George, minister at Edinburgh. 559

Hutcheson, James Theodore. 108
Hutcheson, Lena Edwards. 1439
Hutcheson, Nora Orr. 1858
Hutcheson, Richard G. 1199, 1552
Hutchings, Arthur. 1206
Hutchings, Emily Grant. 2989
Hutchings, Eric. 3886
Hutchings, Margaret. 229
Hutchins, Charles Lewis. 741, 2957, 2962, 2968, 3562
Hutchins, Grace. 3443
Hutchins, William James. 540, 2901
Hutchins, William Norman. 965, 1251
Hutchinson, Aaron. 3341
*Hutchinson, Charles. 1388
Hutchinson, Enoch. 320
Hutchinson, Forney. 3129
Hutchinson, Francis Ernest. 1378, 3039
Hutchinson, George P. 3414
Hutchinson, Horatio Gordon. 1448, 1758
Hutchinson, John Alexander. 1317
Hutchinson, Jonathan. 3129
Hutchinson, Paul. 2421, 924, 1141, 1176, 1525, 3443, 1182
Hutchinson, Paul, 1890-1956. 1176, 1182
Hutchinson, R A. 3280
Hutchinson, Roger. 1722
Hutchinson, Samuel. 3319
Hutchinson, Stuart Nye. 907
Hutchinson, Warner. 1301, 3241
Hutchinson, Winifred Margaret Lambart. 2656, 2661
Hutchison, Becky Rowe. 1367, 1858
Hutchison, Harry. 182, 1095, 1906
Hutchison, James. 1599
Hutchison, James Patterson. 3547
Hutchison, John Alexander. 1086, 1135, 1619, 2833, 3093, 3101, 3117
Hutchison, John Russell. 2920
Hutchison, Joseph B. 1313
Hutchison, Owen. 2264
Hutchison, Patrick. 2174
Hutchison, Robert A. 1830
Hutchison, Stuart Nye. 3369, 313
Hutchison, William R. 2222, 2561, 3708
Huter, Jacob. 37, 1858
Huther, Johann Eduard. 446
Hutley, Walter. 12, 1858
Hutson, Joan. 2389
Huttar, Leora W. 939, 3163
Hutten, Kurt. 1320
Huttenlocker, Keith. 2265, 3353, 3678
Hutter, Irmgard. 85
Hutting, Albert M. 3252, 3690
Huttman, Maude Aline. 1196, 1355
Hutton, Arthur Lafayette. 465
Hutton, Arthur Wollaston. 2328
Hutton, Daniel Mac-Hir. 3396
Hutton, David Graham. 1270
Hutton, Edward. 80
Hutton, Edward Ardron. 348
Hutton, Jean Gertrude. 2550, 3765
Hutton, John Alexander. 35, 1050, 1592, 1995, 2798, 3211, 2931
Hutton, May Arkwright. 1908
Hutton, Orlando. 2849
Hutton, Reginald Ernest. 1912
Hutton, Richard Holt. 738, 1893, 2703, 3066, 3622
Hutton, Samuel Ward. 1419, 2347, 2474, 3003
Hutton, [w. 2675
Hutton, Warwick. 495, 1422, 2711
Hutton, William Holden. 1220
Hutzell, Rita Clark. 3277
Huver, Charles W. 1691
Huxhold, Harry N. 592, 604, 899, 1262, 1448, 2389, 2891
Huxley, Aldous Leonard. 2203, 3101, 3783, 1422, 1756, 2203, 3101, 3783
Huxley, Francis. 1836, 2732
Huxley, Julian Sorell. 3060
Huxley, Sir Julian Sorell. 3060
Huxley, Thomas Henry. 192, 204, 1855, 3075, 3306, 3313, 3341, 192, 1855
Huxtable, William John Fairchild. 277, 2237
Huyghe, Gerard. 2573, 3487
Huyser, Gerrit. 2012
Hyamson, Moses. 3371
Hyatt, Irwin T. 1379
Hyatt, James Philip. 310, 571, 1943, 2950, 516
Hyatt, Thaddeus Pomeroy. 3685
Hybels, Bill. 984
Hyde, Alvan. 3129
Hyde, Ammi Bradford. 2424
[Hyde, Charles]. 3152
Hyde, Charles. 1859
Hyde, Douglas Arnold. 2743
Hyde, Floy (Salls) 3178
Hyde, Gordon M. 277, 1012, 3225
Hyde, Henry Knight. 1859
Hyde, Jabez Backus. 1192
Hyde, John. 2603
Hyde, Joseph Smith. 1859

Hyde, Walter Woodburn. 1192, 1766, 1196, 1766
Hyde, William De Witt. 943, 965, 1050, 1059, 1535, 2836, 3060, 3616
Hyde, William DeWitt. 1535, 3411
Hyder, O. Quentin. 2338
Hydraulic-press brick co., St. Louis. 713
[Hyer, G. W.]. 3728
Hyers, M. Conrad. 1076, 3822, 3893
Hygonet, Bernard. 3540
Hylan, John Perham. 3547
Hyland, James Aloysius. 1150
Hyland, St. George Kieran. 816
Hyma, Albert. 695, 727, 1086, 1143, 1429, 1526, 2274, 2280, 2348, 3215, 3452, 3505
Hyman, Arthur. 2842
Hyman, Jacob David. 911, 3703
Hyman, Joseph Charlap. 32
Hymn of Jesus. English. 1866
Hymn Society of America. 1866
Hynek, Rodolf Maria. 1826
Hynek, Rudolf Maria. 1826
Hynes, Arleen. 2108, 2779
Hynes, Michael J. 1304
Hynes, William J. 743, 893
Hyre, K. M. 2731
Hyren, Frederic. 1050
Hyslop, James Harvey. 2989
Hyslop, James Hervey. 2833, 2989

I

I Ching. English. 1879
*Iamblichus of Chalcis. 1660
Iannucci, Remo Joseph. 195, 2910
IAroslavskii, Emel'ian. 3257
Iatesta, Robert R. 1608
Ibn al-'Arabi, 1165-1240. 3543, 3544
Ibn al-Firkah, Ibrahim ibn 'Abd al-Rahman, 1262-1329. 2635
Ibn al-Kalanisi, d. 1160. 1390
Ibn 'Ata' Allah, Ahmad ibn Muhammad, d. 1309. 3544
Ibn Gabirol Solomon Ben Judah 1021 -- ca. 1058. 1535, 3210
Ibn Gabriol, Solomon ben Judah, ca 1021-ca. 1058. 77
Ibn Kammunah, Sa'd ibn Mansur, 13th cent. 3138
Ibn Kammunah, Sa'd ibn Mansur, 13th cent. 3138
Ibn Tahir al-Baghdadi, 'Abd al-Qahir, d. 1037. 1927
Ibn Tufayl, Muhammed ibn 'Abd al-Malik, d. 1185 or 6. 2841
Ibsen, Sigurd. 2226
Icaza, Rosa Maria. 2136
Ice, Jackson Lee. 1417, 3312
Ice, Orva Lee. 1448, 3886
Ichazo, Oscar. 80
Ickis, Marguerite. 1613
Ide, George Barton. 164, 3672
Ide, George Henry. 1069
Ide, Jacob. 2741
Idelsohn, Abraham Zebi. 2120, 2108, 2111, 2633, 3577
Idelsohn, Abraham Zehi. 2111
Idelson, Abraham Zebi. 2108, 2634
Ideologies de liberation et message du salut. English. 2222
Idinopulos, Thomas A. 3656
Idleman, Finis Schuyler. 20
Idol, Vera. 1448
Idowu, E. Bolaji. 12, 1905, 3868
Idung. 1276
Iersel, Bastiaan Martinus Franciscus van. 1731, 3600
Igeret ha-kodesh. English and Hebrew. 3393
Iglehart, Charles W. 1935, 2954
Iglesias, Margaret G. 1882
Ignatius. 1882
Ihli, Jan. 905
Iino, Norimoto. 2836, 3892
IJsewijn, Jozef. 2199
Ikbal 'Ali Shah. 3268
Ikeda, Daisaku. 708, 710, 1703, 3455
Ikeler, Bernard C. 1014
Ikerman, Ruth C. 663, 1351, 1431, 1439, 1630, 2389, 2625, 2874, 3843, 3856
Ikin, Alice Graham. 1107, 3479, 3540
Ilardi, Mariano Michael. 2360
Ileana. 2706
Ilg, Augustin Maria. 2389
Ilg, John. 1645, 3298
Ilgenstein, Anna (Katterfeld) 2274
[Ilive, Jacob]. 562
Illanes, Jose Luis. 3849
Illingworth, John Richardson. 2823
Illinois. Sesquicentennial Commission. 1883
Illinois synod of the United Lutheran church in America. 3733
Imbakom Kalewold, 1917. 937, 1540

Imber, Samuel Jacob. 3863
Imbert de Saint-Amand, Arthur Leon, 1834-1900. 1638
Imbrie, William. 1210
Imes, William Lloyd. 2932
Imitatio Christi. 1884, 1885
Imitatio Christi. English. 1330, 1404, 1885, 1886, 3129
Imitatio Christi. English. Selections. 1886
Imitatio Christi. English. 1886
Immaculata. 2874, 3419
Immaculata, Sister M. 2573
Improvement Era. 678, 2600, 2609
Imschoot, Paul van. 598
Inama, Adelbert. 835
Inamura, Yeitake. 1844
Inayat Khan, 1882-1926. 3542
Inayat Khan, 1882-1927. 3542, 3544, 3581
Inayat-Khan, Fazal. 3543
Inayat Khan, Pir Vilayat. 1892, 3543
Inayat, Taj. 3544
Inayat Khan. 3542
Inayat Khan, Pir Vilayat. 3542
Inch, Morris A. 578, 606, 1551, 2326
Independent order Brith sholom. Joseph Krohnberg lodge, no. 321. 2101
Index of American Design. 84
India Office Library. 1883, 1895
Indiana. Dept. of Education. 895
Indiana-Kentucky Synod of the United Lutheran Church in America. 2290
Indiana Synod of the United Lutheran Church in America. 3733
Indianapolis. Second Presbyterian church. 2917
Ineson, George. 1364
Infeld, Harry. 2084, 3471
Infeld, Herman Zvi. 2084, 3471
Infield, Henrick F. 174, 3454
Information (New York) 1136
Ingalese, Richard. 1370, 2726
Ingalls, Jeremy. 1095
*Ingalls, Ray Arnold. 1017
Ingarden, Roman. 2738
Inge, William Ralph. 2638, 3443, 310, 751, 943, 1059, 1069, 1281, 1429, 1448, 1456, 1592, 2214, 2639, 2836, 2854, 2978, 3066, 3078, 404, 943, 1226, 2639, 2645, 3067, 3107
Inger, Archie Johnson. 1723, 2005
Ingersoll, Caroline E Lawrence. 3199
[Ingersoll, Charles Jared]. 3740
Ingersoll, Edward Payson. 46
Ingersoll, Robert Green. 19, 199, 670, 1428, 1654, 1655, 1656, 1907, 2218, 2652, 3192, 3234, 3341, 3545, 3568, 3582
Ingersoll, Wendell. 2389
Ingham, Kenneth. 2531
Ingle, Clifford. 896
Ingle, Edward. 1223, 2775
Ingle, M. Bertrand. 1557
Ingle, Sud. 3011
Inglewood, Marian. 1319, 2064
Inglis, Charles. 3373
[Inglis, Charles. 1582, 3744
Inglis, Ervine. 1313
Inglis, Ervine P. 3364
Inglis, James. 2932, 303
Inglis, John. 606
Inglis, Theodora (Marshall) 2509
Ingraham, E V. 3053
Ingraham, Earnest Verner. 3750, 3751
Ingraham, John Phillips Thurston. 277
Ingraham, Joseph Holt. 2005, 1405
Ingram, A B. 1288
Ingram, Ada A. 1911
Ingram, James Henry. 1229
Ingram, John Calvin. 611, 3319
Ingram, Joseph Edward. 2051, 2068
Ingram, Kenneth. 64, 3060
Ingram, Madeline C. 915
Ingram, Thomas Dunbar. 1758
Ingram, Tolbert Robert. 2957, 3184, 3329
Ingrams, Doreen. 1925
Ingvoldstad, Orlando. 2299
Ingwalson, Kenneth W. 2956
Ingzel, Marjorie. 1749, 1750
Inial, Marguerite Felicie. 1404
Inkster, John Gibson. 459
Inman, Lee Bertram. 3663
Inman, Samuel Guy. 2548
Inman, Thomas. 3117, 3573
Inman, W. Richard. 2061, 2942
Innes, Alexander Taylor. 2181
Innes, Brian. 3588
Innes, Christopher. 1478
Innes, Kathleen Elizabeth Royds. 211, 234
Innes review (The) 3042
Innis, George Swan. 3860
Inniss, Ida W. 1448
Innocentius III, 1160 or 61-1216. 2321, 2323
Innocentius III. 1761
Inquire Within. 3322

The Inquiry, New York. 1040, 2978
Inquisition. Albi, France. 1909
Inrig, Gary. 554, 1163, 1405, 1688
Insight, James. 1216
Inskip, James Theodore. 1592
Inskip, John Swanel. 2421
*Inslee, Joseph W. 348
Institoris, Henricus. 3823, 3824
Institute for Christian Learning, Evanston, Ill. 2965
Institute for Creation Research. 1381
Institute for Judaism and Contemporary Thought. 1540
Institute for Religious and Social Studies, Jewish Theological Seminary of America. 1129, 1537, 2190, 3067, 3094, 3573, 3744
Institute for Religious and Social Studies, Jewish TheologicalSeminary of America. 2223
Institute in Basic Youth Conflicts. 313, 950
Institute of Jewish Affairs. 2097, 2099, 2121
Institute of Pastoral Care, Framingham, Mass., 1960. 2780
Institute of Pastoral Care, Framingham, Mass., 1961. 2784
Institute of Pastoral Psychology, 10th, Fordham University, 1975. 2782
Institute of Pastoral Psychology, Fordham University. 1st, 1955. 2784
Institute of Spirituality. 772, 1154
Institute on character education in the summer camp, George Williams college, Chicago. 7th, 1936. 2591
Institute on character education in the summer camp, George Williams college, Chicago. 8th, 1937. 2591
Institute on Contemporary Thought and the Spiritual Exercises of St. Ignatius of Loyola, Loyola University, Chicago, 1962. 2270
Institute on Modern Religious Communication Dilemmas, Syracuse University, 1971. 3002
Institute on Problems That Unite Us, Mundelein College, 1965. 2574
Institute on Religion and Psychiatry, Congregation Adath Israel, Boston, 1947. 2785
Institute on Religion and Psychiatry, Temple Israel, Boston, 1947. 2995
Institute on Religion in State Universities, University of Minnesota. 3757
Institute on Religious Freedom, North Aurora, Ill., 1966. 3774
Institute on Religious Life in the Modern World, St. Louis University, 1966. 2571
The Instructor (Salt Lake City) 2609, 2614
Inter-church conference on federation, New York, 1905. 1044
Inter-varsity Missionary Convention 7th, Urbana Ill., 1964. 2514
Inter-American Conference on Religious, 1st, Mexico City, 1971. 2582
Inter-American Development bank. 29
Interchurch world movement of North America. 1199, 3569
Inter-Collegiate Conference on Students' Religious Activities, 1st, University of Minnesota, 1958. 3537
Interdenominational conference on the city church, Asbury Park, N. J. 1937. 1278
Interdenominational student conference, Evanston, Ill., Dec. 29, 1925--Jan. 1, 1926. 3886
Interdenominational student conference, Evanston, Ill., Dec., 29, 1925-Jan. 1, 1926. 1044
Inter-Lutheran Conference on Worship, Minneapolis, 1973. 3004
Inter-Lutheran Consultation on Worship, Chicago, 1966. 2294
International African Seminar. 3d, Salisbury, Southern Rhodesia, 1960. 13
International African Seminar, 7th University of Ghana 1965. 1073
International Association for Liberal Christianity and Religious Freedom. 34
International Bible students association. 1381
International Buddhist Institute of Hawaii. 706
International Catechetical Congress, 1st, Rome, 1971. 937
International Catholic Conference on Religious Education of the Deaf, Dublin, 1971. 1412
International Christian Broadcasters. 3018
International Committee of Historical Sciences. Commission internationale d'histoire ecclesiastique comparee. British Sub-Commission. 3041

INTERNATIONAL RELIGIOUS BOOKS 1876 - 1982

International Conference for World Peace and Social Reform, Anaheim, Calif., 1976. 3314
International Conference on Taoist Studies, 2d, Chino, Japan, 1972. 3587
International Congregational council. Committee of one hundred. 1344
International congress for the history of religious. 3d, Oxford. 1908. 3093
International Congress of Anthropological and Ethnological Sciences, 9th, Chicago, 1973. 3091
International congress of arts and science, St. Louis, 1904. 3093
International congress of free Christian and other religious liberals. 7th, Boston, 1920. 34
International congress of free Christians and other religious liberals. 4th, Boston, 1907. 3192
International congress of free Christians and other religious liberals. 5th, Berlin, 1910. 965
International Congress of Pastoral Liturgy. 1st, Assisi and Rome, 1956. 843
International congress on Christian education, Mexico, 1941. 3162
International Congress on Mithraic Studies, 1st, Manchester University, 1971. 2560
International Congress on Prophecy, 1st, New York, 1952. 3319
International Congress on Prophecy. 2d, New York, 1955. 3319
International Congress on Religion, Architecture, and the Arts, 3d, Jerusalem, 1973. 78
International congress on Sunday rest. 10th, St. Louis, 1904. 3548
International congress on Sunday rest. 14th, Oakland, Cal., 1915. 3548
International congress on Sunday rest. 7th, Chicago, 1893. 3548
International Congress on 'The Four Gospels in 1957,' Oxford, 1957. 386
International Congress on Vocations to the States of Perfection. 1st. Rome, 1961. 3785
International Congress on Vocations to the States of Perfection. 1st, Rome, 1961. 3785
International Congress on World Evangelization, Lausanne, 1974. 1573
International Consultation on English Texts. 2891
International convention of Christian education. 20th, Columbus, O., 1938. 3162
International Convention on Missionary Medicine. 1st. Wheaton. Ill. 1959. 2539
International Convention on Missionary Medicine. 2d, Wheaton, Ill., 1961. 2539
International Convention on Missionary Medicine. 3d, Wheaton, Ill., 1963. 2377
International Convention on Missionary Medicine, Wheaton, Ill., 1959. 2539
International correspondence schools, Scranton, Pa. 8, 1370
International Council of Religious Education. 1239, 1247, 1498, 1608, 1866, 1915, 3152, 3161, 3162, 3191, 3548, 3784
International council of religious education. American standard Bible committee. 362, 513
International council of religious education. Committee on religious education of youth. 3203
International Ecumenical Congress of Theology (1980. 933
International eucharistic congress. 28th, Chicago, 1926. 1912, 1913
International Hymnological Conference. 2d, New York, 1961. 1204
International Inter-Religious Symposium on Peace, New Delhi, 1968. 2808
International Lonergan Congress, St. Leo College, 1970. 2245, 2376, 3637
International Lutheran Conference on the Holy Spirit, 1st, Minneapolis, 1972. 139
International medical missionary society. Pennsylvania auxiliary. 2486
International missionary council. 2493, 2520, 2540, 3680
International missionary council. 4th meeting, Madras, 1938. 2514, 2520
International Missionary Council. Assembly, Accra, 1957-1958. 2515
International missionary council. Dept. of social and economic research. 1933, 2954
International missionary council. Dept. of social and economic research and counsel. 1933, 2953, 2954
International missionary council. International committee on the Christian approach to the Jews. 1083
International Missionary Council. Theological Education Fund. 3680
International moral education congress. 2d, Hague, 1912. 2592
International Organization for Masoretic Studies. 2364
International Scholars' Conference, 1st, Wayne State University, 1970. 1146
International Society of Christian Endeavor. 1100, 3562, 3736
International Student Missionary Convention, 5th, University of Illinois, 1957. 1069
International Student Missionary Convention. 6th, Urbana and Champaign, Ill., 1961. 2496
International Study Week on Mission and Liturgy. 1st, Nimegen and Uden, 1959. 843
International Study Week on Missionary Catechetics, Eichstatt, 1960. 746
International Sunday-school association. Commission for the study of the adolescent period. 3554
International Sunday-school convention of the United States and British American province. 13th, San Francisco, 1911. 3559
International Sunday-school convention of the United States and British American provinces. 11th, Toronto, 1905. 3561
International Sunday-school convention of the United States and British American provinces. 12th, Louisville, Ky., 1908. 3561
International Sunday-school convention of the United States and British American provinces. 14th, Chicago, 1914. 3559
International Sunday-school convention of the United States and British American provinces. 16th, Kansas City, Mo., 1922. 3561
International Sunday-school convention of the United States and British American provinces. 1st, Baltimore, 1875. 3559
International Sunday-school convention of the United States and British American provinces. 2d, Atlanta, 1878. 3559
International Sunday-school convention of the United States and British American provinces. 4th, Louisville, Ky., 1884. 3560
International Sunday-school convention of the United States and British American provinces. 5th, Chicago, 1887. 3560
International Sunday-school convention of the United States and British American provinces. 7th, St. Louis, 1893. 3554
International Sunday school convention of the United States and British American provinces. 9th, Atlanta, 1899. 3554
International Sunday School Lesson. 1915
International Sunday school lesson committee. 645
International survey committee. 3878
International Symposium on Analytical Astrodynamics, Los Angeles, 1961. 94
International Symposium on the Holocaust, Cathedral of St. John the Divine, 1974. 1825
International Theological Conference, Notre Dame, Ind., 1966. 3774
International workers order. 2104
International workers order. Jewish-American section. Cooperative book league. 2104
Internationaler Kongress fur Lutherforschung. 2d Munster, 1960. 2279, 2281, 2400
Interpretation. 285
Inter-varsity Missionary Convention. 5th, Urbana, Ill., 1957. 2515
Inter-Varsity Missionary Convention, 8th, University of Illinois, 1967. 2515
Inter-varsity Missionary Convention, 11th, Urbana, Ill. 1976. 2515
Inter-varsity Missionary Convention, 10th, Urbana, Ill., 1973. 1997, 2515
Inter-varsity Student Missions Convention, 12th, University of Illinois in Urbana, 1979. 470, 2515
Ioann, Skhi-igumen. 1299, 1918
Ionescu, Petre Gogoneatza. 64
Ions, Veronica. 2652
Iowa conference of spiritualists. 1702, 3505
Iowa. University. Institute of character research. 905
Iowa. University. School of Religion. 3139
Iparraguirre, Ignacio. 1946, 3222
Ipser, Karl. 3768
Iqbal, Afzal. 1460, 2629
Iqbal, Mohammed. 1925
Iqbal, Muhammad. 2565
Iqbal, Sheikh Mohammad. 1925
Irala, Narciso. 2808
Irani, Manija Sheriar. 2400
'Iraqi, Fakhr al-Din Ibrahim. 3544
Iredale, Edith (Brubaker) 1236
Irelan, Elma C. 1464
Ireland, James. 171
Ireland, John. 759, 3086
Ireland, Marion P. 920
Iremonger, Frederic Athelwold. 1211, 3599
Iremonger, Frederick Athelwold. 3599
Irenaeus. 68
Irenaeus, Saint, Bp. of Lyons. 1805
Ireson, Gordon Worley. 3663
Irimie, Cornel. 1881
Irion, Clyde. 3505
Irion, Mary Jean. 1091, 2390
Irion, Paul E. 1693, 3672
Irish, Jerry A. 1413
Irish, Marie. 3277
Irizarry, Carmen. 2979
Irkepman, Ruth C. 3856
Ironmonger, Elizabeth (Hogg) 2433
Irons, William Josiah. 234
Ironside, Henry Allan. 93, 326, 381, 412, 422, 430, 433, 440, 446, 479, 518, 606, 1439, 1557, 1840, 2134, 2809, 2855, 3012, 3218, 3353, 3663, 222, 322, 329, 341, 363, 369, 446, 448, 454, 468, 509, 531, 542, 546, 559, 572, 584, 594, 1069, 1431, 1557, 1575, 1823, 2091, 2874, 3206, 3218, 3271, 3622, 3663
Irvin, Donald F. 747, 1981, 2283, 3184
Irvin, Ida M. 3554
Irvine, Alexander Fitzgerald. 1967, 120
Irvine, Ingram N. W. 44
Irvine, James Elliott. 1059
Irvine, William C. 1804, 3322
Irving, C[hristopher]. 2083
Irving, Christopher. 1286, 2656
Irving, Doreen. 1365, 1920
Irving, George. 1566
Irving, Kate. 3505
Irving, Roy G. 3879
[Irving, Theodore] 1809-1880. 965
Irving, Washington. 25, 1114, 1926, 2129, 2565, 2628
Irwin, Clarke Huston. 222
Irwin, Edwin Franklin. 2533
Irwin, Frank. 2715, 2845
Irwin, John. 2550
Irwin, John Capps. 1095
Irwin, Kevin W. 314, 845, 849, 1262
Irwin, Leonard G. 3568
Irwin, Mary. 931, 1920
Irwin, Paul B. 1260
Irwin, William Andrew. 518, 598
Isaac, Daniel. 3754
Isaac, E. M. 1823
Isaac, Ephraim. 3861
Isaac, F Reid. 408, 1992
Isaac, Jules. 1073, 2013
Isaac of Stella, d. 1169. 863, 1266
Isaac, Reid. 907, 1998
Isaacs, Abram Samuel. 2082, 2402, 3581
Isaacs, Alan. 3082
Isaacs, Evelyn. 3206
Isaacs, Miriam. 2121
Isaacs, Samuel Hillel. 561, 2761
Isaacson, Ben. 2085, 2146
Isabell, Damien. 1648
Isac, Edouard Victor Michel. 2762
Isacksen, Frederick R. 2390
Isacsson, Alfred. 2132
Isais, Juan M. 2537
Isayama, Nobumi. 1238
Isbell, Allen C. 3793
Isbell, Charles D. 558
Isenburg, Merle. 3319
Isenhour, Walter E. 2815
Iserloh, Erwin. 2274
Iserloh, William O. 3239
Isham, Linda. 1253
Isham, Norman Morrison. 2705
Ishee, John A. 993, 2782, 3182, 3829
Isherwood, Christopher. 3774, 3020, 3774
*Isherwood, Margaret. 1592, 3060, 3330
Ishida, Tomoo. 2090, 2177
Ish-Kishor, Sulamith. 294, 1614, 2089, 2094
Ish-Kishor, Sulsmith. 621
Isho'yabh III, d. 657 or 8. 2684
Isho-dadh, of Merv, bp. 343
Ishuan, Shih, d. 867. 3893
Isichei, Elizabeth Allo. 1684
Iskandar, Abkarlyus. 1425
Islam, Khawaja Muhammad. 1698
Isom, Dudley R. 3465
Israel, Ben. 2094
Israel, Gerard. 2094
Israel, Henry. 3254, 3871
Israel, Laviner. 463
Israel, Martin. 1830, 3542
Israel, Menachem. 440
Israel, Raymond. 1316
Israel, Richard J. 1701, 2097
Israelitan, Abraham H. 2084
Israelowitz, Oscar. 2699
Isser, Stanley Jerome. 1477
Isserman, Ferdinand Myron. 2114, 2950
Issett, Lu Nell. 3663
Isutsu, Toshihiko. 1733, 2185
Iswolsky, Helene. 1364, 2750, 3256
Itivuttaka. 709
Iuppenlatz, William L. 3750
Iverach, James. 2798, 3076, 3608
Iversen, John O. 3886
Iversen, John Orville. 1012, 2390, 3018, 3886
Iverson, Gerald D. 3168
Iverson, Jeffrey. 3053
Iverson, Sylva F. 2390
Ives, Charles Linnaeus. 3462
Ives, Florence Lois. 1059, 1995
Ives, Howard Colby. 2, 127
Ivimey, Joseph. 2468
Ivins, Anthony Woodward. 2603
Ivins, Benjamin Franklin Price. 2971
Ivins, Dan. 217, 3353
Ivins, William Mills. 3341
Ivinskis, Zenonas. 2165
Ivison, Stuart. 145
Ivy, Frankie Oliver. 1448
Iwahashi, Takeo. 3095
Iyengar. B. K. S. 3867
Izbicki, Thomas M. 1188, 3704
Izutsu, Toshihiko. 1601, 3893

J

Ja' far Sharif. 2567
Jabay, Earl. 965, 1012, 2323
Jaberg, Eugene C. 2193
Jaberg, Gene. 3594
Jabine, Louis. 1201
*Jablonski, Edward. 2355
Jabusch, Willard. 2901
Jack, Alex. 1393
Jack, Butler. 1115
Jack, James William. 2498
Jackaway, Clarice M. 965
Jackman, Everett E. 2431
Jackman, Sydney Wayne. 738, 3822
Jacks, Lawrence Pearsall. 693, 1128, 1280, 1326, 1592, 2226, 2998, 3060
Jacks, Leo Vincent. 1481, 2183, 2568
Jackson, Abraham Valentine Williams. 2327, 3898
Jackson, Abraham Willard. 2349
Jackson, Alvin R. 3060
Jackson, Benjamin Franklin. 1317
Jackson, Carl T. 92
[Jackson, Carol] 1911. 1282
Jackson, Catherine. 984
Jackson, Charles Davis. 1698
Jackson, Charles L. 1358
Jackson, Charles S. 3734
Jackson, Cortes. 1405
Jackson, Dave. 933, 3027, 3780
Jackson, Donald. 2863, 3012
Jackson, Drury Wellington. 144
Jackson, Edgar Newman. 1170, 1351, 1693, 1774, 2136, 2780, 2784, 2874, 2901, 3182
Jackson, Elizabeth. 1592
Jackson, Esther. 85
Jackson, Frances. 3796
Jackson, Frances I. 965
Jackson, George. 1359, 2064
Jackson, George Anson. 76, 1617, 1618
Jackson, Giovanna R. 1897, 2683
Jackson, Gordon Duffield. 2214
Jackson, Gordon E. 2786
Jackson, Green P. 2943
Jackson, Helen (Barnouski) 1357
Jackson, Henry Ezekiel. 965, 1321, 3141
Jackson, Henry Latimer. 420
Jackson, Herbert C. 1084, 2144, 3117
Jackson, Herbert G. 1942, 3520
Jackson, Irene V. 3522
Jackson, Jeremy C. 1189
Jackson, Jerome Case. 3189
Jackson, Jesse. 1930, 3414
Jackson, John. 2217, 3031, 1295, 1688
Jackson, Joseph Harrison. 1040, 1707, 2500, 2669, 3256, 3850
Jackson, Kathryn. 2022
Jackson, Lois. 602
Jackson, Loulia. 2695
*Jackson, M. Violet. 1608
Jackson, Margaret Austen (Byron) 1931
Jackson, Melvin. 2803
Jackson, Mildred L. 621
Jackson, Myrtle Strode. 1033
Jackson, Neil E. 1171
Jackson, Paul Rainey. 3052
Jackson, Rebecca. 3397, 3631
Jackson, Richard Allen. 164
Jackson, Robert Wyse. 1269
Jackson, Ronald Vern. 2617, 3428
Jackson, Samuel Macauley. 2522, 3042, 3638, 3639, 3900
Jackson, Sheldon. 1899, 2926
Jackson, Sheldon Glenn. 1686

Jackson, Shirley. 3827
Jackson, Thomas. 661, 1781, 2421, 2424, 2442, 2706, 3010, 3798, 1931
Jackson, Thomas Graham. 2755
Jackson, W. T. H. 1521
Jackson, Warner. 3017
Jackson, Warren W. 64
Jackson, William. 2957
Jackson, William Taylor. 2163, 3533
Jacob, Ben. 534
Jacob, Benno. 521
Jacob, Caroline Nicholson. 536, 1677, 1685
Jacob, Edmond. 598
Jacob, Ernest Fraser. 1181, 1186
[Jacob, John]. 1599
Jacob, Margaret C. 1542, 1665, 3085
Jacob, Maude Beeley. 534
Jacob, Micheal. 3886
Jacob, Walter. 2086, 2154
Jacob, William Ungoed. 2057
Jacob ben Hayyim ibn. Adonijah. 2364
Jacob ben Isaac. 516
Jacob ben Isaac, of Janow. 516
Jacobi, Andrea. 1027
Jacobs, Alice. 3554
Jacobs, Barbara Tietjen. 2618
Jacobs, Bela. 3129
Jacobs, Charles Fredrick. 1341
Jacobs, Charles M. 1050
Jacobs, Charles Michael. 1182, 2299, 75, 1095, 1176, 3663
Jacobs, Donald R. 1059, 1423
Jacobs, Francis Warren. 1022
Jacobs, Henry Eyster. 3644, 2274, 2285, 2294, 3663
Jacobs, J. Vernon. 333, 3559, 3565, 3592
Jacobs, James Vernon. 3565, 280, 333, 984, 1251, 1840, 2204, 3152, 3554, 3886
Jacobs, Joan. 1004
Jacobs, Joseph. 2013, 2085, 1952, 2005, 2082, 2093, 2094, 2099, 763, 796, 3265
Jacobs (Joseph) Advertising and Merchandising, inc., New York. 2120
Jacobs, Louis. 1, 505, 1539, 1614, 1789, 2074, 2075, 2080, 2081, 2146, 2885, 2886, 3219, 3584
Jacobs, Margaret Branch (Moore) 1448
Jacobs, Thornwell. 3078, 1091, 3073
Jacobs, William. 2117
Jacobs, William Charles. 1059
Jacobs, William J. 779, 929, 948, 998, 1967
Jacobs, William Plumer. 1931
Jacobsen, David C. 2786, 2874
Jacobsen, Henry. 331, 413, 454, 938
Jacobsen, Jerome Vincent. 1948
Jacobsen, Marion Leach. 984
Jacobsen, Phebe R. 1686
Jacobsen, Thorkild. 2413
Jacobson, Augustus. 1655
Jacobson, Dan. 294, 2096
Jacobson, David. 3439
Jacobson, Edith. 523
Jacobson, Gladys (Slaugh) 2614, 3423
Jacobson, Marsha T. 896, 1231, 1233, 2603
Jacobson, Nils-Olof. 2989
Jacobson, Nolan Pliny. 702, 708
Jacobson, Roger A. 95
Jacobson, Ruth. 2122
Jacobus. 1931
Jacobus de Varagine. 1024, 1931, 3280
Jacobus de Vitriaco, d. 1240. 1583
Jacobus, Donald Lines. 1346
Jacobus, Lee A. 2468
Jacobus, Melancthon Williams. 439, 244, 348, 654
Jacoby, James Calvin. 1608
Jacoby, John E. 2639
Jacoby, Samuel A. 3505
Jacocks, Abel B. 2981
Jacolliot, Louis. 2726, 2732
Jacques, John Herbert. 25
Jacques, Oliver. 2552
Jacques. Oliver. 2552
Jacquett, Josephine. 3286
Jae Jah Noh. 3479
Jaegen, Hieronymus. 998
Jaeger, A J. 2703
Jaeger, Harry J. 425
Jaeger, Lorenz. 3770, 1373, 3770, 3774
Jaeger, Lorenz, Cardinal. 3774
Jaeger, Werner Wilhelm. 1773, 1081
Jaegher, Paul de. 2267, 2390, 2637, 2639, 3487
Jaehn, Klaus Juergen. 3025
Jaenen, Cornelius J. 815, 1899
Ja'far Sharif. 1925
Jaffe, Aniela. 1709
Jaffe, Leonard. 1615
Jaffee, Martin S. 2479, 3702
Jafri, Syed Husain M. 3403
Jagaisa-Chandra, Chattopadhyaya. 3776
Jager, Okke. 1741
Jaggar, Thomas Augustus. 3364
Jagmandar-lal Jaini. 1932

Jagmandar-lar Jaini. d. 1927. 1932
Jahn, Johann. 207
Jahsmann, Allan Hart. 621, 902, 903, 935, 1605, 1981, 2287, 3178, 3563
Jaimini. 2472
Jain, Jyoti Prasad. 1932, 2317
Jaini, Jagmandar Lal. 1932
Jaini, Padmanabh S. 1932
Jairazbhoy, Rafique Ali. 86
Jaki, Stanley L. 2824, 2845, 2862
Jakobovits, Immanuel. 2074, 2139
Jalabert, Henri. 2362
Jalal al-Din Rumi, Mawlana, 1207-1273. 1926
Jalalv-D-Din Muhammad I Rumi, Mavlana. 1933, 3542
Jalland, Trevor Gervase. 1176, 2259, 2769
Jamaica Christian Council. 1933
Jamali, Mohammed Fadhel. 1922
Jamart, Francois. 740, 3487, 3690
Jamblichus. 1501, 1502
James, Arthur Walter. 1086, 2769
James, Ava Leach. 901, 1603
James, Bartlett Burleigh. 674, 2189
James, Bruno Scott. 120, 193, 3487
James, Charles Fenton. 3195
James, David Lewis. 86
James, Donald H. 2780
James, E. O. 2648
James, Edgar C. 459, 606, 1460, 1528
James, Edward. 3505
James, Edward Holton. 2019, 2068
James, Edwin Oliver. 514, 1079, 1107, 1723, 1758, 2624, 2939, 3109, 3117, 3139, 3239, 3271, 3272, 3404, 3423, 3644
James, Fannie B. 318
James, Fleming. 493, 576, 1192, 493, 576
James, Francis Godwin. 2708
James, George Payne Rainsford. 1390
James, George Wharton. 1324, 1646, 3470
James, Gertrude. 877
James, Gladden William. 234
James, Hartwell. 626, 634
James, Henry. 1069, 1535, 1745, 3199
James, Hunter. 2596
James, John. 1745, 749
James, John Angel. 1201
James, John Angell. 965, 1055, 1201, 1324, 1608, 3295, 3672
James, John Thomas. 1422
James, Joseph. 2639
James, Joseph H. 1934
[James, Joshua Marion]. 2849
James, Lena Graham. 1931
James, Mary Dagworthy (Yard) 2631, 3862
James, Maynard G. 1830
James, Minnie (Kennedy) 1799, 3468
James, Montague Rhodes. 462, 491, 2206
James, Muriel. 1586
James, O. Waldo. 343
James, Paul. 2948
James, Powhatan Wright. 3716
James, R R. 463
James, Ralph E. 1788, 2943, 2944
James Stanislaus 1860. 1981
James, Stanley Bloomfield. 3199
James, Sydney V. 1678, 3009
James I. 1423, 1624
James, Thomas Garnet Henry. 2659
James, William. 1751, 1535, 1538, 1586, 1888, 1891, 1934, 3060, 3067
James, William Carey. 2208
James Fleming. 493
James I, King of Great Britain. 1423, 1624
Jameson, Anna Brownell Murphy. 920, 1026, 1957, 2355, 2358, 3280, 3416, 3835
Jameson, Beth. 1934, 2218
Jameson, Vic. 1089
Jamieson, Robert. 222, 223, 534
Jamieson, William F. 1655
Jamison, Albert Leland. 316, 331
Jamison, Alcinous Burton. 3506
Jamison, Daisy. 95
Jamison, David Lee. 2836
Jamison, Leland. 331, 2798
Jamison, Wallace N. 2688, 3736
Jamme, Albert. 1910
Jan. 3244
Janakananda Saraswati, 1939. 3865
Jane, Marie. 1015, 1992
Janelle, Pierre. 1374
Jane Marie. 1176
Janes, Edmund Storer. 294
Janes, George Milton. 3122
Janes, Hugh Paul. 3784
Janet, Paul Alexandre Rene. 1621, 3593
Janeway, Jacob Jones. 405, 466, 800, 2118, 3306
Janeway, James. 895, 896, 1934, 2048
Janeway, Thomas Leiper. 1692, 1934
Janjua, Harbhajan Singh. 3600
Jank, Margaret. 2696, 3862

Jankauskas, John J. 838
Janko, Richard. 1521, 1839
Janney, Oliver Edward. 1675
Janney, Samuel Macpherson. 1637, 1682, 1685
Janning, Edward A. 3506
Janowsky, Oscar Isaiah. 2078, 2099, 2104
Jansen, G. M. A. 3265, 3663
Jansen, John F. 234
Jansen, John Frederick. 135, 287, 348, 431, 2051, 2052, 2258
Jansen, Marius B. 1935
Janss, Edmund W. 1254
Janssen, Johannes. 1129, 1263, 1298
Janssen, Lawrence H. 1278
Janssens, Alois. 3711
Janssens, Louis. 2223
Janssens, Paul Mary. 3411
Jan van Ruysbroeck. 2647
Janvier, Pierre Desire. 78, 2334
Janvier, Thomas Allibone. 1111
Janzen, Abraham Ewell. 606
Janzen, John Gerald. 547
Janzen, John M. 131, 1500, 2209
Janzen, Lester E. 1168
Janzen, Waldemar. 2157
Japan. Bunkacho. 1935
Japan Conservative Baptist Mission. Historical Committee. 2534
Japeth ben Eli. 506
Jaquett, Josephine. 1274
Jardine, Robert Anderson. 3567
Jarman, W. Maxey. 720
Jarratt, Devereux. 1306, 3060, 3644
Jarratt, Elizabeth Ann. 3152
Jarrel, Willis Anselm. 135, 151, 1427
Jarrell, Charles C. 2442, 3848
*Jarrett, Bede. 1936
Jarrett, Bede. 776, 863, 1448, 1622, 1834, 2057, 2214, 3296, 3487, 3633
Jarrett-Kerr, Martin, 1912. 924, 1134, 3071
Jarrett-Kerr, Martin. 1059
Jarrett-Kerr, Martin, Father. 105
Jarstad, Anton. 1772
Jarvis, Frank Washington. 500, 929, 1176, 1967
Jarvis, George Millen. 234, 500
Jarvis, Lucy Cushing. 1222, 2525
[Jarvis, Mary Caroline]. 2891
Jarvis, Robert E[dward] L[ee]. 965
[Jarvis, Samuel Farmar]. 685, 1997, 3627
Jarvis, Stinson. 2989
Jascalevich, Alejandro A. 1911
Jasper, K G. 3374
Jasper, Ronald Claud Dudley. 186
Jaspers, Karl. 111, 114, 1424, 2163, 49, 3716
Jasperson, Robert O. 1672
Jast, Louis Stanley. 3053
Jastrow, Joseph. 2732, 2989, 2732
Jastrow, Morris. 94, 1280, 2119, 3089
Jatakas. 702, 1937, 2206
Jatakas. English. Selections. 2207
Jatakas. English. Selections. 1975. 1632, 1937
Jatakas, Nidana-katha. 2207
Jatho, Charles Conrad. 2957
Jaubert, Annie. 2029
Jauncey, Ernest. 1751
Jauncey, James H. 204, 424, 965, 1566, 1785
Javelet, Robert. 2025
Jay, Carroll E. 1937, 3519
Jay, Eric George. 44, 1187
Jay, John Edwin. 1060
Jay, William. 965, 1284, 1439, 1605, 1692, 3129, 3364, 3631, 3839
Jayme, Luis. 3298
[Jayne, Mary (Salkeld-Robinson)]. 1778
Jayne, Sears Reynolds. 1307
Jayne, Walter Addison. 1742, 1793, 1742
Jaynes, Julian Clifford. 3725
JC139.C3A3 1956 57-799. 2858
Jeaffreson, Herbert Hammond. 2218
Jean de Paris, 1240?-1306. 2863
Jean de Saint-Samson, 1571-1636. 1937, 3490
Jean Marie. 2399
Jean Baptiste. 1741
Jean Maie. 2573
[Jeanne. 2708
*Jeanne Renee, Sister. 895
Jeanneret-Gris, Charles Edouard. 3247
Jean-Nesmy, Claude. 838, 1327
Jebb, Richard Claverhouse. 191, 1526
Jedin, Hubert. 1373, 1176, 1183, 1373, 3710
Jeep, Elizabeth. 940, 3179
Jeeves, Malcolm A. 3082, 1107
Jefferies, Thomas Albert. 595
Jeffers, James A. 46
Jefferson, Alpha. 3142
Jefferson, Charles Edward. 133, 546, 907, 1341, 1888, 3341, 3369, 3886, 57, 543, 907, 1060, 1126, 1288, 1341, 1995, 2563, 2798, 2807, 2901, 3341, 3672

Jefferson, Howard Bonar. 1104
Jefferson, Philip Clarke. 44
Jefferson, Ted. 931, 1939
Jefferson, William. 2317, 3708
Jeffery, Arthur. 1921, 1927, 2185, 2564, 2565, 2629
Jeffery, Graham. 118, 217
Jeffery, H B. 1712, 2409, 2874
Jeffery, Thomas Reed. 3803
Jefferys, Mary Ann. 2497
Jefferys, Ulysses Morgan Grant. 1967
Jefferys, William Hamilton. 2639, 3129
*Jeffrey, Annie L. 1616
Jeffrey, George Johnstone. 1318
Jeffreys, John. 1215
Jeffreys, Raymond John. 1792, 3702
Jeffries, Betty Jean. 756
Jeffries, J Campbell. 1830, 2247
Jeffries, James J. 3597
Jeffries, John. 1543
Jehlicsks, Franz Rudolf. 769
Jeiler, Ignatius. 1848, 3307, 3420
Jellet, Henry. 3341
Jellicoe, Sidney. 529
Jemison, David Herbert. 687
Jemison, T Housel. 3645, 3811, 3886
Jemolo, Arturo Carlo. 1147
Jen, Ch'eng-yian. 2509
[Jencks, E N]. 2858
Jenkens, Charles Augustus. 148, 2025, 148
Jenkens, Millard Alford. 164, 2721
Jenkins, Burris Atkins. 348, 965, 1466, 2976, 3060, 3353, 3744
Jenkins, Claude. 1522, 1762, 2374
Jenkins, Daniel Thomas. 990, 1012, 1119, 1295, 1344, 1491, 1723, 1737, 2874, 3645, 3706
Jenkins, Daphne Smith (Giles) 2856
Jenkins, David. 2545
Jenkins, David E. 2046, 2320, 3622, 3656
Jenkins, David Ernest. 2545
Jenkins, David L. 3186
[Jenkins, Edward]. 1522
Jenkins, Ethel (Stout) 506
Jenkins, Ferrell. 464
Jenkins, Frank Edwin. 1338
Jenkins, Geraint H. 1021
Jenkins, Holt M. 907, 2973
Jenkins, Horace Carroll. 244
Jenkins, Isaac C. 3335
Jenkins, J[ames] H[arvey]. 1448
Jenkins, James Harvey. 3443
Jenkins, Jerry B. 651, 2488, 2533
Jenkins, Leonard Rush. 1840
Jenkins, Lucy Howe. 3886
Jenkins, Mary Jane. 3289
Jenkins, Millard Alford. 164
Jenkins, Newton. 2104
Jenkins, Robert Charles. 737
Jenkins, Sara Lucile. 34, 35, 897
Jenkins, Sephora Bettes. 3506
Jenkins, Thomas. 3252
Jenkins, Thomas J. 805
Jenks, Alan W. 1484
Jenks, Arthur Whipple. 1176, 2382
Jenks, David. 1288, 2482
Jenks, Edward Augustus. 1723
Jenks, Jeremiah Whipple. 687, 2059
Jenks, William. 285, 286, 1303
Jenks William. 102
Jenkyn, Thomas William. 105
Jenner, Katharine Lee (Rawlings) 920, 2358
Jenneskens, Maarten. 2254
Jenness, Mary. 569, 571, 953, 2439, 2527, 2531, 2550, 3764
Jenney, Ray Freeman. 310, 2932, 2976
Jenney, Shirley Carson. 3506
Jennings, Abraham Gould. 204, 1381
Jennings, Don. 2390
Jennings, Frank Leonard. 1566
Jennings, Frederick Charles. 542, 1427
Jennings, Gary. 1423, 1743, 2314
Jennings, Hargrave. 3250
Jennings, Henry C. 2426
Jennings, Ray. 3842
Jennings, Samuel Kennedy. 2459
Jennings, Theodore W. 2874, 3669
Jennings, Vivien. 3844
Jennings, Walter Wilson. 965, 1460
Jennings, William H. 1153
Jenny, Gerald. 2292
Jenny, Henri. 1958
Jens, Arlene Johnson. 523
Jensen, Adolf Ellegard. 3109
Jensen, Andrew. 2617
Jensen, C. Russell. 1638, 1704
Jensen, Clarence H. 1557
*Jensen, Conrad S. 3129
Jensen, De Lamar. 1826, 2274, 2403
Jensen, Erik. 1880
Jensen, Florence (Huntington) 2482
Jensen, Gustav Margerth. 1295
Jensen, Iona (Clark) 2543
*Jensen, Irving L. 554, 1943

Jensen, Irving Lester. 333, 475, 529, 597, 600, 639, 646
Jensen, J C. 1533
Jensen, John Martin. 32, 2302, 3732
Jensen, Joseph. 540, 543, 3704
Jensen, Juliaetta (Bateman) 178
Jensen, Kai. 1351, 2299
Jensen, Kenneth L. 572
Jensen, Margie Calhoun. 1231
Jensen, Mary. 1253
Jensen, Nephi. 2611
Jensen, Richard A. 1712, 2299, 2901
Jensenius, Bertram. 1533
Jenson, Andrew. 1115, 2603, 2610, 2617
Jenson, Robert W. 175, 1060, 1733, 3070, 3263, 3663
Jenson, Ron. 1171
Jent, John William. 3253
Jentges, Damian. 3475
Jenyns, Soame. 59, 1098, 1745
Jepson, John James. 584
Jepson, Sarah Anne. 1431, 1435, 3415
Jepson, Winston F. 1232
Jeremiah, James T. 305
Jeremias, Alfred. 78
Jeremias, Joachim. 334, 477, 1906, 1958, 2008, 2025, 2040, 2049, 2064, 2198, 2247, 2556, 3377
Jeremy, David J. 120
Jerman, H. Noel. 2168, 3277
Jernegan, Prescott Ford. 1723
Jernigan, John C. 3374
Jerphagnon, Lucien. 2891
Jerrold, Douglas. 1086, 3450
Jersey City, N. J. Bergen Reformed church. 1155
Jersey, Edward Drewry. 2430
Jerseyville, Ill. Presbyterian church. 2917
Jersild, Paul T. 64, 1140
Jerusalem Conference on Biblical Prophecy, 1971. 610
Jerusalem. Ecole biblique et archeologique francaise. Bibliotheque. 239, 1944, 2148
Jerusalmi, Isaac. 528
Jervell, Jacob. 426, 2008, 2271
Jervey, Edward Drewry. 1929
Jeschke, Marlin. 1166
Jeske, Richard L. 311
Jess, John D. 55, 885, 3018
Jesse, William. 59, 1098, 1942
Jessett, Thomas Edwin. 2971
Jesske, Waldemar S. 144
Jessop, Harry Edward. 1514, 1823, 2874
Jessop, Thomas Edmund. 192, 946, 3660
Jessopp, Augustus. 2715, 3129
Jessup, Gordon. 2139
Jessup, Henry Harris. 2162, 2552
Jessup, Henry Wynans. 2916
Jesuit Educational Association. 1946
Jesuit philosophical association of the eastern states. 831
Jesuit Research Council Of America. 832, 1949, 3759
Jesuits. 1945
Jesuits. California province. 1948
Jesuits. Letters from missions (North America) 1948, 1949, 2688
Jesus Christ. 2060, 3473
Jeter, Hugh. 1599
Jeter, Jeremiah Bell. 146, 148, 965, 1460, 1461, 2072
Jett, Curtis. 3341
Jette, Fernand. 2334, 3492
Jeudwine, John Wynne. 1542
Jevons, Frank Byron. 3109, 3117
Jewel, Alice. 2695, 2966
Jewel, John. 1216, 1217, 1218, 3629
Jewell, Earle B. 3129, 3539
Jewell, Henry. 2849
Jewell, Horace. 2451
Jewell, John P. 1345, 2072
Jewell, Marianne H. 1603
Jewell, Walter Ellsworth. 3711
Jewett, Dick. 1244, 3385, 3886
Jewett, Edward Hurtt. 1427
Jewett, Frances (Gulick) 1777
Jewett, Henry Erastus. 1341, 1484
Jewett, Paul King. 1906, 2742, 3260, 3391
Jewett, Pendie S. 3506
Jewett, Robert. 403, 1530, 2064, 2803
Jewett, Sophie. 1642
Jewett, Susan W. 3171
Jewish Braille Institute of America. 2075
Jewish Chautauqua society. 2086
Jewish community center, Washington, D.C. 2107
Jewish Community Centers of Chicago. 2098
Jewish community of New York city. Bureau of education. 2101
Jewish education. 187, 2106
Jewish Education Association of Essex County (New Jersey) 2099
Jewish Institute of Religion, New York. 5, 2147
Jewish institute of religon, New York. 5, 2114

Jewish Minorities Research, New York. 2145
Jewish occupational council, New York. 2945
Jewish people's institute of Chicago. 2098
Jewish Publication Society of America. 530
The Jewish quarterly review. New series. 3259
Jewish Statistical Bureau, New York. 3016
Jewish theological seminary of America. 2079, 2080, 2142, 2145, 2164, 3259
Jewish Theological Seminary of America. Jewish Museum. 87, 184, 566, 2101, 3093, 3577
Jewish Theological Seminary of America. Library. 7, 212, 2074, 2331, 2623
Jewish welfare board. 3456
Jewkes, Wilfred Thomas. 1938
Jews. 82, 1780, 2108, 2110, 2111, 2779, 2874, 3240, 3377, 3459
Jews. Liturgy and ritual. 1797, 2108, 2109, 2111, 2139, 2874, 2884, 3455
Jews. Liturgy and ritual. Bar Mitzvah. 1943. 172
Jews. Liturgy and ritual. Benedictions. 2110, 2239
Jews. Liturgy and ritual. Children's services. 2884
Jews. Liturgy and ritual. Daily prayers. 2108, 2110, 2117, 2874, 3456
Jews. Liturgy and ritual. Day of atonement prayers. 1510
Jews. Liturgy and ritual. Festival prayers. 105, 2073, 2108, 2109, 2111
Jews. Liturgy and ritual. Hagadah. 1780, 2110, 2779, 3328
Jews. Liturgy and ritual. Hagadah. 1850. 2779
Jews. Liturgy and ritual. Hagadah. 1907. 2779
Jews. Liturgy and ritual. Hagadah. 1941. 2109, 3022
Jews. Liturgy and ritual. Hagadah. 1943. 2110
Jews. Liturgy and ritual. Hagadah. 1944. 82
Jews. Liturgy and ritual. Hagadah. 1953. 2779
Jews. Liturgy and ritual Hagadah 1964. 1780
Jews. Liturgy and ritual. Hagadah. 1965. 1780
Jews. Liturgy and ritual. Hagadah. English. 1780
Jews. Liturgy and ritual. Hagadah. Mss. 1884
Jews. Liturgy and ritual. Hagadah. Selections. 1964. 1780
Jews Liturgy and ritual. Hagadah. Selections. 1965. 1780, 2779
Jews. Liturgy and ritual. Hagadah. Selections. 1974. 2110
Jews. Liturgy and ritual. Haggadah. 1967. 2110
Jews. Liturgy and ritual. Haggadah. 1965. 2110
Jews. Liturgy and ritual. High holy day prayers. 2081, 2884
Jews. Liturgy and ritual. Mourners' prayers. 1715, 2109
Jews. Liturgy and ritual. New year prayers. 1510
Jews. Liturgy and ritual. Occasional prayers. 2109, 2112
Jews. Liturgy and ritual. Sabbath prayers. 2109, 2111, 3025
Jews. Liturgy and ritual. Sabbath service. 2109
Jews. Liturgy and ritual selections. 901
Jews. Liturgy and ritual. Sephardic. 2097
Jeys, Thomas Henry. 1593
Jezernik, Maksimilijan. 172
Jezreel, James Jershom. 3342
Jick, Leon A. 2155
Jiggetts, J. Ida. 2086
Jinarajadasa, Curuppumallage. 3685
Jinarajadasa, Curuppumallage. 3685
Jinarajadasa, Curuppumullage. 706, 3685, 3689, 3685, 3689
Jindel, Rajendra. 2669
Jirku, Anton. 207
Joad, Cyril Edwin Mitchinson. 1050, 1746, 1060, 1104, 1746, 2839
Joan Mary. 723
Joannes. 1881, 2734
Joannes, Climacus. 3493
Joannes Climacus, 6th cent. 3493
Joannes De Rupella ca. 1190-1245. 2362, 3372
Joannes, of Damascus. 1019
Joannes, Pope 1881-1963. 2123
Joannes XXIII. 2123, 759, 776, 1434, 2123, 2124, 2210, 3018
Joannes XXIII, 1881-1963. 2123, 2861
Joannes XXIII. 2123
Job, John B. 549, 639

Job, Rueben P. 1572
Jobe, Joseph. 1957
Jobes, Gertrude. 2652
Joblin, Kingsley. 414, 1119
Jobson, Orville D. 2558
[Jocelin, Simeon] 1746-1823. 2984
Jocelyn, Beredene. 3479
Jocelyn, John. 95
[Jocelyn, Simeon]. 2984
Jocz, Jakob. 234, 1084, 1377
Joelsson, A G. 2279
Joerndt, Clarence V. 1810, 3274
Joers, Lawrence Eugene Claire. 1060, 2125, 2539, 2874
Johann Jakob Griesbach Bicentenary Colloquium, 1776-1976, Munster, Ger. 351, 1774, 3578
Johann, Robert O. 1729, 2263
Joannes XXIII. 776, 3633
Johannes von Kastl. 3616
Johannis. 1825
Johansson, Rune Edvin Anders. 2867
Johansen, Ruthann Knechel. 3836
*Johansson, Catherine. 1659
Johansson, Catherine B. 484
Johansson, Rune Edvin Andrews. 2711
Johar, Surinder Singh. 3408, 3592
Johlson, Joseph. 2114
[John Berchmans] 3186
John, Bubba Free. 3479, 3483
John, DeWitt. 1033
John, Eric. 2860
John, Erwin E. 2224
John G. Finch Symposium on Psychology and Religion, 1st, Fuller Theological Seminary, 1971. 1587
John G. Finch Symposium on Psychology and Religion, 2d, Pasadena, Calif., 1973. 2986
John, John P D. 1738
John, John Price Durbin. 1069, 1723, 1907, 3161
John, Martin. 3313
John, Mike. 965
John of Salisbury, d. 1180. 1541, 2769
John Paul I, 1920. 776, 787, 788, 793, 863, 998, 1044, 1601, 2126, 2572, 2891, 3364, 3622, 3633, 3890
Catholic Church. 746
John Paul I, 1912-1978. 793, 1884
John Paul II, 1920. 793, 854, 863, 2266, 3223, 3369, 525, 759, 793, 863, 2346, 2390, 3364, 3368, 3369, 3391, 3628, 3890
John, Peter Paul. 474
John, S B. 3050
Johndro, Lorne Edward. 95
Johner, Dominicus. 843, 883
*Johnice, M. 3163
Johnice, Sister. 2014
John of Salisbury. 1541, 2218, 2769
Johnroe, Donan. 691
Johns, Alger F. 78
Johns, Hazel T. 2809
Johns, John, bp. 2376
Johns, June. 3300
Johns, Roger Dick. 2460
Johns, Varner Jay. 3192
Johnsen, Erik Kristian. 2798, 2029
Johnson, Aaaron. 700, 1359
Johnson, Aaron. 1359
Johnson, Abigail (Acker) 3883
Johnson, Alan F. 468, 554, 1314
Johnson, Alan P. 2258
Johnson, Albert. 934, 3145
Johnson, Albinus Alonzo. 3289
Johnson, Alex. 192
Johnson, Alexander Bryan. 1326
Johnson, Alvin D. 1155, 1249
Johnson, Alvin Jewett. 102
Johnson, Alvin Walter. 1129
[Johnson & Johnson]. 3029
Johnson, Andrew. 1553, 1557
Johnson, Anna Jane (Sample) 2019
Johnson, Ashley Sidney. 3325
Johnson, Aubrey Rodway. 578, 588, 658, 1731, 2114, 2950, 3462
Johnson, B. C. 100
Johnson, Barry Lee. 1007
Johnson, Barton W. 437, 463
*Johnson, Ben C. 2885
Johnson, Ben Campbell. 374, 444, 965, 1007, 2128, 2874
Johnson, Byron Lindberg. 1139
Johnson, Carl E. 1566
*Johnson, Carl G. 935, 1840, 3374, 3376
Johnson, Carl O. 2174
Johnson, Cecelia D. 875, 2308
Johnson, Cedric B. 1361
[Johnson, Charles Alfred]. 3333
Johnson, Charles Croxton. 1033
Johnson, Charles D. 3465
Johnson, Charles Ivar. 105
Johnson, Charles R. 1119
Johnson, Christine (Claybourne) 3026
Johnson, Claude M. 3060
Johnson, Cliff Ross. 75

Johnson, Clifton. 621, 3526
Johnson, Clive. 1904
Johnson, Constance Fuller (Wheeler) 1638
Johnson, Daniel E. 3253
Johnson, David. 2390
Johnson, Donald. 1743
Johnson, Doris Miller. 1399
Johnson, Douglas. 234
Johnson, Douglas W. 1242, 1243, 1248, 1251, 1256
Johnson, Duane C. 965
Johnson, Early Ashby. 1608, 2128, 3295, 3616
Johnson, Edgar Nathaniel. 666
Johnson, Edith Henry. 80
Johnson, Edward H. 3289
Johnson, Edwin Clark. 3487
Johnson, Edythe J. 430
Johnson, Elbert Neil. 2637
Johnson, Elias Henry. 1050, 1830, 3479, 3645, 3650
Johnson, Emeroy. 110, 924
Johnson, Emily (Cooper) 3255
Johnson, Emmett V. 965
Johnson, Eola. 422
Johnson, Ethel A. 1981
Johnson, Ethelbert. 3685
Johnson, Eugene J. 2329
Johnson, Florence Miriam. 1324
Johnson, Frances Simington. 1448, 3199
[Johnson, Francis]. 3027
Johnson, Francis Howe. 3073, 3101
Johnson, Frank Roy. 3824
Johnson, Franklin. 1580
Johnson, Frederick A. 800, 2957
Johnson, Frederick Ernest. 1168, 3433, 3443, 3453
Johnson, Frend Irwin. 244, 1060
Johnson, Gary. 3458
Johnson, George. 621, 812, 621, 812, 193, 319
Johnson, George Barent. 26
Johnson, George Ira. 1668
Johnson, George Lindsay. 3506, 3520
*Johnson, Gladys Cordray. 201
Johnson, Gordon G. 142
Johnson, Gustaf E. 2390
Johnson, H. Eugene. 733, 933, 2790
Johnson, Harold L. 720
Johnson, Harriet Everard. 1872
Johnson, Helen M. 3811
Johnson, Henry Theodore. 2242
Johnson, Herrick. 2932, 3672
Johnson, Hildegard Binder. 12
Johnson, Howard Albert. 43, 2170, 2901, 2957
Johnson, Hubert Rex. 1029, 2798, 2696
Johnson, Humphrey John Thewlis. 204, 1211
Johnson, Hunter L. 2064
Johnson, Inman. 2261
Johnson, Irwin C. 1426
Johnson, Ithiel Town. 1575
Johnson, Iver M. 965
Johnson, James Elwin. 984, 2410
Johnson, James Glover. 1104
Johnson, James Leonard. 1075, 1369, 2128, 2244
[Johnson, James R]. 394, 2000
Johnson, James Rosser. 1715
Johnson, James Turner. 2159, 2346
Johnson, James W. 2561
Johnson, James Wager. 3289, 3745
Johnson, James Weldon. 544, 1383, 2680
Johnson, Jan. 1027, 1644
Johnson, Jane. 1678, 1682
Johnson, Jasper W. 1818
Johnson, Jean Dye. 1903
Johnson, Jennie (Bixby) 668
Johnson, Jeremiah Monroe. 135
*Johnson, Jerry Don. 1735, 3173
Johnson, Joe. 1455
Johnson, John. 3294
Johnson, John Barent. 1612
Johnson, John Boman. 2461
Johnson, John Edgar. 2576
Johnson, John Howard. 2699, 2973
Johnson, John Lipscomb. 1593
Johnson, John Rosamond. 2680
Johnson, John Sevier. 3248
Johnson, John Warren. 1086
Johnson, Johnni. 155, 1305, 2484, 2557
Johnson, Joseph. 1110
Johnson, Joseph Andrew. 2682
Johnson, Joseph Mitchell. 1824
Johnson, Josephine Lucas. 2726
Johnson, Judith Anne. 47
Johnson, Kate Nunez. 1506
Johnson, Katharine W. 159
Johnson, Kathryn S. 2183, 2206
Johnson, Keith. 984
Johnson, Keith F. 755
Johnson, Kenneth M. 1249
Johnson, L. D. 171, 311, 549, 2124, 2128, 2390, 3821
Johnson, L. Ted. 1164
Johnson, Lenore. 2047

Johnson, Leslie Leonidas. 690, 3467
Johnson, Lilian D. 3473
Johnson, Lois. 1714
Johnson, Lois Pheips. 3795
Johnson, Lois Walfrid. 902, 931, 1714, 2128, 2891
Johnson, Lorenzo Dow. 2128, 3740
Johnson, Louise Coleman. 2715
Johnson, Luke Timothy. 368, 426, 429, 2946, 3799
Johnson, Lyman Huggins. 1119
Johnson, Margaret. 1351, 1930
Johnson, Margaret Woods. 734, 3847
Johnson, Marian S. 2224
Johnson, Marjorie Guinn. 680
Johnson, Marshall D. 281
Johnson, Mary (Coffin) 1305
Johnson, Mary Parker. 3117
[Johnson, Maud Lalita (Shlaudeman) 3506
*Johnson, Mel. 3097, 3886
Johnson, Melvin Edward. 2323
Johnson, Merle Allison. 984, 1060, 1266, 1295, 2436, 2874, 3353, 3426
Johnson, Nancy Karo. 171, 2129
Johnson, Nathaniel Emmons. 1603
Johnson, Norman Burrows. 488
Johnson, Olive L. 3765
Johnson, Orien. 984, 2786
Johnson, Oscar Francis. 1723
Johnson, P. Adelstein. 1336
Johnson, Paul. 1176, 753, 1176, 2123
Johnson, Paul E. 2823, 3231
Johnson, Paul Emanuel. 924, 2263, 2780, 2995, 2998, 3886
Johnson, Paul Gordon. 2981
Johnson, Paul Samuel Leo. 1522, 1528
Johnson, Pearl (Vennard) 2516
Johnson, Penelope D. 2
Johnson, Peter Leo. 1403, 1803, 2188, 2472, 3274
Johnson, Philip A. 3002
Johnson, Philip C. 479, 506, 509
Johnson, Phillip R. 1574
Johnson, Pierce. 1007
Johnson, Ralph Henry. 2170
Johnson, Ray Neil. 1566
Johnson, Raymond Burgeur. 3152
Johnson, Raynor Carey. 2639, 3027, 3117, 3479
Johnson, Rex E. 3175
Johnson, Robert A. 1359, 2129
Johnson, Robert Clyde. 118, 2040
Johnson, Robert Lee. 380
Johnson, Robert Leon. 1060
Johnson, Roger A. 3082
Johnson, Roswell Park. 2541
Johnson, Roy Lee. 140, 170
Johnson, Ruffus Abraham Reid. 303
Johnson, Ruth I. 616, 924, 1264, 1448, 1455, 2241, 2499
Johnson, Ryder Channing. 3093
Johnson, S. Lewis. 306, 3721
Johnson, Samuel. 2129, 2891, 913, 1896, 2050, 2675, 2776, 2822, 3342
Johnson, Samuel Lawrence. 907, 908, 3369
Johnson, Samuel Lee. 3232
Johnson, Samuel Roosevelt. 3317
Johnson, Sarah Eliza. 3199
Johnson, Sherman Elbridge. 334, 433, 1967
Johnson, Sonia. 2129, 2619
Johnson, Spencer. 1331, 2486, 2832, 3312
Johnson, Talmage Casey. 164, 2338
Johnson, Theodore. 1111
Johnson, Theodore E. 2211
Johnson, Thomas Cary. 727, 1580, 2493, 2603, 2766, 2920, 2928, 3256, 1301, 1399
Johnson, Tilden W. 1134
Johnson, Tom. 3171
Johnson, Torrey Maynard. 3881
Johnson, Vernon Cecil. 788, 3690
Johnson, Vicki M. 2411
Johnson, Victor Eugene. 2552
[Johnson, Virginia Wales]. 2132
Johnson, Walter Nathan. 142, 3465
Johnson, Walton R. 15, 3891
Johnson, Wayne G. 2281, 3669
Johnson, Wilfred Roland. 64, 338
Johnson, Willard L. 3776
Johnson, William Alexander. 3308, 3669
Johnson, William Augustine Bernard. 1268
Johnson, William Bishop. 3342
Johnson, William Clarence. 2470
Johnson, William Franklin. 1795
Johnson, William Hallock. 951, 1580, 2040
Johnson, William Henry. 3817
Johnson, William Samuel. 2896
Johnson, Willie Harry. 3821
Johnson, Woodbridge Odlin. 1893, 2040
Johnson, Zachary Taylor. 1823, 3758
Johnsson, William G. 404, 442
Johnston, Allen W. 800, 1033, 1083, 1496

Johnston, Arthur P. 1566, 1573, 1913
Johnston, Basil. 915
Johnston, Charles. 2165, 3759
Johnston, Donald Kent. 2409
Johnston, Dorothy Grunbock. 901, 903, 2625
Johnston, Edgar Raymond. 1662
Johnston, Faith. 2129
*Johnston, Fran. 2523
Johnston, Francis W. 3285
Johnston, George. 406, 423, 1834
Johnston, Howard Agnew. 180, 234, 1098, 1201, 1967, 3211, 1050, 3182
Johnston, Hugh. 1528
Johnston, J. B. 2984
Johnston, James. 2497
Johnston, James Wesley. 75
Johnston, Jean Hope. 3473
Johnston, Johanna. 1939
Johnston, John Leslie. 3117
Johnston, John Octavius. 2225
Johnston, John T[homas] M[orris]. 1069
Johnston, Jon. 1552
Johnston, Joseph. 527
Johnston, Joseph S. 3220
Johnston, Julia Harriette. 1900, 2048, 2482
Johnston, Julia Michael. 1494
Johnston, Leonard. 294, 295, 563
Johnston, Louisa Mae. 621
Johnston, Mercer Green. 2003
Johnston, Minton C. 2390, 3367
Johnston, Nathan Robinson. 1017
Johnston, Norma. 17, 1936
Johnston, Olaf Raymond. 1608
[Johnston, Reginald Fleming]. 2522
Johnston, Reginald Fleming. 705, 1330, 1331
Johnston, Robert. 1138, 3362
Johnston, Robert K. 1551
Johnston, Robert Matteson. 1176
Johnston, Ruby Funchess. 2682
Johnston, Russ. 984
Johnston, Stephen Morris. 1399
Johnston, Sue Mildred Lee. 41, 3761
Johnston, Thomas J. 1918
Johnston, William. 2639, 1084, 1085, 1304, 2380, 2641, 2643, 2647
Johnston, William Grovenor. 1554
Johnston, William Preston. 536, 1723
Johnston, Charles William. 1551
[Johnstone, Christian Isobel] 1781-1857. 2094
Johnstone, Margaret Blair. 1593
Johnstone, Mildred T. 931, 2129
Johnstone, Parker Lochiel. 1655, 3082
Johnstone, Patrick J. St. G. 3139
Johnstone, Pauline. 1510
Johnstone, Peirce De Lacy Henry. 2629
Johnstone, Richard. 1517
Johnstone, Robert. 3479
Johnstone, Ronald L. 3086, 3886
Johnstone, Verney Lovett. 1214
Joiner, Edward Earl. 150
Joiner, Verna Jones. 1608, 3880, 3886
Joiner, William Lucian. 984
Joines, Karen Randolph. 3376
Joint Board of Christian Education of Australia and New Zealand. 3162
Joint commission on church federation and union of the Church of the United brethren in Christ and of the Evangelical church. 3731
Joint commission on unification of the Methodist Episcopal church and the Methodist Episcopal church, South. 2442
Joint committee of Hopewell Friends. 1688
Joint committee on organic union. 2927
Joint committee on the five-year program of survey and adjustment. 2527
Joint committee on the survey of Christian literature for Moslems. 2540
Joint committee on ways and means to form the United Lutheran church in America. 3733
Joint Committee on Worship. 2929
[Joint distribution committee of the American funds for Jewish war sufferers]. 1673
Joint Liturgical Group. 1262, 3855
Joint Survey Commission of the Baptist Inter-convention Committee. 3613
Joinville, Jean, sire de, 1224?-1317? 74
Joire, Paul Martial Joseph. 2989
Jolivet, Regis. 2418
Jolliffe, Percival. 1483
Jolly, David E. 3060
Jolly, Julius. 689
Joly, Eugene. 1593
Joly, Henri. 2268, 3280
Jomier, Jacques. 2184, 2185
Jonas, Gerald. 1685
Jonas, Hans. 1718, 1709, 1718
Jonas, Larry W. 2611
Jonas Hans. 1718

Jone, Heribert. 948
Jones, A. Jase. 2556
Jones, Abner. 3129
Jones, Alan David. 1790
Jones, Alan W. 3475, 3484
Jones, Alexander. 500, 2208, 2242
Jones, Allen Bailey. 1463
Jones, Alonzo T. 1723, 3034
Jones, Alonzo Trevier. 1095, 1169, 1176, 3192, 300, 463, 809, 1075, 1141, 1619, 3034
Jones, Amanda Theodocia. 513, 3506, 2130, 3521
Jones, Anna May. 2390
Jones, Arnold Hugh Martin. 1192, 1355, 1805, 1807, 2764
Jones, Arthur. 2390
Jones, Arthur Gray. 3342
Jones, Bayard Hale. 2205, 2960
Jones, Billy Walker. 150
Jones, Bob. 2901, 1557, 3758, 592, 1448, 2901
Jones, Carter Helm. 164
Jones, Cave. 1821, 2701, 3089
Jones, Charles Colcock. 2681
Jones, Charles Edwin. 1824
Jones, Charles Lewis. 234
Jones, Charles P. 1860
Jones, Charles Robert Stansfeld. 721, 2726, 3225
Jones, Charles Williams. 1028, 1773, 1780, 2707
Jones, Charlotte Chambers. 3853
Jones, Chris. 688
Jones, Christina H. 1674, 1686, 3438
Jones, Christopher William. 2390
Jones, Clara J. 2509
Jones, Clarence W. 3018
Jones, Claude C. 2061
Jones, Clifford Merton. 408, 537, 639, 1196, 2150
Jones, Crate H. 2390
Jones, Curtis. 1003
Jones, Darius Eliot. 1866
Jones, David. 135, 1500, 2131
Jones, David E. 2773
Jones, David Gareth. 3593
Jones, Donald G. 1138, 2450
Jones, E. Stanley. 1439
Jones, E. Winston. 2901
Jones, Ebenezer Edwin. 1577, 2506
Jones, Edgar. 572, 598
Jones, Edgar De Witt. 1060, 1119, 1466, 2751, 2909, 2910, 3353, 3376, 2909, 2910
Jones, Edgar DeWitt. 1466
Jones, Eli Stanley. 965, 1079, 1090, 1243, 1319, 1359, 1431, 1439, 2174, 2427, 2531, 2813, 3335, 3453, 3540, 3633, 3745, 1007, 1439
Jones, Eliza (Grew) 3129
Jones, Elizabeth B. 901
Jones, Elizabeth Brown. 616, 901, 903, 910, 1162, 2490
Jones, Elizabeth Norton. 3174
Jones, Elizabeth Orton. 2854
Jones, Elwood H. 3275
Jones, Eva McDaniel. 3298
Jones, Ezra Earl. 1166, 1279
Jones, Francis Arthur. 1875
Jones, Francis Price. 2953
Jones, Frank Dudley. 892, 2919
Jones, Franklin. 3334, 3479, 3491
Jones, G. Curtis. 965
Jones, Gary M. 1011
Jones, George. 534, 1967
Jones, George Curtis. 384, 965, 1004, 1165, 1273, 1461, 1466, 1967, 2029, 2390, 2722, 2786, 2874, 3379, 3529, 3600
Jones, George Elliott. 3720
Jones, George Hawkins. 2440
Jones, George Heber. 1050, 2185
Jones, George William. 3403, 3757, 1014, 2627
Jones, Geraint Vaughan. 1818, 2025
Jones, Gladys V. 2263, 3053
Jones, Grace G. 1557
Jones, Griffith Hartwell. 878, 1022
Jones, Harold. 2712
Jones, Harry W. 3742
Jones, Henry. 696, 3101
Jones, Henry Arthur. 3144, 3145
Jones, Henry E. 692
Jones, Henry Wyse. 1894
Jones, Heribert. 2593
Jones, Hosea Williams. 2969
Jones, Howard O. 1132, 2682
Jones, Idris W. 155, 3168, 3550
Jones, Ilion Tingal. 800
Jones, Ilion Tingnal. 1296, 1723, 2901, 2932, 3003
*Jones, Irene. 613, 3060
Jones, J. D. 1413, 3342
Jones, J. Estill. 329
Jones, J Sparhawk. 3342
Jones, James Archibald. 2891

Jones, James William. 1830, 2815, 3082
Jones, Jenkin Lloyd. 2892, 3725
Jones, Jeremiah. 339, 3810
Jones, Jesse Henry. 1782, 2174, 3129, 3608
Jones, Jessie Mae (Orton) 602, 2022, 2757, 2892, 3171
*Jones, Jessie Shaver. 2726
Jones, John. 454
Jones, John (Archdeacon of Merioneth) 3225
Jones, John Cooper. 1351
Jones, John Daniel. 588, 2040, 2263, 3199, 3364, 2214
Jones, John G. 2457, 2559
Jones, John Garrett. 710
Jones, John Gordon. 1455
Jones, John Griffing. 2457
Jones, John Ithel. 164
Jones, John Peter. 2520, 2531
Jones, John Sparhawk. 2932
Jones, John William. 3741
Jones, Joseph Huntington. 1586, 1593, 2686
Jones, Juanita Nuttall. 1418
Jones, Keith Franklin. 2258
Jones, Kenneth. 3325
Jones, Kenneth S. 2426
Jones, Kenneth W. 89
Jones, Laban. 1396
Jones, Larry. 1367, 1631
Jones, Laura (McElwain) 2131
Jones, Lawrence Elmore. 1159
Jones, Leslie Webber. 1395
Jones, Lester Martin. 1675
Jones, Lewis Bevan. 2557
Jones, Lot. 3591
Jones, Louis Thomas. 3093
Jones, Major J. 943, 2682
Jones, Marc Edmund. 2726, 95, 1847, 1848, 2390, 2620, 2726, 3262
Jones, Margaret Jean. 931, 2130
Jones, Marjorie. 2523
Jones, Mary. 901
Jones, Mary Alice. 588, 3152, 313, 587, 621, 629, 898, 901, 903, 1199, 1254, 1315, 1381, 1384, 1723, 1734, 1794, 1952, 1981, 1996, 2007, 2022, 2134, 2249, 3129, 3152, 3165, 3171, 3453
Jones, Mary Gwladys. 887, 888
Jones, Mary Hoxie. 1677, 3028
Jones, Maurice. 342
Jones, Mike. 1012, 2130
Jones, Milton H. 606
Jones, Milton Jenkins. 2611
Jones, Nathan. 941
Jones, Neason. 800, 1849, 2166
Jones, Nellie W. 132
Jones, Nettie Lou. 3563
Jones, O. R. 1823
Jones, Olga Anna. 3797
Jones, Olivia Mary. 903, 3152
Jones, Ora L. 3654
Jones, Orabelle C. 3554
Jones, Orville Davis. 2857
Jones, Owen. 247
Jones, Paul D. 2237
Jones, Percy Kynryn. 1060
Jones, Philip Cowell. 3554
*Jones, Philip Hanson. 2476
Jones, Philip Hanson. 2509
Jones, Philip Lovering. 148
Jones, Putnam Fennell. 182, 2198
Jones, Ralph Ernest. 2591
Jones, Ray O. 2390
Jones, Richard M. 1566
Jones, Richard Uriah. 64
Jones, Robert. 64
Jones, Robert Franklin. 2031
Jones, Robert L. 917
Jones, Rosemary Devonshire. 1526
Jones, Ruby A. 1448
Jones, Rufus. 2131, 3868
Jones, Rufus Matthew. 105, 924, 1050, 1069, 1468, 1637, 1674, 1723, 1790, 1804, 1982, 2130, 2131, 2226, 2639, 2798, 2998, 3060, 3225, 3462, 3479, 3793, 105, 697, 1095, 1468, 1674, 1675, 1679, 1685, 2036, 2645, 3479, 3622, 3794
Jones, Russell Bradley. 1952, 2465, 164, 340, 341, 479, 606, 646, 2057, 2214
[Jones, Sallie Orgain (Blackwell) 669
Jones, Sam. 1557
Jones, Samuel. 153, 1376
Jones, Samuel Calvin. 2130
Jones, Samuel Porter. 33, 1557, 1558, 1840, 2131, 3353, 615
Jones, Spencer John. 1212, 1224
Jones, Stephen D. 3886
Jones, Sylvester. 3129
Jones, Thomas Canby. 1637, 3794
Jones, Thomas Elsa. 2131
Jones, Thomas G. 156
Jones, Tiberius Gracchus. 3672
Jones, Tracey K. 2484, 2554
Jones, Vernon Augustus. 2591

Jones, W. Paul. 2131, 3479
Jones, Walter. 480
Jones, Wesley M. 678
Jones, William. 1847, 3712, 1847, 3712
[Jones, William A]. 854
Jones, William Burwell. 2457
Jones, William Henry Rich. 848
Jones, William Hubert. 3456
Jones, William McKendrey. 3476
Jones, William Northey. 2823
Jones, William Paul. 1060
Jones, William Robert. 151
Jones, William Ronald. 3017
Jones, William Tudor. 2226, 2836
Jones, York F. 877, 2130
Jones-Ryan, Maureen. 3708
Jong, Pieter de. 3656
Jonge, Marinus de. 421, 2011, 2046
Jonsen, Albert R. 3219
Jonsson, Inge. 3570
Jonsson, Jakob. 348
Jopling, Robert Ware. 3809
Joppie, A. S. 42
Joranson, Einar. 1639
Jordan, Alfred McKay. 3506
Jordan, Bernice C. 894
Jordan, Bert. 1599
Jordan, Clarence. 164, 374, 405, 426, 444,
2025, 3335
Jordan, Cynthia. 633, 1406
Jordan, Daniel C. 128
Jordan, David K. 1634
Jordan, David Starr. 3728, 3060
Jordan, Elijah. 2418
Jordan, Franziskus Maria vom Kreuze.
3296
Jordan, George Jefferis. 3308
Jordan, Gerald Ray. 75, 105, 425, 965,
1050, 1319, 1375, 1558, 2247, 2425,
2436, 2874, 2901, 3342, 3479
Jordan, Gerlad Ray. 1319
Jordan, Jerry Marshall. 908
Jordan, Lewis Garnett. 15, 140, 157
Jordan, Louis Henry. 3089, 3094
Jordan, Mickey. 2131
Jordan Of Saxony d. 1237. 3129
Jordan, Philip Dillon. 3287
Jordan, Richard Douglas. 3701, 3707
Jordan, Robert L. 1465
Jordan, Rudolf. 3101
Jordan, Wilbur Kitchener. 1758, 1759,
1760
Jordan, William C. 1060
Jordan, William F. 2517
Jordan, William George. 448, 549, 571
Jordanhill College of Education. 2760
Jorden, Paul J. 493, 1405, 2765
Jordens, J. T. F. 1407
Joret, Ferdinand Donatien. 1476, 2254
Jorgensen, Alfred Theodor. 2274
Jorgensen, Fingar. 459
Jorgensen, Johannes. 663, 749, 1642
Jorgenson, Mildred Bishop. 2512
Jorns, Auguste. 1674, 1675
Jorstad, Erling. 1553, 2286, 2815, 3089,
3232
Joseph ben Meir ibn Zabara, b. 1140?
2075, 2232
Joseph de Dreux, 1629-1671. 1649
Joseph, Eleanor. 1776
Joseph, Emily. 2133
Joseph, Horace William Brindley. 2835
Joseph, Isya. 1429
Joseph, John. 2684
Joseph, Morris. 2114
Joseph, Nathan Solomon. 2114
Joseph, Oscar L. 253, 1100, 2055, 2920,
3554
Joseph, Oscar Loos. 1176, 1566, 3672
Joseph Regenstein Library. 2083
Joseph, Samuel. 174, 2105
*Joseph, Stephen M. 1448
Joseph, William. 3377
Josephine. 2580
Josephson, Elmer A. 317, 1793
Josephson, Emanuel Mann. 3422
Josephson, Marba C. 2603
Josephus, Flavius. 1532, 2083, 2090,
2091, 2094
Josephy, Marcia Reines. 2315
Josey, Charles Conant. 2998
Joshi, Lal, Mani. 705
Joshi, Vasant S. 1778, 3019
Joshua. 3296
Joslin, James Thomas. 3728
Jospe, Alfred. 2109, 2141
Josselin, Ralph. 1292, 2135
Jotin, Brahmachari. 702, 3865
Jouin, Louis. 60
Jounel, Pierre. 1322
Jourdan, Adrien. 3568, 3569
Journet, Charles. 756, 1473, 1746, 1751,
2355, 2862, 3669
Jowett, J. H. 578, 2874, 592, 615
Jowett, John Henry. 1439, 449, 578,
1341, 1439, 1448, 1456, 2135, 2892,
2932, 3540, 3672

Joy, Arthur F. 2205
Joy, Charles Rhind. 2539, 3312, 303,
2539, 3312
Joy, Donald Marvin. 1007, 3152, 3554
Joy, Henry Bourne. 1619
Joy, James Richard. 3803
Joyce, Donovan. 1102, 1978
Joyce, George Hayward. 2338, 2673,
1751, 2673
Joyce, Gilbert Cunningham. 2946
Joyce, J Daniel. 3645, 3853
Joyce, Lester Douglas. 3738
Joyce, Robert F. 1434
Joye, George. 358, 3719, 358, 3719
Joynt, Robert Charles. 3672
Juah Ha-Levi 12th cent. 2144
Juan de la Cruz. 2642
Juan de la Cruz, 1542-1591. 90, 776,
2136, 2637, 2639, 2642, 2643, 3207,
3487, 3629
Juan De La Cruz 1542- 1591. 2642
Juan de la Cruz, 1542-1591. 2642
Juan De Los Angeles 1609. 2642
Juan, Ellen (Li) 2206
Juchen, Aurel von. 2021
Jud, Gerald John. 1119, 1582, 3222, 3540
Judah. 2144, 2115
Judah ben Samuel, d. 1217. 1539
Judah, J. Stillson. 2186, 3325
Judah, Samuel Benjamin Herbert. 3145
Judas, Elizabeth. 3022
Judd, Bertha Grimmell. 2527
Judd, Jesse Oliver. 871
Judd, Lewis Strong. 2697
[Judd, Orange]. 218
Judd, Orrin Grimmell. 693
Judd, Peter A. 3215, 3216, 3267
Judd, Sylvester. 1119
Judd, Tom. 1704
Judd, Wayne. 984
[Judge, Charles Joseph]. 2156, 2500
Judge, Hugh. 2156
Judge, Thomas Augustine. 1593
Judge, William Quan. 196, 3053, 3683,
3685, 3689
Judisch, Douglas. 1713
Judith Montefiore college, Ramsgate, Eng.
Library. 2331
[Judkins, Mary Amelia]. 2758
Judson, Abby Ann. 3506
Judson, Adoniram. 135, 139, 178
Judson, Ann (Hasseltine) 2505
Judson, Edward. 2157, 3672
[Judson, Edward Zane Carroll] 1823-1886.
3199
[Judson, Emily (Chubbuck)]. 2158, 2505
Judy, Ida Mabelle. 2265
Judy, Marvin T. 1240, 2197, 2439
Juel, Donald. 211, 348, 435, 2068
Juergens, Mary. 621, 629, 901
Juergens, Sylvester Peter. 1593, 2703
Juhnke, James C. 1705, 2406
Jukes, Andrew John. 390, 556, 1736,
2218
Jules-Rosette, Bennetta. 76, 3239
Julian. 3861
Julian, John. 1862
Juliana 1343-1443. 1448
Juliana. 1431, 1448, 1449, 2158
[Juliana, 1901. 3274
Juliana, anchoret. 1449
Julianus. 2158
[Julie du St. Esprit, 1868. 1999
[Julie du St. Esprit. 965, 998, 2390, 3015
Jump, Chester. 2513
Jumper, Andrew A. 2924
Jung, Carl Gustav. 2998, 2652, 2998,
3101, 550, 2652, 2995, 2998, 3101
Jung, Leo. 2115, 2144, 1423, 1733, 2082,
2115, 2145, 3371, 3838
Jungblut, Edward Joseph. 1455
Jungel, Eberhard. 175, 176, 1414, 1733
Jungk, Robert. 3312
Jungkuntz, Richard. 135
Jungkuntz, Theodore R. 40
Jungmann, Josef Andreas. 746, 838, 842,
2168, 2236, 2239, 2366, 2789, 2251,
2885
Jungreis, Esther. 1611, 2159
Jungreis, Theodore. 3261
Jung-Stilling, Johann Heinrich. 3475
Juniper, Daniel. 3533
Junker, Bill. 993, 1659
Junkin, David Xavier. 2159
Junkin, George. 135, 174, 403, 2160
Jurgens, W. A. 1018
Jurgensen, Barbara. 569, 965, 984, 991,
1288, 1802, 2509, 2950
Jurgensmeier, Friedrich. 2020
Jurieu, Pierre. 1753
*Jurji, Edward J. 3117
Jurji, Edward Jabra. 1492, 2308, 2679,
3060, 3117
Jurries, Ginger. 1605
Jury, Paul. 3110
Just, Gustav A. 2274
Just, Mary. 851

Justice, William G. 192
Justice, William M. 2052
[Justin Lucian. 2577
Justinus. 68, 69, 3635, 3717
Justus, Emory W. 3458
Justus, Karl B. 1040
Juvenile protective association of Chicago.
896
Jyotirmayananda Saraswati, 1943. 2380

K

K*uijf, T. C. de. 3390
Kaba, Lansine. 3788
Kabir, Muhammad Ghulam. 1816
Kabler, Ciel Dunne. 3594
Kac, Arthur W. 2016, 2119, 2139, 2141,
2414
[Kachline, Susan Ada]. 2596
Kacmarcik, Frank. 1114
Kadel, William H. 2892
Kadison, Alexander. 19
Kadlec, Jaroslav. 2944
Kadowaki, Kakichi. 234, 3893
Kadushin, Jacob Louis. 2074, 2107
Kadushin, Max. 2115, 2139, 3015, 3328,
3855
Kagan, Solomon R. 1798
Kagawa, Toyohiko. 2015, 3636, 965,
1079, 1368, 1836, 2005, 2162, 2265,
2390, 2534, 3029, 2390
Kahan, Aaron. 3371
Kahan, Israel Meir. 3581
Kahan, Samuel. 18, 561
Kahane, Charles Ph. 3371
Kahl, Joachim. 1091
Kahle, Paul Eric. 316
Kahle, Paul Ernst. 724
Kahlefeld, Heinrich. 2025
Kahler, Erich. 3716
Kahler, Heinz. 1929, 2621
Kahler, Martin. 406, 2008
Kahmann, J. 2908
Kahn, David E. 876
Kahn, Dorothy Ruth. 2119
Kahn, Jack H. 1425, 2124
Kahn, Lina. 1425, 1426
Kahn, Robert I. 1314, 1539, 2081, 3370
Kahoe, Walter. 2845
Kain, George Hay. 1668
Kainer, Gordon. 951
Kainz, Howard P. 318, 781, 3616
Kaiser, Albert F. 1999
Kaiser, Edgar P. 1232
Kaiser, Edwin G. 2029, 3265, 1783, 3289,
3660, 3849
Kaiser, Otto. 239, 287, 540, 544, 545,
1416
Kaiser, Paul. 3337
Kaiser, Richard. 984
Kaiser, Robert Blair. 3771
Kaiser, Walter C. 287, 503, 512, 537, 556,
3541
Kaizuka, Shigeki. 1331
Kakar, Sudhir. 2823
Kakhun, Sok. 706
Kakkar, N. K. 2189
al-Kalabadhi, Muhammad ibn Ibrahim.
3544
Kalb, Friedrich. 3855
Kalberer, Augustine. 1024
Kale, Roy Addison. 800
Kalee Paw. 2505
Kalidasa. 1812
Kalir, Joseph. 2139
Kalisch, Isidor. 2116
Kalkstein, Teresa. 682
Kallas, James. 376
Kallas, James G. 401, 1428, 1429, 1967,
2040, 2798, 3663
Kalleel, John G. 2162
Kallen, Horace Meyer. 2104, 2116, 2119,
2142, 3060, 3327
Kallenbach, Walter Dustin. 108, 164,
1095, 2200
Kalor, Earl N. 1324
Kaloria, John B. 253
Kalt, Edmund. 576
Kalt, William J. 1102, 1134, 3117, 3181,
3186, 3394, 3451
Kaltenmark, Max. 2196, 3586
Kalu, Ogbu. 1045
Kalupahana, David J. 710, 712, 1703
Kamal, Ahmad. 2848
Kamei, Marlene. 3479
Kamen, Henry. 1908
Kamen, Henry Arthur Francis. 1910, 3703
Kames, Henry Home. 1535, 1537
Kaminsky, Jack. 2738
Kamm, Josephine. 534, 2084
Kammer, Charles L. 944
Kammerer, Winifred. 1369
Kampf, Avram. 3577
Kampmann, Theoderich. 1262
Kanabay, Donald. 2892

Kanada. 3766
Kanamori, Paul M. 3342
Kandle, George C. 2942
[Kane, Alice L]. 3506
Kane, George Louis. 765, 772, 1364,
2484, 2573, 2577, 2581, 3785
Kane, H. Victor. 908, 1459
Kane, Harnett Thomas. 3761
Kane, J Herbert. 1912, 2482, 2488, 2493,
2501, 2525
Kane, John A. 2031, 2254, 2355, 2811,
3782
Kane, John Francis. 1936, 3093
Kane, John Henry. 3353
Kane, John Joseph. 788, 1603
Kane, Kathleen Dunlop. 2937, 3778
Kane, Liza. 800
Kane, Mark J. 1298
Kane, Robert Joseph. 819, 863, 1723,
1795, 3859
Kane, Thomas A. 999
Kane, Thomas Aloysius. 2792
Kane, Thomas Leiper. 2603
Kane, Thomas S. 390, 2874
Kane, William Terence. 999, 3405, 3524,
3525
[Kane Elizabeth Dennistoun (Wood) 3762
Kanellakos, Demetri P. 3708
Kanellopoulos, Panagiotes. 1414
Kang, C. H. 526, 1381
Kangas, Paul D. 1345
Kania, Ladislao. 3257
Kaniel, Michael. 2073
Kann, Jean Marie. 1642
Kano, Matao. 1615, 3602
Kanof, Abram. 2073, 2234
Kanotopsky, Harold B. 3371
Kansas Baptist Women's Union. 154
Kansas City, Mo. Public library. 868
Kansas City, Mo. St. Andrew's Episcopal
Church. 2967
Kansas. State University of Agriculture and
Applied Science, Manhattan. Library.
3203
Kansas. University. 1854
Kant, Immanuel. 876, 2180
Kant, Immanuel. 876, 1535, 2163, 2164,
2180, 2418, 2591, 2833, 2836, 3506,
3570, 1535
Kantonen, Taito Almar. 1528, 1566, 2286,
3529
Kantonen, Talto Almar. 1060
Kantor, Mattis. 1789
Kantorowicz, Ernst. 2237
Kantowicz, Edward R. 668, 2630
Kantzenbach, Friedrich Wilhelm. 1176
Kao, Charles C. L. 2998
Kapelrud, Arvid Schou. 500, 504, 600,
2679, 3022
Kaper, Ernst. 1328
Kapila. 3301
Kaplan, Aryeh. 2382, 2844
Kaplan, Bert. 1858
Kaplan, Jacob Hyman. 570, 2949
Kaplan, Julius. 3582
Kaplan, Lawrence. 1764
Kaplan, Mordecai Menahem. 2149, 1723,
1822, 2084, 2139, 2141, 3011, 3028
Kaplan, Mordecal Menahem. 3028
Kaplan, Samuel Abraham. 3548
Kaplan, Stuart R. 3588
Kapleau, Philip. 20, 1416, 3493, 3776,
3892, 3894
Kaploun, Uri. 3576
Kapp, Ardeth Greene. 2164, 2618
Kappa sigma pi. 688
Kappen, Sebastian. 1659, 2040
Kaprow, Gordon. 2120
Kapsner, Oliver Leonard. 188, 2578
Karant-Nunn, Susan C. 2284, 2791
Karasick, Joseph. 2145, 3849
Karcher, Joseph T. 759
Karefa-Smart, John. 12
Karff, Joan M. 1615
Karff, Samuel E. 2141
[Karg, George Adam]. 3117
Karim, Fazlul. 1921
Karitzky, Alma L. 3506
Karlin, Alma M. 1904
Karlsruhe. Badische Landesbibliothek.
1884
Karlstadt, Andreas Rudolf. 2165, 3629
Karma. 98
Karma Thinley, Lama Wangchhim. 2164
Karnell, Minnie Karine Lund (Mathisen)
1838
Karney, Arthur Baillie Lumsdaine. 374
Karo, Nancy. 75, 164, 2165
Karolevitz, Robert F. 3862
Karp, Abraham J. 2081, 3749
Karp, Deborah (Burstein) 2075
Karpa, Oskar. 2241
Karpel, Craig. 2726
Karpeles, Gustav. 2089, 2112
Karpf, Maurice Joseph. 2104
Karpinski, Leszek M. 3089
Karr, Margaretta Ayres. 2072

Karraker, William Archibald. 648
Karrer, Otto. 1040, 1169, 1642, 2824, 3117
Karris, Robert J. 329, 426, 428, 430
Karstorp, Lennart. 3406
Kaschmitter, William A. 3628, 3771
Kasdorf, Hans. 1359
Kasemann, Ernst. 334, 350, 370, 424, 468, 1659, 2040
Kasey, J. W. 1324
Kasher, Menachem Mendel. 562, 2142, 2159
Kashima, Tetsuden. 710, 3440
Kashinath. 3775
Kasovich, Israel Isser. 2115
Kasper, Walter. 2040, 2343, 2346, 3651
Kassarjian, Kevork. 2260
Kassiepe, Max. 1298
Kasson, Charles Le Baron. 2226
Kassulke, Karl. 931, 2165
Kaster, Joseph. 2658
Kasulis, T. P. 3893
Kasuya, Masahiro. 1384, 2022
Kater, John. 1086, 1795
Kateregga, Badru D. 1926
Kates, Frederick Ward. 965, 1449, 1456
Kates, George Whitfield. 3506
Kathan, Boardman. 3186
[Katherine Edith. 3289
[Katherine Edith] and Peirce, Grace H. 745
Katju, Shiva Nath. 1635
Kato, Genchi. 3404
Katoppo, Marianne. 2165, 3832
Katsaros, Thomas. 2645
Katsh, Abraham Isaac. 172, 538, 1926, 2139, 2185, 2567, 3745
Katter, Reuben Luther. 1381
Katterhenry, Edwin Andrew. 1440
Katterjohn, Arthur D. 3319
Katz, Aaron Hillel. 2320
Katz, Alexander Raymond. 1796
Katz, Irving I. 1426, 3576
Katz, Jacob. 2110, 1663, 2112, 2153
Katz, Mordecai. 3582
Katz, Paul M. 500
Katz, Peter. 528, 529
Katz, Solomon. 2092
Katz, Steven T. 2080
Katz, Wilber Griffith. 3195
Katzenbach, William H. 1050
Katzenberg, Julius. 534, 629
Katzenellenbogen, Adolf Edmund Max. 889, 3574
[Katzenstein, Julius]. 2089, 3394
Katzoff, Louis. 2086
Kaub, Verne Paul. 1319
Kauffman, Christopher J. 25, 874, 2179
Kauffman, Daniel. 639, 2405, 2666
Kauffman, Donald T. 1022, 1840, 2892, 3092, 3207
Kauffman, J. Howard. 2404, 2408
Kauffman, Luther S. 1150
Kauffman, Milo. 3529, 3531
Kauffman, Paul E. 2509
Kauffman, Reginald Wright. 1756
Kauffmann, Friedrich. 2666
Kaufman, Donald D. 3589
Kaufman, Edmund George. 1704, 2404, 3364, 3645
Kaufman, Gordon D. 944, 1729, 2405, 3645, 3669
Kaufman, James Norman. 2406
Kaufmann, Jean Troxell. 2693, 3809
Kaufman, Reuben. 2080
Kaufman, Robert. 3314
Kaufman, William E. 2141
Kaufman, William Irving. 899
Kaufmann, Peter. 3073
Kaufmann, Walter. 3060, 3213, 883
Kaufmann, Walter Arnold. 1583, 2710, 2836, 3060, 3117, 3129, 3213
Kaufmann, Yehezkel. 545, 2146, 2149, 2150
Kaumans, Gregory. 1639
Kaung, Stephen. 550
Kauper, Paul G. 1280, 3195
Kaushik, R. P. 2381, 3483
Kautsky, Karl. 1050, 1102, 2008, 2112
Kavanagh, Abram Scheckelton. 2421
Kavanagh, Aidan. 137
Kavanagh, Dennis John. 1388, 1696, 2323, 3420
Kavanagh, Joseph William. 27, 838
Kavanagh, Peter. 2664
Kavanagh, William Aloysius. 2049
Kavanaugh, James J. 64, 788, 1014, 1060, 3663, 3886
Kavanaugh, John. 3434
Kay, Hether. 3877
Kay, J Alan. 3853
Kay, Thomas O. 1319
Kay, James R. 199
Kaye, James Ross, 1865. 280, 639, 1514, 1915, 2465
Kaye, John Brayshaw. 2068
Kaye-Smith, Sheila, 1887. 749

Kaye-Smith, Sheila. 749
Kaye-Smith, Sheila, 1887-1956. 749
Kayhle, Alexandra. 95
Kaykavus ibn Iskandar ibn Qabus,' Unsur al-Ma'all. 1021 or 2-1098 or 9. 3880
Kayser, Rudolf. 3472
Kayser, Stephen S. 566
Kazee, Buell H. 1593
Keable, Robert. 2847, 1967
Keach, Benjamin. 314, 2025, 2416, 3129, 3152
Keach, Richard L. 331, 1243, 3799
Kealy, John P. 329, 1196
Kealy, Sean P. 436
Kealy, Thomas Mitchell. 1478
Kean, Charles Duell. 1134, 1066, 1095, 1266, 2031, 2786, 2962, 2964, 3101, 3225, 3295
Kean, Claude. 2573
Kean. Charles Duell. 2972
Keane, John Joseph. 3199, 725
Keane, Philip S. 3393
Kearney, Emilie Fairchild. 3555
Kearney, Flora McLaughlin. 1808
Kearney, John. 3222
Kearns, Francis E. 2426
Kearns, John Chrysostom. 2348
Kearns, Mary Kenneth. 2981
Kearns, Ralph D. 2932
Keary, Charles Francis. 3027, 3109
Keating, Charles J. 953
Keating, Edward M. 829
Keating, John Fitzstephen. 2256
Keating, Joseph Ignatius. 2390
Keating, Sally. 281
Keating, Thomas. 3521
Keator, Eugene H. 1651
Keay, Frank Ernest. 2162
Keble, John. 725, 1265, 1440, 1860, 1866, 3207
Keck, L. Robert. 2166, 2380
Keck, Leander E. 299, 333, 348, 376, 426, 639, 1102, 2008, 2798, 2907, 3311
Kedara-Natha Dasa Gupta. 3117
Keddie, Nikki R. 21, 3199
Kedney, John Steinfort. 3645, 3651
Kedourie, Elie. 21
Kee, Alistair. 3328, 3633
Kee, Howard Clark. 390, 406, 408, 435, 1102, 1119, 1176, 1528, 1798, 1987
Keeble, Samuel Edward. 3439
Keech, William J. 2550, 3529, 3531
Keedy, Edward Everett. 965, 1162, 1201, 3672
Keedy, John Lincoln. 597, 3152
Keefe, Carolyn. 1660
[Keefer, Glen Elgin]. 2465, 3319
Keegan, Gilbert Kearnie. 141, 965
Keegan, Terence J. 433
Keegstra, Jean Connie. 3207
Keel, John A. 2313
Keeler, Bronson C. 736
Keeler, Clyde Edgar. 1396
Keeler, d Clyde Edgar. 1396
Keeler, Ellen (Coughlin) 2458
Keeler, Floyd. 2539
Keeler, Joseph B. 1169
Keeler, Joseph Brigham. 2615
Keeler, R F. 135
Keeler, Ralph Welles. 576, 2454
Keeler, Ronald F. 36, 1251
Keeler, William Frederic. 2695
Keeling, Michael. 944, 946
Keel-Leu, Othmar. 87, 578
Keely, David Fulmer. 965
Keen, John S. 1803
Keen, Mary J. (Palmer) 2166
Keen, Sam. 121, 1324, 2166, 2390
Keen, Samuel Ashton. 1593, 2166
Keen, William Williams. 1580, 2829, 1580, 1888
Keenan, Alan. 3265, 2343
Keene, Carter Brewster. 1664
Keene, Henry George. 2311
Keene, James Calvin. 399
Keene, John Henry. 1033
Keene, Laurence C. 2258
Keene, M. Lamar. 2166, 3520
Keene, Michael James. 2159
Keene, Milton Henry. 17
Keene, Richard Raynal. 2348
Keener, John Christian. 234, 1496
Keeney, Virginia Drysdale. 534
Keeping, Charles. 2022
Keese, George Pomeroy. 1119
Keesecker, William F. 579
Keeseville, N. Y. First Congregational church. 2700
Keesey, Wilbur Ruth. 3061
Keeton, Morris T. 3061
Kefley, James C. 3860
Kegan, Frank R. 1470, 1879
Kegel, Martin. 3117
Kegerreis, Robert B. 2855, 2978
Kegley, Charles W. 698, 2709, 2978, 3699, 2719
Kegley, Frederick Bittle. 3275

Kehl, D. G. 314
Kehoe, Kimball. 1731
Keidel, Levi O. 1359, 2374, 2559
Keightley, Alan. 1593, 3830
Keightley, Thomas. 2658
Keighton, Robert Elwood. 1449, 2257, 2901
Keigwin, Albert Edwin. 1060, 2226
Keikai. 2207
Keil, Karl Friedrich. 497, 540, 546
Keinath, Herman Ottomar Alfred. 1549
Keiper, Ralph L. 214, 984
Keir, Thomas H. 3003
Keirstead, C. Fraser. 1957, 2759
Keiser, Armilda Brome. 3173, 3853
Keister, Elinore. 1004
Keitel, George W. 3874
Keith, Alexander. 606, 1099
Keith, Alphas William. 406
Keith, Arthur Berriedale. 702, 2663, 2718, 3301, 3776, 2664, 2838, 2839, 3776
Keith, Billy. 1387
Keith, Caroline Phebe (Tenney) 2509
Keith, Cassius Clay. 3506
Keith, Edmond D. 153, 1875
Keith, George. 1682
Keith, Noel Leonard. 376, 718, 965, 3111
Keith, W Holman. 3142
Keithahn, Mary Nelson. 644
Keith-Lucas, Alan. 1164, 1254
Kelber, Werner H. 436, 437, 2011, 2176
Kelcher, James P. 114, 3307
*Kelcy, Raymond C. 345
Kelcy, Raymond C. 478, 1273
Keleher, C Woods. 2939
Kelen, Betty. 702, 1330, 1703, 2564, 2629
Kellam, Ida (Brooks) 1269
Kellar, Edgar H. 1566
Kellar, Harry. 1345
Kellaway, William. 1900, 3437
Kelleher, Stephen Joseph. 2343
Kellems, Jesse R. 3342
Kellems, Jesse Randolph. 732, 1461, 1466, 1566, 1633, 2000, 2503, 3222
Kellenberger, James. 2181
Keller, Adolf. 176, 1182, 1542, 2976, 3849
Keller, Charles Roy. 1346
Keller, Edmund B. 376, 2772, 2798
Keller, Edward A. 1136
Keller, Edward G. 965, 3353
Keller, Edward Levi. 1997, 3353
Keller, Ernst. 2476
Keller, Friedrich Paul. 606
Keller, Helen. 3129, 3570
Keller, Helen Adams. 3129, 1593, 3569, 3570
Keller, Hippolyt. 1967
*Keller, James. 999
Keller, James G. 867, 850
Keller, James [Gregory]. 857
Keller, James Gregory. 850, 857, 867, 965, 999, 1115, 1431, 1434, 1440, 3189
Keller, John E. 1253
Keller, Joseph A. 54, 2355, 2476, 3269
Keller, Joseph Anton. 2251
Keller, Mary E. 2323
Keller, Paul F. 1328
[Keller, Paull F]. 1328
Keller, W. Phillip. 984, 1449, 2020
Keller, Weldon Phillip. 2558, 424, 483, 588, 686, 928, 929, 985, 1507, 1967, 2197, 2247
Keller, Werner. 298
Kellermeyer, Josephine M. 1545
Kellersberger, Julia Lake]Skinner. 2537
Kellersberger, Julia Lake (Skinner) 1497, 2513, 3838
Kellet, Ernest Edward. 1516, 3139
Kellett, Arnold. 3322, 3406
Kellett, Ernest Edward. 2096, 3139
Kellett, Frederick William. 1773
Kelley, Alden Drew. 1086, 2191
[Kelley, Alfred Leo]. 769
Kelley, Ann Elizabeth. 3835
Kelley, Balmer H. 519
Kelley, Bennet. 769
Kelley, Carl Franklin. 1491, 1650
Kelley, Dean M. 1242, 3443
Kelley, Donald R. 1639, 1848
Kelley, E G. 3117
Kelley, Edna (Ewing) 903
Kelley, Edward R. 2089
Kelley, Erma W. 2390
Kelley, Frances. 931, 2166
Kelley, Francis Clement. 665, 1147, 1148, 1723, 1826, 667
Kelley, Hugh N. 1244, 3274
Kelley, James Prentice. 28, 3443
[Kelley, Jesse Fillmore]. 2686
Kelley, Maurice. 2472
Kelley, Maurice Willyle. 2472
Kelley, Oscar Allen. 1176, 1528
Kelley, P. J. 1802
Kelley, Page H. 485, 545, 566, 2157
Kelley, Rex C. 1690
Kelley, Ruth E. 1888

Kelley, William Frederick. 1949
Kelley, William Valentine. 1753, 2847
Kelling, Furn. 2886
Kellner, Abraham A. 3370, 3371
Kellner, Esther. 534, 631, 3457
Kellock, Harold. 3801
Kellogg, Amherst W. 2424
Kellogg, Caroline. 616, 910, 3853
Kellogg, Charlotte (Hoffman) 2411
Kellogg, Daniel B. 1283
Kellogg, John Harvey. 3462, 3595
Kellogg, Samuel Henry. 2464, 3061, 3117
Kellogg, William Manley. 1793
Kellow, Norman B. 1431
Kelly, Alfred Davenport. 1395
Kelly, Anthony. 2390
Kelly, Arthur Willard. 280
Kelly, Audrey. 3390
Kelly, Balmer H. 223, 420, 557
Kelly, Bernard J. 1428, 1712, 2576, 2580, 3265, 3487
Kelly, Bernard M. 1290
Kelly, Blanche Mary. 2355
Kelly, Caleb Guyer. 1852
Kelly, Cardinal Lyle. 3122
Kelly, Charles. 3242
Kelly, Earl. 164, 413
Kelly, Ellin M. 3378
Kelly, Faye L. 1765
Kelly, Francis J. 3145
Kelly, Frederic Joseph. 2412
Kelly, George Anthony. 668, 788, 827, 833, 834, 873, 948, 1153, 1248, 2699, 2811, 3275, 3449, 3738, 3739, 3886
Kelly, Gerald A. 1327, 3475
Kelly, Henry Ansgar. 1423, 1803, 3711
Kelly, Herbert [Hamilton]. 1515
Kelly, Herbert Hamilton. 1095
Kelly, Howard Atwood. 204
Kelly, J.N.D. 446
Kelly, J. Thomas. 2569
Kelly, James Patrick. 796, 2811
Kelly, John Bernard. 1792
Kelly, John Frederick. 1269
Kelly, John Norman Davidson. 99, 446, 447, 1385, 1386, 1811, 3657
Kelly, Joseph Patrick. 1716, 3603
Kelly, Josephine. 1288, 1793
Kelly, Kent. 3, 1150
Kelly, Laurence J. 3797
Kelly, M T. 1649
Kelly, Mary Ellen. 3540
Kelly, Mary Gilbert. 874
Kelly, Maurice N. 2470, 2471
Kelly, Michael Aloysius. 999
Kelly, Michael Vincent. 2259
Kelly, Patrick H. 2178
Kelly, Paul A. 1357, 2939
Kelly, Philip Christopher M. 2343
Kelly, Robert Lincoln. 3612
Kelly, Samuel J. 1304
Kelly, Thomas L. 3342
Kelly, Thomas Raymond. 1449
Kelly, Virgil A. 788
Kelly, William. 440, 506
[Kelly, William D]. 1790
Kelly, William L. 857, 3843, 3883
Kelly, William Roswell. 1627
Kelman, Janet Harvey. 1897
Kelman, John. 717, 3199, 1060, 2901, 3793
Kelpien, Lottie Stout. 965
Kelpius, John. 2874
Kelsey, Alice (Geer) 910, 1015, 2490, 2493, 3764
Kelsey, David H. 279, 3656, 3700
Kelsey, George D. 1131, 1135, 3465
Kelsey, Morton. 1731, 935
Kelsey, Morton T. 1088, 1460, 1479, 1586, 1599, 1601, 1696, 1716, 2058, 2158, 2265, 2380, 2648, 2782, 3479
Kelsey, Olivia. 128
Kelso, James Anderson. 567
Kelso, James Leon. 335, 370, 493, 534, 2798
Kelso, John R. 3506
Kelso, John Russell. 100, 234, 1655
Kelton, C. G. 1866
Kelty, Matthew. 2166, 3710
Kemble, Duston. 3191
Kemp, Charles F. 1256, 2786
Kemp, Charles F. 179, 242, 985, 995, 1170, 1254, 1256, 1289, 1604, 2780, 2859, 2901, 3364, 3673, 3680
Kemp, Chester C. 2176
Kemp, Eric Waldram. 736, 1321
Kemp, Franklin W. 102
Kemp, Joseph W. 3462
Kemp, Mabel Duncan. 965
Kemp, Russell A. 3750
Kemp, Thomas L. 863, 1266
Kemper, Clarence Worthington. 164
Kemper, Earskine Gault. 3289
Kemper, Frederick Augustus. 1351
Kemper, Frederick W. 9, 1266, 1308, 1440, 2034, 2236, 2295, 2299, 3353
Kemper, Inez. 1440, 1456

Kemper, Robert G. 1296, 1345, 2167
Kemperman, Steve. 931, 3722
Kempf, Joseph George. 781, 2580
Kempin, Albert J. 209, 507, 966
*Kempis, Thomas A. 1885
Kempker, John F. 819
Kempthorne, John Augustine. 2782
Kempton, A[rthur] C. 3353
Kenawell, William W. 676, 1715
Kendall, Alan. 1022
Kendall, Earline Doak. 938
Kendall, Edith Lorna. 105, 2012
Kendall, Guy. 3101
Kendall, Henry. 3129
Kendall, John. 1682
Kendall, R. T. 404, 405, 553, 727, 729, 730, 3364
Kendall, William Frederick. 170
Kendrck, Klaude. 2814
Kendrick, Asahel Clark. 947, 2158
Kendrick, Blanche V W. 3506
Kendrick, Eliza Hall. 475
Kendrick, Thomas Downing. 1480, 1934, 2333
Kendrick, V. Ben. 2490
Kenellopoulos, Panagiotes. 1414
Kenen, Peter B. 1932. 2675
Kenilworth, Walter Winston. 2695, 2989
Kennard, Edward Allan. 2165
Kennard, Joseph Spencer. 1843, 2167, 1142
Kennedy, Ambrose. 1404, 3847
Kennedy, Annie Richardson. 414, 2699
Kennedy, Charles Johnston. 1337
Kennedy, Dennis James. 1011, 1566, 3663
*Kennedy, Edith Ann. 3317, 3506
[Kennedy, Edith (Arrowsmith) 2167
Kennedy, Edward. 822, 2540
Kennedy, Eugene C. 772, 775, 999, 1060, 1245, 1324, 1431, 1536, 1593, 2263, 2390, 2789
Kennedy, Gail. 3085
Kennedy, Gerald. 1449
Kennedy, Gerald [Hamilton]. 2025
Kennedy, Gerald Hamilton. 399, 966, 1069, 1095, 2025, 2192, 2421, 2427, 2436, 2786, 2901, 2907, 3673, 3745
Kennedy, Harold. 639
kennedy, Harry Angus Alexander. 378, 2798, 2831
Kennedy, Henry Dawson. 514
Kennedy, Hugh Anketell Studdert. 1033, 1050, 1494, 1495, 1210, 1495
Kennedy, James Hardee. 552, 2621
Kennedy, James Henry. 2603
Kennedy, James R. 3111
Kennedy, James William. 966, 1040, 1264, 2211, 2253, 2697, 2786, 2901, 2964, 3850
Kennedy, Jessie (Harper) 1351
Kennedy, John. 398, 507, 2307, 1741, 2786, 2914
Kennedy, John Fitzgerald. 254, 2167
Kennedy, John Joseph. 825
Kennedy, John McFarland. 91
Kennedy, John S. 3286, 3540
Kennedy, Larry. 55, 517, 993
Kennedy, Lureno Nelson. 606
Kennedy, M. G. 3026, 3555
Kennedy, Maurice B. 3248
Kennedy, Melville T. 879, 3766
Kennedy, Minnie E. 1449
Kennedy, Nell L. 915, 2814
Kennedy, Roger. 1162
Kennedy, Theodore. 2202
Kennedy, Walter Joseph. 1440
Kennedy, William Bean. 966, 2956
Kennedy, William Sloane. 2735, 2414
Kenneth. 924
Kennett, Jiyu. 3459
Kennett, Robert Hatch. 500, 510, 2115
Kennett, White Bp. of Peterborough. 29
Kenney, Edward Herbert. 1330, 1331, 3586
[Kenney, Eudorus Catlin. 3568
Kenney, James Francis. 1919
Kenney, Leon Fallis. 17
Kenney, W. Henry. 3593
Kenney, William F. 779
Kenney, William Joseph. 2369
Kenngott, George Frederick. 3152
Kenny, Anthony John Patrick. 1737, 3464, 3636, 3697
Kenny, Denis. 2343, 3771
Kenny, Herbert Andrew. 796
Kenny, John J. 999
Kenny, John Peter. 3295, 3567
Kenny, Virginia Arville. 831
Kenrick, Bruce. 1139
Kenrick, Edward F. 3487
Kenrick, Francis Patrick. 2160, 2167
Kenrick, Peter Richard. 3769
Kenseth, Arnold. 2390, 2892
Kensington, J J. 2874
Kent, Charles Foster. 234, 500, 540, 563, 571, 648, 1069, 1967, 2015, 2089, 2095, 2096, 3439, 406

Kent, Dan G. 553
Kent, Graeme. 2543
Kent, Harold Winfield. 1859
Kent, Herbert Harold. 550, 2021
Kent, Homer A. 380, 416, 2671
Kent, Homer Austin. 2671, 2786, 333, 363, 403, 446, 2786
Kent, John. 1699, 3645
Kent, John, 1923. 2434
Kent, John H. S. 3654
Kent, Juanita Ray. 2509, 2534
Kent, Mark Leo. 2482
Kent, Maxwell. 3851
Kent, Michael. 788
Kent, Peter C. 1147, 1322, 2852
Kent, W. Herbert. 995
Kenton, Edna. 1948
Kenton, Warren. 517, 721, 722
Kentucky Baptist historical society. 3200
Kentucky-Tennessee Synod of the United Lutheran Church in America. 3733
Kenworthy, Leonard Stout. 1676
Kenyon college, Gambier, O. Library. 3681
Kenyon, Don J. 411, 472
Kenyon, Essek William. 966, 2874, 3029, 3289
Kenyon, Floyd Steele. 3807
Kenyon, Frederic George. 207, 284, 290, 351, 174, 277, 290, 1196, 290
Kenyon, John Burnett. 1830
Kenyon, Kathleen Mary. 209
Kenyon, Roger A. 2738
Keough, G. Arthur. 1012, 1119, 3385
Kepelino. 2663
Kephart, Calvin. 1665
Kephart, Cyrus Jeffries. 1992
Kephart, Ezekiel B[oring]. 105
Kephart, Ezekiel Boring. 68, 105
Kephart, Isaiah Lafayette. 951, 2168, 3731
Kepler, Thomas Samuel. 1456, 390, 393, 454, 508, 924, 966, 1440, 1449, 1977, 2046, 2052, 2059, 2390, 2798, 3337, 3645
Keplinger, Lewis Walter. 1732
Kepner, Frank M. 164
Keppel, David. 369, 454, 2126
Kepple, Robert J. 3032
Keppler, Paul Wilhelm von. 966, 1840, 1843, 2029, 3540
Ker, Cecil. 3831
Ker, John. 2909
Kerans, Patrick. 3411
Kerby, William Joseph. 772, 771, 3676
Kerenyi, Karoly. 2661, 11, 1505, 1766, 1806, 2661, 2946, 1459, 1505, 2661, 3895
Kereszty, Roch A. 1417
Kerigan, Florence. 3844
Kerin, Charles Augustine. 717
Kerken, Liberius vander. 2265
Kerlin, Robert Thomas. 1192
Kerman, Joseph. 721
Kermode, John Frank. 1518
Kern, Adam. 2465
Kern, Herbert. 1940
Kern, Horatio G. 3663
Kern, John Adam. 1119, 1240, 1440, 2901, 3673
Kern, John Hewins. 1593
Kern, Louis J. 2737, 3392
Kern, Mary Margaret. 2773
Kern, Milton Earl. 290, 406
Kern, Paul Bentley. 1967, 2064, 2428
Kern, Richard. 3820
Kern, Walter. 857
Kernahan, Arthur Earl. 1201, 1558, 1566, 3353
Kernahan, Coulson. 1888, 3506, 895
Kernan, William Charles. 1364, 1372
Kern County Mental Health Association. 2781
Kernodle, Peter Jefferson. 1705
[Kernot, Henry]. 1429
Kerns, H. J. 2642
Kerns, Joseph E. 948, 2343, 3524
Kerns, Phil. 2817
Kerr, Alva Martin. 3078
Kerr, Annie Barclay. 1588
Kerr, Anthony J C. 1392
Kerr, Cecil. 2769, 2861
Kerr, Clarence W. 1696
Kerr, Clarence Ware. 1608, 1696, 2247, 2338, 3012
Kerr, David W. 3374
Kerr, Edith A. 3597
Kerr, High Thomson. 3325
Kerr, Horace L. 1257
Kerr, Hugh Thomson. 223, 422, 908, 910, 1317, 2006, 2028, 2909, 2914, 3210, 3263, 3342, 3353, 3745, 2932, 2168, 2941, 2976, 2978, 3622, 3636
Kerr, I. C. 3645
Kerr, James. 135
Kerr, James Lennox. 1774, 2486
Kerr, James S. 481, 922, 2258, 3639
Kerr, John Henry. 410

Kerr, John Stevens. 2726, 2815
Kerr, Laura (Nowak) 669
Kerr, Mary Starck. 2798
Kerr, Phil. 1207
Kerr, Phillip Stanley. 1207
Kerr, Robert. 1956
Kerr, Robert Pollok. 1055, 2936, 1375, 2936
Kerr, William Campbell. 1935
Kerr, William Henry. 3221
Kerr, William Shaw. 1918
[Kerrick, Frederick Blazier] 1874. 2390
Kerrigan, William. 2469
Kerrison, Raymond. 668, 3790
Kersey, Jesse. 1675, 3129
Kerschner, Mabel Gardner. 2509, 2550
Kershner, Frederick Doyle. 1041, 2722, 3061, 3611
Kershner, Howard Eldred. 1134, 3353
[Kershner, John J.]. 2310, 3803
Kershner, William J. 3415
Kershner, William Jacob. 3415
Kersten, John C. 3188
Kersten, Lawrence K. 2303
[Kersten, Norbert] d. 1915. 854
Kersting, A. F. 1270
Kerswill, William Dean. 3289
Kertelge, Karl. 468
Kertzer, Morris Norman. 2120, 2139, 2168, 3016, 3454
Kerwin, Jerome Gregory. 1143, 827, 1143
Keshavadas, 1934. 3400
Keshavadas, Swami. 3479
Kesich, Veselin. 2052, 3221
Keskar, Vishwanath. 3479
Kesler, Jay. 983, 3886
Kesselring, Joseph. 3457
Kessler, Harry L. 2078
Kessler, Herbert L. 602, 1883
[Kessler, William George] 1898. 2366
Kestens, Adolph. 90
Keswick Convention, 1976. 2168
Ketcham, Charles B. 1659, 2040
Ketcham, Kneeland Platt. 1041
Ketcham, Robert T. 579
Ketcham, Robert Thomas. 164, 966, 3353, 3720
Ketcham, William Ezra. 1692, 2176
Ketcherside, W. Carl. 1376, 1830, 2174, 2939
Ketchum, Creston Donald. 3129
Ketler, Isaac Conrad. 2767
Ketteler, Wilhelm Emmanuel. 1137, 2168
Kettelkamp, Larry. 99, 2858, 3140
Ketter, Peter. 2353
Kettner, Elmer A. 966, 1015, 1573, 1593, 2214
Kettner, Frederick. 1536
Kettring, Donald D. 915, 3219
Keucher, William F. 1060, 1154, 1566
Kevan, Ernest Frederick. 944, 966, 2201, 3289, 2201
Kevane, Eugene. 114, 769, 1820, 2040, 3182
[Keve, Oliver Morton] 1877. 2436
Kevin, Neil. 627, 2375
Kevin, Robert Oliver. 571
[Kevin, sister]. 1830
Kevorkian, Jack. 2227
Keyes, Charles A. 1575
Keyes, Charles Don. 1060
Keyes, Frances Parkinson (Wheeler) 3690, 48, 723, 1364, 1776, 3460, 3691, 19, 814, 1027, 2525, 3247
Keyes, Francis Parkinson Wheeler. 48
Keyes, Frederick Anthony. 1777
Keyes, Gordon Lincoln. 114, 1819
Keyes, Nelson Beecher. 295, 399, 629, 2025
Keyes, Paul T. 2789
Keynes, Geoffrey Langdon. 192
Keys, Charles C. 1286
Keys, Clara Evans. 2541
Keys, Donald. 103
Keyser, Cassius Jackson. 3081, 3645
Keyser, Herman Julius. 516
Keyser, John H. 1888, 1907
Keyser, Leander Sylvester. 57, 64, 1099, 1360, 1381, 1593, 2561, 2998, 3101, 3414, 3608
Keyser, Paul Edward. 1251, 2204, 1251, 2204
Keyser, Rudolph. 2666
Keyser, William R. 1407
Keyser, Wilma (Sudhoff) 3174, 3185
Keyserling, Hermann Alexander, graf von. 1888
Keysor, Charles W. 584, 585, 985, 1777
Keysser, Christian. 2544
Kezys, Algimantas. 2370
Khadduri, Majid. 2122, 2564
Khan, Gazanfar Ali. 2847
Khan, Muhammad Zafrulla. 2565, 2629 2635
Khan, Naseer Ahmad. 2885
Khan, Sir Muhammad Zafrulla. 2565
Khanna, Madhu. 3862

Kheiralla, Ibrahim George. 128, 185
Kheirallah, George Ibrahim. 2565, 2629
Kherbawi, Basil M. 2746
Khoobyar, Helen. 3152
Khosla, Sarla. 706
Khumayni, Ruh Allah. 1923, 1924
Kidd, Almira. 3506
Kidd, Benjamin. 3439
Kidd, Berenford James. 1176, 1192, 1541, 3034
Kidd, Beresford James. 851, 1196, 1374, 1487, 3042
*Kidd, Elizabeth. 2286, 3164
Kidd, George Eldridge. 1672
Kidd, James Robbins. 8
Kidd, John. 2673
Kidder, Daniel P[arish]. 2884
Kidder, Daniel Parish. 414, 426, 431, 439, 896, 924, 2603, 2902, 2979, 3673, 3682
Kidder, Frank Eugene. 1157
Kiddle, Henry. 3506
Kidner, Derek. 512, 519, 521, 537, 572, 584
*Kidney, Dorothy Boone. 1260
Kieckhefer, Richard. 1805
Kiefer, James S. 739, 2512, 3590
Kiefer, William J. 303, 2216
*Kiefer, James S. 2490
Kieffer, George Linn. 3040
Kiej'e, Nikolas. 1709
Kiely, Martha Meister. 3843
Kiemel, Ann. 985, 1010, 2169
Kienberger, Vincent Ferrer. 189, 1977
Kiene, Paul F. 3579
Kienel, Paul A. 1247, 3189
Kiener, Mary Aloysi. 999, 1347, 1642, 2361, 2703, 3487
Kieninger, Clara Louise. 2169
Kierkegaard, Soren Aabye. 7, 1054, 1055, 1069, 1104, 1619, 2170, 2299, 2390, 2833, 2892, 3101, 3405, 3413, 3479, 3480, 3631
Kierkegaard, Sooren Aabye. 3480
Kierkegaard, Soren Aabye. 1105, 3411, 3413, 3480
Kierkeguard, Soren Aabye. 1070
Kies, Reinhold Friedrich. 52
Kiesewetter, Karl. 2732
Kiesling, Christopher. 838, 877, 3547
Kiesling, Cristopher. 999
Kiessling, Elmer Carl. 2274, 2910
Kietzell, Fritz von. 2058
Kieval, Herman. 2110
Kiger, T[homas] M[arion]. 1314
Kik, Jacob Marcellus. 338, 444, 465, 1141, 1491, 2464, 2932
Kik, Richard. 3312
Kiklin, Joseph Louis J. 3480
Kikumura, Norihiko. 3403
Kilbourn, John Kenyon. 1593
Kilbourn, William. 1066
Kilby, Clyde S. 2219
Kildahl, Harold B. 1440
Kildahl, John Nathan. 1830, 2299
Kildahl, John P. 1717
Kildee, Mary Philomena. 1624
Kilgallen, John J. 334, 3527
Kilgo, Edith Flowers. 1838
Kilgo, John Carlisle. 3537
Kilgore, Elias Gaston. 3129
Kilgore, James E. 885, 1256, 1754
Kilgour, Robert. 655
Kilian, Sabbas J. 2774
Kilinski, Kenneth K. 1199
Kilker, Adrian Jerome. 1587
Killeen, B. D. 838, 3265
Killeffer, David Herbert. 3717
Killen, James Miller. 1795, 1796
Killgallon, James. 796, 999
Killgallon, James J. 796, 999, 1003
Killgore, Robert Fansier. 3129
Killian, Ida F. 2390
Killian, Joseph Aloysius. 788
Killinger, John. 422, 430, 437, 443, 985, 1060, 1170, 1558, 2122, 2480, 2874, 2902, 3003, 3289, 3353
Kilmartin, Edward J. 860, 1046, 2254
Kilpatrick, George Dunbar. 442
Kilpatrick, Thomas Buchanan. 1566
Kim, Hee-Jin. 1472
Kim, Seyoon. 376, 2798
Kim, Yong Choon. 2844
Kim, Young Oon. 709, 1813, 2139, 3329, 3645
Kimball, Caleb. 2040
Kimball, David Tenney. 2741
Kimball, Edward Ancel. 1033
Kimball, Edward L. 2171, 2609
[Kimball, Grace Lucia (Atkinson) 1875-1923. 3506
Kimball, Harriet McEwen. 1597, 1862
Kimball, Heber Chase. 2616
[Kimball, Irving Ellsworth]. 463
[Kimball, Irving Elsworth]. 509
Kimball, James William. 966, 2171
Kimball, Joe. 1324
Kimball, John Calvin. 3078

Kimball, Kate Fisher. 751
Kimball, Spencer W. 1009, 1232, 1633, 2338
Kimball, Stanley Buchholz. 2171, 2617
Kimball, Warren Young. 473, 1802, 3200
Kimber, John Shober. 3579
Kimble, Teena. 1009
Kimbrough, Bradley Thomas. 154
Kimchi, David. 538, 576
Kimchi, Joseph. 1798
Kimhi, David, 1160?-1235? 537, 542, 579
Kimmel, Jo. 985, 2874
Kimmel, William Breyfogel. 3651
Kimp, Bobbie. 2912
Kimpel, Benjamin Franklin. 275, 1105, 1536, 3061, 3102
Kimura, Gibun. 2171, 3197
Kinard, J. Spencer. 1233, 3353
Kincaid, Charles Augustus. 1895
Kincheloe, Raymond McFarland. 454
Kincheloe, Samuel Clarence. 1119, 1278, 3746, 3747
Kinder, Arthur Gordon. 3714
Kinder, Ernst. 1551
Kinderhook, N. Y. Reformed Dutch Church. 3046
Kindred, Charles Granville. 1467
Kindregan, Charles P. 2338
King, Albion Roy. 1746
King, Alonzo. 673, 2505
King, Alta. 2040
King, Archdale Arthur. 838, 851, 2237, 2259
King, Archibald Milroy. 1531
King, Audrey R. 1351
King, Basil. 653, 1593, 1619, 1735, 3069, 3506
King, Betty. 861
King, Beztrice (Tannehill) 2620
King, Bruce. 95, 98, 2313, 2715, 2726, 2946
King, Bucky. 2234
King, Charles David. 606
King, Charles William. 1718
King, Clyde S. 2993
King, Coretta Scott. 2172
King, David. 1705
King, David S. 1244
King, Edith W. 2475
King, Edward. 606, 966, 2172
King, Edward George. 1798
King, Edwin James. 2179, 3317, 1755
King, Eleanor Anthony. 480, 1702
King, Elisha Alonzo. 2461, 3393, 3870
King, Fairley Daniel. 1050
King-Farlow, John. 3102
King, Francis. 95, 1806, 2313, 2314, 2726
King, Francis W. 1307
King, Frankie Jackson. 2390
King, Frederick La Rue. 576
King, Frederick Walter. 3473
King, Geoffrey R. 164, 507, 2006
King, George E. 1655
King, George Walton. 2263
King, George Washington. 1699
King, Georgiana Goddard. 1113, 3778, 2741, 1274
King, Grace. 2442
King, Grace Hamilton. 3204
King, Guy Hope. 588
King, Hannah Tapfield. 2599
King, Harriette. 2490
King, Henry Churchill. 1105, 940, 944, 3177, 966, 1050, 1060, 1070, 1497, 2003, 2064, 3102, 3335, 3443, 3679
King, Henry Melville. 144, 201, 2399, 3192, 143, 153, 277, 398, 684, 1285, 2414, 2984, 3192, 3817, 22
King, Henry Pierson. 2055
King, Henry Safford. 1050
King, Henry Walter. 2726
King, Irving. 2998, 3109
King, J. Norman. 1733, 3019
King, James Norman. 1120
King, James W. 2234
King, Jeff. 2676
King, Jesse. 204
King, Joe Madison. 169
King, John Glen. 2748
King, John H. 3117
King, John N. 1518
King, John Sumpter. 3506
King, Joseph Hillery. 2814
King, Josiah. 673, 1420
King, Julius. 1690
King, Karl C. 2172
King, Kenneth Moffat. 2506, 3376
King, Leonard William. 2654
King, LeRoy. 102
King, Lewis. 465
King, Lillian[Estelle Day]. 3095
King, Maria M. 3506
King, Marian. 1405, 1495, 1957, 2133, 2353
King, Martin Luther. 15, 157, 2323, 146, 2172
King, Morton Brandon. 3453

King, Nell. 3506
King, Noel Quinton. 13, 1073, 1192, 1926, 3111, 3610
*King, Norman. 934
[King, Obadiah Higbee] 1862. 105
King, Patrick. 2178
King, Paul G. 2222
King, Peter King. 74, 1192
King, Rachel Hadley. 204, 1637, 1802, 2647, 2709, 3663
King, Ray A. 93
King, Robert Harlen. 1723
King, Rufus Gunn. 2807
King, Thomas A. 639, 2690, 3095
[King, Thomas Benton] 1838. 3319
King, Thomas Mulvihill. 1836, 3303
King, Thomas Starr. 3725
King, Ursula. 3117, 3593
King, Walter. 384
King, Walter N. 1101, 3399
King, William. 1746, 3003, 3129, 2656
King, William H. 234
King, William Peter. 11, 966, 1723, 3443
King, William Robert. 1838
King, Winston Lee. 704, 711, 1081, 2382, 3061
Kingdom, Hollingworth Tully. 1893
Kingdon, Frank. 3102, 3061, 3129
Kingdon, Robert McCune. 196, 728, 1422, 1852, 3034
Kinghorn, Kenneth C. 985, 1712, 1830, 2321
Kingman, Henry. 886, 1593, 1952, 3342
Kingrey, David W. 3592
Kingsbury, Francis. 1860
Kingsbury, Jack Dean. 390, 442, 444, 2011, 2025
[Kingsbury, Oliver Addison] 1839-1914. 303, 966
[Kingsbury, Oliver Richmond] 1809-1889. 1860
Kingsford, Anna (Bonus) 2726
Kingsford, Hugh Sadler. 844
Kingsford, S. M. 2989
Kingslake, Brian. 1696, 2390, 2690
Kingsland, William. 206
Kingsley, Adelaide Delia (Nichols) 3506
Kingsley, Calvin. 719, 3221
Kingsley, Charles. 563, 1113, 1226, 1806, 1807, 2177, 2652, 2662, 2663, 3342, 3364
*Kingsley, Charles W. 348, 1566
Kingsley, Florence (Morse) 2476
Kingsley, Rose Georgina. 2179
Kingston, Frederick Temple. 1583
Kingston, Jeremy. 3824
Kingston, Kenny. 2177, 2992
Kingston, William Henry Giles. 3280
Kington-Oliphant, Thomas Laurence, 1831-1902. 809, 2978
Kington-Oliphant, Thomas Laurence. 809
Kinkead, Thomas L. 132
Kinloch, Tom Fleming. 3165
Kinn, James W. 2256
Kinnaird, William M. 1351
Kinnaman, J. O. 207
Kinnaman, John Ora. 207
Kinnamon, J. O. 208
Kinnamon, Les. 3880
Kinnane, John F. 3785
Kinne, Clarence James. 2874
Kinnear, Elizabeth Kelsey. 3697
Kinnebrew, J. M. 3645
Kinney, Bruce. 2553, 2490, 2603, 2833
Kinney, Charles B. 1148
Kinney, Dorothy W. 3187
Kinney, Laurence F. 321
Kinney, LeBaron Wilmont. 3575
Kinney, Mary (Martin) 3833
Kinniburgh, L B. 3280
Kinnier Wilson, J. V. 2667
Kinns, Samuel. 2621, 204, 515, 2243
Kino, Eusebio Francisco. 2177, 2849
Kinross, John Patrick Douglas Balfour. 1929
*Kinsella, A. W. 944, 966, 2570
Kinsella, Nivard. 1856
Kinsey, J. F. 3026
Kinsey, Robert Baldwin. 3218
Kinsey, Robert S. 372, 2798
Kinsler, F. Ross. 3332
Kinsley, David R. 1813, 2162, 2186
Kinsley, William Wirt. 2882, 2001, 2874, 3076
Kinsman, Delos Oscar. 1050
Kinsman, Frederick Joseph. 781, 827, 1218, 1364, 2959, 3710
Kinsolving, Arthur Barksdale. 2178
Kinsolving, Wythe Leigh. 3102
Kinzel, Margaret Mary. 2573
Kinzer, Donald Louis. 33
Kip, Abraham Lincoln. 509, 2473, 2690, 3570
Kip, William Ingraham. 745, 1949, 2209
Kiplinger, Charles U. 2695
Kipp, Peter E. 204
[Kipper, Herman Brunswick]. 1967

Kipper, Herman Brunswick. 3314
Kippley, John F. 664
Kirban, Doreen. 2762
Kirban, Salem. 10, 214, 343, 606, 985, 1034, 1428, 1514, 1696, 1940, 2611, 2946, 3018, 3138
Kirby, Clyde. 1014
Kirby, Ethyn (Williams) 2166
Kirby, Ralph. 602
Kirby, Reginald. 164
Kirby, Wallace H. 2436, 3353
Kirby, William. 2673
Kirche im Zeitalter des Absolutismus und der Aufklarung. 1181
Kircher, Clara J. 905
Kirchgassner, Alfons. 2234
Kirchner, Hubert. 2274, 2810
Kirham, E Kay. 1243
Kirieev, Aleksandr Aleksieevich. 2862
Kirk, Albert. 416, 440
Kirk, Albert Emmanuel. 1120, 3492
Kirk, Edward Norris. 2025, 2059, 2771, 3196, 3232
Kirk, Geoffrey Stephan. 2661
Kirk, Geoffrey Stephen. 2661
Kirk, Harris Elliott. 1050, 1060, 1931, 2932, 2977, 3078
Kirk, J. Andrew. 2222, 3234
Kirk, James A. 2663
Kirk, Jane. 3837
Kirk, Jerry. 1843
Kirk, John. 3806
Kirk, Kenneth Escott. 944, 1165, 1536, 3024, 179, 1212, 179
Kirk, Mary Virginia (Lee) 3167
Kirk, Maxie C. 2505
Kirk, Rudolf. 2686
Kirkconnell, Watson. 2232, 2470, 2472
Kirke, Sarah Maria. 3090
Kirkemo, Ronald B. 3740
Kirkendall, Norma Anne. 3179
Kirkfleet, Cornelius James. 1620, 2713, 2912
Kirkham, Arne. 2178
Kirkham, Francis Washington. 678
Kirkham, Oscar A. 2608
Kirkland, Bryant M. 1417, 3480
Kirkland, Henry Burnham. 3462
Kirkland, John Vinus. 2941
Kirkland, Winifred Margaretta. 1090, 1111, 1385, 1593, 1956, 1967, 1977, 2052, 2596, 2874, 1714, 1996
Kirkpatrick, Alexander Francis. 500, 569
Kirkpatrick, Blaine E. 3152
Kirkpatrick, Blaine Evron. 1525
Kirkpatrick, Clifford. 3086
Kirkpatrick, Dow. 2436
Kirkpatrick, Ellis Lore. 1520
Kirkpatrick, Jerald L. 3398
Kirkpatrick, Robert White. 2902
Kirkpatrick, W[illia]m J. 3458
Kirkpatrick, William J. 2815, 3564
Kirkpatrick, William J and Gilmour, H. l. 390
Kirkwood, Aghes E. 3867
Kirkwood, Gordon MacDonald. 2658
Kirkwood, Mossie May (Waddington) 3302
Kirlin, Joseph Louis J. 3200, 824, 857, 1449, 3778
Kirn, George John. 3061
Kirpal Singh, 1894-1974. 2178, 2390, 3197, 3415, 3865
Kirsch, A. Thomas. 92
Kirsch, Augustin Paul. 1091
Kirsch, Felix Marie. 769, 805, 1642, 1645, 3162, 3390
Kirsch, James. 1479, 3800
Kirsch, Paul J. 1083, 1746
Kirschbaum, Engelbert. 2825, 3769
Kirschenbaum, Aaron. 3330
Kirschstein, Arthur J. 2084
Kirshenbaum, David. 1623
Kirtley, James Samuel. 1120, 1910, 148, 1967, 2029
Kirton, John William. 3130
Kirvan, John J. 3537
Kirwan-Mott, Anne. 1208
Kirwen, Michael C. 3814
Kirwin, James Martin]. 1701
[Kirwin, John W.]. 665
Kisch, Guido. 2100, 2107
Kisch, H J. 3061
Kishor, Sulamith Ish. 2106
Kishpaugh, Mary Jerome. 2937
Kiskaddon, Jesse Fulton. 3078
Kissane, Edward J. 576
Kissinger, Dorothy May (Vale) 3767
Kissinger, Warren S. 3335
Kistemaker, Simon. 390, 729, 2025
Kistler, Charles E. 1952
Kitagawa, Daisuke. 1131
Kitagawa, Joseph Mitsuo. 91
Kitagawa. Joseph Mitsuo. 1936
Kitamori, Kazo. 3542
Kitay, Philip Morton. 109
Kitch, Ethel May. 1813

Kitch, M. J. 2978
Kitchen, Kenneth Anderson. 537
Kitchen, Victor Constant. 1359
Kitcher, Philip. 1580
Kitchin, Samuel S. 1060
Kitching, Christopher J. 1212, 1243
Kitel, Ridolf. 1421
Kitov, Eliyahu. 1614, 2120
Kitson Clark, George Sidney Roberts, 1900. 1137
Kittel, Bonnie Pedrotti. 1874, 3605
*Kittel, Gerhard. 313
Kittel, Gerhard. 1768, 1769
Kittel, Rudolf. 493, 595, 2096
Kittel, Rudolph. 1421
[Kittell, Ferdinand]. 1744, 2260
Kittler, Glenn D. 765, 777, 867, 924, 1410, 1937, 2125, 2576, 2989, 3812
Kitto, John. 244, 295, 1605, 1967, 2764, 3130
Kittredge, George Lyman. 3825
Kittredge, Herman Eugene. 1907
Kitts, Eustace John. 2123
Kivengere, Festo. 667, 2178
Kiwleserian, Babgen. 82
Kiyota, Minoru. 3403
Kjaer, Jens Christian. 1401
Kjelgaard, James Arthur. 2615
Kjer, Ludvig Peder. 57
Kjeseth, Peter L. 1830
Kjome, June C. 2540
Klaaren, Eugene M. 3084
Klaasen, Ruth. 2178, 2407
Klaber, Florence Wolff. 2133
Klagsbrun, Francine. 2081, 2621, 2624, 2950
Klah, Hasteen. 2677
Klaiber, Jeffrey L. 824, 2823
Klain, Zora. 1683
*Klammer, Enno E. 686
Klaperman, Gilbert. 555, 2094
Klaperman, Libby M. 6, 629, 1734, 2122, 2151, 3402
Klappholz, Kurt. 2081, 2139
Klaren, Mathias. 1281
Klarmann, Andrew F. 3238
Klarmann, Andrew Francis. 884
[Klarmann, Andrew Francis]. 796, 857, 999, 2378
Klass, Sholom. 1632, 3219
Klassen, Elizabeth Suderman. 1283
Klassen, Peter James. 3034
Klassen, William. 240, 334, 1633, 2332, 2849
Klauder, Alexander L[aurence] A[lphonsus]. 748
Klauder, Alexander Laurence Alphonsus. 770
Klauder, Francis J. 3309, 3593, 3695
Klauser, Theodor. 844
Klausler, Alfred P. 2135, 3784, 3876, 3883
Klausner, Joseph. 1967, 2117, 2414, 2798
Klausner, Joseph Gedaliah. 1967
Klaver, Richard. 2247, 2363
Kleber, Albert. 1936
Kleeberg, Irene Cumming. 1184
Kleen, Tyra af. 704
Klein, Aaron E. 2382
Klein, Arthur Jay. 1146
Klein, Arthur Warner. 1146
Klein, Carol. 2623
Klein, Charlotte. 1073
Klein, Ernst E. 3171
Klein, Felix. 1967, 3712
Klein, Harry Martin John. 2195, 2404, 3048
Klein, Henry. 2299
Klein, Isaac. 1315, 2074, 2120, 2626, 3219
Klein, Moses. 2078
Klein, Ralph W. 505, 598, 1583, 2093
Klein, Sarah Guss. 3174
Klein, Stanley. 1417
Klein, Walter Conrad. 185, 1521, 2057, 2939
Kleine, Glen. 3276
Kleinhans, Theodore J. 686, 1262, 1449, 2274, 3870
Kleinhaus, Theodore J. 1262
Kleinschmidt, Gladys J. 1428
Kleiser, Grenville. 719, 2049, 2902, 3342, 3353
Kleiser, Roy Hagan. 966
Klejment, Anne. 195
Klekotka, Peter John. 1355
Klemke, E. D. 2171
Klemm, Edwin O. 3741
Klemme, Huber F. 1134, 2860, 3439
Klenck, Robert H. 2390
Kleps, Art. 1782
Klett, Guy Soulliard. 2936
Kleuser, Louise C. 1566
Klever, Anita. 616, 2025
Klibanov, A. I. 1038
Kliebard, Herbert M. 1130
Kliever, Lonnie D. 1417, 2708

Kliewer, John W. 195
Kligerman, Aaron Judah. 1623, 2415
Klimisch, Mary Jane. 884, 3781
Klinck, Arthur William. 534, 2765
Kline, George Louis. 3214
Kline, John. 2178
Kline, John Jacob. 2292
Kline, Magdalena. 3506
Kline, Meredith G. 217, 510, 1376, 1377
Klinefelter, Walter. 1712
Klineman, George. 2130
Kling, Christian Friedrich. 322, 326
Kling, Simcha. 1539, 3455
Kling, Smicha. 3455
Klingberg, Frank Joseph. 2542, 3437
Klingberg, Irene. 2178
Klingbert, Frank Joseph. 1150
Klinger, Kurt. 2124
Klingman, George Adam. 100, 101, 1176
Klink, Johanna Louise. 616, 621, 622, 901, 903
Klink, Thomas W. 2781
Klinkerman, Oscar J. 985
Klinsing, P. David. 3868
Klocker, Harry R. 1738, 2843, 3696
Kloetzli, Walter. 1278
Klooster, Fred H. 176, 355, 729, 2008, 2912
Klopfenstein, Janette. 1414
Kloppenburg, Boaventura. 772, 2222, 2789, 3289
Kloppenburg, Bonaventura. 1088
Kloppenburg, Bonaventure. 1188, 2222, 3771
Klopstock, Friedrich Gottlieb. 3095, 3207
Klos, Sarah. 2892
Klose, Ellen. 2760
Klostermaier, Klaus. 1082
Klotsche, Ernest Heinrich. 1386, 1473, 3654
Klotz, John William. 3, 202, 1580, 3069, 3082
Kluber, George Kendall. 2914
Klubertanz, George Peter. 2418, 2738, 3782
Kluckhohn, Clyde. 1901
Klug, Eugene F. 240, 2281, 2282
Klug, Ron. 688, 901, 1112, 1605, 2021, 2892
Klug, Ronald. 3480
Kluger, Rivkah Scharf. 1429
Klykken, O. 1611, 3886
Klyver, Faye Huntington. 3178, 3189
Knapke, Paul Justin. 2940
Knapp, Bliss. 1034, 2178
Knapp, Ezra C. 3555, 3763
Knapp, Forrest Lamar. 1041, 2204, 2548
Knapp, Georg Christian. 3645
Knapp, Grace Higley. 668
Knapp, Ida C. 2639
Knapp, Jacob. 2178
Knapp, Justina. 920
Knapp, Martin Wells. 1359, 3799
Knapp, Peggy Ann. 2908, 3860
Knapp, Shepherd. 538
Knappen, Marshall Mason. 3007, 3009
Knappenberger, James Buchanan. 1034
Knappenberger, Philip. 1091
Knapp-Fisher, E G. 1211
Knauf, Ethel. 2390
[Knauff, Thordore Christian]. 1041
Knebel, Aaron G. 3871
Knecht, Friedrich Justus. 295
Kneeland, Abner. 671, 1091, 1092, 1866, 3176
Knerr, Sylvester Buck. 616
Knesel, Dave. 3004
Knevels, Wilhelm. 1544
Kniffin, Evelyn Gage. 3207
Knigge, Adolf Franz Friedrich Ludwig. 1324
Knight, Alice Marie (Neighbour) 1014, 1840
Knight, Alva. 2717
Knight, Anna A. 2726
Knight, Antonio. 2476
Knight, Cecil B. 3003
Knight, Cecil Bertie Howard. 3161
Knight, David C. 2858
Knight, Douglas A. 505
Knight, Edgar Wallace. 3551
Knight, Frank Hyneman. 1075, 1076
Knight, George Angus Fulton. 537, 516, 543, 545, 557, 598, 1083, 2200
Knight, George Halley. 966, 1351, 1429, 1449
Knight, George Thomson. 744, 1723, 1746
Knight, George W. 2135
Knight, George Wendell. 1608
Knight, George William. 350, 2402
Knight, George Wilson. 1077
*Knight, Goldie. 1723
Knight, Henry. 3382
Knight, Henry Joseph Corbett. 2067
Knight, Herbert Theodore. 1218, 2001, 2476

Knight, Marcus. 3012
Knight, Margaret, Kennedy. 1092
Knight, Paul S. 459
Knight, Plutark S. 1693
Knight, Ralph. 3506
Knight, Richard. 1705
Knight, Richard Payne. 2652, 2828
Knight, Samuel. 1307
Knight, Samuel Kirshbaum. 1218
Knight, Sherwood Sweet. 2227
Knight, Thomas Cornelius. 2178
Knight, Walker L. 1166, 1418, 3232
Knight, Walter Brown. 1431, 1841
Knight, Willard M. 712
Knight, William Allen. 588, 1977, 2021, 2762, 2824
Knight, William Angus. 3608
Knight, William Henry. 2493
Knights of Columbus. Texas state council. Historical commission. 3605
Knights of Columbus, Washington Council no. 224. 2179
Knights of Malta. 2179
Knights of Pythias. Buffalo, N. Y. William McKinley lodge, no. 399. 3205
Knights of Pythias. Iowa. Grand lodge. 3205
Knights of Pythias. Pennsylvania. Grand lodge. 3205
Knights of Pythias, Wisconsin Grand Lodge. 3205
Knights of Tabor. 3205
Knights of the mystic chain. Supreme lodge. 3240
Knights, Ward A. 1258
Knill, Richard. 34
Kniseley, S. Philip. 3568
Knisley, Alvin. 680
Knoch, Adolf E. 234, 343, 506
Knoche, Grace Frances. 2636
Knoche, H. Gerard. 2902
Knoche, Keith. 1012
Knoche, Vikki. 3261, 3379
Knock, Arthur Wilhelm. 1015, 1566
Knoff, Gerald E. 1251, 3561
Knopf, Carl Summer. 214, 348, 410, 534, 571, 3536
Knopf, Eugene. 606
Knopke, Roch Francis. 2341
Knorr, Lester. 3480
Knott, Harold Elkin. 2902
Knott, John C. 2265
Knott, John Ray. 241, 2468, 3008
Knott, Lucy Pierce. 1952, 3292
Knott, Luella (Pugh) 966
Knowles, Andrew. 622
Knowles, Archibald Campbell. 1440, 3263, 2033, 2209, 2971, 3061, 3676
*Knowles, David. 2644
Knowles, David. 188, 1183, 2579, 2582, 2642, 2645
Knowles, David [Michael Clive Knowles]. 2645
Knowles, David [Secular name: Michael Clive Knowles]. 2579, 1183, 3283
Knowles, Dom David. 2579
Knowles, Edward Randall. 2418
Knowles, Ellin J. (Troy) 1455, 3472, 966
Knowles, James Davis. 2158
Knowles, James Purdie. 1686, 3005
Knowles, Joseph W. 1170
Knowles, Leo. 871, 924, 1025, 1026
Knowles, Lucia M. 2064
Knowles, William J. 397
Knowling, Richard John. 394, 2798, 3780
Knowlton, Annie I. 3848
Knowlton, Isaac Case. 3752
Knowlton, Miles Justin. 2520
Knox, Charles Eugene. 578, 673, 1405, 2071, 2251, 2804, 3564
Knox, Edmund Arbuthnott. 951, 2754, 3152
Knox, George William. 1060, 1089, 1936
Knox, Hugh. 730, 2913
Knox, Ian P. 941
Kosters, Israel. 3822
Knox, John. 966, 3042, 64, 105, 234, 339, 447, 472, 1120, 1192, 1281, 1888, 1995, 2003, 2008, 2012, 2040, 2059, 2182, 2332, 2648, 2798, 2902, 3738
Knox, John D. 2182
Knox, John Dunn. 3793
Knox, Loren Laertes. 3645
Knox, Martin Van Buren. 47
Knox, Olive Elsie. 3241
Knox, R. Buick. 3761
Knox, Ronald Arbuthnott. 863, 2182, 64, 73, 344, 376, 655, 756, 763, 788, 796, 863, 924, 1520, 1636, 2182, 2260, 2347, 2370, 2390, 3061, 3667
*Knox, Ronald Arbuthnott. 804, 863, 1298, 2182, 2390, 3222, 3223
Knox, Samuel James. 3710
Knox, Thomas Malcolm. 3067
Knox, Thomas Wallace. 184
Knox, Vicesimus. 2593

Knox, Wilfred Lawrence. 45
Knox, Wilfred Lawrence. 331, 376, 390, 1192, 2798
Knubel, Frederick Hermann. 363, 3733
Knubel, Frederick R. 3673
Knudsen, Carl. 3342
Knudsen, Harold F. 3214
Knudsen, Johannes. 1776, 2290
Knudsen, Ralph Edward. 148, 410, 3663
Knudsen, Raymond B. 1168, 3531
Knudson, Albert Cornelius. 500, 567, 568, 569, 598, 1105, 1586, 1723, 2822, 3061, 3645
Knudten, Richard D. 1715, 3086, 3433
Knutson, Joseph L. 2214
Knutson, Kent S. 1952, 2059, 2285, 2299, 3633, 3645
Ko, Hung. 23
Kobayashi, Takeshi. 3316, 3703
Kobbe, Carolyn Therese (Wheller) 1364
Kober, Adolf. 2098
Koberle, Adolf. 2300, 3368
Kobler, Franz. 3841
Koch, Anton. 2593
Koch, Dietrich-Alex. 435, 2017
Koch, Franz Xavier Jos. 57
Koch, Gustav Adolf. 3745, 3749
Koch, Hans Gerhard. 64
Koch, Klaus. 56, 229, 290, 2950
Koch, Kurt E. 610, 1088, 1423, 1514, 1716, 1928, 2726, 3230, 3231
Koch, Theodore Wesley. 1402
Kocher, Paul H. 1648, 3470
Kocher, Paul Harold. 3084, 3085
Kodell, Jerome. 3487
Kodera, Takashi James. 1472, 2940
Kodesh Church of Immanuel. 2183
Koeberle, Adolf. 2160
Koehler, Alfred W. 3663
Koehler, Edward Wilhelm August. 3663
Koehler, Emma Emilie. 2515
Koehler, John Philipp. 380, 1548
Koehne, John Betts. 720, 1715, 2561
Koehneke, Martin L. 2284
Koenig, John. 348, 1713, 2103
Koenig, John H. 2366
Koenig, Norma E. 903
Koenig, Richard Edwin. 64, 1060
Koenig, Robert E. 639
Koenig, Xavier. 3061
Koenigsberger, Helmut Georg. 2278
Koenker, Ernest Benjamin. 1457, 2234, 2671, 3003
Koerber, Fred. 606
Koester, Mary Camilla. 1304
Koestler, Arthur. 99, 3084
Koether, Luella G. 2509
Kofahl, Robert E. 1381, 1580
Koffler, Jacob. 2091
Kofoid, Carrie Prudence. 3009
Kogan, Michael S. 2143
Koger, Azzie Briscoe. 157
Koger, Nannie Elizabeth. 1593, 3130
Koglin, Anna E. 423
Kohanik, Peter G. 2746, 3257
Kohanski, Alexander Sissel. 699, 2227
Kohaus, Hannah More. 3026
Kohl, Marvin. 1544
Kohl, Percy. 3858
Kohl, Rachel. 2224
Kohler, Hans-Joachim. 124, 3816
Kohler, Irving N. 1099
Kohler, Karl Friederich. 2274
Kohler, Kaufmann. 1402, 1794, 1799, 2080, 2082, 2111, 2115, 2117, 2150, 3371
Kohler, Ludwig Hugo. 598, 1796, 2082
Kohler, Mary Hortense. 1475, 178, 1475, 1476
Kohler, Max James. 2078, 2103
Kohli, Surindar Singh. 7
Kohlmann, Anthony. 2001, 3728, 3729
Kohmescher, Matthew F. 788
Kohn, Eugene. 290, 2104, 2110, 2139, 3028
Kohn, Harold E. 588, 1112, 1351, 1449, 2390, 2844, 3406
Kohn, Jacob. 1381, 1537, 2773
Kohn, Joshua. 2109, 3576
Kohn, Paula M. 910
Kohut, Alexander. 562, 2623
Kohut, George Alexander. 2103, 3409
Kohut, Rebekah (Bettelheim) 2183
Kohut, Rebekah Bettelheim. 2183
Kolakowski, Leszek. 1536
[Kokkinakis, A. T.]. 3455
Kokkinakis, Athenagoras T. 2346
Kokosalakis, N. 2087
Kolarz, Walter. 3257
Kolatch, Alfred J. 3342, 3361, 3584
Kolatch, Mollie. 3261
Kolb, Erwin J. 2874
Kolb, Robert. 40, 1292
Kolbe, Frederick Charles. 1328, 2642
Kolbe, Henry E. 695
Kolbrek, Loyal. 495, 633, 1507
Kolenda, Konstantin. 3102, 3880

Kolesar, John. 2202
Kolesnik, Walter Bernard. 832
Kolig, Erich. 117
Kolitz, Zvi. 503, 2112, 2144
Kolke, Daniel. 3738
Kollek, Teddy. 2848
Koller, Charles W. 1440, 2902, 164, 1440, 2786
Koller, John M. 1896
Kollock, Shepard Kosciuszko. 3673
Kolstoe, Oliver P. 2411
Kolvoord, John. 509
Komroff, Manuel. 244, 247, 629, 1957, 1967, 2652
Kon, Abraham Israel. 2886
Konerding, Volker. 1159
Konig, Adrio. 1723
Konig, Eduard. 290, 1421
Konig, Franz. 2390
Konig, Gustav Ferdinand Leopold. 2274, 3040
Konigmacher, Samuel Martin. 2545
Konijn, Seef. 1060
Konings, Antony. 1327
Konkel, Wilbur. 1870, 1872
Konolige, Kit. 1524
Konrad, Joseph George. 2577
Konstantin. 934, 2852
Kontoglous, Photes. 85
Konus, William J. 584
Konvitz, Milton Ridvas. 1280, 1490
Konz, F. 3269
*Konzelman, Robert. 1111
Koob, C. Albert. 831, 867, 3401
Kooiman, Gladys. 1414
Kooiman, Helen V. 1449, 1633, 1754, 2390, 2625, 3229, 3831
Kooiman, Willem Jan. 284, 2274
Kook, Abrahahm Isaac. 3218
Kook, Abraham Isaac. 2142
Koon, Warren L. 2790
Koons, William George. 2421, 2424, 3152
Koontz, Ida M. 3564
Koontz, Ida Matilda. 3171
Koontz, Paul Rodes. 1553
Koopman, LeRoy. 1620, 1855, 2231, 3480
Koparkar, Mohan. 96
Kopf, Carl Heath. 966, 1332
Koplowitz, Isidore. 1397
Kopp, Clemens. 2014
Kopp, Josef Vitalis. 3593
Kopp, Ruth Lewshenia. 3604
Koppe, William A. 904
Kopper, Philip. 1111
Kopplin, Dorothea (Simons) 303, 1449
Koran. 2183
Koran, English. 78, 2183, 2184
Koran. English & Arabic. 2184
Koran. English. Selections. 2184
Koran. Selections. 2184, 2185
Koran. Selections. English. 2184, 2185
Korchmaryk, Franko Bohdan. 1542
Korem, Danny. 2993
Koren, Henry J. 1332, 1826, 2418, 2495
Koren, Vilhelm. 2300, 3369
Korfker, Dena. 622, 898, 622, 901, 1982
Korn, Bertram Wallace. 2106
Korn, Frank J. 2769
Kornfield, Jack. 2382
Korolevsky, Cyril. 2233
Korper, Ruth. 2750
Kors, Alan C. 3826
Korstjens, Keith A. 171, 2185
Kortendick, James Joseph. 3615
Kortkamp, Ivan. 917
Kortrey, Walter A. 2007
Kory, Robert B. 3708
[Kosanke, Martha]. 3506
Koschade, Alfred. 1548, 2542
Kosicki, George W. 999, 3542
Kosmas ho Aitolos, 1714-1779. 1026, 2185
Kossoff, David. 629, 1967
Kost, John. 1615
Kosten, Andrew. 1375, 1841
Koster, M. D. 517
Kosters, Ludwig. 1120, 2001
Kostlin, Julius Theodor. 2274
Kostof, Spiro K. 876, 3025
Kostyu, Frank A. 1016, 1255, 1356, 2187, 2786, 3732
Kot, Stanislaw. 3439
Koteskey, Ronald L. 1107
Kothen, Robert. 1136, 2343
Kotker, Norman. 406
Kotre, John N. 951, 1301, 1389, 1772, 3451
Kotsuji, Abraham Setsujau. 2952
Kouchagian, Thorgom. 1264
Koulomzin, Sophie. 938, 2186, 2746, 2747
Kourdakov, Sergei. 2186
Koury, Aleah Q. 3216
Kovalevsky, Pierre. 3257, 3334
[Kovar, Edith May]. 1996
Kovesi, Julius. 1536
Kowrach, Edward J. 2377
Koyama, Kosuke. 1097, 2046, 2390, 3622

Kozodoy, Ruth. 1615
Kraabel, Alf M. 3267
Krabill, Russell. 473, 474, 595
Kraeft, Walter O. 2293
Kraeling, Carl Hermann. 1160, 2127, 1483
Kraeling, Emil Gottlieb Heinrich. 71, 282, 344, 504, 505, 548, 2798, 2950
Kraeling, Emil Gottliee Heinrich. 283
Kraemer, Augustus. 1514
Kraemer, Hendrik. 70, 1079, 1095, 1566, 2191, 3061
Kraft, Charles Franklin. 658, 1797
Kraft, Charles H. 1074
Kraft, Frederick A. 3506
Kraft, Heinrich. 25, 1287
Kraft, Marguerite G. 2556
Kraft, Robert A. 590, 1770
Kraft, Vernon Robert. 1460
Kraft, Virgil A. 3195
Kraft, William. 1708, 1820
Kraft, William F. 999, 1836
Krahn, Cornelius. 37, 1705
Krailsheimer, A. J. 2777, 3021
Krajenke, Robert W. 206, 876
Krakovsky, Levi Isaac. 721
Kral, Martin A. 1314
Kramer, A. T. 1264
Kramer, Albert Ludlow. 1359
Kramer, Alice Bishop. 303, 1359, 3289
Kramer, Edward Louis. 1034
Kramer, Frederick Ferdinand. 223
Kramer, Helen Mary. 2847
Kramer, Herbert George. 765, 2186
Kramer, James W. 1558
*Kramer, Janice. 443, 1111, 1747, 2022, 3235, 3580
Kramer, John W. 944
Kramer, Leonard J. 3851
Kramer, Martin S. 1924
Kramer, Paul Stevens. 3289
Kramer, Samuel. 2117
Kramer, Samuel Nathan. 2667
Kramer, Samuel Noah. 2652, 2667, 3545
Kramer, Simon G. 2137
Kramer, Werner R. 376, 2020
Kramer, William Albert. 253, 901, 1328, 3188, 3310
Kramer, William M. 639
Kramp, Joseph. 2366
Krampe, E G. 639
Kramrisch, Stella. 3421
Kranes, Judith Ehre. 2204
Kranidas, Thomas. 2468
Krantzler, Harold I. 2079
Kranz, Gisbert. 3203
Kranzler, George G. 1789
Krasa, Miloslav. 3599
Krasinski, Walerjan Skorobohaty. 3042
Krass, Alfred C. 1566, 2480, 1567
Krass, Elizabeth. 1739
Kratzenstein, Jossef J. 1583
Kratzer, Glenn Andrew. 2320
Kratzer, Glenn Andrews. 1034, 2320, 3227
Kratzig, Henry H. 3364
Kratzker, Glenn Andrews. 1514
Krauch, Edgar William. 712
Kraus, Clyde Norman. 1120, 1467
Kraus, George. 1298, 2297
Kraus, Hans Joachim. 1163, 2902, 3855, 3856
Kraus, Henry. 752
Kraus, Oskar. 3312
Krause, Charles Henry. 2179
Krause, Fred. 2235, 2236
Krause, Victor Clarence. 2293
[Krause, William]. 286
Krauskopf, Joseph. 2103, 2109, 3371
Krauss, Paul H. 3733
Kraut, Benny. 7, 1534
Krauth, Charles Porterfield. 2286, 3034
Krautheimer, Richard. 78
Kravitz, David. 2658
Kravitz, Nathan. 525
Kraybill, Donald B. 1150, 2174, 2405
Kraybill, Paul N. 2403
Kreamer, George W. 3598
Krebs, Ebba Victoria. 2390
Krebs, Engelbert Gustav Hans. 2265
Krebs, Joseph Alois. 3406
Krebs, Joseph Aloysius. 1258, 2892
-Krebs, Stanley Le Fevre, 1864. 1388
Kreckel, Philip George. 812
Kreeft, Peter. 1417, 1794, 1795
Krehbiel, Christian. 1593
Krehbiel, Daniel Edward. 966
Krehbiel, Edward Benjamin. 1912
Krehbiel, Henry Edward. 917, 2740
Krehbiel, Henry Peter. 2404, 3793
Kreidel, George A. 662
Kreider, Alan. 882
Kreider, Carl Jonas. 1006
Kreider, Harry Julius. 2291, 2700, 2755, 3734
Kreider, Robert S. 1704
Kreider, Roy. 2535
Kreipe, Christian Edzard. 2468

Kreischer, Louise. 211, 3527
Kreiser, B. Robert. 2476, 2773
Kremer, Michael Nicholas. 833
Kremer, Nicholas J. 3018
Kreml, Anne Lee. 1608
Kreml, Patricia Banta. 3031
Krentel. Mildred. 1401
Krentz, Edgar. 241, 287
Kresage, Elijah Everett. 3086
Kresh, Paul. 32

Kress, Robert. 2040, 3833
Kretzmann, Adalbert Raphael Alexander. 1298
Kretzmann, Karl. 1549
Kretzmann, Otto Paul. 1449, 2057, 2214, 2297, 3886, 3887
Kretzmann, Paul Edward. 283, 305, 348, 2031, 2211, 2293, 2482, 3117, 3152, 3443
Kretzmann, Reinhard. 2214
Kretzschmar, Karl. 966, 3677
Kreusch, Edmund. 1332, 1636
Kreyche, Robert J. 1440, 2418, 2673
Kreye, Eric. 1366
Kriebel, Oscar Schultz. 1359, 2819
Krieg, Carl E. 3663
Krikorian, Meshach Paul. 588, 3319
Krikorian, Rebecca K. 2186
Krikorian, Yervant Hovhannes. 2675
Krimsky, Joseph Hayyim. 3078
Kring, Donald Walter. 3723, 3725
Kring, James Arthur. 1238, 1584
Kring, Walter Donald. 3061
Krinsky, Fred. 1150
Kripke, Dorothy (Karp) 1615, 1734, 2151
Krishnamurti, J. 3689
Krishnamurti, Jiddu. 1538, 1324, 1536, 1538, 1812, 2187, 2390, 3685, 3686, 3689
Krishnamurti, Jiddy. 1324
Krishnananda, Rishi. 3865
Krishnaswami, Arcot. 3192
Kriss, Marika. 2416
Kristeller, Paul Oskar. 2330, 1286, 2330
Kristos, Kyle. 3787
Krisztinkovich, Maria. 36
Kritzeck, James. 1084, 1820, 1923, 1926, 2566, 2846, 3895
Kriyananda. 2187, 3330
Kriyananda, Swami. 3475
Krock, George L. 2510
Krodel, Gerhard. 331
Kroeber, Alfred Louis. 2165
Kroeker, Nettie. 3815
Kroening, Gottlieb. 2001
Krogh-Tonning, Knud Karl. 1060, 1266
Krol, John Joseph. 759, 793, 3450
Kroll, Harry Harrison. 3803
Kroll, Robert C. 3506
Kroll, Una. 3708
Kroll, Woodrow Michael. 2902, 3234
Kromminga, Diedrich Hinrich. 1024, 1176, 2466
Kromminga, Diedrich Hinrich. 2465
Kromminga, John H. 1024, 1188, 3829, 3850
[Kron, Nils Erik]. 2293
Kroner, Richard. 1394, 1593, 1596, 1740, 3102, 3353, 3651, 3654
Kronkel, Wilbur. 1866
Kropf, Richard W. 241, 2010
Krosnicki, Thomas A. 2865
Kroth, Jerome A. 3426
Krottjer, Ardath Gertrude. 629
Krouse, F. Michael. 2468, 2472
Krshnadasa Kaviraja, b. 1518 or 19. 879
Krueger, Arthur F. 3271
Kruener, Harry H. 3758
Kruer, A. C. 214
Kruger, Gustav. 1019
Kruijf, Th C. 3390
Kruithof, Bastian. 1074
Krull, Vigilius Herman. 1034, 2355, 2415, 3322
Krum, Nathaniel. 1120, 2245, 3386
Krumbholz, Clarence E. 1139
Krumbine, Miles Henry. 185, 966, 2300, 3353, 3364, 3763
Krumm, John McGill. 1804, 2957, 3411
Krummacher, Friedrich Adolf. 1369
Krummacher, Friedrich Wilhelm. 1506, 2029, 2031, 2052
Krump, John. 3890
Krumreig, Edward Ludwig. 164
Krumwiede, Walter. 2020
Krupp, Nate. 1514, 1554
Kruppa, Patricia Stallings. 146, 3523
Kruse, Robert J. 3829
Krutza, Vilma. 2347
Krutza, William J. 413, 639, 966, 985, 1154, 2402, 3887
Krutzky, Paul G. 2561
Krutzky, Paul Gustave. 3374
Krzesinski, Andrew John. 1394, 2520
Krzesinski, Andrzej J. 1394

Ku tsun su yu lu. English. 3893
Kubelbeck, William John. 852
Kubler, George. 1161, 1532
Kubler, George Alexander. 1161
Kubo, Sakae. 270, 316, 2160, 2391, 3260, 3382, 3391
Kubose, Gyomay M. 2182
Kucas, Antanas. 3464
Kucharek, Casimir. 842, 948, 1314, 2236
[Kuegele, Frederick]. 3130, 3342
Kuegele, Frederick. 1328, 2300, 3353
Kuehnel, Reynold. 1826, 2344, 688
Kuehnert, Theodore. 3179
Kuenen, Abraham. 3117
Kuenning, Larry. 234, 1074
Kuenzli, B.E. 3142
Kugel, James L. 579, 1798
Kugler, John Backer. 2916
Kugler, John J. 847
Kuhar, Aloysius L. 2546
Kuhl, Curt. 505, 2950
Kuhlman, John Henry. 1111, 1113
Kuhlman, Kathryn. 1575, 1601, 2187, 2391
Kuhlmann, Edward. 966, 904, 966, 1315, 1449, 2214, 2274, 2282, 2886
Kuhlmann, John Henry. 2450
Kuhn, Alvin Boyd. 671, 1192, 2008, 3109, 3686
Kuhn, Anna. 662, 683, 723, 3460
Kuhn, Barbara. 2202
Kuhn, Clyde L. 1952
Kuhn, Clyde Leslie. 3443
Kuhn, Harold B. 89, 1723
Kuhn, Isobel. 2538, 2553, 2559, 3130
Kuhn, James W. 1075
Kuhn, Julius. 2675
Kuhn, Margaret E. 1060, 1075, 1170
Kuhn, May Cole. 1401, 2128
Kuhn, Roger P. 2366
Kuhn, William Frederick. 1662
Kuhne, Gary W. 985, 1567
Kuhnel, Ernst. 86, 87
Kuhnelt-Leddihn, Erik Maria, 1909. 1102
Kuhner, Hans. 2769
Kuhnhold, Christa. 2170, 3716
Kuhnmuench, Otto James. 1023
Kuhns, Benjamin. 3048
Kuhns, Dennis R. 3832
Kuhns, Frederick Irving. 3698
Kuhns, Levi Oscar. 1857, 2418
Kuhns, William. 676, 1074
Kuiper, Barend Klaas. 727, 1184, 2275
Kuiper, Barend Klass. 1184
Kuiper, Henry J. 3411, 75, 1315, 2249, 3267
Kuiper, Herman. 3289
Kuiper, Rienk Bouke. 105, 176, 1023, 1120, 1567
Kuipers, Cornelius. 1166
Kuist, Howard Tillman. 2798, 304
Kuitert, Harminus Martinus. 234, 244, 1105, 3622
Kuizenga, John E. 2089, 2093
Kukai, 774-835. 3403
Kukkonen, Walter J. 2286
Kulamer, John. 2227
Kulandran, Sabapathy. 1752, 2910
Kulischer, Eugene Michel. 2089
Kulke, Hermann. 1426
Kulow, Nelle Wahler. 3839
Kulp, George Brubaker. 1952
Kulp, Mary Ann Moyer. 2187, 2542
Kumarappa, Bharatan [Name orig.: Benjamin Ebenezer Cornelius]. 1732
Kumm, Hermann Karl Wilhelm. 2497, 2552
Kummel, Sara B. 1532
Kummel, Werner Georg. 351, 410, 476, 2064, 2326
Kumulipo (Hawaiian chant) 1371
Kumulipo (Hawaiian chant). English. 1371
Kumulipo (Hawaiian chant). English and Hawaiian. 1371
Kundakunda. 1932
Kundakunda, Acharva. 1932
Kundakunda, Acharya. 1932
Kundakunda, Acharya. 1932
Kundakunda, Acharya. 1932
Kung, Andres. 2625, 2736
Kung, Hans. 811, 64, 176, 776, 781, 788, 793, 835, 859, 1041, 1120, 1245, 1491, 1673, 1723, 2161, 2188, 2223, 2786, 3012, 3107, 3487, 3622, 3633, 3651, 3652, 3770, 3771
Kunhardt, Dorothy. 2005
Kunkel, Fritz. 440
Kunkel, Paul Aloysius. 3607
Kunneth, Walter. 2052
Kuns, Marian L. 1120
Kuntz, Arnold G. 2214
Kuntz, John Kenneth. 540, 3682
Kuntz, Kenneth A. 2391, 2480, 3529
Kunz, Fritz. 3686
Kunz, Marilyn. 431
Kunze, Johannes. 73
Kunzmann, Jacob Christoph. 1554
Kupfer, Carl Frederick. 913
Kupfer, Fern. 616
Kupferle, Mary L. 2247, 2874

Kupky, Oskar. 2998
Kuppers, Leonhard. 1642, 1706, 2311, 2358
Kurfees, Marshall Clement. 3374
Kurland, Philip B. 1150
Kurland, Samuel. 3897
Kurth, Burton O. 1518, 2471
Kurth, Erwin. 1328, 2279
Kurth, Erwin [William Emil]. 2214
Kurth, Godefroid Joseph Francois. 1176, 677
Kurth, Hanns. 3506
Kurtscheid, Bertrand. 1327
Kurtz, Daniel Webster. 1100
Kurtz, Edward Cuyler. 606, 3027
Kurtz, George Hackett. 1050
Kurtz, H. 3047
Kurtz, Johann Heinrich. 204, 211, 534, 1176, 3289, 3290
Kurtz, John W. 2720
Kurtz, Paul W. 1418
Kurtz, Robert Merrill. 3663
Kurz, Albert L. 1351
Kurzweg, B F. 1005
Kuselewitz, David. 3310
Kuselewitz, Samuel. 562
Kushner, Harold S. 1623, 1723, 1733, 2188, 3610
Kushner, Lawrence. 2151
Kuske, Martin. 505, 676
Kuskin, Karla. 2712
Kuthumi, 19th cent. 117
Kutscher, Austin H. 1353
Kutz, LeRoy. 27
Kutzik, Alfred J. 3454
Kuykendall, Eleanor. 2843
Kuykendall, John W. 2547
Kuyper, Abraham. 454, 730, 966, 1201, 1608, 1698, 1747, 1830, 2033, 2391, 3406, 3669, 3839, 966
Kuyper, Lester Jacob. 451, 1377
Kuyvenhoven, Andrew. 1431
Kuzma, Kay. 938
Kuzniewski, Anthony J. 876
Kuzunishi, Sosei. 2575
Kvamme, Rodney A. 2214, 2300
*Kvande, Carol. 2287
Kvarne, Per. 743
Kwast, Lloyd Emerson. 145
Kybal, Vlastimil. 1642
Kyes, David Henry. 270, 1486
Kyger, John Charles Fremont. 1567
Kyker, Rex P. 1273, 3354
Kyle, Evelyn. 234
Kyle, Louisa Venable. 2304
Kyle, Melvin Grove. 295, 486, 515, 563, 565, 2188, 3594
Kynett, Alpha Jefferson. 1490
Kyriazis, Zaharias J. 1050
Kysar, Robert. 420, 421, 2209

L

La Luzerne, Cesar Guillaume de, 1738-1821. 2033
Labaree, Clara Gray. 897
La Barre, Weston. 2827
La Barre, Weston, 1911. 173, 2827, 3061, 3376
La Barre, Weston. 2827
Labat, Elisabeth Paule. 1737
Labbe, Dolores Egger. 822, 1132, 1133
La Berte, Paul A. 3271
Laberthonniere, L. 805
Labin, Suzanne. 1320
LaBotz, Paul. 594
La Bouillerie, Francois Alexandre Roullet de. 2391
Laboure, Theodore. 2341
Labriolle, Pierre Champagne de. 29, 1018, 1020, 2586
Labuhna bar Sennak. 1018
Lacarriere, Jacques. 2578
Lace, O. Jessie. 473, 537, 595, 2147
Lacey, Thomas Alexander. 1041, 2675, 3039
Lacey, Thomas James. 1943, 2744
LaChapelle, Dolores. 2726, 3186, 3480
La Chevasnerie, Rene de. 2391
Lachs, John. 1457, 2352
Lachs, Samuel Tobias. 2147
Lack, Ernest A. 1440
Lackey, Cleatice (Ingold) 1908
Lackey, James Vernon. 3175
Lackey, Margaret McRae. 3467
Lackington, James. 681
Lackmann, Max. 109
Lackner, Bede K. 1277
Lacko, Michael. 766, 3258
Lacks, Roslyn. 3837
Lacocque, Andre. 506, 552, 1505
LaCorbiniere, Clementine (Le Fer de la Motte) de. 3274
Lacordaire, Jean Baptiste Henri Dominique de. 756

LaCoste, Edward. 966
Lacroix, Jean. 100
Lactantius, Lucius Caecilius Firmianus. 69, 3635
[Lacunza, Manuel]. 52
Lacy, Benjamin Rice. 3230
Lacy, Creighton. 31, 2433, 2515, 2713
Lacy, Donald Charles. 413, 2436, 3354
Lacy, J H. 1120
Lacy, John. 1673
Lacy, Mary Lou. 2265, 3529, 3844
Lacy, Walter Nind. 2430
Ladd, Charles Frederic. 390
Ladd, George Eldon. 2174, 331, 348, 454, 476, 1528, 2052, 2174, 3221, 3319
Ladd, George Trumbull. 185, 234, 2180, 3102
Ladd, James Earl. 1466
Ladd, Parish B. 3717
Ladd, Paul R. 3072
Ladd, Percy C. 2568
Ladd, William Palmer. 2969
Ladell, Arthur Randolph. 179
Ladies' Christian commission, Buffalo. 712
Ladies' home society of the Baptist churches in the city of New York. 169
Ladies' united aid society of the Methodist Episcopal church, in the city of Philadelphia. 2453
Ladner, Gerhart Burian. 3658
LaDouceur, Emile. 726, 3286
Ladriere, Jean. 3070
[La Due, Francia A. 2726, 2727
La Due, John. 966
Lady Sheba. 3824
Laemmlen, Ann. 2598
Laetsch, Theodore Ferdinand Karl. 546, 559, 3652
Laeuchli, Samuel. 735, 1195, 1372, 2196, 2560
Lafarge, John. 3017
La Farge, John. 18, 759, 774, 1845, 1945, 1948, 3017
Lafargue, Paul. 525, 1723, 3462
LaFavre, Robert E. 164
Laferriere, M. 2366
Lafferty, John James. 2455
Lafferty, John Parks. 2064
Lafferty, Theodore Thomas. 2420
Laffineur, M. 3298
La Fontaine, Rachel Adelaide. 2126, 2271, 2361
Laforet, Nicolas Joseph. 1099
Laforgue, Jules. 2594
Lagerkvist, Par. 3200
Lagerlof, Selma Ottiliana Lovisa. 910, 2207
Lago, Mary M. 1139
Lagorio, Valerie Marie. 2644
Lagrange, Marie Joseph. 2978, 3215
Laguerre, Michel S. 3787
LaHaye, Beverly. 3834, 3835
LaHaye, Tim F. 64, 454, 639, 985, 993, 1514, 1609, 2338, 2781, 3391
Lahey, Francis J. 831
Lahey, Thomas Aquinas. 3284
Lai, Bessie C. 3587, 3846
Lai, Chaman. 3204
Lai, Gaetano de. 2029
Laible, Wilhelm. 73
Laidlaw, James S. 1737
Laidlaw, John. 2017
Laidlaw, John R. 667, 765
Laidlaw, Robert A. 64
Lain Entralgo, Pedro. 1892
Laing, Gordon Jennings. 3246
Lair, Loren E. 1461, 1463
Laird, Harold Samuel. 1986
Laird, John. 3608, 3462, 3608
Laird, Margaret. 1034
Laird, Margaret Nicholl. 2191, 2507
Laird, Michael Andrew. 1246
Laistner, Max Ludwig Wolfram. 1192
Lajpat Rai, Lala, 1865. 89
Lajpat Rai, Lala, 1865-1928. 89
Lake, Alexander. 2874
Lake, Benjamin J. 2925
Lake, George G. 869
Lake, Gerard. 1967
Lake, Kirsopp. 102, 315, 410, 1050, 1192, 1888, 2052, 2798
Lake, Peter. 1221, 3009
Lakey, Othal Hawthorne. 1021
Laliberte, Norman. 1388
Lalla, 14th cent. 3422
Lallemant, Louis. 3487
Lallou, William J. 2366
Lallou, William Joseph. 2370
Lally, Francis J. 827
Lally, Frank Edward. 6
Lalone, Emerson Hugh. 3454
Lam, Nora. 1576, 2193
Lama, Fredrich. 2685, 3531
Lama, Friedrich. 2685, 3532
LaMance, Lora Sarah (Nichols) 1967
Lamar, James Sanford. 287, 1527

Lamartine, Alphonse Marie Louis de. 101
Lamask, Milton. 742
Lamb, Alexander. 3832
Lamb, Alexander Mackenzie. 3211
Lamb, Clyde Kern. 1060
Lamb, David Smith. 3456
Lamb, Elizabeth Searle. 1440
Lamb, Francis Jones. 2477
Lamb, George R. 3130
Lamb, George Robert. 2710, 3130
Lamb, Harold Albert. 1390
Lamb, James Riley. 639, 800
Lamb, John Alexander. 584
Lamb, Martin Thomas. 894, 2611, 678, 1567
Lamb, Philip J. 295
Lambdin, Ina (Smith) 141, 3152
Lambdin, Jerry Elmer. 140, 141, 142, 164
Lambdin, Thomas Oden. 1797
Lambek, Michael. 1321
Lambert, Albert Robert. 199
Lambert, Aloysius Albert. 3374
Lambert, Bernard. 3061
Lambert, Bernard J. 173
Lambert, Byron Cecil. 2941
Lambert, Helen Churchill (Smith) 2989
Lambert, Herbert H. 311
Lambert, J Cameron. 2695
Lambert, J R. 3462
Lambert, James Franklin. 2275, 2289
Lambert, John C. 2543
Lambert, John Chisholm. 2493
Lambert, John Christopher. 2497
Lambert, Lance. 610, 1928
Lambert, Louis Aloisius. 1907
Lambert, Malcolm. 1805
Lambert, Norman M. 1199
Lambert, Orlando Clayton. 800, 1940
Lambert, Robert Stanley. 1328
Lamberton, Clark Diven. 420
Lamberton, Helen C. 3506
Lamberts, Lambertus J. 1853
Lambertson, Floyd Wesley. 3183, 3369
Lambertville, N. J. Presbyterian church. 1692, 3536
Lamberty, Manetta. 2360
Lambeth conference, 1920. 2194
Lambeth conference, 1930. 3443
Lambeth Conference 1958. 666
Lambeth Palace. Library. 1242, 2245, 3598
Lambie, Thomas Alexander. 208, 1120, 2020, 2517, 2539, 2552, 208
Lambing, Andrew Arnold. 2338, 1830, 1834, 1835, 2850, 3262
Lamborn, Edmund Arnold Greening. 1159
Lambourne, Alfred. 1388
Lambrecht, Jan. 2025
Lambros, Spyridon P. 2330
Lambuth, Walter Russell. 1050, 2539
Lamirande, Emilien. 1318
Lamm, Maurice. 2139, 2627
Lamm, Norman. 1539, 2751
Lamm, William Robert. 3480
Lammens, Henri. 1921
Lammerts, Walter Edward. 1383
Lamont, Corliss. 1694, 1854, 1889
Lamont, Thomas Johnston. 3290
Lamont, William M. 179, 2466
Lamoreaux, Antoinette Abernethy. 1246, 3152
Lamott, John Henry. 1176
La Mott, Robert L. 1086
Lamott, Willis. 2493, 2534, 2550
LaMotte, Louis Cossitte. 1311
LaMotte, Mary Wilfred. 1630
Lamoureux, Richard E. 22, 2329
Lampe, Geoffrey William Hugo. 138, 313, 1729, 2046, 2052
Lampert, Richard D. 3745
Lamping, A. J. 2862, 3776
Lamping, Severin. 1364
Lampkin, Richard Henry. 1168
Lampkin, William. 908, 2391
Lamprecht, Sterling Power. 2115
Lampton, Edward W. 14
Lamsa, George Mamishisho. 314, 331, 344, 348, 390, 497, 1967, 2064, 3335
Lamson, David Rich. 3396
Lamson, Edna Emma. 2911
Lancashire, A. 2362
Lancaster, George Harold. 567
Lancaster, John. 1248
Lancaster, Kenneth R. 966
Lancaster, Pa. Saint James' church. 1176
Lancaster, Pa. Theological seminary of the Reformed church in the United States. 2195, 3332
Lancaster, Pa. Theological Seminary of the United Church of Christ. 3731
Lancaster, Richard Venable. 1385
Lancaster, Robert Alexander. 3781
Lancaster, Vincentine. 3524
Lance, Derek. 3462
Lance, H. Darrell. 78, 486
Lance, Marion T. 3751

Lanciani, Rodolfo Amedeo. 3245
Lanczkowski, Gunter. 3268
Land, Elizabeth. 1269
Land, Philip S. 3434
Land, Sipke van der. 622
Landaker, Genevieve. 206, 3506, 3507
Landau, Rom. 3130
Landau, Sol. 2081, 2195, 3361
Landay, Jerry M. 1405, 2760
Landeen, William M. 2281
Lander, Richard N. 83
Landero, Victor. 1575, 2195
Landers, Caleb Marshall. 1655
Landers, Lucille. 2718
Landers, Ruth. 2680
Landes, George M. 1797
Landes, Ruth. 915
Landesman, Alter F. 2086
Landini, Lawrence C. 1646
Landis, Abb. 1776
Landis, Benson Young. 311, 827, 1252, 1287, 1375, 3117, 3325, 3329, 3443, 3703, 3740
Landis, Ira David. 1528
Landis, John. 1866, 2048
Landis, Josiah P. 3712
Landis, Paul Henry. 3880
Landis, Robert Wharton. 1821, 3414, 195, 1892, 2048, 3712
Landman, Eva. 2172
Landman, Isaac. 639, 2078, 2950
Landman, Leo. 737
Landon, Donald D. 3216, 3218
Landon, Harold R. 2709, 3264
Landon, Kenneth Perry. 2318
Landorf, Joyce. 985, 1166, 1414, 2195, 2338, 2391, 3835, 3844
Landrum, Eli. 1440
Landrum, L M. 3783
Landsberg, Moses Gercon. 2102
Landsberg, Paul Ludwig. 1414
Landstrom, Elsie H. 2874
Landwehr, Arthur J. 1154
Landwehr, Esther Anna. 2247
Lane, Anne (Wintermute) 3507
Lane, Byron S. 225
Lane, Carlie. 3243
Lane, Charles Arthur. 1759
Lane, Charles Martin. 3507
Lane, Christel. 3453
Lane, Dermot A. 1586, 2040
Lane, George. 893
Lane, Henry Higgins. 1580
Lane, Isaac. 2195
Lane, John Irving. 838
[Lane, Margaret]. 3145
Lane, Mark. 2817
Lane, Myrie (Anderson) 3468
Lane, Ortha May. 2510
Lane, Raymond A. 721
Lane, Sands Harvey. 3379
Lane theological seminary, Cincinnati. 3614
Lane, Thomas Clifford. 2067, 2771
Lane, William Coolidge. 1402, 3653
Lane-Poole, Stanley. 1922, 1944, 3286
Laney, J. Carl. 590
Lang, Andrew. 1631, 1709, 2181, 2195, 2652, 2663, 2989, 3093, 3109
Lang, Celestia Root. 2695
Lang, Celestia (Root) 1580
Lang, Cosmo Gordon. 2017, 2025
Lang, Cosmo Jordon. 2017
Lang, David. 985
Lang, David Marshall. 3283
Lang, Edward M. 89
Lang, Elfrieda Wilhelmina Henrietta. 2626
Lang, George Henry. 601, 507
Lang, Jane. 2244, 3860
Lang, John Dunmore. 2195
Lang, Leonora Blanche. 3280
Lang, Mabel L. 11, 1369
Lang, Martin A. 3628
Lang, Milton Charles. 2539
Lang, Paul H. D. 17, 27, 318, 2295
Langan, Tom. 667, 2685
Langdale, John William. 3444
Langdon, Addison L. 3354
Langdon, Samuel. 459
Langdon, Stephen Herbert. 93, 1878, 2667, 94, 2667
Langdon, William Chauncy. 2758
Lange, Ernst. 1315, 1492, 3850
Lange, Federico. 540
Lange, Johann Peter. 223, 412, 416, 433, 440, 454, 468, 516, 521, 560
Lange, Joseph. 999
Lange, Maurice de. 1074
Lange, Reinhold. 1958
Langenskjold, Margareta. 2708
Langenstein, Rupert. 105, 999
Langenwalter, Jacob Hermann. 1120, 36, 688
Langer, Mordecai Georgo. 3580
Langer, Thomas E. 2343
Langevin, Gene. 1261
Langevin, Jean Marie. 2391

Langford, Alec J. 2391
Langford, Jerome J. 1701, 3084
Langford, Norman F. 3731, 64, 1176, 1982
Langford, Thomas A. 1007, 3656
Langford-James, Richard Lloyd. 2745
Langguth, A. J. 3722
Langham Carter, R. R. 3278
Langhorne, John. 2902
Langland, William. 2012
Langley, Charles K. 3458
Langley, Florence. 3818
Langley, Harold D. 3798
Langley, Noel. 876, 3053
Langlois-Berthelot, Jean Marc. 1649
Langmack, Holger Christian. 3078, 3082
Langmore, Diane. 880
Lango, John W. 2738, 3813
Langone, John. 1417
Langridge, Albert Kent. 2792
Langsdale, Richard M. 2005
Langstaff, John Brett. 295
Langton, Edward. 1428, 1528
Langton, Edward [Frederick Edward Palmer Langton]. 2594
Lanier, Jesse Alvin. 1421
Lanier, John Jabez. 1120, 2874, 3061, 1060, 1120
Lankard, Frank Glenn. 234, 3211, 3561
Lankenau, F. J. 2296
Lankenau, Francis James. 2258, 2722
Lankford, John Anderson. 1158
Lankler, Ralph Conover. 908, 910
Lankvatara-sutra. 711
Lannie, Vincent P. 823, 1851
Lannoy, Richard. 3316
LaNoue, George R. 1142
Lansdail, Henry. 3702
Lansdell, Henry. 3702
Lansing, Dirck Cornelius. 2932
Lansing, Gulian. 2517
Lansing, Ill. First Reformed Church. 1243
Lansing, Isaac J. 800
Lansing, John A. 307
Lanslots, Don Ildephonse. 132, 735, 772, 1192, 3782
Lanslots, Don Ildephonse. 2577
Lansman, Quentin Charles. 1550
*Lanterman, Wilmer D. 3292
Lanternari, Vittorio. 2672
Lantero, Erminie Huntress. 3834
Lantry, Eileen E. 2676, 3812
Lantry, Kimber J. 77, 1021, 2172, 3385
Lantz, John Edward. 613
Lanyon, Walter Clemow. 1927, 2695, 3200
Lanza, Antonio. 948
Lanza del Vasto, Joseph Jean, 1901. 2391
Lanzi. 3270
Lao-tzu. 2196, 2197, 3130, 3586, 2196, 2197, 2199, 2838, 3586, 3587, 2196
Lapati, Americo D. 697, 2703
Lape, Thomas. 105
La Perchia, Alexander. 1314
Lapide, Cornelius A. 2798
Lapide, Phinn E. 860, 2014, 2152, 2952
Lapierre, Eugene. 884
Laplace, Jean. 3475, 2781
Laplace, L. 1403, 2334
Laplante, Mary Cosma. 845, 2369
LaPlante, Mary Cosma. 905
Lapointe, Francois. 2171
Lapomarda, Vincent A. 1949
Laporte, Jean. 3836
La Porte, William Ralph. 687
La Potterie, Ignace de. 1830
Lapp, John Allen. 2403, 2406
Lapp, Paul W. 78, 208, 1817
Lapp, Rhoda Snadeo. 1449
Lappin, Peter. 683, 875, 1028, 2316, 3297
Lappin, Samuel Strahl. 1201, 1462, 2258, 3165, 3374
Lapple, Alfred. 526
Lapple, Alfred Karl. 526
Lapponi, Giusepee. 3507
Lapsanski, Duane V. 1648
Lapsley, James N. 3290
Lapsley, R A. 1823
Lapsley, Robert Alberti. 493, 2527
Lapthorne, Lu James. 1381
Laqueur, Thomas Walter. 3560
Laracy, Hugh M. 850, 2546
Laramie, Edward. 893
Larcom, Lucy. 1324, 1449, 2633, 3200
Lard, Moses E. 1461, 2072
Laredo, Bernardino de. 2639
Large, James. 2020
Large, Johann Peter. 441
Large, John Ellis. 1060, 1599, 2788
Largo, Gerald A. 809, 2235
Larimer, Loyal Herbert. 1266
Larionov, Leonid Fedorovich. 1952
Larkey, Mabel A. 1952, 2636
Larkin, Clarence. 459, 1723, 2055, 3507, 507
Larkin, Edgar Lucien. 3462
Larkin, Emmet J. 819, 820, 1147

Larkin, Francis. 1379, 3269, 3270
Larned, Albert Cecil. 584, 2960
Larned, Augusta. 2663, 2666
Larned, Charles William. 2071
Larned, Josephus Nelson. 1324
[Larned Charles William]. 2071
La Rochefoucauld, Francois, vi. 2375
Larochelle, Stanislas. 2377
La Rocque, Joseph. 2391
La Roe, Wilbur. 1120, 2924
Laros, Matthias. 1328
Larose, Paul F. 3858
Larrabee, Edward Allan. 1541, 1747, 2391
Larrabee, William Clark. 2453, 3803
Larrimer, Mary. 2798
Larrison, C. Owen. 3354
Larry, John Hale. 2048
Larsen, Bernhard. 3102
Larsen, Beverly. 2021, 3258
Larsen, Caroline Dorothea (Jensen) 3130
Larsen, Dean L. 2599
Larsen, Earnest. 939, 999, 1324, 1823, 2040, 2235, 2263, 2391, 3181, 3887
Larsen, Herman Astrup. 2033
Larsen, Jens Peter. 1783
Larsen, Jens Peter Mouritz. 3781
Larsen, John. 2611
Larsen, Lewis H. 1324
Larsen, Ludwig B. 199, 3821
Larsen, Norma Clark. 1009
Larsen, Paul E. 573, 3354
Larsen, Stephen. 2648
Larsen, Vernon Fred. 3537
Larson, Andrew Karl. 3432
Larson, Bob. 1424, 1428, 1816, 3072, 3887
Larson, Bruce. 1011, 1060, 1440, 2932, 3354
Larson, Christian Daa. 1034, 1533, 1835, 2695, 3095, 3848
Larson, Doris Linell. 3883
Larson, Douglas J. 1384, 1698, 2054
Larson, Gustive Olof. 2615, 3762
Larson, J Edor. 110
Larson, James Henry. 1967
Larson, Jeanne R. 1366, 3883
Larson, Martin Alfred. 1102, 1242, 1410, 1532, 1976
Larson, Melvin Gunnard. 121, 2129, 2402, 2484, 3881
Larson, Mildred. 653
Larson, Muriel. 902, 966, 1381, 1443, 2136, 2197, 3842
Larson, Nicholas Christian. 1034
Larson, Orvin Prentiss. 1907
Larson, Philip M. 1199
Larsson, Flora. 2892
Larsson, Raymond Ellsworth. 2892
Larue, Gerald A. 540, 2652
La Rue, William Earl. 2603
La Salle, Jean Baptiste de. 695, 1264, 1498
Lasance, F[rancis] X[avier]. 54
Lasance, Francis Xavier. 854, 1536, 2885, 2892, 3270, 1498, 788, 838, 854, 857, 1440, 1449, 1456, 1714, 2172, 2355, 2391, 2792, 2809, 2884, 2885, 2892, 3006, 3263, 3870, 2362
Lasar, Theodore. 2261
Lascaris, Andrew. 1723
*Lash, Nicholas. 329, 1043, 1473, 2254, 2703, 3622
Lash, William Quinlan. 1741
Lasher, G[eorge] W[illiam]. 3678
Lasker, Bruno. 2105, 2671
Lasker, Daniel J. 1093
Laski, Harold Joseph. 1281
Lasky, William. 1359, 2197
La Sor, William Sanford. 215, 297, 329, 338, 493, 540, 1410, 1411, 1770, 3377
Lassalle, Hugo. 2383, 3892
Lasserre, Jean. 3794
Lassiter, Lelia Boring. 2391
Lassiter, Perry. 2822
Lassus, Jean. 85
Lasswell, William P. 1034
Lastinger, Clayton. 199
Lastinger, Eula Tucker. 1688, 1689
Lasuen, Fermin Francisco de. 726
La Taille, Maurice de. 2040, 2254
Latch, Edward Biddle. 516, 523
Latchaw, Daniel S. 3507
Latchaw, John Roland Harris. 459
Latham, Daisy Lee Carson. 195
[Latham, Henry Jepson]. 2603
Latham, Judy. 3841
Latham, Lenn Lerner. 966
Latham, Robert O. 2241
Latham, S. R. 1774
Lathbury, Clarence. 180, 2690, 2227, 2690
Lathbury, Mary A. 1807, 3534
Lathbury, Mary Artemisia. 629
Lathe, Herbert William. 908
Lathem, Abraham Lance. 329, 639, 990
Lather, A. E. 3833
Lathrop, Elise L. 1271

Lathrop, George Parsons. 1650, 3797
Lathrop, John Howland. 3725
Lathrop, John, jr. 26
Lathrop, Joseph. 135, 365, 1341
[Lathrop, Mary A. 1982
Lathrop, Noah. 2166
Latimer, Elizabeth (Wormeley) 2091
Latimer, George Dimmick. 2040
Latimer, Hugh. 1226, 1227, 3364
Latimer, Robert Sloan. 3256
Latimer-Needham, Cecil Hugh, 1900-1975. 1092, 2050
Latin American Mission. 1574
Latorre Cabal, Hugo. 821
Latourelle, Rene. 390, 2008, 3227, 3616, 2040, 3225
Latourett, Kenneth Scott. 1176
Latourette, Jane. 2260, 2712
*Latourette, Jane R. 2772
Latourette, Kenneth Scott. 400, 702, 1041, 1060, 1100, 1120, 1176, 1182, 1187, 2493, 2510, 2520, 3862, 3871, 817, 1126, 1176, 1182, 1542, 2483, 2746, 2954
La Trobe-Bateman, William Fairbairn. 3130
Latta, James. 2984, 2985
Lattey, Cuthbert. 321, 376, 2040
Lattimore, Richmond Alexander. 1525
Latukefu, Sione. 1152, 2433
Lau, Franz. 2275
*Laubach, Eugene E. 648, 1723, 3858
Laubach, Frank Charles. 966, 1431, 1967, 2517, 2520, 2545, 2637, 2639, 2830, 2874, 3529, 2517, 2874
Laud, William. 1217, 1218, 3630
Lauder, Robert E. 772, 1845, 2199, 2244, 2939
Lauderdale, Beverly. 931
Laudynowa, Stefanja. 2102
Laudynowa, Stefanja. 2102
Lauer, Jean Philippe. 3285
Lauer, Paul Erasmus. 1148
Lauer, Quentin. 1732, 1800
Lauerman, Lucian Leo. 857
Lauf, Detlef Ingo. 88, 3585
Laufer, Calvin Weiss. 1952, 3130, 1872, 639, 3562
Lauferty, Lilian. 966
Laughlin, Charles Parsons. 1558
Laughlin, George G. 1567
Laughlin, Sceva Bright. 1138, 1676
[Laughlin, William J]. 1735
Laun, F. 788
Launay, Louis de. 1095
[Launder, Charles Henry]. 253
Launt, Francis Albemarle Delbretson. 1931
Laur, Elred. 2247
Laurello, Bartholomew J. 1257
Laurence, Theodor. 75, 1428, 3539, 3588, 3589
Laurent, Bob. 985, 1567, 2200
Laurentin, Rene. 2355, 2362, 2816, 3449
Laures, John. 820, 836, 3580
Laurie, David James. 1567
Laurie, Greg. 1403
Laurie, Thomas. 1999, 2520, 2541, 2544
Laurin, Robert B. 540, 600
Laurin, Roy Leonard. 215, 321, 322, 324, 341, 422, 423, 448, 468, 3354, 416
Lauro, Joseph. 1109
Laury, Preston A. 2296, 2474
Lauster, Bobbie. 2200
Lautenschlager, Roy S. 2510
Lauterbach, Jacob Zallel. 25, 2013, 2120
Lauterbach, William Albert. 17, 1258
Lauterbach, William August. 2391, 3406
Lautherbach, William Albert. 11
Laux, John Joseph. 788, 803, 809, 311, 809, 1311, 3152, 3187
La Valle Poussin, Louis de. 702
Lavan, Spencer. 20, 1923, 3730
La Varende, Jean de. 3778
Le Vaseur, Henry Da. 1615
Lavater, Johann Caspar. 55
Lavaud, Benoit. 2570
Lavedan, Henri Leon Emile. 3779
Laveille, E. 1900, 3426
Lavelle, Elise. 2852
Lavelle, Louis. 1642, 1746, 2738, 3299
Lavelle, Louis Jean Jacques. 1746
Lavender, John Allan. 404, 405, 993, 1449, 2874
Lavender, Lucille. 171, 1288, 2200, 2391
Laver, James. 3803
LaVerdiere, Eugene. 331, 368, 473, 1434, 2789
La Vergne, Yvonne de. 3235
Laverty, Rose Maria. 3378
La Vey, Anton Szandor. 3304, 3824
LaVigne, Ruth H. 1292, 1310
Lavik, John Rasmus. 139, 277, 966, 3663
*Lavin, Pat Carey. 1982
Lavine, Sigmund A. 681, 1904

Law, Bimala Churn. 3475
Law, Donald. 96
Law, Edmund. 1930, 3102
Law, Helen Hull. 2662
Law, Howard W. 2554
Law, Lovick Pierce. 1558
Law, Marion. 3342, 3354
Law, Robert. 3200, 420
Law, Samuel Warren. 3342
Law, Thomas Graves. 772
Law, Virginia W. 1717, 2201, 2892
Law, William. 674, 966, 967, 991, 1288, 1449, 2327, 2639, 2874, 3484, 3606, 3630
Lawler, B. F. 164
Lawler, Brendan. 327
Lawler, Justus George. 759, 831, 1519
Lawler, Michael G. 3534
Lawler, Ronald David. 2126
Lawlor, George L. 180, 425, 2040, 3780
Lawlor, Hugh Jackson. 3041
Lawlor, John Irving. 2667
Lawlor, Monica Mary. 2323
Lawlor, Richard V. 794, 949
Lawrence, Bennett Freeman. 1596
Lawrence, Bruce B. 1897
Lawrence, Carl. 693, 1254
Lawrence, Chester Henry. 1762
Lawrence, Clifford Hugh. 1497, 1762
Lawrence county historical society, New Castle, Pa. 3301
Lawrence, D. H. 459
Lawrence, David Herbert. 459
Lawrence, Edgar D. 1257
Lawrence, Edward. 3507
Lawrence, Edward Alexander. 887, 1791, 2502, 2520
Lawrence, Egbert C[harles]. 1817
Lawrence, Emeric Anthony. 399, 788, 838, 846, 1267, 2210, 2977, 3487
Lawrence, Gene H. 1324
Lawrence, Harold Gaines. 3130
Lawrence, Ida (Eckert) 2809, 3507
Lawrence, Irene. 916, 1077
Lawrence, James. 3507
Lawrence, James Bolan. 34
Lawrence, John Benjamin. 164, 454, 639, 1388, 1558, 2550, 3377, 3465, 3466, 3467
Lawrence, John Jones. 1593
Lawrence, Joy E. 1208
Lawrence, L. A. 3507
Lawrence, Margaret Oliver (Woods) 1782, 2227
Lawrence, Marion. 3565, 3548, 3555, 3560, 3303
Lawrence, Peter. 3109
Lawrence, Roy. 2202, 3476
Lawrence, Una Roberts. 2460, 2516, 2527, 3467
Lawrence, Una (Roberts) 2488, 2510, 2516, 2588
Lawrence, William. 694, 750, 2202
Lawrence, William Appleton. 2788
Lawrence, William Irvin. 3153
Lawry, Jon Sherman. 2468
Laws, Romulus Don. 2329
Laws, Samuel Spahr. 2858, 3711
Laws, Sophie. 412
Lawson, A. C. 1449
Lawson, Agnes Rosina (McCarthy) 639
Lawson, Albert Gallatin. 3061, 1034
Lawson, Alfred William. 3142
Lawson, Charles T. 1208, 2594
Lawson, Deodat. 2372
Lawson, E. LeRoy. 697, 1003, 1120
Lawson, Elizabeth. 3878
Lawson, Ernest. 3142
Lawson, George. 572, 589
Lawson, Henry Martin. 1889
Lawson, James Gilchrist. 137, 219, 253, 1586, 1731, 1841, 1952, 2483, 2807, 3014, 135
Lawson, Jo. 734, 2202
Lawson, John. 76, 3645, 3660, 3663
Lawson, John Cuthbert. 1631
Lawson, LeRoy. 2017
Lawson, Lewis A. 2171
Lawson, Martha Knight. 2249
Lawson, Patricia. 298
Lawson, William. 999, 3095, 180, 999
Lawton, George. 3507
Lawton, John Stewart. 2477
[Lawton, Mary Emily]. 1407
Lawton, Stewart. 651
Lawyer, Zelma Wood. 2545
Laxenaire, J. 781, 1696
Lay, Benjamin. 3424
Lay, Henry Champlain. 2203, 2214
[Lay, Matthias]. 3877
Lay, Walter Edwin. 1781
Lay, Wilfrid. 3507
Laycock, George. 2773
Laycock, Samuel Ralph. 2781
Layfield, [Mary Eva (Dice)]. 1551
Layman, Emma McCloy. 710
Laymen's foreign missions inquiry. 2520

Laymen's foreign missions inquiry. Commission of appraisal. 2520
The Laymen's hour (Radio program) 3354
Laymen's Movement for a Christian World. 3849
Laymon, Charles M. 234, 459, 1953, 1967, 2064, 2247, 2440, 2908, 3191
Layne, Norman R. 1548, 3449
Layton, Christopher. 2203, 2603
Layton, Eunice S. 3686
Layton, Mac. 3529
Laz, Medard. 2892
Lazar, Elmer B. 2152, 3771
Lazar, Wendy. 1615
Lazare, Bernard. 2078
Lazareth, William Henry. 967, 2280, 2281, 3171, 3175
Lazaro de Aspurz. 1648
Lazaron, Morris S. 3117
Lazaron, Morris Samuel. 2105, 3117
Lazarus, Emma. 2112, 3458
Lazarus, Josephine. 2142
Lazarus, M. Edgeworth. 3898
Lazarus, Moritz. 1539
Lazarus, Nahida Ruth. 3842
Lazell, David. 3431
Lazell, Frederick John. 1921
[Lazelle, Henry Martyn]. 3076
Lazenby, Marion Elias. 2430
Lazerowitz, Morris. 2418
Le Sage, Wilfred, 1907. 999
Lea, Charles. 1514
Lea, Henry Charles. 1910, 3469, 779, 877, 878, 1176, 1327, 1908, 1909, 1910, 2598, 3469, 3824, 3826
Lea, John William. 105, 270, 3534
Lea, Leonard J. 2608
Leabel, Pius A. 3362, 3535
Leabo, John. 204, 606
Leach, Charles. 616
Leach, Edmund Ronald. 3110
[Leach, Eugene Walter]. 2450
Leach, George. 1599
Leach, Hilma J. 2544
Leach, Joan. 3168, 3174
Leach, Maria. 1381
Leach, Max. 2784
Leach, Robert J. 1678, 3835
Leach, William Herma. 1126
Leach, William Herman. 1199, 10, 1162, 1168, 1251, 1622, 1694, 1747, 2338, 2786, 3354, 3374, 3673
Leacock, Arthur Gordner. 2804
Leacock, Seth. 178
Leacroft, Helen. 1160
Leadbeater, Charles Webster. 2203, 879, 1283, 2187, 2203, 3263, 3686, 879, 1613, 3507, 3686, 3689
Leady, Walter Thomas. 894
Leaf, Horace. 3507
League of Catholic Slovenian Americans. 871
Leahy, J Kenneth. 720, 3487
Leahy, Maurice. 1364, 2668
Leahy, Walter Thomas. 823
Leake, William Samuel. 1034
Leaming, James. 2005
Leaming, Jeremiah. 1522, 1523, 3067, 3122, 3796, 3801
Lean, Florence (Marryat) Church. 3507
Leander, Norman. 3507
Leaney, Alfred Robert Clare. 428, 446
Learned, Ellin (Craven) 1364, 2412
Learned, Marion Dexter. 3790
Learner, Frank Doggett. 3699
Leary, John P. 805, 1945, 1948
Leary, Lewis Gaston. 303, 2977
Leary, Timothy Francis. 1781, 1782
Leary, William. 319, 2230
Leas, Speed. 1199, 2781
Lease, Gary. 1162
Leatherwood, Mattie C. 3555
Leaton, James. 2451
Leavell, Clarence Stanley. 3555
Leavell, Frank Hartwell. 141, 3537, 3829
Leavell, Landrum P. 42, 71, 164, 369, 381, 1836, 3354
Leavell, Landrum Pinson. 3548, 3555, 142, 3555
Leavell, Martha (Boone) 1609, 2040
Leavell, Roland Quinche. 2204, 967, 1558, 1567, 2204, 2798, 3467, 441, 1567, 2798, 2902
Leavell, Zachary Taylor. 156
Leavens, Robert French. 2892
Leaver, Robin A. 1874, 2161, 2281, 3820
Leavitt, Ashley Day. 967
Leavitt, Cyrus Franklin. 2409
Leavitt, Guy P. 940, 3179, 3550, 3555
Leavitt, John McDowell. 1099, 1593
[Leavitt, Percy Metcalf] 1863. 3754
Le Bar, Lois Emogene. 1605, 3153, 3171
Le Bar, Mary E. 3174
LeBar, Mary Evelyn. 185, 904, 3174
Le Bar, Mary Evelyn. 3858
Lebbe, Bede. 2366
Le Beau, Mary. 3507

Leber, Charles Tudor. 1060, 2493, 2954, 3852
Leberman, Josephine Marie. 3153
Lebeson, Anita (Libman) 2105, 2106, 3842
Lebeurier, Pierre Francois. 3275
LeBlanc, Etienne. 3883
LeBlanc, Mary Francis. 2357
Lebon, Henri. 75, 2391
Lebowitz, Regina. 1476, 3210
Lebra, William P. 2735
Le Bras, Gabriel. 817, 2979
Lebret, Leuis Jeseph. 1347
Lebret, Louis Joseph. 1095, 1347
Lebreton, Jules. 1193, 1967, 476, 1193, 1967
Lebreton, Jules Marie Leon. 1193
Le Buffe, Francis P. 2021
Le Buffe, Francis Peter. 854, 857, 1264, 1977, 2361, 2362, 2369, 2391, 3406
LeBuffe, Francis Peter. 2391
Le Camus, Emile. 1967
Lechler, Gotthard Victor. 329
Lechner, Petrus. 188
Leckey, Dolores R. 1609
Leckie, Robert. 874, 3281
Lecky, Robert S. 1243
Lecky, William Edward Hartpole. 3023, 3024
Lecler, Joseph. 1143, 3703
Leclerc, Eloi. 1060, 1642
Leclerc, Ivor. 2418, 3813
Le Clercq, Chretien. 2189, 2506
Leclercq, Jacques. 999
Leclercq, Jacques. 967, 772, 999, 1076, 1077, 1136, 2205, 2718, 3487, 3785, 2321
Leclercq, Jean. 1715, 1807, 2266, 2346, 2570, 2571, 2582
Leclere, Adhemard. 704
Leclerq, Jacques. 3540
Le Compte, Irville Charles. 2980
Lecomte du Novy, Pierre, 1883. 3593
Le Comte, Edward Semple. 2469, 2470, 2661
Le Conte, Joseph. 1580, 3073, 3076
LeCroy, Ruth Brooks. 2798
Lecuyer, Joseph. 2742
Ledbetter, Edith Limer. 3467
Ledderhose, Karl Friedrich. 2400
Le Deaut, Roger. 2142
Lederach, Paul M. 1609, 2405, 3153, 3887
Lederer, William J. 1114
[Ledesma, Andres de]. 2538, 3303
Ledit, Joseph Henry. 822
Ledlie, John Andrew. 3434
Ledlow, William Franklin. 1953
Lednum, John. 2424
Le Du, Jean. 935
Ledyard, Gleason H. 1532, 1612, 3018
Lee, Ada. 1116
Lee, Alfred. 358
Lee, Allan W. 612, 1102, 2540
Lee, Anthony D. 3770
Lee, Arthur C. 1627, 3868
Lee, Bernard. 2944
Lee, Betsy. 2717, 3602
Lee, Carvel. 3555
Lee, Charles Follen. 3050
Lee, Charles Hamilton. 1034
Lee, Charles M. 800
Lee, Charlotte I. 211, 613
Lee, Chauncey. 550, 1503, 3342
Lee, Chin. 1470, 1879
Lee, Clarence Louis. 2034
Lee, Cuthbert. 2190
Lee, Dal. 98
Lee, Dallas. 2131
Lee, E.G. 1060
Lee, E Johann. 1895
Lee, Elizabeth M. 2548
Lee, Elizabeth Meredith. 1408, 2979
Lee, Ernest Eugene. 142
Lee, Ernest George. 1060, 3130
Lee, Florence B. 199, 3171
Lee, Francis Nigel. 1319, 2323
Lee, Frank T. 199, 639
Lee, Frank Theodosius. 408, 493
Lee, Frederick. 1977, 2809
Lee, Frederick George. 3639
Lee, G Avery. 164, 215, 1120, 1449, 2626
Lee, George. 2223, 2352
Lee, Gerald Stanley. 1183, 2415
Lee, Grace Lawless. 1851
Lee, Gustav T. 1150
Lee, Gustav Torgerson. 1351
Lee, Hannah Farnham (Sawyer) 1852, 2275
Lee, Harold B. 2609, 3887, 2609
Lee, Harris W. 1199, 2214, 2300
Lee, Hector. 2684
Lee, Hector Haight. 2684
Lee, J Fitzgerald. 2111
Lee, J[ohn] A. 1860
Lee, J. W. 524

Lee, James Michael. 817, 831, 935, 3153, 3613
Lee, James Wideman. 2424, 3078
Lee, Jarena. 3191
Lee, Jesse. 2206, 2424, 2438
Lee, John. 3194
Lee, John David. 1967
Lee, John Doyle. 2603
Lee, John Francis. 523, 3342
Lee, John Lloyd. 2932
Lee, Joseph. 985
Lee, Judy. 931, 2206
Lee, Julia Tolman. 3531
Lee, Jung Young. 173, 1414, 1729, 1879, 2064, 2323, 3061, 3330
Lee, Knute. 2300
Lee, Kun Sam. 1084
Lee, Leonard C. 3382
Lee, Leroy Madison. 2206, 2451, 2206, 2451
Lee, Luther. 2673, 3228, 3354, 3424, 3645
Lee, Mark W. 2786, 2338, 2341
Lee, Mary. 892
Lee, Mary Virginia. 3153
Lee, Michael A. 3691
Lee, Mrs. Irven. 616
Lee, Olav. 454
Lee, Porter Raymond. 3292
Lee, R.L. 1523
Lee, Robert. 93, 190, 1046, 1075, 1086, 1278, 2481, 2534
Lee, Robert E. A. 2275
Lee, Robert G. 616
Lee, Robert Greene. 164, 215, 133, 139, 143, 164, 165, 169, 215, 324, 346, 1558, 1692, 1841, 2034, 2085, 2327, 2887, 3354, 3652
Lee, Ronald R. 2784
Lee, Roy Stuart. 904, 2998
[Lee, Samuel] 1625-1691. 2412, 3008
Lee, Samuel. 1530
Lee, Umphrey. 1967, 3342, 719, 1150, 1520, 2421, 2424, 3793, 3803, 1520, 2421, 3803
Lee, Walter M. 2463
Lee, William. 305
Lee, William James. 3208
Lee, William Taylor. 235
Lee, Won Sul. 1090
Leeb, David. 596
Leech, Kenneth. 2874, 3475
Leech, Walter Stuart. 2727
Leeder, S. H. 2567
Leeds, Josiah Woodward. 3791
Leeds, Samuel Penniman. 1341
Leedy, Roy B. 1546
Leedy, Walter C. 1157
Leek, Sybil. 672, 1422, 1599, 2206, 2727, 2730, 3053, 3824
Leeming, Bernard. 859, 2719, 3265
Leeming, David Adams. 2658
Leeming, Frank Clifford. 2253
Leen, Edward. 2355, 805, 999, 1141, 1830, 2020, 863
Leen, James. 3222
Leen. Edward. 2571
Leenhardt, Franz J. 468, 1041
Leenhouts, Keith J. 1615, 2206
Lees, Frederic Richard. 3597
Lees, George Robinson. 183, 1967
Leese, Arnold Spencer. 3240
Leeser, Isaac. 184, 2115
Leesmilne, James. 3769
Leeson, Charles Henry. 2029
Leeson, Spencer. 935, 2253, 3153
Leestma, Harold F. 215, 1359, 2391, 3354
Leete, Frederick De Land. 1771, 2762, 3078
Leete, Frederick DeLand. 1440, 1567
Leetham, Claude Richard Harbord. 3251
Leeton, Will C. 122, 633, 1406
Leeuw, Gerardus van der. 3102
Leeuw, J. J. Van der. 3686
Leeuw, Jacobus Johannes van der. 3686
Leeuwen, Arend Theodoor van. 1079, 1154
Lefafa sedeq. 2314
Lefeber, Larry A. 1259
Lefebure, Georges. 2874
Lefebvre, Gaspar. 838, 3029
Lefebvre, Georges. 1735, 2874, 2937
Lefebvre, Vladimir A. 1540
Lefebvre, Xavier. 1627, 3174
Le Feuvre, Amy. 1968
Lefever, Ernest W. 1155, 3850
Lefever, Harry G. 1243, 1787
Le Fevre, Jacques. 2912
LeFevre, Perry D. 1309, 2324, 2885
Leff, Gordon. 688, 1628, 1773, 2810, 2842, 3324
Leffall, Dolores C. 2679
Leffingwell, Charles Wesley. 2884
Lefgren, John C. 2023, 2611
Leflon, Jean. 2376, 2720, 2721
Lefroy, William Chambers. 2
Le Gallienne, Richard. 1095, 2822

LeGant, William. 2836
Legare, Romain. 1935
Legaut, Marcel. 2015
Legendre, Adolph Alphonse Francois. 2762
Leger, Mary Celeste. 850, 1899
Legere, J. Roy. 873, 2208, 3491
Legeza, Ireneus Laszlo. 2314
Legg, John Wickham. 838, 1224, 1249, 1613, 3778
Legg, Leopold George Wickham. 1224
Legge, Francis. 1079
Legge, James. 913, 914, 3523
Leggett, Gary. 479
Leggett, Trevor. 3894
Legrand, Lucien. 3782
Le Grice, Edwin. 2886
Legters, Leonard L. 967, 3409
Legters, Leonard Livingston. 105, 967, 1823, 1878, 3290
Le Guillou, M. J. 2744, 3645
Leh, Leonard Llewellyn. 1100
Lehane, Brendan. 1918
Lehen, Edouard de. 3487
Lehman, Carolyn. 940
Lehman, Celia. 391
Lehman, Chester Kindig. 1830, 651
Lehman, Dale. 967
Lehman, Frederick Martin. 1428
Lehman, H. T. 2902
Lehman, James H. 1236
Lehman, James O. 1389, 2407, 2719, 3239
Lehman, Leo Herbert. 800
Lehman, Louis Paul. 215, 908, 1841
Lehman, Martin Clifford. 2404
Lehmann, Arno. 920
Lehmann, Arnold O. 2236
Lehmann, Helmut T. 2256, 2902
Lehmann, Johannes. 1103, 1410, 2040
Lehmann, Leo Herbert. 794, 800, 1613
Lehmann, Marcus. 2132
Lehmann, Martin Ernest. 2130
Lehmann, Paul. 1633
Lehmann, Paul Louis. 944, 1086
Lehmann, Titus. 967
Lehmberg, Ben F. 215, 2421, 2436
Lehmeier, Ludwig. 2812
Lehn, Cornelia. 622
Lehner, Francis C. 1474, 2380
Lehrburger, Egon. 3322
Lehrman, Irving. 1623
Lehrman, Simon Maurice. 2462
Lehrs, Ernst. 50, 1743
Le Huray, Peter. 1207
Leibert, Edwin Reisinger. 3871
Leibert, Julius Amos. 2227
Leibholz, Gerhard. 1086
Leibniz, Gottfried Wilhelm. 2568, 2833, 3610
Leibowitz, Jacob. 1539
Leibowitz, Nehama. 516
Leibrecht, Walter. 967, 1732, 1782, 3622, 3700
Leiby, Adrian Coulter. 192, 1484, 3047
Leicestershire Education Committee. 3200
Leiderman, Lillian T. 1614
Leidt, Edna J. 2550
Leidt, William E. 44, 3002
Leies, Herbert F. 1776
Leifer; Murray Howard 1902. 2439
Leiffer, Murray Howard. 1278, 1302, 1470, 2440, 3673, 3734
Leigh, Dorian. 931, 2208
Leigh, Margaret Mary. 1364
Leighton, Gerald Rowley. 3073
Leighton, John. 3271
Leighton, Joseph Alexander. 1723, 2003, 2418, 3061
Leighton, Robert. 325, 73, 325, 3630
Leiman, Harold. 3078
Leiman, Sid Z. 495, 2364, 3015
Leinbach, Esther V. 96
Leininger, Louis Lee. 1485
Leinow, Benjamin J. 733
Leiper, Henry Smith. 1060, 1141, 1182, 3849
Leiphart, Elmer Elwood. 1545, 3887
Leipziger, Emil William. 3576
Leiser, Joseph. 2115, 2155
Leishman, Thomas Linton. 290, 286, 290, 451, 565, 1034, 2095, 2950
Leising, William A. 2543, 2721
Leitch, Addison H. 410, 2914, 3650, 3663
Leitch, Flavia Gaines. 2875
Leitch, Clarence Luke. 52
Leith, John H. 1120, 1386, 2915, 3636, 3637, 3679, 3680, 3808, 3809
Leitner, Jerrol. 862
Lekai, Louis Julius. 1276
Lekeux, Martial. 3487, 2875, 3487
Leland, Charles Godfrey. 3824
Leland, John. 1420
Lelen, Joseph Mary. 2784, 390, 857, 999, 1618, 2254, 2938, 3455
Lelyveld, Arthur J. 1733
LeMahieu, D. L. 2675, 2766

Lemaitre, Solange. 1813, 3020
Lemke, Arnold E. 1723
Lemke, Stefan. 495, 633, 1384, 2130, 2712
Lemme, Ludwig. 2013
Lemmi, Charles William. 124, 2656
Lemmon, Clarence Eugene. 1251, 1466, 3537
Lemmon, Sarah McCulloh. 2827
Le Moine, Emanuel Aaron. 2059, 3675
Lemon, Adele Marie. 826
LeMon, Cal. 1315
Lemon, Frank R. 399, 2015
Lemon, John Bunyan. 650
Lemons, Frank W. 405, 1229, 1597, 3354
Lemoyne, Giovanni Battista. 683
Lench, Charles Harris. 3258
Lenchitz, Solomon. 2076, 2083
Le Neve, John. 45, 1215, 1291
L'Engle, Madeleine. 318, 633, 901, 1089, 1264, 2209
Lengyel, Emil. 11
Lenhart, John Mary. 612, 1645, 1894
Lenn, Lottie Helen. 2852
Lenn, Theodore I. 3032, 3016
Lennhoff, Eugen. 1662
Lenning, Larry G. 2557
Lennox, Cuthbert. 1481
Lennox, William Gordon. 2520
LeNoir, Ruth deCormis. 2060
Lenox, James. 717
Lenski, Gerhard E. 2029, 2210
Lenski, Gerhard Emmanuel. 1486, 2345, 3088
Lenski, R. C. H. 3374
Lenski, Richard Charles Henry. 1992, 329, 344, 345, 366, 433, 441, 454, 366, 368, 371, 403, 416, 428, 468, 2902
Lenssen, F A. 1584
Lenta, Clementine. 835, 948
Lentsyk, Vasyl. 756
Lentz, Francis George. 788
Lentz, Harold H. 2281, 2309
Lentz, Richard E. 3168
Lenz, Frederick. 3055
Lenz, Russell H. 2230, 3117
Lenzkes, Susan L. 2216, 2391
Lenzner, Emilie. 3507
Leo. 2189
Leo, Alan. 96
Leo Baeck Memorial Conference on Jewish Social Thought, New York, 1973. 125, 2141
Leo, Franciscan. 1642
Leo I. 2218
Leo X I I I. 110-1903. 3847
Leo XIII, 1810-1903. 1856
Leo I. 2218
Leon, Dorothy. 2021
Leon-Dufour, Xavier. 352
Leon, Philip. 2753
Leonard, Adna Bradway. 2443, 2493
Leonard, Adna Wright. 827, 1554, 1567, 3448
Leonard, Arthur Glyn. 1540
*Leonard, B. G. 3411
Leonard, Bernard F. 455
Leonard, Charles Alexander. 2510
Leonard, Delavan Levant. 2525, 1338, 2520, 2525
Leonard, Donna. 985
Leonard, Emile G. 2978
Leonard, George R. 788, 2366
Leonard, Henry. 2084
Leonard, Jacob Calvin. 1545
Leonard, Jim. 3144
Leonard, John Calvert. 3507
Leonard, Joseph T. 1131
Leonard, Maria. 639
Leonard, Maurice. 671, 3682
Leonard, Mayme (Rolf) 910
Leonard, Oscar. 2105
Leonard, Robert Josselyn. 3733
Leonard, William. 3396
Leonard, William Andrew. 933, 2031
Leonard, William Ellery. 1953
Leonard, William Frederick. 1580
Leonard, William J. 841, 1508, 2239
Leonardi, Dell. 681, 3055
Leonberger, Elinor Ann. 1434
Leon-Dufour, Xavier. 244, 1987, 2052, 3639
Leone, Mark P. 2603
Leoni, Louise. 1005
Leont ev, Aleksei Nikolaevich. 1705
Leo XIII. 1856, 2216
Le Pappe de Trevern, Jean Francois Marie. 2977
Lepicier, Alexis H Marie. 2251
Lepicier, Alexis Henri Marie. 2132, 2255, 2258, 2361, 3269
Lepin, Marius. 390, 1953
Lepitre, Albert. 54
Lepp, Ignace. 1364, 1584, 3449, 101, 1324, 3593
Leppich, John. 1136
Le Prince di Beaumont, Marie. 967

Le Quesne, A. Laurence. 1291, 2171
Le Queux, William. 3600, 3412
Lerberg, Irwin M. 32
Lercaro, Giacomo. 2123, 2239, 2380
Lerhinan, John Patrick. 759
Lerner, Carol. 2853
Lerner, Eric. 712, 2217
Lerner, Martin. 3316
Lerner, Robert E. 691
Lernoux, Penny. 821, 836, 2821
Lerou, Emilie. 2005
Leroux, Jean Marie. 809
Leroy, A. 2233
Le Roy, Albert. 1913
Le Roy, Alexandre. 871, 796, 3109
Leroy, Douglas. 1229
Le Roy, Edouard Louis Emmanuel Julien. 1473
LeRoy, Jean. 896
Leroy, Jules. 2569
Leroy-Beaulieu, Anatole. 2078
Lerrigo, Peter H. J. 3484
Lerrigo, Peter Hugh James. 142, 2202, 2513, 2714, 2875
Lesage, Germain. 3785
Lesage, Robert. 839
Le Sage, Wilfred. 2391
Le Saux, Henri. 2885, 1082
Lesch, Gomer R. 1317, 3002
Lescher, Wilfrid. 3130
Leschnitzer, Adolf. 53
Lescoe, Francis J. 3645, 3722
Lescohier, Don Divance. 2179
Lescrauwaet, Josephus Franciscus. 1249
Lesetre, Henri. 3347
LeShan, Lawrence. 2989
LeShan, Lawrence L. 2380, 2989
Le Shana, David C. 1685
Lesher, W. Richard. 3550
Leslau, Wolf. 1602, 2145
Leslie, Benjamin. 1203
Leslie, Charles. 1419, 2759
Leslie, Charles W. 3663
Leslie, Elmer Archibald. 1525, 542, 546, 567, 568, 576, 2115
Leslie, Elmer Archiblad. 429
*Leslie, John. 211
Leslie, John. 1381
Leslie, John Douglass. 2920
Leslie, Kenneth. 1319
Leslie, Robert Campbell. 1170, 1651, 2050, 2338
Leslie, Samuel Clement. 2151
Leslie, Shane. 1703, 2328, 2703, 2754, 2793
*Lesne, Emile. 1638
Le Sourd, Howard M. 2443
LeSourd, Howard Marion. 1256, 3733
Le Sourd, Leonard Earle. 612
Lessa, William Armand. 3122, 3138
Lessel, William M. 1243, 2734
Lesser, George. 79
Lesser, Graham. 2409
Lessing, Erich. 201, 408, 527, 920, 985, 1968, 2040, 2711
Lessing, Gotthold Ephraim. 3630
Lessius, Leonardus. 1736, 3782
Lessmann, Paul G. 2249
Lester, A. Hoyle. 275
Lester, Andrew D. 1351
Lester, Charles Edwards. 664
Lester, Charles Stanley. 390, 1968
Lester, Gordon. 1609
Lester, H. A. 3555, 3565
Lester, James Adams. 150
Lester, Mildred E. 1588
Lester, Muriel. 2875, 3444
Lester, Reginald Mounstephens. 3507
Lester, Robert C. 704
Lester, W. Sybel. 1092
Lester, William. 3723
Lester-Garland, Lester Vallis. 1850, 3102, 3567
Lestocq, Hubert. 2727
Le Strange, Guy. 2764
Lestschinsky, Jacob. 2090, 3851
Letarouilly, Paul Marie. 3768
Letchford, Peter. 2249, 3354
Letchworth, Thomas. 3010
Lethaby, William Richard. 3808
Lethbridge, Thomas Charles. 1479, 1709, 3824
[Leti, Gregorio] 1630-1701. 2767
Letis, Theodore P. 861, 2955
Letourneau, Emilien. 194
LeTourneau, R. G. 2217, 2391
LeTourneau, Richard. 985
Letourneur, Augustin Jean. 1825
Le Troquer, Rene. 2324
Le Troquer, Rene. 2324
Letson, Samuel Brisbin. 1953
Letts, Harold C. 1075, 1138
Letts, Winifred M. 3281
Leturia, Pedro. 2268
Leuba, James Henry. 1889, 2647, 2998, 3102, 2561, 2647, 2998

Leupold, Herbert Carl. 506, 512, 521, 543, 576, 600
Leuret, Francois. 1599
Leuschner, Albert Edward. 3200
Leute, Karl M. 3507
Leuty, Joseph D. 3716
Levasti, Arrigo. 749
Le Vavasseur, Leon Michel. 839
Leven, Jeremy. 1429
Levensohn, Lotta. 3897
Levenson, Jon Douglas. 519, 550
Leventhal, Herbert. 2733
Lever, Abraham Wolf. 748, 1953
Lever, Jan. 3078, 3082
Lever, Katherine, 1916. 2061
Levere, Rose. 3507
Levermore, Samuel. 2477
Levertoff, Olga. 2073, 2078
Levesque, G Victor. 2477
Levett, Carl David. 2219, 3507, 3521
Levey, Michael. 88
Levey, Samson H. 492, 2415
Levi, Annie Josephine. 2117
Levi, Anthony. 1095
Levi, Carlo. 3061
Levi, David. 2758
Levi, Gerson Baruch. 3371
Levi, Hans. 2072
Levi, Harry. 3370
Levi, Leo. 2139
Levi, Shonie B. 3842
Levi ben Gershon, 1288-1344. 548
Levi d'Ancona, Mirella. 2358
Levie, Jean. 240
Levin, David. 1499, 3827
Levin, Meyer. 1789, 1928, 2081, 2101, 2151, 3166, 3580
Levin, Saul. 2135
Levin, Schmarya. 2102
Levin, Simon S. 317, 1968
Levine, Aaron. 1316
Levine, Daniel H. 835, 3777
Levine, Etan. 556
Levine, Faye. 1786
Levine, Raphael H. 2153
Levine, Robert J. 1853
Levine, Samuel. 2556
Levine, Stephen. 1414, 3780
Levinger, Elma C (Ehrlich) 2094
Levinger, Elma C. (Ehrlich) 2079, 2117, 2121
Levinger, Elma (Ehrlich) 622, 1329, 1506, 2081, 2084, 2094, 2106, 2121, 2207, 3579, 3842
Levinger, Lee Joseph. 2078, 2105
Levinger Elma C (Ehrlich) 625
Levington, John. 135, 2866
Levinson, Henry S. 1934, 3102
Levinthal, Israel Herbert. 2080, 2115, 2116, 3361, 3371
Levisee, Aaron Burton. 1103, 1449
Levison, Leon. 2089
Levison, Wilhelm. 1186
Levison, Wilhelm, 1876-1947. 1186, 2484
Levi-Strauss, Claude. 1903, 2652
Levitan, Elsie. 1780
Levitan, Tina Nellie. 2106, 2144
Levitats, Isaac. 2102
Levitin, Miriam. 2154
Levitt, Albert. 800
Levitt, Zola. 610, 1366, 1367, 1928, 2073, 2219, 2556, 2588
Levtzion, Nehemia. 2635
Levy, Alan. 1754
Levy, Babette May, 1907. 2910
Levy, Bernard Henri. 3072
[Levy, Clifton Harby] 1867. 602
Levy, Gertrude Rachel, 1883. 3109
Levy, J. Leonard. 2884
Levy, Jerome. 2785
Levy, Mark John. 1051
Levy, Maurice. 2227
Levy, Max. 2084
Levy, Paul. 702
Levy, Raphael. 98
Levy, Reuben. 3454
Levy, Richard S. 2858
Levy, Rosalie Marie. 854, 855, 1953, 2355, 2884, 3269, 781, 857, 1364, 1434, 1977, 2132, 2362, 2798, 3269, 3281
Lewalski, Barbara Kiefer, 1931. 2471
Lewi, Grant. 96
Lewi, Grant [William Grant Lewi]. 96
Lewi, Isidor. 3822
Lewin, Isaac. 20, 2142, 3423
Lewin, Leonard. 3543
Lewin, Raphael De Cordova. 2115
Lewinsohn, Lewis. 2082
Lewinsohn, Richard. 2946
Lewis, Abram Herbert. 3547, 2757, 3260, 3388, 3548
Lewis, Agnes (Smith) 317, 2329
Lewis, Alexander. 3362
Lewis, Alice Hudson. 1014, 2510, 2516
Lewis, Alvin G. 17
Lewis, Amzi. 895
Lewis, Arthur. 1532, 2810

Lewis, Arthur H. 554, 3052, 3827
Lewis, Arthur James. 1045, 3896
Lewis, Arthur Morrow. 3313
Lewis, Bernard. 92, 1923, 1927
Lewis, C. S. 967, 1060, 1070, 3622, 3663
Lewis, Charles Clarke. 3887
Lewis, Charles Smith. 951, 3555, 3663
Lewis, Clarence Irving. 1536
Lewis, Clifford. 3210, 3831
Lewis, Clifford Merle. 1949
Lewis, Clive Staples. 1070, 2219, 68, 578, 1060, 1070, 1362, 1521, 1723, 1746, 2219, 2470, 2477, 2758, 3622, 3663, 1061, 1066, 1070, 1217, 1351, 1362, 2263, 2758, 2875, 3200, 3622, 3633
Lewis, David. 2427
Lewis, David L. 2172
Lewis, Dio. 889
Lewis, Dominic Bevan Wyndham. 1625
Lewis, Donald Earle. 2247
Lewis, Douglas. 3777
Lewis, E Arthur. 1514
Lewis, Ebenezer E. 1872
Lewis, Edward Samuel. 3153, 2443
Lewis, Edwin. 57, 277, 951, 967, 1070, 1723, 1953, 2174, 3225, 3663
Lewis, Edwin W. 3507
Lewis, Enoch. 1682
Lewis, Ernest Ridley. 3645
Lewis, Ethel (Clark) 3839
Lewis, Eve. 904
Lewis, Frank Grant. 290, 421, 1919
Lewis, Franklin Fillmore. 235, 1400
Lewis, Frederick White. 2892
Lewis, George. 3300
Lewis, Gordian. 2577
Lewis, Gordon Russell. 64, 69, 3325, 3663, 3708
Lewis, Grant Kirkland. 31, 1461
Lewis, Granville Douglas. 1165
Lewis, Gregory. 1553
*Lewis, H. D. 3117
Lewis, Harve Spencer. 2054, 2411, 2994, 3010, 3053, 3250, 3539, 1968, 2054, 2411, 3053, 3250, 3251
Lewis, Hazel Asenath. 895, 1462, 3153, 3171, 3555
Lewis, Henry Wilkins. 2957
Lewis, Hywel D. 1891, 2040
Lewis, Hywel David. 1105, 1536, 1696, 3102, 3117
Lewis, I. M. 1491
Lewis, Ida Belle. 2220
Lewis, J. D. 3228
Lewis, J. P. 1061
Lewis, Jack Pearl. 270, 298, 560
Lewis, James. 2220
Lewis, James K. 144
Lewis, John. 2810, 3860, 235, 2227, 2913, 1070, 3093, 3436
Lewis, John Masters. 1276
Lewis, John Thomas. 1271, 1463
Lewis, Joseph. 3023, 100, 235, 1314, 1655, 1907
Lewis, Larry L. 1567
Lewis, Margie M. 1609
Lewis, Marvin. 3374
Lewis, Matthew Gregory. 3200
Lewis, Michael Jonathan Tauton. 3600
Lewis, Nettie Edell. 2119
Lewis, Norman. 2483, 3061
Lewis, Ralph Loren. 2902
Lewis, Ralph M. 2727, 3251, 3574
Lewis, Ralph Maxwell. 3251
Lewis, Richard Burton. 3260
Lewis, Richard Welbourne. 253, 1428, 1794
Lewis, Samuel L. 323, 2324, 3542, 3544
Lewis, Tayler. 2675, 3076, 3525
Lewis, Theodore N. 2142
Lewis, Thomas Hamilton. 2459, 277, 2459, 2474, 1288
Lewis, W. Scott. 2322
Lewis, William Henry. 3263, 3095
Lewisohn, Ludwig. 2078, 2082, 2139
Lewison Ludwig. 2139
Lewit, Jane. 172
Lewittes, Mendell. 2074, 2119, 2151
Lewittes, Mordecai Henry. 2094
Lewry, Osmund. 1819
Lewy, Guenter. 818, 3072
Lewy, Immanuel. 500, 563
Lexau, Joan M. 2573
Lexington, Ky. Christ church. 3427
Lexington, Ky. College of the Bible. 1461
Lexington, Va. Lexington Presbyterian Church. 2920
Lexinton, Stephen de. 1292, 2220
Ley, John. 1794
Ley, John Cole. 1630
Leyburn, John. 2944
Leypoldt, Martha M. 938
Leys, Mary Dorothy Rose. 872
Leys, Wayne Albert Risser. 2998
Leysen, Pierre. 1650
Lhamon, William Jefferson. 886, 2483, 331

Lhermitte, Jacques Jean. 1422
L'Heureux, Aloysius Gonzaga. 2334, 2648
L'Heureux, Conrad E. 1743
L'Hoir, F X. 1298
L'Hote, Jean Baptiste. 455
Lhotte, Celine. 3247
Liao, David C. E. 2556
Libackyj, Anfir. 2569
Libanio, J. B. 1086
Libbey, Hubert Cornelius. 1893
Libbey, Scott. 2624, 2804, 3185
*Libby, Raymond H. 3382, 3670
Liber depictus. 1025
Liber, Maurice. 3457
Liber pontificalis. 2770, 2860
Liberal Catholic church. 2220
Liberman, Alexander. 86
Liberman, Maurice. 595
Liberman, Paul. 2073
Libermann, Francois Marie Paul. 3487
Libermann, Francois Marie Paul [Name orig.: Jacob Libermann]. 3488
Liber pontificalis. 2770
Liberty Baptist College. 344
Liberty, Stephen. 2017
Lichfield, Eng. Gild of St. Mary. 2225
Lichius, James. 839
Lichliter, James Marcelius. 1061
Lichliter, James Marcellus. 967
Lichliter, McIlyar Hamilton. 1341, 3673
Lichtenberger, Arthur. 2211, 2788
Lichtenstein, Aharon. 2596
Lichtenstein, Morris. 1324, 2086, 2115, 2116
Lichtenwallner, William A. 3067
Lickey, Arthur E. 1723, 1999, 3382
Licorish, David Nathaniel. 1134
Liddell, Anna Forbes. 24, 3469
Liddell, Brendan E. A. 1536
Liddon, Henry Parry. 133, 374, 468, 702, 1218, 2001, 2056, 2799, 3010, 3342
Lide, Anae Ayers. 24, 2457
Lidgett, John Scott. 1095
Lidz, Charles W. 1480
Lieb, Frederick George. 2727
Lieb, Irwin C. 2418, 3801
Lieban, Richard Warren. 2314
[Lieberkiihn, Samuel]. 2595
Lieberman, Herman. 32, 2076, 2139
Lieberman, Saul. 2101, 2076, 3015
Liebert, Gosta. 1897
Liebert, Sarah L. 534
Liebeschuetz, John Hugo Wolfgang Gideon. 3246
*Liebknecht, Henrietta. 1112
Liebler, H. B. 3244
Liebman, Arthur. 1848
Liebman, Charles S. 2154, 2751
Liebman, Joshua Loth. 1536
Liebman, Seymour B. 1909, 2332
Liederbach, Clarence A. 666, 668, 772, 815, 2343
Liefeld, Theodore S. 474, 2031
Liege, P. A. 999
Liege, Pierre Andre. 999
Liem, Ann. 674
Liemohn, Edwin. 917, 1203, 1209
Lienhardt, Godfrey. 1459
Lierde, Petrus Canisius van. 738, 807
Liesel, Nikolaus. 2237
Liesting, G. T. H. 2255
Lietzmann, Hans. 1193
Lietzmann, Hans [Johannes Carl Alexander Lietzmann]. 1193
Lievegoed, B. C. J. 2636
Lievsay, John Leon. 3303
Lievsay, R. J. 235
Life (Chicago) 3011, 3117, 3118
Life, Nancy. 1359, 2228
Life of the spirit. 760, 772
Liggett, Thomas J. 1138
Lightbody, Charles Wayland. 1938
Lightburne, Teva May (Sparkman) 235
Lighterness, Tony. 985
Lightfoot, Jewel Preston. 1669
Lightfoot, John. 344, 2668
Lightfoot, Joseph Barber. 371, 3061
Lightfoot, Neil R. 290, 403, 2025
Lightfoot, Robert Henry. 435, 431, 435
Lightner, Robert Paul. 64, 105, 241, 606, 897, 1492, 1551, 1716, 1723, 1958, 1959, 2221, 3617
Lighton, William Beebay. 3130
Lignee, Hubert. 3599
Ligon, Bill. 985
Ligon, Ernest M. 3335
Ligon, Ernest Mayfield. 886, 2591, 3335
Ligon, John Washington. 2799
Liguori, Alfonso Maria de. 2259
Liguori, Alfonso Maria de. 2355, 3488, 772, 854, 855, 858, 999, 1417, 1894, 2029, 2031, 2229, 2251, 2259, 2355, 2359, 2380, 2391, 2875, 3294, 3488
Liguori, Alfonso Maris de'. 2031
Liguori, Alfonso Maris de. 2359
Likoudis, James. 788, 870
Liles, Lester R. 3406

Lilienthal, Max. 3130
Lilje, Hanns. 455, 667, 2229, 2275, 2391, 3034
Lilje, Hanns, Bp., 1899. 101
Liljencrants, Johan. 3507
Lilla, Salvatore R. C. 1287
Lillenas, Haldor. 1237, 1872
Lilley, Alfred Leslie. 2561, 2562, 3225, 3263
Lilley, James Philip. 2520, 71
Lilley, James Samuel. 3221
Lilley, M. C., & co., Columbus, O. 1670
Lillie, Amy Morris. 1184, 2535, 3701
Lillie, Arthur. 702, 1081, 2731
Lillie, Harriet E. 3507
[Lillie, James]. 3800
Lillie, John. 447, 2306, 2465
Lillie, R Shepard. 3507
Lillie, William. 378, 2008
Lillingston, Frank. 689
Lilly, David Clay. 2920
Lilly, Edward Charles. 3762
Lilly, Edward G. 888, 1627
Lilly, Eli. 1897
Lilly, John Cunningham. 1736
Lilly, Joseph L. 2190
Lilly, William. 96, 2229
Lilly, William Samuel. 60
Lillycrop, William Arthur. 1248
Lilyers, Jean. 3377
Lim, Catherine. 3200
Limbert, Paul Moye. 1129
Limbert, Paul Moyer. 1128, 1129, 1277, 3757, 3871
Limburg, James. 2950
Limentani, Uberto. 1402
[Limerick, Dudley T]. 639
Limouze, Arthur Henry. 2527, 3153
Lin, Timothy Tian-min. 3203
Lin, Yutang. 967, 1362
Linamen, Harold F. 1165, 1200, 1251
Lincoln, Anthony. 1468
Lincoln, Bruce. 2711
Lincoln, C. Eric. 669
Lincoln cathedral. 2230
Lincoln, Charles Eric. 2172, 2682
Lincoln, Charles Zebina. 1490
Lincoln, Eleanor Terry. 2782
Lincoln, Eugene. 2265
Lincoln, Fredman Ashe. 1419
Lincoln, John Cromwell. 2016
Lincoln, Joseph Colville. 1715, 3713
Lincoln, William C. 639
Lind, Jayne. 2875
Lind, Marie. 924, 2490
Lind, Millard. 500, 2756, 3795, 3855
Lind, Robert W. 3767
Lindaman, Edward B. 1845
Lindars, Barnabas. 416
Lindars, Barnabas [Frederick Chevallier Lindars]. 588
Lindbeck, George A. 3614, 3628, 3770
Lindberg, Conrad Emil. 68, 1473, 606
Lindberg, Paul M. 1486
Lindblad, Frank V. 1830, 2875
Lindblom, Johannes. 235, 569
Lindblom, Myron. 1014
Lindborg, Olga E. 215, 625, 3176
Lindell, Paul J. 2758
Lindeman, Lucile Wells. 459
Lindemann, Frederick Herman. 1267, 1318, 2258, 2260
*Lindemann, Henry. 2675
Lindemann, Henry. 2275
Lindemann, Herbert. 2214
Lindemann, Herbert Fred. 2214, 2295, 2297, 2300
Lindemann, Paul. 1622, 2300, 3673
Linden, Ian. 835, 850, 1108, 1152, 2538, 3812
Linden, Jakob. 756
Linden, James V. 57, 859
Linder, Robert Dean. 1086, 1109
Linder, Ted. 2620, 2683
Linder, Tom. 610
Lindevall, Carl August. 3569
Lindgren, Alvin J. 953, 1200
Lindgren, Anna Josephine. 2391
Lindgren, Carl E. 2720
Lindgren, Donald Norman. 967
Lindholm, Paul R. 3529
Lindhorst, Frank Atkinson. 3153
Lindley, Denton Ray. 732
Lindley, Percy Elliott. 1120
Lindquist, Emory Kempton. 740, 1301
Lindquist, Gustavus Elmer Emanuel. 1900
Lindquist, Raymond Irving. 1011
Lindsay, Alexander Dunlop. 3336, 1280, 2163, 3081
Lindsay, Alexander Dunlop Lindsay. 1282, 2003, 2163, 3336
Lindsay, Anna Robertson (Brown) 953, 2520
Lindsay, Gordon. 610, 690, 952, 2071
Lindsay, Jack. 98, 1502, 1801, 1802
Lindsay, John. 3480
*Lindsay, S. B. 3200

Lindsay, Thomas Martin. 2275, 3034, 3040, 3041
Lindsell, Harold. 944, 277, 305, 985, 1431, 1432, 2230, 2493, 2554, 2734, 2875, 3645
Lindsey, Benjamin Barr. 2338
Lindsey, Edwin Samuel. 890
Lindsey, Hal. 606, 611, 1428, 1845, 1982, 2230, 3290, 3321
Lindsey, Hubert. 2230
Lindsey, J. Allen. 2457
Lindsey, Jonathan A. 3747
Lindsey, Stephen Marcus. 135
Lindsey, Theophilus. 2218
Lindskoog, Kathryn. 1479
Lindskoog, Kathryn Ann. 2219
Lindsley, James Elliott. 2463, 2620
Lindstrom, Dan. 2230, 3493
Lindstrom, David Edgar. 3254, 3195, 3254
Lindstrom, Janet. 130
Lindvall, Ella K. 622
Line, Francis R. 1027, 1642
Lineberger, Lawrence Otto. 338, 2799, 2950
Lineberry, John. 325, 478, 3290
Linedecker, Clifford L. 2586
Linehan, Kevin. 931, 2230
Linehan, Peter. 3469
Lines, John Davis. 3716
Lines, Kathleen. 2022
Linfield, Cornelius S. 3712
Linfield, Harry Sebee. 1248, 2105, 2122
Linford, James Henry. 2230
Linford, Marilynne Todd. 2618
Linforth, Ivan Mortimer. 2744
Ling, Louis. 1426
Ling, Trevor Oswald. 705, 706, 709, 1095, 1543, 2352, 3102, 3139
Lingard, John. 1760
Lingat, Robert. 1457
Linger, O. Afton. 165, 2786
Lingle, Walter Lee. 2936, 3444, 2916, 2936
Lings, Albert A. 1996, 858
Lings, Albert Ad. 2716
Lings, Martin. 21, 3542
Linhares, Margaret. 2727
Link, Bessie A. 3716
Link, Helen Kendall. 904
Link, Henry Charles. 2998
Link, John R. 639
Link, Mark. 431, 1737
Link, Mark J. 534, 929, 1968, 3153, 3187, 3267, 3449, 3880
Linkh, Richard M. 874
Linklater, Eric. 2353
Linn, Clement Huntingford. 1576, 2218
Linn, Edmund Holt. 1635, 2902
Linn, Jan. 1243
Linn, LaVon Parker. 1672
Linn, Mary Jane. 1414
Linn, Matthew. 1599
Linn, Otto Fernand. 416, 433, 476
Linn, Samuel. 2771
Linn, Talford P. 879
Linn, William. 1523
Linn, William Alexander. 2603, 2604
Linnell, Charles Lawrence Scruton. 751
Linnemann, Eta. 2025, 2772
Linnett, Arthur. 3296, 3308
Linneweber, Antony. 1642
Linnik, Philip S. 694
Linscheid, Ruth C. 892, 2178
Linscott, T S. 1051
Linsley, Kenneth W. 2231, 3829
Linssen, Robert. 3894
Lintelo, Jules. 2255, 2256
Linthicum, Blanche. 3171
Linthicum, Robert C. 1243
Lintner, George Ames. 1778
Lintner, Robert Caspar. 3354
Linton, Arthur. 2237
Linton, Charles. 3507
Linton, Elizabeth (Lynn) 3826
Linton, Irwin Helffenstein. 64, 1099
Linton, John. 42, 897, 1558
Lintz, Harry McCormick. 967, 1440
Lion, Aline. 3102, 3778
Liotta, Matthew A. 2378
Liotta, Matthew Alexis. 999
Lipman, Eugene J. 1140
Lippe, Aschwin. 3316
Lippert, Peter. 2124, 863, 1945
Lipphard, William B. 155, 2539
Lipphard, William Benjamin. 2495, 2510
Lippincott, Charles Seward. 1662
Lippincott, Haines Hallock. 1070, 3200
Lippincott, Horace Mather. 1270, 1676
Lippitt, Francis James. 3507
Lippitt, Gordon L. 2156, 2670
Lippitt, Lucile. 3878
Lippman, Thomas W. 1922, 1926
Lippmann, Walter. 1536
Lippy, Charles H. 890, 1333
Lipschitz, Max A. 1789

Lipscomb, Andrew Adgate. 827, 2006, 2824, 3444
Lipscomb, David. 2135, 3290, 416, 2135
Lipscomb, T H. 1347
Lipsky, Abram. 493, 3803
Lipson, Dorothy Ann. 1663
Liptak, David Q. 863, 1025, 1267, 1613, 3267, 3281
Liptzin, Solomon. 1707, 2106
Lischer, Richard. 1567, 2321, 2352, 2902
Lisco, Friedrich Gustav. 2025
Lisemer, Louis. 2990
Lisiero, Dario. 788, 1881
Liske, Thomas V. 2902
Lisle, Dorothy Schwimmer. 2085
Lisle, William McIntire. 1061
Lister, Lincoln Ulysses. 2380
Lister, Louis. 3139, 3310
Liston, Paul. 796, 3488
Liston, Robert A. 3140
Litany of the sun. 3014
Litch, Josiah. 3319, 3796
Litchfield, Beals Ensign. 3507
Litchfield, Grace Denio. 3144
Litchfield, Norman. 2753
Litfin, A. Duane. 3002
Littauer, Florence. 985
Littel, Franklin Hamlin. 36
Littell, Franklin Hamlin. 36, 130, 1073, 1488, 1707, 2403, 2977, 3036, 3342, 3738, 3747
Littell, John Stockton. 1764, 2082, 2962
Littell, Noble K. 1664
Little, Andrew George. 1645, 1647, 1646
Little, Archibald Alexander. 2932
Little, Arthur. 2048
Little, Arthur Wilde. 2957, 2964, 3803
Little, Brooks Bivens. 2422
Little, Bryan D. G. 2579
Little, Carroll Herman. 109, 455, 2286
Little, Charles Eugene. 303
Little, Charles Joseph. 1402, 2422, 3354
Little Compton, R. I. United Congregational church. 2233
Little, Darwin. 500
Little, David. 3191, 3452, 3800
Little, Eliza Adams. 2701
Little, Ganse. 3663
Little, George Albert. 1915
Little, Gertrude. 3153
Little, Jack W. 1371
Little, Jacob V. 1528
Little, James A. 2604
Little, John Andrew. 1593
Little, Lawrence Calvin. 8, 1130, 2592, 2791, 3153, 3162, 3169
Little, Lester K. 2866
Little, Lewis Peyton. 171, 2705
Little, Paul. 2436
Little, Paul E. 64, 985, 1554, 3663, 3829
Little, Robert J. 280
Little, Sara. 639, 933, 1260, 3179
Little, Vilma Gertrude. 1471
Little, William. 2632
Little, William Herbert. 1432, 3660
Little, William John Knox. 2338
Littledale, Freya. 1937
Littledale, Richard Frederick. 594, 800
Littlefair, Duncan E. 3411
Littlefair, Duncan Elliot. 3342, 3521
Littlefield, George Elmer. 3251
Littlefield, Lyman Omer. 2615
Littlefield, Milton Smith. 3555
Littlejohn, Abram Newkirk. 1293
Littlejohn, Carrie U. 743
Littlejohn, Wolcott H. 459, 3260
Littleton, C. Scott. 1482, 2665
Littleton, Mary Brabson. 2981, 3610
Littleton, William H. 1267
Litton, Edward Arthur. 1120
Littorin, Frank T. 2902
Liturgical arts society, New York, comp. 851
Liturgical Conference, 1st, Immaculate Heart Seminary, 1967. 843
Liturgical Conference, Inc. 839, 1157, 1204, 1205, 2240, 3773, 3859
Liturgical Conference, Madison, Wis., 1958. 2233
Liturgical Conference, San Antonio, 1959. 2233
Liturgical Institute. 1st, Valparaiso University, 1949. 2295
Litvag, Irving. 3473, 3859
Litvin, Baruch. 3578
Lively, James Madison. 3078
Livermore, Daniel Parker. 1699
Livermore, George. 212
Livermore, Harriet. 2117, 3191

Liverpool. Public Libraries, Museums, and Art Gallery. Walker Art Gallery. 89, 3235
Liversidge, Douglas. 1642, 2270
Livesay, George Benton. 953
The Living light. 3167
Livingood, Frederick George. 3048
Livingston, David. 1405
Livingston, George Herbert. 565
Livingston, James C. 3659
Livingston, John Henry. 1694, 2347, 2546
Livingston, Paul Yount. 2300
Livingston, Ruth Hull. 1999
Livingston, Vanbrugh. 1751
Livingstone, William Pringle. 1634, 1968, 2499, 2506, 2544, 3425, 3704
Livius, Thomas Stiverd. 76, 2824
Livne, Zvi. 3580
Llamera, Boniface. 2132
Llewellyn Foundation for Astrological Research, Los Angeles. 99
Llewellyn, Joseph Steele. 639
Llorente, Juan Antonio. 1910
Lloyd, Arnold. 1683, 1685
Lloyd, Arthur. 706
Lloyd, Arthur P. 3759
Lloyd, Arthur Selden. 665, 1079
Lloyd, Benjamin. 1866
Lloyd, Bitha (Fox) 925
Lloyd, Ernest. 2886
Lloyd, John William. 2767
Lloyd-Jones, David Martyn. 472, 3364, 470, 472, 584, 3290, 3364
Lloyd, Kent. 953
Lloyd, Marjorie Lewis. 42, 105, 967, 1351, 1856, 2981, 3200, 3207, 3887
Lloyd, Mary Edna. 2022, 2054, 3555
Lloyd, Philip. 2208
Lloyd, Rhys R. 137
Lloyd, Roger Bradshaigh. 3444, 1, 967, 1095, 1220
Lloyd, Sarah. 3185
Lloyd-Jones, D. M. 468
Lloyd-Jones, D. Martyn. 1047
Lloyd-Jones, David Martyn. 118, 365, 366, 584, 1249, 2324, 3290, 3337, 3364, 3365, 472, 3365
Lloyd-Jones, Hugh. 1766
Llwyd, John Plummer Derwent. 2126
Lo Gatto-Perry, Joseph J. T. 1710
Lo, Samuel E. 3176, 3700
Loader, J. A. 512
Loades, D. M. 1021
Loane, Marcus L. 365, 472, 1550, 2006, 2029, 2057, 3193
Loaring-Clark, Ada. 2971
Loavasik, Lawrence George. 2875
Lobb, John. 3582
Lobel, Edgar. 81
Lo Bello, Nino. 807
Lo Bello, Nino D. 827, 1242
Lobingier, Charles Sumner. 1665
Lobingier, Elizabeth Erwin (Miller) 616, 1478, 1479, 2121, 3173
Lobingier, Jhon Leslie. 2550
Lobingier, John Leslie. 3191, 1332, 2550, 3153, 3179, 3555
Lobsang Rampa. 3130, 3699
Lobsang, Rampa T. 3699
Lobsang Rampa, Tuesday. 2727, 3699
Lobseng, Norman M. 1919. 1299
Lobsenz, Norman. 1299
Lobstein, Paul. 3645, 3781
Lochemes, M. J. 2719
Lochemes, Michael Joseph. 805
Lochet, Louis. 756, 2357
Lochhaas, Philip H. 1038, 1082
Lochhead, Marion. 1524
Lochman, Jan Milic. 1012, 1319, 1858, 2247, 2282, 2953, 3290
Locigno, Joseph P. 1481
Lock, Walter. 337, 2166
Lockaby, George W. 2056
Lockard, David. 1754
Locke, Charles Edward. 1037, 2875
Locke, Clinton. 3308
Locke, Don. 2473, 3830
Locke, John. 303, 1054, 2180, 2241, 2593, 3703
Locke, Prescott. 1359
Locker, Mabel Elsie. 1498, 3183
Lockerbie, D. Bruce. 73, 75, 639, 898, 1074, 1089, 1381, 2040, 3566
Lockerbie, Jeanette W. 17, 985, 1449, 1633, 2391, 2462, 2506, 2981, 3843
*Lockerbie, Jeannette W. 1449
Locker-Lampson, Sophie Felicite (De Rodes) 1683
Lockett, Elkin (Lightfoot) 2242, 2542
Lockhart, Clinton. 235, 2415
Lockhart, Jennie Clare (Fagen) 3144
Lockhart, John Gibson. 2227
Lockhart, John Gilbert. 672
Lockhart, Mary E. 2391
Lockhart, William S. 3853
Lockley, Andrew. 933
Lockridge, Ross Franklin. 1786, 2190

Lockridge, S. M. 1070
Lockton, William. 2251, 3221, 390, 1193
Lockward, Lynn Grover. 724
Lockwood, Charlotte Daniels. 1930
Lockwood, Francis Cummins. 2177
Lockwood, Myna. 1982, 2027
Lockwood, William Maynard. 2227, 3507
Lockyer, Herbert. 71, 215, 217, 223, 235, 254, 318, 455, 566, 601, 604, 639, 651, 898, 925, 985, 1351, 1414, 1428, 1429, 1440, 1449, 1514, 1558, 1567, 1623, 1694, 1731, 1737, 1794, 1830, 1986, 2033, 2046, 2057, 2064, 2415, 2477, 2875, 2902, 3354, 3365, 3411, 3540, 3839, 3342
Lockyer, Herbert Henry John. 1737, 2477
Loder, James Edwin. 1107, 2998, 3096
Lodge, David. 3462
Lodge, Oliver Joseph. 1889, 1893, 2833, 2990, 3073, 3078, 3211, 3507, 2990, 3078
Lodge, Richard. 3236
Lodge, Rupert Clendon. 88, 2853
Lodrick, Deryck O. 1378
Lods, Adolphe. 534, 2095, 2151
Loehr, E L. 3026
Loehr, Franklin. 2990
Loen, Arnoldus Ewout. 3327
Loeppert, Adam John. 2562
Loeschcke, Walter. 72
Loeschen, John R. 2281
Loeschke, Naomi. 133
Loessner, Ernest J. 3168
Loetscher, Lefferts Augustine. 1046, 2916, 2925
Loew, Cornelius Richard. 1095, 3212
Loew, Jacques. 754, 1137, 2883
Loew, M. R. 1137
Loew, Ralph W. 1260, 2282, 2300
Loewe, Herbert Martin James. 2112
Loewe, Raphael. 2142, 3252
Loewe, Gertrude. 2718
Loewen, Jacob Abram. 2496
Loewen, M. E. 1152, 3192
Loewenich, Walther von. 2955, 2281
Loewenstein, Hubertus. 2006
Loewenstein, Rudolph M. 53
Loewenstein, Rudolph Maurice. 53
Lofland, John. 2998
Lofquist, Henry Victor. 2807
Lofthouse, William F. 290
Lofthouse, William Frederick. 531, 568
Lofti, Nasser. 1365, 2242
Loftie, William John. 3808
Loftis, Zenas Sanford. 2555
Lofton, George Augustus. 143, 2128, 142, 151, 3102, 3595
Lofts, Norah (Robinson) 1533, 3839
Logal, Nelson William. 712, 788, 796
Logan, Algernon Sydney. 1953, 1968
Logan, Daniel. 99, 2242, 2733, 2948, 2990
Logan, James. 3534
Logan, John. 3342
Logan, Kathrine R. 1324, 3480
Logan, Kathrine Ross. 1696
Logan, Lorna E. 1476, 2556
Logan, Maurice S. 3260
Logan, Patrick. 1838
Logan, Robert William. 2198
Logan, William M. 525
Loganbill, Evangeline E. 2324
Logsdon, S Franklin. 537, 579, 606, 1830, 2034, 3374
Lohe, Wilhelm. 1120, 2295
Lohfink, Gerhard. 229, 305, 331, 2799
Lohfink, Norbert. 484, 503, 1003
Lohkamp, Nicholas. 948, 2064
Lohmann, Hartwig. 3883
Lohmeyer, Ernst. 2247
Lohmeyer, Ernst Johannes. 476
Lohmuller, Martin Nicholas. 735
Lohr, Aemiliana. 844, 1264
Lohr, Ina. 2740
Lohse, Bernhard. 3654
Lohse, Eduard. 341, 390, 408, 410, 435, 2029
Loisy, Alfred Firman. 348
Loisy, Alfred Firmin. 390, 2562, 1095, 1193, 1786, 2562
Loizeaux, A. S. 2136
Lokos, Lionel. 2173
Lollis, Lorraine. 3837
Loman, Mini. 928, 2243
Lomas, Margaret Dager. 3165
Lomask, Milton. 114, 770, 2125, 3778
Lomasney, Eileen. 2249
Lomax, Louis E. 669
Lombardi, Riccardo. 1298, 3294, 3449, 3771
Lombardi, Vincent L. 2346
Lombroso, Cesare. 3507
Lommel, Andreas. 2378
Lomupo, Robert. 2227, 3779
Londis, James J. 1314
London, Allie Spencer. 3555
London Dialectical Society. 3519

London. Eclectic Society. 2243, 3670
London, Lawrence Foushee. 891
London. University. Council for Psychical Investigation. Research Library. 2244, 2992
London. Vita et Pax Convent School. 2022, 2032
Londres, Albert. 2119
Lonergan, Bernard J. F. 776, 1723, 3633, 3645, 3669, 3714
Lonergan, William I. 100, 788, 3222
Lonergan, William Ignatius. 2214
Long, Abram Miller. 3664
Long, Albert Elwood. 1022
Long, Brideen. 3205
Long, Charles H. 1381
Long, David E. 2635
Long, Edward Le Roy. 103, 744, 944, 950, 3078, 3082, 3793
Long, Emil J. 54
Long, Eula Lee (Kennedy) 2505
Long, George. 2758
Long, Haniel. 114
Long, Inez (Goughnour) 1235
Long, Jacob Avery. 3887
Long, James. 985, 3336
Long, James A. 3689
Long, John Cuthbert. 280
Long, John Elbert. 2673
Long, Kenneth R. 915, 1206
Long, Kermit L. 2436
Long, Laura. 1532, 2621
Long, Louise. 2781
Long, Mason. 397, 3090
Long, Max. 2727
Long, Max Freedom. 2314, 2727
Long, Mildred. 2391
Long, Mildred Withers. 235
Long, Nat G. 3887
Long, Orie William. 1800
Long, Richard F. 3437
Long, Robert W. 3444
Long, Rosewell C. 2025
Long, Roswell Curtis. 2025, 2920
Long, S[imon] P[eter]. 2058
Long, Samuel Burman. 1432
Long, Sidney. 1114
Long, Simon Peter. 967, 3342, 2057, 2286, 2300
Long, Stewart. 1957
Long, Valentine. 42, 760, 796, 1449, 2355
Long, Valentine, Father. 760
[Longacre, Charles S]. 3380
Longacre, Charles Small. 3548
Longacre, Lindsay Bartholomew. 510, 540, 1943
Longden, LaRue C. 1009
Longenecker, Harold. 3253
Longenecker, J. Hershey. 2514
Longenecker, Richard N. 241, 2799
Longenecker, Steve. 2942, 3468
Longfellow, Albert Edward. 646
Longfellow, Henry Wadsworth. 1017, 2003
Longford, Elizabeth (Harman) Pakenham. 760
Longford, Frank Pakenham. 1968
Longhurst, John Edward. 1526, 2103, 3704, 3766
Long-Keesing, Elizabeth de. 1892
Longking, Joseph. 402
Longley, Alfred C. 845
Longley, Mary Theresa (Shelhamer) 3507
Longo, Gabriel Anthony. 3130
Longo, Joan. 1582, 2245
Longridge, George. 3507, 2520
Longstaff, Thomas Richmond Willis. 435, 3578
Longstreth, Edward. 558, 622
Longyear, Mary Hawley (Beecher) 1493
Lonning, Per. 2033, 3622
Lonschein, Sam. 3896
Lonsdale, Herman Lilienthal. 2034, 2209, 2973
Lonsdale, Kathleen (Yardley) 3082
Lonsdale, Kathleen Yardley. 1587
Lonsway, Francis A. 3332
Loofbourow, Leonidas Latimer. 660, 2430, 2439, 2686
Loofs, Friedrich. 2040, 2684
Look. 1958, 3325
Look, Henry M. 1666
Lookstein, Joseph Hyman. 3361, 3371
Loomis, Albertine. 2524
Loomis, Augustus Ward. 914
Loomis, Benjamin Bloomfield. 333
Loomis, Benjamin Franklin. 96
Loomis, Bess Bingaman. 1651, 3508
Loomis, Clara Denison. 2245
Loomis, D W. 3432
Loomis, Ernest. 2727
Loomis, Julia Wolfe. 2666
Loomis, Louise Ropes. 1354
Loomis, Samuel Lane. 1277
Loomis, William Farnsworth. 3094
Looney, Floyd. 145
Looney, Myrtle Owens. 3153

Loor, John R. 1430
Loos, Amandus William. 1281, 2320, 3069
Loos, Isaac K. 724, 3287
Loose, Alice Larkin (Wilson) 1061
Lopatin, Ivan Alexis. 1408, 3718
Loper, W. Harold. 3069
Loper, William Campbell. 1818
Lopez, Amy K. 2349
Lopez Trujillo, Alfonso. 821
Loque, Bertrand de. 3793
Lorack, George. 1324
Lorang, Mary Corde. 681
Lorbeer, Floyd Irving. 2229, 3208
Lord, Benjamin. 3810
Lord, Christine. 2695
Lord, Daniel Aloysius. 805, 1014, 1314, 1357, 2020, 2031, 2246, 2259, 2343, 2355, 2370, 2580, 3200, 3675, 3887, 774, 2707
Lord, Daniel Aloysuis. 3488
Lord, David Nevins. 203, 463
Lord, Donald C. 688, 2553
Lord, Eleazar. 2415, 1381
Lord, Eleazer. 1112, 3354
Lord, Fred Townley. 1558, 1889, 3368
Lord, Henrietta Frances. 1034
Lord, John. 3508
Lord, Joseph L. 606
Lord, Myra Belle (Horne) 1495
Lord, Priscilla Sawyer. 1486
Lord, Robert Howard. 606
Lord, Samuel Ebenezer Churchstone. 1723
Lord, Willis. 3319, 3605, 3645
Lord's prayer. English. 2249
Lord's prayer. Polyglot. 2247, 2859
Loredano, Giovanni Francesco. 3200
Lorensen, Larry. 3165
Lorenz, Dona Marie. 99
Lorenz, Edmund Simon. 3458, 1203, 1567, 1872, 1875, 3562
Lorenz, Ellen Jane. 736, 737, 1872
Lorenz, Felix A. 3382
Lorenzen, David N. 1813
Loretz, Oswald. 277
Lorimer, Albert W. 2217
Lorimer, George Claude. 60, 142, 165, 1182, 1324, 1968, 3444
Lorimer, William Laughton. 81
Lorimier, Jacques de. 3887
Loring, Israel. 3354
Loring, James. 1586
[Loring, Louisa Putnam]. 1860
Lorit, S. C. 2123
Lorit, Sergio C. 1297, 1631, 2183
Lornell, Ruby. 1095
Lorrain, Alfred M. 3317
Lorrance, Arleen. 2391, 3436
Lortz, Joseph. 1176, 3034, 3037
Los Angeles (Archdiocese) 1293
Los Angeles Co., Calif. Museum of Art, Los Angeles. 86, 1800
Los Angeles. First Methodist Episcopal church. Pages' club. 2260
[Losa, Francisco de]. 2245
Losch, Henry. 2048
Loserth, Johann. 1857
Losh, Apul T. 3175
Loskiel, George Henry. 2595
Losskii, Nikolai Onufrievich. 2418
Lossky, Vladimir. 179, 2647, 3667
Loth, John H. 2506, 3376
Loth, Moritz. 299
Lothrop, Reuel. 1862
Lothrop, William Henry. 1743
Lotz, Benjamin. 1992
Lotz, David W. 2281
Lotz, H. Winky. 985, 2261
Lotz, Johannes Baptist. 2244, 2380
Lotz, Philip Henry. 925, 2237, 3153, 3190, 3876, 3887
Lotze, Hermann. 2242, 2418, 3102
Loucks, Celeste. 2527, 3467
Loud, Grover Cleveland. 1567
Louden, Michael J. 813
Louden, R. Stuart. 1234
Loudy, Adlai. 1723
Louf, Andre. 2875
Lough, James Perot. 534
Loughborough, John Norton. 10, 3380
Loughhead, LaRue A. 2025, 2214
Louie, Kam. 1330
Louis. 2168, 3787
Louis, Conrad John. 586
Louis, William Francis. 1459
Louise de Marillac, 1591-1660. 2261
Louis-Frederick. 3599, 3600
Louis-Lefebvre, Marie Therese. 1859
Louisiana. Geological Survey. 191
Louisville, Ky. Free public library. 869
Louisville. Ky. Presbyterian theological seminary of Kentucky. 1477
Louisville, Ky. Southern Baptist theological seminary. 3297, 3331, 3332
Loukes, Harold. 1675, 1683
Lounds, Morris. 668

Lounsbery, Grace Constant. 702, 2382
Loup, Robert. 2555, 3704
Loutensock, Sarah. 3430
Louth, Andrew. 2644, 3622
Louthan, Henry Thompson. 165
Louthan, Sheldon. 1254
Louttit, Henry Irving. 2907, 3716
Louvel, Francois. 3265
[Louvet, Simone (Leveque) 727
Loux, Du Bois Henry. 500, 1953, 2836
Loux, Michael J. 3755
Lovasik, Lawrence George. 132, 622, 769, 887, 999, 1298, 1836, 1893, 1977, 1999, 2254, 2262, 2343, 2360, 3284, 3480, 3540
[Lovat, Alice Mary (Weld-Blundell) Fraser. 756
Lovat, Alice Mary (Weld-Blundell) Fraser. 2352
Love, Alonzo Robert. 3023
Love, Emanuel King. 3305
Love, Gladys. 1051
Love, James Franklin. 390, 1105, 2493, 2520
Love, Jeff. 2727
Love, Julian Price. 390, 613, 2504, 3681
Love, Larry. 2932
Love, Thomas T. 2632
Love, William DeLoss. 1999, 2943
Lovegren, Alta Lee (Grimes) 2535
Lovejoy, David Sherman. 1757
Lovejoy, Joseph Cammet. 3705
Lovejoy, Luther Ellsworth. 3529, 3702
Lovejoy, W P. 2433
Lovejoy, William P. 1120
Lovelace, Austin Cole. 915, 916, 1209, 1878, 2743
Lovelace, Delos Wheeler. 2006
Lovelace, Marc. 540
Lovelace, Richard F. 1843, 3233
Loveland, Anne C. 1300
Loveland, Clara O. 2967
Loveland, E Winchester. 2174, 2833
Loveland, Gilbert. 2488
Loveland, J S. 3508
Loveland, Samuel C. 1769
Loveland, Seymour. 622, 626, 629
Loveless, Frances B. 311, 633
Loveless, Wendell Phillips. 468, 594, 967, 1449, 3018
Loveless, William C. 908
Lovell, Alfred Charles Bernard. 99
Lovell, Daisy Washburn. 3274
Lovell, John. 3522
[Lovelle, Albert Clyde] 1887. 1061
Loverdo, Costa de. 2656
Lovern, Thomas Y. 1723
Lovestrand, Harold. 2533
Lovett, C S. 1567
Lovett, W Davis. 3290
Lovette, Roger. 181, 449, 985
Lovgren, Nils. 1176
Lovi, Henrietta. 3519
Loving, Albert L. 2267
Loving, Brady Antoine. 3721
Loving, John W. 2304
Low, Anthony. 2468
Low, John Low. 1483
Lowber, James William. 1051, 1428, 1429, 2836, 1070, 1429
Lowden, Joseph D. 2467, 3233
Lowder, Paul D. 1298, 2267, 2791
Lowe, Arnold Hilmar. 3342, 967, 1070, 1375, 2932
Lowe, Bob. 1295, 2267
Lowe, Chester Carver. 1061
*Lowe, Edith. 584
[Lowe, Edith May (Kovar)]. 622, 901, 1996
Lowe, Edmund Peyton. 204
Lowe, Ephraim Noble. 1506
Lowe, Frank Melville. 1296, 1461
Lowe, Harry William. 83, 1375, 1716, 1751, 3382, 3385
Lowe, Jacques. 754
Lowe, John. 2539, 2824, 2247
Lowe, Louis W. 1120
Lowe, Marmion L. 509, 2040, 2415
Lowe, Martha Ann (Perry) 2267
[Lowe, Paul Emilius]. 1655
Lowe, Samuel Franklin. 3018
Lowell, Abbott Lawrence. 123
Lowell, C. Stanley. 78, 1041, 1150
Lowell, Daniel Ozro Smith. 80, 1936
Lowell, Francis Cabot. 1938
Lowell, James Russell. 750, 2856
[Lowell, John]. 1337
Lowell, Laurel. 96, 99
Lowell, Mass. Eliot church. 1271
Lowell, Mass. First Unitarian society. 2953, 3725
Lowell, Percival. 1936
[Lowell, Robert Traill Spence]. 2939
Lowenthal, Eric I. 528, 2133
Lowenthal, Marvin. 2078, 2092, 2099
[Lower, Thomas]. 1683

Lowery, Daniel L. 999, 3388
Lowery, Irving E. 1577
Lowery, James L. 1296
Lowery, Kathleen. 1582, 2267
Lowie, Robert Harry. 3109, 1389, 3109
Lowith, Karl. 1800, 2843
Lowndes, Arthur Edward Gilbert. 44
Lowndes, Marion S. 1710
Lowndes, Mary E. 2717
Lownsbery, Eloise. 660, 661
Lowrey, Asbury. 3645, 3299
Lowrey, William Tyndale. 1449
Lowrie. 2170
Lowrie, Donald Alexander. 191, 2750
Lowrie, Ernest Benson. 3817
Lowrie, James Gibson. 2015
Lowrie, John Cameron. 2926
Lowrie, John Marshall. 525, 1405, 1506,
    1533, 1977, 2621
Lowrie, Louisa Ann (Wilson) 3130
Lowrie, Randolph W. 1222, 2962
Lowrie, Samuel Thompson. 403, 1612
Lowrie, Walter. 3130, 176, 414, 435, 919,
    1070, 1240, 1249, 1296, 1968, 2170,
    2247, 2257, 2824, 3061, 3652, 920, 2170
Lowrie, Walter Macon. 3130
Lowry, Anna M. 3130
Lowry, Charles Wesley. 1150, 3712
Lowry, Eugene L. 2902
Lowry, Gentry G. 2531
Lowry, Houston W. 2355
Lowry, James Martin. 1467
[Lowry, John]. 1577
Lowry, Lewis A. 1396
Lowry, Oscar. 1567, 3153, 1567, 3393
Lowry, Robert. 3562
Lowry, Walker. 1028, 3603
Lowth, Robert. 567, 1785, 1799
Lowther, Edgar A. 1095
Loy, Matthias. 2160
Loyasik, Lawrence George. 622
Loyola-Baumgarth Symposium on Values
    and Ethics (1980. 950
Loyola, Ignacio de. 3476, 1882, 2268,
    2269, 2380, 2391, 3476, 2268
Loyson, Charles Jean Marie. 1609
Lozier, John Hogarth. 3753
Lozowick, Lee. 1822
Lonning, Per. 9
Lu, K'uan Yu. 1783, 3493, 3892
Lu, K'uan Y. 3892
[Lu, Yen]. 3586
Lubac, Henri de. 967, 1740, 101, 704,
    756, 776, 781, 788, 1120, 1735, 1740,
    3567, 3593, 3633
Lubac, Henri Henri de. 3593
Lubich, Chiara. 807, 999, 1631, 2391,
    2392
Lubienska de Lenval, Helene. 935, 2235
Lubke, Wilhelm. 1160
Luca, Giuseppe de. 399
Lucarini, Spartaco. 2412
Lucas, Abner H. 3342
Lucas, Barbara. 925, 3281
Lucas de San Jose, 1872. 2136, 2571
Lucas, DeWitt Bannister. 2946
Lucas, Edward Deming. 64
Lucas, George Joseph. 19, 3471
Lucas, Isidro. 827, 1817
Lucas, Jerry. 318, 319, 2717
Lucas, John Randolph. 3622
Lucas, Lawrence. 1132
Lucas, Merle J. 10
Lucas of Saint Joseph. 2136, 2571
Lucas, Paul R. 3451
Lucas, Richard Charles. 341
Lucas, Sharalee. 1749, 2270
Lucas, Sidney. 1682, 1685
Lucas, Silas Bradbury. 455
Lucas de San Jose. 3603
Luccock, George Naphtali. 3200
Luccock, Halford Edward. 1432, 332, 374,
    408, 537, 1070, 1432, 1449, 1841, 1905,
    2025, 2424, 2436, 2886, 2902, 3347,
    3444, 3745, 1837, 2392, 2424, 3633
Luccock, Halford Edwards. 1112
Luccock, Naphtali. 2055
Luccock, Robert Edward. 2436, 443,
    1432, 2436, 3354
Luce, Alice Eveline. 3095, 3720
Luce, Arthur Aston. 2585, 192
Luce, Clare (Boothe) 3281
Luce, Harry Kenneth. 2799
Lucey, Dan. 3880
Lucey, William Leo. 822
Luche. 770
Luchs, Alison. 78, 3302
Luchs, Alvin Schanfarber. 2084
[Lucian Alphonsus, 1913. 3187
Lucian Alphonsus. 3187
Lucianus. 2270
Lucianus Samosatensis. 1810
Lucie-Smith, Edward. 1026, 1938
Luciw, Theodore. 1844, 3722
Luck, Burnice. 1362
*Luck, G. Coleman. 345, 413, 519
Luckenbach, William Henry. 3569

Luckert, Karl W. 20, 2677, 2736
Luckey, Leonard Wilson Arnold. 3073
*Luckhardt, Mildred Corell. 3173
Luckhardt, Mildred Madeleine (Corell)
    406, 595, 629, 1120, 1176, 2707
Lucki, Emil. 1187
Luckmann, Thomas. 3086
Luckock, Herbert Mortimer. 390, 2345
Luddy, Ailbe J. 3021, 3709
Luddy, Ailbe John. 3021
Ludeman, Annette Martin. 2171
Luder, Hope Elizabeth. 1685, 3834
Luder, William Fay. 3393
[Ludington, James]. 3508
Ludlow, Arthur Clyde. 2917
Ludlow, Daniel H. 500, 679, 3428
Ludlow, James Meeker. 2639, 1390
Ludlow, John Malcolm Forbes. 1408
Ludlow, Theodore Russell. 1239
Ludlow, Victor L. 500, 2599
Ludovici, Anthony Mario, tr. 2710
[Ludovicka, Mary] 1844. 3421
Ludvigsen, Helena Gebuhr. 682, 2546
Ludwick, Harry M. 3723
Ludwig, Charles. 1229, 381, 681, 682,
    925, 1277, 2033, 2270, 2271, 2490, 2536,
    3301
Ludwig, Charles Shelton. 681, 1841, 2490
Ludwig, David J. 2338, 3480
Ludwig, Emil. 1968
Ludwig, Mileta. 1801, 3421
Ludwig, Minnie E. 1017
Ludwigson, R. 606
Ludy, Claude Edward. 509, 3852
Ludy, Robert Borneman. 1269
Luecke, George. 2282, 2286
Luecke, Richard. 1066
Luecke, Richard Henry. 1279, 2216
Lueckhoff, Friedrich Carl. 1545
Lueker, Erwin Louis. 244, 1120
Lueking, Frederick Dean. 1750, 2296,
    2297
Luff, S. G. A. 999
Luff, Stanley George Anthony. 772, 807,
    999
Luffberry, Henry Benner. 1239, 3733
Lugan, Alphonse. 3450
Lugibihl, Walter H. 2488
Luibheid, Colm. 80, 1544
Luijpen, Wilhelmus Antonius Maria. 100,
    1724, 3102
Luis. 999, 1000
Luis de Granada. 1000, 2981
Luka, Ronald. 2346
Luke, Harry Charles Joseph. 3239
Luke, Helen M. 2649
Lukens, Victor Herbert. 1599
Lukens, W. Dewitt. 967
Luker, R G. 2604
Lukomskii, Georgil Kresent'evich. 3576
Lull, Edward Lawrence. 509
Lull, Ramon. 1355, 2271, 2644, 2648
Lum, Ada. 3415
Lum, Peter. 3525
Lumb, John Reginald. 908, 3174
Lumiere et vie. 137, 2001, 2002
Lumley, Arthur W. 1690
Lummis, Edward William. 429, 3578
Lummis, Eliza O'Brien. 3838
Lumpkin, William Latane. 135, 145, 2258,
    2401, 3130, 3143, 3333
Lums, Dyer Daniel. 3508
Lund, Eric. 287
Lund, Gerald N. 3319, 3887
Lund, Harold Woodhull. 1034, 1037, 3213
Lund, John Lewis. 2618
Lund, Nils Wilhelm. 348
Lund, T. Fenwick. 3370
Lundbom, Jack R. 547
Lunde, Alfred E. 2633
Lunde, Johan. 1440, 17
Lunde, Norman S. 2695
Lundeberg, Knut Olafson. 363
Lundeen, Anton. 2510
Lundeen, Lyman T. 3070, 3813
Lundholm, Algot Theodore. 3839
Lundholm, Helge. 2320
Lundin, Jack W. 1246, 1321, 1605
Lundquist, Amos Theodore. 967, 1434,
    3204
Lundquist, Harold Leonard. 967, 2204
Lundstrom, Emil Ferdinand. 2727
Lundstrom, Gosta. 2064
Lundstrom, Harold. 2611
Lundstrom, Joseph. 679
Lundstrom, Linden John. 916
Lundstrom, Lowell. 3539
Lundwall, Nels Benjamin. 1593, 2604,
    2608, 2611, 3430, 3599
Lunger, Alberta (Huff) 1449
Lunger, Harold L. 732, 1086, 1466, 3444
Lunn, Arnold Henry Moore. 64, 1364,
    3079, 3082, 3803
Lunn, Henry Simpson. 2875, 1041
Lunsford, Otto. 1551
Lunsford, William 3465
[Lunt, Edward D.]. 3508

Lunt, Horace Gray. 1247
Lunt, William Edward. 807, 817, 3589,
    807, 3589
Luntz, Charles E. 96, 3054
Luomala, Katharine. 2374, 2666, 3546
Luongo, Anthony M. 3142
*Lupien, Louis H. 3508
Lupien, Louis H. 3508
Lupo, Joseph F. 1000
Lupton, Daniel E. 613
Lupton, Dilworth. 967
Lupton, Joseph Hirst. 1307, 2123
Lupul, Manoly R. 815, 1144
Lurie, Rose G. 3581
Lurker, Manfred. 1502
Luscombe, David Edward. 1
Luscombe, T. R. 814
Lussier, Ernest. 348, 414, 424, 1742,
    2071, 2255, 2266
Lusson, M. 2946
Lutes, Della Thompson. 633
Luther. 2284
Luther College, Decorah, Iowa Dept. Of
    Religion. 3667
Luther league of America. 2272
Luther league of New York state. 2289
Luther, Martin. 748, 3629, 340, 371, 380,
    386, 447, 468, 521, 748, 1267, 1351,
    1432, 1434, 1440, 1449, 1527, 1658,
    1804, 1873, 1985, 2021, 2034, 2275,
    2278, 2279, 2280, 2281, 2283, 2284,
    2285, 2286, 2297, 2315, 2316, 2392,
    2833, 2892, 3034, 3368, 3579, 3629,
    3637, 3900
Luthera, Ved Prakash. 3088
Lutheran Association, Ithaca, N.y. 2302
Lutheran Church. Book of Concord. 2283
Lutheran Church in America. 2282, 2290
Lutheran Church in America. Board of
    Social Ministry. 1138
Lutheran Church in America. Commission
    on Function and Structure. 2290, 2480
*Lutheran Church in America,
    Commission on Worship. 2295
Lutheran Church in America. Nebraska
    Synod. 2291
Lutheran Church in America. Northeastern
    Pennsylvania Synod. 2292
Lutheran Church in America. South
    Carolina Synod. History of the Synod
    Committee. 2290
Lutheran Church in America. Southeastern
    Pennsylvania Synod. 2292
Lutheran Church in America. Task Group
    for Long-Range Planning. 2791, 3656
Lutheran Church in America. Upper New
    York Synod. 2291
Lutheran church in Norway. Liturgy and
    ritual. 2295
Lutheran church in Sweden Liturgy and
    ritual. 2292
Lutheran Church. Liturgy and ritual. 28,
    2295
Lutheran Church--Missouri Synod. 2289,
    2293, 2296, 2480
Lutheran Church--Missouri Synod. Board
    for Parish Education. 2297, 3184, 3185
Lutheran Church-Missouri Synod.
    Commission on Church Architecture.
    1157
Lutheran Church--Missouri Synod. Dept.
    of Missionary Education. 2483, 2493,
    2504, 2520
Lutheran Church--Missouri Synod.
    Districts. Brazil. 2296
Lutheran Church--Missouri Synod.
    Districts. English. 2296
Lutheran Church--Missouri Synod.
    Districts. Iowa. 2290
Lutheran Church--Missouri Synod.
    Districts. Southern. 2296
Lutheran Church—Missouri Synod.
    Family Life Committee. 2345, 3389
Lutheran Church--Missouri Synod.
    Synodical Centennial Committee. 445
Lutheran churches of the world. 2288
Lutheran Daughters of the Reformation.
    2550
Lutheran Education Association. 1134,
    2293, 3168
Lutheran Evangelism Council. 1573
Lutheran Foreign Missions Conference of
    America. 2296
Lutheran Historical Conference. 2288
Lutheran historical society, Gettysburg.
    Library. 2283
Lutheran world convention. 2282
Lutheran World Federation. Assembly.
    4th, Helsinki, 1963. 2285
Lutheran World Federation. Assembly.
    5th, Evian-les-Bains, France, 1970. 2285
Lutheran World Federation. Commission
    on Education. 1329
Lutheran youth conference. 1st,
    Minneapolis, 1937. 3887
Luthi, Walter. 2902, 416, 468, 509, 2247,
    2902

Lutkin, Peter Christian. 1203, 2633
Lutoslawski, Wincenty. 2418
Luttrell, John Lewis. 3730
Lutyens, 2187, 3683
Lutyens, Mary. 2187
Lutyens, William Enderby. 416
Lutz, A. Fowler. 1976
Lutz, Bernard E. 2670
Lutz, Charles P. 3816
Lutz, Henry Frey. 3130
Lutz, Jessie Gregory. 2510, 3756
Lutz, Lorry. 1706, 2486
Lutz, Milton Charles. 1061
Lutze, Karl E. 1132, 2892
Lutzer, Erwin W. 985, 993, 1534, 3290
Lutzow, Franz Heinrich Hieronymus
    Valentin. 1857, 3038
Lutzow, Franz Heinrich Hieronymus
    Valentin, graf von. 674, 1857
Luxton, David W. 1211
Luxton, Richard. 2375
Luzzatti, Luigi. 3192
Luzzatto, Marco. 500, 2328
Luzzatto, Moses Hayyim. 721, 1539, 2621
Luzzi, Giovanni. 1097
Lwin, Esther. 3179
Lyall, Alfred Comyn. 1896
Lyall, Leslie T. 912, 2493, 2503
Lyall, Leslie T. 2493
Lydgate, John. 1414
Lydon, Patrick Joseph. 736
Lydston, George Frank. 2078
Lyle, Betty. 1776
Lyle, Henry James. 1429
Lyles, Albert M. 2428
Lyles, Jean Caffey. 1046
Lyman, Albert Josiah. 2375, 2902, 3673
Lyman, Albert R. 2304
Lyman, Eugene William. 1105, 1729,
    3102
Lyman, Frederick C. 2380
Lyman, Joseph. 1504
[Lyman, Julia E.]. 1055
Lyman, Mary Redington (Ely) 1414, 410,
    420, 423, 2059, 2502, 2799
Lyman, Sarah Joiner. 2524
Lyman, Stanford M. 1412
Lynch, Adrian. 2341
Lynch, Denis. 329
Lynch, Edward Kilian. 2576, 3306
Lynch, Etta. 2875
Lynch, Flann. 3526
Lynch, Frederick Henry. 967, 2807, 1543,
    3673
Lynch, George Edward. 666
Lynch, Helen M. 3205
Lynch, James Charles. 622
Lynch, John W. 193, 1026, 1449
Lynch, Joseph H. 2583
Lynch, Kilian F. 1328
Lynch, Lawrence E. 1105, 3696
Lynch, Patricia. 3283, 3284
Lynch, Richard. 3751
[Lynch, Thomas P.]. 1041
Lynch, Thomas Toke. 1341
Lynch, Timothy. 1356
Lynch, William E. 386
Lynch, William F. 1593, 1845, 3071, 3328
Lynch, William Francis. 2762
Lynch-Watson, Janet. 928, 3415
Lynch William E. 311
Lynd, Helen (Merrell) 1765
Lynd, Samuel W. 105, 3526
Lynip, G. Louise. 2545
Lynip, Ryllis (Alexander) Goslin. 651
Lynk, Frederick M. 2251, 3717
Lynn. 3887
Lynn, Edwin Charles. 1167
Lynn, Jeannette (Murphey) 1286
Lynn, Mary Loyola. 1650
Lynn, Robert Charles. 1255
Lynn, Robert W. 1130, 3565
Lynn, Thomas. 3374
Lynskey, Elizabeth M. 807
Lyon, Bernice E. 1953, 3171
Lyon, David. 1319, 2352, 3444
Lyon, David Williard. 1039
Lyon, Ernest. 2682
Lyon, Ervin F. 149
Lyon, James. 3718
Lyon, Josephine A. 2688
Lyon, Milford Hall. 694, 951, 2040
Lyon, Oliver Lincoln. 211

Lyon, Quinter Marcellus. 2392, 3118,
    3204
Lyon, Thoburn Cassady. 1736
Lyon, Thomas. 3193, 3194
Lyon, William. 1256
Lyon, William Henry. 3323
Lyone Quinter Marcellus. 3118
Lyonnard, Jean. 3542
Lyons, Alexander. 1329, 2118
Lyons, Arthur. 3304
Lyons, Bernard. 2245, 2774
Lyons, Bob E. 2939
Lyons, Francis X. 1745

Lyons, George Norman. 967
Lyons, Horace G. 967
Lyons, Hugh Peter Carbery. 858
Lyons, James Gilborne. 2973
Lyons, James W. 858, 3406
Lyons, Jeanne Marie. 3243
Lyons, Jenne Marie. 3243
Lyons, John Frederick. 2927
Lyons, Letitia Mary. 824
Lyons, Mark J. 2361
[Lyons, Mary Camilla. 731
Lys, Daniel. 530
Lysnes, Olaf. 3026
Lytch, William Elbert. 195, 2713
Lytle, James Hamlin. 438
Lyttelton, Edith Sophy (Balfour) 2990
Lyttle, Charles Harold. 3808
Lytton, Edward George Earle Lytton
  Bulwer-Lytton. 3200

M

Maahs, Arnold M. 3851
Maas, Anthony John. 1968, 2016, 2415
Maas, Robin. 639
Maat, William Anthony. 1115, 3234
Mabie, Hamilton Wright. 967, 1111, 2652
Mabie, Henry Clay. 105, 1321, 3131, 105,
  1567, 2003, 2493
Mabry, Donald J. 6
Mabry, Gregory. 1288, 1298, 1299
Mabry, J. C. 2068
Mabry, Mildred. 1014
Mabuce, Ethel. 2304, 2505
MacAdam, George. 1150, 1848, 2355,
  2624, 2697
McAdams, Daniel A. 3203, 3204
McAdams, Edward Patrick. 1826
McAdams, Elizabeth E. 2990
McAdoo, H R. 946
McAdoo, Henry Robert. 946, 3655
McAfee, Cleland Boyd. 272, 576, 951,
  1051, 1061, 1120, 1239, 1316, 2520,
  2554, 3336, 3337, 3673, 272, 1070
McAfee, John Armstrong. 1586
McAfee, Joseph Ernest. 2527
McAfee, Sara Jane (Regulus) 1310
McAfee, Sara Jane (Regulus) L. D.
  McAfee. 1310
McAlister, Hazel. 2392
McAlister, Jack. 1455, 1578, 2500, 2517
Macalister, Robert Alexander Stewart.
  1275
McAlister, W., Robert. 1423
McAll, Reginald Ley. 916
McAllaster, Elva Arline. 2304, 3415
MacAllister, Dale E. 1477
McAllister, Frederick Borman. 3887
McAllister, Grace Edna. 3839
McAllister, James Gray. 532, 1776
McAllister, Lester G. 733, 1464, 3572
McAllister, Robert J. 2574
McAlpin, Edwin Augustus. 1061, 3365
MacAlpine, Robert George. 878
MacAlpine, Robert John. 1891
McAnally, David Rice. 2352, 2446, 2447,
  2794
McAndrew, John. 1160
McAndrews, Dunstan. 2188
McAnear, Beverly. 688, 1214
McAnear, Kenneth. 3237
McArdle, Mary Aurelia. 3256
McArdle, Mildred J. 295, 1968, 3171
Macarius. 1018
McArthur, A Allan. 1262
McArthur, Harvey K. 334, 335, 2008,
  3005, 3336
MacArthur, Jack. 1696
MacArthur, John. 277, 985, 1120
MacArthur, John F. 180, 277, 952, 2247,
  2815
Macarthur, John Robertson. 311
MacArthur, John Stewart. 1893, 2685
MacArthur, Kathleen Walker. 3452, 3804,
  2223, 3879
McArthur, Paul. 3508
MacArthur, Robert Stuart. 3342, 3354,
  3409, 3853, 165, 235, 515, 3342, 3409
McCarthy -Shulz. 3233
Macartney, Clarence Edward. 2771, 2902
Macartney, Clarence Edward Nobel. 1841
Macartney, Clarence Edward Noble. 215,
  2932, 64, 71, 73, 215, 493, 561, 604,
  925, 1593, 1841, 1889, 2040, 2250, 2626,
  2771, 2799, 2824, 2887, 2902, 2910,
  2912, 2932, 3342, 3354, 3362, 3839, 604,
  2040, 2064, 2910, 2932, 3354, 2041
McAstocker, David Plant.
McAstocker, David Plante. 2305
McAstocker, David Plante. 763, 1830,
  1945, 1953, 2048, 2132, 2355, 3540
McAstoker, David Plante. 42
Macaulay, David. 750
Macaulay, J. C. 441, 2055

Macaulay, Joseph Cordner. 329, 332, 403,
  423, 800, 1567, 1836
Macaulay, Ranald. 985
Macaulay, Susan Schaeffer. 985
Macaulay, Thomas Babington Macaulay.
  2471
McAuley, Claire. 2343
McAuley, Mary Catherine. 2573, 2580
McAuliffe, Clarence R. 2756, 2812, 3265
McAuliffe, Harold J. 1424
McAuliffe, Marius. 3013
Macauliffe, Max Arthur. 3408
McAvoy, Thomas Timothy. 34, 819, 874,
  819, 833, 874, 2735
Macbain, Alexander. 2655
McBain, John M. 1314, 2064, 3529
McBain, Loren D. 993
MacBeath, Andrew. 551
MacBeth, George. 616, 2130
McBeth, Harry Leon. 149
McBeth, Joseph Phinis. 468
McBeth, Leon. 1393, 1399, 1634, 2483,
  3466, 3834
McBirney, Allegra. 1958, 2875
McBirnie, William S. 611, 3319
McBirnie, William Steuart. 148, 1196,
  1986
McBride, Alfred. 295, 329, 646, 805, 811,
  935
McBride, Andrew Jackson. 3508
MacBride, Andrew Sommerville. 1662
McBride, Charles R. 1609
McBride, Clarence Ralph. 3254
McBride, Cora Emma. 3313
McBride, Genevieve. 2541
McBride, Leda P. 281
McBride, Thomas Garth. 1075
McBridge, Alfred. 1267
McBrien, Richard P. 788, 940, 1187,
  1188, 1245, 1467, 3242
McBurney, Louis. 1298
McCaba, Joseph. 2305, 2542
McCabe, Francis Xavier. 788, 2001, 2642
McCabe, Harriet C. 295
McCabe, Herbert. 948, 1120
McCabe, James Dabney. 2820, 3034
McCabe, James Patrick. 764, 3031, 3032
McCabe, Joseph. 1, 114, 116, 782, 794,
  809, 2769, 3024, 3094, 3434, 1, 3024
McCabe, Joseph E. 9, 1252, 1783, 2237,
  2786, 3673
McCabe, Lorenzo Dow. 1737
McCabe, Margaret Virginia. 3508
Maccabees. 2305
McCafferty, Florence. 3555
McCafferty, Lawrence M. 3118
McCaffery, Ellen. 96, 98
McCaffery, John. 2477, 2849
McCaffery, Richard J. 2370
McCaffree, Joe E. 1470, 1879
MacCaffrey, Isabel Gamble. 2468
MacCaffrey, James. 811
McCaffrey, Patrick Romaeus. 3420
McCain, Walter L. 1304
McCaleb, J. M. 1449
McCaleb, John Moody. 1359, 1953
McCall, Donald D. 11, 1011
McCall, Druie Anselm. 464
McCall, Duke E. 148, 3529
McCall, Emmanuel L. 2683
McCall, Moses Nathaniel. 147
McCall, Oswald Walter Samuel. 1342,
  1449, 1593, 1953, 2902
McCall, Thomas S. 410, 535, 610
Maccall, William. 1542
McCall, Yvonne Holloway. 495, 634,
  2022, 3304
McCalla, Daniel. 1334
McCalla, George Washington. 319, 465,
  2017, 3480
McCallen, James Aloysius. 27
[McCallen Robert Seth]. 3393, 3411
MacCallum, Esther Darbyshire. 1503
McCallum, Eva Beatrice (McNown) 3174,
  3555
McCallum, James Ramsay. 1, 3645
MacCallum, John Archibald. 1593, 1724
McCallum, John Dennis. 2304
McCallum, Martha. 2983
McCallum, William Cecil. 3555
McCammon, Dorothy Snapp. 2510
McCan, Robert L. 465
McCandless, James W. 3871
McCandless, James Wilbur. 3871
McCandless, Oleta R. 1911
McCann, Dennis. 2709, 3452
McCann, Edna. 1432
McCann, Justin. 188, 189, 3221
McCann, Leonard A. 2136, 2639
[McCann, Mary Agnes, 1851. 3378, 3416
McCann, Paul. 1628, 3281
McCann, Richard Vincent. 2784
McCann, Samuel Napoleon. 180
McCants, Dorothea Olga. 1404, 2538
McCarran, Mary L. 2358
McCarrell, William. 461
McCarroll, Tolbert. 2392

McCarron, Hugh Michael. 756
McCartee, Divie Bethune. 2516
*McCarter, Neely Dixon. 1449
McCarter, Neely Dixon. 437, 2892
McCartha, C. L. 1929
McCarthy, Abigail Quigley. 1492
McCarthy, Dan B. 2544, 2771
McCarthy, David S. 985, 991, 3550
McCarthy, Dennis J. 201, 535, 1377,
  2089
McCarthy, Edward Charles. 1372
McCarthy, Elizabeth Edna. 1724
McCarthy, Estelle. 2866
McCarthy, Gerontius. 2850
McCarthy, Helen A. 2245
[McCarthy, J. J.]. 1982
McCarthy, J P. 1794
McCarthy, John. 3012
McCarthy, John M. 863, 2214
McCarthy, Joseph. 1000
MacCarthy, Joseph Patrick. 3061
McCarthy, Joseph. 2211
McCarthy, Justin. 2216
McCarthy, Mary Augustine. 1476
McCarthy, Mary Barbara. 3419
McCarthy, Thomas Patrick. 830, 2581
McCarthy, Timothy. 2939
McCarthy, William. 1655
McCartney, Albert Joseph. 2932
McCartney, Richard Hayes. 52, 2082
McCartt, Clara Anniss. 2734
McCarty, Doran. 235
McCarty, Mary Eva. 3420
McCarty, Richard Justin. 2227
MacCarty, Skip. 3664
McCarty, W. A. 3645
McCary, James Leslie. 200
McCash, Isaac Newton. 2527
McCashland, Selby Vernon. 235
McCaskey, John Piersol. 1114
McCaskill, Charles Wallace. 1034
McCaskill, Joseph Clyde. 688
McCasland, Selby Vernon. 390, 2052,
  235, 1422, 3118, 1968
McCauley, Elfrieda. 1605
McCauley, Leon. 967, 2892
McCauley, MichaelF. 186
MacCauley, Rose Agnes. 586
McCauley, W[illiam] F[letcher]. 295
McCauley, Michael F. 3488
McCaw, Grace Anna (Main) 2513
McCaw, Mabel (Niedermeyer) 3392, 3531
Macchioro, Vittorio D. 2636, 2744, 2799
McClain, Alva J. 218, 468, 1751, 2174
McClain, Charles Allen. 1007
McClain, Dayton E. 3411, 3539
McClain, Roy O. 967
McClain, W. Blair. 2211
McClanahan, John H. 1015
McClary, Clebe. 931, 2306
McClatchey, Diana. 1292
McClelin, John Phillip. 651
McClellan, Albert. 151, 235, 993, 1061,
  1567, 2072, 2507, 3465
McClellan, Foster C. 3750
McClelland, Adam. 1968
McClelland, Clarence Paul. 3758
McClelland, Everett Slater. 1061
McClelland, Margaret Tyrrell. 3181
McClelland, Thomas Calvin. 2071, 338,
  2029, 2064
McClelland, Vincent Alan. 870, 2328
McClelland, W. Robert. 1742, 2306
McClelland, William Grigor. 3434
McClenachan, Charles Thompson. 1660
McClenahan, Sallie Hews (Phillips) 2831
McClendon, Gene. 3327
McClendon, James William. 3102, 3617,
  3669
MacClenny, Wilbur E. 2735
McClintock, James H. 2616
McClintock, John. 244, 1183, 1512, 3798
McClintock, Marshall. 1017
MacClintock, Stuart. 2122
McClinton, Katharine (Morrison) 1157,
  1242
McClinton, Katherine (Morrison) 922
McClorey, John A. 199, 863, 2265, 864,
  1131, 1471, 2214
McCloskey, Joseph Aloysius. 2159
McCloskey, Patrick. 1028, 1646
McCloud, Henry J. 3262, 1249
McClow, Loyd Levi. 3871
McCloy, Shelby Thomas. 1051, 1092,
  1710, 1711
McClung, Floyd. 1260
McClung, Fred W. 3374
McClung, Samuel O. 1496
McClunn, Justin David. 77
McClure, Alexander Doak. 1830
McClure, Arthur F. 1907
McClure, Edmund. 1051
McClure, Haven. 321, 410
McClure, James B. 3572
McClure, James Baird. 1907, 2758
McClure, James Gore King. 967, 3673,
  893, 1794, 2875

McClure, James T. 204
McClure, William Donald. 2552
McClurg, A. C., and company. 199
McCluskey, Neil Gerard. 831, 2328, 2591
McCluskey. Neil Gerard. 833
McClusky, Evelyn (McFarlane) 516, 560,
  3887
Maccoby, Hyam. 2013, 2148
McColgan, Daniel E. 3438
McColgan, Kristin Pruitt. 1933
MacColl, Alexander. 2932, 3645
MacColl, Malcolm. 1218, 1224
MacCollam, Joel A. 1259
McCollister, John. 9, 1100, 2937, 2214,
  2300
McCollough, Charles R. 941
McCollum, Vashti (Cromwell) 1150
McComas, E. W. 876, 2050
McComas, Henry Clay. 2998, 3508
McComb, John Hess. 363, 2932, 3295,
  3664
McComb, Louise. 3161
McComb, Samuel. 248, 1051, 1593, 1724,
  1889, 2409, 2884, 2886, 2892, 2902
MacConastair, Alfred. 2333
McConaughy, David. 2016, 2932, 1260,
  3874
McConaughy, James. 437, 639, 1968,
  1992, 2041, 3555
McConica, James Kelsey. 3039
McConkey, F Paul. 2933
McConkey, James Henry. 459, 606, 967,
  1515, 1830, 2306, 1830
McConkie, Bruce R. 344, 929, 1968,
  2019, 2415, 2599, 2610, 3319
McConkie, Joseph F. 935, 3430, 3493
McConkie, Oscar Walter. 1, 3838, 42
McConkie, Oscar Walter. 1830
McConnachie, John. 176, 1457
McConnell, Charles Melvin. 3254
McConnell, Dorothy Frances. 1621, 2520
McConnell, Francis J. 3342
McConnell, Francis John. 3804, 41, 311,
  1055, 1061, 1070, 1099, 1114, 1168,
  1422, 1593, 1854, 1886, 2306, 2421,
  2734, 2902, 2950, 3092, 3212, 3444,
  3448, 3529, 3616, 3758, 3804, 2734,
  3212, 2306
McConnell, Franz Marsahll. 142
McConnell, Franz Marshall. 2944, 3439
McConnell, John S. J[ames]. 2451
McConnell, John S. Janes. 1912
McConnell, Lela Grace. 3131
McConnell, Lincoln. 1953
McConnell, Margaret. 2573
McConnell, Ray Madding. 28
McConnell,Samuel D. 1051
McConnell, Samuel David. 1061, 1070,
  1889, 2967, 1061, 1095, 1889, 2967,
  2973
McConnell, T. W. 2477
McConnell, Thomas Maxwell. 1986
McConner, John E. 607
McCook, Henry Christopher. 3839
McCool, Gerald A. 3628
McCord, David M. 1003
*McCord, Hugo. 1724
McCord, Hugo. 2247
McCord, Iris Ikeler. 3579
McCord, William J. 3295
McCorkel, Roy James. 2520
McCorkle, Archibald Rea. 451
McCorkle, Henry L. 2548
McCorkle, William P. 1034
MacCormac, Earl R. 3070
McCormack, Arthur. 137, 1137, 2865
McCormick, Anne (O'Hare) 2769
McCormick, Charles Wesley. 1017
McCormick, Donald. 1652
McCormick, John Dale. 639
McCormick, John Newton. 2960
McCormick, John Nicholas. 1823
McCormick, Richard A. 948
McCormick, Rose Matthew. 2550
McCormick, Scott. 2254, 3065
McCormick, Stephen J. 819, 2316
McCormick theological seminary, Chicago.
  2306, 3614
McCormick, William. 687
McCormick, William Patrick Alyn. 3365
McCormick, William Patrick Glyn. 967,
  2307
McCorry, Vincent P. 2581, 366, 367, 384,
  1264, 1714, 2255, 2576, 2581, 2799
McCosh, James. 1580, 19, 1580, 1855,
  2180, 2241, 2418, 2933, 2981, 3102,
  3567
McCoskry, Samuel Allen. 76
MacCoun, Townsend. 2762
McCown, Chester Charlton. 2009, 2064,
  3320, 1818
McCoy, Alan Edward. 1777
McCoy, Charles S. 1127, 2057, 3537,
  3617
McCoy, F. N. 130, 1375
McCoy, Isaac. 1900

McCoy, James Comly. 1947, 1949
McCoy, John Fisher. 519
McCoy, Joseph A. 2554
McCoy, Maurice E. 968
McCoy, Samuel Duff. 2875
McCracken, George Englert. 3669
McCracken, Harold. 3408
MacCracken, Henry Mitchell. 32
McCracken, John. 2538
McCracken, Robert James. 968, 1412, 2902, 3354
McCrady, Edward. 76, 2958, 3079
McCraw, Louis Harrison. 2875
McCraw, Louise Harrison. 2306
McCraw, Mildred C. 3555
McCray, Walter Arthur. 993
McCready, Adelaide M. 1092
McCready, William C. 3747
McCreary, Alf. 1370
*McCreary, W. Burgess. 1264
McCreary, William Burgess. 3883, 218, 280
McCreery, Charles. 2990
McCrie, Thomas. 2179, 2181, 2401, 3042, 3041
McCrossan, Charles Wesley. 1599
McCrossan, Thomas J. 199, 1599
McCrossen, Vincent A. 3118
McCrosson, Mary of the Blessed Sacrament. 2132
McCudden, John. 2774
McCullagh, Archibald. 199
McCulloch, James Edward. 1606
Macculloch, John Arnott. 1186, 2655, 2666
MacCulloch, John Arnott. 878, 1186
McCulloch, Joseph. 1211
McCulloch, William Edward. 3736
McCulloh, Anna Austen. 2392
McCulloh, Gerald O. 82, 83, 1297, 1435, 3614
McCulloh, Gerald W. 3617
McCullough, William Stewart. 1197, 1892, 2091, 3579
McCullough, William Wallace. 3131
McCumber, Harold Oliver. 3381
McCumber, W. E. 441, 1238, 1824, 3299
McCune, William C. 2918
McCunley, Foster R. 537
McCurdy, Convers L. 3026
McCurdy, Mary De Bure. 1672
McCurley, Foster R. 523
McCurry, Bertha B. (Moore) 1254
McCuskey, Dorothy. 23
McCuskey, Roy. 3807
McCutchan, Helen Cowles. 2307
McCutchan, Marjorie Munn. 1254
McCutchan, Robert Guy. 1860, 1875, 2458
McCutchen, Duval Talmadge. 3079
McCutcheon, James N. 2786
McCutcheon, William John. 3019
McDaniel, Allen Boyer. 3818
McDaniel, Audrey. 1449, 1450
McDaniel, Douglass (Scarborough) 1303, 1351
McDaniel, Elsiebeth. 3171, 3174
McDaniel, Ethel Hittle. 1683
McDaniel, George White. 742, 1543, 3342, 3465, 2041
McDaniel, Harold W. 1633, 2182
McDaniel, Ivan G. 2833
McDaniel, Mabel C. 3290
McDaniel, Myrtle Arlene. 968
McDaniel, Walton Brooks. 664
McDaniels, Geraldine. 1724
[McDaniels, Johnson Beauregard] 1862. 2676
McDavid, Mittie Owen. 663
McDearmon, Kay. 1930, 3414
MacDermot, Violet. 90
McDermott, Andrew W. 1562, 3374
McDermott, Beverly Brodsky. 1632, 1744, 2137
McDermott, Charles Henry. 3002
McDermott, Gerald. 3005
McDermott, Hugh Farrar. 2856
McDermott, Irene. 1324
McDermott, Rosarii. 1700, 3420
McDermott, Thomas. 2852, 796
McDermott, Timothy S. 73
McDevitt, Gerald Vincent. 190
McDevitt, Gilbert Joseph. 1883
McDevitt, Herbert. 3535
MacDevitt, John. 1481, 1783
Macdill, David. 563
McDill, Joseph Moody. 1101, 2471
McDill, Wayne. 985, 1567
McDonagh, Enda. 835, 944, 949, 1044, 1086, 3192
McDonagh, John M. 1107
MacDonald, Alexander. 73, 782, 2260, 2366, 2367, 3269
Macdonald, Allan John Macdonald. 192, 1773, 2843, 2861, 3017, 3615
*Macdonald, Angus. 1659
MacDonald, Byrnes. 1322

McDonald, Christina. 280
McDonald, Claude C. 1004
McDonald, Cleveland. 2338
Macdonald, David Ferguson. 2973
McDonald, Donald. 827
McDonald, Donald John. 3745
McDonald, Donald William. 3508
Macdonald, Duncan Black. 211, 2565, 2841, 211, 500, 1922, 1923, 2565, 2841
McDonald, Edwin Lawrence. 2135
MacDonald, Elinor. 3750
Macdonald, Elizabeth Stone. 1813, 3109
McDonald, Erwin Lawrence. 1572, 1841, 1927
Macdonald, Eugene Montague. 1907, 1908
Macdonald, Frederic William. 120
MacDonald, Gail. 1303, 2307
Macdonald, George. 908, 1112, 1432, 2017, 3365, 3622
MacDonald, George Everett Hussey. 1655
Macdonald, George Everett Hussey. 1656, 3717
MacDonald, Gordon. 1615, 2132
McDonald, Grace. 3275
Macdonald, Greville. 3079
MacDonald, Hope. 2719, 2875
McDonald, Hugh Dermot. 341, 476, 3227, 380
Macdonald, James. 12, 191
MacDonald, James Henry. 3228
McDonald, James Ian Hamilton. 2168
MacDonald, James Madison. 413, 463, 2126
McDonald, James Porter. 3645
MacDonald, John. 3296
[Macdonald, Jonathan S]. 2727
Macdonald, Louisa (Powell) 717
McDonald, Mary Reynolds. 622
Macdonald, Murdo Ewen. 64
Macdonald, Murdo Ewen. 1234
McDonald, Osgoode Hamilton. 3153
MacDonald, Robert. 2409
McDonald, Stephen J. 622
McDonald, Stephen James. 622
McDonald, William. 661, 3290, 3508, 48, 1910, 2453, 2818, 3804
MacDonald, William. 363
McDonald, William Joseph. 1373, 3773
MacDonald-Bayne, Murdo. 2307
Macdonell, Anne. 1645
Macdonell, Arthur Anthony. 2663, 3301
McDonell, Ruth. 940
McDonnell, Ernest W. 185
Macdonnell, Frederick Nicholas Ignatius. 763, 788
McDonnell, Graham P. 850, 2488
McDonnell, Kilian. 729, 1000, 2256, 2815, 2816
McDonnell, Killan. 3488
McDonnell, Lois Eddy. 1248, 3171
McDonnold, Benjamin Wilburn. 1396
McDonough, Michael Vincent. 1602, 1841, 3342, 3411
McDonough, Reginald M. 953
McDonough, Sheila. 20, 1925
McDonough, Thomas Joseph. 7
McDonough, Thomas M. 2281
McDonough, Tom. 2355
McDonough, William K. 3712
McDormand, Thomas Bruce. 64, 1871, 3003
MacDougall, Bruce. 449, 1016, 2307
McDougall, David. 2535
MacDougall, Donald. 2542
McDougall, Eleanor. 114
Macdougall, Hamilton Crawford. 1208
MacDougall, Hugh A. 6, 2221
MacDougall, Mary Katherine. 2263, 3539, 3750
McDougall, William. 2473
MacDowall, Charles George. 1634
McDowall, Stewart Andrew. 1582, 3200, 1580, 1582, 3712
McDowell, Alexander. 3029
McDowell, Edith. 3762
McDowell, Edward Allison. 455, 2041, 3458
McDowell, John. 218, 3646, 1051, 3444
McDowell, John Bernard. 904
McDowell, Josh. 68, 277, 563, 2041, 2052, 2711
McDowell, Lowell B. 1329
McDowell Robert Brendan. 1147, 1230
McDowell, William Fraser. 968, 1567, 2443, 3061, 3673, 2041, 3537, 3673
[Macduff, John Ross.] 1818-1895. 192, 215, 1351, 1440, 1450, 1506, 1696, 1953, 1982, 1986, 1999, 2203, 2892, 3456
[Mace, Aurelia Gay] 1835-1910. 3396
Mace, David. 1609
Mace, David Robert. 1303, 2338, 2344, 3391, 3393
[Mace, Elizabeth H. 3508
Mace, Fayette. 3396
Mace, John Wilson. 1287, 2701
Mace, Joseph Willis. 3387

McEachen, Roderick A. 746
MacEachen, Roderick Aloysius. 748, 760, 769, 782, 805, 948, 3061
McEachern, Alton H. 2260, 2741
McEachern, Ted. 3529
McEleney, Neil J. 400, 2951
McElfresh, Franklin. 3555
McElhinney, John J. 1187
McElhinney, Robert Stewart. 2591
McElhone, James F. 2392, 3153
McElhone, James Francis. 2361, 3491
McElligott, C. J. 2822
McElrath, Hugh T. 153
McElrath, William N. 247, 629, 3184, 311, 2157, 2488
McElreath, Walter. 2438
MacElree, Wilmer W. 2068
McElroy, Isaac Stuart. 2261, 2918
McElroy, John Alexander. 2057
McElroy, Lucy (Cleaver) 705, 1450
McElroy, Paul Simpson. 1258, 1354, 1450, 2237, 2392, 2892, 2977
McElvaney, William K. 1007, 2222, 2307, 2786
*McElvany, Harold. 3067
McElveen, Floyd. 1232, 3227
McElwain, Madison E. 2462
McElwain, Thomas. 3332
McEniry, Blanche Marie. 2400, 3417
McEnniry, Christopher David. 1616
McEntee, Georgiana Putnam. 818, 2328
McEntee, Mary Veronica. 3418
McEntire, Adele Tuttle. 406, 532
McEntire, Ralph N. 3555
MacEoin, Gary. 738, 821, 829, 1332, 2597, 3131, 3772
McEvilly, Mary A. 3508
McEvoy, Hubert. 2367, 2369
McEwan, Richard James. 1014
McEwen Elizabeth Clare. 2475
McEwen, James S. 2181
McEwen, Joseph W. 1383
McEwen, William. 607, 3343, 3720
McEwen, William P. 3594
McFadden, Charles Joseph. 2589
McFadden, Elizabeth Spalding. 3387, 3469
McFadden, Michael. 2072
[McFaden, John Duke]. 1999
McFadyen, John Edgar. 3492, 253, 486, 500, 531, 540, 586, 1450, 576
McFadyen, Joseph Ferguson. 2015, 2488
*McFadyen, Mary Jean. 3164
McFadyen. John Edgar. 500
McFague, Sallie. 1077
McFall, Ernest A. 2121, 2716
McFarlan, Donald Maitland. 244, 2506
McFarland, Bertha Blount. 2307, 3405
Macfarland, Charles Stedman. 451, 1041, 1044, 1051, 1145, 1146, 1148, 1335, 1619, 2060, 2866, 3435, 3444, 3617, 3618
McFarland, Horace Neill. 1936
McFarland, John Thomas. 3559
McFarland, William J. 235
Macfarlane, Alan. 1291, 2135
Macfarlane, Claire. 2875
MacFarlane, J. M. 2227
*MacFarlane, K. B. 1469
Macfarlane, Katherine Nell. 1742, 1921
Macfarlane, Kenneth Bruce. 3038, 3860, 3861
McFatridge, Forrest Vernon. 2004, 2875
McFayden, Donald. 73
McFeeters, James Calvin. 1150, 1359, 1794, 2807, 3578
McFerrin, Anderson Purdy. 2324
MacFetridge, Nathaniel S. 730
McGannon, J. Barry. 1946
[McGarr, Mary Frances. 794
McGarrah, Albert Franklin. 1120, 1126, 1168, 1200, 1251
McGarrigle, Francis Joseph. 1000, 3545
McGarry, Michael B. 1084
McGarry, William James. 376, 424, 8
McGarvey, John William. 329, 371, 510
McGaughey, C. E. 1273, 3354
McGaughey, Janie W. 2921
McGaughy, Lane C. 1771
McGavick, Alexander Joseph. 968
McGavick, James E. 871
McGavin, Elmer Cecil. 679, 2604, 2615, 2676, 2772, 3430
McGavran, Donald Anderson. 1171, 2493, 2496, 2554, 2559, 2954, 1171, 1074
McGavran, Grace Winifred. 290, 901, 911, 2490, 3003, 3858
McGaw, Francis A. 1859, 2531
McGeachy, D. P. 1414
McGeachy, Neill Roderick. 888
McGeachy, Pat. 2875, 3529
MacGeary, John Samuel. 2428
*McGee, C. Lincoln. 1724
McGee, Harry F. 1558

McGee, J. Vernon. 223, 514, 589, 3030, 3258, 3354
McGee, James Sears. 45
McGee, James Ellington. 3061
McGee, John Forest. 1649
McGee, John Vernon. 215, 514, 563, 2052, 2247, 3030, 3258, 3354
McGee, Ratha Doyle. 920
McGee, Sarah H. 2307
McGee, Theron Charlton. 1051
McGee, Thomas D'Arcy. 873, 2315
McGeehan, Jude J. 1258, 2307
McGeehan, George. 3508
McGehee, John Boykin. 2457
McGerald, Samuel. 778
McGhie, Anna E. 3480
McGiffert, Arthur Cushman. 1507, 3725, 74, 1177, 1724, 2275, 3213, 3654, 3679, 1499
McGiffert, Michael. 3009
McGill, Anna Blanche. 3416
McGill, Arthur Chute. 3610
McGill, J[ohn]. 1120
McGill, John. 1120
McGill, Mary E. 3281
McGill, Ormond. 2315, 2727, 3824, 1485
McGill, Ralph Emerson. 2762
McGill, Stuart A. 1324
McGill university, Montreal. Library. 1763
McGill University, Montreal. Institute of Islamic Studies. Library. 2307, 2678
McGill, Vivian Jerauld. 3311
MacGillivray, George John. 788, 1364
MacGillivray, J. D. 639
MacGilton, Alice King. 1877
McGilvary, Daniel. 2537
McGinlay, James. 165
McGinley, Anna Matilda Agnes. 28
McGinley, Gerard. 3131
McGinley, John. 3660
McGinley, Laurence J. 390
McGinley, Phyllis. 1024, 3281
McGinn, Bernard. 3464
McGinn, Donald Joseph. 2336, 2813, 3007
McGinn, John T. 3628
McGinnis, Charles Francis. 788, 3281
McGinnis, Howard Justus. 535
McGinnis, Joanna V. 1724
McGinnis, Lillie. 3508
McGinnis, Marilyn. 3415
McGinnis, William Carroll. 2823
McGinty, Claudius Lamar. 2886, 3374, 400, 1419, 3374
McGinty, Park. 1459
McGlade, Joseph. 850, 2533
McGlathery, Roy Munsey. 280
McGlinchey, Joseph Francis. 2531
McGloin, Frank. 1593, 3714
McGloin, John Bernard. 685, 1948, 3298
McGloin, Joseph T. 64, 765, 968, 1000, 1324, 1946, 2059, 2246, 3244, 3393, 3488, 3887, 2367
McGlothin, William Joseph. 1694
McGlothlin, William Joseph. 140, 145, 1906, 3673, 1188
McGlynn, James V. 2738
McGlynn, Thomas Matthew. 1618
McGoey, John H. 760, 772, 2510, 2573, 3393
McGoldrick, Desmond F. 877, 2573, 2574, 2582
McGoldrick, James Edward. 174
MacGonigle, Edwin F. 813
MacGorman, Jack W. 1712
McGovern, Arthur F. 1319
McGovern, James. 2717, 3602
McGovern, James Joseph. 778, 808, 796, 2216, 2309
McGovern, James O. 756, 1188
McGovern, Margaret. 3207
McGovern, Thomas. 2658
McGovern, William Montgomery. 702, 710, 2317
McGowan, Francis Xavier. 3411
McGowan, Herman Craig. 3329
McGowan, Jean Carroll. 1322
Macgowan, John. 1014, 1416, 2132, 2133
MacGowan, Robert. 3343, 3521
McGowen, C. H. 3082
McGowen, Drusilla. 1198
McGown, George. 1664
McGrade, Francis. 1327, 3249
McGrady, Samuel Hugh. 2656
McGrady, Thomas. 1907, 2465
MacGrail, Joseph F. 1177, 3245
MacGrail, Joseph Francis. 800
McGranahan, Ralph W. 2527
McGrann, Albert P. 1440
McGrath, Fergal. 2703, 3545, 3756
McGrath, John Joseph. 1490
McGrath, Joseph Edward. 2994
[McGrath, Marie Cecelia] 1896. 3165
McGrath, Sister Albertus Magnus. 3834
McGrath, Thomas Sylvester. 808, 2884, 3238

McGrath, William Cecil. 1618
McGrath, William R. 3794
McGratty, Arthur R. 1649, 3055, 3270
McGraw, James. 1824, 2909
McGreal, Ian Philip. 1536
Macgregor, Daniel. 2604
MacGregor, Edwin R. 463
Macgregor, G[eorge] H[ogarth] C[arnaby]. 1739
MacGregor, Geddes. 185, 248, 290, 348, 390, 1061, 1088, 1120, 1718, 1724, 1735, 2067, 2181, 2706, 2837, 2862, 2892, 2977, 2998, 3003, 3102
MacGregor, Geddes. [John Geddes MacGregor]. 1855, 2837, 2977
Macgregor, George Hogarth Carnaby. 968, 1968, 2875, 417, 2808
MacGregor-Hastie, Roy. 2769
MacGregor, Jessie G. 1993
MacGregor, Malcolm. 376
Macgregor, Malcolm Blair. 3315
[MacGregor, Mary Esther (Miller) 1876. 2308, 2917
McGregor, Pedro. 2313
Macgregor, William Malcolm. 1070, 2799, 1070, 2799, 3673, 925, 2902
MacGregor-Hastie, Roy. 2124, 2769, 2805
McGroarty, John Steven. 2367, 2757
McGroarty, William Buckner. 24
McGucken, William Joseph. 831, 1946
McGuckin, Jack. 1576, 2308
McGuinness, E. J. 3691
McGuire, Brian Patrick. 1276, 3259
McGuire, Frederick A. 850, 2490
McGuire, Horace. 622
McGuire, John P. 2367
McGuire, Martin Rawson Patrick. 1286
MacGuire, Meade. 968, 1388, 3295, 3540
McGuire, Meredith B. 827, 2816, 3086
McGuire, Murray Mason. 3237
McGuire, Ulysses Melville. 3646
McGurn, Barrett. 827, 2852, 2861
McHale, M. Jerome. 3418
MacHarg, John Brainerd. 3713
McHargue, Georgess. 3508
Machen, John Gresham. 2221, 1070, 3061, 376, 1070, 1593, 2221, 2324, 2799, 2933, 3781
Machen, John Gresham, D.D. 3781
Machen, Minnie (Gresham) 299, 697
Machin, G. I. T. 1760
Machin, Joseph. 277
Macholtz, James D. 1166
MacHovec, Frank J. 1585, 1696, 2380, 3865
Machovec, Milan. 2041
Macht, David Israel. 204, 235, 317
Machtei, Max. 2154
McHugh, Gerald Austin. 1387
McHugh, James T. 2343, 2344
McHugh, John. 2358
McHugh, John Ambrose. 2341, 2593
McHugh, Patrick J. 367, 1000, 1264
MacIagan, David. 1384
McIlhenny, Edward Avery. 2680
MacIlravy, Cora Harris. 594
McIlvaine, Charles Pettit. 60, 1099, 1120, 2160, 2902, 3051
McIlvaine, Edwin Linton. 3211
McIlvaine, James Hall. 1642
McIlwain, Orene. 3003
McIlwaine, Henry Read. 3781
McInerny, Dennis Q. 2412
McInecry, Dennis Q. 2413
McInerny, Ralph M. 3693, 3696
MacInnes, Gordon A. 3858
[MacInnes, (Johnson) 2308
MacInnes, Rev. John. 1550
MacInnis, Donald E. 914
MacInnis, John Murdoch. 2824, 3153
McIntire, Carl. 514, 560, 589, 1134, 1912, 2223, 2563, 2670, 3735
McIntire, James Robert. 1830
McIntire, Russell M. 993
Macintosh, Andrew Alexander. 546
McIntosh, Christopher. 96
Macintosh, Douglas Clyde. 1095, 2181, 3102, 3444, 3646
McIntosh, Ian F. 2786
McIntosh, Maria Jane. 888
MacIntosh, Mike. 3845
McIntosh, William Alexander. 2920
MacIntosh, William Mackenzie. 2055
MacIntyre, Alasdair C. 64, 65, 100
McIntyre, Bonaventure John. 1267
McIntyre, James Lewis. 698
McIntyre, John. 1741, 1818, 1953
McIntyre, Marie. 3179
Mc Intyre, Ralph L. 3555
*McIntyre, Robert W. 968
McIntyre, William Alexander. 968
Maciulionis, Joseph R. 1802, 3419
McIvor, John A. 2915
[McIvor-Tyndall, Alexander J.]. 3686
Mack, Alexander. 1235, 1101, 3207
Mack, Edward. 1731
Mack, Friedrich. 3488

Mack, Silas Franklin. 2520, 2545
McKaig, Robert Newton. 1830
Mackail, John William. 406, 535, 407
McKain, David W. 1080
Mackall, Louis. 3076
McKane, William. 520, 572, 3821
MacKay, Alastair I. 480
McKay, Arthur R. 1061, 3531
Mackay, Brain S. 470
Mackay, Charles H. 2727
McKay, Charles Lloyd. 529, 1574
McKay, Claude Allen. 3534, 2007
McKay, David O. 1426
Mckay, David Oman. 1009
McKay, David Oman. 1009, 2608, 2611, 1009, 2308, 2608, 3887
Mackay, Donald James. 1594
MacKay, Donald MacCrimmon. 2321, 3082
Mackay, Donald Sage. 3049
McKay, Edward James. 459, 498
McKay, Ellen Cotton. 3259
Mackay, George Leslie. 1634
Mackay, Henry Falconar Barclay. 71, 968, 1642, 1968, 925, 1212, 2799
Mackay, James Hutton. 3211
Mackay, John Alexander. 365, 1061, 1105, 1120, 1977, 2548, 2936, 3464
McKay, John William. 2156
Mackay, Joy. 1164, 1373
Mackay, Kris. 1231
McKay, Liewelyn R. 3071
McKay, Lucinda E. 459, 3225
McKay, Richard W. 3181
MacKay, Ruth (Clarage) 2634
McKay, William Alexander. 3228
Mackay, William Mackintosh. 3411
Mackay, William P. 1359
McKean, Frank Chalmers. 1567
Mackean, William Herbert. 2256, 2579
McKeating, Henry. 1777, 1528
McKechnie, James. 2124
McKee, Bill. 985, 1440, 3320, 3887, 1440
McKee, Elmore McNeill. 65, 2892, 3354
McKee, John Edward. 235
McKee, Joseph. 800
McKee, Rose Knisley. 3184
McKee, Ruth (Karr) 2544, 3789
McKeehan, Hobart D. 3343
McKeehan, Hobart Deitrich. 3343, 1545, 3049, 3365
McKeen, Phebe Fuller. 2684
McKeesport, Pa. Evangelical Congregational church. 1546
McKeever, James M. 985, 3711
McKeever, William Arch. 3555
Mackel, John J. 2310
McKellar, Shona. 2712
McKelvey, Gertrude Delia. 1599
McKelvey, Gertrude Della. 182, 1599
McKelvey, John W. 968
McKelvey, R. J. 1163
McKelvey Samuel Willis. 968, 2064
McKelvie, Martha Groves. 1755
McKelway, Alexander J. 3646, 3701
McKendrick, James. 1567
[Mackendrick, William Gordon] 1864. 46
McKendry, James Banford. 1993, 3182
McKenna, Bernard Aloysius. 1886, 3797
McKenna, Charles Hyacinth. 3248
[McKenna, Charles Hyacinth] 1835-1917. 3248
McKenna, Charles Hyacinthe. 2308
McKenna, David Loren. 985, 2050
McKenna, Dennis J. 1879; 2473
McKenna, Lambert Andrew Joseph. 1393
McKenna, Marian Cecelia. 810
McKenna, Mary J. 2859
McKenna, Mary Lawrence. 3836
McKenna, Megan. 597, 941, 1953
Mackenna, Robert William. 2227
McKennan, Frank Blake. 1889
McKenney, Charles R. 3433
Mackensen, Herman. 3225
McKenzie, A Dean. 1881, 3243
Mackenzie, A[lexander] C[ampbell]. 1203
McKenzie, Alexander. 731, 1051, 1968
MacKenzie, Andrew. 1710, 2727, 3321, 3437
McKenzie, Cary Blair. 2658
Mackenzie, Chloris. 2318, 2947
Mackenzie, Compton. 825
McKenzie, David. 2767, 3108
Mackenzie, Donald. 1051, 1997
Mackenzie, Donald Alexander. 2660, 3574, 1904, 2655, 2658, 2659, 2660, 2663, 3574
*McKenzie, E. C. 1163
Mackenzie, Frederick Arthur. 681, 3292
McKenzie, J. Hewat. 3508
Mackenzie, J. N. Landseer. 3462
Mackenzie, Jean Kenyon. 2497, 713, 2497, 3131
Mackenzie, John. 1464
McKenzie, John. 1538
McKenzie, John Grant. 968, 2785, 2995, 3673

McKenzie, John L. 201, 239, 244, 348, 500, 554, 652, 756, 779, 1162, 1776, 2090, 599
Mackenzie, John Stuart. 2418
Mackenzie, Kenneth. 42, 1599, 3686
Mackenzie, Kenneth Donald. 45, 1523, 1041, 1211, 1327, 2237
MacKenzie, Kenneth M. 2438
Mackenzie, Lachlan. 2933, 3365
McKenzie, Leon. 935, 938, 1819, 3449
McKenzie, Maisie. 2433, 2556
McKenzie, Peter Rutherford. 1389, 2487
Mackenzie, R A F. 410
Mackenzie, Robert. 3354
MacKenzie, Roderick A. F. 599
MacKenzie, Roderick Andrew Francis. 599
Mackenzie, Ross. 331, 1120
Mackenzie, William Douglas. 1342, 1889, 1953, 3646
McKenzie, William P. 1860
Mc Kenzie, E. C. 3354
Mckenzie, John L. 788
McKeown, Boyd M. 1168
McKeown, Francis J. 1000
McKernan, James. 864
McKerrow, James Clark. 2420, 2998, 3451
McKerrow, Peter Evander. 144
McKerrow, Ronald Brunlees. 656
Mackey, Albert Gallatin. 1666, 1669, 1671
[Mackey, James Love] 1820-1867. 190
Mackey, James Patrick. 2041, 3102, 3664, 3706
Mackey, Sampson Arnold. 2665
McKibben, Frank Melbourne. 3190, 3153, 3167, 3178
McKibbens, Thomas R. 146, 1500
McKibbin, Alma Estelle (Baker) 333, 596, 1450, 3385
Mackie, Alexander. 1716
Mackie, J. L. 1738
Mackie, Robert C. 1492, 1812, 2626, 3784
Mackie, Robert M. 46
McKiever, Charles Fitzgerald. 1687, 3425
McKillop, Sybil L. 2985
McKim, Audrey. 902
[McKim, Haslett]. 501
McKim, Judson Jackson. 3871
McKim, Randolph Harrison. 563, 801, 2001, 2958, 3354, 3622
Mackin, Theodore. 2346
McKinlay, Kathryn Thorbus. 3732
McKinlay, Lynn A. 2611
McKinley, Charles Ethelbert. 3153
McKinley, Edward H. 3293
McKinley, John. 3168
McKinley, O. Glenn. 83
McKinley, Sybil. 691
McKinley, William. 2438
McKinney, Alexander Harris. 130, 286, 639, 687, 1498, 3153, 3180, 3550, 3592, 3673
McKinney, Baylus Benjamin. 1203
McKinney, Donald. 2392, 2136
McKinney, George Dallas. 1940
*McKinney, Irene T. 1724
McKinney, James C. 917
MacKinney, Loren Carey. 1689
McKinney, Richard Ishmael. 2681
McKinney, William Kerr. 3808
McKinney, William Wilson. 2919
McKinnon, Arch C. 2197, 2513
MacKinnon, Donald MacKenzie. 65, 2418
MacKinnon, Edward Michael. 3716
Mackinnon, James. 476, 727, 1193, 1968, 2275, 2799, 3035, 3038, 727, 2275, 3035
MacKinnon, John G. 3725
MacKinnon, Murdoch. 2227
McKinstry, Arthur R. 2309
McKinstry, Levi C. 3029
[Mackintosh, Charles H.]. 510, 557
Mackintosh, Charles Henry. 562, 3632, 3061, 3686
Mackintosh, Hugh Ross. 1696, 3365, 3652, 1051, 1633, 2041
Mackintosh, Robert. 105, 3411
McKirachan, John Charles. 1603
[McKitrick, David F.]. 1456
Macklin, John. 2727
McKnight, Burr Redding. 1724
McKnight, Edgar V. 311, 387, 405, 1806
McKnight, Felix R. 2032
McKnight, Floyd. 50, 3527
McKnight, George Harley. 1111, 2707
McKnight, Gerald. 3312
McKnight, John. 1594
McKnight, John P. 2768
McKnight, Ozro. 1953, 2875
McKnight, Robert James George. 2055
McKnight, William John. 455, 459
McKown, Edgar Monroe. 3664
Mackowski, Richard M. 1943
McKoy, Henry Bacon. 1772

McKuen, Rod. 2392
Macky, Peter W. 235, 3575
McLachlan, Herbert. 2471, 3212, 426, 1274, 2271, 2471, 2472, 3095, 3212, 3723
Maclachlan, Lewis. 54, 2875
Maclagan, Edward Douglas. 1947
Maclagan, Robert Craig. 1578
Maclagan, William Gauld. 3070
McLain, C. E. 603, 3017
McLane, Edwin D. 2786
McLane, William Ward. 2041, 2227, 1580
MacLaren, A. Allan. 3453
*Maclaren, Alexander. 3374
Maclaren, Alexander. 520
McLaren, Alexander. 71, 165, 181, 223, 300, 368, 417, 429, 435, 442, 510, 515, 520, 573, 576, 577, 590, 592, 658, 1318, 1405, 2247, 3314
Maclaren, Elizabeth. 1594
McLaren, Elizabeth T. 2309
McLaren, Robert Bruce. 944, 1977
McLaren, Rosemary Collyer. 3153
McLaren, William E[dward]. 3200
McLaren, William Edward. 2214, 2875
McLarry, Newman R. 1741, 3540
McLaughlin, Barry. 2998
McLaughlin, Francis A. 44
McLaughlin, G[eorge] A. 1017, 1348
McLaughlin, George A. 417, 441
McLaughlin, George Asbury. 329, 417, 441, 1105, 1348
McLaughlin, Henry Woods. 1374, 3178, 3255
McLaughlin, James Bede Benedict. 748, 3006
MacLaughlin, John. 1904
McLaughlin, Loretta. 2740, 3242
McLaughlin, P. J. 3079
McLaughlin, Raymond. 3096
McLaughlin, Raymond W. 1317, 2902, 2365
McLaurin, Hamish. 3865
Maclaurin, John. 3365
Maclay, K. T. 96
Maclean, Alistair. 2933
MacLean, Angus Hector. 1724, 3131, 3153, 3729
McLean, Archibald. 1465, 1633, 2483, 2493, 2504
Maclean, Arthur John. 1239
Mac Lean, Angus Hector. 1724
MacLean, George F. 1106, 1107, 3107, 1724
McLean, Gordon R. 1255, 3880, 3887, 1359, 2824
McLean, James Hector. 2548
Maclean, John. 1775, 3597
MacLean, John Allan. 2933
MacLean, John Patterson. 3396, 3397, 3398
McLean, Julia Norton. 2864
McLean, Mollie. 2663
Maclean, Norman. 1696
McLean, Robert. 2480, 2527
McLean, Robert Norris. 2460, 2527, 3295
McLean, William Todd. 11, 1841
Maclear, George Frederick. 407, 535, 2483, 2493
McLees, Richard Gustavus. 2913
McLeish, Alexander. 2505, 2516, 2531, 2954
McLeister, Clara. 3131
McLeister, Ira Fofd. 3807
McLeister, Ira Ford. 3807
McLeister, Luther H. 3211
McLellan, George William. 2833
McLellan, Hugh. 3354
MacLellan, Malcolm. 805
McLelland, Joseph C. 968, 1075, 1735, 2227, 3035, 3266, 3777
McLeman, James. 2008, 2052
McLemore, Clinton W. 2781
McLemore, Richard Aubrey. 156
McLendon, Baxter F. 1575
MacLennan, David Alexander. 968, 408, 968, 1267, 1599, 1841, 2392, 2902, 2933, 3354, 3374, 3664, 3731
McLennan, John William. 1051
Maclennan, Kenneth. 1051
MacLennan, Simon Fraser. 2833
McLennan, William Etridge. 1351, 2014, 2762
McLeod, Alexander. 3742
MacLeod, Alexander Benjamin. 2064, 2410
McLeod, Ceil. 2309
MacLeod, Charlotte. 96
Macleod, Donald. 2309, 2239, 2912, 2902, 3003, 3043
Macleod, Donald Malcolm. 1830
MacLeod, Earle Henry. 2392, 2892
Macleod, Flora Abigail. 2892
MacLeod, George Fielden. 1918
MacLeod, Jack M. 928
Macleod, John M. 2918

McLeod, Malcolm James. 1373, 1099, 1567, 1724, 2928, 3131, 3229, 3458
McLeod, Thomas E. 1168
McLeod, W. H. 2668, 3005, 3408
McLeskey, James Meadows. 1092, 1889
McLester, Frances Cole. 886, 1498, 3176, 3180
McLoughlin, Emmett. 794, 1582
McLoughlin, Helen. 1262, 2794
MacLoughlin, James. 782
McLoughlin, Peter P. 2309
McLoughlin, William A. 2358
McLoughlin, William Gerald. 123, 157, 184, 1552, 1755, 3233, 3566, 3747
MacLure, Millar. 2909
McMahan, Myrl (Edwards) 3508
McMahan, Tom. 1755, 3229
McMahon, Edwin M. 2392, 3488
McMahon, Francis Elmer. 1136
McMahon, Franklin. 814, 2309
McMahon, John Francis. 3786
McMahon, John Joseph. 819
McMahon, John Thomas. 948, 1830
McMahon, Martin. 744, 3862
McMahon, Norbert. 695, 2136
McMahon, Thomas. 2367
McMahon, Thomas S. 2309
McManama, Mary Fidelis. 659, 3275, 3419
McManama, Mary Fidelis [Secular name: Maude E. McManama]. 3275
McManis, Lester W. 1278
McMann, Charles Franklin. 1655
McManners, John. 817, 1145, 1416, 1639
McManus, Eugene P. 3017
McManus, Francis. 1311
McManus, Frederick Richard. 844, 848, 1458, 2234, 3772
McManus, Karl C. 463
McManus, Theodore Francis. 2977
McManus, Una. 898, 2309
MacMaster, Eve. 631, 2624
MacMaster, Gilbert. 577, 3427, 3439
MacMaster, Richard Kerwin. 1686, 2407
McMaster, Vernon Cochrane. 2958, 2962, 3178
McMaster, William H. 3260
McMichael, Betty. 2224
McMichael, William. 2450
Macmillan, A. H. 1941
Macmillan, Alice P. 1111
McMillan, Archibald Memory. 2510
Macmillan, David S. 2195
Macmillan, Donald. 2373
McMillan, Duncan Bhann. 2611
McMillan, Duncan Cameron. 1384, 2059
McMillan, Earle. 433, 434
Macmillan, Ebenezer. 2753
Macmillan, Ebenezer. 2933
MacMillan, George Whitfield. 1381
McMillan, Homer. 2501, 2926
McMillan, J. A. 3382
McMillan, Joseph J. 2858
Macmillan, Kerr Duncan. 2978
McMillan, Robert M. 180, 993
McMillen, Sim I. 607
McMillen, Theodore Clark. 3875
McMillin, Joseph L. 3153
McMillon, Lynn A. 2727
McMinn, Edwin. 3200
McMinn, Janie Lancaster. 616
McMinn, Tom. 495, 2952
McMullen, Eleanor. 2480
McMullen, John S. 3529
MacMullen, Ramsay. 3246
MacMullen, Wallace. 3354
McMurray, De Witt. 3061
Macmurray, John. 1586, 3444, 3452
McMurrin, Sterling M. 2611
McMurry, Mildred Dodson. 1260, 2218, 2550
McMurtrie, Tillman Ephraim. 2064
McNabb, Vincent Joseph. 756, 760, 864, 1628, 1920, 1968, 2355, 3450, 760, 776, 858, 2247, 2392
McNabb Vincent Joseph. 1594
MacNair, A Stanley. 461
MacNair, Donald J. 1200, 3678
McNair, Jim. 1712
MacNair, John Van. 2245, 3304
McNair, Philip Murray Jourdan. 3777
McNairy, Philip F. 1609
McNally, Augustin Francis. 2700, 3244, 3245
McNally, James J. 1267, 2355, 2362
McNally, Robert E. 240, 760, 3038, 3710
McNally, Thomas Francis. 908
MacNalty, Arthur Salisbury. 2353
McNamara, Kevin. 2357, 1121, 2041, 3772
McNamara, Marie Aquinas. 116, 1688
McNamara, Robert Francis. 22, 829, 1369, 2910, 3242, 3273, 3737
McNamara, Thomas J. 223
McNamara, William. 2639, 3222, 3488, 819, 1900, 1000
McNamara, Martin. 321

McNamara, Patrick H. 3748
McNamara, William. 1000
MacNamee, James Joseph. 79
McNamee, Mary Dominica. 3419
McNaspy, C. J. 87, 839, 1949
McNaspy, Clement J. 1949, 3772
McNatt, Elmer E. 3555
McNaugher, John. 2041, 2985, 3673, 3736
McNaughton, Jeannette A. 3555
MacNaughton, John H. 3529
McNaughton, Ruth L. 1384, 1734
McNaughton, William. 3586, 1330
McNeal, Patricia F. 2808
McNeal, William H. 1672
McNee, Peter. 2503
McNeely, Jeannette. 2022
McNeely, Richard I. 555
McNeer, May Yonge. 2276, 3804
McNeer, Rembert Durbin. 613
McNeese, Samuel J. 1597
MacNeice, Louis. 96
McNeil, Brian. 585, 3721
McNeil, Jesse Jai. 1278, 1440, 1985, 2402, 2790, 2903
McNeill, John J. 1843
MacNeil, John, Presbyterian evangelist of Australia. 3480
McNeil, Marian W. 2310, 2486
McNeile, Alan Hugh. 474, 2380, 2875, 410, 2799
McNeile, E. R. 3686
McNeile, Hugh. 2119
McNeill, Charles James. 2875, 3262
McNeill, Donald P. 3576
McNeill, Donald Thomas, comp. 1866
MacNeill, Harris Lachlan. 1958, 405, 2009
McNeill, John. 587, 3376
McNeill, John j. 1843
MacNeill, John James. 165, 1696
*McNeill, John T. 1792
McNeill, John Thomas. 730, 878, 1021, 1041, 1046, 1101, 1187, 2812, 3203, 3452
McNeill, Leon Aloysius. 74, 803, 842, 1262, 3263
McNeill, Lois (Johnson) 2129
McNeil, Mayo. 669
McNeill, Robert B. 1132, 1134
*McNeilly, Elizabeth H. 2636
McNeilus, James A. 607
McNeley, James Kale. 2677
McNemar, Richard. 3231, 3396
[McNemar, Richard, 1770-1839. 1866, 3231, 3396, 3398
McNemee, Andrew Jackson. 1295, 2310
McNeur, George Hunter. 2220
McNeur, Ronald W. 1740
MacNevins, Harold A. 1594
McNew, George Jefferson. 2064
[McNicholas, John Timothy] 1877. 1826
McNicholas, Timothy Joseph. 3830
McNickle, Floyd M. 968, 1034
MacNickle, Mary Donatus. 1628, 2757
McNicol, John. 1061
Macnicol, Nicol. 2985, 689, 1896
McNierney, Stephen W. 2257
McNiff, William John. 2604
McNulty, Edward N. 3594, 936
McNulty, Frank J. 1777
McNulty, John Lawrence. 2360
MacNutt, Francis. 1599, 1609
MacNutt, Francis Augustus. 2861
MacNutt, Sylvester F. 2903
McNutt, William Roy. 150, 3003
Macomber, William. 684
*Macon, Leon. 944
Macon, Leon Meertief. 3290
McOuat, Floy (Lewis) Frank McOuat. 639
Macoy publishing and masonic supply company, New York. 1667
Macoy, Robert. 1666
McPeek, Gwynn S. 2777
MacPhail, Ian. 2159, 2731
Macphail, James Russell. 651, 3664
MacPhail, Malcolm Leod. 201, 1866
McPhee, Arthur. 1006, 1567
McPhee, Louise Mapes. 595
McPhee, Norma. 1170, 3887
McPheeters, Julian C. 3343, 1567, 1716, 1823
McPherson, Aimee Semple. 1554, 1567, 3131, 3320, 1912, 2310
McPherson, Anna Talbott. 925
McPherson, Chalmers. 1467
MacPherson, Dave. 3021
Macpherson, Duncan. 428
McPherson, George Wilson. 199, 1127, 1886
McPherson, Goerge Wilson. 3095
Macpherson, Ian. 3374, 607, 1530, 2903, 3365, 3374
Macpherson, Ian [John Cook Macpherson]. 3374
McPherson, Imogene McCrary. 2808, 597

Macpherson, John. 48
Macpherson, Katharine Livingstone. 535
McPherson, Nenien C. 968
McPherson, Thomas. 3102
McQuade, James J. 2269, 3476
Macquarrie, John. 944, 950, 1041, 1076, 1424, 1724, 1733, 1800, 1845, 2392, 2809, 2836, 2843, 3070, 3480, 3637, 3646, 3652, 3664
McQuary, Rodney L. 2392
McQuay, Earl P. 5, 993
MacQueary, Howard. 1580
McQuiddy, J. Clayton. 2231
McQuilkin, J. Robertson. 1171
McQuilkin, Marguerite. 2310
McQuilkin, Robert C. 135, 470, 2026, 2028
McQuilkin, Robert Crawford. 468, 1586, 2247, 2200
McQuirk, John. 1730, 864
MacQuitty, William. 706
MacRae, Alan A. 545
MacRae, George W. 417
McRae,Glenn. 597, 2523, 2799, 3180, 3531
McRae, James Thomas. 2539
McRae, Jane Carroll. 154, 2159
MacRae, Kenneth A. 1300, 2310
Macrae, Norman. 3321
McRae, William J. 1712
Macrakis, Apostolos. 2843
McReavy, Lawrence L. 1632
McReavy, Lawrence Leslie. 3460
McReynolds, Albert B. 3343
McReynolds, Jeannie. 985
MacRitchie, David. 20
McShane, John Francis. 1898, 2233, 2310
McShane, Philip. 1724, 1855, 2245, 2320
McSherry, James. 1948
McSorley, Joseph. 2875, 810, 1000, 1264, 1799, 2392, 2875
McSpadden, Joseph Walker. 2586
McStay, Esther. 1792
McSwain, Larry L. 1165
McSweeney, Thomas Denis. 3298
McSweeney, William. 812
McSwigan, Marie. 2711
McTaggart, John McTaggart Ellis. 1473, 1889, 2738
McTague, Edward Joseph. 864, 2362
McTyeire, Holland Nimmons. 2424, 2455, 2456
McVann, James. 2908
*MacVeagh, Rogers. 2134
MacVeagh, Rogers. 2134
McVeigh, Malcolm J. 12
MacVey, William Pitt. 2421
McWherter, Leroy. 1121, 1968
McWhirter, David I. 159, 2464
Macwhorter, Alexander. 2933
MacWhorter, Alexander. 3591
McWilliams, Anne Washburn. 146, 1744
McWilliams, Bernard F. 855, 1604
McWilliams, Carey. 2078
McWilliams, Le Roy E. 774
Macy, Christopher. 3023
Macy, Paul Griswold. 1045
Macy, S. B. 383, 1968
[Madan, Martin] 1726-1790. 1866
Madden, Alfred. 3508
Madden, Daniel M. 1022
Madden, Edward H. 1551, 2317, 3610
Madden, Frederic William. 481, 2584
Madden, Maude (Whitmore) 1936, 2527
Madden, Myron C. 1107, 1414
Madden, Richard C. 740, 1982
Madden, Ward Ellis. 3154
Madden, William Joseph. 3076, 2939
Maddox, Catherine. 2510
Maddox, Robert. 2401
Maddox, Robert L. 329
Maddry, Charles Edward. 146, 155, 2559
Maddry, Emma (Parker) 149
Maddux, Roy Clark. 571, 586, 596, 600
Madeleine. 2310, 2392
Madeleine, M. 760
Madeleva. 805
Madeley, Dora Ford. 2666, 3407
Madeley, Edward. 1370, 2690
Madigan, Kathleen E. 2160
Madision, Andrew William. 1051
Madison, Ford. 1170
Madison, Wis. Grace Episcopal Church. 1524
Madrigal, Jose A. 3290
Madsen, Carol Cornwall. 1233
Madsen, Erik C. 940
Madsen, Paul O. 1251, 3426
Madsen, Thorvald Berner. 3758
Madsen, Truman G. 1009, 2266, 2324, 2617, 3240
Madsen, William G. 2468
Madson, Norman Arthur. 3614
Maeda, Frances. 2493
Maeder, Gary. 985
Maertens, Marlene. 1264

Maertens, Thierry. 314, 652, 1264, 1588, 1830, 2892, 3832
Maes, Camillus Paul. 820, 2684
Maestri, William. 659, 1000
Maeterlinck, Maurice. 2990, 3118, 1414, 1696, 3118
Maezumi, Hakuyu Taizan. 3493
Maffatt, John Edward. 2581
Maffitt, John Newland. 3143, 3354
Mafteah, Shelomo. 2315
Mafteah Shelomo. English. 2315
Mafteah Shelomo. 2313
Magagna, Anna Marie. 1734
Magan, Percy T[ilson]. 1892
Magan, Percy Tilson. 756
Magana, Jose. 2268
Magaret, Helene. 1620, 1700, 1900, 2229, 2684, 3426
Magary, Alvin Edwin. 338
Magdalene. 1450
Magee, James H. 3131
Magee, John Benjamin. 2875, 3061
Magee, John Calvin. 1121, 2450
Magee, Raymond J. 3222
Magee, William. 105
Mageean, Robert. 1741
Magennis, Peter Elias. 3409
Magevney, Hugh L. 760
Magie, David. 3869
Magill, Frank Northen. 3619
[Magill, Harry Byron] 1872. 1599, 3308
Magill, Hugh Robert. 1051
Maginnis, Andrew. 1000
Magner, James Aloysius. 2789, 3450
Magner, W. C. 3720
Magnes, Judah Leon. 2119, 3756, 3757, 3897
Magnin, Etienne. 1290
Magno, Joseph. 100
Magnus, Katie (Emanuel) 2084, 2091
[Magnus, Laurie] 1872. 2078
Magnuson, Mildred Alberta. 648
Magnuson, Norris. 2860
Magnussen, Julius. 3508
Magnusson, Magnus. 486, 2761
Magonet, Jonathan. 552
Magoulias, Harry J. 2747
Magoun, George Frederic. 1336, 3718
Magoun, Herbert William. 2202
Magre, Maurice. 22, 57
[Magri, Francis Joseph] 1868. 824
Magruder, Edith Clysdale. 3465
Magruder, William H. N. 133
Magsam, Charles M. 1000, 2265, 3853
Maguire, C E. 2310, 2333
Maguire, Clyde (Merrill) 1911, 2938
Maguire, Daniel C. 866, 948
[Maguire, Gabriel Reid] 1871-1931. 2499
Maguire, James George. 1919
Maguire, John. 2817
Maguire, John David. 1095
Maguire, Robert Alfred. 1157
Maguire, Theophane. 2529
Maguire, William Augustus. 3131
Maguire, William Patrick Aloysius. 823
Mahabharata. 196, 2187
Mahabharata. Bhagavadgata. English. 196
Mahabharata. Bhagavadgita. English. 196
Mahabharata. Bhagavadgia. English. 2316
Mahabharata. Bhagavadgita. 196, 3891
Mahabharata. Bhagavadgita. English. 196, 197, 2316
Mahabharata. Bhagavadgita. English & Sanskrit. 197, 2316
Mahabharata. Bhagavadgita. English & Sanskrit. 1972. 2316
Mahabharata. Bhagavadgita. English. Selections. 197, 2316
Mahabharata. Bhagvadgita. English. 197
Mahabharata. English. 2316
Mahabharata. Harivamsa. English. Selections. 689
Mahabharata. Bhagavadgita. English. 197
Mahadevan, Telliyavaram Mahadevan Ponnambalam. 1816, 3020
Mahaffey, Margaret M. 2756
Mahaffy, John Pentland. 2903
Mahan, Alfred Thayer. 968
Mahan, Asa. 1333, 1406, 1658, 1830, 2317, 2818, 3508
Mahan, Milo. 1183, 1193, 1306
Mahan, Wayne W. 3700
[Mahan, William Dennes] 1824-1906. 2069, 3203, 3583
Mahaney, James Erwin. 1051
Mahany, Patricia Shely. 185
Maharaj, Rabindranath R. 1365, 2317
Mahayana sutras. English. 2317
Maher, John Patrick. 114, 1381
Maher, Trafford Patrick. 2571
Mahesh Yogi. 2316
Mahesh Yogi, Maharishi. 3196
Mahin, R. Newton. 3570
[Mahipati] 1715-1790. 1896
Mahler, Raphael. 2112
Mahmood, Syed Tahir. 664
Mahmoudi, Jalil. 125

Mahon, P. J. 833
Mahoney, Albertus. 2232, 2984
Mahoney, Carl K. 2875, 2998
Mahoney, Charles Joseph. 3167
Mahoney, Denis. 2334
Mahoney, Edward J. 2338, 3411
Mahoney, Florence Jerome. 3488
Mahoney, James. 985, 986
Mahoney, William James. 2586
Mahony, Francis Sylvester. 1919
Mahony, Jerome. 810
Mahony, Michael Joseph. 2241, 2843
Mahony, Patrick. 3508
Mahood, John Wilmet. 1830
Mahood, John Wilmot. 65, 1450, 1567, 2380, 2421, 3131
Mahr, August Carl. 1642, 2778
Mahurin, S. 3783
Maida, Adam J. 2341
Maier, Eugene F. J. 2830
Maier, Gerhard. 240
Maier, Hans. 933
Maier, Josef. 1800
Maier, Michael. 3251
Maier, Paul L. 331, 929, 1197, 1301, 1986, 2021, 2302, 2318
Maier, Walter A. 387
Maier, Walter Arthur. 2300, 2338, 3354, 560, 2285, 2300, 3633
Maillard, John May. 1599
Maillefer, Elie. 2189
Mails, Thomas E. 607, 2791
[Maimbourg, Claude]. 3704
Maimonides, Moses. 2479
Main, Arthur Elwin. 639
Main, George Arthur. 3260
Main, John. 188, 2380, 2571
Main, Robert L. 2191
Main, William Holloway. 235
Mainage, Theodore. 1889
Mainage, Thomas Lucien. 1891
Maine. Legislature. Legislative Research Committee. 822
Mainkar, Trimbak Govind. 3775
*Mainprize, Don. 986, 1014
Mainprize, Donald Charles. 3592
Mains, David R. 893, 2481
Mains, Frances Helen. 3878
Mains, George Preston. 1528, 1910, 3131, 305, 700, 1051, 1586, 3079, 3616
Mains, Karen Burton. 986
Mainse, David. 2318, 2817
Mair, John. 3597
Mair, Lucy Philip. 3824
Maisel, John M. 986, 2318
Maisler, Benjamin. 78, 486
Maistre, Joseph Marie. 1910, 2861
Maitland, Brownlow. 60
Maitland, David Johnston. 2318, 2462
Maitland, Frederic William. 1212, 1489
Maitland, Rollo Francis. 736
Maitland, Samuel Roffey. 3039
Maitra, Harendranath. 1813
Maitreyanatha. 3867
Majithia, Surendra Singh. 3865
Majjhima-nikaya. 710
Major, Gertrude Keene. 2604
Major, Henry. 2768
Major, Henry Dewsbury Alves. 386, 1280, 1968, 2561, 3069
Major, Kathleen. 2230
Majumdar, Ramesh Chandra. 3784
Makar, Janos. 1651, 1856
Makarii, Monk. 1010
Makarim, Sami Nasib. 1481
Makemie, Francis. 2318
Makower, Felix. 1219
Makrakes, Apostlos. 455
Makrakes, Apostolos. 344, 386, 576, 795, 1381, 1662, 2392, 2746, 2749, 2836, 2955
Makulec, Louis L. 2700
Malachi, Martin. 3118
Malaise, Joseph. 948
Malalasekera, Geroge Peiris. 708
Malalgoda, Kitsiri. 709
Malan, Cesar. 2371
Malan, Stephen. 1929
Malania, Fae. 1450
Malantschuk, Gregor. 2170
Malard, Suzanne. 2581
Malaska, Hilkka. 2954
Malchus, Marius. 2313
Malcolm, Thomas Walker. 1419
Malcom, Howard. 2338, 105, 244, 245, 3626
Malcomson, William L. 2903
Malden, R. H. 2520
Malden, Richard Henry. 348, 378, 489, 538, 1211, 1225, 1830, 3801
Male, Emile. 3245, 86, 920
Malebranche, Nicolas. 1724
Malech, George David. 2684
Malehorn, Hal. 3555
Malevez, Leopold. 1424
Malfitano, Gilbert Jacques. 2642
Malherbe, Abraham J. 408, 3451

Malik, Charles. 1077
Malik, Charles Habib. 1127, 1738, 2041
[Malin, William Gunn]. 2595
Malina, Bruce J. 348, 2101
Malinowski, Bronislaw. 2652, 3061, 2649, 3109
Malinski, Mieczys aw. 2006
Malinski, Mieczyslaw. 1432, 2126, 2861
Malinverni, Aristide. 1366
Malits, Elena. 2413, 3710
Malko, George. 3314
Mall, E. Jane. 986, 1247, 1351, 2272, 2319, 2625, 3857
Mallalieu, Willard Francis. 1450, 2421, 3228
Mallard, William. 1077
Mallary, Charles Dutton. 685, 2411, 3300
Malle, Quentin Froebel. 3604
Mallery, Richard Davis. 120
Mallery, Samuel S. 3029
Mallett, Frank James. 687
Mallette, Myrtle. 303
M'Allister, M. E. 1450
Malloch, James M. 3639
Mallock, William Hurrell. 1070, 1587, 3102
Malloy, Edward A. 1843
Mallone, George. 558, 1243
Mallory. 3677
Mallory, James D. 986
Mallory, Marilyn May. 2136, 2647
Mallory, Orson E[rskine]. 2790
Mallott, Floyd. 512
Mallough, Don. 92, 404, 405, 1558, 1574, 1597, 3354
Malloy, Edward A. 1843
Malmberg, Constantine F. 2280
Malmin, Dorothy. 49
Malmin, Olaf. 629
Malmsbury, Caleb A. 2849
Malone, A Hodge. 468, 2380
Malone, Dolores Mathis. 644
Malone, Dumas. 1544
Malone, Edward Eugene. 1322
Malone, Henry Thompson. 2966
Malone, Sylvester L. 1294, 2308
Malone, Thomas H. 3343
Malone, Tom. 1567, 3228
Malone, Walter. 2055
Maloney, David M. 772, 2742
Maloney, George A. 3488, 766, 1000, 1417, 1735, 2009, 2041, 2639, 2865, 3667
Malony, H. Newton. 1594
Maloy, Thomas J. 1428, 1729
Maltby, William Russell. 1997, 106, 1953
Malte, Eric C. 449
Malter, Henry. 3131, 3259
Malvern conference, Malvern college, Malvern, Eng., 1941. 3444
Malvern, Gladys. 1533, 3258
Malville, J. Mckim. 881
Maly, Eugene H. 318, 1405, 2093, 2951, 3411
Malz, Betty. 931, 2319, 2875
Mamreov, Anna F. 3200
Manahan, Ambrose. 810
Manas, John H. 3054
Manas, John Helen. 2740, 3054
Manas. John H. 3709
Manasseh ben Joseph ben Israel, 1604-1657. 501
Manasses. 1327
Manchester, Christy Juanita. 1051
Manchester, Henry Montagu. 1528
Manchester, N.H. First Congregational church. 1911, 3789
Manchester, N.H. Mount St. Mary's convent. 3417, 3795
Manchester nonconformist association for the promotion of religious equality. 3118
Mancinus, Dominicus. 1651
Mand, Evald. 295
Mandal, Sant Ram. 2839
Mandel, Arthur. 1650, 2986
Mandel, Henry A. 3508
Mandel, Morris. 2081, 2151
Mandelbaum, Bernard. 1324, 1348
Manderson, Rita. 3362
Mandeville, Bernard. 1536, 3622
Mandeville, Charles Edward. 2454
Mandle, W. F. 54
Mandonnet, Pierre Felix. 1474, 1475
Maness, Edgar A. 1738
Maneval, Solomon H. 2945
Maney, Carlyle. 1837
Manford, Erasmus. 3320
Mangalwadi, Vishal. 1778
Mangan, John Joseph. 1526
Mangasarian, Mangasar M. 3024, 3097
Mangasarian, Mangasar Mugwiditch. 235, 1895, 2008, 3023
Mangum, Oscar Ray. 165, 321, 1450
Manhattan, Avro. 794, 801, 1319
Manhattanville College of the Sacred Heart, New York. 2131
Manikam, Rajah Bhushanam. 1485

Manikka-Vacagar. 3207
Manikyanandi. 1932
Manila (Ecclesiastical province) Council, 1771. 667
Manion, John Murray. 2369
Manire, Benjamin Franklin. 1359
Maniri, Sharaf al-Din Ahmad ibn Yahya. 3542
Maniscalco, Joseph. 3789
Mank, Charles. 2892
[Mankamyer, Orlin Le Roy] 1903. 1568
Manley, G. T. 2052
Manley, George Thomas. 510, 511
Manley, Thomas R. 3601
Manley, William E. 498
Mann, Arthur. 684
[Mann, Cameron, 1851-1932. 1699, 2214
Mann, Charles Eben. 2661
Mann, Charles Holbrook. 1792, 2001
Mann, Christopher Stephen. 274, 331, 1968
Mann, Cyrus. 3597
Mann, Denese Berg. 3837
Mann, Gerald. 993, 3336
Mann, Hames. 3675
Mann, Harold W. 1792
Mann, Horace Kinder. 2861
Mann, J. T. 321
Mann, Jacob. 2092, 2094, 2109, 558, 1706, 2109, 2147, 2462, 3219
Mann, Jesse Aloysius. 1538
Mann, Leonard W. 2436, 3355
Mann, Mary. 235
Mann, Mary Emmanuel. 1811, 2199
Mann, Newton M. 311
Mann, Stella Terrill. 2265, 2808, 2875, 3222, 3716, 3751
Mann, Thomas. 3251
Mann, Thomas Wingate. 563, 2937
Mann, William Julius. 2292, 2629
Manna, Paolo. 850
Mannebach, Wayne C. 2903
Mannes, Marya. 1544
Manning, Al G. 2328, 2727, 2733
Manning, Bernard Lord. 1594, 1468
Manning, Clarence Augustus. 1478
Manning, Francis V. 644
Manning, Frank V. 829, 1137
Manning, Henry Edward. 760, 782, 2328, 2812, 3411, 3769
Manning, James. 3705
Manning, John Joseph. 2938
Manning, Matthew. 2329
Manning, Michael. 864, 1267, 2210
[Manning, Robert]. 872
[Manning, Robert] d. 1730 or 31. 872
Manning, Stanley. 3752
Manning, Timothy. 3613
[Manning, William] d. 1905. 1345, 3240
Manning, William Thomas. 2973, 3095
Mannix, Edward J. 1361
Mannix, Mary Dolorosa. 1632
Mannix, Mary Ellen. 2261
Mannock, John. 788
Manoogian, Sion. 82
Manos, Charley. 895
Manoukian, Serovpe. 1944
Manousos, Demetrius. 1626
Manross, William Wilson. 1222, 2967, 3736
Manschreck, Clyde Leonard. 1177, 2400, 2892, 2977
Mansel, Henry Longueville. 1718, 3102
Mansell, Donald Ernest. 1435
Mansfield, Bruce E. 1527
Mansfield, Elvira S. 9
Mansfield, H. O. 1161
Manship, Andrew. 1568
Manship, David. 1260
Manson, John. 3292
Manson, Thomas Walter. 401, 2064, 311, 1296, 1968, 2016, 2049, 376, 390, 441, 2003, 2064, 2071, 3010
Manson, William. 428, 390, 2016, 335
Mansoor, Menahem. 1411, 3605
Manspeaker, Nancy. 1500
Mansur, Ina G. 183, 1627
Mant, Richard. 1218, 1794
Mantel, Hugo. 3301
Mantle, Eric. 2850
Mantle, John Gregory. 968, 1051, 3343
Manton, Jo. 3312
Manton, Joseph E. 788, 796, 864, 1000, 2392, 2903
Manu. 1812, 3480
Manual of discipline. 3013
Manual of discipline, English. 3014
Manuel, David. 3798
Manuel, Frank Edward. 2705, 3140, 3762
Manuel, Joyce Constance. 896, 1839
Manwaring, Edward. 2199
Manwell, Reginald Dickinson. 3323
Many, Victor. 1751
Manz, James G. 2214, 2300, 3772
Manzoni, Alessandro. 1860
Maol-Iosa. 2489
Mapes, Dora Larue Lewis. 1594

Maple, Eric. 1423, 1424, 1710, 2313, 3824
Maple, James. 3664
Maple, Joseph Cowgill. 157, 3863
Maple, William H. 1092
Maples, Chauncy. 1224
Maples, Evelyn. 313, 3217, 3267
Mara, 1936. 65, 1324
Mara Tautane (Society) 2701
Marah, William Hennessey. 2161, 2233
Maramarco, Phyllis Newcomb. 3185
Maranda, Pierre. 2658
Maranell, Gary Michael. 3749
Marbach, Ethel. 1025
Marbeck, Pilgram. 3629
Marble, Annie (Russell) 3840
Marc, Paul. 1985, 2392
Marcel, Gabriel. 2418, 2834, 1584, 3303, 2418, 3252
Marcel, Gabriel Honore. 2418
Marcel, Pierre Charles Raymond. 2903
Marcelline. 2363, 2556
Marcello, Cristoford, d. 2276, 2768
Marcetteau, Benjamin Felix. 855, 1299, 1886, 3331
March, Daniel. 1342, 1968, 2133, 2673
March, Francis Andrew. 1877
March, Walter William Seymour. 1756
March, William H. 2392
March, William J. 2064
Marchant, James. 663, 925, 1041, 1183, 1211, 1889, 1953, 2355, 3131, 3365, 3508, 1183
Marchant, Leslie Ronald. 2505
Marchant, Ronald Albert. 1490, 3007
Marchbanks, Eleanor. 3310
Marchbanks, John B. 3292
Marchetti, Albinus. 3488
Marchi, Attilio de. 1395
Marchi, Joao de. 1618
[Marchmont, John]. 2338
Marciniak, Ed. 1154
Marcion, 2d cent. 428
Marck, W. H. M. van der. 948
Marcom, Agnes Richeson. 968
Marconis de Negre, Jacques Etienne. 39
Marcu, Valeriu. 2103
Marcum, Elvis. 1753
Marcus, Jacob Rader. 1931, 2094, 2099, 2101, 3131, 3577
Marcus, Ralph. 488
Marcus, Rebecca B. 2623
Marcus, Sheldon. 1372
Marcuse, Ludwig. 2268
Mardsen, Joshua. 2421
Marduel, Henri. 1000
Marechal, Joseph. 2647
Marechal, Paul. 3480
Marenof, Martha. 2085, 2089, 3581
Marett, Robert Ranulph. 3110
Margalit, Avi. 2940
Margaret, Helene. 1900, 3426
Margaret Patrice. 2006, 3285
Margenau, Henry. 3696
Margerie, Bertrand de. 2041, 2268, 3265, 3476
Margil de Jesus, Antonio, 1657-1726. 2333
Margolies, Morris B. 2303, 3309
Margolin, Arnold Davidovich. 2102
Margoliouth, David Samuel. 2629, 1924, 2566, 2629, 2635, 3118
Margolis, Isidor. 1614, 3166
Margolis, Max Leopold. 496, 655, 2115, 2089
Margot, Antoinette. 3818
Margrett, Anne (Sowell) 169
Margulies, Rachel. 543
Margull, Hans Jochen. 1373
Marheine, Allen H. 1201
Maria Alma, 1887. 3421
Maria Antonia, 1900-1939. 765
Maria de Jesus 1602-1665. 2355
Maria del Rey. 2542
Maria Sabina, ca. 1900. 2376
Maria Alma. 805
Maria de Jesus. 2355
Maria del Rey. 1633, 2363, 2490, 2542, 2548, 2573
Maria del Rey, Sister. 1633, 2363, 2490
[Maria Eugenia. 2392
Maria Hestka, Sister. 3420
Marian Congress, Sydney, 1976. 2359
Marianists. 812, 3154
Mariante, Benjamin R. 1121
Marie Angela. 3887
Marie Christopher. 3795
Marie de France, 12th cent. 2793
Marie de la Trinite, 1901-1942. 2639
Marie de l'Incarnation. 2334
Marie de Saint-Pierre, d. 1850. 22, 740
Marie Emmanuel, 1904. 2392
Marie Jean de Pathmos. 3419
Marie, Joseph. 3603
Marie, Josephine. 201
Marie Lucita. 3435
Marie Paula. 1000, 2355

Marie Paula, 1867. 968, 2015
Marie Cecile. 1208
Mariella. 935
Marietta. 884
Marietta, Ohio. First Congregational Church. 1338
Marijnen, P. A. 245
Marin, Louis. 1986, 3720
Marin, Michel Ange. 3418
Marine, Fletcher E. 1808
Marine, Sarah Catharine (King) 2357
Maring, Norman Hill. 30, 150, 158, 170, 1262
Marini, Stephen A. 1038
Marino, Anthony I. 874
Marion, John. 2540
Marique, Joseph Marie Felix. 1110
Marique, Pierre Joseph. 805
Marist brothers. 769
Maritain, Jacques. 42, 756, 760, 1075, 1154, 1355, 1740, 2078, 2276, 2320, 2335, 2739, 3309, 3480, 3610, 3693, 1073, 1121, 1735
Maritain, Raissa. 2247, 2335, 3693
Maritian, Jacques. 1086
Marius, Richard. 2276
Marjoribanks, Thomas. 2071, 3343
Mark Age, 1922. 1324
Mark, Harry Clayton. 1531, 3374
Mark, Harry Thiselton. 2903, 235, 3154
Mark, Julius. 3371
Mark, Matthew. 672
Mark, Thomas Carson. 3472, 3716
Markell, Jan. 1366, 2217
Markham, Clements Robert. 2335
Markham, Ira J. 1009
Markham, Meeler. 993
Markle, Gladys (Jones) 1792
Markley, Mary Elizabeth. 1128
Markley, Mary Mauger. 611
Markoe, Ralston Joshua. 3676
Markoe, William M. 1286
Markowitz, Marvin D. 2559
Markowitz, Samuel Harrison. 2121
Markowitz, Sidney L. 2139, 2892
Marks, Bailey. 733, 1573
Marks, David. 2993, 2335
Marks, Harvey Blair. 1872
Marks, John Henry. 1797
Marks, Joseph. 1288
Marks, Milton. 1724
Marks, Paul F. 2634
Markus, J. Ondrej. 552, 2130
Markus, Robert Austin. 114, 116, 1197, 1820
Markwest, Samuel H. 772, 1582
Marlatt, Earl Bowman. 114
Marlay, John F. 2620
Marle, Rene. 287, 676, 3618, 3656
Marler, Don C. 986, 1107
Marler, Ezra L. 2612
Marlin, Clarence A. 380, 478
Marlin, H C. 639
Marlowe, Christopher. 1351, 2335
Marlowe, George Francis. 1271
Marmion, Columba. 1830, 2392, 3526, 2015, 2335, 3712
Marmonstein, Arthur. 3015
Marmorstein, Arthur. 1724, 2115, 2140, 2412, 3585
Marmorstein, Emile. 3088
Marnack, Adolf von. 3654
Marnas, Melanie. 1968, 2358
Marnell, William H. 1026, 1151
Marnell, William N. 1151
Marney, Carlyle. 968, 165, 968, 1061, 1105, 1837, 2057, 2191, 2912
Marnham, Patrick. 2262
Marolles, Michel de. 2657
Marprelate, Martin. 2336
Marquam, Philip A. 3225
Marquard, Philip. 1649
Marquardt, Mervin A. 339, 632, 2007
Marquess, W. H. 1803
Marquette, David. 2431
Marquette University, Milwaukee. 831
Marquis, John Abner. 3555
Marra, William A. 1785
Marrett, Michael McFarlene. 1524, 2742
Marriage, Margaret S. 889
Marrin, Albert. 1220, 1543, 3793
Marrinan, John J. 3555
Marriott, Alice Lee. 1899, 2671, 2827
Marriott, Horace. 3336
Marriott, Victor Edward. 893
Marrou, Henri Irenee. 114, 1819
Marrow, Stanley B. 390, 474, 788, 3848
Marrs, Elijah P. 2681
Mars, Flla May. 3056
Mars, Gerhart Cornell. 1371
Marsden, George M. 1552, 1691, 2926
Marsden, Joshua. 2507, 3806
Marsella, Elena Maria. 2772
[Marsh, Catherine]. 1568, 2348
Marsh, Charles E. 3411
Marsh, Charles R. 2557
Marsh, Daniel Lash. 685, 2459, 2850

Marsh, Elmer G. 3320
Marsh, F. E. 3480
Marsh, Frank Lewis. 3382, 1580, 1582, 3079, 3082
Marsh, Fredda. 3005
Marsh, Frederick Edward. 1841, 2771, 287, 303, 646, 968, 1841, 3365
Marsh, George Perkins. 801, 2477
Marsh, John. 1177, 3597, 417, 613, 1818
Marsh, Josiah. 1637
[Marsh, Leonard]. 3706
Marsh, Luther Rawson. 3508
*Marsh, Mabel. 2538
Marsh, Michael. 1908, 2348
Marsh, Peter T. 3589
Marsh, Robert Lee. 2348, 2486
Marsh, Robert Thornton. 2267
Marsh, Spencer. 25, 3618
Marsh, W. H. H. 1121
Marshall, Adam. 661
Marshall, Alfred. 1770
Marshall, Catherine. 622
Marshall, Catherine (Wood) 925, 931, 968, 986, 1432, 1609, 1836, 2348, 2875
Marshall, Charles Clinton. 756, 3673, 756
Marshall, Charles F. 184
Marshall, Cyril Baker. 3716
Marshall, David F. 1251
Marshall, Donovan. 1619
Marshall, Dorothy. 3804
Marshall, Edward. 2753
Marshall, Edward A. 1463, 1953
Marshall, Edward Asaph. 3118
Marshall, Effie Lawrence. 2353, 3258
Marshall, Eric. 1724
Marshall, Eugene Francis. 789
Marshall, Frank Hamilton. 1079
Marshall, George. 3312
Marshall, George N. 712, 1418, 1703, 2855, 3312, 3728
Marshall, Gordon. 730, 3800
Marshall, Harry Ignatius. 2505
Marshall, Hugh. 697
Marshall, I. Howard. 329, 369, 428, 2008, 2011, 2041, 2198, 2822, 3660
Marshall, John. 2449, 664, 948
Marshall, John F. 2392
Marshall, John Sedberry. 2041
Marshall, John Turner. 78
Marshall, June Glover. 3523
Marshall, Laurence Henry. 378
Marshall, Logan. 622
Marshall, Mary. 2205, 3396
Marshall, Nathaniel. 1166
Marshall, Peter. 1114, 2029, 2208, 2892, 2933, 3355, 3741
Marshall, Peter James. 1814
Marshall, Richard Maynard. 3102
*Marshall, Robert J. 290, 640
Marshall, Romey P. 3855
Marshall, Thomas Chalmers. 3406
[Marshall, Thomas William]. 1218
Marshall, Walter. 3299, 3300
Marshall, William M. 666, 1845
Marshall, William, of Philadelphia. 2633
Marshall, William Renwick. 1450
Marshall, William W. 2490
Marshall, Zona Bays. 3840
Marshburn, William V. 720
Marsilius, of Padua. 1141
Marsten, Francis Edward. 1034, 1311, 3355
Marstin, Ronald. 1594
Marston, Charles. 486
Marston, Clarence Dean. 1450
Marston, George W. 118
Marston, John. 1014
Marston, Leslie Ray. 968, 1653
Marston, V. Paul. 1609
Marteilhe, Jean. 1852
Martelet, Gustave. 2052, 2255, 3488
Martens, C. G. 607
Marthaler, Berard L. 3154
Martha-Marie. 763
Marti, Fritz. 3103, 3670
Marti, Karl. 2115
Marti, Oscar Albert. 3039
Marti, Retta. 3011
Martimort, Aime Georges. 839, 2240
Martin. 1023, 1440, 1530, 1978
Martin, A J. 1017
Martin, Albert. 2247
Martin, Albert William. 3555
*Martin, Alfred. 3529
Martin, Alfred. 3488, 544
Martin, Alfred Wilhelm. 1968, 2227, 3204, 1193, 1943, 3061, 3118, 3204, 3268
Martin, Alvin. 1690, 2550
Martin, Alvin B. 1575
Martin, Aquinata. 822, 873
Martin, Arthur Davis. 552, 1968
Martin, Asa Roy. 3054
Martin, Bernard. 1258, 1724, 2409, 584, 2111, 2842, 3700
Martin, Bertha D. 910
Martin, Bradford G. 3543

Martin, C. Lewis. 1254
Martin, Carolyn. 1743, 1793
[Martin, Carrie Dehlia (Marshall)] 1872. 2261
Martin, Cecil Henry. 26
Martin, Charles Alfred. 782, 789
Martin, Charles Burton. 3103
Martin, Charles E. 2712
Martin, Clarence S. 1324
Martin, Dan. 15
Martin, Daniel Hoffman. 1414
Martin, David. 32, 2224, 3328
Martin, David A. 1764, 3067, 3327, 3444
Martin, David E. 3857
Martin, David Lorenzo. 215
Martin, Dorothy McKay. 1609, 2587
Martin, E. Osborn. 1743, 1896
Martin, Earl L. 3646, 428
Martin, Earl Leslie. 106, 428, 3646, 3664
Martin, Edward James. 1193, 1880, 2158, 3598
Martin, Edward Osborn. 1896
Martin, Edwin Moore. 338
Martin, Ellen. 3207
Martin, Elmer Good. 1997, 3720
Martin, Ernest Walter. 1429
Martin, Eva M. 3055
Martin, Evan Hartzell. 968
Martin, Everett Dean. 2998
Martin, Fay C. 2875
Martin, Fay Crandal. 1830
Martin, Felix. 1900, 2125
Martin, Florence. 3555, 3764
Martin, Francis A. 2892
Martin, Frank Grant. 2591
Martin, George. 1244
Martin, George Vivian. 1232
Martin, Gerald E. 165
Martin, Gerhard M. 1613
Martin, Gottfried. 2164, 2418
Martin, Harold S. 3290
Martin, Herbert. 1536
Martin, Hugh. 180, 455, 1021, 2026, 2493, 2504, 3203, 3434, 223
Martin, Ira Jay. 1716, 2041, 2799
Martin, Isaac. 2925, 3131
Martin, Isaac Patton. 1848, 2182, 2439
Martin, Issac Patton. 2427
Martin, J. L. 451
Martin, Jacob. 3508
Martin, James. 2006, 2052
Martin, James Alfred. 65, 1105, 3103
Martin, James Perry. 2156
Martin, Jex. 1968
Martin, John Fount. 3480
Martin, John R. 640, 2339
Martin, John Rupert. 1884, 2122
Martin, Kenneth Lewis Price. 2543
Martin, Lena Prather. 2489
Martin, Louis C. 2320
Martin Luther Colloquium, 2d, Lutheran Theological Seminary, 1971. 2279
Martin, Malachi. 778, 811, 1283, 1585, 2041, 2145, 2768, 2770, 2862
Martin, Maria Gratia. 3593
Martin, Marie-Louise. 2171
Martin, Mary Grace. 3154
Martin, Michael. 778
Martin, Noah S. 1121
Martin, Norma. 1471
*Martin, Oliver S. 3225
Martin, Patricia Summerlin. 622
Martin, Paul. 3882, 3883
Martin, Paul Revere. 815, 1649, 2631
Martin, Philip Montague. 1846, 3207
Martin, Rachel. 931, 2349
Martin, Ralph. 1609, 2815
Martin, Ralph P. 341, 348, 376, 410, 434, 448, 449, 1163, 3003, 3028, 3855
Martin, Raymond A. 334, 489, 1769
Martin, Renwick Harper. 3190, 3547
Martin, Richard Byers. 3400
Martin, Richard C. 1922
Martin, Richard Milton. 185
Martin, Robert J. 326, 329
Martin, Samuel Albert. 3211
Martin, Sylvester Mitchell. 1554
Martin, T. T. 1724
Martin, Tenn. First Methodist Church. 2424
Martin, Theodore Krinn. 3759
Martin, Thomas Henri. 2853
Martin, Thomas L. 1271
Martin, Thomas Theodore. 3029, 3295
Martin, Vincent. 1584
Martin von Cochem. 1978, 1985
Martin Von Cochem 1634-1712. 1978
Martin, Walter Ralston. 1034, 1394, 1940, 2612, 3325, 3382, 3664
Martin, William Benjamin James. 1070, 2238, 2722, 3411
Martin, William Clyde. 295, 3673
Martin, William Curtis. 25, 245, 1132
Martin, William Ivan. 901
Martin, William Oliver. 2418
Martin, William T. 2933

Martin, William Wallace. 282, 372, 417, 441, 511, 558, 563, 1157, 3268
Martin. Bernard H. 874
Martindale, Charles O'Neale. 968
Martindale, Cyril Charlie. 191, 578, 626, 789, 845, 864, 889, 1364, 1618, 1702, 1724, 1740, 1937, 2059, 2271, 2324, 2339, 2362, 2367, 3263, 3281, 3285, 3419, 3772, 3774, 789, 1024
Martindale, Elijah. 2349
Martin Descalzo, Jose Luis. 3131
Martineau, Harriet. 2006
Martineau, James. 1055, 2349, 2892, 3061, 3076, 3103, 3365, 3724, 3726, 3728
Martineau, Robert Arnold Schurhoff. 991
Martineau, William Charles. 668, 2216
Martinet, Antoine. 60
Martinez, Angel. 165, 1558
Martinez Dalmau, Eduardo, 1892. 391
Martinez de Toledo, Alfonso, 1398?-1466. 2263
Martinez, Luis Maria. 2639, 1264, 1830, 1999
Martinez, Raymond Joseph. 2200, 3787
Martinez Sierra, Gregorio, 1881. 1113
Martini, Prosdocimus. 3222
Martini, Teri. 2851, 3597
Martinus, Saint, Abp. of Braga. 3635
Martique, L. F. 3131
Martorana, Maria. 1953
[Martorell, Joannot]. 1894
Martos, Joseph. 3265
Martrit, Minna Louise. 311
Marty, Martin. 2791
Marty, Martin E. 235, 2978, 135, 676, 677, 1005, 1041, 1061, 1109, 1177, 1278, 1301, 1314, 1568, 1920, 2251, 2349, 2955, 2956, 2977, 3089, 3214, 3327, 3622, 3623, 3745, 3747
Marty, Myron A. 2298
Martyn, Carlos. 2276
Martyn, Henry. 3815
Martyn, James Louis. 420, 421
[Martyn, Sarah Towne (Smith) 1805-1879. 1982, 3840
Martyrologium Romanum. English. 2350
Martz, Edward E. 1342
Martz, Louis Lohr. 3210, 3774
Marucchi, Orazio. 810, 919
[Marvel, Marie] 1899. 3154
Marvin, Abijah Perkins. 2372
Marvin, Dwight. 1061
Marvin, Dwight Edwards. 2892, 2951, 613, 2773, 2892, 2893, 3207
Marvin, Edward Payson. 1121
Marvin, Enoch Mather. 106
Marvin, Ernest. 1260
Marvin, Francis Merton. 2675
Marvin, Frederic Rowland. 3508
Marvin, John. 2392
[Marvin, Robert B.]. 3791
Marvin, William. 394
Marvin, William Eddy. 968, 2064
Marwick, Max. 3825
Marx, Alexander. 2093, 1796, 2080, 2331
Marx, Jacob. 1825
Marx, Karl. 2865, 3061
Marx, Michael. 2005
Marx, Paul B. 2233, 2461
Marx, Victor. 2145
Marxhausen, Joanne. 904, 1417, 1734
Marxsen, Willi. 348, 410, 435, 2011, 2052, 2256, 2257
Mary. 2695
Mary Adolorata. 2232
Mary Agnes. 472, 2267
Mary Agnes, 1872. 3276
[Mary Agnesine, 1884. 629, 634, 811, 812, 3154
[Mary Alicia, 1873. 2335, 3438
Mary Aloysius. 1332
Mary Aloysius, 1875. 2352
Mary Alphonsus. 3247
Mary Amatora, 1904. 182, 1776, 2359
[Mary Antonia, 1889. 3418
Mary Aurelia, 1881. 805
Mary Barnaba, 1875. 3421
Mary Bartholomeu. 3026
Mary Bernadita, 1932. 2766
Mary Bernard, 1917. 1093, 2041, 2352, 3716
Mary Catherine, 1781, 1982, 3283
Mary Cecilia, 1890. 3493
Mary Celine, S. A. 1645, 2272
Mary Charitas, 1893. 2860, 3284
Mary Charitos. 2352
Mary Christina. 2353
Mary Cornelius, 1901. 3284, 3285
Mary Demetria. 884
Mary Eleanor. 1346, 2353
Mary Eleanor, 1903. 1346, 2490, 2799, 3438
Mary Emmanuel, 1873. 1830, 2132, 2355, 2896, 3270
Mary Estelle. 2332
Mary Ethel, 1890. 2581

[Mary Eustolia. 3790
Mary Eva, 1892. 2392
Mary Fidelis, 1886. 659
Mary Fidelis, 1891. 3284
Mary Florence. 2352, 3415
Mary Florence, 1911. 3454
[Mary Fortunata, 1871. 1347, 3816
Mary Francis. 1644, 2573
Mary Francis, 1921. 180, 1356, 1688, 2571, 2573
Mary Francis Borgia, 1922. 25, 3310
Mary Francis Louise. 2363
Mary Francis. 2573
Mary Frederick. 805, 2573, 3076
Mary Gertrude, 1899. 3761
Mary Gonzaza. 1968
Mary Hester, 1909. 3310
Mary Hilary. 3415
Mary Ignatius. 1387
Mary Immaculate, 1908. 2597
Mary, Immaculate 1908. 2597
Mary Immaculate, 1908. 2012
Mary, Irmina. 1517, 3025
Mary James, 1872-1937. 3416
Mary Jeremy, 1907. 1708, 3416
Mary Joseph. 2198, 3377
[Mary Josephine. 2014
Mary, Just. 2510, 2525, 2750
Mary Laurence. 2573, 2575, 2581
Mary Loretta. 2501, 2893
[Mary Loretto, 1869. 1996
Mary Loyola, 1845-1930. 1000, 1450, 1982, 2255
Mary Madeline. 2031
Mary Magdalene. 2353
Mary Magdela. 901
Mary Marguerite, 1895. 1455
[Mary Maud, 1875. 693
Mary Maureen. 2573
Mary Mauriana. 3163
Mary Michaeline. 2335
Mary Mildred. 3310
[Mary Mildred, 1876. 2360
Mary Minima. 2333
Mary of our lady of the Angels. 2811
Mary of St. Austin. 3006
Mary of Saint Teresita 1902. 3419
Mary of the angels 1897. 2305, 3417
Mary of the Immaculate Heart, 1914. 2355
Mary Oliver. 3795
Mary Paul. 1116, 1399, 2158, 3419
Mary Paula. 42
Mary Paula, 1863. 1111, 2021, 2355
Mary Pauline. 3420
[Mary Petra, 1865. 2720
Mary Phillip. 2258
Mary Reparata, 1892-1927. 2635
Mary Rosalia. 2510
[Mary Rosalia, 1896. 746
Mary Rosalita, 1874. 3783
Mary Rosamond. 2392
Mary Rose de Lima, 1893. 2733
Mary St. Paul. 1540, 2360
Mary Simeon. 2824
Mary Simeon, 1894. 384, 2258
Mary Sylvia. 2772
Mary Teresa. 1750, 2353
Mary Teresa, of St. Joseph, 1855-1938. 740
Mary Theodore, 1856. 826, 1422
Mary Thomas. 1475, 2668
Mary Vera, 1902. 1777
Mary Vianney. 2581
Mary Vincentia. 3419
Mary Vincenza. 3175
[Mary Viola, 1904. 858, 1993
Mary Xavier, 1890. 1370
[Mary Zita, 1905. 2478
Maryanna. 2717, 1000
[Mary Catherine. 3780
Mary Eleanor. 1969
Marygrove College, Detroit. 665, 805, 833, 850, 853, 1948, 2851
Maryknoll Missioners' Conference, Maryknoll, N.Y., 1963. 2515
Maryknoll Sisters of St. Dominic. 779
[Mary Mildred. 3270
MarYosip, Michael. 277
Marzo, Eduardo. 1205
Masa, Jorge O. 2620
Masani, Rustom Pestonji. 3898, 1837
Masaryk, Tomas Garrigue. 2836
Mascall, Eric Lionel. 65, 1041, 1061, 1105, 1249, 1794, 2324, 2673, 2836, 3079, 3242, 3608, 3646, 3656
Mascall, Eric Lionell. 2324, 2357
Mascall, Exic Lionel. 3313
Maser, Frederick E. 2433
Masha, Arnold M. 3851
Mashafa, senkesar. 3283
*Masheck, Charles L. 3191, 3343, 3887
Maskelyne, John Nevil. 3686, 3508
Masliansky, Zebi Hirsch. 3370, 3371
Maslin, Simeon J. 33
Maslow, Abraham Harold. 2998
Maslowski, Stanley J. 864, 1267

Mason, Alfred De Witt. 2525, 2501, 2525
Mason, Arthur James. 3816, 737, 1568, 3692, 111, 1041, 1220, 1759, 2351
Mason, Caroline (Atwater) 1017, 2520, 2525
Mason, Charles Avery. 968
Mason, Clarence E. 594, 607
Mason, David E. 993, 1450, 1883
Mason, Edward. 895
Mason, Ellen (Huntly) Bullard. 2505
Mason, Eveleen Laura. 2990
Mason, Frances (Baker) 1370
Mason, Francis. 2505
Mason, Frank L. 2727
Mason, George Carrington. 3781
Mason, Gershom W. 1249
Mason, Gwen. 2794
Mason, Harold Carlton. 3154
Mason, Henry Lowell. 1860, 1862, 2364
Mason, John. 1450, 1866, 3200, 1324
Mason, John Alden. 3602
Mason, John Brown. 818
Mason, John Mitchell. 1201, 1414, 1754, 2364
Mason, Joseph Warren Teets. 3404
[Mason, Lowell] 1792-1872. 1866, 1867
Mason, Maggie. 3840
Mason, Marcus Clark. 281
Mason, Mary Elizabeth. 2819
Mason, Mary Liguori. 1399, 3419
Mason, Mary Paul. 1144
Mason, Miriam Evangeline. 2022
Mason, Philip. 68, 990, 3017
[Mason, Richard Sharp] 1795-1875. 1930, 2971
Mason, Robert Emmett. 2591
Mason, Robert Lee. 2784
Mason, Rufus Osgood. 2990
Mason, Sumner Redway. 165
Mason, William. 968
Mason, William V. 3880
Mason, Wilmer G. 2813
Mason, Zane Allen. 170
Masonic Service Association of the United States. 1662, 1664, 1670, 1671, 1672
Maspero, Henri. 913
Massabki, Ch. 2041, 3290
Massabki, Charles. 1831
Massachusetts association of the New Jerusalem. 3508
Massachusetts Council of Churches. 1045, 1271
Massachusetts Episcopal association for the promotion of Christian knowledge among the freedmen and other colored persons of the South and South-west. 2541
Massachusetts Universalist Sabbath School Association. 3177
Masse, Benjamin Louis. 1136, 1137
Masse, Henri. 2565
Massee, Jasper Cortenus. 165, 215, 235, 449, 934, 1314, 1558, 1568, 1823, 1831, 2052, 2055, 3131, 3196, 3211, 3232
Masselink, Edward J. 1801
Masselink, William. 1316, 2465
Masserman, Paul. 2105
Masseron, Alexandre. 1645, 3493
Massey, Craig. 2321, 2339
Massey, Floyd. 15
Massey, Gerald. 2652, 2653, 3067, 3110
Massey, James Earl. 986, 1228, 1930, 2875, 2903, 2907, 3003
Massey, Kundan L. 2372, 2557
Massey, Marilyn Chapin. 929, 3535
Massey, Milo Hatch. 384, 2007
Massignon, Louis. 1781, 3543
Massillon, Jean Baptiste. 864, 3673
Massing, Paul W. 54, 2100
Massola, Aldo. 2559
Masson, Francois. 2948
Masson, Gustave. 3236
Masson, Jeffrey Moussaieff. 2646
Masson, Thomas Lansing. 2854, 3200, 3480, 2818, 3521
Masson, Yves Ernest. 90
Masson-Oursel, Paul. 2833
Mast, Daniel E. 2404
Mast, Dolorita. 1706, 3235
Mast, Isaac Newton. 550, 567, 1953, 2227, 3508, 3480
Mast, John B. 2406
Mast, Russell L. 2907, 3296
Masterman, John Howard Bertram. 182, 434, 1051, 1097, 1211, 1141, 1188
Masterman, John Howard Bettram. 460
Masters, Anthony. 1428
Masters, Donald Campbell. 1164
Masters, R. E. L. 3824
Masters, Roy. 2380
Masters, Victor Irvine. 155, 2548, 2558, 3465
Masterson, Mary Adrian. 2374
Masterson, Patrick. 100
Masterson, Reginald. 3681
Maston, T. B. 1538

Maston, Thomas Bufford. 275, 986, 993, 1015, 1134, 1166, 1282, 3329, 3540, 3887
Mastricht, Peter von. 3051
Masud-ul-Hasan. 3842
Masud ibn Umar, Sad al-Din, al-Taftazani. 3722
Masure, Eugene. 772
Mata, Daya. 3480
Matczak, Sebastian A. 176, 1732
Matejic, Mateja. 1028, 2330, 3305
Matera, Frank J. 438, 2055
Matheny, E. Stacy. 2893
Matheny, Ezra Stacy. 2208, 3745
Matheny, Tim. 2557
Mather, Cotton. 130, 684, 968, 969, 1333, 1334, 1335, 1342, 1359, 1372, 1504, 1609, 1613, 1899, 2166, 2261, 2372, 2373, 2399, 2673, 2674, 2687, 2836, 3605, 3680, 3827, 3845
Mather, Edith B. D. 737
Mather, Eleanore Price. 692
Mather, Increase. 42, 77, 180, 1795, 2252, 2372, 2373, 2687, 2733, 2875, 2981, 3343, 3702
Mather, Juliette. 2550
Mather, Kirtley Fletcher. 3313, 3079
Mather, Moses. 1356, 2373
Mather, Richard. 1240
Mather, Samuel. 3720
[Mather, Samuel] 1706-1785. 2372
Mather, Thomas Bradley. 3365
Mathers, S. Liddell MacGregor. 721, 3588
Matheson, Elizabeth Mary. 3812
Matheson, George. 338, 493, 1621, 2392, 3061, 3840
Matheson, Malcolm. 1536
Matheson, Percy Ewing. 3022
Matheson, Peter. 1355, 3024
Matheson, Robert. 1536
Mathew, David. 872
Mathews, Basil Joseph. 408, 969, 1061, 1121, 1281, 1326, 1621, 1913, 1969, 1982, 2078, 2483, 2497, 2502, 2510, 2526, 2531, 2543, 2545, 2626, 2799, 3817, 2526, 2799
Mathews, Donald G. 1108, 2451, 3423
*Mathews, Eleanor Muth. 501, 3191
Mathews, George M. 969
Mathews, George Martin. 2160
Mathews, Horace Frederick. 374
Mathews, James Kenneth. 1066
Mathews, James McFarlane. 204, 205
Mathews, Joseph Francis. 827
Mathews, Loulie (Albee) 3131
Mathews, Marcia M. 26
Mathews, Shailer. 106, 476, 810, 1061, 1121, 1724, 1889, 2016, 2373, 3086, 3092, 3313, 3439, 3444, 3745, 1724, 2064, 2561, 3092, 3313, 3439
Mathews, Stanley G. 1886, 2358
Mathews, Thomas F. 78, 1929
Mathews, Wendell. 969
Mathews, William Barnes. 969, 1004
Mathews, Winifred. 3831
Mathewson, Lester Benjamin. 1841
Mathieson, William Law. 1220
Mathis, Marcian Joseph. 735, 2789
Mathis, Michael Ambrose. 1594, 2531
Mathis, William Thomas. 2455
Mathison, Richard R. 3325
Mathison, Volney G. 3508
Matimore, Patrick Henry. 622, 3281
Matlack, Lucius C. 3423, 3807
Matlock, Charles Rubein. 3365
Matonti, Charles J. 1205
Matsler, Bertha Smith. 1831
Matson, Albert. 2985
Matson, Archie. 430, 1414
Matson, Charles William. 1969
Matson, Edla C. 897
Matson, Howard. 2834
Matson, Louise Klassen. 2373, 2408
Matson, Peter. 1549
Matson, Richard McConnell. 1991
Matson, Theodore E. 1121
Matson, Wallace I. 1738
Matson, William A. 1428
Matsunaga, Daigan. 706, 1802, 3272
Matsunami, Kodo. 702, 708, 2125
Matt, Leonard Von. 88, 189, 683, 1372, 1474, 1475, 1642, 2262, 2268, 2851, 2861, 3460, 3469, 3769, 3779
Matteo da Ferrara. 1811
Matter, Joseph Allen. 28, 3459
Mattes, John Caspar. 2286
Matthew, Donald. 2569
Matthew, Donald James Alexander. 2569
Matthew, Tobie. 2360, 2367
[Matthews, Albert] 1860. 3604
Matthews, Alfred Warren. 114, 2147
Matthews, Arnold Gwynne. 1215, 1468, 1469, 2817
Matthews, Charles D. 2765
Matthews, Charles Evert. 1558, 1568, 3228

Matthews, David. 3233
Matthews, Desmond S. 2545
Matthews, DeWitt. 2786
Matthews, E. L. 523
Matthews, Edward. 905
Matthews, Gomer Benjamin. 2057
Matthews, Honor. 724
Matthews, Isaac George. 535, 2117
Matthews, John L. 235
Matthews, John Vincent. 1000, 1751
Matthews, Joseph B. 1095
Matthews, Joseph Brown. 1095
Matthews, Louise Barber. 2984
Matthews, Lyman. 2864
Matthews, Mark Allison. 1121
Matthews, Mildred. 147
Matthews, Ray A. 3387
Matthews, Robert J. 275, 679, 2127
Matthews, Ronald. 1892
Matthews, Stanley. 300
Matthews, Stanley G. 1280
Matthews, Victor M. 986, 990, 2782
Matthews, Walter Robert. 2247, 391, 969, 1889, 2041, 2244, 2994, 2999, 3623
[Matthews, William B.]. 1940
Matthies, Ron. 1078
Mattill, andrew jacob. 332
Mattingly, Harold. 1193
Mattingly, Mary Ramona. 820
Mattison, Hiram. 1889, 2820, 3299, 3423, 3508, 3520, 3712
Mattison, Judith N. 1714, 2347, 2625, 3409
Mattix, Velva. 172, 2374
Mattoon, Charles Hiram. 159
Mattoon, Laura I. 3853
Mattox, Beverly. 3845
Mattox, Fount William. 1177, 3190
Mattox, Robert. 986
Mattson, Alvin Daniel. 1134, 1547
Mattson, Lloyd D. 733, 1164
Mattuck, Israel Isidor. 571, 1539
Matulenas, Raymond Anthony. 2943
Matulich, Silvano. 2041, 2392, 3270, 3223
Matura, Thaddee. 1000, 1642, 2571
Maturin, Basil William. 180, 1000, 2028, 2057, 3488
Maturin, Edith (Money) 3508
Matzner, Emil W. 1267
*Mauch, Theodor. 640
Mauchline, John. 544
Mauck, Earle L. 3407
Mauduit, Israel. 1468
Mauelshagen, Carl. 2294
Mauldin, Kenneth. 430, 2933, 3355
Maumigny, Rene de. 2887, 2875
Maurer, Arthur James. 205
Maurer, Benjamin A. 1314
Maurer, Charles Lewis. 2292
Maurer, Herrymon. 1676, 2196, 3103
Maurer, Oscar Edward. 1318, 2688
Mauriac, Francois. 2013, 763, 789, 1000, 1070, 1969, 2013, 2332, 2374
Maurice. 626, 1969
Maurice, Charles. 3821
Maurice, Frederick Denison. 493, 756, 1218, 2329, 2374, 3103, 3118, 3343, 3623
Maurice Spertus Museum of Judaica. 2234
Mauricio, Victoria. 668
Maurier, Henri. 2757
Maurin, Peter. 1137
Mauro, Philip. 470, 607, 1051, 1280, 1724, 1993, 2174, 2374, 3200, 3258, 3336, 218, 455, 509, 1121, 1580, 2050, 2174, 3258, 3656, 218, 455
Mauron, Nicholas. 2229, 3031
Maury, Philippe. 1086
Maury, Pierre. 2911
Maury, Reuben. 827
Maus, Charles William. 1920
Maus, Cynthia Pearl. 3887, 535, 1177, 1958, 2360, 3154, 3879
Maus, Cynthis Pearl. 3154
Mauser, Ulrich W. 435
Mavalankar, Damodar K. 3686
Maves, Paul B. 2735, 2995, 3673
Mavis, W. Curry. 969, 1359, 1551
Mavrodes, George I. 1738, 2181, 3108
Max, Peter. 1724, 2265, 2399, 2808
Max Richter Conversation on the History of Judaism, 5th, Providence, 1980. 2146
Max-Wilson, Peter. 3525, 3594
Maxey, Mark. 2374, 2536
Maxfield, Helen A. 3764
Maxfield, Helen Adell. 3764
Maxfield, Heln Adell. 2792, 3579
Maximon, Saadyah. 1784
Maximos IV. 1045
Maximus, ca. 580-662. 2258, 2747
Maximus Confessor, Saint, 580 (ca.)- 662. 90
Maximus Tyrius. 921

Maxson, Charles Hartshorn. 1757
Maxson, Eva. 2230
Maxwell, Arthur Graham. 277, 1724
*Maxwell, Arthur S. 290, 460, 507, 1514, 3380, 3382
Maxwell, Arthur Stanley. 622, 607, 622, 1514, 2543, 2808, 3320, 3380, 3383
Maxwell, C. Mervyn. 506, 1724
Maxwell, Jack Martin. 2236
Maxwell, John. 836
Maxwell, Joseph. 2419
Maxwell, Joseph Raymond Nonnatus. 2826
Maxwell, L E. 969, 3290, 3299
Maxwell, Lawrence. 1014, 1977, 3887
Maxwell, Mary H. 2265
Maxwell, Mervyn. 3887
Maxwell, Neal A. 953, 1009, 1232, 1609, 2392, 2612, 3493
Maxwell, Patricia. 41, 2375, 2483
Maxwell, William. 3235
Maxwell, William Babington. 3200
Maxwell, William Delbert. 1234, 2238, 3853
Maxwell-Scott, Mary Monica. 2168
May, Antoinette. 1817
May, Arthur Sigfrid. 2345
[May, Caroline] b. ca. 1820. 1408, 2961
May, Charles Fremont. 1976
May, Edward C. 1606, 1609, 3406
May, Eugene. 1201
[May, Frederick]. 235
May, George Lacey. 1503
May, George Thomas. 2227
May, Gerald G. 3480
May, Helen. 1260
May, Henry Farnham. 1140
May, Herbert Gordon. 248, 282
May, James Lewis. 2703, 2754, 3079
May, Lynn B. 2669
May, Max Benjamin. 2105, 3822
May, Rollo. 2999, 3574, 3700
May, William E. 944, 1000, 2010, 3391, 3393
May, William F. 3411
May, William J. 493, 622, 3534
May, William John. 493, 616
Maybaum, Ignaz. 2146
Maycock, Alan Lawson. 1291, 1622, 1909
Maycock, Edward A. 321
Mayer, Ambrose M. 2355, 2362
Mayer, Fred. 3257
Mayer, Fred Emanuel. 3325
Mayer, Fred Sidney. 2473, 2690
Mayer, Frederick Emanuel. 3325, 3326
Mayer, Hans Eberhard. 1390
Mayer, Herbert Carleton. 1260, 3154
Mayer, Herbert T. 410, 2788
Mayer, Leo Ary. 3296
Mayer, Mordecal. 2115
Mayerberg, Samuel Spier. 3015
Mayeroff, Milton. 887
Mayers, A. D. H. 510
Mayers, Marvin Keene. 1074, 1127, 2339
Mayers, Ronald B. 3328
Mayerson, Philip. 2657
Mayes, Andrew D. H. 555, 2090
Mayes, Howard. 940
Mayfield, Guy. 1219
Mayfield, L. H. 3406
Mayfield, William H. 1568
Mayhall, Jack. 2339
*Mayhew, Christopher. 3131
Mayhew, Experience. 1753, 1899
[Mayhew, Henry] 1812-1887. 2604, 3428, 3429
Mayhew, Jonathan. 734, 888, 3437, 3726, 3728
Mayle, Peter. 1795
Maylone, W. Edgar. 100
*Maynard, Aurora. 3480
Maynard, Donald More. 1609
Maynard, John Albert. 2699, 3118
[Maynard, Laurens] 1866. 3281
Maynard, Lee Carter. 2258, 3857
Maynard, Michel Ulysse. 1945, 3779
Maynard, Sara. 1643
Maynard, Sara Katherine (Casey) 1643, 3247
Maynard, Theodore. 697, 698, 723, 765, 796, 833, 874, 1403, 1518, 1629, 1643, 1649, 1947, 2198, 2268, 2269, 2270, 2478, 3281, 3307, 3420, 3779, 697, 765, 827, 874, 3281
Maynooth Union Summer School, 1963. 3265
Maynooth Union Summer School 1967. 1155
Mayo, Allen. 3742
Mayo, Amory Dwight. 300, 969, 3176, 3752, 3753
Mayo, Bernard. 1536
Mayo, Elton. 2189
Mayo, Robert. 2653
Mayo, S. M. 599
Mayo, Sarah Carter (Edgarton) 1450
Mayovsky, Mable. 813, 1867

Mayr-Harting, Henry. 1763
Mays, Benjamin Elijah. 990, 1724, 2679, 2680, 2682, 3017
Mays, Carl. 986
Mays, James Luther. 485, 518, 537, 558
Mayson, Barry. 1367, 2376
Mazar, Benjamin. 486
Mazat, Alberta. 3392
Mazer, Sonia. 1623
Mazmanian, Arthur B. 1161
*Mazumdar, Shudha. 3139
Mazure, M. Adeline. 1645
Mazzei, Alfred Maria. 1738
Mazzei, Alfredo Maria. 1738
Mazzeo, Joseph Anthony. 1806
Mazzucchelli, Mario. 2220
Mazzucchelli, Samuel Charles. 827
Mbiti, John S. 12, 13, 1724, 2893
M'Caine, Alexander. 2450, 3804
M'Chesney, James. 1079
M'Cheyne, Robert Murray. 3131, 3365
M'Chord, James. 2912
M'Clune, James. 690
M'Clymont, James Alexander. 348
Meabon, Vera Van Eman. 1061
Meacham, Albert Gallatine. 2424
Meacham, Edgar James. 1293, 1694
Meacham, Henry G. 1670
Meacham, Standish. 3815
Mead, Arthur David. 2542, 3591
Mead, Carl David. 2303
Mead, Charles Marsh. 60, 3462, 3646
Mead, Daniel L. 1200
Mead, Edwin Doak. 2276, 3035
Mead, Eleanor Tyler. 931, 2376
Mead, Emily W. 3508
Mead, Frank Spencer. 142, 215, 303, 925, 1038, 1177, 1318, 2490, 2524, 2527, 2893, 2956, 3002, 3014, 3326, 3355
Mead, George Robert Stow. 674, 1718, 2013, 2744, 3703
Mead, George Whitefield. 1240, 3555
Mead, J. Earl. 1450, 2392
Mead, Jude. 1474, 2032, 2033, 2333
Mead, Loren B. 1244, 2946
Mead, Margaret. 3067
Mead, Matthew. 1017
Mead, Ruth. 986, 2376
Mead, Sidney Earl. 3355
Mead, Sidney Earl, 1904. 1109, 3591, 3739, 3748
Mead, Stith. 1017
Mead, Warren B. 3200
Meade, Everard Kidder. 1652
Meade, Marion. 671, 3682
Meade, Russell J. 1428
Meade, William. 137, 1166, 1328, 1509, 1523, 1606, 2971, 3056, 3781
Meaders, Margaret S. 2392
Meador, Prentice. 2026
Meadowcourt, Richard. 2468
Meadowcroft, Ralph Sadler. 3422
Meadows, Clyde Williamson. 1558
Meadows, Denis. 810, 1947, 3131
Meadows, Denis [George Denis Meadows]. 193, 810
Meadows, Mildred. 480
Meadows, Thomas Burton. 475, 597, 2204
Meadville theological school, Meadville, Pa. Library. 3681
Meagher, George T. 2165, 2859, 3798
Meagher, James L[uke]. 3140
Meagher, James Luke. 3574, 2953, 750, 1613, 1986, 2367, 3076, 3180
Meagher, John C. 1095
Meagher, Robert E. 116, 2324, 3488
Meakin, Frederick. 2836
Meakin, John Phillips. 2604
Means, Elwyn Lee. 2540
Means, Florence (Crannell) 1899
Means, Frank K. 2548, 3529
Means, George H. 135, 1724
Means, Paul Banwell. 1707
Means, Stewart. 3654
Meany, Mary Ignatius. 3419
Mearns, James. 737, 1877
Mears, David Otis. 199, 209, 2178
*Mears, Henrietta C. 321, 482, 2376
[Mears, Henrietta Cornelia] 1890. 648, 1011
Mears, I. 1879
Mears, John William. 1857, 3037
Mease, Clarence. 1594
Mecca, Raymond G. 1243
Mecham, John Lloyd. 821, 1147, 1149
Mechie, Stewart. 1234, 3315
Mechling, George Washington. 1547
Mechthild, of Magdeburg(ca 1212-ca. 1282. 2647
Mecke, Theodore H. 3278
*Meckel, Aaron N. 969
Meckel, Aaron Nathaniel. 1342, 1568
Mecklenburg, George. 1141, 2436, 2452
*Mecklenburg, George, D. D. 2977
Mecklin, John Moffatt. 1469, 2561, 3281, 1469
Mecklin, R. W. 2028, 2933

Medaille, Jean Pierre. 3419
Medaille, Pierre. 1440
Medary, George Philip. 298
Medbury, Charles S. 566, 640
Medbury, Charles Sanderson. 532, 566
Medeiros, Humberto Sousa. 697, 864, 1114, 2377
Medico, Henri E del. 1410
Medicus, Fritz Georg Adolf. 3716
Medler, William H. 2214
Medley, Dudley Julius. 1188
Medlicott, William Gibbons. 657
Medlin, Josephine (Riley) 3529
Medlin, William K. 1149, 2750
Mee, Charles L. 2276, 3035
Mee, Graham. 8
Mee, Keith. 2224
Meecham, Henry George. 368
Meehan, Andrew B. 3784
Meehan, Francis Joseph Gallagher. 2189, 3521
Meehan, Francis Xavier. 3488
Meehan, Thomas A. 2581, 2813
Meehan, Thomas F. 2630
Meehan, Thomas Francis. 2630
Meek, Frederick M. 181, 1342
Meek, George W. 1696
Meek, Jessie. 1969
Meek, Pauline Palmer. 2021, 3164, 3183
Meek, Theophile James. 2111
[Meek, Thomas Sheppard]. 407
Meeker, Ruth Esther. 2458
Meeks, Cathy. 931, 2399
Meeks, M. Douglas. 2568, 3656
Meeks, Rufus Polk. 3355, 2041, 3355
Meeks, Wayne A. 378, 1015, 2098, 2803, 3757
Meer, Frederik Gerben Louis van der. 114
Meer, Frederik van der. 796
Meer, Haye van der. 3834
Mees, Gualtherus Hendrik. 2653
Mees, L. F. C. 2416
Mees, Otto. 3374
Meeter, H. Henry. 730
Meeter, Merle. 211
Meeting of the Monastic Superiors in the Far East, Bangkok, Thailand, 1968. 2578
Mefford, Lila P. 169
Meghdessian, Samira Rafidi. 3834
Meginniss, Ben A. 2033
Megivern, James J. 2256
Mehalick, J. Richard. 3432
Meher, Baba. 2400
Meher Baba. 689, 1381, 1813, 2400, 3200
Meher Baba, 1894-1969. 1381, 2400, 3491, 3492
Mehl, Paul F. 1385, 1386
Mehl, Roger. 944, 1105, 2832, 3444
Mehok, William J. 1946
Mehra, Lal Chand. 1813
Mehta, Phirozshah Dorabji. 3061, 3213
Mehta, Rustam Jehangir. 3600
Mehta, Ved Parkash. 676, 3656
Mei, Yi-pao. 2560
Meiburg, Albert L. 3378
Meier, Carl Anthony. 1290
Meier, Henry Albert. 3336
Meier, Jacob H. 801
Meier, John P. 442, 444
Meier, Paul D. 2339, 2781
[Meier-Smith, Mary Stuart (White)]. 2400
Meikle, James. 1450, 2392, 2419, 3456, 3462
Meilach, Dona Z. 629
Meilach, Michael D. 2041, 3593
Meilaender, Gilbert. 1688, 2220
Meinardus, Otto Friedrich August. 461, 1765, 2127, 2678, 2803, 2804, 3718
Meinhold, Peter. 1141
Meininger, Thomas A. 1882, 2745
Meiring, Bernard Julius. 814
Meiseles, Meir. 1539
Meiselman, Moshe. 3842
Meisenheimer, Thomas. 1267
Meiss, Millard. 3062
Meissner, Sophie (Radford) de. 3508
Meissner, William W. 2574, 2999, 3002
Meister, John W. 135
Mekeel, Arthur Jacob. 1682
Mekler, David Louis. 1789, 1928
Melamed, Deborah (Marcus) 2115, 2140
Melamed, Samuel Max. 2084
Melanchthon, Philipp. 2285, 3629, 3646
Meland, Bernard Eugene. 1061, 1095, 1154, 1281, 1594, 3669, 3745, 3853
Melber, Jehuda. 1306, 2623
Melcher, Marguerite (Fellows) 3398
Melchior, Marcus. 3016
Meldal-Johnsen, Trevor. 1234
Meldau, Fred J. 2477
Meldau, Fred John. 65, 1381, 1580, 2016
Melear, James Melville. 3355
Meletzes, Spyros. 1421
Melgar, Francisco Martin. 818

Melhorn, Nathan Raymond]. 1408
Melia, Pius. 3789
Melick, Edith Moulton. 2529, 2531
Melick, George F. 391, 2335
Meline, Pierre. 1603
Melish, John Howard. 2962, 2131, 3469
Melito. 2034, 3368
Mell, Patrick Hues. 2401
Mellenbruch, Parl Leslie. 3646
Mellert, Robert B. 2944, 3813
Mellinger, Ira Eugene. 1915
Mellinkoff, Ruth. 724, 1847, 2622
Mellis, Charles J. 933
Mellone, Sydney Herbert. 692, 1426, 3213, 3658
Mellor, Enid B. 532
Mellor, Enoch. 135
Mellor, Richard. 1159
Melloy, Camille. 1644
Meloon, Marion. 3471
Meloy, William A. 1488
Melrose, Paul C. 2485
Melton, David. 1381, 1982
Melton, J. Gordon. 1394, 2315, 2431, 3327, 3748
Melton, Julius. 2929
Melton, Roy. 3575
Melton, Sparks White. 165
Melton, William Walter. 165, 332, 1558, 2944, 3200, 3673
Melton, Zora Wofford. 1260
Meltzer, Bernard. 3343
Melugin, Roy F. 545
Melvill, Henry. 1227
Melville, Annabelle McConnell. 742, 892, 1029, 3378, 3417
Melville, Herman. 2762
Melville, J. Keith. 2615, 2619
Melville, John. 1392
Melville, Leinani. 2663
Melville, Thomas. 3244
Melvin, Frank J. 2356
Melyan, Gary G. 1470, 1879
Memmesheimer, Alphonse Louis. 1351
Memon, Muhammad Umar. 1880, 1927
Men and religion forward movement. 687, 2402, 3444
Menager, Francis M. 1532
Menard, Eusebe M. 772, 1000
Menard, William Thompson. 1450
Mencken, Henry Louis. 3062
Mendel, Roberta. 1522
Mendelsohn, Ezra. 3897
Mendelsohn, Isaac. 94, 3118
Mendelsohn, Jack. 13, 882, 3724, 3730
Mendelsohn, Samuel. 2074, 2107
Mendelsohn, Samuel Felix. 2117
Mendelson, E. Michael. 2577
Mendelssohn, Moses. 2155
Mendelssohn, Sidney. 2097, 2098
Mendenhall, George E. 599, 2074
Mendenhall, George Newton. 476
Mendenhall, Harlan George. 2823
Mendes, Frederick de Sola. 2144
Mendes, Henry Pereira. 172
Mendes, Henry Pereirs. 514
Mendl, Robert William Sigismund. 3072, 3095, 3399
[Mendon, Dan]. 3396
Menen, Aubrey. 2645
Menendez, Albert J. 1142, 1148, 3072
Menendez, Josefa. 2643
Menger, Matt J. 850, 2537
Menges, Matthew Clement. 38, 1474
Menges, Robert J. 1298
Menkus, Belden. 2155
Mennenga, George H. 3047
Menninger, Karl. 3411
Menninger, William Claire. 3880
Mennonite church. Board of missions and charities. 2405, 2540, 3646
Mennonite Church. Board of Missions and Charities. Girl's Missionary and Service Auxiliary. 1254
Mennonite church. Church polity committee. 2403
Mennonite Church. General Conference. 2404, 2405, 3086, 3646
Mennonite general conference. 2403
Mennonite general conference. Committee on Christian doctrine. 2405
Mennonite general conference. Music committee. 2406
The Mennonite quarterly review. 187
Menno Simons. 2405
Menon, Y Keshava. 3301
Menoud, Philippe Henri. 477
Mensch, Ernest Cromwell. 3579
Mensching, Gustav. 3703
Mensinga, F. 2050
Mentley, Gertrude B. 2462
Menzel, Addalena. 1953, 2639
Menzel, Emil W. 2531
Menzenska, Mary Jane. 3420
Menzies, Allan. 3118
Menzies, Edna O. 2490

Menzies, Lucy. 1311, 1918, 3285, 3788
Menzies, Robert. 969, 1558
Menzies, William W. 92
Mercatante, Anthony S. 1022, 1746, 2659
[Mercedes. 756, 858, 1364, 3417, 3418
Mercedis, Tusschuna. 3508
Mercer, Alexander Gardiner. 215
Mercer, Edward Clifford Anderson. 3131
Mercer, John Edward. 1381, 3073
Mercer, Lewis Pyle. 434, 1370, 2689, 2690, 3118, 3570
Mercer, Louis P. 3138
Mercer, Robert Hampton. 3355
Mercer, Samuel Alfred Browne. 94, 527, 1502, 1848, 1927, 2094, 2238
Merchant, Jane. 181, 472, 1440, 2392, 2893
Mercier, Anne. 1920
Mercier, Charles Arthur. 876
Mercier, Desire Felicien Francois Joseph. 2242, 3532
Meredith, Anthony. 3706
Meredith, Aubert Lewis. 944
Meredith, Char. 3869
Meredith, Don. 2346
Meredith, Frederic Charles. 3871
Meredith, Isaac H. 3562
Meredith, Isaac Hickman. 910, 3562
Meredith, Lawrence. 1061
Meredith, Ronald R. 588
Meredith, William Henry. 2206, 2424, 3804
Meredith, William V. 3154
Merezhkovskii, Dmitrii Sergeevich. 1969
Merezhkovskil, Dmitril Sergieevich. 1969
Merezhkovskil, Dmltrill Sergieevich. 1969
Mergner, Julie. 1408
Merian, Matthaeus. 601
Meriden, Conn. First Congregational church. 1336
Merideth, Robert. 183
Merikay. 3887
Merion, Pa. Friends Meeting House. 1687
Merivale, Charles. 1359, 2517, 2803
Merizon, Beth. 901
Merjanian, Pepronia. 3171
Merkel, Henry Martin. 2433
Merkens, Guido A. 1251, 1253
Merkley, Christopher. 2604
Merkley, Paul. 2709
Merlaud, Andre. 3171
Merle d'Aubigne, Jean Henri, 1794-1872. 2276, 3035
Merleau-Ponty, Maurice, 1908-1961. 1853, 2739
Merle d'Aubigne, Jean Henri. 1181, 2351, 3035
Mero, Lee. 1958
Merrell, Edward Huntington. 1995
Merrell, James L. 1317, 1462
Merrell, S B. 1568
Merrell-Wolff, Franklin. 2645
Merriam, Charles Wolcott. 2238
Merriam, Edmund Franklin. 143, 156
Merriam, George Spring. 1594, 2015
Merrick, James. 3207
Merrick, Mary Virginia. 1977, 2805
Merrifield, Fred. 2048
Merrill, Amos Newlove. 1324
Merrill, Boynton. 1342
Merrill, Dean. 986
Merrill, Dorothea M. 1478
Merrill, Eugene H. 535
Merrill, George Edmands. 290, 1969
Merrill, Gertrude A. 1910
Merrill, Jenny Biggs. 3765
Merrill Library. Special Collections Dept. 2609
Merrill, Melissa. 2412, 2858
Merrill, Melvin Clarence. 2412
Merrill, S A. 2324
Merrill, Selah. 245, 1944
Merrill, Stephen Mason. 106, 1802, 2004, 2440, 2450, 2477, 3290, 3299
Merrill, Thomas F. 1518
Merrill, Walter McIntosh. 675, 1419
Merrill, William Augustus. 1861
Merrill, William Pierson. 35, 57, 75, 1051, 1594, 2392, 2903, 2933, 2951, 3200
Merriman, Helen (Bigelow) 84
Merriman, Raymond Allen. 96
Merriman, Titus Mooney. 3007, 3817
Merritt, Denny. 334
Merritt, Edward Percival. 685, 814
Merritt, Frank S. 2419
Merritt, George W. 933, 3355
Merritt, Mary Carr. 3131
Merritt, Robert E. 1034
Merritt, Timothy. 2818
Merry, Charles Hamilton. 1724
Merry, Eleanor Charlotte. 50
Merry del Val. 3488
Merry del Val, Raphael. 2753, 2768, 2851
Mersch, Emile. 2020, 3646
Mershon, Katharane Edson. 3239
Mershon, Stephen Lyon. 3480
Merswin, Rulman. 2647

Mertens, Pierre Xavier. 2351
Mertins, Marshall Louis. 157, 1271
Merton, Arthur. 2227, 3821
Merton, Thomas. 584, 2571, 3488, 3492, 584, 760, 1132, 1355, 1708, 1807, 2240, 2255, 2334, 2399, 2413, 2571, 2576, 2578, 3131, 3488, 3709, 3780, 193, 194, 774, 793, 841, 1132, 1356, 1434, 2255, 2380, 2413, 2571, 2572, 2639, 2808, 3488, 3490, 3709, 3710, 3892
*Merton, Thomas [Name in religion, Father Louis]. 3488, 3709
Mertz, Henry August. 648
Mertz, James J. 2270
Merwick, Donna. 773, 1293
Merwin, Wallace C. 1210
Merzger, Bruce Manning. 401
Mes, G. M. 1599
Meschler, Moritz. 1969, 2132
Meschler, Mortiz. 969
Meserve, Harry C. 2380, 2808
Meshack, B. A. 15
Meshi, Ita. 2845
Meslier, Jean. 3091
Mess, Henry Adolphus. 3444
Messenger, Ernest Charles. 1580, 2339, 2343
Messenger, Frank Mortimer. 52
Messenger, Ruth Ellis. 1877
Messent, Claude John Wilson. 2225
Messer, Judy. 1359, 2413
Messer, Mary Burt. 1034
Messer, Thomas Stockton. 282
*Messinger, C. F. 3154
Messiter, Arthur Henry. 2698, 2701
Messler, Abraham. 3047
Messmer, Josef. 2685, 3532
Messmore, J H. 2775
Messsenger, Ernest Charles. 44
Mesters, Carlos. 1496
Metallides, Constantine L. 1450
Metcalf, Anthony. 2604
Metcalf, Frank Johnson. 1210, 1875, 2635
Metcalf, Harold E. 1506, 1507, 3594
Metcalf, Joel Hastings. 3565
Metcalf, Walter. 1969, 1977
Metcalf, William. 640, 1170
Metcalfe, James J. 3285
Metcalfe, James S[tetson]. 2653
*Metcalfe, John J. 2072
Metcalfe, Richard L. 1014
Metcalfe, Richard Lee. 1014, 3183
Metcalfe, William. 218
Metchett, Henry Ludwig Mond. 2119
Methdoist Episcopal church. Liturgy and ritual. 2454
Metheny, Evangeline. 2490
Methodist book concern. 2443
Methodist brotherhood. 694
Methodist brotherhood, Saint Paul chapter, no. 190. 694
Methodist Church (Undted States) Provisional Conferences. Africa. 2438
Methodist church (United States). 2429, 2438, 2440, 2441
Methodist Church (United States). Ad Hoc Committee on E.U.B. Union. 2441
Methodist church (United States) Board of education. Dept. of Christian education of children. 2449
Methodist church (United States) Board of education. Division of educational institutions. 2449
Methodist Church (United States) Board of Education. Editorial Division. 3154, 3876
Methodist Church (United States) Board of Hospitals and Homes. 2439
Methodist Church (United States) Board of Lay Activities. 2402
Methodist Church (United States) Board of Missions. 2433, 2441, 2496
Methodist church (United States) Board of missions and church extension. 2441, 2534
Methodist Church (United States) Board of Missions and Church Extension. Division of Foreign Missions. 2434
Methodist Church (United States) Board of Missions and Church Extension. Division of Home Missions and Church Extension. 2434
Methodist Church (United States) Board of Missions and Church Extension. Division of Home Missions and Church Extension. Section of Home Missions. 2434
Methodist Church (United States) Board of Missions and Church Extention. Joint Division of Education and Cultivation. 2441
Methodist Church (United States) Board of Missions. Joint Commission on Education and Cultivation. 1280
Methodist Church (United States) Board of Missions. Joint Committee on Missionary Personnel. 2434

Methodist Church (United States) Board of Missions. Joint Section of Education and Cultivation. 2493
Methodist Church (United States) Board of Social and Economic relations. 2421
Methodist Church (United States) Co-ordinating Council. 2428, 2439
Methodist church (United States) Commission on courses of study. 2440
Methodist Church (United States) Commission on Ministerial Training. 3669, 3673, 3677
Methodist church (United States) Commission on minsterial training. 3677
Methodist church (United States) Commission on orders of worship, rituals, and aids for the deepening of the spiritual life. 2433, 2441
Methodist Church (United States) Commission on Theological Education. 3614
Methodist Church (United States) Commission to Study the Christian Faith and War in the Nuclear Age. 3793
Methodist Church (United States) Committee Appointed to Study the National Council of the Churches of Christ in the U.S.A. 2670
Methodist Church (United States). Conferences. Baltimore. American Methodist Historical Society. 2431
Methodist church (United States) Conferences. Erie. 2446
Methodist church (United States) Conferences. Louisville. 2439
Methodist Church (United States) Conferences. New Jersey. 2431
Methodist Church (United States) Conferences. North Dakota. Historical Society. 2431
Methodist Church (United States) Conferences. Texas. 2432
Methodist Church (United States) Council of Bishops. 2791
Methodist Church (United States) Crusade Scholarship Program. 2438
Methodist Church (United States) Curriculum Committee. 3154, 3162
Methodist Church (United States) Dept. of Architecture. 1157, 1158, 2777, 3548
Methodist Church (United States) Dept. of Children's Publications. 3188
Methodist Church (United States) Dept. of City Work. 2430
Methodist Church (United States) Dept. of Evangelists. 1558
Methodist Church (United States) Dept. of Ministerial Education. 2439, 3680
Methodist Church (United States) Dept. of Research and Survey. 1132, 1274, 2431, 2439, 2441
Methodist Church (United States) Division of Alcohol Problems and General Welfare. 3597
Methodist Church (United States) Division of Peace and World Order. 1089
Methodist Church (United States) General Board of Christian Social Concerns. 2440
Methodist Church (United States) General Conference. 2441
Methodist Church (United States) General Conference. Commission on Worship. 2441
Methodist Church (United States) General Conference. Commission on Worship. Hymnal Committee. 2442
Methodist Church (United States) Joint Committee on Materials for Training for Church Membership. 2441
Methodist church (United States) Liturgy and ritual. 2433, 2722
Methodist Church (United States) Provisional Conferences. Southeast Africa. 2438
Methodist church (United States) Uniting conference. 2444
Methodist Episcopal church. 1867, 2429, 2430, 2444, 2447, 2448, 2449, 2451, 2454, 3562
Methodist Episcopal church. Board of education. 2757, 3154
Methodist Episcopal church. Board of education for Negroes. 2460
Methodist Episcopal Church. Board of Foreign Missions. 2432
Methodist Episcopal church. Board of home missions and church extension. 2441, 2454
Methodist Episcopal church. Centenary conservation committee. 2442
Methodist Episcopal church city planning committee of one hundred, New York. 2452
Methodist Episcopal church. Commission on worship and music. 916

Methodist Episcopal church. Conferencces. Troy. 2444
Methodist Episcopal church. Conference. 2444
Methodist Episcopal Church. Conference. Erie. 2446
Methodist Episcopal church. Conferences. 2444, 2451
Methodist Episcopal church. Conferences. Alabama. 2444
Methodist Episcopal church. Conferences. Arkansas. 2444
Methodist Episcopal Church. Conferences. Atlanta. 2446
Methodist Episcopal church. Conferences. Austin. 2453
Methodist Episcopal church. Conferences. Baltimore. 2446
Methodist Episcopal church. Conferences. Black River. 2446
Methodist Episcopal church. Conferences. California. 2444
Methodist Episcopal church. Conferences. Central Alabama. 2442, 2444
Methodist Episcopal church. Conferences. Central missouri. 2446
Methodist Episcopal church. Conferences. Central New York. 2444
Methodist Episcopal church Conferences. Central Ohio. 2446
Methodist Episcopal church. Conferences. Central Pennsylvania. 2453
Methodist Episcopal church. Conferences. Central Tennessee. 2453
Methodist Episcopal church. Conferences. Cincinnati. 2453
Methodist Episcopal church. Conferences. Colorado. 2451
Methodist Episcopal church. Conferences. Columbia River. 2444
Methodist Episcopal church. Conferences. Dakota. 2444
Methodist Episcopal church. Conferences. Delaware. 2444
Methodist Episcopal church. Conferences. Des Moines. 2452
Methodist Episcopal church. Conferences. East Genesee. 2444
Methodist Episcopal church. Conferences. East Genesee. Missionary society. 2446
Methodist Episcopal church. Conferences. East Maine. 2446
Methodist Episcopal church. Conferences. Erie. 2446
Methodist Episcopal church. Conferences. Genesee. 2446
Methodist Episcopal church. Conferences. Georgia. 2446
Methodist Episcopal church. Conferences. Gulf. 2452
Methodist Episcopal church. Conferences. Holston. Laymen's association. 2455
Methodist Episcopal church. Conferences. Idaho. 2444
Methodist Episcopal church. Conferences. Illinois. 2444
Methodist Episcopal church. Conferences. Indiana. 2452
Methodist Episcopal church. Conferences. Iowa. 2452
Methodist Episcopal church. Conferences. Kansas. 2446
Methodist Episcopal church. Conferences. Kansas (1914-1939) 2446
Methodist Episcopal church. Conferences. Kentucky. 2452
Methodist Episcopal church. Conferences. Lincoln. 2444
Methodist Episcopal church. Conferences. Little Rock. 2444
Methodist Episcopal church. Conferences. Louisiana. 2445
Methodist Episcopal church. Conferences. Maine. 2446
Methodist Episcopal church. Conferences. Michigan. 2442
Methodist Episcopal church. Conferences. Minnesota. 2452
Methodist Episcopal church. Conferences. Mississippi. 2445
Methodist Episcopal church. Conferences. Missouri. 2446
Methodist Episcopal church. Conferences. Mobile. 2442, 2455
Methodist Episcopal church. Conferences. Montana. 2445, 2452
Methodist Episcopal church. Conferences. Montana state. 2445
Methodist Episcopal church. Conferences. Nebraska. 2445
Methodist Episcopal church. Conferences. New England. 2445, 2451
Methodist Episcopal church. Conferences. New England southern. 2445
Methodist Episcopal church. Conferences. New Hampshire. 2447

Methodist Episcopal church. Conferences. New Jersey. 2445, 2452
Methodist Episcopal church. Conferences. New York. 2445
Methodist Episcopal church. Conferences. New York east. 2445
Methodist Episcopal church. Conferences. Newark. 2445
Methodist Episcopal church. Conferences. North Carolina. 2445
Methodist Episcopal church. Conferences. North Dakota. 2445
Methodist Episcopal church. Conferences. North Indiana. 2452
Methodist Episcopal church. Conferences. North Montana. 2445
Methodist Episcopal church. Conferences. North Nebraska. 2445
Methodist Episcopal church. Conferences. North Ohio. 2445
Methodist Episcopal church. Conferences. Northern Minnesota. 2452
Methodist Episcopal church. Conferences. Northern New York. 2445
Methodist Episcopal church. Conferences. Northwest Indiana. 2452
Methodist Episcopal church. Conferences. Northwest Iowa. 2447
Methodist Episcopal church. Conferences. Northwest Kansas. 2452
Methodist Episcopal church. Conferences. Northwest Nebraska. 2445
Methodist Episcopal church. Conferences. Ohio. 2445, 2446, 2453
Methodist Episcopal church. Conferences. Oneida. 2445
Methodist Episcopal church. Conferences. Philadelphia. 2453
Methodist Episcopal church. Conferences. Philadelphia. Missionary society. 2445
Methodist Episcopal church. Conferences. Pittsburgh. 2447
Methodist Episcopal church. Conferences. Puget Sound. 2445
Methodist Episcopal church. Conferences. Rocky mountain. 2453
Methodist Episcopal church. Conferences. St. Johns River. 3274
Methodist Episcopal church. Conferences. St. Louis. 2446
Methodist Episcopal church. Conferences. Sourthern Illinois. 2452
Methodist Episcopal church. Conferences. South Carolina. 2453, 2455
Methodist Episcopal church. Conferences. South Kansas. 2452
Methodist Episcopal church. Conferences. Southwest Kansas. 2445
Methodist Episcopal church. Conferences. Tennessee. 2455
Methodist Episcopal church. Conferences. Texas. 2445
Methodist Episcopal church. Conferences. Upper Iowa. 2452
Methodist Episcopal church. Conferences. Upper Mississippi. 2445
Methodist Episcopal church. Conferences. Vermont. 2445
Methodist Episcopal church. Conferences. Virginia. 2445
Methodist Episcopal church. Conferences. Washington. 2445
Methodist Episcopal church. Conferences. West Nebraska. 2445
Methodist Episcopal church. Conferences. West Ohio. 2453
Methodist Episcopal church. Conferences. West Texas. 2445
Methodist Episcopal church. Conferences. West Virginia. 2445
Methodist Episcopal church. Conferences. West Wisconsin. 2447
Methodist Episcopal church. Conferences. Western. 2456
Methodist Episcopal church. Conferences. Wilmington. 2445
Methodist Episcopal church. Conferences. Wisconsin. 2447
Methodist Episcopal church. Confernces. Wyoming. 2445
Methodist Episcopal church. Conferences. Florida. 2445
Methodist Episcopal church. Council of Boards of Benevolence. 2442
Methodist Episcopal church. Division of plays and pageants. 3144
Methodist Episcopal church. General conference commission on courses of study. 2449, 2454, 3669
Methodist Episcopal church. General conference. Committee on judiciary. 2449
Methodist Episcopal church. General deaconess board. 1408

Methodist Episcopal church. Liturgy and ritual. 2454
Methodist Episcopal church. Mission conferences. Alaska. 2445
Methodist Episcopal church. Mission conferences. Arizona. 2445
Methodist Episcopal church. Mission conferences. Atlantic. 2454
Methodist Episcopal church. Mission conferences. Black Hills. 2445
Methodist Episcopal church. Mission conferences. Kalispell. 2452
Methodist Episcopal church. Mission conferences. Nevada. 2445
Methodist Episcopal church. Mission conferences. New Mexico English mission conference. 2445
Methodist Episcopal church. Mission conferences. North Montana. 1580
Methodist Episcopal church. Mission conferences. Pacific Japanese. 2445
Methodist Episcopal church. Mission conferences. Wyoming (State) 2445
Methodist Episcopal church. Missions and mission conferences. Utah. 2446
Methodist Episcopal church. Missions and mission conferences. West Nebraska. 2446
Methodist Episcopal church, South. 2442, 2456, 2457
Methodist Episcopal church, South. Conferences. Little Rock, Ark. 2446
Methodist Episcopal church, South. Conferences. North Alabama. 2455
Methodist Episcopal church, South. Conferences. North Arkansas. 2455
Methodist Episcopal church, South. Conferences. West Oklahoma. 2442
Methodist Episcopal church, South. Educational council. 2456
Methodist Episcopal church, South. General Sunday school board. 3555
Methodist Episcopal church, South. Liturgy and ritual. 2455
Methodist Episcopal church, South. Rural work commission. 3254
[Methodist Episcopal church, South. Woman's missionary council. Educational department. 3026
Methodist Episcopal church. Study conference on the significance of Jesus Christ in the modern world, Ohio Wesleyan university, 1931. 3444
Methodist Episcopal church. Womans foreign missionary society. 2454, 2458
Methodist Episcopal Church. Woman's Foreign Missionary Society. Pacific Branch. 2458
Methodist Episcopal church. Woman's home missionary society. 2455
Methodist Episcopal church. Woman's home missionary society. Bureau for deaconess work. 2458
Methodist Episopal church. Conferences. Lexington. 2446
Methodist Protestant church. 2459
Methodist Protestant church. General conference. 2459
Methodist Publishing House, Nashville. 3637
Methodist Society for Medical and Pastoral Psychology. 1601
Methodist Student Workers Association. 3802
Methodist young people's conference, Memphis, 1935. 3887
Methodius. 889
Metraux, Alfred. 3703, 3787
Metropolitan church association. 3144
Metropolitan correspondence Bible college, St. Louis, Mich. 460
Mettinger, Tryggve N. D. 2177
Metts, Wally. 1351, 2393, 3868
Metz, Donald L. 3538
Metz, Johann Baptist. 1066
Metz, Johannes B. 1126
Metz, Johannes Baptist. 65, 2393, 2572, 2866
Metz, Peter. 317
Metzger, Bruce Manning. 201, 229, 241, 315, 321, 337, 351, 473, 479, 489, 1093, 1769, 2760, 2803, 3678
Metzger, Will. 3829
Metzler, Burton. 3336
Metzler, Edgar. 1612
Metzner, Ralph. 2727
Meurer, Moritz. 2276
Meuser, Fred W. 33
Meves, Christa. 611
Mew, James. 1802
Meyendorff, Jean. 2009, 2747, 2749, 3667
Meyendorff, John. 721, 2745
Meyer, Ann Porter. 2990
Meyer, Arnold. 1953
Meyer, Arnold Oskar. 816, 1763
Meyer, Arthur. 1450
Meyer, Audrey May. 1906

Meyer, Ben F. 1121
Meyer, Bernard F. 754, 767
Meyer, Carl Stamm. 1177, 1323, 1508, 1759, 2293, 2297, 2981
Meyer, Carolyn. 35, 622
Meyer, Charles R. 3218, 3693
Meyer, Charles Robert. 1586, 1751, 2939
Meyer, Donald B. 1140, 2709
Meyer, Edith Patterson. 622, 626, 630
Meyer, Eduard. 2604
Meyer, F. B. 165, 215, 2903
Meyer, F[rederick] B[rotherton]. 2820
Meyer, Frank Herman. 1997
Meyer, Fred. 1450
Meyer, Frederick Brotherion. 181
Meyer, Frederick Brotherton. 969, 600, 969, 1450, 2461, 2645, 2824, 2863, 4, 165, 181, 223, 363, 404, 420, 448, 516, 576, 587, 588, 969, 993, 1351, 1405, 1406, 1432, 1943, 2127, 2621, 2799, 2825, 2893, 2903, 3337
Meyer, Fulgence. 756, 1327, 1635, 1649, 3171, 3223, 773, 864, 2057, 2214, 2356, 2762, 3222, 27, 1000, 1351, 1450, 2253, 2581, 3222, 3390
Meyer, Hans. 3693
Meyer, Heinrich August Wilhelm. 329, 363, 371, 380, 417, 434, 441, 468
Meyer, Henry Herman. 2426, 2550, 3556
Meyer, Jack. 3673
Meyer, Jacob Conrad. 1147
Meyer, James. 1643, 1649
Meyer, Johann P. 372
Meyer, John Bleadon. 3154
Meyer, John C. 3664
Meyer, John E. 1318
Meyer, Joseph. 151
Meyer, Kuno. 578
Meyer, Louis E. 3702
Meyer, Louis George. 771
Meyer, Louis Joseph. 2848
Meyer, Lucy Jane (Rider) 1408, 2893
Meyer, Lucy Rider. 2461
Meyer, Majel. 2493
Meyer, Michael A. 2146
Meyer, Michael R. 96
Meyer, Paul E. 133
Meyer, Peter. 2099
Meyer, R Z. 2279, 2281, 3883
Meyer, Ray. 128
Meyer, Rudolph J. 969
Meyer, Ruth Fritz. 2302
Meyer, Samuel. 54
Meyer, Wendelin. 2352, 676, 1885, 3248
Meyer, William F. 3871
Meyer, Zoe. 128
Meyers, Bertrande. 806, 2203, 2573, 2574, 2581, 2848, 3545
Meyers, Carol L. 2408
Meyers, Eric M. 335, 919
Meyers, Harvey. 1816, 2461
*Meyers, Lawrence. 2106
Meyers, Robert Rex. 682, 1271
Meyersdale, Pa. St. Paul's church. Historical committee. 3048, 3816
Meynell, Hugo Anthony. 2181, 2245, 3070
[Meynell, Wilfrid] 1852. 2328
Meyners, Robert. 1418
Meza, Herbert. 2551
Mezers Valdis. 2300
Mezezers, Valdis. 2300, 2846, 3896
Mezieres, Philippe de. 2359, 3605
M'Farland, John. 1201
M'Gavin, William. 801
M'Girr, William. 1655
Mi-la-ras-pa, 1040-1123. 2193
Miall, James Goodeve. 1759
Miao, Chu-seng. 912
Miaskiewicz, Francis Sigismund. 2159
Miceli, Vincent P. 52, 100
Michael, Brother. 1682
Michael, Chester P. 3488
Michael, John Hugh. 448
Michael, Oscar Stewart. 3556
Michael, Phyllis C. 3843
Michael, Sister. 3167, 3178
Michael, William. 2727
Michaels, J. Ramsey. 2041
Michaelsen, Robert. 1130, 3112, 3748
Michalson, Carl. 1107, 1584, 1594, 1818, 3623, 3652, 3659
Michalson, G. E. 1818, 2164
Michaud, Joseph Francois. 1390
Michaux, Lightfoot. 1841
Michel, Albert. 1528
Michel, Jacques. 2393
Michel, Virgil George. 622, 746, 803, 804, 839, 1982, 2367, 3167, 3187
Michelet, Jules. 801, 1938, 1945, 2276, 3824
Michelino. 2393
Michell, George. 3599
Michell, John. 3575
Michell, John F. 3575
Michelmore, Peter. 1594
Michels, Florence. 373, 948, 1659

Michelson, Arthur U. 2016, 2119, 2535
Michelson, Truman. 1637
Michener, Ezra. 1687
Michenfelder, Joseph. 2544, 2771
Michie, Alexander. 2510
Michie, Donald M. 435
Michigan Christian teachers' institute. 3591
Michigan City, Ind. First Methodist Church. 2431
Michigan Synod of the United Lutheran Church in America. 3733
Michigan. Western Michigan College, Kalamasoo. 3161
Michigan. Western Michigan University, Kalamazoo. 3161
Michigan. Western Michigan University, Kalamazoo. Institute of Cistercian Studies. 1276
Michonneau, G. 3676
Michonneau, Georges. 754, 2789, 2903, 3676
Mickelsen, A. Berkeley. 235, 245, 287
Mickelson, A. Berkeley. 287
Mickey, Paul A. 1200, 1552, 2158, 2428, 2786, 2788
Micklem, Caryl. 2783, 2893
Micklem, Edward Romilly. 2017, 2409
Micklem, Nathaniel. 65, 818, 1086, 1145, 1597, 3004, 3031, 3062
Micklem, Philip Arthur. 1240, 1893
Micklethwaite, John Thomas. 2240
Mickley, Richard R. 3391
Micks, Marianne H. 1741, 2321, 3616, 3853
Micou, Mary Dunnica. 1351
Micou, Paul. 1127
Micou, Richard Wilde. 3608
Mid-European Law Project. 1489
Middaugh, Karen. 2382
Middle East Institute, Washington, D.C. 1283
Middlebury, Vt. Congregational church. 1344
Middleditch, Alvarado. 1696
Middlekauff, Robert. 2373, 3009
Middlemann, Udo. 2320
Middleton, Austin Ralph. 1580
Middleton, Caleb Scattergood. 1804
Middleton, Conyers. 801, 2478
Middleton, Edmond. 2949
Middleton, Edwin L. 3556
Middleton, George W. 2833
Middleton, H. W. 3646
Middleton, John. 2654, 3110
Middleton, John Francis Marchment. 3825
Middleton, John S. 2399
Middleton, John Stanislaus. 805, 1299, 2356, 3374
Middleton, Merlissie Ross. 16, 1627
Middleton, Robert Dudley. 1213, 2703
Middleton, Robert G. 1061, 1201, 1296, 2907
Middleton, Robert Lee. 993, 1113, 1450, 1732, 2393, 3237, 3876, 3887, 3888
Middleton, William Vernon. 2427, 2430
Mid-European Law Project. 1145
Midgley, Graham. 1803
Midmer, Roy. 2569
Midrash. English. Selections. 2462
Midrash. Pirke de Rabbi Eliezer. English. 3015
Midrash. 561
Midrash.Tehillim. 2462
Midrash Tehillim. English. 2462
Midwestern Baptist Tehological Seminary, Kansas City, Mo. 2788
Midwestern Institute of Pastoral Theology. 1st, Sacred Heart Seminary, 1961. 2790
Midwestern Institute of Pastoral Theology. 2d, Sacred Heart Seminary, 1962. 2790
Midwestern Institute of Pastoral Theology. 3d, Detroit, 1963. 1261
Midwestern Institute of Pastoral Theology. 4th Sacred Heart Seminary,1964. 2790
Midwestern Institute of Pastoral Theology. 5th, Sacred Heart Seminary, 1965. 2192
Midwestern Institute of Pastoral Theology. 6th, Sacred Heart Seminary, Detroit, 1966. 644
Midwestern Institute of Pastoral Theology. Conference. 2d, Detroit, 1962. 2790
Miegge, Giovanni. 1095, 1424, 2362, 2363, 3192
Miel, Charles Francis Bonaventure. 3191
Mieling, John F. 307
Mielke, Arthur W. 905, 1774, 2463, 2977
Mielziner, Moses. 3583, 3584
Mierow, Charles Christopher. 1811, 3131
Mierzwinski, Theophil T. 774, 2789
Mies, Frank P. 1969
Miethe, Terry L. 111
Mifflin, Mildred. 1351
Mifsud, A. 2179, 2319
Migliore, Daniel L. 1659
Migne, Jacques Paul. 2463

Miguens, Manuel. 398, 1241, 3781
Miguez Bonino, Jose. 3623, 1319, 2222
Mihalcescu, Irineu, Metropolitan of Moldava. 2745
Mihalich, Joseph C. 1584
Mihaly, Joseph. 2749
Mikesell, William Henry. 2781
Mikkelsen, Michael Andrew. 664
Mikolaski, Samuel J. 1751
Milam, John Wesley. 1580
Milans, Henry Foster. 3293
Milburn, Joseph Anthony. 2227
Milburn, Lucy McDowell. 3508, 3509
Milburn, Robert Leslie Pollington. 1818, 1820, 3282
Milch, Robert J. 2155
Mild, Warren. 3880
Mildram, Robert Cecil. 2942
Miles, Delos. 1171
Miles, Frederic James. 607
Miles, George D. 3847
Miles, Henry Adolphus. 314, 2021
Miles, Herbert Jackson. 2339, 3390
Miles, Judith M. 986
Miles, Leland. 1307, 2854
Miles, Margaret Ruth. 674
*Miles, Mary Lillian. 318, 901, 1450
Miles, O. Thomas. 2893, 3735
Miles, Robert Whitfield. 727
Milet, Jean. 3628
Miley, Cora E. 2656
Miley, Jeanie. 986, 2463
Miley, John. 106, 1286, 3646
Miley, Mary Hilda. 2305, 3418
Milford, Conn. Church of Christ Congregational. 1848
Milford, Theodore Richard. 1077, 3652
Milgrom, Jacob. 2755, 3271, 3579
Milham, Richard. 2788
Milhaven, John Giles. 949
Milhouse, Paul W. 1251
Milhouse, Paul William. 215, 1550, 2191, 2752, 3480
Milik, Jozef Tadeusz. 1410
Milindapanha. 3139
Militz, Annie (Rix) 895, 2643, 3336, 1599
Mill, James. 3703
Mill, John Stuart. 192, 1322, 2675, 2865, 3062, 3103, 3608
Millar, William R. 56, 546
Millard, Alan Ralph. 474
Millard, David. 125, 1867, 2041
Millard, David Edmund. 2463
Millard, Frederick Payne. 2227
Millard, Joseph. 876, 877
Millard, Junius William. 30
Millard, William Barrett. 2232
Milledoler, Philip. 2742
Millen, Charles Watson. 1696
Millen, Nina. 2483, 2490
Millen, William Arthur. 2719
Millender, Dharathula H. 2173
Miller, Abraham. 2375
Miller, Adam. 2558, 2439
Miller, Adam William. 410, 540
Miller, Alan W. 2141
Miller, Albert Jay. 1416, 1584
Miller, Albert R. 455
Miller, Albert Robert Herman. 3793
Miller, Alexander. 1128, 3784, 1070, 2160, 3784, 1128
Miller, Alice Gail. 1305
Miller, Allen Jerome. 969
Miller, Allen O. 3664
Miller, Althea S. 1303
Miller, Amos W. 4, 2462
Miller, Amy Bess Williams. 1804, 3396
Miller, Andrew S. 2339
Miller, Avigdor. 2081, 2207
Miller, Barbara. 2460, 2466
*Miller, Basil. 657, 3804
Miller, Basil W. 225, 969
Miller, Basil William. 215, 280, 739, 1575, 1626, 1859, 2048, 2157, 2241, 2276, 2483, 2490, 2510, 2531, 2548, 2622, 2709, 2720, 2875, 2886, 3020, 3242, 3425, 3529, 3556, 3590, 3804
Miller, Bernard Vincent. 1381, 1602, 2367
Miller, C[harles] Armand. 2247
Miller, C. Leslie. 42, 607, 2883
Miller, C. W. 3411
Miller, Calvin. 65, 165, 994, 1568, 1997, 2722
Miller, Carl Wallace. 1105
Miller, Catherine Lanham. 2347
Miller, Cecille. 2488
Miller, Char. 659
Miller, Charles Armand. 1317, 2211
Miller, Charles Edward. 9, 864, 2214, 2722, 3355
Miller, Charles Ervine. 3049
Miller, Charles Henry. 501, 3772
Miller, Charles R. 3244
Miller, Charles Richard. 801
Miller, Clifford R. 159
Miller, Colin F. 1234
Miller, Cyr N. 938

Miller, D. M. 303
Miller, Dale. 435
[Miller, Daniel] b. 1843. 2893, 3049
Miller, Daniel Long. 1616
Miller, Daniel Morrison. 303
Miller, David. 1785, 2120, 3048
Miller, David LeRoy. 2012, 2047, 2854, 2859
Miller, David M. 2572
Miller, David W. 819, 1919
Miller, De Witt L. 1999
Miller, Dessie Rebecca. 1235
Miller, Dianne. 640, 1170
Miller, Donald Eugene. 603, 2221
Miller, Donald Ferdinand. 3405
Miller, Donald G. 277, 1121, 1634, 2799, 2903, 2907
Miller, Earl A. 1997
Miller, Eddie L. 1597, 3103, 3108
Miller, Edna. 1588
Miller, Edward. 1510
Miller, Elfrieda. 1385
Miller, Elizabeth Gore. 726
Miller, Elizabeth M. 2408
*Miller, Ella May. 2339, 2809, 3844
Miller, Ellen Clare. 1686, 2541
Miller, Emily Clark (Huntington) 1982
Miller, Emory. 1738, 1105
Miller, Ernest Albert. 3556, 1111
Miller, Esther. 3090
[Miller, Florence Marion]. 2466
Miller, Francis P. 1121
Miller, Francis Trevelyan. 3118
Miller, Franklin Hoyt. 2048
Miller, Fred. 443
Miller, Frederick Scheibler. 2490, 2536
Miller, Gene Ramsey. 2455
Miller, George Amos. 2241, 914, 2483, 2549, 3480
Miller, George Elmer. 2531
Miller, George Frazier. 3380
Miller, George William. 3709
Miller, Georjean. 1005
Miller, Glenn T. 3195
Miller, Hack. 744, 1366
Miller, Hal. 1121
Miller, Harriet Parks. 742, 2682
Miller, Harvey N. 969
Miller, Haskell M. 969, 1061, 1134
Miller,, Henry K. 3048
Miller, Herb. 953, 1568
Miller, Herbert Sumner. 311, 364, 400, 1834, 1993, 3070, 3720
Miller, Howard. 2923
Miller, Hugh. 203, 1051, 1105
Miller, Ira. 425
Miller, Irving Elgar. 2853
Miller, J. Wesley. 2466, 3051
Miller, James Blair. 1177
Miller, James D. 3509
Miller, James Maxwell. 532
Miller, James P. 661
Miller, James Russell. 1450, 2915, 2936, 180, 725, 969, 1317, 1351, 1432, 1450, 1612, 1977, 1985, 2007, 2133, 2247, 2913, 2933, 3062
Miller, Joaquin. 509, 3458
Miller, John. 277, 468, 1473, 1655, 1889, 2041, 2419
[Miller, John A. 616, 1969
Miller, John Allen. 691, 3646
Miller, John Bleecker. 3450
Miller, John Ezra. 1236
Miller, John H. 839, 849, 3265
Miller, John Leslie. 816, 1764
Miller, John Michael. 1165
Miller, John W. 3336
Miller, Jolonda. 191
Miller, Joseph Hillis. 2875
Miller, Joseph Quinter. 1912
Miller, Joshua Houser. 1753
Miller, June. 986, 2356
Miller, Karl Palmer. 3737
Miller, Keith. 969, 986, 991, 2466
Miller, Ken. 941, 2599
Miller, Kenneth Dexter. 1280, 2698
Miller, L David. 2985
Miller, L G. 789
[Miller, Laurel]. 3575
Miller, Laurence William. 2052
Miller, Lee. 2393
Miller, Leo Francis. 1944, 3859
Miller, Lew. 326, 994, 2875
Miller, Libuse Lukas. 65, 2170
Miller, Lizzie E. 3131
Miller, Louis G. 339
Miller, Lucius Hopkins. 1969
Miller, Madeleine (Sweeney) 245, 1388, 2757
Miller, Madeleine (Sweeny) 2762, 3877, 245, 1388
Miller, Margaret (Ross) 2547
Miller, Marion Mills. 1286
Miller, Mary Janet. 831
Miller, Michael Joseph. 65, 106, 1090, 1450, 2032, 2343, 2356
Miller, Milburn H. 1841, 2886, 3374

Miller, Milton G. 3118
Miller, Minor C. 1807, 3165
Miller, Minor Cline. 290, 3566, 3801
Miller, Neva Pinkham. 1357
Miller, Olive Kennon (Beaupre) 622
Miller, Orlando Dana. 3118
Miller, Osborne Theodore. 2876
Miller, Oscar W. 3107
Miller, Park Hays. 407, 640, 925, 1594, 2912, 3664
Miller, Patrick D. 81, 483, 569, 3413, 3795
Miller, Paul. 3509
Miller, Paul Jerome. 917
Miller, Paul M. 1568, 1585, 1599, 2786, 2791, 2810
Miller, Perry. 1499, 2371, 3007, 1499, 2371, 2466, 3009
Miller, Randolph Crump. 65, 640, 935, 942, 969, 986, 1061, 1121, 1267, 1414, 2006, 2344, 3154, 3165, 3659
Miller, Raphael Harwood. 1466, 2377
Miller, Ray Oakley. 1991
Miller, Raymond J. 853
Miller, Raymond Wiley. 1301, 2229, 2421
Miller, Rex. 2127, 2803
Miller, Richard De Witt. 3054
Miller, Richard Roscoe. 3423
Miller, Robert Bryce. 2973
Miller, Robert Henry. 3336
Miller, Robert James. 91
Miller, Robert Johnson. 420, 2953, 3876
Miller, Robert Mcats. 1140
Miller, Robert Moats. 1140, 3703
Miller, Robert R. 779
Miller, Rufus Wilder. 2306, 3673
Miller, Rutger Blucker. 2701
Miller, Ruth Wagner. 1838
[Miller, S. G.]. 473, 566
Miller, Sadie Louise. 2501, 3802
Miller, Samuel. 686, 1288, 1296, 1523, 2876, 2912, 3243, 3729, 2466, 205
Miller, Samuel Howard. 9, 969, 1066, 1105, 1121, 1602, 2893, 3327
Miller, Samuel Jefferson Thomas. 1045, 3472
Miller, Samuel Martin. 106, 404, 420, 1514, 2064, 2876, 3664
Miller, Sarah Walton. 3005, 3144
Miller, Spencer. 1131
Miller, T. Franklin. 969, 1993, 3556
Miller, Theodore Augustus. 2836
Miller, W. H. B. 3200
Miller, Walter D. 2368
Miller, Walter Henry Baxter. 629
Miller, Waymon Doyne. 1599
Miller, William. 3320
Miller, William A. 1095, 986
Miller, William D. 871, 875, 1407
[Miller, William Haig]. 1632
Miller, William James. 2964, 2967
Miller, William Lee. 1086
Miller, William McElwee. 128
Miller, William Robert. 2173, 3637, 3656, 3679
Millet, Jacques Nicolas Thomas. 1296
Millet, Joshua. 154
Millet, Robert L. 1232, 2401
Millett, Benignus. 820
Milley, C Ross. 2951
Millgram, Abraham Ezra. 1798, 2086, 2111, 2145, 3260, 3261
Millican, Charles N. 1168
Milligan, Anna Augusta. 93, 1803, 2520
Milligan, Ezra McLeod. 1401, 1528
Milligan, Harold Vincent. 1867
Milligan, Oswald Bell. 3003
Milligan, Robert H. 13
Milligan, William. 1506, 2052
Milligram, Abraham Ezra. 2097
*Millikan, Marilyn. 1450
Milliken, Bill. 1260, 3869
Milliken, Ernest Kenneth. 2579
Milliken, Harold Turner. 3276, 3859
Millikin, Jimmy A. 1716
Millikin, Virginia Greene. 908, 1943
Million, Elmer G. 1121, 3785
Millis, William Alfred. 3355
Millman, Daniel. 2467, 3480
Millman, Thomas Reagh. 1144, 2626
Millner, Simon L. 3472
Millon, Judith Rice. 3278
Millot, Rene Pierre. 850
Millroth, Berta. 3545
Mills, Abbie. 1558
Mills, Betty. 862
Mills, Benjamin Fay. 969, 1558
Mills, Charles De Berard. 702, 2653
Mills, Edmund Mead. 1051
Mills, Edward David. 1157
Mills, Edward Laird. 2431, 2455
Mills, Flossie E. 1450
Mills, Frederick V. 665, 1222
Mills, George Thompson. 3303
Mills, Harlow Spencer. 2774
Mills, Henry. 1873

Mills, James Porter. 1348, 2381, 3462
[Mills, Janet Melanie Ailsa] 1891. 3686
Mills, Janet Melanie Ailsa. 3054, 3686
Mills, Jeannie. 2467, 2817
Mills, Job Smith. 1609, 2520, 3731
Mills, John H. 2443
Mills, Laurens Joseph. 1790
Mills, Lawrence Heyworth. 121, 3898, 3899
Mills, Liston O. 1415
Mills, Lois. 1931
Mills, Newt V. 607, 1528
Mills, Philo Laos. 2772, 3110, 3567
Mills, Sanford C. 468
Mills, W. Plumer. 1164, 2953
Mills, Watson E. 1716, 1717
Mills, William. 1889, 3795
Milman, Henry Hart. 48, 71, 810, 1193, 1197, 2089
Milmine, Georgine. 1034, 1495
Milne, Bruce. 1621, 3646
Milne, Christina Hoyer Millar. 398, 425
Milne, James Russell. 2252
Milner, Austin P. 1328
Milner, Jean Shepard. 1061
Milner, John. 290, 295, 717, 789
Milner, Joseph. 1177
Milner, Vincent L. 3118
Milner, Walter Metcalfe Holmes. 611
Milner-White, Eric. 1224, 1308, 2893
Milosevic, Desanka. 2157
Milosh, Joseph E. 1812
Miltner, Charles Christopher. 2419, 2836
Milton, Jennie Lou. 2956
Milton, John. 2468, 1218, 1523, 2330, 2468, 2469, 2470, 2471, 2472, 3297, 3713
Milton, John Peterson. 607, 513, 544, 586, 1095, 1267, 1376, 2286
Milton, Mary Lee Taylor. 1307
Milton, Mass. Public library. 905
Milton, William Hammond. 3462
Milward, Peter. 1516, 1759, 3399
Milwaukee (Archdiocese) 1604
Milwaukee. Public library. 869
Mimpriss, Robert. 1993
Mims, Edwin. 2048, 3071
Minard, Herbert Leslie. 3154, 3171
Minchin, Basil. 1160, 1296, 2255, 2257
Minchin, Gerald H. 3540
Mindel, Nissan. 3702
Mindlin, Valerie. 2305
Mindszenty, Jozsef. 1856, 2624
Mindszerty, Jozsef. 2474
Minear, Paul S. 442
Minear, Paul Sevier. 56, 349, 430, 434, 455, 470, 476, 651, 1121, 1163, 1846, 2052, 2064, 2794, 2799, 2949, 3294, 3785
Miner, Alonzo Ames. 1699
Miner, Bradley. 696
Miner, Caroline Eyring. 2171, 2620
Miner, Edmund Bridges. 2772
Miner, George Washington. 2380
Miner, Luella. 2187, 2510
Miner, Ron. 908
Miner, Samuel Elbert. 1381
Mines, Flavel Scott. 1121, 1362
Ming, John Joseph. 1536
Minghini, Lorraine. 2349
Minich, Roy Linden. 3888
Minister's conference of Greenville college. 1653
Ministers' conference of Greenville college, Greenville, Ill. 1653
Minkin, Jacob Samuel. 5, 1789, 1807, 2103, 2623, 2841
Minneapolis. Salera English Evangelical Lutheran church. 1547
Minnesota. University. Loan Play Library. 1478
Minnesota. State teachers college, Moorhead. 2591
Minnesota. University. 3757
Minnesota. University. Drama Advisory Service. 1478
Minnich, H Spenser. 677
Minogue, Anna Catherine. 1276
Minogue, Anna Catherine. 3417
Minor, Harold D. 1170, 3168
Minor, John D. 300
Minor, John D., et al. 3096
Minor, John D., et al., plaintiffs. 3096
Minor, Maria Sheerin. 2756
Minor, Nell Irene. 2720
Minor Seminary Conference. 3331, 3614, 3615
Minor Seminary Conference. 11th, Catholic University of America, 1960. 3613
Minor Seminary Conference. 12th, Catholic University America, 1961. 3331
Minor Seminary Conference. 1st, Catholic University of America, 1950. 3613
Minor Seminary Conference. 2d, Catholic University of America. 1951. 3613

Minor Seminary Conference. 3d, Catholic University of America. 1952. 3613
Minor Seminary Conference. 4th, Catholic University of America. 1953. 3613
Minor Seminary Conference. 5th, Catholic University of America. 1954. 3613
Minor Seminary Conference. 6th, Catholic University of America, 1955. 3613
Minor Seminary Conference. 7th, Catholic University of America, 1956. 3613
Minor Seminary Conference, 8th, Catholic University of America, 1957. 3613
Minor Seminary Conference. 9th, Catholic University of America, 1958. 3613
Minor Seminary Conference, Catholic University of America. 3614
Minor Seminary Conference. 11th, Catholic University of America, 1960. 3613
Minor, William Sherman. 3815
Minton, Frank D. 165
Minton, Henry Collin. 60
Minton, Wilson P. 1705
Mintz, Jerome R. 1789
Minucius Felix, Marcus. 69, 2475
Minus, Paul M. 861, 1044
Minute of prayer (Radio program) 2876
Mir Hasan Ali, B. 2567
Miranda, Jose Porfirio. 413, 1584
Mirgeler, Albert. 1183
Miriam Auxilium. 3184
Miriam Teresa, 1901-1927. 2478
Miro Ferrer, Gabriel 1879-1930. 2029
Miron, Cyril Harry. 28, 3693
Mirsky, Jeannette. 1160
Mirsky, Mark. 2155, 2478
Mirsky, Norman B. 2155
Mirus, Jeffrey A. 1819
Misca, Frederica E. 3267
Misch, Fannie B. 3718
Mischke, Bernard C. 585, 1434, 2369
Misciattelli, Piero. 3305
Miserandino, Anthony. 474
Miserey, Marie de. 189
Mishima, Yukio. 719, 3862
Mishlove, Jeffrey. 2990
Mishnah. Baba kamma. 3705
Mishnah. Baba mezia. 130
Mishnah. Berakot. English. 1798
Mishnah. Berakoth. 1798
Mishnah. English. 2478
Mishnah. English. Selections. 2478
Mishnah. Selections. 2478, 2479
Mishnah. Sukkah. English. 2109
Mishra, Rammurti S. 3759, 3865
Miskotte, Kornelis Heiko. 530, 2876
Misra, Girija Shankar Prasad. 3779
Missett, Luke. 2903
Mission Helpers of the Sacred Heart, Baltimore, Md. 1412, 3188
Mission inn, Riverside, Cal. 187
Mission Institute, Chicago, 1971. 2496
Mission to London, 1949. 1212
Missionaries of the sacred heart. 858
Missionary conference on behalf of the Mohammedan world. 1st, Cairo, 1906. 2540, 2565
Missionary conference on behalf of the Mohammedan world. 2d, Lucknow, 1911. 2565
Missionary education movement of the United States and Canada. Children's committee. 2490
Missionary Information Bureau. 2505
Missionary Society of Connecticut. 3664
Missions Advanced Research and Communication Center. 1100, 1102, 1505, 1573, 2529, 2539, 2953
Mississippi Synod of the United Lutheran Church in America. 3733
Missouri Bible institute. 540
Missouri. Statewide Adult Basic Education Curriculum Committee. 8
Mistry, Freny. 708, 2710
Mitchel, Jonathan. 1342
Mitchel, Ormsby MacKnight. 212
Mitchel, Valentine Albert. 2362
Mitchell, Anthony. 3315
Mitchell, Antoinette. 283
Mitchell, Basil. 1105, 2838, 3103
Mitchell, Bruce. 1705
Mitchell, Charles Anderson. 2876
Mitchell, Charles Baird. 2973
Mitchell, Charles Bayard. 3343
Mitchell, Charles Caldwell. 2124
Mitchell, Charles Fletcher. 2425
Mitchell, Curtis. 1362, 1755, 1982, 2023, 3230, 3231
Mitchell, Curtis C. 986, 2049, 2876
Mitchell, Dave. 2857, 3578
Mitchell, David. 3509, 3380
Mitchell, David C. 3343
Mitchell, David J. 1947
Mitchell, Edward Craig. 445
Mitchell, Edward Cushing. 378
Mitchell, Elizabeth Ann (Oldacre) 3200
Mitchell, Elsie P. 2560, 3197
Mitchell, H. Brown. 1477
Mitchell, Henry Bedinger. 1051
Mitchell, Henry H. 2682, 2908, 2910
Mitchell, Hinckley Gilbert Thomas. 485, 559, 563, 1539
Mitchell, James. 2324, 3315
Mitchell, James Alexander. 3565
Mitchell, James Alexander Hugh. 1729
Mitchell, James Clayton. 886
Mitchell, James Erskine. 93, 2540
Mitchell, James Young. 2830
Mitchell, Joan. 3888
Mitchell, John. 1337
Mitchell, John D. 1568
Mitchell, John Murray. 1813
*Mitchell, Joseph. 1051
Mitchell, Kenneth R. 885, 1776
Mitchell, Leonel Lake. 139, 2236, 3855
Mitchell, Mary (Hewitt) 2688, 3230
Mitchell, Mike. 2126, 2863
Mitchell, Nasil. 1105
Mitchell, Nathan J. 970
Mitchell, Osborne. 2927
Mitchell, Paul D. 2432
Mitchell, Richard M. 2001
Mitchell, Richard P. 1933
Mitchell, Robert Cameron. 12, 13
Mitchell, Robert H. 1209
Mitchell, Rosamond Joscelyne. 2850
Mitchell, S. H. 154
Mitchell, S. John D. 731, 2820
Mitchell, Samuel S. 2933
Mitchell, Silas Weir. 3207
Mitchell, T Crichton. 3804
Mitchell, Thomas. 1514, 1699, 3300, 3509, 3646, 3076
Mitchell, W A A. 1102
Mitchell, William Fraser. 2903, 2909
Mitchell, William Samuel. 1051, 3848
Mitson, Eileen Nora. 149, 1351, 2393, 2560
Mittermuller, Rupert. 3830
Mittleider, Kenneth J. 3383
Mittmann, Siegfried. 511
Mitton, C. Leslie. 364, 365, 391, 412, 2008, 2176
Miura, Isshu. 2182
Mivart, St. George Jackson. 1580
M'Iver, Colin. 2347
Mix, Rex. 3175
Mixer, Mary E. (Knowlton) 712
Mixter, Russell Lowell. 1580
Miyakawa, Tetsuo Scott. 3807
Miyoshi, Sekiya. 634, 1384, 2130
Mizher, N. S. 379
Mizuki, John. 2953
Mjorud, Herbert. 2560
M'Kee, Joseph. 3754
ML3160.B8B2. 1875
M'Lean, Alexander. 1942, 2450
Moberg, David O. 1134, 1568, 3096, 3444
Moberly, Charlotte Anne Elizabeth. 77, 2334
Moberly, George. 2006, 3654
Moberly, Robert Campbell. 106
Mocatta, Frederic David. 1908, 2103
Mock, Stanley Upton. 1662, 2597
Mockler, Anthony. 1027, 1643
Mockus, Tony. 2560
Mode, Peter George. 3195, 3740
Modern Pilgrim. 399, 1736
Modi, Jivanji Jamshedji. 2777
Modin, Bernhard. 2320
Modras, Ronald E. 1044, 1188, 3700
Moe, Olaf Edvard. 2799
Moe, Terry Allen. 2393
Moede, Gerald F. 2427
Moeder, John Michael. 820
Moehlman, Conrad Henry. 1314, 199, 810, 1083, 1128, 1130, 1151, 1790, 1800, 1997, 2010, 2071, 2977
Moehlmann, F. Herbert. 218, 280
Moeller, Bernd. 3040
Moeller, Charles. 789, 2232
Moellering, Howard Armin. 446, 2855
Moellering, Ralph Luther. 1077, 1132, 3793
Moennich, Martha L. 2494, 2510
Moerner, Otto William. 1203
Moeslein, Mark. 2903, 769, 804, 898
[Moews, Guy Albert] 1904. 2685, 3532
Moffat, James. 3706
Moffat, James Clement. 3118
Moffat, John Edward. 2269
Moffat, John Smith. 3131
Moffatt, Doris. 2380
Moffatt, Gene E. 1288
Moffatt, James. 340, 401, 410, 1193, 1199, 1752, 2001, 2265, 2799, 2912, 2933, 349
Moffatt, John Edward. 855, 970, 1541, 1824, 2015, 2258, 2269, 2361, 2393, 2573, 2576, 2581, 3248, 3270, 3480
[Moffatt, Mary Anne Ursula]. 888, 3031
Moffatt, Nona Stein. 916
Moffett, Grant. 2614
Moffett, Jonas William. 3320
Moffett, Robert. 3343
Moffett, Ruth Jean (Ellis) 128
Moffett, Samuel Hugh. 1110, 2494
Moffitt, Frederick James. 2661
Moffitt, John. 1079
Mofford, Juliet Haines. 2713, 2714
[Mogridge, George] 1787-1854. 3180
Mohammed Ali Alkany. 128
Mohler, James A. 1241, 1601, 2263, 2345, 2572, 3165, 3540, 3697
Mohler, John E. 3712
Mohney, Nell. 932
Mohr, Heinrich. 1267
Mohr, Joseph. 883
Mohr, Louise Maud. 2121
Mohr, Marie Helene. 2831
Mohrman, Dick. 986
Moir, John S. 734, 1148, 2917
Moise, Anutza. 3860
Moise, Penina. 3200
Moister, William. 13
Mojica, Jose. 3143
[Mokotovsky, Abraham]. 2120
Mol, J. J. 117, 3086, 3449
Molan, Dorothy Lennon. 899, 3171
Moldenhawer, Julius Valdemar. 2059
[Moldenke, Charles Edward] 1860-1935. 3562
Moldenke, Harold Norman. 480
Mole, John Witherspoon. 314
Moler, Charles Clyde. 970, 1594
Molin, Lennart. 2327, 2709
Molina, Fernando R. 1584
Molinare, Nicholas. 3073, 3082
Molinari, Gustave de. 3062
Molinari, Paolo. 1455, 2158, 3281
Molinaro, Ursule. 3575
Molinie, Marie Dominique. 1735
Moll, Karl Bernhard. 403, 576
Moll, Willi. 1616, 3832
Molland, Einar. 3323, 2714
Mollat, Guillaume. 2770, 2861
Mollegen, Albert T. 3328
Mollenkott, Virginia R. 944, 986, 2568, 3071, 3832
Moller, Aage. 1070
Moller, Wilhelm Ernst. 1177
Moller-Christensen, Vilhelm. 480
Molloy, Gerald. 203
Molloy, Julia Sale. 2411
Molnar, Enrico S. 925, 3861
Molnar, Ference. 1428
Molnar, Thomas Steven. 811, 1086, 1245, 1855
Moloney, Francis J. 239, 420, 2572, 3458
Moltmann, Jurgen. 676, 1126, 1529, 1845, 1846, 2041, 2046, 2300, 2324, 2326, 2568, 2854, 3368, 3623, 3712
Molton, Warren Lane. 2893
Molzahn, Kurt Emil Bruno. 3090
Mombert, Jacob Isidor. 1487, 2290
Moment, John James. 1386, 1594
Momigliano, Arnaldo. 1193
Mommaers, Paul. 1934, 2647
Monaco, Frank. 2585
Monaghan, Forbes J. 3578
Monaghan, James Philip. 2269, 2393
Monaghan, Patricia. 1742
Monahan, Maud. 2271, 2310, 3438, 3524
Monastier, Antoine. 3789
Monchanin, Jules. 873, 2584
Moncrief, John Wildman. 1177
Moncrieff, Ascott Robert Hope. 2657
Moncrieff, Malcolm Matthew. 1283
Moncrieff, William Thomas. 1017
Moncure, Jane Belk. 495, 632, 634, 1112, 1375, 1844, 2023, 2136, 2172, 2263, 2267, 2983, 3297, 3576
Mondale, Robert Lester. 2786, 3118, 3728
Monday club. 3355
Monden, Louis. 948, 1594, 2477
Mondin, Battista. 3696
Mondini, A. G. 1312, 2498
Monell, Gilbert Chichester. 3076
Money, Walter Baptist. 2775
Monfort, Francis Cassatte. 3664
Mongoven, Anne Marie. 745, 851
Monheim, Gabriel. 2087, 2103
Monica. 41, 890, 1000, 1450, 3277
Monier-Williams, Monier. 3301, 1813, 3301
Monier-Williams, Monier, 1819-1899. 1896
Moninger, Herbert. 384, 475, 640, 3178
Moninger, Herbert H. 644
Monita secreta Societatis Jesu. 1946
Monita secreta Socitatis Jeus. 1946
Monk, Jay Henry. 8
Monk, Maria. 2584, 2585, 2718
A monk of the Eastern Church. 2247
Monk, Robert C. 3007, 3804
Monka, Paul. 2393
Monks, James Lawrence. 1613
Monod, Adolphe. 2799
Monod, Frederic Joel Jean Gerard. 3131
Monod, Wilfred. 1837
Monod-Bruhl, Odette. 3600
Monpuntain, Arthur. 2504, 2505
Monro, Margaret T. 473, 3821
Monro, Margaret Theodora. 473, 523, 596, 1000, 1024, 1304, 3281
*Monroe, Doris. 140
Monroe, Dorothy Fleet. 2864
Monroe, Harriet (Earhart) 2999
Monroe, Herald B. 1166
Monroe, John Walker. 3509
Monroe, Margaret Ellen. 32
Monroe, Robert A. 94
Monsell, Helen Albee. 3590
Monser, Harold E. 1388, 303
Monser, J W. 3639, 3721
Monser, John Waterhaus. 1463
Monsigny, Mary. 2657
Monsky, Jacob. 2699
Monsma, John Clover. 730, 1177, 1738, 3079, 3082, 3829
Monsma, Martin. 1023
Monsma, Peter Halman. 176, 1095, 3225
Monsma, Timothy. 1279
Monson, Charles H. 3609
Monson, Gabriele. 931, 2585
Monson, Leland H. 679, 886
Monson, Thomas S. 1009, 3493
Montagu, Ashley. 118, 1889, 1891, 2653
Montague, George T. 139, 374, 376, 434, 995, 1155, 1834, 2799
Montague, Gerard. 839
Montague, H. Patrick. 1026
Montague, Margaret Prescott. 1359
Montague, William Pepperell. 1889, 3103
Montaigne, Michel Eyquem de. 2585
Montalembert, Charles Forbes Rene de Tryon. 1311, 1508, 2850, 2863
Montandon, Pat. 2586, 2727
Montani, Nicola Aloysius. 813
Montano, Walter Manuel. 801
Montavon, William Frederick. 822
Montcheuil, Yves de. 754, 1121, 1281, 3480
Montclair, N. J. First Congregational church. 1155
Montefiore, Claude Joseph Goldsmid. 2115, 18, 376, 386, 391, 501, 1354, 1539, 2064, 2145, 2799, 3015
Montefiore, Claude Joseph Goldsmith. 2151
Montefiore, Hugh. 403, 3365, 3652
Montell, Gosta. 3599
Monter, E. William. 3826
Montessori, Maria. 2367, 805
Montet, Pierre. 537
Montgesty, G. de. 1303, 2510
Montgomery, A. 1537
Montgomery, Ala. First Baptist church. 143
Montgomery, Ala. First Presbyterian church. 2916
Montgomery, Carrie (Judd) 1599
Montgomery, Dan. 2265
Montgomery, David Kemble. 1162, 3264
Montgomery, Edmund. 2227
Montgomery, Elizabeth Rider. 2845, 3312
Montgomery, G. H. 970
Montgomery, George Redington. 1061, 2180
Montgomery, George Washington. 3755
Montgomery, Harry Earl. 3444
Montgomery, Helen Barrett. 156
Montgomery, Helen (Barrett) 2522, 2494, 2502, 2543, 2876, 3834
Montgomery, Henry Hutchinson. 1121, 2521, 3095
Montgomery, Herbert. 1351
Montgomery, Hugh. 3595
Montgomery, J Dexter. 1461
Montgomery, James. 581, 3207
Montgomery, James Alan. 235, 298, 506, 3118, 3296, 77, 298, 555, 556, 3296
Montgomery, James H. 2545
Montgomery, John. 463
Montgomery, John Harold. 2064, 3439
Montgomery, John Lawrence. 2990
Montgomery, John Warwick. 68, 1043, 1126, 1417, 1724, 1819, 2201, 2278, 2727, 3623, 3667, 3668, 3745
Montgomery, Nancy S. 1488, 3796
Montgomery, Oliver. 3386
Montgomery, Richmond Ames. 2876, 106, 2903, 3673
Montgomery, Riley Benjamin. 1463
Montgomery, Robert. 2393
Montgomery, Ruth (Schick) 1472, 2060, 3473
Montgomery, Ruth (Shick) 1472, 1696, 2306, 3054
Montgomery, Saphronia Geodwin. 3844
Montgomery, William. 114
Montgomery, William Harry. 2007
Montgros, Gabriel de. 1484
The Month. 3281
Montizambert, Eric St. Lucian Percy. 65, 376, 2799
Montoli, Roberto. 2393

Montreal (Ecclesiasti cal Province) Office catechistique provincial. 3184
Montreal (Ecclesiastical Province) Office catechistique provincial. 3184
Montreal, N.C. College. 2928
Montserrat Torrents, Josep. 2343
Monty, Shirlee. 1367, 2399
Moody Bible Institute of Chicago. 227, 1905, 2587, 2979
Moody, Campbell N. 391, 2059
Moody, D. L. 640
Moody, Dale. 138, 365, 369, 1528, 1834, 3646
Moody, Dwight Lyman. 1558, 215, 223, 383, 970, 1316, 1401, 1432, 1440, 1558, 1559, 1562, 1568, 1753, 1794, 1841, 1867, 2393, 2587, 3301, 3343, 3355, 3595
Moody, Granville. 3090
Moody, Ivy M. 648
Moody, Jess C. 146, 165, 1816
Moody, Joel. 1746
Moody, John. 1364, 2703
Moody, Joseph Burnley. 143
Moody, Joseph Nestor. 810, 853
Moody, Loring. 2227
Moody, Paul Dwight. 248, 2587, 2588
Moody, Raymond A. 1698
Moody, Samuel. 2911, 3343
Moody, William Revell. 2588
Moody, William Robert. 2057
Moody, William Vaughn. 3144
Mookerjee, Ajitcoomar. 2187, 3586
Mookerji, Radha Kumud. 2671
Moomaw, Daniel Crouse. 3791, 3793
Moomaw, I W. 1321
Moon, Aileen. 401, 3175
Moon, Floyce (Orr) 2528, 3531
Moon, George Washington. 274
[Moon, James H]. 135
Moon, Margaret. 3473
Moon, Mary Hazel (Ford) 2505
Moon, Robert Barclay. 568
Moon, Robert D. 2944
Moon, Sheila. 1381
Moon, Sun Myung. 3330, 3368, 3623
Mooney, Canice. 819, 3041
Mooney, Christopher F. 1596, 2324, 3593, 3623, 3748
Mooney, F C. 2424
Mooney, James. 1709
Mooney, Mabel Pearson (Schmidt) 1061
Mooney, Patrick. 2893
Mooney, Richard E. 1917
Mooneyham, Walter Stanley. 1090, 1492, 2589
Moor, Edward. 2663
Moore, Addison S. 986
Moore, Albert C. 3141
Moore, Albert Weston. 3073
Moore, Alexander Davis. 1113
Moore, Ambrose Yoemans. 2920
Moore, Arthur James. 65, 2436, 2441, 2496, 2589, 3355
Moore, Asher. 1690, 3755
Moore, Basil. 3623
Moore, Bertha B. 1254
Moore, Brooke Noel. 1696
Moore, Charles Herbert. 1159
Moore, Charles Whitlock. 1670
Moore, Clarence Culver. 1121
Moore, Clement Clarke. 3601
Moore, Clifford Herschel. 1766, 1889
*Moore, Cora. 1443
Moore, David. 3475
Moore, David B. 106
Moore, David Hastings. 3788
Moore, Donald J. 699
Moore, Doraine. 2134
Moore, Edmund Arthur. 2937, 3426
Moore, Edward Caldwell. 339, 1993, 2526, 2836, 3103
Moore, Edward Le Roy. 3062
Moore, Edward Roberts. 773
Moore, Elton E. 970
Moore, Evelyn Garth. 1489, 2990
Moore, Farris F. 2257
Moore, Francis John. 1202
Moore, Frank Lincoln. 2553
Moore, George. 2473
Moore, George Foot. 540, 555, 2115, 3118, 3585
Moore, George H. 1164
Moore, George Rodney. 1382
Moore, George Voiers. 2167, 2220, 3556
Moore, Grace. 3843
Moore, H. L. 1229, 3321
Moore, Harmon D. 3355
Moore, Harvey Daniel. 908
Moore, Hassel Guy. 970
Moore, Helen (Peck) 2810
Moore, Henry. 970, 1629
Moore, Henry Kingsmill. 650, 3154, 1919
Moore, Hight C. 165, 327, 1111, 1993, 2799, 3374, 327, 1993, 2799
Moore, Homer H. 101, 2372
Moore, Humphrey. 3712

Moore, Irene S. 1034
Moore, J. Phillips. 970
Moore, Jack. 1731
Moore, Jack L. 2393
Moore, James. 970
Moore, James Harold. 1756, 2633
Moore, James Richard. 1581
Moore, Jared Sparks. 2739
Moore, Jenny. 1303
Moore, Jesie Eleanor. 629
Moore, Jessie Eleanor. 295, 622, 901, 1479, 2551, 3556
Moore, Jessie Eleanor, comp. 911
Moore, Joan Andre. 99
Moore, Joanna P. 1831
Moore, John Allen. 3203
Moore, John Ferguson. 827, 3871, 3875
Moore, John Henry. 935
Moore, John Milton. 169, 2527, 3131
Moore, John Monroe. 2421, 2440, 2494, 3143
Moore, John Morrison. 1586, 1934
Moore, John Travers. 901, 1776, 2483, 2634
Moore, Joseph. 443
Moore, Joseph Graessle. 1524, 2958
Moore, Judy Hull. 904
Moore, Justin Hartley. 3062
Moore, Karl Hildreth. 1559
Moore, Katharine. 3704
Moore, Kenneth Willoughby. 3132
Moore, Lettie Wheeler. 1309, 1367
Moore, Luther William. 172
Moore, Marcia. 96, 3054
Moore, Margaret Gordon. 3509
Moore, Margaret R. 3284
Moore, Mark Reynolds. 1237, 1249
Moore, Marvin. 1609, 3271
Moore, Mary Anne. 3154
Moore, Mary Elizabeth. 970
Moore, Mary Hunter. 1450, 3385, 3556
Moore, Marylu. 156
Moore, Matthew H. 2423
Moore, Maurice J. 663
Moore, Merrill Dennis. 3529
Moore, Patrick. 2658
Moore, Paul. 1280, 2742, 2962, 1301, 1568, 2589
Moore, Paul L. 1997
Moore, Philip Samuel. 2826
Moore, Ralph. 3003, 3888
Moore, Ralph Westwood. 1177
Moore, Raymond S. 2466, 2539
Moore, Richard E. 1278
Moore, Robert Braden. 2916, 2927, 3646
Moore, Robert Cecil. 815
Moore, Robert Ian. 1805
Moore, Robert Laurence. 3521
Moore, Robert Samuel. 2459
Moore, Samuel W. 2428
Moore, Sebastian. 106, 796, 1000, 1997, 1998, 2245, 2393
Moore, Sidney. 3878
Moore, Stephen N. 673
Moore, Theophilus Wilson. 463
Moore, Thomas. 789
Moore, Thomas Hendrick. 789, 1969, 1985, 2367, 2393, 2876
Moore, Thomas Verner. 1956, 855, 3488
Moore, Thomas Verner [name in religion: Father Pablo Maria]. 3488
Moore, Thomas Verner [Name in religion: Pablo Maria, Father]. 3488
Moore, Virginia. 1414, 3863
Moore, Walter Lane. 1440, 3374
Moore, Walter William. 201, 2913
Moore, Waylon B. 1568
Moore, Willard Burgess. 2568
Moore, William Eves. 1311
Moore, William Joseph. 1296
Moore, William Thomas. 1463, 2008, 3480, 1463, 1466, 3673
Moore, William Walker. 1051
Moore, Willis Luther. 3480
Moorefield, Arthur Albert. 1208, 1701
Moorehead, Lee C. 2903
Moorehead, William Gallogly. 329, 465, 474, 368, 391
Moorhead, James H. 2464
Moorhous, Carl W. 1171
Moorhouse, Geoffrey. 2499, 2571
Moorland, Jesse Edward. 16
Moorman, Charles. 2664, 3817
Moorman, Frederic William. 696, 2783
Moorman, John Richard Humpidge. 428, 1027, 1516, 1643, 1646, 1647, 1759, 1762
Moors, Kent F. 2664, 2853
Moorselaar, Corinne van. 1027, 1644
Moorshead, Robert Fletcher. 2539
Moose, A H. 526, 3462
Moothart, Lorene. 1634
Morais, Herbert Montfort. 1420, 1419
Moral, Herbert Renard. 3406
Moral Re-armament. 2593
Morales, Adam. 2549
Morales, Francisco. 1647

Moralesdorta, Jose. 3520
Moran, Berdice Josephine. 2048
Moran, Gabriel. 277, 805, 935, 938, 1244, 2571, 3225, 3227
Moran, Hugh Anderson. 1385
Moran, John W. 698
Moran, Kieran P. 2362, 2478
Moran, Kieran Philip. 2362, 2478
Moran, Miriam G. 1621
Moran, Owen W. 1203
Moran, Thomas. 311
Morando, Nazarene. 887
Morant, John J. 14
Moravian Church. 2594, 2595
Moravian Church at Oldman's Creek. 3051
Moravian church. Inter-provincial board of Christian education of the Moravian church in America. 2594
Moravian church. Liturgy and ritual. 2594, 2595
Moravian historical society, Nazareth, Pa. 2596
Moravians. 1867, 2595
Moravians. Liturgy and ritual. 1867
Morcock, J W. 496
More, George Voiers. 1239
[More, Hannah] 1745-1833. 944, 970, 1440, 2876
More, Henry. 1520
More, Paul Elmer. 2041, 3658, 349, 1070, 1218, 1969, 2041, 2832, 3103
More, Thomas. 789, 844, 1351, 2276, 2596, 3762
More, Thomas, Saint. 1352, 1522
More, W Robert. 1051
Morea, Andre. 612, 2597
Morea, Dominic. 2332
Moreau, Basile Antoine Marie. 1434
Moreau, Jules Laurence. 2196
Moreau, Roland. 1403
Morehouse, Carrie Warner. 3207
Morehouse, Clifford P. 1224
Morehouse, Clifford Phelps. 1066, 2698, 2964
Morehouse, Frank E. 253
Morehouse, Henry Lyman. 156
Moreira, Eduardo. 2541, 2545
Moreland, Mary L[eona]. 612
Morell, John Daniel. 3103
Morell, Julienne. 1533
Morell, Stephen. 925
Morelli, James. 2333
Morelock, George Leslie. 1239
Morelock, James Capers. 2175
Moreno, Antonio. 2159, 2999
Moreno, Jacob L. 3142
*Morentz, Ethel Irene. 2290
Morentz, Paul Israel. 484
Morenz, Siegfried. 1502
Moreschini, Cesare. 673
Moreton, Bernard. 3262
Moretti, Girolamo Maria. 3281
Morey, Adrian. 177, 2813, 873, 1508, 1631
[Morey, Charles]. 1724
Morey, Charles Rufus. 921
Morey, Robert A. 1480, 96, 1088, 1940, 3829
Morford, M. P. O. 2657
Morgan, Abel. 135, 1625
Morgan, Amon Livingston. 886
Morgan, Angela. 3207
Morgan, Annie (Sewell) 3858
Morgan, Arthur Ernest. 2227
Morgan, Barbara (Spofford) 3103
Morgan, Beatrice Payne. 2399
Morgan, Bernice Bangs. 2500
Morgan, Bruce. 1075
Morgan, Campbell G. 2903
Morgan, Carl Hamilton. 410
Morgan, Carol McAfee. 2559
Morgan, Charles Carroll. 7, 109
Morgan, Charles Herbert. 254, 270, 475, 597, 648, 1193, 2127
Morgan, Clarita Hutchison. 2597
Morgan, Claude M. 1061
Morgan, Dale Lowell. 2608
Morgan, Darold H. 994
Morgan, Dewi. 43, 579, 1362, 2194, 3591, 3664
Morgan, Dewi, ed. 1362
Morgan, Donn F. 3821
Morgan, E. W. 480
Morgan, Edmund Robert. 1224, 1599
Morgan, Edmund Sears. 3007
Morgan, Edmund Sears. 1141, 3007, 3817
Morgan, Edward J. 3336
Morgan, Elise (Nevins) 1450, 2393
Morgan, Ernest. 1414
Morgan, Everett J. 1136, 3623
Morgan, Frederick. 3588
Morgan, G. Campbell. 403, 1314

Morgan, George Campbell. 970, 2004, 71, 199, 201, 223, 235, 403, 417, 428, 434, 435, 441, 444, 460, 468, 521, 522, 538, 543, 546, 548, 550, 558, 559, 567, 640, 970, 990, 1051, 1121, 1316, 1342, 1568, 1724, 1741, 1831, 1969, 2004, 2026, 2064, 2474, 2494, 2597, 2876, 2887, 2903, 3320, 3374, 3673, 223, 224, 235, 332, 345, 403, 550, 558, 576, 600, 970, 2786, 2944, 3200, 1342
Morgan, George W. 2320
Morgan, Geraldine. 2597, 3355
Morgan, H. Daniel. 1241
Morgan, Harry. 463
Morgan, Harry Titterton. 913
Morgan, Hector Davies. 1218
Morgan, Henry Victor. 1070
Morgan, James Logan. 1485
Morgan, Jeremiah James. 1051
Morgan, Jill. 2597
Morgan, John Smith. 1635
Morgan, John Vyrnwy. 3362, 3618
Morgan, Joseph O. 524
Morgan, Kenneth William. 705, 1813, 2565
Morgan, Louis Krafft. 3261
Morgan, Lucy Belle. 970
Morgan, Lucy (Griscom) 2597, 3143
Morgan, Marjorie McCallum. 188
Morgan, Mary Evangelist. 3418
Morgan, Melinda Emily (Boone) 970
Morgan, Nicholas Groesbeck. 3287
[Morgan, P. Brett]. 1861
Morgan, Pliny Brett. 1568
Morgan, Richard. 235, 651, 970, 986, 1061, 1428, 1969, 3271
Morgan, Richard E. 1151
Morgan, Richard Williams. 46
Morgan, Robert. 476
Morgan, Samuel Rowland. 2992
Morgan, Stephen G. 2612
Morgan, Thomas. 1105
Morgan, Thomas Brynmor. 738, 2769, 2852, 2862, 3436
Morgan, William. 1670
[Morgan, William] 1774-ca. 1826. 1670
Morgan, William Ferdinand. 2211
Morgan, William Henry. 3875
Morgan, William Sacheus. 3103, 3343
Morgans, G. J. 166
Morganstern, Julian. 522
Morgenstern, Julian. 81, 486, 522, 543, 1626, 2093
Moriarty, Eugene James. 2719
Moriarty, Francis Edwin. 2812
Moriarty, Frederick L. 540
Moriarty, James Joseph. 1969
Moriarty, James Robert. 2137
Moriarty, Patrick Eugene. 114
Moriarty, Theodore W. C. 3067
Morice, Adrian Gabriel. 1532, 3718
Morice, Charles. 3221
Morice, Henri. 1995, 2356, 2981, 3488
Morich, Randy. 986
Morick, Harold. 2474
Morikawa, Jitsuo. 1171
Morill, Guy Louis. 1724
Morin, Germain. 188
Morin, Jean Baptiste. 98
Morino, Claudio. 29, 1141
Morioka, Kiyomi. 1936
Morison, Ernest Frederick. 177, 2576
Morison, John Hopkins. 438, 441, 1993
Morison, Samuel Eliot. 2371
Morison, Stanley. 2238
Morison, William. 2401
Mork, Wulstan. 2326, 3265, 3488
Morlan, George Kolmer. 2903
Morland, Samuel. 3788
Morley, David C. 2462
Morley, Hugh M. 2805, 2937
Morley, John P. 72
Mormon Festival of Arts, 1st-3d, Brigham Young University, 1969-1972. 87
Mornay, Philippe de. 58
Morneau, Robert F. 1440, 1804, 2393
Morner, Magnus. 1947
Morningstar, Mildred (Whaley) 3171
Moro, Louis. 3574
Morozzo, Carlo Giuseppe. 2643
Morrell, Francis Joseph. 2367
Morrell, Minnie Cate. 315
Morrell, William Parker. 1238
Morrell, Z. N. 170
Morrell, Zenos N. 170
Morrill, Allen Conrad. 2305, 2706
Morrill, Charles. 123
Morrill, G[ulian] L[ansing]. 3343
Morrill, Guy Louis. 3529
Morrill, Jennie Folsom. 970
Morrill, Madge (Haines) 42, 627, 1405, 1982, 2332, 2498, 2825, 3380
Morrill, Sibley S. 1791
Morris, A Wayne. 2918
Morris, Alvin Marion. 2947
Morris, Augustine. 1725
Morris, Benjamin Franklin. 3745

Morris, Bernard Newth. 166
Morris, Byron T. 2167
Morris, Caspar. 3132
Morris, Charles Eugene. 1374
Morris, Charles William. 2227
Morris, Colin. 3154
Morris, Colin M. 1061, 2436, 2903, 3365, 3780
Morris, Daniel Luzon. 3079
Morris, Danny E. 1007, 1121
Morris, David. 2252
Morris, E. C. 15, 2669, 3343
Morris, Ebenezer Joseph. 3355
Morris, Edward Allen. 75
Morris, Edward Dafydd. 118, 692, 2943
Morris, Frederick M. 2903, 2973, 3290
Morris, George E. 1572
Morris, George Sylvester. 1106, 2164
Morris, Henry M. 135, 640
Morris, Henry M 1918. 205
Morris, Henry Madison. 65, 205, 277, 280, 576, 614, 1127, 1382, 1580, 3081, 3082, 3670
Morris, Herbert Newall. 3571
Morris, Herbert William. 205, 1953, 3546
Morris, Hilary. 3459
Morris, J. Wesley. 1275
Morris, James. 1576
Morris, James Kenneth. 1308, 2344
Morris, James Winston. 3272, 3707
Morris, Joan. 3836
Morris, John Gottlieb. 83, 2276, 2282, 2303, 3533
Morris, John J. 1861
Morris, John Webster. 1689
Morris, Kenneth. 3689
Morris, Leon. 106, 107, 321, 420, 425, 428, 445, 455, 478, 1061, 1297, 1831, 2022, 2041, 2157, 2910, 56, 417, 2266, 3225
Morris, Lewis. 1802
Morris, Max. 1319
Morris, Nephi Lowell. 2604, 3429
Morris, Otho Anderson. 3200
Morris, Paul D. 986
Morris, Paul Judson. 3880
Morris, Peter M. K. 557, 562
Morris, Raymond P. 3627
Morris, Richard. 3367
Morris, Robert. 1662
Morris, Robert Hugh. 2620
Morris, Robert Overton. 3509
Morris, Rupert Hugh, 1842 or 3-1918. 891
Morris, Samuel Leslie. 2501, 2528, 2926, 2936
Morris, Scott. 3699
Morris, Thomas Asbury. 2423, 2425
Morris, Thomas V. 65, 3306
Morris, William. 2324, 752
Morris, William Dale. 1177
Morris, William Sparkes. 1249
Morris, Winfield Scott. 1969
Morrisey, Jean. 2420
Morrisey, Kirkie. 1634
Morrish, Furze. 96, 3686
Morrish, George. 529
Morrison, A. B. 3509
Morrison, Abraham Cressey. 3079
Morrison, Abraham Cressy. 3081
Morrison, Al H. 96, 2128
Morrison, Bakewell. 782, 789, 2339, 2343, 2836, 3265
Morrison, Beulah May. 1512
Morrison, Charles Clayton. 135, 1095, 1492, 2956, 3365, 3444, 3793
Morrison, Charles Robert. 1099, 2052
Morrison, Christine Marie (Auchinvole) 3837
Morrison, Clinton. 472, 345, 1769
Morrison, DeLesseps Story. 3741
Morrison, Diana. 1815
Morrison, Eleanor Shelton. 1611, 3154
Morrison, Gay. 2201
Morrison, George Herbert. 3343, 3733, 106, 1108, 3368
Morrison, Henry Clay. 383, 801, 2465, 2521, 2620, 2949, 3320, 3343, 3365, 2620
Morrison, Hugh Tucker. 1532, 1969
Morrison, James Dalton. 1352, 2238, 3207
Morrison, James Horne. 2483
Morrison, John A. 2041
Morrison, John Arch. 2276, 1450, 3673
Morrison, John Cayce. 2591
Morrison, Joseph. 1450
Morrison, Karl Frederick. 1143, 1918, 3707
*Morrison, Lavada R. 2494
Morrison, Martin M. 199
Morrison, Mary Chase. 401, 1995, 3028
Morrison, Max Merritt. 1011
Morrison, Nancy Brysson. 2353
Morrison, Sarah Lyddon. 3824
Morrison, Stanley A. 3194

Morrison, Stanley Andrew. 3194
Morrison, Theodore. 890
Morriss, Frank. 789, 2674, 3284, 3449
Morriss, L. L. 3829
Morro, William Charles. 1168, 2307
Morrow, Abbie Clemens. 613, 1969, 2893
Morrow, Betty. 1615, 1785
Morrow, Charles Malone. 607
Morrow, Ethel Belle. 3313
Morrow, Honore (McCue) Willsie. 23
Morrow, Josiah. 3572
Morrow, Louis La Ravoire. 769
Morrow, Louis LaRavoire. 748, 1627
Morrow, Nancy Clarissa. 1273
Morrow, Ralph Ernest. 2453
Morrow, Thomas Manser. 2427
Morrow, Willard. 1559
Morsch, Vivian Sharp. 1209
Morse, A. L. 3595
Morse, Alfred Handley Chipman. 970, 1450
Morse, Christopher. 2568, 2946
Morse, Eugene. 2505, 2620
Morse, F. Harvey. 3556
Morse, Flo. 3397
Morse, Hermann Nelson. 1273, 1274, 1311, 2528, 2926
Morse, James Johnson. 3509
Morse, James King. 2620, 2687
Morse, Jedidiah. 190
Morse, John E. 1167
Morse, Kenneth. 2023, 2236
Morse, Kenneth S. P. 1679
Morse, Leon. 970
Morse, Richard. 3444
Morse, Richard Cary. 3871
[Morse, Richard Cary] 1841-1926. 2305, 3871
Morse, Samuel Finley Breese. 827
Morse, Tom. 1255
Morse-Boycott, Desmond Lionel. 2754
Morse-Boycott, Desmond Lionel, 1892. 1213, 2754, 3277
Morsey, Thomas Marshall. 2064
Morshead, Owen Frederick. 1158
Morsley, Harold Victor. 209
Morson, John. 2012
Mortensen, Enok. 1401
Mortensen, Karl Andreas. 2666
Mortensen, Mary Alice. 3509
Mortenson, Vernon. 1544
Morteveille, Blanche. 3691
Mortimer, Alfred G[arnett]. 1541
Mortimer, Alfred Garnett. 1327, 181, 578, 1328, 1386, 1486, 2033, 2057, 2964
[Mortimer, Favell Lee (Bevan) 1802-1878. 71, 295, 386, 629, 1982, 2543
Mortimer, Frederic Edward. 2893
Mortimer, Robert Cecil. 2812
Mortimer, Robert Cecil, 1902. 944, 946, 2812
Mortimore, Olive. 2393
Morton, Albert. 3509
Morton, Andrew Queen. 330, 370, 426, 1061, 1771, 2799
Morton, Arthur Leslie. 670, 3095
Morton, Clement Manly. 2876
Morton, Daniel Oliver. 179, 2487, 2777
Morton, Eliza Happy. 3261
Morton, Elizabeth. 253, 814
Morton, Frances McKinnon. 3154
Morton, Francis Torrey. 2227
Morton, Harriet (Cave) "G. E. Morton. 1982
Morton, Henrietta Josephine (Neal) "J. H. Morton. 1479, 2227, 2534
Morton, Henry Canova Vollam. 2762, 2848, 3840
Morton, James Ferdinand. 1241
Morton, Jean Sloat. 205
*Morton, Mildred B. 644
Morton, Nelle. 733, 1121, 3764
Morton, Richard Knowles. 2893
Morton, Robert Kemp. 1151
Morton, Thomas Ralph. 1121, 2014, 2041
Morton, William Albert. 2604, 2951, 3564
Mosbie, Marion, "C. S. Bierce. 1486
Mosby, Ella F. 2227
Moschner, Franz Maria. 2026, 2876
Moseley, Daisy Haywood. 3284, 3468
Moseley, Edward Hilary. 2078
Moseley, J. A. R. 1939
Moseley, James G. 3745
Moseley, Joel Rufus. 3480
Moseley, John Reed. 3480
Moseley, John Watkins. 2914
Moseley, Joseph Edward. 1463, 1573
Moser, Elwood Smith. 1092
Moser, Hans Joachim. 3311
Moser, Kenney Carl. 3290
Moser, Lawrence E. 855, 1604
Moser, Leslie E. 2781
Moses, Adolph Eliezer Asher. 1539, 2115
Moses, Alfred Geiger. 2113
Moses Ben Maiman, 1135-1204. 887, 1312, 2074, 2841

Moses ben Maimon, 1135-1204. 4, 1312, 1539, 2143, 2156, 2318, 2479, 2623, 2841, 3704, 3706
Moses Ben Mainion, 1135-1204. 2074, 2201, 2719, 2841
Moses ben Nahman, ca. 1195-ca. 1270. 562
Moses, Edward P. 2622
Moses, Elijah. 1083
Moses, Jasper Turney. 2624
Moses, Montefiore J. 629
Moses, William Stainton. 3473, 3509
Moses, Wilson Jeremiah. 2415
Moses ben Maimon. 2115, 2242, 2478, 2841
Mosheim, Johann Lorenz. 1177, 1193
Mosher, Arthur T. 2545
Mosher, Helene K. 3764
Mosher, Joseph Albert. 1583
Mosher, Roswel Curtis. 151
Mosier, Bernardine. 3238
Moskin, Marietta D. 3069, 3140
Mosley, Jean (Bell) 480, 3841
Mosley, Nicholas. 3664
Moss, Basil S. 138
Moss, Charles Frederick Arrowsmith. 2538, 2810
Moss, Claude Beaufort. 1041, 1218, 2735, 2964, 3012
Moss, Doley C. 2582
Moss, Harry George. 2247
Moss, James E. 3055
Moss, Lemuel. 3737
Moss, Leslie Bates. 2521
Moss, Peter. 3055
Moss, Robert V. 235, 239
Moss, Rosalind Louisa Beaufort. 2733
Moss, William Dyghum. 2913
Moss, Zeb V. 2369
Mosse, George Lachmann. 1086, 3035
Mosse, Walter M. 3639
Mosshamer, Ottilie. 1259
Mossi, John P. 1541
Mossner, Ernest Campbell. 720, 3212, 720, 1855, 3212
Most, William George. 2361
Motheral, Samuel A. 876
Mothers' correspondence club, Indianapolis. 3317
Mothersill, Mark Henry. 663
Motoyama, Hiroshi. 879
Mott, Edward. 2041
Mott, Francis John. 3438, 3897
Mott, George Scudder. 2944
Mott, Herbert H. 1594
Mott, Joanna (Bowles) 686
Mott, John Raleigh. 2441, 1288, 1568, 2191, 2494, 2512, 2521, 2526, 3673, 3830, 3852, 2521
Mott, Lucretia. 3010
Mott, Sina M. 640
Mott, Stephen Charles. 944
Motte, Gonzague. 864, 1267
Motte, Jean Francois. 1000, 2774
Motte, John Francis. 1649
Motter, Alton M. 9, 2214, 2813, 3355, 3365
Mottern, Hugh Henry. 1390
Motyer, J. A. 449, 485, 1696
Motylewski, Leo F. 1532
Moubarac, Youakim. 74, 651
Mouiren, Trophime. 1382
Mould, Daphne Desiree Charlotte Pochin. 42, 819, 1364, 2582
Mould, Elmer Wallace King. 295, 2064, 295
Mould, Ralph Norman. 1131
Moule, Arthur Christopher. 1110
Moule, C. F. D. 349, 1197
Moule, Charles Francis Digby. 331, 341, 349, 1193, 1771, 1831, 1846, 2011, 2031, 2326, 2477, 3855
Moule, Handley Carr Glyn. 341, 364, 403, 469, 1831, 3365
Moulinier, Louis. 1771
Moult, Margaret Mary. 1357
Moulton, Elizabeth. 2699
Moulton, James Hope. 3898, 3899
Moulton, Joseph Langdon. 33
Moulton, Phillips D. 3847
Moulton, Richard Green. 211, 235, 307, 1798
Moulton, Wilfrid Johnson. 1725
Moulton, William Fiddian. 248
Mounce, Robert H. 447, 455, 469, 476
Mount, Eric. 1347
Mount Holyoke college. 3332
Mount, Ralph H. 1725
Mount, Ralph Holmes. 311, 607, 3579
Mount, RH. 1725
Mount St. Mary's college, Emmitsburh, Md. 870
Mountain, Arthur. 2504
Mountain, James. 135
Mountain, Marian. 3493
Mountcastle, William W. 3111
Mountford, Charles Pearcy. 2654

Mountford, Lydia Mary Olive. 587, 1969
Mountford, William. 1544, 2477, 2735
Mourant, John Arthur. 117, 1892, 3103
Mourer, Charles Calvin. 2847
Mourett, Fernand. 2768
Mouritsen, Dale C. 1232
Mouroux, Jean. 137, 1000, 1594, 2320, 2324, 3701
Mourret, Fernand. 810
Mousel, Eunice. 3421
Mouton, Boyce. 2265
Mouw, Richard J. 65, 603, 1086, 2191
Mouzon, Edwin Du Bose. 2065, 2428, 2483, 2882, 2903, 3439
Mow, Anetta Cordula. 2683, 3405
Mow, Anna B. 18, 640, 970, 986, 1432, 2339, 2393, 2773, 3171
M'Owan, Peter. 3547
Mowinckel, Sigmund Olaf Plytt. 515, 577, 2415
Mowry, Charles E. 1259
Mowry, Lucetta. 1410
Mowshowitz, Israel. 3361
Mowvley, Harry. 569, 2951
Moxcey, Mary Eliza. 1288, 1714
Moyd, Olin P. 16
Moyer, Elgin Sylvester. 334, 925, 2400
Moyer, J Edward. 1875
Moyer, Kenneth Allan. 1290, 2627
Moyer, Robert Le Roy. 2057
Moyer, Robert LeRoy. 2057
Moyer, S T. 2531
Moyer, William Henry Harrison. 607
Moyle, Frank W. 235, 1889
Moynihan, Anselm. 1725
Moynihan, James F. 1946
Moynihan, James H. 1919
Moysey, Charles Abel. 3724
Mozley, Francis Woodgate. 583
Mozley, James Bowling. 501, 2477, 3343
Mozley, James Frederic. 1637, 3719
Mozley, John Kenneth. 74, 108, 1017, 1725, 3654
Mozley, Thomas. 2754
Mozoomdar, Protap Chunder. 2024
Mozumdar, A. K. 3865
Mozumdar, Akhar Kumar. 3462
Mozumdar, Akhoy Kumar. 1794
Mpratsiotes, Panagiotes Ioannou. 2746
Mroz, Mary Bonaventure. 3227, 3399
[Mubashshir ibn Fatik, Abu al-Wafa]. 1894, 2832
Muckenhirn, Charles Borromeo. 1245, 1382, 2573, 2581
Muckle, Coy. 148, 2082, 3851
Muckle, J. Yeoman. 544
Mucklow, William B. 1559
Mudge, Evelyn Leigh. 925
Mudge, Evlyn Leigh. 2999
Mudge, James. 3706, 2442, 2818, 3200, 925, 1440, 1450, 1451, 1587, 1823, 3481
Mudge, Lewis Seymour. 1061, 1066, 1095, 1154, 1402, 3735
Mudge, Lewis W[ard]. 3853
Mudge, Lewis Ward. 3854
[Mudge, Zachariah Atwell]. 1285, 1900, 3402, 3804
Mudroch, Vaclav. 3861
Muedeking, George H. 2995
Muehl, William. 1086, 2393
Muelder, Herman Richard. 1700
Muelder, Walter George. 944, 1075, 1138
Mueller, Arnold Carl. 622, 3161, 3174
Mueller, Charles S. 7, 1253, 1554, 1606, 1609, 3678
Mueller, David Livingstone. 176, 3239
Mueller, Donald A. 2003
Mueller, Elwin W. 1259, 3255
Mueller, Erhart. 1844, 3286
Mueller, Francis John. 71, 338, 789, 2012, 2041, 1000, 2059
Mueller, Franz. 2823, 3450
Mueller, Frederick Ferdinand. 3673
Mueller, Gustav Emil. 3103
Mueller, Herman. 376, 2086
Mueller, J. J. 2400, 2944
Mueller, John Theodore. 322, 2497, 2502, 2510, 2531, 2542, 2792, 3646, 3888
Mueller, Joseph. 2132, 3526
Mueller, Mary Magdeleine. 2216
Mueller, Reuben H. 1247, 1550
Mueller, Therese. 1609
Mueller, Virginia. 443, 444, 632, 633
Mueller, Walter. 1770
Mueller, William A. 1144, 2261, 2276, 2693
Mueller, William Randolph. 1624
Muench, Aloisius Joseph. 1613
Muench, Aoisius Joseph. 1613
Muenscher, Joseph. 287
[Mug, Mary Theodosia]. 1776, 2252, 3419
Mugan, Esther Laurentine. 2179
Mugge, Maximilian A. 2710
Muggeridge, Malcolm. 114, 986, 1070, 1097, 2369, 2487, 2628, 2799, 3602
Mugglebee, Ruth. 1372

Muhaiyaddeen, M. R. Bawa. 3481, 3542, 3544
Muhaiyaddeen, Sheikh Muhammad. 3542
Muhammad. 2565
Muhammad 'Abduh, 1849-1905. 1927
Muhammad ibn'Abd Allan, d. 1329. 2630
Muhammad Ikbal, 1876. 2565
Muhammad, Wallace D. 2345
Muhammad Zaki Badawi. 21, 2635
Muhammad 'Abduh. 1927
Muhammadia, Bi'sana Ta'laha El'shabazziz Sula. 669
Muhlen, Heribert. 3481
Muhlenberg College, Allentown, Pa. Dept. of Sociology. 1548
Muhlenberg, Henry Melchiar. 2629
Muhlenberg, Henry Melchior. 2630
Muhlenberg, William Augustus. 2968
Muilenberg, James. 2148
Muilenburg, Hubert Samuel. 970
Muilenburg, James. 599, 2148
Muir, Augustus. 1982
Muir, Charles Stothard. 290, 2483
Muir, Edwin. 2181
Muir, Gladdys Esther. 1237
Muir, James. 2758
Muir, James Cecil. 247, 407, 535, 537
Muir, Leo Joseph. 970
Muir, Pearson M' Adam. 3608
Muir, Shirley L. 1462
Muir, William. 290, 2494, 2564
Muirhead, Ian A. 3161
Mujeeb, Mohammad. 1925
Mukerjee, Radhakamal. 2639, 2645, 3574
Mukerji, A P. 3865
Mukerji, Dhan Gopal. 3020
Muktananda Paramhamsa. 2380, 2630, 3491
Muktananda Paramhamsa, Swami. 2630, 3491
[Mulchahey, James]. 970
Mulder, Bernard J. 2032
Mulder, J. A. Niels. 712
Mulder, William. 2616
Muldoon, James. 2823
Muldoon, Sylvan Joseph. 94, 2990, 3509
Mulford, Elisha. 3646
Mulford, Prentice. 3484
Mulhern, Philip F. 1475, 2866
Mulholland, John. 3509
Mulholland, John Field. 1791
Mulholland, Kenneth B. 3332, 3681
Mulier. 3054
Mulkey, Abe. 1568
Mulkins, Robert. 96
Mullally, Charles J. 770, 3488
Mullan, Carol. 313, 622, 626
Mullan, Elder. 3454
Mullany, John Francis. 215, 823
Mullany, Katherine Frances. 114, 873, 3603
Mullany, Leo H. 2268
Mullen, James H. 1364
Mullen, Pearson A. 2407
Mullen, Robert James. 1161
Mullen, Robert Rodolf. 2604
Mullen, Thomas James. 991, 1005, 1062, 1134, 2393, 2786
Mullen, William B. 577
Mullendore, William. 3062
Muller, Albert. 1940
Muller, Albert Arney. 3207
Muller, Alois. 780, 1086, 1246
Muller, Eberhard Johannes. 1095
Muller, Frederich Max. 3067
Muller, Fried Max. 3118
Muller, Friedrich Max. 689, 707, 710, 1896, 2196, 2494, 2653, 2673, 2674, 2840, 3020, 3062, 3067, 3110, 3118, 3119, 3122, 3123, 3140, 3200, 3332, 3775, 3776
Muller, G J. 3551
Muller, George. 2876
Muller, Gerald Francis. 1372, 2943
Muller, Gladys (Blanchard) 1167
Muller, Herbert Joseph. 1086, 1854
Muller, Jacobus Johannes. 374, 449
Muller, James Arthur. 731, 3307, 2960
Muller, Johann Baptist. 770, 1702, 839
Muller, John H. 325
Muller, Karl Otfried. 2649
Muller, Marcia. 3589
Muller, Martin M. 763
Muller, Michael. 769, 3290, 1650
Muller, Olga (Erbsloh) 1725
Muller, Robert. 3521
Muller, Wilhelm Max. 2659
Muller-Thym, Bernard Joseph. 1491, 2739
Mullett, Michael A. 1469
Mulligan, James J. 835, 1248, 3488
Mulligan, Joseph. 2222
Mulliken, Frances Hartman. 215, 3840
Mullin, Joseph. 2789
Mullings, Gwendolyn Lydia. 2630, 2855
Mullins, Aloysius. 410, 2026
Mullins, Beverly Schultz. 3056

Mullins, Edgar Young. 2563, 3343, 3465, 118, 148, 341, 364, 1099, 3646
Mullins, Edwin B. 2848
Mullins, Eustace Clarence. 3132
Mullins, George Gatewood. 3534
Mullins, Isla May (Hawley) 2630
Mullins, Terence. 2845
Mullins, William Ritcherdson. 3221
Mullois, Isidore. 1843
Mullowney, John James. 2052, 2695
Mulrenan, Patrick. 872
Mulvey, Mary Doris. 834, 1673
Mumaw, John R. 93, 2052
*Mumford, Bessie Carpenter. 235
Mumford, Bob. 2175, 2339, 2981, 3600
Mumford, Edith Emily Read. 2876
Mumford, James. 789
Mumford, John. 2313
Mumford, Lewis. 2227
Mumma, Howard E. 1568
Munby, D. L. 1075, 1142
Munby, Denys Lawrence. 1075, 1142
Muncey, Raymond Waterville Luke. 29, 450
Munch, Peter Andreas. 2666
Munck, Johannes. 2799, 344, 470
Muncy, William Luther. 1568, 1573
Munday, Anthony. 692, 3245
Munday, William. 3023
Mundelein, George William. 2631, 864
Mundell, Charles Samuel. 3509
Mundinger, Carl Solomon. 1549
Mundy, Jon. 1414
Mundy, Thomas Maurice. 2775
Munger, Robert Boyd. 2933
Munger, Theodore Thornton. 908, 970, 1342, 3347
Munhall, Leander Whitcomb. 2422, 3458, 1362, 3320
Munitz, Milton Karl. 2739
Munk, Arthur W. 65, 1818
Munk, Eli. 525, 1383
Munk, Elie. 562, 2109
Munk, Kaj Harald Leininger. 2300
Munk, William. 1544
Munkres, Alberta. 3154, 3180, 3154
Munnell, Thomas. 3792
Munowitz, Ken. 495, 2023, 2624, 2712
Munro, Bertha. 1432
Munro, Dana Carleton. 1390
Munro, Harry C. 3154
Munro, Harry Clyde. 1460, 1568, 2977, 3154, 3167
Munro, John Josiah. 1387
Munro, Neil Gordon. 20
Munro, William Fraser. 925, 3326
Munsat, Stanley. 3717
Munscher, Wilhelm. 3654
Munsey, William Elbert. 1531, 2436, 3343
Munson, Edwin C. 1267, 1318, 2215
Munson, Helen. 3171
Munson, M. E. 1750
Munson, Sweney. 52
Munson, Thomas N. 3103
Munster, Ernest Greve. 3062
Munster, Ludwig. 1348
Munsterberg, Hugo. 1889, 693
Muntsch, Albert. 1017, 1281, 2576, 3095, 3144, 3450
Munz, Isak. 2623
Munz, Peter. 2653
Mura, Ernest. 2020, 2637
Murakami, Shigeyoshi. 1936
Muraskin, William A. 1667
Murata, Kiyoaki. 3455
Murav'ev, Andrei Nikolaevich. 2750
Murch, Artemas Allerton. 2884, 1214
Murch, James DeForest. 1016, 1914, 646, 1062, 1463, 1464, 2631, 2670, 2876, 2956, 3154, 3677
Murchison, Anne Ferrell. 986, 2631, 2867
Murchison, Carl Allanmore. 2990, 2992
Murchland, Bernard. 1418
Murdick, Olin John. 1364
Murdoch, Benedict Joseph. 1826
Murdoch, Iris. 1537, 1746
Murdoch, William Gordon. 1435
Murdock, Alma. 2631
Murdock, Charles Albert. 3526
Murdock, Kenneth Ballard. 2373
Murdock, Peggy B. 93, 676
Mure, Geoffrey Reginald Gilchrist. 1800
Murnion, Philip J. 773, 2790
Murphet, Howard. 671, 2735
Murphey, Cecil B. 1011, 1257, 1292, 2486, 2631, 2786, 2876
Murphey, James. 1382
Murphree, Jon Tal. 1736
Murphy, Albert John. 2551
Murphy, Andrew Judson. 136
Murphy, Angelina. 2718, 3790
Murphy, Belva (Atkinson) 23
Murphy, Bob. 1367, 2631
Murphy, Bonneau Pernell. 1157, 1242, 2441
Murphy, Carol R. 1414, 1536, 2324, 2380, 2631, 3067

Murphy, Castle H. 2524
Murphy, Charles. 180
Murphy, Charles Kavanagh. 3438
Murphy, Chuck. 991, 3664
Murphy, Denis G. 844, 2718
Murphy, Dennis J. 571
Murphy, Du Bose. 2958, 2974
Murphy, Edmund Stephen. 2479
Murphy, Edward F. 1712
Murphy, Edward Francis. 2200, 2999, 3281
Murphy, Edward J. 867
Murphy, Edward L. 2554
Murphy, Francis Xavier. 866, 880, 1004, 1086, 2123, 2770, 2861
Murphy, Frank. 2329
Murphy, Harry Williams. 1568
Murphy, Ignatius. 820
Murphy, James Gracey. 516, 522
Murphy, John. 3119
Murphy, John Baptist Tuohill. 3223
Murphy, John F. 1478, 3175, 3270, 3782
Murphy, John J. 3253, 3270
Murphy, John Joseph. 2240
Murphy, John L. 1000, 1373, 1480, 2020, 2367, 3706
Murphy, John Nicholas. 2769
Murphy, John P. 136
Murphy, John Prentice. 137, 763
Murphy, Joseph A. V. 884
Murphy, Joseph F. 188, 3274
Murphy, Joseph John. 2673
Murphy, Joseph Stanley. 1070
Murphy, Mabel (Ansley) 925
Murphy, Magdalen B. 1849
Murphy, Margaret Gertrude. 177, 2578
Murphy, Mary Maloney. 2625
Murphy, Miriam. 2876
Murphy-O'Connor, Jerome, 1935. 372, 1411
Murphy, Patricia Shaubah. 2559, 2594
Murphy, Richard Thomas Aquinas. 201, 366, 2029
Murphy, Robert Francis. 2631
Murphy, Robert Wilson. 2322
Murphy, Roland E. 574
Murphy, Roland Edmund. 201, 239, 549, 576, 600, 1410, 3821
Murphy, Roland Edward. 600, 1410
Murphy, Thomas. 461, 3673
Murphy, Thomas J. 2343, 2852
Murphy, Thomas Regis. 864
Murphy, Walter Thomas. 3405
Murphy, Wilkins Harper. 2933
Murphy, William B. 1725
Murphy, William Leo. 1977
Murphy, Willie. 1367, 2632
Murphy-O'Connor, Jerome. 2908
Murran, George. 719
Murray, Andrew. 725
Murray, Albert Leonard. 431
Murray, Albert Victor. 1, 311, 640, 1141, 1586, 3155
Murray, Alexander Stuart. 2653
Murray, Alfred Lefurgy. 1559, 1568, 3155, 3355
Murray, Andrew. 1451, 1599, 1953, 2056, 2393, 2815, 424, 584, 940, 970, 1376, 1432, 1451, 1725, 1823, 1831, 1836, 1856, 2059, 2259, 2494, 2719, 2808, 2818, 2876, 3176, 3481, 3529
Murray, Andrew E. 2917, 2920
Murray, Anna Florence. 3155
Murray, Charles Augustus. 1070
Murray, David Ambrose. 1107, 65, 523, 535, 2055, 3567
Murray, Desmond P. 3281
Murray, Dick. 938
Murray, Ferne H. 3295
Murray, Florence J. 2486, 2632
Murray, George. 2933
Murray, George Lewis. 1181, 2465, 2933
Murray, Gilbert. 1766, 1767, 2221, 2231, 3067, 3533, 1767, 3067, 3093
Murray, Grace. 3026
Murray, Henry Alexander. 2654
Murray, Irving Russell. 2221
[Murray, James] 1732-1782. 1468, 3347
Murray, James Boyles. 65
Murray, James Clayton. 1993
Murray, James R. 3562
Murray, James Ramsey. 3563
Murray, Jane Marie. 602, 796, 1178, 3182
Murray, John. 2939, 3143, 3752
murray, John. 2195, 2922, 3355
Murray, John. 137, 277, 378, 469, 729, 3029, 3414, 2914, 3633, 970
Murray, John Courtney. 827, 1151, 2223, 2632, 3192
Murray, John Lovell. 70, 1016, 2504, 2517, 2521
Murray, John O'Kane. 2849, 3281
Murray, John Owen Farquhar. 417, 1481, 2041
Murray, Joseph A[lexander]. 1812

Murray, Joseph James. 908
Murray, Lindley. 925, 1675, 1682, 3062
Murray, Margaret Alice. 3599, 3824, 3826, 3834
Murray, Marr. 607
Murray, Michael H. 3593
Murray, Michael V 1906. 948
Murray, Nicholas. 801, 1851, 2933, 3585, 3673
Murray, Oliver E. 801
Murray, Paul. 1356
Murray, Ralph L. 166, 422, 434, 526, 570, 1845, 2017, 2247
*Murray, Rev, Andrew. 1725
Murray, Richard D. 2715
Murray, Robert. 1188, 2011
Murray, Robert Henry. 1481, 1526, 2754, 3323, 3703
Murray, Robert J. 1238
Murray, Rosalind. 65, 1105, 1364
Murray, Roy Irving. 2057
Murray, Ruth Shearman (Taber) 1637, 2632
Murray, Sara Van Alen. 1034, 2006
Murray, Verona. 3281
Murray, W[illiam] L[emuel] S[howell]. 3343
Murray, Walter Brown. 3011
Murray, William D. 438, 560, 625, 1969, 3551, 3871, 1993
Murray, William Henry. 53
Murray, William Henry Harrison. 3355
Murray-Aynsley, Harriet Geogiana (Manners-Sutton) 1827?-1898. 3574
[Murray-Ford, Alice May (Harte-Potts) 2733
Murrell, Ethel (Ernest) 3119
Murrell, Gladys (Callahan) 2238
Murrell, Gladys Clarke (Callahan) 2238, 3857
Murrell, Jesse L. 2449
Murrett, John C. 2938
Murrman, Warren Daniel. 2009, 3294
Murry, John Middleton. 1282, 1543, 1725, 1969, 3312, 3365
Murtagh, James G. 117, 814
Murty, K. Satchidananda. 2840
Murvar, Vatro. 1141
Musa, Thomas. 2057
Muscat, Jane Oliphant. 2727
Muschett, Glanville Owen. 2265
Muse, Dan Thomas. 594
Muses, Charles Arthur. 674
Musgrove, Peggy. 215, 3841
Muss-Arnolt, William. 1215
Musselman, G Paul. 1278
Musselman, Hugh Thomas. 30
Musser, Benjamin Francis. 3244, 763, 2183, 1645, 1646
Musser, Daniel. 3050
Musser, Edgar A. 3273
Musser, Joe. 1576, 2307
Musser, Joseph W. 2339, 2612
[Mussey, Benjamin B]. 683, 1757
Mussner, Franz. 414, 657, 1841
Mussolini, Benito. 1857
Mustain, Claud J. 2631
Muste, Abraham John. 2807, 2809
Muston, Alexis. 3789
Musurillo, Herbert Anthony. 1020, 2351
Mutch, William James. 290, 550, 590, 616, 748
Mutchler, David E. 821
Muth, Don. 1506
Muto, Susan Annette. 3488
Mutrux, Robert. 1271
Mutschmann, Heinrich. 1759, 3399, 2469
Muybarac, Youakim. 651
Muyskens, James L. 3103
Muzzey, Artemas Bowers. 1099, 2591
Muzzey, David Saville. 406, 1648, 2951, 3454, 1533
Muzzy, Florence Emlyn (Downs) 3509
Myer, Isaac. 721, 722, 1880
Myer, J. Richard. 610
Myerhoff, Barbara G. 1853
Myers, A. J. William. 625
Myers, Alexander John William. 596, 616, 719, 911, 933, 1062, 1451, 3155, 3180, 3253
Myers, Catherine (Rodgers) 2469, 2471
Myers, Cortland. 1162, 1696, 1831, 1994, 2876, 3062, 1121
Myers, Cortoland. 1568
Myers, David G. 1107, 1746
Myers, Edward. 1121, 1953
Myers, Edward De Los. 3027
Myers, Elisabeth P. 3802
Myers, Elizabeth Fetter (Lehman) 2596
Myers, Ernest R. 1382
Myers, Ernest W. 2893
Myers, Eugene A. 1927
Myers, Franklin L. 596
Myers, Frederic William Henry. 2823, 2990
Myers, Galene J. 3005
Myers, Gerald E. 2834, 2867

Myers, Gustavus. 3509, 3195
Myers, Harry S. 970
Myers, Henry Alonzo. 2419
Myers, Jacob Martin. 26, 201, 537, 589, 596, 1752, 2091, 3623
Myers, James. 3444
Myers, John. 3509, 2198
Myers, John Brown. 1312
Myers, Katie Lea. 1247
Myers, Minor. 726
Myers, Oma Lou. 2348
Myers, Paul Revere. 2762
Myers, Rawley. 662, 773, 774, 2635, 3331
Myers, Richard A. 1270
Myers, Robert Manson. 1783
Myers, T. Cecil. 1007, 1316, 1451, 1609, 2436
Myerson, Abraham. 2099
[Mygatt, Gerald] 1887. 3456
Mygatt, Tracy Dickinson. 71
Myland, David Wesley. 3227
Mylander, Charles. 1171
Myler, Larkin Sylvester. 1663
Myller, Rolf. 281
Mylne, Louis George. 3712
Mylonas, George Emmanuel. 1505
Myra, Harold Lawrence. 3072, 3888
Myrdal, Jan. 87
Myres, William V. 3336
Myrick, Herbert. 2695
Myrvik, Don. 1208

N

N. 3542
Naber, Vera. 3419
Nabers, Charles Haddon. 3365, 970
Nabi Khan, Ahmad. 85
Nabil Zarandi, 1831-1892. 122, 128
Nabil-i-Azam. 25, 128
Nachant, Theresa Elsa. 1062
Nada-Yolanda, 1925. 3473
Nadal, Bernard Harrison. 3355
Nadel, Max. 3166
Nadel, Siegfried Frederick. 2718
Naden, Roy C. 493, 2393
Nader, Sam. 3355
Nadji, Muharrem. 2565
Nadre, Brother, S. C. 1000
Nadzo, Stefan C. 3481
Naes, Vincent L. 867, 1673
Nagaraja Rao$, P., 1910. 3062
Nagarjuna. 2667
Nagarjuna, Siddha. 2867, 3196
Nagel, Ph. 1283
Nagel, Sherman A. 65, 970
Nagel, Thomas. 28
Nageleisen, John August. 3006
Nagelsbach, Carl Wilhelm Eduard. 543, 546
Nagelschmitt, Heinrich Franz. 2215
Nagle, Urban. 904, 2999
Nagler, Arthur Wilford. 1178, 2421, 2846
Nagy, Paul. 3798
Nagy, Paul, jr. 3549
Nahman ben Simhah, 1770?-1810? 1789, 2668, 3581
Nahman Ben Simhah, 1770?- 1810? 3581
Nahman Ben Simhah, 7702-1810? 3581
Nail, Olin Webster. 2432, 2439
Nainfa, John Abel Felix Prosper. 1249
Naipaul, Shiva. 2817
Naipaul, V. S. 1924, 2668
Nairne, Alexander. 25, 410, 501, 535, 1594, 1889
Nairne, Charles Murray. 1739
Nairne, W. P. 2483
Naish, Jack. 339, 632, 2830
Naismith, Archibald. 245
[Naismith, Charles]. 2310
Najib Ullah. 77
Nakamura, Hajime. 712, 1703
Nakosteen, Mahdi Khan. 2822
Nall, Charles J. 463, 601
Nall, James. 100
Nall, Torney Otto. 1352, 2436, 3735, 3888
Nall. Frances (Mahaffie) 3181
Namiat, Rebecca M. 2115
Namiot, Rebecca M. 2115
Nammalvar. 3782
Nance, Ellwood Cecil. 1461, 1463
Nance, Henry C. 3821
Nance, Mabel H. 612
Nanji, Azim. 1927
Nannes, Caspar Harold. 3797
Nanney, Thomas Grady. 1121, 1352
Naogeorgus, Thomas. 52
Naphegyi, Gabor. 2196
Napier, Bunyan Davie. 483, 501, 524, 526, 540, 561, 569, 1062, 1507, 2787
Napoli Prario, Lucy. 2334
Napora, Paul Edward. 1479
Narada. 197
Naranjo, Claudio. 2382

Narayan, R. K. 2316, 2635, 2663
Narayanananda. 3865
Narbutas, Titas. 2362
Nardi, Noach. 2101
Nardone, Nancy K. 916
Nardone, Thomas R. 916
Nares, Edward. 60
Nariman, Gushtaspshah Kaikhushro. 3715
Narot, Joseph R. 3371
Narramore, Bruce. 986, 1777
Narramore, Clyde Maurice. 986, 1260, 2781, 3171, 3880
Narsai. 2684
Nasby, Asher Gordon. 1841, 2300
Nasby, Gordon Asher. 1841
Nash, Arnold Samuel. 2339, 3618, 3679
Nash, Augustus. 1969
Nash, Bessie Hursey. 1626, 1782
Nash, Charles Ellwood. 3029
Nash, Charles Summer. 1126
Nash, E. J. H. 3539
Nash, Gerald R. 3385, 3529, 3560
Nash, Harold L. 3509
Nash, Henry Sylvester. 106, 351, 3433
Nash, J[ohn] J. 767
Nash, John Adams. 686
Nash, John J. 767, 769
Nash, Leonidas Lydwell. 614, 971, 2446
Nash, Robert. 138, 1000, 1945, 2029, 2269, 2377, 2393, 2581, 3331
Nash, Ronald H. 1551, 2181
Nash, Roy. 1625, 2620
Nash, William Verlin. 2608
Nashville. Christ church. 2974
Nason, Donna. 689, 2669
[Nason, Elias]. 1335, 1867, 2588
Nasr, Hossein. 121, 1926
Nasr, Seyyed Hossein. 86, 121, 1371, 1922, 1923, 2181, 3543
Nass, Raoul B. 3103
Nassau, Robert Hamill. 2311, 1624, 2497, 2669
Nast, William. 394, 395
Nastick, Sharon. 1025
Natale, Samuel. 2781
Natas, Eth. 1585
Nathan, Marvin. 2115
Nathan, Walter Ludwig. 921
Nation, Carry Amelia (Moore) 120
National Association of Catholic Chaplains. 1258
National Association of Evangelicals. 3155
National association of evangelicals for united action. 1551, 3155
National Association of Hebrew Day School Pta's. 1611
National association of local preachers of the Methodist Episcopal church. 1580
National cathedral association. 3796
National Catholic alumni federation. 871, 3327
National Catholic Educational Association. 831, 833, 867
National Catholic Educational Association. Special Education Dept. 831
[National Catholic educational association. Superintendents' section]. 2591
National Catholic social action conference. 1st, Milwaukee, 1938. 754
National Catholic Stewardship Council. 3531
National Catholic war council, Washington, D. C. 1543
National Catholic Welfare Conference. 668, 818, 827
National Catholic Welfare Conference. Press Dept. 3770
National Church Growth Convention, Kansas City, Mo., 1978. 1171
National committee of northern Baptist laymen. Committee on survey. 2714
National Committee on Christian Faith and Higher Education Projects. 1128
National Conference and Exhibit on Synagogue Architecture and Art. 3576
National conference for Girl reserve secretaries. 1714
National Conference of Catholic Charities. 8
National Conference of Christians and Jews. Committee on Religion in the Social Studies Curriculum of the Pittsburgh Public Schools. 3096
National Conference of Christians and Jews. Religious Freedom and Public Affairs Project. 1130
National conference of church clubs of the United States. 93
National conference of Methodist students. 1st, Louisville, Ky., 1924. 3444
National conference of preparatory school masters. 2943
National conference of theological students, Indianapolis, 1923. 3875
National Conference on Church and State, 15th, Denver, 1963. 1152

National Conference on Educational Objectives for the Culturally Disadvantaged, Hot Springs, Ark., 1967. 3436
National conference on Jewish welfare. 2106
National Conference on New Styles in Cooperative Evangelism, New Orleans, 1971. 1573
National Conference on Religion and Race, Chicago, 1963. 1132, 3072
National Conference on Religion in Education. 6th, Atlantic City, 1959. 2942
National Conference on Religion in Independent Education. 5th, Atlantic City, 1956. 2942
National Conference on Religion in Independent Education. 6th, Atlantic City, 1959. 2942
National Conference on Religion in Independent Education. 7th, Colorado Springs, 1962. 2942
National Conference on Religion in Secondary Education, Atlantic City, 1946. 2943
National conference on the Christian way of life. Commission on international relations. 1913, 1914, 2494
National conference on the Christian way of life. Commission on the church. 1121
National conference on the Christian way of life, New York. Commission on international relations. 1914
National Conference on the Churches and Social Welfare. 2d, Cleveland, 1961. 1164
National conference on the rural church. 1st, Washington, D. C., 1936. 3255
National conference on the rural church. 2d, Ames, Ia., 1936. 3255
National conference on the rural church. 2d, Ames, Ia., Nov. 1936. 3255
National congress of parents and teachers. Tennessee branch. 896
National Congress of Religious of the United States. 2d, University of Notre Dame, 1961. 2572, 2574
National Congress of Religious of the United States. University of Notre Dame, 1961. 2572
National convocation on the church in town and country. Columbus, O., 1943. 3253
National Convocation on the Church in Town and Country, St. Louis, 1956. 2670
National Council of Catholic Men. 2192, 3772
National council of Catholic women. 1609
National Council of Catholic Women. Nashville Diocesan Council. 873
National council of Congregational churches, Boston, 1865. 2670
National council of Congregational churches, Boston, 1865. Committee on church polity. 1335
National council of Jewish women. Committee on religion. 2076
National council of Jewish women. New York section. 2886
National council of Methodist youth. 2423
National Council of the Churches of Christ in the United States of America. 1134, 1568, 2241, 2750, 2955, 3177
National Council of the Churches of Christ in the United States of America. Bureau of Research and Survey. 1248, 1260
National Council of the Churches of Christ in the United States of America. Committee on Camps and Conferences. 1164
National Council of the Churches of Christ in the United States of America. Committee on Theological Study and Teaching. 3681
National Council of the Churches of Christ in the United States of America. Dept. of Adult Work. 1259
National Council of the Churches of Christ in the United States of America. Division of Foreign Missions. 2670
National Council of the Churches of Christ in the United States of America. Division of Foreign Missions. Committee on World Literacy and Christian Literature. 1319
National Council of the Churches of Christ in the United States of America. Division of Home Missions and Division of Foreign Missions. 2515
National Council of the Churches of Christ in the United States of America. General Board. National Lay Committee. 2670

National Council of the Congregational Churches of the United States. 1041, 1338, 2670
National council of the Congregational churches of the United States. Commission on public worship. 1339
National council of the Congregational churches of the United States. Tercentenary commission. 1344
National council on religion in higher education. 3190, 3191, 3757
National education association of the United States. 1130, 3155
National education association of the United States. National council of education. Committee on moral training in public schools. 2593
National eucharistic congress. 1541
National Federation of Catholic College Students. National Academic Program. 831
National Federation of Catholic College Students. National Catholic Action Study Bureau. 764
National Federation of Catholic College Students. Social Action Secretariat. 1131
National federation of gosepl missions. 2528
National federation of religious liberals. 3d congress, New York, 1911. 971
National federation of religious liberals. 8th congress, Boston, 1917. 3119
National federation of religious liberals. 9th congress, Longwood, Pa., 1919. 2221
National federation of spiritual science churches. 3509
National federation of temple brotherhoods. 2115
National federation of temple sisterhoods. 3416
National Florence Crittenton mission. 1629
National Forum Foundation. 3880
National Funeral Directors Association of the United States. 1691, 3722
National Geographic Society, Washington, D. C. Book Service. 208, 1280, 3119
National Hillel Summer Institute. 19th, Camp B'nai B'rith, 1964. 2145
National Holiness Association. 3623
National Inter-Religious Conference on Peace Washington, D.C., 1966. 2808
National intercollegiate Christian council. National assembly. Oxford, O., 1937-38. 1051
National Intra-decade Conference on Spiritual Well-being of the Elderly, Atlanta, Ga., 1977. 18
National Jewish Music Council. 2633
National Jewish welfare board. 3456
National Jewish Welfare Board. Bureau of Personnel and Training. 1320
National Jewish Youth Conference. 3890
National Library Service for the Blind and Physically Handicapped. 3090
National Liturgical Conference. 1205
National Liturgical Conference. 1st, Madison, Wis., 1958. 2233
National Liturgical Conference, 2d. San Antonio, 1959. 2233
National Liturgical Conference. 3d, Wichita, Kan., 1962. 2233
National liturgical week. 2234
National Lutheran council. 290, 655, 1543, 2276, 2291, 2293, 2463
National Lutheran Council. Advisory Committee for the Church in Town and Country. 3167
National Lutheran Council. Division of American Missions. 2294
National Lutheran Council. Division of Welfare. 2284
National Lutheran Social Welfare Conference. 2284
National Methodist Conference on Industrial Relations. 1st, Cincinnati, 1958. 1130
National Methodist Student Conference. 2426
National Methodist student leadership training conference. 1256
National missionary congress. 1st Chicago, 1910. 2515
National missionary congress. 2d, Washington, D. C., 1916. 2515
National Opinion Research Center. 775, 1302
National Polish committee of America. 2102
National prophecy and prayer conference, Chicago, 1940. 1514
National reform association. 1151
National Research Council. Committee on Occupational Classification and Analysis.
National school of correspondence, Quincy, Ill. 3165

National Sculpture Society, New York. 3333
National selected morticians. 1694
National Service Board for Religious Objectors. 1348
National society of the colonial dames of America. Georgia. 1525
National Society of the Colonial Dames of America. Pennsylvania. 1209
National Spiritual Assembly of the Baha'is of the United States. 128
National Spiritual Assembly of the Baha'is of the United States and Canada. 128, 129
National spiritual association. 1867
National Spiritualist Association. 3509, 3520, 3521
National student conference, Milwaukee. 1926. 3537
National student-faculty conference on religion and education, Detroit, 1930. 1497
National Study Conference on the Church and Ecobomic Life. 3d, Pittsburgh, 1956. 2670
National Study Conference on the Church and Economic Life. 4th, Pittsburgh, 1962. 2671, 3069
National Sunday School Association. 3188, 3556
National Sunday-school convention of the United States. 4th, Newark, N. J., 1869. 3556
National Sunday-school convention of the United States. 5th, Indianapolis, 1872. 3556
National temperance congress, New York, 1890. 3597
National temperance society and publication house, New York. 3596
National Union of Christian Schools. 1023, 1246
National United Methodist Convocation on the Black Church, Atlanta, 1973. 2680
Nations, Gilbert O. 2768
Nations, Gilbert Owen. 735
Nau, Henry. 2542
Nau, Louis J. 2356, 3680
Nau, Louis John. 2341
Nauer, Barbara. 875, 2676
Nauer, Lorenz. 3270
Naughton, James W. 2852
Naughton. Irene Mary. 3188
Nauman, St. Elmo. 1585
Naunidhirama. 1813
Naurois, Louis de. 780
Navagh, James J. 3676
Navantes, S. 3691
Navarra, Fernand. 2711
Nave, Orville James. 640, 3667, 225, 303
Navesink, N.H. 3527
The Navigators. 971
Naville, Edouard Henri. 1502
Naville, Edouard Henri, 1844-1926. 556
Naville, Ernest. 1746
Naville, Henri Edouard. 482
Navone, John J. 1317, 1588, 2042, 3534
Navy Supervisory Chaplains Conference, Washington, D.C., 1966. 2787
Nawyn, William E. 1256
Naylor, Charles Wesley. 11, 971, 1741, 971
Naylor, David. 708
Naylor, Phyllis Reynolds. 35
Naylor, Robert E. 1408
Naylor, Wilson Samuel. 11
NcNair, Jim. 1713
Neal, Bruce W. 994, 1318
Neal, Charles McKendre. 2464, 2465
Neal, Daniel. 3007
Neal, Effie C. 1443
Neal, Emily Gardiner. 1599
Neal, Harry Edward. 3293
Neal, Hazel G. 1229, 1856, 3840
Neal, James H. 2314
Neal, Julia. 3398
Neal, Lucille A. 2393
Neal, Marie Augusta. 3623
Neale, John Mason. 925, 1874, 2168, 2235, 2744, 2747, 2748, 2827
Neale, Mary (Peisley) 2678
Neale, Robert E. 1414
Neale, Rollin Heber. 684
Neale, Sir John Ernest. 753, 1639
Neame, Alan. 2262
Neander, August. 1969, 321, 1008, 1178, 1193, 1969
Nearing, Scott. 3444
Nease, Floyd William. 3355
Neat, Harry R R. 1725
Nebel, Charlotte Elizabeth (Rambach) 2033
Nebel, Long John. 2727
Nebesky-Wojkowitz, Rene de. 3699
Neblett, S. A. 2430
Neborak, Sonja. 2843

Nebreda, Alfonso M. 1317, 2168
Nebreda del Cura, Eulogio. 116
Necheles, Ruth F. 1773
Neches, Solomon M. 2083
Neches, Solomon Michael. 2083
Nederhood, Joel H. 1737, 2339, 2558
Nederlandse Hervormde Kerk. Generale Synode. 311
Nedoncell, Maurice. 1851
Nedoncelle, Maurice. 2876
Nedoncelle, Maurice [Gustave]. 1105
Nee, Watchman. 443, 971
Needham, David C. 986
Needham, George Carter. 3721, 1559, 2324, 2589, 3523
Needham, Joseph. 3073, 3079, 3082
Needham, W P. 1655
Needleman, Jacob. 1095, 2320, 2679, 3067, 3091, 3326
Neel, Isa-Beall (Williams) 3468
Neeley, Deta Petersen. 626, 679, 1982, 3429, 3430, 3432, 3591, 3869
Neely, Nellie Gertrude (Brown) 648
Neely, Thomas Benjamin. 665, 1916, 2903, 2421, 2443, 2455, 2547, 2438, 2547
Neep, Edward John Cecil. 1489
Neerskov, Hans Kristian. 1573, 2679
Neeson, Margaret Graham. 3274
*Nef, E. 1725
Nef, John Ulric. 3086
Neff, Elizabeth Clifford. 1249
Neff, Ethel Maxine. 480
Neff, H. Richard. 3072
Neff, Herbert B. 3173
Neff, LaVonne. 495, 1784, 1785, 2679
[Neff, Lawrence W]. 2561
Neff, Lawrence Wilson. 971, 1103, 1626, 2800
Neff, Merlin L. 65, 296, 622, 1440, 2260, 2311, 3540
Negenman, Jan H. 208
Negev, Avraham. 208, 209, 2761
Negley, Glenn Robert. 3762
Negri, Vitali. 3103
Neher, Andre. 572, 599, 2622, 2646, 2983
Neher, Andrew. 2990
Neibuhr, Barthold Georg. 2661
Neibuhr, Richard R. 3308
*Neiderer, Rodney P. 3462
Neie, Herbert. 2010
Neighbor, Russell J. 936
Neighbors, Aileene. 2876
Neighbour, Ralph Webster. 1244, 1568, 1712
Neighbour, Robert Edward. 224, 413, 552, 594, 1440, 1831, 3200
Neihardt, J[ohn] G[neisenau]. 3207
[Neil, Henry]. 3132
Neil, Samuel Graham. 1568, 3355
Neil, William. 286, 224, 235, 296, 329, 478, 1953, 2071, 3111
Neill, Stephan Charles. 2324
Neill, Stephen. 2526
Neill, Stephen Charles. 43, 245, 351, 476, 944, 1041, 1079, 1080, 1107, 1178, 1182, 1492, 1725, 1823, 1895, 2042, 2494, 2516, 2526, 3673, 2193, 2494
Neill, Thomas Patrick. 760, 765, 810, 1155, 2324, 2807
Neill, William. 1296, 2933
Neilson, Francis. 296, 1183
Neilson, William Allan. 3758
Neilson, William H. 3562
Neimark, Anne E. 877, 1293, 1400, 2993
Neipp, Paul C. 2215, 2300
Neithold, Eugene C. 1168
Nelkin, Dorothy. 205
Nell, Onora. 2648
David-Neel, Alexandra, 1868-1969. 708
Neller, Earl. 3292
Nelli, Rene. 22
Nelms, John Henning. 3797
Nelsen, Hart M. 15, 2679, 2937
Nelson, Amirtharaj. 2954
*Nelson, Boyd. 971
Nelson, Brian A. 166, 2028
Nelson, Byron Christopher. 1421, 2006, 2415
Nelson, Calud D. 1134
Nelson, Carl Ellis. 1314, 1316, 1317, 1347, 1998, 3681
Nelson, Claud D. 1134, 3770
Nelson, Cleland Kinlock. 2318, 2768
Nelson, Clifford Ansgar. 106, 2295, 2393
[Nelson, D.] fl. 1800. 2759
Nelson, Daniel. 2510, 2683
Nelson, David. 3422
Nelson, Dorothy (Nelson) 2523
Nelson, E. Clifford. 1045, 2215, 2288, 2292, 2715
Nelson, Geoffrey K. 3509
Nelson, Harry Tracy. 3073
Nelson, Henry Addison. 1982, 3290
Nelson, J. Robert. 3082
Nelson, James A. 994
Nelson, James Bruce. 944, 1534, 3391

Nelson, James G. 2469
Nelson, Jamet (Fowler) 2339
Nelson, John. 3143
[Nelson, John]. 2914
Nelson, John Oliver. 1252, 1296, 1467, 3785, 3888
Nelson, John Robert. 1041, 1046, 1062, 1121, 1492
[Nelson, John Young]. 1689
Nelson, Joseph A. 3196
Nelson, Joseph Raleigh. 1903, 2683
*Nelson, Lawrence E. 937
Nelson, Lawrence Emerson. 304
Nelson, Lee H. 2829
Nelson, Levi. 3411, 3591, 3616
Nelson, Loveday A. 2023
Nelson, Lowry. 3029
Nelson, Lucy (Green) 2560
Nelson, Marion H. 2378
Nelson, Marlin L. 2502
Nelson, Martha. 1303, 3831, 3832, 3844
Nelson, Mary (De Puy) 971
Nelson, Nels Lars. 607, 1820, 2604
Nelson, P. C. 374
Nelson, P V. 2193
Nelson, Peter Christopher. 92, 235, 374, 1599, 2020, 2800, 3673
Nelson, Ralph Waldo. 2065, 3444
Nelson, Richard Henry. 455, 2962
Nelson, Robert A. 2990
Nelson, Robert Gilbert. 1464, 2513
Nelson, Rosanne E. 986, 3831
Nelson, Ruth Youngdahl. 971, 2303, 2393, 2683, 3843, 3844, 3857
Nelson, Thomas Hiram. 106, 2042, 2074, 2107, 2673, 3234
Nelson, Virgil. 3223
Nelson, W[alter] H[oratius]. 1969
Nelson, Wilbur E. 322, 326, 1008, 1841
Nelson, William. 3471
Nelson, William Hamilton. 682, 3292
Nelson, William Rhame. 1244, 3242
Nelson, William S. 2490
Nelson, William Verner. 3763
Nelson, Zev K. 565
Nelson's picture Bible. 622
Nemec, Ludvik. 879, 1149, 1398, 1906, 2126, 2861
Nemesius, William. 3132
Nemesszeghy, Ervin. 1581
Nemicandra Siddhantacakravartin. 1932
Nemmers, Erwin Esser. 1205, 1206
Nemoy, Leon. 2164
Nemzoff, Samuel A. 1329
Neptune, A Ray. 971
Nepveu, Francois. 2393, 3132
Nersoyan, Hagop. 82
Nervig, Casper B. 1386
Nes, William Hamilton. 1220, 2903
Nesbit, William Marsiglia. 3545
Nesbitt, Charles Maurice Grillett. 611
Nesbitt, Ralph Beryl. 2953
Nesiotes, Nikos A. 1154
Nesmith, William. 3880
Nesper, Paul William. 3376
Nesperling, Delilah Ann. 2876
[Ness, Christopher]. 971
Ness, John H. 1550
[Nesterman, Lewis J.]. 3797
Nestingen, James Arne. 2276, 3037
Nestle, Eberhard. 351
Nestorian Church. 2684
Nestorian tablet of Sian-fu. 2684
Nestorius, fl. 428. 2042
Netanyahu, Benzion. 5, 2332
Neth, John Watson. 3315
Nethercot, Arthur Hobart. 1377, 195
Netram, John W. Richards. 1895
Nettis, Joseph. 3119
Nettl, Paul. 2280
Nettles, Kenneth James. 277
Nettleship, Richard Lewis. 2832
Nettleton, Asahel. 1867
Nettleton, David. 277
Neubau, Walter. 629
Neubauer, Adolf. 544
Neubert, Emile. 2361
Neubert, Emile Nicolas. 1995, 2361, 2363
Neufeld, Vernon H. 1386
Neufer Emswiler, Thomas, 1941. 3003
Neufer Emswiler, Tom, 1941. 1169, 3883
Neugebauer, Otto. 98
Neuhaus, Richard John. 1134, 1296, 3747
Neuhausler, Engelbert. 2033
Neuman, Abraham Aaron. 2103
Neumann, Erich. 2624
Neumann, Friedrich. 2085
Neumann, Henry. 2591
Neumann, John Nepomucene. 1028, 2685
Neumann, Robert. 640, 1388
Neumark, David. 2115
Neumeyer, Murray W. 1296
Neuner, Josef. 782
Neunheuser, Burkhard. 138
Neuser, Heinz. 937

Neusner, Jacob. 172, 1621, 2075, 2079, 2080, 2122, 2125, 2140, 2141, 2143, 2147, 2150, 2154, 2155, 2479, 2828, 2829, 3584, 3585
Neuvecelle, Jean. 778, 807
Nevada. University. 3757
Nevaskar, Balwant. 1675, 1932
Neve, Frederick William. 1121, 3208
Neve, Juergen Ludwig. 109, 1386, 2285, 2286, 2294
[Neve, Juergen Ludwig]. 3654, 3655
Neve, Lloyd R. 2291, 2534
Neve, Rosemary. 45, 2686
Nevil, Susan R. 480
Neville, Edmund. 2973
Neville, Gwen Kennedy. 2235
Neville, Joyce. 3829
Neville, Robert. 3768
Neville, Robert C. 2739, 2944, 3481
Nevils, Coleman. 2743
Nevin, Alfred. 428, 438, 516, 2026, 2920
Nevin, Edwin Henry. 1121
Nevin, George Balch. 49
Nevin, John Williamson. 52, 208, 675, 1568, 2252, 2920, 3048, 3132, 3632
Nevin, Winifred. 741, 3603
Nevin. John Williamson. 2252
Nevins, Albert J. 773, 839, 867, 1477, 2123, 2490
Nevins, John F. 805, 1838
Nevins, William. 801, 971, 2928
Nevins, William Manlius. 139
Nevins, Winfield S. 3827
Nevison, R. L. B. 3103
Nevius, Helen Sanford (Coan) 2686
Nevius, John Livingston. 1424, 2521
Nevius, Richard C. 393, 435, 1736
Nevius, Warren Nelson. 597, 3103
New Braunfels, Tex. 2686
New Brunswick Historical Society. 881, 3274
New Brunswick, N. J. Theological seminary of the Reformed church in America. 1422, 2281, 2304, 2686
New Canaan, Conn. Congregational church. 2686
New Durham, N.J. Grove Reformed church. 1243
New England Methodist centenary convention. 2426
New England Mississippi land company. 1706
New England Tract Society. 3705
New Haven. Congregation B'nai Jacob. 2101
New Jersey Bible society. 612
New Jerusalem church. 2689, 3571
New Jerusalem church. General convention. 1121
New Jerusalem church. Liturgy and ritual. 2689
New, John F H. 3658
New Mexico. University. 2833
New Mexico. University. General Library. 2224
New, N. N. 270
New Orleans. St. Patrick's Church. 1269
New Rochelle, N. Y. College of New Rochelle. 827
New South Wales Humanist Society. 1544
New Ulm, Tex. St. John Lutheran Church. 2696
The New world. 892
New York Academy of Medicine. 2994
New York (Archdiocese) 2583
New York Baptist City Society. 158
New York Bible society. 615
New York. B'nai Jeshurun Congregation. 673
New York board of Jewish ministers. 3576
New York. Brick Presbyterian church. 2913, 2916
New York. Broadway tabernacle church. 2697, 3579
New York. Cathedral free circulating library. 869
New York Catholic protectory, West Chester, N.Y. 2697
New York, Church of Our Lady of Esperanza. 2697
New York. Church of the holy communion. Sunday-school library. 3549
New York. Citizens. 2102
New York (City). B'nai Jeshurun Congregation. 673
New York city Christian science institute. 1034, 3527
New York (City). Metropolitan Museum of Art. 87
New York (City). Missionary Research Library. 2504, 2698
New York (City). Union Theological Seminary. Library. 2698, 3627
New York. Collegiate church. 3045, 3048

New York. Collegiate church. fifth ave. and 48th st. Society for Christian work. 1127
New York. Collegiate Church. Marble Collegiate Church. Marble Club. 2698
New York. Community church. 1310
New York. Congregation Habonim. 1780, 2143
New York ecclesiological society. 1161
New York. Evangelical Lutheran Church of St. Matthew. 2698
New York. Fifth Avenue Presbyterian Church. 2698
New York. First Presbyterian church. 1692, 2831
New York freethinker's association. 1655
New York. French church du Saint Esprit. 3051
New York. Independent liberal church. 1689
New York. Joan of Arc loan exhibition. 1938
New York ladies' home missionary society of the Methodist Episcopal church. 2542
New York. McAuley Water street mission. 2542
New York. Metropolitan museum of art. 1883
New York. Missionary Research Library. 13, 1848, 2485, 2522, 2547, 2953, 2954
New York. Monastery of the Visitation. 2573
New York. Public library. 212, 672, 704, 734, 1112, 1480, 2143, 2564, 2608, 3397, 3678, 3825, 3828
New York. Queen of Angels Church. 1165
New York. Riverside church. 1171, 3568
New York. St. Anselm's church (Catholic) 2775
New York. St. Nicholas of Tolentine Church. 1269
New York. Sanitarium for Hebrew children. 2081
New York State Baptist Convention. 158
New York (State) Laws, statutes, etc. 158
New York state Sunday school association. 3556
New York Sunday school union society. 3564
New York. Temple Emanu-El. 2083
New York times. 2805
New York tribune. 31, 2928
New York. Trinity Church. 2701, 2774
New York. Union theological seminary. 2701, 3331, 3332, 3612, 3615, 3627
New York. Union Theological Seminary. Library. 3627
New York. Unitarian church of the Messiah. Board of trustees. 1310
New York University Institute of Philosophy. 3d, 1959. 2474
New York University Institute of Philosophy, 4th, 1960. 2836
New York University Institute of Philosophy. 7th, 1964. 88
Newall, Venetia. 1477, 2727, 3825
Newark Museum Association, Newark, N. J. 2193
Newark, N.J. North Reformed Dutch church. 1484
Newark, N.J. Trinity Cathedral. 2688
Newberry, Frederick B. 3225
Newberry, Gene W. 971, 986, 1228
Newberry, John Strong. 3110
Newberry library, Chicago. 914, 3123
Newbigin, James Edward Lesslie. 986, 1041, 1045, 1080, 1095, 1122, 1235, 2176, 2480, 2554, 2787, 3295, 3327
Newbigin, Lesslie. 417
Newbolt, Michael Robert. 1497, 1600, 2494
Newbolt, William Charles Edmund. 1215, 2252, 3062, 1227
[Newbrough, John B.]. 1794
[Newbrough, John Ballou] 1828-1891. 120
Newburgh, N.Y. Mt. St. Mary-on-the-Hudson (Dominican convent) 1475
Newbury, Josephine. 1246
Newburyport, Mass. First Presbyterian church. 2701
Newburyport, Mass. St. Paul's parish. 2371
Newby, Elizabeth Loza. 1688, 2701
Newby, Grace V. 2399, 2701
Newby, Henry W. 2409
Newby, J Edwin. 1376
Newby, James R. 1244, 1676, 3491
Newcomb, Arthur. 1478
Newcomb, Charles Benjamin. 2834
Newcomb, Covelle. 2136, 2703, 741, 1711, 2136
[Newcomb, Harvey] 1803-1863. 118, 120, 1099, 1568, 1730, 2516, 2682, 3304
Newcomb, Rexford. 1158
Newcomer, Christian. 3730
Newell, Daniel. 3813

Newell, E Virginia. 2333
Newell, Ebenezer Francis. 20
Newell, Ebenezer Josiah. 2241, 2793
Newell, Ebenzer Josiah. 1759
Newell, James Reginald. 3343
Newell, Norman Dennis. 1382
Newell, Philip Rutherford. 509
Newell, Virginia. 2596
Newell, Wilbur C[harles]. 971
Newell, William. 3132
Newell, William Lloyd. 2645, 3891
Newell, William Reed. 403, 455, 469, 470, 498, 566, 1071
Newell, William Whiting. 1568
Newhall, Nancy (Wynne) 3298
Newhall, Richard Ager. 1390
Newhouse, Flower Arlene (Sechler) 1115, 1837, 2380, 2702
Newhouse, Mildred (Sechler) 42, 1115, 1359, 2024, 3509, 3686
Newington, Conn. Church of Christ. 1269
Newland, Mary (Reed) 296, 749, 1025, 1262, 1609, 3062, 3165, 3169, 3693, 3802
Newland, T. Ernest. 1712
Newlands, G. M. 1735
Newlandsmith, Ernest. 84
Newland-Smith, James Newland. 2706
Newlin, Alexander Willis. 2425, 2702
Newlin, Algie Innman. 1301, 1368
Newlin, Claude Milton. 3213
Newlin, Jay Joel. 686
Newlin, O[ra] A[llen]. 1071
Newlin, Ora Allen. 1559
Newman, Albert Henry. 151, 152, 1178, 1184, 1906
Newman, Aubrey Norris. 2100, 3749
Newman, Barclay Moon. 3079, 349, 455
Newman, Bertram. 2703
Newman, Daisy. 1674, 1675, 3010
Newman, Elias. 2078
Newman Foundation at the University of Minnesota. 760
Newman, Henry Stanley. 3005
Newman, Jacob. 1623
Newman, Jeremiah. 754, 760, 1143, 2191
Newman, John Henry. 789, 1227, 1612, 3449, 80, 206, 305, 306, 738, 774, 776, 782, 789, 790, 816, 836, 858, 864, 934, 1017, 1021, 1193, 1212, 1219, 1227, 1473, 1597, 1715, 2160, 2161, 2166, 2191, 2356, 2393, 2477, 2704, 2740, 2834, 2862, 3201, 3365, 3488, 3489, 3608, 3632, 3646, 3655, 3756, 3769, 774, 864
Newman, John Henry, Cardinal. 2399, 864, 2160, 2356, 3632
[Newman, John Philip. 1451
Newman, John Philip. 60, 2061, 2127, 2704
Newman, Joseph A. 767, 1627
Newman, Julius, 1896. 910
Newman, Louis Israel. 1083, 1789, 1843, 2083, 2146, 2622, 3015, 3162
Newman, Margaret M. 281, 656
Newman, Michael. 8
Newman, Murray Lee. 2148
Newman, Paul S. 282, 2762, 3616
Newman, Robert C. 171
Newman, Robert Chapman. 1382
Newman, Robert George. 2082
Newman, Shirley. 631
Newman, Stewart A. 1346
Newman, William M. 1038, 3088
Newman-Norton, Seraphim. 2744
Newport, David. 2903
Newport, John P. 87, 277, 1078, 3119
Newport, R.I. Trinity church. 1122
Newquist, Jerreld L. 2609, 2610
Newsham, Harold Goad. 215
Newsom, Carroll Vincent. 1103
Newsome, David, 1929. 1760, 2328
Newsome, Dorothy. 901
Newsome, Robert R. 807, 1245
Newton. 3637
[Newton, Alonzo Eliot] 1821-1889. 3509
Newton, Benjamin Gwernydd. 1342
Newton, David F. 971
Newton, Douglas. 3239
Newton, Eric. 921
Newton, Frank. 712
Newton, James Marcus. 2452
Newton, John. 34, 59, 733, 1217, 1291, 1793, 1867, 2705, 2706, 2847
Newton, Joseph Fort. 2474, 725, 925, 971, 1071, 1126, 1441, 1451, 1594, 1662, 1725, 1735, 2032, 2893, 2903, 3119, 3201, 3281, 3343, 3355, 3572, 3793, 925, 1662, 2032, 3196, 3355
Newton, La Vose (Wallin) 2224
Newton, LaVose. 2224
Newton, LaVose (Wallin) 2224
Newton, Louie De Votie. 146, 150
Newton, Louise De Votie. 1451
Newton, Lucilda Adela. 2552
Newton, Percy John. 971
Newton, Richard. 1807, 1982, 3355

Newton, Richard Heber. 523, 640, 871, 1034, 1385, 3422
Newton theological institution, Newton Center, Mass. 2706
Newton theological institution, Newton Centre, Mass. 2706
Newton, Thomas. 607
Newton, W[atson] J[ames]. 1397
Newton, William. 509, 3076
Newton, William Louis. 626, 629, 648, 812, 1376, 648
[Newton, William Wilberforce] 1843-1914. 694, 2627, 2958, 3623
Ng, David. 3858
Ngawang Lobsang Yishey Tenzing Gyatso, 1935. 3698
Nhat Hanh, Thich. 2382, 3893
Niblett, William Roy. 1164, 2591, 3161
Nibley, Hugh. 678, 679, 1691, 2598, 2604, 2608, 2614, 3429
Nibley, Hugh Winder. 2604
Nibley, Preston. 679, 1014, 1231, 2604, 2609, 2615, 2618, 3429, 3869
Niccolls, Samuel Jack. 610
Nicely, Harold Elliott. 2933
Nicetas, 4th cent. 1018
Nichol, Charles Ready. 70, 1273, 1655, 2252, 3840
Nichol, Francis David. 224, 1090, 2467, 3320, 3380, 3383, 3386, 3811, 224
Nichol, John Thomas. 2814
Nicholas, David R. 3837
*Nicholas, Marie-Joseph. 1541
Nicholas, Michael. 2714
Nicholas, Ted. 2382
Nicholas, Tim. 1574
Nicholas, Tracy. 3022
Nicholas, Wayne Alfred. 908
Nicholaus Cusanus, 1401-1464. 2647
Nicholl, Donald. 1823, 3698
Nicholls, David. 1146
Nicholls, William. 2326, 3656, 3854
Nichols, Aidan. 921
Nichols, Beverley. 1090, 2990
*Nichols, Brougham. 1533, 2324
Nichols, C. William. 2393
Nichols, Elizabeth (Barnard) 645, 1810
Nichols, Emmett DeVine. 2227
Nichols, George Warner. 2218
Nichols, Gideon Parsons. 3343
Nichols, Gus. 1272, 1273, 3355
Nichols, Harold. 1408
Nichols, Harry Peirce. 451, 476
Nichols, Ichabod. 391, 2673
Nichols, J[oseph] Marvin. 2494
Nichols, J. Randall. 2903
Nichols, J. W. H. 578
Nichols, James Albert. 106, 1809
Nichols, James Hastings. 1075, 1086, 1187, 2411, 2977, 3049, 3306, 3850, 3855
Nichols, James Robinson. 2320
Nichols, James Thomas. 224
Nichols, Jeannette. 3844
Nichols, John Gough. 2686, 3039, 3846
Nichols, Marie Leona (Hobbs) 2866
Nichols, Peter. 811, 2770
Nichols, R. Eugene. 3481
Nichols, Robert Hastings. 1178, 1188, 2928
Nichols, Roy C. 2436, 3355
Nichols, Roy Franklin. 3745
Nichols, Sallie. 2158, 2159, 3589
Nichols, Samuel. 3355
Nichols, Sue. 1317
Nichols, Thomas. 1867
Nichols, Thomas Low. 1404, 3509
Nichols, Thomas McBride. 2903
Nicholson, Clare Marie. 1938
Nicholson, David. 1205
Nicholson, Dorothy. 3174, 3763
Nicholson, Dorothy (Lamb) Brooke. 1771
Nicholson, Ernest Wilson. 511, 547, 563, 1584
Nicholson, Evelyn Carrie (Riley) 2807
Nicholson, Godfrey Carruthers. 420, 1998
Nicholson, Henry B. 121
Nicholson, John. 3524, 3762
Nicholson, John Angus. 3103
Nicholson, Norman. 3210, 3801
*Nicholson, Reynold A. 2647
Nicholson, Reynold Alleyne. 6, 3542, 6, 657, 1619, 3543
Nicholson, Wallace B. 3579
Nicholson, William R. 342
Nicholson, William Rufus. 342
Nickelsburg, George W. E. 57, 489, 490, 1530
Nickerson, Charles Sparrow. 1122
Nickerson, Converse E. 1710
Nickerson, Converse Ennis. 3520
Nickerson, Hoffman. 3035, 1909
Nickle, Keith Fullerton. 391, 1168
Nicklin, J. Bernard. 607
Nicklin, Thomas. 391
Nicodemus, Donald E. 807
Nicol, William Robertson. 2639

Nicola, John J. 1422
[Nicolaij, Paul Ernst Georg, 1860-1919. 2001
Nicolas, Cusanus [Name originally: Nicolas Krebs (Khrypffs, Chrypffs) of Cues of Cusa.]. 2647
Nicolas, Jean Herve. 1751
Nicolas, Lewis. 2002
Nicolas, Maria Iosephus. 2255
Nicolassen, George Frederick. 452
Nicolaus, Cusanus. 790, 1725, 1846
Nicolay, Helen. 235, 3192
Nicole, Albert. 2156
Nicole, Roger. 36
Nicoll, Maurice. 2026, 2065
Nicoll, William Robertson. 299, 1957, 2876, 3444, 593, 615, 1169, 1796, 3374, 3798
Nicolson, Angus. 2565
Nicolson, C B. 1159
Nida, Clarence. 2339
Nida, Eugene Albert. 47, 275, 290, 652, 655, 1316, 1317, 1554
Nieboer, Joe. 412, 447, 971
Niebuhr, Heimut Richard. 3444
Niebuhr, Helmut Richard. 2585, 3225, 1293, 1394, 2175, 2585, 3225, 3444, 3445, 3680, 3682, 944, 2175, 3445
Niebuhr, Hulda. 623
Niebuhr, Reinhold. 944, 1051, 1071, 1086, 1105, 1289, 1291, 2324, 3434, 3435, 3758, 1071, 1087, 1105, 1294, 2709, 3355, 3435
Niebuhr, Richard R. 2052, 2709
Niedermeyer, Frederick David. 1314, 2762, 2030, 2757
Niedermeyer, Mabel A. 901, 2490, 3531
Nield, Thomas. 3208
Nielen, Josef Maria. 3855
Nielsen, Eduard. 1314, 2740
Nielsen, Ernest D. 1776
Nielsen, Fredrik Kristian. 810
Nielsen, H Skov. 740
Nielsen, Kai. 944, 3103
Nielsen, Niels Christian. 3096, 3119
Nielsen, Rasmus. 1078
Nielsen, Thomas Miller. 3132
Nielson, John B. 376
Nielson, Larry. 2599
Niemoller, Martin. 1458, 2290, 2301
Niendorff, John. 3208
Nies, Frederick C. 1527
Nies, James Buchanan. 89
Nies, Richard. 3290, 3383
Niese, Richard Beall. 10
Niesel, Wilhelm. 801, 3767
[Nietschmann, Hermann Otto]. 2272
Nietzsche, Friedrich Wilhelm. 1092, 1536, 2710, 2834, 3788
Nieuwe katechismus. 770
Niewyk, Donald L. 54, 3469
Nigg, Walter. 1804, 2582
Niggemeyer, Jens-Heinrich. 722, 3329
Nightingale, Reuben H. 1568, 3383
Nijmegen, Netherlands. Hoger Katechetisch Instituut. 767
Nijmegen, Netherlands. Hoger Katechetisch Instituut. 746, 767
Nikhilananda. 1813, 3303, 1813, 3784
Niklas, Gerald R. 773, 2782, 2789
Nikolaj. 3305
Nikolaos. 1929
Niles, Daniel T. 1432, 1569, 2065, 2903
Niles, Daniel Thambyrajah. 462, 523, 613, 1095, 1289, 1569, 1725, 2042, 2554, 2903, 3242, 3829
Niles, Henry Thayer. 702, 1953
Niles, Nathaniel. 1342
Niles, Samuel. 3414, 3591, 3031, 3411
Niles, Susan A. 1903
Nilsen, Maria. 2563
*Nilssen, Jerome. 3166
Nilsson, Martin P. [Nils Martin Persson Nilsson]. 1767
Nilsson, Martin Persson. 1767, 2661, 1395, 1459, 1767, 2661
Nilsson, Martin Persson [Nils Martin Persson Nilsson]. 1767
Nimeth, Albert J. 1000, 1001, 2343, 3132
Nimick, John A. 2695
Nimtz, August H. 3545
[Nind, John Newton]. 2711
Ninde, Edward Summerfield. 1872, 1875, 3813
Nineham, D. E. 434
Nineham, Dennis Eric. 239, 434
Nininger, Ruth. 1203, 1209
Ninomiya, Sontoku. 1538
Nippold, Friedrich Wilhelm Franz. 810
Nisargadatta, Maharaj. 1815
Nisbet, Ebenezer. 205
Nishida, Kitaro. 2834
Nishida, Tenko. 1930
Nissenbaum, Mordecai. 3079
Nissenbaum, Stephen. 1757, 3862
Nissim ben Jacob ben Nissim ibn Shahin, 11th cent. 3585

Nist, Jakob. 1317, 2375
Nitchie, Elizabeth. 1625
Nitobe, Inazo. 719
Nitzsche, Jane Chance. 1705
Niven, Archibald Campbell. 2232, 3790
Niven, William Dickie. 1194
Nivison, David S. 1330
Niwano, Nikkyo. 3272
Nixdorff, George Augustus. 1982
Nixon, Jabez Hunt. 3509
Nixon, Joan Lowery. 1620, 1742, 1747, 1756, 2676, 2945
Nixon, Justin Wroe. 1062, 1100, 2956, 3445
Nixon, Leroy. 727, 3027
Nixon, W Hubert. 1897
Nixon, William G. 3355
Niyazi, Kausar. 2624, 2629, 3196
Nizami, Khaliq Ahmad. 1612, 3088, 3543
Njeim, George A. 455, 2258, 3216
Noall, Claire Augusta (Wilcox) 3235
Noall, Matthew. 3132
Nobbs, Douglas. 730, 1477
Nobile, Philip. 3628
Noble, Charles. 971
Noble, Charles C. 1134
Noble, Christian [?] E. 307
Noble, David A. 2933
Noble, Franklin. 1841, 3343
Noble, Frederic Perry. 2497
Noble, Frederick Alphonso. 1361, 1394, 449, 1361
Noble, George Washington. 1910
Noble, Iris. 1410
Noble, John H. 1362, 1366
Noble, Margaret Elizabeth. 2663, 2712
Noble, Miriam. 1744
Noble, Raymond Goodman. 3119
Noble, Richmond Samuel Howe. 299, 3399
Noble, Samuel. 2690
Noble, Vicki. 3834
Noble, Wilfred Vernon. 1637
Noble, William F P. 215
Noble, William Francis Pringl. 3739
Noble, William Francis Pringle. 215, 216
Noblitt, Loren W. 296
Noblitt, Thomas Lee. 843
Nocent, Adrien. 2234
Nock, Arthur Darby. 1081, 1359, 1361, 2800, 3067
Nockolds, Hilda. 3277
Nodel, Julius J. 2864
Noel, Baptist Wriothesley. 1141, 3406
Noel, Conrad. 1969
Noel, Gerard Eyre. 811
Noel, Napoleon. 2855
Noel, Samuel Lucky. 3673
Noer, Deliar. 1924, 1925
Noerdlinger, Henry S. 1314
Noffs, Ted. 3573
Noffsinger, Jack Ricks. 3829, 3880
Noffsinger, John Samuel. 1128, 1236
Nogar, Raymond J. 1580, 3623
Nogara, Bartolomeo. 3768
Nohl, Frederick. 2280
Noit, Dean. 3201
Nola, Alfonso Maria di. 32, 33, 2893
Nolan, Albert. 2042
Nolan, Hugh Joseph. 852
Nolan, John Gavin. 1811
Nolan, Richard T. 1408
Noland, Cora Mabel (Shaw) 623, 2825
Noland, Emma. 3564
Noland, S. 2028, 2459
Nolde, Otto Fred. 640, 648, 747, 971, 1251, 2279, 2283, 3155
Nolde, Otto Frederick. 3155, 640, 648, 747, 971, 1041, 1077, 1252, 2279, 2283, 2807, 3178
Noldin, Hieronymus. 3270
Noli, Fan Stylian. 22, 2745
Noll, John Francis. 790, 796, 1319, 3190, 796
Noll, Mark A. 3742
Nolte, Evelyn White. 2319
Noonan, Daniel P. 3401
Noonan, Hugh. 2393
Noonan, John Patrick. 2419
Noonan, John Thomas. 663, 664, 2341
Noonan, Richard T. 3330
Noone, Patricia. 2356
Noorbergen, Rene. 699, 1283, 1716, 2711, 3811
Noore, Gerardus Cornelis van. 3646
Noort, Gerardus Cornelis van. 3646
Noppel, Constantin. 3676
Nora-Gon, Evelyn Barrett. 1034
Norbeck, Edward. 1936, 3062
Norberg, Janet Louise. 3606
Norberg, Kaut. 1264
Norborg, Sverre. 338, 493, 1051, 1586
Nordau, Max Simon. 2119, 3896
Nordberg, Robert B. 2646
Norden, John. 1451
Norden, Rudolph F. 561, 971, 2209, 3355, 3664

Nordgren, Julius Vincent. 623, 3766, 3879
Nordgren, Rubye Patton. 910, 3155
Nordheimer, Isaac. 1797
Nordhoff, Charles. 1308, 1320
Nordin, Dayton W. 1203
Nordland, Frances. 1303, 3844
Nordsten, Reuben. 1953
Nordtvedt, Matilda. 932, 1425, 2713, 3857
Norelius, Eric. 3132
Norelli-Bachelet, Patrizia. 455
Norem, Harlan. 3155, 3330
Noren, Paul H. A. 2215
*Norfleet, Mary Crockett. 616, 904
Norfolk, Va. St. Paul's Church (Protestant Episcopal) 2713
Norfolk, Va. St. Paul's church (Protestant Episcopal) Altar guild. 2713
Norlie, Olaf Morgan. 247, 2085
Norman, Albert E. 2719
Norman, Don Cleveland. 314
Norman, Dorothy. 2649
Norman, Edward R. 51, 1088, 1101, 1151, 3452
Norman, Ernest L. 3509
Norman, James Roy. 2238
Norman, Joyce. 1359, 2713
Norman, Ruth. 3226, 3473
Norquist, Marilyn. 180
Norquist, N Leroy. 651, 3191
Norrill, Milo True. 1100
Norris, Albert George Samuel. 96
Norris, Frank B. 1122
Norris, Herbert. 1249
Norris, John. 181, 2180, 2241, 3623
Norris, Judy. 318, 2393, 3843
Norris, Louis William. 3758
Norris, Marion Lela. 3877
Norris, Richard Alfred. 2009, 3610, 3623, 3658, 3664
Norris, Ronald. 2778
Norris, W[illiam] E[dward]. 3201
Norris, William Foxley. 1129
Norris, Zoe Anderson. 3462
North Adams, Mass. First Congregational church. 1332
North America (Diocese) 82
North American assembly of Y.M.C.A. workers with boys. 7th, Cleveland, 1944. 687
North American Assembly on Y. M. C. A. Work with Boys. 8th, Green Lake, Wis., 1947. 687
North American association of boys' work secretaries of the Young men's Christian association. 687
North American Conference on Church and Family, Green Lake, Wis., 1961. 1604
North American Conference on Faith and Order, Oberlin College, 1957. 1044
North American Conference on Muslim Evangelization, Colorado Springs, 1978. 2557
North American Congress of the Laity, Los Angeles, 1978. 2192
North American ecumenical conference, Toronto, 1941. 1044
North American home missions congress, Washington, D. C., 1930. 2528
North American Liturgical Week. 16th, Worcester, Mass., 1955. 2240
North American Liturgical Week. 21st, Pittsburgh, 1960. 1249
North American Liturgical Week. 22d, Oklahoma City, 1961. 2240
North American Liturgical Week. 23d, Seattle, 1962. 1529
North American Liturgical Week. 24th, Philadelphia, 1963. 2240
North American Liturgical Week. 25th, St. Louis, 1964. 2774
North American Liturgical Week. 26th, Baltimore, Portland, Chicago, 1965. 1243
North American radio commission. 3018
North American Student Conference on Christian Frontiers, University of Kansas, 1947-1948. 3537
North American student consultation on the world mission of Christianity, Toronto, 1939-1940. 2521
North Atlantic Treaty Organization. Advisory Group for Aeronautical Research and Development. 11
North, Brownlow. 1470
North Carolina. University. 3818
North Carolina. University. Dept. of Physics. 1469
North Carolina. University. University extension division. 3759
North, Christopher Richard. 3377
North Conway Institute. 23
North, Eric McCoy. 655, 2459, 2523, 2859
North family of Mt. Lebanon, N.Y. 3398

North, Frederick J. 3366
North, Gary. 1075, 2727, 3445
North, Harry Maurice. 1569
North, Louise Josephine (McCoy) 2458
North, Robert Grady. 925, 3243, 3462, 3593
North, Sterling. 2023
North Stonington, Conn. First Baptist church. 147
North Tarrytown, N.Y. First Reformed church. 2714
Northbourne, Walter Ernest Christopher James. 1095
Northbrooke, John. 36
Northcote, Hugh. 3393
Northcott, Reginald James. 2307, 3402, 3809
Northcott, William Cecil. 247, 616, 626, 902, 1073, 1872, 1875, 2499, 2563, 3192, 3850
Northeastern Association of Christian Churches. 1465
Northen, Llewellyn Columbus. 1559
Norther, Llewellyn Columbus. 166
Northern Baptist convention. 149, 150, 156, 172, 1609, 1901, 2494, 2504, 2714
Northern Baptist convention. Board of education. 156, 2714, 3681
Northern Baptist convention. Convention, 1934. 143
Northern Baptist convention (Pre-convention conference, Buffalo, 1920) 149
Northern Baptist convention (Pre-convention conference, Des Moines, 1921) 140
Northey, James E. 1569
Northridge, William Lovell. 2999
Northrip, Irene (Spencer) 3788
Northrop, Henry Davenport. 2820, 640, 1969, 623, 2588
Northrup, Theodore G. 2695
Northwestern university, Evanston, Ill. 2163
Norton, Andrews. 60, 391, 395, 3708, 3728
Norton, Augustus Theodore. 2917
[Norton, Charles Eliot] 1827-1908. 910, 1160
Norton, Daniel Silas. 2657
Norton, Edith (Fox) 2393, 2503, 2714
Norton, Florence E. 2773
Norton, Frank Louis. 2071
Norton, Fred Lewis. 2588
Norton, Frederick Owen. 407
Norton, Herman Albert. 1467, 3601
Norton, Jacob. 3355, 3697, 3712
Norton, John. 1333, 1372, 1682, 3646
Norton, John N[icholas]. 1283
Norton, John Nicholas. 178, 1387, 2829, 2984, 3025, 3788, 3812, 3818
Norton, Lemuel. 1594
Norton, Mabel. 1618
Norton, Perry L. 1278
Norton, Richard F. 2359
[Norton, W. L.]. 3142
Norton, William. 1841
Norton, William Bernard. 10
Norton, William Harrison. 650
Norton, William Joseph. 720
Norvell. 96, 1470, 1879, 2380, 3539
Norvell, Joseph Elgon. 782
Norwegian Lutheran church of America. 2290
Norwegian Lutheran church of America. Centennial commission. 2715
Norwegian synod of the American Evangelical Lutheran church. 3578
Norwich, John Julius Cooper. 102
Norwood, Abraham. 3752
Norwood, Frederick Abbott. 1184, 1187, 1188, 2433, 2438, 2821
Norwood, Frederick William. 3201, 3366, 1342
Norwood, H. Dorothy. 640
Norwood, John Nelson. 2443, 2451, 3423
Norwood, Robert Winkworth. 372, 2800, 1969, 2210, 2973
Noser, A. A. 2393
Nosow, Sigmund. 1826
Noss, Christopher. 2534
Noss, John Boyer. 3119
Noss, Luther M. 1867
Notaro, Thom. 1738, 3767
Notestein, Wallace. 3825, 3826
Noth, Martin. 516, 557, 2764, 484, 516, 557, 561, 563, 2089
Nother, Ingo. 584
Nothstein, Ira Oliver. 2303, 2296
Notovich, Nicolau. 1081, 1976
[Notovich, Nikolai]. 1081, 1976, 1987
Notre Dame Colloquium, University of Notre Dame, 1967. 3328
Notre Dame, Ind. University. 844, 858, 1157, 2715
Notre Dame, Ind. University. Dept. of Economics. 807

Notre Dame, Ind. University. Dept. of Theology. 646
Notre Dame, Ind. University. Institute for Local Superiors. 2583
Notre Dame, Ind. University. Sisters' Institute of Spirituality. 2581, 3489, 3787
Notre Dame, Ind. University. Vocation Institute. 3786
Notre Dame Study of Catholic Elementary and Secondary Schools in the United States. 832
Notredame, Michel de. 2948, 2947, 2948
Notre Dame, Michel de. 2947
Nott, Charles Cooper. 1877
Nott, Eliphalet. 2914
Nott, George Frederick. 1520, 3804
Nott, Josiah Clark. 2680
[Nott, Richard Means]. 2716
Nott, Samuel. 1504, 2903
Nottingham, Elizabeth Kristine. 2431, 3086
Nouet, Jacques. 2015
Nouns homo. 1889
Nourse, Edward Everett. 370, 3879
Nourse, Laura A. (Barney) Sunderlin. 1889, 3509
Nouwen, Henri J. M. 1299, 1414, 2393, 2413, 2716, 2785, 2786, 2876, 3481, 3489, 3490
Novak, Alfons. 511
Novak, David. 3219
Novak, Michael. 186, 874, 1001, 2393, 3062, 3233, 3652, 3770, 3774
Novatianus. 3714
Noveck, Simon. 2084, 2145, 3016, 3526
Novelli, Angelo. 2852
Novotny, Louis Miller. 1167
Novotny, Louise Miller. 2399
Novotny, Louise (Miller) 1623, 3837, 3857
Novotny, Louise [Virgie] (Miller) 3857
Nowack, William H. 2510
Nowak, Andrew Thomas Francis. 2262, 3460
Nowell, Alexander. 1215
Nowell, Ames. 1495
Nowell, Robert. 1408, 2188
Nowell, William Cullen. 455
Nowlan, Connie Wells. 1398, 2485
Nowlin, William Dudley. 154, 3232
Noyce, Gaylord B. 1278, 2480, 2774, 2786, 3538
Noyes, Alfred. 1725, 2896
Noyes, Carleton Eldredge. 2095
Noyes, Edward MacArthur. 908
Noyes, Eli. 1813
Noyes, George Rapall. 34, 3667
Noyes, George Wallingford. 2716, 2737
Noyes, Harriet Newell. 737
*Noyes, Henry Drury. 839
Noyes, John B. 2048
Noyes, John Humphrey. 2737, 3623
Noyes, Morgan Phelps. 1305, 2893, 2903
Noyes, Rufus King. 1655
Nuelsen, John Louis. 2276
Nuelsen, John Louise. 3658
Nuesch, John. 236, 1055, 3027
Nuesner, Jacob. 2149
Nuesse, Celestine Joseph. 1136, 2774
Nugeat, Rosamond. 3781
Nugent, Donald. 2857
Nugent, Francis Edward. 773, 1451, 2356
Nugent, John Peer. 2130
Nugent, Marianna. 2491
Nugent, Rosamond. 1645
Nugent, Vincent Joseph. 2343
Nulman, Louis. 2106
Numbers, Ronald L. 3811
Nunberg, Ralph. 2094
Nunes, Joseph A. 2856
Nunez C., Emilio Antonio. 3290
Nunn, Henry Preston Vaughan. 421, 1525, 1770, 2243, 2561
Nunn, William Curtis. 2394
Nunnally-Cox, Janice. 3840
Nurbakhsh, Javad. 2169, 3543
Nurses Christian Fellowship. 648
Nursi, Said. 2718
Nuthall, Beatrice. 3251
Nutt, Ben. 526
Nutt, Thomas. 185
Nuttall, Clayton L. 1151
Nuttall, Geoffrey Fillingham. 1378, 1520, 1786
Nutting, Herbert Chester. 2199
Nutting, R. Ted. 1609, 2028
Nutting, Willis Dwight. 763, 1426
Nyanaponika. 708, 2382
*Nyberg, Dennis. 9
Nyberg, Kathleen Neill. 1303, 3844
Nyce, A. William. 1750
Nye, Ernest J. 3079
Nye, Rose B. 462
Nye, Thelma M. 1159
Nygaard, Normal Eugene. 2128, 3276

Nygaard, Norman Eugene. 181, 1441, 3456, 89, 682, 1252, 1435, 1441, 2276, 3293, 3590
Nygard, Norman Eugene. 20
Nygren, Anders. 469, 1096, 1122, 2265, 2297, 3103
Nygren, Anders, Bp., 1890. 1122
Nygren, Anders Theodor Samuel. 1096
Nyholm, Paul C. 2302
Nyhus, Paul L. 1648
Nyman, Aaron. 3380
Nyman, Monte S. 543
Nymeyer, Frederick. 1071, 3414
Nyquist, John G. 607
Nystedt, Olle. 17, 1265
Nystrom, Carolyn. 43, 313, 493, 645, 904, 971, 1199, 1405, 1417, 1835, 2765
Nystrom, Daniel. 1318, 110, 1441, 1606
Nystrom, Gertrude Evelyn (Hill) 2129, 2536
Nyvall, David. 3569, 3572

O

O Muirithe, Diarmaid. 1919
Oakes, Dallin H. 1490
Oakes, John P. 640
Oakes, Maud van Cortlandt. 2319, 3703
Oakeshott, Walter Fraser. 1451
Oakesmith, John. 3062
Oakland, Cal. Free public library. 2632
Oakland, Calif. Church of the Ascension (Greek Orthodox) 2719
Oakley, Austin. 2748
Oakley, Francis. 807, 1144, 1186, 1322
Oakley, Thomas Pollock. 2200, 2813
Oakman, Arthur A. 2042, 3215, 3216, 3218, 3355
Oaks, Dallin H. 1490
Oaks, Lewis Weston. 3848
Oates, Bob. 2317, 3708
Oates, James Franklin. 3871
Oates, Wayne E. 3674
Oates, Wayne Edward. 23, 55, 166, 653, 1258, 1289, 1352, 1374, 1831, 2050, 2345, 2781, 2784, 2786, 2790, 2822, 2995, 2999, 3175, 3408, 3674
Oates, Whitney Jennings. 2853
Obayashi, Hiroshi. 1819
Obelkevich, James. 3452
Obenhaus, Victor. 1075, 1076, 1134, 2462, 2671, 3731
Ober, Charles Kellogg. 640, 1359, 3822, 3871
Ober, Douglas. 1514
Ober, Frank W. 3533, 3871
Oberammergau passion-play. 2719, 2720
*Oberfield, William J. 2837
Oberg, Ernest. 1451
Oberg, John Ulrick. 3221
Oberholzer, Emil. 1337
Oberlin Colloquium in Philosophy, 6th, Oberlin College, 1965. 2839
Oberman, Heiko Augustinus. 658, 2356, 3636, 3637, 3659
Obermann, Julian. 1658, 1788
Obermeier, Arnold. 2722
Oberst, Bruce. 511
Oberste, William H. 2179, 3050
Oberste, William Herman. 2333
Obeyesekere, Gananath. 704, 3574
Obolensky, Dimitri. 674
Obolensky, Dmitri. 674
Obrecht, Frances (Harris) 1482
O'Brien, Anthony Henry. 3527
O'Brien, Bartholomew J. 2271, 2380, 3778
O'Brien, Bonnie Ball. 146, 158, 932, 3402, 3524
O'Brien, Charles H. 814
O'Brien, David J. 828
O'Brien, Edward Joseph Harrington. 2710
O'Brien, Elmer. 1492, 2645, 3618
O'Brien, Felicity. 2851, 2861
[O'Brien, Gabriel, 1844-1908. 3418
O'Brien, Isidore. 407, 864, 1643, 1647, 1993, 3132, 407, 1027, 1451, 1643, 1993
O'Brien, James Bernard. 3248
O'Brien, Joachim. 771, 1609, 1646
O'Brien, Joan V. 1382
O'Brien, John. 2232, 2367
O'Brien, John A. 2351
O'Brien, John Anthony. 65, 657, 782, 790, 796, 832, 971, 1044, 1364, 1569, 1580, 1582, 1738, 1909, 1948, 1969, 1982, 2265, 2339, 2343, 3676, 3772
O'Brien, John M. 1186
O'Brien, Joseph D. 2577
O'Brien, Joseph Laurence. 888
O'Brien, Joseph Lawrence. 1516
O'Brien, Kate. 3603
O'Brien, Kevin J. 805
O'Brien, Mary Consilia. 2216, 3450, 3453
O'Brien, Maureen. 1356
O'Brien, May Corita. 2394

O'Brien, Michael J. 2781
O'Brien, Michael John. 2853
O'Brien, Raymond Francis. 6
O'Brien, Robert Yorke. 935
O'Brien, Thomas John. 770, 1541, 767, 770
O'Brien, Virgil Patrick. 1258
O'Brien, William Alexis. 782, 839
O'Brien, William David. 2358
O'Brien, William J. 1810, 1969, 3391
O'Brien, William James. 2649
O'Brien, William Vincent. 103
O'Callaghan, Denis. 2375, 3265
O'Callaghan, Edmund Bailey. 212
O'Callaghan, Jeremiah. 790, 3714
O'Callaghan, Michael C. 2245, 3667
O'Callaghan, Rosaria. 2668
O'Carroll, Michael. 2206, 2360
Occhio, Joseph M. 1071
Occidental D.A.T.A. 99
Occidentalis, Frater. 2048
*Occult review. 2727
O'Ceallaigh, Sean S. 2762
Ocean Grove camp meeting association of the Methodist Episcopal church. 2452
Ochs, Carol. 3389
Ochs, Daniel A. 971, 3380, 3888
Ochs, Robert. 1414, 3019
Ochs, William Benjamin. 971, 1012, 1441, 2042, 3383
Ochsenford, Solomon Erb. 1577, 2030
Ochsenrider, Robert. 2394
Ochshorn, Judith. 3834
Ockenga, Harold John. 321, 365, 471, 478, 479, 1342, 1831, 2215, 2977, 3840
Ockengar, Harold John. 1342, 1836
Ockham, William. 2242, 2252, 2839, 2912, 3469
Ockley, Simon. 2564
O'Collins, Gerald. 1389, 1473, 1845, 1998, 2010, 2052, 2462, 3225, 3226, 3628
O'Connell, Cornelius Joseph. 756, 1541, 2356, 3155, 796
O'Connell, Daniel Patrick. 3236
O'Connell, David. 1638, 2261
O'Connell, David A. 1725, 3193, 3696
O'Connell, Hugh J. 3531
O'Connell, J. B. 2367
O'Connell, Jeremiah Joseph. 823, 824, 3714
O'Connell, John Berthram. 844, 2367
O'Connell, John P. 858, 1977
O'Connell, Kevin G. 517
O'Connell, Laurence J. 832, 839
O'Connell, Laurence John. 832, 844
O'Connell, Margaret F. 3826
O'Connell, Marvin R. 1374
O'Connell, Marvin Richard. 1374, 2754, 3525
O'Connell, Raphael V. 42, 2356, 2361
O'Connell, Robert J. 115, 116, 2327
O'Connell, Timothy E. 948
O'Connell, William Henry. 864, 2734, 2852, 2862, 3132, 2734
O'Connor, Daniel. 1383, 442, 2416
O'Connor, Daniel A. 2852, 3449
O'Connor, Daniel William. 2825
O'Connor, Edward D. 2363
O'Connor, Edward Dennis. 756, 1597, 1835, 1886, 2363, 2805, 2815
O'Connor, Elizabeth. 986, 1238, 1356, 1441, 1712, 3797
O'Connor, James A. 2306
O'Connor, John. 3789, 760, 829
O'Connor, John Bonaventure. 1475, 2576
O'Connor, John Joseph. 816, 1089
O'Connor, Joseph P. 3192
O'Connor, June. 1709
O'Connor, M. 1798
O'Connor, Martin John. 864
O'Connor, Mary Edwardine. 2305, 3418
O'Connor, Mary Loretto. 3418
O'Connor, Mary Paschala. 3420
O'Connor, Nellie Johnson. 702
O'Connor, Robert Francis. 2203
O'Connor, William R. 1268, 2191
O'Connor, William Richard. 2191
O'Conor, John Francis Xavier. 2042, 3281, 3458
*O'Dair, Stan. 3824
O'Daniel, Victor Francis. 820, 825, 1475, 1476, 1622, 2308, 2463, 2721, 3819
O'Day, Rey. 3004
O'Day, Rosemary. 1215, 1291
Odd-fellows, Independent order of . Illinois. Grand lodge. 3205
Odd-fellows, Independent order of. Nebraska. Grand lodge. 3205
Odd-fellows, Independent order of. New York (State) Grand lodge. 3205
Odd-fellows, Independent order of. Pennsylvania. Grand lodge. 3205
Oddo, Gilbert Lawrence. 1364
Ode, James A. 1210
O'Dea, Barbara. 2209
O'Dea, Janet K. 599, 2148

O'Dea, John Coyle. 2342
O'Dea, Paul. 2367
O'Dea, Thomas F. 874, 1062, 1245, 2604, 3086, 3088, 3772
Odeberg, Hugo. 420, 1083
Oded, Arye. 1926
Odegard, Holtan Peter. 2709, 3411
Odegard, Holton P. 1087, 2709
Odegard, Peter H. 1087
Odelain, O. 480
Odell, Edward Albert. 2559
Odell, Jack. 1362
Odell, Margaretta (Grubb) W. H. Odell." 3286
Odell, Margaretta (Grubbs) "W. H. Odell. 3286
Odell, Mary (Clemens) 1609, 3174, 3764
Odell, Mary Elise. 535
Odell, Willis Patterson. 1486
Oden, Margaret (Muse) 2632
Oden, Marilyn Brown. 1007, 1303
Oden, Thomas C. 176, 944, 1244, 1777, 2784, 2999, 3243, 3618
Odenheimer, William Henry. 1219, 2960, 2972
Odenwald, Robert P. 1384
Odgers, J Hastie. 3004
Odhner, C[arl] Th[eophilus]. 2690, 3569, 3570
Odhner, C[arl] Theophilus. 3570
Odhner, Carl Th[eophilus]. 3132
Odhner, Carl Theophilus. 3377
Odhner, Hugo Ljungberg. 3570
Odin, Steve. 1850, 3813
Odle, Don. 2516
Odle, Don J. 2516
Odle, Joe T. 148, 3320
Odman, Charlotte. 2290
Odo, de Deuil. 1392, 2261
O'Doherty, Eamon Feichin. 2571
O'Doherty, Eamonn Feichin. 7, 1107, 2784, 2999, 3171, 3785
Odom, Robert Leo. 3800, 1528, 3260, 3261
Odom, Robert Leon. 3261
O'Donnell, Clement Maria. 852, 1357, 2249
O'Donnell, Elliot. 1710, 3510, 1710
O'Donnell, Elliott. 1710
O'Donnell, Francis Henry Etherington. 3142
O'Donnell, George Edward. 2830
O'Donnell, James Joseph. 744, 928
O'Donnell, John Hugh. 668
O'Donnell, Joseph Dean. 1152, 2200
O'Donnell, Luke. 2030
O'Donnell, Thomas Clay. 629
O'Donnell, William Charles. 3155
O'Donnell, William Charles, jr. 3155
O'Donoghue, Joseph. 808
[O'Donoghue, Martin]. 1051
O'Donoghue, Richard. 2734
O'Donovan, John F. 868
O'Donovan, Leo J. 476, 2010
[O'Donovan, Louis] 1872. 132
O'Donovan, Oliver. 115, 116, 3330
Odor, Ruth. 632, 2054, 2260
Odor, Ruth Shannon. 2023
O'Dowd, James Thomas. 805, 806
O'Dowd, William Bernard. 2903
O'Driscoll, Herbert. 2015, 2361, 2394
O'Driscoll, J. A. 1712
O'Driscoll, Richard. 1615, 2734
O'Dwyer, David T. 2358
O'Dwyer, James F. 1001
Oechslin, Raphael Louis. 2192, 2271, 2876
Oechtering, John Henry. 1184, 1185
OEcumenius. 455
Oehler, Gustav Friedrich. 599
Oehme, Julius. 2760
Oemler, Christian. 1258
Oesterley, William Oscar Emil. 29, 486, 490, 540, 576, 1401, 1531, 2076, 2092, 2115, 2117, 2239, 1400, 2111, 3015
Oesterly, William Oscar Emil. 397, 2026, 578, 2117
Oesterreich, Traugott Konstantin. 1422
Oesterreicher, John M. 599, 860, 1366, 2085, 2152
Oetting, Walter W. 1194
O'Faolain, Sean. 2704
O'Farrell, Patrick James. 814
Offer, Clifford Jesse. 1763
Offermann, Henry Frederick. 1262
Offiler, William Henry. 236
Offner, Clark B. 3324
Offord, Robert M. 2305
O'flaherty, V. M. 3316
O'Flaherty, Vincent M. 1356, 1418, 2268
O'Flaherty, Wendy Doniger. 1747, 2663, 3421
Ofstedal, Rudolph A. 2162
Ogata, Sohaku. 2197, 2199, 3892, 3894
Ogburn, Calvin. 1841
Ogden, Horatio N[elson]. 894

Ogden, Horatio Nelson. 894, 2443
Ogden, R. James. 216
Ogden, Schubert Miles. 713, 1424, 2046, 2222, 3652
Ogden, Uzal. 1420, 2759, 3366
Ogg, Elizabeth. 191
Ogg, George. 1997
Ogilvie, Lloyd John. 2027
Ogilvie, Glencairn Stuart. 3144
Ogilvie, James Nicoll. 1895
Ogilvie, John. 3024
Ogilvie, Lloyd John. 181, 332, 369, 449, 479, 1011, 1435, 1713, 1785, 2258, 2933, 3355, 3356, 3664
Ogilvie, Robert Maxwell. 1286, 2190, 3246
Ogilvy, James A. 2320
Ogle, Arthur. 735, 2304
Ogle, George E. 2486, 2734
Ogle, Mary S. 1927, 2510, 3385, 3431
Oglesby, Stuart Roscie. 449
Oglesby, Stuart Roscoe. 423, 2893, 2933
Oglesby, William B. 971, 987, 2781
Oglesby, William P. 653, 2781
Ogletree, Thomas W. 28, 1417, 1818, 3715
Oglevee, Louis (McArot) 3185
Oglevee, Louise M. 3155, 3564
Oglevee, Louise McAroy. 3155
Oglevee, Louise (McAroy) 911
O'Gorman, James F. 2575
O'Gorman, Thomas. 833
O'Gorman, Walter Ernest Rupert. 782
O'Grady, Anthony Thomas. 790
O'Grady, Desmond. 1153, 1704
O'Grady, John. 829, 887, 1930
O'Grady, John F. 437, 2010, 2042, 2324
O'Guin, C. M. 2722
O'Hagan, Thomas. 2227
O'Hair, Madalyn Murray. 100, 3096
O'Halloran, John L. 2218
Ohan, William Joseph. 2913
O'Hanlon, Assumpta. 1474
O'Hanlon, Daniel. 790
Ohanneson, Joan. 3841
O'Hara, Constance Marie. 1365
O'Hara, Edwin Vincent. 828, 3255
O'Hara, John. 3343
O'Hara, Joseph Michael. 891
[O'Hare, Genoeffa N.] 1906. 1670
O'Hare, Patrick F. 2276
O'Harra, Mileham Leon. 971
O'Heron, Edward J. 318
Ohio anti-saloon league. 3596
Ohio convention of Methodist men. 1915. 1407
Ohio. State University, Columbus. Libraries. 2330
Ohl, Jerimiah Franklin. 2296
Ohlendorf, William Clarence. 3686
Ohlig, Karl-Heinz. 2863
Ohlrich, Charles. 3542
Ohm, Thomas. 1079
Ohmann, Carol Burke. 3276
Ohmann, Richard Malin. 2649
Ohrn, Arnold Theodore. 1096
O'Kearney, Nicholas. 2947
O'Keefe, Maureen. 2573
O'Keefe, Ruth Evans. 3745
O'Keefe, Thomas. 3182
O'Keeffe, Gerald Michael. 2342
O'Keeffe, Henry E. 2399, 3201, 760
O'Keeffe, Timothy J. 372, 1101, 2472
Oken, Alan. 96
Oklahoma Baptist university, Shawnee. 1128
*Oko, Adolph S. 3472
Okwuosa, V. E. Akubueze. 2499
Olan, Levi Arthur. 1892
Olander, Marie Hankla. 2295
O'Laverty, Hugh. 790, 2252
Olcott, Frances Jenkins. 2535, 2762
Olcott, Henry Steel. 671, 702, 3510, 3686
Olcott, William Tyler. 3546
Old Man. 2394
Old Paramus Reformed Church, Ridgewood, N.J. Historical Committee. 2736, 3237
Old, Walter Gorn. 96, 2727, 3575, 3582
Old, Water Gorn. 3575
Oldaker, Wilfrid Horace. 408
Oldemoppen, Bernadette Greenwood. 2560
Olden, Marc. 1909
Oldenbourg, Zoe. 22, 1390
Oldenburger, Teunis. 1090
Oldfather, William Abbott. 1811
Oldfield, Josiah. 1600
Oldfield, Walter Herbert. 2510
Oldham, Dale. 971, 2736
Oldham, Doug. 1359, 2736

Oldham, Joseph Houldsworth. 26, 1096, 3017, 3445, 3017
Oldham, Laura Lee. 1611, 2736
Oldham, Lewis T. 65

Oldham, Pauline E. 1303
Oldham, W. Dale. 1229
Oldham, W Dale. 1229
Oldham, William Fitzjames. 3692
Oldmixon, John. 1309, 3606
Olds, Barbara Moses. 3207
Olds, Charles Burnell. 1096
Oldsen, Armin Charles. 2301
[Oldys, William]. 2
O'Leary, Arthur. 776, 3193
O'Leary, Conrad John. 676, 2320
O'Leary, De Lacy Evans. 77, 1474, 3283
O'Leary, John C. 839
O'Leary, John F. 832
O'Leary, M. 3438
O'Leary, Mary Florence Margaret. 2576, 3438
Olesen, Albert H. 3295
Olf, Lillian (Browne) 2850, 2852
Olford, Stephen F. 166, 422, 1569, 3228, 3232, 3462, 3531, 3721, 3848
Olgiati, Francesco. 3693
Olin, John C. 1374, 1527
Olin, Stephen. 971
Oliphant, Bill. 3380
Oliphant, James Orin. 1627
Oliphant, John. 3132
Oliphant, Laurence. 2762, 3510
Oliphant, Margaret Oliphant (Wilson) 880, 1269, 1405, 1920
Oliphant, Samuel Grant. 1513
Oliphant, William Landon. 1725, 2119
Oliva, Jose Rafael. 2553
Olive branch Evangelical Lutheran synod of Indiana. 1549
Olive, Don H. 2767
Oliveira, Jose Galamba de. 2349
Oliver. 2356
Oliver, Alfred Cookman. 2773
Oliver, C Herbert. 3017
Oliver, C J. 463
Oliver, Charles Alexander. 3556
Oliver, Edmund Henry. 3201
Oliver, Fay Conlee. 2380
[Oliver, Fitch Edward] 1819-1892. 684
Oliver, Frederick Spencer. 2727, 2728
Oliver, French Earl. 1559, 2681
Oliver, George Fletcher. 731, 1569, 2443
Oliver, [Harold Purcell]. 3462
[Oliver, John]. 3290
Oliver, John A. 1287, 1367
Oliver, John Rathbone. 45
[Oliver, Lillie F (Weber)]. 2736
Oliver, Lucille. 987, 1325
Oliver, Peter. 661, 2276, 2371
Oliver, Reginald Campbell Burn. 154
Oliver, Revilo Pendleton. 1062
Oliver, Roland Anthony. 2498
Oliver, William Hosking. 240, 2464
Olivers, Thomas. 2822
Olivier, Bernard. 1845
Olivier, Edith. 1390
Ollard, Sidney Leslie. 1221, 2754
Ollivier, Marie Joseph. 2007, 2030
Olmstead, Albert, Ten Eyck. 1970, 2764
Olmstead, Benjamin Luce. 2800
Olmstead, Clifton E. 3745
Olmstead, Dwight Hinckley. 2977
Olmstead, James Munson. 203
Olmstead, William Backus. 3556
Olmsted, Charles G. 1655
Olmsted, David Lockwood. 1361
Olsen, Alexandra Hennessey. 1778
Olsen, Benjamin David. 1528
Olsen, Charles M. 1244
Olsen, Erling Charles. 423, 585, 1071
Olsen, Kermit Robert. 2876
Olsen, Mahlon Ellsworth. 248, 1970, 3380
Olsen, Peder. 1600, 2784
Olsen, Viggo Norskov. 1188, 1637
Olshausen, Hermann. 344, 386, 2030
Olson, A. V. 3386
Olson, Adolf. 140
Olson, Albert Victor. 3386
Olson, Arnold Theodore. 1361, 1546, 1917
Olson, Bernhard Emmanuel. 3188
Olson, Bruce. 2625, 2736
Olson, Charles. 2867
Olson, David F. 3888
Olson, Eleanor. 88
Olson, Eudora Landstrom. 1982
Olson, Gilbert W. 2546
Olson, Harry E. 318
Olson, John Frederick. 1198
Olson, John Helmer. 3888
Olson, Lois Ellen. 2736
Olson, Mary. 3510
Olson, Mildred Thompson. 91, 2558
Olson, Nathanael. 1569, 1574
Olson, Norman. 646
Olson, Olaf J. 1953
Olson, Oscar Ludvig. 211
Olson, Oscar Nils. 110
Olson, Oscar Thomas. 1071
Olson, Ove Sigfrid. 3180, 3556
Olson, Raymond M. 2279, 3529

Olson, Richard Allan. 936
Olson, Virgil A. 3181
Olson, William George. 2815
Olssen, William Whittingham. 3225
Olsson, Karl A. 648, 987, 1282, 1412, 1546, 1549, 2032, 3239
Olsson, Olof. 106
Olston, Albert B. 1034, 2473
Olt, Russell. 739, 1248, 2999
Olthuis, James H. 2339
Olyphant, Vernon Murray. 3356
Olzendam, Roderic Marble. 1511
O'Mahoney, Katharine A (O'Keeffe) 821
O'Mahony, James Edward. 1001, 1105, 1451, 1646, 1977
O Mahony, Patrick J. 1471
O'Malley, Austin. 2378
O'Malley, John Steven. 2846, 3044
O'Malley, John W. 858, 2910
O'Malley, Lewis Sydney Steward. 1813, 1814
O'Malley, William J. 65, 314, 391, 1945, 2876, 3574, 3888
Oman, Charles Chichele. 1240
Oman, John B. 1775
Oman, John Campbell. 1896, 3272
Oman, John Wood. 1751, 2904, 3646, 2904, 2933, 3062, 3103, 3646
Omarr, Sydney. 96, 3575, 3576
O'Meara and Hills, architects. 1162
O'Meara, John Joseph. 115, 1025
O'Meara, Kathleen. 2755
O'Meara, Thomas A. 2360, 3700
O'Meara, Thomas F. 713, 1062, 1733, 2571, 3618, 3628, 3700, 3717
O'Mikle, Stephen. 2852
Ommen, Lydia. 1725
Ommen, Thomas B. 3669
Onasch, Konrad. 1881
Onderdonk, Benjamin Tredwell. 2737
Onderdonk, Frank Scovill. 2540
[Onderdonk, Henry Ustick]. 1523
Onderwyzer, Joseph. 2115
One (Minneapolis) 2292
O'Neal, James Albert. 607
O'Neal, Margaret. 815, 2506
O'Neall, Freda Schwartz. 1303
O'Neall, Kelly. 2007, 2215
Oneida Community. 2737, 3436
Oneida, N. Y. Presbyterian church. 2918
O'Neil, Charles J. 3693
O'Neil, Daniel John. 828, 2241
[O'Neil, James Louis]. 2774
O'Neil, Josephine M. 1458, 1776
O'Neil, Maud. 1761
O'Neil, Robert P. 948
O'Neile, Charles E. 2215, 3343
O'Neill, Ancilla. 35, 690
O'Neill, Anne (Scannell) 2394
O'Neill, Arthur Barry. 1289, 3201, 3676
O'Neill, Charles A. 3770
O'Neill, Charles Edwards. 822, 1147
O'Neill, Colman E. 2255, 3265
O'Neill, David P. 773, 877, 1001, 1325, 2265, 2774, 3445
O'Neill, Francis Joseph. 3787
[O'Neill, Frederick William Scott. 913
[O'Neill, Henry]. 1388
O'Neill, Hugh. 1920
O'Neill, J. C. 469
O'Neill, James Milton. 828, 832, 1151, 3190
O'Neill, John. 2585
O'Neill, Joseph Eugene. 3329, 3652
O'Neill, Joseph H. 2789
O'Neill, Judith. 2276, 3040
O'Neill, Mary. 3284
O'Neill, Mary Edwin. 2353
O'Neill, Mary (Le Duc) 3284
O'Neill, Michael. 832
O'Neill, Patrick. 3709
O'Neill, Patrick Ireland. 1256
O'Neill, William Henry. 3219
Ong, Walter J. 760, 828, 829, 1403, 3082
*Ongaro, A. Cremonini. 3281
Ong Walter J. 828
Onimus, Jean. 733
Ono, Motonori. 3404
Onstad, Esther. 455
Ooka, Minoru. 3600
Oort, Henricus. 407, 535
Oosborn, Solomon Oliver. 2324
Oosterhuis, Huub. 2893
Oosterink, Henk. 3686
Oosterwal, Gottfried. 2494
Oosterzee, Johannes Jacobus van. 428, 3646
Oosterzee, Johnnnes Jacobus van. 476
Oosthuizen, Gerhardus Cornelis. 1073
[Opdycke, John Baker]. 603
Openshaw, Eunice M. 3278
Opfell, Olga S. 272
Ophiel. 722, 1283, 1470, 2728
Opie, Robert T. 1302, 2740
Opitz, Edmund A. 3069
Opitz, Heinrich. 593
Oppen, Dietrich von. 3445

Oppenheim, Leo. 1479
Oppenheim, Micha Falk. 2144
Oppenheim, Mortiz. 1623
Oppenheimer, Helen. 2344
Oppenheimer, Joseph. 3702
Oppy, John Amandus. 1725
Optatus. 1476
Oquist, Paul H. 3780
Oracula sibyllina. 2740
O'Rafferty, Nicholas. 864, 2362
Orage, Alfred Richard. 2710
O'Rahilly, Alfred. 1985
Oraison, Marc. 948, 1001, 1414, 2227, 2339, 3097, 3176, 3388
Oram, James. 2126, 2861
Orange, Va. St. Thomas' church. 3279
Orchard, Bernard. 224
Orchard, G. H. 152
Orchard, Richard E. 3320
Orchard, Ronald Kenneth. 2554
Orchard, Thomas Nathaniel. 99, 2469
Orchard, William Edwin. 106, 790, 858, 1122, 1342, 1953, 2324, 2783, 2876, 2893, 3062, 3344, 3411, 3481
Orcutt, Franklin B. 2477
Orcutt, William Dana. 1495
Ordal, Zakarias Johannesen. 3221
Order American plowmen. 3239
Order of the amaranth. 3240
Order of the Eastern Star. 2741
Order of the Eastern star. Grand chapter of New York. 2741
Order of the fleur de lis. 1524
Order of the golden seal. 3240
Ordericus Vitalis, 1075-1143? 1178
Ordronaux, John. 1772
Ore, Luis Jeronimo de. 1630
O'Rear, Arthur T. 1831, 2876
O'Reilly, Augustine J. 2351
O'Reilly, Bernard. 2216, 3840
O'Reilly, Elizabeth Boyle. 752
O'Reilly, James D. 663, 2394, 2571
O'Reilly, James P. 3286
O'Reilly, John Boyle. 3201
O'Reilly, John Joseph. 74, 2032
O'Reilly, John Thomas. 2571
O'Reilly, Patrick J. 2026
O'Reilly, Patrick Joseph. 2269, 2394
O'Reilly, Philip. 790, 3012
O'Reilly, Sean. 3390
Orelli, Conrad von. 199
Orendorff, Charles. 1655
Orenstein, Walter. 2081
Orf, Simon J. 1635
Orgain, Alice Lucile (Cartwright) 1034, 1035, 1495, 1496, 2247
Organ, Troy Wilson. 1814, 1815
Organized Bible Class Association. 3560, 3564
[Orgesather, John B]. 3491
O'Rielly, Henry. 53, 2597
Oriental club of Philadelphia. 2743, 3332
Orientius. 2199
Origenes. 594, 878, 1018, 2183, 2743, 2885, 3635
Origo, Iris Margaret (Cutting) 194
O'Riordan, Michael. 819
Orlando, Vittorio Emanuele. 1147
Orleans, France. Bibliotheque municipale. MSS. (Fr. 518) 1938
Orleans, Ilo. 2893
Orleans, Ilo Louis. 2893
Orliac, Jehanne d. 1938
Orlinsky, Harry Meyer. 484, 535, 2096
Orme, William. 179, 2753, 3712, 3761
Ormesson, Wladimir. 2768
Ormond, Alexander Thomas. 2419, 3103
Ormond, Jesse Marvin. 1271, 3255
Ormond, Ron. 91
Ormonde, Paul. 1320
Ormulum. 355
[Orndorff, Frank]. 236
Ornsby, George. 3868
Ornsby, Robert. 1650
O'Rorke, Benjamin Garniss. 2497, 3533
O'Rorke, Lucy Elizabeth (Marshall) 2348
Orosius, Paulus. 3850
O'Rourke, Daniel. 1649
O'Rourke, David K. 775
O'Rourke, Edward W. 1831
O'Rourke, James John. 3051
O'Rourke, Thomas Patrick. 1648
Oroz, Pedro. 1646, 1647
Orozie, Jimenez, Francisco, 1864. 822
Orphanus. 2728
Orpheus. Hymni. 1873
Orr, Charles E[bert]. 1051, 1632
Orr, Charles Ebert. 971, 3095
Orr, Dick. 313, 3888
Orr, Horace E. 944
Orr, J. Edwin. 1740
Orr, James. 3239, 65, 501, 2052, 3225, 3411, 3646, 3655, 3781
Orr, James Edwin. 65, 1182, 1308, 1569, 1824, 3228, 3229, 3230, 3231, 3664

Orr, John. 455
Orr, Robert G. 913
Orr, Robert R. 118, 911
Orr, William Fridell. 3664
Orr, William Mails. 908
Orr, William W. 36, 311
Orrmont, Arthur. 1600, 3326
Orsenigo, Cesare. 739
Orsini, Joseph E. 1001, 1294, 2744, 2815
Orsini, Mathieu. 2356
Orso, Kathryn Wickey. 1609, 2876
Orsy, Ladislas M. 839, 2571, 2812
Ortegon, Samuel M. 2260
Ortenblad, Harald. 2071
Orth, Clement Raymond. 2576
Orth, Mina (Blane) 319
Orthodox-Cistercian Symposium, Oxford University, 1973. 1276, 2583
Orthodox Eastern Church. 1487, 2239, 2240, 2347, 2748, 2749, 2986
Orthodox Eastern church. Liturgy and ritual. 2749
Orthodox Eastern Church. Liturgy and ritual. Apostolos. English. 2748
Orthodox Eastern church. Liturgy and ritual. English. 855, 1487, 2748
Orthodox Eastern Church. Liturgy and ritual. Euchologion. English. 1487, 2745
Orthodox Eastern Church. Liturgy and ritual. Evangelion. English. 2745
Orthodox Eastern Church. Liturgy and ritual. Leitourgikon. 2749
Orthodox Eastern Church. Liturgy and ritual. Leitourgikon. English. 2749
Orthodox Eastern church. Liturgy and ritual.. Leitourgkon. 2749
Orthodox Eastern Church. Liturgy and ritual. Liturgy. English. 2748
Orthodox Eastern Church. : Liturgy and ritual. : Menaion. : English. 2748
Orthodox Eastern church, Russian. 3256
Orthodox Eastern church, Russian. Patriarch. 3256
Orthodox Eastern Church. Synod of Jerusalem, 1672. 1373, 2747
Ortiz, Juan Carlos. 987
Ortlepp, Edmund Ernst. 2032, 2283
Ortlund, Anne. 987, 3835
Ortlund, Raymond C. 1004, 2042
Ortmayer, Roger. 3857
Orton, Azariah Giles. 3076
Orton, Hazel V. 3155
Orton, Job. 18, 3674
Orton, Lawrence D. 1426, 2183
Ory, Joseph Marie. 1541, 3419
Oryu. 3894
Orzell, Laurence. 2742, 2857
Osbeck, Kenneth W. 1872
Osbert. 2218
Osbon, A. M. 509
Osborn, A. C. 2599
Osborn, Albert. 1857
Osborn, Andrew R. 3155, 3308
Osborn, Andrew Rule. 3551, 1062, 3155, 3308
Osborn, Arthur Walter. 1740, 2728, 2990, 3119, 3321
Osborn, Benjamin. 1725, 2419
Osborn, Charles. 1686
Osborn, Charles Virgil. 2050
Osborn, Edwin. 2032
Osborn, Edwin Faxon. 2026
Osborn, Elbert. 2444
Osborn, Eric Francis. 950, 1288, 1616
Osborn, George Edwin. 2238, 3004
Osborn, Henry Fairfield. 699, 1580, 2675
Osborn, Henry Stafford. 480
Osborn, Loran David. 3646
Osborn, Lucy Reed (Drake) 971, 3462
Osborn, Merton b. 1362, 3027
Osborn, Robert T. 1659
Osborn, Ronald E. 933, 941, 1043, 1109, 1122, 1296, 1659, 3745, 3898
Osborn, Sarah (Haggar) 2752
Osborn, Solomon Oliver. 2324
Osborn, Thomas. 56
Osborn, Tommy Lee. 1600
Osborne, Arthur. 3888, 3020
Osborne, Cecil G. 994, 2876
Osborne, Charles Edward. 3674
Osborne, Denis. 3082
Osborne, Dennis. 1814
Osborne, Edward William. 886, 1982
Osborne, Grant R. 640
Osborne, Hubert. 593
Osborne, John H. 1998
Osborne, Josiah. 136
Osborne, Ralph Hills. 640
Osborne, Richard B. 3050
Osborne, Thomas De Courcey. 2564
Osborne, William. 3785
Osborne, William Audley. 1132
Osborne, William Frederick. 3445
Oscarson, R Don. 2618
Oscott, Francesco Luciano. 3473
Osee, Johan. 2357
Osenberg, Hans Dieter. 2394

Osende, Victorino. 1356, 2639
Osgniach, Augustine John, 1891. 1136, 2419
Osgood, Anna Ripley. 3290
Osgood, Charles E. 186
Osgood, Charles Grosvenor. 2469, 2657
Osgood, DeWitt S. 1831
Osgood, Don. 987, 1612, 2752
Osgood, Elliott I. 2510
Osgood, Elliott Irving. 2510, 3403
Osgood, Gilbert C. 1838
Osgood, Phillips Endecott. 1944, 1247, 2221, 3144, 3810
Osgood, Samuel. 607
[Osgood, Samuel]. 507
Osgood, Samuel. 216, 925, 971, 1325
O'Shaughnessy, Mary Michael. 3171
O'Shea, Denis. 2021, 2356, 2762
O'Shea, John Joseph. 2167
O'Shea, Kevin. 1001
O'Shea, William J. 138, 839
Osheim, Duane J. 2270
Osias, Camilo. 2831
Osiek, Carolyn A. 323
Osis, Karlis. 1418, 1696
Osler, William. 1889, 1891
Oslin, S J. 3458, 3459
Osman. 2089
Osman, Betty B. 2204
Osmond, Jonathan. 2920
Osmun, George Wilbur. 115, 934
Osmunson, Robert Lee. 1014, 1435, 1780
Osmunson, Rosemarie. 2374
Osorio, Jeronymo. 790
Oss, John. 2510
Oss, Olga Bertine (Osnes) 2510
Ost, Axel Bo. 206, 1569
Ostby, Ole A. 3510
Ostdiek, Joseph H. 806
Osten, Hans Henning von der. 91
Oster, Henri. 2789
Oster, Kenneth. 1922
Oster, Richard. 329
Ostergaard Christensen, Lavrids 1896. 3312
Osterhammel, August. 971
Osterhaven, M. Eugene. 3646
Osterhaven, Maurice Eugene. 3680
Osterheld, Dudley Oliver. 1630, 3168
Osterwald, Jean Frederic. 2921
Osthathios, Geevarghese. 3445
Ostheimer, Anthony Leo. 790
Ostler, Daniel Eugene. 2718
Ostlin, Melvin T. 3069
Ostling, Richard N. 808, 1658
Ostor, Akos. 1483
Ostow, Mortimer. 2999
Ostrander, Fannie Eliza. 296
Ostrander, Sheila. 2990
Ostrom, Henry. 971, 1017, 1252, 1559, 2082, 2876
Ostrom, Karl A. 1277
Ostroumov, Ivan N. 1622
Ostwald, Wilhelm. 1889
*Ostwalt, Adeline Hill. 3164
O'Sullivan, Jeremiah Francis. 1276
O'Sullivan, Kevin. 314, 366, 576, 864, 1267, 2026
O'Sullivan, Mortimer. 801, 2589
Osuna, Francisco de. 790, 2643, 3603, 2643, 3603
Oswald, Anthony Lewis, 1898. 1858
Oswald, Evan. 688
Oswald, Felix Leopold. 1655
Oswald, Helen K. 2752, 3380
Oswalt, Martin Luther. 2604
Otey, James Hervey. 1289
Otey, William Wesley. 296, 3079
Otheman, Edward. 1942, 2845
Otis, George. 987, 2465, 3745
Otis, Philo Adams. 2913, 1872
O'Toole, Christopher John. 115, 1382
O'Toole, Edward J. 1001
O'Toole, George Barry. 3793
O'Toole, James J. 754
O'Toole, James M. 764
Otsuka, Hisao. 3088, 3800
Ott, Hamilton A. 1549
Ott, Heinrich. 676, 1725, 2904
Ott, Ludwig. 782
Otten, Bernard John. 743, 1051, 1122, 65, 790, 2001, 3265, 3290, 3655
Otten, Herman John. 2563
Ottensen, Carol Clark. 3415
Otterbein, Adam John. 773, 1816
Otterbein, Anna M. 1327
Otterland, Anders. 2815
Otterstad, Robert L. 3541
Ottley, Henry Bickersteth. 2042
Ottley, Robert Lawrence. 501, 2115
Ottman, Ford C. 1725, 1892, 2055
Ottman, Ford Cyrinde. 455, 460, 681, 2415, 3292
Otto, Eberhard. 3599
Otto, Eckart. 1613
Otto, Elinor Sommers. 3278
Otto, Gert. 3679

Otto, Rudolf. 1082, 1970, 2675, 1836, 2175, 2639, 3062, 3067, 3079
Otto, Rudolf [Karl Ludwig Rudolf Otto]. 2643
Otto, Walter Friedrich. 1767, 1459, 1460, 1767
Otto, Walter Gustav Albrecht. 1502
Otts, John Martin Philip. 60, 2708
Otts, John Martin Phillip. 3720
Otwell, John H. 65, 501, 535, 3832
Oudersluys, Richard Cornelius. 629, 3155
Ouellette, Raymond. 1705, 1879
Oughton, Charles Martin. 1035
Oulton, John Ernest Leonard. 106, 1020
Our Lady of Angels Parish, Bronx, New York. 2753
Our Lady of Mount Carmel Church, Bayonne, N.J. Diamond Jubilee Book Committee. 2753
Oursler, Fulton. 535, 1615, 1629, 1970, 2762, 71, 407, 535, 929, 1725, 1970, 1982
Oursler, Grace (Perkins) 1352
Oursler, William Charles. 1062, 1600, 2978, 3062
Oury, Guy Marie. 189
Ouseley, Gideon. 801, 2467
Ouspensky, Leonide. 1880, 3667
Outdoor Writers Association of America. 2135
Outerbridge, Leonard M. 912
Outka, Gene H. 17, 946, 3090
Outlaw, Nell (Warren) 971, 1451, 3840
Outler, Albert Cook. 1041, 1492, 1573, 2428, 2981, 2995, 3664, 3772, 3806
The Outlook. 3119
Overbeck, Julian Joseph. 1225, 2749
Overbey, Edward H. 152
Overbury, Arthur Evill. 474, 1035, 1495
Overbury, Emily Ethel. 3336
Overby, Coleman. 640, 648
Overduin, Jacobus. 2130
*Overholser, Grace McSpadden. 1725
Overholser, James A. 1062
Overholt, William A. 3759
Overland monthly. 2506
Overman, Neal. 1047
Overman, Ralph T. 3082
Overman, Richard H. 1581, 3813
Overmyer, Daniel L. 709
Overstreet, Edward. 2182
Overstreet, Philip P. 971
Overstreet, Phillip P. 1359
Overton, James H. 2436
Overton, John Henry. 1759, 3804
Overton, William Morton. 1451
Owen, A. L. 1480
Owen, A R G. 1710
[Owen, Adeline W]. 2753
Owen, Aloysius J. 2268, 3222
Owen, Bob. 1574, 3664
Owen, David Cymmer. 3110
Owen, Derwyn Randolph Grier. 2324, 3079
Owen, Edward Charles Everard. 2351
Owen, Epenetus. 3132
Owen, Fred Colley. 3278
Owen, George Dickson. 1342, 1347
Owen, George Frederick. 208, 587, 1944, 2764
Owen, George Vale. 3510
Owen, Huw Parri. 1424, 1739, 2374, 3609
Owen, James J. 3510
Owen, Jesse Coleman. 1569
Owen, John. 403, 656, 1633, 1835, 2160, 3030
Owen, John Wilson. 3677
Owen, Joseph Parkes. 2425
Owen, Olin Marvin. 2231
Owen, Ralph Albert Dornfeld. 713, 3119
Owen, Robert Dale. 3510
Owen, Theresa D. 3510
Owen, Thomas Newton. 391
Owen, Trevor A. 2908
Owen, W O. 1751
Owen, William Thomas. 3817
Owens, Claire Myers. 2753, 2999, 3894
Owens, Fern Royer. 2500, 3846
Owens, Gene. 3062
Owens, Harvey W. 1626, 1772
Owens, James Garfield. 2680
Owens, Jimmy. 987
Owens, John Joseph. 517, 527, 1797
Owens, Joseph. 1738, 2419, 2739, 3694, 3695
Owens, Joseph Don. 1388
Owens, Laurella. 2533
[Owens, Lilliana. 2163
Owens, Lilliana. 3417
Owens, Loulie (Latimer) 152, 169, 1787, 3675
Owens, Mary Frances. 585
Owens, Owen D. 2956
Owens, Virginia Stem. 2369, 2394, 2753
Owensboro, Ky. St. Stephen's cathedral. 844, 2774
Owensby, Idus V. 1199

Ownbey, Richard L. 1051, 1569, 3529
Owst, Gerald Robert. 2908, 2909
Oxenden, Ashton. 1329, 971, 2893, 3201
Oxenham, John. 1725, 2262, 2893, 3778, 2262
Oxenhandler, Bernard. 3822
Oxford (Diocese) Bishop, 1845-1869 (Samuel Wilberforce) 3783
Oxford Institute on Methodist Theological Studies, 1962. 1126
Oxford Institute on Methodist Theological Studies. 2d, 1962. 1126
Oxford Institute on Methodist Theological Studies. 3d, 1965. 2050
Oxford Institute on Methodist Theological Studies, 6th, 1977. 3300, 3806
Oxford Institute on Methodist Theological Studies, 5th, 1973. 1833
Oxford society of historical theology. 76
Oxford. University. Bodleian Library. 841
Oxford. University. Socratic Club. 3103
Oxfort, Ursula. 790, 2124
Oxley, J[ames] MacDonald. 3201
Oxley, James Edwin. 3039
Oxnam, Garfield Bromley. 1041, 1062, 1071, 1096, 1131, 2003, 2436, 2904, 3445, 668, 2755, 2904
Oxtoby, Frederic Breading. 640, 597
Oxtoby, Gurdon C. 607, 651
Oyabe, Jenichiro. 3132
Oyer, John Stanley. 37
Ozanam, [Antoine] Frederic. 1402, 1647
Ozanne, C. G. 219
Ozment, Robert Varnell. 971, 1007, 1352
Ozment, Steven E. 1186, 1468, 3037, 3040

P

Paavali, 1914. 2746, 3493
Pable, Martin W. 3785
Pacaut, Marcel. 756
Pace, Charles Nelson. 1101, 3030, 3095
Pace, Charles Robert. 1164
Pace, Dale K. 1255
Pace, Geneva C. 2227
Pache, Boris N. 2756
Pache, Rene. 305, 1492, 1696, 1831, 3320
Pacheco, Elizabeth Condell. 2307
Pachow, W. 709
Pachter, Henry Maximilian. 2772
Pacific coast Congregational alliance for the promotion of education. 1335
Pacific synod of the Evangelical Lutheran church. 3733
Pacific Synod of the United Lutheran Church in America. 3733
Pack, Alice C. 2599
Pack, Frank. 2908
Packard, A. Appleton. 2973
Packard, Dennis J. 640, 2600
[Packard, Frederick Adolphus] 1794-1867. 245
Packard, Joseph. 2756
Packard, Theophilus. 1651
Packer, Athol B. 3216
Packer, Boyd K. 1232, 2344, 3600
Packer collegiate institute, Brooklyn. 2591
Packer, J. A. 143
Packer, J. I. 1554
Packer, James Innall. 1725
Packer, James Innell. 277, 305, 1569, 1690, 3225
Packer, James S. 1178
Packham, E. Richard. 1009
Packull, Werner O. 37
*Paddock, C.L. 1015
Paddock, Charles Lee. 623, 662, 898, 1015, 1451, 2394, 3383
Paddock, Zachariah. 2756
Padelford, Frank William. 156, 2483
Paden, John N. 1923
Padgett, Chester John. 648
Padgett, James E. 3510
Padgett, Leon Vincent. 726
Padgett, Nora. 952
Padmacher. 1122
Padovano, Anthony T. 972, 1001, 1382, 2030, 2235, 3212, 3294
Padwick, Constance E. 2349
Padwick, Constance Evelyn. 653, 2306
*Paetkau, Walter. 3377
Paffarath, Tharasicius. 515
Paffrath, Tharsicius. 515
Pagal Baba. 1896
Paganski, Donald J. 2394
Page, Alexander Leak. 455
Page, Carole Gift. 932, 1321
Page, Charles Grafton. 3510
Page, Charles Nash. 319
Page, Harry Robert. 1168
Page, Henry P. 224

Page, Herman. 1329, 2893
Page, Howard L. 2990
Page, Isaac E. 1751
Page, Isaac Marshall. 193, 2318
Page, James Rathwell. 1214
Page, Jesse. 1389, 2157, 2487
Page, John C. 470
Page, Joseph R. 3242
Page, Kirby. 2757, 3793, 972, 1052, 1441, 1456, 1995, 2065, 3433, 3445, 3793, 2757, 3623
Page, Robert Jeffress. 3618
Page, Roch. 1459
Page, Thomas Frederick. 722
Pagel, Paul Homer. 2145
Pagels, Elaine H. 372, 421, 1718, 1804
Pagel. Walter. 2772
Paget, Elma Katie (Hoare) 2758
[Paget, Fannie Ruthven]. 3510
Paget, Francis. 1214, 1844
Paget, Henry Luke. 2807
Paget, Stephen. 1035
Paiasogli, Giorgio. 2269
Paige, Clara R. 2848, 3811
Paige, Lucius Robinson. 384
Paine, Albert Bigelow. 1938
Paine, Albert Ware. 2990
Paine, Gustavus Swift. 272
Paine, Howard. 2893
Paine, Lauran. 1802, 3824, 3825
Paine, Levi Leonard. 3711, 3712
Paine, Mabel Hyde. 128
Paine, Martyn,, 1794-1877. 203
Paine, Robert. 2308
Paine, Silas H. 1872
Paine, Stephen William. 449
Paine, Thomas. 2758, 589, 2758, 2759, 3023, 3024, 3024, 3023
Paine, Timothy Otis. 1944, 2711
Painter, Franklin Verzelius Newton. 596, 3035, 2276, 3035
Painter, George Stephen. 2067
Painter, J. H. 1463
Painter, John. 423
Painter, Muriel Thayer. 2778, 3862
Painting, Norman. 54, 3281
Pakenham, Elizabeth (Harman) Pakenham. 760
Pakenham-Walsh, Herbert. 1194
Pakkala, Lorraine. 1363, 1658
Pal, Pratapaditya. 87, 693
Palachovsky, V. 3413
Palanque, Jean Remy. 1194
Palau, Gabriel. 2375
Palau, Luis. 987, 2825, 554, 987, 1406, 1575, 2760
Paleario, Aonio. 108
Palermo, Louie. 1749, 2760
Palestine. 2765
Palestine Pilgrims' Text Society, London. 1022
Palestrina, Giovanni Pierluigi. 2371, 2765
Paley, Alan L. 1331, 2832
Paley, William. 59, 373, 1099, 1217, 1227, 2673, 2674, 2766, 3366
Palfrey, John Gorham. 2673, 3596, 3726
Palladino, Lawrence Benedict. 822, 2356, 2362
Palladius. 935, 1115, 2579
Pallascio-Morin, Ernest. 1970
Pallen, Conde Benoist. 806
Pallenberg, Corrado. 808, 2805
Palliere, Aime. 2115
Pallis, Alexander. 421, 430, 436
Pallis, Marco. 709
Pallis, Svend Aage Frederik Dichmann. 2327
Palliser, Palliser & co. 3333
Pallotti, Vincenzo. 777, 2766, 3632
Palm Beach, Fla. Church of Bethesda-by-the-Sea. 1178
Palm, Edith Cling. 3207
Palm, Franklin Charles. 727, 730, 1639, 2586
Palma, Anthony D. 92, 1394, 1831
Palmer. 420
Palmer, A C. 1696
Palmer, Abram Smythe. 3297, 3546
Palmer, Agnes Lizzie (Page) 681, 3290, 3292
Palmer, Albert Gallatin. 2714
Palmer, Albert P. 3801
Palmer, Albert Wentworth. 1725, 2238, 3004, 3344, 3664, 3674
Palmer, Alma Kennedy. 2695
Palmer, Benjamin Morgan. 1606, 3698, 3712
Palmer, Bennett William. 1422
Palmer, Bernard Alvin. 192, 877, 928, 1171, 1385, 2815, 3031, 3704
Palmer, Bertha Rachael. 3598
Palmer, Blanche. 2847
Palmer, Bryon. 3610
Palmer, Byron. 1099
Palmer, C S. 2557
Palmer, Charles E. 1257
Palmer, Clara. 3751

Palmer, Clive W. 1663
Palmer, Donald C. 2814
Palmer, E H. 1738, 3062
Palmer, Earl F. 349, 469, 2266
Palmer, Edward Henry. 282, 2089
Palmer, Edwin H. 730, 1513, 1831
Palmer, Edwin James. 1181
Palmer, Edwin Reuben. 2937
Palmer, Elihu. 1420
Palmer, Everett W. 972, 1007, 2436
Palmer, Florence Ursula. 3556
Palmer, Francis Bolles. 2247, 3567
Palmer, Frank Nelson. 311, 391, 523, 640
Palmer, Frederic. 1889, 1183, 3781
Palmer, Frederick William. 1352
Palmer, Geoffrey. 247, 1411
Palmer, George Herbert. 28, 1540
Palmer, Gordon. 166, 1062, 2238
Palmer, Gretta. 816
Palmer, Henrietta (Lee) 208
Palmer, Horatio Richmond and McCabe, Charles C. and Brouse, M. R. 1861
Palmer, Humphrey. 391, 1725
Palmer, Jim. 1458, 2504
Palmer, Kenyon Alexander. 1711
Palmer, Lala (Caldwell) 3155
Palmer, Larry. 1470
Palmer, Lee A. 2938
Palmer, Leon Carlos. 1569, 3155, 3556, 3879
Palmer, Lloyd. 2065
Palmer, Lois Sedgwick. 3556
Palmer, Louis De Forest. 2432
Palmer, Louis Philander. 2834
Palmer, Margaretta. 2700, 2971
Palmer, Mary. 3095
Palmer, O. R. 3411
Palmer, Pamela. 1167, 2128
Palmer, Parker J. 1154, 3445, 3484
Palmer, Paul F. 2360, 3265, 3266
Palmer, Peter. 629
Palmer, Philip Mason. 1619
Palmer, Phoebe (Worrell) 1594, 1763, 1823, 3295, 3300, 3837
[Palmer, R. A.]. 102
Palmer, Ray. 60, 1861, 3207
Palmer, Robert E. 413, 1316, 2933
Palmer, Robert E. A. 3246
Palmer, Robert Roswell. 872, 3212
Palmer, Russell. 2126, 2806, 2863
Palmer, Samuel. 1606
[Palmer, Simeon]. 1428
Palmer, Spencer J. 1233, 2502
Palmer, Tobias. 42
Palmer, W. Robert. 118, 236, 644, 933
Palmer, Walter Clark. 1783
Palmer, William. 801, 1178
Palmquist, Al. 1255, 2463
Palms, Roger C. 1078, 1741, 2072, 2394
Palmstierna, Erik Kule. 3510
Paltsits, Victor Hugo. 1949
[Palumbo, Anthony] 1879. 2834, 3462
Pan African Conference of Third World Theologians, Accra, 1977. 3653

Pan-Anglican congress, London, 1908. 45
Pana Creation, inc. 526, 1382, 1725
Panagopoulos, Beata Maria. 2569
Panama railroad company. 719
Pancaratra. Naradapancaratra. Jnanamrtasarasamhita. English. 1815
Panchatantra. English. 1897
Pancoast, Blanche Winifred. 1451
Pancoast, Chalmers Lowell. 1665, 3598
Pandey, Dhanpati. 89, 2671
Pandit, Madhav Pundalik. 197, 1812, 3760
Pandita, Indiradevi. 3865
Panel of Scholars. 1461
P'ang, Yun. 3893
Pangborn, Joseph Gladding. 1814
Panichas, George Andrew. 3071
Panikkar, Raimundo. 1082
Panikkar, Raymond. 2649, 3123, 3712, 3854
Panizon, Leo A. Hope. 763
Pank, Oskar. 2215
Pankey, William Russell. 159, 892, 2767, 3286
Pankhurst, Christabel. 607, 3320
Panko, Stephen M. 699
Pannabecker, S F. 1705
Pannabecker, Samuel Floyd. 1705
Panneel, Henry. 2006
Pannell, William E. 1133
Pannenberg, Wolfhart. 74, 946, 1126, 2042, 2175, 2321, 3227, 3616, 3623, 3652
Panneton, Georges. 1794
Pannullo-Parnofiello, Louise. 2359
Panoch, James V. 3096
Panos, Chris. 1576, 2767
Pantin, William Abel. 1516, 1762
Panton, David Morrison. 607
Panunzi, Paul. 3607
*Panzarella, Andrew. 972, 2999, 3161

Panzer, Henry. 2844
Paoli, Arturo. 430, 1659
Paolini, Shirley J. 1402, 3413
Paolo della Croce, 1694-1775. 2767
Paone, Anthony J. 1985, 3132, 3489
Papa, Mary Bader. 3392
Papademetriou, George C. 2760
Papadopoullos, Theodore H. 2746
Papadopoulos, Gerasimos. 2746
Papageorgiou, Athanasios. 1881
Papasogli, Giorgio. 2269, 3603
Papay, Joseph L. 2835
Pape, Dorothy. 1959, 3832
Pape, William H. 338, 493
Papi, Hector. 2577
Papini, Giovanni. 115, 1428, 1725, 1970
Pappenheim, Eugene. 1168
Pappenheim, Shlomo. 2345
Paquier, Richard. 3854
Paracelsus, 1493-1541. 2728, 2772, 2947
Paradis, Adrian A. 1432
Paradis, Grace D. 3880
Paradise, Frank Ilsley. 1077
Paradise, Scott I. 1131, 1426
Paralipomena Jeremiae. English and Greek. 299
Paramananda. 3330
Paramananda, swami. 2772, 2380, 3408
Paramanandas, swami. 3054
Paramanda, swami. 1953
Parampanthi, Puragra. 2380
Paramus, N. J. Reformed Dutch church. 2772
Paranjali. 3865
Parapsychological Association. 2990
Paraskevas, John E. 2747
Parbury, Kathleen. 1026, 2230
Parchment, Samuel Richard. 1671, 2728, 3251
Pardee, Charles Laban. 1317
Pardee, Richard Gay. 3556
Pardee, William H. 137
Pardi, Marco M. 1414
Pardington, G P. 3344
Pardington, George Palmer. 918, 934, 918, 1451
Pardow, William O'Brien. 796, 2773
Pardue, Austin. 972, 1318, 1594, 2209, 2247, 2876
Pardue, Austin [Henry Austin Pardue]. 2253
Pardue, Peter A. 705
Pare, George. 816
Paredi, Angelo. 29
Parente, Pascal P. 42, 90, 179, 2849, 3204, 3475, 3489
Parente, Paschale P. 90, 2643
Parenty, Francois Joseph. 41, 3761
Paret, Barbara. 1441
Paret, William. 3556, 2958, 3556
Paris, Arthur E. 16, 2626
Paris, Charles W. 796
Paris. Saint-Severin (Church) Clergy. 2234, 2367, 2812
Parish, Arlyn John. 2407
Parish, Elijah. 282
Parish, Helen Rand. 1776
Parish, Karl E. 2394
Parish, Samuel Louis. 2436
Parish visitors of Mary immaculate. 1792
Park, Charles Edwards. 1441, 1995, 2893, 3177, 3726
Park, David. 2494
Park, Edwards Amasa. 40, 106, 1511, 1692, 1867, 3533, 3536, 3846
Park, John Edgar. 3336, 2771, 2904
Park, O'Hyun. 91
Park, Olga. 3201
Park, S E. 3473, 3474
Park, Willard Z. 3400
Park, Willard Zerbe. 1903
Park, William. 1035
Park, William Edgar. 3758
Parkany, Betty. 3119
Parke, David B. 3728
Parke, Francis Neal. 3827
Parke, Herbert William. 3895
Parke, Jean. 1953, 3132
Parker, Alice Stuart. 1860
Parker, Alvin P. 2510
Parker, Andrew McClean. 3566
Parker, Caroline Mason (Burditt) 496
Parker, Charles Franklin. 1441
Parker, Clara Hathaway (Stetson) 629
Parker, Clara Hathaway (Stetson) H. C. Parker. 630
Parker, Clyde Norwood. 1559
Parker, D. Coffey. 1609
Parker, De Witt Henry. 2419
Parker, Derek. 2653
Parker, DeWitt Henry. 1585
Parker, Donald Dean. 2775, 2937, 3464
Parker, Edward Harper. 913
Parker, Elsie G (Hill) 455, 1600, 3320
Parker, Eric. 303, 1352
Parker, Evelyn Mildred. 331
Parker, Everett C. 3161, 3594

Parker, Fitzgerald Sale. 3481, 3854
Parker, Francis H. 1597
Parker, Francis J. 1157
Parker, Francis Marion. 3119
Parker, Franklin Ellsworth. 3462
Parker, Franklin Nutting. 2421
Parker, Gary. 202, 1382
Parker, Geoffrey Henry William. 1186
Parker, George. 1878
Parker, Henry Allen. 166
Parker, Hiram. 183
Parker, Ida R. 8
Parker, Inez Moore. 3190, 3736
[Parker, Isabella Grahame. 1942
Parker, J. R. 1594
Parker, Jane(Marsh) 1111, 1953, 2800
Parker, Joel. 3753
Parker, John. 3290
Parker, John William. 3676
Parker, Johns Dempster. 3547
Parker, Joseph. 331, 364, 371, 615, 1333, 2001, 3329, 3374
Parker, Joseph F. 3317
Parker, Kenneth Lawrence. 3732
Parker, Larry. 2775, 3711
Parker, LoRetta C. 733
Parker, Martha Ellen. 96
Parker, Matthew. 2775, 2776
Parker, Orson. 1569
Parker, Paul E. 3407
Parker, Percy G. 2938
Parker, Pierson. 391, 476
Parker, Rebecca J. Arthur Parker." 1110, 3546
Parker, Rebecca Jane. 1110
Parker-Rhodes, Arthur Frederick Parker, 1914. 3491
Parker, Robert Allerton. 131, 2682
Parker, Robert P. 333
Parker, Sarah W. 2711
Parker society, London. 3039
Parker, T F. 1913
Parker, Theodore. 684, 2776, 2893, 3062, 3132, 3344, 3356, 3412, 3434, 3609, 3708, 3723, 3724, 3726, 3728, 3729
Parker, Thomas Henry Louis. 351, 727, 728, 729, 3039
Parker, Thomas Maynard. 1144, 3039
Parker, Thomas Valentine. 65, 2956
Parker, Thomas William. 3598
Parker, William R. 2324, 2876, 2887, 2999
Parker, William Robert. 661
Parkes, Henry Bamford. 1499, 1280, 1345, 1499
Parkes, James William. 1083, 2078
[Parkes, James William] 1896. 1062, 1073, 1083, 1725, 2078, 2089, 2153, 3103, 3119
Parkhurst, Charles Henry. 1041, 2265, 2934, 3674
Parkhurst, Genevieve (Cummins) 1600
Parkhurst, Helen Huss. 1282
Parkhurst, Lucia A. 2529, 3458
Parkin, William. 2012
Parkinson, Merta Mary. 2695
Parkinson, William. 3820
Parkman, Charles McDonogh. 2058
[Parkman, Francis] 1788-1852. 1352
Parkman, Francis. 1948
Parks, Edna. 1872
Parks, Edna D. 1873
Parks, Ella M. 972, 2353
Parks, Isabella Webb. 2134
Parks, J. A. 916
Parks, Joseph Howard. 2858
Parks, Leighton. 1122, 2561, 3132
Parks, M. 284
Parks, Mercer H. 3119
Parks, Robert Keith. 2502
Parks, Thomas David. 1308
Parks, William J. 2800
Parlane, W[illiam] A[lexander]. 3717
Parmele, Mary (Platt) 1035
Parmelee, Alice. 311, 384, 410, 480, 535, 540, 1016, 1178, 2089, 3264
Parmelee, J H. 3647
Parmer, William Tellis. 1664, 1671
Parmiter, Geoffrey de Clinton. 1405
Parmiter, Geoffrey Vincent de Clinton. 1405
Parmon, Kon. 3201
Parot, Joseph John. 813, 2857
Parr, Adolph Henry. 3880
Parr, Lucy. 1231, 2617, 2618
Parr, Margaret S Linn. 3207
Parr, Margaret Sands (Linn) 1052
Parr, Robert H. 2394
Parr, Samuel. 2420
Parr, Susan Resneck. 1624
Parrick, Jerry. 2477, 3801
Parrinder, Edward Geoffrey. 12, 13, 1082, 1395, 1879, 1894, 2013, 2014, 2185, 2643, 3119, 3138, 3242, 3267, 3824
Parrinder, Geoffrey. 197, 1880, 3142
Parris, George Keith. 501
Parris, Percy Elizabeth. 3858

Parrish, Edward. 1683
Parrish, Fred Louis. 3094, 3138
Parrish, George R. 1332
Parrish, Herbert. 3062, 3132, 3745
Parrish, Mary Pratt. 2599
Parrish, Mary Virginia. 987
Parrot, Andre. 4, 122, 395, 1421, 1944, 2762
Parrott, Bob W. 2893, 3069
*Parrott, Leslie. 972
Parrott, Leslie. 972, 1249
Parrott, Lora Lee. 2399
Parrott, Lora Lee (Montgomery) 1303, 3857
Parry, Charles Hubert Hastings. 2777
Parry, David J. 2394
Parry, Edwin Francis. 2605, 3429
Parry, Edwin Satterthwaite. 1287
Parry, Gordon. 1626
Parry, John Burford. 1352
Parsch, Pius. 842, 1264, 2367, 2020, 2367
Parshall, Nelson C. 1581
Parshall, Phil. 2557
Parson, W[illiam] Edward. 174
Parson, William Edwin. 174
[Parsons, Benjamin]. 3713
Parsons, Charles H. 1451
Parsons, Donald J. 2257, 2969
Parsons, E. Spencer. 3829
Parsons, Edward Lambe. 1071, 2033, 2958
Parsons, Edward Smith. 3445
Parsons, Ellen C. 11
[Parsons, Elsie Worthington (Clews) 889
Parsons, Elsie Worthington (Clews) 3005
Parsons, Elsie Worthington Clews. 3838
Parsons, Ernest William. 429, 476
Parsons, Francis B. 2526, 3470
Parsons, Howard L. 1108
Parsons, James B. 3261
[Parsons, James C]. 253
Parsons, John. 2206, 2453
Parsons, John Usher. 303
Parsons, John W. 2876
[Parsons, Julia (Warth) 3132
[Parsons, Levi]. 2920
Parsons, Martin. 1823
Parsons, Reuben. 662, 864, 1178
Parsons, Robert. 790, 816, 872, 1934, 2820
Parsons, Talcott. 3086
Parsons, Theophilus. 2042, 2689, 2691, 3570
Parsons, Thomas William. 1026, 3248
Parsons, Wilfrid. 32, 764, 1147, 1148, 1151
Parsons, William Edward. 81, 908
Parsons, [William Franklin]. 719
Partee, Charles. 728, 2835
Partin, Earl. 987
Partlow, Thomas E. 3545, 3818
Partridge, Edmund B. 3182
Partridge, Eric. 245
Partridge, John A. 3675
Partridge, Mark N. 1377
Parvey, Constance F. 2211
Parvillez, Alphonse de. 1352
Parvin, Robert J. 386
Parvis, Merrill Mead. 315
Parzen, Herbert. 1348
Pascal, Blaise. 58, 791, 1945, 2777, 2778
Pascal, Pierre. 3257
Pascal, Roy. 2276, 3040
Pascal Blaise. 58
Pascalis-Ouviere, Felix. 717
Paschal, George H. 3736
Paschal, George Washington. 158
[Paschall, Ann S.]. 1675
Paschall, Henry Franklin. 148, 224
Paschasius of Our Lady of Mount Carmel, 1867. 2136
Paschasius Radbertus, d. ca. 860. 6
Paschetto, Lodovico. 2533
Pash, Joseph J. 1311
Pasma, Henry K. 216, 3434
Passantino, Robert. 1394
Passebois, Louis Ferdinand. 1852
[Passelecq, Paul]. 650
Passero, Louise. 2376
Passionists. Province of St. Paul of the Cross. Research and Planning Project. 2778
Past, Mary Elizabeth. 3858
Pastanjali. 3867
Pastor, Ludwig. 2862
Pastor, Ludwig, freiherr von, [Full name: Ludwig Friedrich August, freiherr von Pastor von Camperfelden]. 2769
Pastor Nicoli. 2821
Pastorak, John B. 864, 2178
Pastoral psychology. 2995, 3389
Pastorelli, France. 3541
Pastrovicchi, Angelo. 1717
Pat, Emanuel. 2098
Patai, Jozsef. 1809

Patai, Raphael. 1603, 2414, 2624, 2649, 2664, 3389
Patanjali. 3865, 3867
Patch, George H. 607
Patch, Howard Rollin. 1634
Patch, Robert C. 626
Pate, Don. 3682
Paternoster, Michael. 1853
Paterson, Alexander Smith. 3809
Paterson, F. William. 763, 2978
Paterson, John. 550, 570, 578, 600
Paterson, John H. 2050
Paterson, John Harris. 1970
Paterson, Moira. 2143
Paterson, W. P. 3103
Paterson, William Paterson. 118, 2876
Patey, Edward Henry. 991
Pathfinders of America. 2591
Pathway Press. 1096
Patience (Middle English poem) 553
Patimokkha. English. 2577, 3303
Patmont, Louis Richard. 1514
[Patmore, Conventry Kersey Dighton]. 42, 3201
Patmore, Coventry Kersey Dighton. 1594, 3201
Paton, Alan. 1287, 2394, 2887
Paton, David MacDonald. 1043
Paton, Frank Hume Lyall. 2542
Paton, Herbert James. 2163, 3103
Paton, James. 2733, 2792
Paton, John Gibson. 2542, 3132, 3133
Paton, Lewis Bayles. 2115, 513, 3510
Paton, William. 91, 1122, 1481
Patrice, Margaret. 2006
Patricia Jean. 2867
Patrick, 373?-463? 2793
Patrick, Dale. 550, 599, 1731
Patrick, Johnstone G. 2033
Patrick, M. A. 1352
Patrick, Millar. 1875
Patrick, Richard. 2661
Patrick, Sam. 898
Patrick, Simon. 224, 2463
Patrick, Ted. 2793, 3324
Patrick, Walter S. 137
Patrides, C. A. 731, 1101, 2472
Patridge, L. C. 2167
Patrinacos, Nicon D. 2746
Patsch, Joseph. 2358
Patt, Richard W. 916
Patte, Daniel. 56, 287, 349, 505, 3536
Pattee, Fred Lewis. 3155
Pattee, Richard. 825, 2955
Patten, Arthur Bardwell. 1725
Patten, Bebe. 3356
Patten, Donald Wesley. 1421
Patten, Helen (Philbrook) 1889, 1890
Patten, James Alexander. 1294
Patten, Marjorie. 1275
Patten, Priscilla. 2092, 2150
Patten, Simon Nelson. 3445
Patten, William. 1089, 1847, 2759
Patterson, Alexander. 566, 644, 1953
Patterson, Alexander G. 1731
Patterson, Archibald Williams. 140
Patterson, Betsy. 972
Patterson, Bob E. 1244, 2709
Patterson, Charles Brodie. 2320
*Patterson, Charles H. 408
Patterson, Charles Henry. 474, 540, 601
Patterson, Daniel Watkins. 3398
Patterson, David. 2838
Patterson, Dot. 1621
Patterson, F G. 307
Patterson, Frank Willard. 2507
Patterson, George. 2129, 2542
Patterson, George Neilson. 1090, 2555
Patterson, Harriet-Louise Holland. 201, 211, 282
[Patterson, James Herbert]. 3142
Patterson, John Wellington. 2537
Patterson, L. D. 2455
Patterson, Leonard. 2560
Patterson, LeRoy. 3888
Patterson, Lillie. 1111, 1486, 2173
Patterson, Lloyd George. 1820
Patterson, Melville Watson. 1221
Patterson, Paige. 325, 447, 479
Patterson, Rachel Elizabeth. 3459
Patterson, Robert. 1581, 60
Patterson, Robert Leet. 882, 1732, 1819, 3103, 3104, 3107, 3697
Patterson, Robert Mayne. 42, 1506
Patterson, Roberta Turner. 170, 1911
Patterson, Samuel White. 2700
Patterson, Sherwood Hofele. 3018
Patterson, Virginia. 2794, 3843
Patterson, W. Morgan. 152, 3356
Patterson, Ward. 493, 944, 3876
Patterson, Webster T. 2191, 2704
Patterson, William Archie. 1229
Patthana. 708
Pattison, Anthony. 2361
Pattison, E. Mansell. 2786
Pattison, Robert Bainbridge. 3702
Pattison, Robert Everett. 364

Pattison, Samuel Rowles. 203
Pattison, Thomas Harwood. 2904, 2909, 3004, 3344, 3556, 3674
Patton, Carl Safford. 299, 908, 3062, 3370, 391, 2904, 3578
Patton, Cornelius Howard. 2521, 2794, 3439, 2498, 2554, 2876
Patton, Francis Landey. 3609, 1052, 1821, 2920, 3572
Patton, Jacob Harris. 2916, 2924
Patton, John Danie] and others. 3072
Patton, John Daniel. 1861
[Patton, John M]. 1699
Patton, Kenneth Leo. 2639, 3142, 3857
Patton, Leslie Karr. 1128, 1164
Patton, Walter Melville. 523
*Patton, Walter S. 3462
Patton, William. 216, 1970, 3597
Patton, William Weston. 2876
Pauck, Wilhelm. 176, 1786, 2977, 3611, 3617, 3700
Paul. 1891, 2304, 3256, 3611
Paul, Austin. 2513
Paul, Brother. 1891
Paul Carus Memorial Symposium
Peru, Ill.,   1957. 3123

Paul, Cecil R. 1289
Paul, Charles T. 2551
Paul, Harry W. 1145, 3085
Paul, James Albert. 2973
Paul, James Francis. 1044

Paul, John. 80
Paul, John Haywood. 1890, 3484, 3591
Paul, Leslie Allen. 1105, 1221, 1970, 3212
Paul, Louis. 296
Paul, Marie De La Croix. 3484
Paul Marie de la Croix, Father. 424, 3484
Paul, Raymond James. 868
Paul, Robert S. 108, 1062, 1122, 1296, 1387, 1764
Paul, Ronald C. 1576, 1755
*Paul, Saint. 2803
Paul, Shalom M. 208
Paul, William E. 1280
Pauli, Hertha Ernestine. 1310, 2023, 2707, 3284, 3460
Paulicians. Liturgy and ritual. 2805
Paulin, Eugene. 2334
Pauline. 3307
Paulinus. 2218, 3285
Paulinus Mediolanensis. 29
Paulk, Earl P. 1229, 2814
Paulsell, William O. 3491
Paulsen, Dorothy E. 1003
Paulsen, Irwin G. 1168
Paulsen, Irwin Guy. 3858
Paulsen, Jan. 1831
Paulsen, Norman. 2805
*Paulson, Donna. 1725, 2287, 2292, 3164, 3556
Paulson, Eric Edwin. 3633
Paulson, Hank. 612, 1576, 2805
Paulson, Ivar. 1533
Paulson, J. Sig. 460, 1016, 2265, 3750
*Paulson, John F. 2771, 2772
Paulson, Stephen M. 3344
Paulus. 3778
[Paulus, Diaconus Emeriteris]. 2412
Paulus, Nicholaus. 1905
Paulus VI. 760, 1919, 2866, 760, 761, 1001, 1126, 1296, 2042, 2877, 1114, 2866
Paulus VI, 1897. 1833
Paupert, Jean Marie. 391, 1087, 2065
Pauw, Berthold Adolf. 1110, 3719
Pauwels, Louis. 2728
[Pauze, Joseph Alfred]. 839
Pavitt, William Thomas. 3582
Pavlos, Andrew J. 1393
Pavry, Jal Dastur Cursetji. 3898
Pawelzik, Fritz. 2893
Pawley, Bernard C. 1041, 1225, 3770, 3772
Pawlikowski, John. 351, 859, 864, 2153, 2912
Pawson, David. 1906
Pawson, Geoffrey Philip Henry. 731
Pax, Wolfgang E. 1970, 2764
Paxman, Monroe J. 1609
Paxson, Ruth. 364, 972, 3295
Paxton, Geoffrey J. 3381
Paxton, William Edward. 154
Paxton, William Miller. 1808
Paye, Anne. 3418
Payler, Esther (Miller) 2491
Payne, Alex Wesley. 3276
Payne, Charles Edward. 1775
Payne, Charles S. 1052
Payne, D. F. 527
Payne, Daniel Alexander. 14, 2436, 3356
Payne, David Wells. 1636
Payne, Denis. 3088
Payne, Dorothy. 3415
Payne, Ernest Alexander. 3286, 3400

Payne, Harriet Chaffey. 1371, 2227
Payne, John. 1820
Payne, John Barton. 599, 607, 2705, 3320, 1526, 3266
Payne, John Orlebar. 816, 2244
Payne, Leanne. 1835, 1844, 2219
Payne, Marvin. 2394
Payne, O E. 2633
Payne, Philip Francis. 2558
*Payne, Phoebe D. 1283
Payne, Pierre Stephen Robert. 926, 1194, 1617, 2564, 3312
Payne Smith, Robert. 2415
Paynter, Henry Martyn. 1970, 2030, 2052, 2254
Paynter, Richard Henry. 3706
Payson, Anne Byrd. 972, 1359
Payson, Edward. 1342
Payson, George Hubbard. 3019
Payson, George Shipman. 951
Payson, Seth. 1883
Payton, Everett J. 932, 2806
Payton, Jacob Simpson. 2432
Paz, Nestor. 1777, 2806
Paz, Octavio. 3388
Pazhayatil, Harshajan. 2782
Pazzi, Piero. 1240
Peabody, Andrew Preston. 205, 908, 1352, 1354, 2673, 3562, 3724, 3725, 3726
Peabody, David. 4
[Peabody, Elizabeth Palmer]. 23, 882, 2591
Peabody, Emily Clough. 3840
Peabody, Francis Greenwood. 972, 2893, 3062, 3347, 3758, 926, 944, 972, 2065, 2800, 3445, 3706, 3758
Peabody, Frederick William. 1035, 1495
Peabody, Helen. 733
Peabody, Larry D. 1015
Peabody, Lucy (McGill) Waterbury. 895, 2491
[Peabody, Robert Swain]. 2806
Peabody, William Bourn Oliver. 2806
Peace, Richard. 1016, 2263, 3829
Peach, John Vincent. 1371
Peacher, William G. 1671
Peachey, Laban. 3176
Peachey, Paul. 1066, 1278
Peacock, James L. 1925, 2629
Peacock, John. 972
Peacocke, Arthur Robert. 1382, 3082
Peake, Arthur Samuel. 224, 290, 501
Peake, Harold John Edward. 1421
Peale, Norman Vincent. 972, 623, 972, 987, 1325, 1326, 1352, 1970, 2021, 2762, 2788, 2808, 2809, 2994, 2995, 3539
Peale, Ruth Stafford. 3830
Pear, Tom Hatherley. 2999
Pearce, Abigail. 290
Pearce, B. F. 2227
Pearce, Charles William. 2243
Pearce, Ernest Harold. 1305, 3802, 3808, 2244
Pearce, J Winston. 166, 1376, 2071, 2904, 3854
Pearce, Joseph Chilton. 2380, 2630
Pearce, William. 3356
Pearce, William Cliff. 3556
Pearce, William John. 3510
Pearce, William P[eter]. 3229
Pearce, William Peter. 84, 290, 1569, 2071
*Pearce, Winifred M. 2542
Pearce J Winston. 374
Pearcy, Henri Reubelt. 376, 2800
Peare, Catherine Owens. 3847
Pearl, Chaim. 78, 2079, 2154
[Pearl, Cyril]. 3597
Pearl, Leon. 2673
Pearl of Great Price Symposium, Brigham Young University, 1975. 2614, 3429
Pearl, Reuben. 2807
Pearl, Virginia L. 1609
Pearlman, Moshe. 487, 2219, 2305, 2622, 2764, 2951
Pearlman, Myer. 199, 1831, 455, 3647
Pearman, Augustus John. 3242
Pearne, Thomas Hall. 1930
Pears, D F. 2420
Pears, David Francis. 2420
Pears, Thomas Clinton. 1403
Pearsall, Ronald. 3510
Pearse, Mark Guy. 1071, 1428
Pearson, Abel. 2981
Pearson, Andrew Forrest Scott. 743, 3007
Pearson, Andrew Forret Scot. 3007
Pearson, Andrew Forret Scott. 743, 3007
Pearson, Arnold. 1162
Pearson, Benjamin H. 2544
Pearson, Benjamin Harold. 1377, 2586
Pearson, Birger Albert. 323, 1718
Pearson, Carol Lynn. 2609, 2617, 2810
Pearson, Charles William. 1970
Pearson, Donald Stuart. 944
Pearson, E. Norman. 3686
Pearson, Elaine Coleman. 3167

Pearson, Francis Calhoun. 2829
Pearson, Glenn Laurentz. 501, 679, 2599, 2610, 2612
Pearson, Hugh Nicholas. 699
Pearson, J. D. 1924
Pearson, James. 3888
Pearson, John. 74, 1385
Pearson, Lawrence W. 2394
Pearson, Margaret (Crawford) 2807
Pearson, Peter. 2834
Pearson, Roy Messer. 972, 1441, 2071, 2783, 2904, 3664
Pearson, Victor Rosenius. 1993
Pease, Aaron G. 3712
Pease, Alice Campbell. 3840
Pease, Charles G[iffin]. 307
Pease, Dorothy Wells. 1441, 1456
Pease, Eugene Moody. 3062
Pease, George William. 3556
Pease, Jay J. 3674
Pease, Norval F. 1435, 1594, 2161, 3383, 3386
Peaslee, Reuben. 1867
Peaston, Monroe. 2994, 3705
Peat, Frank Edwin. 741
Peatfield, Ernest H. 791
Peatling, John H. 940
Pecher, Erich. 2124
Peck, Alan. 2479
Peck, Arthur Leslie. 1211, 3573
Peck, E J. 1382
Peck, George. 71, 277, 2818
Peck, George Bacheler. 469, 1834
Peck, George Clarke. 1600, 886, 1388, 3281, 290, 3411
Peck, George Terhune. 2644, 3409
Peck, Jesse Truesdell. 1052, 1055
Peck, John. 158
Peck, John Mason. 2560, 1284
Peck, Jonas Oramel. 1569
Peck, Joseph E. 3462
Peck, Kathryn (Blackburn) 1734, 904, 3171
Peck, Melville. 136
Peck, Paul Lachlan. 79
Peck, Sarah Elizabeth. 3385, 648
Peck, Thomas E. 1122, 2936
Peck, W. G. 871
Peck, William George. 756, 871, 1052, 1076, 2754
Peck, Zebulon. 607
Peckham, John. 1673, 2171
Peckham, John Laimbeer. 657
Peckham, Le Roy Bliss. 3412
Pecock, Reginald. 3647
Pedder, Henry C. 2420, 3076
*Peden, Pearle. 1015
Pederick, Alec W. 1620, 2503
Pedersen, Earl C. 2320
Pedersen, Johannes. 2121
Pedersen, Paul Bodholdt. 2552
Pederson, Carl O. 2284
Pederson, Cliff. 987
Pederson, Duane. 1256, 1359, 2072, 2244, 3545
Pederson, Les. 2533
Pederson, Mathew A. 2531
*Pedley, Katharine Greenleaf. 1410
Pedrick, Katharine Francis. 2639
Pedro de Alcantara, 1499-1562. 2877
Pedro de Cordoba, 1460-1525. 770
Peebles, Cora (Rankin) 1696
Peebles, Edwin. 3474
Peebles, Isaac Lockhart. 136, 1752, 3412, 1752, 2521
Peebles, James M. 1993
Peebles, James Martin. 3510, 131, 702, 1933, 3054, 3510
Peeke, George Hewson. 3481
Peel, Albert. 1333, 3193
Peel, Malcolm Lee. 3221
Peel, Robert. 1035, 1038, 1495
Peel, Robert Arthur. 1035
Peeler, Banks J. 1545
Peelman, Nancy. 480
Peelor, Harry N. 1007, 3356
Peerman, Dean G. 3611, 3652
Peerman, Frank. 1774, 2810
Peerman, Nancy. 991, 2394
Peers, Edgar Allison. 741, 1028, 1455, 2136, 2137, 2271, 2648, 3469, 3481, 3603
Peet, Stephen. 3820
Peet, Stephen Denison. 1904
Peeters, Louis. 2269
Peffley, William Edwin. 1201
Pegg, J. G. Broughton. 1528
Pegis, Anton Charles. 2842, 3693, 1105, 3309, 3637, 3694
Pegis, Jessie Corrigan. 779
Pegram, George Allen. 944, 1699
Pegues, A. W. 157
Pegues, Thomas. 3696
Peguy, Charles Pierre. 3207
Peifer, Claude J. 2571
Peifer, John Frederick. 3693
*Peiffer, Marie Venard. 3163

Peil, Rudolf. 2235
Peile, James Hamilton Francis. 1052
Peirce, Bradford Kinney. 236, 332, 515, 686, 1867, 3210
Peirce, Francis X. 2394
Peirce, Isaac Newton. 1913
Peiris, William. 3309
Pekar, Atanasii V. 766
Pekarsky, Maurice Bernard. 2145
Pelcovitz, Ralph. 2751
Pelger, Lucy J. 3842
Pelham, N.Y. Christ church (Protestant Episcopal) 1162
Pelikan, Jaroslav. 801, 1531, 2229, 3062, 3655
Pelikan, Jaroslav A)jan. 1531
Pelikan, Jaroslav Jan. 1128, 801, 1074, 1473, 1531, 1819, 2276, 3035, 3062, 3655, 3659
Pelikan, Jaroslaw. 3035
Pelikan, Jarslav Jan. 100, 2229
Pell, Edward Leigh. 4, 640, 1405, 1890, 1956, 1982, 2127, 2457, 2534, 2588, 2800, 2893, 3062, 3155, 3556, 3564
Pell, Edward Leight. 972
Pell, Walden. 2964, 2965
Pellegrin, Harold Francis. 364
Pellegrino, Michele. 115, 2791
Pelletier, Joseph Albert. 1618
Pelley, Wiley Hall. 3072
[Pelley, William Dudley]. 1621, 2227, 3436
Pelley, William Dudley. 2165, 2728
Pellino, Michael William. 3302
Pellowe, William Charles Smithson. 3804, 2436
[Peloquin, Pierre Joseph. 893
Pelotte, Donald E. 2632, 3611
Peloubet, Francis Nathan. 71, 236, 324, 245, 329, 331, 417, 441, 442, 1451, 3556
Pelt, John. 664
Pelt, Owen D. 2669
Pelton, DeWitt Lincoln. 972
Pelton, Robert D. 1631
Pelton, Robert W. 2728, 1429, 1585, 2313, 3432, 3787
Pelz, Lotte. 2324
Pelz, Werner. 2071
Pember, George Hawkins. 3510
Pemberton, Ebenezer. 1753
Pemberton, Ethel Vera. 360, 646, 937
Pemberton, May. 1113
Pement, Philemon. 2943
Pemsteen, Hans. 2822
Pence, Gilbert Eugene. 2945
Pence, Owen Earle. 3871, 3872, 3875
[Pendarvis, George Henry]. 1077
Pendleton, Charles Rittenhouse. 3469, 3570
Pendleton, James Madison. 106, 148, 150, 2227, 3647
Pendleton, Nathaniel Dandridge. 2689, 2693
Pendleton, Othniel Alsop. 1168
Pendleton, William Frederick. 3344
Pendleton, William Nelson. 205
Pendleton, Winston K. 180
Pendorf, James G. 1200
Pendragon, John. 2990
Penelhum, Terence. 1594, 1890, 3104
Pengelly, John Bradford. 2006
Pengilly, Richard. 136
Penick, Charles Clifton. 2128
Penington, Isaac. 2218, 2639, 3133
Penman, Archibald. 1432
Penn-Lewis, Jessie, 1861-1927. 3832
Penn, W. E. 3072
Penn, William. 1609, 904, 972, 1011, 1609, 1675, 1679, 1682, 1685, 1686, 1919, 3631
Pennell, Alice Maud (Sorabji) 2531, 2813
Pennell, Elizabeth (Robins) 752
Pennell, George E. 531
Pennell, Joseph. 2098
*Pennell, Lucy. 3164
Penner, Archie. 1142
Penner, P. E. 3721
Pennewell, Almer. 3789
Penney, Alfred James. 1122
Penney, Norman. 1684
Pennick, Nigel. 1706
Pennick, Rupert. 3827
Penniman, Alford Brown. 2740
Penniman, Josiah Harmar. 236
Penniman, Josiah Harmer. 236
Penning de Vries, Piet. 386, 2269, 2877, 3492
Penning, Louwrens. 728
Pennington, Chester A. 65, 324, 1007, 1725, 2267, 2904, 3337
Pennington, Edgar Legare. 1223, 1781, 3580, 3869
Pennington, Levi Talbott. 3133
Pennington, M. Basil. 1276, 1356, 2585, 2813, 2877
[Pennock, Ames Castle]. 1746, 3632
Pennock, Dee. 3888

Pennock, Michael. 756, 791, 3265, 3880
Pennsylvania convention of Methodist men. Harrisburg, Pa., 1916. 2459
Pennsylvania historical survey. 1687
Pennsylvania. State University. Center for Continuing Liberal Education. 3670
Pennsylvania. University. Bicentennial Conference. 3618
Pennsylvania. University. Dept. of archoeology. 3093
Pennsylvania. University. Library. 81
Pennsylvania. University. Seybert commission for investigating modern spiritualism. 3510
Penrose, Charles William. 2605
Penrose, John. 60
Penrose Library. 2083
Penrose, Valeria Fullerton. 2539
Penry, John. 1223
Pensatia. 2728
Pentecost, Dorothy Harrison. 1303, 2808
Pentecost, Edward C. 1569
Pentecost, George Frederick. 1164, 2813, 517
Pentecost, J. Dwight. 324, 449, 607, 801, 929, 972, 987, 1428, 1716, 1831, 1970, 3321, 3336, 3356
Pentecostal holiness church. Board of education and publication. 2814
Penter, John. 3063
Penton, M. James. 1940, 3193
Pentz, Croft M. 3374
Pepler, Conrad. 839, 2209, 2643, 2645
Pepper, Clayton. 30, 3255
Pepper, Curtis Bill. 2124
Pepper, Eleuthera I D. 1560
Pepper, Elizabeth. 3824, 3825
Pepper, George Hubbard. 1810
Pepper, George Wharton. 577, 1441, 2904
Pepper, George Whitfield. 885
Pepper, John Robertson. 3556, 3550
Pepper, Stephen C. 3716
Pepper, Stephen Coburn. 2419
Peppert, F. 3344
Peppler, Alice Stolper. 1471
Perce, Warren Raymond. 205
Perceval, Arthur Philip. 76
Percheron, Maurice. 702, 1703
Percival, Harold Waldwin. 1671, 3201, 3686
Percival, Henry Robert. 3285
Percival, Norman. 908
Percy, Frances Coan. 3208
Percy, Laura Helen. 2157
Percy of Newcastle, Eustace Percy, 1887-1958. 2181
Perdelwitz, George. 3290
Perdue-Davis, Vernon. 813, 1877
Perdue, Leo G. 3821
Peregrinatio, Aetheriae. 2762
Peregrinatio Aetheriae. English. 1198
Perera-Wijesinghe, Melissa (Gatling) 1352
Peretz, Don. 1922
Peretz, Isaac Loeb. 2671
Perez deUrbel, Justo, 1895. 1542
Perez Esclarin, Antonio. 1073
Perez, Eugene. 188
Perez, Rene. 2728
Perez Marcio, Braulio. 3383
Perez Vila, Manuel. 1362
Perhac, George. 835
Perin, George Landor. 3344, 3752
Perinbanayagam, R. S. 98
Perinchief, Octavius. 3133
Perinelle, Joseph. 2571
Peritz, Ismar John. 2096
Perkin, Noel. 92
Perkins, Benjamin J. 3374, 3375
Perkins, Benjamin Paul. 2682
Perkins, Dennis N. T. 3011
Perkins, Eunice M. 685
Perkins, Eunice May. 455
Perkins, Faith. 2244
Perkins, Frederic Beecher. 1429
Perkins, George Augustus. 612
Perkins, George William. 3344
Perkins, Henry Martyn. 2820
Perkins, James Breck. 1639, 3236
Perkins, James Scudday. 1414, 3054
Perkins, Jeanette Eloise. 3155, 3165, 3556, 3858
Perkins, Jocelyn Henry Temple. 3808
Perkins, John. 1139, 3786
Perkins, Lynn F. 1662, 1672
Perkins, Mary. 770, 1001, 1609, 2625, 2877
Perkins, Mary Louise. 2963
Perkins, Nathan. 1344, 1504
Perkins, Norah. 972
Perkins, Pheme. 410, 417, 421, 1718, 2026
Perkins, R. L. 3207
*Perkins, Richard F. 1604
Perkins, Robert L. 2170
Perkins, Rufus Lord. 2052
Perkins, Ruth. 733, 3004, 3878
Perkins, Sra. 2485

Perkins, William Allen. 2190
Perkins, William Oscar. 49
Perkins, William Rufus. 2693
Perl, Ruth June. 2556
Perlo, Victor. 3256
Permanand Bhavati, Baba. 2186
Pernicone, Joseph Maria. 2945
Pernoud, Regine. 1390, 1802, 1811, 1938
Perot, Elliston Joseph. 844
Perowne, Stewart. 1038, 1944, 2092, 2667, 2804
Perpetua, Saint. Legend. 1021
Perraud, Charles Alexis. 2058
Perrella, Robert. 2820
Perren, Christopher. 1560, 3375
Perret, Andre. 1414
Perret, Andre S. 1414, 3489
Perreyve, Henri. 1622, 3406
Perrier, Joseph Louis. 3309
Perrin, Daniel A. 1205, 1594, 3459
Perrin, Henri. 3143
Perrin-Jassy, Marie France. 12
Perrin, Jean Paul. 3788
Perrin, Joseph Marie. 749, 754, 1296, 2136, 2191, 2363, 2819, 2877, 3327, 3781
Perrin, Norman. 391, 410, 713, 2011, 2026, 2054, 2065, 2175, 2176
Perrin, Raymond St. James. 3104
Perrin-Jassy, Marie France. 12
Perrins, William Andrew. 166
Perrotta, Antonio. 820
Perrotta, Paul Christopher. 2124
Perroy, Henry. 1372, 3205
Perroy, Louis. 2032
Perry, Alfred Morris. 426
Perry, Bliss. 3481
Perry, Calbraith Bourn. 133
Perry, Charles E. 1298
Perry, Charles Milton. 2419
Perry, Earl. 71, 338
Perry, Edith (Weir) 27
Perry, Edmund. 1079
Perry, George Gresley. 3039
Perry, I. Mac. 65, 277
Perry, James De Wolf. 391, 2211, 2212
Perry, James DeWolf. 2210, 2212
Perry, James H. 2374, 3300
Perry, John. 746, 749
Perry, John D. 1305
Perry, John Gould. 1867
Perry, John T. 60, 1756
Perry, John Weir. 2177
Perry, John Wiley. 2521
Perry, Joseph Earl. 1663
Perry, Lloyd M. 640
Perry, Lloyd Merle. 471, 640, 1165, 1244, 2790, 2904
Perry, Martha Elmina. 517, 597
Perry, Octavia (Jordan) 1811
Perry, Ralph Barton. 1934, 3007, 1934
Perry, Sarah Ann. 1052
Perry, Sarah B. 614
Perry, Theodore Anthony. 1745
*Perry, Thomas Charles. d. 3481
Perry, Thomas D. 1536
[Perry, Thomas W.]. 2820
Perry, Troy D. 1844
Perry, William. 1632, 2754
Perry, William James. 3110
Perry, William Stevens. 1222, 29, 665, 2804, 3431
Perry, Wilma I. 987
Perryman, Edith. 1875
Persenius, Jons Magnus. 2284
Persich, Nicholas C. 2939
Persinger, Michael A. 2845
Person, Amy L. 1841
Person, Peter P. 1260, 3156
Persons, Lee Chandler. 3142
Persons, Stow. 1657
Persson, Axel Wablemar. 1767
Persson, Per Erik. 2286, 3227, 3697
Perth Amboy, N.J. St. Peter's Episcopal church. 1524
Perthes, Friedrich Matthaeus. 1115
Pesch, Christian. 1953, 3270
Pesch, Otto Hermann. 1732, 3628, 3697
Pesikta de-Rab Kahana. English. 593, 3370
Pesikta rabbati. English. 2140
Pessin, Deborah. 2087, 2094, 2106
Pete, Thomas J[efferson]. 1178
Peter, James. 2008
Peter, John Desmond. 2469
Peter Pauper Press, Mount Vernon, N. Y. 2893, 2896, 3894
Peterkin, George William. 2974
Peterman, Mary E. 1600
*Peterman, Richard. 3166
Peterman, Ruth. 2394
Peters, Absalom. 136
Peters, Blanche Marie. 2409
Peters, Camilla W. 2003
Peters, Caroline. 1284, 2168, 3284
Peters, Charles Clinton. 2591
Peters, Clarence H. 626

Peters, Donald L. 3880
Peters, Edward. 1805
Peters, Edward H. 2197
Peters, Edward M. 1390, 1391
Peters, Erna Alma. 2814
Peters, Eugene Herbert. 1105, 3813
Peters, F. E. 2147
Peters, Francis E. 1945, 2700, 2841
Peters, Fred J. 52
Peters, George Llewellyn. 1465
Peters, George Nathaniel Henry. 2175, 607, 2175
Peters, George W. 1171, 1569, 2504
Peters, Gerlach. 3489
Peters, Harry Howard. 1569
Peters, Henry Harrison. 3290
Peters, J. R. T. M. 21, 1927, 2185
Peters, Jensine (Oerts) 2558
Peters, Johannes Arnold Jozef. 2419
Peters, John Leland. 2819
Peters, John Punnett. 1055, 208, 584, 1062, 2096, 2115
Peters, John R. 912
Peters, Lewis Edwin. 3556
Peters, Madison Clinton. 140, 3344, 148, 481, 1696, 3049
Peters, Newton. 3754
Peters, Richard Stanley. 1536
Peters, Ted. 1528, 1062
Peters, Victor. 1858
Peters, Walter H. 190
Peters, William A. M. 2269
Peters, William J. 757, 2343
Petersen, Arnold. 2671
Petersen, Bill. 1530
Petersen, David L. 569
Petersen, Emma Marr. 623, 680, 1197, 1315, 2615, 3430
Petersen, Evelyn R. 3841
Petersen, Gerald A. 3287
Petersen, Henry. 1477, 3043
Petersen, J. Allan. 1609
Petersen, LaMar. 3429, 3595
Petersen, Mark E. 4, 6, 493, 543, 655, 679, 950, 951, 1009, 1232, 1325, 1609, 2127, 2132, 2134, 2339, 2346, 2394, 2599, 2608, 2612, 2614, 2622, 2792, 3304, 3429, 3741, 3880, 3888
Petersen, Melba. 1122
Petersen, Norman R. 349
Petersen, Sigurd D. 1255
Petersen, W. P. 2382
Petersen, William J. 182, 1507, 2513, 2728, 2800, 3701
Petersen, William John. 3707
Petersham, Maud (Fuller) 399, 587, 634, 635, 1996, 2133, 2622, 3258
Petersham, Maud Fuller. 616, 1405, 2133
Petersham, Maud Sylvia (Fuller) 588
Petersilea, Carlyle. 2218, 3510
Peterson, Abbot. 2208
Peterson, Charles Emil. 2829
Peterson, Charles S. 2616
Peterson, Daniel H. 3133
Peterson, Edward. 694
Peterson, Edward C. 1970
Peterson, Edward S. 1737
Peterson, Ephraim. 3030, 3762
Peterson, Erik. 43
Peterson, Eugene H. 520, 579, 585, 1432, 2786, 3888
Peterson, Finis Paul. 1035, 2826
Peterson, Flora (Culp) 3510
Peterson, Frank Loris. 3383
Peterson, Gail. 630
Peterson, Gladys. 1108, 2826
Peterson, Hugh R. 438
Peterson, John. 253, 1547
Peterson, John H. 3476
Peterson, John W. 1749, 2826
Peterson, Lancie Elmer. 180
Peterson, Lewis. 3510
Peterson, Lorraine. 3883
Peterson, Mrs. Fred. 1062
Peterson, Orval D. 1725
Peterson, Orval Douglas. 1467, 1725
Peterson, P. A. 2456
Peterson, Robert. 1429
Peterson, Robert E. 1168
Peterson, Royal F. 139
Peterson, Russell Arthur. 1451, 2287
Peterson, Thomas D. 3331, 3830
Peterson, Thomas Virgil. 1782, 3468
Peterson, Wilferd Arlan. 1325, 1432
Pethrus, Lewi. 1166, 1831
Petiscus, August Heinrich. 2657
Petit, Adolphe. 3222
Petit, Francois, O. Pream. 1746
Petitot, Hyacinthe. 2819, 3460, 3691, 3693
Petitpierre, Ferdinand Oliver. 3610
Petitpierre, Robert. 1585
Petras, James. 2777
Petre, Maude Dominica Mary. 1594, 2243
Petrelli, Giuseppe. 1062, 1122, 1831, 1970, 2015, 2042

Petrie, George. 1147
Petrie, George Laurens. 1931, 2951
Petrie, Irene, A. H. Petrie. 1954
Petrie, Peter Albert. 1463
Petrie, William Matthew Flinders. 1502
Petrovits, Joseph Julius Charles. 2342
Petrullo, Vincenzo. 1420
Petrus, Pictaviensis. 782
Petrus Chrysologus. 3369
Petrus Riga. 224
Petrus Thomae. 782, 3647
Petry, Ann (Lane) 1028
Petry, Ray C., 1903. 1198, 1531, 1643, 2647, 2909, 3344
Petry, Ronald D. 3529
Petr z Mladenovic. 1354, 1857
Petschek, Joyce S. 2731, 2827
Pettazzoni, Raffaele. 1736
Pettee, Julia. 3323
Pettepiece, Thomas G. 2394
Petter, Catherine Hausburg. 461
Petter, Helen Mary. 78
Pettersen, Wilhelm Mauritz. 1790
Pettey, Emma. 3156
Pettey, Richard J. 2816
Pettigrew, George R. 1487, 2042
Pettigrew, Julius Dean. 1062
Pettingell, John Hancock. 1696
Pettingill, William L[eroy]. 1927
Pettingill, William Leroy. 380, 403, 651, 1401, 2373, 2465, 2947, 3225
Pettis, Charles Roberts. 3575
Pettis, Olive G. 2060, 3511
Pettit, Hermon. 404, 3229, 1576, 2827
Pettit, Isabel Lacy. 2531
Pettit, Norman. 3679
Petts, David. 1831
Petty, Carl Wallace. 166, 972
Petty, Jo. 242, 1011, 2893, 3782, 3883
Petty, Orville Anderson. 3609
Pettyjohn, Marie Louise. 3054
Petuchowski, Jakob Josef. 748, 2109, 2140, 2709, 2853, 2886, 3706
*Petulla, Joseph. 1017, 3177
Petulla, Joseph M. 1087, 2352
Petz, Andreas. 1262
Peugnet, Claire Adele. 2995
Peursen, C. A. van. 3462, 3463
Peursen, Cornelis Anthonie van. 1736
Peusch, Leonard. 1998
Peyriguere, Albert. 3489
Peyton, Leslie. 311
Peyton, Patrick J. 1609, 2827, 2877
Peyton, Thomas. 296, 2471
Peyton, Thomas A. 1245
Pezeril, Daniel. 3778
Pfarr, Anthony J. 1264
Pfatteicher, Ernst Philip Henry. 3344, 3452
Pfatteicher, Helen Emma. 1548, 1875, 3875
Pfatteicher, Philip H. 2236
Pfeffer, Leo. 1141, 1151, 3326, 3745
Pfeifer, Carl J. 858, 987, 2394
Pfeiffer, August. 730
Pfeiffer, Charles F. 209, 224, 282, 517, 522, 524, 535, 558, 590, 1410, 2092, 2093, 2096, 2188, 3022
Pfeiffer, Edward. 2494
Pfeiffer, Harold A. 852
*Pfeiffer, Marie Venard. 3163
*Pfeiffer, Mother Marie. 3177
Pfeiffer, Robert Henry. 540, 490, 2092, 2148, 2149
Pfendsack, Werner. 1012
Pffiegler, Michael. 1299
*Pffiffer, Marie Venard. 3163
Pfister, Friedrich. 2661
Pfister, Oskar Robert. 1619
Pfister, Pierre. 2852
Pfleger, Karl. 2232
Pfleiderer, Jean D. 892, 2636
Pfleiderer, Otto. 376, 1178, 1194, 2800, 3104, 3107, 3119, 3617, 3658
Pfliegler, Michael. 2789
Pfnur, Vinzenz. 2788
Pfurtner, Stephanus. 2281, 3294
Phadnis, Urmila. 708
Phares, Ross. 1689, 3749
Pharnes, Henry. 2990
Phayer, J. Michael. 3390
Phelan, David S. 864
Phelan, Edna Beyer. 683
Phelan, Gerald Bernard. 49
Phelan, Josephine. 2190
Phelan, Macum. 2424, 2432, 3323
Phelan, Thomas Patrick. 874, 2722
Phelps, Adaliza (Cutter) 2048
Phelps, Albert H. 1569, 2829
[Phelps, Almira (Hart) Lincoln. 2230
[Phelps, Amos Augustus]. 3177, 3261
Phelps, Arthur Stevens. 201
Phelps, Austin. 1831, 1867, 1875, 2775, 2877, 2904, 3623
Phelps, Edwin Philbrook. 3879
Phelps, Frances Brown. 3183

[Phelps, George Dwight] 1804-1872. 1420, 1472
Phelps, Guy Fitch. 801
Phelps, John Wolcott. 3322
Phelps, Myron Henry. 2, 128
Phelps, Samuel Merrick. 3207
Phelps, Sylvanus Dryden. 166, 3459
Phelps, William Lyon. 349, 501, 613, 3793
Phenix, Philip Henry. 3063, 3190
Phifer, Kenneth G. 630, 3854
Phifer, Lyndon Burke. 640
Phifer, William Everette. 2934
Philadelphia (Archdiocese) Diocesan school board. 807
Philadelphia. Christ church. 1273
Philadelphia. Church of the Epiphany. Members. 3719
Philadelphia Conference on Reformed Theology (1977-1979) 2046, 2321
Philadelphia. Councils. 3546
Philadelphia. First Unitarian church. 2741
Philadelphia. First Unitarian Congregational society. 2375
Philadelphia. Lutheran church of the ascension. 2292
Philadelphia. Lutheran Theological Seminary. 2281
Philadelphia (Mt. Airy) Lutheran theological seminary. 3614
Philadelphia. Overbrook Presbyterian Church. 2936
Philadelphia. St. Agatha's Church. 2830
Philadelphia. St. Peter's church. 2685
Philadelphia. Shiloh Baptist church. 1594
Philadelphia. Tenth Baptist church. 2167
Philadelphia theological seminary of Saint Charles Borromeo. 3331
Philadelphia. Wharton street Methodist Episcopal church. 2453
Philadelphia. Woodland Presbyterian church. 2916
Philadelphia (Archdiocese) Superintendent of Parish Schools. 2774
Philbrick, Minnie Lambert (Smith) 3798
Philbrook, Harry B. 1371, 1725, 1729
Philibert, Helene. 3797
Philibert, Michel Andre Jean. 2904
Philip, James. 508
Philip, Robert. 2467
Philipon, Marie Michel. 3489, 3691, 2335, 2363, 3265, 3489, 3691
Philippe, Marie Dominique. 1741
Philippe, Paul. 1299, 2356, 2716
Philippe, Thomas. 3489
Philippe de la Trinite. 3030
Philipps, Martin. 3560
[Philipps, Martin]. 791, 3184
Philips, Gerard. 754, 2191
Philips, Harvey E. 2567
Philips, Samuel. 672
Philips, T Roland. 3356
Philipson, Clifford Andrew. 3463
Philipson, David. 2100, 2105, 2112, 2116, 3032
[Phillimore, Cecily (Spencer-Smith)]. 2006
Phillippi, Joseph Martin. 3396
Phillips, Allen A. 972
Phillips, Anthony. 599, 1314, 1731, 2042
Phillips, Arthur Angell. 1518
Phillips, Arthur B. 199
Phillips, Arthur Bernicie. 286, 3216
Phillips, Bernard. 3067
Phillips, Bertha Wilson. 994, 2831
Phillips Brooks house association, Harvard university. 3063, 3067
Phillips, Charles Henry. 1203, 1310, 3133, 1021
Phillips, Charles Stanley. 817, 1194, 817, 1215, 1638
Phillips, Clifton Jackson. 31
Phillips, D. Z. 2877
Phillips, Daniel T. 493
Phillips, Dayton. 185
Phillips, Dewi Zephaniah. 2837, 2877, 3107
Phillips, Dorothy Berkley. 3063
Phillips, Dretha. 1853
Phillips, E. Lee. 2783, 2893
Phillips, Emma M. 3215
Phillips, Ethel M. 898, 3171
Phillips, Ewing Lakin. 1609
Phillips, George E. 1759
Phillips, George S. 607
Phillips, Godfrey Edward. 2494, 2531
Phillips, Gordon Lewis. 1616
Phillips, Grace Darling. 3177
Phillips, Harold Cooke. 166, 972, 1995, 2904, 3356
Phillips, Harold L. 1228, 1735, 2800
Phillips, J. B. 1432
Phillips, James. 1158
Phillips, James M. 1101
Phillips, Jim. 349, 1621
Phillips, John. 311, 403, 455, 522, 607, 1880
Phillips, John A. 677, 2009

Phillips, John Albert. 801
Phillips, John Bernard. 108
Phillips, John Bertram. 361, 1062, 1071, 1096, 1227, 1451, 1725, 2252, 2394, 2820
Phillips, John Walter. 166
Phillips, Keith W. 987, 1255
Phillips, Le Roy. 1933
Phillips, Leo T. 29, 2198
Phillips, Leona. 2731
Phillips, Leona Rasmussen. 1112
Phillips, McCandlish. 3567
Phillips, Margaret I. 2394, 2831
Phillips, Margaret Mann. 1526, 3035
Phillips, Maurice. 3776
Phillips, Max Gordon. 1382
Phillips, Mike. 65, 987, 1609
Phillips, Mildred Welshimer. 1461
Phillips, Ordis E. 65, 1514, 2175, 2415, 2762
Phillips, Philip. 1868, 2451, 3563
Phillips, Richard Percival. 3309, 3696
Phillips, S. 1838
Phillips, Samuel. 1594
Phillips, Samuel Louis. 65, 1581
Phillips, Stephen. 1764
[Phillips, Thomas]. 1122
Phillips, Thomas W. 1122
[Phillips, Thomas Wharton] 1835-1912. 1096
Phillips, Wendell. 391, 1970
Phillips, William. 212, 732
Phillips, William B. 3110
Phillips, William J. 742
Phillips, William Presley. 3168, 3556, 3557
Phillott, Henry Wright. 1804
Phillpotts, Eden. 72
Philo. 2839
Philo Judaeus. 535, 208
Philomusus, S. 2201, 3606
Philosophy Conference, 3d, University of Georgia, 1970. 2739
Philostratus, Flavius. 57
Philp, Horace Robert Andrew. 2536
Philp, Howard Littleton. 1746, 2159
[Philp, Robert Kemp]. 286
Philpot, Ford. 1560
Philpot, J H. 3710
Philpot, Joh. 1162
Philpot, John. 1162
Philpot, William M. 3361
Philpott, Anthony J. 1346, 3511
Philpott, J P. 1376, 1602, 2042
Philpott, Kent. 1423, 1428, 1585, 1844
Philpott, Peter Willy. 1729, 2124
Phin, John. 103, 205
Phinney, Frank D. 2409
Phipps, Burton H. 1435
Phipps, Jerome Kenton. 2394
Phipps, John-Francis. 1001
Phipps, Joseph. 136, 1682, 2706
Phipps, William E. 1512, 1954, 1970, 3390, 3392, 3832
Phoebus, William. 3810
Photiadis, John D. 3807
Photius, Patriarch of Constantinople. 2844
Physical Education Society of the Young Men's Christian Associations of North America. Leadership Training Committee. 3872
[Phythian, J Ernest]. 2896
Phythian-Adams, William John Telia Phythian. 236, 501, 1725
Piankoff, Alexandre. 1503
Piat, Stephane Joseph. 1001, 2348, 2356, 3529
Piault, Bernard. 3265, 3714
Picard, George H[enry]. 665
Picard, Max. 1726
Piccarda. 1646, 3489
Pichard, Joseph. 1160
*Pichaske, Donald R. 501, 2282
Pichel, Charles Louis Thourot. 2179
Pichler, Johann Evangelist. 808
Pichon, Almire. 3475
Pichon, Charles. 810
Picht, Werner Robert Valentin. 3312
Pick, Bernhard. 655, 722, 1954, 2747, 3583
Pickard, Samuel. 2178
Pickard, William M. 553
Pickell, Charles N. 342, 1011, 2904
Picken, Stuart D. B. 709, 3404
Pickerill, Grace Gilbert. 3888
Pickering, David. 61, 3754
Pickering, Ernest D. 1468, 1569
Pickering, Hy. 640
Pickering, Wilbur N. 352
Pickett, Jarrell Waskom. 2531, 2555
Pickett, Leander Lycurgus. 828, 2231, 52, 972, 2465
Pickett, Warren Wheeler. 3876
Pickl, Josef. 2030
Pickles, Walter. 3277
Pickman, Edward Motley. 1194, 3655
Pickthorn, William E. 2722

Pickup, Harry Wilson. 1273
Pico della Mirandola, Giovanni Francesco, 1470-1533. 1884
Pico della Mirandola, Giovanni, 1463-1494. 1382
Picolo, Francesco Maria. 1947
Picton, J[ames] Allanson. 3142
Picton, James Allanson. 2767
Picton, Nina. 1479
Pidgeon, George Campbell. 3731
Pidgeon, George S. 1421
Piehl, Mel. 834, 871
Piepenbring, Charles. 1954
Pieper, Franz August Otto. 2286, 3647
Pieper, Josef. 186, 738, 796, 1356, 1414, 1536, 1818, 1819, 2160, 3309, 3693, 3696
Piepkorn, Arthur Carl. 1249, 3324
Pier, Garrett Chatfield. 1584
Pierard, Richard V. 1552
Pierce, Albert C. 870, 1397
Pierce, Alfred Mann. 734, 2430
Pierce, B[enjamin] W[ashington]. 3481
Pierce, Benjamin Washington. 3481
Pierce, Bradford Kinney. 926
Pierce, Carl Horton. 2728
Pierce, Caroline Behlen. 3398
Pierce, Charles C[ampbell]. 3344
Pierce, Charles Clark. 3459
Pierce Christian college, College City, Cal. 1309
Pierce, David Rand. 3207
Pierce, Dorothy. 3511
Pierce, Earle Vaydor. 166, 1122, 2042, 3529
Pierce, Florence. 679
Pierce, George Foster. 2425
Pierce, Henry Niles. 19
Pierce, John. 1504
Pierce, Marilyn Seal. 1502
Pierce, Martin Luther. 1239
Pierce, Ralph Milton. 3366
Pierce, Rice Alexander. 640
Pierce, Robert Fletcher Young. 880, 3716
Pierce, Robert Willard. 2502, 2536, 2551
Pierce, Roderic Hall. 1304
Pierce, Samuel Eyles. 1831
Pierce, Ulysses Grant Baker. 3726
Pierce, William. 1759
Pierce, William Dwight. 1970
Pierhal, Armand. 65
Pierhal, Jean. 3312
Pierik, Marie. 883, 884, 2985
Pierini, Franco. 770
Pierpont, John. 684, 1372
Pierpont Morgan Library, New York. 841, 2021
Pierre. 1354
Pierre, Joseph H. 2639
Pierrel, Gren O. 3872
Pierron, Joseph J. 813
Piersel, Alba Chambers. 2247
Pierson, Arthur T. 615
Pierson, Arthur Tappan. 1726, 3484, 61, 65, 640, 749, 1182, 1569, 1834, 1843, 2491, 2494, 2637, 2904, 3133, 3290, 3320, 3523
Pierson, Delavan Leonard. 2543, 1432
Pierson, George Peck. 106, 2534
Pierson, Hamilton Wilcox. 2483
Pierson, Helen W. 1982
Pierson, Johnson. 3207
Pierson, Paul Everett. 330, 1883

Pierson, Roscoe Mitchell. 739, 1464

Pies, Otto. 2209

Piet, John H. 474, 600, 1122

Pieters, Albertus. 1929, 65, 277, 455, 522, 1376, 3290
Pietrkiewicz, Jerzy. 2186, 2334
Pietro Damiani. 3489
Pietrzyk, Stanley. 1634
Piette, Maximin. 2978, 3804
Piggott, Juliet. 2664
Piggott, Stuart. 1480
Pigott, Grenville. 1493, 2666
Pihl, Herman Gottfrid. 623
Piink, Arthur Walkington. 287
Pike, Albert. 121, 1662, 1671, 3208, 3776
Pike, Diane Kennedy. 1774, 2019, 2042, 2846, 3014
Pike, E[zra] B. 1861
Pike, Edgar Royston. 282, 1420, 1765, 1939, 2241, 2629, 3092
Pike, Esther. 1134
Pike, Eunice V. 2376
Pike, Fredrick B. 1147
Pike, Godfrey Holden. 3523
Pike, Granville Ross. 1738, 3073
Pike, Gustavus D. 2137
*Pike, James A. 972
Pike, James Albert. 66, 944, 991, 1062, 1134, 1151, 1412, 2958, 2965, 2995, 3664, 828, 944, 1096, 1151, 2904, 2995, 3421, 3511, 3664

Pike, James Shepherd. 2371, 2847
Pike, John. 1747, 1911, 2371
Pike, John Gregory. 3063, 904, 3888
Pike, Kenneth Lee. 437, 2563, 2856
Pike, Kermit. 3396
Pike, Morris D. 901
Pike, Nelson. 1533, 1746
Pike, Samuel. 944, 945, 3119
[Pilai, M. Gnauapiakesam]. 2728
Pilch, John J. 460, 1325
Pilch, Judah. 2084, 2106
Pilcher, George William. 1406
Pilcher, James Elijah. 2847
Pilchik, Ely Emanuel. 540, 1812, 2085, 3371
Pilgrim, Geneva R Hanna. 905
Pilgrim, Walter E. 429, 2859
Pilkington, James. 1217
Pilkington, Roger. 1382, 3079, 3082
Pill, David H. 3039
Pillai, C. A. Joachim. 334
Pillai, K. C. 239
Pillar, James L. 822, 2669
Pillar of fire church. 2848
Pillsbury, Agnes. 682
Pilmore, Joseph. 3133
Pinay, Maurice. 861, 2152
Pinch, Frederick. 323
Pinches, Theophilus Goldridge. 501
Pincock, Jenny O'Hara. 3511
Pinder-Wilson, Ralph H. 1883
Pine Bluff, Ark. Congregation Anshe-Emeth. 2089

Pineas, Rainer. 69
Pinegar, Ed J. 1009, 1232, 1616
Pinelli, Luca. 2255
Pines, Burton Yale. 3742
Ping, Charles J. 3070
Pingree, Enoch Merrill. 3754
Pingry, Patricia. 146, 1603
Pink, Arthur W. 52, 236, 420, 523, 1428, 1451, 1726, 2058, 2849, 3481, 1314, 1730
Pink, Arthur Walkington. 106, 180, 287, 306, 374, 403, 423, 516, 553, 604, 656, 1052, 1352, 1377, 1405, 1505, 1506, 1726, 1730, 1831, 2042, 2849, 2981, 3225, 3290, 3300, 3336, 3414, 3481
Pinkerton, Frank C. 1062, 2622
Pinkham, Mildreth (Worth) 3837
Pinkham, Rebekah (Porter) 926, 1306
Pinkham, William P. 108
Pinn, James R C. 455
Pinnell, Lois M. 1672
Pinney, John. 2218
Pinney, Roy. 481
Pinnock, Clark H. 66, 277, 306, 380
Pinnock, Samuel George. 2542
Pinomaa, Lennart. 2281
Pinsent, John. 2661
Pinsk, Johannes. 1001, 1264
Pinsker, Lev Semenovich. 3896
Pinson, Koppel Shub. 2078, 2846
Pinson, William M. 303, 953, 1066, 1140, 1611, 2786, 3181
Pinson, William Washington. 912, 2194, 2494
Pintauro, Joseph. 1308
Pinto, Pio V. 1022
Pinto, Vivian de Sola. 3527
Piolanti, Antonio. 2255
Piot, B. S. 773
Piot, Bertrand Sylvain. 773
Piper, David Roy. 296, 1274, 1321, 1954, 3156, 296, 1015
Piper, F. L. 2052
Piper, Ferdinand. 926
Piper, John. 391, 2065, 2266
Piper, Otto. 1083, 1189, 3388
Piper, Otto A. 1083, 1492, 3393, 3529
Pipes, William Harrison. 2682
Pipkin, H Wayne. 2380, 3900
Pippert, Rebecca Manley. 1569
Pippert, Wesley. 1087
Pippin, Frank Johnson. 1111, 1451, 3356
Pirie, Valerie. 2862
Pirie-Gordon, Charles Harry Clinton. 1542, 1908
Pirke, de-Rabbi Eliezer. 3015
Pirke de-Rabbi Eliezer. English. 3016
Pirkei de-Rabbi Eliezer. 522
Pirkle, Estus W. 212
Pirolo, Nicholas. 791, 2635, 2768
Piron, Paul. 182, 2357
Pirone, Frank John. 3079
Pirtle, Henry. 1670
Pirus, Betty L. 2506, 3376
Pisan, Christian de. 2812
Pisani, Paul. 2576
Pise, Charles Constantine. 3063
Pistis, Sophia. 3437
Pistole, Hollis. 1610
Pitcairn, David. 1849
Pitcairn, Theodore. 2691, 3664
Pitcher, George. 3716

Pitel, Conrad Martin. 640
Pitezel, John H. 7
Pitkin, John Budd. 3356
Pitman, Emma Raymond. 1872, 2488
Pitman, Thomas B. 3868
Pitman, Walter G. 145, 1144
Pitois, Christian. 2314
Pitollet, Camille. 317
Pitrone, Jean Maddern. 1310, 1901, 2556, 3426
Pitrus, John. 1441
Pitt, James E. 695
Pitt, Malcolm. 1814
Pitt, Sherman Grant. 640
Pittard, Barbara Brinsfield. 1316
Pittenger, Norman. 1105
Pittenger, W. Norman. 3647
Pittenger, William Norman. 66, 71, 946, 991, 1062, 1096, 1122, 1696, 1819, 1831, 1843, 1893, 1970, 2042, 2177, 2252, 2253, 2276, 2324, 2800, 2825, 2877, 2904, 2944, 2958, 2981, 3388, 3391, 3412, 3652, 3656, 3664, 3666, 3695, 3712
Pittini, Riccardo. 2544
Pittman, J. C. Ferdinand. 650
Pitt-Rivers, George Henry Lane Fox. 892
Pitts, F. E. 3225
Pitts, John. 1600
Pitts, Lilla Belle. 917, 2634
Pitts, Mildred. 1071
Pitts, Miled. 1071
Pitts, V. Peter. 904
Pittsburgh Calvary church. 1273
Pittsburgh. Carnegie library. 869, 911, 2847
Pittsburgh Catholic. 2850
Pittsburgh (Diocese, Catholic) Board of supervisors. 824
Pittsburgh (Diocese, Catholic) Diocesan school board. 824
Pittsburgh. East Liberty Presbyterian church. 2913
Pittsburgh Festival on the Gospels, 1970. 383
Pittsburgh. First Presbyterian church. 2913
Pittsburgh. Rodef Shalom Congregation. 1660
Pittsburgh. St. John Chrysostom Greek Catholic Church. 1768
Pittsburgh synod of the Evangelical Lutheran church. 1548
Pittsburgh synod of the Evangelical Lutheran church (General council) 1548
Pittsburgh. Third Presbyterian church. 2918
Pittsburgh typewriter & supply company. 10
Pittsburgh. Western theological seminary. 1821, 2850, 3332, 3627
Pittston, Pa. St. Mary's Assumption Church. 1269
Pittwood, Ann. 2728
Pitzer, A[lexander] W[hite]. 972
Pitzer, Alexander White. 2065
Pius a Spiritu Sancto. 2767
Pius Franziskus. 2625
Pius II, 1405-1464. 177, 2861
Pius II, 1405- 1464. 177
Pius II, 1405-1464. 177
Pius X I, 1857. 1817
Pius I I, 1405-1464. 2850
Pius XII. 2343
Pius XII, 1876-1958. 2344
Pius XII, 1857-1939. 739, 1817
Pius XII, 1876. 761, 2853
Pius XII, 1876-1958. 761, 889, 2359, 2894
Pixley, George V. 2176
Pjetursson, Hallgrimur. 1876
Planchart, Alejandro Enrique. 849, 3715
Planhol, Xavier de. 2565
Plank, Hiram. 2156
Plankoff, Alexandre, ed. and tr. 3014
Planque, Daniel. 2344
Plante, Patricia. 1588
Planter, Josephine. 2557
Plantinga, Alvin. 1105, 1729, 1738, 1739
Plantz, Samuel. 3445
Planus, Romain Louis. 3222
Plaquevent, Jean. 904
Plaskow, Judith. 2709, 3834, 3835
Plassmann, Thomas Bernard. 845, 1299, 1886, 2742
Plastaras, James. 565, 1584, 2089
Plater, Charles Dominic. 1543, 757
Plato. 2661, 2834, 2853, 3454, 3762
Platon, 1737-1812. 1469, 2746, 2750
Platt, Frederic. 1886
[Platt, I.L. 397
Platt, Mary (Schauffler) 895, 2483, 2521
Platt, Nancy Van Dyke. 2782
Platt, Smith H. 1506, 3393
Platt, Thomas. 1376
Platt, Ward. 2434, 2443
Platt, William Henry. 61, 66, 3567
Platten, Thomas George. 535

Plattner, Felix Alfred. 819, 1949
Plaut, W. Gunther. 522, 562, 2140, 3032, 3082, 3278
Playfair, Guy Lyon. 1786, 2728, 2858, 2990
Playford, Henry. 917
Ple, Albert. 889
Pleasanton, Louise M. 623
Pleasants, Helene, ed. 2992
Pleasants, Sanderson Alexander. 2001

Plecher, Andrew. 1655
Plekker, Robert J. 1471, 3829
Pleming, Laura C. 550
Plett, C. J. J. M. M. 1428
Plett, Jake. 987, 2854
Pleune, Peter Henry. 2934, 3674
Pleuthner, Willard Augustus. 1252
Plimpton, George. 3598
Ploeg, J. P. M. van der. 1410, 3014
Ploger, Otto. 56
Plopper, Clifford Henry. 913
Plotinus. 2684
Plotkin, Albert. 547, 1943
Plotkin, Frederick. 2080, 3067
Plotz, Helen. 1022
Plotzke, Urban Werner. 3337
Plowden, Alison. 872
Plowman, Edward E. 2712
Plowman, Max G. 291, 311
Plowright, Bernard Clifford. 3445
Plude, Frances Forde. 870
Plueger, Aaron Luther. 607, 1530
Plum, Harry Grant. 1760, 3007, 3008
Plumb, Beatrice. 661
Plumb, Oscar C. 1007
Plumer, William. 573
Plumer, William Swan. 403, 469, 1352, 1369, 1737, 1752, 2042, 2981, 3664, 3674
[Plumley, Gardiner Spring] 1827-1894. 2916
Plumley, Ruth. 1688
Plummer, Alfred. 321, 428, 1194, 3035
Plummer, Charles. 3283
Plummer, Frederick. 3712
[Plummer, George Winslow]. 3251
Plummer, George Winslow. 3251, 3511
Plummer, Goerge Winslow. 3251
Plummer, L. Flora (Fait) 3557
Plummer, L. Gordon. 3687
Plummer, Nellie Arnold. 2854
Plumpe, Joseph Conrad. 1093, 1122
Plumptre, Edward Hayes. 2800
Plumstead, A. W. 1504
Plus, Raoul. 2363, 3300, 138, 1001, 1610, 2032, 2394, 2627, 2637, 2877, 3489, 3782
Plus, Raoul. 1001
Plus Raoul. 2394
Plutarchus. 1765, 1779, 2834, 3246
Plyer, Marion Timothy. 1943
Plyler, A. W. 3699
Plymire, David. 2855 ·
Plymouth, Mass. 1849
[Plymouth, Mass. First Church]. 2855, 3741
Poage, Godfrey Robert. 773, 1028, 1289, 1700, 2333, 3785, 3786
Pobee, J. S. 3653
Pochmann, Henry August. 23, 3708
Pocknee, Cyril Edward. 28, 1221, 1249, 1958
Pocock, David Francis. 1777
Pocock, Nicholas. 1804, 3039
Podach, Erich Friedrich. 2710
Podhradsky, Gerhard. 843, 3855
Podmore, Frank. 3511, 2413, 2990, 3511
Podro, Michael. 88
Podsiadlo, Jack. 3181
Poe, Edgar Allan. 2855
Poe, Elias Dodson. 141, 166
Poehler, Willy August. 2215, 3165
Poel, Cornelius J. van der. 2344
Poellot, Luther. 455
Poelman, Roger. 2209
Poelman, Roger, Abbe. 613
*Poganski, Donald J. 2720
Poggi, Gianfranco. 121, 754
Poggio-Bracciolini. 1857
Pogle, Frances Putnam. 1167
Pohle, Joseph. 1473, 1528, 1529, 1726, 1752, 1954, 2356, 3030, 3263, 3712
Pohlschneider, Johannes. 2939
Poinsenet, Marie Dominique. 1474
Poinsett, Brenda. 2049, 2877
Pointer, Priscilla. 901, 2249
Pointing, Horace Bertram. 1676
Pol, Willem Hendrick van de. 1043
Pol, Willem Hendrick van de. 1062, 2977
Polack, Albert Isaac. 1970, 2092, 2147
Polack, William Gustave. 1549, 1875, 2058, 2241, 2276, 2302, 3790, 3301
Polaert, Andre. 2112
Poland, Burdette C. 2954
Poland, Larry W. 987

Polanyi, Michael. 2376
Pole, Karl Frederick Michael. 1785
Pole, Reginald. 763, 1803, 2161, 3039
Pole, Thomas. 650, 3561
Polen, O. W. 1003
Poley, Irvin C. 1675
Polgreen, John. 2229
Polhamus, William Robert. 456, 1178, 2626
Polhemus, Abraham. 1692
Poling, Daniel Alfred. 908, 1325, 1554, 1954, 1970, 2071, 2394, 2857, 2877, 3012, 3018, 3133, 3344, 3456, 3793, 3888
Poling, David. 384, 1062, 1359, 1576, 1755, 1872
Polish, David. 2140, 3032
Polishook, Irwin H. 3193, 3817
Politella, Joseph. 702, 703, 1129, 1814, 3586
Politi, Leo. 1643, 1644
[Polk, Josiah F. 217, 3259
Poll, Solomon. 565, 1789, 2121
Pollack, Jack Harrison. 1387
Pollak, Michael. 3704
Polland, Madeleine A. 1311
Pollard, Albert Frederick. 3831, 1378, 1948
Pollard, Alfred William. 248
Pollard, Edward Bagby. 3235
Pollard, John Richard Thornhill. 1767
Pollard, Josephine. 253, 296, 406, 532, 626, 630, 911, 1747, 1970, 1983, 3258
Pollard, Ralph J. 1672
Pollard, Robert Spence Watson. 2223
Pollard, Stewart M. L. 1663
Pollard, T. E. 421, 2011
Pollard, William. 1685
Pollard, William Grosvenor. 2981, 3082
Pollen, John Hungerford. 1508, 669, 816, 818, 2269
Pollitt, Levin Irving. 132
Pollock, Algernon J. 1560
Pollock, Bertram. 935, 3366
*Pollock, John. 1569, 1755
Pollock, John Charles. 926, 1292, 1576, 1755, 2588, 2706, 2800, 2821, 2979, 3590, 3813
Pollock, Shirley E. 1260
Pollock, Sylvia. 1111
Polloi, Ch. 2361
Pollom, Noah Doc.]. 3579
Polman, Andries Derk Rietema. 117, 176
Polner, Murray. 3016
Poloma, Margaret M. 2817
Pols, Edward. 2473
Polsey, Austin. 2401

Polston, Don H. 987, 1325, 2394
Polston, Ruth Ann. 3845
Polten, Eric P. 2473
Polycarpus. 2858
Polyzoides, Germanos. 941, 2745, 2747, 2748
Polyzoides, Germanos, Bp. 2745
Polzer, Charles W. 1948, 1949, 2177
Polzin, Robert. 496, 550, 2756, 3536
Polzl, Franz Xaver. 386, 2030
Pomerantz, Alfred. 2568
Pomerantz, Charlotte. 2712
Pomeroy, Ella. 3751
[Pomeroy, Everett]. 783, 791
Pomeroy, John Jay. 3019
Pomey, Francois Antoine. 2657
Pomfret, Conn. First church of Christ. 1269
Pomfret, John. 3208, 3209
Pommer, W H. 1397
Pomona, Calif. First Christian church. Historical committee. 2859
Pomrius, Julianus. 972
Ponce, Charles. 722, 2728
Pond, Douglas V. 2612
Pond, Enoch. 106, 136, 236, 463, 719, 1333, 2373, 2943, 3193, 3570, 3652, 3674, 3814
Pond, Harold Sackett. 1668
Pond, James Burton. 184
Pond, Kathleen. 2648
Pond, Mariam Buckner. 1624
Pond, William Chauncey. 1335
Ponder, Catherine. 494, 1600, 3539
Ponder, Catherine Thrower. 1011
Ponder, James A. 3829
Ponnuthurai, C. S. 1126
Pont, Charles Ernest. 607
*Pontier, Arthur E. 596, 748
Pontifex, Mark. 1738, 2739, 3712
Pontius, Myron Lee. 1352, 1466, 3356
Ponton, Andrew Jackson. 2463
Ponton, Mungo. 3076
Ponton, Mungo Melanchthon. 3718
Pontoppidan, Erik. 1594, 2279, 2283
Ponvert, Simone (De Noaillat) 2712
Pool, David de Sola. 2081, 2101, 2111, 2140, 2162, 2698, 2699, 2700, 3333
Pool, Elizabeth (Routh) 407, 2542

Pool, Elizabeth (Routh) [Alice Elizabeth (Routh) Pool]. 407
Poole, Cecil A. 3251
Poole, Donald R. 1706
Poole, Elijah. 669
Poole, Eva Travers Evered. 1726
Poole, George Ayliffe. 2826
Poole, Reginald Lane. 766, 2769, 2842, 3861, 2769, 2842, 3861
Poole, Stafford. 3614
Pooler, Lewis Arthur Hill Trevor. 2116
Poonen, Zac. 987
Poor, Laura Elizabeth. 2653
Poovey, William Arthur. 8, 66, 299, 365, 443, 471, 1113, 1694, 2003, 2059, 2209, 2210, 2215, 2248, 2301, 2722, 2813, 3012, 3326
Pope, Alexander. 2860
Pope, Charles Henry. 1035
Pope, Charles Wesley. 2528
Pope, Harrison. 1485
Pope, Howard Walter. 1569
Pope, Hugh. 291, 115, 270
Pope, Hugh [Secular name: Henry Vincent Pope]. 115
Pope, Liston. 1703
Pope, Mark Cooper. 1931
Pope, Richard Martin. 1178
Pope, Richard Thomas Pembroke. 794
Pope, Robert G. 1201
Pope, Robert H. 987
Pope, William C. 1178
Pope, William Cox. 1109
Pope, William Kenneth. 2860
Popejoy, Bill. 587, 1600
Popoff, Eli Alex. 1482
Popoff, Haralan. 2820, 2863, 2942
Popoff, Peter. 612, 1576, 2863
Popol vuh. & Quiche. 3013
Popol vuh. English. 3013
Popov, Ladin. 2817, 2863
Popp, Clarissa. 3421
Poppe, Nikolai Nikolaevich. 703
Poppelbaum, Hermann. 50
Poppen, Emmanuel. 2290, 3563
Poppy, Maximus. 1645, 1648, 1649
Popson, Martha. 928
Porlas, Mary Eve. 648
Porrentruy, Louis Antoine de. 179
Porritt, Arthur. 3870, 2135, 3201
Port Society of the City of Boston and its Vicinity. 2411
Portalie, Eugene. 117
Portalis, Jean Etienne Marie. 1145
Portals of prayer. 1434
Portasik, Richard. 1649
Porteous, Alexander. 1632
Porteous, Alvin C. 3650, 2222, 3647
Porteous, David. 3035
Porteous, Norman W. 506
Porter, Albert Davis. 2203
Porter, Alyene. 3675
Porter, Anthony Toomer. 3133
Porter, Arthur Kingsley. 1388
Porter, Blaine R. 1610
Porter, Burton Frederick. 3070
Porter, Charles Talbot. 3076
Porter, David. 136
Porter, David Richard. 1596, 2877, 3857, 3872
Porter, Donald A. 832
Porter, Ebenezer. 2904, 3229
Porter, Edward. 3201
Porter, Eliot. 407, 475, 535, 1198
Porter, Elizabeth Gamble. 3809
Porter, Ellen Jane. 1860
Porter, Elliot. 1201
Porter, Frank Chamberlin. 56, 376, 2042
Porter, Gene (Stratton) 481
Porter, Harold Boone. 1263
Porter, Harry Boone. 3547, 1244
Porter, Harry Culverwell. 3008
Porter, Henry Alford. 166
Porter, Henry Dwight. 2485
Porter, Jack Nusan. 2152
Porter, Jack W. 3278
Porter, James. 1930, 2421, 2443, 3229, 3511, 3674
Porter, Jean Kelleher. 3844
Porter, John William. 1560, 3067, 3292, 3832
Porter, Josias Leslie. 1944, 2864
Porter, Katherine H. 697, 1518
Porter, Larry C. 1233
Porter, Lucius Chapin. 2510
Porter, Mary Harriet. 2864
Porter, Noah. 1946, 2163
Porter, Rose. 1451, 1726, 3406
Porter, Ross C. 2175
Porter, Rue. 3356
Porter, Samuel Judson. 972, 2263, 1071
Porter, W Curtis. 1272
Porter, William Arthur. 3723
Porter, William Stevens. 843
Porterfield, Bruce E. 2504
Porteus, Beilby. 1099, 3317, 3366

Portland, Me. High street Congregational church. 2864
Portland, Me. State street church. 1336
Porton, Gary G. 1921, 3015
Ports, George W. 2304
Portsmouth, N. H. South parish. 3270
Poschmann, Bernhard. 2812
*Posey, A. R. 137, 152
Posey, Walter Brownlow. 169, 2432, 2453, 2548, 2919, 3468
Posner, Zalman I. 2751
Pospishil, Victor J. 1471
Posselt, Teresia Renata de Spiritu Sancto. 3526
Possevino, Antonio. 791, 3257
Possidius. 115
Post, Albert. 1657
Post, Charles Cyrel. 2834
Post, Harry Grant. 2877
Post, Howard Aftan. 1794
Post, Isaac. 3511
Post, Levi Arnold. 2853
Post, Samuel. 3511
Post, Truman Augustus. 2865
Post, Truman Marcellus. 3422
Post, Willard Ellwood. 921
Postal, Bernard. 673
Posterski, Don. 641, 1170
Poston, Charles Dibrell. 2777
Posy, Arnold. 1631, 2646, 3581
Potapenko, Ignatii Nikolaevich. 2939
Pote, Lawrence. 3028
Poteat, Edwin McNeil. 2026
Poteat, Edwin McNeill. 1998, 2247, 3529, 166, 1314, 1986, 1998, 2007, 2030, 2247, 2326, 3104, 3674
Poteat, Edwin McNeill, jr. 166
Poteat, Gordon. 39, 323, 2539
Poteat, Hubert McNeill. 1872
Poteat, William L. 3073
Poteat, William Louis. 1052, 3073, 3079
Poteet, G. Howard. 1418
Pothan, S. G. 3278
Potocek, Cyril J. 1398
Pott, Francis Lister Hawks. 912, 2510
Pott, William Hawks. 332
*Pottebaum, George A. 3163
Pottebaum, Gerard A. 47, 1111, 1726, 2267, 2394, 2894, 3163, 3412
Pottenger, Milton Alberto. 3574
Potter, Bernard. 3063
Potter, C. Burtt. 1569, 3465
Potter, Charles Francis. 2042
Potter, Charles Francis. 1854, 3094
Potter, Charles Francis. 491, 1083, 1410, 1520, 1532, 3090, 3094, 3119
Potter, F L. 2351
Potter, Frederic James. 3227
Potter, George Richard. 3900
Potter, Helen. 1509
Potter, Henry C[odman]. 1730
Potter, Henry Codman. 2865, 3344, 3416, 3445, 3837
Potter, John. 3664
Potter, Lemuel. 106
Potter, Leo Goodwin. 987, 2042
Potter, Mary. 2359, 3476, 3489
Potter, Philip. 990, 3850
Potter, Ralph B. 3793
Potter, Ray. 1478, 1662, 2465, 2822
Potter, Reuben. 3511
Potter, Rockwell Harmon. 1596, 1787
Potter, Samuel L. 623
Potter, Thomas. 3356
Potter, Thomas Joseph. 2904
Potter, William James. 2686
Potterbaum, Charlene. 932, 2865
Potterton, Thomas Edward. 1374
Pottgeisser, Julius. 1267
Potthoff, Harvey H. 1007, 1735, 3616, 3618, 3829
Pottier, Henri. 1498
Pottoff, Harvey H. 333
Potts, Albert M. 1587
Potts, Cyrus Alvin. 245
Potts, Edwin James. 3156
Potts, Eli Daniel. 2546
Potts, George C. 311
Potts, James Henry. 1451, 1529, 1594, 2421, 2437, 2865, 3344
Potts, James Manning. 1456, 2896
Potts, Nancy D. 1256, 2244
Potts, Thomas. 2937, 2938, 3827
Potts, William Stephens. 1946
Pottsville republican, Pottsville, Pa. 2865
Potvin, Raymond H. 3890
Potwin, George Stephen. 1485
Potwin, Lemuel Stoughton. 349
Pouget, Guillaume. 594
Pouillon, Fernand. 2203
Poule noire. English. 3582
Poulet, Charles. 1178
Poullart des Places, Claude Francois. 1679-1709. 777
Poulos, George. 668, 876
Poulson, Omer Bruce. 3463
Pouncey, Temple. 3468

Pound, James Presley. 3366
Pound, Roscoe. 1663
Pounders, Margaret. 3750
Pounds, Jessie Brown. 2483
Pounds, Jessie Hunter (Brown) 2483
Poure, Ken. 987, 1610
Pourrat, Pierre. 90, 2736, 3263, 3545
Pousset, Edouard. 1622
Povah, John Walter. 501, 568, 1249
Povey, Charles. 3235
Powel, Harford Willing Hare. 373, 2800
Powell, Adam Clayton. 2762, 146, 2866, 143
Powell, Arthur Edward. 94, 3079
Powell, Baden. 3706
[Powell, Benjamin]. 1527
Powell, Benjamin F. 3023
Powell, Cyril H. 973, 2244, 2866, 2877
Powell, David. 2689
Powell, David E. 3257
Powell, Edward Lindsay. 1277, 3305, 1466
Powell, Edward Payson. 1581, 3723
Powell, Emma Moody (Fitt) 2588
Powell, Enoch John. 945
Powell, Esther Weygandt. 2348
Powell, F. Ellsworth. 1716
[Powell, Frederick Cecil]. 81
Powell, George C. 2394
Powell, Gideon Little. 1831
Powell, Gordon George. 973, 1356, 1777, 2006, 2021, 2071
Powell, Ivor. 166, 216, 417, 428, 1569, 1841, 3664
Powell, Jacob Wesley. 15
Powell, James Baden. 916
Powell, James M. 1908
Powell, John. 2877
Powell, John Henderson, jr. 1314
Powell, John Joseph. 1122, 1999, 2265, 3664
Powell, John Walker. 973, 501, 600
Powell, Jouett Lynn. 2704
Powell, Lewis. 3201
Powell, Luther P. 1168
Powell, Lyman Pierson. 926, 1035, 1037, 1052, 1495, 2884, 1035
Powell, Mac. 1052, 3463
Powell, Marie (Cole) 3156, 3858
Powell, Milton. 3749
Powell, Newman Minnich. 496
Powell, Newman Wilson. 1204
Powell, Oliver. 1139, 3678
Powell, Paul W. 994, 1171, 3678
Powell, Perry Edwards. 46
Powell, Robert. 2187, 3892, 3894
Powell, Robert Charles. 675, 885
Powell, Robert R. 3557
Powell, Robert Richard. 1170, 2823
Powell, Ruth Marie. 30
Powell, Sidney Waterbury. 11, 1551, 1569, 1610, 3674
Powell, Sumner Chilton. 1282
Powell, T. W. 3557
Powell, Terry. 338, 987
Powell, Thomas. 76, 2817
Powell, W. H. R. 588
Powell, Warren Thomson. 1167, 2854
Powell, Wilfred Evans. 3156
Powell, William Stevens. 3287
Power, Albert. 761, 791, 2132, 2356, 3691
Power, David Noel. 2202
Power, Edmond. 208, 2121
Power, Edward J. 832, 870
Power, Eileen Edna. 1357
Power, Frederick Dunglison. 1462
Power, John. 596, 599, 2555
Power, John Hamilton. 3752, 3753
Power, Marion. 596
Power, Michael. 1707, 1708
Power, P. B. 3406
Powers, Barbara Hudson. 2376
Powers, Bruce P. 953
Powers, Charles W. 1168, 1536
Powers, Edward A. 3163
Powers, Francis Fountain. 2591
Powers, Isaias. 2877
Powers, James Michael. 2586
Powers, John R. 2866
Powers,Joseph M. 2255, 3664
Powers, Laura Bride. 3470
Powers, Oliver Worden. 1569
Powers, Robert Merrill. 3133
Powers, Thomas E. 3481
Powers, William Emmett. 523
Powers, William K. 2734
Power-Waters, Alma (Shelley) 1896. 2190, 2478, 3378, 3379, 3417
Powicke, 2195
Powicke, Frederick Maurice. 3039, 1533, 3039, 1282, 1373
Powley, Edward Barzillai. 1764
Powys, Albert Reginald. 1270
Powys, John Cowper. 2227, 3063
Powys, Llewelyn. 1052, 1726, 2762, 1092
Powys, Theodore Francis. 523, 1807
Poyas, James Kenlock. 120

Poynter, James William. 3041
Poynter, Margaret. 1482, 3717
Poynter, Thomas. 2345
Poyntz, S. G. 3273
Poyser, George K. 1463
Pozdneev, Aleksei Matveevich. 2572
Pozo, Candido. 2806
Prabhavanada. 1815, 2840, 3775
Prabhavananda, 1893. 689
Prabhavananda, Swami. 3336
Pradera, Victor. 1143
Pradervand, Marcel. 3849
Praetorius, E. W. 1328
Praetorius, Elmer Wesley. 973
Praetz, Helen Margaret. 806, 814, 3310
Prager, Dennis. 2751
Prajnaparamitas. Astasahasrika. English. 2819
Prajnaparamitas. Ratnagunasancayagatha. 2867
Prall, William. 1141, 3445, 1141
Pranaitis, IUstin Bonaventura. 2013, 2118
Pranananda. 2316
Prange, Erwin E. 2877
Praptr, Arnold. 2136
Prat, Ferdinand. 377, 1970, 2800
Prat, Ferdinand [Antoine Ferdinand Prat]. 1970
Prater, Arnold. 987, 1007, 1015, 1602, 2136, 2437, 2771, 2786, 2877
Prather, Hugh. 2867, 3481
Prati, Carlo. 2861
Pratney, Winkie. 3888
Pratt, Antoinette Marie. 762
Pratt, Charles Edgar. 3107
Pratt, Dwight Mallory. 1554
Pratt, Helen Marshall. 751
Pratt, Henry Barrington. 523
Pratt, Henry J. 1087, 2670
Pratt, James Bissett. 703, 1096, 1896, 2473, 2675, 2999, 708, 1071, 1597, 2473, 2999
Pratt, James Randall. 1429
Pratt, Jane Abbott. 2329
Pratt, John Barnes. 1868
Pratt, John Webb. 1148
Pratt, Joseph Gaither. 2990, 3520
Pratt, Lillian Louise. 3201
Pratt, Magee. 3133
Pratt, Marsha Whitney. 973, 1594
Pratt, Orson. 2609, 2859, 2867
Pratt, Parley Parker. 2605, 2609, 2612, 2867
Pratt, Samuel Wheeler. 424, 1835, 2001
Pratt, Sarah (Smith) 2962
[Pratt, Stillman]. 1487
Pratt, Waldo Selden. 1203, 2985, 1203
Prawer, Joshua. 1390, 1944
Prebish, Charles S. 703, 710, 3267
Preble, Jedidiah. 2773
Presbyterian church in the United States of America, Board of home missions. Dept. of church and country life. 3435
Predmore, George V. 1205
Predmore, George Vincent. 1205
Predmore, Helen R. 891, 1627
Predovich, Nicholas A. 2571
Preece, Harold. 3326
Pregnall, William S. 2972
Preibisch, Paul. 3245
Preiss, Theo. 335
Preister, Gertrude Ann. 1735
Preller, Victor. 3070, 3697
Prells, Theresa C. 3511
Premananda, 1861-1918. 1814
Premananda. 703, 3330, 3865, 3866, 3867
Preminger, Marion Mill. 1635
Premm, Mathias. 3647
Premm, Matthias. 2367
Prenter, Regin. 1831, 1835, 2276, 2279, 3623, 3647, 3664
Prentice, George. 1628
Prentice, Margaret May. 2510
Prentice, Robert P. 675, 2263
Prentice, Sartell. 750, 921
Prentice, William Kelly. 391
Prentice G. H. 3595
Prentiss, Elizabeth (Payson) 1451, 1999, 3493
Prentiss, George Lewis. 720, 1594, 1612, 2701
Prepositinus d. ca. 1210. 842
Prepositinus Cremonensia, d ca. 1210. 782
Presbyter Anglicanus. 3770
Presbyterian brotherhood of America. 2920
Presbyterian Church in Canada. Presbyteries. Hamilton, Ont. 2917
[McKeever, Harriet Burn] 1807-1886. 1983
Presbyterian Church in the U.S. 1046, 1260, 1603, 2913, 2916, 2919, 2920, 2921, 2923, 2924, 2925, 2926, 2927, 2928, 2971, 3424, 3735, 3808

AUTHOR INDEX PROTESTANT

Presbyterian church in the U. S. A. 687, 692, 891, 926, 1240, 1273, 1560, 1611, 2339, 2521, 2522, 2528, 2818, 2914, 2915, 2916, 2918, 2920, 2921, 2922, 2923, 2924, 2925, 2926, 2928, 2936, 3156, 3435, 3627, 3810, 3854
Presbyterian Church in the U. S. A. Board of Christian Education. 2914, 2923, 2929
Presbyterian Church in the U. S. A. General Assembly. 2922
Presbyterian church in the U. S. A. General assembly. Sustentation committee. 2457
Presbyterian church in the U. S. A. Presbytery of Oneida. 3229
Presbyterian church in the U. S. A. Synod of New York. Committee on religion and public education. 1129
Presbyterian Church in the U.S.A. Board of Christian Education. 1248, 2923, 3759, 3809
Presbyterian Church in the U. S. Board of Christian Education. Dept. of Campus Christian Life. 3537
Presbyterian Church in the U. S. Board of Christian Education. Division of Men's Work. 2915
Presbyterian Church in the U. S. Board of Church Extension. 2925
Presbyterian Church in the U.S.A. Board of Foreign Missions. 2926
[Presbyterian church in the U.S.A. Board of publication and Sabbath school work]. 687, 1482, 1606
Presbyterian Church in the U.S. Board of World Missions. 2926
Presbyterian church in the U.S.A. College board. 2923
Presbyterian church in the U.S.A. Committee on camps and church activities. 3456
Presbyterian Church in the U.S. Council on Theology and Culture. 1844
Presbyterian Church in the U.S. Ecumenical Consultation. 1046, 2927
Presbyterian church in the U. S. Executive committee of Christian education and ministerial relief. 2923
Presbyterian church in the U.S. Executive committee of publication. 1606
Presbyterian church in the U. S. Exevutive committee of Christian education and ministerial relief. 2923
Presbyterian Church in the U.S. General Assembly. 2913, 2914, 2922, 2923, 2925
Presbyterian church in the U.S.A. Liturgy and ritual. 3854
Presbyterian church in the United States of America. 1482, 3627
Presbyterian Church in the U.S.A. (Old School) 2927
Presbyterian Church in the U.S.A. Presbyteries. 3232
Presbyterian church in the U.S.A. Presbyteries. Brooklyn. 3582
Presbyterian Church in the U.S.A. Presbyteries. Carlisle. 2936
Presbyterian church in the U.S.A. Presbyteries. Chicago. 3572
Presbyterian church in the U.S. Presbyteries. East Hanover. 2921
Presbyterian Church in the U. S. Presbyteries. Honover. 2927
Presbyterian Church in the U.S. Presbyteries. Mobile. 2921
Presbyterian Church in the U.S.A. Presbyteries. Oneida. 3232
Presbyterian church in the U.S.A. Presbyteries. West Jersey. 695
Presbyterian Church in the U.S.A. Presbytery of Kanawha. 2927
Presbyterian church in the U. S. Synod of Missouri. Home mission committee. 2928
Presbyterian Church in the U.S. Synods. Florida. 2921
Presbyterian Church in the U.S. Synods. Georgia. 2917
Presbyterian Church in the U.S. Synods. North Carolina. 2928
Presbyterian Church in the U. S. Synods. Virginia. 2928
Presbyterian Church in the U.S.A. Synods. Wisconsin. 2929
Presbyterian college of South Carolina, Clinton, S. C. Surrey commission. 2936
Presbyterian historical society. 2921
Prescott, Edmund E. 3377
Prescott, Hilda Frances Margaret. 1588, 2763, 1022, 1588
Prescott, Houston. 3481
Prescott, Jedediah Brown. 3133
Prescott, Latimer Howard. 2639, 2640
Prescott, Nellie G. 156
Prescott, Reuben. 623
Prescott, William Ray. 2431
Prescott, William W. 934
Prescott, William Warren. 208
*Presentina, Mary. 3163
Pressau, Jack Renard. 3290
Pressense, Edmond Dehault de. 1093, 1970, 2526, 3030
Pressense, Francis de Hault de. 2328
Presser, John Lee. 148
Prestige, George Leonard. 3658
*Preston, Burman H. 224, 614
[Preston, Charles Earl] 1859-1899. 885
Preston, Edward. 2173
Preston, Emily. 1802
Preston, Geoffrey. 1001, 1264, 2015
Preston, James. 881, 1815
Preston, Kerrison. 670
Preston, Mary Frances Johnson. 2204
Preston, Novella D. 1875
Preston, Paul. 1650, 3469
Preston, Samuel. 1359
Preston, South G. 321
Preston, Thomas Scott. 1747, 2033, 2058, 2353
Preston, Virgie Viola (Vail) 47
Preston, William. 1662
Preston, William Hall. 973
Preston, William J. 3566
Prestridge, John Newton. 143, 1122
Prestwich, Eng. 3052
Prestwood, Charles. 1296
Prete, Anthony. 3182
Pretyman, R. D. 2553
Preus, David W. 1765, 3356
Preus, Herman Amberg, 1896. 2276, 2281
Preus, Jacob Aall Ottesen. 277, 1959
Preus, James Samuel. 501, 2165, 2276, 3041, 3669
Preus, Johan Carl Keyser. 1547, 1606, 2528, 3578
Preus, Robert. 306
Preus, Robert D. 2283, 3668
Preuss, Henry Clay. 3207
Prewitt, Cheryl. 932, 2938
PrFrancis, Mary Grace. 3163
Price, Annie Darling. 3050
Price, Carl E. 2394
Price, Carl Fowler. 1861, 1872, 2459
Price, Charles Henry. 918
Price, Charles P. 2235, 2958, 2969
Price, Charles Sydney. 1514
Price, Christine. 87
Price, Daniel. 1227, 2411, 2810
*Price, E. David. 973
Price, E. W. 2877
Price, Eli Kirk. 1510
Price, Ernest Bruce. 3383
Price, Eugenia. 296, 330, 399, 973, 987, 1362, 1367, 1432, 1451, 1726, 2265, 2938, 3012, 3840, 3844, 3845, 3880
Price, Francis Wilson. 2494, 2511
Price, Frederick A. 2538
Price, George McCready. 2938, 66, 465, 506, 1100, 3079, 3313, 3383
Price, Harry. 2990
Price, Henry Habberley. 3079, 3107
Price, Ira Maurice. 487, 535, 291, 487, 291
Price, James Ligon. 410
Price, John. 763
Price, John Milburn. 973, 2061, 2065, 2592, 3156, 3465, 3466
Price, John Richard. 3742
Price, Lucien. 25
Price, Margaret (Evans) 2661
Price, Maude A. 1134
Price, Nelson L. 180, 994, 1881, 3252
Price, Philip B. 3235
Price, Phinehas. 3133
Price, Reynolds. 623
Price, Richard. 1536, 3647
Price, Richard Nye. 2455
Price, Ross E. 1238, 1569
Price, Samuel. 2118
Price, Theodora Hadzisteliou. 2624
Price, Walter K. 52, 53, 444, 471, 509, 552, 610, 1407, 2050, 2415, 3300
Price, Warwick James. 236
Price, Willard. 2521
Price, William Thompson. 174
Prichard, Augustus Bedlow. 579
Prichard, Ernie. 3829
Prichard, Harold Adye. 1052, 1890, 2026, 2904, 2991
Prichard, Harold Arthur. 1537
Prichard, Lucette Marguerite (Hutton) 1451
Prichard, Marianna (Nugent) 1110, 1188
Prichard Marianna (Nugent) 3182
Priddis, Venice. 680
Pride, Ora Lee. 895
Prideaux, Humphrey. 2089
Prideaux, Sherburne Povah Tregelles. 2055, 3375
Pridgeon, Charles Hamilton. 1594, 3220
Priebe, Kenneth. 3888
Prieditis, Arthur. 2715, 2947
Prieditis, Arthur A. 2715, 2947
Priesand, Sally. 3837
A priest. 1441
Priest, Arlis. 932, 2938
Priest, James Eugene. 514, 1460, 1539
Priest, Josiah. 2465
*Priester, Gertrude. 3171
Priester, Gertrude Ann. 634, 898, 2804, 3171
Priestley, Joseph. 59, 227, 1099, 1726, 1855, 2758, 3023, 3655
Priestley, Joshua. 1809
*Prime, Derek. 313, 1108, 2047, 2250, 2867, 2877, 3670
Prime, Ebenezer. 173, 698
Prime, George Wendell. 212, 1894
Prime, Mary Ellen. 3175
Prime, Nathaniel Scudder. 136
Prime, Samuel Irenaeus. 897, 2632, 3210, 3238
Prime, William Cowper. 1389, 1943
Primeaux, Patrick. 2709
Primer, Ben. 2956
Primitive Baptists. 1327
Prince, Aaron E. 166
Prince, Aaron Erastus. 166, 1560, 1784
Prince, Derek. 2877
Prince, Frank Templeton. 2472
Prince, John. 896
Prince, John Conger. 2736
Prince, John Dyneley. 506
Prince, John Francis Theodore. 3450
Prince, John Wesley. 3804
Prince, Leon Cushing. 1035, 3067
Prince, Samuel Henry. 3758
Prince, Thomas. 2941, 3356
Prince, Walter Franklin. 2991, 3859, 2991
Princeton, Ill. Hampshire colony Congregational church. 1274
Princeton, Ind. United Presbyterian church. 3736
The Princeton review. 3623, 3624
Princeton theological seminary. 306, 644, 661, 2800, 2915, 2923, 2941, 3361, 3615, 3619, 3624, 3637, 3682
Princeton theological seminary. Alumni association. 2941
Princeton theological seminary. Class of 1877. 391, 1821
Princeton Theological Seminary. Library. 644, 3627, 3679
Princeton university. 2941
Prindeville, Carlton A. 796, 2356, 2362, 2478, 3331
Pringle, Cyrus Guernsey. 2463
Pringle, John Christian. 3452
Pringle, Patrick. 2241
Pringle, William R. 1668
*Prinz, Harvey L. 3164
Prinz, Joachim. 2861
Prior, Edward Schroder. 751
Prior, Kenneth Francis William. 334, 1076, 1569, 2800, 3300
Prip-Moller, Johannes. 705
Prip-Moller, Johannes, 1889-1943. 3599
Prism (London) 1765
Pritchard, Agnes Camplejohn. 1322
Pritchard, Arnold. 872
Pritchard, James Bennett. 487, 537, 2678, 2743, 3457
Pritchard, John Paul. 349
Pritchard, John W. 3050
Pritchett, Henry Smith. 3536
Pritchett, John Perry. 872
Pritchett, Reuel B. 1300, 2942
Pritt, Stephen. 1215
Probert, John Charles Cripps. 2430
Problemi e prospettive di teologia fondamentale. 3624
Probst, Emile. 54
Procelus, Lycius, surnamed Diadochus. 3616
Prochnow, Herbert Victor. 180, 181, 1315, 1841, 2249, 3014
Proclus, Diadochus. 2944
Procter, Alexander. 1466
Procter, Francis. 1214, 2885
Procter, George. 1390
Procter, Marjorie. 144, 2718
Procter, Rosalie. 626
Proctor, Henry Hugh. 669
Proctor, J. Madison. 1834
Proctor, Jesse Harris. 1924
Proctor, Priscilla. 3835
Proctor, Robert A. 3168
Proctor, William. 1308, 1367, 1553, 2190
Proddow, Penelope. 85, 299, 2822
Proehl, Frederick C. 3737
Progoff, Ira. 1702, 2394, 2647, 3476
Program Development and Financial Planning Seminar for Church-Related Schools, University of Notre Dame. 1967. 832
Progroff, Ira. 1702, 3511
Prohaszka, Ottokar. 399
Prohl, Russell C. 3836
Prokhanov, Ivan Stepanovich. 3788
Prokop, Phyllis Stillwell. 217, 1432, 1506, 3539
Proper, David R. 2166
Prophet, Elizabeth Clare. 1765, 3474
Prophet, Mark. 306, 2361, 3474, 3811
Prophetic Bible conference, Chicago, 1914. 3320
Prose, Francine. 3581
Proserpio, Leone. 1700, 3532
Proskauer, Julien J. 3511, 3520
Prosper, Tiro, Aguitanus. 115, 3331
Prosper, Tiro, Aquitanus. 3295
Protestant Episcopal church in the Confederate States of America. 2972
Protestant Episcopal church in the U. S. A. 2958
Protestant Episcopal church in the U. S. A. Book of common prayer. Psalter. 2986
Protestant Episcopal church in the U. S. A. Church congress. 2958
Protestant Council of the City of New York. 2956
Protestant Council of the City of New York. Dept. of Church Planning and Research. 1786, 1912, 2698
Protestant deaconess society, Indianapolis. 1408
Protestant Church in the U.S.A. 2956
Protestant Episcopal church in the Confederate States of America. 2956, 2958
Protestant Episcopal church in the Confederate States of America. Book of common prayer. 2877
Protestant Episcopal Church in the U.S.A. 1694, 901, 1015, 1285, 2958, 2962, 2966, 2967, 2968, 2970, 2974, 3565
Protestant Episcopal church in the U. S. 1901. 2958
Protestant Episcopal church in the U. S. 1910. 2958
Protestant Episcopal church in the U. S. A. 272, 378, 1090, 1163, 1524, 1993, 2534, 2567, 2583, 2804, 2958, 2960, 2961, 2966, 2967, 2968, 2969, 2975, 3415, 3434, 3557, 3740, 3781, 3837
Protestant Episcopal church in the U. S. A. 1859. 2966
Protestant Episcopal church in the U. S. A. 1865. 2959
Protestant Episcopal church in the U. S. A. 1922. 2961
Protestant Episcopal church in the U. S. A. 1925. 2961
Protestant Episcopal church in the U. S. A. 1927. 2959
Protestant Episcopal church in the U. S. A. 1929. 2959
Protestant Episcopal church in the U. S. A. 1930. 2974
Protestant Episcopal church in the U. S. A. 1931. 2963
Protestant Episcopal church in the U. S. A. 1932. 2959
Protestant Episcopal church in the U. S. A. 1933. 2959
Protestant Episcopal church in the U. S. A. 1934. 2394
Protestant Episcopal Church in the U. S. A. Albany (Diocese) 1131
Protestant Episcopal church in the U. S. A. Army and navy commission. 3456
Protestant Episcopal church in the U. S. A. Board of missions. Domestic committee. 1901
Protestant Episcopal Church in the U. S. A. Book of common prayer. 1868, 2877, 2878, 2879, 2961, 2968, 2972, 3263
Protestant Episcopal church in the U. S. A. Book of common prayer. Commission service. 27
Protestant Episcopal church in the U. S. A. Book of common prayer. Mohawk. 2567
Protestant Episcopal church in the U. S. A. Book of common prayer. Psalter. 883, 2962
Protestant Episcopal Church in the U. S. A. Chicago (Diocese) 2962
Protestant Episcopal church in the U. S. A. Church congress. 2959, 2963
Protestant Episcopal church in the U. S. A. Church congress. 37th, Baltimore, 1922. 2963
Protestant Episcopal church in the U. S. A. Church congress, Richmond, 1926. 2967
Protestant Episcopal church in the U. S. A. Church congress. St. Louis, 1925. 2963
Protestant Episcopal church in the U. S. A. Dept. of religious education. 2965
Protestant Episcopal Church in the U. S. A. Homilies. 2965
Protestant Episcopal Church in the U. S. A. Joint Commission on Architecture and the Allied Arts. 1157

PROTESTANT RELIGIOUS BOOKS 1876 - 1982

Protestant Episcopal Church in the U. S. A. Joint Commission on Church Music. 1209
Protestant Episcopal Church in the U. S. A. Joint Commission on Ecumenical Relations. 1235
Protestant Episcopal Church in the U. S. A. Liturgy and ritual. 2969
Protestant Episcopal Church in the U. S. A. National Council. 3168
Protestant Episcopal Church in the U. S. A. National Council. Dept. of Christian Education. 333, 1601, 1734, 2964, 2965, 3168, 3171, 3174, 3181, 3182, 3188
Protestant Episcopal church in the U. S. A. National council. Dept. of religious education. 2676
[Protestant Episcopal church in the U. S. A. New York (Diocese)]. 2968
Protestant Episcopal Church in the U. S. A. New York (Diocese) Commission on Preparation for Confirmation. 1328
Protestant Episcopal Church in the U. S. A. Niobrara (Missionary District) 2970
Protestant Episcopal Church in the U. S. A. Southwestern Virginia (Diocese) 2974
Protestant Episcopal Church in the U. S. A. Washington (Diocese) 2959, 2966
Protestant Episcopal Church in the U. S. A. Western North Carolina (Diocese) 2959
Protestant Episcopal church in the U.S.A. Book of common prayer. 2879, 2961
Protestant Episcopal church in the U.S.A. Book of common prayer. Psalter. 2962
Protestant Episcopal Church in the U.S.A. Committee on the Observance of the Bicentennial. 33, 2972
Protestant Episcopal church in the U.S.A. Connecticut (Diocese) 1936
Protestant Episcopal Church in the U.S.A. Domestic and Foreign Missionary Society. 27
Protestant Episcopal church in the U.S.A. Forward movement committee. 3407
Protestant Episcopal church in the U.S.A. Georgia (Diocese) 2966
Protestant Episcopal church in the U.S.A. Homilies. 2965
Protestant Episcopal church in the U.S.A. Hymnal. 2968
Protestant Episcopal Church in the U.S.A. Joint Commission on Cooperation with the Eastern and Old Catholic Churches. 2959
Protestant Episcopal Church in the U.S.A. Liturgical Commission. 2961, 2969
Protestant Episcopal Church in the U.S.A. Liturgy and ritual. 366
Protestant Episcopal Church in the U.S.A. Massachusetts (Diocese) Commission on the Ministry. 1298
[Protestant Episcopal church in the U.S.A. National council]. 1116, 2879, 2970
Protestant Episcopal Church in the U.S.A. National Council. Dept. of Chrisian Education. 2965
Protestant Episcopal Church in the U.S.A. National Council. Dept. of Christian Education. 935, 1594, 2959, 2965, 3168, 3172, 3174, 3178, 3763, 3764
Protestant Episcopal church in the U.S.A. National council. Dept. of religious education. 2965, 3188
Protestant Episcopal Church in the U.S.A. National Council. Division of Laymen's Work. 2191
[Protestant Episcopal church in the U.S.A. New York (Diocese)) 2968
Protestant Episcopal church in the U.S.A. New York (Diocese) Cathedral league. 750
Protestant Episcopal church in the U.S.A. New York (Diocese) Mission committee, 1885. 2968
Protestant Episcopal church in the U.S.A. New York (Diocese) Sunday school commission. 3557
Protestant Episcopal church in the U.S.A. New York (Diocese) Survey of the beneficiaries of the program of the church and the assessment. 2971
Protestant Episcopal Church in the U.S.A. Advisory Committee on Theological Liberty and Social Responsibility. 1805
Protestant Episcopal Church in the U.S.A. Oklahoma (Diocese) 2971
Protestant Episcopal Church in the U.S.A. Pennsylvania (Diocese) 2971
Protestant Episcopal Church in the U.S.A. Special Committee on Theological Education. 3680
Protestant Episcopal Church in the U.S.A. Texas. (Diocese) 1524
Protestant Episcopal church in the U.S.A. Western New York (Diocese) 1489
Protestant Episcopal church in the U.S.A. Wyoming (Missionary district) 2975
Protestant Episcopal church in U. S. A. 750
Protestant Episcopal church missionary society for seamen in the city and port of New York. 2959
Protestant Episcopal society for the promotion of evangelical knowledge, New York. 3563
Protestant teachers association of New York city, inc. 3167
Protestant Episcopal Church in the U.S.A. Book of common prayer. 2961
Protestants and Other Americans United for Separation of Church and State. 1151, 1152, 2670
"Protocols of the wise men of Zion." 2078
Proudfit, Alexander Moncrief. 3356
[Proudfit, John Williams]. 74
Proudfoot, Andrea (Hofer) 2023
Proudfoot, John J A. 2904
Proudfoot, Merrill. 3541
Proudfoot, Wayne. 3104
Prout, William. 891
Prouty, Amy. 3405
Prouty, Carrie Burr. 2065
Provera, Paolo. 2571
Providence Baptist Church, Monrovia, Liberia. 2983
Providence evangelical young women's Christian association. 3878
Providence First Congregational Church. (Unitarian) 1612, 1781
Provonsha, Jack W. 66, 1414
[Proyart, Lievain Bonaventure]. 1418, 2203
Prucha, Francis Paul. 1899
Prudden, Theodore P[hilander]. 748
Prudden, Theodore Philander. 1344
Pruden, Edward Hughes. 146, 166, 2984
Prudent, Julia Ann. 3091
Prudentius Clemens, Aurelius. 1878
Pruett, John H. 1292
Prugh, Marcella. 2879, 3183
Prummer, Dominicus M. 948
Pruner, Alfred William. 1666
Prunskis, Joseph. 2265
Pruvost, S. 2262, 3460
Pruyser, Paul W. 2786, 2994, 2999
Pryke, E. J. 437
Prynne, William. 3606
Pryse, James M. 3054
Pryse, James Morgan. 355, 3054
Przybylski, Benno. 442, 1739
Przywara, Erich. 3104
Pseudo-Dionysius. 3266
Psomiades, Harry J. 1152, 1354
Psychotheological Symposium, 4th, Aquinas Junior College, etc., 1978. 775, 2575
Psychotheological Symposium, 5th, Aquinas Junior College, etc., 1979. 775, 2575
Psychotheological Symposium (6th : 1980. 775, 2575
Publication of faith and religious liberty association. 607
Pudney, John. 1292, 3804
Puech, Aime. 1115
Puente, Luis de la. 2394
Pugh, Ernest. 1492
Pugh, Samuel F. 1463
Puglisi Pico, Mario. 2879
Pugsley, Clement H. 1352
Puiseux, J. 1970
Pulgar, Fernando del. 3469
Pulitzer, Walter. 2380, 2394
Pulkingham, Betty. 932, 3005
Pulkingham, W. Graham. 1238, 3005
Pullan, Leighton. 106, 383, 1122, 1186, 1187, 1214
Pullapilly, Cyriac K. 174
Pullen, Alice Muriel. 623, 1996
[Pullen, Henry William]. 1052, 1055
Pullen, John Turner. 2879
Puller, Frederick William. 1213, 2768, 935
Pulley, Frank Easton. 3356, 3742
Pulley, Sande. 710
Pullias, 1907. 2320
Pulpit digest. 3356
Pulzer, Peter G. J. 54
Pumpelly, Mary Hollenback (Welles) 298
Punchard, George. 1344, 1345
Puniet, Jean de. 2367
Puniet, Pierre de. 188
Punshon, William Morley. 2425, 3261
Punt, Neal. 3753
Puranas. Bhagavata purana. 879
Puranas. Bhagavatapurana. English. 3005
Puranas. Bhagavatapurana. English & Sanskrit. Selections. 197
Puranas. Brahmandapurana. Adhyatmaramayana. English. 1816
Puranas. Brahmandapurana. Lalitasaharanama. 1815
Puranas. Brahmavaivartapurana. English. 1816
Puranas. Devibhagavatapurana. English. 3005
Puranas. English. Selections. 2664
Puranas. Matsyapurana. English. 1815
Purce, Jill. 3472
Purcell, Edmund Sheridan. 1407, 2328
Purcell, Harold. 855
Purcell, Mary. 54, 1649, 1938, 2269, 2269, 3580, 3779, 872, 1028, 1882, 3580, 3779
Purcell, William Ernest. 296, 991, 3133
*Purdham, Betty Mae. 3164, 3185
Purdue university, Lafayette, Ind. 3758
Purdue, William J. 2395
Purdy, Alexander C. 990
Purdy, Alexander Converse. 475, 973, 1726, 1954, 3664
Purdy, Susan Gold. 1615
Purdy, William Arthur. 2852
Purdy Alexander C. 3481
Purefoy, George W. 158
Purinton, Carl Everett. 349, 1178, 1970
Purinton, Herbert Ronelle. 410, 1970, 2096
Purkiser, W T. 93, 403, 540, 652, 1352, 1569, 1823, 2818, 3647
Purrington, William Archer. 1035
Purtill, Richard L. 69, 2220, 3104
Purucker, Gottfried de. 3687, 671, 3546, 3687, 3689
Purusottama Pandita. 689
Purves, George Tybout. 1194, 2934, 3344, 3377
Purves, James. 2224, 2939
Purviance, Albert E. 973
Purvis, Cleo. 3356
Purvis, James D. 563, 3296
Purvis, John Stanley. 3639
Purvis, Samuel Warrington. 3344, 3356
Puryear, Herbert B. 93, 877, 2991, 3391
Puryear, Meredith Ann. 2380
Pusey, Edward Bouverie. 507, 1401, 2260
Pusey House, Oxford. 1247
Pushee, Ruth. 1208
Pushpendra Kumar, 1936. 3400
Putman, Jimmy. 1362, 3010
Putnam, Alfred Porter. 1477, 2220
Putnam, Allen. 3511, 2413, 3511, 3827
Putnam, Benjamin. 973
Putnam, C E. 672, 3380
Putnam, Charles Elsworth. 1035, 1052, 1792, 3011
[Putnam, Edward]. 456
[Putnam, Ellen Tryphosa Harrington]. 3323
Putnam, George Haven. 2223, 2224
Putnam, Robert C. 641
Putnam, Roy C. 365, 1007, 2437, 3356
Putnam, Samuel Porter. 1655
Putney, Max C. 1970
Putz, Joseph. 2368
Putz, Louis J. 754, 828, 1264, 2571
Pye, Ernest. 2558, 3816
Pye, John. 2556, 2864
Pye, Michael. 3761
Pyke, Frederick Merrill. 3010
Pylant, Agnes (Durant) 1257, 3028
Pyle, Carl Homer. 1668
Pyle, Charles Bertram. 686
Pyle, Edmund. 2168
Pyle, Eric H. 1096
Pyle, Hugh F. 1717
Pyle, Katharine. 2666
Pyle, Leo. 664
Pym, David. 1077, 1307
Pym, Thomas Wentworth. 2999, 3674
Pyne, Mable Mandeville. 3063
Pyne, Zoe Kendrick. 2766
Pyper, George Dollinger. 1872
Pyramid texts. 3722
Pyron, Harry L. 973
Pyzalski, Leon. 1299, 1741, 2581

Q

Qua-beck, Warren A. 3772
Quackenbos, John Duncan. 1099
Quadfileg, Josef. 3281
Quadflieg, Josef. 75
Quadrupani, Carlo Giuseppe. 3481
Quaife, Milo Milton. 182, 3535
Qualben, Lars Pederson. 1178, 2015, 2294
Qualyle, William Alfred. 2894
Quam, John Elliott. 2136, 3041
Quanbeck, Philip A. 287
Quanbeck, Warren A. 2298, 3772
Quardt, Robert. 2216
Quarles, James Cowardin. 3467
Quasten, Johannes. 1020
Quattlebaum; Paul. 1367
Quay, Eugene. 3
Quayle, William Alfred. 1954, 2192, 2879, 594, 973, 2437, 2894, 2904, 3011
Quebedeaux, Richard. 692, 1551, 1552, 1576, 2816, 3739
Queen, Charles Nicholas. 3201
Queen of Apostles Seminary, Derby, N.Y. 811
Queen, William M. 815, 2333
Queffelec, Henri. 109, 3082
Queller, Donald E. 1391
Quennell, Peter. 685, 1758
Quentin, A. P. 1780, 3586
Quenzel, Carrol Hunter. 1652
Quere, Ralph W. 1569
Querry, B F. 3290
Quesnell, John G. 663
Quesnell, Quentin. 177, 299, 380, 477, 757, 791, 1458
Quetif, Jacques. 1475
Quick, C. 1831
Quick, Cornelius. 1831
Quick, Louise Bowring. 1831
Quick, Oliver Chase. 1052, 1100, 2065, 3104, 3263, 3445
Quick, Robert Hebert. 3013
Quidam, Roger D. 1940
Quiery, William H. 2382
Quigley, Ithamar. 1999
Quigley, Joseph Anthony Michael. 1323
Quigley, Martin. 754
Quigley, Thomas E. 3793
Quill, James E. 3220
Quillen, Robert. 1052
Quillet, Claude. 1541
Quillian, Paul. 2437
[Quillibet]. 2807
Quimby, Chester Warren. 1062, 1971, 2800, 365, 417, 469, 3789
Quimby, Paul Elmore. 570, 2485, 3013
Quimby, Phineas Parkhurst. 2409
Quin, Eleanor. 2717
Quin, George Edward. 896
Quine, Willard Van Orman. 186
Quinlan, David. 757
Quinlan, Edith. 1882
Quinlan, Patrick Thomas. 1262
[Quinlan, Sara-Alice Katharyne]. 3419
Quinley, Harold E. 2956
Quinn, Alexander James. 865, 1264, 1267, 2215
Quinn, Bernard. 829, 2789
Quinn, Eugene F. 1873, 3410
Quinn, Henry. 3023
Quinn, Hugh Gabriel. 1503
Quinn, James. 1541
Quinn, Jane. 696, 2717
Quinn, John M. 3696
Quinn, John Richard. 840, 3265
Quinn, Mary Antonina. 3190
Quinn, Mary Bernetta. 675, 2412
Quinney, Richard. 3445
Quint, Alonzo Hall. 1325
Quintal, Claire. 1938
Quinton, John Allan. 3547
Quispel, Gilles. 456
Quistorp, Heinrich. 728, 1531
Quitman, Frederick Henry. 2313
Quitslund, Sonya A. 182
Quoist, Michel. 1001, 1096, 1451, 2380, 2395
Qutb, Sayyid. 3454

R

Raab, Clement. 1373
Raab, Earl. 3745
Raab, Robert. 3880
Raabe, Evelyn Marie. 2374
Rabalais, Maria. 2812, 3859
Rabbath, Antoine. 2678
Rabbi Isaac Elchanan theological seminary and Yeshiva college. 186
Rabbinical Council of America. 2152
Rabbinowicz, Israel Michel. 2013
Raber, Dorothy A. 2955
Rabin, Albert I. 1308
Rabin, Chaim. 3014
Rabinowicz, Harry M. 1789, 2075, 2627, 3581
Rabinowicz, Oscar K. 2079
Rabinowitsch, Wolf Zeev. 1789
Rabinowitz, Abraham Hirsch. 1312
Rabinowitz, Benjamin. 3876
Rabinowitz, Isaac. 211
Rabinowitz, Jacob J. 2074
Rabinowitz, Louis Isaac. 565, 1811, 3370
Rabinowitz, Louis Issac. 1811
Rabinowitz, Shalom. 2105
Raboteau, Albert J. 17
Rabten, Geshe. 2194, 3017
Rabut, Olivier A. 2181, 3082
Rabuzzi, Kathryn Allen. 3832
Raby, Frederic James Edward. 2199, 3210, 3211
Raccoon, N. J. Swedish Lutheran church. 3572
Race, Martha. 3005

Rachleff, Owen S. 603, 623, 2728
Racine, Jean Baptiste. 299, 514
Rack, Henry D. 2434
Rackauskas, Constantine. 1943
Rackman, Emanuel. 2751, 2752
Rackovsky, Isaiah. 3371
Racovian catechism. 3730
Racz, Istvan. 1731
Rad, Gerhard von. 485, 510, 511, 522, 599, 2622, 299, 503, 572, 2301, 2951, 3370, 3821
Radau, Hugo. 93, 524
Radcliffe, Lynn James. 2252, 2879
Pitt-Watson, Ian, 1881-1955. 2904
Radday, Yehuda Thomas. 529, 543, 555
Raddin, George Gates. 2960, 3816
Radegonde. 3282
Rademacher, Arnold. 3489
Rademacher, William J. 2774
Rader, Paul. 1560, 2521, 3356
Rader, Stanley R. 83, 1144
Rader, William. 3095, 3602
Radford, Benjamin Johnson. 383
*Radhakrishan, Sarvepalli. 3017
Radhakrishnan, Sarvepalli. 1814, 1815, 1881, 2320, 2840, 3063, 3086, 3123, 3760
Radhakrishnan. Sarvepalli. 3119
Radharkrishnan, Sir Sarvepalli. 2840
Radin, Max. 2068, 2121
Radin, Paul. 3110, 3820, 1902, 3110, 3820
Radius, Marianne Catherine (Vos) 630, 1983
Radius, Mariannwe. 1983
Radke, Ken. 1432
Radke, William Julius. 296
Radmacher, Earl D. 994
Radtke, Frederick A. 2395
Radtke, Hans D. 1859
Radtke, Stephen John. 3404
Rae, Daphne. 2487
Rae, Frederick J. 473, 596
Rael, Juan Bautista. 21
Raemers, Sidney Albert. 623, 796, 797, 1178, 1540, 1983
Raemers, Sydney Albert. 623
Raeymaeker, Louis de. 2739
Raffety, William Edward. 1246, 1913, 3156, 3557
Raffles,s Thomas 3471
Raffles, Thomas. 3471
Rafinesque, Constantine Samuel. 501
Raglan, Fitz Roy Richard Somerset. 1807
Raglan, FitzRoy Richard Somerset. 1808
Ragland, Nathaniel M. 2521, 2702
Ragsdale, Bartow Davis. 150
Ragsdale, John Thomas. 3597
Ragsdale, Ray W. 180, 1296, 2067
Raguin, Yves. 878, 1356, 1726, 2879
Rahill, Peter James. 874
Rahlves, Friedrich. 753
Rahm, Harold J. 1776
Rahman, Fazlur. 1922, 2185, 2630
Rahn, Carl Leo. 2999
Rahner, Hugo. 1082, 1126, 2258, 2269, 2361, 2774, 2854, 3647, 1082
Rahner, Karl. 1451, 2223, 2879, 66, 306, 665, 761, 764, 773, 777, 779, 791, 865, 1001, 1073, 1105, 1122, 1126, 1262, 1264, 1299, 1317, 1414, 1473, 1523, 1597, 1659, 1805, 1831, 2033, 2046, 2180, 2223, 2255, 2269, 2324, 2363, 2395, 2571, 2789, 2879, 3104, 3226, 3265, 3266, 3368, 3476, 3491, 3624, 3628, 3633, 3639, 3647, 3695, 3712, 3773, 3783
Rahner Karl. 1264
Rahtjen, Bruce D. 641, 1269
Rahula, Walpola. 703, 704
Railton, George Scott. 682
Raimundus de Agiles. 1391
Rainbow, Bernarr. 1206
Raine, Kathleen. 1519
Raine, Kathleen Jessie. 2649, 3589, 3863
Rainer, Joseph. 3296
Raines, Robert Arnold. 932, 1007, 1155, 1359, 1451, 2192, 2395, 3019, 3539
Raines, Ruth E. 2741
Rainey, George S. 300
Rainolds, John. 1700, 3606, 3607
Rains, Clara Beatrice. 2728
Rains, Paul Boyd. 3019
Rainsford, Marcus. 1451, 424
Rainsford, W[illiam] S[tephen]. 1747
Rainsford, William Stephen. 694, 3067, 951, 2904, 2959, 3133
Raisin, Jacob Salmon. 2102, 2116, 3585, 2117
Raisin, Max. 2089
Raistrick, Arthur. 1636, 1684, 3314, 3868
Raistrick, James. 3511
Raitt, Thomas M. 547
Rajan, Balachandra. 2471
Rajaneesh, Acharya. 1325, 1778, 2007, 2196, 2381, 3019, 3481, 3491, 3543, 3585, 3586, 3760, 3761

Rajaneesh, Archarya. 2792, 3867
Raja-sekhara. 3145
Rajneesh, Bhagwan Shree. 3586
Raju, Poolla Tirupati. 1881, 2840
Rakadazan, Guru. 1778, 2315, 2728
Raleigh, Albert Sidney. 1806, 2835, 3344
Raleigh, N. C. Christ church. 2971
Raleigh, N. C. Edenton Street Methodist Church. Sesquicentennial Committee. 3019
Raleigh, N. C. First Baptist Church. 157, 3019
Raleigh, Thomas. 3315
Raley, Helen Thames. 182, 2539
Rall, Harris Franklin. 1597, 291, 377, 1052, 1096, 1726, 1971, 1993, 2055, 2065, 2177, 2465, 3167, 3290, 3647, 3664
Ralph, Florence. 2531
Ralph, John Robertson. 1071
Ralston, Russell F. 3216
Ralston, Samuel. 732, 1906
Ralston, Samuel S. 464
Ralston, Thomas Neely. 3647, 3652
Ram Dass. 1348, 1816, 2679, 3019, 3481
Rama, 1925. 1415, 3020, 3491, 3760
Ramachandra Aiyar, G. 1814
Ramachandra Rao, Saligrama Krishna, 1926. 3492
Ramachandra Vasu. 1814
Ramachandran, T. P. 1484, 2311
Ramachandsra Vasu. 689, 3020
Ramaker, Albert John. 150
Ramakrishna Ananda. 879, 1778
Raman, K. V. 3523, 3599
Ramana. 3020
Ramana, Maharshi. 3491
Ramanohana Raya 1774-1833. 2071, 3728
Rama-prasada. 2840
Ramaprasada Sena, 1718-1775. 3285
Ramaswami Aiyar, Chetpat Pattabhirama. 2840
Rambach, Pierre. 3403
Ramer, Ernest L. 782
Ramge, Sebastian V. 3603
Ram Gopal. 2635
Ramige, Eldon Albert. 973, 1726, 3701
Raming, Ida. 3842
Ramm, Bernard. 1831, 66, 69, 118, 205, 287, 1127, 1716, 3226, 3656, 3657
Ramm, Bernard L. 66, 176, 287, 517, 947, 1552, 1831, 3669
Ramm, Charles A. 1111
Rammohun Roy, Raja, 1772?-1833. 689
Ramona, Kan. Trinity Lutheran Church. 2291
Ramos, Alex M. 1302, 3021
Rampp, Donald L. 2204
Ramsaur, William Hoke. 2538
Ramsay, DeVere Maxwell. 623, 1185, 1983
Ramsay, E. W. 3511
Ramsay, Emily Mary. 1035, 1495, 1035
Ramsay, Franklin Pierce. 522, 2925, 3781
Ramsay, John Cummins. 886
Ramsay, Sir William Mitchell. 380, 460
Ramsay, William M. 410, 938, 1122, 2042, 3133
Ramsay, William Mitchell. 407, 349, 378, 380, 407, 2800, 2844, 349, 378, 460, 1183, 1184, 1194, 1197, 2003, 2193, 2563, 2800, 1183, 2271
Ramsdell, Edward Thomas. 3647
Ramsdell, Elizabeth. 3511
Ramsdell, Sarah A. 2776, 3511
Ramsden, William E. 1253
Ramsey, Arthur Michael. 951, 1219, 1066, 1071, 1217, 1296, 1434, 1731, 1834, 1835, 2046, 2052, 3633, 3657, 3658, 3659
Ramsey, George Henry. 641
Ramsey, Ian T. 946, 2420, 2838, 3119, 3652, 3669, 3682
Ramsey, James Beverlin. 461
Ramsey, Joyce Sikes. 1971
Ramsey, Paul. 945, 1705, 2708, 3112, 3329, 3652, 3793, 3849
Ramsey, Paul [Robert Paul Ramsey]. 945, 2708, 3329, 3652, 3793
Ramsey, William. 3511
*Ramsey, William M. 3133
Ramseyer, Friedrich August. 2502
Ramseyer, Lloyd L. 887
Ramseyer, Macy (Garth) 3021
Ramstein, Matthew. 735, 2342
Ranade, Ramabai. 3021
Ranaghan, Kevin. 2815
Ranchetti, Michele. 2562
Ranck, Henry Haverstick. 178
Ranck, John Allan. 2551
Rand, Benjamin. 192
Rand, Christopher. 1112
Rand, Edward Augustus. 1862
Rand, Edward Kennard. 3694
Rand, Howard B. 203, 456, 464, 552, 46, 509, 535, 607, 608, 1849, 1943, 2395, 3320

Rand, Willard J. 3785
[Rand, William Wliberforce]. 245
Randall, Claire. 1154
Randall, Daniel Boody. 2446
Randall, Edward Caleb. 3511
Randall, Edwin Jarvis. 1264, 2962
Randall, Edwin T. 35
Randall, George Maxwell. 3201
Randall, Gerald. 1169
Randall, John Herman. 1052, 1451, 2410, 2561, 2695, 2991, 3063, 3119, 1082, 2181, 3063
Randall, John L. 2991
Randall, Mallinson. 1206
Randall, Max Ward. 2559
Randall, Ruth (Kimball) 2319
Randals, Benjamin. 205
Randel, Don Michael. 847, 884
Randles, Marshall. 1594
Randolph, Abigail Graves. 1606
Randolph, Alfred Magill. 1071, 3652
[Randolph, Anson Davies Fitz]. 2588, 3210
Randolph, C. A. 749
Randolph, Corliss Fitz. 2699, 3388
Randolph, David. 314
Randolph, David James. 3004, 287, 2809, 2904, 3004
Randolph, Edwin Archer. 1936, 2683
Randolph, Halvar George. 1831
[Randolph, Henry Fitz,] 1856-1892. 1113
Randolph, Henry S. 3255
[Randolph, Howard Stelle Fitz]. 2304
Randolph, Lois Christian. 1432, 1435
[Randolph, Paschal Beverly]. 3511
Randolph, Paschal Beverly. 1283, 1696
Randolph, Percilla Lawyer. 3095
[Randolph, Richard]. 2419
Randolph, Vance. 2832
Randolph, Wilfrid. 1270
*Raney, L. H. 3564
Rank, Otto. 2653
Ranke, Leopold von. 2769, 2862, 3040
Rankin, Adam. 2167
Rankin, Alexander Taylor. 1689, 2924
Rankin, David O. 3726
[Rankin, George Clark]. 2455, 3595
Rankin, Isaac Ogden. 2894
Rankin, Jeremiah Eames. 1862, 3888
Rankin, John Chambers. 1971
Rankin, Mary Everett. 3156
Rankin, Melinda. 2540
Rankin, Molly K. 2487, 2542, 3021, 3387
Rankin, Oliver Shaw. 600, 2144, 3234
Rankin, Peg. 1726
Rankin, Samuel Meek. 1772
Rankin, William. 2483
Rankin, William Eric Kilmorack. 3273
Ranlett, Louis Felix. 3732
Ranley, Donald p. 1492
Ranney, Darwin H. 1551
Ranney, David James. 3705
Ranney, Irene Belle (McKever) 423
Ranney, Ruth Whitaker. 190
Ransford, Charles Orrin. 3316
Ransil, Bernard Jerome. 3
Ranske, Jutta (Mordt) Bell. 2728
Ransom, John Crowe. 3079, 3081
Ransom, Josephine Maria (Davies) 671, 3687
Ransom, Reverdy Cassius. 2847
Ransome, Harry. 3344
Ransome, William Lee. 166, 3236, 3530
Ranson, Charles Wesley. 2494
Ranson, Stewart. 1291
Ranwez, Pierre. 939, 3165
[Ranyard, Ellen Henrietta (White) 296, 3534
Rao, K. L. Seshagiri. 1701, 3094
Rao, Koneru Ramakrishna. 2991
Rao, Shanta Rameshwar. 2316
Rapaport, Izaak. 2143
Rapaport, Samuel. 2462, 2463
Raphael, Chaim. 1884, 1944, 2110, 2121, 2149
Raphael, D. D. 1540
Raphael, Marc Lee. 2106
Raphael, Pierre. 849
Raphall, Morris J[acob]. 2092
Rapking, Aaron Henry. 3143, 3255, 3375
Rappaport, Solomon. 2143, 2153
Rappaport, Uriel. 1410, 1411
Rappoport, Angelo Solomon. 1976, 2207
Rappoport, Israel Bernard. 1796
Rarick, W. Carl. 473, 596, 597, 648
Ras-chun. 2193, 2461
Rasband, Ester. 1111
Raschid, M. S. 1733, 1918
Raschke, Carl A. 1077, 3063, 3065, 3445
[Ras-chun]. 3511
Rashdall, Hastings. 1954, 2837, 3624
Rashke, Richard L. 1408
Raskas, Bernard S. 1434, 2722
Raskin, Joseph. 3521, 3580
Rasmussen, Albert Terrill. 1076, 1101
Rasmussen, Gerhard. 2395
Rasmussen, Hannah. 3022

Rasmussen, Larry L. 677, 1076
Rasnake, J. Samuel. 92
Rasooli, Jay M. 3272
Rassieur, Charles L. 1298, 2781
Rast, Walter E. 501, 520
Ratcliff, Arthur James John. 1479
Ratcliff, Edward Craddock. 2235
Ratcliff, Richard P. 1688
Ratcliffe, Francis Asbury. 138
Ratekin, George W. 236
Rathbun, Hiram. 652
Rathbun, Job. 3783
Rathe, Gerard. 2500
Rathwick, Clyde W. 2324
Ratiff, Dale Hedrick. 3356
Ratiu, Alexander. 1299, 3025
Ratliff, Dale Hedrick. 3392
Ratliff, Foster. 153
Ratner, Lorman. 53
Ratner, Sidney. 2834
Rato Khyongla Nawang Losang. 2194, 3025
Ratte, John. 2243, 2562
Rattenbury, John Ernest. 2421, 2800, 3804
Ratter, Magnus C. 3312
Ratterman, P. H. 870
Rattey, Beatrice Katharine. 398
Rattey, Beatrice Katharine. 535, 2096
Rattray, Robert Sutherland. 90
Ratzinger, Joseph. 66, 74, 675, 695, 865, 1001, 1126, 1597, 1820, 3715, 3772
Ratzlaff, Lydia Nelson. 2071
Ratzlaff, Ruby. 2804
Rau, Albert George. 1208
Rau, Heimo. 86
Rau, Lois E. 3261
Rau, Sandy. 904
Rauch, Rufus William. 879, 1532, 2626
Raud, Elsa. 608
Raud, Gans Pertel. 1542
Raue, Charles Godlove. 2991
Rauf, Mohammed A. 1924
Raufer. Maria Ilma. 1903, 3277
Rauff, Edward A. 1201
Raughley, Leonard C. 3063
Raughley, Ralph C. 1066
Raupert, John Godfrey Ferdinand. 1971
[Raupert, John Godfrey Ferdinand]. 791, 2999, 3512
Rausch, Jerome W. 1387
Rauschenberg, Lina (Andrews) 1111, 2551, 3063, 3764
Rauschenbusch, Walter. 973, 1062, 2065, 2894, 3087, 3445, 3446
Rauscher, William V. 1109, 2991
Rauws, Johannes. 2516
Raven, Charles Earle. 57, 1052, 1062, 1134, 1831, 1954, 1971, 2756, 3025, 3071, 3079, 3084, 3432, 3793, 3834, 3849, 57
Raven, Edward Earle. 2265
Raven, John Howard. 540
Ravenhill, Leonard. 1109, 2067
Ravenscroft, Trevor. 1820, 1826
Ravensdale, Tom. 3824
Ravi Booth, Vincent 1876. 191, 2381
Ravindranatha, Thakura. 3063
Ravitch, Norman. 1021, 1145
Ravn, Karen. 2395
Rawding, F. W. 712, 1703
Rawidowicz, Simon. 2094, 2842
Rawle, William Henry. 1375, 1376, 1377
Rawlings, James Scott. 1275
Rawlings, Maurice. 1088, 1414, 1696, 3025
Rawlins, C. L. 1399
Rawlinson, Alfred Edward John. 1052, 119, 401, 477, 1211, 1954, 2016, 2042, 3664, 3674, 3713
Rawlinson, George. 77, 1399, 1587, 1920, 2095, 2622, 2800, 3119
Rawlinson, Gerald Christopher. 45
Rawls, Eugene S. 3866
Rawson, Elsie Lewis. 2491, 2531
Rawson, Frederick Lawrence. 2695, 2879
Rawson, Marianna S. 1983
Ray, Ajit Kumar. 3020
Ray, Benjamin C. 12
Ray, Charles Walker. 593
Ray, Charles Wayne. 3011
Ray, David A. 973, 987
Ray, David Burcham. 150, 152
Ray, David R. 3426
Ray, Emma J. 3133
Ray, George McNeill. 3530
Ray, Georgia Miller. 3025
Ray, J. D. 1847, 2752
Ray, Jefferson Davis. 8, 1296, 2136, 2402, 2904, 3674
Ray, John. 2674
Ray, Mary Augustina. 3195
Ray, Randolph. 2962, 3207
Ray, Rex. 2511
Ray, Sandy F. 166
Ray, T Bronson. 140, 156, 2483
Ray, T. Bronson. 3467

Rayan, Samuel. 1836
Rayapati, J. P. Rao. 3775
Rayburn, John. 884
Rayburn, Robert Gibson. 136, 973, 3004
Raychaudhuri, Hemchandra. 3766
Raycroft, Benjamin Joseph. 3566, 865, 2360
Raymond. 765, 1246, 1276, 1483, 1708, 2023, 2122, 2324, 2369, 2813, 3025, 3459, 3527, 3541, 3665, 3709, 3710
Raymond, Earnest Albert. 118, 1052
Raymond, Ernest. 1643, 1646, 1929
Raymond, George Lansing. 2999, 3481
Raymond, Irving Woodworth. 3595
Raymond, Joseph David Flanagan. 1451
Raymond, Louise. 1384, 2023
[Raymond, Louise] 1907. 2023
Raymond,M. 3665
Raymond, Maud Mary (Wotring) 2521
Raymond, Miner. 3647
Raymond, Robert Raikes. 1588
Raymond, Rossiter Worthington. 2229, 2006
Raymond, Walter W. 2695
Raymond Marie. 2305, 3418
Raymont, Thomas. 641
Raymundus de vinies, 1330-1399. 749
Raymundus De Vineis. 749
Raynald, Volanda. 2247
Rayner, Menzies. 1569
Raynolds, Robert. 2263
"Raynor" 1890
Raynor, Wallace Alan. 3287
Rayon, M[esha]. 2640
Rayzor, James Newton. 3530
Raz, Simhah. 2219, 3016
Rea, Lilian. 2864
Rea, W. F. 850, 2559
Read, Christopher. 3257
Read, Conyers. 3039
Read, D. H. C. 66
Read, David Haxton Carswell. 66, 68, 181, 945, 1573, 2248, 2904, 2934, 3356, 3665
Read, Hollis. 122, 2674, 2981, 2982
Read, Katherine L (Henderson) 1803
Read, Leonard Edward. 1432
Read, Maureen Hay. 932, 3025
Read, Newbury Frost. 2700
Read, R. Y. 298
Read, Ralph Harlow. 11, 1126, 3448
Read, Walter E. 3383
Read, William Merritt. 316
Read, William R. 2198, 2505, 2953
Reade, Charles. 216
Reade, William Henry Vincent. 1402
Reading, Benjamin F. 1134
Readington, N.J. Reformed church. 3045
Ready, Dolores. 1029, 2685
Reagan, Joseph Nicholas. 68
Reagin, Ewell K. 1396
Reagin, Ewell Kerr. 3854
Ream, George Franklin. 1253
Ream, Guin. 3857
Ream, Robert J. 3083
Reaman, George Elmore. 1852
Reany, William. 2253, 3463, 3610
Reardon, Bernard M. G. 1639, 1800, 2221, 2562, 3211, 3655
Reardon, David M. 2395
Reardon, James M. 2475
Reardon, James Michael. 3277
Reardon, Robert H. 1228
Reaser, George Washington. 2401
Reasoner, Calvin. 1152, 3605
Reasoner, Charles L. 1662
Reasoner, Norris Jacob. 209, 1041
Reatz, August. 1971
Reaves, Laurie. 307
Reavis, Ralph. 16, 2276
Rebesher, Conrad F. 1360
Rebok, Denton Edward. 3383, 3530
Reccord, Augustus P. 3728
Reccord, Augustus Phineas. 3728
Rece, Ellis Heber. 648
Recejac, E. 2640
Recker, Colane. 858, 2212
Reckett, Maurice Benington. 3449
Reckitt, Maurice Benington. 1137, 3446
Reckitt, Maurice Bennington. 1135, 3446
Rector, G C. 1726
Rector, Hartman. 1366
Rector, William Lee. 1581
[Red, Samuel Clark]. 1849
Red, William Stuart. 3605, 2919
Reddan, Minnie. 2243
Redder, Ronald M. 3883
Reddick, De Witt Carter. 1128
Redding, David A. 74, 216, 338, 576, 926, 929, 945, 1011, 1845, 2013, 2018, 2026, 2894, 2999
Redding, George Walker. 3537
[Redding, James]. 2209
Redding, William A. 2465, 2728, 3094
Reddin Opal. 3877
Reddish, Robert O. 535, 2096
Reddy, Michael. 1001

Rede, Wyllys. 2212
Redeker, Martin. 3308
Redekop, Calvin Wall. 1122, 2408, 2736, 3446
Redekop, John Harold. 1087
Redelheim, Abraham A. 2478
Redfield, Bessie Gordon. 3092
Redfield, Isabella Taylor. 641
Redford, Albert H. 2452
Redford, Courts. 3467
Redford, Jack. 1569
Redford, Robert Ainslie. 2092
Redgrove, Herbert Stanley. 2180, 3570, 2313
Redhead, John A. 181, 216, 217, 973, 1602, 2934, 3012
Rediger, Benjamin E. 1594
Rediger, G. Lloyd. 1293
Redlich, Edwin Basil. 398, 420
Redman, Edward H. 2221
Redmond, Howard A. 1736
Redmond, Nicolaus M. 1267
Redmont, Louis. 934
Rednick, Herman. 2395
Redpath, Alan. 166, 321, 326, 544, 545, 554, 560, 1314, 1405, 1451, 2248, 3356, 3362
Redpath, Helen Mary Dominic. 663
Redwood, Hugh. 2248, 3292, 3293, 1594, 2879
Redwood, John. 1520
Reece, Colleen L. 216, 2609
Reeck, Darrell. 2402
Reed, Albert A. 137
Reed, Andrew. 2854
Reed, Bobbie. 1256, 1610
*Reed, Bruce. 1374
Reed, David Allen. 3647
Reed, Edward. 2807
Reed, Elizabeth (Armstrong) 277, 703, 718, 1184
Reed, Elizabeth Liggett. 3764
Reed, Frank. 1371
Reed, Frank A. 1255
Reed, Gwendolyn E. 6
Reed, Harold W. 1237, 3537
Reed, J Charles. 3174
Reed, James. 1414
Reed, Jane. 1509, 3018
Reed, John Hamilton. 2450
Reed, John J. 3560
Reed, John Sanders. 665
Reed, John Thomas. 3751
Reed, Lewis G[reenleaf]. 2081
Reed, Lewis Thurston. 3344
Reed, Lucas Albert. 99, 3313
Reed, Luther Dotterer. 2236, 2295
Reed, Margaret E. 725
Reed, Marshall Russell. 2818
Reed, Matthew. 2561
Reed, Orville S. 2465
Reed, Orville Sibbitt. 2465
Reed, Rebecca Theresa. 1582, 3031
Reed, Rebecca Theresa, b. ca. 888
Reed, Richard Clark. 2175, 2916
Reed, Ruth Bendure. 2856
Reed, Sampson. 1370, 2473
Reed, Susan Martha. 1147
Reed, Virginia. 1441
Reed, Walter E. 2081
Reed, William J. 2682
Reed, William LaForest. 90
Reed, William Standish. 2377
Reed, William Wellington. 3172
Reeder, Hilda. 2814
Reeder, Lucille Lois. 1595
*Reeder, W. Donald. 2218
Reedy, Edward Napoleon. 1228
*Reedy, William J. 3177
Reem, Harvey Ellwood. 1508
Reeman, Edmund Henry. 1729
Rees, Arthur Dougherty. 934
Rees, Byron Johnson. 1360
Rees, Edward Jeffries. 1267, 1318, 2058
Rees, Howard. 473
Rees, James. 3399, 3607
Rees, Janet Emily (Meagens) Ruutz. 2248, 2809
*Rees, Jean A. 2879, 3281
Rees, Melvin E. 2395
Rees, Paul Stromberg. 325, 327, 449, 1549, 1569, 2496, 2887, 3031, 3715
Rees, Seth Cook. 3031, 3356
Rees, Thomas. 1831
Rees, Thomas Mardy. 1688
Rees, Tom. 1170
Rees, W. G. Edwards. 1299
Rees, Wilbur E. 2395
Rees, William. 2179
Reese, Alexander. 608, 3320
Reese, Clarence Herbert. 3095
Reese, Curtis Williford. 1854, 3357
Reese, J. Irving. 1293
Reese, Lawrence M. 1260
Reese, T. O. 3344
Reeve, Becky. 2618, 3031
Reeve, Jack V. 3531

Reeve, James J. 2561
Reeve, Thomas Ellis. 2513
Reeves, Francis Brewster. 1872, 2830
Reeves, James. 131
Reeves, Jeremiah Bascom. 1872
Reeves, John Baptist. 1475
Reeves, Katherine. 3174
Reeves, Marjorie. 608, 1819, 1820, 2122, 3574
Reeves, Nathaniel S. 1062
Reeves, Richard Ambrose. 604
Reeves, Robert B. 1416
Reformed church in America. 581, 583, 1868, 2238, 2494, 3032, 3043, 3045, 3046, 3047, 3049, 3050
Reformed Church in America. Board of Domestic Missions. Women's Executive Committee. 3047
Reformed church in America Board of publication. 3677
Reformed church in America. Classes. Holland. 2129
Reformed church in America. Classes. Paramus. 3047
Reformed Church in America. Commission on History. 3045
Reformed Church in America. Constitution. 3045
Reformed church in America. General synod. 3043, 3045
Reformed Church in America. Synods. Particular Synod of Albany. 3047
Reformed Church in the United States. 641, 1801, 3044, 3045, 3046, 3047, 3048, 3049, 3308, 3563
Reformed Church in the United States. Classes. North Carolina. 3048
Reformed Church in the United States. Classes. Somerset, Pa. 3047
Reformed church in the United States. Classes. Westmoreland, Pa. 3049
Reformed church in the United States. Liturgy and ritual. 3047, 3049
Reformed church in the United States. Synod of the Northwest. 3047
Reformed Episcopal church. 1868, 2867, 3050
Reformed Presbyterian church in North America. 3050
Reformed Presbyterian congregation of Pittsburgh, Pa. 3050
Reformed society of Israelites, Charleston, S.C. 2109
Regamey, Raymond. 42, 921, 2778, 3489, 3541
Regamy, Raymond [Father Pie Regamey]. 42
Regan, Brian T. 284, 1749
Regan, Cronan. 797, 3670
Regan, George M. 948
Regan, James Wilfred. 804
Regan, John. 3595
[Regan, Mary Barbara. 3545
Regan, Richard J. 1143, 3772
Regardie, Israel. 723, 1782, 1806, 2313, 2695, 3251
Regazzi, John J. 3678
Regehr, Ernie. 3464
Reger, Ambrose. 850
Regester. 748
Regester, John Dickinson. 3312
Reggio, Edwin. 749, 3897
Regional Church Planning Office, Cleveland. 2735
Regis. 868
Regis, Louis Marie. 2180, 3694
Register, Susanne Haines. 1367, 3051
Regnat, William A. 2576
Regnier, Elizabeth Chase. 1451
Regnier, Jerome. 3411
Regula Magistri. English. 2583
Regush, Nicholas M. 117
Rehault, Ludowic. 2187, 3687
Rehberger, Lee. 1035
Rehnborg, C F. 1096
Rehrer, Ronald L. 3881
Rehwinkel, Alfred Martin. 525, 1347, 1382, 1421, 3452
Reich, Emil. 236
Reich, Max Isaac. 586, 2415
Reich, Max Issac. 2116
Reich, Wilhelm. 2050
Reichard, Gladys Amanda. 2677, 2463, 2677, 3300
Reichardt, E. Noel. 3133
[Reiche, Edward H.] 1820-1877. 2595
Reichel, Aaron. 1744, 3016
Reichel-Dolmatoff, Gerardo. 3717
Reichel, George Valentine. 2720
Reichel, Levin Theodore. 2595, 2596
Reichel, O. Asher. 1781, 2751
Reichel, Willy. 3052, 3512
Reichel-Dolmatoff, Gerardo. 1903
Reichelt, Karl Ludvig. 913, 705, 1485
Reichenbach, Bruce R. 1739, 1890
Reichert, Florian. 1365
Reichert, Herbert William. 2710

Reichert, Irving Frederick. 3371
Reichert, Richard. 1701, 3156, 3181, 3266
Reichert, Sara. 939
Reichler, Max. 2082
Reichman, Jacob. 3371
Reichmann, Eva G. 53
Reicke, Bo Ivar. 408, 430
Reid, Albert Clayton. 66, 1071, 1451, 3758
Reid, Alexander James. 2272, 2432, 2557
Reid, Clyde H. 926, 1066, 1170, 1325, 1586, 2904, 3004, 3182
Reid, David P. 2951
Reid, David R. 1308
Reid, Elizabeth. 1755
Reid, Frances P. 2395, 2625
Reid, Frances W. 2347, 3052
Reid, Frances (West) 2347
Reid, Gaines S. 2192
Reid, Gavin. 181, 991, 3660
Reid, Gilbert. 3120
Reid, James. 181, 973, 1451, 1954, 2592, 2934, 205
Reid, Jim. 1573, 3052
Reid, John. 3665, 100
Reid, John Calvin. 338, 398, 570, 585, 623, 908, 2027, 2347, 2676, 2934, 2951
Reid, John Kelman Sutherland. 69, 278, 280, 1046, 2042, 3492
[Reid, John Morrison] 1820-1896. 1849, 3120
Reid, Lizzie Murdock. 296
Reid, Marie L. 973
Reid, Mary Esson. 211
Reid, Numa Fletcher. 2426
Reid, Richard. 724
Reid, Samuel Joseph. 108, 2058
Reid, Stevenson Nathaniel. 157
Reid, Stuart Johnson. 3431
Reid, Thomas. 2675
Reid, Thomas F. 1302, 3052
Reid, William. 1299, 3290
Reid, William Stanford. 2182, 3037, 3083
[Reid, William Thomas] 1843. 3377
Reid, William W. 1016
Reid, William Watkins. 1860, 1861, 2491, 2540
Reidhead, Paris. 987, 2879
Reidt, Wilford H. 2193, 3476
Reidy, Gabriel. 3327
Reidy, Mary. 41
Reif, Stefan C. 2109
Reigstad, Olin Spencer. 2215
Reik, Theodor. 1577, 2097, 2152, 2993, 2999, 3239, 611, 2120, 2999, 3239, 1578, 1908, 1920, 2152, 2993
Reile, Louis. 2577
Reiley, Katharine C. 2834
Reilly, Daniel Flavian. 832
Reilly, Edward Michael. 1467
Reilly, George. 3809
Reilly, Gerald Francis. 177, 1148
Reilly, James. 1868
Reilly, Joseph John. 2704
[Reilly, Mary F.]. 1577
Reilly, Mary Paul. 2581
Reilly, Michael Collins. 2494
Reilly, Robert James. 3203
Reilly, Robert T. 1027, 3284
Reilly, Thomas a Kempis. 1475, 3201
Reilly, Thomas Francis. 2578
Reimann, Henry William. 2283
Reimann, Paul E. 3215, 2344
Reimarus, Hermann Samuel. 2010
Reimensnyder, John Milton. 1062, 3211
Reimer, Gustav Eduard. 1934
Reimer, John B. 3512
Reimer, William Christian. 2227
Reimers, David M. 2683
Reimert, W. D. 26
Rein, Remus C. 11, 1252, 3530, 3531, 3557
Rein, Wilhelm. 2276
Reinach, Salomon. 3140
Reinberger, Francis E. 2879, 2887
Reinboth, Oscar H. 2284
Reine, Francis Joseph. 2256, 3610
*Reiner, D. E. 1052
Reiner, Edwin W. 106, 1377
Reinerman, Alan J. 118, 860
Reiners, Ken. 23
Reinert, Paul Clare. 870
Reinertsen, Peter Amos. 2236
Reinhard, Franz Volkmar. 59
Reinhard, Janet E. 2072
Reinhardt, Madge. 1844
Reinhart, Bruce. 3168
Reinhold, Hans Ansgar. 2368, 840, 921, 2234, 2640, 2939
Reinisch, Leonhard. 3611
Reinitz, Richard. 3008
Reiquam, Oleen T. 987
Reischauer, August Karl. 706, 2534, 3104
Reiser, Oliver Leslie. 2767
Reiser, William E. 1382, 1473
Reishus, Martha. 1548
Reisman, Bernard. 1621, 2079, 2097

Reisman, E. Loretta. 3
Reisman, Frederick W. 80
Reisner, Christian Fichthorne. 587, 1252, 1525, 2894, 2904
Reisner, Christian Fitchthorne. 973, 10
Reisner, Christian Fitchtorne. 1569
Reisner, Edward Hartman. 3142
Reisner, George Andrew, 1867. 1890
Reisner, Sherwood. 2555
Reiss, Joseph. 3067
Reiss, Marguerite. 987, 3055
Reissig, Herman F. 1077
Reissner, Edward A. 1131
Reist, Benjamin A. 677, 3017, 3715
Reith, Herman. 3695
Reitmeister, Louis Aaron. 3120, 1655
Reitz, Rudiger. 1245
Reitzel, Charles F[rancis]. 3133
Reitzel, Charles Francis. 1052, 2803
Reitzenstein, Richard. 1767
Reizenstein, Jennie. 291, 1540
Rekers, George Alan. 1844
[Religions of the cenacle]. 2395
Religionsgeschichtliches Textbuch zum Alten Testament. English. 537, 2679
Religious Education Association. 2324, 2592, 3162, 3176
Religious liberty association. Washington, D.C. 3195
Religious Liberty Conference, 14th, Washington, D.C., 1970. 1469
Religious of the cenacle. 3205
Religious Record Index, Dayton, Ohio. 3271
Religious tract and book society for Ireland, Dublin. 303
Religious tract society, London. 286, 1603
Relly, James. 1954, 2065
Relton, Herbert Maurice. 1052, 2042, 3652
Rem, Oscar. 3290
Rembert, S. S. 3512
Remensnyder, Junius Benjamin. 2286, 3063, 3880, 106, 2276
Remey, Charles Mason. 128, 129, 130, 1269, 3599
Remi, Nicolas. 1423
Remington, Maud. 3512
Remler, Francis Joseph. 90, 2056, 3196, 3541, 3567, 3600
Remmers, John Henry. 3512
Remnant, G. L. 915
Remsburg, John Eleazer. 1655, 2008, 3023
Remy, Jean S. 625, 1983
Remy, Jules. 2605
Renan, Ernest. 71, 811, 1194, 1197, 1954, 1971, 2096, 2122, 2800, 3068, 3123, 3215
Renan, Ernest i.e. Joseph Ernest. 3215
Renard, Alexandre Charles. 1264, 2581
Renard, Henri. 2419, 2739
Renckens, Henricus. 525, 544
Rendall, Norline. 2395
Rendall, Ted S. 3229
Rendell, Elias De La Roche. 3570
Rendtorff, Heinrich. 1299
Rendtorff, Rolf. 540
Rendtorff, Trutz. 1188
Renekens, Henricus. 525, 2148
*Renfrd, Jean Marie. 3163
*Renfrd. Jean Marie. 3163
Renfrew, Jefferson. 166
*Renfro, Jean Marie. 3163
*Renfro, Sister Jean Marie. 3163
Rengers, Christopher. 2030, 2058
Rengstorf, Karl Heinrich. 1290
Renich, Fred. 987, 1857, 2825
Renich, Jill. 3877
Renison, William Thomas. 2939
Renna, Thomas J. 1145
Rennells, Charles Stephen. 3807
Renner, George Thomas. 3110
Renner, Louis L. 1532, 2191
Renner, R Richard. 3305
Renner, Richard. 3305
Rennick, Estella Feller. 236
Reno, Cora A. 202
Reno, Loren Marion. 2505
Renou, Louis. 1814, 1896, 1814, 1896
Renouard, Yves. 2770
Renouf, Peter Le Page. 1502
Renouf, Robert W. 3178
Renwick, A M. 1178, 3042
Reorganized Church of Jesus Christ of Latter-Day Saints. 81, 1239, 1356, 1569, 1861, 2605, 2614, 2791, 3215, 3216, 3217, 3218, 3677, 3881
Reorganized Church of Jesus Christ of Latter-Day Saints. Board of Publication. 3217
Reorganized Church of Jesus Christ of Latter-Day Saints. Children's Division. 3185
Reorganized Church of Jesus Christ of Latter-Day Saints. Committee on Basic Beliefs. 3216

Reorganized Church of Jesus Christ of Latter-Day Saints. Committee on Ministry to College People. 3217
Reorganized Church of Jesus Christ of Latter-Day Saints. Council of Twelve Apostles. 3218, 3357
Reorganized Church of Jesus Christ of Latter-Day Saints. Dept. of Religious Education. 3187, 3217
Reorganized Church of Jesus Christ of Latter-Day Saints. Dept. of Religious Education. Youth Division. 3217
Reorganized Church of Jesus Christ of Latter-Day Saints. Pastoral Care Office. 2791
Reorganized Church of Jesus Christ of Latter Day Saints. Worship Committee. 2345
Reorganized Church of Jesus of Latter Day Saints. Children's Division. 3173
Repp, Arthur Christian. 1329
Repp, George Douglass. 1514
Repplier, Agnes. 2334, 2506, 3377, 3761, 3377, 3438
Reps, Paul. 3892, 3894
Resch, Peter Anthony. 2356, 2358
Rescher, Nicholas. 28, 2841, 3716
Research Seminar in Archaeology and Related Subjects (1980) 1418
Resner, Lawrence. 2097
Ressmeyer, Rudolph Stang. 2301
Rest, Friedrich. 921, 1102, 1875, 1998, 3574, 3857
Rest, Karl. 908, 1606
Rest, Karl H. 908
Rest, Karl H A. 908, 3665
Restarick, Henry Bond. 1289, 2058, 2524
Reston, James. 2130
Retif, Andre. 658, 757, 2127
Retif, Louis. 850
Reu, Johann Michael. 110, 284, 1843, 2276, 2279, 2281, 2292, 2295, 306, 1268, 2277, 2279, 2905
Reumann, John Henry Paul. 270, 291, 477, 1382, 1739, 1971, 3446
Reuss, Eduard Wilhelm Eugen. 406
Reusser, Walter Christian. 1666, 2197
Reuter, Alan. 987
Reuter, Frank Theodore. 828, 3740
Reuter, Frederick. 3370
Reuter, Frederick A. 397, 615, 855, 865, 905, 1318, 1441, 1630, 3204, 3263, 3370
Reuter, Frederick Albert. 865, 908, 1267, 1826, 3888
Reuter, George Sylvester. 2475
Reuter, William Charles. 3567
Reuterdahl, Arvid. 3073, 3079
Revell, Peter. 1455
Revere, Paul. 684
Revesz, Therese Ruth. 3826
Reville, Emile Dalmesse. 1802
Reville, Jean. 1100
Reville, John Clement. 685, 868, 1649
Revilo, Ridge. 1841
Revoir, Trudy West. 1112
Rex, Helmut Herbert. 2052
Rex, Ruth Irwin. 3854
Rex, Ruth (Irwin) 3859
Rex, Walter. 179, 3667
Rex, Walter E. 2778, 2864
Rexine, John E. 721
Rexroat, Stephen. 3557
Rey, Alfonso. 1470, 2260, 2771
Reynes-Monlaur, Marie. 2006, 3201
Reyburn, Hugh Young. 728, 2750
Reyburn, William David. 2506
Reyes, Benito F. 3463
Reymond, Eve A. E. 1021
Reymond, Lizelle. 1814, 2712, 3400
Reymond, Robert L. 176, 306, 698, 2816, 2914, 3657
Reyna, Guglielmo. 1630
Reyna, Ruth. 2375
Reynard the Fox. English. 1588
Reyner, John Hereward. 2395, 2991
Reynolds, Amelia (Stead) 2697
Reynolds, Arthur. 1217
Reynolds, Arthur G. 801
Reynolds, Barrie. 3827
Reynolds, Bede. 791, 1001, 3234
Reynolds, Bernard. 1252
Reynolds, Edward D. 875
Reynolds, Ernest Edwin. 683, 738, 1628, 2704
Reynolds, Ferris E. 3104, 3180
Reynolds, Frank. 2119
Reynolds, Frank E. 709
Reynolds, George. 679, 2598, 2605, 679, 680, 1929, 2605
Reynolds, Isham E. 320, 1203, 2633
Reynolds, James. 1710
Reynolds, James A. 867
Reynolds, James Bronson. 3862
Reynolds, James Seymore. 2421
Reynolds, Jim. 3388
Reynolds, John Clopton. 1466
Reynolds, Joseph William. 3076

Reynolds, Joyce. 3005
Reynolds, Leroy N. 1314
Reynolds, Lillian Richter. 3168, 3188
[Reynolds, Lillie]. 2055, 2175
Reynolds, Loretta. 46
Reynolds, Louis Bernard. 319, 471, 1012, 3357, 3383, 3387
Reynolds, Paul Davidson. 3435
Reynolds, Quentin James. 2793
Reynolds, Ralph Vincent. 3674
Reynolds, Reginald. 3847
Reynolds, Robert L. 2861
Reynolds, Roger E. 2742
Reynolds, Ruth (Sutton) 407, 535
Reynolds, Stephen. 1179
Reynolds, Thomas. 3604
[Reynolds, Thomas Edward] 1898. 3300
Reynolds, William Jensen. 1872, 1875, 2012
Rezek, Antoine Ivan. 2336
Reznikoff, Charles. 2098
Rezy, Carol. 905
Rezzori, Gregor von. 3133
Rhea, Carolyn. 1595, 2395, 2887, 2894, 3541
Rhea, Claude H. 1749, 3234
Rhea, Ralph. 2395
Rhea, Sarah J. 2349
Rhees, Rush. 1971
Rhein, Francis Bayard. 411
Rhie, Marylin M. 1631, 3316, 3718
Rhind, William Graeme. 205
Rhine, Joseph Banks. 2728, 2991, 2728, 2991
Rhinelander, Philip Mercer. 1595
Rhinelander, Phillip Mercer. 1595
Rhoades, Donald H. 1201
Rhoades, Ezra. 2905
Rhoades, F. S. 669
Rhoades, Winfred. 1441, 1512, 1726
Rhoads, David M. 2090, 2134
Rhoads, Samuel G. 3295
Rhodes, Anthony Richard Ewart. 2770, 2852
*Rhodes, Arnold B. 1356
Rhodes, Arnold Black. 3323
Rhodes, Bertha Marilda. 3156
Rhodes, Bertha Marlida. 3763
Rhodes, Daniel D. 517
Rhodes, Harrie Vernette. 3133
Rhodes, Henry Taylor Fowkes. 1429
Rhodes, Jeremiah B.J. 2399
Rhodes, John D. 2791
Rhodes, Mosheim. 449
*Rhodes, Rev. D. L. 3229
Rhodes, Walter. 1843
Rhoides, Emmanouel D. 2122
Rhygyfarch. 1406
Rhymer, Joseph. 520, 540, 565
Rhymes, Douglas A. 2879, 3389
Rhynard, Peter. 3030
Rhys, John. 878
Riach, John M. 1365
Rian, Edwin Harold. 1066, 1130
Riaud, Alexis. 1831
Ribadeau Dumas, Francois. 723
Ribalow, Harold Uriel. 2082
Ribble, Arthur Le Baron. 973
Ricard, Olfert Herman. 2007, 2058
Ricard, Robert. 822, 2460
Riccardo. 987
Riccardo, Martin. 2640
Ricchiuti, Paul B. 10, 2014, 3811
Ricci, Matteo. 1947
Ricci, Scipione de. 1357
Ricciotti, Giuseppe. 1971, 2089, 2351, 2800
Rice, Alice Caldwell (Hegan) 973
Rice, Anna Virena. 1726, 3852
Rice, Austin. 1342
Rice, Charles. 314
Rice, Charles E. 791, 3096
Rice, Charles Lynvel. 2905
Rice, Charles Russell. 2060
Rice, Charles Scott. 2407
Rice, Clarence Edgar. 3376
Rice, Claton Silas. 2557
Rice, Cyprian. 3543
Rice, David. 136
Rice, David Talbot. 86, 922, 1880, 3705, 1881
Rice, Edward. 1038, 3120
Rice, Edward E. 811, 812, 2413, 3138, 3140
Rice, Edward Peter. 2316
Rice, Edwin Wilbur. 437, 442, 1794, 1916, 3551, 3557, 3564, 33, 245, 291, 330, 417, 428, 434, 438, 441, 444, 1570, 3551
Rice, Elaine B. 3463
Rice, F. Philip. 3880
Rice, Fidelis. 106
Rice, Hillery C. 181, 1228, 1741
Rice, Hugh Ashton Lawrence. 1213
Rice, Hugh Smith. 96
Rice, John Andrew. 501, 2437
Rice, John Holt. 2928, 3590

*Rice, John R. 3464
Rice, John R. 66, 166, 201, 306, 330, 441, 652, 994, 1114, 1354, 1360, 1560, 1570, 1831, 2001, 2034, 2465, 2627, 2879, 3012, 3290, 3411, 3836
Rice, Kenneth S. 3557
Rice, Laban Lacy. 1325
Rice, Lillian (Moore) 209, 2765, 3172
Rice, M Leslie. 973
Rice, Madeleine (Hooke) 882, 3424
[Rice, Martin] b. 1814. 157
Rice, Merton Stacher. 1783, 1954, 2426, 2437, 2589, 2740, 3011, 3235, 3344, 1726, 2675
Rice, Nathan Lewis. 1514, 2911
Rice, Patrick William. 2342
Rice, Philip Blair. 1746
Rice, Phillip Blair. 1746
Rice, Rebecca. 2720, 3764, 3766
Rice, Richard. 1737
Rice, Susan Tracy. 1486
Rice, Thomas Jefferson. 1655
Rice, Wallace de Groot Cecil. 1688
Rice, Wayne. 1260
*Rice, William B. 201
Rice, William Carroll. 1208
Rice, William Francis. 2999
Rice, William Henry. 1560
Rice, William North. 1597, 3073, 3313, 3079
Rice. Edward E. 812
Rich, Alice Hamilton. 1971
Rich, Charles. 2395
Rich, Edward Charles. 118
Rich, Elaine Sommers. 1435
Rich, Frank Merritt. 253
Rich, James Walter. 148, 1421, 3080
Rich, Joseph Walter. 587, 2248
Rich, Mark. 3254, 3255
Rich, Russell A. 1233
Rich, Thomas Hill. 576
Rich, Wendell O. 2612
Richard, Claude. 2605
Richard, James. 2834
Richard, James Austin. 1954
Richard, James William. 2284, 2400
Richard, Louis. 3030
Richard, Lucien. 1079, 2043
Richard, Lucien Joseph. 728, 3492
Richard, Marie E. 3471
Richard, Paul. 2012
Richard, Robert L. 3328
Richard, Timothy. 2511
Richard of St. Victor. 1356
Richards, Alberta Rae (Sune) 3840
Richards, Alun. 3627
Richards, Blair. 2238
[Richards, Charles Augustus Lewis] 1830-1914. 694
Richards, Charles Herbert. 1244
Richards, Claude. 2171, 2612, 2619
Richards, Daniel Brigham. 2617
Richards, Edith R. (Pearson) 1451
Richards, Edith Ryley (Pearson) 1451
Richards, Edward H. 3379
Richards, Eugene. 2728
Richards, George. 608
Richards, George Warren. 1052, 1801, 2195, 3213
Richards, Harold Marshall Sylvester. 42, 1432, 1560, 1696, 2052, 2763, 2905, 3069, 3383, 3387
Richards, Harriet M. 3196
Richards, Harry Edward. 3076
Richards, Harry Edwards. 648
Richards, Henry W. 2612, 2634
Richards, Herbert Forest. 2787
Richards, Hubert J. 245, 373, 456, 2801, 3266
Richards, Hubert John. 2052
[Richards, James A.]. 3235
Richards, James Austin. 443
Richards, James McDowell. 3624
Richards, Jean H. 1382, 1983, 2886
Richards, Jean Hosking. 623, 632, 2023
Richards, Jeffrey. 1773, 2770, 2861
Richards, John. 1585
Richards, John Richards. 128
Richards, John William. 1693
Richards, Joseph Addison. 1452
Richards, Joseph Havens. 3235
Richards, Kenneth G. 3312
Richards, Larry. 430, 520, 527, 563, 987, 1041, 1726, 2090, 3888, 988, 3214
Richards, Laura Jane. 3512
Richards, Lawrence O. 333, 378, 381, 444, 446, 472, 530, 544, 556, 641, 940, 942, 945, 951, 953, 995, 1016, 1062, 1170, 1245, 1260, 1713, 1726, 2753, 2782, 2786, 3550, 3888
Richards, Le Grand. 1841, 2119, 2610, 2612
Richards, Le Grand, Bp. 2612
Richards, Leyton Price. 3793
Richards, Lillian P. 236
Richards, Lucy. 3133
Richards, Lysander Salmon. 2834

Richards, Mary Helen. 917
Richards, Norman. 2124
Richards, Philip S. 2320
[Richards, Robert]. 2614
Richards, Stephen L. 2608, 2614
[Richards, Theodore] 1867. 39
Richards, Thomas Cole. 2467, 2879
Richards, William. 1365, 3235
Richards, William Rogers. 2248, 74, 615
Richardson, Alan. 417, 66, 205, 245, 417, 477, 641, 1088, 1818, 2043, 3639, 3657, 3658
[Richardson, Albert Ernest] 1868. 1735, 1835, 2248
Richardson, Alfred Madeley. 1206
Richardson, Alice Marion. 1876
Richardson, Amos W. 136
Richardson, Arthur M. 2599
Richardson, Carl. 1428
Richardson, Caroline Francis. 1215
Richardson, Charles Herbert. 1490
Richardson, Charlotte (Smith) 3209
Richardson, Cyril Albert. 2854
Richardson, Cyril Charles. 1882, 1018, 1179, 1882, 2927, 3713, 1179
Richardson, Don. 2557
Richardson, Donald William. 456
Richardson, E. Allen. 1926
Richardson, Edward Elliott. 2531, 3063, 3104
[Richardson, Eliza (Smith)]. 1357
Richardson, Ernest Cushing. 1931, 3090
Richardson, George Leyburn. 2049
Richardson, George Lynde. 1781
[Richardson, Hannah W.]. 2092
Richardson, Harry Van Buren. 16, 2438, 2682
Richardson, Herbert Warren. 3652
Richardson, Hilary Goode. 199
Richardson, J. Spurgeon. 731, 2169
Richardson, J. T. 1997
Richardson, Jabez. 1670
Richardson, James P. 25, 2375
Richardson, James T. 918
Richardson, John. 1109, 1675
Richardson, John Andrew. 2754
Richardson, John Emmett. 3512, 2728, 2991, 3512
Richardson, John R. 470, 1076
Richardson, John T. 1756, 3694
Richardson, Jonathan. 2469
[Richardson, Joseph]. 1792
Richardson, Julius Miller. 1731
Richardson, Lovella Stoll. 1200
Richardson, Marilyn. 17
Richardson, Mark Wyman. 1378, 2991
Richardson, Mary Kathleen. 3247, 48, 173, 186, 1459, 3235, 3704
Richardson, Merrick Abner. 3463
Richardson, Norman Egbert. 686, 1071, 1167, 1252, 1954, 2061, 2231, 2886, 3156, 3859
Richardson, Oman P. 988
Richardson, Oscar. 1823
Richardson, Peter. 1083, 373, 1659
Richardson, Robert. 732, 1831, 1463
Richardson, Samuel. 3782
Richardson, Simon Peter. 3095, 3133
Richardson, William J. 2480
Richberg, Donald Randall. 1655
Richelieu, Peter. 1696
Richelsen, John. 3191
Richeome, Louis. 1022, 2260
Riches, John Kenneth. 2050
Richet, Charles Robert. 2991
Richey, Eloise May. 3236
Richey, Russell E. 3745
Richey, Thomas. 1181, 2026, 3647
Richmond, Alban Benson. 3512
Richmond, Annette B. 913, 2970
[Richmond. Beth-El congregation]. 1160
Richmond, Central Methodist church. 2198
Richmond, Charles E. 513
Richmond. Congregation Beth Ahabah. 726
Richmond, Cora L. V. (Scott) 3512
[Richmond, Cora Linn Victoria (Scott) 1840-1923. 3512
Richmond (Diocese) Catholic historical society. 3236
Richmond (Diocese). Synod, 4th, 1966. 3578
Richmond, Ernest Tatham. 1944
Richmond, Euphemia Johnson (Guernsey) 616
Richmond, Harry R. 3371
Richmond, Hugh M. 2469
Richmond, Ian Archibald. 1530
Richmond, Isaiah Seth. 296
Richmond, James. 1105, 3104, 3239
Richmond, Legh. 1015, 1302, 2866, 3236
Richmond. Monastery of the Visitation. 2569
Richmond, Olney H. 2729
Richmond, Rebecca (Langworthy) 890
Richmond, S. A. 1600

Richmond, Sonya. 3866
Richmond, Thomas. 3512
Richmond Union Theological Seminary. 2978, 3611, 3612, 3627
Richmond, Va. Second Presbyterian church. 1822
Richmond, Va. Union theological seminary. Library. 3627
Richstatter, Thomas. 735, 840
Richter, Dolle. 3854
Richter, Edward J. 1244
Richter, Friedrich. 2277, 2298
Richter, J. S. 797, 3557
Richter, Johann Paul Friedrich. 3089
Richter, Julius. 2516, 2531, 2552, 2541
Richter, Stephan. 2812
Richtmyer, Bernice D. 973
Ricour, Paul. 3411
Rickaby, John. 1262, 2242, 2399, 2419
Rickaby, Joseph John. 738, 761, 2704, 3133, 3696
Ricker, George M. 74
Ricker, Joseph. 144
Rickerson, Wayne. 1606, 1610, 2339
Rickert, Corinne Holt. 1403, 1585
Rickey, Mary Ellen. 1379
Rickles, Nathan King. 1583
Ricks, Beatrice. 1934
Ricks, Eldin. 680, 2605, 2612
Ricks, Joel. 679
Ricoeur, Paul. 288
Riday, George Emil. 2204
Riddel, John G. 106
Riddell, Newton N. 973, 1052, 1071, 1382, 1554
Riddell, Walter Alexander. 1148
Ridderbos, Herman N. 306, 339, 377, 380, 441, 477
Ridderbos, Nicolaas Herman. 205
Riddle, Donald Wayne. 391, 411, 1093, 1954, 2351, 2801, 2828
Riddle, Marion. 3547
Riddle, Matthew Brown. 360
Riddle, Oscar. 1581
Riddlerbos, Herman N. 2176
Ridenour, Fritz. 205, 278, 471, 945, 988, 1079, 1629, 2854, 3829, 3888
Rideout, Gus. 1062
Rider, Fremont. 3512
Rider, Richard Price. 2332
Ridgaway, Henry Bascom. 1368, 1934
Ridgley, Frank Harris. 2080
Ridgway, William H. 3177
Ridgway, William Hance. 1015, 1595
Ridley, Francis A. 860, 2769
Ridley, Jasper Godwin. 1763, 2182, 3237, 3831
Ridley, Michael. 85
Ridley, Nicholas. 1217
Ridolfi, Roberto. 3305
Ridout, Daniel Lyman. 3674
Ridout, George Whitefield. 1752
Ridout, Lionel Utley. 2204
Ridout, Samuel. 3579
Riede, David Charles. 3310
Riedel, Eunice. 241
Riedel, Johannes. 917
Riedel, Margaret. 2023
Riedemann, Peter. 1859
Riegel, John Ira. 3133
Riegel, Oscar Wetherhold. 2605, 3535
Riegert, Norbert. 623, 688
Riegert, Wilbur A. 1399
Riegle, David D. 1382
Riegler, Gordon Arthur. 2687
Rieke, Marcus. 1260, 3888
Rieker, Hans Ulrich. 2381
Riemer, George R. 1948
Riemer, Jack. 1416
Riencourt, Amaury de. 2640
Rienecker, Fritz. 352
Riepe, Charles K. 1613
Riepe, Dale Maurice. 2675
Riepen, Harry O. 3120
Riesenfeld, Harald. 335
Riess, Oswald. 973, 1005, 2301
Riess, Walter. 2297, 2395, 3888
Rife, John Merie. 1770
Rife, John Merle. 411, 1770
Riffel, Herman H. 306, 994, 3226
Rifkin, Jeremy. 1552
Riforgiato, Leonard R. 1302, 2630
Riga, Peter. 853, 1062, 3411
Riga, Peter J. 853, 854, 1062, 1136, 1151, 1154, 1245, 1831, 2030, 3266, 3336, 3411, 3772
Rigaldus, Odo. 1638
Rigaud, Milo. 3787
Rigaux, Beda. 373, 435, 436, 2801
Rigby, Fred Frankland. 1219
Rigby, N L. 3702
Rigdon, Jonathan. 3073
Rigell, William Richard. 2127, 2905
Rigg, James Harrison. 3804
Riggan, George A. 2016, 2414
Riggenbach, Eduard. 2052, 3221

Riggle, Herbert McClellan. 871, 1122, 1554, 1696, 2014, 2055, 2175, 3261, 3320
Riggs, Alice Claudia (Shepard) 3402
Riggs, James Stevenson. 2065, 2092
Riggs, Ollie L. 2030
Riggs, Ralph M. 92, 608, 3481, 3674
Riggs, Stephen Return. 1399
Riggs, Timberline Wales. 1314, 2599, 2605
Riggs, William G. 2469
Righter, Carroll. 96
Righter, William. 2649
Rightmyer, Levi. 199
Rightmyer, Nelson Waite. 1223
Rightor, Henry Haskell. 1219, 2781
Rigmark, William. 2534
Rigney, Paul. 1062
Rihbany, Abraham Mitrie. 1971, 1983, 2009, 2640, 3578, 3579
Rihn, Roy J. 3223
[Rijckevorsel, E. (Westerwoudt) van]. 850, 3808
Rike, Charles Jesse. 1612
Riley, Arthur Joseph. 823
Riley, Athelstan. 883, 1129, 1875
Riley, Benjamin Franklin. 143, 169, 170
Riley brothers, New York. 3548
Riley, Elihu Samuel. 1017, 2363, 2979
Riley, Frank Lawrence. 643, 3268
Riley, Hugh M. 139, 1398
Riley, Isaac Woodbridge. 1035, 2605, 2640, 3429
Riley, James Whitcomb. 61, 3238
Riley, Lawrence Joseph. 1522
Riley, Marvin P. 1859
Riley, Miles O'Brian. 3362
Riley, Miles O'Brien. 1417
Riley, Nancy Agnes (McNickle) 2231
Riley-Smith, Jonathan Simon Christopher, 1938. 1390
Riley, Walter H. 2421
Riley, Willard D. 2682
Riley, William Bell. 166, 205, 338, 364, 615, 1122, 1372, 1514, 1554, 1560, 1570, 1581, 1954, 2175, 2563, 3232, 3357, 3674, 3740, 3840, 3888, 2787, 2905, 3411
Riley-Smith, Jonathan. 2179
Rilliet, Jean Horace. 3900
Rilling, John William. 430, 2301
Rimaud, Didier. 585
Rimlinger, Herbert Theodore. 2342
Rimmer, Charles Brandon. 66, 1831
Rimmer, Harry. 379, 106, 205, 278, 306, 379, 384, 509, 515, 608, 611, 1134, 1382, 1890, 1986, 1998, 2030, 2248, 2934, 3012, 3051, 3080, 3320, 205, 2043
Rinaldi, Bonaventura. 2356
Rinaldi, Peter M. 1826, 1827
Rinden, Gertrude (Jenness) 2491
Rindge, Fred Hamilton. 2189
Rindge, Frederick Hastings. 1360
Rincer, Harriet Snyder. 3207
Rines, Edward Francis. 1274
Ring, George Cyril. 91, 3140
Ring, John. 3295
Ringel, Erwin. 2995
Ringelblum, Emanuel. 2107
Ringenberg, Loyal R. 296, 324, 423, 648, 995
Ringer, Francis E. 1545
Ringer, Francis Ellsworth. 1545
Ringgold, James Trapier. 3193, 3548
Ringgren, Helmer. 1410, 2148, 2415, 3140, 3332
Ringgren, Helmer [Karl Vilhelm Helmer Ringgren]. 578, 3271
*Ringland, Elinor. 3164
*Ringland, Mabel Crews. 3557
Ringrose, Hyacinthe. 868, 2308
Rinker, Richard N. 1089
Rinker, Rosalind. 973, 988, 1524, 1610, 2880, 2886, 2887, 3238, 3829, 3830, 3888
Rinker, Wilson H. 1726
Rinkliff, George Louis. 973, 3523
Rinpoche, Namgyal. 2819
Rinvolucri, Mario. 2746
Rinzema, J. 3393
Riordan, Joseph W. 1127, 3298
[Riordan, Michael Joseph]. 132
Riou, Roger. 2486, 3238
Ripa, Cesare. 1510
Ripley, Ezra. 1322
Ripley, Francis J. 658, 754, 797, 1299
Ripley, Francis Joseph. 754, 797, 1249, 1299
Ripley, Henry Jones. 1240, 2905
Ripley, M. M. 3599
Ripley, Robert Le Roy. 1397
Riplinger, Thomas. 1188
Rippetoe, Odessa B. 734, 3238
Ripple, Paula. 1471, 1688
Rippy, James Fred. 850, 1903, 1904
Rippy, Mark Leo. 1252
Riquet, Michel. 887

Rische, Henry. 973
Risedorf, Gwen. 3055
Rishabhchand. 1709, 3866
Rishell, Charles Wesley. 61, 1254
Rismiller, Arthur P. 1257
Riss, Richard. 2052
Risser, Emma King. 1809
Rissi, Mathias. 460, 465
Rist, John M. 460
Rist, Martin. 460

Ristoteles. 81
Ristow, Cecil Frederic. 1441
Ristow, Gunter. 1958, 2021
Ristuccia, Bernard Joseph. 2578
Rita Agnes, 1890. 2717
Ritamary. 2573
Ritcher, Stephan. 3218
Ritchie, Andrew. 1389, 926
Ritchie, Arthur. 443, 3344, 420, 436, 428
Ritchie, Carson I. A. 1222, 2558
Ritchie, Carson IA. 1488
Ritchie, Cyril J. 3383
Ritchie, David Ronald. 1007
Ritchie, Frank H T. 3872
Ritchie, Frank Herbert Thomas. 3872
Ritchie, George G. 932, 3238
Ritchie, Jacob Marion. 1514, 2415
Ritchie, James. 1581
Ritchie, John. 1614, 1905
Ritchie, William. 3595
Ritland, Richard M. 3083
Ritschil Dietrich. 1252
Ritschl, Albrecht Benjamin. 2161, 2846, 3156, 3239
Ritschl, Dietrich. 2043, 2905
Rittelmeyer, Friedrich. 1954
Rittenberg, Viola M. 2079
Rittenhouse, Dicie M. 2535
Rittenhouse, Hawley Olmstead. 2592
Rittenhouse, Laurence. 3172, 3185
Rittenhouse, Norman. 3821
Rittenhouse, Stan. 3897
Ritter, Abraham. 2829, 3896
Ritter, Gerhard. 2277, 3037
Ritter, Jacob. 3133
Ritter, Ovid Herbert. 3532
Ritter, Richard Henry. 921
Rittlemeyer, Friedrich. 2248
Riva, Anna. 1804, 2313
Rivadeneira, Pedro de. 1025, 2269
Rivail, Hippolyte Leon Denizard. 3474, 3512
Rivaux. 1632
Rively, William E. 2507
Rivenburg, Sidney W. 2503
Rivenburg, Sidney White. 2503
Rivera, Edith Mary Irvine. 3833
Rivers, Clarence Joseph. 2395, 2722, 3004
Rivers, Edith M. Irvine. 3833
Rivers, Mario E. 801
Rivers, Richard Henderson. 2758
Rivers, William Halse Rivers. 2378
Rives, Elsie. 5, 939, 2793, 3174
Rivest, Michael W. 2265
Rivet, Mary Majella. 2648
Riviere, William T. 2170
Rivkin, Ellis. 2145, 2216, 2829, 3576
Rivoira, Giovanni Teresio. 79
Rix, Harriet Hale. 2695
Rix, Wilton. 1954
Rizk, Helen Salem. 1873
Rizzotto, Mary. 1037
Rizzuto, Ana-Maria. 2994
rNam-par-grol-bahi lam-las sByans-pahi yon-tan bsTan-pa. 2577
Roach, Corwin Carlyle. 299, 1308, 2961
Roach, Fred. 2395
Roadman, Earl A. 3254
Roads, Charles. 3550, 377, 641, 1076, 1107, 2043, 3180, 3254, 3557
Roark, Dallas M. 677, 3660
Roark, Warren C. 1600, 1228, 1831
Roback, Abraham Aaron. 1934, 2082, 3312
Robarts, Edith. 4
Robb, Alfred Arthur. 3469
Robb, Edmund W. 1560, 2437
Robb, James Harry. 2320, 3694
Robb, John Wesley. 1854
Robb, Mary Cooper. 3388
Robb, R. H. 1636, 2430
Robb, Stewart. 2668, 2715, 2947, 2948
Robbins, Anne Manning. 2849, 3512
Robbins, Barney R. 349
Robbins, Chandler. 3357, 685, 1284, 2272, 3204, 3726, 3795
Robbins, Charles Leonidas. 2592
[Robbins, Eliza]. 2657
Robbins, Frank Egleston. 524
Robbins, Howard Chandler. 1441, 2905, 2972, 3357, 3409, 3423
Robbins, Jhan. 3708
Robbins, Joseph Chandler. 673, 2505, 2531
Robbins, Joseph H. 1581
Robbins, Nancy Estelle. 1474

Robbins, Ray F. 456, 1971
Robbins, Robert. 3357
Robbins, Rossell Hope. 3825
Robbins, Sarah (Stuart) 750
Robbins, Shawn. 2993, 3240
Robbins, Thomas. 1342, 2002, 3120, 3133, 3143
Robbins, Wilford Lash. 1595, 66, 1893
Robbins, William. 2704
Robeck, Mildred (Coen) 1712
Robenoff, Janeski. 3716
Roberson, Charles Heber. 245, 2065, 456
Roberson, Harriette Gunn. 2994
Roberson, Lee. 494, 1531, 1560, 3321, 3414
Robert, Andre. 311, 658
Robert, Andre [Marie Edmond]. 311
Robert-Houdin, Jean Eugene. 1345
Roberti, Francesco. 950
Robertis, Nancy. 1710
Roberto. 191, 663, 673, 677, 739, 882, 1304, 1372, 1620, 1629, 1635, 1639, 1649, 1717, 1811, 1908, 1934, 2124, 2183, 2189, 2195, 2269, 2305, 2332, 2348, 2349, 2767, 2810, 2854, 2943, 2946, 3247, 3305, 3317, 3379, 3460, 3526, 3780
Roberts, Ainslie. 2654
Roberts, Alexander. 361, 362, 425, 2014
Roberts, Allen E. 1664, 1671, 2364
Roberts, Alpheus J. 1035
Roberts, Andrew Jackson. 1795
Roberts, Arthur O. 22, 1637, 1676, 1688, 3357
Roberts, Arthur Wayne. 66
Roberts, Benjamin Titus. 3674, 3716, 1004
Roberts, Benjamine Titus. 1823
Roberts, Brigham Henry. 1231, 1179, 1726, 2605, 2612, 2616, 1179, 2608, 2612, 2617, 3591
Roberts, Carl Eric Bechhofer. 671, 3682
Roberts, Cecil A. 994, 1305, 1600, 1786, 3538
Roberts, Charles. 1637, 1677
Roberts, Clarence. 644, 1170
Roberts, Colin Henderson. 1501
Roberts, Dana. 2286
Roberts, Daniel. 3241
[Roberts, David Ellsworth]. 3456, 3459
Roberts, David Everett. 2995, 2934, 1584
Roberts, Donald Llewellyn. 1122
Roberts, Donald S. 901
Roberts, Evelyn. 1303, 1795, 3240
Roberts, Evelyn Harvey. 3201
Roberts, Frank. 548
Roberts, George. 3370
[Roberts, George C M.]. 886
Roberts, George C. M. 2431
Roberts, Guy L. 973, 1421
Roberts, Guy Velope. 1452
Roberts, Irene. 3142
Roberts, Isaac. 1682
*Roberts, J. W. 330
Roberts, J. W. 369, 412, 456
Roberts, James Brendan. 2342
Roberts, James Deotis. 16, 3017, 3647
Roberts, Jane. 3474, 2993, 3241, 3474, 3512
Roberts, Jimmy Jack McBee. 1743
Roberts, John Richard. 1456
Roberts, John Robison. 2265
[Roberts, Jonathan M]. 3512, 3513
Roberts, Joseph. 3073
Roberts, Kenneth F. 757, 3201, 3888
Roberts, Louis. 3019
Roberts, Nancy. 1710
Roberts, Oral. 973, 988, 1007, 1435, 1514, 1560, 1575, 1595, 1792, 2410, 2477, 2808, 3241, 3539
Roberts, Philip I. 2494, 3018
Roberts, Philip Ilott. 24, 2461, 2588
[Roberts, Philip Ilott]. 2307
Roberts, Price. 1464
Roberts, Richard. 1017, 391, 1062, 1141, 1726, 1832, 1986, 2012, 2043, 2065, 2905, 3409
Roberts, Robert. 650
Roberts, Robert Edwin. 936
Roberts, Rufus Putnam. 2342
Roberts, Seldon L. 3156
Roberts, Seldon Low. 3156
Roberts, Susan. 3828
Roberts, Thomas D'Esterre. 791
Roberts, Tom Aerwyn. 190
Roberts, Ursula Wyllie. 1600
Roberts, Verne D. 802, 3237
Roberts, W. Dayton. 1574, 3535
Roberts, Waldemar. 3326
Roberts, Walter Coe. 2212, 2959
Roberts, William. 2395, 2880
Roberts, William Henry. 3627, 3808
Roberts, William Kemuel. 1071, 2321
Roberts, William Nesbit. 3436
Roberts, William O. 1908
Robertson, A. T. 216, 377, 1971, 2801

Robertson, Alec. 84, 89, 123, 883, 885, 1206, 3219
Robertson, Alec Collingwood Cuthbert. 1206
Robertson, Archibald. 322, 2175, 1103
Robertson, Archibald Horace Mann. 1103
Robertson, Archibald Thomas. 3745, 141, 166, 321, 339, 342, 413, 437, 692, 1770, 2356, 3241, 166, 339, 341, 344, 349, 352, 377, 391, 412, 414, 420, 426, 436, 449, 474, 475, 1732, 1770, 1971, 2001, 2043, 2065, 2127, 2128, 2335, 2356, 2801, 2825, 2905, 3241
Robertson, Archilbald Thomas. 449
Robertson, Benjamin Perry. 1832
Robertson, Betty B. 3156
Robertson, Constance (Noyes) 2737
Robertson, D. B. 1242, 2709, 3448
Robertson, David A. 211, 501, 556, 1799
Robertson, Dede. 932, 3241
Robertson, Durant Waite. 1
Robertson, Edwin Hanton. 270, 291, 346, 641, 653, 677, 926, 2325
Robertson, Ella (Broadus) 3840
Robertson, Festus G. 1204
Robertson, Frederick William. 346, 1227, 1441, 3241, 3344, 3366, 3647
Robertson, Hector Menteith. 1076, 3087, 3800
[Robertson, Helen Field]. 3513
Robertson, Irvine. 1394, 3323
Robertson, James. 3513, 2116
Robertson, James Alexander. 1954
Robertson, James Douglas. 1841, 1842, 3004
Robertson, Jenny. 623, 626, 632, 930, 1029, 1983, 1996, 2027, 2032, 2771, 2804
Robertson, John J. 1717, 3383, 3812
Robertson, John M. 3407
Robertson, John Mackinnon. 1655, 1657, 3120
Robertson, Josephine. 17, 973, 1252, 2395, 2676, 3843
Robertson, LaRae Collett. 680
Robertson, Mabel Nixon. 3513
Robertson, Norvell. 3665
Robertson, Pat. 988, 2369, 3241
Robertson, Roland. 3087, 3088
Robertson, Stuart. 973
Robertson, William. 3207
Robertson, William Hall. 224
Robertus. 1029, 3820
Robichaud, Norbert. 1823
Robillard, Edmond. 1088
Robin, 1944-1975. 150, 3241
Robin, Arthur de Quetteville. 665, 1781
Robin, Arthur de Quettevillef. 2820
Robin, Jean. 3526
Robinet, Jean Francois Eugene. 1639
Robinowitz, Chaim. 1312
Robins, Elizabeth. 1362
Robins, Henry Burke. 118, 3679
Robins, John B. 1052
Robins, Sidney Swaim. 1102
Robinson, Albert Ernest. 1062
Robinson, Almadora Mead. 3513
Robinson, Archibald Boaz. 1273
Robinson, Arthur Thomas. 3702
Robinson, Arthur William. 1052, 1735, 973, 991, 1299
Robinson, Benjamin Willard. 408, 417, 1995, 2071, 2801
Robinson, Charles. 1038
Robinson, Charles Alexander. 283
Robinson, Charles Edson. 3398
Robinson, Charles Edward. 122
Robinson, Charles Elmo. 2880
Robinson, Charles Henry. 1954, 2030, 2494, 2526
Robinson, Charles Mulford. 2916
Robinson, Charles Seymour. 429, 436, 1868, 1872, 2825, 2934, 3563
Robinson, Christine Hinckley. 1009, 2608
Robinson, Clarence Cromwell. 3446, 3872
Robinson, Daniel Sommer. 1052
Robinson, David. 119, 1511
Robinson, David James. 1243, 1704
Robinson, Donald Fay. 2008, 3142
Robinson, Donald Ray. 2008
Robinson, Dores Eugene. 3380
Robinson, Edgar M. 687
Robinson, Edna Moore. 299, 3602
Robinson, Edward. 245, 283, 652, 1769, 2763, 3241
Robinson, Ella May (White) 973, 3811, 1015, 1790, 1983, 2134, 2261, 2491
Robinson, Elmo Arnold. 3754, 3755
Robinson, Emma Ameli. 2521
Robinson, Emma Amelia. 211, 595, 632, 635, 939, 1184, 1252, 1957, 2443, 2528, 2531, 3531
Robinson, Ethel Blackwell. 3063
Robinson, Ezekiel Gilman. 2905, 3647
Robinson, Forbes. 1732, 3201
Robinson, Francis. 3762
Robinson, Frank A. 3120

Robinson, Frank Bruce. 1655, 1726, 2986
Robinson, Fred Elmo. 1035
Robinson, G. Clement. 1655
Robinson, George Chester. 303
Robinson, George Livingston. 216, 291, 537, 544, 559
Robinson, George Livingstone. 216, 544, 560, 596, 599, 1096, 2912
Robinson, George Livinstone. 2735
Robinson, George Wade. 108
Robinson, Godfrey Clive. 283, 1253, 2848, 3665
Robinson, Gordon. 349
Robinson, Grant. 2696
Robinson, H. Wheeler. 599
Robinson, Haddon W. 588, 988, 1452, 2905, 3407
Robinson, Harold McAfee. 1993, 1452
Robinson, Henry Wheeler. 291, 501, 540, 599, 1832, 3030, 3541, 291, 599, 1848, 2951, 3541
Robinson, Herbert Spencer. 2653
Robinson, Howard. 179
Robinson, Ian. 1918
Robinson, Jacob. 3851
Robinson, James A. 2737, 2844
Robinson, James Armitage. 1544
Robinson, James C. 3259
Robinson, James E. 3080
Robinson, James H. 281, 641, 905
Robinson, James Herman. 11, 713, 2905, 3133
Robinson, James McConkey. 288, 335, 436, 1018, 1457, 1801, 2008, 2767, 3650, 3657
Robinson, James William. 3463
Robinson, Jane Marie (Bancroft) 1408
Robinson, Jay. 1367, 3241
Robinson, John A T. 377
Robinson, John Arthur Thomas. 212, 349, 377, 379, 470, 946, 991, 1066, 1082, 1096, 1126, 1217, 1529, 1726, 2043, 2257, 3320, 3633, 3665
Robinson, John Bunyan. 3595
Robinson, John Lunsford. 1581
Robinson, John M. 1603
Robinson, John Michael. 1610
Robinson, John Thomas. 2941
Robinson, Joseph Armitage. 321, 3808, 420, 2752, 3457, 3847, 373, 1544, 88, 337, 391, 1715, 1806, 3801
Robinson, Joseph Stanley. 1495
Robinson, L. L. 1983, 1993, 3564
Robinson, Lemuel King. 3226
Robinson, Leonard George. 2105
Robinson, Leonidas. 236
Robinson, Louise A. 2503
Robinson, Lytle W. 877
Robinson, Madeleine J. 2202
Robinson, Marian Dolores. 2571
Robinson, Marion O. 3878
Robinson, Nalbro' Frazier. 2583
Robinson, Norman Hamilton Galloway. 945
Robinson, O. Preston. 283, 1103, 1410, 2043, 2763
Robinson, Olvis Jordan. 166
Robinson, Paschal. 1646
Robinson, Paul M. 1570
Robinson, Peter S. 1168
Robinson, Phinehas. 3207
Robinson, Ras B. 994, 3242
Robinson, Reuben. 2203, 2626, 3242, 1823, 1824, 1302, 1452
Robinson, Richard. 101
Robinson, Richard H. 703, 708, 711, 2311
Robinson, Robert. 166
Robinson, Roland E. 2654, 2655
Robinson, Russell D. 646
Robinson, Ruth (Grace) 3889
Robinson, Samuel Miles. 1602
Robinson, Stuart. 2936
Robinson, Theodore Henry. 403, 443, 484, 498, 1798, 2093, 3140
Robinson, Thomas. 469
Robinson, Thomas Edmond. 2592
Robinson, Virgil E. 41, 682, 1289, 2157, 2487, 2498, 2588, 2792, 3296, 3425, 3788, 3812, 3831, 3882
Robinson, Wayne. 1297, 1716, 3241
Robinson, Wayne Bradley. 3665
Robinson, Willard Haskell. 2026
Robinson, William. 1428, 2259, 1122, 2939
Robinson, William Childs. 93, 1311, 1529, 1595, 2001, 3035, 429
Robinson, William Ellsworth. 3513
Robinson, William Josephus. 1656
Robinson, William Wilcox. 481
Robison, Charles D. 2894
Robison, James. 1287, 994, 1712, 3391, 3742
Robison, John. 1662
Robison, William Ferretti. 66, 757, 865, 2001, 2034, 3263
Robley, Wendell. 988
Robo, Etienne. 397, 3691

Robshaw, Charles P. 2934
Robson, Brian Turnbull. 3566
Robson, George Blenkinsop. 945
Robson, John William. 695
Robson, Vivian Erwood. 96
Robson, Walter. 1685
Robson, William. 2125, 2511
Roby, Mary Linn. 1021
Roca, Paul M. 79
Rocca, Bernard T. 1595
Roccapriore, Marie. 3722
Roche, Aloysius. 1267, 2905, 926, 1001, 2526, 3877
Roche de Coppens, Peter. 3522
Roche, Douglas J. 791, 811, 1245, 2192
Roche, Jean Baptiste. 2361
Roche, Jerome. 2766
Roche, John A. 1483
Roche, John Alexander. 2766
Roche, Joseph Thomas. 719, 2369
Roche, Olin Scott. 2700
Roche, Owen I. A. 1852
Roche, Paul. 1588
Roche, Spencer Summerfield. 1269
Roche, Thomas Bernard. 1314
Roche, William. 2880
Rochelle, Jay C. 1262, 3004
Rochester, Mich. North Central Christian College. 3156
Rochester, N. Y. (Diocese) Superintendent of Schools. 824
Rochester theological seminary, Rochester, N.Y. 3242, 3615
Rocine, Victor Gabriel. 891
Rock, Augustine. 2905
Rockey, Carroll J. 1570
Rockford, Ill. First Lutheran Church. 2290
Rockland, Mae Shafter. 1520, 2120
Rockwell, Anne F. 1630, 3545
Rockwell, Esther (Francis) 3386
Rockwell, Ethel Gesner. 2003
Rockwell, Ethel Theodora. 3145
Rockwell, Katharine Lamberg (Richards) 216
Rockwell, Katharine Lambert (Richards) 1111, 1995
Rockwell, William Walker. 1184
Rockwood, Elizabeth. 2880
Rodd, Laurel Rasplica. 2707, 2940
Rodda, Dorothy. 2224
Rodd. Cyril S. 574
Roddy, Clarence Stonelynn. 405, 2905, 3652
Roddy, Irving Gaines. 2804, 3244
Roddy, Lee. 216, 2009, 2479, 3840
Rodeheaver, Homer Alvan. 2514, 3156, 3563, 3566, 1872, 2559
Rodenbeck, Adolph Julius. 1105
Rodenmayer, Robert N. 991, 1298, 1325, 1756, 2346, 2787
Rodenmayer, Robert N.N. 1756
Roderey, Nicholas. 2228
Rodes, Richard. 933
Rodes, Robert E. 1220, 1489
Rodewyk, Adolf. 1422
Rodger, James George. 3313
Rodger, Patrick Campbell. 1045
Rodgers, Ellen (Davies) 81, 2974
Rodgers, Eugene L. 3276
Rodgers, James B. 2545
Rodgers, William D. 1844
Rodholm, Soren Damgaard. 1862
Rodin, Auguste. 752
Rodino, Amedeo. 111
Rodinson, Maxime. 1923, 2629, 2635
Rodkinson, Michael Levi. 35, 3583
Rodkinson, Michael Lewy. 35, 3583
Rodli, Agnes Sylvia. 100, 2543
Rodney, Clarence O. R. 2419
Rodrigues, Jeanne. 3277
Rodriguez, Alonso. 2885
Rodwell, Warwick. 919
Rodzianko, M. 3258
Roe, Alfred Seelye. 3870
Roe, Edward Reynolds. 3076
Roe, Gordon. 1292, 1484
Roe, John E. 2781
Roe, William Gordon. 1760, 2194
Roebling, Karl. 2815
Roeck, Alan L. 1432
Roeda, Jack. 949, 1314
Roeder, Adolph. 1370, 2401, 3095, 3571
Roeder, Helen. 3281
Roeder, Ralph. 3305
Roehrenbeck, William Joseph. 1111
Roehrs, Walter H. 224
Roellig, Harold F. 296, 1062
Roelofs, Donet Meynell. 1362
Roemer, The. 833
Roemer, Theodore. 77, 2271, 738
Roensch, Roger C. 3187
Roerich, Elena Ivanovna. 1703
Roetzel, Calvin J. 373, 2801
Rogal, Samuel J. 3835
Roger. 1001
Rogers, Adrian. 988

Rogers, Ammi. 3133, 3134
Rogers, Arthur. 543, 1215, 1921
Rogers, Arthur Kenyon. 391, 1971, 3104
Rogers, Cameron. 1907
Rogers, Clement Francis. 68, 1735, 1802, 2001, 2787, 2905, 3674
Rogers, Dale Evans. 897, 901, 928, 973, 1111, 2265, 2395, 3134, 3243, 3407, 3845, 3889
Rogers, Dale Evans [Orig. name: Frances Octavia Smith]. 3243
Rogers, Donald B. 940
Rogers, E. N. 1613
*Rogers, E. W. 1696
Rogers, Ebenezer Platt. 322, 2043, 2667
Rogers, Edward. 106, 1076
Rogers, Edward Coit. 183, 2991, 3513
Rogers, Edward H. 3087
Rogers, Elizabeth Frances. 2826, 3266
Rogers, Eric N. 1613
Rogers, Francis Millet. 1487
[Rogers, George] fl. 1838. 3134
Rogers, Guy. 1216
Rogers, Harold. 1007, 1302, 1424, 2395, 2880, 3013, 3243
Rogers, Harry Clayton. 1441
Rogers, Henry. 306
Rogers, Hester Ann. 2451, 3134, 3201
Rogers, Horatio. 1484, 1687
Rogers, Isaac Wallace. 245
Rogers, Jack Bartlett. 240, 1551, 2009, 3243, 3294, 3680, 3809
[Rogers, James Edwin Thorold] 1823-1890. 1954
Rogers, James Richard. 3009
Rogers, Janet Pierpont. 120
Rogers, Jessie. 1452
Rogers, John. 456, 3605, 2128
Rogers, Joyce. 3845
Rogers, Kristine M. 3734
Rogers, Lewis M. 3108
Rogers, Louis William. 1479, 1726, 2729, 3054, 3687
Rogers, Patrick. 2373
Rogers, Peet & co., New York. 1249
Rogers, Peter V. 1293, 3243
Rogers, Philip George. 2122
Rogers, Reginald Arthur Percy. 1538
Rogers, Robert William. 93, 94, 494
Rogers, Rochester H. 3513
Rogers, Roy. 2023
Rogers, Roy [Name originally: Leonard Franklin Slye]. 2023
Rogers, Samuel. 3134
Rogers, Thomas. 1212
Rogers, Timothy. 1794
Rogers, Truett. 2130
Rogers, Uriah Furman. 1868
Rogers, Virgil McMurray. 1797
Rogers, W. Henry. 2807
Rogers, William C. 1462
Rogers, William Cauldwell. 1062, 3708
Rogers, William F. 1352
Rogers, William Fred. 1352
Rogers, William Henry. 3411
Rogers, William Hubert. 3357, 2043, 608, 3290
Rogers, William L. 3784
[Rogers, William Osgood] 1874. 3557
Rogerson, John William. 501, 2326, 2649, 3567
Roget, Peter Mark. 662
Roggen, Heribert. 1284
Rogness, Alvin N. 2279, 32, 1005, 1352, 1434, 1441, 1452, 1633, 2215, 2301, 2395, 3880, 3889
Rogness, Michael. 1041, 2400
Rogo, D. Scott. 2858, 3243, 3472
Roguet, A. M. 139, 865, 1264, 2368, 3266, 3800
Rohde, Erwin. 1767
Rohde, J. Martin. 2983
Rohde, Joachim. 393
Rohde, John Martin. 2055, 3095, 3446
Rohde, Peter Preisler. 2170
Rohden, L. 2128
Roheim, Geza. 3068
Rohlfing, Charles. 3513
Rohne, John Magnus. 2715
Rohner, Beatus. 2356
Rohrbach, Peter Thomas. 741, 2381, 2905, 3691
Rohrbaugh, Lewis Guy. 2837, 3063
Rohrbaugh, Richard L. 288, 2905
Rohrer, Norman B. 1456, 1576, 1633
Roiphe, Anne Richardson. 2155, 3244
Rojas, Ricardo. 1954
Rokotoff, Natalie. 703
Rolapp, Henry Hermann. 253
Roldan, Alejandro. 3475
Rolfe, Eugene. 66
Rolfe, Mona. 1502
Rolfsrud, Erling Nicolai. 1167, 1257, 1500, 1610
Rolfus, Herman. 3263
Rolfus, Hermann. 74, 770
Roll, William George. 2858

Rolland, Romain. 2840, 3020
Rolle, Richard. 777, 1452, 1807, 2647, 3491, 3636
Roller, Henry B. 3229
Rollet, Henri. 754
Rollings, Elmer James. 608
Rollins, James M. 2068
Rollins, Marion Josephine (Benedict) 501, 1726
Rollins, Wallace Eugene. 1971
Rollins, Wayne G. 391
Rolls, Charles Jubilee. 460, 2020
Roloff, Marie Brady. 170, 3244
Rolston, Holmes. 176, 278, 325, 339, 374, 377, 384, 478, 1405, 1457, 2801, 2934, 3357, 3439, 3808
Rolt, Clarence Edwin. 1696
Rolt, Mary F. 1971
Rolt-Wheeler, Francis William, 1876-1960. 319, 2019
Romain. 747, 748
Romaine, William. 973
Roman Catholic/Presbyterian and Reformed Conversation Group. 3706
Roman Catholic/Presbyterian-Reformed Consultation. 861
Roman Catholic-Protestant Colloquium, Harvard University, 1963. 1044
Roman, LuLu. 932, 3244
Romanes, Ethel (Duncan) 3244
Romanes, George John. 3076, 3609
Romanis, Alfonso Camillo de. 111
Romano, Juanita Napoles. 3244
Romanoff, Moses. 2116
Romanowski, Henry J. 1001
Romanus Melodus. 1874
Romb, Anselm William. 1643, 1648, 2571, 2573, 3332
Romein, Tunis. 2592
Romero, Oscar A. 865, 3369
Romeu, Luis V. 1043
Romeyn, John Brodhead. 3357
Romeyn, Theodore Bayard. 1779
Romig, Edgar Dutcher. 685
Romig, Edgar Franklin. 3045
Romig, Henry Horace. 1041
Romig, Walter. 754, 755
Rominger, Cornelius Augustus. 2055
Romm, Moses. 2116
Rommel, Jon. 3050
Rommel, Kurt. 2248
Romney, Marion G. 1232, 2608
Romney, Rodney R. 2381
Romney, Thomas Cottam. 2617, 2763, 3120, 3432
Romoser, Harold Wolfangle. 2215
Rona, Herbert. 1366
Ronaldson, Agnes Sutherland. 2999
Ronan, Myles Vincent. 48, 3041
Ronander, Albert C. 1876, 3731
Ronayne, E[dmond]. 3134
Ronayne, Edmond. 1664, 1662, 1670
Rondet, Henri. 1473, 1753, 2132, 3411, 3414
Rondthaler, Edward. 3820
Ronen, Avraham. 27, 2756
Roney, Charles Patrick. 296, 386
Roney, H. F. 806
Rongione, Louis A. 9
Ronglone, Louis A. 181
Ronk, Albert T. 691
Ronnegard, Sam. 1527, 3709
Ronning, Halvor Nilson. 3247
Ronning, Nils Nilsen. 1790, 1958, 2192, 2546, 3422
Ronnquist, Ulrik. 2030
Ronsin, F X. 1001, 2573
Rony, Jerome Antoine. 2313
Rood, Paul William. 1560, 1570
Rood, Wayne R. 936, 942, 3180
Roodman, Solomon. 3371
Roof, Simons Lucas. 1896
Roof, Wade Clark. 2222, 2971
Roohan, James Edmund. 828, 1136
Rookmaaker, H. R. 1089
Rookmaaker, Hendrik Roelof. 1089
Rooney, Gerard Jerome. 288, 2032
Rooney, Richard L. 1001
Roop, Eugene F. 649
Roop, Geane A. 3156
Roop, Geane Alice. 3184
Roorbach, Harriet A. 3401, 3764
Roorbach, Rosemary K. 3174, 3180
Roos, Ann. 1286, 1400
Roosen, B. C. 2406
Roosen, P A. 3226
Roosevelt, Franklin Delano. 209
Root, Edward Tallmadge. 247, 945
Root, Frederick Stanley. 1122
Root, George Frederick. 3598
Root, Helen Isabel. 2507
[Root, Jean Christie]. 1730, 1920, 3463
Root, Orrin. 644
Root, Robert. 2681
Root, Sidney. 3134
Roothaan, Joannes Philippus. 2381
Roots, Anne Frances. 3010

Roots, John McCook. 2593
Rooy, Sidney H. 1339
Roozen, David A. 1110
Roper, Albert L. 2052
Roper, Anita. 3295, 3526
Roper, David H. 412, 1377
Roper, Gayle G. 3844
Roper, John Caswell. 1314, 2437, 3156
Roper, William. 2596
Ropes, James Hardy. 392, 412, 1183, 1194
Ropp, Harry L. 2612
Roquette, Ruth. 1027, 2793
Rordorf, Willy. 3547
Rorke, Genevieve A. 917
Rosa, Peter de. 3414
Rosadi, Giovanni. 2068
Rosage, David E. 27
Rosalia. 745
Rosalia, Sister. 745
Rosalita. 3421
Rosati, Joseph. 40
Rosborough, William. 3563
Roscamp, Robert G. 1971, 2944
Roscoe, William. 2216
Rose, Ada (Campbell) 1352
Rose, Albert. 3032
Rose, Anne K. 3297
Rose, Arthur Richard. 1699
Rose, Benjamin Lacy. 1011, 2915
Rose, Cecil. 2754
Rose, Delbert R. 2671, 3430, 3650
Rose, Elise Whitlock. 752
Rose, Elizabeth. 1644
Rose, Elliot. 1469, 1508, 3824
Rose, George Leon. 46
Rose, Goodman Alikum. 2140
Rose, Harold Wickliffe. 1275
Rose, Heloise (Durant) 1402
Rose, Herbert Jennings. 1767, 2657, 2661, 3246, 2661
Rose, Isabel Brown. 2532
Rose, Mary A[nn]. 1861
Rose, Mary Carman. 2838
Rose, Mary Catherine. 1794
Rose, Robert. 1302, 3249
*Rose, Ronald. 2729
Rose, Solomon S[ab'thy]. 565
Rose, Stephen C. 1062, 1066, 1244, 2934, 3357
Rose, Tom. 3446
Rose, Vincent. 392
Roseberry, Robert Sherman. 2500
Rosecrans, Sylvester Horton. 2001
Roseland, Jens Christian. 2303
Rosell, Garth. 1842
Rosell, Mervin E. 973, 1577, 1842, 3889
Roseman, Bernard. 2827
Rosemergy, Jim. 3750
Rosen, Barbara. 3826
Rosen, Bernard Carl. 3882
Rosen, Moishe. 2030, 2556, 2779, 3249
Rosen, Sidney. 2772
Rosenau, William. 240, 530, 2120, 3576, 272, 1517, 2120
Rosenbaum, Samuel. 2151
Rosenberg, Ann Elizabeth. 1673, 3002
Rosenberg, Bruce A. 2910
Rosenberg, Carroll Smith. 1280
Rosenberg, D. 2120
Rosenberg, David W. 544, 551, 561, 586, 1615
Rosenberg, Donna. 2661
Rosenberg, Israel. 589
Rosenberg, Jehiol Mitchell. 3897
Rosenberg, Leon. 3682
Rosenberg, Louis J[ames]. 2376
Rosenberg, Max. 24
Rosenberg, Meyer Joshua. 2087
Rosenberg, Roy A. 722, 3407
Rosenberg, Stuart E. 501, 2140, 2153, 2764, 2986, 3370
Rosenberger, Edward Glen. 3187
Rosenberger, Elizabeth D. 616
Rosenberger, Erwin. 1809
Rosenberger, Harleigh M. 1452
Rosenberger, Ludwig. 2083
Rosenberger, Mary Sue. 2894
Rosenberg Stuart E. 3370
Rosenblatt, Paul. 3847
Rosenblatt, Paul C. 1691
Rosenblatt, Samuel. 2083, 2478, 3016, 3249, 3371, 3800, 3896
Rosenbloom, Joseph R. 544, 2952
Rosenbloom, Noah H. 1817, 2146
Rosenblum, William F. 1784
Rosene, Myrtle Elizabeth. 3764
Rosenfield, Joe. 2808
Rosengrant, John. 1109
Rosengrant, John [ed.]. 1109
Rosenius, Carl Olaf. 1726, 3071
Rosenius, Carl Olof. 1441
Rosenlof, George Walter. 1666, 1667
Rosenstiel, Annette. 2484
Rosenstock-Huessy, Eugen, 1888. 2153

Rosenstock-Huessy, Eugen, 1888-1973. 392, 2009
Rosenstock-Huessy, Eugen. 1062
Rosenstock-Huessy, Eugen Friedrich Moritz 1888. 1063
Rosenthal, David M. 2474
Rosenthal, Earl E. 1755
Rosenthal, Erich. 2098
Rosenthal, Erwin Isak Jakob. 505, 1924, 2154, 2842
Rosenthal, Frank. 2098
Rosenthal, George David. 973, 1890, 3411
Rosenthal, Gilbert S. 2155
Rosenthal, Joel Thomas. 666
Rosenthal, Newman Hirsch. 2100, 3276
Rosenthal Gilbert S. 1539
Rosenwasser, Herman. 1316
Rosenzweig, Efraim M. 2140
Rosenzweig, Franz. 1715, 2087, 2140
Roses, Anthony. 3285
Rosetta stone inscription. 3757
Roseveare, Helen. 404, 405, 1595, 2488, 2513, 3249
Roshwald, Mordecai. 2622
Rosicrucian Fellowship, Oceanside, Calif. 1801
Rosier, Irenaeus. 818
Rosier, Irenaeus [Secular name: Gerardus Ant. Serv. Rosier.]. 818
Rosignoil, Carlo Gregorio. 3786
Rosin, Jacob. 1890
Rosmarin, Aaron. 1539
Rosmarin, Trude (Weiss) 1306, 2837, 1673, 2089, 2116, 2118, 2153, 2585, 3261, 3842
Rosmini Serbati, Antonio. 3513
Rosner, Fred. 317, 2377
Rosner, Jakob. 2764
Rosner, Joseph. 529
Rosoff, Benjamin Wolf. 1252, 2116
Ross, A[bel] Hastings. 3370
Ross, Alan O. 2204
[Ross, Albert Henry]. 2052
Ross, Alexander. 2657, 367, 412
Ross, Alexander Cephas. 96
Ross, Alexander Wendell. 1971
Ross, Anne. 878
Ross, Charlotte. 1303
Ross, Dan. 2097
Ross, David Morison. 1954
Ross, Emma Jewell. 2763
Ross, Emory. 2498
Ross, Eva Jeany. 3450
*Ross, Floyd H. 3142
Ross, Floyd Hiatt. 1079, 2228, 3120, 3404
Ross, Frederick Augustus. 3425
Ross, George Alexander Johnston. 74, 974, 2043, 2908, 3854
Ross, Hugh. 916
Ross, Hugh Gordon. 1954
Ross, Isabel. 1637
Ross, Ishbel. 2697
Ross, James F. 2832, 3104
Ross, Joel H. 3513
Ross, John A. 74
Ross, John Elliot. 865, 974, 1052, 1267, 1595, 2215, 2704, 3344, 66
Ross, John Jacob. 423, 456, 634, 2055, 2175
Ross, John Simpson. 120
Ross, Kenneth Needham. 2636
Ross, Louise Doran. 2368
Ross, Lydia. 2819
Ross, Malcolm Mackenzie. 3210
Ross, Murray G. 3745
Ross, Nancy. 42
Ross, Nancy Wilson. 708, 1110, 1814, 1938, 2122, 3892, 3894
Ross, Pearl. 1971
Ross, Peter. 40
Ross, Peter V. 296, 1037, 1890
Ross, Robert. 3123
Ross, Sir William David. 1746
Ross, William Gordon. 2171, 2320, 3259, 3285, 3590
Ross, Williamson, Hugh. 842, 1365, 3039, 3285, 3590
Rosscup, James E. 420, 988
Rosseau, Olivier. 2234
Rossel, Seymour. 2079, 2151
Rosselot, F. P. 2866
Rosser, George Elijah. 3402
Rosser, Gladys. 1983
Rosser, Harold C. 1063
Rosser, John Leonidas. 150, 2801
Rosser, Leonidas. 136, 896, 1796, 1849, 1906, 2161, 2325
Rosser, Leonidos. 1286
Rosser-Owen, Dawud G. 1922
Rossetti, Christian Georgina. 456
Rossetti, Christina Georgina. 1441, 2212
[Rossetti, Felix Anthony]. 2275
[Rossi, Gaudentius]. 2033, 2381
Rossi, Giovanni, of Assisi. 1452
Rossi, Mario Manlio. 1818
Rossi, Sanna Barlow. 39, 3718
Rossini, Carlo. 813, 883, 1205

Rossiter, Evelyn. 680, 1892
Rossiter, Mary (Henry) 1803
Rossman, Parker. 1493
Rossmoor-Cortese Institute for the Study of Retirement and Aging. 18
Rosso, Antonio Sisto. 2511
Rost, Leonhard. 56, 1410
Rostagno, Sergio. 350
Rosten, Leo Calvin. 3014, 3326
Rostovtsev, Mikhail Ivanovich. 2640
Rostron, Sydney Nowell. 377, 2035
Roszak, Theodore. 3063
Rotberg, Robert I. 2545
Rotenstreich, Nathan. 1854, 2144, 3682
Roth, Alice. 1278
Roth, Arnold C. 1252
Roth, Cecil. 2336, 87, 1910, 2084, 2085, 2090, 2092, 2093, 2100, 2101, 2107, 2327, 2332, 2403, 3014, 1910, 2098, 2327, 2332
Roth, Charles. 1325, 3750
Roth, Charles B. 3750
Roth, Don A. 2546, 2630, 3234
Roth, Francis Xavier. 111
Roth, Helen M. 3400
Roth, John K. 1934, 3108
Roth, Joseph. 49, 52
Roth, Leon. 3472, 303, 2623, 2842
Roth, Leon [Hyam Leon Roth]. 2140
Roth, Paul Hoerlein. 1517
Roth, Paul M. 974
Roth, Robert J. 1735, 3104
Roth, Robert M. 894
Roth, Robert P. 3717
Roth, Samuel. 2019
Roth, Samuel John. 1179
Roth, Sid. 1366, 3252
Roth, Sol. 2144, 2146
Roth, Tobias. 2886
Roth, W M W. 502
Roth, Wolfgang M W. 498
Rothacker, Viola. 3191
Rothenberg, Gunther Erich. 1331, 2098
Rothenberg, Joshua. 657, 2083, 2103, 2154
Rothenburger, William Frederic. 1388
Rothenburger, William Frederick. 1388, 2058
Rothensteiner, John Ernest. 813, 1652, 3276, 813, 818
Rother, Aloysius Joseph. 2739, 3717
*Rothermel, Bertha M. 1262
Rothert, Otto Arthur. 2629
Rothkoff, Aaron. 3223
Rothluebber, Francis Borgia. 3310
Rothrock, George A. 1852
[Rothschild, Robert L.]. 623
Rothuizen, Gerard Theodoor. 583
Rothwell, Allen Edward. 536
Rothwell, Kenneth S. 2974
Rotmann, Bernhard. 3525
Rotondo, Antonio. 54, 729
Rotrou, Jean. 3134
Rottenberg, Isaac C. 2175
Rouch, Mark A. 1297
Rouet de Virles, A. 2395
Rougemont, Denis de. 1066, 1428
*Rouke, Eve. 3192
Roulet, Mary F. (Nixon) 921
Roulin, Eugene Augustin. 1157, 1249
[Roumane, Norman Morand]. 802, 3304
Rounds, Dorothy. 1817
Rounds, James B. 1316
Rounds, James Berley. 1316
[Roundy, William Noble]. 392, 1794, 2265
Rouner, Arthur A. 2880
Rouner, Arthur Acy. 339, 1122, 1344, 1354, 2815, 2894, 3252
Rountree, Horace G. 3134
Rouse, Doris Haver. 939
Rouse, Jordan K. 1271
Rouse, Ruth. 1492
Rouse, William Henry Denham. 3787, 2662, 3787
Rouse, William Thomas. 1832, 2175
Roush, Herbert L. 1735
*Roush, Lester L. 1105
Rousseau, Achille. 757
Rousseau, Christine (McConnell) 2306
Rousseau, Jean Jacques. 1385, 1452, 2839, 3607
Rousseau, Philip. 90
Rousseau, Richard W. 2832
Roustang, Francois. 1947, 3489
Routh, Eugene Coke. 156, 158, 613, 2135, 2511, 3323
Routh, Freda Karsin. 2395
Routh, Harold Victor. 2232
Routh, Porter. 144, 170, 3465
Routley, Erik. 524, 578, 579, 1020, 1044, 1203, 1207, 1208, 1360, 1386, 1468, 1868, 1872, 1876, 2043, 2793
Routtenberg, Hyman J. 485
Routtenberg, Lilly. S. 2345
Routtenberg, Max J. 2143
Roux, Joseph. 3134

Row, Charles Adolphus. 1099, 1699
Row, John. 1234
Rowan, Stephen N. 1772
Rowbotham, Arnold Horrex. 1947
Rowden, Aldred William. 666
Rowden, Marjorie. 2536
Rowe, A T. 2588
Rowe, Alexander Thomas. 974, 3674
Rowe, Claude Watson. 1890
Rowe, David MacClement. 1063
Rowe, Dorothy. 2823
Rowe, Edna B. 625
Rowe, Elizabeth (Singer) 1441
Rowe, Frederick Louis. 311, 2049, 3347
Rowe, Gilbert Theodore. 2421, 3065
Rowe, H. Edward. 1109
Rowe, Henry Kalloch. 40, 926, 1179, 3094, 3156, 152, 926, 3745
Rowe, John F. 3721
Rowe, John Franklin. 1179
Rowe, John Frankoin. 1179
Rowe, John Gordon. 2778
Rowe, Kenneth E. 2422
Rowe, Lois. 1432
Rowe, M. F. 3207
Rowe, William L. 1738, 3108, 3700, 3104
Rowell, Earle Albert. 1099
Rowell, Edmon L. 72, 339
Rowell, Geoffrey. 1531
Rowell, J B. 802, 1570
Rowen, Dolores. 3174
Rowland, Adoniram Judson. 566
Rowland, Benjamin. 926, 86
Rowland, Christopher. 56
Rowland, David Sherman. 1635
Rowland, Henry Hosie. 2521
Rowland, James. 2945
Rowland, Joseph Medley. 3366
Rowland, Kate Hershey. 650
Rowland, Kate Shirley Hershey. 641
Rowland, May. 2395, 3750
Rowland, Stanley J. 945, 3002, 3745
Rowland, Wilmina. 3883
Rowlands, Leo. 916
Rowley, Charles E. 3201, 3563
Rowley, H. H. 596
Rowley, Harold Henry. 78, 1041, 11, 56, 217, 236, 245, 278, 279, 283, 311, 485, 502, 508, 535, 540, 548, 599, 1403, 2560, 2951, 3706, 3856
Rowley, Owsley Robert. 666
Rowley, Peter. 3326
Rowlingson, Donald T. 351, 392, 411, 1987, 2043
Rowlingson, Edna V. 2894
Rowntree, John Stephenson. 1684
Rowntree, John Wilhelm. 2321
Roxbury, Mass. Universalist church. 3754
Roy, Andrew T. 2516
Roy, Cal. 1898
Roy, Charles Eugene. 2685
Roy, Dilip Kumar. 3252
Roy, James. 236
Roy, Joseph. 2395
Roy, Lucien. 878
Roy, Ralph Lord. 3745
Roy, Robindra Lal. 2840
Roy, Rustum. 3083, 3393
Roy, Thomas Sherrard. 1667
Roy, William. 456
Royal. 886
Royal, Claudia. 1726, 3534
Royal Institute of the Architects of Ireland. 1160
Royal order of Tibet fraternity. 3205
Royal School of Church Music. 915
Royce, Andrew. 3752
Royce, G. Monroe. 2622
Royce, George Monroe. 1302
Royce, Josiah. 2674, 1071, 1096, 1536, 1543, 1726, 1890, 1891, 2674, 3104, 3107
Royce, Moses S. 1221
Royden, Agnes Maude. 974, 1071, 1452, 1726, 2880, 3344, 3401
Royer, Fanchon. 1284, 1632, 1647, 2859, 2943, 3455
Royer, Galen Brown. 1237, 1808, 3297
Royer, W M. 2053, 3290
Royle, Edward. 1656
Royo Marin, Antonio. 2819
Royse, Pleasant E. 464, 3379
Rozanov, Vasilii Vasil'evich. 1093
Rozell, Ray. 1916, 3180
Rozell. Ray. 1374
Rozen, Leon Szczekacz. 2345
Rozendaal, Henry Terlouw. 1801
[Rozier, Mary. 131
Rozman, Deborah. 2382
Ruane, Gerald P. 1414
Ruane, Joseph William. 3545
Ruane, Minnie (Halberstadt) 2940
Rubenovitz, Herman H. 1348
Rubenovitz, Mignon (Levine) 1395
Rubenstein, Charles Aaron. 132
Rubenstein, I. H. 1393

Rubenstein, Isadore Harold. 1634
Rubenstein, Richard L. 2080, 2801, 3252
Rubenstein, Shmuel. 1277, 2086, 2165, 3704
rubenz, Sima. 2151
Rubert, Nettie E. 2465
Rubin, Alvan D. 2085
Rubin, Israel. 3304
Rubin, Samuel Aaron. 2083
Rubinoff, Lionel. 1309, 2473
Rubinstein, Arie Leib. 1615
Rubio, David. 2648
Ruble, William. 460
Rucker, Thomas Saunders. 1656
Ruckert, Friedrich. 689
Ruckstuhl, Eugen. 2030
Rudavsky, David. 2148
Rudd, John C[hurchill]. 2959
Rudder, William. 3682
Ruddy, Ella (Giles) 1630
Rudell, George E. 1696
Rudge, Peter Frederick. 1200
Rudhyar, Dane. 96, 97, 2729, 3481, 3689
Rudin, A. James. 1928
Rudin, Arnold James. 1394
Rudin, Cecilia Margaret. 1876
Rudin, Jacob Philip. 3361
Rudin, Josef. 2999
Rudisch, L J. 840
Rudisill, Dorus Paul. 108, 950, 1499
Rudisill, James Jefferson. 3252
Rudloff, Leon von. 797
Rudnick, Milton L. 945, 1690, 2295, 2296
Rudolph, Erwin Paul. 1352, 2201, 3252, 3253
Rudolph, L. 2917
Rudolph, L. C. 89, 3164, 3184
*Rudolph, Mary Baine. 1452, 1726, 3172
Rudometkin, Maksim Gavrilovich. 2568
Rudometkin, Maxim Gavrilovich. 2568
Rudrananda, Swami. 3481
Rudwin, Maximilian Josef. 889, 1428, 3145
Rudy, Charles. 753
Rudy, Esther. 2140
Rudy, Stella M. 2491, 2551
Rue, James J. 1471, 1472
Ruef, John Samuel. 323, 392, 2065
Rueff, Jacques. 693, 2739
Ruemmer, Franz. 1752, 3281
Ruetenik, Herman Julius. 3049
Ruether, Rosemary Radford. 1001, 1073, 1074, 1126, 1141, 1659, 2043, 2356, 3233, 3234, 3253, 3390, 3836
Ruf, Peter. 2071
Ruff, Ethel. 1575
Ruff, G Elson. 1142
Ruffa, Anthony Richard. 1581
Ruffin, Bernard. 1293, 2849
Ruffin, Beverley. 1223
Ruffin, John Demosthenes N. 2832
Ruffini, Ernesto. 3080
Ruffini, Francesco. 3193
Ruffner, Henry. 1748, 2309, 2576
[Ruffner, William Henry]. 1099
Ruffo, Vinnie. 130, 2752
Rufie, Frederick Charles. 1971
Rufinus Tyrannius, Aquileiensis, 345 (ca.)-410. 74
Rugg, Winnifred King. 1858
Ruggles, Eleanor. 2704
Rugh, Arthur. 1052
Ruhlman, John J. 2714
Ruhm von Oppen, Beate. 1145
Ruland, Ludwig. 948, 2248, 2378, 3676
Rule, Ulric Zuinglius. 532
Rule, William Harris. 1909
Ruler, Arnold Albert van. 323, 600, 2395
Rulison, George Ledrew. 2059
Rulison, Nelson Somerville. 1347
Rulof, Jozef. 3513
Rumball-Petre, Edwin Alfred Robert. 212, 1656, 212
Rumbaut, Ruben D. 1028, 2136
Rumble, Leslie. 2605, 3193
Rumbough, Constance. 2534
Rumbough, Constance Hickey. 2426
Rumke, Henricus Cornelius. 3422
Rummel, Leo. 835
Rummerfield, Walter Glen. 2696
[Rumpf, Oscar]. 1063, 3161
Rumple, Jethro. 2918
Rumscheidt, Martin. 176, 3657
Runbeck, Margaret Lee. 2880
Runciman. 1390, 3324
Runciman, Steven. 1149, 1354, 1391, 3324
Runciman, Steven James Cochran Stevenson Runciman. 3324
Rundall, Mary Ann. 296
Rundquist, Alfred. 2668, 3513
Runes, Dagobert David. 53, 54, 2085, 2208, 2832, 3201
Runestam, Arvid. 2784
Rung, Albert. 3332, 3481, 3676
Runia, Klaas. 176, 280, 1385
Runk, Wesley T. 3156

Runkle, Gerald. 1536
Runnalls, Claude Bertram. 2410
Running, Leona Glidden. 23
Runyan, William Marion. 1757
Ruoff, Henry Woldmar. 661
Ruoff, Norman D. 1009, 1010, 3215, 3216
Ruopp, Harold W. 2437
Ruoss, George Martin. 27, 3612
Rupagosvami. 3491
Rupert, Frank F. 3083
Rupert, Greenberry G. 236, 283, 296, 1376, 1514
Rupert, Hoover. 2071, 3665, 3889
Rupp, Augustus. 2313
Rupp, Ernest Gordon. 1318, 1739, 1758, 1764, 1818, 1848, 2277, 2285, 2734, 3035, 3039, 3629
Rupp, George. 3104, 3679
Rupp, Israel Daniel. 3326
Rupprecht, Ferdinand. 649
Rusbuldt, Richard E. 940, 953, 1200, 2480, 3868
Rusch, Harley G. 988, 3255
Rusche, Helga. 3840
Rush, Benjamin. 3481
Rush, Christopher. 14
Rush, Jacob. 1536
Rush, John A. 2729
[Rush, Mary (Wheeler) 3513
Rushdoony, Rousas John. 508, 1076, 1087, 1314, 1386, 1819, 3083, 3767
Rushing, Richard Ray. 2019
Rushmore, Jane Palen. 1684
Rusk, John. 532, 616, 1986
Rusk, Robert R. 3156
Ruskay, Esther J. 2121
Ruskin, Edward V. 3320
Ruskin, John. 35, 2593, 2662, 3201, 3255
Ruskowski, Leo Francis. 874
Russ, Marie. 3877
Russel, Joseph Somers. 527
Russell, Arthur James. 926, 1360, 1432
Russell, Beatrice K. 2230, 3513
Russell, Bertrand Arthur Russell. 3080
Russell, Bertrand Arthur Russell. 3080, 1656, 3068, 3080, 3255, 101, 1656
Russell, C. 2100
Russell, Charles Allyn. 1690
Russell, Charles Frank. 1853
Russell, Charles Howland. 2697
[Russell, Charles Taze]. 1942, 641, 725, 1940, 1941, 2465, 3256, 3579
Russell, Chester. 2809
Russell, D. S. 506
Russell, Daniel. 465, 2402, 2934
Russell, Daniel James. 2459
Russell, David Syme. 56, 2092, 2150
Russell, Edgar Torrey. 2190
Russell, Edward Francis. 974
Russell, Edward Wriothesley. 2729
Russell, Elbert. 2772, 181, 420, 1675, 1685, 1954, 2026, 2772, 3758
Russell, Eric. 97
Russell, Frank. 397, 2071
Russell, Frederick H. 2159
[Russell, George Herbert]. 1338
Russell, George Stanley. 3731, 1122
[Russell, George William]. 3256
Russell, George William. 1348, 3256
Russell, Grace. 3843
Russell, Henry. 774, 2484
Russell, Henry Norris. 3104
Russell, Howard H. 3181
Russell, Howard Hyde. 278
Russell, J. 3793
Russell, James Elmer. 3557
Russell, Jay Vance. 2945
Russell, Jean. 1132
Russell, Jeffrey Burton. 1186, 1429, 1468, 1804, 3826
Russell, John Leonard. 2419
[Russell, John Martin]. 1370
Russell, John X. 3209
Russell, Joseph P. 616
Russell, Josiah Cox. 1971
Russell, Lao. 1726, 3054
Russell, Letty M. 988, 1659, 2321, 3157
Russell, Marjorie. 2381
Russell, Mary (McSorley) 603, 2489
[Russell, Mary St. John, 1874. 2258
Russell, Matthew. 2352, 3256
Russell, Michael. 173, 2760
Russell, Naomi. 2529, 3217
Russell, Olive. 156
Russell, Olive Bernard. 1939
Russell, Olive Ruth. 1544
Russell, Peter. 3708
Russell, Ralph. 3028
Russell, Reginald Charles. 3557
Russell, Riley. 2539
Russell, Robert. 3366
Russell, Ruth W. 199, 1917
Russell, Solveig Paulson. 901
Russell, Stephen. 774
Russell, Walter. 2265
Russell, Walter Bowman. 2729

Russell, Ward. 1971
Russell, William D. 473, 3218, 3357
Russell, William Henry. 782, 806, 1993, 1999, 2043, 3782
*Russell, Wylie H. 3176
Russell-Smith, Hugh Francis. 3193
Russo-Alesi, Anthony Ignatius, 1896. 2351
Russo, Anthony. 939
Russo-Alesi, Anthony Ignatius. 1701, 2351
Rust, Charles Herbert. 30, 1252, 1570, 3097
Rust, Ella Arjenette. 456
Rust, Eric Charles. 1818, 2676, 2905, 2944, 2951, 3083, 3094, 3293, 3609
Rust, George. 2743
Rust, John Benjamin. 1718, 2256, 2401, 2561, 2807
Rust, Paul R. 1214
Rust, Richard Sutton. 3816
Rustad, Richard L. 2825
Rusterholtz, Wallace Palmer. 1656
Ruston, William O. 2917
Ruston, William Otis. 2917
Rutenber, Culbert Gerow. 106, 1096, 3793
Rutenborn, Guenter. 311
Ruter, Martin. 3204
Ruth, C[hristian] W[ismer]. 3300
Ruth, Christian Wismer. 974, 2815
Ruth, Dallas. 623
Ruth, John Adams. 278
Ruth, John L. 1765, 2405, 2408
Rutherford, Adam. 46
Rutherford, James Walter. 3142
Rutherford, Joseph F. 460, 518, 608, 1514, 1939, 1941, 2157, 2175, 2820, 3201, 3513, 3703, 3794
Rutherford, Joseph Franklin. 513, 600, 608, 1514, 1939, 1940, 1941, 3290, 3609, 610, 1941
Rutherford, Mark. 2192
Rutherford, Richard. 840
Rutherford, Samuel. 2218
Rutherford, Thomas. 1109
Rutherford, Thomas G. 536, 3220
Rutherford, Ward. 1480
Ruthven, K. K. 2649
Rutland, Vt. Congregational church. 1339
Rutledge, Archibald Hamilton. 623
Rutledge, Arthur B. 1610, 2528, 3466
Rutledge, Denys. 1082, 1460
Rutledge, Don. 156
Rutledge, Edward. 1221
Rutledge, George Perry. 871, 2001, 3344
Rutledge, Harold Lee. 988
Rutledge, Leslie. 2065, 2209
Rutledge, Loneta (Cessna) 3157
Rutler, George William. 2742
Rutman, Darrett Bruce. 1757, 3009
Rutter, Owen. 880, 2848, 2165
Rutty, John. 1682
Ruud, Brian. 1360
Ruville, Albert von. 1365
Ry van Beest Holle, Carel J. du. 86
Ryall, Edward W. 3054, 3258
Ryan, Archie Lowell. 2454, 3244
Ryan, Arthur Ridgeway. 694
Ryan, Bernard. 1581
Ryan, Charles James. 671, 3682, 3687, 3866
Ryan, Edwin. 734, 825, 2704, 825
Ryan, Finbar Patrick. 2357, 3405
Ryan, George E. 683, 685
Ryan, Gerald Aloysius. 666
Ryan, James Hugh. 806
Ryan, John. 2582, 2793
Ryan, John Augustine. 1142, 1143, 3258, 3434, 3435, 828, 1136
Ryan, John Barry. 1541
Ryan, John James. 132
Ryan, John Joseph. 1188, 2734
Ryan, John Julian. 806
Ryan, John Kenneth. 81, 761, 858, 2259, 2704, 2317
Ryan, Kenneth. 797
Ryan, Leo Raymond. 2700
Ryan, Marah Ellis (Martin) 2894
Ryan, Mary. 848
[Ryan, Mary Imogene] 1867. 1794, 2361
Ryan, Mary Perkins. 584, 797, 806, 942, 951, 1414, 2368, 2880
Ryan, Matthias Bishop. 1093
Ryan, Mery Perkins. 2368
Ryan, Michael D. 3647
Ryan, Oswald. 568
Ryan, Patrick J. 1925
Ryan, Patrick James. 3880
Ryan, Roberta. 3184
Ryan, Rosalie. 335, 1066
Ryan, Stephen Vincent. 76, 1378
Ryan, Thomas. 1613
Ryan, Thomas Richard. 697, 2832
Ryan, William Dennis. 2333
Ryburn, W. M. 3157
Ryburn, William Morton. 3176

Rycaut, Paul. 82, 2746
[Rychnovsky, Ernst] 1879-1934. 2079, 2364
Ryckman, Lucile Damon. 2487, 3259
Rycroft, William Stanley. 1492, 2955, 2979, 3470
Rydbeck, Theodore Luther. 1360
Rydberg, Viktor. 2313, 2666
Ryden, Ernest Edwin. 1876
Ryden, Ernst Edwin. 1876
Ryder, Henry Ignatius Dudley. 761
Ryder, Stephen Willis. 3047
Ryder, Walter Scott. 2192
Rydgren, John. 3889
Rye, N. Y. Community Synagogue. 2076
Ryelandt, Idesbald. 188, 840
Rygh, George Alfred Taylor. 1954
Ryken, Leland. 211, 2469
Rykwert, Joseph. 1160
Rykwert. Joseph. 1160
Rylaarsdam, John Coert. 572, 600
Rylance, Joseph Hine. 3023
Ryland, Garnett. 172
Ryland, John. 1690
Ryland, John A. 2172
Ryland, Robert. 145, 451, 452
Rylander, John V. 611, 2073
Ryle, Effie. 697
Ryle, Herbert Edward. 201, 524
Ryle, John Charles. 991, 417, 441, 974, 1292, 1293, 1824, 1868, 2880
Rymer, J. Sykes. 3259
Rynne, Xavier. 3770, 3772
Ryno, Wakeman. 2653
Ryokan, 1758-1831. 3894
Rypins, Stanley. 241
Ryrie, Charles Caldwell. 465, 272, 275, 278, 477, 608, 652, 974, 1467, 1697, 1752, 1832, 2466, 2683, 3021, 3433, 3836
Ryves, Thomas. 1230, 3702
Rzadkiewicz, Arnold Ladislas. 2223, 3694

S

Saadiah ben Joseph. 2116
Saalman, Howard. 1629, 1630
Saarnivaara, Uuras. 136
Sabatier, Auguste. 106, 2801, 3104, 3120
Sabatier, Auguste i.e. Louis Auguste. 3120
Sabatier, Paul. 1027, 1145, 1643, 1711, 2561, 2562
Sabatini, Rafael. 1910, 3704, 3235
[Sabha-pati Svami] 1840. 3866
Sabiers, Karl George. 319, 1698
Sabin, Elijah Robinson. 1360
Sabin, Frances Ellis. 2657
Sabin, Oliver Corwin. 1035
Sabine, Paul Earls. 3080
Sabini, John. 3742
Sabinus. 2333
Sabiston, Magnus. 614
Sabourin, Justine. 3418
Sabourin, Leopold. 451, 578, 2020, 3721
Sabrames, Demosthenes S. 3389
Sachar, Abram Leon. 2090, 2112
Sachar, Howard Morley. 2091
Sachedina, Abdulaziz Abdulhussein. 2317
Sachse, Julius Friedrich. 1206, 1482, 1521
Sackman, Lana. 1954
Sacks, Benjamin. 1129
Sackville-West, Victoria Mary. 1938, 3603
Saco, Me. First parish Congregational church. 1336
Sacred order of the blue flame. 2729
Sacrum commercium beati Francisci cum Domina Paupertate. English. 1643
Sacutus, Victor. 3868
Saddharmapundarika. 710, 3272
Saddharmapundarika. English. 710, 711
Saddhatissa, H. 705, 711
Sadhu, Mouni. 1393, 2381, 3589, 3866
Sadleir, Michael. 3860
Sadler, Alfred J. 3337
Sadler, Alfred John. 908, 2675
Sadler, George W. 2542
Sadler, Michael Ernest. 2592
Sadler, William Alan. 3001, 3344
Sadler, William Samuel. 2410, 3513, 3761
Sadlier, Agnes. 3378
Sadlier, Mary Anne [Madden]. 218, 3006
Sadofsky, Charles Arthur. 616
Sadony, Joseph A. 3513
Sadowsky, Solomon. 1701, 1812, 2134
Saffen, Wayne. 1170
Saffin, John. 1017
[Safford, Ann Eliza (Bigelow) Turner]. 34, 3272
Safford, George. 2325
Safford, Oscar Fitzalan. 131
Safran, Alexandre. 723
Sagan, Carl. 2729
Sage, Carleton M. 3134
Sage, Janet. 229, 1385
Sage, Michael M. 1398

Sage, Michel. 2849, 3241, 3513
Saggs, H. W. F. 1731
Sahai, Bhagwant. 3316
Sahakian, William S. 3108
Saher, P. J. 2839
Sahi, Jyoti. 1813
Sahlin, Monte. 9, 1308
Sahula-Dycke, Ignatz, 1900. 1092
Said, Edward W. 1925
Sailer, T. H. P. 2551
Sailer, Thomas H. P. 1467
Sailer, Thomas Henry Powers. 2551, 2565, 3181
Sailes, James Thomas. 137
St. Amant, Penrose, 1915. 2918
Saint Andrew's society of the state of New-York. 1179
St. Augustine. Cathedral. 750
St. Benedict's abbey, Atchison, Kan. 2234
St. Boniface. 939
St. Charles Seminary, Carthagena, Ohio. 3438
St. Clair, David. 2731, 2732, 3519
St. Clair, Robert, 1898. 3145
St. Clair, Robert James. 1011, 2784
St. Cyr, Emil, 1865. 3054
St. Cyres, Stafford Harry Northcote, 1869. 1621
Saint Elizabeths Hospital, Washington, D. C. Chaplain Services Branch. 2785
St. Francis College, Loretto, Pa. 2260, 3328
St. Fursy (Church), Peronne, France. 743, 3274
St. George's school. 2969
St. Giles and St. Andrew's priory. 2579
St. Ignatius Church, Oxon Hill, Md. 3274
St. James Catholic Church, Seguin, Tex. 3274, 3329
St. John, Charles Jackson, 1895. 2697
St. John, Henry. 1041
St. John, Martinus. 31, 2143
St. John, Patricia Mary, 1920. 3274
St. John, Robert, 1902. 187, 2084
St. John-Stevas, Norman. 1077
St. John, Wallace. 1762
St. John's and Assumption Seminaries Alumni Association. 3275
St. John's Bicentennial Committee. 3275
[St. John's seminary. 658
[St. John's seminary, Camarillo, Calif. Library, Estelle Doheny Collection. 658
St. John's University, Brooklyn. 3779
St. John's University, Collegeville, Minn. 601
St. John's University, New York. 3779
St. John's University, New York. Mariological Institute, 1958. 2363
Saint Joseph, 1756-1838. 659
St. Joseph's academy, St. Paul. 858
Saint Jure, Jean Baptiste de, 1588-1657. 1452
St. Lawrence college, Mount Calvary, Wis. 3757
St. Lawrence University, Canton, N. Y. Theological School. 1111
Saint-Leger-Vauban, France. Pierre-qui-Vire (Benedictine abbey) 2571
St. Louis (Archdiocese) 1300
St. Louis. Public library. 869
St. Louis university. 3276, 3696
St. Martha's Catholic Parish, Sarasota, Fla. History Committee. 3277
Saint Mary Genevieve. 686
St. Mary's Armenian Apostolic Church, Washington, D.C. Booklet Committee. 3277
Saint Mary's College, Notre Dame, Ind. 1163
St. Mary's college, St Marys, Kan. St. Peter Canisus' writer guild. 852
St. Matthew's parish. 1275
Saint Nectarios Orthodox Conference (2nd : 1980) 2745
St. Nicholas Cathedral Study Group. 2698
St. Patrick, Mother. 1326
St. Paul. 2921
Saint, Paul. 2023
St. Paul. First Baptist church. 170
St. Paul, George A. 1001
St. Paul, Mother. 9, 2395
St. Paul, mother, 1861. 2054, 2361, 2581
Saint Paul, mother, 1861-1940. 1264
St. Paul. Pilgrim Baptist Church. 157
St. Paul. St. Bernard's church. 1179
St. Paul. St. Joseph's academy. 858
St. Paul. St. Mary's church (Catholic) 859
St. Paul Seminary, St. Paul. Library. 3627
St. Paul's Church, Hanover co., Va. 1784
St. Paul's parish, Hanover co., Va. 1784
Saint, Philip. 3278
St. Rose (Dominican Priory) 3278
St. Sava (Serbian Orthodox Church) Gary Ind. 2751
St. Stephen Baptist Church, Kansas City, Mo. History Committee. 2163, 3278
St. Vincent college. 3331

Saint-beuve, Charles Augustin. 1638
Saint Bonaventura. 675
Sainte-beuve, Charles Augustin. 1638
Saint Gregorius. 2644
Saint Ignatius. 1404
Saint Jure, Jean Baptiste de. 2576, 3215, 3489
Saint Paul. 2269, 3223
Saint-Pierre, Jacques Henri Bernardin de. 2676
Saint-Pierre, Michel de. 3460, 3778
Saint Pierre of Jesus. 2741
Saint's herald. 3012
Saint Serapion. 2239
Saint Victor, Paul Jacques Raymond Binsse. 2662
Sajous, Charles Euchariste de Medicis. 3080
Sakkas, Basile. 1163, 2746
Saklatvala, Beram. 397, 1763, 1971
Sakoian, Frances. 97
Sala, Darlene. 2487, 3286
sala, Emeric. 128
Sala, Harold J. 974
Sala, John Robert. 2258, 2909
Salaman, Charles Kensington. 3577
Saldarini, Anthony J. 1539, 3585
Saleeby, Abdallah Assed. 1940
Sale-Harrison, Leonard. 460, 2156, 2763
Salem, A. B. 2098
Salem, Elie Adib. 2169
Salem, Mass. First church. 1334
Salem, Mass. North church. 3286
Sales, Jane M. 2499
Salet, Gaston. 797
Salguero, Jose. 3226
Saliba, John A. 1506, 3094
Saliba, Philip. 1894
Salico, Dale Vincent. 3218
Saliers, Don E. 2887
Saling, Younger. 988
Salisbury, Eng. (Diocese) Bishop, 1297-1315 (Simon of Ghent) 1763
Salisbury, Frank B. 1382, 3083
Salisbury, Helen Wright. 623
*Salisbury, Hugh M. 311, 644, 1352
Salisbury, Pa. New Jerusalem union church of western Salisbury. 2288
Salisbury, William Seward. 3739, 3746
Salit, Charles R. 1890
Salit, Norman. 3371
Sall, Millard J. 611, 1107
Sallaway, George H. 1977
Sallee, Annie (Jenkins) 156, 1942, 2529, 3287
Sallee, James. 1872
Sallee, Lynn. 2894
Salley, Columbus. 3017
Sallmon, William Henry. 2015, 2018, 2801, 2804, 3758
Salls, Betty Ruth. 1352
Salm, Celestine Luke. 652, 949, 3227
Salminen, Esther. 630
Salminen, Immanuel. 3513
Salmon, Edgar Frank. 66
Salmon, George. 1199, 1230, 1718
Salmon, John Hearsey McMillan. 1639
Salmon, Nathan U. 3010, 3032
Salmon, Pierre. 842, 3566
Salmon, Ruth (Barcafer) 3054
Salmon, Victor. 422
Salmon ben Yeruhim, ft. 10th cent. 576
Salmond, Charles Adamson. 1821
Saloff-Astakhoff, Nikita Ignatievich, 1893. 1366
Saloff-Astakhoff, Nikita Ignatievich. 2880, 1514, 2545, 3256, 3788
Salome. 3795
Salotti, Carlo. 2333, 2479, 2511, 1644, 2333
Salpointe, Jean Baptiste. 823, 2548
Salsini, Paul. 774, 1302
Salstrand, George A. E. 3702
Salstrand, George A E. 423, 1103, 1971, 2092, 3530
Salt, Henry Stephens. 3142
Salter, Doris. 218
Salter, Katharine Shepard (Hayden) 797
Salter, William. 2845, 3287
Salter, William Henry. 1697
Saltman, Avrom. 1763, 3609
Saltmarsh, Herbert Francis. 2948
Saltus, Edgar Everston. 3120
Saltus, Edgar Evertson. 3120, 3304
Salvado, Rosendo. 2484, 3287
Salvador, Mario. 1205
Salvation army. 3293
Salvation Army. Men's Social Service. 3293
Salvatorelli, Luigi. 1643
Salvatori, Filippo Maria. 41
Salverte, Eusebe. 2729
Salvianus, 5th cent. 2982, 2983, 3607, 3635
Salyards, Christiana. 3216
Salzmann, Laurence. 2779
Samadhi, Delta. 2991

Samarin, William J. 1716
Samaritans. Liturgy and ritual. 3296
Samartha, S. J. 1080
Samartha, S J. 3017
Saminsky, Lazare. 2634
samlley, Beryl. 240
Sammaciccia, Bruno. 2258
Sammons, Wiley W. 2941
Sampey, John Richard. 166, 482, 502,
    597, 1916, 3297
Sample, Mabel Warkentin. 916
Sample, Robert Fleming. 2015, 3035
Sampley, J. Paul. 365, 377, 1163
Sampson, Ashley. 3366
Sampson, Francis Smith. 403
Sampson, Holden Edward. 2641
Sampson, Tom. 3481
Sampson, Walter Harold. 3897
Sampter, Jessie Ethel. 2119
Samras, Kharaiti Ram. 2840
Samson. 3283
Samson, George Whitefield. 108, 3513,
    3597
Samson, Henri. 3491
Samuel, Athanasius Yeshue. 1410
*Samuel, Edith. 1789
Samuel, Herbert Louis Samuel. 1283
Samuel, Irene. 2471
Samuel, Leith. 3829
Samuel, Maurice. 494, 2082, 2144, 3897,
    494, 503, 2105, 3297
Samuel, Sallie (Brummal) 3185
Samuel, William. 1325, 2808
Samuel, William H. 2180, 2242
Samuels, Ruth. 630
Samuelson, Norbert M. 1735
Samuelsson, Kurt. 1076
Samyutta-nikaya. 1814
San Antonio (Archdiocese) 1274
San Antonio. First Baptist Church. 170
San Diego, Calif. Central Christian Church.
    726
San Francisco (Archdiocese) Dept. of
    Education. 806
San Francisco. Congregation Emanu-El.
    1335
San Francisco. Grace cathedral. Mission of
    healing. 1792
San Francisco. Howard street Methodist
    Episcopal church. 2451
San Francisco. Museum of Art. 84
Sanadi, Lalita. 2329
Sanborn, Franklin Benjamin. 23
Sanborn, Mary Farley (Sanborn) 641
Sanborn, Ruth. 2894
Sanborn, Tracy Lewis. 1666
Sanburn, Isabella. 3207
Sanchez, Anne. 51
Sanchez, Jose Mariano. 51
Sanchez, Pedro. 1294, 2349
Sanchez-Ventura y Pascual, Francisco.
    3298
Sanctis, Luigi de. 802
Sanctis, Santa de. 1360
Sanctuary, Eugene Nelson. 1620
Sand, George. 2228
Sandal, Mohan Lal. 3760
Sandall, Robert. 3293
Sandauer, Artur. 524, 2095
Sanday, William. 2823, 306, 392, 420,
    469, 1971, 1978, 2015
Sandberg, Anne. 1794
Sandberg, Harold William. 3426
Sandberg, Karl C. 179, 1597
Sandberg, Mordechai. 3577
Sandeen, Ernest Robert. 1109, 1690, 1691
Sandel, Irene V. 3380
Sanden, Oscar Emanuel. 205, 3080
Sander, H. W. 1670
Sandercock, Kenneth L. 2058
Sanderlin, George William. 1773, 1811
Sanders, Adam Achad. 1890
Sanders, Charles Finley. 3063
Sanders, Charles H[arvey]. 2204
Sanders, David. 1122
Sanders, E. P. 393, 1411, 3585
Sanders, Ella Katharine. 83, 882, 1650,
    2864
Sanders, Ella King. 517, 3026
Sanders, Ephraim D. 2805
Sanders, Frank Knight. 71, 1928, 2009,
    331, 536, 569, 570, 596, 641
[Sanders, Frederic William] 1864. 2228
Sanders, Henry Arthur. 316, 317, 315,
    316, 2330
*Sanders, J. Oswald. 974, 1595, 2043,
    2883
Sanders, J. Pilant. 2905
Sanders, Jack T. 351, 378, 2043
Sanders, James A. 288, 496, 2934, 3357,
    3706
Sanders, James W. 815
Sanders, Jean Elsie. 623
Sanders, Jim Alvin. 106
Sanders, John Oswald. 417, 216, 953, 974,
    1428, 1741, 1832, 2015, 2880, 3323,
    3336, 3407
Sanders, Joseph Newbould. 417, 420, 477

Sanders, Nicholas. 1884
Sanders, Paul S. 550
Sanders, Peter James. 2483
Sanders, Raymond Ira. 2558
Sanders, Robert Neal. 167, 571
Sanders, Robert Stuart. 1487, 2220, 2261,
    3536, 3777, 3790
Sanders, Tao Tao Liu. 2655
Sanders, Thomas G. 1144
Sanders, Thomas Griffin. 821, 1142, 1144,
    1326
Sanderson, Amanda Cary. 298
Sanderson, Eugene Claremont. 641
[Sanderson, Florence Helen] 1896. 2729
Sanderson, Ivan Terence. 2729
Sanderson, John W. 66, 381, 995
Sanderson, Joseph. 3283, 819, 1693, 2067,
    2793
Sanderson, Leonard. 994, 3557
Sanderson, Ross Warren. 1278, 2194,
    2241, 2735, 3435
Sanderson, Warren. 1392
Sanderson, William Charles. 641
Sandford, Ernest Gray. 3598
Sandford, Ernest Grey. 3598
Sandford, Frank W. 554, 2198, 3300
Sandford, John Loren. 1610, 2949
Sandford, P. P. 1595, 2439
Sandford, Peter P. 278
Sandhu, Swaran S. 1896
Sandiford, Ralph. 3424
Sandilya. 197
Sandison, George Henry. 218
Sandison, Goerge H. 281
Sandlin, James Lee. 1466
Sandlin, John Lewis. 81, 687, 1432, 1452,
    1750, 2347, 2783, 2884, 2894, 3882
Sandmel, Samuel. 125, 211, 349, 485, 502,
    540, 541, 1052, 1807, 2013, 2087, 2103,
    2149, 2153, 2801, 2831, 3063
Sando, Edwin Milton. 3048
Sands, Audrey Lee. 3415
Sands, Elizabeth (Franks) 1623
[Sands, George Washington]. 527
Sands, Percy Cooper. 211, 349, 502
Sandstrom, Peter G. 2281
Sandt, Eleanor E. 2965, 3172
Sandt, George Washington. 1035, 3308
Sandul, Duane G. 177
Sandweiss, Samuel H. 2999, 3304
Sandwich island mirror and commercial
    gazette. 873
Sandys, Edwin. 1227
Sanford, Agnes Mary (White) 494, 991,
    1600, 1601, 2072, 2477, 3301
Sanford, Alexander E. 2377
Sanford, Charlotte. 2937, 3301
Sanford, D. P. 630, 1114, 2962
Sanford, Don. 1872, 2894
Sanford, Edgar Lewis. 1600, 2961
Sanford, Edwin G. 2847
Sanford, Elias Benjamin. 1620, 3035
Sanford, Jack D. 2905
Sanford, James H. 1883
Sanford, John A. 1107, 1294, 1746, 1931,
    2071, 2378, 2994
Sanford, Louis Childs. 2959
Sanford. Agnes Mary (White) 1600
Sangharakshita, Bhikshu. 708
SanGiovanni, Lucinda. 1582
Sangster, James S. 1928
Sangster, Margaret Elizabeth. 281, 1452
Sangster, Margaret Elizabeth (Munson)
    616, 974, 1325, 1983, 3481, 3840
Sangster, P E. 2905
Sangster, W. E. 2905
Sangster, William Edwin. 974, 1452, 1570,
    1842, 2030, 2421, 2754, 2880, 2905,
    3012, 3281, 3674, 1435, 2030, 2437
Sangster, William Edwin Robert. 1842,
    3012, 3674, 2437
Sanjek, Louis. 3740
Sankaracarya. 103, 3775
Sankey, Ira David. 3459, 1861, 1873,
    3230, 3231, 3301
Sankowsky, Shoshanna (Harris) 2119,
    3896
Sannella, Lucia. 202
Sanner, A. Elwood. 434
Sanness, Palmer. 2801
Sano, Roy I. 1133, 3734
Sanqster, William Edwin. 2030
Santa Ana, Julio de. 1153
Santa, George Frederick. 2934, 3876
Santamaria, Bartholomew Augustine. 664
Santaner, Marie Abdon. 3489
Santayana, George. 401, 1500, 2043,
    3201, 3481, 401, 2011, 2230, 2739, 2843
Santen, Herman W. 664
Santesson, Hans Stefan. 1585
Santideva. 703, 710
Santmire, H. Paul. 2676
Santo, Ninguno. 1015
Santoni, Ronald E. 3070
Santucci, James A. 3776
Santucci, Luigi. 1971

Saperstein, Marc. 18, 1920
Saphire, Saul. 1418, 1942, 3457
Sapir, Boris. 2098
Saponaro, Michele. 71
Saporta, Raphael. 2624
Sapp, Phyllis. 1901, 3252
Sapp, Phyllis Woodruff. 939, 974, 2735,
    3180
Sapp, Stephen. 3391
Sappington, Roger Edwin. 1137, 1235,
    1236, 2178
Sarachek, Joseph. 2076, 2414, 5, 2148,
    2414, 2623, 2842
Sarafian, Krikor A. 82
Sarano, Jacques. 2758
Saraydarian, H. 2067, 2381, 2729, 3463
Saraydarian, Torkom. 11, 2732
Sarda y Salvany, Felix, 1844-1916. 2221
Sardar, Ziauddin. 1922
Sardeson, Charles Thomas. 1005, 3682
Sardou, Victorien. 1402
Sarett, Lew R. 1737
Sargant, William Walters. 2999
[Sargent, C. B. 897
Sargent, Daniel. 874, 1284, 1365, 1541,
    1744, 3790, 3899
[Sargent, Epes] 1813-1880. 3513
Sargent, John. 2349, 2350, 2532, 3697
Sargent, John Henry. 908, 909
Sargent, Leonard. 188
Sargent, Lyman Tower. 1518
Sargent, Robert. 1001, 2043
Sarkar, Benoy Kumar. 1631
Sarkissian, Karekin. 82
Sarles, John Wesley. 3295, 3303
Sarna, Nahum M. 522
Sarno, Ronald A. 236, 408, 1123, 1144,
    2043
Sarolea, Charles. 1638
Saron, Gustav. 2097
Sarson, Mary. 2090
Sartorius, Ernst. 2043
Sartory, Thomas A. 1066, 1492
Sartre, Jean Paul. 1584, 2079
Sartre, Joan Paul. 1584
Sasaki, Joseph. 2192
Sasia, Joseph Casimir. 1697
Sasnett, Joseph Randolph. 1168
Saso, Michael R. 1115, 3586
Sasse, Hermann. 2256, 2286
Sasse, Lewis. 974
Sassoon, David Solomon. 2098
Satapathabrahmana. 3139
Satchidananda. 3491
Sateren, Leland B. 917
Sathaye, Shriniwas G. 1536
Sato, Giei. 2575
Sato, Seitaro. 779
Sato, Tasuku. 817
Satolli, Francesco. 828
Satprakashananda. 1082, 1815, 2007,
    2322, 2382, 3020, 3784
Satprem, 1923. 1709
Satre, Elizabeth Dahl. 932, 3304
Satterfield, Carroll E. 1753
Satterfield, Lawrence. 2801
Satterlee, Henry Yates. 1241, 2807, 3796
Satya Bharti, Ma. 3019, 3304, 3482
Satyananda Saraswati, 1923. 2792, 3866
Saucy, Robert L. 278, 1123
Sauer, Chuck. 974
Sauer, Erich. 974, 2325, 3291
Sauer, Val J. 1530
*Saul, John Allen. 2399
Saul, Martha Roper. 470, 994
[Sault, Richard] d. 1702. 100
Saunders, Caroline Kirkland (Ruffin) 3809
Saunders, Daniel J. 66
Saunders, Ernest Dale. 706, 710
Saunders, Ernest W. 417, 478, 1972
Saunders, Frederick. 3210
Saunders, Herbert E. 3261
Saunders, J. Oswald. 18
Saunders, J. Roscoe. 1388, 2494
Saunders, John Joseph. 1391
Saunders, Kenneth James. 703, 705, 2316,
    2999, 703
Saunders, Landon B. 3357
Saunders, Lowell. 697, 1576, 1743
Saunders, Mary Ellen Hawk. 1791
Saunders, Philip K. 46
Saunders, William Trebell. 3304
Saunders, Winnie Crandall. 3702
Saunderson, Henry Hallam. 71, 597, 1430,
    1890, 1972, 2212, 2221, 3008
Saunderson, John de Bedick. 1262
Sauneron, Serge. 2940
Saurat, Denis. 2419, 2733
Sauro, Joan. 2395
Sause, Bernard Austin. 797, 1262, 2344
Sausen, Alphonse. 770, 859
Savage, Alma Helen. 2501, 2004, 2501
Savage, Carol. 1983
Savage, Chester Melvin. 1560
Savage, Courtenay. 1115
Savage, David S. 1859, 2640

Savage, Helen. 2729
Savage, Henry Edwin. 3336, 3783
Savage, Henry Harold. 3291
Savage, Horac C. 2195
Savage, Katharine. 3140
Savage, Mary Lucide. 3419
Savage, Minot Judson. 3063, 61, 236, 725,
    1581, 1726, 1954, 2015, 2065, 3063,
    3076, 3104, 3513, 3514, 3609, 3724,
    3726, 3728, 3729, 3730
Savage, Thomas G. 865, 3758
Savage, William Bowler. 945
Savage, William Edward. 608
Savard, Wilfred. 3063
Savary, Louis M. 990, 1003, 1265, 2046,
    2395, 3482, 3849
Savasis, J. 101
Savery, Christine. 2763
Saville, Henry Martyn. 1868, 3357
Savin, Jacob. 2080, 2143, 3896
Savitsch, Eugene de. 1880
Savoca, Nick. 1574
Savon, Herve. 2568, 2880
Savory, George Washington. 3393
Savory, Jerold. 1154, 2125
Savoy, Gene. 445, 1718, 1912, 1917,
    2729, 3306
Saward, John. 3492
Sawatsky, Walter. 1552
Sawatzky, Harry Leonard. 2407
Sawhill, John Alexander. 1115, 1771
Sawicki, Marianne. 3392
Sawin, Theophilus Parsons. 2034, 2934
Sawyer, Elbert Henry. 1972, 3647
Sawyer, John F. A. 556, 1797, 3293
Sawyer, Joseph Dillaway. 2847
Sawyer, Leicester Ambrose. 288, 311,
    411, 502
Sawyer, Lewis Berdine. 2561
Sawyer, Thomas Jefferson. 1699, 3431
Sawyer, Wesley Caleb. 2206
Saxe, Grace. 333, 516, 520, 554, 555, 556,
    557, 561, 576, 590
Saxon, Kurt. 217, 2948
*Saxton, E. E. 2048
Saxton, N. S. 3463
Say, David Lester. 695
Say, Thomas. 3201
Sayce, Archibald Henry. 93, 94, 502, 543,
    1921
Sayers, Carl R. 3530
Sayers, Dorothy Leigh. 2023, 1105, 3652,
    1105, 2023, 2395, 3652
Sayers, Jane E. 1488
Sayers, John W. 2401
Sayers, Stanley E. 3889
Sayers, Stuart. 739
Sayford, Samuel M. 1702, 3872
Saylor, Dennis E. 2782
Sayre, Claude Enoch. 1100
Sayre, Francis B. 1747, 2973
Sayre, John L. 3090, 3627
Sayre, Leslie C. 1240, 2499
Sayres, Alfred N. 1545
Sayres, Alfred Nevin. 1545, 2905
Sbendle, Arthur James. 307
Scaer, David P. 71, 306, 1957, 2283
Scaff, Marilee K. 1284
Scala, Jacob Israel. 3142
Scalise, Victor F. 693
Scallan, Emeric B. 1483
Scammon, John H. 552, 580
Scanlan, Arthur J. 3276
Scanlan, Charles Martin. 1490
Scanlan, Michael. 1600
Scanlan, Michael James. 1179
Scanlon, A. Clark. 151, 178, 2524
Scanlon, David G. 1129
Scantlan, Sam W. 2865
Scanzoni, Letha. 1844, 3832, 3881
Scarborough, Alma May. 910
Scarborough, Lee Rutland. 1570, 1634,
    2014, 2547, 2813, 3465, 3674, 1560
Scarborough, Peggy. 326, 1003
Scarbourough, Lee Rutland. 1570
Scarlett, John. 3143, 3134
Scarlett, William. 1134, 1135
Scarpati, Rosario. 1245
Scerrato, Umberto. 79
[Schaad, Julius Augustus], 1866. 1079,
    1374, 1554
Schaaffs, Werner. 2477
Schaal, John H. 405, 3557
Schaap, Theodore. 3049
Schaberg, Jane. 445
Schacher, James A. 646
Schachern, Harold. 3772
Schacht, Joseph. 2564
Schachter, Zalman. 1789
Schack, Albert P. 1071
Schack, Albert Peter. 1581
Schade, Sigmund C. 1154
Schaeder, Grete. 699
Schaefer, Aloys. 2356, 2363
Schaefer, James R. 3168
[Schaefer, Joseph] 1848. 3778
Schaefer, Lyle L. 2296

Schaefers, William Henry. 817, 1299
Schaeffer, Charles Edmund. 1545
[Schaeffer, Charles William, 1813-1896]. 1606, 2294
Schaeffer, Edith. 296, 926, 990, 1084, 3306, 3541
Schaeffer, Francis A. 1244
Schaeffer, Francis August. 66, 526, 554, 649, 1063, 1105, 1282, 1853, 2134, 2395, 3357, 3521
Schaeffer, Franky. 1089
Schaeffer, Henry. 2949
Schaeffer, Sue. 720
Schaeffer, William Christ. 2065, 3435
Schafer, Bruno. 1365
Schafer, Charles A. 1978
Schafer, Peter. 43
Schafer, Raymond. 1529
Schaff, David Schley. 1857, 3306, 2977
Schaff-Herzog encyclopedia. 241, 1513, 3639
Schaff, Philip. 115, 344, 352, 380, 559, 1151, 1179, 1385, 1386, 1402, 1995, 2001, 2043, 2977, 3207, 3746, 3756
Schaffer, Ulrich. 2395, 2894
Schaffler, Albert. 3120
[Schagemann, John Henry] 1845. 1325, 3785
Schalk, Carl. 1208
Schall, James V. 1087, 1154, 2126, 3451
Schaller, Jean Pierre. 949
Schaller, John. 2011
Schaller, Lyle E. 658, 1140, 1171, 1200, 1244, 1278, 1279, 1303, 2787, 3761
Schalm, Bernard. 3854
Schamoni, Wilhelm. 1024, 3281
Schanz, John P. 3266
Schanz, Paul. 66
Schaper, Robert N. 550
Schapiro, Jacob Salwyn. 1143
Schapiro, Meyer. 603, 921
Scharf, Betty R. 3087
Scharffs, Gilbert W. 2616
Scharfstein, Ben-Ami. 2640, 1517
Scharfstein, Edythe. 1785, 2779
Scharfstein, Sol. 1784, 2763, 3261
Scharlemann, Martin Henry. 3624, 1600, 2026, 3014
Scharlemann, Robert P. 3694, 3700
Scharp, Heinrich. 808
Scharper, Philip. 791, 2152
Scharper, Philip J. 811, 1245
Scharper, Phillip. 874
Scharpff, Paulus. 1573
Scharsch, Philipp. 1327
Schartau, Henric. 2301
Schatz, Elihu A. 496, 2414
Schatz, Morris. 4
Schatzman, Albert G. 66, 974, 1007
Schauffler, A[dolphus] F[rederick]. 3557
Schauffler, Adolphus Frederick. 3565, 3134, 3557
Schauffler, Alfred Theodore. 3563
Schauffler, Grace Leavitt. 3306
Schauffler, William Gottlieb. 425, 2034
Schauinger, Joseph Herman. 125, 875, 1628
Schauss, Hayyim. 1623, 2120, 1614
Schaya, Leo. 722
Schechter, Abraham Israel. 2109
Schechter, Solomon. 2143, 2080, 3331, 2080, 2083, 2116, 2140, 2143, 2147, 2164
Schechtman, Joseph B. 2863, 3895
Scheck, Joann. 431, 632
Scheck, John F. 2215
Schecter, Jerrold. 708
Schedl, Claus. 536
Schedler, Norbert O. 3107
Scheeben, Matthias Joseph. 782, 1752, 2363, 3647
Scheel, Theodor. 1397
Scheele, Mary Augustine. 116, 3489
Scheer, Gladys E. 2224
Scheetz, Leo A. 791, 2363, 2938
Schefer, Leopold. 2395
Scheffbuch, Winrich. 2821
Scheffczyk, Leo. 1384, 2325
Scheffer, Jacob Gijsbert de Hoop. 1344
Scheffler, Samuel. 1348
Scheiber, Richard B. 761
[Scheible, Johann]. 2315
Scheidt, David L. 17, 311
Schein, Bruce E. 421
Scheiner, Irwin. 1101
Scheler, Max Ferdinand. 2320, 2837
Schelkle, Karl Hermann. 326, 469, 2938, 3840
Schell, Edwin A. 641
Schell, Edwin Allison. 641, 1570
Schell, Mildred. 631, 3203
Schell, William G[allio]. 641
Schell, William Gallio. 3300
Schellenberger, Bernardin. 2571, 3306
Schelling, Friedrich Wilhelm Joseph von. 2739
Schem, Alexander Jacob. 1248

Schemann, Alexander. 2210
Schemmer, Kenneth E. 3541
Schenck, Ferdinand Schureman. 603, 1099, 1185, 1801, 2112, 3601, 3678, 1314
*Schenck, Joann. 508
Schenck, Lewis Bevens. 1906
[Schenck, William Edward]. 897, 1778
Schenectady, N. Y. First Reformed church. 3307
Schenk, Wilhelm. 2857, 3050, 3435
Schenke, Ludger. 436, 2011
Schenkel, Daniel. 1995
Schep, J A. 3221
Schepers, Maurice Bonaventure. 1123
Scher, Bertha. 1452, 2133, 3291
Scherer, Frances Schlosser. 2488, 3308
Scherer, James A. 1063, 2296, 2494
Scherer, James Augustin Brown. 2801
Scherer, Lester B. 3423
Scherer, Margaret Roseman. 3715
Scherer, Melanchthon Gideon Groseclose. 2223
Scherer, Paul. 2905, 545, 2301, 2905
Scherer, Paul [Ehrman]. 1264
Scherling, A R. 1347
Schermerhorn, Elizabeth Wheeler. 2179, 2319
Schermerhorn, John Freeman. 2560
Schermerhorn, Martin Kellogg. 1868, 3268
Schermerhorn, William David. 1194, 2545
Schervier, Franziska. 3307
Scherzer, Carl J. 1258, 1259, 1600, 2395
Scheu, Marina. 81, 2739
Scheub, Harold. 1631
Scheuer, Garry A. 2395
Scheuing, Herman Aloysius. 2001, 2991, 3514
Scheurer, J. B. 2252
Scheuring, Tom. 1610, 3307, 3489
Schevill, Ferdinand. 1854
Schevill, Margaret Erwin. 2677
Schiaparelli, Giovanni Virginio. 212
Schick, Edwin A. 460
Schick, John M. 3043
Schick, Joseph. 2120, 2371
Schieffelin, Samuel Bradhurst. 898, 3157
Schieler, Caspar Erich. 1327
Schieman, Bernard. 115, 116, 2199
Schiff, Alvin Irwin. 2106
Schiffer, Stephen R. 2376
Schiffman, Steve. 1367, 3307
Schilder, Klaas. 2030
Schilder, Klas. 1794
Schillebeecke, Edward Cornelius Florentius Alfons. 3770
Schillebeeckx, Edward. 477, 1752, 2043
Schillebeeckx, Edward Cornelis Florentius. 2043
Schillebeeckx, Edward Cornelis Florentius Alfons. 1729, 2344, 2787, 3266, 3307
Schillebeeckx, Edward Cornelisu Florentinius Alfons. 835
Schillebeeckx, Edward Cornelius Florentinius Alfons. 761, 773, 777, 878, 1123, 1154, 1155, 2363, 3226, 3624, 3634, 3772
Schillebeeckx, Edward Cornelius Florentius Alfons. 477, 1752, 2043, 3226, 3266, 3709, 3770
Schillebeekx, Edward Cornelius Florentinius Alfons. 3226
Schiller, Ferdinand Canning Scott. 186, 1854
Schiller, Gertrud. 1958
Schiller, Mayer. 2751
Schiller, Solomon. 3896
Schiller, Werner. 2763, 2806
Schilling, Harold Kistler. 3083
Schilling, Perry Calhoun. 1881
Schilling, Sylvester Paul. 3452, 100, 543, 1726, 3453, 3610, 3618
Schilling, T C. 156
Schilpp, Paul Arhtur. 1106
Schilpp, Paul Arthur. 2163, 2320, 3018, 3104
Schiltzer, Albert. 1893
Schimberg, Albert Paul. 1307, 1643, 2685, 2755, 3438, 3532
Schimmel, Annemarie. 1918, 2169, 3543, 3544
Schimmel, Harry C. 2075
Schindler, Carl J. 3674
Schindler, Harold. 3242
Schindler, Regine. 2260, 2771
Schindler, Solomon. 1084, 2090, 2414
Schiotz, Fredrik Axel. 974, 1302, 3307
Schisler, John Q. 3157
Schisler, John Quincy. 2428, 3157
Schlabach, Theron F. 2408
Schlamm, Vera. 3038, 3851
Schlarman, Joseph H. 1842
Schlatter, Richard Bulger. 1760
Schleck, Charles A. 2344, 3785
Schleidon, M[atthias] J[acob]. 2082
Schleier, Sylvester Theron. 2834

Schleiermacher, Friedrich. 951
Schleiermacher, Friedrich Ernst Daniel. 1015, 1806, 1972, 3063, 3647, 3669
Schleiter, Frederick. 3110
*Schlenker, Elizabeth D. 1726, 1727
Schlesinger, Arthur Meier. 697
Schlesinger, Julia. 3514
Schlesinger, Max. 1103, 2013
Schlesinger, Sebastian Benson. 3577
Schlesselman, Robert H. 899
Schlette, Heinz Robert. 3104
Schlier, Heinrich. 335, 350, 3475
Schlingman, Edward L. 1167
Schlink, Basilea. 66, 950, 1697, 2033, 2267, 2395, 2735, 3218, 3308
Schlink, Basilea [Secular name: Klara Schlink]. 2735
Schlink, Edmund. 136, 1043, 2072, 2286, 3772
Schlitzer, Albert. 1893
Schlitzer, Albert I. 1893
Schlitzer, Albert L. 1893, 2368, 3266
Schloerb, Rolland Walter. 1727, 2905
Schloss, Ezekiel. 603
Schlosser, Felix. 3785
Schlueter, Henry C. 974
Schmahl, Philipp J R. 1602
Schmaiz, Norbert. 2511
*Schmalenberger, Jerry L. 1164
Schmandt, Henrietta Elizabeth. 97, 2026
Schmandt, Raymond Henry. 1391
Schmauch, Walter W. 1112
Schmauk, Theodore Emanuel. 2284, 3557
[Schmauk, Theodore Emmanual]. 649
Schmaus, Harold E. 1189
Schmaus, Michael. 1096, 2905, 3647
Schmelig, Leddy. 3750
Schmelig, Randolph. 2043, 3750
Schmelzel, Carol. 940
Schmelzenbach, Elmer. 2487, 3308
Schmemann, Alexander. 139, 2551, 2746, 2747, 2748, 2750, 3619
Schmid, Bernard. 1616
Schmid, Calvin Fisher. 1578
Schmid, Evan. 115, 194, 1405, 2596, 2705, 3603
Schmid, Friedrich. 1707
Schmid, Georg. 3063
Schmid, Heinrich Friedeich Ferdinand. 2287
Schmid, Heinrich Friedrich Ferdinand. 2287
Schmid, Jeannine. 939
Schmid, Josef. 434
Schmid, Mark Joseph. 2356
Schmid, Max. 1357, 3270
[Schmid, Placid]. 746, 748, 770, 855, 770
[Schmid, Placid. 770, 859
Schmidt, Albert Marie. 727, 730
Schmidt, Austin Guildford. 57, 66, 1317
Schmidt, Austin Guilford. 66
Schmidt, Dietmar. 2709
Schmidt, Duane A. 2019
Schmidt, Elisabeth. 3043, 3308
Schmidt, Emanuel. 3457
Schmidt, Ernst G. 1005
Schmidt, George Thomas. 782, 840, 1123, 2938
Schmidt, Joel. 2657
Schmidt, John. 108, 1752, 2215, 2283
Schmidt, Karl. 3104
Schmidt, Karl Otto. 1325
Schmidt, Karl Theodore. 2325
Schmidt, Martin. 3804
Schmidt, Nathaniel. 2043, 1798, 3063
Schmidt, Otto Henry. 341, 2516
Schmidt, Paul Frederic. 2181, 3120, 3599
Schmidt, Paul Frederick. 2181
Schmidt, Philipp. 2729
[Schmidt, Placidus. 859
Schmidt, Robert Frederick. 2484
Schmidt, Roger. 3063
Schmidt, Stephen A. 2291, 3681
Schmidt, Steven. 97
Schmidt, Wilhelm. 3110
Schmidt, John. 9
Schmidtmayr, Maria Therese. 896
Schmidt-Pauli, Elisabeth von. 1508, 3691
Schmiechen, Samuel John. 2396, 2783
Schmiedeler, Edgar. 2339, 2344
Schmieding, Alfred. 616
Schmieding, Alfred. 616
Schmiel, David. 1708, 3493
Schmithals, Walter. 56, 71, 346, 368, 1718, 2801
Schmitt, Abraham. 1414
Schmitt, Agnes Mary. 2354
Schmitt, Francis P. 1206
Schmitt, Friedrich. 887
Schmitt, Karl Michael. 821
Schmitt, Myles. 1643
Schmitt, Patricia Ann. 779
Schmitz, Charles Henry. 1441, 1452
Schmitz, Emil. 2851
Schmitz, Joseph William. 2334
Schmitz, Kenneth L. 1383
Schmitz, Robert Morell. 670

schmitz, Walter J. 840, 844, 1837, 2235, 2238, 2368, 2370
Schmoger, Karl Erhard. 1511
Schmoller, Otto. 380, 485, 538
Schmucker, Samuel Mosheim. 3120
Schmucker, Samuel Simon. 1042, 1046, 2287, 2288, 2292, 3035, 3309, 3648
Schnabel, A. O. 278, 3083
Schnackenburg, Rudolf. 137, 417, 477, 1163, 1531, 2175, 2396, 3717
Schneck, Ferdinand Schureman. 75
Schneebeck, Harold N. 2020
Schnecker, Peter August. 1727
Schneid, Hayyim. 1611, 2345
Schneidau, Herbert N. 236, 299
Schneider, Bernard N. 510
Schneider, Carl Edward. 1497, 1550
Schneider, Delano Douglas. 2536, 3309
Schneider, Delwin Byron. 3120
Schneider, Edelhard Louis. 2578
Schneider, Edouard. 188
Schneider, Eliza Cheney (Abbott) 2558
Schneider, Ernest. 2060
Schneider, Frieda Johnetta. 11, 1441
Schneider, Gerhard. 380
Schneider, Herbert Wallace. 1263, 1536, 1787, 2739, 3008, 3063, 3746
Schneider, Herman Peter. 1084
Schneider, Jacob U. 3344
Schneider, Johannes. 403
Schneider, Joseph. 3482
Schneider, Louis. 1455, 3087, 3088
Schneider, Nicholas A. 1716
Schneider, Norris Franz. 1672
Schneider, Reinhold. 1643, 3624
Schneider, Stanley D. 2216, 2905
Schneider, Wilhelm. 1697
Schneiderfranken, Joseph Anton. 422, 1697, 2729
Schneiderman, Harry. 1744, 2091
Schneiderman, Lee. 3000
Schneiders, Nicholas. 2032
Schnell, William J. 1941, 3798
Schneller, Joseph A. 733, 791
Schneller, Ludwig. 2178
Schnepp, Gerald Joseph. 3749
Schneweis, Emil. 43, 2190
Schnittkind, Dana Arnold. 2483
Schnittkind, Henry Thomas. 3090, 3134
Schnitzer, Henry R. 179
Schnitzer, Jeshaia. 2782
Schnitzler, Theodor. 2368
Schnucker, John A. 3254
Schnur, Harry C. 57
Schnurer, Gustav. 1186
Schobert, Theodosia De Witt. 1600
Schochet, Elijah Judah. 1404, 3016
Schodde, George Henry. 2954, 491
Schoen, Max. 1995, 3104
Schoenberg, Wilfred P. 826, 1948, 2305
Schoenberger, Guido. 1891. 87
Schoenberner, Gerhard. 2099
Schoenfeld, Charles. 2228
Schoenfeld, Elizabeth. 3185, 3842
Schoenherr, Irenaeus Martin. 3270
Schoenholtz, Larry. 1879
Schoenl, William J. 807, 2221
Schoeps, Hans Joachim. 377, 1488, 2153, 3140
Schoff, Wilfred Harvey. 594, 3575
Schoffeleers, Matthew. 1484, 3094
Schoffen, Elizabeth. 3416
Schofield, A[lfred] T[aylor]. 1727
Schofield, Alfred Taylor. 3211, 1071, 2410
Schofield, Charles E. 2056
Schofield, Charles Edwin. 1360, 1727, 2421, 2440, 2956
Schofield, Guy. 1194
Schofield, John Noel. 298
Schofield, Joseph A. 3337
Schofield, Joseph Anderson. 909, 898
Schokel, Luis. 201
Schokel, Luis Alonso. 240
Scholastica, Mary. 3271
Scholefield, Harry Barron. 3727
Scholefield, Harry Barron, ed. 3727
Scholem, Gershom Gerhard. 722, 2414, 2646, 3262, 3309, 3310, 3394
Scholes, France Vinton. 1148
Schollgen, Werner. 949
Scholz, G[ustave]. 2980
Schomer, Abraham Shalkewitz. 2079
Schomp, Gerald. 2125
Schoneveld, J. 596, 1498
Schonfeld, Solomon. 2140
Schonfield, Hugh Joseph. 286, 291, 1103, 1197, 1410, 2014, 2053, 2146, 2801, 3072
Schonhovd, Hanna Christine. 3157
Schoo, Jan. 1804
Schoof, T. Mark. 791, 3628
School Sisters of Notre Dame, Milwaukee. 3188
Schooley, Frank Budd. 1399, 3310

Schoolland, John Bernard. 1627
Schoolland, Marian M. 623, 1024, 1734, 2676, 3666
Schoonenberg, Peter. 2325, 3411, 3412
Schoonenberg, Piet J. A. M. 652, 2043, 3648
Schoonhoven, Calvin Robert. 1794
Schoonmaker, Hazel K. 3174, 3763
Schoonmaker, Paul D. 1256, 3252
Schoonover, Melvin E. 990, 1352, 2046, 2698
Schopenhauer, Arthur. 2854, 3068, 3311
Schorsch, Alexander Peter. 2359, 3184
*Schott, Agnes Treick. 2263
Schott, Christian Heinrich. 109
Schott, Walter Edgar. 3389
Schouppe, Francois Xavier. 782, 2058
Schoville, Keith N. 208
Schrader, L. F. 1656
Schrader, Robert William. 3700
Schraff, Anne E. 932
Schraff, Francis. 72, 2825
Schrag, Martin H. 2408
Schrag, Peter. 685
Schramm, John. 1005, 1321
Schramm, Mary. 1712
Schreiber, Albert M. 2775
Schreiber, Clara Seuel. 2272
Schreiber, Emanuel. 2116
Schreiber, Morris. 2664
Schreiber, Otto Louis. 1462
Schreiber, Vernon R. 550, 551, 1931, 2215, 2301, 3357
Schreiner, Samuel A. 3201
Schreiner, Samuel Jonathan. 217, 1433
Schreivogel, Paul A. 898, 1260
Schrenck von Notzing, Albert Philibert Franz, 1862. 2372
Schreyer, George M. 3157
Schrire, Theodore. 35
Schrist, Elizabeth (Hough) 1486
Schrock, Simon. 988
Schroder, Anneliese. 749, 1477
Schroeder, Arnold H. 2783
Schroeder, David. 236, 641, 1727
Schroeder, Frederick W. 2905, 2945, 3854
Schroeder, Friedrich Wilhelm Julius. 518
Schroeder, George W. 3375, 3465
Schroeder, Gustavus Wilhelm. 170
Schroeder, Hermann Henry. 2592
Schroeder, Janet E. 1675
Schroeder, John Charles. 106, 109, 1342
[Schroeder, John Frederick]. 1821
Schroeder, Mary Agnes (Tynan) 3018
Schroeder, Rupert H. 2287
Schroeder, Ruth Jones. 330, 380, 2396, 3857
[Schroeder, Theodore Albert]. 679, 1527, 2223, 3470
Schroeder, Theodore W. 911, 2781
Schroeder, W. Widick. 3446, 3665, 3746
Schroeter, Elizabeth Arlene. 2407
Schroll, Mary Alfred. 189, 190
Schrott, Lambert. 833
Schryvers, Joseph. 1741, 2356, 3223, 3482
Schubert, Hans von. 1179
Schubert, J V. 1315
Schubert, Kurt. 1410, 1411, 3014
Schuch, Ignaz. 2905
Schucking, Levin. 2280
Schucking, Levin Ludwig. 3008
[Schuemacher, Simone]. 3248
Schuen, Joseph. 865
Schuette, Walter Erwin. 974, 1838, 2722, 3674
Schuetze, Armin W. 2787
Schufreider, Gregory. 49, 1739
Schug, Howard Lesher. 1273
Schug, John A. 737, 2849
Schugren, Eric Olof. 2532
Schuh, Charles Gottlob. 2880
Schuh, Lewis Herman. 909
Schuiling, Walter John. 3278
Schuknecht, Joseph J. 3541
Schuler, Anthony W. 203
Schuler, Robert M. 1458
Schuller, David. 1260
Schuller, David S. 1154
Schuller, Robert. 1012
Schuller, Robert H. 2808
Schuller, Robert Harold. 588, 988, 1012, 1433, 2043, 2396, 3330, 3539
Schulman, Arnold. 3304
Schulman, Elias. 2103
Schulte, Augustine Joseph. 189, 840, 1165, 189
Schulte, Karl. 741
Schulte, Paul. 2500, 2501
Schulte, Paul Clarence. 3276
Schultejann, Marie. 3377
Schultheis, Rose May Dawson. 667
Schultz, Charles Henry. 3331
Schultz, Christopher. 3312
Schultz, D Y. 1101
Schultz, Ferdinand Peter. 2407
Schultz, Friedrich Wilhelm. 513, 519
Schultz, Harold Peters. 3407

Schultz, Hermann. 66
Schultz, Howard. 2470
Schultz, John Ahern. 2030
Schultz, Joseph P. 2152
Schultz, Louis R. 974
Schultz, Richard J. 2480
Schultz, Samuel J. 296, 510, 536, 572, 596, 940, 2622, 2951
Schultz, Selina Gerhard. 3312
Schultze, Jurgen. 2803
*Schulz, Florence. 3164, 3174, 3763
Schulze, Andrew. 1133, 2296
Schulze, Frederick. 2790, 3676
Schulze, Gustav Adolf. 2419
Schumacher, Claire W. 3278
Schumacher, Henry. 3439, 312
Schumacher, John N. 1616
Schumacher, Magnus Ambrose. 132, 3184
Schumacher, Matthew Aloysius. 1740, 3157
Schumaker, Albert Jesse Ringer. 3180
Schumann, Hans Wolfgang. 711
Schumm, Robert William. 181, 1452
Schuon, Frithjof. 2565, 703, 2565, 3104, 3543
Schuppert, Mildred W. 3045
Schurch, Maylan. 1012, 1610
Schure, Edouard. 1502, 1532, 1972, 2019, 2622, 2636, 2729, 2744, 3120
Schure. Edouard. 2186, 3019
Schurer, Emil. 2092
Schurhammer, Georg. 1649, 1650
Schurman, Jacob Gould. 19
Schurman, Paul G. 2781
Schurmann, Heinz. 2248
[Schuster, George N.]. 32
Schuster, I'defonso [Alfredo I'defonso Schusters. 19
Schuster, Kay Lathrop. 695
Schuster, Mary Faith. 2626
Schuster, Michael Huldreich. 66
Schutte, Josef Franz. 1949, 2534
Schutz, Albert L. 2733
Schutz, John Howard. 119, 377
Schutz, Roger. 933, 1042, 1316, 1356, 2396, 2571, 3226, 3311, 3772, 3780
Schutze, Alfred. 1746
Schuyleman, John Louis. 3574, 3740
Schuyler, Hamilton. 3344, 3304, 1759
Schuyler, Henry Clement. 1995, 2007, 2255, 2356, 3330
Schuyler, Joseph B. 2699
Schuyler, Montgomery. 3276, 3301
Schuyler, Philippa Duke. 12
Schuyler, Van Koert. 203
Schuyler, William Bishop. 3807
Schwab, Charles F. 1016
*Schwab, Gustav. 2657, 2662
Schwab, Gustav Benjamin. 2352, 2658
Schwab, Jewel Huelster. 2498
Schwab, Laurence Harry. 2175, 3239
Schwab, Paul Josiah. 2632, 3703
Schwab, Ralph Kendall. 1545
Schwager, Friedrich. 850
Schwalm, John George. 1321
Schwalm, May (Barclay) 1910
Schwalm, Vernon Franklin. 3814
Schwartz, Aloysius. 1153, 2537
Schwartz, Charles. 2116, 2140
Schwartz, Christina. 3452
Schwartz, David. 3897
Schwartz, Eduard. 1538
Schwartz, Euphenia (Neil) McGraw. 152
Schwartz, Fanny Schneider. 722
Schwartz, Frederick J. 2553, 3387
Schwartz, Frederick L.B. 612, 613
Schwartz, Gary. 3383, 3454
Schwartz, Helene E. 1387
Schwartz, Hillel. 2464
Schwartz, Howard. 2208
Schwartz, Jacob. 3863, 3577
Schwartz, Paul Waldo. 2314
Schwartz, Samuel. 3143
Schwartz, Stephan A. 2773
Schwartz, Stephen P. 2660
Schwartz, Toby Devens. 3845
Schwartz, Werner. 655, 3035
Schwartzkopf, Louis J. 2290
Schwartzman, Sylvan David. 541, 1328, 3032, 3166
Schwarz, Hans. 1529, 1697, 1727, 2321
Schwarz, Jack. 2381
Schwarz, Jacob David. 2120, 3576
Schwarz, Leo Walder. 2076, 2084, 2100, 2147
Schwarz, Rudolf. 1157
Schwarz, Solomon M. 2103
Schwarzbach, Bertram Eugene. 504, 3786
Schwarzbart, Isaac I. 3851
Schwarzbaum, Haim. 3610
Schwarze, Carl Theodore. 205
Schwarze, William Nathaniel. 1857
Schweid, Eliezer. 2151
Schweinfurth, Philipp. 1880
Schweinsberg, Henry W. 2547

Schweitzer, Albert. 2523, 373, 1079, 1896, 1972, 1979, 2050, 2175, 2194, 2523, 2640, 2801, 3089, 3312, 377, 1529, 1972, 1979, 1993, 2016, 2175, 2176, 2256, 2503, 2523, 2640, 2642, 2801, 3104, 3312, 3368, 3370, 3634
Schweitzer, Leonard J. 879
Schweizer, Eduard. 429, 434, 441, 1832, 2020, 2043, 2254, 3368
Schweizer, Eduard [Robert]. 2012
Schweizer, Eduard Robert. 1166
Schwenckfeld, Caspar. 1012, 3313
Schwenkfelder church. Liturgy and ritual. 3313
Schwer, Wilhelm. 3450
Schwerdtfeger, Hazel Mae. 3313
Schwertner, Thomas M. 1330, 3694
Schwertner, Thomas Maria. 22, 1913, 3025, 3248
Schwickerath, Robert. 1946
Schwickert, Friedrich "Sindbad." 98, 2598
Schwiebert, Ernest George. 2277, 3035, 2277, 3035
Schwieder, Elmer. 35
Schwimmer, Josephine (Betz-Hermann) 3482
Schwirczysnki, Wladyslaw. 2582
Sciater, John Robert Paterson. 3678
Sciens. 2991
Sclater, J R P. 2561
[Sclater, William]. 1194
SCM Press. Editorial Dept. 3627
Scobie, Alastair. 3825
Scobie, Charles Hugh Hope. 2128
Scobie, Geoffrey E. W. 3000
[Scofield, Anna (Bishop) 3463
*Scofield, C.I. 2905
Scofield, Cyrus Ingerson. 253, 479, 974, 199, 641, 1342, 1832, 2905
Scofield, William Campbell. 974, 1834, 2885
Scollard, Robert Joseph. 2330
Scomp, Henry Anselm. 2231
Scorer, Charles Gordon. 3390
Scot, James B. 1666
Scot, Reginald. 3824
Scotford, John. 1042
Scotford, John R. 2474
Scotford, John Ryland. 1157, 1165, 1269, 1290, 3177
Scott. 1392
Scott, A. Brian. 1026, 2318
Scott, Andrew Boyd. 71, 2905
Scott, Anna M. (Steele) 2500, 2970
Scott, Annie J. 313
Scott, Archibald. 1081
Scott, Bernard Brandon. 2026, 2175
Scott, Blair T. 253
Scott, Blair Thaw. 270, 1735
Scott, Catharine Amy (Dawson) 3514
Scott, Charles Archibald Anderson. 372, 377, 378, 477, 2043, 2801, 377, 802, 2801
Scott, Charles Ernest. 2511
Scott, Clinton Lee. 3723, 3755
Scott, Cyril Meir. 1092, 2729
Scott, Delaware Walter. 2535
Scott, Donald M. 1294
Scott, Elizabeth A. 1890, 3514
Scott, Ernest Findlay. 69, 349, 372, 392, 407, 411, 420, 460, 477, 1123, 1194, 1972, 2004, 2175, 2248, 3226, 3439, 321, 469, 1832, 2248
Scott, Eugene Crampton. 2913
Scott, Frank Earl. 1941
Scott, George Ryley. 2339
Scott, Gini Graham. 1908
Scott, Gladys. 1810
Scott, Harvey W. 3142
Scott, Henry Arthur. 734, 2200, 2325
Scott, Herbert Morgan. 3548
Scott, Hugh McDonald. 2706, 3239
Scott, J L. 1697
Scott, Jack B. 541
Scott, Jacob Richardson. 3134
Scott, Jane. 1452
Scott, Jefferson Ellsworth. 3766
Scott, Job. 138, 1290, 3134
Scott, John. 3315, 494, 3134, 3357, 2894
Scott, John Adams. 398, 1987
Scott, John Frank. 2248
Scott, John Martin. 1727, 2244, 2636
Scott, John Pinckney. 3251
Scott, Judith Unger. 3881
[Scott, Mary Elizabeth (Dow)]. 3315
Scott, Melville. 572, 538
Scott, Milton Robinson. 3624

Scott, Nancy Elnora. 3703
Scott, Nathan A. 1415, 2232, 2709, 3069, 3071, 3243
Scott, Niel Courtice. 2442
Scott, Orange. 974, 1868, 2449, 3231, 3423
Scott, Ralph W. 1387
Scott, Reva Lucile (Holdaway) 2605, 2867
Scott, Richard. 100
Scott, Robert. 608, 1123, 1455, 3344
Scott, Robert Balgarnie Young. 569, 578, 2951, 3446, 3821
Scott, Robert M. 2368
Scott, Samuel. 460, 3191
Scott, Thomas. 1071, 2759, 3315, 3648
Scott, Vaile J. 829
Scott, Waldron. 176, 2555
[Scott, Walter. 3120
Scott, Walter. 1113, 1391, 1392, 1423, 2589, 3315, 456
Scott, Walter Sidney. 1938
Scott, William. 392, 1194
Scott, William A. 3679
Scott, William Adolphus. 608
Scott, William Anderson. 74, 1401, 1533, 2001, 2934, 3297, 3357
Scott, William J. 2455
Scott, William Rufus. 2945
Scotti, Juliet. 2178, 3408
The Scottish Episcopal Church. 1524
Scott Moncrieff, George. 1001
Scott-Moncrieff, George [Irving]. 1001
Scott-Moncrieff, George Irving. 825
Scott-Moncrieff, Phillip David. 1501
Scougal, Henry. 974, 3630
Scourby, Alice. 1767, 2747
Scovel, Myra. 2532, 2937, 3315, 3316
Scovell, Bessie Lathe. 3833
Scovil, Elisabeth Robinson. 625, 42, 1452, 1714, 2894
Scoville, Charles Reign. 1560
Scoville, Samuel. 630
Scoville, Warren Candler. 1852
Scragg, Walter. 1013, 3882
Scragg, Walter R. L. 974
Scribner, firm, publishers, New York. (1898. Charles Scribner's sons) 3627
Scribner, Frank J. 3176
Scribner, Robert W. 3035
Scribner, William. 1570
Scriptural Rosary Center. 3249
Scriven, Charles. 1777, 3261, 3665
Scriven, George Benjamin. 1123
Scriven, Gerard F. 1983
Scriven, Michael. 1536
Scrivener, Frederick Henry Ambrose. 272
Scriver, Christian. 1441
Scroggie, W. Graham. 643
Scroggie, William Graham. 434, 278, 296, 297, 323, 447, 460, 470, 554, 604, 990, 2067, 2134, 2266, 2803, 2880, 3030, 3600
Scroggs, Robin. 6, 377, 378, 2011
Scrogin, Michael. 988
Scruby, John James. 2466
Scruggs, Julius R. 1635
Scudder, A M. 940
Scudder, C W. 1134, 1140
Scudder, Delton Lewis. 2894
Scudder, Delton Lewis. 3601, 3609
[Scudder, Eliza]. 3207
Scudder, Jennie W. 3796
Scudder, John Ralph. 1463
Scudder, Moses Lewis. 2438
Scudder, Vida Dutton. 1646, 1856, 2741, 3446
Scudi, Abbie (Turner) 3262
Scull, David. 3291
Scull, Sarah Amelia. 2662
Scullard, H. H. 1624
Scullion, John. 306
Scully, Vincent Joseph. 3692, 79, 3599
Sculthorp, Frederick C. 94
Scupoli, Lorenzo. 2819, 3489
Scutt, Winifred. 911
*Sea, Billie. 1515
Seaborne, Frederick. 3514
Seabough, Ed. 1308
Seabrook, William Buehler. 3824
Seabrook, William Le Vin. 1890
Seabury, David. 2065, 3000
[Seabury, Joseph Bartlett]. 2511, 3317
Seabury, Ruth Isabel. 1895, 1936, 2494, 3455
[Seabury, Samuel]. 2972, 3317, 3357
Seabury, Samuel. 1221
Seabury, William Jones. 3317, 76
Seager, Allan. 3817
Seagle, Nathan A. 2962
Seagrave, Gordon Stifler. 2539
Seagren, Daniel. 216, 2026, 2341, 3870
Seal, Frances Thurber. 1035
Seale, Ervin. 1314, 2026, 2248
Seale, Morris S. 183, 498, 1926, 1927, 2184
Seals, B V. 1452

Sealy, Shirley. 2618, 3317
Seaman, Ralph. 1168
Seaman, T Harvey. 2001
Seaman, William R. 2297, 2894
Seamands, David A. 2339
Seamands, John T. 139, 443, 926, 1317, 1433, 2546
Seamands, Ruth. 2532
Seamans, Herbert Lee. 3872
Search, Pamela. 3293
Searcy, William Everard Hamilton. 3291
[Seares, Alexander] fl. 1720. 684, 3605
Searle, George Mary. 791, 1035, 1495
Searle, Graham William. 1374
Searle, Mark. 138, 836
Searle, Paul. 1326
Searle, Robert Wyckoff. 3357, 1063
Searle, Verna. 932, 3317
Searle, William. 1938
Searles, Herbert Leon. 3190
Sears, Annie Lyman. 3000
Sears, Barnas. 1286, 2277
Sears, Cassius A. 1792
Sears, Charles Hatch. 2158, 1279, 3434
Sears, Clara Endicott. 10, 1788, 2467, 3397
Sears, Edmund Hamilton. 420, 1890, 1972, 2053, 3051, 1978
Sears, Fern. 921
Sears, Jack Wood. 206
Sears, Robert. 216, 297
Sears, William B. 25, 122
Sease, Rosalyn Summer. 2296
Seasholes, Charles Lyon. 167
Seashore, Gladys. 236
Seasoltz, R. Kevin. 844, 1269, 2234, 2235
Seat, W H. 2947
Seath, William. 893
Seaton, Alexander Adam. 3214, 3704
Seats, V. Lavell. 2498
Seattle. Family Counseling Service. 1289
Seattle. Public library. 868
Seaver, Anna Maria. 3817
Seaver, George. 3312, 2241, 3312
Seaver, Horace. 1656
Seaver, Paul S. 3009
Seavey, Burton W. 1600
Seaward, Carl Albert. 3726, 3793
[Seawell, Manon Young (McConnell)[1904. 156
Seay, Frank. 494, 532, 596
Seay, Homer Hoston. 10
Seay, Warren Mosby. 167, 2535
Sebag, Paul. 2162
Sebald, Hans. 3826
Sebaly, Avis Leo. 3178
Sebelius, Sven Johan. 2301
Sebeok, Thomas Albert. 2654
Seboldt, Roland H A. 974, 1983, 2359, 3857
Seboldt, Ronald H. A. 3857
Sebolt, Roland H. A. 1972
SeBoyar, Gerald Edwin. 480
Seccombe, Joseph. 36
Seccombe, Thomas. 1387
Seche, Alphonse. 1954
Sechler, Earl Truman. 2755
Secker, Thomas. 802
Secker, William. 1052, 974
Second Presbyterian Church, Staunton, Va. 3321, 3526
Secret place (The) 2396
Secrist, Henry T. 3728
Secrist, Jacob S. 3080
Seculoff, James F. 757, 3889
Sedding, Edward Douglas. 2880
Seder, A. R. 1546, 2720
Sedgwick, Henry Dwight. 90, 1799, 2269, 2270
[Sedgwick, John] 1742-1820. 1744
Sedgwick, Paulita. 47
Sedore, Marva. 545
Sedore, Marva J. 431, 995
Sedulius. 3635
See, Edwin Francis. 641, 3180
[See, Evelyn Arthur]. 1890
See, Frank Edmund. 1004
See, Ruth Douglas. 312
Seebach, Julius Frederick. 2536, 2956
Seebach, Margaret Rebecca (Himes) 2277, 2528, 2536, 2538, 2630, 3036
Seeberg, Reinhold. 3655
Seeberger, Cosmas Maria. 1329
Seebock, Philibert. 383
[Seebohm, Esther (Wheeler)]. 1678
Seebohm, Frederic. 1071, 1307, 3036
Seeger, Elizabeth. 92
Seehuus, Knut. 3344
Seel, David John. 2486, 2845, 3329
Seeley, Boudinot. 1859
Seeley, Burns K. 422
Seeley, John Robert. 1972, 2004
[Seeley, Robert Benton] 1798-1886. 802, 3134
Seeliger, Wes. 2396
Seely, Amos W. 3665
Seely, Edward D. 937

Seely, Edward Eli. 1510
[Seely, John Robert, 1834-1895. 2674
Seelye, Julius Hawley. 1071
Seeman, Otto. 2657
Seerveld, Calvin. 318
Seese, Mildred N (Parker) 1667
Seesholtz, Anna Groh. 1508, 1674, 2238
Seeyle, Laurenus Clark. 3756
Sefer ha-Yashar. English. 2097
Sefer Yezirah. English. 2189
*Segal, Abraham. 3310
Segal, Abraham. 2154
Segal, Alan. 1805
Segal, Charles M. 2106
Segal, Elizabeth. 281, 623
Segal, Josephine. 2014
Segal, Judas Benzion. 2779
Segal, Moses Hirsch. 564
Segal, Muriel. 3782
Segal, Sameul Michael. 1506, 1631
Segal, Samuel Michael. 3261
Segale, Blandina. 2548
*Seger, Doris Louise. 1479, 3176
Seger, Imogen. 1279
Seger, Valerie. 733
Segerberg, Osborn. 1417
Segerhammar, Carl W. 494
Segerhammar, Carl William. 339, 2301
Segerhammar, Robert E. 2788
Segesvary, Lewis. 2914
Segler, Franklin M. 994, 1296, 1441, 1595, 2790, 3854
Segno, A. Victor. 3104
Sego, James. 1749, 3329
Segovia, Fernando F. 324, 420, 2266
Segraves, Kelly L. 205, 278, 319, 1631
Seguin, P. A. 782
Segundo, Juan Luis. 821, 1123, 1582, 1727, 1752, 2222, 2789, 3266, 3628
Segur, Louis Gaston Adrien de. 2200
Segur, Sophie (Rostophine). 75, 1983
Sehlbrede, G. E. 3040
Seibel, George. 2605, 3429
Seibert, Benjamin Ellis. 1063
Seibert, Earl W. 3718
Seibert, Kenneth Seward. 286
Seidel, George Joseph. 2419
*[Seidel, Lena]. 1595
Seiden, Morton Irving. 2649, 3863
Seidenspinner, Clarence. 1262, 1441, 3004
Seidman, Hillel. 1614
Seifert, Harvey. 945, 1076, 1077, 1134, 1244, 1248, 2781, 3063, 3482
Seiferth, Wolfgang S. 1084
Seigart, William Raymond. 909
Seilhamer, Frank H. 569, 2951
Seiling, Max. 3687
Seippel, Paul. 2162
Seipt, Allen Anders. 1874, 3313
Seisenberger, Michael. 312, 641
Seiss, Joseph A[ugustus]. 3345
Seiss, Joseph Augustus. 99, 136, 403, 404, 461, 462, 557, 1267, 1690, 1972, 2215, 2277, 2301, 3601, 3855
Seitz, Josiah Augustus. 3366
Seitz, Oscar J. F. 1163
Sejourne, Laurette. 2668
Seju ha-Yashar. 562
Sekida, Katsuki. 2383
Selbie, William Boothby. 400, 2044, 3000, 3068, 3308, 3324, 3648
Selborne, Roundell Palmer. 1221, 1285, 1868, 3702
Selby, Donald Joseph. 312, 411, 2801
Selby, Peter. 2053
Selby, Robin C. 2704, 3219
Selby-Lowndes, Joan. 1759
Selden, Charles Albert. 2521
Selden, Edward Griffin. 1179, 1194, 2801
Selden, Eric L. 1727, 3330
Selden, John. 2667
[Selden, Richard Ely] 1797-1868. 2109
[Selder, Jane (Adams) 1867. 245, 641
Seldes, George. 1143, 2768
Seldin, Marian. 2469
Selecman, Charles C. 2808
Selecman, Charles Claude. 66, 2421, 2438, 3804
Self, Carolyn Shealy. 2249, 2880
Self, Jerry M. 422
Self-Realization Fellowship. 2304
Self, William L. 1352, 3375
Selfe, Rose E. 2772
Selig, Harris L. 1614, 2117
Seligman, Charles Gabriel. 3776
Seligman, Paul. 39, 2419
Seligmann, Kurt. 2314
Selkirk, Edward. 22
Selkirk, Thomas Mann. 2473
Sell, Charles M. 1254
Sell, Henry Thorne. 199, 283, 284, 641, 1184, 3157, 3345, 3370, 641, 644, 649, 1972, 1993, 2026, 2801, 2802, 2886, 3840
Sellars, Roy Wood. 2865, 3063, 3068
Sellars, Wilfrid. 2163
Selle, Frank Frederick. 1842

[Selle, Robert L.] 1865. 974, 1824, 3412
Selleck, Alonzo Farrington. 3134
Selleck, George A. 683, 1678
Selleck, Willard Chamberlain. 1282, 3068
Sellers, Charles Coleman. 178, 1478, 1703
Sellers, Ernest Orlando. 641, 1203, 1554, 1575, 3004
Sellers, Hazel Crowson. 1274
Sellers, Horace B. 3190
Sellers, Ian. 1285, 2459
Sellers, James Earl. 945, 1570, 3329, 3541, 3742
Sellers, Ovid Rogers. 1797
Sellers, Robert Victor. 1544
Sellew, Walter Ashbel. 1052, 2206
Sellin, Ernst. 541
Sellmair, Josef. 773
Sellman, Roger Raymond. 1391
Sellon, Walter. 2911
Sells, James William. 3530
Selner, John Charles. 115, 1298, 1619
Selph, John Archer. 286
Selsam, Howard. 1457
Seltman, Charles Theodore. 2662
Seltzer, Lewis B. 3616
Seltzer, Louis Benson. 926
Seltzer, Robert M. 2147
Selwyn, Edward Carus. 349
Selwyn, Edward Gordon. 44, 325, 1052, 1954, 3213, 3624, 3648, 3819, 3854
Selwyn, George Augustus. 3345
Selwyn, Jasper Henry. 219
Semaan, Andrew Nicola. 3142
Semaine d'etudes liturgiques (23rd : 1976. 2236
Sembratovich, Leo I. 766
Semeria, Giovanni. 1541, 2368
[Semeria, Giovanni Battista] 1779-(ca.) 1843. 40
Seminar on Community Conflicts Arising from Religious Controversy Related to the Public Schools, Atlantic City, 1959. 1320
Seminar on Responsibility of Churches to the Aging, Park City, Utah, 1968. 1257
Seminar on Science and the Spiritual Nature of Man. 2d, Rye, N. Y., 1958. 3083
Seminar on Science and the Total Nature of Man. 2d, Rye, N. Y., 1958. 3083
Seminar on Science and the Total Nature of Man. 3d, Rye, N. Y., 1960. 3083
Seminar on the Nature of Guruship, Christian Institute of Sikh Studies, 1974. 1778
Seminars for Clergymen, Cleveland, 1962. 2784
Semmel, Bernard. 2421
Semmelroth, Otto. 2168, 2363, 2905, 3182, 3266
Semmens, Bernard L. 2428
Sempangi, F. Kefa. 1300, 3332
Semper, Isidore Joseph. 763, 2705
Semple, Henry Churchill. 44, 782, 1913, 2693
Semple, Robert Baylor. 172
Sen, Kshitimohan. 1814
Senarclens, Jacques de. 3657
Sencourt, Robert. 921
Sender, Ramon. 2676
Sendy, Jean. 236
Seneca, Lucius Annaeus. 2592, 3533
Seneviratne, H. L. 712, 2162
Senft, Kenneth C. 1005, 1244
Sengel, William Randolph. 24
Senior, Donald. 392, 441, 443, 929, 1972, 2044
Senn, Frank C. 2236
Sensabaugh, Leonidas Franklin. 3557
Sensenig, Barton. 1972
Senter, Ruth Hollinger. 1303, 3333
Senzaki, Nyogen. 3894
Seppelt, Franz Xaver. 2862
Septimus, Bernard. 6, 3016
Serafian, Michael. 2806
Serafim, Archimandrite. 1046, 2749
Serage, Nancy. 1703
Seraphin, Eugene William. 2763
Serapion. 2239, 2327
Sergeant, George. 2763
Sergeant, Lewis. 3861
Sergeant, Philip Walsingham. 3824
Sergio, Lisa. 2894
Serig, Beverly. 1433, 1435
Serl, Elmer Willis. 2199
[Serle, Ambrose] 1742-1812. 2001, 3196, 3714
Sermon on the Mount. English. 3336
Sernett, Milton C. 2662
Serra, Junipero. 2506, 3376
Serraillier, Ian. 1399
Serrell, Jeanne M. 2483
Serres, Michel. 2662
Serrou, Robert. 2717, 3602
Sertillanges, Antonin Gilbert. 2396, 3309, 3694, 1452, 2396, 3309
[Servatia, 1880. 2319

Servetus, Michael. 3713
Service, John. 1234
Serwer, Blanche Luria. 3581
Sesboue, D. 566
Sessions, Alexander Joseph. 1017, 3427
Sessions, Gene Alfred. 1756, 2620
Sessions, Gene Allred. 2609
Sessions, John A. 3872
Sessions, Will. 216, 1986
Sessler, Jacob John. 909, 1198, 2594, 2596, 3665
Sessoms, Robert L. 1257
Seth, Pringle Pattison, Andrew. 3609
Seth, Ronald. 3824, 3826, 3828
Seth Pringle Pattison, Andrew. 1727, 1890, 3104
Seton, Bernard E. 3383
Seton, Elizabeth Ann. 725, 1455, 3417
Seton, Ernest Thompson. 1902
Seton, Walter Warren. 11
Settle, Elkanah. 1309, 3607
Settle, Myron C. 3157
Setton, Kenneth Meyer. 1148, 1391, 1392, 2769
Setzer, J. Schoneberg. 3665
Seubert, Aloysius H. 408
Seume, Richard H. 560, 2683
Seung Sahn. 3197, 3379, 3892, 3893
Seventeen. 1452
Seventh-day Adventists. 603 , 2911, 3180, 3380, 3383, 3385, 3386
Seventh-Day Adventists. General Conference. 1158, 3383
Seventh-day Adventists. General Conference. Biblical Research Committee. 288
Seventh-day Adventists. General conference committee. 3386
Seventh-Day Adventists. General Conference. Committee on Problems in Bible Translation. 288
Seventh-Day Adventists. General Conference Dept. of Eduation. 1983
Seventh-Day Adventists. General Conference. Dept. of Education. 597, 616, 623, 630, 1842, 3185, 3380, 3383, 3386, 3889
Seventh-Day Adventists. General Conference. Historical Research Committee. 519, 724
Seventh-Day Adventists. General Conference. Home Missionary Dept. 1570
Seventh-Day Adventists. General Conference. Lay Activities Dept. 1570
Seventh-Day Adventists. General Conference. Publishing Dept. 3204
Seventh-Day Adventists General Conference Sabbath School Dept. 3380, 3385
Seventh-day Adventists. General conference. Young people's missionary volunteer dept. 1167
Seventh-day Adventists. Mission board. 3387
Seventh-day Baptists. 3388
Severn, Hermon Harrison. 236
Sevier, Marie Christine. 22
Sevre, Leif. 3761
Sewall, Charles G. 312
Sewall, Frank. 3624
[Sewall, Frank] 1837-1915. 3563
Sewall, Jotham. 3388
Sewall, Jotham Bradbury. 205
Sewall, May (Wright) 3514
Sewanee, Tenn. University of the South. 3756
Seward, Desmond. 2463
Seward, Frederick Dwight. 1954
Seward, Roy Holland. 1035
Seward, Theodore Frelinghuysen. 1035, 2982, 3521
Sewel, Willem. 1685
Sewell, Arthur. 2472
Sewell, Benjamin T. 2830
Sewell, Elizabeth Missing. 3883
Sewell, Jesse Londerman. 1705
Sewell, Jesse Parker. 646
Sewell, Lisa. 3783
Sexson, Lynda. 1836
Sexson, W. Mark. 3575
Sexson, William Mark. 3575
Sexton, Ida. 3557
Sexton, Jessie Ethelyn. 1337
Sexton, John E. 2734
Sexton, John Edward. 2734, 3275
Sexton, Mark S. 15, 2687
Sexton, Virgil Wesley. 1063
Sextou gnomai. 1004
Sextus. Pythagoraus. 55
Seybold, Klaus. 1793
Seybold, Theodore C. 879
Seyer, Herman D. 323, 2815
Seyffert, Oskar. 1286
Seymour, Charles. 79, 2716
Seymour, Charles J. 2845, 3514
Seymour, George Franklin. 694

Seymour, Jack L. 940, 942
Seymour, James Cooke. 56
Seymour, Mary Harrison (Browne) 1352, 1441
Seymour, Michael Hobart. 802
Seymour, Mina S. 718, 1283
Seymour, Otto Cleveland. 2934
Seymour, Peter S. 695, 1976
Seymour, Richard A. 68, 3218
Seymour, St. John Drelincourt. 1918, 3783, 3826
Seymour, William Wood. 1388
Seyzinger, Edmund. 3676
Seznec, Jean. 1854, 2657
Sgam-po-pa, 1079-1153. 674
Shack, William A. 1631
Shackelford, John Cockrill. 106
Shackelford, Josephus. 143
Shackford, John Walter. 1252, 3157
Shackleford, John D. 392, 1954
Shacklett, Juanita Purvis. 199
Shacklock, Floyd. 1096, 1745
Shafer, Floyd Doud. 2929, 3854
Shafer, Hazel E. 1452
Shafer, Luman Jay. 2494, 3446
Shafer, Robert. 1306, 3080, 1307, 3081
Shaffer, Albert Monroe. 2201
[Shaffer, Charles Thomas] 1868. 1972
Shaffer, Hiram M. 136
Shaffer, Lucile B. 447
Shaffer, Wilma L. 573, 1452, 3834, 3837, 3843, 3857
Shafran, Avi. 2751
Shaftel, Oscar. 703
Shafto, George Reginald Holt. 2065
Shah, Chimanlal Jaichand. 1933
Shah, Douglas. 3708
Shah, Idries. 2313, 3543, 3544
Shah, Ikbal Ali. 3543
Shah, Ikbel Ali. 2729
Shah, Indries, Sayed. 3543
Shahan, Thomas Joseph. 745, 761, 1194, 2359, 2793
Shahid Bey, Sadik. 2565
Shairp, John Campbell. 1394, 3063
Shakarian, Demos. 3394
Shaked, Haim. 21
Shaker Historical Society. 3397
Shaker Museum, Old Chatham. 3397
Shakers. 1375, 1868, 2205, 2348, 3397, 3398
Shakey, Donald C. 832
Shaku, Soyen. 704, 712
Shalabi, Ibrahim. 669
Shaler, Nathaniel Southgate. 1905, 3076
Shaloff, Stanley. 2536, 2926
Shamblin, J. Kenneth. 2437, 3357
Shamer, Maurice Emory. 2228
Shamir, Yehuda. 2144, 2624
Shamon, Albert J. 74, 3006, 3157, 3489
Shan o yin kuo ching. English & Sogdian. 1812
Shanabruch, Charles. 892, 2475
Shanafelt, Thomas Miles. 169
Shanahan, Louise. 1604
Shands, Alfred Rives. 2234
Shaner, John Junius. 886
Shank, Ezra Abram. 686, 3464
Shank, F O. 464
Shank, Hazel F. 30
Shank, Robert. 1505, 2822
Shank, Robert [Lee]. 2822
Shankel, George Edgar. 1819
Shanklin, Imelda Octavia. 3751
Shankman, Jacob K. 2101, 3599
Shanks, T. J. 2588
Shanley, Walter James. 2262
Shannon, Albert Clement. 2770
Shannon, David T. 536, 995
Shannon, Ellen C. 3639
Shannon, Foster H. 66, 1172, 3735
Shannon, Frederick F. 3345
Shannon, Frederick Franklin. 1071, 3065, 3345, 3357, 3366
Shannon, Harper. 167, 2787
Shannon, Margaret. 1250, 3837
Shannon, Mattie Bayly. 172, 1113, 2757, 3145
Shannon, Richard. 3574
Shannon, Robert. 3182
*Shannon, Robert C. 1052
Shannon, Thomas Anthony. 1143
Shannon, Thomas Washington. 3390
Shannon, William Henry. 664, 763, 1356, 2413
Shapira, Samuel S. 3142
Shapiro, Barbara J. 3085, 3816
Shapiro, David Solomon. 504, 2143
Shaplen, Robert. 184
Shapley, Harlow. 3083
Shapp, Martha. 1615
Sharaf al-Din, 'Abd al-Samad. 742, 1924
Sharda, Sadhu Ram. 3544
Sharf, Andrew. 722, 1477
Sharian, Bedros M. 974, 3401

Shari'ati, 'Ali. 1922, 3454
Sharif, Ja'far. 1925
Sharkey, Donald C. 182, 2262, 2356, 3281, 3460
Sharkey, Mary Agnes. 2400, 3417
Sharkey, Neil. 1773
Sharkey, Owen. 2325
Sharma, Chandradhar. 2840
Sharma, I. C. 877, 3054
Sharma, Ishwar Chandra. 877, 3054
Sharma, Ram Karan. 2316
Sharma, Sri Ram. 2563
Sharman, Henry Burton. 394, 1530, 1993, 2065, 2175
Sharman, John Thomas. 1595
Sharman, Sydney. 2410
Sharon, Douglas. 3400, 3718
Sharot, Stephen. 2149, 2415
Sharp, Alice M. 291
Sharp, Cecil James. 1099, 1169, 1570, 2252
Sharp, Dallas Lore. 1972
Sharp, David G. 1163
Sharp, Dorothea Elizabeth. 2842
Sharp, Frank Chapman. 2592, 1533, 2592
Sharp, Galen. 988
*Sharp, Gladys M. 1452
Sharp, Grace (Hastings) 1325
Sharp, Granville. 425, 2001
Sharp, James Robert. 1861
Sharp, John K. 2905
Sharp, John Kean. 75, 693, 746, 1302, 2905, 3180, 3401
Sharp, Margaret. 3172, 3184, 3857
Sharp, Margaret, comp. 3857
Sharp, Mary. 3283, 3245
Sharp, Roland Hall. 612
Sharp, T. 1822, 3831
Sharp, Watson. 3389
Sharp, Wauban Abram Seward. 154
Sharp, William. 3201
[Sharp, William] 1856-1905. 3095
Sharpe, Alfred B. 2640
Sharpe, Charles Kirkpatrick. 3828
Sharpe, Charles Manford. 278
Sharpe, Dores Robinson. 1134, 3025
Sharpe, Eric J. 3092
Sharpe, William Carvosso. 3394
Sharpe, William Donald. 2784
Sharper, Philip. 1084
Sharpless, Isaac. 1675
Sharrock, David John. 2862
Sharron, Trafford. 2073
*Sharrow, Clarence E. 1727
Sharts, Joseph William. 696
Shatford, Allan Pearson. 974
[Shatford, Sarah Taylor] 2060
Shattock, E. H. 2382
Shaub, Earl L. 550
Shaughnessy, Gerald. 828, 874
Shaver, Edwin Leander. 2946
Shaver, Erwin L. 1497, 2794, 3162, 3176
Shaver, Erwin Leander. 1139, 2204, 2551, 2854, 3157, 3557, 3801, 3859, 3876, 3877
Shaver, John Edward. 2696
*Shaver, Ruth. 2991
Shaw, A[ngus] R[obertson]. 3678
Shaw, Alexander Preston. 2426
Shaw, Avery Albert. 1017, 167
Shaw, Barnabas. 2499
[Shaw, Bradley]. 3514
Shaw, Bynum. 171
Shaw, Charles Gray. 1106, 2228, 3063
Shaw, Daniel Webster. 2460
Shaw, Elton Raymond. 1972
Shaw, Ernest D. 2218
Shaw, George B. 641
[Shaw, George Bernard] 1856. 1052
Shaw, George Bernard. 1071, 1938, 3401
Shaw, Gilbert. 2030
Shaw, Henry B. 1365, 3201
Shaw, Henry K. 1465
Shaw, Horace John. 33, 2209, 3594
Shaw, Irwin. 2764
Shaw, Jacqueline (Meadows) 942
Shaw, James. 3598
Shaw, James Beverly Ford. 2460
Shaw, James Gerard. 2735, 3248
Shaw, Jean. 573, 1015, 1089, 3843
Shaw, John Arthur. 3665
Shaw, John Balcom. 974, 1201, 1697, 2229
Shaw, John K. 3209
Shaw, John MacKay. 1630, 1871
Shaw, Joseph M. 1790, 2161, 2303
Shaw, Leland H. 2175
Shaw, Margaret Rene Bryers. 1391
Shaw, Margaret Renee Bryers. 1391
Shaw, Mark. 2806
Shaw, Moses M. 3876
Shaw, Plato Ernest. 754, 2755, 2956, 754
Shaw, Richard. 667, 1851
Shaw, Robert. 1382, 3076, 3808
Shaw, Roud. 1063, 1466
Shaw, Russell B. 832, 1536

Shaw, Solomon Benjamin. 2880, 3229, 3233
Shaw, Thomas. 1620
Shaw, Wayne. 1154
Shaw, William. 3737
Shaw, William Arthur. 1219
Shaw, William Hudson. 1307
Shawchuck, Norman. 1244
Shayler, Ernest Vincent. 974
Shcherbatskoi, Fedor Ippolitovich. 703, 2711
Shchutsii, IUlian Konstantinovich. 1879
Shea, Daniel B. 3739
Shea, George. 3317
Shea, John. 2044, 3534
Shea, John Dawson Gilmary. 667, 742, 765, 833, 834, 1901, 3282, 3283
Sheahan, Joseph F. 656
Shealy, Julian B. 97
Shealy, Julian Belton. 236
Sheard, Charles. 3134
Sheardown, Thomas Simpson. 3134
Shearer, James William. 383
Shearer, John. 2676
Shearer, John Bunyan. 2640, 3336
Shearer, L. L. 278
Shearer, Roy E. 2954
Shearer, Tony. 1898
Sheares, Reuben A. 2681
Shearme, John. 1215
Sheatsley, Clarence Valentine, 1873. 1548
Shebbeare, Charles John. 3594, 2982, 3594, 3652
Shedd, Arthur B. 3054
Shedd, Charlie W. 641, 1239, 1942, 2396, 2880, 3530
Shedd, Clarence Prouty. 1256, 3537
Shedd, Mary Lewis. 2544, 3401
Shedd, Russell Philip. 373
Shedd, William Ambrose. 2567
Shedd, William G[reenough] T[hayer]. 934
Shedd, William Greenough Thayer. 2905, 2913, 2923, 2934, 3357, 3648, 3652, 3655
Sheddan, Samuel S. 1352
Shedlock, Marie L. 703
Sheed, Francis Joseph. 115, 525, 777, 791, 797, 811, 820, 871, 1001, 1025, 1087, 1320, 1429, 1697, 1793, 1972, 2044, 2228, 2248, 2325, 3282, 3401, 3449, 3634, 3648, 3795
Sheed, Wilfrid. 2132
Sheeder, Franklin I. 3326
Sheedy, Charles Edmund. 2257, 3782
Sheedy, Frank. 794
Sheedy, Morgan M. 1042
Sheehan, Arthur T. 1400, 2198, 2374
Sheehan, Edmund W. 2220
Sheehan, Elizabeth Odell. 2124, 2685
Sheehan, John F. X. 502, 2269, 3476
Sheehan, Patrick Augustine. 865, 3201
Sheehy, John F. 2858
Sheehy, Maurice Stephen. 806, 1001, 1299
Sheeleigh, Matthias. 2277
Sheen, Fulton J. 668, 2265, 2396, 3401
Sheen, Fulton John. 1001, 1972, 66, 181, 384, 668, 737, 757, 761, 763, 793, 797, 865, 929, 930, 949, 974, 1001, 1002, 1021, 1063, 1136, 1452, 1727, 1818, 1972, 1983, 1998, 2020, 2030, 2058, 2228, 2265, 2356, 2396, 2555, 2843, 2939, 3073, 3089, 3104, 3105, 3111, 3212, 3266, 3401, 3412, 3456, 3526, 3594, 3746, 3792, 3793, 3794
Sheen, Harold Edwin. 367
Sheerin, James. 2865
Sheerin, John B. 717, 1044, 1327, 3794
Sheerin, Maria Ward Skelton (Williams) 2339
Sheets, Herchel H. 1986, 2014, 2215, 2437, 3357
Sheets, John R. 3030
Sheets, William B. 3616
Sheetz, Ann Kindig. 932, 3401
Sheetz, Paul H. 988
Sheffield, Eng. University. Institute of Education. 3165
Shehadi, Beshara. 2847
Sheikh, Bilquis. 3402
Sheil, Leonard. 445
Sheil, Michael Timothy. 1890
Sheiner, Ben. 2640
Shek, Kai-nung. 1958
Shelby, Donald J. 2212
Sheldon, Charles Monroe. 623, 657, 2065, 3402, 3434, 3452
Sheldon, David Newton. 3414
Sheldon, Dorothy. 901
Sheldon, Frank M. 312
Sheldon, Frank Milton. 236
Sheldon, Henry Clay. 1052, 1513, 477, 1035, 1179, 1656, 2605, 2636, 2834, 2940, 3320, 3648, 3655, 3687, 3799
Sheldon, Jean. 3383, 3829
Sheldon, Lucy. 3402

Sheldon, Robert Lewis. 2537
Sheldon, Walter Lorenzo. 292, 623, 1540
Sheldon, William. 2657
[Sheldon, William] d. 1871. 3402
Sheldon, William Herbert. 3000
Sheldon, Wilmon Henry. 1597
Shelford, Melvia Thomas. 420
Shelford, Paul K. 1912
Shelhamer, E. E. 1452
Shelhamer, Mary Theresa. 3514
Shelhart, Dwight H. 2528
Shelley, Bruce L. 1189
Shelley, Bruce Lear. 1123
Shelley, Bruce Leon. 118, 994, 1348, 1552, 2350, 2669, 2846
Shelley, Percy Bysshe. 1656
Shelly, Judith Allen. 649, 988
Shelnutt, James Bunkett. 3291, 974, 3291
Shelter, Sanford Grant. 2403
Shelton, Albert Leroy. 2555
Shelton, Barbara. 36, 3402
Shelton, Don Odell. 975, 3459, 2558
Shelton, Flora Beal. 2555, 3402
Shelton, Harriet M. 3514
Shelton, Herbert McGolphin. 3690
Shelton, Lois. 2546
Shelton, Orman Leroy. 1252
Shenk, David W. 2163, 2553
Shenk, Wilbert R. 2404
Shenkel, James Donald. 556
Shenstone, N. A. 184
Shepard, Clara. 1038
Shepard, F. S. 1206
Shepard, Isaac Fitzgerald. 3209
Shepard, James. 2686, 2963
Shepard, John Watson. 372, 1972, 2802
Shepard, Judy. 2763
Shepard, Leslie. 2729
[Shepard, Morgan] 1865. 2894
Shepard, Odell. 23
Shepard, Royal F. 2396
Shepard, Sheldon. 3063
Shepard, Thomas. 748, 1334, 3008, 3201
Shepard, Thomas Griffin. 3336
Shepard, Walter D. 2496
Shepard, William Edward. 2815, 3412, 3422
Shepardson, Daniel. 405, 1560, 3542
Shepardson, George Defrees. 3063
Shepfer, Harold Reed. 1693
Shepfer, William Henry. 205
Shepheard, Harold B. 3072
Shepheard, Harold Beaumont. 1727
Shepherd, Banks D. 2688
Shepherd, Cecil William. 2244
Shepherd, Charles Reginald. 1116
Shepherd, Coulson. 3721
Shepherd, J. Barrie. 2027, 2894
Shepherd, James Walton. 1123
Shepherd, John J. 3609
Shepherd, Margaret Lisle. 1357
Shepherd, Massey Hamilton. 1486, 2233, 584, 2234, 2235, 2238, 2255, 2256, 2259, 2961, 2969
Shepherd, Massey Hamilton, 1918. 2969
Shepherd, Richard Herne. 1307
Shepherd, Robert Perry. 3120, 3557
Shepherd, S. 1022
Shepherd, Silas H. 1662
Shepherd, William C. 2675, 3243
Shepley, David. 1342, 2810
Sheppard, Gerald T. 489, 3821
Sheppard, Hugh Richard Lawrie. 2030, 1071, 3402, 3634
Sheppard, John Augustine. 3358
Sheppard, Lancelot Capel, 1906. 683, 840, 844, 952, 2190, 2234, 2238, 2239, 2257, 2334, 3492, 3784
Sheppard, Roscoe Burton. 1923
Sheppard, William Henry. 2514
Sheppard, William John Limmer. 1868, 3320
Shepperson, Archibald Bolling, 1897. 2937
Shepperson, Mary Fides. 1643
Sheran, William Henry. 1518
Sheraton, William M. 3402
Sherburne, N. Y. Christ Episcopal Church. 2700
Sherer, Michael L. 909
Shergold, William J. 224
Sheridan, Alma Stanley. 3157
Sheridan, Doris. 3691
Sheridan, Earll Cooley. 1730
Sheridan, Harold James. 3157, 3176, 3565
Sheridan, Jo. 1470
Sheridan, John Desmond. 763
Sheridan, John V. 791, 1025, 3012
Sheridan, Michael P. 870, 3772
Sheridan, Ronald. 3316
Sheridan, T. J. 763
Sheridan, Thomas L. 2161, 2704
Sheridan, Wilbur Fletcher. 1525, 1570, 2422
Sheridan, William. 3335
Sherif, Mohamed Ahmed. 21, 3782
Sheriff, John K. 1517
Sherin, Henry. 3291

Sherington, Nick. 38, 3532
Sherlock, Richard. 1442
Sherlock, Thomas. 608, 1420, 2053
Sherlock, William. 1415, 2156, 2982
*Sherman, Alva W. 3226
Sherman, Cecil E. 3358
Sherman, Charles Fayerweather, 1872. 1667
Sherman, David. 1294
Sherman, Eleazer. 3135
Sherman, Franklin. 3, 1138, 1809
Sherman, Franklyn Cole. 1452
Sherman, Harold Morrow. 1283, 1600, 2696, 2880, 3514
Sherman, Homer Henkel. 3157
Sherman, James Edward. 2351, 3694
Sherman, John. 3713
Sherman, Josiah Patterson. 3597
Sherman, Lois. 3514
Sherman, Loren Albert. 3514
Sherman, M. L. 3514
Sherman, Thomas Ewing. 782
Shero, William Francis. 1100
Sheron, Carole. 35, 3403
Sherrard, Philip. 102, 3307
Sherrick, Marvin Manam. 3345, 3375
Sherrill, Henry Knox. 1063, 2202
Sherrill, John L. 2814, 3403, 3604
Sherrill, Lewis Joseph. 895, 975, 1610, 2923, 2929, 3030, 3157, 3165, 3169, 3172
Sherrod, Jennie R. 1581
Sherrod, Paul. 1570
Sherry, Patrick. 3105, 3830
Sherwick, Winston M. 3181
Sherwin, Byron L. 1809, 2137, 3016
Sherwin, Oscar. 3804
Sherwin-White, Adrian Nicholas. 408
[Sherwood, Alexander]. 884
Sherwood, Bill. 3403
Sherwood, Elisha Barber. 2775
Sherwood, Fred C. 460
Sherwood, Grace (Hausmann) 2135, 2720
Sherwood, James Manning. 107, 2921
Sherwood, Jane. 3514
Sherwood, John C. 3331
Sherwood, John R. 3734
[Sherwood, Julia L.] 3403
Sherwood, Mary Martha (Butt) 911, 1215, 3403
Sherwood, Polycarp. 1042
Sherwood, Samuel. 3742
Shestov, Lev. 2843, 3105
Shetler, Samuel Grant. 2720
Shetler, Sanford Grant. 2404, 3403
Shetter, Claire b. 2819
Shevchuk, Tetiana. 3482
Shevill, Ian W. A. 1211
Sheville, John. 1672
Shewmaker, William Orpheus. 2626
Shibayama, Zenkei. 1853, 2182, 3892
Shibles, Warren A. 1415
Shibley, David. 1606, 2815
Shideler, Emerson W. 3083, 3314
Shideler, Mary (McDermott) 74, 1348
Shiel, James. 1082
Shield, Frederic K. 3307
Shields, Charles Woodruff. 61, 3073
Shields, Currin V. 1151
Shields, Elizabeth McEwan. 3157
Shields, Elizabeth McEwen. 623, 901, 3072, 3157, 3174, 3764
Shields, Emily Ledyard. 2159, 3246
Shields, James Kurtz. 3804
Shields, Ried Frampton. 2552
Shiells, Robert. 3703
Shiels, William Eugene. 1948, 3587, 1898, 2794, 3587
*Shifflet, Anne. 916
Shifflett, Alvin. 413
Shilling, Henry. 3709
Shillito, Edward. 313, 1326, 1727, 2494, 2521, 2856, 3751
Shillong, Eric W. 3537
Shiloh, Ailon. 1093, 2050, 3476
Shil-Ponde. 98
Shilstone, Eustace M. 2098
Shilton, Lance R. 3362
Shim, Steve S. 1255
Shimer, William Allison. 3105
Shindler, Mary Dana. 3514
Shindler, Mary Stanley Bunce (Palmer) Dana. 3713
Shindler, Robert. 3523
Shine, Hill. 740
Shinedling, Abraham Isaac. 2098
Shiner, Larry E. 1744, 3657
Shinn, Asa. 3291, 3616
Shinn, Everett. 399, 1996
Shinn, George Wolfe. 2212, 1275
Shinn, Larry D. 3064
Shinn, Roger Lincoln. 1584, 1727, 1818, 2212, 2325, 3157, 3336, 3732, 3794
Shipler, Guy Emery. 3358
Shipley, David O. 1131
Shipley, Maynard. 236, 1582
Shipley, Orby. 2362

Shipman, Jacob S. 3345
Shipman, Raymond M. 2787
Shipman, William Henry. 2449
Shipp, Albert Micajah. 2432, 2453
Shipp, Nelson McLester. 3000
[Shippen, Edward] b. 1820? 3514
[Shippen, Rush Rhees]. 1442
Shippey, Frederick Alexander. 1279, 2440, 3538
Shippey, Josiah. 3207
Shipps, Howard Fenimore. 89
Shipton, Anna. 1452, 1749
Shirah, A. Jason. 909
Shiras, Alexander. 2375
Shires, Henry M. 377, 451
Shirk, Christian Horning. 1052
Shirkey, Albert P. 588, 2248
Shirley, Alfred. 2743
Shirley, Ralph. 94
Shirley, Walter Waddington. 1194
Shissler, Barbara Johnson. 85, 450
Shlemon, Barbara Leahy. 1600
[Shober, Gottlieb] 1756-1838. 2277, 3036
Shoberl, Frederic. 2526
Shockley, Donald G. 1133
Shockley, Norman. 2396, 3404
Shoemaker, Alfred Lewis, 1913. 1486
Shoemaker, Helen Smith. 992, 2880, 2885
Shoemaker, Joseph Shellenberger. 1838
Shoemaker, Robert W., 1924. 2971
Shoemaker, Samuel Moor. 1570, 975, 1087, 1123, 1296, 1360, 1570, 1998, 2058, 2474, 2697, 2973, 3358, 3482, 3674, 992
Shoghi. 125, 128, 129, 130
Shoghi, effendi. 125, 129
Shogi. 129
Shohet, David Menahem. 1375, 2092, 3583
Sholes, Jerry. 3241
Sholl, Anna McClure. 1733
Shonkweiler, James Harvey. 1972
Shook, Charles Augustus. 642, 679, 2605
Shook, Glenn Alfred. 2642
Shook, Laurence K. 870
Shook, William Roen. 224
Shorb, Wil. 2396
Shores, Robert James. 1742
Shorr, Dorothy C. 1958
Shorrosh, Anis. 608
Short, Ernest Henry. 1160
Short, Howard Elmo. 1042
Short, John. 3731
Short, Mark. 994
Short, Robert L. 512, 2060, 3618, 3787
Short, Roy Hunter. 1007, 1249, 1570, 2431, 3734
Short, Ruth Gordon. 926, 1575, 2277, 3039, 3041, 3804, 3813
Short, Thales. 1711
Short, Wallace Mertin. 2474
Short, William. 1035
Shorter, Alan Wynn. 1502
Shorter, Aylward. 12, 13, 1073, 2555
Shortess, John David. 1546
Shortland, Edward. 2332
Shosteck, Robert. 2105, 2106
Shostrom, Everett L. 988
Shotwell, B. M. 312
Shotwell, Forrest L. 1514
Shotwell, James Thompson. 2770
Shotwell, James Thomson. 3120, 2770, 2825
Shotwell, Thomas L. 1675
Shoup, Carl Sumner. 281
Shoup, William J. 1017
Shove, H. P. 253
Showalter, Anthony J. 3563
Showalter, Carol. 2937, 3404
Showalter, George Henry Pryor. 123, 1272
Showalter, J. Henry. 3557, 3754
Showalter, Lewis Pendelton. 3055
Showerman, Grant. 1398
Showers, Paul. 1902
Showers, Renald E. 297, 1819
Shpall, Leo. 2100
Shrader, Wesley. 67, 1289, 2781, 3674
Shrady, M. L. 1111
Shrake, Henry L. 1092
Shreve, Susan Richards. 3253
Shrigley, Eugene Wilford. 3446
Shrigley, George Andrew Cleveland. 2807, 2894, 3794
Shrigley, Homer Theodore. 3142
Shriver, Donald W. 1076, 1132, 3166
Shriver, George H. 1804
Shriver, Peggy L. 1087
Shriver, William Payne. 2528, 2936
Shropshire, Denys William Tinniswood. 133, 3110
Shroyer, Montgomery J. 386, 362, 3665
Shryock, John Knight. 913, 1331, 3064
Shub, Louis. 3403
Shuckburgh, Evelyn Shirley. 183
Shuey, E[dwin] L[ongstreet]. 3730
Shuey, Edwin Longstreet. 2189

Shuffelton, Frank. 1345, 1845
Shuhler, Ralph Vincent. 1327
Shukri, Ahmed. 2345
Shuler, John Lewis. 1013, 1531, 1570, 1972, 2055, 2156, 2161, 2396, 3261, 3291, 3295, 3320, 3383, 3387, 3792
Shuler, Philip L. 392
Shuler, Robert Pierce. 2427, 2437
Shulhan'arukh. 2086
Shull, William Russell, 1899. 975
Shulman, Albert M. 2094, 2154, 3327
Shulman, David. 1392
Shulman, David Dean. 3422
Shulsky, Shelomoh. 905
Shultenover, David G. 2562, 3721
Shultz, James Earl. 2887
Shultz, Joseph R. 2252
Shultz, Lawrence W. 731, 3311
Shultze, David. 3135
Shumaker, Elmer Ellsworth. 2982
Shumaker, Norbert Matthias. 895
Shumaker, Wayne. 2732
Shumate, Aurora (Medford) 3765
Shumway, Harry Irving. 122
Shupe, Anson D. 1394
Shurden, Walter B. 148, 171, 3465, 3467
Shurlock, Aileen Brittain. 1331, 3682
Shurtleff, Alfred Dewey Keegan. 975
Shuster, George. 15
Shuster, George Nauman. 828, 755, 828, 832, 868, 1151, 1320, 1542, 1708
Shuster, Ruth W. 689
Shute, Abraham Lincoln. 1727
Shute, Daniel. 1504
Shute, John Raymond. 1656, 1663, 2221, 3729
Shute, R Wayne. 1009
Shute, William George. 536
Shutter, Marion Daniel. 3080, 3719
Shuttleworth, Philip Nicholas. 278
Shwayder, D. S. 3755
Sibbes, Richard. 1227
Sibley, Celestine. 2396
Sibley, Frank James. 1913
Sibley, Josiah. 2934
Sibley, Julian Scales. 1954, 3226
Sibley, Mulford Quickert. 1697
Sibree, James. 751
Sibthorp, Richard Waldo. 792, 2766
Sibum, L. 2229
Sica, Joseph F. 3019, 3227
Sicard, Augustin. 2368, 840
Sicardo, Jose. 3238
Sickels, Daniel Edgar. 2701
Sickels, Frank E. 3874
Sickle, Sal. 1727
Sickles, Daniel Edgar. 2701
Siddhanta. Selection. English. 1933
Siddhantashastree, Rabindra Kumar. 3421
Siddharta. Selections. English. 1932
Siddons, Philip. 3832
Sider, Ronald J. 247, 1856, 2065, 3780
Siderman, Edward A. 2310
Sides, Dorothy (Smith) 2506
Sidgwick, Henry. 1536
Sidhanta, Nirmal Kumar. 3302
Siebenmann, Paul J. 3208
Siebert, Paul. 332
Siegart, William Raymond. 1352, 3370
Siegel, Abraham M. 594
Siegel, Jonathan Paul. 565, 3711
Siegel, Martin. 3016
Siegel, Meyer D. 3068
Siegel, Richard. 2081, 2120
Siegel, Seymour. 2086
Siegel, William J. 2215
Siegle, Bernard Andrew. 2342
Siegling, Dorothy L. 1304
Siegman, Edward Ferdinand. 2015
Siegmund, Georg. 101, 1081, 2986
[Sieker, Adolphus Theodore] 1872. 642
Siekmann, T. C. 3095
Siekmann, Theodore C. 688, 1529, 3889
Siekmann, Thodore C. 3889
Siemens, David F. 3012
Siemon, Fred. 1709
Sienkiewicz, Henryk. 2857
Sierksma, Fokke. 3699
Sigal, Gerald. 236, 1092
Sigal, Phillip. 2075
Siggins, Ian D. Kingston. 2277, 2279
Sigismund. 3524
Sigismund, Brother. 3524
Sigler, Pearl Nixon. 2763
Sigmon, Charles Alexander. 155
Sigmund, Paul E. 1322, 2708
Signs of the times. 3380
[Sigourney, Lydia Howard (Huntley) 1791-1865. 1630
Sigstedt, Cyriel Sigrid (Ljungberg Odhner) 623, 3570
Sigstedt, Sigrid (Ljungberg Odhner) 624
Sigston, James. 690
Sigsworth, John Wilkins, 1915. 3785
Sih, Paul Kwang Tsien. 1365
Siirala, Aarne. 2279, 2325, 2377, 2378
Sikes, J. R. 3597

Sikes, Jeffrey Garrett. 1
Sikes, Stutely David. 1576, 3345
Sikes, Walter W. 2170
Sikes, William Marion. 392
Sikking, Robert P. 1415, 3750
Sikking, Sue. 975, 1452, 2396, 3750
Sikora, Joseph John. 2739, 3786
Sikorsky, Igor Ivan. 2248, 3482
Silber, Abba Hillel. 2140
Silber, Mendel. 616, 1506, 673
Silberg, Moshe. 2074
Silberger, Julius. 1038, 1495
Silberman, Lou H. 3032, 3050
Silberstein, Solomon Joseph. 2116, 2739
Silcock, Thomas Henry. 1536, 1682
Silcox, Clarice Edwin. 3731, 3746
Silcox, Claris Edwin. 874
Siligardakis, Titus. 3267
Silkwood, Barzillia. 975
Sill, Gertrude Grace. 922
Sill, Louise Morgan (Smith) 1983
Sill, Sterling W. 1009, 1114, 1233, 2396, 2600, 2608, 2617, 2619, 3358, 3408, 3539, 3748
Sillar, Frederick Cameron. 2232
Sillem, Edward Augustus. 192, 1738
Silliman, Charles A. 918
Sills, Finous Hall. 871
Sills, Horace S. 1045
Silsbee, Fred B. 815
Silva, Antone R. Emanuel. 508
Silva, Theodore Joseph. 514
Silvan, Matteo. 875, 3409
Silver, Abba Hillel. 564, 2079, 2140, 2414, 3064, 2145
Silver, Abiel. 1089
Silver, Benno. 2079, 2807
Silver, Daniel Jeremy. 564, 1539, 2143, 2622, 3409
Silver, James Wesley. 1326
Silver, Jesse Forest. 3320
[Silver, Joseph S.]. 1746
Silver, Maxwell. 1539, 2117
Silver, Samuel M. 691, 2140, 2152, 2345, 3014
Silver Spring, Cumberland Co., Pa. Presbyterian church. 2918
Silverman, Althea Osber. 2208, 2951
Silverman, Hillel E. 565, 3361
Silverman, William B. 1539, 2151, 3032, 3064, 3581
Silverstein, Abraham. 1360
Silverstein, Baruch. 3371
Silverstone, Harry. 2082, 3584, 570, 1623
Silverthorne, Elizabeth. 1804
Silvester, Hugh. 1746
Silvey, D. O. 1123, 3557
Simcox, Carroll Eugene. 44, 441, 449, 992, 1314, 1529, 2396, 2959, 2961, 3111, 3264
Simeon, Charles. 3345, 3409
Simhoni, S. 905
Simkhovitch, Vladimir Grigorievitch. 2016
Simma, Maria. 3006, 3409
Simmel, Ernst. 2079
Simmel, Georg. 3064, 3087
Simmonds, A. J. 2616
Simmonds, Shade. 1179
Simmonite, William Joseph. 97
Simmons, Almo Beals. 2111
Simmons, Billy. 413, 994, 3358
Simmons, Billy E. 2020
Simmons, Charles. 303
Simmons, Charles, d. 304
Simmons, Daniel A. 3313
Simmons, Ernest. 792, 1472
Simmons, Ernest Lesley. 1229
Simmons, George Frederick. 3345
Simmons, Henry C. 1689, 3541
Simmons, Henry Martyn. 1382, 3065
Simmons, James P. 3463
Simmons, James W. 2396
Simmons, Joe. 3482
Simmons, John Walter. 3080
Simmons, Marc. 3828
Simmons, Patricia A. 688, 1714, 3845
Simmons, Robert A. 1123
Simmons, Thomas Paul. 3648
Simmons, William James. 3358
Simms, George Otto. 2880
Simms, James Meriles. 3305
Simms, Joseph D. 2455, 3818
Simms, Norman Toby. 1518
Simms, Paris Marion. 291, 655, 2977
Simms, Ruthanna M. 1677, 1901
Simms, William Gilmore. 2109
Simocatta, Theophylactus. 2912
Simon, Alphonse. 1327
Simon, Ann. 1456
Simon, Charlie May (Hogue) 699, 1114, 2162, 3312
Simon, Edith. 2277, 3036, 3282, 3598
Simon, Erika. 1623
Simon, Gerhard. 1148
Simon, Henry William. 742
Simon, Jean Marie. 2529
Simon, John. 1588

Simon, John Mary. 312
Simon, Leon. 2112, 2842
Simon, M Raphael. 1365
Simon, Marcel. 3527, 2080
Simon, Martin P. 653
Simon, Martin Paul William. 624, 1606, 2561
Simon, Maurice. 2140
Simon, Norma. 905, 1784, 2779, 3006, 3249, 3409, 3545, 3867
[Simon, Otto Torney] 1860. 3514
Simon, Paul. 757
Simon, Raphael M. 1365
Simon, Raphael, Secular name: Kenneth Simon. 3489
Simon, Sidney B. 3881
Simon, Solomon. 2103
Simon, Ulrich E. 211, 1794, 3610
Simon, Walter G. 1213
Simon, William Glyn Hughes. 323
Simon, Yves. 2858
Simonde de Sismondi, Jean Charles Leonard, 1773-1842. 22, 23
[Simonds, William] 1822-1859. 3412
Simonds, William Day. 1954
Simoneaux, Henry J. 3475
Simonet, Andre. 773, 2494
Simonhoff, Harry. 2085, 2105
Simons, B. B. 67
Simons, Ezra DeFreest. 464
Simons, Francis. 835
Simons, G. L. 3824
Simons, George E. 1670
Simons, George F. 3482
Simons, George T. 1253
Simons, Joseph B. 3223
Simons, Minot. 3609
Simonsen, Severin E. 1035
Simonson, Conrad. 1727
Simonson, Harold Peter. 1499, 3091
Simonson, Ted. 102
Simonsson, Bengt K D. 119
Simpson, Alan. 3008
Simpson, Albert B. 456, 1388, 2055, 2668, 3410, 975, 1600, 3296, 3410
Simpson, Albert Benjamin. 224, 1442, 1560, 1600, 1824, 2020, 2410, 2494, 2546
Simpson, Albert Edward. 1219
Simpson, Alyse. 2581
Simpson, Bertram Fitzgerald. 2248
Simpson, Cuthbert Aikman. 599, 2151
Simpson, David. 59, 2759
Simpson, David Capell. 564, 578
Simpson, E. P. 1892
Simpson, Edmund Kidley. 364
Simpson, Ervin Peter Young. 1241
Simpson, George. 3313
Simpson, George Eaton. 669, 3400, 3711
Simpson, Hubert Louis. 1071, 2058, 2884, 3366, 3376
Simpson, James Beasley. 43, 2194, 3021
Simpson, James Young. 2320, 2675, 3080, 3085
Simpson, John Ernest. 1168, 1727, 3530, 3531
Simpson, John Francis Minor. 2918
Simpson, John Thomas. 3410
Simpson, John Wells. 1772
Simpson, Matthew. 2421, 2426, 2428, 2905
Simpson, Michael. 1529
Simpson, Michael A. 1416
Simpson, Oscar Livingstone. 1154
Simpson, Patrick Carnegie. 1063, 1123, 1595, 2001
Simpson, Robert. 1375
Simpson, Robert L. 1009, 1198, 1516, 2885, 3624
Simpson, Smauel. 3900
Simpson, Thomas Jefferson. 3073
Simpson, William. 552, 3810
Simpson, William Douglas. 919, 1311
Simpson, William Gayley. 3521
Simpson, William John Sparrow. 111, 2053, 3628, 115, 683, 690, 1211, 1219, 1230, 2044, 2053, 3030, 3221, 3226, 3410, 3804, 2053, 3221
Simpson, William Wynn. 2109, 2120, 2886
Sims, Albert E. 217
Sims, Bennett B. 1330, 2196, 2832
Sims, Charles N. 1496
Sims, Edward R. 437, 2212
Sims, Henry Upson. 1868
Sims, James H. 299, 300, 2335, 2472
Sims, Lydel. 2428
Sims, Mary Sophia Stephens. 3878
Sims, Mary Sophia Stevens. 3878
Sims, Thomas. 1247
Sims, W Hines. 1203
Sims, Walter Hines. 153, 1208
Simson, Eve. 1600
Simson, Otto Georg von. 750, 889, 1161
Simundson, Daniel J. 3541
Sinclair, Caroline Baytop. 3
Sinclair, Donna. 1303

Sinclair, George. 3568
Sinclair, Hannah. 1052
Sinclair, John H. 2954
Sinclair, Keith Val. 859, 1455
Sinclair, Max. 928, 3414
Sinclair, Ronald Sutherland Brook. 1211, 2880
Sinclair, Upton Beall. 1071, 1092, 1727, 1972, 2228, 1092
Sine, Tom. 988
Singenberger, John B. 884, 1877
Singenberger, John Baptist. 885, 1204, 885
Singer, Anna M. 3025, 3446
Singer, Arnold. 2096
Singer, Charles Gregg. 2670, 3746
Singer, Charles Joseph. 3073
Singer, Howard. 2140
Singer, Ignatius. 1595
Singer, Irving. 2263, 3302
Singer, Isaac Bashevis. 5, 1507, 2261
Singer, Isidore. 2079, 2178, 2116
Singer, J. W. 3524
Singer, Joseph I. 1623, 3371
Singer, Milton B. 2186
Singer, Richard E. 550, 3439
Singerman, Robert. 480, 2668
Singh, Harbans. 3408
Singh, Iqbal. 1918
Singh, Ram Bhushan Prasad. 1933
Singh, Sundar. 975, 1697, 2640
Singh, Surjit. 1320, 2044, 3018
Singleton, Esther. 750, 751
Singleton, George A. 14, 3135
Singleton, Gregory H. 2260
Singleton, Janice. 2528
Singmaster, Elsie. 2277, 2296
Singmaster, John Alden. 3648
Sinha, Jadunath. 879, 2840, 3766, 3775, 3779
Sinha, Raghuvir. 1897
Siniscalchi, Liborio. 2270
Sinishta, Gjon. 2820
Sinistrari, Luigi Maria. 1423
Sink, Mary Izetti. 975
Sinkie, Otto A. 28
Sinkler, Lorraine. 1744, 2696, 3482
Sinks, Perry Wayland. 36, 236, 3541
Sinnett, Alfred Percy. 703, 2733, 3602, 3687
Sinnett, Patience Edensor, A. P. Sinnett," 3687
Sinnot, Edmund Ware. 662
Sinnott, Alfred Arthur. 1826
Sinnott, Edmund Ware. 662, 1271, 3080
Sipe, Onjya. 1360, 3415
[Sipple, Simon,] 1875. 26
Siraj ul-Din, Abu Bakr. 3543
Sircar, Dineshchandra. 1895
Sire, James W. 288, 547, 1393, 1882, 3665
Siregar, Susan Rodgers. 178
Sirrell, Lawrence N. 3211
Sisco, L Vernon. 1554
Sisemore, John T. 3161, 3169, 3180, 3550, 3783
Sisk, John P. 1911
Sisler, M. David. 2059
Sisson, Charles Jasper. 1844
Sisson, Edward Octavius. 2592
Sisson, Elizabeth. 3221
Sisson, Richard. 1570
Sissons, Nicola Ann. 2663
Sister Formation Conferences. 2573, 2574, 3196
[Sister of Charity of the Blessed Virgin Mary, Chicago]. 656
A Sister of St. Joseph. 3419
Sisterhood of St Mary. 2968
Sisterhood of the holy nativity. 3416
Sisters' Conference on Spirituality, University of Portland. 2574
Sisters' Conference on Spirituality, University of Portland, 1964. 2574
Sisters' Conference on Spirituality, University of Portland. 6th 1965. 2571, 3772
Sisters Marianites of Holy Cross. Louisiana Province. 3416
Sisters of charity of Nazareth, Nazareth, Ky. 859, 3416
Sisters of Charity of Saint Elizabeth, Convent Station, N.J. 33, 771, 846, 1264
Sisters of Charity of St. Vincent de Paul of New York. 1264
Sisters of charity of the Blessed Virgin Mary, Dubuque, Ia. 3417
Sisters of Christian charity. U.S. 2319
Sisters of mercy, Chicago. 3418
Sisters of mercy. Limerick, Ire. 218
Sisters of mercy, Pittsburgh. 3418
Sisters of Norte Dame, Cincinnati. 1861
Sisters of Notre Dame. Cincinnati. 855
Sisters of Notre Dame, Cleveland. 840, 2259

Sisters of Notre Dame de Namur. 834, 1185
Sisters of Reparation of the Congregation of Mary. 2363
Sisters of Saint Joseph. 3419
Sisters of St. Joseph, Brentwood, N.Y. 859
Sisters of Saint Joseph, Chestnut Hill, Philadelphia. 3177
Sisters of Saint Joseph, Detroit. 813
Sisters of Saint Joseph of Carondelet. 2132
Sisters of Saints Cyril and Methodius. 3416
Sisters of the blessed sacrament for Indians and colored people. 824
Sisters of the divine Savior. 1179
Sisters of the holy cross. 3420
Sisters of the Holy Names of Jesus and Mary. Province of Oregon. 670, 824
Sisters of the Order of St. Dominic. 843, 1264, 3248
Sisters of the Order of St. Dominic, Great Bend, Kan. 3248
Sisters of the Order of St. Dominic, Marywood, Grand Rapids. 806
Sisters of the Order of St. Dominic, Racine, Wis. 843
Sisters of the Order of St. Dominic, San Rafael, Calif. 1475
Sisters of the Presentation of the Blessed Virgin Mary, Fitchburgh, Mass. 3421
Sisters of the Third Franciscan order, minor conventuals, Syracuse, N.Y. 859
Sisters of the Third Order of St. Francis of Assisi. 3111
Sisters of the Third order of St. Francis of Mary immaculate, Joliet, Ill. 859
Sisters of the Third Order of St. Francis of the perpetual adoration. 813
Sisters of the Third order regular of St. Francis, Oldenburg, Ind. 3416
Sisters of the Visitation. Baltimore. 3421
Sisters of the visitation, Chambery, France. 881
Sisters of the visitation, Harrow-on-the-Hill. 691
Sisters of the visitation of Holy Mary, Brooklyn, N.Y. 886, 3421
Sisters of the visitation, Wilmington, Del. 1397
Sisters, servants of the immaculate heart of Mary. 2368
Sisters, servants of the immaculate heart of Mary. 3421
Sit, Amy Wang. 3831
Sit, Hong. 988
Sitchin, Zecharia. 1890
Sites, Evelyn Worthley. 2511
Sites, Sarah (Moore) 2511, 3421
Sitskin, Leon. 3371
Sitterly, Charles Fremont. 321
Sittler, Joseph. 278, 1752, 2285, 2905, 2908, 3634, 3758
Sitwell, Gerard. 1455
Sitwell, Sacheverell. 2569, 1710, 2569
Siu, Ralph Gun Hoy. 1879, 2839, 3586
Sivan, Gabriel. 538
Sivananda. 3867
Sivananda Radha, 1911. 1778, 2188, 2329, 2396
Sivananda, Sri Swami. 3867
Sivarahasya. English. Selections. 3139
Sivaram, Mysore. 3301, 3492
Sivaraman, K. 3422
Sivasamhita. English and Sanskrit. 3867
Sivric, Ivo. 3536
Siwek, Paul. 1746, 2685, 3054, 3532
Siwel, Hplour. 3295
Siwik, Marian. 855
Six, Jean Francois. 1636
Sizer, Sandra S. 3231
Sizoo, Joseph Richard. 278, 975, 1452, 2906, 2934, 3120, 3456
Sjodahl, Janne Mattson. 679
Sjogren, Per-Olof. 2072
Skagen, Edward M[atheson]. 1047
Skaggs, Fred R. 381, 988, 3422
Skard, Bjarne. 1893
Skardon, Alvin Wilson. 2630
Skarga, Piotr. 2255
Skarin, Annalee. 2696
Skattebol, Olaf. 1295, 3422
Skeath, William Charles. 2023, 2058, 2252, 2421
Skeele, Amos. 3358
Skeet, George William. 3164
Skehan, Patrick William. 578, 3821
Skei, Allen B. 3311
Skeireins. 417
Skelly, Andrew M. 3144, 3263, 3345
Skelly, Andrew Maria. 865, 1999, 3223, 3489
Skelton, Eugene. 2951, 3565
Skelton, Frederic. 2880
Skelton, Robert. 2328, 3789
Skene, George. 2887

Skibbe, Eugene M. 2253
Skidmore, Shirley T. 2372
Skidmore, Sydney Tuthill. 3096
Skillen, James W. 1087
Skillin, Joseph H. 2370
Skillman, G. Robinson, inc. 132
Skillrud, Harold Clayton. 2302
Skilton, John Hamilton. 337
Skinner, Betty Lee. 3715
Skinner, Clarence Russell. 2632, 3142, 3358, 1123, 3358
Skinner, Conrad Arthur. 400, 1972
Skinner, Craig. 2906, 3219
Skinner, Dolphus. 3752
Skinner, Florence W. 2757
Skinner, Floyd L. 2466
Skinner, Ichabod Lord. 395
Skinner, James Edward. 154, 1753
Skinner, John. 502, 522, 1943
Skinner, Mary Elizabeth. 3557
Skinner, Otis Ainsworth. 3229, 3534
Skinner, Ralph Burgess. 2220
Skinner, Stephen. 1706, 1621, 1706
Skinner, Thomas Harvey. 2906, 3605, 3652, 2927
Skinner, Thomas Lawrence. 3031
Skinner, Tom. 988, 1096, 1560, 1574
Skinsnes, Casper C. 2529
Skirven, Percy Granger. 1223
Sklare, Marshall. 1348, 2105, 2140
Sklba, Richard J. 1277
Skodacek, August Adolph. 1857, 1878, 2295
Skoglund, Elizabeth. 988, 995, 1108, 2244, 3845, 3881
Skoglund, John E. 2238, 2494, 2555, 3186, 3849, 3854
Skoglund, John R. 3854
Skold, Betty Westrom. 1714
Skolnick, Irving H. 3172
Skoss, Solomon Leon. 2143, 3259
Skottowe, John Coulson. 3068
Skousen, Max Bentley. 988
Skousen, Willard Cleon. 536, 679, 2612
Skovgaard-Petersen, Carl Axel. 1595
Skrade, Carl. 1845
Skrenda, Alfred. 297
Skrine, Francis Henry Bennett. 129
Skrine, John Huntley. 2050, 1385
Skrobucha, Heinz. 1370, 1400, 1880, 1881
Skrupskelis, Ignas K. 1934
Skudlarek, William. 2906
Skulsky, Shelomoh. 905
Skultans, Vieda. 3521
Skutch, Alexander Frank. 1536
Skwarok, J. 3722
Skwirczynski, Wladyslaw. 2940
Skydsgaard, K E. 2955
Skydsgaard, Kristen E. 3770
Skydsgaard, Krister E. 2020
Slaatte, Howard Alexander. 83, 1373, 2437, 3358, 3648, 3804
Slabach, Edwin. 687
Slabaugh, Warren W. 3377
Slack, David B. 3023
Slack, Elvira J. 1994, 2047
Slack, Kenneth. 3736, 3850
Slade, Herbert Edwin William. 1356
Slade, Mary Bridges (Canedy) 3026, 3560
Sladek, John Thomas. 2729
Sladen, Kathleen. 901, 3405
Slafter, Edmund Farwell. 890, 1523, 2371
Slager, Albert L. 2432
Slaght, Lawrence T. 1200
Slaten, Arthur Wakefield. 374, 2065
Slater, Arthur Leslie. 461
Slater, Eleanor Chapin. 691, 1346
Slater, John Rothwell. 1697
Slater, Nelson. 2605
Slater, Peter. 3105
Slater, Peter Gregg. 897
Slater, Philip Elliot. 2729
Slater, Robert Henry Lawson. 1079, 3105, 3123
Slater, Thomas. 3667, 744, 949, 3450, 3676
Slattery, Charles Lewis. 1352, 1587, 1890, 1910, 2248, 2423, 3432, 1289, 1773, 1832, 1890, 1995, 2030, 2880, 2906, 3423
[Slattery, John Richard] 1851-1926. 1286
Slattery, Margaret. 975, 1096, 2175, 3157, 3161, 3434, 3557
Slattery, Sarah Lawrence. 3143
Slaughter, Earl. 1011
Slaughter, Frank G. 1405
Slaughter, Frank Gill. 616, 1405, 1978, 2803
Slaughter, Jean. 742
Slaughter, Philip. 975, 2376
Slaughter, William Bradner. 1371
Slaves of the Immaculate Heart of Mary. 2004, 2356, 3248, 3282, 3283
Slaysman, George Major. 1640
Sledd, Andrew. 291, 330, 436
Sledd, Robert Newton. 3345
Sleeman, John F. 1076

Sleeper, Charles Freeman. 275, 3433
Sleeper, James A. 2112, 2143
[Sleeper, John Fremont]. 1092
Sleeper, William True. 1868
Sleeth, Ronald Eugene. 1586, 2906, 3358
Sleigh, R. C. 3717
Sleigh, William Willcocks. 3639
Slemming, Charles William. 515, 646
Slemp, John Calvin. 1314
Slenker, Elmina (Drake) 236
Slessarev, Vsevolod. 2126
Sletten, Nettie. 2616
Slicer, Henry. 136, 692
Slicer, Thomas Roberts. 2225, 3728
Sligh, John Calhoun. 1954
Slingerland, Howard D. 491
Sloan, David Harvey. 1476
Sloan, Harold Paul. 894, 3616, 74, 1179, 1595, 1893, 1954, 2044
Sloan, Maxine. 594
Sloan, Mersene Elon. 181, 1084, 1814, 3687
Sloan, Patrick James. 1826, 3157, 3202, 3550
Sloan, Robert W. 2605
Sloan, Sarah Bertha. 975
Sloan, Steve. 1800
Sloan, William Niccolls. 3446, 3482
Sloan, William Wilson. 407, 536, 2092
Sloane, Eugene Hulse. 2197
Sloane, James Renwick Wilson. 3425
Sloane, James Robinson. 3208
Sloane, Mary Cole. 1518
Slochower, Harry. 2664
Slonim, Reuben. 2806
Slonimsky, Henry. 2462
Slosser, Bob. 988, 1690, 1832, 2962
Slosser, Gaius Jackson. 1042
Slosser, Galus Jackson. 2924
Slosson, Edwin Emery. 3345

Slouschz, Nahum. 2097

Sloyan, Gerald Stephen. 3182

Sloyan, Gerard Stephan. 1267, 1972

Sloyan, Gerard Stephen. 1267, 315, 436, 783, 806, 840, 865, 936, 1753, 1972, 2011, 2068, 2240, 3157, 3158, 3714, 3773
Sloyan, Gerard Stephen, Stephen, ill. 949
Slusser, Dorothy Mallett. 434, 517, 536
Slusser, Gerald H. 1074, 2787, 3158
Sly, Florence M. 3530
Smagula, Billie J. 2396
Smail, R.C. 1391, 2199
Smail, Thomas A. 1832
Smail, Thomas Allan. 1732
Small, Albert Armstrong. 1514
Small, Annie H. 2532
Small, Charles Herbert. 3326
Small city secretaries' conference, Blue Ridge, N.C., 1924. 3872
Small, Dwight Hervey. 975, 1471, 1906, 2265, 2339, 3391
Small, James Louis. 834, 3675
Small, Jocelyn Penny. 723
Small, John. 1519
Small, John B. 15, 2911
Small, John Bryan. 2911, 3375
Small, Samuel White. 3595
Smalley, Beryl. 199, 240, 1673
Smalley, Gary. 2339
Smalley, John. 1342, 1504, 3412
[Smalley, Julia C. (Marvin) 173, 1365
Smalley, William Allen. 2496, 2555
Smallman, Basil. 123, 2778
Smallwood, E. Mary. 2090
Smallwood, Kate. 1983
Smallwood, Kathleen Ann. 2894
Smallzried, Kathleen Ann. 2894
Smalridge, George. 3366
Smaridge, Norah. 194, 1005, 3192
Smaridge, Norah Antoinette. 1802
Smarius, C.F. 1603
Smarius, Cornelius Francis. 792
Smart. 3105
Smart, George Thomas. 1325
Smart, Henry. 28
Smart, James D. 75, 176, 236, 288, 392, 470, 502, 545, 624, 627, 652, 1296, 1317, 2007, 2934, 2951, 3158, 3657, 3665, 3747
Smart, James S. 2231
Smart, John Jamieson Carswell. 1536
Smart, Kenneth. 140
Smart, Moses Mighels. 3665
Smart, Ninian. 2674, 2837, 3064, 3105, 3120, 3140
Smart, William James. 926, 2953
Smart, Wyatt Aiken. 420, 2059
*Smart. Ninian. 3069
Smaus, Jewel (Spangler) 1495
Smead, Elizabeth. 216
Smeaton, George. 1832
Smeaton, Ronald Colguohoun. 1848
Smedal, Gottfried Athanasius. 1096
Smedberg, Harold V. 631

Smedes, Lewis B. 323, 377, 2044, 2266, 2325, 3393
Smedt, Emile Joseph de. 2339, 2940
Smellie, Alexander. 3036, 1375
Smelser, Fred Lyndon. 2477
Smelser, Ronald M. 1704, 1708
Smeltzer, Wallace Guy. 2432, 2439, 2631, 3810
Smend, Rudolf. 531, 2096
Smertenko, Clara Elizabeth (Millerd) 1767
Smet, Alois de. 196
Smet, Pierre Jean de. 1899, 1902, 3426
Smetana, Judith G. 3
Smetana, Rudolph von. 3223
Smethurst, Arthur F. 3080
Smick, Elmer B. 208, 2131
Smiddy, Thomas W. 1328
Smiles, Samuel. 1325, 1852
Smiley, James Lawrenson. 2156
Smiley, Sarah Frances. 2044
Smiley, Thomas Tucker. 283, 481
Smiley, W B. 3565
Smit, Erasmus. 3135, 3143
Smit, Jan Olav. 2851
Smit, Jan Olay. 2851
Smit, Jan Olva. 2852
Smith. 926
*Smith, A. Richard. 3158
Smith, Ada (Wilcox) 596, 3766
Smith, Alan Gordon. 2837
Smith, Albert Edward. 1711
Smith, Albert Edwin. 123
Smith, Albert Hatcher. 1368
Smith, Alberta. 2696
Smith, Alexander B. 136
Smith, Alfred B. 1954
Smith, Alfred Franklin. 2894
Smith, Almiron. 3095, 3404
Smith, Alson Jesse. 975, 1595, 2845, 3674, 3767
Smith, Amanda (Berry) 1570
Smith, Andre. 3368
Smith, Ann Eliza (Brainerd) 3120
[Smith, Anna (Harris)] d. 1929. 1442
Smith, Anna Lee Kirkwood. 195, 2311
Smith, Anne Whalen. 975
Smith, Annie S (Swan) 1235
Smith, Archie. 15
Smith, Arlis Milton. 71
Smith, Arthur Allen. 897
Smith, Arthur E. 1944
Smith, Arthur Harms. 2906, 3172
Smith, Arthur Henderson. 912, 2511
Smith, Arthur Lionel. 1144
Smith, Arthur Warren. 154
Smith, Asa Dodge. 2205, 2934
Smith, Asbury. 71, 1425
Smith, Audley Lawrence. 1857
Smith, Austin Burns. 3721
Smith, B. B. 3749
Smith, Bailey E. 167, 332, 1570, 3358
Smith, Barbara. 247, 3168
Smith, Barbara (Hawkins) 1442
Smith, Basil Alec. 1246
Smith, Benjamin. 3209
Smith, Benjamin Franklin. 139
Smith, Benjamin Lyon. 732
Smith, Bernard. 3850
Smith, Bernie. 1238, 1362, 2032, 2880
Smith, Bertha. 2494, 2511, 3467
Smith, Bertram Tom Dean. 392, 2026
Smith, Bertrand. 2507
Smith, Betsy Covington. 3835
Smith, Betty. 217, 1972, 1983, 2023, 2067
Smith, Billy K. 579
Smith, Bob. 288, 1108, 2339
Smith, Bradford. 2381, 2524, 1415, 2381
Smith, Brian. 2719
Smith, Brian H. 771, 1143
Smith, Brooke. 2945
Smith, Brooke Williams. 1818, 2335
Smith, Butler Kennedy. 1273, 3296
[Smith, C B. 400
Smith, C Billings. 2982
Smith, C. Henry. 2406
Smith, C Stanley. 3614
Smith, Caleb. 3426
Smith, Callie Margaret. 3514
Smith, Carrie Heckman. 3564
Smith, Cary N. 643
Smith, Catharine Cook. 2313
Smith, Catherine Ruth. 3867
Smith, Cecil Daniel. 3158
Smith, Chard Powers. 2687
Smith, Charles Adam. 494
Smith, Charles Alphonso. 312
Smith, Charles Clark. 1254, 2426
Smith, Charles Edmund. 1668
Smith, Charles Edward. 464, 1595, 1832, 1908, 2342, 1892
Smith, Charles Ernest. 2960, 2363
Smith, Charles H. 626, 2210
Smith, Charles Henry. 2404, 2406, 2404, 2406
Smith, Charles Merrill. 988, 1007, 1025, 1179, 1329, 2788, 3426
Smith, Charles Raimer. 317

Smith, Charles Russell. 1716
Smith, Charles Spencer. 15, 2806
Smith, Charles Stanley. 3614
Smith, Charles William Frederick. 392, 1583, 2026, 2044, 2906
Smith, Charles Zachariah. 181
Smith, Chester Allen. 2437
Smith, Christine. 2849
Smith, Christopher. 2771
Smith, Chuck. 52, 434, 441, 456, 608, 1261, 1514, 1610, 2880, 3021, 3427
Smith, Clarence T. 3172
Smith, Claude William. 688
Smith, Clayton Chaney. 2167
Smith, Clifford Pabody. 1035, 1037, 1495
Smith, Constance Penswick. 3229
Smith, Copeland. 975
Smith, Cora (Kincannon) 3514
Smith, Cushing. 526
Smith, Dana Prom. 9, 74, 422, 1011
Smith, Daniel. 4, 1401, 1405, 1506, 1533, 1587, 1857, 1931, 2127, 2130, 2134, 2622, 2802, 2825, 3297, 3457, 3551, 3675, 2855, 3415
Smith, David. 3815, 1972, 107, 344, 373, 1954, 2072, 2802
Smith, David H. 171, 3427, 190
Smith, David Howard. 913, 1330
Smith, Don Ian. 2396, 2676
Smith, Donald Eugene. 704, 3072, 3088
Smith, Donald P. 1296, 3678
*Smith, Doris J. 3158, 3164
Smith, Dwight Louis. 1665, 1672
Smith, Dwight Moody. 397, 421, 713, 2127
Smith, E. Gilmour. 1015
Smith, Earl C. 975, 375, 975
Smith, Ebbie C. 1101, 1171
Smith, Ebenezer. 460, 464
Smith, Edgar H. 1024, 2542
Smith, Edward Garstin. 1907
Smith, Edward Parmelee. 3737
Smith, Edward W. 3426
Smith, Edwin. 1270
Smith, Edwin William. 133, 2230, 2498, 2499
Smith, Egbert Watson. 975, 2521, 2802, 2914, 2926
Smith, Elbert A. 3135, 3216
Smith, Eleanor. 3563
Smith, Eli. 82
Smith, Elias. 3427
[Smith, Elias] 1769-1846. 1500, 1746, 1868, 2055, 3427
Smith, Eliza Roxey (Snow) 1231, 1983, 2619, 3432
Smith, Elizabeth Oakes (Prince) 1479
Smith, Elizur Goodrich. 2864
Smith, Elliott. 171
Smith, Elmer Lewis. 2407
Smith, Elsie Higdon. 2865
Smith, Elwood F. 3696
Smith, Elwyn Allen. 1142, 1151, 1983, 2922, 3195
Smith, Ervin. 945, 2173
Smith, Esther (Mallory) 3876
Smith, Ethan. 52, 456, 509, 2044, 3713
Smith, Ethel (Sabin) 3064
Smith, Eugene Lewis. 975, 1154, 2521
Smith, Evelyn. 2664
Smith, Everett St. Clair. 3018, 312, 1210
Smith, F. Sherwood. 421, 471
Smith, Florence. 1209
Smith, Foy L. 1210
Smith, Francis Henry. 205
Smith, Francis J. 1023, 1882
Smith, Francis Shubael. 3202
Smith, Frank Wade. 3565, 3889
Smith, Frank Webster. 3158
Smith, Franklin Campbell. 3358
Smith, Fred Burton. 3064, 2807
Smith, Frederic William. 1053
Smith, Frederick Augustus. 2212
Smith, Frederick George. 460, 464, 509, 1100, 1228, 3036
Smith, Frederick Harold. 703
Smith, Frederick Madison. 3216, 3634
Smith, Fredrick W. 1613, 3427
Smith, George. 3624, 739, 1481, 2532, 2654
Smith, George Adam. 502, 547, 559, 1481, 1943, 2764, 2934, 560, 588, 1798, 2764
Smith, George Albert. 1231, 2605, 2619
Smith, George Alexander. 2006
Smith, George Barnett. 2190
Smith, George Dallas. 646
Smith, George Duncan. 792, 1595, 1893, 2044, 2252, 2363
Smith, George Everard Kidder. 1159
Smith, George Gilman. 40, 89, 896, 2178, 2424, 2430
Smith, George Leslie. 2700
Smith, George Williamson. 67
Smith, Gerald Birney. 975, 1071, 1587, 3680

Smith, Gerard. 1106, 1659, 1716, 1740, 2568, 2739, 3717
Smith, Gerrit. 1092, 3064
Smith, Gertrude. 632, 624
Smith, Gladys Watson. 1514
Smith, Goldwin. 1017, 1072, 3068, 3624
Smith, Gordon Hedderly. 2533, 3438
Smith, Grafton Elliot. 1478
Smith, Graham. 3536, 3768
Smith, Gregory. 804
Smith, Gregory Michael. 792, 2944
Smith, H. Alan. 1076, 3218
Smith, H. Daniel. 2331, 2766
Smith, Hannah. 2048
Smith, Hannah (Whitall) 975, 1687, 1727, 3326, 3427
[Smith, Hanover Prescott]. 1035, 1495
Smith, Harmon L. 950
Smith, Harold. 392, 1385
*Smith, Harold D. 1387, 3648
Smith, Harold P. 2120
Smith, Harriet (Lummis) 725
Smith, Harry Denman. 3627
Smith, Harry E. 3328
Smith, Harry Framer. 324, 403, 464
Smith, Harry R. 2626
Smith, Harry Robert. 2959
Smith, Harvey Leigh. 649
Smith, Hay Watson. 1581
Smith, Helen Heath. 1316
Smith, Helen (Reagan) 975, 3541
Smith, Heman Conoman. 179, 2612, 3240
Smith, Henry. 2422
Smith, Henry Allen. 1377, 3429
Smith, Henry Augustine. 1876, 3560
Smith, Henry Boynton. 61, 1189, 3624, 3648, 3660
Smith, Henry Goodwin. 3601
Smith, Henry Griggs Weston. 3674
Smith, Henry James. 3574
Smith, Henry Lester. 3158
Smith, Henry Light. 1473
Smith, Henry Preserved. 236, 590, 1805, 1926, 2096, 2116, 2565
Smith, Henry W. 1203
Smith, Herbert. 2514
Smith, Herbert Booth. 3345, 278, 1697, 2880
Smith, Herbert C. 975
Smith, Herbert F. 1002, 1457, 1844, 2396
[Smith, Herbert Halsey] 1877. 502
Smith, Herbert Heebner. 10
Smith, Herbert Maynard. 1762
Smith, Herman Conoman. 3217
Smith, Hershel. 3304, 3427
Smith, Hester Travers. 3514, 3815
Smith, Hilary. 2574
Smith, Hilary Dansey. 2911
Smith, Hilda Worthington. 699
Smith, Hilrie Shelton. 1132, 3158, 3414, 3740
Smith, Hoder. 3202
Smith, Homer William. 3094
Smith, Horace Greeley. 624
Smith, Huston. 3105, 3121
*Smith, Huston. 3121
Smith, Irene Catherine. 3557
Smith, Isaac. 2428
Smith, Isaac Gregory. 677, 3847
Smith, J. Carpenter. 1179
Smith, J. Fairbairn. 1667
Smith, J[ohn] E[dward]. 1274
Smith, Jacob Brubaker. 345, 456, 1769
Smith, James. 1123, 1179, 1452, 1732, 1954, 2231, 3456, 518
[Smith, James Andrew]. 3753
Smith, James Edward. 518
Smith, James Fairbairn. 1663
Smith, James Henry Oliver. 3345
Smith, James L. 975
Smith, James Lee. 975
Smith, James R. 349
Smith, James Reuel. 3523
Smith, James Roy. 1063, 1837
Smith, James Walter Dickson. 2096
Smith, James Ward. 3121, 3214, 3746
Smith, James Wheaton. 1389
Smith, Jane I. 1531
[Smith, Jane Luella (Dowd), 1847. 3209
Smith, Jay. 2224
Smith, Jay J. 227
Smith, Jean Herron. 3274
Smith, Jean Louise. 2396, 2845
Smith, Jennie. 1576, 3135
Smith, Jesse Guy. 3605
Smith, Jesse Nathaniel. 2605, 3427
Smith, John. 975, 3624
[Smith, John] 1722-1771. 3601, 3792
Smith, John. 3674
[Smith, John] fl. 1748. 1682, 3601
Smith, John B. 218
Smith, John C. 2431
Smith, John C[ross]. 1269
Smith, John Colin Dinsdale. 3846
Smith, John Edward. 1035, 1495
Smith, John Edwin. 1106, 2837, 2838, 3105, 3108

Smith, John Ferris. 3484
Smith, John Holland. 644, 1643, 1938, 3246, 3308
Smith, John Lewis. 2431
Smith, John Merlin Powis. 559, 569, 596, 1539, 2075, 2951, 3064
Smith, John N. 3145
Smith, John Owen. 3446
Smith, John Pye. 203
Smith, John Robert. 1279
Smith, John Talbot. 823, 1179, 2848, 2884, 2215, 2630, 2851, 2862, 3681
Smith, John W V. 1228
Smith, Jonathan Richie. 2325
Smith, Jonathan Ritchie. 421, 3358, 1834
Smith, Joseph. 1677, 3627, 2927, 1231, 1312, 1356, 2598, 2599, 2605, 2612, 2613, 3429, 3430, 3429, 661, 2605
Smith, Joseph Alexander. 3429
Smith, Joseph Fielding. 2606, 2613, 1179, 1231, 1233, 1234, 1506, 2320, 2606, 2608, 2610, 2613, 2616, 2619, 3217, 3429, 3430, 2613, 3430
Smith, Joseph H. 975, 1554
Smith, Joseph Henry. 1832
Smith, Joseph Manton. 3523
Smith, Joseph Martin. 975
Smith, Joseph Tate. 2917
Smith, Joshua. 1869
Smith, Joyce Marie. 217, 589, 988, 2047, 3841
Smith, Judith Florence. 3840
Smith, Julia A. (Norcross) Crafts. 3514
Smith, Juliet C. 1741, 3158
Smith, Justin Almerin. 217, 466, 1187, 1311
Smith, Karl Franklin. 3674
Smith, Katharine Lawrence. 2774, 3273
Smith, Lacey Baldwin. 1759
Smith, Laura (Chase) 889
Smith, Laura Irene (Ivory) 2533, 2559
Smith, Lemuel. 550
Smith, Leon. 1254, 2339
Smith, LeRoy Foster. 1620
Smith, Leslie R. 1352, 2396
Smith, Lloyd E. 2657, 2662
Smith, Lloyd Edwin. 102, 1983
Smith, Louis A. 2480
Smith, Lucius Edwin. 2483
Smith, Lucy (Mack) 3429, 3430
Smith, Lucy Margaret. 1304
Smith, Luther Wesley. 2722
Smith, Lyndsay L. 1260, 3857
Smith, M. Blaine. 1011
Smith, M T. 383
*Smith, Mabel G. 3202
Smith, Macklin. 2984
Smith, Madison Monroe. 136, 3788
Smith, Malcolm. 988, 1294, 1376, 2817, 3431
Smith, Margaret. 2640, 2645, 3017, 3543, 21, 2645, 3543
Smith, Marshall. 278
Smith, Martha. 2218
Smith, Mary Brainerd. 2757
Smith, Mary Constance. 825, 3418
Smith, Mary (Riley) 3208
Smith, Matthew Hale. 300, 2328, 3753
Smith, Matthew J. W. 90, 792
Smith, Matthew John Wilfred. 792, 797, 2356
Smith, Matthew Stephen. 2034
Smith, May. 612
Smith, May C. 281
Smith, May (Riley) 1022, 2856
Smith, Michael. 1401
Smith, Michael Auckland. 1197
Smith, Michael H. 1329
Smith, Michelle. 3304, 3431
Smith, Mildred Nelson. 2718, 3427, 3429
Smith, Miles Woodward. 286, 332
Smith, Milton Asbury. 281
Smith, Mont W. 1377
Smith, Morton. 398, 502, 1288, 1884, 2019, 2149, 3322
Smith, Myrtle]. 3514
Smith, Nancy Anne. 932, 3431
Smith, Nicholas. 1873, 1876
Smith, Noel. 1079, 2917, 1472
Smith, Nora Archibald. 297
Smith, Oberlin. 1890
Smith, Ophia Delilah (Smith) 1179
Smith, Orlando Jay. 3054, 3080, 3313
Smith, Oswald J. 52, 139, 975, 1570, 1873, 2813, 3229, 3482
Smith, Paul B. 1433
Smith, Paul Dewey. 307, 2325
Smith, Paul G. 3530
Smith, Peter. 2419
Smith, Philip. 1186
Smith, Philip Vernon. 414, 1489
Smith, Phineas A. 1727, 3463
Smith, Preserved. 1526, 2277, 2281, 1526, 2277
Smith, R. S. 2685, 3233
Smith, Ralph Lee. 536, 2097
Smith, Ralph M. G. 148, 167, 3484

Smith, Reba S. 2913
Smith, Reginald Anthony Lendon. 737, 3450, 2579
Smith, Reginald Bosworth. 2565
Smith, Rembert Gilman. 1151, 1320, 2755
Smith, Reuben. 3674
Smith, Reuben William. 1282
Smith, Richard. 792
Smith, Richard Bonham. 3087
Smith, Richard Furnald. 2729
Smith, Richard Knox. 2917
Smith, Richard M. 473
[Smith, Richard Morris] 1827-1896. 3142
Smith, Robert Cheney. 3438
Smith, Robert D. 792, 2477
Smith, Robert Edward. 642
Smith, Robert Elmer. 1248, 1869, 2458, 3345
Smith, Robert H. 330
Smith, Robert Houston. 2219
Smith, Robert I. 1187
Smith, Robert John. 39
*Smith, Robert Ora. 3202
Smith, Robert Philip. 3121
Smith, Robert Seneca. 642, 3158, 3859
Smith, Robert Tighe. 2729
Smith, Robert William. 679, 2947, 2948
Smith, Rocksborough Remington. 1603
Smith, Rockwell Carter. 3254, 3681
Smith, Rodney. 1560, 1570, 3135, 3345, 3431
Smith, Roland A. 1167
Smith, Roland Cotton. 2906
Smith, Ronald Gregor. 677, 1595, 1727, 2325, 2326, 3482
Smith, Rosemary Dubpernell. 3892
Smith, Roy L. 2839
Smith, Roy Lemon. 649, 975, 1077, 1252, 1442, 1452, 1972, 2092, 2128, 2422, 2426, 2494, 2627, 2802, 2803, 2906, 3191, 3345, 3358, 3366, 3448, 3530, 1842
Smith, Ruby Kate. 3287
Smith, Ruth. 3204
Smith, Ruth Lyman (Cobb) 3427
Smith, Samuel. 2156
Smith, Samuel B. 465, 802
Smith, Samuel Francis. 30, 1780
Smith, Samuel George. 3446
Smith, Samuel Stanhope. 61, 3648
*Smith, Sandra. 3472
Smith, Sara (Henderson) 1113, 3202
Smith, Sebastian Bach. 735, 835, 1489, 2342
Smith, Seymour A. 885, 3757
Smith, Sherman Meritt. 3166
Smith, Sidney. 545
Smith, Sir George Adam. 2764
Smith, Sir William. 1906
Smith, Stephen Rensselaer. 1660
Smith, Stephen Rensselaer. 3754
Smith, Stephenson Percy. 2664
Smith, Stuart Hall. 3315
Smith, Susy. 94, 1362, 1697, 2216, 2993, 3054, 3431, 3474, 3514, 3824
Smith, Sydney. 3089, 3431
Smith, T. Stratton. 2333, 2717
Smith, Thomas. 2526, 3135
Smith, Thomas Alan. 649, 995
Smith, Thomas I. 1096
Smith, Thomas Jollie. 236
Smith, Thomas Joseph. 437
Smith, Thomas L. 936
Smith, Thomas Vernor. 2843
Smith, Thorne. 665
Smith, Timothy Lawrence. 1237, 2956, 3233, 3739
Smith, Titus Keiper. 3142
Smith, Tom A. 3889
Smith, Travis Edwin. 1626, 2463
Smith, Una (Riddick) 690, 1111, 3557
Smith, Uriah. 456, 465, 506, 507, 634, 1912, 2325, 3721
Smith, Velma. 3174
Smith, Verena. 2349, 2707
Smith, Vincent Edward. 103
Smith, Virgil B. 2599
Smith, W.A. 3514
Smith, W. Douglas. 2504
Smith, W Earle. 149
Smith, W. Robertson. 2951
Smith, Wade Cothran. 314, 975, 687, 688
Smith, Waldo Edward Lovel. 2794
Smith, Walter George. 3533
Smith, Warren. 2729
Smith, Warren Chace. 936
Smith, Warren Sylvester. 3212, 3401
Smith, Warren Thomas. 115, 1025, 1302, 1848
Smith, Wesley E. 1261, 3432
Smith, Wilbur M. 67, 646, 2044
Smith, Wilbur Moorehead. 67, 438, 608, 610, 642, 644, 657, 1114, 1530, 1795, 2002, 2034, 2054, 3203, 3229, 3432, 3627
Smith, Wilbur Moorehead. 312
Smith, Wilbur Morehead. 644

Smith, Wilder. 2908
Smith, Wiley Winton. 975, 1011, 1560
Smith, Wilfred Cantwell. 3105, 1597, 2565, 3068, 3105, 3121
Smith, Willard J. 2613, 3846
Smith, Willard S. 481
[Smith, William]. 1311, 1369, 3358
Smith, William. 1354, 246, 297, 407, 536, 919
Smith, William Benjamin. 1194, 392
Smith, William C. 2443
Smith, William Christie. 136
Smith, William D. 2912
Smith, William Edward. 3713, 1832, 2321, 3291, 3648, 3713
[Smith, William Goodhugh]. 2880
Smith, William Henry. 2561
Smith, William Kyle. 728, 3794
Smith, William L. 2327
Smith, William Martin. 291, 608, 3648, 1462
Smith, William Robertson. 502, 3332
Smith, William Sheppard. 320
Smith, William Walter. 3558, 3565, 2959, 3158, 2764
Smith, William Wiggin. 212
Smith, William Woodford. 1929
Smith, Wistaria. 1954
Smith, Woodrow W. 71
Smith-Durland, Eugenia, 1935. 3409
Smithee, Giles H. 219
Smith. Elias. 700, 1289
Smither, Ethel Lisle. 630, 642, 1983, 2551, 2760, 3172, 3185
[Smith Joseph]. 2613
Smithson, John Henry. 1038, 2691
Smithson, William T. 40, 2437
Smithsonian Institution. Traveling Exhibition Service. 86, 659
Smitty, William H. 593, 3375
Smock, Martha. 1016, 1325, 3750
Smolnikar, Andreas Bernardus. 2320
Smoot, Dan. 3746
Smoot, Thomas Arthur. 975, 3196
Smothers, Elizabeth Marshall. 1871
Smucker, Donovan Ebersole. 3358
Smucker, Jesse N. 1452
Smul, James F. 1536
Smutny, Robert Jaroslav. 3609
Smuts, Jan Christiaan. 1824
Smylie, James. 3315
Smylie, Theodore A. 2396
Smyth, Alexander. 2060, 464
Smyth, Bernard T. 377, 2802
Smyth, Charles Hugh Egerton. 1378, 108, 1378, 1760, 2910, 3039, 3409
Smyth, Clifford. 2813, 3817
[Smyth, Egbert Coffin]. 2002
Smyth, Egbert Coffin, 1829-1904, defendant. 1335, 3432
Smyth, Frank. 1710, 3824
Smyth, Frederic Hastings. 1893, 2253, 3271
Smyth, Hugh P. 3041
[Smyth, Hugh Patrick]. 1727, 3036
Smyth, J Hilton LeBaron. 2852
Smyth, James W. 835
Smyth, John Paterson. 224, 291, 1972, 2340, 2906, 291, 306, 1529, 1731, 1972, 2802
Smyth, Julian Kennedy. 1999, 2020, 2691, 2693
Smyth, Nathan Ayer. 3080
Smyth, Newman. 236, 1042, 1055, 1342, 1595, 1890, 2006, 2562, 2674, 3080, 3202
Smyth, Thomas. 76, 728, 897, 1577, 1652, 2494, 2585
Smyth, William Woods. 199, 46
Smythe, George Franklin. 2959
Smythe, Lewis Strong Casey. 3446
[Smythe, W. Herbert]. 300
Smyth-Vaudry, Telesphor. 2668
Snaith, John. 3105
Snaith, John G. 489
Snaith, Norman Henry. 550, 599, 2096
Snape, John. 3345
Snape, Robert Hugh. 2579
Snare, J P. 3142
Snavely, Guy Everett. 1128
Snavely, John. 936
Snead, Littleton Upshur. 642
Snead, Martha George Tillman. 3783
Sneath, Elias Hershey. 2640, 1385, 1697, 2592, 3158
Sneck, William Joseph. 1712
Sneed, James Richard. 2437
Sneed, Richard Joseph. 431
Snell, Ada Laura Fonda. 1113
Snell, Frederick A. 1691
Snell, Frederick John. 3804
Snell, Heber Cyrus. 2096
Snell, Joy. 3514
Snell, Marvis R. 1713, 2327

Snellgrove, David L. 707, 2193, 2194, 2684
Snelling, Christopher Hanbury William. 2729
Snelling, Joseph. 2940
Snethen, Nicholas. 3358
Sneve, Virginia Driving Hawk. 2974, 3464
Sniadoff, Peter. 1180
Snider, Harold. 3794
Snider, John D. 976
Snider-Pellegrini, Antonio. 1403, 1890
Snipes, A. M. 3202
Snipes, Joseph Franklin. 3514
Snitzer, Jacob Lazarus. 1789, 1928
Snodgrass, Charles Albert. 1670, 1671
Snodgrass, William Davis. 76
Snoeck, Andre. 1327
Snoek, Johan M. 53
Snook, John B. 1325, 3746
Snow, Alpheus Henry. 2704
Snow, Charles Miles. 3193, 3514
Snow, Charles Percy. 3314
Snow, Herman. 3514
Snow, Jimmy. 1575, 3432
Snow, John H. 1066
Snow, Lorenzo. 2859
Snow, Manuel Horn. 1727
Snow, Michael. 2809, 3433
Snowden, James Henry. 871, 976, 1111, 1486, 1727, 1890, 1916, 1954, 1972, 2053, 2474, 2739, 3000, 349, 1035, 1496, 1890, 2466, 2606, 3080, 3158, 3665
Snowden, James Ross. 208
Snowden, John Baptist. 1302, 3433
Snowden, Rita Frances. 324, 346, 1442, 1452, 2396, 3843
Snyder, Albert Whitcomb. 2212
Snyder, Alton G. 3169
Snyder, Dale Norman. 176, 2945
Snyder, G W. 2759
Snyder, Gary. 1780
Snyder, Gerald S. 3746
Snyder, Gerrit. 3463
Snyder, Graydon F. 1155, 1882
Snyder, Harvey Albert. 687, 898
Snyder, Howard A. 1066, 1123, 1292, 3804
Snyder, Joseph Ephrem. 2361
Snyder, Richard L. 626, 642, 1994, 3158
Snyder, Ross. 1260, 1610, 3004, 3881
Snyder, Russell Dewey. 312, 1994
Snyder, W. W. 1913
Snyder, William Cloyd. 2807
Snyder, William Richard. 3574
Soares Prabhu, George M. 443
Soares, Theodore Gerald. 150, 151, 167, 237, 312, 494, 936, 1063, 1325, 2112, 2802, 3158, 3366
Soaring society of America, inc. 1515
Sobel, B. Zvi. 2556
Sobel, Mechal. 16
Sobel, Samuel. 2219, 3743
Sobol, Donald J. 29
Sobosan, Jeffrey G. 1002, 1595, 1777, 3218
Sobrino, Jon. 2044, 2222
Sochen, June. 3842
Social Work Conference, Valparaiso University, 1968. 1138
Society for Old Testament Study. 487, 502, 515, 608, 644, 3242
Society for promoting Christian knowledge, London. 1042, 3296
Society for propagating the gospel among the heathen. 2596
Society for Propagation of the Gospel in New-England. 1507, 2541
Society for Psychical Research, London. Library. 2992, 3437
Society for the promotion of collegiate and theological education. 3680
Society for the propagation of the faith. 3604
Society for the propagation of the faith. U.S. 850
Society for the Propagation of the Faith. U.S. Mission Secretariat. 850, 851, 2515
Society of American Archivists. Church Records Committee. 1243
Society of Biblical Literature. 229
Society of Biblical literature and exegesis. 1530
Society of Catholic Medical Missionaries. 3437
Society of Mary of Paris. 812
Society of retreat conductors. 2880
Society of St. Gregory of America. Music Committee. 1205
Society of Saint John the Evangelist. 2969, 2970
Society of St. Vincent de Paul. U. S. Metropolitan central council of New York. 3438
Society of the Divine Word. 3438
Society of the Holy Child Jesus. American Province. 3438
Society of the rosary altar. 3248

Society of the sisters of the holy names of Jesus and Mary, Oregon. 824
Society of the sons of St. George, Philadelphia. 3196
Sociological Resources for the Social Studies (Project) 3746
Sockman, Ralph Washington. 181, 976, 1063, 1096, 1394, 1452, 1486, 1741, 1983, 2065, 2248, 2426, 2437, 2772, 2906, 3358, 3541
Socrates Scholasticus. 1194
Sodality of the Blessed Virgin Mary. 843, 1869, 2356, 3454, 3455
Sodden, Jesse. 2239
Soderblom, Nathan. 1621, 107, 1998, 3121, 3123, 3226
Soderblom, Nathan, [Lars Olaf Jonathan Soderblom.]. 3123
Soderblom, Nathan [Lars Olof Jonathan Soderblom]. 3123
Sodergren, Carl J. 325, 381, 486, 558, 2561
Sodergren, Carl Johannes. 1697, 2279, 2284
Soderholm, Marjorie Elaine. 895, 937, 3564
Soekmono, R. 682
Soergel, Mary. 932, 3455
Soffin, Joel. 682, 3033
Sofia. Natsionalna khudozhestvena galeriia. Branch for Medieval Bulgarian Pictorial Art. 1881, 3455
Sofield, Loughlan. 1374
Sofranov, Ivan. 815
Sofronii, Archimandrite. 1010
Soggin, J. Alberto. 541, 553, 555
[Sohier, Elizabeth Putnam]. 685
Sohl, Robert. 3892
Sohm, Rudolf. 3238
Sohn, Otto E. 3012
Sohrab, Mirza Ahmad. 2, 6, 11, 129, 3268
Sokolow, Nahum. 2119
Sokolowski, Robert. 1106
Solaryk, Sam. 2948
Solaryk, Sam, 1928. 2948
Solberg, Carl Knutson. 1570
Solberg, Charles Orrin. 2290, 2292
Solberg, Richard W 1917. 1708, 2284
Solberg, Winton U. 3261
Solov'ev, Vsevolod Sergeevich. 671
Solignac, Pierre. 1108
Solis-Cohen, Emily. 1784, 2076
Solle, Dorothee. 107, 1077, 1087, 2049, 2396, 2719, 3541
Sollitt, Kenneth Walter. 84
Sollmann, Friedrich Wilhelm. 1087
Solmsen, Friedrich. 1921
Soloff, Mordecai Isaac. 630, 2094, 2095, 2096, 2120, 3166
Solomon ben Isaac, 1040-1105. 562
Solomon, Charles R. 2781
Solomon, J C. 2127
Solomon, James Cary. 167
Solomon, Paul. 2733, 3482
[Solomon Shelemiel ben Hayyim]. 2272
Solomon, Victor. 1361
Soloukhin, Vladimir Alekseevich. 1881
Soloveitchik, Joseph Dov. 2143
Solov'ev, Vladimir Sergeevich. 3105
Solov'ev, Vladimir Sergeevich. 2807, 3482
Soloviev, Alexandre V. 2750
Solovii, Meletii M. 766, 2236
Soltau, George. 1999
Soltau, Henry W. 3579
*Soltau, T. Stanley. 1405
Soltau, Theodore Stanley. 2480, 2537, 1905, 2044, 2483
Soltes, Avraham. 2112
Soltes, Mordecai. 1614, 1624
Sombart, Werner. 2112
Somboon Suksamran. 709
Somen, Robert W. 3724
Somerndike, John Mason. 642, 2483, 2528, 3558
Somerset, Edward Adolphus Seymour. 1092
Somerville, Robert. 24, 2861
Sommaripa, George. 237
Sommer, Daniel Austen. 297, 1123, 3794
Sommer, Frederick. 2175, 2945
Sommer, Joseph. 664
Sommer, Martin S. 2287
Sommerfeld, Richard Edwin. 1126
Sommerfield, Richard. 1123
Sommerhauser, William B. 2370
Sommers, Charles George. 3524
Sommers, Robert. 2313
Sommers, Ronald K. 2411
Sommerville, Charles John. 1020
Sommerville, William. 579
Song, Ben. 120
Song, Choan-Seng. 1088, 2502, 3616, 3648
Soni, R. L. 2382, 3304
Sonne, Conway Ballantyne. 131
Sonne, Niels Henry. 3213, 3612

Sonnino, Paul. 1638, 2261
Sono, Tel. 3143
Sonquist, David Emmanuel. 3872
Sons and daughters of Jacob of Florida and America, incorporated. 3240
Sons of New Hampshire. 1623
Sontag, Frederick. 802, 1106, 1245, 1730, 1732, 1738, 2163, 2170, 2419, 2640, 3105, 3329, 3610, 3659, 3746
Sontag, Peter J. 1264
Soothill, William Edward. 913, 1331, 2511
Sooy, Josephus Leander. 71
Soper, Alexander Coburn. 79
Soper, David Wesley. 976, 1066, 1362, 1727, 2013, 2977, 2979, 3422, 3611
Soper, Donald Oliver. 2906, 3665
Soper, Edmund Davison. 67, 1063, 2555, 3121, 3849, 3121
Soper, Eunice. 1435
Sopher, David Edward. 3070
Sopherim, Thea El. 394
Sopocko, Michael. 2231
Soppe, Dale. 995
Soras, Alfred de. 1077
Sorely, William Ritchie. 3068
Sorensen, Andrew A. 23, 774
Sorenson, Charles M. 3530
Sorenson, Roy. 3870
Sorenson, Stella. 1455
Sorenson, Stephen. 688, 1005
Sorg, Rembert. 188, 190, 529, 584, 2190
Sork, David A. 941
Soroka, Leonid. 2744
Sorokin, Pitirim Aleksandrovich. 28
Sosebee, W. H. 1928
Sosso, Lorenzo. 2980
Sottek, James J. 2721
Sottovagina, Hugh. 1759
Soule, Caroline Augusta (White) 3464, 3755
Soule, Ella Frances. 3158
Soule, Sherrod. 1748
Soulen, Richard N. 240, 286
Soulsby, Lucy Helen Muriel. 2894
Sourdel, Dominique. 2565
Souter, Alexander. 29, 339, 373, 1769, 2811
Souter, John C. 988
South, Robert. 1227, 3464
Southall, Ivan. 634, 635, 1155
Southard, Carroll O. 2410
Southard, Carroll O'Brien. 2410
Southard, Mabel Madeline. 1955
Southard, Samuel. 994, 1108, 1296, 1570, 2410, 2787, 3679, 3783
Southard, Samuel Lewis. 209, 1675, 2044
Southcott, Ernest William. 3676
Southeastern Pennsylvania Theological Library Association. 3678
Southern, A. C. 1519
Southern Baptist Convention. 3467, 3838
Southern Baptist Convention. Baptist Brotherhood Commission. 1253
Southern Baptist Convention. Education Commission. 3466
Southern Baptist Convention. Executive Committee. 3466
Southern Baptist Convention. Foreign Mission Board. 156
Southern Baptist Convention. Historical Commission. 3090
Southern Baptist Convention. Home Mission Board. 2528
Southern Baptist Convention. Home Mission Board. Division of Evangelism. 1570
Southern Baptist convention. Radio committee. 167
Southern Baptist Convention. Sunday School Board. 150, 153, 1157, 3002, 3163, 3467
Southern Baptist Convention. Sunday School Board. Baptist Training Union Dept. 3465, 3595
Southern Conference on Gerontology, 8th, University of Florida, 1958. 18
Southern, Richard William. 49, 1084, 1186
Southey, Robert. 2424, 3804, 3805
Southgate, Wyndham Mason, 1910. 2072
Southon, Arthur Eustace. 2622
Southwell, Robert. 1354, 1765, 2030, 3489
Southwell Cathedral. 3783
Southwick Congregational Church. Church History Committee. 3468
Southwick, Solomon. 53, 1662
Southworth, Henry W. 107
Southworth, May Elizabeth. 1643
Sovik, Arne. 3291
Sovik, E. A. 2240
Sowards, Jesse Kelley. 1526
Sowder, Zella Mae. 2729
Sowerby, Joseph Henry. 2991
Sowers, Sidney G. 504, 2831

Sowton, Stanley. 1405
Spaan, Howard B. 1023
Spae, Joseph John. 816, 820, 1081, 1090, 2535
Spaeth, Adolph. 2186, 2295
Spaeth, Harriett Reynolds (Krauth) 3469
Spaeth, J. Paul. 1043
Spafford, Belle S. 1233, 3844
Spain, Carl. 446
Spain. Constitution. 3469
Spain, Mildred W. 879
Spain, Rufus B. 1135, 3465
Spainhower, James I. 1087
Spalding, Amos Fletcher. 3796
Spalding, Arthur Whitefield. 8, 314, 624, 1856, 3386, 3534, 3811, 624, 3534
Spalding, B. J. 297
[Spalding, Baird Thomas] 1857. 3202
Spalding, George Burley. 2849
Spalding, Henry Stanislaus. 873
Spalding, James Field. 115, 792
Spalding, John. 1675, 3469
Spalding, John Franklin. 2044, 2973
Spalding, John Howard. 1794, 3570
Spalding, John Lancaster. 828, 1919, 1920, 3064, 3470, 3624
Spalding, Joshua. 3231, 1869, 3648
Spalding, Martin John. 783, 792, 820, 821, 1628, 2167, 2334, 3036, 3470
Spalding, Samuel Charles. 3135
Spalding, Thomas Alfred. 1423, 3399
Spalding, Thomas W. 3470
Spalink, Benjamin H. 2880
Spalink, Benjamin Henry. 2880
Spamer, Claribel. 603
Spande, Norma. 642
Spangenberg, Alice. 1238, 2163
Spangenberg, Leonard M. 1252
Spangler, Bob. 3291
Spangler, J. T. 1325
Spann, John Richard. 67, 1135, 1289, 3300, 3674
Spanner, D. C. 202
Sparkes, Samuel. 509
Sparkes, Vernone M. 3648
Sparkman, Temp. 953, 994, 2238
Sparks, Claude Ezell. 2756
Sparks, Enid. 1004, 1015, 3385
Sparks, Jack. 1393, 1573
Sparks, Jack N. 1394
Sparks, Jacob B., 1886. 1575, 3135
Sparks, James Allen. 2787
Sparks, Lamar. 1452
Sparks, Sam. 616
Sparks, W. A. 608
Sparks, William A. 608
Sparrow, Gregory Scott. 1479
Sparshott, F. E. 1746, 2837
Sparshott, Francis Edward. 1746
Spatz, Don. 2396
Spaude, Paul W. 2293
Spaugh, Herbert. 976
Spaulding, Clarence A. 1011
Spaulding, Dorothy W. 3798
Spaulding, Henry George. 431
[Spaulding, John] 1800-1889. 2913
Spaulding, Jonah. 2820
Spaulding, Solomon. 679
Spayd, Lucian Wilson. 3380
Spayth, Henry G. 3730
Speaight, Robert. 3145, 3593, 3692
Speak, Harold. 28, 3278, 3788
Speakman, Frederick B. 1453, 2934, 2935
Speakman, Thomas Henry. 1685
Speaks, Ruben Lee. 1123
Spear, Charles. 2020
Spear, Richard E. 1474
Spear, Samuel Thayer. 3190
Speare, Eva Augusta (Clough) 1161
Spearing, Edward. 807, 1773
Spearman, Arthur Dunning. 3302
Spearman, Dale. 1063
Spearman, Henry Kuhns. 3345
*Spears, Gene, Jr. 3345, 3732
Spears, Samuel T. 3073
Spears, W. Eugene. 1611
Speas, Ralph. 994
Speck, Frank Gouldsmith. 1420, 1899, 1420, 2669
Speck, Samuel L. 253
Speckhard, Hermann. 552
Specter, Ruth Rachel. 1986, 2140
Spector, Ivar. 741, 1539, 3405
Spector, Shoshannah. 2779
Speculum christiani. 976
Speculum sacerdotale. 1623
Speedy, Graeme W. 3176
Speer, Alfred W. 1697, 3470
Speer, Emma (Bailey) 1838
Speer, Gordon C. 3358
Speer, Jack Atkeson. 228
Speer, James P. 3794
Speer, Leonidas Eli. 1570
Speer, Michael L. 3530

Speer, Robert Elliott. 41, 182, 333, 423, 431, 926, 976, 1053, 1072, 1079, 1194, 1442, 1582, 2002, 2044, 2061, 2066, 2202, 2483, 2494, 2502, 2521, 2532, 2535, 2547, 2802, 2849, 2926, 3471, 926, 1079, 2002
Speer, William. 976
Speers, Theodore Cuyler. 2935
Speers, Thomas Guthrie. 2250
Speers, Wallace Carter. 976, 1072
Speerstra, Karen. 901, 3666
Speeth, Kathleen Riordan. 1778
Speicher, Earl Edmon. 2066
Speicher, Jacob. 2511
Speight, Harold Edwin Balme. 3358
Speiser, Ephraim Avigdor. 2095
Speller, Jon P. 952
Spellman, Francis Joseph, Cardinal. 53
Spellman, Norman W. 667, 3426
Spellman, Norman Woods. 2451
Spellmann, Norman W. 1627
Spence, Basil. 1377
Spence, Hartzell. 1296, 2906, 3326, 3471
Spence, Hersey Everett. 642, 649, 1482
Spence, Inez. 2244
Spence, Irving. 2924
Spence, Lewis. 2653, 94, 878, 1480, 1502, 1898, 2653, 3322, 94, 102, 1480, 1898, 2636, 2653, 2731, 2863, 3013
Spence, Othniel Talmadge. 1824
Spence, Thomas Hugh. 1817, 3242
Spence, Walter, 1867. 2048, 3665
Spence-Jones, Henry Donald Maurice. 224, 752, 1093, 1194, 3204
Spencer, Albert J. 3026
Spencer, Alice. 75
Spencer, Anna (Garlin) 2983, 3202
Spencer, Bonnell. 1180, 1956, 3271, 3665
Spencer, Clarissa (Young) 2606, 3869
Spencer, Claude Elbert. 1462
Spencer, Claudius B. 1486
Spencer, Claudius Buchanan. 2192, 2422, 1529, 2053, 2439
Spencer, Donald Amos. 653, 1873
Spencer, Duane Edward. 730
[Spencer, Dwight]. 1861
Spencer, Edmund. 1869
Spencer, Edna Earle Cole. 3145
Spencer, Floyd Albert. 2802
Spencer, Frederick Augustus Morland. 1697
Spencer, Frederick Joseph. 3548
Spencer, Geoffrey F. 649, 3188
Spencer, Herbert. 1536, 3471
Spencer, Ichabod Smith. 2935, 3291
Spencer, Jesse Ames. 3039
Spencer, John H. 154, 1628
Spencer, Justina K. 1465
Spencer, Katherine. 2677
Spencer, Malcolm. 1610, 3452
Spencer, Morton W. 46
Spencer, Moses. 1861
Spencer, Philip Herbert. 818
Spencer, Robert Stewart. 2535
Spencer, Roswell T. 1664
Spencer, Sidney. 2643, 2644, 3624
Spencer, Solomon Hogue. 1697
Spencer, Steven M. 2539
Spencer, Theodore. 1519
Spencer, Thomas. 75
Spener, Philipp Jakob. 2846
Spens, Will. 119
Spens, Willy de. 3238
Spenser, Edmund. 3471
Sperber, Alexander. 530, 1797
Sperka, Joshua Sidney. 512, 550, 1691, 3015
Sperling, Abraham Isaac. 1614, 2120
Sperna Weiland, Jan. 3657
Spero, Shubert. 1623, 3311
Sperow, Everett H. 1955
Sperry, Paul. 2692
Sperry, Roger Wolcott. 2686
Sperry, Sidney Branton. 558, 568, 598, 679, 2608, 2619, 3430
Sperry, Sidney Bronton. 679
Sperry, Wilard Learoyd. 1194
Sperry, Willard Learoyd. 57, 116, 1063, 1072, 1096, 1130, 1455, 1610, 2895, 2906, 3004, 3068, 3323, 3680, 3739, 3746, 3758, 3759, 3794, 1063, 1096, 1130, 3068, 3323, 3739
Spertus College of Judaica. 2331
Spetter, Matthew Ies. 2396
Speyr, Adrie. 2812
Speyr, Adrienne von. 2358, 2812
Sphujidhvaja. 98
Spice, Marjorie. 3121
Spicer, Dorothy Gladys. 902, 1028
Spicer, Tobias. 3463
Spicer, William Ambrose. 392, 608, 1515, 2494, 2495, 2948, 2982, 3380, 3383, 3386, 3879, 3889
Spicker, Max. 2109, 3576
[Spickler, Charles Abraham] 1880. 1794
Spicq, Ceslaus. 17, 1002, 1299, 2265
Spiegel, Shalom. 5, 2160

Spiegelberg, Frederic. 3121, 3709, 3867
Spiegelstein, Max. 1092
Spiegler, Gerhand. 3308
Spieler, Joseph. 850
Spielman, William Carl. 2016
Spielmann, Richard M. 2167, 3855
Spier, J M. 730, 1584, 2837
Spies, George. 392
Spike, Paul. 3472
Spike, Robert Warren. 976, 1123, 1131, 2528
Spiker, Louise C. 1254
Spillane, Edward Peter. 3767
Spillane, James Maria. 3469
Spiller, Michael R. G. 58, 743
Spillman, James Russell. 1515
Spillman, Sandy. 1577, 1755
Spillmann, Joseph. 3580
Spilman, Bernard Washington. 3180
Spilman, John M. 3080
Spina, Tony. 2124, 3770
Spindler, George Washington. 1632
Spindler, Karl. 1945
Spink, James F. 3456
Spink, John Stephenson. 2839
Spink, Walter. 876
Spink, Walter M. 2186, 2828
Spinka, Matthew. 1042, 1149, 1183, 1188, 1320, 1336, 1857, 2747, 3042, 3256, 3425, 3807, 1149, 1857, 2750, 3038, 3213
Spinka, Matthews. 1188, 1857
Spinks, F Pierce. 3682
Spinks, George Stephens. 1595, 3000
Spinoza, Benedictus de. 1426, 1536, 1537, 2834, 3472
Spinoza institute of America, inc., New York. 3472
Spirago, Franz. 746, 748, 767
Spiritual emphasis conference. 3493
Spiritual emphasis conference. 8th, Mohonk Lake, N.Y., 1932. 1727
Spiritual emphasis conference, New York (City) 1934. 3872
Spiritual Healing Seminar. 1600
Spiro, Jack D. 650, 1354, 1614, 3723
Spiro, Melford E. 709, 718
Spiro, Saul S. 1614, 2140
Spittler, Russell P. 346, 1123, 1731, 3121
Spitz, Lewis William. 3790, 878, 1187, 3037, 3042, 3407
Spivak, John Louis. 1372
Spivey, Charles S. 2437
Spivey, Clark Dwight. 3740
Spivey, Robert A. 411
Spivey, Ted Ray. 1802, 3095
Spivey, Thomas Sawyer. 307, 1078, 1092, 1581, 3221
Spock, Marjorie. 1544
Spoer, Hans Henry. 1524, 44, 2749
Spoerl, Howard Davis. 2994
Spoerri, Theophil. 699, 2593
Spong, John Shelby. 1315, 1972, 2054, 2880
Sponheim, Paul R. 1096, 2170, 2944
Sponseller, Edwin H. 1499, 2714
Spoolman, Jacob. 3300
Spooner, Lysander. 1656
Spottiswood, John. 3315
Spotts, Charles Dewey. 237, 938, 3158
Spotts, Frederic. 1146
Spottswood, Curran L. 2545
Spottswood, Wilson Lee. 2451
Sprading, Charles T. 3073
Spraggett, Allen. 1697, 2729, 2845, 2991
Sprague, Dorothy. 630
Sprague, Eli Wilmot. 2002, 3515
Sprague, Frank Headley. 3482
Sprague, Franklin Monroe. 199
[Sprague, Philo Woodruff] 1852-1927. 1113, 3522
Sprague, Ruth L. 3172
Sprague, William Buell. 1300, 1775, 2307, 2315, 2444, 3229, 3613, 3725, 3840
Spraker, Nettie L. 2364
Sprau, George. 211
Spray, Pauline. 1433
Spread, Ruldolph Alfred Richard. 1600
Spreng, Samuel P. 3291
Spreng, Samuel Peter. 3394
Spretnak, Charlene. 1742
Sprigg, June. 3397
Spriggs, D. G. 600, 1503
Sprigler, Augustine Joseph. 1541
Spring, Elizabeth (Thompson) 3697
Spring, Gardiner. 107, 118, 119, 216, 278, 536, 976, 1353, 1577, 2059, 2467, 2548, 2632, 2917, 3414, 3674, 3158
Spring, Henry Powell. 50, 3527
Spring, Samuel. 2002, 2326, 2412, 2496, 2743, 3587, 3728
Springer, Charles B. 1079
Springer, Fleta Campbell. 1496
Springer, Helen Emily (Chapman) 897, 2514
Springer, John. 138

Springer, John McKendree. 2513, 2514, 3522
Springer, Joseph Arthur. 945
Springer, Max. 884
Springer, Moses. 1869
Springer, Nelson P. 2404
Springer, Rebecca Ruter. 2942
Springfield, Mass. 1165
Springfield, Mass. City library association. 2847
Springfield, Mass. (Diocese) Synod, 2nd, 1957. 1373
Springfield, Mass. St. John's Congregational Church. 1180
Springfield, Mass. Saint Paul The Apostle Church. 1165
Springfield, Mass. South Congregational church. 1337
Springler, Augustine Joseph. 3493
Springsteen, Anne. 2895
Sprinkle, Henry Call. 1658, 2557
Sprinkle, Patricia Houck. 2928
Sproat, Granville Temple. 1861
Sproul, Barbara C. 1384
Sproul, J. Edward. 3872
Sproul, John Welsh. 1600
Sproul, R. C. 67
Sproul, Robert Charles. 67, 642
Sproull, Thomas. 3648
Spruce, Fletcher Clarke. 1238, 2790
Sprunger, Eva F. 194
Sprunger, J[ohn] A. 2949
Sprunger, John Abraham. 1515
Sprunger, Keith L. 34
Sprunt, James. 2935
Spry, John Hume. 1042
Spurgeon, C. H. 1453, 2030, 3347, 3358
Spurgeon, C.H. 3320
Spurgeon, Charles H. 3366
*Spurgeon, Charles H.tSpurgeon's catechism. 748
Spurgeon, Charles Haddon. 586, 1560, 145, 167, 237, 423, 441, 465, 509, 576, 615, 717, 976, 1299, 1433, 1442, 1560, 1570, 1824, 1842, 1986, 2058, 2396, 2906, 2980, 3321, 3336, 3345, 3362, 3367, 3375, 3523, 3632, 3840, 1836
Spurgeon, William Albertus. 456
Spurlock, James Aquila. 3076
Spurr, Frederic Chambers. 2002, 3000
Spurrier, William A. 3665
Spurrier, William Atwell. 945, 3648, 3665
Spykerboer, Hendrik Carel. 545, 1882
Spykman, Gordon J. 1801, 3660
Squier, Ephraim George. 1904
Squier, Miles Powell. 2982, 3412, 3624
Squire, Aelred. 1074, 1533, 3489
Squire, Charles. 2655
Squire, Francis. 1211
Squire, Russel Nelson. 1208, 1464
Squires, Beulah Greene. 2757
Squires, Walter Albion. 1882, 1955, 3135, 3180, 1130, 2061, 3158, 3766
Srawley, James Herbert. 2230, 2240, 2257
Sreenivasa Murthy, H. V. 3301, 3766
Sri Krishna Prem, 1898. 2316
Sri Krishna Prem, 1898-1965. 3866
Sri Ram, Nilakanta. 3688
Srimalasutra. English. 710
Srinivas, Mysore Narasimhachar. 1368
Srinivasa, Chari, S. M. 3775
Srinivasachari, P. N. 2317
Srinivasan, K. R. 3600
Sri Ram, Nilakanta. 3688
Srivastava, A. K. 1732, 3579
Srivastava, Rama Shanker. 3121
Sroka, Barbara. 3415
Srygley, F. B. 1123
Srygley, F. D. 1053
Sogaard, Viggo B. 2844
Ssu shu. 1538
St Amant, Penrose, 1915. 154
Staab, Giles. 761
Staack, Hagen. 494, 2951
Staal, Frits. 19, 2648
Stabler, James W. 1560
Stabler, William. 3524
Stabley, Rhodes R. 2847
Stace, Walter Terence. 2640, 3105, 2419, 2640, 3064, 3105
Stace, Wlater Terence. 3105
Stacey, John. 3861
Stacey, Walter David. 237, 2325
Stach, John Frederick. 1246
Stachen, Lee Garland. 5, 631
Stack, Frank. 1994
Stack, Richard. 331
Stackel, Robert W. 649, 3188, 3889
Stackhouse, Max L. 3446
Stackhouse, Mildred (Orr) 3524
Stackhouse, Perry James. 893, 1842, 2248
Stackpole, Everett Schermerhorn. 2486, 3295
Stacy, Gussie Brown. 3859
Stacy, James. 2949, 2463, 2917
Stacy, Nathaniel. 3135
Stacy, Thomas Hobbs. 123

Stadelman, William Francis Xavier. 1832
Stadler, Johann Evangelist. 1025
Stadsklev, Julius. 690
Stadtler, Bea. 1825
Stadtmauer, Saul A. 2753
Staffeld, Jean. 937
Stafford, Ann. 872, 3460
Stafford, Edward Russell. 1956
Stafford, Geoffrey Wardle. 3336
Stafford, Hazel (Straight) 3763
Stafford, J. M. 1425
Stafford, Leroy Henry. 321
Stafford, Russell Henry. 1727, 392, 976, 1063, 2066
Stafford, Thomas Albert. 921, 1442, 2444
Stafford, Thomas Polhill. 1035, 1832, 3648
Stafford, Tim. 3391, 3889
Stafford, Ward. 2528
Stafford, William S. 3039, 3040
Stagaard, George Hansen. 3524
Stagg, Albert. 1898, 3234
Stagg, Evelyn. 1959, 3832
Stagg, Frank. 18, 330, 381, 430, 477, 1716, 1832, 2325
Stagg, John Weldon. 728, 1907
Stagg, Paul L. 1570
Stagg, Samuel Wells. 3158, 3165
Stahl, Carolyn. 1442
Stahl, Ferdinand Anthony. 1903
Stahl, Friedrich Julius. 2858
Stahl, Thomas K. 1627
Stahlin, Wilhelm. 1123
Stahmer, Harold. 3070, 3087
Stainaker, Leo. 3576
*Stainback, Arthur House. 1916, 3592
Stainer, John. 2634
Stakely, Charles Averett. 2586
Stalcup, Lena (Van Aken). 158, 3524
Staley, Amelia Fargo. 3515
Staley, Cady. 2072
Staley, Daniel Earl. 976
Staley, Ronald. 1320, 3449
Staley, Sue Reynolds. 2551
[Staley, Thomas Nettleship. 39, 2524
Staley, Vernon. 45
Staley, William Wesley. 2475
Stalker, Charles H[enry]. 3135
Stalker, Charles Henry. 2495
Stalker, James. 2802, 489, 1955, 1972, 107, 477, 976, 1595, 1972, 1994, 2004, 2044, 2068, 2127, 2128, 2802, 2804, 2906, 3111, 3782
Stall, Sylvanus. 904, 1168, 1442, 3370
Stallman, Birdie. 3826
Stalnaker, Luther Winfield. 1854
Stam, Cornelius Richard. 330, 377, 1376, 1529
St. Amant, C Penrose. 154
Stamm, Frederick K. 3366
Stamm, Frederick Keller. 181, 1053, 1063, 1342, 1343, 2060, 2072, 2325, 2787, 3049
Stamm, Johann Jakob. 1314
Stamm, John Samuel. 1570
Stamm, Mildred. 1433
Stammler, Eberhard. 1063
Stamp, Josiah Charles Stamp. 3446, 945
Stamps, Drure Fletcher. 464
Stamps, Ellen de Kroon. 932, 3524
Stanard, Mary Mann Page (Newton) 2706
Stanbrook abbey. 884, 2309
Stanbrough, O W. 2340
Stanbrough, Rufus M. 1752
Stanbury, Walter Albert. 2426
Stanchfield, Wilma. 1367, 3524
Stancourt, Louis. 1365
Stancourt, Louis Joseph. 1365
Stander, Thomas F. 713
Standish, Stella Vienna. 1017
Standley, Fred L. 693
Standley, Meredith Goslin. 909, 1560
Stanfield, James Monroe. 3665
Stanfield, Vernon L. 1560, 2906, 3854
Stanford, Charles. 1472
Stanford, Edward V. 763, 832
Stanford, John. 3345
Stanford, Miles J. 988
Stanford, Ray. 2357, 3474
Stanford University. Publications Service. 3524
Stang, Hakon. 1926
Stang, William. 773, 792, 1253, 1826, 2277, 3676
Stange, Douglas C. 1074, 3424
Stanger, Frank Bateman. 1600
Staniforth, Oswald. 1649
Staniland, Hilary. 3755
Staniloae, Dumitru. 2749, 3634
Stanislao di Santa Teresa. 3602
Stanislaw, Richard J. 1870
Stankiewicz, W J. 1639
Stanley, Alfred Knighton. 16
Stanley, Arthur Penrhyn. 909, 1217, 1768, 2090, 2096, 2747, 2763, 3370, 3625
Stanley, Charles F. 2402
Stanley, Clifford L. 1417

Stanley, David Michael. 373, 392, 1188, 1595, 2049, 2269, 2883, 3476
Stanley, E. S. 1529, 3095
Stanley, Reva. 2606, 2867
Stanley, Theodore P. 3202
Stanley, Victor Bland. 1223
Stanley, Walter Edgar. 2396, 2437
Stanley-Wrench, Margaret. 2596
Stannard, David E. 1415
Stannard, William H. 1484
Stan-Padilla, Viento, 1945. 3524, 3862
Stanton, Arthur Henry. 1616
Stanton, Elizabeth Cady. 224, 225, 3840, 3841
Stanton, G. N. 349, 2011
Stanton, Gerald B. 3320
Stanton, Herbert Udny Weitbrecht. 2184
Stanton, Horace Coffin. 1697, 2991
Stanton, Phoebe B. 1749
Stanton, Stephen Berrien. 3463, 2228
Stanton, Vincent Henry. 119, 392
Stanton, William Arthur. 2532
[Stanwood, Eunice H. 2125
Stapfer, Edmond Louis. 1972, 1973, 1977, 1986, 2030
Staples, Edward D. 3165
Staples, Ethlyne Babcock. 2773
Staples, Laurence Carlton. 3796
Staples, M. W. 2936
Stapleton, Ammon. 1546
Stapleton, Michael. 2657
Stapleton, Peter. 1203
Stapleton, Ruth Carter. 1600, 2018
Stapleton, S.I. Immaculate Conception Church. 3525
Stapleton, Thomas. 792
Stapper, Richard. 840
Starbuck, Edwin Diller. 3000
Starbuck, James C. 1162
Starbuck, John C. 2228
Starck, Johann Friedrich. 2396, 2625
Starck, Mary. 1036
Starcke, Walter. 988, 2640, 3482
Stare, Frederick Arthur. 1311
Starenko, Ronald C. 1353, 1415, 2252
Starhawk. 3824
Stark, Alonzo Rosecrans. 76, 2009
Stark, Claude Alan. 3020
Stark, J. Carroll. 1241, 1727
Stark, Lewis Morgrage. 199
Stark, Phyllis. 1303
Stark, Rodney. 3747
Stark, Werner. 3087
Starkes, M. Thomas. 2504, 2815, 3121, 3326
Starkey, Lycurgus Monroe. 470, 950, 1832, 1835, 2895, 3805
Starkey, Marion Lena. 1339, 3827, 3828
Starkie, Walter Fitzwilliam. 1934, 3303
Starkloff, Carl F. 1902
Starkoff, Bernard J. 2100
Starks, Arthur E. 227, 680, 3430
Starling, Lucy. 2553
Starr, Bill. 1735
Starr, Edward Caryl. 144
Starr, Eliza Allen. 2357, 2794
Starr, Frederick. 20, 706, 1331
[Starr, Frederick Ratchford] 1821-1889. 1983
Starr, Homer Worthington. 3158
[Starr, Hyman] 1864-1942. 502
Starr, Irina. 2637
Starr, Lee Anna. 3841
Starr, William Henry. 1595
Starratt, Alfred B. 1096, 3105
Starratt, Rose M. 2699
Starrett, Harry Halsey. 976
Stasheff, Edward. 2910
Statler, Ruth Beeghly. 695, 1236
Staton, Julia. 3834
Staton, Knofel. 181, 237, 988, 1741, 2340
Staub, Jacob J. 1384, 2219
St. Aubyn, Gwendolen (Nicolson) 1365
Staudacher, Joseph M. 480, 2202
Staudacher, Rosemarian V. 885, 2584
Stauderman, Albert P. 1200, 1353, 2288, 2290
Staudinger, Josef. 1697, 2396
Staudt, Calvin Klopp. 3221
Stauffer, Ethelbert. 477, 1195, 1973
Stauffer, Henry. 2467
Stauffer, Joshua. 1595, 1832, 3375
Stauffer, Milton Theobald. 2503, 2511, 2532, 2549, 2551
Stauffer, Milton Theobold. 2535
Stauffer, Richard. 2280, 728, 2280
Staunton, J. Donald. 3331
Staunton, John Armitage. 3309
Stavis, Barrie. 2133
Stead, Estelle Wilson. 3515, 3526
Stead, Francis Herbert. 3446
Stead, George Christopher. 81, 3538
Stead, W. T. memorial center. 3515
Stead, W. T., memorial center, Chicago. 3515
Stead, W. T., memorials center, Chicago. 3515

Stead, William T[homas]. 3526
Stead, William Thomas. 681, 3293, 3515
Stealey, Sydnor Lorenzo. 143
Stearn, Jess. 877, 1283, 2308, 2597, 2729, 3054, 3407, 3515, 3866
Stearns, Ada P. 156
Stearns, Bill. 945, 988
Stearns, Daniel Miner. 465, 936
Stearns, Edward Josiah. 802, 1711, 2348
Stearns, George. 2050, 3023
Stearns, John M[ilton]. 2675
Stearns, Jonathan French. 2701
Stearns, Lewis French. 3427, 3648
Stearns, Monroe. 1757
Stearns, Peter N. 2194
Stearns, Raymond Phineas. 1338, 1764, 2826
Stearns, Samuel. 1513
Stearns, Sharon. 902
Stearns, Wallace Nelson. 2090, 2121, 1616
[Stearns, William Augustus]. 3526
Stebbing, George. 810
Stebbing, Henry. 1219
Stebbins, Charles Matthews. 625
Stebbins, Charles Maurice. 2175, 2948
Stebbins, Edna Willett (Hodgkins) 482
Stebbins, George Coles. 1748, 2632, 1575
Stebbins, Giles Badger. 3204, 3515
Stebbins, Jane E. 926, 927, 1697
Stebbins, John Wesley. 3027
Stebbins, Rufus Phineas. 564, 2187, 2230, 3726
Steck, Francis Borgia. 29, 1148, 1647
Steck, James S. 3008
Steck, Odil Hannes. 1383
Steckley, Anna Marie. 932, 3526
Steckoll, Solomon H. 1944
Stedman, Edmund Clarence. 1689
Stedman, Elaine. 3846
Stedman, Joseph F. 693, 859, 1958
Stedman, Murray Salisbury. 1151
Stedman, Ray C. 323, 324, 332, 334, 365, 404, 424, 437, 438, 444, 471, 526, 529, 547, 551, 608, 988, 1123, 2026, 2049, 2325, 2812, 2880, 3358, 3541
Steed, Ernest H. J. 237, 1483, 2546, 3749
Steedman, Amy. 1973, 3285
Steel, Daniel. 2627, 2818
Steel, David. 2906
Steel, Robert. 3178
Steel, Samuel Augustus. 237, 1289, 1325
Steele, Algernon Odell. 976, 1063
Steele, Daniel. 1956, 2855, 1832, 2818, 2855, 3358
Steele, David. 456
Steele, David McConnell. 1126, 123
Steele, David N. 471, 730
Steele, Eileen Aultman. 3172
Steele, Eliza R. 494, 3841
Steele, Francesca Maria. 2569
Steele, Francis Rue. 2713
Steele, George McKendree. 649
Steele, Harold C. 682, 3293
Steele, Harvey. 3526
Steele, James E. 1261
[Steele, Richard]. 976
Steele, Richard Holloway. 2686
Steele, Robert V. P. 2310
Steele, Thomas J. 3303
Steele, Wayne H. 3142
Steelman, Robert. 1208
Steelman, Robert Bevis. 1396
Steen, Ester A. 2015
Steen, Inez. 3158, 3184
Steen, John Warren. 994
Steen, Robert Service. 2935
Steen, Shirley. 627
Steenberghen, Fernand van. 1738, 2739
Steensma, Juliana. 2845, 3526
Steenweg, Herman. 1053
Steere, Daniel C. 988, 1007
Steere, Douglas van. 976
Steere, Douglas Van. 1005, 1045, 1114, 1356, 1453, 1675, 1682, 2131, 2790, 2880, 3223, 3482
Steere, Dwight. 1209
Steese, Peter B. 513
Steeves, Dimmock. 1254
Steeves, Paul D. 1994, 3665
Steffan, Alice Jacqueline (Kennedy) 2177
Steffen, Albert. 3527
Steffens, Diedrich Henry. 3790
Steffens, Helmut. 2280
Steffens, Joseph Lincoln. 2622
Stegenga, J. 344, 345, 1769
Stegge, Pius aan de. 2134
Steggerda, Morris. 1453
Stehle, Aurelius. 843, 844
Stehle, Hansjakob. 860, 1542
Steibel, Warren. 3471
*Steiger, Brad. 94, 1710, 1900, 1902, 2729, 2949, 2991, 3054, 3055, 3226, 3304, 3589, 3719
Steiger, Henry William. 1036
Steiman, Sidney. 1931, 2100

Steimle, Edmund a. 1486, 2301, 2302, 3358, 3360
Stein, Arnold Sidney. 2471, 2469
Stein, Calvert. 2781
Stein, Edith. 2137, 777
Stein, Edward V. 1127, 1777
Stein, Evaleen. 911, 1453
Stein, Gordon. 1656, 1908
Stein, Henry Binkley. 1742
Stein, Jack. 528
Stein, Robert H. 2026, 2061
Stein, Samuel A. 1168
Stein, Sandra Kovacs. 3576
Stein, William Bysshe. 1815
Steinbach, Alexander Alan. 910, 2118, 2143, 3361
Steinbacher, Nicholas. 794
Steinbauer, Friedrich. 739
Steinberg, Milton. 2093, 2079, 2093, 2116, 2140, 1623, 2116, 2143, 3361, 3372
Steinberg, Moses. 2140
Steinberger, Georg. 1453
Steindorff, Georg. 1502
Steiner, Bruce E. 3317
Steiner, Edward Alfred. 2771, 3191
Steiner, Franklin. 300, 3193
Steiner, Johannes. 2686, 3783
*Steiner, Rudolf. 426, 1078, 1485, 2729
Steiner, Rudolf. 3574, 1498, 2729, 2991, 3475, 3527, 50, 51, 97, 102, 1078, 1079, 1486, 1658, 1912, 2165, 2317, 2640, 2645, 2659, 2729, 3527, 3688
Steiner, Rudolfa. 2710
Steingraeber, John. 2016, 2880
Steinhaeuser, Albert Theodore William. 2033, 2282, 2033
Steinhardt, Irving David. 3389
Steinhauser, Gerard R. 2019
Steinhauser, Gerhard R. 1102, 2019
Steinilber-Oberlin, Emile, 1878. 712
Steinitz, Paul. 123
Steinke, Peter L. 470, 976, 988, 3394, 3889
Steinmann, Friedel. 553
Steinmann, Jean. 312, 1411, 1811, 1973, 2128, 3665
Steinmetz, C. Martin. 32, 1210
Steinmetz, David Curtis. 2277, 3037
Steinmetz, George Harold. 1662, 1670, 1671
Steinmetz, Margaret Bird. 2396
Steinmetz, Urban G. 3393
Steinmueller, John E. 498, 312, 411, 502
Steinsalz, Adin. 722, 3581, 3584, 3585
Steinschneider, Moritz. 2076
Steinweg, Virginia Duffie. 40
[Stelkens, Mary Teheresa. 2884
Stellhorn, August Conrad. 2287, 2297
Stellhorn, August Joseph Conrad. 2297
Stelzer, Theodore George Wilhelm. 3563
Stelzle, Charles. 10, 1279, 3366
Stemman, Roy. 3515
Stemmer, Charles C. 3515
Stenberg, Odin K. 1244
Stendahl, Brita K. 1005, 1314, 2170
Stendahl, Krister. 314, 378, 1028, 1411, 1891, 2742, 2803
Stenerson, Ruth. 3415
Stengel, Paul. 1395
Stenger, Joseph Bernard. 2620
Stenhouse, Fanny. 2606, 2613
Stenhouse, Thomas B H. 2616
Stennett, Samuel. 3468
Stenson, Sten H. 3064
Stepens, John Vant. 3135
Stephan, Eric G. 1604
Stephanos. 2100
Stephanou, Eusebius A. 2744
Stephen, Caroline Emelia. 3416
Stephen college, Columbia, Mo. 3158
Stephen, Dorothea Jane. 2840
Stephen, James. 927
Stephen, Leslie. 19, 1821, 2704
Stephens, Bill. 1164
Stephens, Charles Asbury. 3463
Stephens, Frank Fletcher. 1311
Stephens, George T. 3229
Stephens, Ira Kendrick. 2586
Stephens, James T. 2845
Stephens, John Underwood. 2881, 2895
Stephens, John Vant. 1396
Stephens, Julius Edward. 2175, 2176, 2200
Stephens, Kenneth D. 1232, 2948
Stephens, Madge. 2592
Stephens, Marjorie Gates. 2003
Stephens, Overton. 988
Stephens, Shirley. 349, 3841
Stephens, Simon. 191
Stephens, Thomas. 3158
Stephens, W. Peter. 720, 1835
Stephens, William Richard Wood. 1542, 1759, 1774
Stephenson, Andrew. 2090
Stephenson, Anthony A. 44
Stephenson, Colin. 3527
Stephenson, Frank W. 3535

Stephenson, George Malcolm. 110, 2277, 3572, 3739, 3572, 3739
Stephenson, Gwendolen. 3580
Stephenson, James M. 2175
Stephenson, Maude A. 498
Stephenson, Virginia. 2881
Stephenson, William. 2006
Stepler, John Henry. 3253
Sterck, Leo Clement. 1977
Sterling, Ada. 2085
Sterling, Alice M. 2687
Sterling, Anthony. 3009
Sterling, Chandler W. 1063, 1940, 2788, 3484, 3527, 3665
Sterling, Tamar (Wright) 2532, 2824
Stern, E. Mark. 1106
[Stern, Elizabeth Gertrude (Levin) 3143
Stern, Ellen Norman. 1717, 3309
Stern, Gladys Bronwyn. 1365, 1995
Stern, Harry Joshua. 2083, 2143, 3368
Stern, Henry L. 3515, 3527
Stern, Herman Isidore. 2666
Stern, Horace. 2143
Stern, Jay B. 2106
Stern, Malcolm H. 2106
Stern, Stephen. 2084, 3333
Sterner, R. Eugene. 1003, 1123, 1228, 2192
Sterrett, James Macbride. 57, 3211, 1800, 2561, 3105
Sterrett, T. Norton. 237
Stetler, Roy Herben. 1453
[Stetson, Augusta Emma (Simmons) 3527
Stetson, Augusta Emma (Simmons) 564, 1036
Steuart, Bendict. 840
Steuart, John Alexander. 3296
Steuart, Robert Henry Joseph. 3223, 761, 765, 783, 976, 2175, 765, 3489
Steubenville, O. First Presbyterian church. 1312
Steuding, Hermann. 2657
Steurt, Marjorie Rankin. 3135
Steve, M. J. 283
Steve, Marie Joseph. 283
Steven, George. 3443
Steven, Hugh. 184, 1903, 2128, 2486, 2491, 2542, 3322, 3527, 3721, 3860
Steven, Norma. 3527, 3877
Stevens, Abel. 133, 927, 952, 1241, 1930, 2425, 2427, 2433, 2451, 3806
Stevens, Benjamin. 1504
Stevens, Beulah Fern. 988, 3528
Stevens, Charles Hadley. 3721
Stevens, Charles McClellan. 1890, 2994
Stevens, Clifford J. 765, 930, 1984, 3469
Stevens, Courtenay Edward. 1026, 3407
Stevens, Dan E. 2400, 3482
Stevens, David Harrison. 2469
Stevens, Denis William. 1207
Stevens, Dorothy A. 30, 143, 154, 2551
Stevens, Edmund Harding. 2757
Stevens, Edouard. 1264
Stevens, Edward. 2644, 3105
Stevens, Eldred N. 794
Stevens, Ewing Campbell. 1261
Stevens, George Bakers. 3291
Stevens, George Barker. 326, 373, 377, 414, 477, 2066, 2776, 2804, 3648
Stevens, George Dewey. 2782
Stevens, Georgia. 885
Stevens, Gregory. 1752
Stevens, Halsey R. 3121
Stevens, Henry. 212
Stevens, Henry D. 3482
[Stevens, J Adams]. 3380
Stevens, James Stacy. 253, 642
Stevens, Jesse C. 2119, 2768
Stevens, Jesse Columbus. 3320
Stevens, John. 3545
Stevens, Leon Herbert. 3515, 3528
Stevens, Lillian M N (Ames) 3595
Stevens, Maria. 3482
Stevens, Paul M. 67, 2396
Stevens, Rene. 3439
Stevens, Robert Meredith. 1453
[Stevens, Samuel Eugene]. 1890, 3313, 3568
Stevens, Samuel Nowell. 3000
Stevens, Sherrill G. 522
Stevens, Thelona D. 649
[Stevens, William Bacon, 1815-1887. 1353, 2026, 2972, 3358
Stevens, William Bagshaw. 3135
Stevens, William Bertrand. 2128, 2212, 2708, 2212
Stevens, William Coit. 552, 608, 2466
Stevens, William Oliver. 1479, 1890
Stevens, William Wilson. 407, 424, 536, 3648
Stevenson, Arthur Linwood. 1873, 2427, 2431, 2713, 2826, 3781
Stevenson, Burton Egbert. 304
Stevenson, Charles Goldsmith. 3306
Stevenson, Dwight Eshelman. 299, 411, 423, 537, 989, 1461, 2220, 2763, 2906, 2910, 3182, 3315, 3358

Stevenson, Francis Seymour. 1763, 1775
Stevenson, George John. 1873, 3523, 3806
Stevenson, Gilbert F. 2079
Stevenson, Herbert F. 216, 413, 1561, 1736, 1977, 3484
Stevenson, Ian. 3054, 3055
Stevenson, J. W. 1011
Stevenson, James. 85, 1197, 1544
Stevenson, John. 574, 587, 588, 1998
Stevenson, John Gilchrist. 2802, 3064
[Stevenson, John McMillan]. 2528
[Stevenson, Katharine Lent]. 3598
Stevenson, Kenneth. 1827
Stevenson, Margaret. 1814, 1932
Stevenson, Margaret J. 1984
Stevenson, Marion. 199, 596, 649
Stevenson, Richard T[aylor]. 2425
Stevenson, Richard Taylor. 2495, 728
Stevenson, Robert Louis. 1400
Stevenson, Robert [Murrell]. 1209, 1210
Stevenson, W. Taylor. 1819
Stevenson, Wilfred S. 2325
Stevenson, William. 3036
Stevenson, William Charles. 1941
Stevenson, William Fleming. 927, 2961
Stevick, Daniel B. 736, 1691, 3004
Steward, Charles William. 2345
Steward, George. 3064
*Steward, Gwenda R. 2502
Steward, Mary Alicia. 898, 1984
Steward, Theophilus Gould. 205
Stewardson, Langdon Cheeves. 3366
Stewart, Abel T. 2714
Stewart, Alexander Doig. 2973, 3358
Stewart, Alexander McGinn. 1949, 2402
Stewart, Andrew G. 2533, 3531
Stewart, Annabel (Murray) 3878
[Stewart, Balfour]. 1890
Stewart, Bowyer. 3741
Stewart, Charles Cameron. 21, 1925
Stewart, Charles D. 3023
Stewart, Charles E. 2864
Stewart, Charles Hylton. 1206
Stewart, Charles William. 1296, 1610, 2781, 3889
Stewart, David Alexander. 1080
Stewart, Don. 67
Stewart, Donald Gordon. 1374, 3158
Stewart, Dugald. 1537
Stewart, Eliza (Daniel) 692
Stewart, Elmer Bryan. 3702
Stewart, Eva (Southgate) 3576
Stewart, George. 281, 937, 1123, 1256, 1727, 1893, 1955, 2044, 2895, 2935, 3158, 3162, 3210, 3221, 3531, 3859, 3860
Stewart, George Black. 1955, 1787
Stewart, George Craig. 1837, 3271, 1053, 1955
Stewart, George Shaw. 2881
Stewart, Georgia Metcalf. 3217
Stewart, Gordon. 26, 3231
Stewart, Grover C. 1505
Stewart, H J. 2633
Stewart, Howard R. 150
Stewart, Irma. 424
Stewart, Ivan Robert. 737
Stewart, James. 2498
Stewart, James Alexander. 1570, 306, 1433, 1738, 2813, 3345
Stewart, James H. 2670
Stewart, James Livingstone. 914
Stewart, James Stuart. 377, 1063, 1973, 2555, 2802, 2906, 2935, 3366, 3368, 3714
Stewart, Jane Agnes. 2021
[Stewart, John]. 3434
Stewart, John. 2453, 2684
Stewart, John Alexander. 81
Stewart, John J. 1939, 2018, 2019, 2021, 2606, 2614, 2618, 3429
Stewart, John T. 10, 1291, 3746
Stewart, Joseph. 1325
Stewart, Malcolm. 1869
Stewart, Marjorie. 1570
Stewart, Marshall Bowyer. 1730, 3648
Stewart, Mary. 297, 630, 3869
Stewart, Ora (Pate) 679, 680, 2613, 3430, 3877
Stewart, Robert. 2532
Stewart, Robert Laird. 1689, 1930
Stewart, Robert William. 1995
Stewart, S. A. 2535
Stewart, Samuel J. 3728
[Stewart, W. G.]. 3135
Stewart, Walter Sinclair. 144
Stewart, Wentworth Fall. 1570
Stewart, William. 1082, 3135, 3639
Stewart, William Alexander Campbell. 1683
Stewart, William James. 976
Stewart, William Rhinelander. 2699
Stewart, Willie Jean. 169, 3467, 3765
Stiansen, Peder. 158, 2714
*Stibbs, Alan M. 4
Stibbs, Alan Marshall. 288, 325, 2908

Stibbs, Allen Marshall. 1832
Stibitz, George. 2414
Sticco, Maria. 1293, 1643, 1704
Stickelberger, Emanuel. 728
Stickney, Henry Elmer. 3208
Stidger, William Le Roy. 1360, 1727, 481, 927, 1252, 1485, 1842, 1843, 1890, 2827, 2887, 2895, 2906, 3345, 3347
Stiegele, Paul. 3223
Stieglitz, Heinrich. 1262
Stier, Ewald Rudolf. 412, 2072
Stier, Mark. 1646
Stierli, Josef. 3270
Stiernotte, Alfred P. 2640
Stietenroth, Charles. 2669
Stifler, Francis Carr. 143, 304
Stifler, James Madison. 331, 469, 431, 1994
Stigers, Harold G. 522
Stiles, Ezra. 1338, 3862
Stiles, H Nelson. 2713
Stiles, Isaac. 2743, 3532
Stiles, Jack E. 1832
Stiles, Joseph. 1241
Stiles, Joseph Clay. 732
Stiles, Joseph D. 3515
Stiles, Mervin. 537
Stiles, William Curtis. 2228, 1360, 2178
Still, Florence Shirley (Swetnam) 3158
Still, James Ironside. 331, 2802
Still, William Grant. 2680
Stillingfleet, Edward. 1241, 1759
Stillman, Mildred Whitney. 1955, 3159
Stillman, Mildred (Whitney) 1453
Stillman, Peter. 1756
Stillman, Peter R. 2649
Stillmock, Martin. 3881
Stillpass, Leo Joseph. 3345
Stillwater, Okl. Methodist church. 2432
Stillwell, Richard. 78, 2942
Stillz, Eva M. 3159
Stilson, Max. 281, 874, 1570, 1941, 2613, 3121
Stilz, Eva M. 3159
Stimmel, Howard Lincoln. 976, 1891, 2066
Stimpson, George William. 281
Stimson, Edward W. 878, 1063
Stimson, Henry Albert. 74, 2419, 3345
Stimson, Hiram K. 144
Stimson, John Francis. 2666, 2667, 3717
Stimson, Mary (Sturdivant) 630
Stine, Charles Milton Altland. 1581
Stine, Peter W. 2396
Stinger, Charles L. 1616, 3710
Stinnette, Charles Roy. 1108, 1752
Stinson, Elizabeth. 3765
Stinson, Ernest Claire. 1944
Stinson, James Cyrus. 205
Stinson, John Harrison. 945
Stinson, Roddy. 3184
Stires, Ernest Van R. 2788
Stirling, Betty. 1309, 2677, 3387
Stirling, James. 2771
Stirling, James Hutchison. 3105
Stirling, John. 1984, 3285
Stith, William. 1222
Stitskin, Leon D. 4, 186, 2143, 2751
Stivers, Richard. 3433
Stix, Henry S. 927
Stob, George. 297
Stob, Henry. 1659, 951, 3625
Stob, Ralph. 1282
Stobart, James William Hampson. 2565, 2629
Stobart, Mabel Annie (Boulton) 3520
Stobbe, Leslie H. 616
Stobo, Edward John. 2396
Stock, Augustine. 1529, 1584, 2622, 3291
Stock, Dennis. 1643
Stock, Eugene. 291, 1221, 428
Stock, Frederick. 2545, 2918
Stock, Harry Thomas. 1248, 2551, 2670, 3159, 3453, 3881, 2204, 3186
Stock, Leo Francis. 3741
Stock, R. D. 1518
Stockbridge, John Calvin. 3534, 3535
Stockdale, Allen A. 2895
Stockdale, Fairbank B. 1697, 2426
Stockdale, William. 1940
tocker. 2936
tocker, Harry Emilius. 2595, 2596
tocker, Richard Dimsdale. 1283
Stockhammer, Morris. 3695
tockhardt, George. 364, 2215
Stocking, Charles Francis. 2019, 3135
tocking, Jay Thomas. 895
tockinger, William M. 451, 452
tocklin, Ulrich von Rottach. 1877
tockton, Thomas Hewlings. 278, 2426
tockums, Wilhelm. 773, 1296, 1299
tockwell, Chester Twitchell. 1891
tockwell, Eugene L. 1066
tockwell, Francis Olin. 2942
tockwell, Herbert Grant. 1697
tockwell, Sara (Ward) 1015
tockwell, Spencer Lewis. 2458

Stockwood, Mervyn. 1747
Stoddard, Anne (Glen) 292
Stoddard, Charles Warren. 54, 868, 3135
Stoddard, Francis Hovey. 2636
[Stoddard, John Lawson] 1850-1931. 19
Stoddard, Solomon. 1360, 2161
Stoddard, Whitney S. 1159, 3275
Stoddard, William S. 2396
Stoddart, Jane T. 502, 726, 3515
Stoddart, William. 3543
Stoddart, William Wright. 1287
Stoesz, Samuel J. 994
Stoever, Martin Luther. 2375, 2630
Stoever, William K. B. 1377
Stoffel, Ernest Lee. 456, 1011, 2175, 2935
Stoger, Alois. 428
[Stohr, Fred E.]. 646
Stoke, John H. 1973
Stokes, Anson Phelps. 881, 1151, 2066, 1151
Stokes, Charles J. 1269
Stokes, Ellwood Haines. 2733
[Stokes, George] 1789-1847. 3037
Stokes, George Gabriel. 2674
Stokes, George Thomas. 1918
Stokes, Jeremiah. 2613
Stokes, Kathleen. 1938
Stokes, Mack B. 186, 240, 652, 2428, 3226, 3668, 3805
[Stokes, Olivia Egleston Phelps]. 253
Stokl, Andreas. 1316
Stoldt, Hans-Herbert. 436, 3578
Stolee, Haakon Jacobs. 527, 1716
Stolee, Ingeborg B. 2277, 2021
Stolee, Michael J. 3110
Stolk, Sirkar van. 1892, 3543
Stoll, George. 1252
*Stoll, Joseph. 1017
Stollnitz, Henry Sande. 2105
Stolpe, Sven. 1783
Stoltzfus, Grant M. 2404
Stolz, Alban. 1707
Stolz, Anselm. 115, 2643
Stolz, Benedict. 2574
Stolz, Benedikt. 1332, 2352
Stolz, Karl Ruf. 1581, 2881, 2994, 3000, 2995
Stolzfus, Ruth Brunk. 1604
Stone, Alonzo. 3072
Stone, Baman Nelson. 1123
Stone, Barton Warren. 107, 733, 1461, 1464
*Stone, Betty E. 400
Stone, Darwell. 136, 2194, 2252, 3135, 3266, 2194, 2252
[Stone, E. A.]. 1832
Stone, Edwin Martin. 3819
Stone, Elizabeth Caecilia. 93
Stone, Harry William. 3872
Stone, Henry Morgan. 3345
Stone, Howard W. 2781
[Stone, Jacob L.]. 1306
Stone, James. 1229
Stone, James Kent. 792
Stone, James S[amuel]. 1747
Stone, James Samuel. 193, 1203, 3202
Stone, John Seely. 1123, 1224, 1775, 2467
Stone, John Timothy. 122
Stone, John Timothy. 122, 976, 1453, 1571, 3196, 3345
Stone, Justin. 92, 2381
Stone, Justin F. 3892
Stone, Lee Alexander. 2828
[Stone, Lucy Bradlee]. 1442
Stone, Margaret Manson (Barbour) 2994
Stone, Merlin. 1742, 3834, 3838
Stone, Michael E. 2150
Stone, Nathan J. 599, 1736, 3012
Stone, Phyllis. 2854
Stone, Richard Cecil. 3533
Stone, Robert B. 1261, 2729, 3718
Stone, Robert Hamlin. 2927
Stone, Ronald H. 1087, 1088, 2709, 3088, 3700
Stone, Sam E. 989, 2787
Stone, Stewart. 3412
Stone, William Leete. 1283, 1612, 2373, 2585, 2587
Stonehill, Charles Archibald. 2083
Stonehouse, Ned Bernard. 335, 436, 2308, 2802, 392
Stonelake, Alfred R. 2183
Stoneley, Jack. 2729
Stoner, Carroll. 1393
Stoner, Peter Winebrenner. 205
Stonesifer, Paul Tobias. 1545
Stoney, James Moss. 1524
Stoney, William Shannon. 2598
Stonor, Robert Julian. 3533
Stoody, John Henry. 1282
Stooker, Wilhelmina. 2511, 2551
Stookey, Laurence Hull. 136
Stoop, David A. 3176, 3330
Stoops, Ella. 3515
Stoops, John Dashiell. 2066
Storch, Neil T. 779
Storen, Helen Frances. 3592

Storer, Jacob. 642, 726, 1442
Storer, James W. 3159
Storer, James Wilson. 560, 2937, 3159, 3674
Storey, Del. 1302, 3533
Storey, Frederick Davis. 237
[Storey, William G.]. 1203
Storey, William George. 859, 1264, 1265
Storff, Hugolinus. 2272
Stork, Theophilus. 898, 1610, 2277
Storm, Ida Paterson. 2501
Storm, Marian. 3247
Storm, William Harold. 77
Storms, Albert Boynton. 1072
Storms, Everck Richard. 3735
Storms, Godfrid. 2313
Storr, Catherine. 339, 495, 930, 1984, 2132, 2712
Storr, Gottlob Christian. 3648
Storr, Rayner. 1885
Storr, Vernon Faithfull. 312, 1891, 2951, 3609, 1760
[Storrs, George] 1796. 1453
Storrs, George. 1891
Storrs, Richard S[alter]. 2522
Storrs, Richard Salter. 1772, 193, 1099, 1344, 2522, 2908, 3463, 3609, 3861
Story, J. Lyle. 1302
Story, Ronald. 1401, 1917
Story, Thomas. 1679, 1682, 3534
[Stotesbury, Charles C]. 802, 3426
Stott, Denis Herbert. 2204
Stott, John R. 3665
Stott, John R. W. 237, 322, 326, 364, 369, 411, 461, 472, 989, 1327, 1551, 1571, 1691, 1832, 2481, 2787, 2908, 3336
Stott, Roscoe Gilmore. 1254, 3405
Stott, William Taylor. 153
Stotts, Herbert Edward. 1138, 1139, 3435
Stotts, Jack L. 945, 2809
Stoudt, John Baer. 3046
Stoudt, John Joseph. 674, 3049, 3135
Stouff, Faye. 910
Stoughton, Clarence Charles. 3674
Stoughton, John. 1472, 3008, 3815
Stout, Andrew P. 1997, 2030, 2068
[Stout, Charles B.]. 2701
Stout, George Frederick. 2843
Stout, Hosea. 3762
Stout, John. 237
Stout, John Elbert. 3159, 3763
[Stout, Marie Carol (Tismer)] 1889. 1353
Stout, Percy Ray. 1782
Stout, Walter Milton. 680
Stovall, Charles E. 1252
Stover, Alkin J. 3688
Stover, Ross Harrison. 1697, 2301
Stover, Virginia Handrix. 1575
Stover, Virginia Hendrix. 1575
Stover, Wilbur Brenner. 2495, 2532
Stow, Baron. 145
Stow, Kenneth R. 2152, 3569
Stowe, Calvin Ellis. 411
Stowe, David M. 1080, 1571, 2495, 2551
Stowe, Everett M. 1317
Stowe, Harriet Elizabeth (Beecher) 1973, 3121, 3841
Stowe, Lyman E. 97, 2729
Stowe, Phineas. 3317
Stowe, Walter Herbert. 2971, 45, 1275, 1524, 2967, 3812
Stowe, William McFerrin. 1995, 2437, 2802
Stowell, Earl. 2606
Stowell, Jay Samuel. 1042, 661, 940, 1246, 2459, 2495, 2528, 3740, 3807
Stowell, William Henry Harrison. 1145
Stowers, Stanley Kent. 471, 3234
*Stowman, Knud. 1100
Stoykoff, Todor Philip. 609
Strabo, Mikhail. 2881
*Strachan, James. 199, 603
Strachan, Robert Harvey. 322
Strachan, Robert Kenneth. 3829
Strachey, Giles Lytton. 2329
Strachey, Giles Lytton. 2329
Strachey, Marjorie Colvile. -1020
Strachey, Rachel (Costello) 3816
Strack, Hermann Leberecht. 672, 2109, 3583, 3585
Stradling, Leslie E. 579
Straelen, Henricus van. 814, 850
Strahan, James. 681
Strahan, Thomas W. 932
Strain, Dudley. 1297
Strain, John Newton. 3211
Strait, C. Neil. 1842
Strand, Grace Browne. 3064
Strand, Kenneth Albert. 283, 425, 450, 460, 479, 656, 1512, 2277, 3261
Strand, Ruby. 1486
Strang, Clement J. 1581
Strang, James Jesse. 1234, 3535
Strang, Lewis Clinton. 1036, 3336
Strang, Ruth May. 3174
Strange, Georgianne. 1898
Strange, Marcian. 216

Strange, Roderick. 2010
Stranks, Charles James. 3590
Strasser, Bernard. 1434, 1262, 1434
Strasser, Stephan. 185
Strasser, Stephen. 3463
Stratemeier, Klaas Jacob. 323
Strater, Paul. 3270
Stratford, Jenny. 849, 3668
Strathmann, Ernest Albert. 3019, 3422
Stratman, Chrysostomos H. 2746
Stratmann, Franziskus. 3794
Stratmann, Franziskus Maria. 3794
Straton, George Douglas. 312
Straton, Hillyer Hawthorne. 143, 2825, 167, 2028, 2044, 2895
Straton, John Roach. 167, 1600, 2561, 3135, 3742, 278, 1581, 2002, 2563, 3742, 3781
Stratton, David Hodges. 158
Stratton, Joseph Buck. 1832
Straub, Carl Emil. 1053
Straub, Jacob. 2948
Straub, Walter Lewis. 46, 304
Straube, Carl Frederick. 3515
Straughan, Alice. 2224
Straughn, Harold. 649
Straughn, James Henry. 2440
Straus, Herbert Cerf. 3073
Straus, Raphael. 2102
Straus, Roger Williams. 3193
Straus, Thomas Chalmers. 2049
Strauss, C. T. 703
Strauss, David Friedrich. 1973, 3023, 3308
Strauss, Dorothy H. 1016
Strauss, Dorothy M. 1016, 1252
Strauss, Gerald. 2288, 3040
Strauss, Gerhard Friedrich Abraham. 187
Strauss, Lehman. 324, 369, 380, 412, 444, 449, 456, 507, 609, 1353, 1428, 1453, 1832, 2026, 2059, 2881, 3379
Strauss, Leo. 2672, 3472
Strauss, Richard L. 216, 989, 1610, 2341
Stravinskas, Peter M. J. 792, 832
Straw, Walter E. 474, 596, 3105, 3547
Strawson, P. F. 2419
Strawson, William. 2066
Strayer, James H. 1072
Strayer, Paul Moore, 1871. 1244, 2895
Strayhorn, Lloyd. 3576
Streatfield, George Sidney. 1893
Streator, Martin Lyman. 46
Streebing, Cecilian. 1650, 1854
Street, George Edmund. 1161
Street, Harold Blaine. 3721
Street, J. C. 3515
Street, Julia Montgomery. 1112
Street, Noel. 2381, 3054
Street, T. Watson. 2555, 2925
Streeter, Burnett Hillman. 945, 1081, 1090, 1195, 1727, 3546, 392, 1081, 1832, 3080, 3105
Streeter, Sebastian. 3754
Streibert, Muriel Anne. 3889
Streiker, Lowell D. 1394, 1453, 1755, 2072, 3121, 3329, 3747
Streitfeld, Harold S. 3482, 3535
Stremooukhoff, D. 3457
Streng, Franziskus von. 2344
Streng, Frederick J. 2667, 3064, 3091
Streng, William D. 1080, 1595, 2215, 2295, 3660, 3665
Stresau, Marion. 3515, 3535
Stretton, Hesba. 72, 1973, 1984, 3534, 71, 75, 717, 1973, 1984
Streufert, Frank Charles. 2895
Streufert, Paul William. 1837
Streyffeler, Alan. 3618
Strickland, Arthur Barsalou. 3233
Strickland, Arthur Barsazou. 3233
Strickland, Crump J. 1505
Strickland, Francis Lorette. 3000, 3105
Strickland, Hazel N. 3558
Strickland, Reba Carolyn. 1145, 3064
Strickland, Robert G. 3261
Strickland, Walter William. 2855, 3576
Strickland, William Peter. 31, 89, 2422, 3753
Strickler, Givens Brown. 3345
Strider, Robert Edward Lee. 2826, 2975
Stright, Hayden L. 1045
Striker, William. 1697
Strindberg, August. 3135
Strine, Patricia Balfoure. 1496
String, Margaret Lancaster. 3047
Stringfellow, William. 194, 324, 472, 941, 945, 947, 1087, 1347, 1882, 2822, 2846, 2978, 3541, 3665, 3749
Stringham, Henry David. 1630
Striplin, Clara M. 3174
Strobe, Donald B. 1063
Strobel, Philip A. 1788
Strober, Gerald. 1755
Strober, Gerald S. 1302, 1577, 1603, 1755, 3407
Strobridge, George Egerton. 2169

Strodach, Paul Zeller. 1917, 2297, 227, 2032, 2058, 2212, 2215, 2295, 2297, 2397, 2238
Strode-Jackson, Myrtle Beatrice S. 1036
Stroh, Grant. 1716, 1727
Strom, Kay Marshall. 3841
Strombeck, John Frederick. 93, 976, 1752, 3291
Stromberg, Gustaf. 3080
Stromberg, Ronald N. 3212
Strommen, Merton P. 937, 1260, 1261, 3881, 3889
Strommenberg, Anders Gabriel. 3569
Stromwall, Mary W. 43, 902, 2358
Strong, Anna Louise. 632, 2881
Strong, Augustus Hopkins. 2837, 143, 411, 1072, 2495, 2637, 2837, 3535, 3536, 3611, 3625, 3648, 3649
Strong, Charles O. 3375
Strong, Cyprian. 1334, 2220
Strong, Donald S. 2105
Strong, Edmund Linwood. 1727, 976
[Strong, Elnathan Ellsworth] 1832-1914. 2521
Strong, Esther Boorman. 2495
Strong, Eugenie (Sellers) 3246
Strong, Eugenie (Sellers) "S. A. Strong. 3246
Strong, J. Selden. 730
Strong, James. 225, 227, 228, 536, 1797, 2006
Strong, John Henry. 2881, 67
Strong, Josaih. 2528
Strong, Josiah. 976, 1282, 2528, 3446, 3737, 3742
Strong, June. 1013, 3536
Strong, Kendrick. 71, 494, 1004, 1921, 2248
Strong, Leah A. 3719
Strong, Leon Marshal. 2613
[Strong, Lewis]. 1353
Strong, Patience. 1442, 1453
Strong, Sydney Dix. 976, 1727, 1891, 2881, 3345, 3346
Strong, Thomas Banks. 118, 946
Strong, William. 1490
Strong, William Ellsworth. 31, 2521
Stroop, John Ridley. 278, 3649
Stroud, William. 1998
Stroup, George W. 2044, 3649
Stroup, Herbert Hewitt. 2895, 91, 1144, 1814, 1941, 3135, 1941
Stroup, Herbert W. 2782
Stroup, Ner Wallace. 3412
Stroup, Thomas Bradley. 2472
Stroupe, Henry Smith. 3205
Strousse, Flora. 2188
Strout, Cushing. 3746
Stroyen, William B. 1149, 2750
Strub, Celestine. 1838
Strube, William P. 1320
Struchen, Jeanette. 2124, 2895, 3844
Strugnell, Joseph. 902
Strunk, Orlo. 101, 3000
Strunk, William Oliver. 2632
Struthers, Alice Ball. 2066
Struve, Nikita. 1149
Stryk, Lucien. 711, 3892, 3893
Stryker, Melancthon Woolsey. 291, 312, 1861, 3777, 1869, 2935
Stryker, Peter. 3208
Strype, John. 121, 1378, 1516, 1760, 1775
Strzelec, Karol Wladyslaw. 1130
Strzygowski, Josef. 921
Stuart, Charles Macaulay. 349
Stuart, Douglas K. 530, 1799
Stuart, George Rutledge. 624, 2441, 3346, 2426, 2456
Stuart, George Wilse. 3558
Stuart, Harry Lee. 2019, 2218
[Stuart, Henry Clifford] 1864. 3135
Stuart, Janet Erskine. 806, 1264, 3522
Stuart, Monica. 229
Stuart, Moses. 136, 404, 496, 572, 609, 882, 1797, 2002, 3193, 3597, 3728
Stuart, Reginald Ray. 3298
Stuart, Suzette G. 2697
Stuart, Suzette Grundy. 2697
Stuart, T. McK. 306
Stuart, Vincent. 3482
Stuart, William. 649
Stuart, William David. 3135
Stuart, William Walter. 1663
Stubbe, Ray William. 2472
Stubbes, Phillip. 3607
Stubbings, George Wilfred, 1887-1951. 1206
Stubblefield, Harold W. 1258
Stubbs, Charles William. 21, 1509, 2048
Stubbs, George Edward. 884, 1209
Stubbs, Mattie Wilma. 1101
[Stubbs, Ulysses]. 3139
Stubbs, William. 1213, 1825
Stuber, Stanley Irvin. 802, 1456, 3323
Stuber, Stanley Irving. 802, 1456, 2024, 3204, 3323, 3639, 3772

Stuckenberg, John Henry Wilburn. 2372, 3446
Stucker, Larkin. 1123
Studdert-Kennedy, Geoffrey Anketell, 1883-1929. 1053
Studdert-Kennedy, Geoffrey Anketell. 74, 2061
Student Christian Movement in New England. 3536
Student planning conference on the world mission of the church, College of Wooster, 1943-1944. 2521
Student volunteer movement for foreign missions. 2521, 2523
Student volunteer movement for foreign missions. International convention. 10th, Detroit, 1927-1928. 2515
Student volunteer movement for foreign missions. International convention. 11th, Buffalo, 1931-1932. 2522
Student volunteer movement for foreign missions. International convention. 12th, Indianapolis, 1935-1936. 2515
Student volunteer movement for foreign missions. International convention. 3d, Cleveland, 1898. 3536
Student volunteer movement for foreign missions. International convention. 4th, Ontario, 1902. 2522
Student volunteer movement for foreign missions. International convention. 5th, Nashville, 1906. 2515
Student volunteer movement for foreign missions. International convention. 6th, Rochester, N.Y., 1900-1910. 2515
Student volunteer movement for foreign missions. International convention. 7th, Kansas City, Mo., 1913-1914. 2515
Student volunteer movement for foreign missions. International convention. 8th, Des Moines, 1919-1920. 2515
Student volunteer movement for foreign missions. International convention. 9th, Indianapolis, 1923-1924. 2515
Student Writers Club of Selma. 1269
Studer, Gerald C. 1697
Studiorum Novi Testamenti Societas. 615
-Studniewska, Mary Jeremiah. 1620
Study Conference on the Christian Faith and the Contemporary Middle Eastern World. Asmara, Eritrea, Ethiopia, 1959. 2541
Study, Guy. 28
Stuebel, C. 2667
Stuempfle, Herman G. 1561, 2906
Stuenkel, Omar. 1712
Stuenkel, Walter W. 541
Stuermann, Walter Earl. 1746, 3083
Stuernagel, Albert Emanuel. 1794
Stuff, Grace Hermione. 1714
Stuhlmacher, Peter. 240
Stuhlmueller, Carroll. 9, 429, 543, 545, 569, 579, 859, 1487, 2212, 2895, 3028, 3159, 3484
Stuhr, Walter M. 1293
Stukenbroeker, Fern C. 3715
Stulken, Marilyn Kay. 1876
Stull, Ruth. 1453, 2544
Stultz, Owen Glennard. 1303
Stumme, John R. 3436, 3700
Stump, Edith A. (Harrison) 783
Stump, Gladys Sims. 2134
Stump, Joseph. 649, 3649
Stump, V. L. 691, 3634
Stumpf, Samuel Enoch. 1422
Stuntz, Homer Clyde. 3464
Stuntz, Hugh Clark. 2501
Stupperich, Robert. 2400
Sturge, Charles. 3718
Sturge, Gordon W. 1664
Sturge, Judi Hinchliffe. 897, 3538
Sturges, Philemon Fowler. 2058, 2973
Sturges, Thomas H. 3051
Sturgis, William Codman. 1123, 2881
Sturlaugson, Mary Frances. 3538
Sturm, Christoph Christian. 1285, 1442, 1732
Sturm, George Carl Frederick. 421
Sturney, Alfred Charles. 2177
Sturt, Henry Cecil. 1123
Sturtevant, Mary Rebecca (Clark) 1285
Sturzaker, James. 722
Sturzo, Luigi. 1143, 1738, 3489
Stutenroth, Allen Wert. 3221
Stutley, Margaret. 2315
Styles, John. 689, 1899
Stylianopoulos, Theodore. 1084, 2161
Suares, Carlo. 526, 594, 722, 1704, 3329, 1704
Suares, M R. 167
Suarez, Francisco, 1548-1617. 1142, 2739
Subbamma, B. V. 2556
Subba Row, Tiruvalum. 2317
Subbiah, B. V. 663
Subhadra. 703
Subhan, John A. 3544
Subilia, Vittorio. 802, 3772

Subramaniam, K. 2940
Subramuniya. 121, 1585, 1911, 2397, 3330, 3482
Subramuniya, Master. 2381, 2397
Succop, Margaret Phillips. 1365
Suchocki, Marjorie. 2944
Suda, Jyoti Prasad. 1897
Suddards, William. 3366
Sudenik, Eleazar Lipa. 195
Sudermann, Hermann. 2128
Sudlow, Elizabeth Williams. 3558
Sudlow, Elizabeth (Williams) 3159, 3558, 3841
Sudraka. 1897
Sudweeks, Joseph. 1233, 2819
Sue, Eugene. 3412
Suechting, August G. 1434, 1442
Suelflow, August Robert. 1162, 2296
Suelflow, Roy Arthur. 2296, 2303
Sueltz, Arthur Fay. 421, 989, 1011, 1314
Suelzer, Alexa. 564
Suenens, Leon Joseph. 664, 777, 792, 793, 808, 889, 1002, 1245, 1571, 1729, 1832, 2208, 2363, 2816, 3634
Suenens, Leon Joseph, Cardinal. 761, 2574
Suerken, Ernst Henry. 2895
Suffin, Arnold. 3221
Suffling, Ernest Richard. 690
Sugana, Gabriele Mandel. 706, 2629
Sugar Grove Baptist Church, Davies Co., Ky. 152
Sugarman, Daniel A. 3881
Sugarman, Joan G. 2151
Sugarman, Morris. 3897
Sugden, Christopher. 2712
Sugden, Howard F. 331, 2787
Suger, 1081-1151. 78, 3273
Suggs, M. Jack. 392, 443, 613, 2044, 3821
Sugiura, Sadajiro. 2242
Sugiura, Yoshimichi. 2535
Sugranes, Eugene Joseph. 1284
Sugrue, Francis. 2861
*Sugrue, Thomas. 1283
Sugrue, Thomas, 1907. 828
Suhard, Emmanuel. 1123
Suhard, Emmanuel Celestin. 777, 1123, 777, 3634
Suhr, Elmer George, 1902. 1397, 1767, 3777
al-Suhrawardi, 'Abd al-Qahir ibn 'abd Allah. 3544
Suhrawardy, Abdullah al-Mamun. 1779
Sujata, A. 712
Sukenik, Eleazar Lipa. 3576
Sukul, Deva Ram. 3866
Sulami, Muhammad ibn al-Husayn. 3544
Sullivan, C. Stephen. 3266
Sullivan, Daniel A. 3482
Sullivan, Dennis. 1245
Sullivan, Edward. 317
Sullivan, Edward Taylor. 2705
Sullivan, Eileen. 3474
Sullivan, Ella C. 3470
Sullivan, Florence. 3766
Sullivan, Francis Aloysius. 792, 1712
Sullivan, Frank. 2596
Sullivan, J. C. 1360
Sullivan, James L. 994, 2397, 3545
Sullivan, Jessie P. 3159, 3859
Sullivan, John. 892
Sullivan, John Edward. 3713
Sullivan, John Francis. 757, 763, 792
Sullivan, John J. 765, 2265, 2266, 3489
Sullivan, Joseph Vincent. 1544
Sullivan, Julius. 2523
Sullivan, Kathryn. 531
Sullivan, Kay. 828, 2124, 3460
Sullivan, Leon Howard. 3545
Sullivan, Marion F. 1899, 3377
Sullivan, Mary Rosenda. 806
Sullivan, Michael. 2318
Sullivan, Peter. 2003
Sullivan, Roger J. 81, 1537
Sullivan, Shaun J. 2160
Sullivan, Walter J. 1002, 1453
Sullivan, William Laurence. 1195, 2397, 2561, 3728, 3729
Sulloway, Alison G. 1516, 1846
Sulman, Esther. 2101
Sulzberger, Cyrus Leo. 661, 1415, 2881, 3545
[Sulzberger, David]. 1796
Sulzby, James Frederick. 663
Sulzer, Robert Frederick. 1899
Sumerau, Dorothy Lehman. 1112
Summa izbu. English & Akkadian. 2736
Summerbell, Carlyle. 945
Summerbell, Joseph James. 732, 1180, 2626
Summerbell, Martyn. 976, 3064, 3165, 3323, 3346
Summerfield, Nicholas. 3713
Summerfield, John. 3358
Summers, Jester. 495, 634, 2134, 2588, 3172
Summers, Jo An. 995

Summers, Joseph Holmes, 1920. 2470
Summers, M. M. 205
Summers, Montague. 2640, 3824
Summers, Montague [Alphonsus Joseph Marie Augustus Montague Summers] 1880. 3824
Summers, Ray. 337, 364, 417, 456, 1529, 1770
Summers, Sandra Kay. 2551
Summers, Stanford. 2627
Summers, Thomas Osmond. 225, 2451, 2455, 2982, 3295, 3358, 3550
Summers, William Henry. 2243
Sumner, John Bird. 1099
Sumner, John Daniel. 3135
Sumner, Robert Leslie. 83, 1561, 1571, 1782, 3235
Sumption, Jonathan. 23, 1101
Sumrall, Ken. 1302, 3546
Sumrall, Lester Frank. 802, 1423, 1576, 1736, 2252, 2477, 2491, 2549, 3121, 3390, 3526, 3546, 3710
Sumrall, Tillie Darel. 167
Sumrall, Velma. 1243
Sun Bear (Chippewa Indian) 1902
Sun, Ruth. 642
Sundar, Singh. 3202
Sundar Singh. 1697, 3068
Sunday, Helen Amelia (Thompson) 3566
Sunday school times. 3558
The Sunday times, London. 1412
Sunday, William Ashley. 473, 1522, 1561, 3566, 1561
Sundean, John L. 642
Sundell, Albert F[rank] Oscar. 2834
Sundelof-Asbrand, Karin. 1623, 3560
Sundemo, Herbert. 246
Sunderland, Byron. 3547
Sunderland, Jabez Thomas. 312, 649, 882, 1581
Sunderland, James. 1595
Sunderland, La Roy. 2473, 2606, 3424
Sunderwirth, Wilbert W. 609
Sundkler, Bengt Gustaf Malcolm. 2495, 3897, 3899
Sundquist, Hjalmar. 1099, 1955
*Sundquist, Ralph R., Jr. 895
Sundt, Edwin Einar. 3255
Sung, Z. D. 1879
Sunno Bhikku, 1945. 2382
Sunter, J. Pauline. 1113
Super, Paul. 2228, 3872
Supin, Charles R. 2192
Supler, Albert J. 3515
Supreme Commander for the Allied Powers. Civil Information and Education Section. 1936
Surangamasutra. 711
Surangamasutra. English & Khotanese. 3568
Surburg, Raymond F. 278, 492, 2149
Surface, Bill. 867, 2529
Surface, Ira Edwin. 1595
Surgy, Paul de. 646
Surles, Eileen. 1372, 3205
Surman, Charles E. 1774
Surrey, David S. 3778
Surrey, Peter J. 3426
Surtees, Herbert Conyers. 1483
Surtz, Edward L. 1628
Susek, Ron. 994
Suskind, Richard. 1391, 1392
Suso, Heinrich. 2647
Susott, Albert A. 3004
Susquehanna synod of the Evangelical Lutheran church in the United States. 2630
Sussman, Cornelia Silver. 2413
Sussman, Ellen J. 2411
Sussman, Irving. 1063, 1293
Sussman, Samuel. 1624, 2120
Sustar, Bob R. 2304, 3569
Sutcliffe, B. B. 642
Sutcliffe, Edmund Felix. 502, 3014
Sutcliffe, Joseph. 1053, 1055
Sutcliffe, Thomas Henry. 571
Suter, David Winston. 491
Suter, John Wallace. 1442, 1856, 2961, 688, 1214, 1308, 2895, 2972, 3159, 3665
Sutherland, Allan. 1873
Sutherland, Angelyn B. 3558
Sutherland, E[dward] A[lexander]. 650
Sutherland, Nicola Mary. 1851
Sutherland, Robert T. 904
Sutherland, Stewart R. 100, 1477
Suthpen, William Gilbert van Tassel. 2006, 2030
Sutphin, Stanley T. 3657
Sutphin, Wyn Blair. 2058, 2250
Suttanipata. 707, 710
Suttapitaka. 707, 3779
Suttapitaka. English. Selections. 707, 1856
Suttapitaka, Selections. English. 3779

Sutton, Antony C. 2223

Sutton, Gayle. 1423

Sutton, Harry Trumbull. 1916
Sutton, Hilton. 611, 2073
Sutton, Jack A. 3702
Sutton, Joseph Wilson. 2058, 2881, 2973
Sutton, Katharine Augusta. 1622
Sutton, Katharine Paine. 1353
Suttor, T. L. 814
Suzuki, D. T. 3892
Suzuki, Daisetz Teitaro. 705, 2577, 2640, 3894, 3895, 2317, 2577, 2640, 2867, 3403, 3715, 3892, 3893
Suzuki, Shosan. 3892
Suzuki, Shunryu. 2383
*Svancara-Hloskova, Katarina. 2865
Svarupa Damodara Dasa, Brahmacari, 1941. 2186
Svatmarama. 3867
Svendsen, Kester. 2470
Sverdrup, Georg. 2285
Sverdrup, H[arald] U[lrik]. 748
Sverdrup, Harald Ulrik. 2279, 2283, 2284
[Swaab, Maurice]. 2111
Swaan, Wim. 752
Swabey, William Curtis. 2180
Swadley, Elizabeth. 1113, 3530
*Swafford, Z. W. 3320
Swaim, J. Carter. 1089
Swaim, Joseph Carter. 217, 237, 281, 288, 642, 646, 653, 2473
Swaim, Samuel Budd. 384
Swaim, William. 3569
Swain, Anna (Canada) 2489, 2522
Swain, Clara A. 1895
Swain, Dorothy G. 3178
Swain, Edmund Gill. 2826
Swain, Jasper. 3474, 3569
Swain, Joseph. 3030
Swain, Richard La Rue. 1036, 1727, 2321
Swainson, Charles Anthony. 1768, 2748
Swalm, E. J. 3569
Swan, Able Bernhardt. 3185
Swan, Alexander. 1036
Swan, Alfred Wilson. 392
Swan, Isabella E. 1775
Swan, Jabez Smith. 3233
Swan, William. 1063
Swanberg, John Edwin. 1855
Swanberg, W. A. 3697
Swancara, Frank. 1151, 3195
Swander, Clarence F. 1465
Swander, John I. 3625, 2843, 3076
Swaney, Charles Baumer. 3424
Swaney, Richard A. 471
Swanick, Eric L. 1158
Swank, Calvin P. 1239, 3854
Swank, Calvin Peter. 1994, 2058, 2812
Swank, George W. 2906
Swank, Gerald O. 1574
Swank, Harold Allen. 3193
Swann, Doris Cutter. 3665
Swann, George Betts. 2772, 3346
Swann, Ingo. 2991
Swann, Jeffrey. 3892
Swann, Nathanael Emilius Egerton. 609
Swanson, Harold Roland. 1519
Swansen, Hans Fred. 1286
Swanson, Allen J. 1108
Swanson, D. Verner. 17
Swanson, Guy E. 3036, 3110
Swanson, Harvey. 1343
Swanson, Lawrence F. 3558
Swanson, Mildred Earhardt. 3474
Swanson, Neil H. 2881
Swanson, Steve. 1412, 2301, 3889
Swanson, Swan Hjalmar. 740, 1547, 2296, 2552
Swanston, Hamish F. G. 237, 520, 631, 1386
Swanstrom, Roy. 1819
Swanton, John Reed. 1903
Swantz, Lloyd W. 2553
Swarm, Paul. 1203
Swarthmore college, Swarthmore, Pa. Friends' historical library. 1677
Swartley, Willard M. 437
Swartz, Fred W. 1044
Swartz, Joel. 3136
Swartzbaugh, Constance H. 2969
Swavely, C H. 3733
Swayne, Amelia (Werner) 1486
Swayne, William Shuckburgh. 976
Swayze, Beulah Garland. 734
Swearer, Donald K. 704, 708, 1080, 2382, 3439, 3798
Swearingen, Tilford Tippett. 3159, 3889, 1912
Sweazey, George Edgar. 2935, 1571, 2340, 2481, 2906, 3665
Swedburg, Melva. 3174
Swedenborg, Emanual. 456
*Swedenborg, Emanuel. 1794, 2845
Swedenborg, Emanuel. 2691, 99, 237, 417, 441, 456, 457, 568, 577, 642, 887, 1370, 1371, 1479, 1735, 1794, 1795, 1907, 2156, 2340, 2689, 2691, 2692, 2845, 2982, 2983, 3463, 3570, 3571, 3572, 3631

Swedenborg foundation, incorporated. 3571
[Swedenborg publishing association]. 2689, 3571
Sweeney, David Francis. 3470
Sweeney, Francis W. 1028, 3027
Sweeney, James Norbert. 1267
Sweeney, John F. 3742
Sweeney, Joseph W. 904, 1299, 2574, 3226
Sweeney, Leo. 2419
Sweeney, Nelly K. 2895
Sweeney, Stephen. 2266, 2397
Sweeney, Zachary Taylor. 1832, 3572, 304
Sweeny, Nelson D. 3346
Sweet, Charles Filkins. 1846, 2535
Sweet, Elizabeth. 3515
Sweet, Helen (Firman) 3172
Sweet, Herman J. 1239, 3165
Sweet, John Philip McMurdo. 457
Sweet, Leonard I. 1832
Sweet, Louis Matthews. 57, 270, 392, 642, 1195, 1395, 1581, 1955, 2021, 3674
Sweet, Willia, Warren. 2924
Sweet, William Henry. 2452
Sweet, William Warren. 3089, 152, 1339, 2425, 2433, 2451, 2460, 2924, 3233, 3739, 3740, 3746, 152, 1339, 2460, 3739, 3746
Sweeten, Howard W. 3412
Sweeting, George. 989, 1433, 1611, 2267, 2722, 3358, 3359, 3829, 3848, 3861
Sweetland, Leon Hiram. 2267
Sweets, Henry Hayes. 742, 976, 1127, 1130, 1842
Sweetser, Edwin Chapin. 3346
Sweetser, Lewis Hobart. 3515
Sweetser, Seth. 3674
Sweetser, Thomas P. 815, 2775
Swendenborg, Emanuel. 2692, 3631
Swensen, Russel Brown. 411
Swenson, Carl Aaron. 2397
Swenson, David Ferdinand. 2171
Swenson, Victor E. 2511
Swete, Henry Barclay. 74, 528, 840, 1053, 1618, 1832, 3437
Swiatecka, M. Jadwiga. 1306, 3574
Swichkow, Louis J. 2111, 2895
Swidler, Arlene. 3836
Swidler, Leonard J. 665, 774, 792, 1042, 1043, 1045, 1292, 2460, 3193, 3706, 3837, 3846
Swieson, Eddy. 1011, 1302, 3572
Swift, Albert. 3446
Swift, Arthur Lessner. 3068, 3446
Swift, Clarence F. 615
Swift, David E. 1778
Swift, Elisha Pope. 174
Swift, Emerson Howland. 79, 922
Swift, Grace (Harrison) 1787
Swift, Job. 1343, 3572
Swift, John Edward. 2179
Swift, Jonathan. 2232
Swift, Judson. 2881
Swift, Julia M. 1113
Swift, Marshall S. 2943
Swift, Montgomery. 1891
Swift, Morrison Isaac. 1892, 3096
Swift, Polemus Hamilton. 1561, 3359
Swift, Stephen K. 2474
Swift, William Alpheus. 1063
Swihart, Altman K. 1036, 3527, 1036, 2277, 2288, 3527
Swihart, Judson J. 2340
Swihart, Phillip J. 1415
Swihart, Stephen D. 42, 286, 609, 1515
Swinburne, Richard. 1597, 1730, 1738
Swindle, Lafayette. 1123
Swindoll, Charles R. 953, 989, 1418, 1610, 2340, 2397, 2683, 2822, 3377
Swinehart, Lois Hawks. 2537
Swinford, Frances Keller. 2969
Swing, Albert Temple. 3239
Swing, David. 2936, 3359
Swinnerton, J. G. 1665
Swinney, James Oswald. 2044, 2060
Swinney, Oram Jackson. 1461
Swinstead, John Howard. 2292
Swint, John Joseph. 2255, 792, 1114, 1314, 1453, 2028, 2215
Swiren, David Bernard. 2120
Swisher, Rolla O. 1016, 1442
Swisher, Walter Samuel. 1203, 3064, 3276
Switz, Theodore MacLean. 3145
Switzer, David K. 1297, 2781
Switzer, Ronald R. 3005
Swomley, John M. 1130
Swope, George Washington. 71
Swor, Chester E. 976, 994, 1433, 1783, 3889
Sword, Gustaf A. 1784, 2505
Sword of Moses. 43
The sword of the Lord. 1453
Sword, Victor Hugo. 2503
Swoyer, Grover E. 1453
Swyhart, Barbara Ann DeMartino. 3191

Sydenstricker, Hiram Mason. 1959
Sydnor, James Rawlings. 916, 1203, 1209, 1210
Sydnor, Thomas L. 144
Sydnor, William. 429, 1262, 1329, 1524, 2961
Sydnor.James Rawlings. 1209
Sykes, Christopher. 816, 3405
Sykes, Egerton. 2659
Sykes, Ethel Marie. 609
Sykes, John. 1675
Sykes, Marjorie. 2532, 3438
Sykes, Norman. 1146, 1183, 1213, 1379, 1711, 1759, 1760, 3402, 3788, 1146, 1212, 1221, 1516, 3036
Sykes, Stephen. 44, 3308, 3618
[Sylvain, Adrien] 1826-1914. 1002
Sylvain, Charles. 740
Sylvan. 1459
Sylvest, Edwin Edward. 1648
Sylvester. 1210
Sylvester, Arline. 3515
Sylvester, J. Walter. 3366
Sylvester II. 818
Sylvester I I. 818
Sylvester, Roland. 616
Symanowski, Horst. 1131
Syme, David. 3463
Syme, Eric. 1151, 3384
Syme, George S. 278
Syme, Ronald. 2506, 3425
Symeon. 949-1022. 3636
Symeon Neotheologus. 949-1022. 90
Symes, Thomas. 1210
Symington, Thomas Alexander. 3000
Symon, Benjamin Goodall. 1470
Symond, Ronald. 28, 1955
Symonds, Henry Edward. 1386, 1523
Symonds, John. 671
Symonds, Percival Mallon. 3330
Symonds, Robert Hale. 1804
Symposium on Clerical Celibacy, University of Notre Dame, 1967. 773, 878
Symposium on Islamic Studies, Amsterdam, 1973. 1923
Symposium on Jewish-Christian Relations and Education, Baylor University, 1971. 1084
Symposium on Pacem in Terris by Pope John XXIII, University of Notre Dame, 1965. 853
Symposium on Prayer, Shrub Oak, N.Y., 1968. 2883
Symposium on Seventeenth Century Lutheranism. 2288
[Symposium on the Apologia, Fordham University, 1963]. 2705
Symposium on the Church in Africa, Milligan College, Tenn., 1977. 1073
Symposium on the Culture of Unbelief, Rome, 1969. 186
Synan, Edward A. 1084
Synan, Vinson. 2815
Synave, Paul. 306, 3696
Syndicus, Eduard. 922
Syndicus, Edward. 922
Synge, Francis Charles. 364
Synge, J. M. 3282
Synge, Ursula. 1028
Synod for the Norwegian evangelical Lutheran church in America. 1861
Synod of Ohio of the United Lutheran Church in America. 3733
Synod of the Reformed Presbyterian church of North America. 2306, 2917
Synod of the Reformed Presbyterian Church of North Amrica. 2917
Synon, Mary. 2866, 3420
Sypherd, Wilbur Owen. 1028
Syracuse, N.Y. First Presbyterian church. 2700
Syrdal, Rolf A. 1571, 2526
Syverud, Genevieve Wold. 2297
Szajkowski, Zosa. 2099
Szarecko, Francis. 1583
Szczesniak, Boleslaw. 3256
Szczesny, Gerhard. 3327
Szekely, Edmond Bordeaux. 121, 525, 704, 1092, 1532, 1898, 2019, 2321, 2622, 3899
Szeplaki, Joseph. 2474
Szikszai, Stephen. 531
Szold, Benjamin. 2097
*Szopko, Emey J. 3291
Szostak, John M. 2126, 2861
Szunyogh, Bela. 3064
Szymanowski, Stephen Korwin. 3611
Szymanski, Ladislas. 744

T

T'ai shang kan ying p'ien. English & Chinese. 3587
Taaffe, Thomas. 1020
Tabak, Israel. 1614, 3202
al-Tabataba'i, Muhammad Husayn. 3403
Tabeling, Ernst. 2197
[Taber, Clarence Wilbur] 1870. 3142
Taber, Gladys Leona (Bagg) 1353
Taber, Henry Morehouse. 1656
Taber, Mary Jane Howland. 751
Table prayer league, South Bend, Ind. 2895
Tabor, Edward A. 3870
Tabori, Cornelius. 2732
Tabori, Paul. 2399
Tachibana, Shundo. 1537
Tachikawa, Musashi. 3721, 3766
Tack, Theodoro V. 78, 3220
Tackett, Timothy. 774, 1292
Taegel, William S. 989
Tafel, Johann Friedrich Immanuel. 3571
Taft, Charles Phelps. 1063, 1072
Tager, Aleksandr Semenovich. 185, 3240
Taggart, George H. 1785
Tagore, Rabindranath. 3579, 2840, 3064, 3068, 3579
Tahara, Yoneko. 1360, 3579
Taherzadeh, Adib. 125, 129
T'ai i chin hua tsung chih. 3587
Taillepied, Noel. 77
Taimni, I. K. 2729, 2730, 3422, 3768, 3866
Tainsh, Edward Campbell. 1103
T'ai-shang kan-ying p'ien. 3587
Tait, Archibald Campbell. 3580
Tait, Arthur James. 3263
Tait, Asa Oscar. 1515, 3688
Tait, Leslie Gordon. 3700
Tait, Vera Dawson. 3750
Takada, Koin. 704
Takakusu, Junjiro. 703, 2317
Takenaka, Masao. 1935
Talafous, Camillus D. 3107
Talamonti, Leo. 2991
Talbert, Charles H. 392, 426, 661
Talbert, Daniel H. 3412
Talbert, Horace. 26, 3815
Talbot, C H. 927
Talbot, Carol. 1302, 3580
Talbot, Catherine. 1453
Talbot, Charles H. 2318
Talbot, Edith (Armstrong) 2381
Talbot, Ethelbert. 665
Talbot, Francis Xavier. 1947, 2125, 3275, 3699, 1947, 2125
[Talbot, George Foster] 1819-1907. 2050
Talbot, Gladys Mary. 911
Talbot, Gordon. 118, 522, 989
Talbot, Louis T. 909
Talbot, Louis Thompson. 365, 392, 465, 471, 509, 909, 1515, 1973, 3649, 3721
Talbot, Mabel E. 3329
Talbot, Neville Stuart. 237, 1063, 1595, 1746
Talbot, Percy Amaury. 2828
Talbot, William L. 2167, 3275
Talbott, David N. 3304
Talec, Pierre. 1002, 1253, 2044, 2895
Talford, Frederick A. 509
Taliaferro, Margaret. 1112, 1734
Tallach, John. 48
Tallant, Robert. 3787
Tallet, Jorge. 2739
Talley, Marshall Alexander. 524
Talling, Marshal P. 2881
Talling, Marshall P. 2881, 3482
Tallmadge, Alfred S. 2802
Talmage, Frank. 505, 2171
Talmage, Frank De Witt. 2022
Talmage, James Edward. 2613, 1157, 2606, 2613, 3582, 1232, 1973, 2397, 2606, 2613
Talmage, John R. 3582
Talmage, T. DeWitt. 2935
Talmage, Thomas De Witt. 976, 2935, 3346, 3582
Talmage, Thomas DeWitt. 1973, 2764, 2935, 3833
Talmey, Bernard S. 3389
Talmey, Bernard Simon. 3391
Talmor, Sascha. 1715, 3422
Talmud. Berakoth. 3583
Talmud. Chagigah. 3583
Talmud. English. 3583
Talmud. English. Selections. 18, 3583, 3584
Talmud Minor tractates Semahot. English. 1966. 2627
Talmud, Selections. 2980, 3584
Talmud. Selections. English. 3584
Talmud. Ta'anit. 3584
Talmud Yerushalmi. 2090, 3585

Talmud Yerushalmi. Berakot. English. 3584
Talmud Yerushalmi. English. Selections. 3584
Talmud Yerushalmi. Selections. 724
Talon, Henri Antoine. 2201
Taltavull, Frances. 1611
Tam, Stanley. 1571, 3539
Tamarin, Alfred H. 2094
Tamaron y Romeral, Pedro. 3783
Tambasco, Anthony J. 241, 1538, 3329
Tambimuttu, Francis O. 815
Tamisier, Robert. 312
Tamke, Susan S. 1873
Tan, Paul Lee. 609
Tan, Tai Wei. 2181
Taneyhill, Richard Henry. 1484
Tanghe, Omer. 2895
Tani, Henry N. 1260
Tanis, Edward H. 551
Tanis, Edward J. 802, 3323
Tanksley, Perry. 1453
Tanna debe Eliyahu. English. 1798
Tannehill, James B. 2649
Tannehill, Robert C. 392, 2072
Tannenbaum, Leslie. 241, 300, 670
Tanner, Amy Eliza. 2991
Tanner, Annie Clark. 1284, 3585
Tanner, Benjamin Tucker. 14
Tanner, Eugene Simpson. 1708
Tanner, Florice. 3121
Tanner, George Clinton. 2959, 2166, 2970
Tanner, Jacob. 2279, 107, 1329, 1995, 2287, 2466, 3159, 3665
Tanner, Jerald. 1738, 2606, 2613, 2616, 3429, 2614
Tanner, Joseph M. 1426
Tanner, Nathan Eldon. 2610
Tanner, Obert Clark. 475, 1016, 1973
Tanner, Paul A. 364
Tanner, Ralph E S. 2553
[Tanner, William F.]. 1515
Tanner, William Graydon. 2495
Tanquerey, Adolphe. 90, 3649
Tantras. Candamaharosanatantra. English & Sanskrit. 734, 3586
Tantras. Hevajratantrarajanama. 3585
Tantras. Kularnavatantra. 3586
Tapasyananda, Swami. 879
Tapia, Ralph J. 2046
Tapley, Charles Sutherland. 2718, 3827
Tapley, Harriet Silvester. 3286
Tapman, Lillian Smith. 694, 2944
Tapp, Robert B. 3727
Tapp, Sidney C. 3389
Tapp, Sidney Calhoun. 642, 1956, 3389, 3391
Tappan, David. 1343, 2083, 2327, 3359, 3522
Tappan, Eva March. 1955
Tappan, Henry Philip. 1499, 1658, 1746
Tappan, Luella Rice. 2524, 3587
Tappan, N.Y. Reformed Church. 2700, 3587
Tappan, Sarah (Homes) 3587
Tappan, William B[ingham]. 2484
Tapper, Ruth M. 3247
Tappert, Theodore Gerhardt. 1180, 2252, 2830, 3326, 3668
Tapscott, Betty. 1353, 1600, 3291
Tara, 1921. 3463
Taralon, Jean. 922
Tarbell, Harlan E. 880
Tarbell, Martha. 1917
Tarcov, Edith. 2085
Tardif, Henri. 1616
Tardini, Domenico, Cardinal. 2852
Tardy, William Thomas. 3136
Target, George William. 1063, 2033, 2381
Tari, Mel. 1573, 3232
Tariri. 3400
[Tarkington, John Stevenson] 1832-1923. 1807
Tarlton, Mildred Revelle. 1353
Tarplee, Cornelius C. 3017
Tarr, Charles R. 3229
Tarr, Leslie K. 3403
Tarrants, Thomas A. 1367, 3589
Tarry, Ellen. 1480, 2348
Tarshish, Allan, 1907. 2090
Tarthang Tulku. 2381, 2382
Tartre, Raymond A. 2259, 3774
Tasker, Randolph Vincent Greenwood. 326, 393, 413, 418, 451
Tasker, Randolph Vincent Greewood. 393
*Tassell, Paul. 544, 1942
Tassell, Paul. 167, 587
Tasso, Torquato. 1017
Tate, Allen. 3071
Tate, Bill. 1806
Tate, Charles Spencer. 3589
Tate, Edward Engram. 2961
Tate, Edward Mowbray. 3159
Tate, Jesse. 457, 460
Tate, Judith. 2202, 2574
Tatford, Frederick A. 509, 609, 1428

Tatham, C. Ernest. 1712, 2053
Tatham, Geoffrey Bulmer. 1221, 3136, 3789
Tatic-Djuric, Mirjana. 43
Tatlock, Jessie May. 2657
Tatlock, Richard. 68
Tatnall, Edward. 685
Tatsch, Jacob Hugo. 1672
Tatum, E Ray. 2713
Tatum, Noreen (Dunn) 2457
Tatz, Mark. 3027
Tauben, Carol. 2073
Taubenhaus, Godfrey. 3584
Tauber, Maurice Falcolm. 2080
Tauler, Johannes. 2647, 2819, 3334
Tavard, George H. 2044
Tavard, George Henri. 2266, 3770, 3836
Tavard, Georges Henri. 119, 859, 1123, 2977, 3772, 119, 859, 861, 874, 1225, 1491, 1492, 2192, 2977, 3489, 3665, 3700, 3714, 3770
Tawes, Roy Lawson. 2437
Tawney, Richard Henry. 3112, 3213
Taxay, Marshall. 2107
Tayler. 3136
Taylor, Alfred. 3688
Taylor, Alfred Edward. 1855, 2477, 1738, 2419, 3609
Taylor, Alice. 1303
Taylor, Alva Wilmot. 2495, 3446
Taylor, Ariel Yvon. 3576
Taylor, Arthur F. 489
Taylor, B[ushrod] S. 613
Taylor, Barnard Cook. 502, 2948, 532
Taylor, Benjamin Cook. 3045
*Taylor, Benjamin F. 1325
Taylor, Blaine. 1842, 3589
Taylor, Bob R. 2135, 3176, 3181
Taylor, Bushrod Shedden. 1531, 1571, 1711, 1824
Taylor, C. Tousey. 2730
Taylor, Charles Elisha. 3863
Taylor, Charles Forbes. 3366, 167, 1561, 3229, 3589, 3590
Taylor, Charles L. 655
Taylor, Charles Lincoln. 579
Taylor, Charles Lindsay. 270
Taylor, Charles R. 611
Taylor, Charles Walter. 457
Taylor, Claude Carson. 1731
Taylor, Clifton L. 3384
Taylor, Clyde Willis. 2495, 2537
Taylor, Constance Lindsay. 1345
Taylor, David Bruce. 67
Taylor, David Henry. 2802
Taylor, Edward. 1100, 1189, 1343, 2256, 2260, 3590, 3808
Taylor, Emily. 3208
Taylor, Ernest Richard. 2425
Taylor, Eugene. 3123
Taylor, Eustace Lovatt Hebden. 1076
Taylor, Fennings. 1222, 1689
Taylor, Florence M. 3765
Taylor, Florence Marian Tompkins. 642, 898, 1433, 1610, 1996, 2249, 2397, 3166, 3765
Taylor, Francis Richards. 3305
Taylor, Frank Sherwood. 2372
Taylor, Frederick Eugene. 1571
Taylor, Frederick Howard. 1689, 2511, 3590
Taylor, Frederick William. 99
Taylor, Gardner C. 15, 2908
Taylor, Gary G. 1009
Taylor, George. 3600, 2058
Taylor, George Boardman. 3590
Taylor, George Braxton. 145, 144, 145, 2533
Taylor, George Coffin. 2232, 2469
Taylor, George Floyd. 3320
*Taylor, Gerald J., M.D. 3394
Taylor, Gladys (King) 3811
Taylor, Gordon Rattray. 3394
Taylor, Graham. 3446
Taylor, Harry Milton. 1108
Taylor, Harry T. 672
Taylor, Harvey Boyce. 527
Taylor, Hebden. 202, 1477
Taylor, Henry. 609, 1197, 1710
Taylor, Henry Osborn. 2277
Taylor, Henry W. 509
Taylor, Herbert Hall. 874
Taylor, Herbert John. 976
[Taylor, Isaac] 1787-1865. 1072, 1241, 1520, 1799, 1891, 2422, 2755, 3625, 3805
Taylor, Isaac N. 3832
Taylor, J. 298
Taylor, J. R. 1317
Taylor, Jack R. 560, 994, 1428, 1610, 1858, 2881, 2983, 3229
Taylor, James Barnett. 172, 3235
Taylor, James Brainerd. 3590
Taylor, James Morgan. 2055
[Taylor, Jeremiah Humphre] 1797-1882. 1552, 3191

Taylor, Jeremy. 977, 992, 1217, 1973, 3591, 3630, 3692
Taylor, Jerome. 1851
Taylor, Jesse Paul. 1653, 3300, 3303
[Taylor, John] 1580-1653. 298
Taylor, John. 107, 172, 3591, 2606, 2613, 1880
Taylor, John Bernard. 518, 541, 559, 1922
Taylor, John Ellor. 117
Taylor, John Howard. 1036
Taylor, John Metcalf. 3825
Taylor, John Randolph. 1425
Taylor, John Thomas. 3619
Taylor, John Vernon. 712, 1087, 1491, 1832, 2325, 2500, 2555
Taylor, Joseph. 2552
Taylor, Joseph Judson. 2511
Taylor, Julia Marie. 3845
Taylor, June Filkin. 1774, 3591
Taylor, Kanardy Leslie. 179
Taylor, Kenneth Nathaniel. 202, 430, 445, 471, 531, 565, 586, 601, 624, 902, 904, 977, 1433, 1977, 1991, 3220
Taylor, Key W. 3254
Taylor, Landon. 1903
Taylor, Lawrence E. 2764
Taylor, Lily Ross. 723, 1393, 1396
Taylor, Louis R. 2326
Taylor, Margaret Fisk. 3144, 3172, 3180
Taylor, Marion. 1973
Taylor, Marshall William. 3431
Taylor, Marvin J. 3159, 3190
Taylor, Mary Abigail. 2949
Taylor, Mary Abigail (Mellott) 2949
Taylor, Mary Christine. 823, 2700, 2734
Taylor, Mary Geraldine (Guinness) 2163, 2172, 2511, 3524
Taylor, Mason M. 2044
Taylor, Maude Lambart. 1402
Taylor, Maurice. 2101
Taylor, Melba S. 536
Taylor, Mendell. 1238, 1554, 1571, 2016
Taylor, Michael J. 1155, 2234, 3394, 3412, 3541, 3855
Taylor, Millicent J. 291
Taylor, Nathaniel William. 2983
Taylor, Oliver Alden. 1984, 2205, 3136
Taylor, Oral E. 610
Taylor, Ouvy Wilburn. 152
Taylor, Paul W. 1538
Taylor, Philip A. M. 2616
Taylor, Preston. 449
Taylor, Ralph Penniston. 3278
Taylor, Richard. 1537, 2397, 2419
Taylor, Richard K. 1076, 1133, 1675
Taylor, Richard S. 945, 3375
Taylor, Richard Shelley. 977, 1074, 2906, 3412
Taylor, Robert. 3023, 3024
Taylor, Robert C. 1242
Taylor, Robert N. 3757
Taylor, Robert Oswald Patrick. 3080
Taylor, Robert R. 1610
Taylor, Robert T. 31
Taylor, Rodney Leon. 2164, 2683
Taylor, Ronald William. 2546
Taylor, Ruth B. 3159
Taylor, Samuel Woolley. 1233, 2616, 2617, 2618, 2859, 3591
Taylor, Sarah Elizabeth (Langworthy) 2478
Taylor, Stephen Earl. 2455, 2498
Taylor, T. B. 3616
Taylor, Theophilus. 3612
Taylor, Thomas. 451, 479, 3721, 98, 1505, 1369
Taylor, Thomas Eddy. 1994
Taylor, Timothy Alden. 1072
Taylor, Vincent. 3781, 107, 352, 393, 430, 1973, 2020, 2030, 2044, 430, 2030
Taylor, Willard H. 380, 1973
Taylor, William. 1895, 2499, 2906, 3591
Taylor, William Brooks. 465, 367
Taylor, William Carey. 274, 275, 2547
Taylor, William George Langworthy. 1942, 3515, 3520
Taylor, William J. 1540
Taylor, William James Romeyn. 1704
Taylor, William M. 1252
Taylor, William Mackergo. 1506, 1401, 1405, 1506, 2018, 2026, 2133, 2182, 2622, 2802, 2825, 2935, 3258, 3346, 3572, 3675
Taymaris d'Expernon. 3266
Tcherikover, Avigdor. 2092, 2099
Tchividjian, Gigi. 989, 3591
Tchurmin, Avrhum Yuhzov. 1727
Teaching of the twelve apostles. 71
Teaching of the twelve apostles. English. 950
Teague, Hosea Holcombe. 2978
Teague, Wilbur A. 3087
Teale, A. E. 2163
Teale, William Henry. 1602
Teasdale, Thomas Cox. 2228
Teasley, Daniel Otis. 3391
Tebeau, Charlton W. 2100, 3599

Tedlock, Dennis. 1902
[Teed, Cyrus Reed] 1839-1908. 1929
Teegarden, Kenneth L. 932
Teeling, William. 2852
*Teeple, Douglas M. 2381
Teeple, Howard Merle. 421, 2414, 2711
Tees, Francis Harrison. 2425, 2830
Tefft, Benjamin Franklin. 1581
Tegenfeldt, Herman G. 144
Tehan, Arline (Boucher) 1711
Tehologia deutsch. 1008
Teichman, Jenny. 2473
Teikmanis, Arthur L. 2906
Teilhard de Chardin, Pierre. 1106, 2373, 2643, 2839, 3083, 3541, 3593, 3625, 3891
Teit, James Alexander. 2716
Teiwes-French, Helga. 3298
Teixidor, Javier. 2679
Teja Singh. 3408
Tekippe, Terry J. 1002
Telchin, Stan. 1366, 3593
Telepun, L. M. 3256
Telestic guild, Tampa, Fla. 2731
Telfer, William. 1453, 2816, 665, 745, 1634
Telford, John. 3805
Tellenbach, Gerd. 1144
Teller, Judd L. 2103, 2112
Teller, Woolsey. 99, 101
Temko, Allan. 2774
Temperley, Nicholas. 1207
Templars of honor and temperance. Supreme council. 3598
Temple Beth El of Northern Westchester, Chappaqua, N.Y. 2098, 3598
Temple, Charles A. S. 1080
Temple, Edward Lowe. 199
Temple, Frederick. 3076
Temple, Helen Frances. 1238
Temple, Joe. 904
Temple, Josiah Howard. 3561
Temple, Patrick Joseph. 430
Temple, Robert K. G. 1917
Temple, Robert M. 1360
Temple, Sydney Absalom. 616
Temple, William. 1217, 1042, 1063, 1072, 1106, 1123, 1124, 1227, 1453, 2837, 3366, 3446, 3625, 422, 726, 1072, 1096, 1212, 2210, 2674, 2837, 3446, 3599
Templeton, Charles Bradley. 1571, 2935
Templeton, John M. 3083
Templeton, Mary Ellen. 1275
Ten Boom, Corrie. 681, 928, 1433, 1786, 3601
Ten Boom, Corrie. 681, 928, 932, 989, 1012, 1353, 1433, 1786, 3407, 3601
Tendzin, Osel. 3484
Tenenbaum, Joseph. 2102
Tengbom, Mildred. 445, 551, 902, 1006, 1353, 1750
Tenhaeff, Wilhelm Heinrich Carl. 2991
Tennant, Charles Roger. 1973
Tennant, Frederick Robert. 1602, 2477, 3105, 3412, 1602
Tennent, Gilbert. 3359, 3427, 3601
Tennent, James Emerson. 1927
Tennessee Temple College, Chattanooga. 3229
[Tenney, Edward Payson] 1835. 1325
Tenney, Edward Payson. 1973, 3433, 3807
Tenney, Edward Vernon. 3000
Tenney, Henry Martyn. 2488
Tenney, Jack Breckinridge. 2079, 3897
Tenney, John Ellis. 3385
Tenney, Mary Alice. 2422
Tenney, Mary (McWhorter) 3703
Tenney, Merrill Chapin. 246, 278, 381, 393, 408, 411, 418, 426, 457, 461, 658, 989, 2044, 2053, 3222, 3226, 3653
Tennies, Arthur C. 989
Tennyson, Alfred Tennyson. 3602
Tennyson, Elwell Thomas. 1515
Tennyson, G. B. 3071
Tentler, Thomas N. 2812
Teodorowicz, Jozef. 2686, 3532
Tepper, Joseph L. 2140
Terbovich, John B. 887
Teresa, 1515-1582. 777, 2220, 2249, 2397, 2819, 3489, 3603, 3630
Teresa, 1910. 1002, 2397
Teresa Margaret. 3602, 3691
Teresa of Avila, 1515-82. 3604
Teresita. 82, 3420
Terhune, Albert Payson. 1973
Terhune, Anice Morris (Stockton) 3515
[Terhune, Mary Virginia (Hawes)] 1830-1922. 2182
Terkelsen, Helen E. 3759
Termote, Henri. 90
Terra, Russell. 9, 865, 2722
Terra, Russell G. 2397
Terrasson, Vincent. 1403
Terrell, Ada Knight. 1042
Terrell, John Upton. 1903, 3426

Terrien, Samuel. 297, 312, 548
Terrien, Samuel L. 297, 579, 652, 2210
Terrill, Ada Thurman. 642
Terrille, Joseph Goodwin. 3031
Terry, Alfred Howe. 3516
Terry, Carol. 2532
Terry, Charles Sanford. 123, 916
Terry, Ezekiel. 109
Terry, Jay William. 2176
Terry, Keith. 2616, 3429
Terry, Lindsay. 1203
Terry, Mary. 3829
Terry, Milton Spenser. 502, 3404, 56, 123, 288, 477, 509, 934, 2044, 3191, 3404, 3649
*Terry, R. Harold. 1246
Terry, W. Clinton. 3165
Tertullianus, Quintus Septimius Florens. 69, 1807, 2332, 2344, 2812, 3604, 3635
Terwilliger, Robert E. 278
TeSelle, Eugene. 117, 2044
TeSelle, Sallie McFague. 1077, 3071
Tesh, S Edward. 312
Teske, Robert Thomas. 2749, 3787
Tesniere, Albert. 2253
Tessier, Albert Denis. 3589
Tester, Sylvia Root. 2712
Testerman, Jean. 989, 3604
Tetlow, Elizabeth M. 349, 3835
Tettemer, John Moynihan. 794, 3604
Teulings, C. P. 494
Tevis, Julia Ann (Hieronymus) 120
Tewinkel, Joseph M. 1180
Texas Christian University, Fort Worth. 3604
Texas. University. 3190
Texas. University. Dept. of extension. 3759
Thacher, Delia Tudor. 2856
Thacher, Moses. 1662
Thackeray, Henry St. John. 1084, 1770, 2134, 2802
Thalheimer, Alvin. 2739
Thalman, Norman. 2290
Thanksgiving Workshop on Evangelicals and Social Concern, Chicago, 1973. 1552
Tharaud, Jerome. 2099
Tharp, Constance P. 1756
Tharp, Paul Madison. 977, 2266
Tharp, Zeno Chandler. 1229, 1842
*Thatch, Harrell G. 3136
Thatcher, Adrian. 2740, 3700
Thatcher, Joan. 1245, 3785
Thatcher, John. 144
Thatcher, Oliver Joseph. 854, 1780
Thayer, Alexander Wheelock. 517
Thayer, Caroline Matilda (Warren) 977
Thayer, Earl Harrison. 2397
Thayer, Erastus W. 107, 1973, 2053
Thayer, Erastus William. 107, 1973, 2044, 2053
Thayer, George Augustine. 1275
Thayer, James Henry. 167
Thayer, John. 2177
Thayer, Joseph Henry. 681
Thayer, Lynn W. 1203
Thayer, Mary Dixon. 3526
Thayer, Thomas Baldwin. 1099, 1353, 3753
Thayer, Vivian Trow. 1886. 1130, 3190
Thayer, William Makepeace. 1453, 2200, 3597
Thayne, Mirla Greenwood. 1984, 3321
[The American Lutheran]. 1252
[The Calvary evangel]. 1360
[The Catholic digest]. 1131
Thearch society. 3609
Theas, Pierre Marie. 2262
Thebaud, Augustus J. 828, 1195, 3121
[The Evangel]. 1360
Theiele, Edwin Richard. 496
Theiler, Heinrich. 734, 1836
Thein, John. 3092, 237, 2325
Theisen, Reinold. 2369, 3710
Theiss, Herman C. 1202
Theissen, Gerd. 67, 346, 3451
Theisz, George Elmer. 2006
Thekackara, Matthew Pothen. 2397
Thelen, Mary Frances. 1195, 3412
Themascus, Hazel G. 3520
Themistius. 1151, 2311
Theobald, Morell. 3516
Theocritus. 1771, 3202
Theodor Herzl Institute, New York. 1928
Theodore, John T. 1979
Theodoretus. 1197, 2044
Theodorus. 372
Theologia deutsch. 977, 1008, 3616
Theological Education Association of Mid-America. 3678
Theological Education Consultation Suva Fyi Islands 1961. 3681
Theological Institute for local Superiors University of Notre Dame. 2574, 2581, 2716, 3490, 3787
Theology digest. v. 1. 3677

Theophane. 3490
Theophilus, 2d cent. 69
Theophrastus. 2419
Theosophical society. 3682
Theosophical society. American section. 3682, 3688
Theosophical Society, Blavatsky Lodge. 3688
Theosophical society in America. 3682
Therese 1873-1897. 3282
Therese, 1873-1897. 1026, 2397, 3691
Therese. 2362
Therese Catherine. 3691, 3830
Therese Marie. 2305, 3418
Theron, Daniel Johannes. 1198
Therrien, Vincent. 2816
Thexton, S. Clive. 545
Thibault, B[enoit] C[lovis]. 3294
Thibault, Benoit Clovis. 792
Thibaut, Raymond. 2336
Thickstun, Edmund. 1554
Thiebault, Jules. 3516
Thiel, Rudolph. 2277
Thiele, Edwin Richard. 496, 555, 1115, 1727, 2093
Thiele, Margaret Rossiter. 3812
Thielen, Thoralf Theodore. 1373
Thielicke, Helmet. 1006
Thielicke, Helmut. 2250, 67, 74, 527, 945, 1415, 2028, 2067, 2223, 2250, 2282, 2301, 2710, 2906, 3337, 3368, 3370, 3618, 3625, 3649, 3665
Thieme, Paul. 2560
Thien An, Thich, 1926. 3893
Thierens, A. E. 3589
Thierry, Jean Jacques. 3436
Thiessen, Henry Clarence. 3649, 411, 1515, 3649
Thiessen, John Caldwell. 2495, 2787
Thilo, Hans Joachim. 2784
Thils, Gustave. 1299, 3328
Thind, Bhagat Singh. 3821, 3408
Third Haven Friends' meeting house, Talbot co., Md. 1675
Thirkield, Wilbur Patterson. 2455, 2495, 2823, 2434
Thirlby, Styan. 3810
Thirlwall, Connop. 3202
Thirlwall, John Connop. 3692
Thirtle, James William. 579
Thiry, Paul. 1157
Thoburn, Helen. 1955, 1998
Thoburn, James Mills. 1897, 2532, 2813
Thoburn, Wilbur W[ilson]. 3346
Thoburn, Wilbur Wilson. 3759
Tholuck, August. 418, 469, 2034, 3030, 3368
Thom, William Taylor. 172
Thoma, Clemens. 2145
Thomas. 2645, 3603, 3817
Thomas, 1225?-1274. 792, 3653
Thomas A. Connolly. 826
Thomas A Kempis 1380-1471. 2357, 2896
Thomas, Abel Charles. 1595
Thomas, Abraham Vazhayil. 1110
Thomas, Albert Sidney. 2974
Thomas, Allen Clapp. 1685
Thomas, Alsen Franklin. 1063
Thomas, Anna Lloyd (Braithwaite) 690, 1677
Thomas Aquinas 1225?-1274. 225
Thomas Aquinas. 1225?-1274. 69, 674, 746, 777, 783, 949, 1537, 1728, 1785, 1911, 2047, 2180, 2212, 2266, 2322, 2327, 2397, 2419, 2593, 3463, 3538, 3617, 3636, 3649, 3694, 3695, 3696, 3782
Thomas Aquinas. 1225?- 1274. 2249, 3636
Thomas, Aquinas, Saint. 3649
Thomas Aquines 1225?-1274. 69, 367, 783, 1736, 2180, 2819, 3636, 3782
Thomas, B. J. 1367, 3697
Thomas, Belle. 919
Thomas, Cal. 1367, 1792
Thomas, Cecil K. 361
Thomas, Charles. 919, 1763
Thomas, Charles Drayton. 3516
Thomas, Clyde H. 2112
Thomas, Cordelia. 3482
Thomas, Craig Sharp. 1131
Thomas, D Reginald. 2935, 3359
Thomas, Dana Lee. 2484
Thomas, David. 330, 344, 418, 441, 573, 1433, 2127
Thomas, David M. 1610
Thomas, David Michael. 1610
Thomas, David Owen. 2252
Thomas, David Richard. 3273
Thomas, David Samuel. 1180
Thomas, David Winton. 487
Thomas de Saint-Laurent, Raymond de. 2357
Thomas, Denis. 1958
Thomas, Donald F. 1408
Thomas, E. D. 153
Thomas, Edgar Garfield. 3305, 3665

Thomas, Edith Lovell. 1209
Thomas, Edward. 1543, 1676, 2666
Thomas, Edward Joseph. 703, 705, 703, 705
Thomas, Elbert Duncan. 3741
Thomas, Evan Edward. 1595, 2261, 3027
Thomas, F. 2686
Thomas, Father. 2645, 3603
Thomas, Frank Morehead. 2056
Thomas, Franklin A. 3463
Thomas, Franklin Alonzo. 3516
Thomas, Fred W. 2730
Thomas, George Ernest. 952, 989, 1004, 1007, 1201, 1442, 2004, 2054, 2058, 2437, 2881, 2995, 3482, 3805
Thomas, George Finger. 3463, 945, 1097, 3105, 3108
Thomas, George William Curtis. 107
Thomas, H. J. K. 1728
Thomas, Henry. 3136
Thomas, Hiram Washington. 2426
Thomas, Howard E. 2681
Thomas, Isaac David Ellis. 572
Thomas, Isaac Lemuel. 2459, 2460
Thomas, J. B. 2771
Thomas, J. M. Lloyd. 3801
Thomas, James Bishop. 2163, 3064
Thomas, James David. 68, 278, 1272, 1467, 1752, 2181, 3359
Thomas, James Henderson. 609, 1515
Thomas, James Melton. 1238
Thomas, James Moulton. 1697, 2881
Thomas, Jesse Burgess. 473, 3076
Thomas, Joan. 2340
Thomas, Joan Gale. 1744, 2249
Thomas, John. 457, 609, 1515
Thomas, John Edward. 904, 3806
Thomas, John F. 3516
Thomas, John Frederick. 2991, 3516
Thomas, John Heywood. 2171, 3700
Thomas, John Lawrence. 1603, 2340, 2344, 3012, 3746
Thomas, John Martin. 502
Thomas, Joseph. 2847, 662
Thomas, Joseph Hromas. 3516
Thomas, Keith Vivian. 1764
Thomas, Lately. 2310
Thomas, Latta R. 16, 237
Thomas, Lee. 3566
Thomas, Lee [Obra Lee Thomas]. 3566
Thomas, Leslie Grier. 589, 1272, 3336, 3375
Thomas, Lonnie (Benson) 3468
Thomas, Louise Porter. 2626
Thomas, Lowell Jackson. 2706
Thomas, M A. 2397
Thomas, Madathilparampil M. 1135, 3328
Thomas, Marion. 2443, 3558
Thomas, Martha (Horton) 2397
Thomas, Mary P. 2501
Thomas, Maurice Jacob. 1130
Thomas, Metta Newman. 3841
Thomas, Moses Bross. 1728
Thomas, Nancy White. 2881
Thomas of Strassburg 1357. 2826
*Thomas, Owen C. 1595, 3313, 3665
Thomas, Owen C. 1080
Thomas, Paul Westphal. 2847
Thomas, Reuen. 927
Thomas, Robert Horatio. 333
Thomas, Roger W. 989
Thomas, Roland. 2938
Thomas, Ronald Stuart. 3210
Thomas, Roy L. 1171
Thomas, Roy Wallace. 2881
Thomas S Clarkson Memorial College of Technology, Potsdam NY: Dept. of Industrial Distributionc6. 81
Thomas, Samuel W. 3398
Thomas, Stan. 1941
Thomas, Tay. 1524, 3697
Thomas, W. H. Griffith. 2044
Thomas, W. Ian. 514, 977
Thomas, Warren Ann. 3287
Thomas, Wendell Marshall. 1814, 3080
Thomas, William Henry Griffith. 977, 1752, 2127, 2240, 278, 332, 404, 431, 444, 522, 566, 1212, 1832, 2127, 2825, 3375, 3675, 2045
Thomas, Winburn T. 92, 2495, 2954, 3530
Thomasa, Kempis. 865, 2362
Thomas Aquinas 1225?-1274. 69, 777, 1728, 2839, 3636, 3649
Thomas Aquinas. 2258
Thomas Aquinas, Saint. 3649
[Thomasine, 1872. 840
[Thomason, Adam Peter] 1865. 3609
Thomason, Jean Healan. 2634, 3398
Thomason, William O. 994
Thomasson, William. 349
Thome de Jesus. 1978
The Thomist. 761, 1613
Thompson, Albert Edward. 2535, 3410
Thompson, Alden Lloyd. 488
Thompson, Alexander Hamilton. 751, 1159, 1762, 2569, 3868, 1762, 2569
Thompson, Archie Paul. 1630, 2304

[Thompson, Augustus Charles] 1812-1901. 39, 461, 897, 1693, 1795, 2484, 2881, 3210
Thompson, Bard. 1801, 2238
Thompson, Betty. 1017, 1042, 2325, 3697
Thompson, Blanche Jennings. 868, 3285, 297, 859, 1508, 1650, 2707, 2825, 3285
Thompson, C. A. 2466
Thompson, C A. 2466
Thompson, Carroll. 1805
Thompson, Carroll J. 3476, 3697
Thompson, Charles John Samuel. 2313, 97, 2313, 2378
Thompson, Charles Lemuel. 2926, 657, 1571, 2923, 3121
Thompson, Claude H. 1530
Thompson, Claude W. 1854
Thompson, Colin P. 2137, 2637
Thompson, Conrad M. 1006
Thompson, Craig Ringwalt. 1759
Thompson, David Decamp. 3805
Thompson, David Michael. 1469
Thompson, David W. 1168
Thompson, David Walter. 291
Thompson, David Wilson. 1168
Thompson, E. Margaret. 742
Thompson, Ebenezer. 72, 1973
Thompson, Edward Healy. 3580
Thompson, Edward John. 3208
Thompson, Egbert Herron. 3666
Thompson, Elbert Nevius Sebring. 2469
Thompson, Elizabeth Ann. 898
Thompson, Ellen. 1848
Thompson, Elmer Ellsworth. 642
Thompson, Erik. 444
*Thompson, Ernest Trice. 1180
Thompson, Ernest Trice. 434, 1087, 1153, 2066, 2910, 2921, 2925, 2926, 3336
Thompson, Evelyn Wingo. 3235
Thompson, Francis. 2269
Thompson, Franklin. 2105
Thompson, Fred P. 609, 1832
Thompson, Fred Priestly. 609
Thompson, George B. 743, 3463, 3482
Thompson, George Harry Packwood. 364
Thompson, George Washington. 2068
[Thompson, George Western] 1806-1888. 3105
Thompson, Gjermund S. 2215
Thompson, Gordon. 2437
Thompson, Harry Styles. 977
Thompson, Helen. 3490, 3697
Thompson, Henry Adams. 642, 3841, 3730, 3799
[Thompson, Henry Post] 1831-1891. 2810
Thompson, Henry Yates. 2330
Thompson, Herbert W. 977
Thompson, Hugh Miller. 3095, 3141, 2960
Thompson, Hugo W. 2266
Thompson, J. A. 208
Thompson, J. Larry. 2030
Thompson, James. 326, 404
Thompson, James Edmond. 1100
Thompson, James J. 3466, 3626
Thompson, James Marshall. 4, 1180
Thompson, James Nevill. 1219
Thompson, James Voorhees. 1260
Thompson, James Westfall. 1639, 3202
Thompson, Jean A. 3174
Thompson, Jean McKee. 1112
Thompson, John. 108, 2045
Thompson, John Arthur. 208, 335, 487, 510, 546
Thompson, John Rhey. 3359
Thompson, John Samuel. 3649
[Thompson, Joseph James] 1868-1930. 892
Thompson, Joseph Parrish. 401, 1453, 1484, 1693, 1699, 1777, 1832, 1974, 2066, 2196, 2322, 2541, 2546. 3532

Thompson, Josiah. 2171
Thompson, Karl F. 2232
Thompson, Keith. 940
Thompson, Ken. 2895
Thompson, Kenneth A. 1219, 3446
Thompson, Kenneth W. 1087, 1914
Thompson, L. Buckland W. 1891
Thompson, Laurence G. 914
Thompson, Lawrance Roger. 2401, 3071
[Thompson, Leander] 1812-1896. 1848
Thompson, Leonard L. 314
Thompson, Lewis Nathan. 1378
Thompson, Lewis Olson. 3076
Thompson, Lorne F. 3136
[Thompson, Louise Glenn] 1903. 3159
Thompson, Luther Joe. 324, 977, 2266
Thompson, May Bel. 2511
Thompson, Murray Stewart. 2787, 3698
Thompson, Newton Wayland. 228, 344
Thompson, Noyes L. 184, 693
Thompson, Olive R. 977
Thompson, Olive Ross. 977
*Thompson, Orin D. 3370
*Thompson, Otis. 41, 3412
Thompson, Phyllis. 121, 723, 1784, 2486

Thompson, R J. 3272
Thompson, Ralph Wardlaw. 2125, 2511
Thompson, Reginald Campbell. 1892, 2315
Thompson, Rhodes. 1461
Thompson, Richard Wigginton. 802, 1947
Thompson, Robert Ellis. 72, 1523, 2026, 2924, 3447
Thompson, Roy A. 1021, 1546
Thompson, Samuel Chalmers. 199
Thompson, Samuel Martin. 3105
[Thompson, Samuel N.]. 1656
Thompson, Silvanus Phillips. 1788
Thompson, Thomas K. 3530
Thompson, Tom. 136
Thompson, Virginia. 2397
Thompson, W. Oscar. 3830
Thompson, William D. 299, 1458, 2906
Thompson, William Hertzog. 67
Thompson, William M. 2045
Thompson, William Taliaferro. 1610
Thompson, Wilson. 3136
Thompson, Yancy Samuel. 885
Thoms, Craig S. 306, 1053, 2048
Thoms, Craig Sharp. 502
Thoms, Herbert. 3317
Thomsen, Harry. 3324
Thomsen, Russel J. 317, 1233, 3261
[Thomson Agnes G.]. 237
Thomson, Alexander. 2053
Thomson, Andrews. 2484
Thomson, David Patrick. 1554, 1561
Thomson, Edith Parker. 401
Thomson, Edward. 61, 2532, 3625, 3698
Thomson, James G S S. 2883, 3227
Thomson, John. 3809
Thomson, John A F. 2243, 2770
Thomson, John Arthur. 3080
Thomson, Lucy Gertsch. 1325, 3841
Thomson, Mary. 2669, 3516
Thomson, Mortimer. 1635
Thomson, Paul van Kuykendall. 1365
Thomson, Robert. 119
Thomson, Ronald William. 1860
Thomson, William. 1602
Thomson, William Hanna. 2027, 2415
Thomson, William McClure. 2763
Thomte, Reidar. 2171
Thorbecke, Ellen (Kolban) 2765
Thorburn, Thomas James. 393, 1979
Thoreau, Henry David. 1688
Thoren, Herman H. 3136
Thorkelson, Willmar. 2293
Thorley, Enoch. 3202
Thorman, Donald J. 792, 1002, 1245, 2192
Thorn, Floyd Brantley. 167
Thorn, George W. 460
Thorn, William E. 994, 1842
Thornburgh, George. 1670
Thornbury, John. 1124
Thorndyke, E. P. 3516
Thorne, Charles Greenwood. 3190
Thorne, J[ohn] J[ulius]. 3208
Thorne, Leonard C. 48
*Thorne, Milton. 3330
Thorne, R. A. 2624
Thorne, Rosella A. 2624
Thorne, Sabina. 3020, 3775
Thorning, Joseph Francis. 1136, 3195, 3451
Thornley, Gwendella. 2048
Thornton, David. 989
Thornton, Edward. 2640
Thornton, Edward E. 2781, 2785
Thornton, Edwin William. 1106, 1461, 1842, 3367, 3558, 1467
Thornton, Francis Beauchesne. 738, 2850, 3012, 3248, 3405
Thornton, Jerry. 3727
Thornton, John Wingate. 3742
Thornton, Lionel Spencer. 652, 1893, 3226
Thornton, Martin. 992, 1219, 2166, 2788, 3254, 3484, 3617
Thornton, Mary Crescentia. 815, 1663
Thornton, Robinson. 29
Thornton, Thomas C. 3649
Thornton, Walter Miller. 977
Thornwell, James Henley. 108, 489, 2911, 3698
Thorogood, Bernard. 486
Thorold, Anthony. 2370, 3490
Thorold, Anthony Wilson. 1453
Thorp,Charles Nicholas. 909
Thorp, John. 2218
Thorpe, James Ernest. 314, 876, 1778, 2471
Thorpe, William Homan. 3083
Thorwall, LaReau. 3698
Thoughts of God for boys and girls. 902
Thouless, Robert Henry. 2158, 1081, 3000
Thrall, Margaret E. 1770
Thrapp, Grace R. 481
Thrapp, Grace Romig. 1630
Thrash, Arline Cate. 1610
Thrasher, Marion. 3024

Thrift, Charles Tinsley. 2526, 2430
Throckmorton, Burton Hamilton, 1921. 469, 470, 545, 1383, 1424
Throckmorton, J. Russell. 1571
Throop, Palmer Allan. 1391
Thrower, Arthur H. 2228
Thrower, Bob. 3698
Thrum, Thomas George. 3581
Thrupp, Sylvia Lettice. 2466
Thubten Jigme Norbu. 2193
Thuis, Stephen. 884
Thulin, Oskar. 2277
Thung, Mady A. 3447
Thupten Wangyal. 2193
Thurber, Robert Bruce. 1401, 1955, 2505, 2622
Thureau-Dangin, Paul Marie Pierre. 194, 860
Thurian, Max. 1249, 1328, 2252, 2253, 2358, 3482, 3666
Thurlow, A G G. 2715
Thurlow, Gilbert. 2715
Thurman, Howard. 146, 168, 1112, 1453, 1586, 2066, 2680, 3298, 3698
Thurman, Lloy Duane. 202
Thurman, Thomas D. 395, 930, 1985
Thurneysen, Eduard. 2787, 3336
Thurston, Eli. 3359
Thurston, Herbert. 841, 1710, 1838, 2640, 2643, 3516
Thurston, Howard. 1345
Thurston, John. 3095
Thurston, Joseph Smith. 2066
Thurston, Katherine (Kemp) 2166
Thurston, Lucy (Goodale). 2525
Thurston, Mabel Nelson. 1112, 1595, 2022, 2881
Thurston, Mark A. 93, 877, 2948, 2991
Thurstone, Louis Leon. 1124
Thwaites, Reuben Gold. 2336
Thwing, Charles Franklin. 1289, 3092
Thwing, Edward Payson. 3698
Thwing, Walter Eliot. 1180
Thynne, Roger. 3245
Tibawi, Abdul Latif. 2552
Tibbals, Cyrus F. 3627
Tibbets, Joshua Calvin. 153
Tibbetts, Norris L. 2397
Tibbetts, Orlando L. 1244, 1249, 2895
Tibbitts, Fred Lyman. 3558
Tibbitts, George Franklin. 3367
Tibbutt, Harry Gordon. 183
Tiberghien, Pierre. 754
Tibesar, Antonine. 1647
Tice, Terrence N. 3308
Tichenor, Henry M. 3617
Tichenor, Henry Mulford. 1097, 2654, 3054, 3202, 3244
Tichy, Henrietta. 300
Tickemyer, Garland E. 1842
Ticonius. 457
Ticonius, 4th cent. 288
Tidball, Thomas Allen. 1221, 411, 2045
Tidsworth, Floyd. 1166
Tidwell, Charles A. 2774
Tidwell, Donavon Duncan. 154, 1663
Tidwell, Josiah Blake. 278, 283, 307, 312, 414, 527, 564, 1974, 3550, 3675, 3375
Tidwell, William M. 1842
Tiebout, Harry M. 3123
Tieck, William Arthur. 2698
Tiede, David Lenz. 426, 2622, 3782
Tiedeman, Karl. 3482
Tiedemann, Karl. 1985
Tiele, Cornelis Petrus. 3064
Tien feng. 912
Tierney, Brian. 1144, 1322, 2734
Tierney, Mark. 667, 1387, 2368
Tierney, Mary E. 2397
Tierney, Michael F. 761
Tierney, Terence E. 2341
Tierney, William L. 757
Tietjen, John H. 1045
Tietjen, Mary Louise. 8
Tiffany, Charles Comfort. 2961, 2967
Tiffany, Francis. 174
Tiffany, Joel. 3516, 2325, 3516
Tiffany, Nina (Moore) 2221
Tiffany, Osmond. 216
Tigert, John James. 1053, 2422, 2449, 2451, 3609, 3805, 2310
Tigner, Hugh Stevenson. 1063, 1280, 1097
Tigner, Marcy. 616
Tilak, Lakshmibai (Gokhale) 3143, 3699
Tilburne, Edward Oliver. 2696
Tilcomb, Sarah E. 2664
Tilden, Elwyn E. 1974
Tilden, William Phillips. 3675
[Tileston, Mary Wilder (Foote) 1843. 1442, 1453
Tileston, Mary Wilder (Foote) 1433, 1442, 1453, 2895
Till, Barry. 1045
Tillard, J. M. R. 2255, 2571
Tiller, Carl W. 141, 152
Tillet, Wilbur Fisk. 977, 1053, 2456

Tillett, Gregory. 2203, 3682
Tillett, Wilbur Fisk. 3291
Tillett, Wilbur Risk. 3291
Tilley, Arthur Augustus. 1639
Tilley, Charles J. 3226
Tilley, Ethel. 649, 3188, 3766
Tilley, Terrence W. 3071
Tillich, Hannah. 3611, 3700
Tillich, Paul. 1077, 1106, 2977, 3211, 3212, 3359, 3617, 3655, 3700, 5, 945, 1066, 1067, 1080, 1106, 1595, 2263, 3105, 3359, 3448, 3625, 3649, 3655, 3679, 3700
Tillich, Paul [Johannes Oskar]. 2263, 3359
Tillich, Paul Johannes Oskar. 1080, 1106, 2263, 3359
Tillman, Bonnie. 624
Tillman, Helene. 1908, 2861
Tillmann, Fritz. 949
Tillmanns, Walter G. 2278, 3036
Tillotson, John. 473
[Tillson, Jesse Paxon] 1870. 119
Tillyard, Aelfrida Catharine Wetenhall. 2640
Tillyard, Alfred Isaac. 1581
Tillyard, Eustace Mandeville Wetenhall. 2470
Tillyard, Henry Julius Wetenhall. 2632
Tilmann, Klemens. 2381, 3490
Tilmon, Levin. 3424
Tilroe, William Edwin. 1911
Tilson, Charles Everett. 1394, 3329, 3596
Tilstra, Albertine Klingbeil. 2486, 3701
Tiltman, Marjorie (Hand) Hessell. 927
Tilton, Howard W[inslow]. 3346
Tilton, Theodore. 3208
Tim X. 1424
Timasheff, Nicholas Sergeyevitch. 3257, 1108
Timayenis, Telemachus Thomas. 1808, 2313
Timbrell, John Hamilton. 457, 324
[Timbs, John] 1801-1875. 1513, 2948
Timby, Ruth Jones. 1063
Time, inc. 2806
Time-Life Books. 536, 2095, 2173, 2761
Time-Life Bools. 2173
The Times, London. 312, 313
Timmerman, Samuel Federick. 802
Timmermans, Felix. 1643
Timmons, Ernest Andrew. 2340
Timmons, Tim. 989, 1006, 2340, 3516
Timms, Moira. 2948
*Timms, Noel. 1603
Timofiewitsch, Wladimir. 3777
[Timon, John] 1797-1867. 2542
Timothy, Hamilton Baird. 1718, 1919
Tindal, Matthew. 1420, 3024
Tindall, Gillian. 3824
Tinder, Glenn E. 1615
Tiner, John Hudson. 3073
Ting, K. H. 642
Tingley, Katherine A. (Wescott) 1728
Tingley, Katherine A. (Westcott) 672, 3688, 3689, 3688
Tingley, Katherine Augusta (Westcott) 3688
Tingley, Ralph. 1626, 3415
Tinker, Reuben. 2935
Tinker, Wellington Hutchinson. 3872
Tinling, Christine Isabel. 617, 2502, 3596
Tinling, Christine Isable. 2537
Tinling, James Forbes Bissett. 1842
Tinney, Ethel. 3841
Tinning, Graham. 1164
Tinsley, Ernest John. 995
Tintori, Leonetto. 1643, 3282
Tiplady, Thomas. 1819, 3447
Tippett, Alan Richard. 2504, 2543, 2545, 2547, 2555
Tippett, Donald Harvey. 2250
Tippett, Edward D. 3136
Tippett, Harry Moyle. 977, 1314, 1442, 1453, 1873, 3716
Tippett, James Sterling. 1996
Tippit, Sammy. 3701
Tipple, Bertrand Martin. 757
Tipple, Ezra Squier. 1480, 3701, 89
Tippy, Worth Marion. 2426, 3241, 3447
Tipton, Albert W. 1383
Tipton, L. H. 2220
Tirebuck, William Edwards. 2372
Tirrell, Mary Pierre. 3136
Tiry, Clara Mary. 75, 3407
Tischendorf, Constantin von. 393
Tischler, Franz Seraphicus. 1649
Tischler, Nancy Marie Patterson. 3841
Tisdall, William St. Clair Towers. 3121
Tise, Larry E. 3789
Tisserant, Eugene. 866
Tissot, James Joseph Jacques. 399, 1974
Titcomb, H Everett, 1884. 1204
Titcomb, Sarah Elizabeth. 2410, 3546
Titsworth, Judson. 2215
[Titterington, Sophie (Bronson) 1846. 3209

Tittle, Ernest Fremont. 1126, 1053, 2248, 3359, 3447, 3448, 3482, 3703
Tittle, Ernest Fremont, 1885-1949. 428, 2437, 2896
Tittmann, George Fabian. 67, 1376, 3482
Tittmann, Karl Christian. 1718
Titus, Charles Buttz. 1463, 2485
Titus, Eric Lane. 418, 475
Titus, F. E. 3688
Titus, Justin E. 2730, 3516
Titus, Murray Thurston. 2565
Titus, Pauline Woodruff. 2244
Titus, Timothy Tilghman. 2028
Titzard, Leslie James. 2906
Tixeront, Joseph. 773, 1618, 3655
Tizard, Leslie James. 2906
Tizzard, Leslie James. 2906
Tjader, Marguerite. 663
Tjernagel, Neelak Serawlook. 1225, 1804
Tlapa, Richard J. 1279
To Promote Good Will (Television program) 3142
Toal, M F. 386
Tobey, Carl Payne. 97
*Tobey, Kathrene McLandress. 1254, 3175
Tobias, Robert. 1046, 1542
Tobie, Willard Nathan. 107, 248, 291, 2049
Tobin, James Edward. 868
Tobin, John. 1783
Tobin, Luke. 2718, 3703
Tobin, William. 865
Todd, Charles Mack. 205
Todd, Elbert S. 2495
Todd, Elizabeth. 587
Todd, Floyd. 733, 1164
Todd, Galbraith Hall. 33, 1486, 1623, 2058, 2215, 3359
Todd, J. H. 644
Todd, Jacob. 2175
Todd, James Cameron. 2096
Todd, James Henry. 107, 1955
Todd, James J. 1792
Todd, James Moody. 1339
Todd, Jay M. 3429
Todd, John. 2622, 3136, 3558
Todd, John Adams. 1693, 2189
Todd, John Murray. 119, 1537, 1860, 2192, 2278, 3036, 3037, 3785
Todd, Johnathan. 1504
[Todd, Jonathan] 1713-1791. 1336, 1596, 3240, 3253
Todd, Luther Edward. 2455
Todd, Mary Fidelis. 2190, 2478
Todd, Paul. 764
Todd, Virgil H. 545, 1530
Todd, Wayne E. 2224, 2369
Todrank, Gustave Herman. 3328
Todt, Heinz Eduard. 3458
Toelke, Otto W. 1606
Toennes, William. 1957
Toesca, Pietro. 3777
Toews, Abraham Peter. 2408, 950
Toews, J. B. 2497
Toews, John A. 2403
Toews, John B. 2407, 2408
Tofani, Louise E. 2730
Toffteen, Olaf Alfred. 219, 1584
Toffteen, Olof A. 2666
Toffteen, Olof Alfred. 3064
Together. 2428
[Toher, Eugene]. 767
Toksvig, Signe. 3571
Toland, John. 1480, 2767, 3024
Tolbert, Malcolm. 324, 372, 441, 994
Tolbert, Mary Ann. 2771
Toler, Henry Pennington. 1037
Toles, E. B. 144, 3704
Toliver, Ralph. 1180
Tollenaere, F. de. 229, 1749
Tolles, Frederick Barnes, 1915. 1685, 1687
Tolley, William Pearson. 115, 1728
Tolman, Frank S. 1596
Tolman, Herbert Cushing. 977, 1837
Tolmie, Murray. 1469
Tolson, Chester L. 2881
Tolson, George Tolover. 1053, 1955
Tolstio, Lev Nikolaevich. 3202
Tolstoi, Dmitrii Andreevich. 825
Tolstoi, Lev Nikolaevich. 393, 661, 977, 1055, 1142, 1480, 2000, 2061, 2228, 2756, 2856, 3064, 3095, 3136, 3202, 3794, 3821
Tolstoi, Lev Nikolaevich, graf. 3632
Tolstoi, Lev Nikolaevich, graf, 1828-1910. 1055, 3202
Tomaino, Sarah F. 2822
Tomas, Andrew. 2948
Tomasi, Silvano M. 875, 1929
Tombler, John W. 3021
Tomczak, Larry. 1467, 3391, 3704
Tomkins, Floyd W[williams]. 2397
Tomkins, Floyd William. 2884

Tomkins, Floyd Williams. 1325, 1453, 1442
Tomkins, Oliver S. 1043
Tomkinson, Laura E., "T. L. Tomkinson. 2458
Tomkinson, Thomas. 2047
Tomlinson, Ambrose Jessup. 1229, 1230
[Tomlinson, David Gibson] b. 1799. 2959
Tomlinson, Everett Titsworth. 2714
Tomlinson, Homer Aubrey. 3704
Tomlinson, Irving Clinton. 461, 464, 1496
Tomlinson, Lee Glenn. 1461
Tomlinson, Richard Allan. 3599
Tomlinson, Russell. 1699
Tommasi, Giuseppe Maria. 842
Tompkins, De Loss M. 3565
Tompkins, Iverna. 2881, 3845
Tompkins, Leslie James. 3875
Tonality Group, Salem, Or. 97, 3767
Tondini Melgari, Amelia. 1974
Toner, Helen L. 585, 2397, 2895
Toner, Jules J. 1460, 1882
Tonkin, John. 1188
Tonks, A. Ronald. 3746
Tonna, Benjamin. 1280
[Tonna, Charlotte Elizabeth (Browne) 1790-1846. 692, 3475
Tonne, Arthur. 3375, 1602, 2164, 2185, 3262, 3367
Tonne, Arthur J. 2774, 2775, 3346
Toohey, John Joseph. 2705
Toohey, William. 1002, 1309, 2908
Tooke, Andrew. 2657
Tooke, Mary E. 3564
Tooker, Robert Newton. 1907
Toole, Isaac N. 3202
Toole-Stott, Raymond. 1345
Toombs, Lawrence E. 530, 537, 2149
Toon, Peter. 666, 1124, 1473, 1531, 1552, 1659, 1728, 2175, 2753, 3008, 3259
Tootell, Hugh. 1759
Topel, L. John. 1659
Tophel, Gustave. 462, 1832
Topliss, Patricia. 2778
Topp, Dale. 1209
Toppenberg, Valdemar E. 2498
Topping, Coral Wesley. 1053, 2045
Topping, Eva C. 1025
Topping, Frank. 2895
Topping, Lella Lyon. 3407
Torbert, Albert. 990
Torbet, Robert George. 30, 145, 152, 159, 1468, 2683, 3041
Torchiana, Henry Albert Willem van Coenen. 2685
Torkelson, Ted. 1013
Torkington, Rayner. 727, 2881
Torma, August. 1533
Tormey, John C. 774, 1002, 2789
Torpey, William George. 1490
Torquemada, Juan de. 1169, 3704
Torrance, Thomas Forsyth. 76, 465, 728, 1043, 1106, 1188, 1235, 1383, 1893, 2053, 2327, 2832, 3043, 3084, 3226, 3469, 3653
Torrence, Thomas Forsyth. 1442, 2046
Torrens, R. G. 1806
Torres, Tereska. 1366
Torres, Victor. 2668, 3705
Torrey, Charles Cutler. 330, 393, 398, 488, 518, 519, 543, 2567, 488, 518, 519, 1926
Torrey, Charles Turner. 1693, 3306
Torrey, David Clarence. 2977
Torrey, Mary Ide. 1304
*Torrey, R. A. 139, 1600
Torrey, Reuben Archer. 1917, 199, 318, 642, 643, 1017, 1561, 1793, 1832, 1834, 1974, 2066, 2588, 2881, 3221, 3229, 3293, 3346, 3516, 3705, 219, 237, 278, 324, 615, 642, 652, 977, 1343, 1433, 1561, 1571, 1832, 1842, 1917, 1985, 1995, 2881, 3291, 3375, 3705, 1561, 3320
Torsellino, Orazio. 1025, 1650, 2260
Tortora, Vincent R. 2407
Tos, Aldo J. 541
Tosefta. English. 1798
Tosti, Luigi. 677
Total Environmental Action, inc. 1199
Toth, Tihamer. 1728, 865, 1602, 1730, 2034, 2054, 2066, 757, 1531, 2250, 2344
Totten, Charles Adiel Lewis. 46, 219, 340, 341, 497, 502, 664, 1115, 1955, 1991, 2097, 2466
Totten, John C. 1869
Touey, John P. 3516
Toulmin, Stephen Edelston. 2837
Tourgee, Albion Winegar. 2614
Tournebize, Henri Francois. 1596
Tournier, P. 3000
Tournier, Paul. 977, 1012, 1777, 2378, 2823, 3000, 3002, 3330, 3780
Touron, Antoine. 1475
Tourscher, Francis Edward. 111, 1822, 2830
Tourville, Henri de. 3490, 792

Toussaint, Johann Peter. 3223
Toussaint, Stanley D. 441
Tov, 'Imanu'el. 547
Tovey, Herbert George. 3072
Towart, William George. 634
Tower, Grace Storms. 928, 1730, 2547, 2551, 3188
Tower, Howard E. 109
Towers, Bernard. 3593
Towers, Edward. 1752
[Towgood, Micaiah] 1700-1792. 1906
Towle, Eleanor A. (Taylor) 2678
Towle, Nancy. 120
Towler, Flora. 3474
Towler, Robert. 3087
[Towne, Edward Cornelius] 1834-1911. 1699
Towne, Florence H. 1728
Towne, Florence Hayden. 1527
Towner, Milton Carsley. 2946, 3757
Towner, Vesta. 3859
Towner, Walter. 3558
Towner, Wayne Sibley. 2157
Towns, Elmer L. 927, 936, 989, 1171, 1255, 1256, 1260, 1574, 1626, 2224, 3326, 3558, 3565, 3697
Towns, James E. 3415
Townsend, Allan W. 2278
Townsend, Ann A. 218
Townsend, Anne B. 3889
Townsend, Anne J. 2883
Townsend, Arthur H. 1571, 1575
Townsend, Edgar Jerome. 237
Townsend, Edward Davis. 562
Townsend, George Alfred. 2606
Townsend, Harry Brayton. 3516
Townsend, Janice M. 3216
Townsend, Jewett C. 541
Townsend, John T. 2030
Townsend, John Wilson. 1824
Townsend, L[uther] T[racy]. 1728
Townsend, Leah. 169
[Townsend, Leroy Clifford] 1900. 3379, 3820
Townsend, Luther Tracy. 306, 1383, 3072, 205, 237, 481, 1080, 1421, 1428, 1571, 1699, 1912, 2002, 2130, 3666, 3675
Townsend, Sarah. 473
Townsend, Sibyl Brame. 642
Townsend, Vince M. 14
Townsend, William Cameron. 3705
Townsend, William P. 2230
Townsend, Zella. 2397
Townshend, George. 237, 1360, 125, 129, 237, 125, 129
Towson, Hatton Dunica. 3136
Toy, Crawford. 572
Toy, Crawford Howell. 3140
Toy, Sidney. 2463
Toye, Charles. 2397
Toynbee, Arnold Joseph. 1080, 1103, 1282, 3064, 1698, 3068
Toynbee, Jocelyn M C. 2826, 3769
Toynbee, Philip. 1106
Toyne, Clarice Joy. 3054
Tozer, A. E. 1862
Tozer, Aiden Wilson. 918, 1072, 1931, 3410, 3482, 3522, 918, 1730, 2397, 3634
Tozer, Augustus Edmonds. 813, 884
Tozer, Henry Fanshawe. 721
Tozer, James R. 1011
Trabert, George Henry. 2279, 2303
Tracht, Stephen. 1728
Trachtenberg, Joshua. 1632, 2098, 53
Trachtenberg, Marvin. 1629, 1713
Tracy, David. 2245, 3618, 3649
Tracy, Ebenezer Carter. 1577
Tracy, James D. 1527
Tracy, Joseph. 31, 1529, 1757, 3739, 3813
Tracy, Olive Gertrude. 3706
Tracy, Patricia J. 1333, 1499
Tracy, Robert E. 3772
Tracy, Wesley. 1285, 2908
Trager, Hannah. 897
Trager, Hannah (Barnett) 897
Trager, Helen Gibson. 2506
Traherne, Thomas. 520, 1453, 3782
Trahey, James Joseph. 1332
Trahey, Jane. 3537
Traina, Robert Angelo, 1921. 288
Trakatellis, Demetrius Christ. 2049
Trakiskis, A. 2232
*Tralins, Robert. 1283, 2730
Trall, Russell Thacher. 23
Tralle, Henry Edward. 3565, 1157, 1158, 3534
Transcriptor. 2060
Tranter, Gerald. 1088
Trap, William Martin. 2838
Trapp, Jacob. 3121
Trapp, Maria Augusta. 929, 1610, 1974
Trappes-Lomax, Michael. 880
Trasker, Randolph Vincent Greenwood. 441

Trattner, Ernest Robert. 237, 1728, 1955, 3585
Traum, Samuel Wegner. 2606
Traut, Elise. 1112
Trautmann, Henry. 3710
Traver, Amos John. 977, 1955, 2282, 952, 1201, 2282
Travers, Libbie Miller. 1461
Travis, Arthur E. 1795
Travis, George. 325, 1711, 3713
Travis, John Livingston. 1728
Travis, Joseph. 2457
Travis, M Mitchell. 2097
Travis, Marion M. 565, 2095
Travis, Stephen. 936, 1531
Trawick, Arcadius McSwain. 3447
Trawick, Buckner B. 474, 541, 556
Traxler, Mary Peter. 3837
Traylor, John H. 555
Traylor, Melvin Alvah. 2788
Treacy, Gerald C. 3401
Treacy, Gerald Carr. 3401
Treacy, William. 2219
Treacy, William P. 1948
Treadgold, Donald W. 1180
Treadway, Charles F. 928
Treadway, Oswell Garland. 1663
Treadwell, John H. 2278
Treasure, Geoff. 436, 929, 1974, 3336
Treasure, Geoffrey Russell Richards. 3236
Treat, Roger L. 3402
Treatise on resurrection. English & Coptic. 1718
Treece, Henry. 1392
*Treece, Henry. 1391
Treffry, Richard. 191, 2818, 3427
Trefzger, John D. 312
Trego, Benjamin Brooke Thomas. 2048, 2397, 2048
Trell, Bluma L. 1521
Tremaine, DeWitt Charles. 1124
Tremaine, Guy Everton. 2881
Tremmel, William C. 475, 3064, 3139
Trempelas, Panagiotes Nikolaou. 3257
*Trench, Eichard Chenevix. 2027
[Trench, Maria Marcia Fanny). 3010
Trench, Richard Chenevix. 361, 461, 1771, 2018, 2027
Trench, Richard Chenevix. 2018
Trenchard, John. 2478
Trenholme, Edward Craig. 1214
Trent, Council of, 1545-1563. 3710
Trent, John Scott. 1561
Trent, Kenneth E. 3721
Trent, Robbie. 149, 3166, 292, 627, 630, 902, 1162, 1734, 1984, 2023, 2802, 3166, 3172, 3182, 3549
Trentham, Charles Arthur. 342, 479, 994, 3182
Trepp, Leo. 1614, 2120, 2140, 2147
Tresch, John W. 2881
Trese, Leo John. 1002, 132, 688, 763, 797, 1002, 1299, 3490, 3660
Tresize, Thomas. 941
Tresmontant, Claude. 1616, 1740, 2419, 2802, 2842
Tresp, Alois. 1395
Tressel, Amalia. 2536
Tresselt, Alvin R. 630
Trethowan, Illtyd. 840, 3105
Trettel, Efrem. 1644, 2512
Tretyse of loue. 2266
Trevelyan, George Phillip. 462
Trevelyan, William Bouverie. 2895, 3547
Trever, John C. 1411, 3013, 3710
Trevethan, Thomas L. 342, 2011
Trevett, Reginald Frederick. 3393
Trevino, Jose Guadalupe. 2258, 2349, 3490
Trevor, Meriol. 812, 1629, 2124, 2221, 2704
Trevor, Meriol [Lucy Merial Trevor]. 2704
Trevor, Meriol [Lucy Meriol Trevor]. 2704
Trevor-Roper, Hugh Redwald. 2199
Trewhitt, Paul W. 3516
Trexler, Edgar R. 1244, 1245, 2495
Trexler, Mark K. 1548
Trexler, Samuel G. 2291
Trexler, Samuel Geiss. 2292, 2597, 3675, 3710
Tribble, Harold Wayland. 149, 494, 3291
Tribble, Thomas Preston. 422
Tribe, David H. 1657
Tribe, Reginald Herman. 3447
Trible, Phyllis. 502, 1731
Trice, A N. 802
Trice, Allison Norman. 802, 2563
Triche, Charles W. 1544
Tricht, Victor van. 2032
Trickey, Edna Butler. 3185
Tricot, Alphonse, Elis. 2802
Trilling, Wolfgang. 442
Trimble, Henry Burton. 3531, 1571, 2455
Trimble, John Thomas. 580
Trimble, Malcome Calvis. 3447

Trimble, William Raleigh. 872
Trimingham, John Spencer. 12, 77, 451, 1923, 1924, 1926, 2517, 2552, 2566, 2567, 3543
Trimmer, Ellen McKay. 1603, 3175
Trine, Ralph Waldo. 1907, 2228, 2696, 3136
Trinklein, Frederick E. 3083
Trinterud, Leonard J. 2923, 2924, 3008
Tripitaka. English. Selections. 703, 707, 3715
Tripole, Martin R. 349, 1002, 2045
Tripp, Edward. 2659
Tripp, Robert M. 1376
Trites, Allison A. 3830
Triton, A. N. 3391
Triton, Pseud [Tibetan Dakini]. 2730
Tritton, Arthur Stanley. 726, 2565, 1922, 1927
Trobian, Helen Reed. 2633
Trobisch, Ingrid (Hult) 1853, 2498
Trobisch, Walter. 664, 2340
Trobridge, George. 3571
Trochu, Francis. 2158, 2233, 3460, 3778
Trocme, Andre. 1124, 2045, 2712
Trocme, Etienne. 436, 2045
Troeger, Thomas H. 579, 2381, 2881, 2906, 3291
Troeger, Walter F. 2215
Troeltsch, Ernest. 3452
Troeltsch, Ernst. 1072, 1097, 1138, 2163, 3452, 3625, 3715
Troisfontaines, Roger. 1415
Troki, Isaac ben Abraham. 1092, 2014
Trollope, Anthony. 1215, 3090
Tromp, Sebastiaan [Pieter Cornelis]. 1124
Trooster, Stephanus Gerardus Maria. 3414
Tross, Joseph Samuel Nathaniel. 3090
Trosse, George. 3715
Troth, Dennis Clayton. 2592
Trotter, Jesse M. 3484, 3715
Trotter, Mark. 470
[Trotti de La Chetardie, Joachim] 1636-1714. 2397
Trouncer, Margaret (Lahey) 3460, 3778
Troup, Robert. 2701
Troupe, John Franklin. 2802, 2881
Trout, David McCamel. 3000
Trout, Ethel Wendell. 3167, 3177, 3180, 3184
Trout, Jessie M. 1442
Troutbeck, G. E. 3808
Troutman, Charles. 2495
Troutt, Margaret. 681, 3296
Trovillion, Hal W. 1808
Troward, Thomas. 307, 2696
Trowbridge, Buel. 1063, 1073
Trowbridge, Lydia (Jones) 3816
Trowbridge, Mary Elizabeth (Day) 155
Trowbridge, William Rutherford Hayes. 723
Trowridge, Gertrude Mary (Sherman) 1596
Troy, N.Y. First Presbyterian church. 2918
Troy, N.Y. Sunday school association. 3564
Troyer, Johannes. 1388
Troyer, L. E. 2506
Trubo, Richard. 1544
Trubshaw, Wayne. 2066
Trudel, P. 736
[True, Hiram L.] 1845. 1656, 2053
True, John. 1124
True, Minnehaha Howard. 3516
[Trueb, Carl Theodul] 1872. 3463
Trueblood, David Elton. 434, 3105, 67, 173, 434, 977, 990, 1005, 1064, 1124, 1127, 1314, 1586, 1587, 1676, 1740, 2012, 2049, 2397, 2495, 3105, 3106, 3359, 3491, 3715
*Trueblood, Elton. 1854
Truemper, David G. 2287, 3666
Truesdell, Amelia Woodward. 3470
Truesdell, John W. 3516
Truett, George Washington. 1561, 3359, 168, 1112, 1561, 2722, 2804, 3359, 168
Truett, Jack K. 2730
Truex, H[arvey] E[ldon]. 157
Trufanov, Sergiei Mikhailovich. 3022
Trujillo, Alfonso Lopez. 1143
Trull, George Harvey. 2551, 2921, 3470, 2523, 2551, 3550
Trull, Joe E. 909
Truman, Olivia M. 2845
Truman, Ruth. 1303
Truman, Tom [Thomas Charles Truman]. 814
Trumbull, Benjamin. 1377
Trumbull, Charles Gallaudet. 524, 596, 1571, 3320, 1571
Trumbull, Henry Clay. 199, 237, 1353, 1360, 1376, 1571, 1790, 2484, 2881, 2895, 3422, 3558, 3565, 3574
Trumbull, James Hammond. 25
Trumbull, William. 1581
Trump, Clara K. 3808

Trungpa, Chogyam. 2382, 2194, 3716
Trupo, Anthony. 2381
Truro Parish, Va. Vestry. 3716
Truss, Cyprian. 761, 865, 1842
[Trust, Josephine]. 1955, 2895
[Trust, Josephine de Croix] 1886. 2895, 3121
Truth publishing company, Meridian, Miss. 1321
Trutza, Earl Hester. 149
Trutzschler von Falkenstein, Ingeborg. 3474
Tryon, William Ernest. 2730
Tsai, Christiana. 928, 3717
Tsakonas, Demetrios Gr. 101, 2792
Tsankov, Stefan. 2744
Tsanoff, Radoslav Andrea. 1891, 3106
Tsa To ke, Monroe. 2827
Tschan, Francis Joseph. 194
Tschetter, P P. 216
Tschirhart, Mary J. 543
Tschudy, James Jay. 2781
Tselos, Dimitri Theodore. 848
Tsevat, Matitiahu. 504
Tsirintanes, Alexandros Nikolaos. 1282
Tson-kha-pa Blo-bzan-grags-pa, 1357-1419. 2193
Tsung-kao, 1089-1163. 3892
Tsur, Jacob. 3717
Tu-lun, 1908. 3272
Tu, Wei-ming. 1116
Tubby, Gertrude Ogden. 1878, 2991, 3516
Tubby, Ruth Peckham. 246
Tucci, Douglass Shand. 1158, 1378
Tucci, Giuseppe. 3699
Tuchman, Barbara (Wertheim) 1764
Tuck, Robert. 319
Tuck, William C. 598
Tuck, William P. 1415
Tucker, Alfred Robert. 1224, 2499
Tucker, Angeline. 2514, 3717
Tucker, Beverley D. 2535
Tucker, Beverly D. 2962
Tucker, David M. 16
Tucker, David N. 3596
Tucker, Frank C. 2308, 2431
Tucker, Gene M. 498
Tucker, Gilbert Milligan. 2192
Tucker, Henry Holcombe. 147, 168, 1520
Tucker, Henry St. George. 107, 2212, 2535, 2711
Tucker, Henry William. 1211, 3331
Tucker, Hugh C. 2505
Tucker, Irwin St. John. 3136
Tucker, Iva Jewel. 1575, 2804
Tucker, James A. 3883
Tucker, John T. 2498
Tucker, Johnny. 1300, 1622
Tucker, Joseph Louis. 2682
Tucker, Julius Lafayette. 3359
Tucker, Louis. 626, 1100, 1974
Tucker, Louis Leonard. 1284
Tucker, Michael R. 994, 1244, 1245, 3598
Tucker, Park. 2942
Tucker, Pomeroy. 2606
Tucker, Robert Leonard. 927
Tucker, Sarah. 2545
Tucker, Sarah (Fish) 3136
Tucker, Sussannah Humphreys (Clapp) 977
Tucker, W. Leon. 322, 365, 470
Tucker, Walter Leon. 3017, 457, 1842
Tucker, William. 107
Tucker, William E. 1461, 1702
Tucker, William Edward. 933, 1461, 1702
Tucker, William Jewett. 1124, 2906
Tucker; John T. 2501
Tuckerman, Joseph. 3726
Tuckett, Gain Ream. 902
Tuckett, Guin Ream. 991
Tuckley, Henry. 3653
Tuckwell, James Henry. 3064
Tuckwell, William. 3346
Tudebodus, Petrus. 1391
Tudhope, George Vernon. 124, 1665
Tuell, Harriet [Emily]. 2579
Tuell, Jack M. 3734
Tuggy, Arthur Leonard. 2545
Tuggy, Joy Turner. 2488
Tugwell, Simon. 2815
Tuininga, Margaret Jean. 2491
Tuke, Henry. 1683
Tulga, Chester E. 470
Tulga, Chester Earl. 1619, 2053, 2466, 2563, 2670, 2683, 2714, 3850
Tull, Charles. 1372
Tull, Charles J. 1372
Tull, James E. 107, 149, 2045, 2195, 3466
Tull, Selsus Estol. 151, 168
Tullar, Grant Colfax. 1873
Tulley, Walter J. 870
Tullidge, Edward Wheelock. 2606, 3287, 3429, 3762, 3869
Tullis, Don D. 3359
Tulloch, G. Janet. 879
Tulloch, John. 731, 1759, 1760, 2278, 3036, 3212

Tullock, John. 536
Tully, Bob. 1167
Tully, Norman Ernest. 665
Tulpa, Leonid Vasilievich. 3159
Tulsa, Okl. Temple Israel. 2155
Tulsa, Okla. First Presbyterian Church. 2921
Tuma, George Wood. 2644
Tunink, Wilfrid. 190, 2045, 3490
Tunyogi, Andrew C. 564, 1376
Tunzelmann, George William von. 945
Tupper, Charles B. 3675
Tupper, Elgin Frank. 2767
Tupper, Henry Allen. 888, 2060
Tupper, Kerr Boyce. 927
Turbervill, Edith Picton. 1053
Turberville, Arthur Stanley. 1910, 3324
Turberville, Henry. 792
Turell, Ebenezer. 1310
Turford, Hugh. 977
Turk, Midge. 1582
Turk, Morris Howland. 1891
Turkel, Roma Rudd. 3004, 3091
Turley, Mary Immaculata. 1793
Turlington, Henry E. 430
[Turmel, Joseph] 1859. 810, 1428
Turnage, Mac N. 1612
Turnbull, Agnes (Sligh) 2132
Turnbull, Bob. 989
Turnbull, Coulson. 698
Turnbull, Everett R. 1665, 1670
Turnbull, Grace Hill. 3267, 3268
Turnbull, Ralph G. 332, 339, 436, 494, 536, 596, 977, 1072, 1561, 1573, 2007, 2033, 2045, 2058, 2260, 2787, 2906, 2935, 3136, 3202, 3347, 3367, 3375, 3660, 3675
Turnbull, Robert. 927, 1189, 2045
Turnbull, William W. 1913
Turner, Bryan S. 3454, 3800
Turner, Cuthbert Hamilton. 351, 1195
Turner, Dean. 67, 932, 2244, 3718
Turner, Denise. 1303, 3718
Turner, Denys. 1154
Turner, Dorothy Banker. 978, 1453
Turner, F. Bernadette. 2781
Turner, F. H. 1891
Turner, Frank Miller. 3085
Turner, Frederick C. 821
Turner, George Allen. 404, 421, 2819, 3805
Turner, Harold W. 13, 1237, 3090
Turner, Henry Ernest William, 1907. 107, 337, 1979, 2045, 3658
Turner, Henry McNeal. 14
Turner, Herbert B. 1199
Turner, Herbert Bryant, 1871. 1638
Turner, Herbert Snipes. 195, 1791
Turner, Howard H. 1894
Turner, James Elmer. 642
Turner, John Clyde. 149, 168, 1163, 3666, 168
Turner, John Douglas. 680, 1718
Turner, John Evan. 1586, 1728
Turner, Jonathan Baldwin. 2066
Turner, Kenneth Weston. 3474
Turner, Morrie. 16
Turner, Naomi. 1148
Turner, Nigel. 349, 352, 1769
Turner, Pearl Iva. 1604
Turner, Philip. 624
Turner, Rodney. 3838
Turner, Samuel Hulbeart. 2949
Turner,Samuel Hulbeart. 524, 609, 2076, 2960
Turner, Sharon. 1382
Turner, Sidney Joseph. 2866
Turner, Victor Witter. 1022, 2678
Turner, Wallace. 2606
Turner, William H. 2511
Turner, William Smith. 1036
Turrentine, Francis M. 3136
Turretini, Francois. 108
Turro, James. 2397
Turton, William Harry. 67
Turvey, Vincent N. 1283
Turville-Petre, Edward Oswald Gabriel. 3306
TurvillePetre, Edward Oswald Gabriel. 2666
Tuska, Simon. 2120
Tute, Richard Clifford. 3080, 3081
Tuthill, William Burnet. 751
Tuttle, Alexander Harrison. 516, 3359
Tuttle, Amber M. 2730
Tuttle, C[harles] R[ichard]. 1382
Tuttle, Daniel Sylvester. 2488
Tuttle, Elliotte A[mbrose]. 642
Tuttle, Emma (Rood) 3210
Tuttle, Harold Saxe. 2592
Tuttle, Hudson. 2992, 3094, 3516, 1656, 1728, 2009, 3076, 3516
Tuttle, James Harvey. 3755
Tuttle, John Ellery. 1832
Tuttle, Joseph Farrand. 3719
Tuttle, Penelope T. Sturgis (Cook) 2699
Tuttle, Robert G. 1008, 1833, 2459, 3805

Tuve, Rosemond. 2470
Tuvill, Daniel. 1326
Tuzin, Donald F. 78
Tvedtnes, John A. 502, 2613
Tweddell, Margaret Flavell. 3474
Tweedy, Henry Hallam. 3786
Twelves, J. Wesley. 2971
Twersky, Isadore. 4, 2074, 2623, 3016
Twichell, Joseph Hopkins. 2794, 3862
Twigg, Ena. 3516, 3719
Twigg-Porter, George. 3285
Twing, Carolinn E[dna] S[kinner]. 3482
Twing, Carolinn Edna (Skinner) 3516
Twing, Mary A. E. 2970
Twining, Harry La Verne. 2992
Twiss, Charles Victor. 1819
Twisse, William. 1820, 2911
Twitchell, Paul. 1490, 1491, 1490
Twitchell, Thomas Donn. 1302, 3719
Two Listeners. 1433
Twyman, Mary Eileen. 792
Tyberg, Judith. 3301
Tydings, Judith. 1024
Tydings, Richard. 76, 886
Tyerman, Daniel. 3788
Tyerman, Luke. 1287, 2422, 3805
Tygel, Zelig. 2079
Tying, Ethel Arens. 2511
Tyl, Noel. 97, 98, 1848
Tylar, William. 3516
Tyler, Alice (Felt) 3326
Tyler, Bennet. 2685, 2688, 3231, 3649
Tyler, Charles Mellen. 3106
Tyler, Edward. 2783
Tyler, Frances Landrum. 2881
Tyler, Gladys Beckwith. 2461
Tyler, Hamilton A. 3005
[Tyler, John] 1742-1823. 3291, 3753
Tyler, John Crew. 2373
Tyler, John Mason. 1581
Tyler, John Williamson. 617
Tyler, Joseph Zachary. 3889
Tyler, Wilfred. 1610
[Tyler, William Seymour] 1810-1897. 675, 2241, 2371, 2558, 2881, 2961
Tylor, Edward Burnett. 1282, 3110
Tyms, James Daniel. 157
Tyndale, William. 344, 1219, 2252, 2596
Tyndale, William, d. 3630
Tyndall, Charles Herbert. 3073, 3080, 2720
Tyndall, Henry Myron. 1842
Tyndall, John W[illiam]. 1467
Tyndall, John William. 393, 3180, 3468
Tynder, Paul. 1891
Tynes, Walter Edwin. 1042, 1473
Tyng, Charles Rockland. 3719
Tyng, Dudley Atkins. 2829
Tyng, Stephen Higginson. 182, 286, 332, 1397, 2045, 2200, 2973, 3258, 3558, 3675, 3321, 3720
Tyrrell, Bernard. 1601, 1733, 2245, 2781
Tyrrell, F. G. 3390
Tyrrell, Francis Martin. 67
Tyrrell, George. 761, 783, 793, 1596, 2397, 2412, 2562, 3721
Tyrrell, George Nugent Merle. 77, 2473
Tyson, Joseph B. 1197, 2011, 3578
Tyson, M. Dewey. 2397
Tyson, Stuart Lawrence. 1541, 2340
Tyson, William Ainsworth. 3229
Tytler, James. 2759
Tzangas, George J. 3474

U

Ubaldi, Pietro. 3881
Uber, Guy Lloyd. 304
Uber, Thomas Barclay. 3346
Uchiyama, Kosho. 2383
Udall, John. 1241
Ueda, Daisuke. 708
Uehling, Carl T. 1261, 2783
Uhden, Hermann Ferdinand. 1338
Uhl, Harold J. 423, 627, 909
Uhlhorn, Gerhard. 887, 1053, 1979
Uhlich, Leberecht. 1652
*Uhrig, Gilbert R. 3191
Ujszaszy, Kalman. 2954
Ulanov, Ann Belford. 3000
Ulanov, Barry. 1067, 1416, 3691
Ulbrich, Armand Henry. 3830
Ulery, William Frederick. 2850
Uleyn, Arnold. 2784, 2787
Ulich, Robert. 3165
Ullathorne, William Bernard. 777, 2346
Ullman, Richard K. 1683
Ullman, Walter. 2770
Ullmann, Walter. 2770, 2863, 3308
Ulmer, Louise. 339, 633, 941, 2373
Ulram, Richard. 3438
Ulrich, Bartow Adolphus. 1955
Ulrich, Betty Garton. 1606
Ulrich, Homer. 916

Ulrich, John Oliver. 1974
Ulrich, Louis Edward. 2298
Ulrich, Robert James. 1247
Ultee, Maarten. 3274
Ulyat, Willam Clarke. 978
Umasvati, ca. 135-ca. 219. 1932
Umble, John Sylvanus. 2407
Umen, Samuel. 312, 1103, 2140, 2143, 2829
Umfreville, Joyce. 1652
Uminski, Sigmund H. 2166, 3524
Umphrey, Clyde Ellis. 457
Umphrey, Marjorie. 3000
Unamuno y Jugo, Miguel de, 1864-1936. 1053
Unamuno y Jugo, Miguel de. 1064, 1891
Underdown, Emily. 1402
Underhill, Alice Mertie. 2491
Underhill, Andrew Findlay. 1036
Underhill, Ann Leah. 1636, 3516
Underhill, Ann Leah (Fox) 1636, 3516
Underhill, Edward Bean. 2223, 3194, 149
Underhill, Evelyn. 2641, 2645, 3482, 978, 1103, 2257, 2641, 2707, 3208, 3482, 3483, 3854, 1454, 1736, 2248, 2397, 2641, 2707, 3463, 3483, 3722, 3854, 2212
Underhill, Francis Lees. 978, 2881, 3854
Underhill, Muriel Marion. 1814
Underhill, Ruth Murray. 1902, 2771
Underwager, Ralph C. 1325
Underwood, Alfred Clair, 1885. 149, 1360
Underwood, Almon. 978
Underwood & Underwood. 591, 2851
Underwood, Benjamin Franklin. 101, 1092
Underwood, Horace Grant. 2537, 3587
Underwood, Joseph B. 2491, 3028
Underwood, Kenneth Wilson. 861, 1838, 3452, 3739
Underwood, Lillias (Horton) 2537, 3722
Underwood, Maude Jones. 2707
Underwood, Paul Atkins. 1929
Underwood, Peter. 1710
Underwood, Sara A. (Francis) 3517
Undset, Sigrid. 765, 2022, 3285, 749, 765, 3285
Unger, Carl. 51
Unger, Dominic J. 1635, 3415
Unger, Merrill Frederick. 67, 139, 208, 225, 246, 247, 286, 312, 335, 487, 541, 600, 609, 1411, 1423, 1454, 1717, 1833, 2846, 2906, 3520
Unger, Merrill Frederick. 2907
Ungersma, Aaron J. 3666
Unhjem, Arne. 3700
Union for Christian work, Providence, R.I. Library. 1019
Union of American Hebrew Congregations. 1611, 1796, 2105, 2116, 2140, 2886, 3033, 3723
Union of American Hebrew congregations. Commission on research. 2105
Union of Muslim Organisations of United Kingdom and Eire. 3172
Union of Orthodox Jewish Congregations of America. 2122, 3585
*Union Theological Seminary. New York City. 3627
Union University, Schenectady. Character Research Project. 904, 3159
Unit book A for the primary course. 1728
Unitarian Church, Bloomington, Illinois. 3723
Unitarian church in Washington, D.C. 3725
Unitarian club of California. 3068
Unitarian historical society, Boston. 3730
Unitarian laymen's league. 10
Unitarian Universalist Association. 3727
Unitarian Universalist Association. Committee to Study Theological Education. 3681
United Baptists. Missouri. Central Missouri Association. 157
United Board for Christian Colleges in China. 3756
United boys' brigades of America. 688
United brethren in Christ. 2453, 3730, 3731
United brethren in Christ. Board of administration. 3730
United brethren in Christ. Foreign missionary society. 3731
United Christian Missionary Society. 1465, 3731
United Christian Missionary Society. Division of Church Life and Work. 1462
United Christian Missionary Society. Division of World Mission. 1465
United Church Board for Homeland Ministries. Division of Publication. 3732
United Church Board for World Ministeries. 3732
[United Church of Christ]. 1329, 3389
United Church of Christ. Commission on World Service. 887

United Church of Christ, Conferences Colorado. 1336
United Church of Christ. Council for Church and Ministry. 3732
United Church of Christ. Council for Higher Education. 3732
United Church of Christ. Task Force on Ministries to Military Personnel. 885
United Church of Christ. Uniting General Synod. 3731, 3732
United Church of Christ. Vermont Conference. Dept. of Christian Education. 18
United Danish evangelical Lutheran church in America. Central committee of young people's leagues. 1114
United Dhurch of Christ. 3732
United Free Church of Scotland. 3733
United Jewish appeal. 2112
United Lutheran church in America. 1442, 1547, 1873, 2295, 3548
United Lutheran Church in America. Board of Parish Education. 1260, 2293
United Lutheran Church in America. Board of Publication. 3733
United Lutheran Church in America. Board of Social Missions. 1138
United Lutheran church in America. Committee on German Interests. 1551
United Lutheran church in America. Common service book committee. 3734
United Lutheran church in America. Liturgy and ritual. 2290, 3734
United Lutheran synod of New York. 3733
United Methodist Church (United States) 3734
United Nations Educational, Scientific and Cultural Organization. 1690
United Nations. Office of Public Information. 2806, 2807

The United Norwegian Lutheran church of America. 3177
United Norwegian Lutheran church of America. Liturgy and ritual. 2715
United Presbyterian Church in the U.S.A. 3735, 1257, 2925, 2929, 3735, 3736
United Presbyterian Church in the U. S. A. Board of Christian Education. 1248, 1279, 1408, 3735
United Presbyterian Church in the U.S.A. Board of Christian Education. 978, 1260, 1279, 2914, 2929, 3564, 3735
United Presbyterian Church in the U.S.A. Board of National Missions. 1279
United Presbyterian Church in the U.S.A. Commission on Ecumenical Mission and Relations. 2495, 3736
United Presbyterian Church in the U.S.A. Commission on Ecumenical Mission and Relations. Office for Research. 1883
United Presbyterian Church in the U.S.A. Commission on Ecumenical Mission and Relations. Office of Education. 2915
United Presbyterian Church in the U.S.A. Council on Theological Education. 3681
United Presbyterian Church in the U.S.A. Dept. of Stewardship and Promotion. 2915
United Presbyterian Church in the U.S.A. Division of Evangelism. 1124
United Presbyterian Church in the U.S.A. General Assembly. 3735, 3854
United Presbyterian Church in the U.S.A. General Assembly. Special Committee on Church Membership Trends. 3736
United Presbyterian Church in the U.S.A. General Assembly. Special Committee on Responsible Marriage and Parenthood. 2340
United Presbyterian church of North America. 1658, 2915, 3736
United Presbyterian Church of North America. Board of Christian Education. 3736
United Presbyterian church of North America. Foreign missionary jubilee convention, Pittsburg, 1904. 3736
United Presbyterian Church of North America. General Assembly. 3004, 3736
United Press International. 2863
United Secularists of America. 3024
United society for the spread of the gospel. 156
United sons of America. 3240
U.S. Bureau of Naval Personnel. 3778
United States Catholic Conference. Division of Religious Education—CCD. 1327
United States. Central Intelligence Agency. 912, 1331
U.S. Christian commission. 1089, 3741

United States. Congress. House. Committee on International Relations. Subcommittee on International Organizations. 3194
United States. Congress. Senate. Committee on the Judiciary. Subcommittee to Investigate the Administration of the Internal Security Act and Other Internal Security Laws. 2821
U.S. Dept. of Defense. Armed Forces Chaplains' Board. 3178
United States. General Accounting Office. 1321, 2945
U.S. Joint Publications Research Service. 912
U.S. Library of Congress. Division of Bibliography. 2847

U.S. Military Academy, West Point. Chapel Board. 2232, 2238
United States Presbyterian Church in the U.S.A. 3736
United States. Supreme Court. 1152
United Synagogue of America. 3262
United Synagogue of America. National Women's League. 1348, 3749
United synagogue of America. Women's league. 2122
United synod of the Evangelical Lutheran church in the South. Liturgy and ritual. 2290
United Church Board for Homeland Ministries. Board of Publication. 3731
United Church of Christ. 3732
Unity School of Christianity. 3209, 3750
Unity school of Christianity, Kansas City, Mo. 1479, 2884
Universal Christian conference on life and work, Stockholm, 1925. 1090
Universal Christian Council for Life and Work. 1142
Universal House of Justice. 129
Universalist church. 3754
Universalist church in the U.S. General convention, 1807. 1869
Universalist church in the U. S. General convention, 1870. 3754
Universalist church of America. 3754, 3755
Universalist general convention. 3754
*Unjhem, Arne. 460
Unnik, Willem Cornelis van. 407, 1718
Unopulos, James J. 3226
Unstead, R. J. 2572
Unsworth, Richard P. 3391
Unterman, Alan. 2146
Unterman, Isaac. 568, 1624, 2118, 2842, 3584, 3585
Untermeyer, Louis. 481, 661, 685, 1353
Unwin, Ernest Ewart. 1581
Unwin, Francis Sydney. 921
Unwin, James O. 1084
Unwin, Nora Spicer. 631
Upadhyaya, KashiNath. 197
Upanishads. 3759
Upanishads. Aitareyopanisad. English & Sanskrit. 3760
Upanishads. Brhadaranyakopanisad. English & Sanskrit. 1815
Upanishads. Chandogyopanisad. English & Sanskrit. 3760
Upanishads. English. 2840, 3760
Upanishads. English & Sanskrit. Selections. 3760
Upanishads. English. Selections. 2668, 3760
Upanishads. Isopanisad. English. 3760
Upanishads. Kathaka-upanishad. 1731, 3760, 3761
Upanishads. Maitrayaniyopanisad. English & Sanskrit. 3760
Upanishads. Selections. English. 1454, 3760
Upanishads. Svetasvataropanisad. English & Sanskrit. 1816
Upanishads. Taittiriyopanisad. English & Sanskrit. 3760
Upasak, Chandrika Singh. 3779
[Updike, Daniel Berkeley] 1860-1941. 1275
Updike, Jacob Van. 1561
Updike, L. Wayne. 1353, 3218
Updike, Wilkins. 2972
Upfold, George. 1297
Upham, Caroline E. 3827, 3828
Upham, Charles Wentworth. 1166, 2242, 3286, 3828
Upham, Francis Bourne. 2699
Upham, Francis William. 205, 398, 442, 1100, 2022, 2053, 2311
Upham, Thomas Cogswell. 978, 1335, 1596, 1779, 2637
Uphoff, Walter Henry. 2992
[Upjohn, James A.]. 2019, 3576

Upjohn, James Atchison. 609
Upjohn, Richard. 1158
The Upper room. 1435
Upper Room (The) 1435
Upshaw, William David. 2231
Upson, Stephen H R. 2747
Upton, George Putnam. 2740
Upton, Will Oscar. 1269
Upton, William H. 1667
Upward, Allen. 1064
Urang, Gunnar. 1208
Urban, A. 225, 746, 3565
Urban, Abram Linwood. 2675
Urban, Wilbur Marshall. 1537, 2419, 2420
Urbano, Paul. 2973, 3359
Urbantke, Carl. 120
Ure, Ruth. 3204
Urice, Jay A. 3872
Urlin, Ethel Lucy Hargreave. 1623
Urmy, William Smith. 2027, 3321
Urner, Isaac Newton. 1377
Urofsky, Melvin I. 3016, 3822
Urquhart, Colin. 2815, 3274
Urquhart, John. 515, 609
Urquhart, William Spence. 3775
Ursenbach, Octave F. 2606
Ursenbach, Octave Frederick. 2614
Ursinus, Zacharias. 1801
Ursprung, Otto. 1206
Urtasun, Joseph. 665
Urteaga, Jesus. 1610
Urteaga Lordi, Jesus 1921. 1002
Ury, Zalman F. 2231, 2632
[Usborne, John] 1842. 1454
Usha, Brahmacharini. 3775
Ushenko, Andrew Paul. 2834
Usher, Edward Preston. 2965
Usher, Roland Greene. 1221, 1763
Usher-Wilson. 3448
Usherwood, Stephen. 312
Uspenskii, Petr Dem'ianovich. 3589, 2730
Ussery, Annie (Wright) 2319, 3468, 3531
Ussher, Arland. 2090, 3589
Ussher, Clarence Douglas. 3768
Ussher, Elizabeth. 3136, 3143
Utah Academy of Sciences, Arts and Letters. 2606
Utah. University. Library. 2608
Utica, N.Y. Westminster church. Committee of publication. 1628, 3762
Utley, George Burwell. 1283
Utley, Uldine Mabelle. 3346, 2907
Utt, Charles D. 3012
Utt, Richard H. 281, 2685, 3387
Utt, Walter C. 3789
Utting, Mattie Johns. 2720
Uys, Sue. 644

V

Vaart Smit, H W van der. 2022
Vacandard, Elphege. 1909
Vaccaro, Louis C. 832
Vachon, Brian. 1573
Vadis, John. 2730
Vagaggini, Cipriano. 840, 2327
Vahanian, Gabriel. 1064, 3327, 3657
Vahey, John W. 3076
Vahid, Syed Abdul. 1918
[=Vahle, Joseph]. 1663
Vaiden, Thomas J. 1656, 1822, 3024
Vail, Albert Lenox. 156, 1955, 3136, 3530
Vail, Albert Ross. 1808, 3121
Vail, Charles Henry. 1321
Vail, Isaac Newton. 1421
Vail, Virgie Viola. 129
Vaill, Deborah. 1728
Vaill, Joseph. 3136, 3209
Vaillancourt, Jean-Guy. 866, 2770
Vaillancourt, Raymond. 3266
Vaitkus, Mykolas. 821, 2165
Vajda, Jaroslav. 216
Vajiranana Varoros, 1859-1921. 2940, 3766
Vajta, Vilmos. 1045, 1126, 2283
Val, Sue. 899, 3192
Valavalkar, Pandharinath Hari. 1897
Valcourt-Vermont, Edgar de. 97
Valdez, A. C. 2817, 3766
Valdosta, Ga. First Baptist church. 1124
Vale, Edmund. 750, 752
Vale, Gilbert. 1612, 3768
Vale, Malcolm Graham Allan. 3868
Vale, Walter Sidney. 884
*[Valence, Louis O.]. 464
Valen-Sondstaan, Olav. 3625
Valente, Michael F. 3389
Valentin, Hugo Mauritz. 2079
Valentine, Cyril Henry. 1053, 1728, 3001
Valentine, Ferdinand. 889, 2310, 2719, 2907
Valentine, Foy. 168, 404, 413, 994, 1087, 1133, 3466
Valentine, John Marvin. 2696
Valentine, Mary Hester. 2574

Valentine, Milton. 2674, 3346, 3649, 1537
Valentini, Norberto. 3390
Valero, Anselmo Francisco. 7
Valiente, Doreen. 2313, 3824, 3825
Valitutti, Francis. 1997
Valla, Lorenzo. 1476
Vallance, Aymer. 3316
Valle, Enrico. 2351
Valle, Francisca Javiera del. 1836
Vallier, Ivan. 821
Vallings, James Frederick. 1974
Vallowe, Ed. F. 538, 3229
Vallquist, Gunnel. 1244
Valmiki. 2403, 3139
Valtierra, Angel. 1286
Valyi Nagy, Ervin. 1154
[Van Dyke, Henry] 1852-1933. 2935, 3767
[Van Gelder, Martinus] 1854. 3609
Van Gorder, John Jay, 1881. 2477
Van Rensselaer, Mariana (Griswold) 1851-1934. 751
Van Well, Mary Stanislaus, 1899. 2548
Van Alstyne, Frances Jane Crosby. 1869
Van Amburgh, William Edwin. 2772
Vanamee, Mary Conger. 3768
Vanamee, Mary de Peyster Rutgers McCrea (Conger) 120
Van Amringe, Henry Hamlin. 1053, 1636
Van Antwerp, David D. 1180
Van Antwerp, Eugene Ignatius. 115, 1415
Vanarsdall, David B. 209
Vanasco, Rocco R. 1288
Vanauken, Sheldon. 45, 3768
Van Baalen, Jan Karel. 1353, 978, 1353, 2162, 3326, 3327
Van Baalen, Jay Karel. 3323
Van Bibber, Thomas Emory. 2048
Vanbrugh, John. 1309, 3607
Van Buren, Elizabeth (Douglas) 3604
Van Buren, J. M. 3597
Van Buren, James G. 2867, 989
Van Buren, James Heartt. 3346, 1877
Van Buren, Paul. 729
Van Buren, Paul Matthews. 1064, 3071, 3649, 3653, 1659
Van Burkalow, James Turley. 600
Van Buskirk, James Dale. 2410, 2537
Van Buskirk, Lawrence. 3359
Van Buskirk, William Riley. 3136
Vance, Catherine Stuart. 1714
Vance, Clyde Beauregarde. 97
Vance, James Isaac. 72, 624, 1053, 1318, 1325, 1596, 2250, 2475, 2921, 3191, 3192, 3346, 3359, 72, 472, 2325, 2935
[Vance, James Scott] 1875. 828
Vance, John Adam. 1859
Vance, Joseph Anderson. 107, 1697
Vance, Marguerite. 2006, 2198
Vance, Mary A. 79, 1270
Vance, Thomas L. 1728
Vance, Wilson. 1728
Van Cott, Maggie (Newton) 3233
Van Dalfsen, Patricia. 3407
Vande Vere, Emmett K. 720
Van Dellen, Idzerd. 1023, 3136
Vandeman, George. 1383, 3384
Vandeman, George E. 1013, 1697, 2397, 2992, 3321, 3384
Vanden Burgt, Robert J., 1936. 1934, 3106
Vandenberg, William Ernest. 3047, 3359
Vandenbergh, C. W. 3407
Vandenberghe, Bruno H. 1115
Vandenbroucke, Francois. 840, 2576
Vandenburgh, Mildred. 17
Vandendriessche, Gaston. 1423, 1780
Vander Lugt, Herbert. 1415
Vander Werff, Lyle L., 1934. 2557
Van der Bent, Ans Joachim. 1064
Vanderbyll, Henry Rosch. 1728, 2228
Vanderpool, Herbert Campbell. 144
Vander Donckt, Cyril. 2624
Van der Hart, Rob. 42
Vander Kaay, Dorothy. 3838
VanderKam, James C. 491
Van der Kiel, Aldert. 3074
Van der Kley, Francesca. 2333
Vanderlaan, Eldred Cornelius. 2561, 2563
Vanderlip, George. 421, 424, 469, 989, 1977
*Van Der Meer, F. 115
Vander Meulen, Arnold J. 1756
Vander Meulen, Jacob. 1768
Vandermey, H. Ronald. 538
Vandermey, Mary A. 1004
Vanderpoel, Ambrose Ely. 1666
Van der Poel, Cornelius J. 949
Vanderpool, Herbert Campbell. 144
Vanderpool, James A. 2781, 2782
Vandersloot, Jacob Samuel. 2631, 2632, 3596
Van der Smissen, Betty. 1164
Vander Velde, Frances. 1610, 3841
Vandervelde, George. 3414
Vander Velde, Lewis George. 2923
Van der Veldt, James Herman. 2784, 2995

Van der Veur, Paul W. 1665
Vanderwall, Francis W. 3475
Van der Ziel, Aldert. 524, 3083
Vandeur, Eugene. 8, 120, 1508, 2249, 2258, 2361, 2370
Van Deusen, Dayton G. 2781
Van Devanter, James Nicholas. 110
Van de Vate, Dwight. 2474
Vandevort, Eleanor. 2187, 2552
Van de Water, John. 1756
Van Dijk, Stephen Joseph Peter. 840
Van Dolson, Bobbie Jane. 1435, 2951
Van Dolson, Leo R. 642, 2378, 3384
Van Dolson Leo R. 181
Vandon, Elizabeth. 1365
Van Dooren, L. A. T. 541, 2881
Van Doren, Mark. 579, 503
Van Doren, Robert L. 916
Van'Doren, W. H. 418, 428
Van Doren, William Howard. 428
Van Dusen, Henry Pitney. 1064, 1728, 3649, 978, 1042, 1045, 1064, 1097, 1182, 1183, 1728, 1833, 2221, 2434, 2522, 2543, 3106, 3190, 3889
Van Dusen, Wilson Miles. 3571
Van Duzer, Adelaide Laura. 1714
Van Dyck, Howard. 1110
Van Dyk, Fay Blix. 929, 1974
Van Dyke, Catherine. 2944
Van Dyke, Dick. 895, 3089
Van Dyke, Henry. 3202, 3346, 579, 897, 978, 1053, 1055, 1112, 1114, 1554, 1958, 1996, 2228, 2763, 2907, 2928
Van Dyke, Henry Jackson. 1124
Van Dyke, Joseph Smith. 978, 1533, 1581, 2133
Van Dyke, Paul. 2269, 2770
Van Dyke, Vonda Kay. 1325, 1714, 3881, 2895
Van Dyken, Seymour. 3817
Van Eps, Frank Stanley. 1785
Van Ess, Dorothy. 2557, 3767
Van Etten, Isabel Upton. 2802
Van Eyck, William O. 3046
Van Eyssen, Shirley. 630
Van Gelder, Dora. 1588
Van Gorder, John Jay. 457, 3296, 2477
Van Gorder, Paul R. 323
Van Halsema, Thea (Bouma) 728, 1024
Van Halsema Thea (Bouma) 1024
Van'Harn, Roger. 3680
Van Hock, Kees. 2853
Van Hoof, Mary Ann. 2679
Van Hook, Weller. 3688
VanHoose, Raymond H. 312
Van Horne, Ellsworth S. 1036
Vanier, Jean. 1002, 1003
Van Impe, Jack. 611
Van Impe, Rexella. 1576, 3767
Van Iten, Richard J. 3756
Van Kaam, Adrian L. 3001, 424, 2223, 2462, 2571, 3490
Van Keuren, Floyd. 2340
Van Kirk, Hiram. 1464
Vankirk, John M. 3548
Van Kirk, Walter William. 1042, 2495, 3794
Van Kley, Dale. 1934
Van Lennep, Henry John. 2765
Van-Lennep, Henry John. 2765
Van Linden, Philip. 437, 438
Van Loan, Anna Fitz Gerald. 3447
Van Loan, Samuel Dies. 3263
Van Loon, Hendrik Willem. 624, 661, 3704, 624
Van Marter, Martha. 2536, 3565
Van Meter, Anna Hunter. 3286
Van Meter, Harriet D. 3166
Van Meter, Harriet F. 3833
Van Mildert, William. 288
Vann, Gerald. 949, 3136, 181, 761, 949, 1002, 1454, 2067, 2325, 2643, 3459, 3694, 1002
Vann, Richard T. 1685
Vann, Vicki. 2641
Van Ness, Bethann Beal (Faris) 624
Van Ness, Bethann Beall (Faris) 649
Van Ness, Isaac J. 155, 649, 3465
Van Ness, Isaac Jacobsen. 149
Van Ness, Thomas. 1728, 2687
Van Nest, Abraham Rynier. 195
Van Nest, Garth. 1261
Van Norden, Charles. 1064, 2060
Vannorsdall, John W. 2397, 3756
Van Nuys, Roscoe Golden. 2397
Van Ommeren, H. 423
Van Ormer, Abraham Brower Bunn. 909, 3159
van Over,Raymond. 2381, 2643
Van Paassen, Pierre. 1974, 2848, 3257, 3305
Van Pelt, Gertrude Wyckoff. 2165, 2819, 3688
Van Pelt, John Robert. 642
Van Peyma, P. W. 2420
Van Rensselaer, Cortlandt. 1774
Van Rheenan, Gailyn. 2558

Van Royen, Russell. 2544
Van Ryn, August. 443, 332, 422, 430, 437, 1454
Vansant, Nicholas. 3202
Van Santvoord, Cornelius. 1848, 3049
Van Santvoord, Seymour. 1644
Van Scoyoc, Nancy J. 3836
Van Seters, John. 4, 528
Van Slyke, D. C. 1480
Van Sommers, Tess. 3324
Van Speybrouck, Edouard. 2477, 2794
Van Stone, Doris. 2486, 3767
Van Tassel, George W. 2855
Van Til, Cornelius. 57, 67, 68, 176, 730, 1106, 1399, 1417, 1457, 1477, 1753, 2045, 2153, 2831, 2837, 3070, 3735
Van Til, Henry R. 1394
Van Til, L. John. 2223
Van Treeck, Carl. 921
Van Uchelen, J. Croiset. 3688
Van Vechten, Jacob. 2364
Van Vechten, Schuyler. 1984
Van Vleck, Joseph. 3746
Van Wade, David. 3768
Van Wagoner, Richard S. 2620
Van Woerdan, Peter. 3851
Van Woerkom, Dorothy. 9, 630, 1632, 2023, 2164, 2524
Van Wyk, William P. 3346, 423, 1318, 1693, 2028, 3375
Van Wyk, William Peter. 75, 423, 1316, 1318, 1693, 2028, 2250, 3375
Van Zandt, Abraham Brooks. 685
Van Zandt, Grace Goodspeed. 3136
Van Zella, Hubert. 187, 1002, 2368
Van Zeller, Hubert. 3490
Van zeller, Dom Hubert. 3475
*Van Zeller, Dom Hubert. 2881
Van Zeller, Huber. 187
Van Zeller, Hubert. 120, 188, 190, 507, 560, 580, 630, 859, 1002, 1299, 1415, 1921, 1974, 2397, 2571, 2812, 2881, 3136, 3196, 3300, 3316, 3483, 3490, 3526, 3541, 1002
Van Zeller, Hubert [Secular name: Claude Van Zeller]. 2881, 3300
Van Zeller, Hubert. 1002
Van Zeller, Hubert [Secular name: Claude Van Zeller]. 859
Vanzillotta, Gino. 1650
Van Zyl, Henry. 3558
Vaporis, Nomikos Michael. 285, 1354
Varahamihira, d. 587? 98
Vardaman, E Jerry. 208
Vardys, Vytas Stanley. 822, 2821
Varenne, Jean. 3866
Varg, Paul A. 2512
Varga, Margaret. 1958
Varge, Paul A. 2511
Vargish, Thomas. 2473, 2704
Varillon, Francois. 3666
[Varjabedian, Benjamin Samuel] 1873. 1955
Varker, Philip J. 2423
Varley, Desmond. 3576
Varley, Henry. 1036, 1496, 1561
Varley, Telford. 1943
Varma, Ravindra Sahai. 1519, 2351
Varma, Vishwanath Prasad. 1709
Varner, Chauncey J. 1912
Varner, Paul Nolan. 430
[Varner, W. I.]. 3202
Varro, Marcus Terentius. 3246
Vartooguian, Armayis P. 2502
Varvello, Francesco. 2420
Vasiliev, Alexander Alexandrovich. 1638, 1853
Vaske, Martin, O., S.J. 2420
Vass, Pearl. 2116
Vass, Winifred Kellersberger. 2398, 3768
Vassady, Bela. 1043, 3666
Vassall, William F. 3140
Vassall-Phillips, Oliver Rodie. 2357
Vassar, Thomas Edwin. 3768
Vasu, Srisa Chandra. 1395, 1814, 3760, 3866
Vasudevadas. 3483
Vaswig, William L. 1601, 3768
Vath, Mary Loyola. 1180
Vatican Council. 2d, 1962-1965. 762, 840, 860, 2571, 3159, 3193, 3226, 3770, 3773
Vatican Council. 2d. 860, 1124, 3773
Vatican Council. 2d, 1962-1965. 665, 754, 777, 783, 808, 1124, 1154, 2045, 2192, 2571, 2572, 3182, 3773
Vatican Council, 2d. Constitutio de sacra liturgia. 3773
Vatican Council, 2d, 1962-1965. 3226, 3773
Vatican Council. 2d. 762, 840, 1124
Vatican Council. 2d. 3159, 3773
Vatsayana. 2263
Vaughan, Alan. 2948
Vaughan, Alden T. 3009
Vaughan, Bernard. 1002, 3435, 3774
Vaughan, Charles John. 1606, 2970

Vaughan, Clement Read. 1833
Vaughan, Curry N. 885, 3774
Vaughan, Curtis. 333, 342, 364, 369, 413, 472, 1770
Vaughan, David Davies. 2437
Vaughan, Frank. 1652
Vaughan, Henry. 3774
Vaughan, Herbert. 2884
Vaughan, Herbert Alfred. 2368
Vaughan, Herbert Millingchamp. 2216
Vaughan, John. 2986
Vaughan, John Elwyn. 3217
Vaughan, John Gaines. 3064, 1842
Vaughan, John Stephen. 2768, 3346, 773, 978
Vaughan, Kenelm. 304
Vaughan, Lawrence James. 2263
Vaughan, Louisa. 2511
Vaughan, Patrick H. 503, 1395
Vaughan, Richard Blackmore. 3576
Vaughan, Richard Miner. 2822
Vaughan, Richard Patrick. 2781
Vaughan, Robert. 3861
Vaughan, Roger William Bede. 3694
Vaughan, Samuel S. 3601
Vaughan, Thomas M. 3774
Vaughn, Bill. 1170
Vaughn, Clement Read. 3346
Vaughn, Ray. 3713
Vaughn, Ruth. 932, 989, 1554, 1621, 2398, 3774
Vaughn, Stephen James. 2457
Vaught, Laud Oswald. 1610
Vaught, Louis Allen. 2844
Vaulx, Bernard de. 851
Vaux, James Edward. 1765
Vaux, Kenneth. 1415
Vaux, Roland de. 2097, 485, 3013, 3271, 3013
Vaux, William. 3264
Vawter, Bruce. 306, 398, 522, 569, 644, 652, 2045
Vay, Adelina. 3517
Vaz, August Mark. 793
vCole, Clifford Adair, 1915. 570
Veach, Robert Wells. 978, 1994, 3159
Veatch, Robert M. 3604
Veccia Vaglieri, Laura. 2565
Vecsey, Josef. 2474
Vedanta and the West. 3775
Vedanta Society. 689, 3775
Vedas. 673, 2743, 3267, 3776
Vedas. Atharvaveda. English. 1816
Vedas. Regveda. English. Selections. 3267
Vedas. Selections. 1816
Vedder, Henry Clay. 152, 156, 340, 1180, 2056, 2269, 2278, 37, 152, 333, 414, 1042, 1053, 1850, 2526, 3040, 3211, 3447
Vedral, Joyce L. 312
Veenschoten, Fannie H. 1442
Veenstra, Johanna. 2552
Vega, Angel Custodio. 115, 2835
Vega, Jose M. 3095
Veglahn, Nancy. 743
Vehse, Eduard. 2297, 2303
Veiby, John. 3064
Vekemans, Roger. 1087
Vela, Maria. 2648
Velazco Medina, Jose Luis. 3530
Velimirovic, Nikolaj. 2565
Vella, Bertha F. and Towner, D. B. 320
Venable, Charles Leslie. 457, 1201
Venable, Mary E. 733
Venables, Edmund. 2230
Venard, Jean Theophane. 2351, 3777
Venden, Morris L. 1013, 1435, 1505
Veneziani, Charles. 867
Venkataraman, Balasubrahmanyam. 3600
Venn, Henry. 978, 3291, 2512
Venn, John. 3367
Vera, Augusto. 1800, 2242
Vera, Hernan. 773, 2733
Verba Seniorum. English. 1020
Verband der vereine fur arztliche mission. 2539
Vercruysse, Bruno. 2398
Verdery, John D. 992
Verdesi, Elizabeth Howell. 3837
Verdrie, P. 2592
Verdu, Alfonso. 703, 711
Verduin, John R. 8
Verduin, Leonard. 1144, 2326, 3036
Verey, David. 1158
Verghese, Paul. 1487, 1659
Vergote, Antoine. 1728, 3001
Vergilius Maro, Publius. 11, 3780
Verhalen, Philip A. 3707
Verheyden, A. L. E. 37
Verheylezoon, Louis. 3270
Verhoeven, F. R. J. 2566
Verhovskoy, Serge S. 2745, 3667
Veri, Anthony. 3742
Verity, Arthur Wilson. 2470
Verity, George Bersford. 3649
Verity, Geroge Beresford. 3649
Verkade, Willibrord. 3136

Verkamp, Bernard J. 7, 1221
Verkuyl, Gerrit. 1252, 3159, 1252, 1838, 3190, 3724, 3854, 3859
Verkuyl, Johannes. 1131, 2555, 3234, 3291
Verma, Virendra. 1895, 3404
Vermaseren, Maarten Jozef. 1398, 2560
Vermes, Geza. 4, 505, 1411, 2045, 3014, 3706
Vermes, Pamela. 699, 1733
Vermeule, Emily. 1416
Vermilye, Elizabeth B. 1481
Vermont (town, Dane Co.), Wis. St. James Catholic Church. 835
Vermont. University. 3705
Vermont, Wis. Lutheran Church. 3777
Vernet, Felix. 3483
Verney, Stephen. 1064, 1277, 1377
Vernier, Philippe. 2398
Vernon, Ambrose White. 503, 1180, 1343
Vernon, Frank Lawrence. 1747, 1998
Vernon, Glenn M. 3087
Vernon, Percy L. 2326
Vernon, Samuel Milton. 199
Vernon, Walter N. 1255, 2348, 2430, 2455, 3528, 3734
Verplanck, Gulian Crommelin. 61
Verrill, Alpheus Hyatt. 1909
Verrill, Ethel Bertina (Patten) 2157, 2201
Versefeld, Marthinus. 115
Versenyi, Laszlo. 1801, 2846, 2853, 3717
Versteeg, Dottie. 2398
Versteeg, Harvey. 2608
Versteeg, John M. 3180, 3530, 3881
Versteeg, John Marinus. 911, 1201, 2432, 2813, 3530, 3889
Versteeg, Robert John. 1571, 3337
Verstegen, Richard. 1763
Vertot, Rene Aubert de. 2179
Verwer, George. 989, 1554, 1571
Verwilghen, Albert Felix. 2402, 2403
Verwyst, Chrysostom. 173, 1901
Very, Frank Washington. 3571
Vespasiano da Bisticci, Fiorentino, 1421-1498. 1929
Vespasiano da Bisticci, Fiorentiono. 1929
Vespasino da Bisticei, fiorentino, 1421-1498. 1929
Vessantarajataka. English. 707
Vester, Bertha Hedges Spafford. 1944, 3777
Vetter, Bob. 3415
Vetter, George B. 3001, 3111
Vetter, Robert J. 1353, 3778
[Vetterling, Carl Herman]. 3571
Veuillot, Louis Francois. 1974, 2221
Veuthey, Leon. 1646, 2248, 3526
Via, Dan Otto. 350, 2003, 2027
Vial, Frank Gifford. 1103
Vianney, Jean Baptiste Marie. 865, 745
Viardot, Louis. 19
Viau, Arthur M. 3248
Vicaire, Marie Humbert. 1474, 2583
Vicedom, Georg F. 1080, 2248, 2542, 2555
Vicentini, Francesco. 747
Vick, Edward W. H. 1735, 2045, 2249
Vick G. Beauchamp. 1561
Vickers, Douglas. 2325
Vickers, John Ashley. 666, 1306
Vickery, John B. 1652, 2649
Vickland, Ellen Elizabeth. 2503, 3835
Vickland, William. 3337
Vickrey, Charles Vernon. 1744, 3877
Victor. 12
Victor de la Vierge. 3691
Victorine, Sister. 2581
Victorinus, C. Marius. 3635
Vidler, Alexander Roper. 2243, 2340, 2562, 765, 1187, 1219, 1638, 2194, 2201, 2243, 2562, 3649, 3657
Vidulich, Dorothy. 1397
Vidyarthi, Lalita Prasad. 1812, 2940
Vidyarthi, Pandeya Brahmeshwar. 1897, 3020
Vidyasagar, Iswar Chandra. 3214
Vidyatmananda, Swami. 3020
La Vie spirituelle. 2641
Vielhauer, Philipp. 350, 1020
Viening, Edward. 304
Vienna Presbyterian Church, Vienna, Va. Centennial Committee. 3778
Vier, Peter C. 1483, 1578
Viereck, George Sylvester. 3791
Vierow, Duain W. 2540
Vieth, Paul Herman. 3159, 3180, 3558, 3859
Vietor, Karl. 1743
Viets, Wallace T. 1837, 2215
Vieujean, Jean. 1097, 2266, 3541
Vigeveno, H. S. 8, 471, 646, 1124, 1170, 1353, 1433, 1955, 3323, 3336
Vignat, Louis. 3786
Vignaux, Paul. 2843
Vignoli, Tito. 2649, 2654
Vigourel, Adrian. 840
Villacastin, Tomas de. 3476

Villain, Jean. 1076
Villain, Maurice. 1042
Villaret, Emile, 1876-1952. 1329
Villari, Pasquale. 3306
Villas Boas, Orlando. 1903
Villas, James. 1706
Villehardouin, Geoffroi de. 1391, 2261
Villeneuve, Jean Marie Rodrigue. 840
Villers, Charles Francois Dominique de. 2278, 3036
Villers, Thomas Jefferson. 168, 1956
Villet, Barbara. 2489
Villiers, Elizabeth. 35, 888
Villiers, Marjorie Howard. 930, 1984
Vilnay, Zev. 2207, 2208
Vimalakirtinirdesa. English. 3139
Vinaroff, Gerasim Eetim. 588
Vinayapitaka. 3779
Vincent 1576?-1660. 3417
Vincent, Arthur M. 3800
Vincent, Boyd. 446, 2974
Vincent de Paul, 1581-1660. 1434, 3417
Vincent, Edgar La Verne. 3202
Vincent, Elizabeth Carter. 2357
Vincent, Howell Smith. 3517
Vincent, John Heyl. 3558, 36, 566, 1606, 1994, 3178, 3229, 3558, 3560
Vincent, John J. 989, 2045, 2422, 2712
Vincent, Leon Henry. 3779, 3136
Vincent, Marvin Richardson. 2475, 36, 352, 449, 473, 1180, 1773, 2061, 2945
Vincent, Mary Clare. 2883
Vincent, Thomas. 2156, 2881, 3809
Vincentians. Western Province of the U.S.A. 2398
Vincent Irene (Vongeh) 2631, 3718
Vincentius Ferrerius, 1350 (ca.)-1419. 3490
Vincetn, John Heyl. 1610
Vincentius Lerinensis, 5th cent. 3283
Vine, Aubrey Russell. 2684
Vine, W. E. 246
Vine, William Edwy. 369, 446, 511, 543, 1770, 1921
Vine, William Edwyn. 246, 270, 2127
Vineeth, Vadakethala F. 2571
Viner, Jacob. 1076, 2983
Vines, Jerry. 168, 323, 324, 1561, 2016, 3321
Vinet, Alexandre Rodolphe. 1072, 2907, 3368, 3675
Vining, Elizabeth Gray. 1454, 1676, 2131, 2813
Vinnedge, Hewitt Breneman. 2706
Vino, William Edwyn. 469
Vins, Georgii Petrovich. 153, 3780
Vinton, Alexander Hamilton. 3653
Vinton, Francis. 2969
Vinton, John Adams. 53
Vio, Tommaso de. 3630
Violett, Ebal Eleadah. 1554, 2030, 2765
Violi, Unicio Jack. 474
Virajananda, 1874 or 5-1951. 1732
Virgin, Herbert Whiting. 72, 168
Virgin, Samuel Henderson. 1343
Virginia Council of Churches. 3359
Virginia council of religious education, inc. 3190
[Virginia Marie] sister. 2132
Virginia Museum of Fine Arts, Richmond. 1240
Virginia religious tract society. 3202
Virginia. State Library, Richmond. Archives Division. 1223
Virkler, Henry A. 288
Vishniac, Roman. 2102
Vishnudevananda. 3866
Vishnu-smriti. 3782
Visser 't Hooft, Willem Adolph, 1900. 1492
Visser 't Hooft, William Adolph, 1900. 603, 3214
Visser't Hooft, Welem Adolph, 1900. 603, 3214
Visser'T Hooft, Willem Adolph. 603, 3214
Visser 't Hooft, Willem Adolph. 603, 1064, 1080, 1124, 1492, 2055, 3214, 3452
Visser 't Hooft, William Adolph. 1124
Vita del clarissimo signor Girolamo Miani gentil huomo venetiano. 1943
Vita prima Bernardi. Books 1-3. Portuguese. Selections. 193
Vitae patrum. 3282
Vital, David. 3897
Vitrano, Steven P. 893, 1848, 2911
Vittoria, Theodore J. 1260
Vivekananda, 1863-1902. 2382, 2840, 3020, 3775, 3866, 3867
Vivian, Octavia. 2172
Vizenzinovich, Georgina Mary. 1805
Vizetelly, Francis Horace. 662
Vlasov'skyi, Ivan. 2751
Vlasto, A. P. 3425
Vlastos, Gregory. 1064
Vlerebome, Abraham. 3238

*Voehringer, Erich. 1053
Voehringer, Erich Frederick. 2555
Voelkel, Harold. 2537
Voelkel, Jack. 1256
Voelkel, Robert T. 1808, 3657
Vogel, Arthur Anton. 992, 1586, 1753, 2252, 2325, 3484, 3618
Vogel, Claude Lawrence. 738, 822
Vogel, Linda Jane. 1418
Vogel, Lise. 3768
Vogel, Lois. 1606
Vogel, Max. 1955
Vogel, Stanley M. 3708
Vogel, Traugott. 146, 3786
Vogelstein, Max. 2093
Vogt, Evon Zartman. 3721
Vogt, Hannah. 2090, 2153
Vogt, Paul Leroy. 1321
Vogt, Volrath. 291, 624, 1180, 2715
Vogt, Volrath i.e. Henrik Ludwig Volrath. 291, 1189
Vogt, Von Ogden. 84, 2753, 3854, 1394
Voigt, Andrew George. 1473, 3649
Voigt, Edwin Edgar. 2433
Voigt, Robert J. 2413, 2815, 2846, 3575, 3794
Voigt. Edwin Edgar. 2433
Voillaume, Rene. 1636, 2232, 2398, 2571, 3786
Vokes, Frederick Ercolo. 3592
Volbach, Wolfgang Friedrich. 85
Volbeda, Samuel. 2907
Volden, A. 2715, 2948
Volguine, Alexandre. 97
Volken, Laurent. 2942
Vollebregt, G. N. 2341
Vollert, Cyril O. 2363
Vollmar, Edward R. 834
Vollmer, Philip. 1430, 411, 728, 3439
*Vollmer, Thomas D. 2019
Voltaire, Francois Marie Arouet de. 1092, 1938, 3024, 3091, 3786
Volts, James D. 1392
Volz, Carl A. 1186
[Von Ravn, Clara Iza (Tibbetts)] 1870. 3517
Daniken, Erich von. 319, 1917, 3783
Vondel, Joost van den. 2270
Von der Heydt, Vera. 2159, 2993
Von der Mehden, Fred R. 2671
Von Ende, Richard C. 1204
Von Grunebaum, Gustave E. 1282
Von'Grunebaum, Gustave E. 1282
Von Grunebaum, Gustave Edmund. 1615, 1924, 2566, 1614
Von Hagen, Elizabeth W. 3175
Von Heider, W. M. 1544
Von Hildebrand, Alice M. (Jourdain) 3106
Von Hildebrand, Dietrich. 841, 1537, 762, 773, 783, 793, 841, 878, 889, 949, 1003, 1053, 1283, 1584, 1644, 1649, 3270, 3328, 3389, 3483, 3490, 3782
Von Hilderbrand, Dietrich. 1537
Vonier, Anscar. 43, 777, 1415, 2045, 2255, 3463
Vonk, Idalee Iolf. 3857
Vonk, Idalee Wolf. 2398, 3857, 3876
Von Keler, Theodore Maximilian R. 2184
Von Klenner, Katharine (Evans) 3517
Von Nossack, Ann. 3786
Von Rohr, John Robert. 2977
Von Schenk, Berthold Ernst. 2258
Voobus, Arthur. 367, 1320
Voorhis, Harold Van Buren. 1662, 1667, 1668, 1672, 2741
Voorhis, Horace Jeremiah. 2858
Voorsanger, Jacob. 3346
Vorgrimler, Herbert. 652, 3019
Vorkink, Peter. 677
Vorn Holz, Miranda Morrow (Locke) 3137
Vorreux, Damien. 1027, 1644, 3589
Vorspan, Albert. 2112, 2144, 3454
Vos, Catherine Frances (Smith) 617, 624
Vos, Geerhardus. 564, 652, 2014, 2017, 3321, 405, 652, 1530, 2017, 2802
Vos, Howard F. 278, 520
Vos, Howard Frederic. 405, 208, 380, 411, 437, 444, 450, 522, 642, 1180, 1583, 1974, 3121
Vos, Howard Frederick. 541
Vos, Johannes G. 3121
Vos, K. 3275
*Vosburgh, Adah. 2293
Vosburgh, Joseph Mary. 3378
Vose, James Gardiner. 2983, 2984, 3819
Vos Howard Frederic. 208
Voss, Carl Hermann. 3017, 3121, 3204, 3822
Voss, Louis. 2918
Votaw, Clyde Weber. 333, 473, 474, 398, 661
Voth, M. Agnes. 2736
Vought, Dale G. 2979
[Voysey, Charles] 1828-1912. 2002, 2225
[Vredenburgh, Charles Edwin]. 1092

Vree, Dale. 1319
Vreugdenhil, John. 624
Vries, Ad de. 3574
Vries, Anne de. 624, 617
Vries, Egbert de. 3448
Vries, Jan de. 3111
Vriezen, Theodorus Christiaan. 199, 2148
Vrionides, Christos. 1203, 1206
Vroman, Martin Andrew. 1015
Vroom, Fenwick Williams. 1214
[Vrooman, Charles Elliott]. 149
Vrooman, Hiram. 1620, 2002, 2689, 2692, 3064
Vrooman, William A. 1064
Vruwink, John H. 2136
Vuilleumier, John. 508
Vuilleumier, Marion. 1271, 2398
Vulliemin, Louis. 1745
Vyasa. 1816
Vytell, Virginia Marie. 27, 2778
Vyvyan, John. 2263, 3399

W

Waard, Jan de. 1411
Waardenburg, Jean Jacques. 2206, 3111
Wace, Henry, 1836. 3038
Wace, Henry. 19
Wach, Joachim. 3087, 3121, 3068, 3087, 3121, 3788
Wacholder, Ben Zion. 5, 497, 1115
Wachsmuth, Guenther. 51, 3527
Wachter, Peter. 2368, 2381
Wachtmeister, Constance. 672, 3683, 3688
Waddams, Herbert Montague. 947, 1180, 2707, 3569
Waddel, Moses. 3426
Waddell, David. 3522
Waddell, Helen Jane. 624, 2199, 3282, 624, 1744
Waddell, James. 84
Waddell, Laurence Austine. 2193
Waddell, Lawrence Austine. 2193
Waddell, Thomas. 802
Waddington, George. 1195
Waddle, Oliver M. 1454
Waddy, Cahris. 1922
Waddy, Charis. 1922
Waddy, J. Leonard. 2459
Waddy, Percival Stacy. 579
Wade, Alda Madison. 3517
Wade, David. 86
Wade, Francis C. 1498
[Wade, George N.]. 3208
Wade, John. 1764
Wade, John Donald. 3805
Wade, Joseph D. 878
Wade, Marion E. 720
Wade, Thomas Jefferson. 2161
Wadham, Juliana. 1346
Wadhams, Gordon Butler. 3263
Wadhams, Nellie Content (Kimberly) 437
Wadia, Ardaser Sorabjee N. 1814, 2116, 2566, 2622
Wadley, Susan Snow. 1815
Wadsworth, Benjamin. 1315, 2252
Wadsworth, Charles. 2935
Wadsworth, Cleome Carroll. 197
Wadsworth, Ernest M. 1984
Wadsworth, Lincoln Burdette. 1280
Waetjen, Herman C. 443
Waffle, Albert Edward. 978, 1955, 3137, 288, 1076, 2175
Wagemaker, Herbert. 933
Wagenhauser, Nita. 2006
Wagenknecht, Edward Charles. 1938, 2012, 2910
Wager, Lewis. 2353
Wagers, Charles Herndon. 2837
Wagers, Herndon. 2837
Waggett, John Macphail. 2410, 2763
Waggett, Philip Napier. 1853, 3074, 3314
Waggoner, Ellet Joseph. 380
Wagner, August H. 1415
Wagner, Belle M. 2730
Wagner, C. Peter. 323, 1064, 1171, 1808, 2307, 2495, 2504, 2812, 2814, 3679, 3891
Wagner, Charles. 1325, 978
Wagner, Charles U. 2787
Wagner, Don M. 2597
Wagner, Donald Owen. 3452
Wagner, Ernst. 2983
Wagner, Estry G. 1442
Wagner, H Hughes. 1267, 3523
Wagner, Harold A. 3863
Wagner, Harold E. 2033
Wagner, Harry L. 3384
Wagner, James Edgar. 3666
Wagner, James Elvin. 1571
Wagner, James K. 3476
Wagner, Johannes. 3773
Wagner, Jon. 2479, 2943
Wagner, Mabel Garrett. 897, 898

Wagner, Mary Swain. 3788
Wagner, Oscar Walter. 695, 3453
Wagner, Ruth H. 1454
Wagner, Stanley M. 2143
Wagner, Walter. 885, 1426
Wagner, William L. 150, 1171
Wagnon, Marilyn Simpson. 2551
Wagoner, Walter D. 861, 1297, 2398, 3089, 3359, 3613, 3682, 3732
Wahking, Harold L. 3666
Wahl, Albert J. 1688, 1825
Wahl, Jan. 630, 634, 635, 1458
Wahlberg, Rachel Conrad. 1959
Wahle, Cyril. 2215
Wahlert, Edna. 1306
Wahlert Memorial Library. 892
Wahletka. 2992
Wahlquist, John Thomas. 3159
Wahlstrom, Eric Herbert. 377, 2526, 2804, 3030
Wahr, Mary Huebner. 3095
Waid, George Henry. 155
Waikouaiti, N.Z. St. Anne's Church. Centennial Committee. 3788
Wainright, Samuel Hayman. 2535
Wainwright, Gerald Averay. 1502
Wainwright, Geoffrey. 136, 2252, 3649
Wainwright, Gerald Averay. 1502
Wainwright House, Rye, N.Y. 1676
Wainwright, Jonathan Mayhew. 1523, 1606, 1975
Wainwright, Joseph Allan. 3165
Wainwright, William J. 2644, 3107
Waite, Arthur Edward. 2641, 3277, 722, 1663, 2271, 2313, 2730, 3251, 3589, 3898
Waite, Catharine (Van Valkenburg) 2606, 3869
Waite, Charles Burlingame. 1195
Waite, Richard Alfred. 978
Waite, Richard Alfred, jr. 3196
Waite. Arthur Edward. 722
Waits, Edward McShane. 1309
Waitz, Siegmund. 2398
Wakatama, Pius. 2495
Wake, Arthur N. 1876
Wake, Charles Staniland. 891, 3010
Wake Forest college, Wake Forest, N.C. 1072, 1956
Wakefield, Donam Hahn. 1081
Wakefield, Elizabeth. 2002
Wakefield, Gordon Stevens. 3522
Wakefield, Norman. 989
Wakefield, Samuel. 3649
Wakefield, Walter Leggett. 1638, 1909, 3324
Wakeford, Oneta. 2696
Wakeham, Irene. 951
Wakeham, Richard King. 3375, 1268
Wakeley, Joseph Beaumont. 2452
Wakeley, Joseph Beaumont. 1379, 2168, 2423, 3802, 3813
Wakeman, Henry Offley. 1221, 1759
Wakin, Edward. 828, 829, 832, 874, 949, 1245
[Walahfrid 807?-849. 1701
Walburg, Anthony H. 828
Walchars, John. 2398, 3223, 3788
Walcher, James. 855
Walcott, Gregory Dexter. 3594
Walcott, Philip Cory. 945
Wald, Marcus. 2807
Wald, Oletta. 642
Walden, Treadwell. 3558
Waldenfels, Hans. 1081, 2711
Waldenstrom, Paul Petter. 107
Waldman, Milton. 1938
Waldman, Morris David. 2091
*Waldo, Charlotte E. 3384
Waldock, Arthur John Alfred. 2471
Waldor, Milton A. 2125
Waldron, Daniel Wingate. 2895
Waldrop, W. Earl. 1320, 3746
Waldrup, Earl. 3784
Waldrup, Earl W 1920. 1202, 1253
Waldstein, Abraham Solomon. 2101
Walens, Stanley. 2188
Waley, Arthur. 1850
Walgrave, J. H. 1473, 2704
Walgrave, Jan Henricus. 1473, 2704, 3449
Walgrave, V. 1475, 3773
Walhout, Donald. 3106
Walkem, Charles William. 457
Walker, Aaron. 3609
Walker, Agnes Germain (Briggs) 2000
Walker, Alan. 107, 978, 1279, 1571, 2228, 2430, 2437, 3097, 3362, 1571, 1833, 2398, 2437, 3367
Walker, Albert Henry. 2072
Walker, Allen. 3384
[Walker, Allen W.]. 1974
Walker, Barney. 465
*Walker, Brooke. 2287
Walker, Carl C. 3360
Walker, Charles. 1224
[Walker, Charles]. 1791-1870. 3218
Walker, Charles L. 2618, 3789

Walker, Clarence Earl. 14
Walker, Cornelius. 41, 1353, 1484, 3470, 3649
Walker, Daniel D. 1294
Walker, Daniel Pickering. 69, 1424, 1802, 2314
Walker, Danton. 1710
Walker, David. 3490
Walker, Dick. 2992, 3789
Walker, Doak. 3137, 3143
Walker, Edward Dwight. 3054
Walker, Edward F. 2248
Walker, Edwin C. 1367
Walker, Elmer Jerry. 630, 3889
Walker, Eric Charles. 1421
Walker, Fintan Glen. 819
Walker, Fintan Glenn. 819
Walker, Frank Deaville. 739
Walker, Franklin Trenaby. 1806
Walker, G. S. M. 1186, 1188, 1398
Walker, Gail. 1367, 2859
Walker, Gavin Morton. 149
Walker, George Benjamin. 94, 1815, 2731
Walker, George Bilby. 2895
Walker, George Leon. 1346, 1845
Walker, Gerald Bromhead. 3068
Walker, Grace (Callahan) 2592
Walker, Grace (Mathews) 978
Walker, Granville T. 732, 887, 933, 1467, 2910, 3359
Walker, H. Torrey. 2215, 2301
Walker, Harold Blake. 181, 990, 1265, 1435, 2244, 2245, 2935
Walker, Henry Martyn. 3650, 3653
Walker, James. 3726
Walker, James Barr. 1833, 2674, 2776, 3291, 3422
Walker, James Bradford Richmond. 225, 228
Walker, James D. 2368
Walker, James Perkins. 909
Walker, Jeanne. 3474, 3789
Walker, Jeremy D. B. 2171
Walker, Joe W. 1168
Walker, John Baptist. 797
Walker, John Curry. 909
Walker, John Herbert. 1261
Walker, John Mann. 1208
Walker, John, of Mountpleasant, O. 732, 1906
Walker, Joseph. 1854
Walker, Katharine Kent (Child) 1984
Walker, Kenneth Macfarlane. 2473, 2474, 2644, 2228
Walker, Lawrence D. 818, 3882
Walker, Leslie Joseph. 1047, 2004
Walker, Lucille. 2881
Walker, Martin. 2215
Walker, Michael. 2895
Walker, Mollie (Cullom) 3560
Walker, Norman Lockhart. 699
[Walker, Patrick] 1666?-1745? 2810
Walker, Paul L. 205, 609, 1003
Walker, Raymond B. 2676
Walker, Robert. 3346
Walker, Rollin Hough. 2951, 323, 423, 431, 571, 579, 596, 2066, 2802, 2951, 3789
Walker, Sheila S. 3472
Walker, Thomas. 2014
Walker, Thomas Hamilton B. 3226
Walker, Thomas Holmes. 133
Walker, Thomas W. 933
Walker, Viola M. 2514
Walker, William Bruce. 2881, 3346, 3541
Walker, William David. 1374
Walker, William H. 611
Walker, William Henry, 1913. 611
Walker, Williston. 688, 728, 927, 1180, 1333, 1339, 3036
Walker, Wilmer Russell. 1297
Walker, Winifred. 481
Walkins, Susan M. 3474
Walkley, Charles Thomas. 551
Wall, Bernard. 2768, 3770
Wall, Caleb Arnold. 1686
Wall, Ernest Arthur. 107
Wall, Frank E. 1366, 3381
Wall, Isaac Richert. 67, 404
Wall, James Charles. 1428
Wall, Martha. 1650, 1744, 2500, 2512, 2820, 3539
Wall, Otto Augustus. 2828
Wall, Zeno. 168, 3359
Wallace, Adam. 3697
Wallace, Alfred Russel. 3517, 742, 3517
Wallace, Anthony F. C. 3064
Wallace, Archer. 2484, 927, 1353, 1454, 2398, 2484
Wallace, Arthur. 1738
Wallace, Betty Dollar. 902, 2895
Wallace, Bob N. 2966
Wallace, David Alexander. 2688
Wallace, Dewey D. 3739
Wallace, Ed R. 2453
Wallace, Edwin. 81
Wallace, Edwin Ross. 2325

Wallace, Ethel. 1604
Wallace, Foy Esco, 1896. 457, 1142, 1272, 2466, 3359
Wallace, Gervias Knox. 1906, 1272, 2633
Wallace, Helen Kelsey (Rhodes) 2696
Wallace, Helen Kingsbury. 898, 921, 1252, 3530, 3843
Wallace, Henry Agard. 3447
Wallace, Irving. 2606, 3868, 1728, 2606, 3868
Wallace, J. Sherman. 1955
Wallace, James. 1142, 865, 1024
Wallace, Jerry. 1750
Wallace, John H. 70
Wallace, John Sherman. 1124, 1442, 3859
Wallace, John William. 1477
Wallace, Karl Richards. 124, 2321
Wallace, Kathryn. 1631
Wallace, Lewis. 1996, 2006
Wallace, Lillian Parker. 860, 2216
[Wallace, M. S.]. 3790
Wallace, Mary Bruce. 3517
Wallace, Oates Charles Symonds. 145, 1994, 3465, 3675
Wallace, Philip B. 1161
Wallace, Ray W. 3876
Wallace, Robert. 2675
Wallace, Robert Burns. 211
Wallace, Ronald S. 107, 508, 729, 978, 1315, 1506, 2018, 2027, 2045, 2058, 3227
Wallace, Susan Arnold (Elston) 1996, 2763
Wallace, W J. 3249
Wallace, Wendell. 3790
Wallace, Wilfrid. 3346, 865, 866, 1268
Wallace, William. 1800, 2242, 2674
Wallace, William A. 950
Wallach, Luitpold. 1372, 1882, 2225
Wallack, Morton A. 1693
Wallbrook, William. 3137, 3144
[Wallenhorst, Mary Euphrasia, 1906. 3421
[Wallenstein, Antonius. 1646
Waller, Alfred Rayney. 738, 2704
Waller, Calvin Bernard. 584
Waller, Edward Harry Mansfield. 1042
Waller, George Macgregor. 3008
Waller, John Francis. 1365
Waller, John Lightfoot. 1304
Waller, William Winder. 1515
Wallerstein, Ruth Coons. 1379
Walley, Barbara Ann. 2635
Wallin, Johan Olof. 2857
Wallington, Nellie (Urner) 1275
Wallington, Nellie Urner. 1275
Wallis, Arthur. 1244
Wallis, Charles L. 2210
Wallis, Charles Langworthy. 318, 909, 1262, 1456, 1561, 1693, 1750, 1842, 2210, 2257, 3208, 3359
Wallis, Eleanor. 3517
Wallis, Ethel Emilia. 3705, 3715, 3860
Wallis, Ethel Emily. 1407, 1497, 2517, 2677, 3705, 3860
Wallis, J. L. 1067
Wallis, Jim. 1064, 1360
Wallis, John Eyre Winstanley. 2907
Wallis, Louis. 3087, 291, 536, 649, 2095
Wallis, Reginald. 978, 2045
Wallis, Roy. 1393, 3314
Wallis, Severn Teackle. 3849
Wallis, Wilber Benson. 3765
Wallis, Wilson Dallam. 2414, 3110
Wallman, Joseph. 722
Walls, Ronald. 865, 2636, 3249
Walls, Wesley Lee. 1353
Walls, William Jacob. 15
Wallsend. St. Andrew's Presbyterian Church. 3790
[Walmesley, Charles, 1722-1797. 464
Walmsley, Arthur E. 1067
Walmsley, Edgar Gwillym. 3790
Walmsley, John. 3546
Walmsley, Lewis Calvin. 3812
Walne, Damien. 1618, 2262, 2357
Walpole, Arthur Sumner. 1877
Walpole, Ellen (Wales) 3166
Walpole, George Henry Somerset. 978, 1955, 1053, 3106
Walrath, Douglas Alan. 1171
Walrath, M. E. 3517
Walser, George Henry. 1974
Walsh, Bill. 495, 634, 1406, 1747, 2130, 2711, 2945, 3297
Walsh, Chad. 237, 67, 945, 1064, 1282, 1454, 1996, 2125, 2219, 2220, 3757
*Walsh, Charles. 644
Walsh, Edmund Aloysius. 1148
Walsh, Edward. 2045
Walsh, Eva. 1124
Walsh, Francis Augustine. 853, 855
[Walsh, Francis Edward] 1886. 1157
Walsh, Gerald Groveland. 797
Walsh, Grace. 2304
Walsh, Henry Horace. 1322, 818, 1145, 1322
Walsh, Henry L. 726, 815

Walsh, James. 2645
Walsh, James Anthony. 2351, 2516
Walsh, James Edward. 2310, 867, 2310, 2484, 2511, 3332, 3790
Walsh, James Joseph. 738, 757, 765, 1948, 2198, 2410, 2940, 3064, 3314, 3517, 738, 774, 1948, 2717, 2940
Walsh, Jay. 1362
Walsh, John. 2368, 797
Walsh, John C. 1302, 3790
Walsh, John Evangelist. 1827, 2825
Walsh, John Herbert. 2666
Walsh, John J. 2789
Walsh, John Johnston. 2532
Walsh, John Patrick. 1325
Walsh, John Tomline. 2588, 3292, 3359
Walsh, Louise M. 27
Walsh, Marie de Lourdes. 3417
Walsh, Marion Michael. 3449
Walsh, Mary Ellen. 490, 802
Walsh, Mary Rosamond. 859
Walsh, Michael J. 2770, 3096
Walsh, Michael L. 3346
Walsh, Patrick J. 3790
Walsh, Richard A. 2984, 3273
Walsh, Thomas. 820, 1715, 1919, 755, 868
Walsh, Thomas Tracy. 278, 2959
Walsh, Vincent M. 1443, 2815
Walsh, Vivian Charles. 1746
Walsh, Walter. 1947, 2755
Walsh, William Henry. 2163, 2420, 813
Walsh, William James. 2360, 3404
Walsh, William Pakenham. 2484
Walsh, William Shepard. 3302
Walsh, William Thomas. 2410, 1618, 1909, 2825, 3603, 765, 1618, 1909, 3282
Walsh. Chad. 1328
Walshe, Maurice O'Connell. 703
Walshe, Thomas Joseph. 67
Walsingham, Francis. 764, 2978
Walsingham, Thomas. 2416
Walston, Charles. 2082
[Walston, Charles, 1856-1927. 2082
*Walston, Marie. 2802, 3202
Walter, Daniel. 1533
Walter, Dorothy Blake. 3857
Walter, Emil. 1195, 2415
Walter, Erich Albert. 3757
Walter, Eugen. 1596
Walter, Howard Arnold. 20
Walter, J. A. 3447
Walter, Johnston Estep. 2180, 3469
Walter, Leo J. 1299
Walter, Nehemiah. 1795, 2047, 3359
Walter, Paul H. 1941
Walter, R. Kenneth. 3083
*Walter, Ralph N. 1003
Walter, William Joseph. 1115
Walter, William Wilfred. 1036, 1529, 2420, 3064
Walters, Alexander. 1289
Walters, Annette. 2882
Walters art gallery, Baltimore. 922
Walters, Arthur L. 609
Walters, Carl. 436
Walters, Dick H. 1023, 3159, 3666
Walters, Henry Beauchamp. 2243
[Walters, Henry Guy] 1856. 1512, 2019
Walters, James A. 978, 3202
Walters, John Beauchamp. 1812
Walters, Loren. 940
Walters, Marvin Martin. 1360, 2882
Walters, Orville Selkirk. 1571, 3558
Walters, Raymond. 123, 2634
Walters, Richard P. 43
Walters, Zelia Margaret. 3751
Waltham, Mass. Sacred Heart Church. 1269
Walther, C. F. W. 1164, 1302, 2200, 2285, 2287, 2301, 3368, 3632, 3790
Walther, Carl Ferdinand Wilhelm. 1124, 2200, 2287, 2288, 2295, 2301, 3359, 3790
Walther, James Arthur. 1770
Walther league. 1248
Walthour, John Buckman. 216, 3359
Waltmann, Henry G. 1897
Waltner, James H. 2405
Walton, Alan Hull. 1423
Walton, Alfred Grant. 67, 1090
Walton, John. 1571, 3050
Walton, John H. 497
Walton, Joseph. 1678, 1683
Walton, Mary Ethel. 2359
Walton, Robert Augustus. 1833
Walton, Robert Clifford. 3043
Walton, Rus. 3740
Walton, Thelma. 3185
[Walton, Thomas]. 1479
[Walton, William Claiborne] 1793-1834. 3791
Waltz, Alan K. 3734
Walvoord, John F. 240, 449, 457, 507, 609, 611, 1126, 1833, 1928, 2045, 2466, 2678, 3022, 3321, 3711

Walworth, Clarence Augustus. 1365, 2755, 3788
Walz, Angelus Maria. 3694
Walz, Edgar. 1200
Walz, Max Francis. 672
Walz, Theodore. 2000
Walzer, Michael. 1762
Walzer, Richard. 1700, 2840
Wambach, Helen. 3055
Wamble, G Hugh. 2956, 3466
Wamble, Irving W. 3447
Wampler, John B. 291
Wanamaker, John. 2895
Wand, John William Charles. 1124, 44, 374, 377, 1093, 1124, 1180, 1195, 1211, 1221, 1805, 1819, 1974, 2009, 2067, 2212, 2712, 2802, 3812
Wandell, Samuel Henry. 2598
Wanefsky, David. 568
Wanefsky, Joseph. 566, 3055, 3361
Wanenmacher, Francis. 2342
Wang, Ch'ung-yu. 2735
Wang, Kung-hsing. 1331, 2838
Wang, Mary. 1090, 3791
Wangerin, Theodora Scharffenberg. 2537, 3387
Wangerin, Walter. 624
Wangyal, Geshe. 2311
Wanless, Lillian (Emery) Havens. 3791
Wanless, William. 2928
Wann, John L. 2669
Wansbrough, Elizabeth. 3248
Wansbrough, Henry. 377, 1836, 1894, 2033, 2054
Wansbrough, John. 77, 2184
al-Waqidi, Muhammad ibn 'Umar 747-or 8-823. 2629
War of the Sons of Light against the Sons of Darkness. 3861
War of the Sons of Light against the Sons of Darkness. English. 3014
*Warbler, J.-M. 568, 1994
Warburton, Amy. 2696
Warburton, Ben A. 730
Warburton, George Augustus. 1781
Warburton, John. 168, 3090
Warburton, Stacy Reuben. 2157, 2522, 2526, 2555
Warburton, William. 565, 1698, 3795
Warcollier, Rene. 2992
Ward, Alfred Dudley. 1139, 2481
Ward, Alfred George. 3360, 3463
Ward, Alice Armstrong. 1008, 1353
Ward, Allan L. 2, 130
Ward, Arthur Marcus. 442
[Ward, Arthur Sarsfield] 1883. 2313
Ward, Arthur Sterling. 3456
Ward, Bernard Nicolas. 816, 817, 818
Ward, Bob. 989
Ward, C M. 92, 2944
Ward, Caleb Theophilus. 393
Ward, Charles A. 2715, 2716, 2949
Ward, Clara Mills. 2410
Ward, Clarence. 3774
Ward, Donald. 3719
*Ward, Doris H. 1454
Ward, Duren James Henderson. 1286, 3074, 3080
Ward, Elaine M. 624
Ward, Elizabeth Stuart (Phelps) 1891, 1974
Ward, Ellen E. 3517
Ward, Ernest F. 2532
Ward, Felix. 2778
Ward, Harold B. 3379
Ward, Harry E. 1515
Ward, Harry Frederick. 1554, 2956, 3064, 3447
Ward, Henry Dana. 1388
[Ward, Henry Drana]. 2175
Ward, Hiley H. 952, 1045, 1064, 1287, 3889
Ward, Hortense (Warner) 1370
Ward, James. 3076
Ward, James Edward. 3336
Ward, James Merrill. 486, 538, 569, 2951
Ward, James Thomas. 3376
Ward, Jeannette W. 8
Ward, John Sebastian Marlow. 3517
Ward, John William George. 2771, 72, 181, 587, 909, 939, 1728, 1974, 1998, 2006, 2031, 2935, 2951
Ward, Joseph Neville. 1454, 3248
Ward, Julius Hammond. 3812
Ward, Justine Bayard (Cutting) 885, 2773
Ward, Keith. 2164, 949, 992, 1735
Ward, Kenneth Egerton. 2777
Ward, Leo Paul. 764
Ward, Leo Richard. 806, 828, 832, 949, 2775, 3190, 3594
Ward, Louis B. 188, 1372, 3451
Ward, Maisie. 3282, 384, 764, 765, 872, 1610, 1616, 1742, 2374, 2523, 2705, 3248, 3795
Ward, Margaret S. 3765
[Ward, Maria. 2614
Ward, Marjory Goldfinch. 1443

Ward, Maurine. 1621, 2599
Ward, Mildred M. 1781
Ward, Miley H. 3548
Ward, Nathaniel. 3194
Ward, Patricia A. 3835
[Ward, Reginald Somerset]. 1454
*Ward, Ronald A. 368
Ward, Ronald Arthur. 332, 350, 411, 421, 446, 978, 1770, 3293
Ward, Ruth McRoberts. 1610
Ward, Seth. 2056, 2438
Ward, Susan Hayes. 2697
Ward, Ted Warren. 939, 3889
Ward, Theodora (Van Wagenen) 43
Ward, Thomas. 656, 3258
Ward, Thomas F. 54
Ward, W. R. 1765
Ward, Wayne E. 279, 288, 3030
Ward, Wilfrid Philip. 2755, 762, 816, 872, 1092, 1758, 2705, 2755, 3795, 3822
Ward, William Arthur. 1326, 2882
Ward, William B. 549, 1529, 2915, 3407, 3666
Ward, William Ernest Frank. 1651
Ward, William George. 1124, 1219
Ward, William Thurman. 2887
Warder, Anthony Kennedy. 711
Warder, George W[oodward]. 1370
Warder, Richard C. 1222
Wardin, Albert W. 143, 159
Wardlaw, Ralph. 512, 695, 1906, 3729, 3863
Wardle, Addie Grace. 3159, 3559
Wardle, William Lansdell. 2096
Ware, Charles Crossfield. 1465, 1467, 1636, 2827, 3252, 3533
Ware, Gwen. 3799
Ware, Henry. 978, 1955, 1974, 2045, 2776, 2908, 3726, 3795, 3798, 3848
Ware, James H. 2235
[Ware, John Fothergill Waterhouse] 1818-1881. 3407
Ware, Mary Greene (Chandler) 1353, 1370
Ware, Myrtle (Barber) 1610
Ware, R. M. 34
Ware, Russell. 473
Ware, Sarah Pollard. 1596
Ware, Sedley Lynch. 1219, 2775
Ware, Thomas. 1930
Ware, Timothy. 80, 2744, 2745
Ware, William. 3724
Wareham, James. 2381
Wareing, Ernest Clyde. 1114, 2004, 2228
Warenski, Marilyn. 3838
Warfield, Benjamin Breckinridge. 2477, 1596, 279, 306, 681, 728, 729, 1601, 1907, 2020, 2045, 2477, 2818, 2914, 2935, 2936, 3292, 3360, 3427, 3604, 3634, 3650, 3653, 3714, 3808
[Warfield, Catherine Ann (Ware) 1816-1877. 2856, 2857
Warford, Malcolm L. 942
Wargo, Dan. 1479
Waring, Anna Letitia. 1869
Waring, Edward Graham. 1420
[Waring, George J.] 1872. 1543
Waring, Henry F. 1097
Waring, Henry Fish. 1064, 1097
Waring, Joseph Ioor. 1269
Waring, Luther Hess. 2243, 2278, 2858
Waring, Peter. 1209
Waring, Robert Newton. 219, 304
Wark, Homer Ethan. 2495
Warkentin, Marjorie. 2741
Warlick, C. W. 1297
Warlick, Harold C. 2245
Warlick, Harold G. 1777
Warman, Edward Barrett. 1814, 3517, 2730
Warmath, William Walter. 168, 978, 1412
Warmer, Rose. 3795
Warn, Charles Lathrup. 3202
Warne, Arthur. 1429
Warne, Floyd Lawrence. 1092
Warne, Francis Wesley. 1728, 1893, 2252, 2422, 2776
Warneck, Gustav. 2526
Warneck, Johannes Gustav. 2522
[Warner, Aaron]. 2169
Warner, Almon Mitchell. 1276
Warner, Amos Griswold. 3759
Warner, Anna Bartlett. 1454
[Warner, Anna Bartlett] 1820-1915. 1861
Warner, Anna Bartlett. 36, 588, 1869, 1984
Warner, Beverley Ellison. 74
Warner, D. J. Benson. 3360
Warner, Daniel Sidney. 3720
Warner, David Snethen. 209, 1833
Warner, Gary. 927, 978
Warner, George Henry. 2112
Warner, Harvey C. 1067
Warner, Henry James. 23
Warner, Horace Emory. 3001
*Warner, Hugh C. 3850

Warner, Iva May. 1053
Warner, James A. 2407, 2618
Warner, Louis Henry. 2195
Warner, Marina. 2357
Warner, Olive (Waldron) 2006
Warner, Paul L. 989
Warner, Rex. 2662
Warner, Stephen Alfred. 2244, 2753
[Warner, Susan]. 297
[Warner, Susan] 1819-1885. 253, 297
Warner, Sydney Yantis. 2916
Warner, T. A. 1377
Warner, Wayne E. 81
Warner, Wellman Joel. 1139, 2422, 3805
Warner, William Lloyd. 3746, 3747
Warnke, David. 3881
Warnke, Mabel. 2296
Warnke, Marvin D. 120
Warnke, Mike. 1367, 3796
Warnock, Mary. 3303
Warns, Johannes. 139
Warr, Gene. 1571
Warren, A. E. 197
Warren, Austin. 1379, 2687
Warren, Betsy. 320
Warren, Cornelius J. comp. 2362
Warren, Doug. 1423
Warren, Frederick Edward. 878, 2239
*Warren, Glenn B. 951
Warren, Henry Clarke. 704, 707
Warren, Henry White. 1861, 1504
Warren, Howard Crosby. 3594
Warren, Israel Perkins. 48
[Warren, Jennie (Reed)]. 3517
Warren, Mary. 1406, 1584, 1793, 3532, 3891
Warren, Mary Phraner. 911, 2085, 2763
Warren, Mary Sherburne. 3559, 3765
Warren, Matthew M. 2212
Warren, Max. 1765
Warren, Max Alexander Cunningham. 2495, 2555, 3447
Warren, Meta (Hullihen) 3202
Warren, Michael. 940, 1260
Warren, Ohio. First Baptist Church. 2735
Warren, Ruth. 2629
Warren, Sidney. 1657
Warren, Thomas B. 945, 1272
Warren, Ulysses Grant. 297
[Warren, W. R.]. 1462
Warren, William. 2495
Warren, William F[airfield]. 83
Warren, William Fairfield. 83, 1497, 3121
Warren, William Nixon. 3582
Warren, William Robinson. 2309
Warrick, F. W. 1412, 2992
Warrick, Mancel. 1749
Warriner, Edwin. 694
Warring, Charles Bartlett. 205, 206
Warrington, James. 1870
Warsaw, Isidor. 1315
Warsaw, Philip. 527
Warschauer, Heinz. 1316, 3723
Warshaw, Jospeh. 237
Warshaw, Mal. 2121, 2751
Warshaw, Thayer S. 211, 246, 300, 304, 3092, 3327
Warthin, Aldred Scott. 1400, 2228
Wartick, Wallace W. 405
Warwick, Eng. St. Mary's Church. 3796
Warwick, N.Y. Reformed church. 3046
Warzeski, Walter C. 766, 3891
Wa Said, Dibinga. 1732, 2853
Washburn, Alphonso V. 642, 1571, 3160, 3559
Washburn, Charles Campbell. 1873, 2458
Washburn, Charles Henry. 2686
Washburn, Emory. 2846
Washburn, Francis Tucker. 1343
Washburn, Helen Carpenter. 1046
Washburn, Henry Bradford. 174, 927, 3234, 3447, 927, 3377
[Washburn, Jesse Alvin] 1873. 679
Washburn, Jesse Nile. 679
Washburn, Joseph. 1343
Washburn, Lemuel Kelley. 202
Washburn, Louis Cope. 2829
Washburn, Owen Redington. 2687, 3517
Washburn, Paul. 3734
Washburn, William Ives. 1835
Washington, Booker Taliaferro. 1325
Washington Committee for the Slovenian Chapel. 3797
Washington, D.C. All Souls' church. 3796
Washington, D.C. All Souls' church. Sunday school. Library. 3549
Washington, D.C. Calvary Baptist church. 144
Washington, D.C. Cathedral of St. Peter and St. Paul. 750, 3796, 3797
Washington, D.C. Cathedral of St. Peter and St. Paul. Executive committee. 3797
Washington, D.C. Cathedral of St. Peter and St. Paul. Rare book Library. 656
Washington, D.C. Central union mission. 2479

Washington, D.C. First Congregational church. 1636
Washington, D. C. Founding Church of Scientology. 3314
Washington, D. C. Mt. St. Sepulchre (Franciscan monastery) 1648
Washington, D. C. National cathedral school for girls. 1648
Washington, D. C. New York avenue Presbyterian church. 2913
Washington, D.C. Public library. 868, 905
Washington, D.C. St. Albans parish. 2775
Washington, D.C. St. Mary's Church of the Mother of God. 1180
Washington, D.C. St. Patrick's church. 1180
Washington, D.C. St. Peter's church. 2721
Washington, D.C. Sulpician seminary. 3526
Washington, D.C. Washington Hebrew congregation. 2107
Washington, D.C. Young woman's Christian home. 3878
Washington federation of churches. 3797
Washington, George. 2896
Washington, Joseph R. 2682
Washington Symposium on Catholic Education, 1967. 832
Washinton, D. C. Metropolitan Presbyterian church. 2913
Waskow, Arthur I. 566, 1614, 2110, 2137, 2155
Wass, Meldon Clarence. 24
Wassil, Aly. 2012, 2013
Wassmer, Thomas A. 949
Wasson, Alfred Washington. 2522, 2537
Wasson, Edmond Atwill. 3597
Wasson, John Bourbon. 3517
Wasson, Robert Gordon. 695, 1505, 1898, 3457
Wasson, Samuel Carson. 2935
Watanabe, Yasutada. 3404
Watch Tower Bible and Tract Society. 1940, 1941
Watch Tower Bible and Tract Society of Pennsylvania. 246, 279, 464, 646, 1941
Waterbury, Conn. First Baptist Church. 1819
Waterbury, Jared Bell. 927, 978, 1375, 2000
Waterbury, Maria. 1658
Waterbury, Norma Rose. 2522
Waterbury, William Penfield. 2970
Waterfield, Clough A. 1072, 1112
Waterfield, Robin Everard. 1918
Waterford, N.Y. Grace Church. 1165
Waterhouse, Eric Strickland. 3001, 3675
Waterink, Jan. 3166
Waterland, Daniel. 99
Waterman, Leroy. 545, 1067, 1097, 2066, 3064
Waterman, Lucius. 1596, 3658, 1195
Waters, Clara Erskine Clement. 84, 921, 1025, 3282
[Waters, Cyrus] d. 1853. 3650
Waters, Ethel. 3414, 3798
Waters, F W. 2978
Waters, F. William. 3083
Waters, Frank. 1898
Waters, Harold. 1015
Waters, Nacy McGee. 3064
Waters, Nathaniel Ramsay. 794
Waters, Plummer. 3292
Waters, Walter Nathan. 813
Waters, Wilson. 2335
Waterston, Elizabeth. 1420
Waterston, Robert Cassie. 3160
Watervliet, N. Y. St. Nicholas Church. 1180
Wates, George Frederick. 3064
Wathen, Ambrose G. 189, 3408
Wathen, Edith. 3877
Wathen, James F. 2368
Watkin, Edward Ingram. 757, 793, 817, 842, 1373, 1394, 2641, 2643, 2983, 3068
Watkin, William Ward. 1157, 1162
Watkins, Edgar. 642
Watkins, I. B. 297
Watkins, Keith. 1464, 2238, 2252, 3392
Watkins, Mamie. 139
Watkins, Morris. 613, 2526
Watkins, Oscar Daniel. 2812
Watkins, Owen C. 1676, 3008
Watkins, Peter. 1159
Watkins, Richard Irving. 333
Watkins, William Hamilton. 2401
Watkins, William Turner. 1596, 2422
Watkinson, William L. 2381
Watkinson, William Lonsdale. 615, 886, 1072, 2438, 3346
Watlington, Francis. 1421
Watmough, Joseph Ronald. 1767, 2744
Waton, Harry. 319, 722, 2082, 2758, 3472
Watson, Adam. 3214
Watson, Albert Durrant. 3517
Watson, Alexander, of New York. 2696
Watson, Andrew. 2517

Watson, Arthur. 921, 1958
Watson, Bernard. 682
Watson, Charles H. 2543
Watson, Charles Henry. 107, 1833
Watson, Charles Morell. 1064
Watson, Charles R. 1391, 2495, 2517
Watson, Charles Roger. 2504, 2517, 2566
Watson, Daivd C. K. 1728
Watson, David. 1135, 3447
Watson, David C. K. 67, 989, 992, 1124, 1571, 1833
Watson, David Charles Cuningham. 202
Watson, Edward William. 1211, 1221, 1759
Watson, Elizabeth Elaine. 904, 930, 1384, 1734, 1984
Watson, Elizabeth Sophia Fletcher. 661
Watson, Ellen Batson. 169
Watson, Emerson Cleveland. 151
Watson, Emory Olin. 2455
Watson, Ethel May. 1610
Watson, Eva Margaret (Watson) 3137
Watson, Evelyn Mabel Palmer. 2641
Watson, Frederick. 69
Watson, George D[ouglas]. 978
Watson, George Douglas. 520, 3282, 978, 3282, 460, 978, 1008, 3321
Watson, Goodwin Barbour. 3160, 3219
Watson, Harold. 978
Watson, James Fraughtnan. 3160
Watson, James V. 1571, 3675
Watson, Jane (Werner) 494, 624, 630, 898, 1734, 1895, 2023
Watson, John. 1053, 1055, 291, 1108, 237, 297, 624, 1333, 1752, 1974, 2032, 2066, 2252, 2907, 2935, 3798
Watson, John M. 3080
Watson, John Thomas. 123
Watson, Kenneth. 3069
Watson, Lila. 2305
Watson, Lyall. 2730
Watson, Michael Joseph. 300
Watson, Nancy Dingman. 2634
Watson, Norris Victor. 457, 461
Watson, P. S. G. 609
Watson, Percy. 751, 752
Watson, Philip Saville. 1752, 2278, 2423
Watson, Richard. 59, 237, 279, 1195, 1711, 2759, 237, 386, 3346, 3639, 3650, 3805
Watson, Samuel. 1974, 3517
Watson, Simone. 1776
Watson, Stanley J. 1261
Watson, Thomas. 1405, 181, 613, 1011, 3809
Watson, Thomas Edward. 1779, 2522, 3244, 2522
Watson, Tom. 3202
[Watson, William] d. 1863. 1128
Watson, William Henry. 1036, 2983, 1546
Watt, Donald. 3754
Watt, Gordon. 979, 1388
Watt, Hugh. 880, 1376, 1652
Watt, J. Robert. 9, 1353
Watt, John A. 593, 1147, 2863, 3360
Watt, Reed Loving. 3137
Watt, William Montgomery. 21, 1922, 2629, 3087, 3454
Watterott, Ignaz. 2576, 2581
Watters, Archibald Clark. 1463
Watters, Barbara H. 97
Watters, David H. 1531
Watters, Dennis Alonzo. 3798
Watters, Frank. 1882
Watters, Henry Eugene. 237, 279
Watters, Mary. 3777
Watters, Philip Melancthon. 743
Watters, William. 2475
Watters, William R. 544, 1799
*Watts, Alan W. 3891
Watts, Alan Wilson. 3106, 1053, 1080, 2382, 2641, 2654, 2857, 3068, 3106, 3798, 3892, 3893, 3895, 1080, 1415, 1486, 1728, 2381, 3483, 3587, 3892
Watts, Ewart G. 1008, 3666
Watts, Franklin. 1486
Watts, George Byron. 3789
Watts, Gwendoline. 1443
Watts, Harold Holliday. 312, 3122
Watts, Isaac. 320, 581, 910, 1512, 1697, 1698, 1741, 1869, 1870, 2047, 2242, 2882, 3202, 3209, 3367, 3563, 3799, 3899
Watts, J. C. 3106
Watts, James Washington. 541, 658, 1797, 3465
Watts, John D W. 486, 561, 599, 1797, 2151
Watts, Joseph Thomas. 642, 979, 3559
Watts, Michael R. 1469
Watts, Newman. 279
Watts, Richard G. 1417
Watts. Harold Holliday. 3122
Waugh, Evelyn. 733, 2182
[Waugh, John]. 1523
Waugh, Julia Amy (Davidson) 2452
Waugh, Lorenzo. 3137

Waugh, Raymond A. 52
Wautier d'Aygalliers, Alfred. 1934, 2843
Wavell, Stewart. 3707
Wawrytko, Sandra A. 1621, 2197
Waxman, Meyer. 2076, 2116, 2140, 3842
Waxman, Mordecai. 1348
Way, Robert E. 2771
Way, William. 888
Wayland, Francis. 149, 168, 880, 1537, 2157, 3360, 3675, 3759, 3795
Wayland, Heman Lincoln. 3523
Wayland, John T. 3857
Wayland, John Walter. 1180, 2066, 2802
Waylen, Barbara. 1639
Waylen, Edward. 3740
Wayman, Alex. 706, 3586
Wayman, Alexander Walker. 1289
Wayman, Dorothy (Godfrey) 2734
Wayne, T. G. 2340
Wayner, Walter. 281
Waywood, Robert J. 3490
Wead, Doug. 1302, 1712, 2532, 2815, 3795
Weakland, Rembert. 1265, 3777
Weakley, Clare. 1833, 3336
Wearmouth, Robert Featherstone. 2189, 2431
Wearner, Alonzo Joseph. 1571, 3384
Weatherby, Harold L. 2705, 3095, 3694
Weatherford, Willis Duke. 697, 979, 1587, 2823
Weatherhead, Andrew Kingsley. 3799
[Weatherhead, Elizabeth Maud?]. 2399
Weatherhead, Leslie Dixon. 979, 1360, 1974, 2053, 3541, 55, 107, 587, 589, 979, 1433, 1443, 1601, 1698, 1741, 2032, 2053, 2072, 2398, 2438, 2754, 2763, 3393, 3541, 3650, 3794
Weatherly, Owen Milton. 1315, 2201, 2787
Weathers, Elmer Spalding. 3702
Weatherspool, William W. 102, 168, 2848
Weatherspoon, Jesse Burton. 649, 2907, 3021
Weaver, Anderson. 642
Weaver, Bertrand. 1003
Weaver, Edward Ebenezer. 2410
Weaver, Edwin. 2558
Weaver, Florence Stratton. 911
Weaver, Franklin S. 527
Weaver, Frederic N. 3740
Weaver, George Sumner, 1818-1908. 1596, 1802, 3137
Weaver, Gustine Nancy (Courson) 3251
Weaver, Henry Grady. 2223
Weaver, Horace R. 206, 498, 503, 642
*Weaver, J. Bruce. 3111, 3856
Weaver, Jacob Brown. 1064
Weaver, Jonathan. 3650, 3656, 3799
Weaver, Martin G. 2407
Weaver, Rich. 1064
Weaver, Richard M. 2834
Weaver, Rufus Washington. 904, 1394, 1571, 3193, 3746
Weaver, William B. 879, 1331, 2514
Webb, Aquilla. 1562, 3375, 1842
Webb, Barbara Owen. 365, 1606
Webb, Benedict Joseph. 873
Webb, Beresford. 1160
Webb, Blanche A. 3517
Webb, Charles Thomas. 3453
Webb, Clement Charles Julian. 1730, 45, 2674, 2755, 2778, 2837, 3106, 3111, 3213, 3799, 1728, 2125, 2837
Webb, Eugene. 1836
*Webb, Glenn M. 1005
Webb, Guilford Polly. 1998
Webb, J. F. 3282
Webb, James. 2732
Webb, James Morris. 669
Webb, John Henry. 2887
Webb, K. L. 3186
Webb, Lance. 979, 1008, 1244, 2266, 2438, 2882, 3360, 3413
Webb, Leland. 3467
Webb, Lillian Ashcraft. 1302, 2461
Webb, Maria. 1620, 1676
Webb, Perry F. 168
Webb, R. T. 143
Webb, Richard. 1710, 3054
Webb, Robert Alexander. 3294
Webb, Robert C. 2606
Webb, Robert Lee. 2475
Webb, Robert N. 661
[Webb, Samuel] 1794-1869. 206
Webb, Thomas Smith. 1670
Webb, W. D. 2069
Webb, Wheaton Phillips. 1113, 2215, 2438
Webb, William Walter. 3463
Webbe, Gale D. 90
Webber, Alonzo Bernard. 1842
Webber, C[harles] H[enry]. 97
Webber, Charles. 594
Webber, David. 1515
Webber, Edward Frederick. 3360

Webber, Frederick Roth. 921, 1157, 2238, 2257, 2909, 921
Webber, George W. 1279, 1280, 2481
Webber, Rachel Bevington. 483
Webber, Ralph Ernest. 979, 3889
Webber, Robert. 1317, 1551, 3004, 3447
Webber, Robert E. 946, 2593
Webber, Walter Irving. 3717
Weber, Burton Jasper. 2469
Weber, Carlo A. 2574, 2784
Weber, Edward Joseph. 1157, 1158
Weber, Erwin. 39, 1942, 2288, 2303
[Weber, Eugen]. 2766
Weber, Eugene. 2766
Weber, Francis J. 24, 28, 726, 766, 815, 1322, 1702, 1704, 1898, 1901, 2224, 2329, 2503, 2506, 2586, 2589, 3275, 3279, 3799
Weber, George W. 989
Weber, Gerald P. 1268
Weber, Gerard P. 806, 1268, 3163, 3375
Weber, Hans Ruedi. 1958, 1998, 2192
Weber, Harry Franklin. 2406
Weber, Herman C. 1571
Weber, Herman Carl. 2928, 3530, 1168, 1571
Weber, Jaroy. 1574
Weber, Julius A. comp. 3327
Weber, Leonard J. 1783
Weber, Leonhard Maria. 2344
Weber, Max. 3087, 599, 737, 914, 1330, 1897, 2149, 3087
Weber, Nicholas Aloysius. 3409
Weber, Norbert. 850, 1540
Weber, Oscar Friedolin. 2592
Weber, Otto. 176, 177, 3650
Weber, Otto [Heinrich. 312
Weber, Ralph Edward. 3891
Weber, Theodore R. 1077, 3794
Weber, Thomas. 2460
Weber, Timothy P. 1529, 2464
Weber, William A. 3762
Weborg, John. 3522
Webster, Chauncey. 1151
Webster, Daniel. 1092, 1714, 2847
Webster, Donald A. 979
Webster, Douglas. 2032, 2555, 3681
Webster Groves, Mo. Gallery of living Catholic authors. 869
Webster, Hutton. 1822
Webster, James Benjamin. 2511
Webster, James Bertin. 2559
Webster, John C. B. 1108
Webster, John Calvin. 2620
Webster, John Robinson. 3261
Webster, Loring C. 1737
Webster, Noah. 2592, 2593, 3227
Webster, Rebecca Gair (Russell) 661
Webster, Samuel. 1906, 3412, 3800
Wechsler, Herman Joel. 1743
Wedda, John. 1271
Weddell, Elizabeth Wright. 3237
Weddell, John Weaver. 642
Weddell, Suzanne E. 3047
Wedderspoon, Alexander G. 3165
Weddle, Ethel Harshbarger. 2854
Weddle, Franklyn S. 3217
Wedeck, Harry Ezekiel. 98, 1428, 2314, 2730, 3138, 3520, 2730
Wedel, Alton F. 2215, 2398, 2907
Wedel, Cornelius H. 1180
Wedel, Cynthia C. 3605
Wedel, David C. 24
Wedel, Leonard E. 1200
Wedel, Theodore Otto. 97, 1042, 1097, 1297, 1317, 2907, 98
Wedewer, Hermann. 810
Wedge, Florence. 74, 1454, 1634, 1647, 1856, 2157, 2202, 2210, 2263, 2593, 2792, 2882, 3282, 3285, 3413, 3490, 3600, 3814
Wedgeworth, Ann. 43
Wedgwood, Cicely Veronica. 1389, 1764
Wee, Mons Olson. 951, 2622, 2951, 3297
Weed, George Ludington. 1984
Weed, George Ludlington. 2127
Weed, Henry Rowland. 2922
Weed, Joseph J. 2730, 3251
Weed, Michael R. 314, 447, 2787
Weeden, Theodore J. 436
Weedman, Gary. 431
Weekes, Robert Dodd. 3714
Weekley, James. 1606
Weekley, William Marion. 1168, 3731
[Weeks, Annie Florence] 1882. 2491
Weeks, Dorothy. 2491
Weeks, Genevieve C. 1333, 2307
Weeks, Howard B. 1571, 3384
Weeks, Kent R. 2716
Weeks, Lena (Pittman) 536, 1072
Weeks, Louis. 1109
Weeks, Nan F. 149, 2484, 2549
Weeks, Philip E. 139, 3801
Weeks, S Marion. 3537
Weeks, Stephen Beauregard. 1148, 1686, 2713, 3425
Weeks, William Raymond. 716, 2983

Weeks, William Wellesley. 168
Weems, Ann. 3857
Weems, Benjamin B. 916, 2185
Weenink, Allan J. 1169
Wefer, Marion. 2003
Wegemer, Ludger. 675
Wegener, Gunther S. 291
Wegener, Thomas. 1511
Wegener, William E. 2895
Weger, Hilary R. 3187
Weger, Karl-Heinz. 3019
Wehle, Theodore. 503
Wehrli, Allen G. 536
Wehrli, Eugene S. 518, 1080, 1846, 2027, 2028
Wehrli. Eugene S. 2028
Wei, Cho-min. 1081
Weibel, Johann Eugen. 814, 2848
Weidenbach, Nell L. 3837
Weidensall, Robert. 1102
Weidenschilling, John Martin. 649, 1928, 2295
Weideraenders, Robert C. 2293
Weidmann, Carl Fred. 28
Weidner, Revere Franklin. 2322, 596, 1728, 3660
Weigall, Arthur Edward Pearse Brome. 1053
Weigand, Joseph A. 748
[Weigel, Edward]. 3282
Weigel, Gustav. 3327
*Weigel, Gustave. 3628
Weigel, Gustave. 861, 1067, 1492, 1740, 2977, 3327
Weigel, James. 2654
Weiger, Josef. 2357
Weightman, Richard Hanson. 892
Weigle, Charles Frederick. 3346
Weigle, Luther, Allan. 272, 355, 1343, 2066, 2176, 2287, 3160, 3559, 3565, 3746, 3801
Weigle, Marta. 1806
Weikl, Ludwig. 1299
Weil, Gustav. 199
Weil, Hans. 3879
Weil, Lisl. 495, 631, 634, 1384, 1533
Weil, Samuel. 841, 3517
Weil, Simon. 1741
Weil, Simone. 1730, 1742
Weiland, Duane. 2812
Weilerstein, Sadie (Rose) 630
Weill, Ella. 1036
Weill, Georges Jacques. 2912
Weimar, J. Augustus. 2185, 3592
Weimar, James A. 3517
Weinberg, Albert Katz. 3011
Weinberg, Jacob. 3577
Weinberg, Norbert. 562, 2109
Weinberg, Werner. 1797
Weinberger, Moses. 2101
Weiner, Herbert. 2646
Weiner, Herbert Abraham. 1928
Weiner, Sheila L. 85
Weinfeld, Abraham Chaim. 1658
Weingarten, Henry. 97
Weingarten, Murray. 2765
Weingreen, Jacob. 505, 3706
Weinland, Joseph E. 2596, 3309
Weinlick, John Rudolf. 2594, 3896
Weinmann, Karl. 1208
Weinreber, Tacy. 46
Weinrich, Franz Johannes. 2006
Weinrich, William C. 2350
Weinryb, Bernard Dov. 2112
Weinstein, Donald. 1025, 1629, 3306

Weinstein, Jacob Joseph. 1744, 3017, 3372, 3801, 3897
Weinstock, Harris. 1084, 2083
Weinstock, Stefan. 723, 1512
Weintraub, Ruth (Goldstein) 2105
Weippert, Manfred. 2095
Weir, Forrest Cleburne. 979, 1731, 2325
Weir, James. 3390
Weir, John Ferguson. 2325, 3226
Weir, Leona R. 1777
Weir, Margaret (Bronson) 3801
Weir, Robert. 1802
Weir, Wilbert Walter. 67
Weis, Frederick Lewis. 37, 1271, 1294, 1302, 1809, 1293, 1294, 1302
Weis, J. Max. 2084
Weis, Jechiel Max. 2084
Weisberg, Harold. 2155
Weisberger, Bernard A. 3233
Weisbord, Marvin Ross. 1677
Weisenberg, David H. 2120
Weisenburger, Francis Phelps. 3739, 3746
Weiser, Alfons. 2018
Weiser, Artur. 541, 577
Weiser, Francis Xavier. 684, 1262, 1263, 1486, 1610, 2219
Weiser, Frederick Sheely. 1408, 2376
Weiser, Reuben. 2278, 2686, 3229
Weisfeld, Israel Harold. 3372, 2190, 2622

Weisgal, Adolph J. 3577
Weisgerber, Charles A. 2574
Weisheipl, James A. 3694
Weisheit, Eldon. 3, 555, 909, 1289, 2297, 2895, 2908, 3861
Weisiger, Cary N. 431, 447
Weiskopf, Herm. 192
Weisman, Celia B. 1320
Weiss, Abraham. 2090
Weiss, Albert Maria. 1003
Weiss, Ann E. 1152
Weiss, Benjamin. 3746
Weiss, Bernhard. 370, 411, 477
Weiss, Charles. 1852
Weiss, Edward Benjamin. 3548
Weiss, Francis Joseph. 1632
Weiss, George Christian. 979, 2134, 2555
Weiss, Gerald. 732
Weiss, Jess E. 1697
Weiss, Johannes. 407, 1195, 1197, 2176, 2803
Weiss, John. 2776
Weiss, Louis. 2116, 2414
Weiss, Mary Ethel. 2489
Weiss, Michel P. 802
Weiss, Miriam Strauss. 3762
Weiss, Paul. 3106
Weiss, Sara. 3517
Weisser, Albert. 2634
Weiss-Rosmarin, Trude, 1908. 2146
Weist, Carl Sireno. 909
Weitz, Martin Mishli. 1325, 2121, 2140
Weitzel, Eugene J. 2781, 2789
Weitzman, Alan. 2234
Weitzman, Kurt. 1880
Weitzmann, Kurt. 744, 922, 1881, 3273, 3414, 3768
Weitzner, Emil. 486, 2398
Weizsacker, Karl Heinrich von. 1195
Welbon, Guy Richard. 2711
Welbon, Henry Garner. 1715, 1792
Welbourn, Frederick Burkewood. 1073, 1210
Welch, Adam C. 527
Welch, Adam Cleghorn. 49, 496, 511, 547, 579, 1943, 547, 1943, 2140
Welch, Claude. 1124, 3111, 3112, 3637, 3656, 3713
Welch, Emily H. 909
Welch, Helena. 2671
Welch, Herbert. 120, 2484, 3759, 2484
Welch, Holmes. 705, 2197
Welch, Jane Aikman. 97
Welch, Jerome A. 793, 1245
Welch, John. 2158, 2159, 3492
Welch, Mary Artie Barrington. 989, 2983
Welch, Ransom Bethune. 3077
Welch, Reuben. 405, 424, 428, 1736, 3360
Welch, Stuart Cary. 1883
Welchans, George R. 1665
Weld, Horatio Hasting. 494
Weld, Horatio Hastings. 1974, 3841
Weld, Ralph Foster. 693
Weld, Stanley B. 1787
Weld, Theodore Dwight. 3423
Weld, Wayne. 1171, 3332
Weldon, George Warburton. 61
Weldon, John. 1698
Weldon, Thomas Dewar. 2164
Weldon, Warren. 886
Weldon, Wilson O. 1008, 1454, 2248, 2398
Welfle, Richard A. 2532
Welker, Edith Frances. 3172
Wellborn, Charles. 155, 168
Wellborn, Grace (Pleasant) 1454
Welldon, James Edward Cowell. 1833, 1891
Welldorn, Charles. 168
Welleling, Theodore. 2210
Weller, Charles Henry. 1169
Weller, George. 2466, 3860
Weller, Harvey Americus. 1180
Weller, Katharine J. 1870, 2287, 3175
Welles, Edward Randolph. 2974, 22, 3846
Welles, Noah. 890, 1289
Wellesley, Gordon. 2730
Wellesz, Egon. 883, 2633
Wellesz, Emmy. 657
[Wellford, Clarence]. 3014
Wellford, Edwin Taliaferro. 1387, 2068
Wellhausen, Julius. 2097
Wellington, Paul A. 3217
Wellman, Joshua Wyman. 1335
Wellman, Sterrie A. 2266
Wellman, Sterrie Austin. 3530
Wellner, Catherine. 3517
Wellons, J. W. 3801
Wells, Albert N. 3080
Wells, Amos R[ussel]. 720, 2398, 3208, 3849
Wells, Amos Russel. 199, 202, 216, 218, 613, 643, 979, 1277, 1289, 1750, 1914, 2021, 2398, 2551, 2887, 3370, 3550, 3559, 3565, 3737, 218, 613, 643, 979, 1042, 1750, 1842, 1873, 1914, 3559
Wells, Amos Russell. 646, 649, 3737

Wells, Bob. 1717
Wells, Brooksie (Stillwell) 297
Wells, Charles Arthur. 3064
Wells, Charles Luke. 1195, 888
Wells, D. J. 102
Wells, David F. 802, 3294
Wells, Donald A. 3106
Wells, Edmund E. 2772
[Wells, Geoffrey Harry] 1900. 195
Wells, George Ross. 1101, 3001
Wells, Goldie Ruth. 2514
Wells, Guy Fred. 1247
Wells, Harold Philmore. 936, 2315
Wells, Helen (Butler) 3517, 3518
Wells, Helen (Melchers) 3518
Wells, Herbert George. 794, 1728, 3801, 795
Wells, Joel. 766, 1245
Wells, John A. 934
Wells, John Dunlap. 1259, 2128
Wells, John I. 3794
Wells, John Miller. 2937
Wells, Kenneth Elmer. 710
Wells, Lemuel Henry. 2484
Wells, Mariann Kaye. 3599
Wells, Merle W. 2617
Wells, Preston B. 248
Wells, Reese. 3436
Wells, Robert Dolling. 2739
Wells, Robert J. 3229
[Wells, Seth Youngs]. 3398
Wells, Ursula. 569
Wells, Wesley Raymond. 186
Wells, William W. 1552
Wellwood, John. 2309
Welsby, Paul A. 1227, 2238, 3367
Welsford, Anne Erica. 1195
Welsh, Clement. 2907
Welsh, Frank Manington. 522
Welsh, Mary Gonzaga. 3451
Welsh, Robert Ethol. 2522
Welsh, Wiley A. 3360
Welshimer, Helen. 1714
Welshimer, Mildred. 3191
Welshimer, Pearl Howard. 286, 1464, 3360, 3375
Welsteed, William. 1504
Welte, Jane M. 1321, 1486
Welter, Jean Thiebaut. 1583
Weltge, Ralph. 1154
Weltin, Edward George. 2861
Weltkirche im 20. Jahrhundert. 1182
Weltmer, Sidney Abram. 3698
Welty, Eberhard. 3449
Welty, Hugh Brady. 1772
Welty, Susan. 1644
Welty, Susan Elizabeth (Fulton) 682
Welwood, Andrew. 1795
Welz, Justinian Ernst von. 2296, 3801
Wembridge, Eleanor Harris (Rowland) 1596
Wemp, C. Sumner. 1297, 3579
Wendel, Charles Daniel. 312
Wendel, Francois. 728
Wendell, Barrett. 2372, 3009
Wendell, C. A. 1005, 1581
Wendell, Claus August. 1454, 1185
Wendland, Ernst H. 2296, 2500
Wendling, George Reuben. 2002
Wendt, A. Earnest. 550
Wendte, Charles William. 1180, 2173, 2777, 3137, 3563, 3729, 1112
Wengatz, John Christian. 2498, 2501
Wenger, A. Grace. 2408, 2547, 2549, 3530, 3830
Wenger, Antoine. 3770
Wenger, Eli D. 3799
Wenger, Elwyn D. 1297
Wenger, John Christian. 37, 202, 457, 979, 1006, 1180, 1366, 2403, 2404, 2405, 2406, 2408, 2756, 2809, 3650
Wenger, John Christina. 2404
Wengier, Francis J. 2255
Wengrov, Charles. 1785, 2779, 3261
Wenham, Gordon J. 561
Wenham, John William. 237, 1770, 1959, 3610
Wenhe, Mary B. 604, 2883
Weninger, Franz Xaver. 793, 865, 1268, 3698
Wenley, Robert Mark. 237, 2164, 3239, 3533, 3655
Wenner, George Unangst. 2303, 3160
Wennink, H. 90
Wensinck, Arent Jan. 2566, 1927
Wensinck, Arnet Jan. 2667
Wensing, Michael G. 806, 1261
Wentworth, Elaine. 1482, 3717
Wentz, Abdel Ross. 1408, 1548, 1629, 1652, 1708, 2294, 3309, 3852
Wentz, Frederick K. 1006, 1064, 2293, 2671, 3447, 3785
Wentz, Frederick W. 2298
Wentz, Walter Yeeling Evans. 708, 878, 1631, 3586, 3866
Wentzel, Fred De Hart. 1321
Wenz, Helmut. 2176

Wenzel, Kristen. 1294
Wenzel, Siegfried. 2203
Wenzlick, William. 3483
Wepf, Lewis. 464
Werberig, Robert J. 2215
Werblowsky, Raphael Jehudah Zwi. 741, 2146, 3068
Werguet, Stanislaus. 3031
Werline, Albert Warwick. 1147
Wernaer, Robert Maximilian. 3244
Wernecke, Herbert Henry. 457
Werner, Edward Theodore Chalmers. 2655
Werner, Emily J. 475
Werner, Eric. 841, 1206, 2109, 2634, 3577, 3802
Werner, Hazen G. 979
Werner, Hazen Graff. 979, 1008, 1512, 1603, 2995
Werner, Heinrich. 1284
Werner, Jane. 630, 2134
Werner, Karl. 676, 3667
Werner, Maria Assunta. 1322
Werner, Martin. 3658
Werner, Morris Robert. 2606, 2607, 3869
Werner, Oscar Helmuth. 2679
Werning, Waldo J. 1171, 1201, 3530
Wernle, Paul. 1103
Werr, Donald F. 1604, 3181
Wersell, Thomas W. 2895, 3331
Werstein, Irving. 2130
[Wertenbaker, Green Peyton] 1907. 1812
Wertenbaker, Thomas Jefferson. 2371
Wertheimer, Max. 1429, 1037, 1428, 2085
Wertz, Clara Belle. 2696
Wesberry, James P. 3360
Wesberry, James Pickett. 1561, 2398
Wesche, Percival A. 2620
Wescott, Glenway. 3282
Wesiphal, Barbara Osborne. 2540
Weske, Dorothy (Bruce) 1220
Wesley, Chalres. 2857
Wesley, Charles. 3208
Wesley, Charles Harris. 14, 26, 1668
Wesley, John. 1008, 1292, 1516, 1629, 1870, 2212, 2422, 2427, 2428, 2430, 2434, 2438, 2818, 2819, 2895, 3137, 3144, 3367, 3412, 3631, 3650, 3798, 3805, 3806
Wesley, Samuel. 2048
Wesleyan Church. Office of the General Secretary. 3806
Wesleyan Methodist church. Catechism. English. 2427
Wesleyan university, Middletown, Conn. 2422, 3806
Wessel, Klaus. 85, 2253
Wesseling, Theodore. 841
Wessels, Cletus. 2361
Wessely, Wolfgang. 1443
Wessing, Robert. 1937
Wessler, M. Jenelyn. 2381
Wessler, Martin F. 3391
Wessling, Edward W. 2287
West, Anson. 1408, 1912, 3292, 2430
West, Anthony. 1391
West, Bill G. 994
West Central Africa Regional Conference, Leopoldville, Belgian Kongo, 1946. 2498
West, Charles C. 1064, 1106, 1320, 2497, 3657
West, Cornel. 17
West, David Manuel. 1955
West, Delno C. 2122
West, Donald James. 2262
West, Edward N. 9, 422, 3336
West, Edward William. 3899
West, Emerson Roy. 1231, 2907, 3002
West, Emery Scott. 237
West, Francis Athow. 3305
West, Franklin Lorenzo Richards. 407, 3235
West, George Allen. 2546
[West, George Montgomery]. 22, 3522
West, Georgiana Tree. 1315, 3751
West, Gilbert. 2053
West, Herbert B. 2895
West, Jack H. 604
West, James King. 541
West, Jessamyn. 1679
West, John. 2192
West, John Anthony. 97
West, John W. 1462
West, Judson S. 1053
West, Lillian (Clarkson) 3877
West, Marion B. 989, 3807, 3831
West, Maude De Joseph. 330
West, Morris L. 2342
West, Nathaniel. 228, 304
West New York, N. J. St. John's Evangelical Lutheran Church. 1547
West, Paul. 2232
West, Ray Benedict. 2616, 3869
West, Rebecca. 115
West, Richard F. 946
West, Robert Athow. 2428
West, Robert Cooper. 29

West, Robert Frederick. 732, 1366, 1702, 2674, 3017
West, Roberta B. 2431, 2586
West, Roy A. 679
West, Samuel. 1500, 1658, 3742
West, Samuel Earnest. 2975
West, Serene. 2381
West, Simeon Henry. 3518
West, Stephen. 108, 1334, 1856
West, Steven. 1698
*West, Virginia. 1454
West Virginia Baptist Convention. 1571
West, William. 2823
West, William Garrett. 3533
Westall, Wilfrid. 1583
Westberg, Grange E. 1353
Westberg, Granger E. 1353, 2784, 3434
Westboro, Mass. Evangelical Congregational church. 1546
Westbrook, Richard Brodhead. 1656, 2325
Westburg, Paul A. 1711
Westubyr-Jones John. 1197
Westcott, Arthur. 3807
Westcott, Brooke Foss. 74, 248, 398, 1212, 1543, 3213, 3449, 3807, 3808, 3810
Westcott, F[rank] N[ash]. 1126
Westcott, Frank Nash. 2959, 2965
Westcott, Regina (Hanson) 1610
Westcott, William Wynn. 1921
Westenskow, Melvin. 2614
Wester, Jesse M. 2398
Westerhoff, John H. 936, 939, 1064, 1244, 2235, 3483, 3889
Westerly, R.I. Pawcatuck Seventh day Baptist church. 3388
Westerman, John. 3596
Westermann, Claus. 43, 237, 451, 474, 498, 524, 530, 536, 545, 550, 568, 579, 596, 672, 1382, 1383, 1731, 2045, 2792, 2867
Westermann, Diedrich. 2498
Westermarck, Edward Alexander. 946
Westermeyer, H E. 1708
Western, Helen. 3471
Western Jewish Institute, Los Angeles. 2122
Western Reserve Historical Society, Cleveland. 3397, 3808
[Western Reserve university, Cleveland]. 123, 1820
Westervelt, Josephine Hope. 2533
*Westervelt, Virginia. 3879
Westervelt, William Drake. 2207
Westfall, Richard S. 3085
Westfall, Tom. 2398
Westfield, N.J. Presbyterian Church. 3808
Westgate, Ia. Hope Lutheran church. 2291
Westheimer, Karl. 793, 1283
Westhues, Kenneth. 2576
Westin, Douglass. 1668
Westin, Gunnar. 3323
Westing, Harold J. 3550, 3559
Westman, Heinz. 611
Westman, Paul. 1577, 1753
Westminster assembly of divines. 748, 2913
Westminster City Libraries. 670
Westoctt, Brooke Foss. 3072
Weston, Frank. 3650
Weston, Frank S. 1698
Weston, Henry Griggs. 442
[Weston, Isaac] 1787-1870. 2806
Weston, Jessie Laidlay. 1755
Weston, Joseph Harry. 2607
Weston, Lilla Belle Norton (Folts) 1250
Weston, Sidney A. 1955, 3172, 3190
Weston, Sidney Adams. 644, 979, 1325, 1994, 3360, 3889
Weston, Walter Newell. 1348, 1917
Weston, William. 3137
Westow, Theodore L. 811, 2822
Westphal, Arnold Carl. 909, 3160
Westphal, Barbara (Osborne) 624, 1633, 2505, 2544, 2547, 3387, 3524
Westphal, Clarence. 2810
Westphal, Edward P. 643
Westphal, Edward Pride. 3169
Westropp, Hodder M. 3574
Westropp, Hodder Michael. 2828
Westwood, Horace. 2882, 3483, 3518
Westwood, Thomas Campbell. 469
Wetering, Janwillem van de. 1503, 2383, 2575
Wetherald, Thomas. 1688
Wetherbee, John. 3518
Wetherell, David Fielding. 2984
Wetherill, Charles. 1687
Wetherill, Francis Macomb. 1601, 3122
[Wetmore, Elizabeth (Bisland)]. 1805
Wetsel, David. 58, 2778
Wettstone, Karl Frederick. 2935
Wetzel, Daniel Jacob. 614, 3027
Wetzel, Delia M. 3518
[Wetzel, Elizabeth (Saylor)] 1868. 3463
Wetzel, Franz Xaver. 904

Wetzel, Willard W. 1018, 1064, 1616, 3183
Wetzler, Robert P. 921
Wevers, John William. 518, 579
Wewers, David A. 3322
Weyant, Helen. 3518
Weyer, Frank Elmer. 2918
Weyland, John Matthias. 3137
Weyne, Arthur. 2105, 2134, 3581
Whale, John Seldon. 1042, 1064, 1072, 1124, 1746, 2009, 2977, 3030, 3650
Whalen, Mary Rose Gertrude. 697
Whalen, William Joseph. 1038, 1394, 1663, 1940, 2607, 3122, 3327, 3537
Whaley, Catrina Parrott. 2398, 3842
Whaley, Richie. 495, 634, 3297
Whaley, William Pearson. 1124, 2004, 3483
Whaling, Thornton. 3074
Whalley, Peter. 1817
Whallon, E[dward] P[ayson]. 934
Whallon, Edward Payson. 2782, 1064
Wharey, James. 1180
Wharton, Charles Henry. 2812
Wharton, Conway Taliaferro. 719
Wharton, Francis. 3609
Wharton, Gary. 304
Wharton, Henry Marvin. 2412, 2588
Wharton, Lawrence Hay. 2935
Wharton, Morton Bryan. 494, 3270, 3841
Whately, Arnold Robert. 1106
Whately, Richard. 1100, 1698, 2176, 2755, 3202, 3475, 3704
Whatley Annice. 2491
Whayman, Horace W. 3282
Whealon, John F. 1003
Wheat, Carl I. 3145
Wheat, Ed. 2340
Wheat, Leonard F. 3700
Wheatcroft, Anita. 2625
Wheatley, Dennis. 2730
Wheatley, Melvin E. 2438, 3854
Wheatley, Phillis. 3209
Wheatley, Richard. 753
Wheatly, Charles. 1214, 1224
Whedbee, J. William. 543, 3821
Whedon, Daniel Denison. 1658, 2428, 3632
Whedon, Ralph G. 1508
[Wheeler, Alfred] 1822-1903. 3209
Wheeler, Benjamin Ide. 1460
Wheeler, Bonnie. 932, 3810
Wheeler, Charles Kirkland. 2164, 3027
Wheeler, Clark S. 179
Wheeler, David R. 94
Wheeler, Everett Pepperell. 237
Wheeler, Francis L. 1454, 2895, 3412
Wheeler, Gerald. 1422
Wheeler, Gerald W. 3085
Wheeler, Glen. 3208
Wheeler, Henry. 75, 2443, 2449
Wheeler, Herschel. 2674
Wheeler, J Clyde. 1064, 1467
Wheeler, James Talboys. 536, 1807
wheeler, John S. 3563
Wheeler, Joseph Clyde. 1004, 1064, 1467, 2808
Wheeler, Lee. 3145
Wheeler, Lee S. 1360
Wheeler, Lee Shadduck. 1362
Wheeler, Mary Sparkes. 979
[Wheeler, Mary Sparkes] 1835-1919. 1795
Wheeler, Opal. 195
Wheeler, Post. 3404
Wheeler, Richard S. 3881
Wheeler, Richard Shaw. 1087
Wheeler, Robert Fulton. 3001
Wheeler, Ruth (Carr) 3811
Wheeler, Ruth Lellah (Carr) 291, 2512, 3796, 3811
Wheeler, Susan Anna (Brookings) 2502
Wheeler, Thomas. 2469
Wheeler, William Gordon. 1029, 1628
[Wheeler, William Ogden] 1837-1900. 1525
Wheeler, William Reginald. 2500, 2507, 2540, 2668, 3471, 3817, 2512
Wheeler, Wilmot Henry. 1166
Wheeley, B. Otto. 989, 1200
Wheelock, Effie E. 911
Wheelock, Eleazar. 2589
Wheelock, Robert D. 1259, 2782
Wheelr, Benjamin Ide. 2196
Wheelwright, John. 2371, 3820
Whelan, Basil. 3490
Whelan, Edward H. 3074
Whelan, John A. 111, 2370, 3346
Whelan, Joseph P. 2882
Wheless, Joseph. 237, 802, 1053, 1092
[Whelpley, Samuel] 1766-1817. 730, 2923, 3650
Whelpley, Theresa A. 3520
Whempner, Verna Huber. 898
Wherrit, Elevnora. 2045, 3483
Wherry, Elwood Morris. 2532
Whetzel, Randall. 2503
Whewell, William. 2674

Whibley, Charles. 751
Whichcote, Benjamin. 1217, 1228, 3367, 3630
Whiffen, Marcus. 1159
Whilden, Lula F. 2512
Whinery, Verna. 1113
Whipkey, Andrew J. 927
Whipple, Charles Everett. 3681
Whipple, Charles King. 31, 3423
Whipple, Henry Benjamin. 1901, 2970
Whipple, Nellie Agatha (Downs) 3202
Whipple, Wayne. 1974
Whirley, Carl F. 2498
Whisker, James B. 3249
Whisler, Ezra Leroy. 1235
Whiston, Charles Francis. 2016, 2248, 2882, 3810
Whiston, Lionel A. 422, 437, 438, 979, 1004
Whiston, William. 497, 1384, 3810
Whitaker, C. B. 3300
Whitaker, David B. 179
Whitaker, Edward Charles. 136
Whitaker, N[icholas] T[illinghast]. 2953
Whitaker, Nathaniel. 3822
Whitaker, O'Kelley. 1415
Whitaker, Robert. 1016
Whitaker, Robert C. 2815
Whitaker, Walter Claiborne. 2945, 2960, 3818
Whitaker, William. 186, 217, 238
Whitcomb, Helen. 3877
Whitcomb, Ida Prentice. 1996, 1955
Whitcomb, John Clement. 508, 514, 556, 1403, 1422
Whitcomb, Paul. 865
White, Alan R. 2473
[White, Albert C.]. 892, 3024
White, Alex Sandri. 3615
White, Alexander Newton. 2866
White, Alma. 1423, 1928, 3811, 3812
White, Alma (Briduell) 2848
White, Alma (Bridwell) 802, 2848, 3137, 3811
White, Amos Jerome. 2498
White, Andrew Dickson. 3074, 3085, 3314
[White, Anna] 1831-1910. 1577, 3397
White, Anne S. 979, 992, 1433
White, Anne Terry. 630, 2662
White, Annie Randall. 645, 1984
White, Anthony G. 1279
White, Arthur Kent. 802, 2848, 3811
White, Benjamin Franklin. 3718
White, Blanche Sydnor. 149, 159, 172
White, Bouck. 2027
[White, Catherine Ann] 1825-1878. 624, 1180, 2654
White, Charles Ignatius. 3378, 3379
White, Charles J. 2016
White, Charles Lincoln. 156, 2714, 2528
White, Clara L. 3160
White, Despina Stratoudaki. 1028, 2844
White, Donald Cedric. 3433
White, Dorothy Margaret. 899
White, Dorothy Vernon (Smith) 1254
White, Douglas. 1633
*White, Douglas M. 1842
White, Douglas Malcolm. 168, 517, 1576, 1791, 2907
White, E. G. 2045
White, Edith Denny. 3236
White, Edith Hamilton. 3833
White, Edward Arthur. 3085, 3314
White, Edward Joseph. 203
White, Edwin Augustine. 1490
White, Edwin E. 2526
White, Edwin Elverton. 2526
*White, Elena G. de. 1955, 3137, 3384
White, Elijah. 1585
*White, Ellen G. 1325
White, Ellen Gould (Harmon) 199, 979, 1013, 1053, 1433, 1436, 1443, 1459, 1572, 1955, 1974, 1984, 1998, 2019, 2027, 2066, 2067, 2135, 2378, 2488, 2539, 3160, 3166, 3292, 3300, 3336, 3337, 3380, 3381, 3384, 3385, 3386, 3435, 3530, 3677, 3811, 3812, 2887
White, Emma Jane. 1258
White, Ernest. 1361, 2341
White, Erskine Norman. 138
White, Eugene Edmond. 1520
White, Florence Meiman. 2233, 2681
White, Floyd Edward. 1015
White, Frank Stonewall. 1588
White, Freda Dunlop. 297
White, George Edward. 39, 3706
White, George Miles. 1360
White, George Starr. 3518
White, Goodrich Cook. 3559
White, Greenough. 1305, 2167
White, Hamilton. 3668
White, Helen Chappell. 1353, 1415
White, Helen Constance. 1455, 1760, 1455
White, Henry Alexander. 2912, 564

White, Henry E. 1353, 2341
White House conference on child health and protection. Sect. III: Education and training. Committee on special classes. 1419
White, Hugh C. 1067
White, Hugh Vernon. 1064, 2522, 3660
White, Hunter C. 3814
White, Isabella. 2666
White, Jack. 2979
White, James. 2467, 3380
White, James A. 142
White, James Addison. 870
White, James Ana. 142, 169, 3160
White, James D. 1826
White, James Edson. 473, 2056, 2132, 3026, 3321, 3812
White, James F. 1274, 1490, 2235, 3004, 3854
White, Jerry E. 946, 2462, 3849
White, Jesse Eugene. 168, 2035
White, John. 3708, 989, 1064, 2773, 2883, 3393
White, John Bradley. 594, 2263
White, John Lee. 373, 1771
White, John Warren. 1415, 1485, 2381, 2641, 3708
White, John Wesley. 52, 67, 609, 611, 1360, 1429, 1561, 2945, 3321
White, John White. 2927
White, Joseph Blanco. 720, 802, 3137, 3144
White, Joseph L. 3074
White, Julius Gilbert. 3384
White, Kenneth Owen. 538, 547, 560
White, Lillian. 3453
White, Lloyd Smith. 443
*White, Louise. 1728
White, Margaret Rossiter. 1803
*White, Marian. 3172
White, Mary (Chapin) 3184
White, Mary Culler. 2512, 102, 2512, 3890
White, Mary Michaels. 899
White, Mary Sue. 1199, 1756
White, Mel. 2272
White, Nelson. 2311
White, Paul Hamilton Hume. 2480, 2539, 2540, 2552
White, Percy. 979
White, Pliny Holton. 1339
White, Prescott Cushing. 238, 3202
White, R. E. O. 473, 615
White, Ralph Jerome. 2290
White, Ray Bridwell. 802, 2848
White, Ray L. 953
White, Reginald E. O. 137, 168, 275, 324, 342, 443, 604, 950, 979, 994, 1433, 1834, 1985, 2033, 2787, 2802, 2883, 2907, 3375
White, Reginald James. 191
White, Rhea A. 2992
White, Richard. 1443
White, Richard C. 3375
White, Richard Clark. 3639
White, Robert Andrew. 1572
White, Ruth. 2, 129
White, Ruthe. 2398, 3812, 3845
White, Sam Jordan. 802, 1845, 3227
White, Sheryl. 2616
White, Stewart Edward. 3518, 3474, 3518
White, Theodore H. 2730
White, Thomas. 1268, 941
White, Timothy. 1942
White, Tom. 1021, 3812
White, Victor. 762, 3001, 762, 2159, 3001
White, Wallace. 2547
White, Wilbert Webster. 423, 596, 3221
White, William. 3571, 2962, 2967, 3812, 3611, 3768
White, William Allen. 3484
White, William Boyce. 3242
White, William Charles. 2100
White, William Luther. 2219, 2327
White, William Parker. 200
White, William Prescott. 2918
White, William Richardson. 149, 169
White, William Spottswood. 3675
White, Willie W. 3360
Whitefield, George. 1757, 2935, 3346, 3375, 3813
Whitehead, Alfred North. 3064, 2834, 3065
Whitehead, Carleton. 3483
Whitehead, Evelyn Eaton. 989
Whitehead, George. 3137
Whitehead, Henry. 1742, 1743
Whitehead, Henry St. Clair. 1454
Whitehead, Hubert. 2006
Whitehead, James D. 1297
Whitehead, John. 3292, 3806, 1036
Whitehead, John W. 1152
Whitehead, K. D. 3, 866
Whitehead, O. Z. 129
Whitehill, James. 2381
Whitehill, Michel. 253, 3459
Whitehouse, Donald S. 1606

Whitehouse, Elizabeth S. 3202
Whitehouse, Elizabeth Scott. 624, 630, 1994, 2398, 3172, 3766
Whitehouse, Walter Alexander. 177, 3083, 3626
Whitelaw, Thomas. 3346
Whiteley, Charles Douglas. 67
Whiteley, Charles Henry. 2420
Whiteley, Denys Edward Hugh. 377
Whiteley, Peter. 44
Whiteley, W H. 3580
Whitell, Evelyn. 587, 979
Whitelocke, Lester T. 2829
Whiteman, Kalman. 2110
Whiterig, John. 2398
Whitesell, Faris Daniel. 216, 304, 332, 537, 979, 1572, 2907, 3346, 3375, 3841
Whitesell, Frank Louis. 1053
Whitesell, Jack R. 1562
Whiteside, Elena S. 3799
Whiteside, Robertson Lafayette. 1273, 609
Whiteside, William B. 3874
Whitfield, Frederick. 1228
Whitfield, Joseph. 3521, 3813
Whitfield, Thomas. 1363, 3813
Whitgift, John. 743, 1220
Witham, Alfred Edward. 1454
Whitham, Arthur Richard. 2741
[Whiting, Albert Bennet] 1835-1871. 1656, 3518
Whiting, Charles C. 3227
Whiting, Charles Edwin. 1468, 1469
Whiting, George Wesley. 2472
Whiting, Isabel Kimball. 3145
Whiting, Isabel (Kimball) 3859
Whiting, Lilian. 3095, 3518, 2135, 3483, 3518, 2696
Whiting, Lillian. 3483
[Whiting, Lillian] 1859-1942. 3518
Whiting, Rachel Augusta. 3518, 3814
Whiting, Thomas A. 2438, 2945, 3360
Whiting, William. 1786
Whitla, William. 697, 1893
Whitley, Charles Francis. 512, 547, 2093, 2096, 2148
Whitley, Elizabeth. 2182
Whitley, Henry Charles. 2200
Whitley, Jesse T. 1795
Whitley, John E. 2130
Whitley, Mary Theodora. 895, 2551, 3172
Whitley, Oliver Read. 1124, 1464, 3087
Whitley, William Thomas. 2495, 2526
Whitlock, Elias D. 2446
Whitlock, Glenn E. 1290, 2782
Whitlock, Pamela. 3184
Whitlow, Brian. 1412
Whitman, Alan. 1038
Whitman, Allen. 2882
Whitman, Bernard. 3193, 3536, 3568, 3726, 3753
Whitman, Charles Huntington. 3471
Whitman, Eleanor Wood. 598, 601
Whitman, Evelyn Ardis. 2381
Whitman, Howard Jay. 1728
Whitman, Jason. 3814
Whitman, John Alexander. 1275
Whitman, John Pratt. 2048
Whitman, Peleg Spencer. 494, 1977
Whitman, Roger C. 1242
Whitman, Walt. 1796
Whitmer, David. 679, 2607
Whitmer, John. 1233, 2616
Whitmer, Thomas Carl. 3814
Whitmont, Edward C. 1742
Whitmore, Clara Helen. 3518
Whitmore, James Herman. 1995
Whitmore, Orin Beriah. 3597
Whitney, A. Clarence. 509
Whitney, Adeline Dutton (Train) 565, 1036
[Whitney, Charles Frederick]. 1899, 3574
Whitney, Dudley J. 3756
Whitney, Dudley Joseph. 206, 1382
Whitney, Frank B. 1386, 3750, 3751
Whitney, George Henry. 283
Whitney, Harold J. 67
[Whitney, Harvey Greene] 1891. 2730
Whitney, Helen Mar (Kimball) 2607
Whitney, James Pounder. 3036
Whitney, Janet. 3847
Whitney, Janet (Payne) 3847
Whitney, John Raymond. 646, 3015
Whitney, Lorenzo Harper. 3898
Whitney, Lorenzo Harper. 2018
Whitney, Norman Jehiel. 1521
Whitney, Orson Ferguson. 1791, 2171, 2607, 3137
Whitney, William T. 2592
Whitney, Wilson. 2636
Whiton, James Morris. 3202
[Whiton, James Morris] 1833-1920. 1092, 2477, 3713
Whitsitt, William Heth. 152, 1464, 3818
Whitson, Robley Edward. 1124, 2053, 2644, 3122

Whittaker, Edmund Taylor. 1371
Whittaker, Frederick William. 1787, 3611
Whittaker, John Edwin. 139
Whittaker, John H. 2181
Whittaker, Otto. 1302, 1811
Whittaker, Thomas. 2420, 2684, 2944, 3065
Whittaker, William Gillies. 123
Whitteker, John Edwin. 2002
Whittelsey, Charles M. 1572, 2325
Whittemore, Carroll E. 1054
Whittemore, George Henry. 1779
Whittemore, Lewis Bliss. 1882, 1891, 2959
Whittemore, Mildred C. 1860
Whittemore, Thomas. 131, 2027, 3753, 3814
Whittier, A. Gerald. 2398
Whittier, Arthur Gerald. 2398
Whittier, Isabel Mary Skolfield. 3789
Whittier, John Greenleaf. 253, 1017, 1773, 1807, 2857, 3568
Whittingham, George Napier. 2763
Whittingham, R. 979
[Whittingham, William]. 1651, 3009
Whittingham, William Rollinson. 2974
Whittington, Earle Ligon. 2402
Whittle, Arthur Ernest. 2974
Whittle, Donald Carey Grenfell. 84
Whittles, Thomas Davis. 1811
Whittlesey, Federal Lee. 1209
Whittlesey, John. 2820
Whitty, Michael James. 3688
Whitwell, Dewey. 1561
Whitwell, Nevada Miller. 3859
Whitwell, Nevada (Miller) 3160, 3857
Whitwell, Richard. 1644
Whitworth, John Ford. 3222
Whitworth, John McKelvie. 3397
Whone, Herbert. 922
Whorton, John Lacy. 169
Whybray, R. N. 3822
Whybray, Roger Norman. 484, 545, 573
Whyte, Alexander. 1974, 3065, 665, 2705, 2887, 2935, 3202
Whyte, H. A. Maxwell. 1423
Whyte, John Henry. 820, 875, 1147
Whyte, Paul Courtright. 2228
Whyte, Robert Bisset. 586, 2216
Wibbelt, Augustin. 1353, 1415
Wicher, Edward Arthur. 2917
Wick, Barthinius Larson. 2406
Wick, Warner Arms. 2420
Wicke, Myron F. 1127
Wickenden, Arthur Consaul. 1064
Wickens, Stephen B. 609, 3798
Wicker, Brian. 1074, 1087, 1131, 3449
Wicker, Evelyn Lowes. 3202
Wicker, John Jordan. 2983
Wickersham, Henry C. 1180
Wickes, Dean Rockwell. 430
Wickes, Edward Zeus Franklin. 2223, 2844
Wickes, Lewis Alfred. 1572
Wickes, Thomas. 465, 1974
Wickey, Gould. 2287, 2294, 2671
Wickey, Harold J. 2368
Wickham, Archdale Kenneth. 1270
Wickham, Edward Ralph. 1067
Wickizer, George Edward. 3027
Wickizer, Willard Morgan. 1467
Wickland, Carl August. 3474, 3518
Wicklein, Edward C. 2929
Wickline, W. A. 3609
Wicklow, William Cecil James Philip John Paul Howard. 1365, 1529, 860, 2852
Wicks, Henry J. 57, 490
Wicks, Jared. 2281
Wicks, Robert Russell. 979, 1603, 2325
Wicks, Robert S. 3637
Wicks, Sidney F. 1644, 1646
Wickser, Josephine Wilhelm. 2757
Wickwar, John Williams. 3825
Widber, Mildred. 1339
Widber, Mildred, C. 1167
Widdowson, Gregory. 1025
Widdrington, Roger. 793, 2863
Widengren, Geo. 1718, 2328
Widgery, Alban Gregory. 3122
Widmer, Eric. 2512
Widmer, Frederick W. 1610, 1611, 2921
Widmer, R. Rubin. 3295
Widney, Joseph Pomeroy. 3122, 3142, 3292
Widney, Robert M. 1383
Widtsoe, John Andreas. 679, 2600, 2608, 2614, 2615, 3429, 3430, 3717, 3814, 3848, 2614, 2615, 3215, 3429, 3814
Widtsoe, Osborne J. P. 3220
Wieand, Albert Cassel. 423, 2066, 2882
Wieand, David J. 457, 1235
Wiebe, David V. 2408
Wiebe, Donald. 2181
Wiebe, Katie Funk. 1006, 2404, 2408, 3814
Wiebe, Peter Jesse. 475
Wiedemann, Alfred. 1502, 1891

Wiederkehr, Dietrich. 3294
Wieger, Leo. 3587
Wieger, Leon. 914
Wieman, Henry Nelson. 979, 1325, 1659, 1728, 3001, 3065, 3106, 3107, 3815
Wieman, Regina (Hanson) Westcott. 1611
Wiemer, Rudolf Otto. 2130, 2134, 2711, 2945
Wien, Johan. 307
Wienandt, Elwyn Arthur. 1208
Wienandt, Elywn Arthur. 1208
Wiener, Harold Marcus. 503
Wiener, Peter F. 2278, 2671
Wiener, Sita. 3304
Wienpahl, Paul. 2382, 3893
Wier, Frank E. 3393, 3083
Wiernik, Peter. 2105
Wiersbe, Warren W. 181, 213, 364, 381, 413, 442, 449, 469, 478, 989, 995, 1290, 1393, 1454, 2027, 2398, 3459, 3484, 3889
Wiersma, J T. 75
Wierwille, Victor Paul. 279, 331, 979, 989, 995, 1698, 1833, 3889
Wiese, Walter. 3670
Wiesel, Elie. 18, 494, 1788, 2462, 2624, 2844
Wiesel, Eliezer. 1789
Wiesenberg, Charles. 3483
Wiesendanger, Emil Ulrich. 2160
Wiesinger, Alois. 2730
Wiesner, William. 122
Wiest, Elam G. 1252
Wiest, W Irvine. 1666
Wiest, William James. 3309
Wietzke, Walter R. 365, 1125
Wifall, Walter. 483, 2951
Wigal, Donald. 3183
Wigan, Bernard. 2257
Wigder, Shabsie. 1539, 2303
Wigdoer, Devorah. 2952
Wiggers, Gustav Friedrich. 2811
Wiggin, Frederick Alonzo. 3518
Wiggin, James Henry. 1036, 1792
Wiggins, James Bryan. 1629
Wigglesworth, Edward. 890, 1523, 3413
Wigglesworth, Michael. 2156, 3815
Wiggs, Lewis D. 3202
Wight, Edward Van Dyke. 2177
Wight, Francis Asa. 1596, 2176, 460, 1833, 3282, 3321
Wight, Fred Hartley. 169, 208, 1572, 2045, 3218, 3721
Wight, Jarvis Sherman. 3815
Wight, Joseph K. 522
Wight, Levi Lamoni. 2598
Wight, Maxine C. 1254, 3217
Wight, Paul Stone. 469
Wightman, William May. 737
Wighton, R W. 169
Wigle, E[li]. 3292
Wigle, Hamilton. 1843
Wigley, John. 3548
Wigmore, A. H. 979, 1064
Wigmore-Beddoes, Dennis George. 692
Wigoder, Devorah. 2952
Wigram, George V. 344, 498, 1797
Wigram, William Ainger. 93, 2585
Wijngaards, J. N. M. 2045, 3490
Wikenhauser, Alfred. 377, 411
Wikenhauser. Alfred. 377
Wikgren, Allen Paul. 272, 1103, 3818
Wilansky, Dena. 2116, 3822
Wilberforce, Edward. 1402
[Wilberforce, Samuel, 1805-1873. 1015, 3424
Wilberforce, William. 1054
Wilbert, Warren N. 938
[Wilbur, Asa]. 1833, 2045
Wilbur, Earl Morse. 2376, 2864, 3439, 3724, 3729
Wilbur, Helen S. 1715
Wilbur, Henry Watson. 1810
Wilbur, John. 1687
Wilbur, Mary Aronetta. 3160
Wilbur, Sibyl. 1496
Wilbur, William Allen. 171, 1772
Wilburn, James R. 1612
Wilburn, Ralph Glenn. 1461, 1819, 2977
Wilby, Thomas William. 1036
Wilckens, Ulrich. 2053, 3221
Wilcock, Michael. 428, 457
Wilcox, Alanson. 1465
Wilcox, Asa. 1906, 2245
Wilcox, Brad. 2618, 3815
Wilcox, Elmer Harry. 2544
*Wilcox, Ethel Jones. 979
Wilcox, Francis McLellan. 979, 1606, 2378, 3087, 3380, 3384, 3385, 3812
Wilcox, Llewellyn A. 1529, 3385
Wilcox, Mark F. 2499, 3815
Wilcox, Max. 331
Wilcox, Milton Charles. 200, 3385
Wilcox, Pearl. 2617, 3217
Wilcox, Robert K. 1827
Wilcox, Tamara. 2773
Wilcox, William C. 2499

[Wilcoxon, Mitchell Haney] 1852. 3247
Wilczak, Paul F. 192
Wild, Doris. 1880
Wild, John Daniel. 1106, 1584
Wild, Joseph Charles. 2721
Wild, Laura Hulda. 211, 238, 248, 286, 528, 630, 1054, 1994, 2096, 2763, 3208, 3861
Wild, Philip Theodore. 1812
Wild, Robert. 2815
Wilde, Arthur. 3572
Wilde, Carolyn. 1576, 3815
Wilde, Jean T. 1584
Wilde, Oscar. 3287
Wilde, Oscar [Fingall O'Flahertie Wills]. 3287
Wilde, Robert. 2118
Wildenstein and Company, inc., New York. 1743
Wilder, Amos Niven. 288, 397, 425, 1097, 1530, 2027, 2066, 3071, 3190, 3626, 3653
Wilder, Charlotte Frances (Felt) 1984
Wilder, Elmer Lavern. 909, 910
Wilder, Franklin. 1292, 3802, 3806
[Wilder, George Albert] 1855. 2500
Wilder, Grant Beardsley. 2455
Wilder, Harriet. 2538
Wilder, John B. 802, 1289
Wilder, John Bunyan. 802, 1289, 1843, 3881
Wilder, John Watson. 1984
Wilder, Lesley. 1433
Wilder, Martha L. (Thornton) 2563
Wilder, Mitchell A. 921, 3303
Wilder, Robert Parmelee. 1814, 3536, 3872
Wilder, Royal Gould. 2532
Wilder-Smith, A. E. 3541
Wilder, Thornton Niven. 722
[Wildermann, Charles.] 859
Wilder-Smith, A. E. 202
Wildes, Harry Emerson. 1637
Wildmon, Donald E. 1008
Wildridge, Thomas Tindall. 1775
Wilds, Louis Trezevant. 3541
Wilds, Nancy A. 1169
Wildschut, William. 1389
Wildsmith, Brian. 1826
Wildung, Dietrich. 1743
Wiles, Charles Peter. 3889
Wiles, Gordon P. 374
Wiles, Maruice F. 1473
Wiles, Maurice. 1019
Wiles, Maurice F. 67, 373, 421, 1473, 1616, 3653, 3655, 3658, 3669
Wiley, Elizabeth. 1550
Wiley, Frederick Levi. 3021
Wiley, Henry Orton, 1877. 404, 1106, 1238, 3650
Wiley, Isaac William. 1611
Wiley, Lulu Rumsey. 320, 481
Wiley, Samuel Wirt. 3874, 3875
Wilf, Alexander. 2321
Wilfley, Xenophon Pierce. 2803
Wilhelm, Anthony J. 797
Wilhelm, Hellmut. 881, 1879
Wilhelm, Richard. 1331, 1879, 2839
Wilhelmsen, Frederick D. 2321
Wilk, Gerd. 283, 1984
Wilk, Harold. 1258, 1259
Wilke, Richard B. 2250, 2260, 2345, 2438, 3360
Wilken, Robert Louis. 1084, 1180, 1398
Wilkerson, Barbara. 3859
Wilkerson, David. 1255, 2056
Wilkerson, David R. 609, 979, 989, 1255, 2398, 2823, 2948, 3321, 3597, 3816, 3881
Wilkerson, Don. 979, 1255, 1572
Wilkerson, Pauline DeGarmo. 3208
Wilkerson, Ralph. 1088, 1698, 2245
Wilkerson, Thelma B. 1911
Wilkes, Alphaeus Nelson Paget. 1596
Wilkes, Gerald Alfred. 2469
Wilkes, Keith. 3592
Wilkes, Lanceford Bramblet. 1746
Wilkie, James Wallace. 1148
Wilkie, William E. 860, 1763
Wilkin, Eloise. 902
Wilkin, Eloise (Burns) 1734, 2249
Wilkin, Esther. 1054, 3202
Wilkin, Vincent. 3030, 3390
Wilkins, Chester. 1572
Wilkins, Eithne. 3248
Wilkins, Henry John. 1471
Wilkins, John. 2675
Wilkins, Robert p. 2971
Wilkins, Ronald J. 3182
Wilkins, William Joseph. 1814
Wilkinson, Benjamin D. 291
Wilkinson, Benjamin George. 1181
Wilkinson, Burke. 3236
Wilkinson, Frances. 979, 1611
Wilkinson, George Howard. 2212
*Wilkinson, Henrietta T. 979, 1005, 2224
Wilkinson, Henrietta (Thompson) 1728

Wilkinson, Holland Reid. 1454
[Wilkinson, Horace]. 3011
Wilkinson, John Donald. 288, 2257
Wilkinson, John Thomas. 686
Wilkinson, Marjorie. 979, 2398
Wilkinson, Raymond S. 1211
[Wilkinson, Rebecca]. 910
Wilkinson, Violet. 431, 586
Wilkinson, William Cleaver. 2803, 3208, 3304, 83, 84, 704, 2803, 2909
Wilkinson, Winifred. 1016
[Wilks, Mark]. 1398
Wilks, Michael. 2768
Wilks, Samuel Charles. 1055
Will, Allen Sinclair. 1711
Will, James E. 1097
Will, Josef. 754
Will, Joseph Stanley. 2979
Will, Stanley S. 940, 3385
Will, Theodore St. Clair. 2965, 3254
Willam, Franz Michel. 3248
Willard, Frances Elizabeth. 3833, 3835
Willard, George Washington. 1801
Willard, John Dayton. 2371
Willard, Mine Eugene. 306
Willard, Samuel. 1335, 1343, 1613, 2772, 3809
Willard, Warren Wyeth. 2775, 3596
Willard, Winifred. 3518
Willcocks, William. 536
Willcox, Giles Buckingham. 2061, 2944, 3675
Willcox, Helen Lida. 603, 2489, 2757, 3145
Willcox, Kathleen Mary. 2177, 2763
Willcutt, William Purcell. 1905
Willeke, Bernward Henry. 2512
Willems, Boniface A. 176, 3030
Willems, Emilio. 2953
Willer, Earl C. 1843
Willes, Maurice F. 374
Willet, Nathaniel Louis. 3080
Willets, Alfred. 1634
[Willett, Franciscus]. 40, 41, 189, 194, 442, 1909, 2125, 2127, 2305, 2804, 2825, 3761
Willett, Herbert L[ockwood]. 733
Willett, Herbert Lockwood. 1072, 238, 291, 411, 571, 732, 1602, 1955, 1975
Willett, Robert Albert. 1578
Willett, William Marinus. 1975, 3546
Willetts, Alfred. 1634
Willetts, Jacob. 1706
Willetts, R. 1387
Willetts, R. F. 1387
Willey, Basil. 67
Willey, John Heston. 643, 1072, 1115, 3203
Willey, Samuel H[opkins]. 2917
Willging, Eugene Paul. 829, 852
William, Clinton. 460
William, Father. 3223
William, Franz Michel. 1975, 2357, 3183
William S. Carter Symposium on Church Growth, Milligan College, Tenn., 1974. 2515
Williamowsky, Charles. 496
Williams. 879
Williams, Aaron. 1870
Williams, Albert Nathaniel, 1914. 208, 209, 246, 313, 2335, 2803
Williams, Alfred E. 3890
Williams, Alice L. 1518
Williams, Alvin Peter. 2197
Williams, Arnold. 524
Williams, Arthur Lukyn. 69, 559, 2116
Williams, Augustus Warner. 2588
Williams, Bascom Warren. 2512
Williams, Bertrand. 688, 1714
Williams, Blanche Colton. 1717
Williams, Carl Carnelius. 1229, 1561, 3666
Williams, Carol M. 1742
Williams, Caroline. 1024
Williams, Charles. 1163, 1181, 1265, 3825
Williams, Charles Bray. 292, 615, 350, 1955, 3160, 372
Williams, Charles David. 1054, 2336, 3447, 3675
Williams, Charles Henry. 3483
Williams, Charles Stephen Conway. 330
Williams, Charles Walter Stansby. 1181
Williams, Chester Sidney. 3193
Williams, Cicely. 1303
Williams, Clayton Edgar. 2035
Williams, Colin W. 3806
Williams, Colin Wilbur. 1572, 1125, 1154, 1572, 1944, 3806
Williams, D. L. 3292
Williams, Daniel Day. 40, 1097, 2266, 2782, 3657, 3659, 2266, 3657
Williams, Daniel Jenkins. 730, 3817
Williams, Daniel T. 669
Williams, David Forest. 3360
Williams, David Rhys. 1855, 3122
Williams, David Riddle. 693
Williams, Don. 381, 447, 450, 1261

Williams, Edward. 1471
[Williams, Edward C.]. 3234
Williams, Edward Franklin. 1054
Williams, Edwin Marshall. 602
Williams, Effie Mae (Hency) 1228
Williams, Ernest Swing. 3375, 3650, 3675
Williams, Esther. 3074
Williams, Ethel (Hudson) 3830
Williams, Ethel L. 17, 2680, 2683
Williams, Francis Emmett. 3276
Williams, Frank Chenhalls. 1955, 3137
Williams, Frederick Vincent. 2351
Williams, Frederick Wells. 2512, 3818
Williams, Gail. 3518
Williams, George. 2747, 225
Williams, George Huntston. 49, 731, 1184, 1788, 2126, 3036, 3755, 3815
Williams, George M. 3455
Williams, George Mason. 3784
Williams, George Walton. 888, 1379, 2960
Williams, Gershom Mott. 3360
Williams, Gertrude Leavenworth (Marvin) 195, 672
Williams, Glanmor. 1184, 3039, 3789
Williams, Granville Mercer. 2974, 3263, 3360
Williams, H. 1596
Williams, H. C. N. 1064
Williams, Harold Aubrey. 2053
Williams, Harold Page. 2340
Williams, Harry Abbot. 3221
Williams, Harry Abbott. 992, 1228, 1837, 2882, 3221
Williams, Harvell P 1922. 979
Williams, Hayward A. 101
Williams, Henry Clay. 3227
Williams, Henry Francis. 2926
Williams, Henry Jonathan. 404
Williams, Henry Llewellyn. 898
[Williams, Henry T.]. 2730
Williams, Herbert Lee. 67, 279
Williams, Herman. 1016
Williams, Horace Blake. 1054
Williams, Horace W. 3453
Williams, Howard. 3666
Williams, Hugh. 1761
Williams, Hugh Richardson. 1497
Williams, Ira E. 989
Williams, Irene Aldridge. 2859, 3052
Williams, Irwin. 97
Williams, Isaac. 2755
Williams, Isabella Burgess (Riggs) 2512
Williams, Jane. 624
Williams, Jay G. 541, 599, 1315, 2067, 2147, 2649
Williams, Jerome Oscar. 169, 1562, 1843, 2907, 3375, 3376
Williams, Jesse. 206
Williams, Jessie (Tandy) 3160, 3172
Williams, John. 1228, 1304, 1318, 2545
[Williams, John, 1817-1889. 1870
Williams, John. 331, 2018, 1833
Williams, John Adrian. 2332
Williams, John Alden. 2566
Williams, John Alfred. 2173
Williams, John Bickerton. 3305
Williams, John Bigelow. 1290
Williams, John Clark. 1325
Williams, John Gordon. 3083
Williams, John Hargreaves Harley. 2477
Williams, John Milton. 3653
Williams, John Paul. 2422, 2443, 3160, 3746, 3747
Williams, John Rodman. 1584, 1833, 1835, 3666
Williams, John West. 2992
Williams, Joseph John. 1454, 2097, 2398, 3826, 3828
Williams, Joseph Louis. 3799
Williams, Joseph W. 3360
Williams, Kathleen. 1526
Williams, L. Griswold. 3220
Williams, Lacey Kirk. 2722
Williams, Laura. 3097
Williams, Laurence Frederic Rushbrook. 2
Williams, Leewin Bell. 1168, 1529, 1843
Williams, Loren R. 916, 1862
Williams, Loyd Elmo. 2398
Williams, Margaret. 3538
Williams, Margaret Anne. 1785, 2311, 3270, 3438
Williams, Marion Moffet. 2607
Williams, Martha (Noyes) 1353
Williams, Maxine. 3161
Williams, Mel. 941
Williams, Melvin D. 2682
Williams, Melvin J. 3454
Williams, Michael. 3206, 757, 1543, 1644, 3195, 3691, 757, 3204
Williams, Milan Bertrand. 1537, 1561, 1572, 3389
Williams, Nancy Clement. 2607, 3817
Williams, Nathan. 136
Williams, Norman Powell. 1042, 1602, 1752, 2755
Williams, Norman V. 1611

Williams, Oliver Emmet. 1956
Williams, Pat. 1360, 3817
Williams, Patti. 2340
Williams, Paul Edgar. 3872
Williams, Paul L. 2, 1537
Williams, Peter W. 3746
Williams, Philip. 2535
Williams, Philip Leland. 1797
Williams, Philip W. 192, 1417
Williams, R. E. 2233, 3233
Williams, Reese F. 2002
Williams, Rheinallt Nantlais. 67
Williams, Richard E. 1930, 2829
Williams, Richard John. 2935
Williams, Robert A. 989
Williams, Robert Folkestone. 738
Williams, Robert G. 1575
Williams, Robert Henry. 2079
Williams, Robert Hugh. 3817
Williams, Robert R. 1732, 3308, 3658
Williams, Robert S. 3346
Williams, Roger. 979, 3194, 3818
Williams, Ronald Colvin. 2895
Williams, Ronald Ralph. 653
Williams, Rowan. 3492
[Williams, Rudolph,] 1844. 2692
Williams, Samuel. 2321
Williams, Samuel Jacob. 2119
Williams, Samuel Porter. 2701
Williams, Samuel Wesley. 2432
Williams, Schafer. 1181, 1774
Williams, Selma R. 2371, 3827
Williams, Smallwood Edmond. 656, 3360
Williams, Solomon. 1343
Williams, Sophia. 3707
Williams, Stephen Bassanno. 3293
Williams, Stephen Douglas. 203
Williams, Stephen West. 1419, 3817
Williams, Sylvester Vernon. 579
Williams, T. James. 1928
[Williams, Thomas]. 2834
Williams, Thomas. 1511, 1512, 1693, 3346, 3362
Williams, Thomas Andrew. 1354
Williams, Thomas David. 297, 304, 480, 1736, 2258, 3279, 3416, 3817
Williams, Tom M. 2863
Williams, Vivian May. 1036
Williams, Walkin Wynn. 193
Williams, Walter B. 2538
Williams, Walter Dakin. 793
Williams, Walter George. 562, 2951, 209, 2951
Williams, Walter L. 2500
Williams, Walter Rollin. 1408, 1676, 2512
Williams, Watkin Wynn. 193
Williams, William. 2592
Williams, William Carlos. 3203
Williams, William George. 137, 470, 2674
Williams, William Proctor. 3203, 3591, 3617
Williams, William R. 672, 2248, 3296, 3632, 3782
Williams, William Thomas. 979
Williams, Wolcott B. 3190
Williamson, Adolph Ancrum. 2622
Williamson, Audrey J. 1303, 3890
Williamson, Benedict. 1700, 2474, 2641, 2643, 3244, 3691
Williamson, Clark M. 1073, 1596
Williamson, Claude Charles H. 765, 3282
Williamson, E. Stanley. 169, 3531, 3564
Williamson, Eugene L. 84
Williamson, Frank. 1601
Williamson, Geoffrey. 2593
Williamson, Gerald Irvin. 3809
Williamson, Isaac Dowd. 1699, 3346, 3666, 3753, 3755
Williamson, John Jacob. 2730
Williamson, John Rutter. 2539
Williamson, Joseph. 1617
Williamson, Lamar. 2937
[Williamson, M. J.]. 3518
Williamson, Margaret. 684, 3878
Williamson, Mary (Heald) 3832
Williamson, Mary Paula. 2333
Williamson, Norma. 3835
Williamson, Rene de Visme. 1087, 1088, 3700
Williamson, Robert Donald. 3531
Williamson, Robert L. 2783
Williamson, Robert Wood. 2859
Williamson, Sydney George. 2500
Williamson, Wayne B. 1172, 2959
Williamson, William B. 1299, 2959
Williamson, William Bedford. 3107, 3176
Williamson Robert Wood. 2859
Willibald. 677
Willie, Charles Vert. 2481
Willigan, Walter Luke. 3451
Willimon, William H. 137, 477, 1008, 2236, 2253, 2907, 3004
Willing, Jennie (Fowler) 3818
Willing, Ora Mae (Campbell) 2942
Willingham, Elizabeth Walton. 3818
Willingham, Ronald L. 3539

Willink, M. D. R. 3762
Willink, Margaret Dorothea Rose. 436
Williram. 594

Willis, Anthony Armstrong. 1760

Willis, Avery T. 1171
Willis, Cecil. 2752
Willis, Charles DuBois. 609, 1529
Willis, Edith H. 1871
Willis, Edward David. 2882
Willis, Ellen. 121
Willis, Frederick Milton. 1958, 3054, 3221, 3483, 3688
Willis, Garry. 811
Willis, Hugh Evander. 3447
Willis, Janice Dean. 2193
Willis, John Randolph. 1018, 3658
Willis, John T. 522, 536, 543, 586, 2952
Willis, Mary Farley. 1284, 3818
Willis, Nathaniel Parker. 298
Willis, Richard Storrs. 1203, 1204
Willis, Ron. 1280
Willis, Thomas. 1683, 1810
Willis, Wayne. 939
Willis, Wesley, R. 3559
Willison, John. 1353, 2253, 3548
Williston, Arthur Lyman. 3074
Williston, Mary Denny. 1456
Williston, Ralph. 1870
Williston, Samuel. 1791, 3235
Williston, Seth. 133, 2067, 2176, 2688, 2935, 3261
[Willits, Alphonse Albert] 1821. 2018
Willits, Alphonso Albert. 2018
Willitts, Ethel R. 1601
Willman, Leon Kurtz. 630
Willman, Reinhold. 2410
Willmann, Agnes. 2333
Willmann, Dorothy Julia. 1248
Willmington, H. L. 279, 1530
Willock, Edward. 1003
Willoughby, Edwin Clifford Holland. 1891
Willoughby, Frank. 3762
Willoughby, Harold Rideout. 2636, 274, 316, 2636
Willoughby, Victor (Boomer) 238
Willoughby, William. 1552, 2593
Willoughby, William Charles. 133
Willoughby, William G. 2308
Wills, Ann McCelvey. 980
Wills, Arthur J. 3519
Wills, Frank. 1159
Wills, Garry. 481, 811, 2223, 3457
Wills, Henry O. 3137
[Wills, Joshua E.]. 1181
Wills, Joshua Edwin. 1187, 3799
Wills, Samuel. 461
Wills, Theodore O. M. 2935
Willson, Arabella M (Stuart) 2157
Willson, Beckles. 2992
Willson, Marcius. 297
Willson, Thomas Benjamin. 1148
Willyard, Warren Hastings. 1463
Wilm, Emil Carl. 3160, 3106, 3160
Wilmer, Wilhelm. 783
Wilmers, Wilhelm. 808
Wilmington, Del. First Swedish Baptist church. 3569
[Wilmington, Del. St. Andrew's church. Committee of the vestry]. 2205
Wilmore, Augustus Cleland. 3730
Wilmore, Gayraud S. 2682, 3447
*Wilmot, John. 238, 306
Wilmot-Buxton, Ethel Mary. 1391, 1644
Wilms, Jerome. 1474
Wilnai, Zeeb. 2208
Wilson, Alfred. 1327
Wilson, Alpheus Waters. 2803, 2045
Wilson, Alton H. 2896
Wilson, Amos Lincoln. 462, 507, 3247
Wilson, Arthur. 3137
Wilson, Arthur Edward. 3234, 3432, 3819
Wilson, Bert. 1252, 2532, 3530
Wilson, Bill. 1260
Wilson, Birbeck. 2859
Wilson, Bird. 3812
Wilson, Bruce M. 2896
Wilson, Bryan. 1067
Wilson, Bryan R. 918, 1154, 1507, 2204, 3087, 3323
Wilson, C. Vincent. 313
Wilson, Carl. 989
Wilson, Caroline (Fry) 643, 980, 3160
Wilson, Charles H. 3031
Wilson, Charles Reagan. 1108
Wilson, Clarence True. 1833, 3410
Wilson, Clifford A. 209, 367, 384, 487, 505, 552, 1405, 1488, 1506, 2045, 2053, 3457
Wilson, Colin. 2206, 2730, 2858, 2992, 3022
Wilson, Daniel. 61, 2674
Wilson, David L. 79
Wilson, Derek A. 304, 3039
Wilson, Dorothy Clarke. 690, 2486, 2539, 2557, 2758, 3316, 3569

Wilson, Dorothy Frances. 3160
Wilson, Douglas James. 734
Wilson, Dwight. 2464
Wilson, Ealon V. 3431
Wilson, Earl D. 2773
Wilson, Ebenezer. V. 3519
Wilson, Edmund. 1411, 1928, 3819
Wilson, Edward Raymond. 1688, 2241
Wilson, Elijah. 195, 2936
Wilson, Elizabeth. 2458, 2529, 3841, 1700, 2447, 3879
Wilson, Elizabeth A Galley. 2498
Wilson, Ella Calista (Handy) 1994, 2027
Wilson, Epiphanius. 752
Wilson, Ernest C. 1072, 1356, 1454, 3055, 3751
Wilson, Ernest Charles. 1986, 3055, 3750, 3751
Wilson, Evon Leroy. 1670
Wilson, Floyd Baker. 2696, 3463
Wilson, Frank Elmer. 445, 597, 886, 1106, 1181, 1214, 1263, 2882, 2967, 2974, 3666, 2967
Wilson, George. 464, 2529
Wilson, George Herbert. 2498, 3759
Wilson, George Washington. 2449, 3321
Wilson, Gilbert Lord. 1997, 3261
Wilson, Grace Hannah. 3447, 3879
Wilson, H. W., firm, publishers. 656, 2224
Wilson, Harry Robert. 916
Wilson, Hazel Thorne. 1443, 2896, 3843
Wilson, Henry. 314, 3819
Wilson, Henry Albert. 1523, 67, 1219, 2006
Wilson, Henry Blauvelt. 1741, 1793, 3229, 1601, 3519
Wilson, Henry (Marble dealer) 3333
Wilson, Herman O. 573
Wilson, Howard A. 3122
Wilson, Howard McKnight. 2927, 3701
Wilson, Ian. 1827
Wilson, J. Christy. 2566, 3615, 3899
Wilson, J M. 1092
Wilson, J. Maley. 1036
Wilson, Jacob. 1656
Wilson, James. 98, 1241, 3713, 483, 1671
Wilson, James I. 980, 989
Wilson, James Maurice. 1072, 3626, 3675
Wilson, James Orville. 1015
[Wilson, James Patriot]. 3292, 3414
Wilson, James Rodman. 1064
Wilson, Jerry B. 1544
Wilson, Jesse Rodman. 1125, 1454, 2522, 2526
Wilson, John. 3367, 46, 3729
[Wilson, John] 1804-1875. 1507, 1901
Wilson, John. 1106, 1537, 2592, 2837, 3065, 3087
Wilson, John Boyd. 2837
Wilson, John Churchwood. 3036
Wilson, John Dover. 2336, 3818
Wilson, John F. 1209
Wilson, John Francis. 3065
Wilson, John Frederick. 1109, 1152, 3008
Wilson, John K. 3519
Wilson, John Laird. 3861
Wilson, John Maley. 716
Wilson, John Mills. 649
[Wilson, Joseph] 1797-1878. 1500
Wilson, Joseph Anselm. 1800
Wilson, Joseph Erwin. 275, 1497
Wilson, Joseph Robert. 991
Wilson, Kenneth L. 1458, 2523
Wilson, Kenneth Lee. 994
Wilson, Laurie. 1880
Wilson, Lawrence Ray. 279, 803, 1273, 1975
Wilson, Leland. 1003, 1235, 2398, 3819
Wilson, Lewis Gilbert. 3172, 3191, 3346, 3726
Wilson, Lilly (Dever) 1515
Wilson, Lois. 1252
Wilson, Louis. 2758
Wilson, Louis C. 137, 3346
Wilson, Louis Charles. 137, 1467
Wilson-Ludlam, Mae R. 97
Wilson, Luther Halsey. 509
Wilson, Lycurgus A[rnold]. 2607
Wilson, Lycurgus Arnold. 2614, 2794
Wilson, Mabel Aureola. 3160, 3177
Wilson, Mabel Ponder. 21
Wilson, Mabel Reed. 3819
Wilson, Madele. 3819
Wilson, Margery. 990
Wilson, Matthew Hale. 2066
Wilson, Monica (Hunter) 12
Wilson, Oliver G. 1454
Wilson, Peter Lamborn. 43
Wilson, Philip Whitwell. 331, 464, 681, 1064, 1955, 1975, 2031, 2588, 3203, 3293
Wilson, R. Marshall. 1572, 3890
Wilson, R. P. 3519
Wilson, Raymond Edward. 946
Wilson, Robert Anton. 2730, 2731, 3819
Wilson, Robert Dick. 508, 515, 503, 508, 515

Wilson, Robert H. 667, 2685
Wilson, Robert Leroy. 1125, 3734
Wilson, Robert McLachlan. 350, 1718
Wilson, Robert R. 281, 569, 2951
Wilson, Robert S. 1546
Wilson, Robert Smith. 2332
Wilson, Roger Cowan. 1678
Wilson, Ron. 2369, 2979
Wilson, S. A. 1289
Wilson, Sadie Mai. 2512
Wilson, Samuel Graham. 129, 2566
Wilson, Samuel Tyndale. 2626
[Wilson, Sara W]. 1443
Wilson, Stephen G. 426, 1705
Wilson, Theron D. 1072
Wilson, Thomas. 1224, 1443, 2253
Wilson, Thomas Ernest. 350, 424, 2415, 2501, 2636
Wilson, Thomas Frew. 2069
Wilson, Thomas Herod. 1833
Wilson, Waitman. 3203
Wilson, Walter Lewis. 422, 1360, 3574
Wilson, Warren H. 3255
Wilson, Warren Hugh. 1125, 3254, 3255
Wilson, William. 3346, 3831, 498, 1517, 519, 928
Wilson, William Bender. 3875
Wilson, William Croft. 2882
Wilson, William Dexter. 1490
Wilson, William Gilbert. 1230
Wilson, William Joseph. 866, 2481
Wilson, William Riley. 2031
Wilson, William Teasdale. 3688
Wilson, Winefride. 921, 922
Wilson, Wlater Lewis. 3574
Wilson, Yvonne M. 2859
Wilstach, Josph Walter. 2586
Wilt, Dorah W. 1601, 2325
Wiltgen, Ralph M. 2523, 3769, 3773
Wilton, Dean Thayer. 1975
Wiltse, May Barnard. 2733, 3519
Wiltshire, Mollie (Roberson) 3237
Wimberly, Charles Franklin. 56, 650, 927, 1428, 1561, 2053, 2620, 2710
Wimberly, Edward P. 2782, 2787
Wimberly, Vera L. 2886
Wimbledon, R. 3368
Wimmer, Joseph F. 350, 1613
Wimmer, R. 1289
Wimms, J. H. 3565
[Wimsey, Josepha] 1893. 2190, 2478
Winans, George Woodruff. 1933
Winans, Ross. 3065
Winbigler, Charles Fremont. 2410, 1036
Winburn, Oscar Edgar. 3106
Winchester, Benjamin Severance. 598, 3160
Winchester, Caleb Thomas. 3806
Winchester, Charles Wesley. 2979
Winchester, Elhanan. 465, 3030, 3753
Winchester, Eng. (Diocese) 1763
Winchester, Olive May. 3300
Winchester, Samuel Gover. 1611
Winchester Eng. (Diocese) 1221
Winckley, Edward. 2248, 2774
Wincoff, John Eugene Lee. 803
Wind, Edgar. 87
Wind, Gerhard Lewis. 624
Wind, Henry F. 2216
Windeatt, Mary Fabyan. 189, 1618, 1775, 1859, 1936, 2190, 2194, 2348, 2372, 2803, 3247, 3286, 3437, 3455, 3691, 3694, 3778
Windeatts Mary Fabyan. 749
Winder, Blanche. 624
Winder, Francis Joseph. 1572
Windham county association of Congregational ministers, Windham co., Conn. 1611, 3535
Windham, Joan. 2803, 3283, 3285
Windisch, Hans. 424, 1834
Windle, Bertram Coghill Alan. 757, 2755, 3080, 3122
Windsor Castle. St. George's Chapel. 3820
Wine, Joseph Floyd. 726
Wine, Sherwin T. 2141
Winebrenner, John. 1273
Winecoff, John Eugene Lee. 1711, 1805
Winehouse, Irwin. 92
Wines, Abijah. 3412
Wines, Enoch Cobb. 1377, 1737, 3218, 3600
Wines, Frederick Howard. 1907
Winfrey, L. S. 200
Winfrey L. S. 200
Wing, Conway Phelps. 739
Wing, R. L. 1470, 1879
Wingart, Norman Ambrose. 2405
Wingert, Norman Ambrose. 1362
Wingfield, Marshall. 1072, 1343
Wingo, Earl L. 2069
Wingo, Earle L. 2069
Wingo, Nancie. 897
Wingren, Gustaf. 659, 1383, 1384, 1386, 1919, 2281, 2325, 2718, 2907, 3650, 3657, 3659, 3820

Wingren, Gustaf Fredrick. 2325
Wingren, Gustaf [Fredrik]. 2907
Wink, Walter. 393, 643, 1170, 2128
Winkler, Gershon. 1744, 2137
Winkler, Ken. 1577, 3309
Winkler, Maria Lydia. 1454
Winkler, Martin. 1880, 1958
Winkley, Samuel Hobart. 1994, 3564
Winklhofer, Alois. 1529
Winkworth, Catherine. 1873, 1874, 3459
Winkworth, Douglas Eric. 1054
*Winn, Albert Curry. 3166
Winn, Albert Curry. 421, 2504, 3786
Winn, Arthur Harmon. 3724
Winn, Dick. 2157
Winn, Douglas. 1561
Winn, Laura Rocke. 911
Winn, Ralph Bubrich. 1584
Winn, Viola Schuldt. 3820
Winner, Anna Kennedy. 3688
Winner, William Lane. 1054
Winnett, Arthur Robert. 1471
Winnett, Frederick Victor. 564
Winninge, Ingrid. 2517
Winnington-Ingram, Arthur Foley. 67,
    503, 992, 1212, 1634, 1728, 3432, 3820
Winquist, Charles E. 3071
Winrod, Frances. 3579
Winrod, Gerald B. 1054
Winrod, Gerald Burton. 206, 609, 611,
    1054, 1072, 1955, 2278, 2803, 2882,
    3852
Winsbey, Herbert Andrew. 3816
Winsborough, Hallie (Paxson) 2488, 2928
Winship, Albert Edward. 3565
Winski, Norman. 2644
Winslow, Carolyn V. 2512
Winslow, Francis Joseph. 1471, 1588
Winslow, Harriet Wadsworth (Lathrop)
    2507
Winslow, Hubbard. 3650, 3713
Winslow, Octavius. 1454
Winslow, Ola Elizabeth. 1499, 1500,
    1507, 2687
Winslow, Raymond A. 1808
Winslow, Wentworth Byron. 1036
Winsor, Laura Ellen. 1698, 2730
Winsor, Wiley. 3872
Winston, Alexander Porter. 980
Winston, Alice. 57
Winston, Annie Steger. 3095
Winston, Carleton. 1459, 1854
Winston, Martin Bradley. 3005
*Winter, Bob R. 344
Winter, David Brian. 1003, 1433, 1698
Winter, Frank H[enry]. 2321
Winter, Gibson. 947, 1279, 3142, 3538,
    3568
Winter, Jerry Alan. 3087
Winter, John Garrett. 1804, 2667
Winter, Lovick Pierce. 2278
Winter, Michael. 3394, 3544
Winter, Michael M. 489, 1246, 2770,
    2825
Winter, Miriam Therese. 3004, 3857
Winter, Nathan H. 187, 2106
Winter, Paul. 2069, 917
Winter, Paul M. 828, 2187
Winter, Ralph D. 1064, 2515
Winter, Rebecca J. 1553, 3587
Winter, Roberta H. 3737
Winterbauer, Thomas Aquinas. 1474
Winterborn, Benjamin. 1003
Winterbotham, Rayner. 2066, 2176
Winterburn, Katherine. 3576
Wintermeyer, Herbert Herman Henry.
    3254
Winternitz, Moriz. 91, 3302
Winters, Roy Lutz. 2194
Winthrop, Edward. 609
Winthrop, James. 52, 609
Winton, George Beverly. 486
Wintz, Jack. 871
Winwar, Frances. 1938
Winward, Stephen F. 570, 2882, 3666,
    3854
Winzen, Damasus. 922
Wipper, Audrey. 1459
Wire, Edith. 2758
Wireker, Nigellus. 1762
Wireker, Nigellus, ca. 1130-ca. 2577
Wirgman, Augustus Theodore. 1772, 13,
    2863
Wirt, Loyal Lincoln. 3137
Wirt, Sherwood Eliot. 181, 368, 587, 720,
    990, 1755, 2866, 3014, 3203, 3230, 3232,
    3360, 3447, 3637, 3820
Wirt, Winola Wells. 1454
Wirth, Augustine. 2216
Wirth, Edmund John. 1752
Wirth, Louis. 2082, 2098
Wirth, William G. 1036
Wirth, William George. 2561
Wirthlin, Joseph Leopold. 2619
Wirz, Corbinian. 2254
Wisbey, Herbert Andrew. 3293, 3816
Wischnitzer, Rachel (Bernstein) 3577

Wisconsin Association of School
    Librarians. Audiovisual Cataloging
    Manual Committee. 2225
Wisconsin. University. University extension
    division. 3759
[Wisdom, William M.]. 3256
Wise, Aaron. 2120
Wise, Carroll A. 1374, 2378
Wise, Carroll Alonzo. 2782, 2787, 2995
Wise, Charles C. 339, 1985, 2033
Wise, Daniel. 718, 743, 980, 1975, 2422,
    2427, 3890
Wise, Gene H. 2505
Wise, George C. 3242
Wise, Isaac Mayer. 2014, 2090, 2092,
    2105, 2116, 2156, 2834, 3822
Wise, James Waterman. 2079, 2100, 2105,
    2116
Wise, Jennings Cropper. 3781
Wise, Jeremiah. 3360
Wise, John. 1338
Wise, Judah L. 172
Wise, Karen. 990, 3822
Wise, Robert L. 3535
Wise, Stephen Samuel. 2119, 3897, 3144
Wise, Thomas James. 1307
Wise, William. 2585
Wise, William Herman. 3346
[Wiseley, Francis Marion]. 1064
Wiseman, Adam John. 3065
Wiseman, Donald John. 209 206
Wiseman, Frederick Luke. 3802
Wiseman, George W. 3095
Wiseman, Nicholas Patrick Stephen. 842,
    865, 2851, 3077
Wiseman, Peter. 279
Wiser, Leslie S. 1561
Wiser, William Henricks. 2495
Wishard, S[amuel] E[llis]. 1701
Wishard, Samuel Ellis. 200, 2607, 1651
Wishart, Alfred Wesley. 3065, 3435, 2569,
    3080
Wishart, Charles Frederick. 460, 1072
Wishart, John Elliott. 2882
Wishlade, R. L. 3324
Wishnietsky, Dan H. 2145
Wisloff, Carl Johan Fredrik. 2256, 2281
Wisloff, Fredrick. 585
Wisloff, Fredrik. 1833, 3407
Wisloff, Hans Edvard. 17
Wismar, Adolph Louis. 1924, 2566
Wismar, Don Roy. 728
Wismer, Don. 1926, 2013
Wisner, Benjamin Blydenburg. 1856
Wisplinghoff, Erich. 3407
Wisse, Frederick. 431
Wissel, Joseph. 3031
Wissler, Clark. 3408
Wissmann, Erna E. 1325
Wissowa, Georg. 3246
Witcher, Walter Campbell. 67, 2053
Witcutt, William Purcell. 803
Wither, George. 579, 584, 1870, 2853
Witherington, Henry Carl. 3001
Withers, Ammon Barnes. 1004
Withers, Frances H. 806
Withers, Harlston Reed. 107
Witherspoon, John. 2914
Witherspoon, Thomas Dwight. 927, 2168
Witherspoon, Thomas E. 1625
Withington, Leonard. 594
Withrow, Pat B. 888
Withrow, William Henry. 745, 1182,
    2422, 2427, 745
Witkov, Harold. 52, 611, 1778
Witley L. V. H. 3519
Witmer, Safara Austin. 219, 1572
Witmore, Nyla. 3830
Witsell, William Postell. 1181, 1759, 2013,
    2882, 2970
Witsius, Herman. 1377
Witt, Elmer N. 3883
Witt, Karl. 2207
Witt, Lydia Workman. 537
Witt, Raymond H. 893
Witt, Reginald Eldred. 1921
Witte, Kaaren. 3830, 3890
Witte, Paul W. 861, 2955
Witte, Raymond Philip. 3254
Witten, Robert R. 2439
Wittenauer, Josephine Carole. 1799, 3273
Witter, Evelyn. 2121, 2763
Wittgenstein, Ludwig. 1652, 2654
Witthaus, Hazel. 627
Witting, Alisoun. 2663
Wittke, Carl Frederick. 2669
Wittkofski, Joseph Nicholas. 980, 2784
Wittkower, Rudolf. 1160
Wittman, E. C. 318
Witty, Claud Francis. 610
Witty, Robert Gee. 1833, 3783
Witzenmann, Herbert. 51
Wiznitzer, Arnold. 3027
Wlodyga, Ronald R. 1078
Wobbermin, Georg. 3106, 3308
Woburn, Mass. First Congregational
    church. 1337

Wobus, Paul A. 1550
Wodehouse, Ernest Armine. 3142
Wodehouse, Helen. 3027, 3548, 3106
Woelfel, B LaSalle. 1151
Woelfel, James W. 677, 1106
Woelfkin, Cornelius. 1072, 3065, 3463
Woelfl, Genevieve. 2992
Woellner, Fredric Philip. 3337
Woertendyke, James H. 2561
Wofford College, Spartanburg, S.C.
    Library. 1871
Wogaman, J. Philip. 946, 2440, 3193
Wogen, Norris L. 2815, 3831
Wohlfeil, John Carl. 917
Wohlgemuth, Paul W. 1204
Wohlstein, Herman. 55
Wojcik, Stanley L. 3474
Wojniak, Edward J. 2400
Wokrman, Herbert Brook. 3861
Wolber, David A. 9
Wolcott, Carolyn Muller. 1734, 1996,
    2886, 2983
Wolcott, Leonard T. 365, 1015, 3122
Wold, Erling. 3831
Wold, Joseph Conrad. 2538
Wold, Margaret. 3845
Wold, Marge. 990, 2347, 3845
Wolf, Arnold Jacob. 2080, 2143, 2322
Wolf, Barbara. 3666
Wolf, Betty Hartman. 2131
Wolf, Carl George. 2302
Wolf, Donald J. 1142, 3618
Wolf, Edmund Jacob. 393, 2282, 2293
Wolf, Edwin. 2101
[Wolf, Frederick Ellsworth] 1883. 1252
Wolf, Herbert. 529
Wolf, Herbert C. 2009, 2171
Wolf, Luther Benaiah. 2296
*Wolf, Richard. 2291
Wolf, Richard C. 2291, 2293
Wolf, William J. 44, 107, 861, 1109, 1740,
    1844, 2230
Wolfard, Nathan Dordwin. 3617
Wolfe, Betty. 1240
Wolfe, David L. 2181
Wolfe, Don Marion. 2470
Wolfe, Jack Seymour. 2100
Wolfe, John Marcus. 762, 866
Wolfe, Mary Catherine. 2398
Wolfe, Napoleon Bonaparte. 3519
Wolfe, Paul Austin. 3004
[Wolfe, Percy C.]. 319
Wolfe, Rinna. 2126, 2861
Wolfe, Rolland Emerson. 485, 2951
Wolfenbuttel. Herzog-August-Bibliothek.
    2634
Wolfenbuttel, Herzog-August-bibliothek,
    Mss. (677(Helmst. 628). 2634
Wolfenbuttel Herzog-August-Bibliothek.
    Mass. (Aug. 11.2) 367
Wolfenstein, E. Victor. 669, 2233
Wolferstan, Bertram. 2512
Wolff, Bernard. 3422
Wolff, Christian M. 304
Wolff, Hans Walter. 35, 503, 538, 541,
    552, 558, 2326
Wolff, Joseph. 675, 2502, 3532
Wolff, Mizanna. 2696
Wolff, Otto. 2753
Wolff, Pierre. 1003
Wolff, Richard. 425, 413, 425, 529, 953,
    1417, 2245
Wolff, Robert Paul. 2163
Wolff, Werner. 1383
Wolfgang, Ralph T. 2966
Wolfram, Gertrude (Metlen) 2848
Wolfson, Abraham. 3472
Wolfson, Harry Austryn. 2837, 2831,
    2837, 3658, 1927, 2831, 3108
Wolhorn, Herman. 1636, 2696
Wolk, Daniel S. 3400
[Wolkenfeld, Aaron] 1910. 3142
Wolkovich-Valkavicius, William Lawrence,
    1929. 1294, 3891
Wollaston, John Ramsden. 3137
Wollaston, William. 1537, 2675
Wolleh, Lothar. 3773
Wollman-Tsamir, Pinchas. 2094
Wollstein, Dewey H. 1663
Wolman, Judith. 1620
Wolpert, Leo. 1843
Wolseley, Charles. 279
Wolseley, Roland Edgar. 2135, 3002,
    3203
Wolsey, Louis. 3372
Wols-Schon, Greta. 1728
Wolter, Allan Bernard. 1646
Wolter, Marius. 2571
Wolter, Martin. 1648
Wolterstorff, Nicholas. 186, 1089
Wolthuis, Enno. 3083
Wolverton, Robert E. 2658
Womach, Merrill. 3831
Womack, David A. 202, 992, 1171, 1572,
    2814
Womack, Don L. 1561

Woman's Christian Temperance Union.
    3598
Woman's Christian temperance union,
    New York. 3833
Women, Parley Paul. 2056, 3065, 3346
Women's correspondence Bible class,
    Oakland, Cal. 3845
Wong, Richard. 2896
*Wood, A. Skevington. 3483
Wood, Alfred Harold. 2458
Wood, Allen Tate. 3846
Wood, Allen W. 2164, 3106
[Wood, Annie E. 2410
Wood, Arthur Skevington. 240, 241, 472,
    609, 1181, 1572, 2281, 2907, 3806
Wood, Barry. 67, 2674
Wood, Bertha Vivian. 994
Wood, Britton. 1256
Wood, Charles. 1017
Wood, Charles James. 3653
Wood, Charles Monroe. 288
Wood, Charles T. 677, 1638
Wood, Charles Travers. 1698
Wood, Chester. 980, 1729
Wood, Christine. 2855, 3846
Wood, Clarence Ashton. 643
Wood, Clarence E. 2540
Wood, Clement. 483, 1910, 2090, 2122,
    3704
Wood, E[zra] M[organ]. 665, 1596, 3314,
    3475
Wood, Edward Cope. 1891, 3519
Wood, Ella N. 314, 669, 880
Wood, Ella Nancy. 643, 880, 2720
Wood, Ernest. 109, 1615, 1918, 3688,
    109, 3775, 3866, 3895, 3301, 3689, 3775,
    3866, 3867
Wood, Eugene Halsey. 3065
Wood, Francis Lloyd Ferguson. 2936
Wood, Frank Louis. 1072, 2250
Wood, Fred M. 216, 381, 547, 560, 646,
    994, 1943
Wood, Frederic C. 3394, 3626
Wood, Frederic Herbert. 3519
Wood, Frederick Ponsonby. 3600
Wood, George. 1676
Wood, George O. 181
Wood, Henry. 238
Wood, Henry Alonzo. 610
Wood, Henry Wellington. 1572
Wood, Herbert George. 67, 1067, 1072,
    1282, 1717, 1764, 2009, 3193, 1282,
    3193, 3213
Wood, Horace G. 2758
Wood, Irving Francis. 483, 643, 1833,
    211, 238, 643, 3160
Wood, J[ohn] A[llen]. 3203
Wood, James. 246, 1290, 1752
Wood, James Edward. 1142, 1151, 2671,
    2916
Wood, James Playsted. 1500
Wood, Jean H. 598
Wood, Jeremiah. 1693, 3862
Wood, John Allen. 1824
Wood, John George. 481
Wood, John Goerge. 481
Wood, John Sumner. 1077, 2128
Wood, Joseph. 307
Wood, Joshua Gibson. 1036
Wood, June Smallwood. 2398
Wood, Katharine Marie, 1910. 43, 75,
    902, 1575, 2825
Wood, Kenneth H. 1436
Wood, Laurence W. 1587
*Wood, Leland Foster. 3675
Wood, Leon J. 495
Wood, Leon James. 503, 507, 522, 536,
    555, 569, 1507, 1834, 2093, 2951, 3321
Wood, Letitia W. 3857
Wood, Louis Aubrey. 54, 2472
Wood, Lynn H. 2248
Wood, Lynn Harper. 1443
Wood, M. D. 2532
Wood, Mary S. 1676
Wood, Mattie Pegues. 2586
Wood, Miriam. 1303, 1574, 1800, 2130,
    2487, 2542, 2707, 2820, 3386, 3387,
    3388, 3846, 3881
Wood, Nathan Eusebius. 152, 684
Wood, Nathan Robinson. 1097, 1371,
    1729, 3412
Wood, Nathaniel Milton. 169
Wood, Presnall H. 141, 144
Wood, R. H. 3026
Wood River, Ill. First Baptist church. 143
Wood, Robert. 949, 1042, 2537
Wood, Robert E. 699
Wood, Ross. 1515
Wood, S. R. 1984
Wood, Samuel. 3702
Wood, Samuel Hamill. 200
Wood, Susan. 2569
Wood, Thomas. 1383, 3890
Wood, Violet. 655
Wood, Wilford C. 2607, 3429
[Wood, William] 1770-1841. 61
Wood, William Carleton. 3145

Wood, William Hamilton. 3074
Wood, William. (of Lexington) 52, 2053
Wood, William W. 2814
Woodall, Elizabeth Grey. 1362
Woodall, William Live. 902
Woodall, William Love. 739, 902
Woodard, Arvle. 2484
*Woodard, Carol J. 939
Woodbridge, Charles Jahleel. 330, 3012
Woodbridge, Frederick James Eugene. 2420
Woodbridge, Jahleel Ligon. 1377
Woodbridge, John D. 240, 1553, 3243, 3680
Woodbridge, Warren Samuel. 980
Woodburne, Angus Stewart. 3001, 3074
Woodbury, Helen. 1353
Woodbury, W. H. 1707
Woodcock, Brian Lindsay. 1488
[Woodcock, Catherine Mary Antony]. 2850
Woodcock, George. 1482
Woodcock, Irene G. 2962
Woodcock, Percival George. 2659
Woodcox, Benjamin Franklin. 3474, 3483
Wooden, Kenneth. 897, 2817
Woodfield, Andrew. 3594
Woodfin, Yandall. 2837
Woodforde, James. 1292, 2755, 3846
Woodgate, Mildred Violet. 1323, 1650, 2203, 2778, 3377, 3779
Woodhall, Ralph. 1893
Woodhouse, Arthur Sutherland Pigott. 2470
Woodhouse, Frederick Charles. 2463
Woodhull, George H. 3347
Woodhull, Will Scranton. 2109
Wooding, Dan. 35, 2821
Wood-Legh, Kathleen Louise. 883, 1759
Woodlock, Francis. 757, 1748, 2561
Woodlock, Thomas Francis. 797
Woodman, Charles M. 1683
Woodman, Charles Mellen. 1676, 2048
Woodman, J. M. 206, 3226
Woodman, Jabez C. 1484, 3519
Woodrew, Greta. 2992
Woodroffe, John George. 3400, 3867
Woodroffe, Sir John George. 3866
Woodrow, James. 1399, 3077, 3137
Woodrow, Ralph. 319, 609, 656
[Woodruff, Albert]. 3559
Woodruff, C. Roy. 1253
Woodruff, Douglas. 1143
Woodruff, Helen. 2942
Woodruff, Hezekiah. 3296
Woodruff, Julia Louisa Matilda (Curtiss) 1698
Woodruff, Leola. 1366, 3846
Woodruff, Wilford. 2614
Woods, B. W. 3541
Woods, Bobby W. 2808
Woods, C. Stacey. 990, 1911
Woods, Clyde M. 498, 522
Woods, Dalton J. 1139
Woods, David F. 1602
Woods, Edward Sydney. 980, 1065, 3196
Woods, Francis Frederick. 775
Woods, Francis Henry. 1596
Woods, Frank Theodore. 1214, 3675
[Woods, Franklin] 1827. 292
Woods, George Frederick. 946
Woods, Grace Winona (Kemp) 3229, 3852
[Woods, Grace Winona (Kemp) "Henry M. Woods"] 1871. 3229, 3852
Woods, Guy N. 137, 1272, 1770, 3670
Woods, Henry. 115, 793, 1581
Woods, Henry McKee. 803, 3852
Woods, Henry, Presbyterian Minister. 2925
Woods, James Haughton. 3065, 3111
Woods, James L. 726, 2913, 2917
Woods, John. 3397
Woods, John Franklin. 2847
Woods, John Purvis. 3321
*Woods, Leon P. 1833
Woods, Leonard. 40, 306, 882, 1334, 1906, 2689, 2818, 2966, 3412, 3729, 3795
Woods, Margaret. 3137, 3144
Woods, Matthew. 2804
Woods, Patrick. 1181
Woods, Ralph Louis. 210, 869, 1479, 1957, 3014, 3111, 3208, 3405, 3637
Woods, Richard. 1078, 1843, 2641
Woods, Sheila D. 3859
Woods, Thomas Edward Peck. 216, 515, 593, 646, 3051
Woods, William Colcord. 1893
Woods, William Howard. 1428, 3825
Woodsmall. 3852
Woodson, Carter Godwin. 2682
Woodson, Carter Goodwin. 2682
Woodson, Hortense. 2129
Woodson, Leslie H. 522, 609, 652, 1042, 1471, 1572, 1802, 1837, 2018
Woodson, Meg. 1398, 3847

Woodson, Sue Terry. 2536
Woodstock College of Baltimore County, Md. 3847
Woodward, Clifford Salisbury. 980, 1955
Woodward, David B. 1544, 1651
Woodward, Eugene A. 304
Woodward, George William Otway. 2579, 2584
Woodward, H. G. 3387
Woodward, Hugh McCurdy. 3122
Woodward, Ian. 1428
Woodward, James D. 916
Woodward, John J. 48
Woodward, Luther Ellis. 3001
Woodward, Mary Ann. 2165
Woodward, Thomas B. 990
Woodward, Walter Carleton. 2708
Woodward, William W. 3229
[Woodward, William Wallis]. 3233
Woodworth, Hugh M. 3892
Woodworth, Maria Beulah. 1554
Woodworth, Ralph. 1280, 2736
Woodworth, Reginald O. 3559
Woodworth, Robert Bell. 2927, 3820
Woodworth, Ruth A. 3847
Woodworth, Samuel. 30, 3459
[Woodworth, William Norman]. 1407, 1730
Woody, Robert Henley. 2943
Woody, Thomas. 1687, 1683
Woodyard, David O. 67, 990, 1065, 1733, 1845
Woolam, John. 1676
Woolcock, E. C. Rundle. 238
Woolever, Harry Earl. 2442
Woolf, Mildred E. 2270
Woollard, A. G. B. 1088
[Woollard, Edwin Johnston] 1867. 464
Woollen, C J. 1712, 2020
Woolley, Charles Leonard. 5, 3761
Woolley, Davis C. 158, 1184, 3193
Woolley, John G[ranville]. 980
Woolley, John Granville. 1282, 3596
Woolley, Milton. 238, 2019
Woolley, Reginald Maxwell. 1541, 2238, 1851
Woolman, John. 1679, 1778, 3296, 3424, 3847
Woolsey, Elijah. 1307
Woolsey, John Martin. 2654, 2711
Woolsey, Raymond H. 609, 1436, 1572, 1833, 2340, 3022
[Woolsey, Sarah Chauncey] 1835-1905. 1357
Woolsey, Theodore Dwight. 3065
Woolston, Clarence Herbert. 643, 2720, 3160
Woolston, Thomas. 2018
Woolton, John. 980, 992
Woolworth, Laura (Fowler) 1636, 2453
Worboys, James Samuel Alphaeus. 169
Worcerter, Elwood. 2410
Worcester, Benjamin. 3571
Worcester, Dean Conant. 1540
Worcester, Elwood. 1956, 2410, 2974, 524, 1055, 2410, 3065, 3781
Worcester, Eng. (Diocese) Bishop, 1308-1313 (Walter Reynolds) 3783
Worcester, Henry Aiken. 2250
Worcester, John. 443, 524, 1370
Worcester, John H. 2241
Worcester, Mass. First church. Ecclesiastical council. 1820. 1748
Worcester, Noah. 2002, 3412, 3713, 3714, 3729
Worcester, Samuel. 882, 1343, 1870, 3729
Worcester, Samuel Austin. 891, 1862
[Worcester, Samuel Austin] 1799-1859. 1862
Worcester, Samuel Melanchthon. 3286, 3848
Worcester, William Loring. 2006
Worden, Hazel Irene. 509
Worden, Ian P. 2744, 3574
Worden, James Avery. 3160
Worden, Oliver Norton. 159
Worden, Thomas. 579
Wordley, Dick. 2717, 2865
Wordsworth, Christopher. 803, 1211
Wordsworth, Ephraim Edward. 588, 3295
Wordsworth, John. 1129, 3848, 1165, 3569, 3848
Wordsworth, William. 2857, 3210
Worgul, George S. 3266
Work, Edgar Whitaker. 238, 980, 1572, 1632
Work, John Wesley. 2680
*Workman, Edgar John. 238
Workman, George Coulson. 3028, 3347, 1956
Workman, Herbert B. 2576
Workman, Herbert Brook. 2820, 1186, 2425, 2821, 3038, 3212, 3861
Workman, Katherine A. 1897
Workman, William Hay. 2925

Workshop for Baptists on Deafness and Rehabilitation, University of Tennessee, 1965. 1257
Workshop in Pastoral Counseling, University of Florida, 1959. 2782
Workshop on Catholic College Integration, Catholic University of America, 1949. 88
Workshop on Discipline and Integration in the Catholic College, Catholic University of America, 1950. 2409
Workshop on Home, Church, and School Relations in the Religious Education of Children and Youth, University of Chicago, 1954. 3162
Workshop on Our Lady in Education, University of Dayton, 1958. 2357
Workshop on Pastoral Problems and Clinical Understanding, Gearhart, Or., 1959. 2784
Workshop on the Administration of the Catholic Secondary School, CatholicUniversity of America, 1947. 832
Workshop on the Christian Education of Adults, University of Pittsburgh, 1958. 3169
Workshop on the Curriculum of Christian Education for Adults, University of Pittsburgh, 1961. 3169
Workshop on the Philosophy of Catholic Higher Education, Catholic University of America, 1947. 832
Workshop on Vatican Council II: its Challenge to Education, Catholic University of America, 1966. 806
World conference on Christian fundamentals, Philadelphia, 1919. 1054
World conference on church, community and state, Oxford, 1937. 1142, 1143
World conference on faith and order. 1042
World conference on faith and order. 2d, Edinburgh, 1937. 927, 1044, 1443
World conference on faith and order. 2d, Edinburgh, 1937. Commission on the church's unity in life and worship. 1044, 1318
World conference on faith and order. 2d, Edinburgh, 1937. Commission on the ministry and sacraments. 1044
World Conference on Faith and Order. 4th, Montreal, 1963. 1044
World conference on faith and order. Continuation committee. 1045, 1125, 1249, 3849
World conference on faith and order, Lausanne, 1927. 1045
World conference on faith and order. Preliminary meeting, Geneva, 1920. 1045
World Congress of the Lay Apostolate. 2d. Rome, 1957. 754
World Congress on Evangelism, Berlin, 1966. 1573
World Council of Christian Education and Sunday School Association. 1383
World Council of Christian Education and Sunday School Association. North American Administrative Committee. 2627
World Council of Chuches. 1st Assembly, Amsterdam, 1948. 3850
World Council of Churches. 279, 1133, 1433, 3850
World Council of Churches. 2d Assembly, Evanston, Ill., 1954. 1125, 3850
World Council of Churches. 3d Assembly, Delhi, 1961. 1492
World Council of Churches. 3rd Assembly,Dehli, 1961. 3850
World Council of Churches. Commission on Faith and Order. 1042, 1125
World Council of Churches. Commission on Faith and Order. Commission on Ways of Worship. 3854
World Council of Churches. Commission on Faith and Order Study Commission on Institutionalism. 1911
World Council of Churches. Commission on Faith and Order. Theological Commission on Intercommunion. 1912
World Council of Churches. Commission on Faith and Order. Theological Commission on the Church. 1125
World Council of Churches. Commission on Faith and Order. Theological Commission on Worship. North American Section. 3855
World Council of Churches. 1st Assembly, Amsterdam. 1948. 1045
World Council of Churches. Library. 1043
World Council of Churches. Advisory Commission on the Main Theme of the Second Assembly. 3850
World Evaluation Conference on Christian Education, Geneva, 1969. 3162

World Federation of YMHA's and Jewish Community Centers. Council. 3872
World fellowship of faiths. International congress. 1st, Chicago and New York, 1933-1934. 3138
World Jewish Congress. 3851
World Jewish congress. Economic bureau. 2100
World Methodist Council. 2422
World Methodist Council Consultation on Evangelism, Jerusalem, 1974. 1573
World missionary conference, Edinburgh, 1910. 2495
World missionary conference, Edinburgh, 1910. Continuation committee. 2502
World order magazine. 125, 129
World Young Women's Christian Association. 643
World's Christian citizenship conference. 2d, Portland, Or., 1913. 3347
World's Columbian Catholic Congress, Chicago, 1893. 1137, 3852
World's Parliament of Religions, Chicago, 1893. 2143, 3122
World's religious parliament extension. 3122
World's student Christian federation. 3190
World's Sunday-school convention. 10th, Los Angeles, 1928. 3560
World's Sunday-school convention. 11th, Rio de Janeiro, 1932. 3560
World's Sunday-school convention. 12th, Oslo, 1936. 3560
World's Sunday-school convention, 4th, Jerusalem, 1904. Central committee. 2763
World's Sunday-school convention. 5th, Rome, 1907. 3559
World's Sunday-school convention. 7th, Zurich, 1913. 3559
World's Sunday-school convention. 8th, Tokyo, 1920. 3560
World's woman's Christian temperance union. 3598
World's Young women's Christian association. 3447
Worley, Robert C. 1125, 2909
Worley, Win. 1423
Worlledge, Arthur John. 2882
Worlton, Lois F. 2264
Worm, Piet. 627, 630, 631
Worman, Alwin Emmanuel. 3050
Worman, Eugene Clark. 3872, 3874
*Worman, Theresa. 2491
Worman, Theresa. 2491
Wormley, Augustina Elizabeth. 1929
Worob, Avraham. 699, 2143
Worrall, Benjamin A. 1601, 2202, 2992
Worrall, Arthur J. 1687
Worrell, Edward K. 1247
Worrell, George E. 3830
Worrell, William Hoyt. 315, 1700, 2330
Worsley, Peter. 2400
Worth, Grant A. 2882
[Worth, Horace]. 1289
Worthington, Anne. 3253
Worthington, Edward William. 2884, 1454, 2258
Worthington, Marjorie (Muir) 1
Worthley, Harold Field. 1337
Wortman, Arthur. 899, 2882
Worton, Stanley N. 3195
*Wossilek, Joseph. 313
Wotherspoon, H. J. 1289
Wotherspoon, Henry Johnstone. 1234, 1368, 2884
Woudstra, Marten H. 81, 553
Wouk, Herman. 2140
*Woychuck, N. A. 3295
Woychuk, N A. 322, 326, 345
Woywod, Stanislaus. 775, 735, 775
Woznicki, Andrew N. 2126, 2322
Wrather, Eva Jean. 732
Wray, Angelina W. 3559
Wray, Elizabeth. 1937, 2631
Wray, Newton. 238, 550
Wray, Winifride. 1498
Wrede, William. 406, 436, 2017, 2803
Wren, Christopher. 79, 2243, 2244, 2589
Wren, H. 462
Wren society, London. 2244, 3860
Wren, Thomas E. 1537
[Wrenn, E. E.]. 1578
Wrenn, Lawrence G. 2344
Wright, Abiel Holmes. 3347
Wright, Addison G. 2462
[Wright, Alfred] 1788-1853. 915, 1862
Wright, Alfred Askin. 3519
Wright, Alfred Augustus. 1771
Wright, Anthony David. 682, 1374
Wright, Arthur F. 705, 1331
[Wright, Asher] 1803-1875. 3332, 3333
Wright, Barton. 2165
Wright, Bernard Arker. 2471
Wright, Brooks. 84, 704
Wright, Bruce S. 1443, 1602, 1737, 3203

Wright, Bruce Simpson. 895, 980, 1054; 1836, 2210, 3360
Wright, Carter. 3530
Wright, Charles Henry Hamilton. 286, 541, 643, 803, 3639
Wright, Charles James. 2477
Wright, Conrad. 3725, 3729, 3730, 3748
Wright, Cuthbert. 810
Wright, D. B. 464
Wright, David. 3533
Wright, David Sands. 643
Wright, Elbert Joseph. 141
Wright, Emily Dudley. 2050
Wright, Eula Lena (Ryan) 238
Wright, Frank C. 174
Wright, Frank Lloyd. 3860
Wright, Georg Henrik von. 1746
Wright, George E. 2992
Wright, George Ernest. 23, 209, 283, 313, 503, 599, 652, 1731, 2678
Wright, George Frederick. 61, 206, 1626, 2943, 3077
Wright, H. Elliott. 927, 2160
Wright, H. Norman. 938, 1512, 1611, 2340
Wright, Harry B. 3825
Wright, Henry Burt. 1741, 3698
Wright, Henry Clarke. 238, 1729, 2228, 2631
Wright, Henry Wilkes. 1596, 3106
Wright, Howard Foster. 1793
Wright, J. Clegg. 3519
Wright, James Elwin. 1572, 1620, 1690
Wright, James Frederick Church. 1482
Wright, James Roy. 3166
Wright, John. 28, 213, 2884, 3264
Wright, John F. 3013
Wright, John H. 2882
Wright, John Joseph. 762, 1143, 2058, 2059, 3029, 3360
Wright, John, (of Washington) 3424
Wright, John Stafford. 216, 556, 2325
Wright, John W. 1976
Wright, Joseph. 1749
Wright, Julia (MacNair) 216, 217, 1759, 1899, 2926, 3110
Wright, Kathryn S. 2633, 3160
Wright, Larry. 3590, 3594
Wright, Lawrence. 1561, 3360
Wright, Leoline L. 1415, 3055
Wright, Linda Raney. 1611
Wright, Louis Booker. 2485, 2505, 2543
Wright, Louis Clinton. 3890
Wright, Luella Margaret. 1676
Wright, Marcenus R. K. 3519
Wright, Marcenus Rodolphus Kilpatrick. 1330, 2838, 3519
Wright, Marcia. 2552
Wright, Martha J. 1656
Wright, Mary Emily. 3467
Wright, Melton. 3137
Wright, Michael. 990
Wright, Naomi Taylor. 643, 1259
Wright, Nathan. 2253
Wright, Otis Olney. 1378
Wright, Paul. 72, 927, 1975, 1978
Wright, Paul S. 1503, 2915
Wright, Ralph B. 834
Wright, Ralph Justus. 3137
Wright, Richard Robert. 14, 2451
Wright, Richard Roberts. 2066
Wright, Richardson Little. 339, 1443, 2212
Wright, Robert Joseph. 3666
Wright, Robert Roy. 1195, 2398
Wright, Robert William. 1383
Wright, Ronald Selby. 866, 1054, 1234, 1235, 3367, 3456
Wright, Ruth V. 318
Wright, Samuel. 3051
Wright, Sara Margaret. 297
Wright, Theodore Francis. 516, 3106
Wright, Thomas. 928, 1510, 2313, 2818
Wright, Walter, Coleman. 364, 404, 3271
Wright, Walter Page. 1702
Wright, William Arter, 1857. 107
Wright, William Burnet. 2803, 1343, 3337
Wright, William Clarence. 910
Wright, William James Payling. 1402
Wright, William Kelley. 3106
Wright, Worthington. 3483
Wrighton, William Hazer. 1752, 2000, 2266, 3030, 3292
Wrightson, Keith. 3604
Wrigley, Louise Scott. 624, 1015, 1326, 3844, 3845
Writers' program, Arizona. 3298
Writers' program, Illinois. 893
Writers' program, Texas. 117
Wroblewski, Sergius. 676, 1003, 1644, 1646, 1648, 2210, 3244, 3490
Wrong, Margaret. 2498
Wroughton, Oliver Loraine. 2730
Wu, Chao-Kwang. 2512
Wu, Ching-hsiung. 1081, 1365, 2266
Wuellner, Bernard. 1113, 2006, 2228, 3309

Wuellner, Flora Slosson. 2882, 3483
Wuellner, Wilhelm H. 1628
Wuenschel, Edward A. 1827
Wuerl, Donald W. 773, 1021, 1616, 2938
Wuest, John Berchmanns. 2261
Wuest, Joseph. 841, 2240, 841
Wuest, Kenneth Samuel. 325, 340, 364, 381, 404, 425, 446, 449, 469, 1768, 3321
Wulf, Maurice Marie Charles Joseph de. 2843, 3694, 2843, 3309, 3696
Wulff, Robert M. 2553
Wunder, Clinton. 3463
Wunderli, Richard M. 1488
Wunderlich, Friedrich. 2430
Wunderlich, Lorenz. 1833
Wunsch, William Frederic. 2689, 3571
Wuppermann, Carlos. 1596
Wurm, Alois. 3767
Wurm, Shalom. 3897
Wurmbrand, Richard. 1073, 1320, 1433, 2556, 2821
Wurmbrand, Sabina. 2821
Wurthwein, Ernst. 505
Wurzer, Joseph Clement. 68
Wust, Klaus German. 1491, 3260
Wust, Louis. 2348, 2349
Wuthnow, Robert. 3747
Wyand, Fred B. 1065
Wyatt, Clair L. 1231, 3323
Wyatt, Edward Gerald Penfold. 1541
Wyatt, Mary Moore. 1736
Wyatt, Thomas. 219, 625
Wyatt, William. 2426
Wyatt, William W. 298
Wyburn, Susie May (Patterson) 2305, 2699
Wyche, Charles David. 3080
Wyche, Cyril. 238
Wyckoff, Albert Clarke. 1036, 1108
Wyckoff, Capwell. 2501
Wyckoff, D. Campbell. 1087, 2551, 3160, 3163
Wyckoff, William Henry. 655, 1803
Wycliffe, John. 1729, 2739, 3636, 3861
Wycoff, Mary Elizabeth. 3890
Wycott, Sara Jean (Clark) 3137
Wyeth, John. 1204
Wyeth, Walter N. 2158
Wygal, Winnifred. 980, 3878, 3092, 3878
Wykeham-George, Kenneth. 1936
Wyker, Bertha Park. 2488, 3861
Wyker, Mossie Allman. 3837
[Wyl, W.]. 2607, 3430
Wyland, Fred Bloom. 1065
Wylie, James Aitken. 3789
Wylie, James Hamilton. 1354, 1857
Wylie, Macleod. 2506
Wylie, Richard Cameron. 2056, 3548
Wylie, Samuel Brown. 1377
Wylie, Samuel J. 1042, 1067, 3264
Wylie, William P. 2340
Wyllys, Rufus Kay. 2177
Wyman, Albert Lincoln. 2561
Wyman, Charles A. 2896
Wyman, Edwin Allen. 3292
Wyman, Leland Clifton. 2677, 2678
[Wymetal, Wilhelm von. 2607, 3430
Wynants, Miche. 2711
Wyngaarden, Martin J. 609
Wyngarden, Martin Jacob. 609
Wynhoven, Peter Mathias Hubertius. 1299
Wynhoven, Peter Mathias Hubertius. 771, 869
Wynkoop, Elizabeth W. 3292
Wynkoop, Mildred Bangs. 83, 3806
Wynn, Daniel Webster. 1072, 2438, 2954, 3360
Wynn, John Charles. 2347, 2787, 936, 2782
Wynne, John Joseph. 1948
Wynne-Edwards, Grace. 571
Wynne-Tyson, Esme. 1891
Wynne-Tyson, Esme, 1898. 2560
Wyon, Olive. 2882, 980, 2033, 2253, 2583, 2882, 3491
Wyrick, Herbert McNultie. 3323
Wyrick, Neil. 1454
Wyrtzen, Jack. 1362, 3389, 3394, 3830
Wyschogrod, Edith. 1415
Wyschogrod, Michael. 2171, 2739
Wysham, William Norris. 1103
Wyszynski, Stefan. 866
Wythe, Joseph Henry. 2444, 3077, 2048

X

Xaverian brothers. American province. 832
Xavier. 1423, 3691
Xavier alumni sodality. 841, 3861
Xavier, Francisco Candido. 120

Y

Yacovsky, F. Jacob. 611
Yadin, Yigael. 1411, 1792
Yager, Thomas C. 3122
Yaggy, Levi W. 602, 1958
Yahuda, Abraham Shalom. 565
Yahuda, Joseph. 2074, 2107
Yajnavalkya. 1812
Yale, Alfred W. 375, 2803
Yale, Cyrus. 1781, 3231
Yale, John. 3775
Yale university. 1483, 1870, 1911, 3862
Yale university. Catholic club. 869
Yale university. Divinity school. 3626
Yale university. Divinity school. Day missions library. 2522
Yale university. Graduate school. 1469
Yale university. Library. 272, 748, 1344
Yamada, Koun. 1853, 2182
Yamagami, Sogen. 711
Yamaguchi, Susumu. 2317
Yamamori, Tetsunao. 1171, 2954
Yamamoto, J. Isamu. 708, 3329
Yamamoto, Kosho. 3403
Yamaoka, Haruo. 1634
Yamauchi, Edwin M. 209, 335, 408, 515, 919, 1892, 2148, 2327, 1718 *206*
Yancey, Philip. 991, 2342, 3541
Yandell, Keith E. 3106, 3108
Yang, Ch'ing-k'un. 914
Yang, Samuel. 1879
Yang, Yung-ch'ing. 914
Yang, Yung-ch'ing. 914
Yannai. 2109
Yanoff, Morris. 1914, 2187
Yarbo, Chelsa Quinn. 3474
Yarbro, Chelsea Quinn. 3474
Yarbrough, Caesar Augustus. 3244
Yarbrough, Robert Clyde. 980
Yarden, Leon. 2408
Yardley, Thomas Henry. 2022
Yarker, John. 1665
Yarmolinsky, Avrahm. 2103
Yarn, David H. 2608, 2614
Yarnes, Thomas D. 2460
Yarnes, Thomas David. 2432
Yarnold, Edward. 3414
Yarnold, Greville Dennis. 2053, 2054, 2253, 3080
Yaron, Reuven. 2074
Yarrington, Roger. 951, 3215
Yarrow, Phillip. 3742
Yarrow, William H. 3523
Yarwood, A. T. 2347, 2485
Yashar, Sefer ha. 564
Yates, David O. 611, 2823
Yates, Elizabeth. 898, 1353, 1443
Yates, Elizabeth McGreal. 898, 2896
Yates, Frances Amelia. 698, 2732, 3251
Yates, Freeman. 3754
Yates, Graem. 1873
Yates, James. 3724, 3795
Yates, John Clyde. 1572
Yates, Kyle M. 486
Yates, Kyle Monroe. 169, 299, 422, 494, 570, 586, 1797
Yates, Miles Lowell. 2259, 90, 1454
Yates, Otis Webster. 325
Yates, Walter L. 2938
Yatman, Charles Henry. 1572
Yavis, Constantine George. 28
Yaxley, Grace. 3879, 3890
Ydur, Rudy. 609
Ye-ses-mtsho-rgyal, 8th cent. 2194, 2756
Yeager, Randolph O. 345, 1768
Yeakel, Mary Agnes. 1403
Yeaple, Whitney Starr Kunz. 169
Year. 3140, 3141
Yearley, Lee H. 2705
Yeater, Samuel Horatio. 3074
Yeaxlee, Basil Alfred. 3001, 3160
Yee, Min S. 2203, 2817
Yeh, Theodore T. Y. 912
Yeiser, John Green. 3347
Yeiser, John Otho. 1892
Yeiser, Noah Emanual. 1816
Yellin, David. 2623
Yellowlees, David. 3001
Yelverton, Eric Esskildsen. 3037
Yelvington, Jesse Leonard. 425
Yelvington, Ramsey. 3145
Yeo, Margaret. 739, 1649, 1650
Yeo, Margaret (Routledge) 1310, 1649, 1650
Yeomans, Lilian Barbara. 1454

Yereance, Robert A. 319, 2322
Yerkes, James. 2010
Yerty, Oscar L. 1602
Yerushalmi, Yosef Hayim. 2110
Yeshiva Synagogue Council. 3576
Yesudian, Selva Raja. 3866
Yinger, John Milton. 3065, 3087

Yingling, Emma Katherine, 1888. 3519
Ylvisaker, Carl B. 340
Ylvisaker, Nils Martin. 107, 2031, 3295, 3456, 3666, 3890
Yochum, Harold Leland. 1329
Yoder, Edward. 2405, 2807
Yoder, Gideon G. 1254
Yoder, Glee. 904, 1385, 3807
Yoder, James D. 316
Yoder, John Howard. 176, 1152, 2046, 3433, 3630, 3794
Yoder, John Oscar. 2014
Yoder, Joseph Warren. 2405, 2406, 2407, 3863
Yoder, Perry B. 643
Yoder, Sanford Calvin. 570, 1799, 2406
Yoder, Thomas. 1393
Yoga-vasishtha-ramayana. Selections. English. 3866
Yogananda. 3065, 3866, 3137, 3330, 3137, 3866
Yogananda, Paramahansa. 2948, 3331, 3866
Yogananda, Paramhansa. 1730, 3137, 3483, 3866
Yogesvara Dasa. 2186, 3005
Yogiji, Harbhajan Singh Khalsa. 3408
Yohn, David Waite. 473, 503, 1377, 2907, 3360
Yohn, Rick. 609, 990, 1712, 1739, 3600
Yokoi, Yuho. 1472, 3459
Yolen, Jane H. 1637, 3398
Yonan, Isaac Malek. 2544, 3272
Yoneda, Soei. 3776
Yonge, Charlotte Mary. 292, 625, 632, 1443, 2166, 2398, 2484
Yonge, Julia J. 2813
Yonge, Stanley. 740
Yonker, Nicholas J. 1729
Yonkers, N.Y. Saint John's Evangelical Lutheran Church. 3868
Yoo, Yushin. 704, 709
Yoosuf, Abraham Arthur Kevork. 2566
Yorgason, Blaine M. 1009, 2609, 2620, 3868
Yorgason, Brenton G. 2347
York, Eng. (Diocese) Archbishop, 1480-1500 (Thomas Rotherham) 3868
York quarterly. 3483
York, Raymond. 2266, 2813
York, Thomas Lee. 1363, 3868
York, William E. 3830
Yorke, Margaret. 1428
Yorke, P[eter] C. 3181
Yorke, Peter Christopher. 28, 2368, 793, 804, 806, 841, 3360
Yoshor, Moses M. 2116, 2162
Yost, Casper Salathiel. 397, 1975, 2135, 3519, 3859
Yost, Frank H. 3261
Yost, Martha England Murphey. 3203
Youard, Henry George. 3069
Young, A. Beatrice. 1425
Young, Alexander. 1054
Young, Alfred. 793
Young, Andrew. 1975
Young, Ann Eliza (Webb) 2607
Young, Anna Eliza (Webb) 3868
Young, Arthur Milton. 2662
Young, Arthur Morgan. 1936
Young, Brigham. 2607, 2609, 2619, 3869
Young, Cecelia Mary. 1275
Young, Cecilia Mary. 2262
Young, Charles Alexander. 1463
Young, Charles R. 1850
Young, Charlotte A. 2551
Young, Chester Smith. 3137
Young Christian Workers. 754, 3244, 3869
Young, Dan. 3137
Young, Davis A. 203
Young, Duncan McNeill. 2181, 2696
Young, Edith Mae. 2502, 2551
Young, Edward. 1891, 3213
Young, Edward Joseph. 503, 507, 509, 520, 527, 541, 543, 544, 599, 1797, 1911, 2951
Young, Egerton Ryerson. 1577, 1901
Young, Emanuel Sprankel. 283, 364, 470, 646, 1554
Young, Emerson K. 393
Young, Frances Margaret. 3271
Young, Frances Merle. 3749
Young, Frank Rudolph. 2992, 3539
Young, Fred L. 2615, 2888
Young, George Henry. 2066
Young, George Lindley. 331
Young, Geroge Lindley. 2046
Young, H. Edwin. 169, 588, 994
Young, Helen. 3172
Young, Helen, of Wayne, Neb. 2495
Young, Henry. 1737
Young, Henry A. 3560
Young, Henry J. 16, 17
Young, Howard Palmer. 2963, 3890, 2803
Young, J. Terry. 1998
Young, Jacob. 1596

Young, James H. 3519
Young, James Oliver. 2560
Young, Jesse Bowman. 210, 2002, 2426
Young, John. 156, 3819, 1956, 2002, 2329, 3024, 3610, 2002
Young, John B. 813
Young, John Freeman. 1861
Young, John M L. 1935
Young, John R. 2607
Young, John Terry. 1126, 1833
Young, Karl. 1479
Young, Karl E. 2617
Young, Kimball. 2859
Young, Lois Horton. 614, 643, 3180, 3184, 3765, 3766
Young, Loren. 2398
Young, Loyal. 2914
Young, Lucinda (Smith) 3203
Young, Mary Blamir. 3819
Young men's Christian association. Buffalo. Library. 3874
Young men's Christian association. International committee. 3875
Young men's Christian associations. 687, 980, 1164, 2844, 3872, 3873, 3875
Young men's Christian associations. Association of secretaries. 3873
Young men's Christian associations. Association of secretaries. 47th conference, Toronto, 1939. 3873
Young men's Christian associations. Association of secretaries. 48th conference, Cleveland, 1942. 3873
Young Men's Christian Associations. Association of Secretaries. 50th Conference, Grand Rapids, 1948. 3873
Young Men's Christian Associations. Association of Secretaries. 51st conference, Cleveland, 1951. 3873
Young Men's Christian Associations. Association of Secretaries. 53d conference, Kansas City, Mo., 1956. 3873
Young Men's Christian Associations. Auburn University. 3874
Young men's Christian associations. Business secretaries' association. 3873
Young men's Christian Associations. Chicago. 980
Young men's Christian associations. Colgate university, Hamilton, N.Y. 3874
Young men's Christian associations. Commission on advertising and promotion. 3873
Young men's Christian associations. Committee on discussion courses for high school boys. 687
Young men's Christian associations. Drew theological seminary, Madison, N.J. 3873
Young Men's Christian Associations. Hi-Y Manual Committee. 688
[Young men's Christian associations. Internatina committee]. 687
Young men's Christian associations. International committee. 643, 688, 3254, 3873, 3874, 3875
Young men's Christian associations. International committee. Army and navy dept. 3455
Young men's Christian associations. International committee. Bureau of records, studies and trends. 3029
Young men's Christian associations. International committee. Commission on materials for Christian education and training. 687
[Young men's Christian associations. International committee] Committee on counsel and guidance of the Christian citizenship program. 687
Young men's Christian associations. International committee. County work dept. 1374, 1375, 3255, 3873
Young men's Christian associations. International committee. Educational council. 2823
Young men's Christian associations. International committee. Educational dept. 3592, 3873, 3875
Young men's Christian associations. International committee. Industrial dept. 3873
Young men's Christian associations. International committee. Railroad department. 3873
Young men's Christian associations. International committee. Religious work dept. 886
Young men's Christian associations. International committee. Secretarial bureau. 3875
Young men's Christian associations. International committee. Student department. 3873, 3875
Young men's Christian associations. Le Mans region. 1543

Young men's Christian associations. Mexico (City) Railroad branch. Library. 3875
Young men's Christian associations. Michigan university. 3873
Young men's Christian associations. Minneapolis. 3875
Young Men's Christian Associations. National Board. 3873, 3874
Young Men's Christian Associations. National Board. Bureau of Records, Studies and Trends. 3029, 3873
Young Men's Christian associations. National Committee on Work with High-School Youth. 3876
Young men's Christian associations. National council. Bureau of records, studies and trends. 3873
Young Men's Christian associations. National Jr. Hi-Y Commission. 688
Young men's Christian associations. New Jersey. 3873
Young men's Christian associations. New York. 3455
Young men's Christian associations. Town and country and community manual committee. 1375
Young men's Christian associations. Virginia. University. 3874
Young men's Christian associations, Washington, D.C. War work council. 1543
Young men's era publishing company. 3874
Young men's Hebrew association, New York. 3876
Young, Mildred Binns. 1676, 3847
Young, Norman James. 1383, 1818
Young, Pauline (Vislick) 2568
Young people's Luther league]. 473
Young people's Luther league. 11th convention, Billings, Mont., 1941. 3890
Young people's Luther league. 3d convention, Minneapolis, 1925. 3881
Young people's Luther league. 4th convention, Seattle, 1927. 3881
Young people's Luther league. 5th convention, Duluth, 1929. 3881
Young people's Luther league. 8th convention, Sioux Falls, S.D., 1935. 3881
Young people's missionary movement of the United States and Canada. 2515
Young, Percy Marshall. 917, 1783
Young, Perry Deane. 1087, 2593
Young, Philip Norton Frushard. 2532
Young, Richard K. 1259, 2782
Young, Robert. 2526, 1360, 225, 226, 228, 1797, 3528, 3055
Young, Robert Doran. 1297
Young, Robert Render. 2498
Young, Robert T. 2438, 3360
Young, Rosa. 2302, 2303
Young, Samuel. 3530, 1454
Young, Samuel Chien-Sheng. 1013
Young, Samuel Edward. 2936
Young, Seymour Dilworth. 2614, 3869
Young, T. W. 2616
Young, Theodore Cuyler. 1282
Young, Thomas Shields. 3160
Young, Thomas W. 2614
Young, Valentine. 3331
Young, Vashni. 1326
Young, W. Harold. 3362
Young, Walter Milton. 1237
Young, Warren Cameron. 1456, 2834, 3160
Young, William. 3213
Young, William Allen. 2543
Young, William Edgar. 495, 634, 2624
Young, William Harold. 3367
Young, William Henry. 2911, 1572, 2907
Young, William Tate. 2961
Young Women's Christian Assocations. U.S. National Board. 3878
Young women's Christian association. Binghamton, N.Y. 3878
Young women's Christian association, Chicago. 3878
Young women's Christian association, New York City. 3878
Young women's Christian association, Washington, D.C. 3878
[Young women's Christian associations]. 1443, 1715
Young women's Christian associations. Brooklyn, N.Y. 3878
Young women's Christian associations. New York. 3878
Young women's Christian associations. U.S. National board. 1715, 3873, 3878, 3879
Young women's Christian associations. U.S. National board. Dept. of research and method. 1715

Young women's Christian associations. U.S. National board. Division of community Y.W.C.A.'s. 3879
Young women's Christian associations. U.S. National speakers bureau. 3841
Young women's Christian associations. Washington, D.C. (Colored) 3878
Youngberg, Norma R. 2491
Youngblood, Ronald. 169
Youngblood, Ronald F. 599
Youngdahl, Reuben K. 1433, 1434, 1435, 1443, 2302
Younger, George D. 1279, 3453
Younger, Paul. 1814, 1897
Younghusband, Francis Edward. 3065, 3849, 2641
Youngman, Bernard R. 297, 1195
Youngman, Elmer Haskell. 1065
Young-O'Brien, Albert Hayward, 1898. 3425
[Youngs, Benjamin Seth] b. 1773? 3397
Youngs, Bill. 2267
Youngs, James. 2422
Youngs, John William Theodore. 1338
Youngs, Robert W. 1011, 1065, 1435
Youngwood, Pa. Holy Cross Church. 1165
Yount, William R. 1257
Yourd, Robert Wilson. 1181
Yours truly. 3024
Youtz, Herbert Alden. 1735, 3522, 1729
Yowa. 2952
Yperman, Joseph. 2255
Yram. 94
Yram, pseud. 94
Yu, Chun-fang. 1115, 2940
Yu, Pin. 816
Yuhaus, Cassian J. 2778
Yukteswar, 1855-1936. 3330
Yule, George Udny. 1885, 3692
Yule, Goerge Udny. 1885, 3692
Yungblut, John R. 1683, 2046, 2641, 2882, 3001
Yusut ibn taghri-birdi. 1501
Yzermans, Vincent Arthur. 1837, 2540, 3770

Z

Zabel, James A. 1145, 1426
Zabkar, Louis Vico. 3014
Zablocki, Benjamin David. 698
Zabriskie, Alexander Clinton. 691, 1042, 1551, 2241, 3244
Zabriskie, Francis Nicoll. 2944
Zacatecas, Mexico (City). Apostolico Colegio de Nuestra Senora de Guadalupe. 2553
Zacchello, Joseph John. 803
Zachar, Louis A. 3574
Zacharias, Alfred. 630
Zacharias, Gerhard P. 3304
Zachary, James W. 1836
Zachman, Harry L. 3666
Zadeik, Peter A. 2287
Zadokite documents. 3891
Zaehner, R. C. 3069
Zaehner, Robert Charles. 1080, 1457, 1709, 1731, 1782, 1814, 1816, 2325, 2329, 2641, 2644, 2645, 3122, 3899
Zagorsk, Russia. Gosudarstvennyi istoriko-khudozhestvennyi muzei. 1881, 3891
Zahan, Dominique. 12
Zahm, John Augustine. 206, 1581, 1811, 3077
Zahn, Gordon Charles. 818, 1931, 1932, 3794
Zahniser, Arthur De France. 2428
Zahniser, Charles Reed. 3447, 1042, 1572, 3675
Zahniser, Clarence Howard. 3240
Zahrnt, Heinz. 2009, 3618, 3679
Zakatarious. 2859
Zakich, Rhea. 1008, 3891
Zald, Mayer N. 3874
Zalitach, Myron. 2253
Zalman, Shneur. 1789
Zamboni, Camillo. 3877
Zamoyta, Vincent. 2010
Zamperini, Louis. 1362
Zanchi, Giorolamo. 2911
Zanchi, Girolamo. 2911
Zandee, Jan. 1530
Zander, Valentine. 3334
Zander, Walter. 3405
Zandstra, Sidney. 600
Zangwill, Israel. 2079, 2082, 2087, 2119
Zapffe, Carl. 689
Zappulli, Cesare. 173, 2717
Zarchin, Michael Moses. 2100, 2102, 2103
Zarchy, Harry. 877, 3575
Zaremba, Theodore Anthony. 1736, 2352
Zaretsky, Irving I. 3519, 3749
Zarnecki, George. 2230, 2576, 3316
Zart, Gustav. 1956

Zartman, Rufus Calvin. 1698, 1833, 3412
Zastrow, Nancy B. 3845
Zatko, James J. 824, 825, 3626
Zatkovich, Theophile Akos. 766
Zatlin, Linda Gertner. 1517
Zawart, Anscar. 1644
Zayek, Francis M. 2717, 3025
Zdenek, Marilee. 2896, 3004
Zdepski, Stephen. 152
Zearfoss, Robert Newell. 2398, 2399
Zebedee, Donald Henry John. 2230
Zedtwitz, Mary Elizabeth (Caldwell) von. 803
Zeeden, Ernst Walter. 2278, 2288
Zehavi, A. M. 3122
Zehnle, Richard F. 332, 3451
Zehr, Paul M. 2046, 3579
Zehring, John William. 990, 3785, 3849
Zeidler, Clemens H. 108, 2783
Zeigler, Earl Frederick. 3160, 3169
Zeigler, Earle F. 3106
Zeigler, William Abraham. 3138
Zeilinger, George J. 1549
Zeiller, Jacques [Marie Joseph Charles Jacques Zeiller]. 1195
el Zein, Abdul Hamid M. 1925
[Zeisberger, David] 1721-1808. 1421
Zeitlin, Joseph. 2155, 3016
Zeitlin, Solomon. 1411, 1998, 2092, 2097, 2112, 2134, 2148, 2623
Zeitschrift fur Theologie und Kirche. 3678
Zeldner, Max. 596
Zeligs, Dorothy F. 2090
Zeligs, Dorothy Freda. 494, 625, 1624, 2090, 2094, 2763, 3897
Zelinsky, Wilbur. 1198
Zelle, Margaretha Geertruida. 3138, 3144
Zeller, George W. 438, 1717
Zeller, Harry K. 1237, 3360
Zeller, Renee C. T. 2132
Zellers, George Andrew. 279
Zeluff, Daniel. 1298
Zema, Demetrius. 2561
Zenor, Richard. 3474
Zenos, Andrew Constantinides. 477, 946, 2923, 238
Zentarra, Oskar. 97
Zentmyer, George Aubrey. 1627
Zeoli, Anthony. 107, 1367, 3321, 3541, 3721, 3895
Zeoli, Billy. 990, 1633, 2896
Zepp, Arthur C. 1125, 3300
Zepp, Arthur Carroll. 1125, 1347
Zepp, J. Albert. 3405
Zerahiah, ha-Yewani. 1539
Zerbe, Alvin Sylvester. 176, 3650, 564, 1581, 3074
Zerfass, Samuel Grant. 1521, 3388
Zerin, Edward. 564, 2140, 2151
Zernov, Nicolas. 2169, 2745, 2746, 2750, 3214, 3256, 3334
Zerr, Edward Michael. 225
Zervos, Christian. 2986
Zerwick, Maximilian. 364
Zeydel, Edwin Hermann. 1826
[Zhitnik, Abraham J.]. 2103
Zia-ba-Bsam-'grub, Kazi, 1868-1922. 708
Ziefle, Helmut W. 3639
Ziegenhals, Walter E. 1279
Ziegler, D. Paul. 1929
Ziegler, David Paul. 46, 991
Ziegler, Dewey Kiper. 696
Ziegler, Donald Jenks. 3042
Ziegler, Edward Krusen. 1302, 2907, 3409, 3854, 3895, 3854
Ziegler, Gregor Thomas. 2124
Ziegler, Jesse H. 1237, 3176
Ziegler, John Henry. 1327
Ziegler, John Sherman. 1385
Ziegler, Sandra. 1112, 1673
Ziegler, Wesley Moody. 679, 2614, 3430
Ziehe, Heinz Carl. 2292
Zielinski, Stanislaw A. 1683, 3001
Zielinski, Tadeusz. 1767
Ziemer, H B. 803
Ziemke, Donald C. 887, 2278
Ziesler, J. A. 90, 377, 2161
Ziff, Larzer. 1372
Ziglar, Zig. 995, 3895
Zigler, D. H. 3094
Zilboorg, Gregory. 3825
Zilinski, Joseph. 904
Zilonka, Paul. 471
Zimmels, Hirsch Jakob. 1825, 3333
Zimmer, Allen E. 2399
Zimmer, Frank J. 1582
Zimmer, Heinrich Robert. 2664, 2840
Zimmer, Luke B. 793, 859, 1003
Zimmer, Norma. 1749, 3896
Zimmerli, Walther. 503, 518, 599, 1846, 3377, 3850, 3851
Zimmerman, Benedict. 741
*Zimmerman, Eleanor. 2282, 3175
Zimmerman, Jeremiah. 980, 1596, 1746, 1814, 2035
Zimmerman, John Edward. 2659

Zimmerman, Leander M. 980, 1443, 2896, 3675
Zimmerman, Martha. 1611
Zimmerman, Paul Albert. 202, 1403, 1581
Zimmerman, Wendell. 1562
Zimmermann, Felix H. 507
Zimmermann, Frank. 392, 512, 529
Zimmermann, Mary Theola. 741
Zimmermann, Odo John, 1906. 189
Zimmermann, Otto. 3900
Zimmermann, Paul Albert. 1403, 1581
Zimmermann, Wolf Dieter. 677
Zimmern, Alfred Eckhard. 1282
Zimmern, Alice. 2666
Zimpfer, George. 2575, 2581
Zinberg, Israel. 1789
Zincke, Foster Barham. 2908
Zink, Heidi. 1606, 3172
Zink, Jorg. 3890
Zinkiewicz, Crystal. 1611
Zinzendorf, Nicolaus Ludwig. 2595, 3367
Ziolkowski, Thaddeus Stanislaus. 1165
Zionist organization in America. 3897
Zionist organization of America. 3897
Zionist organization of America. Dept. of youth and education. 3897
Zionist Organization of America. National Education Dept. 3897
Zion's Hope. 911

Zion's printing and publishing company, Independence, Mo. 2607
Ziprin, Nathan. 1354
Zittel, Christian A. 813
Zizola, Giancarlo. 2124, 2861
Zlotowitz, Bernard M. 547, 1736
Znosko, Vladimir. 1622
Zobell, Albert L. 1843, 2607, 2617, 2619, 2720
Zockler, Otto. 496, 507, 512, 549, 572, 594
Zodhiates, Spiros. 413
Zodiates, Spyros. 181, 323, 324, 422
Zoff, Otto. 1852
Zoghby, Samir M. 1923
Zohar. English. Selections. 722, 3898
Zollars, Ely Vaughan. 123, 473, 646, 565, 609, 3296
Zollikofer, Georg Joachim. 2592, 3347
Zollikofer, Johannes, 1633-1692. 3049
Zollinger, Camma Larsen. 1231, 3267
Zollmann, Carl Frederick Gustav. 1490
Zollner, Johann Evangelist. 1843
Zollner, Johann Karl Friedrich. 3519
Zook, Noah. 297
Zook, Pat. 3141
Zorab, George. 2992
Zorn, Carl Manthey. 3196, 2287

Zorn, H. M. 3895
Zorn, Raymond O. 2176
Zornan, John. 2287
[Zschokke, Heinrich] 1771-1848. 1417, 1454, 3252
Zubek, Theodoric J. 825
Zubly, John Joachim. 928
Zuck, Roy B. 549, 689, 3160, 3890, 3899
Zuck, William Johnston. 2004
Zucker, Norman L. 1928
Zuckermann, Benedict. 3262
Zuckmayer, Carl. 119
Zucrow, Solomon. 2074, 2107, 2074, 2107
Zueblin, Charles. 3065
Zuesse, Evan M. 12
Zuidema, Sytse Ulbe. 2171
Zumbro Valley Medical Society. Medicine and Religion Committee. 2378
Zumbrunnen, Albert Clay. 1321
Zundel, Maurice. 797, 2135, 2357, 2368
Zundel, William Arter. 3896, 2288
Zunkel, Charles. 995
Zunkel, Cleda. 2399
Zunser, Eliakum. 3055
Zunser, Miriam Shomer. 2121
Zuntz, Gunther. 373, 475, 1512, 3405
Zunz, Leopold. 2093
Zurbonsen, Anthony. 814
Zurcher, E. 705

Zurcher, Erik. 705
[Zurcher, George] 1852. 2863
Zurcher, George. 2576
Zurcher, Jean. 460, 2046
Zurcher, Jean R. 3463
Zuurdeeg, Willem Frederick. 2321, 2710
Zuurdeeg, Willem Frederik. 3106
Zuver, Dudley. 3106
Zuzic, Marko. 2127
Zweig, Ruth G. 6, 2099
Zweig, Stefan. 889, 1526, 2410, 2413, 890
Zweizig, William H[enry]. 1125
Zwemer, Amy E. (Wilkes) 2566
Zwemer, Samuel Marinus. 2502, 2566, 21, 47, 494, 904, 980, 1092, 1572, 1736, 1893, 2054, 2202, 2271, 2501, 2504, 2540, 2566, 2882, 3065, 3841, 3899, 2498
Zwerin, Raymond A. 1316
Zwierlein, Frederick James. 824, 1370, 2310, 3036, 2700
Zwingli, Ulrich. 3042, 3044, 3630, 3653, 3900
Zwingli. Ulrich. 3044
Zwingll, Ulrich or Huldreich. 940
Zybura, John S. 1065
Zychlinaski, Aleksander. 3490
Zymonidas, Alessandro. 3519

Title Index

A

A-A method for the cumulative endowment of churches. 1167
A. Bronson Alcott. 23
A. C. Dixon, romance of preaching. 2899
A. J. Gordon. 163
A.M.E. church book of discipline. 2442
A. M. E. Church ecclesiastical judicial practice. 1488
A. M. Mackay. 2308, 2558
A.P.A. movement. 33, 826
A. T. Robertson. 3241
A-visiting we will go. 3063
A. W. L.'s catechism. 748
A. W. Tozer, a twentieth century prophet. 3705
AAR Seminar in Dialectic. 177, 1458
Aaronic priesthood. 1
Aaronic priesthood through the centuries. 2938
Aaron's riming Bible. 561
AATS directory 1964. 3612
Abaddon, and Mahanaim. 3475
Abailard's Ethics. 942
Abandon earth. 3318
Abandon hope! 92
Abandoned spouse. 2343
Abandomed to Christ. 969
Abandonment. 2642
Abandonment to divine providence. 2642
Abarbanel and the expulsion of the Jews from Spain. 5, 2103
Abba. 2248, 3475
Abba, father. 2247, 2398, 2892, 3060
Abbe Gregoire, 1787-1831. 1773
Abbe Huvelin, Apostle of Paris, 1839-1910. 1859
Abbe Pierre speaks. 759
Abbe Pierre speaks; speeches collected by L. C. Repland, translated by Cecily Hastings and George Lamb. 759
Abbee Pouget discourses. 2865
Abbey & bishopric of Ely. 1510
Abbey of St. Gall as a centre of literature & art. 3274
Abbey of St. Germain des Pres in the seventeenth century. 3274
Abbey psalter. 849, 2986
Abbeys and churches of England and Wales. 1270
Abbeys and priories in England and Wales. 2579
Abbeys, Priories and Cathedrals. 752

Abbie's God book. 1734
Abbot Columba Marmion. 2336
Abbot in monastic tradition. 3566
Abbot Suger on the Abbey Church of St.-Denis and its art treasures. 78, 3273
Abbot's house at Westminster. 3808
Abbott's Comments on the Revelation of Jesus Christ. 452
Abbreviated Bible [with the Apocrypha. 200
ABC. 3090
ABC catechism. 314
A.B.C. History of Palmyra and the beginning of "Mormonism," 2600
ABC of Acts 2:4. 332
A.B.C. institute of the holy faith. 3063
ABC of Bible lands. 242
ABC of commercial letters of credit. 2218
A. B. C. of occultism. 2845
A B C of palmistry. 2766
ABC of the Bible. 245
ABC of the New Testament. 161
ABC of the spiritual life. 3493
ABC of witchcraft past & present. 3824
ABC of your religion and mine. 3119
ABC religion. 3165
ABC stories for Jewish children. 627
ABC's for young LDS. 2618
ABC's in the Bible. 198
ABC's of Christian faith. 3665
ABC's of modern catechetics. 747
ABC's of salvation. 3296
ABC's of the miracles. 2477
ABC's of the prophetical scriptures. 605
ABC's of the Revelation. 457
Abd Allah, teacher, healer. 1927
Abdul Baha and the promised age. 2
Abdul Baha on divine philosophy. 125
Abdul Baha's grandson. 11
Abe Mulkey's budget. 1568
Abel being dead, yet speaketh. 1333, 1372
Abelard and Heloise. 1
Abelard and St. Bernard. 1
Abelard's Christian theology. 1, 3645
Abhandlungen zur romischen Religion. 3246
Abide above. 988
Abide in Christ. 970
Abiding Comforter. 1378, 1822
Abiding gift of prophecy. 3379
Abiding hope, a devotional guide. 1433
Abiding in Christ: studies in John 15. 420, 988
Abiding life. 1834
Abiding past. 1546
Abiding presence of the Holy Ghost in the soul. 1834
Abiding spirit. 1829, 1834
Abiding value of the Old Testament. 596, 599
Abiding values in Christian education. 3154
Abiding values of evangelicalism. 1552
Abiding word. 3652
Abindgon Bible commentary. 222
Abingdon Bible handbook. 308
Abingdon Church. 3
Abingdon funeral manual. 1694
Abingdon glossary of religious terms. 246, 3092

Abingdon marriage manual. 2336
Ablaze for God. 3387
Abnormal Christians. 1107
Abolished rites. 1100
Abolishing of death. 3506
Abolition of God. 64
Abolition of ,poverty. 1703, 3436
Abolition of religion. 1061
Aboriginal mission stations in Victoria: Yelta, Ebenezer, Ramahyuck, Lake Condah. 2559
Aboriginal myths and legends. 2654
Abortion? 3
Abortion and the early church. 3
Abortion and the meaning of personhood. 3
Abortion counseling and social change from illegal act to medical practice. 3
Abortion, the American holocaust. 3
Abortion, the development of the Roman Catholic perspective. 3
Abortion, the moral issues. 3
About Advent. 8
About an old New England church. 1183
About by books, Concerning my name, and other texts. 2729
About Christ. 1072
About extraordinary. 740
About face. 3698
About Hebrew manuscripts. 2331
About hoping. 1845
About learning. 628
About loving. 2265
About Mormonism. 2614
About my father's business. 1302, 1303, 2461
About people. 962
About Saint Francis. 1640
About the Bible. 233, 235
About the Holy Bible. 199
About the Holy Spirit. 1836
About the New English Bible. 274
About the old faith. 3662
About the Old Testament. 539
"About to come forth" 3856
About vocations. 2570
About yoga. 3864
About your state in life. 1645
About Zionism. 2118
Above all a shepherd. 2123
Above all else. 984, 1856
Above every name. 3449
Above or within? 941
Above ourselves. 1785
Above rubies. 3860
Above the battle? 231
Above the blue. 1794
Above the noise. 1209
Above the tumult in China. 2509
Above the wind's roar. 3455
ABQ book. 313, 3011
Abraham. 4, 5, 492, 2792, 3761
Abraham and David. 528, 1377
Abraham and his times. 4
Abraham and the contemporary mind. 4, 2995
Abraham Cowley. 1377
Abraham, father of believers. 4
Abraham, friend of God. 4, 493, 2792

Abraham Geiger and liberal Judaism. 1704, 3032
Abraham: his heritage and ours. 4
... Abraham, his life and times. 4
Abraham in history and tradition. 4, 528
Abraham Isaac Kook. 2142
Abraham Joshua Heschel. 1809
Abraham Lincoln returns. 3514
Abraham, loved by God. 4
Abraham, man of faith. 5, 2793
Abraham the patriarch. 5, 631
Abraham to Allenby. 2764
Abraham to the Middle-East crisis. 2764
Abraham was their father. 2147
Abraham Weiss jubilee volume. 2090
Abrahamic promises fulfilled. 646
Abraham's children. 637
Abridged catechism of Christian doctrine. 767
Abridged edition of "Grace and truth," 1359
Abridged Euchologion. 1487
Abridged history of the sodalities of Our Lady. 1329
Abridged prayer book for Jews in the Armed Forces of the United States. 2884
Abridgement of The secret doctrine. 3683
Abridgment by Katharine Hillard of the Secret doctrine, a synthesis of science, religion and philosophy. 3683
Abridgment of Milner's Church history. 1177
Abridgment of Mr. Locke's Essay concerning human understanding. 2180
Abridgment of the Book of martyrs. 2350
Abridgment of the Church history of New-England. 2687
Abridgment of the Interior spirit of the Religious of the visitation of Holy Mary. 2741
Abridgment of the Interior spirit of the Religious of the visitation of the Blessed Virgin Mary. 2741
Absence of the Comforter described and lamented, in a discourse on Lam. I. 16. 3353
Absolute being. 2739
Absolute is in the dark. 3749
Absolute life on trial. 1890
Absolute nothingness. 1081, 2711
Absolute surrender and other addresses. 1451
Absolute unlawfulness of the stage-entertainment fully demonstrated. 3606
Absolutely null and utterly void. 44, 853
Absoluteness of Christianity and the history of religions. 1097
Absolutes in moral theology? 947, 949
... The absolution of recidivists in the sacrament of penance. 6
Abstract history of the Mississippi Baptist Association for one hundred years. 156
Abstract of a new theory of the formation of the earth. 1381
Abstract of systematic theology. 3641
Abstract of the journal of Rev. Dan Beach Bradley, M. D., medical missionary in Siam. 2546

Abstract of the minutes of the annual meeting. 1550
Abstract of the proceedings of the Antimasonic state convention of Massachusetts. 52
Abstract of the proceedings of the Corporation. 1222
Abstracts of selected doctoral dissertations on adult religious education. 3169
Abstracts on life (Stewart, William James) 976
Absurdity of Christianity, and other essays. 1103
Abts zu Wessobrunn, 1438-1443. 1877
Abu Bakr. 6, 726
Abundant life. 1341, 2610
Abundant life in changing Africa; report of the ... conference. 2498
Abundant life through Aldersgate. 3805
Abundant living. 1439
Abusing science. 1580
Abyss of despair (Yeven metzulah) The famous 17th century chronicle depicting Jewish life in Russia and Poland during the Chmielnicki massacres of 1648-49. 915, 2102
Academic course Bible doctrines. 3381
Academic freedom and the Catholic university. 830
Academic illusion. 3756
Academic man in the Catholic college. 831
Academic study of Judaism. 2075, 2122
Academic study of religion. 3112
Academy scrapbook. 726
Accent. 2634
Accent on laughter. 1346
Accent on purity. 889
Accent on the Ascension! 1958
Accents in Luther's theology. 2280
Accents of life. 3887
Acceptable minister of Christ. 2938
Acceptance. 3028
According to Amos. 2803
According to Cardinal Newman. 789
According to John. 420
According to John, through the loud speaker. 416
According to knowledge. 277
According to Luke. 426
According to Mark. 433
... "According to my Gospel" 3702
According to Paul. 377
According to plan, "I will build my church" 2508
According to promise. 167
According to Saint John. 419
According to St. Paul. 374
According to Scripture. 473
According to the flesh. 1496
According to the pattern. 2309, 3437
According to the Scriptures. 476, 2031
According to Thy promises. 991
According to Thy Word. 1549
"According to your faith," 1595
Account of our religion, doctrine, and faith. 1859
Account of the conduct of the Shakers. 3395
Account of the convincement, exercises, services and travels, of that ancient servant of the Lord, Richard, Davies. 1684
Account of the creation of the world according to Hawaiian tradition. 1371
Account of the executors of Richard, Bishop of London, 1303. 1756
Account of the experience of Hester Ann Rogers. 2451
Account of the gospel labours. 3812
Account of the gospel labours and Christian experiences of John Churchman. 1109
Account of the infancy, religious and literary life, of Adam Clarke...written by one who was intimately acquainted with him from his boyhood to the sixtieth year of his age. 1109
Account of the life. 1109
Account of the life and travels, in the work of the ministry, of John Fothergill. 1674
Account of the life of that ancient servant of Jesus Christ. 1675
Account of the Lord's dealings with the Rev. Thomas Rutherford. 1109
Account of the people called Shakers. 696, 3394
Account of the people called Shakers: their faith, doctrines, and practice, exemplified in the life, conversations, and experience of the author during the time he belonged to the society. 3395

Account of the reasons why a considerable number (about fifty, whereof ten are members in full communion) belonging to the New North congregation in Boston, could not consent to Mr. Peter Thacher's ordination there. 684, 3605
Account of the religious and literary life of Adam Clarke. 1109
Account of the religious and literary life of Rev. Adam Clarke. 1109
Accounting for parishes. 1168
Accounts of religious revivals in many parts of the United States from 1815 to 1818. 3228
Accounts rendered by papal collectors in England, 1317-1378. 807, 3589
Accuracy of the Bible. 565
Accuracy of the Old Testament. 514
Achievement. 2819
Achievement of a century. 3421
Achievement of Bernard Lonergan. 2245
Achievement of Israel. 2096
Achievement of John C. Bennett. 190
Achievement of Karl Rahner. 3019
Achievement of Nazareth. 1893
Achievement of the Master. 1970
Achievements of Vatican II. 3771
Achieving Christian character. 886
Achieving Christian maturity. 754
Achieving Christian perfection. 2818
Achieving peace of heart. 2808
Achieving promises. 999
Achieving results in church finance. 1168
Achieving the impossible with God. 1634
Achitophel. 484, 1225, 3363
Acimnos ceiphr to a correct." and complete work. 1669
Acimnos ceiphr to a correct and complete work and messages of truth. 1669
Acknowledging my stewardship. 3530
Acolytes and altar guilds. 2236
Acquaintance with God. 3292
Acquainted with grief. 1352
Acquainting youth with Christ. 1525
Acquiring and developing church real estate. 1241
Acquitted! 2160
Acredios, the veil lifted. 3509
Acres of diamonds. 3538
Across a world. 849
Across the bridge. 2548
Across the churchyard. 2573
Across the continent of the years. 964
Across the desert. 2621
Across the editor's desk. 2135
Across the line. 3515
Across the night. 2639
Across the pastor's desk. 3012
Across the prairie in a motor caravan. 2506
Across the threshold. 3842
Across the unknown. 3518
Across three centuries. 1404
Acrostic Bible. 6, 319
Act and being. 1457
Act of becoming. 1251
Act of contrition. 3218
Act of love. 1592
Act of marriage. 3391
Act of mercy: euthanasia today. 1544
Act of the Apostles. 330
Act of the Associate presbytery of Pennsylvania, concerning public convenanting, unanimously agreed to at Philadelphia, April 29, 1791 ... To which is added an act concerning the admission of church members to communion. 2918
... The act of uniformity. 1046
Acta Pilati. 2069
Acta Stephani Langton Cantuariensis Archiepiscopi A. D. 1762
Actes of Englysh votaryes. 2579
Acting on principle. 2163
Acting on the Word. 2570
Acting out the truth. 3144
Action dramas for the young church. 1211
Action in the liturgy. 2257
Action in waiting. 673
Action priest. 1109
Actions, gestures & bodily attitudes. 778, 1708
Activating the passive church. 1244
Activation of energy. 3083
Active life and contemplative life. 2819
Active life and contemplative life, a study of the concepts from Plato to the present. 2819
Active man and the Christ. 2931, 3353
Active method. 748
Activities for active Bible classes. 3552
Activities for Christian family. 1607
Activities in child education for the church school teacher. 3173
Activities in the religious school. 3166
Activities of the rabbi. 3015
Activity programs for junior groups. 935, 3735

Acton-Newman relations. 6, 2221
Acts. 327, 329, 330, 331
Acts, a study guide. 333
Acts--adventures of the early church. 198
Acts, an exposition. 330
Acts, an expositional commentary. 332, 2930, 3348
Acts: an inductive study. 333
Acts analyzed. 327
Acts and Apocalyptic literature. 333
Acts and decrees of the Synod of Jerusalem. 1373, 2747
Acts and letters of the Apostles. 197
Acts and monuments of John Foxe. 1637, 2350
Acts and proceedings of the General synod of the Evangelical and Reformed church. 1545
Acts and proceedings ... of the General synod of the Reformed church in America. 3045
Acts and proceedings of the General synod of the Reformed Dutch church, in North America, at Albany, June, 1817. 3043
Acts and proceedings of the General synod of the Reformed Protestant Dutch church in North America. 3043
Acts and the history of earliest Christianity. 330, 1197
Acts and words of Our Lord and Saviour, Jesus Christ. 2070
Acts, Epistles, Revelation and reference passages. 320
Acts, God working with us. 333
Acts in prayer. 2877
Acts in the Revised standard version. 328
Acts of devotion. 1436
Acts of faith. 2097
Acts of the Apostles. 70, 71, 198, 327, 328, 329, 330, 331, 332, 343, 344, 891, 1434
...The Acts of the apostles and Bible doctrines. 333
Acts of the apostles and reference passages. 198
Acts of the Apostles: commentary. 328
Acts of the Apostles explained. 343
Acts of the Apostles for children. 75
Acts of the apostles in present-day preaching. 332
Acts of the Apostles in the proclamation of the Gospel of Jesus Christ. 199
Acts of the apostles of the sea. 3317
... The Acts of the Apostles (i-xiv) 328
Acts of the apostles, the Epistles and the Revelation of St. John, the Divine. 198
Acts of the Apostles. 328
Acts of the Christian martyrs. 2351
Acts of the Holy Spirit. 1834
Acts of the pagan martyrs. 2330
Acts of worship. 2238
Acts story. 330
Acts, the birth of the Church. 328
Acts then and now. 331, 333
Acts: working together in Christ's mission. 329
Actual grace. 1752
Actual spirit messages from life beyond. 3515
Acute and chronic unbelief. 1108
Acute cases in moral medicine. 744, 1107
Acvaghosha's Discourse on the awakening of faith in the Mahayana. 709
Ad Autolycum. 69
Ad limina apostolorum. 797
Ada Beeson Farmer. 2485
Adalia. 3197
Adam, Abraham and the Apocalypse. 56, 605
Adam and Cain. 53
Adam and Christ. 1377
Adam & Eve & The city. 3203
Adam and Eve, history or myth? 481
Adam and his times. 525
Adam and the family of man. 2326
Adam and the first Sabbath. 6
Adam Clarke, controversialist. 1285, 2459
Adam, Eve, and the ape. 63
Adam Schall. 3306
Adam Schall, a Jesuit at the Court of China. 109
"Adam, where art thou?" 2433
Adam, who is he? 6, 1232
Adamant & stone chips. 3071
Adamnani Vita S. Colombae. 1310
Adam's apple and other stories. 617
Adam's fall refuted, by earth's rocky records. 202
Adam's fractured rib. 3836
Adam's haunted sons. 492
Adam's new friend, and other stories from the Bible. 615, 617
Adam's rib; essays on Biblical medicine. 317
Adaptation of the religious life to modern conditions. 2574

Adaptive way of teaching confraternity classes. 745
Adat, Islam, and Christianity in a Batak homeland. 178
Adath Israel. 3577
Add life to your years. 1324
Add them to the church. 1357
Addicted to mediocrity. 1089
Adding life to our years. 3371
Additional hymns. 3046
Additional speeches, addresses and occasional sermons. 3729
Address by the ministers of the original Association of the county of Windham, to the heads of families in their respective societies, on the duty of family religion. 1611
Address commemorative of the life and character of the Rev. Daniel Elliott, D.D., LL.D. 1509
Address delivered before the American Whig and Cliosophic societies of the College of New Jersey. 209
Address delivered on the two hundredth anniversary of the organization of the First Baptist church. 684
Address from the clergy of New-Jersey, to the Episcopalians in Virginia. 1222
Address on the internal evidence of divine authorship, in nature and revelation. 3076
Address to all believers in Christ. 679, 2607
... Address to Origen. 2743
Address to persons of fashion, relating to balls. 36
Address to the living. 2211
Address to the ministers and congregations of the Presbyterian and independent persuasions in the United States of America. 2972
Address to the Quakers. 1681
Address to the Roman Catholics of the United States of America. 784, 3809, 3810
Address to the seven churches of Asia. 457
Addressed to Christians. 1079
Addressed to youth. 805
...Addresses. 3620
Addresses and historical papers before the centennial council of the Protestant Episcopal church in the diocese of Virginia. 3781
... Addresses and lectures of D. L. Moody. 1558
Addresses and lectures on various occasions. 2116
Addresses and papers (Mott, John Raleigh) 2512
... Addresses and papers presented at the Diamond jubilee, 1827-1902, May 11-14. 1332
Addresses and records (Purdue university, Lafayette, Ind) 3758
Addresses and sermons (Cicognani, Amleto Giovanni) 758
Addresses and sermons (Cicognani, Anteto Giovanni) 758
Addresses and sermons of His Excellency of the Most Reverend Archbishop Amleto Giovanni Cicognani. 758
Addresses and sermons of His Excellency the Most Reverend Archbishop Amleto Giovanni Cicognani. 758
Addresses and sermons to students. 123
Addresses at the celebration of the two hundred and fiftieth anniversary of the Westminster assembly. 3808
Addresses at the inauguration of Rev. Archibald A. Hodge, D. D. 1821
Addresses at the inauguration of Rev. Charles E. Knox. 1707
Addresses at the International Hymnological Conference. 1204
Addresses at the thirtieth meeting of the Unitarian club of California. 3068
Addresses before the Alumni association of Princeton theological seminary, at its annual meeting in Princeton, April 25th, 1876. Pub. at the request of the association. 2941
Addresses (Brooks, Phillips) 2230, 2972
Addresses by Henry Drummond. 3620
Addresses by the Right Reverend Phillips Brooks. 2230, 2972
Addresses delivered at the centennial celebration of the diocesan missionary society of the Protestant Episcopal church in the Diocese of Virginia. 2958
Addresses delivered at the ... conference. 730
Addresses delivered at the fortieth anniversary of the boards of home missions. 2296

Addresses delivered at the inauguration of the professors in the Danville theological seminary. 3612
Addresses delivered at the quarter-century anniversary of the reunion of the Old and New school Presbyterian churches. 2925
Addresses delivered in New-York by Rev. Wm. Arthur, A.M., with a biographical sketch of the author. 2434
Addresses for women workers. 3837
Addresses for young people. 3887
Addresses, lectures, expositions on Timothy. 446
Addresses on foreign missions delivered before the American board of commissioners for foreign missions. 2522
Addresses on notable occasions. 2422
Addresses on Romans (Talbot, Louis Thompson) 471
Addresses on the Acts of the Apostle. 327
Addresses on the book of Joshua. 2134
Addresses on the duties, dangers, and securities of youth. 3885
Addresses on the Epistles of John, and an Exposition of the Epistle of Jude. 369
Addresses on the First and Second Epistles of Thessalonians. 479
Addresses on the First and Second epistles of Timothy. 446
Addresses on the First Epistle to the Corinthians. 322
Addresses on the Gospel of John. 422
Addresses on the Gospel of Luke. 430
Addresses on the Second epistle to the Corinthians. 326
Addresses on the Song of Solomon. 594
Addresses (Phillips, Mildred Welshimer) 1461
Addresses to the dispersed of Judah. 2117
Addresses to women engaged in church work. 3837
Adelaide de Cice, foundress of the Society of the Daughters of the Heart of Mary. 1275
Adepts in the Western esoteric tradition. 2732
Adepts of the five elements. 95
Adequacy of Judaism. 2113
Adequate man. 449
Adequate religion. 1342
Adhyatma Ramayana. 1816
Adjust or self-destruct. 2321
Adjustment of law to life in rabbinic literature. 2074, 2107
Adjustment to Jesus. 971
Adler Special Manuscript Collection from the Library of the Jewish Theological Seminary. 7, 2331
Administering a vacation Bible school. 3762
Administering Christian education. 3552
Administering Christian education in the local church. 3149
Administering church training. 953
Administering God's gifts. 973
Administering the Bible teaching program. 642, 3559
Administering the ministry. 1199
Administering the senior department of the church school. 3553
Administering the vacation church school. 3763
Administering the young people's department of the local church. 3158
Administration in the Y.W.C.A. 3879
Administration of the Catholic secondary school. 832
Administration of an institutional church. 2699
Administration of instruction in Southern Baptist colleges and universities. 3759
Administration of Islam in Indonesia. 1924
Administration of religion in universities and colleges: personnel. 3756
.. The administration of seminaries. 3613
.. Administration of the church school. 3556
Administration of the sacraments. 3265
Administration of Y.M.C.A. boys' work. 687
Administrative handbook of elementary and secondary schools and the Confraternity of Christian Doctrine. 806
Administrative legislation in the new Code of canon law. 735
.. Administrative recourse. 77
Admirable Heart of Mary. 3270
Admirable life of S. Francis Xavier, 1632. 1025, 1650
Admirable life of Saint Wenefride. 1029, 3820
Admission to vows. 3787
Admitted to the mysteries; a history of Freemasonry and its hidden rites. 1661

Admonition controversy. 3007
Admonition to the people of England. 1589. 2336
Adner Ward. 3795
Adnodan dyrys'y Testament Newydd. 343
Adolescence and religion. 3882
Adolescent conflicts. 1260
Adolescent freedom and responsibility. 3394
Adolescent religion. 3889
Adolescent worship, with emphasis on senior age. 3854
Adolescents in search of a new church. 939
Adominant Romanism. 801
Adomnan's Life of Columbia. 1310
Adoniram Judson. 2157
Adoniram Judson, apostle of Burma. 2157
Adoniram Judson Gordon. 1748
Adonis, Attis, Osiris. 8
Adopted in love. 470
Adoption of Christianity in Bulgaria. 713
Adoption practices in Catholic agencies. 8
Adoptive rite ritual. 2741
Adoratio crucis: the Regularis concordia and the Decreta Lanfranci. 844, 2195
Adoration. 1441, 1446
Adoration of the blessed sacrament. 2253
Adore the Lord. 1742
Adoremus. 1877
Adoro te. 8
... Adrein Jourdan's Susanna. 3568
... Adrien Jourdan's Susanna. 3568
Adsum. 2939
Adult baptism and the catechumenate. 138
Adult Bible class. 641, 3556
Adult Bible classes and how to conduct them. 643
Adult Bible teacher and leader. 3168
Adult catechesis. 938
Adult Christianity. 3662
Adult class manual. 804, 1328
... Adult class study. 3160
Adult department. 3147
Adult department of the Sunday school. 3556
Adult devotions for public and private use. 1438
Adult division in the church school. 805
Adult education in Christian Churches. 3168
Adult education in the church. 938, 3157, 3169
Adult education in The Methodist Church. 3168
Adult guide on the Churche's mission town and country. 3253
Adult Jewish Education. 2086
Adult ministries in the church and the world. 1253
Adult program in the church school. 3552
Adult religious teaching. 3149
Adult Son. 435
Adult Sunday school work. 938
... The adult worker and his work. 3551
... The adult worker and work. 2449
Adults and the art of learning. 3146
Adults as learners. 8
Adults at worship. 1438
Adults continuing to learn. 3168
Adults in church training. 3182
Adults in the school. 3168
Adults in the Sunday school. 3168, 3552
Adults learn and like it; how to teach adults in the church. 3168
Adults teaching adults. 8
Advaita and Visistadvatta. 3775
Advance: a history of Southern Baptist foreign missions. 3466
Advance guard of missions. 2482
Advance in the Antilles. 2515
Advance of Baptist associations across America. 171
Advanced B.Y.P.U. methods. 142
Advanced Bible history for Lutheran schools in the words of Holy Scripture. 618
Advanced catechism of Catholic faith and practice. 747, 767, 770
Advanced choir. 917
Advanced course for Catholic living; teacher's manual. 3181
Advanced course in Yogi philosophy and oriental occultism. 2722
Advanced course in yogi philosophy and Oriental occultism, by Yogi Ramacharaka [pseud.]. 2722
Advanced Mariology. 2362
Advanced soul science. 3510
Advanced thought on electrical and spiritual voltage. 2986
Advanced vocalist. 917
Advancement of theological education. 3682
Advancing church. 2455

Advancing church in Latin America. 2548
Advancing dignity of woman in the Bible. 3832
Advancing the smaller local church. 1250, 1268
Advantage of a handicap. 1783
Advantages and means of union in society. 1503
Adveniat regnum tuum. 3416
Advent. 8, 9, 2037
Advent and ascension. 2021
Advent Christian manual. 9
Advent Christmas. 314
Advent, Christmas, New Year, Easter, and other sermons. 3354
Advent landmarks. 9
Advent message in Inter-America. 2559
Advent message in the Golden West. 3381
Advent, ministry and works of Our Lord Jesus Christ. 399
Advent of divine justice. 128, 129
Advent of God. 2393
Advent of salvation. 2037
Advent of women. 3843
Adventism and the Bible. 8
Adventism answered (the Sabbath question) 3380
Adventist evangelism in the twentieth century. 1571, 3384
Adventual essays delivered at the congress of the Parliament of religions. 9
Adventure. 77, 2334, 3080
Adventure beautiful. 3483
Adventure book for younger girls. 1715
Adventure for God. 2959
Adventure for God on Okinawa. 2543
Adventure in analysis. 231
Adventure in architecture. 3275
Adventure in discipleship. 983
Adventure in dying. 75, 164, 2165
Adventure in evangelism. 1554
Adventure in faith. 2937, 3778
Adventure in freedom. 2106
Adventure in insight. 1449
Adventure in love. 1610
Adventure in missions. 2936
Adventure in oothodoxy. 2751
Adventure in prayer. 2874
Adventure in religious education. 3177
Adventure in renewal. 1250
Adventure in the will of God. 977
Adventure in understanding. 3703
Adventure in unity. 1210
Adventure into the reality of you. 2694
Adventure inward. 3479
Adventure of becoming one. 2337
Adventure of being a man. 2225
Adventure of being a wife. 3830
Adventure of being you. 1011
Adventure of faith. 1595
Adventure of fasting. 1613
Adventure of finding God. 62
Adventure of growing. 3764
Adventure of growing (The) 1498
Adventure of Judaism. 1329
Adventure of life. 2227
Adventure of living. 3330
Adventure of Paul of Tarsus. 2799
Adventure of prayer. 2868, 2881
Adventure of the Christian ministry. 2474
Adventure of the church. 2492
Adventure of the hereafter. 1695
Adventure with Catholic verse. 917
Adventure with people. 3180
Adventurer saints. 764
Adventurers for God. 2496
Adventurers with God. 3314
Adventures for a better world. 3833
Adventures in brotherhood. 34, 695
Adventures in Christian journalism. 2135
Adventures in Christian leadership. 3152
Adventures in Christian living. 993, 3884
Adventures in Christian living and learning. 3185
Adventures in Christian stewardship. 3530
Adventures in consciousness. 2730
Adventures in evangelism. 1554, 1573
Adventures in faith. 4, 923
Adventures in faith and freedom. 3732
Adventures in faith in foreign lands. 2457
Adventures in friendliness. 3147
Adventures in missionary cooperation. 2521
Adventures in other lands. 2489
Adventures in prayer. 2875, 2876, 2889
Adventures in radiant living. 965
Adventures in recreation. 1166
Adventures in religion. 3069
Adventures in reputation. 1758
Adventures in Samoa. 2618
... Adventures in service. 3442
Adventures in soul-winning. 1564
Adventures in survival. 3499
Adventures in synagogue administration. 3576
Adventures in the Holy Land. 2762

Adventures in the land of Canaan. 615
Adventures in the philosophy of religion. 3107
Adventures in the South seas. 2543
Adventures in the spirit world. 3518
Adventures in the spiritual life. 3477
Adventures in training the ministry. 3332, 3681
Adventures in visitation evangelism. 1566
Adventures in world friendship. 2550
Adventures into the psychic. 2729
Adventures of a deserter. 2130
Adventures of a missionary. 2500, 2563
Adventures of a modern Huguenot. 1852
Adventures of a modern occultist. 2733
Adventures of a preacher. 3201
Adventures of a Protestant in search of a religion. 1365
Adventures of a spiritual tramp. 3199
Adventures of Adam. 1615
Adventures of an angel. 1001
Adventures of Catherine of Siena. 749
Adventures of healing. 3476
Adventures of John Hawkins, Restoration pioneer. 1791
Adventures of Kado. 2491
Adventures of men of Maryknoll. 867
Adventures of Mr. Friend. 2527
Adventures of Mottel, the cantor's son. 2105
Adventures of Peter and Paul. 72, 2825
Adventures of Saint Paul. 2803
Adventures of the black girl in her search for God. 1052
Adventures of the Christian soul. 2999
Adventures of the Greek heroes. 2663
Adventures of the mind. 2312
Adventures with Abraham's children. 628
Adventures with children. 938
Adventures with Christ in Latin America. 2549
Adventures with God. 899, 2540
Adventures with the Bible. 2490
Adventures with the Bible in Brazil. 2504
Adventures with the Krus in West Africa. 2538
Adventuring for Christ. 2296
Adventuring for Christ in changing times. 2631
Adventuring for Christ; Lutheran missionary leaders. 2296
Adventuring for Jesus. 911
Adventuring in peace and goodwill. 903
Adventuring in the church. 1329
Adventuring into the church. 1201
Adventuring with amateur adults. 3888
Adventuring with Christ. 3342
Adventuring with Disciple pioneers. 1464
Adventurings in the psychical. 2987
Adventurous future. 1235
Adventurous God. 1727
Adventurous preaching. 2905
Adventurous religion, and other essays. 1069
Adventurous religion and others essays. 1069
Adventurous youth. 3879
Adversaries of the sceptic. 2843
Adversary. 1427
Adversary, his person, power and purpose. 1428
Adversus Judaeos. 69
Adversus Marcionem. 69, 2332
Advertising Jesus. 3338
... Advertising methods for young people. 10
Advertising the church. 10
Advertising the local church. 10
Adverturing with gospel literature. 3203
Advice for boys. 688
Advice from the field. 2554
Advice to a desolate France. 2223
Advice to communicants. 2259
Advice to the young Christian, on the importance of aiming at an elevated standard of piety. 978
Advisory study. 2929, 3736
Advocacy of the Gospel. 2906
Advocate for God. 2231, 3829
Advocates of reform, from Wyclif to Erasmus. 3042
Aelred of Rievaulx. 1533
Aeneas, Sicily, and Rome. 11
Aerial bombardments. 1273
Aesthetic dimensions of religious education. 936
Aesthetic element in morality and its place in a utilitarian theory of morals. 1533
Aesthetic philosophy of peace. 2840
Aestheticism and decadence. 1518
AFA astrological atlas of the United States. 99
Affable enemy. 1058
Affectionately, Dad. 688
Affectionately inscribed to the memory of Elder Frederic W. Evans. 1577
Affectionately yours, John Wesley. 3804

Affiliation of Swedish and American churchmen. 1178
Affinity no bar to marriage. 1472, 2347
Affirm the best in yourself. 1777
Affirmation. 2435
Affirmation of immortality. 1888
Affirmations. 61
Affirmations, by a group of American Anglo-Catholics, clerical and lay. 61
Affirmations of God and man. 1016
Affirmations of Judaism. 2114
Affirmations of our faith. 61
Affirmative religion. 3059
Affirming the human and the holy. 2996
Affirming the human personality. 1003
Afflicted man's companion. 1353
Affliction. 3541
Affliction worketh. 11
Afghani and 'Abduh. 21
Afiong. 2490
Aflame for God. 1302, 1544, 1603, 1651
Africa and Christianity. 2498
Africa and the American Negro. 2497
Africa and the making of books. 2498
Africa answers. 2552
Africa, apostolic pilgrimage. 863, 3364
Africa—arrows to atoms. 2498
Africa at the crossroads. 11
Africa called us. 2552
Africa has my heart. 2498
Africa in five hours. 2497
Africa is waiting. 720
Africa of Albert Schweitzer. 2539, 3312
Africa or death. 1312, 2498
Africa: past, present, and future. 11
Africa south of the Sahara. 13
Africa today. 2497
African adventurers. 2497
African apostles. 76, 3239, 3812
African bridge builders. 2489
African Christian spirituality. 1073
African Christian theology. 12
African Christianity. 1073
African churches among the Yoruba. 2559
African churches among the Yoruba, 1888-1922. 2559
African civilisations in the New World. 2681
African culture and the Christian church. 1073
African diary. 2500
African holocaust. 2351
African independence and Christian freedom. 3088
African Methodism in the South. 14
African Methodist Episcopal Zion Church. 15
African missionary heroes and heroines. 2497
African missions. 2497
African oral narratives, proverbs, riddles, poetry, and song. 1631
African origins of the major "Western religions" 12
African primal religions. 12
African reactions to missionary education. 2500
African religions. 12
African religions & philosophy. 12
African religions of Brazil. 690
... The African society becomes Emmanuel African Methodist Episcopal church, Portsmouth, Virginia. 2864
African systems of thought. 13
African theology en route. 3653
African traditional religion. 12
African trail. 713
African triumph. 2303, 2351
African triumph; life of Charles Lwanga. 1021, 2303
African widows. 3814
Africans on safari. 2499
Africa's Bible. 2552
Africa's Mountain Valley. 1268
Africa's three religions. 12
Africa's twelve apostles. 774, 2484
Afro-American religion and church and race relations. 1897, 2683
Afro-American religious music. 3522
Afro-American religious studies. 2683
After a hundred years. 2521
After Auschwitz; radical theology and contemporary Judaism. 2080
After Bernadette; the story of modern Lourdes. 2262, 3460
After C. T. Studd. 3536, 3852
After Christianity--What? 1049
After confirmation what? 3884
After Damien. 1400
After death. 1696, 3515
After death: the immortality of man. 1696
After death--what? 66, 1415, 1529, 1696, 1697, 3507
After death--what then? 1695
After dogmatic theology, what? 3515
"After eighty years. 1311

After fifty years. 918, 1652, 3671
After fundamentalism. 176, 3669
After God's heart. 589
After He had risen. 2006
After her death. 3518
After his likeness. 168
After His passion. 2052
After Kilvert. 1291, 2171
After life in Roman paganism. 3246
... After materialism--what? 3080, 3081
After nine hundred years. 3307
After ninety years. 3551
After Nostradamus. 2715, 2948
After one hundred and fifty years. 1231
After 100 years. 2607, 3817
After one hundred years, 1844-1944. 3386
After our pilgrimage. 1698
After our present trials—the coming victory. 3446
After Pentecost. 1192
After Pentecost (the Alexandrian chronicle of Cleophas) 24, 2335
After Pentecost, what! 1827
After revival comes. 993
After-sermon prayers of Newell Dwight Hillis. 2891
After seventy-five years. 110, 1772
After seventy-five years, 1860-1935. 110
After the Council. 3772
After the cross. 2053
After the feast. 2944
After the flowers have gone. 1257, 1418
After the New Testament. 1020
After the primary; what? 639
After the rapture. 1529
After the sacrifice. 403
After the spirit comes. 994
After the storm, the restoring fire. 1421
After the war. 605
After the wedding. 2342
After therapy, what? 2986
"After this" 1051
After this manner pray ye. 2249
After twenty years. 2833
After we die, what then? 1696
After you receive power. 139, 3801
After you've said, "I believe" 3888
Afterdeath journal of an American philosopher. 3474
Afterglow. 2939, 3230, 3479, 3820
Afterlife. 1696
Aftermath. 2651
Afternoon. 3844
Afternoons in the College chapel. 3347
Afterpiece to the Comedy of convocation. 802, 2348
Afterworld effects. 3507
Aga Khans. 1927, 2165
Agada. 2141
Again pioneers. 2528
Against all reason. 2571
Against fate. 1615
Against Julian. 1750, 3413
Against the Academics. 3422
Against the clock. 713, 2485
Against the gates of hell. 83, 1144
Against the goad. 1364
Against the grain. 2318, 2462
...Against the Manichees. 2327
Against the powers. 989
Against the stream. 3618
Against the tide. 146, 2866
Against the world for the world. 77
Agape. 17, 419, 2263
Agape and Eros. 2265
Agape and history. 1819
Agape and the Eucharist in the early church. 2256
Agape in the New Testament. 17
AGARDograph. 11
Agasha, master of wisdom. 3474
Agashan discourses. 3474
Age and grace. 1257
Age and you. 2301
Age group objectives of Christian education. 2293, 3150
Age of absolutism. 808
Age of adventure. 2844
Age of belief. 2842
Age of Catherine de Medici. 753, 1639
... The age of Charlemagne. 888
Age of disunity. 2434
Age of enlightenment. 1520
Age of fable. 2650
Age of faith. 1719
... The age of Hildebrand. 1180, 1773
Age of idolism. 1583
Age of infidelity. 2834
Age of lay sanctity. 1403
Age of Luther. 2272, 3215
Age of martyrs. 2351
Age of miracles. 1599
Age of reason. 2758, 2759, 3023
Age of reason & revelation. 2758
Age of reason, being an investigation of true and fabulous theology. 3023
Age of reason unreasonable. 2759

Age of reform (1250-1550) 1186
Age of Reformation. 3034
Age of revelation. 276, 2758
Age of schism. 3307
Age of technology. 3592
Age of the crusades. 1390
Age of the Fathers. 1189, 1196
... The age of the great western schism. 3308
Age of the person. 3445
Age of the Reformation. 3033
...The age of the renascence. 2770
Age of the saints in the early Celtic Church. 878
Age of the spirit. 974, 1106
Age of the world. 3084
Age of Torquemada. 2103, 3704
Age of vinaya. 3779
Age-temptation of American Christians. 3600
Aged pilgrim's triumph over sin and the grave. 2847
Ageless Borobudur. 712
Ageless story of Jesus. 1957
Ageless wisdom of life. 3684
Agencies for the religious education of adolescents. 3167
Agency and urgency. 1537
Agenda for American Jews. 2084
Agenda for Anglicans. 43
Agenda for Biblical people. 1064
Agenda for the "sexual revolution" 3
Agenda for theology. 3618
Agent for change. 3526
Agents of reconciliation. 1117
Ages before Moses. 520
Ages in tension. 1819
Ages of the world. 2739
... The ages of the world, translated with introduction and notes by Frederick de Wolfe Bolman, jr. 2739
Ages to come. 1527
Aggressive evangelism. 1565
Aggressive work in the church of Christ. 1568
Agharta. 701
Aght'amar. 1237
Aght'amar, Church of the Holy Cross. 1237
Aging and the human spirit. 1257
Agnes and the key of her little coffin. 1349
Agnes and the litle key. 1349
Agnes and the little key. 1349
Agni, the Vedic ritual of the fire altar. 19
Agnostic. 19
... An agnostic looks at life. 19
Agnosticism. 19
... Agnosticism, and other essays. 19
... Agnosticism and religion. 19, 3471
... Agnosticism of Hume and Huxley. 19, 1855
Agnostic's apology. 19, 2704
AGO survey report. 32, 1210
Agobard of Luons, churchman and critic. 19
Agonists, a trilogy of God and man. 1017
Agony. 1093, 2041
Agony at Galloway. 1133, 1930
Agony of Christianity. 1053, 1064
Agreement. 2881
Agreement of consolidation including constitution and by-laws. 2290
Agreement of evolution & Christianity. 1581
Agreement of science and revelation. 3077
Agricola. Or, The religious husbandman. 968
Agricultural activities of the Jews in America. 2105
Agrippa. 1575
Ah Ya, I still remember. 3587, 3846
Ahead of myself. 2993, 3240
Ahiman rezon. 1661, 1669
Ahimsa (dynamic compassion) 20
Ahmadivyah. 2566
Ahmadiya movement. 20
Ahmadiyah movement. 20, 1923
Ahmadiyyah. 2566
Aid for churchmen. 44, 2749
Aid for churchmen, Episcopal and Orthodox, toward a mutual understanding. 1524
Aid to Bible understanding. 242, 246
Aid to the Heidelberg catechism. 3043
Aida of Leningrad. 2821, 3423
Aids for grade school religion teachers. 3179
Aids to a theological library. 3626
Aids to Christian belief. 1070
Aids to faith. 1602
Aids to preaching and hearing. 2906
Aids to will training in Christian education. 3816
Aids to worship. 2238

Ailred of Rievaulx and his biographer Walter Daniel. 1533
Aim of Jesus Christ. 1951
Aims and methods in teaching religion. 3180
Aims of interpretation. 1806
... The aims of teaching in Jewish schools. 2086
Ainos. 20
... The Ainsworth psalter. 2985
Ainu creed and cult. 20
Ainu group at the Saint Louis exposition. 20
Aion-aionios. 3752
Airwaves proclaim Christ. 2300
Aishah, the beloved of Mohammed. 20
Aitareya Brahmanam of the Rigveda, containing the earliest speculations of the Brahmans on the meaning of the sacrificial prayers, and on the origin, performance and sense of the rites of the Vedic religion. 3775
Aitareya Upanisat. 3760
Ajanta. 85
Ajanta to Ellora. 876
Akan religion and the Christian faith. 2500
Akiba. 20
Akiba, scholar, saint and martyr. 20
Akkadian Namburbi texts. 93
Al Baghdadi. 1924
Al Conquistadora. 3302
"Al-Islam," 2564
Al-'Uqlah texts. 1910
Alabaster and spikenard. 3777
Alabaster tombs of the pre-reformation period in England. 3333
Alamo chain of missions. 2546
Alarm to unconverted sinners. 1357
Alarm to unconverted sinners in a serious treatise on conversion. 1357
Alarms and visions. 1062
Alaska. 659, 1532
Alaska, and missions on the north Pacific coast. 1899, 2926
Alaska--assignment accomplished. 2500
Alaskan diary of a pioneer Quaker missionary. 1686, 2500
Alba House New Testament. 320
Albany protocol. 2291
Albany religious spectator. 3197
Alberic of Monte Cassino and the hymns attributed to Saint Peter Damian. 22, 1876
Albert Camus and Christianity. 733
Albert Cassel Wieand. 3814
Albert Schweitzer. 2486, 3311, 3312
Albert Schweitzer, a vindication. 3312
Albert Schweitzer, an introduction. 3311
Albert Schweitzer, Christian revolutionary. 3312
Albert Schweitzer, great humanitarian. 2845, 3312
Albert Schweitzer jubilee book. 3311
Albert Schweitzer, man of mercy. 3311
Albert Schweitzer: reverence for life. 3312
Albert Schweitzer, the man and his mind. 3312
Albert Schweitzer's gift of friendship. 3311
Albert Schwitzer. 3311
Alberti's Church of San Sebastiano in Mantua. 22, 2329
Albertus Magnus. 2311
Albigensian Crusade. 23
Albigensian heresy. 23
Album of language. 2196
Album of Methodist history. 2425
Album of the Armenian Monastery of Jerusalem. 1944
Alchemy and the occult. 2159, 2731
Alchemy, medicine, and religion in the China of A.D. 320. 23
Alchemy of awareness. 3482
Alchemy of happiness. 23
Alchemy of the word. 1077
Alcohol, a dangerous and unnecessary medicine. 23
Alcohol and Christian influence. 3595
Alcohol and science. 23
Alcohol and the scriptures. 3597
Alcohol in and out of the church. 23
Alcohol problems and general welfare. 3597
Alcohol the destroyer. 3595
Alcoholic priests. 23, 774
Alcoholics are God's children, too. 23
Alcoholism and Christian experience. 1253
Aldersgate and after. 1360
Aldhelm, the prose works. 23
Aletheia. 3396
Aletheia: spirit of truth. 3396
Alex and the good news. 2536
Alexander Campbell. 732
Alexander Campbell and Christian liberty. 732

Alexander Campbell and his Christian system today: the "Christian church", the "Church of Christ", the "Disciples of Christ." 732
Alexander Campbell and his new version. 361
Alexander Campbell and natural religion. 732, 2674
Alexander Campbell and the Disciples. 732, 1461
Alexander Campbell, preacher of reform and reformer of preaching. 732
Alexander Campbell's theology. 732
Alexander Campbell's tour in Scotland. 732, 1465
Alexander Duff. 1481
Alexander Gregg, first bishop of Texas. 1773
Alexander James Grieve, M. A., D. D., 1874-1952. 1774
Alexander Taylor Rankin, 1803-1885, his diary and letters. 1689, 2924
Alexander the Corrector. 1390
Alexander III and the twelfth century. 24, 1143
Alexander's Space, time and deity. 24, 3469
Alexandria controversy. 780
Alexandrian Christianity. 1020
Alexandrian Halakah in apologetic literature of the first century C. E. 2098, 2134
... The Alexandrine gospel. 25
Alfred Gandier. 1701
Alfred Lee. 2205
Alfred Loisy. 2243
Alfred Tennyson. 3602
Algebra of conscience. 1540
Alhambra. 25
Alias oves habeo. 850
Alice in Bibleland. 233
Alien baptism and the Baptists. 139
Alien Christ. 929, 2062
Alien Rome. 757
Alienated Christian: a theology of alienation. 25
Alienation, atheism, and the religious crisis. 1062
Alienation of church wealth in Mexico. 1242
Alive. 3353
Alive again. 2944
Alive and running. 1437
Alive in Christ. 992, 2384, 3163, 3492
Alive to God. 2384, 2885
Alive to God through prayer. 2871
Alive unto God. 959
Alive with God. 796, 3488
All about angels. 42
All about Bible study. 639
All about children's church. 3859
All about Eve ... and Adam and Jane and Johnnie. 1604
All about fast and abstinence. 1613
All about infant baptism. 134
All about Japan. 2533
All about Jesus. 1956
All about Jewish holidays and customs. 1614, 2121
All about nothing. 934
All about repentance. 3218
All about the baby and preparations for its advent. 1907
All about the baby and preparations for its advent, together with the homeopathic treatment of its ordinary ailments. 1907
All about the Bible. 308
All about the junior. 3159
All about the primary. 3558
.. All about the Sunday school. 3553
All about witnessing. 326, 329
All-age Bible quizzes. 280
All-Britain crusade of 1967. 1755, 3230
All call me Blessed. 2359
All coherence gone. 1514, 1747
All colour book of Greek mythology. 2661
All day long. 3164
All day with God. 859
All for Christ. 2817
All for her. 2827
All for Jesus. 2063, 2435, 3349, 3486, 3526
All for love. 1969
All for the King's delight. 889
All for the love of God. 2957
All God's children. 1301, 1393, 1500, 3189
All God's children ... six stories of Christians in many lands. 2536
All God's chillun. 2680
All God's chillun got soul. 16
All hail. 637
All heart. 682, 2546
All His benefits," 1017
All I have seen. 2309
All in God's family. 1044

All in good time. 1365
All in the day's work. 2494
All in the name of God. 3194
All kindreds and tongues. 2714
All-knowing God. 1736
All lost in wonder. 862
All loves excelling. 3838
All men are brothers. 3312
"All my days for Jesus" 2466, 3051
All my dusty babies. 2542, 3387
All my liberty. 2269
All nations in God's purpose. 2504
All nations of the earth blessed in Christ. 686, 2567
All occasion talks for children. 909
All of the women of the Bible. 3839
All on fire. 1700
All one body we. 1188, 3850
All or nothing. 1363
All originality makes a dull church. 1171
All our days. 3882
All our days—laugh & praise. 901
All out for God. 1377
All over the world. 1017
All-present God. 114, 1737
All religions and religious ceremonies: in two parts. 3120
All round ministry. 1299
All round the world. 2551
All Saints' Chapel in Centralia, Anne Arundel County, Maryland, being a short history of the first quarter-century (1875-1901) of the work of the Protestant Episcopal Church at Annapolis Junction, Maryland. 25
All Saint's Church, Waccamaw. 3788
All saints' day, and other sermons. 1226
All Saints Episcopal Church. 3236
All Saints' Memorial Church in the Highlands of Navesink, 1864-1964; [a centennial history. 3527
"All Scripture is inspired of God and beneficial." 646
All shall be well. 2158
All slave-keepers that keep the innocent in bondage. 3424
All souls are mine. 1016
All Souls Congregational Church (United Church of Christ) 3732
All-stars of Christ. 925
All-sufficient Christ. 341
All that we are we give. 983
All that you are. 2695
All the animals of the Bible lands. 480, 3898
All the apostles of the Bible. 71
All the bandits of China. 1802, 2509
All the Bible says about tongues. 1717
All the Bible's men of hope. 214, 1846
All the birds of the Bible. 480
All the books and chapters of the Bible. 219, 223
All the Catholic people. 1001
All the children of the Bible. 898
All the children of the world. 2490
All the cloudy days were made bright. 1859
All the damned angels. 2393
All the day long. 3790
All the days. 1354, 1431
All the days of my life. 3416
All the divine names and titles in the Bible. 1731, 2046
All the doctrines of the Bible. 651
All the families of the earth. 3047
All the good gifts. 3529
All the holy days and holidays. 1623
All the kingdoms of the earth. 567
All the kings and queens of the Bible. 215
All the Master's men. 71
All the men of the library of more than 3000 Biblical characters. 217
All the messianic prophecies of the Bible. 2415
All the miracles of the Bible. 2477
All the miracles we hope for. 2397
All the parables of Jesus. 2024
All the parables of the Bible. 601
All the people and places of the Bible. 242
All the plants of the Bible. 481
All the prayers of the Bible. 604
All the promises of the Bible. 254, 1737
All the promises of the Bible;a unique compilation and exposition of divine promises in Scripture. 1737
All the sayings of Jesus as recorded in the New Testament. 2070
All the spiritualism of the Christian Bible. 3515
All the things you aren't ... yet. 3330
All the trees and woody plants of the Bible. 480
All the way. 2643
All the way to Calvary. 3720
All the way to heaven. 870
All the way with God. 623

All the world in all the World. 2549
"All-the-year-round" activities for young people. 1166
All these. 660
All these things shall give thee experience. 1009
All things and stuff. 2388
All things are possible. 3232
All things are possible through prayer. 2867
All things bright and beautiful. 1860
All things common. 1858
All things considered ... ; trials, tribulations, temptations, and triumphs of being Christian in modern-day America. 994
All things in Christ. 2851
All things made new. 377, 2044, 2325
All things new. 462, 663, 1005, 1564, 2570
All things new ... youth ministry in a technological society. 2474
All things to all men. 2785
All things weird and wonderful. 518
All things work together for good to them that love God. 3807
All through the day. 588
All through the year. 901
All Thy mercies. 1736
All to the good. 944
All truth is God's truth. 1597
All we're meant to be. 3832
All ye who labor. 3784
All you lonely people, all you lovely people. 1170
All you who are burdened. 66
Allah, the God of Islam. 2564
Alleged Bible contradictions explained. 232
Alleged discrepancies of the Bible. 230
Alleged socialism of the church fathers. 3435
Allegion. 3142
Allegoriae poeticae. 2657
Allegorical visions of the pathways of life. 2642
Allegorical works of John Bunyan. 713
Allegories of Genesis. 639
Allegories of the virtues and vices in mediaeval art from early Christian times to the thirteenth century. 3574
Allegories of the virutes and vices in mediaeval art. 3574
Allegory and event. 240
Alleluia affair. 2384
Allied Masonic groups and rites. 1672
Allies of religion. 2974
Allness of good. 3064
Allnutt of Delhi. 26
All's right with the world. 2834
Alluring the soul along the pathway of nature's beauty. 3142
Alma White's evangelism. 2848, 3811
Almah—virgin or young woman? 3780
Almanac. 2302
Almanac and year-book. 3047
Almanac of missions. 2559
Almighty. 1728
Almighty God's prescription for peace and everlasting life. 1719
Almost Christian discovered. 1017
... Alms-gathering by religious. 771
Alone. 2408, 3814
Alone and beginning again. 171, 2129
Alone at high noon. 3456
Alone of all her sex. 2357
Alone until tomorrow. 192
Alone with God. 1263, 1434, 1715, 1719, 1807, 2873, 2893, 3222
Alone with Thee. 1826
Along a little way. 1364
Along civilization's trail. 2727, 3251
Along kingdom highways. 155
Along kingdom highways, A special edition. 156
Along life's highway. 2932, 3354
Along life's way. 1440
Along Masonic trails. 1672
Along the friendly way. 2639
Along the highway of service. 3740
Along the Indian road. 2531
Along the King's Highway. 2538
Along the mission trail. 850
Along the trail of the friendly years. 2638
Along the water's edge. 3533
Along the way. 2638
Along the years. 2757
Along Thimblelane trails. 617
Along with Christ. 2210
Alpha. 1381
Alpha and Omega. 175, 522, 2708, 2730, 3713
Alpha and the omega. 461, 1528
Alpha the myths of creation. 1381
Alphabet of creation. 3898
Alphabet of God's love. 268
Alphabet of thought. 2416

Alphabetic biographical catalog. 1389
Alphabetical arrangement of main entries from the shelf list. 2698, 3627
Alphabetical arrangement of main entries from the shelf list, Union Theological Seminary Library, New York; 10v. 3627
Alphabetical subject index and index encyclopaedia to periodical articles on religion, 1890-1899. 3090
Alphabetical compendium of the various acts which have appeared in the world from the beginning of the Christian era to the present day. 3091
Alpheus Cutler and the Church of Jesus Christ. 1230
Alpheus W. Wilson. 3818
Altar. 28, 961
Altar and priest. 28
...Altar and sanctuary. 2370
Altar and the world. 2257
Altar at home. 1604
Altar book. 27
Altar boys' ceremonial. 27
Altar boy's complete ceremonial. 27
Altar chants. 884
Altar egos. 3089
Altar fire. 27, 2253
Altar fires. 309
Altar fires for family worship. 1433
Altar fires of faith. 1439
Altar fires relighted. 1033
Altar, gift, and Gospel. 399
Altar guild manual. 27
Altar guild workbook. 27
Altar hour. 2237
Altar in the wilderness. 3685
Altar of God. 2805
Altar of the household. 1439
Altar prayers. 27
Altar prayers (Enchiridon precum) 27
Altar prayers for the church year. 2783
Altar service book of the Lutheran Church in America. 28
Altar stairs. 2893
Altar steps. 1438
Altar wreath. 28
...Altars according to the Code of canon law. 27
Altars from Genesis. 526
Altars of my fathers. 1395
Altars of the East. 91
Altars under the sky. 1441
Alter boys' ceremonial. 27
Alter Christus. 1298
... The alterations in the ordinal of 1662. 44
Alternate lifestyles. 1259
Alternate realities. 2989
Alternative altars. 3747
Alternative church. 2712
Alternative classification for Catholic books. 1286
Alternative goals in religion. 3098
Alternative readings from the New Testament. 344
...Alternative readings in the Hebrew of the books of Samuel. 590
Alternative teaching strategies. 2943
Alternative to futility. 1064
Alternative views of the Bible. 231
Alternatives. 3750
Alternatives to Christian belief. 3212
Altitude of prayer. 2872
Altizer-Montgomery dialogue. 1417
Altruism. 28
Altruistic love. 28
Alumni catalogue of the Union theological seminary. 3331
Alumni catalogue of the Union theological seminary in the city of New York, 1836-1936. 3332
Alumni directory. 3331
Alumni directory, 1836-1958. 2701
Alumni re-union of the Western theological seminary. 3331
... Alumni record. 3331
Alumni record of Drew theological seminary. 3331
Alvah Hovey, his life and letters. 1849, 2706
Always an answer. 1014
Always becoming. 1749, 2270
Always God's people. 1003
Always in prayer. 2873
Always in triumph. 2310
Always, Karen. 3474, 3789
Always springtime. 3545
Always the poor. 2717, 3602
Always the priest. 3235
Always young for liberty. 881
A.M. 2382
Am I a Christian? 1586
Am I a human radio? 3496
Am I intelligent! 63
Am I living a spiritual life? 3488
Am I losing my faith? 1592
Am I not here. 1776

Am I of the chosen. 3288
Am I ok—if I feel the way I do? 756, 3885
Am I running with you, God? 2888
Amalgamation. 3418
Amateur philosopher. 2833
Amateur spirit. 3481
Amazing Christ. 2212
Amazing cross. 2214
Amazing Dead Sea scrolls and the Christian faith. 1410
Amazing discoveries in the words of Jesus. 2071
Amazing discoveries within the book of books. 319
Amazing grace. 1292, 1752, 1753, 2706
Amazing heritage. 3837
Amazing man of Galilee. 1969, 1977
Amazing Saints. 3278
Amazing secrets of the masters of the Far East. 3864
Amazing secrets of the psychic world. 2987
Amazing world of Kreskin. 2186, 2989
Amazonia. 2501
Amazons of Greek mythology. 29
Ambassador. 2900, 3343
Ambassador for Christ. 2795
Ambassador in chains. 374, 721
Ambassador in chains, and other sermons. 1465
Ambassador of Christ. 772
Ambassador of the King. 911, 2513
Ambassador supreme. 2519
Ambassador to the saints. 2557
Ambassadors for Christ. 2910
Ambassadors of Christ. 3673
Ambassadors of God. 2898
Ambiguity of religion. 3100
Ambitious dreams of youth. 3884
Amelia Sheldon. 3402
Amen. 2653
Amen, amen. 958
Amen: the diary of Rabbi Martin Siegel. 3016
Amens of Christ. 2070
America. 757, 1700, 3333, 3746
America and Palestine. 3896
America and the American church. 2967, 3740
America and the future of theology. 3651
America and the story of the prophets. 611
America and world evangelization. 1554
America as a field for the exertions of the Christian scholar. 1673
America at the crossroads. 3742
America awakening. 1655
America bewitched. 2242, 2733
America educates for Antichrist. 52
America, God shed His grace on thee. 3748
America in history and Bible prophecy. 610, 3748
America in the coming crisis. 1359
America in theological perspective. 3748
America is too young to die. 1109
America, its destiny. 3740
America; its not too late. 942
America must be Christian. 2558
America on trial before a prostrate world. 1150
America, one nation under God. 3744
America prays. 1441
America tomorrow. 156
America triumphant under God and His Christ. 3057
America, turn to Christ! 2300
America vindicated from European theologico-political and infidel aspersions. 1656, 1822
American abundance. 2670
American Academy of Religion, annual meeting, San Francisco, California, December 28-December 31, 1977. 3091
American ambassadors to Lourdes. 2262, 3460
American amen. 1845
American and Catholic. 874
American and the Bible. 642
American apocalypse. 2464
American apostolate. 828
American apostle. 2721
American astrology tables of houses, for latitudes 0o to 600 north and south, including rules for the proper calculation of higher latitudes. 96
American Baptist pulpit at the beginning of the twentieth century. 165
American Baptist register, for 1852. 172
American Baptists; whence and whither. 30, 170
American Baptists with a Spanish accent. 2549
American Bible. 199
American bible and the American God. 1654

American Bible society and the Baptists. 655, 1803
American bishop at the Vatican Council. 3772
American bishops, 1964-1970. 667, 771
... The American board. 31
American Board year book and calendar of prayer. 2559
American Book of common prayer. 1214
American book of days. 1822
American Buddhism. 710
American Calvinism. 730
American Calvinism;a survey. 730
American cathedral. 750
American Catholic. 874
American ... Catholic almanac and year book. 866
American Catholic almanar and year book ...1931. 866
American Catholic catalog. 787
American Catholic catechism. 780, 3628
American Catholic Church and the Negro problem in the XVIII-XIX centuries. 3423
American Catholic convert authors. 32
American Catholic crossroads. 760, 829
American Catholic crossroads; religious-secular encounters in the modern world. 760
American Catholic dilema. 874
American Catholic dilemma. 874
American Catholic exodus. 760, 829
American Catholic horizons. 757
American Catholic leadership. 2670
American Catholic opinion in the slavery controversy. 3424
American Catholic peace movement, 1928-1972. 2808
American Catholic social ethics. 834, 3451
American Catholic thought on social questions. 3449
American Catholicism. 833
American Catholicism and European immigrants, 1900-1924. 874
American Catholicism and social action. 1135
American Catholicism and social action: a search for social justice, 1863-1950. 1135
American Catholicism and the intellectual ideal. 873
American Catholicism: where do we go from here? 826
American Catholics. 874
American Catholics and the intellectual life. 874
American Catholics and the social question, 1865-1900. 828, 1136
American Catholics and Vietnam. 3793
American Catholics face the future. 792
American Catholics in the war. 1543
American children of Krsna. 1914, 2186
American Christian missionary society and the Disciples of Christ. 31, 1461
American Christianity. 3740
American church. 2967
... The American church almanac and year book. 2975
American church building of today. 1162
American church dictionary and cyclopedia. 2964
American church history series. 3737
American church law. 1490
American church law considered in relation to the law of the Church of England and the administration of the civil law in the United States. 1490
American church of the Protestant heritage. 3325
American churches. 1161, 1162, 3325, 3746
American churches, beliefs practices. 3325
American churches in the ecumenical movement, 1900-1968. 1492
American churches: the bulwarks of American slavery. 3423
American churchmen visit the Soviet Union. 2750, 2955
American city and its church. 1278
... American civil church law. 1490
American civil religion. 3745
American college chaplaincy. 885
American constitutions and religion. 1151
American contacts with the Eastern churches, 1820-1870. 2956
American convert movement. 1361
American culture and Catholic schools. 794
American culture and religion. 3746
American culture and the quest for Christ. 3294
American denominational organization. 3454
American devotion. 3745
American dialogue. 2955

American dialogue: a Protestant looks at Catholicism and a Catholic looks at Protestantism. 1321
American doctor at work in India. 2928
American Dominicans. 1475
American ecclesiastical and educational almanac, for ministers and laymen. 1274
American ecclesiastical year-book. 1248
American education and religion: the problem of religion in the school. 1129
American Episcopal church in China. 913, 2970
American Episcopal clergy. 2962
American essays for the Newman centennial. 761, 2704
American evangelicals, 1800-1900. 1552
American evangelists. D.L. Moody and Ira D. Sankey. 2587
American evangelists, Dwight L. Moody and Ira D. Sankey. 2588
American faith. 3740
American foundations of religious liberty. 3195
American foundations of the Sisters of Notre Dame de Namur. 3418
American free thought, 1860-1914. 1657
American freedom and Catholic power. 798
American freethought. 1657
American Friends in world missions. 1686
American Greek Testaments. 337
American harmony. 1870
American heretics and saints. 1656
American heroes on mission fields. 2484
American Holiness movement. 1824
American Holy week manual, the liturgy from Palm Sunday through Easter day together with tenebrae. 2969
American hymns old and new. 32, 1862
... American idealism. 3746
American impact: Judaism in the United States in the early nineteenth century. 3032, 3050
American Indian ceremonial dances. 1903
American Indian policy in crisis. 1899
American Indians and Christian missions. 1901
American infidel: Robert G. Ingersoll. 1907
American interests in Syria. 2552
American Jesuits. 1948
American Jew. 2104
American Jew in search of himself. 3032
American Jewish community. 2154
American Jewish cyclopedia. 2085
American Jewish ritual. 3240
American Jewish woman. 3842
American Jewry. 2104
American Jewry and Judaism in the twentieth century. 2154
American Jewry comes of age. 2699
American Judaism. 2115, 2154, 2155
American Judaism: adventure in modernity. 2155
American Judaism reader. 32
American Judaism: the next century. 2155
American lectionary. 2205
American lectures. 3685
American liberty enlightening the world. 1913
American Lutheran almanac and year-book. 2302
American Lutheran biographies. 2303
American Lutheran Church. 2288, 2292
American Lutheran Church 1964 Year-book. 2302
*American Lutheran Church elementary curriculum. 2293
American Lutheran hymnal. 2288
American Lutheran preaching. 3364
American Lutheranism surrenders to forces of conservatism. 2294
American martyrs. 1948
American Mennonite worship. 2408
American messiah. 3050
American Methodism. 2421, 2438
American Methodist bicentennial, 1766-1966. 2431
American millennial message. 3142
American mission in Egypt, 1854 to 1896. 2517
American missionaries in China. 2484, 2501
American missionary. 2156, 2500
American missionary community in China, 1895-1905. 2509
American missionary memorial. 2483
American missionary to Meiji Japan. 1775, 2534
American missions in Bicentennial perspective. 2501
American montage. 2527, 3467
American movement to develop Protestant colleges for men in Japan, 1868-1912. 1164
American mysticism. 2648
American needs God. 161

American Negro songs and spirituals. 2680
American nun in Taiwan. 1116
American nuncio: Cardinal Aloisius Muench. 2627
American of Jewish faith. 2103
American opinion of Roman Catholicism in the eighteenth century. 3195
American oracle. 1513
American origin of the Augustana synod, from contemporary Lutheran periodicals, 1851-1860. 1546
American overture. 2104
American parish and the Roman liturgy. 840
American participation in the second Vatican Council. 3773
American pastor in Rome. 774
American patriotic devotions. 2208, 3745
American philosophies of religion. 3106
American philosophy pragmatism critically considered in relation to present day theology. 2867
American physician in Turkey. 3768
American pilgrimage. 1413
American pluralism and the Catholic conscience. 1143
American political-antimasonry, with its "Good-enough Morgan." 53, 2597
American preacher. 3347
American preachers of to-day. 2910
American priest. 2938
American priests. 775, 1302
American promise. 2106
American Protestant thought: the liberal era. 2222
American Protestant women in world mission. 3838
American Protestantism. 2955, 2956
American Protestantism and social issues. 1140
American Protestantism and social issues, 1919-1939. 1140
American Protestantism's response to Germany's Jews and refugees, 1933-1941. 1256
American psalmody. 1210
American Psalter. 986
American pulpit. 693, 3337, 3365
American pulpit series. 3347
American Puritanism. 3009
American Quakers today. 1674
American rabbi. 1748, 3016
American Reform rabbi. 3032
American religion and philosophy. 1109
American religion as I see it lived. 3744
American religions and the rise of Mormonism. 2615
American religious depression, 1925-1935. 3746
American religious experience. 3659
American religious experiment. 3748
American religious heretics. 1804
American religious history. 3748
American religious movement. 1464
American religious philosophy. 3104
American religious thought. 3743
American religious values and the future of America. 3748
American republic and human liberty foreshadowed in Scripture. 607
American Revolution and religion; Maryland 1770-1800. 2363
American saints & seers. 1038
... An American satyr. 1017
American scholar. 3723
American school hymn book. 1865
American seances with Eusapia Palladino. 2766
American search for soul. 3748
American Shakers; from neo-Christianity to presocialism. 3395
American spirit in theology. 3659
American spiritual autobiographies. 3126
American standard program for boys. 687
American state papers and related documents on freedom in religion. 3548
... American state papers bearing on Sunday legislation. 3548
American state papers on freedom in religion. 3548
American synagogue as a leavening force in Jewish life, and a collection of select writings. 2145
American synagogue directory. 3578
American text book of popery. 798
American text-books of popery: Being an authentic compend of the bulls, canons and decretals of the Roman hierarchy. 797
American theology in the liberal tradition. 2221
American theory of church and state. 1149
American theosophical society lodge procedure. 3682

American thought and religious typology. 3721
American Tract Society documents, 1824-1925. 33
American tradition in religion and education. 1149
American Unitarian biography. 3724
American Universalism. 3755
New Testament of Our Lord and Saviour Jesus Christ. 361
American vision of the church. 1188
American war Congress and Zionism. 3897
American way. 3743
American writers and compilers of sacred music. 2635
American year-book and national register for 1869. 3197
Americanism and Catholicism. 827
Americanism and the Bible. 1655
Americanism versus Christianity. 1321
Americanism vs. Roman Catholicism. 756, 1321
Americanization of a congregation. 1824
Americanization of the Danish Lutheran churches in America. 2302
Americanization of the Synagogue, 1820-1870. 2155
Americans all. 2105
American's guide to English parish churches, including the Isle of Man. 1270
Americans in Africa. 34
Americans of Jewish descent. 2106
Americans who have been reincarnated. 3055
America's boys and girls. 2528
America's Catholic heritage. 828
America's fastest growing churches. 1171
America's first Bibles. 212
America's first Christmas. 1310
America's forgotten priests. 829
America's future religion. 1697
America's hour of decision. 1754, 3232
America's invisible guidance. 2725
America's Ju-deal. 2105
America's Lutherans. 2292
America's mission. 3202
America's real religion. 3744
America's schools and churches. 1128
America's spiritual culture. 3745
Americas spiritual recovery. 3744
America's thousand bishops: from 1513 to 1974. 668, 772
America's triumph. 2103
America's way in church. 1150
America's way in church, state, and society. 1150
AmeriChristendom. 1174
Amethyst Gray. 3600
Amicable discussion on the Church of England and on the reformation in general. 2977
Amillennialism today. 2465
Amische lieder, written and compiled by Joseph W. Yoder. 2406
Amish family. 35
Amish folk of Pennsylvania Dutch country. 2407
Amish life. 2407
Amish Mennonites. 2406
Amish people. 35, 2407
Amish society. 2408
Amish traditions. 2405
Amish year. 2407
Amityville horror. 1423, 2303
"Ammi--my people;" 1017
Ammi Rogers and the Episcopal Church in Connecticut, 1790-1832. 3243
Among central African tribes. 2513
Among India's students. 1814
Among industrial workers. 3873
Among industrial workers (ways and means) a hand book for Associations in industrial fields. 3873
Among missions in the Orient and observations by the way. 2502
Among South American friends. 2547
Among the Alaskans. 1899, 2926
Among the believers. 1924, 2668
Among the dervishes. 3542
Among the Franciscan tertiaries. 1649
Among the Gospels and the Acts. 384, 472
Among the heretics of Europe. 143
Among the Mescalero Apaches. 55, 690
Among the minarets. 2540
Among the Mormons. 2603, 2616
Among the mystics. 2645
Among the stars. 2332
Among the Telugoos. 1705
Amongst the Shans, by Archibald Ross Colquhoun ... With upwards of fifty whole-page illustrations, and an historical sketch of the Shans. 1905
Amorous astrologer. 96
Amos. 35, 486

Amos; a commentary. 485
Amos; a study guide with questions for discussion. 486
Amos among the Prophets. 35, 485
Amos and his message. 485
Amos and his message, an expository commentary. 485
Amos & Isaiah: prophets of the word of God. 486
Amos, Hosea. 486
Amos of Tekoa. 485
Amos, prophet of justice. 34, 35
Amos studies. 486
Amos, the prophet. 35
Amos versus Amaziah. 2160
Amos's oracles against the nations. 486
Amplified Bible, containing the amplified Old Testament and the amplified New Testament. 198
Amplified New Testament. 320
Amplified Old Testament. 481, 482
Amsterdam to Nairobi. 1155, 3850
Amulets. 35
Amulets and birthstones. 95
Amulets and superstitions. 35
Amulets, talismans, and fetishes. 35
Amurru. 2113
Amusements. 36
Amusements, in the light of reason and Scripture. 35
Ana Stahl of the Andes and Amazon. 2544, 3524
Anabaptism; a social history, 1525-1618. 37
Anabaptism and asceticism. 36
Anabaptism in Flanders. 37
Anabaptism in Flanders, 1530-1650. 37
Anabaptist baptism. 137
Anabaptist beginnings (1523-1533) 37
Anabaptist book confiscations in Hungary during the eighteenth century. 36
Anabaptist story. 37
Anabaptist view of the church. 36
Anabaptists and religious liberty in the sixteenth century. 36
Anabaptists and Thomas Muntzer. 37, 2631
Anabaptists four centuries later. 2404, 2408
Anabaptists in south and central Germany, Switzerland, and Austria, their names, occupations, places of residence, and dates of conversion, 1525-1618. 37
Anacalypsis. 3093
*Analecta Hymnica Medii Aevi. 1876
Analects of Confucius. 1537
Analogical imagination. 3649
Analogy. 1725
Analogy and symbolic meaning of the Bible doctrine to nature, to human nature and to human acquirements. 639
Analogy and the scope of its application in language. 2196
Analogy of experience. 1106
Analogy of religion. 38
Analogy of religion, natural & revealed. 38
Analogy of religion, natural and revealed, to the constitution and course of nature. 38, 2674
Analogy of religion, to the constitution and course of nature. 38
Analogy of science. 3076
Analyses of fraternal societies and illustrations of premium computations. 1776
Analysis and summary of Old Testament history and the laws of Moses. 536
Analysis and translation of selected documents of Napoleonic Jewry. 2080
Analysis of Holy Writ. 636
Analysis of Malay magic. 2315
Analysis of man and his philosophy. 2834
Analysis of moral man. 2994
Analysis of objects. 2419
Analysis of religious belief. 3112
Analysis of Revelation. 452, 3224, 3226
Analysis of the Articles of faith. 2614, 3430
Analysis of the Book of Mormon. 679
Analysis of the book of Revelation. 459
Analysis of the Hawaii Mission of the Methodist Church. 2431, 2441
Analysis of the Institutes of the Christian religion of John Calvin. 727, 3640
Analysis of the principles of the divine government. 2981
Analysis of the racial adjustment activities and problems of the Filipino-American Christian Fellowship in Los Angeles. 1625, 2556
Analysis of the restored Holy Week rites for pastoral use. 844
Analysis of the Sravakabhumi manuscript. 706
Analysis of Vatican 30. 2462

Analysis of Watson's Theological institutes. 3798
Analytics of a belief in a future life. 1888
Analytic-synthetic distinction. 3717
Analytical approach to the New Testament. 411
Analytical concordance to the Bible. 225, 226, 228
Analytical concordance to the Bible on an entirely new plan. 228
Analytical concordance to the Bible on an entirely new plan containing about 311,000 references, subdivided under the Hebrew and Greek originals, with the literal meaning and pronunciation of each. 228
Analytical concordance to the Holy Scriptures. 302
Analytical concordance to the Revised Standard Version of the New Testament. 345
Analytical guide to the bibliographies on Islam, Muhammad, and the Quran. 657
Analytical guide to the bibliographies on modern Egypt & the Sudan. 657
Analytical guide to the bibliographies on the Arab Fertile Crescent (with a section on the Arab-Israeli conflict) 657
Analytical guide to the bibliographies on the Arabian Peninsula. 657
Analytical Holy Bible, self-pronouncing, self-interpreting, self-explanatory. 225
Analytical index to the Book of common prayer, and a brief account of its evolution. 577
Analytical interpretation of Martin Buber's I and Thou. 699, 2227
Analytical linguistic key-word-in-context concordance to the book of Judges. 555
Analytical linguistic key-word-in-context concordance to the books of Haggai, Zechariah, and Malachi. 529
Analytical lingustic concordance to the book of Isaiah. 543
Analytical manual of the English Bible. 225
Analytical philosophy of religion. 3106
Analytical studies in the Psalms. 577
Analytical study of the Abhidharmakosa. 3, 3768
Analyzed Bible. 223, 417, 441, 468, 521, 543, 548, 567
Ananda and the three great acharyas. 3301, 3492
Anaphora. 1487, 2240
Anaphoras of the Ethiopic liturgy. 2237
Anastasis. 3220
Anatolia. 609
Anatomie of abuses. 3607
Anatomy of a church. 2746
Anatomy of a hybrid. 1144
Anatomy of anti-semitism. 3017
Anatomy of athesim. 101
Anatomy of evil. 1427
Anatomy of faith. 2143
Anatomy of God. 722, 3407
Anatomy of hymnody. 1878
Anatomy of prophecy. 2948
Anatomy of saints. 339
Anatomy of society. 1765
Anatomy of the body of God. 3225
Anatomy of the Catholic Church. 811
Anatomy of the ministry. 1288
Anatomy of the New Testament. 411
Anatomy of the occult. 2723
Anatomy of the soul. 3464
Anatomy of witchcraft. 3823
Ancestor worship in contemporary Japan. 39
Ancestors. 39
Ancestry of our English Bible. 291
... The ancestry of the Harklean New Testament. 475
Anchor Bible. 220
Anchor of hope. 3406
Anchor of the soul. 1589
Anchor post. 2129
Anchored in God. 102
Anchored to the Rock. 3200
Anchors of the soul. 3725
Ancient aliyot. 2101
Ancient America and the Book of Mormon. 2598
Ancient America speaks. 679
Ancient and accepted Scottish rite of freemasonary. 1665
Ancient and modern initiation. 2636
Ancient apostles. 1426
Ancient art and ritual. 88
Ancient astrology. 98
Ancient beliefs in the immortality of the soul. 1889
Ancient British and Irish churches. 1761
Ancient Christian writers. 1019
Ancient Christianity, and the doctrines of the Oxford tracts. 2755

Ancient Christianity exemplified in the private, domestic, social, and civil life of the primitive Christians, and in the original institutions, offices ordinances, and rites of the church. 1190
Ancient chronology. 219
Ancient church orders. 1239
Ancient cipher. 3576
Ancient Coptic Churches of Egypt. 919, 1368
Ancient devotions to the Sacred Heart of Jesus. 3269
Ancient Edom. 1497
Ancient Egypt, the light of the world. 3110
Ancient Egyptian art. 3599
Ancient Egyptian Book of two ways. 1501
Ancient Egyptian doctrine of the immortality of the soul. 1891
Ancient Egyptian magic. 2314
Ancient Egyptian religion. 1501
Ancient English ecclesiastical architecture and its principles. 1159
Ancient epic. 1521
Ancient facts and fictions concerning churches and tithes. 1285, 3702
Ancient faith in conflict. 1271
Ancient faiths and modern. 3117
Ancient Fathers of the desert. 1115, 3493
Ancient fires for modern men. 2436, 3353
Ancient fires on modern altars. 1567
Ancient Gods. 3139
Ancient Greek religion. 1767
Ancient Hebrew literature. 481, 482
Ancient Hebrews. 2096
Ancient history of universalism. 3752
Ancient hymns of holy church. 1870
Ancient Indian asceticism. 89
...Ancient Indian fables and stories. 1897
Ancient Indian magic and folklore. 2315
Ancient Indian rituals and their social contents. 3239
Ancient Israel. 2096
Ancient Israel from patriachal to Roman times. 2096
Ancient Israel; its story and meaning. 2096
Ancient Israel's criminal law. 1314
Ancient Italy and modern religion. 3246
Ancient Jerusalem. 1944
Ancient Jewish and Greek encouragement and consolation. 1354
Ancient Jewish philosophy. 2841
Ancient journey. 1733
Ancient Judaism. 599, 2149
Ancient Judaism and the New Testament. 347, 1083
Ancient library of Qumran and modern Biblical studies. 1409, 3013
Ancient liturgies of the Gallican Church. 2237
Ancient liturgy of the Church of England according to the uses of Sarum, York, Hereford and Bangor, and the Roman liturgy. 2237
Ancient liturgy of the Church of England, according to the uses of Sarum, York, Hereford, and Bangor, and the Roman liturgy arranged in parallel columns with preface and notes. 2237
Ancient masters and Jesus. 2060
Ancient, medieval, and modern Christianity. 1175
Ancient mirrors of womanhood. 1742
Ancient missions and churches of America. 2501
Ancient monasteries of Kiev Ru's. 2569
Ancient mysteries. 2322
Ancient mysteries and modern revelations. 3566
Ancient mysteries of Delphi: Pythagoras. 2636
Ancient mysteries of the East: Rama/Krishna. 2186, 3019
Ancient mystic oriental masonry. 2638, 3821
Ancient myth and modern man. 2652
Ancient myths. 2651
Ancient Near East. 487, 537, 2678, 2743
Ancient Near Eastern texts relating to the Old Testament. 537
Ancient operative masonry. 1671
Ancient Orient and Old Testament. 537
Ancient oriental history. 2114
Ancient pagan and modern Christian symbolism. 3573
Ancient pagan symbols. 3573
Ancient patterns in modern prayer. 2865
Ancient peoples at new tasks. 2521
... Ancient philosophers. 2832
...The ancient platforms of the Congregational churches of New England. 1344
Ancient Popes. 2861
Ancient portraits in modern frames. 215
Ancient prehistoric wisdom. 3821
Ancient records and the Bible. 514

Ancient religions. 3115
Ancient religious cults. 3268
Ancient Roman religion. 3246
Ancient science of geomancy. 1706
Ancient sermons for modern times. 3337
Ancient stones cry out. 207
Ancient symbol worship. 2828, 3574
Ancient synagogue of Beth Alpha. 195
Ancient synagogues in Palestine and
Greece. 3576
Ancient synagogues of the Iberian
peninsula. 3577
Ancient synagogues, the state of research.
3576
Ancient testimony of the Religious society
of Friends. 1681
Ancient testimony of the religious Society
of Friends, commonly called Quakers,
respecting some of their Christian
doctrines and practices: revived and
given forth by the Yearly meeting, held
in Philadelphia in the fourth month,
1843. 1681
Ancient text of the New Testament. 352
Ancient theology. 69
Ancient thoughts in modern perspective.
565
Ancient truths for modern days. 592
Ancient truths for today's needs. 1267
Ancient way. 298, 2679
Ancient wisdom. 3683
Ancient wisdom for modern man. 3821
Ancient wisdom revived. 3689
Ancient wives and modern husbands.
3839
Ancren riwle. 2579, 2580
Ancrene riwle. 2580
Ancrene wisse. 2580
And a cast of thousands. 2527, 3466
And a new earth. 3434
And a pair of warm socks. 3112
. . . and a time to laugh. 2937
And after this? 1528
And all the dark make bright like day.
1114
"... and be baptized" 134
And be ye saved. 1555
... "And behold, the camels were coming"
(Genesis 24: 63) by Edward Cuyler
Kurtz. 3027
"And certain women," 3840
And cleanse my lips. 1264
And gladly learn. 3545
...and gladly serve. 1239
And God bless me. 1022
And God caught an eel. 3698
And God created. 1381
"And God remembered ..." 1560
And God spake these words. 278
And God wants people. 2265
And, God, what about ...? 3670
... and great shall be your reward. 3294
And he gave pastors. 2790
And he had compassion. 2017
And he is lifted up. 421
And he prayed. 1506
And heaven and nature sing. 2384
"And hell laughed," 230
"And I John saw." 2206
And I look for the Resurrection. 2059
And i shall be healed. 1598, 2262
And I will make of thee a great nation.
3581
And in all Judea. 155
"And in Samaria" 879
... and into the light. 2729
And it came to pass. 609, 742, 1406
And it shall come to pass. 45
And it was told of a certain potter. 3200
And Jesus said. 2024, 2071
And Jesus said... The Master's answers to
human needs. 2071
And Judas Iscariot. 1556
And let us reason together. 1438
And light new fires. 3698
And me, coyote! 1384
And more about God. 3108
And none would believe it. 950
And Nora said yes. 2581
And now a word from our Creator. 865,
3758
And on this rock. 2824, 2862
'And other pastors of thy flock. 186, 3619
And our defense is sure. 3355
And peace at the last. 1413
And pilate asked. 2215
And Pilate wrote a title. 2006
And Sarah laughed. 501, 3832
And see the people. 3731
And she was called Magdalen. 2353
And sleep in the woods. 1363, 3868
And smoking flax shall he not quench.
445
And so I preached this! 2722
And so they came to Bethlehem. 1478
And so you never pray! 2882
... and spare me not in the making. 2580

And still He speaks. 2006
And still is ours today. 929, 1967
And the answer is yes! 983
And the greatest of these: the power of
Christian love. 2267
And the last shall be first. 1029
And the life everlasting. 1886
And the light shines in the darkness. 3270
And the Lord said. 628
And the new earth. 3073
And the other Mary. 1888
And the prophets. 2950
... and "the spoken word," 2607
And the third day. 2012, 3204
"And the two shall become one flesh" 365
And then a cathedral. 3276
And then comes the end. 347, 1530
And then I pray, goodnight. 621
And they all sang hallelujah. 731
And they shall teach their children. 1607
And they went forth. 2929
And this is how it is. 987
And this is the Torah. 500
And thou shalt die in a polluted land.
1853
And thy neighbor as thyself. 3454
And to the Eskimos. 1532
And was crucified. 2056
And was made man. 390, 1952
And we are whole again. 2995
And worship him. 3386
And would you believe it! 2706
And ye visited me. 1258
And yet it moves. 1492, 3850
And yet so new. 1364
And you visited me. 1258, 2782
And young men shall see visions. 998
And your neighbor. 2060
Anders Nygren. 2718
Andover hersy. 1335, 3432
Andover liberals. 40, 3659
Andover theological seminary. 3331
Andreae and the Formula of concord. 40,
1292
Andreas. 40
Andreas and The fates of the apostles. 40
Andrew Hunter Dunn, fifth bishop of
Quebec. 1483
Andrew Law, American psalmodist. 2201
Andrew Melville. 2401
Andrew Murray year book. 725
Andrew of Galilee, apostle of Christ. 40
Andrew Potter, Baptist builder. 2865
Andrew, the apostle. 40
Androcles and the lion. 1071
Andromedans & other parables of science
and faith. 3082
Anecdote-sermonettes for children's mass.
865, 908, 3370
Anecdotes and characters of the times.
740
Anecdotes and examples illustrating the
Catholic catechism. 767
Anecdotes and illustrations. 1841, 1842
Anecdotes and illustrations of D. L.
Moody. 1841
Anecdotes and illustrations of the Christian
ministry. 3675
Anecdotes, illustrations and incidents.
1841
Anecdotes of Henry Ward Beecher. 184
Anecdotes of the Puritans. 3006
Anecdotes of the Wesleys. 3802
Angel adjutant of "twice born men," 2206,
3292
Angel and the donkey. 131
Angel and the vision. 330
Angel at her shoulder. 1458, 2523
Angel band. 42
Angel book. 43
Angel children: those who die before
accountability. 897, 1812
Angel city. 43
Angel food. 906
Angel food for Jack and Jill. 906
Angel food time. 906
Angel for his guide. 3703
Angel from hell. 1429
Angel-guardian's clock, 1630. 41, 785,
997
Angel in ebony. 2620
Angel in my house. 42
Angel in the cloud. 42
Angel in the flame. 3354
Angel in the house. 3201
Angel in the house. The espousals. 42
Angel in the soul. 3355
Angel in the streets. 2348
Angel in the sun. 2229
Angel of death. 2857, 3474
Angel of light. 42
Angel of mercy. 855
Angel of peace. 1508
Angel of the Andes. 3247
Angel of the judgement. 3780
Angel of the ragpickers. 2195
Angel spreads her wings. 3243

Angel stories of the Bible. 42
Angel unaware. 3243
Angel voices from the spirit world. 3507
Angel whispers; or, The echo of spirit
voices. 1347
Angel with a slingshot. 3356
Angel world. 41
Angela. 41
Angela Merici. 41
Angelic doctor. 3309, 3693
Angelic guide. 854, 3692
Angelic orders. 42
Angelic overtures of Mary Baker Eddy's
"Christ and Christmas," 1034, 1496
Angelic shepherd. 2852
Angelic wisdom about divine providence.
2983, 3570
Angelic wisdom concerning divine love
and wisdom. 2983
Angelic wisdom concerning the divine love
and the divine wisdom. 1735, 2982,
2983, 3570
Angelic wisdom concerning the divine
providence. 2982, 3570
Angelic wisdom concerning the opening of
the first of the seven seals. 41
Angelic wisdon concerning the divine
providence. 2982
Angelique of Port Royal. 83, 2864
Angelographia. 42
Angelology of the Old Testament. 42
Angels. 42, 43
Angels and demons according to
Lactantius. 43, 2190
Angels and dirt. 3099
Angels and man. 3473
Angels and me. 43
Angels and men. 41
Angels and ministers of grace. 43, 588
Angels and principalities. 375, 2866
Angels and the liturgy. 43
Angels and their ministrations. 42
Angels and their mission. 41, 43
Angels and us. 41
Angels, angels, angels. 42
Angels, angels, everywhere. 42
Angels' diary and celestion study of man.
2399
Angels, God's secret agents. 42
Angels--good and bad. 42
Angels in faded jeans. 3830, 3890
Angels in heaven and earth. 42
Angels in religion and art. 42
Angels in the mountains. 1575
Angels messages, through Mrs. Ellen E.
Ward. 3517
Angels must have smiled. 871
Angels of God. 42, 43
Angels over Elisabethville. 2270, 3388
Angels, secret agents of God and Satan.
42
Angels then and now. 42
Angels' whispers; or, Echoes of spirit
voices. 1350
Angels' wings. 904
Angels within call. 3506
Anger and assertiveness in pastoral care.
2779
Anger—yours & mine & what to do about
it. 43
Angkor. 87
Angle-American Bible revision. 274
Anglican and Puritan. 3658
Anglican career of Cardinal Newman.
2702
Anglican Church in Canada. 43
Anglican Church in Delaware. 1223
Anglican Church in New Jersey. 2971
Anglican Church in New Zealand. 1238
Anglican church principles. 1220
Anglican climate in Connecticut. 2963
Anglican communion. 44
Anglican Communion, past and future. 43
Anglican communion throughout the
world. 1224
Anglican Episcopate in Connecticut (1784-
1899) 2963
Anglican episcopate and the American
colonies. 44, 1222
Anglican episcopate of Canada and
Newfoundland. 666
Anglican essays. 44
Anglican Eucharist in ecumenical
perspective. 2253
Anglican evangelicalism. 1551, 3244
Anglican humanitarianism in colonial New
York. 2542, 3437
Anglican liberalism. 2220
Anglican liturgies. 2257
Anglican low mass. 1214
Anglican-Methodist conversations: a
comment from within. 1321
Anglican moods of the eighteenth century.
3212
Anglican mosaic. 44
Anglican mosaic. 44
Anglican orders. 44

Anglican orders and defect of intention.
44
Anglican ordinations. 44
Anglican pulpit to-day. 44
...The Anglican reformation. 3041
Anglican revival. 2754
Anglican/Roman Catholic dialogue. 1224
Anglican study in Christian symbolism.
1249
Anglican turning point. 44
Anglican view of the Vatican Council.
1041, 3770, 3772
Anglican view of the Vation Council.
3770
Anglicanism. 43, 45, 1218, 1220
Anglicanism and episcopacy. 1211, 3573
Anglicanism by Stephen Neill. 43
Anglicanism for parents. 1219
Anglicanism in ecumenical perspective.
1043
Anglicanism in history and today. 44
Anglicanism in South Carolina, 1660-1976.
2974
Anglicanism in transition. 1211
Anglicanism and unity. 1043
Anglicans and unity. 1043
Anglo-American Bible revision. 274
Anglo-French sequelae. 3333
Anglo-Saxon cross. 1388
Anglo-Saxon, saints and heroes. 3283
Anglo-Vatican relations, 1914-1939:
confidential annual reports of the British
Ministers to the Holy See. 860, 1763
Anglo-American alliance in prophecy. 46
Anglo-American preaching. 3365
Anglo-Catholic ideals. 45
Anglo-Catholic revival. 2754
Anglo-Catholicism. 1218
Anglo-Catholic's thoughts on religion. 45
Anglo-Israle and the Jewish problem. 46
Anglo-Israel mysteries unmasked. 46
Anglo-Roman relations, 1558-1565. 860,
1763
Anglo-Saxon and Slovak-Avar patterns of
Cuthbert's Gospel. 843
Anglo-Saxon-charms. 888
Anglo-Saxon Congregationalism in the
South. 1338
Anglo-Saxon influence on Western
Christendom, 600-800. 1185
Anglo-Saxon Israel. 46
Anglo-Saxon magic. 2313
Anglosaxon missionaries in Germany.
927, 2318
Anglo-Saxon saints and scholars. 23
Anglo-Saxon towers. 3705
Angola beloved. 2501
Angry king. 495, 634, 3304
Anguish and joy of the Christian life.
1000
Anguish of preaching. 2908
Anguished men of God. 1289
Anima eroica. 663
Animadversions on a pamphlet, entitled "A
series of letters on this question. 3280
Animadversions on "The substance of two
sermons. 1334, 2220
Animal and vegetable physiology. 662
Animal ghosts. 2772
Animal kingdom. 2845
Animal symbolism in ecclesiastical
architecture. 920
Animals and birds redeemed from death.
47
Animals and the ark. 2712
Animals, birds, and plants of the Bible.
481
Animals in the Bible. 313, 481
Animals of the Bible. 313, 480, 481
Animated junior sermons. 910
Animated object talks. 2720, 3376
Ann H. Judson. 2158
Ann [!] illustration of the character &
conduct of the Presbyterian church in
Virginia. 2928
Ann Judson. 2157
Ann Lee (the founder of the Shakers)
2205, 3395
Ann of Ava. 2157, 2158
Ann the Word. 2205
Anna Brinton. 692
Annals and growth of the First Baptist
Church of Fort Payne, Alabama, 1885-
1963. 1634
Annals and growth of the First Baptist
Churct of Fort Payne, Alabama, 1885-
1963. 1634
Annals of a life of faith. 1595
Annals of Ebenezer. 1487
Annals of King's chapel from the Puritan
age of New England to the present day.
684
Annals of loyalty. 3286
Annals of St. Luke's church. 1116
Annals of Southern Methodism. 2458
Annals of the American pulpit. 1300,
2444

Annals of the American Unitarian pulpit. 3725
Annals of the Baptist churches in New-Hampshire. 147
Annals of the church in Scotland. 3315
Annals of the classis of Bergen. 3045
Annals of the earlyRiends. 2777
Annals of the Evangelical association of North America. 1546
Annals of the first African church, in the United States of America. 2681
Annals of the First Presbyterian Church, Lexington, Kentucky, 1784-1959. 2220
Annals of the Good Shepherd, Philadelphia, 1850-1925. 3420
Annals of the Methodist Episcopal church, of Seymour, Conn. 3394
Annals of the Nyingma lineage in America. 3589
Annals of the parish. 3199
Annals of the poor. 1015, 2866
Annals of the Reformation and establishment of religion. 1760
Annals of the Society of the Holy Child Jesus, American Province, 1862-1882 [by] Mother M Mildred. 3438
Annals of the United States Christian commission. 3737
Annals of Trinity church, Newport, Rhode Island. 1122
Annals of witchcraft in New England, and elsewhere in the United States. 3827
Anne. 48
Anne de Xainctonge. 3761, 3861
Anne de Xainctonge, her life and spirituality. 3761, 3861
Anne Hutchinson, troubler of the Puritan Zion. 53, 1858
Annie Besant. 195
Annie Laurie mine. 3197
Annihilation of the wicked scripturally considered. 48
Anniversary and Sabbath school hymns. 3561
Anniversary gems. 3026
Anniversary leaves. 3026
Anniversary of the foundation of the Diocese of El Paso, March 3, 1914, and of the consecration of the Most Reverend Sidney M. Metzger, Bishop of El Paso, April 10, 1940. 1503
Anniversary of the Pennsylvania Baptist convention. 159
Anniversary speaker. 3026
Anno Domini. 1176
Anno santo, Holy year, 1925. 2848
Annotated, analytical bibliography of Tirso de Molina studies, 1627-1977. 3594
Annotated Bible. 198
Annotated bibliography in classical Eastern psychology. 3123
Annotated bibliography in religion and psychology. 2785, 3002
Annotated bibliography of cryptography. 1392
Annotated bibliography of John Bunyan studies. 716
Annotated bibliography of philosophy in Catholic thought, 1900-1964. 1106
Annotated bibliography of research studies on the education of sisters. 3205
Annotated bibliography of studies relating to spelling. 1517
Annotated bibliography of the writings of William James. 1934
Annotated bibliography of writings on Judaism published in the Soviet Union, 1960-1965. 2103

Annotated bibliography on the Amish. 2404

Annotated bibliography on the medical, legal, and moral/ethical dimensions of euthanasia. 1544

Annotated Book of common prayer. 2870

Annotated catalog of documentary-type materials in the Wilford C. Wood Collection. 2616, 3846

Annotated constitution and canons for the government of the Protestant Episcopal Church in the United States of America, adopted in general conventions, 1789-1952. 2966

Annotated New Testament. 343
Annotated Scottish communion office. 2257
Annotations from John. 424
Annotations of the Hymnal. 2968
Annotations upon popular hymns. 1872

Announcement of courses of study. 3331
Announcing Christ through Scripture to the church. 3666
Announcing the good news. 864, 3355
Announcing the word of God. 2789
Annual announcement. 1309, 3875
Annual assembly. 82
... Annual catalog. 3332
Annual catalogue. 3332
Annual catalogue of the officers and students. 3332
Annual catalogues of the teachers and pupils of the Mount Holyoke female seminary. 3332
Annual Catholic information guide and business directory, complete. 2864
Annual Catholic missal for Sundays and Holydays. 845
Annual convention. 3576, 3598
... Annual convention American section T. S. 3682
Annual convention. [Minutes]. 2296
... Annual convention of the Theosophical society in America. 3682
... The annual cycle of redemption. 842
Annual directory. 143
Annual lecture on revival and evangelism. 3229
Annual lesson commentary [on the] National Sunday School Association uniform lessons. 3188
Annual meeting of the Massachusetts Episcopal society for the religious instruction of freedmen. 2541
Annual minutes, year book, Wyoming annual conference. 2445
Annual of the Northern Baptist convention 1908. 2714
Annual official Catholic directory and calendar. 842
Annual report. First. 2923
Annual register. 3332
Annual register of the Baptist denomination. 142
Annual regular meeting, acts and proceedings of the Lehigh synod of the Evangelical and Reformed church. 1545
Annual report. 33, 101, 154, 169, 615, 683, 824, 1083, 1127, 1131, 1210, 1408, 1458, 1544, 1551, 1657, 1796, 2081, 2085, 2086, 2098, 2452, 2453, 2457, 2479, 2486, 2505, 2518, 2542, 2546, 2913, 2923, 2942, 2959, 3556, 3705, 3756, 3833, 3876, 3878
... Annual report. 19. 3756
Annual report, 1928. 1332
Annual report. 1st-101st; 1827-1927. 1343
Annual report. 1st- 1883/84. 2923
...Annual report. 1st- 1918. 1343
...Annual report ... and the proceedings at the annual meeting. 2546
... Annual report, no. 2107
Annual report of the American Bible society. 30
... annual report of the Board of inspectors of the Sunday school association of the city of Troy. 3564
... Annual report of the board of managers. 2455, 3571
... Annual report of the Board of missions for freedmen of the Presbyterian church in the United States of America. 2926
Annual report of the directors of the American Congregational association. 1345
Annual report of the Evangelical education society of the Protestant Episcopal church. 2965
Annual report of the Executive committee. 33
Annual report of the missionary bishop of Niobara. 2970
Annual report of the Missionary society of the East Genesee conference. 2446
Annual report of the National Lutheran council. 1543
... Annual report of the New-York Sunday school union society ... 1st (Feb. 1817) 3564
Annual report of the Philadelphia conference missionary society. 2445
Annual report of the president. 34, 1277
Annual report of the rector. 870
Annual report of the Young women's Christian association of the city of New York. 3878
Annual reports. 1st- Feb. 1905. 3878
Annual reports and list of members. 2101
Annual reports of the American Bible society with an account of its organization. 30
Annual retreat mediations. 2398
Annual session. 2446
Annual session. Minutes. 154
Annual session of Central New York conference. 2444

Annual session of the Baptist congress. 140
Annual session ... Provincial program. 1901. 154
Annual session. [Report]. 2458
Annual survey, religious work, Young men's Christian associations. 3874
Annuals of the Southside Baptist Church. 663
Annulment. 2341
Annunciation. 2361
Annunciation from the right. 920, 2357
Annunciation of the Eden age. 1496
Annunciation, visitation. 854, 2361
Anointed to preach. 2898
Anointed to serve. 92
Anointing of the Holy Spirit. 1833
Anointing of the sick and the elderly. 3722
... The anointing of the sick in Scripture and tradition. 935
Anonymous apostle. 1308
Anonymous Christian. 3295
Anonymous hypothesis of creation. 1380
Anos; an essay in exegesia. 485
Another brown bag. 908
Another cathechism. 769
Another chance. 986
"Another comforter" 1830
Another day, another miracle. 2309
Another essay for investigation of the truth. 134
Another gospel. 386
Another hand on mine. 182, 2513
Another kind of love. 1843
Another look at Seventh-Day Adventism. 3382
Another pair of shoes. 1016
Another path. 1353
Another will gird you. 1676
Another wonder in heaven. 463
Another world and yet the same. 1017
Another year's talks to children. 906
Anscar Vonier, abbot of Buckfast. 3786
Anselm. 49, 1739
Anselm and a new generation. 49
...Anselm and his work. 49
Anselm and Nicholas of Cusa. 49
Anselm and talking about God. 49, 1733
Anselm, fides quaerens intellectum. 48, 49, 1739
Anselm's discovery. 49, 1739
Anselm's theory of the atonement. 104
Answer. 2082, 3436
Answer for agnostics. 1094
Answer from Amsterdam. 3850
Answer in defence of the truth against the Apology of private mass. 2365
Answer is God. 3243
Answer is the spirit. 1834
Answer me this. 3012
Answer of faith. 2299
Answer of God. 912
Answer of history. 46
Answer to a pamphlet entitled Priest-craft detected. 1017
Answer, to a paragraph contained in the United States Catholic miscellany. 869
Answer to anxiety. 2808
Answer to Dr. Perry's Reply to the Calm review. 2820, 3299
Answer to Dr. Priestley's appeal. 2939
Answer to Father Coughlin's critics. 1372
Answer to Hugh Miller and theoretic geologists. 202, 2466
Answer to humanistic psychology. 64
Answer to Job. 550, 3101
Answer to Mr. Joseph Methodist. 135, 2589
Answer to modern religious thinking. 3383
Answer to Sir Thomas Moore's Dialogue. 2252, 2596
Answer to Six months in a convent. 888, 3031
Answer to skeptics. 110
Answer to some late papers, entitled, The Independent Whig. 1211
Answer to the ages. 1695
Answer to the question, (Why are you a Christian?) 1098
Answer to the Word. 475
Answer to Thomas Bels late challeng. 792
Answer to war. 2756
Answer wisely. 763
Answer without ceasing. 2880
Answerable style: essays on Paradise lost. 2469
Answered. 705, 2889
Answered by the Master. 160
Answered or unanswered. 2511
Answered or unanswered! miracles of faith in China. 2511
Answered prayer in China. 2511
Answering Christ's call. 959
... Answering distant calls. 2482
Answering God's call. 164

Answering the tough ones. 63
Answering your questions. 3012
Answers. 3011
Answers, a book of Catholic information on religious topics. 770
Answers for inquiring Christians. 3012
Answers for young Latter-day Saints. 1232, 3890
Answers of Jesus to Job. 550
Answers of the ages. 3014
Answers on the way. 3385
Answers to Book of Mormon questions. 679
Answers to ever-recurring questions from the people. 3499
Answers to gospel questions. 2613
Answers to objections. 3380, 3383
Answers to praise. 982
Answers to questions. 280, 3011
Answers to seventeen objections against spiritual intercourse and inquiries relating to the manifestations of the present time. 3494
Answers to the cultist at your door. 1394
Answers to 343 bible questions. 3012
Answers to tough questions skeptics ask about the Christian faith. 68
Answers to your questions. 794, 949
Answers to your questions about the Bible. 281
... Ante-Nicene exegesis of the Gospels. 392
Ante-Nicene fathers. 1018, 1019
...Ante-Nicene exegesis of the Gospels. 392
Anthem angelic. 3348
Anthem in New England before 1800. 1209
Anthems and anthem composers. 49
Anthology. 3680, 3724
Anthology of atheism and rationalism. 101
Anthology of Buddhist tantric songs. 743
Anthology of Christian literature. 3204
Anthology of I ching. 1878
Anthology of Jesus. 1953
Anthology of Kongo religion. 131, 1500
Anthology of mediaeval Hebrew literature. 1798
Anthology of mysticism. 2639
Anthology of prayers. 3310
Anthology of religious verse designed for the times. 3210
Anthology of the Bible. 303
Anthology of the love of God. 1736
Anthology of Zen. 3894
Anthrology and religion. 2859
Anthropography or Bible phrenology of the nations and tribes that sprang from Abraham. 483
Anthropological approaches to the study of religion. 3085
Anthropological religion. 3062
Anthropological studies in Theravada Buddhism. 3110
Anthropology and religion. 2859
Anthropology and the missionary. 2484
Anthropology and the Old Testament. 2326
Anthropology for the people. 2585
Anthropology of the Old Testament. 503, 2326
Anthropology; or, The science of man. 2228
Anthropomorphism dissected, and spiritualism vindicated. 3500
Anthropos. 2322
Anthroposophy. 3097
... Anthroposophy and the human gemut. 50
Anti-Christian cults. 3495
Anti-Judaism in Christian theology. 1073
Anti-masonry. [n.p. 1661
Anti-Mormonism in Idaho, 1872-92. 2617
Anti-Mortonus. 763
Anti-popery, or History of the popish church. 756
Anti-Semite and Jew. 2076, 2079
Anti-Semitism and the British Union of Fascists. 54
"Anti-Semitism can never find a basis in the Catholic religion." 53
Anti-Semitism in the New Testament? 2103
Anti-Semitism yesterday and tomorrow. 2078
Anti-anthropomorphisms of the Greek Pentateuch. 50
Anti-"black" magic. 2312
Anti-Calvinism. 730
Anti-Catholicism in America, 1841-1851. 803
Anti-Catholicism in Victorian England. 51
...Antichrist. 49, 51, 52, 604, 1092
Antichrist and some mistakes concerning him. 52

ANTICHRIST AND THE

RELIGIOUS BOOKS 1876 - 1982

Antichrist and the last days of the world. 1514
Antichrist and the millenium. 2464
Antichrist and world destiny revealed. 52, 611, 1778
Antichrist identified. 52, 2053
Antichrist in history. 52
Antichrist in seventeenth-century England. 52
Antichrist in the Middle Ages. 52
Antichrist, including the period from the arrival of Paul in Rome to the end of the Jewish revolution. 1194
Anti-Christian supernaturalism. 3686
Anti-Christianity of Kierkegaard. 2170
Anticipation of the Civil War in Mormon thought, and Joseph Smith and the West. 2600
Anticlericalism. 51
Anticlericalism; conflict between church and state in France, Italy, and Spain. 1143
Antidote. 3226
Antidote for deism, or, Scripture prophecy fulfilled. 608
Antidote for Tom Paine's theological and political poison. 2758
Antidote to backsliding. 70
Antidote to Christian science. 1033
Antidote to deism. 1420, 2759
Antidote to Mormonism. 1079
Antidote to the poison of popery. 800, 3306
Antient and modern stages survey'd. 1309, 3606
Anti-Janus. 1474
Antimasonry; the crusade and the party. 53
Anti-Methodist publications issued during the eighteenth century. 2422, 2428
Anti-missionary criticism with reference to Hawaii. 2524
Antinomian controversy. 1858, 2371
Antinomian controversy of 1637. 53
Antinomian controversy, 1636-1638. 53, 1858
Anti-Paedo-Rantism. 135, 1625
Anti-Paedo-Rantism defended. 135, 1625
Antiphonal readings for free worship. 3220
Antiphons, responsories, and other chants of the Mozarabic rite. 847, 884
Antipope. 190
Antique drum. 2420
Antiquities of the Christian church. 1190
Antiquity of Hebrew writing and literature. 564
Antiquity unveiled. 3512, 3513
Antireligious propaganda in the Soviet Union. 3257
... Antisemitism. 2078
Anti-semitism, a social disease. 2079
Anti-Semitism and emotional disorder. 53
Anti-Semitism and the Christian mind. 1083
Antisemitism and the foundations of Christianity. 1073
Antisemitism historically and critically examined. 2079
Antisemitism in modern France. 53, 1480
Anti-Semitism in the United States in 1947. 2076
Anti-Semitism [organized anti-Jewish sentiment]. 2077
Anti-semitism, the voice of folly and fanaticism. 2077
Antologia de la poesia religiosa de La Avellaneda. 28
Anton T. Boisen, 1876-1965. 675, 885
Antonio and Mellida & Antonio's revenge. 1014
Antonito, a Spanish boy of to-day. 2474
Anutu conquers in New Guinea. 2541
Anvil. 2744, 2815
Anxiety in Christian experience. 55
... The anxious bench. 1568
Anxious enquirer after salvation. 3295
Anxious inquirer after salvation. 3295
Anxiously engaged. 1008
Any Christian can. 3829
Any news of God? 999
Any saint to any nun. 2580
Anybody here know right from wrong? 945
Anyone can prophesy. 2949
Anyone can teach (they said) 3161
Anytime book for busy families. 1611
Apart with Him. 2626
Apart, yet not afar. 3495
Apartheid and the archbishop. 1287
Apeiron of Anaximander. 39, 2419
Apella. 2078
Aphorisms of Sandilva. 197
Aphorisms of Swami Sivananda Radha. 2396
Aphorisms on man. 55
Aphraates and the Jews. 55, 2153
Apistophilon. 1589
Apocalypse. 458, 459, 460, 461
Apocalypse explained. 456
Apocalypse explained according to the spiritual sense. 456
Apocalypse explained for readers of to-day. 459
Apocalypse in art. 462
Apocalypse in Latin and French. 2331
Apocalypse interpreted. 465
Apocalypse of Abraham. 491
Apocalypse of Adam. 55
Apocalypse of Baruch. 488
Apocalypse of Jesus Christ. 459, 3319
Apocalypse of John. 452, 2127
Apocalypse of St. John. 451, 452, 453
Apocalypse of St. John, or Prophecy of the rise, progress, and fall of the Church of Rome. 463
Apocalypse; or, Absolute Christian science. 1034
Apocalypse revealed. 456, 457
Apocalypse today. 465
Apocalypse unsealed. 129, 452, 458
Apocalypse unveiled. 452
Apocalyptic. 56
Apocalyptic, ancient and modern. 56
Apocalyptic angel. 2762
Apocalyptic dispensation. 451
Apocalyptic gnomon points out eternity's divisibility rated with time, pointed at by gnomons sidereals. 218
Apocalyptic movement, introduction & interpretation. 56
Apocalyptic sketches. 451, 461
Apocalyptic spirituality. 3321
Apocalyptic vision in Paradise lost. 2469
Apocalyptic vision of the book of Daniel. 507
Apocalyptic vision revealed to John. 1515
Apocalyptic writings. 453
Apocalyptical key. 463
Apocatastasis; or, Progress backwards. 3706
... The Apocriticus of Macarius Magnes. 1018
... The Apocrypha. 56, 489, 490
Apocrypha and Pseudepigrapha of the Old Testament in English. 56, 487
Apocrypha and pseudepigrapha of the Old Testament in English, with introductions and critical and explanatory notes to the several books. 491
Apocrypha anecdote. 488
Apocrypha, bridge of the Testaments. 489
Apocrypha of the Old Testament. 487, 489
Apocryphal and legendary life of Christ. 336
Apocryphal books of the New Testament. 336
Apocryphal literature. 488
Apocryphal New Testament. 335, 336
Apocryphal revelations. 337
Apogee. 3466
Apoligia pro vita sua. 789
Apollinarianism. 57
Apollonius. 2845, 2987
Apollonius of Tyana. 57
Apologetic of modern missions. 70
Apologetic of the New Testament. 69
Apologetica. 68
Apologeticall narration. 1344
Apologetics. 61, 63, 68, 1097
Apologetics and evangelism. 62
Apologetics and the Biblical Christ. 276
Apologetics and the eclipse of mystery. 61, 3018
... Apologetics; or, Christianity defensively stated. 59
Apologetics; or, The rational vindication of Christianity. 61
Apologia. 59
Apologia pro vita sua. 789, 790
Apologia pro vta sua. 790
Apologies, good friends ... an interim biography of Daniel Berrigan, S. J. 194, 774
Apologies of Justin Martyr. 68, 69
Apology. 61
Apology against a pamphlet called A modest confutation of the animadversions upon the remonstrant against Smectymnuus. 1523
Apology and polemic in the New Testament. 68
Apology for actors. 1809, 3606
Apology for African Methodism. 14
Apology for Christianity. 1195, 1711
Apology for Christianity, 1776, and An apology for the Bible, 1796. 59, 279, 1711
Apology for the Bible. 237, 279, 2759
Apology for the book of Psalms, in five letters. 577
Apology for the Christian divinity. 1680
Apology for the doctrine of apostolical succession. 76
Apology for the Episcopal church. 1522
Apology for the true Christian divinity. 58, 1680
Apology for wonder. 121
... An apology made by George Joy. 358, 3719
Apology made by George Joy, to satisfy, if it may be, W. Tindale. 1535. 358, 3719
... The Apology of Aristides on behalf of the Christians. 68
Apology of the Church of England. 1218
Apologye of Syr Thomas More, knyght. 789
Aposles of deceit. 3743
Apostacy of the present day Christian church. 1120
Apostasy from the divine church. 2610
... The apostle. 2803
Apostle: a life of Paul. 2800
Apostle and apostolate. 2503
Apostle and bishop. 1155, 1295
Apostle bas-relief at Saint-Denis. 3273
Apostle extraordinary. 2802
Apostle for our time. 2805
Apostle for our time, Pope Paul VI. 2805
Apostle in a top hat. 2755
Apostle John. 2127
Apostle of Alaska. 3329
Apostle of charity. 1403, 3779
Apostle of China, Samuel Isaac Joseph Schereschewsky. 3307
Apostle of culture. 119, 1511
Apostle of freedom. 732
Apostle of liberty: Starr King in California. 2173
Apostle of New Jersey, John Talbot. 3580
Apostle of Norway, Hans Nielsen Hague. 1790
Apostle of peace. 2853
Apostle of reality. 1481
Apostle of reason. 2186
Apostle of Rome. 1629
Apostle of the Amazon. 2504, 2683
Apostle of the Chilean frontier, William D. T. MacDonald. 2307
Apostle of the Chippewas. 172
Apostle of the ice and snow. 3329
Apostle of the North. 675, 2307
Apostle of the North, Rev. James Evans. 1577, 1901
Apostle of the western church. 2167
Apostle of two worlds: Father Frederic Janssoone, O.F.M., of Ghyvelde. 1935
Apostle Paul. 2796, 2798, 2799, 2801, 2804
Apostle Paul and the modern world. 2800
Apostle Paul and the Roman law. 2795, 3244
Apostle Paul speaks to this age. 2804
Apostle Paul speaks to us today. 377, 2801
Apostle Peter. 2825
Apostle Peter speaks to us today. 325, 2934, 3357
Apostle to inland China. 2512, 3590
Apostle to Islam. 3899
Apostle to the Chinese communists. 2510, 2683
Apostles. 70, 71, 406
Apostles and evangelists. 72
Apostles and the primitive church. 407
Apostles as everyday men. 72
Apostles' creed. 72, 73, 74, 75
Apostles creed and the New Testament. 73
Apostles Creed for everyman. 72
Apostles' creed in modern worship. 74
Apostles' creed in the light of modern discussion. 74
Apostles' Creed in the light of today's questions. 74
Apostles' creed in the twentieth century. 75
Apostles' Creed interpreted in words and pictures. 75
Apostles' creed to-day. 75
Apostles' doctrine. 1462
... Apostles, fathers. 1172
Apostles for our time. 2494
Apostles in the home. 3171
Apostles, including the period from the death of Jesus until the greater mission of Paul. 71
Apostles, Jesus' special helpers. 72, 339
Apostles of discord. 3745
Apostles of India. 1895
Apostles of Jesus Christ. 72
Apostles of light. 3145
Apostles of mediaeval Europe. 2483
Apostles of Shri Ramakrishna. 3020
Apostles of the front lines; looking ahead with Catholic action. 754
Apostles of the Lord. 625
Apostleship of suffering. 3542
Apostolate and ministry. 1290
Apostolate of chastity. 889
Apostolate of Christian renewal. 859, 1003
Apostolate of moral beauty. 3488
Apostolate of suffering. 3540
Apostolate to Negro America. 2541
Apostolate to the sick. 1258
... Apostolic administrators. 7
Apostolic age. 1183, 1189, 1190
Apostolic age and the New Testament. 346
Apostolic age in the light of modern criticism. 1183, 1194
Apostolic' age of the Christian church. 1195
... The Apostolic camera and Scottish benefices, 1418-1488. 807
Apostolic Church. 1163, 1173, 1190
Apostolic church and the apostasy. 1228
Apostolic Church: founding, nature, polity, worship, impact. 1163
Apostolic church government displayed. 1241
Apostolic church in the New Testament. 1188
Apostolic constitution. 2578
Apostolic constitution 'Sponsa Christi' and instruction of the Sacred Congregation of Religious. 2581
Apostolic delegate speaks. 758
Apostolic dimensions of the religious life. 2571
Apostolic exhortation. 1563
Apostolic exhortation of the Supreme Pontiff Paul VI to the members of every religious family in the Catholic world on the renewal of the religious life according to the prescriptions of the Second Ecumenical Vatican Council. 2570
Apostolic faith restored. 1596
... The Apostolic fathers. 76, 1018, 1019, 1617
Apostolic Fathers; a new translation and commentary. 76
...Apostolic fathers, and the apologists of the second century. 76
Apostolic interpretation of history. 334
Apostolic itch. 753
Apostolic legations to China of the eighteenth century. 2511
Apostolic letter, Sabaudiae gemma, of Pope Paul VI. 2771
Apostolic life. 331, 2569, 2583
Apostolic message. 103
Apostolic ministry. 2474, 3675
Apostolic optimism, and other sermons. 1341
Apostolic organism. 1121, 2450
Apostolic origin of episcopacy asserted. 1522
Apostolic parish. 3676
Apostolic preaching and its developments. 1530
Apostolic preaching of the cross. 425, 2910
Apostolic renewal. 793, 1003
Apostolic renewal in the seminary in the light of Vatican Council II. 3614
Apostolic sanctity in the world. 3327
Apostolic Scriptures. 71, 306
Apostolic spirituality of the nursing sister. 2718
Apostolic succession. 77
Apostolic succession and the problem of unity. 76
Apostolic tradition. 1239
Apostolic tradition of Hippolytus. 1239
Apostolic woman. 3274
Apostolical and primitve church. 1241
... The Apostolical constitutions and cognate documents. 77
Apostolical succession in the Church of England. 76
Apostolos. 2748
Apostolos Makrakis. 2318
... Apostrophe to the skylark. 868
Apotheosis and after life. 3246
Appalachian ghosts. 1710
Appalachian Presbyterian: some rural-urban differences. 2937
Apparel of high magick. 2312
Apparitions. 77
Apparitions and haunted houses. 77
Apparitions and precognition. 1709
Apparitions and shrines of heaven's bright Queen. 2360, 3404
Apparitions and shrines of heaven's bright Queen in legend, poetry and history. 2360
Apparitions in late Medieval and Renaissance Spain. 2357, 3783
Apparitions of Garabandal. 3298
Apparitions of Our Lady, their place in the life of the Church. 2357
Appeal for negro bishops. 665
Appeal for the ancient doctrines of the religious society of Friends. 1681

Appeal from tradition to Scripture and common sense. 277
Appeal in behalf of the views of the eternal world and state. 2690
Appeal in the Briggs heresy case before the General assembly of the Presbyterian church in the United States of America. 692
Appeal of India. 2531
Appeal of medical missions. 2539
Appeal of the Bible to-day. 235
Appeal of the child. 940
Appeal to all the world for "a chapel in every home," 991
Appeal to life. 1342
Appeal to matter of fact and common sense. 3410, 3413
Appeal to reality. 3027
Appeal to reason. 1597
Appeal to the American churches. 1046
Appeal to the candid. 3729
Appeal to the candid of all denominations, in which the obligation, subjects, and mode of baptism are. 136, 692
Appeal to the Christian women of the South. 3424
Appeal to the gospel. 1218
Appeal to the Methodists. 2376, 2450
Appeal to the public. 1942, 2450
Appeal to the public for religious liberty. 3193
Appearance and reality. 2416, 2839
... Appellatio Flaviani. 1191, 1521
Appelman's sermon outlines & illustrations. 3372
Appendix to the New Testament. 52, 609
Apple and Eve. 2047, 3414
Apple is my symbol. 3199
Apple of discord. 2863
Apples of gold. 3201
Apples of immortality from the Cuna tree of life. 1396
Application of Christianity. 1234
Application of redemption by the effectual work of the word and spirit of Christ, for the bringing home of lost sinners to God. 3029
Applied Christianity. 1051, 3442
Applied cybernetics; atomic energies of the mind. 1325
Applied evolution. 3080
Applied religion. 3197, 3200
Applied religious psychology. 2994
Applied theology. 3664
Applying ethics. 3433
Applying the Gospel. 1140
Appointment Congo. 2201
Appointment for Andy. 3466
... The appointment of parochial adjutants and assistants. 1290
Appointment with God. 2252
Appraising the summer camp. 2591
Appreciation of Eastern Christianity. 861
Appreciations and historical addresses. 2913
Apprentice to the King. 1425
Apprentices in love. 997
Approach to Calvary. 3526
Approach to christian education. 936
Approach to Christian ethics. 146, 2372
Approach to Christian sculpture. 3316
Approach to Christianity. 3648
Approach to Jesus. 2000
Approach to monasticism. 2571
Approach to penance. 2812
Approach to philosophy. 2833
Approach to plainsong through the office hymn. 883
Approach to prayer. 2881
Approach to prayer & approach to penance. 2881
Approach to preaching. 3674
Approach to reality. 3688
Approach to religious education in Sunday school and day school. 3160
Approach to the Book of Mormon. 679, 2598
Approach to the Episcopal Church. 2959
Approach to the New Testament. 349
Approach to the psychology of religion. 1636, 2997, 2999
Approach to the religious geography of the United States. 1198
Approach to the study of Book of Mormon geography. 679
Approach to the teaching of Jesus. 2062
Approach to the theology of the sacraments. 3262
Approach to Vedanta. 3774
Approach to Zen. 2383
Approaches to a theology of history. 1818
Approaches to ancient Judaism. 2149
Approaches to Christian unity. 1491
Approaches to God. 1735, 1740, 2335
Approaches to meditation. 2379
Approaches to morality. 1538

Approaches to Old Testament interpretation. 504
Approaches to the Bible. 541
Approaches to the Cross. 3539, 3540
Approaches to the philosophy of religion. 3098
Approaches to the true church. 3201
Approaches to the understanding of God. 1729
Approaches towards church unity. 1042
Approaching advent of Christ. 608, 3320
Approaching Christian marriage; a course for eleventh and twelfth grades. 2337
Approaching crisis. 719, 3566
Approaching end of the age viewed in the light of history, prophecy and science. 1514
Approaching Subud. 3139
Approaching the Gospels. 401
Approaching the Nuer of Africa through the Old Testament. 2121, 2716
... The approbation of religious institutes. 2576
Approved list of church music for the archdiocese of Dubuque. 1205
Aprayer for every meeting. 2783
April sixth. 2023, 2611
Apron-pocket book of meditation and prayer. 3843
Apt illustrations for public addresses. 1842
Apt to teach. 940
Aquarian age of man. 3027
Aquarian gospel of Jesus the Christ. 1975, 2005
Aquarius Wayfarer. 3473
Aqueduct papers. 1696, 2690
Aquinas. 1738, 3694, 3695, 3697
Aquinas; a collection of critical essays. 3694
Aquinas and problems of his time. 3694
Aquinas ethicus. 3695
Aquinas On being and essence. 2737
Aquinas reader. 777, 3636
Aquinas Scripture series. 225
Aquinas' search for wisdom. 3692
Aquinas to Whitehead. 3609
Arab Campaign against American Jews. 2073
Arab historians of the Crusades. 1390
Arab-Islamic bibliography. 77
Arab painting. 2759
Arabia and the Bibel. 298
Arabia and the Bible. 77, 298
Arabic commentary of 'Ali ben Suleiman the Karaite on the book of Genesis. 522
Arabic commentary on the book of Psalms, chapters 42-72. 576
Arabic thought and the Western world in the golden age of Islam. 1927
Arabische Quellenbeitrage zur Geschichte der Kreuzzuge. 1392, 3286
Arabula: or, The divine guest. 3499
Aradia; the gospel of the witches. 3824
Aramaic approach to the Gospels and Acts. 383
Aramaic of the Old Testament. 78
Aramaic origin of the four Gospels. 392
Aramaic origin of the Fourth gospel. 414
Aramaic texts from Qumran. 1409
Aramaic version of Lamentations. 556
Arbitrary power, poperty, Protestantism. 784
Arc of civilization. 463
Arcana coelestia. 2691
Arcana of Christianity. 525, 3303
Arcana of spiritualism. 3516
Arcane secrets and occult lore of Mexico and Mayan Central America. 1898
Arcane teaching. 3138
Archaelogical writings of the Sanhedrin and Talmuds of the Jews. 3583
...The archaeolgoy of Palestine and the Bible. 1583
Archaeological and the historical writings of the Sanhedrin and Talmuds of the Jews. 3583
Archaeological encyclopedia of the Holy Land. 209, 2761
Archaeological writings of the Sanhedrin and Talmuds of the Jews. 3583
Archaeologist follows the Apostle Paul. 370, 2798
Archaeologist looks at the Gospels. 335
Archaeology and Bible history. 207
Archaeology and Biblical studies: retrospects and prospects. 207
Archaeology and Old Testament study. 487
Archaeology and our Old Testament contemporaries. 493
Archaeology and the after-life in pagan and Christian imagery. 1530
Archaeology and the Bible. 206, 208, 2678
Archaeology and the Book of Mormon. 678

Archaeology and the Dead Sea scrolls. 3013
Archaeology and the living word. 208
Archaeology and the New Testament. 335
Archaeology and the Old Testament. 487, 537
Archaeology and the Old Testament world. 486
Archaeology and the pre-Christian centuries. 487
Archaeology and the religion of Israel. 514, 2150
Archaeology, historical analogy & early Biblical tradition. 487
Archaeology, historical analogy & eary Biblical tradition. 487
Archaeology in Bible lands. 208, 1583
Archaeology in Biblical research. 209
Archaeology in India, with especial reference to the works of Babu Rajendralala Mitra. 2560, 3599
Archaeology in the land of the Bible. 208, 2761
Archaeology of New Testament cities in western Asia Minor. 335, 919
...The archaeology of Palestine and the Bible. 1583
Archdiocese of San Antonio, 1874-1949. 1274
Archaeology of the Bible. 207, 486, 2761
Archaeology of the English church. 919
Archaeology of the Jordan Valley. 208, 2131
Archaeology of the New Testament. 335
Archaeology of the New Testament [by] R. K. Harrison. 335
Archaeology of the Old Testament. 486, 556
Archaeology, the rabbis, and early Christianity. 335, 919
Archaic fictile revetments in Sicily and Magna Graecia. 3604
Archaic Roman religion, with an appendix on the religion of the Etruscans. 3246
Archaology and the Bible. 208
Archbishop and the lady. 1621, 1779
... Archbishop Bramhall. 690
Archbishop Grindal, 1519-1583. 666, 1775
Archbishop Lamy. 2195
Archbishop Laud. 2199
Archbishop Laud commemoration, 1895. 2199
Archbishop of the Reformation. 3037
Archbishop Pecham. 2810
... Archbishop Peckham as a relious educator. by John Laimbeer Peckham. 657
Archbishop Romero, martyr of Salvador. 666, 3247
Archbishop Stepinac. 3527
Archbishop Thomas and King Henry II. 1763, 3692
Archbishop's test. 3196
Archdeacon Francis Wrangham. 3860
Archdeacon Paley's View of the evidences of Christianity. 1099
Archdiocesan demographic study. 873
Archdiocese of Chicago, antecedents and development. 892
Archeology and the Old Testament. 487
Archeology of the New Testament. 335, 2399
Archeology of world religions. 3139
Archeology series. 810
Archeology's solution of Old Testament puzzles. 515
Archer saint. 1850
Arches and spires. 1159
Archibald the Arctic. 1532
Archiepiscopal and patriarchal autonomy. 766, 2792
Architects of Conservative Judaism. 1348
Architectural compositions in the Indian style. 3599
Architectural study of Arch Street Meeting House, Fourth and Arch Streets, Philadelphia, Pennsylvania. 2829
Architecture and the church. 1155, 1156, 1157
Architecture for worship. 2240
Architecture in worship. 1155
Architecture of dissent. 1274
Architecture of Jeremiah 1-20. 547
Architecture of Scottish post-Reformation churches, 1560-1843. 1161
Architecture of the European synagogue. 3577
Architecture of the monastic library in Italy, 1300-1600. 2575
Architecture of truth. 2203
Architecture of truth; the Cistercian abbey of Le Thoronnet in Provence. 2203
Archive of Hor. 1847, 2752
Archives of the Case Memorial Library. 1788
Archivum franciscanum historicum. 3011

Archaology and the ancient testament. 534
Archko library. 3203
Archko volume. 3583
Archko volume or, The archeological writings of the Sanhedrim and Talmads of the Jews (intra secus) 2069
Archko volume; or, The archeological writings of the Sanhedrim and Talmuds of the Jews. 2069
Archko volume; or, The archeological writings of the Sanhedrin and Talmuds of the Jews. 3583
Archpriest controversy. 772
Arctic gateway. 2500
Arctic wings. 2543, 2721
Arden House Conference on Family Living. 1604
Ardent pilgrim. 1918
Are Americans a chosen people? 3067
Are Anglo-Saxons Israelites? 1929
Are Catholic schools progressive! 832
"Are foreign missions done for!" 2521
Are mediums really witches. 3516
Are missions a failure? 2521
Are premillennialists right? 2464
Are Southern Baptists "Evangelicals"? 1552, 3465
Are the dead alive? 3512
Are the dead alive now? 1698
Are the heathen really lost? 2525
Are the New Testament documents reliable? 378
Are there chords in the harps of humanity? 1017
Are there too many churches in our town? 1040
Are these the last days? 605, 3319
Are we a Christian nation? 1017
Are we of Israel? 1929
Are we spiritually dead? 1828
Are you an evangelist. 1566

Are you for real? 3888
Are you fun to live with? 979
Are you in the picture? 901
Are you listening. 2398
Are you looking for God? 2301
Are you Mormons ignoramuses? 2612
Are you nobody? 2325
Are you running with me, Jesus? 2888
Are you saved? 3291
Are you the Christ? 438, 2068
Are you the Christ? And other questions asked about Jesus. 2435, 3352
Are Your running with me, Jesus? 2888
Aretalogy used by Mark. 436
Arguing with God. 550, 1746
Argument for Christianity. 60
Argument for the perpetuity of the Sabbath. 3261
Argument for the truth of Christianity. 3755
Argument of Aristotle's Metaphysics. 80
Argument of Hon. Emory Washburn. 2846
Argument of Samuel L. Southard. 1675
Argument of the Hon. Daniel E. Sickles, in the Senate of the state of New York. 2701
Argument of the Hon. Daniel E. Sickles, in the Senate of the state of New York, April, 1857, on the Trinity church bill. 2701
Argument on the duties of the Vice-President of the U. States. 726
Argument to prove that death is not obligatory on Christians. 3709
Arguments against the doctrine of general redemption, considered. 2911
Arguments and doctrines. 2141
Arguments for the existence of God. 173/
...The arguments of Romanists from the infallibility of the church and the testimony of the fathers in behalf of the Apocrypha, discussed and refuted. 489
Arguments of the counsel of Joseph Hendrickson. 1676
Arian controversy. 80
Arians of the fourth century. 80
Arise and go in peace. 2257
Arise and walk. 1952, 2695, 3540
Arise! Awake! 3477
Arise Jerusalem! 855, 1604
Arise my love. 602
Arise take thy journey. 1037
Arising call for every man and every nation. 3203
Arising from the Psalms. 579
Aristeas to Philocrates. 528
Aristeas to Philocrates (letter of Aristeas) 528
Aristocracy. 3205
Aristotle. 80
Aristotle and Anglican religious thought. 1218
Aristotle and the Arabs. 2841

Aristotle Desensu and Dememoria. 80
Aristotle on his predecessors. 2416
Aristotle texts and commentaries to 1700 in the University of Pennsylvania Library. 81
...Aristotle's Metaphysics. 2416
Ark and a rainbow. 2711
Ark file. 2711
Ark of God. 1775
Ark of Noah. 2711
Ark of the convenant. 2428
Ark of the Covenant from conquest to kingship. 81
Ark, the ephod and the "tent of meeting," 81
Arm of compassion. 2427
Armageddon. 462, 606, 609, 1514, 1528, 2678
Armageddon and you. 1941
Armageddon around the corner. 1940
Armageddon, dead ahead. 605, 3021
Armageddon has come. 1514
Armageddon now! 2464
Armageddon 198? 609, 1515
Armageddon, when & where? 607
Armand-Jean de Rance, Abbot of La Trappe. 3021
Armed for crisis. 3183
Armed Forces manual. 81
Armed Forces prayer book. 3456
Armed neutrality, and An open letter. 1055
Armed with love. 75
Armenian Apostolic Church. 82
Armenian awakening. 82
Armenian church. 82
Armenian Church and her teachings. 82
Armenian Church, founded by St. Gregory the Illuminator. 82
Armenian Evangelical Union of America. 82
Armenian translation of Deuteronomy. 510
Armenian version of the letters of Athanasius to Bishop Serapion concerning the Holy Spirit. 1835
Armenian version of the Testament of Joseph. 2133
Armenia's ordeal. 2502
... Armeniun [mythology]. 2654
Armies of God. 2616
Arminian arm of theology. 83
Arminius; a study in the Dutch Reformation. 83
Armor of faith. 81
Armor of God. 3348, 3456
Armor of light. 3349
Armor of righteousness. 957
Armor of youth, talks to children. 3197
Armorial windows erected, in the reign of Henry VI. 2686, 3846
Armour of light. 2961
Arms and the monk! 2693
Armstrong empire. 3852
Armstrong error. 83
Armstrongism. 83
Armstrongism's 300 errors exposed by 1300 Bible verses. 83
Armstrong's Church of God. 3018
Army drum. 3292
Army hymn-book. 1860, 2916
Army in battle array. 1475
Arnold Damen, S.J. 893, 1400
Arnold of Brescia. 83, 928
Arnold's practical Sabbath-school commentary on the international lessons. 1914
... Around a Mexican patio. 2551
Around old St. Bridget's. 1898
Around the corner from sixty. 18
Around the cross. 160
Around the home table. 1608
Around the Lord's table. 2251
Around the manger. 1111
Around the Mediterancan with my Bible. 282
Around the Meditteranean with my Bible. 282
Around the wicket gate. 976
Around the wide world. 694
Around the world. 2926
Around the world with a magician and a juggler. 1345
Around the world with Jack and Janet. 2522
Around the world with the Bible. 2491
Around the world with the gospel light. 1229
Around the year with the Trapp family. 1610
Arousing the sleeping giant. 1199
Arrangement of the psalms, hymns, and spiritual songs, of the Rev. Isaac Watts, D.D. 1869
Arrest and liberation of Rabbi Shneur Zalman of Liadi. 3404

Arrest, trial and conviction of Jesus Christ from a lawyer's standpoint. 2068
Arrogance of piety. 1063
Arrow and the cross. 1903
Arrow by day. 1790, 2539
Arrow to the sun. 3005
Arrows from my quiver. 1556
Arrows of His bow. 2844, 3237
Arrows of light. 1342
Arrows of light from the Egyptian tarot. 3588
Arrows of the Almighty. 2124
Arsenal for skeptics. 1653
Arshko volume. 3583
Art and architecture in Medieval France. 1159
Art and architecture of Christianity. 1165
Art and architecture of India. 86
Art and architecture of India: Buddhist, Hindu, Jain. 86
Art and cities of Islam. 86
Art and craft of preaching. 2902
... Art and ethics--things artistic. 1537
Art and meaning in Berceo's Vida de Santa Oria. 1745
Art and philosophy. 88
Art and philosophy; [proceedings of] a symposium, edited by Sidney Hook. 88
Art and practice of Caballa magic. 722, 2728
Art and practice of clairvoyance. 1283
Art and practice of the occult. 2728
Art & religion. 84, 2753
Art and religion as communication. 84
Art & science of meditation. 2381
Art and Tao. 88
Art and the future. 85
Art and the message of the church. 921
Art and the occult. 2314
Art and the Reformation. 84
Art and the Reformation in Germany. 86
Art and thought of John. 419
Art and truth of the parables. 2025
Art and wisdom of living. 2994
Art forms in sacred music. 1208
Art in action. 1089
Art in Judaism. 2073
Art in the early church. 920
Art in the light of mystery wisdom. 50
Art in the vatican. 88
Art, love and life. 84
Art magic. 3496
Art, mind, and religion. 2839
Art, mind, and religion; proceedings. 2839
Art needs no justification. 1089
... The art of accompanying plain chant. 884
... The art of accompanying plain chart. 884
Art of becoming a whole person. 994
Art of being. 1323
Art of being a Jew. 2139
Art of being a member missionary. 2618
Art of being a sinner. 3411
Art of being human. 3488
Art of Benin. 88
Art of Biblical narrative. 556
Art of building worship services. 3003
Art of candidating. 1289
Art of Christian alchemy. 3477
Art of Christian caring. 3783
Art of Christian doubt. 1103
Art of Christian listening. 2810
Art of Christian living. 964
Art of Christian promotion. 1568
Art of Christian relationship (The) 33
Art of church canvass. 1169
Art of church cooperation. 1912
Art of church management. 1251
Art of conducting public worship. 3004
Art of contemplation. 1355, 2382, 2644
Art of counseling. 2781
Art of dying. 1413, 1414
Art of dying well. 1416
Art of dynamic preaching. 2905
Art of enjoying the Bible. 640
Art of friendship. 162
Art of God incarnate. 921
Art of group worship. 3859
Art of happy Christian living. 972
Art of illustrating sermons. 2898, 2903
Art of India. 3600
Art of interesting. 2899
Art of Islam. 86
Art of lands in the Bible. 87
Art of lands in the Biple. 87
Art of listening to God. 980
Art of living. 972, 1003, 3865
Art of living, day by day. 1432
Art of living joyfully. 996
Art of living today. 964
Art of living treasure chest. 1325
Art of living . . . when you're young. 3881
Art of living with God. 1750
Art of making choices. 1536

Art of management for Christian leaders. 952
Art of mental prayer. 2379
Art of ministering to the sick. 1258
Art of Newman's Apologia. 2703, 2705
Art of pastoral conversation. 2780, 2786
Art of pastoral counselling. 447
Art of personal evangelism. 1571
Art of personal prayer. 2882
Art of persuasion in pastoral theology. 3676
Art of prayer. 2875, 2881
Art of preaching. 2896, 2898, 2907, 2908, 2910
Art of preaching in the light of its history. 2899
Art of public worship. 3003
Art of real happiness. 2995
Art of soul-winning. 1562, 1567
Art of Southeast Asia: temples and sculpture. 3599
Art of spiritual achievement. 962
Art of spiritual healing. 2694
Art of spiritual snakehandling, and other sermons. 3363, 3732
Art of staying off dead-end streets. 512
Art of staying sane. 3723
Art of teaching children. 2614
Art of teaching Christian doctrin. 746
Art of teaching Christian doctrine. 746
Art of teaching Christianity. 3180
Art of teaching intermediates. 3152
Art of teenage living. 3881
Art of the American folk preacher. 2910
Art of the Anglo-Saxon age. 85
Art of the Arab World. 86
Art of the Christian world, A.D. 200-1500. 922
Art of the Copts. 85
Art of the dark ages. 85
Art of the Hebrew tradition; Jewish ceremonial objects for synagogue and home. An exhibit at the Metropolitan Museum of Art, New York City, commemorating the American Jewish tercentenary; arranged by the Jewish Museum of the Jewish Theological Seminary ofAmerica, January 20, 1955 to February 27, 1955. Stephen S. Kayser, editor; Guido Schoenberger, associate editor. 87
Art of the late antique from American collections. 88
Art of the Odyssey. 1839
Art of the rhythmic choir. 1400, 3144
Art of war for the Christian soldier. 554
Art of winning folks. 1573
Art of worship. 3003
Art of Zen meditation. 2383
Art projects for the mentally retarded child. 2411
Art responds to the Bible. 602
Art studies in the life of Christ. 1957, 2759
Art tells a story, the Bible. 85, 299
Art thou the Christ? 3198
Art treasures of the Vatican. 3768
Artaxerxes iii Ochus and his reign. 88, 2822
Arthur A. Oakman. 3218, 3355
Arthur C. A. Hall. 1781
Arthur Ford speaks from beyond. 3474
Arthur Selden Lloyd, missionary-statesman and pastor. 2241
Arthurian triptych. 2664, 3817
Articles of association of the African Methodist Episcopal Church of the city of Philadelphia in the Commonwealth of Pennsylvania. 13
Articles of faith. 2598, 2613
Articles of faith and practice, with the covenant, that is confessed by the separate churches of Christ in general in this land. 3535
Articles of religion of the Methodist Church. 2427
Articles of the Synod of Dort. 2919
Articles of the Synod of Dort and its rejection of errors. 2919
Articles on antiquity in Festschriften. 1817
Artist and the Pope. 2124
Artist within. 2381
Artistic expression. 88
Artistotle on his predecessors. 2416
Artistry in living. 982
Arts and their mission. 50
Arts in early England. 86
Arts in early England/by G. Baldwin Brown. New, rev. ed. 86
Arts in the churches and synagogues of North Carolina. 84
"Arts of His ways" 1442
Arts of Islam. 86
Arts of Orpheus. 2744
Arts of Shinto. 88
Arts of the church. 921

Artus Desire: priest and pamphleteer of the sixteenth century. 1426
Arya dharm. 89
Arya samaj. 89
Arya Samaj and Indian nationalism, 1875-1920. 89, 2671
Aryan sun-myths. 2664
Aryan sun-myths the origin of religions. 3546
Ary's conferences. 2359
As a Jew sees Jesus. 1955
As a lawyer sees Jesus. 2035
As a living oak. 1540, 3421
As a magnet. 741
As a man thinketh. 2693
As a mighty stream. 2093
As a roaring lion. 1744, 2512
As a tale that is told; recollections of many years. 120
As a tree grows. 1449
As among the Methodists. 1408
As angels of light. 2129
As between brothers. 2284
As childred worship. 3858
As children of light. 3888
As children worship. 3858
As Christians face rival religions. 1078
As Christians teach. 3177
As close as the telephone. 2228
As far as I can see. 1090
As far as I can step. 1717
As for me and my family. 1610
As gold in the furnace. 659
As he journeyed. 3871
As He passed by. 2007
As He said. 3211
As I live and breathe. 686
As I lived it. 3863
As I look back. 2507
As I recall my past century. 120
As I remember. 120
As I saw it. 1319
As I see religion. 3059
... As I was saying. 960, 2581
As I was thinking. 1450
As if he had seen the invisible. 754
As it is. 1034, 1035, 1495
As it is in heaven. 1795, 3200
As it is to be. 3499
"As it is written"; the use of Old Testament references in the documents of Vatican Council II. 501, 3772
As it was in the beginning. 531, 2037
As it was--so shall it be. 1513
As Jesus grew. 644
As Jesus passed by. 1560, 1979
As long as the sun gives light. 1677, 1901
As Lord Acton says. 6
As Matthew saw the Master. 443
"As much as in me is ..." and other sermons. 1466
As never before. 2384
As of a mustard seed. 1590
As one of them. 2573
As one who serves. 2299, 3332
As one who speaks for God. 2905
As one without authority. 2899
As others saw Him. 2005, 2013
As others see us. 996, 1293
As others see us, and as we are. 1461, 1463
As pilgrims and strangers. 3487
... As protestant Latin America sees it. 2549
As seeing the invisible. 462
As showers on tender grass. 33
As stars for all eternity. 3592
As tall as my heart. 2625
As the day begins. 901
As the eagle. 720, 3487
As the fields ripened. 3045
As the lightning flashes. 2494
As the morning star. 1641
As the morning star; the life of St. Dominic. 1474
As the river flows. 119
"As the small rain," 1448
As the spirit leads us. 139
. . . as the stars they shall shine. 1387
As the twig is bent. 3145
As the way opens. 3835
As the years go by. 3702
'As the years go by. 1303
As thy days so thy strength. 1440
As translated correctly. 655
"As 'twas told to me" 2083
As we ought. 2576
As we remember Him. 1986, 3352
As we see it from here. 3473
"As ye sow." 3594
As yesterday when it is past. 1275
As you tithe so you prosper. 3702
Asa Turner. 1336, 3718
Asbury and his coadjutors. 2453
Asbury Wilkinson: pioneer preacher. 3816
Asbury Wilkinson: pioneer preacher. [1st ed.]. 3816

TITLE INDEX ATLAS OF THE

Ascending flame, descending dove. 3707
Ascending life. 1986
Ascension at the cross roads. 1548, 3449
Ascension of Isaiah. 490
Ascensions. 3200
Ascent. 180
Ascent of Calvary. 2032
Ascent of life. 2989
Ascent of Mount Carmel. 2642
Ascent of Mount Sion. 2639
Ascent of Olympus. 1743
Ascent of the mountain, flight of the dove. 3062
Ascent of the soul. 3461
Ascent through Christ. 3029
Ascent to faith. 1414
Ascent to God. 1595
Ascent to the cross. 579
Ascent to the tribes. 2553
Ascent to truth. 1355, 1356
Ascent to Zion. 3853
Ascese et vie modern. 90
Ascetic life. 90
... The ascetic works of Saint Basil. 177
Ascetical conferences for religious. 90
Ascetical life. 90
Ascetical works. 90
Asceticism and eroticism in the mythology of Siva. 3421
Ascetics, authority, and the church in the age of Jerome and Cassian. 90
Asclepius. 11, 1395
Asgard & the Norse heroes. 2665
Asherah in the Old Testament. 90
Ashes for breakfast. 1132, 2310
Ashes from the cathedral; liturgical reflections for the lenten weekdays. 865, 2215
Ashes of tomorrow. 3206
Ashkenazim and Sephardim. 3333
Asia looks at Western Christianity. 1079
Asian Christian theology. 3619
Asian journal of Thomas Merton. 3488
Asian religions: 1971. 91
Asian voices in Christian theology. 3657
Asiatic Arcadia. 2772
Asiatic fields. 2454
Asiatic mythology. 2666
Asiatic studies, religious and social. 1896
Asimov's guide to the Bible. 292
Ask and receive. 2870
Ask Him anything. 3664
Ask me a Bible question. 281
Ask me, Lord, I want to say yes. 1524, 3238
Ask me to dance. 1011
Ask the awakened. 710
Ask the Bible. 995
Ask the cards a question. 3589
Ask the kids. 902
Ask the Master. 990
Ask the prophets. 3670
Ask the prophets, a Bible study manual. 571
Ask the rabbi; two thousand questions and answers about the Jew. 3011
"Ask what ye will" 2875
Asked and answered. 2061
Asking for trouble. 120
Asking questions. 639
Asking the fathers. 3489
Asking them question. 3011
Asking them questions. 1056, 3011, 3669
Asking why. 1054
Asklepios; archetypal image of the physician's existence. 11
Asleep in Jesus. 1692, 1698, 2299, 3220
Asma'ul-Husna. 1733
Aspasio vindicated and the Scripture doctrine of imputed righteousness defended, in eleven letters from Mr. Hervey to Mr. John Wesley, in answer to that gentleman's remarks on Theron and Aspasio. 1809, 2161
Aspects and houses in analysis. 97
Aspects of authority in the Christian religion. 118
Aspects of belief. 1103
Aspects of Biblical inspiration. 304
Aspects of Buddhism. 704
Aspects of Christ. 2004, 2044
Aspects of Christian character. 182
Aspects of Christian social ethics. 3443
Aspects of death in early Greek art and poetry. 1416
Aspects of ethical religion. 1537
Aspects of Freemasonry in modern Mexico. 1667
Aspects of humanity, brokenly mirrored in the everswelling current of human speech. 2419
Aspects of Indian religious thought. 1896
Aspects of Islam. 1923, 2565
Aspects of Islamic civilization. 1927
Aspects of Jewish belief. 2138
Aspects of Jewish power in the United States. 2104
Aspects of Judaism. 2119
Aspects of monasticism. 2570
Aspects of pentecostal-charismatic origins. 2816
Aspects of rabbinic theology. 2080, 2116
Aspects of religion in the Soviet Union, 1917-1967. 3257
Aspects of religion in the United States of America. 3743
Aspects of religious and scientific thought. 3066
Aspects of religious belief and practice in Babylonia and Assyria. 94
Aspects of religious propaganda in Judaism and early Christianity. 69
Aspects of reunion. 1041
Aspects of revelation. 3224
Aspects of the Bible. 200
Aspects of the church. 1121
Aspects of the Crusades. 1391
Aspects of the Hebrew genius, a volume of essays on Jewish literature and thought. 2842
Aspects of the infinite mystery. 1049
Aspects of the Jewish question. 2078
... Aspects of the Old Testament considered in eight lectures. 501
Aspects of the religious behavior of American Jews. 2154
Aspects of the rise of economic individualism. 1076, 3087, 3800
Aspects of the rise of economic individualism; a criticism of Max Weber and his school. 3087, 3800
Aspects of the rise of economic individualsm. 3085, 3800
Aspects of the theology of Karl Barth. 175
Aspects of the thought of Teilhard de Chardin. 3593
Aspects of the Way. 1968
Aspects of theism. 3608
Aspects of wisdom in Judaism and early Christianity. 451, 2831, 3821
Aspects ofthe church. 1118
Aspirations of nature. 787
Assassination of Malcolm X. 669, 2233
Assassins. 92
Assassins: a radical sect in Islam. 92
Assemblies of God, a popular survey. 92
Assembly at Westminster. 3808, 3809
...The assembly of gods. 1414
Assent of faith. 185
Assertio septem sacramentorum; or, Defence of the seven sacraments. 3263
Assertive Christian. 92
Assessment of candidates for the religious life. 3785
Assessment of morality. 2592
Assignment. 1109, 1110
Assignment: overseas. 1109
Assignment: race; report of inventory. 1133
Assignments of Antonio Claret. 1284
Assimilating new members. 1171
Assisi papers. 843
Associate creed of Andover theological seminary. 40
Associate plan for youth in the liberal church. 1261
Association accounting. 3874
Association administration. 3871
Association advertising. 3872
Association and Christianity. 1053, 1636
Association and church training. 953
Association records. 3873
Association secretaryship. 3871
Associational Baptist training union manual. 141
Associational church music guidebook. 1204
Associational music ministry. 1204
Associational Sunday school work. 3551
ASsociationalism among Baptists in America, 1707-1814. 171
Des associations religieuses chez les Grecs, thiases, eranes, orgeons. 1766
Assorted gems of priceless value. 2611
Assumption and faith. 66
Assumption of the Virgin. 2359
Assurance of divine fellowship. 415
Assurance of faith. 1589
Assurance of immortality. 1888
Assurance of salvation. 93, 993
Assurance of salvation and other evangelistic addresses. 3292
Assyrian and Hebrew hymns of praise. 578
Assyrian Apostolic Church prayer, hymn and liturgical service book. 93
Asteroid ephemeris. 99
Astounding errors. 3380
Astounding facts from the spirit world. 3503
Astounding new discoveries. 319
Astral body and other astral phenomena. 94
Astral journey. 94
... The astral light. 3685
... The astral plane. 3686
Astral projection. 94
Astral world, higher occult powers. 3516
Astrea, or Goddess of justice. 3516
Astrologers almanac and occult miscellany. 95
Astrologer's electronic calcuator manual. 97
Astrologer's handbook. 97
Astrologer's manual. 95
Astrological directory. 98
Astrological keywords. 95
Astrological mandala. 96
Astrological timing. 96
...The astrological works of Abrham ibn Ezra. 98
Astrology. 95, 96
Astrology 14. 97
Astrology: a recent history including the untold story of its role in World War II. 98, 2186
Astrology according to Shakespeare. 95, 3399
Astrology and alchemy. 98
Astrology and foretelling the future. 95
Astrology and marriage. 96
Astrology and prediction. 97
Astrology and religion among the Greeks and Romans. 3058, 3114
Astrology and the modern psyche. 97
Astrology & the tarot. 3589
Astrology as taught by the Lotus Group. 95
Astrology at-a-glance. 94
Astrology for skeptics. 96
Astrology guide annual forecast. 99
Astrology in a nutshell. 97
Astrology in Roman law and politics. 99
Astrology, its history and influence in the Western world. 98
Astrology: mundane, astral, and occult. 97
Astrology of America's destiny. 96
Astrology of change. 96
Astrology of human relationships. 97
Astrology of I Ching. 95, 1878
Astrology of inner space. 97
Astrology of personality. 96
Astrology of relationship. 96
Astrology of the ancient Egyptians. 98
Astrology of the Old Testament. 95
Astrology, palmistry, and dreams. 96
Astrology primer for the millions. 97
Astrology, psychology, and the four elements. 97
Astrology: sense or nonsense? 95
Astrology, the divine science. 96
Astrology, the space-age science. 95
Astrology; the stars and human life. 96
Astrology; wisdom of the stars. 99
Astronomical and commercial discourses. 99
Astronomico-theological lectures of the Rev. Robert Taylor. 3023
Astronomy and general physics considered with reference to natural theology. 2674
Astronomy and the Bible. 99, 211
Astronomy in the Bible. 99
Astronomy in the Old Testament. 212
Astronomy of Milton's Paradise lost. 99, 2469
Astronomy of the Bible. 212
Astropsychiatry. 95
Astropsychology. 95
Astrosynthesis. 98
Astrotheology for the cosmic adventure. 3469
Asvalayana grhyasutram, with Sanskrit commentary of Narayana. 1815
At all times and in all places. 2256
At all times, in every age. 772, 1000
At any cost. 1844
At Camp Kee Tov. 1539
At Christmas time. 1112
At dawn of day. 1265, 1438
At ease! 3455
At ease in Zion. 1135, 3465
At eventide. 1339, 2735
At home and abroad. 3857
At home in the Bible. 637
At home in the world. 1003, 1802
At home with Jesus. 978
At home with the Hebrews. 2084
At life's crossroads. 215
At-one-ment of Christian science and single tax. 1037
At one with the invisible. 2640
At onement. 3028
At-onement by the Christian Trinity. 3711
At our own door. 2501
At school with the great Teacher. 3155, 3169
At sea and in port. 1629
At Sinai. 1329
At sundry times. 3122
At sunset; or, After 80. 166, 3357
At the beautiful gate. 1449, 2633
At the beautiful gate, and other religious poems. 3210
At the bedside of the sick. 2718
At the center of the world. 2770
At the court of His Catholic Majesty. 25, 3469
At the cross. 2033, 3210
At the crossroads of faith and reason. 179, 1597
At the dawn of civilization. 2095
At the desk next to mine. 1254
At the door knocking. 2395
At the door of the church. 2433
At the edge of hope. 2192
At the end of the Santa Fe trail. 2548
At the feet of Jesus. 2041, 3355
At the feet of Paul. 370, 2794
At the fiftieth milestone. 2290
At the foot of Dragon Hill. 2486, 2632
At the foot of the mountain. 517
At the foot of the rainbow. 2535
At the foot of the tree. 2320
At the fountain. 2619
At the fountains of living waters. 2381
At the gate of Asia. 2534
At the gates. 3863
At the gates of mercy. 2887
At the hour of death. 1696
At the Lord's table. 1318, 2252, 2258, 2260
At the Lord's treasury. 3528
At the Master's feet. 3202, 3337
At the name of Jesus. 45, 2686
At the risk of idolatry. 1117
At the Shrine of the Master. 3517
At the sign of the Flying Angel. 2557
At the table altar. 1606
At the turning. 2138
At Thine altar. 2896
At wit's end. 2808
At work for a Christian world. 2549
At work in the homeland. 2527
At work with Albert Schweitzer. 3312
At work with children in the small church. 3170
At worship. 1862
At your best. 963
At your ease in the Catholic church. 770
Athanasia. 1890, 2053
Athanasian creed. 99
Athanasian creed and its early commentaries. 99
Athanasian creed vindicated and explained. 99
Athanasius. 100
Atharva-veda Samhita. 2743
Atheism. 101
Atheism among the people. 101
Atheism and alienation. 100
Atheism & Christianity. 100
Atheism and liberation. 1073
Atheism and other addresses. 1655
Atheism and pantheism. 1739
Atheism and the rejection of God. 100, 1477
Atheism, humanism, and Christianity. 101
Atheism in Christianity. 1073
Atheism in our time. 101
Atheism in our universities. 1579
Atheism in philosophy, and other essays. 101
Atheism in the English renaissance. 100, 101
Atheism is dead. 1733
Atheism of astronomy. 99
Atheism of Brownson's review. 3714
Atheism's faith and fruits. 101
Atheist debater's handbook. 100
Atheist epic: Bill Murray, the Bible, and the Baltimore Board of Education. 3096
Atheist magazines. 101
Atheist manifesto. 100
Atheistic humanism and the Biblical God. 1154
Atheist's values. 101
Athelete of Christ: St. Nicholas of Flue. 2711
Athenagoras. 1093, 3634
Athens and Jerusalem. 3105
Athens or Jerusalem? 2221
Atheos. 3024
Athlete of Christ: St. Nicholas of Flue, 1417-1487. 2711
Athletes of the Bible. 647
Athos. 102
Athos: miraculous icons. 1881
Athos, the mountain of silence. 102
Atid bibliography. 2083, 2144
Atishwin. 1899
Atlantic district of the Evangelical Lutheran synod of Missouri, Ohio. 1549
Atlantis. 102
Atlantis, fact or fiction? 102, 876
Atlas of man and religion. 1488
Atlas of textual criticism. 348
Atlas of the Bible Lands. 283

Atlas of the Biblical world. 281, 2678
Atlas of the Methodist Episcopal church. 2444
Atmanushasana (Discourse to the soul) 1932
Atom-smashing power of mind. 3751
Atom speaks. 103
Atomic apostle. 2400
Atomic energy plus. 205
Atoms, men, and God. 3080
Atonement. 103, 104, 105, 106, 107, 108, 348, 2029
Atonement and forgiveness. 107
Atonement and law. 103
Atonement and modern thought. 106
Atonement and personality. 106
Atonement and psychotherapy. 103
Atonement and the modern mind. 104
Atonement and the modern mind, iii. 104
Atonement and the sacraments. 108
Atonement and the social process. 106
Atonement in Christ. 106
Atonement in history and in life. 104
Atonement in literature and life. 104
Atonement in our time. 105
Atonement in the death of Our blessed Lord and Savior. 105
Atonement in the light of history and the modern spirit. 107
Atonement of Christ. 106
Atonement of George Fox. 1684
Atonement viewed as assumed divine responsibility. 108
Atoning Christ. 2213
Atoning death of Christ. 107, 2045
Atoning gospel. 107, 2045
Atoning life. 106
Atoning work of Christ. 107
'Atsa Louie, I'ma Phil. 1749, 2760
Attack from the spirit world. 1423
Attack upon 'Christendom. 68
Attack upon the American secular school. 1130
Attacking on all fronts. 912
Attaining Jewish manhood, Bar-Mitzvah addresses. 2110
Attainment through cosmic vibrations. 2409
Attempt at a critique of all revelation. 3224
Attempt to answer the important queston, What must I do to be saved! 3288
Attempt to exhibit the true theory of Christianity. 2323
Attempt to explain God's gracious covenant with believers. 1376
Attempt to prove the truth of Christianity from the wisdom displayed in its original establishment. 60
Attic festivals of Demeter and their relation to the agricultural year. 1422
Atticus Green Haygood. 1792
Atticus Greene Haygood. 1792
Attitude education. 1016
Attitude of Jesus toward woman. 1955
Attitude of the Catholic Church towards witchcraft and the allied practices of sorcery and magic. 762
Attitude of the Christians towards war. 3791
Attitude of the church to some of the social problems of town life. 3434
Attitude of the early Christian Latin writers toward pagan literature and learning. 1020
Attitude of the Jewish student in the colleges and universities towards his religion. 2115
... The attitude of Wolfgang Musculus toward religious tolerance. 2632, 3703
Attitudes and consequences in the restoration movement. 1272
Attitudes of educators toward exceptional children. 3592
Attitudes of Seventh-Day Adventist college students toward missions. 1309, 3387
Attitudes to the body in Western Christendom. 2321
Attitudes toward changing organizational goals. 1826
Attitudes toward other faiths. 1079
Attitudes toward other religions. 1080
Attraction of the cross. 107, 1055
Attractions of the ministry. 2474
Attractive Christ. 165
Attractive church. 1121
Attractive truths in lesson and story. 940
Attractive way. 962
Attractiveness of God. 3644
Attributes of God. 1721, 1730
Attributes of love. 1626
Attributes of the Christian woman. 3844
Aubrey messages. 2809, 3507
Auburn seminary record. 109
Auchincloss' chronology of the Holy Bible. 496

Auction. 3764
Audacity of faith. 1592
Audacity of preaching. 2897
Audience adaptations in the sermons and speeches of Paul. 298, 2804
Audience criticism and the historical Jesus. 387, 1505, 2007
Audio-Visual discussion guides. 3161
Audio-visual man. 3161
Audio-visual media. 936
Audiovisual idea book for churches. 1253
Audiovisual media in Christian education. 1253
Audio-visuals in the church. 1253
Auditorium. 3215
Auditory processing and learning disabilities. 2204
Augsburg confession. 109, 110
Augsburg confession; a contemporary commentary. 109
Augsburg Confession and Catholic unity. 109
Augsburg sermons. 592, 1265, 2298
Augsburg sermons; sermons on Gospel texts from the new lectionary and calendar. 1265, 2298
Augsburg sermons; sermons on Gospel texts from the new lectionary and calendar: series C. 1265, 2298
Augusta Parish, Virginia, 1738-1780. 1223
Augustana annual. 2302
Augustana heritage. 110
Augustana Lutheran Church in America. 110
Augustana ministerium. 110, 1300
Augustana synod. 110
Auguste Forel and the Baha'i Faith. 125
Augustin und der antike Friedensgedanke. 114, 2806
Augustine. 114, 116, 3635
Augustine; a collection of critical essays. 116
Augustine and evolution. 115, 1581
Augustine and the Latin classics. 116
Augustine, his life and thought. 115, 1025
Augustine Laure, S. J., missionary to the Yakimas. 2200, 3862
Augustine of Hippo. 113, 114
Augustine on immortality. 117, 1892
Augustine, philosopher of freedom. 113
Augustine reader. 3635
Augustine, saint for today. 114
Augustine sunthesis. 3634
Augustine synthesis. 3634
Augustine the bishop. 114, 115
Augustine the educator. 114
Augustine, the theologian. 117
... Augustine: the thinker. 115
Augustine's quest of wisdom. 111, 113
Augustine's view of reality. 116
Augustinian bibliography, 1970-1980. 111
Augustinian manual of Saint Rita of Cascia, O.S.A. 3238
Augustinian mission manual. 854
Augustinian sermons. 111
Augustinian studies. 111, 804
Augustinian studies; papers read at recent Augustinian educational conferences. 112
Augustinians. 111
Augustinians in seventeenth century Japan. 111
Augustus Caesar's world. 1282
Augustus Conant, Illinois pioneer and preacher. 1322
Augustus to Constantine. 1191
Aunt Charlotte's stories of Bible history for young disciples. 632
Aunt Charlotte's stories of Bible history, told for the 52 Sabboths of the year. 625
Aunt Fannie's miracle. 2489
Aunt Hope's kitchen stove and the girls around it. 3877
Aunt Jane's verses for children. 632
Aunt Mary's delightful Bible stories for every day in the week. 632
Aunt Ruth's delightful Bible stories for every day in the week. 632
Aurora. 224
Aurora documents. 3122
Auschwitz, beginning of a new era? 1825
Austin Presbyterian Theological Seminary. 117
Australia; the Catholic chapter. 117, 814
Australian adventure. 1775, 2484
Australian & New Zealand theological library directory. 3612
Australian Labor Party and the aid to parochial schools controversy. 2190, 3525
Australian religions. 117
Austria and the papacy in the age of Metternich. 118, 860
Austrian aid to American Catholics, 1830-1860. 873

Authentic account of the persecutions and trials of the Rev. John Whittlesey, of Salem, Connecticut. 2820
Authentic Christianity. 988
Authentic history of the missions under the care of the Missionary society of the Methodist Episcopal church. 2454
Authentic Jew and his Judaism. 2138
Authentic literature of Israel freed from the disarrangements, expansions and comments of early native editors. 499
Authentic living. 1431
Authentic narrative of some remarkable and interesting particulars in the life of John Newton. 2705
Authentic narrative of some remarkable and interesting particulars in the life of the Rev. Mr. John Newton. 2705
Authentic New Testament. 320
Authentic notes of discussions and talks given by Krishnamurti [at] Ojai and Sarobia, 1940. 3685
Authentic pastor. 2785
Authentic preaching. 2900
Authentic report of eight talks. 3685
Authentic report of seventeen talks given in 1936. 3685
Authentic report of the controversial discussion between the Rev. Richard T. P. Pope, and the Rev. T. Maguire. 794
Authentic report of the testimony in a cause at issue in the Court of chancery of the state of New Jersey, between Thomas L. Shotwell, complainant, and Joseph Hendrickson and Stacy Decow, defendants. 1675
Authentic witness. 1120
Authentic writings of Ignatius. 1882
Authenticity of the Scriptures. 230
Author and added entry catalog of the American Missionary Association archives. 33, 2526
Author and title catalogue of the Cathedral library, of New York. 869
Author catalog of Disciples of Christ and related religious groups. 1462
"Author of liberty," 2223
Authordoxy. 892, 3024
Authorised daily prayer book. 2884
Authoritative Christianity. 1373, 1521, 2706
Authoritative life of General William Booth. 682
Authority. 118, 1162
Authority and freedom. 119, 3000
Authority and institution. 779, 1162
Authority and interpretation of the Bible. 240, 3680
Authority and ministry. 119
Authority and person of Our Lord. 1995
Authority and power in the free church tradition. 30
Authority and reason in the early middle ages. 2843
Authority and rebellion. 791
Authority and resistance in the Investiture Contest. 1918
Authority and spiritual power. 3216
Authority and the church. 118
Authority and the individual. 1905
Authority and the renewal of American theology. 119
Authority, ecclesiastical and Biblical. 118
Authority in Protestant theology. 118
... Authority in religion. 118
Authority in the church. 118, 779, 1162
Authority of religious experience. 1587
Authority of Scripture. 278, 280
Authority of the altar. 3677
Authority of the Bible. 276, 277
Authority of the Bible in Christian belief. 3665
Authority of the Biblical revelation. 276
Authority of the New Testament Scriptures. 339
Authority of the New Testaments. 378
Authority of the old testament. 530
Authority of the past. 20, 1925
Authority of the word of God. 951
Authorized and authentic life and works of T. De Witt Talmage. 3582
Authorized catechism of Christian doctrine. 766
Authorized cipher. 1669
Authorized daily prayer book. 2112
Authorized edition of the English Bible (1611) 272
Authorized literature of the Sacred order of the blue flame. 2729
Authorized ritual of the Order of the amaranth. 3240
Authorized ritual of the Order of the amaranth, inc. 3240
Authorized standard ritual of the Order of Eastern star in the state of New York. 2741
Authorized version of the Apocrypha. 487

Authorized version of the Bible and its influence. 271
Authorised version of the English Bible, 1611. 271
Authorship of the book of Deuteronomy. 510
Authorship of the four Gospels. 394
Authorship of the Fourth Gospel. 418, 421
Auto ride to heaven. 962
Autobiografia de San Juan Neumann, C.S.S.R., cuarto obispo de Filadelfia. 1028, 2685
Autobiographical notes. 1591, 1593
Autobiographical reminiscences of Henry Ward Beecher. 183
Autobiographical sketches and recollections, during a thirty-five years' residence in New Orleans. 2693
Autobiographical writings. 774
Autobiography. 116, 184, 740, 1333, 1505, 1570, 1596, 2317, 2776, 3093, 3691
Autobiography and journal of Rev. Heman Bangs. 133
Autobiography and reminiscences of Rev. John Graham. 84, 2931
Autobiography and sermons of Elder Elijah Martindale. 2349
Autobiography, correspondence, etc., of Lyman Beecher, D. D. 184
Autobiography of a Campaigner for Christ. 755
Autobiography of a cathedral. 750
Autobiography of a fallen "Christ" 772
Autobiography of a hunted priest. 872
Autobiography of a New churchman. 1593
Autobiography of a pioneer. 1596, 2178
Autobiography of a plain preacher. 3129
Autobiography of a Shaker. 463, 1577
Autobiography of a Shaker, and Revelation of the Apocalypse. 463, 1577, 3395
Autobiography of a yogi. 3137
Autobiography of Adin Ballou, 1803-1890, containing an elaborate record and narrative of his life from infancy to old age. 131
Autobiography of an African. 2555, 2627
Autobiography of an Elizabethan. 872, 3137
Autobiography of an old breviary. 842
Autobiography of Augustus Hopkins Strong. 3535, 3611
Autobiography of Beals E. Litchfield. 3507
Autobiography of Bishop Isaac Lane, LL. D. 2195
Autobiography of Charles Force Deems. 1692
Autobiography of Charles G. Finney. 1333, 1625
Autobiography of Christopher Layton. 2603
Autobiography of Dan Young. 3137
Autobiography of Dr. D. B. Kellogg. 1283
Autobiography of Elder Henry Kendal. 3129
Autobiography of Elder Jacob Knapp. 2178
Autobiography of Elder Samuel Rogers. 3134
Autobiography of Elder Wilson Thompson. 3136
Autobiography of Erastus O. Haven. 3128
Autobiography of Frank G. Allen. 3123
Autobiography of George A. Singleton. 3135
Autobiography of George L. Robinson. 2912
Autobiography of God. 1467, 1728, 2027
Autobiography of Hosea Stout, 1810-1844. 3762
Autobiography of Isaac Williams, B.D. 2755
Autobiography of James Henry Linford, Sr. 2230
Autobiography of Jesus. 1967
... Autobiography of John Cuthers, 1876-1946, seventy years a Mormon. 3125
Auto-biography of Lemuel Norton. 1594
Autobiography of Lorenzo Waugh. 3137
Autobiography of Madame Guyon. 872, 1779, 3127
Autobiography of martyrdom. 1947
Autobiography of O. P. Alderman. 1589
Autobiography of Parley Parker Pratt. 2867
Autobiography of Peter Cartwright. 743
Autobiography of pioneer John Brown. 2601
Autobiography of prayer. 2870
Autobiography of Rev. Abel C. Thomas. 1595
Autobiography of Rev. Eugene Bononcini, D.D. 1756

Autobiography of Rev. J. B. McGehee,
D.D. of South Georgia conference. 2457
Autobiography of Rev. James B. Finley.
1689
Autobiography of Rev. Samuel D. Davis.
3388
Autobiography of Richard Baxter. 178
Autobiography of St. Ignatius. 1882
Autobiography of St. Ignatius Loyola.
2268
Autobiography of St. Therese of Lisieux.
3691
Autobiography of the Blessed Mother
Anne of Saint Bartholomew. 741
Autobiography of the Blessed Virgin. 2356
Autobiography of the first forty-one years
of the life of Sylvanus Cobb, D. D., to
which is added a memoir. 1305
Autobiography of the life and works of
Rev. D. W. Jackson. 144
Autobiography of the Rev. David Powell.
2689
Autobiography of the Rev. Dr. Alexander
Carlyle. 740
Autobiography of the Rev. Enoch Pond,
D. D. 1333
Autobiography of the Rev. John H. Mills.
2443
Autobiography of the Rev. Joseph Travis,
A.M., a member of the Memphis annual
conference. 2457
Autobiography of the Rev. Samuel H.
Turner, D. D. 2960
Autobiography of the Rev. Samuel Huber.
3730
Autobiography of Venerable Marie of the
Incarnation, O.S.U. 2334
Autobiography of William Neill, D. D.
2933
Autobiography, the life of Prince-Patriarch
Vajirana of Siam, 1860-1921. 2940,
3766
Autobiography, the life of Prince-Patriarch
Vajiranana of Siam, 1860-1921. 2940,
3766
Autocephaly of the Metropolia in America.
3257
Autograph of God. 2398
Autographs of Saint Paul. 2795
Automatic or spirit writing. 3517
Autonomy of reason. 2163
Autonomy of religious belief. 3071
Autumn days. 2962
Auxilium. 840
Availability of religious ideas. 3100, 3107
Available mind. 2380
Availing prayer. 2875
Avarice--Anger. 3412
Avatar. 2400
Avatar and incarnation. 1894
Avatara, the humanization of philosophy
through the Bhagavad Gita. 2316, 2840
Ave Maria. 120, 755, 857, 2859, 3248
Ave Maria hymnal. 813
Ave Maria; or, The Mother of Jesus in
verse. 1205
Ave Maria; prayers and devotions for
Catholics with Epistles and Gospels. 857
Avenel dictionary of saints. 1025
Average boys and girls. 3153
Average man. 866, 3066
Zend-Avesta. 120
Avesta eschatology compared with the
books of Daniel and Revelations. 3898
Avesta eschatology compared with the
books on Daniel and Revelations. 3898
Avesta: the religious books of the Parsees.
120
Avestan hymn to Mithra. 2560
Avicenna on theology. 121, 1927
Avicenna's de anima (Arabic text) 3461
Avignon papacy, 1305-1403. 2770
Avrg. 109
Awake, Christian scientists! 1030
Awake in a nightmare. 2817
Awake in heaven. 761
Awake, my heart. 1430
Awake, O America! 2930
Awake the courteous echo. 2232, 2472
Awake the sleeping giant within you. 987
Awake to a perfect day. 1030
Awakened heart. 3889
Awakened one. 1778, 3019
Awakened worship; involving laymen in
creative worship. 3003
Awakening. 3331, 3362
Awakening in Asia. 733, 1573
Awakening mystical consciousness. 2694
Awakening of faith. 1589
Awakening of faith, attributed to
Asvaghosha. 3302
Awakening of India. 2532
Awakening of Kundalini. 2187
Awakening of St. Timothy's league. 1248
Awakening of the soul. 2638
Awakening of Zen. 3892
Awakening sermons. 3362

Awakening that must come. 1243
Awakening to community. 50
Awakening to God. 1827
Awakening to the good--psychological or
religious? 2999
Awakening to the universe. 3510
Award winning sermons. 160
Aware person in today's church. 984
Awareness. 2988
Awareness of self discovery. 1325
Away with God and Christianity. 1736
Awful disclosures. 2584
Awful disclosures, by Maria Monk, of the
Hotel Dieu nunnery of Montreal. 2584
Awful disclosures of Maria Monk. 2584
Awful disclosures of the Hotel Dieu
Nunnery. 2584
Awful disclosures of the Hotel Dieu
Nunnery of Montreal. 2585, 2718
Awful exposure of the atrocious plot
formed by certain individuals against the
clergy and nuns of Lower Canada,
through the intervention of Maria Monk.
2584
Awful thoughts. 3509
Awkward questions on Christian love.
3652
Awman translations. 3063
Ax must fall. 2125
Axiomatics and dogmatics. 3668
Axioms of religion. 148
Axis and the rim. 3119
Axis of Eros. 2828
Axling: a Christian presence in Japan.
121, 2534
"AZ you were!" 2594
Aztirc. 3053
Azusa Street. 177, 2817

B

Bab. 122
B. A. U. manual. 140
B. F. Lamb, ecumenical pioneer. 2194,
2735
B. W. Spilman, the Sunday school man.
3472
B. Y. P. U. manual. 142
B. Y. P. U. story hour. 3534
B'riha: flight to the homeland. 192, 3050
Baal, Christ, and Mohammed. 12
Baal or God. 2563
Baba. 3304
Baba of Karo, a woman of the Muslim
Hausa. 122, 1790
Baba's grace; discourses of Shrii Shrii
Anandamurti. 3476
Babel and Bible. 207, 486
Babel and Bible;two lectures on the
significance of Assyriological research for
religion, embodying the most important
criticisms and the author's replies. 486
Baboon chase, and other new missionary
stories. 2490
Baby Bible stories. 632
Baby born in a stable. 2022
Baby Jesus. 2022, 2023
Baby just now? 664
Baby Moses. 2621
Babylon. 607, 2635, 2768
Babylon by choice. 1278
Babylon is falling. 610
Babylon reborn. 1424
Babylon the Great has fallen! 1941
... Babylon within Jehovah's monarchy.
1054
Babylonia epic of creation restored from
the recently recovered tablets of Assur.
1380
Babylonian and Assyrian religion. 94
Babylonian and oriental excavations and
early Bible history. 1421
Babylonian captivity and Deutero-Isaiah.
545, 2149
Babylonian dragon. 630
Babylonian excavations and early Bible
history. 1421
Babylonian Genesis. 1370
Babylonian religion and mythology. 2654
Babylonian Talmud. 3583
Babylonian Talmud in selection. 3583,
3584
Baby's life of Jesus Christ. 1971
Baby's prayer at twilight. 901
Baccalaureate and convocation sermons.
123
Baccalaureate messages. 3537
Baccalaureate sermons. 122
Baccalaureate sermons and addresses. 123
Baccalaureate sermons and essays. 123
Bach. 123
Bach: the cantatas and oratorios. 123
Bach: The passions. 123
Bachelor of divinity. 3682
Bach's chorals. 123, 916

Bach's Passions. 123
Back from the edge. 2396, 3404
Back of beyond. 2540
Back of God. 2868
Back side of Satan. 1427
Back to basics. 3742
Back to Benedict. 188
Back to Bethel. 166, 2461
Back to Bethlehem. 1072
Back to Christ. 967, 1065, 1218, 1950,
2001, 2040, 3665
Back to creationism. 1579
Back to Eden. 3389
Back to God. 1327
Back to God and His church. 406
Back to Holy church. 1365
Back to Jesus. 999, 1594, 1950, 2064
Back to Methodism. 2420
Back to Methuselah. 3401
Back to Oxford. 2421
Back to Pentecost. 2813
Back to square one. 1005
Back to the Bible. 66, 201, 2938
Back to the sources. 1188
Back to Wesley. 3803
Back to Yahweh. 1736
Back where you belong. 3219
Background of Luther's doctrine of
justification in late medieval theology.
2161, 2280
Background of Passion music. 123, 2778
Background of the Bible. 231
Background of the life of Jesus. 408
Background of the New Testament and its
eschatology. 334
Background of the Old Testament. 534
Background of the social gospel in
America. 3452
.Background to morality. 759
Background to the Bible. 311
Background to the New Testament. 408
Backgrounds to dispensationalism. 1467
Backslider. 961
Backsliders of the Bible. 214
Backstage missionary. 2246
Backward look -- with a forward hope.
2913
Backwoods boy who became a minister. 7
Bacon Masonry. 124, 1665
... Bacon's Novum organum. 124
Bad Christian. 3410
Bad Popes. 2860
Badger kirk. 2929
Baedae Opera historica. 1761
Bag without holes. 3528
Bagbys of Brazil. 125
Baggy pants and other stories. 1016
Bagster art Bible. 271
Bah a i. 128
Baha i world faith. 127
Baha'u'llah and the new era. 125, 127
Baha u'llah and the new era. 125, 127
Baha 'U'llah's Hidden words [the glory of
God]. 126
Baha'i prayers and tablets for the young.
130
Baha'u'llah and the new era. 125, 127
Baha'i administration. 128
Bahai answers. 128
Baha'i centenary, 1844-1944. 129
Bahai community. 128
Baha'i faith. 127
Baha'i faith: its history and teachings. 128
Bahai leads out of the labyrinth. 129
... The Bahai movement. 128
Baha'i prayers for children. 130
Bahai procedure. 128
Bahai religion and its enemy. 129
Bahai revelation. 127
Bahai revelation and reconstruction. 128
Baha'i scriptures. 126
Bahai, the spirit of the age. 127
Bahai world. 127
Bahai world faith. 126, 127
Baha'i: world faith for modern man. 127
Baha'i writings. 126
Baha'i youth. 3879
Baha'ism. 128
Bahaism and its claims. 129
Bahaism; the modern social religion. 127
Bahaism, the religion of brotherhood and
its place in the evolution of creeds. 129
Bahaullah and the new era. 125, 127,
1700
Bahir. 721
Baidawi's commentary on surah 12 of the
Qur'an. 2185
Bailie's activities in China. 130, 2507
Baker James Cauthen. 146, 876
Baker's Bible atlas. 282
Baker's dictionary of Christian ethics. 950
Baker's dictionary of practical theology.
3679
Baker's dictionary of theology. 3637
Baker's pictorial introduction to the Bible.
309

Baker's pocket atlas of the Bible. 282
Baker's pocket bible concordance. 225
Baker's pocket dictionary of religious
terms. 3092
Baker's pocket harmony of the gospels.
287
Bakht Singh of India. 3415
Balag-compositions. 3545
Balance. 3080, 3752, 3753
Balance sheet of extermination. 3851
Balance the fundamental verity. 3313
Balance wheel. 2458
Balance wheels. 1324
Balanced life. 2227
Balancing country life. 1375
Balancing the Christian life. 974
Baldur and the mistletoe. 2665
Baldwin lectures for 1904-1905. 1067
Baldwin lectures for 1902-1903. 1067
Baldwin-Slocum lectures. 3065
Baleful legacy. 2683
Bali. 131
Bali: temple festival. 131
Balinese temple festival. 131
Ballads, lyrics, and hymns. 743
Balthasar Hubmaier. 37, 1850
Balthsar Hubmaier. 1850
Baltimore catechism. 767
Baltramiejus Vilentas' Lithuanian
translation of the Gospels and Epistles,
1579. 366
Bamboo cross. 2559
Bamboo hospital. 1803
Bampton lectures for the year
MDCCCXXIV. 287
Banaras, City of Light. 1815
Bandlet of righteousness, an Ethiopian
book of the dead. 2314
Banished king and his kingdom. 621
Banker meets Jesus, by Rowland
Hegedues. 1110, 1999
Banker's views on religious and other
important subjects. 3065
Bangkok '73. 3851
Banner-bearers. 2505
Banner book. 122
Banners of light. 3508
... The banns of marriage. 2342
Banquets & beggars. 2003
Bantu prophets in South Africa. 3899
Baptism. 133, 134, 135, 137, 138, 139,
2349
Baptism: a practical treatise for plain
people. 139
Baptism according to the Scriptures. 137
Baptism and Christian unity. 137
Baptism and confirmation. 138
Baptism and conversion. 3051
Baptism and faith. 139
Baptism & fullness. 1832
Baptism and gifts of the Holy Spirit. 139
Baptism and the Lord's supper. 134
Baptism, and the terms of communion: an
argument. 134
Baptism as taught in the Scriptures. 137
Baptism, Christ's act in the church. 136
Baptism, confirmation and commitment.
138
Baptism: conscience and clue for the
church. 134
Baptism: divine birth. 137
Baptism, filling & gift of the Holy Spirit.
139
Baptism for the dead. 3216
Baptism; foundation for Christian unity.
138
Baptism in fire. 1832
Baptism in its mode and subjects. 134
Baptism in spirit and in fire. 138
Baptism in the Demonstrations of
Aphraates, the Persian sage. 55, 138
Baptism in the Holy Ghost. 1831
Baptism in the Holy Spirit. 139
Baptism in the Holy Spirit made plain.
139
Baptism in the New Testament. 133, 134,
137, 138
Baptism in the thought of St. Paul. 137
Baptism, its doctrine and mode. 137
Baptism, its importance, its subjects, its
mode. 137
Baptism; its mode, subjects and design.
135
Baptism: its nature, obligation, mode,
subjects, and benefits. 136
Baptism of Christ. 138, 1958
Baptism of fire. 1652
Baptism of infants a reasonable service.
1906
Baptism of Roger Williams. 3817
Baptism of the ages and of the nations.
138
Baptism of the Holy Ghost. 1830
Baptism of the Holy Ghost "and more"
1828
Baptism of the Holy Ghost "and more",
copyright. 1828

Baptism of the Holy Spirit for salvation. 1829
Baptism of the Spirit. 2815
Baptism reconsidered. 133
Baptism through the centuries. 138
Baptism today and tomorrow. 133
Baptism with the Holy Spirit. 139, 1832
Baptismal anointing. 139
... Baptismal fonts, classified and illustrated. 1632
Baptismal instructions. 138
Baptismal liturgy. 136
Baptismal records of Apple's Church. 2169
Baptismal regeneration. 135, 136
Baptismal ritual. 836
Baptismal sacrifice. 134
Baptist adult union manual. 140
Baptist advance. 158
Baptist almanac and repository of indispensable knowledge. 171, 3466
Baptist annals of Oregon. 159
Baptist atlas. 143
Baptist beginnings in education. 1694
Baptist beliefs. 148
Baptist bibliography. 144
Baptist bibliography, being a register of printed material by and about Baptists. 144
Baptist biography. 144
Baptist brotherhood manual. 3465
Baptist builders in Louisiana. 154
Baptist campus directory. 2714
Baptist church directory. 148
Baptist Church discipline. 150
Baptist Church in the lower Mississippi Valley seventeen seventy-six--eighteen forty-five. 169
Baptist Church manual. 150
Baptist church perpetuity. 151
Baptist concepts of the church. 1119
Baptist confession of faith. 140
Baptist confessions of faith. 140, 145
Baptist convictions. 148
Baptist councils in America. 150
Baptist deacon. 1408
Baptist denomination: its history. 142
Baptist directory. 148
Baptist distinctive and objective. 148
Baptist distinctives. 149
Baptist doctrines. 140, 148
Baptist ecclesiology. 171, 3466
Baptist education study task. 3466
Baptist encyclopaedia. 147
Baptist faith. 148
Baptist faith and martyrs' fires. 151
Baptist family in foreign mission fields. 156
Baptist foundations in the South. 3333
Baptist fundamentals. 149
Baptist fundamenatals. 149
Baptist generation in Cuba. 147
Baptist handbook. 151
Baptist heritage. 140, 147
Baptist history. 151
Baptist history of South Dakota. 169
Baptist history of the north Pacific coast. 158, 171
Baptist history vindicated. 151
Baptist home missions. 155
Baptist home missions in North America. 155
Baptist hymn and tune book. 152
Baptist hymn and tune book for public worship. 153
Baptist hymn writers and their hymns. 1875
Baptist hymnal. 140, 152, 153
Baptist in history. 151
Baptist intermediate union manual. 142
Baptist journalism in nineteenth-century Texas. 2937
Baptist Junior union manual II. 3707
Baptist leaders in religious education. 3465
Baptist library. 146
Baptist looks back. 2560
Baptist manual. 150, 151
Baptist manual of polity and practice. 150
Baptist march in history. 151
Baptist message. 149
Baptist milestones. 152
Baptist ministry: then and now. 145
Baptist missions in the South. 2548
Baptist opportunity. 142
Baptist people from the first to the twentieth century. 151
Baptist praise book. 152
Baptist preachers with social consciousness. 1635
Baptist principles. 149
Baptist principles reset. 148
Baptist pulpit speaks. 162
Baptist relations with other Christians. 159
Baptist situation of Boston proper. 154
Baptist songs, with music. 153

Baptist source book. 152
Baptist story. 151, 152
Baptist student union manual. 141
Baptist student union methods. 141
Baptist succession. 150, 152
Baptist successionism. 152
Baptist Sunday school standard manual. 3552
Baptist system examined. 136, 1690
Baptist trail-makers of Michigan. 155
Baptist trailblazers. 144
Baptist training union manual. 141
Baptist treasury. 143
Baptist trophy. 142
Baptist way-book. 142
Baptist way of life. 142, 151
Baptist waymarks. 147
Baptist, why and why not. 147
Baptist witness. 148, 152
Baptist world alliance, Second congress, Philadelphia, June 19-25, 1911. Record of proceedings pub. under the auspices of the Philadelphia committee. 141
Baptist year book. 145
Baptist young people at work. 141
Baptist young people's union administration. 141
Baptist young people's union handbook. 142
Baptistery of Pisa. 2849
Baptists. 142, 143, 147, 151, 152
Baptists and Christian unity. 1043
Baptists and ecumenism. 1043
Baptists and local autonomy. 150
Baptists and public affairs in the Province of Canada, 1840-1867. 145, 1144
Baptists and the American experience. 171
Baptists and the American Republic. 170
Baptists and the American tradition. 171
Baptists and the Bible. 119, 306
Baptists and the Oregon frontier. 159
Baptists and their doctrines. 140
Baptists and unity. 142
Baptists around the world. 144
... Baptists councils in America. 147
Baptists establishes of religious liberty. 151
Baptists in America. 170
Baptists in Assam. 2503
Baptists in Burma. 2505
Baptists in Europe. 145
Baptists in history. 142
Baptists in Kentucky, 1776-1976. 154
Baptists in Kingwood, New Jersey. 152
Baptists in Massachusetts. 154
Baptists in Missouri. 157
Baptists in New Jersey. 158
Baptists in Oregon. 159
Baptists in southern California. 145
Baptists in Thailand and the Philippines. 170
Baptists in transition. 149
Baptists in Upper and Lower Canada before 1820. 145
Baptists mobilized for missions. 156
Baptists North and South. 170
Baptists of New Hampshire. 157
Baptists of Shelby County. 143
Baptists of Tierra Blanca. 170
Baptists of Virginia. 172
Baptists, 1783-1830. 152
Baptists, the Bible, church order and the churches. 149, 279
Baptists: the passionate people. 3465
Baptists under the Cross. 30
Baptists who dared. 144
Baptists who shaped a nation. 170
Baptists; who they are and what do they believe? 147
Baptized in blood. 1108
Baptized into Christ. 139
Baptizing, Biblical and classical. 138
Baptizing community. 134
Baptizing work of the Holy Spirit. 1833
Baptizo-dip-only: the worlds' pedobaptist Greek scholarship. 135
Bar/Bat Mitzvah planbook. 172
Bar mitzvah. 172, 2110
Bar mitzvah book. 2143
Bar mitzvah companion. 172
Bar-mitzvah for boyhood. 172
Bar-mitzvah for boyhood, youth, and manhood. 172
Bar mitzvah illustrated. 172, 2139
Bar-mitzvah pulpit. 172
Bar Mitzvah treasury. 172, 2145
Barabbas. 172
Barabudur, history and significance of a Buddhist monument. 682
Baralam and Yewasef. 700
"Barb, please wake up!" 689, 3899
Barbara. 173
Barbe Acarie. 2334
Barbed arrows. 3358
Barclay's apology in modern English. 1680

Bards of the Bible. 1799
Bare ruined choirs. 811, 2579
Barefoot days of the soul. 1006
Barefoot in the church. 1244, 1787
Barefoot journey. 1307
... Barhebracus' scholia on the Old Testament. 497
Barlam and Yewaseef, being the Ethiopic version of a Christianized rescension of the Buddhist legend of the Buddha and the Bodhisattva. 700
Barley told Bible stories for bigger children. 617
Barnabas bible. 118, 217
Barnabas gospels. 316
Barnabas, Hermas and the Didache. 337, 1806
Barnabas in Pittsburgh. 1783
Barne's bible encyclopedia, biographical, geographical, historical, and doctrinal. 242
Barnes' notes on the New Testament. 343
Barns of the Abbey of Beaulieu. 182
Baron Friedrich von Hugel. 1851
Baron Friedrich Von Hugel and the modernist crisis in England. 1850, 2562
Baron Paul Nicolay. 2708
Barren fig-tree. 174
Barren fig trees doom. 2772
Barrett. 175, 928
Barriers. 2104
Barriers to belief. 64
Barriers to Christian belief. 63
Barron's simplified approach to the New Testament. 411
Bartered birthright. 1931
Barth. 176
Barthian theology and the man of to-day. 176, 1457
... Bartholomaeus Ziegenbalg. 3895
Bartholomew of Exeter, bishop and canonist. 177, 2813
Barth's soteriology. 176
Barton Warren Stone. 3533
Barton Warren Stone, pathfinder of Christian union. 3533
Baruch Spinoza. 3472
Bas Mitzvah treasury. 2145
Bas Mitzvah treasury, ed. by Azriel Eisenberg, Leah Ain Globe. 2145
Basal beliefs of Christianity. 3665
Basal concepts in philosophy. 2419
Base church. 1244
Baseball, popcorn, apple pie, and liberty. 3193
Baseball's sermon on the mound. 165
Bases of religious belief, historic and ideal. 3106
Bases of the temperance reform. 3594
Bases of world order. 1087
Basic belief. 1235
Basic beliefs. 3115, 3644
Basic beliefs of Christians. 3660
Basic beliefs of Jesus. 2064
Basic beliefs of the reformed faith. 2914
Basic Bible doctrines. 3641
Basic Bible studies. 649
Basic bibliography for ministers. 3627
Basic book list for church libraries. 3626
Basic books for the minister's library. 3626
Basic catechetical prespectives. 746
Basic catechism. 769, 3011
Basic Christian beliefs. 1072, 3182, 3662
Basic Christian convictions. 3645
Basic Christian doctrines. 3651
Basic Christian ethics. 945
Basic Christian teachings. 1050, 2286, 3660
Basic Christian values. 951
Basic Christian writings. 1456
Basic Christianity. 1094, 1676, 3665
Basic community in the African churches. 12
Basic convictions. 1072
Basic ecclesial communities. 933
Basic ecclesiastical statistics for Latin America. 825
Basic education for children with learning disabilities. 2204
Basic elements of Biblical history. 296
Basic encyclopedia for youth ministry. 1261
Basic evangelism. 1562
Basic forms of prophetic speech. 568
Basic formula for church union. 1040
Basic Gregorian chant and sight reading. 884
Basic guide to Judaism. 2137
Basic history of Lutheranism in America. 2294
Basic ideas in religion. 3608
Basic ideas of Calvinism. 729, 730
Basic ideas of occult wisdom. 3688
Basic introduction to the New Testament. 322
Basic issues in Christian thought. 1105

Basic issues in the philosophy of religion. 3106
Basic Jewish beliefs. 3011
Basic Jewish encyclopedia. 2146
Basic Jewish ethics and freedom of will. 1658
Basic Judaism. 2116
Basic leader skills. 953
Basic modern philosophy of religion. 1387, 3099
Basic patterns in Old Testament religion. 599, 2151
Basic principles in pastoral counseling. 2781
Basic principles of astrology. 95
Basic principles of Biblical counseling. 1107
Basic principles of education and expression. 3160
Basic principles of effective teaching. 934
Basic questions about Christian behaviour. 951
Basic questions about the Bible. 648
Basic questions for Christian educators. 940
Basic questions in theology. 3652
Basic readings in theology. 3636
Basic reform Judaism. 3032
Basic sources of the Judaeo-Christian tradition. 3204
Basic statements and health treatment of truth. 1471
Basic teacher skills. 940
Basic teachings for Catholic religious education. 784, 3148
Basic teachings of the New Testament. 476
Basic teachings of the New Testament. [1st ed.]. 476
Basic thoughts of Confucius. 2838
Basic truths of the Christian faith. 1072
Basic types of pastoral counseling. 2780
Basic values in Jewish religion. 3028
Basic writings. 914
Basic writings in Christian education. 3162
Basic writings of Saint Augustine. 3634
Basic writings of Saint Thomas Aquinas. 3694
Basics for communication in the church. 3179
Basics for teaching in the church. 3177
Basics of Bible interpretation. 288
Basil Anthony Mary Moreau. 1332, 2597
Basil Lee Lockett. 2242, 2542
Basilica of St. Mary of Minneapolis. 2475
Basilica on Jackson Square and predecessors. 2693
Basis for brotherhood and kindred themes. 694
Basis for study. 3537
Basis of Anglican fellowship in faith and organization. 1218
... The basis of assurance in recent protestant theologies. 3679
Basis of belief. 3105
Basis of Christian faith. 63, 951
Basis of Christian faith; a modern defense of the Christian religion. 63, 68
Basis of Christian unity. 1047, 1249
Basis of Israelite marriage. 2345
Basis of millennial faith. 3319
Basis of religious liberty. 3192
Basis of Roman Catholicism. 795
Basis of the premillennial faith. 2466
Basket in the reeds. 2624
Baskets of silver. 160
Bastion of faith. 562
Batak blood and Protestant soul. 2552
Batek Negrito religion. 178
Bath-kol. 2922
Battle. 3293
Battle and Brother Louis. 2577
Battle for Africa. 1073
Battle for the American church. 833, 834, 3738, 3739
Battle for the Bible. 305
Battle for the Gospel. 240
Battle for the mind. 64
Battle for the soul. 1361
Battle for world evangelism. 1573
Battle for your Faith. 1589
Battle-ground. 885, 3774
Battle-ground of the spiritual reformation. 3496
Battle manual for Christian survival. 981
Battle of Armageddon. 1514
Battle of Hudson's bay. 2543
Battle of the ages. 1061
Battle of the churches. 2561
Battle of the cross. 2058
Battle over Genesis. 202, 522
Battle over the Bible. 278
Battle to save. 3595
Battlefield of faith. 3077
Battlefield reviewed. 1903
Battleground. 3382

Battles of peace. 2973, 3341
Battles of the Bible. 558
Battling the hosts of hell. 1423
Baxter McLeadon. 2309
Bay Psalm book. 581
Bay View. 179
Bay windows into eternity. 3479
Bayle the sceptic. 179
Bazaar of Heracleides. 2042
BBC hymn book. 1864
Be! 3889
Be a better parent. 2773
Be a leader people follow. 953
Be a real teenager! 3889
Be a saint in spite of yourself. 3280
Be a spirit lifter. 1512
Be a wonder to yourself. 968
Be alive! 1005
Be all you can be. 1006
"Be-attitudes" 3175
"Be-attitudes" for the church. 3678
Be filled with gladness. 3348
Be filled with the Spirit. 1832
Be free. 381, 995
Be glad you're a Protestant! 2977
Be good to yourself. 2438, 3360
Be joyful. 449
Be mature. 413, 989
Be more than you are. 987
Be my guest. 1848
Be my son. 873, 2208
Be not afraid. 1002
Be not anxious. 969
Be not conformed to this world. 3348
Be not dismayed. 1349
Be not solicitous; sidelights on the
   providence of God and the Catholic
   family. 1610
Be of good cheer. 2307, 2437
Be of good courage. 3750
Be of good heart. 1000
Be one. 1041
Be opened! 1257
Be perfect? 2818
Be ready. 478
Be real. 989
Be rich. 364
Be right. 469
Be somebody ... God doesn't take time to
   make a nobody. 2386
Be sons of your father. 3336
Be still and know. 1433, 1439, 2695
Be strong in the Lord. 164, 2973
Be swift to love. 1605, 3218
Be the leader you were meant to be. 953
Be the woman you want to be. 3844
Be thou an example. 1009, 1232
Be thou made whole. 1598
Be what you are. 3735
Be wise as serpents. 987
Be ye also ready; evangelistic sermons.
   1558
Be ye perfect. 2819
Be ye renewed. 3222
Be ye thankful. 2259
Be your best self. 3493
Be your whol self. 1006
Beacon Bible commentary. 219
Beacon Bible expositions. 219
Beacon fires. 2726, 2727
Beacon lights. 2301, 3572
Beacon lights of faith. 927
Beacon lights of grace. 923
Beacon lights of prophecy. 568, 569, 3383
Beacon lights of prophecy in the latter
   days. 606
Beacon-lights of the reformation. 3035
Beacon search-lights on pioneers and
   millionaires. 1300
Beacons of light. 2722
Beams from Meher Baba on the spiritual
   panorama. 2400
Bearers of the torch. 2549
Beargrass Christian Church. 179
Bearing of archaeology on the Old
   Testament. 537
Bearing of psychology upon religion. 2997
... The bearing of recent discovery on the
   trustworthiness of the New Testament.
   349, 378
Bearing witness. 1645
Bearing witness to the truth. 2904
"Bears" of the Bible. 906
Beast, modernism and the evangelical faith.
   1596
Beasts and saints. 3282
Beasts and sevens of Revelations. 3226
Beasts, birds, and fish of the Bible. 480
Beatitude. 3695
Beatitudes. 179, 180, 181
Beatitudes; a contemporary meditation.
   181
Beatitudes and modern life. 182
Beatitudes and the Lord's prayer. 180
Beatitudes and the Lord's prayer for
   everyman. 179, 180
Beatitudes are for today. 180

Beatitudes for today. 180
Beatitudes, Jesus' pattern for a happy life.
   180
Beatitudes of Christ. 180
Beatitudes of Jesus. 180
Beatitudes of the Old Testament. 180
Beauduin, a prophet vindicated. 182
Beauties of Hervey. 1808
Beauties of home and the life beyond.
   2624
Beauties of nature delineated. 1442
Beauties of Rev. George Herbert, A.M.
   1804
Beauties of sacred literature. 625
Beauties of Sir Walter Scott, and Thomas
   Moore, esquire. 2589, 3315
Beauties of the Bible. 472, 473, 590, 592
Beauties of the late Rev. Dr. Isaac Watts.
   3799
Beauties of the late Reverend Dr. Isaac
   Watts. 3799
Beautiful Bible stories. 296
Beautiful Bible stories containing
   captivating narratives of the most striking
   scenes and events in the Old Testament.
   623
Beautiful childhood. 1960
Beautiful city, and the King of glory. 2174
Beautiful eternal now. 2695
Beautiful garden. 622
Beautiful gift book. 249
Beautiful gleaner. 589
Beautiful land, Palestine. 2761
Beautiful on the earth. 2677
Beautiful poems on Jesus. 2048
Beautiful songs of Zion. 3459
... Beautiful stories about Jesus. 2760
Beautiful stories from the Bible. 616
Beautiful stories from the good old Book.
   615
Beautiful story. 619
Beautiful story of Jesus and the lives of
   His apostles. 72, 75, 1973, 1984
Beautiful story of the Bible told for young
   and old. 210
"Beautiful thoughts" from Henry
   Drummond. 1481
Beautiful thoughts from the Holy Bible.
   725
Beautiful way. 1910
Beautiful word pictures of the Epistle to
   the Ephesians. 222
Beauty and bands, and other papers. 1212
Beauty and mystery of holiness. 1823
Beauty and truth of the Catholic church.
   787
Beauty care for the ears. 2231
Beauty care for the eyes. 3480
Beauty care for the feet. 1620
Beauty care for the hands. 3480
Beauty care for the tongue. 1855
Beauty crowned. 1532
Beauty for ashes. 1446, 1691
Beauty in religion. 1071
Beauty in the Bible. 206
Beauty in your own backyard. 2389
Beauty is God's word. 963
Beauty of daily duties and others. 805
Beauty of every day. 969
Beauty of God. 1726, 1742
Beauty of holiness. 1822
Beauty of Immanuel. 1966
Beauty of Jesus. 1570, 2455
Beauty of strength. 907
Beauty of the beatitudes. 181
Beauty of the King. 1966
Beauty of the New Testament. 348
Beauty of wisdom. 3821
Beauty's pilgrim, a portrait of Jesus. 1962
Beautyway. 2677
Beautyway: a Navaho ceremonial. 2677
"Because--" for the children who ask why.
   3684
Because God cares. 2299, 3351
Because He lives. 1700, 1749
Because we have good news. 1565
Beckonings; moments of faith. 3488
Becomers. 986
Becoming a Catholic Christian. 749
Becoming a Christain. 2929
Becoming a Christian. 982
Becoming a Christian person. 3182
Becoming a lover. 2264
Becoming a mature Christian. 3487
Becoming a person in the whole Christ.
   3488
Becoming a prophetic community. 2480
Becoming a whole family. 1608
Becoming and being. 1733, 1788
Becoming Catholic even if you happen to
   be one. 1003
Becoming Christian. 137
Becoming family. 1607
Becoming God's people today. 1278
Becoming human. 944, 2321
Becoming of Ruth. 2952
Becoming of the Church. 2944

Becoming one in the spirit. 1041
Becoming transformed. 984
Becoming you. 3879
Bed-time Bible stories for little children.
   632
Bedae Venerabilis Expositio Actuum
   apostolorum et Retractatio. 327
Bede Jarrett anthology. 776, 3633
Bede Jarrett of the Order of Preachers.
   1936
Die Bedeutung der Wundererzahlungen fur
   die Christologie des Markusevangeliums.
   435, 2017
Bedrock of belief, the foundations of
   religion. 66
Beds of pearls. 324, 346
Bedside Bible. 317
Beecher: Christian philosopher. 183
Beecher-Tilton investigation. 183
Beer-sheba: the excavation of a Biblical
   city. 184
Beesley's illustrated guide to St. Michael's
   church, Charleston, So. Ca. 1274
Befo' de war spirituals. 2680
Before and after. 3232
Before and after Zachariah. 616
Before, behind (and bigger than) the Bible.
   200
Before Christ came. 629
Before death comes. 1414, 3025
Before His face. 1298
Before I forget. 3432
Before I go to sleep. 619
Before I sleep. 2506, 3376
Before it slips my mind. 692
Before Jesus came. 3538
Before making important decisions. 955
Before many witnesses. 659
Before Olympos. 1397, 1767
Before philosophy, the intellectual
   adventure of ancient man. 3212
Before the bawdy court. 2734
Before the beginning. 525, 1383
Before the dawn. 2768
Before the deluge. 2393
Before the Earth arose. 1003, 2183
Before the foundation of the world. 3227
Before the holy table. 2255
Before the lost arts. 3075
Before the offering. 2383
Before the sun goes down. 994, 3242
Before the Synod of Illinois, North. 2920,
   3572
Before the times. 2092, 2150
Before they are three. 3174
Before they start to leave. 3888
Before you build your church. 1167
Before you marry ... for men only. 2339
Before you marry them. 2345
Before you teach children. 2287, 3169
Before you teach teen-agers. 3167
Beggar to king. 207, 2733
Beggars and prayers. 3581
Beggars in velvet. 968
Begin today with God. 1431
Begin with these. 3856
Begining at Jerusalem. 2535
Beginner Bible teacher and leader. 3177
Beginner Sunday school work. 3558
Beginners and primary plan book. 3155
Beginner's Bible. 619
... The Beginner's book in religion. 3163
Beginner's book of yoga. 3864
Beginners' course in Bible study. 645
Beginner's course in the Sunday school.
   3155
Beginners' department. 3559
Beginner's grammar of the Hebrew Old
   Testament. 1797
Beginner's handbook of Biblical Hebrew.
   1797
Beginner's handbook to Biblical Hebrew.
   1797
Beginners in God's world. 3157
Beginners workbook to biblical Hebrew.
   1797
Beginning. 526, 1381, 1382
Beginning a new pastorate. 1296
Beginning; a study of Genesis. 522
Beginning again. 3750
Beginning and end in the Bible. 1383
Beginning and end of the world. 1381
Beginning and growth of the Christian life.
   963
Beginning and the end. 2416
Beginning at home. 1609
Beginning at Jerusalem. 1943
Beginning at the end. 2213
Beginning from Jerusalem. 1189
Beginning Greek book. 1770
Beginning in Jerusalem. 1573
Beginning life in Christ. 3170
Beginning now. 525
Beginning of a nation. 3167
Beginning of Christian philosophy. 1616
Beginning of Christianity. 406
Beginning of eternal life. 1601, 3697

Beginning of history. 522
Beginning of hope. 1845
Beginning of sorrows. 442
Beginning of the end. 1514
Beginning of the English Reformation.
   3039
Beginning of the gospel. 1968
Beginning of the New Testament translated
   by William Tyndale, 1525. 358
Beginning of the rainbow. 2712
... The beginning of the Society of St.
   Sulpice in the United States. 3545
Beginning of the world. 1384
Beginning of things in nature and in grace.
   522
Beginning of wisdom. 62, 3821
Beginning or the end, where are we going?
   2946
Beginning the day. 2890
Beginning the Old Testament. 524
Beginning to meditate. 2381, 2397
Beginning to see. 712
Beginning to see the light. 121
Beginning vocalist. 917
Beginning with God. 3665
Beginning your marriage. 2344
Beginning your ministry. 1296, 1634,
   2788
Beginnings. 526, 1379, 1383
Beginnings, early American Judaica. 2155
Beginnings: earth, sky, life, death. 3185
Beginnings for the newly married. 2347
Beginnings in Bible archaeology. 208
Beginnings in church history. 1180
Beginnings in Jewish philosophy. 2151
... Beginnings in social service. 1525
Beginnings in spiritual life. 3487
Beginnings in the life of Christ. 1974
Beginnings in the Old Testament. 541
Beginnings in theology. 3662
Beginnings of a people. 565
Beginnings of American Methodism. 2433
Beginnings of Bible archaeology. 208
Beginnings of Buddhist art and other
   essays in Indian and Central-Asian
   archaeology. 85
... The beginnings of Catholicism in South
   Dakota. 825
Beginnings of Christian art. 922
Beginnings of Christian philosophy. 404
Beginnings of Christian Science in Ireland.
   1037
Beginnings of Christian theology. 3654
Beginnings of Christianity. 1103, 1191,
   1194
Beginnings of Christology. 2011
Beginnings of Christology, together with
   The Lord's Supper as a Christological
   problem. 2011, 2257
Beginnings of dialectic theology. 1457
Beginnings of earth and sky. 2664, 2667
Beginnings of faith and science. 1596,
   3314
... The beginnings of gospel story. 432
Beginnings of history according to the
   Jews. 2562
Beginnings of Indian philosophy. 1816
Beginnings of life and death. 2229
Beginnings of Lutheranism in New York.
   2291
Beginnings of Methodism in England and
   in America. 2425
Beginnings of our religion. 532, 1192
Beginnings of Presbyterianism in the
   Southwest. 2918
Beginnings of Quakerism. 3010
Beginnings of religion. 3109
Beginnings of seership. 1283
Beginnings of the Christian Church. 1193,
   1194
Beginnings of the Christian religion. 309
Beginnings of the church. 1194, 3163
Beginnings of the Church in the New
   Testament. 1004
Beginnings of the Hebrew people. 2097
Beginnings of the temporal sovereignty of
   the popes, A.D. 754-1073. 2770
Beginnings of the Theological seminary of
   the Reformed church in the United
   States, from 1817 to 1832. 3048
Beginnings of the Wesleyan movement in
   America and the establisment therein of
   Methodism. 2423
Beginnings of Unitarianism in America.
   3725, 3730
Beginnings of western Christendom. 1189
Beginnings without end. 2166, 2390
Begone, Satan! 1422
Der Begriff des Sprunges und der Weg des
   Sprachdenkens. 2170, 3716
Beguines and Beghards in medieval culture.
   185
Beguines in medieval Strasburg. 185
Beha 'Ullah (The glory of God) 128
... Behavior and destiny. 974
Behavior patterns in children's books. 905

Behavioral problem children in the schools. 2943
...The behaviour problem child in the Catholic school. 895
Behind barbed wire. 2752
Behind convent walls. 1357
Behind curtains of darkness a new fire is blazing. 612, 1576, 2863
Behind history. 444, 2026
Behind shuttered windows. 749
Behind that wall. 1455, 3481
Behind the Big hill. 3369
Behind the church curtain. 1564
Behind the church curtains. 1575
Behind the clouds--light. 3406
Behind the dictators. 794, 1613
Behind the garden of Allah. 2552
Behind the Gospels. 387
Behind the iron altar. 2260
Behind the opened hedge. 551
Behind the purple curtain. 801
Behind the scenes. 2926
Behind the scenes with the mediums. 3494
Behind the scenes with the metaphysicians. 1030
Behind the Third gospel. 430
Behind the veil. 454
Behind the world and beyond. 2419
Behold. 2051
Behold a people. 2207
Behold a sower! 3165
Behold! Genesis. 526
Behold God's love. 3883
Behold, He cometh! 46, 3320
Behold, He cometh; an exposition of the book of Revelation. 454
Behold He cometh in the clouds. 1910
Behold Him! 2036
Behold His love. 2033, 2395
Behold, I make all things new. 955
"Behold, I say unto you, I cannot say the smallest part which I feel." 1009
Behold life. 2227
Behold light beameth down from the spirit land of love. 3511
Behold my glory. 296
Behold my messengers! 2951
Behold sPilgrim Holiness Church--Sermons. 3353
Behold, the Bridegroom! A life of Christ. 1966
Behold the Christ. 1957, 2695
Behold the church. 2965
Behold the glory. 1454
Behold the King. 441
Behold the Lamb. 103, 417
Behold the Lamb of God! 107, 2033, 2036, 2213, 2610
Behold the Lamb of God, aspects of Our Lord's personality from the Gospels. Chosen by Robert Murrary. 2036
Behold the man. 105, 123, 1954, 1957, 1962, 1969, 1985, 1997, 2005, 2068
"Behold the man!" A review of the trials and crucifixion of Jesus. 2068
Behold the morning! 2053
Behold the Savior in sacred art. 2034, 2299
Behold the sign. 3574
Behold the son of man. 1990
Behold the spirit. 2641
Behold this heart. 21
Behold: thy King cometh to thee! 1317
Behold thy Mother. 2262
Behold your God. 1600
Behold your King. 441, 1407, 2055
Behold your mother, woman of faith. 2354
Behold your queen! 1533
Being. 2739
Being a Christ! 2990
Being a Christian. 954, 1015
Being a Christian in today's world. 967
Being a Christian on the campus. 1256
Being a Christian today. 996
Being a Christian: what it means and how to begin. 962
Being a Christian when the chips are down. 1006
Being a church member. 1201
Being a disciple. 994
Being a kid ain't easy. 907
... Being a preacher. 2475
Being and attributes of God. 1722
Being and becoming. 2418
Being and being known. 2180
Being and believing. 1218
Being and death. 1413
Being and existence in Kierkegaard's pseudonymous works. 2171
Being and God. 2738
Being and the Messiah. 413, 1584
Being and time. 2738
Being and transcendental awareness. 2737
Being Christian. 1001
Being Christian in our time. 3444

Being Christian in our town. 163
Being Christlike. 3666
Being, evolution, and immortality. 1708
Being good enough isn't good enough. 3295
Being human. 985
Being Jewish in America. 2141
Being joyous. 2135
Being known and being revealed. 2737
Being made over. 1340
Being of God. 2982, 3609
Being of the sun. 2676
Being the community of Christian love. 1123
Being the people of god. 1126
Being there for others. 3529
Being where you are. 3339
Beings and their attributes. 2624
Bektashi order of dervishes. 185
Bel, the Christ of ancient times. 93
Belief and behavior. 1601
Belief and faith. 186
Belief and history. 1597
Belief and life. 400
Belief and practice. 119
Belief and practice in the Orthodox Church. 2744
Belief and unbelief. 186
Belief and unbelief since 1850. 1764
Belief and work of Seventh-day Adventists. 3379, 3383
Belief and worship in native America. 1902
Belief, existence, and meaning. 185
Belief in a personal god. 3097
... Belief in Christ. 1952, 2038, 2042
Belief in God. 1602, 1722, 1737, 2181, 3609
Belief in God and immortality. 1889
Belief in God and mental health. 2986
Belief in human life. 972
Belief in man. 2320
Belief in personal immortality. 1888
Belief in redemption. 3294
Belief in the New Testament. 2396
Belief in the Trinity. 3712
Belief of Catholics. 784, 788
Belief of the first three centuries concerning Christ's mission to the underworld. 1999
Belief of the Jewish people and of the most eminent gentile philosophers, more especially of Plato and Aristotle, in a future state, briefly considered. 1889, 3795
Belief today. 1001
Belief unbound. 3103
Beliefs about man. 3726
Beliefs about the Bible. 236
Beliefs and practices of Judaism. 2138
Beliefs for Baptist young people. 148
Beliefs have consequences. 2932
Beliefs of a United Methodist Christian. 3734
Beliefs of Baptists. 148
Beliefs of Orthodox Christians. 2745
Beliefs of unbeliefs. 2474
Beliefs that are basic. 167
Beliefs that count. 3662
Beliefs that live. 3666
Beliefs that matter. 1048, 3663
Believe & behave. 322, 994
Believe and belong. 2932, 3354
Believe and know. 1590
Believe and live. 1545
Believe His prophets. 3383
Believe it or not. 1397
Believe it or not; the world of religion. 1397
Believe the good news. 2210
Believer free from the law. 3071
Believer in hell. 1107
Believer-priest in the tabernacle furniture. 3721
Believers and builders in Europe. 149
Believer's Christ. 2001
Believers' church. 2976
Believer's critique of the Bible. 234
Believer's daily renewal. 1432
Believer's experience. 984
Believer's golden chain. 3363
Believer's hand-book. 1823
Believers incorporated. 365, 1125
Believer's life of Christ. 1971
Believers only. 1917
Believer's pocket companion. 968
Believer's school of prayer. 2876
Believer's unbelief. 3664
Believest thou this. 3206
Believing. 930, 1593, 2202, 2707
Believing and knowing. 3083, 3314
Believing & obeying Jesus Christ. 470, 2515
Believing, deciding, acting. 945
Believing God. 404, 405
Believing in God. 1723
Believing in the church. 1219

Believing Jew. 2140, 3361
Believing people; literature of the Latter-Day Saints. 1231
Believing the impossible before breakfast. 1011
Believing world. 3113
Believing youth. 3158
Beliver's unbelief. 3664
Bell and the river. 2132
Bell street chapel discourses. 3202
Bell witch. 1709
Bellarmine theolotical lectures. 757
Les belles histoires de la Bible. 290
Bells above the Amazon. 2408, 2631
Bells and crosses of the Mission inn and the Ford paintings of the California missions. 187
Bell's New pantheon. 2658
Bells of heaven. 1937
Bells of India. 2530
Bells of Is. 2461
Bells on two rivers. 3242
Bells still are calling. 2530
Belmont school chapel service. 3377
Belonging. 3182
Belonging and alienation. 3066
Belonging, issues of emotional living in an age of stress for clergy and religious. 775, 2575
Belonging to the people of God. 3111, 3856
Beloved. 2400
Beloved community. 3444
Beloved community, America! 2385
Beloved disciple. 2126
Beloved disciples. 422
Beloved Jew. 2005
Beloved leaders. 3383
Beloved mendicant. 2183
"Beloved of the Lord." 3457
Beloved physician. 2271
Beloved physician of Teheran. 2544, 3272
Beloved rabbi. 192
Beloved son. 26, 1393
Beloved unbeliever. 3830
Beloved world. 296
Ben Asher's creed. 1, 2164
Ben-Gurion looks at the Bible. 484
Ben-Hur. 2006
Ben Nelson, defender of the faithful. 2620, 2683
Ben-Onic. 2085
Ben Roland gospels. 3056
Ben Sira and the nonexistence of the Synagogue. 3576
Bench-ends in English churches. 2827
Bench marks. 1313
Bench marks of faith. 3666
Beneath the cross of Jesus. 105, 2033
Beneath the cross of Jesus; meditations for Lent and Holy week suggested by the hymn, "Beneath the cross of Jesus," 2213
Beneath the moon and under the sun. 1898
Beneath the Southern Cross. 2499
Beneath the surface. 565
Beneath two flags. 3292
Benedicenda. 189
Benedictine Abbey of New Norcia, Western Australia. 187
Benedictine almanac and guide to abbeys. 188
Benedictine and Moor. 3705
Benedictine bibliography. 188
Benedictine contributions to church architecture. 1159
Benedictine idea. 188
Benedictine martyrology. 188
Benedictine monachism. 187
Benedictine monasticism. 188, 189, 190
Benedictine monasticism as reflected in the Warnefrid-Hildemar commentaries on the Rule. 189
Benedictine nun, her story and aim. 187
Benedictine peace. 188
Benedictine pioneers in Australia. 188
Benedictine spirituality. 188
Benedictines. 188
Benedictines, a digest for moderns. 188
Benedictines in Britain. 188
Benedictinism through changing centuries. 188
Benediction. 189
Benediction from solitude. 189
Benedictions taken from Genesis to Revelations of the King James version of the Bible. 188
Die Benediktinerabtei Siegburg. 3407
Beneficent euthanasia. 1544
Beneficium Christi. 108
Benefit of a well-ordered conversation. 1424
Benefit of Christ's death. 108
... Benefit of clergy in England in the later middle ages. 1291

Benefits annexed to a participation in the two Christian sacraments, of baptism and the Lord's supper. 3264
Benefits of His passion. 2031
Benevolence. 2669
Benga primer. 190
Bengal temples. 3600
Benham Club of Princeton, New Jersey. 3144
Benign influence of religion on civil government and national happiness. 1504
Benito Arias Montano. 80
Benjamin coleman's Some of the glories of Our Lord and Saviour Jesus Christ. 1340, 1978
Benjamin; essays in prayer. 2882
Benjamin Franklin and the zealous Presbyterians. 1651, 2937
Benjamin Furly and Quakerism in Rotterdam. 1688, 1694
Benjamin Goodall Symon, Jr., his biography and letters. 1470
Benjamin Wisner Bacon, pioneer in American Biblical criticism. 124
Benjamite king. 3304
Bennett law of 1899. 1247
Bennett's Guide to the Bible. 600
Bennie Brighton. 660
Bent-knee time: a bit for every day of the year. 2890
Bent world. 1853, 3069
Bentley. 191
Benziger brothers' publications. 869
Bequests for masses for the souls of deceased persons. 2365
Beraysheeth. 3338
Berdyaev's philosophy of hope. 191, 1530
Berean. 2737, 3623
Berengar and the reform of sacramental doctrine. 192, 3615
Beresheet; a kindergarten guide. 3175
[Bereshit (romanized form)] Genesis. 522
Der Begriff des Politischen und der politischen Theologie. 1085
Berkeley. 192
Berkeley bussei. 707
Berkeley, Hume and Kant. 2843
Berkeley journal; Jesus and the street people—a firsthand report. 1261
Berkeley version of the New Testament from the original Greek. 479
Berkeley's American sojourn. 192
Berlin and its treasures. 192
Bernadette. 3460
Bernadette and Lourdes. 3460
Bernadette and the Lady. 193
Bernadette of Lourdes. 193, 2262, 3460
Bernadette of Lourdes, shepherdess, Sister, and Saint, [Rev. version, with new material added. 3460
Bernadette, Our Lady's little servant. 3460
Bernadette—the only witness. 193, 1026
Bernard. 194
Bernard Haring replies. 3012
Bernard Lonergan's philosophy of God. 1733, 2245
Bernard Meltzer's Guidance for living. 3343
Bernard of Clairvaux. 193
Bernard of Clairvaux: studies presented to Dom Jean Leclercq. 194
Bernard of Clairvaux, the times, the man, and his work. 193
Bernard Revel: builder of American Jewish orthodoxy. 3223
Bernard Vaughan, S.J. 3772, 3774
Bernardine Realino, Renaissance man. 3027
Bernardines. 194
Bernardino Ochino, of Siena. 2734
Bernhard Felsenthal, teacher in Israel. 1621
Bernie becomes a nun. 2573
Berrigan brothers. 194
Berrigans. 194, 195
Berry's Greek-English New Testament lexicon with synonyms. 1768
Bertha and her baptism. 133, 1905
Bertha Fidelia. 660
Bertran Russell's philosophy of morals. 3255
Bertrand Russell's philosophy of morals. 3255
Beschworungsformeln aus dem "Buch der Geheimnisse" (Sefar ha-razim). 722, 3329
Beside all waters. 918, 1545
Beside Galilee. 2761
Beside still waters. 2301, 2676
Beside the beautiful Willamette. 2206, 2453
Beside the cross. 2031
Beside the house. 1369
Beside the new-made grave. 1891
Beside the sea of glass. 465
Beside the Shepherd's tent. 1452

Beside the Syrian sea. 2005
Besieged city; the church in the world. 1116
Besieging spirit. 2385
Best Bible tales. 626, 629
Best Bible verses. 301
Best Black sermons. 3361
Best books for the Catholic people. 869
Best books on spirit phenomena, 1847-1925. 3519
Best church hymns. 1874
Best church plays. 934, 3145
Best from Pulpit digest. 3356
Best I remember. 3201
Best is yet to be. 17, 2735
Best is yet to come. 608
Best Jewish sermons. 3370
Best Jewish sermons of. 3370
Best-loved hymn stories. 1871
Best loved hymns and prayers of the American people. 1867
Best-loved Unity poems. 3209
Best man I know. 943
Best modern illustrations. 1840
Best of A. W. Tozer. 2397
Best of Alexander MacLaren. 165
Best of Billy Sunday. 1561
Best of both worlds. 996
Best of Charles E. Jefferson. 1341
Best of Chester Swor. 994
Best of Church & state, 1948-1975. 1142
Best of Cry pax! 871
Best of D. L. Moody. 1558
Best of Dick Sheppard (H. R. L. Sheppard) 3634
Best of Elton Trueblood. 3491
Best of John A. Hutton. 2931
Best of John Henry Jowett. 1448, 1456
Best of luck. 2729
Best of New creations. 1005
Best of Open windows. 1436
Best of Sybil Leek. 2206, 2730, 3823
Best of the good news. 2436, 3355
Best of the Sanctuary. 1435
Best of times, the worst of times. 1301, 1772
Best of Walter A. Maier. 2285, 3633
Best of your life is the rest of your life. 1005
Best plays for the church. 3145
Best sermons. 3338, 3348
Best sermons. 1944. 3338
Best stories from the best book. 3026
Best texts for soul winners. 1572
Best things in the Bible. 650
Best way. 1360
Best wishes for common days and special days. 2390
Beth-El lite. 1160
Beth El story. 1426
Beth Israel hymnal. 2097
Beth Sar Shalom hymnal. 1860
Bethada naem nErenn. 3283
Bethany college sermons. 3363
Bethany junior department manual. 3170
Bethel Among the Oaks. 1943
Bethel and Aurora. 3436
Bethel and her ministers, 1746-1946. 195
... Bethel and Penuel. 2934
Bethel chimes. 3458
Bethel Presbyterian Church at Madonna, Maryland, 1769-1969: two hundredth anniversary. 195, 2311
Bethlehem. 1981, 2021
Bethlehem Bach Choir. 123, 2634
Bethlehem church and its pastor. 195
Bethlehem diary. 2595
Bethlehem drama (in five acts) 3144
Bethlehem nights. 1111, 2021
Bethlehem revisited. 1114
Bethlehem star. 1984
Bethlehem tree. 8
Betrayal of Father Coughlin. 1372
Betrayed! 1366, 3593
Betrothed, The highland widow. 1392
Betrothment and marriage. 196
Betsy Ross, Quaker rebel. 1287
Better a day. 1945
... Better Americans. 1839
... Better Americans, no. 3. 1838
Better Baptist churches. 143
Better Bible study. 3720
Better Bible teaching for intermediates. 3167
Better Bible teaching for juniors in the Sunday school. 3172
Better chalk talks. With devotions by Quentin M. Perreault and Reve Stewart Perreault. 880
Better Christmas. 1111
Better church finance. 1167
Better church leaders. 1239
Better church leadership. 1199
Better church school. 3555
Better country. 3475
Better covenant. 3029

Better day is dawning. 1173
Better endeavor, for officers, committees, pastors. 1910
Better half of the ministry. 1303
Better hope. 2435
Better land. 1795
Better leaders for your church. 1250
Better life. 404
Better life; the true meaning of tertiarism. 3692
Better living through Christ. 405
Better meetings. 1248
Better men for the better times. 3439
Better music in our churches. 1208
Better music in the church. 1203
Better not. 36
Better part. 1001, 1052, 2478
Better preaching. 2899
Better primary teaching. 3171
Better readings. 3026
Better Testament. 641
Better than gold. 1861, 3459
Better than I was. 931, 2166
Better than seven sons. 589
Better things. 2459
Better vacation Bible schools. 3763
Better way. 955, 1823
Better world. 3381
Betterment, individual, social, and industrial. 3330
Betty Baxter story. 1598
Betty book. 3474, 3518
Betty's proof of spirit return. 3514
Between an atom and a star. 2388, 3199
Between belief and transgression. 3536
Between Black and white. 669
Between Caesar and Jesus. 1135
Between Christ and Satan. 2726
Between christian parent and child. 1608
Between community and society. 1141
Between earth and heaven. 1101, 3399
Between faith and tears. 3541
Between faith and thought. 3651
Between faith and unfaith. 1056
Between God and history. 1683
Between God and man. 1062, 1473, 2139, 3391
Between God and ourselves. 3490
Between God and ourselves; aids to spiritual progress. 3490
Between God and Satan. 2067
Between heaven and earth. 3625
Between honesty and hope. 821
Between man and man. 1457
Between ourselves. 1001
Between pleasure and pain. 3864
Between reason and faith. 3022
Between ring & temple. 2347
Between science and religion. 3085
Between the Americas. 3807
Between the covers of the Book of Mormon. 678
Between the covers of the Doctrine and covenants. 3217
Between the covers of the Old Testament. 595
Between the eagle & the dove. 3740
Between the generations: a Jewish dialogue. 3882
Between the lines of the Bible. 1312
Between the Testaments. 2091, 2092, 2150
Between time and eternity. 2147, 3201
Between two centuries. 2502
Between two cities. 1281
Between two wars. 2851, 2861
Between two worlds. 643, 681, 1010, 1954, 2323, 3203
Between you and me. 956
Between you and me, God. 1714
Between you & me, Lord. 2892
Beulah land. 119
Beverly's quest. 1714
Beware familiar spirits. 3509
Beware of these days, light your lamps. 3198
Bewitching jewelry. 3582
Bexley Hall, 150 years. 2167
Beyond. 2989, 3337
Beyond a miracle. 1452
Beyond agnosticism. 1047, 1056
Beyond all horizons. 1949
Beyond all horizons; Jesuits and the missions. 1949
Beyond and back. 1698
Beyond androcentrism. 3834
Beyond anxiety. 2995
Beyond any kind of God. 2227
Beyond belief. 1056, 1722, 3087
Beyond believing. 987
Beyond birth control. 3391
Beyond brokenness. 2480
Beyond Buddhism. 708
Beyond call. 992
Beyond commitment. 965
Beyond conflict. 710
Beyond conformity. 1551

Beyond conversion. 994
Beyond Cotabato. 2545
Beyond cynicism; the practice of hope. 1845
Beyond Damascus. 2802
Beyond death. 1528, 1695
Beyond death's door. 1696, 1698
Beyond despair. 3479
Beyond dialogue. 2317
Beyond dilemmas. 1138, 1676
Beyond disbelief. 2045, 3483
Beyond disenchantment. 1060
Beyond diversity to a common experience of God. 2131
Beyond doubt. 3507
Beyond East and West. 1365
Beyond existentialism and Zen. 3104
Beyond fundamentalism. 1691
Beyond fundamentalism and modernism. 1052
Beyond futility. 512
Beyond gates of gold. 1696
Beyond guilt. 1777
Beyond heartache. 1351
Beyond high school. 3536
Beyond humanism. 806
Beyond humiliation. 968
Beyond ideology. 1090
Beyond ideology, religion and the future of Western civilization. 3123
Beyond individualism. 3481
Beyond loneliness. 2244
Beyond love. 924, 1783
Beyond mere obedience. 2719
Beyond mythology. 3057
Beyond normal cognition. 2991, 3516
Beyond one man. 870, 1397
Beyond our selves. 968
Beyond our tribal gods. 1594
Beyond personality. 1723
Beyond petition. 2879
Beyond pledging. 2192
Beyond politics. 1085, 3436
Beyond positive thinking. 981
Beyond prison walls. 2716, 2942
Beyond questions and answers. 73
Beyond religion. 1119
Beyond renewal. 1121
Beyond revolution. 1244
Beyond romance. 2531
Beyond romance, a true story from the heart of India. 2529
Beyond science. 3566
Beyond sorrow. 1351
Beyond space. 42
Beyond spiritual gifts. 990
Beyond statistics. 2518
Beyond the altar rail. 2367
Beyond the atom. 63
Beyond the bar. 72
Beyond the battle for the Bible. 277
Beyond the blue Pacific. 2490
Beyond the body. 94
Beyond the borderline of life. 3509
Beyond the burning bush. 888, 1627
Beyond the classics? 3112
Beyond the commandments. 999
Beyond the cross and the switchblade. 1255, 3816
Beyond the darkness. 3222
Beyond the eight horizons. 1116
Beyond the either-or church. 1566
Beyond the exit door. 1353, 3778
Beyond the eyes of man. 3517, 3518
Beyond the facts. 2437
Beyond the gates of death. 1697
Beyond the gods. 2637
Beyond the grave. 1939
Beyond the Himalayas. 2307
Beyond the horizon of science. 3074
Beyond the Kikuyu Curtain. 2536
Beyond the lighthouse. 3473
Beyond the Milky Way. 3717
Beyond the mind. 3477
Beyond the natural order. 3197
Beyond the new theism. 3100
Beyond the ranges. 3862
Beyond the rat race. 3409
Beyond the river. 3510
Beyond the road to Rome. 1363
Beyond the rummage sale. 3857
Beyond the shadows. 1351
Beyond the sunset. 1697, 1890, 3509
Beyond the time barrier. 2948
Beyond the tomb. 1696
Beyond the vail. 3509
Beyond the valley. 3499
Beyond the veil. 3354
Beyond the wall. 612, 1576, 2805
Beyond theology. 1080
Beyond this darkness. 3794
Beyond this God cannot go. 992
Beyond this land of whoa. 3527
Beyond this present. 2114
Beyond thyself. 3361
Beyond TM. 2379
Beyond tradition and modernity. 3068

Beyond tragedy. 1105
Beyond tragedy--what? 1238
Beyond Trinity. 3711
Beyond words. 3491
Beyond words and thoughts. 2694
Beyond yesterday. 3724
Bezae codex cantabrigiensis. 398
Bezels of wisdom. 3544
Bhafavad-gita. 196
Bhagavad Gita. 196, 197, 2316, 3891
Bhagavad-Gita and Hymn to Narayena. 196
Bhagavad Gita and the Epistles of Paul. 2317
Bhagavad Gita as it is. 2316
Bhagavad Gita for daily living. 2316
Bhagavad gita; or, The Lord's lay. 196
Bhagavad gita; or The message of the master. 196
Bhagavad gita "The songs of the master" 196
Bhagavadgita. 196, 197
Bhagavadgita in the Mahabharata. 197
Bhagavadgita; or, The battle of life. 196
Bhagavadgita, the book of devotion. 196
Bhagvat-geeta, 1785. 196
Bhagwan Mahavira and his relevance in modern times. 1932, 2317
Bhakti-ratnavali. 197
Bhakti sutras of Narada. 197
Bharavi's peom Kiratarjuniya. 3206
Bhaskar and his friends. 897
Bi-centennial. 3279
Bi-centennial anniversary of the Friends' Meeting-House. 1687
... The bi-centennial celebration of the founding of the First Baptist church of the city of Philadelphia, 1898. 2829
Bias and the pious. 1131
Bible. 199, 209, 210, 224, 232, 249, 260, 278, 289, 290, 300, 307, 309, 311, 312, 352, 418, 472, 500, 514, 528, 538, 543, 603, 614, 624, 637, 639, 1370, 1655, 3383
Bible A B C. 3026
Bible a missionary message. 2503
Bible: a modern Jewish approach. 538
Bible: a modern understanding. 235
Bible, a sustaining presence in worship. 477, 3004
Bible ABC's. 623
Bible acrostic puzzles. 281
Bible against slavery. 3423
Bible alive. 2386
Bible allegories. 500
Bible almanac. 298, 3439
Bible alphabet word puzzles. 281
Bible among the nations. 653
Bible, an American translation. 261
Bible analyzed in twenty lectures. 234
Bible and archaeology. 207, 208
Bible and astronomy. 204, 211
Bible and Babylon. 290, 1421
Bible and business. 719, 994
Bible and character. 806
Bible and Christ. 451, 3721
Bible and Christian science. 1033, 1496
Bible and church history stories for the Primary department of the Sunday School. 2615
Bible and church history stories for the primary department of the Sunday school. 643
Bible and civilization. 538
Bible and college theology. 3159
Bible and common sense. 653
Bible and democracy. 526, 1422
Bible and drug abuse. 1480
Bible and early man. 204
Bible and English prose style. 210
Bible and ethics in the Christian life. 275, 942
Bible and evangelism. 636
Bible and flying saucers. 232
Bible and history. 298
Bible and history studies. 641
Bible and how to read it. 310
Bible and human rights. 2223
Bible and Islam. 1926
Bible and Islami. 2565
Bible and its books. 210, 312
Bible and its Christ. 615
Bible and its interpreter. 835
Bible and its interpreters. 234
Bible and its literary associations. 210
Bible and its story. 308
Bible and its use. 653
Bible and labor. 2189
... The Bible and life. 209
Bible and men of learning. 204, 205
Bible and mission stories. 615
Bible and missions. 2494
Bible and modern belief. 536
Bible and modern criticism. 229
Bible and modern doubt. 186, 652
Bible and modern life. 200, 637

Bible and modern literature, comparing the literature of today with the ancient Jewish scriptures. 240
Bible and modern man. 201
Bible and modern medicine. 317, 3073
Bible and modern scholarship. 174, 277, 1196
Bible and modern science. 205, 635
Bible and modern science. [Rev. ed.]. 203
Bible and modern thought. 304
Bible and money. 2584
... Bible and nature stories. 619
Bible and nature versus Copernicus. 205
Bible and other ancient literature in the nineteenth century. 237
... Bible and other stories. 619
Bible and our Christian beliefs. 651
Bible and our common life. 3439
Bible and our national life. 206
Bible and our social outlook. 3454
Bible and our social responsibility. 3439
Bible & people who lived and wrote it. 535
Bible & polygamy. 2859
Bible and prayer. 2887
Bible and property with applications to present times of land possessing, railroad tyranny, Standard oil, sugar, leather, beef, whisky, and other trusts. 247
Bible and rationalism. 237
Bible and recent archaeology. 209
Bible and rural life. 3454
Bible and science. 205, 3077
Bible and sex ethics today. 3390
Bible and social living. 3453
...The Bible and social problems. 3444
... Bible and spade. 208, 486
Bible and spiritual life. 3484
Bible and sword. 1764
Bible and Talmud stories. 620
Bible and the ages. 232
Bible and the ancient Near East. 23, 485, 503, 2678
Bible and the Anglo-Saxon people. 269
Bible and the Bermuda Triangle. 193, 319
... The Bible and the Bible country. 649
Bible and the Bible school. 647
Bible and the child. 3169
Bible and the church. 312, 1590
Bible and the closet. 613
Bible and the common reader. 203, 210
Bible and the common schools, or The question settled. 300
Bible and the cross. 199
Bible and the faiths of men. 206, 3115
Bible and the family. 1603
Bible and the future. 1530
Bible and the gold rush. 290, 1336
Bible and the historical design. 309
Bible and the human quest. 1063
Bible and the Jews. 1083
Bible and the Koran. 2184, 2185
Bible and the liturgy. 838, 2240
Bible and the nations. 209
Bible and the origin of man. 2323
Bible and the problem of poverty. 2865
Bible and the public schools. 638, 3096
Bible and the quest of life. 647
Bible and the role of women. 2742
Bible and the schools. 3096
Bible and the spade. 197
Bible and the Sunday school. 637
Bible and the tarot. 234, 721
Bible and the teacher. 635
Bible and the universe. 1817
Bible and the world. 1381
Bible and things to come. 1531
Bible and today's headlines. 3439
Bible and tomorrow's news. 608
Bible and woman. 3832
Bible and you. 613
Bible and your child. 638
Bible animals. 481
Bible answers for today's questions. 319, 1012
Bible answers us with pictures. 611
Bible anthology. 252
Bible, archaeology, and faith. 207
Bible as a community book. 1321
Bible as a document of the university. 239
Bible as English literature. 210
Bible as good reading. 210
Bible as history. 298
Bible as history in pictures. 298
Bible as I see it. 234, 307
Bible as/in literature. 210
Bible "as is" 601
Bible as it is. 644, 650
Bible as literature. 210, 211, 230, 234, 238, 275, 541, 556, 649
... The Bible as literature. 238
Bible as read and preached in the old synagogue. 558, 2109, 2462
Bible as religion and literature. 499
Bible as the Church's book. 276
Bible at a single view. 307
Bible atlas. 282

Bible atlas and a new system of chronological and pictorial charts. 283
Bible autobiographies and other Bible stories. 210
Bible babies. 624, 898
Bible background. 2096
Bible ballot. 1087
Bible baptism. 135
Bible basketball. 637
Bible beautiful. 654, 922
Bible belt Catholicism. 824, 2735
Bible belt mystique. 3468
Bible between fundamentalism and philosophy. 276
Bible biographies (bibelbiografier) for use in the intermediate department of Sunday schools. 215
Bible biography. 216
Bible book by book. 307, 312, 649
Bible book of medical wisdom. 317
Bible book study. 638
Bible books outlined. 645
Bible boys and girls. 313, 898
Bible calls for action. 3453
Bible cameos. 216
Bible catechism. 217
Bible catechism and questionnaire. 217
Bible-centered devotions on fulfillment and splendor. 318
Bible-centered devotions on purity and hope. 318
Bible-centered devotions on resurrection and glory. 318
Bible-centered devotions on silence and remembrance. 318
Bible-centered Sermon Starters. 3373
Bible challenges. 280
Bible character stories. 493
Bible characters. 213, 215, 216
Bible characters and doctrines. 647
Bible chats. 3353
Bible children. 897, 906
Bible Christian. 1054
Bible, church, and God. 1655
Bible class and the community. 650
Bible class directory. 3560
... Bible classics. 614
Bible clippings. 301
Bible college story. 219
Bible comes alive. 211
Bible commentary. 225, 426, 546, 559
Bible commentary: the minor prophets. 559
Bible comments for home reading. 497
Bible communism. 2737
Bible companion. 285, 286
Bible companion for pastors evangelists and teachers and all seekers after truth. 248
Bible comparatives. 159
Bible course for Southern Bible institute. 3468
Bible crafts. 229
Bible criticism and the average man. 234
Bible cyclopedia. 242
Bible dates itself. 496
Bible days. 207
Bible defended. 1598
Bible definition of religion. 3061
Bible designed to be read as living literature. 210
Bible devil. 307
Bible devotions for Ash Wednesday and the six weeks of Lent. 242
Bible dictionary. 246
Bible dictionary. Drawings by Robert F. Ramey. 247
Bible dictionary for boys and girls. 244
Bible dictionary for boys and girls, by Manuel and Odette Komroff. 247
Bible dictionary for young readers. 247
Bible difficulties. 229
Bible difficulties and their alleviative interpretation. 515
Bible digest. 646
Bible digest charts. 646
Bible directory. 3426
Bible doctrine. 1473, 2405, 3181, 3646
Bible doctrine of devotion. 1473
Bible doctrine of immortality. 1889
Bible doctrine of the great salvation. 1473
Bible doctrine of the soul. 3462
Bible doctrine study outline for a six hour college course, with suggestive adaptations for a four hour course. 3382
Bible doctrines. 92, 3641, 3648
Bible doctrines for teenagers. 3660
Bible doctrines study outline for a six hour college course, with suggestive adaptations for a four hour course. 3382
Bible does not teach close communion. 650
Bible: dogma, myth, or mystery? 644
Bible economy of plenty. 247
Bible elements of a good character, and good success maxims. 886
Bible emblems. 1510

Bible encyclopedia for children. 247
Bible. English. 254
Bible. English. 1965. 270, 274
Old and the New Testaments of the Holy Bible. 266
New World translation of the Holy Scriptures. 265
Holy Bible, containing the Old and New Testaments. 265
Bible epitaphs. 215
Bible etchings of immortality. 1887
Bible examined. 307
Bible exposed. 235
Bible expositions. 592
Bible expositor. 206
Bible, fact, fiction, fantasy, faith. 309
Bible facts and precis. 291
Bible facts and precis, regarding the dates of writing, authorship, dates of events, historical value, sources, and contents of each book of the Holy Bible. 311
Bible facts with questions and answers. 612
Bible family life seminar. 982
Bible festivals and holy days. 1614
Bible fires. 215
Bible firsts. 623
Bible football. 612, 644
Bible footlights. 198
Bible footlights for the pilgrim's path. 198
Bible for all the world. 291
Bible for boys and girls. 313
Bible for children. 313, 616, 621, 622
Bible for ethics. 241, 1538, 3329
Bible for everyone. 310
Bible for family reading. 251
Bible for school and home. 224
Bible for students of literature and art. 210
Bible for students of literature and art. Selected with an introd. 210
Bible for the humanities. 251
Bible for the liberal. 250
Bible for the sick. 252, 3406
Bible for to-day. 2755
Bible for today. 603
Bible for today's church. 230
Bible for today's world. 614
Bible for young Christians. 625, 628
Bible for young folks. 313
Bible for young people. 313, 481, 625, 627
Bible for young readers: the Old Testament. 628
Bible forget me nots. 725
Bible: four hundred years after 1538. 201
Bible from the beginning. 291
Bible fun book. 281
Bible gallery. 602
Bible gems. 724
Bible geography. 283
Bible: God's word to man. 308, 648
Bible guidebook. 311
Bible hand-book. 308, 635
Bible hand-book, theologically arranged. 303
Bible handbook. 285, 286, 650
Bible handbook for freethinkers and inquiring Christians. 233
Bible handbook for young learners. 314
Bible harp. 1867
Bible has the answer. 280, 3670
Bible healing prayer book. 1793
Bible hero classics. 213
Bible hero devotions for boys and girls. 898
Bible heroes. 629, 1807
Bible heroes, kings & prophets. 630
Bible heroines. 3841
Bible highpoints. 311
Bible highway. 619
Bible highways. 166
Bible history. 219, 289, 292, 293, 532, 620, 621, 622, 624, 648, 649
Bible history and brief outline of church history. 291, 1189
Bible: history and culture of a people. 201
Bible history commentary, Old Testament. 533
Bible history digest. 295
Bible history for home and school. 624
Bible history for schools and the home. 617, 620
Bible history for schools, confirmation classes and homes. 618
Bible history for the use of elementary schools. 623
Bible history in outline: Genesis-Esther. 596
Bible history of answered prayer. 2885
Bible history of the Holy Land. 2764
Bible history of the Old and New Testaments. 292, 297
Bible history of world government. 291, 608

Bible history of world government and a forecast of its future from Bible prophecy. 608
Bible history--Old Testament. 515
Bible history [Old Testament] after the results of historical criticism. 534
Bible history outlines. 253
Bible history references. 649
Bible history with a history of the church. 622
Bible history with an epitome of church history. 291, 1180
Bible hockey. 637
Bible holiness. 1823
Bible homes and families. 619
Bible homes and homes today. 3764
Bible; how to understand and teach it. 636
Bible ideals. 211
Bible illustrations. 2760
Bible in a thousand tongues. 655
Bible in a year. 318
Bible in America. 655
Bible in American education. 241, 650, 1130
Bible in art. 566, 602
Bible in Basic English. 267
Bible in Brazil. 2505
Bible in brief. 296
Bible in Britain. 270
Bible in Browning. 299, 697
Bible in Browning, with particular reference to The ring and the book. 299, 697
Bible in China. 289
Bible in Christian teaching. 278
Bible in court. 203
Bible in current Catholic thought. 201, 1776
Bible in dialogue with modern man. 235
Bible in early English literature. 299, 304, 1811
Bible in East Germany. 653
Bible in eight ages. 1376
Bible in English drama. 1517
Bible in everyday living. 643
Bible in harmony with nature. 2675
Bible in human transformation. 643
Bible in the light of modern science. 204
Bible in India. 612
Bible in Israeli education. 596, 1498
Bible in its ancient and English versions. 291
Bible in its literary milieu. 238
Bible in lesson and story. 625
Bible in living English. 1940
Bible in Masonic ritual. 1670
Bible in Milton's epics. 299, 300
Bible in mission lands. 612
Bible in modern light. 232, 313
Bible in modern scholarship. 229
Bible in New York. 2696
Bible in order. 218
Bible in our day. 200
Bible in our modern world. 236, 312
Bible in our public schools. 300
Bible in pastoral care. 653
Bible in pictures. 602
Bible in pictures for little eyes. 624
Bible in pocket, gun in hand. 1689, 3749
Bible in questions and answers. 311, 648
Bible in schools plans of many lands. 637
Bible in sermon. 614
Bible in Shakespeare. 299, 3399
Bible in song. 319
Bible in Spain. 3469
Bible in story. 295
Bible in story and art. 297
Bible in story and pictures. 618
Bible in symbols. 645, 1810
Bible in the age of science. 205, 3080
Bible in the balance. 233, 305, 2230
Bible in the British scene. 653
Bible in the building of life. 648
Bible in the church. 240, 644
Bible in the counting-house. 719, 3426
Bible in the counting-house; a course of lectures to merchants. 719
Bible in the early Middle Ages. 240
Bible in the hands of its creators. 2114
Bible in the Levant. 3238
Bible in the light of modern science. 204
Bible in the light of religious science. 2695
Bible in the local church. 653
Bible in the making. 290
Bible in the making in the light of modern research. 291
Bible in the making of ministers. 2696, 3812
Bible in the modern world. 230
Bible in the nineteenth century. 240
... The Bible in the public schools. 300, 3096
Bible in the pulpit. 299, 2907
Bible in the Wesleyan heritage. 240, 3668, 3805

Bible in the world of today. 230
Bible in type and antitype. 607
Bible in worship and ministry. 653
Bible in your life. 2287
Bible index pocketbook. 301
Bible indispensable in education. 300
Bible inerrancy primer. 276
Bible inspiration; orthodox point of view. 306
Bible instructor in personal and public evangelism. 1566
Bible interpretation. 238, 307
Bible interpreter. 302
Bible is a special book. 313
Bible is different. 306
Bible is for you. 501
Bible is human. 536
Bible; is it the word of God? 276
Bible is not the ultimate authority. 1099
Bible is the Word of God. 277
Bible, its origin and interpretation. 290
Bible, its origin, and interpretation. 232
Bible, Jesus, and the Jews. 2087, 2103
Bible Jesus read is exciting! 535
Bible jewels. 614
Bible jingle rhymes. 313
Bible journeys, experiences for Christian growth. 313, 3888
Bible key words. 313
Bible key words, from Gerhard Kittel's Theologisches Worterbuch zum Neuen Testament. 1768
Bible lamplighters and their messages for boys and girls. 313
Bible lamps for little feet. 314
Bible landmarks in a changing land. 2763
Bible lands. 2765
... Bible lands and places with their Biblical connections. 283
Bible lands illustrated. 282
Bible learning activities: children, grades 1 to 6. 3169
Bible legend book. 2207
Bible lessons. 621, 636
Bible lessons and lectures. 313
Bible lessons for foreigners beginning English. 635
Bible lessons for little beginners. 645
Bible lessons for the Christian year. 496
Bible lessons for the Sunday evenings of the Christian year. 636
Bible lessons for the Sunday mornings of the Christian year. 636
Bible lessons for youth. 3187
Bible lessons on Christian duty. 1015
Bible lessons on the creed. 73
Bible, life, and worship. 2240
*Bible, life and worship series. 319, 3184, 3188
Bible light for daily life. 1315
Bible light on daily life. 964
Bible light on everyday problems. 275
Bible-light on life's pathway. 233, 1431
Bible lights for little folks. 313
Bible lights on baptism. 140
Bible literature. 651
Bible, liturgy, and dogma. 651
Bible lives today. 514
Bible looking-glass. 219, 1013
Bible looks you over. 201
Bible lore. 1996
Bible lovers illustrated library. 226
Bible made plain. 636, 3382
Bible makes sense. 231
Bible manual. 46, 639
Bible marksman. 646
Bible marvel workers. 3511
Bible mastery. 636, 643
Bible meanings. 243
Bible meets you where you are. 641, 1170
Bible men and things with their gospel meanings. 3720
Bible men of prayer. 213
Bible message for modern manhood. 306
Bible messages. 306
Bible messages for the modern mind. 313
Bible miniatures. 216
Bible morals. Twenty crimes and vices sanctioned by Scripture. 1655
Bible music. 320
Bible must be retaught. 651
Bible mysteries revealed. 307
... Bible mystery and Bible meaning. 307
Bible: myth or reality? 500
Bible myths and their parallels in other religions. 232, 2651
Bible name quiz contests relating to famous Bible characters. 218
Bible names, pronunciations and meanings, alphabetically arranged. 480
Bible natural history. 480
Bible nature stories in chalk. 880
Bible needs no apology: or, Watson's system of religion refuted. 234
Bible news. 2002, 3713, 3714
Bible nights. 1285

Bible nines of power. 2063
Bible not of man. 278
Bible notebook. 643
Bible: now I get it! 229
Bible now. 200
Bible number quiz. 281
Bible object book. 643
Bible of bibles. 1654, 3268
Bible of humanity for supreme wisdom. 3821
Bible of Jesus. 499, 1952
Bible of mankind, compiled and edited by Mirza Ahmad Sohrab. 3268
Bible of nature and the Bible of grace. 1753
Bible of pure spiritualism. 3478
Bible of reason. 3023
Bible of superhuman origin. 237, 279
Bible of the expositor and the evangelist. 615
Bible of the middle way. 272
Bible of the religion of science. 3314
Bible of the world. 3268
Bible of to-day. 231, 308
Bible on asceticism. 90
Bible on Christian unity. 1249
Bible on conversion. 1361
Bible on light. 2229
Bible on marriage. 2341
Bible on miracles. 2477
Bible on revelation. 3226
Bible on sexuality. 3390
Bible on suffering. 3541
Bible on temperance. 3597
Bible on the childhood of Jesus. 1977
Bible on the church. 1163
Bible on the exodus. 1584
Bible on the life hereafter. 1695
Bible on the living God. 1731
Bible on the preaching of the World. 2908
Bible on the salvation of nations. 2503, 3293
Bible on the temptations of man. 3600
Bible 1, 2, 3's. 650
Bible, or organic evolution. 1579
Bible or Word of God uncovered and explained after the revelation given through Emanuel Swedenborg. 231
Bible our heritage. 198
Bible outline. 646
Bible outline studies. 645
Bible outlined in a hundred lessons. 646
Bible outlines. 645
Bible outlines for vacation Bible schools. 3765
Bible pageant. 622
Bible parables in pantomime. 601
Bible paradoxes. 3347
Bible parts to learn by heart. 251
Bible people. 217
Bible people and places. 293
Bible personalities. 638
Bible personalities, teacher's book for use with 10 year olds. 638
Bible phrases used as book titles, in English novels, plays, and books of poetry. 3702
Bible picture A B C book. 3026
Bible picture book. 619, 627
Bible picture stories. 313
Bible picture stories from the Old and New Testaments. 622
Bible picture word puzzles. 281
Bible pictures. 164
Bible pictures and their stories. 293
Bible pinnacles. 216
Bible places. 283
Bible plants for American gardens. 480, 1702
... The Bible play workshop. 3146
Bible plays for juniors. 603
Bible poem. 248
Bible prayer book. 603
Bible prayers. 603
Bible precepts for home and school. 650
Bible primer. 310
Bible primer for foreigners. 311
Bible primer for the tiny tots. 2940
Bible primer, New Testament. 410
Bible primer, Old Testament. 539
Bible principles. 216
Bible problems solved. 233
Bible proof that America is God's chosen nation. 46
Bible prophecies. 609
Bible prophecies and the plain man. 607
Bible prophecies fulfilled today. 2118
Bible prophecy. 604, 611, 1531
Bible prophecy for our time. 604
Bible prophecy notes. 604
Bible prophecy of today's events. 606
Bible punchers. 238
Bible puzzle book. 281
Bible question bee. 280
Bible question book. 3011
Bible questions. 3011
Bible questions answered. 651, 3011

Bible questions explained. 3649
Bible questions for the study of church, ladies', and young people's organizations. 3011
Bible quiz and answers. 281
Bible quiz and cross word puzzle book. 218
Bible quiz book. 280, 281
Bible quiz program book. 280
Bible quizbook. 281
Bible quizzes. 280
Bible quizzes and questions. 280
Bible quizzes for everybody. 280
Bible quizzle book for boys and girls from 6 to 12. 612
Bible quotes & comments. 2386
Bible read as literature, an anthology. 211
Bible reader. 650
Bible readers' aids. 285, 286, 643
Bible-reader's help. 286
Bible readers's companion. 286
Bible-reader's life of Christ. 1962
Bible reading-book. 618
Bible reading for the home fireside. 636, 1228
Bible readings. 302, 304, 500, 614
Bible readings and hymns for school use. 319
Bible readings and sermon outlines on the Christian plea. 615
Bible readings and spiritual essays. 613, 1824
Bible readings for Bible students and for the home and fireside. 253
Bible readings for boys and girls. 618
Bible readings for Christian workers. 225
Bible readings for couples. 2347
Bible readings for schools. 249
Bible readings for schools and colleges. 250
Bible readings for singles. 3415
Bible readings for the family hour. 624
Bible readings for the home. 3381
Bible readings for the home circle. 301
Bible readings for the responsive service in Christian worship. 252
Bible readings for the synagogue. 251
Bible readings for the use of teachers and schools. 249
Bible readings in character and citizenship. 886
Bible readings on the double heart and kindred truths. 253
Bible readings on the Holy Spirit. 1834
Bible records. 198
Bible records: Brinneshults, Glendinning, Smith. 198
Bible-related curriculum materials. 300
Bible religion. 651
Bible, religion, and the public schools. 300, 3095
Bible revelation of the Holy Spirit. 1830
Bible revival. 1557
Bible riddles in rhyme. 313
Bible rule of temperance. 3596
Bible says. 277
Bible says you can expect these things. 604
Bible-school. 286
Bible school book. 642
Bible school manual. 451
Bible school on the mission field. 2517
...Bible school pedagogy. 3153
Bible school teacher's handbook. 3553
Bible-school vision. 286
Bible science. 1471
Bible, science, and creation. 203
Bible, science, and faith. 206
Bible search. 285
Bible search light thrown onto mormonism. 2611
Bible selections and original poems for primary classes. 313
Bible selections arranged for many uses. 250
Bible selections for daily devotion. 725
Bible sermon outlines. 3374
Bible service. 838
Bible services for a parish mission. 839
Bible sharing. 231, 996
... The Bible: should it be in the school room? 300
Bible sketches (a connected series) 298
Bible snap-shots. 199
Bible societies, American missionaries, and the national revival of Bulgaria. 612, 713
Bible songs. 319, 3271
Bible soul-winners. 304
Bible speaks. 304, 651, 3382
Bible speaks about faith. 1430
Bible speaks again. 311
Bible speaks on aging. 18
Bible speaks to daily needs. 1439
Bible speaks to our day. 304, 1067
Bible speaks to our generation. 234
Bible speaks to our times. 3356
Bible speaks to you. 231, 3661

Bible status of woman. 3841
Bible stories. 619, 621, 623, 627, 628, 629, 641
Bible stories about Jesus. 1980
Bible stories and character building. 618
Bible stories and how to tell them. 616, 3534
Bible stories and modern science. 204
... Bible stories and poems. 618
... Bible stories and religious classics. 3204
Bible stories and you. 620
Bible stories arranged according to the church year. 647
Bible stories as they are recorded in the Bible. 623
Bible stories as told to very little children. 617
... Bible stories every child should know. 625
Bible stories every one should know. 621
Bible stories everyone should know. 621
... Bible stories for a little child. 3185
Bible stories for boys. 620
Bible stories for boys and girls. 620
Bible stories for children. 292, 617, 621, 625, 626, 630
Bible stories for everyone. 619
Bible stories for foreigners. 633
Bible stories for Jewish children. 628, 629
Bible stories for Jewish children, from Joshua to Queen Esther. 630
Bible stories for little children. 616, 621, 629
...Bible stories for little children in words of one syllable. 625
Bible stories for little folk. 625
Bible stories for little folks. 618
Bible stories for me. 619
Bible stories for parochial and Sunday-schools. 620
Bible stories for primary classes. 625
Bible stories for the cradle roll. 628
Bible stories for use in the primary department of the Sunday school. 625
Bible stories for very little people. 625
Bible stories for young Latter-Day saints. 623
Bible stories for young people. 619
Bible stories for young readers. 617, 619, 622
Bible stories from the Old and New Testaments. 618
Bible stories from the Old and the New Testament. 618
Bible stories from the Old Testament. 629, 633
Bible stories: God at work with man. 621
Bible stories in Bible language. 618
Bible stories in easy rhyme. 298
Bible stories in easy words. 1982
Bible stories in rhyme and rhythm. 632
Bible stories in rhyme, rhymes and illustrations. 5
Bible stories my children love best of all. 621
... Bible stories (New Testament) 625
Bible stories of boys and girls. 898
Bible stories of the Old and New Testaments, simply told. 295
Bible stories retold for adults. 536
Bible stories that live. 622
Bible stories then and now. 623
... Bible stories to read. 295
Bible stories to read and tell. 618
Bible stories to tell. 624
Bible stories to tell children. 625
Bible stories told again. 294
Bible stories told to "Toddles," 625
Bible stories you can't forget, no matter how hard you try. 619
Bible stories you've never heard. 616
Bible story. 296, 308, 310, 617, 618, 621, 622, 623
... The Bible, story and content. 639
Bible story and its teaching for children. 625
Bible story book. 293, 615, 619, 620, 624
Bible story book for boys and girls. 625
Bible story for boys and girls. 619
Bible story for Jewish young folks. 625
Bible story from the American standard edition of the revised Bible. 625
Bible story hour. 621
Bible story in pictures. 625
Bible story in religious education. 638
Bible story in the Bible words. 597, 633
Bible story in verse. 621
Bible story library. 292, 621
Bible story library (The) 618
Bible story of the creation. 1381, 1384
Bible story picture book. 619
Bible story primer. 3026
Bible story retold for young people. 618
Bible story sermonettes for the children's mass for the Sundays of the ecclesiastical year. 615, 865, 908
Bible story told. 621

Bible story with living pictures. 602
Bible story word puzzles. 281
Bible storybook. 630
Bible student's companion. 301
Bible students' cyclopaedia. 642
Bible student's English-Greek concordance and Greek-English dictionary. 344
Bible student's primer in the science of truth. 635, 2896
Bible studies. 215, 640
Bible studies for teacher training. 641
Bible studies in Christian doctrines. 3645
Bible studies in missions. 640
Bible studies in the epistle of James. 412
Bible studies in the King James and inspired versions. 649
Bible studies in the life of Christ. 1993
Bible studies in the life of Christ, historical and constructive. 1972
Bible studies in the life of Paul. 2801
Bible studies in the life of Paul, historical and constructive. 2802
Bible studies in vital questions. 641
Bible studies on Jesus, the King. 637
Bible studies on sanctification and holiness. 639
Bible studies on the Sabbath question. 639
Bible study. 309, 642
Bible study and devotion. 642
Bible study and marking systematized. 642
Bible study and the Christian life. 640
Bible study by books. Rev. ed. 641
Bible study by doctrines. 641, 649
Bible study by periods. 641, 644
Bible study can be exciting! 638
Bible study for Bible students. 637
Bible study for busy women. 638
Bible study for grownups. 527
Bible study for the 21st century. 240
Bible study helps for the International Sunday school lessons for 1930. 1915
Bible study in the work of life. 637
Bible study in the YWCA. 643
Bible study made easy. 636
... A Bible study on prayer. 638
Bible study outlines for the use of schools. 643
Bible study popularized. 639
Bible study songs for junior societies. 320
Bible study source. 643
...Bible study through educational dramatics. 603
Bible subjects and texts. 640
Bible survey, a treasury of Bible information. 310
Bible survey outlines. 646
Bible symbols. 617, 640, 3573
... Bible symbols designed and arranged to familiarize the child with the great events of Bible history and to stimulate interest in Holy Writ. 638
Bible tales for the very young. 533
Bible tales for very young children. 628
Bible talk outlines. 3372
Bible talks. 641
Bible talks for heart and mind. 1376
Bible talks on the new life in Christ. 650
Bible teachings. 304, 596, 649, 3665
Bible teachings as to a future life in the kingdom of God upon earth, with a history of the temples at Jerusalem. 650
Bible tells it like it is. 640
Bible tells me. 3549
Bible tells me so. 620
Bible temperance. 3596
Bible temperance is not total abstinence. 3596
Bible terminology relative to the future life. 1696
Bible text-book. 301
Bible text stories for boys and girls. 911
Bible texts. 650
Bible that was lost and is found. 3569
*Bible (The): book of faith. 651
Bible: the Book of God and of man. 235
Bible, the church, and the reason. 118
Bible, the Koran, and the Talmud. 199
Bible; the living word of revelation. 278, 3226
Bible, the rod, and religion, in common schools. 300, 2328
Bible, the supernatural, and the Jews. 3567
Bible the word of God. 230
Bible themes. 652
Bible themes from Matthew Henry. 615
Bible theology. 651
Bible theology and Christian union. 652
Bible therapy. 318
Bible through a telescope. 642
Bible through the ages. 289
Bible through the centuries. 291
Bible throughout the world. 655
Bible to-day. 232
Bible today. 232, 312, 313
Bible today for those who teach it. 639

Bible topics. 635
Bible tragedies. 290
Bible trails for children. 899
Bible training for Christian workers. 639
Bible translating. 655
Bible translation in India, Pakistan and Ceylon. 612
Bible treasures. 216
Bible treasury. 725
Bible triumphant. 277, 718
Bible true. 204
Bible truth for today's youth. 639
Bible truth illustrated. 1839
Bible truth in person. 216
Bible truth presented in prose and poetry. 3641
Bible truth through eye and ear. 2720
Bible truths. 218
Bible truths for today. 3182
Bible truths illustrated. 650
Bible truths with Shakspearian parallels. 299, 3399
... The Bible unauthorized; or, The true text of the Bible. 526
Bible under fire. 231
Bible universal. 636
Bible unlocked. 230, 231
Bible unmasked. 235, 1653
Bible unveiled. 3024
Bible verified. 275
Bible verses for the little ones. 724
Bible verses to remember. 318, 899
Bible versus Christian science. 1029
Bible vs. Communism. 1319
Bible vs. modernism. 2563
Bible versus Romanism. 802
Bible versus the secretary. 199
Bible vs. tradition. 48
Bible view of the Jewish church, in thirteen lectures. 2113
Bible views of creation. 1382
Bible vigils. 656
Bible vignettes. 656
Bible vindicated against the aspersions of Joseph Barker. 276
Bible way. 1462
Bible weeks. 641
Bible when you need it most. 1352
Bible when you want it. 303
Bible who's who. 291
Bible windows. 1841
Bible wines vs. the saloon keeper's Bible. 3597
... Bible women. 640, 648
Bible women of faith. 3840
Bible wonders and aids to Bible study. 285, 638
Bible word book. 271
Bible word book, concerning obsolete or archaic words in the King James version of the Bible. 271
Bible, word of God. 233
Bible, word of God in words of men. 240
Bible words in living language. 272
Bible words that guide me. 1446
Bible work and play. 3310
Bible year. 637, 643
Bible year-book for children. 725
Bible year book of the new thought. 638
... Bible youth in modern times. 214
Bible zoo. 480
Bibles & battle drums. 2130
Bible's authority today. 118, 276
Bible's best. 250
Bibles in many languages. 199
Bibles in the Caxton exhibition mdcclxxvii. 212
Bibles in the public schools. 300
Bible's legacy for womanhood. 3839
Bibles of the churches. 291
Bibles of yore. 213
Bible's secret of full happiness. 993
Bible's seeming contradictions. 232
Bibles, Testaments, Episcopal prayer books and hymnals, pulpit and family Bibles and Catholic prayer books. 1901-1902. 199
Biblia innocentium. 406, 535
Biblical account of the creation. 614
Biblical affirmations of woman. 3846
Biblical allegorism. 643
Biblical analysis. 303, 304
Biblical and historical background of Jewish customs and ceremonies. 1614, 2119
Biblical and historical background of the Jewish holy days. 1588
Biblical and historical researches. 291
Biblical and Near Eastern studies. 238, 2197, 3332
Biblical and other studies. 2141
Biblical and patristic studies in memory of Robert Pierce Casey. 744, 3657
Biblical and post-Biblical defilement and mourning. 1416

Biblical and practical theology. 3642
Biblical and psychological perspectives for Christian counselors. 2783
Biblical and Semitic studies. 2087
Biblical and theological dictionary. 3639
Biblical and theological studies. 3624, 3653
Biblical anthropology compared with and illustrated by the folklore of Europe and the customs of primitive peoples. 275
...Biblical antiquities. 206
Biblical antiquities of Philo. 208, 535
Biblical apocalyptics. 56
Biblical Apocrypha and the early Irish. 56
Biblical approach to personal suffering. 556, 3541
Biblical approaches to pastoral counseling. 231, 2780
Biblical archaeologist reader. 206, 209
Biblical archaeology. 207, 208, 209
Biblical archaeology and history. 208, 1817
Biblical archaeology in focus. 208
Biblical astronomy. 212
Biblical authenticity. 278
Biblical authority. 240, 306, 3243, 3680
Biblical authority for modern preaching. 2906
Biblical authority for today. 279
Biblical backgrounds. 281
Biblical backgrounds for the rural message. 309
Biblical backgrounds of the Middle East conflict. 533, 2073
Biblical basis for infant baptism. 1906
Biblical basis for ministry. 2788
Biblical book. 251
Biblical books translated from the Aramaic. 529
Biblical-catechetical homilies for Sundays and holy days (ABC) 863, 1267
Biblical chant. 319
Biblical Christian marriage. 2337
Biblical Christology. 2011
Biblical chronology from the sacred Scriptures, by revelation to man. 219
Biblical commentary on the New Testament. 344
Biblical commentary on the Old Testment. 497
Biblical companions. 318
Biblical concept of power. 2866
Biblical cosmology and modern science. 614
Biblical criticism. 231, 238, 240, 287, 312
Biblical criticism and heresy in Milton. 240
Biblical criticism and preaching. 240
Biblical demonology. 1423
Biblical diary and quiz book. 612, 613
Biblical dimensions of church growth. 1171
Biblical discovery. 523
Biblical doctrine. 3662
Biblical doctrine of grace. 1752
Biblical doctrine of heaven. 1795
Biblical doctrine of initiations. 137
Biblical doctrine of judgment. 2157
Biblical doctrine of man in society. 636
Biblical doctrine of original sin. 3414
Biblical doctrine of the church. 1122
Biblical doctrine of virginity. 3782
Biblical doctrines. 3650
Biblical dogmatics. 3649
Biblical encyclopedia. 222
Biblical encyclopedia and concordance. 225, 242
Biblical encyclopedia and museum. 222
Biblical errancy. 279, 2843
Biblical eschatology. 1528
Biblical ethics. 275, 1538
Biblical ethics and social change. 944
Biblical exegesis. 530, 3011
Biblical exegesis in the apostolic period. 241
Biblical exegesis in the Qumran texts. 504
Biblical expositor. 221
Biblical expositor (The) 221
Biblical faith and Christian freedom. 277
Biblical faith and social ethics. 943
Biblical faith and the Black American. 16, 237
Biblical faith of Baptists. 140, 147
Biblical family. 1609
Biblical flood and the ice epoch. 1421
Biblical foundations. 3653
Biblical foundations for belief and action. 651
Biblical foundations for Christian worship. 3855
Biblical foundations for church music. 1202
Biblical games. 499
Biblical garden. 2853
Biblical Hebrew for beginners. 1797
Biblical heritage of American democracy. 538, 3745

Biblical hermeneutics. 288
Biblical hermeneuties. 287
Biblical history familiarized by questions. 218
Biblical history for Israelitish schools. 533
Biblical history for Jewis religious schools. 291
Biblical history for Jewish religious schools. 291
Biblical history for school and home. 534, 629
Biblical history in the words of Holy Scripture for intermediate and higher classes. 618
Biblical homilies. 865, 3368
... The Biblical idea of God. 1728
Biblical ideas of atonement. 104
... Biblical idyls. 319
Biblical illustrator. 222
Biblical image of the family. 1603
Biblical images. 234
Biblical influences in English literature. 300
Biblical inspiration. 306
Biblical interpretation. 287
Biblical interpretation in religious education. 241, 1820
Biblical interpretations in preaching. 299, 2301, 3370
Biblical interpreter. 288, 2905
Biblical introduction to the Old Testament. 539
Biblical law. 203
Biblical lectures. 233
Biblical life of Jesus Christ. 1988
Biblical lights and side-lights. 303
Biblical literature and its backgrounds. 311
Biblical manuscripts and books in the library of the Jewish theological seminary. 212
Biblical meaning of man. 2326
Biblical meditations for Advent and the Christmas season. 9
Biblical meditations for lent. 2212
Biblical meditations for the Easter season. 859, 1487
Biblical message of Marc Chagall. 566
Biblical messengers of encouragement. 214
Biblical mosaic. 504
Biblical motifs. 484
Biblical museum. 222
Biblical myth and legend in Jewish education. 2086
Biblical nature studies. 2675
Biblical notes for the Sunday lectionary. 314
Biblical novel, a checklist with an introductory essay. 298
Biblical numerology. 2716
Biblical pedagogy. 3146
Biblical period. 537
Biblical period from Abraham to Ezra. 2095
Biblical perspective of science. 206
Biblical perspective on the race problem. 3017
Biblical perspectives on death. 1416
Biblical philosophy of history. 1819
Biblical preaching. 2905
Biblical preaching for today's world. 2904
Biblical predestination. 2911
Biblical problems and Biblical preaching. 298
Biblical prophecy. 604
Biblical psychology. 601
Biblical questions. 647
Biblical quotations. 301
Biblical quotations in old English prose writers. 612
Biblical quotations in Old English prose writers. 2d series. 612
Biblical reader. 647
Biblical realism confronts the Nation. 1066
Biblical reason why. 286
Biblical reason why prohibition is wrong. 3597
Biblical reflections on crises facing the church. 784
Biblical religion and the search for ultimate reality. 1106
Biblical researches in Palestine, Mount Sinai, and Arabia Petraea. 283, 2763, 3241
Biblical revelation. 3226
Biblical revelation and inspiration. 3224
Biblical revelation, the foundation of Christian theology. 306
Biblical review. 498
Biblical scholarship and inspiration. 305
Biblical semantic logic. 314
Biblical separation. 1468
Biblical separation defended. 1045
Biblical sermon guide. 2904
Biblical shape of hope. 1845
Biblical sites in the Holy Land. 2763

Biblical spiritualism. 206
Biblical spirituality of St. John. 424, 3484
Biblical standpoint. 1833, 2045
Biblical story of creation in the light of the recently discovered Babylonian documents. 1379
Biblical structuralism. 550, 3536
Biblical studies. 173, 238
Biblical studies in final things. 1530
Biblical studies in memory of H. C. Alleman. 26, 201
Biblical studies, meeting ground of Jews and Christians. 238, 1084
Biblical studies today. 241
Biblical study. 636
Biblical subject index. 303
Biblical Sunday school commentary. 1914
Biblical teachings concerning the Sabbath and the Sunday. 3260
Biblical text in the making. 505, 2364
Biblical text of Clement of Alexandria in the four Gospels and the Acts of the apostles. 1287
Biblical texts. 3376
Biblical texts for special occasions. 252
Biblical themes for pastoral care. 653, 2781
Biblical theology. 651, 652
Biblical theology and Christian education. 640
Biblical theology in crisis. 651
Biblical theology of missions. 2504
Biblical theology of sacrifice. 3271
Biblical theology of the New Testament. 476, 477
Biblical theology of the secular. 1155
Biblical thoroughfare. 237
Biblical thought and the secular university. 3148
Biblical tradition in Blake's early prophecies. 241, 300, 670
Biblical treasury of the catechism. 769
Biblical truth and modern man. 641
Biblical view of sex and marriage. 3393
Biblical view of the church. 650
Biblical witness and the world. 645
Biblical women. 3838
Biblical words for time. 3701
Biblical world. 209
Biblical zoo. 480
Biblico-theological lexicon of New Testament Greek. 1768
Bibliographia Augustiniana. 116
Bibliographia Catholica Americana. 32, 764
Bibliographic history of dispensationalism. 1467
Bibliographical and historical description of the rarest books in the Oliveira Lima collection at the Catholic university of America. 658
Bibliographical essay on the history of the Society of Jesus. 1945
Bibliographical guide to New Testament research. 474
Bibliographical guide to the history of Christianity. 1183

Bibliographical outline of New Testament research and interpretation. 351
Bibliographical studies and notes on rare books and manuscripts in the library of the Jewish Theological Seminary of America. 1796, 2080, 2331
... Bibliography. 3627
Bibliography and index to the works of Theodore Parker. 2777
Bibliography for Christian formation in the family. 868
Bibliography for Jewish vocational agencies. 2945
Bibliography for Old Testament exegesis and exposition. 492
Bibliography for study of New Testament Greek. 474
Bibliography of aesthetics and of the philosophy of the fine arts from 1900 to 1932. 1533
Bibliography of American doctoral dissertations, 1885 to 1959. 3161, 3162
Bibliography of American Presbyterianism during the colonial period. 2923
Bibliography of Anabaptism, 1520-1630, a sequel, 1962-1974. 37
Bibliography of antimasonry. 1661
Bibliography of Bible study for theological students. 644
Bibliography of bibliographies in religion. 657
Bibliography of books on conjuring in English from 1580 to 1850. 1345
Bibliography of Christian philosophy and contemporary issues. 1107
Bibliography of Coleridge. 1307
Bibliography of college, social, university and church settlements. 3435

[Bibliography of Cornell University's holdings of materials relative to the anti-Masonic movement. 1663
Bibliography of cryptography. 1392
Bibliography of dissertations in nineteenth century theology, 1960-1976, accepted by doctoral institutions in the United States and Canada. 3617
Bibliography of doctoral dissertations. 1142
Bibliography of doctoral dissertations in character and religious educatiion. 2592
Bibliography of doctoral dissertations undertaken in American and Canadian universities. 1142
Bibliography of English conjuring, 1581-1876. 1345
Bibliography of foreign missions. 2522
Bibliography of fund raising and philanthropy. 1690
Bibliography of George Berkeley. 192
Bibliography of George Berkeley, Bishop of Cloyne. 192
Bibliography of Greek myth in English poetry. 2662
Bibliography of literature concerning Yemenite-Jewish music. 2634
Bibliography of literature written in the People's Republic of China during the campaign to criticize Lin Piao and Confucius, July 1973-December 1974. 912, 1331
Bibliography of new religious movements in primal societies. 3090
Bibliography of New Testament bibliographies. 657
Bibliography of parapsychology. 2992
Bibliography of philosophical bibliographies. 657
Bibliography of post-graduate masters' theses in religion. 3626
Bibliography of practical theology. 3679
Bibliography of progressive literature. 2696
Bibliography of psychological and experimental aesthetics. 1533
Bibliography of psychological and experimental aesthetics, 1864-1937. 11
Bibliography of publications and other resources on Jewish music. 2634
Bibliography of Samuel Taylor Coleridge. 1307
Bibliography of sex rites and customs. 2828
Bibliography of Shaker literature. 3397
Bibliography of studies in metaphysical poetry. 1519
Bibliography of the architecture, arts, and crafts of Islam to 1st Jan. 1960. 79
Bibliography of the cataloged books of the Augustana college library. 2282
Bibliography of the churches of the dispersion. 2608
Bibliography of the Consultation on Church Union. 1043, 1355
Bibliography of the genus Fundulus. 1691
Bibliography of the Judaica studies materials in the Penrose Library, University of Denver. 2083
Bibliography of the pentecostal periodical holdings in the Oral Roberts University Pentecostal Collection. 2816
Bibliography of the Reform, 1450-1648, relating to the United Kingdom and Ireland for the years 1955-70. 3041
Bibliography of the Samaritans. 3296
Bibliography of the Sanskirt drama. 3301
Bibliography of the theology of missions in the twentieth century. 2504
Bibliography of the Theophrastan character in English. 887
Bibliography of the Theophrastan character in English with several portrait characters. 887
Bibliography of the works of John Bunyan. 716
Bibliography of the writings in prose and verse of Samuel Taylor Coleridge. 1307
Bibliography of the writings of Henry James. 1933
Bibliography of the writings of Jeremy Taylor to 1700. 3591
Bibliography of theses and dissertations in sacred music. 1204
Bibliography on Buddhism. 704
Bibliography on Cardinal Mindszenty (1892-1975) 2474
Bibliography on death, grief, and bereavement II, 1975-1980. 1416
Bibliography on Judaism & Jewish-Christian relations. 2144
Bibliography on spirit possession and spirit mediumship. 3519
Bibliography on the Jewish woman. 3842
Bibliophilic odyssey. 2224
Bibliotheca anti-Quakeriana. 1677, 3627
Bibliotheca diabolica. 1429

Bibliotheca lutherana. 2282
Bibliotheca sacra. 652
Bibliotheca symbolica ecclesiae universalis. 1386
Bibliotheca symbolica ecclesise universalis. 1385
Bibliotheca theologica. 3626
Bibliotheca Wiffeniana. 656, 3470
Bicentennial centennial history, Sacred Heart Church, Hebron, Nebraska, 1876-1976. 1799, 2282
Bicentennial history of Chestnut Grove Baptist Church, 1773-1973. 892
Bickersteth's Treatise on the Lord's supper. 658, 2250
Bidding prayers. 1475
Big bender. 1358
Big Bible puzzle book. 280, 313
Big book. 624
Big book of favorite Bible stories. 621
Big change. 1243
Big difference. 955, 2535
Big enough to help. 2490
Big Fisherman. 2825
Big golden book of Bible stories from the Old and New Testaments. 619
Big ideas for small sunday schools. 3555
Big jobs for little churches. 1152
Big kids' Mother Goose. 986
Big little school. 3565
Big men and cargo cults. 739
Big Peanuts. 2552
Big picnic, and other meals in the New Testament. 1459
Big saints. 3284
Big search. 3662
Big six of the Bible. 615
Big three, then the big job. 305, 620
Big treasure book of prayers and grace. 901
Big treasure book of prayers and graces. 901
Bigallo. 1629
Bigger and better Sunday school. 3553
Bigger than yourself. 2607
Biggest business of life and other addresses. 305
Bilal. 658, 1925
Bill and Betty learn about God. 1733
Bill Wallace of China. 3790
Billion dollar bait. 3520
Billows of song, for the song service. 3562
Billy. 896
Billy Graham. 1361, 1577, 1753, 1754, 1755
Billy Graham: a mission accomplished. 1754
Billy Graham, a parable of American righteousness. 1576, 1754
Billy Graham, and seven who were saved. 1361, 1362, 1754
Billy Graham and the New York crusade. 1754, 3231
Billy Graham, Euro '70. 1754, 3230
Billy Graham, evangelist to the world. 1576, 1755
Billy Graham, his life and faith. 1577, 1755
Billy Graham London crusade. 1755, 3231
Billy Graham, performer?, Politician?, Preacher?, Prophet? 1576, 1754
Billy Graham, prophet of hope. 1576, 1755
Billy Graham religion. 1552, 1754
Billy Graham, revivalist in a secular age. 1755
Billy Graham, saint or sinner. 1755
Billy Graham story. 1754
Billy Graham; the authorized biography. 1755
Billy Graham, the man and his ministry. 1576, 1754
Billy Graham: the personal story of the man. 1754
Billy Graham, the preacher. 1754
Billy Sunday. 3566
Billy Sunday, his tabernacle and sawdust trials. 3566
Billy Sunday meetings. 3566
Billy Sunday speaks! 1522, 1561
Billy Sunday story. 3566
Billy Sunday, the man and his message. 3566
Billy Sunday was his real name. 3566
Billy Sunday's doctrine conerning the second coming exposed by the voice of Scripture. 3566
Biluim. 3897
Binding of Isaac. 494, 1920, 2792
Binding the Devil. 1585
Binding with briars. 786, 3393
Binney's Theological compend improved. 1047
Binney's Theological compend improved, containing a synopsis of the evidences, doctrines, morals and institutions of Christianity. 3640

Bioethical decision-making. 3191
Bioethics—a parish resource. 659
Biographers of Christ. 392
Biographic etchings of ministers and laymen of the Georgia conferences. 2455
Biographical and literary studies. 923, 1402
... Biographical catalogue. 661
Biographical catalogue of the Princeton theological seminary. 2941
Biographical dictionary. 662
Biographical dictionary; comprising a summary account of the lives of the most distinguished persons of all ages, nations, and professions; including more than two thousand articles of American biography. 661
Biographical dictionary of ancient, medieval and modern freethinkers. 3024
Biographical dictionary of parapsychology. 1964-66. 2992
... Biographical dictionary of the Franciscans in Spanish Florida and Cuba. 1647
Biographical dictionary of the saints. 1025, 3280
Biographical directory of clergymen of The American Lutheran Church. 32
Biographical directory of Negro ministers. 2680
Biographical directory of pastors of The American Lutheran Church. 32
Biographical directory of pastors of the Evangelical Lutheran Church. 1547
Biographical memoir of the Rev. John Williams, first minister of Deerfield, Massachusetts. 1419, 3817
Biographical memoirs of Saint John Bosco. 683
... Biographical notes. 659
Biographical notices of some of the most distinguished Jewish rabbies, and translations of portions of their commentaries. 2076
Biographical preaching for today. 2897
Biographical process. 3090
Biographical record of the Lutheran Theological Seminary at Philadelphia. 2281
Biographical record, Theological seminary, New Brunswick, 1784-1911. 2281, 2686
Biographical remains of Rev. George Beecher. 659
Biographical sketch of Colonel Arthur Latham Conger. 1331, 3682
Biographical sketch of Henry Clay Morrison, p.p., editor of "The Pentecostal herald" 2620
Biographical sketch of Mother Margaret Mary Hallahan, O. S. D. Abridged from her life. 869, 1781
Biographical sketch of Rev. James Lowry Fowler. 1636, 2430
Biographical sketch of Richard G. Spurling, Jr. 3523
Biographical sketch of Right Reverend Francisco Garcia Diego y Moreno. 1702
Biographical sketch of Right Reverend Joseph Sadoc Alemany. 24
Biographical sketch of the Most Rev. John Carroll. 742
Biographical sketch of the Most Rev. John Hughes, D. D., archbishop of New York. 1851
Biographical sketch of the Rev. Thomas Davies, A.M. 1406
Biographical sketches and selected verses. 660
Biographical sketches and sermons, of some of the first ministers of the Associate church in America. 661
Biographical sketches of eminent itinerant ministers distinguished. 2455
Biographical sketches of eminent itinerant ministers distinguished, for the most part, as pioneers of Methodism within the bounds of the Methodist Episcopal church, South. 2455
Biographical sketches of Gospel preachers. 1462
Biographical sketches of Grand high priests of the Grand Royal arch chapter of North Carolina. 1670
Biographical sketches of James Embree, Philip Price, and Eli K. Price. 1510
Biographical sketches of Joseph Smith, the prophet. 3430
Biographical sketches of Joseph Smith the prophet and his progenitors for many generations. 3429
Biographical sketches of our pulpit. 157
Biographical sketches of the founder, and principal alumni of the Log college. 2937

Biographical sketches of the past masters of Hannibal Lodge no. 550, F. & A. M. from 1824-1960. 1664
Biographical sketches of the pioneer preachers of Indians. 1293
...Biographical studies in Scottish church history. 3315
Biographical studies in the Bible ... in the next text of the American revised Bible. 213
Biographies and sermons of pioneer preachers. 1466
Biographies of ancient and modern celebrated freethinkers. 3024
Biography. 2304
Biography & bibliography of Edgar Johnson Goodspeed. 1748
Biography and family record of Lorenzo Snow. 1231, 3432
Biography and miscellany. 660
Biography as theology. 3669
Biography of a cathedral. 2773
Biography of a church. 731
Biography of a country church. 2736
Biography of a great planet. 605
Biography of a prayer. 2247
Biography of Christopher Merkley. 2604
Biography of Dr. A. U. Boone, thirty-two years pastor of the First Baptist church, Memphis, Tennessee. 681, 2401
Biography of Dr. Friedrich Bente. 659
Biography of Dr. W. A. Belding. 185
Biography of Donna Olimpia Maldachini. 2767
Biography of Eld. Barton Warren Stone. 1461
Biography of Eld. Barton Warren Stone, written by himself. 1461
Biography of Elder J. T. Johnson. 2128
Biography of Ezra Thompson Clark. 1284
Biography of Father James Joseph Conway of the Society of Jesus. 1367
Biography of Francis Schlatter. 1599, 3308
Biography of Gospel song and hymn writers. 1749
Biography of J. S. Buckminster, S. C. Thacher and J. E. Abbot. 700
Biography of Jesus. 1972
Biography of Jonathan Weaver, D.D. 3799
Biography of Mrs. L. E. Fassett. 1613
Biography of Mrs. Rebecca Gair Webster. 661
Biography of Parley P. Pratt. 2605, 2606, 2867
Biography of Rev. A. Cedarholm, with a sketch of his labors among the Scandinavian population of the United States, and as first missionary of the M. E. church in Sweden. 660
Biography of Rev. David Smith of the A.M.E. Church. 3815
Biography of Rev. Elhanan Winchester. 3819
Biography of Rev. Henry Ward Beecher. 659
Biography of Rev. Hosea Ballou. 131
Biography of Rev. Jacob Smith Kessler, of the Church of the United brethren in Christ, compiled from his autobiography, by Rev. I. L. Kephart, with a sermon by the compiler. 2168, 3731
Biography of Richard Furman. 660
Biography of Saint Sava. 1028, 3305
Biography of Satan. 1427
Biography of the brothers Davenport. 1404, 3509
Biography of the gods. 3116
Biography of the Rev. Daniel Parish Kidder. 2169
Biography of the Rev. Robert Finley, D.D., of Basking Ridge, N.J. 31, 1625
Biography of the Saviour, and his apostles with a portrait of each. 1960
Biological basis of religion and genius. 3059
Biological foundations of belief. 186
... Biology. 662
Biology and Christian belief. 3078
Biology and the soul. 1853
Biology of God. 1582, 3082
Biology of the cross. 1388
Biology of the Holy Spirit. 983
Biology of the spirit. 662
Biosophy and spiritual democracy. 1536
Birchism was my business. 2125
Bird gods. 47
Bird life in Wington. 908
Bird tail. 2541
Bird walk through the Bible. 480
Birdfeather astrological space book. 95
Bird's eye view of exegetical studies. 372
Bird's-eye view of Jewish history. 2090
Bird's-eye view of the Bible. 311
Birds of the Bible. 480, 481
Birkbeck and the Russian church. 1768

Birth a new chance. 3052
Birth, an anthology of ancient texts, songs, prayers, and stories. 664
Birth and growth of religion. 3118
Birth and infancy of Jesus Christ. 392, 2021
Birth and rebirth. 1908
Birth, care, and feeding of a local church. 1200, 3678
Birth control and conscience. 663
Birth control and natural law. 664
Birth control debate. 664
Birth control encyclical. 663
Birth control in Jewish law. 3389
Birth from above. 3050
Birth of a book. 742
Birth of a kingdom. 590
Birth of a movement. 2583
Birth of a people. 2097
Birth of a reformation. 3796
Birth of a revolution. 1154
Birth of Christ. 2023
Birth of Christianity. 1191
Birth of churches. 1166
Birth of God. 9, 1060
Birth of Jesus. 2021
Birth of man. 1060
Birth of Messiah. 443, 2021
Birth of Methodism in America. 2421
Birth of Methodism in England. 2424
Birth of missions in America. 2501
"The birth of modern spiritualism" (the message of Hydesville) 3520
Birth of Mormonism in picture. 2618
Birth of pleasure. 2854
Birth of popular heresy. 1805
Birth of the Bible. 307
Birth of the Bible, a new approach. 500
Birth of the body. 332, 3358
Birth of the Catholic Tubingen School. 1480, 3717
Birth of the Christian religion. 1193
Birth of the church. 332
Birth of the gods. 3110
Birth of the Gospel. 392
Birth of the Jewish people. 2097
Birth of the living God. 2994
Birth of the Messiah. 443
Birth of the New Testament. 349, 1193, 1197
Birth of the Torah. 564
Birth pangs of a new age. 1514
Birth, parentage, life and experience of Jedidiah Preble. 2773
Birth that we call death. 1413
Birth through death. 3517
Birth to birth. 1414
Birthday and the age of Christ discovered. 1997
Birthday book. 2928
Birthday of little Jesus. 2023
Birthday remembrance. 981
Birthdays, holidays, and other disasters. 2393
Birthright. 986
Births -- baptisms (3683) of the First Lutheran Church, Westmoreland County, Greensburg, Pennsylvania, 1792-1853. 139
Bishop. 33, 665, 2209, 3013, 3594
Bishop among his flock. 665
Bishop and chapter. 779
Bishop and his boss. 2424
Bishop Barlow and Anglican orders, a study of the original documents, by Arthur Stapylton Barnes. 174
Bishop beloved. 2128
Bishop Berkeley. 192
Bishop Brent, crusader for Christian unity. 691, 1042
Bishop Bury, late bishop of North and Central Europe. 719
Bishop Butler. 665, 720
Bishop Butler and the age of reason. 720, 3212
Bishop Butler's Analogy of religion, natural and revealed, to the constitution and course of nature. 38
Bishop Butler's challenge to modernism. 720, 2561
Bishop Challoner. 880
Bishop Chandler. 881
Bishop Charles Betts Galloway, a prince of preachers and a Christian statesman. 1701
Bishop Chase's Reminiscences. 2137
Bishop-elect. 666
Bishop for the Hottentots. 2529
Bishop Fulbert and education at the school of Chartres. 1689
Bishop George F. Pierce. 665
Bishop has kept his word. 2460
Bishop Healy. 1793
Bishop Healy, beloved outcast. 1793
Bishop Healy: beloved outcaste. 1793
Bishop Hill Colony. 664
Bishop Holland Nimmons McTyeire. 2310

Bishop in Christian initiation. 665
Bishop in Honan. 3812
Bishop J. G. Strossmayer. 3536
Bishop Jonathan H. Hale of Nauvoo, his life and ministry. 1781
Bishop Joseph Blount Cheshire. 891
Bishop Joseph Hall, 1574-1656. 666, 1781
Bishop jots it down. 667
... Bishop Laval. 734, 2200
Bishop of Africa. 2500, 3591
Bishop of Everywhere. 3401
Bishop of Heard County. 7, 2459
Bishop of Heard County preaches. 2434
Bishop of Heard County; the story of J. C. Adams, Georgia circuit rider. [3d ed.]. 668
Bishop of the Great Plains. 664
Bishop of the penal times. 819
Bishop of the winds. 664
Bishop on horseback, the story of Francis Asbury. 89
Bishop Pierce's sermons and addresses. 2425
Bishop Pike affair. 2846
Bishop Reginald Pecock. 2810
Bishop Richard Allen and his spirit. 26
Bishop Sarapion's prayer-book. 2239
Bishop Sheen story. 3401
Bishop Sheil and the CYO. 3402
Bishop speaks his mind. 665
Bishop Tamaron's visitation of New Mexico. 3783
Bishop to all peoples. 2589
Bishop Walsh of Maryknoll. 668, 3790
Bishop who dared. 667, 1424
Bishop Wilberforce. 3815
Bishop Wilberforce's visitation returns for the Archdeaconry of Oxford in the year 1854. 3783
Bishop Wilson Seeley Lewis. 2220
... Bishoprick papers. 1212
Bishops and legislation. 665
Bishops and people. 665
Bishops and reform. 667
Bishops and the supervisional system of the Methodist Episcopal church. 665
Bishops at large. 3322
Bishop's blue book. 665
Bishops by ballot. 665, 1222
Bishop's candlesticks. 665
Bishops come to Lambeth. 2194
Bishop's English. 274
Bishop's jaegers. 665
Bishop's message. 665
Bishop's move. 665
Bishop's niece. 665
Bishop's nightmare. 665
Bishops of the African Methodist Episcopal Church. 14
Bishops of the American church, past and present. 665
Bishops of the United States of Irish birth or descent. 668
Bishop's register. 1763
Bishop's rostrum. 757
Bishops' synod. 735
Bishops: their status and function. 665
Bishops versus Pope. 785, 2862
Bishop's wife, but still myself. 1303
Bit of honey. 1842
Bit of living, learning, and believing. 970
Bit of reasoning and believing. 1594
Bite a blue apple. 994
Biting on granite. 2083
Bits of evergreen. 3018
Bits of precious ore. 1441
Bits of truth. 2602
Bitter atonement. 54
Bitter harvest. 1148
Bitter herbs and honey. 3897
Bitter road. 2028
Bitter sacred cup. 2459
Bitter waters. 2819
Bittersweet. 1418
Bittersweet grace. 3089
Black Americans and the evangelization of Africa, 1877-1900. 2500
Black Americans and the missionary movement in Africa. 16
Black and free. 1574
Black and Mennonite. 669, 696
Black and trying. 1367, 2632
Black and white. 516
Black and white together. 1132
Black apostles. 16
Black apostles at home and abroad. 16
Black awareness. 2682
Black bearded barbarian. 2308, 2917
Black belief. 2682
Black bishop, Samuel Adjai Crowther. 1389, 2487
Black box. 2845
Black characters and references of the Holy Bible. 669
Black Christian experience. 2683
Black Christian nationalism. 669
Black Christians' tragedies. 2682

Black church. 2679
Black church gang. 1092
Black church in America. 2679
Black church in the sixties. 15
Black church in the U.S. 2681
Black church vs. the system. 16, 1627
"black convent" slave, the climax of nunnery exposures; awful disclosures, the "Uncle Tom's cabin" of Rome's "convent slavery," 3423
Black eagle. 2523
Black experience in religion. 2682
Black folks and Christian liberty. 993
Black gods of the metropolis. 2681, 2682
Black gospel/white church. 17, 1524
Black gown and redskins. 668, 1948
Black International. 794
Black magic, white magic. 2314
Black man in the Old Testament and its world. 2680
Black man, the father of civilization. 669
Black man's religion, and Extracts and comments from the Holy Black Bible. 230, 2681
Black Messiah. 2024, 2681
Black messiahs and Uncle Toms. 2415
Black militancy and the university. 1131
Black Muslims in America. 669
Black Muslims in the United States. 669
Black nationalism. 2567
Black nations in action. 966
Black pastors and leaders. 16
Black pastures, an American pilgrimage in two centuries. 2932
Black Pentecostalism. 16, 2626
Black political theology. 3647
Black pope. 801
Black popes. 791
Black power and Christian responsibility. 275, 3433
Black power and white Protestants. 1132
Black preacher in America. 2680
Black preaching. 2910
Black priest/white church. 1132
Black pullet. 3582
Black redemption. 17, 3751
Black religion. 2682
Black religion and American evangelicalism. 2682
Black religion and Black radicalism. 2682
Black religions in the new world. 669
Black River and Northern New York conference memorial. 2446
Black River conference memorial. 2446
Black robe. 3426
Black robe and buckskin. 872
Black robe peacemaker, Pierre de Smet. 1900, 1901, 3426
Black-robed Samson. 3426
Black robes and Indians on the last frontier. 1903, 3277
Black rubric 1965. 2970
Black Samson. 1359, 2374
Black sects and cults. 2682
Black song. 3522
Black spot in the sun. 186
Black theology and black power. 1131
Black theology II. 669
Black theology of liberation. 3642
Black treasure. 2497
Black woman in search of God. 2499
Black women and religion. 17
Blackboard catechism. 747
Blackboard illustrations and beacon lights from God's word. 602
Blackboard in Sunday-school. 669
Blackboard lectures on Matthew. 169
Blackboard outlines. 3559
Blackout of civilization and beyond. 1514
Blade of grass. 1435
Blaiklock's Handbook to the Bible. 308
Blaise Pascal. 2777
Blasting the rock of ages. 18
Blavatsky and The secret doctrine. 672
Blavatsky, Besant and co. 671, 3682
Blaze of evangelism across the equator. 2547
Blaze of noon. 2468
Blazing a gospel trail to Alaska. 2500
Blazing fountain. 1784
Blazing new trails. 2484
Blazing star. 721, 3471
Blazing the Gospel trail. 1509
Blazing the missionary trail. 2482
Blazing the trail. 2599
Blazon of episcopacy. 1804
Blending lights. 204
Blending of the divine with the human, fundamentalism versus modernism. 2562
Bless the Lord, O my soul. 1694, 2815
Bless this desk. 2895
Bless this house. 1607
Bless this mess, & other prayers. 2889
Bless we the Lord. 1262
Bless your dirty heart. 2230
Blessedness of the inner life. 3330
Blessed and poor. 3778

Blessed angels. 42
'Blessed are the merciful. 2363
Blessed are the peacemakers. 3356
Blessed are the pure in heart. 181, 3534
Blessed are they. 180
Blessed are they that hunger. 998
Blessed are they who teach. 3179
Blessed are ye. 181, 3337
Blessed are ye: talks on the Beatitudes. 181
Blessed are you. 180, 181
Blessed art Thou. 2239
"Blessed art thou among women" 2354
Blessed be Egypt my people. 2567
Blessed be God. 836, 856
Blessed company of all faithful people. 1597
Blessed Diana and Blessed Jordan of the Order of preachers. 1458
Blessed Edmund Campion. 733, 1947
Blessed friend of youth. 683
Blessed friend of youth, Saint John Bosco. 683
Blessed Giles of Assisi. 11
Blessed hope. 3319
Blessed hope and the tribulation. 3711
Blessed hope of His glorious appearance. 972
Blessed hope of the Lord's return. 972
Blessed is the daughter. 3842
Blessed is the spot. 130
Blessed James Salomoni. 3287
Blessed John Neumann. 2685
Blessed Joseph Pignatelli. 1945, 2846
Blessed Kateri Tekakwitha, Mohawk maiden. 2567, 3592
Blessed life. 584, 973
Blessed Margaret Clitherow. 1304
Blessed missionaries. 2499
Blessed Mother Seton. 3378
Blessed peace of death. 1353, 1415
Blessed rage for order, the new pluralism in theology. 3618
Blessed Raymund of Capua. 3025
Blessed Robert Southwell. 3468
Blessed sacrament. 2251, 2254
Blessed Sacrament and the Mass. 2258
Blessed sacrament book. 3263
Blessed Sacrament missal. 3262
Blessed simplicity—the monk as universal archetype. 2578
Blessed Spinoza. 3472
Blessed Therese of the Child Jesus "The Little sister of missionaries" 3604
Blessed to be a blessing. 3476
Blessed Trinity. 3711
Blessed Trinity and the sacraments. 3266
Blessed Vincent Maria Strambi. 3535
Blessed Virgin. 2355
Blessed Virgin and social reconstruction. 2357
Blessed Virgin and the priesthood. 1299, 2356
Blessed Virgin in the catacombs. 745, 2359
Blessed Virgin Mary. 2355, 2357, 2362
Blessed Virgin Mary as mediatrix. 2360
... The Blessed Virgin Mary as mediatrix in the Latin and Old French legend prior to the fourteenth century. 2360
Blessed Virgin's book. 2479
Blessed Virgin's silence. 2361
Blessedness of a nation whose God is Jehovah. 3346
Blessing and ban from the cross of Christ. 2056, 2972
Blessing in mosque and mission. 2557
Blessing in the Bible and the life of the church. 672
Blessing of believing, and other addresses. 160
Blessing of the Holy Spirit. 1828
Blessings. 632
Blessings for blah days. 983, 1775
Blessings in illness. 3405
Blessings of a soul in health and prospering to be supremely wish'd for. 3351
Blessings of suffering. 3540
Blessings out of buffetings. 321, 326
Blessings unlimited. 989
Blessingway. 2678
Blest be the tie that frees. 195, 981
Blight or bloom. 1282
Blind Bartimeus. 177
Blind canary. 2856
Blind friend of the poor. 3329
Blind man's creed, and other sermons. 2934
Blind man's stories. 3404
Blind minister and the difficulties met by the helpless. 660
Blind seer: George Matheson. 2373
Blind spot in American public education. 3189
... The blind spot (sequel to Fantastic uncle) 2530
Bliss Knapp, Christian Scientist. 2178

Blocksberg tryst. 2845
Blood against blood. 672
Blood and fire! 682, 3292
Blood atonement, as taught by leading elders of the Church of Jesus Christ of latter-day saints. 2605
Blood, bread, and fire. 163
Blood brothers in Christ. 1376
Blood covenant. 1376
Blood-drenched altars. 1147, 1148
Blood heart. 2190
Blood hunters. 2533
Blood libel at Tiszaeszlar. 672
Blood of Jesus. 3290
Blood of the lamb. 672
Blood on the tail of a pig. 2986
Blood-stained cross. 2047
Blood, sweat & love. 1261
Bloodwitness for peace and unity. 774, 1292, 2460
Bloody footprints. 3256
Bloody sacrifice. 107, 2053
Bloody theatre. 2350
Bloom where you are. 1303, 1850
Bloom where you are planted. 981
Bloomfield College. 672
Blooming desert. 170
Blossoms gathered from the lower branches. 2720
Blossoms of the cross. 1388
Bloudy tenent, washed, and made white in the bloud of the Lambe. 2223, 3817
Blow away the black clouds. 985
Blow the man down. 2794
Blow the trumpet at the new moon. 2581, 3522
Blow, wind of God! 1754
Blue angels with white hats. 2261
Blue badge of courage. 3534
Blue book, and A friendly guide. 2923, 2954
Blue book of missions for Henry Otis Dwight. 2522
Blue cliff record. 2182
Blue flag. 1375
Blue Galilee. 167
Blue jeans theology of James. 413
Blue laws of Connecticut. 2201
Blue light: Christian dimensions in marriage. 2337
Blue Lodge. 1670
Blue lodge enlightment. 1668
Blue prints for great living. 1265
Blue River Baptist Association, Missouri. 157, 1271
Bluebook of free and inexpensive resources for religious, character, and citizenship education. 1652
Blueprint and structure. 2323
Blueprint for a balanced Sunday school. 3564
Blueprint for a Catholic university. 806
Blueprint for a Christian world. 2422
Blueprint for a working church. 1246
Blueprint for abundant living. 957
Blueprint for humanity. 1074, 3699
Blueprint for quality. 1164
Blueprint for teaching. 3180
Blueprint for teen-age living. 3880
Blueprint for worship. 840
Blueprint of creation. 3371
Blueprint of the missionary vocation. 2484
Blueprints for building a better way of life. 994
Blueprints for living. 3838
Blueprints of God. 610
Blues of the sky. 586
Bluestone on Romanism. 799
Blundering into paradise. 3353
B'nai B'rith. 673
B'nai B'rith in the Southland. 673
B'nai B'rith manual. 673
Boardman of Burma. 673, 2505
Boasting in the Lord. 373, 2883
Bob and Betty wonder. 903
Bob Harrington: God's happy hero. 1786
Bob Shuler met these on the trail. 2427
Bobbed hair, bossy wives and women preachers. 3836
Bobbing around songster. 30
Bodily healing and the atonement. 1599
Bodily worship of the Living God. 699, 3859
Body. 375, 377
Body and mind. 2473
Body and mind and their possibilities. 2725
Body and soul. 2324, 2409, 3519
Body as spirit. 1107
Body is one. 1123
Body life. 1123, 2812
Body-mind and creativity. 2584
Body, mind and spirit. 2410
Body of Christ. 2019, 2020
*Body of Christ (The) 2228
Body of God. 1739, 2837
Body of practical divinity. 3809
Body, soul, and spirit. 2473

Body, soul, spirit. 3462, 3463
Body theology; God's presence in man's world. 1586
Bogatzky's golden treasury for the children of God. 1436
Bogeyman. 1654
Bogomils. 674
Bogomils,.a study in Balkan Neo-Manichaeism. 674
Bohras. 1927
Bokotola. 1690, 2559
Bold frontier preacher. 1379
Bold heart. 2190
Bold in the spirit. 2286, 2815
Bold ones on campus. 1308
Bold preaching about Christ. 168
Bold to say. 2247
Bolenge. 2513, 3534
Boles Bible questions. 280
Bolshevism and religion. 3257
Bombshells for wets and reds. 2231
Bon secours sisters in the United States. 3416
Bonaventure. 775, 3636
Bonaventurian theology of prayer. 676, 1648
Bonclarken. 93, 676
Bond of honour. 2337
Bond of marriage. 2344
Bond of peace. 788
Bond of perfection. 2267
Bond of power. 2380, 2630
Bondage of the will. 1527, 1658
Bondsmen and bishops; slavery and apprenticeship on the Codrington Plantations of Barbados, 1710-1838. 3424
Bone and the star, two perspectives on the scene of time. 3099
Bone of his bone. 105, 964
Bone of space. 3893
Bones and verdure. 204
Bones of St. Peter. 2825
Bonganga. 696, 3862
Bonhoeffer. 676, 2909
Bonhoeffer, exile and martyr. 676, 1108
Bonhoeffer in a world come of age. 677
Bonhoeffer; the man and his work. 676
Bonhoeffer's theology. 677
...Boniface. 677
Bonifacius. 968
Bonifacius: an essay. 968
Bonifacivs. 968
Boo Hoo bible. 1782
Book, a group, and you. 1776
Book about Jesus. 3549
Book about praying. 2876
Book about the Bible. 281
Book about the English Bible. 236
Book above all. 278
Book and its story. 3534
Book and the map. 680
Book by my side. 313
Book for Bible study. 648
Book for boys. 688
Book for boys and girls. 688
Book for catechumens. 749
Book for Passover and other holidays, adapted for young people, edited and collated by W. A. Alexander. 2778
Book God made. 237
Book in the light of its books. 232
Book-Miller debate on instrumental music in worship. 2633
Book nobody knows. 230
Book of a thousand tongues. 655, 2859
Book of Acts. 329, 330, 333
Book of Acts in history. 332
Book of Advent. 8
Book of all nations. 233
Book of altruism. 28
Book of American Negro spirituals. 2680
Book of Ammon. 38
... The book of Amos. 35, 485, 486
Book of angels. 41, 42
Book of answered prayer. 2884
Book of asseverations. 2719
Book of assurance. 126
Book of assurance (The book of Ighan) 126
Book of Baruch. 488
Book of beliefs and opinions. 2116, 2138
Book of Bible animals. 481
Book of Bible prayer. 603
Book of black magic and ceremonial magic. 2313
Book of black magic and of pacts. 2313
Book of books. 290, 309, 533, 536, 555, 648, 1128
Book of books and its wonderful story. 3534
Book of Books in art. 566
Book of Books; Old Testament. 536
Book of Boumi. 39
Book of Catholic authors. 754
Book of Catholic authors (fifth series) 754

Book of Catholic authors (sixth series) Informal self-portraits of famous modern Catholic writers. 755
Book of Catholic names & numbers. 830
Book of Catholic quotations. 869
Book of Catholic worship. 2233, 3859
Book of ceremonial magic. 2730
Book of ceremonies. 836, 839
Book of certainty. 3543
Book of changes, with Biblical references. 1879
Book of Chanukah. 1785
Book of chapel talks. 3758
Book of charms. 888
Book of charms and talismans. 3582
Book of Christ Jesus. 3507
Book of Christian faith. 3670
Book of Christian prayer. 2888
Book of Christian worship for voluntary use among the Disciples' of Christ and other Christians. 1109
Book of Christmas and Epiphany. 1110
Book of church history. 809
Book of church law. 1489
Book of church order of the Presbyterian Church in the United States. 2925
Book of church services with orders of worship. 1339
Book of Clifford. 3495
Book of comfort. 1352, 3206
Book of comfort for those in sickness. 3406
Book of commandments for the government of the Church of Christ. 2612, 2613
Book of Commandments of the government of the Church of Christ organized according to law. 1312
Book of commemoration of the one hundreth anniversary of the consecration of the present church edifice. 2774
Book of common praise. 1222, 1868, 2867
... The Book of common prayer. 680, 1868, 2567, 2868, 2870, 2877, 2878, 2879, 2884, 2960, 2968
Book of common prayer among the nations of the world. 1215
Book of common prayer and administration of the sacraments. 2879, 3263
Book of common prayer and administration of the sacraments and other rites and ceremonies of the church. 3262
Book of common prayer and administration of the sacraments and other rites and ceremonies of the church togther with the form and manner of making. 3262
Book of common prayer, 1559. 2870
Book of common prayer with the additions and deviations proposed in 1928. 3262
Book of common worship. 2236, 2929, 3852, 3853, 3854
Book of common worship, as authorized by the synod, 1962. 3853
Book of common worship (revised) 3854
Book of Concord. 2283
Book of consolations. 2684
Book of counsel. 3013
Book of courage. 1375
Book of daily devotion. 1437
Book of daily texts for all Christians. 2595
... The book of Daniel. 506, 507, 508, 509
Book of Daniel from the Christian standpoint. 507
Book of Daniel unlocked. 508
Book of David; or, "I am" in the Bible. 1405
Book of day. 460
Book of days. 1430
Book of days for Christians. 1443
Book of dedications. 1419
Book of delight. 2232
Book of destiny. 455
Book of Deuteronomy. 510
Book of Deuteronomy; Hebrew text and English authorized version. 510
Book of devotional readings from the literature of Christendom. 511
Book of devotions. 511
Book of devotions for men and boys. 2971
Book of devotions for women and girls. 2971
Book of discipline of the United Methodist Church, 1972. 3734
Book of discipline of the United Methodist Church, 1976. 3734
Book of divine consolation of the Blessed Angela of Foligno. 2646
Book of divine prayers and services of the Catholic Orthodox church of Christ. 855
Book of doctrine and covenants. 1356
Book of Doctrine and Covenants carefully selected from the revelations of God, and given in the order of their dates. 3215

Book of doctrine and covenants of the Church of Jesus Christ of latter-day saints. Carefully selected from the revelations of God, and given in the order of their dates. 1356
Book of doctrines. 1273
Book of dreams and ghosts. 1709
Book of Easter. 1486
Book of Ecclesiastes. 512
Book of elements. 2393
Book of Elias. 1
Book of English collects. 1308
Book of Enoch. 491
Book of Enoch the prophet. 567
Book of Ephesians. 364
Book of essays. 191
Book of Esther. 513, 514
Book of Esther, a new translation. 513
Book of everyday prayers. 2888
Book of Exodus. 515, 516, 517
Book of Exodus in the revised version. 515
Book of Ezekiel. 518
Book of Ezra. 519
Book of facts. 1653
Book of faith. 1596
Book of faith in God. 1590
Book of family prayer. 1605
Book of family worship. 1605, 1606, 1611
Book of fate. 95
Book of fate and fortune. 2723
Book of First Corinthians. 322
Book of gems. 1651
Book of gems, or Choice selections. 1651
Book of Genesis. 520, 521, 522
Book of Genesis, complete. 520
Book of Genesis for Bible classes and private study. 527
Book of Genesis, for the use of divinity students. 527
Book of Genesis in the light of modern knowledge. 524
Book of Genesis in the Revised version. 521
Book of Genesis of the Holy Scriptures. 527
Book of God. 627
Book of God and man. 549
Book of goddesses and heroines. 1742
Book of God's command. 473
Book of God's gifts. 899
Book of God's love. 3481
Book of God's people. 313
Book of God's providence. 2980
Book of good fellowship. 1621
*Book of good news (The) 3163
Book of good tidings from the Bible. 527
Book of gratitude. 1756
Book of Haggai. 529
Book of Hanukkah. 1784
Book of heavenly death. 1796
Book of heavenly teachings. 3495
Book of Hebrews. 402
Book of Holiness. 2201
Book of Hosea. 538
Book of hours. 1443, 1848
Book of human destiny. 497
Book of human nature. 2473
Book of hymns for young persons. 910
... The book of Ighan. 126
Book of Indian beauty. 1621
Book of installation services. 1911
Book of invocations for use throughout the year. 2891
Book of Isaiah. 541, 542, 544, 602
Book of Isaiah from the New international version. 541
Book of Isaiah in fifteen studies. 544
Book of Isaiah: the English text. 542
Book of Isaian in fifteen studies. 544
Book of Isaiah, chapters (one-thirty-nine) 543
Book of James. 412, 3474
Book of Jasher. 562
Book of Jeremiah. 546, 547, 1942
Book of Jeremiah and Lamentations. 546
Book of Jesus. 1965
Book of Jewish concepts. 2146
Book of Jewish holidays. 1615
Book of Jewish knowledge. 2146
Book of Jewish thoughts. 2084
Book of Jewish thoughts selected and arranged. 2075
... The book of Job. 548, 549, 550, 551, 602
Book of Job, and the prophets. 547
Book of Job as a Greek tragedy. 549
Book of Job from the King James Bible. 551
Book of Job in its time and in the twentieth century. 550
Book of Job in poetry. 551
Book of Job in the revised version. 550
Book of Job in two versions. 551
Book of Joel. 552
Book of Johannes. 3500
Book of Jonah. 552

Book of Jonah: Jonah speaks again. 552
Book of Joseph. 2132
... Book of Joshua. 531, 553
Book of Joshua, books of Judges to II Samuel. 531
Book of Joshua with English translation. Linear system. 553, 554
Book of Jubilees. 490
... The book of Judges. 554, 555
Book of Judges, with introduction and notes, and Notes on the Hebrew text of the books of Kings, with an introduction and appendix. 554
Book of Kashruth. 2086
Book of Kells. 317
Book of Kings 1. 483
Book of knowledge. 3495
Book of knowledge, psychic facts. 3495
Book of Kuzari. 2115
Book of legends. 2207
Book of Lent. 2211
Book of Leviticus. 557, 558
Book of Leviticus in the revised version. 557
Book of life. 254, 292, 312, 406, 647, 2225, 2226, 2227, 2401, 2695
Book of life and death. 2226
Book of Life, arr. and edited. 292
Book of life; mind and body. 2228
Book of life opened. 462
Book of life, services and ceremonies observed at the death bed, house of mourning and cemetery, together with prayers on visiting the graves. With an appendix containig the laws, rites and cermonies concerning the dying and the dead, and the usages of mourning. 2226
Book of magical art, Hindu magic and Indian occultism. 2724
Book of martyrs. 2350
Book of Mary. 2354
Book of Matthew. 588
Book of meditations. 2394
Book of memories. 2103
Book of memories, 1842-1920. 2401
Book of mercies. 1446
Book of Micah. 558, 559
Book of miracles. 1684, 2475, 2476
Book of missionary heroes. 2483
Book of modern Catholic prose. 1518
Book of modern prayers. 2892
Book of Mormon. 2598, 3428
Book of Mormon: an account written by the hand of Mormon, upon plates taken from the plates of Nephi. 2598
Book of Mormon commentary. 2598
Book of Mormon compendium. 679
Book of Mormon evidences in ancient America. 678, 2598
Book of Mormon guide book. 678
Book of Mormon, key to conversion. 2612
Book of Mormon: lands and times. 679
Book of Mormon message and evidences. 2598
Book of Mormon personalities. 679
Book of Mormon practical geography. 680
Book of Mormon speaks for itself. 678
Book of Mormon stories for children. 680
Book of Mormon stories for children. Illus. by Edith Brockway. 680
Book of Mormon stories for little children. 680
Book of Mormon stories for young Latter-Day Saints. 680
Book of Mormon story. 680
Book of Mormon testifies. 679
Book of Mormon treasury. 678
Book of Mormon, true or false? 678
Book of Mormons. 2620
Book of mythology. 2657
Book of myths. 2650, 2664
Book of Nahum. 560
Book of needs of the Holy Orthodox Church. 2748
Book of Nehemiah. 560
Book of Numbers. 560, 561
Book of Numbers in the revised version with introduction and notes. 560
Book of Obadiah. 561
Book of offices. 1524, 2969
Book of offices and prayers for priest and people. 2971
Book of offices; services for certain occasions not provided in the Book of common prayer. 2969
... A book of offices; services for occasions not provioded for in the Book of common prayer, comp. by a committee of the House of bishops. 2958
Book of Old Testament. 601
Book of Old Testament lessons for public reading in churches. 2240
Book of one. 3588
Book of Onias. 2611
Book of opening the mouth. 1691
Book of our heritage. 1614

Book of parables. 558
Book of Passover. 2778
Book of Passover ; by Edythe and Sol Scharfstein. Pictures by Siegmond Forst. 2779
Book of pastoral prayers. 2896
Book of peace. 3574
Book of praise. 579, 1868
Book of praises. 2867
Book of prayer. 2884
Book of prayer according to the custom of the Spanish and Portugese Jews, edited and translated by David de Sola Pool. 2108
Book of prayer for everyman. 2890
Book of prayer for Jewish girls. 2886
Book of prayer for use in the churches of Jesus Christ. 2912
Book of prayers. 2884, 2888, 2891, 2892
Book of prayers for boys. 688
Book of prayers for church and home. 2893
Book of prayers for public and personal use. 2884
Book of prayers for various seasons and sundry occasions. 1224
Book of prayers for young people and all who are interested in them. 2893
Book of prayers for youth. 2891, 3882
Book of private devotion. 1440
Book of private prayer. 859
Book of prophecy. 2946, 2948
Book of Protestant saints. 924
Book of Proverbs. 254, 572, 590
Book of Proverbs; a commentary. 572
Book of proverbs, containing seven thousand gems. 2979
Book of Proverbs, from the authorized King James version. 590
Book of Psalms and the First psalm of David. 592
Book of Psalms. 29, 573, 574, 575, 576, 577, 579, 582, 583, 2917
Book of Psalms and the First psalm of David. 591
Book of Psalms arranged for use in a college chapel. 3220
Book of Psalms for the modern reader. 583
Book of Psalms [from the] Authorized King James version. 582
Book of Psalms. Hebrew text and English version. Translation rev. by Alexander Harkavy. With exegetical notes by the reviser. 530
Book of public worship. 2237
Book of religion and empire. 2564
Book of religion for Catholic elementary schools. 647
Book of religions. 3322
Book of religious advertisements. 10
Book of religious holidays and celebrations. 1613
Book of remembrance. 1338, 2557
Book of remembrances. 2557
Book of Revelation. 452, 453, 454, 455, 457, 458, 459, 460, 461, 463, 464, 465
Book of Revelation explained by history. 455
Book of Revelation expounded. 455
Book of revelation from the ethereal plane. 3507
Book of Revelation in plain language. 453
Book of Revelation, its message and meaning. 459
Book of Revelation not a mystery. 454
Book of Revelation revealed in the great drama. 457
Book of Revelation speaks to us. 457
Book of revelations. 3504
Book of rings. 3474
Book of ritual. 1550
Book of Romans. 469
Book of rules of Tyconius newly edited from the mss. 288
... The book of Ruth. 530, 589, 2856
Book of Ruth and the book of Esther. 59 2
Book of Ruth in the revised version. 589
Book of sacramental basics. 3262
Book of Saint Valentine. 3281
Book of saints. 3279, 3283, 3284
Book of saints and friendly beasts. 47, 1028
Book of saints and heroes. 3280
Book of saints and wonders. 764, 1026
Book of saints (The) 3283
Book of seasons. 2201
Book of sermons. 3359
Book of sermons for all occasions. 3370
Book of service. 2454
Book of services for group worship. 1443
Book of shadows. 3824
Book of silent prayer. 2884
Book of similitudes. 3113
Book of simple words. 1999
Book of spiritual instruction. 2642
Book of student prayers. 3537

Book of Sufi chivalry. 3544
Book of Sunday sermons. 3354
Book of table graces. 1750
Book of talismans, amulets and zodiacal gems. 3582
Book of Tao. 3587
Book of tarot. 3588
Book of temple service. 2201
Book of the acts of God. 313
Book of the ages. 649
... The book of the Ancient and accepted Scottish rite of freemasonry. 1660
Book of the Apocalypse. 462
Book of the beginning. 523
Book of the beginnings, containing an attempt to recover and reconstitute the lost origines of the myths and mysteries, types and symbols, religion and language, with Egypt for the mouthpiece and Africa as the birthplace. 2652
Book of the Bible. 241, 293
Book of the chapter. 1669
Book of the Christ child. 1996
*Book of the Convenant people (The) 3163
Book of the craft of dying. 1412
Book of the craft of dying and other early English tracts concerning death. 1416
Book of the dead. 680, 1892
Book of the epic. 1521
Book of the Epistles. 2205
Book of the fortieth year. 1748
Book of the gods and rites and The ancient calendar. 121
Book of the Goetia of Solomon the King. 2312
Book of the Gospels. 2205
...The Book of the gradual sayings (Anguttara-nikaya) 47
Book of the Holy Child. 3026
Book of the junior sodalists of Our Lady. 3454
...The Book of the kindred sayings (Sanyutta-nikaya) or grouped suttas. 1814
Book of the law. 238, 510, 511
Book of the law found again. 236
Book of the law of the Lord. 1234
Book of the law <technically called Liber al vel legis sub figura CCXX as delivered by XCIII = 418 to DCLXVI. 3473
Book of the Lord. 929, 1960
Book of the lover and the beloved. 2648
Book of the Master. 1501
Book of the miraculous medal. 2478
Book of the mysteries of the heavens and the earth and other works of Bakhayla Mikael (Zosimas) 1540
Book of the poor in spirit. 2647
Book of the Popes. 2770, 2860
... The book of the popes (Liber pontificalis) i. 2860
Book of the promises of God. 1739, 3188
... The book of the prophecies of Isaiah. 542
Book of the prophet Daniel. 507
... The book of the prophet Ezekiel. 517, 518, 519
Book of the prophet Isaiah. 541, 542, 544
Book of the prophet Jeremiah. 546, 547
Book of the Prophet Jeremiah, chapters 1-25. 547
Book of the prophet Jeremiah together with the Lamentations, in the Revised version. 546
Book of the prophet Jeremiah, chapters 26-52. 547
Book of the prophet Jermiah. 546
Book of the Psychic society. 2997
Book of the Revelation. 455, 456
Book of the Revelation of Jesus Christ, which God gave unto him. 456
Book of the Revelation of Jesus Christ, which God gave unto him, to shed unto His servants things which were to come to pass. 456
Book of the Revelation, outlined studies. 456
Book of the Sabbath. 3261
Book of the sacred magic of Abra-Melin the mage. 2311
Book of the sacred magic of Abramelin the mage, as delivered by Abraham the Jew unto his son Lamech, A.D. 1458. 2311
Book of the saints of the Ethiopian church. 3283
Book of the secret -I. 3586
Book of the secrets. 3585, 3586
Book of the secrets of Enoch. 490
Book of the Seeker. 1539
Book of the sesqui-centennial of American Methodism. 2423
Book of the twelve apostles. 75
Book of the twelve Minor prophets. 558
Book of the twelve prophets. 559
Book of the twelve prophets, commonly called the minor ... With introds. 560

Book of the vision quest. 3239
Book of the ways of God. 548
Book of the weird. 2731
Book of Thirty Centuries. 241
Book of Thomas the Contender, from Codex II of the Cairo gnostic library from Nag Hammadi (CG II, 7) 680, 1718
Book of Thoth. 3588
Book of Tobit. 488, 490
Book of tokens. 721
Book of Torah readings. 565
Book of truth. 3141
Book of unlikely saints. 1024, 3281
Book of visions. 3783
... The book of Wisdom. 488, 490, 3544, 3821
Book of Wisdom; the Greek text, the Latin Vulgate, and the Authorised English version; with an introduction, critical apparatus, and a commentary. 490
Book of wisdom unsealing the mental, social and physical life of man. 3821
Book of witchcraft. 3822
Book of witches. 3823
Book of witnesses. 1967
Book of world religions. 3119
Book of worship. 1236, 1237, 1339, 1545, 1604, 2289, 2290, 2689
Book of worship for church and home. 2433, 2441, 3313
Book of worship for village churches. 3854
Book of worship of the church school. 3562
Book of Yahweh. 592
Book of Yashar. 2097
Book of Young men's Christian association buildings. 3874
Book on life beyond. 1697
Book sealed with seven seals and the sounding of seven angels. 459
Book sealed with seven seals and the sounding of the seven angels. 459
Book study of the Bible. 647
Book that is alive. 600
Book they couldn't ban. 612, 2597
Book-to-book survey of the Old and New Testaments. 223
Book to commemorate the golden jubilee of Holy Name of Mary Church. 2700
... The book to know. 639
Book we love. 233
Book we study. 209
Book we teach. 649
Book written by the spirits of the so-called dead. 3504
Book you always meant to read: the Old Testament. 533
Books. 905
Books and the parchments. 289, 317
Books and their use. 681
Books by Catholic authors in the Carnegie library of Pittsburgh. 869
Books for Catholic colleges. 656
Books for Catholic students. 869
Books for New Testament study. 473, 474
Books for Old Testament study. 596
Books for religious sisters. 656
Books for the church library. 3089
Books in English on Islam, Muhammad, and the Qur'an. 1924
Books of American Negro spirituals. 2680
Books of Amos, Hosea and Micah. 485
Books of Books in art. 566
Books of chants. 883
... The books of Chronicles. 496
Books of Chronicles in relation to the Pentateuch and the "higher criticism." 496
Books of Deuteronomy. 510
Books of Ecclesiastes, Song of Solomon, Daniel and the Minor prophets, translated into the Mpongwe languge at the Gaboon and Corisco mission, Gaboon, West Africa. 2627
Books of Esther. 592
Books of Esther & Judith. 513
Books of Exodus. 515
... The books of Exodus and Leviticus. 515, 592
Books of Ezekiel. 592
.. The books of Ezra and Nehemiah. 519
Books of Ezra-Nehemiah. 519
Books of faith and power. 1021, 3203
Books of Genesis. 2627
Books of Genesis and Exodus unveiled. 500
Books of Genesis, Exodus, Leviticus, Numbers, and Deuteronomy. 915
Books of Haggai and Zechariah. 529
Books of Haggai, Zechariah, and Malachi. 529
Books of history. 532
Books of Isaiah and Jeremiah. 592

Books of Job, Psalms, Proverbs, Ecclesiastes, and the Song of Solomon. 248
... The books of Joel and Amos with introduction and notes. 552
Books of Joel, Obadiah, Jonah, and Micah. 558
Books of Joel, Obadiah, Jonah, Nahum, Habakkuk, and Zephaniah. 559
Books of Joshua, Judges, and Ruth, translated into the Choctaw language. 915
Books of Joshua, Judges, Ruth, i and ii. Samuel, i and ii. Kings. 591
Books of Kings. 556
... The books of Nahum, Habakkuk and Zephaniah. 558
... The books of Numbers to Ruth. 531, 592
Books of Ruth and Esther. 589
Books of Ruth & Tobit. 592
Books of Ruth, Esther, Ecclesiastes, the Song of Songs, Lamentations. 519
Books of Samuel. 589, 590
Books of the Bible. 290
Books of the Chronicles. 496
Books of the Kings. 555
Books of the kings of Judah and Israel. 531
Books of the law. 562
Books of the Minor prophets. 559
Books of the New Testament. 410
Books of the Old Testament. 540, 541
...The books of the Pentateuch. 565
Books of the Pilgrims. 658, 2847
... The Books of the prophet Jeremiah. 546, 591
Books on Buddhism. 709
Books on Catholic subjects chiefly by Catholic authors. 868
Books on devotion. 3089
... Books on proverbs, quotations and toasts. 2943
Books to read. 3626
Books were opened. 604
Boot and saddle in Africa. 2517
Boother and sister saints. 3280
Bootstrap fallacy. 1010
Borachio's bo-peep; or, The drunkard's play with children. 1913
Borderland. 3515
Borderland Christianity; critical reason and the Christian vision of love. 1106
Borderland of psychical research. 2989
Borderland of right and wrong. 7, 3237
Born a snake fighter. 1384
Born again. 1310, 1363, 1367, 3053
Born again & living up to it. 993
Born again, but still wet behind the ears. 932, 3401
Born-again Christian catalog. 1553
Born again radical. 187, 1300
Born againism, perspectives on a movement. 1361
Born at midnight. 2517
Born Catholics. 871
Born crucified. 3299
Born for a purpose. 688, 3293
Born for friendship. 2596
Born for victory. 1340
Born in Bethelehem. 2022
Born in Bethlehem. 2022
Born in Tibet. 915, 2194, 3698, 3716
"Born of the needs of the people" 3297
Born of the spirit. 1009, 3051, 3482
Born of the Virgin Mary. 2362
Born out of conflict. 120
Born remembering. 685
Born to battle. 3293
Born to burn. 3790
Born to climb. 2482
Born to grow. 987
Born to live. 1005
Born to lose, bound to win. 119, 1706, 2486
Born to music. 2307
Born today, born yesterday. 3055
Born twice. 3054, 3258
Borneo, past. 1217
Borrowed axes. 3350
Borrowed Bible. 1013
Borrowed glow. 1437
Boso's life of Alexander III. 24
Bossuet. 683
Bossuet and Vieira. 683, 2910
Boston (Botolph's Town) 683
Boston preachers. 3363
Boston priests, 1848-1910. 773, 1293
Boston Y.MC.A. and community need. 3874
Boston young men's Christian union. 1046
Bostonian Ebenezer. 684
Boston's awakening. 3231
Boswell-Hardeman discussion on instrumental music in the worship. 2633

Botanical memoirs. 1162
Both feet in the water. 92, 930
Both sides. 2130
Both sides of the circle. 712, 1856
Both sides of the music question discussed. 2633
Both sides of the veil. 2849, 3512
Botolph of Boston. 683, 685
Bottles of heaven. 1841
Bottom facts concerning the science of spiritualism. 3516
Bottom line catechism for contemporary Catholics. 764
Bought by the blood. 164, 169
Bought with a price. 2299, 3352
Bound in the bundle of life. 2236
Bound in the Spirit. 2916
Boundaries unlimited. 1454
Boundless horizons. 1454
Bountiful living. 969
Bouquet. 1588
Bo[u]quet of love. 3865
Bouquet of spiritual flowers. 3498
Bourdalou at Versaile, 1670. 3368
Bourgeois mind and other essays. 1281
Bourges Cathedral. 686, 3316
Bow in the cloud. 1351, 1353, 1354, 3540
Bow in the clouds. 1376, 2983
Bowing the preacher out politics. 1141
Bowl of heaven. 94
Bowl of saki. 3544
Box of God. 1737
Boy and the Christ. 1014
Boy and the church. 687
Boy and the Sunday school. 3551
Boy called Rashi. 3456
Boy for sale. 3370
Boy hears about Jesus. 1981
Boy hears stories from the Old Testament. 633
Boy in a hurry. 3305
Boy Jesus. 1983, 1994, 1996
Boy Jesus and His companions. 1982
Boy meets Luther. 2279
Boy named Jesus. 632, 2023
Boy named Nelson. 2505
Boy of Cordova. 2622
Boy of Galilee. 1955
Boy of Wilna. 1506
Boy once lived in Nazareth. 1996
Boy preacher. 1787, 3232
Boy problem solved. 687
Boy prophet. 2950
Boy-savers' guide. 896
Boy scout movement applied by the church. 686
Boy-talks. 687
Boy, the man, and the Bishop. 3470
Boy thirteen. 1413
Boy who came home. 3501
Boy who changed his name. 2027
Boy who gave his lunch away. 422
Boy who ran away. 2945
Boy who saved his family. 634
Boy who saw the world. 1649
Boy who stayed cool, and other stories of young people in the Bible. 213, 619
Boy who threw away his gold. 1641
Boy who wanted to fly. 911
Boy who worked wonders. 54
Boy with a mission. 2349
Boy with a sling. 1406
Boy with a sling: 1 Samuel 16: 1-18:5 for children. 1406
Boy with a song. 3164
Boy with the blue ears and 49 other object lessons for children. 2720
Boyhood consciousness of Christ. 430
Boyhood of Christ. 1996
Boyhood of Jesus. 626, 1983
Boyhood's highest ideal. 688, 2591
Boys. 3889
Boys and Brothers. 2189
Boys and girls at worship. 3858
Boys and girls in China. 2509
...Boys and girls in other lands. 2551
Boys and girls life of Christ. 1972
Boys and girls living as neighbors. 3453
... Boys and girls of the Bible. 632, 898
Boys' and girls' prayer book. 854
Boy's book of prayers. 687, 688, 2884, 2888
Boy's choice. 2271
Boy's congress of missions. 2515
Boy's-eye views of the Sunday-school. 3557
Boys for Christ. 687
Boy's life; its spiritual ministry. 3482
Boys' life of Christ. 2014
Boy's lunch. 627
Boys made good and other sermons. 2848
Boys of Princeville. 3597
Boys of the Bible. 632, 687, 898
Boy's offering. 622
Boy's prayer book. 688
Boys' prayers. 688
Boy's religion. 2421

Boy's religion from memory. 3060
Boys will be men. 3310
Boys' work message. 687
Bradwardine and the Pelagians. 688, 2810
... Bragers Chant service book. 1205
Brahma Sutra. 3774
Brahma-vaivarta puranam. 1816
Brahmadarsanam. 1813
... Brahman. 2839
Brahmans, theists, and Muslims of India. 1896
Brahmin priest of Tamil Nadu. 2940
Brahmo samaj & Arya samaj in their bearing upon Christianity. 689
Brahmoism. 689, 3020
Brahmopanisat-sara sangraha. 1816
Brain and the Bible. 1653
Brain building and soul growth. 973
Brainard's Monsignor Klein. 2178
Braj, the Vaishnava Holy Land. 3766
Bramble. 3596
Branch of almond. 1942
Branch of today and tomorrow. 3881
Branches of the banyan. 2547
Branches of the vine. 962, 3488
Brand from the burning. 3382, 3515
Brand of Dominic. 1909
Brand plucked from the burning. 48
Brands from the burning. 944
Brass instruments in church services. 1210
Brave adventures. 2482
Brave boys and girls of long ago. 928
Brave men of the Bible. 619
Brave men to the battle. 3788
Brave rebels. 1677
Bray's university dictionary of mythology. 2658
Brazen serpent. 1593, 2214
Brazen serpent, or Faith in Christ illustrated. 1593
Brazil. 863, 3369
Brazil in five hours. 814
Brazil 1980: the Protestant handbook. 2953
Brazil; where the action is. 2504, 3387
Breach with Rome. 1220
Bread and the liturgy. 690
Bread and the word. 1264
Bread & wine in the now generation. 2370
Bread blessed and broken. 1541
Bread broken and shared. 795, 2254
Bread for each day. 1430
Bread for each day ; 365 devotional meditations. 1431
Bread for her day. 956
Bread for the journey. 3856
Bread for the wilderness, wine for the journey. 2874
Bread from Bellevue oven. 133, 139, 164
Bread from heaven. 725, 2070, 2255
Bread in the desert. 2895
Bread in the wilderness. 584
Bread of heaven. 2250
"The bread of life" 766, 3289
... The bread of the eucharist. 1541
Bread on the waters. 156
... Bread-pills: a study of mind-cure. 2409
Bread upon the waters. 1076, 3129
Bread which we break. 2253
Break down the walls. 1131
Break out and become a new creature in Christ. 987
Break those fetters of fear. 3716
Break through! 989, 1170
Break thru. 1454
Break up the night. 2929
Breakdown of authority. 118
Breakers! 2422
Breakfast table autocrat. 1389
Breakfast with the risen Lord. 2051
Breaking bread. 834, 871
Breaking bread together. 1435
Breaking down Chinese walls. 2510
Breaking down Chinese walls, from a doctor's viewpoint. 2510
Breaking down the walls. 2420
Breaking of bread. 1464, 2254, 2365
Breaking of the image. 3444
Breaking of traditions: theological convictions in colonial America. 3086
Breaking the bread. 864, 3355
Breaking the seals. 456
Breaking the stained-glass barrier. 1572
Breaking the Tablets. 2084
Breaking through. 3834
Breaking through the maturity barrier. 1324
Breaking with the past. 3036
Breakout. 3888
Breakthrough. 926, 3749
Breakthrough; Christ's journey for everyman. 2033
Breakthrough into renewal. 1244, 1806
Breakthrough, Meister Eckhart's creation spirituality, in new translation. 2647
Breakthrough: rediscovery of the Holy Spirit. 1833

Breakthrough to life. 1324
Breakup of Solomon's kingdom. 631
Breath and name. 3477
Breath and spirit of God. 1830
Breath in the winds. 3357
Breath is life. 3863
Breath of God. 42
Breath of God with man. 3141
Breath of life. 1323
Breath of the mystic. 2639
Breathings of the better life. 1324
Breeze of the spirit. 1301, 3404
Breezes of the Spirit. 999
Breife meditations. 2255
Brethren along the Snake River. 1235
Brethren bibliography. 1235
Brethren builders in our century. 1235
Brethren, hang loose. 1243
Brethren, hang together. 1243
Brethren hymnal. 1236
Brethren in colonial America. 1236
Brethren in northern Illinois and
　Wisconsin. 1236
Brethren in Virginia. 1236
Brethren lesson commentary on the
　International Sunday-school lessons for
　1903. 3564
Brethren of the Common Life. 695
Brethren preaching today. 1237
Brethren social policy. 1137
Brethren story caravan. 1236
Brethren trail blazers. 1235
Brethren writers. 2855
Brethren's tune and hymn book. 1236
...Breviary. 841
Breviary and missal prayers. Edited and
　compiled from approved sources by John
　C. Selner. 1298
Breviary and the laity. 842
Breviary explained. 842
Breviary through the centuries. 842
Breviloquium. 3641
Brhad-devata. 1816
Brian Wildsmith's illustrated Bible stories.
　624
Brick church and parish house. 713
Brick church hymns. 2917
Brick church memorial. 2913
Bricks from Babel. 3110
Bride. 1116
Bride for His Son. 208
Bride of Christ. 2207
Bride of the Lamb and other essays. 1069
Bride on the Amazon. 2505
Bride unveiled. 459
Bridegroom and bride. 2347
Bridehood saints. 3282
Bride's manual. 857
Brides of Christ. 3489
Bride's prayer book. 855
Bridge. 1034, 1060, 1082, 1592
Bridge across four centuries. 1293
Bridge across the years. 2929
Bridge between the Testaments. 2091,
　2149
Bridge between two worlds. 3506
Bridge builders. 1213, 3235
Bridge building. 168
Bridge is love. 3017
Bridge of criticism; dialogues among
　Lucian, Erasmus, and Voltaire on the
　Enlightenment. 1520, 2270
Bridge of love. 1820, 3517
Bridge of love by a lover. 3518
Bridge of the new dawn. 95
Bridge over the world. 2366
Bridge (The) 1082
Bridge to Africa. 2506
Bridge to brotherhood. 2153
Bridge to Heaven. 3226
Bridges--not walls. 3117
Bridges to a holy time. 2109
Bridges to hope. 2395
Bridges to the unknown. 3101
Bridges to the world. 1573
Bridges to tomorrow. 2204
Bridges to understanding. 1544
Bridges we cross. 1444
Bridging Israel and America through music
　and honoring four American Jewish
　composers. 2633
Bridging the gap. 1260
Bridging the generation gap and bringing it
　back to God. 3889
Bridging the great divide between the
　physical and the spiritual worlds. 2991
Bridging two worlds. 2195, 3361
Bridled tongue. 251
Brief account of associated presbyteries.
　2689, 2919
Brief account of the Associated
　presbyteries. 1240
Brief account of the life and work of
　Emanuel Swedenborg. 3569
Brief account of the life of the late Rev.
　Caleb Smith, A.M., minister of the
　gospel, at Newark mountains. 3426

Brief account of the military orders in
　Spain. 2741
Brief account of the rise and progress of
　the people called Quakers, in which their
　fundamental principle, doctrines, worhsip,
　ministry and discipline are plainly
　declared. 1675
Brief account of the rise progress and
　present state of the Theological seminary
　of the Presbyterian church in the United
　States at Princeton. 2915
Brief annals. 2451
Brief apology in behalf of the people in
　derision call'd Quakers. 1674
Brief Bible history. 289
Brief Biblical history, New Testament. 406
Brief Biblical history, Old Testament. 533
Brief biographical dictionary. 662
Brief biographical sketches of deceased
　Welsh Baptist ministers who have
　laboured in northeastern Pennsylvania
　from 1832 to 1904. 159
Brief biographical sketches of some of the
　early ministers of the Cumberland
　Presbyterian church. 1396
Brief biographies of some members of the
　Society of Friends. 1678
Brief chronological account of the Catholic
　educational institutions of the
　archdiocese of New York. 823
Brief commentary on Paul's letter to the
　Church at Rome. 467
... A brief commentary on the little office
　of the immaculate conception of the
　Blessed Virgin Mary. 1886
Brief commentary on the text of the
　Roman breviary. 841
Brief concordance to the Holy Scriptures.
　226
Brief concordance to the Holy Scriptures
　of the Old and New Testaments. 225,
　226
Brief concordance to the Holy Scriptures,
　of the Old and New Testamets. 226
Brief course in mediumship. 3511
Brief dictionary of the denominations.
　3326
Brief discourses on the Gospel for all
　Sundays and festivals of the year. 383
Brief dissertation on the three first
　chapters of Genesis. 525
Brief essay about the gods and my friends.
　1655
Brief examination of the practice of the
　times. 3424
Brief explanation of the book of
　Revelations in chronological order. 463
Brief explanatory commentary and lexicon
　on the New Testament. 224
Brief exposition of the doctrine of the New
　church, which is meant by the New
　Jerusalem in the Apocalypse. 2691
Brief exposition, with practical
　observations, upon the whole Book of
　Canticles. 593
Brief funeral meditations. 1693
Brief guide to abstracting and indexing
　services relevant to the study of religion.
　3096
Brief historical sketch of St. Johns
　Methodist Episcopal church. 2452
Brief historical sketch of the Catholic
　church on Long island. 872
Brief historical sketch of Wakefield
　Presbyterian church and Sunday school.
　2830
Brief history of Aghalee Parish to
　commemorate the three hundredth
　anniversary of the consecration of
　Aghalee Parish Church, 1st May, 1677-
　1st May, 1977. 18
Brief history of Beha Ullah, the founder of
　Behai Religion. 125, 127
Brief history of Calvary Baptist Church,
　compiled by Mrs. Roy Cookston and the
　1965 Historical Committee of Calvary
　Baptist Church, Alexandria, Louisiana,
　1965. 24
Brief history of First Presbyterian church.
　1849
Brief history of Islam. 1924
Brief history of Joseph Smith, the prophet.
　3429
Brief history of Lyles Baptist church,
　Fluvanna County, Virginia. 2304
Brief history of our English Bible. 248
Brief history of preaching. 2908
Brief history of Rocky Springs Baptist
　Church, organized 1845. 3242
Brief history of St. Bernadette's Roman
　Catholic shrine church. 694
Brief history of St. Paul's Parish, Grosse
　Pointe Farms, Michigan. 3278
Brief history of the Baptist. 152
Brief history of the Bible Presbyterian
　Church and its agencies. 2916

Brief history of the Catholic Church in
　New Jersey. 823
Brief history of the Catholic church in the
　United States, compiled for use in
　Catholic schools. 834
Brief history of the Christian church. 933
Brief history of the church. 1180
Brief history of the Church in West Texas.
　2975
Brief history of the Church of God
　reformation movement. 1228
Brief history of the Church of Jesus Christ
　of latter-day saints. 2600
Brief history of the Church of Jesus Christ
　of Latterday saints, from the birth of the
　prophet Joseph Smith to the present
　time. 2602, 3428
Brief history of the diocese of Fall River,
　Mass. 1602
Brief history of the First Presbyterian
　church of Baltimore. 2917
Brief history of the Foreign Missionary
　Department of the Pentecostal
　Assemblies of the World. 2814
Brief history of the Huguenots and three
　family trees. 1851
Brief history of the Lutheran church in
　America. 2294
Brief history of the Main street Methodist
　Episcopal church. 2452
Brief history of the Methodist Episcopal
　church in Wellfleet, Massachusetts. 3801
Brief history of the Minnesota Woman's
　Christian temperance union. 3833
Brief history of the Moravian church.
　3286
Brief history of the parish of Trinity
　church, Albany, N.Y., from its
　organization, September 4, 1829, to the
　consecration of the church edifice, Sept.
　10, 1849. 22
Brief history of the Presbyterians. 2916
Brief history of the Presbytery of Geneva
　and a tribute to some early ministers.
　2919
Brief history of the Riverside Church.
　2699
Brief history of the trial of the Rev.
　William A. Scott, D.D. 3315
Brief history of the Universalist church for
　young people. 3754
Brief history of the Universalist society of
　Hartland, Vermont. 3752
Brief history of the Woman's Christian
　temperance union. 3598
Brief history of Trinity Church,
　Towsontown, 1860-1960. 3705
Brief illustration and confirmation of the
　divine right of infant baptism. 1905
Brief introduction to the Old Testament.
　540
Brief introduction to the philosophy of
　religion. 3106
Brief Jewish biographies in Biblical, post-
　Biblical and Talmudical times. 2084
Brief life of Paul. 2800
Brief lives. 2856
Brief memoir concerning Abel Thomas.
　3692
Brief memoir of Maria Fox. 3127
Brief memoir of Rev. Joseph Bancroft Hill.
　1811
Brief memoirs of the pious. Prepared for
　the Presbyterian board of publication.
　926
Brief miscellaneous narrative of the more
　early part of the life of L. Tilmon. 3424
Brief narrative of the life of Jacob Lindley.
　2230
Brief notes on the ceremonial of bishops.
　665
Brief notes on the Old Testament, copied
　from the margin of my Bible and from
　commentaries. 498
Brief on historical use of the symbol and
　words "red cross." 3029
Brief outline on the study of theology.
　3669
Brief prayers for Bread and Cup. 2259
Brief recollections of the late Rev. George
　W. Walker. 3789
Brief sketch of Greek church history.
　2747
Brief sketch of life from childhood to fifty
　years. 3360
Brief sketch of the Church of England.
　1210
Brief sketch of the history of the Catholic
　church on the island of New-York. 823
Brief sketch of the life and labors of the
　Rev. Maurice M. Jones. 2130
Brief sketch of the life of the Reverend
　Francis Sebastian Job. 2124
Brief sketch of the present state and future
　expectations of the Jews. 2117
Brief sketches of the last scenes. 2156

Brief story of the Augsburg confession told
　for young people. 109, 117
Brief study of Christian science. 1035
Brief study of customs and civilization in
　Bible lands. 524, 1280
Brief summary of the history and doctrine
　of the Holy Scriptures. 290, 295
Brief summary of the Ten commandments.
　1313
...A brief survey of present-day religious
　and moral education in the schools of
　countries other than the United States of
　America. 3158
Brief survey of southern Africa. 762
Brief survey of the Bible. 297
Brief topical index of the Book of common
　prayer. 2957
Brief treatise on the atonement. 105
Brief view of Christian doctrine. 3665
Brief view of Greek philosophy, from the
　age of Socrates to the coming of Christ.
　2835
Brief view of Greek philosophy up to the
　age of Pericles. 2835
Brief view of the doctrines of the Christian
　religion as professed by the Society of
　Friends. 1681
Brief view of the figure. 314
Brief view of the heavenly doctrines. 3570
Brief view of the heavenly doctrines
　revealed in the theological writings of
　Emanuel Swedenborg. 3570
Brief views of the Saviour. 1984
Briefe answere. 787
Brieff discours off the troubles begonne at
　Franckford in Germany, Anno Domini
　1554. 1651, 3009
Briefs for church builders. 1156
Briefs on prophetic themes. 2946
Brigham Young. 2604, 2606, 2607, 3868,
　3869
Brigham Young and his Mormon empire.
　2601, 3868
Brigham Young at home, by Clarissa
　Young Spencer with Mabel Harmer.
　2606, 3869
Brigham Young, modern Moses, prophet of
　God. 2619, 3869
Brigham Young, the colonizer. 2603, 3869
Brigham's destroying angel. 3762
Brigham's destroying angel: being the life,
　confession, and startling disclosures of
　the notorious Bill Hickman, the Danite
　chief of Utah. 3762
Bright beautiful bells. 2633
Bright cloud. 651
Bright essence. 2471
Bright future. 3254
Bright future of Sunday School. 936
Bright galaxy. 3725
Bright is the shaken torch. 1234
Bright light of death. 886, 3521
Bright pathways. 2489
Bright-shining place. 932, 2938
Bright side and the other side. 1895
Bright side of death. 1350
Bright side of life. 1612
Bright wind of the spirit: Pentecostalism
　today. 2814
Brighten the corner, and 45 other women's
　devotions. 3843
Brighter side. 1351
Brighter than the sun. 1982
Brihadaranyaka Upanisad. 1815
Brihajjatakam of Varaha Mihira. 98
Brimstone bargains in the marriage market.
　3390
Brimstone Corner. 685
Bring forth justice. 2555
Bring him to me. 3030
Bring hither the timbrel. 583
Bring me an ax! 677
Bring me my bow. 960
Bring on the puppets! 3005
Bring them in! 1565
Bring your loved ones to Christ. 1572
Bringing back the King. 3318
Bringing Christ back. 2029
Bringing in sheaves. 1564
Bringing our world together. 871
Bringing souls to Christ. 1569
Bringing the Mass to the people. 2368
Bringing the mother with you. 2360
Bringing the sacraments to the people.
　3266
Bringing the sheaves. 1564
Bringing up children in the Christian faith.
　939
Bringing up John. 3155
Bringing your child to God. 3174
Brink of mystery. 1226, 3363
Britain's remembrancer. (cI' I[reverse c]
　cxxviii) 2853
British and American utopian literature,
　1516-1975. 1518
British Baptist missionaries in India. 2546

British Baptist missionaries in India, 1793-1837. 2546
British Baptists. 149
British cathedrals. 753
British churches. 1270
British discovery of Hinduism in the eighteenth century. 1814
British empire under fire. 1758
British Israel theory. 45
British Museum manuscript Egerton 3307. 2777

British preachers. 3363
British pulpit. 3366
British teaching techniques in adult education. 8
Broad church theology. 3628
Broadcast. 1839
Broadcasting religion. 3018
Broadcasting the advent message. 3018
Broadcasts to America from unseen friends. 3506
Broadening Church. 2925, 3679
Broader Bible study. 566
Broadly speaking. 61
Broadman Bible commentary. 221
Broadman church manual. 150
Broadman comments on the International Bible lessons for Christian teaching. 643, 1914
Broadman devotional annual. 1445
Broadman minister's manual. 2790
Broadman sermon outlines. 3373
Broadway tabernacle church. 2697
Broken beams from the summer-land. 3498
Broken bits of old China. 3135
Broken bread for serving disciples. 1559
Broken bread in a broken world. 2251
Broken but loved. 1000, 2041
Broken center. 3071
Broken circle. 2726
Broken cup. 1237
Broken earthenware. 1585
Broken image. 1844
Broken lamp; a story of Edith Stein. 3526
Broken links. 1048, 2217, 3022
Broken pillars, a study of the Ten commandments. 1312
Broken platform. 2285
Broken silence, the story of today's struggle for religious freedom. 129
Broken tablets (a photograph of life) 1315
Broken things. 1350
Broken vase. 3164
Broken wall. 364
Broken walls of Jerusalem. 297
Bronson Alcott at Alcott house. 23
Bronson Alcott, teacher. 23
Bronze age God in the space age. 1720
Bronzes of Kashmir. 693
Brook Kerith. 2005
... Brooklyn church year book ... 19. 693
Brooks by the traveller's way. 2932
Brooksiana. 1242
Brosamlein von des Herrn Tisch. 1264
Brother and the brotherhood. 2931
Brother Andre, C. S. C., the apostle of Saint Joseph. 1598
Brother Andre of Monreal. 40
Brother Andre of Montreal. 40
Brother Andre of Mount Royal. 40
Brother Andre of Saint Joseph's oratory. 40
Brother Azarias. 2630
Brother Berthold tells a story. 1843
Brother Bonsack. 677
Brother Earth. 2676
Brother Francis. 1027, 1640, 1644
Brother Fred Chicken, superpastor. 2788
Brother in the church. 695
"Brother McGarvey"; the life of President J. W. McGarvey of the College of the Bible, Lexington, Ky. 2307
Brother Mack, the frontier preacher. 1295, 2310
Brother Nicholas, a life of St. Nicholas of Flue. 2710
Brother Norbert's masterpiece. 2186
Brother of the birds. 1641
Brother Solomon. 3457
Brother to a dragonfly. 145, 733
Brother to brother. 2264
Brother Van. 2481, 3767
Brother wolf. 931, 2129
Brother Zero. 2136
Brotherhood. 695
Brotherhood & civilisation. 3443
Brotherhood and the church. 2920
Brotherhood economics. 1368
Brotherhood guidebook. 3465
Brotherhood in our apartment-size world. 695
Brotherhood of men. 694
Brotherhood of the burning heart. 1318
Brotherhood of the Rosy Cross. 3251

Brotherhood of thieves. 3424
Brotherhood through religion. 1104
Brotherly community—the highest command of love. 1859
Brotherly faithfulness. 37, 1858
Brotherly love. 695, 3197
Brothers all. 2457, 3182
Brothers East and West. 2749
Brothers in Christ. 37
Brothers in deed to brothers in need. 2408
Brothers of Braemore. 188
Brothers of holy cross. 1332
Brothers of light. 1806
Brothers of light, brothers of blood. 1806
Brothers of men. 1636, 2232
Brothers of the Bible. 695
Brothers of the Christian Schools. 695
Brothers of the faith. 1492
Brow of the hill above the Warrior. 1825
Brown bag. 908
Brown goes. 3124
Browning and the Christian faith. 697, 1047
Browning as a philosopher and religious teacher. 696
Browning as a philosophical and religious teacher. 696
Browning of America. 827, 1817
Brownists in Norwich and Norfolk about 1580. 697
Brownson-Hecker correspondence. 697, 1365
Bruce Olson. 2625, 2736
Bruchko. 2625, 2736
Bruised for our iniquities, meditations for Lent. 2034
Bruised reed. 208, 2627
Bruised reeds. 2893
Brunner's dialectical encounter. 698
Bryan and Darrow at Dayton. 202, 698, 1578
Buber on God and the perfect man. 699, 1733
Buckeye Disciples. 1465
Bud and the flower of Judaism. 2140
Bud, blossom and fruit. 1747, 2371
Bud Robinson. 3242
Buddha. 705, 706, 709, 712, 1703, 3128, 3144
... Buddha and Buddhism. 702
Buddha and early Buddhism. 702
Buddha and five after-centuries. 705
Buddha and his doctrine. 703
Buddha and his religion. 700
Buddha and the Christ. 705
Buddha and the gospel of Buddhism. 701
Buddha; Buddhist civilization in India and Ceylon. 706
Buddha eye. 709
Buddha, his life and teachings. 701
Buddha in the palm of your hand. 3484
... The Buddha-karita of Asvaghosha. 706
Buddha Maitrya-Amithaba has appeared. 130
Buddha, Marx, and God. 709, 3102
Buddha, the Prophet, and the Christ. 3128
Buddha, the quest for serenity. 712, 1703
Buddha, truth, and brotherhood. 706
Buddha way. 707
... Buddhadatta's manuals. 711
Buddha's philosophy. 700
Buddha's teachings. 707
Buddha's way. 705
... Buddhavamsa. 707
Buddhism. 85, 700, 701, 702, 703, 704, 705, 707, 708, 710, 711
Buddhism—a modern perspective. 703
Buddhism: a "mystery religion"? 702
Buddhism—a non-theistic religion. 710
Buddhism, a philosophy of the spirit and a way to the eternal. 703
Buddhism: a subject index to periodical articles in English, 1728-1971. 704
Buddhism, a way of life and thought. 708
Buddhism and Buddhists in China. 702
Buddhism and Buddhists in Japan. 706
Buddhism and Buddhists in southern Asia. 703
Buddhism and Christianity. 1081
Buddhism and Christianity face to face. 702
... Buddhism and immortality. 700
Buddhism and its Christian critics. 701
Buddhism and psychotherapy. 706
Buddhism and society. 705
Buddhism and society in southeast Asia. 3439
Buddhism and the claims of Christ. 1095
Buddhism and the race question. 708
Buddhism and the spirit cults in north-east Thailand. 3605
Buddhism and Zen. 3894
Buddhism and Zen in Vietnam in relation to the development of Buddhism in Asia. 3893
Buddhism, Christianity, and the future of man. 2323

Buddhism for the West. 711
Buddhism for the West: Theravada; Mahayana and Vajrayana. 711
Buddhism for today. 703, 3272
Buddhism in Afghanistan and Central Asia. 85
Buddhism in America. 710, 3440
Buddhism in China. 704, 709
Buddhism in Chinese history. 705
Buddhism in Hawaii. 705
Buddhism in India, Ceylon, China and Japan. 704
Buddhism in Japan. 706
Buddhism in Japan, with an outline of its origins in India. 710
Buddhism in Sinhalese society, 1750-1900. 709
Buddhism in the modern world. 703, 708
Buddhism in transition. 704
Buddhism in translations. 704, 707
Buddhism, its doctrines and its methods. 707
Buddhism; its essence and development. 701
Buddhism, Japan's cultural identity. 709
Buddhism of Tibet and The key to the middle way. 707
Buddhism of Tibet, or Lamaism. 2193
Buddhism or communism. 708
Buddhism primitive and present in Magadha and in Ceylon. 701
Buddhism, the first millennium. 708
Buddhism: the religion of analysis. 708
Buddhism under Mao. 705
Le buddhisme au Cambodge. 704
Buddhist and Christian gospels. 1080
Buddhist and Quaker experiments with truth. 706
Buddhist and Taoist studies. 708
Buddhist art and architecture in Pakistan. 85
Buddhist art in its relation to Buddhist ideals. 85
Buddhist bible. 707
Buddhist Bible, the favorite scriptures of the Zen sect. 704
Buddhist birth stories. 2206, 2207
... Buddhist birth-stories (Jataka tales) 2207
... A Buddhist catechism. 702, 703
Buddhist China. 705
Buddhist-Christian empathy. 1081
Buddhist concept of hell. 1802, 3272
Buddhist conception of spirits. 3475
Buddhist conquest of China. 705
Buddhist ethics. 711
Buddhist experience. 700
Buddhist Himalaya. 707, 2193
Buddhist leader in Ming China. 1783, 2940
Buddhist Mahayana texts. 707
Buddhist meditation in the Southern school. 702, 2382
Buddhist monastic discipline. 2577, 3303
Buddhist monk, Buddhist layman. 2572
Buddhist monks and monasteries of India. 2577
Buddhist nirvana and its Western interpreters. 2711
Buddhist paintings from shrines and temples in Ceylon. 2760
Buddhist parables. 2206
Buddhist philosophy. 710
Buddhist philosophy in India and Ceylon. 702, 2838
Buddhist philosophy in theory and practice. 2838
Buddhist practice of concentration. 701
Buddhist praying-wheel. 3810
Buddhist religion. 703, 708
Buddhist revival in China. 705
Buddhist revival in India. 709
Buddhist scriptures. 710
Buddhist sects of Japan. 712
Buddhist sermons. 702
Buddhist spectrum. 709
Buddhist stories. 701
Buddhist stories for children. 706
Buddhist students' manual. 709
Buddhist studies in honour of I. B. Horner. 704, 1847
Buddhist suttas. 707
Buddhist Tantras. 3586
Buddhist temples in Japan. 3600
Buddhist texts from Japan. 707, 710
Buddhist texts through the ages. 707
Buddhist thought and Asian civilization. 708, 1776
Buddhist thought in India. 701, 710
Buddhist tradition in India, China & Japan. 705
Buddhist way of life. 703
Buddhist wisdom. 702
Buddist temples in Japan. 3600
Budget. 13
Buds and blossoms. 996, 2529

Buds and blossoms; missionary stories for children. 2529
Buenos dias. 155
Buffalo church directory. 712
Bugle. 3504
Bugle call. 956
Bugler for Sallateeska. 2528
Bugles in the afternoon. 2436, 3365
Bugs, floods, and fried rice. 2487, 3286
Build an approved Sunday Bible school. 3558
Build my church. 1904, 2527
Build on the rock. 3335
Builder of dreams. 880
Builders. 894, 1662, 2455, 3387
Builders and crusaders. 814
Builders by the sea. 3761
Builders of a new Africa. 2484
Builders of a new world. 3440
Builders of men. 3875
Builders of our foundations. 1550, 1702
Builders of the Bay colony. 2371
...Builders of the church. 927
Builders of the Conservative movement. 1348
Builders of the Jewish people from ancient times to present times. 2089
...Builders of the kingdom. 2443
Builders of the Quaker road 1652-1952. 1677
Builders of the social order. 1136, 3451
Building. 3206
Building a better Sunday school. 3552
Building a Christian home. 1607, 1609
Building a church people. 916
Building a church training program. 141
Building a community. 3440
Building a country Sunday school. 3556
Building a just society. 1319
Building a life. 964, 3884
Building a moral reserve. 1277
Building a new world. 3448
Building a school system. 806
Building a standard Sunday school. 3553
Building a successful men's Bible class. 3168
Building a successful Sunday school. 3552
Building a young adult ministry. 1259
Building a young people's society program. 3876
Building an effective church school. 3551
Building an intermediate program. 3167
Building and care of Methodist church property. 1157, 1242
Building and equipment for Christian education. 3548
Building and equipping for Christian education. 3548
Building & maintaining a church staff. 1200
Building better Bible classes. 3177
Building better churches. 3671
Building Bible names. 3010
Building brotherhood: what can elementary schools do? 695
Building character. 938, 2590
Building character from within. 948
Building Christian communities. 1245
Building Christ's body. 995, 2799
Building Christ's church in a crumbling world. 918
Building church membership through evangelism. 1563
Building churches through income financing. 1167
Building eras in religion. 1068
Building for religious education. 1157
... Building for to-morrow. 3765
Building juniors. 937
Building leaders for church education. 935
...A building memorial of the Roman Catholic church of St. Anthony of the Desert, Fall River, Mass., U.S.A., 1930. 1602
Building missionaries in Hawaii. 2599
Building of a diocese. 3358
Building of a great church. 1549
Building of churches. 1269
Building of the Bible. 406
Building of the church. 1126
Building of the city of God. 2615
Building of the cosmos. 1932
Building of the Kingdom. 3186
Building of the Mother Church. 684
... Building on rock. 886
Building on the back forty. 2462
Building on the Rock. 2529
Building people, through a caring, sharing fellowship. 1620
Building sermons. 3345
Building sermons to meet people's needs. 2898
Building spritual foundations in the family. 1609
Building templar masonry. 1665
Building the integrated curriculum. 830
Building the Americas. 2543

Building the church. 1121, 2925
... Building the church of Christ as described in the New Testament. 3150
Building the city. 996
Building the congregation. 2421
Building the dispensations. 1376
Building the Escorial. 1532
Building the faith community. 3149
Building the home Christian. 1608
Building the house of God. 1156
Building the kingdom. 1016, 3148
Building the kingdom of God in the countryside. 3255
Building the medieval cathedrals. 751, 752
Building the new age. 3441
Building the new church. 1156
Building the sermon. 3342
Building the Sunday School. 3557

Building the word. 2903
Building town and country churches. 3253
Building up one another. 983
Building up the mid-week service. 2887
Building up your congregation. 1252
Building with buses. 3253
Building with India. 2530
Building your spiritual strength. 3540
Buildings of the South Church, Bergenfield, New Jersey. 192
Built on a rock. 764
Built on the rock, 1869-1969. 3868
Built upon the cornerstone. 1180
Buk in Jenesis. 198
Bulfinch's Mythology. 888, 2650, 2655
Bulfinch's mythology: The age of fable, The age of chivalry, Legends of Charlemagne. 2650
Bulgakov anthology. 2750, 3632
Bulgaria, churches and religion. 1489
Bull at a new gate. 1089
Bullet stopped me. 1575
Bulletin. 615, 871, 3190, 3757
Bulletin board ideas. 713
... Bulletin ... Fall conference number. 2941
... Bulletin Joseph Krohnberg lodge, no. 321. 2101
Bulletin no. [1-]. 101
Bulletin of reports of constituting convention. 2282
Bultmann-Barth and Catholic theology. 3628
Bulwark never failing. 163
Bunch of daisies. 1609
Bunch of everlasting. 3348
Bundle of life. 3497
Bunyan's awakening works. 713
Bunyan's Grace abounding to the chief of sinners. 713
Bunyan's inviting works. 713
Bunyan's Pilgrim in verse. 717
Bunyan's Pilgrim's progress. 716
... Bunyan's Pilgrim's progress, etc. 717
Bunyan's Pilgrim's progress illustrated. 716
Burden bearing, and other sermons. 3359
Burden is light! 1362, 1367, 2938
Burden made light. 3406
Burden of belief. 763
Burden of freedom. 1659
Burden of ill-health. 3407
Burden of Soren Kierkegaard. 2169
Burden of the Lord. 2903
Burden of the time. 2237
Bureaucracy and Church reform. 1219, 3446
Burial services. 1693
Burial services, rite one and rite two. 1694
Buridan's mule. 1731
Buried alive for Christ and other missionary stories. 2490
Buried cities recovered. 1419, 2761
Buried life. 1582
Buried wheat. 1645
Burke Culpepper. 1393
Burma prisoner. 2157, 2529
Burma through alien eyes. 2506
Burmese supernaturalism. 718
Burn a little! 3488
Burned-over district. 2700
Burning, burning bush. 535, 2096
Burning bush. 533, 649, 733, 2714, 3188
Burning bushes. 3
Burning bushes & moon walks. 165
Burning coals. 3356
Burning conscience. 103
Burning-glass. 2253
Burning heart. 1001, 2043, 2929, 3806
Burning hearts. 2006
Burning light. 2127
Burning questions in historic Christianity. 1174
Burning questions of the life that now is and that which is to come. 3651
Burning themes and heavenly manna. 1071
Burning thirst. 2428

Burning water. 2668
Burnout in ministry. 1298
Burnt offerings. 2771
Burnt out incense. 1708
Burro and the Bibles. 612, 2540
Burrows on the Dead Sea scrolls. 1409
Bursting of new wineskins. 3445
Bus them in. 2625
Bus aglow. 2587
Bush is burning! Radical Judaism faces the pharaohs of the modern superstate. 2155
Bush is still burning. 2933, 3355
Bush still burns. 3484
Bushido: the soul of Japan. 719
Bushnell rediscovered. 719
Business administration of a church. 3671
Business and the church. 719
Business aspect of Christian stewardship. 3529
Business girl chooses. 3877
Business girls. 3832
Business guide for priests. 773, 1253
Business handbook for churches. 1200, 1251
Business in the Bible. 197
Business man and the church. 719
Business man of Syria. 2019
Business man's religion. 720
Business men of the Bible. 247
Business of living. 3569
Business of missions. 2554
Business of salvation. 3290
Business side of religion. 719
Businessman looks at the Bible. 720
Busy Bible. 229
Busy books. 229
Busy Christians. 1385
Busy feet. 904
Busy man's Bible. 200
Busy man's Old Testament. 589
Busy pastor's book on matrimony. 2341
Busy people's Bible course. 254, 270
But as for me. 1505
But as yesterday. 3306
But Christ did rise! 2215
But deliver us from evil. 1585
But for our grief. 1774, 3591
But for the grace of God. 1751
But God. 241, 2197
. . . but God can. 971
But God comes first. 3591
But God has promised. 2486, 2631
But he hit me first! 1610
But I have called you friends. 1688
... But I must decrease. 214
But that I can't believe! 3665
But time and chance. 774, 2349
"But, until seventy times seven" 2305, 2699
But with the dawn, rejoicing. 3540
But you don't know Harry. 3844
Butler's moral philosophy. 720
Button's inn. 2614
Buy me. 1323
Buynyan's devotional works. 713
Bvzantine east and Latin west. 3307
Bwiti. 1612
By all means. 3466
By an unknown disciple. 2006
By clipper plane. 3467
By courage and faith. 739
By deed and design. 1251
By faith. 1589
By faith alone. 2161
"By faith"; Henry W. Frost and the China inland mission. 1689
By faith I live. 1014
By freedom's holy light. 166
By grace alone. 3289
By grace through faith plus nothing. 380
By His Spirit. 1430
By His stripes. 1599
By Jacob's well, a planned retreat. 3222
By John Calvin. 3044
By John Calvin, a reflection book introduction to the writings of John Calvin. 3044
By life and by death. 3524
By life or by death. 2559
By light, light. 2118
By love compelled. 2491
By man rejected. 2033
By means of death. 2057
'By my spirit. 2509
By oath consigned. 1376
By one spirit. 1546
By paths in the Bible country. 318
By-paths to forgotten folks. 155
By post to Rome. 763
By post to the apostles. 70
By post to the apostles. 71
By railway or rainbow. 3419
By saddle and sleigh. 3812
By Shaker hands. 3397
By sundown shores. 3095
By the finger of God. 1422
By the great wall. 2512

By the obedience of one. 2213
By the power of God. 3482
By the power of the Holy Spirit. 1830
By the River of No Return. 2396
By the rivers of Babylon. 2300
By the rivers of Babylon: studies in the Book of Daniel. 508
By the still waters. 1447
"By the sweat of thy brow" 862
By the time you count to 10. 2983
By the waters of Babylon. 634
By the waters of Bethesda. 3255
By the way. 1447
By the way of Scripture interpretation. Theism: a prophecy: or, Prophetical dissertation. 606
By the way, Sister. 2573
By their blood. 1021
By their fruits. 3398
By their fruits you shall know them. 995
By these faiths. 3140
By these names I am known. 2021
By these things men live. 954, 2385
By this shall all men know. 2265
By Thy holy cross. 3526
By unknown ways. 1013
By water and the Holy Spirit. 137, 2969
By way of illustration. 1839
By way of remembrance. 3852
By way of response. 1301, 2349
By ways I knew not. 2756
By ways to highways. 3159
By Waysides in India. 2530
By what authority? 118, 119, 3216, 3739
By what standard? 3767
By Whom is the world to be converted! 1577
By word and prayer. 1298, 2297
By-laws of Boston Commandery of Knights Templars and the appendant orders. 1665
Bypaths in the Greek New Testament. 425
By-products of the rural Sunday school. 3558
Byways. 1015
Byways in Quaker history. 1684, 1853
Byways of blessing. 1454
By ways to highways. 3159
Byzantine architecture and decoration. 1156, 1158
Byzantine chant of the Greek Orthodox Church. 1203, 1206
Byzantine Christianity: emperor, church, and the West. 2747
Byzantine church of Hagia Sophia. 1161, 1929
Byzantine churches of Istanbul. 1929
Byzantine divine liturgy. 766
Byzantine East and Latin West. 1622, 3307
Byzantine East and Latin West: two worlds of Christendom in Middle Ages and Renaissance. 1622, 3307
Byzantine legacy in the Orthodox Church. 721, 2745
Byzantine liturgy. 2239
Byzantine missions among the Slavs. 1398, 2546
Byzantine music and hymnography. 2632
Byzantine patriarchate. 2747
Byzantine patriarchate, 451-1204. 2747, 3307
Byzantine rite Rusins in Carpatho-Ruthenia and America. 766, 3891
Byzantine sacred art. 85
Byzantine seraphic typicon. 2239
Byzantine-Slav liturgy of St. John Chrysostom. 842, 2236
Byzantine theocracy. 1149
Byzantine theology. 3667
Byzantine tradition in church embroidery. 1510
Byzantium and the Roman primacy. 861, 2862

C

C. 3465
C. England of Lapeer. 1515
C. F. M. inquiry program. 951
C. H. Dodd, interpreter of the New Testament. 2693
C. H. Spurgeon's autobiography. 3523
C. H. Spurgeon's Sermon illustrations, gold and arrows from the prince of preachers. 167
C. H. Spurgeon's Sermon notes, Genesis to Revelation. 3375
C. H. Spurgeon's Treasury of David. 576
C. M. Ward story, with Doug Wead. 1302, 3795
C. R. Nichol. 2707
C. S. Lewis. 2219, 2220
C. S. Lewis: apostle to the skeptics. 2219

C. S. Lewis, defender of the faith. 62, 2219
C. S. Lewis; five best books in one volume. 1217, 3633
C.S. Lewis, mere Christian. 2219
C. S. Lewis on Scripture. 306, 2219
C.S. Lewis's case for the Christian faith. 69, 2220
C. S. S. S. 1332, 2307
C. T. Studd. 2513, 3536
C. U. S., 1867-1967, a centenary record. 871, 2335
Cabala. 722
Cabbalists and other essays. 2142
Cabin boy's locker. 3317
Cactus. 2856
Cacus and Marsyas in Etrusco-Roman legend. 723
Cadence. 2388
Cadet chapel sermons. 3356
Caesar. 1703
Caesar and God; the priesthood and politics. 1087
Caesar Baronius, Counter-Reformation historian. 174
Caesar's court. (A wonderful book.) 2069
Caesar's or God's? 1141
Caged light. 2125
Cagliostro. 723
Cagliostro and his Egyptian rite of freemasonry. 723
Cain, come home! 25
Cain's lamentations over Abel, in six books ... 3d ed. 723
Cain's lamentations over Abel, in six books ... The 4th ed. 723
Cairo connection. 610, 2073
Cairo geniza. 316, 724
Cajetan responds. 3630
Calabar. 1234, 2506
Calamy revised. 1468
Calas affair. 724, 1852
Calas affair; persecution. 724, 1852
Calculated goodness. 2391
Caleb Maccabee. 2005
Caledonia's bard. 718, 1671
Calendar and lectionary. 1262
Calendar of Christianity. 1262
Calendar of faith and flowers. 1630
Calendar of hymns. 1865
Calendar of love. 1432
Calendar of prayer for missions. 2879, 2970
Calendar of prayer for 1922. 2454
Calendar of saints. 3283
Calendar of saints for unbelievers. 3282
Calendar of the papers of Charles Thomas Longley, Archbishop of Canterbury, 1862-1868, in Lambeth Palace Library. 2245
Calendar of the Reformation. 3035
Calendar question. 1163, 2746
Calendar saints. 3283
Caliban in Grub street. 3061
Califonria missions. 2506
California Catholicism. 726, 815
California cult. 186, 2328
California digest of masonic law. 1666
California League of youth. 1253
California Masonic code. 1666
California missions and landmarks and how to get there. 3470
California pilgrim. 726
California pilgrimage. 3470
California pioneer decade of 1849. 726, 2913, 2917
California plan for the education of migrant children. 898
California poets. 33
California state evangelistic-stewardship conference seromsn. 3241
California superquake, 1975-77? 2948
California utopia. 3701
Californian Crusoe. 2614
Californians and Mormons. 726
California's Catholic heritage. 815
California's mission heritage. 815, 2506
California's missions. 834
California's old missions. 1648, 3470
California's pioneer Sister of Mercy, Mother Mary Baptist Russell. 3256
California's reluctant prelate. 28
California's Spanish missions. 3470
California's Spanish missions yesterday and today. 3470
Caliphate. 726
Caliphs and their non-Muslim subjects. 726
Call. 3241
Call Adonoi. 2733
Call and challenge of the unseen. 2645
Call and response. 3785
Call and the answer. 3785
Call collect. 2125, 2874
Call drum. 2549
Call for colleagues from leaders in the younger Christian churches. 2521

Call for God. 3049
Call for me? 3785
Call for new Churches. 2441
... The call from Africa. 2497
Call from beyond. 3223
... The call from India. 2530
... The call from the Far East. 2516
... The call from the Moslem world. 2540
Call her Blessed. 2359, 3842
Call me Joe! 1000
Call me John. 2123
Call of all nations. 3295
Call of China and the Islands. 1238, 3731
Call of China's great north-west. 2163
Call of Christ in an age of dilemma. 3215
Call of Christ, unto thirsty sinners, to come to Him and drink of the waters of life. 2067
Call of heaven. 718, 875
Call of Israel. 501
Call of Jesus to joy. 2067
Call of Korea, political--social--religious. 2537
Call of Lent. 2214, 2300
Call of St. Clare. 1284
Call of the blessed sacrament. 2259
Call of the Christ. 1955
Call of the Congo. 2220, 2514
Call of the forgotten man. 2455
Call of the harvest. 1574
Call of the Master. 2067
Call of the minaret. 2564
Call of the new era. 2494
Call of the soul. 3698
Call of the Torah. 562
Call of the Virgin at San Damiano. 2357
Call of the waters. 3738
Call of the world; or, Every man's supreme opportunity. 2492
Call of to-day. 3342
Call the witnesses: perspectives on evangelism in the Church of the Brethren. 1570
Call to action. 829, 990, 1137
Call to advance. 2453, 2496
Call to adventure. 3222
Call to America to build Zion. 546, 1755, 2119
Call to Catholic action. 870
Call to Christian action. 1134
Call to Christian character. 2846
... The call to Christian perfection. 2818
Call to Christian stewardship. 3528
Call to Christians. 966
Call to commitment. 3797
Call to commitment in the school of St. Francis. 1648
Call to contemporary discipleship. 1015
Call to conversion. 1360, 1554
Call to courage. 1776
Call to discipleship. 987
Call to glory. 2037, 2946
Call to holiness. 1823
Call to integration. 2571
Call to Istanbul. 653, 2306
Call to laymen. 1790, 2192
Call to mission. 2494
Call to parents, and children. 955
Call to praise. 3561
Call to prayer. 2880, 3347
Call to prophetic service. 2949
Call to reflection. 2398
Call to remember. 1273, 2669
Call to seriousness. 1551
Call to service. 2292
Call to the country. 2526
Call to the heights. 3685
Call to the laity. 754
Call to the nations. 129
Call to the sacred office. 1290
Call to the streets. 1261
Call to the unconverted. 1357
Call to the unconverted to turn and live. 1358
Call to the unfaithful professors of truth. 1651
Call to total consecration. 2569
Call to unity. 3095
Call to virginity? 3781
Call to what is vital. 1095
Call to witness. 3828
Call to worship. 2234
Call to youth. 3888
Callaway Baptist preachers. 726
Called and chosen. 1930, 2829
Called & committed. 989·
Called by Christ to heal. 2168
Called, in honor. 3675
Called of God. 1288, 2577
Called to action. 1733
Called to be Christian. 3187
Called to be free. 982, 1659
Called to be friends. 1688
Called to be saints. 2932
Called to be sent. 2403
Called to care. 1006
Called to Cathay. 2509

Called to freedom. 1659
Called to heal. 1460, 3476
Called to holy worldliness. 2191
Called to maturity. 955
Called to minister. 3378, 3734
Called to serve. 1295
Called to service. 999
Called to teach. 870, 3158
Called to the colors. 2536
Called unto holiness. 1237
Called unto liberty. 2375
Calling. 3786
Calling all Christians. 2215
Calling life's signals. 1800
Calling men for the ministry. 1295
Calling of a diocesan priest. 773
Calling on eternity. 1533
Calling program of the local church. 1250
Calling youth to Christ. 1557
Callings! 3784
Callipaedia. 1541
Calls and vacancies. 2284
Calls of the Conqueror. 1747
Calm delight. 1437
Calm down. 982
Calm of mind. 2467
Calm review of the inaugural address of Prof. Charles A. Briggs. 118, 692
Calmet's Dictionary of the Holy Bible. 242
Calming the mind and discerning the real. 2193
Calvary. 1747
Calvary and community. 2366
Calvary and its victim. 107, 2044
Calvary and the mass. 2058
Calvary attitudes. 2214
Calvary Christ. 1998
Calvary church in action. 2697
Calvary church, Pittsburgh, Pennsylvania. 1273
Calvary church, yesterday and today. 2697
Calvary covers it all. 1563
Calvary in China. 2509
Calvary life insurance. 3295
Calvary; or, The death of Christ. 1997, 2047
Calvary, "quiet talks" 2031
Calvary 's cross. 3339
Calvary selection of spiritual songs for the church and the choir. 1868
Calvary selection of spiritual songs for use in social meetings. 1868
Calvary to-day; the words from the cross to modern men and women. 1999
Calvary to Pentecost. 969
Calvary's cross. 3343
Calvary's wondrous cross. 105
Calvert daily lesson outlines. 814
Calvert handbook of Catholic facts. 814
Calvert School daily lesson outlines. 814
Calvin. 727
Calvin: a life. 728
Calvin and Augustine. 729
Calvin and Calvinism. 728
Calvin and Calvinism: sources of democracy? 728, 1422
Calvin and classical philosophy. 728, 2835
Calvin and English Calvinism to 1649. 727, 730
Calvin and his enemies. 728
Calvin and the Anabaptist Radicals. 36, 727
Calvin and the Italian anti-Trinitarians. 54, 729
Calvin and the reformation. 727
Calvin: commentaries. 221
Calvin memorial addresses. 2913
Calvin on Scripture and divine sovereignty. 277, 729
Calvin; the origins and development of his religious thought. 728
Calvin treasury. 729
Calvin, Twisse and Edwards on the universal salvation of those dying in infancy. 728, 1907
Calvin Wilson Mateer. 2372
Calvinism. 729, 730
Calvinism and evangelical Arminianism. 729
Calvinism and Scholasticism in Vermigli's doctrine of man and grace. 2327, 3777
Calvinism and the Amyraut heresy. 728, 730
Calvinism and the philosophy of nature. 729
Calvinism and the political order. 1142
Calvinism and the religious wars. 727, 730
Calvinism in history. 730
Calvinism: its history and basic principles, its fruits and its future, and its practical application to life. 730
Calvinism versus democracy. 730, 1484
Calvinist preaching and iconoclasm in the Netherlands, 1544-1569. 1294
Calvinist temper in English poetry. 1519

Calvinistic and Socinian systems. 729
Calvinistic and Socinian systems examined and compared. 729
Calvinistic concept of culture. 1394
Calvinistic controversy. 729
Calvin's Calvinism. 729
Calvin's doctrine of man. 728, 2327
Calvin's doctrine of predestination. 355, 729, 2912
Calvin's doctrine of the Christian life. 978
Calvin's doctrine of the knowledge of God. 729
Calvin's doctrine of the last things. 728, 1531
Calvin's doctrine of the Word and sacrament. 729, 3227
Calvin's ethics of war. 728, 3794
Calvin's New Testament commentaries. 351, 727
Cambridge and Saybrook platforms of church discipline. 1335
Cambridge bede book. 1224
Cambridge Bible for schools and colleges. 221
Cambridge Greek Testament for schools and colleges. 342, 343
Cambridge history of the Bible. 289
Cambridge hymnal. 1865
Cambridge movement. 1490
Cambridge platform of church discipline. 1344
Cambridge platform of 1648. 1337
Cambridge Platonists. 731
Cambridge Platonists and their place in religious thought. 731
Cambridge sermons. 1226
Cambridge shorter Bible. 198
Cambro-American pulpit. 3362
Came liberty beyond our hope. 1785
Cameo of Angela. 41
Cameos, being over one thousand practical illustrations. 1843
Cameos from Calvary. 1998
Cameos of prophecy. 1514
Cameos, women fashioned by God. 3831, 3846
Camilla, a biography of Camilla Eyring Kimball. 2171, 2620
Camillus. 731, 2667
Camillus de Lellis. 731
Caminos de renovacion. 3290
Camp fires in the Congo. 897, 2514
Camp meeting manual. 731
Campa cosmology. 732
Campaigners for Christ handbook. 786
Campaigning for Christ. 786, 958
Campaigning for Christ in Japan. 2535
Campaigning with Christ's church. 2214
Campanile of Florence Cathedral: "Giotto's tower." 1629, 1713
Campbell and the colleges. 732, 3759
Campbellism examined. 1460
Campbellism exposed. 732, 2197
Campbellism is rebellion. 732
Campbellism re-examined. 1461
Campbell's baptismal remission an unscriptural doctrine. 732
Campfire tales from Africa. 2489
Camping for Christian youth. 1164
Camping guideposts. 733
Camping in covenant community. 1164
Campion college sodality manual for the use of members of the sodalities of Our Lady. 3244
Campus aflame; dynamic of student religious revolution. 1308
Campus Christian fellowship. 1620
Campus Christian Witness. 1911
Campus clergyman. 885
Campus evangelism in theory and practice. 1553
Campus gods on trial. 3757
Campus ministry. 1127
Campus prayers for the '70s. 3756
Campus reports. 831
Can a man be a Christian to-day? 3079
Can a religious democracy survive? 1141
Can America survive??? 3744
Can an evolutionist be a Christian? 1581
Can Catholic schools survive? 870
Can Christ help me? 2059
Can Christ save society? 3442
Can Christianity save civilization? 1281
Can Christianity survive? 1065
Can Christians be educated? 935
Can Christians fight? 3792
Can Christians learn from other religions? 1079
Can Christians preserve peace? 2806
Can church & industry unite? 1130
Can ethics be Christian? 943
Can faith survive? 2142
Can God--? 1569
Can God be trusted? 1724
Can I believe in God the Father? 1720
Can I believe in miracles? 434, 2017
Can I forgive God? 1633

Can I help it if they don't learn? 940
Can I know God? 2425, 2437
Can I know God? and other sermons. 2437
Can I make it one more year? 1298
... Can I teach my child religion? 3158
Can I trust my Bible? 280
Can I trust the Bible? 278
Can man hope to be human? 1153
Can persecution arise in America? 3548
... Can prayer be answered? 2868
Can Protestantism win American? 2956
Can Quakerism speak to the times? 1681
Can Quakerism speak to this generation? 1675
Can religious education be Christian? 3149
Can telepathy explain? 3513
Can the Christian now believe in evolution? 1580
Can the church survive in the changing order? 881
Can the church think again? 3213
... Can the churches unite? 1042
Can the dead communicate with the living? 3503
Can? The living talk with the dead?? 3513
Can these bones live? 24, 1056, 1243
Can we be sure of mortality? 1887
Can we believe? 1098
Can we believe in immortality? 1890
Can we break bread together? 1912
Can we expect a world-wide revival? 1560
Can we explain the poltergeist? 1710
Can we find God? the new mysticism. 1725
Can we keep the faith! 1096
Can we repeat the creed? 73
Can we still be Christians? 1711
... Can we still believe in immortality? 1888
Can we trust Bible history? 277
Can we trust the New Testament? 379
Can you help me! Sermons addressed to individuals. 1466
Can you really talk to God? 2871
Can you run away from God? 552
Cana movement in the United States. 2342
... Canaan parish, 1733-1933, being the story of the Congregational church of New Canaan, Connecticut. 2686
Canaanite god Resep. 3219
Canaanite myth and Hebrew epic. 499, 733
Canada. 734
Canada's bishops from 1120 to 1975 ... from Allen to Yelle. 666, 815
Canadian experience of church union. 1043, 3731
Canarian. 1358
Cancer chemotherapy. 1952
Candamaharosana Tantra, chapters I-VIII. 734, 3586
Candid examination of Dr. Mayhew's Observations on the charter and conduct of the Society for the propagation of the gospel in foreign parts. 2375, 3437
Candid examination of the question whether the pope of Rome is the great antichrist of Scripture. 52
Candid examination of theism. 3609
Candid reasons for renouncing the principles of anti-psedobaptism. 1905
Candid reply to the Reverend Doctor Hemmenway's Remarks on a dissertation on the Scriptural qualifications for admission and access to the Christian sacraments. 1803, 3262
Candidates for sainthood. 871, 924
... Candide. 3786
Candide and other philosophical tales. 3786
Candle as a symbol and sacramental in the Catholic church. 734
Candle burns for France. 3285
Candle by night. 170
Candle flames. 961
Candle for the dark. 1448
Candle light stories; eight little tales for Chanuko. 1784
Candle love feast. 1112
Candle of comfort. 3095
Candle of the Lord. 731, 2012, 2607, 2972, 3856
Candle of vision. 1348, 3256
Candlelight kingdom. 2750
Candles in the city. 1466, 3379
Candles in the dark. 1839
Candles in the dark boreen; writings. 3403
Candles in the night. 2395
Candles in the Roman rite. 734
Candles in the sun. 1787, 3683
Candles in the wind. 957
Candles on the glacier. 1446
Cane Ridge meeting-house. 3009
Cannibal island. 2542

Cannibal valley. 2541
Cannon shots for Christ in art and poetry. 2012
Cannot and can fall from grace. 1752
Canon and authority. 515, 3896
Canon and Masorah of the Hebrew Bible. 2364
... Canon and text of the New Testament. 339
Canon law. 735, 736
Canon law, a handbook. 736
Canon law digest. 775
Canon law for religious women. 2581
Canon law governing communities of sisters. 2577
Canon law in mediaeval England. 735, 2304
Canon law of the papal throne. 735
Canon law on civil action in marriage problems. 2341
... The canon law on sermon preaching. 2908
Canon Muratorianus. 339
Canon of history, secular in particular. 1115
Canon of reason and virtue. 2197
Canon of Scripture. 217
Canon of the Mass. 842
Canon of the Mass and liturgical reform. 840
Canon Sheehan. 3401
Canon Sheehan of Doneraile. 3401
Canon text and manuscripts of the New Testament. 321
Canonic sayings of Jesus the Christ chronologically arranged. 320
Canonical and civil status of Catholic parishes in the United States. 2775
... Canonical cause for matrimonial dispensations. 2345
Canonical decisions of the Holy Sea. 775
Canonical elections. 1503
Canonical employer-employee relationship. 1131
Canonical evidence in marriage cases. 2342
...Canonical norms governing the deposition and degradation of clerics. 1290
Canonical obligation of preaching in parish churches. 2908
Canonical procedure in disciplinary and criminal cases of clerics. 779
Canonical procedure in matrimonial cases. 2341
Canonical procedures in matrimonial cases. 2341
Canonical status of priests in the United States. 1290
... The canonical status of the Orientals in the United States. 851
Canonization and authority in the western church. 736
Canonization of Hebrew scripture. 495, 3015
Canonization of the synagogue service. 2110, 2885
Canons and decrees of the Council of Trent. 3710
Canons and decrees of the sacred and oecumenical Council of Trent. 3710
Canons of Dort. 1477, 3043
... The canons of 1571 in English and Latin. 735
Canons of the Council of Sardica, A. D. 343. 3303
Can't help wondering. 2492
Can't you here me calling! 1244
Cantata no. 4. 736
Cantata texts. 737
Cantatas of Johann Sebastian Bach. 123
... "Cantate Domino" 1205
Cantate Domino; a selected collection of sacred songs. 917
... Canterbury. 737
Canterbury administration. 1219
Canterbury cathedral priory. 737
Canterbury pilgrim. 1217, 3633
Canti[c]o espiritual of San Juan de la Cruz. 2136
Canticle for the harvest. 3310
Canticle of canticles. 594
Canticle of creatures. 1642
Canticles of the Christian church. 737
Cantiones bohemicae. 1876
Cantiones et muteti. Lieder und Motetten des Mittalalters. 1877
Cantor: an historic perspective. 737
Cantorial anthology of traditional and modern synagogue music,arr. for cantor and choir with organ acc. 3577
Cantorial art. 883
Cantors at the crossroads. 720, 1204
Caoitular masonic code of the Grand chapter of Ohio, 1914. 1669
Cap and gown. 3758
Capers of the clergy. 2786

Capital funds campaign manual for churches. 1168
Capitalism and the Reformation. 2978
Capitalism and socialism. 3436
Capitalists without capitalism. 1675, 1932
Capitular masonic code of the Grand chapter of Ohio, 1921. 1669
Capsules of wisdom. 1840
Captain Bickel of the Inland Sea. 658, 2534
Captain Ducky & other children's sermons. 3369
Captain of our faith. 3354
Captains of the host. 3386
Captive flames. 924
Captive on the Ho Chi Minh Trail. 2537, 2740
Captive to the Word. 241, 2281
Captives of the Word. 1464
... The captivity and the pastoral epistles. 446
Captivity Epistles. 371
Captivity; 1 Kings 21:9-Malachi. 629
Captured by mystery. 1452
Capturing a community for Christ. 1563
Capturing a town for Christ. 1574, 3697
Capuchin century book. 738
Capuchins; a contribution to the history of the Counter-Reformation. 737, 1374
... The Capuchins in French Louisiana. 738
Capuchins in French Louisiana (1722-1766) 738, 822
Carcich at 7:30. 3349, 3387
Cardijn story. 739, 3869
Cardinal Archbishop of Westminster. 2328
Cardinal Bainbridge in the court of Rome. 130
Cardinal characters in the New Testament. 338
Cardinal Consalvi and Anglo-papal relations, 1814-1824. 860, 1347
Cardinal Contarini at Regensburg. 1355, 3024
Cardinal Cushing of Boston. 1397
Cardinal from Oxford. 2705
Cardinal Gasquet, a memoir. 1703
Cardinal Gibbons. 1711
Cardinal Hayes. 3821
Cardinal Hayes, one of ourselves. 1792
Cardinal ideas of Isaiah. 543
Cardinal ideas of Jeremiah. 546
Cardinal in armor. 3236
Cardinal Lavigerie and the African slave trade. 2200, 2498, 3423
... Cardinal Lavigerie, primate of Africa. 2200
Cardinal Lorenzo Campeggio, legate to the courts of Henry viii and Charles v. 733
Cardinal Manning. 1881, 2328
Cardinal Manning, his life and labours. 2328
Cardinal Mercier. 2411, 3532
Cardinal Mindszenty. 2474
Cardinal Moran and the A.L.P. 2190, 2594
Cardinal Newman. 738, 2703
Cardinal Newman and William Froude, F.R.S. 790
Cardinal Newman in his age. 2705
Cardinal Newman's best plain sermons. 1227
Cardinal Newman's Dream of Gerontius. 1021
Cardinal O'Connell. 2734
Cardinal O'Connell of Boston. 2734
Cardinal of charities. 1792
Cardinal of Lorraine and the Council of Trent; a study in the counter-reformation, by H. Outram Evennett. 2260, 3710
Cardinal of Spain; the life and strange career of Alberoni. 22
Cardinal protectors of England. 860, 1763
Cardinal Quiroga. 3013
Cardinal Richelieu and the development of absolutism. 3236
Cardinal said no! St. John Fisher. 2125
Cardinal Spellman story. 3471
Cardinal Spellman, the man. 3471
Cardinal Stritch story. 3535
Cardinal truths. 162
Cardinal truths of the Gospel. 3199
Cardinal Wiseman. 3822
Cardinals of faith. 1593
Cardinal's story. 2474
Cardiphonia. 1793, 2705
Cards--Bible--church--religion. 3092
Care and counseling of the aging. 1257
Care and counseling of youth in the Church. 1257
Care and education for exceptional children in Tennessee. 896
Care and feeding of ministers. 1303
Care and feeding of volunteers. 1251

Care and maintenance for the Christain life. 992
Care for God's fruit trees. 1557
Care for God's fruit-trees, and other messages. 1557
Care for the dying. 2782
Care of all the churches. 2959
Care of the earth. 3758
Care of the earth, and other university sermons. 3758
Career and significance of Jesus. 1962
Career development for priests and religious. 3785
Career of a cobbler. 739
Career of Jesus Christ. 2019
Career of John Cotton. 1372
Career of religious ideas. 1656
Career of the Christ-idea in history. 2009
Career of the God-idea in history. 1728
Career of the reformer IV. 2273
Career of the Right Reverend John Lancaster Spalding, bishop of Peoria, as president of the Irish Catholic colonization association of the United States, 1879-1892. 1920
Career opportunities in religion. 1253
Career women of the Bible. 3841
Careers for you. 3784
Careers in Jewish communal service. 2084
Careers in religious journalism. 2135
Careers of service in the church. 1252
Careful and strict enquiry into the modern prevailing notions of that freedom of will, which is supposed to be essential to moral agency, virtue and vice, reward and punishment, praise and blame. 1657
Careful and strict examination of the external covenant. 1376, 2373
Careful and strict inquiry into the modern prevailing notions of that freedom of will, which is supposed to be essential to moral agency, virtue and vice, reward and punishment, praise and blame. 1657
Carey memorial lectures. 3619
Caribbean Quakers. 1678
Caribbean quest. 2507
Caricatures & Christians. 998
Carillon. 2394
Caring. 2265, 3576
Caring enough to confront. 1006
Caring God. 2981
Caring in crisis. 649, 988
Caring Jesus. 420, 2011
Carl Heath Kopf. 2183
... Carlisle. 1016
Carlos and the green car. 2545
Carlotina and the Sanfedesti. 1945
Carlstadt's ordinaciones and Luther's liberty. 2165, 3041
Carlyle B. Haynes speaks to young ministers. 1288
Carlyle Marney, a pilgrim's progress. 145, 2336
Carlyle's fusion of poetry, history, and religion by 1834. 740
Carmarthen Road United Reformed Church, Swansea, 1876-1976. 740
Carmel. 111, 740, 1363
Carmel in America. 741
Carmel in England. 741
Carmelite devotions and prayers for special feasts of the liturgical year. 741
Carmelite Monastery of Cristo Rey. 740
Carmel's call. 741
Carmen Christi. 449
Carmina coeli. 3206
Carmina for social worship. 3853
Carmina for the Sunday school. 3854
Carmina Mariana. 2362
Carmita of Cuba. 2515
Carnal mind. 3138
Carnival of souls. 1259
... Carol junior choir book with optional descants. 3723
Carol to a child. 2634
Carolina Quakers; our heritage, our hope. 1687
Carols of today. 917
Carols old and carols new. 741
Carols; their origin, music, and connection with mystery-plays. 742
Carpenter. 2132
Carpenter and His kingdom. 1967
Carpenter and the rich man. 2027
Carpenter at prayer. 2246
Carpenter of Nazareth. 397, 1970, 1975
Carpenter prophet. 1970
Carpenter's method of preaching. 2899
Carpenter's Son. 165, 2060
Carrie F. Butler Thwing. 3698
Carrie; or, The child of the parsonage. 3533
Carry a little honey, and other addresses. 2425
Carry on. 169, 965
Carrying the Christian message. 953

Carta enciclica Mater et magistra [por] S.S. Juan XXIII. 1135
Cartaphilus. 2465
Carthusian order in England. 742
Carthusians. 742
Cartoons of the eternal compassion. 1072
Cartoons that live. 1010
Cartulary of Cirencester Abbey. 743
Cartulary of Creake Abbey. 1379
Cartulary of Dale Abbey. 743
Carving out a kingdom. 171, 740
Casanova's book of numbers and the daily horoscope. 98
Case against dogma. 1473
Case against modernism. 2563
Case against modernism in foregin missions. 2714
Case against Mormonism. 2606, 2613
Case against neo-orthodoxy. 2683
Case against original sin. 3410, 3413
Case against siritualism. 3515
Case against the church. 1092
Case against the Federal Council of Churches. 1619
Case against the National Council of Churches. 2670
Case against the pagans. 68
Case against the social gospel. 2563
Case against the World Council of Churches. 3850
Case and comment. 1448
Case as it is. 2754, 3010
Case book of the unknown. 2727
Case book on Christian responsibility for freedom. 1658
Case conference problems in group guidance. 2592
Case for a new reformation theology. 2683
Case for an afterlife. 3494
Case for an auxiliary priesthood. 772, 1289
Case for and against psychical belief. 2990, 2992
Case for astral projection. 2990
Case for astrology. 97
Case for believing. 2387
Case for biblical Christianity. 3632
Case for Calvinism. 730
Case for Christianity. 1068, 1070
Case for creation. 1380
Case for divine healing. 1600
Case for due process in the church. 2721
Case for episcopacy. 1523
Case for evangelical modernism. 3661
Case for exorcism. 1585
Case for freedom. 783, 1659
Case for immortality. 1697
Case for liberal Christianity. 2221
Case for liberal religion. 2221
Case for life after death. 2990
Case for orthodox theology. 1093
Case for pastoral clinical training. 1372, 2783
Case for religious naturalism. 3057
Case for spirit photography. 3500
Case for spiritual healing. 2409
Case for the chosen people. 2140
Case for the Jews. 2118
Case for the resurrection of Jesus Christ. 2053
Case for theology in liberal perspective. 3642
Case histories from the files of Dr. Luke. 430
Case histories of tentmakers. 1297, 2962
Case method in pastoral and lay education. 2791
Case of a middle class Christian. 988
Case of Cornelia Connelly. 1346
Case of D. M. Canright. 1403, 1585
Case of John Darrell. 1403, 1585
Case of Patience Worth. 2991, 3859
Case of Rev. Gilbert P. Williams in the ecclesiasical court of the Diocese of Washington. 1488
Case of Satan's fiery darts in blasphemous suggestions and hellish annoyances. 3303
Case of the Book of Mormon witnesses. 680
Case of the dissenting ministers. 1468
Case of the door-openers vs. the fence-builders. 694
Case of the General assembly of the Presbyterian church in the United States of America. 2919
Case of the Rev. E. B. Fairfield. 1588
Case of Therese Neumann. 2685, 3531
Case studies bearing upon survival. 3516
Case studies for teachers of religion. 3160
Case studies in Christ and salvation. 2009, 3294
Case studies in classroom teaching. 3166
Case studies in spirit possession. 3472

TITLE INDEX CATECHISM OF THE

Case studies in the campus ministry. 1257, 3400
Case studies of present-day religious teaching. 3151
Case work evangelism. 1572
Case work in preaching. 2905
Casebook: Exorcism and possession. 1423
Casebook for Christian living. 1010
Casebook in pastoral counseling. 2780
Casebook of military mystery. 1709
Casebook of witchcraft. 3825
Casebook on church and society. 3679
Cases in the Muhammadan law of India and Pakistan. 1926
Cases of conscience. 1469, 1508
Cases of conscience for English-speaking countries. 744
Cases of the reincarnation type. 3055
Cases on church and state in the United States. 1152
Casino of Pius IV. 3536, 3768
Caspar Schwenckfeld von Ossig (1489-1561) spiritual interpreter of Christianity, apostle of the middle way, pioneer in modern religious thought. 3312
Cassadaga. 3520
Cassell's Dore gallery. 84
Cassell's illustrated Bible: containing the Old and New Testaments, with references, numerous critical and explanatory notes, and a condensed concordance. Illustrated with more than 900 highly finished engravings. 197
Cassian and the Fathers. 2412
Cassiodori Senatoris Institutiones. 3668
Cassiodorus. 744, 928
Cast off the shadow. 958
Castaneda's The teachings of Don Juan, A separate reality & Journey to Ixtlan. 744, 3862
Castaneda's the teachings of Don Juan, a separate reality, & journey to Ixtlan notes. 744
Castaway. 165
Casting out anger. 3580
Casting the net. 1564
Castings from the Foundry mold. 3797
Castle of Zion. 633
Castle of Zion-- Hawaii. 2524
Castle on the hill. 1622
Castles and churches of the crusading kingdom. 744
Castles in the air. 2931
Casuist. 744
Cat in the musteries of religion and magic. 876
Cat in the mysteries of religion and magic. 876
Catacombs. 85
Catacombs and the Colosseum. 3246
Catacombs of Rome. 745
Catacombs of Rome and their testimony relative to primitive Christianity. 745
Catacombs of Rome as illustrating the church of the first three centuries. 745
Catalog. 3166
Catalog of authors, subjects and titles in the Catholic union of the city of Albany circulating library, together with list of newspapers, magazines and works of reference. 868
Catalog of Bible entries represented by Library of Congress printed cards issued to July 31, 1942. 212
Catalog of capital needs. 1465
Catalog of Catholic paperback books. 868, 869
Catalog of Concordia publishing house [1931-1932]. 2282
Catalog of missionary literature, June 1922. 2504
Catalog of the art and design of utopian and religious communities in the index of American Design. 84
Catalog of the Emma B. King Library of the Shaker Museum. 3397
Catalog of the Foster Stearns Collection on the Sovereign Military Order of St. John of Jerusalem, called, of Malta. 2179
Catalog of the Lititz Congregation collection. 1208
Catalog of the Salem congregation music. 1208
Cataloging, processing, administering AV materials. 2225
Catalogue. 2587, 2927, 2965, 3333, 3627, 3681
Catalogue, Announcements. 3681
Catalogue de la Bibliotheque de l'Ecole biblique et archeologique francaise. 239, 1944, 2148
Catalogue of a collection of books. 657
... Catalogue of a collection of works on ritualism and doctrinal theology. 3653
...Catalogue of all Catholic books in English. 869
... Catalogue of an exhibition held in the Day missions library. 1344
... Catalogue of an exhibition illustrating some phases of popular religious education before 1800. 748
... Catalogue of an exhibition illustrative of the history of literature. 868
Catalogue of an exhibition of books, portraits, and facsimiles illustrating the history of the English translation of the Bible. 272
Catalogue of author sins. 3411
Catalogue of books. 869, 3627
Catalogue of books & manuscrips in the Estelle Doheny collection. 658
Catalogue of books & manuscripts in the Estelle Doheny collection. 658
Catalogue of books belonging to the library of the theological seminary of the diocese of Ohio, Kenyon college and the preparatory schools. MDCCCXXXVII. 3681
Catalogue of books chiefly relating to English and American history and antiquities together with a collection of historical, ecclesiastical, and political tracts (from 1624) 1763
Catalogue of books contained in the library of the American Bible society. 212, 213
Catalogue of books in the library of the Presbyterian historical society. 2921
...Catalogue of books in the library of the Sunday-school of the Church of the holy communion. 3549
Catalogue of books in the Sunday school library of the First Baptist church, Groton, Mass. 2953
Catalogue of books, library Railroad Young men's Christian association, Mexico city, Mexico. 3875
Catalogue of books of the Parish library. 2953
Catalogue of books relating to, or illustrating the history of the Unitas fratrum, or United brethren. 2595
Catalogue of Catholic and other select authors in the Enoch Pratt free library, Baltimore, Md., comp. 869
Catalogue of Catholic and other select authors in the Public library of the District of Columbia. 868
Catalogue of Catholic books in Milwaukee public library. 869
Catalogue of Catholic literature. 868
Catalogue of Church ornaments. 1169
... Catalogue of church ornaments, statues, vestments, material for vestments, and regalia. 1169
Catalogue of doctoral dissertations. 3619
Catalogue of East Asiatic books on religion, history, literature and arts. 914
Catalogue of editions of the Holy Scriptures in various languages. 212
Catalogue of Friends' historical library of Swarthmore college, Swarthmore, Pa. 1893. 1677
Catalogue of manuscripts in Lambeth Palace Library. 3090
Catalogue of misericords in Great Britain. 915
Catalogue of music by American Moravians, 1742-1842. 1208
Catalogue of resources. 1132
Catalogue of selected editions of the Book of common prayer both English and American. 2884
Catalogue of short plays for schools, clubs, churches, and other community groups. 1478
Catalogue of the American philosophical society library. 745
Catalogue of the books and manuscripts in the library of the Baptist historical society. 143
Catalogue of the books and maps belonging to the library of the Board of foreign missions of the Presbyterian church. 2522
Catalogue of the books, pamphlets, and manuscripts belonging to the Huguenot society of America. 1851
... Catalogue of the Buddhist Sanskrit manuscripts in the University library, Cambridge. 2331
Catalogue of the Byzantine and early mediaeval antiquities in the Dumbarton Oaks collection. 87
Catalogue of the Christian hall library of Chestnut Hill. 2224
Catalogue of the entire library of the late Rev. Samuel Farmar Jarvis ... of Middletown, Connecticut. 3627
... Catalogue of the entire private library of the late Rev. Rufus W. Griswold. 2224
... Catalogue of the Foreign mission library of the Divinity school of Yale university, New Haven, Conn. 2522
Catalogue of the General theological library, Boston, Massachusetts. 3626
Catalogue of the Greek manuscripts on Mt. Athos. 2330
Catalogue of the Hindustani manuscripts in the library of the India office. 2331
Catalogue of the Jackson Collection of manuscript fragments in the Royal Library Windsor Castle. 849, 3668
Catalogue of the Jewish Braille Library. 2075
Catalogue of the Lake library. 869
Catalogue of the library belonging to the theological institution in Andover. 3626
Catalogue of the library belonging to the Union theological seminary in Prince Edward, Va. 3627
Catalogue of the library of All Soul's Sunday school, Washington, D.C. 3549
Catalogue of the library of Princeton theological seminary. 3627
Catalogue of the library of Rev. Thomas Prince. 2687
Catalogue of the library of the American Bible union. 212
Catalogue of the library of the late Bishop John Fletcher. 29
Catalogue of the ... library of the late George Livermore. 212
Catalogue of the library of the late Rabbi Emanuel Eckstein of Cleveland. 1798
Catalogue of the library of the late Rev. E. H. Chapin, D. D., of New York. 2953
Catalogue of the library of the late Rev. J. S. Buckminster. 3626
Catalogue of the library of the late Rev. Joseph M. Finotti. 869
Catalogue of the library of the Meadville theological school. 3681
Catalogue of the Library of the Society for Psychical Research, London, England. 2992, 3437
Catalogue of the library of the Theol. seminary in Andover, Mass. 40, 3627
Catalogue of the Lutheran historical society's collection of books, pamphlets, photographs, etc. deposited in the theological seminary at Gettysburg, Pa. 2283
... Catalogue of the McAlpin collection of British history and theology. 3627
Catalogue of the manuscripts in the Hebrew character collected and bequeathed to Trinity college library by the late William Aldis Wright. 2331
... Catalogue of the Married men's sodality library. 934
Catalogue of the officers and students of the Theological seminary of the Presbyterian church at Princeton, N. J. 3682
Catalogue of the officers, faculty, and students of St. Vincent college and seminary. 3331
Catalogue of the Phaenogamous and filicoid plants of Newcastle county, Delaware. 685
[Catalogue of the Poe collection of Robert B. Kegerreis. 2855, 2978
Catalogue of the printed books and of the Semitic and Jewish mss. in the Mary Frere Hebrew library at Girton College, Cambridge, by Herbert Loewe. 2076
Catalogue of the South Congregational Sunday school library. 3549
Catalogus of the Southern Baptist theological seminary. 3331
Catalogue of the Talfourd P. Linn collection of Cervantes materials on deposit in the Ohio State University Libraries. 879
... Catalogue of the theological library. 3626
Catalogue of the Tibetan collection and other Lamaist articles in the Newark Museum. 2193
... Catalogue of the valuable theological, scientific and miscellaneous library of the late Rev. Dr. William Rudder, of St. Stephen's church, Philadelphia. 3682
... Catalogue of vestments, banners and regalia. 1250
Catalogue of works in refutation of Methodism. 2422
Catalogue or bibliography of the Library of the Huguenot Society of America. 1851
Catalogue provinciae Californiae Societatis Jesu. 1948
Catalogus translationum et commentariorum: mediaeval and Renaissance Latin translations and commentaries. 1286
Catalpa bow. 3400
Catalyst. 47, 930
Catastrophe of the Presbyterian church, in 1837. 2925
Catch a red leaf. 2386
Catch the bright dawn. 3379, 3883
Catch the little foxes that spoil the vine. 994
Catch the new wind. 3004
Catch the spirit of hope. 988
Catch us those little foxes. 740
Catching men. 1563
Catching the rainbow. 1259
Catching up on catechetics. 3157
Catching up with the Church. 796, 3772
Catching up with the church: Catholic faith and practice today. 796
Catechesis of revelation. 3227
Catechesis, realities and visions. 939
Catechetical documents of Pope Pius X. 745, 2851
Catechetical evangelization. 745, 2279
Catechetical exercises upon the testimony of the Associate church. 745
Catechetical experience. 3175
Catechetical helps. 1328, 2279
Catechetical instructions of St. Thomas Aquinas. 746
Catechetical instructor. 145
Catechetical lectures. 745
Catechetical lectures, with a rev. translation, introd., notes and indices. 3635
Catechetical methods. 745
Catechetical oration of Gregory of Nyssa. 747, 3644
Catechetical preparations. 747
Catechetical question book. 439
Catechetical sermon-aids. 1842
Catechetical stories for children. 1840
Catechetics and prejudice. 859, 2912
Catechetics for the future. 936
Catechetics in context. 3154
Catechetics in the New Testament. 745, 2061
...Catechism. 767, 1215, 2848
Catechism and confession of faith. 747, 1678
Catechism based on the Bible and Luther's Small catechism. 2284
Catechism comes to life. 745
Catechism explained. 746, 748, 767
Catechism for adults. 747, 748, 767
Catechism for divorced catholics. 1471, 1472
Catechism for non-Catholics. 748
Catechism for the Catholic parochial schools of the United States. 748, 769
Catechism for the Catholic parochial schools ot [!] the United States. 747
Catechism for theologians. 3660
Catechism for youth. 2921
Catechism in Christian worship. 3854
Catechism in stories. 132
Catechism lessons on vocation. 747, 3786
Catechism made easy. 767
Catechism of Catholic education. 806
Catechism of Catholic social teaching. 3449
Catechism of Catholic teaching. 748
... A catechism of Christian doctrine. 747, 767, 768, 769
Catechism of Christian doctrine as taught in the United evangelical church. 3732
... Catechism of Christian doctrine, no. 1-4. 768
Catechism of Christian doctrine, no. 3. 768
... Catechism of Christian doctrine, no. 4 Revised according to the code of 1918. 768
Catechism of general information about the Bible. 748
Catechism of Gregorian chant. 883
Catechism of health. 1859
Catechism of Hindu dharma. 1814
Catechism of life. 1059
Catechism of modern man. 783, 3182
Catechism of mottos of unity, peace, love and good will. 747
Catechism of mythology. 2651
Catechism of natural theology. 2673
Catechism of perseverance. 767
Catechism of Rodez explained in form of sermons. 770
Catechism of Scripture history. 218
Catechism of the Armenian Apostolic Holy Church. 82
Catechism of the Bible. 562
Catechism of the Blessed Virgin Mary for use in parochial schools and academies. 769
Catechism of the Catholic religion. 769, 915
Catechism of the Catholic religion for Catholic schools and Catholic homes. 748, 770
Catechism of the Christian doctrine. 747
Catechism of the Council of Trent for parish priests. 768
Catechism of the Eastern orthodox church. 2745

Catechism of the Eastern Orthodox Church; a Sunday school primer. 2745
Catechism of the religious profession. 2578
Catechism of the steam plant. 748
Catechism of the "Summa theologica" of Saint Thomas Aquinas. 3696
Catechism of the Third order of St. Francis. 1649
Catechism of the vows. 3787
Catechism of the vows for the use of religious. 3787
Catechism of Thomas Becon. 1217
Catechism of Vatican II. 770
Catechism on church government. 2456
Catechism on the religious state in conformity with the Code of canon law. 2570
Catechism stories. 1840
Catechism theology. 748
Catechism today. 1215, 2962
Catechisme. 1215
Catechisms of the Wesleyan Methodists. 2427
Catechist and the catechumen. 748
Catechist as minister. 748
Catechist formation book. 941
Catechist's handbook. 748
Catechist's manual. 745, 748
Catechist's manual for first communicants. 1627
Catechumen's counselor for the edification of baptized members of the Reformed church. 3043
Categorical imperative. 2163
Categorical imperatives of the Christian faith. 1051
...The categories of being in Aristotle and St. Thomas. 81, 2739
Catharine and Craufurd Tait, wife and son of Archibald Campbell, archbishop of Canterbury. 3580
Catharine of Siena, an ancient lay preacher. 749
Cathars and reincarnation. 3055
Cathechism of the religious profession. 2578
Catecism in stories. 132
Cathedral. 750, 1282, 3298
Cathedral and crusade. 1185, 1186
Cathedral builders. 79, 750, 753, 1312
Cathedral builders in England. 751
... The cathedral church of England. 751
... The cathedral church of Hereford. 1804
Cathedral church of Saint John the Divine. 750
Cathedral Church of Saint Luke, Portland, Maine. 2864
Cathedral churches of England. 751
Cathedral churches of England, their architecture, history and antiquities, with bibliography, itinerary & glossary. 751
Cathedral craftsman - past and present. 1199, 2230
Cathedral daily missal. 2883
Cathedral France. 752
Cathedral in the nation's capital, a pictorial. 750
Cathedral of Christian truth. 471
Cathedral of Granada. 1755
Cathedral of Mary Our Queen. 132
Cathedral of Palermo. 2760
Cathedral of the Royal City of the Holy Faith of Saint Francis. 3302
Cathedral of the soul as horoscope perspectives. 97
Cathedral on California Street. 3298
Cathedral paragraph Psalter. 2985
Cathedral pilgrimage. 1516
Cathedral prayer book. 2883
Cathedral records from the beginning of Catholicity in Baltimore to the present time. 132
Cathedral series. 3765
Cathedral sermons. 3357
Cathedral: the story of its construction. 750
La cathedrale de Bourges. 686
Cathedrals. 750, 752, 753
Cathedrals, abbeys, and churches of England and Wales. 751
Cathedrals and abbey churches of the Rhine. 1161
Cathedrals and abbeys of Great Britain and Ireland. 753
Cathedrals and churches of Italy. 1160
Cathedrals and churches of northern Italy. 1160
Cathedrals and churches of Rome and southern Italy. 753
Cathedrals and churches of the Rhine and north Germany. 752
Cathedrals and cloisters of midland France. 752
Cathedrals and cloisters of northern France. 752

Cathedrals and cloisters of the Isle de France. 752
Cathedrals and cloisters of the south of France. 752
Cathedrals and monasteries of Spain. 753
Cathedrals' crusade. 752
Cathedrals in Britain and Ireland. 752
Cathedrals in the wilderness. 1628
Cathedrals of Britain. 752
Cathedrals of central Italy. 753
Cathedrals of England. 751
Cathedrals of England and Wales. 751
Cathedrals of Europe. 750
Cathedrals of France. 752
Cathedrals of Great Britain. 752
Cathedrals of Italy. 753
Cathedrals of northern Spain. 753
Cathedrals of southern France. 752
Cathedrals of southern Spain. 753
Cathedrals of Spain. 753
Cathedrals of the Church of Ireland. 1269
Cathedrals of the Old world. 750
Catherine. 749
Catherine Marshall's Story Bible. 622
Catherine of Siena. 749
Catherine Winkworth. 1874, 3820
Catholc teachers's companion. 805
...Catholic action. 753, 754
Catholic action and politics. 814
Catholic action and the laity. 753
Catholic action and the parish. 754
Catholic action handbook. 754
Catholic Action in Italy. 121, 754
Catholic action in practice. 754
Catholic activism and the industrial worker. 1131
Catholic adult education. 829
Catholic Albany. 813
Catholic almanac. 26
Catholic America. 826, 874
Catholic American. 782
Catholic and his church. 967
Catholic and Manichaean ways of life. 2327
Catholic and Manichaen ways of life. 2327
Catholic and Protestant. 2959
Catholic and Protestant countries compared in civilization, popular happiness, general intelligence, and morality. 793
Catholic and Protestant elements in Christianity. 1052
Catholic and Reformed. 3048, 3632
Catholic & Jewish approach to sex & their relative influence upon the cultural character of our society. 3389
Catholic anthology. 755, 868
... Catholic apologetical literature in the United States. 827
Catholic apologetical literature in the United States (1784-1858) 827, 869
Catholic apostolic church, sometimes called Irvingite. 754
Catholic approach to Protestantism. 1492
Catholic approaches to modern dilemmas and eternal truths. 760
Catholic art and culture. 1394
Catholic as citizen. 1085, 3449
Catholic at war. 3792
Catholic authors. 754, 755, 1822
Catholic authors of the past and present. 32
Catholic avant-garde. 817, 3449
Catholic baby book. 138
Catholic beginnings in Kansas City, Missouri. 873
Catholic belief and practice. 871
Catholic belief and practice in an ecumenical age. 785, 1044
Catholic Bible in pictures. 602
Catholic Bible play book. 644
Catholic Bible stories from the Old and New Testaments. 615
Catholic Bible symbols. 638
Catholic Biblical encyclopedia. 242, 352
Catholic Bicentennial profiles. 829, 3737
Catholic bishops and archbishops of America. 665
Catholic book of marriage. 2343
Catholic booklist 1960 (The) 868
Catholic booklist (The) 868
Catholic bookman's guide. 868
... The Catholic boy-choir manual. 1205
Catholic builders of the nation. 826
Catholic campus. 832
Catholic case against segregation. 3329
... Catholic catechism. 767, 768, 787, 3181, 3186, 3628
Catholic catechism 1. 768
Catholic catechism, drawn up. 769
Catholic catechism for the parochial and Sunday schools of the United States. 769
Catholic catechism 2. 768
Catholic centenary, 1808-1908. 3244
Catholic center, an abridgement. 793

Catholic Central Union. 755
Catholic centre. 757, 793
Catholic charismatics: are they for real? 2815
Catholic charities in the United States. 829
Catholic child's Bible. 624
Catholic child's book of prayers. 899
Catholic child's missal and prayerbook. 899
Catholic child's picture dictionary. 779
Catholic child's prayer book. 902
Catholic choirmasters correspondence course. 2634
Catholic choirmaster's diary. 2632
Catholic Christian instructed. 768, 2462
Catholic Christian instructed in the sacraments, sacrifice, ceremonies, and observances of the church. 768, 770, 2462
Catholic Christian instructed in the sacraments, sacrifices, ceremonies and observances of the church. 768, 2462
Catholic Christianity and the modern world. 1060, 1266
Catholic Church. 755, 756, 757, 828, 829
... The Catholic church and adult education. 805
Catholic church and bolshevism. 1131
Catholic church and confession. 1326
Catholic Church and conversion. 1358
Catholic Church and current literature. 755
Catholic Church and freedom. 2343, 3771
Catholic Church and German Americans. 826
Catholic church and healing. 757
Catholic church and history. 780
Catholic church and its reactions with science. 757
Catholic Church and modern Christianity. 790
Catholic Church and Nazi Germany. 818
Catholic church and philosophy. 756
Catholic church and social order. 3450
Catholic Church and social welfare. 1135
Catholic Church and the American idea. 827, 874
Catholic Church and the American poor. 1153
Catholic church and the appeal to reason. 764
Catholic Church and the Bible. 289, 291
Catholic church and the citizen. 1142
Catholic church and the home. 756
Catholic Church and the Knights of Labor. 1131, 2179
Catholic church and the modern mind. 789
Catholic Church and the modern state. 1142
Catholic Church and the Soviet Government, 1939-1949. 860, 1149
Catholic church and the struggle for Zimbabwe. 835, 1152
Catholic Church and you. 795
Catholic church buildings. 1157
Catholic Church, dissent, and nationality in Soviet Lithuania. 822, 2821
Catholic church from within. 756
... Catholic church hymnal. 813
Catholic Church in a changing America. 827
Catholic church in action. 757
Catholic Church in Alaska. 813
Catholic Church in America. 834
Catholic Church in Australia. 814
Catholic church in Chicago, 1673-1871. 815
Catholic church in China from 1860 to 1907. 2512
Catholic church in Clinton County. 822
Catholic church in Connecticut. 816
Catholic church in contemporary Europe, 1919-1931. 817
Catholic Church in Detroit, 1701-1888. 816
Catholic church in Englewood. 823
Catholic Church in Fort Wayne. 817
Catholic Church in Greencastle, Putnam County, Indiana, 1848-1978. 3278
Catholic church in Indiana, 1789-1834. 819
Catholic Church in Japan. 820, 836
Catholic Church in Louisiana. 822
Catholic Church in Lynchburg. 2304
Catholic Church in Maine. 822
Catholic Church in Mississippi. 2669
Catholic Church in Mississippi, 1837-65. 822, 2669
Catholic Church in modern Africa. 2789
Catholic church in New Jersey. 823
Catholic church in New York. 823
Catholic Church in Oregon and the work of its archbishops. 667, 765
... The Catholic church in Paducah, Kentucky. 824

Catholic church in Rhode Island. 824
Catholic church in Russia to-day. 825
Catholic Church in South Africa: from its origins to the present day. 825
Catholic church in the city and diocese of Richmond. 824
Catholic Church in the Diocese of St. Paul. 3277
Catholic church in the meeting of two frontiers. 819
Catholic Church in the meeting of two frontiers: the southern Illinois country (1763-1793) 819
Catholic Church in the modern world. 808, 809
Catholic church in the United States. 833
Catholic church in the United States of America. 826, 866
... The Catholic church in Virginia (1815-1822) 835
Catholic church in Wisconsin. 835
Catholic Church in world affairs. 809
Catholic Church invites you. 859
Catholic Church music. 915
Catholic church of the diocese of Trenton, N. J. 823
Catholic Church of the future. 782
Catholic Church on the Kentucky frontier (1785-1812) 820
Catholic Church on the Nebraska frontier (1854-1885) 822, 873
Catholic Church on the northern Indiana frontier, 1789-1844. 819, 1900
Catholic Church story, changing and changeless. 809, 1174
Catholic church, the mystic body of Christ, animated by the spirit of God, the teacher of the world. 2642
Catholic Church, the mystical body of Christ. 755
Catholic church the true church of the Bible. 756, 796
Catholic Church through the ages. 809, 1175
Catholic Church today: Western Europe. 817
Catholic Church U S A. 828
... Catholic church working through its individual members in any age and nation. 3452
Catholic churchs and institutions. 1162
Catholic college in the world today; some duties of educated Catholics. 805
Catholic colleges and the secular mystique. 870
Catholic colonial Maryland. 873
Catholic commentary on Holy Scripture. 224
Catholic companion to the Bible. 210
Catholic concise dictionary. 778
Catholic concise encyclopedia. 778
Catholic controversy in the New Testament light. 778
Catholic crisis. 1143, 1245, 3772
Catholic cult of the Paraclete. 2814
Catholic curriculum and basic reading instruction in elementary education. 830
Catholic customs and symbols. 920
Catholic devotional life. 3487
Catholic dictionary. 778
Catholic dictionary (A) 778
Catholic dictionary of theology. 3638
Catholic dictionary of theology (A) 3638
Catholic digest Christmas book. 1110
Catholic digest reader. 758
Catholic dimension in higher education. 831
Catholic directory. 766
Catholic directory and telephone guide. 1304
Catholic directory for the dioceses of Savannah-Atlanta. 3305
Catholic doctrine in the Bible. 784
Catholic doctrine of a Trinity. 1847, 3712
Catholic doctrine of a Trinity, proved by above an hundred short and clear arguments, expressed in the terms of the Holy Scripture ... and digested under the four following titles. 1847, 3712
Catholic doctrine of grace. 1751
Catholic doctrine of the Church of England. 1212
Catholic doctrine on justification. 2160
Catholic doctrine on race relations. 3017
Catholic dogma. 3290
Catholic Eastern churches. 851
Catholic ecclesiology. 1158
Catholic education. 820, 830, 832
Catholic education—a new dawn? 832
Catholic education faces its future. 831
Catholic education in a changing world. 832
Catholic education in America. 833
Catholic education in Australia, 1806-1950. 814
Catholic education in New Jersey and the Nation: history, status, and outlook. 823

Catholic education in St. Louis. 825
Catholic education in the Archdiocese of St. Louis: allocation and distribution of human and financial resources. 807
Catholic education in the Western World. 817
Catholic education today and tomorrow. 832
Catholic elementary school principal. 830
Catholic elementary school program for Christian family living. 1607
Catholic emancipation. 816
Catholic emancipation crisis in Ireland, 1823-1829. 867
Catholic emancipation, 1829 to 1929. 816
Catholic encounter with world religions. 850
Catholic encyclopedia. 735, 778
Catholic encyclopedia for school and home. 778, 3638
Catholic encyclopedia for school and home (The) 778
Catholic epistles. 340
Catholic ethics and Protestant ethics. 944
Catholic evidence training outlines. 764
Catholic experience. 833
Catholic faith. 768, 769, 1070, 1591
Catholic faith and modern theologies. 698
Catholic faith and practice. 808, 2964
Catholic faith based on the Catholic catechism as drawn up by His Eminence Peter cardinal Gasparri and. 769
Catholic faith in a process perspective. 3647
Catholic faith in outline. 782
Catholic faith in practice. 787
Catholic faith today. 769
Catholic family. 1603
Catholic family book of novenas. 2716
Catholic family edition of the Holy Bible. 198, 1329
Catholic footprints in California. 815
Catholic gentleman. 1540
Catholic German Bibles of the Reformation era. 656
Catholic girl's guide. 788, 1714
Catholic girl's manual and Sunday missal. 1714
Catholic heritage encyclopedia. 779
Catholic heritage of Saint Louis. 3276
Catholic hierarchy of the United States, 1790-1922. 668
... The Catholic high school curriculum. 831
Catholic high schools and minority students. 867
Catholic higher education in America. 870
Catholic highlights of Europe. 817
Catholic history of Alabama and the Floridas. 814, 826
Catholic home library. 2224
Catholic hymnal. 812
... Catholic hymns. 1862
Catholic immigrant colonization projects in the United States, 1815-1860. 874
Catholic imperialism and world freedom. 794
Catholic in America. 874
Catholic in secular education. 832
Catholic in the modern world. 1000
Catholic Indian missions in Maine (1611-1820) 850, 1899
Catholic influence on American colonial policies, 1898-1904. 828, 3740
Catholic joke book. 34
Catholic journalism in the Midwest. 755
Catholic journey through Ohio. 824
Catholic laity in Elizabethan England. 872
Catholic landmarks in London. 2243
Catholic layman and holiness. 3485
Catholic layman speaks. 759
Catholic layman's book of etiquette. 1167
Catholic left. 826
Catholic Left in Latin America. 1138
Catholic library practice. 2224
... Catholic life and action. 998
Catholic life annual. 866
Catholic life in the West Indies. 835
Catholic life, U.S.A. 828
Catholic literary revival. 869
Catholic liturgics. 840
Catholic liturgy, its fundamental principles. 838
Catholic living in a nutshell. 962
Catholic looks at Billy Graham. 1754
Catholic looks at his world. 3448
Catholic looks at life. 757
Catholic looks at the world. 1136
Catholic loyalism in Elizabethan England. 872
Catholic map directory of the Chicago metropolitan area. 819
Catholic marriage and child care. 2343
Catholic medical missions. 2539
Catholic memoirs of Vermont and New Hampshire. 1849
Catholic mind through fifty years. 758

Catholic ministries in our time. 773, 2789
Catholic missal. 2883
Catholic missions. 849
Catholic missions among the Indian tribes of the United States. 1901
Catholic missions in Canada: 1721. 2545
Catholic missions of north-east Arkansas. 814
Catholic modernists. 2562
Catholic moral theology in dialogue. 947
Catholic movement in the American Episcopal church. 45
Catholic Negro bishops. 875
Catholic Negro education in the United States. 875
Catholic nonsense. 3628
Catholic northwest progress. 826
Catholic origins of Minnesota. 2540
Catholic orthodoxy and Anglo-Catholicism. 1225, 2749
Catholic parent's guide to sex education. 3390
Catholic pattern. 797
Catholic pentecostalism. 2816
Catholic pentecostals. 2815
Catholic periodical index. 852
Catholic picture Bible. 622
Catholic picture dictionary. 852
Catholic pioneers in West Africa. 813
Catholic pioneers of America. 2849
Catholic Pittsburgh's one hundred years. 2849
Catholic Pittsfield and Berkshire. 873
Catholic pocket dictionary and cyclopedia. 778
Catholic policemen's and firemen's companion. 808
Catholic politics. 1145
Catholic politics in China and Korea. 816, 1144
Catholic position in the United States. 1151
Catholic post-secondary education in English-speaking Canada, a history. 870
Catholic power in the Netherlands. 875, 2165
Catholic power today. 794
Catholic practice at church and at home. 770
Catholic prayer book, for every Catholic, for every day. 856
Catholic priest. 775
Catholic priest and the changing structure of pastoral ministry. 773, 2790
Catholic priest in the modern world. 2789
Catholic priesthood. 771, 2939
... Catholic priests distinguished Protestants have known. 771
Catholic primer on the ecumenical movement. 1492
Catholic primer on world peace. 2808
Catholic principles and our political parties. 2858
Catholic principles as illustrated in the doctrine, history, and organization of the American Catholic church in the United States. 2959
Catholic principles of politics. 1143
Catholic principles of social justice. 3449
Catholic- Protestant conflicts in America. 788
Catholic Protestant dialogue. 794
Catholic-Protestant mind. 810
Catholic pulpit. 1266
Catholic quest for Christian unity. 859
Catholic quiz book. 796
Catholic radicals in Brazil. 2627
Catholic reaction in France. 817
Catholic reading. 868
Catholic reading list. 869
Catholic rebels. 2167
Catholic red book of Baltimore-Washington and environs. 132
Catholic red book of western Maryland including Cumberland, Frostburg, Lonaconing, Mt. Savage, Midland, Westenport, Barton. Hagerstown, Hancock, Frederick and Oakland. 2363
Catholic rediscovery of Protestantism. 861, 1044
Catholic Reformation. 1374
Catholic reformation: Savonarola to Ignatius Loyola. 1374
Catholic reformer. 724
Catholic register and official directory of the diocese of Providence. 824
Catholic religion. 45, 782, 789, 871
Catholic religion and the Protestant faith. 1711
Catholic religious orders. 2578
... The Catholic religious vacation school. 3762
Catholic Reporter, The. 3769
Catholic reunion. 1224
Catholic revival in England. 816

Catholic revival in Episcopal Connecticut (1850-1925) Enl. ed. with an index. 2957
Catholic revival in Mexico. 822
Catholic revivalism in the United States, 1830-1900. 833, 2774
Catholic revolution. 811, 1245
Catholic rule of life. 45
Catholic runs for President. 2937, 3426
Catholic school system in the United States. 830
Catholic schools in a declining church. 831
Catholic schools in action. 832
Catholic scripturist. 789
Catholic secondary education. 831
... Catholic secondary education in the diocese of Brooklyn. 823
Catholic secondary school administration. 867
Catholic serials of the nineteenth century in the United States. 852
Catholic shrines in the United States and Canada. 3405
Catholic shrines of Europe. 3405
Catholic social action. 753, 1135
Catholic social doctrine. 2852, 3449
Catholic social Locke. 2852
Catholic social principles. 1135, 3449
Catholic social principles; the social teaching of the Catholic Church applied to American economic life. 1136
Catholic social teaching on liberation themes. 2222
Catholic social theory. 3450
Catholic social thought. 3454
Catholic sociology. 2216, 3453
Catholic soldiers' and sailors' companion. 808
Catholic soldiers by sixty chaplains and many others. 1543
Catholic speaks his mind on America's religious conflict. 828
Catholic spirit. 757
Catholic spirit in America. 828, 1151
Catholic story of Liberia. 2537
Catholic stronghold and its making. 822
Catholic subjects of Elizabeth I. 873, 1508
Catholic Sunday missal. 837
Catholic Sunday missal and simplified prayerbook. 837
Catholic Sunday preaching. 829, 2910
Catholic Sunday school. 3553
Catholic teaching for children. 1498
Catholic teachings. 787
Catholic telegraph almanac and directory. 779
Catholic telephone guide and directory, central and western Pennsylvania. 824
Catholic theology. 132
Catholic theology and the human race. 2554, 3294
Catholic theology in dialogue. 861, 3628
Catholic theology in the nineteenth century. 3628
Catholic theories of Biblical inspiration since 1810. 306
Catholic thought and papal Jewry policy, 1555-1593. 2152, 3569
Catholic thought in crisis. 1062
Catholic thought on contraception through the centuries. 664
... Catholic topics and authors in the Public library of the District of Columbia. 868
Catholic tourist guide. 828
Catholic truth in survey. 3150
Catholic university. 870
Catholic verse for secondary schools. 33
Catholic viewpoint. 3017
Catholic viewpoint on censorship. 879
Catholic viewpoint on church and state. 1143
Catholic viewpoint on education. 831
Catholic viewpoint on marriage and the family. 2340
Catholic viewpoint on race relations. 3017
Catholic vote. 874
Catholic way. 796
Catholic way in education. 830, 831
Catholic way of life. 796
Catholic way of life (an explanation for non-Catholics) 62
Catholic wocekiye wowapi. 855
Catholic women of Tennessee, 1937- 1956. 873
Catholic worship. 770
Catholic writer's magazine market. 852
Catholic year book of New England for 1902. 823
Catholic youth directory. 866
Catholic youth's guide to life and love. 3886
Catholic youth's hymn book. 812
Catholicism. 755, 759, 781, 784, 786, 788, 797
Catholicism against itself. 800
Catholicism; an historical survey. 809

Catholicism and American freedom. 828, 1151
Catholicism and crisis in modern France. 817
Catholicism and criticism. 787
Catholicism and history. 2769, 3768
Catholicism & life. 941
Catholicism and mental deficiency. 762
Catholicism and modernity. 811
Catholicism and political development in Latin America. 821
Catholicism and reason. 763
Catholicism and Roman Catholicism. 871
Catholicism and Scotland. 825
Catholicism & society. 948
Catholicism and the American mind. 827
Catholicism and the Franco regime. 825, 1149
Catholicism and the modern mind. 757
Catholicism and the progress of science. 3084
Catholicism and the world today. 670, 763
Catholicism between Luther and Voltaire. 811
Catholicism, capitalism, or communism. 756
Catholicism charitably exposed. 800
Catholicism, communism and dictatorship. 3450
Catholicism confronts modernity. 799, 2562
Catholicism in America. 826, 875
Catholicism in American culture. 827
Catholicism in England, 1535-1935. 872
Catholicism in English-speaking lands. 818
Catholicism in Japan. 820
... Catholicism in New England to 1788. 823
Catholicism in questions and answers. 804
Catholicism in Rhode Island. 824, 3234
Catholicism, nationalism, and democracy in Argentina. 825
Catholicism on the march, the California missions. 2506, 3376
Catholicism, Protestantism and capitalism. 737
Catholicism: religion of tomorrow? 759
Catholicism, social control, and modernization in Latin America. 821
Catholicism today. 788, 793, 1245
Catholicism U.S.A. 874
Catholicism under the searchlight of the Scriptures. 798
Catholicity. 871
Catholicity and progress in Ireland. 819
Catholicity in Mississippi. 822
Catholicity in Philadelphia from the earliest missionaries down to the present time. 824
Catholicity in Tennessee. 825
Catholicity in the Carolinas and Georgia. 823, 824
Catholicity in the Carolinas and Georgia: leaves of its history. 824
Catholicity of Protestantism. 2976
Catholicity's bar sinister. 1802
Catholics and birth control. 663
Catholics and broken marriage. 2342
Catholics and Canadian socialism. 3436
Catholics and divorce. 1471
Catholics and Jews. 2077
Catholics and Orthodox: can they unite? 861
Catholics and protestants. 792
Catholics and Protestants, separated brothers. 794
Catholics and scholarship. 832
Catholics and the International labor organization. 1913
Catholics and the practice of the faith. 1248
Catholics and the practice of the faith, 1967 and 1971. 873
Catholics and the welfare state. 872
Catholics & unbelievers in eighteenth century France. 872, 3212
Catholics courageous. 764
Catholic's guide to social and political action. 1135
Catholics in America. 874
Catholics in Caroline England. 872
Catholics in Colonial America. 834
Catholics in colonial days. 874
Catholics in colonial law. 834
Catholics in controversy. 1151
Catholics in conversation. 827
Catholics in England, 1559-1829. 872
Catholics in revolution. 1320
Catholics in the early Platte purchase (to 1845) and in Nodaway county (to 1930) 873
Catholics in the promised land of the saints. 875
Catholics in western democracies. 875

Catholics, Jews, and Protestants. 874, 3746
Catholic's manual. 808
Catholics, marriage, and contraception. 664
Catholics, meet the "mike," a radio workbook giving professional guidance to the amateur. 3018
Catholics on campus. 3537
Catholics, peasants, and Chewa resistance in Nyasaland, 1889-1939. 850, 2538
Catholic's pocket prayer-book. 856
Catholic's question box. 770
Catholic's ready answer. 781
Catholic's Ripley's believe it or not! 868
Catholics/U.S.A. 875
Catholic's work in the world. 753
Catholicism in Japan. 820
Cats. 876
Cats and bats and things like that, and other wonderful things about God's world. 2983
Cats and dogs together, and other children's sermons. 907
Caught with my hands full. 1153
Caught with my mouth open. 636
Cauldron of witches. 3826
Cause and cure of infedility. 3422
Cause and cure of infidelity. 3422
Cause and cure of war. 2756
Cause of death. 1939
Cause of God and truth. 1722
Cause of our joy. 2357
Cause of world unrest. 2077
Cause, principle, and unity. 2417
Causes and cure of unbelief. 1099
Causes, evils, and cures, of heart and church divisions. 954, 955
Causes of religious declension. 957
Causes of the clericalization of the order of Friars Minor, 1209-1260 in the light of early Franciscan sources. 1646
Caution. 984
Caution—God at work. 2981
Cautions for the times. 2755
Cavalcade of the supernatural. 3498
Cavalry of Christ on the Rio Grande. 2721
Cave of poison grass. 2867
Cave of riches. 1410, 1411
Cave of the oracle. 2724
Cave temples of Maichishan. 2318
Caves, conversions, and creatures. 3285
Caves of God. 876
Caves to cathedrals. 1270
Cayce, Karma, & reincarnation. 877, 3054
CB for Christians. 1277
CCD methods in modern catechetics for use in leadership courses in the catechetical renewal. 3179
Ceaseless circle. 2931
Cebuano sorcery. 2314
Cedar block. 2005
Cedar of Lebanon. 2649
Celebrant's guide to the new sacramentary. 314, 845, 849, 1262
Celebrant's manual. 2969
Celebrate joy! 991
Celebrate the feasts of the Old Testament in your own home or church. 1611
Celebrate the temporary. 1325
Celebrate while we wait. 9
Celebrate with drama. 2301, 2722
Celebrate with song— every parish can. 1205
Celebrate your existence. 1325
Celebrate your freedom. 381
Celebrate yourself. 734, 1010
Celebrated case. 2590
Celebrating advent. 8
Celebrating family prayer services. 856, 1605
Celebrating joy. 2389
Celebrating mass with children. 905
Celebrating St. Patrick's day. 3277
Celebrating Thanksgiving. 3605
Celebrating the dawn. 2317, 3708
Celebrating the medieval heritage. 3697
Celebrating the saints. 1265
Celebrating your church anniversary. 1155
Celebration. 2394, 2722
Celebration of death. 3333
Celebration of discipline. 3493
Celebration of life. 2225, 2236
Celebration of mass. 2367
Celebration of the Consecration, October, 29, 1960. 3011
Celebration of the Eucharist. 2255
Celebration of the Eucharist facing the people. 2253
Celebration of the fiftieth anniversary of the American Congregational association. 1336
Celebration of the gospel. 2237
Celebration of the Mass. 27

Celebration of the one hundredth anniversary of the birthday of William Ellery Channing. 890
Celebration of the one hundredth anniversary of the church building. 1269
Celebrations for special days and occasions. 1605
Celebrations of life. 2237
Celebrities of our time, interviews. 659
Celestial connection. 2615
Celestial cycle. 2232, 2470
Celestial fire. 1443
Celestial homespun. 1799
Celestial magnet. 3023
Celestial marriage. 2611
Celestial message. 3502
Celestial or plural marriage. 2339
Celestial showers, no. 2. 3563
Celestial symbol interpreted. 1953, 3546
Celestial telegraph. 3473, 3497
Celestial visitors. 41
Celestical phones. 3480
Celibacy. 773, 878
Celibacy and the crisis of faith. 773, 878
Celibacy for our times. 878
Celibacy in the church. 877
Celibacy, ministry, church. 771, 877
Celibacy of the priest. 877
Celibacy of the priest; meaning and basis. 877
Celibacy, prayer, and friendship. 877
Celibacy: the necessary option. 773, 878
Celibate love. 877
Celibate passion. 983
Cell of self-knowledge. 1446, 2644
Celt looks at the world. 878
Celtic and Scandinavian religions. 878
Celtic Britain and the pilgrim movement. 1022
Celtic Christianity. 878
Celtic Christianity of Cornwall. 1369
Celtic church in Britain. 878
Celtic Church in Dunblane. 670, 878
Celtic churches. 878
Celtic Druids. 1480
Celtic Gospels. 398
Celtic invocations. 1873
Celtic monasticism. 1919
Celtic myth and legend. 2655
Celtic myth & legend, poetry & romance. 2655
... Celtic [mythology]. 2655
Celtic mythology and religion. 2655
Celtic mythology and religion, with chapters upon Druid circles and Celtic burial. 2655
Celtic prayers. 2889
Celtic psaltery. 3209
Celtic saints. 878
Cemetery and bible records, in volumes III and IV. 1704
Cemetery records of Stanislaus County, California. 1247
Censorship and freedom of expression in Jewish history. 879
Censorship of the Church of Rome and its influence upon the production and distribution of literature. 2223, 2224
Centenary. 755
Centenary cameos. 2426
Centenary celebration. 3438
Centenary edition, the Pittsburgh Catholic. 2850
Centenary history. 140
Centenary history as related to the Baptist General Conference of America. 140
Centenary Methodist church of St. Louis, the first hundred years, 1839-1939. 3276
Centenary missionary addresses. 2496
Centenary of American Methodism. 2451
Centenary of Catholicity in Kentucky. 873
Centenary of Relief society, 1842-1942. 2609
... Centenary of St. Peter's church. 2721
Centenary of the birth on 8th November 1846 of the Reverend Professor W. Robertson Smith, the University of Aberdeen, 8th November 1946. 3432
Centenary of the see of Boston. 779
Centenary of Wesleyan Methodism. 2424, 2442
Centenary pictorial album, being contributions of the early history of Methodism in the state of Maryland. 2431
Centenary record. 1945
Centenary singer. 3562
Centenary souvenir commemorative of the completion of a century by the First Presbyterian church of Dayton, Ohio. 2918
Centenary survey of the Board of home missions. 2441
Centenary ... the story of a church. 2432
Centenary translation of the New Testament. 353
Centennial. 1701, 3275

Centennial advances for Y.M.C.A. work with boys. 687
Centennial annals of St. Luke's church. 3242
Centennial book, one hundred years of Christian civilization in Hawaii, 1820-1920. 2524
Centennial celebration. 1663
Centennial celebration of the parish of St. Stephen's cathedral. 2774
Centennial celebration of the Theological seminary of the Presbyterian church in the United States of America, at Princeton. 2923
Centennial ceremonies held in Christ church parish, Raleigh, North Carolina, A. D. 1921. 2971
Centennial commemoration. 1547, 2715
Centennial directory of the College of the Bible (Lexington Theological Seminary) 2220
Centennial discourse on the one hundredth anniversary of the First Baptist church, Warren, R.I., November 15, 1864. 3796
Centennial, 1853-1953. 2854
... Centennial encyclopedia of the African Methodist Episcopal church. 2451
Centennial essays for the Milwaukee archdiocese, 1843-1943. 2472
Centennial general catalogue of the trustees, officers, professors and alumni of Union theological seminary in Virginia. 3612
Centennial history. 1848
... Centennial history [1836-]1936 of the Michigan Baptist convention. 155
Centennial history, 1856-1956. 1820
Centennial history, Lincoln Lodge No. 19, Ancient, Free and Accepted Masons, June 25, 1868-June 25, 1968. 1666
Centennial history of Arkansas Methodism. 2457
Centennial history of Camden Methodism. 2450
Centennial history of Hiawatha Lodge 434. 1667
Centennial history of Jerusalem chapter no. 8 of Royal arch masons of New York 1799-1899. 1819
Centennial history of Littleton Fowler Lodge, No. 305 A.F.A.M. 1664
Centennial history of Mountain City Lodge No. 67. 1666
Centennial history of Rahway Methodism. 2424
Centennial history of Saint Bartholomew's church. 2699
Centennial history of Saint Edward Church, Providence, Rhode Island, 1874-1974. 2984, 3273
Centennial history of St. Mary of the Assumption Church, Northampton, Massachusetts, 1866-1966. 2714
Centennial history of St. Paul's Episcopal Church. 890
Centennial history of Salt Springs Lodge No. 520, F. & A. M. 1671
Centennial history of the American Bible society. 31
Centennial history of the archdiocese of Dubuque. 1481
Centennial history of the Associate Reformed Presbyterian church. 2915
... Centennial history of the First Baptist church of Waterville, Maine. 3798
Centennial history of the First Baptist Church, Woodbridge, Virginia, 1876-1976. 1626
Centennial history of the First Congregational United Church, Washington, D. C., 1865-1965. 1818
... Centennial history of the first Methodist Episcopal church of New Bedford, Fairhaven abd Acushnet, Massachusetts. 1818
Centennial history of the first Methodist Episcopal church of New Bedford, Fairhaven and Acushnet, Massachusetts. 1819
Centennial history of the First Presbyterian church and society, Westfield, N. Y. 3808
Centennial history of the Lower Deer Creek Mennonite Church, 1877-1977. 2267
Centennial history of the Mennonites of Illinois. 2406
Centennial history of the Presbyterian church of New Windsor, Maryland, 1839-1939. 2696
Centennial history of the Protestant Episcopal church in the diocese of New York. 2958
Centennial history of the Shadyside Presbyterian Church. 2850

Centennial history of the Steuben Baptist association and of its original churches and pioneer pastors. 3527
Centennial history of the Webb Horton Memorial Presbyterian Church. 2462
Centennial jubilee number April 6, 1830-April 6, 1930 Salt Lake City beobachter. 1230
Centennial memorial. 2232, 3790
... Centennial memorial, English Presbyterian congregation. 1787
Centennial memorial of the First Baptist church of Hart ford, Connecticut, March 23d and 24th, 1890. 1819
Centennial memorial of the First Baptist church of Hartford, Connecticut. 1269
Centennial memorial of the Presbytery of Carlisle. 2936
Centennial 1974. 3778
Centennial of Grace, 1868-1968. 1750
... Centennial of home missions. 2528
Centennial of New England Methodism. 2423
Centennial of the First Reformed Church of Lansing, Illinois. 1243
Centennial of the Grand lodge. 1672
... The centennial of the Grove Reformed church, North Bergen, New Jersey, April twelfth, nineteen forty-three, Rev. Miner Stegenga, D. D., pastor. 1243
Centennial of the New York avenue Presbyterian church, Washington, D.C., 1803-1903. 2913
... Centennial of the Theological seminary of the Reformed church of America. 1422
Centennial of the village church in Chatham, known as the Ogden memorial Presbyterian church, Chatham, New Jersey. 890
Centennial pageant of Auburn theological seminary. 2758
Centennial papers. 1336
Centennial, Pilgrim Baptist Church, 1863-1963. 157
... Centennial register. 2195
Centennial report of education. 816
Centennial sketch of the history of the Presbytery of Chicago. 2927
Centennial story. 2290
Centennial story, 1873-1973. 3274, 3329
Centennial story of Texas Baptists. 141, 170
Centennial story of the Lutheran Church in Texas. 2292
Centennial survey of foreign missions. 2519
Centennial survey of the Episcopal Diocese of Bethlehem, 1871-1971. 2960
Centennial Thanksgiving sermon. 3761
Centennial, the First Evangelical Lutheran Church. 2290
Centennial volume of the First Presbyterian church of Pittsburgh, Pa. 1784-1884. 2913
Center of Christianity. 64
Center-shots at Rome. 871
Center-shots at sin. 1554
Centering moment. 1453
Centering prayer. 1356
Centers of Christian renewal. 2583
Centers on belief. 3142
Centinel, warnings of a revolution. 1222, 1523
Central African diaries of Walter Hutley, 1877 to 1881. 12, 1858
Central certainties. 65
Central Christian Church, Lexington, Kentucky. 2220
Central church treasury. 1168
Central conception of Buddhism. 703
Central idea of Christianity. 1052, 1055
Central message of the New Testament. 334, 477
Central Presbyterian church. 2586, 2687
Central records of the Church of England. 1212, 1243
Central teaching of Jesus Christ. 424
Central themes of American life. 3743
Central truth. 697, 1682, 1893
Centrality and commonality. 1116
Centrality of Christ. 1072, 1442, 2046
Centrality of preaching in the total task of the ministry. 2902
Centrality of the resurrection. 425, 3221
Centre of history. 431
Centurial history of the Mendon association of Congregational ministers. 2403
Centuries. 1453
Centuries ago. 534
Centuries of Nostradamus. 2715
Centuries, poems, and thanksgivings. 1453
Century and a quarter. 2291
Century at St. Bernard's. 3798
Century beckons. 3152

Century closes, the church continues. 1627
Century cyclopedia of history and biography of Pennsylvania. 2813
Century for Cornwall. 1222, 1369
Century in Ceylon. 2507
Century in Eden. 1792
Century in Nigeria. 2542
Century in North DeKalb. 881, 1626
Century in the Madura mission. 2538
Century of American Protestantism, 1846-1946. 2953
Century of Anglican theology. 45
Century of Baptist achievement. 151
Century of Bibles. 292
Century of caring. 2296
Century of Catholicism in western Massachusetts. 822
Century of change. 693
Century of charity. 3438
Century of Christian Science healing. 1030
Century of church history. 1172
Century of Congregationalism in Kansas. 1336
Century of endeavor, 1821-1921. 2695, 2957
Century of faith. 156
Century of faith and service. 1594
Century of God's grace. 892
... A century of gospel-work. 3739
Century of grace. 120, 1369, 1549
Century of growth: the Kachin Baptist Church of Burma. 144
Century of history. 3316
Century of history in the First Baptist Church in Waterbury, Conn. 1819
Century of Jewish life. 2081, 2092
Century of Jewish missions. 2535
Century of Judaism in New York. 2696
Century of life and growth. 110
Century of Lutherans in Ohio. 2291
Century of Masonry in Albany. 1663
Century of miracles. 3387
Century of missionary effort. 1370
Century of missions in the Empire state. 141
Century of Moravian sisters. 2596
Century of "Mormonism" in Great Britain. 2616
Century of Old Testament study. 504
Century of persecution under Tudor and Stuart sovereigns from contemporary records. 816
Century of progress, 1846-1946. 2439
Century of progress being the history of First Baptist Church, Greenville, South Carolina. 1772
Century of Protestant Christianity in Japan. 2954
Century of Protestant theology. 3656
Century of religion at the University of Michigan. 3056
Century of sacrifice. 1370
Century of service. 1426, 3237, 3849
Century of service, 1854-1954. 3874
Century of Unitarianism in the national capital, 1821-1921. 3796
Century of Voltaire study. 3786
Century of witness. 1705
Century of worship, 1872-1972. 1627
Century of worship and work. 862
Century readings in the Bible. 250
Century readings in the New Testament. 355
Century; Salem Lutheran Church. 893
Century with Christ. 1463
Century with Christian women in Virginia. 3837
Century with Iowa Jewry. 2100
Century with Texas Baptists. 170
Century with youth. 3870
Century's change in religion. 1182
Century's changes of outlook. 1283
Century's progress. 2699
Cerebrations on coming alive. 1007
Ceremonial. 814
Ceremonial art in the Judaic tradition. 2234
Ceremonial curiosities and queer sights in foreign churches. 3238
Ceremonial for the use of the Catholic churches in the United States of America. 826
Ceremonial spirit possession in Africa and Afro-America. 3472
Ceremonialism of the Tepecan. 3602
Ceremonies and processions of the cathedral church of Salisbury. 749, 750
Ceremonies at the holy places. 3239
Ceremonies at the installation of Rev. Dr. Kaufmann Kohler. 2183
Ceremonies in modern Jewish life. 2120
Ceremonies of a choral eucharist. 916
Ceremonies of Holy week. 840
Ceremonies of Holy Week, solemn rite and simple rite. 844

Ceremonies of Judaism. 2120
Ceremonies of the Easter virgil. 848
Ceremonies of the Founding Church of Scientology. 3314
Ceremonies of the Roman rite described. 838, 3238
... Ceremonies proper for Discalced Carmelites, taken from new edition of Manual. 740
Ceremony and celebration. 2295
Ceri Richards and the Metropolitan Cathedral of Christ the King. 89, 3235
... Cermonial of the Discalced nuns of the Order of Our Blessed Lady of mount Camel. 740
Certain difficulties felt by Anglicans in Catholic teaching considered. 790
Certain life. 2015, 2394
Certain people of the Book. 494
Certain principles in Evanson's "Dissonance of the four generally received evangelists", &c. 394, 1577
Certain sermons or homilies appointed to be read in churches in the time of the late Queen Elizabeth. 1225
Certain spirtual practices. 2238
Certain women. 3840
Certain young man of Assisi. 1643
Certaine articles or forcible reasons, 1600. 928, 1510
Certaine sermons or Homilies, appointed to be read in churches, in the time of Queen Elizabeth I, 1547-1571. 1225, 3363
Certainity of life after death. 1528
Certainly, I'm a Catholic! 796
Certainties for today. 1353
Certainties of faith. 1238
Certainties of the Advent movement. 3380
Certainties of the gospel. 93
Certainty of God. 1721, 1725
Certayne reasons and arguments proving that it is not lawfull to heare or have any spiritual communion with the present ministerie of the Church of England. 3027
Certified gospel. 3359
Certitude. 3717
Ces inutiles. 2577
C'est la fin! 3382
Cestello, a Cistercian church of the Florentine renaissance. 78, 3302
Cesvs Klist, em-opunvkv-hera. Maro coyvte. 1386
Ch'an and Zen teaching. 3892
Ch'i: a neo-Taoist approach to life. 3586
Ch'u silk manuscript: translation and commentary. 98
Chahta vba isht taloa holisso. 915, 1862
CHAI-ways. 2146
Chain of error in Scottish history. 3315
Chain of jewels from James and Jude. 412
Chain of prayer across the ages. 2890
Chain that saves. 3643
Chain, with its concomitants. 2428
Chains are strong. 1139
Chains of the spirit. 3516
Chair of Peter. 2769
Chair-talks on perfection. 2818
Chairman's final report to the members of the National Lay Committee. 2670
Chaitanya movement. 879, 3766
Chakras. 879
Chalcedon. 1893, 2685
... The Chalcedonian decree. 2706
Chaldean account of Genesis. 2654
Chalice and the covenant. 15, 2687
Chalice of the heart. 3685
Chalk; or, We can do it. 669
Chalk talks. 880
Chalk talks for Sunday schools. 880
Chalk talks with boys and girls. 880
Challenge. 201, 858, 1056, 1155, 1557, 2618
Challenge and conformity. 1060
Challenge and crisis in missionary medicine. 2486, 3329
Challenge and power, meditations and prayers in personal and social religion for individual and group use. 1436
Challenge and response. 2495, 3772
Challenge and response, a handbook of Christian apologetics. 64
Challenge and response in the city. 1278
Challenge and witness. 3191
Challenge and witness in revelation. 457
Challenge for evangelical missions to Europe. 2954
Challenge of a liberal faith. 3728
Challenge of basic Christian communities. 933
Challenge of Black theology in South Africa. 3623
Challenge of Burma. 1578
Challenge of Central Asia. 2503
Challenge of change. 881, 2527

Challenge of child evangelism. 3169
Challenge of Christ. 3356
Challenge of Christian stewardship. 3529
Challenge of Christian unity. 1492
Challenge of church membership. 155
Challenge of eternity. 1539, 2303
Challenge of existentialism. 1584
Challenge of Israel's faith. 1731
Challenge of Jesus. 422, 2044
Challenge of Kagawa. 2162
Challenge of Kagawa to the church and nation. 2162
Challenge of Lent. 2215
Challenge of liberation theology. 2222
Challenge of life. 2226
Challenge of Marxism. 1457, 2352
Challenge of Mater et magistra. 853
Challenge of missions. 2494
Challenge of modern church-public relations. 3002
Challenge of New Testament ethics. 378
Challenge of our culture. 1394, 1395
Challenge of our times. 2612
Challenge of perfection. 943
Challenge of Pierre Teilhard de Chardin. 3592, 3593
Challenge of Pittsburgh. 2850
Challenge of radical renewal. 2571
Challenge of redemptive love. 3029
Challenge of reincarnation. 3054
Challenge of religion today. 3107
Challenge of religious studies. 639
Challenge of Schweitzer. 3312
Challenge of single adult ministry. 1256
Challenge of suffering. 3540
Challenge of the ages. 544, 3377
Challenge of the church. 1070, 1121
Challenge of the church, rationalism refuted. 3022, 3024
Challenge of the council; person, parish, world. 2774
Challenge of the cults. 3325
Challenge of the hills. 2501
Challenge of the impossible. 893
Challenge of the prophets. 568
Challenge of the scrolls. 1410
Challenge of the sects. 3141
Challenge of the space age. 3069
Challenge of the universe. 3594
Challenge of the unknown. 2986
Challenge of the war. 1888
Challenge of the world religions. 1080
Challenge of to-day. 1407
Challenge of vacation Bible school evangelism. 3766
Challenge to action. 2125
Challenge to change. 759, 1059
Challenge to Christian missions. 2522
Challenge to confirmands. 2080
Challenge to fundamentalism. 2561
Challenge to Jewry. 2140
... A challenge to life service. 355
Challenge to love. 997
Challenge to modern man. 999
Challenge to pray. 2879
Challenge to religious life today. 1950, 2572
Challenge to reunion. 1046
Challenge to the Church. 817, 870, 1066, 1458
Challenge to the Darwinians. 1578
Challenge to think. 50, 3527
Challenge to you. 1060
Challenge, trust, and faith. 1594
Challenger of the most high God. 1428
Challenges of life. 1324
Challenges to kingdom building. 3217
Challenges to the cross. 161
Challenging a god. 1728
Challenging careers in the church. 1252
Challenging Christ. 1951
Challenging hours, messages of inspiration and hope. 2435
Challenging object lessons. 3156
Challenging youth for Christ. 3889
Challoner's Catholic Christian instructed in the sacraments, sacrifice, ceremonies, and observances of the Catholic church. 769
Chamber in the heart. 3078
Chamber music. 1365
Chamber of peace, and other religious poems. 3210
Chambers of the soul. 3463
Chaminade. 881, 2334
Champaklal's treasures. 3866
Champion of reform. 1
Champion of reform, Manuel Abad y Queipo. 1
Champion of the apostolate. 2766
Champion of the cross. 1846
Champion of youth. 2246
Champions all. 928
Champions of Christianity. 923
Champions of religious freedom. 3193
Champions of religious liberty. 3193
Champions of the church. 923

Champlain and the St. John, 1604-1954, edited. 881, 3274
Ch'an and Zen teaching. 3892
Chance and life. 2227
Chance and providence. 2981
Chance for change. 3722
Chance, luck, & destiny. 2732
Chance or the dance? 3327
Chance to change. 2325, 3697
Chancel. 27
Chancel of English churches. 27
Chancel windows. 3360
... The chances of surviving death. 1889
Chand of India. 2490
Chandi Borobudur. 682
Chandler's choice series sermon outlines. 3372
Change. 881, 1879
Change and challenge. 3747
Change and the Catholic Church. 760
Change and the changeless. 3624
Change and the church. 1120
Change and the Muslim world. 1922
Change, chaos, and Christianity. 1058
Change, conflict, and self-determination. 3176
Change in Smithville. 1228
Change in the Church. 1125
Change not changes. 1949
Change of key. 2236, 2295
Change of the Sabbath. 3260
Change points, when we need Him most. 2195, 3835
Change the world from your parish. 999
Change the world through. 2359
Change, witness, triumph. 2514
Change your life through faith and work! 3716
Change your life through love. 3751
Change your life through prayer. 3751
Change your thoughts and alter your life. 2696
Changed cross, and other religious poems. 3210
Changed cross, and The shadow of the rock. 3210
Changed life. 959
Changed men of our time. 1362
Changeless Christ. 3350, 3881
Changeless Christ, and other sermons. 3351
Changes. 3464
Changes in Joseph Smith's History. 2606, 3429
Changes in moral reasoning through the high school years. 7
Changes in the liturgy. 837
Changing Africa and the Christian dynamic. 12
Changing aims in religious education. 3164
Changing American family. 1607
Changing backgrounds in religion and ethics. 2835
Changing Catholic college. 805, 831, 3759
Changing church. 758, 1157
Changing church in Europe. 1542
Changing climate of religion. 3725
Changing concept of the universe. 99
Changing conceptions in Jewish education. 2086, 2087, 2103
Changing conceptions of original sin. 3414
Changing conceptions of religion. 2451
Changing concepts of the Bible. 1383
Changing emphases in American preaching. 2910
Changing esoteric values. 2723
Changing expectations and ethics in the professional ministry. 1302
Changing face of Catholic Ireland. 820
Changing face of theology. 795
Changing foreign missions. 2554
Changing heart. 1640, 3218
Changing man: the threat and the promise. 1853
Changing mind. 3482
Changing of the gods. 3834
Changing patterns in Christian education. 3160
Changing patterns in Christian programs. 1139
Changing perspectives in the scientific study of religion. 3111

Changing scene. 3276, 3859
Changing scene in China. 2559
Changing scenes. 1003
Changing Sister. 2573
Changing South and the Presbyterian Church in the United States. 2921
Changing Vatican. 807
Changing view-point in regligious thought. 3619
Changing world, and lectures to theosophical students. 3683
Changing world of Mormonism. 2614

Channel. 238, 3385
Channels for power. 3300
Channels of challenge. 2386
Channels of devotion. 1429, 3857
Channels of grace. 683
... Channels of redemption. 3263
Channels of revelation. 3224
Channels of spiritual power. 966
Channels of Thy peace. 2390
Channing centenary in America, Great Britain, and Ireland. 881
Channing, the reluctant radical. 882, 3730
Chanonry of Ross. 1634
Chant and service book. 2957
Chants of the Divine liturgy of the Armenian Apostolic Orthodox Church. 884
Chants of the Vatican gradual. 843
Chanukah. 1784
Chanukah is here. 1784
Chanukah treasure chest. 1785
Chaos and a creed. 1385
Chaos in Mexico. 1148
Chaos of cults. 3326
Chapel at Ronchamp. 3247
Chapel hour. 3758
Chapel hymn book, with tunes, for the worship of God. 2916
Chapel hymnal. 1865, 2916
Chapel in the sky. 962
Chapel messages. 160
Chapel of Princeton University. 2942
Chapel of the Cardinal of Portugal. 1629
Chapel of the hermits. 1807
Chapel prayer book. 3756
Chapel readings. 250
Chapel talks. 3337, 3537
Chapel talks delivered before the student body of The College of the Bible in 1910 and 1911. 1466
Chapel talks for school and camp. 3889
Chapel time. 3758
Chapel vespers. 1440
Chapels. 2527
Chaplain Duffy of the Sixty-ninth regiment, New York. 1482
Chaplain of St. Catherine's. 3273
Chaplain on the waterfront. 2245, 3304
... Chaplain service in a mental hospital. 1258
Chaplain Smith and the Baptists. 3427
Chaplain speaks. 1072
Chaplain's experience ashore and afloat. 3742
Chaplains in action. 885
Chaplains of the general government, with objections to their employment considered. 3740
Chaplain's prayers. 2895
Chapman's Choice outlines and illustrations. 3372
Chapman's pocket sermons. 3339
Chappell's special day sermons. 2721, 3339
Chapter of Franciscan history. 3421
Chapter of unwritten history. 2957
Chapters, councils, commanderies and Scottish rite in New Hampshire. 1667
Chapters from my life. 1041
Chapters from the bible of the ages. 3204
Chapters from the religions history of Spain connected with the Inquisition. 3469
Chapters from the religious history of Spain connected with the Inquisition. 1910, 3469
Chapters in a life of Paul. 2798
Chapters in Christian doctrine. 796
Chapters in church history. 1174, 1180, 1182
Chapters in religion. 796
...Chapters in religious institutes. 2577
Chapters in the history of New Testament textual criticism. 241
Chapters of Bible study. 234
Chapters of the Fathers. 886
Chapters on church-going. 886
... The characer outcome of present-day religion. 1047
Character. 886
Character and best exercises of unregenerate sinners. 3359
Character and Christian education. 3148
Character and citizenship training in the public school. 2591
Character and conduct of the apostles considered as an evidence of Christianity, in eight sermons preached before the University of Oxford, in the year MDCCCXXVII., at the lecture founded by the late Rev. John Bampton. 71
Character and doctrines of Jesus Christ. 3422
... The character and history of Pelagius' Commentary on the Epistles of St. Paul. 2811
Character and leadership. 886

Character and power. 886
Character and the Christian life. 886
Character and value of an evangelical ministry. 3672
Character and work of Jesus Christ. 1994
Character book for the grade. 3026
Character builder. 886
...Character building for junior high-school grades. 2590
Character building in a democracy. 3189
... Character building in New York public schools. 2591
Character calendar. 3284
Character diploma an incentive to moral conduct and good citizenship in public school training. 2592
Character education. 2590, 2591
... Character education by state and church. 2592
Character education in the junior high school. 2590
Character education methods. 2590
Character education through Bible study. 648
Character emphasis in education. 2591
Character-glimpses of Most Reverend William Henry Elder, D. D. 1503
Character grams. 3576
Character in human relations. 2591
Character, not creeds. 3678
Character of a Christian leader. 953
Character of Anna, the prophetess, consider'd and apply'd. 3761
Character of Christ. 1994, 1995
Character of Christ as man's spiritual example. 1995
Character of Christ considered. 2037
Character of forming in school. 2590
Character of Jesus. 1995, 2000
Character of Jesus forbidding his possible classification with men. 2000
Character of Jesus portrayed. 1995
Character of Mencius. 2402
Character of Our Lord and Saviour Jesus Christ. 2047
Character of Paul. 2798
Character of the candidates for civil government. 1504
Character-portrayals in the Ramayana of Valmiki. 3767
Character sketches from the pages of Scripture, illustrated in the world of nature. 313, 950
Character studies in Genesis. 886
Character through creative experience. 2590
Character training. 2590, 2591
Characteristics from the writings of Archbishop Ullathorne. 777
Characteristics from the writings of John Henry Newman. 776, 3632
Characteristics of a caring home. 1611
Characteristics of charity. 887
Characteristics of Jesus. 1995
Characteristics of the Christian life. 886
Characteristics of the early church. 1190
Characteristics of true devotion. 1429
Characters in the Gospels. 384
Characters of the Inquisition. 765, 1909
Characters of the passion. 384, 2030
Characters of the reformation. 3037
Characters, scenes, and incidents, of the reformation. 3038
Charge of the church of Jesus Christ to you. 1120
"Charge that to my account" 3353
Charge to keep. 143
Charge to keep; history of the First Baptist Church of Kenova, West Virginia. 2167
Charge to the clergy of the Protestant Episcopal church in the commonwealth of Pennsylvania. 2962
Charges, and extracts of charges, on moral and religious subjects. 1536
Charges of Jean Baptiste Massillon. 3673
Chariot of fire. 183, 3214
Chariot of Israel. 1928
Chariot of the sun. 2665
Chariots of fire. 215
Chariots of God. 2388
Chariots of the Gods? 1917
Charism and sacrament. 1358
Charismata. 1713
Charismatic approach to social action. 2814
Charismatic catechism. 748
Charismatic Christ. 1834, 2046
Charismatic church. 2815
Charismatic figure as miracle worker. 2622, 3782
Charismatic gift of tongues. 1717
Charismatic leader and his followers. 444, 2004
Charismatic movement. 2816, 2817
Charismatic prayer group. 2885
Charismatic reader. 1585, 3005

Charismatic renewal. 2815
Charismatic renewal among Lutherans. 2816
Charismatic renewal and ecumenism. 2816
Charismatic renewal and social action. 2816
Charismatic social action. 2814
Charismatic spiritual gifts. 1712
Charismatic theology. 3481
Charismatic truce. 2815
Charismatica, the Holy Spirit in the Bible. 1835
Charismatics. 2815
Charisms and charismatic renewal. 792, 1712
Charisms in the church. 1712
Charities of St. Vincent de Paul. 887, 3779
Charity. 887
Charity and liberty in the New Testament. 2265
Charity and our three vows. 2267
Charity begins at home. 887
Charity Cook. 1301, 1368
Charity for the suffering souls. 3006
Charity, morality, sex, and young people. 3391
Charity never faileth. 1009
Charity of Christ. 1995
Charity of Christ presses us. 2572
Charity of the primitive churches. 887
Charity school movement. 887, 888
Charity's reward. 2489
Charlemagne's cousins. 6
Charlemagne's cousins; contemporary lives of Adalard and Wala. 6
Charles A. Briggs heresy trial. 692, 3711
Charles Betts Galloway. 1701
Charles Bowen. 686, 928
Charles C. Rich, Mormon general and Western frontiersman. 3235
Charles Chapin Tracy. 39, 3706
Charles Coulson Rich. 2602, 3235
Charles D. Helmer. 1802
Charles de Condren. 1323
Charles E. Cowman. 1377
Charles E. Maddry. 146
Charles Elwood. 3422
Charles F. Coffin, a Quaker pioneer. 1305
Charles Fillmore: herald of the new age. 1625
Charles Francis Barnard. 174
Charles Freer Andrews. 41
Charles G. Finney. 657, 1626
Charles Gallaudet Trumbull. 3716
Charles Gordon Ames. 657
Charles Gore. 1748
... Charles Grandison Finney. 1626
Charles H. Spurgeon. 3367, 3523
Charles Haddon Spurgeon. 146, 3523
Charles Harold Dodd, 1884-1973. 1472
Charles Hartshorne. 1788
Charles Henry Brent. 691
Charles Henry Brigham. 657
Charles John Seghers. 3329
Charles Kingsley, a references guide. 2177
Charles L. Allen treasury. 1006
Charles Lemuel Thompson. 657
Charles Lewis Slattery. 3423
Charles M. Sheldon. 657
Charles McEwen Hyde. 1859
Charles Peirce and scholastic realism. 2810
Charles Perry, Bishop of Melbourne. 2820
Charles Porterfield Krauth. 2186
Charles Raven. 3025
Charles S. Longacre. 2245
Charles S. Medbury. 2377
Charles Simeon of Cambridge. 1292, 3409
Charles W. Abel of Kwato. 2, 2537
Charles Wesley. 3802
Charles Wesley and his colleagues. 3802
Charles Wesley seen in his finer and less familiar poems. 2857
Charles Wesley, the first Methodist. 3802
Charleston papers. 2974
"Charlie" Alexander. 24
Charlie's "be kind" day. 185
Charlotte R. Willard, of Merzifon. 2558, 3816
Charm. 3877
Charm of Jesus. 1956
Charm of the chapel. 685
Charms and counter-charms. 888
Charms of the Bible. 210
Charms of winning. 1566
Chart and compass for Christian laymen. 957
Chart Bible. 199
Chart messages on the history and prophecy of the Bible. 1376
Chart of mind. 2845
Charters of St-Fursy of Peronne. 743, 3274
Charting a course for the church. 1061
Charting the future course of Christian adult education in America. 3169

Chartism and the churches. 888
Chartres. 889
Chartres Cathedral. 889
Chartres, the masons who built a legend. 749
Chasidic dance. 1789
Chasidic tales retold. 1789
Chasing rainbows. 2310
Chassidic insights. 1789
Chastity. 889
Chastity and the affective life. 889
Chastity, sexuality & personal hangups. 878
Chats and stories about the blessed sacrament. 2251
Chats by the fireside. 2227
Chats from a minister's library. 3203
Chats on Christian names. 2668
Chats with children of the church. 906
Chats with Jesus. 1999

Chats with Pope Paul. 2805
Chats with prospective converts. 795
Chats with St. Anne. 48
Chats with St. Anne for children. 3273
Chats within the fold. 758
...Chauetas of Majorea. 1909
Chautauqua. 890
Chautauqua normal guide. 3178
Chauvinist or feminist? 375, 3832
Chavurah. 1621
Check list of Rosicrucian literature in the Library of Congress. 3251
Check list of some of the books and authors quoted or referred to in the two volumes of "The secret doctrine" 3685
Check your character. 181
Checkered state of the gospel church. 1613
Checking up on the Bible by facts of science. 3080
Checklist of four-shape shape-note tunebooks. 1870
Cheer for life's pilgrimage. 2820
Cheer up. 1454
Cheerful ascetic: the life of Francis Xavier Seelos. 3329
Cheerful to-days and trustful to-morrows. 974
Cheerful warrior. 1702
Cheering views of man and Providence. 3610
Cheese and the worms. 1689, 3306
Chefoo. 912
Cheiro book of fate and fortune: palmistry, numerology, astrology. 2766
Cheiro's book of numbers. 3575
Chela and the path. 1765, 3474
Chemical diagnosis. 891
Chemical ecstasy. 1782
Chemical history of the six days of creation. 205
Chemical illustrations. 2720
Chemistry, meteorology, and the function of digestion. 891
Chemistry of the blood and other stirring messages. 3350
Cherished experiences. 2608
Cherished experiences, from the writings of President David O. McKay. 2308, 2608
Cherokee hymn book. 1862
... Cherokee hymns. 891, 1862
Cherokee messenger. 891, 3848
Cherokee pictorial book. 891
Chester. 891
Chester (N.Y.) Presbyterian Church. 891, 1627
Chester's century of Catholicism, 1842-1942. 891
Chesterton continued. 892
Cheyenne. 892
Chhandogya Upanisad. 3760
Chiasmus in the New Testament. 348
... Chicago and its Jews. 2098
Chicago and the Baptists. 893
Chicago churches and synagogues. 893
Chicago declaration. 1552
Chicago papers. 2959
Chicago pinkas. 894
Chicago primer. 893
Chicago Sunday school extension. 893
Chicago's Catholics. 892, 2475
Chicken coops or sky scrapers. 1229, 1561
Chicorel index to parapsychology and occult books. 2993
Chief end of revelation. 3224
Chief evils of the times. 2215
Chief points of difference between the Catholic and Protestant creeds. 788
"chief rabbi" of Rome becomes a Catholic. 3015
Chief sources of sin. 3411
Chief steward. 1251
Chiesa del Redentore. 3777
Child. 895

Child and adult before God. 3001
Child and church. 2428
Child and God. 894
Child and his religion. 3149
Child and religion. 3158
Child and the bishop. 694
Child and the Christian faith. 3170
Child and the Christian mystery. 3171
Child and the church. 894
Child and the emperor; a legend. 2006
Child and the mystery of death. 1418
Child and the problem of faith. 3170
Child and the serpent. 1813
Child as God's child. 1254
Child for Christ. 3153
Child guidance. 3166
Child in Christian worship. 2293
Child in the church. 805, 894, 2443
Child in the congregation. 895
Child in the midst. 895
Child in the temple. 894
Child is born. 1996
Child is born: messages for Advent,
   Christmas, Epiphany. 9
Child Jesus. 1996
Child kneels to pray. 900
Child life and religion. 3150
... Child life and religious growth. 3763
Child life in Bible times. 898
... Child life in mission lands. 894
Child of Calvary, myrtyr [sic] of Satan.
   2712
"Child of gentleness." 2758
Child of God. 803, 2962
Child of God, the Lord be with you. 3858
Child of happiness. 2530
Child of many wonders. 1906
Child of Mary. 855
Child of rage. 1367, 1809
Child of Satan, child of God. 102, 1363
Child of the flood. 894
Child psychology and religion. 746
Child psychology and religious education.
   3160
Child religion in song and story. 894
Child study for teacher-training. 3180
Child, the wise man, and the devil. 895
Child unfoldment. 895
Childen together. 1254
Childern of the Devil. 3413
.. Childhood and character. 3151
Childhood and conversion. 896
Childhood conversions. 896
Childhood education in the church. 3170
Childhood in exile. 2102
Childhood in the Moslem world. 904
Childhood of Christ as seen by the
   primitive masters. 1961
Childhood of Jesus. 1996
Childhood of Jesus Christ. 1996
Childhood of Jesus Christ according to the
   canonical gospels. 1996, 3780
Childhood of religions. 3114
Childhood's songs of long ago. 3799
Children. 1917, 1941
Children against witches. 3826
Children and adolescents, our teachers.
   3171
Children and churches in Latin America.
   2460
Children and conversion. 896
Children and God: communion, confession,
   confirmation. 903
Children and priest at Mass. 2369
Children & Puritanism. 937, 3167
Children & Quakerism. 903, 1683
Children and religion. 3170, 3555
Children and the Bible. 642
Children and the Christian faith. 938
Children and the church. 3189
Children and their religion. 904
Children are God's favorite people. 1736
Children ask. 905
Children ask about God and everything.
   905
Children at worship. 3858
Children can worship meaningfully at
   church and home. 3858
Children, celebrate! 3859
Children, crayons, and Christ. 1385
Children for Christ. 3176
Children, go where I send thee. 3522
Children in a Christian home. 2773
Children in Amish society. 2408
Children in Christ. 105
Children in church. 3150
Children in community. 3172
Children in heaven. 897
Children in our urban world. 896
Children in paradise. 1907
Children in radioland. 2298
Children in the Bible. 617
Children in the Bible school. 3171
Children in the church. 3170
Children in the New England mind. 897
Children in the school. 3170

Children in the worshipping community.
   3858
Children is crying. 16
Children learn from Jesus. 3764
Children of Abraham. 2147
Children of Bible times. 898
Children of darkness. 3881
Children of destiny. 1615
Children of doom. 898
Children of Fatima. 1618
Children of freedom. 1659
Children of God. 898, 986, 1741
Children of God, and other story sermons.
   909
Children of God and Union with Christ.
   898
Children of gospel days. 2006
Children of India. 1897
Children of Jonestown. 897, 2817
Children of La Salette. 3286
Children of light. 1684, 2131
Children of Mary. 3580
Children of our Father. 3163
Children of promise. 1905
Children of sea and sun. 898
Children of the Bible. 897, 898
Children of the Bible. With eight
   illustrations. 898
Children of the bush country. 2543
Children of the cave: a tale of Israel and of
   Rome. 3580
Children of the Conestoga. 1297, 1704
Children of the covenant. 927, 2168
Children of the Devil. 3413
Children of the font. 3170
Children of the kingdom. 3163
Children of the light in India. 1110
Children of the New Testament. 898
Children of the parsonage. 910
Children of the promise. 592
Children of the rainbow. 2663
Children of the Reformation; the story of
   the Christian Reformed Church, its origin
   and growth. 1024
Children of the resurrection. 3798
Children of the second birth. 1360
Children of the wilderness. 298
Children of the world. 2490
Children we teach. 3172
Children's Advent and Christmas. 2022
Children's adventures with nature and
   people. 911
Children's Bible. 250, 252, 619, 621, 624
Children's Bible history. 623
Children's Bible stories from the Old
   Testament. 628
Children's Bible story book. 629, 911
Children's Bible (The) 619
Children's Bible: the Old Testament, the
   New Testament. 619
Children's bishop. 1793
Children's book of Bible stories. 619
Children's book of hymns. 1862
Children's book of religious pictures. 922
Children's book of the Holy Mass. 2369
Children's books for Sunday school
   libraries. 905
Children's challenge to the church. 3554
Children's chapel song book. 3562
Children's church. 3858
Children's covenant. 3146
Children's devotions. 899
... Children's division yearbook. 2449
Children's education in community. 697,
   938
Children's eucharist. 2253
Children's everyland story-sermons. 908
Children's favorite Bible stories. 628
Children's friend. 625, 628, 896, 1980
Children's gateway to Bible-story-land.
   896
Children's Gospel commentary. 384
Children's great texts of the Bible. 907
Children's history of Israel from the
   creation to the present time. 2094
Children's history of Isreal. 2094
Children's hour. 910
Children's hymnal. 3563
Children's hymnary. 1865
Children's illustrated Bible dictionary. 247
Children's King and other plays for
   children. 3144
Children's kingdom. 1443
Children's lectionary. 2205
Children's Lent and Easter. 2032
Children's life of Jesus. 1981
Children's Master. 911
Children's missionary library. 2482
Children's moment. 906
Children's music ministry. 1208
Children's new mission book. 837
Children's new mission book of the
   Congregation of the most holy
   Redeemer. 900
Children's New Testament. 354
Children's parable story-sermons. 908,
   2028

Children's parish. 1254
Children's Paul. 2802
Children's prayer book. 899
Children's prayers. 900
Children's prayers and praises. 902
Children's prayers for every day. 901
Children's prayers for today. 902
Children's prayers from other lands. 902
Children's prayers, praises & pledges. 902
Children's Psalm-book. 573
Children's pulpit. 908
Children's religious concepts. 904
Children's retreats. 895
Children's saint. 2310
Children's Saint Anthony. 54
Children's Saint Francis. 1639
... The children's Saviour. 895, 1982
Children's sermons in stories. 906
Children's sermons, outlines, and
   illustrations. 906
Children's service book for the Sundays of
   the church year and special occasions.
   2971
Children's shepherd. 1481, 2481
Children's six minutes. 895
Children's Stations of the Cross. 895
Children's stories. 911
Children's stories from The dawn-breakers.
   128
Children's story Bible. 618
Children's story of Jesus. 1983
Children's story of the Bible. 294
Children's story of Westminster abbey.
   3808
Children's story-sermons. 910
Children's story sermons for today. 908
Children's Sunday school work. 3170
Children's talks for Sundays and holidays.
   895
Children's time in worship. 3857
Children's version of the Hly Bible. 513
Children's version of the Holy Bible. 253,
   513
Children's version of the Holy Old
   Testament. 528
Children's work in the church. 3557
Children's workship in the church school.
   3858
Children's worship in the church school.
   3858
Children's worship story-sermons. 908
Children's year. 895
Child's approach to religion. 3150, 3165
Child's Bible. 250, 254, 292
Child's Bible in Bible words. 626
Child's Bible in colour. 627
Child's Bible in rhyme. 298
Child's Bible reader. 625
Child's book of Bible stories. 630
Child's book of character building. 3782
Child's book of great popes. 2769, 2861
Child's book of prayers. 898, 900
Child's book of Psalms. 583, 901
Child's book of saints. 3279, 3284
Child's book on repentance. 3218
Child's book on the soul. 3462
Child's cabinet of things. 2921
Child's Christ-tales. 2023
Child's commentator on the Bible, for the
   home circle. 619
Child's dictionary of Jewish symbols.
   3575
Child's first Bible. 633
Child's first book of Bible stories. 629
Child's garden of Bible stories. 894
Child's garden of religion stories. 622
Child's garden of song. 3563
Child's grace. 899, 900
Child's guide to mythology. 2651
Child's guide to the Bible. 894
Child's happiest moments when Jesus
   comes. 858
Child's history of Daniel. 1401
Child's history of Jewish life. 2090
Child's history of Jewish life for the first
   sixteen centuries of the common era.
   2090
Child's history of King Solomon. 3457
Child's history of the Hebra people. 2094
Child's introduction to the early Prophets.
   631
Child's introduction to Torah. 631
Child's life of Christ. 1980, 1981, 1982
Child's life of Jesus. 1982, 2225
Child's life of Luther. 2273
Child's life of Mary. 2225
Child's life of Mary Baker Eddy. 1494
Child's life of Our Lord. 1983
Child's look at the Twenty-third Psalm.
   588
Child's picture Hebrew dictionary. 2845
Child's portion. 1343
Child's praise. 901
Child's prayers. 898, 2884
Child's ramble through the Bible. 894
Child's religion. 2996, 3160
Child's religious life. 3152

Child's rule of life. 804
Child's Scripture, question-book. 217
Child's story Bible. 617, 624
Child's story Bible. Illustrators; Dirk
   Gringhuis [and] Norman Mathesis. 624
Child's story of Jesus' friends. 2007
Child's story of Saint Frances Cabrini.
   723
Child's story of the baby who changed the
   world. 1962
Child's story of the beautiful life of Jesus
   told in simple language. 3534
Child's story of the Bible. 619, 3534
...A child's story of the Bible in words of
   one syllable. 294
Child's story of the Book of Mormon. 679
Child's story of the life of Christ. 1966
Child's story of the nativity. 2023
Child's story of the New Testament. 626,
   3534
... A child's story of the Old Testament.
   3534
Child's story of the Pearl of great price.
   3430
Child's story of the prophet Brigham
   Young. 3869
Child's story of the prophet John Taylor.
   3591
Child's story of the prophet Joseph Smith.
   3429
Child's story of the prophet Lorenzo
   Snow. 3432
Child's storybook of Bible people. 620
Child's storybook of Jesus. 1982
Child's storybook of Peter and Paul. 2825
Child's thought of God. 1733
Child's treasury of Bible stories. 617
Child's way of the cross. 3526
Child's world in story-sermons. 906
Chilean Christian Democracy. 2777
Chimaera of his age. 194
Chime of the bells. 187
Chimes and the children. 895
Chimes of Salem. Golden jubilee, 1889-
   1939. 1547
Chimes of truth. 3716
Chimham and his khan. 621
Chin up. 2398
China--1925. 2510
China, a new day. 1090
China, American Catholicism, and the
   missionary. 849, 2507
China and Christian responsibility. 2512
China and Christianity. 1090, 2510
China and Methodism. 2454
China and the Christian colleges, 1850-
   1950. 3756
China and the cross. 912
China as a challenge to the church. 912
China calling. 912
China centenary missionary conference
   records. 911
China centenary missionry conference
   records. 2508
China Centennial Documents. 911
China; Christian students face the
   revolution. 1090
China Coast family. 911
China cry. 1576, 2193
China doctor. 2466, 2539
... China from within. 2511
... China her own interpreter. 2511
China in action. 912
China in revival. 2508
China in the sixteenth century. 1947
China inside out. 914
China marches toward the cross. 2508
China martyrs of 1900. 912
China, the emerging challenge. 2509
China two generations ago. 1782
Chinaman as we see him. 2556
Chinaman's chance. 2855
China's borderlands and beyond. 2508
China's challenge to Christianity. 2510

China's Christian army, a story of Marshal
   Feng and his soldiers. 1109, 1622
China's first preacher. 2220
China's religious heritage. 914
Chinese altars to the unknown God. 913
Chinese appeal to Christendom concerning
   Christian missions. 2522
Chinese astrology. 98
Chinese Buddhism. 704, 709
Chinese Buddhist bronzes. 693
Chinese Buddhist monasteries. 3599
... Chinese Buddhist monasteries, their plan
   and its function as a setting for Buddhist
   monastic life. 705
Chinese Buddhist verse. 711
Chinese church that will not die. 1090,
   3791
Chinese classical work commonly called
   the Four books (1828) 1538
Chinese classics. 914, 3523
Chinese culture and Christianity. 914
Chinese Empire. 2508

CHINESE GARDEN OF RELIGIOUS BOOKS 1876 - 1982

Chinese garden of serenity. 711
Chinese gateways. 2512
Chinese ginger jars. 3315
Chinese heart-throbs. 2509
Chinese horrors and persecutions of the Christians. 2820
Chinese humanism and Christian spirituality. 1081
Chinese in dispersion. 2503
Chinese Jews. 2100
Chinese lama temple, Potala of Jehol. 3599
Chinese literature. 914
Chinese magic and superstitions in Malaya. 2314
... The Chinese mind. 1331, 2838
Chinese missions. 2511
Chinese mystics. 2643
...Chinese [mythology]. 2655
Chinese mythology, Japanese mythology. 2655
Chinese religion. 914
Chinese religion seen through the proverb. 913
Chinese religions. 913
Chinese renaissance. 912
Chinese story-teller. 2509, 3403
Chinese symbols and superstitions. 913
Chinese teen-agers--and God! 2511
Chinese temples in California. 3599
Chinese transformation of Buddhism. 704
Chinese twice-born. 2511
Chinese way in religion. 914
Chinigchinix: an indigenous California Indian religion. 2137
Chipped dishes, zippers & prayer. 3843
Chips from a German workshop. 3113, 3118, 3119
Chips of wisdom from the rock of Peter. 2771
... Chips of wisdom from the rock of Peter, a collection of brief papal utterances bearing on modern social questions. 787
Chirst is born. 2003
Chirst, the leader. 1993
Chirst the Son of God. 1964
Choice. 3401, 3592
Choice before us. 2174
Choice called atheism. 101
Choice chuckles. 1290
Choice consolation for the suffering children of God. 1349
Choice dialogues. 3560
Choice illustrations and quotable poems. 1842
Choice is always ours. 3063
Choice of a state of life. 3786
Choice of conscience. 3778
Choice of God. 3490, 3493
Choice of the pew. 162
Choice passages in the Holy Scriptures; a teacher's guide. 3591
Choice pickings. 1841
Choice proverbs for grammatical analysis. 2980
Choice selection of evangelical hymns. 1870
Choice selection of hymns and spiritual songs. 1867
Choice selection of hymns and spiritual songs for the use of the Baptist Church and all lovers of song. 153
Choice selection of psalms, hymns, and spiritual songs, for the use of Christians. 1464
Choice sermon notes. 3375
Choice sermon outlines. 3372
Choice stories. 1013
Choice to love. [1st ed.]. 2263
Choicemaker. 2226
Choir clinic manual. 917
Choir ideas for choir members. 1204
Choir loft and the pulpit. 3004
Choir school. 916
Choir service book. 1209
Choir stalls of Lincoln Minster. 915, 2230
Choirmaster's guide to Holy Week. 1204
... The choirmaster's guide to the selection of hymns and anthems for the services of the church. 1206
Choirmaster's notebook on Anglican services and liturgical music. 1204
Choix de cantiques extraits du recueil de cantiques de la Science chretienne (Christian science hymnal) y compris sept poemes de Mary Baker Eddy. 1037
Choma, a boy of Central Africa. 2491
Choose life. 2138, 2823
Choose once again. 1636
Choose to win! 1005
Choose ye this day. 1566
Choose your tomorrow. 3785
Choosing a sex ethic. 3392
Choosing God's way. 3764
Choosing life. 1077, 1517, 3486
Choosing of bishops. 665
Choosing our memories. 1449
Choosing riches or ruin. 1939
Choosing the Christian way. 1237
Choosing to love. 2347
Choosing well. 1536
Choral echoes from the church of God in all ages. 1865
... Choral music and the oratorio. 916
Choral music of the church. 1208
Choral music of the world. 917
Choral reading for worship and inspiration. 3220
Choral readings for teen-age worship and inspiration. 917
Choral readings from the Bible. 3220
Choral responses. 916, 3219
Choral revival in the Anglican Church (1839-1872) 1206
Choral service book. 916
Choral teaching at the junior high school level. 917
Choral tradition. 917
Chorale through four hundred years of musical development as a congregational hymn. 917
Choralia. 916
Chores and the altar. 27
Chorister's companion. 2984
Chorister's pocket book. 915
Chorus of faith as heard in the Parliament of religions. 3122
Chorus of life. 2227
Chose Catherine. 1399, 3419
Chosen and sent: calling the church to mission. 2480
Chosen boy. 2621
Chosen by God. 2088
Chosen, communicating with Jews of all faiths. 2141
Chosen days. 561, 1615
Chosen families of the Bible. 1603
Chosen for leadership. 144, 3465
Chosen for peace. 187
Chosen for riches. 363
Chosen highway. 127
Chosen people. 532, 2091, 2099, 3811
Chosen people question box. 231, 280
Chosen peoples. 1116, 2087
Chosen to serve: the deacon. 2924
Chosen vessel. 331, 1780
Chosen women of the Bible. 3841
Chosen Word. 254
Chretien de Troyes, the man and his work. 918
Chrisitanity, politics and power. 1086
"Chrissie, I never had it so bad ... " 3880
Christ. 864, 1061, 1102, 1319, 1343, 1350, 1951, 1965, 1971, 2008, 2018, 2020, 2036, 2041, 2043, 2681, 3023, 3648
Christ a friend. 1994
Christ;a poetical study of His life from Advent to Ascension. 2047
Christ above all. 164
Christ above all, and other messages. 164
Christ acts through the Sacraments. 3262
Christ acts through the sacraments. Translated by Carisbrooke Dominicans. 3266
Christ after chaos; the post-war policy of the Methodist church in foreign lands. 2441
Christ all in all. 2047, 3364
Christ alone. 3456
Christ among men. 1992, 2041
Christ among us. 797
Christ and Adam. 472
Christ and Apollo. 3071
Christ and architecture. 1156
Christ and Baha'u'llah. 125, 129
Christ and Baha'u'llah. 125
Christ and Buddha. 706
Christ and Caesar in Christian missions. 2514
Christ and Catholicism. 800
Christ and Christian education. 3147
Christ and church. 3645
Christ and community. 1116
Christ and counter-Christ. 1529
Christ and crisis. 1077
Christ and crisis in Southeast Asia. 1090
Christ and culture. 1048, 1394
Christ and divorce. 2341
Christ and evolution. 3640
Christ and Freud. 1586, 1673
Christ and his Apostles. 71
Christ and His bride. 594
Christ and His church. 160, 1122, 1972
Christ and His Church in the Book of Psalms. 577, 3720
Christ and his companions. 2007
Christ and His cross. 106, 1997, 2064
Christ and His fisherman. 431
Christ and His friends. 2434
Christ and His men. 2007
Christ and His message. 242, 1959
Christ and his mission. 2009, 2012
Christ and His salvation. 1340
Christ and His teaching. 2063
Christ and His time. 1972
Christ and history. 1818
Christ and human needs. 2059
Christ and human personality. 165
Christ and human suffering. 3540
Christ and human values. 1071
Christ and humanity. 2037, 2038, 2323, 3644
Christ and international life. 1053
Christ & Israel. 344, 470
Christ and Japan. 2534
Christ and life. 976, 998, 2063
Christ and littleness. 1976
Christ and man's dilemma. 1093
Christ and men. 1950
Christ and Methodism. 2422
... Christ and modern thought. 3619
Christ and modern unbelief. 2001
Christ & moral theology. 947
Christ and oriental ideals. 1953
Christ and original sin. 2037, 3413, 3414
Christ and other masters. 3116
Christ and our country. 1052, 2441
Christ and our crises. 2385
Christ and our liberties. 163
Christ and ourselves. 963, 1952
Christ and power. 2039, 2866
Christ and prayer. 2868
Christ and progress. 1065
Christ and Prometheus. 3328
Christ and Renan. 3215
Christ and revolution. 3441
Christ and science. 205
Christ and selfhood. 2050
Christ and social change. 3441
Christ and society. 2060, 3442
Christ and spirit in the New Testament. 1834, 2011
Christ and the apostles. 1957
Christ and the believer in the Song of songs. 594
Christ & the Bible. 237, 1959
Christ and the Caesars. 1195
Christ and the carols. 2012
Christ and the Catholic college. 806
Christ and the cherubim. 3720
Christ and the Christian faith. 1893
Christ and the church. 365, 652, 797, 2040, 3225
Christ and the church in the Old Testament. 1163
Christ and the city. 166
Christ and the common man. 3356
Christ and the cosmos. 2049
Christ and the creed. 73
Christ and the eastern soul. 2024
Christ and the end of the world. 657
Christ and the eternal order. 1950
Christ and the even balance. 1690
Christ and the fine arts. 1958
Christ and the forked tongue of man. 2019
Christ and the gospel. 390, 1953
Christ and the hiddenness of God. 2832
Christ and the hill-men. 2556
Christ and the Hindu heart. 324
Christ and the hope of glory. 1888
Christ and the human life. 961
Christ and the human race. 2012
Christ and the inheritance of the saints. 2015
Christ and the inner life. 1009
Christ and the Jews. 2153, 2831
Christ and the kingdom of God. 2014
Christ and the man in the street. 1593
Christ and the meaning of life. 2301
Christ and the media. 2369
Christ & the modern mind. 1074
Christ and the modern opportunity. 1134
Christ and the modern woman. 3843
Christ and the moral life. 943, 2059
Christ and the nations. 2465
Christ and the new consciousness. 3119
Christ and the new nations. 1134
Christ and the powers. 375, 2866, 3475
Christ and the priest. 1299, 2399
Christ and the problems of youth. 3881, 3889
Christ and the sailor. 3316
Christ and the Scriptures. 308
Christ and 'the Spirit. 1834
Christ and the Teacher of Righteousness. 3591
Christ and the universe: Teilhard de Chardin and the cosmos. 2010
Christ and the world religions. 1078
Christ and the world today. 2492
Christ and the young people. 1958
Christ and this crisis. 2973
Christ and time. 3642
Christ and tomorrow. 460
Christ and us. 2037
Christ and violence. 2065, 3780
Christ and your job. 3784
Christ applied psychology and the kingdom of heaven on earth. 2050
Christ as a teacher. 2061, 2066
Christ as authority. 2285
Christ as John knew Him. 420
Christ as organizer of the church. 792
Christ as Prophet and King. 409
Christ at every turn. 2935
Christ at the bamboo curtain. 2508
Christ at the door. 1229
Christ at the hearth. 1610
Christ at the phone. 2025
Christ at the Round table. 1079
Christ at work. 2072
Christ-based teachings. 3749
Christ be with me. 2384
Christ before Calvary. 424
Christ Bible. 355
Christ book. 2063
Christ brotherhood. 2434
Christ builds His church. 1169
Christ came again. 3321
Christ can make you fully human. 2321
Christ-centered life. 2042
Christ-centered spirituality. 3490
Christ child. 399, 1996
Christ child in art. 1958
Christ Child in devotional images in Italy during the XIV century. 1958
Christ-child in legend and art. 1955
Christ-child in story. 1996
Christ child missal. 3202
Christ, Christianity and communism. 62
Christ, Christianity and the Bible. 1050, 1058, 2000
Christ Chruch, 1706-1959. 888
Christ church. 1158, 3427
Christ, church, and communism. 1319
Christ church at Pelham. 1162
Christ church, Ballston Spa, N. Y. 132
Christ Church, Cincinnati, 1817-1967. 1275
Christ church Gardiner, Maine. 1702
Christ Church, Greensburg. 1772
Christ church, Nashville. 2974
... Christ church parish and cathedral, 1762-1942. 1787
Christ church parish, Pensacola, Florida, 1827-1927. 2813
Christ church, Philadelphia. 2829
Christ comes to the Indians. 2261
Christ comes to the village. 2521
Christ, communism, and the clock. 1319
Christ crucified. 1273, 1999, 2030
Le Christ dans l'Apocalypse. 465
Christ down east. 2243
Christ dream. 2434
Christ Emphasis New Testament of Our Lord and Saviour Jesus Christ. 361
Christ encountered. 1973
Christ enthroned in man. 2323
Christ enthroned in the industrial world. 1076
Christ eternal. 3357
Christ, faith and history. 2037
Christ, faith and history: Cambridge studies in Christology. 2037
Christ finds a rabbi. 2085
Christ first. 3881
Christ for a world like this. 962
Christ for America. 3228
Christ for every crisis! 2300
Christ for Jamaica. 1933
Christ for me! 167
Christ for the moving millions. 2463
Christ for the nation! 2300
Christ for the world. 2041, 2546
Christ for the world--now. 3881
Christ for us in the theology of Dietrich Bonhoeffer. 677, 2009
Christ forever. 1999
Christ frees and unites. 2282
'Christ frees and unites . . . for responsible service. 2285
Christ from without and within. 416, 419
Christ healing. 1598
Christ heals today. 2409
Christ himself. 1968
Christ, his own witness. 2035
Christ, hope of the world. 1965
Christ I know. 168
Christ ideal. 2063
Christ ideal for world peace. 2809
Christ impulse and the development of ego consciousness. 51
Christ in a changing world. 943, 2038
Christ in a pluralistic age. 2037
Christ in all the Scriptures. 2040
Christ in American education. 3190
Christ in Bangladesh. 2503
Christ in Bethlehem; Christ in the Eucharist. 2023
Christ in Christian tradition. 2010, 2011
Christ in chronology and science of the Sabbath. 1997, 3261
Christ in contemporary thought. 2010
Christ in context. 2044
Christ in creation and ethical monism. 3625

Christ in Eastern Christian thought. 2009, 3667
Christ in eclipse. 1001, 2044
Christ in everyday life. 956
Christ in far countries. 2491
Christ in Genesis. 527
Christ in Hades. 1764
Christ in high school life. 688, 957
Christ in His church. 1176, 1178, 3163
Christ in His consecrated virgins. 1348
Christ in his mysteries. 2015
Christ in His mystical body. 2020
Christ in his sacraments. 3262
Christ in His suffering. 2030
Christ in history. 1189
Christ in India. 1082
Christ in Jesus. 474
Christ in literature. 2012
Christ in Main Street. 2059
Christ in man-making. 2063
Christ in marriage. 2343
Christ in me. 2370
Christ in modern English literature. 2012
Christ in modern life. 980, 3363
Christ in our hearts. 3295
Christ in our lives. 941
Christ in our place. 729
Christ in our time. 1001
Christ in our world. 3266
Christ in perspective. 2045
Christ in promise, in person and in his church, by Sister Mary Thaddeus . . . and others. 2015
Christ in prophecy. 2415
Christ in Psalm CXIX. 579
Christ in Russia. 2750
Christ in the army. 3737
Christ in the Bible. 224
Christ in the Book of Daniel. 509, 2415
Christ in the Book of Mormon. 2019
Christ in the camp. 3741
Christ in the centuries. 3340
Christ in the church. 2019, 3197
Christ in the classroom. 1001, 2044
Christ in the common ways of life. 980, 1955
Christ in the communist prisons. 2821
Christ in the country club. 1367, 2219
Christ in the daily meal. 961
Christ in the drama. 1517, 2012
Christ in the four Gospels. 388, 1961
Christ in the Gospels. 389, 401, 1951, 1960, 1988, 2016
Christ in the gospels and the church. 626
Christ in the great forest. 2489
Christ in the haunted wood. 1096
Christ in the home. 963, 1610, 1838
Christ in the industries. 1134
.. Christ in the life. 980
Christ in the liturgy. 840
Christ in the marvelous Book. 2900
Christ in the Mass. 2369
Christ in the New Testament. 411, 1953, 2045
Christ in the old and the New Testament. 1968
Christ in the Old Testament. 499, 2415, 3682, 3720
Christ in the Passover. 2030, 2779
Christ in the Pentateuch. 564
Christ in the Psalms. 585, 3721
Christ in the rosary. 3248
Christ in the Scriptures. 3721
Christ in the silence. 3476
Christ in the silver lands. 3467
Christ in the tabernacle. 3721
Christ in the theology of St. Paul. 375
Christ in the thought of Teilhard de Chardin. 3592
Christ in the Tombs. 1387
.. Christ in the under-world. 995
Christ in the universe. 963
Christ in the wilderness. 435
Christ in the world of to-day. 2959
Christ in type and prophecy. 2016, 2415
Christ in us. 2015
Christ in war time. 3792
Christ in word and work. 976
Christ in you. 342
Christ in your life. 399, 981
Christ in your shoes. 993
Christ is alive! 1096
Christ is all! 1466, 1560, 2045
Christ is all and other sermons. 3340
Christ is coming. 3318
Christ is God. 2047
Christ is God's middle name. 1721
Christ is here. 1403
Christ is in our midst. 1299, 1918
Christ is losing his world. 763
Christ is our strength. 1555
Christ is our victory. 1435
Christ is passing by. 863, 3369
Christ is the answer. 168, 1229
Christ is the gospel. 1265
Christ is victor. 1999
Christ Jesus. 382

Christ Jesus our King. 2259
Christ Jesus the physician. 1503
"Christ-killers" 1083, 2034
Christ knocking at the door of sinners' hearts. 1358
Christ law. 2201
Christ-law in the star of Bethlehem. 1793
Christ leads the way. 3163
Christ legends. 2207
Christ, liberation of the world today. 2041, 3290
Christ life. 975, 1824
Christ life from Nativity to Ascension. 390, 2067
Christ light. 206
Christ lives in me. 2913
Christ liveth in me, and Game with minutes. 2637
Christ, lord of battles. 3792
Christ, Lord, Son of God. 376, 2020
Christ lore. 920
Christ-man in type as prefigured by Biblical persons from Adam to David. 3720
Christ matters! 1007
Christ men need. 2213
Christ, model and reward of religious. 2569
Christ my friend. 1985
Christ myth. 2050
Christ now. 1263
Christ of all nations. 1990
Christ of Anglo-Israel. 1515
Christ of chaos. 66
Christ of Christianity. 431, 1994
Christ of Cynewulf. 1022, 1398
Christ of English poetry. 2048
Christ of every road. 2813
Christ of experience. 2038
Christ of faith. 1590, 2035
Christ of faith and the Jesus of history. 3308
Christ of God. 1956, 2001, 2037
Christ of God; sermons on the poet eternal. 3357
Christ of history. 1956, 2002
Christ of Lent. 2215
Christ of nineteen centuries. 1950
Christ of our novelists. 1624, 2005
Christ of our poets. 2047
Christ of promise in Homer, Hesiod, Vergil, Ovid, Horace, etc. 2019
Christ of the ages. 1172, 1893, 2044
Christ of the ages in words of Holy writ. 1987
Christ of the American road. 3745
Christ of the Apostles' creed. 74, 2001
Christ of the Bible. 199
Christ of the byways. 3340
Christ of the centuries. 160
Christ of the Christian faith. 1953
Christ of the church. 3339
Christ of the class room. 1954, 2061, 3156
Christ of the countryside. 1962
Christ of the Cross. 1061, 1969
Christ of the dawn. 2974
Christ of the earliest Christians. 2042
"The Christ of the eternities" 2041
Christ of the Gospels. 1987, 1990, 3343
Christ of the Gospels, an exegetical study. 1972
Christ of the human heart. 1954
Christ of the Indian road. 2531
Christ of the Korean heart. 2536
Christ of the Logia. 391, 2043
Christ of the Mount. 3335
Christ of the New Testament. 349, 1969
Christ of the poets. 2048
Christ of the Revelation, His message to the church and the world. 460, 2046
Christ of to-day. 970, 2038
Christ of Vatican II. 2045
Christ on campus. 3537
Christ on the American road. 2994
Christ on the cross. 587, 1998
Christ on the Jewish road. 2556
Christ on the road of today. 3462
Christ on the throne of power and Antichrist. 462
Christ on trial. 2030
Christ or Caesar. 1140, 3793
Christ or chaos. 66, 2808
Christ or clergy.? 1290
... Christ or confusion. 2215, 2301
Christ or Mary? 2359
Christ or Napoleon--which? 2806
Christ our Brother. 1950, 2035
Christ our coming King. 3318
Christ our creditor ("How much owest thou") 3702
Christ our devotional example. 2004
Christ our example. 980, 2004
Christ our high priest. 2049
Christ, Our Lady, and the Church. 2009
Christ--our life. 458, 1252, 1959, 3356
Christ our light. 636

Christ our Lord. 2047
... Christ our penal subtitute. 104
Christ our righteousness. 1602
Christ our Savior. 3163
Christ our Saviour. 1974, 1984
Christ outside Christianity. 3295
Christ over the seven seas. 1015
Christ pre-eminent. 2240
Christ preaching to spirits in prison. 1999
Christ preeminent. 378, 2041
Christ, present and coming. 1531
Christ present and yet to come. 770, 3852
Christ, priest and redeemer. 1951
Christ-principle and true-Christianity to be. 2054
Christ proclaimed Christology as rhetoric. 2035
Christ prophecy and Gospel exposition. 386
Christ question settled. 1993
Christ receiving sinners. 1358
Christ reflected in creation. 1384, 2059
Christ rejected. 2051
Christ revealed. 451, 1518, 3721
Christ, St. Francis and to-day. 3274
Christ, set the world aright! 2300
Christ speaks from Calvary. 2058
Christ speaks from the Cross. 2056
Christ standard key to life. 1371
Christ story. 399, 1094, 1955, 1996
Christ story for boys and girls. 1983, 3578
Christ supreme. 1596
Christ teaches us today. 3187
Christ that is to be. 1058
Christ, the anchor. 404
Christ the answer. 2003
Christ the apocalypse. 56
Christ, the avatar of sacrificial love. 2067
Christ the builder. 1449
Christ, the center. 1956, 2046
Christ, the center of life. 2038
Christ, the Christian and the church. 1892, 2019
Christ, the church, and man. 3619
Christ, the church, and the end. 341
Christ, the church, and the poor. 1152
Christ the controversialist. 1551
Christ the crisis. 2038
Christ, the divine one. 1972
Christ the educator. 1004
Christ, the experience of Jesus as Lord. 477, 1752, 2043
Christ, the fountaine of life. 324, 1340
Christ the grand subject of gospel-preaching. 3582
Christ, the great deceiver. 2019
Christ, the healer. 1598, 1792
Christ, the hope of glory. 1529
Christ the hope of the future. 1845, 2039
Christ, the hope of the world. 3560
Christ the incomparable. 1954
Christ the key to Bible knowledge. 642
Christ: the key to interpreting the Bible. 287
Christ, the key to Scripture. 643
Christ the King. 2211, 2212
Christ, the leader. 1993
Christ the liberator. 1911, 2514
Christ the life and light. 2209
Christ, the light of the world. 1953
Christ the Lord. 426, 1530, 1972, 2271
Christ the Lord; the meaning of Jesus in the early church. 2040
Christ, the man God. 2042
Christ, the man God, our redeemer. 2042
Christ, the master of all diseases. 1602
Christ, the master speaker. 2049, 2902
Christ the meaning of history. 1818
Christ the one priest, and we His priests. 1298, 2049
Christ, the redeemer and judge. 457
Christ the representative. 107, 2049
Christ, the sacrament of encounter with God [by] E. Schillebeeckx. 3266
Christ, the sacrament of the encounter with God. 3266
Christ the Savior. 2038, 3696
Christ the Savior of the world. 1837
Christ the seed. 3438
Christ, the Son of God. 1964
Christ the sparrow. 3721
Christ the spirit. 2019
Christ the teacher. 2063
Christ, the teacher of men. 2065
Christ the tiger. 1473
Christ the true prototype of man. 1580
Christ the truth. 1106, 1453
Christ the Victorious. 954
Christ the way. 177, 2012
Christ the Word. 2041, 3658
Christ, thy Captain. 3356, 3742
... Christ to-day. 1015
Christ transcendent. 2174
Christ triumphant. 167
Christ triumphant and Christian ideal. 1881
Christ unconquered. 2048

Christ unmasked. 929, 3535
Christ unveiled. 2019
Christ versus Christianity. 1050
Christ versus Hitler. 1708, 1820
Christ victorious over all. 3220
Christ way. 2024
Christ we forget. 1975
Christ we know. 1964, 2015
Christ we love. 1952
Christ we need. 161
Christ who is all. 1955
Christ who lives in me. 3249
Christ whom we worship. 1951
Christ with us. 2250, 2253, 3163
Christ within. 5, 1054
Christ without myth. 713, 1424
Christ yet to come. 3319, 3796
Christ you'll have to know. 162
Christain belief in immorality in the light of modern thought. 1890
Christian missionaries and the creation of Northern Rhodesia, 1880-1924. 2545
Christan way in a modern world. 3664
Christand the Christian. 997
Christanity and the new situation. 1060
Christendom. 1172, 3323
Christendom and Islam. 1084
Christendom anno Domini mdccci. 1182
Christendom astray. 650
Christendom divided. 3034
Christendom in Dublin. 1913
Christendom revisited. 2170, 3744
Christening. 138
Christentum in der Gesellschaft. 1176
Christhood and adeptship. 2201
Christi imago. 977
Christian unity. 1039
Christian. 686, 1056, 1463, 1549
... The Christian according to Paul. 374
Christian action in Africa. 2497
Christian action in economic life. 1075
Christian adventure. 962
Christian adventures in South Africa. 2499
Christian advices. 1680, 3475
Christian affirmations. 3352, 3652
Christian affirmations in a secular age. 1095
Christian after death. 1696
Christian agnostic. 3650
Christian agnosticism as related to Christian knowledge, the critical principle in theology. 3680
Christian altar in history and today. 28
Christian alternative to socialism. 3436
Christian alternative to church chaos. 3446
Christian alternatives within marriage. 2337
Christian ambassador. 3796
Christian ambassador and other addresses. 1561
Christian America. 3738
Christian America; protestant hopes and historical realities. 3738
Christian Americanization. 2488
Christian and amusements. 36, 955
Christian and Catholic. 2964
Christian and civic economy of large towns. 1277
Christian and conscription. 2405
Christian and deist, and The prophets. 1419
Christian and Gnostic Son of Man. 3458
Christian and Hebrew atomic bomb. 1429
Christian and his America. 3745
Christian and his Bible. 234
Christian and his Bible. [1st ed.]. 234
Christian and his decisions. 950
Christian and his money. 3529
Christian and his money problems. 3530
Christian and Jew. 2078
Christian and Mohammedan. 1084
Christian and Muslim in Africa. 1073
Christian and politics. 1085
Christian and revolution. 3448
Christian and secular education. 3190
Christian and social action. 1139
Christian & temptation. 3600
Christian and the cults. 3325
Christian and the government. 1142
Christian and the law. 3029
Christian and the nations. 1076
Christian and the occult. 1078
Christian & the supernatural. 1088
Christian and the war. 3793
Christian and the world. 1065
Christian and the world of unbelief. 65
Christian and the world (The) 1065
Christian and warfare. 2809
Christian and world integration. 1076, 1077
Christian annual. 1016
Christian answer. 1064
Christian answer to communism. 1319
Christian answer to life's urgent questions. 3665

CHRISTIAN ANSWER TO
RELIGIOUS BOOKS 1876 - 1982

Christian answer to the problem of evil. 1746
Christian answers to teenage sex questions. 3394
Christian answers to war questions. 3792
Christian anthropology. 2324, 2325, 2327
Christian anthropology and ethics. 2321
Christian antiquities in the Nile valley. 919
Christian apologetic. 66
Christian apologetics. 63, 66, 69, 762, 785
Christian apologetics of the second century in their relation to modern thought. 1018
Christian apology. 66
Christian approach to culture. 1394
Christian approach to Islam. 2564
Christian approach to Islam in the Sudan. 2552
Christian approach to Muslims. 1925
Christian approach to philosophy. 2834
Christian approach to science and science teaching. 3083
Christian approach to the Bible. 313
Christian approach to the Bible (La lecture chretienne de la Bible) 308
Christian approach to the Moslem. 1925, 2540
Christian archaeology. 918
Christian architecture. 1158
Christian art. 921
Christian art in Africa and Asia. 920
Christian art of the 4th to 12th centuries. 85
Christian as a businessman. 720
Christian as a doctor. 2845
Christian as citizen. 1085
Christian as communicator. 3829
Christian as witness. 3731
Christian asceticism. 90
Christian asceticism and modern man. 89
Christian at the crossroads. 3624
Christian attitude to other religions. 1078
Christian attitude toward the emperor in the fourth century. 1148
Christian attitude toward war. 3792
Christian attitude towards democracy. 3444
Christian attitude towards the emperor in the fourth century. 1148
Christian attitude towards the emperor in the fourth century, especially as shown in addresses to the emperor. 1148
Christian attitudes toward war and peace. 3794
Christian auto-suggestion. 936
Christian baptism. 134, 135, 137, 139, 178
Christian bases of world order. 1135, 3441
Christian basis of a new society. 3447
Christian basis of the world democracy. 400
Christian, be a real person! 983
Christian beginnings. 409, 1195
Christian behavior. 1005, 3445
Christian behavior: does it matter what you do, or only what you are? 1001
Christian behaviour. 942
Christian being and doing. 412
Christian belief. 3649
Christian belief about Christ. 2035
Christian belief and Christian practice. 2064
Christian belief and science. 3081
Christian belief and this world. 3619
Christian belief in God. 1737, 3106
Christian belief in God in relation to religion and philosophy. 1721
Christian belief interpreted by Christian experience. 1058
Christian beliefs. 3645, 3663
Christian beliefs: a brief introduction. 3660
Christian beliefs about life after death. 1694
Christian beliefs and anti-Semitism. 1073
Christian beliefs and modern thought. 1047
Christian beliefs and teachings. 3664
Christian believing. 64, 238, 3626
Christian biography. 661, 1781
Christian biopolitics. 1057
Christian blessedness, 1690. 181, 2180, 2241
Christian Book of concord. 2283
Christian boy's problems. 688
Christian Brahmun. 122
Christian Brother in the United States, 1848-1948. 695
Christian Brothers 1868-1968. 695
Christian Buddhism of St. John. 419, 706
Christian building. 1158
Christian Bunsen and liberal English theology. 713
Christian business ethics. 1905
Christian business on the air. 1562
Christian calendar. 1163, 1262
Christian calendar in the free churches. 1262
Christian calling and vocation. 3784
Christian capitalism. 347, 1491
Christian case against poverty. 1152
Christian castle building. 3542
Christian catalogue. 1100
Christian catechism. 2283
Christian: celebrate your sexuality. 3391
Christian centuries. 811, 1173, 1183
Christian centuries from Christ to Dante. 1194
Christian century, 1843-1943. 1100, 2917
Christian century in Japan. 1935
Christian century in Japan, 1549-1650. 1935
Christian century reader. 1065, 1066
Christian certainties. 747
Christian certainties of belief. 2691
Christian challenge. 64
Christian challenge in Latin America. 2548
Christian challenge to the modern world, with special reference to Christian education. 3162
Christian character. 944
Christian character building with boys and young men. 886
Christian charity in action. 887
Christian charity in action, from the beginning to St. Vincent de Paul. 887
Christian charity in the ancient church. 887
Christian child development. 938
Christian church. 1096, 1117
Christian church and church federation. 1095, 1169
Christian church and education. 3150
Christian Church and liberty. 3192
Christian Church and missions in Ethiopia. 2517
Christian church art through the ages. 922
Christian church as social process. 1122
Christian church at Dura-Europos. 1483
Christian Church (Disciples of Christ) 1460
Christian Church (Disciples of Christ) and its future. 1463
Christian Church (Disciples of Christ) in West Virginia. 1467
... Christian church discipline (Kristen forsamlingstukt) 1166
Christian church in Communist China. 1144
Christian church in Communist China, to 1952. 1144
...The Christian church in the epistles of St. Jerome. 919
Christian church in the modern world. 1065
Christian church in these islands before the coming of Augustine. 1761
Christian church plea. 933
Christian churches and their work. 1461
Christian Churches (Disciples of Christ) of Southern California, a history. 1462
Christian churches of America. 3324
Christian churches of the East. 1487
Christian citizen. 980
Christian citizenship. 963, 1150, 1326, 3444
Christian citizenship and visitation evangelism. 1566
Christian citizenship in high school. 1810
Christian college. 3759
Christian college in a secular age. 1127
Christian college in a world of change. 1164
Christian college in developing India. 1127
Christian college in India. 1127
Christian college in the post-war world. 1128
Christian college in the twentieth century. 1127
Christian collegians and foreign missions. 2514
Christian comfort. 1354
Christian commission for the army and navy of the United States of America. 1089
Christian commitment. 62, 2789
Christian commitment to God and to the world. 998
Christian communes. 933
Christian communicator's handbook. 3002
Christian-Communist dialogue. 1319
Christian community. 2521
Christian community and American society. 3440
Christian Community and change in nineteenth century north India. 1108
Christian community, biblical or optional? 1121
Christian community: response to reality. 62
Christian concept of freedom. 1659
Christian concept of history in the chronicle of Sulpicius Severus. 1820, 3388
Christian conception and experience. 3191
Christian conception of God. 1719
Christian concepts in social studies in Catholic education. 806
Christian conduct. 971
Christian confederacy. 1047
Christian confrontation with Shinto nationalism. 1084
Christian conquest of Asia. 91
... The Christian conquest of India. 2532
Christian conquests. 955
Christian conquests in the Congo. 2513, 2514
Christian conscience. 1347
Christian conscience and Negro emancipation. 1132
Christian consciousness. 1103
Christian consolations. 1352, 1354
Christian contemplated in a course of lectures. 965
Christian content of the Bible. 233
Christian contract. 3441
Christian conversation. 1434
Christian conversationalist. 1571
Christian conversion. 1361
Christian conversion in context. 1359
Christian converts and social protest in Meiji Japan. 1101
Christian conviction. 1051
Christian cooperation in Latin America. 2548
Christian corridors to Japan. 2535
Christian counsel on divers matters pertaining to the inner life, and Spiritual letters. 997
Christian counseling. 2780
Christian counseling and occultism. 2726
Christian counseling in the light of modern psychology. 2783
Christian counselling. 1374
Christian counselling and occultism. 1088
Christian counselor's casebook. 2779
Christian counter culture. 65, 3336
Christian couple. 2337
Christian courage for everyday living. 1375
Christian credentials. 1593
Christian creed. 3686
Christian creeds. 1385
Christian criticism. 1518
Christian criticism of life. 1281
Christian critique of American culture. 1074
Christian critique of culture. 1061
Christian critique of the university. 1127
Christian crusade. 957, 3872
Christian crusade for a warless world. 2807
Christian crusade for world democracy. 2455
Christian debate. 1082, 3242
Christian decides. 3164
Christian decision and action. 946
Christian decision in the nuclear age. 1077
Christian declaration of human rights. 1127
Christian demand for social justice. 1134
Christian democracy. 879
Christian democracy for America. 2454
Christian democracy in Italy and France. 933, 2777
Christian democracy in Western Europe. 933
Christian democracy in Western Europe, 1820-1953. 933
Christian Democratic movement in Nicaragua. 933
Christian denominations. 3322
Christian design for sex. 2342
Christian Deuteronomy. 511
Christian deviations. 3141
Christian deviations: the challenge of the new spiritual movements. 3141
Christian devotion. 3362
Christian devotion, addresses. 3362
Christian dialogs and recitations. 1166
Christian differential. 164
Christian dimensions of family living. 1604
Christian disciplines. 2387, 2388
Christian discourse. 3682
Christian discourses. 1069, 1070
Christian discrimination. 1281
Christian doctrin of salvation. 3753
Christian doctrine. 3650
Christian doctrine for beginners. 748
Christian doctrine for Sunday school teachers. 3664
Christian doctrine for the instruction and information of the Indians. 770
Christian doctrine harmonized and its rationality vindicated. 3645
Christian doctrine; lectures and sermons. 691, 3646
Christian doctrine of forgiveness of sin. 1633, 1634
...The Christian doctrine of God. 1720
Christian doctrine of grace. 1751
Christian doctrine of health. 3478
Christian doctrine of history. 1818
Christian doctrine of justification and reconciliation; the positive development of the doctrine. 2161
Christian doctrine of peace. 2807
Christian doctrine of prayer. 933, 2870, 2872, 2873
Christian doctrine of reconciliation. 104
... The Christian doctrine of salvation. 3291
Christian doctrine of the church, faith, and the consummation. 1117
Christian doctrine of the Godhead. 1721
Christian doctrine of the soul. 3461
Christian doctrines. 3642, 3647, 3650
Christian dogmatics. 3646, 3647
Christian dogmatics and notes on the history of dogma. 1473
Christian doubt. 185
Christian duty. 1484
Christian dynamic in a nuclear world. 1065
Christian economics. 1076
Christian economy. 1076, 1445
Christian education. 178, 804, 935, 936, 3146, 3149, 3155, 3156
Christian education and evangelism. 3158
Christian education and some social problems. 161
Christian education and the image of the church; the four-year program of the National Sunday School and Baptist Training Union Congress [1962-1965] -- study-resources handbook. 941
Christian education and the inarticulate age. 942
Christian education and the local church. 3148, 3154
Christian education and the national consciousness in China. 2511
Christian education and the world today. 2449
Christian education and world evangelization. 3162
Christian education as engagement. 1467
Christian education; being eight lectures delivered before the University of Oxford, in the year 1944, on the foundation of the Rev. John Bampton, Canon of Salisbury. 3153
Christian education by Congregationalists in the seven Pacific coast states. 1335
Christian education catalog. 937
Christian education committee in action; a study manual. 3564
Christian education for emotionally-disturbed children. 1254
Christian education for liberation and other upsetting ideas. 936
Christian education for retarded children and youth. 3173
Christian education for socially handicapped children and youth. 3175
Christian education for the local church. 3148
Christian education handbook. 937, 3148
Christian education in a democracy. 3155
Christian education in a secular society. 3161, 3162
Christian education in action. 3157
Christian education in Africa. 1129
Christian education in family clusters. 941
Christian education in Japan. 3160
Christian education in local Methodist churches. 2428
Christian education in mission. 3157
Christian education in the 70's. 935
Christian education in the church today. 3149
Christian education in the home. 3170
Christian education in the local church. 3149, 3558
Christian education in theological focus. 3157
Christian education in your church. 3154
Christian education objectives. 3160
Christian education of adults. 3169
Christian education of older youth. 3175
Christian education of young adults. 3168
Christian education of youth. 940
Christian education reviewed. 935, 3153
Christian education through the church. 3153
Christian education thru music. 2633
Christian education week. 940
Christian education where the learning is. 3150
"Christian efficiency," 2242, 3027
Christian Egypt: church and people. 1501

Christian emphasis in Y.M.C.A. program. 3871
Christian empiricism. 2838
Christian employee. 986
Christian endeavor edition of Gospel hymns no. 6. 3230
Christian Endeavor essentials. 1100, 1914
Christian endeavor in all lands. 937
Christian endeavor in every land. 1914
Christian endeavor manual. 1914
Christian Endeavor playlets, short, bright, different. 3144
Christian England. 1515
Christian enterprise among rural people. 3254
Christian entrepreneur. 1006
Christian epic. 410
Christian epoch-makers. 2526
Christian equivalent of war. 1039
Christian eschatology and social thought. 1531
Christian essays. 1055
Christian essays in psychiatry. 2986
Christian essentials. 1051
Christian ethic as an economic factor. 945
Christian ethicks. 3782
Christian ethics. 943, 944, 945, 946, 948, 949, 950
Christian ethics and nuclear warfare. 943
Christian ethics and contemporary philosophy. 946
Christian ethics and economics. 1075
Christian ethics and modern problems. 943
Christian ethics and moral philosophy. 945
Christian ethics and social policy. 942
Christian ethics and the community. 946, 949
Christian ethics and the dilemmas of foreign policy. 1087
Christian ethics and the sit-in. 3329
Christian ethics for Black theology. 943
Christian ethics for practical living. 944
Christian ethics for today. 945, 949
Christian ethics in the African context. 943
Christian ethics in the modern age. 943
Christian ethics; sources of the living tradition. 950
Christian ethos. 950
Christian Eucharist and the pagan cults. 2251
Christian Europe today. 1542
Christian evangel. 1061
Christian evangelism. 1553, 1564
Christian Evangelist index, 1863-1958. St. Louis, Mo. 1554
Christian evidence movement. 69
Christian evidences. 59, 63
Christian evidences and ethics. 1099
Christian executive. 952
Christian executive in a secular world. 984
Christian existence in the New Testament. 477
Christian experience. 1000, 3488
Christian experience & teachings of Ellen G. White. 3811
Christian experience of forgiveness. 1633
... The Christian experience of life. 1068
Christian experience of the Holy Spirit. 1832
Christian experiences. 1585
Christian faces his world. 977, 3347
Christian fact and modern doubt. 62
Christian facts and forces. 1342
Christian failure. 3449
Christian faith. 951, 1094, 1104, 1180, 1218, 1335, 3441, 3640, 3642, 3647, 3649, 3660, 3665, 3666
Christian faith and war in the nuclear age. 3793
Christian faith and Communist faith. 65
Christian faith and criminal justice. 1387
Christian faith and democracy. 1064
Christian faith and economic change. 3444
... The Christian faith and eternal life. 1888
Christian faith and Greek philosophy. 1081
Christian faith and higher education. 1127
Christian faith and history. 1818, 3715
Christian faith and its cultural expression. 1049
Christian faith and life. 1063, 1227, 3044, 3186, 3366
Christian faith and man's religion. 3662
Christian faith and modern theology. 3617
Christian faith and my job. 3784
Christian faith and natural science. 3078
Christian faith and non-Christian religions. 1078
Christian faith and other faiths. 1079
Christian faith and pastoral care. 2786

Christian faith and philosophical inquiry. 2837
Christian faith and practice. 951, 3663
Christian faith & public policy, thinking and acting in the courage of uncertainty. 1134
Christian faith and secularism. 67
Christian faith and social action. 1135
Christian faith and the campus mind. 64
Christian faith and the Christian life. 2962
Christian faith and the church. 1118
Christian faith and the interpretation of history. 114, 1819
Christian faith and the liberal arts. 1127
Christian faith and the Marxist criticism of religion. 1319
Christian faith and the modern state, an ecumenical approach. 1141
Christian faith and the new day. 951
Christian faith and the new psychology. 65, 1107
Christian faith and the Old Testament. 502
Christian faith and the question of history. 1819
Christian faith and the social revolution. 3435
Christian faith and the space age. 3083
Christian faith and the spirit of the age. 64
Christian faith and the state university. 1127
Christian faith and war in the nuclear age. 1089
Christian faith and way. 3664
Christian faith and youth today's. 2942
Christian faith at the nation's capital. 3746
Christian faith, bulwark of freedom. 1085
Christian faith, bulwark of freedom. [Reissue. 1085
Christian faith for men of today. 951
Christian faith for today. 951, 3665
Christian faith in a day of crisis. 3617
Christian faith in a religiously plural world. 1081
Christian faith in action. 168
Christian faith in an age of science. 3079, 3313
Christian faith in modern light. 1048
Christian faith in our time. 1057
Christian faith in the doctrinal documents of the Catholic Church. 780
Christian faith in the modern world. 1070, 3644
Christian faith personally given in a system of doctrine. 3642
Christian faith speaks to children. 1254
Christian faith to-day. 951
... The Christian faith under modern searchlights. 951
Christian family. 1603, 1607, 2344
Christian family activities for families with children. 1610
Christian family activities for families with preschoolers. 1610
Christian family activities for families with teens. 1606
Christian family altar. 1430
Christian family and home. 2337
Christian family and its money. 1603
Christian family annual. v. 1. 1711
Christian family education in the local church. Manual. 2921
Christian family in action. 1609
Christian family in conflict. 1607
Christian family life education. 1608
Christian family living. 1609
Christian family planning and sex education. 663
Christian family prepares for Christmas. 1609
Christian family today. 1603
Christian fath in focus. 3660
Christian fathers. 1616, 3658
Christian father's present to his children. 1324
Christian fellowship. 1040, 1201, 1621
Christian fellowship among the nations. 2806
Christian fellowship and modern industry. 3443
Christian fellowship in action. 2970
Christian fellowship in thought and prayer. 1621
Christian feminism. 3392
Christian focus. 3342, 3758
Christian freedom. 1070, 2799, 3193
Christian freedom for women and other human beings. 3836
Christian freedom in a permissive society. 946
Christian friendship; youth devotions that lead to action. 3882
Christian frontiers. 3537
Christian fundamentals for academy students. 938

Christian fundamentals in the light of modern science. 3313
Christian funeral. 1693
... The Christian future. 1062, 1063
Christian gentleman. 1015
Christian giving. 951, 3702
Christian girls and their problems. 1714
Christian girl's problems. 1714
Christian global strategy. 2495
Christian go-givers. 923
Christian God. 1726
Christian God and other addresses. 3357
Christian gospel and the parish church. 2964
Christian government. 3072
Christian government and the Sabbath. 3547
Christian greatness in the minister. 2678
Christian growth. 989, 1004
Christian growth and conduct. 3730
Christian growth in family life. 1607
Christian growth through meditation. 2380
Christian guidance. 3265
Christian guide to your child's sex life. 3390
Christian Hall of Fame. 927
Christian healing. 1030, 2409
Christian healing rediscovered. 2202, 3476
Christian heritage. 165, 809, 1174, 1774
Christian heritage in America. 3325
Christian heroes of today. 1014
Christian heroism in heathen lands. 1808
Christian history and interpretation. 2182, 3619
Christian history in its three great periods. 1172
Christian holiness. 1823
Christian holiness restudied and restated. 3299
Christian home. 1607, 1838, 2780
Christian home and family living. 1610
Christian home, as it is in the sphere of nature and the church. 1838
Christian home in a changing world. 1608
Christian home in a rural setting. 1609
Christian home in the 70's. 1608
Christian home making. 1838
Christian home training. 3165
Christian hope. 1528, 1845, 1887
Christian hope & the future. 1531
Christian hope and the future of humanity. 1845
Christian hope and the Lordship of Christ. 2055
Christian hope and the Second Coming. 1846
Christian hope and the secular. 3328
Christian hope and the task of the church. 1125
Christian hope for world society. 3452
Christian household. 1604
Christian humanism. 762, 976, 1855, 2126, 2322
Christian humanism and the Reformation. 1525, 1854, 1855
Christian humanism of Flannery O'Connor. 1855, 2734
Christian husband. 1857
Christian hymnody. 1875
Christian hymns. 1867, 1875
Christian hymns for church, school, and home. 1861
Christian hymns, poems, and spiritual songs. 1868
Christian hypothesis. 1103
Christian idea in the modern world. 1057
Christian idea of sin and original sin in the light of modern knowledge. 3410
... The Christian ideal and social control. 3444
Christian ideals for young disciples. 1882
... Christian ideals in industry. 3453
Christian identity on campus. 3757
Christian image. 1519
Christian image of woman. 3832
Christian imagination. 759, 1089
Christian impact in English. 806
Christian imperative. 1085
Christian imprint. 3148
Christian in business. 1076
Christian in East Germany. 2282
Christian in his blindness. 960
Christian in his world. 1155
Christian in Hungarian romance. 2129
Christian in mid life. 2462
Christian in modern style. 2846
Christian in politics. 1086, 2858
... The Christian in social relationships. 1074
Christian in society. 1138, 2191, 3449
... A Christian in the countryside. 3253
Christian in the market place. 2789
Christian in the material world. 2866
Christian in the modern world. 1015

Christian in the theology of St. Paul. 375
Christian in the world. 3186, 3187
Christian in the world. (The) 3186
Christian in the world. [Translated by S. Page]. 957
Christian in today's world. 3446
Christian in war time. 1543
Christian India. 819, 1895
Christian information directory. 1253
Christian inheritance. 3184
Christian initiation. 136, 137, 139, 762, 1398
Christian initiation in Spain, c. 300-1100. 138
Christian inscriptions. 1525
Christian insights for marriage. 2344
...Christian institutions. 1172, 3625
Christian institutions; essays on ecclesiastical subjects. 3625
Christian intellectual. 875, 1074
Christian internationale. 2549
Christian internationalism. 1051
Christian interpretation of marriage. 2336
Christian interpretation of religion. 3060
Christian interpretation of sex. 3388
Christian interpretation of the cabala in the renaissance. 721
Christian introduction to religions of the world. 3121
Christian is the name of the church. 1463
Christian island. 1763
Christian issues in southern Asia. 1108
Christian-Jewish tragedy. 1083, 1997
Christian journalism for today. 2135
Christian joy. 2136
Christian Knowledge of God. 1740
Christian Knowledge Society and the revival of the Episcopal Church in New Jersey. 2971
Christian laborer--the Christian hero. 3070
Christian law of amusement. 36
Christian layman. 994, 3713
Christian layman and his church. 2192
Christian layman's guide to public speaking. 2911
Christian layman's handbook. 3663
Christian leader. 3755
Christian leaders of the eighteenth century. 1293
Christian leaders of the last century. 1292
Christian leadership. 953, 2204
Christian leadership in Indian America. 1898
Christian league of Connecticut. 1045
Christian lesson commentary. 941
Christian letters on sex and marriage. 1860
Christian letters to a post-Christian world. 3652
Christian liberal arts education. 727
Christian liberty. 3193
Christian liberty and church unity. 2223
Christian library. 3198
Christian life. 951, 955, 957, 963, 965, 970, 985, 1003, 1005, 2391
Christian life a nomal experience. 979
Christian life and character of the civil institutions of the United States. 3745
Christian life and how to live it. 977
Christian life and salvation. 958
...The Christian life and the spiritual life. 90
Christian life and the unconscious. 1361
... Christian life & theology. 961
Christian life and worship. 3266
Christian life and worship. 838, 3266, 3267
Christian life calendar (The) 766
Christian life curriculum. 3162
Christian life day by day. 1002
Christian life in song, the Christian year. 3072
Christian life in the Book of common prayer. 2961
Christian life in the community. 933
Christian life in the light of the cross. 963
Christian life in the Middle Ages, and other essays. 1282
Christian life in the modern world. 972, 978
Christian life in the primitive church. 1190
Christian life lived experimentally. 1587
Christian life made plain. 960
Christian life of faith, love, and duty. 1015
Christian life patterns. 989
Christian life problems. 3186
Christian life series. 796, 3182
Christian life, social and individual. 955
Christian life songs. 3072
Christian life-style. 991
Christian life, teacher's book. 942
Christian lifestyle. 472, 995
Christian literature in Moslem lands. 2540
Christian lives by the Spirit. 1830
Christian living. 965, 974, 1015

Christian living from Isaiah. 544
Christian living sermon outlines. 3372
Christian living today. 1002
Christian look at secular society. 1074
Christian looks at himself. 2323
Christian looks at the Jewish question. 1073, 2078
Christian love. 2263
Christian love and human sexuality. 889
Christian love: campus style. 1308
Christian love contrasted with the love of the world. 2265
Christian love in action. 2744
Christian love in everyday living. 2264
Christian love in religious life. 2573
Christian maiden. 1809, 3877
Christian man. 1021, 2323
Christian manhood for adolescents and young men. 3870
Christian manifesto. 57, 1057, 1244
Christian man's world. 3529
Christian manual. 980
Christian manual; or, Of the life and manners of true Christians. 992
... Christian marriage. 2338, 2339, 2343, 2344
Christian marriage today. 2337
Christian married love. 663, 853
Christian martyrs of the world. 2350
Christian-Marxist dialogue. 1319
Christian mass movements in India. 2531
Christian materialism. 3529
Christian maturity. 997, 998, 1439, 2931
Christian maturity and Christian success. 1012
Christian maturity and the theology of success. 990
Christian meaning of money. 3529
Christian meaning of the Old Testament. 484
Christian meditation, its art and practice. 2380
Christian meditation the better way. 2380
Christian meditations. 2398
Christian memorials of the war. 3741
Christian men in a modern world. 1238
Christian message and myth. 1424
Christian message and program. 1061
Christian message for the world today. 1057, 3441
Christian message in a non-Christian world. 70
Christian message in a scientific age. 3080
Christian metaphysics. 2419
Christian method of moral judgment. 946
Christian Miller, an American pioneer. 2849
Christian mind. 3327
Christian mind healing. 2695
Christian minister. 2787
Christian minister's manual. 3677
Christian ministry. 953, 1289, 1295, 1297, 3670
Christian ministry a work for the gospel's sake. 2474
Christian ministry and social problems. 3447
Christian ministry and the social order. 3444
... The Christian ministry at the close of the nineteenth century. 1293
Christian mission and social justice. 2481
Christian mission in the world of today. 2522
Christian mission in Africa. 2498
Christian mission in America. 3745
Christian mission in our day. 2494
Christian mission in reconstruction—an Asian analysis. 2502
Christian mission in rural India. 2529
Christian mission in the modern world. 2481, 2545
Christian mission in theological perspective. 2433, 2496
Christian mission of the General Conference Mennonite Church. 1705
Christian mission stations in Africa, 1920's. 12
Christian mission to Muslims. 2557
Christian mission today. 2493
Christian missionaries and the creation of Northern Rhodesia. 2545
Christian missions. 2481, 2526
Christian missions and a new world culture. 2518
Christian missions and social progress. 2519
Christian missions in Biblical perspective. 2493
Christian missions in China. 2510
Christian missions in Nigeria. 2542
Christian missions in Nigeria, 1841-1891. 2542
Christian missions in the nineteenth century. 2495
Christian missions in today's world. 2554
Christian monarchy. 1169

Christian monasticism. 2576, 2582
...Christian monasticism in Egypt to the close of the fourth century. 2579
Christian moral principles. 943
Christian moral reasoning. 947
Christian morality. 946
Christian morality & you. 947
Christian morality today. 947
Christian morals today. 946
Christian mortalism from Tyndale to Milton. 3464
Christian mother. 78, 2625
Christian motherhood and education. 2624
... The Christian motive and method in stewardship. 3531
Christian mourning. 1414, 1754
Christian music. 1026
Christian music in contemporary witness. 1207
Christian must have an answer. 64
Christian mysteries. 2636
Christian mysticism. 2136, 2639, 2647
Christian mysticism and other essays. 2643
Christian mysticism and Subud. 2643
Christian mysticism considered in eight lectures delivered before the University of Oxford. 2639
Christian myth and ritual. 2648, 3239
Christian mythology. 2207
Christian natural theology. 2672, 3813
... Christian nature series, course ... prepared for the General board of religious education. 2676
... Christian neighborliness. 1321
Christian neurosis. 1108
Christian new morality. 3421
Christian Newcomer. 3730
Christian non-resistance. 1578
Christian non-resistance, in all its important bearings. 1578
Christian nurture. 1015, 3147, 3148
Christian nurture and the church. 1121
Christian nurture for the nursery school child. 3173
Christian nurture of children. 3170
Christian nurture of youth. 3167
Christian nurture series. 3188
... Christian nurture series. 3188
Christian nurture through the church. 3150
Christian occasions. 1038
Christian of the future. 761
Christian opportunity. 1066, 1068
Christian orator. 3026
Christian ordinances and social progress. 3442
Christian origins. 1194
Christian origins and Judaism. 1190
Christian origins in sociological perspective. 1102
Christian origins of social revolt. 1177
Christian outlook. 1060
Christian outlook in the modern world. 1049
Christian pacifism. 2809, 3433
Christian pacifism re-examined. 2756
Christian pagan. 1091
Christian panoply. 68
Christian paradox. 1092
Christian parenting, the adolescent. 2792
Christian parenting, the young child. 939
Christian parish. 2788
Christian pastor. 1289, 2786, 3674
... The Christian pastor and the working church. 3672
Christian pastor in the new age, comrade-- sponsor--social mediator. 3673
Christian pastorate. 3673
Christian paths to self-acceptance. 2996
Christian patriarch. 3814
Christian patriotism. 1141
Christian patriotism in temperance reform. 3595
Christian pattern. 1097
Christian pedagogy. 2591
Christian perfection. 1449, 2818, 3478
Christian perfection and American Methodism. 2819
Christian perfection and married life. 2819
Christian perfection as taught by John Wesley. 2818, 2819
Christian perfection for the layman. 1003
Christian perfection for the married. 2347
Christian perfection; selections. 2818
Christian periodical index. 1958. 3678
Christian persecutions. 2820
Christian person. 2325
Christian personal ethics. 943
Christian personalism of Pope John Paul II. 2126
Christian perspective. 3647
Christian perspective of knowing. 2180
Christian perspectives. 3043
Christian perspectives in contemporary culture. 1282

Christian perspectives on psychology. 2994
Christian persuader. 1565
Christian philosopher. 2673, 2674, 3075
Christian philosopher triumphing over death. 1748
Christian philosophy. 1048, 1105, 3099, 3696
Christian philosophy and religious renewal. 1106
Christian philosophy and intellectual freedom. 1105
Christian philosophy and its future. 1106
Christian philosophy and religious renewal. 1106
Christian philosophy and science. 1463
Christian philosophy discussed under the topics of absolute values, creative evolution and religion. 2836
Christian philosophy, God. 3099
Christian philosophy in the college and seminary. 2835
Christian philosophy in the twentieth century. 1104
Christian philosophy of education. 3098
Christian philosophy of existence. 1584
Christian philosophy of life. 1341, 2228
Christian philosophy of Saint Augustine. 116, 1740
Christian philosophy of St. Thomas Aquinas. 3695
Christian pilgrim. 1022
Christian Platonists of Alexandria. 2743, 2831, 2854
Christian poems. 1017
Christian poet in Paradise lost. 2469
Christian point of view. 595
Christian political theology. 1087, 2352
Christian political theory and church politics in the mid-twelfth century. 736, 1756
Christian power plan. 987
Christian practice. 959
Christian praise. 1865
Christian prayer. 2868, 2872, 2876
Christian prayer through the centuries. 2885
Christian prayers and holy meditations. 2889
Christian preacher. 2899, 2900
Christian presence in the neighborhood. 1253
Christian priest of to-day. 3674
Christian priest today. 1296
Christian priesthood. 771
Christian primer. 3661
Christian principles. 990
Christian priorities. 991
Christian proficiency. 1219
Christian program for the rural community. 3253
Christian progress. 965
Christian progress by oblivion of the past. 3366
Christian progress in Burma. 2505
Christian prospect in eastern Asia. 2516
Christian psalmist. 1865
Christian psalmody, in four parts. 1870
Christian psychology. 1107, 3111
Christian psychology of Paul Tournier. 2996, 3705
Christian public worship. 3003
Christian pursuit. 1000
Christian race. 649
Christian rationalism. 3023
Christian reader. 1456
Christian reader's guide to the New Testament. 473, 3360
Christian reader's guide to the Old Testament. 503, 1377
Christian realism. 1103
Christian realism and liberation theology. 2709, 3452
Christian realism and political problems. 1087
Christian realities. 1072
Christian reality & appearance. 1061
Christian reconstruction of modern life. 1057
Christian reflections. 1066
Christian reformed church. 1023, 1024
Christian Reformed Church government. 1023
Christian reformed church in North America. 1023
Christian Reformed church order. 1023
Christian Reformed tradition. 1024
Christian religion. 1054, 1060
Christian religion and human progress. 3619
Christian religion & its competitors to-day. 1078
Christian religion explained (The) 1212
Christian religion in growing life. 3152
Christian religion in its doctrinal expression. 3646

Christian religion in the Soviet Union. 3453
Christian religion, its meaning and proof. 1095
Christian religious education. 935, 3149
Christian religious experience. 3191
Christian religious tradition. 1179
Christian remembrancer. 3196
Christian renaissance. 1077, 1429, 3215
Christian renewal in a changing world. 998
Christian renewal in the changing world. 998
... Christian researches in Asia. 1847
Christian response to the atomic crisis. 103
Christian response to the Holocaust. 1825
Christian response to the sexual revolution. 3391
Christian responsibility and world poverty. 1137
Christian responsibility in economic life. 1076
Christian responsibility in one world. 44
Christian responsibility in the emerging world economic stituation. 1075
Christian responsibility to society. 3441
Christian retrospect and register. 1181
Christian reunion. 1044
Christian reunion: historic divisions reconsidered. 1042, 2009
Christian reunion in ecumenical light. 1040
Christian revelation. 3224
... The Christian revolution. 3443
Christian revolution for church renewal. 1243
Christian revolutionary. 2469, 3233
Christian rite and Christian drama in the Middle Ages. 844, 1478
Christian ritual and the world of Shakespeare's tragedies. 1101, 3400
Christian role in today's society. 948
Christian roots of democracy in America. 1086
Christian Sabbath. 3260
Christian sabbath, its history, authority, duties, benefits, and civil relations. 3546
Christian sacraments. 3263
Christian sacraments and Christian personality. 3264
Christian sacraments and Christian pesonality. 3264
Christian sacrifice. 2253, 3271
Christian saga. 1173
Christian salvation. 3294, 3296
Christian salvation and human temporal progress. 3289
Christian school: why it is right for your child. 1247
Christian science. 1029, 1030, 1032, 1033, 1034, 1035, 1037, 1495
Christian science against both science and the Bible. 1033
Christian science against itself. 1029
Christian Science and its discoverer. 1035, 1495
Christian science and its enemies. 1033
Christian science and its real author. 1035
Christian science and kindred subjects. 1036
Christian science and kindred superstitions. 1036
Christian science and legislation. 1038
Christian Science and liberty. 1034
Christian science and organized religion. 1033, 1210, 1494
Christian science and other superstitions. 1029
Christian Science and philosophy. 1036
Christian science and the Bible. 1036, 1792
Christian science and the Catholic faith. 1029
Christian science and the ordinary man. 1038
Christian science as a religious belief and a therapeutic agent. 1033
Christian Science association addresses. 1037
Christian science church. 1034
Christian Science church edifices. 1269
Christian Science class instruction. 1030, 1494
Christian science dissected. 1033
Christian science examined. 1036, 1496
Christian science exposed. 1029, 1034
Christian science exposition of the atonement. 103
Christian science falsely so called. 1029, 1036
Christian science healing. 1034
Christian science hymnal. 1037
Christian science in Germany. 1035
Christian science in the light of Holy Scripture. 1033

Christian science in the light of reason. 1030
Christian science: its legal status. 1035
Christian science made plain. 1035
Christian Science myth. 1034
Christian science: no and yes. 1030
Christian science of health. 1036
Christian Science re-explored. 1034
Christian Science re-explorrd. 1034
Christian science so-called. 1035
Christian science theory and practice. 1035
Christian Science today. 1029
Christian science under the searchlight. 1030
Christian science unmasked. 1029, 1034
Christian science versus pantheism. 1030
Christian science versus pantheism, and other messages to the mother church. 1030
Christian Science way of life. 1033
Christian science, with notes containing corrections to date. 1030
Christian (?) science X-rayed. 1030, 1036
Christian scientist who never made a demonstration. 1033
Christian sculpture. 3316
Christian sects. 3322
Christian sects in the nineteenth century. 1038
Christian seed in Western soil. 1100
Christian seets. 3322
Christian service and the modern world. 3444
Christian sex & family planning. 2340
Christian sex ethics. 3389
Christian sexuality. 3391
Christian sharing of possessions. 3531
Christian shepherd. 2780
Christian simplicity in St. Therese. 3690
Christian singers of Germany. 1874
Christian social conscience (The) 3449
Christian social consciousness. 1134
Christian social ethics. 946, 1101, 1133
Christian social ethics in a changing world. 3447
Christian social hygiene. 1859
Christian social manifesto. 853
Christian social principles. 3450
Christian social reformers of the nineteenth century. 3434
Christian social responsibility. 1138
Christian social science. 3452
Christian social teachings. 1016
Christian social tradition. 3447
Christian social union addresses. 3072
Christian society. 1178, 3443
Christian society and the Crusades, 1198-1229. 1390
Christian sociology. 3446
Christian sociology for to-day. 3449
Christian soldier. 365, 366, 3364
Christian souvenir, and missionary memorial for 1851. 2492
Christian spiritualist catechism. 1038
Christian spirituality. 90, 3492
Christian spirituality East & West. 3521
Christian spirituality in geologic perspective. 3522
Christian spirituality to-day. 3483
Christian stake in science. 3081
Christian stance in a revolutionary age. 1059
... Christian standards in life. 1016
Christian state. 3443
Christian state of life. 863
Christian Stewardship. 3528, 3529
Christian stewardship and church finance. 3528
Christian stewardship and Negro Baptists. 3530
Christian story. 3643
Christian story-telling and stories for parents, teachers, and students. 3534
Christian storytelling. 3534
Christian strategy for a struggling world. 1154
Christian students and world problems. 2515
Christian student. 1942
Christian symbolics. 1386
Christian symbolism. 920, 3573
Christian symbolism in the evangelical churches. 921
Christian symbols, ancient and modern. 919
Christian symbols and how to use them. 920
Christian system. 732, 1462
Christian task. 1091
Christian teacher. 1309, 3178
Christian teacher in Sunday schools. 3178
Christian teaching. 476, 977
Christian teaching and life. 476
Christian teaching and the Christian year. 3373
Christian teaching in the churches. 3157

Christian teaching of kindergarten children. 938, 3173
Christian teaching on social and economic questions confronting older boys and young men. 3446
Christian teachings. 748, 2286
Christian technocracy. 53
Christian, the church, and contemporary problems. 1134
Christian, the state, and the New Testament. 1142, 3072
Christian theatre. 3145
Christian theistic ethics. 3070
Christian theology. 3640, 3641, 3642, 3643, 3644, 3647, 3649, 3650, 3651, 3653, 3656
Christian theology and metaphysics. 1103
Christian theology and modern skepticism. 1092
Christian theology and natural science. 3079, 3313
Christian theology for the people. 3645
Christian theology in outline. 3641
Christian theology of Judaism. 2145
Christian theology of the Old Testament. 598
Christian theology, systematic and Biblical. 3640
Christian theory of knowledge. 67
Christian therapy for a neurotic world. 2780, 2784
Christian thinking on friendship and marriage. 2344
Christian thought. 3098
Christian thought from Erasmus to Berdyaev. 3213
Christian thought, its history and application. 1072
Christian thought to the Reformation. 3212
Christian thoughts for the journey of life. 3211
Christian today. 3485
Christian tradition. 1122, 3655
Christian tradition and the unity we seek. 1491, 1492
Christian treasures. 1094
Christian Trinity. 3713
Christian trugh and life. 3346
Christian truth. 62
Christian truth and modern opinion. 3074, 3075
Christian truth and religious delusions. 1386
Christian truth in history. 1105
Christian under pressure. 997
Christian understanding of atonement. 104
Christian understanding of existence. 999
Christian understanding of God. 1721
Christian understanding of human nature. 2324
Christian understanding of man. 2323, 2352
Christian understanding of the human person. 2321
Christian union. 1040
Christian unity. 134, 1039, 1042, 1491, 1912, 2246
Christian unity and Christian diversity. 1041
Christian unity and Disciples of Christ. 1491
Christian unity and religion in New England. 2687
Christian unity and the Gospel. 1039
Christian unity at work. 1046
Christian unity doctrinally and historically considered. 1042
Christian unity in effort. 1079
Christian unity in North America. 1041
Christian unity in practice and prophecy. 1041
Christian unity in the making. 1619
Christian unity is our business. 1042
Christian unity: its relevance to the community. 1912
Christian universe. 65
Christian use of emotional power. 1512
Christian use of the Bible. 653
Christian use of time. 3701
Christian values and economic life. 1075
Christian victory instruction. 2695
Christian view of abortion. 3
Christian view of being and knowing. 2840
Christian view of history? 1819
Christian view of homosexuality. 1844
Christian view of life. 990, 1439
Christian view of man. 2324, 3183
Christian view of men and things. 62
Christian view of science and Scripture. 205
Christian view of sex education. 3391
Christian view of sexual behavior. 2177, 3388
Christian view of the Old Testament. 482
Christian view of the world. 1103

Christian views science. 3083
Christian virtues. 3782
Christian vision. 760, 1002
Christian vocation. 3191, 3784
Christian voices in China. 912
Christian war on Anti-Semitism. 1073
Christian watchman. 2324
Christian way. 992, 1048, 2971, 3153, 3184, 3336
Christian way of death. 1413
Christian way of liberty. 2223
...The Christian way of life for young people. 3885
Christian wholeness. 1007, 3484, 3715
Christian wisdom. 3462
Christian wisdom and Christian formation. 1946
Christian witness in a secular age. 69
Christian witness in an industrial society. 1131
Christian witness in communist China. 912
Christian witness in the secular city. 3623
Christian witness on campus. 3828
Christian witness to the State. 1152
Christian witnessing. 3828, 3829
Christian woman. 3843, 3844
Christian woman as a social worker. 3443
Christian woman in the Christian home. 3843, 3844
Christian woman in the working world. 3832
Christian womanhood. 1578
Christian woman's search for self-esteem. 3835
Christian women at work. 3835
Christian word book. 3638
Christian words. 352, 1769
Christian words and Christian meanings. 3682
Christian work as a vocation. 3786
Christian work in Latin America. 2548
Christian work in South America. 2547
... Christian workers Bible. 198
Christian workers' commentary on the Old and New Testaments. 222
Christian worker's handbook. 1252, 3677
... Christian workers' Holy Bible. 197
Christian workers' manual. 3070
Christian worker's manual of practical knowledge. 3674
Christian worker's New Testament. 479
Christian workship by families. 3853
Christian world. 1282
Christian world action. 1077, 2807
Christian world-builders. 3877
Christian world facts. 2523
Christian world mission. 2491, 2554
Christian world mission in our day. 1187
Christian world neighbors. 2549
Christian world of C. S. Lewis. 2219
Christian worship. 2236, 2238, 2306, 3004, 3853
Christian worship and church education. 3853
... Christian worship and its future. 3854
Christian worship by families. 1607
Christian worship for America youth. 3857
Christian worship in transition. 3004
Christian worship, its making and meaning; [revised edition]. 3853
Christian worship, its theology and practice. 3854
Christian worship, studies in its history and meaning, by members of Mansfield college. 3004
Christian worshiping. 3854
Christian writer's handbook. 3203
Christian year. 725, 1262, 1265, 1268, 1433, 1860, 1866, 2946
Christian year for schools and the isolated. 1262
Christian year in human story. 726
Christian year, its purpose and its history. 1262
Christian year (The) 2883
Christian yes or no. 3829
Christian yoga. 2379
Christian young people and world-friendship. 2551
Christian youth, an in-depth study. 3890
Christian youth at song. 3562
Christian youth fellowship. 1166, 3876
Christian youth fellowship worship manual. 3858
Christian youth in action. 3882, 3886
Christian Zen. 1084, 1085, 2380
Christiana follows on (witness #2) 3783
Christiana Tsai. 928, 3717
Christianica. 696
Christianity. 61, 1047, 1048, 1051, 1052, 1080, 1092, 1098, 1172, 1176, 1184, 1189, 1654, 2072, 2266, 2554, 3060
Christianity; a biologic fact. 3074
Christianity: a historical religion? 1819, 2009

Christianity a national law. 1141
Christianity, a personal mission. 2554
Christianity according to John. 424
Christianity according to Paul. 375
... Christianity according to St. John. 414
Christianity according to St. Luke. 430
Christianity according to St. Paul. 377, 2801
Christianity across cultures. 2529
Christianity against infidelity. 1099
Christianity against Jesus. 1093, 2050
Christianity American style. 3743
Christianity amid rising men and nations. 2515
Christianity among the Arabs in pre-Islamic times. 77
Christianity among the religions. 1078
Christianity among the religions of the world. 1080
Christianity among the religious. 1078
... Christianity, an inquiry into its nature and truth. 1096
Christianity; an interpretation. 1095
Christianity, an outline of dogmatic theology for laymen. 3662
Christianity and African education. 3161
Christianity and agnosticism. 19
Christianity and agnosticism: a controversy. 19
Christianity and American capitalism. 1136
Christianity and American education. 1130
Christianity and American freemasonry. 1663
Christianity and America's social problems. 1135
Christianity and amusements. 36
Christianity and animism in Taiwan. 3580
Christianity and anti-Semitism. 53
Christianity and anti-Christianity in their final conflict. 51
Christianity and autosuggestion. 1107
Christianity and Barthianism. 176
Christianity and Christ. 1049
Christianity and civilisation. 1281, 1282, 3066
Christianity and civilization. 1069
Christianity and civilization in the south Pacific. 2543
Christianity and classical civilization. 1282
Christianity and classical culture. 1281
Christianity and coercion. 3448
Christianity and colonialism. 1310
Christianity & commerce. 1077
Christianity and common sense. 1048, 1593
Christianity and communication. 2554
Christianity and comparative religion. 1078
Christianity and cosmopolitan civilization. 1065
Christianity and culture. 1070, 1182, 2557, 3442
Christianity and democracy. 1075
Christianity and economic problems. 1075
Christianity and economics. 1075, 3446
Christianity and education. 3149
Christianity and est. 988
Christianity and ethics. 942
Christianity and evolution. 3076, 3625
Christianity and existentialism. 1584
Christianity and false evolutionism. 3074
Christianity and fear. 1619
Christianity and freedom, a symposium. 2223
Christianity and Greek philosophy. 2834
Christianity and history. 1098, 1817, 1818, 3653
Christianity and humanism. 1854
Christianity and humanity. 3725
Christianity and idealism. 1053, 1055, 2837
Christianity and immortality. 1891
Christianity and industry. 3440
Christianity and industry in America. 3446
Christianity and infidelity. 1050
Christianity and international peace. 2807
Christianity and Islam. 1082
Christianity and Islam in Spain, A.D. 756-1031. 1108
Christianity and Islam under the sultans. 1084, 1926
Christianity and its Bible. 1064
Christianity and its contrasts. 1098
Christianity and its Judaic heritage. 1178
Christianity and Judism compare notes. 1052
Christianity and justice. 2065, 3445
Christianity and liberalism. 2221
Christianity and medical science. 1047
Christianity and mental health. 2784
Christianity and mental hygiene. 2996
Christianity and militarism. 1089
Christianity and modern crises. 1134
Christianity and modern culture. 1106

Christianity and modern man. 3328
Christianity and modern thought. 1049,
3211, 3621, 3723
Christianity and modernism. 2561
Christianity and money. 1136
Christianity and morals. 946
Christianity and mythology. 1078
Christianity and naturalism. 1306, 1307,
3080, 3081
Christianity and non-Christian religions
compared. 3118
Christianity and other religions. 1079,
1080
Christianity and other world religions.
1053
Christianity--and our world. 1056
Christianity and pagan culture in the later
Roman Empire. 1192
Christianity and pagan culture in the later
Roman Empire together with an English
translation of John Chrysostom's
Address on vainglory and the right way
for parents to bring up their children.
1192
Christianity and paradox. 2836
Christianity and personality. 2822
Christianity and philosophy. 2836
Christianity and political responsibility.
1086
Christianity and politics. 1086, 1087,
1143, 3441
Christianity and politics in Africa. 1087,
1144
Christianity and positivism. 3102
Christianity and power politics. 1086
... Christianity and problems of to-day.
3097
... Christianity and progress. 1049
Christianity and property. 1075, 1076
Christianity and race. 3017
Christianity and real life. 2202
Christianity and reasons. 3027
Christianity and revolution. 1085, 3042
Christianity and rival religions. 1079
Christianity and Romanism. 1078
Christianity and scholarship. 3083
Christianity and science. 205, 3079, 3084
Christianity and sex. 3392
Christianity and sex problems. 3393
Christianity and sin. 3411
Christianity and social adventuring. 3441
Christianity and social justice. 1135
Christianity and social order. 3441, 3446
Christianity and social problems. 3440
Christianity and social process. 3086
Christianity and social progress. 1136
Christianity and social science. 3442
Christianity and socialism. 3436
Christianity and society. 3442
Christianity and some living religions of
the East. 1078
Christianity and statesmanship. 1069
Christianity and statesmanship, with
kindred topics. 1069
Christianity and success. 1059
Christianity and symbolism. 3407
Christianity and the affluent society. 1075
Christianity and the age of the earth. 203
... Christianity and the American
commonwealth. 3738
Christianity and the arts. 84
Christianity and the Asian revolution.
1485
Christianity and the bourgeoisie. 3087
Christianity and the children of Israel.
1083
Christianity and the class struggle. 3433
Christianity and the commonplace. 3057
Christianity and the contemporary scene.
3617
Christianity and the cultural crisis. 1134
Christianity and the encounter of the
world religions. 1080
Christianity and the existentialists. 1584
Christianity and the family. 1603
Christianity and the gamut of evolution.
3314
Christianity and the individual in a world
of crowds. 1905
Christianity and the Japanese. 2533
Christianity and the Jew. 2535
Christianity and the labor movement.
3440
Christianity and the machine age. 3442
Christianity and the man of to-day. 2326
Christianity and the modern chaos. 1052
Christianity and the modern mind. 1051
Christianity and the modern world view.
1059
... Christianity and the nations. 2521
Christianity and the nature of history.
1072
Christianity and the new Africa. 1073
Christianity and the new age. 1051
Christianity and the new idealism. 1881,
3099

Christianity and the problem of history.
1818
Christianity and the race problem. 3017
Christianity and the religions. 1079
Christianity and the religions of the world.
1079
Christianity and the religious drama. 934,
3145
Christianity and the Roman government.
3245
Christianity and the scientist. 3081
Christianity and the social crisis. 3087,
3445
Christianity and the social order. 3441
Christianity and the social range. 3440
Christianity and the social revolution.
3436
Christianity and the social state. 3444
Christianity and the state. 1140
Christianity and the supernatural. 3642
Christianity and the survival of the West.
1062
Christianity and the Trinitarian doctrine.
3713
Christianity and the United States. 1109
Christianity and the world of thought.
1074
Christianity and the world order. 1088
Christianity and traditional religion in
western Zimbabwe, 1859-1923. 3234
Christianity and war. 3792
Christianity and world democracy. 1050
Christianity and world issues. 1134
Christianity and world order. 1056
Christianity and world revolution. 1066
Christianity and Xhosa tradition. 1110
Christianity and you. 166
Christianity as history and faith. 1177
Christianity as mystical fact and The
mysteries of antiquity. 1078, 1079
Christianity as old as the creation. 1420
Christianity as old as the creation, 1730.
3024
Christianity as taught by Christ. 2066
Christianity at Rome in the apostolic age.
2824, 3245
Christianity at the centre. 64
Christianity at the cross-roads. 2562,
2563, 3465
Christianity at the crossroads. 1601
... Christianity at work. 3180
Christianity between Sundays. 1059, 1821
Christianity, capitalism and communism.
3452
Christianity challenges the university.
1074
Christianity, communism, and history. 64
Christianity confronts communism. 1320
Christianity confronts culture. 1074
Christianity cross-examined. 1654
Christianity crucified. 3052
Christianity designed and adapted to be a
universal religion. 1054
Christianity, diplomacy and war. 1085
Christianity divided. 2955
Christianity does make sense. 1058
Christianity explained to Muslims. 2557
Christianity for pious skeptics. 337, 1028,
2795
Christianity for the tough-minded. 68
... Christianity for to-day. 3663
Christianity goes to press. 612
Christianity in a changing world. 1093
Christianity in a new world. 3706
Christianity in a revolutionary age. 1182
Christianity in a world of science. 3078
Christianity in action. 976
Christianity in Africa. 1073
Christianity in Africa as seen by Africans.
1135
Christianity in America. 3744
Christianity in an age of science. 3077
Christianity in chains. 1060, 3449
Christianity in China, Tartary and Thibet.
850
Christianity in Communist China. 1090
Christianity in conflict. 2976
Christianity in context. 1103
Christianity in crisis. 65
Christianity in crisis: new hope. 3623
Christianity in culture. 1074
Christianity in early Britain. 1761
Christianity in education. 1128, 1129
Christianity in England. 1758
Christianity in European history. 1097,
1542
Christianity in Israel. 1101
Christianity in its modern expression.
1058
Christianity in Japan. 1101
Christianity in modern Japan. 2533
Christianity in peril. 1062
Christianity in Roman Britain to AD 500.
1763
Christianity in Russia. 3256
Christianity in science. 3078
Christianity in Somerset. 3457

Christianity in southeast Asia. 1090
Christianity in Talmud and Midrash. 1101
Christianity in the apostolic age. 1194
Christianity in the Asian revolution. 2502
Christianity in the computer age. 1061
Christianity in the daily conduct of life.
970
Christianity in the Eastern conflicts. 91
Christianity in the home. 1603
Christianity in the light of reason. 3027
Christianity in the light of reason and
revelation. 1051
Christianity in the modern world. 1048,
1068
Christianity in the new age. 1059
Christianity in the nineteenth century.
1182
Christianity in the non-Western world.
1090
Christianity in the non-western world.
1090
Christianity in the Roman Empire. 1193
Christianity in the Roman world. 1197
Christianity in the Southern Hemisphere.
1101
Christianity in the Soviet Union. 1108
Christianity in the twentieth century.
1059
Christianity in the United States. 3738
Christianity in the United States from the
first settlement down to the present time.
3738
Christianity in thought and practice. 2837
Christianity in tropical Africa. 1073
Christianity in world history. 1079
Christianity in world perspective. 1074
Christianity is Christ. 864, 2044, 2045
Christianity is for you. 2295
Christianity is Jewish. 296, 1084
Christianity is life. 958
Christianity is personal. 147
Christianity is revolutionary. 809
Christianity, Islam and the Negro race.
2680
Christianity, Judaism, and revolution.
3441
Christianity marches on! 1198
Christianity meets Buddhism. 1080
Christianity mobilizing. 1058
Christianity: mystery of love. 2266
Christianity never survived. 1051
Christianity not a temperance religion.
3596
Christianity not mysterious. 3024
Christianity of Christ. 2060
Christianity of Christ and His apostles.
1053
Christianity of Ignatius of Antioch. 1882
Christianity of Main Street. 1097
Christianity of St. Paul. 3277
Christianity of to-morrow. 1051
Christianity old and new. 124
Christianity on the march. 1183
Christianity on trial. 62
Christianity or Christ. 3260
Christianity or religion? 3059
Christianity; or, Why I became a non-
sectarian. 1091
Christianity our citadel. 3467
Christianity, past and present. 67, 1175
Christianity reborn. 1100
Christianity rediscovered. 1094
Christianity restored. 2464
Christianity rightly so called. 1094
Christianity rubs holes in my religion.
1367, 2631
Christianity: some non-Christian
appraisals. 1080
Christianity supernatural. 60
Christianity takes a stand. 1135
Christianity tested. 923, 2502
Christianity the final religion. 1092
...Christianity--the paradox of God. 1051,
1997
Christianity the perfection of true
manliness. 1323
Christianity the religion of nature. 2673
Christianity, the science of manhood. 61
Christianity the state in the light of
history. 1144
Christianity the true theology. 1089, 2759
Christianity the way. 1095
... Christianity the world-religion. 1047
Christianity through Jewish eyes. 2154
Christianity through the ages. 1176
Christianity through the centuries. 1173
Christianity through the thirteenth century.
1197, 1198
Christianity to-day. 1069
Christianity today. 1090, 1182, 3651
Christianity today reader. 1090
Christianity today. Symposium The
challenge of the cults. 3325
Christianity triumphant. 60
Christianity unveiled. 1091, 2129

Christianity vs. communistic atheism. 610
Christianity vs. freemasonry. 1661
Christianity vs. militarism. 3792
Christianity versus orthodox theology.
1103
Christianity vs. railroading. 957, 3070
Christianity versus religion. 1179
Christianity vs. selfishness. 3087
Christianity versus the cults. 3323
Christianity versus war. 3791
Christianity vindicated. 60
Christianity where men work. 1131
Christianity where you live. 3739
Christianity, which way? 1122
Christianity with nature. 2676
Christianity's China creations. 2508
... Christianity's compelling conviction.
3295
Christianity's contributions to civilization.
1049
Christianity's greatest peril. 1049
Christianity's problem in the Far East.
2520
Christianity's storm centre. 1279
Christianity's unifying fundamental. 1097
...The Christianization of American life.
1108
Christianization of the European East and
messianic aspirations of Moscow as the
"Third Rome" 1542
Christianized rationalism. 3022
Christianizing a nation. 133
Christianizing community life. 1139, 3447
Christianizing our community. 1139, 3176
Christianizing the social order. 3445
Christians. 1189
Christians active in the world. 776, 3632
Christians alive. 962
Christians alive; handbook for spiritual
growth. 987
Christian's alternative to war. 3793
Christians and Jews. 53, 1083, 2535
Christians and Marxists. 1319
Christians and mental health. 1108
Christians and power politics. 1076
Christians & prayer. 941
Christians and race relations in South
Africa. 1108
Christians & sociology. 3444
Christians and the Church in the German
Democratic Republic. 1146
Christians and the crisis in sex morality.
3389
Christians and the good earth. 1348
Christians and the great commission. 2518, 25
Christians and the state. 1140
Christians and the world of nations. 1086
Christians and world freedom. 1076
Christian's appreciation of other faiths.
3120
Christians are citizens. 1085
Christians are not for lions. 938
Christians around the alter. 2365
Christian's aspirations. 968
Christians at prayer. 2882
Christians at worship. 3856
Christians awake. 862, 1057, 1139, 1941
Christian's Bible--New Testament. 353
Christian's business. 1567
Christian's calling. 3784
Christians can conquer. 1592
Christians' claim about Jesus of Nazareth,
perfect God and Perfect Man. 2001
Christians, claim your heritage. 1103
Christian's companion. 2685
Christians confront communism. 1319
Christians courageous. 926, 932
Christian's daily manna. 995
Christian's day. 2383
Christian's defence against the fears of
death. 1413
Christian's defensive dictionary. 3639
Christian's dictionary. 3639
Christian's Dr. Jekyll and Mr. Hyde. 983
Christian's duty and kindred sermons.
2931
Christian's education. 1497
Christian's experience in the conquest of
sin. 3384
Christians face issues of high moment in
our changing economy. 1075
Christians, fellow-helpers to the truth.
3339
Christians' God. 1725
Christian's God and his family. 1058
Christian's great interest. 1779, 3289
Christians' guide. 941
Christian's guide to Bible study. 637
Christian's guide to effective jail & prison
ministries. 1255
Christian's guide to piety. 856
Christian's guide to prayer. 2877
Christian's guide to the New Testament.
473
Christian's guide to the Old Testament.
541
Christian's habits. 1053

Christian's handbook on communism. 1319
Christians have troubles, too. 2780
Christian's home in glory. 1793, 1838
Christians in a new era. 784
Christians in a rapidly changing economy. 1075
Christians in a technological era. 1067
Christians in action. 2508, 3764
Christians in an unchristian society. 3447
Christians in China before the year 1550. 1110
Christians in conflict. 25, 1132
Christians in contemporary Russia. 1149
Christians in conversation. 794
Christians in crossfire. 2785
Christians in Persia: Assyrians, Armenians, Roman Catholics and Protestants. 1918
Christians in racial crisis. 1290
Christians in secular India. 1110
Christians in the American Revolution. 3742
Christians in the Arab East. 1109
Christians in the arena. 2820
Christians in the shadow of the Kremlin. 3257
Christians in the world. 999, 1074
Divine man or magician? 1742, 2046
Christian's instructor. 3663
Christian's last end. 1531
Christian's life and program. 963
Christian's magazine. 3677
Christian's manual. 2818
Christian's mission. 2480
Christian's model. 1986
Christians near and far. 1074
Christians of Korea. 1110
Christians of the East. 851, 2516
Christians of to-day. 937
Christians on the right. 1086
Christians only. 1464, 2077
Christians organizing for political service. 1087
Christian's patriotism. 2794
... The Christian's personal religion. 3097
Christian's philosophy of religion. 3099
Christians, politics and violent revolution. 1085, 3233
Christian's power. 2866
Christian's prayer book. 1265
Christian's recreation. 2854
Christian's relation to evolution. 1580
Christian's religion. 1051
Christian's rule of marriage. 2338
Christian's saving interest. 1361
Christian's secret of a happy life. 975
Christian's secret of a happy life for today. 984
Christians, the church, and property. 1075
Christians together. 3732
Christians togethers. 3732
Christian's triumph. 922
Christians two chiefe lessons, viz. selfe-deniall and selfe-tryall. 964
Christians under the hammer & sickle. 2821
Christian's undoing. 1091
Christians will go through the tribulation. 3711
Christians with courage. 924
Christians with secular power. 2191
Christians worship. 3855
Christians you should know. 924
Christians you would like to know. 924
Christiantiy and democracy. 1086
Christianus per ignem. 2399
Christic reign. 3342
Christina doctrine of prayer. 2873
Christina Forsyth of Fingoland. 1634, 2499
Christina worship, some meanings and means. 3853
Christioan college. 1128
Christisanity and cosmopolitan civilization. 1065
Christisis. 3461
Christisis; a course of study in higher soul culture. 3461
Christlike Christian (The) 3090
Christlike Christianity. 1049
Christlike God. 3092
Christlikeness. 2581
Christly life. 961
Christmas. 1110, 1111, 1112, 1113, 2021, 2022
Christmas ABC book. 1111
Christmas and the saints. 3284
... Christmas and Twelfth night. 2022
Christmas around the world. 1111
Christmas at home. 1113
Christmas bells. 1113
Christmas book. 1112, 2021
Christmas books. 1112, 1712
Christmas carols. 741, 742
Christmas chimes. 1113, 1114
Christmas chronicle. 1111
Christmas companion. 1111

Christmas crib. 1387
Christmas cycle. 9
Christmas Day. 1113
Christmas-day anthem. 1113
Christmas dictionary. 1111
Christmas entertainments for Sunday schools. 1112
Christmas Eve; dialogue on incarnation. 1015
Christmas every day. 1112
Christmas every Friday, and other Christmas stories. 1114
Christmas feasts and festivals. 1111
Christmas festival illustrated through illuminated manuscripts and drawings in the Pierpont Morgan library, New York, December 16, 1935 to January 31, 1936. 2021
Christmas gift to the American home. 1112
Christmas here and everywhere. 1111
Christmas in Bethlehem. 1112
Christmas in Bethlehem, and Holy Week at Mount Athos. 1112
Christmas in heart and home. 1112
Christmas in old New England. 1114
Christmas in our hearts. 1110
Christmas in song, sketch, and story. 1114
Christmas in the olden time. 1113
Christmas is a happy time! 1112, 2023
Christmas is always. 1111
Christmas is here. 1113
Christmas is today. 1112
Christmas joys. 1111
Christmas kalends of Provence and some other Provencal festivals. 1111
Christmas letter. 3822
Christmas light and the Easter hope. 1111
... Christmas list, 1906. 905
Christmas literature through the centuries. 1112
Christmas masque of Saint Roch, Pere Dagobert, and Throwing the wanga. 1113
Christmas messages. 1112, 1114
Christmas miracle and God bless this house. 1113
Christmas of the purple pugassus. 1111
Christmas pageant. 2022
Christmas plays for children. 1113
Christmas, prepared by the members of a seminar in religious education. 1111
Christmas promise. 2021
Christmas road. 1112, 2022
Christmas sermons. 1114, 1233
Christmas sermons of Bl. Guerric of Igny. 1114
Christmas shrine. 1111
Christmas sky. 3525
Christmas stories. 1114
Christmas stories of George MacDonald. 1112
Christmas stories that never grow old. 1114
Christmas story. 2022, 2023
Christmas story; a book of paintings. 1958
Christmas story from the Gospels of Matthew & Luke. 2024
Christmas testament. 1111
Christmas-tide in song. 1113
Christmas tidings. 1110, 2021
Christmas to-day. 1111
Christmas treasures. 1114
Christmas treasury. 1111
Christmas voices. 1114
Christmas wonder. 741
Christmas workshop for the church family. 1112
Christmastide. 1111
Christo-paganism. 3578
Christobel. 1021
Christographia. 1343
Christological controversy. 2010
Christological perspectives. 2046
Christologies ancient and modern. 1971
Christology. 1954
Christology after Auschwitz. 1084
Christology and a modern pilgrimage. 435, 2820
Christology and criticims. 2045
Christology and personality. 2044, 3018
Christology at the crossroads. 2044, 2222
... The Christology in the Apostolic fathers. 76, 2009
Christology in the making. 1894
Christology of Hegel. 2010
Christology of Jesus. 477, 2044
Christology of St. Paul. 377, 2035
Christology of the Epistle to the Hebrews. 1958
Christology of the Espistle to the Hebrews. 405, 2009
Christology of the later Fathers. 2009
Christology of the New Testament. 475, 1951, 2010
Christology of the Old Testament. 2415

Christopaganism or indigenous Christianity? 2515
Christoph Blumhardt and his message. 2298
Christopher. 2260
Christopher Layton. 2203, 2603
Christopher prayers for today. 2888
Christopher Sauers. 2942, 3468
Christopher the giant. 1114
Christotherapy. 1601
Christotherapy II. 2781
Christs. 2012, 2047
Christ's acted parables. 2017
Christ's adequacy for human needs. 3493
Christ's adventurers who changed history. 2483
Christ's alternative to communism. 1090, 1319, 3453
Christ's ambassadors. 2899
Christ's appeal for love to His humble servant Josefa Menendez. 2643
Christ's battles with the Pharisees. 1953
Christ's cabinet. 71
Christ's call to commitment. 161
Christ's career woman. 2581
Christ's challenge, and other evangelistic sermons. 1561
Christ's challenge to man's spirit in this world crisis. 2972
Christ's Christianity. 2070
Christ's church. 1043, 1048
Christ's church bride. 301
Christ's coming and His kingdom. 2464
Christ's coming kingdom. 519
Christ's cure for the world. 2012
Christ's darkest hours. 2031
Christ's discourse on love. 424
Christ's economy. 731, 2004
Christ's eternal gospel. 1103, 2043
Christ's eternal invitation. 2033
Christ's expendables. 155
Christ's experience of God. 959, 2014
Christ's famous titles. 1742
Christ's famous titles, and The believer's golden chain, handled in divers sermons. 3363
Christ's farewell discourse. 424, 2071
Christ's gift, the mass. 2365
Christ's gift to the churches. 3465
Christ's glorious achievements. 3358
Christ's glorious church. 737
Christ's hall of fame. 384, 2007
Christ's headship of the church. 36
Christ's idea of the supernatural. 1951
Christ's ideals for living. 1016
Christ's image. 399, 1957
Christ's keys to happiness. 181
Christ's kingdom and coming. 2174
... Christ's kingdom and reign. 2014
Christ's kingdom not of this world. 2176
Christ's last message to His church. 459
Christ's life and ours. 1992
Christ's life, Our life. 929, 1976
Christ's little ones. 896
Christ's lordship and religious pluralism. 1081
Christ's love will make you live. 2395
Christ's masterpiece. 757
Christ's memorial. 1318
Christ's message to the churches. 2018
Christ's message to us today. 3365
Christ's messengers. 331
Christ's messengers; studies in the Acts of the apostles. 331
Christ's militant kingdom. 2014
Christ's mould of prayer. 2246
Christ's "No!" 2215
Christ's object in life. 2016
Christ's object lessons. 1955, 2027, 2066
Christ's offspring. 1033
Christ's one church forever. 1463
Christ's one sacrifice in its threefold mode. 104
Christ's own church. 757
Christ's parables for today. 2024
Christ's pathway to power. 3885
Christ's people. 1284, 2817
Christ's place in history. 2050
Christ's preachers. 1295
Christ's preachers, according to the New Testament. 1295
Christ's preaching, and ours. 2904
Christ's promise fulfilled. 125
Christ's redemptive sacrifice. 3031
Christ's second coming. 2055
... Christ's second coming and what will follow. 2055
Christ's secret of happiness. 1785
... Christ's service of love. 1318
Christ's seven letters to his church. 461
Christ's shining way. 1953
Christ's social remedies. 3444
Christ's soul-searching parables. 2024
Christ's strange work. 2201
Christ's suburban body. 2480

Christ's sudden and certain appearance to judgment. 2156
Christ's table talk. 2063
Christ's teaching on creation vs. evolution. 1382
... Christ's temptation and ours. 2067, 3600
Christ's theory and resurrection power. 1515
Christ's trumpet-call to the ministry. 3672
Christ's twelve. 71
Christ's valedictory or, Meditations on the fourteenth chapter of John. 2015
Christ's victory and ours. 1747, 2057
Christ's vision. 2771
Christ's way and the world's, in church, state, and society. 1060
Christ's way of winning souls. 1954
Christ's witchdoctor. 1508, 2505
Christ's word to this age. 2063
Christ's words as related to science, law, government, history, philosophy, religion, and universal human experience. 2066
Christ's words from the cross. 2058
Christus. 2003
Christus auctor. 1098
Christus consolator. 1350
Christus Dominus. 665
Christus emptor. 962
Christus liberator. 11
Christus Mediator. 2038
Christus redemptio. 2543
Christus victor. 108
Christward. 1359, 2024
Chronicle and sketch of the church of Saint Ignatius of Loyola. 132
...A chronicle history of Saint Patrick's parish. 888
Chronicle of Ahimaaz. 20, 2087
Chronicle of an American crusader. 3015
Chronicle of Christ Church. 2688
Chronicle of events between the years 1623 and 1733, relating to the settlement of the Order of Carmelites in Mesopotamia (Bassora); a contribution to the history of Christian missions in the East, written by Agathangelus of St. Theresa and others. 741
Chronicle of Methodism in Van Diemen's Land 1820-1840. 2553
Chronicle of the Catholic history of the Pacific Northwest. 826
Chronicle of two hundred years of St. John's Church. 2713
Chronicler's history of Israel. 1927
... Chronicles. 496, 590, 1178
Chronicles of an old Missouri parish. 818, 1652
Chronicles of Calvary Baptist church in the city of Washington. 171
Chronicles of Christ church parish, Williamsport, Pa., 1840-1896. 1523
Chronicles of Emanu-El. 1335
Chronicles of Jerahmeel. 2207
Chronicles of the Crusades. 1391
Chronological and background charts of the New Testament. 402
Chronological aspects of the life of Christ. 1996
Chronological charts of Bible history and prophecy. 218, 610
Chronological charts of the Old Testament. 497
Chronological harmony of the Gospels. 396
Chronological harmony of the Gospels using the revised text of the Challoner-Rheims version of the New Testament. 396
Chronological introduction to the history of the church. 1997
Chronological key to Bible study. 219
Chronological list of reports of committees of both houses of the convocation of Canterbury, 1847-1921 (April) 1220
Chronologie de la premiere croisade, 1094-1100. 1391
Chronology and historical narratives of Foundry's 150 years, 1814-1964. 3797
Chronology and recensional development in the Greek text of Kings. 556
Chronology of Christ's life. 1997
Chronology of Ezra 7. 519, 724
Chronology of Paul's life. 2803
Chronology of the Bible. 218
Chronology of the Hebrew kings. 555, 2093
Chronology of the last days of Jesus. 2030
Chronology of the life of Christ. 1997
Chronology of the public ministry of Jesus. 1997
Chruch manual of the First church of Christ, Scientist, in Boston, Massachusetts. 1030
Chrysalis, "a journey into the new spiritual America" 1476, 3747
...Chrysostom. 1115

Chrysostomus and his message. 1115
Chuang tsu: Inner chapters. 914
Chuang Tzu. 2188
Chuang tzu: mystic, moralist, and social reformer. 2838
Chuetas of Majorca. 1909
Chuma. 2490
Chuma finds a baby. 2490
Chumash artifacts collected in Santa Barbara County, California. 50
Chums and their powwows. 3870
Chundra Lela. 1116
Church. 760, 804, 811, 812, 1117, 1119, 1120, 1122, 1123, 1124, 1125, 1126, 1187, 1188, 1200, 1228, 1240, 1254, 3157
Church, a believing fellowship. 1120, 2915
Church a composite life. 1122
Church, a divine mystery. 1119
Church a field of service. 1252
Church, a pictorial history. 812
Church and Scottish social development, 1780-1870. 1234, 3315
Church abroad. 1465
Church across the street. 3323
Church action in the world. 2481
Church activities for young couples. 1259
Church: Acts-Revelation. 1198
Church administration. 1126, 1251
Church administration in Black perspective. 15
Church advertising. 10
Church after the Council. 792, 3773
Church after the war. 1061
... The church-after the war--what? 1619, 3470
Church against itself. 1126
Church against the world. 1117
Church alive. 329, 3674
Church alive and growing. 1126
Church almanac. 26
Church amid revolution. 3448
... The church among Tamils and Telungus; reports of some aspect studies. 1897
Church: an organic picture of its life and mission. 1116
Church and a Christian society. 3168
Church and a village grow up. 2462
Church and Black liberation. 1123
Church and campus. 1128
Church and campus in Pennsylvania. 1127
Church and chapel. 49
Church and children under two. 1254
Church and China, towards reconciliation? 816, 1090
Church and Christian belief. 3182
Church and Christian prayer. 2880
Church and Christian union. 1041
Church and civilization. 1075, 1281, 2425
Church and clergy in the American Revolution. 3738
Church and colonialism. 1137
Church and communications arts. 3002
Church and community. 1117, 2775
Church and community organization. 1134
Church and community, 1675-1975. 3432
Church and community survey of Pend Oreille County, Washington. 1275
Church and community survey of Salem County, New Jersey. 1271, 3286
Church and contemporary change. 1062
Church and contemporary culture. 3700
Church and contraception. 664
Church and country life. 3253
Church and creed. 1385
Church and culture in the Middle Ages. 1186
Church and demobilization. 1259
Church and ecumenism. 1491
Church and ecumenism (The) 1491
Church and education. 1130
Church and English life. 3366
Church and evangelism. 1569
Church and faith in Mid-America. 2462
Church and Freemasonry in Brazil, 1872-1875. 815, 1663
Church & gnosis. 1717
Church and God's people. 1119
Church and government in the Middle Ages. 891, 1187
Church and healing. 1600
Church and her children. 133, 1253
Church and her prophets. 2951
Church and her walls. 3738
Church and her work. 3733
Church and homosexuality. 1844
Church and human society at the threshold of the third millennium. 1065
Church and I. 3401
Church and industrial reconstruction. 3441
Church and industry. 1130, 1131
Church and infallibility. 1199, 3304
Church and infants and toddlers. 904
Church and its American opportunity. 2958

Church and its changing ministry. 1117
Church and its culture. 1178
Church and its elders. 1251, 1288
Church and its function in society. 1124
Church and its laity. 2191
Church and its ministry. 1116
Church and its mission. 1117
Church and its organization in primitive and Catholic times. 1240
Church and its teaching today. 1123, 1124
Church and its young adults. 1259
Church and Jesus. 1184, 1987
Church and kingdom. 2176
Church and mankind. 1116, 1117, 1123, 3770
Church and mankind (The) 1117
Church and manor. 2329
Church and marriage. 2343
Church and medical missions. 2538
Church and mental health. 2995
Church and metropolis. 1278
Church and ministry. 1117
Church and mission in Japan in January, 1941. 2534
Church and mission in modern Africa. 813, 2497
Church and missionary education. 2515
Church and missions. 2521
Church and modern life. 1118
Church and modern men. 1118
Church and modern problems in the light of the teaching of Paul in First Corinthians. 1134
Church and modern science. 3079
Church and modern society. 759, 3086
Church and modern youth. 1260
Church and my life. 3175
Church and newspapers. 10
Church and non-profit housing: a survey. 1849
Church and only a church. 3153
Church and organized movements. 1121
Church and parish. 3809
Church and Parliament. 1140
Church and people, 1450-1660. 1515
Church and people in New Guinea. 2542
Church and people, 1789-1889. 1220, 1748
Church and politics. 835, 1086
Church and politics in Chile. 771, 1143
Church and popular education. 1128
Church and power in Brazil. 814, 1144
Church and primitive peoples. 133, 3110
Church and printer's ink. 10
Church and psychotherapy. 2995
Church and race in South Africa. 13
Church and religion. 1187
Church and residential desegregation. 2681
Church and revolution. 1154
Church and revolution in Rwanda. 1108, 3812
Church and sacrament. 3266
Church and science. 3080
Church and Scottish social development, 1780-1870. 3315
Church and sect in Canada. 734
Church and sex. 3393
Church and sex education. 3390
Church and slavery. 3425
Church and social change in Latin America. 821
Church and social justice. 3449
Church and social progress. 1137
Church and social reforms. 3443
Church and social relations. 3453
Church and social responsibility. 1135
Church and social welfare. 1164
Church and socialism. 3434
Church and society. 810, 3443
Church and Society Conference. 2405, 3086
Church and society in Catholic Europe of the eighteenth century. 817
Church and society in eighteenth-century Devon. 1429
Church and society in England. 1516
Church and society in England 1770-1970. 3452
Church and spiritualism. 3516
Church and state. 1141, 1143, 1146, 1148, 1150, 1152, 3007, 3605
Church and state and other essays, including Money; Man and woman: their respective functions. 1142
Church and state behind the Iron Curtain. 1145
Church and state behind the Iron Curtain: Czechoslovakia, Hungary, Poland, Romania. 1145
Church & state from Constantine to Theodosius. 1144
Church and state in American history. 1152
Church and state in American law. 1490
Church and state in Britain since 1820. 1146

Church and state in Canada West. 1148
Church and state in confrontation. 1144
Church and state in contemporary America. 1149
Church and state in Czechoslovakia. 1149
Church and state in early Maryland. 1147
Church and state in education. 1128, 3189
Church and state in England. 1146
Church and state in England in the XVIIIth century. 1146, 1221
Church and state in England to the death of Queen Anne. 1146
Church and state in English education. 1129
Church and state in English education, 1870 to the present day. 1129
Church and state in Europe, 1864-1914. 1145
Church and state in Fascist Italy. 1147
Church and state in France, 1300-1907. 1145
Church and state in France, 1870-1914. 817, 1145
Church and state in French colonial Louisiana. 822, 1147
... Church and state in Germany under Otto the Great (936-973) 1145
Church and state in Guatemala. 1146
Church and state in Italy, 1850-1950. 1147
Church and state in Latin America. 821, 1147, 1149
Church and state in Luther and Calvin. 1143, 1144, 2273, 2276
Church and state in massachusetts. 1147
Church and state in Massachusetts from 1740 to 1833. 1147
Church and state in medieval Europe, 1050-1314. 1145
Church and state in Mexico. 1147
Church and state in modern Ireland, 1923-1970. 1147
Church and state in New England. 1148
... Church and state in New Mexico, 1610-1650. 1148
Church and state in North Carolina. 1148
Church and state in Revolutionary Virginia, 1776-1787. 1152
Church and state in Russia. 1148
Church and state in scripture, history, and constitutional law. 1142
... Church and state in Silesia under Frederick II (1740-1786) 1148, 1673
Church and state in social welfare. 1139
Church and state in the Middle Ages. 1144
Church and state in the modern world. 1140
Church and state in the teaching of St. Ambrose. 29, 1141
Church and state in the United States. 1151
Church and state in Tonga. 1152, 2433
Church and state in Tudor Ireland. 819, 1146, 1147
Church and state in your community. 1151
Church and state in Yugoslavia since 1945. 1152
Church and state, their relations considered. 1141
Church and state through the centuries. 1144
Church and state under God. 1150
Church and state under the Tudors. 1146
Church and Sunday-school buildings. 1156
Church and Sunday school hymnal. 3177
Church and Sunday-school work in Yonkers. 3867
Church and synagogue in Boston renewal. 3761
Church and synagogue library resources. 2224
Church and synagogue library standards. 2224
Church and the age. 756, 1281
Church and the age of reason. 1181
Church and the age of reason, 1648-1789. 1181
Church and the aging. 1257
Church and the agricultural situation. 3255
Church and the amateur adult. 1260
Church and the Bible. 233, 644
Church and the black man. 1132
Church and the body politic. 3747
Church and the Catholic. 759
Church and the challenge of to-day. 3674
Church and the change. 1136
Church and the changing order. 1121
Church and the children. 3152, 3179
Church and the Christian. 1121
Church and the church school. 3148
Church and the churches. 1116
Church and the city. 1279
Church and the city, 1865-1910. 1279
Church and the civil law. 1490

Church and the community. 1133, 3442
Church and the computer. 1505
Church and the confessions. 2283
Church and the country community. 828, 3255
Church and the crisis in the Dominican Republic. 826
Church and the crowd. 964
Church and the Eastern empire. 721
Church and the ecological crisis. 2676
Church and the empire. 1188
Church and the era. 1188
Church and the ever-coming kingdom of God. 3086
Church and the exceptional person. 1257
Church and the exploding metropolis. 1278
Church and the fine arts. 1177
Church and the four-year college. 1128
Church and the future. 2959
Church and the gentile world at the first promulgation of the gospel. 1195
Church and the Good Samaritan. 1126
Church and the gospel. 763
Church and the Gospels. 390
Church and the greater sacraments. 3263
Church and the homosexual. 1843
Church and the hour. 3446
Church and the immigrant. 3740
Church and the Jewish people. 3773
Church and the Jews in the XIIIth century. 2077
Church and the kingdom. 473, 1118
Church and the laity. 2192, 2702
Church and the laity: from Newman to Vatican II. 2192
Church and the law. 1490
Church and the layman. 2192
Church and the liturgy. 3773
Church and the liturgy (The) 3773
Church and the man. 1119
Church and the ministry. 76, 1118
Church and the nation. 1140, 1760
Church and the national security state. 2222
Church and the nations. 873
Church and the Negro. 2618
Church and the new generation. 1259
Church and the new knowledge. 1117
Church and the new world mind. 1085
Church and the nineteenth century. 808
Church and the older person. 1257
Church and the papacy. 2769
Church and the political problem of our day. 1145
Church and the prisoner. 2942
Church and the problems of to-day. 1123
Church and the public conscience. 3452
Church and the Puritans. 1759
Church and the reality of Christ. 2008
Church and the reconstruction of the modern world. 1135
Church and the returning soldier. 1259
Church and the rights of man. 1127
Church and the Roman empire. 1190
Church and the rural poor. 2860
Church and the Russian revolution. 3256
Church and the sacramental system. 1119
Church and the sacraments. 3265
Church and the second sex. 3835, 3836
Church and the secular order in Reformation thought. 1188
Church and the slum. 1138
Church and the social problem. 3445
Church and the suburbs. 1118, 3538
Church and the twentieth century. 1212
Church and the twentieth century (The) 1212
Church and the two nations in medieval Ireland. 1147
Church and the urban challenge. 1278
Church and the urban racial crisis. 2681
Church and the urban racial crisis (The) 2681
Church and the visual arts. 84
Church and the workingman. 1130, 1131
Church and the world. 791, 1121, 1126, 3655
Church and the world parish. 2457
Church and the world. (The) 1125
Church and the world's farmers. 2550
Church and the young people. 1260
Church and theology. 1188
Church and Third World revolution. 1155
Church and truth. 2967
Church and urban power structure. 1279
Church and urban renewal. 1279
Church and war. 3793, 3794
Church and world. 1116
Church and world conditions. 1122
Church and world encounter. 1544
Church & world mission. 2496
Church and world peace. 2806
Church & young men. 3869
Church & youth. 3886
Church annual. 3731
Church anthem book. 49

Church apostolic. 2554
Church architecture. 1156, 1157
Church architecture and liturgical reform. 1156
Church around the world. 1184
Church as a political factor in Latin America. 821
Church as a prophetic community. 1153
Church as a school. 3154
Church as a social institution. 3444
Church as dialogue. 1154
Church as educator. 1128
Church as employer, money raiser, and investor. 1168
Church as evangelist. 2481
Church as institution. 3440
Church as it ought to be. 1123
Church as mission. 2554
Church as moral decision-maker. 3443
Church as teacher. 3153
Church as the body of Christ. 2020
Church as the body of Christ (The) 2019
Church at Corinth. 322
Church at Eucharist. 2254
Church at Franklin, Louisiana, before 1940. 1651
... The church at play. 1167
Church at prayer. 2237
Church at the campus gate. 2302
Church at the center. 1125
Church at the end of the 20th century. 1063
Church at the heart of the world Christian community. 2495
Church at the turning points of history. 1176
Church at the university. 1256
Church at work. 1250, 1251, 2163
Church at work and worship. 3173
Church at work and worship; a vacation church school course for junior groups. 1120
Church at work in college and university. 1127
Church at work in the modern world. 3678
Church at work in the world (The) 3667
Church at work: organization and duties of the agencies of the Southern Presbyterian church; Excutive committee of foreign missions. 2920
Church at worship. 3003, 3854
Church beautiful; a practical discussion of church architectures. 1157
Church before Pilate. 1141
Church before the watching world. 66
Church bells in the forest. 2291
Church benevolences for the Junior league course of study. 2443
Church between revolution and restoration. 811
Church between temple and mosque. 1078
Church beyond division. 1117
Church Bible study handbook. 639
Church book. 2289
Church book for the use of Evangelical Lutheran congregations. 2289
Church book of the Evangelical Lutheran Augustana synod in North America. 1546
Church-book of the Woodland Presbyterian church, Philadelphia. 2916
Church brotherhood guidebook. 3465
Church budget development. 1168
Church buildings and furnishings. 1157
Church builder. 1156
Church builders of the nineteenth century. 1158
Church building. 1156, 1160
Church-building and things to be considered, done, or avoided in connection therewith. 1157
Church building in Boston, 1720-1970. 1158, 1378
Church bulletin bits. 2135
Church business methods. 1200
Church business policies outlined. 1168
Church by daylight. 1221
Church calendar for the year of Our Lord For the use of the clergy and laity. 1163
Church calendar for use in vestry or study. 27
Church camp counselor's manual. 1163, 1164
Church camp program. 1164
Church camp program guide. 1164
Church camping. 1164
... The church can save the world. 1123
Church cannot ordain women to the priesthood. 772, 2742
Church cantatas of J. S. Bach. 123
Church catechism. 1215
Church catechism and the living Word. 2962
Church, Catholic and Protestant. 1039
Church, change or decay. 1244
Church choir management. 915

Church choir-trainer. 915
Church Christ approves. 992
... Church chronology. 1115
Church city planning. 1279
Church, college, and nation. 1127
Church college in today's culture. 1127
Church college of the old South. 1127
Church college today. 1127
Church comity. 2955
Church communications. 1316
Church communion. 2251
Church community. 1118
Church, community and state in relation to education. 1128
Church conferences for youth and adults. 1200
... The church congress journal. 2959
Church conqueror over humane wit, [1639?]. 786
Church continuity & unity. 1117
Church cooperation. 1041
Church cooperation and unity in America. 1046
Church cooperation in community life. 1321
Church cooperation in the United States. 2241
Church courts and the people during the English Reformation, 1520-1570. 1488
Church covenant. 155, 1240, 1376
Church covenant idea. 1376
Church creative. 1250
Church creeds and party platforms. 1122
Church custodian's manual. 1199
Church cyclopaedia. 2963, 3637
Church dedications of the Oxford Diocese. 1165
Church defence. 1218
Church--depression--Christianity. 1124
Church: design for survival. 1119
Church dictionary. 3638
Church directory. 2953, 3216
Church directory, First Methodist church, fifty-first anniversary of the church's organization. 2432
Church directory of the Churches of Christ of the United States and Canada. 1272
Church disestablishment, 1870-1970. 1230
Church dogmatics. 3640
Church [Ecclesia]. 673, 1116
Church edifice and its appointments. 1156
Church education for family life. 1607
Church education for tomorrow. 3150
Church educational agencies. 3148
Church educational ministries. 936
Church efficiency. 1124
Church efficiency movement. 1117, 1250
Church emerging. 1117, 2292
Church enchained. 1118
Church encounters Asia. 1233, 2502
Church error. 3072
Church etiquette for the layman. 1167
Church executive: building the kingdom through leadership development. 953
Church faces liberalism. 2221
Church faces the challenge. 1137
Church faces the isms. 3323
Church faces the problem of juvenile delinquency. 1255
Church faces the world. 367, 1117
Church facts and principles. 2959
Church family camps and conferences. 1164, 1254
Church family gatherings. 1254
Church, fascism and peace. 1613
Church fathers speak. 1616
Church federation and the kingdom of God. 1619
Church federation, Inter-church conference on federation. 1044
Church-fellowship. 1119
Church fights; managing conflict in the local church. 1199
Church finance. 1167, 1168
Church finance and social ethics. 1168
Church financing by financial institutions in the United States,1946-1952. 1168
Church folklore. 1765
Church folks. 1333
Church follows its students. 1256
Church for Americans. 2956
Church for an open future. 1246, 1321
Church--for everyone. 1117, 1277
Church for our time. 2787
Church for sinners, seekers, and sundry non-saints. 989
Church for the new age. 1249
Church for these times. 1043
Church for you. 2959
Church founders of the Northwest. 2246
Church functioning effectively. 1252
Church functions with purpose. 1122
Church fund raising. 1168
Church furnishing & decoration in England and Wales. 1169
Church furnishings. 1165
Church furniture. 1169

Church, God's people. 1123
Church goes down and out. 2304
Church goes West. 3739
Church-going pays. 1162
Church goods. 1248
Church government. 1240
Church grounds and gardens. 1169
Church group activities for young married people. 1248
Church grows. 1198
Church grows in Canada. 734
Church grows on a tree claim. 1238
Church growth. 1171
Church growth, a mighty river. 1171
Church growth and Christian mission. 2554
Church growth and group conversion. 1170
Church growth and methods of evangelism in Asia-South Pacific. 1573
Church growth and the whole Gospel. 1171
Church growth and the word of God. 2504
Church growth in Burundi. 3324
Church growth in central and southern Nigeria. 2542
Church growth in Japan. 2954
... Church growth in Korea. 2537
Church growth in Mexico. 2954
Church growth in Sierra Leone. 2546
Church growth in West Utkal. 2530
Church growth is not the point. 1059
Church growth that counts. 1170
Church growth through Evangelism-in-depth. 1563
Church guides children's work. 1254
Church handbook. 1251
Church handbook for teacher training classes. 636
Church harmonies. 3754
Church; her ministry and sacraments. 1124
Church historians. 1184
Church history. 809, 812, 1172, 1173, 1176, 1180, 3181
Church history and modern revelation. 2616, 3429
Church history by non-Catholic historians. 811
Church history for busy people. 1176
Church history for the use of schools and colleges. 1176
Church history for the use of secondary schools. 1178
Church history from Nero to Constantine. 1198
Church history handbooks. 1180
Church history in a Puritan colony of the middle West. 1700
Church history in future perspective. 1184
Church history in plain language. 1189
Church history in rhyme. 1189
Church history in the age of science. 1184
Church history in the light of the saints. 809, 1174
Church history in the modern Sunday school. 1173
... Church history, mediaeval and modern. 1185, 1187
Church history of Britain. 1758
Church history of New England. 2687
Church history of Scotland. 3315
Church history of the first seven centuries. 1183
Church history of the first seven centuries to the close of the sixth general council. 1193
Church history through biography. 764
Church: hope of the world. 762
Church hymn book, with tunes, for the worship of God. 2916
Church hymnal. 2968, 3386, 3731
Church hymnal, revised. 2968
Church hymnary. 1199
Church hymns and tunes. 1199
Church ideals in edcation. 2965
Church ideals in education. 2965
Church in a changing world. 1196
Church in a diverse society. 1255
Church in a Marxist society. 2953
Church in a secularised society. 811
Church in a society of abundance. 1067
Church in a working world. 1130
Church in a world that won't hold still;-general and group reports. 2671
Church in action against the saloon (revised) 51
Church in Africa. 866
Church in Africa, 1977. 1073
Church in Africa (The) 825
Church in America. 3738
Church in America and its baptisms of fire. 3738
Church in an age of revolution. 1187
Church in an age of revolution, 1789-1870. 1187

Church in Anglo-Saxon England. 1761
Church in Asia. 1090
Church in Brazil. 690, 765
Church in changing Africa. 1043
Church in Christian faith and life. 1248, 3735
Church in Christian faith and life (The) 3165
Church in Communist China. 2953
Church in community action. 1134
Church in community organization. 25, 1133
Church in contemporary Ireland. 1489
Church in council. 1373
Church in crisis. 1373
Church in dialogue. 761
Church in disrepute. 1056
Church in early Irish society. 1918
THe church in earnest. 3730
Church in eastern Ohio. 1174
Church in England. 1758
Church in Estonia. 1533
Church in experiment. 1245
Church in fellowship. 1045
Church in France, 1789-1848. 817, 1638
Church in France, 1848-1907. 817, 1638
Church in frenzy. 1109
Church in Gaelic Ireland. 819
Church in God. 479
Church in God's program. 1123
Church in Great Britain. 1272
Church in history. 693, 1173, 1178, 1184, 3093
Church in Italy in the fifteenth century. 820, 1929
Church in its teaching work. 3159
Church in many lands. 1153
Church in mission. 2497, 2554
Church in mission (The) 2496
Church in modern times. 811
Church in northern Ohio and in the diocese of Cleveland. 824
Church in our community. 3801
Church in our town. 3254
Church in our world. 3732
Church in perspective. 3182
Church in politics. 1150, 3548
Church in prophecy. 1126
Church in Puerto Rico's dilemma. 2954
Church in Rome in the first century. 3245
Church in rural America. 3253
Church in rural life. 3254
Church in Saint Paul. 1109
Church in search of itself. 1122
Church in social welfare. 1138
Church in social work. 1215
Church in Southeast Asia. 92
Church in Soviet Russia. 1149, 2750
Church in the age of absolutism and enlightenment. 1181
Church in the age of feudalism. 1186
Church in the age of liberalism. 811
Church in the age of Orthodoxy and the Enlightenment. 1181
Church in the British era, from the British conquest to confederation. 734
Church in the Canadian era. 734
Church in the changing city. 1278
Church in the changing world. 1180
Church in the churches. 756, 1188
Church in the city. 1278
Church in the commonwealth. 1141
Church in the community. 2791
Church in the Confederate States. 2956
Church in the country town. 3253
Church in the Dark Ages. 1185
Church in the eighteenth century. 1181
Church in the English lordship, 1216-1307. 820
Church in the fort. 718
Church in the industrial age. 811, 1182
Church in the making. 1202
Church in the middle ages. 1185
Church in the modern age. 1182
Church in the modern world. 812, 1122
Church in the new Jamaica. 1933
Church in the New Testament. 1163
Church in the New Testament and today. 3191
Church in the next decade. 1153
Church in the old fields. 1791
Church in the present crisis. 1165
Church in the purpose of God. 1042
Church in the racially changing community. 1132
Church in the Roman empire. 1191, 1196
Church in the Roman empire before A. D. 170. 1194, 1197
Church in the service of liberty. 1135
Church in the seventeenth century. 1181
Church in the 60's. 44
Church in the social order. 1146
Church in the South American republics. 825
Church in the theology of St. Paul. 1163
Church in the theology of the reformers. 1187

Church in the thought of Bishop John Robinson. 1188, 3242
Church in the thought of Jesus. 1169, 2062
Church in the United States history. 833
Church in the universities. 3872
Church in the university. 3756
Church in the way. 2785
Church in the wilds. 1904
Church in the world. 809, 1117, 1119, 1153, 1154, 1163, 1188, 3066, 3067
Church in the world of radio-television. 3018
Church in three tenses. 1121
Church in thy house; how home and church can work together. 1610
Church in today's catacombs. 2821
Church in today's world. 3765
Church in transition. 1245, 3771
Church in travail. 1545
Church in travail; story of Philadelphia Synod, Evangelical and Reformed Church, 1939-1962. 1545
Church in University. 1303
Church in urban America. 1277, 1278
Church in war and peace. 2608
Church incarnate. 1157
Church inside out. 1125
Church inventory handbook. 3435
Church is a communion. 1249
Church is a who. 1199
Church is born. 2528
Church is different. 757
Church is families. 1254
Church is for the birds. 3091
Church is mine. 2426
Church is not expendable. 2480
Church is people. 1116
Church, kingship, and lay investiture in England, 1089-1135. 1146
Church kneelers. 1165
Church, law and society. 1116
Church leader in the cities: William Augustus Muhlenberg. 2630
Church leader training handbook. 952
Church lesson-books. 748
Church library. 2224
Church library guide; [proceedings] from the Third Church Library Conference. 2224
Church library handbook. 2224
Church life and thought in North Africa A. D. 200. 1183
Church, life-giving union with Christ. 793
Church life in England in the thirteenth century. 1516, 1762
Church life in Norway, 1800-1950. 2714
Church life in the rural South. 1274, 3254
Church, light of all mankind. 1126
Church loans by commercial banks. 1167
Church lobbying in a western state. 828, 2241
Church lobbying in the Nation's Capital. 1150
Church location directory for the Wesleyan Church—United States, Canada, & British Isles. 3806
Church looks ahead. 2956
Church looks forward. 1212
Church loyalty. 973
Church made relevant. 1154, 3772
Church, maintained in truth. 835, 1120
Church maintenance manual. 1242
Church management guidelines. 2786
Church management profession: a descriptive analysis. 1199
Church manual. 150
Church manual of the First church of Christ, Scientist, in Boston, Massachusetts. 1030, 1032
Church manual of the First Church of Christ, Scientists, in Boston Massachusetts. 1030
Church meetings that matter. 1200
Church meets Judaism. 1083
Church members' book. 2167
Church member's guide. 1201
Church-members' hand-book of theology. 3665
Church member's manual. 3217
Church-membership. 2295
Church membership as a Catholic and ecumenical problem. 1118
Church membership in the Methodist tradition. 2433
Church militant. 57, 2434, 2957
Church Militant and Iberian expansion, 1440-1770. 825
Church ministries in New Testament times. 1241
Church: mirror or window? 1124
Church, mission, and state relations in pre and post independent Tanzania (1955-1964). East Africa in the modern world. 2553

Church Missionary Society archives relating to Africa and Palestine, 1799-1923. 1202, 2499
Church, monastery, cathedral. 922
Church music. 1202, 1203, 1204, 1206, 1208
Church music and musical life in Pennsylvania in the eighteenth century. 1209
Church music and the Christian faith. 1208
Church music and theology. 1203
Church music and worship. 1202
Church music comes of age. 1209
Church music for adults. 1204
Church music for children. 1204
Church music for the whole church. 1203
Church music for youth. 1204
Church music handbook. 1203
Church music in America. 1210
Church music in America, comprising its history and its peculiarities at different periods. 1210
... Church music in history and practice. 1207
Church music in the light of the motu proprio. 1205
Church music in the nineteenth century. 1206
Church music in transition. 1209
Church music manual. 1208
Church music, musical and hymnological developments in Western Christianity. 1208
Church music of William Billings. 659
Church music of yesterday, to-day and for to-morrow. 1202
Church music pamphlet series. 1209
Church music regulations for the Archdiocese of San Francisco. 1202
Church music through the ages. 1202
Church music transgressed. 1206
Church musick vindicated in Estwick, Sampson, a, 1739. 1202
Church must modernize men. 3448
Church must win! 3852
Church needlework. 2679
Church-night service. 1210
Church nobody knows. 1041
Church not in darkness. 3199
Church not made with hands. 1059
Church now. 808
Church nurtures faith. 2408
Church nurtures faith, 1683-1963. 2408
Church of apostles and martyrs. 1190
... The church of Christ. 757, 763, 780, 1096, 1116, 1122, 1123
Church of Christ a firm and durable house. 1247
Church of Christ and the problems of the day. 1059
Church of Christ as measured by the Bible. 1123
Church of Christ in Corea. 1118
Church of Christ, in its idea, attributes, and ministry. 1120
Church of Christ in Japan. 1210
Church of England. 1211, 1219, 1220, 1221, 1759, 1760
Church of England and episcopacy. 1220
Church of England and reunion. 1040
Church of England and social reform since 1854. 3452
Church of England and the American Episcopal Church. 2972
Church of England and the church of Christ. 1211
Church of England and the ecumenical movement. 1043
.. Church of England and the Reverend Clement Hall im colonial North - carolina. 1223, 1781
Church of England. Book of common prayer. 1213
...Church of England doctrine. 1212
... The Church of England in colonial Virginia. 1223
Church of England in Nova Scotia and the Tory clergy of the revolution. 1223
Church of England in pre-Revolutionary Connecticut. 1222
Church of England in the twentieth century. 2295
Church of Erin. 820
Church of God and her adversaries. 464
Church of God as an essential element of the Gospel. 2936
Church of God, Body of Christ, and Temple of the Spirit. 1187
Church of God of Prophecy history & polity. 1229
Church of Haghia Sophia at Trebizond. 3705
Church of Ireland, 1869-1969. 1147, 1230
Church of Ireland—why conservative? 1230
Church of Israel. 2115

Church of Jesus. 148
Church of love. 2264
Church of our fathers. 1184
... Church of Our Lady of esperanza. 2697
Church of Pentecost. 2813
Church of Rome. 800, 803
Church of Rome, in her primitive purity, compared with the Church of Rome, at the present day. 800
Church of Rome the apostasy. 798
Church of St. Andrew, Richmond, Staten island. 3237
Church of St. Anthony of Padua, 1870-1919. 3273
...The Church of St. Bernard of Saint Paul, Minnesota; a record of fifty years. 1179
Church of St. Bunco. 1030
Church of Saint Eirene at Constantinople. 1354
Church of St. Helen, Bishopsgate. 2243
Church of Saint John Baptist, Burford. 717
Church of St. John the Evangelist. 2686
Church of St. Mary the Virgin, Oxford. 2755
Church of Saint Peter in the Great valley, 1700-1940. 3278
Church of St. Stanislaus Bishop and Martyr. 2700
Church of San Marco in Venice: history, architecture, sculpture. 3777
Church of Santa Trinita in Florence. 1630
Church of silence in Slovakia. 825
Church of the 21st century. 1123, 1126
Church of the Advent. 663
... The Church of the atonement and the Chapel of the cross at Chapel Hill, North Carolina. 885
Church of the Brethren. 1235
Church of the Brethren and war, 1708-1941. 1236, 3792
Church of the Brethren in Northeastern Ohio. 1235
Church of the catacombs. 1194
Church of the covenant. 1303, 2829
Church of the early centuries. 1189
Church of the early fathers. 1194
Church of the eastern Christians. 2746
Church of the Epiphany. 2697
Church of the fathers. 1192, 1193
Church of the Founding Fathers of New Jersey. 1508
Church of the future. 1118
Church of the Holy Sepulchre in Jerusalem. 1943
Church of the Holy Sepulchre, Jerusalem. 1237
Church of the living God. 1178, 3755
Church of the living Lord. 363
Church of the living waters. 1121
Church of the Lord. 1119
Church of the Lutheran Reformation. 2288
Church of the Madonna dell'Orto. 894, 1160
Church of the Middle Ages. 1186
Church of the Old Testament. 502, 2613
Church of the Pilgrim Fathers. 2855
Church of the poor. 854, 1136
Church of the queen country. 3255
Church of the reconstruction. 1047
Church of the Redeemer. 3309
Church of the Renaissance and Reformation. 3215
Church of the spirit. 3706
Church of the T'ang dynasty. 912
Church of the United Brethren in Christ. 3730
Church of the United Brethren in Christ in Sierra Leone. 1238, 2546
Church of the Visitation. 1238
Church of the Word Incarnate. 756
Church of to-day. 1118, 1048
Church of today--and tomorrow. 1250
Church of tomorrow. 1118, 1157
Church officers. 1239
Church officers at work. 1239
Church on earth. 756
Church on Lafayette Square. 3797
Church on Main Street. 1930
Church on mission. 850
Church on the changing frontier. 1271
Church on the green. 3796
Church on the hill. 3275
Church on the move. 333, 1154, 2852
Church on the urban frontier. 1278
Church on the western waters. 2927
Church on wheels. 30
Church order commentary. 1023
Church order in the New Testament. 1166
Church order of the Christian reformed church. 1023
Church organization. 1200
Church organization and methods. 151
Church organization and work. 1117
Church organized and functioning. 150

Church ornaments and their civil antecedents. 1249
Church pageantry. 2757
Church parking lot. 1273
Church Peace Mission pamphlet. 1. 2809
Church pictorial directory of New York City. 2698
Church planning and management. 1200
Church plans for kindergarten children. 3175
Church planting in Uganda. 2558
Church plays and how to stage them. 3145
Church poetry. 2968
Church politics. 1085
Church, politics, and society. 1134
Church polity. 1240
Church polity of the Pilgrims. 1335
Church portals. 2935
Church posters and publicity. 10
Church prayer book. 854
Church prayers for war-time. 2891
Church principles. 1123
Church problems and their solution. 1165
Church proclaiming and witnessing. 1572, 1927
Church profit-making. 1167
Church program guidebook. 1964/65. 1253
Church promotion handbook. 10
Church property and its management. 1241
Church property in Cuba. 1242
Church psalmody. 1866
Church psalter. 2962
Church public relations at work. 3002
Church public relations committee. 3002
Church publicity. 10
Church publicity; basic principles and practices for churches and church-related organizations. 1243
Church purchasing procedures. 1243
Church quarrels. 1240
Church reaching out. 1569
Church reader for Lent. 2213
Church reclaims the city. 1280
Church records. 6, 3533
Church records, 1805-1910. 1243
Church recreation. 3028
Church redemptive. 1201
Church reform of Peter the Great. 1148, 2824
Church reforms in Russia, 1905-1918. 1373, 2750
[Church register of] Robinson's Run United Presbyterian Church. McDonald, Pennsylvania. [commencing April 1, 1878]. 1243
Church-related college. 1127
Church related higher education. 1164
Church renewed. 1245, 3772
Church resource library. 2224
Church responds. 1245
Church revival. 3228
Church says . . . welcome! 1251
Church school. 3146, 3558
Church-school administration. 3553
Church school and its officers. 3558
Church school and parish house building. 1156
Church school and the Sunday-school normal guide. 3558
Church school and worship. 3858
Church-school blue-print. 3555
Church school book of prayer and praise. 440
Church school chats for primary teaching. 3169
Church school comes to life. 3554
Church school curricula and education for Protestant church unity. 3159
Church school graded courses. 1913
Church school hymnal for youth. 3562
Church school improvement. 1246
Church school in action. 3554
Church school in the Book of common prayer. 2960
Church-school leadership. 1246
Church school looks at Christian unity. 1046
Church school methods. 3175
Church school objectives, "bigger and better Sunday schools" 3552
Church school of citizenship. 3151
Church school of missions. 2550
Church school organization and administration. 3556
Church school planning. 3548
Church school prayers. 3564
Church school program, "better and bigger church schools" 3552
Church school superintendent. 3554
Church school teacher's guide for youth in Burma (ages twelve through fourteen) 3179
Church-school teacher's job. 3179
Church school teaching can be fun! 940

Church schools of today. 3151
Church seasons. 1261
Church seasons (The) 1261
Church secretary. 1247
Church serves the changing city. 3435
Church serves the world. 1125
Church service. 3856
Church service book. 3856
Church service book and ministerial acts of the Evangelical Lutheran Augustana synod of North America. 1547, 1546
Church services and service-books before the reformation. 840
Church silver of Colonial Virginia. 1240
Church since emancipation: Church reorganization. 819
Church since Pentecost. 1198
Church song. 2289
Church speaks to the modern world. 1135, 2768
Church-sponsored higher education in the United States. 1127
Church staff administration. 1200
Church staff and its work. 1251
Church stands corrected. 323
Church, State. 1141
Church, state, and Christian society at the time of the investiture contest. 1144
Church, state, and education in Africa. 1129
Church, state, and freedom. 1151
Church, state, and nation in Ireland, 1898-1921. 819, 1919
Church, state, and opposition in the U.S.S.R. 1148
Church, state, and public policy. 1152
Church, state, and Rome. 782
Church, state, and study. 1142
Church, state, and the American Indians. 1149
Church-state policies and the National Council of Churches. 2670
Church/state problem has been handed on to you; a guide for community groups. 1140
Church-state relations. 1142
Church state relations and religious instruction in the public elementary schools of Switzerland, West-Germany and US. 3095
Church-state relations in ecumenical perspective. 1142
Church-state relationships in education in Connecticut. 1144
Church story. 1233
Church street. 3254
Church Street Methodists, children of Francis Asbury. 2182
Church struggle in South Africa. 3464
... Church support in the United States. 833
Church swept out. 1154
Church symbolism. 921
...The church takes root in India. 2531
Church teachers. 780
Church teachers' life of Christ. 197
Church teaches. 1248
Church teaches nines to twelves. 3167, 3170
Church teaching children grades one through six. 3172
Church teaching through Scripture. 644
Church that dared to change. 1245, 3598
Church that Jesus built. 1197
Church that produced a President. 169, 742
Church that takes on trouble. 2197
Church that was and is to be. 2423
Church that was founded on lies and forgeries. 802
Church (The;) 1125
Church, the Bible, and the creed. 1118
Church, the body of Christ. 364, 1120, 2020
Church, the churches and the kingdom. 1121
Church: the continuing quest. 1188
Church, the falling away, and the restoration. 1123
Church, the gospel and war. 3793, 3794
Church, the layman, and the modern world. 2192
Church, the liturgy, and the soul of man. 2258, 2747
Church, the ministry, and reunion. 1122
Church, the people and the age. 1123
Church, the people of God. 1120
Church the pillar and ground of the truth. 1121
Church, the schools and evolution. 1579
Church, the state, and education in Virginia. 942, 3190
Church, the university, and social policy. 1256
Church, the university, and urban society: focus on the church. 3445
Church through half a century. 696, 1187

Church through the ages. 1176, 1179, 1180
Church through the centuries. 1179
Church-time for four's and five's. Learning God's Word. 3175
Church time for preschoolers. 939
Church to believe in. 1125
Church to-day and to-morrow. 1057
Church today. 777, 1123, 1124, 1153, 3771
Church today and tomorrow. 1235
Church tomorrow. 3770
Church tomorrow [by]. 3770
Church training intermediates. 3176
Church training juniors. 3172
Church training young people. 3175
Church trap. 3747
Church treasurer's handbook. 1168
Church triumphant. 1118, 1120, 1793
Church troubles. 3673
Church truly catholic. 1066
Church unbound. 1154
Church under communism. 1128
Church under siege. 1197
Church under the Cross. 2820
Church under the law. 1490
Church union. 1492
Church union at midpoint. 1355
Church union consultation and various churches. 1043
Church union in Canada. 3731
Church union in focus. 1046
Church union in South India. 1042
Church: united or untied? 1042
Church unity. 363, 1039
Church unity and church mission. 1041
Church unity movements in the United States. 1040
Church universal. 1120, 1123
Church universal and the see of Rome. 1523
Church upon the rock. 797
Church use of audio-visuals. 109
Church usher. 1249
Church ushers. 1249
Church ushers' manual. 1239
Church using its Sunday school. 3551
Church vacation school. 3762
Church vacation school guide. 3763
Church vacation school handbook. 3763
Church; Vatican II's dogmatic constitution on the church. 1124
Church vestments, their origin & development. 1249
Church victorious. 1057
Church visible. 2957
Church visitation: theory and practice. 3783
Church vocations. 3785
Church vocations—a new look. 3785
Church we cannot see. 1121
Church we forget. 331
Church we love. 1120
Church wealth and business income. 1242
Church wealth in Mexico. 822, 1147
Church -- what and why. 3182
Church—who needs it? 163
Church without a bishop. 1241
Church without God. 1059
Church without priests? 771
Church without walls. 1244
Church women at work. 3834, 3836, 3837
Church women in the scheme of things. 3837
Church work. 1252
Church work in the city. 1279
Church work with boys. 687
Church work with intermediates. 3150
Church work with juniors. 1253
Church work with young people. 3159
Church worker's handbook. 1253
Church working with young adults. 1252
Church, world, mission. 2746
Church worship. 3852
Church worship book. 2238
Church worships. 841
Church worships (The) 841
Church year. 1261, 1917
Church year and calendar. 1163
Church year and home life. 1262
Church year book. 815, 866
Church year book and budget directory for Manhattan, Bronx, Queens [and] Staten island. 2698
Church year sermons. 1247
Church year sermons for children. 1247
Church years. 1262
Church yesterday & today. 791
Churchand Sunday school publicity. 10
Churched and the unchurched in America. 1110
Churches. 1155, 1156
Churches allied for common tasks. 1619
Churches and church membership in the United States. 1248
Churches and abbeys of Ireland. 1160
Churches and cathedrals. 1160

Churches and change. 2671
Churches and chapels. 1157
Churches and Christian unity. 1043
Churches & church membership in the United States. 1248
Churches and churchgoers. 1171
Churches and educated men. 1128
Churches and educated men; a study of the relation of the church to makers and leaders of public opinion. 1256
Churches and how they grow. 1170
Churches and mental health. 2784
Churches and planning controls. 1270
Churches and politics in Germany. 1146
Churches and politics in Latin America. 1147
Churches and public buildings. 78
Churches and rapid social change. 1085, 1133
Churches and sects of Christendom. 1386
Churches and sects of the United States. 3325
Churches and states. 3087
Churches & temples. 1157
Churches and the campus. 3757
Churches and the church. 859
Churches and the Indian schools, 1888-1912. 1899
Churches and the kingdom. 2175, 2176
Churches and the nations. 1077
Churches and the public. 1085
Churches and the Soviet Union. 3256
Churches and the Y. M. C. A. at work with boys. 1253
... The churches and war. 3792
Churches at work. 2528, 2714
Churches' handbook for spiritual healing. 1598, 2409
Churches in cooperation. 3190
Churches in crisis. 1165
Churches in cultural captivity. 1135, 3465
Churches in Delaware during the revolution. 1420
Churches in Episcopal Connecticut. 1270, 2963
Churches in Ireland. 3324
Churches in North America. 3327
Churches in rock. 876
Churches in the modern state. 1141, 1211
Churches in the nineteenth century. 1181
Churches in the State of Washington. 1248
THe churches militant. 3747
Churches of Africa. 813
... The churches of Allentown. 26
Churches of Cambridgeshire and the isle of Ely. 1270
Churches of Christ. 1173
Churches of Christ in Mississippi. 1273
Churches of Christ in Owen county, Indiana. 2753
Churches of Christ in time of war. 1543
Churches of Davie County, North Carolina. 1271
Churches of eastern Christendom from A.D. 451 to the present time. 851, 1487
Churches of El Dorado county, California. 1269
Churches of Fluvanna County, Virginia. 1630
Churches of France. 1270
Churches of Lakewood. 2735
Churches of Martin County, Indiana. 1270
Churches of Mexico, 1530-1810. 1161
Churches of old New England. 1271
Churches of Rome. 3245
Churches of Rye, New Hampshire, 1725-1959. 1271
Churches of Salem County. 1274, 3286
Churches of Somerset. 1270
Churches of the Federal council. 1619
Churches of the Holy Land. 2761
Churches of the Isle of Wight. 1275
Churches of the Presidents, a television series. 3797
Churches of the Presidents in Washington. 3797
Churches of the West. 756
Churches of today and yesterday in southern Lancaster County. 1273
Churches of today in the light of Scripture. 1461
Churches on Cape Cod. 1271
Churches on the move. 1244
Churches quarrel espoused (1713) 1338
Churches the Victorians forgot. 1274
Churches: their riches, revenues, and immunities. 1242
Churches, 253,762. 3324
Churches working together. 1251
Churchill returns. 3473
Churchin the world. 1117
Churching the small city. 79
Churchless Protestants. 1063

Churchman's glossary of ecclesiastical terms. 3031
Churchman's guide. 1217
Churchman's guide to faith and piety. 1224
Churchman's heritage. 1211
Churchman's manual of methods. 3166
Churchman's ready reference. 2964
Churchman's treasury of song. 3458
Churchman's year book and American church almanac. 2975
Churchmanship. 2915
Churchmanship and character. 1117
Churchmanship of St. Cyprian. 1188, 1398
Churchmember's guide and complete church manual. 3167
Churchmen and the condition of England, 1832-1885. 1137
Church's amazing story. 809
Church's attitude towards truth. 2965
Church's best state. 1565
... The church's certain faith. 1054
Church's colleges of higher education. 1164
Church's concern for communities with a rural nonfarm population in the northeast U.S.A. 3167
Church's confession under Hitler. 174
Church's debt to heretics. 1804
Church's faith. 3664
Church's first thousand years. 1195
Church's flight into the wilderness. 3742
Church's holiness and religious life. 3488
Church's life. 1123
Church's Magna charta for migrants. 1511
Church's ministry. 1296
Church's ministry in mental retardation. 1258
Church's ministry in our time. 1063
Church's ministry of healing. 1598
Church's ministry of healing for young people and children. 1601
Church's ministry of reconciliation in the field of education. 3162
Church's ministry to the older unmarried. 1256
Church's ministry to youth in trouble. 1260
Church's ministry with senior highs. 1253, 1259
Church's ministry with senior highs; a guide for adult workers. 1259
Church's mission in the world. 850
Church's mission to the educated American. 2558
Church's mission to the mountaineers of the South. 2547
Church's number 1 problem. 1202
Church's one foundation. 1169
Church's opportunity in adult education. 3169
Church's play. 2370
Church's program for young people. 3154
Church's real work. 3672
Church's singular task. 1563
Church's stake in urban renewal. 1133
Church's task under the Roman empire. 1172
*Church's teaching for small church schools (The) 2966
*Church's teaching in the [closely graded church schools (The) 2966
Church's teaching ministry. 3148
Church's way. 2962
... The church's work for men at war. 1543
Church's worldwide mission. 2514
Church's worship. 3773
Church's year. 1261
Churton, Ralph. 1225, 2050
Cicero in the courtroom of St. Thomas Aquinas. 3694
CICOP working papers. 1138
Ciencia y salud, con clave de las Escrituras. 1030

Cincinnati papers. 2963
Cinders and ashes. 1445
Cipher of Genesis. 526, 1704
Circle and the Cross. 107
Circle book of charts. 1847
Circle of faith. 923
Circle of life. 2228
Circle of sanctity. 3281
Circle of seasons. 3005
Circle of strength. 1004
Circles of faith. 3113
Circuit-rider days along the Ohio. 2446
Circuit rider dismounts. 2456, 3468
Circular letters (selected) of Redemptorist generals. 2229, 3031
Circulation and character of the volumes of the American tract society. 34
Circum praecordia. 1026
Circumcision covenant. 1376

CIRCUMSTANTIAL EVIDENCE. RELIGIOUS BOOKS 1876 - 1982

Circumstantial evidence. 3063
Cistercian and mendicant monasteries in medieval Greece. 2569
Cistercian heritage. 1276
Cistercian ideals and reality. 1276
Cistercian nunnery in medineval Italy. 3237
Cistercian settlements in Wales and Monmouthshire, 1140-1540. 1276
Cistercians. 1276
Cistercians and Cluniacs. 1276
Cistercians in Denmark. 1276
Cistercians in the late Middle Ages. 1276
Cistereians in Yorkshire. 1276
Citadel of faith. 129
Citadel of Wisdom. 2359
Cities and bishoprics of Phrygia. 2844
Cities and churches. 1278
Cities in New Testament times. 381, 1277
Cities of our faith. 1068
Cities of Paul. 2803
Cities of St. Paul. 2796
"Cities of the dead"—New Orleans cemetery architecture. 2693
Cities of the New Testament. 1277
Citizen Christian. 3749
... Citizen, jr. 1277
Citizen of no mean city: Archbishop Patrick Riordan of San Francisco (1841-1914) 3238
Citizens for the new world. 1139
Citizens in training. 1277
Citizens of the cosmos. 3479
Citizens of to-morrow. 2527
Citizens of two worlds. 615
Citizenship and conscience. 3703
Citizenship and moral reform. 3444
Citizenship for Christians. 1087
Citizenship ideals for Christian youth, including, the citizenship workshop of practical plans for young people's societies. 1277
Citizenship in the post-war kingdom of God. 1277
City. 3358
City and church in transition. 1278
City and the sign. 552
City centres of early Christianity. 1189
City challenges the church. 1278
City church and its social mission. 3447
City church--death or renewal. 1278
City churches and the cultural crisis. 1277
City institute for religious teachers. 3146
City of God. 112, 1121, 1248, 2173, 2355
City of God against the pagans. 2173
City of God and the church-makers. 1116
City of God and the politics of crisis. 113, 116, 1085
City of God, books VII-XVI. 3790
City of God (De civitate Dei) in two volumes. 112
City of gold and other stories from the Old Testament. 628
City of New Jerusalem. 3350
City of perfection. 2818
City of revelation. 3575
City of the gods. 1416
City of the King. 1996, 2763
City of the saints. 3762
City of women. 2680
City of wrong. 2013
City of Zion. 2745
City on a mountain. 2849
City parish grows and changes. 1277
City set on a hill. 1548
City Sunday-school. 3552
City Temple sermons. 1340
City within the heart. 3069
City without a church. 959
City's church. 1278
Civic Christianity. 3445
Civil church law. 1489
Civil disobedience and political obligation. 1749
Civil government and religion. 1075
Civil government and religion, or, Christianity and the American Constitution. 1075
Civil government the foundation of social happiness. 1503
Civil law and the church. 1490
Civil magistrates power in matters of religion modestly debated, impartially stated according to the bounds and grounds of Scripture. 1140
Civil rights. 1280
Civil rulers the ministers of God, for good to men. 1504
Civilisation and religious values. 1280, 3069
Civilization and religion. 1281
Civilization by faith. 1282
Civilization of right relationships. 979
Civilization on the march. 803
Civilization on trial. 1281
Civilization's builder and protector. 790
Civilized religion. 3063
De civitate Dei. 3447
Claim of Jesus Christ. 104
Claim these victories. 1467
Claim your inheritance. 984
Claimed by God. 3185
Claimed by God for mission. 1066
Claims and opportunities of the Christian ministry. 1288
Claims in conflict. 1136
Claims of a Protestant Episcopal bishop to apostolical succession and valid orders disproved. 76, 1378
Claims of Jesus. 2045
Claims of religion upon the young. 3884
Claims of the common life. 614
Claims of the established church to exclusive attachment and support. 1212
Clairvoyance. 1283
Clairvoyance and materialisation. 1283
Clairvoyance & thoughtography. 1283
Clairvoyant. 3715
Clairvoyant strangers. 1283
Clairvoyant theory of perception. 1283
Clap your hands! 3704
Clara Leffingwell. 2206
Clare Vaughan. 2353
Clarel. 2762
Clarence Pickett. 2845
Clarified New Testament. 344
Clarifying Jewish values. 2079
Clarity in prayer. 2874
Clarity in religious education. 935
Clarity of the science of Christian Science. 1034
Claros varones de Castilla. 3469
Clash. 3440
Clash between Christianity and cultures. 1074
Clash of the cymbals. 681, 3292
Clash of the Titans. 2822
Class-book of New Testament history. 407
Class-book of Old Testament history. 533, 535
Class devotions. 1438
Class devotions for use with the 1981-82 International lessons. 1913, 3560
Class leader. 643, 1285
Class-leader's manual. 1286
Class lessons, 1888. 1033
Class-meeting. 1286
Class meetings: embracing their origin, nature, obligation, and benefits. 1286
Class notes on sacred history. 647
Class notes on the Epistle to the Hebrews and the Epistle of James. 405
Class-room lectures on the Apostles creed. 73
Classbook of Old Testament history. 534
Classic baptism. 134
Classic Christian creeds. 1386
Classic Christian faith. 745, 2299
Classic christian townsite at Arminna West. 2716
Classic creeds & living faith. 1385
Classic deities in Bacon. 124, 2656
Classic Hassidic tales. 1928, 3580
Classic myth and legend. 2657
Classic myth-lore in rhyme. 2658
Classic mythology. 2207
Classic myths in English literature. 2656
Classic myths in English literature and in art. 2656
Classic myths in English literature and in art, based originally on Bulfinch's "Age of fable" (1855) 2656
Classic of spiritism. 3508, 3509
Classic stories from the lives of our prophets. 1232
Classical and contemporary metaphysics. 2417
Classical and contemporary readings in the philosophy of religion. 3108
Classical approaches to the study of religion. 3111
Classical dictionary of Hindu mythology and religion, geography, history, and literature. 2664
Classical evangelical essays in Old Testament interpretation. 503
Classical gods and heroes. 2656
Classical Hindu mythology. 2664
Classical law of India. 1457
Classical mythology. 2657
Classical mythology in literature, art, and music. 2657
Classical mythology of Milton's English poems. 2469, 2657
Classical myths. 2656
Classical myths in English literature. 2657
Classical myths in sculpture. 2649
Classical myths that live today. 2657
Classical statements on faith and reason. 1597
Classical studies. 1286
Classics, Greek & Latin. 1286
Classics in philosophy and ethics. 2839
Classics of Christian missions. 2496
Classics of free thought. 1656
Classification of religions. 1286
Classification of religious. 3138
Classification system for libraries of Judaica. 1286
Classified and descriptive catalogue of new and standard works in all departments of religious literature. 3627
Classified Bible studies. 645
Classified bibliography of literature on the Acts of the Apostles. 332
Classified bibliography of youth materials that can be used by youth groups and their leaders in the church and in the field of informal education in other social and fellowship groups. 3203
Classified catalog of the ecumenical movement. 1043
Classified Psalter arranged by subjects. 2985
Classis Holland. 2129
Classroom creativity. 940, 3179
Claude Dubuis, bishop of Galveston. 1481
Claude's book, ed. 3494
Clausen's commentaries on morals and dogma. 1671
... The clausulae of St. Hilary of Poitiers. 1811, 2199
Clavis universalis. 2417
Clay and fire. 2225
Clean and strong. 3393
Clean oblation. 2259
Clean water. 135
Cleaning up the Christian vocabulary. 3682
Cleanse my heart. 367
Cleansing of the sanctuary. 3720
Cleansing of the temple. 2210
Clear light from the spirit world. 3505
Clear mind. 3501
Clear of the brooding cloud. 960
Clear white light. 1585
Clearest and surest marks of our being so led by the Spirit of God. 3347
Clearing the passageways. 964
Clee of the lighted tower. 1287, 2701
Cleland. 1287
Clement of Alexandria. 1287
Clement of Alexandria and a secret Gospel of Mark. 1288, 3322
Clement of Alexandria's treatment of the problem of evil. 1287, 1745
Clergy a source of danger to the American republic. 1655
Clergy and clients. 2784
Clergy and family service collaboration. Alderbrook Inn, Union, Washington, April 29-May 1, 1964. Sponsoring groups. 1289
Clergy & laity. 774, 2192
Clergy and the Great Awakening in New England. 1757
Clergy and the pulpit. 1843
Clergy and what they do. 1296
Clergy in Maryland of the Protestant Episcopal church since the independence of 1783. 2956
Clergy in the cross fire. 1296
Clergy, ministers and priests. 1291
Clergy of Litchfield County. 1288
... The clergy of the established church in Virginia and the revolution. 1223
Clergyman and the psychiatrist—when to refer. 2784
Clergyman's fact book (The) 1783
... The clergyman's looking-glass. 700, 1289
Clergyman's psychological handbook. 2781
Clergymen of the Church of England. 1215
Clergymen's attitudes toward Black Africa. 1294
Clerical bead roll of the diocese of Alton, Ill. 814
Clerical courtesy. 3676
Clerical dress and insignia of the Roman Catholic Church. 1249
... Clerical education in major seminaries. 3613
Clerical exodus. 1582
Clerical obligations of canons 138 and 140. 1290
Clerical studies. 3680
Clerical system. 3671
Clerical types. 3675
... Cleveland Congregationalists 1895. 1304
Click in the clock. 3883
Cliffs of fall. 2027
Climax of revelation. 1954, 3226
Climax of the ages. 509
Climax of the Bible; the book of the Revelation. 453
Climb along the cutting edge. 187
Climb every mountain. 690, 2486
Climb the highest mountain. 306, 951
Climb to God. 2894
Climber. 903
Climbing. 2509
Climbing higher. 1430
Climbing Jacob's ladder. 3883
Climbing the heights. 1430
Climbing up the mountain, children. 3336
Climbing up to nowhere. 122
Climbing upward. 3888
Clinic of a cleric. 3671
Clinical approach to the problems of pastoral care. 2785
Clinical education for the pastoral ministry. 1258
Clinical training for pastoral care. 2783, 2995
Clinton family. 3597
Clippings from my notebook. 1012, 3601
Clock of the passion of Our Lord Jesus Christ. 2031
Clock struck one. 3517
Clock struck three. 3517
Clock struck two. 3517
Clock wise. 981
Clock work image. 3082
Cloister and the world. 2580
Cloister book. 3349
Cloisters Apocalypse. 602
Close of the ministry. 1952
Close your eyes when praying. 621
Closed faith. 1156
Closeness of God. 552, 1886
Closer than a brother. 1003
Closer than my shadow. 1835
Closer walk with God. 1015
Closer you look, the greater the book. 278
Closet and altar. 2889
Closing century's heritage. 3620
Closing scenes of the life of Christ. 1988
Cloture of Notre-Dame and its role in the fourteenth century choir program. 2773, 2774
Cloud-hidden, whereabouts unknown. 3068
Cloud of unknowing. 2644, 2646, 2647
Cloud of unknowing, and other treatises. 2646
Cloud of unknowing, and other works. 2646
Cloud of unknowing and The book of privy counseling. 2646
Cloud of unknowing and the Book of privy counselling. 2646
Cloud of unknowing, (The) 2646
Cloud of witnesses. 338, 1849, 2797, 3500, 3793
Clouded hills. 2384
Clouds and rainbows. 1238
Clouds for chariots. 3354
Clouds without water. 425
Clough, kingdom-builder in south India. 1304, 2530
Clovis Chappell. 886, 1301
Clown and the crocodile. 2227
Clowning in Rome. 3490
"The Club" of life. 8
Clue to Christian education. 3154
Clue to history. 3452
Clue to Pascal. 2777
Clues to the kingdom. 1448
Cluniac monasticism in the central Middle Ages. 2582
Cluniacs and the Gregorian reform. 1304
Cluny under Saint Hugh, 1049-1109. 1304
Cluster of church prayers. 2873
Clyde company papers. 1305
Co-operation between the Young women's and the Young men's Christian associations. 3877
Co-operative revision of the New Testament. 358
... Coadjutors and auxiliaries of bishops. 666
Coast Salish spirit dancing. 2713
Coat of many colors. 2133
Cobbin's commentary on the Bible for young and old. 293
Cobble stones of Galilee. 1977
Cobb's Baptist church manual. 30
Cobra's den. 2530
Cochem's Life of Christ. 1978
Cock Lane and common-sense. 2989
COCU, the official reports of the four meetings of the Consultation. 1039
Code of Christ. 180
Code of international ethics. 2852
Code of Jewish law. 2155
Code of Jewish law (Kitzur Schulcan Aruch) 2114
Code of Jewish law (Kitzur Shulchan Aruch) 2074, 2107
Code of joy. 180
Code of life to health, wealth, happiness. 1324
Code of Maimonides. 2074, 3704
Code of Maimonides. bk. 3. 2074
Code of Oriental canon law. 1490

Code of Oriental canon law, the law on marriage. 2342
Code of the spirit. 3601
Code on the discipline of the African Methodist Episcopal Zion church. 15
Codex 2400 and its miniatures. 316
Codex Bezae. 315
Codex Christi. 2062
Codex Climaci rescriptus Graecus. 393
Codex furis canonici Pii X pontificis maximi issue digestus. 735
Codex iuris canonici Pii X pontificis maximi iussu digestus. 735
Codex juris ecclesiastici anglicani. 1489
Codex 1 of the Gospels and its allies. 315
Codex purpureus Petropolitanus. 383
Codex rosae crucis. 3251
Codex (G) gamma of the Ecumenical Patriarchate of Constantinople. 1354
Coercion and perversion. 3410
Coeur d'Alenes. 1908
Coffee house manual. 979
Coffee house ministry. 1305
Coffee table book of witchcraft and demonology. 3823
Coffee-time prayers. 2894
Coffer of jewels about our infallible, eternal Word of God, the Bible. 201
Coffin texts. 1502
Cognitive structures and religious research. 3446
Coherence of theism. 1730
Coherence theory of truth. 3716
Coincidence of opposites. 675
Coins of Bible days. 481
Coins of the Bible. 208
Cokesbury funeral manual. 1694
Cokesbury marriage manual. 2338
Col. Robert G. Ingersoll as he is. 1907
Coleccion de bulas, breves y otros documentos relativos a la iglesia de America y Filipinas. 814
Colenso's fallacies. 1306
Coleridge and Christian doctrine. 1307
Coleridgeiana, being a supplement to the Bibliography of Coleridge. 1307
Collaboration with tyranny in Rabbinic law. 99
Collapse of Christless civilizations. 2056
Collapse of nonpublic education: rumor or reality? 2942
Collapses in adult life. 805
Collated constitutions of the Grand lodge of Free and accepted masons of the state of New York. 1668
Collateral Bible. 499
Colleciton of hymns and anthems adapted to public worship. 3398
Collect for the day. 2295
Collectanea Anglicana Ordinis Fratrum Eremitarum S. Augustini. 111
Collectanea evangelica. 2017
Collectanea Franciscana. 1646
Collected articles of Jacob Mann. 2147
Collected letters (Therese) 3691
Collected papers in church history. 1172
Collected papers of Evelyn Underhill. 2641
Collected papers (Smith, Reginald Anthony Lendon) 2579
Collected works. 777, 2643
Collected works of Georges Florovsky. 2745, 3633
Collected works of Joseph Glanvill. 3100
Collected works of Ramana Maharshi. 3020
Collected works of St. Teresa of Avila. 777, 3630
Collected writings (Blavatsky, Helene Petrovna (Hahn-Hahn)) 3689
Collected writings of James Henley Thornwell. 3698
Collected writings of John Murray. 2914, 3633
Collectio rituum. 837
Collection. 776, 1168
Collection made by Committee on antiquities of the Grand lodge Free and accepted masons, of the state of New York. 1667, 1668
Collection of articles on free churches. 1117
Collection of certain letters and conferences lately passed betvvixt certaine preachers & tvvo prisoners in the Fleet. 697
Collection of eastern stories and legends. 703
Collection of English hymns of Creek Baptists. 1864
Collection of essays and fugitive writings on moral, historical, political and literary subjects. 2593
Collection of family prayers. 1606
Collection of family prayers, with various occasional forms. 1606

Collection of faux-bourdons and descants for the french ecclesiastical melodies. 883
Collection of hymns. 320, 1421, 1864, 1867, 2429, 2595
Collection of hymns adapted to the use of the Methodist Episcopal church. 2429
Collection of hymns, and A liturgy, for the use of Evangelical Lutheran churches. 2289
Collection of hymns for the use of native Christians of the Mohawk language. 1878, 2567
Collection of hymns, for the use of the people called Methodists. 1870
Collection of hymns for the use of the Protestant church of the United brethren. 2594, 2595
Collection of interesting tracts. 2447
Collection of interesting tracts, explaining several important points of Scripture doctrine. 2447
Collection of many select and Christian epistles, letters and testimonies. 1679
Collection of memorials concerning divers deceased ministers and others of the people called Quakers, in Pennsylvania, New Jersey, and parts adjacent. 1677
Collection of millenial hymns. 3398
Collection of millennial hymns adapted to the present order of the church. 1868, 3398
Collection of miscellaneous pieces. 3204
Collection of miscellaneous poems, moral, religious, sentimental, and amusing. 3209
Collection of papers on political, literary, and moral subjects. 2592
... Collection of prayers and good works to which the Roman pontiffs have attached indulgences in favor of all the faithful or of certain groups of persons 1899 to 1928. 854
Collection of prayers from the ancient Armenian Book of office and divine liturgy. 82
Collection of private devotions. 1224
Collection of psalm and hymn tunes, chants, anthems, and sentences. 2968
Collection of psalm and hymn tunes sung at the chapel of the Lock hospital. 1866
Collection of Psalms and hymns. 3754
Collection of psalms and hymns for public worship. 1862
Collection of rare books, manuscripts, paintings, etc., relating to Utah and the Mormons offered for sale. 2608, 3762
Collection of Sabbath school hymns. 2634
Collection of sacred hymns. 1233
Collection of sacred hymns; adapted to the faith and views of the Church of Jesus Christ of Latter day saints. 1233
Collection of sacred music for the use of the South parish in Portsmouth. 3270
Collection of sacred songs for the use of the Baptist native Christians of the Six nations. 1878
Collection of select biography. 923
Collection of the acts, deliverances, and testimonies of the supreme judicatory of the Presbyterian church from its origin in America to the present time. 2919
Collection of the epistles from the Yearly meeting of Friends in London to the Quarterly and Monthly meetings in Great-Britain, Ireland and elsewhere, from 1675 to 1805. 1685
Collection of the essays on the subject of episcopacy. 1523
Collection of the promises of Scripture. 301, 302
Collection of the several writings of that true prophet. 1678
Collection of the sweet assuring promises of Scripture. 302
Collection of the works of Thomas Chalkley. 1679
Collection of the world's great masterpieces of Christian art. 919
Collection of theological essays. 34
Collection of theological essays from various authors. 34, 3667
Collectioon of Scriptural and miscellaneous poems. 2856
Collectivism challenges Christianity. 1319
Collectivism in the churches. 2955
Collector's Bach. 123
Collects and prayers for use in church. 3734
Collects, epistles, and gospels for the lesser feasts and fasts. 2969
College and religion. 1308
College and the higher life. 122
College apologetics. 762
College Bible. 250
College dogmatic theology. 3659
College guide for Jewish youth. 2106

College handbook to Newman. 2704
College hymnal for divine service at Yale college in the Battell chapel. 1870
College is a question mark. 1308
College man in doubt. 1127
College man's religion and other studies in religion and life. 1309
College men and the Bible. 1308
College moral theology. 947
College of apostles. 72
College of colleges. 2588
College reading & religion. 3756
College readings on Africa. 12
College record. 2406
College sacramental theology. 3264
College seeks religion. 3757
College sermons. 3337, 3366
College situation and student responsibliity. 3873
College students at Northfield. 2588
College teaching and Christian values. 3757
College warden. 1588
College year. 3777
Colleges and academies of the Council for Higher Education. 3732
Collegiate church and parish of S. Mary, Port Elizabeth. 2863
Collegiate Reformed Protestant Dutch church of the city of New York. 2698
Collegium Divi Johannis Evangelistae. 3756
Collier Mythology of Greece and Rome. 2650
Collier tracts, 1703-1708. 3606
Collier tracts, 1698. 3606
Collingridge. 1309
Collingwood and the reform of metaphysics. 1309, 2473
Collins-Craig auditorium meeting. 1556
Collins gem dictionary of the Bible. 243
Collins Street Baptist Church, Melbourne, 1843-1968. 2401
Collision course. 1302, 3533
Colloquium of the seven about secrets of the sublime. 859, 3113
Colloquy. 3366
Colloquy on baptism, by the twin brothers Alpha and Omega. 136
Colloquy on Christian education. 936
... Collossians, Ephesians and Hebrews. 371
... Cologne. 2098
Colombia; land of conflict and promise. 2512
Colonel Bob Ingersoll. 1907
Colonial Baptists and southern revivals. 2209, 3333
Colonial Baptists, Massachusetts and Rhode Island. 154, 1825
Colonial church in Virginia. 1223
Colonial churches and meeting house. 1161
Colonial churches and the colonial clergy of the middle and southern colonies, 1607-1776. 1271
Colonial churches in Virginia. 1275
Colonial churches of Tidewater Virginia. 3781
Colonial clergy and the colonial churches of New England. 1294
Colonial clergy of Maryland, Delaware, and Georgia. 1293
Colonial clergy of the Middle Colonies. 1294
Colonial clergy of the middle colonies, New York, New Jersey, and Pennsylvania, 1628-1776. 1294
Colonial clergy of Virginia. North Carolina, and South Carolina. 1302
Colonial evangelism. 2556
Colonial houses of worship in America. 1275
Colonial meeting-houses of New Hampshire compared with their contemporaries in New England. 1161
Colonial parson of New England. 1294, 2687
Colonial Spanish art of the Americas. 7, 85
Colonialism and Christian missions. 2494
Colony leader: Anne Hutchinson. 1858
Color and the Edgar Cayce readings. 877, 3575
Color, ebony. 1363
Color me legitimate. 3663
Color of his soul. 3462
Color of the night. 551
Colored Catholics in the United States. 875
Colored light. 1311
Colored man in the Methodist Episcopal Church. 2442, 2460
Colorful and eventful life of St. Clair W. Smith. 3431
Colors of my days. 3485
Colors of the mind. 988, 3422

Colossian and Philemon studies. 341
Colossians. 341, 342
Colossians and Philemon. 341, 342
... Colossians, Ephesians and Hebrews. 371
Colossians, Philippians, 1 & 2 Thessalonians, 1 & 2 Timothy, Titus, Philemon. 372
Colossians speaks to the sickness of our times. 163, 342
Colporteur reports to the American Tract Society. 2688
Columba Marmion. 2335
Columban church. 1311, 1918
Columban, saint, monk, and missionary 539-615, A.D. 1311
Columbia basin project area and its churches. 3435
Columbia theological seminary and the Southern Presbyterian church. 1311
Columbian family and pulpit Bible. 219
Columbian miscellany. 3176
Columbus tabernacle sermons. 1466
Column of Antoninus Pius. 3768
Colum's other island. 1761
Combat myth in the Book of Revelation. 458, 1312
Combination reference. 2605
Combined Biblical dictionary & concordance [for the New American Bible. 243
Combined chronology for use with The Mahatma letters to A. P. Sinnett and The letters of H. P. Blavatsky to A. P. Sinnett. 671, 2317
Combined gospels of Matthew, Mark, Luke and John. 1990
Come. 2014, 2970
Come alive. 1324, 2064, 3186
Come and follow. 1176, 1967
Come and see. 2269, 3184, 3186, 3475, 3875
Come and see, a cooperative text. 3186
Come and see the symbols of my church. 922
Come as you are. 2383
Come aside and rest awhile. 856
Come, be reconciled. 2812
Come blow your mind with me. 810, 827
Come build my church. 1776
Come clean! 584, 1777
Come closer to me, God! 1005
Come down, Zacchaeus. 201
Come everyone and worship. 3853
Come, fill the cup. 305
Come, follow Me! 1886, 1980, 2215, 3188
Come, hear, and see. 229
Come help change the world. 733, 3537
Come, Holy Ghost. 1828, 1834, 1835
Come, Holy Spirit. 1828, 1835, 1836, 3049
Come Holy Spirit, meditations for apostles. 3486
Come home—the door is open. 785
Come, Immanuel. 9, 2299
Come into His presence. 3857
Come into my parlor. 1367, 1629
Come, let us adore. 854
Come, let us adore Him. 3856
Come, let us celebrate. 1614, 2238
Come let us eat. 1626
Come, let us reason together. 3361
Come, let us worship. 2235, 2236, 2239, 3004, 3854
Come, let us worship God. 2783
Come! Live! Die! The real revolution. 989
Come, Lord Jesus. 3163, 3222
Come Lord Jesus, come quickly. 2211
Come, Lord Jesus; devotions for families with children. 1604
Come, meet Abraham, God's friend. 5, 495, 2792
Come, meet Abraham, the pioneer. 5, 495, 2792
Come, meet Isaac. 495, 1920, 2792
Come, meet Jacob, God's prince. 495, 631, 1931
Come, meet Jacob, the grabbing twin. 495, 631, 1931
Come, meet Jesus, the baby. 627, 632, 2022
Come, meet Jesus, the boy. 627, 1996
Come meet my friend. 1367, 1788
Come, meet Ruth. 495, 631, 3258
Come north! 3251, 3416
Come, O breath! 306
Come on, let's pray! 2892
Come out—or stay in? 1360
Come out the wilderness. 1139
Come pray with me. 2887
Come see a Man. 1985
Come share the being. 1010
Come sit with me. 908
Come sweet death. 524, 526
Come, take up your cross. 3526
Come the end. 1529
Come: the inspiring word of grace. 1751

Come to Christmas! 1112
Come to Jesus. 1358, 1999
Come to me. 2258
Come to the family meal. 845, 2369
*Come to the Father. 3163
Come to the Father series. 3184
Come to the Father series. 1. 3184
Come to the feast of the Lord; "Bible Living" studies for men. 995
Come to the holy table. 905
Come to the party. 987
Come unto me. 1435, 1440, 1441, 1555, 1999, 2000
Come unto me [a religion manual and workbook for teachers and parents of the mentally handicapped child, in collaboration with Henry Bedessen. 3183
Come unto these yellow sands. 1544
Come up higher. 1435
Come visit God's house. 747
Come walk the world. 2589
Come what may. 1364, 2505
Come wind, come weather. 912, 2753
Come with faith. 1318
Come with me and see Jesus. 1999
Come worship. 3857
Come ye apart. 725, 1432, 1439, 1977, 1985
Comeback. 1367, 3241
Comedie humaine. 100
Comedy of convocation in the English church. 1218
Comet. 1485
Comfort. 1373, 1374
Comfort and counsel. 1374
Comfort and strength from the Shepherd psalm. 587
Comfort crumbs. 1349
Comfort for Christians. 1352, 1451
Comfort for hours of sorrow. 1349
Comfort for the Jews. 608, 610
Comfort for the people. 1939
Comfort for the sick. 1351, 3407
Comfort for those who mourn. 1349, 1353
Comfort from Calvary. 2056
Comfort my people. 545, 772, 2789
Comfort of God. 321
Comfort of the catholic faith. 1373, 2706
... Comfort to spare. 1353
Comfort words for those who mourn. 1374
"Comfort ye my people," 1352, 3406
Comfortable faith. 1373
Comfortable pew. 1065
Comforter. 1350, 1374, 1693, 1828
Comforting of Christ. 998
Comforting those who grieve. 1257
Comfortings. 1350
Comic vision and the Christian faith. 1076
Coming age and the Catholic church. 755
Coming and kingdom of Christ. 3320
Coming antichrist. 52, 53
Coming back. 1369, 2128
Coming catastrophe. 2946
Coming Christ, and events preceding and following. 2055
Coming Christ and the coming church. 1043
Coming collapse and other sermons. 1238
Coming conflict. 2055
Coming convergence of world religions. 3122
Coming creed. 2056, 3346
Coming creed of the world. 3023
Coming crisis. 1514, 2465, 3384
Coming crisis in Israel. 1928
Coming day. 2055
Coming events. 2055
Coming events, a handbook of Bible prophecy. 606
Coming events in prophecy. 1513
Coming faith. 1061, 2055
Coming forth by day. 1501
Coming free Catholicism. 871
Coming generation. 3512
Coming God. 9
Coming great church. 1042
Coming home. 3491
Coming into being among the Australian Aborigines. 118
Coming judgement. 2156
Coming king. 2056, 3320, 3321
Coming king and the last times. 2055
Coming king; the world's next great crisis. 2055
Coming kingdom. 605, 2055, 2177, 2436, 2465, 3318
Coming kingdom of Christ. 2465
... The coming league and the Roman dream. 509
Coming light. 3517
Coming Lord Jesus Christ. 462
Coming man. 2055
Coming-of- age of Christianity. 1183
Coming of age: problems of teen-agers. 3880

Coming of Christ. 319, 1957, 1958, 3319
Coming of Christianity to England. 1763
Coming of His Kingdom. 1529
Coming of Jesus. 2055
Coming of Shiloh. 2118
"Coming of the Bridegroom." Sacred cantata. 736
Coming of the Christ child. 2023
Coming of the Comforter. 1828
Coming of the demons. 3225
Coming of the Friars minor to England & Germany. 1647
Coming of the King. 2021, 2055, 3320
Coming of the kingdom. 2176
Coming of the Lord. 463, 2466, 3319
Coming of the Messiah. 2055
Coming of the Mormons. 2615
Coming of the peasant. 3740
Coming of the perfect. 1466
Coming of the Russian Mennonites. 2404, 2406
Coming of the Slav. 2926, 3425
Coming of the third church. 810, 1057, 1155
Coming One. 2055
Coming one; Israel in the last days. 610, 1928
Coming presence. 2056
Coming Prince. 508
Coming-- ready or not. 2513
Coming reformation. 2977
Coming religion. 3063, 3141
Coming revival. 1567, 3232
Coming revival of religion. 3228
Coming Russian invasion of Israel. 610
Coming science. 2987
Coming superman. 52
Coming, the world's greatest crisis. 1514
Coming to Christ. 2048
Coming to earth! (Very very soon) 3318
Coming to life. 417
Coming to terms with life. 2931
Coming to terms with the universe. 3104
Coming to the communion. 1317
Coming to the King. 1439
Coming together. 3836
Coming twice. 3318
Coming war and the rise of Russia. 611
Coming world crisis. 3719
Coming world dictator. 52, 609
Command to love. 2258
Commanded to live. 1623
Commanded to preach. 2907
Commandment of love. 2262, 2265
Commandment of love; the first and greatest of the Commandments explained according to the teaching of St. Thomas Aquinas. 2266
Commandment seven. 3392
Commandments. 1312
Commandments & promises of Jesus Christ. 2062
Commandments and sacraments. 1313
Commandments and sacraments explained. 3265
Commandments and the new morality. 2064
Commandments explained according to the Munich or psychological method. 747
... The commandments in sermons. 1315
Commandments of Christ. 2071
Commandments of God. 1314
Commandments of Jesus Christ Our Lord. 2069
Commandos for Christ. 2504
Commands and promises for daily meditation. 725
Commands of Christ. 2064
Commemorating St. Andrew's 75th anniversary and dedication of our new church. Westwood, New Jersey. 3809
Commemorating the dedication of St. Patrick's Church, Springfield, Massachusetts. 1165
Commemorating the dedication of Saint Paul the Apostle Church. Springfield, Massachusetts. 1165
Commemorating the one hundredth anniversary of the foundation of the Brothers of Saint Francis Xavier. 832
Commemorating the opening of the new sanctuary and the 114th anniversary of the founding. 152
Commemorating the 25th anniversary of St. Thomas More Church, Braintree, Massachusetts. 1261
...Commemoration of forty-five years of service. 1822
... Commemoration of the bicentenary of the revocation of the Edict of Nantes. 1497
Commemoration of the one hundred fiftieth anniversary of the founding of Grace Church, Waterford, New York. 1165

Commemorative discourses preached in the Beneficent Congregational church. 2983, 3819
Commemorative exercises of the two-hundredth anniversary of the Friends' meeting-house, at Third Haven. 1675
Commemorative history of the Presbyterian church in Westfield, New Jersey, 1728-1928. 3808
Commemorative history of the Presbyterian Church in Westfield, New Jersey, 1728-1962. 3808
Commemorative services at the twenty-fifth anniversary of the pastorate of the Rev. John Pike, Rowley, Mass., November 19, 22, 23, 1865. 1911
Commemorative services of the First Baptist church of Boston, Massachusetts. 154
Commemorative services on the semi-centennial anniversary of pastorate of Rev. John Chambers, D. D. 880
... Commencement number. 1390
Commencement sermons delivered in Asbury college chapel. 3365
Commentar on the Gospel according to John. 415
Commentaries. 221
... The commentaries of Ishodad of Merv, bishop of Hadatha. 343
... The Commentaries of Pius II. 2850
*Commentaries on doctrinal themes. 769
Commentaries on Hebrew and Christian mythology. 3717
Commentaries on living. 1536, 1538, 1812
Commentaries on living, from the notebooks of J. Krishnamurti. Edited by D. Rajagopal. 1538
Commentaries on living, from the notebooks of J. Krishnamurty. Second series. 1538
Commentaries on t on the Epistle of Paul the apostle tothe Romans. 467
Commentaries on the book of Joshua. 553
Commentaries on the book of the prophet Daniel. 506
Commentaries on the book of the prophet Jeremiah and the Lamentations. 546
Commentaries on the Catholic Epistles. 340
Commentaries on the Epistle of Paul the apostle to the Hebrews. 402
Commentaries on the Epistles of Paul the apostle to the Philippians, Colossians, and Thessalonians. 371
Commentaries on the Epistles of Paul to the Galatians and Ephesians. 371, 379
Commentaries on the Epistles to Timothy, Titus, and Philemon. 446
Commentaries on the first book of Moses. 521
Commentaries on the first twenty chapters of the book of the prophet Ezekiel. 518
Commentaries on the four last books of Moses, arranged in the form of a harmony. 562
Commentaries on the twelve minor prophets. 559
Commentarium medium in Aristotelis De generatione et corruptione libros. 81
Commentary. 371
Commentary, critical and explanatory, on the Old and New Testaments. 222, 223
... A commentary, critical and explanatory, on the whole Bible. 223
Commentary, critical and grammatical, on St. Paul's Epistle to the Galatians. 379
Commentary, critical, experimental, and practical, on the Old and New Testaments. 223
Commentary, critical, expository, and practical, on the Gospel of John. 415
Commentary, critical, expository, and practical, on the Gospel of Luke. 427
Commentary, critical, expository, and practical, on the Gospels of Matthew and Mark. 439
Commentary, explanatory, doctrinal, and practical, on the Epistle to the Ephesians. 364
Commentary of David Kimhi on Isaiah. 542
Commentary of Levi ben Gerson (Gersonides) on the book of Job. 548
Commentary of Rabbi David Kimhi on Hosea. 537, 538
Commentary of Rabbi David Kimhi on Psalms CXX-CL. 579
Commentary of the Catechism of Rev. W. Faerber for the Catholic parochial schools of the United States. 746, 1588
Commentary of the epistles to the seven churches in Asia. 461
Commentary of the original text of the Acts of the apostles. 329
Commentary on 1 and 2 Peter and Jude. 447

Commentary on 1 Maccabees. 488
Commentary on a harmony of the Evangelists, Matthew, Mark, and Luke. 386, 3057
Commentary on Acts of apostles. 329
Commentary on Acts of the apostles. 328
Commentary on Colossians & Philemon. 341
Commentary on Daniel. 495
Commentary on Ecclesiastes, with other treatises. 512
Commentary on Ephesians. 363
Commentary on Exodus. 516
Commentary on 1 & 2 Corinthians. 345
Commentary on 1 & 2 Timothy & Titus. 446
Commentary on I Corinthians. 322
Commentary on First Peter. 325
Commentary on Galatians. 379
Commentary on Genesis. 521, 522
Commentary on Hebrews. 403
Commentary on Isaiah. 542
Commentary on Jeremiah. 546
Commentary on Luke. 428
Commentary on Mark thirteen. 438
... Commentary on Paul's Epistle to the Romans. 468
Commentary on Paul's Epistle to the Romans. 469
Commentary on Romans. 469
Commentary on Saint Ignatius' Rules for the discernment of spirits. 1460, 1882
Commentary on Saint John the apostle and evangelist. 422
Commentary on St. Paul's Epistle to the Galatians. 371, 380
Commentary on St. Paul's Epistle to the Romans. 371, 467
Commentary on St. Paul's Letter to the Ephesians. 364
... Commentary on the Acts. 330
Commentary on the Acts of the Apostles. 327, 329, 330
Commentary on the American prayer book. 2957
Commentary on the American scene. 2104
Commentary on the Apostles' Creed. 74
Commentary on the apostolic faculties. 1588
Commentary on the Bhagavad Gita. 2316
Commentary on the Bible. 221, 224
... A commentary on the book of Daniel. 506
... Commentary on the book of Deuteronomy. 510
... Commentary on the book of Job. 548
Commentary on the Book of Leviticus. 557
Commentary on the Book of Mormon. 678
Commentary on the book of Proverbs. 572
Commentary on the book of Psalms. 575
Commentary on the book of Psalms. Translated from the original Latin, and collated with the author's French version. 575
Commentary on the book of Revelation. 452, 454
Commentary on the book of the Acts. 328
Commentary on the book of the prophet Isaiah. 542
... A commentary on the books of Amos, Hosea, and Micah. 559
Commentary on the catechism of Rev. W. Faerber. 769, 1588
Commentary on the Catholic epistles. 340
Commentary on the Confession of 1967 and an introduction to The book of confessions. 3735
Commentary on the Constitution and on the Instruction on the sacred liturgy. 3771
Commentary on the creed of Islam. 3722
Commentary on the cult of the most blessed sacrament of the altar. 2253
Commentary on the decree "Ne temere" 2346
... A commentary on the Doctrine and covenants. 3215, 3430
Commentary on the documents of Vatican II. 3771
Commentary on the Epistle of James. 412
Commentary on the Epistle of Jude. 425
Commentary on the Epistle of Paul, the apostle, to the Hebrews. 403
... Commentary on the Epistle of Paul to the Galatians. 379
... Commentary on the Epistle of Paul to the Romans. 466
Commentary on the Epistle to the Ephesians. 363
Commentary on the Epistle to the Galatians; a new abridged translation by Theodore Graebner. 380

Commentary on the Epistle to the Hebrews. 403, 404
Commentary on the Epistle to the Philippians. 448
Commentary on the Epistle to the Romans. 466, 467, 468
Commentary on the Epistles of Paul the apostle to the Corinthians. 345
Commentary on the epistles of Peter and of Jude. 447
Commentary on the Epistles of St. Paul to the Thessalonians. 478
Commentary on the Epistles to the Ephesians and the Colossians. 364
... Commentary on the First book of Samuel. 483
Commentary on the First Epistle to the Corinthians. 322, 345
Commentary on the five scrolls. 498
Commentary on the general epistle of James. 412
Commentary on the Gospel according to John. 328, 416, 417
... Commentary on the Gospel according to Luke. 428
Commentary on the Gospel according to Mark. 432, 437
...Commentary on the Gospel according to Matthew. 439, 440, 441, 442
Commentary on the Gospel according to Saint John. 417
Commentary on the gospel according to St. Luke. 428
Commentary on the Gospel according to St. Mark. 433
Commentary on the Gospel according to St. Matthew. 440, 441
Commentary on the Gospel by John. 415
Commentary on the Gospel by Luke. 427
Commentary on the Gospel by Mark. 432
Commentary on the Gospel by St. John. 417
Commentary on the Gospel of John. 416, 419
Commentary on the Gospel of Luke. 428
Commentary on the Gospel of Mark. 432, 433
Commentary on the Gospel of Matthew. 439, 440
Commentary on the Gospel of St. John. 418
... A commentary on the Gospel of St. Luke. 428
Commentary on the Gospels. 344, 385, 386
Commentary on the Gospels of Matthew and Mark, critical, doctrinal, and homiletical, embodying for popular use and edification the results of German and English exegetical literature, and designed to meet the difficulties of modern skepticism. 394
Commentary on the harmony of the Gospels. 386
Commentary on the Heidelberg catechism. 1801
Commentary on the Holy Bible. 220, 221, 222
Commentary on the Holy Bible, containing the Old and New Testaments according to the authorized version. 220
Commentary on the holy communion. 2961
Commentary on the Holy Scriptures. 223
Commentary on the Johannine Epistles. 369
Commentary on the Lord's Sermon on the Mount. 3334
Commentary on the Minor Prophets. 559
Commentary on the new Code of canon law. 775
Commentary on the new lectionary. 315
Commentary on the new Little office. 847
Commentary on the New Testament. 342, 343
Commentary on the New Testament Epistles. 367
Commentary on the New Testament from the Talmud and Hebraica, Matthew — I Corinthians. 344, 2668
Commentary on the Nicomachean ethics. 1537
Commentary on the original text of the Acts of the apostles. 329
Commentary on the Pastoral Epistles. 446
Commentary on the Pauline Epistles. 372
Commentary on the present Index legislation. 879
Commentary on the prophecies of Isaiah. 541
Commentary on the prophets. 497
Commentary on the Psalms. 575, 577
Commentary on the Psalms from primitive and mediaeval writers. 575
Commentary on the Psalms of David. 576
Commentary on the Psalms, Psalms i-l. 574

Commentary on the Revelation of John. 454
Commentary on the Revelation of St. John, the Divine. 452, 453
Commentary on the science of organization and business development. 719
Commentary on the Song of Solomon. 593
Commentary on the Song of songs. 594
Commentary on the Sunday lectionary, first Sunday of Advent to last Sunday of the year, year C. 595
Commentary on the Torah. 562
Commentary on the whole Bible. 222
Commentary on the whole Bible, Genesis to Revelation. 222
Commentary on true and false religion. 3653
Commentary, practical and explanatory, on the whole Bible. 223
Commentary to Mishnah Aboth. 4
Commentary to Union Prayer Book. 2239
Commentary upon the Epistle of Paul the apostle to the Galatians. 380
Commentary upon the Epistle to the Hebrews. 403
Commentator's lectionary. 2368
Commenting and commentaries. 237
Comments at the cross. 2214
Comments on Daniel. 507, 508
Comments on the Revelation. 451
Commission, conflict, commitment. 2496
Commission, conflict, commitment: messages. 2496
Commission executed. 473
Commission of Moses and the Christian calling. 2621
... The commission plan for realizing the ideals of the Christian life program through the young people's society. 3877
Commissioned by the Lord himself. 3491
Commitment. 3884
Commitment and indifference. 992
Commitment and the school community. 2942
Commitment on campus. 1309
Commitment to care. 67
Commitment to truth. 3703
Commitment without ideology. 1585
Commitments and consequences. 1103
Commitments of confirmation. 1328
Committed communities. 933
Committed locally, living globally. 1565, 2433
Committed marriage. 2336
Committed to Christ. 3537
Committed to whom? 1012
Committed unto us. 2493
Committee report. 2811
Common catechism. 3643
Common creed of Christians. 75
Common cross. 3540
Common diseases of the skin. 3422
Common experience. 3483
Common expositor. 524
Common faith. 3058
Common faith of common men. 1596
Common faith, uncommon people. 2087, 3028
Common ground. 1316, 2105
Common life. 1068
Common mystic prayer. 2379
Common objections to Christianity. 57
Common order of morning worship. 2884
Common prayer in nine services. 1223
Common quest. 3668
Common roots. 1551
Common sense. 1000, 1104, 1106
Common sense about Christian ethics. 942
Common sense about religion. 57, 3119
Common sense about yoga. 3866
Common sense and God. 3609
Common sense applied to religion. 3097
Common-sense Christianity. 1053, 1325
Common-sense hell. 1699
Common sense in church building. 1156
Common-sense in religion. 1048, 1105
Common sense of Bible salvation. 3288
Common sense of God. 1103
Common sense philosophy for modern man. 2320
Common-sense philosophy of spirit or psychology. 3502
Common-sense religion, what's it good for? 1106
Common sense theology of Bishop White. 3812
Common-sense view of Christian science. 1034
Common service book of the Lutheran church. 2290
Common ventures of life. 1854
Commonism. 3434
... The Commonitory of St. Vincent of Lerins. 3283

Commonplace-book to the Holy Bible. 303
Commonplace prodigal. 2869
Commonsense of Christianity. 1057
Commonsense religion. 3141
Commonweal (The) 2192
Commonwealth. 2492
Commonwealths and the kingdom. 2483
Communal Catholic. 874
Communal life. 2570
... The communal organization of the Jews in the United States, 1927. 2105
Communal pietism among early American Moravians. 2594, 2596
Communicant's companion. 2251, 2258
Communicant's spiritual companion; or, An evangelical preparation for the Lord's supper. 2259
Communicating Christ. 1317
Communicating Christ cross-culturally. 1316
Communicating Christ in the inner city. 939
Communicating issues in thanatology. 1413
Communicating love through prayer. 2880
Communicating reality through symbols. 1317
Communicating the Gospel. 2902
Communicating the mystery. 3178
Communicating with God. 2885
Communicating with junior highs. 3167
... Communication, a source of privileges. 2943
Communication as commitment. 1316
Communication for churchmen series. 1317
Communication for the church. 1317
Communication in pulpit and parish. 1316
... Communication in religious worship with non-Catholics. 1316
Communication in the church. 810, 1317
Communication: key to your marriage. 2340
Communication of the board of directors of the Panama railroad company to the stockholders. 719
Communication of the Christian faith. 1566
Communication of the gospel. 2904
Communication with the spirit world. 3503
Communications from the spirit world. 1345
Communicators for Christ. 1404
Communio: church and papacy in early Christianity. 1196
Communion. 1304, 1318, 1450, 1781, 2252
Communion counsel and prayers. 2258
Communion devotions for religious. 2259
Communion handbook. 2257
Communion manual. 2258
Communion meditations. 1318
Communion, meditations, and prayers. 1318, 2258
Communion messages. 1318
Communion of communions. 2972
Communion of possibility. 3071
Communion of prayer. 2883
Communion of saints. 1317, 1318, 2276, 3281
Communion of saints: sanctity through the centuries. 3282
Communion of the Christian with God. 1592
Communion of the Christian with God described on the basis fo Luther's statements. 2286
...The communion prayer book. 1825
Communion service as it might be. 2250
Communion thoughts and prayers. 2259
Communion through preaching. 2899
Communion tokens, their origin, history, and use, with a treatise on the relation of the sacrament to the vitality, and revivals of the church. 3703
Communion wine and Bible temperance. 2200, 3597
Communion with Christ. 2255, 2258
*Communion With God. 1445, 2881, 2887, 2892
Communion with the spirit world. 3475
Communion with young saints. 1608, 2128
Communism and Christianism. 1319
Communism and Christianity. 1319
Communism and fascism destroyed at Christ's second coming. 3321
Communism and man. 1320
Communism and the churches. 1319, 3745
Communism and the theologians. 1320, 3657
Communism, Christianity, democracy. 1320
Communism vs. Christianity. 1319

Communism versus creation. 1319
Communist-Christian encounter in East Europe. 1542
Communist encounter. 1319
Communist exploitation of religion. 2821
Communist menace. 1320
Communist Russia and the Russian Orthodox Church, 1943-1962. 1149, 2750
Communistic societies of the United States. 1308, 1320
Communities in Britain. 1765
Community action; a handbook for Catholic high schools. 867
Community and Christian education. 1912
Community and commitment. 1118
Community & growth. 1002
Community and liturgy. 809, 2235
Community and message of Isaiah 56-66. 544
Community and the Y. M. C. A. 3872
Community called church. 1123
Community church. 1321
Community churches, the community church movement. 1321
Community daily vacation Bible school. 3763
Community forces for religious education, early adolescence. 3150
Community health program for the Y.W.C.A. 3877
Community in a Black Pentecostal church. 2682
Community in the Lord. 998
... The community industries of the Shakers. 3398
Community journey. 1364
Community leadership and social change in Cali, Colombia. 726
Community life for women. 1321
Community mental health. 1321
Community of believers. 155, 1166, 1201
Community of character. 943
Community of faith. 1121
Community of the beloved disciple. 413, 1163
Community of the free. 2858, 3451
Community of the King. 1123
Community of the mind. 3461
Community of the new age. 435
Community of the saved. 197, 2814
Community of the spirit. 1120
Community on campus. 3757
Community organization. 1140
Community organization in religious education. 3189
Community programs for cooperating churches. 1040, 1369
Community psychiatry and the clergyman. 3434
Community school visitor. 3783
Community, state, and church. 3043, 3618
...The community survey in relation to church effciency. 3435
Community, the church and the mentally retarded. 1255
Community witness. 237
Community work and the churches. 1321
Community work of the Young men's Christian association. 3872
Communsity & commitment. 2222, 2971
Compact Bible. 653
Compact commentary on the New Testament. 343
Compact concordance. 226
Compact guide to Bible-based beliefs. 304, 3327
Companion Bible. 653
Companion characters. 214
Companion for American Catholic hymnals. 1862
Companion for daily communion. 855
Companion for the festivals and fasts of the Protestant Episcopal church in the United States of America, principally selected and altered from Nelson's Companion for the festivals and fasts of the Church of England. 1613
Companion for the young people of North-America. 3885
Companion of eternity. 2320
Companion of prayer for daily living. 2889
Companion of the crucified. 2269
Companion of the way. 3682
Companion to Baptist hymnal. 1875
Companion to Biblical studies. 232
Companion to Hymnbook for Christian worship. 1876
Companion to John. 414
Companion to neo-Latin studies. 2199
Companion to Paul. 370
Companion to Scripture studies. 312
Companion to the Authorised daily prayerbook. 2109
Companion to the Bible. 242, 311, 595

Companion to the Bible [Reissue]. 595
Companion to the book of Genesis. 524
Companion to The book of worship. 2440
Companion to the clams. 2393
Companion to the communion service. 2259
Companion to the font and the pulpit. 137
Companion to the Good news Old Testament. 540
Companion to the Greek Testament and the English version. 352
Companion to the Hymnal. 2430
Companion to the missal for Sundays and principal feasts. 845
Companion to The new Scofield reference Bible. 232
Companion to the New Testament. 411
Companion to the Old Testament. 498
Companion to the prayer book. 1308, 2960
Companion to the revised version of the New Testament. 361, 362
Companion to the Spiritual exercises of Saint Ignatius. 3484
Companion to the study of St. Augustine. 113
Companion to the study of St. Anselm. 49
Companion to the Summa. 3696
Companion to the temple. 1211
Companion to world mythology. 2664
Companion to your study of the Book of Mormon. 679
Companion to your study of the Doctrine and covenants. 3428
Companion to your study of the Old Testament. 500
Companions along the way. 2060, 3473
Companions of the sorrowful way. 2032
Companions of the unseen. 2399
Companions of the way. 1057
Companionship with the Master. 934
Company of Heaven. 2543
Company of strangers. 1154
Company of the committed. 1064
Comparation of vyrgin and a martyr (1523) 3781
Comparative and rational Christian science. 1038
Comparative excellence and obligation of moral and positive duties, 1730, and A discourse concerning reason, 1731. 3022
Comparative harmony of the four Gospels. 1988
Comparative history of religions. 3118
Comparative liturgy. 2236
Comparative miracles. 2477
Comparative mythology. 2653
Comparative philology and the text of the Old Testament. 505, 1797
Comparative philosophy. 2833
Comparative religion. 3113, 3114, 3117, 3119, 3121
Comparative religion and the religion of the future. 3061
Comparative religion, its adjuncts and allies. 3089
Comparative religions. 3117
Comparative religious ethics. 3191
Comparative religious literature. 646, 3015
... Comparative studies in religion. 3728
Comparative study of religions. 3121
... A comparative study of some high school religion texts. 803
Comparative study of the four Gospel records. 391
Comparative study of the Old Testament text in the Dead Sea scrolls and in the New Testament. 1411
Comparative view of the Gospels. 397
Comparison of religions. 3122
Comparison of youth and adult reactions to Lutheran youth problems and sources of assistance. 1261
Compass. 3211
Compass for conscience. 983
Compass for prayer. 2875
Compass points for Old Testament study. 540
Compassion, a reflection on the Christian life. 3576
Compassion and community. 1134
Compassion of God and the passion of Christ. 2210
Compassionate and free. 2165, 3832
Compassionate Christ. 427
Compassionate God. 3616
Compassionate touch. 2532
Compelled by the cross. 1998
Compelled to speak. 2778
Compelling indwelling. 424
Compend of Alexander Campbell's theology. 732
Compend of baptism. 135
Compend of Bible truth. 3661
Compend of Christian divinity. 3752
Compend of Luther's theology. 2281, 2286

Compend of the Institutes of the Christian religion. 3044
Compend of Wesley's theology. 3650
Compendicus book of godly and spiritual songs, (A) 1878
Compendious abstract of the history of the church of Christ. 1174
Compendious critical life of St. Therese of Lisieux. 3691
Compendious ecclesiastical history. 1178
Compendious history of the rise and progress of the Methodist church. 2424
Compendious introduction to the study of the Bible. 310
Compendious narrative. 2348, 3395
Compendious system of geography. 1706
Compendium explained. 1801
Compendium guide. 1023
Compendium helper. 1023
Compendium maleficarum. 1423
Compendium of Baptist history. 152
Compendium of Biblical texts and topics for every Sunday of the year. 642
Compendium of Christian doctrine. 934
Compendium of church history, comp. for use in Catholic schools. 1185
Compendium of ecclesiastical history. 1174
Compendium of first and second years academic religion. 3111
Compendium of first and second years academic religion, according to the requirements of the Catholic University. 3186
Compendium of liturgical music terms. 1206
Compendium of Methodism. 2421
Compendium of occult laws. 2724, 3250
Compendium of religious and scientific reflections. 3211
Compendium of religious faith and practice. 1675, 1682
Compendium of Scriptural truths. 278
Compendium of temperance truth. 3595
Compendium of the chief doctrines of the true Christian religion. 2690
... A compendium of the faith and doctrine of the Reorganized church of Jesus Christ of latter day saints. 3216
Compendium of the faith and doctrine of the Reorganized Church of Jesus Christ of Latter Day Saints. 3216
Compendium of the history of the Cistercian order. 3709
Compendium of the life of Saint Nicholas of Tolentine, priest of the Order of Saint Augustine, patron of the holy souls in purgatory. 2707
Compendium of the religious doctrines, religious and moral precepts, historical and descriptive beauties of the Bible. 231
Compendium of the system of divine truth. 3641, 3642
Compendium of the theological and spiritual writings of Emanual Swedenborg. 2691
Compendium of the theological writings of Emanuel Swedenborg. 2691, 3570
Compendium of theology. 755, 3649
Compendium of third and fourth years high-school religion. 3111
Compendium of third and fourth years high-school religion, according to the requirements of the Catholic University. 3186
Compensation. 305, 1510
... Compensation, self reliance, and other essays. 1510
Competency and creativity in language arts. 2475
Competent church. 1250
Competent ministry. 1297
Competent to lead. 953
Compilation & digest of decisions and relevant matter. 1666
Compilation & digest of descisions and relevant matter contained in proceedings of the Grand lodge of Free and accepted masons of the state of New York. 1666
Compilation and history of National Baptist Memorial Church (formerly Immanuel Baptist Church), Washington, D.C., 1906 to about 1976. 2669
Compilation containing the Lectures on faith as delivered at the School of the prophets at Kirkland, Ohio, with added references on the Godhead and the Holy Ghost, also an historical sketch of the same by Dr. John A. Widtsoe, also a treatise on True faith by Orson Pratt, also a bibliography on Melchizedek by Ariel L. Crowley. 1593
Compilation for the use of the members of the Protestant Episcopal church, in Maryland. 2958
Compilation of Christian beliefs. 3322

Compilation of passages derived from Holy Scripture. 253
Compilation of proposals for Christian unity. 1045
Compilation of public records. 145
Compilation of public records [of] 42 of the Unitarian clergymen and 450 rabbis. 3724
Compilation of public records of 658 clergymen and laymen connected with the National Council of Churches. 1300
Compilation of the healings of Christ and His apostles as recorded in the New Testament. 2017
... Compilation of the holy utterances of Baha'o'llah and Abdul Baha. 126
Compilation of the lectures given by the spirit-band through the mediumship of Mrs. Magdalena Kline. 3506
Compilation of the litanies and vespers hymns and anthems as they are sung in the Catholic church. 812
Compilation of the litanies, vespers, hymns and anthems as sung in the Catholic Church. 812
Complaint. 3213
Complaint of the Rev. Thomas H. Skinner, against the action of the presbytery of Cincinnati, at its fall meeting, 1876, with the argument. 2927
Compleat body of divinity. 1335, 3809
Compleat witch. 3824
Complete alphabetically arranged Biblical biography. 213
Complete analysis of the Holy Bible. 228, 304
Complete and practical method of the Solesmes plain chant. 883
Complete art of witchcraft. 3824
Complete Bar-Mitzvah book with all haftorahs. 172
Complete Bible, an American translation. 653
Complete bibliography of the scholarship on the life and works of Saint John Chrysostom. 1115
Complete book of Bible stories for Jewish children. 628
Complete book of church growth. 1171
Complete book of Hanukkah. 1784
Complete book of Jewish observance. 1614, 2120
Complete booke of white magic. 2313
Complete candlelight services for Christmas. 1114
Complete catachism of Christian doctrine. 769
Complete catalogue of Catholic literature. 869
Complete catechism of Christian doctrine. 746
Complete catechism of the Catholic religion. 746, 767, 769, 770
Complete commentary. 455
Complete commentary of Oecumenius on the Apocalypse. 455
Complete concordance of the Book of Mormon. Edited and arr. by Philip C. Reynolds. 680
Complete concordance to Miscellaneous writings. 1493, 1494
Complete concordance to Science and health. 1493, 1494
Complete concordance to the American standard version of the Holy Bible. 225
Complete concordance to the Bible. 228
... A complete concordance to the Book of Mormon. 679, 680
Complete concordance to The Chester mystery plays. 892, 2636
Complete concordance to the doctrine and covenants. 3430
Complete concordance to the Holy Scripture of the Old and New Testament. 226
Complete concordance to the Holy Scripture of the Old and New Testaments. 226
Complete concordance to the Holy Scriptures of the Old and New Testament. 226
Complete concordance to the Holy Scriptures of the Old and New Testaments. 226
... A complete concordance to the Old and New Testamemt. 226
Complete concordance to the Old and New Testament. 226
Complete concordance to the Old and New Testaments. 227
Complete conspiracy trial book. 140
[Complete daily prayers]. 2110
Complete daily prayers with a revised translation according to the custom of Ashkenasim. 2109
Complete dictionary of astrology. 98

Complete directory of Orthodox Catholic churches in the United States. 2751
Complete duty of men. 978
... A complete expose of Eddyism or Christian science and the plain truth in plain terms regarding Mary Baker G. Eddy. 1035, 1495
Complete funeral manual. 1693
Complete group guidance for Catholic high schools. [Ed. by Francis A. Quinn et al.]. 867
Complete guide to church building. 1156
... Complete guide to St. Patrick's, New York. 2700
Complete guide to the Christian's budget. 3530
Complete guide to the tarot. 3588
Complete hand book for S. S. teachers and Bible classes. 438
Complete handbook of church accounting. 1168
Complete handbook of religious pictures. 2959
Complete history of Methodism as connected with the Mississippi Conference of the Methodist Episcopal Church. 2457
Complete history of Methodism as connected with the Mississippi conference of the Methodist Episcopal church, South. 2457
Complete history of Mississippi Baptists. 156
Complete home study course in ontology. 2174
Complete illustrated book of divination and prophecy. 1470
Complete illustrated book of the psychic sciences. 2725
Complete illustrated book of yoga. 3866
Complete index of books by Max Heindel. 1801
Complete index of the Summa theologica of St. Thomas Aquinas. 3696
Complete index to the thought and teachings of Christ. 397, 2063
Complete integrated version of the four Gospels for reading and study. 1960
Complete lessons. 1916
Complete magick curriculum of the secret order G. .B. .G. 1765, 2733
Complete missionary programs. 2549
Complete musical service for Day of atonement. 3577
... The complete poems of John Milton. 2468
Complete poetical and prose works of Robert Burns. 718
Complete poetical works of James Russell Lowell. 2856
Complete poetical works of John Greenleaf Whittier. 2857
Complete poetical works of John Milton. 2468
Complete poetical works of Robert Burns. 718
Complete poetical works of Thomas Campbell. 2855, 2856
Complete poetical works of William Cowper, esq. 2856
Complete prayers. 2894
Complete prophecies of Nostradamus. 2947, 2948
Complete religious and theological works of Thomas Paine. 2758
Complete Rosary. 3248
Complete sayings of Jesus. 2070
Complete Sermon outlines. 3373
Complete source book for the Lord's Supper. 2257
Complete speaker and reciter for home, school, church and platform. 3170
Complete spiritual doctrine of St. Therese of Lisieux. 3487, 3690
Complete story of Tishrei. 3702
Complete system of Catholic education is necessary. 830, 3258
Complete system of Christian theology. 3649
Complete testimony of the early fathers proving the universal observances of Sunday in the first centuries. 276
Complete with commas. 2388
Complete woman. 573, 3844
Complete works. 3603
Complete works (Josephus, Flavius) 2083
... The complete works of Charles Dickens (in sixteen volumes) 2856
Complete works of Chuang Tzu. 2856
Complete works of Count Tolstoy. 2856
Complete works of Count Tolstoy. [Limited edition. Translated from the original Russian and edited by Leo Wiener]. 2856
...The complete works of Nathaniel Hawthorne. 2856
Complete works of Robert Burns. 718

Complete works of Saint John of the Cross, doctor of the Church. 776
Complete works of Samuel Taylor Coleridge. 1306

Complete worship services for the college age. 3856
Complete writings (Menno Simons) 2405
Complete writings of Charles Dickens. 2856
Complete writings of Elbert Hubbard. 2856
Complete writings of Nathaniel Hawthorne. 2952
Complete writings of Ralph Waldo Emerson. 1510
...The complete writings of Robert Burns. 718
Complete writings (Pallotti, Vincenzo) 777, 3632
Complete writings (Williams, Roger) 3818
Completeness of Christ. 2059
Completer light: a gospel of Americanism. 3434
Completing the course. 1575, 1715
Completing the reformation. 2939
Completion of Coleridge's Christabel. 1306
Complex vision. 2227
Composer's point of view. 916
Composite administrative report to the Board of home missions and church extension. 2454
Composite annual report. 2434
Composite Gospel. 1990
Composite Gospel of Our Lord and Savior, Jesus Christ. 1989
Composite report of the secretaries. 2441
Composition and corroboration in classical and Biblical studies. 515
...The composition and date of Acts. 330
Composition and order of the fourth Gospel. 421, 713
Composition of the Hexateuch. 531
Comprehensive account of the rise and progress of the blessed reformation of the Christian church. 2277, 3036
Comprehensive analysis of the Bible. 302
Comprehensive Baptist young people's union manual. 142
Comprehensive Bible concordance. 226
Comprehensive Bible index. 302
Comprehensive Bible study course. 645
Comprehensive bibliography of modern African religious movements. 13
Comprehensive bibliography of the thanatology literature. 1416
Comprehensive catalogue of Catholic books in the English and German languages. 868
Comprehensive commentary of the Holy Bible. 220
... The comprehensive commentary on the Holy Bible. 220
Comprehensive commentary on the Quran. 2184
Comprehensive concordance of the New World translation of the Holy Scriptures. 229
Comprehensive concordance to the Holy Scriptures. 225, 228
Comprehensive confession of faith. 1327
Comprehensive dictionary of Freemasonry. 1663
Comprehensive dictionary of the Bible. 246
Comprehensive guide to children's literature with a Jewish theme. 2107, 2151
Comprehensive handbook of Christian doctrine. 3645
Comprehensive history of Jainism, up to 1000 A.D. 1933
Comprehensive history of the Church of Jesus Christ of latter-day saints, century i. 2605
Comprehensive history of the Disciples of Christ. 2008
Comprehensive index to biennial convention minutes of the United LutheranChurch in America 1918-1952. 3733
Comprehensive index to the writings of Ellen G. White. 3812
Comprehensive lexicon and concordance; a complete key to the Greek Scriptures and their English translations in the Concordant version. 344
Comprehensive outline of prophecy. 1514
Comprehensive pastoral care. 2787
Comprehensive program of church music. 1209
Comprehensive supplement to the Machzor for the Yamim noraim. 2110
Comprehensive teachers' Bible. 647
Comprehensive view of Freemasonry. 1661

Comprehensive view of the leading and most important principles of natural and revealed religion. 3648
Compressed view of the religious principles and practices of the age. 1218
Compulsion of love. 3347
Compulsive Christian. 993
Compulsory dancing. 3483
... The computation of time in a canonical novitiate. 3701
Computer Bible. 498
Comrades in service. 659
Comrades in the great cause. 450
Comrades of the Carpenter. 1999
Comrades of the cross. 2006
... Comrades of the way. 348, 410
Comrades round the world. 2520
Comradeship hour. 429
Comte de St. Germain. 3274
Comus. 2468
... Comus, L'allegro, Il penseroso, and Lycidas. 2468
Concealed map of the land of Israel. 283
Concelebration. 1322
Concentration. 109, 3866
Concentration and meditation. 2380, 2382
Concentration camp hero. 2709
Concentration methods and helps. 2727
Concentric circles of concern. 3830
Concept and quality. 2419
Concept development and the development of the God concept in the child. 904
Concept in Thomism. 3693
Concept of a limited God. 2822
Concept of a university. 2302
Concept of anxiety. 3413
Concept of belief in Islamic theology. 1601
Concept of benevolence: aspects of eighteenth-century moral philosophy. 190
... The concept of clerical immunity. 1892
Concept of correlation. 3669, 3699
Concept of deity. 1723
Concept of dread. 3413
Concept of existence in the Concluding unscientific postscript. 2170
Concept of God. 1735
Concept of grace. 1752
Concept of holiness. 1823
... The concept of ingratitude in renaissance English moral philosophy. 1908
Concept of man. 2320
Concept of man in the Bible. 2326
Concept of Maya from the Vedas to the 20th century. 2375
Concept of newness in the New Testament. 2162
Concept of peace. 2809
Concept of prayer. 2877
Concept of sacred theology. 3659
Concept of sin. 3412
Concept of state and law in Islam. 1923
Concept of the diocesan priesthood. 771
Concept of the guardian spirit in North America. 1902
Concept of the secular state and India. 3088
Concept of univocity regarding the predication of God and creature according to William Ockham. 38, 1474
Concept purpose. 3593
Conception: a history of the first century of the Conception colony, 1858-1958. 1322
Conception, birth and infancy in ancient Rome and modern Italy. 664
Conception of Buddhist nirvana (along with Sanskrta text of Madhayamaka-karika) 2711
Conception of God. 1726
Conception of God in the philosophy of Aquinas. 1732, 3697
... The conception of immortality. 1890, 1891
Concepts and values. 566
Concepts of deity. 3609
Concepts of freedom in the Old Testament. 484, 1659
Concepts of God in Africa. 1724
Concepts of Judaism. 2080
Concepts of self and morality. 3
Concern and response. 1164
Concern for benevolence among Disciples of Christ. 2669
Concern for social justice in the Puritan Revolution. 3050, 3435
Concern for unity. 1682
Concerning heretics. 1805
Concerning hymn tunes and sequences. 1875
Concerning infants in heaven. 897
Concerning Isabel Carnaby. 1999
Concerning life. 3725
"Concerning natural experimental philosophie" 58, 743

Concerning our duties to God. 2745
Concerning preachers. 3675
Concerning scandals. 1012, 3044
Concerning sin and grace. 2299
Concerning the Book with the greatest plan. 309
Concerning the Christ. 1951
Concerning the City of God against the pagans. 2173
Concerning the collection. 1167
Concerning the Disciples. 1464
Concerning the earths in our solar system which are called planets. 1371
Concerning the faith. 1597
Concerning the future. 1696
Concerning the inner life. 978, 3463
Concerning the ministry. 2904
... Concerning the philosophical defensibility of a limited indeterminism. 1658
Concerning the prophet Frederick Madison Smith. 3427
Concerning the teacher (De magistro) and On the immortality of the soul (De immortalitate aminae) 3460
Concerning the teacher (De magistro) and On the immortality of the soul (De immortalitate animae) 3460
Concerning them which are asleep. 1414
Concerning worship. 3853
Concerns of a continent. 2713
Concerns of a world church. 1117
Concerns of household workers. 3877
Concerns of religion. 1064
Concert harmony. 1203
Concessions of "liberalists" to orthodoxy. 3642
Das Concil und die getreuen kinder der kirche. 3769
Conciliar-evangelical debate. 2496
Conciliator of R. Manasseh ben Israel. 501
Concise account, of church history. 1173
Concise account of the religious Society of Friends, commonly called Quakers. 1681
Concise and faithful narrative of the various steps which led to the unhappy division. 2921
Concise Bible. 653, 654
Concise Bible commentary. 221
Concise Bible concordance. 227
Concise Bible dictionary. 243
Concise Catholic dictionary. 778
Concise code of Jewish law. 2074, 2119
Concise commentary on the whole Bible. 222
Concise dictionary of Christian ethics. 950
Concise dictionary of Eastern religion. 91
Concise dictionary of ecclesiastical terms. 2963
Concise dictionary of existentialism. 1584
Concise dictionary of Judaism. 2085
Concise dictionary of religion. 3638
Concise dictionary of religious knowledge and gazetteer. 3638
Concise dictionary of religious quotations. 3111
Concise dictionary of the Christian world mission. 2516
Concise encyclopedia of living faiths. 3122
Concise exegetical grammar of New Testament Greek. 1770
Concise Hebrew and Aramaic lexicon of the Old Testament, based upon the lexical work of Ludwig Koehler and Walter Baumgartner. 1796
Concise history of Catholicism. 810
Concise history of church music. 1208
Concise history of foreign Baptists. 152
Concise history of Freemasonry. 1665
Concise history of Israel. 2095
Concise history of Israel from the earliest times to the destruction of the Temple in A.D. 70. 2095
Concise history of Methodism, in England and America, of its origin, founders, development and institutions. Written for the publishers. 2424
Concise history of the Catholic Church. 808, 1173
Concise history of the Christian church, from its first establishment to the present time. 1100, 1175
Concise history of the introduction of Protestantism into Mississippi and the Southwest. 2559
Concise history of the Kehukee Baptist association. 2166, 2941
Concise history of the Kehukee Baptist Association, from its original rise down to 1803. 2941
Concise history of the United Society of Believers called Shakers. 3398
Concise Jewish Bible. 3704

Concise Oxford dictionary of the Christian Church. 3638
Concise system of theology. 3809
Concise treasury of Bible quotations. 612
Concise view of the doctrine and practice of the ecclesiastical courts in Doctors' commons. 2345
Concise view, of the principal religious denominations, in the United States of America. 3322
Conco-dant ve-s)on. 226
Concomitance and communion. 2256
... The Concord anthem book. 49
Concord lectures on philosophy. 1510, 3708
Concord of ages. 1719
Concordance of Bible events. 225
Concordance of Bible readings. 303
Concordance of Bible readings, compiled. 303
Concordance of Prudentius. 2984
Concordance of the Pearl of great price. 3428, 3430
Concordance of the Prayer Book Psalter. 577
Concordance of the proper names in the Holy Scriptures. 480, 1736
Concordance of the Septuagint. 529
Concordance of the Septuagint and the other Greek versions of the Old Testament. 498
Concordance supplement for the inspired version of the Holy Scriptures. 227
Concordance to Christian science hymnal and hymnal notes. 1210
Concordance to Pascal's Les provinciales. 2777
Concordance to Pascal's Pensees. 2778
Concordance to Q. 3010
Concordance to the Apocrypha/Deuterocanonical books of the Revised Standard Version. 489
Concordance to the Bible. 228
Concordance to the book of Doctrine and covenants of the Church of Jesus Christ of latter-day saints. 3430
Concordance to "The Christian year." 2166
Concordance to the distinctive Greek text of Codex Bezae. 316
Concordance to The doctrine and covenants. 3430
Concordance to the English poems of Thomas Gray. 1757
Concordance to the Hidden words of Baha' u'llah. 125
Concordance to the Historia ecclesiastica of Bede. 182, 2198
Concordance to the Holy Scriptures. 227
Concordance to the Holy Scriptures of the Old and New Testaments. 225, 226
Concordance to the Latin original of the four books known as De imitatione Christi. 1885
Concordance to The Lutheran hymnal. 2302
Concordance to the Methodist Hymnal. 2425, 2442, 2458
Concordance to the New English Bible, New Testament. 344
Concordance to the Old and New Testaments. 225
Concordance to the Peshitta version of Ben Sira. 489
La concordancia analitica greco-espanola del Nuevo Testamento greco-espanol. 345, 1769
Concordant commentary on the New Testament. 343
Concordant discord: the interdependence of faiths. 2644
Concordant literal New Testament. 357
Concordant literal Old Testament: the book of Daniel. 506
Concordant studies in the book of Daniel. 506
... Concordant version. 356
Concordant version, the Sacred Scriptures. 226
Concordat of 1801. 1322
Concordat of 1801: a study of the problem of nationalism in the relations of church and state. 818, 1145, 1322
Concordia Bible. 220
Concordia Bible dictionary. 243, 244
Concordia Bible story book. 620
Concordia Bible with notes: the New Covenant. 358
Concordia commentary: Acts. 330
Concordia commentary: 1 Timothy, 2 Timothy, Titus. 446
Concordia commentary: Jeremiah, Lamentations. 546
Concordia commentary: 1 and 2 Samuel. 590
Concordia commentary: Romans. 467
Concordia cyclopedia. 3092

Concordia hymnal. 2288
... The Concordia New Testament. 343
Concordia self-study commentary. 224
Concordia Seminary. 1322
Concrete Christian life. 3522
Concrete God. 1788, 2943, 2944
... Condemned societies. 1323
Condemned to the mines. 666, 2734
Condensed Bible. 268
Condensed formulary of prayers for the use of the Sisters of St. Joseph, diocese of Brooklyn. Containing community daily prayers. 859
Condensed history and manual of Maverick Congregational church. 3853
Condensed history of the Church of God from the days of John the Baptist under the present time. 2941
Condition of Jewish belief. 2080
Condition of society. 3395
Condition of the Christian philosopher. 1105
Condition or Jewish belief. 2080
Conditionalist faith of our fathers. 48
Conditions of conversion, and other sermons. 615
Conditions of philosophhy. 2834
Conditions of success in preaching without notes. 2908
Condor of the jungle. 1808, 2504
Conduct. 1325
Conduct of life. 2226, 2227, 2838
Conduct of the schools of Jean-Baptiste de La Salle. 1498
Conduct stories. 910
Confederate morale and church propaganda. 1326
Confederate poets, physician and priest. 3699
Confederate States of America in prophecy. 2947
... Conference for religious workers. 2492
Conference matter for religious. 3486
Conference of Baptist theological seminaries. 3681
Conference of bishops of the Anglican communion. 2194
Conference of the birds. 3542
Conference on American-Jewish dilemmas. 2155
Conference on the world-wide expansion of the Young men's Christian association held at the White House. Proceedings Ocotber 20, 1910. 3872
Conference with God. 2300
Conferences after Wesley, an attempt to keep the record straight. 2428
Conferences for boys. 688
Conferences for Franciscan religious. 1645
Conferences for married men. 3222
Conferences for married women. 2344
Conferences for men. 1826
Conferences for religious. 676
Conferences for religious communities. 2576, 3144
Conferences in Catholic action. 754
Conferences of Christian workers among Moslems, 1924. 2540
Conferences of St. Vincent de Paul to the Sisters of Charity. 3417
Conferences on the beatitudes. 181
Conferences on the Blessed Trinity. 3714
Conferences on the interior life for sisterhoods. 3144, 3489
Conferences on the religious life. 2570
Conferences on the religious life for sisterhoods. 3144
Conferences to children on practical virtue. 2592
Confess your sins. 1327
Confessing one faith. 110
Confessing the Gospel Mark preached. 1999
Confession. 1327, 2000, 2077, 2081, 2811, 2812
Confession and absolution. 1326, 1327
Confession and forgiveness. 584
Confession and pastoral psychology. 1327
Confession and psychoanalysis. 1327
Confession and the service of penance. 2811
Confession and What I believe. 2000
Confession as a means of spiritual progress. 1327
Confession; meaning and practice. 2812
Confession of a Roman Catholic. 865
Confession of an octogenarian. 1326
Confession of Christ. 3263
Confession of faith. 145, 748, 1333, 1336, 1590, 1654, 2936
Confession of faith for the average Christian. 1386
Confession of Faith of the Presbyterian Church in the United States. 2913

Confession of faith owned and consented to be the elders and messengers of the churches in the colony of Connecticut in New England. 1336
Confession of faith owned and consented to by the elders and messengers of the churches in the colony of Connecticut in New England. 1333
Confession of faith, owned and consented unto by the elders and messengers of the churches, assembled at Boston in New England, May 12, 1680. 1336
Confession of 1967, its theological background and ecumenical significance. 3735
Confession of our Christian faith. 99
Confession of Pontius Pilate. 2847
... The confession of S. Augustine. 112
Confession, the encounter with Christ in penance. 2812
Confessional history of the Lutheran church. 2284
Confessional principle and the confessions of the Lutheran church. 2284
Confessional statement and The book of government and worship. 3736
Confessional statement and The book of government and worship [of] the United Presbyterian church of North America. 2915
Confessions. 112, 113, 2638, 3635, 3796
Confessions and criticisms. 1326
Confessions and Enchiridion. 3667
Confessions; in thirteen books. 112
Confessions of a catechist. 940
Confessions of a Catholic Worker. 875, 1703
Confessions of a clergyman. 1251
Confessions of a conservative Evangelical. 1551, 3243
Confessions of a convert. 1363
Confessions of a converted infidel. 1326
Confessions of a happy Christian. 995, 3895
Confessions of a heretic. 1856
Confessions of a medium. 3498
Confessions of a moonlight writer. 3203
Confessions of a pentecostal. 696, 2817
Confessions of a psychic. 2993
Confessions of a puzzled parson, and other pleas for reality. 101, 1069
Confessions of a religionless Christian. 3062
Confessions of a totaled woman. 990, 3822
Confessions of an agnostic clergyman. 1597
Confessions of an inquiring spirit. 305
Confessions of an old priest. 1061
Confessions of Augustine. 112, 1024
· Confessions of Augustine in modern English. 1024
... Confessions of St. Augustine. 112, 113, 114, 1885
Confessions of St. Augustine, book VIII. 112
Confessions of St. Augustine (books one to ten) 111, 1024
Confessions of Saint Augustine; selections. 113
Confessions of sin and love in the Middle Ages. 1402, 3413
Confessions to a counselor. 2782
Confessor after the heart of Jesus. 1327
Confident children and how they grow. 1610
Confident Christian. 326
Confident faith. 3358
Configurations of Christian living. 1015
Confirmation. 1328, 1329
Confirmation and education. 1329
Confirmation in the church today. 1826
Confirmation in the Lutheran Church. 1329
Confirmation in the modern world. 1328
Confirmation instruction for eleven- to fourteen-year-olds; leader's guide for a confirmation course. Produced under the auspices of the Department of Christian Education, Protestant Episcopal Church. 1329
Confirmation interviews. 1328
Confirmation made interesting. 1328
Confirmation of history. 340
Confirmation practices. 1328
Confirmation reader. 1329
Confirmation sermons. 1329
Confirmation service sampler. 1329
Confirmation: the power of the Spirit. 1328
Confirming our faith. 1328, 3731
Confirming the faith. 1595
Confirming your call in church, home, and vocation. 1011, 2915
Conflict. 1151
Conflict and change in the church. 2706, 3538

Conflict and compromise. 2619
Conflict and conquest in holiness. 1823
Conflict and conscience. 1347
Conflict and consensus. 3772
Conflict and continuity at m abbey. 3259
Conflict and courage. 1433
Conflict and harmony in science and the Bible. 206
Conflict and resolution. 2788
Conflict and the victory of life. 2509
Conflict at Colossae. 342
Conflict between capital and labor. 2190
Conflict between church and state in Latin America. 1147
Conflict between Hellenism and Judaism. 1206
Conflict between paganism and Christianity in the fourth century. 1193
... The conflict between Pope Boniface viii and King Philip iv, the Fair. 677, 860
Conflict in a voluntary association. 1329, 1627
Conflict in community. 2574
Conflict in religious thought. 3100
Conflict ministry in the church. 1165
Conflict of ages. 2322
Conflict of centuries. 3411
Conflict of Christianity with heathenism. 1053
Conflict of Christianity with its counterfeits. 2563
Conflict of naturalism. 3027
Conflict of religions. 3112
Conflict of religions in the early Roman Empire. 1191, 1196
Conflict of the ages. 46, 2200
Conflict of the church and the synagogue. 1073
Conflict of the kingdoms. 3288
Conflict with Rome. 798
Conflict within. 2837
Conflict within my self. 166
Conflicting concepts of holiness. 1823
Conflicting images of man. 2326
Conflicting reports about God. 1417
Conflicts about the Holy Spirit. 1833
Conflicts in religious thought. 3100
Conflicts in the narrow way. 305
Conflicts of the clergy. 1298
Conflicts of the early church. 1194
Confraternity of Christian Doctrine in the United States. 1330
Confraternity school year religion course. 3183
Confratternity comes of age. 1330
Confrontation. 1013, 2067
Confrontation at Worms: Martin Luther and the Diet of Worms. 2274
Confrontations with the Devil! 1429
Confronted by Jesus. 1999
Confronting Christ. 434
Confronting death. 1413
Confronting popular cults. 3326
Confronting the Bible. 647, 941, 3187
Confronting the cults. 3325
Confronting young men with the living Christ. 3830
Confucian notebook. 1330, 1331
Confucian personalities. 1331
Confucian persuasion. 1331
Confucian vision. 1330
Confucianism. 1331, 2839
Confucianism and Christianity. 1330
Confucianism and its rivals. 1330, 1331
Confucianism and modern China. 1330, 1331
... Confucianism and Taoism. 913
Confucianism, Christianity & China. 912
Confucianism in action. 1330
Confucius. 1330, 1331
Confucius, ancient Chinese philosopher. 1331, 2832
Confucius and Chinese humanism. 1330, 1854
Confucius and Confucianism. 1331, 2839
Confucius and the Chinese classics. 914
Confucius and the Chinese way. 1331, 2839
Confucius, his life and time. 1330, 1331
Confucius: in life and legend. 1330
Confucius, the man and the myth. 1330
Confucius—the secular as sacred. 1330
Confucus. 1331
Confusion and hope. 1065
Confusion, call, commitment. 2268, 3885
Confusion of tongues. 1323, 3744
Confusion twice confounded. 1149
... Confusion untangled from Eden to glory. 1051
Confutation of a booke intituled An apologie of the Church of England. 2072
Confutation of two tracts. 3822
Congo as I saw it. 2513
Congo chattel. 3832, 3838
Congo chocolate drops. 2514
Congo crisis and Christian mission. 2513
Congo crosses. 3838

Congo drumbeat. 2432
Congo jungle preachers. 1290
Congo, past and present. 2183
Congo, the first Alliance mission field. 2513
Congratulations—God believes in you! 181, 1785
Congratulations, graduate! 3880
Congregation Albert, 1897-1972. 1331, 2098
Congregation and its older members. 1257
Congregation as church. 2480
Congregation at work. 1252
Congregation B'nai Torah, the first 50 years. 1332, 2100
Congregation in mission. 1279
Congregation named Saint John's. 2376
Congregation of Saint Joseph of Carondelet. 3419
Congregation of the Sisters of charity of the Incarnate word of San Antonio, Texas. 3417
Congregational administration. 1126
Congregational centennial, 1869-1969. 1425
Congregational Christian churches. 1332
Congregational church of Three Oaks. 3698
Congregational churches. 1338
Congregational churches of Vermont and their ministry. 1339
Congregational churches of Vermont and their ministry, 1762-1941. 1339
Congregational churches of Vermont and their ministry, 1762-1942. 1339
Congregational creeds and covenants. 1333
Congregational heritage. 2715
Congregational house churches. 1848
Congregational hymn book. 1335
Congregational manual. 1335
Congregational missionary work in Porto Rico. 2545
Congregational Nebraska. 1337
Congregational prayers for the children's mass. 854
Congregational readings from the Scriptures ..., hymns, inspirational writings. 3218, 3220
Congregational way. 1339, 1343
Congregational way of life. 1344
Congregational year-book. 1339
Congregationalism. 1344
Congregationalism: a restatement. 1344
Congregationalism and Methodism. 1344
Congregationalism as a social action pioneer. 1137
Congregationalism, betrayed or fulfilled? 1344
Congregationalism in the Dutch Netherlands. 1338
Congregationalism of the last three hundred years. 1344
Congregationalism of the last three hundred years, as seen in its literature; with special reference to certain recondite, neglected, or disputed passages. 1344
Congregationalism, slavery, and the Civil War. 1337
Congregationalism: what it is; whence it is; how it works; why it is better than any other form of church government; and its consequent demands. 1344
Congregationalists. 1339, 1343, 1344
Congregationalists and unity. 1044
Congregations alive. 3678
Congregations in change. 1244, 2946
... The congregations of priests from the sixteenth to the eighteenth century. 2576
Congress of arts and science, Universal exposition. 3093
Conjectures of a guilty bystander. 2413
Conjugal sins against the laws of life and health and their effects upon the father, mother and child. 3392
Conjugates Christ-Church in the Hexaemeron of Ps.-Anastasius of Sinai. 38
Conjugal love and its chaste delights. 2340
Conjunctions and disjunctions. 3388
Conjurer's coffin. 1345
Conklin's the world's best proverbs and epigrams. 1521
Connected view of the principles and rules by which the living oracles may be intelligibly an certainly interpreted. 1462
Connecticut churchmanship. 2963
Connection between religion and medicine. 2378
Connop Thirlwall, historian and theologian. 3692
Conquering. 1007
Conquering and to conquer. 458
Conquering Christ. 456, 1999

Conquering family stress. 1609
Conquering forces of the kingdom. 2438
Conquering forces of the kingdom and
    other sermons. 2056
Conquering frontiers. 2671
Conquering horseman. 1739
Conquering inner space. 994
Conquering Jew. 2112
Conquering loneliness. 2245
Conquering Oubangui-Chari for Christ.
    2558
Conquering personal problems. 2994
Conquering the fear of death. 324
Conquering the seven deadly sins. 3413
Conquering with Christ. 3890
Conqueror in chains. 2799
Conqueror of the world. 1739
Conquerors of the continent for Christ and
    His church. 1821, 2970
Conquest and crisis. 553, 2090
Conquest and triumph of divine wisdom
    and love in predestination. 2911
Conquest and victory. 554
Conquest of Canaan. 1584
Conquest of chaos. 604
Conquest of death. 1889, 2473
Conquest of fear. 1619
Conquest of grief. 2136
Conquest of illusion. 3686
Conquest of life. 758, 2434
Conquest of mind. 2723
Conquest of the continent. 2970
Conquest of the cross in China. 2511
Conquest of the kingdom of God. 2642
Conquest of the world by the Jews. 2089
Conquest of trouble. 1349
Conquest or failure? 2713
... Conquests for God. 3165
Conrad Celtis, the German arch-humanist.
    878
Conrad Grebel, son of Zurich. 1765
Conrad Grebel's programmatic letters of
    1524. 37
Conrad Noel and the Thaxted Movement.
    2712
Conscience. 1347
Conscience alone not a safe guide. 1347
Conscience and action. 1138
Conscience and commitment. 3807
Conscience and compromise. 744
Conscience and concessions. 1347
Conscience & confession. 1327
Conscience and its culture. 1347
Conscience and its right to freedom. 1347
Conscience and liberty. 2223
Conscience & obedience. 472, 1087
Conscience and responsibility. 1347
Conscience and success. 1347
Conscience—development and self-
    transcendence. 1347
Conscience, government, and war. 3851
Conscience in conflict. 2560, 3075
Conscience in crisis. 1686, 2407
Conscience in today's world. 1347
Conscience of a Christian. 986
Conscience of a king. 2596
Conscience of culture. 1394
Conscience of Israel. 569
Conscience of the nation. 2950
Conscience of the state in North America.
    1151
Conscience on trial. 1091
Conscience: theological and psychological
    perspectives. 1347
Conscientization and deschooling. 1883,
    3451
Conscientization for liberation. 821, 1138
Conscious clay. 3105
Conscious interlude. 3251
Conscious union with God. 2694
Consciousness. 1348
Consciousness and sacrifice. 2329
Consciousness and the brain. 2473
Consciousness & the ultimate. 2038, 3059
Consciousness creative. 3438
Consciousness of battle. 1348
Consciousness of God. 2380, 3492
Consciousness of Jesus. 2038, 2039
Consciousness of the atom. 2722, 2723
Consciousness unfolding. 2694
Consecranda. 840, 1165
Consecranda: the rite observed in some of
    the principal functions of the Roman
    pontifical and the Roman ritual. New ed.
    fully rev. and with some additions by J.
    B. O'Connell. 1165
Consecrate every day. 3842
Consecrated leadership. 977
Consecrated life. 3127, 3135
Consecrated talent. 1577
Consecrated talents. 2364, 3561
Consecrated unto me. 2345
Consecrated women. 924
Consecration. 1561
... The consecration and blessing of
    churches. 1165
Consecration and purity. 979

Consecration and service. 2570, 3771
Consecration of genius. 921
Consecration of the layman. 1328
Consecration of the most reverend
    Humberto Medeiros [bishop of
    Brownsville]. 697, 2377
Consecration services of Trinity church.
    1348
Consecutive missal of the mystical body.
    846
Consecutive questions on the Gospel of
    John. 414
Consecutive questions on the Gospel of
    Luke. 426
Consecutive questions on the Gospel of
    Mark. 431
Consecutive questions on the Gospel of
    Matthew. 439
Conseils pour la vie quotidienne. 1325
Consensus in theology? 2188, 3622
Consequences: truth and. 1056
Conservation and restoration of churches.
    1270
Conservation of freedom. 1086
... Conservation of national ideals. 2558
Conservation of the spiritual life as taught
    by St. John. 1324
Conservative Baptists. 1348
Conservative character of Martin Luther.
    2277
Conservative imperative. 789
Conservative introduction to the New
    Testament. 409
Conservative introduction to the Old
    Testament. 538
Conservative Judaism. 1348, 2114
Conservative Judaism and Jewish law.
    1348
Conservative looks to Barth and Brunner.
    176, 1457
Conservative millenarians. 814, 2464
Conservative reformation and its theology.
    2286, 3034
Conservative reformers. 1136
Conservative Sabbath and holiday prayer
    book. 2111
Consider. 2410
Consider Africa. 2497
Consider Christ Jesus. 3049
Consider Christian maturity. 999
Consider Him. 1439, 2015, 2033, 3407
Consider ... interpretations of selected
    scriptural texts. 2410
Consider Nippon (Incidents from my life.)
    1238
Consider Paul, apostle of Jesus Christ. 377
Consider the days. 1452
Consider the lilies. 251
Consider the years. 2098
Consider what God is doing. 1013
Considerate priest. 3676
Consideration of the Sermon on the
    Mount. 3335
Considerations for Christian teachers. 940
Considerations on eternity from the Latin
    of Jeremias Drexelius, S.J. 1533
Considerations on keeping Negroes. 3296
Considerations on the sacred priesthood.
    773
Considerations respecting the recognition
    of friends in another world. 1654, 1999
Consistency of the sinner's inability to
    comply with the gospel. 3412
Consistent Christianity. 962
Consitution of the American Bible society.
    30
...Consolation. 1349, 1350, 1351
Consolation from Homar. 1354
Consolation in bereavement. 1691, 2364
Consolation in discourses on select topics,
    addressed to the suffering people of God.
    1349
Consolation of philosophy. 1350, 2835
Consolations of Catholicism. 869
Consolations of the afflicted. 1351
Consolations of the cross. 2056
Consoler. 1830
Consolidated history of the fifteen
    churches of the Framingham Baptist
    association. 1271
Consoling thoughts of St. Francis de Sales.
    1354
Conspectus of cooperative missionary
    enterprises. 2519
... A conspectus of modern Catholic
    thought on the essence of the eucharistic
    sacrifice. 2259
Conspectus of the Revised lectionary.
    2205
Conspectus to the self-study project of
    University College, the University of
    Chicago. 894
Conspiracy against democracy. 1941
Conspiracy of God. 1829
Conspiracy that failed. 1148
Constancy amid change. 2607
Constant cross. 999

Constant fire. 1590
Constantine and religious liberty. 1355,
    3194
... Constantine and the beginnings of
    Christianity. 1097
Constantine and the conversion of Europe.
    1192, 1355
Constantine the Great. 1196, 1355
Constantine the Great and the Christian
    church. 1195, 1355
Constantinople, Canterbury & Rome, a
    criticism of Bishop Gore's theory of the
    Catholic church. 757, 1748
Constellational astrology according to the
    Hindu system. 98
Constitution & by-laws adopted 1958.
    1459
Constitution and canons for the
    government of the Protestant Episcopal
    Church in the Diocese of Pennsylvania.
    2971
Constitution and canons for the
    government of the Protestant Episcopal
    church in the United States of America.
    2966
Constitution and canons for the
    government of the Protestant Episcopal
    Church in the United States of America.
    2966
Constitution and canons of the diocese of
    Western New York. MDCCCLXXXIV.
    1489
Constitution and canons of the Diocese of
    Washington of the Protestant Episcopal
    Church. 2966
Constitution and canons of the Protestant
    Episcopal church in the United States.
    2966
Constitution and discipline of the
    Methodist Protestant church. 2459
Constitution and government of the
    Congregational Methodist Churches of
    the United States of America. 1343,
    2439
Constitution and religious education. 3190
Constitution and standards of the
    Associate-Reformed church in North-
    America. 3044
Constitution, by-laws and ritual of the
    Methodist brotherhood. 694
Constitution, by-laws and rituals. 694
Constitution for Congregationalism? 1344
Constitution for the United Methodist
    Church, with enabling legislation and
    other historic documents. 2441
Constitution of man, physically, morally,
    and spiritually considered. 3100
Constitution of the church. 763
Constitution of the church in the new
    Code of canon law. 807
Constitution of the Cumberland
    Presbyterian church. 2919
... The constitution of the human soul.
    3463
Constitution of the Methodist Episcopal
    church. 2447
Constitution of the Methodist Episcopal
    churches in America. 2456
Constitution of the Presbyterian church in
    the United States. 2921
Constitution of the Presbyterian church, in
    the United States of America. 2920,
    2921, 2922, 2923
Constitution of the Reformed church in
    America. 3045
Constitution of the Reformed Dutch
    church of North America. 3045
Constitution of the Spanish monarchy.
    3469
Constitution of the United Presbyterian
    Church in the United States of America.
    3735
Constitution of the United Societies, of
    Believers (called Shakers) 3397

Constitution on the church. 1124
Constitution on the sacred liturgy of the
    Second Vatican Council and the Motu
    proprio of Pope Paul VI. 840
Constitution or covenant of the United
    society of believers called Shakers. 1375
Constitutional amendment. 3260
Constitutional and governmental rights to
    the Mormon. 2601
Constitutional and parliamentary history of
    the Methodist Episcopal church. 2450
Constitutional church government in the
    dominions. 1219
Constitutional free speech. 2223
Constitutional history and constitution of
    the Church of England. 1219
Constitutional history of American
    Episcopal Methodism. 2451
Constitutional history of the Presbyterian
    church in the United States of America.
    2925

Constitutional powers of the General
    Conference. 2449, 3423
Constitutional prohibition. 3595
Constitutions and canons ecclesiastical.
    1489
Constitutions & canons ecclesiastical, 1604.
    1489
Constitutions and canons for the
    government of the Protestant Episcopal
    church in the United States of America.
    2958
Constitutions of canon 1125 and their
    application in the United States. 775
Constraining love. 2550
Construction of Gothic cathedrals. 78
Construction of junior church school
    curricula. 3145, 3169
Construction of life and death. 2823
Construction of Paradise lost. 2469
Construction of the Bible. 307
Constructive evangelism. 1553, 1563
Constructive modernism. 2561
Constructive natural theology. 2674
Constructive principles of the Bahai
    movement. 128
Constructive revolution of Jesus. 3234
Constructive revolutionary. 728
Constructive studies in the life of Christ.
    388, 1961
Consul. 682
Consul of God. 1773, 2861
Consular relations between the United
    States and the Papal states. 3741
Consultation on church union 1967. 2954
Consultation on Church Union, 1967.
    1039, 1355
Consultation on World Missions, October
    13-19, 1962, Montreat, N.C.
    Recommendations. 2926
Consumer's guide to Christian counseling.
    2781
Consuming fire. 1570
Contact with the other world. 2989
Contacts with non-Christian cultures.
    1394
Contagious congregation. 1566
Contardo Ferrini. 1622
Contemplating now. 1355
Contemplation and leisure. 1356
Contemplation in a world of action. 2571
Contemplation; liberating the ghost of the
    Church: churching the ghost of
    liberation. 1355
Contemplation of Christ. 1356
Contemplations. 1355, 1446
Contemplations on the night. 2710
Contemplative Christianity. 3478
Contemplative community. 1356
Contemplative life. 972, 2570, 2694
Contemplative life ; The giants ; and,
    Selections. 2839
Contemplative nuns speak. 1356
Contemplative prayer. 2380, 2873
... Contemporary American literature. 32
Contemporary American Protestant
    thought, 1900-1970. 3679
Contemporary American theologies. 3667
Contemporary American theologies II.
    3620
Contemporary American theology. 3611
Contemporary and his soul. 2843
Contemporary antiquities. 31
Contemporary approach to classical
    metaphysics. 2419
Contemporary approaches to Christian
    education. 940
Contemporary Catholic theology. 3628
Contemporary Catholic thought. 1067
Contemporary Catholicism in the United
    States. 826
Contemporary celebration. 3004
Contemporary Christ. 1062, 2059
Contemporary Christian. 1065
Contemporary Christian communications,
    its theory and practice. 1358
Contemporary Christian philosophy of
    religion. 1062
Contemporary Christian thought. 3618
Contemporary Christian trends. 1066
Contemporary Christologies. 2010
Contemporary church art. 1156
Contemporary concepts of time and the
    idea of God. 1726, 3701
Contemporary continental theologians.
    3618
Contemporary continental theology. 3658
Contemporary conversions. 1362
Contemporary critiques of religion. 3103
Contemporary culture and Christianity.
    1074
Contemporary evangelical thought. 3617
Contemporary evolution. 1580
Contemporary evolution of religious
    thought in England America and India.
    3141
Contemporary existentialism and Christian
    faith. 1584

CONTEMPORARY EXPLOSION OF RELIGIOUS BOOKS 1876 - 1982

Contemporary explosion of theology. 3647
Contemporary forms of faith. 1096
Contemporary godlessness. 1065
Contemporary gospel. 164
Contemporary halakhic problems. 2074
Contemporary High Holiday service for teenagers and. 3377
Contemporary icons. 84
Contemporary illustrations for speakers & teachers. 1839
Contemporary insights from Bible characters. 217
Contemporary introits for the revised Church calendar. 1917
Contemporary Islam and the challenge of history. 1922
Contemporary issues. 1139, 2746
Contemporary issues and Christian values. 1065
Contemporary Jewish ethics. 1539
Contemporary Jewish philosophies. 2141
Contemporary Jewish thought. 2145
Contemporary Judaic fellowship in theory and in practice. 1621
Contemporary look at the Formula of Concord. 2288
Contemporary meditation on doubting. 186
Contemporary meditation on the everyday God. 2386
Contemporary missiology. 2555
Contemporary moral theology. 947
Contemporary New Testament interpretation. 351
Contemporary Old Testament theologians. 600
Contemporary options in eschatology. 2465
Contemporary pastoral counseling. 2781
Contemporary pastoral prayers for the Christian year. 2783
Contemporary philosophy and Christian faith. 3103
Contemporary philosophy and religious thought. 3099
Contemporary prayer. 2889
Contemporary prayers for public worship. 2783
Contemporary preacher and his task. 2907
Contemporary preaching. 2897
Contemporary problems in moral theology. 949
Contemporary problems in religion. 3065, 3066
Contemporary Protestant thought. 3679
Contemporary reading of The spiritual exercises. 2268, 3475
Contemporary reflections on the medieval Christian tradition. 1102, 2826
Contemporary Reform Jewish thought. 3032
Contemporary Reform responsa. 3219
Contemporary relevance of Sri Aurobindo. 1709
Contemporary religion and social responsibility. 3088
Contemporary religious issues. 3212
Contemporary religious thinkers from idealist metaphysicians to existential theologians. 3637
Contemporary religious thinking. 3357
Contemporary religious thought. 3645
Contemporary sexual morality. 3392
Contemporary sister in the apostolate of home visitation. 3783
Contemporary social spirituality. 3488
Contemporary Spanish literature in English translation. 3470
Contemporary spirituality. 3486
Contemporary synagogue art. 3577
Contemporary Testament studies. 335
Contemporary theology and psychotherapy. 2784
Contemporary theology and theism. 3239, 3655
Contemporary theology of grace. 1751
Contemporary thinking about Jesus. 390, 393, 2046, 2059
Contemporary thinking about Paul. 2798
Contemporary transformations of religion. 1067
Contemporary trends in studies on the Constitutions of the Society of Jesus: annotated bibliographical orientations. 1946
Contemporary world theology. 3656
Contemporary worship services. 3856
Contending for the faith. 1462, 1593
Contending the grade in India. 1895
Contendings of the apostles. 75
Contendings of the apostles (Mashafa gadla hawaryat) 75
Contennial history of American Methodism. 2432, 2433
Content of the advanced religion course. 3057
Contentious community. 1165
Contents of Calvary's cup. 106
Contents of the New Testament. 410
... The contest for liberty of conscience in England. 1762
Contestation in the church. 810
Contested highway. 2508
Context for discovery. 3616
Context of contemporary theology. 2208, 3618
Context of decision. 944
Context of pastoral counseling. 2780
Context versus principles. 943
Contexts of Dryden's thought. 1481
Contextualization of theology. 3668
Continence. 113
Continental harmony. 917
Continental pietism and early American Christianity. 2846
Continental rationalists. 1425, 3022
Continental reformation in Germany, France and Switzerland from the birth of Luther to the death of Calvin. 3035
Continual burnt offering. 1431
Continuation committee conferences in Asia, 1912-1913. 2502
Continuation of Letters concerning the constitutions and order of the Christian ministry. 686, 1296
Continuation of the Calm and dispassionate vindication of the professors of the Church of England. 1821
Continuation of the Letters to the philosophers and politicians of France on the subject of religion, and of the Letters to a philosophical unbeliever in answer to Mr. Paine's Age of reason. 2758, 3023
Continuation of the Reverend Mr. Whitefield's journal. 3813
Continuation of the Reverend Mr. Whitefield's journal from Savannah, June 25, 1740 to his arrival at Rhode-Island, his travels in the other governments of New-England to his departure from Stanford for New-York. 3813
Continuing Christ in the modern world. 3451
Continuing Easter. 2052
Continuing education for ministry. 1298
Continuing evangelism in Brazil. 2953
Continuing in Christ. 1006
Continuing light. 3237
Continuing quest. 1297
Continuing quest for God. 2582
Continuing search for the historical Jesus. 2008
Continuing spirit. 1037
Continuing study of outcomes. 3614
Continuing the quest. 2607
Continuities in the sociology of religion. 3087
Continuity and change. 1220
Continuity and change in Roman religion. 3246
Continuity of Christian doctrine. 1473
Continuity of Christian thought. 3615, 3667
Continuity of early Christianity; a study of Ignatius in relation to Paul. 1155, 1882
Continuity of human and spiritual life. 3508
Continuity of life. 3495
Continuity of life a cosmic truth. 2227
Continuity of the Bible. 565, 2095, 2950
Continuity of the Church of England in the sixteenth century. 1221
Continuity of the prohpets. 127
Continuous creation. 1578
Continuum. 744, 1590
Contours of faith. 3617
Contra amatores mundi of Richard Rolle of Hampole. 2647
Contra Celsum. 878
Contra gentes. 69, 2046
Contraception. 663, 664
Contraception; a history of its treatment by the Catholic theologians and canonists. 664
Contraception and Catholics. 664
Contraception and holiness. 663
Contraception and the natural law. 664
Contraception; authority and dissent. 119, 783
Contraception; refelections on the Pope's ruling. 664
Contraception vs. tradition. 664
Contract at Mount Horeb. 3742
Contract with God. 2081
... Contracts between bishops and religious congregations. 1356
Contradiction of Christianity. 3622
Contradictions of orthodoxy. 3288
Contrary winds, and other sermons. 2935, 3346
Contrast. 1224
Contrast between Calvinism and Hopkinsianism. 729, 1847
Contrast between good & bad men. 216
Contrast: evangelicalism and spiritualism compared. 3505
Contrasts in social progress. 3433
Contrasts in spirit life. 3516
Contrasts in the character of Christ. 886
Contrasts: the arts & religion. 84, 89
Contribution of Belgium to the Catholic Church in America (1523-1857) 185, 823
Contribution of German Catholicism. 818
Contribution of religion to social work. 3435
Contribution of the Society of friends to education in Indiana. 1683
Contribution to Biblical lexicography. 505, 1797
Contribution to conjuring bibliography. 1345
Contribution to education by the Pentecostal Assemblies of Canada. 2814
Contribution to the history of the Presbyterian churches, Carlisle, Pa. 1812
Contributions of science to religion. 3313
Contributions of the Quakers. 1676
Contributions to a Milton bibliography, 1800-1930. 2469
Contributions to a Milton bibliography, 1800-1930, being a list of addenda to Stevens's Reference guide to Milton. 2469
Contributions to a systematic study of Jewish music. 2633
Contributions to Fox ethnology. 1637
Contributions to the bibliography of the "Lettres edifiantes" 1949
Contributions to the ecclesiastical history of Connecticut; prepared under the direction of the General association. 1346
Contributions to the ecclesiastical history of Essex County, Mass. 1532
Contributions to the science of mythology. 2653
Contributions to the scientific study of Jewish liturgy. 2109
Control of parenthood. 663
Controversial conversations with Catholics. 1245
Controversy. 377
Controversy between M. B. [pseud.] and Quaero [pseud.]. 780
Controversy between Senator Brooks and "John," archbishop of New York. 1242
Controversy in the twenties. 2562
Controversy on the translation of the Scriptures into modern Greek and its effects, 1818-1843. 285
Convenant of the First church in Dedham. 179
Convenant with God's poor. 1644
Convent. 2581
Convent and the world. 2581
Convent boarding school. 831
Convent choir book for female voices. 915
Convent cruelties. 1357
Convent hypocrisy. 805
Convent in the modern world. 2573
Convent life. 2573
Convent life of George Sand. (From "L'histoire de ma vie") Tr. by Maria Ellery MacKaye. 2228
Convent mirror. 2580
Convent readings and reflections. 2573
Convention adult Bible classes. 642
Convention essays. 2285, 3632
Convention militant. 2963
Convention normal manual for Sunday-school workers. 3552
... Conventionalization and assimilation in religious movements as problems in social psychology. 1081
Conventual buildings of Blackfriars, London, and the playhouses constructed therein. 2243
Convergence of traditions, Orthodox, Catholic, Protestant. 3654
Convergence of traditions; Orthodox, Catholic, Protestant. 1492
Convergent spirit towards a dialectics of religion. 2325
Conversation in faith. 1016, 3183
Conversation on faith. 1095
Conversation with children. 3183
Conversation with Christ. 2381
Conversation with God. 2891, 3490
Conversation with the Bible. 308
Conversational Bible studies. 646
Conversational word of God. 2267, 3492
Conversations. 1679
Conversations about the Babe of Bethlehem. 2022
Conversations at Little Gidding. 1013
Conversations at Malines, 1921-1925. 1039
Conversations: Christian and Buddhist. 1081
Conversations for the young. 237
Conversations in Umbria according to St. Francis. 1022, 1640
... The conversations of Jesus. 2072
Conversations of Jesus Christ with representative men. 337, 2061
Conversations on Christian re-union. 1041
Conversations on Christian responsibility. 1024
Conversations on growing older. 18
Conversations on love and sex in marriage. 3392
Conversations on religious subjects between a father and his two sons. 1682
Conversations on the attributes of God. 1730
Conversations on the Bible. 236
Conversations on the edge of eternity. 1005
Conversations on the memoirs of pious children. 889, 895
Conversations on the present age of the world, in connection with prophecy. 463
Conversations with an unrepentant liberal. 2220
Conversations with Archbishop Marcel Lefebvre. 787
Conversations with children on the Gospels. 384
Conversations with Christ. 2061, 2704
Conversations with giants. 217
Conversations with God. 1446
Conversations with Luther. 3579
Conversations with Ogotemmeli. 1473
Conversations with prophets. 1506
Conversations with Seth. 3474
Conversations with the crucified. 1998
Conversative introduction to the Old Testament. 539
Converse with God, an aid to meditation. 2381
Conversion. 1359, 1360, 1361
Conversion: a series of sermons. 1359
Conversion and Christian character. 994
Conversion and religious experience. 1359
Conversion: Christian and non-Christian. 1360
Conversion experience in Axum during the fourth and fifth centuries. 20
Conversion of a high priest into a Christian worker. 1358
Conversion of a Klansman. 1367, 3589
Conversion of a psychic. 1362, 3431
Conversion of a skeptic. 131
Conversion of Augustine. 114
Conversion of children. 903
Conversion of children; can it be effected? 903
Conversion of Constantine. 1197, 1355
Conversion of Constantine and pagan Rome. 1189, 1355
Conversion of Europe. 2526
... The conversion of Hamilton Wheeler. 1359
Conversion of India. 2532
Conversion of Marie-Alphonse Ratisbonne. 3025
Conversion of Mr. Banks. 1358
... The conversion of Mormonism. 1360
Conversion of St. Paul. 331, 2799, 2803
Conversion of the church. 1123
Conversion of the Maoris. 2542
Conversion of the northern nations. 2517
Conversion of the pagan world. 850
Conversion of the Roman empire. 1359
Conversion of the Slovenes. 2546
Conversion of the world. 1358
Conversion of Western Europe, 350-750. 1187
Conversion, perspectives on personal and social transformation. 1360
Conversion through personal Christian effort. 1358
Conversion to Islam. 1924
Conversion to Judaism. 2952
Conversions to the Catholic church. 1364
Convert. 784, 1362, 1363
Convert and his relations. 1362
Convert-making. 1360
Convert-pastor explains. 784
Converted church. 1570
Converted Jew. 2085
Converts. 1366
Convert's basic guide. 796
Convert's helper and expositor. 2447
Convert's homeward guide. 1362
Convert's manual. 797
Convert's vade mecum. 797
Convictions. 1305, 3619
Convictions to live by. 955
Convincing the world. 3343
Convocation, and Edward Dodd's share in its revival. 1219, 1472
Convocation of the clergy. 1220
Conyent in the modern world. 2573
Cooks Creek Presbyterians. 1368
Cool arm of destruction. 103

Cool it or lose it! 3889
Cool of the day. 1072
Coon Prairie. 2715
Co-operating Southern Baptists. 3465
Co-operation and human values. 1534
Cooperation and the world mission. 2521
... Cooperation in crime. 6
Cooperation without compromise. 1368
Cooperative church extension planning. 1270
Cooperative churches. 1620
Cooperative parish in nonmetropolitan areas. 2197
Cooperative religion at Cornell university. 1369
Coping. 775, 995, 2575
Coping with anxiety. 55, 885
Coping with being single again. 3415
Coping with clergy burnout. 1293
Coping with counseling crises. 2779
Coping with criticism. 980
Coping with life and its problems. 988
Coping with physical disability. 1783
Coping with stress in the minister's home. 1303
Coptic apocrypha in the dialect of Upper Egypt. 56
Coptic apocryphal Gospels. 337
Coptic art. 85
Coptic art and archaeology. 85
Coptic Biblical texts in the dialect of Upper Egypt. 656, 1369
Coptic bibliography. 1369
Coptic gnostic treatise contained in the Codex Brucianus. 1717
Coptic homilies in the dialect of Upper Egypt. 3362
Coptic manuscripts in the Freer collection. 315, 1700, 2330
Coptic martyrdoms, etc., in the dialect of Upper Egypt. 1018
Coptic morning service for the Lord's day. 1368
Coptic office. 1369
Coptic palimpsest. 531
Coptic Psalter in the Freer collection. 1369
Coptic texts. 1369
Coptic version of the Acts of the apostles. 315
Coptic version of the New Testament in the northern dialect. 315
Coptic version of the New Testament in the southern dialect otherwise called Sahidic and Thebaic. 229
"Copy." 2960, 3095
Coral and Christian. 2847
Coral in the sand. 2543
Cordial and dispassionate discussion on predestination. 2911
Cords of Adam. 1446
Cords with heaven. 2856
Core of the Bible. 251
Corespensibility in the church. 808, 1245
Coretta. 2172
Corinthian catastrophe. 2816
Corinthian church. 323, 346
Corinthian church, a Biblical approach to urban culture. 346
Corinthian correspondence. 346
Corinthian letters of Paul. 345
Corinthian mirrow. 323
... Corinthians. 345
Corinthians, i and ii. 345
Corinthians 1 and 2. 346
Cork Hill Cathedra. 1404
Cork Hill Cathedral. 1404
Cornbread and milk. 2399
Corned beef, knishes and Christ. 2219
Cornelia Connelly. 1346, 3438
Cornelius Shyne, S.J. 3405
Cornelius the centurion. 1369
Corner in India. 2503
Corner-stone. 954
Corner stone of Christianity. 2008, 3432
Corner-stones of faith. 3326, 3665
Cornerstone; a history of Beaumont and Methodism, 1840-1968. 182
Cornerstones of astrology. 98, 2598
Cornerstones of religious freedom in America. 3194
Cornish crosses, Christian and pagan. 1388
... The coronation of the Queen. 1224, 3778
Corporate worship in the reformed tradition. 3049, 3855
Corporation sole. 668, 2630
Corporations and morality. 1905
Corpus Christi. 1120, 1249, 3298
Corpus Christi, quod est ecclesia. 1124
Corpus dictionary of Western churches. 3638
Corpus of religious material from the civilian areas of Roman Britain. 1764
Corpus papyrorum Judaicarum. 2099

Corpus scriptorum ecclesiasticorum latinorum. 1617
Corpus unum. 1044
Correct, full and impartial report of the trial of Rev. Ephraim K. Avery before the Supreme judicial court of the state of Rhode-Island, at Newport, May 6, 1833, for the murder of Sarah M. Cornell. 1369
Correct view of that part of the United States which lies west of the Allegany mountains. 2560
Corrected English New Testament. 353
... The correlation of church schools and public schools. 3146
Correlatives. 1494
Correspondence and records of the S.P.G. relating to Wales, 1701-1750. 1181
Correspondence between the First church and the Tabernacle church in Salem. 1334
Correspondence course in Luther's Small catechism. 2279, 2284
Correspondence for children of the New church. 1370
Correspondence of Descartes and Constantyn Huygens. 1425
Correspondence of Erasmus. 1527
Correspondence of Fraulein Gunderode and Bettine von Arnim. 1624
Correspondence of Gerrit Smith with Albert Barnes. 1868. 1092
Correspondence of interest to the members of the Choral society of the New York city Christian science institute. 3527
Correspondence of James Logan and Thomas Story. 3534
Correspondence of John Henry Newman with John Keble and others, 1839-1845. 2166

Correspondence of John Owen (1616-1683): with an account of his life and work. 656
Correspondence of Matthew Parker. 2775, 2776
Correspondence of Pope Gregory VII. 2860
Correspondence of Pope Gregory vii. 2860
Correspondence of Rev. Louis Baroux, missionary apostolic of Michigan, to Rev. M. J. De Neve, superior of the American College at Louvain. 849, 2865
Correspondence of William Ellery Channing, D. D. 881
Correspondence on church and religion of William Ewart Gladstone. 1715
Correspondence on infallability [!] between a father Jesuit and General Alexander Kireeff. (An eastern Orthodox) 2862
Correspondence school. 2086
Correspondences of the Bible. 1370
Corrie ten Boom, the authorized biography. 923, 3600
Corrie, the lives she's touched. 928, 3600
Corrupt the young. 3880
Corruptions of the New Testament. 378
Corruptors. 982
Corrymeela. 1370
Corydon Presbyterian Church through 150 years (oldest continuous church in Corydon) 1819-1969, the church of the Governor. 1370
Cosmic book on the mechanics of creation. 1385
Cosmic center. 1074, 2040
Cosmic chants. 3330, 3331
Cosmic Chirst and the new ethical order, by Alpha jefferson. 3142
Cosmic Christ. 2009, 3029
Cosmic consciousness. 3474, 3686
Cosmic continuum. 3509
Cosmic drama. 454
Cosmic geometry. 3575
Cosmic God. 2834
Cosmic influence. 95
Cosmic influences on human behavior. 95
Cosmic language. 3542
Cosmic law. 3462
Cosmic love and human wrong. 3412
Cosmic memory. 50, 102, 1485
Cosmic mountain in Canaan and the Old Testament. 2626
Cosmic mysteries of the universe. 1371
Cosmic plan. 1380
Cosmic reformation. 1049
Cosmic relations and immortality. 2989
Cosmic religion. 3061
Cosmic revelations. 2730
Cosmic Shakti Kundalini (the universal mother) 3400
Cosmic theology. 1460
[Cosmic theory of primes. 1898
Cosmic trigger. 2731, 3819
Cosmic unfoldment. 2019

Cosmic view of religion. 3059
Cosmic womb. 1740
Cosmogonies of our fathers. 1370
Cosmogony. 3076
Cosmogony and evolution. 1370
Cosmogony, or, The mysteries of creation. 1380
Cosmological argument. 1738, 1739
Cosmological argument from Plato to Leibniz. 1738
Cosmological arguments. 1737
Cosmology. 1371
Cosmology and Christianity. 1371
Cosmology and social behavior in a West Javanese settlement. 1937
Cosmonics of worlds and forces. 1578
Cosmos and man. 3073
Cosmotheologies. 1382
Cost in Pentecost. 1001
Cost of a new world. 1051
Cost of Christian conquest. 956
Cost of commitment. 989
Cost of discileship. 3334
Cost of discipleship. 3335
Costly harvest. 2512
Costs and benefits of Catholic elementary and secondary schools. 830
Costume of prelates of the Catholic church. 1249
Cotswold churches. 1158
Cottage Bible, and family expositor. 220
Cotton Mather. 2372, 3009
Cotton Mather, the Puritan priest. 2372
Cotton patch evidence. 2131
Cotton patch parables of liberation. 2025
Cotton patch version of Hebrews and the general Epistles. 405
Cotton patch version of Luke and Acts. 426
Cotton patch version of Matthew and John. 444
Cotton patch version of Paul's Epistles. 374
Couch and the altar. 2999
Could it be you? 140, 3340
Could you explain Catholic practices? 770
Council. 3773
Council and reunion. 859
Council and the future. 3771
Council and the Mass. 2368
Council day book. 3770
Council daybook. 3770
Council fathers and atheism. 762
Council in action. 3770, 3771
Council of Chalcedon and the Armenian Church. 82
Council of Constance. 1354
Council of Constance to the death of John Hus. 1354, 1857
Council of Nicaea. 2706
Council of the gods. 2662
Council of Trent. 3710
Council of Trent and Anglican formularies. 1386
Council of Trent, the Spiritual exercises, and the Catholic reform. 3710
Council on the campus. 870, 3772
Council over Pope? 807, 1322
Council, reform, and reunion. 859, 1041, 3771
Council speeches of Vatican II. 762
Councils. 1372
Councils and assemblies. 1373
Councils and ecclesiastical documents relating to Great Britain and Ireland. 1762
Councils & synods. 1373
Councils of the church. 1373
Counsel and comfort spoken from a city pulpit. 1374, 2930
Counseling. 2781
Counseling and health care. 2782
Counseling and theology. 2780, 2995
Counseling Christian parents. 1604
Counseling for church leaders. 2780
Counseling for church vocations. 1296
Counseling for liberation. 2780
Counseling for ministers. 2781
Counseling in Catholic life and education. 1373
Counseling skills for church leadership. 2780
Counseling the dying. 1258
Counseling the serviceman and his family. 1255
Counseling the unwed mother. 3759
Counseling with college students. 1256
Counseling with confidence. 1713
Counseling with senior citizens. 1257
Counseling with single adults. 1256
Counseling with teen-agers. 1259
Counseling with the mind of Christ. 2781
Counseling with youth. 1260
Counseling with youth at church, school, and camp. 1260
Counselling the Catholic. 2780

Counselor and religious questioning and conflicts. 3884
Counselor in counseling. 2995
Counselor, state your case! 64
Counsels of light and love. 2639
Counsels of light and love of Saint John of the Cross. 90
Counsels on diet and foods. 1459
Counsels on education, as presented in the nine volumes of Testimonies for the church. 3385
Counsels on health, and instruction to medical missionary workers. 2488
Counsels on Sabbath school work. 3385
Counsels on stewardship. 3530
Counsels to editors. 2135
Counsels to religious superiors. 3513
Counsels to Sunday school teachers. 3552
Counsels to teachers, parents and students regarding Christian education. 3160
Counsels to writers and editors. 2135
Count it all joy. 324
Count of Saint Germain. 3274
... Count Robert of Paris. 1391
Count your numbers. 3575
Count your numbers and make your numbers count. 3575
Count Zinzendorf. 3896
Countdown. 2873
Countdown, a newsman looks at the rapture. 3021
Countdown of history. 3318

Counter culture and the vision of God. 1060
Counter Reformation. 1374
Counter reformation 1559-1610. 1374
Counter Reformation, 1559-1610. 1374
Counter-revolution for peace. 2357
Counterattack, scapegoats or solotions. 3703
Counterfeit Christ. 3343
Counterfeit miracles. 2477
Counterfeit or genuine? 438
Counter-Reformation, 1550-1600. 1374
Counting stars. 900
Counting the cost. 2308
Country beyond. 3514
Country church. 1374, 3253
Country church and community cooperation. 3254
... The country church and its program. 3254
Country church and our generation. 3255
Country church and public affairs. 3255
Country church and rural welfare. 3254
Country church and the rural problem. 3254
Country church as it is. 3253
Country church in colonial counties. 1275
... The country church in colonial counties as illustrated by Addison county, Vt., Tompkins county, N. Y., and Warren county, N. Y. 1275
Country church in industrial zones. 1273, 1311
Country church in North Carolina. 1271
Country church in the new world order. 1374
Country counting house. 1291, 2806
Country faith. 3357
Country life leadership. 1374
Country parson. 1375
Country parson looks at religion. 1052
Country parson ; The temple. 1023
Country preacher. 3674
Country priest in English history. 3255
Country road home. 3778
Country sermons. 3390, 3353
Country sermons on free texts. 3342
Country town Sunday school. 3553
Countrywoman and her church. 3832
County-by-county. 2294
County-by-county church distribution study, related to Lutheran churches. 2302
Couples in the Bible. 216, 2341
Couples of the Bible. 216
Courage. 400, 1375
Courage and confidence from the Bible. 1440
Courage and submission. 589
Courage, church! 1125
Courage covenant. 2620
Courage for crisis living. 1003
Courage for dialogue. 1080
Courage for the crisis. 2808
Courage for today, hope for tomorrow. 455
Courage in both hands. 1013
Courage in Christ. 2300
Courage of Christ. 1995
Courage of the coward. 159
Courage that propels. 1375
Courage to be brothers. 695
Courage to care. 1007, 1138

Courage to change. 2708
Courage to choose. 1775, 2572
Courage to conquer. 102
Courage to live. 965, 1006
Courage to love. 2265, 3049, 3350
Courage to pray. 2868, 2882
Courageous adventures. 630
Courageous Catherine. 2305, 3418
Courageous children. 896
Courageous prophet. 2178
Courageous prophet, chapters from the life of John Kline. 2178
Courageous shall conquer. 1375
Course for beginners in religious education, with lessons for one year for children five years of age. 3156
Course in apologetics. 68
Course in precious Epistles in 365 devotional studies. 368
Course in psychic unfoldment. 2988
Course in religion. 3184
Course in religion for Catholic high schools and academies. 788, 803, 3152, 3187
Course in religion for the elementary schools. 3184
Course in religious instruction for grammar grades and high school. 3192
Course in social and civic relations. 2592
... Course of Christian doctrine. 933, 934
Course of Christian missions. 2525
Course of creation. 1705
Course of critical lectures, or, Systematical theology, in four parts, viz: Theology, Demonology, Christology, and Anthropology. 3649
Course of lectures in defence of the final restoration. 3220
Course of lectures on the Jews. 2155
Course of lectures on the Scripture types. 3720
Course of lectures on the subject of hell. 1802
Course of man, as brought to light by the gospel. 2323
Course of modern Jewish history. 2091
Course of my life. 3527
Course of religious instruction for Catholic youth. 786
Course of sermons on early piety. 2846
Course of studies on Bogra, Ulubaria, and Europe. 2530
Course of study. 807
Course of study for Christian schools. 1246
Course of study in religion. 3148
Course of study in religion for grade three. 3162
Course of study in religion for teachers of Catholic children who attend public schools. Grades I [-VIII] Developed as a manual for the use of priests, religious and lay teachers in religious vacation school classes. 3762
Course of study in religion for the Catholic schools and academies of the diocese of Baker City, grades I.-VIII. and high school. 3162
Course of study on Jewish prayer. 2076
Course outlines in dogmatic theology for college students. 3162
... Courses in the history of the Christian church. 1188
Court and camp of David. 1405
Court history of Israel. 483
Court of conscience. 1347
Court of final appeal. 1489
Court of the Queen. 764
Courts of appeal in causes ecclesiastical. 1490, 3241
Courtship and marriage. 2337, 2339
Covenant. 1356, 1376, 1377, 2104
Covenant and community. 240, 2332
Covenant and creation. 652
Covenant and hope. 2951
Covenant and promise. 571, 2093, 2949
Covenant and sacrifice. 2257
Covenant and the kingdom. 520, 1376
Covenant, articles of faith, and rules of High street Congregational church, Portland, Me., with a catalogue of its members. January, 1858. 2864
Covenant by sacrifice. 1575
Covenant, Christ, and contraception. 664
Covenant community. 517
Covenant frontiers. 1549
Covenant group for lifestyle assessment. 3409
Covenant idea in New England theology, 1620-1847. 2688
Covenant in Canada. 2917
Covenant in the Old Testament. 1377
Covenant-interest, of the children of believers, illustrated and proved. 895
Covenant-keeping God. 1728
Covenant missions in Japan. 2534
Covenant of peace. 2236, 2756

Covenant of salt as based on the significance and symbolism of salt in primitive thought. 3574
Covenant people. 2096, 3166
Covenant people of God. 1377
Covenant prayers. 2889
Covenant renewal in religious life. 2570
Covenant sealed. 3266
Covenant story of the Bible. 615
"A covenant with death," An "Agreement with hell," "The refuge of lies." 1802
Covenant with stones. 3419
Covenanters in America. 3578
Covenants. 1376, 1377
Covenants of the Pentateuch. 298
Coverdale Psalter and the quatro-centenary of the printed English Bible. 272
Covering Islam. 1925
Coward's guide to witnessing. 3828
Cowards or conquerors. 163
Cowboy and the Bible. 1721
Cowboy missionary in Kwangsi. 2511
Cowley & Whitney on doctrine. 2611
Cowley Fathers in America. 3438
Cowman handbook of the Bible. 285
Crack in the Bible. 233, 1091
Cracks in the steeple. 871
Cradle days of St. Mary's at Natchez. 2669
Cradle of God. 1726
Cradle of Mississippi Methodism. 2457
... The cradle of the Bible. 2762
Cradle roll department of the Sunday school. 3175, 3555
Cradle roll department visitor. 3173
Cradle roll lessons. 3185, 3564
Cradle roll of the church school. 1246
Craft and its symbols. 1671
Craft of dying. 1455
Craft of prayer. 2247
Craft of sermon construction. 2905
Craft of sermon illustration. 1842
Crafts in the Bible. 1784
Craftsman's Bible. 1660
Craftsmen all. 2521
Craftsmen of the soul, and other addresses. 3460
Craighills of China. 1378
Cranmer & the Reformation under Edward VI. 1378, 3039
Cranmer and the English Reformation. 1378, 3039
Cranmer & the reformation under Edward VI. 1378
Cranmer, Archbishop of Canterbury 1533-1556. 1378
Cranmer's first litany. 1210
Cranmer's godly order. 843, 2236
Crash landing. 1014
Crative evolution. 2416
Crawford-Musgrave debate. 134
Crawling out. 1498
Crayon and character. 880
Crayon talks. 880
Crazes, credulities and Christian science. 1035
Crazy for God. 1498
Crazy pigs and other Bible stories. 624
Creacion of the world. 2636
Create and celebrate! 3004
Create and make new. 2209
Created to praise. 2867
Creating a successful Christian marriage. 2338
Creating an intentional ministry. 2787
Creating children's sermons. 2911
Creating Christian personality. 3167
Creating fresh images for preaching. 2906
Creating programs for the gifted. 1712
Creating; reflections during pregnancy. 2625
Creating the caring congregation. 1258
Creation. 204, 602, 1379, 1380, 1381, 1382, 1383, 1384, 1941, 3078, 3500
Creation; accident or design? 204
Creation and catastrophe. 1379
Creation and covenant. 565, 2089
Creation & deluge, according to a new theory. 206
Creation and development of the universe. 1381
Creation and evolution. 202, 1382, 3078
Creation and fall. 525, 1380
Creation and Gospel. 1384, 3820
Creation and law. 2325
Creation and man. 1381
Creation and me. 3763
Creation and method. 1383, 2046
Creation & new creation; the past, present, and future of God's creative activity. 1382
Creation and providence. 1384
Creation and redemption. 1380, 3647
Creation and salvation in ancient orphism. 1459
Creation and science. 1380

Creation and the early developments of society. 3074
Creation and the flood. 203
Creation and the world of science. 1382
Creation book for children. 1384
Creation by the word. 545, 1383
... Creation by thinking. 1382
Creation, Christ, and culture. 3620, 3704
Creation condition, and destiny of man. 2323
Creation continues. 440
Creation controversy. 205
Creation, evolution, and God's word. 202
Creation ex nihilo. 1380
Creation explanation. 1381
Creation; Genesis 1:1—Exodus 19:20. 527
Creation in Christ. 3365
Creation legends of the ancient Near East. 1384
Creation myths. 1384
Creation; nature's designs and designer. 1380
Creation-not evolution. 1379
Creation of a cathedral. 3716
Creation of a future. 1244
Creation of a God. 3074
Creation of death and life. 204
Creation of sacred literature. 503
Creation of the Bible. 304
Creation of the human soul. 3463
Creation of the universe. 1380
Creation of the world according to Gersonides. 1384, 2219
Creation of woman. 1577, 1578, 2993
Creation or evolution? 1382, 3079
Creation; or, The power behind evolution. 1381
Creation revealed. 204
Creation, science, and theology. 177, 3626
Creation story. 1380
Creation story and modern man. 3079
Creation-story of Genesis i. 524
Creation, the facts of life. 1382
Creation: the impact of an idea. 1383
Creation, time and eternity. 3080
Creation versus chaos. 598
Creation vs. evolution handbook. 202
Creation waits. 991
... Creations in ecclesiastical art. 28
Creative activities. 1385, 2720
Creative advance. 1105, 3813
Creative Bible study. 641
Creative Bible study methods. 635
Creative Bible teaching. 641
Creative brooding. 1451
Creative camping. 1164
Creative centre of Quakerism. 1681
Creative Christ. 1892, 1950
Creative Christian communication. 1317
Creative Christian living. 3484
Creative Christianity. 1061, 1094
Creative church administration. 1200
Creative churchmanship. 1243
Creative conflict in religious education and church administration. 1165
Creative congregationalism. 2719
Creative congregations; tested strategies for today's churches. 1244
Creative controversies in Christianity. 3213
Creative counseling for Christian camps. 1373
Creative counterpart. 3831
Creative delivery of sermons. 2902
Creative designs with children at worship. 905
Creative dislocation. 696, 3611
Creative edge of American Protestantism. 2955
Creative encounter. 1586
Creative energy. 1879
Creative era between the Testaments. 2150
Creative evolution. 2416
Creative faith. 1592, 3726
Creative family worship. 1609
Creative formation of life and world. 3490
Creative freedom in action; Alexander Campbell on the structure of the church. 732
Creative freedom, vocation of liberal religion. 1659, 3815
Creative gift. 1089
Creative giving. 952
Creative hymn-singing. 1860
Creative image. 944
Creative imagination in preaching. 2900
Creative Judaism. 2084, 2138
Creative leadership; programme ideas and leadership techniques for boys' club leaders, girls' club leaders, teachers, and all interested in giving a leadership which will be creative in the development of Australian youth. 1260
Creative learning. 2204
Creative living. 3857

Creative loneliness. 2244
Creative love. 1170
Creative meditation. 3483
Creative meditation and multi-dimensional consciousness. 2382, 2383
Creative men. 2443
Creative methods for adult classes. 3168
Creative mind. 193, 2834
Creative minds in contemporary theology. 3617
Creative ministries. 1251
Creative ministry. 2786
Creative minority. 1060
Creative personality and evolution. 1580
Creative personality in religious life. 2571
Creative power of silence. 3408
Creative prayer. 2873
Creative preaching. 2896, 2897
Creative procedures for adult groups. 3168
Creative psychics, the art of regeneration. 2988
Creative religion, as seen by a social scientist. 3066
Creative religion involvement programs. 3175
Creative religious literature. 299
Creative revolution. 3450
Creative revolution of Jesus. 2065
Creative role of interpersonal groups in the church today. 1170
Creative science. 3142
Creative self-transformation through meditation. 2380
Creative society. 3444
Creative stewardship. 3528
Creative suffering. 3541
Creative sunday schools. 3553
Creative task. 2902
Creative teaching. 3159
Creative teaching in Christian education. 805, 935
Creative teaching in the church. 3154
Creative teaching in the church school. 3180
Creative theology of P. T. Forsyth. 3633
Creative unity. 2840
Creative ways to worship. 3856
Creative word. 495, 934
Creative worship. 1674, 3852
Creativity and God. 2944
Creativity and method. 758, 3620
Creativity and Taoism. 3586
Creativity in Henry Nelson Wieman. 3815
Creator and cosmos. 1382
Creator and cosmos illustrated. 1382
Creator and creation. 3100
Creator and His workshop. 3382
Creator and man. 499, 1730
Creator and the Adversary. 1723
Creator and the created. 3103
Creator and the creature. 1587, 1721, 1741
Creator, creation, and faith. 1383
Creator Spirit. 1831
Creatures of Arcadia, and creatures of a day. 2660
Credenda: being a treatise of thirteen Bible doctrines. 30
Credentials of Christianity. 66
Credentials of Jesus. 1099, 1955
Credentials of science the warrant of faith. 3075
Credentials of the church. 1118
Credibility of the book of the Acts of the apostles. 330
Credibility of the church today. 784
Credibility of the virgin birth. 3780
Credo. 72, 73, 871
Credo; a practical guide to the Catholic faith. 795
Credo; a short exposition of Catholic belief. 796
Credo hoc. 1324
Credo of Maimonides. 2623
Credo of the People of God. 2806
Credo, the Christian view of faith and life. 1386
Creed. 1385
Creed and catechetics ; a catechetical commentary on the creed of the people of God. 769
Creed and curriculum. 3155
Creed and deed: a series of discourses. 3065
Creed and its credentials. 72
Creed and modern thought. 73
Creed and personal identity. 73
Creed and the creeds. 1385
Creed and the prayer. 75
Creed before the creeds. 1386
Creed explained according to the psychological method. 745, 1419
Creed explained according to the psychological or Munich method. 1385
Creed for a Christian skeptic. 74
Creed for a young Catholic. 74, 767
Creed for college men. 1385

Creed for free men. 1422
Creed for the twentieth century. 2706
Creed in Christian teaching. 75
Creed in slow motion. 73
Creed of a biologist. 2228
Creed of a Catholic. 73
Creed of a churchman. 1211
Creed of a layman. 1385
Creed of a modern agnostic. 19
Creed of a priest of Savoy. 1385
Creed of a slave. 2935
Creed of Buddha. 702, 706, 1703
Creed of Buddha, by the author of "The creed of Christ" 702
Creed of Christ. 1385, 2063, 2247
Creed of Christendom. 1654
Creed of Christendom as expressed in the Nicene creed. 2706
Creed of half Japan. 706
Creed of Jesus. 2249
Creed of kinship. 3142
Creed of our hope. 72
Creed of Presbyterians. 2914
Creed of the dauntless. 1386
Creed or chaos? 3652
Creed or charter, which? 231
Creed, ritual and discipline of the Evangelical congregational church. 1385
Creed that changed the world. 73
Creeds. 1385, 1386
Creeds and confessions. 1386
Creeds and loyalty. 1385
Creeds and platforms of Congregationalism. 1333
Creeds and religious beliefs as they appear to a plain business man. 3116
Creeds, councils, and controversies. 1197
Creeds in collision. 63
Creeds in collision. 63
Creeds in competition. 3326, 3745
Creeds in the Bible. 1386
Creeds in the making. 3658
Creeds of Christeddom. 1386
Creeds of the churches. 1386, 3636, 3637
Crescent in north-west China. 2567
Cretan cults and festivals. 1387
Cribratio Alchorani. 2708
Cries from the cross. 1388
Cries from the half-world. 1136
Cries from the heart. 586
Cries of the Christ from the cross. 2057
Crime against Christ and a sermon to the Sunday evening club of Chicago. 3342
Crime and community in Biblical perspective. 2160
Crime and cure. 1387, 2068
Crime, character, education. 2590
...The crime of abortion in canon law. 3
Crime of Christendom. 1073
Criminal and illegal trial of the Nazarene peasant. 2068
Criminal jurisprudence of the ancient Hebrews. 2074, 2107
Crises in morality. 1140
Crises in the early church. 1191
Crises in the history of the papacy. 2769
Crises of the Christ. 1969
Crisis. 1939
Crisis and creed. 3735
Crisis and decision. 2112
Crisis and faith. 2080
Crisis and response. 558
Crisis and story. 595
Crisis, catastrophe and survival. 2090
Crisis counseling. 2781
Crisis experience in modern life. 2780
Crisis experiences in the Greek New Testament. 3300
Crisis for baptism. 138
Crisis in American Lutheran theology. 2294
Crisis in Christendom. 761
Crisis in church and college. 1127
Crisis in church music? 1204
Crisis in church work. 1252
Crisis in communication. 1564
Crisis in history. 1818
Crisis in Lutheran theology. 3667, 3668
Crisis in marriage. 2346
Crisis in Methodism. 2447
Crisis in priestly ministry. 2789
Crisis in religion. 3064
Crisis in the Armenian church. 82
Crisis in the church. 827, 1058, 1065, 1477
Crisis in the life of Jesus. 1972
Crisis in the pulpit. 2901
Crisis in the reformed churches. 1477
Crisis in unity and witness. 1121
Crisis in Watertown. 1135, 1627
Crisis of authority. 668, 827
Crisis of Christian rationalism. 3024
Crisis of church & state, 1050-1300. 1144
Crisis of civilization. 1281
Crisis of cultural change. 1065
Crisis of faith. 802, 1104, 1245, 3167
Crisis of liturgical reform. 841, 2236

Crisis of moral authority. 62
Crisis of piety. 956
Crisis of religious language. 1317
Crisis of religious life. 2571
Crisis of the church. 1122
Crisis of the churches. 1122
Crisis of the Reformation. 3036
Cristobal Rojas y Spinola, cameralist and irenicist, 1626-1695. 1045, 3472
Criswell's forbidden predictions. 2715, 2948
Criswell's guidebook for pastors. 2788
Criteria for the evaluation of Catholic elementary schools. 830, 1247
Criteria of diverse kinds of truth as opposed to agnosticism, being a treatise on applied logic. 2180
Criterion for the church. 1062
Critical analysis of the historicity of the Book of Daniel. 508
Critical analysis of the Jewish educational philosophy in relationship to the Epistles of St. Paul. 376, 2086
Critical and candid analysis of Christian science. 1036
Critical and constructive essays. 758
Critical and doctrinal commentary on the Epistle of St. Paul to the Romans. 466
Critical and doctrinal commentary upon the Epistle of St. Paul to the Romans. 467
... A critical and exegetical commentary on Amos and Hosea. 485
... A critical and exegetical commentary on Genesis. 522
... A critical and exegetical commentary on Haggai, Zechariah, Malachi and Jonah. 559
... A critical and exegetical commentary on Judges. 555
... A critical and exegetical commentary on Micah, Zephaniah, Nahum, Habakkuk, Obadiah and Joel. 559
... A critical and exegetical commentary on Numbers. 560
Critical & exegetical commentary on the Book of Amos. 485
... A critical and exegetical commentary on the book of Daniel. 506, 507
... A critical and exegetical commentary on the Book of Esther. 513
Critical and exegetical commentary on the book of Exodus. 516
Critical and exegetical commentary on the book of Genesis. 522
Critical and exegetical commentary on the book of Genesis. With a new translation. 522
... A critical and exegetical commentary on the book of Isaiah, i-xxxix. 542
Critical and exegetical commentary on the book of Job. 548
Critical and exegetical commentary on the book of Job, together with a new translation. 548
Critical and exegetical commentary on the book of Leviticus, with a new translation. 557
... A critical and exegetical commentary on the book of Proverbs. 572
Critical and exegetical commentary on the book of Psalms. 575
... A critical and exegetical commentary on the books of Chronicles. 496
Critical and exegetical commentary on the books of Ezra and Nehemiah. 519
Critical and exegetical commentary on the Books of Kings. 555, 556
...A critical and exegetical commentary on the books of Samuel. 590
... A critical and exegetical commentary on the Epistle of St. James. 412
...A critical and exegetical commentary on the Epistle to the Galatians. 379
... A critical and exegetical commentary on the Epistle to the Romans. 469
... A critical and exegetical commentary on the Epistles of St. Paul to the Thessalonians. 478
Critical and exegetical commentary on the epistles of St. Peter and St. Jude. 378
... A critical and exegetical commentary on the epistles to the Ephesians and to the Colossians. 341, 362
... A critical and exegetical commentary on the Epistles to the Philippians and to Philemon. 449
... A critical and exegetical commentary on the First epistle of St. Paul to the Corinthians. 322
Critical and exegetical commentary on the Gospel according to St. John. 415
... A critical and exegetical commentary on the Gospel according to St. Luke. 428
... A critical and exegetical commentary on the Gospel according to St. Mark. 433, 435

Critical and exegetical commentary on the Johannine epistles. 369
... A critical and exegetical commentary on the Second epistle of St. Paul to the Corinthians. 321
Critical and exegetical hand-book to the Epistle to the Ephesians. 363
Critical and exegetical hand-book to the Epistle to the Galatians. 380
Critical and exegetical hand-book to the Epistle to the Romans. 468
Critical and exegetical hand-book to the Epistles to the Philippians and Colossians, and to Philemon. 371
Critical and exegetical hand-book to the epistles to Timothy and Titus. 446
Critical and exegetical hand-book to the Gospel of John. 417
Critical and exegetical hand-book to the Gospel of Matthew. 441
Critical and exegetical hand-book to the Gospels of Mark and Luke. 434
Critical and exegetical handbook to the Acts of the Apostles. 329
Critical and exegetical handbook to the General epistles of James. Peter, John, and Jude. 340
Critical and exegetical handbook to the Revelation of John. 453
...Critical and exegtical commentary on the book of Isaih, I-XXXIX. 542
Critical and grammatical commentary on St. Paul's Epistles to the Philippians, Colossians, and to Philemon. 371
Critical and historical introduction to the canonical scriptures of the Old Testament. 539
Critical and historical review of Fox's Book of martyrs. 2350
Critical anthology of English recusant devotional prose, 1558-1603. 1456
Critical bibliography of existentialism (the Paris School) 1584
Critical bibliography of religion in America, by Nelson R. Burr in collaboration with the editors: James Ward Smith and A. Leland Jamison. 3748
Critical commentary and paraphrase on the Old and New Testament and the Apocrypha. 224, 2463
Critical commentary on the book of Daniel. 506
Critical commentary on the Epistle to the Hebrews. 403
Critical commentary on the Songs of the return. 574
Critical concordance to the Acts of the Apostles. 330
Critical confessions. 32, 2195
Critical disquisitions on the eighteenth chapter of Isaiah. 546
Critical dissertation, with notes, on Milton's Paradise regained. 2468
Critical essays on Jonathan Edwards. 1500
Critical examination of the belief in a life after death. 1892
Critical examination of the Peshitta version of the Book of Ezra. 519
Critical exposition comprising all that is said in the New Testament relating to the Holy Supper. 2254
Critical faith. 67
Critical guide to Catholic reference books. 764, 3031, 3032
Critical handbook of the Greek New Testament. 378
Critical history and defence of the Old Testament canon. 496
Critical history of free thought in reference to the Christian religion. 1654, 1656
Critical history of Sunday legislation from 321 to 1888 A. D. 3548
Critical history of the Athanasian creed. 99
Critical history of the doctrine of a future life. 1694
Critical history of the evolution of trinitarianism. 3712
Critical history of the life of David. 1404
Critical history of the Sabbath and the Sunday in the Christian church. 3260
Critical hours in the preacher's life. 2228
Critical introduction to the Gospels. 398
Critical introduction to the Old Testament. 539
Critical investigation of the works of Rabbi Isaac Baer Levinsohn (R I Ba L) 2219
Critical investigation of the works of Rabbie Isaac Baer Levinsohn (RIBaL) 2219
Critical issues in modern religion. 3082
Critical look at religion. 1054
Critical meaning of the Bible. 231
Critical moment. 3844

Critical paraphrase of the New Testament. 354
Critical quests of Jesus. 1978
Critical remarks on the books of Job, Proverbs, Psalms, Ecclesiastes, and Canticles. 499
Critical review of Wesleyan perfection, in twenty-four consecutive arguments. 2818
Critical reviews. 681
Critical study of Adi Granth, being a comprehensive and scientific study of Guru Granth Sahib, the scripture of the Sikhs. 7
Critical study of Book of Mormon sources. 678
Critical study of Hinduism. 1813
Critical study of sacred texts. 3267
Critical theology of Theodore Parker. 2776
Critical way in religion. 2181
Critical word book of Leviticus, Numbers, Deuteronomy. 557
Critical word book of the Pentateuch. 562
Critical years. 2967
Criticism and faith. 234
Criticism of Christian dogma. 1387, 3648
Criticism of the crusade. 1391
Criticism of the Fourth gospel. 420
Criticism of the New Testament. 1387
Criticism on Milton's Paradise lost, from 'The spectator.' 31 December, 1711-3 May, 1712. 2467
Criticisms of life. 1068
Criticisms on Paradise lost. 2467
Critique by eternity. 1676
Critique of design-arguments. 2673
Critique of Msgr. Pospishil's The quest for an Ukrainian Catholic Patriarchate. 766, 2865
Critique of Paradise lost. 2469
Critique of practical reason, and other writings in moral philosophy. 1535
Critique of pure Kant. 2164
Critique of pure reason. 876, 2180
Critique of religion and philosophy. 3058, 3060
Critique of the psycho-physical identity theory. 2473
Critique of the theory of vital atonement. 106, 1809
Critiques of Confucius in contemporary China. 1330
Critiques of God. 1729
Critque of pure reason. 876
Critter chronicles. 1588
Crocodile and cassowary. 3239
Croiset, the clairvoyant. 1387
Croke of Cashel. 667, 1387
Cronica de los Colegios de Propaganda Fide de la Nueva Espana. 1647
Cronica franciscana de las Provincias del Perd. 1648, 1744
Crook in the lot. 1234
Crooked spire of Chesterfield. 892
Crookes and the spirit world. 3498
Crosby street synagogue (1834-1860) of the Congregation Shearith Israel (founded in the city of New York--1655) 2700
Crosier family. 1387
Crosier on the frontier. 1803
Cross. 105, 1388, 1998, 2048, 2215
Cross above the crescent. 2540
Cross against the sky. 2597
Cross and affliction. 11
Cross and crescent. 1392
Cross and crisis in Japan. 1935
Cross and crown. 2820, 3034
Cross & crown hymnal, Church of the Pillar of fire. 2848
Cross and crucifix in Christian worship and devotion. 1958
Cross and crucifix in mission. 2513
Cross and flame. 2350
Cross and great living. 2934
Cross and its shadow. 3720
Cross and passion. 1388
Cross and sanctification. 3295
Cross and swastika. 1426, 1707
Cross and sword. 2559, 3273
Cross and the altar. 2366
Cross and the Beatitudes. 181, 2058
Cross and the Christian. 3541
Cross and the common man. 104
Cross & the Creed. 2059
Cross and the cries of human need. 2299, 3349
Cross and the crisis. 757, 1063
Cross and the crown. 1037, 1628, 2541
Cross and the Dragon. 2508
Cross and the eternal order. 104
Cross & the flag. 1550
Cross and the garden. 1342
Cross and the prodigal. 431, 603
Cross and the reconstruction of the world. 1388
Cross and the scalpel. 2539

Cross and the switchblade. 1255
Cross-annunciation. 2355
Cross as symbol & ornament. 1388
Cross athwart the sky. 2213
Cross before Calvary. 2435
Cross builders. 338, 2029
Cross-currents. 53, 54
Cross-currents in the personality of Martin Luther. 2280
Cross destroys. 108
Cross examined. 2214
Cross fire. 980
Cross for Napoleon. 1293, 2196
Cross from coast to coast. 2300
Cross in agony and ecstasy. 2214, 2300
Cross in Christian experience. 104
Cross in faith and conduct. 1388
Cross in hymns. 1875, 1998
Cross in iconography, archaeology, architecture, and Christian art. 1388
Cross in Japan. 2534
Cross in symbol spirit and worship. 1388, 2058
Cross in the light of to-day. 2041
Cross in the marketplace. 168
Cross in the New Testament. 107
Cross in the Old Testament. 1388, 3541
Cross in the sand. 817
Cross in the sunset. 2439
Cross in the valley; the history of the establishment of the Catholic Church in the northern San Josquin Valley of California up to 1863. 3532
Cross in the West. 835
Cross in the wilderness. 890, 3277
Cross in tradition, history, and art. 1388
Cross-index of indices of books on thanatology. 1416
Cross is heaven. 2640
Cross is the key. 106
Cross is urgent. 2215
Cross, its history & symbolism. 1388
Cross-lots. 1388
Cross, meditations on the seven last words of Christ. 2058
Cross of Christ. 106, 107, 1388, 1954, 2034
Cross of Christ, our soul's panacea. 2214
Cross of Christ - the throne of God. 1388
Cross of Golgotha. 1388
Cross of Hosea. 1848
Cross of Jesus. 3485
Cross of sorrow. 1388
Cross on the mountain. 181
Cross on the range. 2975
...The cross or the pound. Which? 1814
Cross or the star? 2145
Cross, our hope. 2058, 2973
Cross over Africa. 2497
Cross over Mount Kenya. 1238
Cross-reference Bible. 1388
Cross-reference Bible, containing the Old and New Testaments. 1388
Cross-reference digest of Bible references. 1388
Cross-reference study of Acts. 333
Cross, the cow, or the prayer rug. 3113
Cross through the open tomb. 2050
Cross through the Scriptures. 105
Cross to glory. 2215
Cross today. 1389
Cross upon cross. 2850
Cross versus the crescent. 1388
Cross without velvet. 955
Cross words; sermons and dramas for Lent. 2059
Crosscurrents. 2502
... The crosses and culture of Ireland. 1388
Cross-eyed bear and other children's sermons. 907
Crossing Jordan at flood tide. 1568, 3383
Crossing over; a study of death and the future life. 1413
Crossing the Kidron. 2213
Crossings. 2219, 3521
Crossings, a transpersonal approach. 2219, 3507
Crossroad children's Bible. 622
Crossroads in missions. 2492
Crossroads of Lent. 2212
Crossroads of the cross. 2007
Crossroads on life's highway. 1559
Crosswinds. 1389, 3239
Crow Indian medicine bundles. 1389
Crowded church, through modern methods. 1250
Crowded detours. 92, 3354
Crowded to Christ. 3290
Crowded ways. 1280
"Crowds of souls" 3463
Crowe-Kleran debate on the Church of Christ and Roman Catholicism. 1272
Crown and clergy in colonial Mexico, 1759-1821. 1147
Crown and glory of a Christian. 971
Crown and the cross. 1978

Crown for the butcher's wife. 1304
Crown for the schoolboy. 191
Crown of brotherhood. 694
Crown of character. 886
Crown of fire. 3305
Crown of glory. 2605, 2852, 3535
Crown of Hinduism. 1813
Crown of jewels for the Little secretary of Jesus. 1622
Crown of life. 1453, 2686, 2822, 3755
Crown of service. 2457
Crown of sorrow, Lent. 2032
Crown of thorns. 1961
Crowned. 2631
Crowned and discrowned. 3304
Crowned in palm-land. 2497, 2669
Crowned victors. 2443
"Crowned with glory and honor" 146, 3817
Crowning decade, 1949-1959. 3298
Crowning glory. 1558
Crowning triumph. 3562
Crowns and crosses. 1351
Crowns of Christ, and other sermons. 165
Crucial dimensions in world evangelization. 2496
Crucial experiences in the life of D. L. Moody. 1576, 2587
Crucial issues in Bangladesh. 2503
Crucial issues in mission today. 2495
Crucial issues in missions tomorrow. 2496
Crucial problems in Christian perspective. 1139
Crucial questions about the kingdom of God. 2174
Crucial questions in apologetics. 68
Crucial questions on problems facing the church today. 758
Crucial task of theology. 3616
Crucial words from Calvary. 2057
Cruciality of the Cross. 1634
Crucible. 3874
Crucible of Calvary. 384, 2030
Crucible of change. 2789
Crucible of Christianity. 1103
Crucible of love. 2642, 3603
Crucible of redemption. 1837
Crucified and risen. 105
Crucified answer. 2210
Crucified God. 2041
Crucified; Good Friday addresses on the seven last words from the cross. 1747
Crucified Jew. 1997
Crucified Lamb. 3109
Crucified Messiah, and other essays. 1997
Crucified with Christ. 765
Crucifiers. 2028
Crucifiers, then and now. 164
Crucifix. 104
Crucifixion. 1532, 1998, 3526
Crucifixion and the resurrection of Jesus, by an eye-witness. 1998
Crucifixion in our street. 3531
Crucifixion of Christ. 1997
Crucifixion of superiority. 1747
Crucifixion of the Jews. 1073
Cruden's Complete concordance of the Old and New Testaments. 227
Cruden's complete concordance to the Old and New Testamants. 227
Cruden's Complete concordance to the Old and New Testaments. 227
Cruden's Concordance to the Holy Scriptures. 227
Cruden's pocket dictionary of Bible terms. 243
Cruden's useful concordance of the Holy Scriptures. 227
Cruel Caesars. 408, 1144
Cruel persecutions of the Protestants in the kingdom of France. 2979
Cruise of the eight hundred to and through Palestine. 2763
Crumbling walls. 1061
Crumbs and character. 3371
Crumbs from heaven. 1794
Crusade at the Golden Gate. 1755, 3232
Crusade, commerce, and culture. 1390
Crusade for life. 3079
Crusade for souls. 3376
... Crusade for the anemone. 2761
Crusade hymn stories. 1871
Crusade in the city. 3232
Crusade in the later middle ages. 1392
Crusade of brotherhood. 33
Crusade of compassion for the healing of the nations. 2538
Crusade of Fatima. 1618
Crusade '66. 1569, 1755
Crusader for creation. 2938
Crusader for freedom. 2718
Crusader in Great Britain. 692
Crusaders. 1390, 1392
Crusaders for Christ. 1541
Crusaders for God. 2483, 2484
Crusaders; in Syria and the Holy Land. 2199

Crusaders in the Holy Land. 1944
Crusaders' kingdom. 1944
Crusaders of the jungle. 850, 1903, 1904
Crusaders of the twentieth century. 2291
Crusades. 1390, 1391, 1392
Crusades, a documentary survey. 1390
Crusades, and other historical essays; presented to Dana C. Munro by his former students. 1390
Crusades, motives and achievements. 1392
Crusades; origin of an ecumenical problem. 1391
Crusading Taylors. 3590
Crusading warfare. 1391
Crusading warfare (1097-1193) 1391
... Crux ansata. 794, 795
Crux imperatorium philosophia. 1304
Crux of chronology. 1997
Crux of pastoral medicine. 2378
...A cry for justice. 486
Cry for the world. 987
Cry from the North. 2217
Cry in the night. 2710
Cry in the wilderness. 2127
Cry in the wilderness: "Hear ye the voice of the Lord," 2501
Cry jubilee! 3421
Cry justice! 1077
Cry of despair from Moscow churchmen. 2749
Cry of the human heart. 987
Cry of the people. 821, 836, 2821
Crying stones. 379
Crypt conference on Sunday schools. 3557
Crypt conference on Sunday schools, held under the auspices of the Sunday school commission, diocese of New York, May, 1901. 3557
Crystal chalice. 3544
Crystal-gazing. 1392
Crystal gazing and clairvoyance. 1392
Crystal mountain. 987
CSMC study guide. 1322
Cteni o Moravskych bratrich. 2596
Cub creek church and congregation. 1392
Cuba, church and crisis. 816
Cuba for Christ. 2516
Cuban church in a sugar economy. 2953
Cuchama and sacred mountains. 1902
Cuckolds, clerics, & countrymen. 1588
Cuddesdon College, 1854-1904. 1392
Cuddesdon College office book. 3756
Cues for church camping. 731
Cues for collectors. 1345
... Culavamsa. 3816
Cullom lantern. 1393
Cullom Mennonite Church. 1393
Cult and conscience. 3271
Cult and countercult. 1908
Cult and culture. 1394
Cult and myth of Pyrros at Delphi. 3010
Cult & occult. 2729
Cult experience. 1393, 1394
Cult explosion. 1393
Cult of Kibo-tumn. 3717
Cult of Our Lady of Guadalupe. 1776
Cult of revolution in the church. 3233
Cult of Tara. 3588
Cult of the dead among the natives of the Amur Basin. 1408, 3718
Cult of the dead in a Chinese village. 39
Cult of the goddess. 881, 1815
Cult of the Heavenly Twins. 744
Cult of the mother-goddess. 2624
Cult of the seer in the ancient Middle East. 90
Cult of the sun. 1501
Cult that died. 2130
Le culte des heros et ses conditions sociales. 1807, 2793
Cultic prophet and Israel's psalmody. 578, 2950
Cultic prophet in ancient Israel. 567, 2114, 2950
Cultism to charisma. 689, 1363
Cultivating the fruit of the Spirit. 1827
Cultivating the presence. 3481
Cultivation of Christian character. 974
Cultivation of sagehood as a religious goal in Neo-Confucianism. 2164, 2683
Il culto privato di Roma antica. 1395
Cults and creeds in Graeco-Roman Egypt. 1502
Cults and isms. 3121
Cults and isms ancient and modern. 3323
Cults and new faiths. 1393
Cults and the family. 1394
Cults and the occult. 1038
Cults are coming! 1394, 3329
Cults, myths, oracles, and politics in ancient Greece. 1395
Cults of America. 3324
Cults of Dacia. 1395
Cults of the Greek states. 1395
Cults of the Sabine territory. 3246

Cults of unreason. 3322
Cults, world religions, and you. 3113
Cultural anthropology. 1074
Cultural concept of Christianity. 1394
Cultural crisis of our time. 3749
Cultural history of religion in America. 3745
Cultural resources of the Black River-St. Lawrence region. 89
Cultural significance of the Reformation. 3034
Cultural subversion of the Biblical faith. 3747
Cultural system. 3688
Culture and conscience. 2765
Culture and faith. 1394
Culture and human values. 2496
Culture and liturgy. 3449
Culture and mental disorders. 1858, 2823
Culture and personality aspects of the Pentecostal Holiness religion. 2814
Culture and religion in some of their relations. 1394, 3063
Culture and the cross. 3359
Culture, crisis, and creativity. 3689
Culture of a sacred town. 2669
Culture of ancient Israel. 2084
Culture of Christian manhood. 3758
Culture of religion. 3160
Culture of unbelief. 186
Culture-protestantism. 3679
Culture shock. 2696, 3862
Cultus of the sacramental presence in the eucharist and in the reserved sacrament. 1395
Cumberland Presbyterian digest, 1975. 1396
Cumberland Presbyterian pulpit. 3365
Cumberland's hallowed heritage. 1396
Cumorah--where? 678
Cumorah's "Gold Bible," 679
Cumulative index of Gregorian chant sources. 884
Cuneiform parallels to the Old Testament. 93
Cup. 3523
... The cup of demons, and other sermons. 2930
Cup of fire. 1069
Cup of grief. 1747
Cup of life. 2092, 2147, 2252
Cup of wonder. 2258
Cupid and creeds. 1397
Cupid & Psyche. 1396, 1397
Cupid in Arcady. 1397
Curate. 973
Curbed sinner. 2372
Cure and cult in ancient Corinth. 11, 1369
Cure d'Ars. 3778
Cure for anxiety. 960
Cure for crime. 1387
Cure for depression. 1053
Cure for troubled hearts. 985
Cure of Ars and his cross. 3778
Cure of Ars; the priest who outtalked the devil. 3778
Cure of Ars to his people. 745
Cure of souls. 2907, 3462, 3463, 3633
Cure of souls, a socio-psychological approach. 3672
Curiosities of physical research. 2845
Curiosities of superstition, and sketches of some unrevealed religions. 3112
Curiosities of the hymnal. 1872
Curious Christians. 2934, 3356
Curious facts, myths, legends, and superstitions concerning Jesus. 1976
Curious layman. 3069
Curious questions. 3098
Currency of the invisible. 3529
Current challenge to church-state separation. 2670, 1152
Current Christian thinking. 975
Current comments on timely topics. 734
Current concepts and practices of confirmation in Lutheran churches. 1329
Current discussions in theology. 3631
Current issues in Biblical and patristic interpretation. 200, 3601, 3667
Current issues in New Testament interpretation. 334, 2849
Current list of serials with significant theological or religious content. 3678
Current perspectives in the psychology of religion. 3001
Current problems in religion. 3066
Current questions-Catholic answers. 789
Current Reform responsa. 3219
Current religious perils. 1368
Current religious thought. 3618
Current theological thinking. 3616, 3618
Current trends in theological libraries. 3612
Current trends in theology. 3618
... Current week-day religious education. 3153

Curriculum for Jewish religious schools. 2086
Curriculum guide. 3163
Curriculum guide for the kindergarten. 2106
Curriculum guide for the local church. 3162
Curriculum guide. 1960-1963/4. 3163
Curriculum of religious education. 3147, 3162
Curriculum of the Catholic college, integration and concentration. 3756
Curriculum of the minor seminary. 3611, 3612, 3613
Curriculum of the minor seminary: religion, Greek, and remedial reading. 3613
Curriculum of the minor seminary: social studies, Greek, and the general curriculum. 3613
Curriculum of worship. 3149
Curriculum of worship, for the junior church school. 3858
Curse of Cain. 634
Curse of Rome. 800, 1177, 3245
Curse of septic soul-treatment. 3461
Curse of the cannibals. 2487, 2792
Curses, hexes & spells. 672
Curses, lucks and talismans. 672
Cursus Sanctae Mariae. 18, 2331
Cushing of Boston. 1397
Custom and myth. 1631, 2652
Custom and survival. 1931, 2100
Customary of the Sisters of Saint Dominic. 843
Customs and ceremonies in Israel. 2120
Customs and folkways of Jewish life. 2121
Customs and traditions of Israel. 2120
Cut from the loaf. 1438
Cuthbert Tunstal. 3718
Cutnumbered, and other stories. 1014
Cutting edge. 1133
Cutting through spiritual materialism. 3484
Cuttle-fish. 2079
Cybele and Attis. 1398
Cycle of Christ. 1264
Cycle of prayer. 2873
Cycle of the ages. 643
Cycles and renewal trends in Protestant lay education. 938
Cycles: the first year. 1265
Cyclomancy, the secret of psychic power control. 2992
Cyclopaedia of Biblical literature. 244
Cyclopaedia of Biblical, theological, and ecclesiastical literature. 244, 1183, 1512
Cyclopaedia of Methodism. 2421, 2428
Cyclopedia of African Methodism in Mississippi. 2426
Cyclopedia of Bible illustrations. 1840
Cyclopedia of commencement sermons and baccalaureate addresses. 122
Cyclopedia of eminent Christians of various denominations. 923
Cyclopedia of evangelism. 1565
Cyclopedia of funeral sermons and sketches, with ministrant's manual. 1692
Cyclopedia of missions. 2516
Cyclopedia of moral and religious anecdotes. 41
Cyclopedia of pastoral methods. 2891
Cyclopedia of religious anecdotes. 1841
Cyclopedia of sermon outlines. 3375
Cyclopedia of sermon outlines for special days and occasions. 3373
Cyclopedia of sermons ... Five volumes complete in one. 3360
Cyclopedia of the colored Baptists of Alabama. 157
Cyclopedia of twentieth century illustrations. 1842
Cynic's meditations. 2380, 2394
Cypress wreath. 1350
Cyprian. 1398
... Cyprian De unitate ecclesiae. 1398
...Cyprian; the churchman. 1398
Cyprus passion cycle. 2778
Cyril Bardsley. 173
Cyril of Jerusalem and Nemesius of Emesa. 745
Czars, Soviets & Mennonites. 2408
Czech Catholics at the 41st International Eucharistic Congress held August 1-8, 1976 in Philadelphia, USA. 872, 1913
Czech mate. 612, 1790, 2942
Czechoslovak heresy and schism. 879, 1398

D

D.C.E., a challenging career in Christian education. 3161
D. D. Home, his life and mission. 1838, 3520
D. D. Home, the man who talked with ghosts. 1838, 2399
D.d's for ministers. 3671
D. L. Moody. 2587, 2588
D. L. Moody; a worker in souls. 2587
D. L. Moody at home. 2588
D. L. Moody year book. 1440
D. Martin Luther's Werke. 3629
D.R.E. book. 937
... Dachau sermons. 2301
Daddy Darwin's dovecot. 935, 1016
Daddy King. 146, 2172
Daemonologia. 3823
Daemonologie. 1423, 1624
Daemonologie, 1597. 1423, 1624
Dag Hammarskjold. 1783
Dag Hammarskjold, a spiritual portrait. 1783
Dag Hammarskjold's white book. 1783
Dagger and the cross. 2756, 3793
Dagger John. 667, 1851
Dagon of Calvinism. 729
Daily assignment. 1449
Daily Bible commentary. 343, 497
Daily Bible illustrations. 295, 1605
Daily Bible memory verses, arranged topically for fifty-two weeks. 198
Daily Bible readings from the Revised standard version. 1430
Daily Bible studies. 1442
Daily blessing. 1435
Daily bread. 1433, 1435
Daily breath. 1811, 2389
Daily breviary meditations. 1263
Daily celebration; devotional readings for every day of the year. 1430
Daily cheer for all the year. 1441
Daily Christian living. 1430
Daily communion. 1438
Daily companion. 1436
Daily compline. 2239
Daily delights. 1433
Daily devotion. 1437, 1605
... Daily devotional Bible readings. 725
Daily devotional study of the Bible. 1442
Daily devotions for individual and family use. 1437
Daily devotions for juniors. 1455
Daily devotions for Lutheran youth. 2297
Daily devotions for Lutheran youth, by twelve pastors of the Augustana synod. 2297
Daily devotions from the Jerusalem Bible. 1444
Daily diamonds. 1455
Daily digest of the Sunday-school lessons in the International improved uniform series for. 643
Daily discoveries. 902
Daily duties inculcated in a series of letters, addressed to the wife of a clergyman. 1323
Daily evening and morning offering (Agnihotra) according to the Brahmanas. 19
Daily food for Christians. 725
Daily food in Negro spirituals. 2680
Daily glow. 1438
Daily gospel. 1433, 1434, 1985
Daily gospel, evangelistic meditations for every day of the year. 1433
Daily guidance. 198
Daily guide for the sanctified. 935
Daily guide to knowing God. 1431
Daily heavenly manna and devotional service for the house hold of faith. 725
Daily help for daily need. 725
Daily inspiration. 2888
Daily life devotions for youth. 3882
Daily life in Bible times. 2765
Daily life in the time of Jesus. 2765
Daily life of early Christians. 1004
Daily life of the Christian. 970
Daily life prayers for youth. 3882
Daily light and strength. 1442
Daily light on the daily path. 725, 1430
Daily light on the daily path, morning and evening hour. 1430
Daily manna. 253, 317, 1430
Daily manual of the precious blood. 672, 856
Daily meditations. 1432, 1433, 1434, 1448
Daily meditations for seminarians. 3331
Daily meditations for the family altar. 2383
Daily meditations on the Christian life for every day in the year. 2399

Daily meditations on the seven last words. 2058
Daily meditations upon the epistle lessons of the church year. 2399
Daily meditations upon the Gospel lessons of the church year. 2399
Daily meditations with F. B. Meyer. 1432
Daily miracle in a name. 2668
Daily missal meditations. 846
Daily missal meditations; meditations for every day of the year based on the liturgy of the Mass. 1264
Daily missal of the mystical body. 2237
Daily office. 2297
Daily practice of the Hindus, containing the morning and midday duties. 1395
Daily praise and prayer. 1442
Daily prayer. 2893
Daily prayer and praise. 1430
Daily prayer companion. 2894
Daily prayer for family and private use. 2297, 2894
Daily prayer with English direction. 2874
Daily prayers. 2297, 2874
Daily prayers for children. 898
Daily prayers with English directions. 1797
Daily prime. 843
Daily promises from Holy Scripture. 725
Daily reading for school and home. 1430
Daily readings. 726, 3148
Daily readings from the works of Leslie D. Weatherhead. 1433
Daily readings from W. E. Sangster. 1435
Daily readings from William Temple. 3850
Daily readings in the Gospel of Mark. 438
Daily reminders from the Gospel of John. 423
Daily sacrifice. 1439
Daily secrets of Christian living. 1432
Daily service. 2972
Daily strength for daily needs. 1433, 1442
Daily study Bible series, revised edition [by] William Barclay. 1399
Daily thought. 1434
Daily thought for Lent. 2211
Daily thought from the writings of Mother Seton. 725
Daily thoughts for disciples. 1430
Daily thoughts for priests. 856
Daily thoughts from Phillips Brooks ... [and Henry Drummond] With an estimate and tribute [of Phillips Brooks] by Archdeacon Farrar. 1437
Daily thoughts of Mother Seton. 1455
Daily thoughts on living free. 1430
Daily vacation Bible school. 3762
... The daily vacation church school, how to organize and conduct it. 3763
Daily walk with God. 1434
Daily we touch Him. 2877
Daily will I praise Thee. 1431
Daily with the King. 1431
Daisy. 2936, 3427
Dake's annotated reference Bible: The Holy Bible, containing the Old and New Testaments of the Authorized or King James version text ... and a complete concordance and cyclopedic index. 614
Dake's annotated reference Bible--the New Testament. 320
Dakota Wowapi Wakan. 197
Dalai Lama. 2706
Dalton's tables of houses. 99
Damascus chronicle of the Crusades. 1390
Damien, the leper. 1400, 2568
Damien, the leper priest. 1293, 1400
Damned art. 3825
Damned children. 3436
Damned through the church. 1126
Damsel from afar. 3258
Dan Bosco. 683
...Dan of Nazareth. 634
Dan, the pioneer of Israel. 45
Dana's date with trouble. 3385
Dance in Christianity. 1401
Dance in steps of change. 1321
Dance of death. 1400
Dance of love. 1778, 2400
Dance of the pilgrim. 1095
Dancing at my funeral. 1006
Dancing madly backwards. 3480
... The danegeld in France. 1639
Danger ahead. 608, 1134
Danger and opportunity. 2751
Danger, duty, and delight of life. 166
Danger! Fraud ahead! 3742
Danger signals for new century manhood. 3870
Danger to Elizabeth. 872
... Dangerous opportunity. 2507
Dangers of Jesuit instruction. 1946
Dangers of the day. 978
Daniel. 505, 506, 507, 509, 1401
Daniel, a model for young men. 1401

Daniel and Minor prophets, with Wycliffe Bible commentary. 506
Daniel and Revelation. 506
Daniel and the atomic equations of the loaves. 509
... Daniel and the inter-Biblical period. 506, 633
Daniel and the latter days. 508, 2465
... Daniel, and the Minor prophets. 633
Daniel and the Revelation. 506, 507, 634
Daniel, Darius the Median, Cyrus the Great. 1401
Daniel, decoder of dreams. 506, 1401, 2952
Daniel Edwin Bushnell, a memorial. 719
Daniel, Esther, and Jeremiah. 489
Daniel for today. 507
... Daniel, his life and times. 1401
Daniel in Babylon. 507
Daniel in the critics' den. 507
Daniel Lammot and his role in the New Church in Delaware. 1179
Daniel Mannix: Archbishop of Melbourne 1917-1963. 2329
Daniel speaks to the church. 509
Daniel the beloved. 1401
Daniel, the key to prophetic revelation. 507
Daniel, the man and his visions. 506
Daniel, the man greatly beloved and his prophecies. 509
Daniel the prophet. 507, 509, 1401
Daniel the prophet in the latter days. 509
Daniel verified in history and chronology. 509
Daniel, who dared. 494, 633, 1401
Daniel's half-week now closing. 634
Danish Luteran Church in America. 1401
Danish Lutheran Church in America. 1401
Danish rebel. 1776
Danites. 509
Danners discussion. 3753
Dante. 1141, 1401, 1402
Dante and Catholic philosophy in the thirteenth century. 1402
Dante and Milton. 2471
Dante and the Divina commedia. 1402
Dante and the Divine comedy. 1402
... The Dante collections in the Harvard college and Boston public libraries. 1402
Dante's Divine comedy. 1402
... Dante's Inferno. 1401
Dante's Inferno and other translations. 1402
Dare I love? 3393
Dare to be different. 900
Dare to believe! 2395
Dare to care like Jesus. 993, 2004
Dare to defy. 1006
Dare to live. 1316, 3884
Dare to reconcile. 1467
Dare we be Christians. 973, 1062
Dare you face facts? 3444
Daring discipleship. 3182
Daring of Jesus. 2012
Daring prayer. 2882
Daring to draw near. 2883
Daring to live. 764
Darius the Mede. 508, 1403
Darius the Mede and the four world empires. 508, 1403
Dark Africa and the way out. 1331, 2550
Dark ages. 2092
Dark center. 3017
Dark cloud in between. 1017
Dark dove. 1836
Dark glory. 2682
Dark night of the soul. 2323, 2642
Dark road to triumph. 2035
Dark salvation. 16, 2438
Dark shepherd. 1288, 1793
Dark side of history. 2732
Dark symphony. 1363
Dark threads the weaver needs. 3540
Dark Virgin. 1776
Dark world of witches. 3824
Darkening valley. 103
Darker drink. 3494
Darker superstitions of Scotland. 3567
Darkness and light. 776, 2034, 2719, 3070, 3629, 3830
Darkness discovered. 3214
Darkness is passed. 1985
Darkness of the sun. 1935
Darkness or light. 1355
Darshan: the vision of light. 3477
Dartmouth Bible. 198
Darvishes. 1425
Darvishes; or, Oriental spiritualism. 1425
Darwin and the human situation. 3081
Darwin and the modern world view. 3084
Darwin: before and after. 1403
Darwin, evolution, and creation. 1403, 1581
Darwinism and determinism. 1581

Darwinism in morals, and other essays. 3066, 3619
Darwinism in Texas. 202
Darwin's vision and Christian perspectives. 1403, 3082
Das Register Innocenz' III. 1826
... The Dasarupa. 3301
... Dat boexken vander missen. 845
Data book. 2528
Data of modern ethics examined. 1536
Date of Easter and other Christian festivals. 1163
Date of the Last Supper. 2029
Date with destiny. 1394
Dated events of the Old Testament. 496
Datelines and by-lines; a sketchbook of Presbyterian beginnings and growth in Arizona. 2917
D'Aubigne's "History of the great reformation in Germany and Switzerland," reviewed. 2334, 3036
D'Aubigne's Martyrs of the reformation. 2351
Daughter of Africa. 3455
Daughter of Coventry Patmore, Sister Mary Christina, S. H. C. J. 2792
Daughter of destiny. 1575, 2187
Daughter of heaven. 3094
Daughter of the gods. 1801
Daughter of Zion. 2603
Daughters of charity in Milwaukee, 1846-1946. 1403
Daughters of Dominic on Long Island. 3420
Daughters of Dominic on Long Island, the Brooklyn Sisters of Saint Dominic. 3420
Daughters of Dorcas. 3838
Daughters of Eve. 3839
Daughters of Islam. 3842
Daughters of the church: proceedings of two inter-province institutes on renewal and adaptation. 1403
Daughters of the faith. 3838
Daughters of the King. 3845
Daughters of the Puritans. 3328
Daughters of Zion. 3839
Daughters who prophesy. 3832
Dauntless women. 3831
Dave Ranney. 3705
Davenport brothers the world-renowned spiritual mediums. 1404, 3499
David. 616, 1404, 1405, 1406
David, a Bible study. 640
David and Goliath. 495, 633, 634, 1404, 1405, 1406
David and Goliath, or a treatise on water baptism. 136
David and his friends. 1555
David and his harp. 1405
David and his mighty men. 492, 493, 1404
David and the giant. 1017
David and the Psalms. 640
David Brainerd, his life and diary. 689
David Brainerd, the man of prayer. 1900
David. Drawings by R. M. Sax. 1406
David Friedrich Strauss and his place in modern thought. 3535
David Friedrich Strauss and his theology. 3535
David Gomes. 146, 1744
David Henkel against the Unitarians. 2039, 3729
... David, his life and times. 1404
David Hume & the miraculous. 1855, 2477
David Hummell Greer. 1773
David James Burrell. 718
David Kimhi, the man and the commentaries. 505, 2171
David, king of Israel. 1405
David Livingston, explorer-missionary. 2241
David Livingstone. 2240, 2241, 2499
David Livingstone, foe of darkness. 2240
David Livingstone: the story of one who followed Christ. 2241
David Morton. 2620
David, my Jewish friend. 2151
David, shepherd. 1405
David, shepherd and king. 493, 1404
"David," shepherd, poet, warrior, king. 1404
David: shepherd, psalmist, king. 1406
David Stanton Tappan, Grandfather's China story, 1906-1950. 2524, 3587
David Swing. 3572
David Swing's sermons. 3359
David, the biography of a king. 1404
David the giant killer. 2076
David the king. 578, 1405
David, the shepherd king. 1405
David: warrior and king. 1405
David, warrior, poet, king. 633
David, when only God's grace will do. 1404
David Wolffsohn, Herzl's successor. 3831

David's son is born. 1112
Davis' notes on Matthew. 440
Davis parallel Gospels. 385
Davis, soldier missionary. 1406
Davva-samgaha (Dravya-samgraha) 1932
Dawn and the day. 702, 1953
Dawn and twilight of Zoroastrianism. 3899
Dawn-breakers. 25, 128
Dawn-breakers; Nabil's narrative of the early days of the Baha'i revelation. 122, 128
Dawn brings glory. 2943
Dawn in Bantuland. 2498
Dawn in the Dark continent. 2498
Dawn is come. 3494
Dawn of a brighter day. 3383
Dawn of a consecration. 2572
Dawn of a conviction. 3509
Dawn of a new day. 163, 1513, 3501
Dawn of a new religious era, and other essays. 2752
Dawn of another life. 3494
Dawn of apocalyptic. 56, 544
... The dawn of Christianity. 333, 1193
Dawn of conscience. 1538
Dawn of day. 3321
Dawn of devotion. 1431
Dawn of God's day. 3491
Dawn of heaven. 1793
Dawn of life. 63
Dawn of light. 1598, 3202
Dawn of modern thought. 1426
Dawn of the awakened mind. 3506
Dawn of the Catholic revival in England, 1781-1803. 816
Dawn of the Christian life. 939
Dawn of the Middle Ages. 1194
Dawn of the Reformation. 3038
Dawn of the scarlet age. 452
Dawn of time. 2654
Dawn of truth. 2668
Dawn on the hills of Tang. 2507
Dawn over Amazonia. 1904, 3860
Dawn over Mount Hira, and other essays. 129
Dawn over temple roofs. 2553
Dawn-thought on the reconciliation. 2767
Dawn without darkness. 1001
Dawning of the great day of revelations. 3225
Daws. 3715
Day. 3547
Day after Christmas. 1302, 3790
Day after day. 1445
Day after tomorrow. 2489
Day after tomorrow, and other sermons. 3387
Day at a time. 1430, 1431, 2402
Day book of meditations. 1431
Day book of meditations. 2389
Day book of the Bible. 1431
Day brighteners. 471
Day by day. 1431, 1437, 1456, 1606, 1609, 2385, 2870, 2873, 3189
Day by day we magnify thee. 1432, 1440
Day by day with Amy Bolding. 1433
Day-by-day with Andrew Murray. 1432
Day by day with Jesus. 400, 1983
Day by day with My daily visitor. 1434
Day by day with the Master. 321
Day Christ died. 929, 1997
Day Christ was born. 929, 2005, 2021
Day dawn. 1695
Day dawn in Africa. 2500, 2970
Day dawn in Yoruba land. 2559
Day dawns in fire. 3743
Day death died. 2051
Day for God-called men. 168
Day for meditation. 2380
Day God died. 2059
Day God laughed. 3015
Day God made it rain. 495, 633, 1507
Day in Capernaum. 637, 1951
Day in the Lord's court. 1445
Day is at hand. 2788
Day is dawning. 1458
Day of a stranger. 2413
... The day of atonement. 3577
Day of disaster. 2404
Day of doom. 2156
Day of His coming. 9, 389
Day of Jesus Christ. 449
Day of light. 3547
Day of miracles. 1359
Day of our Abraham. 3252
Day of resurrection. 2054
Day of solemn thanksgiving. 1208
Day of the country church. 3253
Day of the cross. 2034
Day of the lamb. 459
Day of the lion. 485
Day of the Lord. 1513, 3318
Day of worship. 3547
Day of wrath. 1514, 3202
day of wrath and other sermons. 1561
Day of Yahweh. 2114

Day office of the monastic breviary. 3415
Day star of salvation. 3198
Day that changed the world. 1997
Day the cat jumped. 3321
Day they martyred the prophet. 3429
Day to day. 1456
Day to remember. 3384
Day unto day. 1434, 1435
Day with Jesus (A) 1985
Day with Jesus and Mary. 3248
Day with the Good Shepherd. 3200
Day with the Pope. 2852
Day with yoga. 3867
Day X. 1514
Dayananda Sarasvati, his life and ideas. 1407
Daybreak in Korea. 2536, 2537
Daybreak in Livingstonia. 2498
... Daybreak in the Dark continent. 11
Daybreak in the soul. 2880
Daykeeper, the life and discourse of an Ixil diviner. 1930, 2182
Daylight. 1431
Daylight materilization and psychic power. 2372
Daylight must come. 3249, 3407
Days aglow. 2389
Days and customs of all faiths. 1407
Days and the nights. 856, 3843
Days and ways. 1614, 1623
Days before Christmas. 8
Days before Easter. 2209
Days demanding courage. 990
Day's end. 902
Days in an Indian monastery. 2570
Days of awe. 1623
Days of Christ's coming. 2023
Days of delusion. 10, 2467
Days of destiny. 3382
Days of glory. 2029
Days of heaven on earth. 1442
Days of heaven upon earth. 1442
Days of His flesh. 1954
Days of hope and promise. 776, 3633
Days of humiliation, times of affliction and disaster. 1342
Days of joy. 2006
Days of June. 2512
Days of Martin Luther King, Jr. 2172
Days of my years. 3016, 3094, 3249
Days of Noah and their prophetic message for today. 1513
Days of our life. 1454
Days of our pilgrimage. 2847
Days of our years, 1812-1962. 3611
Days of Pentecost. 2813
Days of sorrow and pain. 125, 3016
Days of the Lord. 1264, 1265
Days of the upright. 1852
Days of the week. 1407
Days to remember. 2721
Days with Albert Schweitzer. 3311
Day's worship. 2297
Dayspring. 1433
Daystar. 2597
Daystar at midnight. 3350
Dayuma story. 1407, 2517
Dazzling darkness. 2868
De apostolatu laicorum. 754
De archana deorum. 2416
... De beata vita. 1785
De civiate Dei. 113
De civitate Dei. 113, 2173
De consensv evangelistarvm libri qvattvor. 387
De contemptu mundi, 1488? 2576
De deis gentium. 3215
De divina releatione. 3226
De divina revelatione. 3226
De ecclesia. 1124
De ecclesia in mundo huius temporis. 1154
De ecclesia; the Constitution on the Church of Vatican Council II proclaimed by Pope Paul VI, November 21, 1964. 1124
De educatione Christiana. 3159
De gestis Concilii Basiliensis commentariorum. 177
De gestis Concilii Basiliensis commentariorum: libri II; edited and translated [from the Latin]. 177
De haeresibus of Saint Augustine. 1805
... De immortalitate animae. 1886
De incarnatione of Athanasius. 1894
De incarnatione Verbi Dei. 1893
De kolonie. 1024
De La Salle. 695, 2189
De lapsis. 1166
... De libero arbitro (libri tres) 1657
De ordine. 1295
... De quantitate animae. 3461
De-Romanization of the American Catholic Church. 828, 829, 874
De Romanorum precationibus. 2887
(De sacerdotio) of St. John Chrysostom. 1295

De sacramentis in genere. 3265
De sacramento altaris. 2252
De sacramento altaris of William of Ockham. 2252
De sapientia veterum. 2660
Deacon and his ministry. 92, 1408
Deacon and the Jewess. 54
Deacon at work. 1408
Deacon in a changing church. 1408
Deacon in search of identity. 1408
Deacon in the Church; past time and future. 1408
Deacon problem solved. 1408
Deacon wore spats. 1291, 3746
... Deaconess. 1408
Deaconess and her work. 1408
... Deaconesses. 1408
Deaconesses in Europe and their lessons for America. 1408
Deacon's life and his wife. 1239
Deaconship. 1239, 2741
Dead. 3502, 3503
Dead and the living and other sermons. 3340
Dead do not talk. 3511
Dead men tell tales. 515
Dead or alive. 1116, 2214
Dead or alive, a series of sermons for Lent and Easter. 2214
Dead Sea community. 1410, 3014
Dead Sea community: its origin and teachings. 1411, 3014
Dead Sea Isaiah scroll: a literary analysis. 544
Dead Sea manual of discipline. 2080
Dead Sea Psalms scroll. 1409
Dead Sea scriptures. 1409
Dead Sea scrolls. 1409, 1410, 1411, 3013, 3014, 3710
Dead Sea scrolls, 1947-1969. 1411
Dead Sea scrolls, a preliminary survey. 1410
Dead Sea scrolls and modern scholarship. 1411
Dead Sea scrolls and original Christianity. 1410
Dead Sea scrolls and primitive Christianity. 1409, 1411
Dead Sea scrolls and the Bible. 1409, 1410
Dead Sea scrolls and the Christian faith. 1410
Dead Sea scrolls and the early church. 1410
Dead Sea scrolls and the living church. 1410
Dead Sea scrolls and the New Testament. 1411
Dead Sea scrolls and the originality of Christ. 1102, 1410
Dead Sea scrolls and the origins of Christianity. 1409
Dead Sea scrolls. English. 1411
Dead Sea scrolls in English. 1409
Dead stones with living messages. 206
Deadly magic. 2313
Dealing squarely with God. 2941
Dealing with conflict. 2435, 3352
Dealing with death—a Christian perspective. 1413
Dealing with double-mindedness. 1418
Dealing with doubt. 62
Dealing with the devil. 1427
Dealings of God. 1477, 1478
Dealings with the dead. 3511
Dean Church. 1246
Dean Inge. 1907
Dean Stanley with the children. 907, 3525
Dear Agnos. 64
Dear atoms. 2717
Dear Bishop. 1136
Dear Bob. 3671
Dear Charles. 3674
Dear daughter, letters from Eve and other women of the Bible. 3839
Dear Dawn, Dear Dad. 3877
Dear Ellen. 1287
Dear Father. 771
Dear Father in heaven. 899
Dear feast of Lent. 2211
Dear Fiyon. 2881
Dear Frances. 3844
Dear Georgia. 988, 3528
Dear gift of life. 1415
Dear God. 3843
Dear God, where are you? 2435
Dear Jesus. 2717
Dear Jesus ... I'm so human. 986
Dear Jesus, love Sandy. 3885
Dear land of home. 680
Dear Lord. 3883
Dear Lynn, I have a problem. 3879
Dear Margaret. 156
Dear Mr. Brown. 1058
'Dear Mom. 2541
Dear newlyweds. 2344
Dear ones at home. 2508

Dear parents. 2106
Dear Pastor. 1011
Dear Philippine. 1481
Dear Seminarian. 3331
Dear shut-in. 3405
Dear Sister. 2580
Dear Superniki Purple. 980
Dear Tim. 3661
Dear Vonda Kay. 3881
Dearest Debbie. 897, 3243
Dearest Debbie: In Ai Lee. 897, 3243
Dearest Kate. 3877
Dearest mother. 3520
Dearly beloved. 1266
Death. 1413, 1414, 1415, 1416
Death; a book of preparation and
    consolation. 1416
Death, a vision. 1416
Death, afterlife, and eschatology. 3140
... Death--and after? 195, 1531
Death--and afterwards. 1412
Death & beyond. 1695, 1698
Death and beyond in the Eastern
    perspective. 173, 1414
Death and birth of the parish. 2791
Death and creativity. 1413
Death and dying. 1418
Death and Eastern thought. 1416
Death and eternal life. 1695, 1696
Death and hope. 1415
Death and immortality. 1414
Death and judgement. 1415
Death and life. 1353, 1415, 1416, 1887
Death and life of Bishop Pike. 2846
Death and life of Malcolm X. 669, 2233
Death and ministry. 1415
Death and reincarnation: eternity's voyage.
    1416
Death and resurrection. 1695, 1837
Death and resurrection of Christ. 1747,
    1998
Death and resurrection of Jesus Christ.
    2030
Death and the after-life. 3499
Death and the afterlife in pre-Columbian
    America. 1904
Death & the caring community. 2782
Death and the Christian. 3264
Death and the Christian answer. 1414
Death and the Devil. 1413
Death and the enlightenment. 1416
Death and the future state. 1697
Death and the hereafter. 1226
Death and the life beyond. 1414
Death and the life hereafter. 1794
Death, and then what? 1414
Death and Western thought. 1413
Death as a speculative theme in religious,
    scientific, and social thought. 1415
Death as an enemy according to ancient
    Egyptian conceptions. 1530
Death as departure. 420, 1998
Death-blow to spiritualism. 2162, 3499,
    3520
Death by bread alone. 2396
Death by decision. 1544
Death by enchantment. 3823
Death Christ died. 105
Death comes dancing. 3304, 3482
Death comes home. 191
Death, dying, and grief. 1416
Death, dying, and the biological revolution.
    3604
Death education. 1418
Death, grief, and bereavement. 1416
Death, hell and judgment. 1531
Death in American experience. 1415
Death in disguise. 3594
Death in every now. 1414, 3019
Death in other words. 1415
Death in the city. 1063
Death in the family. 191
Death in the pot. 1620
Death in the secular city. 1412
Death into life. 1697
Death is a noun. 1417
Death is all right. 1417
Death is my parish. 2620
Death is no dead end. 1352
Death—Jesus made it all different. 1415
Death loses the game. 146
Death; meaning and mortality in Christian
    thought and contemporary culture. 1413
Death not life. 48
Death not life: or. 48
Death of a Christian. 840
Death of a church. 3735
Death of a dogma? 663
Death of a guru. 1365, 2317
Death of a myth. 2548
Death of a nation. 547
Death of Abel. 723
Death of Abel, in five books. 724
Death of Adam. 1582
Death of Adam and of non-intelligent
    animals. 1602, 2042
Death of Cain. 723

Death of Christ. 104, 105, 1633, 1997,
    3029
Death of Christ at Calvary. 1940
Death of classical paganism. 3246
Death of death. 1699
Death of death in the death of Christ.
    3030
Death of God. 3327
Death of God controversy. 28, 1417
Death of God debate. 1417
Death-of-God movement. 1417
Death of Jesus. 1102, 2029
Death of man. 1417
Death of Mary, Queen of Scots. 2353
Death of the custodian. 1376
Death of Virgin Mary. 2354
Death row chaplain. 885
Death shall have no dominion. 1416
Death, the gate of life? 2635, 2987
Death -- the gateway to life. 1891
Death: the glorious adventure. 1413
Death, the meaning and result. 3519
Death, the riddle and the mystery. 1414
Death-thorn. 1904
Death trails in Bolivia. 1413
Death unveiled. 3502
Death vanquished. 324
Deathbed observations by physicians and
    nurses. 1418
Deathless book. 199, 209
Deathless preacher. 1343
Deaths duell. 1226, 1418
Debatable land between this world and the
    next. 3510
Debate about the Bible. 276
Debate between Judge Ben Lindsey and G.
    C. Brewer on "Companionate marriage."
    2338
Debate between Rev. A. Campbell and
    Rev. N. L. Rice, on the action, subject,
    design and administrator of Christian
    baptism. 1462
Debate between W. L. Oliphant ... and
    Charles Smith. 1725
Debate held at Lena, Ind., May 24, 25 and
    26, 1892. 3290
Debate on Christian baptism, between Mr.
    John Walker, a minister of the secession,
    and Alexander Campbell. 1905
Debate on spiritualism between Moses
    Hull (representing spiritualism) and Eld.
    W. R. Covert (representing Christianity)
    3505
Debate on the destiny of the wicked.
    3753
Debate on the doctrines of atonement,
    universal salvation, and endless
    punishment. 3753
Debate on universalism. 3753, 3754
Debate on Universalism and the
    resurrection of the dead, between Rev.
    John Hughes...and Eld. John R. Daily.
    3752
Debates and proceedings of the National
    council of Congregational churches.
    2670
Debates that made history. 732
Debbie in dreamland. 1615
Debbie in dreamland, her holiday
    adventures. 1615
Debonaire disciple. 1011
Deborah. 1418
Deborah, the woman who saved Israel.
    1418
Debs, dolls & dope. 1255
Debt and grace. 3053
Debt and grace, as related to the doctrine
    of a future life. 1696
Debtors monitor, directory & comforter:
    or, The way to get & keep out of debt.
    3343
Decade of objective progress in church
    unity, 1927-1936. 1044
Decade of the best. 2607
... The decadence of Christianity and its
    cause. 1655
Decadence of the orthodox church. 2751
Decades of Henry Bullinger. 3049
Decalogue in a new key. 1315
Decalogues for our day. 1325
Decapolis. 1565
Decay of czarism. 185, 3240
Decay of modern preaching. 2903
Decay of the Church of Rome. 809
Deceptions and myths of the Bible. 233,
    1091
Deceptions of anti-Semitism. 2077
Decet meminisse fratrum. 1290
Decide for yourself. 279, 3663
Decide to love. 980
Decides. 2013
Deciding for myself. 3171
Deciding voice of the monuments in
    Biblical criticism. 515
Decimon Huydas, a romance of Mars.
    3517
Decision and destiny. 213

Decision and the condition of man. 1418
Decision at dawn. 2821
Decision; church, teacher's introduction
    with idea-lines. 3181
Decision in crisis. 1094
Decision in paradise. 1497
Decision maker. 1064
Decision-makers. 1200
Decision making and the Bible. 275, 1418
Decision making and the will of God.
    1740
Decisions. 949, 1314
Decisions, decisions. 275, 942, 1418
Decisions for successful living. 3887
Decisions in philosophy of religion. 3107
Decisive battles of the Bible. 558
Decisive days in social and religious
    progress. 3448
Decisive hour of Christian missions. 2521
Declamations and dialogues. 3026
Declamations and dialogues for the
    Sunday-school. 3026
Declaration and address for today. 733
Declaration of dependence. 2721, 3793
Declaration of faith. 2921
Declaration of interdependence; the church
    and the churches. 1124
Declaration of the faith professed in the
    Palatinate. 3044
Declaration of the Lord's own religion--
    church--nation or, for short, Renation
    with His real peace. 3058

Declaration on certain questions
    concerning sexual ethics. 777, 3392
Declaration on religious freedom of
    Vatican Council II. 3193
Declaration on the relation of the Church
    to non-Christian religions. 3773
Declarations on the rule of our holy father
    St. Benedict. 190
Declare his glory among the nations. 2515
Decline and fall of radical Catholicism.
    811, 827
Decline and fall of the Hebrew Kingdoms.
    484, 498, 2093
Decline and fall of the Roman church.
    778, 2768
Decline and revival of the social Gospel.
    1139
Decline and revival of the social gospel;
    social and political liberalism in
    American Protestant churches, 1920-
    1940. 1139
Decline in American democracy. 3087
Decline of hell. 1802
Decline of nations. 1319
Decline of the Medieval Church. 1185,
    1186
Decline of the medieval Cistercian
    laybrotherhood. 1276
Decline of the sacred in industrial society.
    3085
Decoded New Testament, authorized
    version. 445, 1731
Decoding the Rabbis. 18, 1920
Decolonizing theology. 669
Decomposition of Catholicism. 811, 1245
Deconstruction and theology. 3618
...The decorative arts in the service of the
    church. 921
Decree on ecumenism of the Second
    Vatican Council. 860
Decree on priestly training. 3773
Decree on the pastoral office of bishops in
    the church. 665, 808
Decree on the renewal of religious life of
    Vatican Council II. 2571
Decree on the renewal of religious life of
    Vatican Council II promulgated by Pope
    Paul VI, October 28, 1965. 2571
Dedicated. 2712
Dedicated poverty: its history and
    theology. 2866
Dedicated to you for meaningful living.
    1323
Dedication. 3210
Dedication and blessing of the Church of
    St. Benedict and Convent of St.
    Benedict's Parish, Throggs Neck, Bronx,
    New York. 188
Dedication, April 13, 1958. 3274
Dedication Ceremonies, April 29, 1956.
    3274
Dedication of Rollins chapel and Wilson
    hall. Dartmouth college, June, 24, 1885.
    1403
Dedication of St. Aloysius Church,
    Leonardtown, Maryland, March 18,
    1962. 2216
Dedication of the new buildings of the
    Union theological seminary in the city of
    New York, November 27, 28 and 29,
    1910. 3612

Dedication of the restored Old First
    church of Bennington. 191
Dedication Service, Sunday, March 22,
    1959. 1459
Dedication services. 1419
Dedication services for all occasions. 1419
Dedication, what it's all about. 982
Dedications and patron saints of English
    churches. 919
Dedicatory services at the Publishing
    house of the A. M. E. church Sunday
    school union, Nashville, Tenn. 15
Dedicatory services of the new edifice of
    the Third Presbyterian church, of
    Pittsburgh, Penn'a. 2918
Deeds and rules in Christian ethics. 945
Deeds done for Christ. 925
Deeds of Christ. 1985
Deeds of daring. 2484
Deeds of faith. 866
Deeds of gods and heroes. 2651
Deeds of the Franks and the other pilgrims
    to Jerusalem. 1391
Deep furrows. 1321
Deep in the heart. 1133
Deep is the hunger. 1453
Deep Mende. 2402
Deep river. 2680
Deep river and The Negro spiritual speaks
    of life and death. 2680
Deep roots. 2400
Deep-sea canoe. 2543
Deep South. 724, 2955, 3468
Deep the roots of hope. 2536, 3309
Deep things of God. 1093, 1447, 3624
Deepening the spiritual life. 959
Deeper Christian life. 970
Deeper experiences of famous Christians.
    1586
Deeper faith. 1596
Deeper into John's Gospel. 421
Deeper Life. 2641
Deeper life for you. 1557
Deeper meaning of stewardship. 3530
Deeper mysteries. 3685
Deeper voice. 3095
Deeper yet. 2387
Defeat of death, and other sermons. 2930
Defeat of fear. 3353
Defeat of the bird god. 2812, 3891
Defeat triumphant. 54
Defeating despair & depression. 1425,
    2713
Defects of the Negro church. 16
Defence, not defiance. 2144
Defence of a book lately re-printed at
    Boston, entitled, A modest proof of the
    order and government settled by Christ
    and his apostles in the church. 1522
Defence of Armageddon. 3225
Defence of Catholic principles. 786, 787
Defence of Christianity. 59, 1517
Defence of dramatick poetry. 1309, 3607
Defence of modern spiritualism. 3517
Defence of "Our fathers", and of the
    original organization of the Methodist
    Episcopal church, against the Rev.
    Alexander McCaine, and others. 2305,
    2376, 2442, 2450
Defence of "our fathers", and of the
    original organization of the Methodist
    Episcopal church, against the Rev.
    Alexander M'Caine and others. 2376,
    2450
Defence of plays. 1309, 3606
Defence of Professor Briggs before the
    Presbytery of New York. 2922
Defence of Professor Briggs before the
    Presbytery of New York, December 13,
    14, 15, 19, and 22, 1892. 692
Defence of religious liberty. 3492
Defence of the Catholic faith concerning
    the satisfaction of Christ. 108
... A defence of the Christian religion.
    1092, 1714
Defence of the Church of England against
    disestablishment. 1221
Defence of the dialogue intitled, A display
    of God's special grace. 1458
Defence of the doings of the reverend
    Consociation and association of New-
    Haven county. 1336, 3240
Defence of the episcopal government of
    the church. 1522, 3801
Defence of the Gospel in the New
    Testament. 69, 475
Defence of the Observations on the charter
    and conduct of the Society for the
    propagation of the gospel in foreign parts
    against an anonymous pamphlet. 734,
    3437
Defence of the Old Testament. 2758
Defence of the principles of the "Summer-
    morning's conversation concerning the
    doctrine of original sin." 1285, 3413
Defence of the Protestant Bible. 217,
    3259

Defence of the Short view of the profaneness and immorality of the English stage. 1345, 3605
Defence of the sincere and true translations of the Holy Scriptures into the English tongue. 270, 2348
Defence of the Trinitarian system. 3714
Defence of theological ethics. 946
Defender of peace. 1141
Defender of the faith. 2617, 3240
Defenders of our faith. 765
...The defenders of the faith. 69
Defense and a refuge. 1232
Defense of Biblical infallibility. 277
Defense of Christian perfection. 2627, 2818
Defense of Galileo. 1700, 3084
Defense of St. Augustine. 115, 3331
Defense of the Answer to Mr. Whiston's suspicions. 3810
Defense of the Bible against the charges of modern infidelity. 60
... The defense of the Catholic church. 785, 1963
Defense of the faith. 57
Defense of the unity of the church. 1803, 3039
Defense rests its case. 63
Defense to Galileo of Thomas Campanella. 1701, 3084
Defensorium obedientiae apostolicae et alia documenta. 2862
Deferred revolution. 826, 1245
Defining America. 3743
Definite signs of this age closing. 3319
Definition of good. 1745
Defrost your frozen assets. 961
Degrees of Jewish benevolence. 887
Degrees of the zodiac. 96
DeHoff's Bible handbook. 645
... The deification of abstract ideas in Roman literature and inscriptions. 3245
Deification of Alexander the Great. 24, 77
Deification of Man. 2319
Deism; an anthology. 1420
Deism and natural religion. 1420
Deism in eighteenth century America. 1419, 1420
Deist's manual, 1705. 1420
Deist's reply to the alleged supernatural evidences of Christianity. 1656
Deity analyzed. 100
Deity and law. 2614
Deity and morality. 3070
Deity of Christ. 9, 2002
Deity of Christ, and other sermons. 3049
Deity of Christ, briefly considered. 2000, 3711
Deity of Jesus, and other sermons. 1466, 2000
Deity of Jesus Christ according to the Gospel of John. 424, 2001
Deity of Jesus Christ essential to the Christian religion. 2002
Delight in the Lord. 9
Delights of life. 1446
Delights of wisdom concerning conjugial love. 2340
Delights of wisdom pertaining to conjugial love. 2340
Delilah. 482
Delineation of Roman Catholicism, drawn from the authentic and acknowledged standards of the Church of Rome. 799
Delinquent saints. 1337
Deliver us from evil. 2246, 3540
Deliver us from fear. 983
Deliverance. 1939
Deliverance book. 1585
Deliverance from fear and from sickness. 2410
Deliverance from the penalty and power of sin. 3411
Deliverance of Sister Cecilia. 2717
Deliverance prayer. 2882
Deliverance to the captives. 2942
Delivered unto Satan. 1583, 3050
Delphi: sanctuary and museum. 1421
Delphic oracle. 1421, 2740
Delphic oracle, its responses and operations, with a catalogue of responses. 1421
Delta Ministry. 1132, 1421
Deluge. 1421, 1422
Deluge and its cause. 1421
Deluge story in stone. 1421
Demand and the supply of increased efficiency in the Negro ministry. 16
Demand for Christ, addresses and sermons. 3338
Demands for Chirstian renewal. 2481
Demands of discipleship. 3334
Demands of freedom. 1088
"The demands of Rome," 3416
Demands on ministry today. 1288
Demaundes of the Holy Scripture. 3670
Demeter and Persephone. 2822

De-miracleized Bible. 198
Democracy and Catholicism in America. 1151
Democracy and civilization. 1818
Democracy and the church. 1422, 3446
Democracy and the churches. 1075, 1086
Democracy can succeed-how? 1134
Democracy in the church. 1240
Democracy is self-government. 3686
Democracy of Methodism. 1422
Democratic Christianity. 1422
Democratic church. 807
Democratic living. 3434
Democratic manifesto. 1422
Democratic methodism in America. 2459
Democratic movement in Asia. 2502
Democratic opinions and experience. 1422
Democratization of the church. 1241
Demon bowler and other talks to schoolboys. 908
Demon of Padeng. 1366, 1850
Demon possession. 1424
Demoniality. 1423
Demonic possession. 1423
Demonolatry. 1423
Demonologist. 1424, 3796
Demonology or spiritualism. 3504
Demonology, past and present. 1423
Demonosophy unmasked in modern theosophy; whence? what? whither? 3687
Demons. 1423
Demons and tongues. 1423, 2848
Demons, demons, demons. 1078
Demons, devils, and djinn. 1424
Demons have had it. 3665
Demons in the world today. 1423
Demon's notebook. 1423
Demons, yes—but thank God for good angels. 1428
Demonstrating Christ. 3249
Demonstration of the truth and divinity of the Christian religion. 59
Demonstration of the truth of that discipline, which Christ hath prescribed in His word, for the government of His church, in all times and places, until the end of the world. 1241
Demythologizing and history. 347, 1818
Denehy's Catholic directory of clergymen and institutions in the New England states. 823
Denial of death. 1412, 2169
Denigration of capitalism. 1074
Dennis C. Benson's Recycle catalogue. 3679
Denomination looks at itself. 30
Denominational policies in the support and supervision of higher education. 1129
Denominational policies in the support of supervision of higher education. 1128
Denominational schools. 1130
Denominational society. 3744
Denominationalism. 3327
Denominations -- how we got them. 3323
Departed gods. 1542
Departed Lord. 1952
Department of pastoral care. 1259
Department supervisor. 3557
... Departmental teachers' manual for the elementary school. 3176
Departmentally graded vacation Bible school textbooks. 3765
Departure. 1655
Departure ceremonies. 1647
Departure ceremonies for Franciscan missionaries. 1647
Deposition of a disciple. 1009, 1232
Depth discipleship. 3492
Depth of God. 1726
Depth perspectives in pastoral work. 2781
Derelict saint and other sermons. 1467
Desatir. 1918
Descending light. 3496
Descent into darkness. 825
Descent into hell. 1055
Descent of the Dove. 1181
Description of the Church of the Holy Apostles at Constantinople. 1929
Descriptive catalogue of books on missions and mission lands. 2481
Descriptive catalogue of fourteen illuminated manuscripts, nos. xcv to cvii and 79a. 2330
Descriptive catalogue of genizah fragments in Philadelphia. 2331
Descriptive catalogue of Greek New Testament manuscripts in America. 315
Descriptive catalogue of New Church books and tracts, American and foreign. 2689, 3571
Descriptive catalogue of seventeenth-century English religious literature in the Kansas State University Library. 3203
Descriptive catalogue of seventeenth century English religious literature in the Kansas State University library. 3203

Descriptive catalogue of the Book of common prayer and related material in the collection of James R. Page. 1214
Descriptive catalogue of the Hebrew mas. of the Montefiore library. 2331
Descriptive catalogue of the library of the Sunday-school attached to the First Ref. Dutch church. 3549
Descriptive catalogue of the McClean collection of manuscripts in the Fitzwilliam museum. 2330
Descriptive catalogue of the Milton Collection in the Alexander Turnbull Library, Wellington, New Zealand. 2469
Descriptive catalogue of the publications of the Presbyterian board of publication. 3627
Descriptive catalogue of the publicatons of the Presbyterian board of publication. 3627
Descriptive catalogue of the second series of fifty manuscripts (nos. 51 to 100) 2330
Descriptive catalogue of twenty illuminated manuscripts, nos. LXXV to XCIV. 2330
Descriptive exhibition of four prophetical horses. 2949
... The desecration and violation of churches. 3272
Desecration of Christ. 84
Deseret's sons of toil. 1131, 1230
Desert and the city. 3522
Desert Bible: nomadic tribal culture and Old Testament interpretation. 183, 498
Desert calling. 1635
Desert Christian. 1019
Desert democracy. 2092
Desert Fathers. 3282
Desert in the city. 3485
Desert is fertile. 3435
Desert padre. 2177
Desert pilgrim. 723
Desert saints. 2615
Desert wisdom. 1008
Desiderii Erasmi Roterodami Colloquia familiaria nonnulla selecta. 1525
Desiderius Erasmus of Rotterdam. 1525
Design for a journey. 1165
Design for a just society. 3449
Design for adult education in the church. 3168
Design for Christian education. 1246, 3731
Design for Christian living. 2932
Design for church growth. 1170
Design for dedication. 2593
Design for destiny. 2729
Design for discipleship. 987
Design for evangelism. 1565
Design for family living. 1604
Design for good living. 968
Design for happiness. 3336
... A design for living. 1060, 1324, 2140, 3336
Design for personal living. 3887
Design for religion. 805, 935
Design for teaching-learning. 3162
Design in "Christ and Christmas" 1496
Design of baptism. 134
Design of Darien. 1403
Design of my world. 44, 1362, 1419
Design of the Scriptures. 651
Designed for duty. 1449
Designed for worship. 1169
Designing a theological education by extension program. 3332
Designing education in values. 3870
Designing the sermon. 2903
... Designs and drawings. 2244
... Designs by Sir Chr. Wren for Westminster abbey. 79, 2589
Designs for Christian living. 967
Designs for monuments. 3333
Designs for parish churches. 1158
Designs for progress. 3449
Designs upon the trestleboard. 1666
Desirable government. 1939
Desire and the universe. 3064
Desire body. 3250
Desire of ages. 1955, 1974
Desire of all nations. 2521
Desires of a religious man. 2250
Desk drawer devotions. 1436
Despair; a moment or a way of life? 1426
Despair and hope for our time. 1154
Destination—Green Hell. 1802
Destination life. 3384
Destination Palestine. 1584
Destined to overcome. 981
Destiny. 1615
Destiny and disappointment. 3739
Destiny bible. 95
Destiny for Congregationalism. 1335
Destiny of a king. 2664
Destiny of America, with an appendix. 46
Destiny of Britain and America, with an appendix. 46

Destiny of man. 1534
Destiny of man viewed in the light of his origin. 1887
Destiny of man viewed in the light on his origin. 1887
Destiny of modern woman in the light of papal teaching. 3836
Destiny of the nations. 2723
Destiny of the soul. 1694, 1698, 3460
Destiny of the species, and other messages. 165
Destiny of the warrior. 1807
Destroyer of Jesus. 84
Destruction of the kingdom. 2093
... A desultory examination of the reply of the Rev. W. V. Harold to a Catholic layman's rejoinder. 1786, 2830
Det Nya Testamentet of War Harre och Fralsare Iesus Christus. 320
Detached branch, the olive branch of peace. 1035, 1495
Detailed planning. 1157
Detente and Papal-Communist relations, 1962-1978. 860, 1542
Deterioration of the Puritan stock and its causes. 1419
Determined to live. 1215
Detroit Industrial Mission. 1131, 1426
Deus destroyed. 1101
Deus est caritas. 771
Deus homo: God-man. 2042
Deus-semper. 3105
Deus visibilis. 1739
Deutero-Isaiah. 543, 545
Deuteronomium 1:1-6:3 literarkritisch und traditionsgeschichtlich untersucht. 511
... Deuteronomy. 509, 510, 511
Deuteronomy, a favored book of Jesus. 510
... Deuteronomy and Joshua. 510
Deuteronomy and the Decalogue. 510
Deuteronomy and tradition. 511
Deuteronomy, Jeremiah. 510
Deuteronomy: the gospel of love. 510
Deutscher Katholizismus. 818
... The devachanic plane. 3686
Devaraja cult. 1426
Devastated vineyard. 793
Devata. 1743
Development of the Sunday-school. 3561
Developing a Christian mind. 61
Developing a giving church. 952
Developing Christian education in the smaller church. 934
Developing Christian personality. 1015
Developing Christian personality and building a Christian society. 3871
Developing dynamic stewardship. 3531
Developing human community. 1134
Developing moral-spiritual values in the schools. 2590
Developing skills for church leaders. 954
Developing spiritually sensitive children. 902
... Development. 1580
Development and purpose. 1580
Development hypothesis. 1580
Development of a curriculum of religious education. 3152
... Development of a religious inventory for a specific study in higher education. 3537
Development of Chinese Zen after the Sixth Patriarch in the light of Mumonkan. 1853
Development of Christian doctrine. 1473
Development of Christian worship. 840
Development of Christianity. 1178
Development of Christianity in the Latin Caribbean. 2559
Development of doctrine in the church. 1473
... The development of doctrine in the Epistles. 378
Development of English theology in the later nineteenth century. 1760
Development of English theology in the nineteenth century. 1760
Development of first Presbyterian Church of Cuero. 1392
Development of fundamental theology. 3628
Development of Jewish religious thought i the inter-testamental period. 2829
Development of Kant's view of ethics. 2164
Development of mediumship. 3515
Development of Methodism in the old Southwest. 2453
Development of Methodism in the old Southwest, 1783-1824. 2432
Development of modern Catholicism. 45
Development of modern Christianity since 1500. 1187
... Development of Muslim theology. 256

Development of Muslim theology, jurisprudence and constitutional theory. 1922
Development of Negro religion. 2682
Development of Neo-Confucian thought. 2683, 1330
Development of personality. 804
Development of religion. 2998, 3109
Development of religion and thought in ancient Egypt. 1501, 1502
... The development of religion in Japan. 1936
Development of religious liberty in Connecticut. 1346
Development of religious toleration in England. 1759, 1760
Development of religious toleration in England from the accession of James I to the convention of the Long parliament (1603-1640) 1758
Development of St. Augustine, from Neoplatonism to Christianity, 386-391 A.D. 114
Development of social ideas among the Disciples of Christ. 1138, 1460
Development of the Canaanite dialects. 733
Development of the early Christian church. 327, 1196
Development of the idea of God in the Catholic child. 904
Development of the missionary and philanthropic interest among the Mennonites of North America. 2404
Development of the papacy. 2769
Development of the social thought of Walter Rauschenbusch. 3025, 3440
Development of the understanding of the Mass in children in Catholic schools. 2370
.. The development of the United church of northern India. 3732
Development of the young people's movement. 1247
Development of theology in Germany since Kant. 3617
Development of theology in Germany since Kant and its progress in Great Britain since 1825. 3617
Development of trinitarian doctrine in the Nicene and Athanasian creeds. 3711
Developmental disabilities. 2411
Device. 276
Devil. 1427, 1428, 1429
Devil and all his works. 2730
Devil and God. 1428
Devil and I. 977
Devil and Mr. Smith. 3304, 3427
Devil and the Jews. 53
Devil at my heels. 1362
Devil at the wheel. 1359, 2824
Devil, demonology, and witchcraft. 1423
Devil did not make me do it. 1585
Devil in Britain and America. 1426, 1427, 3826
Devil in legend and literature. 1428
Devil in Massachusetts. 3827
Devil in modern society. 1428, 1429
The devil in robes" 3411
Devil in Scotland. 1427
. The devil in the church. 802
Devil-puzzlers and other studies. 1429
Devil, seven wormwoods, and God. 66
Devil unmasked. 958, 1427
Devil-ution. 827
Devil worship. 1429
Devil, you say? 1423
Devilish but true. 2988
Devils. 1428, 1429
Devils and demons. 1424
Devils and evil spirits of Babylonia. 1892
Devil's bride. 1585
Devil's diary. 1427, 1428
Devil's dominion. 1428
Devil's dropout. 1360, 3415
Devil's empire. 51, 605
Devil's greatest counterfeit. 800
Devils of Loudun. 1422, 1756
Devil's picturebook. 3588
Devil's pulpit. 3023
Devil's repertoire. 103
Devil's shadow. 3827
Devil's share. 1428
Devil's work. 1428
Devolution in mission administration. 2492
Devotedly yours. 2848
Devotion. 1446
Devotion to Mary is the 20th century. 2359
Devotion to Our Lady. 2359
Devotion to the Sacred Heart: object, ends, practice, motives. 3270
Devotion to the Sacred heart of Jesus. 3270

Devotional aids for the chamber of sickness. 3406
Devotional, alphabetical indexed family Bible. 636
Devotional Bible. 445
Devotional Bible studies. 1841
Devotional classics. 1445, 1455
Devotional commentary on Philippians. 448
Devotional commentary on the Acts of the apostles. 329
Devotional commentary on the Bible. 224
Devotional commentary on the Gospel of St. John. 222
Devotional commentary on the Gospel of St. Matthew. 440
Devotional exercises. 1437
Devotional exercises for the use of Jewish women, on public and domestic occasions. 1443
Devotional guide to Bible lands. 178, 283, 1928
Devotional guide to John. 422
Devotional guide to Luke. 430
Devotional guidebook for board and committee chairpersons. 1298
Devotional interpretation of familiar hymns. 1871
Devotional introduction to Job. 548
Devotional introductions. 1454
Devotional leadership. 3854
Devotional life of the Sunday school teacher. 1450
Devotional life of the Sunday-school worker. 1445
Devotional life of young people. 3884
...Devotional offerings. 1445
... Devotional offices for general use. 1442
Devotional passages from the Hindu Bible. 1454
Devotional poems. 1445
Devotional poems for First-day schools. 1446
Devotional prayers for personal and family use. 1605
Devotional programs about people and places. 3856
Devotional programs for every month. 1439
Devotional programs for special days and occasions. 1264, 1448
Devotional programs for the changing seasons. 3856
Devotional programs for women's groups. 2399, 3857
Devotional programs for young adults. 1445
Devotional readings for use in schools. 1446
Devotional readings from Luther's works for every day of the year. 1449
Devotional selection. 2392
Devotional selections. 2392
Devotional somnium. 2890
Devotional studies in Galatians and Ephesians. 380
Devotional studies in Philippians. 449
... Devotional studies in St. John's Gospel. 423
Devotional studies in the Epistle to the Hebrews. 403
Devotional studies of Old Testament types. 3721
Devotional talks for children. 906
Devotional talks for women's organizations. 1448
Devotional talks from familiar things. 1842
Devotional talks on everyday objects. 1439
Devotional thoughts for youth. 3882
Devotional thoughts from the Holy Land. 2389
Devotional treasury from the early church. 1447
... The devotional use of the Bible. 613
Devotionals by a physician. 241
Devotionals for modern men. 2402
Devotionals for nurses. 1449
Devotionals for today's women. 3842
Devotionals on flowers of the Bible. 1454
Devotionals on trees of the Bible. 1454
Devotionarie book of John Evelyn of Wotton, 1620-1706. 2259
Devotions, a family affair. 1610
Devotions and dialogs for women. 1452, 3857
Devotions and prayers. 1436, 2297, 2889
Devotions and prayers for the sick room. 2892, 3406
Devotions and prayers of John Wesley. 2434
Devotions for adult groups. 1438
Devotions for boys and girls. 902
Devotions for children. 902
Devotions for church groups. 3047, 3359

Devotions for church school teachers. 3550
Devotions for dieters. 1459
Devotions for dynamic living. 1443
Devotions for every day. 1434
Devotions for everyday. 1434
Devotions for families. 365, 1606
Devotions for families: fruit of the spirit. 1606
Devotions for junior highs. 898
Devotions for juniors. 901
Devotions for Lutheran schools. 3310
Devotions for personal and group renewal. 1438
Devotions for the children's hour. 902
Devotions for the home. 2388
Devotions for the middle years. 2461
Devotions for the sick room, and for times of trouble. 3406
Devotions for the single set. 3415
Devotions for women at home. 3843
Devotions for women's groups. 3842
Devotions for young teens. 3882
Devotions for your family. 437, 1604
Devotions for youth. 3883
Devotions from a grateful heart. 992
Devotions from around the world for women. 3842
Devotions in honor of Saint Teresa of Jesus. 3603
Devotions in honor of the Infant Jesus. 2237
Devotions upon emergent occasions. 2386
Devotions with a difference. 3882
Devotions with Julie and Jack. 1450
Devout Christian's vade-mecum. 856, 937
Devout exercises of the heart, in meditation and soliloquy, prayer and praise. 1441
Devout exercises of the heart in meditation and soliloquy, prayer and praise. 1441
Devout humanism as a style. 1650, 1854
Devout life. 2387
Devout soldier. 718
Dew drops from the rifted clouds. 3094
... Dew on Jordan. 3326
Dews of Tabor. 1434
Dhahr Mirzbaneh tombs. 78
Dhamapada. 701
Dhamma of Gotama the Buddha and the gospel of Jesus the Christ. 700
Dhammapada. 701, 704, 711, 2193
Dharma. 1457
Dharma, or The religion of enlightenment. 701
Diabolic root. 1420
Diabolical possession and exorcism. 1422
... Diabolology. 1427
Diaconate—a full and equal order. 1408
... The diaconate according to the apostolic tradition of Hippolytus and derived documents. 773, 1816
Diaconate now. 1408
Diagnosing the rural church. 3254
Diagnosing to-day. 2589
Diagnosis of man. 2473, 2474
Diagrams for living. 233, 1323
Diakka, and their earthly victims. 3499
Dial 911. 3027, 3780
Dialectic in practical religion. 3110
Dialectic materialism. 2209, 3234
Dialectical aspects in Buddhist thought. 703
Dialectical Christianity and Christian materialism. 1457
Dialog mass, a book for priests and teachers of religion. 2365
Dialogic style in preaching. 2906
Dialogue. 2646
Dialogue and destiny. 1590
Dialogue and tradition. 2094, 2153
Dialogue at Calvary. 2057
Dialogue between a minister and his neighbour, about the Lord's supper. 2252
Dialogue between a tutor and his pupil, 1768. 1419
Dialogue between Christians: Catholic contributions to ecumenism. 1043
Dialogue between theology and psychology. 2997
... A dialogue concerning witches and witchcrafts. 3823
Dialogue for reunion. 1042
Dialogue gap. 1062
Dialogue in despair. 548, 2780
Dialogue in medicine and theology. 2377
Dialogue in the desert. 2067
Dialogue of Christians and Jews. 1084
Dialogue of comfort against tribulation. 1351, 1352
...The dialogue of Palladius. 1115
Dialogue of religions. 3120
Dialogue on church and state; unabridged addresses. 1150
Dialogue on destiny. 1527
Dialogue on the way. 3770

Dialogue preaching. 1458
Dialogue, the key to understanding other religions. 1080
Dialogue; the state of the church today. 811
Dialogue with death. 1414
Dialogue with God. 2868
Dialogue with God, being a series of studies on the principle of prayer in human life. 2871
Dialogue with myself. 758
Dialogue with the other. 1675
Dialogues. 189, 760, 3284
Dialogues and ideologues. 811, 1245
Dialogues and recitations. 3026
Dialogues concerning natural religion. 2673, 2674, 2676
Dialogues concerning natural religion and the posthumous essays, Of the immortality of the soul and Of suicide. 2674
Dialogues concerning natural religion; edited with introduction. 2672
Dialogues, letters, and essays, on various subjects. 3643
... The Dialogues of Athanasius and Zacchacus and of Timothy and Aquila. 1083
Dialogues of creatures moralised. 1588
Dialogues of devils. 1014
Dialogues of G. de Purucker. 3687
Dialogues of Gregory the Great. 189
Dialogues of Plato. 2853
Dialogues of the Buddha. 705
Dialogues on morality and religion. 1534
Dialogues on the supersensual life. 956
Dialogues with God. 2893
Diamond crown for Christ the King. 3421
"Diamond-diggers and their mine" 635
Diamond in the dust. 1372
Diamond Jubilee, 1881-1956, Assumption Church. 93
... Diamond Jubilee, 1847-1922, of the diocese of Galveston and St. Mary's cathedral. 1701
Diamond Jubilee of St. Alphonsus Church, 1882-1957. 3272
Diamond jubilee of the consecration of the Chapel of the Immaculate Conception. 1407
Diamond jubilee of the General association of colored Baptists in Kentucky. 154
Diamond jubilee, St. Martin parish, 5870 Princeton, Chicago, Ill. 893
Diamond light. 2193
Diamond shield. 2263
Diamondola. 91, 2558
Diamonds from Daniel. 506
Diamonds in the rough. 3206
Diamonds, persimmons, and stars. 3353
Dianetics and scientology technical dictionary. 3314
Dianetics, the original thesis. 1458
Diaries and correspondence of David Cargill, 1832-1843. 739, 2487
Diaries, prayers and annals. 2304
Diario: the journal of Padre Serra. 2506
Diary. 3535, 3590
Diary and visitation record of the Rt. Rev. Francis Patrick Kenrick. 2167
Diary of a circuit rider. 1467
Diary of a country parson. 1292, 3846
Diary of a country parson, 1758-1802. 1292, 3846
Diary of a country priest. 807
Diary of a deacon. 1408
Diary of a dean. 751
Diary of a disciple. 1976
Diary of A. J. Tomlinson. 1229, 1230
Diary of a mystic. 2640
Diary of a nun. 2582
Diary of a parish priest. 774
Diary of a psychic. 2988
Diary of a saint. 3279
Diary of a spiritualist. 3512
Diary of a warrior king. 2661
Diary of a widow. 1412
Diary of a witch. 3824
Diary of an exile nun. 1357
Diary of an old soul. 1432
Diary of, and poems. 3137, 3144
Diary of another Ann. 3786
Diary of Charles L. Walker. 2618, 3789
Diary of daily prayer. 2894
Diary of Erasmus Smit. 3135, 3143
Diary of Fra Junipero Serra, O.F.M. 2506
Diary of Isaac Backus. 123, 1300
Diary of Jean Evarts. 3135
... The diary of John Comer. 159
Diary of John Young, S.T.P. 3819
Diary of Kenneth A. MacRae. 1300, 2310
Diary of Mata Hari. 3138, 3144
Diary of meditations. 1431
Diary of Michael Wigglesworth, 1653-1657. 3815
Diary of Peter Parson pseud. 1070
Diary of prayer. 1431, 2027, 2894

DIARY OF PRAYERS
RELIGIOUS BOOKS 1876 - 1982

Diary of prayers, personal and public. 2889
Diary of private prayer. 2888
Diary of Ralph Josselin 1616-1683. 1292, 2135
Diary of readings. 1436
Diary of Richard L. Burtsell, priest of New York. 719, 1294
Diary of Robert Rose. 1302, 3249
Diary of some religious exercises and experience. 3191
Diary of the Holy Spirit. 1438
Diary of Thomas Robbins, D. D., 1796-1854. 3133, 3143
Diary of William Bentley, D. D. 3286
Diary of William Plumer Jacobs. 1931
Diatessaron. 1988
Diatessaron of Tatian and the synoptic problem. 3589
Diatribe and Paul's letter to the Romans. 471, 3234
Dick Gregory's Bible tales, with commentary. 318
Dick Sheppard and St. Martin's. 3402, 3809
Dictes and sayings of the philosophers. 1894, 2832
Dictionary catalog of the Missionary Research Library, New York. 2504, 2698
Dictionary catalogue of the Byzantine collection of the Dumbarton Oaks Research Library, Washington, D.C. 721, 1482
Dictionary, concordance, and collation of Scriptures in The Bible companion. 225
Dictionary-index. 778
Dictionary of all religious and religious denominations. 3091
Dictionary of all scriptures and myths. 3574
Dictionary of American religious biography. 3124
Dictionary of angels, including the fallen angels. 43
Dictionary of astrology. 98
Dictionary of Bible proper names. 245
Dictionary of Bible topics. 243
Dictionary of Biblical theology. 244, 3639
Dictionary of Buddhism. 705, 709
Dictionary of canon law. 736
Dictionary of Catholic biography. 765, 3703
Dictionary of Chinese mythology. 2655
Dictionary of Christ and Gospels. 243
Dictionary of Christ and the Gospels. 243
Dictionary of Christian antiquities. 919
Dictionary of Christian biography, literature, sects and doctrines. 926
Dictionary of Christian ethics. 950
Dictionary of Christian theology. 3639
Dictionary of church music. 1206
Dictionary of church terms and symbols. 3638
Dictionary of classical antiquities, mythology, religion, literature [and] art. 1286
...A dictionary of classical mythology. 2657, 2659
Dictionary of comparative religion. 3138
Dictionary of Congregational usages and principles. 1344
Dictionary of Congregational usages and principles according to ancient and modern authors. 1344
Dictionary of correspondence, representatives, and significatives, derived from the Word of the Lord. 3571
Dictionary of correspondences, representatives, and significatives. 1370, 3570, 3571
Dictionary of demonology. 1424
Dictionary of early Buddhist monastic terms based on Pali literature. 3779
Dictionary of ecclesiastical terms. 3092, 3639
Dictionary of English church history. 1221
Dictionary of esoteric words. 3092
Dictionary of Greek and Roman mythology. 2657
Dictionary of hymnology. 1862
Dictionary of illustrations. 1840
Dictionary of illustrations for pulpit and platform. 1839
Dictionary of important names, objects, and terms, found in the Holy Scriptures. 244, 245
Dictionary of Islam. 1922, 1924
Dictionary of life in Bible times. 209
Dictionary of liturgical Latin. 843
Dictionary of liturgy and worship. 2236
Dictionary of magic. 2314
Dictionary of Mary. 2359
Dictionary of miracles. 2476, 2477
Dictionary of miracles, imitative, realistic, and dogmatic. 2478
Dictionary of modern theological German. 3639
Dictionary of moral theology. 950
Dictionary of mysticism. 3092
Dictionary of mythology. 2659
Dictionary of mythology, mainly classical. 2658
Dictionary of New Testament Greek synonyms. 1771
Dictionary of non-Christian religions. 3138
Dictionary of Orthodox theology. 2745
Dictionary of pagan religions. 3138
Dictionary of papal pronouncements, Leo XIII to Pius xii, 1878-1957. 2771
Dictionary of pastoral psychology. 2995
Dictionary of phrase and fable. 1588
Dictionary of proper names and places in the Bible. 480
Dictionary of Protestant church music. 1209
Dictionary of religion. 3637
Dictionary of religion and ethics. 3092
Dictionary of religious knowledge, for popular and professional use. 3637
Dictionary of religious terms. 3092
Dictionary of saints. 1025, 3283
Dictionary of Satanism. 2731
Dictionary of scholastic philosophy. 3309
Dictionary of scientific illustrations and symbols, moral truths mirrored in scientific facts. 3314
Dictionary of sects, heresies, ecclesiastical parties, and schools of religious thought. 3637
Dictionary of spiritualism. 3520
Dictionary of symbols and imagery. 3574
Dictionary of symbols, attributes, and associations in classical mythology. 2657
Dictionary of the American hierarchy. 829
Dictionary of the American hierarchy, 1789-1964. 3244
Dictionary of the apostolic church. 244
Dictionary of the Bible. 243, 244, 246
Dictionary of the Bible, comprising its antiquities, biography, geography, and natural history. 246
Dictionary of the Bible dealing with its language. 244
Dictionary of the Biblical Gothic language. 284, 1749
Dictionary of the Book of Mormon. 680, 2598
Dictionary of the Bulgate New Testament. 425
Dictionary of the Council. 3774
Dictionary of the Eastern Orthodox Church. 2745
Dictionary of the Episcopal Church. 2963
Dictionary of the Episcopal Church, compiled from various authentic sources. 2963
Dictionary of the Holy Bible. 245, 246
Dictionary of the Holy Bible, for general use in the study of the Scriptures. 245
Dictionary of the Jewish religion. 2085, 2146
Dictionary of the most important names, objects, and terms, found in the Holy Scriptures. 245
Dictionary of the New Latin Psalter of Pope Pius XII. 584
Dictionary of the New Testament. 352
Dictionary of the occult and paranormal. 2731
Dictionary of the Psalter. 848
Dictionary of the tarot. 3588
Dictionary of theology. 779, 3637, 3639
Dictionary of world mythology. 2658
Dictum of reason on man's immortality. 1888
Did Christ really live! 67, 2009
Did Genesis man conquer space? 526, 2854
Did God make the devil? 1428, 1729
Did I say thanks? 1756
Did I say that? 788
Did Jesus change? 1995
Did Jesus command immersion? 135, 137
Did Jesus go to church, and 51 other children's sermons. 907
Did Jesus live 100 B.C.? 2013, 3703
Did Jesus mean it? 3334
Did Jesus really live? 2008
Did Jesus rise? 2051
Did Jesus rise from the dead? 2052, 2053
Did Jesus write this book? 491, 1520
Did man just happen? 202, 3077
Did man make God; or, Did God make man. 1723, 1907
Did Paul know of the virgin birth? 2796, 3780
Did the early church baptize infants? 139
Did the Jews kill Jesus? 1997
Did the light go out? 798
Did you receive the Spirit? 2815
Didascalia apostolorum. 1239
Diderot's treatment of the Christian religion in the Encyclopedie. 1458, 1513
Die Psalmen des koniglichen Propheten Davids mit einer einleitung von W. G. Marigold. 583
Diegesis. 3024
Dies irae. 1458
Dietrich Bonhoeffer. 677
Dietrich Bonhoeffer; man of vision, man of courage. 676
Dietrich Bonhoeffer: reality and resistance. 677
Dietrich Bonhoeffer, theologian of reality. 676
Dieu des athees. 101
Difference between the present and former days. 512
Difference Christ is making. 1957
Difference God makes. 983
Difference in being a Christian. 944
Difference in being a Christian today. 991
Difference that Jesus makes. 2040
Differences between old and new school Presbyterians. 2914
Different dream. 2712
Different drum. 3139
Different drums. 1329, 3426
Different heaven and earth. 3835
Different kind of gentleman. 1291
Different New Testament views of Jesus. 1987, 2012
Difficult Bible questions answered. 218
Difficult commandment. 889
Difficult sayings of Jesus. 2071
Difficult star. 1936, 3437
Difficulties for Christian belief. 3651
Difficulties in Christian belief. 64, 65
Difficulties in mental prayer. 2379
Difficulties in religious thinking. 3211
Difficulties in the way of discipleship. 71
Difficulties of becoming the Living ECK Master. 1490
Difficulties of infidelity. 57, 59, 60
Difficulties of Romanism. 799
Difficulty of being Christian. 2170
Diffusion of Sufi ideas in the West. 3543
Diffusion of the Reformation in southwestern Germany, 1518-1534. 3041
Diffusions. 3068
Digest. 2928
Digest and index of the minutes of the General Synod of the Reformed Church in America, 1958-1977. 3045
Digest for Christ' s parables for preacher, teacher, and student. 2772
Digest of Catholic mission history. 851
Digest of Christian theology. 3643
Digest of Christian thinking. 3618
Digest of constitutional and synodical legislation of the Reformed church in America. 3045
Digest of masonic law and usage. 2364
Digest of Methodist law. 2440, 2450
Digest of minutes of meetings 1931-1965. 1335
Digest of regulations and rubrics of Catholic Church music. 1205
Digest of rulings and decisions of the bishops of the African Methodist Episcopal church. 14
Digest of St. Augustine's City of God. 2173
Digest of studies and lectures in theology. 3644
Digest of the acts and deliverances of the General assembly of the Presbyterian church in the United States of America. 2922
Digest of the acts and proceedings of the General Assembly of the Presbyterian Church in the United States. 2922
Digest of the acts and proceedings of the General assembly of the Presbyterian church in the United States. 2922
Digest of the Bible, the authorized version condensed for easy reading. 296
Digest of the canons for the government of the Protestant Episcopal church in the United States of America. 2966
Digest of the canons for the government of the Protestant Episcopal church in the United States of America, passed and adopted in general conventions. 2966
Digest of the canons for the government of the Protestant Episcopal Church in the United States of America, passed and adopted in the General Conventions of 1859, 1862, and 1865, together with the Constitution. 2966
Digest of the decisions and legislation of the Grand lodge, Grand encampment and Rebekah assembly of the Independent order of Odd fellows of Colorado, from their organization to 1904. 3205
Digest of the decisions of the Grand lodge of the Independent order of odd fellows of the state of Michigan. 3205
Digest of the divine law. 203
Digest of the Grand lodge, I.O.O.F. 3205
Digest of the laws of the I.O.O.F. for Illinois. 3205
Digest of the laws of the Independent order of Odd fellows of the state of Pennsylvania. 3205
Digest of the laws of the order of Knights of Pythias in the state of Pennsylvania. 3205
Digest of the principal deliverances of the General assembly of the United Presbyterian church of North America. 3736
Digest of the proceedings, laws, decisions and enactments of the Grand lodge of Nebraska. 3205
Digest of the proceedings of the conventions and councils in the diocese of Virginia. 2974
Diggers for facts. 207, 208
Digging up Biblical history. 2760
Digging up the Bible. 487, 2764
Digging up the Bible lands. 209, 1583
Dignitarian way. 3141
"Dignitas decani" of St. Patrick's Cathedral, Dublin. 1481
... Dignity and duties of the priest; or, Selva. 772
Dignity and duty of the civil magistrate. 1504
Dignity & exploitation. 3391
Dignity and happiness of marriage. 2344
Dignity of life. 2589
Dignity of man. 1094
Dignity of man as shown in his creation, redemption and eternal destiny. 2321
Dignity of the despised of the earth. 1131
Dignity of the human person. 2319
Dignity of the undefeated & other sermons suggested. 1341
Dilemma. 1423
Dilemma of church and state. 1142
Dilemma of contemporary theology. 3622
Dilemma of contemporary theology prefigured in Luther, Pascal, Kierkegaard, Nietzsche. 3622
Dilemma of modern belief. 3327
Dilemma of Protestantism. 2976
Dilemma of religious knowledge. 3056
Dilemmas and decisions. 3890
Dilemmas of contemporary religion. 3067
Dilemmas of euthanasia. 1544
Dilemmas of Jesus. 1956
Dilemmas of tomorrow's world. 1136
Diligently compared. 513
Diluvium. 1421
Dimension of depth. 166
Dimension of future in our faith. 1529
Dimensions beyond the known. 2727
Dimensions for happening. 643, 3180
Dimensions in religious education. 3620
Dimensions in salvation. 3381
Dimensions of authority in the religious life. 2581
Dimensions of belief and unbelief. 1590
Dimensions of Christian writing. 3203
Dimensions of dying and rebirth. 1698
Dimensions of faith. 1601, 3651
Dimensions of human sexuality. 3391
Dimensions of Jewish existence today. 2145
Dimensions of Job. 549
Dimensions of life. 1008
Dimensions of love. 2266
Dimensions of love, East and West. 2263
Dimensions of man. 3091
Dimensions of mind. 2474
Dimensions of prayer. 2880
Dimensions of spirituality. 1846
Dimensions of the church. 1118
Dimensions of the future. 3593
Dimensions of the priesthood: theological, Christological, liturgical, ecclesial, apostolic, Marian. 774, 2789
Dimly burning wicks. 2397
Din dan don, it's Christmas. 742
... Dinabandhu. 1895
DIO, "dictionary of illustrations and outlines." 1840
... Diocesan archives. 1459
Diocesan clergy. 771
Diocesan consultors. 1355
Diocesan pastoral council. 1459
Diocesan priest. 1299
Diocesan priest saints. 3280
Diocesan service book. 2722
Diocese and Presbytery of Dunkeld, 1660-1689. 1482
Diocese of California. 2958
Diocese of Louisiana. 2970
Diocese of Rochester, 1868-1968. 3242
Diocese of Western New York. 2975

Dionysiac mysteries of the Hellenistic and Roman age. 1459
... Dionysius, the Areopagite. 1460
... Dionysius, the Areopagite, on the Divine names and the Mystical theology. 1460
Dionysos and immortality. 1460
Dionysos; archetypal image of the indestructable life. 1459
Dionysos slain. 1459
Dionysus. 1459
Dionysus, myth and cult. 1460
Diplomacy and dogmatism. 1826, 2403
Diplomacy and God. 1913
Diplomatic studies in Latin and Greek documents from the Carolingian Age. 1372, 1882, 2225
Direct and fundamental proofs of the Christian religion. 1089
Directed survey and visitation evangelism. 1566
Directing boys and students; retreats, mediations, conferences. 3223
Directing the learner. 3179
Direction and destiny. 1006
Direction in prayer. 2880
Direction of conscience. 2781
Direction of nuns. 2572
Directional signals. 3380
Directions. 1013
Directions and helps. 1408, 2454, 3669
Directions and helps for the first[-fourth] year. 2449, 3669
Directions for living. 1316, 2933
Directives to lay apostles. 754
Director of Catholic facilities for exceptional children in the United States. 831
Director of Christian education in the local church. 1460
Director of religious education. 1460, 3154
Directorium sponsae. 2574
Directory. 707, 1946, 3205, 3727
Directory and calendar of prayer. 2559
Directory and calendar of prayer. 1961/62. 3732
Directory and church register ... Fairview Presbyterian church, Glen Moore, Pa. 2915
Directory and manual of the First Baptist church. 143
Directory and statistics of the Moravian Church in America. 2594
Directory of American Catholic theologians. 3611
Directory of Catholic charities in the United States. 887
... The Directory of Catholic clergymen, New England (province of Boston), New York, New Jersey and Detroit dioceses. 823
Directory of Catholic clubs, Holy name societies, Catholic clergy and institutions of Greater New York for. 830
Directory of Catholic colleges and schools. 831, 832
Directory of Catholic facilities for exceptional children in the United States. 831, 897
Directory of Catholic special facilities and programs in the United States for handicapped children and adults. 831
Directory of centers for the study of society. 93
... A directory of ceremonial. 1224
Directory of church and synagogue libraries in Maryland. 2224
Directory of church libraries. 2224
Directory of churches and other religious organizations in metropolitan Detroit. 1426
Directory of churches and other religious organizations in metropolitian Detroit. 1426
Directory of churches in Chicago and suburbs. 893
Directory of counseling centers for priests and religious in the United States 1973. 1374
Directory of fellowship awards for the Rockerfeller Brothers Theological Fellowship Program, the Rockefeller Doctoral Program, the Protestant Fellowship Program. 1497
Directory of foreign mission boards, societies, colleges, cooperative councils, and other agencies of the Protestant churches of the world. 2522
Directory of gospel missions in the United States of America. 2528
Directory of independent Catholic churches. 1894
Directory of Jewish archival institutions. 79, 2083
Directory of Lutheran agencies and institutions. 2284

Directory of ministry of the undenominational fellowship of Christian churches and Churches of Christ. 1272
Directory of missionary agencies in North America. 2522
Directory of Protestant medical missions, compiled by Arthur W. March [research associate]. 1848
Directory of religious archival and historical depositories in America. 1962. 1243
Directory of religious bodies in the United States. 3748
Directory of religious organizations in the United States of America. 3749
Directory of Sabbath-observing groups. 3260
Directory of the Armenian Church in North America. 82
Directory of the Augustinians in the United States, Province of St. Thomas of Villanova. 111
Directory of the churches of Chapel Hill, North Carolina. 885
Directory of the devout life. 969
Directory of the Nazarene churches in Australia, British Isles, Canada, Mexico, and the United States. 1237
Directory of the occult. 2731
... Directory of the religious press of the United States ...[3d ed.]. 3205
Directory, Universalist churches and ministers. 3755
Disestablishment of the Church of Ireland in 1869. 1918
Disadvantaged early adolescent. 3592
Disappearance of Aimee Semple McPherson. 2310

Discern these times. 607
Discerning God's will. 2194
... Discerning the Lord's body. 2253
Discerning the signs of the times. 3758
Discerning the spirit. 2570
Discerning the times. 1154
Discerning the way. 3649
Discernment. 1460
Discernment of spirits, according to the life and teachings of St. Ignatius of Loyola. 2269, 3492
Discernment of vocations. 3785
Disciple. 987, 1093
Disciple and his Lord. 1967
Disciple assemblies of eastern North Carolina, by Wm. Joseph Barber. 1465
Disciple down under. 1102
Disciple in prison. 1359, 2129
Disciple of Plato. 2854
Disciple preaching in the first generation. 1461, 2910
Disciple thought. 1460
Disciple thought: a history. 1463
Disciple winners. 1569
Discipler's manual. 968
Disciples. 71, 1460
Disciples and prophets. 239, 2572
Disciples and religious education. 1463
Disciples and the Church universal. 1045
Disciples are made-not born. 984
Disciple's commentary on the New Testament. 344
Disciples in action. 330
Disciples in Canada. 1462
Disciples in Christ's school. 1463
Disciples in Kentucky. 1464
...The Disciples of Christ. 1464
Disciples of Christ in Argentina, 1906-1956. 1461
Disciples of Christ in Georgia. 1463
Disciples of Christ in Indiana. 1464
Disciples of Christ in Jamaica, 1858-1958. 1464
Disciples of Christ in Kentucky. 1464
Disciples of Christ in Missouri. 1465
Disciples of Christ in Texas. 1467
Disciples of Jesus. 1006
Disciples of the Way. 435, 995
Disciples of the wise. 2155, 3016
Disciples' prayer. 2247
Disciple's profile of Jesus. 430
Disciples to such a Lord. 432
Discipleship. 985, 990, 2004, 2754
Discipleship and priesthood. 2938
Discipleship for the 70's. 1008
Discipleship in the new age. 2723
Disciplinary, moral, and ascetical works. 3635
Discipline. 1226
Discipline and integration in the Catholic college. 2409
Discipline of Genesee Yearly meeting of Friends. 1679
Discipline of sorrow. 1350
Discipline of the Church of God. 1228
Discipline of the Evangelical Methodist Church. 1549

Discipline of the Evangelical United Brethren Church. 1550, 3731
Discipline of the Metropolitan church assn. of Wisconsin. 3144
Discipline of the religious Society of Friends of Ohio Yearly Meeting. 1680
Discipline of the Society of Friends of Indiana Yearly Meeting. 1680
Discipline of the Yearly meeting of Friends. 1680
Discipline of the Yearly Meeting of Friends, held in New-York. 1680
Discipline Study Committee. 2405
Discipline, the glad surrender. 983
Disciplined by grace. 976
Disciplined heart. 1439
Disciplined life. 977
Disciplined life-style. 1074
Disciplines for life in the Age of Aquarius. 1008
Disciplines of liberty. 1063, 1072
Disciplines of life. 960
Disciplines of the beautiful woman. 3835
Disciplines of the Christian life. 1007
Disciplines of the high calling. 3672
Disciplines of the holy quest. 1115
Disciplines of the spirit. 1453
Disciplines of the spiritual life. 3482
Disciplines of the United brethren in Christ. 3730
Discipling of a nation. 2545
Discipling of Timothy. 2800, 3701
Discipling of West Cameroon. 145
Discipling the brother. 1166
Discipling the city. 1279
Discipling through theological education by extension. 3332
Disclosure of the ultimate. 2832
Disclosures of the universal mysteries. 2739
Discontented optimist. 2740
Discontinued L.D.S. periodicals. 1233, 2819
Discord, dialogue, and concord. 2282
Discours de la religion des anciens Romains illustre. 3246
Discourse. 378, 1477
Discourse about true happinesse. 1225, 3295
Discourse addressed to the alumni of the Princeton theological seminary, April 30, 1862. 3613
Discourse commemorative of Rev. Rufus Anderson, D.D., LL.D., late corresponding secretary of the American board of commissioners for foreign missions. 39, 1693
Discourse commemorative of the Reverend Talbot Wilson Chambers, S.T.D., LL.D. 881, 2698
Discourse concerning faith and fervency in prayer. 2875
Discourse concerning the church. 1125
Discourse concerning the divine providence. 2982
Discourse, concerning the inventions of men in the worship of God. 3003
Discourse concerning the maintenance due to those that preach the gospel. 3702
Discourse concerning the nature and design of the Lord's-supper. 2251
Discourse concerning the wonderfulness of Christ. 2047, 3359
Discourse considerations in Translating the Word of God. 184, 654
Discourse, delivered at Plymouth, December 22, 1820. 2847
Discourse delivered ... at the Church of the Annunciation, city of New York, on the 25th day of June, A. D., 1873, in memory of Samuel Seabury, D. D., presbyter of the diocese of New York, professor of Biblical learning and interpretation of Scripture in the General theological seminary. 3317
Discourse delivered at the funeral of Professor Moses Stuart. 1692, 3536
Discourse delivered at the one hundredth anniversary of the organization of the First Baptist church in North Stonington, September 20, 1843. 2714
Discourse delivered at the opening of the Synod of New Jersey in the First Presbyterian church of Elizabeth, N. J. 3318
Discourse delivered before His Excellency George N. Briggs, governor. 1504
Discourse delivered in the North Reformed Dutch church (Collegiate) in the city of New-York. 2698
Discourse in commemoration of Rev. William Parsons Lunt, D. D. 2272, 3726
Discourse in commemoration of the glorious reformation of the sixteenth century. 3035
Discourse in memory of Archibald Alexander Hodge. 1821

Discourse in memory of William Hague. 1780
Discourse of civill life. 1326
Discourse of free-thinking. 1309, 1654
Discourse of matters pertaining to religion. 2776, 3728
Discourse of natural theology. 2672
Discourse of reason. 3331
Discourse of the glory to which God hath called believers by Jesus Christ. 1342
Discourse of the grounds and reasons of the Christian religion. 588, 1091, 3810
Discourse on free will. 1658
Discourse on meekness, and quietness of spirit. 1856
Discourse on method. 1426
Discourse on psalmody. 2984, 2985
Discourse on religion. 3103
Discourse on sanctification versus Christian perfection. 2819
Discourse on the Christian union. 1338
Discourse on the incomprehensibleness of God. 1720
Discourse on the latest form of infidelity. 60
Discourse on the life and character of the Rev. Joseph Tuckerman, D. D. 3718
Discourse on the life and services of Professor Moses Stuart. 3536
Discourse on the nature and design of the eucharist, or sacrament of the Lord's supper. 2250
Discourse on the nature and subjects of Christian baptism. 135
Discourse on the nature, design, and institution, of the holy eucharist, commonly called the sacrament of the Lord's supper. 2250
Discourse on the official character of Nathanael Emmon. 1511, 1693
Discourse on the order and propriety of divine inspiration and revelation. 3396
Discourse on the traffic in spirituous liquors. 3596
Discourse on the true idea of the state as a religious institution, together with the family and the church, ordained of God. 3525
Discourse on theological education. 3680
Discourse on thinking. 2738
Discourse on true magnanimity addressed particularly to young men. 2315
Discourse, preached at the dedication of the Second Congregational Unitarian church. 3729
Discourse preached at the ordination of Mr. Robert C. Waterston. 3798
Discourse preached before the Second church and society in Boston. 3795
Discourse preached in the Center Church, in New Haven, August 27, 1828. 91, 2223
Discourse proving that the Christian religion is the only true religion. 2372
Discourse reviewing a ministry of fifty years. 1296
Discourse utter'd in part at Ammauskeeg-Falls in the fishing season, 1739. 36
Discourses. 2612, 3724, 3727
Discourses addressed to mixed congregations. 864, 3365
Discourses against Judaizing Christians. 2145
Discourses and addresses. 1911
Discourses and addresses at the ordination of the Rev. Theodore Dwight Woolsey, LL.D. 1911
Discourses and discussions in explanation and defence of Unitarianism. 3727
Discourses and dissertations on the scriptural doctrines of atonement & sacrifice. 105
Discourses and essays. 758, 881
Discourses and sayings. 90
Discourses and sayings of Our Lord Jesus Christ. 2062
Discourses and sermons for every Sunday and the principal festivals of the year. 863, 1266
Discourses,chiefly biographical, of persons eminent in sacred history. 2932
Discourses commemorative of the life and work of Charles Hodge. 1821
Discourses delivered extempore at several meeting houses of the people called Quakers. 1688
...Discourses from the spirit-world. 3519
Discourses of B. H. Roberts of the First Council of the Seventy. 2608
Discourses of Brigham Young. 2607, 2619
Discourses of Rev. Charles Backus, D. D. of Somers, Conn. on the Scripture doctrine of regeneration. 3050
Discourses of Rumi. 1455, 1926
Discourses of warre and single combat. 3793
Discourses of Wilford Woodruff. 2614

Discourses on Christian communion and baptism. 1304
Discourses on Christian doctrine. 3664
... Discourses on grace and the sacraments. 3264
Discourses on human nature. 1853
Discourses on intemperance. 3596
Discourses on miracles. 2477
Discourses on Our Lady. 864, 2362
Discourses on priesthood. 2939
Discourses on religious subjects. 1343, 3572
Discourses on Romanism and the reformation. 3034
Discourses on Scripture mysteries. 1218
Discourses on Scripture psalmody in praising God. 2633
Discourses on several important subjects. 3317, 3359
Discourses on several subjects. 3317, 3357
... Discourses on the Apostles creed. 75
Discourses on the apostolical succession. 76
Discourses on the beatitudes. 180
Discourses on the Christian spirit and life. 3727
Discourses on the credibility of the Scripture. 276
Discourses on the doctines of Christianity. 3727
Discourses on the doctrines of Chrisitanity. 3727
Discourses on the doctrines of Christianity. 3727
Discourses on the Epistle of Paul to the Philippians. 449
Discourses on the Holy Ghost. 1828, 2608
Discourses on the love of God. 1741
Discourses on the most important doctrines and duties of the Christian religion. 1775
Discourses on the nature, evidence, and moral value, of the doctrine of the Trinity. 3713
Discourses on the nature of faith. 1595
Discourses on the offices and character of Jesus Christ. 2045, 3726
Discourses on the parable of the sower. 3468
Discourses on the rectitude of human nature. 2322
Discourses on the scope and nature of university education, addressed to the Catholics of Dublin. 3756
Discourses on the temptations of Christ. 2067
Discourses on various important subjects, nearly concerning the great affair of the soul's eternal salvation. 1343
Discourses on various points of Christian doctrine and practice. 2930
Discourses, on various subjects. 3755
Discourses on various subjects and occasions. 1227
Discourses relating to the evidences of revealed religion. 1099
Discourses, reviews, and miscellanies. 3724
Discourses through the mediumship of Mrs. Cora L. V. Tappan. 3512
Discourses to the aged. 18
Discover life. 1313
Discover the power within you. 2062
Discover the word in print. 1317
Discover your destiny. 956
Discover your spiritual gift and use it. 1712
Discover yourself. 3864
Discovered country. 3517
Discoverie of witchcraft. 3824
Discoveries for peaceful living. 987
Discoveries made from living my new life. 1362
Discovering a Christian life-style. 989
Discovering an evangelical heritage. 1552
Discovering discipleship. 649, 995
Discovering freedom. 1659
Discovering God within. 2641
... Discovering how to live. 3149
Discovering how to pray. 2875
Discovering Jesus. 418, 1994
Discovering love. 2266
Discovering myself. 3880
... Discovering our church. 3183
Discovering the Bible. 313
Discovering the Bible, book by book. 312
Discovering the Biblical world. 293
Discovering the boy of Nazareth. 1996
Discovering the depths. 982
Discovering the holy fellowship. 3170
Discovering the joy of obedience. 2719
Discovering the lands of the Bible. 3765
Discovering the quality of success. 3539
Discovering the unshakeable through psalmists' eyes. 585
Discovering the world of the Bible. 2678

Discovering wayside treasures. 965
Discovering your real self. 2437, 3358
Discovery and correct philological analysis of the original human speech is the path to perception of an ideal earthly condition. 318
Discovery Bible handbook. 1008
Discovery in celebration. 3181
Discovery in drama. 934
Discovery in politics. 3186
Discovery in prayer. 2873
Discovery in song. 3886
Discovery in the Judean desert. 1411
Discovery in the press. 3434
Discovery in word. 3886
Discovery of a missing Chinese Torah scroll. 3704
Discovery of discoveries. 2990
Discovery of Genesis. 526, 1381
Discovery of God. 1727, 1735, 1740
Discovery of Noah's ark, final and decisive. 2711
Discovery of the church. 1465
Discovery of the East. 1485
Discovery of the self. 2753
Discovery of the soul. 3463
Discovery of the soul and the law of its development. 3462
Discovery patterns. 3181
Discretion and valour. 1108
Discussing death. 1413
Discussing religion creatively. 3146
Discussion. 2633
Discussion and program suggestions for adults on Latin America, based primarily on On this foundation. 2955
Discussion between Newton Peters, predestinarian Baptist ... and M. A. Peters, Universalist. 3754
Discussion guide for Consecrated unto me. 2081
Discussion: Is the Roman Catholic religion inimical to civil or religious liberty? 794, 3192
Discussion of the cause, character and operations of the creator. t. 1729
Discussion of the conjoint question. 3754
Discussion of the conjoint question, is the doctrine of endless punishment taught in the Bible? 3753
Discussion of the facts and philosophy of ancient and modern spiritualism. 3496
Discussion of the subject of Universalism, held in Laport, Lorain county, Ohio. 3752
Discussion on Methodist Episcopacy, between Rev. E. J. Hamill ... and Samuel Henderson. 2450
Discussion on revision of the holy oracles. 31
Discussion on the automatic powers of the brain. 183, 3513
Discussion on the order of the Sons of temperance. 3459
Discussion on the Trinity, church constitutions and disciplines, and human depravity. 3713
Discussion programs for junior highs. 3887
Discussion. Shall Christians go to war? 3792
Discussion starters for youth groups. 1467
Discussions and arguments on various subjects. 2703
Discussions and summaries of the third general assembly of workers with boys. 687
Discussions held in Lebanon, Pa., on Monday, Tuesday, and Wednesday, the 17th, 18th and 19th of October, 1842. 794
Discussions in history and theology. 3621
Discussions in theology. 3652
Discussions of theological questions. 3643
Discussions on the life of Jesus Christ. 1992
Discussions on the Styx. 3066
Disease and remedy of sin. 3411
Disestablishment in France. 1145
Disguises of the demonic. 1427
Disinherited daughter. 83
Disintegrating church. 1125
Disintegration of Islam. 2566
... The dismissal of religious in temporary vows. 3787
...Dispelling the spirtual gloom in South American forests and pampas. 2547
... Dispensation from private vows. 1467
Dispensational key to the Holy Scriptures. 643
Dispensational theology. 3640
Dispensational truth. 1723
Dispensationalism. 1376
Dispensationalism in America. 1467
Dispensationalism today. 1467
Dispensations and ages of Scripture. 1735

Dispensations of the eternal program of God. 1730
Display of God's special grace. 1753
Display of the religious principles of the Associate presbytery of Pennsylvania. 2922
Disputation and dialogue. 2152
Disputation on Holy Scripture. 238
Disputation on Holy Scripture, against the papists, especially Bellarmine and Stapleton. By William Whitaker ... Translated and edited for the Parker society, by the Rev. William Fitzgerald. 186, 217
Disputed doctrines. 2286
Disputed questions. 760, 1001, 3253
Disputed questions in education. 831
Disquisitions and notes on the Gospels. 438, 441
Dissent and reform in the early Middle Ages. 1804
Dissent in American religion. 3214
Dissent in and for the church. 785
Dissent in church and state. 1469
Dissent on Bonhoeffer. 676
Dissenter in a great society. 3749
Dissenter in Zion. 3756, 3757, 3897
Dissenters. 1469
Dissentient voice. 1023
Dissenting tradition. 740, 1469
Dissertation. 2049, 3720
Dissertation concerning liberty & necessity. 1658, 3807
Dissertation, historical and critical on the Christian ministry. 1295
Dissertation of the mysteries of the Cabiri. 723
Dissertation on Christian baptism. 136
Dissertation on miracles. 2478
Dissertation on native depravity. 3414
Dissertation on prophecies. 508
Dissertation on the coincidence between the priesthoods of Jesus Christ and Melchisedec. 2049
Dissertation on the marriage of a man with his sister in law. 2347
Dissertation on the nature and genius of the kingdom of Christ. 2174
Dissertation on the prophecies relative to Antichrist and the last times. 52, 509
Dissertation on the rule of faith. 118, 119
Dissertation on the Scriptural authority. 1906
Dissertation on the sixth vial. 462
Dissertation, wherein the strange doctrine lately published in a sermon. 2252
Dissertations on subjects connected with the incarnation. 1893
Dissertations on the character, death & resurrection of Jesus Christ, and the evidence of His gospel. 1994, 2758
Dissertations on the nature and effect of Christian baptism. 136
Dissertations on the prophecies. 607
Dissertations on the prophecies relative to the second coming of Jesus Christ. 605
Dissertations received and in progress including Th. D., D.R.E., Th. M., and M.C.M., April, 1962. 1469
Dissertations upon several fundamental articles of Christian theology. 3640
Dissertations upon various subjects. 3067, 3122
Dissident Eastern churches. 1487
Dissolution of the monasteries. 2579, 2584
Dissolution of the religious orders in Ireland under Henry VIII. 1803, 2582
Dissolution of the trio. 1655
Dissolving views in the history of Judaism. 2090
Distant grief. 1300, 3332
Distinction of the indistinguished. 2426
Distinctive customs and practices of the Moravian Church. 2594
Distinctive doctrines and customs of the Lutheran church. 2286
Distinctive doctrines and usages of the general bodies of the Evangelical Lutheran church in the United States. 1547, 2285
Distinctive emphases of Asbury Theological Seminary. 89
Distinctive emphasis of Asbury Theological Seminary. 3299
Distinctive ideas of Jesus. 1047, 2061
Distinctive ideas of the Old Testament. 599
Distinctive principles of Baptists. 148
Distinctive principles of the Presbyterian church in the United States. 3424
Distinctive teachings of the restoration. 2612
Distinctive translation of Genesis. 527
Distinctiveness of Christian ethics. 946

Distinguishing characteristics of Mary Baker Eddy's progressive revisions of Science and health. 1494
Distinguishing marks of a work of the Spirit of God. 1835
Distinguishing traits of Christian character. 976
Distressing days of the judges. 555, 2093

Distribution of Catholic priests in the United States, 1971. 829
District superintendent, asset or liability? 1470
District superintendent. 2440
Disturbed about man. 990
Disturbed by joy. 2301, 3358
Disturbing Christ. 405
Diuturnity. 3074
Divers orders of ministers. 1193
Diverse elements of religion. 3122
Diversity in holiness. 765
Diversity of Scripture. 651
Dives and pauper. 1315
Divided kingdom. 2093
Divided mind of modern theology, Karl Barth and Rudolf Bultmann, 1908-1933. 176, 3657
Divided people of God. 1045
Divided vision, Eugene O'Neill and Oriental thought. 2737, 2844
Divided we stand. 171, 1588
Dividing of Christendom. 3307
Dividing the people. 1939
Diviens. 393
Divination and the historical and allegorical sources of the I ching, the Chinese classic. 1470, 1879
Divination and the historical and allegorical sources of the I ching, the Chinese classic, or. 1470
Divine adventures. 3208
Divine and contingent order. 1383
Divine and human rights. 1151
Divine and moral songs. 910
Divine apostle. 373, 374
"Divine arithmetic" a subject long since forgotten. 3616
Divine armory of Holy Scripture. 304
Divine art of living. 125, 126, 128, 2228
Divine art of preaching. 2900, 2904
Divine authority of Holy Scripture asserted, from its adaptation to the real state of human nature, in eight sermons preached before the University of Oxford, in the year MDCCCXVII, at the lecture founded by the late Rev. John Bampton. 277
Divine authority of Paul's writings. 376
Divine authority of the Bible. 119
Divine being and other realities of the Scriptures. 3645
Divine birth. 137
Divine book of holy and eternal wisdom. 3394
Divine challenge. 551
Divine character vindicated. 183, 2322
Divine child is born. 3145
Divine collaborators. 1709
Divine comedy. 1402
Divine comedy of Dante Alighieri. 1402
Divine Comforter. 1831
Divine comforts. 1011
Divine command. 2200
Divine command morality. 1537
Divine commands and morality. 3070
Divine commission. 1181
Divine conquest. 3482
Divine constitution. 181
Divine Counsellor. 1452
Divine courtship. 1819
Divine covenants. 1377
Divine creation and perfection of man. 2321
Divine credentials of the Bible. 277
Divine creed. 1463
Divine crucible of purgatory. 3006
Divine descent. 1717, 1816
Divine destroyer. 1746
Divine dimension. 63
Divine direction or chaos? 1034
Divine disobedience: profiles in Catholic radicalism. 764, 1468
Divine dividends. 181
Divine drama. 565, 1738, 2095
... The divine drama of Job. 549
Divine economy. 2174
Divine educator. 2255
Divine election. 1504
Divine enchantment. 3207
Divine endowment. 1833
Divine Family. 3712
Divine flashes. 3544
Divine force in the life of the world. 1051
Divine Friend. 2007
Divine gift. 3145
Divine gift of mediumship. 3496

Divine grace. 1752
Divine grace and man. 1751
Divine guidance, that voice behind you. 982
Divine healing. 1598, 1599, 1600, 1792, 1793, 2409
Divine healing according to the Scriptures. 1600
Divine healing and health for soul, mind, and body through the merits and in the name of Jesus, the Christ. 1601
Divine healing mind, and faith cure. 1600
Divine healing of the body. 1598
Divine healing today. 1600
Divine healing under the lens. 1598
Divine healing under the searchlight. 1598
Divine helmsman. 239, 2983, 3408
Divine hierarchy. 1815
Divine-human encounter. 1457, 3709
...Divine-human society. 3453
Divine humanity. 2012
Divine humanness. 2279, 2325
Divine hymns. 1869
Divine hymns on the sufferings of Christ. 1865
Divine illumination. 3502
Divine image. 949
Divine impartiality. 375, 1733
Divine imperative. 942
Divine indwelling. 1886
Divine inspiration. 305, 1910
Divine inspiration of the Bible. 236, 306, 2849
Divine inspiration, psychic research of the great beyond. 2992
Divine inspiration vs. the documentary theory of the higher criticism. 306
Divine institutes, books I-VII. 69
Divine institution of preaching the gospel considered. 698
Divine intimacy. 1263
Divine intimacy; meditations on the interior life for everyday of the year. 1263
Divine invasion. 1727, 2215
Divine journey. 954, 3476
Divine judgment in human history. 2980
Divine key of the revelation of Jesus Christ. 458
Divine law and the Sabbath in all ages. 3261
Divine law applied. 203
Divine law as to wines. 3597
Divine law of beneficence. 952
Divine law of birth. 3393
Divine legacy. 2251
Divine legation of Moses demonstrated. 565, 1698
Divine library. 212
Divine library of the Old Testament. 500
Divine life. 107, 962, 1834
Divine life for the body. 1599
Divine liturgies of our holy fathers John Chrysostom and Basil the Great. 2749
Divine liturgy. 82, 766
Divine liturgy of our father among the saints, John Chrysostom, of the Holy Orthodox Catholic and Apostolic Church. 2748
Divine liturgy of St. Chrysostom of the Eastern Orthodox Church. 2749
Divine liturgy of St. John Chrysostom of the Eastern Orthodox Church. 2749
Divine liturgy of the Armenian Apostolic Orthodox Church. 82
Divine logos. 2242
Divine Lord and Saviour. 3290
Divine love and the possibilities of life. 3518
Divine love and wisdom. 2691
... The divine love story. 804
Divine luminous wisdom that dispels the darkness. 3479
Divine Man. 1960
Divine masterpieces. 765
Divine milieu. 1106
Divine minstrels. 1639
Divine mother. 2641
Divine mystery. 1064
Divine name and presence, the memra. 562, 2402
Divine names and attributes of animals. 47
Divine names in Mark. 435, 1736
Divine nescience of future contingencies a necessity. 1737
Divine office. 841, 842
Divine opportunity. 2426
Divine order and the immortalization of man. 1061
Divine order of degrees in man, exemplified in the order of the four Gospels. 399
Divine origin of Christianity, indicated by its historical effects. 1099

Divine origin of prophecy illustrated and defended in a course of sermons preached before the University of Oxford. 608
Divine origin of the Bible. 278
Divine pedigree of man. 3075
Divine penology. 1699
Divine perfection. 1732
Divine personality. 2838
Divine personality and human life. 2837
Divine Physician. 3407
Divine Physician; devotions for the sick. 3407
Divine pictures of the Christian centuries. 464
Divine pity. 181
Divine plan of man's salvation. 2435
Divine plan of the ages. 1940
Divine poems and essays. 3208
Divine politician. 1368
Divine power. 307
Divine praises. 855, 1826
Divine presence and guidance in Israelite traditions. 563, 2937
Divine principle. 3642
Divine principles. 2171, 3141
Divine priorities. 3353
Divine problem. 876
Divine program. 3029
Divine propagandist. 2062
Divine Providence. 2689, 2980, 2981, 3571
Divine providence and human destiny. 2980
Divine providence and human progress series. 3182
Divine providence and the problem of evil. 2980
Divine purpose. 2980
Divine purpose in us. 1009
Divine pymander, and other writings of Hermes Trismegistus. 2638
Divine pymander of Hermes Mercurius Trismegistus. 2638
Divine quest in music. 3072
Divine reason of the cross. 105
Divine relativity. 1722
Divine remedies. 1600
Divine residue. 238
Divine revelation and the limits of historical criticism. 3223
Divine revelations. 3503
Divine reward. 2190
Divine right of church government. 2915
Divine right of individuality in religion. 3192
Divine right of missions. 1321
Divine romance. 3401
Divine rule of faith and practice. 276
Divine Savior. 1952
Divine scheme. 72
Divine science. 1033, 1496, 3513
Divine science and healing. 1793
Divine science and metaphysics. 2418
Divine science and the science of God. 3070, 3697
Divine science discloses evil's impersonality. 1035
Divine seal. 1736
Divine selection. 3608
Divine Service. 1234, 2257, 2971, 3855
Divine soliloquies of Gerlac Petersen. 3489
Divine songs. 910
Divine songs attempted in easy language. 3799, 3899
Divine songs attempted in easy language for the use of children. 910
Divine songs of Zarathushtra. 3898
Divine sovereignty and human freedom. 1658
Divine sovereignty and human responsibility. 423, 2983
Divine sovereignty in the salvation, and damnation of sinners vindicated. 3357
Divine staircase. 1004, 1921
Divine story. 1981
Divine substance. 81, 3538
Divine synthesis. 829
Divine theory. 3648
Divine time table. 610
Divine tragedy. 2006
"Divine tragedy of the Christ." 2003
Divine transplant. 1007
Divine Trinity. 3712
Divine triunity. 3712
Divine twilight. 592, 627
Divine twins. 3719
Divine unfolding. 3029
Divine upliftings. 966
Divine vengeance. 3227, 3399
Divine vision. 3256, 3685
Divine warrior in early Israel. 3795
Divine wisdom. 600, 3408
Divine yes. 1007
Diviner. 1470
Diviner immanence. 1886

Diviners. 3144
Diving deep and surfacing. 3834
Divinity and experience. 1459
Divinity and man. 2321
Divinity as the eternal feminine. 3142
Divinity of Christ. 2000, 2001
Divinity of Christ in the Gospel of John. 420, 2001
Divinity of Jesus Christ. 2000, 2002, 3659
Divinity of Jesus Christ considered. 2002
Divinity of Jesus Christ scientifically stated. 2002, 2692
Divinity of marriage. 1609
Divinity of our Lord. 2000, 2038
Divinity of Our Lord and Savior Jesus Christ. 2001
Divinity of Our Lord and Saviour Jeses Christ. 2001
Divinity of Our Lord and Saviour, Jesus Christ. 2001
Divinity of the Roman emperor. 723, 1393, 1396
Divinity within us. 3483
Divinization of man according to Saint Hilary of Poitiers. 1812
Divinty of Our Lord and Saviour, Jesus Christ. 133, 2001
Division in the Protestant house. 3679, 3735
Divisions in the Society of Friends. 1685
Divorce, a Christian dilemma. 1471
Divorce and remarriage. 1471, 2339, 2342
Divorce and remarriage for Catholics? 2343
Divorce and remarriage in Anglicanism. 1471
Divorce and remarriage in the Catholic Church. 2344
Divorce and remarriage in the church. 1471
Divorce & the Christian. 1471
Divorce and the faithful church. 1471
Divorce and the gospel of grace. 1471
Divorce in the New Testament. 888, 2336
Divorce in the parsonage. 1291
Divorce problem fully discussed. 1471
Divorce, the church, and remarriage. 1471
Divorced and Christian. 1471
Divorced and separated Catholics. 1471
Divorced Catholic. 1471
Divus Julius. 723, 1512
DNA, RNA and the atom. 3073, 3082
Do a loving thing. 324, 2267
Do and tell: engagement evangelism in the '70s. 1564
Do be practical. 960
Do black patent-leather shoes really reflect up? 2866
Do both Bible Testaments harmonize. 450
Do dogmas change? 1473
Do fundamentalists play fair! 2562
Do I have to be me? 980
Do I really believe? 75
Do-it-yourself destiny. 1231, 3885
Do it yourself ...in devotions. 1455
Do-it- yourself retreat. 3223
Do Jehovah's Witnesses and the Bible agree? 1940
Do not sin against the cross. 108
Do not test us. 2992, 3789
Do religious claims make sense? 3098
Do the Bible and Christian science agree? 1033
Do the dead depart? 3495
Do the dead return? 3500, 3506
Do the dead still live? 1416
"Do they love us yet!" 3507
Do we know the others? 860
Do we live after death? 3054
Do we live again? 3500
Do we need a new idea of God? 1729
Do we need a new religion? 3104
Do we need Christ for communion with God? 2013
Do we need the church? 1187
Do we still need religion? 1063
Do you believe? 422, 3349
Do you believe in God? 66
Do you believe in miracles. 2475
Do you believe it? 3567
Do you ever have questions like these? 1734
Do you hear me, God? 2894
Do you know about angels? 43
Do you know Jesus? 903
Do you know who you are? 3883
Do you know your Bible! 218
Do you really know the Church? 764
Do you see what I see. 3479
Do you sometimes feel like a nobody. 3889
Do you understand the Bible? 288
Do you understand what you read? 234
... Do you want a Christian world? 2550
Do you want to be healed? 1598
Do you worry about the future? 2389

Do your prayers bounce off the ceiling? 2882
Do yourself a favor: love your wife. 2340
Do'a. 128
Dobbie, defender of Malta. 1472
Doctor Apricot of "Heaven-below." 2508
Doctor at Calvary. 1997
Dr. B. H. Carroll, the colossus of Baptist history, pastor First Baptist church, Waco, Texas, and first president of S. W. B. T. seminary, Fort Worth, Texas. 742
Dr. Balaam's talking mule. 2384
Dr. Becker's brownies rummaging among the mediums of modern spiritualism. 3495
Dr. Bentley. 191
Doctor Bob Hockman. 1821
Doctor Carl Ferdinand Wilhelm Walther. 3790
Doctor carries on. 2539
Dr. Channing's note-book. 881
Dr. Coxe's claims to apostolicity reviewed. 76, 1378
Dr. David Livingstone and Sir Henry Morton Stanley. 2241
Dr. Drummond's da-fun-mental. 1371
Dr. Edward McGlynn. 1294, 2308
Dr. Evans' question box. 637
Dr. Frank. 2204
Doctor Fraser and his sermons. 3362
Doctor from Lhasa. 3130, 3699
Dr. Grant and the mountain Nestorians. 2541
Dr. Gray at Moody Bible institute. 1757
Dr. Gregory's History of the Christian church. 1175
... Dr. Guthrie. Father Mathew. 3130
... Dr. Harry Emerson Fosdick's book. 1635
Dr. Henry of Assiut, pioneer medical missionary in Egypt. 93, 1803
Dr. Hyde and Mr. Stevenson. 1859
Dr. Ida. 2539, 3316
Doctor in an old world. 182, 2539
Dr. Ironside's Bible. 222
Dr. Isaac Watts, "The bard of sanctuary," 3799
Dr. James Woodrow. 3137
Dr. John Clifford, C. H. 3131
Dr. John Walker and the Sufferings of the clergy. 1221, 3136, 3789
Doctor Johnson's prayers. 2891
Dr. L. L. Gwaltney, TH. M., S. T. D., LITT. D., editor emeritus of the Alabama Baptist. 1779
Doctor looks at miracles. 2477
Doctor Luther. 2273
Dr. McLaren of Manchester. 2309
Dr. Mannix. 2329
Dr. Martin Luther's Church-postil. 1267
Dr. Martin Luther's Small catechism. 2279
Dr. Martin Luther's Small catechism graded, with Bible verse. 2279
Dr. Martin Luther's Small catechism with explanation. 2283, 2284
Dr. Mason's speech. 2364
Doctor-merchant. 1451
Doctor-merchant, his inspirational letters. 1451
...Dr. Mublenberg. 2627
Doctor of the happy landings. 2537
Doctor Paracelsus. 2772
Dr. Pierson and his message. 3133
Dr. Poling's radio talks with questions and answers. 3018
Dr. Rice, here is my question. 3012
Dr. Samson Benderly, leader in American Jewish education. 187, 2106
Dr. Samuel Clarke. 1285
Dr. Schweitzer of Lambarene. 3311
Dr. Sheldon's scrap book. 3402
Doctor Sparks. 2401, 3130, 3143
...Dr. Theodore H. White's higher courses and complete system of occult science. 2730
Doctor upstairs. 1013
Dr. Watts' imitation of the Psalms of David. 580
Doctor Watts's Imitation of the Psalms of David. 269, 580
Dr. William Smith's Dictionary of the Bible. 246
Doctor without a country. 2539
Doctor's best love story. 422
Doctor's casebook in the light of the Bible. 2378
Doctors courageous. 2539
Doctor's great commission. 2552
Doctors of philosophy of Yale university. 1469
Doctors of the church. 3611
Doctor's soliloquy. 3078
Doctor's widow. 2333
Doctrinal aspects of Christian experience. 3290

Doctrinal conflict between Roman Catholic and Protestant Christianity. 798
Doctrinal declarations. 2285
Doctrinal discourses. 1273
Doctrinal guide. 3661
Doctrinal instruction of religious sisters. 2580
Doctrinal meaning of prophecy. 2949
Doctrinal New Testament commentary. 344
Doctrinal pluralism. 3645
Doctrinal preaching for today. 2897
Doctrinal sermon outlines. 3347
Doctrinal sermons for children. 908
Doctrinal standards of Methodism. 2421
Doctrinal standards of the Christian Reformed Church consisting of the Belgic Confession, the Heidelberg catechism, and the Canons of Dort. 1023
Doctrinal survey of selected Protestant groups in Portland Oregon and vicinity. 2864
Doctrinal test. 2449
Doctrinal theology of the Evangelical Lutheran church. 2287
Doctrinal theology of the Evangelical Lutheran church. 2287
Doctrinal thoughts. 3665
Doctrinal treatises and introductions to different portions of the Holy Scriptures. 1219
Doctrine and administration of the church. 3052
Doctrine and convenants and the future. 3430
Doctrine and covenants. 2610, 3428
Doctrine and covenants compendium. 3430
Doctrine and covenants of the Church of Jesus Christ of Latter-day Saints. 2599, 2612
Doctrine and covenants of the Church of Jesus Christ of latter-day saints; containing revelations given to Joseph Smith, the prophet, with some additions by his successors in the presidency of the church. 2599
Doctrine and covenants, of the Church of Jesus Christ of latter-day saints containing the revelations given to Joseph Smith, jun., the prophet, for the building up of the kingdom of God in the last days. 2599
Doctrine and covenants of the Church of the Latter Day Saints. 2612
Doctrine and covenants of the Church of the Latter day saints: carefully selected from the revelations of God, and compiled by Joseph Smith, junior, Oliver Cowdery, Sidney Rigdon, Frederick G. Williams, (presiding elders of said church) Proprietors. 2599
Doctrine and covenants, our modern scripture. 2610, 3428
Doctrine and covenants speaks. 3430
Doctrine and discipline of the A.M.E. church. 13, 14
Doctrine and discipline of the African Methodist Episcopal Church. 14
Doctrine and discipline of the Colored Methodist Episcopal church in America. 1310
Doctrine and discipline of the Methodist Episcopal church. 2447
Doctrine and discipline [1] of the A.M.E. church. 14
Doctrine and duty made plain and attractive. 1484
Doctrine and function of revelation. 3225
Doctrine and life. 1466, 3648
Doctrine and practice of the eucharist as deduced from Scripture and the ancient liturgies. 2252
Doctrine and principles of the people called Quakers, explained and vindicated. 1683, 1810
Doctrine explanations. 767, 769
Doctrine for 3's to 5's. 3175
Doctrine in the Church of England. 1212, 1217
Doctrine of absolute predestination stated and asserted. 2911
Doctrine of atonement. 108
Doctrine of baptism. 136
Doctrine of Christ. 934
Doctrine of Christianity, as held by the people called Quakers, vindicated: in answer to Gilbert Tennent's sermon on the lawfulness of war. [Twelve lines of Biblical quotations]. 3601, 3792
Doctrine of Christianity, as held by the people called Quakers, vindicated: in answer to Gilbert Tennent's sermon on the lawfulness of war. 1682, 3601
... The doctrine of cycles. 2819
Doctrine of decress. 2936

Doctrine of election in tannaitic literature. 2087
Doctrine of eternal punishment. 934, 1699
Doctrine of future and endless punishment. 1699
Doctrine of God. 175, 1719, 1723, 1725, 1727, 1730, 3645
Doctrine of God in the Jewish apocryphal and apocalyptic literature. 57, 490
Doctrine of grace. 1751
Doctrine of grace in the Apostolic Fathers. 76
Doctrine of Holy Scripture respecting the atonement. 4th ed. 104
Doctrine of Jehovah's Witnesses. 1940
Doctrine of justification. 2160
Doctrine of justification according to the Scriptures. 1389
Doctrine of justification by faith. 2160
Doctrine of life for the New Jerusalem. 2691, 3571
Doctrine of man. 2322
Doctrine of man in classical Lutheran theology. 2326
Doctrine of merits in old rabbinical literature. 2412, 3015
Doctrine of modernism and its refutation. 2562
Doctrine of original sin. 1821, 3414
Doctrine of our redemption. 3031
Doctrine of our salvation. 3289
Doctrine of predestination truly and fairly stated. 2911
Doctrine of probation examined with reference to current discussions. 2943
Doctrine of reconciliation. 175
Doctrine of redemption. 3645
Doctrine of revelation. 3225
Doctrine of St. John. 414
Doctrine of salvation. 3290
Doctrine of sanctification. 3300
Doctrine of spiritual perfection. 115, 2643
Doctrine of the atonement. 105, 108
Doctrine of the atonement and its historical evolution and Religion and modern culture. 106
Doctrine of the atonement in Jonathan Edwards and his successors. 108, 1499
Doctrine of the atonement in the theology of Wolfhart Pannenberg. 2010
Doctrine of the Buddha. 701, 702
Doctrine of the church. 1124, 1126, 1187
Doctrine of the church and Christian reunion. 1040
Doctrine of the church in American Lutheranism. 2294
Doctrine of the covenants. 1376
Doctrine of the divine indwelling. 1508, 2636
Doctrine of the Holy Spirit. 1830, 1832, 1833
Doctrine of the incarnation. 1892
Doctrine of the infallible Book. 276
Doctrine of the law & grace unfolded. 1752
Doctrine of the law and grace unfolded and I will pray with the Spirit. 1753
Doctrine of the Mennonites. 2405
Doctrine of the Messiah in medieval Jewish literature. 2076, 2414
Doctrine of the mystical body of Christ. 1950
Doctrine of the New Jerusalem concerning the Lord. 2691
Doctrine of the New Jerusalem concerning the Sacred Scripture. 2691
Doctrine of the original sin, according to Scripture. 3412
Doctrine of the passions. 1512
Doctrine of the person of Christ. 2037
...The doctrine of the person of Jesus Christ. 2041
Doctrine of the prophets. 569, 2950
Doctrine of the resurrection of the body. 3220
Doctrine of the self-existent Father. 3713
Doctrine of the subtle body in Western tradition. 674
Doctrine of the Sufis. 3544
Doctrine of the Trinity. 175, 176, 1733, 3711, 3712, 3713
Doctrine of the Trinity; Croall lectures, 1942-1943. 3711
Doctrine of the twelve apostles. 950
Doctrine of the universal decrees and agency of God. 2983
Doctrine of the universal priesthood. 2939
Doctrine of the void. 2136, 2639
Doctrine of the will. 1658
Doctrine of the Word in the structure of Lutheran theology. 278
Doctrine of the Word of God (Prolegomena to Church dogmatics ...) ... Authorized translation by G. T. Thomson. 175
Doctrine of the work of Christ. 108
Doctrine of time in St. Thomas. 3696

Doctrine of universal restoration carefully examined. 3799
Doctrine of universal restoration examined and refuted; and the objections to that of endless punishment considered. 3754
Doctrines and descriptions of the present great religions of the world. 3116
Doctrines and disciple of the Christian Methodist Episcopal Church. 1022
Doctrines and discipline. 1550, 1652, 2440
Doctrines and discipline of the A.M.E. church. 14
Doctrines and discipline of the African Methodist Episcopal church. 14
Doctrines and discipline of the African Methodist Episcopal church in America. 14
Doctrines and discipline of the Evangelical association of North America. 1546
Doctrines and discipline of the Free Methodist church. 1653
Doctrines and discipline of the Free Methodist church of North America. 1653
Doctrines and discipline of the Kodesh church of Immanuel. 2183
Doctrines and discipline of the Methodist church. 2440
Doctrines and discipline of the Methodist Church, 1960. 2447
Doctrines and discipline of the Methodist Episcopal church. 2447, 2448, 2449
Doctrines and discipline of the Methodist Episcopal church, 1924. 2449
Doctrines and discipline of the Methodist Episcopal church in America. 2449
Doctrines and discipline of the Methodist Episcopal church, South. 2456
Doctrines and discipline of the Methodist Episcopal church, South, 1894. 2456
Doctrines and discipline of the Methodist Episcopal church, South, 1898. 2456
Doctrines and discipline of the Methodist Episcopal church, South, 1902. 2456
Doctrines and discipline of the Methodist Episcopal church, South, 1914. 2456
Doctrines and discipline of the Methodist Episcopal church, South, 1922. 2456
Doctrines and discipline of the Methodist Episcopal church, South, 1926. 2456
Doctrines and discipline of the Methodist Episcopal church, South, 1934. 2456
Doctrines and discipline of the Methodist Episcopal church, South, 1938. 2456
Doctrines and discipline of the Pillar of fire church. 1918. 2848
Doctrines and disciplines of the Methodist Episcopal church. 2449
Doctrines and disipline of the Methodist Episcopal church. 2449
Doctrines and ordinances of the New Testament. 1485
Doctrines and polity of the Methodist Episcopal church, South. Part first. 2456
Doctrines do grow. 3628
Doctrines for the times. 3645
Doctrines from the beloved disciple. 423
Doctrines from the prophets. 2609, 2610
Doctrines of Christianity. 3646
Doctrines of demons. 2727
Doctrines of devils. 3138
Doctrines of divine revelation, as taught in the Holy Scriptures, exhibited, illustrated, and vindicated. 3644
Doctrines of election and justification. 1505
Doctrines of Friends. 1681
Doctrines of Friends: or Principles of the Christian religion. 1681
Doctrines of glorious grace unfolded, defended, and practically improved. 1635, 1753
Doctrines of grace. 1750, 1752, 1753
Doctrines of modern Judaism considered. 2116
Doctrines of modernism. 2561
Doctrines of our faith. 140, 147
Doctrines of salvation. 2610
Doctrines of the Bible. 2405
Doctrines of the book of Acts. 331
Doctrines of the Christian religion. 3648
Doctrines of the Mennonites. 2405
Doctrines of the Methodist Episcopal church in America. 2449, 3805
Doctrines of the Society of Friends as set forth in the life and writings of Thomas Story. 1682
Doctrines of Unitarians examined, as opposed to the Church of England. 3724
Documentary annals of the reformed Church of England. 1219
Documentary history of the American Bible union. 31
Documentary history of the Evangelical Lutheran ministerium of Pennsylvania and adjacent states. 1548

Documentary history of the Protestant Episcopal church in the diocese of Vermont. 2974
Documentary history of the Protestant Episcopal church in the United States of America. 1222
Documentary history of the struggle for religious liberty in Virginia. 3195
Documentary reports on early American Catholicism. 834
Documentary story of a century of the Jewish community center, 1854-1954. 1320
Documentary studies. 607
Documented history of the Franciscan order. 1646
Documents bearing on the problem of Christian unity and fellowship, 1916-1920. 1042
Documents concerning baptism and church membership. 137
Documents concerning the life and character of Emanuel Swedenborg. 3571
Documents from Old Testament times. 487, 515
Documents illustrating papal authority, A.D. 96-454. 2770
Documents illustrative of English church history. 1762
Documents illustrative of the continental reformation. 3034, 3042
... Documents illustrative of the history of the church. 1176
Documents in early Christian thought. 1019
Documents inedits pour servir a l'histoire du christianisme en Orient. 2678
Documents: Nerinckx—Kentucky—Loretto, 1804-1851. 2684
Documents of American Catholic history. 834, 835
Documents of California Catholic history. 766
Documents of California Catholic history, 1784-1963. 766
Documents of dialogue. 1045
Documents of Jewish sectaries. 2164
Documents of Jewish sectaries ... ed. from Hebrew manuscripts in the Cairo Genizah collection now in the possession of the University library, Cambridge ... by S. Schechter. 2080
Documents of Lutheran unity in America. 2293
Documents of the Christian church. 1198
Documents of the Christian church, selected and edited by Henry Bettenson. 1198
Documents of the Jewish pious foundations from the Cairo Geniza. 724, 887
Documents of the primitive church. 393
Documents of the 31st and 32nd general congregations of the Society of Jesus. 1945
Documents of Vatican II. 777, 3773
Documents on Christian unity. 186, 1039
Documents on Christian unity, 1920-4. 1039
Documents on instrumental music. 319
Documents on renewal for religious. 2572
Documents relating to the foundation and antiquities of the Collegiate Church of Middleham, in the County of York. 1309
Documents study of the Gospels. 395, 3246
Dodd's Church history of England, from the commencement of the sixteenth century to the revolution in 1688. 1759
Dodging the commandments. 1313
Doers of the word. 2180, 2857
Does America need the Moral Majority? 1552, 2593
Does anyone care how I feel? 902
Does anyone here know God? 924
Does Christ heal today? 1599
Does Christ still heal? 1601, 1793
Does Christianity make sense? 65
Does civilization need religion? 1051
Does God answer prayer? 2875
Does God care? 2882, 3540
Does God care? or, The face of God as seen in the story of Esther. 514
Does God confort? 1730
Does God exist? 1723, 1738, 3609
Does God have a nature? 1729
Does God matter for me? 1724, 1740
Does God punish? 1742
Does God send trouble? 1745
Does God still guide? 2980
... Does Hellenism contribute constituent elements to Paul's Christology. 2803
Does inspiration demand inerrancy? 306
Does Jesus make a difference? 2046
Does man survive? 3506
Does my father know I'm hurt? 2845
Does prayer avail? 2882

Does religion pay? 3232
Does science confront the Bible? 205
Does science support the Scriptures? 205
Does sex morality matter? 3393
Does telepathy explain spiritualism? 3495
Does the Bible contradict itself. 229
Does the Bible really work? 279
Does the Bible sanction war? 3794
Does the Bible teach pacifism? 3792
Does the church know how to teach? 936
Does the modern papacy require a new
  evaluation! 2768
Does the reformation need reforming?
  1057
Does your pet have a sixth sense? 2773
Dogen Kigen, mystical realist. 1472
Dogen's formative years in China. 1472,
  2940
Dogma. 3647
Dogma and compulsion. 611, 2999
Dogma and pluralism. 758, 1386
Dogma for the layman. 796
Dogma of the Immaculate Conception.
  1886
Dogma of the immaculate conception,
  historical development and dogmatic
  fulfillment. 1886
Dogmatic and mystical theology of John
  Donne. 1476
Dogmatic canons and decrees. 781
Dogmatic Constitution on the Church.
  1124
Dogmatic series. 782
Dogmatic theology. 2923, 3646, 3648
Dogmatic theology for the laity. 3647
Dogmatic theology on the intention of the
  minister in the confection of the
  sacraments. 3264
Dogmatic vs. Biblical theology. 652
Dogmatics. 3641
Dogmatics in outline. 3640
Dogon masks. 1473
Dogsled apostles. 2501
Doing and believing. 1055
... Doing as God wants. 3183
Doing Christian education in new ways.
  935
Doing, dance & drama. 1478
Doing evil to achieve good. 946
Doing likewise, three vital Southern
  Baptist ministries. 3465
"Doing" or "done" 284
Doing right and wrong. 1325
Doing the Eucharist: a guide to trial use.
  2257
Doing the faith. 1006
Doing the Gospel in Southeast Asia. 2503
Doing the impossible; chaple talks to
  young men and women. 3175
Doing the truth. 944, 949
Doing theology in a revolutionary
  situation. 2222
Doing theology in new places. 3620
Doing what comes supernaturally. 1010
Doing what is Christian. 956
Dojo. 3545
Doktor Luther. 2273
Doleful state of the damned. 2911
Dolorous passion of Our Lord Jesus Christ.
  2031
Dom Helder Camara. 731
Domain of being, ontology. 2737
Domain of devils. 1423
Dome and the rock. 2564
Dome of the Rock in Jerusalem. 1944
Domenichino. 1474
Domenico Bollani, Bishop of Brescia. 667,
  675
Domesday book. 1474
... Domesday studies being the papers read
  at the meetings of the Domesday
  commemoration 1886. 1474
Domestic portraiture. 3236
Domesticating the clergy. 3039, 3040
... Domicile and quasi-domicile. 1474
Dominant ideas and corrective principles.
  1748
Dominant Romanism. 3244
Dominic Giacobbi. 1710
Dominican architecture in sixteenth
  century Oaxaca. 1161
Dominican ceremonial for mass and
  benediction. 843
Dominican incunabula in the Library of
  Congress. 1475
Dominican life. 1476
Dominican mission. 2774
Dominican mission prayer book and
  manual of special devotions. 854
Dominican nuns in their cloister. 1476
... The Dominican order in England before
  the reformation. 1475
Dominican province of Saint Joseph. 1476
Dominican self-appraisal in the light of the
  council. 1475, 3773
Dominican sisters' office book. 843
Dominican spirituality. 1474, 1475, 1476

Dominican tertiaries' guide. 2308
Dominican tertiaries' manual. 1476
Dominicans. 1475
... Dominicans in early Florida. 1475
Dominicans of Illinois. 1475
Dominicans of San Rafael. 1475
Dominion. 275
Dominion over demons. 1423
Dominion rhymes. 3208
Dominion within. 1034
Don Bosco. 683
Don Camillo and his flock. 3127, 3143
Don Francisco. 1649
Don Isaac Abravanel. 5
Don Isaac Abravanel, statesman and
  philosopher. 5
Don Juan, Mescalito, and modern magic.
  744, 3400
Donatist Church. 1476
Donet. 3647
Donjon of demons. 1857
Donne at sermons. 1476, 2909
Donne's Prebend sermons. 1226, 3363
Donovan Memorial Church in the Singers
  Glen community. 1477
Don't be afraid of the dark. 2438
Don't be an oyster! 997
Don't bug me, preacher! 1288
Don't bury me 'til I'm dead. 150, 3241
Don't call me preacher. 1132, 1485
Don't die on trial. 1558
Don't disappoint God! 3887
Don't divorce the Holy Spirit. 237
Don't fall out the window. 3485
Don't go overseas until you've read this
  book. 2501
Don't just stand there! 2492, 3887
Don't kid yourself! 975
Don't limit God! 1457, 2229
Don't look now. 955
Don't lose that fish. 1569
Don't park here. 960, 3540
Don't sleep through the revolution. 2496
Don't turn me off, Lord, and other jail
  house meditations. 2384
Don't waste your time in worship. 3853
Don't wrestle, just nestle. 989
Don't you belong to me? 3486
Don'ts for boys. 687
Donum gentilicium. 350, 1403
... Doom and resurrection. 2364, 3212
Doom of dogma and the dawn of truth.
  1473
Doom of the dictators. 1319
Doom of the majority of mankind. 1699
Doomed religious. 3120
... The doomed Turk, the end of the
  "Eastern question;" 2949
Doomsday Cult. 2998
Door ajar. 1349
Door of heaven opened and shut. 961
Door of hope. 1480, 2781
Door of liberation. 2193, 2311
Door of salvation. 756
Door opened. 2323
Door that has no key. 3362
Door to the future. 1283
Doors into life through five devotional
  classics. 1453
Doors of eternity. 1413
Doors of God, and other addresses. 3065
Doors of perception and Heaven and hell.
  3783
Doors to perception. 3484
Doors to the sacred. 3265
Doorway papers. 652
Doorway to a new age. 470
Doorway to heaven. 1440
Doorway to meditation. 2384
Doorways. 2489
Doorways to devotion. 2238
Doorways to spiritual living. 3480
Dora. 1418
Doran's minister's manual. 3373
Dore Bible gallery. 602
Doric temple. 3599
Dorie, the girl nobody loved. 2486, 3767
"Dorio" 3506
Dork Walker, three-time all-American.
  3137, 3143
Dorner on the future state, being a
  translation of the section of his System of
  Christian doctrine comprising the
  doctrine of the last things, with an
  introduction and notes. 1528
Dorothy. 1477
Dorothy and David explore Jewish life.
  2101
Dorothy Day. 875, 1407
Dorset churches. 1158
Dortch's Gospel voices. 1860
Dositheans. 1477
Dostoevsky, Kierkegaard, Nietzsche, and
  Kafka. 1477, 1583
Double cross. 1412, 2301
Double cure. 1824

Double doctrine of the Church of Rome.
  803
Double honour due to the laborious gospel
  minister. 3021
Double mind. 411
Double minded man. 205, 278
Double search. 105
Double yoke. 2539, 2712
Doubleday devotional classics. 1455
Doubt and religious commitment. 2179,
  2705
Doubters and their doubts. 3211
Doubting castle. 928, 1810
Doubting Thomas today. 1190
Doubts & difficulties. 1097
Doubt's boundless sea. 3215
Doubts, loneliness, rejection. 1602
Douglass devotional. 1431
Douglass Sunday School lessons 1961
  (The) 1914
Douglass Sunday school lessons 1962
  (The) 1914
Douglass Sunday school lessons, 1964
  (The) 1914
Douglass Sunday school lessons, 1965
  (The) 1914
Douglass Sunday School lessons (The)
  1915
Doukhobors. 1482
Doukhobors of British Columbia. 1482
Doukhobors, their history in Russia, their
  migration to Canada. 1482
Dove and the Messiah. 1632
Dove in harness. 68, 990
Dove in the cleft. 2333
Dove of gold, and other signposts of the
  spirit. 3225
Doves in the dust. 168
Dowie. 1478
Dowley Bible atlas. 217
Down grade. 30
Down hill and up hill. 954
Down holiday land. 1623
Down in Water street. 2305, 2699
Down into the arena. 2299, 3352
Down nature's paths. 1450
Down, peacock's feathers. 1133, 1214
Down through the ages. 248
Down to earth. 991, 1075, 2354, 3666
Down way up. 932, 1321
Down with anxiety! 55
Downfall of the anti-Semitic political
  parties in imperial Germany. 2858
Downfall of the Hebrew nation. 3180
Downward ascent. 2321
... Dowry of women religious. 1478
Doxology. 3649
Dozen daring Christians. 338
Draft of a book in religion tentatively
  entitled For the love of God. 3106
Draft proposed Book of Common Prayer
  and administration of the sacraments and
  other rites and ceremonies of the Church.
  2961
Dragon and the beasts. 458
Dragon bound. 456
Dragon cast out of heaven, by Michael and
  his angels, into the earth. 463
... The dragon, image, and demon. 913
Dragon killer. 1706
Dragon net. 1090
Dragon teeth. 912
Dragons, gods & spirits from Chinese
  mythology. 2655
Drama and liturgy. 2636
Drama and the symbols. 1719
Drama come true. 3237
Drama goes to church. 3144
Drama in the church. 3144
Drama of ancient Israel. 533
Drama of atheist humanism. 101
Drama of incarnation. 1837
Drama of Job. 548
Drama of life. 235
Drama of life after death. 3507
Drama of our religion. 292
Drama of redemption. 3029, 3030
Drama of salvation. 3145
Drama of the ages. 3381
Drama of the Apocalypse. 461
Drama of the Apocalypse in relation to the
  literary and political circumstances of its
  time. 458
Drama of the Bible. 295
Drama of the book of Revelation. 453
Drama of the cross. 168, 2035
Drama of the end-time. 1514
Drama of the face, and other studies in
  applied psychology. 2994
Drama of the medieval church. 1479
Drama of the Psalms. 577
Drama of the spiritual life. 3000
Drama of Vatican II. 3771
Dramas for church services. 3144
Dramas of salvation. 200
Dramas of the Bible. 549

Dramatic and symbolic elements in
  Gregorian chant. 884
Dramatic calendar for churches. 3145
Dramatic illustrations of passages from the
  second part of The pilgrim's progress by
  John Bunyan, arranged in the year 1877
  by Mrs. George MacDonald. 717
Dramatic images [plays] for the church.
  3145
Dramatic instinct in religious education.
  3150
... The dramatic method in religious
  education. 3145
Dramatic moments in the life of Jesus.
  2003
Dramatic narrative in preaching. 3533
Dramatic personality of Jesus. 1951
Dramatic preludes and services of worship.
  3859
Dramatic providence in Macbeth. 1101,
  3399, 3400
Dramatic services of worship. 3145
Dramatic silences of his last week. 2215,
  2438
Dramatic stories for missionary programs.
  924
Dramatic stories of Jesus. 1950
Dramatic stories of the Bible. 297
Dramatic story of early American
  Methodism. 2433
Dramatic story of Old Testament history.
  535
Dramatic studies from the Bible. 637
Dramatic uses of Biblical allusions in
  Marlowe and Shakespeare. 300, 2335
Dramatic works of a new author ...
  Individual American sentiments. The
  drama. Poetry, verse, prose, moral,
  immoral, characteristics, humor, satire,
  philosophy, loyalty. 119
Dramatics for creative teaching. 3166
Dramatics in the Christian school. 1479
Dramatization in the church school. 1478
Dramatization of Bible stories. 1479
Dramatized missionary stories. 2489
Dramatized sermons. 3352
Drastic discipleship. 3363
Drastic discipleship, and other expository
  sermons. 3363, 3365
Draughts of remembrance. 2724, 3052
Dravidian gods in modern Hinduism.
  1813
"Draw me after Thee, O Lord." 2884
"Draw near to Him," 3487
Draw near with faith. 2253
Draw up a chair. 1015
Draw your strength from the Lord. 1001
Drawing down the Moon. 3828
Drawing near Him with confidence. 370
Drawing nigh to God. 1437
Drawing toward God. 1010
... Drawings and models of the
  construction of St. Paul's cathedral.
  2244, 3860
Drawings at the second Vatican Council.
  3773
Drawings, designs, illustrations, borders,
  alphabets, pithy sayings, etc., for church
  bulletins. 10
DRE reader. 937
Dream a new dream. 1350, 1701
Dream and a promise. 2134
Dream by the river; two centuries of Saint
  Louis Catholicism, 1766-1967. 3276
Dream come true. 1920, 3237
Dream feather. 3524, 3862
Dream lives forever. 2699
Dream of Gerontius. 2703
... The dream of Gerontius by Cardinal
  Newman. 2703
Dream of Heaven. 1795
Dream of the future. 508
... The dream of the soldier saint. 2268
Dream power of youth. 3151
Dream your way to success. 915, 2814
Dreamer cometh. 3235, 3465
Dreamer in the desert. 1717, 3309
Dreams. 1479
Dreams and myths. 1479
Dreams & omens revealed. 1479
Dreams and premonitions. 1479
Dreams and visions. 2426
Dreams come true. 956
Dreams, dungeons, diadems. 151
Dreams in the life of prayer. 876, 1479
Dreams of a spirit seer. 2418, 3570
Dreams of destiny. 1001
Dreams: the dark speech of the spirit.
  1479
Dreams, visions, and oracles. 609
Dreamtime. 2654
Drew sermons. 3701
Drew sermons. First series. 3701
Drew sermons on the golden texts for
  1908. 3701
Drew sermons on the golden texts for
  1909. 3701

DREW SERMONS ON RELIGIOUS BOOKS 1876 - 1982

Drew sermons on the golden texts for 1910. 3701
Drew theological seminary, 1867-1917. 1480
Drift, from the shore of the hereafter. 3498
Drift of Western thought. 63
Driftwood. 1842
Drillmaster of Methodism. 2421
Drink at Joel's Place. 165
... Drinker library of choral music. 916
Drinking. 3596
Drinking at the sources. 2152
Drinking the mountain stream. 2193
Driven from home. 2085
Driving out the devils. 1422
Droopy flower mystery, and other object lessons for children. 908
Dropping ashes on the Buddha. 3379, 3892
Dropping in; putting it all back together. 3879
Drops of gold. 943
Drugs and magic. 2773
Drugs and the life of prayer. 2868
Drugs, drinks & morals. 950
Druids. 1480
Druids and druidism. 1480
Druids and their heritage. 1480
Drum and candle. 3519
Drum call of hope. 2537
Drumbeat of love. 332, 2933, 3356
Drummond year book. 1438
Drummond's address. 3620
Drummond's addresses. 959, 3620
Drums in the darkness. 2498
Drunk on the divine. 3019
Drunkenness of Noah. 523, 2711
Druze faith. 1481
Dry blockade. 3833
Dry bones can live again. 1564
Dry bones; living worship guides to good liturgy. 3003
Dry messiah. 735
Dry side of a wet subject. 3597
Du Bose as a prophet of unity. 1481, 2041
Dual mind. 2990
Dualism of eternal life. 1528
Duality of human existence. 2996
Duality of physical truth and cause. 3716
Duality of the Bible. 642
Dubious heritage. 3107
Dublin Apocalypse. 1884
Dudley's dog days. 988, 3255
Dugger-Porter debate. 3260
Dulin from saddlebags to satellites. 1603
Duly and scripturally qualified. 2790
Duncan's Masonic ritual and monitor. 1669
Dunkers. 1236
Duplicating and publicity manual for Christian workers. 2734
... Durham. 1483
Durham book. 1213
Durham diocesan records. 1483
Durham jurisdictional peculiars. 1483
Durham Priory, 1400-1450. 1483
Durkheim on religion. 3066
Dust and destiny. 2437
Dust of her sandals. 3603
Dust on my toes. 2490
Dust, remember thou art splendor. 1001
Dutch Anabaptism. 37
Dutch Anabaptists. 1477
Dutch Reformed Church in the American colonies. 3046
Dutch tiles. 1979
Dutchman bound for paradise. 2486, 3701
Duties of a Christian. 1484
Duties of a pastor to his church. 3672
Duties of the mind. 699, 2143
Duties of the ruling elder. 1503, 2915
Dutiful child. 904
Duty. 1325, 1484, 3870
Duty and conscience. 2172
Duty & property of a religious householder. 2372
Duty and the discipline of extemporary preaching. 2908
Duty of all Christians. 1340
Duty of altruism. 28
Duty of imperial thinking. 1072
Duty of parents to transmit religion to their children. 2592
Duty of private Christians to pray for their ministers. 1343
Duty unto death. 1779
Dux Christus. 1935
Dvaita Vedanta. 1484, 2311
Dwell in peace. 2712
Dweller on two planets. 2727
... A dweller on two planets; or, The dividing of the way. 2728
Dwight E. Stevenson. 3528, 3615
Dwight L. Moody. 1562, 2587, 2588
Dwight L. Moody, American evangelist, 1837-1899. 2587
Dwight Lyman Moody's life work and gospel sermons as delivered by the great evangelist in his revival work in Great Britain and America. 1568, 3301
Dwight Lyman Moody's life work and latest sermons as delivered by the great evangelist. 2587
Dyaloge called Funus. 1416
Dyer's psalmist. 1865
Dying and living Lord. 2032
Dying, death, and destiny. 1414
Dying exercises of Mrs. Deborah Prince. 2941
Dying for enlightenment. 2379, 3019
Dying hours. 923
Dying hours of, good and bad men contracted. 924
Dying into life. 1007
Dying legacy to the people of his beloved charge. 2933
Dying lights & dawning. 3060
Dying Lord. 2057
Dying thoughts of the Rev. Richard Baxter. 1444
Dying thoughts of the reverend, learned and holy Mr. Richard Baxter. 178
Dying to live. 1108
Dymanic Christian living. 967
Dynamic approach to church education. 3158
Dynamic approaches to teaching high school religion. 804, 937
Dynamic Christian fellowship. 1621
Dynamic Christianity. 1058
Dynamic church: spirit and structure for the seventies. 150
Dynamic contemplation. 1355
Dynamic devotionals for men. 2402
Dynamic difference. 1831
Dynamic discipleship. 985
Dynamic element in the church. 1126
Dynamic evangels. 1569
Dynamic faith. 1596
Dynamic force of example. 127
Dynamic imaging. 3539
Dynamic in Christian thought. 3620
Dynamic interpersonalism for ministry. 2129, 2784
Dynamic laws of healing. 1600
Dynamic leadership. 953
Dynamic living for difficult days. 994
Dynamic ministry. 3672
Dynamic of all-prayer. 2871
Dynamic of Christianity. 1057
Dynamic of faith. 1596
"The dynamic of the printed page" in EFC history. 1021, 1546
Dynamic out of silence. 699, 2593
Dynamic power of our sacraments. 3264
Dynamic preaching. 2899
Dynamic psychology of early Buddhism. 2867
Dynamic psychology of religion. 2994, 2999
Dynamic redemption. 2960
...Dynamic religion. 1992, 3058
Dynamic religious movements. 1393
Dynamic sermon outlines. 3373
Dynamic stability. 3256
Dynamic Sunday talks to children. 909
Dynamic transcendence. 651, 3644
Dynamic word. 347
Dynamic worship programs for young people. 3857
Dynamics of a city church. 1279
Dynamics of belief. 1592
Dynamics of Christian adult education. 3168
Dynamics of Christian discipleship. 962
Dynamics of Christian unity. 1492
Dynamics of church growth. 1171, 2555
Dynamics of community. 2569
Dynamics of confession. 1326
Dynamics of discipleship training. 985
Dynamics of doubt. 3700
Dynamics of evangelism. 1563
Dynamics of faith. 1595
Dynamics of forgiveness. 1633
Dynamics of liturgy. 2234
Dynamics of morality. 947
Dynamics of personal follow-up. 1567
Dynamics of religion. 3105
Dynamics of sanctification. 3299
Dynamics of small groups within the church. 1170
Dynamics of spiritual gifts. 1712
Dynamics of spiritual life. 3233
Dynamics of the faith. 3620
Dynamics of the psychic world. 3689
Dynamics of worship. 3854
Dynamism of Biblical tradition. 200
Dynamite of God. 3011

E

E. G. White and church race relations. 1133, 3811
E. Y. Mullins lectures on preaching, with reference to the Aristotelian triad. 1485
Each day. 1438
Each hour remains. 2580
Each month with Christ. 838
Each new day. 1433
Each one his own priest. 1735
Each with his own brush. 920
Eager feet. 3230
... The eagle and the dove. 3603
Eagle and the Rising Sun. 1936
Eagle life and other studies in the Old Testament. 592, 615, 2135
Eagle of Avila. 3603
Eagle of God. 2127
Eagle of the wilderness. 2630
Eagle story. 3890
Eagle's gift. 744, 1782
Eagle's wings. 989, 3604
Eagle's word. 418
... The Ear of Dionysius. 3494
Ear of God. 2877
Earl Blue report on clergy disaffection. 1582
Earlier writings. 3634
Earliest Christian church. 1192
Earliest Christian confessions. 1386
Earliest Christian liturgy. 3855
Earliest Christianity. 407, 1197
Earliest editions of the Hebrew Bible. 530
Earliest Gospel. 347, 433, 435
Earliest Latin commentaries on the Epistles of St. Paul. 29, 373
Earliest life of Gregory the Great. 1773
Earliest lives of Jesus. 2010
Earliest records of Jesus. 385, 1950
Earliest saints' lives written in England. 952
Earliest semitic pantheon. 1743
Earliest sources for the life of Jesus. 388, 1987
... The earliest translation of theOld Testament into the Basque language. 482
Early American Christianity. 3740
Early American churches. 1162
Early American interest in Vedanta. 3775
Early American Jewry. 2101
Early American Jews. 2106
Early and latter rain. 3385
Early and medieval Christianity. 1197
Early Anglicanism in Connecticut. 2967
Early architectural history of the cathedral of Santiago de Compostela. 3303
Early Arianism—a view of salvation. 80, 2010
... Early Baptist missionaries. 144
Early Baptists defended. 153, 1285
Early Baptists of Virginia. 171
Early Bible illustrations. 601, 603
Early Bibles of America. 213
Early Brahmanical system of gotra and pravara. 689
Early Buddhism and the Bhagavadgita. 197
Early Buddhist monachism. 2577
Early Buddhist rock temples. 876
Early Byzantine churches in Macedonia and southern Serbia. 1160
Early Catholic Americana. 32, 764
Early Catholic missions in old Oregon. 824
Early Catholicity in Kansas. 820
Early Chola art. 3599
Early Christian and Byzantine architecture. 78
Early Christian and Byzantine art. 85, 922
Early Christian and Byzantine world. 85
Early Christian apologists and Greek philosophy. 1718, 1919
Early Christian archaeology of North Britain. 919
Early Christian architecture of Syria. 78
Early Christian art. 85, 921, 922
Early Christian art and symbolism. 86
Early Christian art in Rome. 88
Early Christian attitude to war. 1089, 3791
Early Christian biographies. 1020, 1616
...The early Christian books. 1020
Early Christian church. 1190, 1196
Early Christian creeds. 1385, 1386
Early Christian doctrine of God. 1732
Early Christian doctrines. 3657
Early Christian epoch. 930, 2060
Early Christian fathers. 1018, 1020, 1616
Early Christian hymns. 1877, 1878
Early Christian interpretations of history. 1818, 1820
Early Christian Ireland. 1919
Early Christian Latin poets from the fourth to the sixth century. 1023
Early Christian life as reflected in its literature. 1093
Early Christian origins. 1103, 3818
Early Christian prayers. 2891
Early Christian rhetoric. 425
Early Christian Sabbath. 3261
Early Christian thinkers. 25, 1287
Early Christian thought and the classical tradition. 1287, 2161
Early Christian worship. 419, 3260, 3855
Early Christian writings. 1018, 1019
Early Christianity. 330, 1189
Early Christianity and Greek paideia. 1081
... Early Christianity and its rivals. 1078
Early Christianity and paganism. 1194
Early Christianity and society. 3451
Early Christians. 330, 1093, 1196
Early Christians after the death of the apostles. 1018
Early Christians in Rome. 1093
Early Christians of Rome. 919
Early Christians of the 21st century. 1282
Early Christians speak. 1196
Early church. 328, 334, 1190, 1191, 1196, 1197
Early church and Africa. 329, 1196
Early church and the coming great church. 1192
Early Church and the state. 1152
Early church from ignatius to Augustine. 1192
Early church history to A.D. 313. 1196
Early church in Britain. 1759
Early church in the light of the monuments. 918
Early church portrait gallery. 1616
Early church speaks to us. 1433
Early churches and towns in South Dakota. 3464
Early churches in Palestine. 1273
... Early churches in Syria. 1161
Early churches of Constantinople: architecture and liturgy. 78
Early churches of Rome. 3245
Early churches of Venango county. 1273
Early churches of Washington State. 1162
Early clergy of Pennsylvania and Delaware. 1293
Early communar and pitancer rolls of Norwich Cathedral Priory with an account of the building of the cloister. 2715
Early Connecticut meetinghouses. 1269
Early conversion. 1783
Early conversion of children. 896
Early crowned. 2714
... The early days of Christianity. 1049, 1191
Early days of Elisha. 1506
... The early days of Israel. 483
Early days of monasticism on mount Athos. 102
Early days of Mormonism, Palmyra, Kirtland, and Nauvoo. 2603
Early days of St. Gabriel's. 1347
Early days of the church in the Helderberg. 1690, 3215
Early days of Thomas Whittemore. 3814
Early dead. 896
Early development of Mohammedanism. 1924
... The early development of Mohammedinism. 2566
Early Dominican laybrother. 1475
Early Dominicans. 1475
Early English church. 1758
Early English churches in America 1607-1807. 1162
Early English dissenters. 1468
Early English dissenters in the light of recent research (1550-1641) 1468
Early English hymns. 1873
Early Episcopal Sunday schools. 2965
Early Franciscan classics. 1641, 1646
Early Franciscan government. 1505, 1646
Early Franciscans & Jesuits. 933
Early freemasonry in Pennsylvania. 1668
Early freemasonry in Williamsburg. Virginia. 1672
Early friends of Christ. 338
Early gentile Christianity and its Hellenistic background. 1081
Early Greek elegists. 1505
Early harvest. 896
Early Hebrew history. 596
Early Hebrew stories. 628
Early Hebrew story. 2096
Early history of Christianity. 1192
Early history of Free Will Baptists. 1658
Early history of Israel. 2097
Early history of Linton Church. 3277
Early history of the Church of the United Brethren (United Fratrum) 2595

Early history of the Disciples in the Western Reserve, Ohio. 1465
Early history of the liturgy. 2240, 2257
Early history of the Lutheran church in America. 2294
Early history of the monastery of Cluny. 1304
Early history of the Reformed church in Pennsylvania. 3048
Early history of Zionism in America; papers presented at the conference on the early history of Zionism in America, convened by the American Jewish Historical Society and the Theodor Herzl Foundation, in New York City, on December twenty-sixth and twenty-seventh, nineteen hundred and fifty-five. Edited by Isidore S. Meyer. 3897
Early iconography of the tree of Jesse. 921, 1958
Early impressions. 1682
Early Indian religions. 1897
Early Indian religious thought. 1897, 3020, 3213
Early Indian sculpture. 3316
Early Irish myths and sagas. 1521
Early Israel in recent history writing. 499
Early Jewish hermeneutic in Palestine. 56, 505
Early Judaism. 2146
Early Kansas churches. 1270
Early Latin hymnaries. 1877
Early Latin hymns. 1877
Early Latin song-book. 1876
Early Latin theology. 1020
Early Latter Day Saint history. 1233, 2616
Early letters of Thomas Carlyle. 740
Early life and later experience and labors of Elder Joseph Bates. 3379
Early life and times of the First Congregational church of Pocatello. 2855
Early life of Jesus and new light on Passion week. 1977
Early liturgy, to the time of Gregory the Great. 2236
Early lost, early saved. 1349
Early Low-German Bibles. 283
Early Lutheran education in Pennsylvania. 2292
Early Madhyamika in India and China. 2311
Early manhood. 937
Early medieval music. 2633
Early medieval theology. 3669
Early Methodism in the Carolinas. 2432
Early Methodism in the Miami Valley 1798-1920. 2432
Early Methodist Church buildings in the Pittsburgh Conference. 2447
Early Methodist people. 2423
Early Methodist women. 2427
Early Methodists under persecution. 2440
Early Middle Ages. 1185, 1186
Early ministers at St. Michael's, Charleston. 2960
Early missionary preaching. 334
Early monastic Buddhism. 1704
Early monastic rules. 2583
Early morning light. 1228
Early morning scenes in the Bible. 614
Early mystic of Baghdad. 21
Early narratives of Genesis. 524
Early New England and catechisms. 748
Early New England catechisms. 748
Early New England psalmody. 1208
Early newspaper accounts of freemasonry, in Pennsylvania, England. Ireland and Scotland. from 1730 to 1750. 1664
Early Norman secular musicians on the church of Barfreston in Kent. 173, 2634
Early Old Testament stories. 630
Early persecutions of the Christians. 2821
Early piety. 910
Early piety exemplified in the life and death of Mr. Nathaniel Mather. 2373
Early poems of Ralph Waldo Emerson. 1510
Early poetry of Israel in its physical and social origins. 1798
Early portraits of Jesus. 1995
Early prayer books of America. 2884
Early Presbyterianism in Wisconsin. 2929
Early puritan writers. 32
Early Quaker education in Pennsylvania. 1683
Early Quaker writings, 1650-1700. 1678
Early reading of Pierre Bayle. 179
Early religion of Israel. 2115, 2116
Early religious education considered as the divinely appointed way to the regenerate life. 3149
Early religious poetry of the Hebrews. 1798
Early Russian architecture. 1161
Early Saxons. 1761

Early sermons of Luther and their relation to the pre-reformation sermon. 2274, 2910
Early 17th century missions of the Southwest. 3470, 2526
Early Sikh tradition. 3005
Early sixteenth century Roman Catholic theologians and the German Reformation. 3628
Early sources of the liturgy. 2239
Early Soviet saint. 3891
... The early spread of religious ideas especially in the Far East. 3115
Early stained glass of Canterbury Cathedral, circa 1175-1220. 737, 1715
... Early steps in the fold. 785
Early stone temples of Orissa. 3600
Early teachings of the masters. 3685
Early teen pack. 937
Early temples of the Mormons. 3600
Early Tennessee Baptists. 152
Early theological works. 3637
Early tractarians and the Eastern church. 2755
Early traditions about Jesus. 1960, 1986, 2007
Early trail and centennial history of Methodist Episcopal church. 2452
Early trope repertory of Saint Martial de Limoges. 849, 3715
Early versions of the New Testament. 479
Early Victorian Methodism. 713
Early will I seek thee. 899, 1362
Early will I seek Thee, journal of a heart that longed and found. 1362
Early works of Thomas Becon. 1216
Early writings of Ellen G. White. 3384
Early writings of John Hooper. 1216, 1702
Early writings of Mrs. White. 3384
Early years. 687
Early years of Christianity. 1093, 2526
Early years of Isaac Thomas Hecker. 1799
Early years of the Christian church. 626
Early Zoroastrianism. 3899
Earnest Christian. 3240
Earnest entreaties and appeals to the unconverted. 1358
Earnest inquiry into the true Scriptural organization of the Churches of God in Christ Jesus. 1273
Earnest ministry the want of the times. 3672
Earnest search for truth. 1396

Ears of Midas, and other radio sermonettes. 2425
Earth. 293
Earth and sky. 1733
Earth and the Word. 203
Earth and the world. 204
Earth festivals. 2726
Earth has no sorrow. 1353
Earth in the heavens. 95
Earth is enough. 3098
Earth is full of His riches. 3766
Earth is the Lord's. 938, 1022, 2075, 3164, 3530
Earth is the Lord's and The Sabbath. 2075
Earth mass. 1308
Earth might be fair. 1853, 2323, 2374
Earth, moon, and beyond. 3069
Earth speaks to Bryan. 699, 1580
Earth, the temple, and the gods. 79, 3599
Earth, the theater of the universe. 1485
Earth wisdom. 3480
Earth with heaven. 2062
Earthen vessel. 3503
Earthen vessel;a volume dealing with spirit-communication received in the form of books-tests. 3503
Earthen vessels. 3299
Earthkeeping, Christian stewardship of natural resources. 2672
Earthly and temporal power. 3525
Earthly blooms from heavenly stems. 1436
Earthly footprints of our risen Lord. 399, 1988
Earthly paradise. 3785
Earthly problems in heavenly light. 2692
...Earthly stories with heavenly meanings. 3204
Earthly things. 63
Earthly trials and glory of the immortal life. 1697
Earth's earliest ages and their connection with modern spiritualism and theosophy. 3510
Earths in our solar system, which are called planets. 1371
Earths in the universe, and their inhabitants. 1371
Earthward pilgrimage. 3729
East African Christian. 1073
...The East African question. 2119

East and West. 1913
East and west in religion. 3119
East Bay and Eden. 1339
East Burlap parables. 1089
East Christian paintings in the Freer collection. 921
East from Burma. 2503
East is East. 1082
East Liberty Presbyterian church. 2913
East meets West. 3689
East to Eden? 3086
East wind. 2230, 3851
East window, and other sermons. 2436
East Windsor heritage. 1485
Easter. 314, 1486
Easter and its customs. 1485
Easter and lilies. 1486
... Easter as a chapter in the mystery wisdom of man. 1486
Easter book. 1486
Easter chimes. 1485
Easter eve. 1323
Easter faith and history. 2051
Easter garland. 1486
Easter helper. 1486
Easter hope. 1891
Easter idea book. 1485
Easter in the Sunday school. 1485
Easter, its story and meaning. 1486
Easter lilies. 2054
Easter meditations. 2051
Easter message today. 2051
Easter moment. 2054
Easter people. 2596
Easter proclamation: remembrance, and renewal. 162, 2054
Easter radiance. 1485
Easter reflections. 1486, 1529, 2053
Easter sermons by representative preachers. 3366
Easter story. 632, 2032, 2054
Easter story for children. 1486, 1983
Easter story from the Gospels. 1985
Easter the world over. 1486
Easterglow. 2211
Eastern branches of the Catholic church. 851
Eastern Catholic Church and Czar Nicholas I. 756
Eastern Catholic liturgies. 2237
Eastern Catholic worship. 2236
Eastern Christendom. 2745
Eastern Christianity in India. 866
Eastern church in the Western World. 1487, 2970
Eastern churches and Catholic unity. 1045
Eastern churches review. 1487
Eastern definitions. 3138
Eastern elements in Western chant. 2633
Eastern liturgical theology. 2236
Eastern liturgies. 1487
Eastern manners illustrative of the Old Testament history. 534
Eastern mysticism. 2642
Eastern Orthodox catechism. 2745
Eastern Orthodox Church. 2744, 2745, 2747
Eastern Orthodox Church directory of the United States, 1968. 2751
Eastern Orthodox Church, its thought and life. 2744
Eastern paths and the Christian way. 1082
Eastern philosophy for western minds. 3865
Eastern politics of the Vatican, 1917-1979. 860, 1542
Eastern question in prophecy. 610
Eastern religions. 92
Eastern religions and western thought. 3123
Eastern religions in the electric age. 3880
Eastern sketches. 1686, 2541
Eastern Star. 2741
Eastern thoughts Western thoughts. 2187
Eastern wisdom and Western thought. 2839
Easter's path to Pentecost. 1267
Eastertide in Pennsylvania, a folk cultural study. 1486
Eastward! The story of Adoniram Judson. 2157
Eastward to the sun. 2530
Easy Christman book by various authors. 1111
Easy essays. 1137
Easy finding Bible index. 304
Easy grammar of sacred history. 296
... The easy instructor; or, A new method of teaching sacred harmony. 2632
Easy journey to other planets. 3867
Easy journey to other planets, by practice of supreme yoga. 3867
Easy keys for busy teachers. 3557
Easy lessons on Scripture history. 915

Easy notation for singing the proper of the mass for all feasts of "double" rite (1st class, 2nd class, major) Sundays, ember and rogation days, vigils and the forty hours. 883
Easy object lessons (to get and give) 909
Easy plays for church and school. 2161
Easy programs for church holidays. 1623
Easy steps for little feet from Genesis to Revelation. 645
Easy steps in the Bible story. 628, 644
Easy Sunday school entertainments for Easter, Christmas, Mother's day, Father's day, Children's day and Rally day. 3560
Easy to use installation services. 1911
Eat, drink and be merry! 2252
Eat from God's hand. 1153, 1704
Eating and drinking with Jesus. 2254
Ebell lectures on spiritual science. 2695
Eberhard Arnold. 83
Eberhardt's Bible thesaurus. 302
Ebla tablets. 1488
Ebony jewel box, and other sermons. 2933
Ebony saint. 2620
Ecce Agnus Dei. 106
Ecce clerus. 3672
Ecce Deus. 1194, 2001, 3329
Ecce Filius. 2044
"Ecce homo"? 788, 1957, 1972, 1978, 2001, 2004, 3503
Ecce Homo; a survey of the life and work of Jesus Christ. 2004
Ecce homo! or, A critical inquiry into the history of Jesus of Nazareth. 1978
Ecce orienti. 1669
Ecce terra. 2980
Ecce veritas. 1951
Ecclesiastical history. 1194
Eccentric preacher. 1478
Eccleastictical opposition to the Bible. 278
De ecclesia. 1118
Ecclesia Dei. 1118
Ecclesial cybernetics. 807
Ecclesial dimension of the sacrament of Penance from a catechetical point of view. 2812
Ecclesial man. 1104, 1858
Ecclesial reflection. 3668
Ecclesial women. 2572
Ecclesiam Suam. 755, 2805
... Ecclesiastes. 511, 512, 513, 602, 3394
... Ecclesiastes and the Wisdom of Solomon. 489, 511
Ecclesiastes anglicana. 2900
Ecclesiastes; or, Koheleth. 512
Ecclesiastes speaks to us today. 512
Ecclesiastes: stories to live by. 512, 3015
Ecclesiastes, with an essay. 511
Ecclesiastes, words of Koheleth, son of David, king in Jerusalem. 511
Ecclesiastical administration in medieval England. 1220, 1489
Ecclesiastical amusements. 1121
Ecclesiastical and liturgical year. 2391
Ecclesiastical and political history of the popes of Rome during the sixteenth and seventeenth centuries. 2862
Ecclesiastical art in Germany during the middle ages. 1160
Ecclesiastical authority and spiritual power in the church of the first three centuries. 1162
Ecclesiastical barony of the middle ages. 179
... Ecclesiastical censure at the end of the fifteenth century. 1583
Ecclesiastical class book. 1175
Ecclesiastical courts of York. 1488
Ecclesiastical crafts. 2234
Ecclesiastical dictionary. 3092
Ecclesiastical empire [from the fall of Rome to the present day]. 1176
Ecclesiastical hierarchy. 3266
Ecclesiastical history. 1173, 1190, 1191, 1524
Ecclesiastical history, ancient and modern. 1177
Ecclesiastical history, ancient and modern, from the birth of Christ, to the beginning of the present century. 1177
Ecclesiastical history and the Martyrs of Palestine. 1190
Ecclesiastical history book III, text. 1761
Ecclesiastical history of England and Normandy. 1178
Ecclesiastical history of Orderic Vitalis. 1178
Ecclesiastical history of the English nation. 1397, 1761
Ecclesiastical history of the English people. 1760
Ecclesiastical Japanese. 779
Ecclesiastical law and discipline. 1166
Ecclesiastical law and rules of evidence. 1490

ECCLESIASTICAL LAW AND RELIGIOUS BOOKS 1876 - 1982

Ecclesiastical law and rules of evidence, with special reference to the jurisprudence of the Methodist Episcopal church. 1490
Ecclesiastical laws of Pennsylvania. 1490
Ecclesiastical octopus. 1619
Ecclesiastical office and the primacy of Rome. 1248, 1287
... Ecclesiastical pensions. 190
Ecclesiastical polity. 1240, 1335
Ecclesiastical polity, book VIII. 1146
... The ecclesiastical prohibition of books. 2945
... Ecclesiastical records. 1762
Ecclesiastical reminiscences of the United States. 3740
Ecclesiastical shields for the interior of churches. 1804
Ecclesiastical sonnets of William Wordsworth. 3210
Ecclesiastical tradition. 3706
Ecclesiastical vocabulary and apocryphal code. 307
Ecclesiastical year. 1262
Ecclesiastical year for Catholic schools and institutions. 1262
Ecclesiasticall history [of] Theodoret. 1197
... Ecclesiasticus. 489
Ecclesiasticus, or the wisdom of Jesus son of Sirach. 489
Ecclesiatical polity of Methodism defended. 2450
[Ecclesiology. 147, 1118, 1248
Ecclesiology, a study of the churches. 2d and carefully rev. ed. 1118
Echo of the Nazi holocaust in rabbinic literature. 1825
Echo of tradition. 3371
Echoes along the shore. 298
Echoes eternal. 3480
Echoes from Bharatkhand. 2532
Echoes from Edinburgh, 1910. 3851
Echoes from eternity. 2725
"Echoes from hell," 2939
Echoes from Indonesia. 2533
Echoes from peak and plain. 2451
Echoes from the altar, sermons. 1466
Echoes from the Oratory. 2703
Echoes from the Orient. 3685
Echoes from the past. 1444
Echoes from the spirit world. 3506
Echoes of Assisi. 1640, 1645
Echoes of Christian education. 15
Echoes of memory and emotion. 2401, 2697
Echoes of Pauline concepts in the speech at Antioch. 334
Echoes of Pinebrook. 3350
Echoes of the cosmic song. 2725
Echoes of the Orient. 3689
Echoes of thunder. 3053
Echoes of wisdom. 3584
Eck-Vidya. 1490
Eckankar dictionary. 1491
Eclipse of Biblical narrative. 241
Eclipse of Christianity in Asia. 91
Eclipse of Christianity in Asia from the time of Muhammad till the fourteenth century. 91
Eclipse of God. 3098
Eclipse of God; studies in the relation between religion and philosophy. 2835
Eclipse of symbolism. 3573
Eclogue. 537
Ecology and human need. 1853
Ecology of faith. 2905
Economic activities of the Jews of Amsterdam. 2098
Economic anxiety & Christian faith. 1076
Economic background of the Gospels. 389, 394
Economic basis for downtown renewal. 1929
Economic basis of the evangelical church in Mexico. 2954
Economic basis of the Evangelical church in Mexico. 2954
Economic causes of the reformation in England. 3039
Economic consequences of the size of nations. 3525
Economic crisis. 1076
Economic destruction of German Jewry by the Nazi regime, 1933-1937. 2100
Economic Eden. 3345
Economic ethics of John Wesley. 3452, 3804
Economic morals of the Jesuits. 1944, 3241
Economic order and religion. 1075, 1076
Economic problems of the church. 1219
... Economic survey of Wilmington, North Carolina. 3818
Economics and the Gospel. 1076
Economics of Christianity. 3443
Economics of the kingdom of God. 3441
Economics of the Zambezi missions, 1580-1759. 850, 2559
Economy and policy of a Christian education. 3151
Economy and society. 3450
Economy of Methodism illustrated and defended. 2422
Economy of the animal kingdom. 2845
Ecountering truth. 3227
Ecritures grecques chretiennes. 320
Ecstasies of Thomas De Quincey. 2638
Ecstasy. 1491
Ecstatic religion. 1491
Ecuador. 2517
Ecumencial studies: baptism and marriage. 134
Ecumenic Psalm 87. 584
Ecumenical beginnings in Protestant world mission. 1912
Ecumenical breakthrough. 1044
Ecumenical confession of faith? 1386
Ecumenical council. 1373, 3770
Ecumenical council, the church and Christendom. 3770
... The ecumenical councils. 1372, 1373
Ecumenical councils of the Catholic Church. 1373
Ecumenical dialogue at Harvard. 1044
Ecumenical dialogue in Europe. 1045
Ecumenical directory of retreat and conference centers. 1164
Ecumenical era in church and society. 1492, 2308
Ecumenical experiences. 1043
Ecumenical foundations. 1913
Ecumenical mirage. 1041
Ecumenical missionary conference, New York, 1900. 2519
Ecumenical movement. 1045, 1491, 1492, 3849
Ecumenical movement in bibliographical outline. 1492
Ecumenical movement, what it is and what it does. 1040
Ecumenical patriarchate under the Turkish Republic. 1152, 1354
Ecumenical progress. 1491
Ecumenical revolution. 861, 1492
Ecumenical scandal on Main Street. 1039
Ecumenical student workbook. 1493
Ecumenical testimony. 1046
Ecumenical theology no. 2. 1039
Ecumenical theology today. 1042, 1046
Ecumenical trends in hymnody. 1875
Ecumenical vanguard. 1045, 2460
Ecumenicity and evangelism. 1571
Ecumenicity, evangelicals, and Rome. 1043
Ecumenics. 1120
Ecumenism. 1468, 3061
Ecumenism and charismatic renewal. 2816
Ecumenism and religious education. 1043
Ecumenism and the evangelical. 1491
Ecumenism and the future of the Church. 1043
Ecumenism and the Reformed Church. 1046, 3046
Ecumenism and the Roman Catholic Church. 1042
Ecumenism and universalism. 1039
Ecumenism and Vatican II. 3770
Ecumenism: boon or bane? 1039
Ecumenism in the age of the Reformation. 2857
Ecumenism or new reformation? 811, 1245
Ecumenism, the spirit, and worship. 1043
Ecumenism, unity, and peace. 1043
Ecumenopolis U.S.A. 2480
Edda. 1493, 2665
... Eddic [mythology]. 2666
Eddyism. 1037
Edel Quinn, beneath the Southern Cross. 2499, 3013
Eden and Easter. 1382, 2030
Eden and evolution. 204
Eden, golden age or goad to action? 1496
Eden Revival. 1497, 1894
Eden road. 2694
Eden tableau. 526
Edenton Street in Methodism. 3019
Edgar Cayce. 876, 877
Edgar Cayce; mystery man of miracles. 877
Edgar Cayce on prophecy. 2946, 2948
Edgar Cayce on reincarnation. 3052, 3053
Edgar Cayce on religion and psychic experience. 876, 3072
Edgar Cayce on the Dead Sea scrolls. 1410, 2989
Edgar Cayce reader. 2992
Edgar Cayce readings. 2993
Edgar Cayce, the sleeping prophet. 877
Edgar Cayce's photographic legacy. 876
Edgar Cayce's story of Jesus. 2060
Edgar Cayce's story of karma. 2165
Edgar Gardner Murphy, gentle progressive. 2631, 3468
Edgar Young Mullins. 2630
Edge of adventure. 986, 2466
Edge of contingency. 3085
Edge of death. 1415
Edge of judgment. 556
Edge of paradise. 2767
Edge of the edge. 1121
Edge of the ghetto. 1131, 1132
Edge of tomorrow. 2539, 2948
Edge of wisdom. 3637
Edges of language. 3071
Edict of Nantes. 1497
Edicts. 707
Edifying discourses. 3479, 3480
Edith Stein. 1363, 3526
Edith Stein: thoughts on her life and times. 3526
Editio princeps of the Epistle of Barnabas. 337
Editions of the Bible and parts thereof in English, from the year mdv to mdccl. 212
Editorial comments on the life and work of Mary Baker Eddy. 1493
Editorial subjects and viewpoints of life. 2225
Editorially speaking. 1003
Editorials from Lehre und Wehre. 2285, 3632
Edmund A. Walsh, S. J. 3790
Edmund Campion. 733
Edmund Gibson, bishop of London, 1669-1748. 1711, 1759
Edmund Rich. 1497
Edmunds law. "Unlawful cohabitation," as defined by Chief Justice Chas. S. Zane, of the territory of Utah, in the trial of Angus M. Cannon, esq., in the third District court, Salt Lake City, April 27, 28, 29, 1885. 2858
Edouard Seguin. 3329
Educating children for peace. 2808
Educating emotionally disturbed children. 2411
Educating for Christian missions. 936, 3467
Educating for civic responsibility. 1277
Educating for missions in the local church. 2551
Educating the children of the poor. 3436
Educating the good man. 2592
Educating to purity. 3393
Educating youth in missions. 1260
Education. 806
Education adequate for modern times. 1497
Education among the Mennonites of America. 2405
Education and evangelism. 1164
Education and marginality in the communal society of the Hutterites. 1858
Education and practical common sense. 1323
Education and railroad men. 3592
Education and religion. 3157
Education and responsibility. 2592
Education and the faith of America. 2591
Education and the liturgy. 18th North American Liturgical Week, St. John's Abbey, Collegeville, Minn., August 19-22, 1957. 2240
Education and the worship of God. 3190
Education curriculum for the moderately, severely, and profoundly mentally handicapped pupil. 2411
Education for change. 3146
Education for character. 2592
Education for Christian living. 3154, 3176
Education for Christian marriage. 2339
Education for Christian service. 3626
Education for churchmanship. 3168, 3169
Education for decision. 2942
Education for life with God. 3156
Education for ministry. 2474
Education for mission. 2551
Education for moral growth. 2591
Education for renewal. 3168
Education for successful living. 3148
Education for supervised ministries. 685, 1297
Education for the culturally disadvantaged. 3436
Education for the real world. 1127
... Education for world-mindedness. 2551
Education handbook of parents of handicapped children. 2773
Education in church music. 1203
Education in religion and morals. 2590
Education in the Christian religion. 3157
Education in the city church. 1279
Education in the city church: the city church project, 1964-1967. 1279
Education in the New Testament. 3161
Education in the Society of Friends past, present, and prospective. 1683
Education into religion. 3155
Education of a Black Muslim. 669
Education of a civilized man. 1129, 1226
Education of American Jewish teachers (The) 3166
Education of American ministers. 1471, 3612
Education of an urban minority. 815
Education of boys. 806
Education of Catholic Americans. 831
Education of Catholic girls. 806
Education of children from the standpoint of theosophy. 1498
Education of Christ. 2003
Education of dull children at the primary stage. 2411
Education of ministers of Disciples of Christ. 1463
Education of missionaries' children. 898
Education of Negro ministers. 2681, 3612
Education of sisters. 2581
Education of the Jewish child. 3166
Education of the novice. 2716
Education question. 1129
Education that educates. 2086
Education that is Christian. 3153
Education: to whom does it belong? 1481
Education toward adulthood. 938
Education under penalty. 818
Education with a tradition. 3438
Educational activities for boys. 3870
Educational activities of New England Quakers. 1683
Educational aspects of spiritual writings. 116, 3489
Educational aspects of the legislation of the Councils of Baltimore, 1829-1884. 814
Educational aspects of the missions in the Southwest. 2548
Educational blue book and directory of the Church of the brethren, 1708-1923. 1236
Educational classes and other service with working-men. 2189
Educational convention papers. 1023
Educational evangelism. 3153
Educational foundations of the Jesuits in sixteenth-century New Spain. 1948
Educational function of the church. 1128
Educational ideal in the ministry. 3671
Educational ideals of Blessed Julie Billiart. 659
Educational ideas and related philosophical concepts in the writings of Maimonides. 2622
Educational instructions overseas. 2915
Educational-jubilee. 1498
Educational lectures. 806
Educational ministry of the church. 1128
Educational mission of our church. 3157
Educational mission of the church. 3161
Educational missions. 2518
Educational movements of to-day. 1130
... Educational of defectives in th public schools. 895
Educational policy and the mission schools. 2517
Educational principles in the curriculum. 3154
... Educational supervision in our Catholic schools. 804
Educational systems of the Puritans and Jesuits compared. 1946
Educational task of the local church. 3147
...Educational work for men, its field, organization, and supervision in the Young men's Christian associations. 3873
Educational work of the church. 1460, 3151
Educational work of the Felician Sistors of the Province of Detroit in the United States, 1874-1948. 1620
Educational work of the small church. 3157
Edward Christian Jesperson-Ida Martineau book of golden memories, 1911-1916. 1944
Edward Gayer Andrews. 41
Edward Hicks, Friends' minister. 1810
Edward Irving" 1920
Edward Judson, interpreter of God. 2158
Edward King: Bishop of Lincoln, 1885-1910. 2172
Edward Leen. 2206
Edward O. Guerrant. 1776
Edward Schillebeeckx, O.P. 777, 3634
Edward Stuart Talbot. 3580
Edward Taylor. 3590

Edward Taylor vs. Solomon Stoddard. 2256, 3590
Edward Taylor's "Church records," and related sermons. 1343, 3808
Edward Williams, D.D., 1750-1813. 3817
... The Edwardian inventories for Bedfordshire. 1242
... The Edwardian inventories for Buckinghamshire. 1242
... The Edwardian inventories for Huntingdonshire. 1242
Edwin Arnold as poetizer and as paganizer. 83, 84, 704
Edwin Bainbridge. 130
Edwin Diller Starbuck, pioneer in the psychology of religion. 2996, 3525
Edwin Vincent O'Hara. 2735
Edwin Vincent O'Hara: American prelate. 2735
Eerdman's concise Bible encyclopedia. 285
Eerdmans' concise Bible handbook. 285
Eerdman's family encyclopedia of the Bible. 285
Eerdmans' handbook. 3661
Eerdmans' handbook to Christian belief. 3666
Eerdmans' handbook to Christian history. 1184
Eerdmans' handbook to the Bible. 285
... The effect of reading on moral conduct and emotional experience. 681
Effect of the Shaker conversions on the Christian Church in Kentucky and Ohio. 3398
Effect of the teaching of evolution upon the religious convictions of undergraduate students as evidenced by theses upon this subject. 1580
Effective adult class. 3154
Effective Bible study. 638, 642
Effective biblical counseling. 1107
Effective Christian college. 1127
Effective church. 1251
Effective church planning. 1200
Effective city church. 1278
Effective communication. 1316
Effective evangelism. 1571
Effective evangelistic messages. 1560
Effective evangelistic preaching. 2906
Effective father. 1615
... Effective illustrations. 1842
Effective leadership for today's church. 952
Effective missionary. 1233, 1564
Effective parent. 552, 2773
Effective pastor. 1295
Effective prayer. 2870, 2883
Effective prayer life. 2880
Effective praying. 2872
Effective preaching. 2897, 2902
Effective public prayer. 2783
Effective readings for special days and occasions. 1446
Effective use of church space. 1167
Effective work with intermediates in the Sunday school. 3167
Effective workers in needy fields. 2240
Effective year-round Bible ministries. 937
Effectiveness of Lutheran elementary and secondary schools as agencies of Christian education. 3886
... Effectiveness of Prebyterian college programs in developing leadership for religious education. 3176
Effects of divine manifestation on the reader's perspective in Vergil's Aeneid. 3780
Effects of religion. 2113
Effectual fervent prayer. 604
Effectual prayer. 2409
Efficiency in the spiritual life. 3493
Efficiency in the Sunday school. 3553
Efficiency points. 2492
Efficient church. 1118, 2442
Efficient church business management. 1250
Efficient church officer. 1239
Efficient Epworthian. 1525
Efficient layman. 958
Efficient religion. 3065
Efficient young people's society. 1248, 3877
Egeria: diary of a pilgrimage. 1198
Egermeier's Bible story book. 620
Egermeier's favorite Bible stories. 620
Ego and the self. 3330
Ego in faith. 2280
Egoism. 3087
Egotism in German philosophy. 1500
Egypt and Israel. 1501
Egypt and the Bible. 537
Egypt and the books of Moses, or, The books of Moses illustrated by the monuments of Egypt: with an appendix. 526

Egypt and the Christian crusade. 1391, 2517
Egypt and the Exodus. 517
Egypt in biblical prophecy. 610
Egypt myth and legend. 2659
Egypt to Canaan. 516
Egyptian belief and modern thought. 1501
Egyptian book of the dead. 1503
... The Egyptian conception of immortality. 1890
Egyptian elements in the legend of the body and soul. 3461
Egyptian heaven and hell. 1530
Egyptian ideas of the future life. 1501, 1698
Egyptian initiation. 1660
Egyptian magic. 1501, 2314
Egyptian myth and legend. 2659
Egyptian mythology. 2659
Egyptian myths and mysteries. 2659
Egyptian religion. 1501, 1502
Egyptian religious texts and representations. v. 1. 1501
Egyptian revival. 2726
Egyptian saints. 1743
Egyptian temples. 3599
Egypt's princes. 2517
Eheofpiaubos: or, The triumph of mercy in the chariot of praise. 2412
Eight American praxapostoloi. 316
Eight bags of gold. 3580
Eight Beatitudes. 180
Eight Boyle lectures on atheism. 101, 862
Eight days of glory. 1837
Eight days' retreat for religious. 3222
Eight days that rocked the world. 1837
Eight days with Bob Harrington. 1786, 3230
Eight days with the spiritualists. 3503
Eight first words of the risen Saviour, John 20-21. 2006
Eight friends of the great. 1758
8 happy people. 179
Eight hundred colleges face the future. 1164
Eight hundred years of journeys to the Holy Land, from Benjamin of Tudela to the present. 2847
Eight keys to happiness. 180
Eight keys to success. 3539
Eight leading churches. 1268
... Eight lectures. 3866
Eight lectures on miracles. 2477
Eight lights. 1784
Eight-minute sermons. 1266
Eight points of the Oxford group. 2753
Eight sermons preached before the University of Oxford. 1226
Eight sermons preached before the University of Oxford, in the year 1783, at the lecture founded by the Rev. John Bampton. 1225
Eight studies of the Lord's day. 3260
Eight translation New Testament. 357
Eight vital relationships for the growing Christian. 988
Eight women of the YWCA. 3878
Eight-year teacher. 3549
Eight years in Kaffraria, 1882-1890. 1224, 2536
Eighteen centuries of the church in England. 1758
Eighteen centuries of the Orthodox Greek church. 1768
1888-1925. History of the Woman's Christian temperance union of Indian Territory, Oklahoma Territory, state of Oklahoma. 3833
1855-1885. Our India mission. 2530
1853 1903; anniversary services of the first Presbyterian church Bridgeport, Connecticut, October 25th-November 1st. 2915
1853-1953: one hundred years of achievement by the Catholic Church in the Diocese of Burlington, Vermont...Centenary memorial book. 717
1804-1904; the record of a century of church life of the Reformed church. 3046
1806-1906. The centennial volume of Missouri Methodism. 2457
1819-1849 abstradex of annual returns: Mississippi Free and Accepted Masons. 1667
1896 and five redemption years. 1563
Eighteen sermons on great themes. 1561, 3360
Eighteen sermons preached by the late Rev. George Whitefield. 2935
1810-1910; centennial celebration of the United Presbyterian church Princeton, Indiana. 3736
1833-1933. One century for Christ. 712
Eighteen years in Uganda & East Africa. 1224, 2499

Eighteenth century confronts the gods. 3140
18th century creche. 1387
Eighteenth century English aesthetics. 11
Eighteenth century piety. 3437
Eighteenth century pulpit. 2909
Eighteenth century Reformed church schools. 3048
Eighth-century Gelasian sacramentary. 3262
Eighth century prophets. 544
Eighth day of creation. 1712
Eighth fear. 2434
Eighth square. 3665
88 evangelistic sermons. 1561
80 talks for Orthodox young people. 941
Eighty-three different questions. 3669, 3670
Eighty-three years. 2586
Eighty-two family letters to the western family of lovers and followers of Meher Baba. 2400
Eighty years. 2917
Eighty years of Fidelity no. 163, U.G.L. of N.S.W. 1668
Eighty years of history of St. John's Evangelical Lutheran Church of West New York. 1547
Eighty years of Swedish Baptist work in Iowa, 1853-1933. 154
88 children's sermons for all occasions. 3370
89 evangelistic sermons. 1561
89 modern mission stories. 2489
87 years behind the black curtain. 14
82 family letters to the western family of lovers and followers of Meher Baba. 2400
Eileen Garrett and the world beyond the senses. 1702
... Eileithyia. 1509
Eistles general of Peter. 447
Either way, I win. 931, 2128
Eivind Berggrav. 192
Eivind Berggrav, God's man of suspense. 192
Ekstasy. 94
El discurso maestro de Jesucristo. 1955, 3137
El Dorado. 2757
Elder Aaron Leland. 2209
Elder and younger brothers. 1083
Elder brother. 2203, 3682
Eldership. 1503
Eldridge Cleaver reborn. 1287, 1367
Elect in the Son. 1505
Elect ladies of Centenary. 3236
"The elect lady" 685
Elect nation. 1637
Election and consensus in the church. 665, 759
Election and conversion. 1360
Election and reprobation. 2911
... The election of bishops in the letters of Gregory the Great. 666, 1773
Elections in the church. 808
Electives for revitalizing high school religion. 3175
Electric church. 3018
Electric evangelism. 3018
Electric liturgy. 3003
Electric love. 981

Electrical merchandising classified directory of appliance. 1505
Electricity. 1505
Electricity and Christianity. 1505
Electricity and its similitudes. 3080
Electro magnetic principle of creation. 1383
Electrograms from Elysium. 3501
Electronic Christian. 793
Electrons of inspiration. 3018
Elegant and learned discourse of the light of nature. 3099
Elegant composition concerning relief after adversity. 3585
... An elegy in a country churchyard. 1757
Elegy of faith. 3095, 3602
Element of child study and religious pedagogy. 3158
Elemental forces in home missions. 2526
Elemental religion. 3060
Elemental theology. 3640
Elemental theology, doctrinal and conservative. 3640
Elementary Bible history. 292
Elementary Christian metaphysics. 2419
Elementary Christianity. 1047
Elementary course of Biblical theology. 3643, 3648
Elementary division organized for service. 3552
Elementary ethics. 1534
Elementary forms of the religious life. 3108, 3109

Elementary grade children in the school manual. 3178
Elementary grammar of Gregorian chant. 883
Elementary homiletics. 2900
Elementary introduction to religion and Christianity. 3056
Elementary schools. 1129
Elementary schools and religious education of the people. 1129
Elementary studies in the life and letters of Paul. 372
Elementary theosophy. 3685, 3687
... The elementary worker and his work (treating the beginner's and primary departments only.) 3554
Elements in Baptist development. 151
Elements of astrology. 95
Elements of Biblical interpretation. 288
Elements of Christian belief. 67
Elements of Christian philosophy. 2836, 3695, 3697
Elements of dispensational truth. 3717
Elements of divinity. 3624, 3647, 3652
Elements of dogmatic history. 3654
Elements of ecclesiastical law. 735, 1489
Elements of Franciscan formation. 1646
Elements of general and Christian theology. 3666
Elements of Hindu iconography. 2663
Elements of intellectual philosophy. 2833
Elements of logic. 2242
Elements of medium theology. 3661
Elements of metaphysics. 2419
Elements of moral science. 1534, 1537
Elements of moral theology. 946
Elements of mythology. 2657
Elements of New Testament Greek. 1770, 1771
Elements of pain and conflict in human life, considered from a Christian point of view. 3541
... Elements of personal Christianity. 1051
Elements of poetry in the Mahabharata. 2316
Elements of popular theology. 3648
Elements of practical pedagogy. 3592
Elements of religion. 3663
Elements of religion and religious teaching. 3165
Elements of religious pedagogy. 3155
Elements of spiritual philosophy. 3494
Elements of spirituality. 3478
Elements of the Christian religion. 2285
Elements of the higher criticism. 238
Elements of the Jewish faith. 2113, 2138
Elements of the science of religion. 3064
Elements of the spiritual life. 89
Elements of theology. 3643, 3662
Elements of theology, or, An exposition of the divine origin, doctrines, morals and institutions of Christianity. 3645
Elements of truth. 3139
Elena G. de White y la Iglesia Adventista del Septimo Dia. 3126
Elephant in the dark, and other writings on the diffusion of Sufi ideas in the West. 3543
Elephant's ballet. 1345, 2167
Eleusinian and Bacchic mysteries. 1505
Eleusis. 1505
Eleusis and the Eleusinian mysteries. 1505
Eleusis;archetypal image of mother and daughter. 1505
Elevation to Krsna consciousness. 2186
Eleven and one other. 72
Eleven Christians. 923
Eleven discourses. 1688
Eleven gentlemen of Charleston. 1672
Eleven Lourdes miracles. 2262
Eleven Marian sermons. 2362, 3372
Eleven months in Horeb. 562
11 o'clock news & other experimental sermons. 3351
Eleven o'clock Sunday morning. 2935
Eleven religions and their proverbial lore. 3114
Eleven who dared. 660
Eleven-year teacher, book one. 3549
Eleven years of Bible bibliography. 644
Eleventh-century background of Citeaux. 1277
Eleventh commandment. 3601
Eleventh hour; explosion of a church. 1245
Eleventh wing. 1878
Eli and Sybil Jones. 2130
Elias Hicks. 1810
Elijah. 1506, 1507, 1631
Elijah and Elisha. 1506
Elijah, brave prophet. 494, 633, 1507
Elijah; confrontation, conflict, and crisis. 1506
Elijah Embree Hoss, ecumenical Methodist. 1848
Elijah; God's mighty witness. 1507
... Elijah, his life and times. 1506

ELIJAH MUHAMMAD THE RELIGIOUS BOOKS 1876 - 1982

Elijah Muhammad the false prophet. 669
Elijah, prophet of God. 1507
Elijah, prophet of power. 483, 1507
Elijah, prophet of the one God. 1506
Elijah speaks today. 570, 1506
Elijah task. 2949
Elijah, the favored man. 1506
Elijah, the man who went to heaven. 1506
Elijah, the pilgrim prophet. 1506
Elijah the prophet. 1506
Elijah the prophet and his mission. 1506, 2613
Elijah the Slave. 1507
Elijah vindicated. 1506
Elijah's sacred keys to heaven. 285
Eliminator; or, Skeleton keys to sacerdotal secrets. 1656
Eliphas Levi, master of occultism. 1354
Elisama. 2091
Elisha, man of God. 1506
Elisha the man of God. 1506
Eliza Chappell Porter. 2864
Eliza R. Snow. 2619
Eliza Scott Ross. 3251
Elizabeth. 1508
Elizabeth and the English Reformation: the struggle for a stable settlement of religion. 1220, 1759
Elizabeth Ann Seton, mother, teacher, saint for our time. 1029, 3379
Elizabeth Bayley Seton. 3378, 3417
Elizabeth Bayley Seton, 1774-1821. 1029, 3378, 3417
Elizabeth Day McCormick Apocalypse. 315
Elizabeth I and the religious settlement of 1559. 1508, 1759
Elizabeth of Dijon. 1508
Elizabeth Seton. 3378
Elizabeth Seton's two Bibles, her notes and markings. 304, 1029, 3378
Elizabeth I and the Puritans. 1508, 3008
Elizabethan cardinal. 26
Elizabethan cardinal, William Allen. 26
Elizabethan clergy and the settlement of religion. 1220
Elizabethan demonology. 1423, 3399
... Elizabethan episcopal administration. 1220
Elizabethan life: morals & the church courts. 1489
Elizabethan parish in its ecclesiastical and financial aspects. 1219, 2775
Elizabethan prayer-book & ornaments. 2884
Elizabethan Puritan movement. 1764
Elizabethan Puritanism. 3008
Elizabethan recusant prose, 1559-1582. 1519
... Elizabeth's mission (faithful and true) 2771
Ella Adams: or, The demon of fire. 3199
Ellen. 10, 3811
Ellen G. White and her critics. 3383, 3811
Ellen G. White and the Seventh-Day Adventist Church. 3811
Ellen G. White in Europe, 1885-1887. 3811
Ellen G. White, prophet of destiny. 3811
Elliott O'Donnell's Casebook of ghosts. 1710
Eloheim. 3711
Elohist and north Israelite traditions. 1484
Eloquence of Christian experience. 2898
Eloquent Indian. 685
Elpis Israel. 1515
Elusive presence. 652
Ely Vaughn Zollars. 3898
Ely volume. 2520
Elysium. 3509
Emancipation and adjustment. 2148
Emancipation of a freethinker. 1363
Emancipator. 1034
Emanuel B. Hoff, Bible teacher. 1822
Emanuel Swedenborg. 3569, 3570, 3571
Emanuel Swedenborg and the New Christian church. 2689, 3570
Emanuel Swedenborg: scientist and mystic. 3571
Embark for tomorrow. 2489
Embassy for the Christians. 68
Embattled saint. 1629
Embattled wall. 78, 1150
Embattled witness. 1786, 3851
Embers. 1861
Emblems in the Gospels. 2299
Emblems of saints. 3282
Emblems of the Holy Spirit. 314
Embodiment. 3391
Emergence of a Mexican church. 93, 2540
Emergence of a world Christian community. 1041
Emergence of Christian Science in American religious life. 1210
Emergence of Conservative Judaism. 1348
Emergence of Conservative Judaism; the historical school in 19th century America. 1348
Emergence of Emily. 3136
Emergence of liberal Catholicism in America. 34
Emergence of philosophy of religion. 3108
Emergence of philosophy of religion, by James Collins. 3108
Emergence of the church in the Roman world. 1193
Emergence of the Jewish problem, 1878-1939. 2078
Emergency in China. 912, 2510
Emergent church. 1066
Emergent evolution and the incarnation. 1893
Emergent Gospel. 1155
Emerging Catholic university. 870
Emerging Christian faith. 1100
Emerging church. 1060, 3181
Emerging civilization. 1818
Emerging issues in religious education. 936
Emerging lay ministry. 2789
Emerging layman. 2192
Emerging order. 1552
Emerging perspective. 2670
Emerging revival. 1558
Emerging role of deacons. 1408
Emerging self. 3750
Emerging shapes of the church. 1154
Emerging woman. 3830
Emerson's complete work. 1510
Emerson's complete works. 1510
Emerson's earlier poems. 1510
...Emerson's essays, selected and edited with an introduction. 1510
Emil Brunner. 698
Eminence of love. 2264
Eminence of teaching in Disputed questions in education. 3592
Eminent authors on effective revival preaching. 1556
Eminent Christian workers of the nineteenth century. 2190
Eminent dead. 926
Eminent men I met along the sunny road. 1289
... Eminent missionary women. 2488
Eminent opinion regarding the cathedral at Washington. Representative Americans state their views. 3797
Eminent opinion regarding the cathedral at Washington. 3796
Eminent Victorians. 2329
Emissary: the key heaven. 3438
Emm Lou. 2524
Emmanuel. 3199
Emmanuel Episcopal Church, 1868-1968. 185
Emmanuel Mounier and the new Catholic left, 1930-1950. 872, 1532, 2626
... Emmanuel, the Savior of the world. 2038
Emmet Fox's golden keys to successful living & reminiscences. 1636, 2696
Emory J. Rees language pioneer. 2242, 3031
Emotional problems and the Bible. 2995
Emotional problems and the Gospel. 611, 1107
Emotionally free. 991
Emotions Jesus stirred. 2437
Emotions of God's people. 611, 1107
Emperor and the Pope. 2850, 2861
... The Emperor Julian. 1193, 2158
Emperor Theodosius and the establishment of Christianity. 1192, 3610
Emperors, popes, and general councils. 1372
Emphasized Bible. 264
Emphasized Gospel of John. 414
Emphasized Gospel of St. John. 414
Emphasized New Testament. 357
Emphasizing missions in the local church. 2551
Emphatic diaglott. 320
Empire and papacy—a search for right order in the world? 1144
Empire of love. 2264
Empire of silence and selected sermons. 2932
Empirical philosophies of religion. 3103
Empirical philosophies of religion, with special reference to Boodin, Brightman, Hocking, Macintosh and Wieman. 3103
... An empirical study of the development of religious thinking. 2999
Empirical theology of Henry Nelson Wieman. 3815
Empirical theology of Henry Nelson Wieman (The) 3815
Empowered! 2868
Empowered to care. 2791
Empowerment. 1136
Emptiness. 2667
Empty churches. 1268
Empty churches, and how to fill them. 1251
Empty Cloud. 1850
Empty crib. 1350, 1398
Empty mirror; experiences in a Japanese Zen monastery. 2575
Empty pulpit. 2904
Empty room. 3118
Empty shoes. 1235
Empty tomb. 1486, 2006, 2052
Emptying. 2382
Emptying empire. 805, 2573
EN-DON: the ageless wisdom. 3684
Ena Twigg, medium. 3516, 3719
Enchanted boundary. 2991
Enchanted cross. 1056
Enchanted garden. 526
Encharistic faith & practice. 2256
Enchiridion. 1008
Enchiridion of commonplaces against Luther and other enemies of the church. 785, 2978
Enchiridion of Erasmus. 1008
Enchiridion precum, altar prayers. 843
Enchiridion Theologicum Sancti Augustini. 111
Encircled serpent. 3376
Encounter. 2145
Encounter between Christianity and science. 3081
Encounter in the non-Christian era. 66
Encounter of religions. 3114
Encounter of the faiths. 1078
Encounter with Christ. 2434
Encounter with early teens. 3890
Encounter with Erikson. 1527, 3138
Encounter with God. 1586, 3484, 3652
Encounter with modern society. 1067
Encounter with Scripture. 644
Encounter with Spurgeon. 2906
Encounter with terminal illness. 3604
Encounter with the divine in Mesopotamia and Israel. 1731
Encounter with the Holy Spirit. 1833
Encounter with the New Testament. 410
Encounter with the text. 288
Encounter with Zen. 3893
Encountering Christ. 2191
Encountering darkness. 1132, 1624
Encountering God. 1466
Encountering Marx. 1319
Encountering myself. 2384
Encountering New Testament manuscripts. 351
Encountering the unseen. 1088
Encountering truth. 3225
Encounters between Judaism and modern philosophy. 2144
Encounters in yoga and Zen. 3894
Encounters: poems. 194
Encounters with Christ. 2017
Encounters with silence. 1451
Encounters with the Jewish people. 2121, 2149
Encounters with the past. 3055
Encouragements to religious effort. 168
Encourager. 990
Encouraging faith. 1059
Encyclical "Humani generis" 784
Encyclical letter from the bishops. 666, 3443
Encyclical letter of His Holiness Pius xii on the sacred liturgy (Vatican Library translation) 837
Encyclical letter of His Holiness Pope Paul VI on the development of peoples. 1137
... Encyclical letter of Pope Pius xii, October 20, 1939. 786
Encyclical letter of Pope Pius XI on social reconstruction. 1512
Encyclical letter on the regulation of birth (Humanae vitae) of Pope Paul VI. 663, 853
Encyclicals and other messages of John XXIII. 1512
Encyclopaedia biblica. 243
Encyclopaedia of missions. 2516
Encyclopaedia of occultism. 2731
Encyclopaedia of psychic science. 2993
Encyclopaedia of religion and ethics. 3092
Encyclopaedia of religion and religions. 3092
Encyclopaedia of the Presbyterian church in the United States of America. 2920
Encyclopaedia on the evidences. 3639
Encyclopeadia of superstitions folklore, and the occult sciences of the world. 3567
Encyclopedia of American Quaker genealogy. 1684
Encyclopedia of American religions. 3327
Encyclopedia of ancient and forbidden knowledge. 2726
Encyclopedia of archaeological excavations in the Holy Land. 209, 2761
Encyclopedia of Bible creatures. 480
Encyclopedia of Bible difficulties. 280
Encyclopedia of Bible life. 245
Encyclopedia of Bible stories. 623
Encyclopedia of Biblical examples & illustrations demonstrated by the Scriptures. 3638
Encyclopedia of Biblical interpretation. 562
Encyclopedia of Biblical prophecy. 607
Encyclopedia of Biblical spiritualism. 3505
Encyclopedia of Biblical theology. 242
Encyclopedia of Catholic saints. 1024
Encyclopedia of Christian parenting. 2773
Encyclopedia of Christianity. 1513
Encyclopedia of classical mythology. 2658
Encyclopedia of death and life in the spirit-world. 3502
Encyclopedia of devotional programs for women's groups. 3856
Encyclopedia of entrepreneurship. 1520
Encyclopedia of etiquette. 1540
Encyclopedia of Jewis knowledge. 2085
Encyclopedia of Jewish knowledge. 2085
Encyclopedia of living divines and Christian workers of all denominations in Europe and America. 1513
Encyclopedia of mentalism and allied arts. 2990
Encyclopedia of missions. 2492, 2516
Encyclopedia of modern Christian missions. 2516
Encyclopedia of mysticism and mystery religions. 2644
Encyclopedia of occult sciences. 2731
Encyclopedia of occultism & parapsychology. 2731
Encyclopedia of preaching. 862
Encyclopedia of prophecy. 2949
Encyclopedia of psychic science. 2845
Encyclopedia of religion. 3092
Encyclopedia of religions. 3092
Encyclopedia of religious knowledge. 3091
Encyclopedia of religious quotations. 3014
Encyclopedia of sacred theology. 3669
Encyclopedia of Sunday schools and religious education. 3150, 3561
Encyclopedia of tarot. 3588
Encyclopedia of the Bible. 245
Encyclopedia of the Bible (The) 243
Encyclopedia of the Book of Mormon. 680
Encyclopedia of the Jewish religion. 2146
Encyclopedia of the Lutheran Church. 2285
Encyclopedia of the Papacy. 2769
Encyclopedia of the unexplained: magic, occultism, and parapsychology. 2723
Encyclopedia of theology. 3638
Encyclopedia of witchcraft and demonology. 3825
Encyclopedia of witchcraft & magic. 1477, 2727, 3825
Encyclopedic dictionary of Christian doctrine. 3638
Encyclopedic dictionary of the Bible. 243
Encyclopedic history of the Church of Jesus Christ of latter-day saints. 2610
Encyclopedic outline of Masonic, Hermetic, Qabbalistic, and Rosicrucian symbolical philosophy. 2732
Encylopadia of religions. 3092
Encylicals of Pope John XXIII. 1512
End. 454, 3318, 3385
End draws near. 3320
"The end from the beginning" 608, 1737
End of a road. 1090
End of all things is at hand. 1515
End of Christendom. 1097
"The end of controversy," controverted. 800, 2467
End of conventional Christianity. 1062
End of days, 1971-2001. 609, 1529
End of man. 1226, 3363
End of our era. 2948
End of our exploring. 3478
End of philosophy. 2418
End of religion. 3059
End of religious controversy friendly corrspondence between a religious society of Protestants and a Catholic divine. 789
End of religious controversy, in a friendly correspondence between a religious society of Protestants, and a Roman Catholic divine. 717, 789
End of Roman Catholicism. 3244
End of the age. 606, 1514, 1515
End of the age themes. 1513
End of the beginning. 3048
End of the days. 508
End of the historical-critical method. 240
End of the line? 3654
End of the search. 1730
End of the world. 1514
End of the world and the opening of the book of life. 1514

End of the world and the world to come. 3663
End of this present world. 609
End of time. 1818, 1819
End of youngblood Johnson. 700, 1359
End, re-thinking the Revelation. 454
End times. 608, 1514, 1530
Endeavor hymnal for young people's societies. 3562
Endeavors after the Christian life. 2349, 3726
Endeavors after the spirit of religion. 3211
Endings & beginnings. 22, 1004
Endless future of the human race. 1699
... The endless life. 2620
Endless line of splendor. 2424
Endless punishment: in the very words of its advocates. 1699
Endless quest. 964
Endtime. 1530
Enduring faith. 3077
Enduring memory. 3333
Enduring message of the Bible. 307, 1057
Enduring religion of Japan. 2183
Enduring salvation and other sermons. 162
Enduring satisfaction. 3594
Enduring significance of Emerson's divinity school address. 1511
Enduring witness. 2917
Enduring Word. 1229, 3216, 3860
Endymion in England. 2661
Enemies. 1939
Enemies and evidences of Christianity. 1099
Enemies of youth. 36
Enemy of the people, antisemitism. 2078
Enemy; Satan's struggle for two boy's souls. 1424
"An enemy sowed cockle" 2977
Enemy versions of the Gospel. 1986, 3357
Energy & vitality book. 981
Energy conservation manual for congregations. 1270
Energy-efficient church. 1199
Energy ethics, a Christian response. 2866
Energy of God. 2031
Enfolded in love. 1431
Enfoque arqueologico del mundo de la Biblia. 486, 2760
Engagement and marriage. 2345
Engaging the aging in ministry. 1257
Engigmas of psychical research. 2989
Engineer of the soul. 1306
England and Holland of the pilgrims. 1516
England and Rome. 1758
England and the Catholic Church under Queen Elizabeth. 816, 1763
England and the church. 1515
England and the Continent in the eight century. 2488
England and the continent in the eighth century. 1186
England and the Holy See. 1212
England: before and after Wesley. 1762, 3802
England in the eighteen-eighties. 1765
England's cardinals. 738
England's conversion and reformation compared. 872
England's earliest Protestants, 1520-1535. 3038
England's greater churches. 1159
England's ideal, and other papers on social subjects. 3434
Englands' reawakening. 2754
English abbey. 2
English abbeys and priories. 2
English Austin friars in the time of Wyclif. 111, 3860
English Baptist literature on religious liberty to 1689. 149
English Baptist reformation. 151
English Bible. 210, 248, 249, 252, 253, 269, 270, 642
English Bible, 1534-1859. 268
English Bible as literature. 210
English Bible before the King James. 212
English Bible, from KJV to NIV. 270
English Bible in America. 247
English Bible studies. 1993
English Bible versions. 254
English cabalah. 721, 3575
English cathedral journey. 751
English cathedral music. 1206
English cathedral through the centuries. 751
English cathedrals. 751
English cathedrals illusttated. 753
English cathedrals in colour. 751
English Catholic books, 1641-1700. 868
English Catholic enlightenment. 1520, 2230
English Catholic nonjurors of 1715. 1763
English Catholic revival in the nineteenth century. 860

English Catholics in the reign of Queen Elizabeth. 818, 1508
English chantries. 882
English Church. 1143, 1221, 1758, 1759
English Church a new look. 1143
English church ales as seen in English churchwardens' accounts. 24
English Church and its bishops, 1700-1800. 666, 1220
... The English church and the ministry of the reformed churches. 1211
English church & the papacy. 1146
English church and the papacy in the Middle Ages. 1762
English church and the reformation. 3038, 3041
English church architecture. 1158
English church brasses from the 13th to the 17th century. 690
English church composers. 1321
English church design. 1159
English church from its foundation to the Norman conquest (597-1066) 1758
English church from the accession of Charles I to the death of Anne. 1220
English church from the Norman conquest to the accession of Edward i. 1759
English church furniture. 1169
English church history for American children. 1222
English church in other lands. 1211
English church in the eighteenth century. 1221
English church in the fourteenth and fifteenth centuries. 1761
English church in the fourteenth century. 1516, 1762
English church in the reigns of Elizabeth and James i. 1758
English church in the sixteenth century. 1758, 1759
English church in the sixteenth century from the accession of Henry VIII to the death of Mary. 1759
English church music, 1650-1750. 1206
English church, 1000-1066. 1516
English church plate, 597-1830. 1240
English church reform, 1815-1840. 1220
English church screens. 3316
English church, 1000-1066. 1761
English church, 1066-1154. 1516
English Church under Henry I. 816, 1516
English churches. 1158
English churches in a secular society. 1220, 3451
English Cistercian monasteries and their patrons in the twelfth century. 1276
English clergy. 1215, 1291, 1762
English clergy and their organization in the later Middle Ages. 1762
English collegiate churches of the Middle Ages. 1270
English conferences of Ernest Renan. 1194
English correspondence of Saint Boniface. 677
English country churches. 1159
English district. 1549
English ecclesiastical studies. 2579
English Episcopal acta. 1516
English Free Churches. 1468
English friars and antiquity in the early fourteenth century. 1673
English Gothic churches. 1158
English hearts and English hands. 1568
English-Hebrew dictionary. 1517
English hero, 1660-1800. 1517
English hexapla. 358
English humanists and Reformation politics under Henry VIII and Edward VI. 3039
English hymn. 1871
English hymnal. 1865
English Hymnal service book. 1223
English hymns. 1871
English hymns, their authors and history. 1871
English in the liturgy. 2196
English Jesuits. 1947
English lands of the Abbey of Rec. 188
English-Latin Roman missal for the United States of America. 845
English-Latin Sacramentary for the United States of America. 849
English letter-writer. 2217
English liturgical colours. 1310
English liturgy hymnal. 837
English Lutheranism in the Northwest. 2303
English madrigal composers. 2311
English magical and scientific poems to 1700. 1458
English martyrology. 2351
English mediaeval monasteries, 1066-1540. 2569
English mediaeval parish church. 1270
English mediaeval recluse. 1807

English messiahs. 1892
English metrical homilies. 1519
English metrical homilies from manuscripts of the fourteenth century. 1519
English modernism, its origin, methods, aims. 2561
English monasteries. 2569
English monasteries and their patrons in the thirteenth century. 2569
English monastic finances in the later Middle Ages. 2579
English monastic life. 2579
English monasticism yesterday and today. 2579
English mystical tradition. 2644, 2645
English mystics. 2638, 2645, 2648
English mystics of the fourteenth century. 2645
English New Testament. 355
English New Testament from Tyndale to the Revised standard version. 355
English of the pulpit. 1843
English parish and diocese. 878
English parish church. 1270
English parish churches. 1270
... English penitential discipline and Anglo-Saxon law in their joint influence. 2200, 2813
... English prayer books. 2238
English preachers and preaching, 1640-1670. 1215
English Presbyterians, from Elizabeth Puritanism to modern Unitarianism. 2917
English primers (1529-1545) 248, 2941
English primers, 1529-1545. 2941
English prose translation of stanzas selected from the Breviary and the Missal. 1876
English prose writings of John Milton. 2471
English pulpit. 3363
English pulpit oratory. 2909
English pulpit oratory from Andrewes to Tillotson. 2903
English Puritan tradition. 3008
English Puritanism from John Hooper to John Milton. 3637
English Puritans. 3008
English Reformation. 3038, 3039
English Reformation, 1529-58. 3039
...The English reformation and its consequences. 3038
English reformation and Puritanism. 1758
English Reformation literature. 1518
English Reformation to 1558. 3039
English reformers. 3039
English religious dissent. 1468
English religious heritage. 2645
English religious life in the eighth century as illustrated by contemporary letters. 1758, 1760
English religious tradition. 1516
English ritual explained. 838
... The English River congregation of the Church of the brethren. 1520
English Roman Catholics and higher education, 1830-1903. 870
English Roman life. 692, 3245
English romanesque architecture. 1158
English romanesque architecture after the conquest. 1158
English romanesque architecture before the conquest. 1158
English satire; papers read at a Clark Library Seminar, January 15, 1972. 2336, 2860
English school and family reader. 3025
English sects. 3324
English secular cathedrals in the Middle Ages. 886
English secularism. 3327
English sermon. 1226, 3363
English sermons of John Foxe. 1226, 3367
English-speaking hymnal guide. 1872
English-speaking peoples. 2495
English spiritual writers. 1455
English synodalia of the thirteenth century. 1516, 1761
English text of the Ancrene riwle. 2579, 2580
English thought. 1758, 1760
... The English version of the polyglott Bible. 308
English versions of the Bible. 270
English versions prior to King James. 272
English view of American Quakerism. 1685
English view of Christian science. 1033
English village church. 1159
English way. 765, 872
English works of Raja Rammohun Roy. 689
English writings of Richard Rolle, hermit of Hampole. 1807
Englishman's Greek concordance. 344

Englishman's Greek concordance of the New Testament. 344
Englishman's Hebrew and Chaldee concordance of the Old Testament: being an attempt at a verbal connection between the original and the English translation. 498, 1797
... Engravings of St. Paul's cathedral and part II of the building accounts for the years 1685-95. 2244
Enigma of evil. 1746
Enigma of faith. 1734
Enigma of life. 2225
Enigma of out-of-body travel. 94
Enigma of reincarnation. 3055
Enigma of the Bay Psalm book. 580, 581
Enigma of the hereafter. 3054
Enigma of the poltergeist. 1709
Enigma of the stigmata. 3531
Enigma of the unknown. 2727
Enjoy the Bible's beauty. 211
Enjoy the Lord. 1355
Enjoying intimacy with God. 1741
Enjoying the New Testament. 473
Enjoying the wisdom books. 3821
Enjoyment of Scripture. 211, 502
Enkindling of love. 3485
Enlargement of life. 967
Enlargements upon meditations made in time of retreat. 2399
Enlarging conception of God. 1729, 1735
Enlightenment. 1517, 1520
Enlightenment, an interpretation. 1520
Enlightenment of the whole body. 3477
Enlist, train, support church leaders. 953
Enlisting and developing church leaders. 1251
Enlisting for Christ and the church. 1201
Enlisting laymen. 2202
Enlisting Sunday school. 3557
Enough is enough. 1491
Enquiries into religion and culture. 3066
Enquiry concerning human understanding, and selections from A treatise of human nature. 2180
Enquiry concerning the design and importance of Christian baptism and discipline. 136
Enquiry concerning the promises of the gospel. 2375
Enquiry into goodness. 1746
Enquiry into goodness and related concepts. 1746, 2837
Enquiry into the evidential value of prophecy. 605
Enquiry into the fundamental principles of the Roman Catholics. 798
Enquiry into the ideas of space, time, immensity, and eternity. 1930, 3102
Enquiry into the truth of the imputation of the guilt of Adam's first sin to his posterity. 3413
Enriching many. 2319
Enriching worship. 1451
Enriching your New Testament studies. 474
Enriching your teaching. 940
Enrichment of life. 3758
Enrichment of prayer. 2877
Enroute of a soul. 3517
Ensign to the nations. 1233
Enter at your own risk. 993
Enter into life. 961
Enter Saint Anthony. 3132
Enter the crocus. 1837
Enter the quiet. 2381
Enter the temple called Beautiful. 1324
Enter with joy. 3852
Entering the kingdom. 954
Entering the path of enlightenment. 710
Entertaining, moral, and religious repository. 960
Entertaining programs for the assembly in the Jewish religious school. 2117
Entertainments. 3560
Enthroned. 1954
Enthronement of the sacred heart. 1379, 3269
Enthronement of the Sacred Heart of Jesus. 3269
Enthusiasm. 1520
Enthusiasm in the Spirit. 2815
Enthusiasmus triumphatus. 1520
Enthusiasts of Port-Royal. 2864
Entire Bible on holiness. 3805
Entire sanctification. 3300
Entire sanctification a second work of grace. 3300
Entrance to the tree of life. 721
Entrepreneur. 1520, 1521
Entrepreneuring. 1520
Entrepreneurship and the outlook for America. 123, 1521
Enthronement of the Sacred Heart of Jesus. 3269
Entrusted with spiritual leadership. 3368
Entrusted with the gospel. 2902

Entry of the Slavs into Christendom. 3425
Envious? Who, me? 3413
Environment of early Christianity. 407
Environmental factors in Christian history. 743, 744, 1182
Environmental man. 1074
Envoy to Africa. 3013
Envoys of peace. 2491
Envy. 3412
Eoce Homo. 2015
Epher Whitaker of Southold. 3810
Ephesian Gospel. 363, 419
Ephesian letter. 363
Ephesian studies. 364
Ephesian tradition. 419
Ephesians. 363, 364, 365, 3367, 3731
Ephesians, an exposition. 161, 365
Ephesians and Colossians in the Greek New Testament for the English reader. 364
... Ephesians, Colossians, Philemon & Philippians. 370
Ephesians, Colossians, 2 Thessalonians, the Pastoral epistles. 365
Ephesians: pattern for Christian living. 364
Ephesians, Philippians, Colossians. 365
Ephesians, the epistle of Christian maturity. 363
Ephesians; the glory of the church. 363
Ephesians, the mystery of the church. 363
Ephod. 1521
... Ephod and ark. 2113
Ephraim Bowles: his Quaker heritage. 686
Ephraim Holding's homely hints. 3180
Epic mythology. 2316, 2663
Epic of a people. 2087
Epic of earth. 1485
Epic of Hades. 1802
Epic of Moses. 3208
Epic of Paul. 2803
Epic of revelation. 3226
Epic of Saul. 3304
Epic of the Crusades. 1390
Epic of the inner life. 549
Epic of the Maccabees. 2305
Epic of the Old Testament. 592
Epic of the preacher. 1288
Epic of the starry heaven. 1787
Epic of Unitarianism. 3728
Epic poem. 2599
Epigrams to live and die by. 1522
Epilegomena to the study of Greek religion. 1395
Epilogues and prayers. 3856
Epiphanies of the risen Lord. 1956
Epiphany of the cross. 2174
Epiphany story. 1425
Epiphany studies in the Scriptures. 1522
Episcopacy ancient and modern. 1522
Episcopacy and the royal supremacy in the Church of England in the XVI century. 1219, 3252
Episcopacy and unity. 1219, 1523
Episcopacy examined. 1523
Episcopacy examined and re-examined. 1523
Episcopacy in the Lutheran Church? 2288
Episcopacy in the present day. 2439
Episcopacy tested by Scripture. 1523
Episcopal and Anglican history. 1221
Episcopal appointments and patronage in the reign of Edward II. 2794
Episcopal bishops in Indiana. 2962
Episcopal bishops, the successors of Apostles. 76
Episcopal ceremonies for Holy Week. 844
Episcopal church. 1523, 1524, 2956, 2964, 2965, 2967
Episcopal church and early ecclesiastical laws of Connecticut. 2963
Episcopal Church and education. 2965, 2966
Episcopal Church annual (The) 2975
Episcopal Church annual (The) 1963. 2975
Episcopal Church annual (The) 1968. 2975
Episcopal Church comes to Arizona. 1750
Episcopal church defended. 2966
Episcopal Church in Colorado. 2963
Episcopal Church in Colorado, 1860-1963. 2963
Episcopal Church in Fulton County. 2969
Episcopal Church in Georgia. 2966
Episcopal Church in Georgia, 1733-1957. 2966
Episcopal Church in northern Texas. 2956
Episcopal Church in Oklahoma. 2971
Episcopal church in the American colonies. 1508
Episcopal Church in the United States, 1789-1931. 2966
Episcopal church in the United States, 1800-1840. 2967
Episcopal Church in the United States and the National Council of Churches. 2670

Episcopal Church in the United States, 1789-1931. 2967
Episcopal church in town and country. 2957
Episcopal church in Wyoming. 2975
Episcopal church, its faith and order. 2964
Episcopal church, its teaching and worship. 1523
Episcopal Church since 1900. 2967
Episcopal Church welcomes you. 2957
Episcopal colleges. 1164, 2965
Episcopal common praise. 2968
Episcopal controversy reviewed. 1522, 2737
Episcopal Curch in the Diocese of Texas. 1524
Episcopal Methodism. 2450
Episcopal Methodism and slavery. 3424
... Episcopal Methodism, as it was, and is. 2450
Episcopal Scotland in the nineteenth century. 1524
Episcopal series of the Protestant hour (The) (Radio program) 3351
Episcopal silver-jubilee of the Most Reverend Patrick John Ryan. 3259
Episcopal theological school. 731
Episcopal young churchmen's notebook. 1522
Episcopalian way of life. 2958
...The Episcopalians. 1523, 2957
Episcopalian's dictionary: church beliefs, terms, customs, and traditions explained in layman's language. 2964
Episcopalians united. 2957
Episcopate and Christian unity. 1523
Episcopate and the primacy. 1523
Episcopate in the church. 1522
Episcopate in the kingdom of Leon in the twelfth century. 1459
Episcopate of Charles Wordsworth, Bishop of St. Andrews, Dunkeld, and Dunblade 1853-1892. 3848
Episcopate of Charles Wordsworth, bishop of St. Andrews, Dunkeld, and Dunblane 1853-1892. 3848
Episode in anti-Catholicism. 33
Episode in the struggle for religious freedom. 2718
Episodes at the olive press. 3682
Epistemology. 2179, 2419
Epistemology, an introductory essay. 2181
Epistemoloyg, or the theory of knowledge. 2179
Epistles of Paul the apostle to the Thessalonians. 1, 2 Timothy, Titus. 478
Epistle. 2536
Epistle congratulatory to the right reverend the bishops of the Episcopal court at Camden. 1472
Epistle exhortatory of an English Christian. 3605
Epistle general of James. 412
Epistle homilies. 864
Epistle lectionary of the Eastern Orthodox Church. 2748
Epistle of Christ. 3339
Epistle of Christian courage. 325
Epistle of comfort. 1354
Epistle of James. 412
Epistle of James and the life of faith. 413
Epistle of Jude. 425
Epistle of Paul. 364, 471
Epistle of Paul the apostle of the Galatias. 379
Epistle of Paul the apostle to the Colossians. 341
Epistle of Paul the apostle to the Ephesians. 363
Epistle of Paul the apostle to the Galatians. 379
... The Epistle of Paul the Apostle to the Hebrews. 402
Epistle of Paul the Apostle to the Hebrews and the First and Second espistles of St. Peter. Translator: William B. Johnston. 404
... The Epistle of Paul the apostle to the Romans. 466, 467
Epistle of Paul to the churches of Galatia. 379, 380
Epistle of Paul to the Ephesians. 363
... The Epistle of Paul to the Galatians. 379, 380
Epistle of Paul to the Philippians. 448
Epistle of Paul to the Phillippians. 448
Epistle of Paul to the Romans. 466, 467, 468
Epistle of Paul to the Thessalonians. 478
Epistle of St. Jude and the Second epistle of St. Peter. 269, 447, 425
Epistle of St. Jude and the Second epistle of St. Peter. Greek text with introd., notes, and comments. 425
... The Epistle of St. Paul to the Colossians. 342
Epistle of St. Paul to the Galatians. 379

Epistle of St. Paul to the Philippians. 448
Epistle of the apostle Paul to the Romans. 466
Epistle of the Gallican churches. 2350
Epistle selections of the ancient church. 366
Epistle to Diognetus. 2161
Epistle to Rheginos. 3221
Epistle to the Colossians. 342
Epistle to the Ephesians. 362, 363, 364, 365, 561
... The Epistle to the Galatians. 379, 380
Epistle to the Galatians and the Epistle to the Romans. 379
... The Epistle to the HBrews with some interpretative suggestions. 402
... The Epistle to the Hebrew. 402, 403
Epistle to the Hebrews. 270, 402, 403, 404, 405, 2112
Epistle to the Hebrews: a commentary. 403
Epistle to the Hebrews, an introduction and commentary. 403
Epistle to the Philippians. 448
Epistle to the Philippians [and] the Epistle to the Colossians. 448
Epistle to the Phillipians. 448
... The Epistle to the Philippians. 448
Epistle to the Romans. 466, 467, 468, 469, 470
... The Epistle to the Romans in the revised version. 467
Epistle to the skeptics. 3422
Epistle to the Son of the Wolf. 126
Epistles. 1684
Epistles and Apocalypse of John. 413
... The Epistles and Gospels. 366
Epistles and Gospels for pulpit use. 366
Epistles and Gospels for pulpit use on Sundays and holy days. 366
Epistles and gospels for Sundays and festivals of the year. 366
Epistles and gospels for Sundays and holydays. 366
Epistles and gospels for Sundays and holydays throughout the year. 366
Epistles and Gospels for the Sundays, holydays, various intentions and special occasions in the Catholic church of the Greek rite. 366
Epistles and Gospels together with lessons from the Old Testament. 366
Epistles and testimonies issued by the Yearly meetings of Friends. 1681, 2038
Epistles and testimonies issued by the Yearly meetings of Friends, in North America. 1687
Epistles as I know them. 366
Epistles (complete) 269
Epistles from prison. 372
Epistles from prison; Philippians, Ephesians, Colossians, Philemon. 372
... The epistles general of I. and II. Peter and I. John. 368
Epistles in focus. 327
Epistles/now. 445
Epistles of James and John. 367, 412
Epistles of James, John, and Jude. 340
Epistles of James, Peter, and Jude. 340
Epistles of John. 368, 369
Epistles of John and Jude. 368
Epistles of John: light, love, life. 369
Epistles of Paul. 370, 371, 446, 3879
Epistles of Paul in modern English. 374
Epistles of Paul the apostle to the Colossians and to Philemon. 341
Epistles of Paul the apostle to the Corinthians in the revised version. 345
Epistles of Paul the apostle to the Ephesians, Philippians, Colossians and to Philemon. 363
Epistles of Paul the Apostle to the Galatians, Ephesians, Philippians and Colossians. 379
Epistles of Paul the apostle to the Romans and to the Thessalonians. 469
Epistles of Paul the apostle to the Thessalonia. 478
Epistles of Paul the apostle to the Thessalonians. 478
Epistles of Paul to the Colossians and Philemon. 341
Epistles of Paul to the Colossians and to Philemon. 341
Epistles of Paul to the Colossians, to Philemon and to Philemon. 341
Epistles of Paul to the Colossians, to Philemon and to the Ephesians. 372
Epistles of Paul to the Galatians, Ephesians, Philippians, Colossians, and Thessalonians. 371
Epistles of Paul to the Philippians and to Philemon. 374
Epistles of Paul to the Phillippians and to Philemon. 449
Epistles of Paul to the Romans, Corinthains, Hebrews, and Ephesians. 372
Epistles of Paul to the Thessalonians. 478

Epistles of Paul to the Thessalonians; an introduction and commentary. 478
Epistles of Peter. 447
Epistles of Peter, John and Jude. 447
... The Epistles of S. John. 368, 369
... The Epistles of S. John, ed. 369
Epistles of St. Clement of Rome and St. Igatius of Antioch. 1093
... The epistles of St. Ignatius. 1882
... The epistles of St. Ignatius, bishop of Antioch. 1882
Epistles of St. John. 369
Epistles of St. John: the Greek text. 368
Epistles of St. Paul. 370
Epistles of St. Paul explained. 371
Epistles of St. Paul to the Galatians and to the Romans. 379
Epistles of St. Paul written after he became a prisoner. 371
Epistles of St. Peter and St. Jude preached and explained. 447
Epistles of St. Peter, St. John and St. Jude. 340, 367
Epistles of Saints James, Jude. 340
Epistles of the New Testament. 378
Epistles to the Colossians and Thessalonians. 371
... The epistles to the Colossians and to Philemon. 341
... The Epistles to the Colossians and to the Ephesians. 341
Epistles to the Colossians, Thessalonians and Timothy. 370
Epistles to the Corinthians. 345, 346
... The epistles to the Corinthians and Galatians. 345
Epistles to the Galatians and Ephesians. 381
Epistles to the Galatians, Ephesians, and Philippians. 370
Epistles to the Hebrews, Colossians, Ephesians, and Philemon, the Pastoral epistles, the Epistles of James, Peter, and Jude, together with a sketch of the history of the canon of the New Testament. 367
Epistles to the Philippians, Colossians, and Philemon. 449
... The Epistles to the Thessalonians. 477, 478, 479
Epistles to Timothy. 479
Epistles to Timothy and Titus. 445, 446
Epistles to Timothy, Titus, and Philemon. 446
Epistles to Titus and Philemon. 479
Epistola de tolerantia. 3703
Epitaphs for eager preachers. 2785
Epitome et collectorium ex Occamo circa quatuor Sententiarum libros. 2826
Epitome of aspersions cast at civilians. 1489
Epitome of general ecclesiastical history. 1177
Epitome of Greek and Roman mythology. 2656
Epitome of history. 1820
Epitome of Rev. Dr. Erick Pontoppidan's Explanation of Martin Luther's Small catechism. 2279, 2283
Epitome of spiritualism and spirit magnetism. 3504
Epitome of Swedenborg's science. 3571
Epitome of the doctrines and practice of the old Waldenses and Albigenses. 3788
Epitome of the history of the world. 294
Epitome of the New Testament. 1768
Epitome of the priestly life. 2752
... Epoch makers of modern missions. 2483
Epoch of creation. 1381
Epoch of Negro Baptists and the Foreign Mission Board. 15, 2669
Epochs in Buddhist history. 705
Epochs in the life of Apostle John. 414, 2127
Epochs in the life of Jesus. 1971
Epochs in the life of Paul. 216, 2801
Epochs in the life of Simon Peter. 216, 2825
Epochs in the life of the Apostle John. 216
Episcopal Church in Texas, 1838-1874. 2974
... The Epworth engine. 1525
Epworth hymnal. 3562
Epworth league Bible studies. 641
... Epworth Methodist church, golden jubilee. 3579
Equal rights in religion. 1143
Equality and submission in marriage. 2338
Equality of all Christians before God. 1039
Equilibrium; fidelity to nature and grace. 3484
Equinox of the gods. 3473
Equipped for good work. 2788
Equipping of disciples. 995

Era in Anglican theology. 3658
Era in Anglican theology, from Gore to Temple. 3659
Era of the church fathers. 1193
Era of the Protestant revolution. 3036
Era of the Spirit. 1835
Eranistes. 2044
Erasmus. 1525, 1526
Erasmus; a study of his life, ideals, and place in history. 1526
Erasmus Against war. 3791
Erasmus and his age. 1527
Erasmus and Luther. 1526, 2277
Erasmus & Luther: their attitude to toleration. 1526, 3703
Erasmus and the age of Reformation. 1525, 1526
Erasmus and the northern Renaissance. 1526, 3035
Erasmus and the "other" Pope Julius. 1526
Erasmus and the seamless coat of Jesus. 1526
Erasmus and the Spanish Inquisition. 1526, 3766
Erasmus: his theology of the sacraments. 1526, 3266
Erasmus of Christendom. 1525, 3037
Erasmus of Rotterdam. 1526
Erasmus on language and method in theology. 1525, 3071
Erasmus; the Rede lecture delivered in the Senate-House on June 11, 1890. 1526
... Erasmus; the scholar. 1526
Erasmus, Tyndale, and More. 1525, 3038
Erastus Snow; the life of a missionary and pioneer for the early Mormon Church. 3432
Eric Graham, 1888-1964. 1754
Erich Fromm. 1689, 2976
Erichtonius and the three daughters of Cecrops. 1527
Ernest C. Wilson's master class lessons. 1072
Ernest Holmes: his life and times. 1825
Ernst Troeltsch and the future of theology. 3715
Eros and evil. 3824
Eros defiled. 3393
Erosion of faith. 3656
Erotic aspects of Hindu sculpture. 1896
Errand of mercy. 1551
Errata of the Protestant Bible. 656, 3258
Error and eccentricity in human belief. 2732
... Error invalidating matrimonial consent. 2342
Error's chains. 3115
Errors chains: how forged and broken. 3115
Errors of evolution. 1581
Errors of Hopkinsianism detected and refuted. 3640
Errors of mind healing compared with the miracles of Christ and His disciples in the healing of the afflicted as viewed by a physician. 2410
Errors of Russellism. 3256
Errors of the Bible demonstrated by the truths of nature. 238
Escape. 931, 2349, 3820
Escape from emptiness. 3018
Escape from rage. 1576, 3768
Escape from terror. 2085
Escape from the coming tribulation. 3711
Escape from the money trap. 1075
Escape from witchcraft. 670, 3822
Escape to the kingdom. 1514
Escaped nun. 1357
Escaping the web of deception. 66
Eschatological expectation of Isaiah 40-66 with special reference to Israel and the nations. 545, 1530
Eschatology. 464, 1528, 1529, 1530
Eschatology and ethics. 1529
Eschatology and ethics in the teaching of Jesus. 1530, 2066
Eschatology handbook. 1530
Eschatology in Luke. 429, 1530
Eschatology in Maimonidean thought. 1531, 2318
Eschatology of Paul. 377
Eschatology of Paul in the light of modern scholarship. 377
Eschatology of victory. 444, 2464
Eschatology, the doctrine of a future life in Israel, Judaism, and Christianity. 1530
Escorial. 1531
Esdranalda. 2722
Esoteric art of living. 1325
Esoteric Buddhism. 703, 3687
Esoteric Christianity. 1102, 3683
Esoteric cosmic yogi science. 3866
Esoteric keys to personal power. 3481
Esoteric lessons. 2725
Esoteric reading of Biblical symbolism. 3575
Esoteric tradition. 3687

Esoteric writings of Helene Petrovna Slavatsky. 3683
Esotericism of the Popol Vuh. 2863, 3012
ESP in the Bible. 319, 3072
ESP or HSP? 1088
ESP, seers & psychics. 2723
Especially for mother. 2625
... The Espurgatoire Saint Patriz. 2793
Essaei transcripts. 1912
Essai sur les rapports du pouvoir politique et du pouvoir religieux chez Montesquieu. 2586, 3088
Essay. 3427, 3439
Essay concerning human understanding. 2180
Essay concerning the restoration of primitive Christianity. 1681
Essay concerning the unlawfulness of a man's marriage with his sister by affinity. 2347
Essay for the recording of illustrious providences. 2733
Essay in aid of a grammar of assent. 3608
Essay in Christian philosophy. 1104
Essay in practical philosophy. 2227
Essay in which the doctrine of a positive divine efficiency exciting the will of men to sin. 3410
Essay Let us think it over. 3054
Essay on apostolical succession. 76, 2817
Essay on baptism. 136
Essay on Catholicism, authority and order considered in their fundamental principles. 3436, 3449
Essay on Catholicism, liberalism and Socialism considered in their fundamental principles. 3436
Essay on church polity. 1241
Essay on creation. 1383
Essay on education in the Society of Friends. 1683
Essay on intolerance. 3193
Essay on man. 2860
Essay on man, in four epistles. 2860
Essay on mediumship. 3508
Essay on metaphysics. 2417
Essay on miracles. 2478
Essay on native depravity. 3412
Essay on Scripture prophecy. 604
Essay on temptation. 3600
Essay on the action proper for the pulpit. 2900
Essay on the bases of the mystic knowledge. 2640
Essay on the composition of a sermon. 2899
Essay on the Decalogue, or Ten commandments. 1315
Essay on the development of Christian doctrine. 790, 934, 1473, 3654, 3655
Essay on the divine authority of the New Testament. 378
Essay on the doctrine of divine influence upon the human soul. 1827
Essay on the fall of angels and men. 1500, 1746
Essay on the fundamental principles of operative occultism. 2725
Essay on the gospel ministry. 1295
Essay on the human character of Jesus Christ. 1994
Essay on the identity and general resurrection of the human body. 3220
Essay on the importance of considering the subject of religion. 3059
Essay on the inspiration of the Holy Scriptures of the Old and New Testament. 305
Essay on the kingdom of Christ. 2014
Essay on the manner of writing history. 1817
Essay on the nature and immutability of truth. 3717
Essay on the origin of evil. 1746
Essay on the pastoral office. 2444
Essay on the plan of salvation. 3291
Essay on the prize-question. 3597
Essay, on the probation of fallen men. 3292
Essay on the real deity of Jesus Christ. 2002
Essay on the spirit and influence of the reformation by Luther. 2278, 3036
Essay on the union of church and state. 1141
Essay on the warrant, nature, and duties of the office of the ruling elder, in the Presbyterian church. 2912
Essay on theological method. 3669
Essay on truth. 3624
Essay on war. 3794
Essay toward faith. 1595
Essay towards promoting all necessary and useful knowledge, both divine and human. 2224
Essaying Montaigne. 2585
... Essays. 1510, 1511

Essays and addresses (Brooks, Phillips) 694
Essays and addresses (Drummond, Henry) 1481
Essays and addresses (Liddon, Henry Parry) 702, 2799
Essays & addresses on the philosophy of religion. 2016, 3100, 3101
Essays and addresses (Wilson, James Maurice) 1072, 3626
Essays and letters on orders & jurisdiction. 1213
Essays and miscellanies. 567
Essays and reviews, chiefly on theology, politics, and socialism. 697
Essays & sketches (Fullerton, Kemper) 3621
Essays and sketches (Newman, John Henry) 776, 3632
Essays & sketches, Oberlin, 1904-1934. 2720, 3621
Essays by Ralph Waldo Emerson. 1511
Essays Catholic & critical. 44, 3624
Essays catholic and missionary. 1224
Essays, civil, and moral, and The new Atlantis. 696
Essays, critical and historical. 2703
Essays, debates, and proceedings. 2292
Essays, educational and historic. 755
Essays (Emerson, Ralph Waldo) 1510, 1511
... Essays from the Sketch-book. 2129
Essays / (Godwin, William. 3621
Essays in American theology. 3019
Essays in ancient & modern philosophy. 2835
Essays in applied Christianity. 1071
Essays in appreciation (Douglas, George William) 479
Essays in Biblical culture and Bible translation. 484
Essays in Biblical Greek. 529
Essays in biblical interpretation. 235, 236, 239
Essays in Christian philosophy. 1104, 2838
Essays in Christian politics and kindred subjects. 3625
Essays in Christian unity. 1041
Essays in classical and modern Hindu law. 1812
Essays in comparative religion. 3123
Essays in culture (Wolfe, John Marcus) 762
Essays in divinity (Donne, John) 3642
Essays in ecclesiastical biography. 927
Essays in existentialism. 1584
Essays in Greco-Roman and related Talmudic literature. 2154
Essays in history (Pius X I) 1817
Essays in history, written between the years 1896-1912. 739, 1817
Essays in honor of George Ernest Wright. 503, 3860
Essays in honor of Joseph P. Brennan. 691, 3620
Essays in honor of Solomon B. Freehof. 1660
Essays in Indian philosophy and religion. 3062
Essays in Jewish intellectual history. 2147, 2403
Essays in Jewish sociology, labour and cooperation in memory of Dr. Noah Barou, 1889-1955. 174, 3454
Essays in Jewish thought. 2147, 3899
Essays in later medieval history. 1181
Essays in medical sociology. 3392
Essays in metaphysics. 2420
Essays in metaphysics (Heidegger, Martin) 1881
Essays in metaphysics: Identity and difference. 1881
Essays in ministry (Wagoner, Walter D. 1297
Essays in modern English church history. 1762, 3573
Essays in modern English church history, in memory of Norman Sykes. 1762
Essays in modern theology and related subjects. 692, 3636
Essays in morality and ethics. 1537
Essays in occultism, spirtism, and demonology. 2725
Essays in Old Testament ethics. 514, 1859
Essays in ontology (Allaire, Edwin B. 2739
Essays in order. 759
Essays in pastoral medicine. 2378
Essays in radical empiricism. A pluralistic universe. 1585
Essays in reconstruction. 3028
Essays in religion and morality. 3067
Essays in religion (Frieder, Emma) 3066
Essays in seminary education. 3613

Essays in the American Catholic tradition. 828
Essays in the conciliar epoch. 1186
Essays in the history of religious thought in the West. 1543, 3213, 3810
Essays in the philosophy of religion: based on the Sarum lectures, 1971. 3107
Essays in Thomism. 3693, 3696
Essays in traditional Jewish thought. 2141
Essays in Zen Buddhism, first series. 3892
Essays in Zen Buddhism (Suzuki, Daisetz Teitaro) 3894
Essays in Zen Buddishm (Suzuki, Daisetz Teitaro) 705
Essays, moral and divine. 3065
Essays, moral and literary. 2593
Essays, moral and religious. 3625
Essays moral, political, and literary. 1855, 2834
... Essays of a Catholic. 758
Essays of a Catholic (Belloc, Hilaire) 758
Essays of a modern mystic. 3250
Essays of an atheist (Teller, Woolsey) 101
Essays of Michel de Montaigne. 2585
Essays of Montaigne. 2585
Essays of today (Newton, William Wilberforce) 3623
Essays on a science of mythology. 2652
... Essays on antisemitism. 2078
Essays on Biblical interpretation. 288
Essays on biblical theology. 652
Essays on Bonhoeffer. 677
Essays on Catholic education in the United States. 830, 831
Essays on Christ Jesus with excerpts from different writers. 1955
Essays on church and state. 1140
Essays on church music. 1204
Essays on divine metaphysics. 1037
Essays on faith and immortality. 1596
Essays on French history. 3039
Essays on Gladstone and the Vatican. 1715
Essays on human science. 50, 3527
Essays on Islamic philosophy and science. 2840
... Essays on Jesus. 1952
Essays on Jewish chronology and chronography. 5, 497, 1115
Essays on John Milton, history and Samuel Johnson. 2471
Essays on Judaism (Silverstone, Harry) 2082
Essays on Kierkegaard (Gill, Jerry H.) 2170
Essays on liberty and necessity. 1500, 1658
Essays on liturgiology and church history. 2235
Essays on Luther (Strand, Kenneth Albert) 2277
Essays on Maimonides. 2622
Essays on music in the Byzantine world. 2632
Essays on nature and grace. 1752
Essays on New Testament Christianity. 350, 1464
Essays on New Testament themes. 334, 350
Essays on Old Testament hermeneutics. 530
Essays on Old Testament history and religion. 484, 2096
Essays on Pierre Bayle and religious controversy. 179, 3667
Essays on prayer. 2871
Essays on religion and the ancient world. 3067
Essays on religion (Clutton-Brock, Arthur) 3619
Essays on renewal / (Suenens, Leon Joseph. 793
Essays on Romanism ([Seeley, Robert Benton]) 802
Essays on segregation (Ingram, Tolbert Robert) 3329
Essays on some select parts of the liturgy of the Church of England. 1223
Essays on some theological questions of the day. 1053
Essays on subjects connected with the reformation in England. 3039
Essays on the church of God. 1201
Essays on the distinguishing traits of Christian character. 976
Essays on the formation and publication of opinions. 185
... Essays on the friends of Jesus. 1952
Essays on the Gita. 2316
Essays on the Gita (Ghose, Aurobindo) 2316
Essays on the Greek Christian poets and the English poets. 1772
Essays on the Heidelberg catechism. 1801
Essays on the logic of being. 2738
Essays on the love commandment. 2066, 2266

Essays on the most important subjects in religion. 1071, 3648
Essays on the nature and uses of the various evidences of revealed religion. 61
Essays on the New Testament. 350
Essays on the occasion of the seventieth anniversary of the Dropsie University, 1909-1979. 503, 2093, 2147
Essays on the priesthood [offered to St. Meinrad Archabbey on the occasion of its centenary (1854-1954) 3277, 3675
Essays on the principles of morality and natural religion. 1535
Essays on the principles or morality and natural religion. 1537
Essays on the Scottish Reformation. 3042
Essays on the Semitic background of the New Testament. 350
Essays on the social gospel. 1251
Essays on the supernatural origin of Christianity. 60
Essays on the Trinity and the incarnation. 3713
Essays on the truth of the Christian religion. 1047
Essays on the work entitled Supernatural religion. 3061
Essays on the works of Erasmus. 1527, 3620
Essays on typology. 3720
Essays on various subjects. 3501
Essays (Parsons, Theophilus) 2689, 2691
Essays philosophical and practical. 3494
Essays, philosophical and theological. 3619
Essays politic and moral, and Essays moral and theological. 1326
Essays, practical and speculative. 1070
Essays presented at the First Liturgical Institute. 2295

Essays, reviews, and addresses. 3724
Essays, reviews, and discourses. 2428, 3632
Essays (Ryder, Henry Ignatius Dudley) 761
Essays (Slonimsky, Henry) 2462
Essays, theological and miscellaneous. 3623
Essays to do good (Mather, Cotton) 969
Essays upon some controverted questions. 3313
Essence and substance. 2737
Essence of Anglo-Catholicism. 45
Essence of Buddhism. 1812
... The essence of Catholicism. 785
Essence of Christianity. 1047, 1048, 1096, 1104, 1507, 3099
Essence of faith. 3104
Essence of faith according to Luther. 1591, 2273
Essence of Hinduism. 1813
Essence of Judaism. 2113, 2114, 2115, 2116, 2137
...Essence of life in psychic phenomena. 3513
Essence of our faith. 1396
Essence of Plotinus. 2854
Essence of prayer. 2875
Essence of religion. 3057, 3059
Essence of religions. 3117
Essence of spiritual religion. 3105
Essence of the Bible. 209, 614
... The essence of the Koran. 2184
... The essence of the Talmud. 3583, 3584
Essence of wisdom. 3821
Essence of yoga. 3864
Essene book of creation. 525, 2622
Essene Christ. 1978
Essene-Christian faith. 1410, 1532, 1976
Essene code of life. 2321
Essene gospel of peace. 1092, 2019
Essene heritage. 1410, 1532
Essene plan. 1532
Essene writings from Qumran. 1410
Essenes. 1532
Essenes and Christianity. 1532
Essential Augustine. 3634
Essential books for a pastor's study. 3626
Essential books for a pastor's library. 3627
Essential Calvinism. 730
Essential changes. 1879
Essential Christianity. 1047, 1050, 3664
Essential Erasmus. 1527
Essential Eusebius. 1191
Essential greatness. 72, 3367, 3731
Essential mysticism. 2638
Essential nature of New Testament preaching. 476
Essential Newman. 3632
Essential place of religion in education. 3155
Essential spirit of Jesus. 968, 2064

Essential Swedenborg: basic teachings of Emanuel Swedenborg, scientist, philosopher, and theologian. 2692, 3631
Essential Talmud. 3584, 3585
Essential Torah. 562, 2109
Essential unity of all religions. 3058
Essentials. 1060
Essentials and non-essentials in religion. 3729
Essentials and non-essentials of the Catholic religion. 756
Essentials in church history. 1179, 1231, 1233, 2616, 2619
Essentials in the development of religion. 1586
Essentials of an effective ministry. 3671
Essentials of astrological analysis. 95
Essentials of Bible history. 295
Essentials of Bible history. 3d ed. rev. by N. Neil Richardson, Robert F. Berkey. 295
Essentials of Biblical Hebrew. 1797
Essentials of Buddhist philosophy. 703, 2317
Essentials of Christian belief. 1591
Essentials of Christian salesmanship. 3204
Essentials of Christianity. 1052, 1053
Essentials of church administration. 1199
Essentials of discipleship. 1010
Essentials of evangelical theology. 1552
Essentials of evangelism. 1566, 1567
Essentials of leadership. 2592
Essentials of Methodism. 2421
Essentials of mysticism and other essays. 2641
Essentials of new life. 1010
Essentials of New Testament Greek. 1770
Essentials of New Testament study. 475
Essentials of prayer. 2868
Essentials of preaching. 2900
Essentials of religious education. 3151
Essentials of spirituality. 3476
Essentials of successful living. 3887
Essentials of the Christian faith. 1051
Essentials of the Dharma blossom sutra. 3272
Essentials of theism. 3608
Essentials of Wesleyan theology. 1552, 2158, 2428
Essentials of Zen Buddhism. 3892, 3894
Essentials of Zen Buddhism, selected from the writings of Daisetz T. Suzuki. 3892
Essex lad who became England's greatest preacher. 3523
Essex story; a history of the Jewish community in Essex County, New Jersey. 2099
... Established present truth. 1554
Establishing the converts. 1564
Establishing values. 980
... The establishment of Christianity. 1355
Establishment of Christianity and the proscription of paganism. 1196, 1355
Establishment of the Anglican Church in the Leeward Islands. 1224, 2537
Establishment of the English Church in continental American colonies. 1222
...Establishment of the university of being in the doctrine of Meister Eckhart of Hochheim. 1491, 2739
Estate documents at Lambeth Palace Library. 1242
Estate of glory. 954
Estetica gregoriana. 838, 884
Esther. 495, 513, 514, 634, 693, 1366, 1532, 1533
Esther and Harbonah. 514
Esther and her times. 1533
Esther becomes a queen. 1532
Esther, courage in crisis. 513
Esther for such a time as this. 514
Esther, the romance of providence. 514
Esther, the triumph of God's sovereignty. 514
Esther Wheelwright, Indian captive. 2223
Estimate of the religion of the fashionable world. 970
Estranged God. 3212
Etchings of the Master. 3559
Eternal answers for an anxious age. 971
Eternal Architect. 2048
Eternal atonement. 108
Eternal books retold. 539
Eternal burning a scandal against the almighty. 1699
Eternal Christ. 2474
Eternal companion. 689
Eternal covenant. 3308
Eternal crucible. 1371
Eternal energy. 2942
Eternal epistle. 3342
Eternal evangel. 1553
Eternal faith, eternal people. 2147
Eternal flame. 3256
Eternal flame; the story of a preaching mission in Russia. 3256
Eternal fount. 2117

Eternal fountain. 701
Eternal fruits of knowledge. 3251
Eternal Galilean. 1972
Eternal glory of Christ. 2056
Eternal God. 2000
Eternal goodness, and other sermons. 1226, 3342
Eternal gospel. 3100, 3225
Eternal hope. 1528, 1699, 3363
Eternal hunger. 3191
Eternal in man. 2325, 3191, 3192
Eternal inheritance. 3196
Eternal King. 2040
Eternal kingdom. 1177
Eternal legacy from an upper room. 424
Eternal life. 1691, 1695, 1698, 1889, 3505
Eternal life, how attained, how and where served. 3195
Eternal life in action. 3196
Eternal life of mankind. 1886
Eternal light. 2098, 2152
Eternal love. 2344
Eternal man. 2324
Eternal message of Muhammad. 2564, 2628
Eternal now. 3359
Eternal people. 2082, 2115, 2151
Eternal progress. 1008, 1232
Eternal promise. 1449
Eternal prosperity and success. 1324
Eternal punishment. 1699
Eternal purpose. 1349, 1740, 3489
Eternal quest. 1623, 2237, 2602, 2607
Eternal retribution. 1531
Eternal sacrifice. 2368
Eternal security. 3290
Eternal security of the believer. 3196
Eternal Shepherd. 1969, 1985
Eternal son. 2036, 3848
Eternal soul. 3688
Eternal spirit in the daily round. 2386
Eternal stranger. 2097, 2100
Eternal teacher. 2061
Eternal testament. 2251
Eternal thoughts from Christ the teacher. 1985
Eternal triumphant Christ. 230
Eternal values in religion. 1071
Eternal verities. 3504, 3685
Eternal verities, for the teachers of children. 3685
Eternal voice. 2438
Eternal war. 3793
Eternal why. 529
Eternal wisdom. 747
Eternal wisdom and health. 3195, 3196
Eternal witness. 850
Eternal word in the modern world. 366
Eternal year. 1262
Eternalism. 3054
Eternity. 1059, 1533
Eternity here and now. 120
Eternity in the heart. 2437
Eternity is now. 1533, 2324
Eternity shut in a span. 1450
Ethelbert Talbot, 1848-1928. 3580
Etheric body of man. 117
Ethic for Christians and other aliens in a strange land. 947
Ethic of Jesus in the teaching of the church. 2003
Ethic of Jesus in the teaching of the church: its authority and its relevance. 2003
Ethica. 945
...Ethical and moral instruction in schools. 1540
... Ethical and religious significance of the state. 2857
Ethical confrontation in counseling. 2780
Ethical dilemmas of ministers. 3673
Ethical end of Plato's theory of ideas. 2853
Ethical ideals of Jesus in a changing world. 2003, 3445
Ethical in the Jewish and American heritage. 1539
Ethical issues confronting world Christians. 2519
Ethical issues in human genetics: genetic counseling and the use of genetic knowledge. 1853
Ethical issues in nursing. 2718
Ethical issues in social science research. 3435
Ethical issues in social work. 3435
Ethical mysticism in the Society of Friends. 2644
Ethical patterns in early Christian thought. 950
Ethical philosophy. 1535
Ethical philosophy of life presented in its main outlines. 2843
Ethical philosophy of the Gita. 2317
Ethical readings from the Bible. 249
Ethical religion of Zoroaster. 3898

Ethical resources for international relations. 1077
Ethical Sunday school. 1540
Ethical teaching of Jesus. 942, 2004
Ethical teaching of Paul. 373
...The ethical teaching of the Gospels. 394
Ethical teachings in the Latin hymns of medieval England. 1877
Ethical teachings of Jesus. 2061
Ethical treatises of Berachya. 1538
Ethical world-conception of the Norse people. 1534
Ethical writings of Maimonides. 1539
Ethics. 942, 946, 951, 1534, 1535, 1536, 1537
Ethics: an introduction to moral philosophy. 1534
Ethics and belief. 3069
Ethics and etiquette of the pulpit, pew, parish, press and platform. 1535
Ethics and metaethics. 1538
Ethics and nuclear deterrence. 103
Ethics and reference services. 3032
Ethics and regulations of clinical research. 1853
Ethics and social science research. 3435
Ethics and the Gospel. 2003
Ethics and the moral life. 1536
Ethics and the New Testament. 378
Ethics and the theology of liberation. 949
Ethics and the urban ethos. 3446
Ethics and world politics. 1914
Ethics as a religion. 1533
Ethics, crime, and redemption. 945
Ethics for an industrial age. 1075, 1076
Ethics for the young. 3880
Ethics from a theocentric perspective. 943
Ethics from Sinai. 4
Ethics in a business society. 1075
Ethics in a Christian context. 944
Ethics in a permissive society. 942
Ethics in America. 3742
Ethics in the New Testament. 378
Ethics of Aristotle. 80
... the ethics of Bishop Butler and Immanuel Kant. 1538, 2163
Ethics of Buddhism. 1537
Ethics of Confucius. 2838
Ethics of decision. 943
Ethics of enjoyment. 3433
Ethics of freedom. 2223
Ethics of human subject research. 1853
Ethics of India. 1812
Ethics of Jesus. 2003
Ethics of Jesus and social progress. 2003, 3442
Ethics of Jonathan Edwards. 1500
Ethics of Judaism. 1539
Ethics of Judaism from the aspect of duty. 1539
Ethics of Martin Luther. 2280
Ethics of Martin Luther King, Jr. 945, 2173
Ethics of Paul. 2796
Ethics of persuasive preaching. 2902
Ethics of St. Paul. 942
Ethics of smuggling. 992
Ethics of spiritualism. 3516
Ethics of the Christian life. 943
Ethics of the fathers. 4
Ethics of the fathers in the light of Jewish history. 4
Ethics of the law and proverbs. 1539
Ethics of the Old Testament. 1539
Ethics of the rabbis. 1539
Ethics of the Shulhan 'aruk. 741, 1539, 3405
Ethics of tolerance applied to religious groups in America. 3703
Ethics on a Catholic university campus. 950
Ethics without God. 944
Ethik der Griechen. 1538
Ethiopian Church. 3861
Ethiopian Orthodox Church. 3861
Ethiopic Book of Enoch. 489
Ethiopic Didascalia. 1239
Ethiopic liturgy. 2238
... The Ethiopic vesion of the book of Enoch. 1540
... The Ethiopic version of the Hebrew Book of Jubilees. 1540
Ethnic and social background of the Franciscan Friars in seventeenth century Mexico. 1647
Ethnic identity and religion. 2087
Ethnic realities and the church. 1171
Ethnic trinities and thier relations to the Christian trinity. 3711
Ethnicity. 1135
Ethnicity, denomination, and inequality. 3748
Ethos of the Bible. 1538
Ethusiasm makes the difference. 3539
Etiquette and milk. 1540
Etudes de sociologie religieuse. 817, 2979
Etudes sur la peinture postbyzantine. 1880

Etudes sur le Timee de Plato. 2853
Euangelium secundum Iohannem. 47
Euangelium secundum Johannem. 47
Euangelium secundum Lucam. 654
Euangelium secundum Marcum. 654
Euangelium secundum Mattheum. 654
Eucharist. 2254, 2255, 2366, 3709
Eucharist and Christian life. 2254
Eucharist and church fellowship in the first four centuries. 2256
Eucharist and education. 2254
Eucharist and eschatology. 2252
Eucharist and human liberation. 2254
Eucharist and institution narrative. 2257
Eucharist and life. 2254
Eucharist & liturgical renewal. 2233
Eucharist & ministry. 2298, 2787
Eucharist and the confessional. 2254
Eucharist and the hunger of the world. 2254
Eucharist and you. 2253
Eucharist as sacrifice. 2255
Eucharist in Catholic life. 2254
Eucharist in ecumenical dialogue. 2253
Eucharist in St. Paul. 1541
Eucharist in the New Testament. 2254
Eucharist in the New Testament (The) 2254
Eucharist in the primitive church. 2254
Eucharist (law and practice) 2251
Eucharist of the early Christians. 2256
Eucharist-sacrament. 2255
... The eucharist, the mystery of Holy Thursday. 2374
Eucharist: theology and spirituality of the eucharistic prayer. 2256
Eucharist today. 2254, 2259
Eucharistia. 2366
Eucharistic apostolate of St. Ignatius Loyola. 2256, 2267
Eucharistic chats. 2254
Eucharistic Christ. 2253
Eucharistic congress in reality and in miniature. 2253
Eucharistic controversy of the eleventh century. 2257
... A eucharistic day. 839
Eucharistic doctrine and liturgy of the mystagogical catecheses of Theodore of Mopsuestia. 2256, 3610
Eucharistic doctrine in England from Hooker to Waterland. 2250
Eucharistic doctrine of the Oxford movement. 2256
Eucharistic Emmanuel. 3340
...The eucharistic fast. 2254
Eucharistic hours for priests and people. 2253
Eucharistic life. 2250
Eucharistic lilies. 2252
Eucharistic liturgies. 838, 2368
Eucharistic liturgies of the Eastern churches. 2237
Eucharistic liturgy in the Roman rite. 1541, 2368
Eucharistic liturgy of Taize. 2257
Eucharistic memorial. 2252
Eucharistic miracle of Lanciano, Italy. 2258
... The eucharistic prayer. 1541
Eucharistic prayer, and The meaning of Sunday. 842
Eucharistic prayers for children. 900
Eucharistic prayers from the ancient liturgies. 2257
Eucharistic priest. 2251, 2255
Eucharistic renaissance. 1913
Eucharistic reservation in the western church. 2259
Eucharistic sacrifice. 1541, 2367
Eucharistic sacrifice and the Reformation. 2259
Eucharistic springtime of the Church. 1317
Eucharistic teaching of Ratramn of Corbie. 3025
Eucharistic theology. 2255
Eucharistic Words of Jesus. 1541, 2198
Eucharistica. 812
Eucharistics. 2259
Euchology. 2748
Euclea; works. 2856
Eudemon, spiritual and rational. 2903
Eugene Carson Blake, prophet with portfolio. 670, 1300
Eugene Carson Blake, the chief church spokesman for leftist causes. 2670
Eugene de Mazenod. 2376, 2720, 2721
Eugene Russell Hendrix, servant of the kingdom. 1803
Eugenio Pacelli, Pope of peace. 2852
Eulogies. 1693
Eulogy on the life and character of Rev. Zachariah Greene. 1772
Eunice. 3196
Eureka. 457
Eureka carols. 3458, 3459

Europe—a mission field? 2517
Europe and America. 1491
Europe and Methodism. 2420
Europe and the faith. 1542
Europe and the gospel. 3466
Europe and the Jews. 2111
Europe at the crossroads. 1552
Europe at this minute. 609
Europe in the Reformation. 3034
Europe in torment: 1450-1550. 86
... Europe in transition. 2954
Europe in travail. 1543
Europe, whither bound! 149
European civilization. 1542
European financing of Latin America's economic development. 29
European history (1525-1874) of the Swiss Mennonites from Volhynia. 2408
European Jewry ten years after the war. 2099
European Jewry ten years after the war; an account of the development and present status of the decimated Jewish communities of Europe. 2099
European missions in Texas. 2553
European thought in the eighteenth century, from Montesquieu to Lessing. 1503
European witchcraft. 3826
Eurythmy. 1543, 1544
Eusapia Palladino and her phenomena. 2766, 3497
Eusebius. 1191
Eusebius of Caesarea and the Arian crisis. 80, 1542
Eustathius of Antioch and his place in the early history of Christian doctrine. 1544
Eustratios Argenti. 80
Euthaliana. 1544
Euthaliana, studies of Euthalius. 373, 1544
Euthanasia. 1544
Euthanasia and the right to death. 1544
Euthanasia and the right to die. 3238
Euthanasia, (compassionate death) 1544
Euthanasia controversy, 1812-1974. 1544
Euthanasie. 1544
Euthanasy. 1544, 2735
Eutychus and his pin. 1008
Eutychus and his pin, edited with an apology. 1008
Eutychus and his relations. 1008
Evaluating the charismatic movement. 2814
Evaluating versions of the New Testament. 351
Evaluation of claims to the charismatic gifts. 1713
Evaluation of the vocabulary content of twelve series of primary readers. 3025
Evaluations of audio-visual materials for Jewish schools. 2154
Evan Fry. 3218, 3352
Evangel. 1554, 1990
Evangel of a new world. 2174
Evangel of religion. 2931
Evangel of the strait, gate. 2930
Evangel reader. 1229
Evangel sermons. 1229, 3353
Evangel Wiseman, or, The mother's question. 1905
Evangelical academies in Germany. 1544
Evangelical action! 1551
Evangelical agenda, 1984 and beyond. 1553
Evangelical and Reformed Churches and World War II. 3851
Evangelical awakenings in Africa. 3229
Evangelical awakenings in Eastern Asia. 3230
Evangelical awakenings in Latin America. 3231
Evangelical awakenings in southern Asia. 3231
Evangelical awakenings in the South Seas. 3231
Evangelical book of worship. 1550
Evangelical challenge. 1551
Evangelical Christianity. 3648
Evangelical Christianity in the Philippines. 2831
Evangelical church. 1551
Evangelical Church in Ohio. 1546
Evangelical commentary on the Bible. 220
Evangelical Convenant Church. 1549
Evangelical economy developed. 3356
Evangelical faith. 3642, 3649
Evangelical faith for today. 3663
Evangelical heritage. 1552
Evangelical humanism. 1551
Evangelical invasion of Brazil. 1546
Evangelical Lutheran church, providentially how great and where unique. 2286
Evangelical Lutheran hymn book. 2289
Evangelical Lutheran hymnbook. 2289

Evangelical mind and the new school Presbyterian experience. 1552, 2926
Evangelical missions tomorrow. 2514
Evangelical movement in the Highlands of Scotland. 1550
Evangelical offices of worship and meditation derived chiefly from the New Testament. 2969
Evangelical pioneers. 1550
Evangelical primer. 747
Evangelical primer, containing a minor doctrinal catechism. 748, 1550, 1551
Evangelical primer, containing a minor doctrinal catechism; and a minor historical catechism. 747
Evangelical Protestant movement. 1549
Evangelical pulpit. 3353
Evangelical rationalism. 3645
Evangelical renaissance. 1550
Evangelical response to Bangkok. 2515
Evangelical responsibility in contemporary theology. 3617
Evangelical revival in the eighteenth century. 1759
Evangelical roots. 239, 1551, 3432
Evangelical sermons of our day. 1555
Evangelical socio-spiritual development. 1137
Evangelical Sunday school lesson commentary. 3188
Evangelical synod in India. 2531
Evangelical theologians of Wurttemberg in the sixteenth century. 3626
Evangelical theology. 3659
Evangelical theology, 1833-1856. 1552
Evangelical theology of missions. 2554
Evangelical-Unification dialogue. 1552, 3330
Evangelical; what does it really mean? 1551
Evangelical witness. 1569
Evangelicalism and Anabaptism. 1551
Evangelicalism and social responsibility. 3442
Evangelicalism in America. 1552, 2669
Evangelicals. 1551, 1553
Evangelicals and Jews in conversation on scripture, theology, and history. 2153
Evangelicals and unity. 1043
Evangelicals at an impasse. 1551
Evangelicals at the brink of crisis. 1551, 3849
Evangelicals face the future. 1553
Evangelicals in search of identity. 1552
Evangelicals in the White House. 1553
Evangelicals, revolutionists and idealists. 2734, 3212
Evangeline Booth. 681
Evangelisation in der Erwartung des Reiches Gottes. 1573
Die evangelische Kirchenmusik. 1207
Evangelisches Liederbuch fur Gemeinde, Schule, Haus. 1551
Evangelism. 1565, 1568, 1569, 1572, 1573, 3228
Evangelism: a graphic survey. 1571
Evangelism according to Christ. 423
Evangelism and baptism. 1553
Evangelism and change. 1566
Evangelism and Chrisitan experience. 1570
Evangelism and contemporary issues. 1562
Evangelism and contemporary theology. 3656
Evangelism and social service. 1553
Evangelism and the present world-order. 1563
Evangelism and the revival work of Rev. G. W. Wilson. 1563, 3819
Evangelism and the sovereignty of God. 1554, 1569
Evangelism, Christ's imperative commission. 1567
Evangelism -- commitment and involvement. 1573
Evangelism evangelized. 1554
Evangelism explosion. 1566
Evangelism for our day. 1564
Evangelism for teen-agers for a new day. 1574
Evangelism for teenagers for a new day. 1574
Evangelism for the world today. 1568
Evangelism for today. 1563, 1566
Evangelism for today's church. 1572
Evangelism for tomorrow. 1571
Evangelism handbook. 1572
Evangelism in a changing America. 1564
Evangelism in a changing world. 1562
Evangelism in a contemporary context. 1563
Evangelism in a tangled world. 1567
Evangelism in action through Christ-centered messages. 1556
Evangelism in Christian education. 1569
Evangelism-in-depth. 1574, 2979

... Evangelism in Korea. 2536
Evangelism in perspective. 1572
Evangelism in sermon and song. 1575
Evangelism in the Acts. 332
Evangelism in the church. 1554
Evangelism in the congregation. 1562
Evangelism in the early church. 330, 1573
Evangelism in the local church. 1568
Evangelism in the new age. 1564
Evangelism in the remaking of the world. 1554
Evangelism in the Sabbath school. 3385
Evangelism in the Sunday church school. 1564
... Evangelism in the Sunday school. 1563
Evangelism in the Wesleyan spirit. 1573, 3806
Evangelism in your church school. 1562
Evangelism men. 1556, 3829
Evangelism now. 1573
Evangelism of Jesus. 2004
Evangelism of youth. 1565
Evangelism old and new. 1564
Evangelism on purpose. 2480
Evangelism: the church on fire. 1571
Evangelism, the ministry of the Church. 3216, 3678
Evangelism through the local church. 1570
Evangelism through the localchurch. 1570
Evangelism through the Sabbath school. 3385
Evangelism today: message not method. 1572
Evangelism without apology. 1570
Evangelism's open secrets. 1568
Evangelist. 3233
Evangelistic addresses. 1560
Evangelistic awakening. 1570
Evangelistic church. 1571
Evangelistic comments on the Gospel according to St. Luke. 1556
Evangelistic congregation. 1568
Evangelistic cyclopedia. 1565
Evangelistic entreaties. 1561
Evangelistic illustrations. 1555, 1839
Evangelistic illustrations, for pulpit and platform. 1839
Evangelistic illustrations from the Bible. 304
Evangelistic message. 1554
Evangelistic message of Protestantism. 2976
Evangelistic messages. 1557
Evangelistic note. 1068
Evangelistic preaching. 2904
Evangelistic preaching and the Old Testament. 537
Evangelistic preaching, with sermon outlines and talks to children and young people. 1562
Evangelistic sermon outlines. 1562
Evangelistic sermonettes. 1555
Evangelistic sermons. 1555, 1556, 1557, 1558, 1560, 1561, 1562
Evangelistic sermons by great evangelists. 1556
Evangelistic sermons hotline. 1562
Evangelistic sermons of Clovis G. Chappell. 1556, 2435
Evangelistic sermons, together with practical suggestions for the conduct of the after-meeting. 1560
Evangelistic spirit and the laymen's task. 1571
Evangelistic talks by Gipsy Smith. 1560
Evangelistic work in principle and practice. 1569
Evangelists manual. 3754
Evangelists to the poor. 1574
Evangelium secundum Mattheum. 654
Evangelization. 1572
Evangelization and catechesis. 1566
Evangelization and justice. 2789
Evangelization in America. 76, 826
Evangelization in the American context. 829, 2790
Evangelization in the world today. 1572
Evangelization of the world in this generation. 2521
Evangelization today. 1565
Evangelize or fossilize. 1567
Evangelize thru Christian education. 1574
Evangelized America. 1567
Evangelizing Europe. 2517
Evangelizing neopagan North America. 1567
Evangelizing of the Roman Empire. 1554
Evangelizing the American Jew. 2556
Evanston, an interpretation. 3850
Evanston report, the Second Assembly of the World Council of Churches. 3850
Eve of Catholic emancipation. 817
Eve of the Reformation. 1516
Evelyn Underhill, 1875-1941. 3722
Evelyn Underhill reader. 3483
Even as you and I. 963, 3839

Even if I'm bad? 3370
Even so, believe. 1007
"Even unto Bethlehem" 1112
Even unto death. 37, 2003
Even when I cry. 2398
Evening. 1860
Evening altar. 972
Evening and morning in China. 2511
Evening bells at Bethany. 3614
Evening exercises for the closet. 1439
Evening meditations. 3206
Evening of life (compensations of old age) 2735
Evening prayers for every day of the year. 2888
Evening sacrifice. 1452
Evening service for Sabbaths and festivals. 2108
Evening thoughts for every day in the year. 1450
Evening with God. 18
Evenings with famous Christians. 926
Evenings with Grandfather Braddock. 1929
Evenings with the Bible. 232
Evenings with the Bible and science. 205
Evenings with the doctrines. 3639
Evenings with the Master. 1445
Evenings with the sacred poets. 3210
Event in eternity. 545
Eventful narratives. 2614
Eventful nights of August 20th and 21st, 1854. 3501
Eventful years and experiences. 2106
Events and epochs in religious history. 1173
Events and their afterlife. 1402, 3720
Events of the last days. 1513
Ever-living life. 2227
Ever open door. 3368
Ever since Sinai. 2140, 3706
Ever timely thoughts. 997
Ever-widening circle. 643, 1259
Everbody is a somebody. 3330
Everflowing streams. 3270
Evergreen things. 2390
Everlasting covenant. 503, 3289
Everlasting covenant, content and value of the Old Testament. 498
Everlasting evangel and its program. 1569
Everlasting goodwill and glory. 1006
Everlasting gospel. 670, 3095, 3340, 3351, 3463
Everlasting gospel versus Babylon the great. 3381
Everlasting harmony. 1726
Everlasting life. 2848
Everlasting life, a creed and a speculation. 1888
Everlasting life after death. 1695
Everlasting light. 251, 736
Everlasting man. 762, 3057
Everlasting now. 1417
Everlasting priest. 771
Everlasting salvation. 3590
Everlasting spires. 3287
Everlasting things. 2607
Every body's book. 1727, 3463
Every boy needs a man. 146
Every child's Pilgrim's progress. 3198
Every Christian a soul winner. 1571
Every Christian's job. 1568
Every church its own evangelist. 1564
"Every cloud has a silver lining ..." 3
Every community survey of Maine. 1274
Every creature. 1567
Every day. 1441
Every day a prayer. 1437
Every day; Bible readings for each day of the year. 1430
Every day Bible stories. 253
Every-day evangelism. 1567
Every day I have a journey. 1323
Every-day life illustrated by the life of Jesus. 1994
Every-day religion. 975, 980, 3196
Every-day science for the Christian. 204
Every day Scripture readings. 249
Every day with God. 1606
Every day with Jesus. 2016
Every end exposed. 2182
Every fourth Tuesday. 1256
Every good desire. 3750, 3751
Every good gift. 2392
Every head bowed. 995
Every knee shall bow. 2046
Every man a Bible student. 301
Every man a brother. 1136
Every man heart lay down. 2022
Every man in his ministry. 1296
Every man my brother. 1028, 3027
Every man's Bible. 230, 251
Every man's book. 304
Every man's challenge. 923
Every man's story of the New Testament. 410

Every man's story of the Old Testamet. 535
Every man's story of the Oxford movement. 2754
Every member canvass. 1168
Every-member evangelism. 1553
Every member evangelism for today. 1564
Every minister his own evangelist. 1572
Every moment an Easter. 75
Every morning. 1605
Every need supplied. 3324
Every one that believeth. 471
Every pastor a counselor. 2995
Every pastor needs a pastor. 1298
Every place a voice. 3850
Every thing in Christ. 322, 2043
Every tribe and tongue. 2515
Every wind of doctrine. 3640
Every woman can be more beautiful. 3844
Everybody calls me Brother. 2577
Everybody calls me Father. 772
Everybody can know. 2395
Everybody needs somebody sometime. 1399, 1917
Everybody wins. 1008, 3891
Everybody's afraid in the ghetto. 1255
Everybody's bishop. 1602
Everybody's book. 289
Everybody's favorite sacred songs. 253, 3459
Everybody's Pope. 2123
Everybody's St. Francis. 1641
Everyday and its possibilities. 2385
Everyday beginnings. 3844
Everyday Bible. 250
... An everyday Christian. 3196
Everyday counsel for everday living. 976
Everyday devotions for youth. 3882
Everyday evangelism. 1565
Everyday faith. 1264
Everyday, five minutes with God. 1431
... Everyday lessons in religion. 617, 3146
Everyday life in Bible times. 208, 1280
Everyday life in New Testament times. 407, 2765
Everyday life in Old Testament times. 486
Every-day objectives for older boys. 687
Everyday philosophy of Jesus and his brother James. 1323
Everyday prayers. 901, 2888
Everyday prayers for all sorts of needs. 2890
Everyday religion. 975, 3196, 3340
Everyday religious living. 3355
Everyday saints. 3283
Everyday science for the Christian. 3078
Everyday spiritual perception. 956
Everyday talks for everyday people. 761
Everyday work of the Westminster assembly. 3808
Everyland children. 895
Everyman a priest. 2939
Everyman's adventure. 1116, 1598
Everyman's book of saints. 1024, 3279
Everyman's dictionary of non-classical mythology. 2659
Everyman's goal. 1598
Everyman's history of the Jews. 2089
Everyman's history of the prayer book. 2960
Everyman's life of Jesus. 1989
Everyman's Mass. 2369
Everyman's mission. 1598
Everyman's problems and difficulties. 67
Everyman's religion. 1059, 3196
Everyman's road to heaven. 3490
Everyman's saint. 54
Everyman's St. Paul. 366, 2799
Everyman's search. 1598
Everyman's Talmud. 2074, 3582, 3585
Everyman's theology. 797
Everyman's world. 2227
Everynun. 3200
Everyone a minister. 3678
Everyone in the Bible. 217
Everyone needs a church. 1248
Everyone's St. Paul's. 2244
... Everything counts. 3181
Everything happens with kids. 896
Everything is yours. 1007
Everything Jesus taught. 2064
Everything to gain. 786
Everything you always wanted to know about sorcery. 3823
Everything you ever wanted to know about heaven— but never dreamed of asking. 1795
Everything you need to grow a Messianic synagogue. 2073
Everything you need to know for a cassette ministry. 2844
Everything you want to know about astrology, numerology, how to win. 95
Everything you want to know about: black magic, revelations by Zolar, metaphysical astrology, mediumship, crystal gazing. 2313

Everything you want to know about nature's mysteries, the prophets, Nostradamus, tea leaf readings, herbs, candle burning. 2715, 2946
Everything you want to know about the mission field, but are afraid you won't learn until you get there. 2495
Everything you want to know about TM - including how to do it. 3708
Everything you want to know about TM, including to do it. 3708
Everything you wanted to know about the Catholic Church but were too pious to ask. 795
Everywhere God. 3137
Everywhere I go. 3164
Everywhere people waiting. 2333
Everywhere the light. 692, 3473
Eves of faith. 651
Evgippii Vita Sancti Severini. 3388
Evidence and its function according to John Duns Scotus. 1483, 1578
Evidence for God. 1721
Evidence for immortality. 1888
Evidence for our faith. 62
Evidence for the resurrection of Jesus Christ. 2052
Evidence from Scripture and history of the second coming of Christ. 3320
Evidence in science and in religion. 1738
Evidence of Christianity, derived from its nature and reception. 1099
Evidence of conflation in Mark? 435, 3578
Evidence of eternity. 1887
Evidence of God in an expanding universe. 1738, 3079
Evidence of immorality. 1886
Evidence of prophecy. 606
Evidence of salvation. 3295
Evidence of Satan in the modern world. 1427
Evidence of the truth of the Christian religion. 1099
...Evidence of the truth of the Christian religion, derived from the literal fulfilment of prophecy. 1099
Evidence of things not seen. 1592
Evidence of tradition. 1198
Evidence on Christianity and evolution. 1654
Evidence that convicted Aida Skripnikova. 2821, 3423
Evidences against Christianity. 1654
Evidences and reconciliations. 2614
Evidences for immortality. 1890
Evidences of catholicity. 783
Evidences of Christianity. 59, 60, 61, 68, 1047, 1098, 1099, 1100
Evidences of Christianity from impartial sources. 67
Evidences of Christianity, in their external. 60
Evidences of Christianity, in their external, or historical, division. 60
Evidences of divine being. 1738
Evidences of immortality. 3517
Evidences of modern spiritualism. 3518
Evidences of religion. 60
Evidences of revealed religion. 58, 61
Evidences of romantic treatment of religious elements in late eighteenth-century minor poetry (1771-1800) 3210
Evidences of the authenticity, inspiration, and canonical authority of the Holy Scriptures. 59, 275
Evidences of the Christian religion. 58, 1097
Evidences of the Christian religion, briefly and plainly stated. 1097
Evidences of the divinity of Jesus Christ. 2000
Evidences of the genuineness of the gospels. 391, 395
Evil. 1745, 1746
Evil and danger of stage-plays. 3605
Evil and suffering. 1746
Evil and the Christian faith. 1745
Evil and the concept of God. 3610
Evil and the God of Love. 3610
Evil eye. 1578
Evil eye in the western Highlands. 1578
Evil in modern myth and ritual. 3433
Evil religion does. 3096
Evil, suffering, and religion. 1745
Evils of infant baptism. 1906
Evoltion of a Christian. 957
... Evolution. 1579, 1580, 1582, 3073
Evolution and Christian faith. 202, 1580
Evolution and Christian hope. 1582
Evolution and Christian thought today. 1579, 1580
Evolution and Christianity. 1579, 1581
Evolution and Christians. 1579
Evolution and dogma. 1581, 3077
Evolution and Genesis. 1581

Evolution and guilt. 1582
Evolution and Jesus Christ. 1579
Evolution and man. 1092
Evolution and man here and hereafter. 1579
Evolution and modern thought. 3080
Evolution and Presbyterianism. 1581
Evolution and redemption. 1579, 3029
Evolution and religion. 1579, 1580, 1581, 3080, 3085
Evolution and religion in education. 1580
Evolution and spiritual life. 1582
Evolution and the Bible. 1579
... Evolution and the Christian concept of God. 3079
Evolution and the Christian doctrine of creation. 1581, 3813
Evolution and the doctrine of original sin. 3414
Evolution and the doctrine of the Trinity. 3712
Evolution and the earthly destiny. 1709, 1814
Evolution and the fall. 1579
Evolution and the high school student. 202
Evolution and the immanent God. 1579
Evolution and the inward light. 1681, 2242
Evolution and the modern Christian. 3081, 3082
Evolution and the need of atonement. 1582
Evolution and the orthodox church. 1579
Evolution and the reformation of biology. 202, 1477
Evolution and theology. 1580
Evolution and true light. 1579
Evolution as revelation. 1381
Evolution, as taught in the Bible. 1580
Evolution at the bar. 1580
Evolution contrasted with Scripture truth. 1579
Evolution, creation and science. 1580, 3079
Evolution examined in the light of revelation and reason. 1581
Evolution from space. 1580
Evolution, God and immortality. 3074
Evolution in a nutshell. 1581
Evolution in Christian doctrine. 3654
Evolution in my mission views. 2519
Evolution in religion. 1580, 1709
Evolution in science and revolution in religion. 1578
Evolution in the afterlife. 1888
Evolution of a churchman. 3196
Evolution of a great literature. 311
Evolution of a life. 3027
Evolution of a missionary. 1407
Evolution of a theologian. 3611
Evolution of an Endeavor. 3737
Evolution of an old New England church. 1485
Evolution of beliefs. 185
Evolution of Bible study. 637
Evolution of Buddhist architecture in Japan. 79
... Evolution of Christian doctrines. 3654
Evolution of Christian thought. 3653
Evolution of Christianity. 1047, 1093, 1100
Evolution of Christology. 2046
Evolution of church building. 1158
Evolution of church music. 1207
Evolution of Congregationalism. 1344
Evolution of Dutch Catholicism, 1958-1974. 826
Evolution of early Christianity. 1190
Evolution of immortality. 1889, 1891, 3250
Evolution of Jewish thought. 2107, 2146
Evolution of love. 1105
Evolution of man. 1581, 3473
Evolution of man and Hristianity. 1580
Evolution of man-s mind. 3683
Evolution of new China. 2507
Evolution of New Testament Christology. 350, 1955
Evolution of Newman's conception of faith. 1590, 2702
Evolution of our Christian hymnology. 1872
Evolution of religion. 3059
Evolution of religions. 3113
Evolution of spiritual man. 1061
Evolution of the atmosphere as a proof of design and purpose in the creation, and of the existence of a personal God. 103
Evolution of the Buddha image. 85
Evolution of the Christian year. 1262
Evolution of the conception of God. 1722
Evolution of the dragon. 1478
Evolution of the earth. 3250
Evolution of the English hymn. 1871
Evolution of the God. 3094

Evolution of the Greek Orthodox church in America and its present problems. 2746
Evolution of the Hebrew people and their influence on civilization. 2096
Evolution of the human soul and the future life scientifically demonstrated. 1694
Evolution of the idea of God. 1742, 3093
Evolution of the kingdom. 2175
Evolution of the monastic ideal. 2576
Evolution of the Sikh community. 3408
Evolution of the soul. 3463
Evolution of the soul, and other essays. 2989
... The evolution of the sunday school. 3561
Evolution of the universe. 1612, 3501
Evolution of theology in the Greek philosophers. 2834
Evolution on trial. 202
... Evolution or Christianity, God or Darwin? 1579
Evolution or creation. 202, 1380, 1383
Evolution theory. 1579
Evolution versus creation. 1581
Evolutionary astrology. 96
Evolutionary naturalism. 2865
Evolutionary philosophies and contemporary theology. 2944
Evolutionary philosophy. 1579
Evolutionary self. 1403, 1517
Evolutionist and missionary, John Thomas Gulick. 2482
Evolutionist looks at religion. 1579
Evolutionistic spiritualism. 3495
Evolving church. 1245
Evolving church and the Sacrament of Penance. 839, 2812
Evolving religious careers. 3785
Evolving world and theology (The) 1581
Ex-nuns. 1582
Ex oriente lux. 3250
Ex-prelate's meditations. 3128
Ex-priest and the riddle of religion. 800
Exact science of Christianity. 1891
Exactly how you may receive your healing--through faith. 973
Exalt His name. 3562
Exalted fisherman. 2824
Exalted life. 2610
Exalted name, a study of the name "Lord Jesus Christ" 1952
Examen. 1347
Examen of witches. 3826
Examens for retreat time. 1347
Examination into and an elucidation of the great principle of the mediation and atonement of Our Lord and Savior Jesus Christ. 2613
Examination of a pamphlet entitled The misrepresentations of Anna Braithwaite, in relation to the doctrines preaches by Elias Hicks. 1810
Examination of Canon Liddon's Bampton lectures on the divinity of Our Lord and Saviour Jesus Christ. 2002, 2225
Examination of certain recent assaults on physical science. 1399, 3077
Examination of certain statements in Macaulay's History of England. 1220
Examination of conscience. 1347
examination of conscience for modern Catholics. 1347
Examination of dispensationalism. 1467
Examination of Dr. Washington Gladden's New theology. 1715
Examination of President Edwards' inquiry into the freedom of the will. 1500, 1657
Examination of President Edwards's Inquiry on the freedom of the will. 1657
Examination of the Bible. 3023
Examination of the Bliss imbroglio, both in its spiritual and legal aspect. 672, 3504
Examination of the Council of Trent. 3710
Examination of the divine testimony concerning the character of the Son of God. 2039
Examination of the doctrine of endless punishment. 1699
Examination of the doctrine of future retribution. 1699
Examination of the doctrine of perfection. 2818
Examination of the essays Bacchus. 1775, 3597
"Examination of the late Rev'd President Edwards's Enquiry on freedom of will" 1500, 1657
Examination of the late Reverend President Edwards's 'Enquiry on freedom of will. 1500, 1657
Examination of the origin, progress and unity of the church of God. 3642
Examination of the passages in the New Testament. 589

Examination of the Pelagian and Arminian theory of moral agency as recently advocated. 184, 1658
Examination of the principles contained in the Age of reason. 2758
... The examination of the qualities of the ordinated. 2741
Examination of the Reverend John Anderson's Discourse, on the divine ordinance of singing psalms. 39, 2984
Examination of the so-called American missal. 33
Examination of the system of new divinity. 2447, 3617
Examination of the testimony of the four evangelists. 2067
Examinations and writings of John Philpot. 1162
Examiner, examined. 3601
Examiners examined. 2758
Example of Jesus Christ (Imago Christi) 2004
Example of Our Lord, especially for His ministers. 1952
Example of the passion. 2033
Examples of the glories of heaven. 1793
Examples of youthful piety. 3196
Excavating Kirjath-Sepher's ten cities. 486, 2188, 3594
...The excavation of Armageddon. 2400
Excavations at Qumran. 1410, 3014
Excavations at Tell en-Nasbeh, 1926 and 1927. 3594
Exceeding worth of joining the church. 1201
Excellence of exposition. 2907
Excellence of our calling. 2898
Excellence of the rosary. 3248
Excellency of the word. 2903
Excellency of virture, contrasted with the deformity of vice. 956
Excellent sayings of the Prophet Muhammad (may the peace and blessings of God be upon him) and Hazrat Ali (upon whom be peace) 1780
Excell's male quartets and choruses. 3458
Excelsior. 1421
Except . . . for fornication. 3411
Except ye be born again. 1048
Except ye repent. 3218
Exceptional children: a special ministry. 1254
Exceptional stories from the lives of our apostles. 1231
Excepts of Our Lord. 2071
Excerpts from the Paul Solomon tapes. 2733
Excerpts from The testimony of the evangelists. 1574
Ontology. 2738
Exciting Christianity. 325
Exciting church. 641, 1942, 2880
Exciting church where they give their money away. 3530
Exciting object lessons and ideas for children's sermons. 3859
Ecclesiology of Vatican II. 1188, 3771
Exclusion of women from the priesthood. 3842
Exclusive by-path. 2855, 3846
Exclusiveness and tolerance. 2112, 2153
Excursions to the spirit world. 94
"Excuse me!" 1360
Excuse me, Sir. 2895
Excusiveness and tolerance. 2153
Execution of Jesus. 2031
Executive director on the job in a membership organization, the YWCA 3877
Executive role in Y.M.C.A. administration. 3872
Exegesis. 288
Exegesis of life. 2738
Exegetic homilies. 525
Exegetical analysis of the Epistles. 346, 378
Exegetical analysis of the Epistues. 346
Exegetical and analytical commentary on Paul's epistle to the Romans. 467
Exegetical and practical commentary on the Epistle to the Romans. 468
Exegetical commentary on the gospel according to S. Matthew. 440
Exegetical method. 239, 287
Exegetical method of the Greek translator of the Book of Job. 551
Exempla of the rabbis. 1583
Exempla or illustrative stories from the sermones vulgares of Jacques de Vitry. 1583
Exemplar. 2647
Exemplary life of the pious Lady Guion. 1779
Exemplum in the early religious and didactic literature of England. 1583
Exemplum in the early religious and didatic literature of England. 1583

Exempting the churches. 1241
Exemption of religious in church law. 2577
Exercise in compassion. 1548, 2499
Exercises. 2647
Exercises at the dedication of the Backus monument, North Middleboro, Mass., June 30, 1893. 123
Exercises at the meeting of the First Congregational Unitarian society. January 12, 1875. 2741
Exercises at the ninety-third anniversary and dedication of building and campus of the Hartford seminary foundation]1834-1927. 1788
Exercises commemorating the one hundred fiftieth anniversary of the organization of St. Andrews royal arch chapter, Boston, Massachusetts. 1670
Exercises commemorative of the two-hundredth anniversary of the founding of the First Congregational church in Cheshire, Connecticut, 1724-1924. 1336
... Exercises connected with the inauguration of the Rev. Daniel Johnson Fleming. 3612
Exercises in Bible history. 648
... Exercises in commemoration of the one hundred and seventy-fifth anniversary of the Silver Spring Presbyterian church. 2918
Exercises in connection with the inauguration of the Rev. Walter W. Moore, DD., LL.D. 3612
Exercises in interpreting Scripture. 287
Exercises in religious understanding. 3098
Exercises upon the first Psalme. 584
Exeter Cathedral, its life and work. 1583
Exhaustive concordance of the Bible. 225, 227, 228
Exhibition of Bibles. 212
Exhibitionism. 1583
Exhortations and admonitions of our venerable father and founder. 3296
Exile. 2508, 3573
Exile and Biblical narrative. 499
Exile and restoration. 532
Exile and return. 2092
Exile and tenderness. 1642
Exile ends in glory. 2334
Exile heart. 2933
Exile of the Word, from the silence of the Bible to the silence of Auschwitz. 599, 2983
Exile to exile. 2091
Exiled by the Czar. 1934
Exiles. 2979
Exiles in Babylon. 234, 1074
Exilic age. 547, 2093, 2096, 2148
Existence and analogy. 3608
Existence and attributes of God. 1730
Existence and being. 1800
Existence and faith. 1589
Existence and logic. 2739
Existence and presence. 1720
... The existence of a children's limbo according to Post-Tridentine theologians. 2229
Existence of God. 1738
Existence of God as confessed by faith. 1737
Existential approach to theology. 3663
Existential aspects of the writings of Fyodor Dostoevsky. 1583
Existential metaphysics. 2739
Existential psychoanalysis. 1584
Existential structure. 2738
Existentialism. 1583, 1584
Existentialism and human emotions. 1583, 1584
Existentialism and Indian thought. 1583
Existentialism and religious belief. 1584
Existentialism and religious liberalism. 2221
Existentialism and the new Christianity. 2689
Existentialism and theology. 1583
Existentialism and Thomism. 1584
Existentialism as philosophy. 1584
Existentialism from Dostoevsky to Sartre. 1583
Existentialist ethics. 3303
Existentialist posture. 1584
Existentialist prolegomena. 2163, 2419
Existentialist theology. 1076, 1800, 2836
Existentialist theology of Paul Tillich. 3700
Existentialists. 661
Existentialists and God. 2737
Exit the Devil. 1291, 1412
... The Exodus. 515, 516, 517, 1797
Exodus; a commentary. 516
Exodus, a hermeneutics of freedom. 287, 1659
Exodus; an introduction and commentary. 516

Exodus and Sinai in history and tradition. 563, 1584
Exodus for the church. 1060
Exodus from Concordia. 1322
Exodus from death. 3341
Exodus into the world. 1066
Exodus, Moses and the Decalogue legislation. 2097, 2621
Exodus of the Church of Scotland. 1652
Exodus pattern in the Bible. 499, 1584
Exodus theology. 659, 3659
Exodus to a hidden valley. 2505, 2620
Exorcising devils. 1585
Exorcism. 1585
Exorcism as a Christian ministry. 1585
Exorcism: New Testament style! 1428
Exorcism of Anneliese Michel. 1585, 2461
Exorcism through the ages. 1585
Exoteric philosophy presents the rhythmic rite. 3239
Expanded life. 179
Expanded panorama Bible study course. 1467
Expanded paraphrase of the Epistles of Paul. 374
Expanded present. 97
Expanded translation of the Greek New Testament. 356
Expanding church. 1233
Expanding faith. 2934, 3356
Expanding horizons. 1072, 3689
Expanding life in the Christian faith with junior highs. 3181
Expansion for the sake of God, love and civilization. 1892
Expansion of awareness. 2990
Expansion of Christianity in the first three centuries. 1192, 1196
Expansion of God. 1079
Expansion of the Anglican communion. 43
Expansion of the Catholic Church in Pennsylvania. 824
Expansion of the Christian church. 1174
Ex-pastors; why men leave the parish ministry. 1582
Expect to win. 1323
Expectation of Siam. 2546
Expectations for endowed living. 1008
Expectations westward. 2616
Expected church. 3344
Expecting. 1301, 1782
Expendable Mary Slessor. 2487, 3425
Experience. 63, 2387
Experience and God. 3105
Experience and gospel labors of the Rev. Benjamin Abbott. 3123
Experience and gospel labours of the Rev. Benjamin Abbott. 3123
Experience and language of grace. 1750
Experience and ministerial labors of Rev. Thomas Smith. 3135
Experience and religion. 3664
Experience and substance. 1585
Experience and the Christian faith. 1104
Experience and travels of Mr. Freeborn Garrettson. 1702
Experience and trials of Edward D. Tippett, preceptor; or, 44 years of his life: containing strange and mysterious events whilst the teacher of the Eastern free school, Washington, D.C. 3136
Experience, existence and the good. 2418, 3801
Experience facing death. 1412
Experience, inference, and God. 3609
Experience into words. 1519
Experience of celibacy. 877, 1285
Experience of death. 1414
Experience of death ; The moral problem of suicide. 1414
Experience of dying. 1415
Experience of faith. 1592
Experience of German Methodist preachers. 2439
Experience of God. 1000, 1586, 1590
Experience of God and his peace. 3476
Experience of God in modern life. 1729
Experience of God's presence. 1725
Experience of grace. 1357
Experience of Hester Ann Rogers. 3134
Experience of inner healing. 1600
Experience of praying. 2869
Experience of several eminent Methodist preachers. 2430, 2431
Experience with the supernatural in early Chrisian times. 3566
Experience with the supernatural in early Christian times. 3566
Experience worketh hope. 2931
Experiences and observations by the way. 3126
Experiences facing death. 1412
Experiences from "Over there" 3514
Experiences in community. 2571

Experiences in spiritualism with Mr. D. D. Home. 1838, 3501
Experiences in the church school kindergarten. 3556
Experiences in witnessing for Christ. 1566
Experiences of a pioneer minister of Minnesota. 3128
Experiences of David Dare in Bible research. 1099
Experiences of God. 1846, 2568
Experiences of Samuel Bowles ... in spirit life. 3482
Experiences of the higher Christian life in the Baptist denomination. 3299
Experiences, struggles, and hopes of the Black church. 3482
Experiencing commitment. 1007
Experiencing God. 3643
Experiencing Jesus. 2045, 3490
Experiencing, living, sharing Christ. 162
Experiencing reincarnation. 3054
Experiencing the Christian faith. 976
Experiencing the Holy Spirit. 1712
Experiential Bible study. 637
Experiential catechetics. 935
Experiential education, X-ED. 935
Experiment hope. 1846
Experiment in liberty. 933, 1659
Experiment in mindfulness. 2382
Experiment of faith. 1049, 1570, 1591
Experimental handbook for Christian involvement. 965
Experimental investigation of the effectiveness of selected motion pictures integrated with a unit of church school literature. 3161
Experimental investigation of the spirit manifestations, demonstrating the existence of spirits and their communion with mortals. 3504
Experimental liturgy book. 2368
Experimental logic of Jesus. 2065, 3444
Experimental object lessons. 650
Experimental parapsychology. 2991
Experimental preaching. 3353
Experimental psychology. 2988
Experimental religion. 3130
Experimental religion: embracing justification, regeneration, sanctification, and the witness of the Spirit. 2161
Experimental spiritism. 3512
Experimental telepathy. 2992
Experimentation and measurement in religious education. 3160
Experimentation in American religion. 3747
Experimenting with truth. 3083
Experiments in a search for God. 93, 2991
Experiments in community: Ephrata. 1521
Experiments in growth, spiritual growth, that is. 941
Experiments in personal religion. 1586
Experiments in psychical science. 2987
Experiments in psychics. 1412, 2992
Experiments in telepathy. 2992
Experiments of spiritual life and health. 979
Expert endeavor. 1914, 3737
Explaining Judaism to Jews and Christians. 2140
Explaining the Gospels. 398
Explanation and pious reflections on the Little office of the Blessed Virgin. 847
Explanation of Dr. Martin Luther's Small catechism. 2284
Explanation of Luther's small catechism. 748, 2284
Explanation of some of the prophesies which have predicted the rise, the power and tyranny. 607
Explanation of the Apocalypse. 464
Explanation of the Baltimore catechism of Christian doctrine. 132
Explanation of the Baltimore catechism of Christian doctrine for the use of Sunday-school teachers and advanced classes. 132
Explanation of the book of Revelation. 455
Explanation of the catechism. 2279, 2283
Explanation of the common service. 2294, 2295
Explanation of the Epistle of the Hebrews. 403
Explanation of the Epistle to the Hebrews. 403
Explanation of the holy rule of Carmel. 22, 740
Explanation of the holy sacrifice of the mass. 2366
Explanation of the mystical words used by John. 458
Explanation of the rule of the Friars minor. 1645
Explanation Psalmorum XII. 574

Explanatory analysis of St. Paul's Epistle to the Romans. 468
Explanatory Bible atlas and Scripture gazetteer. 102
Explanatory notes and remarks on Milton's Paradise lost. 2469
Explicated Tao. 2196
Explication of an engraving called The origin of the rites and worship of the Hebrews. 2120
Explication of the Shorter catechism. 3809
Explicatory catechism. 2881, 3809
Explicatory catechism: or, An explanation of the Assembly's Shorter catechism. 2881, 3809
Explo story. 1573, 1914
Exploding church. 826, 1302, 3052
Exploding mystery of prayer. 992
Exploits of faith. 1599
Exploratio philosophica. 2833
Exploration into contemplative prayer. 1356
Exploration into God. 1726
Exploration of Egypt and the Old Testament. 1501
Exploration of outer space. 99
Exploration of the inner world. 2995
Explorations in altruistic love and behavior, a symposium. 28
... Explorations in Hittite Asia Minor. 91
Explore. 1253
Explore the Book. 647
Explore the word! 640
Explore your own inner space. 3477
Explore your psychic world. 2202, 2992
Explorers. 1714
Explorer's life of Jesus. 391, 1970
Exploring a theology of education. 805
Exploring Africa. 2497
Exploring Beginnings. 1588
Exploring Buddhism. 702
Exploring Christian education. 935
Exploring Christianity. 3012
Exploring evangelism. 1554, 1571
Exploring Genesis. 522
Exploring God's answers. 3381
Exploring God's out-of-doors. 3764
Exploring God's word. 3665
Exploring God's world. 3766
Exploring Hebrews. 403
Exploring life. 3185
Exploring mysticism. 2648
Exploring old British churches. 1160
Exploring our Christian faith. 3647
Exploring our neighborhood. 3149
Exploring paths of church unity among Christians where they live. 1040
Exploring religion. 3063
Exploring religion with eight year olds. 3172
Exploring religious ideas: the great Western faiths. 3670
Exploring religious meaning. 3058
Exploring Revelation. 455
Exploring spiritual direction. 3475
Exploring the Bible. 233, 637, 638
Exploring the Bible with children. 638, 903
Exploring the Christian way. 342, 993
Exploring the Christian world mind. 1066
Exploring the deeps. 3642
Exploring the faith. 3216
Exploring the faith we share. 861
Exploring the great beyond. 3685
Exploring the heritage of John Calvin. 729
Exploring the human aura. 117
Exploring the logic of faith. 1589
Exploring the Messianic Psalms. 2415
Exploring the New Testament. 474
Exploring the next world. 1696
Exploring the occult. 2726
Exploring the Old Testament. 540, 3537
Exploring the parables. 2027
Exploring the philosophy of religion. 3107
Exploring the Psalms. 578
Exploring the Scriptures. 311
Exploring the silent shore of memory. 2535
Exploring the Talmud. 2075, 2087, 3584
Exploring the trail with the Master Guide. 3763
Exploring the world of psychic powers. 1878
Exploring Unification theology. 3330
Exploring Vatican 2. 997, 3771
Exploring your Bible. 640
Exploring your Bible; a comprehensive and useful handbook, a complete study-method manual. 640
Explosion of people evangelism. 2814
Explostion and defense of Universalism, in a series of sermons delivered in the Universalist church, Baltimore, Md. 3753

Exponents and philosophy of religious Zionism, an anthology. 3896
Expose. 3510
Expose of polygamy in Utah. 2606
Expose of religious fraud. 1656
"Expositio in Cantica canticorum" of William, abbot of Ebersberg, 1048-1085. 594
"Expositio in Cantica canticorum" of Williram, abbot of Ebersberg. 594
Expositio Psalmi CXVIII. 574
Exposition and defense of the scheme of redemption. 3030
Exposition and explanation of the modern phenomena called spirit manifestations. 3498
Exposition in the form of question and answer of the Westminster assembly's Shorter catechism. 3809
Exposition of a portion of the Epistle to the Romans. 466
Exposition of Aristotle's treatise on generation and corruption. 81
Exposition of Bible doctrines. 471
... Exposition of Christian doctrine. 780
Exposition of Daniel. 506
Exposition of Ecclesiastes. 512
Exposition of Ephesians. 363
Exposition of Ezekiel. 518
Exposition of Genesis. 521
Exposition of heavenly truths. 236, 1055
Exposition of heavenly truths through the revelation of the Holy Scriptures and the testimonies of the world's history. 236
Exposition of Hebrews. 403
Exposition of I and II Thessalonians. 478
Exposition of Isaiah. 543
... An exposition of modern spiritualism. 3511
Exposition of Reformed doctrine. 3043
Exposition of St. Paul's Epistle to the Romans. 469
Exposition of Second Timothy, inspirational and practical. 326
Exposition of selected Psalms by the late Rev. Frederick La Rue King. 576
Exposition of the Apocalypse. 463, 465
Exposition of the Apocalypse of St. John the apostle. 456
Exposition of the Bible. 222
Exposition of the Bible, chapter by chapter in one volume. 224
Exposition of the Book of Proverbs. 572
Exposition of the Book of Revelation. 458
Exposition of the church, catechism. 1215
Exposition of the Confession of faith of the Westminster assembly of divines. 3808
Exposition of the Creed. 74, 1385
Exposition of the dangers of interment in cities. 717
Exposition of the epistle of Paul the Apostle to the Galatians. 380
Exposition of the Epistle of Paul to the Romans. 470
Exposition of the Epistle to the Ephesians. 365
Exposition of the Epistle to the Hebrews. 403
Exposition of the Epistle to the Hebrews, in the form of questins and answers. 405
... An exposition of the Epistle to the Philippians. 449
... An exposition of the Epistle to the Romans. 469
Exposition of the Epistle to the Romans, in the form of questions and answers. 466
Exposition of the Epistles of Paul to the Galatians, Ephesians, Philippians, Collossians, Thessalonians. 371
Exposition of the faith of the Religious Society of Friends. 1681
Exposition of the form of government and the rules of discipline of the Presbyterian church in the United States. 2925
Exposition of the Gospel according to John. 416
Exposition of the Gospel of John. 416, 420, 423
Exposition of the Gospel of Luke. 428
Exposition of the Gospel of Mark. 433
Exposition of the Gospel of Matthew. 440
Exposition of the Gospels of St. Matthew and St. Mark. 386
Exposition of the gospels of the church year. 393
Exposition of the law of baptism. 134
Exposition of the litany. 2239
Exposition of the minor prophets: Obadiah, Johan, Micah, Nahum, Habakkuk, Zephaniah. 559
Exposition of the Old and New Testament. 222
Exposition of the parables in the Bible. 2025

Exposition of the peculiarities, difficulties and tendencies of Oberlin perfericionism. 2818
Exposition of the prophecies of the Apocalypse. 463
Exposition of the Psalms. 576
Exposition of the Reformed standards for young people. 1801
Exposition of the Revelation. 460, 464
Exposition of the Revelation, ch. 4-22. 460
Exposition of the Revelation of Jesus Christ. 456
Exposition of the Revelation of Jesus Christ to John. 453
Exposition of the second epistle to the Corinthians. 326
Exposition of the Sermon on the Mount. 3336
Exposition of the Thirty nine articles of the Church of England. 1212
Exposition of the xxxix Articles of the Church of England. 1212
Exposition of the trinities of the Sacred Scriptures. 3711
Exposition of Titus. 479
Exposition of Universalism. 3752, 3753
Exposition of views respecting the principal facts, causes, and peculiarities involved in spirit manifestations. 3494
Exposition of Zechariah. 600
Exposition on the book of Esther. 514
Exposition on the Epistle to the Romans. 468
Expositions and notes on sundry portions of the Holy Scriptures, together with The practice of prelates. 344
Expositions of heavenly truths. 236
Expositions of Holy Scripture. 223
Expositions of Ruth and Esther. 514
Expositions on the creed, the Lord's prayer, and the Ten commandments. 73
Expositon of the First epistle to the Corinthians. 322
... The expositor. 3
Expositor's Bible. 222, 225
Expositor's dictionary of texts. 299
Expositor's Greek Testament. 343
Expositor's harmony of the synoptic Gospels. 394
Expositor's ministers annual. 3373
Expository analysis of the various systems of sacramental causality. 3265
Expository commentary on Acts. 329
Expository commentary on Hebrews. 403
Expository commentary on John. 423
Expository dictionary of New Testament words with their precise meanings for English readers. 243, 246
Expository dictionary of Old Testament words. 511
Expository discourses on the First Epistle of the Apostle Peter. 325
Expository lectures on Paul's letter to the Philippians. 449
Expository lectures on the principal passages of the Scriptures which relate to the doctrine of the Trinity. 3711
Expository messages on the Epistle to the Galatians. 381
Expository messages on the whole Bible. 471
Expository method of G. Campbell Morgan. 2597
Expository notes on Ezekiel. 518
Expository notes on Ezekiel, the prophet. 518
Expository notes on the Epistles of James and Peter. 412
Expository notes on the Gospel of Mark. 433
Expository notes on the Gospel of Matthew. 440
Expository notes on the prophet Isaiah. 542
Expository notes, with practical observations upon the New Testament of Our Lord and Saviour Jesus Christ. 343
Expository outlines on the gospel of John. 3374
Expository outlines on the whole Bible. 3345
Expository preacher's notebook. 1226
Expository preaching. 2903, 2904
Expository preaching for today. 2897
Expository preaching without notes. 2902
Expository sermon outlines. 3375
Expository sermons on Revelation. 464
Expository sermons on Revelation volume two. 464
Expository sermons on the book of Daniel. 509, 3350
Expository sermons on the Epistle of James. 161, 413
Expository sermons on the Epistles of Peter. 161, 447, 3350

Expository sermons on the Heidelberg catechism. 1801
Expository studies in 1 Corinthians. 323, 3358
Expository studies in 1 John. 324, 3358
Expository studies in Job. 551, 3541
Expository studies in the life of Christ: His early days. 1977
Expository thoughts on the Gospels. 417, 441
Expostition of the late controversy in the Methodist Episcopal church. 2459
Exposure of millennial dawnism the preacher's imperative duty. 1939
Expounding God's word. 2908
Expulsion of the Jesuits from Latin America. 1947
... The expulsion of the Jews from Spain. 2103
Extemporaneous discourses. 3755
Extempore preaching. 2908
Extended family. 1608
Extension arm of the Sunday school; a new study of the enlarged field of the Home department. 3552
Extension department. 3555
Extension department of the Sunday school. 3559
Extension movement in theological education. 3332
Extension seminary primer. 3680
Extent and efficacy of the atonement. 105
Extent of salvation. 3220
Extent of the atonement, in its relation to God and the universe. 105
External fragrance. 2386
External reality in the Lockian philosophy. 2180, 2242
External religion: its use and abuse. 761
Externals of the Catholic Church. 792
Extinction of the ancient hierarchy. 1759
Extinction of the Christian churches in North Africa. 1183
Extirpation of idolatry in Peru. 1904
Extra-Biblical sources for Hebrew and Jewish history. 2094
Extra-canonical life of Christ. 1975
... Extra-judicial procurators in the Code of canon law. 18
Extra-sensory perception. 2991
Extra-sensory perception after sixty years. 2990
Extract from Mr. Law's Serious call to a holy life. 966
Extract from the journal of Mr. John Nelson. 3143
Extract of Minutes of the 129th annual convention of the Ev. Luth. ministerium of New York and adjacent states and countries. 1547
Extract of the life of Monsieur de Renty, a late nobleman of France. 3215
Extract of the Rev. Mr. John Wesley's journals. 3137, 3144
Extracts from Abu l-Mahasin ibn Taghri Birdi's Chronicle. 1501
...Extracts from Blanco White's Journal and letters. 3137, 3144
Extracts from from the Pentateuch compared with similar passages from Greek and Latin authors. 1771
Extracts from One religion: many creeds. 3065
Extracts from the Book of Jasher. 564
Extracts from the flying roll. 3342
Extracts from the journal of the late Margaret Woods from the year 1771 to 1821. 3137, 3144
Extracts from the letters of Elizabeth, Lucy, and Judith Ussher. 3136, 3143
Extracts from the minutes of the proceedings. 93
Extracts from the writings of Francis Fenelon, archbishop of Cambray. 3126
Extracts on politics and government from the Supreme Pontiff from Third general controversy. 2767
Extracts: politics and government from Defense of the faith. 1142
... The extrajudicial coercive powers of ecclesiastical superior. 2159
... The extraordinary absolution from censures. 2812
Extraordinary black book. 1764
Extraordinary blessings of an ordinary Christian. 1509
Extraordinary Christianity. 3780
Extraordinary living for ordinary men. 992
Extraordinary living for ordinary people. 981
Extras from Exodus. 516
Extra spiritual power. 1004
Extreme center. 3351
Extreme unction. 1587
Extreme untion. 1587
Extremely spiritual man. 1823

Exuberant years. 1253
... The Exultet rolls of south Italy. 1884
Eye of love. 3316
Eye of newt in my martini. 2328, 2733
Eye of Shiva. 2640
Eye of the storm. 664, 1349
Eye of the storm; the great debate in mission. 2496
Eye salve for church goers. 1180
"Eye to "aye" 3289
Eye witness. 1014
Eye witness at Fatima. 1618
Eye-opener. 1654
Eyes east. 816
Eyes for Eric, and other stories. 911
Eyes have it. 3161
Eyes of faith. 651, 1059
Eyes of the blind. 2695
Eyes on Europe. 2517
Eyes on the modern world. 1066
Eyes to behold him. 1704
Eyes to see God. 1385
Eyes upon the cross. 2003
Eyewitness: John's view of Jesus. 423
Eyewitnesses at the cross. 2214
... Ezekiel. 269, 517, 518
Ezekiel among the prophets. 518
... Ezekiel and Daniel. 517
Ezekiel, Second Isaiah. 518
Ezekiel speaks today. 518
Ezra. 519
Ezra Abbot. 2
Ezra and Nehemiah. 519, 1587
Ezra, Nehemiah. 519
... Ezra, Nehemiah and Esther. 531
... Ezra, Nehemiah, Esther. 531
Ezra Squier Tipple. 3701
Ezra Stiles Gannett. 1701
Ezra Stiles Gannett, Unitarian minister in Boston, 1824-1871. 1701
Ezra studies. 519

F

F. B. Meyer. 165
F. B. Meyer, preacher, teacher, man of God. 2461
F.D. Maurice. 2374, 3626
F. J. Sheed. 777, 3634
F.M. Smith. 2619, 3427
F. X. Durrwell, C.S.S.R. 776, 3633
Faber. 1587
Fabian essays in socialism. 3436
Fable of the bees. 1536
Fables and proverbs from the Sanskrit. 3302
Fables of infidelity and facts of faith. 60
Fabri conciones. 1266
Fabric and finance. 1167
Fabric of Paul Tillich's theology. 3700
Fabricated man. 1705
Fabulous Flemings of Kathmandu. 1629, 2684
Fabulous Freddie and the Saints and Sinners. 190
Fabulous gods denounced in the Bible. 2667
Face beyond the door. 1888
Face in the flames. 663
Face of Benedictus Spinoza. 3472
Face of Christ. 1837, 1957, 1958
Face of faith. 1789
Face of God. 3731
Face of Jesus. 2690
Face of love. 2030
Face of my parish. 1562
Face of our Lord. 1549
Face of silence. 3020
Face of sin. 3412
Face of the deep. 456, 1382
Face of the Heavenly Mother. 2624
Face of the saints. 1024, 3281
Face to face. 2152
Face to face with God. 2883
Face to face with the Church of the Nazarene. 1238
Face to the sky. 2895
Face to the world. 1649
Face up with a miracle. 2476
Faces about the Christ. 384
Faces about the cross. 1826, 2034, 2435
Faces among the faithful. 1235
Faces of death. 1416
Faces of fear. 876, 1619
Faces of Findhorn. 1625
Faces of freedom. 1659
Faces of God. 217, 787, 1066, 2386
Faces of Israel. 2864
Faces of Jesus. 1957
Faces of love. 887
Faces of prayer. 2889
Faces toward God. 3890
Faces toward the light. 1442
Facet of life in Keswick, 1757-1975. 2168, 2431

Facets of ecumenicity. 1039
Facets of our faith. 1340
Facets of Taoism. 3587
Facets of the faith. 1524, 3352
Facets of the future. 2572
Facing a new day. 1051
Facing adult problems in Christian education. 3152
Facing Calvary. 2031
Facing death and grief. 1418
Facing death and grief. 1415
Facing facts in modern missions. 2554
Facing God. 2382
Facing grief and death. 1415
Facing life. 3886
Facing life and getting the best of it. 2932
Facing life with Christ. 973
Facing life with Jesus Christ. 3887
Facing life's experiences. 992
Facing life's questions. 2930
Facing north. 964
Facing Old Testament facts. 502
Facing ourselves. 3182
Facing our day. 3441
Facing problems as Christian parents. 1607
Facing Protestant-Roman Catholic tensions. 794
Facing student problems. 3537
Facing the crisis. 3086, 3087
Facing the crisis in the light of Bible prophecy. 3382
Facing the cross. 2216
Facing the facts. 1072
Facing the field; the foreign missionary and his problems. 2483
Facing the future. 1254
Facing the future in Indian missions. 1900
Facing the future unafraid. 1071
Facing the gods. 1743
Facing the issues. 1154
Facing the new world, and other sermons. 164
Facing the next day. 991
Facing the people. 2386
Facing the situation. 2928
Facing the sphinx. 3573
Facing the sun. 2227
Facing the truth. 3793
Facing the unbeliever. 3828
Facing the unfinished task. 2514
Facing the world with Christ. 3881
Facing today's demands. 1056
Facing today's frontiers. 3187
Facing turbulent times. 2132
Facing your nation. 966
Facsimiles and descriptions of minuscule manuscripts of the New Testament. 315, 2330
Facsimiles of early Episcopal Church documents (1759-1789) 2967
Fact and fable in psychology. 2989
Fact and faith. 2051, 2476
Fact and faith in the kerygma of today. 1424, 2009, 2168
Fact and fancy about the future life. 1695
Fact and fancy in spiritualism, theosophy, and psychical research. 671, 3505
Fact book. 1465
Fact, fiction, & faith. 65
Fact not fiction. 2231, 3232
Fact of a future life. 1696
... The fact of Christ. 2001
... The fact of conversion. 1359
Fact of God. 1738, 3665
Fact of prayer. 2882
Fact of some consequence. 1893
Fact of the Christian church. 1123
Factors in the effectiveness of articulation therapy with educable retarded children. 2411
Factors influencing Catholic high school enrollment. 832
Factors related to Sunday school growth and decline in the Eastern Synod of the Reformed Church in the United States. 3048, 3564
Factors related to Sunday school growth and decline in the Eastern synod of the Reformed church in the United States. 3554
Factory people and their employers. 2189
Facts about Luther. 2276
Facts about Lutheran congregations. 2294
Facts about our Bible. 305
Facts about our churches and a changing America. 1467
Facts about the Bible. 312
Facts about the Bible[by]. 199
Facts about the Catholic Church. 762
Facts about the faith. 794
Facts against fancy. 2701
Facts and documents. 1628
Facts and documents, exhibiting a summary view of the ecclesiastical affairs, lately transacted in Fitchburg. 1337

Facts and fables of Christian science. 1034
Facts and faith. 68, 1272
Facts and fallacies regarding the Bible. 199
Facts and fancies in modern science. 3075
Facts and fictions of mental healing. 2409
Facts and folks in our fields abroad. 2520
Facts and mysteries of spiritism. 3504
Facts and mysteries of the Christian faith. 65
Facts and the faith. 74
Facts and visions; twenty-four baccalaureate sermons. 123
Facts concerning salvation. 3291
Facts concerning the Mexican problem. 822
Facts concerning the work and progress of the instrumentalities toward the fulfillment of our Christian world mission. 3732
Facts, fables, and fantasies of Freemasonry. 1661
Facts for Freemasons. 1662
Facts, frauds, and phantasms. 3508
Facts of faith. 799, 1595
Facts of life in relation to faith. 1063, 1595
Facts of the Chelsea Baptist church, Atlantic City, New Jersey, December, nineteen twenty-one. 102
Facts of the faith. 795, 3341
Facts that call for faith. 2931
Facts that undergird life. 2301
Facts we hate to face. 1238
Faculties of pastors and confessors for absolution and dispensation according to the Code of canon law. 1588
Failing wine. 2356
Failure and the hope. 1132
Failure in the Far East. 815
Failure of Jesus and his triumph. 2048
Failure of the American rabbi. 3016
Failure of the "higher criticism" of the Bible. 236
Failure of the sexual revolution. 3392
Fair as the moon. 2356
Fair haven. 2036
Fair play the Christian way. 803
Fair wind for Troy. 2661
Faire and easie way to heaven. 1377
Fairest flower. 3299
Fairest flower of paradise. 2361
Fairest Lord Jesus. 2059, 3764
Fairest of all. 3365
'Fairest star of all. 2356
Fairfield experiment. 2978
Fairhope. 1119
Fairy-faith in Celtic countries. 878, 1631
Faith. 1003, 1593, 1597, 2494, 3654, 3888
Faith according to St. John of the Cross. 1601, 2126
Faith active in love. 2273, 3452
Faith after the holocaust. 1825
"Faith against life's storms" 1595
Faith alive! 1342
Faith amid the Amorites. 1855
Faith and a fishhook. 3284
Faith and appreciative awareness. 2400, 2944
Faith and behavior. 945
Faith and belief. 1597
Faith and certainty. 1595
Faith and character. 964
Faith and Christian living. 3660
Faith and Christian living, four-volume religion program. 3660
Faith and commitment. 3153
Faith and community. 1592
Faith and courage for today. 367, 1439
Faith and creativity. 961
Faith and culture. 1594
Faith and destiny of man. 3371
Faith and doctrine. 780
Faith and doubt. 1597, 2181, 2702, 2751
Faith and doubt in the century's poets. 1518
Faith and doubt of Holocaust survivors. 1825
Faith and duty. 945
Faith and ethics. 2708, 3652
Faith and fact. 1075
Faith and facts. 2508
Faith and fatherland. 876
...The faith and fire within us. 1592
Faith & form. 2374, 3577
Faith and fraternalism. 874, 2179
Faith and fratricide. 1073
Faith and freedom. 731, 1659, 2221, 2222, 2283, 3667, 3802
Faith and freedon. 3363
Faith and health. 2378, 2409
Faith and history in the Old Testament. 599
Faith and immortality. 1695, 3340
Faith & its counterfeits. 62
Faith and its difficulties. 1589
Faith and its effects. 1594

Faith and its furtherance. 147
Faith and its psychology. 1592
... Faith and its rational justification. 1589
Faith and justice. 1077
Faith and justification. 2160
Faith and kindred subjects. 1594
Faith and knowledge. 2148, 2181
Faith and learning. 1128
Faith and life. 1596, 2935, 3344, 3360
Faith and logic. 1105
Faith and love. 2143
Faith and modern error. 63
Faith and modern man. 763
Faith and modern thought. 3077
Faith and moral authority. 1536
Faith and morality in the secular age.
  3327
Faith and morals. 1592, 3239
Faith and my friends. 3141
Faith and nurture. 3158
Faith and order. 1045
Faith and order findings. 3620
Faith and perseverance. 2822
Faith and philosophical enquiry. 2837
Faith and philosophy. 1105, 2838, 3104,
  3624
Faith and practice. 1591, 3666
Faith and practice of the Five years
  meeting of Friends in America. 1681
Faith and practice of the Philadelphia
  Yearly Meeting of the Religious Society
  of Friends. 1681
Faith and practice of the Quakers. 1590
Faith and practice of the Religious society
  of Friends of Philadelphia and vicinity.
  1681
Faith and Prayer. 1594
Faith and prejudice. 3188
Faith and prejudice, and other unpublished
  sermons. 864
Faith and process. 2944
Faith and rationalism. 60, 1098
Faith and reality. 3623
Faith and reason. 57, 66, 1590, 1597,
  2142, 2148, 2623, 2832, 2842, 3067.
  3099, 3121, 3198
Faith and reflection. 3099
Faith and reform. 786
Faith and religious life. 1595
Faith and revealed truth. 1595
Faith and revelation. 1601
Faith and sanctification. 1589
Faith and science. 1103
Faith & sexism. 3392
Faith and sight. 1594
Faith and social service. 3448
Faith and society. 3446
Faith and speculation. 2832
Faith and success. 1593
Faith and technology. 3592
Faith and the act of faith. 1589
Faith and the adolescent. 3167
Faith and The faith. 1590, 1592
Faith and the future. 1597
Faith and the human person. 1601, 3306
Faith and the life of reason. 3102
Faith and the mystery of God. 67
Faith and the philosophers. 175, 2836,
  3002
Faith and the physical world. 3082
Faith and the prospects of economic
  collapse. 1075
Faith and the vitalities of history. 3239,
  3668, 3669
Faith and the world. 1058
Faith and the world of politics. 1087
Faith and theology. 1590
Faith and truth. 1589
Faith and understanding. 651, 3619
Faith and understanding in America. 861
Faith and violence. 3780
Faith and virtue. 3782
Faith and work. 1589
Faith and works. 2160, 3800
Faith and works at Middle Octorara since
  1727. 2462
Faith and works of Christian science.
  1035
Faith and youth. 3175
Faith applied. 996
Faith as related to health. 1589
Faith at the blackboard. 1497
Faith at the cross. 1594
Faith at the frontiers. 1066
Faith at work. 1360, 1596
Faith, authenticity, and morality. 951
Faith beyond humanism. 1855
Faith builds a chapel. 130
Faith built on reason. 1589
Faith by which the church lives. 1059
Faith by which we live. 3059
Faith; can man still believe? 1594
Faith can master fear. 2995
Faith, Christ and truth. 3514
Faith, Christ, or Peter. 444
Faith despite the KGB. 1110
Faith enacted as history. 652

Faith eternal and the man of today. 785
Faith explained. 132
Faith, fact, and fantasy. 1066
Faith, facts, history, science, and how they
  fit together. 67
Faith, fancies, and fetich. 3868
Faith for a dark Saturday. 617
Faith for a secular world. 61
Faith for a time of storm. 1451
Faith for all seasons. 862, 1265, 2398
Faith for complicated lives. 1005
Faith for daily living. 1446
Faith for fallibles. 2137
Faith for fellowship. 1201
Faith for life. 803
Faith for modern man. 3661
Faith for moderns. 3059
Faith for new frontiers. 3216
Faith for our generation. 1133
Faith for personal crises. 1107
Faith for the college man. 3346
Faith for the future. 33, 1134
Faith for the job. 3879
Faith for the nations. 1094
Faith for the new generation. 1591
Faith for the space age; three sermons.
  3345
Faith for the times. 545, 3356
Faith for the times/deliverance. 545, 3362
Faith for these times. 62, 2301, 3367,
  3731
Faith for this one world? 1095
Faith for today. 9, 61, 3664, 3665, 3744
Faith for tomorrow. 63
Faith for tough times. 1069
Faith for you. 3661, 3743
Faith founded on fact. 68
Faith, freedom, and selfhood. 1108
Faith, freedom, and the future. 3038
Faith fulfilled. 3797
Faith healer. 1600, 3144
Faith healing. 1598, 1600, 2409, 3476
Faith healing and religion. 1599
Faith healing and the Christian faith. 2377
Faith healing: finger of God? 1598
Faith, hope and charity. 1589, 3667
Faith, hope, and charity in primitive
  religion. 3110
Faith, hope, and clarity. 951
Faith, hope and hilarity. 895
Faith, hope, and love. 1589, 1601
Faith, hope, love. 3064, 3615
Faith, hope, love, these three. 340
Faith I found. 1061
Faith in a changing culture. 1074
Faith in a day of unbelief. 2608
Faith in a secular age. 1154
Faith in a secularized world. 3707
Faith in action. 1000, 3186, 3885
Faith in an age of fact. 3142
Faith in Christ. 1594
Faith in conflict. 1105
Faith in ferment. 1705
Faith in focus. 3660
Faith in God and heaven. 1596
Faith in God is the victory. 1594
Faith in God's love. 1741
Faith in history and society. 65
Faith in Jesus Christ. 2037
Faith in Jewish survival. 1811
Faith in practice. 787
Faith in the center ring. 1589
Faith in the divine fatherhood. 1723
Faith in the face of doubt. 1596
Faith in the future. 2607
Faith in the mysteries. 1592
Faith in the Synoptic Gospels. 1597
Faith in these times. 1238
Faith is a family affair. 3182
Faith is a star. 1014
Faith is a weapon. 3436
Faith is not a feeling. 130, 930
Faith is power for you. 2877
Faith is still there. 66
Faith is the answer. 2995, 2996
Faith is the password. 471
Faith is the substance. 1392
Faith is the victory. 141, 324, 1593, 1595,
  2973
Faith: its life and growth. 1589
... Faith justified by progress. 1596
Faith letters. 67
Faith made them champions. 962
Faith magnificent. 2972, 3369
Faith makes sense. 763
Faith makes the difference. 1596
Faith meets faith. 1080
Faith, mighty faith. 1912
Faith moves mountains, an autobiography.
  3125
Faith must be lived. 1108
Faith no fancy. 2000
Faith of a Hassid. 1789
Faith of a heretic. 2836, 3129
Faith of a layman. 3445
Faith of a liberal Jew. 3371
Faith of a Methodist. 2421

Faith of a middle-aged man. 1593
Faith of a modern Christian. 65, 3615
Faith of a modern Protestant. 1056
Faith of a pagan. 3660
... The faith of a Protestant. 3662
Faith of a Quaker. 1675
Faith of a scientist. 3083
Faith of a worker. 1592
Faith of America. 1822
Faith of an English Catholic. 3135
Faith of an unrepentant liberal. 3725
Faith of ancient Egypt. 1590
Faith of Baha'u'lah. 3115
Faith of Billy Graham. 299, 1754
Faith of Catholics. 784, 3628
Faith of centuries. 1069
Faith of Christendom. 1385
Faith of experience. 322
Faith of fact. 1656
Faith of great scientists. 3077
Faith of Israel. 599, 2114
Faith of Japan. 1935
Faith of Jesus. 2041, 3381, 3713
Faith of Jesus and the commandments of
  God. 3381
Faith of John Knox. 2181
Faith of man speaks. 1353
Faith of men. 3593
Faith of millions. 782, 790
Faith of modern man. 68
Faith of modernism. 2561
Faith of morn. 1454
Faith of other men. 3121
Faith of our children. 3152
Faith of our families. 1611
Faith of our father. 1591, 1772
Faith of our fathers. 74, 160, 786, 1023,
  1528, 1594, 2286, 2744, 2920
Faith of our fathers. A centennial history
  of the First Congregational Church of
  Sabetha, Kansas, 1858-1958. 3262
Faith of our forefathers. 802, 1711
Faith of our own. 985, 1590
Faith of our pioneer fathers. 2609
Faith of Paul. 2799
Faith of Qumran. 1410
Faith of reason. 1520, 3066
Faith of Robert Browning. 696, 697
Faith of secular Jews. 2141
Faith of the ages. 75
Faith of the Apostles' Creed. 73
Faith of the atheist. 100
Faith of the Catholic church. 73, 796
Faith of the Christian church. 3640
Faith of the Church. 73, 75, 2964, 2965,
  3646
Faith of the cross. 1595
Faith of the early fathers. 1018
Faith of the Episcopal church. 2964
Faith of the Finns: historical perspectives
  on the Finnish Lutheran church in
  America. 1625, 1626
Faith of the free. 3066
Faith of the gospel. 1594, 3339
Faith of the little shepherd. 2005
Faith of the millions. 761
Faith of the New Testament. 475, 1594
Faith of the Old Testament. 501
Faith of the people of God. 3664
Faith of the psalmists. 578
Faith of the Roman Church. 789
Faith of the Russian Evangelicals. 2979
Faith of the saints. 2745
Faith on the frontier. 1310
Faith on the march. 1941
Faith on tiptoe. 967, 1012
Faith on trial. 584
Faith on trial in Russia. 2821
Faith once delivered. 2932, 3350
Faith once given. 74
Faith, or an act of faith, which? 1592
... Faith papers. 1593
Faith, peace, and purpose. 2607
Faith power. 2693
Faith precedes the miracle. 1009, 1232
Faith promoting stories. 1014
Faith, psychology & Christian maturity.
  1107
Faith, reason, and civilization. 1281
Faith, reason, and existence. 3101
Faith, reason, and the Gospels. 1592
Faith recycling. 989
Faith; response to the dialogue of God.
  761
Faith, science, and the future. 3083
Faith seeking understanding. 3653
Faith seeks understanding. 1597
Faith shaping. 3886
Faith, skepticism, and evidence. 2180
Faith, stars, and stripes. 3746
Faith takes a name. 3358
Faith that conquers fear. 1595, 3381
Faith that demonstrates. 1590
Faith that does justice. 1077
Faith that enquires. 3101
Faith that fulfills. 1056
Faith that has come to me. 3142

Faith that makes faithful. 1591
Faith that makes sense. 3664
Faith that overcomes the world. 1591
Faith that persuades. 65
Faith that propels. 2425
Faith that rebels; a re-examination of the
  miracles of Jesus. 2017
Faith that satisfies. 3347
Faith that saves. 161, 1594, 1596, 3383
Faith that sings. 3368
Faith that wins. 1589
Faith that works. 413, 980, 1435, 3348
Faith, the Church and the university.
  3757
Faith, the falsity and the failure of
  Christian science. 1035
Faith the greatest power in the world.
  1593
Faith through reason. 2140
Faith through reason, a modern
  interpretation of Judaism. 2116
Faith to act. 942
Faith to affirm. 1058
Faith to doubt. 2976
Faith to grow on. 3662
Faith to keep. 941
Faith to live by. 364, 960, 981, 1070,
  1095, 1595, 1677, 2383, 3381
Faith to move mountains. 2296
Faith to proclaim. 1063
Faith to procliam. 1063
Faith to see. 2387
Faith triumphant. 1435
Faith triumphant and others poems. 3206
Faith, truth, destiny, decrees, works. 1662
Faith unafraid. 164
Faith under challenge. 1591
Faith under fire. 1063, 1433, 3541, 3661
Faith under scrutiny. 64, 763
Faith victorious. 1487, 2281, 2290
Faith victorious in the Kentucky
  mountains. 3131
Faith walks with me. 3207
Faith we affirm. 933, 941
Faith we declare. 1070
Faith we hold. 2746, 3493
Faith we live. 1590
Faith we live by. 73, 785
Faith we proclaim. 1545
Faith we share. 149
Faith we teach. 1595
Faith wins! 1590
Faith without dogma. 1592
Faith without fantasy. 993
Faith without prejudice. 2152
Faith work under Dr. Cullis. 1393
Faith works! 1009
Faith, works and grace. 1590
Faithful. 1590
Faithful also in much. 3530
Faithful and fair. 3392
Faithful at Mass. 2364
Faithful church. 937
Faithful city. 1277
Faithful elder. 1691, 3818
Faithful for ever. 1594
Faithful guide to peace with God. 1726
Faithful in Christ Jesus. 365
Faithful minister. 3675
Faithful mother's reward. 2624
Faithful narrative, of the proceedings, of
  the First society and church in
  Wallingford, in their calling, and settling
  the Rev. Mr. James Dana, in the pastoral
  office over them. 1596
Faithful narrative of the remarkable revival
  of religion. 1346, 3228
Faithful narrative of the surprising work of
  God in the conversion of many hundred
  souls in Northampton, and the
  neighbouring towns and villages of the
  county of Hampshire, in the province of
  the Massachusetts-Bay in New-England.
  1757, 3231
Faithful preacher. 2196
Faithful rebels. 1277, 3056
Faithful servant. 3409, 3485
Faithful shepherd. 2791
Faithful Shirley. 1590
Faithful to the Lord. 169, 3531
Faithful unto death. 37, 1413, 3886
Faithful witnesses. 2350
Faithing oak. 2395
Faithlifters. 1449
Faiths, cults, and sects of America. 3325
Faiths, cults, and sects of America: from
  atheism to Zen. 3325
Faiths for a complex world. 3115
Faiths for the few. 3327
Faiths in fellowship. 3849
Faiths men live by. 3112, 3119
Faiths of famous men in their own words.
  1593
Faiths of man. 3092
... The faiths of mankind. 3121
Faiths of the Far East. 709
Faiths of the world. 3116

Faith's testimony. 1600
Faith's unclaimed inheritance. 964, 1592
Faithsong. 2633
Fakers. 2993
Fakes, frauds, and fools. 67
Falasha anthology. 1602
Falasha antrology. 2145
Fall and rise of Israel. 2088
Fall conference, chaplain supervisors. 2780
Fall from the sky. 1399
Fall of Babylon. 462
Fall of Christianity. 3792
Fall of David's tabernacle. 3579
Fall of great Babylon. 2807
Fall of man. 1602
Fall of man and original sin. 1602
Fall of the German gods. 1708
Fallacies of Christian science. 1036
Fallacy. 2611
Fallen angel. 1367, 2376
Fallen angels in Jewish, Christian, and Mohammedan literature. 1423
Fallen sinners of men able to do well. 1635
Fallible forms and symbols. 3669
Falling angels. 1427
"falling away" 1179
Falling fire. 1626
Falling off cloud nine and other high places. 3883
Falls Church Presbyterian Church, 1873-1973. 1602
False and the true. 3221
False churches and how they got that way. 1805
False gods. 3115
False messiahs. 2414
False presence of the kingdom. 1153
False prophet. 2906
False prophets. 660
Familiar Bible quotations. 252
Familiar Bible verses. 584
Familiar dialogues on Shakerism. 3396
Familiar discourses on the way of salvation. 3296
... Familiar explanation of Christian doctrine. 769
Familiar failures. 886
Familiar illustration of Christian baptism. 136
Familiar lectures on the Pentateuch. 563
Familiar letters. 2752, 3402, 3711
Familiar letters and poems. 3752
Familiar letters to a gentleman. 1098
Familiar letters to John B. Fitzpatrick. 799
Familiar letters, to the Rev. John Sherman. 3403, 3711
Familiar prayers, their origin and history. 841
Familiar survey of the Christian religion. 1175
Familiar talks on sermon building. 3347
Familiar talks on that boy and girl of yours. 3441
Familiar talks with students of the Greek New Testament. 1768
Families and friends. 3164
Families in the church. 1608
Families in trouble. 1603
Families sharing God. 1606
Families with purpose. 1611
Family. 1611
Family, a church challenge for the 80's. 1607
Family advent book. 8, 2023
Family album of favorite hymns. 1866
Family altar. 1603, 1605, 1606
Family altar and Faith primer. 1605
Family altar readings. 1434
Family altar stories for children. 1603
Family and church. 1610
Family and Franciscan ideal. 1603
... The family and its Christian fulfilment. 1608
Family and mental illness. 2410
Family and the Bible. 296
Family and the church. 1609
Family and the corporation man. 1612, 2752
Family and the Cross. 3525
Family and the fellowship. 348, 1163
Family apostolate and Africa. 1603, 1610
Family at prayer. 1606
Family Bible encyclopedia. 245, 247
Family Bible study book. 647
Family book of favorite hymns. 1862
Family centered projects of St. Paul through the workers eyes. 1603
Family chronicle. 1389
Family, church, and community. 1254
Family clinic. 3012
Family cluster programs. 1609, 2028
Family commentary on the Holy Bible. 1603
Family companion. 1606

Family culture. 1462
Family customs. 1262
Family customs, Easter to Pentecost. 1262
Family devotional Bible. 1604
... Family devotions. 2972
Family devotions idea book. 1604
Family devotions with school-age children. 1605
Family E and its allies in Luke. 1603
Family E and its allies in Matthew. 438
Family evening activity devotions. 1605
Family expositor. 347
Family faith and fun. 1609
Family first. 1608
Family followship. 168, 324
Family for families. 2004
Family foundations. 2339
Family ghosts and ghostly phenomena. 1710
Family God chose. 631
Family guide to Sabbath nature activities. 2676
Family healing. 1254, 1611
Family idea book. 1611
Family II and the Codex alexandrinus. 436
Family II [i.e. pi] in Matthew. 443
Family II in John. 421
Family II in Matthew. 438
Family in crisis or in transition. 1611
Family instructor: in three parts. 1607
Family life. 1603, 1608
Family life and the church. 1610
... Family life in Christ. 1609
Family life of Ralph Josselin, a seventeenth-century clergyman. 1291, 2135
Family lives its religion. 1610, 1611
Family living in the Bible. 1603
Family looks at itself. 1608
Family looks at one world. 1339
Family, love, and the Bible. 1603
Family man. 1616
Family manual of the broad church. 1603
Family memorial. 925
Family ministry. 1254, 1611
Family ministry in today's church. 1254
Family monitor. 1608
Family monitor, or A help to domestic happiness. 1608
Family of believers. 786, 1040
Family of Bethany. 424
Family of God. 110, 756, 1003, 3746, 3747
Family of Joseph Smith. 3430
Family of martyrs. 2351
Family of the forgiven. 1005
Family of the Rev. James Wilson. 3819
Family ofGod. 958
Family Passover. 2779
Family pastoral care. 1254
Family pictures from the Bible. 1603
Family planning. 664
Family planning dilemma revisited. 663
Family power! 1609, 2599
Family prayer. 1605, 1609
Family prayer and sermon book. 1606
Family prayer for morning and evening and the festivals of the church year. 1606
Family prayers. 1604, 1605, 1606, 2884, 2892
Family preacher. 1607
Family relationships. 1610
Family Rosary edition of the Holy Bible. 778
Family Seder. 2110
Family service book. 1442
Family story. 1609
Family talk. 1607
Family temperance meeting. 3597
Family that never died. 1620
Family therapy in pastoral ministry. 2782
Family 13 (the Ferrar group) the text according to John. 421
Family 13 (the Ferrar group) the text according to Mark with a collation of Codex 28 of the Gospels. 436
Family 13 (the Ferrar group) 436
Family treasury of inspiration and faith. 3014
Family vacation idea book. 3766
Family well-ordered. 1609
Family worship for every day in the year. 1610
Family worship idea book. 1606
Family worships together. 1605

Famous cathedrals as seen and described by great writers. 750
Famous couples of the Bible. 214, 2341
Famous Druids. 1480
Famous English sermons, edited, with an introduction. 3366
Famous ex-priests. 1582
Famous figures of the Old Testament. 492
Famous firsts in Minnesota Lutheranism. 2291
Famous forerunners of Christ. 628
Famous Hebrew Christians. 1366
Famous hymns. 1864
Famous hymns and their authors. 1875
Famous hymns and their story. 1875
Famous hymns and their writers. 1870
Famous hymns of the world. 1873
Famous infidels who found Christ. 1360, 1362
Famous Mather Byles. 721
Famous men of the Old Testament. 494
Famous messages, mostly hitherto unpublished. 1071
Famous missionaries. 2483
Famous mothers from the Bible and history. 2624
Famous Negro sermons. 2681
Famous New York fundamentalist-modernist debates. 2561
Famous reformers of the Reformed and Presbyterian churches. 3034
Famous shrines of Our Lady. 3394
Famous singles of the Bible. 214, 3415
Famous stories of inspiring hymns. 1875
Famous women of the New Testament. 3841
Famous women of the Old Testament. 3841
Famulus Christi. 182, 1760
Fan vaulting. 1157
Fanaticism. 1612
Fanaticism; its source and influence. 1612, 3768
Fannie E. S. Heck. 1799, 3468
Fanny. 3218
Fanny Crosby speaks again. 1869
Fantasies for fantastic Christians. 1004
... Fantastic uncle. 2519
Far above rubies. 1303, 3815
Far East journey of peace and brotherhood. 793, 3364
Far from home. 2945
Far hence. 2502
Far horizon. 1478
Far horizons of Scripture. 2504
Far-off hills. 54, 875
Far-out facts of the Bible. 319
Far-out saints of the Jesus communes. 3889
Far peoples. 3177
Far round the world. 2490
Far side of consciousness. 2987
Far-spent night. 9
Farel the firebrand. 1612
Farewell address to the Payson church, South Boston. 1612
Farewell dinner to Francis Ellingwood Abbot. 2
Farewell discourse and final prayer of Jesus. 424
Farewell ministry of Christ. 424
Farewell sermon, and oration and poem. 1812
Farewell sermon, delivered September 26th, 1802, in the North Dutch church, Albany. 1612
Farewell to Abington. 1612
Farewell to innocence. 669
Farm boy and the angel. 2601
Farm sermons. 167
Farmer boy who became a bishop. 665
Farmer gives thanks. 1612
Farmer's church. 3254
Farmers, machanics & servants' magazine. 967
Farming and gardening in the Bible. 480
Farming the inner city for Christ. 171, 1612
Farmington. 1612
Farther into the night. 2533
Farther shore. 1888
Farthing in her hand. 3528
Fascinating facts about American Jewish history. 2106
Fascination of faith. 2386
Fascination of the Book. 238
Fascism or freedom. 1941
Fashion me a people. 1245
Fashions in church furnishings, 1840-1940. 1169
Fast by the road. 1364
Fast falls the eventide. 17
Fast hold on faith. 1592
Fasti. 3733
Fasti ecclesiae anglicanae. 45, 1291
Fasti ecclesiae Anglicanae, 1300-1541. 1291

Fasti Ecclesiae anglicanae, or A calendar of the principal ecclesiastical dignitaries in England and Wales, and the chief officers in the universities of Oxford and Cambridge, from the earliest time to the year M.DCC.XV. 1215
Fasting. 1613
Fasting changed my life. 39, 1613
Fasting in the New Testament. 350, 1613
Fasting rediscovered. 1613
Fate and faith. 2084
Fate and freedom. 3104
Fate and Justice. 2160
Fate of the nations. 2715, 2947
Fate or destiny? 2990
Father, a son, and a three-mile run. 1615, 2206
Father Abraham's children. 46
Father Agapius Honcharenko. 1844, 3722
Father and fatherhood. 1616
Father and His family. 3289
Father and son Y-Indian guides. 3870
Father Baker. 131, 2190
Father Billy. 1616
Father Bishop. 664
Father Bond of Kohala. 3300
Father Brennan's favorite stories. 906
Father Charles E. Coughlin. 1372, 3451
Father Clark. 2305
Father Connell answers moral questions. 3011
... Father Connell's The new Baltimore catechism. 768
Father Connell's The new Baltimore catechism no. 3. 768
Father Constant Lievens. 1947, 2225
Father Coughlin. 1372, 3441
Father Coughlin and the New Deal. 1372
Father Coughlin of the Shrine of the Little Flower. 1372
Father Coughlin, the radio priest, of the Shrine of the Little Flower. 1372
Father Coughlin's radio discourses. 862
Father Coughll and the New Deal. 1372
Father Damien. 1400
Father Damien and the bells. 1400
... Father Damine. 1400
Father Dave. 2305
Father De Smet. 1900, 3426
Father DeSmet. 1900, 3426
Father DeSmet, pioneer priest of the Rockies. 1900, 3426
Father Divine. 131
Father Divine, holy husband. 131
Father Dominic Barberi. 1474
Father Douglass of Behala. 1477
Father Dujarie: pastor of Ruille-sur-Loir, Canon of Le Mans, founder of the Communities of the Sisters of Providence, and the Brothers of St. Joseph, now the Brothers of Holy Cross, 1767-1838. 1482
Father Finn. 1615
Father Flanagan of Boys Town. 1615, 1629
Father Gavazzi's lectures in New York. 781
Father Gemelli. 1293, 1704
Father Hand. 1481, 1783
Father Hecker. 1799
Father Hecker and his friends. 1799
Father Herman, Alaska's saint. 1707
Father Huntington. 1856, 2741
Father Joe. 1617
Father John Sullivan, S.J. 3545
Father Jose Burgos priest and nationalist. 1616
Father Joseph Kundek. 2188
Father Junipero Serra. 3376
Father Junipero's holy family. 1616
Father Kosmas, the apostle of the poor. 1026, 2185
Father Lukas Etlin, O.S.B. 1540
Father McGuire's new study help. 766
Father McGuire's The new Baltimore catechism and Mass. 768
Father McGuire's The new Baltimore catechism. Official rev. ed.,illustrated, study helps, word meanings, phoneticized vocabulary. 768
Father McNabb reader. 776
Father McShane of Maryknoll. 2310
Father Madden's life of Christ. 1982
Father Marquette. 2292
Father Mateo speaks to priests on priestly perfection. 1298
Father Maturin, a memoir, with selected letters. 2374
Father Moreau. 1332, 2597
Father of Joshua/Jesus. 2135
Father of Little women. 23
Father of the church in Tennessee. 825, 2463
Father of the family. 1616
Father of the Little Flower (Saint Therese of the Child Jesus) 1823-1894. 2348
Father of the Wesleys. 3806

FATHER O'HARA OF

RELIGIOUS BOOKS 1876 - 1982

Father O'Hara of Notre Dame. 2735
Father Olier. 2736, 3545
Father Pat; a hero of the Far West. 1920
Father Paul and Christian unity. 1044
Father Paul, apostle of unity. 1673, 2794
Father Paul of Graymoor. 1673, 2794
Father Payne. 2225
Father Penn and John Barleycorn. 3597
Father Pierre Bouscaren, S. J. 1616
Father Price of Maryknoll. 2938
Father Ravalli's missions. 1615
Father Reeves, the Methodist class-leader. 3031
Father Scott's radio talks. 761
Father Shealy. 3401
Father Shealy--a tribute. 3401
Father Smith instructs Jackson. 796
Father Stanton's sermon outlines from his own manuscript. 1616
Father Taylor. 3590
Father ten Boom, God's man. 681, 1786
Father, the Son, and the Holy Spirit. 445
Father Theobald Mathew. 2373
Father Thurston. 3698
... Father Tim. 1424
Father Tim's talks with people he met. 1616
Father to the immigrants, the servant of God. 3306
Father Tom. 2309
Father Tompkins of Nova Scotia. 3704
Father Vincent McNabb, O. P.; the portrait of a greatDominican. 2310
Father Wainright. 3788
Father, we thank Thee. 899, 1605
Fatherhood. 1616
Fatherhood of God. 1727, 1732
Fatherhood of God and the Victorian family. 3025, 3433
Fatherhood of St. Joseph. 2132
Fathering-forth. 772
Fatherly rule of God. 1141
Fathers, a fresh start for the Christian family. 1608
Fathers according to Rabbi Nathan. 1538
Fathers and Doctors of the church. 1472
Fathers and founders. 1549
Fathers and heretics. 3658
Fathers and sons, the Bingham family and the American mission. 659
Fathers are special. 1618
Father's faith. 1616
Father's mantle. 1301, 2708
Fathers of the Bible. 1616
Fathers of the church. 1616
Fathers of the covenant. 524
Fathers of the desert. 2576
Fathers of the early church. 1018
Fathers of the Greek Church. 1617
Fathers of the kirk. 1234
Fathers of the Latin Church. 1618
Fathers of the primitive church. 1020
... The fathers of the third century. 1618
Fathers of the Victorians. 1551
Fathers of the Western Church. 926
Fathers on celibacy. 878
Fathers on Christology. 2011
Fathers still speak. 2431
Fathers without theology. 1020
Fatima and you. 1618
Fatima, hope of the world. 1618
Fatima or world suicide. 1618
Fatima: pilgrimage to peace. 1618
Fatima prophecy; days of darkness, promise of light. 2357, 3474
Faust. 1618, 1619
... Faust, part one. 1619
Faust revisited. 1427
Faust revisted. 1427
Faust: sources, works, criticism. 1619
Faustus Socinus. 3433
Favored people. 1939
Favorite and favors of the Sacred heart of Jesus. 3269
Favorite Bible verses. 249
Favorite Christian poems. 1022
Favorite gospel songs. 3458
Favorite hymns and their authors. 1860
Favorite Newman sermons, selected from the works of John Henry cardinal Newman. 3365
Favorite novenas and prayers. 2716
Favorite object talks. 3337
Favorite poems faith and confort. 3207
Favorite poems of faith and comfort. 3207
Favorite Psalms. 575
Favorite Psalms for children. 575
Favorite Scripture texts of famous people. 230
Favorite sermons of John A. Broadus. 160
Favorite son. 2133, 2371
Favorite stories and illustrations. 1842
Favorite stories from the Bible. 620
Fear and trembling. 1104, 1105, 1619
Fear and trembling, and The sickness unto death. 1104
Fear, faith, and the future. 1062
Fear God in your own village. 3442, 3444
Fear, love, and worship. 3852
Fear not. 3716
"Fear not, little flock," 2575
Fear not the crossing. 3518
Fear of God. 1619
Fear of hell as an instrument of conversion. 1802
Fear of the dead in primitive religion. 1408, 1409
Fearfully and wonderfully made. 1116
Feast day. 1938, 3280
Feast days and fast days. 1623
Feast for a time of fasting. 2211
Feast for a week. 2363, 3845
Feast in honor of Yahweh. 1588
Feast of fools. 1623
Feast of history. 1884, 2110
Feast of hope. 1845
Feast of joy. 2252
Feast of lights. 2229
Feast of lights, comprising The vision of Judas the Hammer, The story of Gaspar, The epistle of Nicodemus, A night with Gamaliel. 2006
Feast of quails and other sermons. 1340
Feast of the family on the birthday of the King. 1110
... The feast of the presentation of the Virgin Mary in the temple. 2937
Feasting and social oscillation. 92
Feasting upon the word. 640, 2600
Feasting with cannibals. 2188
Feasts and fasts of Israel. 1623
Feasts of Jehovah. 1614
Feasts of Our Lady. 2361
Feathered Serpent and Smoking Mirror. 121
Feathered trip-hammer. 3898
Feathers on the moor. 1067
Fede e ricerca filosofica nel pensiero di S. Agostino. 113
Federal aid and Catholic schools. 830
Federal harmony. 2632
Federal Street pastor. 882
Federation of religions. 1620, 3064
Federico Borromeo and Baronius. 682, 1374
Feed my lambs. 910, 938, 2788
Feed my sheep. 2905, 3557
Feed whose sheep? 2267, 2791
Feeding among the lilies. 2442
Feeding and leading. 1295
Feeding and management of live stock. 1620
Feeling good. 1500, 1576
Feeling good about feeling bad. 989
Feeling good about your feelings. 980
Feeling kind of temporary. 1004
Feeling low? 1351
Feelings! 1004
Feelings are facts. 1512
Felipe, being the little known history of the only canonized saint born in North America. 1620
Felix Adler and ethical culture. 7, 1533
Felix Westerwouldt, missioner in Borneo. 850, 3808
Fellow workers for God. 2282
Fellowship. 960
...Fellowship, a means of building the Christian social order. 1121
Fellowship evangelism through church groups. 1568
Fellowship hall planning. 1157
Fellowship in the life eternal. 369
Fellowship of discontent. 924
Fellowship of faiths. 3204
Fellowship of the church. 3264
Fellowship of the holy spirit. 1829
Fellowship of the saints. 1449
Fellowship of the veld. 13
Fellowship of toil. 3444
Fellowship prayers. 1621, 2890
Fellowship with God. 321
Fellowship with the Father. 2890
Fellowships from A to Z. 1166
Fellowships of concern. 1248
Fells of Swarthmoor hall and their friends. 1620, 1676
Female convents. 1357
Female experience and the nature of the divine. 3834
Female Pentecost. 202
Female preacher. 2627
Female Scripture biography. 3839
Feminine. 3838
Feminine aspects of divinity. 3834
Feminine crises in Christian faith. 3835
Feminine crisis in Christian faith. 3835
Feminine dimension of the Divine. 1621
Feminine faces. 3839, 3843
Feminine spirituality. 3845
Feminism. 3832
Feminism & Christianity. 3831
Feminist mystic, and other essays on women and spirituality. 3834
Fenelon, his life and works. 1621
Fenian catechism; from the vulgate of St. Lawrence O'Toole. 1622
Ferdinand Christian Baur on the writing of church history. 1184
Ferial Gospels of Lent. 2213
Ferial Menaion. 2748
Ferment in the Church. 1094, 1095
Ferment in the ministry. 2785
Ferment on the fringe. 3253
Fermenting universe. 881
Fermin Francisco de Lasuen (1736-1803) 726, 2198
Fernand Portal (1855-1926) 2319, 2864
Fertile soil. 2093
Fervent in spirit. 686, 3464
Fervent novice. 3418
Fervent prayer. 3228
Fessenden & co's Encyclopedia of religious knowledge. 3091
Fessenden & co's Encylcopedia of religious knowledge. 3091
Fest. 1613
Festal Menaion. 2748
Festal year. 1613
Festival. 3311
Festival and joy. 1613
Festival days. 1622
Festival joy, a book for Jewish children. 1615
... Festival mass for soli and chorus. 1623
Festival of Christmas. 1111
Festival of the Sons of New Hampshire. 1623
Festival prayer book. 2108
Festival prayers. 2108
Festival shrines. 2109
Festival stories of child life in a Jewish colony in Palestine. 897
Festivals and ceremonies of the Roman Republic. 1624
Festivals, holy days, and saints' days. 1623
Festivals of Attica. 1623
Festivals of the Jewish year. 1614
Festschrift in honor of the 36th anniversary of Congregation Beth Hillel of Washington Heights, New York, New York, 1940-1976. 1331, 2142
Festschrift, Theodore Hoelty-Nickel. 1204
Festschrift zu Israel Lewy's siebzigstem Geburtstag. 2147, 2220
Fetich in theology. 1473
Fetichism and fetich worshippers. 1624
Fetichism in West Africa. 1624
Fetish folk of West Africa. 13
Fetishism in West Africa. 1624
Few among many. 2544
Few historic records of the church in the diocese of Texas. 1773
Few kind words. 2396
Few lines to tell you. 740
Few notes on prayer. 2875
Few select specimens of the sculptors art in stations of the way of the cross. [Catalogue]. 3525
Few summer ceremonials at the Tusayan Pueblos. 1846
Few thoughts for Lent. 2211
Few thoughts on Revelation. 3225
Few words about the devil. 1653
Few words on verse translation from Latin poets. 2199
Fibres of faith. 1592
Fichte's science of knowledge. 1624, 2179
Fidelis of the Cross. 3533
Fidelity. 775, 2575
Fidelity to truth. 2421
Fides Trumpet books. 617
Fidistoria. 1589
Field and the fruit. 3755
Field and work of the Young men's Christian associations of North America. 980
Field god. 1722
Field-Ingersoll discussion. 19
Field of broken stones. 1348
Field of diamonds. 1455
Field of the hidden treasure. 1810
Field of theology. 3216
Field of Zen. 3892
Field work and its relation to the curriculum of theological seminaries. 3612
Fields at home. 2527
Fields of glory. 1368
Fields of service in the church. 1259
Fields of the Lord. 3306
Fields of the Wood. 1230
Fiery chariot. 1506
Fiery-flying serpent slender, and the brazen serpent charity, delineated. 3423
Fife's revival sermons. 3232
Fifteen eventful years. 140
Fifteen hundred Bible questions with Bible answers. 648
Fifteen hundred facts and similes for sermons and addresses. 1842
1500 themes for series preaching. 3376
Fifteen saints for girls. 3285
Fifteen sermons. 2974
Fifteen sermons preached before the University of Oxford between A. D. 1826 and 1843. 1227, 3365
Fifteen sermons preached on various important subjects. 3346
1517-1917. Jubilee volume. 2291
Fifteen years among the Mormons. 2602, 3431
Fifteen years amont the Mormons. 2602, 3431
Fifteen years in the senior order of Shakers. 3395
Fifteen years in the senior order of Shakers: a narration of facts, concerning that singular people. 3395
15th anniversary, memorial history, Beth Tfiloh congreations. 3577
Fifteenth century Bibles. 212, 1894
Fifteenth-century English prayers and meditations. 1455
XVth century guide-book to the principal churches of Rome. 3245
Fifteenth station. 3526
Fifth avenue sermons. 2930
Fifth book of Moses, called Deuteronomy. 509
Fifth decade. 2463
Fifth Gospel. 12, 377, 816, 2043
Fifth gospel; the miracle of the holy shroud. 305
Fifth grade teachers plan book and manual. 812
Fifth horseman. 2620
Fifth International (tenth national) Sunday school convention of the United States and British North America provinces. 3560
Fifth National Sunday-school convention. 3556
Fifth sun. 121
Fifth testament. 2014
Fifth week. 1945
Fifth World congress of free Christians and other religious liberals at Berlin, Germany, August 5-11, 1910. 965
Fifth World Congress of Free Christians and Other Religious Liberals at Berlin, Germany, August 5-11, 1910. 34
Fiftieth anniversary book of the Albanian Orthodox Church in America, 1908-1958. 22
50th anniversary, Holy Trinity Russian Orthodox Church, Brooklyn, New York. 2749
Fiftieth anniversary of the founding of the First congregational church. 1636
Fifty animal stories of Saint Francis, as told by his companions. 47, 1640
Fifty chalk talk programs. 880
Fifty character stories. 928
50 children's sermons. 907
50 craft projects. 229
Fifty-four years of African Methodism. 14
Fifty fruitful years, 1891-1941. 3467
Fifty golden years. 150, 2527
Fifty golden years in central Illinois. 717
50 golden years in the Church of the Nazarine, 1908-58. Scriptural holiness, heritage, vision, task. 1237
Fifty key words: comparative religion. 3092
Fifty key words in theology. 3682
50 key words, the Bible. 243
50 key words: the church. 3639
Fifty lessons in training for service. 3178
... Fifty litarary evenings for Epworth leagues and the home cirle. 1525
Fifty lives for God. 923
Fifty meditations on the Passion. 2377
50 meditations. 2390
Fifty missionary heroes every boy and girl should know. 2482
Fifty missionary programmes. 2491
Fifty new devotional programs. 1455
Fifty notable years. 3751
50 object lessons. 2720
Fifty object talks for your junior congregation. 906
Fifty outstanding religious books. 3203
... Fifty pictures of Gothic altars. 28
Fifty plus. 2462
50 progressive messages from Armageddon to new earth. 3319
Fifty psalms. 575
Fifty radio sermons. 3350
50 ready-cut sermons. 3373
Fifty reasons why the Roman Catholic religion ought to be preferred to all others. 786
Fifty select sermon outlines. 1321

Fifty sermon outlines on conversion. 3373
Fifty sermon outlines on forgiveness. 3373
50 sermon-talks for boys and girls. 909
Fifty sermons and evangelistic talks. 2587
Fifty short sermons. 3350, 3582
Fifty stories for the bedtime hour. 910
50 strange stories of the supernatural. 2731
50,000 miles of missionary miracles. 2549
Fifty-two evangelistic illustrations. 1839
Fifty-two Gospel meditations. 399
Fifty-two sermons. 1652
Fifty-two workable junior high programs. 3856
Fifty-two worship programs on Christian living. 3857
Fifty wonderful years 1878-1928. 2547
Fifty wonderful years, missionary service in foreign lands. 3306
50 worship talks for children. 906
Fifty years. 1148, 2202
Fifty years an editor. 2495
Fifty years ... and beyond. 1237
Fifty years and seventy places. 734, 1546
Fifty years in Brown county convent. 3277
Fifty years in buckles and saddle. 3804
Fifty years in China. 1379, 2509
Fifty years in Christian missions. 2509
Fifty years in conflict and triumph. 3861
Fifty years in Congo. 2514
Fifty years in foreign fields. 3047
Fifty years in psychic research. 3514
Fifty years in the Church of Rome. 798, 1148
Fifty years in the magic circle. 1345
Fifty years in Western Africa. 2524
Fifty years in Yorkville, or, Annals of the parish of St. Ignatius Loyola and St. Lawrence O'Toole. 2698
Fifty years of association work among young women, 1866-1916. 3879
Fifty years of attack and controversy. 1464
Fifty years of church work in the diocese of Minnesota, 1857-1907. 2166, 2959, 2970
Fifty years of Faith and Order. 3849
Fifty years of federation of the Young men's Christian associations of North America. 3871
Fifty years of freethought. 1655, 1656, 3717
Fifty years of Hume scholarship. 1855
Fifty years of Methodism. 2451
Fifty years of National Sojourners. 1672
Fifty years of Nazarene missions. 1238
Fifty years of preaching at the Palace. 161
Fifty years of Protestant theology. 3656
Fifty years of psychical research. 2990
Fifty years of service, a challenge to womanhood; an appreciation of Anne C. Spellman, missionary. 3471
Fifty years of the Young men's Christian association of Buffalo. 3874
50 years on the battle front with Christ. 1782
Fifty years on the Nebraska frontier. 2736
Fifty years on the skirmish line. 2775
Fifty years on the trail. 1689
Fifty years, thirteen centuries. 2208
Fifty years to atheism. 101
Fifty years will be long enough! 1704
Fifty years with our Mexican neighbors. 1464
Fifty years with the Sabbath schools. 3552
Fifty years' work in London (1889-1939) 3820
Fifty years' work of the Hebrew education society of Philadelphia, 1848-1898. 1796
5500 questions and answers on the Holy Bible. 289
Fifty-five years, the Young Men's Christian Association of Chicago. 980
59 programs for pre-teens. 939
57 stories of saints for for boys and girls. 3284
53 more Sunday talks to children. 909
53 nature Sunday talks to children. 909
53 object Sunday talks to children. 909
53 Sunday talks to children. 909
52 complete young people's programs. 3876
52 devotional programs for primary children. 899
... Fifty-two memory hymns to enrich diction, enlarge thought, strengthen memory, give wings to faith. 1861
52 parables. 909
52 planned programs for youth and adults. 3876
52 practical programs for young people. 3857
Fifty-two prayer meetings. 2887
Fifty-two primary missionary stories. 2491
52 primary workshop programs. 3857
52 seed thoughts for Christian living. 994

52 sermon outlines on the titles of Our Lord. 2021
52 sermon trails for boys and girls. 909
52 sermonettes for the church year. 1266
52 simple invitation illustrations. 1839
52 simple sermon outlines. 3374
52 special-day invitation illustrations. 2721
52 story sermons. 906
Fifty-two story sermons for children. 908
Fifty-two story talks to boys and girls. 906
52 three minute talks to children. 907
Fifty-two ways to make the church go spiritually, financially, numerically. 1118
52 weeks to a great new life. 3330
52 workable young people's programs. 3856
52 workable youth object lessons. 2720
52 worship services (with sermon outlines) 3857
Fifty-two years in Florida. 1630
Fig tree blossoms. 2073
Fight. 989
Fight, faith, and crown. 1774
Fight for character. 3758
Fight for dominion. 3791
Fight for freedom. 3192
Fight for God. 809
Fight for God, 1870-1939. 809
Fight of faith. 3794
Fight of the Norwegian church against nazism. 2714
Fight on! Fear not! 3355
Fight the good fight. 969, 973
Fight with Rome. 799
Fighter and prophet. 3895
Fighters for freedom, heroes of the Baptist challenge. 140, 144
Fighting Africa's black magic. 2332, 2498
Fighting angel. 2508, 3572, 3579
Fighting church. 1122
Fighting Father Duffy. 1481
Fighting for faith. 2813
Fighting Jew. 2094
Fighting parson. 120
Fighting the debauchery of our girls and boys. 3742
Fighting the devil in modern Babylon. 3742
Fighting the stars. 1238
Fighting the stars, and other sermons. 1238
Figurae of Joachim of Fiore. 2122, 3574
Figurative representation of the Presentation of the Virgin Mary in the temple. 2359, 3605
Figures in our Catholic history. 683
Figures in the drama of salvation. 863
Figures of speech used in the Bible. 307, 314
Figures of the passion of Our Lord. 2029
Figures or types of the Old Testament. 3720
Fiji revisited. 1472, 2486
Filial tribute to the memory of. 1849
Filing your sermon ideas. 2899
Filings of light. 2388
Filioque. 2047
Filipino playmates. 898
Filippo's dome. 1630
Fill a blank page. 3306
Fill He come. 2258
Fill my cup, Lord. 445
Fill your days with life. 17
Filled hands. 2227
Filled with new wine. 2815
Filled with the spirit. 330, 1828, 1831
Fillmores' Sunday-school songs. 3554
Film use in the church. 3161
Final act. 1830
Final causes. 3593
Final Christian understanding of science, religion, and survival of mankind. 1035
Final conclave. 2862
Final countdown. 1012
Final events on planet Earth. 1528
Final failure of Christianity. 1103, 2800
Final faith. 3646
Final home of the redeemed. 1698
Final invasion of God. 3321
Final mystery. 1417
Final outcome of Hitler's mad dream. 610
Final outcome of the Jew. 610
Final outcome of the Jew and the duty of Christians. 610
Final report. 830
Final report on the survey for contemplatives. 2575
Final science. 2372
Final testimonies. 3619
Final theology. 411
Final war. 1939
Finality of Christ. 1080, 3344
Finality of faith. 1590, 1591
Finality of faith and Christianity among the world religions. 1591

... The finality of Jesus Christ. 1079, 2002
Finality of Jesus Christ in an age of universal history. 1819
Finality of the Christian religion. 1049
Finality of the higher criticism. 1581
Finally. 2798
Finally home. 3414, 3798
Finances of the Church. 807
Financial recovery for the local church. 1167
Financial relations of the papacy with England. 3589
...Financial relations of the papacy with England to 1327. 807
Financial security for the synagogue. 3576
Financing of the Young men's Christian associations. 1620
Financing the kingdom. 1168
Find happiness in your name. 2717
Find out for yourself. 3880
Find your self in the Bible. 648
Find your own faith. 640
Findhorn garden. 2732
Finding a religion to live by. 957
Finding a soul. 120
Finding a way to follow. 982
Finding and filing Bible facts and features. 637
Finding Christ. 1950
Finding each other. 1003
Finding God. 1727, 2395
Finding God among us. 1722
Finding God in a new world. 2928
Finding God in all things. 2267, 3485
Finding God in human life. 1721
... Finding God in our homes. 3185
Finding God through Christ. 3621
Finding God through the beautiful. 1721
Finding God's best. 993
Finding God's comfort. 1612
Finding God's healing power. 1599
Finding his world. 2597, 3143
Finding holy ground. 1466
Finding hope again. 2782
Finding is the first act. 1810
Finding Jesus through the Gospels. 390, 2008
Finding list of the Y.M.C.A. library, Buffalo, N.Y. 3874
Finding meaning in the Beatitudes. 181
Finding of God. 1719
Finding of the 'third eye. 2722
Finding our father. 1719, 2050
Finding ourselves. 1340, 3371
Finding out about God. 3164
Finding out God's secrets. 3534
... Finding out what Jesus expects of us. 3765
Finding the comrade God. 3456
Finding the goal posts. 3879
Finding the historical Jesus. 2008
Finding the light. 3380
Finding the living Christ in the Psalms. 585
Finding the lost prophetic witnesses. 1689
Finding the Old Testament in the New. 451
Finding the real you. 1006
Finding the trail of life. 2131
Finding the truth about God. 1976
Finding the way. 1364, 2063, 2395, 2412
Finding the will and power of the living God. 1727
Finding your self. 2996
Findings and decisions. 1045
Findings of conferences held under the leadership of Dr. John R. Mott. 2513
Fine art of meditation. 2397
Fine art of preaching. 2897
Fine art of public worship. 3003
Fine art of soul-winning. 1565
Fine gold of Newman. 2703, 2704
Fine gold of the Old Testament. 5 91
... The finest album of religious songs. 3271
Fingal's quest. 1311
Finger of God. 1077
Finger plays and songs for church, home, and day schools. 910
Fingerposts to children's reading. 905
Fingerposts to children's readings. 905
Fingerprints of Bible people. 647
Fingerprints of God. 908
Fingers. 2095
Fingertip devotions. 1436
Finished! 2059
Finished kingdom. 5
Finite and infinite. 1907, 3099
Finney lives on. 1625
Finney on revival. 3228
Finney's systematic theology. 3651
Finno-Ugric. 2659
Fire and blackstone. 2912
Fire and the cloud. 3522
Fire and the hammer. 1569
Fire and the rose are one. 1000, 1997
Fire by night and cloud by day. 1419

Fire flares anew. 2815
Fire from heaven. 3031
Fire from strange altars. 3116
Fire from the throne; race relations in the church. 1133
Fire in Coventry. 1377
Fire in his name. 2227, 3779
Fire in my bones. 547, 1943, 3361, 3469
Fire in the brand. 3804
Fire in the church. 3229
Fire in the fireplace. 2815
Fire in the hills. 1638, 1803
Fire in the pulpit. 1561
Fire in thy mouth. 2903
Fire is his name. 3779
Fire of contemplation. 3489
Fire of creation. 3686
Fire of Francis Xavier. 1649
Fire of little Jim. 413
Fire of love. 1008, 1452, 1830, 2427, 3631
Fire of love and The mending of life. 3491
Fire on a drumhead. 909
Fire on Azusa Street. 2817, 3766
Fire on the earth. 763, 1136, 1551, 3450, 3779
Fire on the mountains. 2517
Fire on the prairie. 2431
Fire upon the earth. 1176, 3477
Fire was lighted. 2198
Fire we can light. 3745
Firebrand. 1379
Firecracker Christians. 906
Firehundredaarig Lutherdom. 2288
Fires to warm us. 3361
Fireside Bible stories. 629
Fireside chats. 305, 2398
Fireside discussion group of the Anti-defamation league of B'nai Brith. 2111
Fire-side piety. 1606
Fireside prayers. 2892
Fireside stories. 961
Firm faith for today. 3641
Firm union of a people represented. 1503
Firmicus Maternus: the error of the pagan religions. 69
First International (sixth national) Sunday school convention. 3559
First 108 hymns from the revised and enlarged hymnal. 2968
First account of creation. 1381
First African Baptist church of North America. 3305
First age of Christianity. 407
First amendment. 1151
First American. 3737
First American Catholic missionary congress. 851, 2514
First American diocese: Connecticut. 2963
First American itinerant of Methodism. 3798
First American peace movement. 2807
First among the unafraid. 2003
First and fundamental truths. 2418
First and last freedom. 3685
First and second books of Samuel. 590, 915
First and second books of the Chronicles. 496
First and second books of the Kings. The First and second books of the Chronicles. 555
First and Second Books of the Maccabees. 488
First and second epistles of St. Paul to the Corinthians--Commentaries. 345
First and second Epistles to the Thessalonians. 478
I & II Kings. 555
1 & 2 Kings, 2 Chronicles. 555
First and second letters of Paul to the Corinthians. 345
First and second letters of Paul to the Thessalonians. 478
First and Second Peter. 447
First and second prayer-books of King Edward the Sixth. 1213
First and second Samuel. 590
I and II Samuel, a commentary. 590
1-2 Thessalonians and Galatians. 478
First and the last. 1595
First authorized English Bible, and the Cranmer preface. 274
First Baptist Church. 737, 1612
First Baptist Church at Boone, North Carolina. 681, 1626
First Baptist Church, Miami, Florida, 1896-1961. 3798
First Baptist church, North Stonington, Connecticut. 147
First Baptist Church of Dallas. 1399
First Baptist Church of Nashville, Tennessee, 1820-1970. 2669

First Baptist church, Saint Paul, Minnesota; seventy-five years, 1849-1924; seventy-fifth anniversary, October 5 to 9, 1924. 170
First Baptist Church, Wilmington and Morgan Street, Raleigh, N.C., 1812-1962. 157
First Bible. 618
First Bible lessons. 645
... First Bible stories. 629, 630
First biography of Joan of Arc. 1938
First Bishop of Sonora. 1898, 3234
... The first book about Jesus. 3764
First book of ancient Bible lands. 283
First book of Bible heroes. 629
First book of Chanukah. 1784
First book of Chronicles. 496
First book of Jewish holidays. 1615
First book of Kings. 483, 555
First book of Maccabees. 487, 488
First book of Maccabees with introduction and notes. 488
First book of Moses. 520
First book of Moses called Genesis. 520, 522, 524
First book of mythology. 2657
First book of Psalms. 584
First book of saints for little Catholics. 3284
... The First book of Samuel. 483, 589
First book of Samuel in Hebrew. 1797
First book of the Bible: Genesis. 521
First book of the Christian religion. 73
... The first book of the Kings. 483
First book of the Kings, in the revised version. 483
First book of the Torah, Genesis. 521
First came the wings. 1007
First cardinal of the West. 815, 2631
First carols. 741
First catechetical instruction. 745
First Catholics. 626
First centenary of the North church and society, in Salem, Massachusetts. Commemorated July 19, 1872. 3286
First century, 1855-1955. 26
First century A.D. literary culture and early Christian literature. 1020
First century Christianity. 1093
First century Judaism in crisis. 2125, 2150
First century message to twentieth century Christians. 460
First century of Baptists in New Mexico, 1849-1950. 158
First century of Congregationalism in Iowa, 1840-1940. 1336
First century of Italian humanism. 1854
First century of Scottish Rite masonry in Texas, 1867-1967. 1672
First chapter of Genesis as the rock foundation for science and religion. 204
First chapters in religious philosophy. 3099
First Christian. 1102, 2796, 2797
First Christian century. 349, 2563
First Christian century in Judaism and Christianity. 2149
First Christian daily paper, and other sketches. 3402
First Christian drama. 453
First Christian school, the teacher and the pupils. 934
First Christians. 331, 1197
First Christmas. 2021, 2023
First Christmas; from the Gospels according to Saint Luke and Saint Matthew. 2024
First Christmas; the true and unfamiliar story in words and pictures. 2021
1 Chronicles. 481
First church chronicles, 1815-1915. 2916
First church collection of sacred musick. 1335
First church in Newark. 2701
"The first church." Its origin and manual of practice as revealed in the New Testament. 321
First church of Christ, Scientist, and miscellany. 684
First Church of Christ, Scientist, Belvedere, California. 187
First Church of the Ascension. 2719
First Colored Baptist church in North America. 3305
First commandment. 1315
First Communion. 2250
First communion catechism. 768
First Congregational Church of Brainerd. 689
First Congregational church of Great Barrington, 1743-1943. 1757
First Congregational Church of Marietta, Ohio. 1338
First Congregational Church of Moline. 2568
First Congregational church (Unitarian) of Cincinnati. 1275

First Congregational society in New Bedford, Massachusetts. 2686
1 Corinthians. 322, 323, 345
First Corinthians for today. 323
1 Corinthians, 2 Corinthians. 345
1 Corinthians. 322
First Council of the Vatican. 3769
First Crusade. 1391
First Crusade; the accounts of eye--witnesses and participants. 1391
First day of the new creation. 2052, 3221
"The first decade." 1230
First desert hero. 2805
First disciples of Saint Dominic. 1475
First Easter. 929, 1986, 2029, 2052, 2226
First encounter with Francis of Assisi. 1027, 1644
First English New Testament and Luther. 358
... The first English printed Protestant Bible and its significance. 612
First epistle general of Peter. 325
...The first Epistle of Clement to the Corinthians. 1093
First epistle of John. 324, 416
First epistle of John, practically explained. 321
First epistle of Paul the apostle to the Corinthians. 321, 322, 345
First epistle of Paul to the Corinthians. 321, 322, 346
First epistle of Peter. 325
... The First epistle to the Corinthians. 322, 323, 345
First establishment of the faith in New France. 2189, 2506
First Evangelical Congregational church, Cambridgeport, Mass. 731
First Evangelical Lutheran church of Springfield. 3523
First fifty years. 1273, 1465
First fifty years; a history of University Unitarian Church. 3317
First fifty years of the Pacific Synod, 1901-1951. 3733
First five centuries of the church. 1193
First five lives of Annie Besant. 195
First Franciscans and the Gospel. 1648
First freedom. 1151
First Fridays with the Sacred heart. 3270
First fruits. 3531
First fruits in Korea. 2536
First fundamental: God. 1723
First genesis. 3082
First glance at Adrienne von Speyr. 3471
First Gospel. 441
First Gospel, being the Gospel according to Mark. 432
First graces. 2884
First grad teachers plan book and manual. 1628
First Haggadah. 2779
First half century of St. Ignatius church and college. 1127, 3298
... The first half century of the Northumberland Baptist association, situated in Northumberland, Montour, Columbia, Sullivan, Lycoming, Clinton, Union and Snyder counties, Pennsylvania. 159
First-hand religion. 2637
First Holy Communion for little Catholics. 1626
First Holy One. 1330, 1331
First hundred and twenty-five years. 6, 2099
First hundred years. 1187, 1304, 1790, 3388
First hundred years, a history of the Mennonite church in Adams county, Indiana, 1838-1938. 194
First hundred years of Central Presbyterian Church, Denver, Colorado, 1860-1960. Compiled and edited by James H. White. 1425
First hundred years of the Central church in Worcester, 1820-1920. 3847
First hundred years of the New Hampshire Bible society. 2688
First hundred years of the Second Conpregational Church of Holyoke. 1838
First hundred years of the Southwest Texas Conference of the Methodist Church, 1858-1958. 2439
First hundred years, Trinity Church, Solebury, Pennsylvania. 3714
First hymns. 1860
First impact of the Reformation. 3041
First inter-collegiate conference on students' religious activities. 3537
First interpreters of Jesus. 476
First Jesuit. 2269
First Jesuit: St. Ignatius Loyola. 2269
First Jesuit, St. Ignatius Loyola (1491-1556) 1028, 1882

First khedive. 2133
First lesson on the Bible. 648
First lessons in the Gospels. 384
First lessons in the science of the saints. 969
First lessons on the Bible. 648
First life of Christ for little Catholics, in the words of Mary, the Mother of Jesus. 1981
First, man—then, Adam! 204, 526
First, man,tthen, adam! 526
First martyr of the German reformation. 2178
First martyrs of North America. 657, 1948, 2351
First millennial faith. 107
First movable church. 885
First negro priest on southern soil. 2219
First New Testament. 1411, 2721
First ninety years of the Parish of the Holy Apostles. 2830
First Noel. 1113
First Occult review reader. 2726, 2727
First of the Puritans and the Book of common prayer. 1214
First of three generations of White Wolves in China. 3010
First 150 years. 1304
First 150 years of St. John's Church. 3717
First one hundred and fifty years of the First United Methodist Church, Hamilton, Ohio. 1782
First 100 years. 2197, 2630, 2957
First one hundred years in the life of Friendship Baptist Church, 1875-1975. 1688, 1689
First 100 years of the First Baptist Church, Dention, texas, 1858-1958. 1425
First page of the Bible. 1379
First parish, Newbury, Massachusetts 1635-1935. 2701
First parishes of the province of Maryland. 1223
First person. 1453
1 Peter. 325, 447
1 Peter, estrangement and community. 325
First Peter in the Greek New Testament for the English reader. 325
First philosophy; an introductory text in metaphysics. 2418
First picture dictionary for little Catholics. 779
First Polish colonies of America in Texas. 2857
First prayers. 854, 900, 2884
First prayers for children. 2893
First prayers for little children. 901
First prelude. 1023, 1882
First Presbyterian church, 1833-1913. 2913
First Presbyterian Church, Fulton, Missouri. 1690
First Presbyterian Church of Claremore, Oklahoma 1889-1964. 2913
First Presbyterian Church of Franklin, Indiana. 2912
First Presbyterian church of Jamaica, New York, 1662-1942. 1933
First Presbyterian Church of Royal Oak, Michigan. 3252
First Presbyterian church of Webb City, Missouri, commemorating sixty-five years of its history, 1877-1942. 3799
First Presbyterian Church of Westfield, New York, 1808-1968. 3808
First Presbyterian church, Staunton, Virginia. 2912
...A first primary course for the vacation church school. 3762
... First principles. 1745
First principles of a new system of philosophy. 3471
First principles of Christian citizenship. 3446
First principles of faith. 1594
First principles of knowledge. 2242
First principles of philosophy. 2732
First principles of religion. 3063
First principles of theosophy. 3685
First principles of theosophy. 10th ed. Madras, Theosophical Pub. House; [on label. 3685
First principles of theosophy. 9th ed. Madras, Theosophical Pub. House; [on label. 3685
First Protestant Church, New Braunfels, Texas. 2686
"The first publishers of truth." 1684
... First quarter century of the Woman's Christian temperance union, Salem, New Jersey. 3833
First questions on the life of the Spirit. 3481
First rainbow. 2711
First register of Saint Mary's church. 3051

First religion. 3065
First religious instructions for little ones. 3120
First resurrection and the reign of Christ with his saints on earth. 3221
First ripe fruit gathered. 1396
I Samuel. 483
First 7000 years. 219
First[-seventh] reader. 3025
First six hundred years. 1196
First sixty years of the First Christian Church. 2270
First Southern Baptists. 888, 3316
First spiritual aid to the sick. 838
First standard manual of teacher training. 635, 3551
First step in God realization. 2379
First steps. 3174
First steps for new & used Christians. 1016
First steps in Christian renewal. 1492
First steps in church government. 2615
First steps in faith. 3186
First steps in occultism. 671
First steps in prayer. 2876
First steps in program building. 2339
First steps in religious education. 3154
First steps in the Bible. 615, 651
First steps in the religious life. 2580
First steps in theology. 3662
First steps to sanctity. 3006
First steps to the priesthood. 3331
First steps toward church unity. 1041
First sunrise. 2654
First Swedish Baptist church, Wilmington, Delaware, 1889-1939. 3569
... The first ten years of Hope. 2530
First the political kingdom. 1087
First things. 536
First things first. 1313, 2385
First thirty years, 1927-1957. 1663
First three Gospels. 397
First three hundred years. 1772
First Timothy. 321, 479
First tome or volume of the Paraphrase of Erasmus upon the Newe Testament. 343
First tome or volume of the Paraphrase of Erasmus upon the Newe Testamente. 343
First twenty years of Ministers and missionaries benefit board of the Northern Baptist convention. 2714
First two Dominican priories in the United States. 3278
First 200 years. 1627, 1689
First 2000 years. 679
First United Methodist Church of Salem, Oregon. 1627
First Ursuline. 41
First ward historical review. 2604
First Wesley Foundation. 3802
First white women over the Rockies. 31, 2488
First words from God. 205, 2053
First work book study on the Offices of instruction. 2962
First year New Testament Greek. 1770
First year of priesthood. 775
First year with Jesus. 1994
First years of the life of the redeemed after death. 978
First Zen reader. 3894
Firstborn Son. 2041
Firsts of American Jewish history. 2106
Fish—a ministry of love. 1627
Fish for my people. 1627
Fisher of men. 1476, 2537, 3304
Fisher prince. 2825
Fisherman of Galilee. 1444
Fisherman saint. 2825
Fisherman's ring. 2851
Fisherman's surprise. 430
Fishermen's saint. 40
Fishers of boys. 687
Fishers of men. 71, 1562, 1564, 2764, 3674, 3828
Fishin' fer men. 637
Fishing for me. 1564
Fishing for men. 1563, 1564
"Fit and proper"? 8
Fitly framed together. 2744
Fitting God into the picture. 996
Five addresses and devotional poems. 1443
5 ancient sins. 3414
Five Biblical portraits. 494
Five Bohemian windows. 925
Five books of Joses, a catechism of rational religion. 747
Five books of Maccabees in English. 487
Five books of Moses. 563, 564
Five books on consideration. 2767
Five centuries of religion. 193, 1185
Five children. 182, 2357
Five Christian leaders of the eighteenth century. 1293
Five cries of youth. 3881

Five dark days in history. 2172
... Five deans. 1307
Five decades. 3420
Five decades and a forward view. 2526
Five discourses on Hell! 1284, 1699
Five discourses on the Sabbath. 3261
Five essays on the Bible. 200
Five experiments in campus Christian community. 3536
Five for sorrow, ten for joy. 1454, 3248
Five Franciscan churches of Mission Santa Clara, 1777-1825. 3302
Five German Roman Catholic parishes. 2699
Five great encyclicals. 3450
Five great healers speak here. 3476
Five great philosophies of life. 1535
Five great religions. 3120
508 answers to Bible questions. 280
540 little known facts about the Bible. 319
501 Adventist illustrations and stories. 1841
Five hundred and one sermon illustrations. 1840
Five hundred Bible story questions and answers on the Old Testament. 630
500 Bible study outlines. 303
500 plans and ideas for church officers. 1251
500 questions & answers in religion. 2962
500 selected sermons. 2935, 3346
Five hundred sermon themes. 3373
500 sketches and skeletons of sermons. 3372
Five hundred thousand of a hundred million. 2921
500th anniversary pictorial census of the Gutenberg Bible. 314
Five in search of wisdom. 1366, 2085
Five interpretations of Jesus. 2009
Five jewels of the orient. 3839
Five kings--three judgments. 608
Five lanterns at sundown. 2480
Five laws that govern prayer. 2872
5 little pennies and how they grew. 3528
Five loaves and two fishes. 1620
Five makers of the New Testament. 409
Five Marys. 3839
Five men named John. 1749
Five metaphysical poets: Donne, Herbert, Vaughan, Crashaw, Marvell. 1476, 1519
... Five minute Bible readings from Genesis to Revelation. 725
Five minute object sermons to children. 3370
Five-minute parish talks. 2774, 2775, 3367
Five minute sermons. 865, 1267, 3344
Five-minute sermons in objects, for young folks. 3345
Five minute sermons in stories for young folks. 3345
Five-minute talks for Sunday school leaders. 908
Five minutes a day. 1442
Five minutes a saint. 3280
Five minutes daily with Luther. 2275
Five minutes to twelve. 3849
Five minutes with the Master. 1433
Five missionary minutes. 2551
Five Mountains. 2584
Five "musts" of the Christian life. 2461
Five pebbles from the brook. 1578
Five petals. 3346
Five points in faith. 3023
Five points of Calvinism. 729, 730
Five portraits of Jesus. 1951
Five present-day controversies. 2563
Five reasons why Methodists don't dance. 1400
5 secrets of living. 989
Five sermons. 3726
Five sermons against popery. 802
Five sermons and a tract. 3354
Five sermons on the following subjects. 3351
Five sermons preached at the Rolls Chapel. 1225
Five smooth stones for pastoral work. 520, 2786
Five stages of Greek religion. 1766, 1767, 3093
Five symbols, Revelation, twelfth chapter. 457
Five theological orations of Gregory of Nazianzus. 1542
Five thousand best modern illustrations. 1840
Five thousand five hundred questions and answers on the Sacred Scriptures. 280
Five times ten. 3468
5-15 minute talks. 1663
Five tracts of Hasan Al-Banna' (1906-1949) 1922, 1933
Five upon the altar. 1626
Five ways. 1737, 3697
Five-year-olds in the church. 3174

Five years in Christian science. 1036
Five years in the Alleghanies. 34
Five years of theosophy. 3689
Fives stages of Greek religion. 1767
Fixed stars and constellations in astrology. 96
Flag that flies highest of all. 1240
Flagellant on horseback. 689, 1900
Flair & the fire. 2975
Flame. 749
Flame and the light. 3775
Flame for the altar. 1562
Flame in the mind. 1616
Flame in the night. 1650
Flame in the snow. 3334
Flame in the wilderness. 1713, 3420
Flame of beauty, culture, love, joy. 11
Flame of faith. 1602
Flame of fire. 659, 3539
Flame of love. 2668
Flame of prayer. 2880
Flame of white. 2851
Flame of white ; & The rose of life. 2728
Flame still burns. 2332
Flame still burns; a story of St. Margaret of Cortona. 2332
Flamed by the Spirit. 1834
Flames for the bride; a story of Saint Agnes. 19
Flames over Battle Creek. 28
Flaming center. 2480
Flaming fagots. 954
Flaming hearts and other sermons. 1466
Flaming spirit. 2397
Flaming sword. 971, 3374, 3375, 3588
Flaming tongue. 3230
Flash lights. 2305
Flashes along the Burma road. 2505
Flashes from the eternal semaphore. 970
Flashes of light from the spirit-land. 3511
Flashes of light on obscure lives, being a series of sketches grouped about little known Bible characters. 214
Flashlights from history. 1236
Flashlights on the future. 463
Flavius Josephus: selections from his works. 2091
Flaxman, Blake, Coleridge, and other men of genius influenced by Swedenborg. 3571
Flesh and matter. 1034
Flesh and spirit. 381
Flesh, instrument of salvation. 840, 2327
Flesh is weak. 1221, 1516
Flesh of the gods. 1782
Flickering desire. 3887
Flickering light. 870
Fliedner the faithful. 1408, 1629
Flight and the nest. 2609
Flight from creation. 1383
Flight from God. 1726
Flight into Egypt. 2048
Flight of a wandering sparrow. 26, 1256
Flight of Feathered Serpent. 1471
Flight of the eagle. 2187
Flight of the wild gander. 2649
Flight to destiny! 3875
Flood. 1421, 1422
Flood and Noah's ark. 1421
Flood in the light of the Bible, geology, and archaeology. 1421
Flood reconsidered. 1421
Flood, the fact of history. 219
Florence Allshorn and the story of St. Julian's. 26
Florence Nightingale's nuns. 3418
Florence Simms. 3409
Florentine portrait: Saint Philip Benizi, 1233-1285. 1625
Florida Christians. 1463
Florissant heroines. 3417
Flow of religious instruction. 3153
Flower does not talk. 3892
Flower for sign. 1365
Flower grows in Ireland. 2979
Flower hill; human failures and spiritual triumphs. 998
Flower of a mortal soul. 1579
Flower of Fatima. 1618, 2349
Flower of grass. 62
Flower of Her Kindred. 2668
Flower of peace. 1447
Flowering of mysticism. 1674
Flowering tree. 3053
Flowers and fruits from the wilderness. 170
Flowers and fruits in the wilderness. 170
Flowers by the way-side. 33
Flowers for the living. 3814
Flowers from Gethsemane and other sermons. 2933
Flowers from St. Francis. 1641
Flowers of emptiness. 2832, 3019
Flowers of inspiration in God's garden. 3843
Flowers of the Bible. 481, 1630
Flowers of the cloister. 1630

Flowers of the Midrash for the schools and homes. 1630
Flowers of the sanctuary. 1630
Flowers of the soul. 1630
Flowers of the spirit. 1630
Flowers of the wind. 1899, 1903
Flowers of thought. 1630, 3507
Flute solo. 2166, 3709
Flux and fidelity. 1059
Flying high Children's mission study. 2535
Flying missionary. 2500
Flying priest over the Arctic. 2501
Flying saucers in the Bible. 1631
Flying worms. 3051
Fo-kuang ssu. 1631, 3316, 3718
Fo-sho-hing-tsan-king. 700
Focal points of Christian history. 1173
Focolare after 30 years. 1631
Focus. 868, 1563, 3847
Focus: Building for Christian education. 1167
Focus of belief. 1106
Focus of freedom. 1659
Focus of history. 340, 1955
Focus on doctrine. 3628
Focus on fact. 277
Focus on Hinduism. 1816
Focus on infinity. 694
Focus on life. 3182
Focus on living. 1016
Focus on people in church education. 3153
Focus on prophecy. 610
Focus on religion in teacher education. 3161
Focus on the Christian family. 1610
Focus on the family. 3871
Focus on the unknown. 2723
Focus on Watergate. 3798
Focusing on fundamentals. 1012
Focusing the Bible on current problems. 1071
Foes of the Spirit. 2561
Folded hands. 3209
Folewer to the Donet. 3647
Folger Library edition of the works of Richard Hooker. 1216, 3629
Folk and faith. 1329
Folk arts in renewal. 1088
Folk Buddhist religion. 709
Folk-element in Hindu culture, a contribution to socio-religious studies in Hindu folk-institutions. 1631
Folk elements in Burmese Buddhism. 702, 709
Folk-lore of Ireland. 1631
Folk religion in Japan. 1935
Folk-lore in the Old Testament. 1631
Folklore of wells. 1837
Follow Christ. 1037
"Follow me" 399, 440, 1294, 2070, 2386, 3431, 3786
Follow me: be human. 1977
Follow me; stories from the Bible for children, by H. G. Pihl, K. Beckman. [Tr. by Edward Carney]. 623
Follow the Christ. 360, 646
Follow the King. 216
Follow the Leader. 2490
Follow the leadership and other skits. 3877
Follow the rubrics. 2235
Follow the saints. 3284
Follow those women. 3837
"Follow thou Me" 1561, 3359
Follow thou Me, junior high course of study. 3217
Follow up evangelism. 1563
Followers in the way. 925, 1212
Followers of Christ. 2572
Followers of Jesus. 1003, 3164, 3185, 3766
Followers of the gleam. 1747
Followers of the new faith. 2953
Followers of the way. 964, 2395
Following after Jesus. 3722
Following Christ. 969, 2892, 3423
Following Francis. 3244
Following God through the Bible. 1731
Following in His train. 3468
Following Jesus. 434, 992, 995, 1003
Following Mary today. 1608, 2355
Following of the Holy Spirit. 1829
Following of the saints. 3279
Following our divine model; meditations for those who are called. 2392
Following the Christian way. 1201
Following the dramatic instinct. 1478
Following the fire. 1425, 1576
Following the King. 650
Following the liturgical year. 1262
Following the living Christ. 3559
Following the Master. 959
Following the pioneers. 2531
Following the saints. 1025
Following the sunrise. 156

Following the way. 421
Folly of bigotry. 3703
Folly of profanity. 3569
Folly of the cross. 2032
Folly of the three wise men. 1632
Folly or power? 1169
Font and the table. 133
Font of truth. 796
Fonts and font covers. 1632
Foochow missionaries, 1847-1880. 2517
Food for fasting. 2436
Food for God's children. 983, 2086
Food for lambs; or, Leading children to Christ. 1253, 1632, 1992
Food for the lambs. 1632
Food for the million. 3511
Food for thinking Christians. 1632
Food for thought day by day. 1439
Food in the Bible. 1632
Fool has said God is dead. 67
Fool hath said. 1090, 1097
Fool of love. 2271
Foolishness of God. 3660
Foolishness of peaching, and other sermons. 3703
Foolishness to the Greeks. 3652
Fools for Christ. 3062
Foot-notes to St. Paul. 372
Foot of pride. 2111
Foot of the cross. 3459
Foot-prints of an itinerant. 2452, 2453
Foot prints of Christ. 2062
Footfalls on the boundary of another world. 3510
Footings for faith. 57
Footnotes. 1446
Footnotes and headlines. 2394
Footnotes for the atom. 103
Footprints and waymarks for the help of the Christian traveller. 1683
Footprints in a darkened forest. 865
Footprints in Palestine. 2762
Footprints in the sand. 2383
Footprints of a dream. 3298
Foot-prints of an itinerant. 2452
Footprints of Gautama the Buddha. 701
Footprints of God. 101
Footprints of Prince Hall Masonry in New Jersey. 1668
Footprints of providence. 985
Footprints of the Jesuits. 1947
Footprints of the pioneers. 3386
Footprints of the Saviour. 1999
Footprints on the Mendocino coast. 120
Footprints on the sands of time. 120
Footsteps in a parish. 122
Footsteps in the sea. 668, 876, 2436, 3355
Footsteps of Mary Baker Eddy's progressive interpretations of the Lord's prayer. 2247
Footsteps of our forefathers. 1759
Footsteps of the flock. 2941
Footsteps of the Master. 1973
For a better religious life. 2570
For a child's day. 614
For a deeper life. 3492
For a little child like me. 1984, 3285
For a new America. 2527
For a time like this. 3289
For a world like ours. 323
For adult Catholics only. 795
For all eternity. 322
For all God's people. 1433
For all men; Catholic teaching for today based on Vatican II. 797
For all of life. 2495
For all sorts and conditions. 2961
For all that lives. 2228, 3312
For all the saints! 3788
For all the world. 2555
... For all to live by. 1977
For all who seek. 3473
For all your seasons. 1010
For behold ye are free. 2611
For better church members. 1201
For better, not for worse. 2338
For children mainly. 909
For Christ and country. 2300
For Christ and the church. 155
For Christ and the kingdom. 3673
For Christ in China. 2510
For Christ will come tomorrow. 1237, 2620
"For Christ's crown," and other sermons. 3349
For Christ's sake. 1094, 3242
For church builders, a recall to basics. 2240
For conscience sake. 2406
For days and for seasons. 862
For days of crisis. 2890
For each day a prayer. 2883, 2890
For each new day. 1432
For every young heart. 3880
For everything a season. 1263, 1349
For everything there is a season. 512
"For example ..." 1839

For faith and freedom. 1104
For faith and science. 1596
For family worship. 2
"For fear of the Jews" 3897
For freedom and belief. 3724
For God and C. M. E. 2260, 2311
For God and country. 3746
For God and democracy. 3450
For God and Texas. 1812
For God and the people. 2894
For God so loved the world. 2021
For God was with them. 216
For God's sake. 2536, 3365
For God's sake, be human. 985
For good or evil. 1746
For goodness sake. 3173
For goodness' sake, an informal treatise on
  being good. 999
For greater things. 3524
For happier families. 951
For hearts that hope. 1794
For heaven's sake. 906
"For heaven's sake!" Forty-six variations
  on the theme: how to react to the
  conditions of life on earth in such a way
  as to prepare oneself for life in the
  Kingdom of Heaven. 2390
For heretics only. 1091
For His name's sake. 3349
For His name's sake, a book for daily
  devotions, taking the worshipper through
  the New Testament in a year. 1439
For I am with you. 1454
'... for I have sinned. 795
For inner peace and strength. 2889
For instance. 1840
For Jesuits. 1949
For lack of a meddlesome preacher. 1063
For laymen and other martyrs. 2192
For love, for life. 971
For man's sake. 3186
For me to live is the church. 2570
For men of action. 754, 3480
For mercy's sake. 2305, 3418
For missionaries only. 2492
For one hundred years active with voice
  and with pen to crusade for the Church
  in our land: Paulist Fathers centennial
  year, 1958. 2805
For our age of anxiety. 163
For peace within. 2213
For people who fidget in church. 1189
For preachers and other sinners. 2907
For priests. 3487
For pulpit and platform. 2899
For remembrance. 3438
For rent. 2986
For righteousness' sake. 2394
For sceptics also. 3473
For self-examination and Judge for
  yourselves! 3101
For self-examination. 2299
For self-examination and Judge for
  yourselves! 3101
For shine and shade. 3404
For singles only. 3415
For sinners only. 1360, 2251, 2796
For students and others fed up. 1323
For such a time. 3216
For such a time as this. 143, 514, 692,
  3845
For such a time as this; inspirational
  messages for 20th century Christians.
  2301
For such a time: Bishop James H.
  Straughn, A.B., B.S.T., D.D., LL.D.
  3535
For the ark. 2711
For the children's hour. 3369
For the dispossessed. 181
For the faith, life of Just de Brentenieres,
  martyred in Korea, March 8, 1866. 691,
  2536
For the glory of the Father, Son, and Holy
  Spirit. 1024, 2745
...For the healing of the nations. 2522
For the heart of Africa. 2506
For the honor of the King. 3767
For the honor of the nation. 2104
For the life of the world. 2551
For the life that now is. 951
For the living of these days. 960
For the love of singles. 3415
For the making of ministers. 192
...For the millions of men now under arms.
  3875
For the open door. 3276
"For the power is in them ... " Mormon
  musings. 2392
For the reputation of truth. 1687
For the sake of divine truth. 37
For the sake of heaven. 1788
For the sake of simple folk. 3035
For the support of the ministry. 1462
For the time of tears. 1692
For the work of the ministry. 3674
For the world. 1572

For Thee alone. 3485
For them also. 768
For them also, a resume of Catholic
  doctrine. 768
For these fragile times. 2391
For they shall be comforted. 1353
For thinking teens. 3880
For this cause. 1266, 3468
For this cross I'll kill you. 2625, 2736
For this day. 1432
For this I was born. 1302, 3580
For those who grieve. 1774
For Thy great glory. 3796
For times of crisis. 250
For times out of joint. 167
For to-day. 1432
For two hundred years the same. 891
For uncomplicated Christians. 2267
For victorious living. 3456
For we have this treasure. 2905
For what do we live! 2226
For what purpose? 3794
For what purpose assembled. 3216
For when tomorrow comes. 3462
For whom did Christ die? 105, 176
For whom the rabbi speaks. 3371
For women only. 3841
For your pilgrimage. 1438
For Zion's sake; a biography of Judah L.
  Magnes, first chancellor and first
  president of the hebreW University of
  Jerusalem. 2315
"Forbid them not;" 896, 3098, 3884
Forbidden fruit. 298
Forbidden Gospel. 1717, 1975
Forbidden land. 3698
Forbidden universe. 2991
... Force and fear in relation to delictual
  imputability and penal responsibility.
  1777
Force of intercession. 2872
Force of mind. 2410
Force of truth. 3315
Forces in foreign missions. 2295
Forces of destiny, and other addresses.
  1072
Forefathers' day sermons. 3341
Foregleams and foreshadows of
  immortality. 1890, 2053
Foregleams in nature of redemption in
  Christ. 3481
Foregleams of glory. 3221
Foreign biographies. 1542
Foreign-born Americans and their children.
  2970
Foreign conspiracy against the liberties of
  the United States. 827
"Foreign countries" 1671
Foreign mail annual. 3875
Foreign mission work of Pastor Louis
  Harms. 2296
Foreign missionaries in action. 2493
Foreign missionary. 2518, 2520, 3736
Foreign missionary and his work. 2488,
  2519
Foreign missionary enterprise and its
  sincere critics. 2520
Foreign missionary, today and yesterday.
  2518
Foreign missionary work of the Christian
  Church. 1465
Foreign missions. 2518, 2520, 2521
... Foreign missions after a century. 2522
Foreign missions conference of North
  America. 2523
Foreign missions conference of North
  America, Committe of reference and
  counsel. 2523
Foreign missions controversy in the
  Northern Baptist Convention. 2714
Foreign missions convention at
  Washington, 1925. 2519
Foreign missions exposed. 2522
Foreign missions of the Protestant
  churches. 2518
Foreign missions of the Russian orthodox
  church. 2750
Foreign missions under fire. 2521
Foreign policy in Christian perspective.
  1913
Foreign policy is your business. 1077
Foreign Protestants and the settlement of
  Nova Scotia. 2716
Foreigner. 3258
Foreigners or friends. 2970
Foreknowledge. 2948
Foreknowledge of God. 1737
Foreknowledge of God, and cognate
  themes in theology and philosophy.
  1737
Foremothers. 3840
Forerunner of Saint Francis and other
  studies. 2583
Forerunners. 2127, 2612
Forerunners and rivals of Christianity.
  1079
Forerunners of a new age. 1326

Forerunners of Christ. 492
Forerunners of Jesus. 545
Forerunners of Saint Francis and other
  studies. 1185
Forerunners of the Reformation. 3636,
  3637
Foreshadows. 2024
Forest folklore, mythology, and romance.
  1632
Forest hospital at Lambarene. 2523
Foretokens of immortality. 1888
Forever after. 2618, 3317
Forever and ever. 1230, 2344
Forever beginning, 1766-1966. 2432, 2433
Forever building. 2348
Forever is now. 1695
Forever principle. 984
Forever triumphant. 964
Forever yes. 1027, 2270
Foreword. 2288
Foreword to the Old Testament. 539
Foreword to the Old Testament books.
  540
Forge and the crucible. 2416
Forgery in Christianity. 1053, 1092
Forgive, forget, and be free. 1633
Forgive our forgettings, Lord! 2892
Forgive them. 2162
Forgive us our prayers. 2247
Forgiveness & confession; the keys to
  renewal. 1633
Forgiveness and hope. 3662
Forgiveness and law. 1633
Forgiveness and suffering. 1633
Forgiveness; decisive issue in Protestant
  thought. 1633
Forgiveness in action. 1633
Forgiveness of Jesus Christ. 1633, 2061
Forgiveness of sin. 1633, 2811
Forgiveness of sins. 1633, 1634, 2934
Forgiving Christ. 1327
Forgiving community. 1633
Forgotten books of Eden. 491
Forgotten Christians. 885
Forgotten faces. 886
Forgotten Father. 1732
Forgotten Founding Fathers of the
  American church and state. 1301
Forgotten God. 1723
Forgotten gospel. 2174
Forgotten Hume. 1855
Forgotten Madonna. 2946
Forgotten patriot. 1710
Forgotten purpose. 1412
Forgotten religion. 3064
Forgotten religions. 3115
Forgotten religions, including some living
  primitive religions. 3122
Forgotten revelation. 2674
Forgotten saints. 925
Forgotten secret. 2870
Forgotten shrines of Spain. 2569
Forgotten truth. 3105
Forgotten truths. 1453, 2087, 3318
Forgotten women. 2581
Forgten saints. 925
Forks of Elkhorn Church. 1634, 2167
Form-analyisis and exegesis. 2479
Form and freedom in worship. 3004
Form and function of the body of the
  Greek letter. 373, 1771
Form and meaning. 552
Form and meaning of the fall narrative.
  521
Form and order of the service that is to be
  performed and the ceremonies that are to
  be observed in the coronation of Her
  Majesty Queen Elizabeth II. 1508
Form and origin of Milton's antitrinitarian
  conception. 54, 2472
Form and spirit. 3056
Form criticism. 388, 389
Form criticism; a new method of New
  Testament research. 389
Form criticism of the Old Testament. 498
Form-criticism of the synoptic healing
  narratives. 390
Form criticism reexamined. 387
Form, fire, and ashes. 1623
Form of a Christian congregation. 2288
Form of a servant. 1892
Form of baptism explained. 134
Form of baptism in sculpture and art. 134
Form of consecration of St. George's
  chapel. 2969
Form of discipline. 2449
Form of government, the discipline. 2927
Form of the servant. 3226
Formal policy statements of the American
  Council for Judaism. 2111
Formal study of myth. 2648
Formation of character. 867
Formation of Christendom. 1281
Formation of Christian dogma. 3658
Formation of Christian understanding. 288
Formation of faith. 1602

Formation of historical theology. 178,
  1819
Formation of Isaiah 40-55. 545
Formation of Islamic art. 86
Formation of lay Franciscans. 1649
Formation of social policy in the Catholic
  and Jewish traditions. 3749
Formation of the American Catholic
  minority, 1820-1860. 874
Formation of the American Lutheran
  Church. 33
Formation of the Bible. 289
Formation of the Christian Bible. 217
Formation of the Christian character. 978
Formation of the Christian character,
  addressed to those who are seeking to
  lead a religious life. 978
Formation of the Gospel according to
  Mark. 436
Formation of the gospel tradition. 393
Formation of the Lutheran Church in
  America. 2290
Formation of the New Testament. 339,
  410, 411
Formation of the Old Testament. 498
Formation of the Resurrection narratives.
  2054
Formative factors in character. 1536
Formative factors in Christian character.
  2592
Formative ideas in the Y.M.C.A. 3872
Formed by the word. 1267
Forming a Christian mentality. 998
Forming catechists. 748
Forming of an American tradition. 2924
Forming the faith of adolescents. 3167
Forms and techniques of altruistic and
  spiritual growth, a symposium. 28
Forms of Christian life. 3785
Forms of prayer for Jewish worship. 2108
Forms sacra, or, A sacred platform of
  natural and revealed religion. 2912,
  3641
Formula criticism and the poetry of the
  Old Testament. 544, 1799
Formula divine. May man enter heaven
  while he lives? 3751
Formula of Jesus Christ. 355
Formula of prescriptions. 1459
Formula quotations in the infancy
  narrative of Matthew. 443
Formulators of the Formula of concord.
  40
Forsaken fountain. 65
40th Anniversary and Rededication. 2291
Fortieth anniversary of Rev. Robert Stuart
  MacArthur, D.D., LL. D., as pastor of
  Calvary Baptist church, New York city,
  May 15-20, 1910. 1870-1910. 2304
Fortified cities of India. 2463
Fortune for your thoughts. 2473
Fortune of eternity. 3506
Forty centuries of law and liberty. 3192
Forty days. 2006
Forty days after Our Lord's resurrection.
  2051
Forty days at the cross. 1436
Forty days of the risen life. 2006
Forty-four fun fables. 3533
Forty fruitful years. 2193
Forty happy years in Japan, 1888-1928.
  2534
Forty hours. 1635
Forty-hours' devotion to Jesus in the
  blessed sacrament. 855
Forty Martyrs. 1021
Forty missionary stories. 2489
Forty-ninth star, Alaska. 2501
Forty-ninth star, Alaska. Illus. by Rus
  Anderson. 2501
40 object sermons for children. 909
40 objects lessons. 2394
Forty of the twentieth. 143
40+, 3. 1858
Forty prophetic wonders predicted in
  Daniel and Revelation. 508
40 proven ways to a successful church.
  1200
Forty sermon studies from the book of
  Jonah. 553
Forty-six select Scripture narratives from
  the Old Testament. 1420
Forty steps to Easter. 2211
Forty stories for the church, school and
  home. 1014
40 stories for you to tell. 911
Forty-two years amongst the Indians and
  Eskimo. 1847, 1899
Forty ways to say thank you, Lord. 1756
40 year English-Jewish calendar. 724
Forty year on the tiring line. 1272
Forty years after. 853
Forty years an evangelist. 3431
Forty years at Raritan. 3047
Forty years behind the wall. 3025, 3710
Forty years' experience in Sunday-schools.
  3558

Forty years in south China. 3582
Forty years in the church of Christ. 1210
Forty years in the land of tomorrow. 2504
Forty years in the lap of Methodism. 2421
Forty years in the Philippines. 2545
Forty years in the Turkish empire. 2515
... Forty years in the United States of America. 828
Forty years of parish life and work, 1883-1923. 2700
Forty years of pioneer life. 2560
Forty years of psychic research. 2988
Forty years on the spiritual rostrum. 3498
Forty years with Christ in Tanzania, 1928-1968. 1401, 2487
Forty years with Russian. 3875
Forty-eight plus! 2500
Forty-eight primary worship services. 3853
48 simple sermon outlines. 3374
Forty-five sermons written to meet objections of the present day. 864
Forty-five years in China. 2511
Forty-five years in New Guinea, memoirs of the senior missionary. 2541
49 worship stories for children. 911
...Forty-one facsimiles of dated Christian Arabic manuscripts. 2329
Forty-seven identifications of the Anglo-Saxons with the lost ten tribes of Israel. 1929
Forty-six years in the Methodist ministry. 1756, 2427
42 sermons for children. 907
Forum. 3748
Forward in faith sermons. 1229
Forward march of faith. 2715
Forward movements of the last half century. 1182
Forward the layman. 2191
Forward through the ages. 2526
Forward with Christ. 850, 3183, 3881
Fossils and the word of God. 3848
Fostering development. 2582
Found faithful. 3529
Foundation and orders of Sannerz and the Rhon Bruderhof. 697
Foundation and the superstructure. 1590
Foundation builder. 3409
Foundation for missions. 2504
Foundation for reconciliation. 180
Foundation for the Advancement of Sephardic Studies and Culture, inc. presents four reviews on Stephen Birmingham's book The grandees. 663
Foundation for tomorrow. 2296
Foundation guide for religious grant seekers. 1168
Foundation letters and teachings. 3684
Foundation of Biblical authority. 276
Foundation of Christian education. 3150
Foundation of faith and morals. 3109
Foundation of Japanese Buddhism. 706
Foundation of modern religion. 1186
Foundation of moral goodness. 3782
Foundation of the Partai Muslim in Indonesia. 2777
Foundation, organization and development of the Catholic Audio-Visual Association. 754
Foundation report. 99
Foundation rites with some kindred ceremonies. 3238
Foundation stones of truth. 1471
Foundations. 2561
Foundations for a philosophy of Christian education. 3153
Foundations for a psychology of grace. 2999
Foundations for Christian education in an era of change. 936
Foundations for Christian family policy. The proceedings of the North American conference on church and family, April 30-May 5, 1961. 1604
Foundations for educational ministry. 936, 2287
Foundations for freedom. 149
Foundations for purposeful church administration. 1200
Foundations for reconstruction. 1314
Foundations for youth. 1328
Foundations must stand! 305
Foundations of a faith. 2142
Foundations of belief. 185, 3099
Foundations of Bible history. 553
Foundations of Biblical faith. 651
Foundations of Biblical spirituality. 3484
Foundations of Buddhism. 703, 1703
Foundations of Catholic belief. 780
Foundations of Catholic theology. 3182
Foundations of Christian belief. 763, 3105
Foundations of Christian faith. 791, 3647
Foundations of Christian knowledge. 118
Foundations of Christianity. 1050, 1102, 1173, 2008, 2112

Foundations of doctrine in Scripture and experience. 1823
Foundations of dogmatics. 3650
Foundations of ecumenical social thought. 1143
Foundations of empiricism. 2417
Foundations of faith. 63, 1060
... The foundations of faith and morals. 3061, 3109
Foundations of Jewish ethics. 1538
Foundations of Jewish life: three studies. 1716, 2090
Foundations of Judaism. 2114, 2115
Foundations of Judaism and Christianity. 1083
Foundations of metaphysics in science. 2417
Foundations of mission theology. 2514
Foundations of morality. 948, 1535
Foundations of Mormonism. 2603
Foundations of New Testament Christology. 2010
Foundations of our faith. 3050
Foundations of religion. 3099
Foundations of religious education. 937
Foundations of sacred study. 3668
Foundations of social order. 1386
Foundations of spiritualism. 3497
Foundations of the Christian faith. 61, 477
Foundations of the Christian mission. 2554
Foundations of the conciliar theory. 1322
Foundations of the faith. 3643
Foundations of the metaphysics of morals. 1535
Foundations of the millennial kingdom of Christ. 2610, 3427
Foundations of the Seventh-Day Adventist message and mission. 3379
Foundations of theology. 2245, 3226, 3637
... Foundations of Thomistic philosophy. 3309, 3694
Foundations of Tibetan mysticism. 2193
Foundations of Wesleyan-Arminian theology. 83
Foundations of world order. 2926
Foundations of world unity. 125
Founded on a rock. 809
Founded upon a rock. 3335
Founder of Christianity. 2037
Founder of Mormonism. 2605, 3429
Founder of St. Ansgar. 1286
Founders and pew renters of the Unitarian Church in Charleston, S.C., 1817-1874. 888, 3051
Founder's manual. 1636
Founders of Christian movements. 925
Founders of great religions. 3124
Founders of great religions, being personal sketches of famous leaders. 3124
Founders of living religions. 3135
Founders of the message. 3380
Founders of the Seventh day Adventist denomination. 3382
Founding of a new world. 1190, 1636
Founding of Califf Haven. 870
Founding of Pacific Garden mission. 1636
Founding of the Augustana synod. 110
...The founding of the Christian church. 1636
Founding of the church. 1169
Founding of the church universal. 1193
Founding of the Jesuits, 1540. 1946
Founding of the kingdom. 332
Founding Presbyterianism in South Dakota. 2937
Founding the church in South Dakota. 3464
Founding the life divine. 1708, 3864
Foundress in nineteenth century Italy (Blessed Paola Frassinetti and the Congregation of the sisters of St. Dorothy) 1652
Fount of our joy. 2359
Fountain of life. 805, 2931
Fountain of life in manuscripts of the Gospels. 603
Fountain of life opened. 2931
Fountain of living water. 1830
Fountain of living waters. 760, 965
Fountain of wisdom. 2120
Fountain of youth. 2855, 3338
Fountain of youth, and other revival sermons. 1558
Fountain-source of occultism. 3687
Fountain: with jets of new meanings. 3499
Fountains of faith. 1326
Fountains of joy. 3798
Fountains of streams and public schools. 300
Four Americans. 1322, 3247
4 1/2 years in the Italy mission. 2486
Four and twenty elders. 458
Four apostles. 71

... Four books of Pope's Iliad I, VI, XXII, XXIV. 2860
Four cardinal virtues. 738
Four centuries of silence. 2092
Four centuries of the English Bible. 270
Four centuries of witch-beliefs. 3825
Four chapters on freedom. 2792, 3866
Four churches, one church. 3274
Four conferences touching the operation of the Holy Spirit, delivered at Newark, N. J. 1828
Four cosmical lectures. 3076
Four decades with men and boys. 3871
Four-dimensional man. 2196, 3776
Four doctrines. 2691, 3631
Four doctrines with the Nine questions. 2691
Four essays on love. 2266
Four evangelists. 1575
Four evangelists in classic art. 2126
Four existentialist theologians. 3100
Four faces, and other sermons. 3341
Four faces of Christian ministry. 3621
Four faces of Rozanov. 1093
Four first things. 783
Four-fold Gospel. 3410
Four fundamental questions. 3483, 3491
4 Gospel keys t. 1969
Four gospels. 381, 382, 383, 385, 386, 387, 392, 398, 2627
Four Gospels according to the Eastern version. 382
Four Gospels and Acts. 388
Four Gospels and the Christian life. 959
Four Gospels and the Revelation. 381, 383
Four Gospels, arranged in the form of a harmony. 383
Four Gospels as one. 1990
Four Gospels as one; the ministry, and mission of Jesus Christ: an arrangement of the Gospels York. 1990
Four Gospels (Authorized version) 382
Four Gospels esoterically interpreted. 3251
Four Gospels examined and vindicated on Catholic principles. 394
Four gospels from a lawyer's standpoint. 387
... The four Gospels from the Codex corbeiensis. 316
... The four Gospels from the Codex veronensis. 383
... The four Gospels from the Munich ms. 2631
Four Gospels (in epitome) transcribed by the disciples of the Venerable Bede's school at Jarrow or Wearmouth. 381
Four Gospels in one. 1988
Four Gospels in one made plain. 1989
Four Gospels in one narrative. 1988
Four Gospels in one story. 1990
Four Gospels in Syriac. 383
Four Gospels in the original Greek. 383
Four Gospels of Karahissar. 393
Four Gospels of Matthew. 383
Four Gospels of our Lord and Savior Jesus Christ. 382
Four Gospels of Our Lord Jesus Christ. 3401
Four Gospels of the New Testament. 383
Four Gospels shortened for children. 626, 627
Four Gospels: their age and authorship. 398
Four Gospels united into one. 397
Four great encyclicals. 2189
Four great encyclicals of Pope Pius XII. 3710
Four great heresies. 1805
Four Hasidic masters and their struggle against melancholy. 1788, 2844
Four historical booklets regarding the American province of the most precious blood. 2940
Four hitherto unpublished gospels. 2005
450 stories from life. 1840
405 worship illustrations. 1839
440 more snappy sermon starters. 3373
445 additional difficult Bible questions answered. 642
431 quotes from the notes of Henrietta C. Mears. 1011
Four hundred silent years. 2091
400 years after Valdivia. 2507
400 years of freethought. 1655
Four in one. Christ in the Gospels. 1988
Four independents. 1365
Four institutions under Catholic auspices. 2161
Four institutions under Catholic auspices accepting commitments from the New York City Children's Court. 2161
Four keys to prayer. 2396
Four lamas of Dolpo. 2194
Four last things: Death. Judgment. Hell. Heaven. 1530

Four Latin plays of St. Nicholas from the 12th century Fleury play-book. 2707
Four leading doctrines of the New Church. 642, 2689, 2691, 3631
... Four lectures delivered in the Church of the Holy Trinity, Philadelphia, in the year 1877. 3653
Four lectures on the offices and ceremonies of Holy week, as performed in the papal chapels. 842
Four-letter words that are good. 2389
Four letters of Pelagius. 2811
Four loves. 2263
Four major cults. 3325
Four Marian encyclicals and the apostolic constitution Munificentissimus Deus. 2361
Four marks of a total Christian. 994
Four martyrdoms from the Pierpont Morgan Coptic codices. 1021
Four metaphysical poets. 1476, 1519
Four minor prophets. 561
Four-minute talks for laymen. 3354
Four minute talks for superintendents. 3186
Four modern religious movements. 3212
Four mysteries of the faith. 2642
Four northern lights. 3253
Four Northwest fundamentalists. 1295
Four of the earlier Epistles of the apostle Paul. 371
Four old Greeks. 2662
Four-part chorals of J. S. Bach. 917
Four pastorates. 1341
Four paths to one God. 2155
Four philosophical problems. 2673
Four pictures of Christ. 1999
Four pillars. 1099
Four pillars of democracy. 3100
Four portraits of the Lord Jesus Christ. 1999
Four princes. 2801
Four prophets: Amos, Hosea, First Isaiah, Micah. 654
Four prophets of our destiny. 1583, 2170
Four psalms. 588
Four reformers. 2272, 3037
Four religions of Asia. 91
Four religious essays. 3068
Four riders of the Apocalypse. 464
Four rivers of Eden. 1496
Four sacred seasons. 3546
Four saints. 3299
Four sermons, on important subjects. 3366
Four sermons on the wisdom of God in the permission of sin. 3609
Four sermons to young men, from Titus ii. 6. 3350
Four-square. 738
... Four stages of Greek religion. 1767
Four standard works of the Church of Jesus Christ of latter-day saints. 2610
Four steps in the evolution of religious thought. 1037, 3213
Four steps to pure iman. 3542
Four strange books of the Bible: Jonah, Daniel, Koheleth, Esther. 552
Four temperaments. 50, 3065
4000 questions and answer on the Bible. 280, 643
Four thousand years ago. 532
Four thousand years of Indian education. 705
Four translation New Testament. 357
Four translation New Testament: King James. 357
Four translation New Testament: King James; New American standard Bible; Williams, in the language of the people; Beck, in the language of today. 357
Four views of Christ. 390
Four-wheel brakes. 3191
Four witnesses. 397
Four-year report [April 27, 1954-June 30, 1958] of the Continuing Committee on Muslim-Christian Cooperation Incorporated. 1925
Four years' campaign in India. 1895
Four years in Ashantee. 2502
Four years in the Old world. 1763
Four years on wheels. 1503
Four years struggle of the Church in Hungary. 818
Fourfold challenge of to-day. 3451
Fourfold Gospel. 381, 394, 1988
Fourfold pilgrimage. 1518
Fourfold story. 398
Fourfold test of Mormonism. 2605, 3799
Fourscore. 2389, 3135
Foursquare Christian. 934, 1064
Foursquare gospel. 1912
Fourteen for teens. 1015
Fourteen hours. 2805
Fourteen journeys to Unitarianism. 3728
Fourteen lessons in Yogi philosophy and Oriental occultism. 3863
Fourteen men who knew Christ. 71

Fourteen of Meaux. 2377
Fourteen sermons on Christian science. 1033
Fourteen years a Jesuit. 1945
Fourteen year's work among "erring girls" 1629
Fourteenth century English Biblical version. 357
Fourteenth century English mystics. 2644
14th-century English mystics. 2644
Fourth American faith. 3744
Fourth Baptist world congress. 142
Fourth book of catechism stories. 1840
Fourth book of Ezra. 654
Fourth candle. 9
Fourth Crusade. 1391
Fourth dimension. 915, 982
Fourth dimensional man. 2948
Fourth evangelist and his Gospel. 421
Fourth gospel. 414, 415, 420, 421, 422, 1972
Fourth Gospel and Jewish worship. 419
Fourth gospel and some recent German criticism. 420
Fourth Gospel and the Jews. 20, 418
Fourth gospel and the life of to-day. 420
Fourth gospel and the logos-doctrine. 419
Fourth gospel in research and debate. 418
Fourth gospel in the early church. 420
Fourth grade teachers plan book and manual. 634
Fourth in the furnace. 2228
Fourth International (ninth national) Sunday school convention of the United States and British American provinces. 3560
Fourth Lutheran hour. 2300
Fourth man. 1560
... The 4th man, and other famous sermons exactly as Oral Roberts preached them from the revival platform. 3241
Fourth man in the fire. 160
Fourth paper presented by Major Butler. 3194
Fourth R. 3189
Fourth R in American education. 3190
Fourth "R", the forgotten factor in education. 3237
Fourth report of the Joint commission on the Book of common prayer, appointed by the General convention of 1913. 2960
Fourth session. 3772
Fourth Synod of the Diocese of Richmond. 3578
Fourth thousand years. 536
Fourth wise man. 2834
Fourth witness. 423
... The fowre hymnes. 1869
Fox and Hoyt's quadrennial register of the Methodist Episcopal churchh. 2438
Fox-Taylor automatic writing, 1869-1892. 2478
Foxe's Book of English martyrs. 1021
Foxe's Book of martyrs. 2350
Foxe's Christian martyrs of the world. 2350
Fox's Book of martyrs. 2350, 2351
Fractured questions. 3880
Fragile craft. 3815
Fragile presence. 2232
Fragile universe. 3098
Die Fragmente der griechischen Kultschriftsteller. 1395
Fragmented layman. 3453
Fragments. 2010, 3090, 3689
Fragments from the Cairo genizah in the Freer collection. 2329
Fragments of a faith forgotten. 1718
Fragments of a future scroll. 1789
Fragments of an unknown gospel and other early Christian papyri. 1018
Fragments of Heracleon. 416
Fragments of my life. 871, 1473
Fragments of spiritual knowledge pertaining to the spiritual world. 3474
Fragments of thought upon theology, science, morals and men. 3632
Fragments of truth. 2726
Fragments that remain from the ministry of Maltbie Davenport Babcock. 2929
Fragrance of beauty. 3844
Fragrance of Christian ideals. 1099
Fragrance of the Lord. 2734
Framework of the New Testament stories. 334
Framley parsonage. 3090
France alive. 1638
France pagan? 1742, 2523
France under Mazarin. 1639, 3236
Frances Schervier, mother of the poor. 3307
Frances Warde and the first Sisters of Mercy. 3795
Frances Willard. 3816
Frances Willard, from prayers to politics. 3816

Frances Willard of Evanston. 3816
Francesca Cabrini. 723
Francesco. 1642
Francia's masterpiece. 2270, 3019
Francis. 1640, 1644
Francis, a biography of the Saint of Assisi. 1640
Francis and Clare. 1642
Francis and Clare, Saints of Assisi. 1642
... Francis and Dominic and the mendicant orders. 1642, 1673
Francis and the animals. 1027, 1644
Francis Asbury. 89
Francis Asbury, the prophet of the lond road. 89
Francis Asbury's reading of theology. 89
Francis Asbury's silver trumpet. 3432
Francis Bacon on the nature of man. 124, 2321
Francis, Bible of the poor. 1027, 1640
Francis book. 1644
Francis E. Clark year-book. 1288
Francis Goodwin of Hartford. 1748
Francis Lambert of Avignon: (1487-1530) 2194
Francis Marion Rains. 3019
Francis Mora; last of the Catalans. 2589
... Francis Murphy gospel temperance hymns. 3598
Francis Norbert Blanchet and the founding of the Oregon missions (1838-1848) 824
Francis of Assisi. 1027, 1640, 1641, 1642, 1643, 1644
Francis of Assisi, apostle of poverty. 1643
Francis of the Crucified. 1643
Francis, Saint of Assisi and of the world. 1644
Francis Schaeffer's apologetics. 65, 3306
Francis, the poor man of Assisi. 1027, 1640
Francis Thompson, & other essays. 760
Francis Tregian. 3710
Francis Xavier; his life, his times. 1650
Franciscan adventure. 1646
Franciscan beginnings in colonial Peru. 1647
Franciscan book of saints. 1646
Franciscan calling. 1648
Franciscan centenary. 1649
Franciscan charism in the church. 1643, 1648
Franciscan concept of mission in the High Middle Ages. 1648
Franciscan crown. 1644
*Franciscan daily missal and hymnal. 838
Franciscan days of vigil. 1645
Franciscan education. 1642, 1645
Franciscan financial administration. 1646
Franciscan formation conferences. 1646
Franciscan life in Christ. 1646
Franciscan literature. 1646
Franciscan manual of prayer for the Sisters of the Third Franciscan order of Syracuse, New York. 859
Franciscan message in authentic texts. 1645
Franciscan mission architecture of Alta California. 1158
Franciscan missionaries in Hispanic California, 1769-1848. 1647
Franciscan missionary sisters of the Sacred heart in the United States. 2489
Franciscan missions in Texas (1690-1793) 1648
Franciscan monastery. 3797
Franciscan mystic. 10
... Franciscan mysticism. 2646
Franciscan nun in China. 1647
Franciscan order from its origins to the year 1517. 1646
Franciscan parish prayerbook. 1648
Franciscan Pere Marquette. 2401, 2688
Franciscan perfection. 1640, 1645
Franciscan philosophy at Oxford. 2842
Franciscan philosophy at Oxford in the thirteenth century. 2842
Franciscan pictorial. 856
Franciscan pictorial book. 856
Franciscan poets. 1645
Franciscan poets in Italy of the thirteenth century. 1647
Franciscan readings. 1648, 2387
Franciscan saint of the day. 1028, 1646
Franciscan spirituality. 1645
Franciscan supplement to the daily missal. 845
Franciscan symbol, the Tau. 1644, 3589
Franciscan view of the spiritual and religious life. 2570
Franciscan women. 2859
De re Franciscana. 1646
Franciscans. 1645, 1646
Franciscans and Italian immigration in America. 1649, 1929
Franciscans and the Protestant revolution in England. 1647
Franciscans came first. 1647

Franciscan's climb to God. 2388
Franciscans in Arizona. 1646
Franciscans in California. 1646
... The Franciscans in medieval English life (1224-1348) 1647
Franciscans in Nebraska. 1647
Franciscans in South Germany, 1400-1530. 1648
Franciscans: love at work. 1645
Francisco Fulgencio Soren, Christ's interpreter to many lands. 3459
Franco codex of the Cathedral of Mexico. 917
Franco-Judaica. 2099
Francois Dardan d'Isturitz, martyr des Carmes (1733-1792) 1403
Francois de Fenelon. 1621
Francois de Sales. 1650
Francois Hotman. 1639, 1848
Frank answers to youth questions. 3887
Frank Buchman's secret. 699, 2593
Frank C. Porter, pioneer in American Biblical interpretation. 2864
Frank H. Nelson of Cincinnati. 2683
Frank Higgins, trail blazer. 1811
Frank Laubach's prayer diary. 1431
Frank Mason North. 2713
... Frankfort. 2099
Franklin Clark Fry. 1689
Franklin Spencer Spalding. 3469
Frankly feminine. 3835
Frankness in religion. 3070
Franz Rosenzweig: his life and thought. 1715
Franz Rosenzweig's philosophy of existence. 2138, 3249
Fraser of Trinity and Achimota. 1651
Fraternal appeal to the American churches. 1046
Fraternal appeal to the American churches, with a plan for catholic union on apostolic principles. 1046
Fraternal camp-meeting sermons. 3352
Fraternal charity. 887
Fraternal sermons and addresses, by outstanding ministers of various denominations. 3352
Fraternalism and the church. 1323
Fraternitatis Rosae Crucis. 3250
Fraternity and other addresses. 1325
Fraternity of the Rosicrucians. 3250
Fratris Johannis Pecham . . . Tractatus tres de paupertate. 1673, 2171
Fraud of modern "theosophy" exposed. 3686
Fraudulent gospel. 3850
Fray Jose G. Mojica, O.F.M., mi guia y mi estrella. 2568
Fray Pedro de Aragon, O. S. A. 78, 3220
Freaks and follies of fabledom. 2649
Fred Francis Bosworth (the joybringer) and continued story of Joybringer Bosworth; his life story. 685
Frederic Henry Hedge. 1800
Frederic Ozanam. 2755
Frederic Ozanam and his world. 2755
Frederick Baraga; a portrait of the first bishop of Marquette. 172
Frederick Bohn Fisher. 1628
Frederick Denison Maurice and the new reformation. 2374
Frederick Denison Maurice, rebellious conformist. 2374
Frederick Ernest Emrich. 1512
Frederick May Eliot. 3723
Frederick Parish, Virginia, 1744-1780. 1652
Frederick Temple. 3598
Fredericksburg Lodge No. 4. 1664
Free and faithful in Christ. 947, 948
Free as the wind. 2224
Free at last. 1002, 1256, 3350, 3387
Free-born John. 2229
Free choice. 1657
Free Christian. 957
Free church. 1463, 2977
Free church and seductive culture. 3446
Free church in a free state? 820, 1143, 1150
Free church through the ages. 3323
Free church today. 1122
Free churches and Christian unity. 1491
Free churches and re-union. 1040
Free conversation on the unpardonable sin. 3414
Free enterprise and Jewish law. 1316
Free for the taking. 1751
Free forever. 1367, 3895
Free grace of God displayed in the salvation of men. 1750
Free in obedience. 2822, 3665
Free inquiry into the miraculous powers. 2478
Free inquiry into the nature and origin of evil. 1745
Free land and fire from the altar. 1448, 3443

Free love and heavenly sinners. 184
Free man's almanac. 1432
Free man's faith. 1104
Free man's legacy. 1105
Free masonry: a poem. 52
Free men. 1658, 1659
Free Methodist church. 2428
Free Methodist hymnal. 2429
Free organ accompaniments to festival hymns. 1861
Free publicity. 3004
Free pulpit in action. 3358
Free religion. 1657
Free religion, an American faith. 1657
Free religious. 3193
Free speech in the church. 2223
Free speech, press, and mails, the divine right of man. 2223
Free the child in you. 981
Free thought. 1653
Free thoughts concerning religion. 1654
Free thoughts on religion, the church, and national happiness. 3622
Free to be Christian. 1658
Free to be Christian in high school. 963
Free to be, free to give. 1237, 3360
Free to be me. 994
Free to be single. 2304, 3415
Free to choose. 939
Free to do right. 3237
Free to grow. 2996
Free to live, free to die. 2384
Free to obey. 1659
Free, white, and Christian. 1133
Free will. 1657
Free will, responsibility, and grace. 1657
Freed from witchcraft. 1365, 1920
Freed spirit. 3499
Freedom. 879, 1659
Freedom, a guarantee for everybody. 469
Freedom after ejection. 1220
Freedom and advance. 1100
Freedom and authority. 119
Freedom and authority in religion. 118
Freedom and Catholic power in Spain and Portugal. 798
Freedom & discipline in the education of young people. 804
Freedom and faith. 1087, 3148
Freedom and fellowship in religion. 3192, 3066
Freedom and fulfillment. 1708, 1927
Freedom and grace. 1551, 2317, 3622
Freedom and healing. 999
Freedom and liberty. 2223
Freedom and man. 2223
...Freedom and restraint. 1657
Freedom and the churches. 1180
Freedom and the moral life; the ethics of William James. 1934
... Freedom and the spirit. 61, 3097
Freedom and truth, and other sermons in King's chapel. 3349
Freedom bound. 1659
Freedom bridge. 867, 2529
Freedom, civil and religious. 3380
Freedom dream. 1367, 1792
Freedom for all, a practical application of the Bible. 299
Freedom for me and other human creatures. 1660
Freedom for ministry. 1296
Freedom for the peoples. 1940
Freedom from a self-centered life/dying to self. 991
Freedom from depression. 984
Freedom from sinful thoughts: Christ alone breaks the curse. 980
Freedom from want. 588
Freedom, grace, and destiny. 1104
Freedom in Christ. 3163
Freedom in faith. 380
Freedom in God. 191
Freedom in meditation. 2379
Freedom in modern theology. 1659
Freedom in Molina. 1659, 2568
Freedom in the church. 792, 2964, 3193
Freedom is never free. 164
Freedom letter. 468
Freedom, love and truth. 1456
Freedom made flesh. 821, 2480
Freedom moves west. 3808
Freedom of a Christian man. 2286
Freedom of authority. 57
Freedom of choice in education. 1129
Freedom of Christ. 3355
Freedom of conscience and religious freedom. 2223
Freedom of faith. 970, 3347
Freedom of forgiveness. 1633
Freedom of God. 1505
Freedom of God's sons. 380
Freedom of man. 1657, 1659
Freedom of man in myth. 2648
Freedom of religion. 3195
Freedom of religion in America. 3195
Freedom of science. 3077

TITLE INDEX

FROM JUSTINIAN TO

Freedom of simplicity. 3409
Freedom of the Christian. 470
Freedom of the Christian man. 2223
Freedom of the preacher. 2903
Freedom of the pulpit. 2903
Freedom of the soul. 1281
Freedom of the will. 1657, 2162
Freedom of the will as a basis of human responsibility and a divine government. 1658
Freedom of thought in religious teaching. 1654
Freedom of will. 1657, 2162
Freedom or tolerance? 3192
Freedom revolution and the churches. 1131
Freedom Road. 563
Freedom seder. 2110
Freedom story. 3195
Freedom, suffering and love. 3610
Freedom through Christ. 380
Freedom through right thinking. 1036
Freedom through the cross. 105
Freedom through the truth. 26
Freedom to be free. 1659
Freedom to die. 1544
Freedom to fail. 1007
Freedom to starve. 690, 1701
Freedom today. 2223
Freedom versus slavery. 1057
Freedoms and mental fitness. 1325
Freedom's ferment. 3326
Freedom's holy light. 1109, 3194

Freely. 658
Freeman's morals. 1749
Freemasnry in Staunton, Virginia. 1671
Freemason at work. 1664
Freemasonry. 1662, 1671
Freemasonry and Catholicism. 3250
Freemasonry and the American Indian. 1902
Freemasonry in American courts. 1666
Freemasonry in Brownwood. 1663
Freemasonry in Federalist Connecticut. 1663
Freemasonry in Highland Springs. 1664
Freemasonry in Indonesia from Radermacher to Soekanto, 1762-1961. 1665
Freemasonry in Shelby County, Texas 1846-1900. 1671
Freemasonry in the Holy Land. 1662
Freemasonry in the thirteen colonies. 1672
Freemasonry made plain. 1661
Freemasonry of the ancient Egyptians. 1665
Freemasonry's movie picture drama. 1671
Freemasonry's servant, the Masonic Service Association of the United States. 2364
Freemasons. 1662
Freemason's monitor. 1670
Freemason's pocket dictionary. 1664
Freemason's pocket reference book. 1664
Freeport Presbyterian church, 1833-1933. 1672
Freer gospels. 383
Freer Indian sculptures. 3316
... The freethinker's pictorial text-book. 1654
Freethought in the United Kingdom and the Commonwealth. 1656
Freethought in the United States. 1656
Freewheeling. 2891
Freewill Baptist selection of spiritual songs. 153
French cathedrals. 752
French cathedrals, monasteries and abbeys. 752
French Catholic missionaries in the present United States (1604-1791) 834, 1673
French church architecture. 1159
French churches in the war zone. 1270
French convert. 799, 1361
French Creek Presbyterian Church. 1672
French devotional texts of the Middle Ages. 859, 1455
French diocesan hymns and their melodies. 1221
French emigre priests in the United States (1791-1815) 874
French existentialism. 1583
French free-thought from Gassendi to Voltaire. 2839
French Jesuits in lower Louisiana (1700-1763) 822, 1947
French laic laws (1879-1889) 1145
French laic laws, 1879-1889. 1145
French profiles. 1638
French prophets. 2464
French Protestantism and the French Revolution. 2954
French Protestantism and the French Revolution; a study in church and state, thought and religion. 2954
... French Protestantism, 1559-1562. 1852
French pulpit oratory, 1598-1650. 2908
French renascence. 1638
French Revolution and the Church. 1639
French secondary education, 1763-1790. 867
French text of the Ancrene riwle. 2580

French wars of religion. 1639
French wars of religion: their political aspects. 1639
Frequent communicant's prayer-book. 2259
Frequent communion. 2213
Frequent communion for busy men. 2256
Frequent confession. 1327
Frequent journeys to Calvary. 3525, 3526
Frere Jacques missal. 905
Fresco cycle of S. Maria di Castelseprio. 744
Frescoes of Saint-Savin. 3278
Fresh approach to the New Testament. 410
Fresh approach to the New Testament and early Christian literature. 409, 1019
Fresh approach to the Psalms. 578
Fresh bait for fishers of men. 2897
Fresh every morning. 2436
Fresh leaves in the Book and its story. 296
Fresh new insight into love is now. 983
Fresh perspectives on program planning. Guide for studying the role of a YWCA in its local community. 3878
Fresh start. 421
Fresh wind of the Spirit. 1830
Freshman mentor. 1373
Freshness of the spirit. 990, 3820
Freud and Christianity. 2998
Freud and future religious experience. 1673, 2993, 2994
Freud and religious belief. 1673, 2994
Freud and Saint Paul (an exploratory study of two great men who have had a profound influence upon Western civilization) 1673
Freud and the problem of God. 1673, 3107
Freud on ritual ; reconstruction and critique. 1673, 3240
Freudian theory and American religious journals, 1900-1965. 1673, 3002
Friar Bringas reports to the King. 1648, 1898
Friar Felix at large. 1022, 1588, 2763
...Friar Jerome's beautiful book. 3197
Friar Thomas D'Aquino: his life, thought, and work. 3694
Friars and German society in the thirteenth century. 1708
Friars and the dead weight of tradition, 1200-1400 A.D. 2582
Friars and the Jews. 53
Friars in medieval France. 1673
Friars Minor Conventual Penitentiaries in the Basilica of St. Peter in the Vatican. 852, 1357
Friday evening and special services. 2108
Friday evening late service. 2109
Friedens church at the Little Schuylkill. 1180
Friedrich Nietzsche. 2710
Friedrich Schleiermacher. 3308
Friend. 1637
Friend at church. 3392
Friend of God. 1942
Friend of life. 2131
Friend of mine. 1953
"Friend of Moses;" 565
Friend of sinners. 1951
Friend on the road and other studies in the Gospels. 1448
Friend to friend. 903, 1231
Friendly chats of the Friendly hour. 3351
Friendly dialogue, in three parts, between Philalethes & Toletus, upon the nature of duty. 2326, 3587
Friendly heritage; letters from the Quaker past. 1678
Friendly invaders. 700, 1678
Friendly letters to a Universalist on divine rewards and punishments. 3753
Friendly philosopher, Robert Crosbie (1849-1919) 3684
Friendly visit to the house of mourning. 1349
Friendly words with fellow-pilgrims. 966
Friends, a handbook about getting along together. 1673
Friends and community service in war and peace. 1674
Friends and friendship for Saint Augustine. 116, 1688
Friends and neighbors. 2551, 3763
Friends & the racial crisis. 1133, 1675
Friends and their children. 1683
Friends are my story. 952
Friends at home and in the community. 3764
Friends at work. 3763
Friends down under. 169
Friends everywhere. 3766
Friend's family. 1675
Friends for 300 years. 1684
Friends in Bedfordshire and West Hertfordshire. 183, 1677
Friends in Palestine. 1674, 3438
Friends in the Bible. 620
Friends in the seventeenth century. 1684
Friends in the underground church. 472, 2213, 2298
Friends, let us pray. 2874
Friends' library. 1679
Friends' meeting-house. 2829
Friends of Africa. 2497
Friends of Christ in the New Testament. 2006
Friends of God. 1447, 1674
Friends of God, friends of mine. 764
Friends of Jesus. 217, 2007, 3164, 3766
Friends of St. Francis. 1644, 1646
Friends of the caravan trails. 2550
Friends of the road. 2385
Friends, Romans, countrymen. 2964
Friends. Romans, Protestants. 64
Friends search for wholeness. 3491
Friends wherever we are. 3549
Friends with all the world. 3172
Friends with life. 2225
Friends world conference official report. 1679
Friendship. 1688
Friendship, a study in theological ethics. 1688
Friendship Center in China, a junior missionary project. 2511
Friendship evangelism. 1567
Friendship house. 2541
Friendship in the Lord. 1688
Friendship of Christ. 862, 3177
Friendship of God. 3344
Friendship of Jesus. 978
Friendship with God. 44
Friendship with Jesus. 999
Friendship's meaning. 1446
Friendships of Jesus. 2007
From a Black brother. 167
From a boundless basis. 1030
From a Christian ghetto. 1061
From a convent tower. 3415
From a far country. 1363
From a hostel veranda in Bengal. 2754
From a listening heart. 2393
From a morning prayer. 953
From a mustard seed. 1626, 1782
From a parson's diary. 3675
From a philosopher's scrap-book. 2677
From a shepherd's heart. 2390
From Aaron to Zerubbabel. 214
From Accadia to Machpelah. 4
From Adam to Abraham. 526
From Adam to Japheth. 319
From Adam to me. 293
From Adam to Moses. 494
From Adam's rib to women's lib. 1621, 2599
From age to age a living witness. 1653
From among men. 2609
From an abundant spring. 761, 1613
From Babel to Cumorah. 679
From Babylon to Bethlehem. 2091, 2149
From Baca to Beulah. 1576
From backwater to mainstream. 870
From baptism to the act of faith. 137
From Becket to Langton. 1761
From belief to understanding. 49, 1739
From Berlin to Jerusalem. 3309, 3310
From Bethlehem to Calvary. 1969, 2067
From Bethlehem to Olivet. 1967, 1993
From Bethlehlem to Calvary. 2067
From beyond. 3502
From beyond the veil. 3336
From Bible to Mishna. 505, 3706
From Bonaventure to Bellini. 186, 922
From bondage to freedom. 161, 3161
From bondage to freedom; God's varied voices. 544
From bondage to liberty in religion. 3123
From Bossuet to Newman. 781, 1473
From Brahma to Christ. 3699
From building to neighborhood. 3870
From call to service. 1290
From Cana to Calvary. 1986, 2934
From Canaan to Egypt. 528, 2133
From carabao to clipper. 2545
From cave to cathedral. 3404
From chaos to catholicism. 756
From chaos to character. 968
From chaos to covenant. 546
From Christ to Constantine. 1193
From clay to rock. 72, 338, 2824
From clerk to cleric. 1288, 1291
From Confucius to Christ. 1364, 1365
From confusion to certainty. 1342
From Constantine to Hitler. 2100
From Constantine to Julian. 1193
From cover to cover. 163, 614
From Dan to Megiddo. 2094
From Daniel to Daniel. 1308
From Daniel to St. John the Divine. 56
From darkness to light. 1062, 2229, 2231, 3126, 3298
From dawn to dusk. 2914
From dawn to sunrise. 3120
From day to day. 725, 1431
From day to day; book of daily devotions. 1439
From death to birth: sermons. 2301, 3358
From death to life. 975, 1359
From death to life through Christ. 164
From deep roots. 3878
From Descartes to Kant. 2843
From desert to temple. 598
From ditches to discipleship. 1007
From doubt to faith. 1448, 1596
From dream to vision of life. 3483
From dugout to steeple. 2423
From dusk to dawn. 3420
From dust to divinity. 1461
From earth to heaven. 1050
From earth to sky. 1450
From Eden to Calvary. 623
From Eden to eternity. 450
From Eden to glory. 3610
From Eden to the Jordan. 566
... From Egypt to Canaan. 517
From Egypt to the Golden Horn. 2763
From eternity to eternity. 3291
From everlasting to everlasting. 2397
From every nation without number. 1133, 3734
... From every tribe and nation. 2481
From evolution to creation. 202
From exile to freedom. 144
From existence to life. 1348
From Exodus to Advent. 1013
From experience to faith. 1056
From Ezra to the last of the Maccabees. 2091
From faith to faith. 239, 501, 790, 2466, 3621
From famine to fruitage. 3806
From far Formosa. 1634
From fashions to the Fathers. 1363
From fertility cult to worship. 3855
From fetish to God in ancient Egypt. 1502
From fetters to freedom. 819

From first Adam to last. 375
From Florence to Brest (1439-1596) 861, 2749
From football field to mission field. 2544
From freedom to formula. 1541
From garden to city in seven days. 1376
From gaslight to dawn. 127
From gaslight to dawn, an autobiography. 127
From generation to generation. 2634, 3371, 3802
From Genesis to Revelation. 230
From Germantown to Steinbach. 2407
From Gethsemani to Calvary. 2032
From gloom to gladness. 1533
From glory to glory. 975, 1302, 1454, 2644, 3546
From gods to dictators. 2997
From goo to you by way of the zoo. 1381
From Gospel to life. 1649
From guilt to glory. 471, 3358
From heart to heart. 3361
From hearth to cloister in the reign of Charles I I. 3796
From Hegel to Nietzche. 1800, 2843
From Hegel to Nietzsche. 1800, 2843
From here to maturity. 993, 1598
From here to the pinnacles. 2407
From here to the pinnacles memoris of Mennonite life in the Ukraine and in America. 2407
From heresy toward truth. 3754
From house t house. 737
From house to house. 737
From housewife to heretic. 2129, 2619
From idols to God. 1359, 1449
From incarnation to re-incarnation. 2726
From India to the planet Mars. 3427, 3502
From infidelity to Christianity. 3124
From information to action. 1199
From intellect to intuition. 2379
From Japan to Jerusalem. 2502
From Jerusalem to Jerusalem. 2522
From Jerusalem to Rome. 473
From Jesus to Christianity. 1103
From Jesus to Paul. 2117, 2798
From Joseph to Joshua. 535, 3706
From Joshua to David. 493
From Judaism to Christianity. 2138
From Justinian to Luther. 1186

FROM KARL MARX RELIGIOUS BOOKS 1876 - 1982

From Karl Marx to Jesus Christ. 1364
From Kirtland to Salt Lake City. 2604
From life to life. 1839, 3516
From Liffey to Jordan. 2762
From limbo to heaven. 3030
From limbo to heaven; an essay on the economy of the redemption. 3030
... From love to praise. 2932
From Luther to Chemnitz. 240, 2281
From Luther to 1580. 2288, 2303
From Luther to Kierkegaard. 3655
From machismo to mutuality. 3389
From magic to metaphor. 3266
From make-believe to reality. 1358, 3240
From manger to throne. 1973, 2764
From me to thee. 1910
From millions to happiness. 1359
From mine pit to pulpit. 1290
From mission to mission. 2954
From missions to mission. 2954
. . . From missions to mission in Latin America. 2548
From morality to religion. 1534
...From Moses to Elisha. 497, 531
From Moses to Qumran. 485
From mouth to ear. 1668
From movies to ministry (and victory over alcohol) 146, 1694
From my generation to yours...with love! 3886
From my window. 3406
From my world to yours. 3474, 3569
From mythical to mediaeval man. 1282
From nation to nation. 2494
From newsboy to evangelist. 1551
From night to light. 1446
From night to sunlight. 1363, 3813
From now to Adam. 295
From nowhere to Beulahland. 1358
From office to profession. 1294
From Oklahoma City to Ogbomosho. 3788
From one convert to another. 1365
From one generation to another. 2926
From one to multiplication. 121, 1687
From opposition to appropriation: the resolution of Southern Baptist conflict with dramatic forms, 1802-1962. 3606
From order to omega. 2041
From Orpheus to Paul. 2636, 2744, 2799
From out of the west. 1315, 3337
From Pachomius to Ignatius. 2582
From pagan to Christian. 967, 1362
From Palmyra, New York, 1830, to Independence, Missouri, 1894. 678, 2611, 3428
From paradise lost to paradise regained. 1941
From Passover to Pentecost. 2814
From Patmos to the Holy City. 463
From patriarch to prophet. 536
From Pentecost to Patmos. 327, 2799
From Peter to John Paul II. 2769
From Pharaoh to Hitler. 2077
From Philo to Spinoza. 2831, 3108
From place to place. 3611, 3700
From Planet Pluto with brotherly love. 3502
From plight to power. 1260
From plowboy to prophet. 2951
From politics to piety. 2828
From primitives to Zen. 3140
From prison in Rome. 448
From prison to pulpit. 971, 3341
From pulpit to people. 2903
From Puritanism to the age of reason. 1221
From Quaker to Latter-Day Saint. 2609, 3847
From rabbinism to Christ; the story of my life. 2085
From Reform Judaism to ethical culture. 7, 1534
From religion to grace. 2159, 2160
From religion to philosophy. 2835
From religious experience to a religious attitude. 3176
From rock bottom to mountaintop. 988
From romance to reality. 3131
From Romanism to Pentecost. 1823
From Sabbath to Lord's Day. 3547
From Sabbath to Sunday. 3546
From sacred to profane America. 3738, 3744
From saddle to city by buggy, boat and railway. 2898
From saddlebags to satellites. 2430
From St. Augustine to William Temple. 924
From St. Francis to Dante. 3286, 3287
From Saul to Paul. 2802
From Saul to Solomon. 534
From scenes like these. 1604
From science to God. 3104
From science to souls. 205
From science to theology. 3592
From Scripture to prayer. 374
From sea to shining sea. 1332
From shadow into everlasting light. 1486
From shadow to promise; Old Testament interpretation from Augustine to the young Luther. 501, 2276, 3669
From shadow to substance. 404
From shadows to reality. 3720
From shadowy types to truth. 2468
From Sheldon to Secker. 1760, 3402
From ship to pulpit. 3123
From sin to wholeness. 1412
From Sinai to Calvary. 1360
From skepticism to faith. 2973
From slave to priest. 3704
From slavery to the bishopric in the A.M.E. Church. 13
From so small a dream. 3387
From Solomon to Malachi. 494
From Solomon to the captivity. 531
From soul to soul. 3210
From Sphinx to Christ. 2729, 3120
From state church to pluralism. 3738
From State church to pluralism: a Prostestant interpretation of religion in American history. 3738
From statesman to philosopher. 675, 1419
From strength to strength. 130, 3467
From Sunday school to church school. 942
From Sunday to Sunday. 845
From sunset to dawn. 1352
From survey to service. 1838
From Swedenborg. 3570
From symptom to reality in modern history. 51
From talk to text. 1444
From Tarsus to Rome, the story of the first Christian hierarchy. 2798
From tepees to towers. 2432
From text to sermon. 405, 2897
From the Apostles' faith to the Apostles' Creed. 72
From the Apostolic community to Constantine. 1189, 1195
From the ashes of Christianity. 1091
From the beginning. 526, 540
From the beginning of our priesthood. 1298, 3778
From the book of life. 3206
From the caves and jungles of Hindostan, 1883-1886. 671, 1895
From the cenacle to the tomb. 2034
From the cradle to the grave. 1460, 1849
From the creation of man to eternity. 638
From the crib to the cross. 1984
From the cross: the seven last words. 2056
From the crossroads. 2608
From the dust of decades. 2616, 3429
From the epic of Chicago. 186
From the Exile to Christ. 2148
From the farm to the bishopric. 3133
From the fiery stakes of Europe to the Federal courts of America. 2408
From the flag to the cross. 3741
From the footlights of the theatre unto the light of the cross. 1551
From the garden of Eden to the crossing of the Jordan. 536
From the Gospel to the creeds. 1195
From the ground up; the story of 'Brother Van,' Montant pioneer minister, 1848-1919. 3767
From the heart. 2101
From the high Middle Ages to the eve of the Reformation. 1186
From the hillside. 3334
From the housetops. 1264
From the Jordan to the throne of Saul. 532, 640
From the land o' the leal. 3508
From the land of Sheba. 2107
From the Mennonite pulpit. 2404
From the Methodist pulpit into Christian science and how I demonstrated the abundance of substance and supply. 1035
From the mill to the mission field. 2530
From the mines to the pulpit. 1445, 3350
From the morning watch. 2005
From the mountains of L'Abri. 2190
From the Nile to Mount Pisgah. 2622
From the Nile to the waters of Damascus. 2764
From the other side. 756
From the pen of Bishop W. A. Patterson. 1229
From the pilot's seat. 865
From the pinnacle of the temple. 1590
From the pit to the pulpit. 1784
From the plains to the pulpit. 3347
From the plow to the pulpit. 2913
From the pulpit to the palm-branch. 3523
From the pulpit to the poor-house, and other romances of the Methodist itinerancy. 2435
From the pyramids to Paul. 3241
From the rabbis to Christ. 2117
From the rainbow to the cross. 539
From the rising of the sun. 1101
From the rock to the gates of hell. 1247
From the Sacred Heart to the Trinity. 771, 3602
From the seen to the unseen. 3072
From the sermons of Rabbi Milton Steinberg. 1623, 3372
From the seventh plane. 3518
From the shadow of insight. 566, 3361
From the ship to the pulpit. 1562
From the snare of the fowler. 957
From the stage coach to the pulpit. 144
From the stone age to Christianity. 2585
From the study window. 2385
From the tablets of my heart. 2427
From the the stone age to christianity. 2585
From the throne of Saul to Bethlehem. 532, 640
From the underside. 849, 1562
From the upper room to the empty tomb. 2029
From the usher's desk to the tabernacle pulpit. 3523
From the wisdom of Mishle. 572
From the world of the Cabbalah. 721, 2137
From then to now. 606
From theosophy to Christian faith. 3686
From this day forward. 2337
From this world to the next. 1455
From throne to cross. 2213
From time to time. 3700
From Tokyo to Jerusalem. 2952
From tradition to gospel. 387, 389
From tradition to mission. 2195
From traditional to rational faith. 3728
From tragedy to triumph. 548, 2213
From twilight to dawn. 2108
From two to one. 2347
From, understanding the Resurrection. 2054
From Union square to Rome. 1363
From Ur to Nazareth. 296
From week to week. 565
From Wesley to Asbury. 2438
"From whence came we?" 1672
From whence cometh, 1767-1977. 1302, 3433
From whence cometh my help. 1342
From where I stand. 2142
From why to yes. 744, 1301
From within. 1448
From word to life. 643
From wrecks to reconciliation. 3189
From youth into manhood. 3393
Front line of the Sunday school movement. 3556
Frontier bishop. 698, 3241
Frontier bishop, Simon Gabriel Brute. 698
Frontier evangelism. 1600
Frontier mission. 44, 2548
Frontier missionary. 130
Frontier missionary problems. 2553
Frontier parish. 1222, 2558
Frontier peoples in Central Nigeria and a strategy for outreach. 1574
Frontier peoples of India. 2531
Frontier spirit in American Christianity. 3195
Frontiers for Christian youth. 155
Frontiers for the church today. 1117
Frontiers in American Catholicism. 828
Frontiers in missionary strategy. 2495
Frontiers in modern theology. 3617
Frontiers of Christian thinking. 1058
Frontiers of faith and reason. 760
Frontiers of healing. 2988
Frontiers of hope. 2119
Frontiers of the after life. 3511
Frontiers of the Christian world mission since 1938. 2199, 2525
Frontiers of the spirit. 2992
Frontiers of theology in Latin America. 2222
Frontiersmen of the faith. 170
Frontline theology. 3652
Frozen assets. 1555
Frugality in the spiritual life. 2381
Fruit from the garden of spices. 616
Fruit from the jungle. 2532
Fruit in the seed. 1364
Fruit of deliverance. 544, 3356
Fruit of His compassion. 2353
Fruit of lips. 392, 2009
Fruit of the spirit. 381, 995, 1712, 1713, 2815
Fruit of the spirit, joy. 252
Fruit of the spirit, peace. 252
Fruit of the sycamore tree. 3354
Fruit of the sycamore tree, and other sermons. 3354
Fruit-yielding vine. 1218
Fruitage of spiritual gifts. 3386, 3811
Fruitful activity. 3485
Fruitful and responsible love. 854, 2266
Fruitful confessions. 1327
Fruitful ideal. 1648
Fruits of a father's love. 1609
Fruits of contemplation. 1356
Fruits of enduring faith. 3017
Fruits of faith. 3300
Fruits of Mormonism. 2602, 2605
Fruits of silence. 3099
Fruits of the devotion to the Sacred Heart. 3340
Fruits of the Shaker tree of life. 3394
Fruits of the spirit. 1451, 1454, 2248, 3483
Fuel for missionary fires. 2491, 3564
Fugitive. 2817, 2863
Fulfill thy ministry. 3673
Fulfilled promise. 2820
Fulfilled prophecies that prove the Bible. 605
Fulfilled prophecy. 276
Fulfilled woman. 2336
Fulfilling the ministry. 1218
Fulfillment in Christ. 3163
Fulfillment of life. 2201
Fulfillment: the epic story of Zionism. 3897
Fulfilment of Scripture prophecy. 609
Fulham papers in the Lambeth Palace Library. 1222
Full and true statement of the examination and ordination of Mr. Arthur Carey. 739
Full assurance. 93
Full blessing of Pentecost. 1831, 2815
Full church, empty rectory. 775, 2192
Full circle. 893, 2404, 2481
Full course of instruction in explanation of the catechism. 746, 749
Full gospel in action. 383
Full history of the wonderful career of Moody and Sankey in Great Britain and America. 1565, 2587
Full life for empty men. 967
Full of grace. 2361
Full refutation of the doctrine of unconditional perservance. 2822
Full report of the case of Stacy Decow, and Joseph Hendrickson, vs. Thomas L. Shotwell. 1674
Full report of the trial of Rev. John W. White for heresy. 2927
Full surrender to God. 1357
Full time effort of man. 1078
Full-time living. 980
Full years. 3247
Fullness & freedom. 341
Fullness of Christ. 956
Fullness of joy. 3885
Fullness of life. 674
Fullness of the blessing of the gospel of Christ. 2421
Fully alive. 1002, 2161
Fully furnished. 968
Fulness of Christ. 2059
Fulness of God. 363
Fulness of grace: the believer's heritage. 1751
Fulness of Israel. 501
Fulness of sacrifice. 2254
Fulness of the gospel. 383
Fulness of time. 1818
Fulton J. Sheen Sunday missal. 845
Fulton J. Sheen treasury. 3401
Fulton J. Sheen's guide to contentment. 1001
Fulton Oursler's Greatest. 535, 929, 1970
Fulton Sheen reader. 793
Fulton's footprints in Fiji. 1690, 2517
Fun & names. 1484, 2617
Fun from the Bible. 281
Fun ideas for family devotions. 1605
Fun plans for church recreation. 3028
Fun with Bible geography. 229, 283
Funality of Christ. 2050
Function and structure. 2290, 2480
... The function of divine manifestations in New Testament times. 321
Function of religion in man's struggle for existence. 3059
Function of spirit in matter. 3498
Function of teaching in Christianity. 3160
Function of the church in modern society. 1124
Function of the public schools in dealing with religion. 3189
Function of theology. 3617
Functional approach to religious education. 3148
Functional asceticism. 2570
Functional objectives for Christian education. 2287
Functional philosophy of religion. 3099
Functioning faith. 413, 3358

Functions of faith and reason in the theology of Saint Hilary of Poitiers. 1811
Functions reserved to pastors. 1290
Fundament of all teaching. 2675
Fundamental biology. 3382
Fundamental Catholic teaching on the human race. 3017
Fundamental Christian faith. 73
Fundamental Christianity. 1052
Fundamental Christology. 2046
Fundamental concepts of moral theology. 947
Fundamental differences between the Reorganized Church and the Church in Utah. 3216
Fundamental doctrines of the Christian faith. 1561
Fundamental ends of life. 2226
Fundamental facts of spiritualism. 3505
Fundamental facts of the faith. 3662
Fundamental ideas of the Roman Catholic church. 799
Fundamental liberties of a free people. 1280
Fundamental liberties of a free people: religion, speech, press, assembly. 1280
Fundamental moral attitudes. 3782
Fundamental moral theology. 942
Fundamental pastoral counseling. 2780
Fundamental principles of the Yi-king, Tao, and the Cabbalas of Egypt and the Hebrews. 3575
Fundamental questions. 1060
Fundamental religious principles in Browning's poetry. 697
Fundamental religious teachings of Christian science. 1034
Fundamental revelation in dramatic symbol. 234
Fundamental rubrics. 839
Fundamental theology. 3628
Fundamental virtues. 3782
Fundamentalism. 1691
Fundamentalism and American culture. 1691
Fundamentalism and evangelism. 1691
Fundamentalism and the church. 1690
Fundamentalism & the Missouri Synod. 1690, 2296
"Fundamentalism" and the word of God. 1690
Fundamentalism vs. evolution at Dayton, Tennessee. 3084
...Fundamentalism versus modernism. 2563
Fundamentalism versus modernism, a layman's viewpoint. 2561
Fundamentalist controversy. 2562
Fundamentalist phenomenon. 1690
Fundamentalists and modernists. 2561
Fundamentally speaking. 2384
Fundamentals. 3636
Fundamentals and programs of a new catechesis. 746
Fundamentals and their contrasts. 1068
Fundamentals for daily living. 642
Fundamentals in the philosophy of God. 2672
Fundamentals of Bible doctrine. 3384
Fundamentals of Catholic action. 754
Fundamentals of Catholic belief. 763
Fundamentals of Catholic dogma. 781, 782
Fundamentals of Christian sociology. 3449
Fundamentals of Christian statesmanship. 1142
Fundamentals of Christianity. 1053, 1069
Fundamentals of dispensationalism. 1376
Fundamentals of early Christianity. 347
Fundamentals of esoteric philosophy. 3687
Fundamentals of ethics. 1537
Fundamentals of faith. 3643
Fundamentals of faith in the light of modern thought. 1054
Fundamentals of freethought. 1654
Fundamentals of Hindu faith and culture. 2840
Fundamentals of human spirituality. 3478
Fundamentals of Judaism. 2140
Fundamentals of Lutheran church government. 2288
Fundamentals of Mariology. 2362
Fundamentals of Methodism. 2428
Fundamentals of missiology. 2554
Fundamentals of new individualism. 2739
Fundamentals of our faith. 3663
Fundamentals of Protestantism. 2953
Fundamentals of religion. 57, 2607
Fundamentals of religious belief. 1595
Fundamentals of the Christian religion. 796, 1069
Fundamentals of the everlasting gospel. 3382
Fundamentals of the faith. 991, 3651
Fundamentals of the liturgy. 839

Fundamentals of the religious life. 961, 2576
Fundamentals of yoga. 3865
Funeral. 1693
Funeral, a source book for ministers. 1693
Funeral and the mourners. 3672
Funeral encyclopedia, a source book. 1693
Funeral mediations. 1691
Funeral meditations. 1691
Funeral message. 1843
Funeral orations. 1692
Funeral orations by Saint Gregory Nazianzen and Saint Ambrose. 1692
Funeral sermon. 1326, 1692, 1817
Funeral sermon on the death of Rev. Spencer Houghton Cone, D.D. 1326, 1691
Funeral sermon outlines. 1691
Funeral sermons and outline addresses. 1692, 2176
Funeral sermons and outlines. 1692
Funeral service. 3722
Funeral service, or Meditations adapted to funeral addresses. 1694
Funeral services. 1693
Funeral services for today. 1693
Funeral services of Rev. Henry L. Hitchcock, D.D., of Western Reserve college. 123, 1820
Funeral sourcebook. 1694
Funeral: vestige or value? 1693
Funk and Wagnalls new Standard Bible dictionary. 244
Funky. 1694
Funny thing happened on the way to church. 1289
Funny thing happened on the way to heaven. 963, 2788
Funny thing happened on the way to the crusade. 1755
Funny thing happened to the church. 766, 1245
Funny, you don't look Christian. 1014
Furnace of renewal. 558, 1243
Furnace of the Lord. 1943
Furta sacra. 3056
Further chronicles of Therese Neumann. 2685, 3531
Further communications from the world of spirits. 3502
Further Discourses on the Holy Ghost. 1828
Further Greek epigrams. 1522
Further insights into holiness. 1824
Further journey. 1364
Further lives of the saints. 3280
Further pages of my life. 1212
Further paradoxes. 788
Furtherance of the gospel. 1177, 2549
Fury of God. 3792
Futher dialogues of the Buddah. 710
Futile sermons. 1406, 2899
Futterer's shorthand Bible method. 1992
Future as the presence of shared hope. 1529
Future belongs to you. 3879
Future course of Christian adult education. 3169
Future events revealed. 445
Future evolution of man. 1579
Future explored. 1529
Future for the historical Jesus. 2008
Future for youth catechesis. 940
Future growth and development of higher education in the Reorganized Church of Jesus Christ of the Latter Day Saints. 3217
Future hope. 1561
Future is before us. 992, 3464
Future is now. 3321
Future is upon us. 1077
Future kingdom. 640
Future leadership of the church. 1288
Future life. 1695, 1696, 1697, 1887, 3515
Future life demonstrated. 3515
Future life in the light of ancient wisdom and modern science. 1694
Future life in the light of modern inquiry. 1889
Future of Africa. 2499
Future of an illusion. 1104, 2997
Future of belief. 1720
Future of belief debate. 1456
Future of canon law. 735
Future of Catholic Christianity. 1066
Future of Christianity. 1068
Future of church-related higher education. 1164
Future of creation. 1529
Future of ecumenism. 1492
Future of empirical theology. 1512
Future of Europe. 462
Future of faith. 1057
Future of freedom. 1086, 3450
Future of God. 3641

Future of hope. 1529, 1846
Future of Israel. 2079
Future of John Wesley's Methodism. 2434
Future of man, meta-pschic. 3511
Future of marriage as institution. 2343
Future of metaphysics. 2420
Future of Muslim civilisation. 1922
Future of our religious past. 3621
Future of philosophical theology. 2832
Future of religion. 1084, 3056
Future of religions. 1066, 1067, 3700
Future of Roman Catholic theology. 3628
Future of the American church. 3747
Future of the American past. 3743
Future of the Bible. 269
Future of the Christian. 1064
Future of the Christian Church. 1066
Future of the Christian Sunday. 3547
Future of the Christian world mission. 2496
Future of the church. 1246, 3784
Future of the Church of England. 1211
Future of the churches; historic and economic facts. 1116, 1182
Future of the great planet earth. 606
Future of the human mind. 2473
Future of the Jew in America. 605
Future of the kingdom in prophecy and fulfillment. 609
Future of the liturgy. 2234
Future of the United States by divine appointment. 464
Future of the world. 465
Future of theology. 1106, 3628
Future of unbelief. 3327
Future parish. 2774
Future people: Christianity, modern culture and the future. 1074
Future present. 3853
Future probation and foreign missions. 2484
Future probation examined. 2943
Future punishment. 1699
Future retribution. 1699
Future retribution viewed in the light of reason and revelation. 1699
Future science. 2730
Future shape of ministry. 2785
Future shape of preaching. 2900
Future shapes of adult religious education. 938
Future significance of civilization, nature, and religion. 3069
Future to hope in. 1058
Future unrolled. 508
Future way. 3688
Future with hope. 2735
Future won't wait. 1259
Futures, human and divine. 1528
Futurist option. 3651
Fuuture of partnership. 988
Fuzzy tells the Easter story. 1486
Fuzzy-Wuzzy tales. 2533

G

G. A. R. patriotic and semi-religious poems. 3206
G. A. Selwyn, D. D., bishop of New Zealand and Lichfield. 3331
G. Harry Agnew. 19, 2433
G. Harry Agnew, a pioneer missionary. 19
G. Hovah explains. 1655
G. K. Chesterton. 892
Gaa nah shoh neh de o waah'sao'nyoh gwah Na'wenni'yuh. 3333
Gaa nah shoh neh deo waah'sao'nyoh'gwah na'wenni'yuk. 3333
Gabriel and Michael, the archangel, their prominence in Bible prophecy ... A message for our times answering vital questions in the light of the Bible. 1700
Gabriel Marcel on religious knowledge. 2181, 2332
Gabriel's wing. 1918
Gadarene. 3495
Gadgets, gimmicks, and grace. 936
... Gailhac of Beziers. 1700
Gain by loss. 3406
Gaina sutras, translated from Prakrit. 1933
Gaines S. Dobbins. 1472, 1498
Gaining a radiant faith. 2212
Gaining the faith you need. 1104
Gaining through losing. 3540
Galatians. 379, 380, 381
Galatians; a letter for today. 381
Galatians, dialogical response to opponents. 381
Galatians, Ephesians. 380
Galatians in Greek. 381
Galatians in the Greek New Testament for the English reader. 381

Galatians/Romans. 381
... Galatians, Romans, Philippians, Philemon. 371
Galaxy of saints. 216
Galen on Jews and Christians. 1700
Galilean. 1968, 2005
Galilean fishermen. 1572
Galilean gleam. 1181
Galilean way. 1095
Galilee doctor. 2544, 3704
Galileo, science, and the church. 1701, 3084
Gallant life. 3877
Gallery of Bible stories. 602
Gallery of ghosts. 1710
Gallery of living Catholic authors is the Catholic literary center of the world. 869
Gallery of New Testament rogues. 338, 3243
Gallery of portraits of the Old Testament. 494
Gallery of spirit art. 3520
Gallery of the saints. 3280
Gallican rite. 843
Gallitzin's letters. 787
Galloping Gospel. 3131
Galloway Memorial Methodist Church, 1836-1956. 1930
Gallup opinion index. 3002
Galut. 2085
Gamblers at Golgotha. 2215
Game of chess. 100
Game of life. 3782
Game of wizards. 2728
Games Zen masters play. 3891
Gaming: the fine art of creating simulation/learning games for religious education. 1701
Gandhari Dharmapada. 701
Gandhi's letters to a disciple. 3405
Ganesa. 1701
Ganga Dass. 2489
Ganging sermon effectiveness. 2903
Ganta United Methodist Mission, 1926-1976. 2433, 2537
Gaon of Wilna. 1506
Garbage and the goddess. 699
Garden. 3764
Garden and the graveyard. 527, 2212, 2298
Garden and the wilderness. 1150
Garden enclosed. 2392
Garden meditations. 2676
Garden of Bible verses. 621
... The garden of Eden. 526, 629
Garden of Eden and the flood. 1496
Garden of hope. 1449
Garden of Methodism. 2439
Garden of nuts. 2639
Garden of pomegranates. 723
Garden of praise. 2757
Garden of prayer. 2890
Garden of prayers. 900
Garden of sorrows. 1349
Garden of temptation. 3
Garden of the beloved. 2771
Garden of the heart. 126
Garden of the Little Flower. 2638
Garden of the Lord. 1454, 1687
Garden of the soul. 856
Garden spots in the Old Testament. 1444
Gardener looks at the fruits of the spirit. 985
Gardens and gleanings; along life's way. 1453
Gardens, flowers and trees of the Bible. 480
Gardens of Adonis. 7, 84
Gardens of green. 1448
Gardens of life. 167
Garenganze. 2513
Garfield Bromley Oxnam, revolutionist? 2755
Gargoyles and grotesques. 3316
Garland of gladness. 181
Garland of praise. 813
Garland of saints for children. 3284
Garments of power. 1446
Garo jungle book. 1702
Garuda purana (Saroddhara) 1813
Garveyism as a religion movement. 16, 1703
Gatakamala. 700
Gate and the cross. 469
Gate of death. 1444
Gate of Heaven. 3294
Gate of horn. 3109
Gate of life. 2214
Gate of the kingdom. 1060
Gate to the Gospel. 1447
Gateless gate. 702, 1853, 2182
Gates and keys to Bible books. 236
Gates Mills and a history of its village church. 1703
Gates of Dannemora. 1860, 2942
Gates of hades" 1802

Gates of Jerusalem. 1944
Gates of knowledge. 2729
Gates of new life. 2935, 3366
Gates of the mind. 3513
Gates shall not. 3382
Gates to the Old City. 18, 556, 2207, 3581
... The gateway of liberation. 3685
Gateway of understanding. 3518
Gateway to God. 1730
Gateway to Judaism: encyclopedia home reference. 2094, 2154
Gateway to power. 3432
Gateway to the Mishnah. 2479
Gateway to Tibet. 2555
Gateway to wisdom. 2383
Gateways into light. 2380
Gathas of Zarathushtra. 121
Gather up the fragments. 2388, 2425
Gathered church. 1469
Gathered for power. 3005
Gathered fragments. 144, 2435
Gathered gold. 1447, 2396
Gathered in 1707. 689
Gathered leaves of Sunday school song. 3562
Gathered lilies. 897
Gathered memories. Eastern Star ceremonies. 2741
Gathered together. 1839
Gathered together: readings on religious themes. 3200
Gathering. 3798
Gathering a people. 1024
Gathering jewels. 1569, 2181, 2696, 2829
Gathering of strangers. 1125
Gathering storm in the churches. 1154
Gaucho land boy. 2547, 3387
Gautama Buddha in life and legend. 702, 1703
Gautama the Buddha. 1080, 1703
Gautama; the story of Lord Buddha. 701
Gauvin-Olson debates on God and the Bible. 3023
Gay church. 1254, 3751
Gay gods and merry mortals. 1742
Gay invasion. 1844
Gay legends of the saints. 3284
Gay theology. 1844
Gayan ; Vadan ; Nirtan. 3542
Gayety of grace. 1751
Gazetteer of British ghosts. 1710
Gearing into life; youth examines its relationships; a manual for leaders. 687
Geheimnis und Geheimhaltung im rabbinischen Judentum. 3322
Die Geheimwissenschaften. 2732
Gelebter Glaube. 3382
Gem cyclopedia of illustrations. 1842
Gem of Christ. 1700
... Gemma caelestia. 189
Gemma Galgani. 1700
Gemma of Lucca. 1700
Gems and minerals of the Bible. 318
Gems from Genesis. 521
Gems from Genesis, an outlined study. 521
Gems from Genesis. [n.p. 527
Gems from James. 413, 2436, 3354
Gems from Scripture. 249
Gems from the Bible. 252, 614
Gems from the Equinox. 2314
Gems from the Gita. 197
Gems from the Midrash. 1519
Gems from the Psalms. 575, 576
Gems from the pulpit. 3340
Gems from the sacred mine. 219
Gems from the Sunday gospels in the Orthodox Church. 2751, 3363
Gems from the Veda. 1812
Gems of Aryan wisdom. 2839
Gems of devotion. 1455
Gems of gold. 1440
Gems of immortality. 1349
Gems of thought from leading intellectual lights. 2988
Gems of thought from Saint Margaret Mary. 3279
Gems of truth. 2395
Gems of wisdom. 1839
Gems of wisdom from the Bible. 250
Genealogical research. 1704
Genealogical sources for Utah and L.D.S. Church surveys and research. 1704
Genealogy and history in the Biblical world. 281
Genealogy and life of Asa Gilbert Eddy. 1493
Genealogy of morals. 1536
Genealogy of the gods. 3139
... Geneisis. 524
General and connected view of the prophecies. 567
General B. Y. P. U. manual. 142
General benevolence agencies of the Methodist Church. 2440
General Biblical introduction. 311

General biographical catalogue. 2850
General biographical catalogue of Auburn theological seminary, 1818-1918. 109
General biographical dictionary. 661, 662
General catalog of Hartford theological seminary. 3614
... General catalog of the Crozer theological seminary. 1390
General catalogue. 2941, 3614, 3615
General catalogue 1850 to 1900. 3242
... General catalogue, 1850 to 1910. 3615
General catalogue of Andover theological seminary. 3614
General catalogue of Lane theological seminary. 3614
General catalogue of the Auburn theological seminary. 109
General catalogue of the Divinity school of Harvard university. 3614
General catalogue of the McCormick theological seminary. 893, 3614
General catalogue of the McCormick theological seminary of the Presbyterian church, Chicago, Illinois. 2306, 3614
... General catalogue of the Newton theological institution. 40
General catalogue of the Presbyterian theological seminary. 3614
General catalogue of the Theological seminary. 3614
General catalogue of the Union theological seminary in the city of New York, 1836-1918. 3615
General catalogue of Union theological seminary. 3615
General catechetical directory. 934
General Conference Mennonite pioneers. 1704
General conference powers under the Constitution of the Methodist Episcopalchurch. 2449
General confession made easy. 1327
General Convention of the Episcopal Church. 2966
General council. 1373, 3773
General councils of the church. 1373
General course of study for Lutheran elementary schools. 1549
General course of study for Lutheran elementary schools, with supplement. 2297
General Epistle of James. 412, 413
General Epistle of James and the Epistle of Paul the apostle to the Hebrews. 412
General Epistle of Jude [and the Revelation of John]. 891
General Epistle of Paul the Apostle to the Romans from the text of the Authorized King James Version of 1611, with some differences in capitalization and punctuation. 470
... The general Epistle of St. James. 412
General Epistles. 339, 340
General epistles, James, Peter, and Judas. 340
General epistles of James & Jude. 413
... The general Epistles of St Peter and St. Jude. 447
... The general Pistles. 339, 340
General Evangeline Booth. 681, 3293
General Evangeline Booth of the Salvation Army. 681, 3293
General evidences of catholicity. 783
General explanation of The Buddha speaks, The sutra in forty-two sections. 3523
General features of the moral government of God. 2981
General history of the Baptist denomination in America, and other parts of the world. 151, 170
General history of the Catholic church. 809
General history of the Christian church. 464
General history of the Christian religion and church. 1178
General idea of the college of Mirania. 1311
General index to Parker's People's Bible. 224
General index to the names and subject-matter of The sacred books of the East. 91
General index to the publications of the Parker society. 1211
General intercessions. 839
General introduction, by a Committee of the Christian Brothers Educational Association. 934
General introduction to the Bible. 309
General introduction to the Old Testament. 495, 1798
General introduction to the Sacred Scriptures. 637
General introduction to the study of Holy Scripture. 231

General introduction to the study of the Holy Scriptures. 309
General legislation in the new Code of canon law; general norms. 735
General Leonidas Polk, C.S.A., the fighting bishop. 2858
General Menaion. 2748
General metaphysics. 2419
General Mickey, a true story. 2316
... General monumental work. 3333
General next to God. 682
... The general norms of dispensation. 1467
General practice of the churches of New-England, relating to baptism, vindicated. 134
General principles of the Kabbalah. 721
General principles of the religious life. 3196
General report of the deputation sent by the American board to China in 1907. 911
General report of the Survey of the beneficiaries of the program of the church and / or the assessment in the diocese of New York. 2971
General revelation. 3224
General superintendency in American Methodism, 1784-1870. 2451
General survey of Hebrew literature in translation- the Biblical period. 1798
General survey of psychical phenomena. 2989
General theory of secularization. 3328
General view of the geology of Scripture. 202
General view of the history of the English Bible. 248
General was a lady. 681, 3296
General who rebuilt the Jesuits. 3243
General without a gun. 682
Generation of decision. 2106
Generation of excellence. 1261
Generation of giants. 1947
Generation of opportunity. 3785
Generation of the third eye. 828
Generation to generation. 936
Generation without memory. 2155, 3244
Generations in crisis. 1539
Genes and Genesis. 3470
Genes, genesis, and evolution. 202, 1580
Genesee diary. 2716, 3489
Genesis. 520, 521, 522, 524, 525, 527, 658, 891, 1797, 3368, 3389, 3391
Genesis 1-11. 525
Genesis; a devotional commentary. 524
Genesis: a new interpretation of the first three chapters. 525
Genesis and archaeology. 520
Genesis & ecology. 525, 1853
Genesis and evolution. 204, 523
Genesis and evolution of Islam and Judaeo-Christianity. 3122
Genesis and exodus of the human spirit. 2409
Genesis and geology. 203, 204, 3084
Genesis and growth of religion. 3061
Genesis and modern science. 205
Genesis and science. 523, 2743
Genesis and scientific inquiry. 524
Genesis and Semitic tradition. 523, 526, 2667
Genesis and the Christian life. 1438
Genesis and yourself. 524
Genesis disclosed. 523
Genesis-Exodus. 522, 527
Genesis, Exodus, Leviticus, Numbers. 523
Genesis Flood. 1422
Genesis I-II. 1380
Genesis in space and time. 526
Genesis, mother of sciences. 527
Genesis octapla. 524
Genesis of Christ Church, Stratford, Connecticut. 3535
Genesis of Genesis. 522, 523
Genesis of religion. 3110, 3834
Genesis of the Baptist churches in Virginia. 171
Genesis of the Cumberland Presbyterian church. 1396
Genesis of the heavens and the earth and all the host of them. 204
Genesis of the New England churches. 3009
Genesis of the social conscience. 3433
Genesis of the social gospel. 2064
Genesis 1. and modern science. 205
Genesis one & the origin of the Earth. 1382
...Genesis I-II. 525
Genesis, outlines and notes for Bible classes. 527
Genesis printed in colors. 522
Genesis re-read. 205
Genesis regained. 525
Genesis: the first book of Moses. 527

Genesis, the first book of Moses. Drawings by Saul Raskin. 520
Genesis to Deuteronomy: notes on the Pentateuch. 562
Genesis 12-50. 528
Genesis versus evolution. 206, 3756
Genetic engineering. 1705
Genetic history of the New England theology. 2688
Genetic history of the New England theology of Chicago press. 2688
Geneva and the consolidation of the French Protestant movement, 1564-1572. 196, 1852
Geneva Bible. 653
Genius and mission of Methodism. 2422
Genius and spirit of the Hebrew Bible. 501
Genius and theory of Methodist polity. 14
Genius figure in antiquity and the Middle Ages. 1705
Genius of Christ. 2062
Genius of Christianity. 1048
Genius of creation. 3720
Genius of Geneva. 728
Genius of Israel. 2095
Genius of Methodism. 2421
Genius of Paul. 2801
Genius of public worship. 3003
Genius of the apostolate. 3613
Genius of the Gospels. 392
Genius of the prophets. 2950
Genre for the Gospels. 393
Gentile comes to Cache Valley. 2616
Gentiles and the Gentile mission in Luke-Acts. 426, 1705
Gentilism. 3121
Gentle breeze of Jesus. 3232
Gentle cynic. 511, 512
Gentle people. 2407
Gentle revolutionary. 1027, 1644
Gentle war. 3293
Gentle way. 982
Gentleman and the Jew. 503, 2105, 2144, 3297
Gentleman from Heaven. 2724
Gentleman's pocket register. 26
Gentlemen theologians. 3666
Gentleness of Jesus. 1071
Genuine epistles of the Apostolic fathers. 1617
Genuine epistles of the Apostolic fathers, St. Clement, St. Polycarp, St. Ignatius, St. Barnabas. 1019
Genuine epistles of the Apostolical fathers. 1617
Genuine words of Jesus. 1962
Genuinely human existence. 1107
Genuineness and authenticity of the Gospels. 394
Geoffrey Chaucer's The prologue to the book of the tales of Canterbury, The knight's tale, The nun's priest's tale. 1519
Geognosy. 203
Geographic influences in Old Testament masterpieces. 528, 2763
Geographical companion to the Bible. 281
Geographical publishing company's Commercial atlas of the world; new census. 102
Geography and atlas of Protestant missions. 2518
... The geography of Bible lands. 282
Geography of religion. 3070
Geography of the Bible. 281, 282
Geography of the Book of Mormon. 678
Geography of witchcraft. 3824
Geology and revelation. 203
Geomancy. 1706
Geometry and faith. 2673
Geonica. 1706
Geordie life of Jesus. 1963
George. 1706
George Alonzo Hall. 1781
George and Mary Schlosser. 2488, 3308
George Batten's directory of the religious press of the United States. 3205
George Bell. 186
George Berkeley and the proofs fot he existence of God. 192, 1738
George Borrow: God's picaro. 682
George Bourne and The Book and slavery irreconcilable. 686, 3424
George Bowen of Bombay. 2491
George Bowen, D. D., pioneer-missionary and explorer, an autobiography. 696, 2485
George Burman Foster, religious humanist. 1635
George C. Stebbins. 1748
George C. Stebbins: reminiscences and gospel hymn stories. 1575
George Cannon, the immigrant, Isle of Man, 1794-St. Louis, U.S.A., 1844. 734
George Catlin vs. the Philobiblon Society. 876

George Crumley family of Sullivan County, Tennessee. 1390
George F. Pentecost. 2813
George Fox. 1637
George Fox, an autobiography. 1677
George Fox and the light within, 1650-1660. 1637, 2647
... George Fox, Seeker and Friend. 1637
George Fox's attitude toward war. 1637, 3794
George Hay Forbes. 1632
George Hodges. 1822
George Hooper, 1640-1727, Bishop of Bath and Wells. 666, 1845
George Joye, 1495?-1553. 2136
George K. Little, and his revival work. 2233, 3233
... George Keith (1638-1716) 2166
George of Lydda, the patron saint of England. 1706
George Pepperdine college lectures. 1272
George Reichert. 3052
George Santayana. 3302
George Santayana and the endless comedy. 3302
George Santayanna. 3302
George seeks a reason. 3752
George Street Synagogue of Congregation B'nai Jacob. 2101
George Sylvester Morris. 2620
George Thomas Montgomery. 2586
George Tyrrell. 2562, 3721
George W. Truett. 3716
George W. Truett, Biography. 3716
George Warren Field. 1332
George Whitefield. 34, 3813
George Whitefield and the Great Awakening. 3813
George Whitefield, prophet-preacher. 3813
George Whitefield, the awakener. 1549, 3813
George Whitefield, the life and times of the great evangelist of the eighteenth-century revival. 1293, 3813
George Whitefield, trumpet of the Lord. 1575, 3813
Georgia Baptists. 150
Georgian metalwork, from antiquity to the 18th century. 87
Gerald Massey's Lectures. 3067
Gerard de Nerval. 1706
Gerard Manley Hopkins and the Victorian temper. 1516, 1846
Gerhard von Rad. 3017
German Baptists in North America. 150
German Bibles before Luther. 283
German cathedrals. 752
German Catholics and Hitler's wars. 818
German church conflict. 1707
German church on the American frontier. 1550
German church struggle and the Holocaust. 1146
German churches under Hitler. 1146
German-English prayer-book for children. 854
German Evangelical Church and the Jews, 1879-1950. 54
German gospel sermons with English outlines. 3370
German Jew. 2099
German Kantian bibliography. 2163
German liberty authors. 3307
German literary influences on the American transcendentalists. 3708
German Methodist Episcopal Church of Lawrence, Kansas. 1707, 2201
German missions in Tanganyika, 1891-1941. 2552
German phoenix. 1707
German phoenix; men and movements in the church in Germany. [1st ed.]. 1707
German religious life in colonial times. 3195
German sectarians of Pennsylvania. 1482, 1521
Germany, England, and Scotland. 1181
Germany; its universities, theology and religion. 3756
Germany-pilgrimage of unity and peace. 759, 3368
Germany's new religion. 1708
Germany's stepchildren. 1707
Germs of thought. 3890
Gershom Scholem. 2646, 3309, 3310
Geru Tegh Bahadur. 3408, 3592
Gesammelte Abhandlungen zur romischen Religions- und Stadtgeschichte. 3246
Geschichte der katholischen theologie. 3667
Geschichte der Munchener Freimaurerei des 18. [i.e. achtzehnten] Jahrhunderts. 1667
Geschichte der protestantischen theologie. 2954

Geschichte der urchristlichen Literatur. 350, 1020
Geschichte des neueren Occultismus. 2732
Gesta Christi. 1048
Gesta Pilati. 2069
Gesta Romanorum. 3340, 3581
Gesture of balance. 2381
Get growing, Christian! 984
Get high on yourself. 2393
Get it together with God. 2384
Get me a tambourine. 880, 982
Get off the fence! 951
Get off the fence! Morals for moderns. 951
Get on with living. 988
Get out there and do something about injustice. 1060
Get out there and reap! 991
Get ready! Get called! Go! 1233
Get set! 687
Get the facts. 3880
Get the m[a deleted e inserted above letter]ssage? 991
Get thee behind me; my life as a preacher's son. 2906
Get up and go. 3883
Get with it, man. 3886
Get your hands off my throat. 3881
Gethsemane. 3289
Gethsemane to Calvary. 2215
Gethsemani. 1708, 1747, 2033
Getting a church started in the face of insurmountable odds with limited resources in unlikely circumstances. 1171
Getting acquainted with God. 1436, 1720, 1724
Getting acquainted with Jewish neighbors. 2121
Getting acquainted with the Bible. 310
Getting acquainted with the New Testament. 347, 473, 474
Getting acquainted with the Old Testament. 595
Getting along with difficult people. 887
Getting and giving. 1168
Getting back to God. 1102
Getting better acquainted with your Bible. 312
Getting down to cases. 3672
Getting help from religion. 962
Getting help from the Bible. 653
Getting inside the Bible. 311
Getting into God. 636, 2869
Getting into Luther's Large catechism. 2275
Getting into the act. 1006
Getting into the Bible. 637
Getting into the Formula of Concord. 2282
Getting into the story of Concord. 2283
Getting into the theology of Concord. 2283
Getting it all together. 365
Getting more from your Bible reading. 231
Getting on top of your troubles. 994
Getting publicity. 3005
Getting ready for a revival. 1567
Getting ready for Christmas. 9, 1113
Getting ready for heaven. 3288
Getting rich. 1452
Getting started in adult religious education. 938
Getting straight about the Bible. 206, 642
Getting the Bible's message; teacher's guide. 643
Getting the church on target. 1244
Getting the gold out of the word of God. 642
Getting there. 1015
Getting there from here. 1011
Getting things from God. 2868
Getting through to adults. 938
Getting through to God. 2887
Getting through to the wonderful you. 2880
Getting to know Christ. 1992
Getting to know God. 2934
Getting to know God, and other sermons. 2934
Getting to know Mary. 2361
Getting to know the Bible. 308
Getting to know the Eucharist. 2255
Getting to know your Bible. 311
Getting to know your faith. 3665
Gezangboek van Christian science (Christian science hymnal) Waaronder zeven gezangen van de Reverend Mary Baker Eddy. 1037
Ghana Assembly of the International Missionary Council. 2515
Ghazali's theory of virtue. 21, 3782
Ghebers of Hebron. 3115
Gheranda samhita. 3867
Ghetto. 2082, 2098

Ghetto and the Jews of Rome. 2102
Ghetto of indifference. 1134
Ghost and ghoul. 1709
Ghost dance. 3061
Ghost dance Messiah. 1902, 3860
Ghost-dance religion and the Sioux outbreak of 1890. 1709
Ghost-dance religion and Wounded Knee. 1709
Ghost hunter's strangest cases. 1709
Ghost in my life. 1361
Ghost land. 3496
Ghost of Caesar walks. 1141
Ghost of Royal Oak. 1372
Ghost story index. 1709
Ghostly bibliography. 1710
Ghosts? 1709, 3519
Ghosts about us. 1709
Ghosts and hauntings. 1709
Ghosts and poltergeists. 1710
Ghosts and witches aplenty. 3580
Ghosts are everywhere. 3474
Ghosts, devils, angels and sun gods. 3568
Ghosts I have talked with. 3508
Ghosts in American houses. 1710
Ghosts in Irish houses. 1710
Ghosts I've met. 1709
Ghosts of bigotry. 793
Ghosts of Borley. 1710
Ghosts of London. 1710
Ghosts of the Bible. 1710
Ghosts of the Carolinas. 1710
Ghosts or gospels. 3519
... Ghosts that still walk, real ghosts of America. 1710
Ghosts the Indians feared. 1904
Giant against the sky. 734
Giant at the ford. 1028
Giant for God. 3137
"A giant in the earth," a biography of Dr. J. B. Boddie. 674
Giant in the land. 2129
Giant in the wilderness. 2684
Giant judge. 3297
Giant of the Lord. 2601
Giant saint. 1115
Giants along my path. 2736
Giants in action. 2439
Giants of faith. 3016, 3382
Giants of the faith. 1364
Giants of the missionary trail. 2482
Gibbon's antagonism to Christianity. 1051, 1092, 1710, 1711
Gibeon and Israel. 531, 1711
Gibeonites. 1711, 1824
Gideon's band. 1711
Gideon's gang. 1332, 3433
Gift and call. 944
Gift—creation. 1383
Gift (dorea) of the Holy Spirit. 253
Gift for God. 2397
Gift for mourners. 1350
Gift from God's fingers. 1380
Gift of a golden string. 1444
Gift of a sound mind. 2410
Gift of administration. 1200
Gift of belonging. 1305, 2557
Gift of Christmas. 632, 1114. 2023
Gift of communion. 2256,
Gift of conversion. 1360
Gift of doubt. 987
Gift of dreams. 1479
Gift of Easter. 2054
Gift of gentians. 1022
Gift of gifts. 1831
Gift of God. 1724, 1830, 3339
Gift of grace. 1753
Gift of healing. 1601
Gift of healing and spiritual science. 3494
Gift of his heart. 1013
Gift of hope. 961
...The gift of immortality. 1890
... The gift of influence. 2930
Gift of inner healing. 1600
Gift of inner peace. 2808
Gift of joy. 2135
Gift of life. 1455, 3361
Gift of light. 2757
Gift of love. 2264, 2265, 2393
Gift of mind to spirit. 2227
Gift of oneself. 3482
Gift of piety. 2388
Gift of power. 999, 1832, 3157
Gift of prayer. 2886, 2890
Gift of prophecy. 606, 1472
Gift of prophecy in 1 Corinthians. 323, 2949
Gift of retirement. 17
Gift of self. 1009
Gift of Shalom. 995
Gift of suffering. 165, 3540
Gift of the Father. 1349
Gift of the healer. 2539
Gift of the Holy Spirit. 1832
Gift of the Holy Spirit today. 1833
Gift of the King. 2366
Gift of the Spirit. 1831, 3484

Gift of time. 8
Gift of tongues. 1716
Gift of wholeness. 1006, 1498
Gift packages. 2388
Gift that abides (I John ii:27) 3480
Gift to be simple. 3398
Gifted in socioeducational perspective. 1712
Gifts and fruit of the spirit. 1712
Gifts and graces. 323
Gifts and ministries. 1712
Gifts for men. 313
Gifts for the graduate. 3883
Gifts from the Bible. 318
Gifts of civilization and other sermons and lectures. 1281
Gifts of grace. 181, 1712
Gifts of life and love. 2073
Gifts of power. 3397, 3631
Gifts of silence. 2381
Gifts of the Holy Ghost. 1829
... The gifts of the Holy Ghost in the Dominican saints. 1475
Gifts of the Holy Spirit to unbelievers and believers. 1833
Gifts of the lotus. 1431
Gifts of the spirit. 1712
Gifts of the spirit and the body of Christ. 2814
Gifts that differ. 2202
Gifts that never wear out. 985
Gilbert Foliot and his letters. 1631
Gilbert Haven, Methodist abolitionist. 1790, 3424
Gilbert Keith Chesterton. 892
Gilbert's manual for choir-loft and pulpit. 1204
Gild of St. Mary, Lichfield. 2225
Gilgamesh epic and Old Testament parallels. 1713
Gilgamesh epic and Old Testment parallels. 1713
Gingerbread church. 737
Gingerbread man: Pat Williams—then and now. 1360, 3817
Giordano Bruno. 698
Giordano Bruno and the Hermetic tradition. 698, 2732
Giordano Bruno: philosopher and martyr. 698
Giovanni Pierluigi da Palestrina, his life and times. 2766
Gipsy for Jesus. 930, 1673
Gipsy Smith. 3135, 3431
Gipsy Smith: from the forest I came. 3431
Gipsy Smith missions in America. 3431
Gipsy Smith's best sermons. 3345
Girded with gladness. 1054
Girdling the globe for God. 3788
Girl and the grotto. 3460
Girl Friday to Gladys Aylward. 121, 2744
Girl in the stable. 1707
Girl in white armor. 1938
Girl of an Indian garden. 2531
...The girl reserve movement. 1715
Girl Reserve movement of the Young Women's Christian Association. 1714
Girl who had everything. 931, 2208
Girl who laughed at Satan. 3247
... Girlhood and character. 1714
Girlhood today. 1714
Girlhood's highest ideal, helpful chapters to Catholic girls at the parting of the ways. 935, 3785
Girl's book of prayers. 2884
Girls' book of saints. 3284
Girl's daily life. 1714
Girl's every day book. 935
Girls of the Bible. 290, 898
Girls who made good. 1714
Girls who talked to ghosts. 1942, 3521
Girl's prayer book. 1714
Girl's year book. 725
Gist. 2492
Gist of Christian doctrine. 3051
Gist of it. 3607
Gist of spiritualism. 3498
Gist of the Bible. 642
Gist of the Bible book by book. 635
Gist of the cults. 3327
Gist of the lesson. 1915, 1917
*Gist of the lesson (The) 638
Gist of the lessons. 1917
Give Christ back to us! 995
Give comfort to my people. 1258
Give God equal time! 2392
Give heed unto reading. 3645
Give it to me straight, doctor. 982
Give me another chance. 1340
Give me back my soul. 3356
Give me souls. 2412
Give me souls! : Life of Don Bosco. 683, 1028
Give me that old-time religion. 1576, 1855

Give me that prime-time religion. 3241
Give me this mountain. 2513
Give me tomorrow. 971
Give the whole gospel a chance. 3446
Give the winds a mighty voice. 1690
Give them their dignity. 1261
Give this man place. 1557, 2135
... Give this man place; chapters on the life and character of Saint Joseph. 2132
Give unto Caesar what are God's. 1151
Give up your gods. 934
Give up your small ambitions. 2484
Give us this day. 900, 1017, 1431, 1440, 2249
Give us this day our daily bread. 2871
Give us this mountain. 2534
Give ye! 3529
"Give ye them to eat" 3375
Give your guilt away. 3295
Give your life a lift. 1438
Give yourself a chance. 3539
Giver and his gifts. 346, 2855
Giving a good invitation. 1554
Giving a reason for our hope. 1845
Giving and growing. 1250
Giving and living. 3530
Giving God what you are. 992
Giving—God's way. 952
Giving testimony. 3343
Giving the answer. 795
Giving wings to a warm heart. 2427
Glacial period and the deluge. 349
Glad Easter day. 2054
Glad game. 1369, 2487
Glad moments with God. 1606
Glad tidings. 380, 1558
Glad tidings; centennial history of Saint Gabriel's Episcopal Church, Marion, Massachusetts, 1871-1971. 3274
Glad tidings to perishing sinners. 1358, 3288
Glad tidings to the meek. 2300
Gladness in Christian living. 970
Gladness of His return. 3319
Gladstone, church, state and Tractarianism. 1715, 1764
Glamour; a world problem. 2723
Glances over the field of faith and reason. 1103
Glanvill. 1715, 3422
Glass, stones & crown. 3545
Glasse of time, in the first age. 296, 2471
Gleams of glory. 1437
"Gleams of grace." 161
Gleams over the horizon. 1655
Gleanings. 806, 1266, 2574
Gleanings among the wheat sheaves. 2973
Gleanings from Elisha. 1506
Gleanings from God's word. 317
Gleanings from my scrap book. 2830
Gleanings from old Shaker journals. 1788, 3397
Gleanings from Paul. 374
Gleanings from the New Testament. 334
Gleanings from the Scriptures. 3414
Gleanings from the writings of Baha'u'llah. 126
Gleanings in Exodus. 516
Gleanings in Genesis. 523
Gleanings in Joshua. 553
Gleanings in the Godhead. 1726, 2042
Gleanings of a mystic. 3250
Gleanings of fifty years. 824
Gleanings of fifty years; the Sisters of the Holy Names of Jesus and Mary in the Northwest, 1859-1909. 670, 824
Gleanings of religion. 3114
Gleig's wonderful book concerning the most wonderful book in the world. 294
Glenn Clark. 1284, 2385
... A glimpee at Mexico. 2540
Glimpse behind the veil. 1268
Glimpse into glory. 2187, 2391
Glimpse of India. 1895
Glimpse of nothingness. 2383
Glimpse of Saint Joseph. 2132
Glimpse of world missions. 2495
Glimpses heavenward; led to Jesus. 2000
Glimpses of a Mormon family. 2600
Glimpses of Baptist heritage. 171
Glimpses of Bible climaxes from "the beginning" to "the end" 232
Glimpses of Bible lands. 2763
Glimpses of Christ in Holy Scripture. 1999
Glimpses of God, and other sermons. 1342
Glimpses of God meditative essays. 1448
Glimpses of God's presence. 2395
Glimpses of grace. 2238
Glimpses of grandeur. 1950
Glimpses of great fields. 3075
Glimpses of Jewish life in San Francisco. 2103
Glimpses of life in soul-saving. 3461

Glimpses of life of Lord Krishna, from the discourses of Rev. His Holiness Shastri Shri Pandurang V. Athavale. 2186
Glimpses of light. 3339
Glimpses of Mennonite history. 2406
Glimpses of Mennonite history and doctrine. 2406
Glimpses of the beyond. 3506
Glimpses of the celestial country. 897
Glimpses of the Christ. 2048
Glimpses of the life and work of George Douglas Watson. 3137
Glimpses of truth. 996, 1446
Global broadcasts of His grace. 2300
Global Christ. 2437
Global justice & development. 1155
Global living here and now. 1063
Global mission of God's people. 2550
Global mission of the church. 850
Global odyssey. 43
Global view of Christian missions from Pentecost to the present. 2525
Globe-trotting for the gospel. 2516
Gloria. 2692
Gloria Christi. 2520
gloria" hymnal. 812
Gloria Patri. 3713
Gloria psalter. 2985
Glories and virtues of Mary. 2353
Glories of Czestochowa and Jasna Gora. 1399
Glories of divine grace. 1752
Glories of Mary. 2355, 2359
Glories of Mary in Boston. 3252
Glories of Mays. 2359
Glories of Our Lord. 2039
Glories of the Catholic church in art, architecture and history. 1156
Glories of the Cross. 1556
Glories of the Holy Ghost. 1832
Glories of the love of Jesus. 1999
Glories of the Sacred Heart. 3269
Glories of the sacred heart of Jesus. 3269
Glorification. 2693
Glorified Christ. 736
Glorious afflictions. 1752
Glorious appearing. 3319
Glorious Assumption of the Mother of God. 2358
Glorious body of Christ. 1120
Glorious church. 365
Glorious company. 71
Glorious Galilean. 2006
Glorious gospel. 1229
Glorious gospel hymns. 1237
Glorious heritage, 1885-1965. 3833
Glorious imperative. 2436
Glorious kingdom of the Father foretold. 129
Glorious Koran. 2184
Glorious liberty. 967
Glorious living. 2488
Glorious Maccabees. 2305
Glorious names of Jesus. 2021
Glorious praise. 3553
Glorious presence. 3775
Glorious purpose. 2619
Glorious revival under King Hezekiah. 3229
Glorious ride. 2309, 3253
Glorious St. Joseph, guardian of God's lilies. 2132
Glorious Ten commandments. 1314
Glory and the Way of the Cross. 436, 2011
Glory and the wonder of the Bible. 231
Glory at the right hand: Psalm 110 in early Christianity. 579
Glory awaits me. 1350
Glory beyond all comparison. 1006
Glory days. 1343, 3801
Glory, hallelujah! 1872
Glory in the church. 3228
Glory in the Cross. 106
Glory, jest, and riddle. 1818
Glory of a nation. 3193
Glory of Christ. 2047, 2059, 2482
Glory of Christian worship. 3004
Glory of Galatians. 381
Glory of God. 1716, 1732, 3206
Glory of God and the transfiguration of Christ. 1731
Glory of God in the Christian calling. 363
Glory of God is intelligence. 2149
Glory of going on and other life studies. 3199
Glory of Golgotha. 2215
Glory of grace. 472
Glory of His grace. 1752
Glory of His rising. 2051
Glory of His robe. 2396
Glory of Israel. 865, 2636
Glory of man. 2046
Glory of Mormonism. 2606
Glory of priesthood. 3676
Glory of the cross. 1389
Glory of the empty tomb. 2054

Glory of the God-head in the Gospel of John. 420, 2000
Glory of the immortal life. 1697
Glory of the impossible. 2537
Glory of the Jewish holidays. 1614
Glory of the manger. 1893
Glory of the ministry. 2905
Glory of the sun. 2608
Glory of the triune God. 3711
Glory of Thy people. 1365
Glory plain. 1229
Glory road. 107, 2031
Glory to Thy name. 3236, 3715
Glory today for conquest tomorrow, significant sermons. 164
Glory within you: modern man and the spirit. 3521
Glory woods. 734, 1773
Glorying in the cross. 1466
Glorying in the cross, and other sermons. 3342
Glossary of important symbols. 3573
Glossary of Jewish terms. 2085
Glossary of liturgical and ecclesiastical terms. 3639
Glossary of Sanskrit from the spiritual tradition of India. 1815
... A glossary of the West Saxon Gospels. 47
Glossolalia. 1716
Glossolalia in the Apostolic church. 1716
Glossolalia phenomenon. 1716
Gloucester fragments. 3572
Gnesio-Lutherans, Philippists, and Formulators. 879, 3668
Gnigma of the Bay Psalm book. 581
Gnomic poetry in Anglo-Saxon. 1717
Gnosis. 348, 1717, 1718
Gnosis and the New Testament. 350, 1718
Gnosis: divine wisdom. 3104
Gnosis or ancient wisdom in the Christian Scriptures. 206
Gnostic attitude. 1718
Gnostic dialogue. 1718
Gnostic ethics and Mandaean origins. 2327
Gnostic gospels. 1718
Gnostic heresies. 1718
Gnostic Paul. 372, 1718
Gnostic problem. 1718
Gnostic religion. 1709, 1718
Gnostic treatise on resurrection from Nag Hammadi. 1718
Gnosticism. 1717, 1718
Gnosticism and agnosticism. 1718
Gnosticism and early Christianity. 1717, 1718
Gnosticism in Corinth. 346, 1718
Gnostics and their remains, ancient and mediaeval. 1718
Go! 348, 1566
Go, Abraham, go. 5, 993
Go & make disciples. 1573
Go back, you didn't say "May I" 1931
Go-between God. 1832
Go! Champions of Light. 2535
Go for the gold. 985
Go forth. 2577
Go free. 2160
Go from your father's house. 1015, 3757
Go gentle into the night. 2881, 3545
Go Gospel. 435, 436
Go-groups. 2480
Go home and tell. 2511
Go in peace. 1327, 2811
Go inquire of the Lord. 1069
Go, make disciples. 1571
Go on singing. 585, 982
Go out in joy! 893, 1806, 1808
Go placidly amid the noise and haste. 933, 1467, 3359
Go quickly and tell. 1431, 2300
Go tell it everywhere. 867
Go tell the people. 2900
Go till you guess. 218
Go to heaven. 974, 1001
Go to Joseph, our unfailing mediator. 2132
Go to the mountain. 2815
Go up higher. 3725
Go 'wana gwa'ih sat'hah yon de'yas dah'gwah. 3332
Go with God. 2888
Go with the gospel. 1765, 3356
Go ye and teach. 934
'Go ye' means you! 2483
Go ye therefore. 1563
Goal and the glory. 102
Goal and the way. 2322
Goal of creation. 455
Goal of life. 2723
Goal posts. 3887
Goals. 1008

Goals and guidelines for use in strenghtening and expanding interchurch cooperation in Massachusetts as a whole, in clusters of towns and cities, in neighborhoods and towns. 1045
Goals of Jesus. 2066
"God," 131, 967, 1473, 1720, 1722, 1724, 1725, 1726, 1728, 1730, 3207, 3774
God a present help. 1720, 3751
God; a timely consideration of what the Bible says about God and his relationship to you. 1719
God, a woman, and the way. 3459
God—after all. 1445
God after God. 175, 1733
God against slavery. 3425
God—alive! 3627
God, Allah, and Ju Ju. 13
God always says yes. 975
God amid the shadows. 3375
God among men. 795
... God among the Germans. 1707
God and a mouse. 902
God and America's future. 3746
God and atheism. 1738
God and Caesar. 1142
God and Caesar in East Germany. 1708
God and children. 1610
God and church apart. 3616
God and company. 1722
God and country. 2228
... God and creation. 785, 1371, 1722
God and creatures. 3643
God and evil. 1746, 3610
God and evolution. 1580, 1581
God and Freud. 1673, 2997
God and gods in Hinduism. 1743
God and Gog. 1513
God and government. 1152, 3446
God and His Bible. 236
God and His covenant people. 1726
God and His creation. 1725
God and his friends in the Old Testament. 504, 2679
God and His helpers. 1721
God and his image. 651
God and His infinite perfections. 785
God and His people. 482, 597, 616, 654, 1119
God and His works. 1728, 3694
God and His world. 3765
God & history. 1818
God and history in early Christian thought. 1820
God and history in the Old Testament. 500, 503, 1731
God and human anguish. 3610
... God and human progress. 1725
God and human suffering. 3540
God and I. 1440, 1722, 2284, 2881
God and I are partners. 3383
God and I through seance. 3317, 3506
God and Incarnation in mid-nineteenth century German theology. 3637
God and intelligence in modern philosophy. 1727
God and its relation with the finite self in Tagore's philosophy. 1732, 3579
God and Jack Wilson. 1453
God and little children. 897
God and mammon. 1076, 3443
God and man. 62, 253, 270, 1725, 1729, 1730, 1731, 1735, 2300, 2982, 3206
God and man in history. 1819
God and man in Judaism. 2137
God and man in missions. 2492
God and man in the Koran. 1733, 2185
God and man in the Old Testament. 303
God and man in the Sefer hasidim. 2137
God and man in the thought of Hamann. 1732, 1782
God and man in time. 1818
God and man in Washington. 1149
God and man in Washngton. 1149
God and mankind versus Satan. 2616
God and man's destiny. 3097
God and marriage. 2336
God and me. 1734
God & men. 1094, 1721
God and Mr. Wells. 3801
God and music. 2632
God and my heart. 858
God and myself. 782, 2702
God & nature. 2843
God and one redhead: Mary Slessor of Calabar. 2506, 3425
God and other gods. 3064
God and other minds. 1738
God and our parish. 3857
God and ourselves. 1719, 1723, 1731, 2945
God and personality. 1728, 1730
God and Peter. 2824
God and philosophy. 1740, 2672
God and politics. 1085, 1087
God and rationality. 1106
God and reality. 1730, 2673

God and reality in modern thought. 2843
God and reason. 1720, 1730, 3103, 3607
God and secularity. 1733
God and sons. 3664
God and temple. 1944
God and the astronomers. 3078
God and the atom. 64
God & the Bible. 83
God and the celebration of life. 1735
God and the census. 2527
God and the city. 1730
God and the common life. 3098
God and the cosmic order. 1730
God and the cosmos. 100
God and the day's work. 957, 3784
God and the family. 1603
God and the future. 507, 1528
God and the golden rule. 1735
God and the good. 3532, 3621
God and the grotesque. 1845
God and the H-bomb. 103
God and the himan condition. 3648
God and the interior life. 3489
God and the modern mind. 1740
God and the negro, synopsis of God and
  the negro; or, The Biblical record of the
  race of Ham. 275
God and the new knowledge. 1734
God and the people. 1730, 2930
God and the permission of evil. 3610
God and the problem of evil. 2335, 3610
God and the rhetoric of sexuality. 502,
  1731
God and the rich society. 1075
God and the self. 3104
God and the soul. 1267, 3066
God and the Soviets. 3257
God and the story of Judaism. 2151
God and the story of Judaism [by]
  Dorothy K. Kripke, Meyer Levin.
  Stephen Kraft: art ed.; Lorence F.
  Bjorklund: illustrations. 2151
God and the struggle for existence. 3099
God and the supernatural. 780, 781
God and the teenager. 757, 3889
God and the unconscious. 2159, 3001
God and the universe. 945, 3078, 3079,
  3158
God and the universe of faiths. 3107
God and the ways of knowing. 1720
God and the world. 1735, 3651
God and the world of man. 787
God and these times. 1340
God and this troubled world. 3623
God and three shillings. 695
God and timelessness. 1533
God and utopia. 1064
God and war. 3791, 3794
God and word. 3620
God and world in early Christian theology.
  3658
God and world order. 3594
God and you. 1095, 3885
God and your family. 1606
God around us. 899
God as Christians see him. 1720
God as first principle in Ulrich of
  Strasburg. 3645, 3722
God as form. 1743
God as I understand Him. 1723
God as mother: a feminine theology in
  India. 3005
God as spirit. 1729, 2046
God as woman, woman as God. 3833
God at large. 1064
God at my elbow. 215, 1359
God at work. 1720
God at work in His world. 733
God at work in Israel. 503
God at work in science. 3103
God at your door. 1555
God, authority, and salvation. 3641
God B.C. 599, 1731, 2042
God being my helper. 1829
God beyond doubt. 2998
God beyond knowledge. 1729
God beyond nature. 1737
God bit. 1520
God bless America. 162
God bless U, daughter. 3474
God blesses you real good. 1754
God, blood and society. 672
God breaks in. 2385
God-breathed book. 3575
God builds the church in Latin America.
  2549
God builds the church in South Asia.
  2547
God builds the church through
  congregational witness. 3830
God, but I'm bored! 983
God-called man. 1727
God called the play. 2307
God calling; a devotional classic. 1433
God calls. 1719
God Calls me. 1722
God can do anything. 2490

God can do it. 1036
God can heal you now. 1599
God can make it happen. 984
God can transform the world. 979
God; can we find him? 1738
God can work through you. 989
God cares. 506, 2287
God cares for me. 1734
God cares for us. 3181
God cares for you. 2981
God, carpenter and man. 1450
God-centered evangelism. 1567
God-centered faith. 2914
God-centered living. 729
God-centered religion. 727, 729
God-centered therapy. 2781
God chose them. 338
God, Christ, and pagan. 1393
God, Christ, and the church. 781
God, Christ, and the church; Catholic
  doctrine and practice explained, with
  answers to objections and examples. 787
God, Christ, and the world. 3657
God, Christ, Church. 2944
God confronts man in history. 1094
God, conscience and the Bible. 1731
God-controlled lives. 338
God created me. 3185
God, creator and sustainer. 3171
God day by day. 2396
God dealing with slavery. 3512
God demands doctrinal preaching. 217,
  2907
God demands reparation. 1483
God, demons, and others. 2635, 2663
God did it, but how? 204
God did not ordain silence. 1110
God didn't put elephants in trees. 1384
God died at three o'clock. 2032
God does guide us. 2754
God doesn't live here any more. 1090
God, dreams, and revelation. 1479
God dwells with his people. 2046, 3579
God enthused man. 1406
God-evaders. 1066
God, evolution, and mind healing. 3077
God exists. 1730
God-experience. 2999
God experience: essays in hope. 1729
God explosion in my life. 39, 1357
God, family, country. 1232, 1603
God—fellowship or frustration. 986
God-filled life. 1454
God fixation. 1092
God for all seasons. 1264
God for every day. 1000
God for science? 3081
God, freedom, and evil. 1738
God gave the growth. 110
God gave the increase. 2535
God gets in the way of a sailor. 3136
God given. 1720
God-given messages. 1072
God-given mother. 2356
God gives new life. 1384
God giveth the increase. 2971
God glorified in his works of providence
  and grace. 3810
God goes to Golgotha. 2215
God goes to high school. 3881
God goes to murderer's row. 2813
God, gold and government. 1134
God, gold and government; the
  interrelationship of Christianity, freedom,
  self-government and economic well-
  being. 1134
God, grass, and grace. 1415
God guides us. 3181
God has a communication problem. 2904
God has a plan for you. 976
God has a story too. 288, 2934, 3357
God has many names. 1079, 1100
God has special places. 2983
God has spoken. 277, 539, 3225
God has the answer. 955, 1238
God has the answer for you! 1360
God hath chosen. 3848, 3861
God hath spoken. 1054, 1273, 3356
God hath spoken at sundry times and in
  divers manners. 1727
God help me! 3064
God, help me understand. 1734
God—here and now! 956, 990, 1728, 3650,
  3693
God: his names and nature. 1723
God, his prophets and his children. 3542
God, His Son Jesus, and man. 622
God, His world, and me. 2965
God, history, and historians. 1819
God, history, and the end of the world.
  604
God holds your tomorrows. 1741
God I don't believe in. 1456
God, I don't understand. 3661
God I love. 1012
God I serve. 988

God I want. 1729
God idea. 1723
God-idea of the ancients. 3389
God in a Rolls Royce. 131
... God in a world at war. 1725
God in action. 1457, 1724, 1725, 1828,
  2225, 2973
God in action. [1st ed.]. 1725
God in Africa. 12
God in all seasons. 1623
God in American history. 3746
God in an age of atheism. 100
God in an evolving universe. 3082
God in Christ. 104, 2036
God in contemporary thought. 1729
God in creation. 2675
God in creation and evolution. 1580
... God in creation and evolution, and the
  church of every age in light and shade.
  1379
God in disease. 2980
God in education. 3096, 3190
God in everything. 3073
God in evolution. 3073
God in exile: modern atheism. 101
God in freedom. 3192
God in Greek philosophy to the time of
  Socrates. 2835
God in his Providence. 2980
God in His world. 1542, 1719, 3644
God in history. 1189, 1192, 1732
God in Hollywood. 1824
God in human thought. 2672
God in man's experience. 576
God in modern philosophy. 1720, 1732
God in my day. 2383
God in my family. 1604
God in my home. 1447
God in my kitchen. 1439
God in my unbelief. 1011
God in nature. 1719
God in nature and revelation. 3226
God in our daily life. 998
God in our home. 1606
God in our house. 1263
God in our lives. 1727, 2395, 3765
God in our public schools. 3189
God in our street. 1727, 2044
God in our widening world. 935, 1728
God in our work. 958
God in public: political theology beyond
  Niebuhr. 1085
God in reason and intuition. 1737
God in search of man. 2138, 2139, 3489
God in the American schools. 3189
God in the classroom. 3096
God in the Constitution. 1151
God in the dock; essays on theology and
  ethics. 3622
God in the Garden. 1755, 3231
God in the hands of man. 2211
God in the heart of things. 3621
God in the modern world. 1722
God in the New Testament. 1730
God in the Old Testament. 1719
God in the present. 1722
God in the shadows. 3292, 3359
God in the slums. 3293
God in the space age. 1722, 3069, 3073
God in these times. 1064, 1728
God in three Persons. 3711
God in unexpected places. 989
God in us. 90, 1104, 1674
God in us: we in God. 1585
God in you. 1137
God incarnate. 1892, 1893, 2001, 2036
God incognito. 1726, 2213
God infinite. 3608
God infinite and reason. 1720, 1730
God is. 100, 101, 1720, 1726, 1737, 1738,
  1739
God is a good friend to have. 1724
God is a good God. 2808
God is a millionaire. 3325
God is a new language. 796
God is a sea. 3490
God is a spirit. 3663
God is a verb! 2896
God is able. 1599
God is always greater. 2735
God is at the organ. 1727
God is at work. 1728
God is beautiful, man. 619
God is dead. 1417
God is doing it. 1036
God is dying. 864, 2057
God is everywhere. 1720, 1733, 1737
God is for everybody. 998
God is for real, man. 619
God is good. 1721, 1734
God is good, by Mary Alice Jones in
  collaboration with Kate
  Smallwood.tIllustrated by Elizabeth
  Webbe. 1734
God is good; teacher's manual for
  perform-a-text 1. 3181
God is great, God is good. 1604, 2957

God is here; let's celebrate! 585
*God is in many places. 2172
God is inescapable. 1727
God is light. 66, 3288
God is light, God is love. 324
God is love. 414, 624, 1735, 1736, 1741,
  2263, 2266, 3602
God is mercy. 2231
God is my adventure. 3130
God is my captain. 1060
God is my friend. 617, 1435
"God is my fuehrer," 2301
God is my helper. 617
God is my landlord. 1792, 3702
God is my life. 1708
God is my pilot. 81
God is my record. 3545
God is near. 3406
God is never absent. 1596
God is no fool. 2385
God is no island. 2299
God is no more. 2071
God is not dead. 1056, 1557, 1721
God is not yet dead. 3091
God is one. 1724
God is real. 1719
God is red. 1091
God is the answer. 1724, 3751
God is there. 1450
God is up to something. 1845
God is waiting to meet you. 67
God is where you are. 3362
God is with us. 66, 2012, 3150
God, I've got a problem. 983
God, Jesus, and man. 1722
God, Jesus, and Spirit. 3651
God Juggernaut and Hinduism in India.
  1814
God Juh! 1113
God keeps an open house. 966
God keeps His promise. 622
God knowable and unknowable. 1735
God knows you. 1734
God leads us to witness at home. 2408
God lifts my sights. 2301
God lives! 644, 983
God lives in his city. 1728
God lives in word and world. 1005
God longs for family. 1610, 3307
God love you. 1452, 2396
God loved the muddle. 631, 1383
God loves all people. 941
God loves and plans for me. 3164
God loves everybody. 3172
God loves like that! 1425
God loves me. 901, 1734, 3158
God loves me, too. 1736
God loves my kitchen best. 3830
God loves the dandelions. 1626
God loves the pagans. 2559
God loves us. 3163
God loves you. 1609
God made me new. 1362
God made me ... to be responsible. 3763
God made the sea, the sand, and me.
  1384
God made the violet too. 1650
God made the world. 296, 1726, 1733
God made them great. 48
God made this lovely, lovely world. 1734
God! Make me a man! 3031
God make me brave for life. 2399
God makes a difference. 1454
God makes the difference. 3104
God makes the rivers to flow. 2387
God makes the world. 631
God-man. 1080, 1720, 2002, 2035, 2048
God, man, and Archie Bunker. 25, 3618
God, man, and atomic war. 103
God, man and church growth. 1171, 2307
God, man, and disaster. 1460
God, man & epic poetry. 2232
God, man, and history. 1733
God, man, and philosophy. 1854
God, man, and religion. 3108
God, man & salvation. 652, 3647
God, man and Satan. 1428, 2470, 3094
God, man, and sin. 3412
God, man and society. 3442
God, man and the absolute. 5
God, man and the church. 3482
God, man, and the planetary age. 1729
God, man, and the thinker. 3106
God, man and the universe. 762
God, man, and time. 3659
God meets man. 3260, 3382
God meets us where we are. 1004, 1806
God, money, and you. 987
... God, nature and attributes. 1730
God, nature, man. 3249
God never fails. 2388
God news from Matthew. 443
God nobody knows. 1726
God of a hundred names. 2890
God of all comfort. 1727
God of all: Sri Ramakrishna's approach to
  religious plurality. 3020

God of all the earth. 3549
God of battles, a soldier's faith. 1543
God of Buddha. 1703, 1721
God of Daniel S. 2141
God of evil. 1738
God of Exodus. 1584
God of faith and reason. 1106
God of forgiveness and healing in the theology of Karl Rahner. 1733, 3019
God of fundamentalism. 1690
God of great surprises. 1011
...The God of Israel. (Rev. and enl.) 1731
...The God of Israel. (Rev. and enl.) (Abridged ed.) 1731
God of Israel (The), the God of Christians. 3720
God of Jane. 2993, 3241
God of Jesus Christ. 865, 3715
God of love. 787
God of our faith. 3647
God of our fathers. 563, 1727
God of reason. 2673
God of science. 3073, 3083
God of space and time. 651
God of the beginnings. 1732
God of the bible. 1723, 3117, 3516
God of the Christians. 1725
God of the deaf adolescent. 939
God of the early Christians. 1724
God of the impossible. 986, 2356
God of the liberal Christian. 1052
God of the living. 3105
God of the lucky. 3344
God of the Old Testament in relation to war. 501, 1719, 1726
God of the oppressed. 2222
God of the philosophers. 1737
God of the present age. 1727, 3330
God of the scientists. 3081
God of the scientists, God of the experiment. 3081
God of the untouchables. 1365, 1778
God of the witches. 3824
God on Main Street. 1036
God on our minds. 984
God on the Bowery. 2697
God on the gridiron. 102
God on the secular campus. 3756
God on trial. 101, 3371
God or chaos. 1723
God or Christ? 3628
God or Ichabod? 1060
God? or Lucifer? 1721
God or man? 2998
God our contemporary. 1062, 1341
God our help. 1721, 2980
God our loving enemy. 1742, 2306
God our Savior. 3295
God our Saviour. 3295
God owns my business. 3539
God, pain, and evil. 3540
God passes by. 129, 130
God planned it that way. 2983
God plans for happy families. 901
God planted five seeds. 1903
God-players. 2323
God-pointed life. 1405
God portrays more women. 3839
God portrays women. 3839
God, power, and evil. 3610
God prays. 3207
God present. 2937
God present as mystery. 3628
God probably doesn't know I exist. 984
God question and modern man. 1056
God question in Thomas Aquinas and Martin Luther. 1732, 3697
God reigns. 543, 3076
God rejected. 100
God, religion and faith. 763
God, religion, and family life. 1611
God remembers. 600
God revealed. 1721
...God revealed in the process of creation. 2674
God revealed through His world. 3182
God reveals himself. 1739
God, revelation, and authority. 1552
God runs my business. 2217
God s secret agent. 2943
God said, Let there be woman. 3832
God, Satan, Messiah ... and? 524, 2095
... God save our noble Union! and other poems for the times. 3207
God save the home? 1838
God, science, and the Bible. 3080
God, secularization, and history. 3431, 3616
God seekers for a new age. 1417
God sees a beautiful you. 470, 994
God sent a man. 2133
God sent his son. 3164
God sent me to Korea. 2537, 3387
God, sex and war. 946
God, sex, & youth. 3388
God so loved. 1113, 1562, 3286
God so loved, He gave. 1113

God so loved the world. 293, 1965, 3019, 3164, 3227
God so loves the world. 1064
God, some conversations. 1722
God sovereign and man free. 2911
God spake by Moses. 562
God speaking. 198
God speaking in the first person in His kingdom. 500
God speaks. 604, 1437, 2287, 3207
God speaks again in Palestine. 2763
God speaks from the sky in open vision. 3318
God speaks in daily work. 2287
God speaks in my life. 1725, 2292
God speaks in the Bible. 3556
God speaks Navajo. 1497, 2677
God speaks; the theme of creation and its purpose. 1381
God speaks through nature. 2676, 2931
God speaks through suffering. 3540
God speaks through the Bible. 647
God speaks to an X-rated society: are the Ten commandments still valid? 1314
God speaks to man. 305
God speaks to me. 1450, 1734, 3158, 3183
God speaks to men. 309
God speaks to modern man. 3382
God speaks to women today. 3844
God speaks today. 168, 323
God spoke one word. 863, 1266
God Squad. 885, 1305, 1426
God stalk. 1447
God still answers prayer. 2890
God still guides. 3143
God still helps. 1452
God still lives. 1062
God still loves my kitchen. 3843
God still makes sense. 1722
God still speaks. 1317
God still speaks in the space age. 1063
God struck me dead. 2682
God-talk. 3070
God that Jesus saw. 1722
God that Job had. 549
God the almighty, man, and Satan. 742, 1924
God the anonymous. 1735
God, the atom, and the universe. 205
God, the Bible, truth and Christian theology. 1049
God, the Christlike. 2036
God—the cornerstone of our life. 759
God the Creator. 1381, 3150
God the Creator; on the transcendence and presence of God. 2739
God the creator; the Hastie lectures in the University of Glasgow, 1935. 1740
God, the disturber. 2437, 3367
God, the eternal paradox. 2215
God, the eternal torment of man. 1719
God the Father. 476, 1232, 1729, 1731, 2063
God the Father, meditations. 2388
God, the future of man. 1154
God the greatest poet. 1737
God the Holy Ghost. 1827, 1828
God, the invisible king. 1728
God the loving Father. 3147
God the of the beginnings. 1732
God the problem. 1729
God the redeemer. 1602, 2036
... God the redeemer, the redemption from sin as wrought by Jesus Christ, the son of God. 3151
God, the rod, and your child's bod. 1467
God the Son. 929, 1972
God the stranger. 1486, 2301
God, the substance of all form. 2694
God -- the supreme steward. 1727
... God, the universal reality. 3865
God the unknown. 762
God the unknown, and other essays. 762
God the worshipful. 1741
God to glorify. 3531
God to glorify, through Christian stewardship. 3531
God tomorrow. 1579
God transcendent. 2933
God translated. 1721
God trip. 1587, 2731
God unknown. 1719
God up close. 399, 2015
God up there? 3707
God used sermons. 3345
God ventures. 924
God wants me to learn. 3538
God wants you. 3184
God wants you to be well. 1598
God wants you to smile. 3844
God was, God is, God shall be. 1721
God was in Christ. 2035
God was in Christ, an essay on incarnation and atonement. [New ed.]. 2035
God was there. 1453
God wash the world and start again. 1422

God we need. 1728
God we seek. 3106
God, we thank You. 903
... The God we trust. 74, 1722
God we worship. 1741
God, what people have said about Him. 1731
God who acts. 651, 652
God who cares. 296, 1062, 2139
God who comes. 2385
God who dares to be man. 3665
God who is there. 66
God who likes me. 2274
God who loves. 1739
God who loves us. 1268
God who makes a difference. 66
God who redeems. 3030
God who saves us. 198
God who shows himself. 1066
God who speaks. 1090, 1727, 3848
God who speaks and shows. 3616
God whom we ignore. 1741
"God, why am I so afraid?" 1619
God, why did You do that? 3610
God will do it. 1036
God will help you. 2980
God will not let me go. 981
God will work with you but not for you. 1726
God wills it. 3420
God wills us free. 1132
God winning us. 2690
God with men. 216
God with us. 1104, 1983, 1999, 2040, 2935, 3644, 3857
God with us [study book]. 637
God within. 1738, 2225, 2386, 3058, 3094
God within process. 2943
God without thunder. 3079, 3081
God, woman & ministry. 1422, 3836
... God working through mankind. 3159
God works through medicine. 1599
God writes straight with crooked lines. 1006
God wrote His gospel in His nature. 3500
God you can know. 1720
God, you've got to be kidding. 1315
Goddena, the unknown god. 3518
Goddess. 1742
Goddess faith. 2723
Goddess of love. 55
Goddesses of Sun and Moon. 2661
Godless Christians. 1417
Godly and the ungodly. 1071
Godly exhortation by occasion of the late judgement of God. 3606
Godly kingdom of Tudor England. 1021, 1221
Godly man in Stuart England. 45
Godly pastor. 1781, 3231
Godly rebellion. 772, 1292
Godly union and concord. 1226
Godman. 3415
Godmanhood as the main idea of the philosophy of Vladimir Solovyev. 3105
Godmen of India. 1778
Gods. 3092, 3098
Gods, a dictionary of the deities of all lands. 3092
God's adventures. 927
God's agents--the prophets, and other Biblical tales. 2949
...God's amazing world. 1728
God's amazing grace. 1436
God's ambassadress. 663
Gods and demons. 2652
Gods and games. 2854
Gods and goddesses in art and legend. 1743
Gods and goddesses of ancient Greece. 2660
Gods and heroes. 1631, 1743, 2352, 2656, 2657, 2658, 2662
Gods & heroes from Viking mythology. 2665
Gods and heroes of the Bhagavad-gita. 2663
Gods and heroes of the Greeks. 2660, 2661
...Gods and heroes of the North. 2666
Gods and heroes of war. 2650
Gods and men. 1280, 1897, 3110
Gods and mortals in classical mythology. 2658
Gods and myths of northern Europe. 2659
Gods, and other lectures. 1654
Gods and rituals. 3110
Gods and spacemen in ancient Israel. 533, 1917, 2018
Gods and spacemen in the ancient East. 3069
Gods and spacemen of the ancient past. 318, 1917
Gods & spacemen throughout history. 1917
Gods and symbols of ancient Egypt. 1502

Gods and the kings. 693, 2739
God's angels need no wings. 43
God's angry men. 2950
God's angry side. 1742
God's animals. 481
God's answer. 1436
God's answer for the unequally yoked. 2337
God's answer to anxiety. 2808
God's answer to evolution. 1580
God's answer to juvenile delinquency. 2161
God's answer to man's question. 164
God's answer to man's sin. 1555
God's answers to human dilemmas. 517, 993
God's answers to man's doubts. 2562
God's approbation of our labours necessary to the hope of success. 3363
God's architecture. 3290
Gods are good. 3145
Gods await. 1728, 3688
God's awesome challenge. 2546
God's awful warnings to a giddy, careless, sinful world. 1734
God's back pastures, a book of the rural parish. 3253
God's "bad boys." 2680
God's balance of faith and freedom. 1596
God's bandit, the story of Don Crione, Father of the Poor. 2743
God's bandit, the story of Don Orione. 2743
God's basic law. 1313
... God's battle ax. 1720
God's best for my life. 1435
God's best secrets. 1432, 1725
God's better thing. 1719
God's Biblical sacrificial blueprints and specifications for reconciling the world into Himself. 235, 986
God's Biblical sacrificial blueprints and specifications for reconciling the world unto himself. 970
God's big little words. 2228
God's big promise. 1726
God's blessed man. 3356
God's blueprints. 3397
God's board. 2259
God's book. 234
God's Book for me. 618
God's book speaking for itself. 1720
God's boycott of sin, a consideration of hell and pacifism. 1802
God's breath in man and in humane society. 694
God's bullies. 1087, 2593
God's business. 1076
God's calendar on the wall of time from creation to the consummation. 607
God's call to public responsibility. 1077
God's calling. 1393, 2486
God's candle. 1725
God's care is everywhere. 2983
... God's care of mankind. 3159
God's challenge for today. 955
God's challenge to modern apostasy. 1090
God's challenge to youth. 956
God's channel of truth. 3383
God's charge unto Israel. 1504
God's child. 1054
God's children. 1734
God's children at prayer. 2886
God's children at work and play. 3164
God's children in glory land. 1794
God's children living together. 3764
God's children pray. 2249
God's choice of men. 615
God's chosen people. 511, 629
God's Christmas. 1111
*God's Church and my life. 3161
God's church for today. 1124
God's church is everywhere. 1199
God's city in the jungle. 39, 3718
God's claim on you. 3187
God's clock of the Bible. 318
God's colony in man's world. 1280
God's communicating door. 2991
God's contact man, a story of pastoral evangelism. 1563
God's control. 975
God's country. 1061
God's covenant faithfulness. 2975
God's covenant of blessing. 1376
God's covenants and our time. 1376
God's covenent. 644
God's created speech. 21, 1927, 2185
God's creation. 1381
God's creation and salvation. 3648
God's cross in our world. 1721
God's cure for anxious care. 1354
God's day, today and everyday. 900
Gods, demons, and others. 2663
God's discipline. 471
God's dispensations. 1719
God's doing. 158

God's drama in seven acts. 2059, 2299
God's dynamite. 2875
God's eagles. 3282
God's early heroes. 494, 627
God's education of man. 1050
God's encounter with man. 2876
God's engineer. 3899
God's eonian purpose. 1723
God's estimate of man. 3338
God's eternal design. 1528, 3216
God's eternal good pleasure. 470, 2975, 3353
God's eternal power. 468
God's eternal purpose revealed. 2981
God's everlasting sign. 3261
God's everlasting "yes" 2932
God's failure or man's folly! 2320
God's faith in man. 3345
God's family. 631, 1722, 3554
God's family in god's world. 1725
God's fantastic creation. 1381
God's fellow-workers. 967
God's final message to the nations of the world. 1210
God's final messengers; or, Pharaoh's cup refilled. 2465
God's finger wrote freedom. 1314
... God's first children. 630
God's first words. 520
God's fool. 1640, 2555
God's fools. 3370
God's footprint on my floor. 181
God's forever family. 1573
God's forgetful pilgrims. 1119
God's formula for success and prosperity. 3539
God's free-lancers. 3860
God's freedom. 471
God's friend. 4
God's friendly world. 3764
God's friendship. 2394
Gods from outer space. 1917
God's frozen people. 2191
God's gambler. 1366, 1702
God's garage. 3359
God's garden of segregation. 3329
God's gentlemen. 1224, 2540
Gods, ghosts, and ancestors. 1634
Gods, ghosts, and men in Melanesia. 3109
God's gift. 1721
God's gift baby. 495, 1784, 1785
God's gift of tongues. 438, 1717
God's gift, the Holy Spirit! 1833
*God's gifts to us. 1722, 3163
God's glory displayed. 345
Gods, goddesses, and myths of creation. 3140
God's gold. 145
God's gold in my hand. 3530
God's gold mines. 160
God's good gifts. 3150
God's good news. 2901, 3164
God's good will. 963
God's goodness and severity. 1699, 1728
God's got a better idea. 1633, 2896
God's grace and man's hope. 1097
*God's grace and my need. 3161, 3187
*God's grace for God's people. 1329
God's grace in Galatians. 380
God's grace in history. 1153
God's gracious design; a new look at Catholic doctrine. 3661
God's grade in history. 1153
God's great gift. 1833
... God's great plan. 648, 1723, 3385
... God's great plan for mankind. 3159
God's great plan for you. 2322
God's great plan of salvation. 3290
God's great searchlight, and other sermons. 1555
God's great secret. 2175
God's great soul winners. 1575
God's greatest gift. 1232, 1695, 2266
God's greatest hits. 254
God's guerrillas. 1572, 3890
God's guests of tomorrow, a mystical visit to purgatory and a consideration of the sabbatine privilege. 3006
God's guide for man's faith and practice. 302
God's guiding hand. 879
God's hall of mirrors. 1313
God's hand I see. 2388
God's hand in America. 3743
God's hand in my life. 1012, 3380
God's hand in our lives. 2980
God's happy people. 181
God's healing community. 1600
God's healing power. 1600
God's heart-touch. 141, 166
God's Heartbreak Hill. 1445
God's hedge. 3542
God's heralds. 568
God's heroes. 3284
Gods, heroes and men of ancient Greece. 2662
God's highways. 2571

God's history. 540
God's hour. 899
God's house and the old Kingsbridge Road. 2698
God's hurry. 3529
God's ideal woman. 3831
God's image and man's imagination. 1722
God's image in us. 3336
God's images. 317, 318, 2952
God's impatience in Liberia. 2538
God's impatient builder. 1851
Gods in exile. 3686
God's in His heaven--but all's not well with the world. 1513
Gods in plain garb. 3101
Gods in the making. 3821
Gods in the making, and other lectures. 1726
God's incomparable plan. 459
God's incomparable word. 277
God's incredible plan. 2983
God's inerrant Word. 279
God's inescapable nearness. 3368
God's infinite love and ours. 1741
God's infinite mercy. 1736
God's jester. 2943
God's joy in my heart. 2303, 2683
God's joyful people—one in the spirit. 1119
God's junkie. 1255
God's key to health and happiness. 317, 1793
God's kingdom. 2176
God's kingdom for today. 2175
God's kingdom in the New testament. 445
God's kingdom in the Old Testament. 561
God's knotty log. 1720
God's lamb. 2214
God's last letter to man. 458
God's last word. 403
God's last word to man. 403
God's law and God's grace. 2200
God's law of life. 3348
God's law of love. 1735
... God's library. 459
God's light as it came to me. 3478
God's little children. 903
God's little crumbs. 970
... God's little hope. 1845
Giotto's lively people. 2191
God's living oracles. 1726
God's living room. 1261
God's living truths. 1443
God's living word. 2208, 2242
God's lost cause. 1132
...God's love and God's children. 470
God's love for a sinning world. 1556
God's love in human language. 2344
God's love letters. 267, 1737
God's love story. 1555
God's loving-kindness. 901
God's man. 1292, 2709
God's man in Manhattan. 121
God's many houses. 1722
God's marvelous grace to me. 2847
God's master builders. 3178
God's masterpiece. 364
God's masterpieces. 214
God's meaning in life. 1724
Gods, men & monsters from the Greek myths. 2661
God's men, from all nations to all nations. 2515
God's men of color. 875
Gods mercy. 1288
God's message. 1431, 1438
God's message and the messengers. 1061
God's message in troubled times. 160, 547
...God's message to the human soul. 237
God's messengers. 1338
God's method with man. 3289
God's methods for holy living. 955
God's methods with man in time. 1724
God's middlemen. 2131
... God's minute. 1605
God's minutemen. 970
God's minutes. 1451
God's miracle of marriage. 2340
God's miracles. 1101
God's miraculous plan of economy. 2983
God's mission--and ours. 2521
God's missionary plan for the world. 2518
God's moment. 1007
God's mother and ours. 2355
God's my friend. 902
God's new age. 3351
God's new society. 364
God's new thing.Lectures and sermons on revival. 3345
God's news behind the news. 697, 1576, 1743
God's no and God's yes. 2200
God's oath. 1725, 2415
Gods of air and darkness. 1917

Gods of atheism. 100
Gods of generation. 2827
Gods of goodness. 1056
Gods of India. 1743, 1896
Gods of India: their history, character, & worship. 1743
Gods of life. 3604
Gods of love. 2827
Gods of men. 1342
Gods of Mexico. 1898
Gods of myth and stone. 2827
Gods of Northern Buddhism. 702, 1743, 2317
Gods of Olympos. 2657
Gods of our fathers. 2666
Gods of prehistoric man. 3109
Gods of the ancient Northmen. 2665
Gods of the campus. 3537
Gods of the Egyptians. 2659
Gods of the Gentiles. 3140
Gods of the Greeks. 2661
Gods of the North. 2665
God's open. 3346
God's order. 365, 1722
God's out-of-doors. 2675
God's outdoors; a unit for use with nursery children in the church study course. 3173
God's outlaw. 928, 3719
God's own Magna charta. 3337
God's own people. 1122
God's parable. 601, 1719, 1950
God's party. 3004
God's pattern for the home. 1608
God's peace for this new era. 308
God's people. 901, 2814
God's people are different. 964
God's people at work in the parish. 1253
God's people in Christ. 450, 1163
God's people in God's world. 1061, 3442
God's people in transition. 217, 3353
God's people on the march. 757
God's perfect will. 1741
God's picked young men. 216
God's picture gallery. 3374
God's plan. 1049, 3289, 3482, 3535, 3663
God's plan and me. 3649
God's plan for His friends. 3549
God's plan for man. 3660
God's plan for marriage. 2337
God's plan for me. 904, 3549
God's plan for Russ. 3524
God's plan for social security. 2395
God's plan for the future. 609
God's plan for this planet. 607, 1530
... God's plan for world evangelism. 1564
God's plan for world redemption. 2495, 2504
God's plan for your life. 3382
God's plan of salvation. 3288
God's plan of the ages. 1515
God's plan unfolded. 541
God's plan with men. 1724, 3295
God's plot. 3008
God's power for me. 973
God's power to triumph. 1013
God's power within. 1361
God's presence in history. 2138
God's presence in my life. 178, 1006
God's present kingdom. 2174
God's prison gang. 1254
God's program of the ages. 609
God's promise for children. 555, 909
God's promise for today. 2386
God's promises. 623, 1719
God's promises and our prayers. 1606
God's promises come true. 619
God's promises for you. 2394
God's prophecies for plain people. 2947
God's prophetic plan through the ages. 604
God's prophetic word. 1272, 2466
God's prophets versus soothsayers like the Philistines. 605
God's providence unfolded in the Book of Esther. 514
God's provision for Christian living. 967
God's provision for normal Christian living. 966
God's provision for victorious living. 1823
God's psychiatry. 954
God's purpose. 1438
God's purpose in planting the American church. 2546
God's purpose in this age. 3664
God's questions and answers. 558
God's ravens. 2513
God's reach. 957
God's reach for man. 3289
God's regard for the widow and fatherless. 1350
God's remedy for the world's tragedy. 2161
God's requirements, and other sermons. 3755
God's rescues. 3296
God's restless servants. 3185

God's revelations of Himself to men. 3224
God's revolution and man's responsibility. 1065
God's rule and kingdom. 2175
God's rule for Chrstian giving. 976
God's rules for the game of life. 791
God's sabbath. 1723
God's savings and trust co. 1724
God's search for man. 3049
God's secret agent. 2943
God's secret armies within the Soviet Empire. 1110
God's seven abominations. 3411
Gods, sex, and saints. 2600
God's silent preachers. 2675
God's smile. 3508
God's smuggler. 2517
God's soldier. 682
God's Son. 1983
God's Son and God's world. 2395
God's son on earth. 1972, 1983
God's song in my heart. 3843
Gods sovereign government among the nations. 3339
God's special book. 313
God's spirit in the church. 331
God's spirit in you. 1836
God's spiritual universe. 3216
God's spotlight on tomorrow. 1950
God's spy. 1576, 2767
God's stars. 212
God's statesman: the life and work of John Owen. 2753
God's stewards. 3528
God's strategy in human history. 1819
God's sun-lit road to health. 1793
God's super salesman. 1575
God's surprises. 2438, 3360
God's table. 1318
God's tabernacle in Israel's wilderness journey. 1725
God's tent. 517, 2037, 3579
God's time and ours. 1266
God's treasure-house unlocked. 2880
God's tribesman. 3005
God's trobadour. 1642
God's trombones. 3360
God's troubadour. 1642
God's troubadour; the story of Saint Francis of Assisi. With paintings by Giotto. 1642
God's troublemakers. 2555
God's trustees, to whom much is given. 3528
God's trustworthy plan. 1730
God's truth. 789
God's truth made simple. 1721
God's turf. 1255
God's turn. 2930
...God's twenty unclean birds. 480
God's two books. 3079
God's two witnesses and their search for a Christ, told. 1951
God's ultimate purpose. 365, 3364
God's ultimate victory. 1445, 1720
God's ultimatum. 1528
God's underground. 3256
God's underground in Asia. 816
God's unfolding purpose. 293
God's unspeakable gift, the Jesus Paul preached. 376, 2039
God's voice in the stars. 202
God's war. 1728
God's warrior. 2803
God's way. 301, 643, 2929
God's way and ours. 2973
God's way in evolution. 1581
God's way in his world. 1726, 1727
God's way in the New Testament. 348
God's way in the Old Testament. 501
God's way of life. 3513
God's way of reconciliation (studies in Ephesians, chapter 2) 365, 3364
God's way out. 1720
God's way out of futility. 470
God's way to be human. 1001, 2015
God's way to the good life. 1012
God's way with man. 1721, 2056, 2981
God's way with men; a study of the relationship between God and man in providence, "miracle," and prayer. 2981
God's wayfarer. 1363
God's ways. 968, 2015
God's ways, not as our ways. 3848
God's wayside beauty. 1446
God's white throne. 3610
Gods who walk the rainbow. 1778
God's will. 1740
God's will and how to know it. 1741
God's will and our life. 1741
God's will and ours. 2911
God's will and your life. 993
God's will for the world. 1741
God's wisdom and the Holy Bible. 233
God's wisdom in Christ's cross. 1837
Gods with bronze swords. 2656

God's woman. 3840
God's wonder book and an approach to it. 234
God's wonder world. 899, 3148
God's wonderful world. 3186
God's wonderful world of words. 1606
God's wonders of fifty years. 1724
Gods woord in mensenhandon. 3848
God's Word--and man's! 995, 3596
*God's word and my faith. 309
God's word & work; the message of the Old Testament Historical books. 531
God's word at Mass. 2366
God's word for God's world. 2292, 3164
God's word for to-day. 1605
God's Word in man's language. 290
God's word in today's world. 3661
God's word into English. 254
God's Word or the woman's. 799
God's word through preaching. 2900
God's Word to His people. 3225
God's word to Israel. 540
... God's word to man. 3848
God's Word to men. 287, 513, 3224
God's word to women. 3848
God's word to women. Forty-eight Bible lessons of the Women'scorrespondence Bible class. 3845
God's word today. 3148
God's word written. 202
God's words—our prayer. 585
God's words to his children. 908
God's work in God's way. 1904
God's workshop. 2694
God's world. 3439, 3515
God's world and God's people. 616, 625
God's world and Johnny. 902
God's world and mine, revised teacher's manual. 3171
God's world and other sermons. 1558
God's world and ours. 3765
God's world and ours; course for intermediates or junior high school groups in vacation church schools. 3765
God's world and word. 2929
God's world in the making. 2325
God's world of tomorrow. 1513
God's world of wonder. 3766
God's world-program. 1727
God's world through young eyes. 899
God's young church. 337, 1195
Godward. 1448
Godward side of life. 1719
Godwin's Cabalistic encyclopedia. 722
Godwrestling. 566, 2137
Goethe. 1743
Goethe's Faust. 1743
Goforth of China. 1744, 2509
Going further; life-and-death religion in America. 3746
Going God's way. 1443
Going her way. 2938
Going His i[Westwood, N. J.]. 2438
Going His way. 906, 2438
Going home. 932, 3019
Going on in the Christian faith. 966
Going public with one's faith. 216
Going sideways. 3545
Going steady with God. 1432
Going straight. 1576, 1849
"Going, therefore, teach ..." 775
Going to God. 1627
Going to God our Father. 3163
Going to Jerusalem. 2535
Going up? 977
Gold coast at a glance. 1744
Gold Coast mission history. 2523
Gold Coast missions history, 1471-1880. 2523
Gold cord. 1474
Gold dust. 1443
Gold dust: a collection of golden counsels for the sanctifications of daily life. 2398
Gold, frankincense and myrrh. 2575
Gold from God's mint. 1721
Gold from Golgotha. 164, 2057
Gold in Alaska. 2500
Gold in Korea. 2536
Gold is God. 1724
Gold mountain. 2558
Gold of the witches. 3824
Gold ring. 2337
Gold seal Holy Bible. 197, 198
Gold town church. 1338
Gold tried by fire. 691
Gold tried in the fire. 945, 3478, 3817
Gold under the grass. 969
Gold was the mortar. 752
Golden age. 1133
Golden age of Justinian, from the death of Theodosius to the rise of Islam. 85
Golden age of myth & legend. 2650
Golden age sermons for juniors. 906
Golden anniversary. 2179
Golden Anniversary 1910-1960. 3221

Golden anniversary and solemn re-dedication of newly decorated St. John Chrysostom Greek Catholic Church ... 1960. Pastor: Very Rev. Msgr. John Bilock. 1768
Golden anniversary book of the Lutheran Church of the Good Shepherd. 693
Golden arrows. 3206
Golden Bible. 627, 678
Golden Bible atlas. 297
Golden Bible for children. 472
Golden book of Bible stories. 623
Golden book of B'nai Zion congregation, Chattanooga, Tennessee, 1888-1938. 2098
Golden book of Eastern saints. 3279
Golden book of faith. 3209
Golden book of immortality. 1887
Golden book of Oswald Chambers. 1437
Golden book of prayer. 2888
Golden book of religious verse. 3209
Golden book of Tillotson. 473
Golden book on true devotion to Mary. 2354, 2359
Golden booke of the leaden gods. 2655
Golden booklet of the true Christian life. 957
Golden bough. 2312, 2651
Golden bridge. 2694
Golden censer. 2247, 2889
Golden chain. 298, 3295
Golden city. 2690
Golden cow. 1064
Golden dawn. 1656, 1806, 2095
Golden dawn of man. 275
Golden days. 17, 318
Golden deeds in character education. 2590
Golden door. 1480
Golden epistle. 3487
Golden fleece. 722
Golden Fleece and the heroes who lived before Achilles. 80
Golden gate of prayer; devotional studies on the Lord's prayer. 2247
Golden gleams from the heavenly light. 3516
Golden gleanings from the Holy Scriptures. 251
Golden gleanings to comfort the afflicted and help the toiler. 3208
Golden god, Apollo. 57
Golden Gospels of Echternach. 317
Golden Gospels of Echternach, Codex aureus Epternacensis. 317
Golden grove. 3591
Golden harvest. 3735
Golden harvest (Zlote zniwa) 1620
Golden Heart. 179, 182
Golden heritage. 2145
Golden hoard. 2725
Golden hours. 3493
Golden Jubilee. 1747
Golden jubilee history of the Minnesota District of the Wisconsin Evangelical Lutheran Synod and its member congregations, 1918-1968. 3821
Golden jubilee history of the Sacred heart parish. 2628
Golden jubilee of St. Nicholas Ukrainian Catholic Church. 1180
Golden jubilee of the New world. 892
Golden jubilee, St. Matthias' Parish, 1913-1963. 1856
Golden jubilee souvenir, 1870-1920. 1284
Golden jubilee, the Luther league of America. 2272
Golden key. 989
Golden key to Bible interpretation. 201
Golden key to worldly and eternal happiness. 971
Golden ladder. 3500
Golden ladder of stewardship. 3528
Golden Latin Gospels in the library of J. Pierpont Morgan. 317
Golden legend. 3280
Golden legend of Jacobus de Voragine. 1024, 1931
Golden legend of the slums. 3277
Golden legend of young saints. 3280
Golden legends. 3204
Golden light. 2638
Golden light upon the two Americas. 2198, 3300
Golden lyre. 1861
Golden man. 3285
Golden memories. 2697
Golden memories of an earnest life. 3518, 3814
Golden milestone. 2501
Golden milestone in Japan. 2534
Golden moments of religious inspiration. 1445
Golden mountain. 1789, 1928
Golden nuggets. 3373

Golden nuggets from the Greek New Testament. 425
Golden nuggets from the New Testament. 269
Golden nuggets of wisdom. 1450
Golden oil. 1828
Golden parable. 2944
Golden passional, and other sermons. 3349
Golden path to successful personal soul winning. 1570
Golden pot. 2930
Golden prayers. 2893
Golden prologue to the future. 1399
Golden quest of worship. 3853
Golden rule. 1744
Golden rule city. 3147
Golden rules. 1539
Golden rules of world religions. 1744
Golden sands. 1002
Golden sayings of the Blessed Brother Giles of Assisi. 1443
... The golden scripts. 1621
Golden sequence. 3482, 3483
Golden sparrow. 2530
Golden straws and chaff in the wind. 987
Golden string. 1363, 1364
Golden sunset. 3432
Golden tapestries. 1639
Golden thoughts. 997
Golden thread. 2672, 3119, 3473
Golden threads in the tapestry of history. 3689
Golden treasures from the Greek New Testament for English readers. 348
Golden treasury. 1436
Golden treasury, for the children of God. 1436
Golden treasury for the children of God whose treasure is in heaven. 1436
Golden treasury of Bible stories. 624
Golden treasury of myths and legends. 2651
Golden Treasury of prayers for boys and girls. 900
Golden treasury of Psalms and prayers for all faiths. 2890
Golden treasury of Puritan quotations. 3111
Golden treasury of texts for every day in the year. 956, 1430
Golden treasury of the Bible. 253, 268, 269
Golden truth. 302
Golden twigs. 2724
Golden well. 3573
Golden Word. 216
Golden words. 1443
Golden words for every day. 1431
Golden words from the book of wisdom. 269
Golden words of faith, hope & love. 3014
Golden words of Moses. 521
Golden wreath for the month of Mary. 2360, 3248
Golden years. 499, 1977
Golden years of the Hutterites. 1398, 1858
Golden zephyr. 3196
Goldlen rule. 1744
Gold's happy people. 181
Golem. 1632, 1744, 2137
Golem of Prague. 1744, 2137
Golgotha. 1388, 3339
Gommatsara jiva-kanda (The soul) 1932
Gommatsara karma-kanda. 1932
Gone the golden dream. 1366, 2217
Gone west. 3503, 3517
Gongs in the night. 2533
Gonzalo de Tapia (1561-1594) 1898, 1948, 3587
Good American vacation lessons. 2590
Good and a bad government. 1142
Good and evil. 1745, 1746, 1747
Good and evil: a new direction. 1537
Good and evil spirits. 1528
Good as gold. 3562
Good as gold hymn book. 3562
Good beginnings. 3370
Good book. 1994
Good-bye, Old South, good-bye! 3848
Good Cardinal Richard. 3235
Good cheer. 969
Good child's Sunday book. 3564
Good Christian. 863
Good Christian men. 1174
Good Christian men rejoice. 180
Good confessor. 1327
Good father in Brittany. 2374
"A good fight" 2804
Good food from a Japanese temple. 3776
Good Friday. 2057
Good Friday addresses on the seven last words of Our Lord. 2057
Good Friday at St. Margaret's. 108
Good Friday meditation. 1747

Good Friday to Pentecost Sunday. 74, 2032
... Good God. 1725, 3609
Good grief. 1353
Good hand of our God. 1820, 2509
Good housekeeping in the church. 1242
Good is good. 3186, 3189
Good King Wenceslas. 3802
Good life. 472, 995, 2390, 2459
Good life; Epistle of James. 413
Good Lord, where are You? 583
Good man gone wrong? 122
Good man making a good end. 130
Good manners in God's house. 1540
Good men without faith. 935
Good minister of Jesus Christ; an interpretation of the Reverend Charles Bauman Schneder, D.D. 3309
...Good ministers of Jesus Christ. 3673
Good morals and gentle manners. 2591
Good morning. 1451
Good morning, boys and girls! 907
Good morning forever. 1267
Good morning, good people. 2580
Good morning, Lord. 17, 733, 898, 1439, 2388, 3592, 3882
Good morning, Lord; devotions for college students. 1308
Good morning, Lord; devotions for everyday living. 1439
Good morning, Lord; devotions for servicemen. 81
Good morning, Lord: devotions for shut-ins. 3407
Good morning, Lord; devotions for women. 3843
Good-natured man. 1517
Good new days. 3758
Good news. 32, 269, 391, 619, 1071, 1557, 1939, 1962
Good news about Jesus. 1991
Good news about Jesus as told as Mark. 437
Good news about trouble. 1011
Good news according to Mark. 434, 435
Good news according to Matthew. 441, 442
Good news across the continent. 2550
Good news and its proclamation. 746
Good news Bible. 268
Good news by John. 418
Good news for bad times. 325, 1063
Good news for children. 621, 836, 955
Good news for every person. 1565
Good news for everyone. 275
Good news for Grimy Gulch. 942
Good news for rich and poor. 1076
Good news for Russia. 1574
Good news for the liturgical community. 1263
Good news for today. 2901
Good news for you. 3380
Good news for young and old. 1601
Good news from God. 1728
Good news from John. 423, 909
Good news from Luke. 429, 430, 907
Good news from Matthew. 441, 444, 907
Good news in Acts. 333
Good news in bad times. 3229
Good news is bad news is good news. 2222
Good news is for sharing. 1565
Good news of a spiritual realm. 387
Good news of God. 1226, 3342
Good news of Jesus. 3660
Good news of Jesus Christ. 418
Good news of suffering. 3542
Good news on the frontier. 1396
Good news people in action. 1566
Good news to make you happy. 1941
Good news to the poor. 429, 1153, 2859
Good news yesterday and today. 2168
Good night. 902
Good night book. 900
'Good-night' thoughts about God. 1726
Good night too soon. 3812
Good of marriage. 2336
Good of the order. 1913
Good old plastic Jesus. 3887
Good old way. 969
Good pagan's failure. 1105
Good Pope John. 2124
Good report. 2211
... The good saint. 48
Good Saint Joseph. 2132
Good Samaritan. 1747
Good Samaritan and other Biblical stories. 3145
Good sense; or Natural ideas opposed to supernatural. 3567
Good Shepherd. 619, 1999, 2787
Good Shepherd calleth His sheep. 3380
'A good shepherd he was. 2851
Good Shepherd's fold. 2811, 3419
Good shepherds of Ireland. 1913
Good side of Christian science. 1034

Good society: Jewish ethics in action. 1539
Good soldier of Christ Jesus. 325
Good stewards. 3529
Good templarism illustrated. 1894
... The Good templars. 1913
Good templars' hand-book. 1913
Good things for humanity. 1855
Good thoughts in bad times. 1446
"Good tidings of great joy" 269
Good times for boys. 687
Good times in the rural church. 1167
Good times together. 1166
Good to be a Jew. 2139
Good was there. 1453
Good way. 2959, 3686
Good ways. 3112
Good without God. 3022
Good word. 1238, 2395
Good word for the devil. 1428
Good-by, my son. 1352, 3252, 3253
Goodbye, beloved Brethren. 3591
Goodbye, Jehovah. 3656
Goodbye, World. 607
Goodly company. 3171
Goodly fellowship. 3733
Goodly fellowship of the prophets. 570
Goodly heritage. 1653, 1665, 2101, 2775, 2966, 2974
Goodness is not enough. 1454
Goodness of God. 1719, 1732, 3610
Goodness of God in the conversion of youth. 3345
Goodness of God in view of the facts of nature and the supernatural. 1723, 1746
Goodness, you're following me! 587
Goodwill memorial. 2586
Gopal the Invincible. 2186, 3005
Gorakhnath and the Kanphata Yogis. 2163
Gordian knot. 65
Gordon 75th anniversary war. 3621
Gosepl and law. 2200
Gospel. 1058, 1120, 1990, 2612, 2614
Gospel according to. 164
Gospel according to Billy. 1754
Gospel according to Isaiah, seven sermons on Isaiah 53 concerning the Passion and death of Christ. 544
Gospel according to Jesus. 394, 2063
Gospel according to John. 415, 416, 417, 418, 420, 421
Gospel according to John, in Greek. 307
Gospel according to John in the Revised standard version. 416
Gospel according to Luke. 427, 428, 891
Gospel according to Luke in the Revised Standard Version. 427
Gospel according to Luke, I-IX. 427
Gospel according to Mark. 431, 432, 433, 434, 435, 437, 439
Gospel according to Mark and its meaning for today. 434
Gospel according to Matthew. 439, 440, 441, 891
Gospel according to Matthew in the revised standard version. 440
Gospel according to Moses. 565
Gospel according to Mother Goose. 2772
Gospel according to Paul. 471, 988
Gospel according to Revelation. 453
Gospel according to S. Matthew. 440
Gospel according to St. John. 414, 415, 416, 417, 418, 424, 2567
Gospel according to St. John 11-21 and the First Epistle of John. 424
Gospel according to St. John. 418
... The Gospel according to St. Luke. 427, 428, 429, 431
Gospel according to St. Luke, in Greek. 427, 429
... The Gospel according to St. Mark. 432, 433, 435
Gospel according to St. Mark; a text and commentary for students. 432
Gospel according to St. Mark: the Greek text with introduction, notes, and indexes. 433
Gospel according to Saint Matthew. 46, 439, 440, 442, 443, 2461
Gospel according to St. Matthew. 441
Gospel according to St. Paul. 376, 389
Gospel according to science fiction. 318, 3069
Gospel according to St John. 416
Gospel according to strange evangelists. 2215
Gospel according to superman. 1010
Gospel according to the enemy. 391
Gospel according to the Scriptures. 3295
Gospel according to the Wall Street journal. 1075, 3789
Gospel according to these times. 392
Gospel according to Thomas. 388
Gospel according to you, and other sermons. 2973
Gospel according to Zen. 3892

Gospel accoring to Matthew. 444
Gospel among the slaves. 2541, 2557
Gospel anchors aweigh! 3387
Gospel and authority. 3633
Gospel and Christian education. 3160
Gospel and church. 3650
Gospel and conflicting faiths. 1080
Gospel and culture. 1075
Gospel and epistle hymns for the Christian year. 2968
Gospel and Epistles of John. 413
Gospel and frontier peoples. 2514
Gospel and government. 1140
Gospel and human life. 387
Gospel and human needs. 1069
Gospel and India's heritage. 1082, 2061
Gospel and Islam. 2557
Gospel and its earliest interpretations. 2062, 3657
Gospel and its ministry. 3287
Gospel and law. 2200
Gospel and letters of John. 414
Gospel and myth in the thought of Rudolf Bultmann. 1424
Gospel and our world. 1059
Gospel and the ambiguity of the Church. 1126
Gospel and the Catholic church. 1219
Gospel and the church. 390, 1095, 1786
Gospel and the churches. 801
Gospel and the gay. 1843
Gospel and the Gospels. 390
Gospel and the land. 2765
Gospel and the modern man. 1061
Gospel and the modern mind. 391
Gospel and the new world. 2494
Gospel and the plow. 2530
Gospel and the Sermon on the Mount. 1096
Gospel and unity. 1043
Gospel appeals. 1556
Gospel as history. 3621
Gospel at Corinth. 391
Gospel at work. 3247
Gospel at work in modern life. 1016
"The gospel awakening." 1559
Gospel before Mark. 391
Gospel before the Gospels. 389
Gospel behind bars. 1255
Gospel blimp. 1550, 1562
Gospel by Mark. 3471
Gospel by Moses, in the book of Genesis. 521
Gospel chains. 967
Gospel characters. 384, 2007
Gospel cheer messages. 1561
Gospel Christianity. 1068
Gospel, church, mission. 2285, 3633
Gospel-criticism and historical Christianity. 388
Gospel crown of life. 3646
Gospel dawn in Africa. 2497
Gospel day. 1051
Gospel development. 393
Gospel doctrine. 1234, 2613
Gospel-doctrine of justification by faith, explained and vindicated. 1594
Gospel doctrine; selections from the sermons and writings of Joseph F. Smith. 2606
Gospel echo. 389
Gospel fishing. 389
Gospel for a world of sin. 1053
Gospel for an age of doubt. 1053, 2907
Gospel for an age of thought. 1340
Gospel for an exploding world. 148
Gospel for Asia. 2316
Gospel for both worlds. 3340
Gospel for children. 627, 909
Gospel for kids, series A. 909
Gospel for kids, series B. 909
Gospel for kids, series C. 909
Gospel for Main street. 388
Gospel for the cities. 1280
Gospel for the eye. 390
Gospel for the ghetto. 167
Gospel for the laity. 2056
Gospel for the layman's age. 392
Gospel for the new age. 388
Gospel for the person who has everything. 1008
Gospel for the social awakening. 3445
Gospel for the whole of life. 470
Gospel for three worlds. 393
Gospel for to-day. 1561
Gospel for young christians. 1986
Gospel fountain. 1752
Gospel from the Mount. 3334
Gospel from the mountains. 163
Gospel gallery for Lent. 2210
Gospel gems. 1985
Gospel gleanings. 391
Gospel graffiti. 1011
Gospel guide. 401
Gospel harmony. 384
Gospel harmony, chronologically arranged in separate lessons. 384

Gospel harmony using the Confraternity edition of the New Testament. 387
Gospel history. 391, 1821
Gospel hour sermons. 1557
Gospel hymnal. 152
Gospel hymnal for Sunday school and church work. 3562
Gospel hymns and sacred songs. (Words only.) 3230
Gospel hymns and social religion. 3231
Gospel hymns combined. 3230
Gospel hymns consolidated. 1864, 1865, 3230
Gospel hymns no. 2. 1864, 3230
Gospel hymns no. 3. 3230
Gospel hymns no. 4. 3231
Gospel hymns no. 5. 3231
Gospel hymns no. 6. 3231
Gospel hymns nos. 1 to 6. 3230, 3231
Gospel hymns nos. 5 and 6 combined. 3231
Gospel ideals. 2611
Gospel in a broken world. 1066
Gospel in a pagan society. 334, 1569, 2800
Gospel in a strange, new world. 1317
Gospel in action. 1649, 3178
Gospel in Alaska. 2500
... The Gospel in all the world. 392
Gospel in America. 1553
Gospel in art. 399, 919, 1957
Gospel in athletic phrases. 3196
Gospel in brief by Count Lyof N. Tolstoi. 393
Gospel in Burmah. 2506
Gospel in dispute. 1079
Gospel in Enoch. 1520
Gospel in experience. 1217
Gospel in Ezekiel. 518
Gospel in Ezekiel, illustrated in a series of discourses. 518
Gospel in hymns. 1871
Gospel in Isaiah. 543
Gospel in Korea. 2490
Gospel in Leviticus. 557, 3855
Gospel in miniature. 2247
Gospel in modern poetry. 3210
Gospel in other words. 1974
Gospel in our day. 3337
Gospel in slow motion. 863
Gospel in Solentiname. 388
Gospel in the book of Numbers. 561
Gospel in the Christian year and in Christian experience. 3354
Gospel in the church. 299, 748, 757
Gospel in the early church. 476, 2799
Gospel in the feasts of Israel. 3720
Gospel in the Gospels. 401
Gospel in the Hebrew tabernacle, priesthood, and offerings. 3720
Gospel in the King James version. 413
Gospel in the Old Testament. 450
Gospel in the Pentateuch. 566
Gospel in the South Pacific. 2533
Gospel in the stars. 99
Gospel in the ten commandments. 1314
Gospel in the twentieth century. 3081
Gospel in type and antitype. 3721
Gospel initiations for each Sunday of the year. 366
Gospel initiations for Lent. 2213
Gospel insights. 2619
Gospel Jesus preached. 2063
Gospel kingdom. 2606
Gospel lectionary of the Eastern Orthodox Church. 2745
Gospel life of Francis of Assisi today. 1000, 1642
Gospel light. 2064
Gospel: love it & live it. 3664
Gospel manual. 1988
... The Gospel manuscripts of the General theological seminary. 315
Gospel meditations. 1985
Gospel melodies. 1865, 3207
Gospel message of Jesus Christ. 929, 1991
Gospel message of St. Mark. 431, 435
Gospel messages for boys and girls. 3884
Gospel minister. 3675
Gospel ministry. 3675
Gospel miracles. 2018
Gospel miracles in their relation to Christ and Christianity. 2018
Gospel music encyclopedia. 1748
Gospel-mystery of sanctification. 3299, 3300
Gospel of a country pastor. 390, 2784
Gospel of a Covenant God. 168
Gospel of Apollonius of Tyana. 57
Gospel of baptism. 135
Gospel of Barnabas. 2506
Gospel of beauty. 1071
Gospel of Buddha. 701, 1703
Gospel of Buddha according to old records. 701, 1703
Gospel of cause and effect. 3234
Gospel of Christ. 1453, 2056

Gospel of Christ, and other addresses. 169
Gospel of Christian atheism. 1417
Gospel of Christian freedom. 380
Gospel of common sense as contained in the canonical Epistle of James. 413
Gospel of consolation. 389
Gospel of contradiction. 392
Gospel of divine action. 3104
Gospel of divine providence. 2981
Gospel of eternal life. 414
...The gospel of fellowship. 2336
Gospel of giving. 3531
Gospel of gladness. 3349
Gospel of God. 1095, 2297
Gospel of good and evil. 1746
Gospel of good will as revealed in contemporary scriptures. 965
Gospel of grace. 3342
Gospel of healing. 1600
Gospel of health. 2378
Gospel of history. 1991
Gospel of hope. 392
Gospel of industry. 155
Gospel of irreligious religion. 3121
Gospel of Isaiah. 545
Gospel of Jesus. 387, 1989, 2056
Gospel of Jesus and the problems of democracy. 2056, 3447
Gospel of Jesus the Christ. 201
Gospel of Jesus the son of God. 1060
Gospel of John. 415, 416, 417, 418, 419, 421, 423, 2127
Gospel of John and Judaism. 418, 2103
Gospel of John for today. 422
Gospel of John in Christian history. 421
Gospel of joy. 388, 2136, 3725
Gospel of law. 3728
Gospel of liberation. 2300, 3368
Gospel of love. 387
Gospel of Luke. 427, 428, 429, 430, 431
Gospel of Mark. 431, 432, 433, 434, 435, 437
Gospel of Mark for growing Christians. 434
Gospel of Mark for men in service. 438
Gospel of Matthew. 439, 440, 441, 443, 444
Gospel of Matthew for growing Christians. 441
Gospel of Moses. 296, 2622
Gospel of nature. 3514
Gospel of now. 1264
Gospel of opportunity. 2056
Gospel of Our Lord and Savior Jesus Christ. 397, 2071
Gospel of Our Lord and Saviour Jesus Christ. 2056
Gospel of Our Lord and Saviour Jesus Christ according to Saint Matthew. 2567
Gospel of our sufferings. 3479
Gospel of Paul. 323, 376
Gospel of peace and justice. 1137, 2123
Gospel of Philip. 268
Gospel of prayer. 2882
Gospel of redemption. 3642
Gospel of relativity. 988
Gospel of St. John. 50, 417, 418, 421
Gospel of St. John and the Johannine Epistles. 415
Gospel of St. John and the Synoptic gospels. 418
Gospel of St. John in its relation to the other three Gospels. 50
Gospel of St. Luke. 426, 427, 429
Gospel of St. Mark. 50, 433, 434, 435, 436, 437
Gospel of St. Matthew. 440, 441, 443
Gospel of St. Paul. 372
Gospel of salvation. 1555
Gospel of service, and other sermons. 162
Gospel of signs. 419
Gospel of spiritual insight. 416
Gospel of Sri Ramakrishan. 3020
Gospel of St John. 417
Gospel of the church's infancy. 332
Gospel of the Comforter. 1832
Gospel of the cross. 2299
Gospel of the divine sacrifice. 105
... The gospel of the grace" 1750
Gospel of the grace of God. 168
Gospel of the Hellenists. 418
Gospel of the herafter. 1529
Gospel of the Holy Spirit. 329, 1835
Gospel of the Incarnation. 1893
Gospel of the kingdom. 440, 441, 2063, 2174, 2175, 2176, 3336
Gospel of the kingdom and the gospel of the church. 1048
Gospel of the kingdom of God. 391
Gospel of the life beyond. 1794
Gospel of the lilies. 389
Gospel of the living Jesus. 389
Gospel of the Lord. 428
Gospel of the Lord Jesus. 400, 1972
Gospel of the Pentateuch. 563
Gospel of the Pentateuch, a set of parish sermons. 1226

Gospel of the red man. 1902
Gospel of the Redman. 1902
Gospel of the second coming. 3319
Gospel of the secular life. 1226
Gospel of the Sp1rit. 1831
Gospel of the Spirit. 419
Gospel of the Word. 415
"The gospel of truth" 387, 3142, 3767
Gospel of work. 3848
Gospel of youth in the God-man. 1996
Gospel on campus. 3537
Gospel on Skid Row. 1566
Gospel on the air. 388
Gospel origins. 390
Gospel parables. 397, 2026
Gospel parables in verse. 2771
Gospel paradox. 2025
Gospel parallels. 387, 3147
Gospel-perspective on Jesus Christ. 392, 1987
Gospel pioneering. 1335
Gospel plan. 2611
Gospel plan of salvation. 3288
Gospel plea. 1051
Gospel plea for Christian unity. 1051
Gospel poverty. 2866
Gospel power. 2898
Gospel praises , no. 2. 390
Gospel preacher. 1466
Gospel preacher and his preaching. 2907
Gospel preaching for the day. 1266
Gospel priesthood. 1299, 3632
Gospel principles. 1232
Gospel project. 1093, 2035
Gospel records. 392, 395
Gospel records in the light of recent research. 392
Gospel records of the message and mission of Jesus Christ. 387
Gospel romance in the huts of the Punjab. 2529
Gospel seed for busy sowers. 2899
Gospel selections of the ancient church. 366
Gospel sermons. 2933
Gospel song writers biography. 1749
Gospel songs. 1865
Gospel sound. 1749, 2680
Gospel spirituality. 996
Gospel standards. 2609
Gospel story. 392, 1965, 1981, 1990
Gospel story, in easy words for children. 1982
Gospel story of Jesus. 399, 1989, 2056
Gospel studies. 3368
Gospel teacher, or. 3721
Gospel teachings in the Book of Mormon. 2601
Gospel teachings the Book of Mormon. 2601
Gospel-telling. 2911
Gospel temperance. 3597
Gospel text of Epiphanius of Salamis. 393, 1522
Gospel that has saved 16,000 souls. 1560
Gospel, the church and society. 1344
Gospel, the church and the world. 1126
Gospel through the ages. 2611
...The gospel to all the world. 333
Gospel to every creature. 1571
Gospel today. 1062, 2601
Gospel tradition. 335
Gospel tragedy: an epic poem. 3206
Gospel trail blazers. 1466
Gospel truth. 1681, 2325, 2609, 2848
Gospel truth; discourses and writings of president George Q. Cannon. 2609
Gospel versus Gospel. 2408
Gospel wagon. 3589
Gospel we preach. 1265
Gospel without compromise. 997
Gospel woes. 2213
Gospel work. 1572
Gospel workers. 3677
Gospel worthy of all acceptation. 1591
Gospels. 305, 383, 385, 388, 390 , 391
Gospels, a translation. 401
Gospels and Acts. 398
Gospels and contemporary biographies in the Greco-Roman world. 398, 661
Gospels and Epistles for every Sunday. 855
Gospels and epistles of the Sundays and feasts. 1268
... The Gospels and the Acts of the apostles. 70
Gospels and the critic. 388
Gospels and the Jesus of history. 1987
Gospels and the life of Christ. 1974
Gospels and the teachings of Jesus. 2065
Gospels as a mandala of wisdom. 390, 2067
Gospels as historical documents. 392
Gospels combined. 1988, 1989
Gospels for Lent and the passion of Christ. 2209, 2211
Gospels for Sundays and feasts. 398

Gospels in current study. 390
Gospels in study and preaching. 367
Gospels in study and preaching (The) 366
Gospels of Matthew and Luke. 441, 442
Gospels of Saint Matthew, Saint Mark, Saint Luke & Saint John. 450
Gospels reconsidered. 386
Gospels without myth. 389
... Gotama Buddha. 703, 712, 1703
Gothard. 1300, 1749
Gothic architecture. 78
Gothic architecture in England. 79
Gothic cathedral. 750, 752, 889
Gothic cathedral: origins of Gothic architecture and the medieval concept of order. 750, 889
Gothic cathedrals and sacred geometry. 79
Gothic commentary on the Gospel of John. 417
Gothic image. 86, 920
Gothic revival & American church architecture. 1749
Gothic version of the Epistles. 368
Gothic version of the Gospels. 395
Gothic vs. classic. 1160
Gotthold's emblems. 1441
Gould's history of freemasonry throughout the world. 1664
Government. 3609
Government & improvement of mirth. 1340
Government, discipline, and worship of the Presbyterian church in theUnited States of America. 2921
Government in the Missouri Synod. 1549
Government of God. 1723
Government of God the true source and standard of human government. 1503
Government of religious communities. 2577
Government of the Catholic Church. 807
Government of the Methodist Episcopal Church. 2450
Governmental and judicial ethics in the Bible and rabbinic literature. 514, 1539
... Governments-in-exile on Jewish rights. 3852
Gracanica. 1749
Grace. 1751, 1752, 3696
Grace abounding. 984, 1439, 1753
...Grace abounding and The pilgrim's progress. 1750
Grace abounding to the chief of sinners. 714, 1750
Grace, actual and habitual. 1752
Grace all the way home. 470
Grace and common life. 1751
Grace and faith in the Old Testament. 598, 1752
Grace and forgiveness in ministry. 2787, 3698
Grace and glory. 1752, 1794
Grace and judgment. 3290
Grace and mercy in her wild hair. 3285
Grace and personality. 1751, 3646
Grace and power. 1752
Grace and prayer explained according to the Munich or psychological method. 1750
Grace & race in the Lutheran Church. 1751
Grace and reason. 2281
Grace and the human condition. 1752
Grace and the searching of our heart. 1752
Grace and torah. 1752
Grace and truth. 1752, 3720
Grace at point zero. 1058
Grace before meals. 1750
Grace before meat. 1750
Grace Church. 3762, 3868
Grace church, Albany. 22
Grace church and old New York. 2699
Grace church in Newark. 2701
Grace defended, in a modest plea for an important truth. 1753
Grace displayed. 2507
Grace divine. 3458
Grace Episcopal Church, Madison, Wisconsin; a history of the parish. 1524
Grace filling an earthen vessel with glory. 2973
Grace for grace. 1751, 3578
Grace for today. 3540
Grace-gifts. 1712
Grace greater than sin. 2435
Grace grows best in winter. 3540
Grace, guts & goods. 1057
Grace, hymns and blessings. 2112
Grace in experience and theology. 1752
Grace in freedom. 791, 1659
Grace in Galatians. 381
Grace in the New Testament. 1752
Grace in the wilderness. 3350
Grace is not a blue eyed blond. 993
Grace King. 2442

Grace McBride, missionary nurse. 2305
Grace magnified. 1750
Grace notes and other fragments. 2285, 3634
Grace of Christ. 1752, 1753
Grace of giving. 952, 3531
Grace of god. 1751, 1752, 3664
Grace of God in faith and philosophy. 1751
Grace of God in the Gospel. 63
Grace of Guadalupe. 1776
Grace of law. 2201
Grace of the Passion. 2033
Grace of the way. 1000
Grace of Zen. 3894
Grace; six lenten discourses preached in the parish church of Saint Martin's at Freiburg. 1753
Grace to act now. 838
Grace under pressure. 1750, 2399
Grace unlimited. 1752
Grace upon grace. 652, 2188
Gracechurch. 1750
Graceful giving. 952
Graceful living. 3265
Graceful reason. 2672
Graceful reason; the contribution of reason to theology. 2672
Graces and powers of the Christian life. 969
Graces and prayers. 2894
Graces for children. 899
Graces of Christmas. 1113
Graces of the risen Christ. 2006
Gracious adventurers. 3467
Gracious calling of the Lord. 1571
Gracious presence of God. 1503
Gracious years. 1364
Graded Bible stories. 616
Graded catechism, according to the instruction of the motu proprio "Orbem catholicum" of Pius xi, June 29, 1923. 769
Graded choir handbook. 916
Graded church. 3555
Graded course of instruction for Jewish religious schools. 639
Graded lessons on the catechism. 747
Graded memory course for Lutheran Sunday-schools and other institutions. 3184, 3185
Graded missionary education in the church school. 2549
Graded series of Home Mission studies. 2528
Graded social service for the Sunday school. 1251
Graded Sunday school. 3551
... The graded Sunday school in principle and practice. 3556
Graded text books for the modern Sunday school. 3162
Grading the Sunday school. 3551
Gradual awakening. 3780
Graduate directory. 2700
Graduate education in religion. 3111
Graduate Theological Union. 1753, 3613
Graduate theses and dissertations written in the field of education. 1469
Graduate theses of Southern Baptist Theological Seminary. 3332
"Graduated with honor." 1790
Graduate's guide to success. 3887
Graduation—a new start. 1308
Graduels. 883
Graham. 1755, 3407
Grain of mustard. 2948
Grain of mustard seed. 2635
Grain of wheat. 3341
Grains of gold. 3782
Grains of incense for the thurible of prayer. 2386
Grains of sand. 3843
Grammar of belief. 63
Grammar of biblical Hebrew. 1797
Grammar of faith. 3622
Grammar of New Testament Greek. 1769
Grammar of prophecy. 605
Grammar of Septuagint Greek. 1770
Grammar of the Benga language. 190
Grammar of the Gothic language, and the Gospel of St. Mark. 1749
Grammar of the Greek New Testament in the light of historical research. 1770
Grammar of the Old Testament in Greek according to the Septuagint. 1770
Grammatical aids for students of New Testament Greek. 1770
Grammatical analysis of selections from the Hebrew scriptures. 1797
Grammatical insights into the New Testament. 349
Grand commandery of Knights templars, Massachusetts and Rhode Island. 1805-1905. 3598
Grand constitution and grand status. 3205

Grand constitution and grand statutes of the Grand lodge, Knights of Pythias, domain of Iowa. 3205
Grand constitution and grand statutes of the order of Knights of Pythias. 3205
"Grand grimore;" 2312
Grand Lodge recognition. 1661
Grand Lodge, 1717-1967. 1664
Grand man of God, James Edward Freeman. 1660
Grand Priory of the Order of the Hospital of St. John of Jerusalem in England. 1755
Le Grand Richards speaks. 2610
Grandees. 3333
Grandeur and misery of man. 2934
Grandfathers, God's gift to children. 903
Grandma goes gadding. 92, 1856, 2482
Grandmother's book. 1756
Grandmothers, God's gift to children. 903
Grandpa as a polygamist. 2600
Grandpa was a polygamist. 2600
Granite for God's house. 697
Granny Brand, her story. 690, 2486
Grapes from Gospel vines. 164
Grapes of Canaan. 2524
Grapes of Eshcol. 1696
Graphic astrology. 96
Graphic Bible. 281
Graphic Bible from Genesis to Revelation. 281
Graphic history of the Jewish heritage. 2094
Grass roots church. 1244
Grassroots ecumenicity; case studies in local church consolidation. 1045
Grassroots evangelism. 1574
Gratz College, anniversary volume. 2093, 2147
Grave. 1757
Grave of God. 1153
Graven images. 1537
Graven in the rock. 515
Graver thoughts of a country parson. 2930
Gravestones of early New England and the men who made them, 1653-1800. 3333
Gray and Adams Bible Commentary. 222
"Graybeard's" lay sermons. 3662
Great achievements. 3132
Great Advent movement. 3379
Great adventure. 75, 333
Great affirmations of religion. 3728
Great ages and ideas of the Jewish people. 2147
Great American Catholic Missionary Congresses. 851
Great American Catholics. 829, 3737
Great American foundresses. 2717, 3415
Great American revival. 3233
Great and humble soul, Mother Therese Couderc. 1372, 3205
Great and Little One of Prague. 1906
Great anguish. 2493
Great apostasy. 2606
Great apostasy, considered in the light of scriptural and secular history. 2606
Great apostolic blunder machine. 1058
Great archbishop of Dublin, William King, D.D., 1650-1729. 3129
Great architect. 187, 3074, 3076
"Great are the words of Isaiah" 543
Great argument. 2415
Great art and children's worship. 2845
Great Asian religions. 91
Great assize. 2156
Great Awakening. 1757, 3230, 3289, 3739, 3813
Great Awakening, 1720-1760. 1757
Great Awakening and the American Revolution. 3214
Great awakening at Yale College. 1757, 3862
Great Awakening: documents illustrating the crisis and its consequences. 1757
Great awakening in Columbus, Ohio, under the labors of Rev. B. Fay Mills and his associates. 2467
Great Awakening in New England. 1757
Great Awakening in Nova Scotia. 1757
... The great awakening in the middle colonies. 1757, 3232
Great awakening in Virginia. 3233
Great awakening of 1740. 1757
Great awakening on temperance. 3596
Great Basin Kingdom. 3762
Great battles of Biblical history. 558
Great beliefs of the church. 3664
Great betrayal. 2119, 3897
Great beyond. 1697
Great Bible questions. 614
Great Bible renowns. 614
Great Bible stories and master paintings. 603, 623
Great Bible truths for human problems. 3539
Great Bible words. 245

Great big boat. 2712
Great Black Robe. 1901, 3426
Great book: Calvary Protestant Episcopal Church, 1832-1972, Memphis, Shelby County, Tennessee. 2401
Great book of magical art. 2724
Great books on religion and esoteric philosophy. 3089
Great Bournemouth mystery. 3516
Great brain robbery. 202
Great Britain: England and Wales. 818, 1920
Great Britain Palestine and the Jews, Jewry's celebration of its national charter. 3896
... The great Brooklyn romance. 184
Great Canadian preaching. 3362
Great Canadian preaching, edited, with introduction and biographical notes. 3367
Great cathedrals. 750
Great cathedrals and most celebrated churches of the world. 750
Great cathedrals of the world. 750
Great Catholic festivals. 1613
Great Catholics. 765
Great Catholics in American history. 874
Great challenge. 3481
Great chapters of the Bible. 223
Great characters of the New Testament. 338
Great characters of the Old Testament. 494
Great choices of the last week. 1837
Great Christian books. 1021, 3203
Great Christian doctrine of original sin defended. 3410
... Great Christian hymns. 1860
Great Christian plays. 3145
Great Christian teachings. 3663
Great Christians. 1050
Great Christina doctrine of original sin defended, evidences of its truth produced, and arguments to the contrary answered. 3413
Great church awakes. 1181
Great church fights. 1165
Great Church in captivity. 1354
Great church-state fraud. 1150
Great church towers of England, chiefly of the perpendicular period. 3705
Great churches of America. 1274
Great cloud of witnesses. 137, 404, 405
Great commandment and the royal law. 1091
Great commandments of God. 1313
Great commission. 2519
Great commission for today. 1765
Great commitment. 1589
Great Companion. 1719
Great concern. 1357
Great concern of salvation. 3294
Great concern of salvation in three parts. 3294
Great conflict. 2751
Great conjecture, who is this Jesus? 1956
"great conquest" 2519
Great conspiracy against our American public schools. 807
Great consummation. 2465
Great contest. 2605
Great contest of faith and reason. 1597
Great contest, truth and knowledge versus falsehood and ignorance. 1057
Great controversies. 792
Great controversy. 3325
Great controversy between Christ and Satan. 1053, 3384
Great controversy between Christ and Satan during the Christian dispensation. 1053, 3384
Great controversy between Christ and Satan; the conflict of the ages in the Christian dispensation. 3384
Great controversy between God and man. 2981
Great controversy between God and man, its origin, progress, and end. 2981
Great crisis in American Catholic history. 34
Great crisis in American Catholic history, 1895-1900. 34
Great crisis in the life of Christ. 1972
Great date wait, and other hazards. 3882
Great day. 464
Great day of atonement. 2033
Great days and seasons. 1433
Great days for the family. 1606
Great days of the last week. 1837, 2029
Great debate. 1339
Great debate on miracles. 1855, 2476
Great debate today. 1106, 2045
Great debates of the Reformation. 3042
Great demonstration. 508
Great design. 1370
Great dialecticians in modern Christian thought. 1457

Great dicourse of Jesus the Christ, the Son of God. 2071
Great dilemma. 2042
Great discourse of Jesus Chirst the Son of God. 2071
Great discourse of Jesus Christ the Son of God. 2071
Great discourse of Jesus the Christ the Son of God. 2071
Great discovery. 1410
Great discussion of modern spiritualism, between Prof. J. Stanley Grimes and Leo Miller. 3503
Great divide. 2855, 3576
Great divorce. 1746
Great doctrines of our faith. 649
Great doctrines of the Bible. 161, 232, 614, 651, 3643, 3662
Great doctrines relating to salvation. 3292
Great dynamic. 1831
Great efficacy of simple faith in the atonement of Christ. 1999
Great elm tree. 2969
Great empire of silence. 2210
...Great English churchmen: or, Famous names in English church history and literature. 1212
Great enigma. 60
Great enterprises. 3874
Great epic of India. 1521, 2316
Great epic of Israel. 1798
Great escape. 1584
Great essentials of the Christian life. 968
Great evangel. 1566
Great evangelical preachers of yesterday. 2909
Great evangelism. 1568
Great evangelistic opportunity. 1571
Great events in the Bible recorded on maps. 528
Great events in the life of Christ. 1968, 2016
Great exemplar. 1973
Great exorcism. 1745
Great expectations realized. 2505
Great expository sermons. 3346
Great expressions of human rights. 2223
Great figures and events in Jewish history. 2092
Great forty years in the diocese of Chicago. 2962
...The great friend: Frederick Ozanam. 2755
Great friendship and other sermons of the Little brown church of the air. 2436
Great fundamentals of the Bible. 3382
Great Galilean. 1967
Great Galilean returns. 3440
Great German mystics: Eckhart, Tauler, and Suso. 1491, 2644
Great globe. 3073
Great God. 1730
Great God, here I am. 1445
Great gospel. 2300
Great gospel sermons. 1557
Great harmonia. 2833, 2987, 2988
Great harmony. 3111
Great Healer's prayer. 2248
Great heresies. 1804
Great heresies and church councils. 1182
Great heresines. 1804
Great hero. 2804
Great hero, St. Paul the apostle. 2804
"Great hymns and modern instances," 1872
Great hymns and their stories. 1868
Great hymns of the church. 1861
Great hymns of the middle ages. 1877
Great 'I am's' of Jesus. 161
Great I came's of Jesus. 2072
Great Ideal. 1723
Great ideas of the Bible outlined for moderns. 651
Great importance of a religious life considered. 969
Great importance of the Sabbatic number seven. 3379
Great in church history. 1188
... The great Indian religions. 1895
Great initiates. 3120
Great inspirers. 1811
Great interviews of Jesus. 2932
Great invitation, and other sermons. 3049
Great iron wheel examined. 1756
Great is the company. 655
Great is the Lord. 3652
Great is your reward. 182
Great issues. 1063
Great issues concerning theism. 3609
Great Jewish books. 2145
Great Jewish books and their influence on history. 2145
Great Jewish debates and dilemmas. 2112, 2144
Great Jewish ideas. 2145
Great Jewish personalities in ancient and medieval times. 2084

Great Jewish thinkers of the twentieth century. 2145
Great Jewish women. 3842
Great Jews since Bible times. 2084
Great joy. 1559
Great judgment day in the light of the sanctuary service. 2156
Great Knight of the Crimsoned Cross. 1993
Great known. 3512
Great known; what natural science knows of the spiritual world. 3512
Great Lambeth Bible. 317, 1883
Great leaders in human progress. 660
Great leaders of Hebrew history. 214
Great leaders of the Book of Mormon. 679
Great leaders of the Christian church. 925
Great legacy. 3288
Great Lent. 2210
Great light. 2300, 3033
Great living system. 3081
Great logicians. 2832
Great love stories of the Bible and their lessons for today. 473
Great Magdalens. 764, 3831
Great mantle. 2851
Great march. 3581
Great means of salvation and of perfection. 2875
Great men and movements in Israel. 493, 2096
Great men as prophets of a new era. 660
Great men in Israel. 2084
Great men of God. 215, 216
... Great men of the Bible. 213, 215
Great men of the Bible and the women in their lives. 215
Great men of the Christian church. 927
Great men search for God. 1722
Great message. 2728
Great migration. 2111
Great ministry. 1966
Great miracle. 1785
Great missionaries. 2484
Great missionaries of the church. 2481, 2482
Great missionaries to Africa. 2497
Great missionaries to China. 2510
Great missionaries to India. 2531
Great missionaries to the Orient. 2502
Great modern sermons. 3343
Great moments in Catholic history. 811
Great moments in church history. 1188
Great moments in spiritualism. 3494
Great moral leaders. 1943
Great morning of the world. 175
Great Mosque of Kairouan. 2162
Great mother. 2624, 3838
Great mother of the gods. 1398
Great mysteries. 3662
Great mysteries of the Bible. 346, 2636
Great mystery of the great whore unfolded. 1681
Great mystics. 2645
Great Naropa poetry wars. 2194, 3716
Great nations of to-day. 463
Great necessity and advantage of public prayer. 3003
Great neglected Bible prophecies. 609
Great New England churches. 1271
Great news. 294
Great Ngee. 2129
Great nights of the Bible. 2932
Great painters and their famous Bible pictures. 920
Great painters' gospel. 2760
Great paradox. 63
Great parenthesis. 606
Great partnership; God and man. 1724
Great peace motto. 2401, 2807
Great penitents. 1363, 2813
Great people of the Bible and how they lived. 214
Great personalities of the Bible. 215
Great personalities of the New Testament. 338
Great personalities of the Old Testament. 493
Great phrases of the Christian language. 1447
Great Physician. 2004, 3405, 3751
Great Physician and His healing ministry. 3444
Great pilgrimage of the Middle Ages. 2848
Great polyglot Bibles. 603
Great portraits of the Bible. 2434
Great prayer. 842, 2248
Great prayer: concerning the Canon of the Mass. 842
Great prayers. 604
Great preachers of today. 1273
Great preaching. 3360
Great preaching today. 3365
Great problem. 3349, 3440
Great prologue. 1232, 3741

Great promise. 5, 427, 634
Great promises of the Bible. 604
Great prophecies for our time. 607
Great prophets. 3112
Great prophets: Moses, Zoroaster, Jesus. 3112
Great Protestant festivals. 1262
Great psychic. 2988
Great question: will you consider the subject of personal religion? 1358
Great questions of the last week. 1837
Great reading from Decision. 3637
Great realities. 1105
Great reality. 978, 1955
Great red dragon. 799
Great Redeemer. 865, 2034
Great redemption. 469, 1559, 2587
Great reform. 952
"The great reformation," 783, 791
Great refusal. 1557
Great religions. 3114, 3118
Great religions. [1st ed.]. 3118
Great religions by which men live. 3120, 3142
Great religions of the Holy Land. 2764
Great religions of the modern world. 3117
Great religions of the world. 3116, 3119
Great religious leaders. 3094
Great religious stories. 923
Great religious teachers of the East. 3118
Great revelation. 3224
Great reversal. 1568
Great revision. 3142
Great revival. 1149, 2750
Great Revival, 1787-1805. 3232
Great revival at Roberts Park M. E. church and other churches. 3232
Great revival in the west. 3738
Great revival in Wales. 3233
Great revivals and the great republic. 1563
Great Roman-Jewish war. 2091, 2094
Great sacrilege. 2368
Great Saint Augustine. 115
Great saints and saintly figures. 925, 3281
Great saints of the Bible. 213
Great salvation. 3296
Great Schism, 1378. 3308
Great schisms in Jewish history. 2080
Great second advent movement. 10
Great Second Advent movement, its rise and progress. 10, 3380
Great secret. 2228, 3118
Great secret of the saints. 3281
Great sects and schisms in Judaism. 2080
Great sermon. 3335
Great sermons by great American preachers. 3351
Great sermons by great preachers. 3364
Great sermons by young preachers. 3353
Great sermons for growing disciples. 3353
Great sermons from master preachers of all ages. 3340
Great sermons of the world. 3340, 3342
Great sermons on evangelism. 1558
Great sermons on the birth of Christ. 1114
Great sermons on the death of Christ by celebrated preachers. 2034
Great sermons on the Resurrection. 2054
Great sermons on the Resurrection of Christ. 2054
Great sermons on the Resurrection of Christ, by celebrated preachers. 2054
Great sermons on world peace. 2807
Great servant of God, Mother Paola Frassinetti, foundress of the Sisters of St. Dorothy, 1803 [i. e. 1809]-1882. 1652
Great sinners of the Bible. 213
Great soul-winning churches. 1171
Great souls at prayer. 2870
Great South African Christians. 13
Great Southern Baptist doctrinal preaching. 165
Great Southern Baptist evangelistic preaching. 165
Great southern preaching. 3363
Great sphinx speaks to God's people. 46
Great step. 2259
Great stewards of the Bible. 3530
Great stories from the Bible. 623, 628
Great stories of the Bible. 313
Great stories of the Bible, for children. 313, 620
Great story. 399, 1989
Great supper of God. 2256
Great surprise! 616, 3897
Great teacher. 865, 2066
... The great teachers of Judaism and Christianity. 648
Great teachings of Masonry. 1662
Great texts from Romans. 471, 3357, 3387
Great texts of the Bible. 222
Great themes from the Book of Mormon for family activities. 1607

GREAT THEMES FROM RELIGIOUS BOOKS 1876 - 1982

Great themes from the Old Testament. 503, 1003
Great themes of Jesus. 2063
Great themes of life. 127
Great themes of the Bible. 651
Great themes of the Christian faith. 3351
Great themes of the New Testament. 346
Great themes of the Old Testament. 599
Great things of the Bible, Sunday morning messages. 1559
Great three-sixteens of the New Testament. 1238
Great time to be alive. 3351
Great tradition of the American churches. 1150, 1274
Great treasury of Christian spirituality. 3491
Great trek of the Russian Mennonites to Central Asia, 1880-1884. 2407
Great tribulation. 3318
Great tribulation, the church's supreme test. 2466
Great twentieth century Jewish philosophers: Shestov, Rosenzweig, Buber, with selections from their writings. 2842
Great unity. 3146
Great universe. 3476
Great unveiling. 460
Great Upanishads. 3760
Great verses from the Psalms. 576
Great voices of the Reformation. 2978
Great warfare. 607
Great Week. 844
Great Western mystics. 2637
Great White Brotherhood in the culture history and religion of America. 1765, 3474
Great white light. 3496
Great women of faith. 3834
Great women of the Bible. 3839
Great women of the Christian faith. 3831, 3834
Great words of the Christian faith. 991
Great words of the gospel. 3663
Great work. 2728
Great world crisis. 1514
Great writers as interpreters of religion. 3071
Great yogic sermon. 3865
Greater Anglo-Saxon churches. 1159
Greater Atlanta church guide. 1270
Greater awareness. 2729
Greater Christ. 955
Greater church of the future. 3141
Greater dividends from religion. 2611
Greater English church in the middle ages. 1158
Greater English church screens. 3316
Greater extension and development of church influence. 827
Greater freedom. 3330
Greater generation. 886
Greater glory. 1628, 2757
Greater happiness. 964
Greater Judaism in the making. 2149
Greater Key of Solomon. 2315
Greater life and work of Christ as revealed in Scripture, man, and nature. 1953
"Greater love..." 2057, 2213, 2258
Greater love hath no man. 2215
Greater men and women of the Bible. 214, 216
Greater mysteries. 2726
Greater perfection. 2478
Greater poems of the Bible. 603
Greater revelation. 3517
Greater task. 3435
Greater than Adam is here. 487, 2045
Greater than David is here. 1405
Greater than Elijah is here. 1506
Greater than Jonah is here. 552, 2053
Greater than Joshua is here. 209
Greater than our hearts. 2894
Greater than Solomon. 164
Greater than Solomon is here. 3457
Greater-truth from the Great Spirit. 1727
Greater-truth of the universe from the GreatSpirit, the supreme Lord God, Jehova-Ahura-Mazda. 1727
Greater victory. 1235
Greater way of freedom. 3474
Greatest Bible doctrines explained. 638
Greatest Bible stories. 407
Greatest book ever written. 356, 535
Greatest book in the world. 232, 270
Greatest calling. 773, 2398
Greatest Catherine. 749
Greatest chapter. 209
Greatest English classic. 272
Greatest errors of Christianity in this present day. 1064
Greatest faith ever known. 71, 407
Greatest gift. 626
Greatest good of mankind. 3483
Greatest help. 982
Greatest is love. 602, 2266
Greatest kidnapping event! 1513
Greatest life. 1967
Greatest life ever lived. 1977
Greatest life; Jesus tells his story. 1967
Greatest men of the Bible. 3354
Greatest mystery of the ages revealed. 1952, 2636
Greatest name. 1979
Greatest object in the universe. 3479
Greatest of hese. 2264
Greatest of the Borgias. 1649
Greatest of the prophets. 506
Greatest of these. 323, 887, 1440, 2263
Greatest of these is love. 323, 2264, 2896
Greatest possibility thinker that ever lived. 988, 2043
Greatest power in the world. 1052
Greatest prayer. 2370
Greatest question of the bible and of life. 2932
Greatest questions of the Bible and of life. 2932
Greatest saint of France. 2349
Greatest sermons. 3733
Greatest song. 2740
Greatest story ever told. 929, 1970
Greatest story never told. 2140
Greatest texts of the Bible. 2932
Greatest thing in the universe. 3575
Greatest thing in the world. 588, 959, 2263, 2264
Greatest thing in the world Henry Drummond's inspirational classic in a modern, readable edition, with other selected essays. Ed. by William R. Webb. Illus. by James Hamil. 2264
Greatest things in religion. 954
Greatest thinkers. 660
Greatest thoughts about God gleaned from many sources. 1731
Greatest thoughts about Jesus Christ. 1952
Greatest thoughts about the Bible gleaned from many sources. 219
Greatest thoughts on immortality. 1888
Greatest week in history. 1837
Greatest word in the world. 1735
Greatest words in the Bible and in Human speech. 2932
Greatest work in the world. 2485, 3360
Greatheart of the border. 697, 2487
Greatheart of the Bowery. 2542
Greatheart of the South. 39, 2539
Greatly to be. 2212
Greatness. 971
Greatness and grace of God. 3077
Greatness and simplicity. 975
Greatness & the decadence of the Jews. 2145
Greatness of Christ. 1970, 2050
Greatness of Christ, and other sermons. 2056
Greatness of the kingdom. 2174
Greatness of the soul [and] The teacher. 3461
Grecian and Roman mythology. 2655, 2656
Greece, gods, and art. 86
Greedk-English lexicon to the New Testament. 1769
Greek altars, origins and typology. 28
Greek and Christian concepts of justice. 2159
Greek and Eastern churches. 1486
Greek and English lexicon of the New Testament. 1769
Greek and Roman ghost stories. 1709
Greek and Roman [mythology]. 2656, 2657, 2662
Greek and Roman religion. 1766
Greek and Roman stoicism and some of its disciples. 1521, 3533
Greek and Russian icons and other liturgical objects in the Collection of Mr. Charles Bolles Rogers. 1881, 3243
Greek and Syrian miniatures in Jerusalem. 1884
[Greek characters for Elthon (romanized form)]-sayings in the synoptic tradition. 387, 2069
Greek culture and the Greek Testament. 1768
Greek divination. 1470
Greek East and the Latin West. 3307
Greek elements. 1770
Greek-England lexicon of the New Testament. 1769
Greek-English analytical concordance. 344
Greek-English analytical concordance [of the Greek-English New Testament. 344, 345
Greek-English concordance to the New Testament. 345, 1769
Greek-English lexicon of the New Testament. 1769
Greek-English lexicon of the New Testament and other early Christian literature. 479, 1768
Greek English lexicon to the New Testament. 1769
Greek-English lexicon to the New Testament after the latest and best authorities. 1769
Greek-English lexicon to the New Testatment after the latest and best authorities. 1769
Greek-English New Testament. 307
Greek-English New Testament. Being the original Greek text ... with a literal ... interlinear translation. 284
Greek fathers. 1616, 1617
Greek fictile revetments in the archaic period. 3604
Greek folk religion. 1767
Greek gods and heroes. 2661, 2662
Greek grammar of the New Testament. 1770
Greek grammar of the New Testament and other early Christian literature. 1769
Greek hero cults and ideas of immortality. 1395
Greek heroes; stories translated from Neibuhr. 2661
Greek horoscopes. 98
Greek in Jewish Palestine. 2101
Greek into Arabic; essays on Islamic philosophy. 2840
Greek legends. 2661
Greek lexicon. 1769
Greek liturgies. 1768
Greek liturgies, chiefly from original authorities. 2748
Greek love mysteries. 2263
Greek manuscripts of Aristotle's poetics. 81
Greek mythology. 2660, 2661
Greek mythology systematized. 2662
Greek myths. 2661
Greek myths and Christian mystery. 1082
Greek myths and their art. 2661
Greek New Testament. 269, 285
Greek of the Fourth gospel. 422
Greek oracles. 2740
Greek origin of Freemasonry. 1664
Greek Orthodox catechism. 2747
Greek orthodox church. 1768, 2744, 2746
Greek Orthodox Church of the Ascension ... Architecture 2N, May 11, 1961. 2719
Greek Orthodox Church of the Ascension, Hellenic community of Oakland and vicinity. 2719
Greek Orthodox prayer book. 3455
Greek particles in the New Testament. 1770
Greek piety. 1767
Greek popular religion. 1767
Greek religion and its survivals. 1766
Greek religious thought from Homer to the age of Alexander. 1766
Greek sanctuaries. 3599
Greek temples. 2698, 3599
Greek Testament. 284, 343
Greek text of Judges. 555
Greek text of the epistles to Timothy and Titus. 479
Greek the language of Christ and His apostles. 425, 2014
Greek thought and the rise of Christianity. 1082
Greek thought in the New Testament. 347
Greek to me. 1770
Greek votive offerings. 3787
Greek words and Hebrew meanings. 1769
Greeks and the irrational. 2732
Greeks and their gods. 1743, 1766
Greeks bearing gifts. 2660
Greeks, gods and heroes. 1743
Green Bay Plan. 3162
Green book. 2970
Green gods. 2533
Green letters. 988
Green olive branch. 2736
Green pastures. 1440
Greenboro Masonic Museum. 1667
Greening of Mrs. Duckworth. 931, 1481
Greening of the church. 1243
... The Greenville Baptist church in Leicester, Massachusetts. 1772
"Greenwood memorial church" (Methodist Episcopal) Dorchester. Massachusetts. 1477
Greet God in the morning. 251
Greet the man. 1259
Greeting. 1113
Gregorian chant. 883, 884, 885
Gregorian chant accompaiment. 884
Gregorian chant analyzed and studied. 884
Gregorian chant for church and school. 883
Gregorian chant rhythm. 884
Gregorian chant, volume two. 885
Gregorian epoch: reformation, revolution, reaction? 1181, 1774
Gregorian Kyriale (requiem mass included) with organ accompaniment. 837
Gregorian music. 884
Gregory of Rimini. 1773
Gregory of Tours. 3635
... Gregory the Great. 1773
Gregory the Great, his place in history and thought. 1773
Gret mystery. 167
Gretchen, I am. 1937, 3519
Grey book. 53
Grey dawns and red. 3126
Grey eminence. 2203
Grey friars. 1641
Grey Friars in Cambridge. 1647
Grey friars in Oxford. 1647
Grey friars of Canterbury, 1224 to 1538. 1647
Grey ladye. 3508
Greyfriars Parish Church, Aberdeen, 1471-1971. 1774
Griechische Mythologie und Religionsgeschichte. 1766
Die griechischen Kultusaltertumer. 1395
Grief and mourning in cross-cultural perspective. 1691
Grief observed. 1349, 1351
Grief's slow wisdom. 1350
Griffith John. 2125, 2511
Griffith John, founder of the Hankow Mission, central China. 2125, 2511
Grihya-sutras. 3239
Grimoire of Lady Sheba. 3824
Gringo volunteers. 2544, 2771
Grinnell vespers. 971
Grip that holds. 1560
Grist for the mill. 3019, 3481
Griswold's Life of Henry Ward Beecher. 184
Grit to grapple with life. 160
Groans of a damned soul. 1470, 1699
Groote Eylandt Mission. 1775, 2523
Grosse Pointe Memorial Church. 2918
Grotesque in church art. 1775
Les grottes de Murabba'at. 1409
Ground and goal of human life. 2228
Ground and grammar of theology. 3084
Ground and nature of the right. 1536
Ground of certainty. 2835
Ground of evil-doing. 1745
Ground of growth. 988
Ground of the heart. 1756
Ground on which Jews will accept Christianity. 1083
Ground plan of the Bible. 312
Ground plan of the English parish church. 1159
Ground to stand on. 65
Ground work for comparative metatheology. 3668
Grounded faith for growing Christians. 989
Grounded in love. 3264
Grounds of a holy life. 977
Grounds of an old surgeon's faith. 3791
Grounds of Christianity examined. 3022
Grounds of Christianity examined by comparing the New Testament with the Old. 3022
Grounds of secession from the M. E. Church. 2449, 3423
Grounds of theistic and Christian belief. 60, 1098
Groundwork of Christian ethics. 945
Groundwork of the metaphysic of morals. 2591
Group. 1170
Group activities for church women. 3837
Group counseling. 1170
Group counseling in the church. 1775
Group discussion in religious education. 3149
Group dynamics in evangelism. 1568
Group dynamics in the religious life. 2574
Group leader as counselor. 1374
Group leaders and boy character. 687
Group leaders' guide. 3873
Group leadership. 2204
Group movement. 2753
Group movements throughout the ages. 2754, 3323
Group readings for the church. 613
Group theories of religion and the individual. 3106
Group workshop way in the church. 1250
Groups alive—church alive. 1170
Groups movement. 2754
Groups that work. 1170
Grow in grace. 1432
Growing a Christian personality. 1015
Growing a church. 1250
Growing a musical church. 1203
Growing a soul. 667, 3347, 3426
Growing as Christians. 960, 977, 3163
Growing as Jesus grew. 896

Growing Christian. 969, 979, 3477
Growing church. 1120
Growing church lobby in Washington. 1149
Growing church school. 3561
Growing churches for a new age. 2956
Growing congregation. 1170
Growing disciples through preaching. 163
Growing edge. 168
Growing edges in home missions for Disciples of Christ. 1464
Growing edges in the psychology of religion. 3001
Growing in Christ. 2284
Growing in Christian faith. 3480
Growing in faith. 3168
Growing in faith and knowledge. 3478
Growing in grace. 295
Growing in love. 3181
Growing in perfect union. 2569
Growing in stature. 3857
Growing in the fellowship. 3174
Growing in the life of prayer. 2872
Growing in the priesthood. 1232, 2401
Growing knowing Jesus. 1430
Growing love in Christian marriage. 2339
Growing menace of the "social gospel," 3441
Growing minister. 2785
Growing minister, his opportunities and obstacles. 2785
Growing miracle. 567, 2948
Growing new churches. 1171
Growing old, and how to cope with it. 18
Growing pains. 3886
Growing pastor. 3673
Growing person. 3176
Growing places. 3886
Growing season. 1810, 2460
Growing, sharing, serving. 3843
Growing spiritually. 1439
Growing storm. 1186
Growing through problems. 2592
Growing together. 2241, 2347
Growing toward God. 963
Growing toward wholeness. 1011
Growing up Christian. 947
Growing up in Christ. 979, 1611, 3888
Growing up in mission. 2551
Growing up in religion. 3884
Growing up in the church. 3185
Growing up in the family. 1611
Growing up isn't easy, Lord. 688
Growing-up stories for four's and five's. Bible teaching for everyday living. 185
Growing up straight. 1844
Growing up to God. 1527, 2997
Growing up with Jesus. 3174
Growing with nursery and kindergarten children. 3170
Growing world mission of Disciples of Christ. 1465
Growth. 2228
Growth and achievement. 684
Growth and contents of the Old Testament. 500, 540
Growth & decline in the Episcopal Church. 1172, 2959
Growth and development of the Catholic School system in the United States. 830
Growth and development of the Young women's Christian association. 3878
Growth and life in the local church. 1244
Growth & structure of the Gospels. 398
Growth counseling. 2780
Growth crisis in the American church. 1172, 3735
Growth in Christ. 972, 2210, 3161
Growth in Christ through the Gospels. 1264
Growth in grace. 990
Growth in holiness. 3478, 3486
Growth in holiness toward perfection. 1823
Growth in ministry. 2787
Growth in partnership. 988
Growth in prayer. 2872
Growth in religion. 3176
Growth in the Holy Spirit. 3487
Growth in the knowledge of our Lord. 1263
Growth in the spirit. 3489
Growth in worship. 3876
Growth of a Christian. 954
Growth of a work of God. 1911
Growth of Christ. 2392
Growth of Christian personality. 3156
Growth of Christianity. 1173
Growth of Japanese churches in Brazil. 2953
Growth of medieval theology (600-1300) 3659
Growth of papal government in the Middle Ages. 2769, 2770
Growth of religion. 3106
Growth of religious and moral ideas in Egypt. 1502

Growth of sacrificial ideas connected with the holy eucharist. 2252
Growth of spiritual power. 3512
Growth of the Biblical tradition. 229
Growth of the body. 334, 3358
Growth of the Christian church. 1178
Growth of the church in Africa. 2497
Growth of the church in Buganda. 712
Growth of the churches in America, 1926-1950. 1275
Growth of the early church. 333, 1197
Growth of the Gospels. 389, 400
Growth of the idea of God. 1724
... Growth of the missionary concept. 2482, 2519
Growth of the Old Testament. 540, 595, 596
... The growth of the papacy. 2769
Growth of the Pentateuch. 563
Growth of the soul. 2641, 3687
Growth of the spiritual life. 3478
Growth or decline? 1123
Growth through groups. 1169
Growth to selfhood. 3542
Guadalupe to Lourdes. 2262
Guaranteed deposits. 2930
Guard drills of the Ladies of the Maccabees of the world. 2305
Guard our unbelief. 3180
Guard the Gospel. 326
Guardian of the faith. 740
Guardian spirits, a case of vision into the spiritual world. 1284
Guardians of liberty. 802
Guarding the outposts. 968
Gubulawayo and beyond. 1948
Guess what, God! 688
Guesses at the riddle of existence. 1017
Guesses at the riddle of existence, and other essays on kindred subjects. 3624
Guessing at truth. 1291, 1786
Guest for souls. 168
Guest of solitude. 1806
Guests of God. 2258
Guia de informacion sobre las instituciones catolicas estadounidenses. 3756
Guidance and cheer for the whole year. 253
Guidance by God. 965
Guidance for Christian home life. 1607
Guidance for religious. 3475
Guidance for the new age. 1448
Guidance for the young. 2592
Guidance from Galatians. 379
Guidance from men of God. 216
...Guidance in associations with limited staff. 2823
Guidance in prayer. 2891
Guidance memo. 3455
Guidance of God. 1740
Guidance of Jesus for to-day. 942
Guidance of religious. 2576
Guidance through life's contradictions. 975
Guidance to the study of the New Testament. 475
Guidance to the study of the Old Testament. 597
Guide against seducing spirits. 3496
Guide and teaching suggestions. 2634
Guide and test sheets for denominational history. 3386
Guide book. 81, 3796, 3797
Guide book for Catholic church choirmasters. 916
Guide book for the Sacred heart cathedral, Richmond, Virginia. 3236
Guide book for volunteers. 3878
Guide book for young people's organizations. 1247
Guide book in catechetical instruction. 747, 2279
Guide-book in the administration of the discipline of the Methodist Episcopal church. 2442
Guide book of the Cathedral of all saints. 22
Guide book of the Little Church Around the Corner. 2697
Guide book of the Little church around the corner, New York city. 2697
Guide book on Baptist institutions in Texas. 170
Guidebook to the Biblical literature. 210
Guide book to Trinity Church and the Parish of Trinity Church in the city of New York, founded 1697. 2701
Guide book to Trinity church in the city of Boston. 2697
Guide for a college course in Christian marriage. 1604
Guide for Catholic young women. 3877
Guide for Catholic young women, Specially for those who earn their own living. 959
Guide for church school teachers. 3154
Guide for genealogical research. 1704

Guide for good priesthood ministry. 2791
Guide for lay readers. 2191
Guide for little footsteps. 724
Guide for modern life. 996
Guide for New Testament study. 407
Guide for Old Testament study. 536
Guide for Reform Jews. 2119, 3032
Guide for religious administrators. 2582
Guide for senior teenage groups on the contribution of the church to the development of Canada. 1252
Guide for social action. 1281
Guide for soul winners and How to be healthy. 1570
...A guide for teachers and parents for use with. 3155
Guide for the Christian assembly. 314, 1264
Guide for the Christian homemaker. 1609
Guide for the daughter of charity. 1403
Guide for the Jewish homemaker. 3842
Guide for the lay preacher. 2910
Guide for the misguided. 231
Guide for the perplexed. 2115, 2623, 2841, 2842
Guide for the preplexed. 2841
Guide for victim souls of the Sacred heart. 3270
Guide for writing the history of a church. 1184
Guide for young disciples of the Holy Saviour, in their way to immortality. 3888
Guide for youth choirs. 915
Guide in church finance. 1168
Guide lines for young men and women. 1324
Guide of Judaism. 2146
Guide of the perplexed. 2841
Guide of the preplexed. 2841
Guide-posts along the way. 3368
Guide-posts on the foot-path to peace. 3207
Guide-posts to immortal roads. 3508
Guide texts for Mass commentators. 846
Guide through Bible history. 297
Guide to America-Holy Land studies. 34
Guide to America-Holy Land studies, 1620-1948. 2765
Guide to American Catholic history. 834, 3739
...A guide to an exhibition of Islamic miniatrue painting and book illumination. 1883
Guide to an Irish gentleman in his search for a religion. 801, 2589
Guide to awareness and tranquillity. 2808
Guide to better living. 3379
Guide to better teaching in the Buddhist Sunday school. 3172
Guide to Bible study. 293, 648
Guide to Bibles in print. 212
Guide to Bibles in print. 1966. 212
Guide to biblical preaching. 298, 2899
Guide to biblical resources. 637
Guide to Buddhist religion. 709
Guide to Catholic college administration. 832
Guide to Catholic literature, 1888-1940. 869
Guide to Catholic literature (The) 869
Guide to Catholic reading. 764
Guide to Catholic reading ... [v. 1. 869
Guide to CFM. 1608
Guide to child activity, for teachers and mothers. 3159
Guide to Christ. 1360
Guide to Christian colleges. 1164
Guide to Christian living. 964
Guide to Christian unity. 1046, 1047
Guide to church building and fund raising. 1268
Guide to church-centered Jewish evangelism. 2556
Guide to church furnishing and decoration. 1169
Guide to church furniture. 1169
Guide to church planting. 1566
Guide to church ushering. 1249
Guide to church woodcarvings. 3846
Guide to Cistercian scholarship. 1276
Guide to confident living. 972, 2995
Guide to curriculum construction for the religious school. 3172
Guide to daily prayer. 1430
Guide to early Oregon churches. 1273
Guide to effective Bible events, historical value, sources, and contents of each book of the Holy Bible, by Max G. Plowman. 311
Guide to effective Bible teaching. 644
Guide to eternal life as taught by the spirit in the new covenant. 1795
Guide to faith. 1705
... A guide to Franciscan studies. 1645
Guide-to-God New Testament. 361
Guide to gods and goddesses. 1742

Guide to gold in Bible mines. 615
Guide to Greetings! For teachers and leaders of preinduction discussion groups. 3456
Guide to Hassidism. 1789
Guide to Hindu religion. 1815
Guide to horoscope interpretation. 1847
Guide to immortality. 1005
Guide to indexed periodicals in religion. 3678
Guide to Islam. 2565
Guide to Jewish history under Nazi impact. 3851
Guide to Jewish holy days. 1614
Guide to Jewish knowledge. 2079, 2154
Guide to Jewish religious practice. 2074, 2120
Guide to Jewish themes in American fiction, 1940-1980. 32, 2087
... Guide to Kant. 2163
Guide to life. 2627
Guide to literature for character training. 905
Guide to living power. 3476
Guide to Marxist philosophy. 1457
Guide to modern versions of the New Testament. 358
Guide to morals. 943
Guide to Mormon diaries & autobiographies. 2608
Guide to Mount St. Sepulchre. 1648
Guide to music for the church year. 1208
Guide to mythology for young readers. 2651
Guide to Nazareth literature, 1873-1973. 3420
Guide to Old Testament study. 595, 596
Guide to Orthodox America. 2751
Guide to Pacem in terris for students. 853
Guide to Pacem in terris for students (with discussion questions) 853
Guide to palmistry. 2766
Guide to pastoral care. 2787
Guide to philosophy. 2833
Guide to piety. 2846
Guide to practical pastoring. 1297
Guide to prayer. 2871, 2882
Guide to preaching. 2907
Guide to Quaker practice. 1684
Guide to reading in aesthetics and theory of poetry. 1533
Guide to reading the Bible. 613
Guide to reading the entire Bible in one year. 613
Guide to religious education. 3615
Guide to research in Quaker records in the Midwest. 1686
Guide to Saint John's Seminary, Camarillo, California. 3275
Guide to St. Mark's Gospel. 433
Guide to Shaker manuscripts in the Library of the Western Reserve Historical Society. 3396
Guide to Sidrot and Haftarot. 566, 2107
Guide to Sunday School enlargement. 3558
Guide to survival. 606, 1514
Guide to the archives and manuscripts of the Diocese of Duluth. 779
Guide to the archives and records from Protestant Christian missions from the British Isles to China. 2505
Guide to the Archives of the Archdiocese of Boston. 764
Guide to the Bible. 285, 311, 650
Guide to the Book of Amos. 486
Guide to the Book of Exodus. 516
Guide to the British Cathedrals. 752
Guide to the cathedral. 1377
Guide to the Cathedral church of Saint John the Divine. 750, 2697
Guide to the Cathedral Church of Saint John the Divine in the City of New York. 2697
Guide to the Catholic sisterhoods in the United States. 2581
Guide to the Christian faith. 3648, 3665
Guide to the Christian faith, an introduction to Christian doctrine. 3665
Guide to the church. 1211
Guide to the churches of Rome. 3245
Guide to The city of God. 115
Guide to the Colorado Woman's Christian Temperance Union papers, 1878-1975. 3833
Guide to the debate about God. 3656
Guide to the diocesan priesthood in the United States. 830
Guide to the Divine liturgy in the East. 2749
Guide to the encyclicals of the Roman pontiffs from Leo xiii to the present day (1878-1937) 1512
Guide to the Epistles of Saint Paul. 374
Guide to the Fathers of the Church. 1616
Guide to the Franciscan monastery, Mt. Saint Sepulchre. 1648

Guide to the Franciscan monastery, Washington, D.C. 1648
Guide to the General Assembly of the Church of Scotland. 1234
Guide to the gods. 1742
Guide to the good life. 945
Guide to the Holy Land. 2763
Guide to the I Ching. 1470, 1878
Guide to the kingdom. 2026
Guide to the knowledge of God. 1732
Guide to the literature of asthetics. 11
Guide to the literature of rural life. 1375
Guide to the New Testament. 410
Guide to the official publications of the European Communities. 1543
Guide to the Old Testament and the Apocrypha. 540
Guide to the parables. 2028
Guide to the parables of Jesus. 2028
Guide to the Pilgrim hymnal. 1876, 3731
Guide to the Prophets. 570
Guide to the Prophets and the Apocrypha. 570
Guide to the psychic life. 2988
Guide to the religions of America. 3325
Guide to the revised Baltimore catechism . . . according to the St. Paul catechism of Christian doctrine. 1404, 3278
Guide to the Revised Baltimore catechism for first communion. 1626
Guide to the Revised Baltimore Catechism for grades 7, 8. 747
Guide to the Savior. 3295
Guide to the study and practice of Judaism. 2144
Guide to the study of church history. 1188
Guide to the study of Revelation. 452
Guide to the study of the Bible. 646
Guide to the study of the Christian religion. 3680
Guide to the study of the development of thought in the New Testament. 475
Guide to the study of the English Bible. 642, 649
Guide to the study of the holiness movement. 1824
Guide to the study of the Old and New Testaments. 639
Guide to the Talmud. 3584
Guide to the teachings of the early church Fathers. 3658
Guide to the thought of Saint Augustine. 117
Guide to the United States for the Jewish immigrant. 3737
Guide to the Victor series of lantern slides for Catholic instruction. 806
Guide to the world's religions. 3141
Guide to Thomas Aquinas. 3693
Guide to three spiritual classics. 1621
Guide to true peace. 3013
Guide to true religion. 1181
Guide to understanding the Bible. 651
Guide to Washington cathedral. 750
Guide to worship in camp and conference. 3858
Guide to Zionism. 2119
Guidebook for developing the church youth program. 1259
Guidebook for the new Christian. 983
Guidebook for the study of psychical research. 2986
Guidebook to astrology. 96
Guidebook to church music promotion. 1204
Guidebook to discipleship. 984
Guidebook to the Bible. 311
Guidebook to the Summa. 3696
Guidebook to the true secret of the heart. 3542
Guidebook to worship services of sacred music. 1209
Guided by God. 1446
Guided by visions. 1283
Guidelines. 2390
Guidelines and syllabus on Islamic education. 3172
Guidelines for a Texas Mission. 2716, 3298
Guidelines for evaluation of the local urban church. 1277
Guidelines for family worship. 1607
Guidelines for high school CCD teachers. 1330, 3179
Guidelines for living. 974
Guidelines for mystical prayer. 2637
Guidelines for parents. 1608
Guidelines for survival. 966
Guidlines for urban church planting. 1278
Guidelines for women's groups in the congregation. 3837
Guidelines for world evangelism. 2496
Guidelines to courageous living. 1375
Guidepost. 2584
Guideposts. 962
Guideposts anthology. 1014

Guideposts Christmas treasury. 1112
Guideposts Family topical concordance to the Bible. 227
Guideposts for the church musician. 1203
Guideposts for worship. 3856
Guideposts for youth. 2935
Guideposts to a stronger faith. 2808
Guideposts to creative family worship. 1608
Guideposts to happiness. 3387
Guideposts treasury of faith. 1602
Guideposts treasury of hope. 1845
Guideposts treasury of inspiration. 1447
Guideposts treasury of love. 983
Guideposts trilogy. 1014
Guides to the higher life. 3366
Guiding a church school. 3558
Guiding a growing life. 3150
Guiding ... along the trail. 2599
Guiding children. 939
Guiding children in Christian growth. 3129, 3171
Guiding children in the nursery class. 3173
Guiding children in worship. 3859
Guiding hand. 2981
Guiding individual growth. 3147
Guiding intermediates. 3169
Guiding intermediates in worship. 3857
Guiding Jewish youth. 2086
Guiding junior boys and girls in the Sunday school. 3153
Guiding kindergarten children in the church school. 3174
Guiding light. 3509
Guiding light on the great highway. 289
Guiding nursery children in home and church (successor to the author's The nursery class of the church school) 3555
Guiding power. 3518
Guiding preschoolers. 939
Guiding star to a higher spiritual condition, sequel number two to "Rending the vail" 3509
Guiding the experience of worship. 3858
Guiding the little child in the Sunday school. 3157
Guiding the nursery class. 3173
Guiding the primary child in the Sunday school. 3156
Guiding thoughts to success and achievement. 3537
Guiding workers in Christian education. 3178
Guiding young people in Bible study. 3179
Guiding youth. 939, 3879
Guiding youth in Christian growth. 3175
Guido and Julius. 3030
Guild of Saint Apollonia. 1777
Guilt. 775, 1777, 2575
Guilt and freedom. 1777
Guilt & grace. 1777
Guilt and grace ; The meaning of persons ; The person reborn ; To understand each other. 1777
Guilt and redemption. 3030
Guilt and the Christian. 1777
Guilt, anger, and God. 61
Guilt free. 1777
Guilt, grace, and gratitude. 1801
Guilt of sin. 3414
Guilt of slavery and the crime of slaveholding. 231, 3425
Guilt: where religion and psychology meet. 1327
Guilty, O Lord; yes, I still go to confession. 1326
Guitars and water jars. 2547
Guitton at the Council. 3769
Guns, guts, and God! 1368, 1573
Gupta sculpture. 1778, 3316
Gurdjieff, seeker of the truth. 1778
Guru. 1778
Guru, by his disciple. 1778
Guru: Chitshaktivilas. 2630, 3491
Guru Gobind Singh. 1749
Guru Nanak and the Sikh religion. 2668, 3408
Guru Tegh Bahadur. 3408, 3592
Gurus, swamis, and avataras: spiritual masters and their American disciples. 3322
Gustavo Gutierrez. 1779
Gutenberg Bible, landmark in learning. 314, 1778
Guthlac of Croyland. 1778
Gutter and the ghetto. 1255
Guy de Fontgalland. 1632
Gwinnett churches. 1270
Gyana yoga. 3867

H

H. A. Ironside, ordained of the Lord. 1920
H.A.R.; the autobiography of Father Reinhold. 2939
H. C. Early, Christian statesman. 1485
H. G. Wells. 3801
H. M. S. Richards, man alive. 3235
H. P. B. 671
H. P. Blavatsky. 671, 3687
H. P. Blavatsky and The secret doctrine. 672
H. P. Blavatsky and the theosophical movement. 671, 3682, 3687
H. P. Blavatsky to the American conventions, 1888-1891. 3689
H. Richard Niebuhr. 2708
H. T. W. S. S. T. K. S. and his followers. 1668
Ha! Ha! among the trumpets. 2299, 3351
Ha! Ha! amoung the trumpets. 2299
Habakkuk in the ancient commentary from Qumran. 1779
Habaqquq III and Selah. 529
Habit talks and missionary stories. 3765
Habitation of dragons. 986
Habits and virtues. 3782
Habitual drinking and its remedy. 3595
Hacaritama (ah-kah-ree-tah-mah). 39, 2512
Had you been born in another faith. 3112
Hadassah: Esther the orphan queen. 630, 1533
Hadassah, the Jewish orphan. 33, 1532
Hagadah. 1780
Hagadah for Passover. 3022
Hagadah for Pesach. 1780
[Hagadah shel Pesah (romanized form)]. 1780
Hagarism. 1924
Haggada. 1780
Haggadah. 1780
Haggadah and history. 2110
Haggadah for a secular celebration of Pesach. 1780
Haggadah for Passover. 2110
Haggadah for the school. 1780
Haggadah of Passover. 1780
Haggadah: past and present. 2110
Haggadah"Me-ir Ay-ni-yim" 2110
Haggai and Malachi. 529
... Haggai and Zechariah. 529
Haggai, Zechariah, Malachi. 529
Hagia Sophia. 1929, 2621
Haifa. 2762
Hail, holy Queen. 854, 3296
Hail Mary. 120, 2361
Hail Mary for little Catholics. 2360
Hail Mary, full of grace. 3248
Hail! The altar boy. 27
Hainuwele. 2664
Haircuts and holiness. 2385
Haiti diary. 2524
Haiti, status of Christianity. 1100
Hajj studies. 2635
Hajj today. 2635
Hal, "a young life of real worth." 888
Halcyon days. 3274
Hales Owen Parish Church, St. John Baptist. 1781
Half a century. 2427
Half a century of Lutheranism among our colored people. 2295
Half a century's labors in the gospel. 3134
Half a hero and Father Stafford. 3128
Half a lifetime in Korea. 2536
Half can never be told. 3229
Half century among the Siamese and the Lao. 2537
Half-century discourse. 2702
Half-century history of Rebekah odd fellowship of the I. O. O. F. from its organization in 1851 to 1901. 3027
Half century messages to pastors and people. 2436
Half-century of the Unitarian controversy, with particular reference to its origin, its course, and its prominent subjects among the Congregationalists of Massachusetts. 3727
Half century of theology. 3656
Half century of Union Theological Seminary. 2701
Half hours with college students. 3355
Half-hours with St. John's epistles. 3358
Half hours with the Bible. 1450
Half hours with the lessons of 1883. 1915
Half-known God. 1833
Half time. 1121
Half-truths or whole Gospel? 1007
Half-way covenant. 1201
Half-way to faith. 1058
Half-year in the prayer book. 2969
Halford Luccock treasury. 3633

Halfway to heaven. 928, 3414
Half way to noon. 885
Halfway up the mountain. 1325, 2462, 3750
Hall of magic mirrors. 671
Al Hallaj. 21, 3543
Hallelujah anyway, Tim! 326, 1003
Hallelujah Army. 3293
Hallelujah hole. 1407
Hallelujah Jack. 1576
Hallowed be this house. 1608
Hallowed flame. 3131
Hallowed songs. 1868
Hallowed were the gold dust trails. 726, 815
Hallowing the time. 1264
Hallucinogens and shamanism. 1782
Halo for a housewife. 3844
Halo for father. 1618
Halo of the cross. 2757
Halo on the sword. 1938
Halting kingdom. 12
Ham and Japheth. 1782, 3468
Hamadsha. 1782
Hamer's Bible animals. 480
[Hamesh megilot ve-sefer Yonah (romanized form)]. 519
Hamlet's divinity. 872
Hamlet's mill. 2648
Hamlet's search for meaning. 1101, 3399
Hammer and fire. 3489
Hammer and sparks. 1839
Hammer of the Lord. 2436, 3154, 3365
Hammer on the mountain: life of Henry Steel Olcott (1832-1907) 2735
Hammer on the rock. 547, 2462, 3481
Hammered as gold. 2512
Hammers in the fire. 2397
Hampshire colony Congregational church, its first hundred years, 1831-1931. 1274
Hampshire churches. 1783
Hampton Adams. 6
Hand. 1783
Hand and the spirit. 84
Hand-book of Christ church, Philadelphia. 1273
Hand-book of freemasonry. 1664
... Hand book of instructions for healing and helping others. 2410
Hand book of plans & programs for the community council. 3168
Hand-book of prophecy. 2949
Hand-book on Mormonism. 2601
Hand clasps with the holy. 3281
Hand in hand. 903
Hand in hand with the wise men. 3564
Hand me another brick. 953, 2683
Hand of a child. 3207
Hand of God. 782, 1449, 1550, 3663
Hand of God in American history. 3351
Hand of God in history. 2948, 2981, 2982
Hand of God in human experience. 529
Hand of God in my life. 3126
Hand of God in the Sudan. 2552
Hand of God on the wall. 3224
Hand of mercy. 756
Hand of the Lord. 81, 483
Hand that intervenes. 2982
Hand book on infant baptism. 135, 2105, 3033, 3191
Handbook for American Catholic hymnals. 813
Handbook for Bible students. 321
Handbook for Bible study. 640
Handbook for Board of Christian Education and its staff. 3735
Handbook for Catholic parents. 896, 898
Handbook for Christian believers. 3666
Handbook for Christian homemakers. 1838
Handbook for Christian writers. 3203
Handbook for church recreation leaders. 1166
Handbook for church secretaries. 1247
Handbook for church weddings. 3800
Handbook for committees of congregations of the Lutheran Church in America. 2290
Handbook for congregational officers. 1239
Handbook for conscietious objectors. 1348
Handbook for elders and deacons. 1239
Handbook for engaged couples. 2345
Handbook for Episcopalians. 2959
Handbook for followers of Jesus. 3888
Handbook for Forty hours' adoration. 1635
Handbook for guide patrol leaders. 2599
...Handbook for high school and boarding school Girl reserves, Y.W.C.A. 1715
Handbook for hospital chaplains. 1258
Hand-book for inquirers and converts. 1358
Handbook for leaders. 642
...A handbook for leaders of younger girls. 1715
Handbook for lectors. 2202

Handbook for mission groups. 1169, 3797
Handbook for missionary workers among
   the American Indians. 1900
Handbook for new Catholics. 770
... Handbook for Orthodox Sunday schools.
   620
Handbook for personal soul-winning. 1572
Handbook for Presbyterian pioneers. 687
Handbook for Presbyterians. 2920
Handbook for primary teachers in church
   Sunday schools. 3155
Handbook for senior highs in the church.
   2459
Handbook for sisters. 1357
Hand-book for soul winners. 1567
Handbook for special preaching. 2897
Handbook for spiritual survival. 983
Hand-book for Sunday-school teachers.
   3550
Handbook for Sunday-school workers.
   3556
Handbook for teachers of religion in grades
   3, 4, 5. 746
Handbook for teaching the Bible in
   literature classes. 211
Handbook for the beginner's home study
   in the word of God. 2287
Handbook for the Catholic choir. 1205
Handbook for the church office. 1200
Handbook for the church secretary. 1247
Handbook for the congregational school
   board member. 2086
Handbook for the humanistic astrologer.
   96
Handbook for the leadership education
   curriculum. 3177
Handbook for the lectionary. 298, 1261
Handbook for the new rubrics. 848
Handbook for the preacher at work. 2785
Handbook for the study of the English
   Bible. 648
Handbook for today's Disciples. 932
Handbook for vestrymen. 1239
Hand-book for workers. 302
... Handbook for workers with young
   people. 1260
Handbook of all denominations. 3323
Handbook of association business
   administration. 3873
Hand-book of Bible biography. 213
Handbook of Bible games for all ages. 281
Handbook of Bible geography. 283
Handbook of Bible history. 297
Handbook of Bible lands. 282, 2678
Hand-book of Bible manners and customs.
   207
Hand-book of Bible reading. 613
Handbook of Bible types and symbols.
   243
Handbook of Biblical chronology. 218
Handbook of Biblical criticism. 240, 286
Handbook of Biblical personalities. 217
Handbook of canon law. 735
Handbook of canon law, for congregations
   of women under simple vows. 2577
Handbook of Catholic practices. 808
Handbook of ceremonies for priests and
   seminariana. 839
Handbook of ceremonies for priests and
   seminarians. 770, 839, 1702
Handbook of Christian doctrine. 1849,
   3644
Handbook of Christian etiquette. 1540
Handbook of Christian feasts and customs.
   1262, 1263
Handbook of Christian meditation. 2381
Handbook of Christian psychology. 2998
Handbook of Christian realism. 1052
Handbook of Christian social ethics. 3449
Handbook of Christian symbols. 921
Handbook of Christian symbols and stories
   of the saints as illustrated in art. 921
Handbook of Christian theologians. 3611
Handbook of Christian theology. 3638,
   3648
Handbook of Christian theology (A) 3638
Handbook of Christian truth. 648, 3645
Handbook of church administration. 1250
... Handbook of church advertising. 10
Handbook of church correspondence.
   1165
Handbook of church finance. 1168
Handbook of church history. 1175, 1176
Handbook of church law for the clergy.
   1489
Handbook of church management. 2786
Handbook of church music. 1208
Handbook of classical mythology. 2658,
   2659
Handbook of comparative religion. 3061,
   3117
Handbook of concepts for living. 3661
Handbook of contemporary theology.
   3656, 3657
Handbook of denominations in the United
   States. 1038, 3326

Handbook of ecclesiology and Christology.
   1117, 2037
Handbook of effective church letters.
   1165
Handbook of Egyptian religion. 1501
Handbook of English cathedrals. 751
Handbook of eschatology. 1530
Handbook of evangelism for laymen. 1563
Handbook of French and Belgin
   Protestantism. 2954
Handbook of fundamental theology. 62
Handbook of Good templary. 1913
Handbook of Greek religion. 1766
Handbook of heresies. 1804
Handbook of information. 2422
Handbook of Judaism. 2116
Handbook of legendary and mythological
   art. 84
Handbook of masonic law of New York.
   1666
...Handbook of medical ethics for nurses,
   physicians and priests. 2377
...Handbook of medical ethics for nurses,
   physicians and priests. Preface by the
   Most Reverend James C. McGuigan.
   2377
Handbook of moral theology. 948, 2593
Handbook of mythology. 2651, 2655
Handbook of New Testament Greek. 1770
Handbook of Newman. 2702
Handbook of Norse mythology. 2666
Handbook of notes on theology. 2593
Handbook of parish music. 1206
Handbook of patrology. 1616, 1618
Handbook of preaching resources from
   English literature. 1841
Handbook of preaching resources from
   literature. 1842
Handbook of prophecy. 2948
Handbook of psi discoveries. 2990
Handbook of public prayer. 2783
Handbook of religious instruction for week
   day and Sunday schools. 640
Handbook of revivals. 1564
Handbook of school policies and practices
   of the diocese of Pittsburgh. 824
Handbook of Scripture study. 312
Handbook of St. Paul. 2802
Handbook of standards, principles and
   policies. 3293
Handbook of stewardship procedures.
   3530
Handbook of symbols in Christian art. 922
Handbook of the American Lutheran
   Church. William Larsen, secy. 32
Handbook of the Bible. 480
Handbook of the Catholic faith (The
   triptych of the kingdom) [by] N. G. M.
   van Doornik. 762
Handbook of the Christian religion for the
   use of advanced students and the
   educated laity. 783, 808
Handbook of the community church
   movement in the United States. 1274
Handbook of the Confraternity of Christian
   doctrine. 805
Handbook of the Congregational
   foundation for education. 1338
Handbook of the financial law. 2614
Handbook of the Gospels. 398
Handbook of the life of the apostle Paul.
   2796
Handbook of the liturgy. 2235
Handbook of the Lutheran Church --
   Missouri Synod. 2296
Handbook of the Methodist protestant
   church. 2459
Handbook of the militant Christian. 960
Handbook of the National Catholic war
   council. 1543
Handbook of the new thought. 2694
Handbook of the Northern Baptist
   convention. 2714
Handbook of the Religious Society of
   Friends. 1679
Handbook of the restoration. 2607
Handbook of the revolution. 3233
Handbook of the science of
   correspondences. 1370
Handbook of the Third Order Secular of
   St. Francis of Assisi. 1649
Handbook of the United brethren in
   Christ. 3730
Handbook of the world's religions. 3122
Handbook of the Young women's
   Christian association movement. 3879
Handbook of the Young womens Christian
   associations of the United States of
   America. 3879
Handbook of theological terms. 3638
Handbook of theosophy. 3684
Hand book of Washington cathedral. 3796
Handbook on administration for Catholic
   institutions of higher education in the
   United States. 830
Handbook on Bible study. 473
Handbook on Brethren hymns. 1236

Handbook on children's evangelism. 1253
Handbook on Christian dating. 1403
Handbook on Christian education in the
   inner city. 1278
Handbook on conversions to the religions
   of the world. 1361
Handbook on deliverance. 1428
Handbook on evangelism. 1570
Handbook on the origin and history of the
   International uniform Sunday-school
   lessons from 1825 on and 1872-1924.
   1916
Handbook on witches. 3824
Handbook, Senior High Fellowship. 1260
Handbook to Catholic historical New York
   city. 873
Handbook to the Bible. 207
Handbook to the Christian liturgy. 2238
Handbook to the Church hymnary. 1199
Handbook to the Hymnal. 2925
Handbook to the life and times of St.
   Teresa and St. John of the Cross. 741,
   3603
Handbook to The Lutheran hymnal. 2302
Handbook to the Mennonite hymnary.
   2406
Handbook to the New Testament. 474
Handbook to the Old Testament. 596
Handbook to the textual criticism of the
   New Testament. 351
Handel's Messiah. 9, 1783
Handel's Messiah; origins, composition,
   sources. 1783
Handful of certainties. 897
Handful of nuggets. 1450
Handful of pearls. 413, 982
Handful of quietness. 3013, 3243
Handfuls of purpose. 1445
Handicapped. 664
Handing on the faith. 746
Handle and the axe. 872
Handles of power. 960
Handling life. 2932
Handling special materials in libraries.
   2225
Handling the church's money. 1168
Handlist of anarchist material in the library
   of the University of Stirling. 38, 3532
Handlist of parish register transcripts in
   the Borthwick Institute of Historical
   Research. 682, 1243
Handlist of the records of the Bishop of
   Lincoln and of the Archdeacons of
   Lincoln and Stow. 2230
Handmaid of the Divine Physician. 1258
Handmaid of the holy rosary, Mother
   Mary Alphonsus of the Rosary, first
   foundress of an Arab congregation.
   1332, 2352
Handmaid of the Lord. 2358
Handmaid to theology. 3659
Handmaidens of the King to foreign lands.
   3466
Hands at rest. 1479, 2534
Hands for others. 2376
Hands full of honey. 3347
Hands, hands, hands, thank you, God for
   hands. 3166
Hands that care. 2718
Hands to the needy. 1774, 3890
Handwork for junior societies. 3563
Handwork in religious education. 3159
Hand-work in the Sunday-school. 3555
Handy book. 1167
Handy companion, dedicated to our
   soldiers and sailors, and to the honor and
   glory of the cross and flag. 3455
Handy concordance. 227
Handy-dandy evolution refuter. 1580
Handy dictionary of the Bible. 243, 246
Handy helps for busy workers. 1570
Handy Scripture guide. 2610
Handyman of the Lord. 682, 2681
Hang in there. 2815
Hang on to the Lord's prayer. 2247
Hang on to your heritage. 2914
Hang tough in a hostile world. 404, 405,
   993
Hanging in there with Christ. 3490
Hannah. 1780
Hannington of Africa. 1784
Hans Egede. 1500
Hans Kung. 776, 3633
Hans Kung and reunion. 2188
Hans Kung, his work and his way. 2188,
   3621
Hans Memlinc's paintings for the Hospital
   of Saint John in Bruges. 922, 2401
Hans Nielsen Hauge, his life and message.
   1790, 3655
Hans Urs von Balthasar. 775, 3632
Hanserd Knollys. 2179
Hansi's new life. 1817
Hanukkah. 1784, 1785
Hanukkah ABC. 1784
Hanukkah anthology. 1784
Hanukkah book. 1784

Hanukkah crafts. 2073
Hanukkah in song and story. 1785
Hanukkah story. 1784, 1785
Haphtoroth. 529
Happen stance. 983, 1003
Happening at Lourdes. 2262
Happiest day. 632, 2054
Happiest people on earth. 3394
Happiness. 163, 181, 584, 1438, 1785,
   3707
Happiness and Christian hope. 1785
Happiness and contemplation. 1356
Happiness and health in Christ. 1599
Happiness can be a habit. 3750
Happiness can be a havit. 3750
Happiness for patients. 3405
Happiness in Christian living. 971
Happiness in holiness. 1649
Happiness in the cloister. 2570
Happiness is. 1445, 1785
Happiness is a family time together. 1607
Happiness is a family walk with God.
   1607
Happiness is a habit. 973
Happiness is God's gift. 180
Happiness is not an accident. 1785
Happiness is still home made. 1609
Happiness of the blessed considered as to
   the particulars of their state. 1794
Happiness outside the state. 2146
Happiness over the hill. 1000
Happiness through prayer. 2879
Happiness through victory. 1450
Happiness unlimited. 3336
Happiness wall to wall. 1013
Happiness with God. 3490
Happy Acres. 1610
Happy are ye. 966
Happy are you who affirm. 999
Happy ascetic. 2826
Happy birthday, baby Jesus. 2023
Happy bondage. 1071
Happy book of happy stories. 1114
Happy Christ. 1950
Happy crusaders. 868
Happy day. 3835
Happy days for shut-ins. 725
Happy family made happier. 2203
Happy hang up! 3887
Happy heart. 2319
Happy home stories. 1015
Happy hours with Christ. 3407
Happy housewife. 3830
Happy in hell. 1785
Happy is the man. 1007
Happy issue. 879
Happy life. 1785
Happy m0ments with God. 1604
Happy man. 2933, 3165
Happy medium: the life of Caroline
   Randolph Chapman. 886
Happy memories of a Sister of charity.
   3416
Happy moments with God. 1604, 3882
Happy path. 3887
Happy Purim night. 3006
Happy Sam, the converted miner. 3292
"Happy seeker, happy finder," 2933
Happy talk. 1605
Happy talks. 974
Happy those who believe. 996
Happy times in our church. 3764
Happy warriors. 3293
Happy warriors: the story of the social
   work of the Salvation Army. 3293
Happy was my youth. 1700
Happy year. 3506
Har-Magedon, before and after. 463
Haralds of a passion. 1049
Harbinger of the millennium. 958
Harbinger's testimony. 1052
Harbin's notes on the Epistle to the
   Hebrews. 405
Harbor Jim of Newfoundland. 955
Hard commands of Jesus. 2071
Hard life. 3884
Hard look at adult Christian education.
   3168
Hard questions. 3621
Hard rain and a cross. 1057
Hard sayings of Jesus. 2072
Hard times. 978
Hard-to-teach child. 2204
Hardeman-Bogard debate, held at Little
   Rock, Arkansas, April 19-22, 1938,
   between N. B. Hardeman ... and Ben M.
   Bogard. 1829
Hardeman's Tabernacle sermons. 1273,
   3352
Hardest journey. 1682
Hardness of heart. 3410
Hare Krishna and the counterculture.
   2186
Hariakhan Baba, known, unknown. 1786
Hariyana. 1816, 2461
Hark to the trumpet. 571

HARKNESS PIANO METHOD

RELIGIOUS BOOKS 1876 - 1982

Harkness piano method of evangelistic hymn playing. 1861
Harlem. 2973
Harlem-Upper Manhattan church and community study. 1786
Harlot and the Virgin. 3024
Har-Moad; or The mountain of the assembly. 3118
... Harmonia evangelica. 396
Harmonia sacra. 917
Harmoniae caelestes. 3206
Harmonial man. 3499
Harmonic arrangement of the Acts of the apostles. 333
Harmonics in astrology. 94
Harmonious vision. 2469
Harmonist. 2451
Harmonized and subject reference New Testament. 356
Harmonized exposition of the four Gospels. 386
Harmonizing of science and the Bible. 204, 606
Harmony. 981
Harmony and commentary on the life of St. Paul according to the Acts of the Apostles and the Pauline Epistles. 2797
Harmony and discord. 1204
Harmony and numbers in Latin and English. 2199
Harmony between the Old and New Testamens respecting the Messiah. 2414
Harmony of ages. 183
Harmony of being. 1034
Harmony of reason. 2163
Harmony of religious truth and human reason asserted in a series of essays. 1098
Harmony of science and Scripture. 205
Harmony of science and the Bible. 205
Harmony of science and the Bible, and the relation of man to each. 206
Harmony of science and the Bible on the nature of the soul and the doctrine of the ressurection. 3462
Harmony of sermons. 166
Harmony of the Bible with science. 204
Harmony of the books of Samuel, Kings and Chronicles. 3297
Harmony of the four Gospels in English. 395
Harmony of the four Gospels in Greek. 396
Harmony of the Gospel narratives of Holy week. 1988
Harmony of the Gospels. 396, 1989
Harmony of the Gospels for historical study. 395, 396
Harmony of the Gospels for students. 396
Harmony of the Gospels for students of the life of Christ. 396
Harmony of the Gospels in Greek. 396
Harmony of the Gospels in modern English. 1987
Harmony of the Gospels in the revised version. 396
Harmony of the Gospels in the words of the American standard edition of the revised Bible. 396
Harmony of the Holy Scriptures. 236
Harmony of the kings. 2095
Harmony of the life of St. Paul according to the Acts of the Apostles and the Pauline Epistles. 2795
Harmony of the life of St. Paul according to the Acts of the apostles and the Pauline epistles. 2797
Harmony of the prophetic word. 567
Harmony of the religious life. 998
Harmony of the synoptic Gospels for historical and critical study. 396
Harmony of the synoptic Gospels in Greek. 397
Harmony of the three commissions. 2047
Harmony of the Westminster Presbyterian standards, with explanatory notes. 2913
Harmony of the words and works of Jesus Christ. 395
Harmony oif the Gospels. 395
... A harmony study of Exodus. 517
... A harmony study of Judges, Ruth, i and ii Samuel, and Psalms. 597
Harnack and Troeltsch; two historical theologians. 1786
Harnessed for service. 3876
Harnessing God. 1560
Harold S. Bender, educator, historian, churchman. 187
Harold St. John. 3274
Harp and psaltery. 581
Harp of David. 2208
Harp of God. 1941
Harp of Zion. 142, 2048
Harper book of Christian poetry. 1022
Harper study Bible. 274

Harper study Bible: The Holy Bible. Rev. standard version. Translated from the original tongues, being the version set forth A.D. 1611, rev. A.D. 1881-1885 and A.D. 1901, compared with the most ancient authorities and rev. A.D. 1952. Reference ed. with concordance and maps. 274
Harper's annotated Bible. 220
Harper's Bible commentary. 224
Harper's Bible dictionary. 245
Harper's encyclopedia of Bible life. 245
Harper's introduction to the Bible. 310
Harper's topical concordance. 303
Harper's world of the New Testament. 408, 2148
Harps of God ... and the chords they play. 1150
Harriet Starr Cannon. 3415
Harrisonburg Baptist church, 1869-1944. 1275
Harry Denman. 1302, 1424
Harry Emerson Fosdick's art of preaching. 1635, 2909
Harry Hosier, circuit rider. 1302, 1848
Harry Orchard, the man God made again. 1363
Harry P. Stagg. 146, 3524
Harry Woollcombe, bishop. 3847
Harsh and dreadful love. 871, 1407
Hartford papers. 2959
Hartford seminary foundation; training for religious leadership. 953
Hartford theological seminary. 1788
Hartford's First church. 1787
Hartmann's international directory of psychic science and spiritualism. 2731
Hartmann's who's who in occult, psychic and spiritual realms. 2731
Hartwick seminary conference on the social mission of the Lutheran church. 1138
Harvard Divinity School. 1788
Harvard divinity school bulletin; issue containing the annual lectures and book reviews. 3621
Harvard theological review. 3677
Harvest. 3371
Harvest and the reaper. 3233
Harvest and the reapers. 1568, 1569
Harvest festivals. 450
Harvest field. 1273
Harvest in the desert. 3897
Harvest is great. 3331
Harvest is rich. 3415
Harvest 1960. 867
Harvest of faith. 17
Harvest of happy years. 2202
Harvest of hearts; missionary experiences. 1756
Harvest of iniquity. 462
Harvest of light. 2992
Harvest of medieval theology. 658, 3659
Harvest of the spirit. 164, 381, 955, 963
Harvest on the prairies. 153
Harvest recitations. 3560
Harvest: sermons, addresses, studies. 3371
Harvest within. 968
Harvey Vonore. 3143
Has Christianity a revelation? 3224
Has Christ's return two stages? 3318
Has God called you? 3784
Has God rejected his people? 1073
Has God spoken? 278, 3083
Has man an immortal soul? 2372
Has Rome converted? 759
Has science discovered God? 3081, 3084
Has sin changed? 3410
Has spiritualism any foundation in the Bible? 3501
Has the church a future? 1119
Has the ecumenical movement a future? 1492
Has the immigrant kept the faith? 828, 874
Has the new liturgy changed you? 2368
Hasidic anthology. 1789
Hasidic community of Williamsburg. 1789, 2121
Hasidic prayer. 2885, 2886
Hasidic tales of the Holocaust. 1825
Hasidic thought. 1789
Hasidism and enlightenment (1780-1820) 1789
Hasidism and modern man. 1788
Haskalah movement in Russia. 1789, 2102
Hasmonean hoax. 609
Hassocks for your church. 1488, 3277
Hasten to take away the spoils: make haste to take away the prey. 543
Hastening the day of God. 3319
Hastings' illustrations. 1840
Hatching chickens for the hawks. 1444
Hatha yoga. 3867
Hatha yoga pradipika. 3867
Haunted Britain. 1710
Haunted house. 3347

Haunted house and other sermons for the family service. 907, 2973
Haunted houses and wandering ghosts of California. 1817
Haunted mind. 1709
Haunted people. 1709
Haunting of America. 1710
Haunting of Bishop Pike. 2846, 3520
Have a good day, and other sermons. 2301
Have a lively faith. 3662
Have a wonderful time! 1004
Have faith in God. 1593, 2876
Have faith without fear. 994
Have it His way. 3877
Have mercy upon me. 584
Have no fear. 2808
Have this mind. 2436
Have time and be free. 1323
Have we lived before? 3055
Have we outgrown religion! 1048
Have you a religion? 3059
Have you been saved? 3288
Have you ever asked yourself these questions? 2751
Have you felt like giving up lately? 989
Have you lived on other worlds before? 3473
Have you lived other lives? 3055
Have you lost God? 1726
Have you met these women? 3840
Have you seen my father? 318
Have you talked to Him? 3474
Have you tried this? 3173
Haven house for the once born. 966
Haven of my salvation. 835
Haverford symposium on archaeology. 1582
Hawaii and its gods. 1791
Hawaii, lei of islands. 826
Hawaii, 1778-1920, from the viewpoint of a bishop. 2524
Hawaiian folk tales. 3581
Hawaiian mythology. 2663
Hawaii's religions. 1791
Hawks of the sun. 78
Hazard of the die. 1612
Hazor; the rediscovery of a great citadel of the Bible. 1792
Hazy moon off enlightenment. 3493
He author. 22
He became like us. 2057
"He being dead yet speaketh." 3755
He calls me by my name. 941
He came from Galilee. 1961, 1970
He came to me. 970
He cares for me. 11
He cares, He comforts. 1353
He celebration of the Eucharist facing the people. 2255
...He cometh. 8
He died as He lived. 2059
[He epikeimene pale]. 3384
"He ezpounded" 2907
He gave some prophets. 570
He grew in wisdom. 2048
He had to preach. 1846
He had to preach;an informal biography of Hampton C. Hopkins. 1846
He has come! 1114
He has done marvelous things. 3164
He has never left us. 1452
He history of Jesus Christ. 1961
He is able. 974, 2437
He is in heaven. 2514, 3717
He is Lord. 2040
He is Lord of all. 2059
He is not here. 2051
He is risen. 1486
He is there and He is not silent. 1105
He is worthy. 990, 2046
"He knoweth not how" 2507
He knows how you feel. 2399
He lapsed. 1166
He leadeth me. 617, 1277, 3851
He leads, I follow. 678
He led me through the wilderness. 1446, 3143
He lives. 1318, 2053
He made planet Earth! 1382
He made the stars also. 168
He opened the Book. 3672
He opened to us the Scriptures. 230
He pasa ekklesia; an original history of the religious denominations at present existing in the United States. 3326
He prayed. 1953, 2875
He reigns from the cross. 2057
He restoreth my soul. 979, 1439, 1447, 1587, 2619
"He sent His word and healed them" 268
He sent leanness. 2873
He sent two. 25, 3310
He sets the captive free. 928, 3601
"He shall speak peace." 253
He social thought of John XXIII: Mater et magistra. 853

He speaks from the cross. 2057
He speaks the word of God. 2809
He spoke, now they speak. 2938
He spoke to the ages. 165
He spoke to them in parables. 2027, 2434
He started from nowhere, and other stories. 3370
"He stirreth up the people" 3443
He story of his life as recorded in the Vita prima Bernardi by certain of his contemporaries, William of St. Thierry, Arnold of Bonnevaux, Geoffrey and Philip of Clairvaux, and Odo of Deuil. A first translation into English by Geoffrey Webb and Adrian Walker. 193
He suffered. 1837
He taught them saying. 2067
He that cometh. 954, 2415
"He that giveth" 3530
"He that hath an ear" 461
He that is spiritual. 1828
He that liveth. 1965
He that winneth souls. 1563
He took it upon himself. 3434
He touched her. 1598, 3809
He touched me. 2877
He upset the world. 2795
He was called Jesus. 3188
He wears orchids. 2979
He wears orchids, & other Latin American stories. 2979
He who has no sword. 1065
He who hunted birds in his father's village. 1780
He who is. 3218, 3608
He who lets us be. 1735
"He whom a dream hath possessed" 966
He will abundantly pardon. 2300
He will answer. 1010
He will come. 3320, 3321
"He yet speaketh" 2973
Head and face masks in Navaho ceremonialism. 2676
Head of the corner. 1195, 1955
Head of the family. 1615
Head over heels. 1001
Heading for the center of the universe. 974
Headline news. 2301
Headlines. 606
Headmaster. 3535
Heads above the stars. 761
Heads bowed together. 1456
Heads of religious houses, England and Wales, 940-1216. 2582
Heal my heart O Lord. 2389
Heal the sick. 1598, 1792
Heal thyself through Christ-Messiah. 1792
Heal yourself. 2728
Healed of Cancer. 734, 2202
Healer of the mind. 924
Healing. 1599, 1600, 2784
Healing and Christianity. 1601
Healing and missions. 2538
Healing and occult science. 3688
Healing and redemption. 1600
Healing and religious faith. 1598
Healing and the conquest of pain. 1600
Healing and wholeness. 2378
Healing and wholeness are yours! 1600
Healing at Lourdes. 2262
Healing Christ. 1070
Healing devotions. 1433
Healing en masse. 1600
Healing evangel. 923
Healing for you. 1258
Healing forces. 3515
Healing fountain. 1017
Healing gifts of the Spirit. 1600
Healing gods of ancient civilizations. 1742, 1955
Healing in His wings. 3541
Healing in Jesus' name. 1601
Healing in the church. 1229
Healing in the churches. 1601
Healing in the family. 1611
Healing is yours. 1599
Healing leaves. 2390
Healing life's hurts. 1599
Healing life's sore spots. 1016
Healing love. 988
Healing ministry in the church. 2409
Healing of Christ in His church. 1599, 1792
Healing of Harry Landers. 2409
Healing of memories. 1599
Healing of "Sam" Leake. 1034
Healing of sorrow. 1352
Healing of souls. 1555, 3673
Healing of the mind. 694, 981
Healing of the nations. 2539, 3058, 3507, 3602
Healing of the soul. 1589
Healing ourselves. 2526
Healing potential of transcendental meditation. 3708
Healing power of Christ. 1599

Healing power of faith. 1600
Healing power of love. 2265
Healing power of the Bible. 494, 2477
Healing prayer. 1600
Healing, prayer, and the revelation. 2987
Healing question. 1598
Healing relationship. 3406
Healing shadow. 2437
Healing the dying. 1414
Healing the emotions. 2783
Healing the fracture. 1713, 3798
Healing the sick and casting out devils. 1600
Healing the whole man. 2377
Healing the whole person. 1600
Healing through meditation & prayer. 2380
Healing through prayer. 1600
Healing touch. 3476
Healing touch in mission lands. 2539
Healing words. 1792
Healing your hurts. 1354
Healing yourself. 2695
Healings of Jesus and the apostles. 473
Healings of the Bible. 317
Health and happiness. 1785
Health and life. 1939
Health and turnover of missionaries. 2520
Health care and the church. 2377
Health care ethics. 2377
Health care ministries. 2782
Health for mind and spirit. 2999
Health/medicine and the faith traditions. 2377
Health shall spring forth. 1597
Health through leisure-time recreation. 3877
Health through will power. 2410
Healthy Christian. 958
Healthy, happy, holy. 2378, 3384
Healthy personality and the Christian life. 175, 1107
Hear His voice. 1712
Hear His voice today. 308
Hear me, Father. 900
Hear me, Lord. 2895
Hear my confession. 1294, 2744, 2815
Hear now the word of the Lord. 241
Hear, O Israel. 2151
Hear, oh Israel. 3370
Hear our grace. 898, 899
Hear our prayer. 898, 902, 2783
Hear the word of the Lord. 1449
Hear ye Him! 1013, 1101
Hearers of the word. 3104
Hearing for eternity. 3347
Hearing His voice. 1740
Hearing the parables of Jesus. 2026
Hearing the unheard. 2426
Hearst Castle. 1743, 1793
Heart. 3270
Heart afire. 749
Heart aflame, thoughts on devotion to the Sacred heart. 3269
Heart after God. 1406
Heart and blood in the Bible. 317
Heart and home truths. 979
Heart and mind of John XXIII. 2123
Heart and voice. 3563
Heart-beats. 1450
Heart-cry for revival. 3228
Heart first. 965
Heart garden. 969
Heart has its seasons. 1113
Heart in pilgrimage. 991, 2869
Heart in the desert. 1635
... Heart messages from the Psalms. 576
Heart of a father. 3504
Heart of an optimist. 3752
Heart of Asbury's journal. 89
... The heart of Buddhism. 703
Heart of Buddhist meditation (Satipattana) 2382
Heart of Catholicity. 2965
Heart of Christ. 1999
Heart of Christianity. 1051
Heart of Christ's religion. 2265
Heart of Confucius. 1116
Heart of flesh. 2679
Heart of healing. 2696
Heart of Hebrew history. 534
Heart of history. 497
... The heart of India. 1895
... The heart of Jainism. 1932
Heart of Job. 549
Heart of John Wesley's Journal. 1292, 3798, 3805
Heart of man. 1534, 2325
Heart of man, its genius for good and evil. 1534
Heart of Mary. 3270
Heart of Mary, sacrificial altar of Christs' love. 3270
Heart of missionary theology. 2555
Heart of Missouri. 2296
Heart of Mormonism. 2602

Heart of N-England rent at the blasphemies of the present generation. 1682
Heart of Newman. 3646
Heart of Newman's Apologia. 790
Heart of Pascal. 2777
Heart of Paul. 374
Heart of prayer. 2874
Heart of Reformation faith. 3617
Heart of religion. 3061
Heart of revelation. 3269
Heart of St. Jane Frances de Chantal. 2385
Heart of Saint Therese. 3690
Heart of the Bible. 249, 251, 292
Heart of the Christian faith. 3642
Heart of the Christian message. 1018
Heart of the Christian year. 1265
Heart of the church. 3269
Heart of the creeds. 1018, 1054
Heart of the fathers. 862
Heart of the gospel. 104, 237, 1017, 3662
Heart of the Gospel (studies in the Beatitudes) 181
Heart of the Gospel, traits of the sacred heart. 3269
Heart of the King. 2041, 3270
Heart of the Levant, Palestine-Syria. 2544
Heart of the mass. 2365
Heart of the matter. 2373
Heart of the moral law. 2593
Heart of the New Testament. 107, 410
Heart of the Old Testament. 502, 597
Heart of the prayer book. 2960
Heart of the Rihbu [i.e. Ribhu] gita. 3139
Heart of the rosary. 3247
Heart of the Saviour. 3270
Heart of the world. 1736, 3521
Heart of the Yale lectures. 2897
Heart of things. 2377, 2725
Heart of truth. 3621
Heart of wisdom. 1434
Heart of woman. 3878
Heart prepared. 3679
Heart reaching object lessons. 909
Heart religion. 123
Heart religion, as described by John Wesley. 3806
Heart remembers, too. 2385
Heart searching talks to ministers, by various writers. 1452
Heart sermons in outline. 3375
Heart side of God. 1060
Heart talks. 971
Heart talks from the Word. 1558
Heart talks on Bible themes. 1455
Heart talks with Jesus. 854, 1953, 2884, 3269
Heart talks with Mary. 855, 857, 2355, 2362
Heart to heart. 164, 858, 2394
Heart to heart letters. 1437
Heart-to-heart talks with mothers. 2773
Heart to heart with you. 2299
Heart to know thee. 3485
Heart-touching sermon outlines. 3372
Heartbeats. 2890
Heartening messages. 168, 3359
Hearth and altar. 253
... Hearth and home essays. 2121
Hearth-stone. 971
Hearts afire. 1565
Hearts aflame. 2482
Hearts aflame in a world on fire. 918
Hearts aglow. 2890
Hearts and hands uplifted. 1548
Hearts and structures. 2327, 2709
Hearts at attention. 3352
Hearts, cupids, and red roses. 3279
Heart's ease for heart trouble. 1354
Hearts made glad. 3429, 3595
Hearts of iron, feet of clay. 554
'Hearts shall be enlightened. 1347
Heart's true home. 3122
Heartsease hymns. 1860
Heartsease miracle. 2699
Heartwarmers. 163
Heath in the wilderness. 3355
Heathen. 2492
Heathen religion in its popular and symbolical development. 3116
Heathen world and St. Paul. 1399, 2800, 2803
Heathens. 3109
Heather. 3823
Heaven. 1793, 1794, 1795
Heaven: a place, a city, a home. 1793
Heaven and Charing cross. 2260
Heaven and Hades. 1429
Heaven and hell. 1794, 1795, 3783
Heaven and hell in comparative religion. 1402, 1794
Heaven and hell in Western art. 1795
Heaven and its wonders. 1794
Heaven and its wonders and Hell. 1794, 1795, 2689

Heaven and its wonders and hell, from things heard and seen. 1795
Heaven and its wonders, the world of spirits, and hell. 1795
Heaven, and other sermons. 1795
Heaven and purgatory. 1939
Heaven at Bay; the Jewish Kulturkampf in the Holy Land. 3088
Heaven bound. 17
Heaven, earth, and man in The book of changes. 1879
Heaven for those who can't believe. 897
Heaven happens here. 978
Heaven has a floor. 1795
Heaven help me. 2625
Heaven help the home! 2338
Heaven help us. 941
Heaven help us (the Holy Spirit in your life) 1830
Heaven in a wildflower. 1624
Heaven in the Christian tradition. 1794
Heaven is my home. 3663
Heaven knows what. 96
Heaven lies within us. 3864
Heaven, man and a carrot. 2081
Heaven of the Bible. 1793
Heaven on earth. 161, 2604, 2695, 2890, 3285
Heaven on your head. 18, 561
Heaven open to souls, love for God above all things, and perfect contrition easy and common in souls resolved to avoid mortal sin. 782
Heaven opened. 456, 1793
Heaven or hell. 1794
Heaven or hell-which? 1470
Heaven revealed. 3503
Heaven, the heart's deepest longing. 1794
Heaven was not enough. 1365
Heaven, what is it? 1794
... Heaven: where it is, its inhabitants, and how to get there. 1794
Heaven? Yes! Hell? No! 2784
Heavenly alibi. 3023
Heavenly bridegrooms. 1527
Heavenly City. 1793, 1794
Heavenly converse. 2642
Heavenly counsellor in Isaiah xl 13-14. 545
Heavenly days. 2721
Heavenly deception. 1834
Heavenly destiny. 2588
Heavenly doctrine of the New Jerusalem. 3571
Heavenly echoes. 1871
... The Heavenly Father and His children. 3146
Heavenly footman. 1018
Heavenly friends. 3281
Heavenly guest. 416
Heavenly harmonies. 2928
Heavenly heretics. 926
Heavenly history. 1793
Heavenly Jervsalem. 1943
Heavenly life. 978
Heavenly light for earthly firesides. 3644
Heavenly muse. 2470
Heavenly octave. 180
Heavenly or divine government. 148
Heavenly pearls set in a life. 971
Heavenly pilgrim, and other poems. 3207
Heavenly places in Christ. 1556
Heavenly prospect. 1529
Heavenly recognition. 1795
Heavenly road. 781
Heavenly secrets. 2691
Heavenly sisters. 1822, 3831
Heavenly sunlight. 1865
Heavenly sunshine. 1690, 2736
Heavenly vision and other sermons. 2930
Heavenly voice. 2072
... The heavenly wisdom of the saints. 3490
Heavens alive. 3082
Heavens and earth declare. 3073
Heaven's antidote to the curse of labor. 3547
Heavens are opened. 2383
Heavens declare. 203, 204
Heaven's hall of heroes. 213
Heaven's jewelry. 165
Heaven's own doorstep. 2695
Heaven's recent wonders. 2262
Heavens speak in astrology marvelous things. 97
Heaven's window. 278, 2181
Heavenward. 1831, 3563
Heavenward, a choice collection of sacred songs. 3562
Heavenward, a guide for youth. 3880
Heavenwards. 1450
... Heavenwords. 906
Heavy bread. 251
Heavy questions. 3885
Heavyweight champion who lost his title. 1560
Heber C. Kimball. 2171, 2617

Heber J. Grant. 1756
Heber J. Grant, man of steel, prophet of God. 1756, 2617
Hebraic literature. 1798
Hebraisms in the Authorized version of the Bible. 272, 530, 1517
Hebrew alphabet book. 2940
Hebrew amulets. 35
Hebrew and Aramaic dictionary of the Old Testament. 1796
Hebrew and Babylonian traditions. 1280
Hebrew and English lexicon of the Old Testament. 1796
Hebrew and English lexicon of the Old Testament, with an appendix containing the Biblical Aramaic, based on the lexicon of William Gesenius as translated. 1796
... Hebrew beginnings. 482
... The Hebrew Bible. 530
Hebrew Bible in Christian, Jewish and Muslim art. 566
Hebrew Christian looks at Romans. 468
Hebrew Christianity. 2073, 2556
Hebrew-Christians. 1966
... Hebrew education in America. 2106
Hebrew ethical wills. 3818
Hebrew fragments of Pseudo-Philo's Liber antiquitatum Biblicarum preserved in the Chronicles of Jerahmeel. 2207
Hebrew glosses and notes. 500, 2328
Hebrew goddess. 2624
Hebrew goddess. 2624
Hebrew grammar. 1797
... Hebrew history. 597
Hebrew home life. 2121
Hebrew honey. 511
Hebrew humanism. 2139
Hebrew humanism of Martin Buber. 699
Hebrew idolatry and superstition: its place in folk-lore. 2765
Hebrew Iliad. 2096
Hebrew impact on western civilization. 2085
Hebrew kindergarten manual. 2086
Hebrew kingdoms. 497, 2093
Hebrew kings. 2095
Hebrew lawgiver. 2621
Hebrew life and thought. 500
...Hebrew life and times. 597, 2121
Hebrew literary genius. 211, 500
Hebrew literature of wisdom in the light of to-day. 600
Hebrew looks up to God. 1731
Hebrew man. 2082
Hebrew manuscripts in the Houghton Library of the Harvard College Library. 1788, 2331
Hebrew men and times. 532, 2095
... The Hebrew monarchy. 531
Hebrew Moses. 1673, 2585
Hebrew mythology. 238
Hebrew myths. 523, 2664
Hebrew origins. 2111
Hebrew Passover. 2779
Hebrew Pentateuch analyzed. 565
Hebrew philosophical genius. 2841
Hebrew poetry. 1799
Hebrew prophecy. 609
Hebrew prophet and his message. 567
Hebrew prophets. 568, 571
Hebrew prophets and the church. 609
Hebrew prophets for English readers in the language of the Revised version of the English Bible. 567
Hebrew religion. 2117
Hebrew religion to the establishment of Judaism under Ezra. 2113
Hebrew religious education treated historically. 2086
Hebrew sanctuary. 3579
Hebrew Scriptures. 540, 541
Hebrew Scriptures in the making. 496
Hebrew scrolls. 2331
... Hebrew tales. 1798, 3581
Hebrew text of Sirach. 489
Hebrew text of the Old Testament. 530
Hebrew thought compared with Greek. 2841
Hebrew union college. 1799
Hebrew union college annual. 2075
Hebrew union college annual [1904]. 1799
Hebrew Union College-Jewish Institute of Religion at one hundred years. 1799
Hebrew Union College jubilee volume, 1875-1925. 2093, 2148
Hebrew verse structure. 1798
Hebrewisms of West Africa. 2097
... Hebrews. 402, 403, 404
Hebrews: a commentary. 402
Hebrews and hermeneutics. 404
Hebrews and the Red sea. 517
Hebrews handbook for world revival. 404, 3229
Hebrews in the Greek New Testament. 404
Hebrews, James, 1 and 2 Peter, Jude, Revelation. 404

... Hebrews, James, and i. and ii. Peter. 366
Hebrews, James, 1 & 2 Peter. 404
Hebrews, James, Peter. 403
Hebrews--the beauty of Christ unveiled. 321
Hebrews, the epistle of warning. 403
Hebridean in Goethe's Weimar. 2307
Hechalutz. 2118
Hechalutz builders and fighters. 3897
Hegel. 1800
Hegel's concept of God. 1732, 1800
Hegel's logic. 1800, 2242
Hegel's philosophy of mind. 2473
Hegel's philosophy of religion. 1800
Heian temples. 3006
Heidegger. 1801, 3717
Heidegger memorial lectures. 1801
Heidelberg catachism. 3043
Heidelberg Catechism. 1801, 3043, 3047
Heidelberg Catechism (an exposition) 1801
Heidelberg catechism (an exposition) The triple knowledge. 1801
Heidelberg catechism for today. 1801
Heidelberg catechism with commentary. 3043
Heidelberg catechism, with proof-texts and explanations as used in the Palatinate. 1801, 3043
Heidelberg story. 1801
Heidelbergh catechism. 3043
Heights of Christian blessedness. 180
Heights of Christian devotion. 2247
Heights of Christian living. 3335
Heights of Christian love. 2264
Heights of Christian unity. 1040
Heights of living and dying in pure spiritualism. 3497
Heights of manhood. 955
Heil, Hebrew! 2082
Heine and his heritage. 3202
Heinrich Bullinger and the covenant. 713, 1377
Heinrich Pesch and his theory of Christian solidarism. 2823, 3450
Heinrich Schutz. 3311
Heinrich Schutz, a guide to research. 3311
Heirloom edition of the Holy Bible, containing the Old and New Testaments(Authorized on King James version) 198
Heirs of St. Teresa of Avila. 741, 3603
Heirs of the gods. 318, 1280
Heirs of the kingdom. 1266
Heirs of the Pharisees. 3706
Heirs of the prophets. 2566
Heirs of the Reformation. 3657
Heirs to eternity. 3054
Heirs together. 2338
Helen E. Moses. 2624
Helen of Troy. 1801, 1802
Helen Potter's impersonations. 1509
Helena. 1802
Helena Petrovna Blavatsky. 672
Helicopter bird. 662
Heliotropium. 3486
Hell. 1802
Hell and amen. 1654
Hell and salvation. 1802
Hell and the heaven. 1802
Hell and the Victorians. 1531
Hell demolished. 1653
Hell is no joke. 1561
Hell of it. 3410
Hell on earth. 1428
"Hell upon earth" made heaven. 3393
Hell--will the wicked burn forever? 1802
Hellenic spirit, Byzantine and post Byzantine. 721
... Hellenism. 1802
Hellenism and Christianity. 1081
Hellenism in Jewish Palestine. 2076
Hellenistic civilization and the Jews. 2092
Hellenistic magic and the synoptic tradition. 390, 2314
Hellenistic mystery-religions. 1767
Hellenistic philosophies. 2832
Hellenistic religions. 3116
Hellenistic ways of deliverance and the making of the Christian synthesis. 1082
Hello, God! 902, 3143
Hello/goodbye. 2394
Hello, I'm God & I'm here to help you. 981
Hello, lovers! 943
Hello toddler. 3165
Hell's ramparts fell. 2632
Helmet and spear. 1765
Heloise. 1802
Heloise and Abelard. 1, 1802
Help. 2191
Help for bereaved parents. 1353
Help for the poor souls in purgatory. 855
Help for the tempted, and that means all of us. 979
Help from beyond. 3515, 3527

Help from the hills. 1437, 3356, 3742
Help! I believe in tongues. 1716
Help! I don't know how to pray. Amen. 2249, 3354
Help! I run a Sunday school. 3553
Help! I'm a layman. 2191
Help! I'm a Sunday school teacher. 3550
Help! I'm a woman! 3845
Help! I'm in college. 1308
Help in daily living. 1013
Help in time of need. 1013
Help in time of trouble, and other dial-a-prayer meditations. 1436
Help in troubled times. 2396
Help in understanding the Bible. 639
Help in understanding theology. 3661
Help is only a prayer away. 2875
Help it all make sense, Lord! 3883
Help, Lord! 2875
Help, Lord, I blew it again. 1012, 2130
Help me adapt, Lord. 3409
Help me, Father. 3475
Help me, Jesus. 3882
Help me understand, Lord. 437, 2892
"Help those women" 3836
Help thou my unbelief. 276, 1779
Help thou my want. 1435
Help to faith. 278, 1595
Help to the study of the Holy Spirit. 1827
Help to Zion's travellers. 963, 1447
Help wanted: faith required. 2190
Help when tempted and tried. 980
Help your boy or girl to be Christian. 1254
Help your minister to do his best. 2787
Helper. 1836
Helpers all! 2550
Helpers at my church. 1199
Helpers in God's world. 3160
Helpful hints for daily living as-I-find-it. 962
Helpful material for all Christians. 964
Helpful material for all Christians, from a life of 25 years as pastor then 25 years as teacher. 1014
Helping a child understand death. 1418
Helping adolescents grow up in Christ. 3167
Helping boys. 687
Helping children accept themselves and others. 2590
Helping children know doctrine. 3171
Helping children know the Bible. 638
Helping children worship. 903
Helping church workers succeed. 1251
Helping churches through associational Sunday school work. 3564
Helping each other be human. 993
Helping God at His job. 2295
Helping hand. 1444
Helping handicapped children in school. 895
Helping human beings. 943
Helping others to become Christians. 1567
Helping people grow. 2519
Helping people in need. 3181
Helping the Bible speak. 612
Helping the helpers to help. 2783
Helping the helpless in lower New York. 3833
Helping the retarded to know God. 939
Helping your child appreciate the Mass and the sacraments. 2370
Helping your child discover faith. 938
Helping your child know right from wrong. 941
Helping yourself with numerology. 3575
Helping youth and adults know doctrine. 3175
Helping youth and adults know the Bible. 648
Helping youth in conflict. 1255
"Helps along the way" 2693
Helps and entertainments for juvenile and young people's miissionary socities. 3890
Helps and entertainments for juvenile and your people's missionary societies. 3027
Helps by the way. 1443
Helps for Bible readers. 3665
Helps for soul-winners. 1562
Helps for the busy minister. 3373
Helps for the day. 725
Helps for the scrupulous. 3316
Helps from Hebrews. 403
Helps on the road. 2299
Helps to a better Christian life. 2212
Helps to a life of holiness and usefulness. 1556
Helps to a spiritual life. 3482
Helps to Bible study. 199, 245, 286, 641, 3383
Helps to faith. 1058
Helps to happiness. 1785
Helps to health and purity. 3870
Helps to prayer. 2884
Helps to the Christian life. 962

Helps to the holy communion from the writings of Phillips Brooks, with prayers adapted from the Book of common prayer. 1825
Helps to the promotion of revivals. 1571
Helps to the study of classical mythology. 2657
Helps to the study of Presbyterianism. 2936
Helps to the study of the Bible. 285
... Helps to the study of the versions of the New Testament. 474
Helps toward nobler living. 1325
Hemlandssanger. 2288
Hemlock and the cross. 1855
Henri de Lubac, S.J. 776, 3633
Henric Schartau and the order of grace. 2301
Henrician reformation. 666, 1217
Henrietta Mears story. 2376
Henry Alline 1748-1784. 26
Henry and Antonio. 1547
... Henry Boynton Smith. 3427
Henry Charles Lea. 2203
Henry Charles Lea's historical writings. 2203
Henry Clay Morrison. 2620
Henry Codman Potter. 2865
Henry Codman Potter, an American metropolitan. 2865
Henry Cohen. 1305
Henry Drummond. 3631
Henry Edward Manning, his life and labours. 2328
Henry Jackson Van Dyke. 2935, 3767
Henry James. 1934
Henry James, 1917-1959. 1933
Henry Loomis, friend of the East. 2245
Henry Luke Paget. 2758
Henry Lyman Morehouse. 2597
Henry Martyn. 2349
Henry Melchior Muhlenberg. 2629
Henry More. 2596
Henry Morse. 2620
Henry Newman's Salzburger letterbooks. 3296
Henry Schomberg Kerr, sailor and Jesuit. 2168
Henry Sloane Coffin, the man and his ministry. 1305
Henry VIII and the English monasteries. 2582
Henry VIII and the Lutherans. 1225, 1804
Henry viii and the Reformation in the relation to the Church of England. 1803
Henry Ward Beecher. 183, 184, 1333
Henry Ward Beecher's art of preaching. 184, 2899
Henry Wilder Foote, hymnologist. 1632
Henry Wilson, one of God's best. 3819
Hepburn of Japan and his wife and helpmates. 1804
Heptaplus. 1382
Her children call her blessed. 3841
Her door of faith. 694
Her dream came true. 2194
Her glimmering tapers. 1365
Her heart and home. 1604
Her invisible spirit mate. 2988
Her life for His friends. 875, 2308
Her little way. 3690
Her silence speaks. 2356
Her works praise her. 3844
Herald of Christ, Louis Bourdaloue, S.J. 685
Herald of the Evange. 124, 1068
Herald of the Evangel. 124, 1068
Herald sermons. 3353
Heralds of a brighter day. 1228
Heralds of a liberal faith. 3727
Heralds of Christ. 1297, 3829
Heralds of Christ, the King. 826, 1422
Heralds of freedom. 151
Heralds of God. 2906
Heralds of salvation. 1574
Heralds of the good news. 3150
Heralds of the Gospel. 2902
Heralds of the king. 764, 1024, 1172, 1648, 2021, 3280, 3318
Heralds of the morning. 1515, 3688
Herbert Booth. 681, 3292
Herbert Butterfield. 1819
Hercules' labors. 1804
Herder's commentary on the Psalms. 576
Here am I. 922, 1723, 2287, 3175
Here am I, a Christian autobiography. 922
Here am I—send Aaron. 516, 981
Here am I! Send me. 880
Here and beyond. 3461
Here-and hereafter. 974, 1001, 2325, 3054
Here & now. 3328
Here and there a leaf. 964
Here and there in the Greek New Testament. 349
Here and there with the Bible. 2489
Here are more answers. 1115
Here are your saints. 3285

Here at thy table, Lord. 2260
Here begins the Gospel. 400, 437
Here comes Elijah. 1483
Here for a purpose. 3351
Here for a reason. 3368
Here I am, God, where are you? 3407
Here I am, Lord. 581
Here I stand. 2272
Here in this house. 2388
Here is Brigham. 3869
Here is help for you. 962
Here is my method. 2902
Here is the answer. 3665
Here lies our hope. 1064
Here stand I! 2301
Here, there, and above. 2142
Here they stand. 3341
Here we stand. 2286
Hereafter. 1696, 1698, 1890, 1939, 2061, 3500
Hereafter and heaven. 1695
... The hereafter of sin. 1699
Hereafter: what happens after death? 1698
Heredity; a study in science and the Bible. 205
... Hereford. 1804
Herein is love. 324, 2264
Here's a faith for you. 972
Here's how and when. 3173
Here's how to win souls. 1564
Here's how youth meetings. 3890
Here's money for churches and societies. 1168
Here's the church. 1159
Here's to life! 2229
Here's your answer. 280
Heresies exposed. 1804, 3322
Heresies of the high Middle Ages. 3324
Heresy. 1635
Heresy and authority in medieval Europe. 1805
Heresy and inquisition in Narbonne. 22, 1909
Heresy and obedience in Tridentine Italy. 1374, 2857
Heresy, crusade, and inquisition in southern France, 1100-1250. 1638, 1909
Heresy in the later Middle Ages. 3324
Heresy of Antioch. 2800
Heresy of Job. 551
Heresy of monasticism; the Christian monks: types and anti-types. 2572
Heresy of Pope John XXIII. 790, 2124
Heresy of the free church in the later Middle Ages. 691
Heretic. 1688, 1804, 1805, 3724
Heretical imperative. 3617
Heretics. 1804
Heretic's defense. 1805
Heretic's religion. 3067
Heretics, saints and martyrs. 1183
Heritage. 1614, 3420
Heritage and destiny. 1105, 1464
Heritage and history of the East St. Louis Baptist Association, 1787-1917-1967. 1485
Heritage and promise. 1235
Heritage book, 1977. 1432
Heritage book, 1979. 1432
Heritage design understood. 95
Heritage of Bay View, 1875-1975. 179
Heritage of beauty. 1156
Heritage of Biblical faith. 310
Heritage of Christian thought. 3620
Heritage of dedication; one hundred years of the National Woman's Christian Temperance Union. 3833
Heritage of devotion. 1438
... The heritage of eastern Asia. 1283
Heritage of faith. 2285, 2619, 3418
Heritage of holiness. 1824, 3293
Heritage of John Calvin. 727, 729
Heritage of peace. 2037
Heritage of prayer for boys and girls. 899
Heritage of Saint Matthew's Parish of Black Brook, New York, 1832-1876-1976. 3277
Heritage of the bhikkhu. 704
Heritage of the Blackfeet. 3408
Heritage of the cathedral. 750
Heritage of the Fathers. 1801
Heritage of the First Presbyterian Church of Metuchen, N.J. 2460
Heritage of the Reformation. 2977, 3650
Heritage of the Sikh. 3408
Heritage of those that fear Thy name. 2472
Heritage seekers. 16, 2743
Heritage to hold in fee, 1817-1917. 132
Heritage without end. 2430
Herman J. Ruetenik. 3253
Herman Lauster. 2200
Hermann Cohen's philosophy of Judaism. 1306
Los Hermanos Penitentes. 1806
Hermeneutic of dogma. 3669
Hermeneutic of Erasmus. 240, 1525

Hermeneutic of the idea of revelation. 288, 1806
Hermeneutical manual. 405
Hermeneutics. 287, 288, 1806
Hermeneutics of Philo and Hebrews. 504, 2831
Hermes guide of souls. 1806
Hermes—literature, science, philosophy. 2662
Hermes the thief. 2412
Hermetic and alchemical writings of Aureolus Phillippus Theophrastus Bombast of Hohenheim. 2728
Hermetic fundamentals. 3251
Hermetic philosophy. 2727
Hermetica. 2661
Hermit in the Himalayas. 3477
Hermit of Capri. 1807
Hermit of Cat Island. 1791
Hermit of Lebanon. 2318
Hermit philosopher of Liendo. 2586
Hermitage journals. 875, 1775
Hermits. 1806, 1807
Hermits and anchorites of England. 1807
Hero. 1807, 1808
Hero and the king. 1521
Hero: myth, image, symbol. 2649
Hero-myths & legends of the British race. 3244
Hero of Babylon. 1401
Hero of faith and prayer. 2178
Hero of heroes. 2014
Hero of the gallows, a story of blessed Edmund Campion. 733
Hero of the hills. 189
Hero pattern and the life of Jesus. 393, 929, 1976
Hero stories from the Old Testament. 629
Hero stories of the Old Testament. 629
Hero tales from mission lands. 2483
Hero tales of Congregational history. 1344
Hero tales of the Bible. 314
Hero with a thousand faces. 2650
Herod. 1807
Herod, King of the Jews. 1807
Herod the Great. 1807
Herodotus. 1807
Herods of Judaea. 1807, 2764
Heroes. 2662, 2663
... The heroes and crises of early Hebrew history from the creation to the death of Moses. 2096
Heroes and gods. 1807
Heroes and heroines of the Christian church. 926
Heroes and heroines of the church. 924
Heroes and heroines of the cross. 3095
Heroes and martyrs of the modern missionary enterprise. 2483
Heroes from every walk of life. 871
Heroes, gods and monsters of the Greek myths. 2660, 2661
Heroes, kings, and men. 296
Heroes of Bohemia; Huss, Jerome and Zisea. 1857, 3037
Heroes of early Israel. 483
Heroes of faith. 405
... Heroes of faith in Japan. 2534
Heroes of faith on pioneer trails. 2482
Heroes of God. 2482
Heroes of God's church. 3281
Heroes of Greece and Troy. 2661
Heroes of Heaven. 482
Heroes of Israel. 494, 597, 1807
Heroes of Israel's golden age. 1807
Heroes of Jewish history. 2094
Heroes of Jewish thought. 2075
Heroes of Methodism. 2423
Heroes of missions and their work. 2482
Heroes of modern Jewish thought. 2075
... Heroes of modern missions. 2483
Heroes of the Bible. 494, 622, 629
Heroes of the Bible and Bible lands. 214
Heroes of the Book of Mormon. 679
Heroes of the campus, the records of a few of those knightly souls who, burning out for God, kindled unquenched fires in the lives of their fellow students. 1807
Heroes of the church. 925
Heroes of the cross. 1647
... Heroes of the cross in America. 2558
Heroes of the early church. 1807
Heroes of the faith. 493, 923, 1807
Heroes of the five books. 630
Heroes of the Greeks. 2661
Heroes of the hinterlands; the Bressilac story. With a foreword. 2335, 3437
Heroes of the Reformation. 3050
Heroes of the saddle bags. 3605
Heroes of the South seas. 2733
Heroes of the trail. 834
Heroic age of India. 3302
Heroic Aloysius. 2271
Heroic brothers. 2577
Heroic colonial Christians. 3739
Heroic faith of pioneers. 2757
Heroic knowledge. 2471

Heroic life and exploits of Siegfried, the dragonslayer. 2666, 3407
Heroic life of Saint Vincent de Paul. 3779
... Heroic lives. 1807, 1808, 3235
Heroic lives in universal religion. 1808
Heroic Methodists of the olden time. 2427
Heroic nuns. 764
Heroic sanctity and insanity. 3488
Heroic women of the Bible and the church. 3840
Heroin, deviance, and morality. 1480
Heroine of charity, Venerable Mother d'Youville. 1774
Heroines of charity. 3416
Heroines of Christ. 765
Heroines of Methodism. 2422, 2423
Heroines of missionary adventure. 2488
Heroines of modern religion. 3831
Heroines of olden time. 3839
Heroines of sacred history. 3841
Heroines of the church. 2488
Heroines of the crusades. 1390
Heroines of the household. 3831
...Heroines of the mission field. 2488
Herosim and romance. 2432
Herrmann the Great. 1345, 1808
Herrmann the magician. 1345, 1808
Herrmann's little jokes. 1345, 1808
Herrman's black art. 2312
Herrnhuterian pietism in the Baltic, and its outreach into America and elsewhere in the world. 2846, 3896
Herself. 2355
Hertel's standard reference indexed Bible. 197
Herzl as I remember him. 1809
He's man. 1706
Hesburgh papers. 870
Hesed in the Bible. 598, 1809
Hesiod and Theognis. 1809
Hesitant pilgrim. 829
Hester's Easter morning. 1486
Het geheim der eeuwen. 234
Heterodox London. 2243
Hevajra Tantra. 3585
Hex. 3052, 3827
... The hexaemeral literature. 524
Hexameron, Paradise, and Cain and Abel. 1616
Hexaplar Psalter. 2986
Hexateuch. 530
Hey, God! Hurry! 900
Hey, God, what about ...? 3670
Hey, God: What is Christmas? 1112
Hey, God! Where are you? 1734
Hey- lets talk it over! 3537
Hey, Mom! 2625
Hey, Preach—you're comin' through! 1255
Hey, that's our church! 1200
Hey, why don't we try Christianity? 3488
Hey, you! 2873
Heyday of a wizard. 1838
Heyday of spiritualism. 3521
Heydegger's letter to the Bishop of London. 3606
Hi-Y today. 3874
... Hibernica minora. 578
Hickslee separation. 1684
Hid in my heart. 267
Hidatsa shrine and the beliefs respecting it. 1810
Hidden apostles. 2721
Hidden Bible. 319, 3251
Hidden books. 482
Hidden center. 2011
Hidden discipline. 1314
Hidden disciplines. 986
Hidden door to reality. 2395
Hidden face of pain. 2758
Hidden glory of the inner man. 3463
Hidden God. 1738, 2322
Hidden handicap. 2204
Hidden highwave. 2543
Hidden history of reincarnation. 876, 3053
Hidden in plain sight. 2379
Hidden kingdom. 434, 2176
Hidden life. 969, 3095
Hidden life of a Christian. 977
Hidden life of Christ. 1977
Hidden life of the soul. 3462
Hidden manna. 1822
Hidden manna, being the Revelation called Apocalypse of John the Divine with complete text and commentaries. 455
Hidden meaning in the New Testament. 350, 1770
Hidden meanings of the world's great stories. 615
Hidden motives of pastoral action. 821, 2789
Hidden mystery of the Bible. 229, 3573
Hidden path. 3518
Hidden patterns and the grand design. 514

Hidden power. 2696
Hidden question of God. 3625
Hidden records of the life of Jesus. 56
Hidden revolution. 2829
Hidden riches of secret places. 2392
Hidden rocks. 425
Hidden secret. 1533
Hidden secrets of creation revealed. 3500
Hidden side of Christian festivals. 1613
Hidden story of scientology. 3314
Hidden stream. 763
... The hidden teaching beyond Yoga. 2417, 2418
Hidden things of God's revelation. 238, 3227
Hidden treasure. 900
... The hidden truth. 1030, 3510
Hidden truths. 3474
... Hidden unit. 1049
Hidden valley. 1584
Hidden way across the threshold. 3515
Hidden wells of comfort. 2434, 3337
Hidden wisdom in the Holy Bible. 526, 3575
Hidden words of Baha'u'llah. 127
Hidden world. 2733
Hidden years. 1991
Hiding place. 1454
Hidushe rabi Reuven. 3584
... Hierarchies: the ladder of life. 3688
Hierarchy and democracy in Australia. 814
Hierarchy and the plan. 2729
Hierarchy of heaven and earth. 1371
Hierarchy of hell. 1802
Hierarchy of the Roman Catholic church in the United States. 668
Hieroglyphic vocabulary to the Theban recension of the Book of the dead, with an index to all the English equivalents of the Egyptian words. 680
Hieroglyphick Bible. 1810
Hieronimus Bosch. 683
Hierophant. 1505
Hieroschemamonk Feofil, fool-for-Christ's-sake. 1622
Higgins. 1811
High above the sun. 2596
High adventure. 2461, 2695
High adventure in Korea. 2537
High adventure in Tibet. 2855
High and law mass in the Roman Catholic church. 2366
High call, high privilege. 1303, 2307
High calling. 937
High calling; meditations on St. Paul's letter to the Philippinas. 449
High Church schism. 2712
High cost of growing. 985
High cost of holy living. 975
High cost of living. 3478
High cost of loving. 2265
High country. 2933
High endeavor. 3506
High endeavours. 129
High fellowship set. 1545
High green hill. 761
High heritage. 3560
High holiday Bible themes. 1811
High Holiday liturgy. 2110
High holiday prayer book. 2884
High Holy Day prayer book, for the Jewish personnel in the Armed Forces of the United States. 82
High Holy Days. 2110
High hours of Methodism in town-country communities. 3254
High lights from the book of Revelation. 457
High lights of the New Testament. 475
High lights on hymnists and their hymns. 1875
High mysticism. 2638
High points in the higher life. 3665
High priest. 1782
High priest of rebirth. 2183
High priesthood and sacrifice. 482
High road to Christ. 1017
High roads and cross roads. 1016
High school work-study program for mentally subnormal students. 2411
... The high school's cure of souls. 2592
High science of Jesus Christ. 1953
High walk of discipleship. 3864
High wind at noon. 1094
... The higher aspects of Greek religion. 1766, 1767
Higher aspects of spiritualism. 3509
Higher Biblical criticism: an analysis and a critique. 235
Higher Christian education. 3149
Higher Christian life. 956
Higher consciousness. 1579
Higher criticism. 232
Higher criticism and the new theology. 1017

Higher criticism and the new theology, unscientific, unscriptural, and unwholesome. 237
Higher criticism and the Old Testament. 499
"higher criticism" and the verdict of the monuments. 502
Higher criticism cross-examined. 237
Higher criticism of the Hexateuch. 530, 531
Higher criticism of the Pentateuch. 563
Higher critic's Bible. 198
Higher critics criticised. 564, 2187
Higher education in the Evangelical United Brethren Church, 1800-1954. 1550
Higher education of Southern Baptists. 3465
Higher freedom. 2140
Higher goals. 1171
Higher ground. 1715
Higher happiness. 181
Higher individualism. 3758
Higher law and the rights of man in a revolutionary society. 1280
Higher life. 1022, 3095
"higher life" doctrine of sanctification, tried by the word of God. 3299
Higher living. 2225
Higher manhood. 965
Higher mathematics, to help you along. 973
Higher path. 167
Higher plane. 975
Higher psychical development (Yoga philosophy) an outline of the secret Hindu teachings. 3864
Higher ritualism. 2442
Higher rock. 2282
Higher sacrifice. 3728
Higher significance of the gospel. 1095
Higher spiritualism. 3507
Highest culture and Christianity. 1051
Highest in us. 1009
Highest life. 3479
Highest office. 1296
Highest state of consciousness. 2641
Highland Agnes. 40
Highland second-sight. 3321
Highland shepherds. 3672
Highlands of the mind. 3337
Highley commentary [for] 1964. 1915
*Highley commentary [for] 1965. 1915
*Highley commentary [for] 1966. 1915
Highley's Sunday school lesson commentary. 1915
Highlights along the road of the Anglican church. 1211, 2974
Highlights in Mormon political history. 2615
Highlights of archaeology in Bible lands. 208
Highlights of Christian missions. 2525
Highlights of early church history. 1182
Highlights of Hebrew history. 533
Highlights of Jewish history. 2089
Highlights of templar history. 1665
Highlights of the Bible. 529
Highlights of the Book of Revelation. 458
Highlights of the story of Christianity. 1178
Highroad of Methodism. 2442
Highroads of the universe. 1104
Highlights of the 968 World Conference. 3216
Highway. 1050
Highway and the way. 2175
Highway helps. 2612
Highway of God. 2906, 3365
Highway of life. 3342
Highway of mission thought. 2483
Highway of praise, an introduction to Christian hymnody. 1875
Highway of print. 3204
Highway shall be there. 3885
...The highway to God. 769, 803
Highway to happiness. 2932
Highway to heaven. A new colleciton of gospel songs. 3563
Highways and by-ways in the spiritual life. 3522
Highways and byways of Appalachia. 2928
Highways and hedges. 1565, 2453
Highways in the desert. 2501
Highways of Christian doctrine. 3653
Highways of Christian living. 334
Highways of the spirit. 956
Highways of worship. 2388
Highways that lead to God. 1837
Highways to faith. 2979
Highways to happiness. 3383
Highways to heaven. 2027
High ways to perfection of Abraham Maimonides. 2075
Highways to truth. 3382
*Higley commentary. 1915
Hilandar Slavic manuscripts. 2330

Hildebrand. 1773, 2861
Hildebrand and his times. 1542, 1774
Hill. 2003
Hill ablaze. 720, 2485
Hill called Moon. 2542
Hill of discernment. 3689
Hill of stoning. 3320
Hill of the Lord. 622
Hillel. 1812
Hillel, the book against the sword. 1812
Hillel, the elder. 1812
Hillel's calendar. 1615
Hillel's happy holidays. 1615
Hills beyond the hills. 1291
Hills of creation. 1379
Hills of God. 3341
"Hills to climb" 3370
Hillside thoughts. 968
Hilltop verses and prayers. 1437
Him again. 1736
Him--His. 2042
Him we declare. 61
Himalayan heartbeat. 2208
Himalayan pilgrimage. 2684
Himnos de Sion de la Iglesia de Jesucristo de los santos de los ultimos dias, publicado por la Mision mexicana. 1233
Himself. 763, 2048, 3021
Hindu. 1816
Hindu and Muslim mysticism. 2645
Hindu astrology (Joytisha-shastra) 98
Hindu-Christian meeting point, within the cave of the heart. 1082
Hindu conception of the deity as culminating in Ramanuja. 1732
...Hindu ethics. 1538
Hindu ideal. 1814
Hindu literature. 3302
... Hindu logic as preserved in China and Japan. 2242
Hindu manners, customs and ceremonies. 1897
Hindu monastic life. 2572
Hindu monism and pluralism as found in the Upanishads. 2584
Hindu mysticism. 2638, 2645
Hindu myths. 2663
Hindu pantheon. 2663
Hindu philosophy. 2839
... Hindu philosophy in a nutshell. 1814
Hindu philosophy popularly explained. 1814
Hindu places of pilgrimage in India. 2848
Hindu polytheism. 1743
Hindu quest for the perfection of man. 1814
Hindu religious tradition. 1813
... The Hindu religious year. 1814
Hindu scriptures. 689, 1816
Hindu social institutions. 1897
Hindu social system. 1897
Hindu sound. 1813
Hindu temple. 3599
Hindu theology. 1814
Hindu tradition. 1812
Hindu view of Christ. 2024
Hindu view of life. 1813, 1814
Hindu views and ways and the Hindu-Muslim interface. 1815
Hindu world. 1815
Hindu-Yogi science of breath. 3863
Hinduism. 1813, 1814, 1815, 1895
Hinduism, a cultural perspective. 1813
Hinduism, a religion to live by. 1813
Hinduism and Buddhism. 1813
Hinduism and Christianity. 1082, 1815, 2007
Hinduism in Europe and America. 1814
Hinduism invades America. 1814
Hinduism; its historical development. 1815
Hinduism: its meaning for the liberation of the spirit. 1813
Hinduism or Christianity? 1813
Hinduism: the world ideal. 1813
Hinge of history. 1818
Hinges of destiny. 2300
Hinterlands of the church. 3253
Hints and helps in pastoral theology. 3674
Hints and helps in the study of some of the neglected parts of the Bible. 500
Hints and observations for investigating the phenomena of spiritualism. 3498
Hints concerning church music, the liturgy and kindred subjects. 1203
Hints on Bible study. 635
Hints on extemporaneous preaching. 2908
Hints on metaphysics. 2409
... Hints on prayer, revivals, and Bible study. 1572
Hints on the formation of religious opinions. 60
Hints on the interpretation of prophecy. 609
Hints to Bible study. 639
Hints to parents on the religious education of children. 3158

Hints to preachers. 2900
Hints to self-educated ministers. 3674
Hints to young men from the parable of the prodigal son. 2944
Hints to young students of occultism. 2729, 3687
Hiouen-thsang in India. 1850
Hippies, Hindus and rock & roll. 1816
His Apocalypse. 457
His body the church. 1122
His book. 233
His by choice. 3438
His church. 1247, 1550
His continued witness. 3349
His cross and mine. 1388
His cross and ours. 2032
His Cross in your life. 1003
His crown, or His cross. 1351
His darling wife, Evelyn. 1303, 3240
His days and ours. 2213
His death and ours. 1417
His decease at Jerusalem. 2033
His deity hence His day. 3261
His end up. 1721
His everlasting love. 1009
His eye is on the sparrow. 3414, 3798
His eye is on the sparrow so ... this is really for the birds. 932, 2865
His Father's business. 1447
His father's house. 2183
His finest week. 1837
His five smooth stones. 192
His footsteps; studies for edification from the life of Christ. 1992
His fortunate grace. 1750
His friends. 1460
His fullness. 964
His gifts & promises. 2933
His glorious appearing. 3319
His glorious body. 372
His glorious name. 2020
His glory. 1716
His golden cycle. 698, 2508
His good and perfect will. 1741
His Gospel of life, love and light. 419, 2125
His Grace. 3201
His great apostle. 2795
His great journey. 1967
His grey eminence. 2203
His guide to evangelism. 1572
His guide to sex, singleness & marriage. 3393
His hand upon me. 964
His/hers devotionals. 2347
His hidden grace. 287
His Holiness Pope Pius XII. 2852
His honor the heretic. 3729
His in a life of prayer. 2873
His in mind and heart. 611
His indwelling presence. 2937
His initials were F. D. N. 2707
His kingdom is forever. 2175
His last Thursday. 2029
His last week. 2031, 2035
His last words. 2058
His life. 1960
His life and our life. 1977
His life and ours. 1974
His life in the words of the four gospels. 1960
His life is mine. 1010
His life our pattern. 958
His many mansions. 3322
His mercy endureth forever. 3418
His messenger. 3811
His messengers went forth. 3114, 3125
His mind, his heart. 2719
His mother. 1950
His mother, the life history of Mary, the mother of Christ. 2354
His name among all nations. 2553
His name is Jesus. 1984
His name is Wonderful. 2398
His name was Jesus. 1981
His name was John. 1305, 2123
His only Son our Lord. 1952
"His only Son," the truth of the divinity of Christ. 2001
His own good daughter. 2596
His own received Him not. but. 1950
His part and ours. 1444
His passion forever. 2031
His power in you. 437
His presence in the world. 2254
His quiet splendor. 1735
His religion and hers. 3846
His return. 2055
His Reverence--his day's work. 3676
His right to rule. 1514
His salvation. 199, 472
His servants speak. 1009, 1232
His servants speak; excerpts from devotional addresses given at Brigham Young University. 1009
His servants, the prophets. 571
His side versus our side. 381

"His Son" 322
His story. 929, 1965, 1991
His story in Georgia W. M. U. history. 3468
His struggle. 2099
His stubborn love. 2338
His sure return. 2055
His ten wives. 2859
His things of power. 963
His touch is love. 929, 1974
His truth endureth. 537
His truth is marching on. 609
... His unchanging word. 647
His vengeance. 1940
His very own. 365
His way. 982, 1313
His way out. 517
His will. 1740
His will is our peace. 1454
His witnesses. 330
His Word endures. 791
His word through preaching. 2901
His Word was with power. 1972
His words on happiness. 2437
His works. 1939
Hiscox guide for Baptist churches. 148
Hiscox standard Baptist manual. 148
Hispano-Jewish culture in transition. 6, 3016
Hisperica famina. 3094
Histoire de la divination dans l'antiquite. 1470
Histoire de la poesie liturgique au moyen age. 849
Histoire de la propriete ecclesiastique en France. 1638
Histore du mouvement bulgare vers l'Eglise catholique au XIXe siecle. 815
Historia de Hierosolymitano itinere. 1391
... Historia destructionis Troiae. 3715
Historia Francorum qui ceperunt Iherusalem. 1391
Historiae rhythmicae. 812
Historian and character. 1183
Historian and the believer. 241, 1819, 3617
Historians and the English reformation. 1764
Historian's approach to religion. 3064, 3068
Historians of Israel. 531
Historic Bibles in America. 213
Historic chapters in Christian education in America. 3561
Historic Christ in the faith of to-day. 1965
Historic Christianity and the Apostles' creed. 74
Historic Christianity and the new theology. 3616
Historic church. 1174
Historic church and modern pacifism. 3793
Historic churches of America. 1274, 1275
Historic churches of Fairfield County. 1269
Historic churches of the South. 1274
Historic churches of the United States. 1274
Historic churches of the world. 1269
Historic episcopate. 1523
Historic essay. 1686
Historic exodus. 1584
Historic faith and a changing world. 1062
Historic faith, short lectures on the Apostles' creed. 74
Historic Jesus. 390, 1968
Historic martyrs of the primitive church. 2351
Historic meaning of prophecy. 2949
Historic mission of Jesus. 2062, 2176
Historic origin of the Bible. 289
Historic patterns of church growth. 1171
Historic Protestantism and predestination. 2912
Historic reality of Christian culture. 1074, 1394
Historic reality of Christian culture; a way to the renewal of human life. 1074
Historic reality of Christianity. 1096
Historic records of Christ church, Cooperstown, N. Y. 1119
Historic St. Luke's Episcopal Church. 1931
Historic St. Mary's Church, Albany, New York. 22
Historic St. Peter's Episcopal church. 1524
Historic St. Stephen's. 3798
Historic sketch of the Reformed church in North Carolina. 3045, 3048
Historic story of St. Mary's Albany, N. Y. 22
Historic tales of the old missions for boys and girls. 3470
Historic theories of atonement. 105
Historic Virginia homes and churches. 3781

Historical illustrations of the social effects of Christianity. 1048
Historical account of Christ church, Boston. 683
Historical account of Jamaican Freemasonry. 1665
Historical account of some of the more important versions and editions of the Bible. 212
Historical account of the Apostolic Faith, a Trinitarian-fundamental evangelistic organization. 76
Historical account of the belief in witchcraft in Scotland. 3828
Historical account of the building of Altalaha Lutheran Church, Rehrersburg, Pa. in 1808 and the bell tower of 1849. 3052
Historical account of the First Presbyterian church and society in Newburyport, Massachusetts, addressed to the congregation, worshipping in Federal street, July 9, 1826. 2701
Historical account of the heathen gods and heroes. 2656
Historical account of the incorporated Society for the Propagation of the Gospel in Foreign Parts. 2543, 3437
Historical account of the Protestant Episcopal Church in South-Carolina. 2974, 3464
Historical account of the Protestant Episcopal Church in South Carolina, 1820-1957. 2974
Historical account of the Protestant Episcopal church in South Carolina, from the first settlement of the province, to the war of the revolution. 2974
Historical account of the rise and development of Presbyterianism in Scotland. 2915
Historical address delivered at the dedication of the remodelled church of the First Unitarian society, Hudson. 3728
Historical address delivered at the fiftieth anniversary of the Newton theological institution, June 8, 1975. 2706
... Historical addresses delivered on the one hundred and fiftieth anniversary of the First Congregational church, Concord, N.H., November 18th, 1880. 1337
Historical and analytical bibliography of the literature of cryptology. 1392
Historical and bibliographical sketches of the early churches and pioneer preachers of the Christian church in Missouri. 1465
... A historical and bibliographical survey of the German religious drama. 3145
Historical and biographical introduction to accompany the Dial. 1457
Historical and biographical papers. 1037, 1495
Historical and descriptive sketches of the women of the Bible. 3839
Historical and expository notes on the patriarchs, kings and prophets of Israel. 1928
Historical and literary outlines of the Old Testament. 481
Historical and literary studies. 201, 1093
Historical and religious value of the fourth Gospel. 420
Historical approach to evangelical worship. 3003
Historical approach to the New Testament. 347
Historical atlas of religion in America. 1488
Historical atlas of the religions of the world. 3115
Historical background of early Methodist enthusiasm. 1520
Historical background of the Bible. 298
... The historical background of the church-state problem in Mexico. 1148
Historical background of the Dead Sea scrolls. 3014
Historical backgrounds of Bible history. 298
Historical backgrounds of early Methodist enthusiasm. 1520, 3803
Historical bases of religions. 3108
... The historical books of the Old Testament. 532
... Historical catalogue. 109, 2706
... Historical catalogue 1816-1901. 133
Historical catalogue of the printed editions of Holy Scripture in the Library of the British and Foreign Bible Society, London. 212
Historical catalogue of the Theological institute of Connecticut. 1788
Historical catalyst. 1180

... Historical celebration in recognition of the eightieth year of the origin of the seminary. 2306

Historical character of St. John's Gospel. 321, 420

Historical Christ. 1978, 2013

Historical collections of Richland Baptist Church. 3236

Historical collections of the life and acts of the Right Reverend Father in God, John Aylmer. 121

Historical collections relating to the American colonial church. 1222

Historical commentaries on the state of Christianity during the first three hundred and twenty-five years from the Christian era. 1193

Historical commentary on St. Paul's epistle to the Galatians. 380

Historical commentary on the eleventh chapter of Daniel. 509

Historical Committee series. 1705

Historical credibility of Hans Kung. 2188

Historical-critical method. 287

Historical criticism and theological interpretation of Scripture. 240

Historical deluge in its relation to scientific discovery and to present questions. 1421

... The historical development of Christianity. 1176

Historical development of Hebrew education from ancient times to 135 C. E. 2087

Historical dimensions of a rational faith. 1818, 2164

Historical dimensions of Irish Catholicism. 820

Historical directory of the Reformed Church in America. 3045

Historical directory of the Reformed Church in America, 1628-1978. 3045

Historical discourse. 2460, 2686, 2714, 2984, 3234

... Historical discourse and addresses delivered at the 175th anniversary of the Reformed church Readington, N. J. October 17th, 1894. 3045

Historical discourse delivered at the Centennial anniversary of the Congregational church, Candia, N.H., April 5, 1871. 734

Historical discourse delivered at the semi-centennial celebration of Christ church, St. Louis, on All-saints' day, 1869. 3276

Historical discourse delivered on occasion of the re-opening and dedication of the First reformed (Dutch) church. 1779

Historical discourse delivered on the fiftieth anniversary of the organization of the Emmanuel Baptist church, (formerly Pearl street) Albany, N.Y., by the pastor, Henry Melville King, October 27, 1884. 22, 684

Historical discourse delivered on the occasion of the semi-centennial year of the Reformed church, Utica, N. Y. 3047

Historical discourse delivered on the one hundredth anniversary of the Piscataqua association of ministers, at the North church, Portsmouth, N.H., October 26, 1881. 2849

Historical documents, advocating Christian union. 1463

Historical evidence for the resurrection of Jesus Christ. 2052

Historical evidence for the virgin birth. 3781

Historical evidence of the New Testament. 1097

Historical evidences of the truth of the Scripture records. 277

Historical examination of some non-Markan elements in Luke. 429

Historical exposition on the origin and evolvement of the basic tenets of the Doukhobor life-conception. 1482

Historical facts about the churches of Wythe county. 1275

Historical Foundation and its treasures. 1817

Historical Foundation holdings of eighteenth-century American publications. 2923, 3627

Historical foundation of Christianity. 394, 2000

Historical geography of the Bible. 282

Historical geography of the Holy land. 2764

Historical growth of the English parish church. 1159

Historical in Kant's philosophy of religion. 2163

Historical information for New Testament students. 407

Historical inquiry in regard to the Grand constitutions of 1786. With a foreword by Luther A. Smith. 1671

Historical introduction to the Christian religion. 1195

Historical introduction to the Marprelate tracts. 1759

Historical introduction to the New Testament. 409

Historical introductions to the Book of concord. 2283

Historical investigations. 1183

Historical Jesus. 1954, 1978, 2009

Historical Jesus and the kerygmatic Christ. 2008

Historical Jesus and the kingdom of God. 1530, 2063

Historical Jesus in the Gospel of St. John. 414

Historical Jesus of Nazareth. 1103, 2013

Historical leaflets. no. 1-9. 3042

Historical lectures and addresses. 1817

Historical lectures on the life of Our Lord Jesus Christ, being the Hulsean lectures for the year 1859. 1963

... Historical lessons on the nature of the kingdom of God. 2176

Historical life of Jesus of Nazareth. 2060, 3511

Historical Man of Nazareth. 2008

Historical memoirs relating to the Housatonic Indians. 3334, 3532

Historical memorial of the centennial anniversary of the presbytery of Huntingdon held in Huntingdon, Pa., April 9, 1895. 1273

Historical memorials of Ely cathedral. 21, 1509

... Historical method in Bible study. 635

Historical narrative of Bethel Presbyterian church. 195

Historical notes. 2319

Historical notes about Christ Church, West Haven, Connecticut. 3807

Historical notes on St. Benedict's Rule for monks. 190

Historical notes on the apostolic leaders. 71, 331

Historical notes on the life of Christ. 2009

Historical notes relating to the Pennsylvania Reformed church. 3048

Historical open questions among American Lutherans. 2286

Historical pamphlet. 174

Historical perspective. 2329

Historical poem. 298

Historical poetry of the ancient Hebrews. 1799

Historical presentation of Augustinism and Pelagianism from the original sources. 2811

Historical problems of church renewal. 1183

Historical Protestantism. 3679

Historical recollections of St. Paul's chapel, New York. 2699

Historical records concerning Jesus the "Christ" Messiah. 2069

... Historical, religious and economic texts and antiquities. 89

Historical resources of the Episcopal Diocese of Connecticut. 1269, 2963

Historical revelations of the relation existing between Christianity and paganism. 2158

Historical road of Anglicanism. 44

Historical road of Eastern Orthodoxy. 2747

Historical role of the Catholic Church in times of mental chaos & moral decay. 793, 1283

Historical Saint Columba. 919, 1311

Historical scenes from the old Jesuit missions. 1949

Historical selections in the philosophy of religion. 3105

Historical setting of the early gospel. 347

Historical shape of faith. 1819

Historical sketch of Christ Reformed church. 1508

Historical sketch of Ebenezer Reformed Presbyterian Church, Jessamine County, Kentucky. 1487

Historical sketch of First Baptist church of Valdosta, Georgia. 1124

Historical sketch of Grace church, Morganton, North Carolina. 2598

Historical sketch of Massaponax Baptist church of Spotsylvania county, Virginia. 2371

Historical sketch of New Hope church. 2688

Historical sketch of sacerdotal celibacy in the Christian church. 877

... Historical sketch of St. John's church. 1791

... Historical sketch of St. Joseph's provincial seminary, Troy. N. Y., by the Right Rev. Henry Gabriels. 3275

Historical sketch of the Baptist council of Richmond. 140

Historical sketch of the Baptist missionary convention of the state of New York. 158

Historical sketch of the Brethren movement. 2855

Historical sketch of the Catholic church in New Mexico. 823

Historical sketch of the China mission of the Protestant Episcopal church in the U.S.A. 2970

Historical sketch of the church and missions of the United brethen, commonly called Moravians. 2595

Historical sketch of the Church of the Good Shepherd, Rosemont, Pennsylvania, 1869-1934. 3249

Historical sketch of the Congregational churches in Massachusetts, from 1620 to 1858. 1343

Historical sketch of the Convent and Academy of the Sisters of St. Francis in Oldenburg, Indiana, and of the work of their community in the United States. 3416

Historical sketch of the First Presbyterian church. 3788

Historical sketch of the First Presbyterian Church of Milledgeville. 2463

... Historical sketch of the First Presbyterian church of Rahway, N. J. 3019

Historical sketch of the freedmen's missions of the United Presbyterian church, 1862-1904. 1658

Historical sketch of the Independent congregational church, Meadville, Pennsylvania, 1825-1900. 2376

Historical sketch of the Massachusetts Baptist missionary society and convention, 1802-1902. 2370

Historical sketch of the origin and organization of the Reformed church in America and of the Collegiate church of the city of New York. 3045

Historical sketch of the origin and progress of the Society of the Sons of St. George. 3196

Historical sketch of the parish of St. Rose, Chelsea, Massachusetts. 1179

Historical sketch of the Pittsgrove Baptist church, Daretown, Salem County, New Jersey. 1187

Historical sketch of the rise, progress, and decline of the Reformation in Poland, and of the influence which the scriptural doctrines have exercised on that country in literary, moral, and political respects. 3042

Historical sketch of the Saint Andrew's society. 1179

Historical sketch of the Second Baptist church of Baltimore, Maryland. 1181

Historical sketch of the Sisters of mercy in the diocese of Buffalo. 2626, 3418

...An historical sketch of the Unitarian movement since the reformation. 3727

Historical sketch of the work of foreign missions of the Reformed Church in the United States. 3048

... An historical sketch of thePresbyterian church of Ballston Centre, N.Y. 132

Historical sketches. 1684, 2917

Historical sketches and incidents. 3754

Historical sketches, from the life of Mary Baker Eddy. 1037, 1495

Historical sketches of Iowa Baptists. 154

Historical sketches of the Bible Standard Churches Inc. in 1919 before merging with the Open Bible Churches Inc. in 1935. 615

Historical sketches of the Catholic church in Oregon, during the past forty years. 824

Historical sketches of the Evangelical Lutheran Synod of South Carolina from its formation in 1824. 2292

Historical sketches of the missions of the American Board. 2491

Historical sourcebook of the Japan mission of the Reformed church in America (1859-1930) 3047

Historical souvenirs of Martin Luther. 2274

Historical studies in the cult of the goddess Manasa. 2327

Historical studies of church-building in the Middle Ages. 1160

Historical studies of church-building in the Middle Ages: Venice, Siena, Florence. 1160

Historical study of African religion. 13

Historical study of Southern Baptists and race relations, 1917-1947. 1133, 3466

Historical study of the educational agencies of the Southern Baptist Convention. 3465

Historical study of the educational agencies of the Southern Baptist Convention, 1845-1945. 3466

Historical survey of the Old Testament. 535

Historical text book and atlas of Biblical geography. 282

Historical textbook and atlas of Biblical geography. 282

Historical theology. 1616, 3653, 3655

Historical tradition in the Fourth Gospel. 419

Historical transcendence and the reality of God. 1719

Historical tribute to St. Thomas' seminary. 3279

Historical tribute to St. Thomas' seminary at Poplar Neck, near Bardstown, Kentucky. 3279

Historical value of the first eleven chapters of Genesis. 525

Historical vindication of the abrogation of the plan of union by the Presbyterian church in the United States of America. 2925

Historical waymarks of the Church of God, (headquarters, Oregon, Illinois) 1228

... The historical writings of John Fiske. 2835, 2836

Historically speaking on Lewiston-Auburn, Maine, churches. 2220

Historicism and faith. 1820

Historicity of Jesus. 2008

Historico-critical introduction to the canonical books of the New Testament. 409

Historie of the Kirk of Scotland. 1234

Histories. 520

Histories and prophecies of Daniel. 507

Histories of Baptist churches in Burlington and Alamance County, North Carolina. 144

Histories of Rabban Hormizd the Persian and Rabban Bar-'Idta. 1847

Histories of United Church of Christ in Burlington and Alamance County, North Carolina. 3732

Historiographer. 2967

Historiographical sketch of pioneer Catholicism in the Californias: missions and missionaries. 1901

... The historiography of the American Catholic church. 834

Historiography of the American Catholic Church, 1785-1943. 833

History. 1668, 2769

History and activities of Congregation Anshe-Emeth, Pine Bluff, Arkansas, 1867-1917. 2089

History and advocacy of the Christian church. 1174

History and antiquities of the Anglo-Saxon church. 1760

History and background of St. George's Episcopal Church. 1652

History and beliefs of Mormonism. 2598

History and character of American revivals of religion. 3232

History and character of Calvinism. 730

History and characteristics of the Reformed Protestant Dutch church. 3046

History & Christianity. 3623

History and criticism of the Marcan hypothesis. 436, 3578

History and customs of the Amish people. 2404

History and destiny of the Jews. 2089

History and directory of Temple Presbyterian church. 2830

History and directory of the First Presbyterian church. 2916

History and eschatology. 1817

History and evolution of Freemasonry. 1664

History and existential theology. 1818

History and exposition of the twenty-five articles of religion of the Methodist Episcopal church. 2449

History and future of religious thought. 3112

History and God. 1818

History and guide to Judaic bibliography. 657, 2083

History and hermeneutics. 287, 1818

History and literature of Christianity from Tertullian to Boethius. 1018, 1020

History and literature of the New Testament. 406, 409, 1093

History and literature of the Palestinian Jews from Cyrus to Herod, 550 B.C. to 4 B.C. 2091

HISTORY AND MANUAL RELIGIOUS BOOKS 1876 - 1982

History and manual of the First Congregational church, Concord, New Hampshire, 1730-1907. 1337
History and manual of the First Congregational church, Norwich, N. Y. 1119
History and message of hymns. 1871
History and motives of literary forgeries. 2231
History and mystery of Methodist episcopacy. 2450, 3804
History and origins of Druidism. 1480
History and philosophy of marriage. 2858
History and philosophy of the metaphysical movements in America. 3325
History and pictures of the fifty Churches of Christ in Maury County. 1272
History and pictures of the fifty Churches of Christ in Maury County, Tennessee. 1272
History and power of mind. 2726
History and practice of magic. 2314
... History and present condition of the Barbary states. 173
...The history and principles of Mennonite relief work, an introduction. 2404
History and published records of the Midway Congregational Church, Liberty County, Georgia. 2463
History and record of the Protestant Episcopal church in the diocese of West Virginia. 2974
History and rededication of Saint John Evangelical Lutheran Church of 1867 on October 26th, 1958, Meyersville, Texas. 3274
... The history and religion of Israel. 2096, 2148
History and reminiscences of the Monumental church, Richmond, Va., from 1814 to 1978. 3237
History and repository of pulpit eloquence. 3340
History and stories in the Book of Mormon. 680
History and teachings of the Eastern Greek Orthodox Church. 941, 2747
History and the Gospel. 389
History and the theology of liberation. 2198
History and theology in Second Isaiah. 545
History and theology in the Fourth Gospel. 420
History and Torah. 2143
History and use of hymns and hymn-tunes. 1874
History, annals and sketches of the Central church of Fall River, Massachusetts. A. D. 1842-A. D. 1905. 1602
History as myth. 1819
History compiled for First Methodist Episcopal church. 2865
History, criticism & faith. 1819
History, diocese of Belleville. 1172
History, essays, orations, and other documents of the sixth general conference of the Evangelical alliance. 1551
History in Christian perspective. 1819
History in miniature of the holy years. 1838
History in the making. 1819
History, Mount Vernon Place United Methodist Church, 1850-1976. 2626
History, nature and use of epikeia in moral theology. 1522
History, object, and proper observance of the holy season of Lent. 2209
History of a penitent. 3218
History of African Christianity, 1950-1975. 1073
History of African Methodism in Virginia. 2433
History of all religions. 3113, 3120
History of All Saints' Church, Ockbrook: including a brief account of the early origins of the village and parish. 25, 2734
History of All Saint's parish in Frederick county, Maryland, 1742-1932. 1652
History of American Baptist missions. 143, 156
History of American Baptist missions in Asia, Africa, Europe and North America. 155
... A history of American Christianity. 3737
History of American church music. 1210
History of American Congregationalism. 1338
History of American Methodism. 2423, 2438
History of American Methodism (The) 2424
History of American missions to the heathen. 2522
History of American revivals. 3227, 3228, 3232
History of American slavery and Methodism from 1780 to 1849. 3423, 3807
History of amulets, charms and talismans. 35
History of an African independent Church. 1237
History of Andover theological seminary. 40
History of anti-pedobaptism, from the rise of pedo baptism to A.D. 1609. 1906
History of Antony Bek. 185
History of apologetics. 69
History of apostasies. 1179
... A history of Armenian Christianity from the beginning to our own time. 82
History of astrology. 98
History of Asylum Hill Congregational Church, Hartford, CT. 1787
History of Auborn theological seminary. 109
History of auricular confession and indulgences in the Latin Church. 779, 1327
History of avarice. 120
History of Baltimore Yearly Meeting of Friends. 1677
History of Bangor theological seminary. 3614
History of baptism. 138
History of Baptist churches in Maryland connected with the Maryland Baptist union association. 154, 1175
History of Baptist Indian missions. 1900
History of Baptists in America, prior to 1845. 171
History of Baptists in Michigan. 155
History of Baptists in New Jersey. 158
History of Bedford church. 183
History of Benedictine nuns. Translated by M. Joanne Muggli, edited by Leonard J. Doyle. 187
History of benefices. 190
History of Bethesda Presbyterian Church, 1765-1965, Caswell County, N.C. 195, 2713
History of Betsey Green, a Sunday scholar. 33
History of Biblical literature. 291
History of bigotry in the United States. 3195
History of Black religion in Northern areas. 2683
History of Black religion in southern areas. 2683
History of Brethren hymnbooks. 1236
History of Brethren missionary movements. 691
History of British Churches of Christ. 1463
History of Brooklyn Jewry. 2098
History of Brown memorial Presbyterian church. 132
History of Buddhism in Kashmir. 706
History of Buddhist thought. 705
History of Buffalo Presbyterian church and her people Greensboro, N. C. 1772
History of California Southern Baptists. 145
History of Calvary church, Americus, Georgia. 34
History of Calvary Church of the Brethren, Front Royal Road, Winchester, Virginia, 22601. 726
History of Calvary Church, Stonington. 726
History of Carver School of Missions and Social Work. 743
History of Catholic Church music. 1205
History of Catholic education in Connecticut. 816
History of Catholic education in Kansas. 820
History of Catholic education in the United States. 830
... The history of Catholic elementary education in the diocese of Buffalo. 1247
History of Catholic higher education in the United States. 832
History of Catholicism in the north country. 2734
History of Catholicity in northern Ohio and in the diocese of Cleveland from 1749 to December 31, 1900. 1304
History [of] Central City Chapter, No. 70, Royal Arch Masons,1821-1962. 1671
History of Central Methodist Church, Asheville, North Carolina, 1837-1967. 90
History of Central Methodist church, Thirteenth and Porter streets. Richmond, Va. 2198
History of Cheatham Memorial United Methodist Church, Edgewood, Texas. 890
History of chivalry. 1390
History of Christ. 1988
History of Christ, according to inspiration. 1960
History of Christ Church. 1716
History of Christ Church, Guilford, New York, 1830-1955. 1777
History of Christ Church (Old Sweedes) 1172
History of Christ church parish. Macon. Georgia. 2310
History of Christ Episcopal Church. 2700
History of Christ Evangelical Lutheran Church. 3542
History of Christ Reformed church. 918
History of Christ Reformed Church at Indian Creek (Indianfield) 918
History of Christian doctrine. 934, 3643, 3654, 3655, 3657
History of Christian doctrine, A.D. 90-1517. 3655
History of Christian doctrines. 1473
History of Christian education. 3165
History of Christian ethics. 950
History of Christian-Latin poetry. 2199
History of Christian-Latin poetry from the beginnings to the close of the Middle Ages. 2d ed. 3210, 3211
...History of Christian missions. 2494
History of Christian missions in China. 2510
History of Christian missions in South Africa. 2499
History of Christian philosophy in the Middle Ages. 2840
History of Christian preaching. 2909
History of Christian spirituality. 3492
History of Christian thought. 3213, 3654, 3655, 3658
History of Christian thought, from its Judaic and Hellenistic origins to existentialism. 3655
History of Christian worship. 3853, 3855
History of Christianity. 1100, 1172, 1176, 1180, 1191, 1196, 1198, 2794, 3238
History of Christianity from Saint Paul to Bishop Brooks. 1100
History of Christianity from the birth of Christ ot the abolition of paganism in the Roman empire. 1193
History of Christianity, from the birth of Christ to the abolition of paganism in the Roman empire. 1193, 1197
History of Christianity from the origin of Christianity to the time of Gregory the Great. 2090
History of Christianity in America. 3737
History of Christianity in England. 1758
History of Christianity in Japan. 2533, 2534
History of Christianity in the apostolic age. 1177
History of Christianity in the Balkans. 2747, 3425
History of Christianity in the Middle Ages. 1185
History of Christianity in the world. 1177
History of Christianity in West Africa. 13
History of Christianity, 1650-1950. 1187
History of Christianty in Japan. 2533
History of church discipline in Scotland. 1234
History of church music. 1207, 1208
History of Church of Christ (Holiness) U.S.A., 1895-1965. 1210
History of Cleveland Presbyterianism with directory of all the churches. 2917
History of Coffee creek Baptist association, southern Indiana. 153
History of colored Baptists in Alabama. 157
History of conferences and other proceedings connected with the revision of the Book of common prayer. 1213
History of confession. 2811
History of Congregation Anshe Amonium. 2082
History of Congregationalism from about A. D. 250 to 1616. 1345
History of Congregationalism in Nebraska. 1337
History of Connecticut Baptist state convention, 1823-1907. Philip S. Evans. 151
History of conservative Baptists. 1348
History of Conservative Friends. 1679
History of Cosmopolite. 3091
History of creation and origin of the species. 1381
History of Criterion lodge, no. 68 Knights of Pythias (of Cleveland, Ohio) 2639, 2640
History of Crow River Lutheran Church, Belgrade, Minnesota, 1861-1961. 1389
History of Daniel. 1401
History of deeds done beyond the sea. 1390
History of Deer Creek Harmony Presbyterian Church, 1837-1972. 1419
History of Disciple theories of religious education. 1463
History of divorce and re-marriage for English churchmen. 1471
History of dogma. 3654
History of dogmas. 3655
History of early Christian literature. 1020
History of early Christian literature in the first three centuries. 1019
History of early Methodism in Texas, 1817-1866. 2424
History of early missions to India. 2529
History of eastern Christianity. 1486
History of Eastern Shore Chapel and Lynnhaven Parish, 1642-1969. 2304
History of Ebenezer Missionary Baptist Assocation (of Georgia) 1814-1964. 150
History of Eleanor Vanner. 3768
History of Emmanuel Baptist Church, Amherst County, Virginia. 34
History of English nonconformity. 1468
History of episcopacy. 1522
History of episcopacy, in four parts, from its rise to the present day. 1522
History of Episcopal churchwomen in Montana. 2970
History of Erie conference. 3093, 3139
History of Evangelical missions. 1546
History of evangelism. 1573
History of evangelism in the United States. 1573
History of evangelistic hymnody. 1872
History [of] Evans Avenue Baptist Church, Fort Worth, Texas, 1908-March, 1963. 151
History of Fifth street Baptist church. 1784
History of First Christian Church. 1858
History of First Christian Church, Greencastle, Indiana, 1830-1972. 1626, 1772
History of First Methodist Church. 3301, 3402
History of First Methodist Church, Martin, Tennessee, 1874-1960. 2424
History of First Methodist Church, Wichita Falls, Texas. 1627
History of Florida Baptists. 150
History of Forestdale Evangelical United Brethren Church. 1633, 2182
History of forty choirs. 915
...The history of Franciscan preaching and of Franciscan preachers. 1644
History of Frankford lodge. 1668
History of freedom of thought. 1653, 1656
History of Freemasonry in Michigan. 1667
History of freemasonry in Princeton. 1665
History of freemasonry in South Carolina. 1671
History of freemasonry in Tennessee, 1789-1943. 1671
History of freethought in the nineteenth century. 1655
History of fundamentalism. 1690, 2562
History of fundamentalism in America. 1691
History of Georgia Methodism from 1786 to 1866. 2424
History of Gettysburg classis of the synod of the Potomac, Reformed church in the United States. 3048
History of gospel music. 1748
History of gospel tents and experience. 1568
History of Grace Church. 888
History of Grace Episcopal church. 1523
History of Grace Episcopal Church, Hartford, Connecticut. 1787
History of Grace reformed church, Northampton, Pennsylvania. 3046
History of Grassy Creek Baptist Church from its foundation to 1880. 1756
History of Great Bend lodge no. 15, A. F. & A. M., 1873-1956. 1664
History of Greek religion. 1767
History of Har Sinai congregation of the city of Baltimore. 132
History of Head of Christiana Presbyterian church, the second oldest Presbyterian church in Delaware. 1792
History of Heidelberg college. 1801
History of heresy. 1805
History of Highland Baptist Church, Shreveport, Louisiana, 1916-1966. 3404
History of Holy Trinity Parish, Bloomington, Illinois. 673
History of Holy Trinity parish, Washington, D.C. 3797
History of Home missions council. 1838
History of Howard congregational church. 183

History of Huron presbytery. 2916, 2927
History of Illinois Congregational and
Christian Churches. 1336
History of Immanuel Church, 1824-1967.
1787
History of Independent royal arch lodge,
no. 2, F. & A. M. of the state of New
York. 1664
History of Indian literature. 3302
History of Indian philosophy. 2839
History of interpretation. 240
History of interpretation of Hebrews 7, 1-
10 [seven, one to ten] from the
reformation to the present. 404, 405
History of Iowa Baptist schools. 3756
History of Irish Catholicism. 820
History of Islam in West Africa. 1923,
2566
[History of Islamic civilization]. 1283
[History of Islamic philosophy]. 2841
History of Israel. 2088, 2089, 2095
History of Israel from Moses to Christ.
1928
History of Israel in Old Testament times.
534, 2096
History of Israel. Translated by Clement
Della Penta and Richard T. A. Murphy.
2089
History of Israel. Translated by Clement
Della Penta and Richard T.A. Murphy.
2d ed. 2089
History of Israelite religion. 598, 2150
History of Jacob. 1931
History of Japanese religion. 1935
History of Jemima Wilkinson. 3816
History of Jerusalem Lutheran and
Reformed church of western Salisbury,
Lehigh Co., Penna. 2288
History of Jesus. 1964
History of Jesus Christ. 1961
History of Jewish coinage, and of money
in the Old and New Testament. 481
History of Jewish coinage, and of money
of the Old and New Testament. 2584
History of Jewish education in America.
2106
History of Jewish education in the Soviet
Union. 2103
History of Jewish life in modern times for
young people. 2090
History of Jewish literature. 2076
History of Job. 550
History of Jonah, for children and youth.
2130
History of Joseph. 2133
History of Joseph Smith. 3429
History of Josiah. 2135
History of Judaism. 2146
History of Judaism, the next ten years.
2146
History of Kansas Baptist Women, 1828-
1960. 154
History of Kansas Baptists. 154
History of Kansas Masonry. 1665
History of Kentucky Baptists. 154
History of King Edward VI School. 3524
History of Lake Shore Chapel, Douglas,
Michigan. 2193
History of Laramie Lodge No. 3, A.F. &
A.M. of Wyoming, 1870-1970. 1666
History of Latin Christianity. 810
History of Lodge no. 43, F. and A. M.
1785-1910. 1665
History of Long Branch Baptist Church,
Fauquier County, Virginia. 2245
History of Louisville Presbyterian
Theological Seminary. 2261
History of Lutheran missions. 2296
History of Lynchburg's pioneer Quakers
and their meeting house. 1686
History of Madison lodge no. 93 of Free.
1666
History of magic. 2313, 2314
History of magic, including a clear and
precise exposition of its procedure, its
rites, and its mysteries. 2314
History of marriage, Jewish and Christian,
in relation to divorce and certain
forbidden degrees. 2345
History of Mars Hill Presbyterian Church.
102, 2347
History of Marsh lodge no. 188 of Free
and accepted masons, "The mother-lodge
of old Williamsburgh" from its institution
on May 12th, 1847 to July 5th, 1900.
1665
History of Maryland classis of the
Reformed church in the United States.
3048
History of Mattaponi Baptist church, King
and Queen County, Virginia. 2373
History of Maud United Methodist
Church, 1874-1974. 2374
History of mediaeval philosophy. 2843
History of medieval Christianity. 1186

History of Memorial United Methodist
Church, founded 1884, Lynchburg,
Virginia. 2304, 2401
History of Mendelssohn's oratorio "Elijah"
2402
History of Mennonites in Virginia. 2408
History of Messianic speculation in Israel
from the first through the seventeenth
centuries. 2414
History of Messianic speculation in Isral.
2414
History of Methodism. 2423, 2424
History of Methodism in Alabama. 2430
History of Methodism in Alabama and
West Florida. 2430
History of Methodism in Arkansas. 2451
History of Methodism in Bridgeport. 691
History of Methodism in Georgia. 2430
History of Methodism in Georgia and
Florida, from 1785 to 1865. 2430
History of Methodism in Illinois. 2451
History of Methodism in Kentucky. 2431,
2452
History of Methodism in Maine, 1793-
1886. 2431
History of Methodism in Minnesota. 2452
History of Methodism in North Carolina.
2432
History of Methodism in northwest
Kansas. 2452
History of Methodism in Pensacola,
Florida. 2813
History of Methodism in Providence,
Rhode Island, from its introduction in
1787 to 1867. 2453
History of Methodism in South Carolina.
2432, 2453
History of Methodism in Southern
California and Arizona. 1929, 2430
History of Methodism in the United
States. 2433
History of Methodism in Troy, N. Y.
2433
History of Methodism in Utah. 2433
History of Methodism within the bounds
of the Erie annual conference of the
Methodist Episcopal church. 2446
History of Methodist churches and
institutions in middle Tennessee, 1787-
1956. 2432
History of Methodist missions. 2441
History of Methodist reform, synoptical of
general Methodism. 2423
History of Methodists in the United States.
2438
History of middle Tennessee Baptists. 170
History of Mission House-Lakeland. 2193
History of missions. 2522
History of missions in India. 2531
History of Mississippi Baptists, 1780-1970.
156
History of Missouri Baptists. 156
History of modern thought. 2241, 2843
... The history of Montgomery classis, R.
C. A. 3045
History of Monumental Methodist Church,
1772-1966. 2864
History of Mother Seton's daughters.
3416
History of my life. 3201
History of Nebraska Epworth assembly.
1525
History of Nebraska Methodism. 2431
History of New England. 157
History of New England theology. 2688
History of New Mexico Spanish and
English missions of the Methodist
Episcopal church. 2454
... History of New Testament criticism.
351
History of New Testament times. 490,
1191, 2092, 2149
History of North Carolina Baptists. 158
History of North Mississippi Methodism.
2455
History of North Parish Church of North
Andover, 1645-1974. 2713, 2714
History of Northwest Regular Baptists.
2714
History of Nuestra Senora de la leche y
buen parto. 750
History of Ohio Methodism. 2452
History of old Pine street. 2830
... History of Old Testament criticism. 504
History of old Zion Evangelical Lutheran
church in Hempfield Township,
Westmoreland County, Pennsylvania.
3896
History of Olivet Congregational Church,
Columbus, Wisconsin. 1311
History of Orange Presbytery, 1770-1970.
2927
History of Oregon Methodism. 2432,
2460
History of Orthodox theology since 1453.
3667
History of our B. Lady of Loreto. 2260

History of Our Blessed Lord and Saviour
Jesus Christ. 72, 1973
History of Our Lady of Mount Carmel
Parish, Baden, Missouri. 124, 2753
History of Our Lord. 1968
History of Our Lord and Saviour Jesus
Christ. 2007, 2008
History of our Lord as exemplified in
works of art. 920, 1957
History of Padgett's Creek Baptist Church.
2756
History of Palestine and Syria to the
Macedonian conquest. 2764
History of Palestine, from the patriarchal
age to the present time. 2764
History of Pamela. 3782
History of Paris lodge no, 27, A. F. & A.
M. 1668
History of penance. 2812
History of Pencader Presbyterian church
(Welsh in origin) of Glasgow, Delaware.
1715
History of Pentateuchal traditions. 563
History of Perth Amboy, Jersey, Young
Men's Christian Association, 1912-1957.
3874
History of philosophy. 2840
History of philosophy in Islam. 2840
History of Pickering Lodge No. 472. 1668
History of Plymouth church. 184, 693
History of Pope Boniface VIII and his
times. 677
History of preaching. 2909
History of preaching in Britain and
America. 2909
History of Presbyterianism in North
Carolina. 2918
History of Presbyterianism on Prince
Edward Island. 2918
History of priestcraft in all ages and
nations. 2939
History of primitive Christianity. 1190,
1195
History of Prince Hall Freemasonry (1775-
1945) 1667
History of Protestant divines. 1215, 1291
History of Protestant missions in the near
East. 2516, 2541
History of Protestant theology. 3679
History of Protestantism. 2978
History of Providence Presbyterian
Church, Mecklenburg County, North
Carolina. 2984
History of pues. 2827
History of Purity Presbyterian church of
Chester, South Carolina. 892
History of Quakerism. 1685
History of rationalism. 3023, 3024
History of reformatory movements
resulting in a restoration of the Apostolic
Church. 1179
History of religion. 3093, 3094, 3118
History of religion East and West. 3139
History of religion in the United States.
3094, 3745
History of religions. 3111, 3115, 3116,
3118, 3139
History of religions. v. 1. 3141
History of religious architecture. 1160
History of religious education. 3165
History of religious education in
Connecticut. 937, 3162
...A history of religious education in recent
times. 3147
History of religious education in the
Episcopal church. 2965
History of religious education in the
Episcopal Church to 1835. 942, 2965
History of religious educators. 1498
History of religious ideas. 3093
History of religious orders. 2575
History of religious sectarianism in Russia,
1860s-1917. 1038
History of Reynard the Fox. 1588
History of Richland Baptist Church,
Richland, Mississippi. 3236
History of Rochester presbytery from the
earliest settlement of the country. 2920
History of Rodeph Shalom Congregation,
Philadelphia, 1802-1926. 2829
History of Romanism. 799
History of Royal Arch Masonry. 1670
History of Royal Arch Masonry in
Alexandria, Virginia. 1663
History of Rt. Rev. Michael Egan. 1500
History of Russian-Soviet music. 2634
History of Sabatai Sevi, the suppos'd
Messiah of the Jews (1669) 3394
History of sacerdotal celibacy in the
Christian Church. 877, 878
History of Sacred Heart Cathedral,
Rochester, New York, 1911-1961. 3242
History of Saint Agnes' Episcopal Church
Washington, D. C. 3797
History of St. Alphonsus church,
Murrinsville, Pennsylvania. 2632

History of St. Andrew's church, Ann
Arbor, Michigan. 1173
History of Saint Andrew's society of the
state of New York. 1179
History of Saint Augustine of Canterbury
Parish, 1824-1974. 1799, 3273
History of St. Clement's church, El Paso,
Texas, 1870-1925. 1503
History of St. Dominic. 1474
History of Saint Francis Xavier Church
and Bohemia Plantation, now known as
Old Bohemia, Warwick, Maryland. 674,
3274
History of St. Francis Xavier Roman
Catholic Church (Old Newtown) the
Manor of Little Bretton, St. Mary's
County, Maryland [1662-1962. 3274
History of St. George's church in the city
of New York. 2699
History of St. George's parish, Flushing,
Long Island. 1179
History of Saint James' church in the city
of New York, 1810-1860. 2698
History of St. James' church (Protestant
Episcopal) 1744-1944. 2195
History of St. John the Evangelist church,
Antigo, Wisconsin. Golden jubilee, 1880-
1930. 52
History of Saint John's church. 1788
History of St. John's church, Newark.
1187
History of St. John's Congregational
Church. 1180
History of St. John's Episcopal Church,
Norwood Parish, 1874-1965. 892
History of St. John's Lodge No. 24. 1671
History of Saint John's Methodist Church,
1922-1960. 3252
History of St. John's Parish Whiting,
Indiana. 1783
History of Saint John's seminary, Brighton.
3275
History of St. Joseph, 1856-1956. 1175
History of St. Joseph's Old Cathedral.
712
History of St. Lucas Evangelical Lutheran
Church, Milwaukee, Wisconsin... in
commemoration of the 85th anniversary
of its founding, October, 1957. Comp. by
Albert G. Nickel and Selma M. Koehler.
2472
History of Saint Luke's church in the city
of New York. 2699
History of St. Luke's church, in the town
of Darien, Noroton, Conn., 1855-1930.
1403
History of Saint Luke's church, Marietta,
Ohio. 2335
History of Saint Mark's church, New
Britain, Conn., and of its predecessor
Christ church, Wethersfield and Berlin,
from the first Church of England service
in America to nineteen hundred and
seven. 2686
History of Saint Martin of Tours parish.
2830
History of St. Mary's church. 1173
History of Saint Mary's church, Govans.
133
History of St. Mary's Church of the
Mother of God. 1180
History of St. Mary's Parish, 1867-1967.
2560
History of St. Mary's Parish, Glens Falls,
New York,, 1848-1919. 1716
History of St. Matthew's church,
Francisville, Philadelphia, 1822-1925.
2830
History of St. Michael's church, Crydon.
1389
History of St. Michael's Parish. 3277
History of Saint Norbert. 2713, 2912
History of Saint Norbert, founder of the
Norbertine (Premonstratensian) order.
2713, 2912
History of Saint Patrick parish. 2163
History of St. Patrick's cathedral. 2700
History of St. Patrick's church, Carlisle,
Pennsylvania. 1174
History of St. Patrick's church,
Washington, D.C. 1180
History of St. Paul's Cathedral. 2244
History of St. Paul's Cathedral and the
men associated with it. 2244
History of St. Paul's Church. 1174
History of St. Paul's church, Alton,
Illinois. 28
History of St. Paul's church, Buffalo, N.Y.
712
History of Saint Paul's Evangelical
Lutheran Church, Fort Atkinson,
Wisconsin. Affiliated with the Wisconsin
Evangelical Lutheran Synod, 1861-1961.
1174
History of Saint Paul's lodge, no. 11.
1666

History of Saint Paul's protestant Episcopal church in the city of East Cleveland. 1304
History of Saint Peter's church. 22, 893, 3237
History of St. Peter's church, Auburn, N. Y. 109
History of St. Peter's Church in Oxford, Connecticut. 2753
History of St. Peter's Church in Perth Amboy. 2823
History of St. Peter's Church in Perth Amboy, New Jersey, 1685-1956. 2823
History of Saint Peter's Church, Morristown, New Jersey. 2620
History of St. Philip's church in the Highlands. 1173
History of St. Philip's Parish, 1897-1975. 3278
History of St. Stephen's Church, Millburn, New Jersey, 1851-1963. 2463
History of St. Thomas Episcopal Church. 3697
History of Saint Thomas parish, Ann Arbor. 48
History of St. Thomas's Episcopal church, New Haven, Connecticut, 1848-1941. 2688
History of St. Vincent de Paul. 3779
History of Salem Baptist Church. 892, 3286
History of Salonitan Christianity. 1190
History of Salt Lake City and its founders. 3287
History of salvation. 596
History of Scottish Congregationalism. 1338
History of SDA church-state relations in the United States. 1151, 3384
History of secular Latin poetry in the Middle Ages. 2199
History of Seventh-Day Adventist education. 3385
History of Seventh day Baptists in West Virginia including the Woodbridgetown and Salemville churches in Pennsylvania and the Shrewsbury church in New Jersey. 3388
History of seventy-five years of funeral service in Iowa. 1693
History of Shearn church. 1173
History of Sikh gurus. 3408
History of simony in the Christian church. 3409
History of South Carolina Baptists. 169
History of South Carolina Methodism. 2432
History of South Congregational church, Springfield, Massachusetts. 1337
History of Southern Baptist Landmarkism in the light of historical Baptist ecclesiology. 2195, 3466
History of Southern Baptist Theological Seminary. 2261
History of Southern Methodism in New Orleans. 2457
History of Southern Methodist missions. 2457
History of spiritualism. 3500, 3520
History of sprinkling. 137
History of St Mary's Church, Garforth. 3277
History of Sugar Grove Baptist Church, 1861-1961. 152
History of Synod of N.C., Presbyterian Church in the U.S. 2928
History of Taylor's Chapel, 1770-1968. 133
History of temperance in Saratoga County, N.Y. 2231
History of Temple Israel of New Rochelle, New York. 2101, 3599
History of Temple-Noyes lodge no. 32. 1664
History of ten Baptist churches. 172, 3591
History of Texas Baptists. 170
History of Texas Methodism, 1900-1960. 2432
History of thanatology. 1412
History of the A. M. E. Zion Church. 15
History of the Abbey of Aberconway. 2
History of the abbey of St. Alban. 2
History of the Abington Baptist association, from 1807 to 1857. 151
History of the African Methodist Episcopal Church. 14
History of the African mission of the Protestant Episcopal Church. 2500, 2970
History of the African mission of the Protestant Episcopal church in the United States, with memoirs of deceased missionaries, and notices of native customs. 2500
History of the African Orthodox Church. 15
History of the African union Methodist Protestant church. 2459

History of the Afro-American group of the Episcopal church. 1524
History of the Albany cathedral of the Immaculate conception. 22
History of the Alleghany Evangelical Lutheran synod of Pennsylvania, together with a topical handbook of the Evangelical Lutheran church, its ancestry, origin and development. 1548
History of the Allentown conference of the Ministerium of Pennsylvania. 2474
History of the American Bible society. 31
History of the American board of commissioners for foreign missions. 31
History of the American college of the Roman Catholic church of the United States Rome, Italy. 3245
History of the American Episcopal church. 2967
History of the American Episcopal church from the planting of the colonies to the end of the civil war. 2967
History of the American Province of the Society of the Precious Blood. 2940
...A history of the American Sunday school curriculum. 3561
History of the Anabaptists in Switzerland. 37
History of the ancient accepted Scottish Rite in Illinois, 1846-1965. 1665
History of the Ancient Accepted Scottish Rite in Ohio. 1668
History of the Andover theological seminary. 40
History of the Apostles creed. 74
History of the Apostolic church. 1179
History of the Arabian mission. 2501
History of the archbishops of Hamburg-Bremen. 1707
History of the archdiocese of Boston in the various stages of its development, 1604 to 1943. 683
History of the archdiocese of Cincinnati. 1176
History of the archdiocese of St. Louis in its various stages of development from A. D. 1673 to A. D. 1928. 3276
History of the Armenian Church. 82
History of the Armonk Methodist church of North Castle. 83
History of the art of magic. 1808, 2313
History of the Articles of religion. 3093
History of the Associate Reformed Presbyterian Church. 93
History of the attempts to establish the Protestant reformation in Ireland. 873
History of the Auglaize annual conference of the United brethren church, from 1853 to 1891. 3730
History of the Augusta church. 110
History of the Baptist Church at the Stamping Ground, Ky., 1795. 3524
History of the Baptist church in Middletown Springs Vermont. 2462
History of the Baptist church of Ira, Vermont. 1918
... A history of the Baptist churches in the United States. 151, 152
History of the Baptist denomination in Georgia. 150
History of the Baptist young people's union of America. 142
History of the Baptists. 151, 152
History of the Baptists at Iredell, Texas. 154
History of the Baptists in Maine. 154
History of the Baptists in New England. 157
History of the Baptists in Norway. 158
History of the Baptists in the middle states. 152
History of the Baptists in the southern states east of the Mississippi. 169
History of the Baptists in Vermont. 151
History of the Baptists in Virginia. 172
History of the Baptists of Alabama. 143
History of the Baptists of Alabama: from the time of their first occupation of Alabama in 1808, until 1894: being a detailed record of denominational events in the State during. 143
History of the Baptists of Hill County, Texas. 170
History of the Baptists of Louisiana. 154
History of the Baptists of Oak Ridge, Louisiana, 1797-1960. 158
History of the Baptists of Texas. 170
History of the Baptists on the Eastern Shore of Virginia. 149
History of the Baptizers movement. 1468
History of the Baron de Hirsch fund. 174, 2105
History of the Beckley Jewish community. 2098
History of the Bell street chapel movement. 2983

History of the Bethel Baptist Association. 169
History of the Bethel Methodist Church, 1814-1965. 195
History of the Bible. 289, 290, 294
History of the Bible in English. 269
History of the Blessed Virgin Mary and The history of the likeness of Christ which the Jews of Tiberias made to mock at. 3093
History of the Blood River association of Baptists. 154
History of the Blue river Baptist association of Missouri. 157
History of the Book of common prayer. 1214, 2885
History of the Book of common prayer with a rationale of its office. 1214
History of the Bordentown Baptist Church. 682
History of the Brethren. 2855
History of the Brethren Church; its life, thought, mission. 691
History of the Brethren in Christ church. 691
History of the Brethren in Virginia. 3094
History of the Brethren movement. 2855
History of the Brighton church. 3242
History of the Broad Run Baptist Church. 692
History of the Broadway tabernacle church. 2697
History of the Broadway tabernacle of New York city. 3579
History of the Brooklyn and Queens Young Men's Christian Association, 1853-1949. 3874
History of the Catholic church. 808, 809, 810, 812, 1174
History of the Catholic church for the use of colleges, seminaries, and universities. 1178
History of the Catholic Church from the Renaissance to the French Revolution. 811
History of the Catholic church in California. 815
History of the Catholic church in Indiana. 819
History of the Catholic church in Iowa. 819
History of the Catholic church in Jamaica, B. W. I. 820
History of the Catholic Church in Nebraska. 823
History of the Catholic church in the diocese of Brooklyn. 693
History of the Catholic church in the dioceses of Pittsburg and Allegheny. 2850
History of the Catholic church in the New England states. 823
History of the Catholic church in the United States. 833
History of the Catholic Church in Wisconsin. 835
History of the Catholic church in Woonsocket and vicinity. 835
History of the Catholic Church within the limits of the United States. 667, 742, 834
History of the Catholic missions among the Indian tribes of the United States, 1529-1854. 1901, 834, 1901
History of the Catholic missions in northeast India 1890-1915. 851, 2532
History of the Catholic Total Abstinence Union of America. 870
History of the Catholicity in Richmond and Wayne co., Ind. 819
History of the Celtic Church from its inception to 1153. 1761
History of the Celtic religion and learning: containing an account of the Druids. 1480
History of the Central conference Mennonite church. 879
History of the Central Ohio conference of the Methodist Episcopal church...1856-1913. 2446
History of the Central Pennsylvania conference of the Evangelical church 1839--Centennial ed.--1939. 1546
History of the Cherrydale Masonic Lodge. 1663
History of the Chestnut Hill chapel. 892
History of the Chilhowee Baptist Association. 911
History of the Chillicothe presbytery. 2919
History of the choir and music of Trinity church. 2698
History of the choir and music of Trinity Church, New York. 2701
History of the Choral Union of the Evangelical Lutheran Church, 1847-1960. 1547

History of the Christian Church. 1174, 1175, 1176, 1177, 1178, 1179, 1180
History of the Christian Church and Church of Christ in Minnesota. 1464
History of the Christian church during the first six centuries. 1190
...The history of the Christian church during the middle ages with a summary of the reformation, centuries XI to XVI. 1186
History of the Christian church, from its origin to the present time. 1179
History of the Christian church from the earliest time to A. D. 461. 1191
History of the Christian Church in the West. 1464
History of the Christian Church, Maysville, Kentucky. 2376
History of the Christian Churches of Hendricks County, Indiana. 1463
History of the Christian denomination in America. 1100
History of the Christian movement. 1174
History of the Christian people. 1179
History of the Christian religion and church. 1193
History of the Christian religion to the year two hundred. 1195
History of the Christian science movement. 1033
History of the church. 1173, 1174, 1175, 1176, 1183, 2941
History of the church and her organizations, commemorating the one hundred fiftieth anniversary of the organization of the First Congregational church, Walton, New York, 1793-1943. 3791
History of the church and state in Norway. 1148
History of the church from Christ to Constantine. 1191
History of the church from the birth of Christ to the present time. 1180
... A history of the church, from the earliest ages to the reformation. 1195
History of the church in Burlington, New Jersey. 717
History of the church in England. 1759
History of the church in general. 1546
History of the church in Latin America. 2198
History of the church in the eighteenth and nineteenth centuries. 1181
History of the church in the fifth centruy. 1192
History of the church in Venezuela, 1810-1930. 3777
History of the church, in verse. 1189
History of the Church in Wales. 3789
History of the church known as the Moravian Church, or the Unitas Fratrum, or the Unity of the Brethren, during the eighteenth and nineteenth centuries. 2594
History of the Church Missionary Society of Australia. 1202, 2503
History of the church of Christ. 1177, 1189
History of the Church of Christ, from the days of the Apostles, to the year 1551, abridged from the first five volumes of Milner's Church history. 1177
History of the Church of Denmark. 1401
History of the Church of England. 1220, 1221
History of the Church of England in India. 1223
History of the church of God. 1175, 1229
History of the Church of God (Holiness) 1229
History of the Church of God in the United States of North America. 1229
History of the Church of Ireland. 1918
History of the Church of Jesus Christ. 1230
History of the Church of Jesus Christ of Latter-Day Saints in North Carolina. 1233
History of the Church of Our Saviour, Protestant Episcopal; in Longwood, Massachusetts, from its founding in 1868 to 1936, written and compiled at the request of the Parish council of the church. 693
History of the Church of Russia. 2750
History of the Church of Scotland. 1234, 3315
History of the Church of the brethen of the Southern district of Ohio, by the Historical committee. 1236
History of the church of the Brethren. 1236
History of the Church of the Brethren, Eastern Pennsylvania, 1915-1965. 1237
History of the Church of the brethren in Kansas. 1236

History of the Church of the brethren in Maryland. 1237
History of the Church of the brethren in Michigan. 1237
History of the Church of the brethren in Southern district of Pennsyvania, by the Historical committee. 1237
History of the Church of the brethren in the First district of West Virginia. 1235
History of the Church of the brethren of the Eastern district of Pennsylvania. 1237, 1236
History of the Church of the brethren of the Southern district of Ohio by the historical committee. 1236
History of the Church of the Holy Apostles. 2697
History of the Church of the Holy Trinity, Hertford, North Carolina. 1808
History of the Church of the Mediator, Kingsbridge, New York. 1173
History of the Church of the Messiah, 1834-1934. 3276
History of the Church of the United Brethren in Christ. 3730
History of the church of the United brethren in Christ, Virginia conference. 3731
History of the church of York, 1066-1127. 1759
History of the Church of Zion and St. Timothy of New York 1797-1894. 2697
History of the church through the ages. 1173
History of the church to A.D. 461, by B. J. Kidd. 1192
History of the church to A.D. 461. 1196
History of the churches and ministers. 1651
History of the churches and ministers connected with the Presbyterian and Congregational convention of Wisconsin. 1198
History of the churches in the United States and Canada. 2713
History of the churches, of all denominations, in the city of New York. 2698
History of the Churches of Christ in Texas. 1273
History of the churches of New Bedford. 2686
History of the churches of the Pittsburgh Baptist association. 159
History of the Clarksburg Baptist Church, Clarksburg, West Virginia. 1285
History of the classis of Lancaster of the Eastern synod of the Reformed church in the United States. 3048
... A history of the classis of Paramus of the Reformed church in America. 3047
History of the Clear Creek Baptist Association 1874-1957. 143
History of the Coffeeville Methodist Church, 1824-1970. 1305
History of the Colorado Baptist General Convention. 147
History of the Colored Methodist Episcopal Church in America. 1021, 1310
History of the Columbia district of the Tennessee Conference of the Methodist Church. 2438
History of the Commission on Ecumenical Mission and Relations of the United Presbyterian Church in the U.S.A. 1492
History of the conflict between religion and science. 3072, 3084
History of the Congregational association of Oregon and Washington territory. 1332
History of the Congregational association of southern Illinois. 1332
History of the Congregational Church in Ann Arbor. 48
History of the Congregational church of Blooming Grove. 673
History of the Congregational church of Middlebury, Vt. 1790-1913. 1344
History of the congregational churches in Maine. 1336
History of the Congregational churches in Orleans county, Vt. 1339
...A history of the Congregational churches in the United States. 1339
History of the Congregational Methodist Church. 1343
History of the corruptions of Christianity, 1782. 3655
History of the Council of Bishops of the United Methodist Church, 1939-1979. 3734
History of the Council of Florence. 1622
History of the Council of Trent. 3710
History of the councils of Baltimore. 829
History of the councils of Baltimore, 1791-1884. 829

History of the councils of the church, from the original documents. 1372
History of the Coventry Brethren church in Chester county, Pennsylvania. 1377
History of the creeds. 1386
History of the criticism of the Acts of the Apostles. 331
History of the cross. 1388
History of the crusades. 1390, 1391, 1392
History of the crusades against the Albigenses, in the thirteenth century. 22
History of the crusades against the Albigtnses in the thirteenth century. 23
History of the cryptic rite. 1670
History of the Cumberland Presbyterian church. 1396
History of the Cumberland Presbyterian church in Texas. 1396
History of the cure of souls. 1792
History of the deaconess movement in the Christian church. 1408
History of the decline and fall of the medieval Papacy. 2769
History of the destruction of Jerusalem, and the desolation of Palestine. 2088
... History of the development of devotion to the Holy name. 1826
History of the devil. 1428
History of the devil and the idea of evil, from the earliest times to the present day. 1427
History of the devil, both ancient and modern. 1427
History of the Diocese of Albany. 2957, 2960
History of the Diocese of Ardagh. 79
History of the diocese of Boise. 675
History of the diocese of Buffalo. 712
History of the Diocese of Cleveland. 1304
History of the Diocese of Cork from the earliest times to the Reformation. 779
History of the Diocese of Crookston. 829
History of the diocese of Fond du Lac and its several congregations. 2957
History of the Diocese of Harrisburg Protestant Episcopal Church. 2966
History of the Diocese of Killaloe. 779
History of the Diocese of Massachusetts, 1810-1872. 1175
History of the diocese of Ogdensburg. 1179
History of the diocese of Ohio until the year 1918. 2959
History of the Diocese of Pennsylvania of the Protestant Episcopal Church in the U.S.A., 1784-1968. 2971
History of the diocese of Sault Ste. Marie and Marquette. 2336
History of the diocese of Syracuse, established 1886, with an introduction by the Rt. Rev. Mgr. J. S. M. Lynch ... story of the parishes, 1615-1909. 1175
History of the Disciples of Christ in Illinois, 1819-1914. 1464
History of the Disciples of Christ in Ohio. 1465
History of the discipline of the Methodist Episcopal church. 2447
History of the division of the Presbyterian church in the United States of America. 2925
... The history of the doctrine of Christian perfection in the Evangelical association. 1545
History of the doctrine of the holy eucharist. 2252
History of the doctrine of the soul, among all races and peoples, ancient and modern, including theologians, philosophers, scientists, and untutored aboriginees. 3461
History of the doctrine of the work of Christ, in its ecclesiastical development. 2009, 2038
History of the Dominican liturgy. 843
History of the Dominican Order. 1475
History of the Dominican Sisters of the Perpetual Rosary. 1332
History of the Donatists. 1476
History of the early Christian church. 1194
History of the early church. 1193
History of the early church to A.D. 500. 1195
History of the earth's formation. 3517
History of the East Black River Association of Free Will Baptists, 1891-1896. 1485
History of the East Hickman Baptists Church, 1787-1962. 2220
History of the East Michigan conference. 1652
History of the East Pennsylvania Conference of the Church of the United Brethren in Christ. 1238
History of the Eastern diocese. 1172

History of the Eastern synod of the Reformed church in the United States, prepared by. 3048
History of the ecumenical movement, 1517-1948. 1492
History of the Emmanuel movement from the standpoint of a patient. 684
History of the English Baptists. 149
History of the English Bible. 248, 269
History of the English Bible as shown in facsimile pages from 1525 to 1611. 248
History of the English Church and people. 1760
History of the English church and people in South Africa. 13
History of the English church during the civil wars and under the Commonwealth, 1640-1660. 1219
History of the English clergy. 1215
History of the English hymn. 1871
History of the English Lutheran church of Pottsville, Pa. 1547
... The history of the Episcopal church in Japan. 2535, 2711
History of the Episcopal church in Narragansett, Rhode Island. 2972
History of the Episcopal Church of Bethesda-by-the-Sea, documented from authentic and contemporary sources. 2766
History of the Episcopal parish of Saint Andrew at Cripple Creek. 1387
History of the establishment and progress of the Christian religion in the islands of the South sea. 2543
History of the Evangelical and Reformed Church. 1545
History of the Evangelical church. 1546
History of the Evangelical churches of the valleys of Piemont. 3788
History of the Evangelical Congregational Church. 1546
History of the Evangelical Lutheran church in the United States. 2294
History of the Evangelical Lutheran church of Frederick, Maryland, 1738-1938. 1652
History of the Evangelical Lutheran church of the Trinity, Norristown, Pa., 1848-1938. 2713
History of the Evangelical Lutheran district. 1547
History of the Evangelical Lutheran joint synod of Ohio. 1548
History of the Evangelical Lutheran synod and ministerium of North Carolina, in commemoration of the completion of the first century of its existence. 1549
History of the Evangelical Lutheran synod of East Pennsylvania. 1548
History of the Evangelical Lutheran synod of Kansas (General synod) 1549
History of the Evangelical Lutheran synod of Maryland of the United Lutheran church in America, 1820-1920. 1548
History of the Evangelical Lutheran synod of West Pennsylvania of the United Lutheran church in America, 1825-1925. 1548
History of the Evangelical party in the Church of England. 1551, 1554
History of the Evangelical United Brethren Church. 1550
History of the expansion of Christianity. 1100, 1176
History of the expansion of Methodism in Texas, 1867-1902. 2432
History of the expedition to Jerusalem, 1095-1127. 1391
History of the fall and dissolution of Christendom. 1100
Angola. 2501
History of the Fifth avenue Presbyterian church of New York city, New York. 2916
History of the Finnish Congregational churches in North America. 1345
History of the First African Baptist church. 3305
History of the First Baptist church and some of her pastors. 3236
History of the First Baptist church, Chicago. 145
History of the First Baptist Church, Columbia, South Carolina. 1311
History of the First Baptist Church in New Haven, 1816-1966. 2688
History of the First Baptist church of Boston (1665-1899) 152, 684
History of the First Baptist Church of Griffin, Georgia, 1841-1977. 1626
History of the First Baptist Church of Milledgeville, Ga. 2463
History of the First Baptist Church of Milledgeville, Georgia, 1811-1975. 1626, 2463

History of the First Baptist church of Montgomery, Alabama. 2586
History of the First Baptist church of Newport News, Virginia. 2705
History of the First Baptist church of Norristown, Pa., from the organization. 2713
History of the First Baptist Church of Taylors, South Carolina. 3591
History of the First Baptist Church, Tuskegee, Alabama, 1839-1971. 3718
History of the First Christian church of Pomona, California. 2859
History of the First church in Dunstable-Nashua, N.H. 2669
History of the First Church in Malden. 2319
History of the First church in Roxbury, Massachusetts. 1630-1904. 1180
History of the First Church of Christ, Congregational. 3807
History of the First Church of Christ, Congregational, West Hartford, Conn. 3807
History of the First church of Stafford, Connecticut. 3524
History of the First Congregational Church, Keene, New Hampshire. 2166
History of the First Congregational Church of Ridgefield. 3237
History of the first Council of Nice. 1355, 2706
History of the First English evangelical Lutheran church in Pittsburgh. 1547
History of the First English Presbyterian church in Amwell. 2916
History of the First Evangelical and Reformed Church. 1545
History of the First Methodist Church [Marshall, Texas. 2348
History of the First Methodist church of Loveland, Colorado. 2267
... The history of the First Methodist Episcopal church. 1477
History of the First Methodist Episcopal church of Lawrence, Kansas. 2202
History of the First Methodist Episcopal church of Saranac, Clinton County, N. Y. 3303
History of the First Methodist Episcopal church of the city of Lancaster Pa., from 1807 to 1893. 2451
History of the First Methodist Episcopal church, Racine, Wisconsin. 2450
History of the First Parish Church in Brunswick, Maine. 698
History of the first pastorate of the Howard Presbyterian church. 2917
History of the First Presbyterian Church. 1811, 2916
History of the First Presbyterian Church, Danville, Virginia, 1826-1976. 1627
History of the First Presbyterian Church, Frankfort, Kentucky. 1650
History of the First Presbyterian Church, High Point, North Carolina, 1859-1959. 1811
History of the First Presbyterian Church in Greenville, South Carolina. 1772
History of the First Presbyterian church of Carlisle, Pa. 739
History of the First Presbyterian church of Columbus, Georgia. 1311
History of the First Presbyterian Church of Greensboro, North Carolina, 1824-1945. 1772
History of the First Presbyterian Church of Heuvelton. 1627, 1809
History of the First Presbyterian Church of Monpoe. 2585
History of the First Presbyterian Church of Natchez, Mississippi. 1627
History of the First Presbyterian Church of Rock Hill, South Carolina. 3242
History of the First Presbyterian Church of Tulsa, Oklahoma, 1885-1960. 2921
History of the First Presbyterian Church of Yorktown from 1906 to 1975. 1627, 3868
History of the First Presbyterian church, Salem, New Jersey. 3286
History of the First Presbyterian society. 2936
History of the First Reformed church, Lancaster, Pa., 1736-1904. 2195
History of the first Sabbath school in Framingham, Mass., from 1816 to 1868. 3561
History of the First Unitarian church, of Portland, Oregon. 1867-1892. 2864
History of the First United Methodist Church of Cuyahoga Falls, Ohio, 1830-1969. 1398
History of the Firt Presbyterian church of Chicago, 1833-1941. 893

HISTORY OF THE RELIGIOUS BOOKS 1876 - 1982

History of the Fisher s River Primitive Baptist Association from its organization in 1832, to 1904. 2941
History of the Fisher's River primitive Baptist association from its organization. 2941
History of the Foreign Christian missionary society. 1465, 1633
History of the formation and growth of the Reformed Episcopal church, 1873-1902. 3050
History of the foundations of Catholicism in Northern New York. 823, 2700
History of the founders and early organization of Scottish Rite Freemasonry in Sacramento. 1670
History of the Franciscan Order from its origins to the year 1517. 1646
... History of the Franks. 1651
History of the Free Baptist woman's missionary society. 1652
History of the Free church of England. 1652
History of the Free churchmen called the Brownists, Pilgrim fathers and Baptists in the Dutch republic. 1344
History of the Free Methodist church of North America. 2408
History of the Free Presbyterian Church of Scotland (1893-1933) 1653, 3315
History of the Freewill Baptists. 1658
History of the French Protestant refugees. 1852
... A history of the Friends in America. 1685
History of the General or Six Principle Baptists, in Europe and America. 1705
History of the Genesee annual conference of the Methodist Episcopal church. 2446
History of the Georgia-Alabama Synod of the United Lutheran Church in America, 1860-1960. 1706
History of the Georgia Baptist Convention, 1822-1972. 150
History of the Georgia Woman's Christian temperance union from its organization. 3833
History of the German Baptist Brethren in Europe and America. 698, 1235, 1236
History of the German Bptist Brethren in Europe and America. 1236
History of the German Congregational churches in the United States. 1339
History of the Gettysburg theological seminary of the General synod of the Evangelical Lutheran church in the United States and of the United Lutheran church in America, Gettysburg, Pennsylvania, 1826-1926. 1708
History of the Goshenhoppen Reformed charge, Montgomery County, Pennsylvania (1727-1819) 3048
History of the Grand Commandery of Knights Templar of Pennsylvania. 1668
History of the Grand Commandery of Knights Templar of the State of Illinois. 3598
History of the Grand Encampment of Knights Templar of the United States of America. 1672
History of the Grand Lodge of A.F.&A.M. of Oregon. 1664
History of the Grand Lodge of Ancient. 1666
History of the Grand Lodge of the Most Ancient and Honorable Society of Free and Accepted Masons for the State of New Jersey; commemorating the 175th anniversary, 1786-1961. 1667
History of the great reformation in England, Ireland, Scotland, Germany, France, and Italy. 3033
History of the great reformation of the sixteenth century. 3035
History of the great secession from the Methodist Episcopal church in the year 1845. 2456
History of the great temperance reforms of the nineteenth century. 3598
History of the half century celebration of the organization of the First Presbyterian church of Franklin, Indiana. 1651
History of the Harriet Hollond memorial Presbyterian church of Philadelphia, Pa. 2918
History of the Harvard church in Charlestown. 888
History of the heathen gods, and heroes of antiquity. 2657
History of the Hebrew commonwealth. 2087
... A history of the Hebrew people from the earliest times to the year 70 a. d. 2095
History of the Hebrews' second commonwealth. 2092
History of the Hebron Lutheran church. 1799
History of the hereditary government of the Sovereign Order of Saint John of Jerusalem, Knights of Malta. 2179
History of the higher criticism of the New Testament. 351
History of the holy catholic Bible. 274
History of the Holy Eastern Church. 2744
History of the holy eucharist in Great Britain. 2250
History of the holy Jesus. 2048
History of the Holy Land. 2764
History of the Home Mission Board. 3466
History of the Hongwanji mission in Hawaii. 1844
History of the Howson Fellowship Bible Class. 894
History of the Huguenot emigration to America. 1852
History of the Huguenots. 1852
History of the Hyde Park Baptist church. 893
History of the iconoclastic controversy. 1880
History of the Immaculate Conception Parish in the Colville Valley. 1311
History of the Independent or Congregational Church of Charleston, South Carolina, commonly known as Circular Church. 888
History of the Independent order of Good templars. 1913
History of the Indian Creek Baptist Church and related events. 1897
History of the Indian wars of New England. 1903
History of the Indiana-Kentucky Synod of the Lutheran Church in America: its development, congregations, and institutions. 1897
History of the Inquisition in the Middle Ages. 1909
History of the inquisition of Spain. 1910
History of the Inquisition of the middle ages. 1908, 1909
History of the institution of the Sabbath Day. 3547
History of the International order of the King's daughters and sons, year 1886 to 1930. 1913
History of the Irish hierarchy. 1919
History of the Iron County mission and Parowan, the mother town. 2618
History of the Islamic Center. 3797
History of the Islamic peoples. 2564
History of the Israelitish nation. 2090
History of the James City and the James River Baptist Churches. 1933
History of the Japan mission of the Reformed church in the United States, 1879-1904. 3048
History of the Jermain Memorial Church Congregation of Watervliet, New York, 1814-1974. 1943
History of the Jewish church. 2096
History of the Jewish experience: eternal faith, eternal people. 2120, 2147
History of the Jewish nation. 2089
History of the Jewish nation after the destruction of Jerusalem under Titus. 2092
History of the Jewish people. 2089
History of the Jewish people during the Maccabean and Roman periods. 2092
History of the Jewish people in the time of Jesus. 2092
History of the Jewish people in the tine of Jesus. 2092
History of the Jews. 2088, 2089, 2090, 2146
History of the Jews, from the earliest period down to modern times. 2089
History of the Jews in America. 2106
History of the Jews in America, from the period of the discovery of the new world to the present time. 2105
History of the Jews in America from the period of the discovery of the New World to the present time. 2105
History of the Jews in Baghdad. 2098
History of the Jews in England. 2100
History of the Jews in modern times. 2089
History of the Jews in Russia and Poland. 2102
History of the Jews in Spain. 2103
History of the Jews in the United States. 2105
History of the Jews of Italy. 2100
History of the Jews of Petersburg. 2101
History of the Jews of Philadelphia from colonial times to the age of Jackson [by] Edwin Wolf, 2d [and] Maxwell Whiteman. [1st ed.] 2101
History of the Jews of the middle ages. 2092
History of the Kickapoe mission and parish. 2169
History of the Kingston Presbyterian Church. 2177
History of the Knights Hospitallers of St. John of Jerusalem. 2179
History of the Lancaster conference of the Evangelical Lutheran ministerium of Pennsylvania and the adjacent states. 2291
History of the law of tithes in England. 3702
History of the legal incorporation of Catholic Church property in the United States (1784-1932) 826, 1242
History of the Liberty (East) Baptist association of Alabama. 143
History of the life and acts of the Most Reverend Father in God, Edmund Grindal. 1775
History of the life and sufferings of the Reverend and learned John Wiclif, D.D. 3860
History of the life, writings, and doctrines of Martin Luther. 2272
History of the literature of ancient Israel from the earliest times to 135 B. C. 539
History of the Little Church on the Circle. 1897
History of the Little sisters of the poor. 2233
History of the lives, sufferings, and triumphant deaths, of the primitive as well as the Protestant martyrs. 2351
History of the London Missionary Society. 2243
History of the Long run Presbyterian church. 1920
History of the Lutheran church in America. 2294
History of the Lutheran church in Japan. 2538
History of the Lutheran church in New Hanover, Montgomery County, Penna. 2292
History of the Lutheran Church in South Carolina. 2290
History of the Lutheran church in Virginia and east Tennessee. 2302
History of the Lutheran church of the ascension, Mount Airy, Philadelphia, Pa; 1889-1939. 2292
History of the Lutheran schools of the Missouri synod in Michigan, 1845- 1940. 1246
History of the Lutheran Theological Seminary at Philadelphia, 1864-1964. 2830
History of the M. W. Grand Lodge of Ancient, Free and Accepted Masons of Delaware. 1663
History of the McCormick theological seminary of the Presbyterian church. 2307
History of the Marion Methodist Church. 2335
History of the Marranos. 1910, 2332, 2336
History of the mass. 2367, 2368
History of the mass and its ceremonies in the eastern and western church. 2367
History of the mediaeval Jews. 2092
History of the Mennonite Brethren Church. 2403
History of the Mennonite brethren in Christ church. 2406
History of the Mennonite Community of Hamburg and Altona. 2406
History of the Mennonites. 2405
History of the Mennonites of the Franconia conference. 2404
History of the Methodist Church at Hendersonville, Tenn. 1803
History of the Methodist Church in North Dakota and Dakota Territory. 2431
History of the Methodist Episcopal church. 2450
History of the Methodist Episcopal church in Mexico. 2452
History of the Methodist Episcopal church in Omaha and suburbs. 2432
History of the Methodist Episcopal church on Port Republic and Smithville charge. 2864
History of the Methodist Episcopal church South, in Cumberland Maryland. 2450
History of the Methodist mission home of Texas, San Antonio. 2458
History of the Miami Baptist association. 158
History of the Michigan conference. 3807
History of the Michigan conference of the Evangelical church, 1838-1940. 1546
History of the Middle District Association, 1794-1958. 172
History of the Middle district Baptist association. 172
... History of the mission of the American board of commissioners for foreign missions to the Sandwich islands. 2524
History of the missions. 851
History of the missions in Japan and Paraguay. 2533
History of the missions of the American board of commissioners for foreign missions. 2529
History of the missions of the American board of commissioners for foreign missions, in India. 2529
... History of the missions of the American board of commissioners for foreign missions to the oriental churches. 2516
History of the missions of the American board of commissioners forforeign missions, in India. 2529
History of the missions of the Moravian church. 2595
History of the Missouri Methodist Church of Columbia, Missouri, and its Columbia predecessors. 1311
History of the Mizrachi movement. 2560
History of the Moravian Church. 2594, 2595
History of the Moravian church in Philadelphia. 2829, 3896
History of the Moravian mission among the Indians in North America, from its commencement to the present time with a preliminary account of the Indians. 2595
History of the Mormons. 2604, 3428
...History of the Mormons: or Latter-day saints. 2604, 3429
History of the most interesting events in the rise and progress of Methodism. 2422
History of the most interesting events in the rise and progress of Methodism in Europe and America. 2422
History of the most wonderful promise ever made. 2395
History of the Musar movement, 1840-1945. 2632
History of the Muscle shoals Baptist association from 1820 to 1890. 143
History of the Negro Baptists of Maryland. 157
History of the Negro Baptists of Tennessee. 157
History of the Negro church. 2682
History of the Neshannock Presbyterian church, New Wilmington, Pennsylvania, together with some account of the settlement of that part of northwestern Pennsylvania in which the church was organized. 2696
History of the New Bethel Methodist Church. 2686
History of the New England conference of the Methodist Episcopal church. 2451, 2442
History of the New England spiritualist campmeeting association. 2688
History of the New Hampshire conference of the Methodist Episcopal church, edited. 2446
History of the new school, and of the questions involved in the disruption of the Presbyterian church in 1838. 2925
History of the New Testament in words of one syllable. 406
History of the New York Bible society. 2696
History of the North American Young men's Christian associations. 3871
History of the North Carolina annual conference of the Methodist Protestant church. 2459
History of the North Carolina Chowan Baptist association, 1806-1881. 158
History of the North Dakota district. 2291
History of the North Indiana conference of the Methodist Episcopal church, from its organization, in 1844, to the present. 2450
History of the North Indiana Conference of the Methodist Episcopal Church, from its organization in 1844 to the present. 2439
History of the Norwegian Baptists. 158
History of the Norwegian Baptists in America. 158, 2714
History of the old Baltimore conference from the planting of Methodism in 1773 to the division of the conference in 1857. 2446
History of the old covenant. 534
History of the old hundredth psalm tune, with specimens. 2736
History of the "Old Scots" church of Freehold. 3601
History of the Old South church of Boston. 685

History of the Old Testament. 532, 534, 536

History of the Old Testament in words of one syllable. 532

History of the old Waldenses, anterior to the Reformation. 3788

History of the Orangeville Evangelical and Reformed Church, Orangeville, Pennsylvania. 2740

History of the order of Assassins. 92

History of the Order of St. John of Jerusalem in Wales and on the Welsh border. 2179

History of the Order of the Hospital of St. John of Jerusalem. 2179

History of the organization of the Methodist Episcopal church, South. 2457

History of the origin and establishment of the Inquisition in Portugal. 1910

History of the origin and progress of adult schools. 650, 3561

History of the origin and progress of Seventh-day Adventists. 3380

History of the origin of all things. 3494

History of the origin of the Free Methodist church. 2428

History of the orthodox church. 2747

History of the Ozark division mountain mission schools of the home mission board Southern Baptist Convention. 3465

History of the Palmyra Church of the Brethren. 2766

History of the Palmyra Church of the Brethren, 1892-1967. 2766

History of the papacy from the great schism to the sack of Rome. 808, 2769, 2862

History of the papacy in the 19th century. 2769, 2850

History of the papacy in the xixth century. 810

History of the parish of Christ Church. 2714

History of the parish of Immaculate Conception on the occasion of the 75th anniversary, 1887-1962. 3525

History of the parish of St. Joan of Arc, Harrowgate, Philadelphia. 2830

History of the parish of Trinity Church in the city of New York. 2701

History of the Paritans, of Protestant Nonconformaists. 3007

History of the passion, death, and glorification of Our Saviour, Jesus Christ. 2028

History of the passion of Our Lord Jesus Christ. 2029

History of the patriarch Jacob. 1931

History of the Pennsylvania conference of the Church of the United brethren in Christ. 3730

History of the Pennsylvania Mennonite Church in Kansas. 1809

History of the Pennsylvania railroad department of the Young men's Christian association of Philadelphia. 3875

History of the People Church. 877

History of the people of Israel. 2096

History of the people of Israel, c. 1800 B.C.-A.D. 1980. 535, 2089

History of the people of Israel in pre-Christian times. 2090

... History of the persecutions of the Jews in Russia. 2102

History of the Pilgrims and Puritans, their ancestry and descendants. 2847

History of the planting and training of the Christian church by the apostles. 1193

History of the popes. 2769, 2862

History of the Presbyterian and Congregational churches and ministers in Wisconsin. 3820

History of the Presbyterian church and other sketches of Gerrardstown, West Virginia. 1708

History of the Presbyterian church in Georgia. 2917

History of the Presbyterian Church in Louisiana. 2918

History of the Presbyterian Church in Michigan. 2918

History of the Presbyterian church in South Carolina. 2919

History of the Presbyterian church in South Carolina since 1850. 2919

History of the Presbyterian church in Texas. 2919

History of the Presbyterian church in the forks of Brandywine, Chester county, Pa., (Brandywine manor Presbyterian church.) from A.D. 1735 to A.D. 1885. 690

History of the Presbyterian church, in the state of Illinois. 2917

History of the Presbyterian church in the state of Kentucky. 2917

History of the Presbyterian Church in Winchester, Virginia, 1780-1949, based on official documents. 3820

History of the Presbyterian Church of Fredericksburg, Virginia, 1808-1976. 2915

History of the Presbyterian church of Rome, Pennsylvania 1844-1942. 3245

History of the Presbyterian church of Wysox, Pennsylvania, 1791-1938. 3861

... A history of the Presbyterian churches in the United States. 2924

History of the Presbyterian churches of the world. 2916

History of the Presbyterian controversey. 2925

History of the presbyterian of Indianapolis. 2920

History of the Presbytery of Blairsville and its churches. 2927

History of the Presbytery of Hudson. 2920

History of the Presbytery of Kanawha, 1895-1956. 2927

History of the presbytery of Luzerne, state of Pennsylvania. 2920

History of the Presbytery of Westminser and its antecedents, 1732- 1924. 2927

History of the Presbytery of Winchester (Synod of Virginia) 2927

History of the Primitive Baptists of Mississippi. 2941

History of the primitive church. 1193

History of the Prince Hall Grand Lodge of Free and Accepted Masons of the State of Ohio. 1668

History of the Prince Hall Grand Lodge of Free and Accepted Masons of the State of Ohio, 1849-1971. 1668

History of the progress and suppression of the Reformation in Italy in the sixteenth century. 3041

History of the progress and suppression of the Reformation in Spain in the sixteenth century. 3042

History of the Protestant church in Hungary. 1856

History of the Protestant Episcopal Church. 2967

History of the Protestant Episcopal church in Alabama, 1763-1891. 2960

... A history of the Protestant Episcopal church in the United States of America. 2967

History of the Protestant reformation. 3036

History of the Protestant reformation in England & Ireland. 3038

History of the Puritans, or Protestant non-conformists. 3007

History of the Puritans, or Protestant nonconformists. 3007

History of the Quakers in Wales and their emigration to North America. 1688

History of the recent developments in spiritual manifestations, in the city of Philadelphia. 3504

History of the Red River Valley Conference of the Augustana Lutheran Church. 110

History of the reformation. 2272, 3033, 3034, 3035, 3036, 3038

History of the reformation in England. 3039

History of the reformation in Europe in the time of Calvin. 3035

History of the Reformation in Germany. 3040

History of the Reformation in Scotland. 3042

History of the reformation in Sweden. 3042

History of the reformation in the church of Christ. 3034

History of the reformation in the sixteenth century. 3035

History of the reformation of the Church of England. 3038

History of the reformation of the sixteenth century. 3033, 3035

History of the Reformed church at Peapack, N.J. 2810

History of the Reformed church in America. 3045

History of the Reformed church in Reading, Pa. 3049

History of the Reformed church in the United States. 3048

History of the Reformed church of Germany. 3047

History of the Reformed church of Tappan, N. Y. Prepared for its two hundredth anniversary. 3587

History of the Reformed church within the bounds of the Westmoreland classis. 3049

History of the Reformed churches in Chester county. 3048

History of the Reformed Presbyterian church in America. 3050

History of the Reformed Presbyterian church of New Alexandria, Pa. 2686

History of the religion of Israel, from the Babylonian captivity to the end of prophecy. 2149

History of the religious beliefs and philosophical opinions in China from the beginning to the present time. 914

History of the religious movement of the eighteenth century. 2425

History of the religious movement of the eighteenth century, called Methodism. 2425

History of the religious Society of Friends. 1685, 1687

History of the Reorganized Church of Jesus Christ of Latter Day Saints. 3217

History of the restoration plea. 1464

History of the Reverend John Simpson. 3410

History of the revisions of the discipline of the Methodist Episcopal church, South. 2456

History of the rise and influence of the spirit of rationalism in Europe. 3023, 3024

History of the rise and progress of the Baptists in Virginia. 172

History of the rise, increase, and progress, of the Christian people called Quakers. 1685

History of the rise of Methodism in America. 2424

History of the rise of the Huguenots of France. 1852

History of the rise, progress, genius, and character of American Presbyterianism. 2925

History of the robe of Jesus Christ. 1825

History of the Roman breviary. 841

... A history of the Roman Catholic church in the United States. 833

History of the Russian Church abroad and the events leading to the American Metropolia's autocephaly. 3258

History of the Rye Presbyterian Church. 3259

History of the Sabbath. 3261

History of the Sabbath and first day of the week. 3260

History of the Sacred Scriptures of the New Testament. 406

History of the saints. 2600, 3428

History of the Sakta religion. 3400

History of the Salem Church of Honey Creek. 1844, 3286

History of the Saluda Baptist association. 169

History of the Salvation Army. 3293

... History of the Sandwich islands mission. 2524

History of the Sandy Creek Baptist association. 158

History of the Sandy Creek Baptist Association, from its organization in A.D. 1758, to A.D. 1858. 158

History of the Saracens. 2564

History of the Sarepta Baptist association of Georgia and historical sketches of churches composing the association. 1270

History of the Scandinavian mission. 2617

History of the Scottish Rite bodies in the District of Columbia. 1664

History of the seal of confession. 1327

History of the Second church, or Old North, in Boston. 685

History of the Second Congregational church and society in Leicester, Massachusetts. 2208

History of the Second Presbyterian church, Columbus, Ohio, from 1839 to 1876. 1311

History of the Second Presbyterian Church, Lexington, Kentucky, of the United Presbyterian Church in the U S A. 2220

History of the Second Presbyterian Church, Staunton, Virginia, 1875-1975. 3321, 3526

History of the Seneca Baptist association. 158

History of the separation in Indiana Yearly meeting of Friends. 1686

History of the settlement of German Mennonites from Russia. 2407

History of the settlement of Jews in Pauducah and the lower Ohio valley. 2100

History of the Sikhs. 3408

History of the Sisters of Divine Providence, San Antonio, Texas. 3417

History of the Sisters of Providence of Saint Mary-of-the-Woods. 3419

History of the Sisters of Saint Anne. 3419

History of the Sisters of St. Francis of the diocese of Pittsburgh, Pennsylvania, 1868-1938. 3421

History of the Sisters of Saint Joseph of Carondelet in the Troy province. 3419

History of the Sisters of St. Mary of St. Louis, Mo. 3420

History of the sixteen Karmapas of Tibet. 2164

History of the Slovak Evangelical Lutheran Church in the United States of America. 3426

History of the Smithburg charge composed on Trinity, Smithburgh, Md., Mt. Moriah, Foxville, Md., St. Paul's Greensburg, Md. 3432

History of the so-called Jansenist Church of Holland. 2168

History of the Society of Friends in America. 1684

History of the Society of Jesus. 1946

History of the Society of Jesus in North America, colonial and federal. 1948

History of the South Carolina Conference of the Wesleyan Methodist Church of America. 3807

History of the Southern conference of the Pittsburg synod of the Evangelical Lutheran church. 2850

History of the Southern Illinois Conference, the Methodist Church. 2439

... A history of the Southern Presbyterian church, with appendix. 2920

History of the Spanish inquisition. 1910

History of the Stanton street Baptist church, in the city of New York. 2701

... History of the strange sounds or rappings. 3500

History of the suffering and death of Jesus Christ. 390, 2029

History of the Sugaw Creek Presbyterian Church. 888

History of the Sunday school movement in the Methodist Episcopal church. 3559

History of the supernatural in all ages and nations and in all churches. 3567

History of the Supreme Council, 330. 1672

History of the Supreme Council, 33. 1672

History of the Swedish Baptists in Sweden and America. 170

History of the Swiss reformed church since the reformation. 3047

History of the Sycamore Associate reformed church. 3572

History of the Synod of Washington of the Presbyterian church in the United States of America. 2928

History of the synoptic tradition. 386, 387

History of the synoptic trandition. 387

History of the Syrian nation and the old evangelical-apostolic church of the East. 2684

History of the Tahitian Mission. 2552

History of the Talmud. 3583

History of the Tenessee Conferences and a brief summary of the general conferences, the Methodist Church, from the frontier in middle Tennessee to the present time. 2439

History of the Tennessee Baptist Convention. 170

History of the textual criticism of the New Testament. 352

History of the Theological Seminary fo the Reformed Church in the United States, 1825-1934. 2195

History of the Theological seminary in Virginia and its historical background. 24

History of the Theological seminary of the Evangelical church. 1497

History of the translation of the blessed martyrs of Christ, Marcellinus and Peter. 2332

... History of the Trappist abbey of New Melleray, Dubuque county, Iowa. 2693

History of the true church. 1228

History of the Tunkers and the Brethren Church. 1235

History of the Ukrainian Catholic parochial schools in the United States. 766, 3310

History of the United church of New Haven. 2688

History of the United Lutheran Synod of New York and New England. 3734

History of the United Missionary Church. 3735

History of the United Synagogue of America. 3749

History of the Universities' Mission to Central Africa. 2498, 3759

HISTORY OF THE RELIGIOUS BOOKS 1876 - 1982

History of the Upper Iowa conference of the Methodist Episcopal church, 1856-1906. 2447
... A history of the use of incense in divine worship. 1894
History of the use of the Shorter catechism in the Presbyterian church in the United States of America. 3809
History of the Vaudois church from its origin. 3789
History of the venerable English college, Rome. 3245
History of the Vulgate in England from Alcuin to Roger Bacon. 398
History of the Wake Baptist Association, its auxiliaries and churches, 1866-1966. 3788
History of the Waldenses. 3789
History of the Waldenses of Italy, from their origin to the Reformation. 3788
History of the Walnut Hills Congregational church of Cincinnati, 1843-1935. 1276
History of the warfare of science and theology in Christendom. 3085
History of the warfare of science uith theology in christendom. 3085
History of the warfare of science with theology in Christendom. 3085
History of the Wellesley Congregational church. 3801
History of the Welsh Baptists. 172
History of the Wesley M. E. church of Brooklyn, L. I. 694
History of the Wesleyan Methodist Church of America. 3807
History of the Westminster assembly of divines. 3808
History of the Wetumpka Methodist Church. 3809
History of the White Brotherhood and its teachings. 3811
History of the White River conference of the church of the United brethren in Christ. 3730
History of the Wilhelms and the Wilhelm charge. 3048, 3816
History of the William Taylor self-supporting missions in South America. 2547
History of the Wisconsin Synod. 1548
History of the Woman's foreign missionary society, M. E. church, South. 2457
History of the Woman's missionary society in the Colored Methodist Episcopal church. 1310
History of the work in the Washington, D.C., district. War work council, Y.M.C.A., from July 1st, 1917, to July 1st, 1919. 1543
History of the work of redemption. 3029, 3030
History of the World's Young Women's Christian Association. 3852
History of the Y. M. C. A. in North America. 3871
History of the Y.M.C.A. in the Le Mans area. 1543
History of the Young men's Christian association. 3874
History of theological education in the United Presbyterian church and its ancestries. 3736
History of theology. 3654
History of theosophy. 3684
History of tithes. 3702
History of training for the ministry of the Church of England in England and Wales from 1875 to 1974. 1216
History of Trinity church. 712
History of Trinity church, Portland, Connecticut, 1788-1938. 2864
History of Trinity church, Woodbridge, New Jersey, from 1698 to 1935. 3846
History of Trinity Episcopal Church and Norborne Parish, Martinsburg, Berkeley County, West Virginia, Diocese of West Virginia. 185th anniversary, 1771-1956. 2349
History of Trinity Episcopal Church, Fredonia, New York, 1822-1967. 1652
History of Trinity Evangelical and Reformed Church, 1853-1953, Mount Vernon, Indiana. 2626
History of Trinity Lutheran church, Germantown, Philadelphia, 1836-1936. 2830
History of Trinity Lutheran church, Reading, Pa. 3027
History of Trinity Lutheran church, Shamokin, Pennsylvania, 1840-1940. 3400
History of Trinity parish, Newton Centre, Massachusetts. 2705
History of Trinity Parish, Scotland Neck [and] Edgecombe Parish, Halifax County. 3315
History of Tugalo Baptist association. 150
History of Union Presbyterian church, Walnut township, Montgomery county, Indiana, 1834-1934. 3723
... History of Union United Presbyterian church. 3723
History of Unitarianism. 3439, 3724
History of United Methodism in Greene and Washington Counties, Pennsylvania (mainly the Washington District of the Western Pennsylvania Conference) 3735
History of United Methodism in Western Pennsylvania. 2432
History of Unity Baptist church, Muhlenberg County, Kentucky. 2629
History of University Park Methodist church, Dallas, Texas, 1939-1959. 3759
History of vicarages in the Middle Ages. 1241
History of Walnut Hill Presbyterian Church, Fayette County, Kentucky. 3790
History of Walnut street church. 1577
History of Wasco Lodge No. 15, A.F. & A.M, and allied organizations. 1672
History of Western Christianity. 1177
History of Western morals. 2589
History of Westminster Presbyterian church of Minneapolis, Minnesota. 2475
History of Wheat Swamp Christian Church, including the conditions in Europe and the colonies. 3810
History of Windy Cove Presbyterian church, Millboro Springs, Virginia, 1749-1929. 2463
History of witchcraft and demonology. 3824
History of witchcraft in England from 1558 to 1718. 3825, 3826
History of witchcraft, sorcerers, heretics, and pagans. 3826
History of Woman's Missionary Union. 3468
History of woman's work in East Hanover Presbytery. 2927
History of world religions. 3140
History of worship in the Church of Scotland. 1234
History of Y.M.C.A.-church relations in the United States. 3874
History of Zen Buddhism. 3893, 3895
History of Zion church of the city of Baltimore, 1755-1897, pub. in commemoration of its sesqui-centennial, October 15, 1905. 133
History of Zion Reformed church, Allentown, Pennsylvania, 1762-1937. [By Simon Sipple, D.D.] pastor. 26
History of Zionism, 1600-1918. 2119
History of Zion's or Old organ church. 3897
History of Zoroastrianism. 3898
History, principles, and practice of symbolism in Christian art. 920
History, religion, and spiritual democracy. 671, 3107
History sacred and profane. 1818
History Sandy Creek, 1858-1958. 152
History: self-understanding of the Church. 1125
History: the Idylwood Presbyterian Church. 1882
History, time, and deity. 1819
History's crowded climax. 1514
History's greatest prince! 204
Histrio-mastix. 3606
Histriomastix. 3606
Hitchcock's new and complete analysis of the Holy Bible. 234, 302
Hitchhiking on Hope Street. 1367, 3796
Hitherto. 158
Hitler and the Christians. 1707
Hitler youth and Catholic youth, 1933-1936. 818, 3882
Hitler's first foes. 818
Hitler's ten-year war on the Jews. 2099
Hits and misses. 2931
Hittites. 1820
[Hizuk emunah (romanized form)] or. 1092, 2014
Ho for heaven! 1414
Ho i'wiyos'dos hah neh cha ga'o hee dus, gee ih' niga'ya dos'ha gee, neh nan'do wah'gaah he'ni a'di wa'noh daah. 3332
Hobart's Analysis of Bishop Butler's Analogy of religion, natural and revealed, to the constitution and course of nature. 2673
Hobbes. 1821
Hobnails for rugged paths. 160
Hogan schism and trustee troubles in St. Mary's church, Philadelphia, 1820-1829. 1822, 2830
Hold hands and die! 2817
Hold me tight. 1934, 2218
Hold me up a little longer, Lord. 3843
Hold your tongue! 2220
Holdeman people. 1229
Holdings of the University of Utah on Utah and the Church of Jesus Christ of Latter-Day Saints. 2608
Holiday concert. 3026
Holiday devotionals. 1822
Holiday frame of mind. 980
Holiday night dreams. 1631
Holiday work and play. 1615
Holidays and festivals. 1614
Holidays are nice; around the year with the Jewish child. 1615
Holidays for American Judaism. 1614
Holidays of the Church. 1880, 1958
Holidays or the Church. 1958
Holiness. 1823, 1824, 3300
Holiness and happiness. 1449
Holiness and high country. 1823
Holiness and justice. 2846, 2853
Holiness and radicalism in religious life. 2571
Holiness, and some mistakes about it. 1823
Holiness and the will of God. 3604
Holiness for all. 1823, 3486, 3771
Holiness illustrations. 1843
Holiness in action. 3279, 3280
... Holiness in the church. 3300, 3490
Holiness in the prayers of St. Paul. 1824
Holiness is where you find it. 3282
Holiness is wholeness. 997
Holiness of life. 2580, 3489
Holiness of sex. 3389
Holiness of the priesthood. 2396
Holiness of Vincent de Paul. 3779
Holiness-Pentecostal movement in the United States. 2815
Holiness pulpit. 1824
Holiness revival of the nineteenth century. 1824
Holiness teachings. 1823
Holiness the birthright of all God's children. 1823
Holiness, the finished foundation. 3303
Holiness to the Lord. 1823
Holism and evolution. 1824
Holland N. McTyeire. 2310
Holland, the birthplace of American political, civil and religious liberty. 2685
Holley's visual Bible. 646
Hollis street church from Mather Byles to Thomas Starn King. 1732-1861. 684
Hollow globe. 3514
Hollow of His hand. 1351
Holman topical concordance. 303
Holocaust. 1825
Holston Methodism. 2455
Holy and the daemonic from Sir Thomas Browne to William Blake. 1518
Holy and the profane. 1631
Holy angels. 42, 43
Holy apostles. 2825
Holy baptism. 136
... The Holy Bibl (self pronouncing) containing the Old and New Testaments, translated out of the original tongues and with the former translations diligently compared and revised. Authorized (King James) version. 1660
Holy Bible. 30, 219, 242, 247, 254, 255, 256, 257, 258, 259, 260, 261, 262, 263, 264, 265, 266, 267, 268, 272, 273, 274, 275, 354, 358, 359, 482, 580, 582, 585, 601, 614, 624, 655, 656, 778, 1660, 1665, 1808, 1884, 2197, 2370, 2740
Holy Bible abridged. 200, 292, 618
Holy Bible, according to the authorized version. 219
Holy Bible and International Bible encyclopedia and concordance. 229
Holy Bible and the law. 203
Holy Bible at the University of Texas. 315
Holy Bible authenticated. 790
Holy Bible. Authorized King James version with illus. by celebrated old masters. 263
...Holy Bible (authorized or King James version) 260, 266
Holy Bible (Authorized or King James version) The new standard alphabetical indexed Bible. School and library reference ed. Containing the Old and New Testaments translated out of the original tongues and with all former translations diligently compared and revised. 614
Holy Bible (Authorized or King James version) The new standard alphabetical indexed Bible. Scholl and library reference ed., containing the Old and New Testaments translated out of the original tongues and with all former translations diligently compared and revised; to which are added many unique features of the Bible: pictorial pronouncing dictionary and other interesting instructive features. 614
Holy Bible containing both the Old and New Testaments. The entire Sacrifice of the Mass in pictures and explanatory text in accord with the Constitution on Sacred Liturgy of Vatican Council II; the Way of the Cross; and a complete Catholic dictionary keyed to the Bible and its use. Family and library references ed. 655
Holy Bible, containing the Holy Name version of the Old and New Testaments, critically compared with ancient authorities, and various manuscripts. 230
Holy Bible, containing the Old and New Testament. 255, 256, 257
Holy Bible, containing the Old and New Testaments. 219, 220, 230, 242, 247, 255, 256, 257, 258, 259, 260, 261, 265, 266, 267, 268, 358, 359, 611, 1330, 1660, 2741, 2755
Holy Bible containing the Old and New Testaments and the Apocryha. 650
Holy Bible, containing the Old and New Testaments and the Apocrypha. Translated out of the original tongues. 264
Holy Bible, containing the Old and New Testaments (Authorized or King James version). To which is added an alphabetical and cyclopedic index, a unique set of charts from Adam to Christ, leading doctrines, harmony of the gospels, parables and miracles, Bible dictionary, all alphabetically arranged for practical and everyday use. 266
Holy Bible, containing the Old and New Testaments in the authorized King James version. 264, 265, 266, 267
Holy Bible. Containing the Old and New Testaments in the King James version. The living word; the family library. 266
Holy Bible, containing the Old and New Testaments. King James version, 1611. 266, 267
Holy Bible, containing the Old and New Testaments. Revised Standard version, translated from the original tongues. 265
Holy Bible, containing the Old and New Testaments, the text carefully printed from the most correct copies of the present authorized translation, including the marginal readings and parallel texts. 220
Holy Bible: containing the Old and New Testaments, together with the Apocrypha. 256
Holy Bible, containing the Old and New Testaments, tr. out of the original tongues and with the former translations diligently compared and revised. Authorized King James version. 266
Holy Bible containing the Old and New Testaments. Tr. out of the original tongues, and with the former translations diligently compared and rev. by His Majesty's special command. Appointed to be read in churches. Authorized. King James version. 264
... The Holy Bible, containing the Old and New Testaments, translated from the original tongues; and with the former translations diligently compared and revised. 256
Holy Bible. Containing the Old and New Testaments. Translated out o- the original tongues and with the former translations diligently compared and revised by His Majesty's special command. Authorized King James version. Appointed to be read in churches. New Garnet text. 266
... The Holy Bible containing the Old and New Testaments translated out of the original tongues. 259, 267
Holy Bible, containing the Old and New Testaments. Translated out of the original tongues, and with the former translations diligently compared and revised. 265, 266
Holy Bible, containing the Old and New Testaments: translated out of the original tongues: and with the former translations diligently compared and revised, by His Majesty's special command. Appointed to be read in churches. 226
Holy Bible, containing the Old and New Testaments, with the Apocrypha. 255
... The Holy Bible, containing the Old and New Testamnenbts. 259
Holy Bible containing the Old and the New Testaments. 267
Holy Bible, containing the Old Testament, and the New. 257, 260
Holy Bible, conteyning the Old Testament, and the New. 254
Holy Bible, Douay version. 274
... The Holy Bible (Douny version) 273

Holy Bible explained. 280
Holy Bible for children. 614
Holy Bible for young readers. 407
Holy Bible from ancient Eastern manuscripts. 650
Holy Bible, illustrated. Ed. by the Daughters of Saint Paul. 601
Holy Bible, illustrated from the works of Michelangelo Buonarroti, 1475-1564. Conceived by Vincent Price expressly for Sears, Roebuck and Co. and Simpsons-Sears, ltd. Designed by Jack Carter, Mary Grant Price and Curtis S. Ruddle. Illustrated reproduced by Skira, art publishers, Geneva. 266
Holy Bible in brief. 268
Holy Bible in giant print. 267
Holy Bible in miniature. 298
Holy Bible in modern English. 261
Holy Bible in the language of today. 275
Holy Bible index book. 310
... The Holy Bible marked on temporal belssings. 635
... The Holy Bible marked on temporal blessings. 635
Holy Bible, Old Testament. 482
Holy Bible repudiates "prohibition" 3596
Holy Bible repudiates "prohibition"; compilation of all verses containing the words "wine" or "strong drink," proving that the Scriptures commend and command the temperate use of alcoholic beverages. With comment by George G. Brown. 3596
Holy Bible, revised standard version containing the Old and New Testaments. 247, 265
Holy Bible. Revised standard version containing the Old and New Testaments. Translated from the original tongues; being the version set forth A.D. 1611, revised A.D. 1881-1885 and A.D. 1901; compared with the most ancient authorities and revised A.D. 1946-1952. Self-pronouncing ed. 265, 266
Holy Bible, Revised standard version, containing the Old and New Testaments. Translated from the original tongues; being the version set forth A.D. 1611, revised A.D. 1881-1885 and A.D. 1901; compared with the most ancient authorities and revised A.D. 1946-1952. Reference ed. 254
... The Holy Bible, self-pronouncing, containing the Old and New Testaments. 635
Holy Bible: the Old and New Testaments. 267
Holy Bible, translated from the Latin Vulgate. 272, 273
Holy Bible translated from the Latin Vulgate and diligently compared with the Hebrew, Greek and other editions in divers languages. 273
Holy Bible, with the Confraternity text. 655, 1329
Holy Bible. With the Confraternity text. Catholic action ed. Published with the Approbation of Walter A. Coggin. 655
Holy Book and holy tradition. 3267
Holy book of Revelation. 462
Holy book of Revelation interpreted. 462
Holy catechism. 2745
Holy Catholic faith. 1017
Holy Child. 1113, 2048
Holy Christian church from its remote origins to the present day. 1176
Holy City. 1944
Holy Comforter. 1832
Holy common sense. 2248
Holy communion. 2250, 2252, 2253, 2259
Holy communion cyclopedia. 2251
Holy communion in the reformed Church of Scotland. 2255
Holy company. 927
Holy cross. 1389, 3482
Holy Cross Church dedication, April 21, 1963. 1165
Holy cross parish and Lone mountain district of San Francisco. 3298
Holy Cross service book. 1487
Holy day sermons. 3341
Holy days and holidays. 1022, 1624, 1839, 2120
Holy eucharist. 424, 1541, 2251, 2254, 2255, 2258
"The holy eucharist a comfort to the penitent." 2260
Holy eucharist and Christian life. 2251
Holy Eucharist and Christian unity. 1249
Holy eucharist and frequent and daily communion. 1541
Holy eucharist devotionally considered. 2258
Holy Eucharist in art. 2254
Holy Eucharist, rite two. 2257, 2969
Holy Family. 2004, 2384

Holy family: Jesus, Mary, and Joseph. 2004
Holy Family School dedication, Sunday, September 24, 1961. 3151
Holy family sisters of San Francisco. 3420
Holy Father speaks to newlyweds. 2343
Holy fire! 1571, 1617
Holy fires for unholy days. 1557
Holy flower. 3208
Holy garments. 1267
Holy Ghost. 1827, 1828, 1829, 1830
Holy Ghost and fire. 92
Holy Ghost and His work in souls. 1830
Holy Ghost manual. 1836
Holy Ghost prayer book. 1836
Holy Gospel. 284, 394
Holy Gospel according to Saint Luke. 427
Holy Gospel children. 626
Holy Gospel for children. 626
Holy Gospels. 284
Holy Grail. 3602
Holy Grail, and other poems. 3602
Holy Grail revealed. 2732, 3304, 3305
Holy ground. 517
Holy Holy Land. 318, 3208
Holy hour. 864, 1541, 1826
Holy hour for priests. 1826
Holy hour in Gethsemane. 47
Holy hour manual. 1826
Holy hour meditations. 1826
Holy hour of adoration. 1826
Holy hours in the Holy Land. 2761
... The Holy house of Loreto. 2260
Holy icons in the religious art of the Eastern Church. 1880
Holy images. 1882
Holy in Christ. 1823
Holy incense. 235
Holy infection. 1823
Holy Innocents. 81
Holy Island. 2211
Holy Jerusalem voyage of Ogier VIII, Seigneur d'Anglure. 47, 1022
Holy Kabbalah. 722
Holy Koran. 2184
Holy Koran of the Moorish-American school and temple of religious sciences. 2183
Holy Land. 2219, 2764, 2765, 3200
Holy Land and its inhabitants. 2764
Holy land hymns. 1864
Holy Land in American Protestant life, 1800-1948. 2979
Holy Land in geography and in history. 2762
Holy Land in pictures. 2764
Holy Land in the time of Jesus. 406
Holy Land missions and missionaries. 2118, 2544
Holy Land -- then and now. 2762
Holy laughter. 3822
Holy letter. 3393
Holy life. 1823, 1970
Holy life of Armelle Nicolas. 2708
Holy man: Father Damien of Molokai. 1400
Holy man of Santa Clara. 745
Holy mass. 2366, 2368
Holy Mass according to the the Syrian rite of Antioch, with Anaphora of the Twelve Apostles. 3578
Holy Mass and life. 2365
Holy matrimony. 2337, 2338
Holy matrimony and common-sense. 2338
Holy men of God. 923
Holy moments in the Holy Land. 1928
Holy morality: a religious approach to modern ethics. 1536
Holy Moscow. 2749
Holy mother. 3303
Holy mountain. 2153
Holy murder. 3242
Holy Name Bible. 266
Holy names. 2020
Holy nation. 1824
Holy night. 1113, 2021, 2757
Holy nudges. 987, 3055
Holy orders. 2741
Holy orders and ordination. 773
Holy Orthodox church. 2748
Holy places of Christendom. 1038
Holy places of the Gospels. 2014
Holy pretence. 1086
Holy priest. 3200
Holy Qur-an. 2183
Holy restraint. 2573
... The holy resurrection. 2052
Holy Roman Empire. 1826
Holy Roman empire in German literature. 1826
Holy Roman Republic. 1186, 1826
Holy rosary. 3247, 3249
Holy rule. 190
Holy Russia. 2750
Holy sacrifice. 2368
Holy sacrifice of the Mass. 2366, 2368, 2370, 3139

Holy science. 3330
Holy Scripture. 230
Holy Scriptures. 200, 309, 511, 558, 2599, 2600
Holy Scriptures according the the Masoretic text. A new translation, with the aid of previous versions and with constant consultation of Jewish authorities. 530
Holy Scriptures according to the Masoretic text. 530
Holy Scriptures, containing the Old and New Testaments. 2600
Holy Scriptures; Deuteronomy. 510
Holy Scriptures; Numbers. 560
Holy Scriptures of the Church of Jesus Christ of Latter-Day Saints. 2601
Holy Scriptures (Old Testament) English version. 513
Holy See at work. 807, 852
... Holy sorrow. 2030
Holy souls book reflections on purgatory. 3006
Holy Spirit. 1827, 1828, 1829, 1830, 1831, 1832, 1833, 1834, 1836
Holy Spirit, a layman's conception. 1835
Holy Spirit; a study. 1835
Holy Spirit acting in our souls. 1831
Holy Spirit and Christian experience. 1835
Holy Spirit and contemporary man. 1831
Holy Spirit and His gifts. 1832
Holy Spirit and me. 1835
Holy Spirit and modern thought. 1828
Holy Spirit and our faith. 1830
Holy Spirit and power. 1833, 2815
Holy Spirit and the art of living. 1712
Holy Spirit and the Gospel tradition. 1827
Holy Spirit and the holy life. 1830
Holy Spirit and the Prayer book. 1836
Holy Spirit and the priest. 1828
Holy Spirit and you. 139, 1007
Holy Spirit at work in the church. 1832
Holy Spirit baptism. 139
Holy Spirit, His gifts and power. 1835
Holy Spirit in Acts. 1834
Holy Spirit in Acts. 2d ed., rev. 1834
Holy Spirit in Christian education. 1829
Holy Spirit in Christian life. 1712
Holy Spirit in Christian theology. 1829
Holy Spirit in doctrine and life. 1829
Holy Spirit in five worlds. 1831
Holy Spirit in life and service. 1828
Holy Spirit in me. 1835
Holy Spirit in power. 1831
Holy Spirit in the Acts of the Apostles. 334, 1834
Holy Spirit in the ancient church. 1832
Holy Spirit in the devout life. 951
Holy Spirit in the Gospels. 1834
Holy Spirit in the Holy Scriptures. 1834
Holy Spirit in the life of the church. 1834
Holy Spirit in the life of today. 1828
Holy Spirit in the New Testament Scriptures. 1834
Holy Spirit in the Old Testament. 503, 1834
Holy spirit in the theology of Martin Bucer. 720, 1835
Holy Spirit in thought and experience. 1831
Holy Spirit in today's church. 2815
Holy Spirit in today's world. 161, 1836
Holy Spirit in your life. 2930
Holy Spirit in your teaching. 3160
Holy Spirit, Lord and Life-giver. 1833
Holy Spirit of God. 1830, 1832
Holy Spirit, our helper. 961
Holy Spirit our teacher in prayer. 1833
Holy Spirit, state, church, and school. 1832
Holy Spirit, the key to supernatural living. 1827
Holy Spirit--the seal of God. 1835
Holy Spirit then and now. 1830
Holy Spirit today. 1832
Holy Spirit versus modern tongues. 1830
Holy Spirit, your retreat director. 2268, 3222
Holy Spirit's ministry. 1572
Holy Spirit. 1829
Holy state and the profane state. 1535
Holy sword. 2564
Holy table, name and thing. 1318
Holy teaching of Vimalakirti. 3139
Holy temple. 1232, 3600
Holy terror. 1085
Holy the firm. 2386
Holy theatre. 1478
Holy triangle. 2339
Holy Trinity. 3711, 3712, 3714
Holy Trinity book of prayers. 858
Holy Trinity parish, Boston, Mass., 1844-1944. 684
Holy types. 557
Holy vessels and furniture of the Tabernacle. 3579

Holy viaticum of life as of death. 2254
Holy war. 714, 1391
Holy war, a philsophy of redemption. 716
...The holy war and The heavenly footman. 714
Holy war made by King Shaddai upon Diabolus. 714
Holy war made by Shaddai upon Diabolus. 714
Holy war "made in Germany," 3718
Holy water and its significance for Catholics. 1836
Holy Week. 844, 863, 1837, 2057
Holy Week and Easter. 1837, 2295
Holy Week and Easter, a liturgical commentary. 844
Holy Week book. 1837
Holy Week in large and small churches. 844
Holy Week manual for priests. 844, 1837
Holy Week manual for servers. 844
Holy Week masses. 844, 845
Holy Week offices. 2969
Holy wells of Ireland. 1838
Holy wind in Navajo philosophy. 2677
Holy wisdom. 90
Holy Word in its own defence. 1089
Holy work. 188, 190
Holy Writ or Holy Church. 119, 861
Holy Year of jubilee. 1838
...The holy year of the Guards of honor and friends of the Sacred heart of Jesus. 3270
Holy years of Mary. 2358
... Holyday prayers. 2139
Homage to the ancient child. 2197
Home. 1608, 1838
Home altar. 1838
Home Altar treasures. 1434
Home and church. 3171
Home and church tithing. 3702
Home and church working together. 1608
... The home and family in the light of Bible teaching. 3165
Home and happiness. 1939
Home and its inner spiritual life. 1606
Home and the children. 2773
Home before dark. 1417, 1930
Home Bible. 268
Home Bible study by mail. 647
Home book of Bible quotations. 304
Home can be a happy place. 2340
Home celebrations. 855, 1604
Home, church, and school relations in the religious education of children and youth. 3162
Home circle. 1675
Home classes and the home department of the Sunday-school. 3554
Home coming. 1696
Home department. 1838
Home enterprise. 2527
Home evangelization. 612
Home evening handbook for use of parents and older children. 2605
Home folks. 1607
Home for God's family. 628
Home for good. 1000
Home for the homeless. 325, 3439
Home front of Jewish missions. 2535
Home God meant. 3200
Home helpers far and near. 3152
Home in Honduras. 673, 2529
Home in world missions. 1610
Home is the place. 1608
Home is where God is. 1605
... Home lessons in religion. 3158, 3165
Home life and reminiscences of Alexander Campbell. 732
Home life in Bible times; a study in Biblical antiquities. 2765
Home-life in the Bible. 208, 2765
Home memories of President David O. McKay. 3071
Home mission heroes. 2482
Home mission history. 2596
Home mission investments. 2527
Home mission trails. 2528
Home missions. 2527
...Home missions in action. 2526
Home missions in the mother synod. 2296
Home missions in the new world. 3467
Home missions on the American frontier. 2553
Home missions on the American frontier, with particular reference to the American Home Missionary Society. 1343, 2553
Home missions today and tomorrow. 2527
Home nurture for the little ones of the church. 3071
Home of fadeless splendour. 2763
Home of God's people. 2762
Home of the countryside. 1374
Home of the Eddic poems. 1493, 2665
Home of the monk. 2579
Home of the redeemed and other discourses. 3071

Home of the rural pastor. 2777
Home of the soul. 978
Home prayers. 2892
Home, resources for family sharing. 1605
Home scenes. 3208
Home-scenes of the New Testament. 1610
Home school. 3170
Home service. 2972
Home sweet fishbowl. 1303, 3718
Home sweet home, here and hereafter. 1608
Home-talks. 2737
Home talks about the Word. 1982
Home team wears white. 927
Home: the savior of civilization. 1606
Home to Bethphage. 3235
Home to our valleys! 3789
Home training, the secret of character building. 1838
Home virtues. 1838
Home, where life makes up its mind. 1610
Home with the open door. 2483
Home work. 1250
Home work of D. L. Moody. 2588
Home world. 1607
Homegrown Christian education. 936
Homeland harvest. 2527
Homely homilies. 1843
Homely spirituals. 996
Homemade Christians. 1609
Homemade church. 877
Homer. 1839
Homer and the Homeric problem. 1839
Homer, Hesiod, and the Hymns. 1521, 1839
Homeric gods. 1767
Homes of the first Franciscans in Umbria. 1647
Homes of the Psalms. 579
Homes that last. 1610
Homespun. 961
Homestead Methodism (1830-1933) 2631, 3810
Homeward bound. 3499
Homiletic sermonettes on the Gospels of the Sundays of the ecclesiastical year. 397, 865, 1267
Homiletic thesaurus on the Gospels. 400
Homiletic thoughts and counsels. 1843
Homiletical and pastoral lectures. 2901
Homiletical innovations of Andrew W. Blackwood. 669, 1839
Homiletical plot. 2902
Homiletics. 1843, 2901, 2905, 2907
Homiletics, and pastoral theology. 2905
Homiletics and preaching. 1843
Homilies for the celebration of baptism for children. 139
Homilies for the celebration of marriage. 865, 3800
Homilies for the liturgical year. 864, 1267
Homilies for the new liturgy. 1267
Homilies for the year and prayers for the faithful. 1267
Homilies, hymns and harmonies. 2633
Homilies in homespun. 1466
Homilies of Ælfric. 3362
Homilies of Saint Jerome. 586, 3369
Homilies of St. John Chrysostom on the letters of St. Paul to Titus and Philemon. 479, 1115
Homilies of science. 3074
Homilies on all the Sunday Gospels of the ecclesiastical year. 397
Homilies on Christmas and Epiphany. 1114
Homilies on the Sunday gospels. 863, 1266
Homilist: a series of sermons for preachers and laymen. 3364
...A homily of Clement of Alexandria. 1287
Homily on the passion. 2034
Homing in the presence. 2388
Hominisation. 2324
Homo faber. 2473
Homo religiosus. 3087
"Homo religiosus" in Mircea Eliade. 1506, 3094
Homo vistor. 2834
Homosexual crisis in the mainline church. 1843
Homosexual way, a Christian option? 1843
Homosexuality, a Biblical view. 1844
Homosexuality and the Christian faith. 1844
Homosexuality and the Christian way of life. 1843
Homosexuality and the Church. 1843
Homosexuality and the Judeo-Christian tradition. 1844
Homosexuals in the Christian fellowship. 1843
Honest answers to honest questions. 3885
Honest debtors. 3352
Honest liberty in the church. 2963

Honest love and human life: is the Pope right about contraception? 854
Honest prayer. 2872, 2880
Honest religion. 3103
Honest religion for secular man. 3327
Honest search for a righteous life. 163
Honest sex. 3393
Honest to God. 1096
"Honest to God" debate. 3242
Honest to man. 1092
Honesty. 1844
Honesty in the church. 2223
Honesty, morality & conscience. 946
Honesty with the Bible. 238, 3202
Honey and salt [second portion]. 2388
Honey from many hives. 1440
"Honey in the rock," 3242
Honey out of the rock. 3090, 3202
Honeymoon is over. 681, 930
Honeywell plans. 1158
Honeywell plans for modern and moderate priced church and Sunday school buildings. 1158
Hong Kong digest. 2529
Hongry catch the foolish boy. 632, 2945
Honi and his magic circle. 1844, 3581, 3584
Honolulu. 3198
Honor of the church. 1117
Honor thy father and mother. 1315
Honor to whom honor is due. 670
Honorable Japanese fan. 2533
Honorable youth. 1323
Honoring the deaconship. 1239
Honour thy father. 2794
Honouring God the true way to honour. 1503
Hoof beats to heaven. 743
Hooked on a good thing. 1358
Hooked—on God! 1255, 2177
Hooker's Ecclesiastical polity. 1146
Hooker's polity in modern English. 1488
Hooker's theology of common prayer. 1214
Hooker's theology of common prayer; the fifth book of the Polity paraphrased and expanded into a commentary on the prayer book. 1214
Hookerton history. 1465
Hooks in their jaws. 2465
Hoosier heritage, 1874-1974: Woman's Christian Temperance Union. 3833
Hoosier parson. 3090
Hoosier rabbinate. 1624, 2100
Hoosier Zion. 2917
Hop, skip, hop. 3164
Hope. 1846
Hope against hope. 1846, 2568
Hope and courage. 3407
Hope and planning. 3623
Hope and resurrection of the dead. 3221
Hope and the future of man. 1846
Hope beyond the darkness. 3220
Hope for a despairing world. 3610
Hope for healing. 1599
Hope for man. 1536
Hope for our broken world. 695
Hope for the church. 1846, 2568
Hope for the future? 3890
Hope for the hopeless. 34
Hope for the Jews. 2118
Hope for the leper. 2537
Hope for the victims of alcohol, opium, morphine, cocaine, and other vices. 2668
Hope for your church. 1626
Hope in an age of nihilism. 1845
Hope in grief. 1691
Hope in the ruins. 2524
Hope in time of abandonment. 1845
Hope is an open door. 2718, 3703
Hope is my house. 2952
Hope is the remedy. 1845
Hope Lutheran church, Westgate, Iowa. 2291
Hope of glory. 472, 1528, 2964, 2972, 3339, 3350
Hope of his calling. 3090
Hope of His coming. 3318
Hope of history. 2466
... The hope of immortality. 1887, 1889, 1891
Hope of Israel, what is it! 607
Hope of Isreal, what is it? 607
... Hope of life. 1450
Hope of our calling. 2016, 3200
Hope of the ages. 3202, 3319
Hope of the gospel. 3199
Hope of the great community. 1543
Hope of the harvest. 3777
Hope of the race. 3383
Hope of the world. 1273, 2757, 3318, 3351, 3354, 3746
Hope or despair. 1845
Hope or hindrance? 1245
Hope that is in us. 1845
Hope that sets men free. 1845

Hope, the Christian response to Chicken Little. 1845, 2199
Hope thou in God. 1350
Hope triumphant. 3319
Hope unlimited. 2826
Hopes for English religion. 1764
Hopes of the human race, hereafter and here. 3198
Hopes that perish. 3355
Hopewell Friends history, 1734-1934, Frederick county, Virginia. 1688
Hopi kachina dolls. 2165
Hopi Kachinas. 2165
Horace. 2199
Horace Bushnell. 1333, 3090
Horace Bushnell and religious education. 719, 3155
Horace Mann and religion in the Massachusetts public schools. 1129, 2328
Horae Beatae Mariae Virginis. 1848
Horae germanicae. 1873
Horae Paulinae. 373
Horae solitaire. 2001
Horae solitariae. 3714
Horae synopticae electronicae. 389, 1771
Horary. 97
Horary astrology. 95
Horary astrology and the judgment of events. 97
Horatio Stebbins. 3526
Horatius Bonar, D. D. 3090
Horizon book of great cathedrals. 750
Horizon, First Methodist Episcopal church, Los Angeles, June, 1938. 2260
Horizon history of Christianity. 1172
... Horizon of American missions. 2527
Horizon of light. 1448, 3199
Horizons. 3354, 3493
Horizons for older people. 1257
Horizons of Christian community. 1121
Horizons of consciousness. 2694
Horizons of hope. 1572, 2213
Horizons of immortality. 3510
Horizons of science. 3083
Horizons of stewardship. 3530
Horizons of theological education. 3590, 3680
Horizons of thought. 2179
Horn and the sword. 713
Horned Moses in medieval art and thought. 1847, 2622
Horns and halos in human nature. 1094
Horologion. 842, 2748
Horoscope construction. 1848
Horoscopes and the Christian. 96
Horrified and the glorified. 3220
Horsburgh affair. 1848
Horse bibleiae. 289
Horse lyricae. 3209
Horse lyricae and Divine songs. 1869
Horse Mosaicae. 564
Horse named Amber. 3531
Horse synopticae. 3578
Hort and the Cambridge tradition. 1848
Hortus conclusus. 1877
Horus. 1848
Hosanna. 3562, 3563
Hosanna in the whirlwind. 1449
... Hosea. 537, 538
Hosea, a commentary. 537
Hosea, a new translation with introduction and commentary. 537
Hosea and his message. 537
Hosea Ballou. 131, 3752
Hosea: prophet of God's love. 537
Hosea, the heart and holiness of God. 538
Hospital chaplain. 885
... Hospital chaplains. 885
Hospital prayer book. 3406
Hostage in Djakarta. 2533
Hostage to the devil. 1585
Hostages of civilisation. 53
Hot line to heaven. 2874
Hou to give away your faith. 3829
Hound of God. 1474
Hour after midnight. 2545
Hour before sunset. 2830
Hour cometh! 3320
Hour has come. 425, 1720
Hour is now. 2390
Hour of God's judgment. 606
Hour of good news. 893, 1848
Hour of our death. 1412
Hour of power. 2886
Hour of prayer. 1438
Hour of St. Francis of Assisi. 1643
Hour of the dragon. 3777
... An hour on Christianity. 1052
Hour to the stone age. 2556
Hour with Jesus. 2572
Hour with the Little flower. 3690
Hourglass. 1449
Hours among the Gospels. 1961
Hours before the altar. 2391
Hours of devotion. 1454

Hours of the divine office in English and Latin. 842
Hours of the Passion. 2033
Hours of thought on sacred things. 3365
Hours with the Bible. 499
Hours with the evangelists. 391
Hours with the ghosts. 671, 3501
House built on rock. 2766
House by the bo tree. 2532
House by the side of the road. 1006
House church. 1848
House church evolving. 1848
House church in the twentieth century. 1243, 1787
House divided. 2173
House for hope. 2943
House for tomorrow, and other sermons. 2302
House God built. 1598
House in Chicago. 2588
House not made with hands. 1324, 2963
House not made with hands: Love's Methodist Church, 1791-1966. 3789
House of bread. 1363
House of Christmas. 2021
House of David. 1405
House of friendship. 1621
House of God. 761, 1118, 1269, 3744
House of God and the child. 3208
House of happiness. 980, 1785
House of Hapsburg. 1779
House of Islam. 1921
House of Israel. 45, 297
House of Martha at Bethany. 1198
House of Nasi: Dona Gracia. 2093, 2403
House of pilgrimage. 3363
House of the Lord. 1157, 2606
House of the Master. 163
House of understanding. 3630
House on Logan Square. 2685
House on the rock. 2772
House on the roof. 3545
House on the soul. 3482
House upon a rock: about Southern Baptists in Louisiana. 154
House with a hundred gates. 1363
Household consecration. 1603
Household of faith. 1069, 1121, 1625, 3750
Household of God. 1122, 1125
Household of power. 3678
Household reading. 1344, 1456
Household salvation, and other sermons. 1558
Houses built upon the sand. 1029
Houses of Antioch. 78
Houses of God. 1160
"The houses of peace", being a historical, legendary, and contemporary account of the Moravians and their settlement of Salem in North Carolina. 2595
Houses: their signs and planets. 97
... Housing the Sunday school. 3548
How! 2558
How a Dane became an American. 3132
How a master works. 2400
How a small church can have good Christian education. 3150
How about Christianity? 63
How adults learn. 8
How am I doing, God? 2319
How am I supposed to love myself? 3831
How and what the church teaches. 2961
How and why I became a spiritualist. 3499
How and why of third world missions. 2502
How and why wonder book of the Old Testament. 555
How are we led? and Who is it that leads us? 2204
How are you programmed? 2322
How Baptists work together. 3182
How beautiful. 3368
How beautiful upon the mountains; an anthology of poetry about Jesus. 2048
How Biblical is the church growth movement? 1171
How big is God? 1734
How big is your world. 3188
How black is the Gospel? 1096
How book of evangelism. 2443
How Buddhism left India. 702
How came our faith. 2113, 2138
How came the Bible? 289
How came the Bible into the Garo language? 281
How can a Jew speak of faith today? 2141
How can God answer prayer? 2868, 2882
How can I find God? 1360
How can I find you, God? 984, 2389
How can I lead my pupils to Christ? 3155
How can I live. 1430
How can Jew, Catholic, Protestants agree on religion, evolution. 1039
How can local churches come together? 1040

How can these be? 3353
How can we believe? 62
How can we get Lily Rose to settle down? 2384
How can we still speak responsibly of God? 1734
How Catholics look at Jews. 941
How Christ lived and labored in Palestine. 1953
How Christ said the first mass, or, The Lord's last supper. 2367
How Christian unity came to Alpha. 1016
How Christians grow. 984
How Christmas came to the Sunday-schools. 1111
How churches fight poverty: 60 successful local projects. 1153
How churches grow. 1171
How churches grow in an urban world. 1170
How come, God? 549, 2983
How come it's taking me so long to get better? 1010
How come we're alive? 1003
How dependable is the Bible? 278
How did a fat, balding, middle-aged Jew like you become a Jesus freak? 1366, 2307
How did the universe originate and when did the world become a habitable earth? 1381
How different are people who attended Lutheran schools. 2293, 2303
"How do I change my man?" (For women only) 1324
How do I fit in? 3888
How do I know I'm doing right? 949
How do I look from up there? 3885
How do I pray? 2882
How do we know? 3062
... How do we know God? 1740
How do we know there is a god? 1724
How do you do? 966
How do you do, and why? 3166
How does God reward. 986
How does God teach us morals? 948
How does the Christian confront the Old Testament? 530
How does the death of Christ save us? 2003
How Donald kept faith. 1592
How Europe was won for Christianity. 1101
How far is it to Bethlehem? 2854
How far to the nearest doctor? 2538
How firm a foundation. 160, 407, 763, 1426, 1856, 3298
How France built her cathedrals. 752
How glorious is youth. 2611
How God acts. 1728
... How God calls men. 214
How God can use nobodies. 4
How God deals with evil. 2157
How God heals. 1599
How God helps. 1446
How God inspired the Bible. 306
How God made you. 1384
How God meets needs. 3549
How God speaks to us. 3224
How good are Catholic schools? 832
How Granny told the Bible stories. 3534
How green is green? 3883
How green is my mountain. 2178, 2407
How home and church can work together. 1610
How I became a non-Catholic. 1362
How I became a Unitarian. 3728
How I believe. 3625
How I can be real. 3888
How I can experience God. 1726
How I can fit in. 3888
How I can make decisions. 3888
How I can make prayer more effective. 2875
How I changed my mind. 3124
How I changed my thinking about the church. 1119
How I discovered my mediumship. 3498
"How I found God's will for my life" 3785
How I know God answers prayer. 2872
How I know that the dead are alive. 3510
How I know that the dead return. 3515
How I learned to meditate. 2817, 3431
How I lost my job as a preacher. 2898
How I reached the celestial heaven. 2641
How I used truth. 3749
How in the world? 1566, 3735
How in the world do Americans? 3737
How in this world. 3467
How in this world can I be holy? 993
How is God populating heaven? 1906
How it all began. 1102
How Jesus became God. 2010
How Jesus came. 2022
How Jesus dealt with men. 2004

How Jesus heals our minds today. 2065, 3000
How Jesus helped people. 2437
How Jesus met life questions. 400
How Jesus showed God to the people. 1972
How life came upon the earth. 1385
How love can change your life. 2262
How love will help. 1451
How Luke was written. 429, 3578
How many loaves? 894
How many miles to Babylon? 1325
How many ways to heaven? 3381
"How may I win my unsaved friend to Christ?" 3292
How men are saved. 3288
How men worship. 3855
How Mennonites came to be. 2406
How Methodism came. 2423
How militarism murders Christ. 1997
How modern should theology be? 2301, 3368
How much faith does it take? 1602
How much is left of the old doctrines? 3643
How my mind has changed. 3211
How nations share. 3763
How not to be uptight in an uptight world. 1011
How not to go crazy. 3535
How not to raise a Cain. 904
How odd of God. 2077
"how" of divine revelation, its method and technique. 3519
How of vacation church school. 3763
How of volunteer training in the Y.W.C.A. 3877
How old is Christ's Gospel? 1410
How one man changed the world. 1950, 1979
How our Bible came to us. 290
How our church came to our country. 3743
How our religion began. 3094
How persons grow in Christian community. 904
How Peter became pope. 2768
How philosophy shapes theology. 3105
How prayer helps me. 2875
How Protestants differ from Roman Catholics. 802
How readest thou! 2401
How real is religion? 67
How relevant is the Bible? 239
How St. Francis tamed the wolf. 1644
How secure these rights? 2105
How senior citizens can save our country. 18
How shall I learn to teach religion? 3179
How shall man be just with God? 2160
How shall they hear without a preacher? 3703
How shall they preach. 2908
"How shall we escape?" 1559, 1560
How shall we escape if we neglect... so great salvation. 3289
How shall we keep Sunday? 3547
How shall we meet troble? 11
How shall we worship God? 3859
How should I love you? 2265
How should we then live? 1282
How silently. 2377
How Southern Baptists do their work. 3466
How the animals got their names. 47
How the Baptists got their doctrines. 3654
How the Bible came to us. 290, 292
How the Bible grew. 290
How the Catholic Church is governed. 808
How the church began. 333
How the church can help where delinquency begins. 1421
How the church can minister to the world without losing itself. 1058
How the church grew. 3217
How the church grows. 3217
How the church grows in Brazil. 2953
How the codex was found. 317
... How the Disciples began and grew. 1190
How the early Hebrews lived and learned. 2087
How the gospel spread through Europe. 2526
How the gospels work. 391
How the great religions began. 3116, 3139
How the Jewish people grew up. 2095
How the Jewish people lives today. 2094
How the New Testament came to be written. 409
How the Pope became infallible. 2850, 2862
How the Reformation came. 3037
How the Reformation came. [Tr. from German by Ott M. Knab. 3037

How the reformation happened. 3033, 3034
How the swans came to the lake. 710
How the tarot speaks to modern man. 3588
How the world began. 527
How they brought the good news of Methodism to north Montana. 2431, 2586
How things began. 3185
How to achieve past life recalls. 3508
How to achieve personality through prayer. 2868
How to achieve security, confidence, and peace. 981
How to administer programs for disadvantaged adults. 3436
How to advertise a church. 10
How to analyze and overcome your fears. 2808
How to answer a Jehovah's Witness. 1940, 3829

How to be a Christian. 1012
How to be a Christian in an unchristian world. 988
How to be a happy Christian. 971
How to be a minister's wife and love it. 1303
How to be a pastor. 3671
How to be a pastor in a mad, mod world. 1295
How to be a preacher's wife and like it. 1303
How to be a real Christian scientist. 1033
How to be a seminary student and survive. 3332
How to be a successful bus pastor or bus captain. 2625
How to be a transformed person. 1439
How to be a victorious Christian. 1012
How to be a winner. 931, 984, 1811
How to be an American Jew. 2155
How to be an effective church woman. 3836
How to be an effective Sunday School teacher. 3565
How to be born again. 3051
How to be Christian without being religious. 471
How to be enriched by giving. 952
How to be fully alive. 1003
How to be happy in the non-electric church. 3426
How to be happy though married. 2338
How to be nervous and enjoy it. 1323
How to be really with it. 996
How to be saved. 3289, 3291, 3292
How to be saved, and how to be lost. 3293
How to be the Lord's prayer. 2246
How to be your best. 962
How to be your own selfish pig. 985
How to beat the blahs. 987
How to become a bishop without being religious. 2788
How to become a Christian. 977, 1360
How to become a Christian, and other sermons. 167
How to become a Christian and stay one. 2375
How to become a clairvoyant. 1283
How to become a Masonic lodge officer. 1666
How to become a successful Christian leader. 953
...How to become an efficient Sunday school teacher. 3555
How to begin the Christian life. 989
How to behave in the parish. 2962
How to believe. 1096
How to believe again. 2301, 3370
How-to-book. 990
How to bring men to Christ. 1571
How to build a church. 3672
How to build a church choir. 915
How to build a church library. 2224
How to build an evangelistic church. 1563, 1564
How to build an evangelistic church music program. 1203
How to build expository sermons. 2896
How to build up an adult Bible class. 640
How to build up your church school. 3149
How to burn your candle. 1013
How to carry out God's stewardship plan. 3528
How to change your world in 12 weeks. 3539
How to choose a guru. 1778
How to combat anti-Semitism in America. 2104
How to combat communism. 1320
How to comfort the sick. 1258
How to conduct a church vacation school. 3763
How to conduct a funeral. 1693

How to conduct a primary department. 3555
How to conduct a Sunday school. 3555
How to conduct an installation service. 1911
How to conduct religious radio programs. 3018
How to consider the church evangelist. 1571
How to consult the I ching. 1470, 1878
How to contact soul voices. 120
How to control your emotions. 2380
How to converse continually and familiarly with God. 2380
How to cure scruples. 3316
How to deal with controversial issues. 953
How to deal with doubts and doubters. 1360, 3422
How to deal with how you feel. 994
How to deal with Jehovah's witnesses. 1941
How to deal with Mormons. 2613
How to deal with Roman Catholics. 874, 1570
How to decorate your church. 1165
How to demonstrate Christian Science. 1034
How to develop a better self-image. 3330
How to develop a praying church. 2880
How to develop a tithing church. 3530
How to develop faith that heals. 2695
How to distinguish the saints in art by their costumes, symbols, and other attributes. 919
How to do all things. 1324
"How to do" stewardship and church finances using the S. S. and other church organization. 1167
How to do things right. 1324
How to dramatize Bible lessons. 603
How to enjoy reading the Bible. 233
How to enjoy studying the Bible. 638
How to enjoy supernatural prosperity. 3539
How to enjoy the Bible. 232, 237
How to enjoy the Christian life. 986
How to enter God's kingdom. 983
How to establish a jail and prison ministry. 1256
How to evaluate your Christian education program. 3160
How to face your fears. 1619
How to fail successfully. 692, 1588
How to feel like a somebody again. 983
How to finance your church building program. 1167
How to find comfort in the Bible. 1351
How to find God. 1727
How to find happiness. 2872
How to find health through prayer. 1598
How to find out who you are. 1881
How to find the good life. 966
How to find time for better preaching and better pastoring. 2786
How to follow Jesus. 403
How to foresee and control your future. 1283
How to gain health, happiness, prosperity. 978
How to gain tranquillity & the pleasures of internal contentment & emotional balance without the taking of pills. 997
How to gather and order a Congregational Christian Church. 1250
How to get acquainted with God. 1035
How to get along with people in the church. 2204
How to get more from your Bible. 640
How to get more out of the mass. 2367
How to get the best out of life. 2226
How to get the most out of bible study. 642
How to get through your struggles. 1007
How to get to heaven. 3505
How to get to heaven from your house. 1435
How to get what you want from God. 1002
How to get your church news in print. 10
How to get your share of industrial business. 1370
How to give a devotion. 1443
How to give a retreat. 3222
How to give away your faith. 3829
How to give away your life. 985
How to give the spiritual exercises of St. Ignatius to lay apostles. 2269, 3476
How to grow a church. 1171
How to grow an effective Sunday school. 3558
How to grow new Christians. 988
How-to handbook of massive tax reduction. 1370, 3751
How to handle life's hurts. 994
How to handle pressure. 986
How to have a family altar. 1611
How to have a giving church. 952

How to have a good marriage. 2338
How to have a revival. 3229
How to have a soul winning church. 1564
How to have a successful Christmas entertainment. 1111
How to have better health through prayer. 3406
How to have family prayers. 1610
How to heal one's self and others. 1599
How to help through understanding. 1252
How to help your child have a spiritual life. 903
How to hold circles for developing mediumship at home. 3516
How to improve. 3881
How to improve adult education in your church. 3168
How to improve church music. 1203
How to improve my church's school. 3555
How to improve your preaching. 2901
How to improve your Sunday school. 3552, 3565
How to increase church attendance. 1162
How to increase church income. 1167
How to increase church membership and attendance. 1564
How to increase memorial giving. 1168
How to increase Sunday night attendance. 3548
How to increase your Sunday-school attendance. 3561, 3565
How to interest the young in Bible truths. 3885
How to interest your Sunday school in missions. 2551
How to interpret our Bible. 236
How to interpret the New Testament. 405
How to involve children in worship services. 905
How to keep a spiritual journal. 3480
How to keep the family that prays together from falling apart. 1606
How to know and be your self forever. 1003
How to know and use your Bible. 653
How to know God. 1735, 3865
How to know the Bible. 635, 638
How to know the Holy Bible. 639
How to know the will of God. 1741
How to know when God speaks. 1735
How to know your Bible. 311
How to lead a Bible school. 3557
How to lead Moslems to Christ. 1358
How to lead Roman Catholics to Christ. 1570
How to learn astrology. 95
How to learn how. 59
How to listen when God speaks. 636, 2379
How to live. 1324
How to live a Christian. 985
How to live a Christian life. 966, 1011
How to live a holy life. 1010
How to live a prosperous life. 1011
How to live above & beyond your circumstances. 214, 985
How to live above your problems. 988
How to live beyond your means. 984
How to live effectively. 2437
How to live for health and spiritual attainment. 2695
How to live in a layman's order. 1649
How to live in the circle of prayer and make your dreams come true. 2875
How to live like a king's kid. 984, 1811
How to live the Bible like a king's kid. 931, 1811
How to live the Christ life. 958
How to live the Christian life. 1010
How to live with a tiger. 1013
How to live with yourself. 973, 1324
How to live your faith. 2437
How to love your enemies. 2263
How to love your neighbor. 2265
How to maintain your church buildings and grounds. 1242
How to make a friendly call. 3783
How to make a good mission great. 2618
How to make a grand success of the Christian life. 994
How to make chalk talk. 880
How to make chruch school equipment: it's easier than you think! 3310
How to make church school equipment. 3310
How to make friends for your church. 10
How to make pastoral calls. 3783
How to make perfection appear. 2639
How to make the church go. 1199
How to make the league "go;" 1525
How to make the mission. 2774
How to make the Sunday school go. 3552
How to make the wheel go. 1525
How to make up your mind. 1418
How to make us want your sermon. 2896
How to make your church hum. 3678

How to make your marriage exciting. 2338
How to make your teaching count. 3153
How to manage yourself and others. 1583
How to marry a minister. 1303
How to master the English Bible. 638, 645
How to meditate. 2379, 2380, 2381
How to meditate perfectly: develop spiritually, unfold psychically. 2381
How to meditate without attending a TM class. 2379
How to meet and master adversities. 11
How to meet your troubles. 11
How to minister to families in your church. 1254
How to minister to senior adults in your church. 1257
How to murder a minister. 1295
How to operate a Sunday school. 3559
How to organize a music department for a church. 916
How to organize and direct the church choir. 1203
How to organize the education program of your church. 3146
How to organize your church library. 2224
How to organize your church office. 2734
How to organize your church staff. 1252
How to orient one's own life. 3881
How to overcome stress and tension in your life. 984
How to overcome temptation. 3600
How to pay church debts. 1168
How to picture hymns with chalk. 1874
How to plan. 1714
How to plan a lesson. 3179
How to plan and conduct a primary church. 3858
How to plan and conduct Sunday school worship services. 3565
How to plan informal worship. 3853
...How to plan, prepare and present devotional programs and promote the crusade of prayer. 3858
How to plan the rural church program. 3254
How to plant and organize New Testament churches. 1169
How to pray. 2248, 2872, 2879, 2880, 2881, 2887, 2890
How to pray always without always praying. 2871
How to pray for healing. 604, 2883
How to pray for spiritual growth. 3486
How to pray for Vietnam. 3778
How to pray for your children. 2877
How to pray the Psalms. 585
How to pray today. 2879
How to pray well. 2877
How to preach from the Gospel of John. 423
How to preach the Word with variety. 2902
How to preach to people's needs. 2901
How to preach with power. 2907, 2911
How to prepare an expository sermon. 2902
How to prepare Bible messages. 2898
How to prepare sermons. 2900
How to prepare sermons and gospel addresses. 3347
How to produce miracles. 2727
How to promote & conduct a successful revival. 3229
How to promote Christian union. 1041
How to protect yourself against black magic and witchcraft. 2729
How to psychoanalyze the Bible. 1654
How to publicize church activities. 3002
How to put church members to work. 1250
How to raise a Christian family. 1606
How to raise funds for Wesley foundations. 3802
How to raise your children for Christ. 940
How to raise your parents. 3880
How to reach men, to hold men, to teach men, to win men. 3161
How to reach the Jew for Christ. 2535
How to reach the ones you love. 3830
How to read and enjoy the Psalms. 586
How to read and remember the Scriptures. 637
How to read St. Paul. 374
How to read tarot cards. 3588
... How to read the Bible. 235, 613, 637, 638
How to read the Bible aloud. 612
How to read the Bible for all it's worth. 637
How to read the Bible in the twentieth century. 613
How to read the New Testament. 475
... How to read the Revelation of Jesus Christ. 452

How to rear a happy Christian family. 1608
How to reason infallibly. 3027
How to recognize the Antichrist. 51
How to recruit and keep Sunday school teachers. 3177
How to reform mankind. 1907
How to respond ... the occult. 1078
How to respond to ... the cults. 1393
How to respond to ... the Eastern religions. 1082
How to respond to ... the Jehovah's Witness. 1940
How to respond to ... the Latter Day Saints. 1232
How to respond to ... "the new "Christian" religions" 1038
How to run a church. 3672
How to run a little Sunday school. 3553
How to run a Sunday school. 3558
How to save time in the ministry. 1199
How to say no to a stubborn habit, even when you feel like saying yes. 985
How to say yes to life. 2347
How to search the scriptures. 640
How to serve God in a Marxist land. 1110
How to serve in simple, solemn, and pontifical functions. 836
... How to set the church in order. 1239
How to share your faith without being offensive. 3829
How to share your spiritual discoveries. 3829
... How to sing the choral service. 884
How to sleep on a windy night. 3534
How to slove your problems. 979
How to solve mysteries of your mind and soul. 2696
How to solve your problems by prayer. 2869
How to spark gospel learning. 2599
How to speak in church. 1231, 3002
How to speak with the dead. 2991
How to stand up for what you believe. 3880
How to start counseling. 1373
How to stay alive all your life. 1004
How to study and use the Bible. 640
How to study Ephesians. 365
How to study I Corinthians. 321
How to study John. 423
How to study Luke. 431
How to study Philippians, Colossians, and Philemon. 374
How to study the Apocalypse. 460
How to study the Bible. 636, 638, 639, 642
How to study the Bible for the greatest profit. 642
How to study the Bible for yourself. 639
... How to study the city church. 1278
How to study the life of Christ. 3564
How to study the Old Testament. 596
How to study the Psalms. 575
How to study the Revelation. 465, 474
How to study your association and the community. 3872
How to study your Bible. 640
How to succeed in business without being a pagan. 3538
How to succeed in the Christian life. 977, 3539
How to survive & live in heaven on earth. 980
How to take the worry out of witnessing. 3830
How to talk to God when you aren't feeling religious. 1007
How to talk with God. 1734, 2871
How to tangibilitate. 1007
How to teach. 3558

How to teach Bible stories. 644
How to teach evangelical Christianity with special reference to the word of God. 3151
... How to teach in Sunday-school. 3557
How to teach in the church school. 3159
How to teach John. 423
How to teach junior high. 3168
How to teach junior highs. 3168
How to teach morals. 2591
How to teach one and win one for Christ. 2517
How to teach Philippians, Colossians, and Philemon. 374
How to teach religion. 746, 935, 3111, 3147
How to teach senior highs. 3175
How to teach seniors. 3157
How to teach the Bible. 637, 638
How to teach the catechism. 132
... How to teach the life of Christ. 1993
How to teach the little folks. 3554
How to teach the New Testament. 473

How to teach the Old Testament. 596
How to teach the Revelation. 465
How to teach the word of God. 3156
How to teach young people and adults in the Sunday school. 3149
How to teach your children about God. 903
How to tell a church (as in recognize) 1121
How to tell Bible stories. 3534
How to think about evolution & other Bible-science controversies. 202
How to think about God. 1719
How to think of Christ. 2036
How to train the Sunday school. 3178
How to train the Sunday school teacher. 3178
How to treat and prevent the crisis in the priesthood. 775
How to treat your family as well as you treat your friends. 2340
How to understand and influence children, ages five, six, seven, and eight. 3171
How to understand and use the Bible. 636
How to understand the Bible. 236, 310, 635, 644
How to understand the Gospels. 389
How to understand the words of Christ. 647
How to understand your Bible. 237
... How to understand your Bible, a philosopher's interpretation of obscure and puzzling passages. 318, 319
How to understand your Bible better. 201
How to unlock the power of your mind with hypnosis, and Explore the riddle of reincarnation. 1878
How to use a hymnal. 153
How to use the Bible. 641, 653
How to use the Bible for help today. 3183
How to use the Bible story. 653
How to use the Greek New Testament. 1770
How to use the hymnal. 3217
How to use the power of prayer. 2880
How to use your church. 1201
How to use your healing power. 1599
How to usher. 1249
How to value life. 993
How to visit the English cathedrals. 751
How to vitalize young adult classes. 3168
How to wait for Jesus. 984
How to wake up singing. 3539
How to win a soul. 1572
How to win a Sunday school contest. 3554
How to win boys, a book of information and inspiration for the Sunday school worker. 1254
How to win in a crisis. 2783
How to win over communism. 1319
How to win over loneliness. 2244
How to win over worry. 2808
How to win souls. 1565, 1566
How to win souls and influence people for heaven. 3829
How to win souls today. 1564
How to win the war. 992
How to win them. 1572
How to win to Christ. 1563
How to win your family to Christ. 1569, 1574
How to witness successfully. 3829
How to work. 3849
How to work for Christ. 1571
How to work with church groups. 3179
How to work with juniors in the Sunday school. 3172
How to work with parish groups. 1169
... how unsearchable His ways. 2830
How we become moral. 2592
How we can help children to pray. 2876
How we got our Bible. 289, 291, 312, 3549
How we got our denominations. 3323
How we got the Bible. 290
How we got the Book of Mormon. 679
How we got the New Testament. 474
How would Jesus teach? 1954, 3156
How would you like to see the slides of my mission? 2599
How you can be sure you are a Christian. 982
How you can broadcast religion. 3018
How you can help other people. 3674
How you too can teach. 3178
How Yung Fu saved a Bible. 2509
Howard Robert Weir, rector. 3801
Howard University bibliography of African and Afro-American religious studies. 17
Howel Harris. 1786
Hroswitha of Gandersheim. 1849
Hrough the needle's eye. 2866
Hsiang-Ya journal. 1772, 1850, 2488
Hte inside story of the Hollywood Christian Group. 1824
Hte power of dynamic faith. 1591

Hua-yen Buddhism. 120, 2166
Hubert Walter, Lord of Canterbury and Lord of England. 1850
Huck Finn goes to church. 3887
Huck's Synopsis of the first three Gospels. 394
Hudson Taylor. 2508, 3590
Hudson Taylor and Maria. 3590
Hudson Taylor and the China inland mission. 2511, 3590
Hudson Taylor in early years. 3590
Hudson Taylor's spiritual secret. 3590
Hugh. 191
Hugh Blair. 670
Hugh Bourne. 686
Hugh Capet of France and Byzantium. 1638, 1853
Hugh Davey Evans, LL. D. 1577
Hugh Latimer. 2198
Hugh Latimer and the sixteenth century. 2198
Hugh Latimer, apostle to the English. 666, 2198
Hugh McLellan's sermons. 3354
Hugh of Saint-Victor. 3493
Hugh Wilson, a pioneer saint. 3819
Hugo Distler and his church music. 1470
Hugo Gurgeny, prisoner of the Lisbon $inquisition. 1778
Huguenot. 1851, 3227
Huguenot ancestors represented in the membership of the Huguenot Society of New Jersey. 1852
Huguenot ancestors represented in the membership of The Huguenot Society of New Jersey. 2d. ed. 1852
Huguenot church of New York. 2699
Huguenot galley-slave. 1852
... A Huguenot saint of the twentieth century. 2162
Huguenot settlements in Ireland. 1851
Huguenot struggle for recognition. 1851
Huguenots. 1852
Huguenots and Henry of Navarre. 1803, 1852
Huguenots and the revocation of the Edict of Nantes. 1497, 1852
... The Huguenots, fighters for God and human freedom. 1852
Huguenots in France and America. 1852
Huguenots of colonial South Carolina. 1852
Huguenots: their settlements, churches, and industries in England and Ireland. 1852
Huldreich Zwingli. 3042, 3900
Huldreich Zwingli, 1484-1531. 3042, 3900
Huldreich Zwingli, the reformer of German Switzerland, 1484-1531. 3042, 3900
Huldrych Zwingli. 3044, 3630
Human achievement and divine vocation in the message of Paul. 375
Human adventure. 1000
Human adventure, four world views. 3140
Human adventures in happy living. 927
Human and its relation to the divine. 3106
Human and the holy. 2321
Human ascent. 1095
Human body. 2327
Human brotherhood and a Psalm of faith. 3208
Human but holy. 1002
Human chain for divine grace. 1557, 2299
Human charter. 126
Human Christ. 2012
Human church. 758
Human destinies as taught in the Bible. 232
Human destiny. 947, 1615, 3593, 3753
Human destiny and the new psychology. 2999
Human destiny in the light of revelation. 2325
Human dimension of catechetics. 935
Human documents of the Lloyd George era. 1765, 2241
Human dynamo. 3060
Human element in the church of Christ. 757
Human element in the inspiration of the Sacred Scriptures. 305
Human element in the making of a Christian. 1553
Human exile. 2833
Human face of God. 2043
Human footprints on the divine highroad. 1061
Human freedom and social order. 1106
Human gods. 3059
Human heritage. 3688
Human history and the word of God. 1817
Human identity in Christian faith. 2046, 2326
Human immortality. 1888, 1891

Human immortality and pre-existence. 1889
Human liberation in a feminist perspective—a theology. 1659
Human life. 2227, 2782
Human life and its conditions. 3363
Human life of Jesus. 1963
Human like me, Jesus. 2888
Human living in Christ. 3485
Human love. 2262
Human love, existential and mystical. 2262
Human miracle. 2379
Human moral problems. 3413
Human nature. 1498, 2226
Human nature and Christian marriage. 2340
Human nature and progress. 2320
Human nature and the church. 1120
Human nature and the gospel. 349
Human nature, election, and history. 2321
Human nature in Christian work. 3180
Human nature, in its fourfold state. 2322, 3288
Human nature in the Bible. 501
Human nature in the Christian tradition. 2321
Human nature of the saints. 3280
Human nature under God. 2996
Human needs and world Christianity. 3444
Human personality and its survival of bodily death. 2823, 2990
Human predicament: dissolution and wholeness. 2320
Human problems of the minister. 1294
Human process for enlightenment and freedom. 80
Human progress through missions. 2553
Human purpose of Catholic education. 831
Human puzzle. 1107
Human quest. 748, 795, 3081
Human quest and the divine plan. 3030
Human questions and divine answers. 3360
Human quintessence. 2226
"The human race" and other sermons. 3366
Human reality of Sacred Scripture. 201
Human reality of Sacred Scripture (The) 201
Human relations and the South African scene in the light of scripture. 3017, 3047
Human relationships and the church. 3442
Human religion. 3060
Human response to the Holocaust. 1825
Human rift. 965
Human rights. 1280
Human rights and the liberation of man in the Americas. 1280
Human science & human dignity. 2321
Human sexuality. 3389, 3393
Human sexuality in our time. 783, 3390
Human side of the ministry. 2788
Human soul and its relations with other spirits. 3463
Human spirits. 1321
Human touch. 156, 1304, 2487
Human values and Christian morality. 947
Human values in a secular world. 1537
Human venture. 3100
Human way. 3099
Human wisdom of St. Thomas. 3694
Humane imperative. 1528
Humane religion. 3061
Humanism. 1854
Humanism and Christianity. 1088, 1854
... Humanism and human dignity. 1854
Humanism and the church fathers. 1616, 3710
Humanism as a way of life. 1854
Humanism in action. 1854
Humanism in New England theology. 1855
Humanism in the contemporary era. 1854
Humanist funeral service. 1694
Humanist meditations and paraphrases. 2398
Humanist pulpit. 3725
Humanist sermons. 3357
Humanistic existentialism. 1583
Humanistic Judaism. 2141
Humanistic psychology. 1107
... Humanistic studies. 1854
Humanistic values in the Bible. 595
Humanist's "trew imitation": Thomas Watson's Absalom. 1405
Humanist's view of religion. 1102
Humanitarian individualism; an outline for tomorrow. [1. ed.]. 1905
Humanitas; human becoming & being human. 2319
Humanities, religion, and the arts tomorrow. 3089
Humanity. 2321, 2324

Humanity and divinity. 2417
Humanity and divinity of Christ. 2012
Humanity and its four visions. 2320
Humanity at the cross-roads. 1052
Humanity, benevolence and charity legislation of the Pentateuch and the Talmud. 2084
Humanity immortal. 3029
Humanity in the city. 3349, 3755
Humanity of Christ. 2012
Humanity of God. 1720, 1730, 3655, 3656
Humanity of man. 2319
Humanity of the Christ. 2012
Humanity to honey bees. 185
Humanity's greatest need. 3122
Humanizing Biblical religion. 233
Humanizing Jewish life. 2081, 3598
Humanness of John Calvin. 728
Humanum genus. 1663
Humble address to every Christian of every nation and denomination of people under Heaven. 3792
Humble approach. 3083
Humble, earnest, and affectionate address to the clergy. 1288
Humble harvest. 3438
Humble hours of solitude. 3208
Humble inquiry into the rules of the Word of God. 1201
Humble inquiry into the Scripture-account of Jesus Christ. 2002, 3727
Humble supplication to Her Maiestie. 1765
Humboldt years, 1930-1939. 1293, 3791
Hume. 192, 1855
Hume, Newton, and the design argument. 2705, 3594
Hume on religion. 3107
Hume's Dialogues concerning natural religion. 2673
Hume's moral epistemology. 1855, 2180
Hume's philosophy of religion. 1855
Hume's Treatise of morals. 1855
[Humiliations followed with deliverances. 1899
Humiliated Christ in modern Russian thought. 3214
Humiliation and celebration. 3617
Humiliation of Christ. 3348
Humiliation of Christ in its physical, ethical. 2012
Humiliation of the church. 1059
Humiliation of the church, by Albert H. vanden. 1059
Humiliations follow'd with deliverances. 1613
Humility. 1856
Humility of God. 2392
Humor and warmth of Pope John XXIII. 2124
Humor of Christ. 2012
Humor of Jesus. 2012
Humorous tales of latter day rabbis "as 'twas told to me" 2083
Humour and irony in the New Testament. 348
Humours of a parish. 2775
Huna code in religions. 2727
Hunan harvest. 2529
Hundred letters. 3542
Hundred songs of God and His kingdom, compiled and edited by Cephas Guillet. 1865
Hundred years in His house. 2829
Hundred years *in house. 2829
Hundred years in the homeland. 2528
Hundred years of Catholic emancipation (1829-1929) 816
Hundred years of China Methodism. 2430
Hundred years of missions. 2525
Hundred years of the faith. 835
Hundred years of the First Presbyterian church of Ann Arbor, Michigan. 48
Hundredth anniversary 1867-1968. 2696
Hundredth Archbishop of Canterbury. 3021
Hundredth century philosophy. 3027
Hungarian Jewish catastrophe. 3851
Hungarian Protestantism yesterday and today. 2954
Hunger and hope. 2492
Hunger for experience. 3144
Hunger for wholeness. 2389
Hunger for wholeness, man's universal motive. 2321
Hunger of the heart for faith. 3344
Hunger, the thirst. 1139
Hungering dark. 2384
Hungers of the heart. 1447
Hungers of the human heart. 2436
Hungry Christ. 2426
Hungry for God. 2815
Hungry generation. 1308
Hungry inherit. 3289

Hungry sheep. 763
Hunted heretic. 3377
Hunters of souls. 1475
Hunting the divine fox. 3661
Hurdles to heaven. 1412
... Hurlbut's handy Bible encyclopedia. 244
Hurlbut's story of Jesus for young and old. 2005
Hurlbut's story of the Bible. 294
Hurlbut's story of the Bible for young and old. 294
Hurlbut's story of the Bible told for young and old. 294
Hurlbut's story of the Christian church. 1100
Hurlbut's teacher-training lessons for the Sunday school. 3554
Hurrah for the process. 449
Hurrell Froude. 660
Hurry before sundown. 2495
Hurry call of Jesus. 1956
Hurry home where you belong. 2299
Hurt and healing. 3002
Hurting parent. 1609
Husband and father. 997
Husband and wife. 2338, 2345, 3391
Husband prays. 1858
Husband-wife equality. 2339
Husbands. 2340
Husbands, wives, parents, children. 1609
Hush! hush! 2869
Hustle won't bring the kingdom of God. 166, 2028
Hustler for the Lord. 1367, 1631
Hustling parson. 3701
Hutterian brethren. 1859
Hutterian Brethren, 1528-1931. 1578, 1859
Hutterite Brethren. 1859
Hutterite society. 1308, 1858
Hutterites. 1858
Hutterites in Montana: an economic description. 1859
Hutterites in North America. 1859
Hutton's book of nature laid open. 2675
... Hvmanism. 1854
Hyacinth Marie Cormier. 1369
Hyacinths to feed the soul. 2383
Hydesville in history. 2162, 3497
Hymn and congregational singing. 1210
Hymn and Scripture selection guide. 653, 1873
Hymn and tune book for the church and the home. 1862
Hymn as literature. 1872
Hymn-book for children. 1862
Hymn-book for the army and navy. 1862
Hymn book for the use of Evangelical Lutheran schools and congregations. 2289
Hymn-book of the church. 2985
Hymn-book of the Free Methodist church. 1865
Hymn book of the United evangelical church. 1865
Hymn festivals. 1860
Hymn gems. 1869
Hymn homilies. 1875
Hymn interpretations. 1873
Hymn is born. 1874
Hymn "Jesus of Nazareth passeth by." 1874
Hymn lore. 1872
Hymn of hate and The law of love. 3208
Hymn of Jesus. 1866
Hymn of the early church. 1873
Hymn of the universe. 2643
Hymn playing. 1862
Hymn stories. 1871, 1873, 2458
Hymn stories of the twentieth century. 1871
Hymn studies. 2429
Hymn to joy. 2135
Hymn to the cross. 675
Hymn tune names. 1860
Hymn tune names: their sources and significance. 1860
Hymn-tunes of Lowell Mason. 1860, 1862, 2364
Hymn writers of the Christian church. 1860
Hymnal. 1860, 2916, 2926, 3217
Hymnal and order of service. 110, 1547, 1865
Hymnal companion. 1872
Hymnal companion to the Lutheran book of worship. 1876
Hymnal concordance. 1873, 3410
Hymnal for Evangelical Lutheran missions. 2289
Hymnal for joyous youth. 3562
Hymnal for juniors in worship and study. 3563
Hymnal for Scotland. 1524
Hymnal for youth. 1866

Hymnal handbook for Standard hymns and gospel songs. 1872
Hymnal 1940 companion. 2967, 2968
Hymnal of the Evangelical church. 1865
Hymnal of the Evangelical Lutheran Augustana synod. 110
Hymnal of the Methodist Episcopal church. 1867
Hymnal of the Protestant Episcopal church in the United States of America, 1940. 2968
Hymnal of the Protestant Episcopal church in the United States of America. 2967
Hymnal of the Reformed church in the United States. 3044, 3046, 3048
Hymnal of the Reformed Episcopal church. 3050
Hymnal [of the] reorganized Church of Jesus Christ of Latter Day Saints. 3217
Hymnbooks at Wittenberg. 1862, 3830
Hymnes and songs of the church. 1870
Hymni inediti. 812
Hymni latini antiquissimi LXXV. 1877
Hymnic affirmation of divine justice. 485, 2867
Hymnodia hiberica. 1877
Hymnody of the Christian church. 1874
Hymnographi latini. Lateinische Hymnendichter des Mittelalters. 1877, 3210
Hymns. 905, 1221, 1587, 1862, 1868, 1869, 2704, 3398, 3725, 3754
Hymns, ancient and modern, for use in the service of the church. 1866
Hymns, and anthems. 1867
Hymns and choirs. 1867, 1875, 2775
Hymns and church music. 1875
Hymns and epigrams. Lycophron, with an English translation. 1873
Hymns and human life. 1876
Hymns and hymn tunes found in the English metrical Psalters. 1872
Hymns and hymn writers of the church. 2451
Hymns & hymnody. 1871
Hymns and hymnwriters of Denmark. 1862
Hymns and meditations. 1869
Hymns and poems. 3811
Hymns and poetry of the Eastern church. 2747
Hymns and prayers for the use of the army and navy. 1862
Hymns and sacred pieces. 3207
Hymns and sacred pieces, never before published. 1866
Hymns and songs of praise for public and social worship. 1865
Hymns and songs of the Spirit. 1866
Hymns and sonnets. 3207
Hymns and spiritual songs. 125, 1862, 1866, 1867, 1869, 3799
Hymns and spiritual songs in three books. 1870
Hymns and the faith. 1872
Hymns and tunes. 1876
Hymns and tunes selected from "In Excelsis;" 1862
Hymns and verses. 1869
Hymns, &c. 1860
Hymns at heaven's gate. 1773
Hymns for children. 1860
Hymns for Christian devotion. 3754
Hymns for divine worship in churches and Sunday schools. 2288
Hymns for infant minds. 1865
Hymns for primary worship. 3562
Hymns for public and social worship. 1862
Hymns for schools and families. 2451
Hymns for social worship selected from Watts, Doddridge, Newton, Cowper, Steele, and others. 1860
Hymns for special services. 2968
Hymns for Sunday-schools. 3563
Hymns for Sunday schools, youth & children. 1866
Hymns for the camp. 3741
Hymns for the drowning. 3782
Hymns for the Lord's supper. 1865
Hymns for the use of the Evangelical Lutheran church. 2289
Hymns for the use of the Methodist Episcopal church. 1867, 2429
Hymns for the use of the New Jerusalem church. 2692
Hymns for today for Sunday schools. 3562
Hymns for youth. 3563
Hymns from the harps of God. 1875
Hymns from the land of Luther. 1874
Hymns from the Latin. 1878
Hymns from the Vedas. 1816
Hymns, fun songs, worship resources. 1862
Hymns historically famous. 1876
Hymns; how to sing them. 1878

Hymns in Christian worship. 1872
Hymns in human experience. 1875
Hymns in prose for children. 1862
Hymns in the lives of men. 1875
Hymns of childhood for primary and junior grades. 910
Hymns of help and hope. 1862
Hymns of His grace. 1862
Hymns of hope and courage. 1864
Hymns of joy, and songs of faith. 1862
Hymns of my holy hours. 1861
Hymns of our faith. 1872
... Hymns of prayer and praise. 3046
Hymns of Qumran. 1874, 3605
Hymns of spiritual devotion. 1865
Hymns of the ages. 1860
Hymns of the Alvars. 1860
Hymns of the Atharva-veda. 673, 1816
Hymns of the breviary and missal. 1876
Hymns of the church. 3046
Hymns of the church militant. 1861
Hymns of the Dominican missal and breviary. 1876
Hymns of the Eastern Church. 1874, 2747
Hymns of the higher life. 1867
Hymns of the living faith. 2429
Hymns of the North. 1862
Hymns of the Roman liturgy. 1876, 1877
Hymns of the Russian church. 2747
Hymns of the spirit for use in the free churches of America. 3724
... Hymns of the Tamil Saivite saints. 1860
Hymns of worship and service. 1866
Hymns of Zarathustra. 3899
Hymns of Zoroaster. 121
Hymns old and new. 1871
Hymns on the collects for every Sunday in the year. 2961
Hymns pro patria, and other hymns. 1862
Hymns, selected and original for public and private worship. 2289
Hymns selected from Dr. Watts. 1865
Hymns selected from Faber. 1587
Hymns selected from Frederick William Faber, D. D. 1587
Hymns selected from the Christian science hymnal. 1037
Hymns selected from various authors, for the use of young persons. 1865
Hymns that are immortal. 1875
Hymns that endure. 1875
Hymns that every child should know. 1862
Hymns that live. 1871
Hymns to St. Geryon, and other poems. 3208
Hymns to the goddess. 3400
Hymns to the gods. 3208
Hymns to the Holy Spirit. 1832
Hymns today and tomorrow. 1872
Hymns unbidden; Donne, Herbert, Blake, Emily Dickinson, and the hymnographers. 1875
Hymns we love. 1875
Hymns we sing. 153
Hymns you ought to know. 1872
Hyms attributed to John Dryden. 1481, 1877
Hymus of the Roman liturgy. 1877
Hypatia. 2177, 3144
Hyper-Calvinism and the call of the Gospel. 1751, 2975
Hypersentience. 3054
Hyphenated priests. 773
Hypnotism and spiritism. 3507
Hyponoia. 454
Hypostatic union and created actuation by uncreated act. 2040
Hyrum Smith, patriarch. 3427

I

I: a Christian concept of man. 2323
I, a sinner. 3143
I accept these facts. 2262, 2475
I also send you. 789
I always wore my topi. 2304, 2505
I am. 214, 3295
I am a beggar. 187
I am a child of God. 1384
I am a Christ. 973
I am a Christian. 285, 1064
I am a Protestant. 2976
I am a rabbi's wife. 3016
I am a Sioux Indian. 1399
I am a tree. 904
"I am a vestryman" 1239
I am a woman. 3844
I am a woman--and a Jew. 3143
I am a woman by God's design. 3834
"I am" adorations and affirmations. 1444
I am an Orthodox Jew. 2081
I am Andrew. 3164
I am come. 2003

"I am" discourses. 1444
I am food. 2365
I am grateful. 2390
I am, I can. 1007
I am in iambics. 1431
"I am Jesus" 1558
I am Joseph. 494, 2134, 2792
I am Lucifer. 1429
I am my brother. 695
"I am, O Lord, wholly and forever Thine." The life of Rev. John S. Inskip. 1910
"I am" of the fourth Gospel. 419
I am on fire. 1802, 3426
I am ... people. 904
I am persuaded. 2934, 2997
"I am that I am" 5
I am: the ascent of mankind. 50
I am the Lord thy sex. 523
"I am the resurrection and the life." 1691
I am the sun. 904
I am the truth. 2019, 2218
I am the vine. 3184
I am the way. 2071
I am what I do. 3486
I AMs of Christ. 2038
I & II Peter and Jude. 447
I and that. 3057
I and the people. 611
I and thou. 699, 2225, 2646
I become an evangelist. 1553
"I believe— 73, 74, 166, 763, 956, 1095, 1594, 2052, 2141, 2695, 3082, 3661, 3662, 3665, 3666
I believe because. 61
"I believe, but ...!" 3661
I believe in angels. 42
I believe in evangelism. 1571
I believe in ghosts. 1710
I believe in God. 74, 75, 1385, 1722, 1726, 3170
I believe in God and in evolution. 1580
I believe in God the Father. 1341, 3184
I believe in hope. 1091, 1459
I believe in immortality. 1887
I believe in Jesus Christ. 1956, 3188
I believe in justice and hope. 665, 743
I believe in love. 3486
I believe in man. 2321, 2325
I believe in revelation. 3225
I believe in Satan's downfall. 1427
I believe in the Bible. 278
I believe in the church. 1116, 1119, 1124
I believe . . . in the communion of teenage saints. 3155
I believe in the Creator. 1381
I believe in the great commission. 1765
I believe in the historical Jesus. 2008
I believe in the Holy Ghost. 1830
I believe in the Holy Spirit. 1829, 1832, 1833
I believe in the holy spirit and the church. 3188
I believe in the living God. 75
I believe in the resurrection of Jesus. 2052, 3221
I believe in visions. 1956, 3783
I believe--so what? 2706
I belong. 3182
I belong to God. 3183
I belong where I'm needed. 1755
I bring you joy. 3289
I called Jesus and He came leaping over mountains and skipping over hills. 3783
I came here to pray. 2889
I can choose: leader's guide. 3763
I can make my own prayers. 2886
I can pray, you can pray. 2869
I-can-read-it-myself Bible stories. 930, 1980
I can talk with God. 2886
I can tell you anything, God. 3883
I cannot go back. 1575, 3432
I challenge you. 3885
I changed gods. 1362
I ching. 1470, 1879
I ching and its associations. 1470, 1879
I Ching and mankind. 1470, 1879
I ching and modern man. 1879
I Ching and you. 1470, 1879
I Ching; Book of changes. 1879
I ching coin prediction. 1470, 1879
I ching numerology. 3400, 3575
I ching primer. 1470, 1879
I Ching! Taoist book of days. Calendar-Diary 1975-Year of the Rabbit, selectively structured by Khigh Alx Dhiegh. Foreword by Jose A. Arguelles. Calligraphy by Chen Hsi. 1879
I Ching workbook. 1470, 1879
I choose. 3143
I choose all. 3691
I chose a parson. 1303
I Chronicles. 483
I Chronicles [and] II Chronicles. 496
"I confess" 2811
I Corinthians. 322, 2795
I cover God. 1446

I cried ... and He answered. 172, 2374
"I cried, He answered" 2867
I crucified the Lord. 2211
I cry Joseph. 3428
I dared to call him Father. 3402
I didn't ask to be baptized. 138
I didn't know that! 1229
I discover the Orient. 2508
I do. 3477
I do believe because. 1591
I do my best. 3192
I do not die. 1415
I don't feel called (thank the Lord!) 2484
I don't live there anymore. 1359, 2736
"I feel" formula. 1010
I felt God's presence in the nation's Capital. 164
I find my joy in the Lord! 581
I follow after. 3143
I follow Christ above all. 1967
I follow Saint Patrick. 1919, 2793
I follow the road. 972
I found Francis in Assisi. 1642
I found God in Soviet Russia. 1362, 1366
I found it! 692, 1576
I found the ancient way. 1362
I found the key to the heart of God. 3308
I found the way. 3382
I, Francis. 1640
I give myself unto prayer. 3222
I give up God. 931, 1010, 1483
I give you a new land. 2914
I go to mass with God's family. 2369
I had to know. 1363
I have a dream. 2172, 2173
I have a ghetto in my heart. 1261
I have a question, God. 8
I have a stewardship. 1437
I have believed. 3663
I have called you Friends. 1687, 2007
I have chosen His glory. 3143
'I have chosen you. 3223
I have considered the days. 3143
I have fought a good fight. 31
I have heard the rainbow. 2387
I have kept the faith. 2798
I have learned. 2390
I have met Him: God exists. 1358
I have only one life to live. 2434
I have planted thee in this land. 143
I have seen God do it. 2980
I have seen God work in China. 2508
I have six wives. 2859
I hear St. Francis singing. 2394
"I heard a voice" 3505
I heard singing. 2542, 3387
I, Heracles. 1804
I hurt inside. 1325
I, John. 2127
I, John, Take thee, Mary. 2346
I knew Dietrich Bonhoeffer. 677
I know. 3505
I know who god is. 1371
'I know whom I have believed. 65
I know why we give thanks. 1756
I leap for joy. 2352
I leap over the wall. 2580
I learn about Jesus. 902, 1980
I learn about sharing. 3401
I learn about the Bible. 313, 971
I learn about the gifts of the Holy Spirit. 1713
I leave you my heart. 980
I lie on my mat and pray. 2893
I lift my lamp. 1948, 2696
I like Christmas. 3192
I live by faith. 1575
I live in the world. 3166
I live on an island. 997, 1473
I looked for God's absence. 818
I looked for God's absence: France. 818
I love America. 974, 3401
I love being married to a grandma. 195, 930
I love Christmas. 1114
I love every-people. 2267
I love Idi Amin. 667, 2178
"I love life!" said Pope John XXIII. 2123
I love the trail. 3522
I love the work impossible. 985
I love Thy house. 2219, 3743
I love to tell the story. 3550
I love you, I hear you. 2339
I loved this people. 3219
I, Luke, being a summary of eyewitness reports concerning Jesus Christ. 430
I, Mark. 436
I married a minister. 1303
I married a missionary. 2545
I married a preacher. 1303
I married a priest. 84, 797, 1582, 2245
I married a witch's love. 2727
I married you. 2340
I meet God through the strangest people. 902
I met a man; imagined remembrances of Jesus. 2029

I met a man with a shining face. 1823
I met a traveller. 2831
I met God there. 164
I, Nathaniel, knew Jesus. 2006
I never promised you a Disneyland. 3886
I never said I didn't love you. 1775, 2388
I offered Christ. 2366
I once spoke in tongues. 1716
I owe my life to Jesus—you also? 985, 2261
I, Paul. 2803
I pick up hitchhikers. 146, 1399
I pledge allegiance. 2794
I pledge you my troth. 2339
I pray the mass. 846
I prayed, He answered. 1601, 3768
I preached in those hills. 2900
I predict. 2946
I promise. 969
I promise God. 1013
I protest. 668, 2755
I recommend the Bible. 232
I remain unvanquished. 1353
I remember Flores. 817
I remember, I remember. 2504
I remember Jesus. 2006
I remember Maynooth. 2375
I saw a new earth. 455
I saw an angel. 1639
I saw God. 1445
I saw Gooley fly. 1013
I saw heaven opened. 457
I saw Israel. 2762
I saw the holy shroud. 1826
I saw the light. 1362
I saw the Welsh revival. 3233
I see 4. 1401
I see what God wants me to know. 904
I seen him when he does it. 1167
I serve the God of miracles. 1426, 3476
I serve the King. 1649
I serve through Christian discipleship. 3886
I shall glorify him. 2139
I shall not want. 579
"I shall return" - Jesus. 3321
I should have seen it coming when the rabbit died. 673, 875
I sing of a Maiden; the Mary book of verse. 2362
I speak. 2389
I speak again. 1955
I speak for myself. 3128
I still believe in God. 62
I stood upon a mountain. 1384
I talked with Noah. 493
I talked with Paul. 338
I talked with spirits. 3520
I teach catechism. 1
I, the prophet. 570, 2298, 3362
I. The reformers and the persecutions of heretics. II. William Tyndale and the English Bible. III. The English Bible in pre-reformation times. 289
I, the story of the self. 3330
I think about God. 899, 1734
I think about Jesus. 1983
I think I'll be. 3181
I, too, am man. 1107
I turned my collar round. 1216
I. W. W. trial. 1905
I wager on God. 3660
I walk a joyful road. 3243
I walk the glory road. 1362
I want happiness now! 981
I want my church to grow. 1170
I want somebody to know my name. 931, 2399
I want that mountain! 2626
I Want to be good. 903
"I want to be like Stalin," 2590
I want to enjoy my children. 2773
I want to live. 1219
I was a Catholic priest. 1366, 1420
I was a Communist prisoner. 2942
I was a monk. 794, 3604
I was a Mormon. 2610
I was a pagan. 1359
I was a stranger. 682, 2596, 3293
I was a teen-age communicant. 978
I was an Algerian preacher. 1365
I was born again. 1362
I was born tomorrow. 961
I was called— to be a layman. 1007, 1778
"I was in prison" 1145
I was made a minister. 1290
I was raised a Jehovah's Witness. 1809, 1940
I was sick and You visited me. 3406
I went to church in New York. 2698
I will be called John. 2123
I will be your God. 535
I will build by church. 1024
I will build my church. 1024, 1184, 1238, 2531
I will come again. 3318
"I will come again"--Jesus. 3319

I will lift up mine eyes. 1349, 2870
I will tell you about God. 620
I wonder. 903
I wonder about Japan. 2534
I-wonder-why stories. 906
I won't be crippled when I see Jesus. 932, 2806
I would do it again. 3671
"I write in anguish". The vivid true-life story of an American family and a boy refugee portrays the human drama of a European tragedy. 2111
Iabal. 1918
"Ian Maclaren" 3798
Ian Ramsey. 1586, 3021
Ian Ramsey, Bishop of Durham; a memoir. 3021
I& II Kings. 555
Iations of Jamaica and I Rastafari. 3022
Iban and their religion. 1880
Iberian fathers. 1018
Ibn Kammuna's Examination of the three faiths. 3138
Ibn Tufayl's Hayy ibn Yaqzan. 2841
Ice cutter. 1901, 3252
Icelandic church saga. 1880
Icelandic meditations on the passion. 1876
Ich dien. 2169
Icon. 1880
Icon and pulpit. 1046, 2746
Icon and swastika. 1149, 2749
Icon painting. 1880
Iconographic dictionary of the Indian religions. 1897
Iconography of Christian art. 1958
Iconography of minor Hindu and Buddhist deities. 3316
Iconography of religions. 3141
Iconography of the Immaculate Conception in the Middle Ages and early Renaissance. 2358
Iconography of Tibetan Lamaism. 2193
Iconography: St. Birgitta of Sweden. 663
Iconologia. 1510
Icons. 1880, 1957
Icons and their history. 1881
Icons from the Elvehjem Art Center. 1509, 1881
Icons in Czechoslovakia. 1881
Icons of angels and prophets. 1881
Icons of Cyprus. 1880, 1881
Icons of St. Nick. 2707
Icons of the Mother of God. 2357
Icons; the Natasha Allen Collection. 26, 1881
I'd gladly go back. 3055
I'd like to ask Sister White. 3811
I'd take this way again. 3125
Idea of a Catholic college. 806
Idea of a Christian college. 1127
Idea of a Christian society. 3448
Idea of a free church. 1123
Idea of a secular society. 1142
Idea of a secular society, and its significance for Christians. 1142
Idea of biblical poetry. 579, 1798
Idea of Catholicism. 755, 780
Idea of Christ in the Gospels. 401, 2011, 2043
Idea of development of the soul in medieval Jewish Philosophy. 2841
Idea of disarmament! 103
Idea of God. 1729
Idea of God and human freedom. 3652
Idea of God as affected by modern knowledge. 1721
Idea of God, historical, critical, constructive. 1732
Idea of God in early religions. 3109
Idea of God in Protestant religious education. 1724
Idea of God in the light of recent philosophy. 1727
Idea of God in the philosophy of St. Augustine. 115, 1728
Idea of immortality. 1890
... The idea of immortality and western civilization. 1887
Idea of perfection in Christian theology. 2818, 2819
Idea of personality in Sufism. 3542
Idea of progress in American Protestant thought, 1930-1960. 2945
Idea of reform. 3658
Idea of revelation in recent thought. 3224
Idea of the church. 1187
Idea of the church, aspects, forms, activities. 1119
Idea of the holy. 1836, 2998, 3062
Idea of the laity. 1243
Idea of the resurrection in the ante-Nicene period. 3221
Idea of the soul. 3462
Idea of the supernatural. 3567
Idea of the symbol. 1306, 3574
Idea takes wings. 2593
Idea to win the world. 2593

Ideal adult class in the Sunday-school. 3565
Ideal Christian home. 1838
Ideal church. 1125
Ideal city for an ideal people. 3762
Ideal Franciscan brother. 1646
Ideal Holy Bible, self-pronouncing, self interpreting, self-explanatory. 271
Ideal life. 1481, 2227
Ideal ministry. 3672
Ideal of a Christian Church considered in comparison with existing practice, containing a defence of certain articles in the British critic in reply to remarks on them in Mr. Palmer's "Narrative" 1124, 1219
Ideal of Christian worship. 2253
Ideal of humanity. 2319
Ideal of Jesus. 1048
Ideal of the monastic life found in the apostolic age. 188
Ideal of the priesthood as illustrated by the life of John Coassini, of the German-Hungarian college in Rome. 1305
Ideal persistent. 3343
Ideal teacher. 805
Ideal world from a Bible standpoint. 3762
Idealist view of life. 1881, 3017
Idealistic conception of religion. 3102, 3778
Idealistic thought of India. 1881, 2840
Ideals. 1537
Ideals and aspirations. 1069
Ideals and realities of Islam. 1923
Ideals for Christian service. 3674
Ideals for earnest youth. 974
Ideals for juniors. 903
Ideals of a young Lutheran. 3884
Ideals of asceticism. 89
Ideals of life. 1534, 3204
Ideals of Mother McCauley and their influence. 2305, 3418
Ideals of St. Francis of Assisi. 1641
Ideals of science & faith. 3078, 3313
Ideals of the Jewish prayer book. 2108
Ideals that have helped me. 2422
Ideals to live by. 2269
Ideas and feelings necessary to national greatness. A sermon delivered before the executive and legislative departments of the government of Massachusetts. 1504
Ideas and ideals. 3624
Ideas and ideals of the Hassidim. 1789
Ideas for a successful church program. 1199
Ideas for a successful pastorate. 3672
Ideas for better church meetings. 1200
Ideas for church embroidery. 1488
Ideas for sermons and talks. 3374
Ideas for the midweek service. 2886
Ideas for young people's programs. 3876
Ideas for youth outreach. 1260
Ideas from nature. 3075
Ideas have consequences. 2834, 3727
... Ideas have legs. 2753
Ideas of Newman. 2705
Ideas of religious toleration at the time of Joseph II. 814
Ideas of revelation. 3227
Ideas of the apostle Paul. 375, 2796
Ideas of the fall and of original sin, a historical and critical study. 1602
... The ideas of the Old Testament. 648
Les Idees maitresses de l'Ancien Testament. 598
Identifying Christianity. 3618
Identity. 1034
Identity and difference. 1881
Identity and distinction in Petrus Thomae, O.F.M. 1881, 2826
Identity and faith in young adults. 3887
Identity and the sacred. 3086
Identity crisis in Black theology. 669
Identity of Jesus Christ. 2038
Identity of primitive Christianity and modern spiritualism. 3498
Identity of the New Testament text. 352
Identity of the priest. 772
Identity of the true Baptist Church. 2941
Identity of the two Apocalyptic witnesses, their character, death and resurrection, as connected with the introduction of the millennium, to which is added, Pious relfections. 465
Identity theory of mind. 2474, 3259
Ideologics of religion. 3099
Ideologies of religion. 3099
Ideology, reason, and the limitation of war. 2159
Idiom book of New Testament Greek. 1771
Idioms in the Bible explained. 314
Idle word. 962, 3071
Idolatry in America. 3745
Idols and ideals. 3122
Idylls of Theocritus. 1771

If a man die. 1413, 1886
If a man die shall he live again? 1531, 1890
If any man thirst. 2258
If any man will. 1561
If being a Christian is so great, why do I have the blahs? 982
If Brother Paul were there: answering Who is teaching heresy? 800
If calmly you listen. 46
If Christ came to Congress. 3737
If Christ had not come. 1555
If Christ is the answer, what are the questions? 988
If Christ were king. 1955, 2175, 3137
If God be for us. 2161, 2436
If God be for us! and other sermons. 1549
If God does not die. 1724
If God is God. 64
If God loves me, why can't I get my locker open? 3883
If God talked out loud. 3886
If God won the war, why isn't it over. 2157
If he should fail. 1560
If I be lifted up. 1998, 3358
If I believe. 3661
If I could find God. 552
If I could pray again. 2894
If I could preach just once. 3364
If I die at thirty. 1398, 3847
"If I forget thee ..." 2099
If I go down to hell. 1056
If I had a bigger drum. 1856
If I had a wish. 492, 3822
If I had my ministry to live over, I would. 1297, 3465
If I had not come. 1069
If I had one sermon to preach. 3350, 3387
If I had only one sermon to preach. 3365, 3366, 3367
If I had only one sermon to preach on immortality. 1890
If I had only one sermon to prepare. 2903
If I have twelve sons. 3387
If I marry outside my religion. 2346
If I perish, I perish. 514
If I should die before I live. 1011
If I should die, if I should live. 1417
If I were a Christian. 955
If I were a Jew. 2085
If I were an angel. 3192
If I were an atheist. 1008
If I were God. 1656, 3354
If I were in my thirties. 2131, 3868
If I were to preach. 862, 1266
"If I were you" 3369
If I were young. 2435
If I'm so free, how come I feel boxed in? 983
If it be of God. 1045
If it matters. 3437
If Jesus came back to earth. 2063
If Jesus came to my house. 1744
If man is to live. 104
If my people. 975, 987, 3218
...If not a united church--What? 1039
If one be lifted up. 2806
If only he knew. 2339
If only I could fly. 2889
If sinners entice thee. 3600
If teaching is your job. 3179
If the Church is to survive. 1118
If the churches want world peace. 1076
If the devil wrote a bible. 1428
If the grain does not die. 1629, 1645
If the minister is to succeed. 3671
If the prophets were alive today. 3439
If, then, and when. 1472
If there is a God, why are there atheists? 67
If they don't come back. 1890
If this be heresy. 3664
If this be religion—. 1063
If thou shalt confess. 978
If thou shalt confess. 978
If today you hear His voice. 1263
If two agree. 2455
If we dared! 976
If we had lived in Bible times. 3765
If we were Christians. 962
If with all your heart. 967
If ye continue. 3288
If ye fulfil the royal law. 1064
If ye love me. 2064
If ye shall ask. 2869
If you ask me. 964
If-you form in Israelite law. 2075
If you love me. 981
If you need healing do these things. 2410
If you want to walk on water, you've got to get out of your boat. 1006
If You were the creator. 3383
If you're there, show me. 1366, 2219
IFA. 1882
Ifa divination. 1882
Ifa divination poetry. 1882

Iglesia Presbiteriana. 2557, 2919
Ignatian approach to divine union. 2269
Ignatian retreat for priests, in five days. 2269, 2394
Ignatian thoughts in sonnet form. 2278
Ignatian way to God. 2267, 3475
Ignatiev and the establishment of the Bulgarian Exarchate, 1864-1872. 1882, 2745
Ignation methods of prayers. 2269, 2379
Ignatius his conclave. 1946, 2268
Ignatius Loyola. 1945, 2268, 2269, 2270
Ignatius Loyola and Francis de Sales. 2267, 3492
Ignatius of Loyola. 2270
Ignatius the theologian. 2269
Ignorance, faith and conformity. 944
Ignorance of certainty. 2653
Igrot tsafon. 2139
I'll die laughing! 1946, 3244
I'll let you taste my wine if I can taste yours. 3885
"I'll make a world" 1383
"I'll not be a traitor!" 3535
Illegal trial of Jesus. 2069
Illimitable one. 1450
Illinois believes. 1883
Illinois conference, Methodist Episcopal church, South. 2455
Illinois conference of the Methodist Episcopal church. 2455
Illnesses of the modern soul. 2783
Illuminated Bible. 271
Illuminated Bible story book for young people. 253
Illuminated Brahmanism. 689
Illuminated faith. 442
Illuminated lessons on the life of Jesus. 1992
Illuminated New Testament. 473
Illuminated way. 3208
Illumination and love. 3251
Illumination on Jacob Bcehme. 674
Illumination on Jacob Boehme. 674
Illumined cross. 1388
Illumined life. 962
Illusion of immoratality. 1889
Illusion of immortality. 1889
Illusions of Christian science, its philosophy rationally examined. 1036
Illustrate! 1915
Illustrate! The 1966 Sunday school lesson. 1915
Illustrate! The 1967 Sunday school lesson. 1915
Illustrate! The 1968 Sunday school lessons. 1915
Illustrated anthology of sorcery, magic and alchemy. 2312, 2725
Illustrated Bible and church handbook. 3639
Illustrated Bible biography. 214
Illustrated Bible for children. 622
Illustrated Bible history and brief outlines of church history. 2715
Illustrated Bible scenes and studies. 3204
Illustrated Bible stories. 294
Illustrated Bible stories for young and old. 624
Illustrated Bible story book. 622, 626
Illustrated Bible story books. 629
Illustrated Bibles from Tours. 602, 1883
Illustrated book of all religions from the earliest ages to the present time. 3117
Illustrated book of Christian ballads and other poems. 3209
Illustrated book of Jewish knowledge. 2085
Illustrated catalogue of the private library of the late Charles Roberts of Philadelphia. 1637, 1677
Illustrated catechism. 769
Illustrated catechism for little children. 770
Illustrated commentary on the Gospel according to St. John. 415
Illustrated commentary on the Gospels. 385
Illustrated commentary on the Gospels according to Mark and Luke. 432
Illustrated dictionary of Bible manners and customs. 209
Illustrated edition of the Revised New Testament. 361
Illustrated encyclopaedia of mysticism and the mystery religions. 2644
Illustrated encyclopaedia of traditional symbols. 3574
Illustrated explanation of the Apostles' creed. 74
Illustrated explanation of the holy sacraments. 3263
Illustrated family hymn book. 1866
Illustrated golden bough. 2651
Illustrated guide to abbreviations, for use in religious studies. 3619

Illustrated guide to ghosts & mysterious occurrences in the Old North State. 1710
Illustrated hand-book to all religions. 3092
Illustrated history of Methodism. 2424
Illustrated history of the Bible. 926
Illustrated history of the Holy Bible. 295
Illustrated history of the Popes. 2770
Illustrated history of the Reformation. 3034
Illustrated life of Jesus. 919, 1957
Illustrated New Testament. 450
Illustrated notes on English church history. 1759
Illustrated prayers, blessings and hymns. 2110
Illustrated Psalms of the Jerusalem Bible. 583
Illustrated Scripture history for the young. 621
Illustrated stories about the New Testament. 626
Illustrated stories from church history. 1233
Illustrated Story Bible. 619
Illustrated study Bible. 614
Illustrated symbols and emblems of the Jewish, early Christian, Greek, Latin, and modern churches. 3574
Illustrated treasury of Bible stories. 623
Illustrated world of the Bible library. 207
Illustrating mirror; or A funndamental illustration of christ's Sermon on the Mount. 3335
Illustrating Sabbath songs for tiny tots-- cradle roll. 3458
Illustrating the lesson. 1916, 3592
Illustration in sermon, address, conversation and teaching. 1841
Illustration of The heavenly ladder of John Climacus. 1884, 2122
Illustration of the types, allegories, and prophecies of the Old Testament. 607
Illustrations and meditations. 2396
Illustrations Chinese Christians. 1109
Illustrations for preachers and speakers. 1839
Illustrations for preachers and teachers. 1839
Illustrations for preaching. 1839
Illustrations for sermons. 3376
Illustrations from art. 1839
Illustrations from biblical archaeology. 209
Illustrations from great literature. 1840
Illustrations from literature. 1841
Illustrations from mythology. 1839
Illustrations from nature. 1842, 1843
Illustrations in choir accompaniment. 2634
Illustrations in the manuscripts of the Septuagint. 1884
Illustrations of Bible truth. 1840
Illustrations of masonry. 1662, 1670
Illustrations of Old Testament history. 486
Illustrations of positivism. 2864
Illustrations of the divine government in remarkable providences. 2981
Illustrations of the history of medieval thought and learning. 2842
... Illustrations of the liturgy. 1223
... Illustrations of the occasional offices of the church in the middle ages from contemporary sources. 844
... The illustrations of the Utrecht psalter. 1884
Illustrations of universal progress. 3471
Illustrations on the moral sense. 1535
Illustrative anecdotes for preachers, Sunday school teachers and the family circle. 1842
Illustrative answers to prayer. 2881
Illustrative lesson notes. 1915, 1916
Illustrative stories for pulpit and platform. 1839
Illustrative teachings of Jesus. 2066
Illustrious gentile Asiatics. 91
Illustrious life of T. De Witt Talmage, the greatly beloved divine. 3582
Illustrious women of Bible and Catholic church history. 3840
Illustrissimi. 793, 1884
I'm a good man, but. 3888
I'm glad you asked that. 3843
I'm glad you called. 2896
I'm gonna fly. 3795
I'm human—Thank God! 993
I'm in love with a married man. 8
"I'm learning from Protestants how to be a better Catholic" 2560
I'm listening, Lord, keep talking. 131, 2383
I'm no hero. 492, 981
I'm no spring chicken, but it's fun being over forty. 1368, 2462
I'm not mad at God. 979
I'm out to change my world. 2169
I'm saved, you're saved—maybe. 3290

I'm still me. 931, 1786
Image and likeness of God. 2323, 2386
Image and pilgrimage in Christian culture. 1022
Image and symbol in the sacred poetry of Richard Crashaw. 1379
Image and the word. 1880
Image-breaking/image-building. 3004
Image of a Christian. 1604
Image of a Christian family. 1604
Image of an oracle. 1702, 3511
Image of God. 1884, 2036, 3346, 3713
Image of God in creation. 1382
Image of God in man. 1884, 2323
Image of God in sex. 3390
Image of his Maker. 2322
Image of joy. 2391
Image of man in C. S. Lewis. 2219, 2327
Image of Mary according to the Evangelists. 2358
Image of the angels. 43
"Image of the beast" 465
Image of the heavenly. 104
Image of the Jews. 2154
Imagery and thought in the metaphysical poets. 1519, 2351
Images and symbols. 3573
Images & themes in five poems by Milton. 2470
Images for self recognition. 2323
Images of authority. 118
Images of divinity. 3316
Images of faith. 969, 1593
Images of hope. 1845
Images of Jesus. 442, 2416
Images of man. 2832
Images of Moses. 564, 2622
Images of religion in America. 3743
Images of the Black preacher. 16
Images of the Christ. 2044
Images of the church in the New Testament. 1163
Images of the future. 3734
Images of women in mission. 2575
Images or shadows of divine things. 38
Imagination and religion. 1884
Le imagini ... degli dei. 2655
Imago Christi. 2004
Imago Dei. 2159, 3002
Imale. 1925
Imitating Christ. 2004, 3492
Imitation of Christ. 1404, 1884, 1885, 1886
Imitation of Christ, in four books. 1886
Imitation of Chrsit. 1885
Imitation of God in Christ. 995
Imitation of Mary. 2354, 2357
Imitation of St. Therese of the Child of Jesus. 3691
Imitation of the Sacred heart of Jesus. 3269
Immaculate conception. 2272
Immaculate conception in the divine plan. 1886
Immaculate deception. 3389
Immaculate Heart. 1618
Immaculate Mother, help! 855
Immaculate perception. 1953, 3132
Immanence: a book of verses. 3208
Immanence and Christian thought. 1886
Immanence & incarnation. 1886
Immanence of God. 1886
Immanence of God in rabbinical literature. 1886
Immannuel Kant. 2163
Immanuel. 1071, 1963, 1971, 1984
Immanuel Kant. 2163
Immanuel Kant's Critique of pure reason. 2180
Immanuel, our King. 400
Immateria medica. 3406
Immensity. 3077
Immersion essential to Christian baptism. 134
Immigrant church. 873
Immigrant pastor. 675
Immigrant saint. 723
Immigrant school learner. 2760
Immigrants and religion in urban America. 3748
Immigrants, Baptists, and the Protestant mind in America. 170
Imminent appearing of Christ. 3320
Imminent prophecies for today's world. 1531
Immobilized Christian. 943
Immolation. 1403, 2334
Immortability. 1889
Immortaility. 3207
Immortal aim. 1887
Immortal chaplain. 1637
Immortal fire. 2525
... The immortal friend. 2187
Immortal garland. 3285
Immortal hope. 1351
Immortal hymns and their story. 1874
Immortal life. 1887

Immortal life, an Easter choir cantata for mixed voices. 736
Immortal longings. 3363
Immortal lovers: Heloise and Abelard. 1
Immortal man. 2694
Immortal master. 3500
Immortal pilot. 1047
Immortal profile. 1970
Immortal rebels. 527
Immortal rebels; freedom for the individual in the Bible. 527
Immortal seven. 2157, 2482
Immortal survival of the human personality. 1888
Immortal tidings in mortal hands. 2496
Immortal words of Christ and the apostles. 472
Immortality. 1527, 1886, 1887, 1888, 1889, 1890, 1891, 2377, 3209, 3515, 3619
Immortality; a rational faith. 1887
Immortality and happiness. 1890
Immortality and how attained. 1889
Immortality and modern thought. 1887
Immortality, and our employments hereafter. 3510
Immortality and resurrection. 1891
Immortality and salvation in Indian religions. 1888
Immortality and the cause of spiritualism. 3502
Immortality and the cosmic process. 1889
Immortality and the future. 1696
... Immortality and the modern mind. 1888
Immortality and the new theodicy. 1888
Immortality and the unseen world. 1531
Immortality established through science. 1892
...Immortality in post-Kantian idealism. 1887
Immortality in the light of modern thought. 1887
Immortality in the light of reason. 3053
Immortality inherent in nature. 3206
Immortality of the soul. 1888, 1889, 1890, 3505
Immortality of the soul and the final condition of the wicked carefully considered. 1892
Immortality of the soul philosophically demonstrated. 3462
Immortality of the soul, religiously and philosophically considered. 1887
Immortality or extinction? 1694
Immortality, religion, and morals. 1891
Immortality triumphant. 1098
Immortality victorious. 3504
Immortals. 2653
Immortals by my side. 696, 3497
...The immortals, who they are. 181
Immutability of Christ and Justinian's condemnation of Theodore of Mopsuestia. 2035
Immutable law. 3497
Impact of American religious liberalism. 2221
Impact of atomic energy. 103
Impact of Christianity on the non-Christian world. 2553
Impact of computers on society and ethics. 1505
Impact of history on theology. 1817
Impact of Israel on the American Jewish community. 1928
Impact of renewal on priests & religious. 772
Impact of science and scriptures on delinquency. 1421
Impact of the church upon its culture. 1183
Impact of the Dead Sea scrolls. 1410
Impact of the future. 1244
Impact of Vatican II (The) 3771
Impact, the exploration of an idea. 2528
Impactivity: youth program resources. 1260
Impaled; the story of Brian Dunn. 1483, 2546
Impartial Christ. 1950, 3125
Impartial narrative of the proceedings of nine ministers, in the town of Cornwall. 1744
Impartial review of testimonies in favor of the divinity of the Son of God. 2002, 3713
Imparting the Christian message. 745, 935, 3151
Imparting the Word. 637
Impassibility of God. 1725
Impatience of a layman. 1050
Impatience of a parson, a plea for the recovery of vital Christianity. 3402
Impeachment of the Bible. 237
Implementing Vatican II in your community. 3772
Impelling need of the hour. 2591

Impending crisis of 1860. 3423
Impending drama. 1513
Impending peril. 2447
Imperative is leadership. 1462, 3681
Imperfect disciple. 994
Imperial Christ. 168
Imperial church from Constantine to the early Middle Ages. 1196
Imperial cities and the Reformation. 3040
Imperial cult under the Flavians. 1395
Imperial government and Catholic missions in China during the years 1784-1785. 2512
Imperial hope. 2055
Imperial intellect. 2702
Imperial ritual of magic. 2312
Imperial voice. 3341
Imperial voice, and other sermons and addresses. 2436
Imperialism and Christ. 1892
Imperialism and religion. 2093, 2152
Imperialistic religion and the religion of democracy. 2996
Imperialism versus the Bible, the Constitution,and the Declaration of independence. 1892
Imperishable dreams. 3341
Imperishable heart. 3338
Imperium and sacerdotium according to St. Basil the Great. 177, 1148
...The impersonal judgment. 2833
Impersonal life. 2225
Impersonation game. 1697
Implementing Vatican II in your community. 3772
Implications, case studies for ethical and spiritual development. 990
Implications of public confession. 1201
Implications of renewal. 1245
Imporovement of the understanding, Ethics, and Correspondence of Benedict de Spinoza. 3472
Importance and value of proper Bible study. 643
Importance of being human. 2323, 2324
Importance of being ourselves. 2932
Importance of being sick. 3407
Importance of family religion. 1611
Importance of inspiration. 305
Importance of prayer. 2872
Importance of teaching. 1309
"Important correspondence," concerning the Presbyterian theological seminary of the North-west, between Rev. Willis Lord ... Jesse L. Williams. 3614
Important historical disclosures about the real manner of the death of Jesus. 1532, 1998
Important office of immense love. 755, 2202
Important questions. 3456
Important religious truths. 3126
Important to me. 975
Impossible community. 1308, 1911
Impossible dream. 665, 731
Imposters of God. 1882
Impregnable rock of Holy Scripture. 201
"Impressions." 1359
Impressions and opinions. 3124
Impressions of a layman. 3676
Impressions of great naturalists. 2675
Impressive inquiries. 2064
Impressive service. 3756
Impressive talks. 3341
Imprison him! 2820
Imprisoned in the brotherhood. 986, 1107
Imprisoned preachers and religious liberty in Virginia. 171
Imprisoned splendor. 1011
Imprisoned splendour. 3027
Improper opinion. 1568
Improprieties of Noah. 631
Improve your church bulletins. 10
Improved funeral manual. 1694
Improved missal-manual. 856
Improved phreno-chart and compass of life. 2844
Improved question-book, and studies on the parables and other instructions of the Saviour. 2028
Improved question-book on the life of Christ. 1992, 3564
Improvement of college, worship. 3756
Improvement of teaching in the Sunday school. 3553
...The improvement of the moral qualities. 77, 1535
Improvement of the understanding. 3472
Improving church education. 934
Improving our leadership. 2204
Improving religious education through supervision. 3153
Improving the small church school. 3556
Improving your church school. 3557
Improving your serve. 3377
Improving your Sunday school. 3558
Improving your teaching. 3153

Imprudence in St. Thomas Aquinas. 3693
Impudent dreamer. 1287
Imputation of Adam's sin. 3414
Imputed rights. 1280
In a barley field. 3030, 3258
In a college chapel. 3340
... In a day of social rebuilding. 3441
In a far country. 30
In a great tradition. 2309
In absolute confidence. 404
In affectionate memory of the Reverend Doctor Lewellyn Pratt of Norwich, Connecticut, who in the fullness of his years passed into the eternal light, onJune the fourteenth in the year nineteen hundred and thirteen. 2867
In after days. 1698, 1888
In aid of faith. 1589
In Albert Schweitzer's realms. 3312
In all His offices. 2041
In all things charity. 3417
In America for America. 1705
In American vineyards. 2584
In an age of revolution. 1281
In and around the book of Daniel. 122, 507
In and out the Andes. 2548
In anybody's town. 3183, 3188
In awe and wonder. 3800
In awe of the ordinary. 993
In behalf of children. 3172
In-between. 3488
In Bible days. 621
In but not of the world. 1123
In but still out. 3837
In case you get homesick. 3886
In charity unfeigned. 2849
In Christ. 376, 1439, 1446, 2637, 2798
In Christ a sketch of the theology of Saint Paul. 376
In Christ, in Canaan. 1950, 3124
In Christ Jesus. 2637, 3163, 3188, 3290
In Christ, my Lord. 2392
In Christ we live. 3264
In Christian love. 3378
In Christ's company. 2384
In Christ's place. 1296
In clearer light. 3646
In clover. 2937, 3316
In commemoration of the fiftieth anniversary of the National council of the Congregational churches of the United States. 1041
In commemoration of the seventy-fifth anniversary of the founding of the First Unitarian Church, Salt Lake City, Utah, 1891-1966. 3287
*In communication with God. 3166
In crossfire of hate. 1650, 2820
In David's town. 2021
In days of old. 535
In debt to Christ. 2032
In defence of Christian prayer. 2868
In defence of free will, with other philosophical essays. 1537
In defence of purity. 889
In defense of God. 1728
In defense of life. 1089
In defense of magic. 2313
In defense of Martin Luther. 2278
In defense of purity. 889
In defense of the faith. 161
In denim and broadcloth. 2284
In Deo veritas: the Catholic Educational Association of Pennsylvania, 1919-1969. 867
In divers manners. 761
In divided and distinguished worlds. 696
In essentials, unity. 1043
In every corner sing. 1209, 1875
In every land. 2549
In face of anguish. 3610
In favor with God and man. 904
In fealty to Apollo. 1518
In four continents. 2926
In full assurance. 963
In garments all red. 1028, 2333
In God we should trust. 3478
In God we trust. 3616, 3716
"In God we trust" (cries the little red penny) 1595
In God we trust; everyday essays on life and philosophy. 3716
*In God's care. 3296
In God's community. 1125
In God's crucible. 3136
In God's defense. 1314
In God's garden. 3285
In God's image. 1890, 2325
In God's presence. 1438
In God's sacred cave. 3222
In gods we trust. 1882, 3747
In good spirits. 3480
In grateful remembrance. 1353
"In green pastures" 3885
In guest of beauty. 3136
In habit. 2581

In hard times. 3050
In harvest fields by sunset shores. 3419
In haven we shall rest. 2766
In heavenly places. 1436
In Him is life. 2637, 3660
In Him the fullness. 168, 342
In Him was life. 1266
In Him was light. 2545
In Him we live. 1440
In His Father's name. 2113
In His footsteps. 1600, 2014, 2018, 2762, 2816
In His healing steps. 1598
In his holy temple. 3859
In His image. 699, 1068, 2322, 2323, 3175, 3585
In his image, but. 1132
In his light. 767
In His likeness. 2004
In His name. 1030, 2894, 3685
"In His name" (poetry and prose) 3199
In His presence. 2387, 2391, 2874
In His service. 1095
In his spirit. 3487
...In His steps. 2014, 2762, 3452
In His steps to-day. 3434
In His steps today. 3402
In Hitchcock, Roswell Dwight. 227
In hoc ligno. 2081
In hoc signo? 833
In holy marriage. 2340
In honor of St. Basil the Great. 177
In honor of Saints Benedict and Scholastica (b. 480) 189
... In honour of Apollonius of Tyana. 57
In hope of God's glory. 376
In human presence - hope. 1323
In Jesus' day. 2121, 2763
In Jesus' name. 2501, 3802
In journeyings often. 1648
In King David's footsteps: decision in Israel - a personal account. 1928
In league with the stones. 1802
In letters of gold. 3531
In loving memory of Rev. William Force Whitaker, D. D. 1508, 3810
In man we trust. 2095, 3821
In many lands. 2121
In many pulpits. 2905
In many pulpits with Dr. C. I. Ingerson. 1342
In many pulpits with Dr. C. I. Scofield. 2905
In memoriam. 40, 102, 672, 1285, 1310, 1399, 1414, 1482, 1483, 1630, 1706, 1748, 1778, 1847, 1921, 2307, 2401, 2422, 2630, 2716, 3315, 3396
In memoriam: Francis Cardinal Spellman, Archbishop of New York. 3471
In memoriam; Minneva J. Neher, Alva C. Harsh, Mary Hykes Harsh. 2683
In memoriam of the Rev. John Kendrick Converse. 1357
In memoriam of the Rev. R. D. Harper, D. D. 1786
In memoriam. Rev. Cyrus Hamlin. 1782
In memoriam, Rev. Frederick R. Gallaher, D.D. 1701
In memoriam. Rev. George H. Atkinson. 102
In memoriam. Rev. John W. Dulles, D. D. 1482
In memoriam, Rudolf Steiner. 3527
In memoriam. Tributes to the memory of Rev. C. P. Gadsden, late rector of St. Luke's church, Charleston S. C. 1700
In memory of a beloved wife and mother. February 26, 1864. 3401
In memory of her. 347, 1102
In memory of me. 3029
In memory of Rev. John Chester Backus, D. D., LL. D. 124
In memory of the life and ministry of the Rev. William Pratt Breed, D. D. 691
In memory of the Rev. George D. Baker, D. D. 131
In modern scientific language defined. 276
In my behalf. 341
In my Father'as house are many mansions. 1071
In my father's house. 2203, 2817
In my Father's house are many mansions. 1071
In My Name shall they cast out devils. 1585
In my own way. 3798
In my soul I am free. 94, 3719
In my understanding. 2880
In my upstairs room. 984, 1845
In no one's pocket. 1090
In no strange land. 1363
In one spirit. 2551
In other words. 3648
In our image. 566
In Our Lady's library, character studies of the women of the Old Testament. 3840
In our midst. 1675

In our time, 1947-1957. 3731
In Palestine at the empty tomb. 2030
In Palestine with the Twenty-third psalm. 2765
In parables. 2024
In pastures green and by waters still. 588
In perilous paths. 2325
In perils oft. 2544
In place of sacraments. 3262
In plain paths. 252
In Potiphar's house. 3392
In praise of Baal Shem Tov [Shivhei ha-Besht]. 3580
In praise of chaos. 996
In praise of folly. 1526
In praise of learning. 940
In praise of Mary. 2882
In praise of Our Lady. 1618, 2359
In praise of Saint Paul. 2804, 3368
In praise of the Blessed Virgin Mary. 865, 2362
In praise of women. 573, 3832
In praise of zero. 3098
In prison ... and visited me. 2942
In pulpit and parish. 2898
In pursuit of Dietrich Bonhoeffer. 676
In pursuit of perfection. 2819
In quest of a kingdom. 2438
In quest of a ministry. 3681
In quest of God. 881, 2508
In quest of God's power. 954
In quest of heaven. 3566
In quest of integrity and other discourses. 3370
In quest of life. 122, 3884
In quest of life's meaning. 978
In quest of light. 3068
In quest of the absolute. 873, 2584
In quest of the best, and other Christ-centered revival sermons. 1555
In quest of the shared life. 191, 1010
In quest of the soul of civilization. 3124
In quietness and confidence. 1448
In remembrance of creation. 87, 601
In remembrance of Me. 839, 1318
In remembrance of Reu. 3223
In retreat with the Sacred Heart. 3269
In retrospect. 656, 697
In royal service. 3466
In sacristy and sanctuary. 839
In search. 2101
In search of a beginning. 1672
In search of a lost people. 2102
In search of a plot. 1012
In search of a religion. 3142
In search of a responsible world society. 1133, 3849
In search of a soul. 2326
In search of a way. 1638, 1851, 1950
In search of a yogi. 1082
In search of ancient gods. 1917
In search of balance. 944
In search of foundations. 3656
In search of ghosts. 1709
In search of God. 501, 1727, 3093, 3140
In search of God and immortality. 1723
In search of God's gold. 2430
In search of God's ideal woman. 1959, 3832
In search of historic Jesus. 2009
In search of humanity. 1520
In search of Israel. 2535
In search of Lehi's trail. 679, 2208
In search of meaning. 3121
In search of mission. 2514
In search of Noah's ark. 2711
"In search of our Sephardic roots." 2376
In search of religious maturity. 2997
In search of the beyond. 996
In search of the hereafter. 3507
In search of the historical Jesus. 2008
In search of the self. 2170
In search of the unknown God. 797
In search of tomorrow. 1282
In search of true wisdom. 675, 2575
In search of truth. 3717
In search of twentieth-century Pauls. 2798
In search of ultimates. 3660
In search of white crows. 3521
In season. 908
In season, out of season. 3620
In-service training for Christian leaders. 953
In-service training study. 953
In silence. 3740
In silence I speak. 1320
In silence I speak; the story of Cardinal Mindszenty today and of Hungary's 'New Order. 1320
In silence they return. 120, 683, 3473
In silence with God. 3479, 3485
In six days. 3082
In soft garments. 763, 804
In soft garments, a collection of Oxford conferences. 3667
In solitary witness. 1931, 1932
In sorrow's lone hour. 1352

In spirit and in truth. 1308, 3485
In spirit and in truth, a book of worship programs. 3856
In spite of danger. 2510, 3431
In spite of dungeon. 2502
In step with Christ. 1013
In step with God. 1446
In step with Jesus. 166, 3883
In step with the infinite for health and happiness. 2389
In step with time. 2527
In such a night as this. 1449
In such harmony. 1311
In terms of life. 3346, 3759
In that case. 3673
In the African bush. 2498
In the Amazon jungles. 1903
In the arena. 3130
In the arena of faith. 974
In the beginning. 4, 203, 204, 523, 525, 536, 627, 630, 1379, 1382, 1383, 1384, 1385, 1496, 1990, 3083, 3508
In the beginning: a handbook for parents. 939
In the beginning, astrology. 95
In the beginning ... Genesis I-III. 525
In the beginning God. 505, 525, 558, 1176
In the beginning God created the heaven and the earth. 534
In the beginning God stands forth. 1381
In the beginning, love. 503
In the beginning there were the parents. 1607
In the beginning was the word. 656
In the beginning was the world. 3473
In the beginnings. 3109
In the Biblical preacher's workshop. 299
In the blowing out of a flame. 709
In the breaking of the bread. 1318
In the bright Syrian land. 2762
In the cauldron of Russia. 3788
In the choir loft. 3577
In the Christian spirit. 997
In the city of confusion. 2211
In the cloudy and dark day. 1351
"In the cross of Christ I glory" 1997
"In the cult kindgom" 2601, 3256
"In the day when I cried Thou answeredst me", Psalms 138:3. 579
In the days of giants. 2665
In the days of Mordecai and Esther. 1532
In the days of Origen. 2743
In the days of the first temple. 2095
In the days of the second temple. 2091
"In the days of thy youth." 3340, 3882
In the early days. 400
In the early days, pages from the annals of the Sisters of charity of the Blessed Virgin Mary, St. Joseph's convent, Mount Carmel, Dubuque, Iowa, 1833-1887. 3417
In the end, God. 1529
In the eyes of others. 786
In the face of death. 1413
In the final days. 509
In the fire. 1822
In the flow of life. 1323
In the footprints of the Good Shepards, New York, 1857-1907. 823
... In the footprints of the Lamb. 1453
In the footsteps of Arminius. 83
In the footsteps of Arminius. A delightsome pilgrim age. 83
In the footsteps of Jesus. 1970, 2764
In the footsteps of Martin Luther. 2280
In the footsteps of Pope John Paul II. 2126, 2861
In the footsteps of Saint Teresa of the Child Jesus. 3691
In the footsteps of the Buddha. 705
In the footsteps of the Master. 399, 434, 1263
In the footsteps of the prophets. 2951
In the fullness of time. 1053
In the fullness of time; the Gospel of St. Matthew explained. 440
In the fulness of time. 1107, 3197
In the gap. 2492
In the Garden. 2132, 3544
In the garden of His love. 1443
In the garden of the Lord. 1446
In the gospel net. 3814
In the gospel net the story of Anna Karine Gaarden Widtsoe. 3814
In the grip of bandits and yet in the hands of God. 2510
In the hands of God. 1067, 2383
In the heart of Hindustan. 1897
In the heavenlies. 363
In the high Andes. 2516
In the hills of Galilee. 626
In the hollow of His hand. 1309, 1351
In the Holy Land. 283, 2848
In the Holy Land with Dr. and Mrs. Martin Hegland. 2762
In the homes of martyrs. 2351

In the hope of His coming. 1043
In the hope of nibbana. 711
In the hour of silence. 1450, 3492
In the house of the Lord. 2108
In the image of Christ. 1000
In the image of God. 2336, 3390
In the interest of Lutheran unity. 2292
In the kingdom of the lonely God. 1775
... In the King's service. 3736
... In the land of new Acadie. 2538
In the land of sweepers and kings (medical missionary work in India) 2531
In the land of the Aztecs. 2540
In the land of the salaam. 2532
In the land of the Santals. 2531
In the land where Jesus lived. 209, 2765
In the lands of pagodas, temples and mosques. 2518
In the light of faith. 3341
In the light of myth. 2649
In the light of the Bible. 996
In the light of the cross. 1995
In the light of the Spirit. 1835
In the light of the supernatural. 3642
In the light of the Trinity. 659
In the likeness of men. 2047
In the lion country. 2545
In the Lord's due time. 1366, 1660
In the manner of Jesus. 1316, 2061
In the margins of the Gospel. 397
In the Master's vineyard. 2284
... In the matter of the presentation of Bishop William Montgomery Brown. 696
In the middle of the world. 1119
In the midst. 962, 1275
In the midst of men. 1636
In the midst stands Jesus. 409, 1961
In the minister's workshop. 2902
In the morning. 1441
In the morning, bread. 1433
In the morning hour. 2397
In the mother's light. 1709, 3866
In the name of Christianity. 2499
In the name of God. 1623, 3069
In the name of the devil. 3828
In the night His song. 1451
In the one spirit. 3133
In the paradise of Krishna. 1082
In the paradise of the Sufis. 3543
In the pillory. 682
In the presence. 2258, 2297
In the presence of God. 1606
In the presence of my Father. 604
In the redeeming Christ. 3486
In the refiner's fire. 3541
In the sanctuary. 2249
In the school of Christ. 179, 3061, 3673
In the school of prayer. 2891
In the school of Saint Francis. 1641
In the second hundred years of Mackville. 2309
In the secret of His presence. 1429
In the secret place. 3851
In the secret place of the Most High. 2872
In the service. 959
In the service of God. 3591
In the service of the King. 806, 3131, 3671
In the service of the lepers. 2537
In the service of the Lord. 1458
In the shade of the juniper tree. 3376
In the shadow of death. 3406
In the shadow of Gomer. 3391
In the shadow of His hand. 130, 170, 3406
In the shadow of Our Lady of the cenacle. 3205
In the shadow of Peter. 1365
In the shadow of the cross. 2031, 2060
In the shadow of the Enlightenment. 2733
In the shadow of the Himalayas. 2529
In the shadow of the Mosque of Omar. 2761
In the shadow of the tabernacle. 1014
In the sight of the Lord. 2211
In the spirit, in the flesh. 999
In the spirit of Saint Francis; conferences for Franciscans. 1645
In the spirit of wonder. 1111
In the steps of Jesus. 2764
In the steps of John Wesley. 1237
In the steps of Moses. 1501, 2621
In the steps of Moses the lawgiver. 2621
In the steps of Pope Paul. 2806
In the steps of St. Francis. 1643, 1646, 1929
In the steps of St. Joan of Arc. 1938
In the steps of the Master. 2762
In the stillness is the dancing. 1737
In the storm. 3716
In the strangest places ... God. 1453
In the swelling of Jordan. 2930
In the tavern of ruin. 3543
In the third place. 1154
In the time of harvest. 2143, 3409

In the time of Paul. 1194, 2801
In the track of the Gospel. 2526
In the track of the storm. 1543
In the tracks of Buddhism. 703
In the twilight of Christendom. 1800
In the unity of the faith. 1046
In the upper room. 419, 2213
In the valley of the Mekong. 850, 2537
In the valley of the Nile. 2517
In the whole Christ. 2388
In the workshop of St. Joseph. 2005
In the world. 1420
"In the world celestial" by T. A. Bland. 3496
In their own way. 904
In these last days. 340
In this free land. 1085
In this generation. 3815
In this moment. 2383
In this name. 3713
... In this sign conquer! 3798
'In Thy courts. 3786
... In Thy light. 2282
In Thy presence. 2388
In time...for eternity. 1266
In time of sorrow. 1352, 1693
In time of temptation. 3600
In time of trouble. 11
In times like these. 163
In touch; selections from Living light. 3883
In touch with Christ. 973, 1954
In touch with God. 1435, 3265
In touch with heaven. 1456
In tribulation. 1353
In tune. 1367, 3697
In tune with God. 1435
In tune with the Infinite. 1907
In two minds. 1592
In unbroken line. 2535
In understanding be men. 3644
In wartime and after. 3473
In Wembo-Nyama's land. 2513
In what life consists and other sermons. 3340
In whom we live. 1266
In wisdom and the spirit. 939
In yellow light. 3504
In your midst. 2496
Inasmuch. 1134
Inaugural address and defense, 1891/1893. 276, 2922
Inaugural sermons, preached at the opening services of St. Ann's on the heights. Brooklyn, N.Y. Published by the vestry. 2972
... Inauguration of George Tybout Purves, D.D., as professor of New Testament literature and exegesis. 306, 2800
... Inauguration of Rabbi Samuel Belkin, PH.D. as president. 186
Inauguration of the Rev. Wm. Van Vranken Mabon, D. D. 2304
Inayat Khan. 1892
Inca gold. 2547
Incarnate Lord. 1893
Incarnate Word. 416
Incarnated and redemmed. 3206
Incarnation. 1892, 1893, 1894, 1977, 3053
... The incarnation a revelation of human duties. 3807
Incarnation and myth. 1894, 2649
Incarnation and principles of evidence. 1893
Incarnation and re-incarnation. 3053
Incarnation and recent criticism. 1892
Incarnation, birth and infancy of Jesus Christ. 1894
Incarnation in our street. 1893
Incarnation in religion and literature. 1893
Incarnation in the sermons of Saint Peter Chrysologus. 1894, 2824
Incarnation in the university. 1893
Incarnation of the Lord. 1892
Incarnation of the Son of God. 1893, 2039
Incarnation of the Word of God. 1894
Incarnation to ascension. 3666
Incendiary fellowship. 1124
Incendium amoris of Richard Rolle of Hampole. 1452
Incense-bearers of Han. 2509
Incense of prayer. 2880
Inchiquin, the Jesuit's letters, during a late residence in the United States of America. 3740
Inchristed men. 3206
Incident at Massena. 672
Incidental illustrations of the economy of salvation. 3295
... Incidents and anecdotes of Rev. Edward T. Taylor. 3590
Incidents and reflections. 1683
Incidents illustrating the doctrines and history of the Society of Friends. 1683
Incidents in a busy life. 3124
Incidents in my life. 3505

Incidents in the life of Madame Blavatsky. 671
Incidents in the life of President Dwight, illustrative of his moral and religious character. 1484
Incidents in the life of the Rev. J. Asher. 3123
Incidents of my later years. 3125
Incidents of the United States Christian commission. 3737
Include me out! Confessions of an ecclesiastical coward. 1061
Inclusive dictionary-concordance. 242
... The incoming millions. 2527
Incomparable Book. 279, 646
Incomparable book, to guide you as you read it through. 312
Incomparable Christ. 1952, 2020, 2043, 3130
Incomparable Paul. 2801
Incomparable salvation. 3295
Incomparable story. 233
Incompatibility in marriage. 3476
Increase and multiply. 1476, 2909
Increase Mather. 2373
Increase Mather vs. Solomon Stoddard. 1166
... Increase of faith. 1070, 1593
Increase of piety. 3233
Increase of piety, or. 3233
Increase of true religion. 3066
Increasing Christhood. 2973
Increasing church attendance. 1162
Increasing church school attendance. 3553
Increasing the effectiveness of the field sales force. 3331
... Increasing values in Jesus. 1951
Incredible alliance. 1507, 3473
Incredible cover-up. 3021
Incredible Dr. Matrix. 3575
Incredible I Ching. 1470, 1878
Incredible messiah. 131, 2682
Incunabulum incunabulorum. 314
Indebted to Christ's resurrection. 2006
Indefinite boundary. 2990
Independence and involvement. 1087
Independence for the third world church. 2495
Independence of the Celtic church in Ireland. 1918
Independence through submission. 2573
Independent Bible study. 639
Independent credends in theology. 3642
Independent or democratic church government, the divinely appointed constitution of the churches of our Lord and Saviour Jesus Christ. 1241
Indescribable Christ. 2020
Indestructible faith. 2113
Index. 1233
Index and reference volume to The Lemegeton of Solomon. 2311
Index canonum. 735, 736
Index-concordance to Emerson's sermons; with homiletical papers. 1511
Index guide to periodicals of the Church of Jesus Christ of Latter-day Saints. 2618
Index Islamicus. 1924
Index of articles on the New Testament and the early church published in Festschrifren. 337
Index of articles on the New Testament and the early church published in Festschriften. 337
Index of Christian art at Princeton university. 2942
Index of Festschriften in religion in the Graduate Seminary Library of Phillips University. 3090
Index of graduate theses in Baptist theological seminaries, 1894-1962. 3090
Index of Gregorian chant. 884
Index of Middle English verse. 1519
Index of Presbyterian ministers. 2922
Index of the pamphlet collection of the Diocese of Connecticut. 3627
Index: the Holy Bible. 300
Index to American Catholic pamphlets. 829
Index to Catholic pamphlets in the English language. 764
Index to Expositions of Holy Scripture. 300
Index to fairy tales, myths and legends. 1589
Index to festschriften in Jewish studies. 1624, 2083
*Index to Jewish periodicals. 2076
Index to occult sciences. 2693, 2731
Index to periodical literature on Christ and the Gospels. 401
Index to periodical literature on the Apostle Paul. 2803, 3678
Index to psychic science. 2992

Index to references to churches, clergymen and religious subjects mainly on the Pacific Coast, in The Pacific, organ of the Northern California Congregational Conference, 1851-1868, made at the San Francisco Theological Seminary, San Anselmo, California, under the direction of the Reverend Clifford M. Drury. 3096
Index to religious periodical literature. 3096
Index to St. Nicholas. 2707
Index to stories of hymns. 1876
Index to the Bible. 227
Index to the Brown, Driver and Briggs Hebrew and English lexicon of the Old Testament. 695
Index to the chant of the Mozarabic rite. 847
Index to the holy Bible. 301
Index to the letters and papers of Frederick Temple, Archbishop of Canterbury, 1896-1902 in Lambeth Palace Library. 3598
Index to the Millennial harbinger. 159, 2464
Index to the New Testament and The topical analysis to the New Testament. 408
Index to the principal works in every department of religious literature. 3626
Index to the prophecies. 301
Index to the records of the Moravian mission among the Indians of North America. 2595
Index to the subjects of obituaries (Sterbfalle, Todesanzeigen) abstracted from Der Christliche Botschafter of the Evangelical Church, 1836-1866. 1546, 2720
Index to the works of John Henry cardinal Newman. 2704
Index to the writings of Saint Francis de Sales. 1650
Indexed Bible. 301
Indexed synopsis of the "Grammar of assent" 2705
Indexed teachers' Bible. 301
Indexes to first periodicals of the Church of Jesus Christ of Latter-day Saints. 1233
Indexes to the Bible. 300
India. 1895
India a problem. 2532
India and Christendom. 1081
India and Christian opportunity. 1895
India and its faiths. 1896
India and its millions. 1814
India and its missions. 2530
India and Malaysia. 1897
India and southern Asia. 1897
India and the Latin captivity of the Church. 3659
India at the threshold. 2529
...India awakening. 1896
India, give me thine heart. 2531
India in conflict. 2532
India in five hours. 819
India mission source book. 2530
India--1925. 2531
Indian and Christian miracles of walking on the water. 2476
Indian and Far Eastern religious traditions. 1895
... Indian and Spanish neighbours. 1900
Indian and white in the Northwest. 822
... An Indian approach to India. 2532
Indian Buddhism. 711
Indian Buddhist sculpture in American collections. 3316
Indian Christ, the Indian king. 2375
Indian Christians of St. Thomas. 3278
...Indian conceptions of immortality. 1895
Indian designs and symbols. 1899, 3574
Indian festivals. 1902
Indian logic and atomism. 2718
Indian menace. 1814
Indian Muslims. 2635
Indian myth and legend. 2663
... Indian [mythology]. 2663, 2664
Indian myths. 1902
Indian philosophy. 2840
Indian philosophy and modern culture. 2839
Indian priest, Father Philip B. Gordon, 1885-1948. 915, 1748
Indian priestess, the life of Chundra Lela. 1116
Indian puberty rites. 3002
Indian realism. 2840
Indian saint. 702
Indian Shakers. 1897, 1901
Indian summer of the heart. 3010
Indian temples. 3600
Indian theism from the Vedic to the Muhammadan period. 1896

Indian theogony. 2664
Indian thought and its development. 1896
Indian thought through the ages. 2839
Indian underworld. 2315
Indian way. 1896
Indiana Baptist history, 1798-1908. 153
Indiana Conference of the Methodist Church, 1832-1956. 2439
Indiana Methodism. 2431, 2452
Indiana survey of religious education. 3166
... Indians and missions. 1903
Indians and white in the Northwest. 822
India's hood unveiled. 2728
India's hurt, and other addresses. 2530
India's outlook on life. 3775, 3776
India's problem Krishna or Christ. 2531
India's religion of grace and Christianity compared and contrasted. 1082
India's religious frontier. 1082
India's religious quest. 1813
Indications of the Creator. 2674
Indications of the first book of Moses. 523
Indications of the second book of Moses called Exodus. 516
Indifferent mean. 7, 1221
Indifferentism. 1904
Indigenous church. 1905, 2550
Indigenous church and the missionary. 2493
Indigenous church principles in theory and practice. 1905
Indirect testimony of history to the genuineness of the Gospels. 394
Indirect testimony to the Gospels, and Christ's mission to the underworld. 394
Indispensable book. 201
Indispensable Christ. 1454
Indispensable soul. 3461
Individual. 1905
Individual and community. 32
Individual and his Orthodox Church. 2746
Individual and his religion. 2996, 3096
Individual and the nature of mass events. 3474
Individual and the social gospel. 3444
Individual evangelism. 1562
Individual in our present-day world. 2997
Individual prayer as a working force. 2872
Individual work for individuals. 1571
Individual worth in a social crisis. 3442
Individualist. 3234
Individualist; a biography of Bert Rhoads. 3234
Individualistic gospel. 3097
Individuality. 71
... Individuality and immortality. 1889
Individuals; an essay in descriptive metaphysics. 2419
Indivisible Isaiah. 543
Indo-Aryan deities and worship as contained in the Rig-Veda. 3776
Indomitable Baptists. 170
Indonesia: church & society. 1101
Indonesia in five hours. 819
Indonesian adventure for Christ. 2533
Indonesian revival. 1171
Inductive approach to biblical study. 650
Inductive method of Bible study. 644
Indulgences. 1905
Indulgences as a social factor in the middle ages. 1905
Industrial agitation. 1905
Industrial chaplaincy. 885
Industrial influence on the psychology of Jesus. 1950
Industrial peace. 1131
Industrial village churches. 3253
Industrial work of the Y. W. C. A. 3878
Industrialization: Brazil's catalyst for church growth. 2953
Indwelling Christ. 2636, 3731
Indwelling God. 1886
Indwelling of the Holy Spirit in the souls of the just. 1828
Indwelling of the Trinity. 2636, 3693
Indwelling Spirit. 1829
Ineffable glory. 3220
Inerrancy. 279
Inerrancy and common sense. 279
Inescapable calling. 3829
Inevitable choice. 67
Inevitable cross. 106
Inevitable encounter. 2931
Inevitable voyage. 3500
Inexhaustible Christ. 3351
Inextinguishable blaze. 1181
Infallibility. 2862
Infallibility and the evidence. 835
Infallibility and the resurrection. 3221
Infallibility debate. 835
Infallibility of the church. 1199
Infallibility of the laity. 2192, 2702
Infallibility of the Pope at the Covncil of Constance. 1857
Infallible? An inquiry. 835

Infallible logic. 2242
Infallible proof. 1997
Infallible Word. 305
Infancy. 857, 1977
Infancy narratives. 1977, 2023
Infancy of religion. 3110
Infant baptism. 1905, 1906
Infant baptism and adult conversion. 1358, 1906
Infant baptism and the covenant of grace. 1906
Infant baptism in the first four centuries. 1906
Infant baptism under cross-examination. 1906
Infant Christ. 1996
Infant class. 3553
Infant King. 1906
Infant of Prague. 1906
... Infant salvation. 1906
Infant salvation according to the Bible. 1906
Infant salvation in its relation to infant depravity. 1906
Infant school teacher's assistant. 3146
Infanticide and the handicapped newborn. 1907
Infernal conference. 1014
Inferno. 3135
Infidel. 3214
Infidel death-beds. 1656
Infidel scourge of God. 3718
Infidel testimony concerning the truth of the Bible. 277
Infidel tradition from Paine to Bradlaugh. 3024
Infidelity: comprising Jenyn's Internal evidence, Leslie's method, Lyttelton's Conversion of Paul, Watson's reply to Gibbon and Paine, A notice of Hume on miracles, and An extract from West on the resurrection. 1098
Infidelity of the times. 1406, 3498
... Infidels and heretics. 19
Infidel's text-book. 232
Infiltration, quotation, notation and illustration used by the late W. Leon Tucker, D. D. 1842
Infinite affection. 1051, 1335
Infinite artist, and other sermons. 3345
Infinite contact. 3509
Infinite God and the Summa fratris Alexandri. 24
Infinite in trinity and unity. 3712
Infinite Presence. 2417
Infinite way. 2694
Infinitely happy. 1012
Infinity of God. 1719
Infinity of questions. 1631, 2638
Inflated self. 1746
Inflation, deployment, and the job prospects of the clergy. 1215
Influence of animism on Islam. 47
Influence of Buddhism on primitive Christianity. 1081
Influence of Calvin and Calvinism upon the American heritage. 727, 729
Influence of Christ in modern life. 1050
Influence of Christ in the ancient world. 3862
... The influence of Christianity of fundamental human institutions. 3522
Influence of Christianity on civilization. 1092
... The influence of Cicero upon Augustine in the development of his oratorical theory for the training of the ecclesiastical orator. 2474
Influence of Greek ideas on Christianity. 1192
... The influence of Islam on a Sudanese religion. 1790
Influence of Islam upon Africa. 1923
Influence of Jesus. 1089, 2012, 2013
Influence of John Dewey in religious education. 1456, 3160
Influence of man on animal life in Scotland. 1581
Influence of prophecy in the later Middle Ages. 608, 1820, 2122
Influence of Puritanism on the political & religious thought of the English. 3006, 3008
Influence of religion in American history. 3745
Influence of Saint Bernard. 194
Influence of spiritual beings upon man. 50
Influence of the apostle Paul on the development of Christianity. 1194, 2800
Influence of the Bible on civilisation. 304
Influence of the Bible on history, literature, and oratory. 1819
Influence of the church on modern problems. 2963
Influence of the Enlightenment on the Catholic theory of religious education in France. 3164

Influence of the Enlightenment on the Catholic theory of religious education in France, 1750-1850. 937, 3164
Influence of the Holy Spirit. 1834
Influence of the Irish on the Catholic Church in America in the nineteenth century. 1920
Influence of the Jews upon civilization. 2084
... The influence of the Spanish mystics on the works of Saint Francis de Sales. 2648
Influence of the synagogue upon the divine office. 2239
Influential theologians on woman. 3832
Informal groups in the church. 1170
Information and illustration. 1839, 3338
Information and inspiration. 3374
...Information, statistics and suggestions. 3875
Informe on the new province of California. 1947
Informe on the new province of California, 1702. 1947
Informed ministry. 2791
Ingathering of members. 1201
Ingersoll. 1907
Ingersoll; a biographical appreciation. 1907
Ingersoll the magnificent. 1907
Ingersoll's Christmas sermon. 1907
Ingersoll's greatest lectures, containing speeches and addresses never before printed outside of the complete works. 1656
Ingersoll's new departure. 3572
Ingham lectures. 2674
Ingri and Edgar Parin d'Aulaire's Book of Greek myths. 2662
Inherit the promise. 476
Inheritance of the saints. 1448
Inheritance: what Catholics believe. 3628
Inigo de Loyola. 2268
Iniquity unfolded! 685, 1406
Initial life. 2325
Initiate consciousness. 3688
Initiation. 2723
Initiation by the Nile. 1502
Initiation, human and solar. 2722, 2723, 2726
Initiation into occult consciousness. 2730
Initiation into yoga. 3866
Initiation to adulthood. 1908
Inititiation and its results. 3688
Ink in his blood. 2182
Inklings of grace. 2393
Inner chamber. 1452, 2880
Inner chamber and the inner life. 2808
Inner chapters. 914
Inner circle. 70
Inner circles. 2856
Inner crusade. 3222
Inner ecstasy. 1716
Inner elite. 738
Inner eye. 2142
Inner eye of love. 2639
Inner growth, outer change. 1244
Inner guidance. 3480
Inner healing. 1598, 1600
Inner healing through healing of memories. 1600
Inner history of the Great Schism of the West. 3308
Inner journey of the poet, and other papers. 1519
Inner kingdom. 1049
Inner land. 954, 3491
Inner life. 35, 970, 1218, 2131, 3489, 3689
Inner life and the Tao-teh-king. 914
...Inner life night thoughts. 1479
Inner life of an inn. 3788
Inner life of the Catholic. 781
Inner life of the soul. 3461
Inner life of worship. 3853
Inner light. 253, 1451, 1825
Inner light, first series. 1443
Inner light, second series. 1451
Inner loneliness. 2245
Inner mission. 2296
Inner mission services on the territory of the Ministerium of Pennsylvania. 1548
Inner mystery. 3500
Inner radiance. 2641, 2740
Inner revolution. 3888
Inner search. 1635, 3490, 3709
Inner sentinel. 3060
Inner signature. 2723
Inner splendor. 1598
Inner story. 2649
Inner teachings of the philosophies and religions of India. 2839
Inner traditions of magic. 2312
Inner victory. 1441
Inner vision, dreams and their interpretation. 1479
Inner visions. 2724

INNER VOICE REVEALS. RELIGIOUS BOOKS 1876 - 1982

Inner voice reveals. 3515
Inner way. 2379
Inner words for every day of the year. 1430
Inner world. 1103, 2823
Inner world of Qohelet. 512
Innere Worte fur jeden Tag des Jahres. 1430
Innermost room. 2393
Innkeeper of Bethlehem. 2006
Innocence and ignorance. 3390
Innocent the Great. 1542, 1908
Innocent III. 1908
Innocent III, church defender. 1908
Innocent I I I Vicar of Christ or lord of the world? 1908
Innocent III, Church defender. 1908
Innovations of the Roman Church. 795
Innovator and other modern parables. 1014
Input/output. 2389
Inquirer's guide. 755
Inquiries. 3633
Inquiries and suggestions in regard to the foundation of faith in the Word of God. 1097
Inquiring faith; an exploration in religious education. 3149
Inquiry. 1891
Inquiry concerning the most important truths. 3664
Inquiry concerning the principles of morals. 1855
Inquiry concerning the relation of death to probation. 2943
Inquiry into being. 2739
Inquiry into faith. 1592
Inquiry into meaning and truth. 3255
Inquiry into our need of the grace of God. 1750
Inquiry into the accordancy of war. 3792
Inquiry into the accordancy of war with the principles of Christianity. 1089, 3791, 3792
Inquiry into the causes of the infidelity and scepticism of the times, 1783. 3024
Inquiry into the consistency of popular amusements with a profession of Christianity. 36
Inquiry into the constitution and discipline of the Jewish church. 1201
Inquiry into the constitution, discipline, unity, and worship, of the primitive church, that flourished within the first three hundred years after Christ. 1192
Inquiry into the deity of Jesus Christ. 1091
Inquiry into the ecclesiastical constitution. 1240
Inquiry into the general principles of Scripture-interpretation. 288
Inquiry into the heresies of the apostolic age, in eight sermons. 1805
Inquiry into the laws of organized societies as applied to the alleged decline of the Society of Friends. 1684
Inquiry into the merits of the Reformed doctrine of "imputation," 1751
Inquiry into the nature of sin. 3410
Inquiry into the nature of the sinner's inability to make a new heart, or to become holy. 3412
Inquiry into the nature of true holiness. 1823
Inquiry into the original of our ideas of beauty and virtue. 1535
Inquiry into the right to change the ecclesiastical constitution of the Congregational churches of Massachusetts. 1337
Inquiry into the Scriptural doctrine concerning the devil and Satan. 1427
Inquiry into the Scriptural import of the words sheol, hades, tartarus, and gehenna. 1699
Inquiry into the scriptural views of slavery. 3424
Inquiry [into the secondary causes which Mr. Gibbon has assigned for the rapid growth of Christianity] (1786) 1196, 1710
Inquiry into the sources of the history of the Jews in Spain. 2094
Inquiry into the truth of dogmatic Christianity. 1654
Inquiry into the usage of bazipo. 134
Inquiry of the United Jewish appeal. 2112
Inquiry program. 753, 951
Inquiry respecting the self-determining power of the will. 1657
Inquisitio de fide. 3033, 3034
... The inquisition. 1908, 1909
Inquisition and Judaism. 1910
Inquisition and liberty. 1908
Inquisition at Albi. 1909
Inquisition at Albi, 1299-1300. 1909
Inquisition from its establishment to the Great Schism. 1909
Inquisition in Spain, and other countries. 1908
Inquisition in the Spanish dependencies. 1908, 1909
Inquisition of the Middle Ages. 1909
Inquisitors and the Jews in the New World. 1909, 2332
Ins and outs of Romanism. 803
Inscape. 1610
Inscriptions of Asoka. 1895
Inscriptions on tombstones and monuments in the burying grounds of the First Presbyterian church and St. Johns church at Elizabeth, New Jersey. 1525
Insearch—discovering the real you. 3477
Insearch; psychology and religion. 2784
Insecurity of freedom. 2139, 2142
Inside Buchmanism. 2593
Inside facts on Europe. 1542
Inside Methodist union. 2440
Inside out. 2355
Inside scientology; how I joined scientology and became superhuman. 3314
Inside story. 354, 932
Inside story of Jehovah's Witnesses. 1941
Inside story of Mormonism. 2610
Inside the husk. 2393
Inside the medium's cabinet. 3501
Inside the occult. 671
Inside the outside. 967
Inside the parsonage. 2777
Inside the synagogue. 3032
Inside the synod, Rome, 1967. 866
Inside the Vatican. 808
Inside the wall. 1109
Inside view of the Vatican Council. 3769
Inside views of mission life. 2481
Insight. 3499
Insight of the Cure d'Ars. 3778
Insight; uncommon sense for common people. 567
Insights and heresies. 3463
Insights for the age of aquarius. 3098
Insights from the Psalms. 586
Insights into holiness. 1823
Insights into modern Hinduism. 1813
Insights into reality. 2702
Insights into religious life. 2569
Insights into the book of Revelation. 455
Insipirational Bible. 263
Inspiration. 306, 1910
... The inspiration and authority of Holy Scripture. 3203
Inspiration and canonicity of the Bible. 305
Inspiration and interpretation. 240
Inspiration and revelation in the Old Testament. 599, 2951
Inspiration and wisdom from the writings of Thomas Paine. 3023
Inspiration explains itself. 305
Inspiration for daily living. 2
Inspiration for today. 3204
Inspiration in common life. 2438
Inspiration in the Bible. 306
Inspiration of Holy Scripture. 305
Inspiration of Holy Scripture, its nature and proof. 305
Inspiration of ideals. 2722
Inspiration of our faith. 2935
Inspiration of prophecy. 2946
Inspiration of responsibility. 691, 1067
Inspiration of responsibility, and other papers. 1067
Inspiration of Scripture. 304, 306
Inspiration of the Bible. 199, 305, 538
Inspiration of the Scriptures. 305
Inspiration or evolution. 205
Inspiration plus revelation equals the Bible. 306
Inspiration Point and its personalities. 1911, 2627
Inspiration under the sky. 1456
Inspirational gleanings. 1910
Inspirational meditations for Sunday school teachers. 3550
Inspirational missionary stories. 1233, 2485
Inspirational reader. 251
Inspirational readings for church and home. 3204
Inspirational short sermons. 1229
Inspirational talks for women's groups. 3844
Inspirational talks for youth. 2604
Inspirational think-it-overs. 2396
Inspirational thoughts for every day. 1435
Inspirational thoughts on the Beatitudes. 181
Inspirational thoughts on the Lord's Prayer. 2249
Inspirational thoughts on the Ten commandments. 1315
Inspirational truths from the doctrine and covenants. 1009
Inspiration's enigma. 593
Inspirations: radio talks and travel sketches. 1069
Inspired children. 3152
Inspired history of the nations, past and future. 296
Inspired letters. 354
Inspired principles of prophetic interpretation. 238, 306
Inspired psalms, selected, and literally translated. 581
Inspired Scriptures. 304, 305
Inspired word. 200, 201
Inspired word: Scripture in the light of language and literature. 200
Inspired words for the inspired life and man's privilege. 3201
Inspired youth. 903
Inspiredp rophetic warnings to all inhabitants of the earth. 2611
Inspiring develotional programs for women's groups. 3856
Inspiring devotional programs for women's groups. 1443, 3856
Inspiring fingertip devotions. 1436
Inspiring lives of sixty famous men. 659
Inspiring messages for daily living. 972
Inspiring stories for children. 908
Inspiring talks to juniors. 907
Inspiritor of the community. 3566
Inspriation and authority of Scripture. 305
Installation, dedication, funeral and other ceremonies. 3598
Installation of Rev. Joseph May as pastor of the First Unitarian Congregational society of Philadelphia, January 12, 1876. 2375
Installation services for all groups. 1911
Installation services for arious occasions. 1911
Instant answers for King's kids in training. 995
Instant Bible. 646
Instant creation—not evolution. 1379
Instant inspiration. 1000
Instant who's who in the Bible. 217
Instead of death. 941, 945
... Instead of "wild oats", a little book for the youth of eighteen and over. 3393
Instinct in religion. 2997
Instincts and religion. 2997
Institute annual. 1956. 2121
Institute on Religion in State Universities. 3757
Institutes of Biblical criticism. 233
Institutes of Biblical law. 1314
... Institutes of Christian history. 1173
Institutes of ecclesiastical history, ancient and modern. 1177
Institutes of ecclesiastical history, ancient and modern ... much corrected, enlarged and improved, from the primary authorities. 1177
Institutes of the Christian religion. 3044, 3643
Institutes of Vishnu. 3782
Institution of the Archpriest Blackwell. 669, 816
Institution of the Christian religion. 3044, 3641
Institutional church. 3672
Institutional nature of adult Christian education. 3168
Institutional work for the country church. 1251
Institutionalism and church unity. 1911
Institutions connected with the Japan mission of the American church. 2970
Instructed heart. 1793, 3795
Instruction and encouragement for Lent. 2209
Instruction and instructional facilities in the colleges of the United Lutheran Church in America. 3733, 3759
Instruction for the ignorant ; Light for them that sit in darkness ; Saved by grace ; Come, & welcome, to Jesus Christ. 3294
Instruction in Christian love, 1523. 957
Instruction in faith (1537) 3661
Instruction in the Christian religion. 3156
Instruction in the Mosaic religion. 2114
Instruction on mixed marriages. 2346
Instructions and prayers for Catholic youth. 838
Instructions for mixed marriages. 2346
Instructions for non-Catholics before marriage. 790
Instructions how to enter the kingdom of God. 3056
Instructions of Saint Louis. 1638, 2261
Instructions of the Prudential committee of the American board of commissioners for foreign missions to the Sandwich islands mission. 2524
Instructions on Christian doctrine. 747
Instructions on Christian morality. 780
Instructions on the Christian family for Sundays and holy days. 1604
Instructions on the prayers and ceremonies of the holy sacrifice of the mass. 2365
Instructions on the religious life. 2577
Instructions on vows for the use of the Brothers of the Christian schools. 3787
Instructions to the living, from the condition of the dead. 1359
Instructive and entertaining fables of Pilpay. 1587
Instructive communications from spirit life. 3473, 3474
Instructor's manual for Luther's Small catechism. 747, 2279
Instrument of thy peace. 2394, 2887
Instrument of Your peace (An) 2805
Instrumental ensemble in the church. 2633
Instrumental music and New Testament worship. 2633
Instrumental music in the church. 1203
Instrumental music in the public worship of the church. 2633
Instrumental music is scriptural. 2633
Insuppressible book. 3471
Insurgent spring. 1086
Intangible inheritance. 2206
Integral yoga. 3864
Integrated curriculum at work. 830
Integrated program of religious education. 3151
Integrated transits. 97
Integrating arts and crafts in the Jewish school. 2073
Integrating psychology and theology. 1107
Integration in Catholic colleges and universities. 88
Integration of human knowledge. 1854
Integration of psychology and theology. 1107
Integration of religion and psychiatry. 2996
Integrative preaching. 2907
Integrity. 1911
Integrity of Anglicanism /Stephen W. Sykes. 44
Integrity of Christian science. 1036
Integrity of church membership. 1201
Integrity of I Maccabees. 488
Integrity of mission. 2555
Integrity of preaching. 2902
Integrity of the church. 1119
Integrity of worship. 2235
Intellectual adventure of ancient man. 3212
Intellectual crisis confronting Christianity. 3344
Intellectual crisis in English Catholicism. 807, 2221
Intellectual foundation of faith. 3106
Intellectual honesty. 3758
Intellectual honesty, and other addresses. 3758
Intellectual honesty and religious commitment. 3060
Intellectual interests of Engelbert of Admont. 1515
Intellectual legacy of Paul Tillich. 3699
Intellectual milieu of John Dryden. 1481
Intellectual mysticism. 2640
Intellectual pleasures of the Puritans. 3008
Intellectual tradition in the Old Testament. 3822
Intelligent agnostic's introduction to Christianity. 66
Intelligibility and the philosophy of nothingness. 2834
Intelligible religion. 3063
Intelligible world. 2419, 2420
Intended for pleasure. 2340
Intent of Jesus. 1340, 1994
... The intention of Jesus. 2036

Inter-communion with God. 2881
Inter-related analysis of the Bible. 645
Intercession of Our Lord. 1950
Intercession services for congregational use in public worship. 1338
Intercessory prayer. 2868
Interchurch Center. 2698
Interchurch community programs. 1042
Interchurch cooperation in Kentucky, 1865 to 1965. 2167
Interchurch government. 1169
Interclass competitive tests in Christian doctrine. 769
Intercommunion. 1912, 3849
Interdenominational conference. 1912
Interdenominational survey of metropolitan Louisville, Kentucky, January 1944. 3435
Interdict. 1912

Interdisciplinary approaches to learning disorders. 2204
Interest of the Bible. 500
Interesting extracts, from the journals of the Rev. John Wesley, A. M. 3805
Interesting facts of the Russian revolution. 2545, 3788
Interesting views of Christianity. 1097
Interests of young men. 3872
Inter-faith organizations, 1893-1979. 3111
Intergerini parietis septum (Eph. 2:14) 177, 3622
Intergrity of preaching. 2902
Interim report on the books Jesus & Christ. 3307
Interior Carmel. 2266
Interior castle. 3489, 3603
Interior life. 3485, 3487
Interior life of St. Thomas Aquinas. 3693
Interior life of the social worker. 856, 857
Interior life simplified and reduced ot its fundamental principle. 3487
Interior of Jesus and Mary. 1966
Interior prayer: the exercise of personality. 2380
Interlinear Aramaic-English Old Testament. 492
Interlinear Bible. 306
Interlinear literal translation of the Greek New Testament. 1768, 1769
Interlinear literal translation of the Hebrew Old Testament. 307, 538
Interludes. 1440
Interludes in a woman's day. 1454
Intermediate B.Y.P.U. manual. 142
Intermediate Bible narratives. 250
Intermediate department. 3553
Intermediate department of the Sunday school. 3555
Intermediate expressional services. 3160
Intermediate fishers. 3181
Intermediate historical catechism on the Old Testament. 496
Intermediate leadership manual. 3167
...Intermediate method in the church school. 3167
Intermediate plans and methods. 142
Intermediate spiritual metaphysics. 79
Intermediate studies of the human aura. 117
Intermediate Sunday school work. 3153, 3167
...The intermediate worker and his work. 2443
Intermediate world. 1912
Intermediate worship services. 3859
Intermediates in action, through the Sunday school. [Teacher's ed.]. 3181
Intermediates in the learning fellowship. 1015
Intermediates in training. 3181
Intermediates' worship programs. 3858
Internal Christ. 3819
Internal evidence of inspiration. 306
Internal evidences of the genuineness of the Gospels. 395
International aspect of the missionary movement in China. 2512
International aspects of Christianity. 1407
International aspects of German racial policies. 2078
International Bible commentary. 222
International Bible dictionary. 246
International book of sacred song. 3271
International brotherhood through service clubs. 3141
"international" Christian worker's New Testament. 352, 479
International church worker. 2517
International Conference for World Peace and Social Reform & Human Rights Prayer Day, 1976. 3314
International convention, Disciples of Christ. 1461
International Convention on Missionary Medicine in review. 2539
International curriculum guide for the development of a comprehensive program in Christian education. 3152
International directory of religious information systems. 3096
International esoteric and illuminated Bible lessons. 654
International golden rule Sunday. 1744
International lesson annual (the) 1968. 1915
International Lesson annual 1960 (The) 1915
International lesson annual. 1956. 1915
International lesson annual (the) 1915
International lesson annual (The) 1963. 1915
International lesson annual (The) 1965. 1915
International lesson system. 1916
International morality. 1077

International "mystery schools" directory. 3138
International Nietzsche bibliography. 2710
International problems and the Christian way of life. 1914, 1913, 1914
International relations. 1913
International revision commentary on the New Testament. 344
International standard Bible encyclopaedia. 244
International standard Bible encyclopedia. 244
International Sunday school lessons. 1915
International survey of the Young men's and Young women's Christian associations. 3878
International teachers' handy Bible encyclopedia and concordance. 244, 247, 1512
International theological library. 3612
Internationalization of Jerusalom. 1943
Interpleader. 2561
Interpretation and belief. 3620
Interpretation and community. 288
Interpretation and Dionysos. 1459
Interpretation and imagination. 2905
Interpretation of Biblical history in the Antiquitates Judaicae of Flavius Josephus. 2134, 2144
Interpretation of Christian ethics. 944
Interpretation of cosmic and mystical experiences. 2987
Interpretation of dreams. 1479
Interpretation of dreams in the ancient Near East. 1479
Interpretation of existence. 2739
Interpretation of four regal Psalms (Pss. 2, 110, 45, and 72) 576
Interpretation of Genesis. 522, 523
Interpretation of India's religious history. 1896
Interpretation of Islam. 2565
Interpretation of life. 1371
Interpretation of nature. 3076
Interpretation of plainchant. 883, 885
Interpretation of prayer in the early church. 2885
Interpretation of prophecy. 609
Interpretation of religion. 3056
Interpretation of St. John. 416
Interpretation of St. John's gospel. 344, 416
Interpretation of St. John's Revelation. 454
Interpretation of St. Luke's Gospel. 428
Interpretation of St. Mark's and St. Luke's Gospels. 433
Interpretation of St. Matthew. 440
Interpretation of St. Matthew's Gospel. 441
Interpretation of St. Paul's Epistle to the Romans. 468
Interpretation of St. Paul's Epistles to the Colossians, to the Thessalonians, to Timothy, to Titus and to Philemon. 371
Interpretation of St. Paul's Epistles to the Galatians, to the Ephesians and to the Philippians. 371
Interpretation of St. Paul's First and Second epistle to the Corinthians. 345
Interpretation of Scripture. 236
Interpretation of the Acts of the apostles. 329
Interpretation of the Bible. 233
Interpretation of the Bible in the Mishnah. 2478
Interpretation of the English Bible. 221
Interpretation of the entire New Testament. 344
Interpretation of the Epistle to the Hebrews and of the Epistle of James. 403
Interpretation of the epistles of St. Peter, St. John and St. Jules. 368
Interpretation of the Fourth Gospel. 419
Interpretation of the Gospel law and commentary on the Epistle tc the Hebrews (both in extenso) including historical theological knowledge of great benefit to the Jews and a supplementary monograph on baptism. 386
Interpretation of the New Testament. 351
Interpretation of the New Testament, 1861-1961. 351
Interpretation of the Revelation of St. John the Divine. 455
Interpretation of the Scriptures. 287
Interpretation of the Scriptures by the Scriptures. 252
Interpretation of the spiritual philosophy. 2836
Interpretation of the symbols of the book of Revelation. 3224
Interpretation of Whitehead's metaphysics. 2417, 3813
Interpretations and forecasts. 3439

Interpretations for the weekly Torah reading. 562, 658
Interpretations of the attributes of the principal fabulous deities. 2655
Interpretative statistical survey of the world mission of the Christian church. 2520
Interpreted by love. 1339
Interpreter. 1341
Interpreter of Buddhism to the West. 84, 704
Interpreter with his Bible. 288
Interpreter's Bible. 222
Interpreter's dictionary of the Bible. 244
Interpreters needed. 166
Interpreters of God. 3675
Interpreters of Luther. 2279
Interpreter's one volume commentary on the Bible. 222
Interpreting basic theology. 3663
Interpreting God's word for today. 288
Interpreting God's word today. 239
Interpreting Jewish life. 3370
Interpreting Luther's legacy. 2278
Interpreting Paul's gospel. 376
Interpreting prophecy. 606
Interpreting religion. 3106
Interpreting religious experience. 1585
Interpreting Revelation. 457
Interpreting the atonement. 104
Interpreting the Beatitudes. 180
Interpreting the Bible. 237, 287, 310
Interpreting the Bible to youth. 636
Interpreting the Book of Revelation. 460
Interpreting the church through press and radio. 3002
Interpreting the doctrine of God. 1473
Interpreting the Gospels. 388
Interpreting the Gospels for preaching. 397
Interpreting the Hebrew Bible. 503, 3249
Interpreting the Lord's Supper. 2251
Interpreting the miracles. 2017, 2476
Interpreting the New Testament. 405, 410
Interpreting the New Testament today. 346
Interpreting the Old Testament. 500
Interpreting the parables. 2025
Interpreting the prophetic tradition. 568, 2950
Interpreting the resurrection. 2051, 3220
Interpreting the scriptures. 311
Interpreting the Sunday Mass. 2365
Interpreting the word of God. 288
Interrelation of the Old and New Testaments. 451
Inter-religious encounters in West Africa. 1389, 2487
Interrobang. 3883
Interruption of eternity. 3065
Intersections. 1004, 2042
Interspersed harmony of the life and journeys of Christ. 382
... The interstices required for the promotion to orders. 2741
Interview with the Dalai Lama. 699
Interviewing God. 2881
Interviews. 880
... Interviews with spirits, Joan of Arc.-- Napoleon Bonaparte [and others]. 3516
Interwoven Gospels. 382
Interwoven Gospels and Gospel harmony. 382
Intimacy. 2785
Intimacy and ritual. 3521
Intimacy with Jesus. 2048
Intimate disciple. 3235
Intimate glimpses of the rabbi's career. 192
Intimate Gospel. 420
Intimate view of Robert G. Ingersoll. 1907
Intimations of immortality. 1889, 1890
Intimations of immortality: and ode. 2857
Intimations of immortality from recollections of early childhood and other poems. 2857
Into a nation. 734
Into a new age and other sermons. 2930, 3350
Into all the world. 1195, 2502, 2518, 2549
"Into all the world." the great commission: a vindication and an interpretation. 2504
Into Aztec land. 2540
Into covenant life. 966
Into His likeness. 968, 1968
Into his splendid light. 1263
Into meditation now. 2379
Into my storehouse. 3530
Into the arena. 1012
Into the clouds. 1513
Into the deep. 2741
Into the glory. 11, 2159
Into the high country. 2340
Into the highways and hedges. 1563
Into the holiest. 403
Into the light of Christianity. 1941

Into the mind of God. 1720
Into the new age. 1064
Into the strange unknown. 91
Into the unknown. 2726
Into the whirlwind. 654
Into the wilderness. 2067, 3600
Into the woods, and other favorite verses. 1448
Into this land. 1304
Into this world and out again. 2855
Into Thy hands. 2305, 3418
Intolerance. 2820, 3703
Intolerance in the reign of Elizabeth, Queen of England. 1146
Intolerance of Christianity. 1050
Intoxication of power. 1109
Intrareligious dialogue. 3123
Intrigue in Santo Domingo. 155
Introduccion al Antiguo Testamento, por F. Lange. 540
Introducing Aldersgate Biblical series. 3152
Introducing animism. 47
Introducing Biblical literature. 314
Introducing Buddhism. 702, 708, 2125
Introducing Christian ethics. 942
Introducing Christianity. 1096
Introducing church growth. 1171
Introducing contemporary Catholicism. 811
Introducing Hinduism. 1814
Introducing Islam. 2566
Introducing Jacques Ellul. 1509
Introducing New Testament theology. 476
Introducing religion. 3058
Introducing the Bible. 311
Introducing the Christian faith. 951
Introducing the lessons of the church year. 314
Introducing the New Testament. 410
Introducing the Old Testament. 539, 540, 541
Introducing the Orthodox Church, its faith and life. 2745
Introducing the proposed Book of common prayer. 2958
Introducing the saints. 3281
Introductin to yoga. 3864
Introducting the Bible. 636
Introduction. 331, 490, 540
Introduction and use of the graded lessons. 2426, 2443, 3551
Introduction copy of The power that lies in right thinking. 2695
Introduction in the Baptist faith. 148
Introduction of Christianity into the Hawaiian Islands. 2524
Introduction to A Catholic catechism. 755
Introduction to a course of lectures on the early Fathers. 1293
Introduction to a devout life. 2387
Introduction to a devoute life, 1613. 2387
Introduction to a philosophy of religion. 3106
Introduction to a scientific system of mythology. 2649
Introduction to African religion. 13
Introduction to Anglican polity. 44
Introduction to Anselm's argument. 49, 1739
Introduction to Asian religions. 3142
Introduction to Augustine. 116
Introduction to Barth's Dogmatics for preachers. 175, 177
Introduction to Bible archaeology. 207, 208
Introduction to Bible study. 596, 637
Introduction to Biblical archaeology. 207
Introduction to Biblical astrology and modern world problems. 1513
Introduction to Biblical Christian education. 935
Introduction to Biblical chronology. 218
Introduction to Biblical Hebrew. 1797
Introduction to Biblical literature. 597
Introduction to books of the Old Testament. 540
Introduction to Buddhist psychology. 710
Introduction to catechetics. 746
Introduction to Catholic action. 753
Introduction to Catholicism. 782
Introduction to christian apologetics. 57, 62
Introduction to Christian camping. 1164
Introduction to Christian doctrine. 767, 3660, 3661
Introduction to Christian economics. 1075
Introduction to Christian education. 934, 3156, 3159
Introduction to Christian faith. 3651
Introduction to Christian missions. 2493
Introduction to Christian philosophy. 2837
Introduction to Christian theology. 1106, 3660
Introduction to Christian theology today. 3618
Introduction to Christian worship. 2235

Introduction to Christianity. 66, 74, 1053, 1055, 1094, 3640
Introduction to church history. 811
Introduction to church music. 1209
Introduction to classical scholarship. 1286
Introduction to college theology through sacred Scripture. 646
Introduction to college theology through sacred Scripture, a course designed for college students. 646
Introduction to comparative mysticism. 2643
Introduction to contemporary preaching. 2897
Introduction to divine and human readings. 3668
Introduction to dogmatic theology. 3644, 3660
Introduction to education. 805
Introduction to Egyptian religion. 1502
Introduction to English canon law. 1489
Introduction to English church architecture from the eleventh to the sixteenth century. 1160
Introduction to English liturgical colours. 1310
Introduction to Ethiopic Christian literature. 1540
Introduction to evangelical Christian education. 3151
Introduction to freemasonry. 1661
Introduction to French church architecture. 1159
Introduction to general metaphysics. 2418
Introduction to Hegel. 1800
Introduction to hermeneutics. 287, 3656
Introduction to holiness. 2819, 3691
Introduction to homiletics. 2899
Introduction to icons. 1880
Introduction to Indian religious thought. 1897
Introduction to Islam. 1921
Introduction to Islamic civilization. 1283, 2184
Introduction to Islamic cosmological doctrines. 1371, 1926
Introduction to Islamic theology and law. 1921
Introduction to Jesuit life. 1946
Introduction to Jesus for the twentieth century. 1995
Introduction to Jewish Bible commentary. 504
Introduction to Johannes Galliculus. 1208, 1701
Introduction to John and the Acts of the apostles. 422
Introduction to Judaism. 2118, 2139, 2146, 2154
Introduction to Jusaism. 2113
Introduction to Kant's Critique of pure reason. 2164
Introduction to Karl Barth. 175, 3641
Introduction to Kings, Later Prophets, and Writings. 631
Introduction to liturgical theology. 2748
Introduction to Lutheran symbolics. 2285
Introduction to Mahayana Buddhism. 702, 2317
Introduction to Mennonite history. 2406
Introduction to metaphysics. 2416, 2418, 2419, 2420, 2738
Introduction to missionary service. 2482
Introduction to moral theology. 948
Introduction to myth. 2649
Introduction to mythology. 2653
Introduction to natal astrology. 95
Introduction to natural theology. 2673
... An introduction to Navaho chant practice. 1901
Introduction to New Testament. 351
Introduction to New Testament Greek. 1770
Introduction to New Testament literature. 211, 348, 350
Introduction to New Testament study. 411
Introduction to New Testament textual criticism. 351
Introduction to New Testament thought. 476
Introduction to Old Testament Study. 504
Introduction to Old Testament times. 537
Introduction to ontology. 2738
Introduction to parish church architecture. 1159
Introduction to pastoral care. 2783
Introduction to pastoral counseling. 2781
Introduction to Paul. 2799
Introduction to Pharisaism. 2828
Introduction to Philo Judaeus. 2831
Introduction to pneumatology. 2998
Introduction to prayers and holidays for the student. 901
Introduction to prophecy. 608
Introduction to Protestant dogmatics. 3645

Introduction to psychology and counseling. 2781
Introduction to Puritan theology. 3008
Introduction to Rabbi Samson Raphael Hirsch's Commentary on the Torah. 562
Introduction to Radhakrishnan. 3017
Introduction to religion. 3061
Introduction to religions of the East. 3267
Introduction to religious counseling. 2781
Introduction to religious education. 3156
Introduction to religious philosophy. 3101, 3102
Introduction to Sacred Scripture. 310
Introduction to Saint Gregory Palamas. 2760
Introduction to Saint Thomas Aquinas. 3636
Introduction to scholastic philosophy. 3309
Introduction to scholastic philosophy, medieval and modern. 3309
Introduction to Scripture. 311
Introduction to speculative logic and philosophy. 1800, 2242
Introduction to spirituality. 3485
Introduction to Sufi doctrine. 3542
Introduction to Swedenborg's religious thought. 2689, 3570
Introduction to Tantric Buddhism. 3586
Introduction to the Acts of the apostles and the Epistles of St. Paul. 331
Introduction to the Apocrypha. 489
Introduction to the Apocryphal books of the Old and New Testament. 488
Introduction to the Bible. 294, 308, 309, 310, 311, 312
Introduction to the Bible as literature. 211
Introduction to the Bible for teacher of children. 636
Introduction to the Bible for teachers of children. 636
Introduction to the Book of Mormon. 679
Introduction to the books of the Apocryphias. 490
Introduction to the books of the New Testament. 409
Introduction to the books of the Old Testament. 540
Introduction to the canonical books of the Old Testaments. 539
Introduction to the Christian religion. 1328
Introduction to the Code of Maimonides (Mishneh Torah) 2074, 2623
Introduction to the critical study. 310
Introduction to the critical study and knowledge of the Holy Scriptures. 310
Introduction to the critical study of the text of the Hebrew Bible. 505
Introduction to the devotional study of the Holy Scriptures. 638
Introduction to the devout life. 2387
Introduction to the Episcopal Church. 2956
Introduction to the Epistles. 1262
Introduction to the Epistles and Gospels of the church year. 1262
Introduction to the faith of Catholics. 3628
Introduction to the fifth book of Hooker's treatise Of the laws of ecclesiastical polity. 1214, 1844
Introduction to the first three Gospels. 397
Introduction to the Fourth gospel. 420
Introduction to the geography of the New Testament, comprising a summary chronological and geographical view of the events recorded respecting the ministry of Our Saviour. 381
Introduction to the Gospel. 2610
Introduction to the great creeds of the church. 1385
Introduction to the great religions. 3114
Introduction to the history of Christianity, A.D. 590-1314. 1185
Introduction to the history of early New England Methodism. 2431
Introduction to the history of early New England Methodism 1789-1839. 2431
Introduction to the history of mysticism. 2645
Introduction to the history of religions. 3140
Introduction to the history of the Assyrian church. 93
Introduction to the history of the Christian church. 1172
Introduction to the history of the Church of England, from the earliest times to the present day. 1221
Introduction to the Holy Land, based on modern tour routes. 2762
Introduction to the Ignatian exercises. 2269, 2384
Introduction to the intertestamental period. 492, 2149

Introduction to the law of Christ. 947
Introduction to the law of the Aramaic papyri. 2074
Introduction to the life of Christ. 389, 1966, 1987
Introduction to the life of Jesus. 1986
Introduction to the literature and thought of the Bible. 312
... An introduction to the literature of the New Testament. 410
Introduction to the literature of the Old Testament. 539
Introduction to the liturgical year. 840
Introduction to the liturgy. 2235
Introduction to the liturgy of the Lord's Supper. 2257, 2961
Introduction to the Massoretico-critical edition of the Hebrew Bible. 530
Introduction to the metaphysics of St. Thomas Aquinas. 2419
Introduction to the Negro churches in the Church of God Reformation Movement. 1228
Introduction to the new hermeneutic. 405, 1689, 3070
Introduction to the New Testament. 408, 409, 410, 411, 658
Introduction to the New Testament through behavioral objectives. 474
Introduction to the non-Pauline epistles. 368
Introduction to the Old Testament. 311, 539, 540, 541
Introduction to the Old Testament as Scripture. 539
Introduction to the Old Testament, from its origins to the closing of the Alexandrian canon. 541
Introduction to the Old Testament: "Hear, O Israel." 541
Introduction to the Old Testament in Greek. 528
Introduction to the Old Testament Prophets. 568
Introduction to the parables of Jesus. 2026
Introduction to the philosophy of being. 2418
Introduction to the philosophy of Bernard Lonergan. 2245
Introduction to the philosophy of mind. 2474
Introduction to the philosophy of religion. 3097, 3098, 3100, 3101, 3103, 3104
Introduction to the philosophy of Saint Augustine. 3634
Introduction to the philosophy of St. Thomas Aquinas. 3695
Introduction to the poetic books of the Old Testament. 1798
Introduction to the Prayer-book. 1214, 2960
Introduction to the principles of religious education. 3149
Introduction to the Psalms. 584
... Introduction to the psychology of religion. 2997, 3000
Introduction to the Rabbinic Bible. 2364
Introduction to the reformed tradition. 3679, 3680
Introduction to the Revised standard version of the New Testament, by members of the revision committee. Luther A. Weigle, chairman. 362, 513
Introduction to the right understanding of the oracles of God. 231
Introduction to the Saints Church. 3216
Introduction to the science of comparative mythology and folklore. 2651
Introduction to the science of metaphysics. 2418
Introduction to the science of missions. 2491
Introduction to the science of religion. 3122
... An introduction to the study of Christian apologetics. 63
Introduction to the study of Christian missions. 2492
... An introduction to the study of comparative religion. 3109
Introduction to the study of foreign missions. 2520
Introduction to the study of pastoral theology. 2787, 3674
Introduction to the study of religion. 3067
Introduction to the study of the Bible. 635, 642
Introduction to the study of the Book of Mormon. 679
Introduction to the study of the books of the New Testa- ment. 410
Introduction to the study of the Gospel of St. John. 418
Introduction to the study of the Gospels. 398
Introduction to the study of the Holy Scriptures. 310

Introduction to the study of the New Testament. 410
Introduction to the study of the tarot. 3588
Introduction to the symbolical books of the Lutheran church. 2286
Introduction to the Talmud. 3583, 3584
Introduction to the Talmud and Midrash. 3583, 3585
Introduction to the teaching of Jesus. 2066
Introduction to the textual criticism of the Greek New Testament. 351
Introduction to the Theological summa of St. Thomas. 3696
Introduction to the theology of Albrecht Ritschl. 3239
Introduction to the theology of the New Testament. 477
Introduction to the theosophy of Christ. 3684
Introduction to the Thessalonian epistles. 478
Introduction to the works of Bonaventure. 675
Introduction to the writings of Andrew Jackson Davis. 3499
Introduction to the writings of Saint Teresa. 3603
Introduction to the Yoga philosophy. 3866
Introduction to theology. 3615, 3616, 3650, 3665, 3669
Introduction to Zen Buddhism. 3895
Introduction to Zen Buddhism, including "A manual of Zen Buddhism. 3892
Introductions east & west. 3490
Introductions to the Bahai revelation. 127
Introducton to metaphysics. 2416
Introductory Bible studies. 641
Introductory bibliography for the study of Scripture. 644
Introductory grammar of New Testament Greek. 1769
Introductory guide to the Old Testament. 541
Introductory lectures in systematic theology. 3649
Introductory lectures on the Oxford reformers, Colet, Erasmus and More. 1307
Introductory lessons on Christian evidences. 1100
Introductory metaphysics. 2417
Introductory New Testament Greek course. 1770
Introductory preface of the people's new covenant. 474
Introductory sketch to the Martin Marprelate controversy. 1588-1590. 2336
Introductory studies in contemporary theology. 3657
Introductory studies in Newman. 2704
Introductory theological wordbook. 3638
Introits and graduals for the church year. 1917
Introits and hymns. 1917
Introits for the church year. 1917
Intruders. 2586, 2727
Intuition. 1917
Intuition of the will. 1918
Intuitive cognition. 3309
Invaded church. 1153
Invading gospel. 1094
Invasion from the East. 3122
Invasion of demons. 1423
Inventory of church archives. 1687
Inventory of church archives of Virginia. 171
Inventory of large additions to the correspondence of Samuel Farmar Jarvis (1786-1851) historian, internationalist, Connecticut churchman, friend to literature, and collector of rare books and paintings. 1936
Inventory of the records of the particular (Congregational) churches of Massachusetts gathered 1620-1805. 1337
Inventory of unpublished material for American religious history in Protestant church archives and other repositories. 3740
Investigating the Book of Mormon witnesses. 680
Investigation of that false, fabulous and blasphemous misrepresentation of truth. 2759
Investigations in occultism. 2729
Investiture controversy. 1918
Investment. 3529
Investment of truth. 3339
Investment, the miracle offering. 3529
Invincible advance. 2522
Invincible Christ. 2931
Invincible company. 2510
Invincible cross. 104

Invincible Jew. 373, 2800
Invincible power. 2264
Invisible Christ. 1954
Invisible encounter. 3482
Invisible halos. 1368
Invisible helpers. 2203
Invisible landscape. 1879, 2473
Invisible presence. 502, 3509
Invisible religion. 3086
Invisible road to peace. 1133
Invisible things. 2932
Invisible things, and other sermons. 3342
Invisible war. 1427
Invisible way. 3542
Invisible world. 2843, 2987
Invisibles. 2726, 2732, 3518
Invisibles and I. 958
Invisibles, realities, demonstrated in the holy life and triumphant death of John Janeway. 1934
Invitation committee. 252
Invitation from the planet Venus. 3505
Invitation of God. 2300, 3368
Invitation to a great experiment. 3481
Invitation to Acts. 329
Invitation to adventure. 473, 615
Invitation to Ahmadiyyat. 20
Invitation to Bible study. 286
Invitation to discipleship. 991, 1562
Invitation to faith. 64
Invitation to hope. 759
Invitation to John. 417
Invitation to joy. 181, 2135
Invitation to Luke. 428
Invitation to Mark. 431
Invitation to Matthew. 441
Invitation to pilgrimage. 61, 1562
Invitation to prayer. 2872
Invitation to the Book of Revelation. 453
Invitation to the Buddhist way of life for Western readers. 702
Invitation to the kingdom. 253
Invitation to the New Testament. 409
Invitation to the New Testament Epistles, I. 380
Invitation to the New Testament Epistles IV. 402
Invitation to the New Testament Epistles, I. 380
Invitation to the New Testament Epistles III. 368
Invitation to the New Testament, Epistles II. 368
Invitation to the Old Testament. 596
Invitation to the Talmud. 3584
Invitation to theology. 3664
Invitation to worship. 2295
Invitations of Our Lord; notes of meditations. 2383
Invited guests. 3519
Invited to faith. 236, 1727
Invitiation heeded. 792
Invocation. 2112
Invocation of saints treated theologically and historically. 3285
Invocations. 2111, 2895
Invocations and "D'var Torah" supplement. 2895
Involved. 1199
Inward cross. 2031
Inward journey. 1453
Inward light. 701, 3477
Inward peace. 3489
Inward pilgrimage. 1021
Ioannis Saresberiensis Historiae pontificalis quae supersunt. 1541, 2769
Iowa Catholic historical review v. one-January, nineteen thirty. 873
Iowa pulpit of the Church of Christ. 1463
Iqbal. 1918
Iqbal's concept of God. 1733, 1918
Ira D. Sankey centenary. 3301
Ira Oscar Knapp and Flavia Stickney Knapp. 1034, 2178
Iran. 3403
Iranian Christian. 1365, 2242
Irano-Aryan faith and doctrine as contained in the Zend-Avesta. 121
Iraq. excavations of the Oriental Institute 1932/33. 894
Ireland and the Celtic church. 1918
Ireland and the pope. 1919
Ireland, harbinger of the Middle Ages. 1918
Ireland, "In the footsteps of St. Patrick" 3622
Ireland; its saints and scholars. 1026
Ireland, liberation, and theology. 2222
Irenaeus testimony to the Fourth gospel. 421, 1919
Irenic apocalypse. 56, 1402
Irenic theology. 3646
Irenicum. 1241
Irina, a love stronger than terror. 169, 3455
Irish and Catholic power. 819, 1919
Irish Anglicanism, 1869-1969. 1230

Irish boy and God. 1786
Irish Carmelites of New York City and the fight for Irish independence, 1916-1919. 741
Irish Catholic colonization association of the United States. 1920
Irish directory on ecumenism. 1044
Irish Druids and old Irish religions. 1919
Irish monasticism. 2582
Irish monasticism; origins and early development. 2582
Irish monks in the golden age. 2582
Irish mythological cycle and Celtic mythology. 2655
Irish mythology, a dictionary. 2664
Irish pilgrimage. 819
Irish prince and the Hebrew prophet. 1663
Irish saints. 1027, 3284
Irish visions of the other-world. 3783
Irish way. 820
Irish witchcraft and demonology. 3826
Irishman in the jungles of Africa. 2499
Irma. 3274
Iron Curtain Christians. 1320
Iron duke of the Methodist itinerancy. 3699
iron flute. 3894
Iron shoes. 122, 160
Irony in the Old Testament. 499
Irony in the Old Testatment. 499
Irrational man. 1583
Irrational season. 1264
Irrationalism and rationalism in religion. 3104
Irreconcilable records. 202
Irreligious reflections of the Christian church. 3644
Irrepressible conflict. 3076
Irrepressible conflict in religion. 2561
Irreversible decision, 1939-1950. 103
Irrigation and religion. 1269
Irritated oyster & other object lessons for children. 908
Irving's catechism of classical biography. 1286
Irving's Catechism of Jewish antiquities. 2083
Irving's Catechism of mythology. 2656
Irwin's Bible commentary. 222
"Is any sick among you. 1792
Is anybody driving? 2397
Is anybody listning when I pray? 2886
Is anybody up there? 61
Is anyone for real? 990
Is anyone out there? 2729
Is anyone there? 1728
Is celibacy outdated? 877
Is Christ coming soon? 3320
Is Christ divided? 1041, 1042
Is Christ for John Smith? 3829
Is Christ possible? 1955
Is Christ the end of the law? 1753, 2011
Is Christian science Christian? 1035
Is Christianity a failure? 1094
Is Christianity Christian! 1050
Is Christianity credible? 64
Is Christianity practicable? 696
Is Christianity the only true religion? 1092
Is Christianity the only way? 1096
Is Christianity true? 1091
Is death for real? 1414
Is death the end? 1529, 1888, 3512
Is "eternal" punishment endless? 1092
Is faith obsolete? 1589
Is for Advent. 3682
Is for angels. 2023
Is God a person? 1719
Is God a white racist? 3017
Is God alive? 1066
Is God at home? 1451
Is God dead? 101, 1417
'Is God dead?' controversy. 1417
Is God dead?iNew York. 101
Is God emeritus? 1724
Is God evident? 2673
Is God for real. 1719
Is God for sale? 1553
Is God God? 1729
Is God good? 1732
Is God in history? 3100
Is God in there? 1060
Is God limited? 2306
Is God necessary? 1726
Is God still speaking to men? 1729
Is God supernatural? 287
Is He not able? 2393
Is hell eternal. 3220
... Is immortality desirable! 1887
Is it God's word? 237
Is it I, Lord? 2787
Is it love? 2346
Is it morning yet? 2436
Is it, or isn't it? 61
Is it too late? 3744
Is it true? 2295

Is it true what they say about Edgar Cayce? 877
Is it worth while? 2689
Is Jesus God? 2001, 2059
Is Jesus of Nazareth the son of God? 2001, 2991
Is legalism a heresy? 942
Is life worth living? 512
Is man immortal? 1887
Is man the Phoenix? 1890
... Is Mark a Roman gospel? 124
... Is Mary relevant? 2362
Is Masonry a religion? 1661
Is metaphysics possible? 2416
Is modern culture doomed? 1394
Is Mormonism Christian? 2611
Is Moses scientific? 204
Is my church what God meant it to be? 3678
Is my head on straight? 3843
Is original sin in Scripture? 3413
Is preparedness for war unchristian? 1089
Is religion dying? 61
Is religion enough? 3482
Is revolution change? 3234, 3448
Is Roman Catholicism in America identical with that of the popes? 3244
Is suicide a sin? 3545
Is that in the Bible? 301
"Is that in the Book of Mormon?" 680
Is the antichrist at hand? 52
Is the Baptist Church relevant to the Black community. 15
Is the Bible a human book? 279
Is the Bible really the word of God? 279
Is the Bible the inerrant word of God, and was the body of Jesus raised from the dead. 3705
Is the Bible the word of God? 278, 307
Is the Bible true? 275, 276
Is the Bible what it claims to be? 307
Is the Bible worth reading, and other essays. 202
Is the coming of Christ before or after the millennium? 3341
Is the day of the denomination dead? 3326
Is the devil a myth? 1428
Is the end near? 3320
Is the family here to stay? 2341
Is the higher criticism scholarly? 503
Is the homosexual my neighbor? 1844
... Is the Jewish race pure? 2082
Is the kingdom age at hand? 1401
Is the kingdom of God realism! 2174
Is the Last Supper finished? 2252
Is the Lord among us? 965
Is the mode of Christian baptism prescribed in the New Testament? 136
Is the New Testament anti-Semitic? 1082
Is the rapture next? 3321
Is the whole body a tongue.? 1716
Is the world going red? 3448
Is the young man safe? 3128
Is theology a science? 3615
Is there a Christian philosophy? 1105
Is there a conflict between Genesis 1 and natural science? 205
Is there a God? 1654, 1723, 1728, 1737
Is there a man in the house? 2402
Is there a millennium? 2466
Is there a personal God? 1738
Is there an answer? 2081
Is there hope for the city? 1277
Is there life after death? 1698
Is there life after high school? 3868
Is there life after thirty? 988
Is there really a God? 65
Is there really only one way? 64
Is there salvation after death? 2943
Is there salvation outside the Catholic church? 3288
Is this a Christian country? 1764
Is this religion? 1054
Is this the last century? 1515
Is this the same church? 811
Is this Wilson? 3514
Is your child exceptional. 895
Is your God big enough? 1006
Is your soul progressing? 3461
Isa, Kena, Katha, Prasna, Mundaka and Manduka Upanisads. 3760
Isaac Ambrose, Lancashire nonconformist. 29, 1469
... Isaac and Jacob. 1920
Isaac Backus and the American pietistic tradition. 123
Isaac Backus on church, state, and Calvinism. 146
Isaac Halevy, 1847-1914: spokesman and historian of Jewish tradition. 1781, 2751
Isaac Loeb Peretz. 2671
Isaac M. Wise. 3822
Isaac Mayer Wise and Emanu-El. 3822
Isaac Mayer Wise, the founder of American Judaism. 2105, 3822
Isaac Newton Clark. 3125

Isaac W. Wiley. 3816
Isaac Watts, his life and works. 3799
Isaac Watts's Hymns and spiritual songs, 1707. 1870, 3799
Isacc Mayer Wise. 3822
Isaiah. 161, 541, 542, 543, 544, 1921, 2895
Isaiah 1-39. 544
Isaiah 1-39: introduction and commentary. 544
Isaiah 40-66. 545
Isaiah; a study guide. 544
Isaiah and the Assyrian crisis. 1920
... Isaiah and the nature cults. 543
Isaiah & wisdom. 543, 3821
Isaiah as a nature-lover. 1921
Isaiah as read by a clairvoyant. 206
Isaiah fifty-three, a devotional and expository study. 544
Isaiah for today. 543, 2599
Isaiah XL-LXVI. 542
Isaiah 40-66. 545
Isaiah, messenger for God. 493, 1921, 2952
Isaiah 1-12: a commentary. 544
Isaiah,I-XXXIX. 542
Isaiah, prince of Old Testament prophets. 542
Isaiah, scroll of prophetic heritage. 543
Isaiah speaks. 543
Isaiah. 'the salvation of Jehovah. 544
Isaiah 13-39. 545
Isaiah 24-27 and the origin of apocalyptic. 56, 546
Isaias. 1921
Isaiah XXI. 546
Iscariot. 72, 2156, 2778
Ishmael and the church. 2567
Isiac tablet. 1921
Isidore of Seville on the pagan gods (Origines VIII:11) 1742, 1921
Isis among the Greeks and Romans. 1921
Isis in the Graeco-Roman world. 1921
Isis unveiled. 3683, 3684
Isis unveiled: collected writings, 1877. 3689
Islam. 79, 1282, 1921, 1922, 1925, 2564, 2565, 2566, 2629
Islam, a cultural perspective. 1922
Islam, a general picture. 1921
Islam, a survey of the Muslim faith. 1921
Islam and Africa. 2564
Islam and capitalism. 1923
Islam and Christianity. 20, 1926
Islam and Christianity in India and the Far East. 2532
Islam and development. 1922
Islam and international relations. 1924
... Islam & its founder. 2565, 2629
Islam and medieval Hellenism. 1924
Islam and missions. 2565
Islam and modernism in Egypt. 1922, 2628
Islam and Pakistan. 1925
Islam and Pan-Africanism. 2680
Islam and politics in East Africa. 3545
Islam and power. 1923
Islam and revolution. 1924
Islam and social order in Mauritania. 21, 1925
Islam, and the Arabian prophet. 2565, 2629
Islam and the confluence of religions in Uganda, 1840-1966. 1926
Islam and the integration of society. 3454
Islam and the oriental churches. 2567
Islam and the perennial philosophy. 3543
Islam and the plight of modern man. 1922
Islam and the transformation of culture. 1922
Islam and the West. 2566, 2598
Islam: beliefs and observances. 1921
Islam from within. 1921
Islam in Africa. 1923, 2564
Islam in China. 2567, 2635
Islam in East Africa. 12, 1923
Islam in Egypt today. 1924
Islam in Ethiopia. 1924, 2567
Islam in India. 1925, 2567
Islam in modern history. 2565
Islam in sub-Saharan Africa. 1923
Islam in the modern national state. 1924
Islam in the modern world. 1283
Islam in the Soviet Union. 1926
Islam in the Sudan. 1926, 2567
Islam in the world. 1921
Islam in transition. 1922
Islam in Uganda. 1926
Islam in West Africa. 2567
Islam, its meaning for modern man. 2565
Islam observed. 1925
Islam, our guide. 3196
Islam—politics and religion in the Muslim world. 1926
Islam reconsidered. 1922
Islam: the straight path. 2565

Islam, the true faith. 1921
Islam, Turkey, and Armenia, and how they happened. 2565
Islamic Africa. 1923
Islamic architecture. 79
Islamic architecture in Libya. 79
Islamic art. 86, 1800
Islamic art across the world. 86
Islamic art and architecture. 86
Islamic art from the Collection of Edwin Binney 3rd. 86, 659
Islamic art in the Metropolitan Museum of Art. 87
Islamic civilization in the Middle East. 1282
Islamic cultures in North America. 1926
Islamic doctrine of economics and contemporary economic thought. 1923
Islamic government. 1923
Islamic influence on Indian society. 1925
Islamic Jesus. 1926, 2013
Islamic life and thought. 1923
Islamic literature. 77
Islamic messianism. 2317
Islamic metalwork of the eighth to the fifteenth century in the Keir Collection. 87, 1407
Islamic modernism in India and Pakistan, 1857-1964. 1925
Islamic patterns. 86
Islamic philosophical theology. 1927
Islamic philosophy and mysticism. 2841
Islamic philosophy and the classical tradition. 2841, 3791
Islamic rationalism. 21, 1926
Islamic response to imperialism. 3199
Islamic space. 1921
Islamic sufism. 3543
Islamic tradition. 1921
Islamic understanding of death and resurrection. 1531
Islamic view of women and the family. 1611
Island churches of the South Pacific. 2533
Island of forgotten men. 2541, 2740
Island of menstruating men. 1540
Island of my life. 2486, 3238
Islands of Titicaca and Koati. 3702
Isle of Palms, sketches of Hainan. 2512, 2929
Isle of Patmos. 459
Isms and ologies. 3322
Isms new and old. 3324
Isn't it a wonder! 1384
Isn't one wife enough? 2859
Israel. 297, 1929, 2078, 2088, 2121, 2763, 3377
Israel, a secret documentary. 610, 1928
... Israel after the exile. 531
Israel after the exile, sixth and fifth centuries, B.C. 568
Israel among the nations. 2078
Israel: an echo of eternity. 2765
Israel and the ancient world. 293
Israel and the church. 2152
Israel and The Dead Sea scrolls. 1411, 1928, 3819
Israel and the holy places of Christendom. 3405
Israel and the nations. 2095
Israel and the nations, from the Exodus to the fall of the Second Temple. 2095
Israel and the nations in prophecy. 605, 610
Israel and the new covenant. 1376
Israel and the world. 2141
Israel and the world, essays in a time of crisis. 2082
Israel and Zionism. 3896
Israel at the center of history & revelation. 611
Israel at the crossroads. 2151
Israel at the end of this age. 463
Israel before Christ. 2095
Israel Bettan memorial volume. 196, 2910
Israel diary. 2761
Israel! Do you know? 2119
Israel Edson Dwinell, D. D. 1341, 1484
Israel for Christians. 1928
Israel, from its beginnings to the middle of the eighth century. 534, 2095, 2151
Israel: God's peculiar treasure. 610
Israel in agony. 610, 1928
Israel in ancient Near Eastern setting. 534, 2095, 2150
Israel in Canaan. 2096
Israel in Christian religious instruction. 860
Israel in exile, a theological interpretation. 598, 1583, 2093
Israel in prophecy. 611, 1928
Israel in revolution, 6-74 C.E. 2090, 2134
Israel in the apostolic Church. 1083
Israel in The decline of the West. 2084, 3471
Israel in the period of the judges. 555, 2090

Israel in the ranks. 2116
Israel in the spotlight. 610, 2118
Israel Jacobson. 1931, 3131
"Israel--Jehovah's covenant people." 1927
Israel, land of Zion. 294, 1928
Israel of God. 599, 2973
Israel of the Alps. 3789
Israel of tomorrow. 2082
Israel returns home according to prophecy. 2118
Israel revisited. 2762
Israel saga. 210
Israel speaks. 1931
Israel speaks for democracy. 2084
Israel, the Biblical people. 2077
Israel, the reality: people, places, events. 1928
Israel under Babylon and Persia. 498, 2149
Israel vindicated. 1083
Israel way to peace. 2118
Israel without tears. 2762
Israel, yesterday and to-day. 1929
Israeli/Arab conflict, and the Bible. 608
Israeli kibbutz. 1308
Israeli tales and legends. 3581
Israelis, Jews, and Jesus. 2014
Israelite and Judaean history. 534, 2096
Israelite religion. 2148
Israelite wisdom. 569, 3604, 3821
Israelites. 536, 2095, 2761
Israel's account of the beginnings. 523
Israel's Bible lands. 283, 2763
Israel's Black Hebrews. 668
Israel's concept of the beginning. 525
Israel's destiny. 610
Israel's faith. 2114
Israel's fate and faith. 3371
Israel's final holocaust. 611
... Israel's historical and biographical narratives. 532
Israel's hope encouraged. 579, 1846
... Israel's laws and legal precedents from the days of Moses to the closing of the legal canon. 2073, 2107
Israel's Messianic hope to the time of Jesus. 2415
Israel's period of progress. 536, 2097
Israel's praise! 586
Israel's prophetic heritage. 484, 2630
Israel's prophetic tradition. 6, 569, 2951
Israel's prophets. 2951
Israel's religious development. 597
Israel's sacred songs. 578
Israel's wisdom. 3821
Israel's wisdom in modern life. 2115
Israel's Wisdom literature. 600, 3234
Issac Abravanel. 5
Issue one: evangelism. 1572
Issues. 759
Issues and answers. 3467
Issues in American Protestantism. 2978
Issues in Christian ethics. 174, 946
Issues in Christian thought. 3100
Issues in Jewish education. 2086
Issues in religion. 3090, 3108
Issues in sexual and medical ethics. 949
Issues in the Jewish-Christian dialogue. 1376, 2087
Issues in the labor-management dialogue— church perspectives. 867
Issues in theological education, 1964-1965. 3680
Issues of immortality. 1889
... The issues of life. 1325
Issues of the age. 2420
Issues of theological conflict. 2221
Issues of theological warfare: evangelicals and liberals. 2222
Issues that divide the church. 759
Issues we face ... and some biblical answers. 1140
It ain't been easy, Charlie. 893
It ain't gonna reign no more. 981
It all began with God. 2437
It began in an upper room. 330
It began in Burma. 2505
It began in Galilee. 2173
It began on the cross. 1194
It began thus. 474
It came in handy. 2539
It came to pass in the San Juan Islands. 1511
"It came to pass in those days" 3704
It can happen between Sundays. 1210
It can happen in the church. 1120
It couldn't happen, but it did. 2983
It depends on you. 2555
It didn't just happen, and other talk-about Bible stories. 617
It does add up. 964
It feels good to forgive. 1633
It happened at night. 623
It happened in Brazil. 690, 3467
It happened in Palestine. 2763
It happened in Paraguay. 2544

It happened in Syria. 2552
It happened this way. 3181
It hurts so bad, Lord! 1351
It is always spring! 3202
It is dear persuasion. 3378, 3417
..."It is finished" 1084
It is happening. 604
It is hard to be a Christian. 980
It is His own blood. 2255
It is I. 2003
It is not lawful for me to fight. 3794
It is Paul who writes. 286, 326, 2795
It is required of stewards. 3529
It is the Christmas-time. 1113
It is the Lord! 1326
It is time. 163
It is time to rebuild: our faith, our character, our America. 1343
It is to share. 1168
It is toward evening. 1447
It is written. 277, 617, 1959
It is you I beckon. 3331
It just doesn't make sense. 1324
It might be you. 2490
It must have been an angel. 42
It only happens to preachers. 3675
It pays to praise spiritual praise. 2867
It takes time to love. 2491
It took a miracle! 2844
It was done. 102
It was for you. 2214
It was for you; Lenten sermons by Lutheran pastors. 2214
It will be worth it all. 3234
'It will be your duty. 1239
It works. 2994
Italian-Americans and religion. 1929
Italian element in Milton's verse. 2472
Italian evangelical pioneers. 2558
Italian lordship. 2270
Italian Methodist mission in the Little Italy of Baltimore, Md. 3127
Italian pioneer in America. 1710
Italian reformers. 3041
Italian reformers, 1534-1564. 3041
Italo-Vatican accord. 1322
Italy and the Reformation to 1550. 3041
Items by and about Mary Baker Eddy. 1494
Itestamente lipya nya pfumu yatu Jesu Kristu. 479
Itinerancy; its power and peril. 1929
Itinerant on foot. 3134
Itinerary. 3710
It's a great life. 3384
*It'S a great time to be a Christian. 3176
It's a Playboy world. 1067
It's a sin to bore a kid. 3869
It's a two-way street. 1316
It's a whole new scene. 2391
Its a woman's privilege. 3843
It's alive. 639
It's all about Jesus. 902, 1981
It's all in the day's work. 944
It's all in the family. 1610
It's better to believe. 992
It's bright in my valley. 2788
It's dynamite. 1560
It's faster to heaven in a 747. 3402
It's fun to teach. 3179
It's getting late. 478
It's good to know. 713, 1358
It's great to pray. 2876
It's happening with youth. 1261
It's here. 604
"It's incredible!" 1010
It's me O Lord! 2814, 2891, 2895, 3247
*It's my congregation, too! 3191
It's my turn. 1754, 2388
It's O.K. to be single. 1256
It's possible. 3539
It's smart to be a Latter-Day Saint. 1009
It's startling! 97, 3767
It's still lion vs Christian in the corporate arena. 980
It's the Lord's Supper. 2254
It's time for Easter. 1486
It's time to live. 1353
It's time to talk to God. 2886
It's time to tell them the truth. 2077
It's too bad we didn't know it before. 2409
It's tough growing up. 3879
It's up to you. 787, 2695
It's worth your life. 993
It's your business, teen-ager! 3884
It's your choice. 578, 2959, 2965
It's your day. 1434, 2396
It's your education [by] Philip Harris, William J. McMahon [and] James J. Cribbin. Editorial consultant, Sister Barbara. 805
It's your future. 804
It's your mass too. 2365
It's your souls we want. 1708
It's your turn. 3467
It's your turn now! 3880

Ivan Spencer, willow in the wind. 3471
I've got to play on their court. 3252
I've got to talk to somebody, God. 3842
I've had me a time! 3135
I've met Jesus Christ. 2380, 2395

J

J. Alberione: thoughts. 995
J. B. Dykes (1823-1876), priest & musician. 1292, 1484
J. B. Tidwell plus God. 3699
J. Christian Bay at seventy. 179
J. D. Sumner: Gospel music is my life. 3135
J. E. Klingberg, adventurer in faith. 2178
J. G. Dodge's lectures on man, present and future. 2323
J. Golden Kimball. 2171, 2619
J. Gresham Machen. 1301, 2308
J. Gresham Machen, a biographical memoir. 2308
J.H. Garrison and Disciples of Christ. 1461, 1702
J. H. Ingram. 1908
J. Howard Williams. 3817
J. Howard Williams, prophet of God and friend of man. 3817
J. Hudson Taylor. 2511, 3590
J. J. Griesbach, synoptic and text critical studies, 1776-1976. 351, 1774, 3578
J. Leonard Levy, prophetic voice. 3361
J. M. Price; portrait of a pioneer. 2938
J. P. Migne. 2463
Jachin and Boaz. 1669
Jacinta. 2349
Jack and Jill stay for church. 3163
Jack Gillen predicts. 2948
Jack-in-the-pulpit. 1017
Jack Wyrtzen story. 3848, 3861
Jacob and the angel. 3086
Jacob Boehme. 674
Jacob Boehme: His life and thought. 3135
Jacob Boehme's The way to Christ. 2637
Jacob Hamblin. 1689, 1782, 2600, 2601, 2602
Jacob Hamblin, a narrative of his personal experience, as a frontiersman, missionary to the Indians and explorer, disclosing interpositions of Providence, severe privations, perilous situations and remarkable escapes. 1689
Jacob Hamblin, buckskin apostle. 1782, 2600
Jacob Mountain, first lord bishop of Quebec. 1144, 2626
Jacob's ladder. 3129, 3338, 3511, 3854
Jacob's ladder, theology and spirituality in the thought of Austin Farrer. 1613
Jacob's night. 1638, 2810
Jacob's sons. 1931
Jacob's well. 3335
Jacob's well of life. 3135
Jacob's well; some Jewish sources and parallels to the Sermon on the Mount. 3335
Jacopo Sadoleto, 1477-1547. 3272
Jacques Benigne Bossuet. 1650
Jacques Ellul. 1509
Jacques Maritain, antimodern or ultramodern? 1818, 2335
Jadoo. 2313
Jahin and Boaz. 1669
Jahn's Biblical archaeology. 207
Jahn's Biblical archaeology. 207
Jailhouse rock. 334
Jain directory. 1933
Jain philosophy. 2841
Jaina iconography. 3316
Jaina path of purification. 1932
Jaina Sutras. 1932
Jainism. 1932
Jainism in early medieval Karnataka, c. A.D. 500-1200. 1933
Jainism in north India. 1933
Jamaa. 1933
Jamaa and the Church. 835, 1933
James. 412
James, a practical faith. 413
James; a practical primer for Christian living. 164, 413
James; a study guide. 413
James Addison Ingle (Yin Teh-sen) 3129
James Bond's world of values. 950
James Cooper, presbyter in the church of God. 1368
James: Faith in action. 413
James Fraser, second bishop of Manchester. 1651
James Freeman Clarke. 3125
James G. Blaine on the money question, and other psychic articles. 3506
James G. Endicott. 1515, 2485
James Gibbs as a church designer. 1711
James H. Brookes. 693

James H. Hyslop--X. 1878, 3516
James H. McConkey. 2306
James Hannington, D.D., F.L.S., E.R.G.S.,
first bishop of eastern equatorial Africa.
1784
James Hannington, D. D., F. L. S., F. R
G S., first bishop of eastern equatorial
Africa; a history of his life and work,
1847-1883. 1856
James Henry Chapin. 3137
James Hervey and eighteenth-century
taste. 1808
James Hudson Taylor. 3590
... James, I and II, Thessalonians and I and
II Corinthians. 412
James Jays takes a case. 2002
James Laynez, Jesuit. 2191
James Martineau. 2349
James Mercer Kirkham: highlights of his
successful life. 2178
James Mill. 2463
James Mill, a biography. 1882. 2463
James Monroe Buckley. 700
James Robb. 3240, 3466
James Sherman Kimball. 2171
James Shirley. 3404
James speaks for today. 413
James Stokes. 3533, 3871
James Stokes Dickerson. 1458
James Stokes, pioneer of Young men's
Christian association. 3533, 3871
James: the epistle of reality. 2374
James the Lord's brother. 76, 1933
James Ussher, Archbishop of Armagh.
3761
James W. Bashford. 177
James White. 3812
James, your brother. 412
Jamil, the child Christ. 1912
Jane Bailey. 130
Jansenists and the expulsion of the Jesuits
from France, 1757-1765. 1934
Janua coelestis. 3295
...Janus in Roman life and cult. 1935
Jap. 3136
... Japan. 2534
Japan advancing--Whither? 2534
Japan and its rescue. 2534
Japan begins again. 1935
Japan; God's door to the Far East. 2291,
2534
Japan in five hours. 1935
Japan mission. 2535
Japan mission of the American church.
2533
Japan on the upward trail. 2533
... Japan speaks for herself. 2535
Japanese and Sun Yat-sen. 1935
Japanese Buddhism. 706, 2707
Japanese contributions to Christian
theology. 3659
Japanese fortune calendar. 98
Japanese grotesqueries. 1709
Japanese mythology. 2664
Japanese religion. 1935
Japanese religion and philosophy. 1936
Japanese religion in the modern century.
1936
Japanese religion: unity and diversity.
1935
Japanese religious attitudes. 1936
Japanese Robinson Crusoe. 3132
Japanese witnesses for Christ. 1110
Japanese youth faces life. 2534
Japan's new Baptists. 154
Japan's new Buddhism. 3455
Japan's religions; Shinto and Buddhism.
1935
Japan's religious ferment. 1935
... The Jarvis centenary. 1936
Jason Lee. 2205, 2544
Jason's quest. 80, 1936
Jataka. 1937
Jataka tales. 1632, 1937
Jay Bain, junior boy. 3564
Jean de Brebeuf, 1593-1649. 691, 1857
Jean de La Fontaine. 2189
... Jean Jacques Rousseau and education
from nature. 3252
Jean LeClerc. 2203
Jean Lefebvre de Cheverus. 892
Jean Rotrou's Saint Genest and Venceslas.
3134
Jeane Dixon. 1472, 2948
Jeane Dixon: my life and prophecies.
2948
Jeane Dixon: prophetess or fraud? 1472
Jeane Dixon: the Washington prophetess.
1472
Jeanne d'Arc. 1937, 1938, 1939
Jeanne Jugan. 2158, 2233
Jedidiah Morse. 2620, 2687
Jeep tracks. 2529
Jeff Ray I knew; a pioneer preacher in
Texas. 3025
Jefferson Bible. 400

Jefferson Bible. With the annotated
commentaries on religion of Thomas
Jefferson. Introd. by Henry Wilder
Foote. Forward by Donald S. Harrington.
400
Jefferson on religion in public education.
1939, 3189
Jehovah. 535, 1940
Jehovah and other gods. 1728
Jehovah-Jesus. 3346, 3714
"Jehovah-jireh." 1269, 2981
Jehovah, not the serpent, thy God. 531
Jehovah of the Watchtower. 1940
Jehovah's finished work. 1725
Jehovah's man. 35
Jehovah's war against false gods, and other
addresses. 1461
Jehovah's Witnesses. 1939, 1940, 1941
Jehovah's witnesses in American prisons.
1940
Jehovah's Witnesses in Canada. 1940,
3193
Jehovah's Witnesses in Central Africa.
1942
Jehovah's Witnesses in the divine purpose.
1940
Jenny Lind Chapel. 39, 1942
Jenny's prayer diary. 2891
Jensen Bible study charts. 600, 646
Jensen's Survey of the New Testament.
475
Jensen's survey of the Old Testament.
597
Jeptah and his daughter. 1942
... Jeremiah. 269, 546, 547, 1943
... Jeremiah [and Lamentations]. 546
Jeremiah, Bible study commentary. 546
Jeremiah-Ezekiel prophecies of promises to
chosen people. 558
Jeremiah for today. 1942
... Jeremiah, his life and times. 1942
Jeremiah, his time and his work. 547,
1943
Jeremiah: man and prophet. 1942
Jeremiah, meet the 20th century. 547
Jeremiah: mighty man of God. 1942
Jeremiah, prophet of courage and hope.
1943
Jeremiah, prophet of disaster. 1943
Jeremiah, prophet under siege. 546
Jeremiah: spokesman out of time. 546,
1943
Jeremiah, the iron prophet. 492, 1942
Jeremiah the prophet. 1942
Jeremiah the prophet, by George A.
Birmingham (J. O. Hannay) 1942
Jeremy. 1942
Jeremy and Judy say the Sh'ma. 3402
Jeremy and the Torah. 2151
Jeremy learns about God. 1734
Jeremy Taylor. 1217, 3590, 3630
Jeremy Taylor, 1700-1976. 3591, 3617
Jeremy Taylor and the Great Rebellion.
3590
Jeremy's and Judy's Hanukah. 1784
Jerome. 1811
Jerome and Jovinian. 1811
Jerome Biblical commentary. 221
Jerome's commentary on Daniel. 506
Jerry Falwell. 1603
Jerry Falwell, man of vision. 146, 1603
Jerry McAuley. 2305
Jerry McAuley, an apostle to the lost.
2305
Jerry McAuley and his mission. 2305
Jerusalem. 1943, 1944, 2155, 2186, 2762
Jerusalem, a history. 1944
Jerusalem and Athens. 3622, 3767
Jerusalem & Bethlehem. 1944
Jerusalem and Rome. 1241, 2091
Jerusalem, Athens, and Oxford. 3655
Jerusalem, Bethany and Bethlehem. 1944,
2864
Jerusalem Bible. 266, 268
Jerusalem Bible. general editor Alexander
Jones. 266
Jerusalem, city of Jesus. 1943
Jerusalem delivered. 1017
Jerusalem meeting of the International
missionary council, March 24- April 8,
1928. 2493
Jerusalem mission under the direction of
the American Christian Missionary
Society. 1465, 2535
Jerusalem pilgrims before the Crusades.
1022
Jerusalem sinner saved. 714
Jerusalem the golden. 1888
Jerusalem to Rome. 328, 333
Jerusalem tragedy. 2030
Jeshurun sermons. 3371
Jesse Herman Holmes, 1864-1942. 1688,
1825
Jesse Lee. 2206
Jesse tree. 9
Jesu, joy of man's desiring. 1443

Jesuit. 1945
Jesuit child. 1945
Jesuit code of liberal education. 1946
Jesuit education. 1946
Jesuit education in Philadelphia. 3275
Jesuit educational quarterly. 1946
Jesuit enigms. 1944
Jesuit heritage in New England. 1949
Jesuit in focus. 1945
Jesuit martyrs of North America. 1948
Jesuit Martyrs' Shrine. 2462
Jesuit missions of St. Mary's County,
Maryland. 1949
Jesuit order and higher education in the
United States. 1949
Jesuit relations and allied documents.
1949, 2688
Jesuit relations and allied documents;
travels and explorations of the Jesuit
missionaries in North America, 1610-
1791. 1948
Jesuit relations, and other Americana in
the library of James F. Bell. 1949
Jesuit relations of Canada, 1632-1673.
1947, 1949
Jesuit religious life today. 1949
Jesuit schools. 1946
Jesuit spirit in a time of change. 1949
Jesuit theological library. 764
Jesuit thinkers of the renaissance. 2306
Jesuitism in Methodism. 1945
Jesuits. 1944, 1945, 1946, 1947, 2267,
2268
Jesuits, 1534-1921. 1946
Jesuits, a history. 1947
Jesuits, a self-portrait. 1945
Jesuits and education. 1946
Jesuits and the Great Mogul. 1947
Jesuits by the Golden Gate. 1948, 3298
Jesuits, 1534-1921. 1946
Jesuits for the Negro. 875
Jesuits go East. 1949
Jesuits in Great Britain. 1947
Jesuits in history. 1947
Jesuits in modern times. 1945
Jesuits in Montana. 1948
Jesuits in North America in the
seventeenth century. 1948
... The Jesuits in old Oregon. 2543
Jesuits in Oregon. 1948
Jesuits in Poland. 1948
Jesuits in the Philippines, 1581-1768.
1948
Jesuits of the middle United States. 1900,
1948, 1949
Jesuits: their spiritual doctrine and
practice. 1945
Jesus. 347, 384, 400, 431, 929, 930, 1056,
1064, 1950, 1956, 1959, 1961, 1962,
1964, 1965, 1966, 1967, 1968, 1970,
1972, 1973, 1978, 1980, 1981, 1984,
1991, 1994, 1995, 2005, 2015, 2022,
2037, 2039, 2043, 2059, 2060, 2062,
2392, 3269, 3407, 3622
Jesus; a dialogue with the Saviour. 2015
Jesus, a Gospel portrait. 392, 2044
Jesus, a myth. 2008
Jesus; a new biography. 1961
Jesus, a pictorial history of the New
Testament. 2008
Jesus—a savior or the Savior? 1078, 2035
Jesus according to a woman. 1959
Jesus according to Luke. 429
Jesus according to Mark. 433
Jesus according to S. John. 417
Jesus according to St. Mark. 435
Jesus after nineteen centuries. 3448
Jesus against the rapture. 1530, 2064
Jesus ahead. 2384
Jesus alias Christ. 1968
Jesus all great. 1999
Jesus all holy. 1964
...Jesus among His neighbors. 3179
Jesus and a boy's philosophy of life. 687
Jesus and Aimee. 2310
Jesus and broken personalities. 297
Jesus and Christian origins. 2007
Jesus and Christian origins outside the
New Testament. 1102, 1986
Jesus and citizenship. 1952, 2066
Jesus and discipleship. 2004
Jesus and earthquakes. 1485
Jesus and ethics; four interpretations. 950,
2003
Jesus and freedom. 1659, 2040
Jesus and God's new people. 390
Jesus and his adversaries. 390, 1956
Jesus and his apostles. 1967
Jesus and His Bible. 450
Jesus and His biographies. 1964
Jesus and His cause. 437, 438
Jesus and His Church. 1163
Jesus and His coming. 3320
Jesus and his contemporaries. 1964
Jesus and His cross. 3458
Jesus and His friends. 2007, 3764
... Jesus and His lollowers. 3146

Jesus and His methods. 1953
Jesus and His ministry. 1971
Jesus and His mother. 1999
Jesus and His people. 1121
Jesus and his pets. 3171
Jesus and his sacrifice. 107, 2030
Jesus and His story. 1973
Jesus and His teachings. 389, 1957, 2038,
2066
Jesus and His times. 1962
Jesus and human personality. 2823
Jesus and I. 626, 627, 904
... Jesus and I, together with the complete
text of the First communion catechism
prepared from the official revised
Baltimore catechism. 626
Jesus and Israel. 1073, 2013
Jesus and Judas. 2156
Jesus and life. 2015
Jesus and logotherapy. 1651, 2050
Jesus and man's hope. 383
Jesus and Mary. 865, 1999
Jesus and me. 236
Jesus and modern life. 2065, 3726
Jesus and modern religion. 1656
Jesus and our friendships. 1955
... Jesus and our generation. 2063
Jesus and our human needs. 1012
Jesus and our human problems. 2066
Jesus and our pressing problems. 2066,
3789
Jesus and ourselves. 979
Jesus and Paul. 2006
Jesus and politics. 3072
Jesus and the American mind. 3745
Jesus and the children. 898, 1958
Jesus and the Christian. 335
Jesus and the Christian religion. 1050
Jesus and the constraints of history. 2008
Jesus and the disinherited. 2066
Jesus and the educational method. 2066,
2176
Jesus and the Eucharist. 2039, 2251
Jesus and the first three Gospels. 388
Jesus and the four Gospels. 389, 929,
1963
Jesus and the future. 438, 2063, 2176
Jesus and the future life. 2066
Jesus and the gospel. 383, 389, 1951,
2008, 2010, 2824
Jesus and the gospel of love. 1052, 1954
Jesus and the Gospel tradition. 387, 2035
Jesus and the historian. 334, 1311
Jesus and the human conflict. 1951
Jesus and the hunger for things unknown.
1002, 2044
Jesus and the kingdom. 2174
Jesus and the language of the kingdom.
2026, 2065, 2175, 2176
Jesus and the law in the synoptic tradition.
1958, 2201
Jesus and the liberal mind. 166
Jesus and the men about him. 338
Jesus and the new age, according to St.
Luke. 427
Jesus and the new age of faith. 1096
Jesus and the nonviolent revolution. 2045,
2712
Jesus and the Old Testament. 1958
Jesus and the origins of Christianity.
1191, 1965
Jesus and the Pharisees. 1954, 2068, 2828
Jesus and the politics of violence. 2038,
3780
Jesus and the poor. 1153
Jesus and the power of Satan. 401, 1429,
1967
Jesus and the problem of human life. 962
Jesus and the problems of life. 979, 1955
Jesus and the prophets. 451
Jesus and the resurrection. 1486, 2053
Jesus and the revolutionaries. 2037
Jesus and the rising generation. 957
Jesus and the Son of Man. 3458
Jesus and the spirit. 1587, 2060
Jesus and the transformation of Judaism.
2050
Jesus and the Trinity. 3714
Jesus and the unemployed. 1952
Jesus and the woman of Sychar. 3572
Jesus and the word. 1457, 2062
Jesus and the world. 1980
Jesus and the world's quests. 1950
Jesus and the young man of to-day. 1992
Jesus and the Zealots. 3891
Jesus and what He said. 400
Jesus and you. 2047
Jesus and your nice church. 1244
Jesus and youth. 2062
Jesus, as a child and among children.
1981
Jesus as a controversialist. 1966
Jesus as a friend. 1955
Jesus as a soul-winner. 166
Jesus as a teacher and the making of the
New Testament. 321, 1952
Jesus as He was and is. 2059

Jesus as judged by his enemies. 1954
Jesus as men saw him. 2043
Jesus as others saw Him. 1952
Jesus as precursor. 3071
Jesus, as problem, teacher, personality, and force. 1960, 2036
Jesus as seen by his contemporaries. 2045
Jesus as teacher. 937, 1989, 2061
Jesus as they remembered Him. 1971
Jesus as they saw Him. 2010
Jesus at Nain. 2018
Jesus at the well. 3572
Jesus before Christianity. 2042
Jesus before Pilate. 2069
Jesus before Pilate, a monograph of the crucifixion. 2069
Jesus before the bar. 2016, 2535
Jesus begins his work. 339, 930, 1984
Jesus's audience. 2121, 2326
Jesus book. 445
Jesus brought back. 2414
... Jesus came preaching. 2898
Jesus Christ. 1951, 1963, 1965, 1970, 1971, 1974, 1990, 2013, 2015, 2029, 2038, 2039, 2047, 2384, 3326, 3506
Jesus Christ among the ancient Americans. 2602
Jesus Christ an example to His ministers. 3670
Jesus Christ and His Cross. 104
Jesus Christ and His kingdom. 2174
Jesus Christ and history. 3319
Jesus Christ and human freedom. 1659, 2040
Jesus Christ and human life. 2214
Jesus Christ and mythology. 1424
Jesus Christ and the Christian character. 944, 2003
Jesus Christ and the civilization of to-day. 2003
Jesus Christ and the faith. 477
Jesus Christ and the human quest. 1953
Jesus Christ and the modern challenge. 2002
Jesus Christ and the social question. 2065, 3445
Jesus Christ and the temple. 3599
Jesus Christ and the world today. 3443
Jesus Christ at the crossroads. 1951, 2562
Jesus Christ, before he became a superstar. 63, 2038
Jesus Christ before His ministry. 1972, 1977
Jesus Christ! Deity or demoniac? 164
Jesus Christ during His ministry. 1973, 1986
Jesus Christ for today. 429, 1577, 2044
Jesus Christ, God and man. 1893, 2044
Jesus Christ--God or man? a vital question. 2000
Jesus Christ heals. 1598
Jesus Christ, heir to the astronauts. 1102, 2019
Jesus Christ, His life, His passion, His triumph. 1960
Jesus Christ--His pre-existence, deity, humanity and ministry. 2045
Jesus Christ in a changing world. 147
Jesus Christ in his homeland. 1969
Jesus Christ in human experience. 1956, 2014
Jesus Christ in man's conflicts. 1956
Jesus Christ in Matthew, Mark, and Luke. 390, 2011
Jesus Christ in our world. 2039
Jesus Christ in the Talmud, Midrash, Zohar, and the liturgy of the synagogue. 2013, 3015
Jesus Christ is alive. 2052
Jesus Christ is alive and well and living in His church. 2383
Jesus Christ is Lord. 348, 1742, 2044, 2055
Jesus Christ liberator. 2036
Jesus Christ, Light of the World. 3326
Jesus Christ: Lord of the universe, hope of the world. 1997, 2515
... Jesus Christ our hope. 2300
Jesus Christ our Lord. 2000, 2045, 3440
Jesus Christ Our Saviour's person, mission, and spirit. 1963
Jesus Christ: prophet priest. 1953, 2056
Jesus Christ, Redeemer of mankind. 1956
Jesus Christ reforms his Church. 1243
Jesus Christ science of healing and living. 1792
Jesus Christ solid rock. 3321
Jesus Christ solidrock. 2056
Jesus Christ, Son of God. 2287
Jesus Christ, the divine man. 1974
Jesus Christ, the exiled King. 793
Jesus Christ, the gate of power. 999, 2040
Jesus Christ, the God-man. 2037
Jesus Christ, The King of our hearts. 3269
Jesus Christ the master soul winner. 1953
Jesus Christ the proof of Christianity. 2044, 2973

Jesus Christ, the risen Lord. 476
Jesus Christ the same. 2001
Jesus Christ, the same yesterday, today and forever. 2041
Jesus Christ the teacher. 2062
Jesus Christ, the unique revealer of God. 1951
Jesus Christ through history. 2008
Jesus Christ today. 403
Jesus Christ yesterday and today. 2004
Jesus' Christianity. 1049, 2117
Jesus' Christo niya tawa-mani. John tsidyatrani. 320
... Jesus Christ's men. 1017
Jesus Christus, meditations. 863
Jesus comes for everybody. 1996
Jesus community. 1263
Jesus compared. 2047
Jesus confronts life's issues. 1959
Jesus crucified. 2031
Jesus' design for living. 3337
Jesus died for me. 1982
Jesus died in Kashmir. 1976, 2165
Jesus, dollars and sense. 2973, 3530
Jesus establishment. 1103
Jesus event and our response. 349, 1002, 2045
Jesus experience. 2385
Jesus exultant. 1956
'Jesus family' in Communist China. 1319, 3863
Jesus' first trip. 2023
Jesus for a no-God world. 63, 2039
Jesus for Jews. 2019
Jesus for the men of today. 3073
Jesus freaks. 1816
Jesus, friend and teacher. 1994
Jesus, friend of boys and girls. 1958
Jesus generation. 3885
Jesus: God and man. 2000, 2042
Jesus: God, man or myth? 2008
Jesus, God's way of healing and power to promote health. 2193, 3476
Jesus goes to school. 1996
Jesus goes to the market place. 1996
Jesus goes to the synagogue. 1980
Jesus has a man in Waikiki. 1261, 3718
Jesus has come. 930, 1984
Jesus has many names. 2021
Jesus helps everybody. 1979
"Jesus himself." 2059
Jesus himself drew near. 1950
Jesus, his life and times. 929, 1965
Jesus: his mission on earth. 3291
Jesus: His opinions and character. 2050
Jesus, His story. 1990
Jesus; history and culture of the New Testament. 408, 920, 1968
Jesus, history and you. 1964, 2008
Jesus, human and divine. 1954
Jesus' idea. 1959
... Jesus' ideals of living. 2063
Jesus in action. 1995
Jesus in bad company. 2039, 2040
Jesus in Bethany. 1982
Jesus in Christian devotion and contemplation. 2009
Jesus in contemporary historical research. 2010
Jesus in danger. 632, 2032
Jesus in Genesis. 521
Jesus in Gethsemane. 392, 2049
Jesus in His homeland. 1967
Jesus in his time. 397, 1975
Jesus in history. 390, 1987
Jesus in literature and art. 3069
Jesus in modern life. 1953, 1968
... Jesus in our teaching. 1951
Jesus in our time. 2008
Jesus in pagan and other texts. 1986
Jesus in portraits of verse. 2047
Jesus in the background of history. 1970
Jesus in the church's Gospels. 1971
Jesus in the Eucharist. 1541
Jesus in the experience of men. 1058, 2038, 2063
Jesus in the Gospel. 930, 1991
Jesus in the Gospel of Matthew. 444
Jesus in the Gospels. 1972
Jesus in the Jewish tradition. 2013
Jesus in the light of history. 1970
Jesus in the memory of the early church. 350, 2011
Jesus in the midst. 999
Jesus in the Qur'an. 2013, 2014, 2185
Jesus in the records. 1993
Jesus in the Synoptic Gospels. 386
Jesus in the Talmud. 1954, 3583
Jesus: inspiring and disturbing presence. 2046
Jesus, interpreter of the eternal. 1970
Jesus is. 2047
Jesus is alive and well (what Jesus People really believe) 3664
Jesus is born. 1994, 2021, 2022
Jesus is coming. 3318
Jesus is coming again. 3320

Jesus is coming this week to reign on earth. 1515
Jesus is coming to earth again. 2051
Jesus is coming to that great meeting in the air. 1051
Jesus is His name. 3766
Jesus is Lord. 2045, 2795, 3490
Jesus is my guide. 618
Jesus is my teacher. 618
Jesus is victor! 175, 3294
Jesus is victory. 1689
Jesus' Jerusalem expedition. 2016
Jesus-Jeshua, studies in the Gospels. 388, 2070
Jesus, Jews and gentiles. 1083
Jesus, joy of the suffering. 3540
Jesus kids. 2072
Jesus, King most wonderful. 2039
Jesus, King of kings. 1969
... Jesus, King of love. 3269
Jesus life. 1005, 1969
Jesus lights the Sabbath lamp. 1996
Jesus live in me, through Blessed Virgin Mary in the spirit of St. Teresa. 855
Jesus living in the priest. 1296
Jesus living the Father's values. 941, 1953
Jesus Lord. 1020
Jesus, Lord and Christ. 2010, 2040
Jesus, Lord and Savior. 2045
Jesus, Lord and Saviour. 3622
Jesus, Lord for all times. 2037
Jesus, love in action. 420, 2011
Jesus, lover of men. 1954
Jesus loves me. 2035
Jesus loves me, this I know. 899, 1735
Jesus makes me laugh. 1011
Jesus: man and master. 1995
Jesus; man for today. 2041
Jesus, man of genius. 1969
Jesus manifest. 1969
Jesus, Mary, and Joseph, daily missal. 846
Jesus, master and Lord. 1979
Jesus; Matthew-John. 1981
Jesus means freedom. 1659, 2040
Jesus' measure of a Christian. 1052
Jesus' mission to Jerusalem. 430
Jesus model. 985, 2050
Jesus, my forever friend. 395, 930, 1980
Jesus, my love. 857
Jesus my Saviour, being brought nigh by His blood. 108
Jesus mystery. 1895, 1975
Jesus myth. 2039
Jesus Nazareth. 1970
Jesus never fails. 1052
Jesus now. 1283, 2041
Jesus of fact and faith. 1978
Jesus of faith. 2037
Jesus of Galilee. 928, 1959
Jesus of history. 1951, 2008
Jesus of Israel. 1980
Jesus of Mark's Gospel. 434
Jesus of Nazareth. 437, 928, 929, 1959, 1960, 1961, 1965, 1967, 1969, 1970, 1971, 1974, 1979, 1982, 1989, 2005, 2015, 2036, 2038, 2060, 3177
Jesus of Nazareth; a course for fifth and sixth grades. 1994
Jesus of Nazareth and His disciples. 2007
Jesus of Nazareth in New Testament preaching. 349, 2011
Jesus of Nazareth in the light of to-day. 1954
Jesus of Nazareth in word and deed. 2037
Jesus of Nazareth passeth by. 399
Jesus of Nazareth, Saviour and Lord. 3656
Jesus of Nazareth, the annointed of God. 1962
Jesus of Nazareth: the hidden years. 2003
Jesus of Nazareth, who was He? 1971
Jesus of our fathers. 1952
Jesus of Palestine. 388
Jesus of psychoanalysis. 2050
Jesus of St. Mark. 435, 1952
Jesus of the parables. 2025, 2026
Jesus of the poets. 2048, 3209
Jesus of the spirits. 2313
Jesus of yesterday and today. 2037
Jesus on Calvary. 108
Jesus on earth. 1983
Jesus on His second coming. 2051
Jesus on social institutions. 2064, 3439
Jesus on the holy mount. 2067
Jesus on trial. 420, 2068
Jesus on trial to-day. 1998
Jesus only. 163, 1058, 1955, 2039
Jesus only, songs and hymns. 1860
Jesus option. 399
Jesus or Christianity. 1052
Jesus or Paul? 1102, 1953
Jesus, our best friend. 3180
Jesus our brother in suffering. 2212
Jesus our contemporary. 1055, 2035
Jesus, our Friend. 627, 1981, 2016
Jesus our ideal. 2004

Jesus our Savior. 1982
Jesus--our standard. 2004
Jesus our table guest. 2872
Jesus' own words. 2070
Jesus' parables and the war of myths. 397, 2027
Jesus party. 1103
Jesus' pattern of prayer. 2247
Jesus, Paul and Judaism. 347
Jesus Paul preached. 376
Jesus People. 2072
Jesus people come alive. 3232
Jesus people speak out! 2072
Jesus performs miracles. 1620
Jesus' personal campaign among. 2056
Jesus, persons, and the kingdom of God. 2039, 2174
Jesus, Pilate, and Paul. 2013, 2847
Jesus, politics, and society. 429
Jesus power. 2866
Jesus prayer. 2072
Jesus prayer for today. 992
Jesus prays. 2049, 2869
... Jesus' principles of living. 2015
Jesus' proclamation of the kingdom of God. 2176
Jesus' promise to the nations. 1958, 2064, 2556
Jesus, prophecy, and the Middle East. 608
Jesus' prophetic sermon. 444, 2050
Jesus rediscovered. 1070
Jesus revolution. 1053, 2045, 2072, 3232
Jesus said. 400, 2071
Jesus said "I am" 2935
Jesus saves. 3296
Jesus says to you. 2071
Jesus scroll. 1102, 1978
Jesus' second family. 339, 632, 2007
Jesus shall have pre-eminence. 1954
Jesus, Shelley, and Malthus. 1653
Jesus showed God's love. 1966
Jesus silent. 2388
Jesus. son of David. 1969
Jesus, Son of God. 985, 2040
Jesus, son of Joseph. 2008
Jesus, Son of Man. 1995, 2035
Jesus, son of Mary. 930, 1983
Jesus, Son of Mary: fallacy and factuality. 2007
Jesus speaks. 2018
Jesus speaks of his death. 108
Jesus speaks to me. 3217
Jesus speaks to you. 3877
Jesus spells freedom. 1659, 2039
Jesus' spiritual journey--and ours. 1977
Jesus spreads His Gospel. 1982
Jesus stood by us. 3541
Jesus, stories for children. 627
Jesus story. 1962, 1963, 1964, 1979, 2042, 3534
Jesus, stranger from heaven and Son of God. 421, 2011
Jesus: superstar or savior? 2039
Jesus, symbol-maker for the kingdom. 2026, 2175
Jesus talked with me. 1362
Jesus taught me to cast out devils. 1585
Jesus, teacher and Lord. 1977
Jesus--teacher, principles of education for both pupils and Bible school teachers. 3158
Jesus teaches on prayer. 2049, 2880
Jesus' teaching in its environment. 2062
Jesus' teaching on the use of money. 2062, 3799
Jesus' teachings. 2060
... Jesus' teachings and the use of leisure. 2065, 2209
Jesus' teachings for young people. 3172, 3889
Jesus tells a story. 2027
Jesus the carpenter. 3341
Jesus, the carpenter of Nazareth. 1960
Jesus, the carpenter's son. 2005
Jesus the child. 1996
Jesus the Christ. 161, 396, 1951, 1952, 1953, 1967, 1973, 1993, 2037, 2040, 2045, 2050, 2613, 3179, 3582
Jesus the citizen. 1954
Jesus the divine layman. 1961
Jesus, the divine teacher. 2043
Jesus; the eternal dilemma. 2039
Jesus: the face of man. 990, 2046
Jesus: the fact behind the faith. 2008
Jesus; the four Gospels, Matthew, Mark, Luke and John, combined in one narrative and rendered in modern English. 1991
Jesus, the Friend. 3764
Jesus the Good Shepherd. 2037
Jesus, the great teacher. 2061
Jesus, the ideal teacher. 2061
Jesus, the invading God. 398
Jesus the Jew. 2045, 2050, 2073
Jesus the Jew and other addresses. 1084, 2083
Jesus—the Jew's Jew. 2556

Jesus the joyous comrade. 1950
Jesus the King is coming. 610
Jesus, the king of truth. 1991
Jesus the last great initiate. 1532, 1972
Jesus the leader. 930, 952, 1983, 2036
Jesus, the Light of the world. 1989, 3177, 3295
Jesus the Lord. 2039
Jesus the magician. 2019
Jesus the man. 1952, 1995, 2045
Jesus the man and Christ the spirit. 1956
Jesus, the man and the myth. 2041
Jesus, the man of Galilee. 1994, 2047
Jesus the man of prayer. 2881
Jesus—the man, the Christ. 2043
Jesus: the man, the mission, and the message. 1962
Jesus the master teacher. 2061
Jesus the mediator. 106
Jesus, the Messiah. 390, 1963, 1966, 2016
Jesus the Messiah in prophecy and fulfillment. 3849
Jesus the Nazarene. 1951, 1966
Jesus the Nazarene is certainly the Messiah of Jewish prophecy. 2016, 2414
Jesus, the new Elijah. 400, 1507, 3721
Jesus the pagan. 1971
Jesus the patriot. 1962
Jesus the pioneer. 1963
Jesus, the pioneer, and other sermons. 3342
Jesus the preacher. 2049
Jesus, the religious ultimate. 2043
Jesus the revolutionary. 1955
Jesus the Saviour. 1977
Jesus the servant. 437
Jesus the Son of God. 1978, 2007
Jesus the Son of man, His words and His deeds as told and recorded by those who knew Him. 2005
Jesus, the story of His life. 1959
Jesus, the storyteller. 2027, 2771
Jesus, the stranger. 862, 3363
Jesus, the teacher. 1953, 2061, 2065, 3171
Jesus the unknown. 1969
Jesus, the way. 430, 1954, 2047, 3350
Jesus, the Word of God. 395
...Jesus the worker. 2003
Jesus the world's perfecter. 1958
Jesus then and now. 1194, 2008
Jesus thing. 989
Jesus through many eyes. 476, 2042
Jesus through the centuries. 1957, 2009
Jesus' title to the throne of David. 2007
... Jesus; told by the Wandering Jew. 2019, 3791
Jesus told me to ... tell them I am coming. 931, 1488
Jesus touch. 3829
Jesus trip; advent of the Jesus freaks. 2072
Jesus upon earth. 1981
... Jesus wants them all. 3185
Jesus was. 1954
Jesus was a Jew. 2038
Jesus was a single adult. 3415
Jesus was not Jew. 2007
Jesus was their friend. 338
Jesus' way. 1059
Jesus' way of living. 965
Jesus' way with people. 973, 1954
Jesus went about doing good. 1246, 3179
Jesus: what manner of man is this? 1981
Jesus, where are you taking us? 139
Jesus: where it all began. 1961, 2764
Jesus who helped people. 1981
Jesus; who is he? 2039
Jesus, why? 2213
Jesus with us. 930, 1984
Jesus - word and presence. 2039
Jesus years. 395, 930, 1985
Jesus: "yesterday and today, and forever" 1984
Jet Cadets. 3876
Jew. 958, 2121
Jew and Christian. 2118
Jew and Christianity. 1083
Jew and civilization. 2085
Jew and Gentile. 2113, 2153
Jew and Greek. 1190
Jew and his destiny. 2078
Jew and his duties: the essence of the Kitzur Shulhan arukh. 2138
Jew and his home. 2120
Jew and his mission. 2082
Jew and his neighbour. 2078
Jew and his religion. 2114
Jew and his world. 2139
Jew and human sacrifice. 672, 2109
Jew and Mormon. 2619
Jew and Palestine in prophecy. 610
Jew and the Christian missionary. 236, 1092
Jew and the cross. 54
Jew and the universe. 2622, 2623, 2841
Jew and the world. 2082

...The Jew and the world ferment. 2078
Jew at home. 2098
Jew baiting. 187, 2077
Jew, essays from Martin Buber's journal Der Jude, 1916-1928. 2142
Jew faces a new world. 2082
Jew, God's timepiece. 2119
Jew has come home. 2119
Jew-hate as a sociological problem. 53
Jew; his contribution to modern civilization. 2084
Jew in American life. 2105
Jew in English fiction. 2100
Jew in history. 2089
Jew in London. 2100
Jew in love. 3371
Jew in the contemporary world. 2112
Jew in the medieval world. 2094
Jew in the new world. 2077
Jew in the plan of God. 2118
... The Jew of Malta. 2335
Jew of Tarsus, an unorthodox portrait of Paul. 2801
Jewel in the lotus. 704
Jewel ornament of liberation. 674
Jewels from green hell. 2489, 3387
Jewels from the Orient. 2518
Jewels of masonic oratory. 1663
Jewels of promise. 167
Jewels of the valleys. 2614
Jewels of the wise. 3588
Jewels of thought for daily reading. 1437
Jewels the giant dropped. 2544
... The Jewess. 1017
... Jewis Emancipation. 2112
Jewish activities in the United States. 2104
Jewish adventures in America; the story of 300 years of Jewish life in the United States. Designed by William Steinel. 2106
Jewish altar. 3271
Jewish Americans and their backgrounds. 657, 2083
Jewish and Christian ethics with a criticism on Mahomedism. 942
Jewish and Christian self-definition. 1197
Jewish and Hebrew onomastics. 480, 2668
Jewish and Mandaean incantation bowls in the Royal Ontario Museum. 1892
Jewish and Moslem versions of some theodicy legends. 3610
Jewish and Roman acquittal. 2068
Jewish and Roman law. 2074
Jewish and Roman law, a comparative study. 2074
Jewish antecedents of the Christian sacraments. 2110, 3262
Jewish anthology. 2075
Jewish art. 87
Jewish art: an illustrated history. 87
Jewish art in European synagogues. 3576
Jewish art treasures in Venice. 3577
Jewish audio-visual review. 2154
Jewish background. 2239
Jewish background of the Christian liturgy. 2239
Jewish bard. 3 138
Jewish beginning. 628, 631
Jewish Bible guide. 639
Jewish Biblical commentators. 240
Jewish biblical exegesis. 505
Jewish Billy Sunday. 1744, 3016
Jewish book annual. 2076
Jewish caravan. 2076
Jewish carol and The insuperable barrier. 741
Jewish catalog. 2081, 2120
Jewish ceremonial art. 87, 2073
Jewish ceremonial art and religious observance. 2073
Jewish ceremonial institutions and customs. 2120
Jewish child is born. 1276
Jewish child's Bible stories. 627
Jewish child's Bible stories told in simple language. 627
Jewish-Christian argument. 2153
Jewish-Christian relations. 2153
Jewish-Christian relations in today's world. 1084
Jewish Christianity. 343, 1488
Jewish code of jurisprudence. 2073, 2074, 2107
Jewish communal survey of Greater New York. 2101
... The Jewish community. 2111
Jewish community directory of Greater New York. 2101
Jewish community in Russia, 1772-1844. 2102
Jewish community life in America. 2104
Jewish community of Cuba. 2098
Jewish community of Pittsburgh, December, 1938. 2101
Jewish community organization in the United States. 2104

Jewish community relations. 2308
Jewish concepts and reflections. 2140
Jewish consciousness raising. 2079
Jewish contribution to civilization. 2083, 2084, 2085
Jewish court in the Middle Ages. 1375, 2092, 3583
Jewish culture. 2113
Jewish customs and ceremonies. 2120
Jewish day school in America. 2106
Jewish dietary laws. 2086
Jewish dietary laws, their meaning for our time. 2086
Jewish dilemma. 2077
Jewish disabilities in the Balkan states. 2103
Jewish education. 2079
Jewish education in a pluralist society: Samson Benderly and Jewish education in the United States. 187, 2106
Jewish education in democratic society. 2106
Jewish education in France, 1789-1939. 2099
Jewish education in New York city. 2086
Jewish education register and directory. 1951. 2106
Jewish educator. 2096
... Jewish emancipation under attack. 2112
Jewish encyclopedia. 2085
Jewish ethical idealism. 2080
Jewish ethics. 1539
Jewish ethics & Catholic doctrine. 2145
Jewish ethics and values. 1538
Jewish ethics, philosophy and mysticism. 1539
Jewish eugenics, and other essays. 2082
Jewish evangelism, a study. 2535
Jewish experiences in America. 2105
Jewish experiential book. 2079, 2097
Jewish expression. 2080
Jewish expressions on Jesus. 2014
Jewish fairy book. 3581
Jewish family. 1611
Jewish family book. 1611
Jewish family celebrations. 2145
Jewish family papers. 2114
Jewish family solidarity; myth or fact? 2121
Jewish feasts and fasts. 1614
Jewish festivals. 1614, 1623
Jewish festivals in the religious school. 2079
Jewish forerunners of Christianity. 2082
Jewish foundation of Islam. 1926, 2567
Jewish Gnostic Nag Hammadi texts. 2154
Jewish heroes. 630
Jewish history. 534, 2088
Jewish history and literature. 2088
Jewish holiday book. 1615
Jewish holiday crafts. 2073
Jewish holiday party book. 1614
Jewish holidays. 1614, 1615, 1624
... The Jewish holidays, a guide to their origin, significance and observance. 1624
Jewish holidays and festivals. 1614, 1623
Jewish holy days. 3721
Jewish holyday stories. 2081
Jewish holydays and minor holidays and fasts. 1623
Jewish home beautiful. 1623
Jewish horizons. 2143
Jewish idea of community. 2146
Jewish ideals. 2082
Jewish ideals and interpretations. 3370, 3371
Jewish ideals, and other essays. 2093
Jewish identity games. 1701, 2097
Jewish identity in an age of ideologies. 2097, 2148
Jewish image of man. 2097
Jewish influence in modern thought. 2082
Jewish influence on Christian reform movements. 1083
Jewish influences in American life. 2104
Jewish interpretation of the book of Genesis. 522
Jewish Jesus. 1977
Jewish kindergarten. 2087
Jewish law. 2074
Jewish law and Jewish life. 3219
Jewish law faces modern problems. 2074
Jewish law in ancient and modern Israel. 2074
Jewish law: its influence on the development of legal institutions. 2074
Jewish laws and customs, some of the laws and usages of the children of the Ghetto. 2121
Jewish leaders. 2144
Jewish legends of the Middle Ages. 2207
Jewish legion of valor. 2083
Jewish library. 2082, 2145
Jewish life. 2081, 2120
Jewish life in America. 2104
Jewish life in art and tradition. 2234, 2635

Jewish life in modern times. 2081
Jewish life in our community. 2121
Jewish life in our times. 2084
Jewish life in South America. 2103
Jewish life in the middle ages. 2081, 2121
Jewish life in Turkey in the XVIth century. 2107, 2378
Jewish literature between the Bible and the Mishnah. 57, 489
Jewish literature from the eighth to the eighteenth century. 2076
Jewish literature since the Bible. 2075
Jewish liturgy and its development. 2111
... Jewish magic and superstition. 1632
Jewish Marriage, Source of Sanctity. 2338
Jewish martyrs of the inquisition in South America. 2103, 3409
Jewish matrimonial law in the Middle Ages. 2345
Jewish Medieval and Renaissance studies. 2148
Jewish merchants in colonial America. 2104
... Jewish migrations. 2089
Jewish mind. 2075
Jewish monitor and guide to the Holy Land. 2119
Jewish music in its historical development. 2108, 2633, 2634
Jewish mystical testimonies. 2646
Jewish mystical tradition. 2646
Jewish Mysticism. 2646
Jewish nation. 2080
Jewish New Year. 3249
Jewish notables in America, 1776-1865. 2105
Jewish panorama. 2082
Jewish parent. 1611
Jewish party book. 1520, 2120
Jewish people. 2089, 2094
Jewish people and Jesus Christ after Auschwitz. 1084
Jewish people and their faith. 2113
Jewish people, faith, and life. 2146
Jewish people, Jewish thought. 2147
Jewish people, past and present. 2089
Jewish peril and the hidden hand. 2078
Jewish philosophers. 2842
Jewish philosophical polemics against Christianity in the Middle Ages. 1093
Jewish pioneers and patriots. 2106
... Jewish pioneers in America. 2105
Jewish polity completely overturned and the sceptre reserved for Jesus Christ. 2014
Jewish population of Chicago, Illinois. 2098
Jewish population of Greater Washington in 1956. 2107
Jewish portraits. 2084
Jewish post-Biblical history through great personalities. 2083
Jewish prayer and worship. 2109, 2886
Jewish prayers and songs. 2697
Jewish problem. 2077
Jewish problem and theology in general in accordance with the economical affairs of the present time and with the whole modern science and philosophy. 2116
Jewish problem in the modern world. 2078
Jewish prophets. 570
Jewish quarterly review. 2151
Jewish question. 2077
Jewish question and answer book on the Bible. Jewish lore and holidays. 2139
Jewish question and the great tribulation. 2079
Jewish question and the key to its solution. 2118
Jewish question and the mission of the Jews. 2082
Jewish quiz book. 2082
Jewish reader. 1455
Jewish reflections on death. 1416
Jewish religion. 2114
Jewish religion in the Soviet Union. 2154
Jewish religious conflicts. 2140
Jewish religious education for the retarded child. 2079
... Jewish religious life. 2113
... Jewish religious life after the exile. 2113
Jewish religious polemic of early and later centuries. 2144
Jewish reply to Christian evangelists. 1083
Jewish research literature. 657, 2083
Jewish return into history. 1825
Jewish rights at international congresses. 2078
Jewish rights at the congresses of Vienna (1814-1815) and Aix-la-Chapelle (1818) 2078
Jewish Sabbath. 3261
Jewish schools in Poland. 2102
Jewish schools under czarism and communism. 2103

Jewish science. 2113
Jewish science and health. 2086
Jewish Scriptures. 499
Jewish sects at the time of Jesus. 2080
Jewish self-government in the middle ages. 2112
Jewish services in synagogue and home. 2107
Jewish situation in eastern Europe including Russia and the work of the Joint distribution committee. 2102
Jewish social studies. 2111
Jewish song book for synagogue, school and home, covering the complete Jewish religious year. 3577
Jewish soul on fire. 1611, 2159
Jewish sources of the Sermon on the Mount. 3335
Jewish spectre. 2112
Jewish spirit triumphant. 2083
Jewish spiritual heroes. 2083
Jewish state. 3896
Jewish student's companion. 2086
Jewish studies at American and Canadian universities. 2122
Jewish studies in American colleges and universities. 2154
Jewish studies in memory of Israel Abrahams. 5, 2114, 2147
Jewish survival. 2116, 2146, 3371
Jewish survival in the world today. 2112
Jewish tales and legends. 3581
Jewish teacher training schools in the United States. 3166
Jewish teaching on peace. 2807
Jewish teenagers in Wilkes-Barre; a survey of attitudes and values conducted under the sponsorship of the Wilkes-Barre chapter of the American Jewish Committee and the Jewish Community Center of Wilkes-Barre. Research consultant: Irving Jacks. 3882
Jewish theology. 2080
Jewish theology, systematically and historically considered. 2080, 2115
Jewish tradition in the modern world. 2142
Jewish understanding of the New Testament. 348, 349, 408, 2153
Jewish understanding of the New Textament. 349, 2153
Jewish Utopia. 2114
Jewish values. 2081
Jewish values and social crisis. 2144
Jewish values for modern man. 2752
Jewish view of Jesus. 2013
Jewish view of prayer and worship. 2886
Jewish views of Jesus. 2014
Jewish war. 2091
Jewish war, and other selections from Flavius Josephus. 2091
Jewish Washington. 2683, 2794
Jewish way. 2120
Jewish way in death and mourning. 2627
Jewish way of life. 1538, 2081
Jewish way of life and thought. 2081
Jewish way to life. 2137
Jewish wedding. 2345
Jewish wedding book. 2345
Jewish woman and her home. 2121
Jewish woman in Jewish law. 3842
Jewish woman in Judaism. 3837
Jewish woman, 1900-1980. 3842
Jewish women and Jewish law bibliography. 3842
Jewish women through the ages. 3842
Jewish world in the time of Jesus. 408, 2091, 2149
Jewish worship. 2111
Jewish year. 1623
Jewish youth, challenge and promise. 3897
Jewish youth in America. 2118
Jewry-law in medieval Germany. 2107
Jews. 2013, 2077, 2088, 2153
Jews: a chronicle for Christian conscience. 2090, 2153
Jews among the nations. 499, 2087
Jews, ancient, medieval, and modern. 2088
Jews and Christians. 1083
Jews and Christians after the Holocaust. 1084
Jews and Christians in Antioch in the first four centuries of the common era. 2098
Jews and Christians in dialogue. 348, 2103
Jews and Christians in Egypt. 100, 1501, 2099
Jews and divorce. 1471
Jews and Freemasons in Europe 1723-1939. 1663
Jews and gospel. 1082
Jews and Jesus. 2219, 2556
Jews and "Jewish Christianity" 2144
Jews and Judaism. 2092
Jews and Judaism during the Greek period. 2092

... Jews and Judaism in the nineteenth century. 2112
Jews and Judaism in the United States. 2106
Jews and minority rights. 2078
Jews and modern capitalism. 2112
Jews and Moors in Spain. 2103
... The Jews and other minor nationalities under the soviets. 2103
Jews and Palestine. 610
Jews and Palestine in the light of prophecy. 2119
Jews and the cults. 2152
Jews and the gospel. 1082
Jews and the Mosaic law. 184, 2115
Jews and the passion for Palestine in the light of prophecy. 2118
Jews and world affairs. 2078
Jews behind the Iron Curtain. 2098
Jew's Christian. 2073
Jews come to America. 2105
Jews for Jesus. 2556, 3249
Jews from Alexander to Herod. 2092, 2150
Jews from Cyrus to Herod. 2096
Jews from Germany in the United States. 2104
Jews, Gentiles, and the church. 1079
Jews, God and history. 2088
Jews, Greeks and Christians. 350, 1406, 2149
Jews in a Christian social order. 2078
Jews in a free society. 2142
Jews in a gentile world. 2077
Jews in America. 2104, 2106, 2155
Jews in American Alaska, 1867-1880. 2098
Jews in American history. 2104, 2107
Jews in American wars. 2104
Jews in American wars, by J. George Fredman and Louis A. Falk. 2104
Jews in Egypt and in Palestine under the Fatimid caliphs. 2092
Jews in Louisiana. 2100
Jews in Maerican life. 2104
Jews in medieval Germany. 2100
Jews in Nazi Germany. 2099
Jews in New England. 2101
Jews in Poland. 2102
Jews in Russia. 2102
Jews in South Africa. 2097
... The Jews in Spain. 2103
Jews in the East. 1651, 2761
Jews in the post-war world. 3028
Jews in the province of Posen. 2102
Jews in the Soviet satellites. 2099
Jews in the Soviet Union. 2103
Jews in the Visigothic and Frankish kingdoms of Spain and Gaul. 2092
Jews, let us stop dreaming! 2079
Jews of Africa. 2097
... The Jews of Angevin England. 2099
Jews of Asia. 2098
Jews of Charleston. 2098
Jews of Des Moines. 2098
Jews of eastern Europe. 2102
Jews of Germany. 2099
Jews of medieval Oxford. 2101
Jews of modernity. 2107, 2141
Jews of Russia and Poland. 2102
Jews of Spain and Portugal and the Inquisition. 1908, 2103
Jews' reasons for believing in one God only. 2117
Jews; social patterns of an American group. 2105
Jews' success. 2112
Jews: their history, culture, and religion. 2088, 2146
Jews, their religious beliefs and practices. 2146
...The Jews today; a call to Christian action. 2077
Jews transition. 2100
Jews under Hitlerism. 2100
Jews under Roman rule. 2090
Jews, unite! 2111
Jews: views and counterviews. 860, 2141
Jewthink. 2751
Jim Crow comes to church. 822, 1132, 1133
Jim Handy, the wandering preacher. 3135
Jim, I need you. 1377
Jimmy Moss. 3 132
Jingles of humor, sarcasm, and facts, to tingle the priest. 2081
Jingo. 3064
Jnana-yoga. 3775
Jo, the Indian friend. 3518
Joab Powell. 2866
Joachim of Fiore and the prophetic future. 1819, 2122
Joachim of Fiore in Christian thought. 2122
Joachim of Flora. 2122
Joan, maid of France. 1938
Joan, Maid of Orleans. 1938

Joan of Arc. 1026, 1110, 1937, 1938, 1939, 2122
Joan of Arc and her companions. 1938
Joan of Arc and the recovery of France. 1937
Joan of Arc loan exhibition catalogue. 1938
Joan of Arc, the life story of the Maid of Orleans. 1938
Joan of Arc. 1938
Joan the saint. 1937
Job. 547, 548, 549, 2124
Job: a study guide. 551
Job, a vision of God. 549, 2124
Job a world example. 2124
Job and Solomon. 600
Job and the mysteries of wisdom. 548
Job: defense of honor. 549
Job and his old friends and his new friend. 551
Job, hated but hedged. 2124
Job, his old friends and his new friend. 551
Job, moral hero. 2124
Job, our contemporary. 550
Job: poet of existence. 548
Job, Song of songs, Ruth and Ecclesiastes. 482, 591
Job speaks. 551
Job speaks to us today. 549
Job speaks to us today. 549
Job, the hero par excellence. 2124
Job the man speaks with God. 2124
Job's encounter. 550
Job's illness. 1425, 2124
Jock, Jack, and the corporal. 1364
Joel and Amos. 552
Joel Drury Miller, in that land where only true unselfish service counts. 2466
Joel finds out. 2151
Joel, Obadiah, Jonah and Malachi. 552
Joel's prophetic message and warning. 552
Joey finds out how his church works. 3386
Johann Adam Mohler. 2568
Johann Christian Edelmann. 1496, 3024
Johann Conrad Beissel. 185, 1521
Johann Conrad Beissel, mystic and martinet, 1690-1768. 185
Johannean problem. 419
Johannes. 2127, 2128
Johannes in eremo. 1333, 1372
Johannine Christology and the early Church. 421, 2011
Johannine circle. 419, 2125
Johannine Council. 3769
Johannine Council, witness to unity. 3769
Johannine epistles. 369
Johannine Gospel in gnostic exegesis: Heracleon's commentary on John. 421, 1718, 1804
Johannine lessons in the Greek Gospel lectionary. 421
Johannine literature and the Acts of the apostles. 413
Johannine school. 414, 2125
Johannine Son of Man. 420, 3458
Johannine studies. 413
Johannine synopsis of the Gospels. 1990
Johannine theology. 414
Johannine writings, a study of the Apocalypse and the Fourth gospel. 413
Johannine writings and the Johannine problem. 414
Johannis Wyclif Summa de ente. 1729, 2739
John. 421, 2123
John A. Morehead who created world Lutheranism. 2597
John Albert Bengel's Gnomon of the New Testament. 342
John Alexander Dowie and the Christian catholic apostolic church in Zion. 932, 1478
John Alexis Edgren, soldier, educator, author, journalist. 1497
John and Betty Stam, martyrs. 3524
John and Charles Wesley. 2427, 3631
John and his five books. 414
John and his friends. 3337
... John and his writings. 414, 2126
John and Jesus in their day and ours. 1963, 2127
John, apostle of peace. 2126
John Bale, mythmaker for the English Reformation. 131
John Baptist de La Salle. 695, 2189
John Baptist Scalabrini, apostle to emigrants. 667, 3306
John Baptist's decreasing and Christ's increasing witnessed. 134, 2127
... John Binney. 659
John Brockenbrough Newton. 2706
John Bull considers his church. 1220
John Bunyan. 716
John Bunyan's dream story. 717
...John Bunyan's Pilgrim's progress. 717

John Bunyan's The pilgrim progress. 717
John Calvin. 727, 728, 729, 1854, 2256, 2976
John Calvin and John Wesley. 727
John Calvin and the Calvinistic tradition. 727, 730
John Calvin and the Genevan reformation. 727
John Calvin, contemporary prophet. 727
John Calvin in New England. 2687
John Calvin on God and political duty. 2858
John Calvin: selections from his writings. 3044, 3629
John Calvin, the organiser of reformed Protestantism. 728
John Calvin, the organiser of reformed Protestantism, 1509-1564. 728
John Calvin versus the Westminster Confession. 3808
... John Calvin's "Instruction in Christianity," 3044
John Calvin's sermons on the Ten commandments. 1315
John Calvin's teachings on human reason. 727, 3027
John Carroll, bishop and patriot. 742
John Carroll of Baltimore. 742
John Carroll papers. 742
John Cassian. 744, 2575, 2578
John celebrates the Gospel. 417
John Chambers. 880
John Charles Ryle. 666, 3259
John Checkley. 890, 1523, 2371
John Chrysostom and his time. 1115
John Clark Archer. 78
John Cobb's theology in process. 1305
John Colet and Marsilio Ficino. 1307
John Colet and the Platonic tradition. 1307, 2854
John Cotton. 1372
John Cotton on the churches of New England. 1334
John Counsellor's evolution. 3319
John Courtney Murray. 2632, 3611
John defends the gospel. 419
John, disciple, evangelist, apostle. 419, 2126
John Doe, disciple. 2933
John Donne. 1476
John Donne and the metaphysical poets. 1476, 3210
John Donne treasury. 1016
John Dunmore Lang. 2195
John Duns Scotus, 1265-1965. 2837
John Dury, advocate of Christian reunion. 1045, 1484
John E. Green and his forty years in Houston. 3127
John E. Williams of Nanking. 2668, 3817
John Eliot, apostle to the Indians. 1507
John Eliot's Indian dialogues. 1507, 2370
John Ellard the newsboy. 1508
John Ellerton. 3198
John England. 1516
John England, bishop of Charleston. 1516
John F. Kennedy and American Catholicism. 874, 2167
John F. Kennedy and his church. 826
John Fletcher Hurst. 1857
John fourteen. 2127
John Foxe and his book. 1637
John Foxe and the Elizabethan church. 1188, 1637
John Frederic Oberlin. 2720
John Frederick Starck's Daily hand-book in good and evil days. 2396
...John Freeman and his family. 3124
... John Freeman Young. 3869
John G. Paton. 2792
John G. Paton, hero of the South Seas. 2792
John G. Paton, missionary to the New Hebrides. 3132, 3133
John G. Paton, missionary to the New Hebrides. 2542, 2792
John Gilmary Shea. 3401
... John (Gospel, letters, Revelation) 355
John Greenleaf, minister. 3132
John H. Scheide Biblical papyri. 518
John Hales of Eton. 1781
John Hall. 1781
John Henery Newman. 2702
John Henry. 2704
John Henry Barrows, a memoir. 3124
John Henry, Cardinal Newman. 738, 2702, 2704
John Henry Jowett, C. H., M. A., D. D. 2135
John Henry Newman. 2703, 2704
John Henry Newman and the Abbe Jager. 206
John Henry Newman, the romantic, the friend, the leader. 2703
John Heyl Vincent. 3136
John Heyl Vincent; a biographical sketch. 3779

John, his record of Christ. 2127
John Hughes. 1851
John Humphrey Noyes. 2716, 2737
John Hus. 1857
John Hus, a biography. 1857, 3038
John Hus and the Czech reform. 1857
John Hus at Constance. 1857
John Hus at the Council of Constance. 1354, 1857
John Hus' concept of the church. 1188, 1857
John Hus, the martyr of Bohemia. 1857
John Huss. 1857
John in the isle of Patmos. 458
John Jasper. 1936
John Jewel and the problem of doctrinal authority. 2072
John Kebel [by]. 2166
John Keble. 2166, 2754
John Kenneth Mackenzie. 2309
John Kline, a brother in reality. 1235, 2178
John Knox. 2181, 2182
John Knox and the Reformation. 2181
John Knox: portrait of a Calvinist. 2181
John Knox, the hero of the Scottish Reformation. 2181
John La Farge, gentle Jesuit. 2188
John La Farge reader. 759
John Lancaster Spalding. 3469
John, life eternal. 416
John Leland story. 2209
John Locke. 2241
John Locke, a biography. 2241
John McCullough, "grandfather," 3131
John McMillan. 2309
John McMillan, the apostle of Presbyterianism in the West, 1752-1833. 2309
John Mark. 2335
John Mark and the origin of the gospels. 390, 2335
John Mason Neale, D.D. 2678
John Mill and Richard Bentley. 351, 2463
John Milton. 2469
John Milton, his life and times, religious and political opinions. 2468
John Milton: Paradise lost. 2469, 2471
John Milton: topical bibliography. 2469
... John Milton's last thoughts on the Trinity. 3713
John Monteith and Detroit Presbyterianism. 2586
John Morgan Walden. 3788
John Neumann. 667, 2685
John Nevins Andrews, flame for the Lord. 41
John Newton, author of the song "Amazing grace," 2705
John of God. 1028, 2136
John of Salisbury. 2125
John of the Golden Mouth. 1115
John of Torquemada, O. P. 1169, 3704
John Paul II, catechist. 746
John Paul II in our Nation's Capital. 2126, 2863
John Paul II. 2126, 2861
John Paul II, a pictorial celebration. 2126, 2863
John Paul II, pilgrimage of faith. 2863
John Paul II, the Pilgrim Pope. 2126, 2861
John Penry and the Marprelate controversy. 2336, 2813
John, Peter, and the Fourth gospel. 419
John R. Mott. 2625
John R. Mott, world citizen. 2626
John R. Mott, 1865-1955. 2625, 3874
John Robinson and the English separatist tradition. 3241, 3653
John Ronge, the holy coat of Treves. 1707
... John Ruskin. 3255
John Ruskin, preacher. 3255
... John Ruskin; The two boyhoods. 3255
John Saffin. 1017
John Scripps. 3316
John 17. 388, 424
John shines through Augustine. 422
John Smith Moffat, C.M.G. missionary. 3131
John Strachan, 1778-1867. 3535
John Sung. 912
John Tay, messenger to Pitcairn. 2487, 3589
John the Baptist. 2127, 2128, 2952
John the Baptist, forerunner of Jesus. 339, 632, 2128
John the Baptist in the gospel tradition. 393, 2128
John the Baptist, the forerunner of Our Lord. 2127
John, the Gospel of belief. 418
John, the Gospel of life. 421
John, the gospel of the Word, the gospel of the only Beloved Son. 417
John, the interpreter of Christ. 2127

John, the intrepid. 3387
John, the loyal. 2128
John, the maverick Gospel. 420
John the Presbyter. 414, 2126, 2127
John the Twenty-Third. 2123
John XXIII and the city of man. 853
John XXIII; simpleton or saint? 2123
John XXIII. 2123, 2861
John XXIII and American Protestants. 861, 2954
John XXIII and the city of man. 853
John, the universal Gospel. 417
John Todd. 3136
John 12 12ff. and the question of John's use of the Synoptics. 2127
John Walmsley, ninth bishop of Sierra Leone. 3790
John Welch, the man who couldn't be stopped. 1300, 3801
John Wesley. 1291, 2428, 2459, 3007, 3631, 3802, 3803, 3804, 3805
John Wesley among the scientists. 3077, 3803
John Wesley and his world. 1292, 3804
John Wesley and modern religion. 2421, 3803
John Wesley and the Church of England. 1211, 3802, 3804
John Wesley and the eighteenth century. 3803
John Wesley as a social reformer. 3805
John Wesley, friend of the people. 3804
John Wesley in the evolution of Protestantism. 2978, 3804
John Wesley, master in religion. 3804
John Wesley prayer book. 2433
John Wesley: spiritual witness. 3803
John Wesley the Methodist. 3803
John Wesley treasury. 2428, 3631
John Wesley's awakening. 3803
John Wesley's England. 1516, 3805
John Wesley's first hymn-book. 2430
John Wesley's Journal. 3805
John Wesley's New Testament. 356
John Wesley's New Testament, compared with the Authorized version. 356
John Wesley's religious quest. 3803
John Wesley's theology. 2428, 3650
John Wesley's theology today. 3806
John Wheelwright: his writings. 2371, 3820
John White of Mashonaland. 3812
John Whitgift and the English Reformation. 3813
John Wiclif's Polemical works in Latin. 3861
John Wilbur Chapman. 886
John Wilkins, 1614-1672. 3085, 3816
John William Carter. 3129
John Williams, the shipbuilder. 2545, 3817
John Winebrenner: nineteenth century reformer. 3820
John Wise. 3822
John Wise, early American democrat. 3822
John woolman. 3847
John Woolman, American Quaker. 3847
John Woolman: child of light. 3847
John Wyclif. 3860, 3861
John Wyclif and reform. 3861
John Wyclif and the English Bible. 248
John Wyclif, last of the schoolmen and first of the English reformers. 3861
John Wycliffe and the beginnings of English noncomformity. 3038, 3860
John Wycliffe and the beginnings of English nonconformity. 3860
John Wycliffe and the first English Bible. 3861
John Wycliffe, patriot and reformer. 3861
Johndro's theory of planetary rulerships of aspects per se. 96, 2128
John's Gospel. 423
John's letters—light for living. 369
John's witness to Jesus. 423
John's wonderful Gospel. 417
Johnson's New illustrated family atlas of the world ... with physical geography, and with descriptions, geographical, statistical and historical, including the latest federal census, and the existing religious denominations in the world. 102
Johnson's sermons. 2129, 3367
... Johnson's worker's Bible. 258
Join us for the holidays. 1614
Join your right hands. 3800
Joint festival celebration of the seventy-fifth anniversary, jew's college. 2243
Joke of Christianizing China. 2512
Joking apart. 1211
Jolly old St. Nicholas. 2707
Jon and the little lost lamb. 2260
Jonah. 495, 552, 553, 633, 2129, 2130, 3364

Jonah and the big fish. 634, 2130
Jonah and the great fish. 633, 2130
Jonah and the Lord. 616, 2130
Jonah and the whale. 495, 634, 1653, 2129, 2130
Jonah Bondi Wise. 3822
Jonah complex. 552
Jonah, go to Nineveh! 633, 2130
Jonah in fact and fancy. 552
Jonah legend. 552
Jonah, living in rebellion. 552
Jonah, messenger of the eleventh hour. 552
Jonah speaks. 553
Jonah, the reluctant prophet. 2129
Jonah, verse by verse. 552
Jonah's journey. 633, 2130
Jonah's trip to Tarshish. 163
Jonas and the whale. 2130
Jonas King. 2172
Jonathan. 2130
Jonathan Edwards. 1498, 1499
Jonathan Edwards, 1703-1758. 1499
Jonathan Edwards; a profile. 1499
Jonathan Edwards, a retrospect. 1499, 1500
Jonathan Edwards Adams, D. D., and Maine Congregationalism. 7, 1336
Jonathan Edwards & the visibility of God. 1498
Jonathan Edwards, bibliographical synopses. 1500
Jonathan Edwards; his life and influence. 1499
Jonathan Edwards on Evangelism. 1564
Jonathan Edwards, pastor. 1333, 1499
Jonathan Edwards, 1703-1758. 1500
Jonathan Edwards, the fiery Puritan. 1345, 1499
Jonathan Edwards the Younger, 1745-1801. 1500
Jonathan Edwards, theologian of the heart. 1499
Jonathan Edwards's moral thought and its British context. 950, 1499
Jonathan Fisher, Maine parson. 1628
Jonathan loved David. 1844
Jonathan, you left too soon. 658, 1774
Jones character movement (to help our children) 2591
Jorgen Eriksson. 2136, 3041
Joseph. 633, 634, 2132, 2133
Joseph and Asenath. 488
Joseph and Benjamin. 60
Joseph and Emma Smith, companions for seventeen and a half years, 1827-1844. 2609, 3428
Joseph and his brethren. 2134
Joseph and his brothers. 495, 616, 2132, 2133, 2134
Joseph and his brothers, from the story told in the book of Genesis. 634, 2133
Joseph and Jesus. 2132
Joseph Carlebach and his generation. 739
Joseph Dutton. 2568
Joseph E. Ramseyer--"yet speaking," 3021
Magic. 2725
Joseph Fielding Smith; a prophet among the people. 3430
Joseph Glanvill. 58, 1715
Joseph, God's man in Egypt. 492, 2133, 2792
Joseph H. Kennard, D. D.; a memorial. 2167
Joseph Hopkins Twichell. 3719
Joseph ibn Kaspi's Gevia' kesef. 505, 744, 2841
Joseph in Egypt. 2134
Joseph John Gurney. 1778
Joseph John Gurney: banker, reformer, and Quaker. 1778
Joseph Karo, lawyer and mystic. 741
Joseph Lewis--enemy of God. 1654, 2220
Joseph Most Just. 2132
Joseph narrative in Genesis. 528, 2133
Joseph Nichols and the Nicholites. 2708
Joseph of Egypt. 2132, 2614
Joseph Sadoc Alemany. 24
Joseph Smith. 2602, 2606, 3428, 3429
Joseph Smith and his Mormon empier. 2600, 3428
Joseph Smith and the restoration. 1233
Joseph Smith and world government. 3428
Joseph Smith as scientist. 3429
Joseph Smith begins his work. 2607, 3429
Joseph Smith chronology. 2617, 3430
Joseph Smith, democracy's unknown prophet. 3429
Joseph Smith, martyr, prophet of God. 2617, 3428
Joseph Smith: prophet of the restoration. 3428
Joseph Smith, prophet-statesman. 3429
Joseph Smith, the first Mormon. 2609, 3428
Joseph Smith, the man and the seer. 3428

... Joseph Smith, the prophet, his family and his friends. 2607, 3430
Joseph Smith III and the Restoration. 2605, 661
Joseph Smith's first vision. 2619, 3428, 3782
Joseph Smith's New England heritage. 3427
Joseph Smith's new translation of the Bible. 268
Joseph Smith's teachings. 3430
Joseph son of David. 2133
Joseph, the dreamer. 633, 2133
Joseph the forgiver. 495, 634, 2134
Joseph, the Jew. 2132
Joseph, the just. 2132
Joseph, the just man. 2132
Joseph: the man closest to Jesus. 2132
Joseph the prime-minister. 2133
Joseph the prophet. 3428
Joseph the seer. 678, 3428
Joseph the silent. 2132
Joseph; the story of twelve brothers. 2133
Joseph Williams and the pioneer mission to the southeastern Bantu. 2499, 3817
Joseph's harvest. 3371
Josephus and the Jews. 2134
Josephus on Jesus. 2134
Josephus, the man and the historian. 2134
Josh, excitement of the unexpected. 1576, 2307
Joshua. 553, 2134
Joshua: a commentary. 553
Joshua and the flow of Biblical history. 554, 2134
Joshua, Bible study commentary. 553
Joshua Bloch memorial volume. 672, 2143
Joshua Davidson, Christian. 3129
... Joshua, his life and time. 2134
Joshua in the light of the New Testament. 554, 990, 2134
Joshua-Judges. 554, 2096, 2764
Joshua, Judges, Ruth. 497, 553
Joshua, Judges, Samuel, Kings. 520
Joshua, leader of a united people. 2134
Joshua, man of faith. 2134
Joshua: rest-land won. 554
Joshua roll. 3768
Joshua, the Hebrew and Greek texts. 553
Joshua, the redeemer. 2134
Joshua Wiggins and the king's kids. 899
Joshua's long day and the dial of Ahaz. 502
... Josiah Bushnell Grinnell. 1775
Jottings from life. 3125
Journals, 1737-1741. 1757
Journal. 1636, 2445, 2446, 2455, 2594, 3805, 3847
Journal (abridged) of Wm. Edmondson, Quaker apostle to Ireland & the Americas, 1627-1712. 1497
... The journal and essays of John Woolman. 1778
Journal and essays on religious subjects. 1674
Journal and letters. 89
Journal and letters of the Rev. Henry Martyn. 3815
Journal and major essays of John Woolman. 3424
Journal and minutes of the ... session of the West Texas annual conference. 2445
Journal and records of the ... session of the Illinois annual conference. 2444
Journal and year book of the...sesion of the Erie Annual conference. 2446
Journal and year book of the...session of the Erie Annual Conference. 2446
Journal diary of a Baha'i teacher in Latin America. 130
Journal diary of Baha'i travels in Europe. 129
Journal-diary of European Baha'i travels. 129
Journal for life. 3482
Journal for Mary. 2354
Journal for renewal. 1014
Journal for the theology and the church. 3677
Journal for theology and the church. 3616, 3677, 3678
Journal into faith. 2704
Journal of a Catholic bishop on the Oregon trail. 668, 670
Journal of a fast. 1613, 3427
Journal of a happy woman. 3536
Journal of a Jewish traveller. 2103
Journal of a late vocation. 774
Journal of a parish priest. 774, 2635
Journal of a psychoanalyst-priest. 3110
Journal of a rabbi. 2139
Journal of a soul. 2123, 2861
Journal of a southern pastor. 774
Journal of a tour on the "Indian territory" 1901
Journal of an itinerant artist. 123, 875
Journal of an ordinary pilgrim. 960

Journal of Ann Branson. 1674
*Journal of Biblical literature. 211
Journal of discourses digest. 2608
Journal of ecclesiastical history (The) 1189
Journal of Father Adam Marshall, 1824-1825. 661
Journal of George Fox. 1636
Journal of Heber C. Kimball, an elder of the Church of Jesus Christ of latter day saints. 2616
Journal of Jesse N. Smith, compiled and edited by Nephi Jensen. 2605, 3427
Journal of John Wesley. 3805
Journal of John Woolman. 3847
Journal of Joseph Pilmore, Methodist itinerant, for the years August 1, 1769, to January 2, 1774. 3133
Journal of Leo Tolstoi. 661
Journal of proceedings of the ... annual council of the diocese of Lexington. 2958
Journal of proceedings of the ... annual session. 673
Journal of proceedings of the ... annual session of the most worthy District grand lodge, no. 4. 673
Journal of that faithful servant of Christ, Charles Osborn. 1686
Journal of the 1st- annual meeting of the Board of missions. 2441
Journal of the Alabama annual conferences of the Methodist Episcopal church. 2444
Journal of the annual convention. 2959
Journal of the ... annual convocation of the missionary district of Utah and Idaho. 2958
Journal of the annual council. 2974
Journal of the ... annual council of the Protestant Episcopal church, in the diocese of Western New-York. 2975
Journal of the annual meeting of the convention together with reports. 2971
Journal of the ... annual session of the New Mexico English mission. 2445
Journal of the ... annual session of the Northwest Nebraska conference. 2445
Journal of the ... annual session of the Puget Sound conference. 2445
Journal of the ... annual synod of the diocese of Quincy ... 1st. 2958
Journal of the bishops, clergy and laity. 2958
Journal of the Columbia River annual conference. 2444
Journal of the Florida annual conference ... Session. 2445
Journal of the General convention of the Prostestant Episcopal chruch in the United States of America. 2966
Journal of the Idaho annual conference ... Session. 2444
Journal of the life. 3134
Journal of the life and religious labors of Sarah Hunt. 3129
Journal of the life and religious labours of Elias Hicks. 1810
Journal of the life and religious labours of John Comly. 3125
Journal of the life and religious services of William Evans, a minister of the gospel in the Society of Friends. 3126
Journal of the life, gospel labours, and Christian experiences, of that faithful minister of Jesus Christ, John Woolman. 3847
Journal of the life of gospel labors. 3847
Journal of the life of Joseph Hoag. 3128
Journal of the life of that ancient servant of Christ. 3127
Journal of the life, religious exercises, and travels in the work of the ministry of Rufus Hall. 3127, 3128
Journal of the life, travels and gospel labours of that faithful servant and minister of Christ. 3134
Journal of the life, travels, and labours in the work of the ministry. 1675
Journal of the life, travels, labours, and religious exercises of Isaac Martin. 2925, 3131
Journal of the primary convention of the clergy and laity of the Protestant Episcopal Church in the Diocese of Illinois, held in Peoria ... March 9, 1835. 2962
Journal of the proceedings of the ... annual convention of the Protestant Episcopal church in the diocese of Western Michigan. 2958
Journal of the proceedings of the General council of the Protestant Episcopal church in the Confederate States of America. 2956, 2958
Journal of the ... quadrennial session of the General conference of the Methodist Protestant church. 2459

Journal of the Rev. Francis Asbury. 2444
Journal of the Rev. John Wesley. 2422, 3137
Journal of the Rev. William Bagshaw Stevens. 3135
Journal of the Reverend John Wesley. 3137
Journal of the ... session. 2444
Journal of the ... session of the Montana annual conference. 2445
Journal of the ... session of the New York east annual conference. 2445
Journal of the ... session of the Pacific Japanese mission. 2445
Journal of the ... session of the Texas annual conference. 2445
Journal of the ... session of the Washington conference. 2445
Journal of the sixtieth annual session of the General convention of the New Jerusalem in the United States of America. 1121
Journal of the Southern Indian Mission. 1903
Journal of the stated preacher to the hospital and alms-house, in the city of New-York, for the year of Our Lord 1811. 1911
Journal of the Uniting conference of the Methodist Episcopal church. 2444
Journal of Thomas Chalkley. 1679
Journal of voyages and travels by the Rev. Daniel Tyerman and Goerge Bennet, esq. 3788
Journal of William Edmundson, 1627-1712 (abridged and designed for daily devotional reading) 1497
Journal or historical account of the life, travels, sufferings, Christian experiences, and labour of love in the work of the ministry, of that ancient, eminent, and faithful servant of Jesus Christ, George Fox. 1637
Journal with other writings of John Woolman. 1676
Journalist's prayer book. 2135
Journals and diaries (Wollaston, John Ramsden) 3137
Journals and letters of Mother Theodore Guerin. 3419
Journals and papers of Chauncy Maples. 1224
Journals and papers (Shultze, David) 3135
Journals (Kierkegaard, Soren Aabye) 2170
Journals of Eric Norelius. 3132
Journals of general conventions of the Protestant Episcopal church. 2967
Journals of Henry Melchior Muhlenberg. 2630
Journals of Jim Elliot. 1509, 2485
Journals of Soren Kierkegaard. 2170
Journals of the annual conventions of the Protestant Episcopal church, in the diocese of Ohio. Diocese organized, A. D. 1818. 2958
Journals of the conventions of the Protestant Episcopal church in the diocese of New York. 2958
Journals of the general conventions of the Protestant Episcopal church, in the United States of America. 2958, 2967
La journee des malades. Daily life of the sick. 3406
Journey. 3795
Journey away from God. 203
Journey beyond. 3191
Journey from Babylon to Jerusalem. 2672
Journey from Egypt to Jerusalem. 1360
Journey from sense to soul. 3191
Journey Godward of a servant of Jesus Christ. 3191
Journey in faith. 933, 3666
Journey in the night. 2137, 2642
Journey into Christ. 3484
Journey into faith. 2390
Journey into fullness. 985
Journey into His presence. 3295
Journey into joy. 986
Journey into light. 1366, 3477
Journey into light; a study of the long search for truth in a world darkened by dogma, and an examination of first century Christianity as the only solution for the moral dilemmas of the nuclear age. 3064
Journey into light and joy. 1023
Journey into mission. 2535
Journey into the void. 1081
Journey into truth. 1364
Journey into usefulness. 986
Journey inward, journey outward. 3797
Journey inwards. 2379
... The journey of a white gift. 1114
Journey of insight meditation. 712, 2217
Journey of Jesus. 1989
Journey of love. 2124, 3460, 3526

Journey of Luther and their important relation ot the work of the reformation. 2274
Journey of the heart. 390, 2874
Journey of the human spirit. 3478
Journey of the soul and the ethereal world. 2724
Journey of the three kings. 1522
Journey of Western spirituality. 3522
Journey that men make. 1006
Journey through a wall. 1674
Journey through the Bible. 224, 293
Journey through the Bible lands. 537
Journey through the Holy Land. 2131
Journey through the Old Testament. 532
Journey to Bethlehem. 2006
Journey to Calvary. 2032
Journey to Carith. 741
Journey to Easter. 2211
Journey to fulfillment. 984
Journey to Gorakhpur. 1079
Journey to Great-Salt-Lake City. 2605
Journey to inner space. 2381
Journey to Jerusalem. 2003
Journey to joy. 2215
Journey to the Lord of Power. 3544
Journey to the other side. 94
Journey to the other world. 1696
Journey toward freedom. 2222
Journey toward joy. 449
Journey toward renewal. 1244, 2570, 3242
Journey toward wholeness. 3490, 3697
Journey towards self-realization. 3330
Journey with David Brainerd. 689, 2888
Journey with the saints. 924
Journeying in South America. 2547
Journeying through a jungle. 166
Journeyings of Jesus. 1988
Journeyman in Jordan. 2491
Journeys. 765, 3611
Journeys beautiful. 626, 1969
Journeys of Jesus. 1981, 2014
Journeys of St. Paul. 2804
Journeys on the razor-edged path. 1896
Journeys out of the body. 94
Journeys through space. 3499
Journeys to glory. 1615
Journeys to the planet Mars. 3517
Journeys with Jesus and Paul. 283, 1984
Journeys with Mary. 2357
Journeys without maps. 3882
Joy. 1003, 2054, 2135, 2136
Joy and power. 978
Joy and rejoicing. 613
Joy and strength for the pilgrim's day. 1442
Joy before us. 3216
Joy begins with you. 2136
Joy beyond grief. 1349
Joy beyond sorrow. 1528
Joy comes with the morning. 1351
Joy every morning. 2136
Joy in believing. 864, 1445
Joy in church membership. 155
Joy in creation and judgment. 3643
Joy in His presence. 2388
Joy in service. 3377
Joy in sorrow. 1452
Joy in stone. 3052
Joy in the face of death. 1352
Joy in the Lord. 2974, 3360
Joy in the morning. 1436
Joy in the spiritual life. 3487
Joy is. 2136
Joy maker. 3477
Joy of being human. 1431
Joy of belonging. 1201
Joy of caring. 3576
Joy of discipleship. 159
Joy of discovery. 2488, 3191
Joy of discovery in Bible study. 642
Joy of discovery in Bible study, in Bible teaching. 642
Joy of fellowship. 324
Joy of freedom. 1487
Joy of Jewish humor. 3014
Joy of Jewish living. 1614
Joy of life. 2116
Joy of life through yoga. 3866
Joy of living. 449, 974, 1325
Joy of revelations. 3191
Joy of salvation. 3290
Joy of service. 969
Joy of serving God. 3487
Joy of sorrow. 3540
Joy of study. 334
Joy of teaching. 3171
Joy of the plain life. 3409
Joy of worship. 1741
Joy robbers. 2135
Joy that endures. 2619
Joy that no man taketh from you. 2135
Joy to my heart. 2509, 3422
Joy to my youth. 3186
Joy to the world. 1566
Joybells of life. 2299, 3352

"Joyce I feel like I know you" 985
Joyce Jackson's so happy "if" book. 3880
Joyful Christian. 1217, 3633
Joyful community. 698
Joyful hours of Jesus. 2015
Joyful journey, highlights on the high way. 2485
Joyful kingdom of Raj Anandpur. 2545
Joyful life. 974
Joyful mysteries of the Rosary. 3248
Joyful mystery. 2023
Joyful songs. 1113
Joyful sound. 1875
Joyful voices. 1865
Joyful wedding. 2347
Joyfully expectant. 2625
Joyfully ready. 2308
Joyous adventure. 1267
Joyous birth. 1417
Joyous day. 1910
Joys beyond the threshold. 1695
Joys of Easter. 1485
Joys of Jesus. 162
Joys of meditation. 2381, 3892
Joys, sorrows. 3248
Joys that live. 2135
Jr. Hi-Y. 688
Juan Diego and the lady. 1458
Jubilee! 1576, 2827, 3622
Jubilee, a monk's journal. 1276, 2585
Jubilee at Mount Saint Mary's, October 6, 1858. 870
Jubilee book of the Brooklyn Jewish center. 2098
Jubilee essays. 1325
Jubilee gems of the Visitation order. 3421
Jubilee history of Latter-day saints Sunday schools. 1849-1899. 2614
Jubilee history of Latter-day saints Sunday schools. 2614
Jubilee in '53. 154
Jubilee lay lectures. 2200
Jubilee memorial. 1500
Jubilee memorial of the Throop avenue Presbyterian church and mission. 1632
Jubilee of the world. 3261
Jubilee of work for young men in North America. 3872
... Jubilee souvenir of the First Presbyterian church of Rahway, N. J. 3019
Jubilee souvenir of Temple Sinai, 1872-1922. 2693
... Jubilee voluem. 2082
Judaea weeping. 2090
Judaean scrolls. 1409
Judaeo-Christian tradition. 2139
Judah. 3144
Judah's sceptre and Joseph's birthright. 45, 2087
Judaic heritage. 2138
Judaic law. 523, 2138
Judaic tradition. 2112, 2150
Judaica. 2083
Judaica reference materials. 657, 2083
Judaica research at Yale university. 3862
Judaid. 3207
Judaism. 1084, 2073, 2113, 2115, 2116, 2137, 2138, 2140, 2145, 2146, 2147, 2149, 2151, 2154
Judaism, a way of life. 2138
Judaism and change. 108, 2696
Judaism and Christian beginnings. 349, 2149
Judaism and Christianity. 1083, 2118, 2151, 2153
Judaism and Christianity; perspectives and traditions. 1083
Judaism and Christianity, the two outstanding religions. 1083
Judaism and Christianity: what we believe. 2151
Judaism and cities in crisis. 2144
Judaism and ethics. 1539
Judaism and healing. 2377
Judaism and Hellenism. 2154
Judaism and human rights. 1280
Judaism and immortality. 1892
Judaism and Islam. 1926, 2154, 2185
Judaism and its history. 2117
Judaism and its traditions. 2114
Judaism and modern man. 2138, 2139
Judaism and prayer. 2885
Judaism and progress. 3371
Judaism and psychiatry. 3072
Judaism and psychical phenomena. 2144
Judaism and psychoanalysis. 2144
Judaism and St. Paul: two essays. 376, 2799, 3015
Judaism & the American Jew. 3371
Judaism and the American mind in theory and practice. 2113, 2138
Judaism and the Christian predicament. 2152
Judaism and the Christian seminary curriculum. 1084

Judaism and the early Christian mind. 1084, 1398
Judaism and the Gentile faiths. 2152
Judaism and the Jewish school. 2106
Judaism and the modern mind. 2114
Judaism and the modern world. 2116
Judaism and the new woman. 3837
Judaism and the scientific spirit. 3082
Judaism and the space age and other sermons. 3370
Judaism & tragic theology. 2080
Judaism as a civilization. 2084, 3028
Judaism as a philosophy. 4
Judaism as a religion. 3371
Judaism as creed and life. 2114
Judaism at bay. 2116, 2142
Judaism at the World's Parliament of Religions. 2143
Judaism, Christianity and Germany. 9
Judaism, Christianity, and Islam. 599, 2148
Judaism, Christianity and modern social ideals. 1083
Judaism confronts contemporary issues. 2074
Judaism despite Christianity. 2153
Judaism: development and life. 2140
Judaism for non-Jews. 2143
Judaism for the modern age. 2138
Judaism for today. 2138
Judaism in a changing civilization. 2104, 3028
Judaism in a changing world. 2082
Judaism in a Christian world. 2141
Judaism in America. 2155
Judaism in German Christian theology since 1945. 2152
Judaism in Islam. 1926, 2185, 2567
Judaism in the American humanities. 2154
Judaism in the first centuries of the Christian era. 2115, 3585
Judaism in the Greek period. 529, 567
Judaism in the secular age. 2141
Judaism in the war of ideas. 2083
Judaism in theory and practice. 2113, 2119, 2138, 2139
Judaism in transition. 2084
Judaism, Jewish-Christian relations, and the Christian mission to the Jew. 2144
Judaism meets Christ. 2535
Judaism meets Christ; guiding principles for the Christian-Jewish encounter. 2153
Judaism of Karl Shapiro. 3400
Judaism on trail. 1091
Judaism or Jewish nationalism. 2139
Judaism outside the Hebrew canon. 56, 1410
Judaism outside the Holy Land. 2085
Judaism, postbiblical and Talmudic period. 2145
Judaism speaks to the modern world. 3371
Judaism, the evidence of the Mishnah. 2479
Judaism, thought and legend. 1539
Judaism today and yesterday. 2141
Judaism under freedom. 3028
Judaism without supernaturalism. 3028
Judaistic Christianity. 1192
Judas. 2156
Judas (a study of possibilities) and Jude (a study of contrasts) 2156
Juda's jewels. 578
Judas, the betrayer. 2156
Jude, the Acts of the Apostles. 332
Judea from Cyrus to Titus. 2091
Judea in her desolations. 2092
Judeo-Christian heritage. 599
Judeo-Christian vision and the modern corporation. 1369
Judge among his candlesticks. 461
Judge for yourself; a workbook on contemporary challenges to Christian faith. 64
Judge Woodward and the Catholepistemaid, by William W. Bishop. 3847
Judgement and acquittal. 2214
Judgement seat of Christ. 2156
Judgements of Father Judge. 2156
Judgements of Joan. 1938
... The Judges. 269, 274, 554
Judges, a commentary. 555
Judges and a permissive society. 555
Judges and kings. 629
... Judges and Ruth. 554
Judges, Bible study commentary. 554
Judges look at themselves. 2156, 2670
... The judges of faith. 805
Judgment. 2157
Judgment and destiny. 3371
Judgment and mercy: or, Aaron dead and lamented, and Eleazar in his office. 3253
Judgment and redemption in Isaiah. 545, 2157

Judgment begun at the house of God. 2157
Judgment day for everybody. 2156
Judgment in pastoral counseling. 2780
Judgment in the church. 2156
Judgment of a Catholicke English-man living in banishment for his religion (1608) by Robert Persons. 816, 1934
Judgment of God. 3793
Judgment of Jonah. 2130
Judgment of the dead. 2157
Judgment of the nations. 1085
Judgment of the world. 2157
Judgment seat of Christ. 2157
Judgments of God upon the nations. 2157
Judgments: right or rash? 2157
Judicial acts of the General synod. 93
Judicial decisions of the General conference of the Methodist Episcopal church. 2444
Judicial doctrines of religious rights in America. 1490
Judiciary department of the diocean curia. 1488
Judiciary department of the diocesan curia. 1488
Judicious marriage of M'Hooker and the birth of The laws of ecclesiastical polity. 1844
Judicious marriage of Mr. Hooker and the birth of The laws of ecclesiastical polity. 1844
Judith, martyred missionary of Russia. 1366
Judson centennial, 1814-1914. 30
Judson concordance to hymns. 1871
Judson of Burma. 2157
Judson, the hero of Burma. 2157
Judson the pioneer. 2157
Judsons of Burma. 2157
Juges/Ruth. 554
Juggernaut. 1036
Juggling with Jesus. 1092, 2050
Juicing. 3894
Juju gods of West Africa. 2500
Julian and her Norwich: commemorative essays and handbook to the exhibition "Revelations of Divine Love" 1807, 2158
Julian of Norwich. 1448, 1455, 2158
Julian the Apostate. 2158
Julie Billiart. 659
Juliette Derricotte. 1425

Julius exclusus. 2158
Jumping beans. 2460
June prayers. 3253, 3270
Jung and St. Paul. 2159, 2160
Jung and Tarot. 2158, 2159, 3589
Jung and the problem of evil. 1746, 2159
Jung, gods, & modern man. 2159, 2999
Jungle call. 2504
Jungle doctor. 2539
Jungle Doctor series. 2539, 2540, 2552
Jungle heroes. 897
Jungle magic. 2314
Jungle Pilot. 2517, 3277
Jungle saints. 12
Jungle stories. 2505
Jungle thorn. 2491
Jung's hermeneutic of doctrine. 2159, 2993
Junior. 895, 936, 937
Junior; a handbook for his Sunday school teacher. 3564
Junior and his church. 3156, 3184
Junior and intermediate leaders' manual (revised 1942) 141
Junior and the church. 1117
Junior assembly programs. 3858
Junior Bible. 250
Junior Bible archaeology. 209
Junior Bible encyclopedia. 247
Junior boys write their life of Christ. 1992
Junior character sermons. 909
Junior choir leadership manual. 917
Junior Christian endeavor songs. 3459
Junior church. 1118
Junior church choir year-book of anthems for soprani and alti. 49
Junior church in action. 1253
Junior church manual. 905
Junior citizen. 896
Junior class manual. 3565
Junior confirmation book. 1329
Junior congregation. 906
Junior department. 3171
Junior department of the church school. 3557
Junior department organization and administration. 3564
Junior endeavor in theory and practice. 896, 1914
Junior folks at mission study--India. 2529
Junior-hi. 3876
Junior high ministry. 1260

Junior high school boys and girls in the church. 3167
Junior highs. 1261
Junior highs and their MYF. 905
Junior history of Methodism. 2421, 2424
Junior hour; a junior guidance manual of sermons and prayer band outlines for ministers. 908
Junior hymnal. 2288, 3561
Junior Jewish encyclopedia. 2085
Junior leader's guide on the contribution of the church to the development of Canada. 734
Junior leadership manual. 141
Junior magic sermon-talks. 909
Junior manual for missionary volunteer workers. 2550
Junior manual for those who plan for and work with junior-age boys and girls in the church. 3172
... Junior method in the church school. 3156
Junior missionary stories. 3046
Junior nature sermons. 909
Junior object sermons. 909
Junior pageants. 2757
Junior parish. 908
Junior plan book. 3155
Junior prayer book. 2108
Junior sermon stories. 909
Junior sermons for special occasions. 909
Junior society in action. 169
Junior stewards of the Bible. 898
Junior stories with Bible outline study. 632
Junior story talks. 907
Junior studies in the life of Christ. 2014
Junior Sunday school work. 3171
Junior surprise sermons. 909
Junior talks for special days. 3160
Junior teacher's guide on Christian concerns of North American neighbors. 1108
Junior teacher's guide on Churches for new times. 1254
Junior teacher's guide on South America. 2547
Junior teacher's guide to accompany. 3121
Junior teacher's text books. 648
Junior text-book. 3737
...The junior worker and his work. 2443
Junior workers' hand book. 3160
Junior workers' manual, including helps for Bible study, worship themes, projects, special selections for junior workers in Sunday school, worship services, vacation Bible schools, week-day religious schools [and] the home circle. 3172
Junior worker's note-book. 3736
Junior worship. 3560
Junior worship guide, of special value to schools using the Church school closely graded courses. 3853
Junior worship materials in program form. 3858
Juniors. 3169
Juniors in training. 3184
Junipera Serra. 3377
Junipero Serra. 2506, 3377
Junipero Serra in his native isle (1713-1749) 2318, 3376
Juno. 2159, 3246
Junor history of Methodism. 2424
Jupiter: the preserver. 96
Jura sacerdotum vindicata. 1290
... The juridic effects of moral certitude on pre-nuptial guarantees. 2346
Juridical aspect of incorporation into the church of Christ--Canon 87. 137
Juridical status of churches. 1141
Jurisdiction of the confessor according the Code of canon law. 2811
Jurisdiction of the patriarchs of the major sees in antiquity and in the Middle Ages. 2792
Jurisprudence of Freemasonry. 1666
Just a half-a-minute. 1438
Just a minute! 2387
Just a minute, Lord. 1714
Just a moment. 967
Just a taste of honey. 2395
Just a touch of drama. 3837
Just across the street. 971
Just among Friends. 1674
Just as I am. 1451
Just because. 1250, 3837
Just between God & me. 3883
Just call me Pastor. 2788
Just defence of the slandered priestes. 771, 1291
Just five days till Friday. 3835
Just for juniors. 906
Just for today. 1431, 1434, 1437, 2216
"Just going to" 908
Just Jennie. 102
Just law of compensation. 3251

... Just like you. 2491
Just off Chicken Street. 1260
Just one more story. 906
Just one of us. 1700
Just plain bread. 2246
Just take it from the Lord, brother. 2981
Just the greatest. 1998
Just think, Mr. Berton. 1065
Just think, Mr. Berton, a little harder. 1065
Just to help; some poems for every day. 3208
Just to illustrate. 1841
Just war in the middle ages. 2159
Just weight, and other chapel addresses. 2306
Just why? 1438
Just You and me, God. 1441
Justice. 2160
Justice and Judaism. 3454
Justice and mercy. 3249, 3355
Justice by the book. 1387
Justice church. 3617
Justice for all. 1136
Justice for my people. 2077
Justice for the Russian Jew. 2102
Justice in social relations. 1139
Justice, justice shalt thou pursue ; papers on the occasion of the 175th birthday of the Reverend Dr. Julius Mark, as an expression of gratitude of the Jewish Conciliation Board with whose services and leadership Dr. Mark has long been identifies. 2147, 2335
Justice of God in the teaching of Jesus. 2061
Justice of Zeus. 1766
Justifiable abortion. 3
Justification. 176, 2160, 2161
Justification by an imputed righteousness. 2160
Justification by faith. 2160
Justification by success. 1058
Justification of God. 3610
Justification of religious belief. 3103
Justification of the ungodly. 2160
Justification; Pauline texts interpreted in the light of the Old and New Testaments. 375, 2161
Justin Martyr. 3717
Justin Martyr and the Mosaic law. 1084, 2161
Justin Martyr: his life and thought. 2161
Justinian Welz. 2296, 3801
Justus Jonas, loyal reformer. 2130
Jusus. 1977
Juvenile piety. 3791
Juvenile round table. 867
Juvenile speaker and songster. 3026
Juxta crucem, the life of Basil Anthony Moreau. 2597

K

Kaatsbaan church records, Ulster county, N.Y.: marriages 1735-1838. 2165
Kabala of numbers. 3575
Kabala of numbers, a handbook of interpretation. 3575
Kabalah, from its inception to its evanescence. 722
Kabbalah. 721, 722, 723
Kabbalah and criticism. 722, 1387
Kabbalah and Exodus. 517, 721
Kabbalah and Spinoza's philosophy. 722, 3472
Kabbalah decoded. 722
Kabbalah for the modern world. 721
Kabbalah, tradition of hidden knowledge. 721
Kabbalah unveiled. 721
Kabbalistic aphorisms. 722
Kabbalistic numerology. 3575
Kabballistic and Eloimic magic. 2315
Kabir. 2162
... Kabir and his followers. 2162
Kachinas: a Hopi artist's documentary. 2165
Kaddish. 2111, 2162
Kaddish, its power for good. 2120
Kagawa. 2162
Kagawa in Lincoln's land. 2162
Kagawa, Japanese prophet. 3636
Kagawa the Christian. 2162
Kahunas; the black and white magicians of Hawaii. 1791
Kalam cosmological argument. 1733
Kalidasa's Sakuntala. 1812
Kaliya, king of serpents. 2187
Kalpa sutra and Nava tatva. 1932, 2317
Kalumburu. 188
Kama sutra; the Hindu ritual of love. 2263
Kansas Mennonites during World War I. 2407
Kansas Methodist pulpit. 2434

Kansas monks. 3273
Kant. 2163
Kant and Spencer. 2163
Kant and the problem of metaphysics. 2163, 2418
Kant, moral legislation and two senses of will. 2163, 3816
Kant on the foundation of morality. 1536
Kant, ontology & the a priori. 2164
Kantharos. 1395
Kantian ethics. 2163
Kant's aesthetic theory. 2163
Kant's critical philosophy for the English readers. 2180
Kant's criticism of metaphysics. 2163, 2420
Kant's Critique of pure reason. 2164
Kant's ethics. 2163
Kant's metaphysics and theory of science. 2164
Kant's moral religion. 2164, 3106
Kant's pre-critical ethics. 2163
Kant's Prolegomena to any future metaphysics. 2418
Kapalikas and kalamukhas. 1813
Kapitene of the Congo steamship Lapsley. 2197, 2513
Karaite anthology. 2164
Karaite studies. 2164
Karaites in Byzantium. 2164
Karen Ann Quinlan. 3013, 3604
Karen! Karen! 986
Karive Djami. 1929
Karl Barth. 175, 176, 3611
Karl Barth and Christian unity. 176
Karl Barth & evangelicalism. 175, 1550
Karl Barth and radical politics. 176, 3436
Karl Barth and the Christian message. 175
Karl Barth and the future of theology. 176
Karl Barth and the problem of war. 176, 3794
Karl Barth in re-view. 176
Karl Barth on God. 176, 1732
Karl Barth, preaching through the Christian year. 3640
Karl Barth-Rudolf Bultmann letters, 1922 to 1966. 175, 3611
Karl Barth theology. 176, 3650
Karl Barth's Church dogmatics. 176, 177
Karl Barth's doctrine of election. 175, 1505
Karl Barth's doctrine of Holy Scripture. 176, 280
Karl Barth's idea of revelation. 176, 3225
Karl Barth's struggle with anthropocentric theology. 176, 2945
Karl Barth's table talk. 175
Karl Barth's theological method. 175, 3668
Karl Barth's theology of mission. 176, 2555
Karl G. Maeser, Mormon educator. 2311, 2614
Karl Marx. 1319, 2352
Karl Marx and religion in Europe and India. 1543, 2352
Karl Rahner. 3019
Karl Rahner, an introduction to his theology. 3019
Karl Rahner, S.J. 777, 3633
Karlstadt's battle with Luther. 2165, 3629
Karma. 2165
Karma and dharma. 2165
Karma and rebirth in classical Indian traditions. 2165
Karma/Nirvana. 2165
Karma, the universal law of harmony. 2165
Karma-yoga and Bhakti-yoga. 3867
... Karman. 2165
Karmenia. 2729
Karmic theater. 98
Karok myths. 2165
Kashf al-mahjub. 3544
Kassulke. 931, 2165
Katalog der Lehranstalten. 2293
Kate Luther. 2272
... Katha unpanishad, dialogue of death and vision of immortality. 3760
Katha upanishad. 1731, 3761
Katharine Drexel. 1480, 2532, 2533
Katharine Drexel, friend of the neglected. 1480
Katharine von Bora, Dr. Martin Luther's wife. 2272
Kathayan slave. 2505
Katherine. 2272
Katherine Luther of the Wittenberg parsonage. 2272
Katherine Neel Dale, medical missionary. 1399
Kathleen, a record of a sorrow. 670, 1774
Die katholische kirchenmusik. 1206
Kathryn Kuhlman. 1576, 2187
Kathy. 2460, 2466
Kathy Ann, kindergartner. 3173
Kathyrn Kuhlman. 2187

Katie Fox. 1942, 3520
Katie Malone. 3524
Katolik anamihan, ene ka. 2413
Keen delight. 3095, 3694
Keen look at the last book of the Bible. 455
Keep 'em flying; sermons to men in the air forces. 20
Keep in touch. 3882, 3883
Keep my commandments. 3184
Keep on counting. 3575
Keep telling the story. 3184
Keep the faith, baby! 143
Keep the gate, guarding the soul against sin. 2398
Keep your faith. 2931
Keeper of the door. 2935
Keeper of the gate. 2006
Keeper of the keys. 2852
Keeper of the law. 1713
Keeper of the law: Louis Ginzberg. 1713
Keeper of the temple. 3059
Keepers of the Eucharist. 1299
Keepers of the Lighthouse. 1743
Keepers of the poor. 1152
Keepers of the springs. 2933
Keeping a spiritual journal. 3884
Keeping close to God. 956
Keeping men on their feet. 1342
Keeping power of God. 985
Keeping score on modern prophets. 2948
Keeping the Christian year, and a Christian year glossary. 1262
Keeping the church year. 1263
Keeping the covenant. 3172
Keeping the faith. 164, 1466, 2287, 2722, 3666
Keeping the foundations. 160
Keeping the spirit of Christmas. 1110
Keeping the Sunday school alive. 3161
Keeping up with our Catholic faith. 871
Keeping your church in the news. 10
Keeping your church informed. 10
Keeping your cool in a world of tension. 985
Keepsake. 1809
Keith and the cactus patch. 3261, 3379
Keithian controversy in early Pennsylvania. 2166, 2813
Kena Upanisad. 3759
Kendra. 682, 1349
Kennedy explosion. 1573, 2167
Kenneth Forbes. 639
Kenotic Christology. 2043
Kenotic theory. 1893
Kent chantries. 882
Kentucky Baptist atlas. 154
Kentucky Baptist history. 154
Kentucky revival. 3231, 3396
Kentucky Shakers. 3398
Kentucky spring. 3469
Kentucky Town and its Baptist church. 2167
Kentucky's Fox Creek. 1636
Kenyon Palmer's scrapbook. 1711
Kepelino's Traditions of Hawaii. 2663
Kept by the power of God. 166, 2822
Kept for the Master's use. 963, 2873
Kept from the hour. 3320
... Kerala, the gem of India. 3387
Kerry. 2167
Kerygma and comedy in the New Testament. 350
Kerygma and counseling. 2784, 3243
Kerygma and didache. 2168
Kerygma and dogma. 1473
Kerygma and myth. 346, 348
Kerygma in crisis. 1317
Kerygma in crists? 1317, 2168
Kerygma or Gospel tradition--which came first? 386
Kesatuan Kebaikan. 1031
Keshub Chunder Sen. 689, 3332
Keswick seventysix. 2168
Keswick's triumphant voice. 1561
Ketubah. 2168
Keturi ganytojai. 821
Key Bible words. 614
Key concepts of St. Paul. 375, 3287
Key concepts of the Old Testament. 598
Key in the hand. 2871
Key in your hand. 977
Key next door. 2438
Key of David. 456, 1091, 1387, 2952
Key of heaven. 857, 859, 2884
Key of history. 497
Key of life. 1747, 2056
Key of Solomon the King (Clavicula Salomonis): now first translated [from Latin, French and Italian]. 2315
Key of truth. 2805
Key problems of Genesis. 526
Key steps in local church planning. 1200
Key to a loving heart. 986
Key to a successful church library. 2224
Key to charismatic renewal in the Catholic Church. 2815

Key to "Christ and Christmas" 1033, 1496
Key to Christian Science and the Bible. 1032
Key to communication. 3515
Key to Daniel. 507
Key to Ephesians. 364, 2737
Key to faith. 598
Key to ghostism. 3509
Key to God's program. 453
Key to happiness. 3540
Key to heaven. 857, 859
Key to heaven: edifing tales from Holy Scripture to serve as teaching and warning. 1536
Key to inductive Bible studies. 635
Key to inner power. 978
Key to life with Scriptural phrasings. 1323
Key to Nostradamus. 2715
Key to original Gospels. 390
Key to our God given heritage. 236
Key to revelation. 444, 462
Key to succession in the presidency of the church and a complete ready reference for the missionary. 2483
Key to Sunday school achievement. 3177
Key to the Apocalypse. 462
Key to the Bible. 247, 287, 310, 319
Key to the Bible and our looking glass. 199
Key to the development of your psychic powers. 3514
Key to the doctrine of the Eucharist. 2255
Key to the door of divine reality. 2639
Key to the full life. 971
Key to the Good news. 474
Key to the Gospels. 395
Key to the important things in the Bible. 225
Key to the kingdom. 181, 1765
Key to the laws of the occult psyche science. 2723
Key to the lost treasures of the Bible. 200
Key to the Missal. 845
Key to the missionary problem. 2494
Key to the mysteries of God's laws. 2201
Key to the mystery of iniquity. 2192
Key to the new liturgical constitution. 3774
Key to the New Testament. 473
Key to the Old Testament. 499
Key to the parables. 2025
Key to the Pentateuch explanatory of the text and the grammatical forms. 563
Key to the prophecies of the Old & New Testaments, which are not yet accomplished. 605
Key to the Psalms. 579, 584
Key to the Revelation. 456
Key to the Revelation of St. John. 463
Key to the riddle of your life. 3576
Key to the science of theology. 2612
Key to the secret vault. 2322
Key to the spiritual palace. 3509
Key to the spiritual treasures. 1329
Key to the study St. Thomas. 3693
... Key to the treasury. 639
Key to the universe. 2740
Key to the world's progress. 755
Key to the writings of the principal fathers of the Christian church. 1617
Key to theosophy. 3684
Key to triumphant living. 994
Key, to unlock the door, that leads in, to take a fair view of the religious constitution, established by law, in the colony of Connecticut. 1346
Key to victory. 1012
Key truths of occult philosophy. 2726
Key-words and phrases of the New Testament. 321
Key words for Lent. 2210
Key words in Christian thinking. 3682
Key words in church music ; definition essays on concepts, practices, and movements of thought in church music. 1206
Key words of Lent. 2211
Key words of the Bible. 246
Key-words of the inner life. 363
Key words to Bible truth. 243
...Keynote studies in keynote books of the Bible. 312
Keys of heaven. 857, 1939
Keys of power. 1895
Keys of the kingdom. 2396, 3467
Keys of the kingdom and other sermons. 1340
Keys that unlock the Scriptures. 285
Keys to Christian living. 966
Keys to conquest. 3879
Keys to creative faith. 985
Keys to effective motivation. 953
Keys to inner space. 2725
Keys to life. 3690
Keys to richer living. 2435
Keys to spiritual growth. 985
Keys to successful Bible study. 640

Keys to the third floor. 3486
Keys to truth. 2393
Keystone graded Sunday-school lessons. 3564
Keystone of Christianity, and other addresses. 1072
Keystone of Mormonism. 678
Keystones of faith. 3661
Keywords in the teaching of Jesus. 2065
Kharshedji Rustamji Cama. 730
Khont-hon nofer, the lands of Ethiopia. 2552
Khotanese Buddhist texts. 711
Khotanese Surangamasamadhisutra. 3568
Kiamichi Baptist Assembly, its origin and early development. 731, 2169
Kibbutz studies. 1308
Kid Keepers. 1260
Kierkegaard. 2169, 2170, 2171
Kierkegaard: a collection of critical essays. 2171
Kierkegaard and Bultamnn. 2009, 2171
Kierkegaard and Bultmann. 2009, 2171
Kierkegaard and Christendom. 1104, 2170
Kierkegaard and Faulkner: modalities of existence. 2169
Kierkegaard and Heidegger. 2171, 2739
Kierkegaard and radical discipleship. 2169
Kierkegaard as theologian. 2169
Kierkegaard critique. 2170
Kierkegaard handbook. 2170
Kierkegaard, Heidegger, Buber and Barth. 3615
Kierkegaard, Heidegger, Buber and Barth: Subject and object in modern theology. 3615
Kierkegaard on Christ and Christian coherence. 2170
Kierkegaard studies. 2169, 2170
Kierkegaard the cripple. 2170
Kierkegaard's attack upon "Christendom," 1054, 1055
Kierkegaard's attack upon "Christendom," 1854-1855. 1054
Kierkegaard's authorship. 2169
Kierkegaard's Concluding unscientific postscript. 1104
Kierkegaard's dialectic of existence. 1583, 2169
Kierkegaard's Fear and trembling. 1106, 2170
Kierkegaard's philosophy of religion. 2171
Kierkegaard's presence in contemporary American life. 2171
Kierkegaard's way to the truth. 2170
Killing giants, pulling thorns. 2397
Killing in defense of private property. 2160
Kilwinning Crosse Lodge Number 2-237. 1663
Kimbangu. 2171
Kin Chan and the crab. 2549
Kind of praying. 2015, 2889
Kind words for sad hearts, for times of bereavement. 1349
Kind words series. 145
... Kindergarden method in the church school. 2171
Kindergarten course for Sunday schools. 3146
...Kindergarten course for the daily vacation church school. 3764
Kindergarten lessons for church Sunday schools. 3565
Kindergarten manual for administrators and teachers in the church school kindergarten. 3174
Kindergarten manual for Jewish religious schools. 2172
Kindergarten of the church. 3565
Kindergarten stories for the Sunday school and home. 625, 3198
Kindergarten story time. 3184
Kindle a blaze for Christ. 1454
Kindled flame. 324, 346
Kindling. 3559
Kindling for revival fires. 1558
Kindlings; outlines and sermon starters. 3374
Kindly light. 738, 858, 2702
Kindness. 887, 2172
Kindness, the bloom of charity. 2172
King. 2172
King Alcohol in the realm of King Cotton. 2231
King Alfred's West-Saxon version of Gregory's Pastoral care. Edited by Henry Sweet. 3676
King among men. 3869
King and church. 2794
King and His cross. 1837
King and His kingdom. 1241, 1727, 1994, 2055
King and Messiah. 2177
King and Queen County, Virginia. 2172
King and the Kingdom. 647
King and the kingdom of heaven. 443

King and you. 2175
King came riding. 2032
King David. 1405
King ever glorious. 1837
King for ever. 2935, 3368
King God didn't save. 2173
King in His beauty. 1454
King is coming. 1530
King James Bible stories. 620
King James Bible translators. 272
King James version. 254, 271
King James version debate. 270
King James version of the English Bible. 271
King James version of the Holy Bible. 261
King Jesus. 2005
King Jesus is coming. 3320
King Jesus' manual of arms for the 'armless. 3795
King nobody wanted. 1982
King of glory. 1968
King of Israel. 2633
King of kings. 623
King of love. 588
King of men. 1956
King of the castle. 3099
King of the earth. 2325
King of the ends of the earth. 425
King of the golden city. 2255
King of the harem heaven. 3009
King of the Jews. 441
King of the Jews, a sacred drama. 934
King of the shepherds and His psalm, lecture. 587
King of the witches. 3300
King or shepherd! 593
King reigning in righteousness, and princes ruling in judgment. 1504
King shall reign! 2003
King Solomon. 3457
King Solomon and his followers. 1669
... King Solomon and his followers. Lone star. 1669
... King Solomon and his followers. Mo. 1669
King Solomon's "first" temple. 3579
King Solomon's goat. 3457
King Solomon's Temple. 1669, 3599
King Strang story. 182, 3535
King Tut's tomb. 1696, 2052
King was no fool. 572, 3457
King who couldn't preach. 1021, 2172
Kingdom. 474, 2175
Kingdom and a cross. 2229
Kingdom and church. 1188
Kingdom and community. 3451
Kingdom and the farm. 2174
Kingdom and the golden calves. 251
Kingdom and the nations. 2523
Kingdom and the power. 476, 3500
Kingdom, and the power, and the glory. 251
Kingdom at hand. 2174
Kingdom (Basileia) 2173
Kingdom citizens. 3335
Kingdom come. 792, 1062, 1838, 2248
Kingdom cometh. 3120
Kingdom, cross, and community. 1074, 2403, 2405
Kingdom here and now. 988
Kingdom in action. 1125
Kingdom in history and prophecy. 2174
Kingdom in Mark. 437, 2176
Kingdom in mystery. 2175
Kingdom in the cradle. 1253
Kingdom in the states. 156
Kingdom is. 2024
Kingdom is yours. 657, 2176
Kingdom living. 180
Kingdom of Christ. 756, 1218, 2176
Kingdom of Christ delineated. 2176
Kingdom of darkness. 2730
Kingdom of God. 249, 251, 253, 597, 622, 2173, 2174, 2175, 2176, 2374, 3144, 3239, 3496
Kingdom of God and history. 2174
...The Kingdom of God and peace essays. 3794
Kingdom of God and primitive Christianity. 2176
Kingdom of God and the one thousand years' reign. 2175
Kingdom of God and the Son of Man. 2175
Kingdom of God developed according to the inspired records and predictions. 464
Kingdom of God established, invaded and restored from invasion. 2175
Kingdom of God in America. 2175
Kingdom of God in the New Testament. 2175
Kingdom of God in the synoptic tradition. 390, 2176
Kingdom of God in the teaching of Jesus. 2064, 2175
Kingdom of God in the writings of the Fathers. 2174

Kingdom of God is at hand. 1993
Kingdom of God is now. 2174
Kingdom of God is within you. 1055, 2175
Kingdom of God restored. 2615
Kingdom of God today. 1040
Kingdom of God visualized. 2173
Kingdom of God's dear Son. 1950
Kingdom of happiness. 3685
Kingdom of heaven. 617, 1529, 2174, 3666
Kingdom of Heaven as seen by Swedenborg. 1794
Kingdom of heaven here and hereafter. 2066, 2176
Kingdom of heaven in parables. 2026
Kingdom of heaven is at hand. 1794
Kingdom of heaven is like. 3218
Kingdom of inner meaning. 969
Kingdom of Israel and house of Judah. 463
Kingdom of Jesus. 2066
Kingdom of light. 3351
Kingdom of love. 956, 1960, 2014
Kingdom of love and knowledge. 1212, 3667
Kingdom of love and the pride of life. 62
Kingdom of priests. 2404, 2939
Kingdom of promise and prophecy. 609
Kingdom of Saint James. 182, 3535
Kingdom of self. 2323
Kingdom of song. 3561
Kingdom of the Crusaders. 1390
Kingdom of the cults. 1394, 3325
Kingdom of the Messiah. 2174
Kingdom of the saints. 2616, 3869
Kingdom of the seal. 1532
Kingdom of the shining ones. 42, 1115
Kingdom of the world in prophecy. 607
Kingdom on earth. 3335
Kingdom or nothing. 2616, 3591
Kingdom parables and their teaching. 444
Kingdom pathfinders. 2482
Kingdom revisited. 944
Kingdom seekers. 984
Kingdom stories. 1562
Kingdom stories for juniors. 630, 3202
Kingdom that is being built. 2175
Kingdom that must be built. 2174
Kingdom, the power and the glory. 2969
Kingdom within. 1107, 2071, 3453, 3865
Kingdom without end. 1104
Kingdom without frontiers. 2493, 2504
Kingdom without God. 1086
Kingdom's coming. 431
Kingdoms of Christ from the days of the apostles to the Middle Ages. 1198
Kingdoms of God. 130
Kingdoms of Judah and Israel. 1928
Kingdoms of man and the kingdom of God. 2174
Kingly Christ. 1266
... Kings. 555, 556
King's advocate. 2712
Kings and prophets. 535, 536, 631, 2089
... The kings and prophets of Israel and Judah, from the division of the kindgom to the Babylonian exile. 2089
... The kings and prophets of Isreal and Judah, from the division of the kingdom to the Babylonian exile. 2095
King's business. 2521
King's chapel sermons. 3726
King's cross. 2057
King's daughters' dairy. 2383
Kings depart. 2305
King's garden. 1698
King's Handbook of notable Episcopal churches in the United States. 1275
King's highway. 2502, 3289, 3387
King's hostage. 2333
Kings in shirtsleeves. 492
King's invitation. 444, 632
King's message. 745
King's message in song. 3561
... The kings of Israel and Judah. 2095
Kings on parade. 494
King's own honors roll. 460
King's penknife. 2561
Kings, prophets, and history. 534
King's steward. 967
King's stewards. 3348
... Kings to Esther. 531
King's trumpeter. 3780
Kingship and the gods. 2177
Kingship and the gods; a study of ancient Near Eastern religion as the integration of society & nature. 2177
Kingship and the gods: the Western apostasy. 1144
Kingship and the psalms. 578, 2177
Kingship of Christ. 1492, 2055, 3849
Kingship of God. 2173
Kingship of Jesus ; composition theology in Mark 15. 438, 2055
Kingston Presbyterian Church. 1367
Kink and I. 986

Kino guide. 2177
Kino's Historical memoir of Pimeria Alta. 2177, 2849
Kinships. 1452
Kirban's book of charts on prophecy. 606
Kirban's prophecy New Testament, including Revelation visualized, King James version. 343
Kirby Page and the social gospel. 2757, 3623
Kirche und Amt. 2788
Kirchenbau. 1156
Kirk on Rutgers farm. 2697
Kirkbride conversations. 62
Kirkpatrick memorial. 2178, 3348
Kirpal Singh. 2178, 2390, 3408
Kirtland economy revisited. 2178, 2617
Kiss of Judas. 2930
Kiss the son. 584
Kitab al-maghazi of al-Waqidi. 2629
Kitab-i-iqan. 126
Kitty! Come quickly! 2305
Kitty, my rib. 2272
Kivie Kaplan. 2144, 2164
Kloster Loccum. 2241
Knaves, fools, madmen, and that subtile effluvium. 2464
Knaves or knights? 2495
Knee of listening. 3491
Kneeling Christian. 2874
Kneeling in the bean patch. 759
Knight-errant of Assisi. 1641
... Knight of Christ. 2269, 2393
Knight of Molokai. 1400
Knight of the burning heart. 3802
Knight of the Kingdom. 131
Knight of the sanctuary. 1299
Knight without armor, a story of St. Thomas Aquinas. 3693
Knights Hospitallers of the ven. Tongue of England in Malta. 2179, 2319
Knight's Illustrations for today. 1841
...The knights of Anytown. 3801
Knights of Christ. 2576
Knights of Columbus, illustrated. 2178
Knights of Columbus in peace and war. 2178
Knights of Columbus in Texas, 1902-1952. 2179
Knights of God. 3283, 3284
Knights of St. Crispin, 1867-1874. 2179
Knights of St. John in Jerusalem and Cyprus, c. 1050-1310. 2179
...Knights of service. 1246, 3765
Knights of the cross (Krzyzacy) historical novel. 2857
Knights of the Eucharist. 1299
Knights of the labarum. 2157
Knights Templar history. 1665, 3598
Knights Templars. 3598
Knights Templars in England. 3598
Knoche's law: "If something can go wrong, it will. 1012
Knock and enter. 1328
Knock and it shall be opened unto you. 2670
Knock!knock! 3164
Knock wood! 3567
Knothole glimpses of glory. 1716
Know about the Crusades. 1392
Know and grow. 2389
Know and live the Mass. 2367
"know-how" of Christian living. 955
Know Jewish living and enjoy it. 2146
Know- so salvation. 3290
Know the Bible. 280, 595
Know the Latter-Day Scriptures. 2610
Know the marks of cults. 3324
Know the truth. 231, 1782, 3608, 3646, 3661
Know thyself. 1445, 3509
Know what you believe. 3663
Know why you believe. 64
Know your Bible. 313, 643
Know your Bible better. 280, 535
Know your Bible series. 649
Know your child. 904
Know your Christian life. 3662
Know your church! 2920, 3735
Know your enemy. 2079
Know your festivals and enjoy them. 1615
Know your hymns. 153, 1871
Know your karma. 2165
Know your King. 1977
Know your local church. 1252
Know your New Testament. 474
Know your numbers. 3575
Know your religion. 2612
Know your scriptures. 613
Know your synod. 2290
Know yourself. 948
Know yourself and live. 1029
Knowableness of God. 1740
Knowing and helping youth. 3890
Knowing children better. 895
Knowing Christ. 930, 1985

Knowing Christ through Mark's gospel. 438
Knowing God. 1725, 1727, 3207
Knowing God through His creation. 1384
Knowing God's secrets. 964
Knowing God's will. 1011 ·
Knowing God's will—and doing it. 1740
Knowing Jesus. 2014
Knowing Jesus through His friends. 2007
Knowing Scripture. 642
Knowing the doctrines of the Bible. 3647
Knowing the future. 609
Knowing the living God. 1734, 1735
Knowing the Master through John. 419
Knowing the New Testament. 410
Knowing the Old Testament. 499
Knowing the Scriptures. 640
Knowing the unknown God. 1735
Knowing where you stand with God. 993
Knowledge. 65
Knowledge and life. 2226
Knowledge and love in rabbinic lore. 1733, 2115
Knowledge and the sacred. 2181
Knowledge & virtue. 1853
Knowledge, belief, and transcendence. 3100
Knowledge beyond understanding. 3060
Knowledge is power. 2608
Knowledge of God. 175, 1586, 1734, 1740, 3641
Knowledge of God and the service of God according to the teaching of the Reformation, recalling the Scottish confession of 1560. 3044, 3315
Knowledge of God in ancient Israel. 1735
Knowledge of God in Johannine thought. 423
Knowledge of God, its meaning and its power. 1727
Knowledge of life. 3141
Knowledge of reality. 2418
Knowledge of religious truth, and other papers. 3096
Knowledge of the Bible. 286
Knowledge of the higher worlds and its attainment. 50
Knowledge of the holy. 1730
Knowledge of things hoped for. 3070
Knowledge unto salvation. 2293
Known and unknown life of Jesus,the Christ. 97
Known Bible and its defense. 276
Knox brothers. 1515, 2182
Knoxville's first graveyard. 2182
Koheleth. 512, 513
Koheleth (romanized form) 512
Koheleth, the man and his world. 512
Koheleth, the man and his world. [2d augm. ed.]. 512
Koinonia ministries guidebook. 1169
Korada. 2531
Koran. 2183, 2184, 2185
Koran, an edition prepared for English readers. 2184
Koran Christ. 2564
Koran commonly called Al Koran of Mohammed. 2184
Koran, commonly called the Alcoran of Mohammed. 2184
Koran in the light of Christ. 1082, 2184
Koran interpreted. 78
Koran (Qur'an) 2184
Korea. 2185
Korea calls! 2537
Korea for Christ. 2536
Korea in transition. 2536
Korea, land of the dawn. 2537
Korea the hermit nation. 2537
Korean Buddhism, history--conditions--art. 706
Korean Catholicism in the 1970s. 821
Korean church and the Nevius methods. 2929
Korean immigrant churches today in Southern California. 1255
Korean Pentecost and the sufferings which followed. 670, 2486
Korean young folks. 2536
Koreshanity, the new age religion. 2185, 3592
Kosher code of the orthodox Jew. 2086, 2377
Kourotrophos. 2624
Kramer family song booklet. 2117
Kremilin, the Jews, and the middle East. 2103
Kremlin and the church. 64
Kremlin, the Jews, and the Middle East. 2103
Krieg Buchlin des Friedes. 2809
Krinkle nose. 932, 3718
Krishna, master of all mystics. 2187, 2663
Krishna; myths, rites, and attitudes. 2186
Krishna: the cowherd king. 693
Krishnamandala, a devotional theme in Indian art. 2186

Krishnamurti. 2187, 3687
Krsna. 2186, 3005
Krsna consciousness. 3864
Krsna consciousness, the matchless gift. 3864
Kukai: major works. 3403
Kularnava tantra. 3586
Kulikuwa hatari. 2498
Kulikuwa hatari: a way, a walk, and a warfare of faith. 2498
Kumuhonua legends. 2207
Kumulipo. 1371
Kundalini. 2188, 3864
Kundalini, evolution and enlightenment. 2188
Kundalini, secret of the ancient yogis. 3330
Kundalini, the arousae of the inner energy. 2187
Kundalini West. 2187
Kundalini, yoga for the West. 2188
Kung Fu meditations & Chinese proverbial wisdom. 2389
K'ung Fu Tze. 1330
Kung in conflict. 788
Kuntres Uma'ayon mibais haShem. 1779
Kurdish prayer book done on the multiplex Hammond writing machine. 1876
Kuzari (Kitab al Khazari) 2144
Kuzari (Kitab at Khazari) 2144
Kvutza. 3897
Kwangsi. 2537
Kyabram Methodism. 2188, 2431
Kybalion. 2726
Kyrie eleison. 837
Kyrie eleison ("Lord, have mercy") 2884
Kyrios Christos. 2010

L

L. D. S. reference encyclopedia. 2610
L. R. I. ching. 1470, 1878
L. Wilbur Messer, an appreciation. 2413
La charite dans l'enseignement de saint Augustin. Dossier rassemble par M. Huftier. 114
... La divina commedia. 1402
La Madre. 3604
La Salle. 2189
Laba zeme. 3198
Labadist Colony in Maryland. 674, 2189
Labor and tomorrow's world. 1131
Labor education in the U.S. 2189
Labor, industry, and the church. 1131
Labor legislation in the Bible and Talmud. 2190
Labor problems in Christian perspective. 1131
Laboratory and pulpit. 3073, 3079
"Laborers together" 3467
Labor's defiant lady. 2130
Labors of the apostles. 70
Labor's relation to church and community, a series of addresses. 2190
Labrador logbook. 1447
La Breeska. 1749, 1803
Labyrinth. 1395, 1786, 2190
Labyrinth of the world and the paradise of the heart. 958, 1273, 1274
Lacordaire. 2190
Lad of Lima. 2348
Lad who hiked to heaven. 3524
Ladder. 3052
Ladder of angels. 318, 633
Ladder of divine ascent. 3493
Ladder of initiation. 3052
Ladder of learning. 3179
Ladder of life. 3052
Ladder of light. 181
Ladder of monks. 3487
Ladders to the sun. 908
Ladies' aid manual. 1248
Ladies of the Covenant. 1375
Lady Fourth Daughter of China. 2509
Lady general. 681
Lady hymn writers. 1872
Lady in the pulpit. 669
Lady in white and her marvellous mission. 1033
...The Lady Julian. 2158
Lady of Guadalupe. 1776
Lady of the Tboli. 1634, 2488
Lady Poverty. 1643, 2865
Lady preacher. 3031
Lady said come to Lourdes. 2262, 2357
Lady unafraid. 1903, 2683
Lady was a bishop. 3836
Lady was a skipper. 3819
Lady with the magic eyes. 671
Ladybird New Testament. 626
Lady's life among the Mormons. 2606
Lafayette avenue church. 1398
Lagrange and Biblical renewal. 201
Lagrange lectures. 219
De laicis. 2858

Laila of Lebanon. 897
Laity and liturgy. 2972
Laity, church, and world. 2191
Laity mobilized. 2554
Laity: The people of God. 2192
Lake of fire, and consummation. 1802
Lalibela. 876
Lamarck, the mythical precursor. 1578, 2193
Lamb and the blessed. 2034
Lamb in the midst of the throne. 107
Lamb of God. 108, 1983, 3291
Lamb, the woman and the dragon. 455
Lamb who is the lion. 454
Lambeth and unity. 43
Lambeth conference. 44
Lambeth Conferences. 1043, 2194
Lambeth Conferences and women priests. 1524, 2742
Lambeth conferences of 1867, 1878, and 1888. 2194
Lambeth, unity and truth. A reply to the pastoral letter issued by the House of Bishops meetings in General Convention, Miami Beach, Florida, October 1958. 2957
Lambs among wolves. 3295
Lambs in wolfskins. 683, 3286
Lame and lovely. 3066
Lame man who walked again. 1793
Lamennais and England. 1760, 2194
Lamentations. 556
Lamentations, Ezekiel, Daniel. 556
Lamp and the lantern. 304
Lamp-lighters across the sea. 2518
... A lamp of burnished gold. 3733
Lamp of prophecy. 606
Lamp of the soul. 2833
Lamp to our feet. 644
Lamp unto my feet. 1438, 3352
Lamp unto our faith. 2399, 2701
Lamplight. 1842
Lamps. 2901
Lamps and paths. 908
Lamps are for lighting. 2586
Lamps for the journey. 1449
Lamps for worship. 3858
Lamps in the darkness. 2437
Lamps of liberty. 2436
Lamps of the Roman period. 2195
Lamps of western mysticism. 2641
Lamps without oil. 2435
Lamy of Santa Fe, his life and times. 2195
Lan Ta-te. 2195, 2508
Lancelot Andrewes. 2908
Land. 651, 2195
Land and destiny. 3896
Land and leaders of Isreal. 595
Land and people of Israel. 2762
Land and the Book. 2763
Land and the promise. 616
Land beyond the Nile. 2552
Land born in a day. 311
Land in search of God. 3745
Land of all nations. 2528
Land of Canaan. 2089
Land of Christ; archaeology, history, geography. 395, 2762
Land of Christmas. 2085, 2763
Land of Eldorado. 2955
Land of faith. 3481
Land of milk and honey. 177, 1367
Land of promise. 2761
Land of sojourn. 494
Land of stones and saints. 814
Land of the Bible. 281, 282, 528, 2095, 2762
Land of the lighthouse. 2546
Land of Zeus. 2660
Land shadowing with wings. 680
Land, wildlife, and peoples of the Bible. 480
Land within. 1934, 2647
Landmark history of the United brethren church. 3731
Landmarks for Christian scientists from Bow to Boston. 1038
Landmarks from Bow to Boston. 1038
... Landmarks in Christian history. 3156
Landmarks in the history of early Christianity. 1192
Landmarks in the struggle between science and religion. 3085
Landmarks of church history, to the Reformation. 1173
Landmarks of faith. 1304
Landmarks of freemasonry. 1662, 1666
Landmarks of Old Testament history-- Samuel to Malachi. 532
Landmarks of the Reformed-fathers. 3046
Landrum Pinson Leavell, D. D. 2204
Lands and peoples of the living Bible. 297
Lands of fire and ice. 2164, 2524
Lands of sunshine. 2548
Lands of the Bible. 282, 297
Landscape; a bundle of thoughts about the Psalms. 583

Landscape with churches. 1159
Landscapes of history. 2844
Landscapes of the Bible. 282, 2219
Lanfranc of Bec. 666, 2195
Language and belief. 3070
Language and Christian belief. 1106
Language and concepts in Christian education. 3176
Language and cultural diversity in American education. 2475
Language and faith. 655, 1317, 3027
Language and imagery of the Bible. 314
Language and ontology. 2738
Language and religion. 3102
Language and religious language. 2196
Language and style in Milton. 2470
Language, existence & God. 38
Language for madness. 1386
Language gap and God. 935
Language, hermeneutic, and word of God. 2025, 3656
Language in religious practice. 3071
Language in worship. 3004
Language, logic, and God. 2242
Language, myth, and man. 3067
Language needs of minority group children. 2475
Language of faith. 1590, 2076, 2117, 2196, 3615
Language of faith: a selection from the most expressive Jewish prayers. 2076
Language of heaven. 464
Language of Judaism. 2146
Language of morals. 1535
Language of religion. 3070
Language of the Book of common prayer. 1213
Language of the Christian community. 933
Language of the cross. 2031, 3541
Language of the Gospel. 425
Language of the heart. 2890
Language of the King James Bible. 271, 1517
Language of the New Testament. 1770
Language of the Pentateuch in its relation to Egyptian. 565
Language of Uranian astrology. 95
Language, persons, and belief. 2196, 3830
Language proficiency in the multi-racial junior school. 2475
... Language studies in the Franciscan order. 1645
Language, truth, and meaning. 2245, 2376
Languages. 2230, 2836
Lantern for mine anointed Jesus. 3783
Lantern in Tokyo. 1754, 3232
Lantern to our children. 3147
Lao tze. 2196
Lao tze's Tao teh king. 2838
Lao Tzu. 2196
Lao Tzu and Taoism. 2196, 3586
Lao-Tzu and the Tao te Ching. 2196, 2832
Laodicean messenger. 3256
Laotzu's tao and wu wei. 2197, 3586
Lappin's sermon outlines. 3374
L'archeologie et les manuscrits de la mer Morte. 3013
Large catechism. 2284
Large type prayer book. 2197
Larger catechism. 769, 2913
Larger Christ. 1341, 2059
Larger church. 1120
Larger evangelism. 1568
Larger faith. 1589
Larger parish and group ministry. 2197
Larger than the sky. 1711
Larger view. 2894
Larger vision. 199, 1581
Larger way for women. 3166
Lark. 1938
Larks of Umbria. 1643
Larousse encyclopedia of mythology. 2652
Larousse Greek and Roman mythology. 2657
Larousse world mythology. 2651
Lars O. Skrefsrud. 2546, 3422
L'art gregorien. 884
Last abbot of Glastonbury, and other essays. 872, 3814
Last Adam. 6, 377, 2011
Last and future world. 604
Last apostle. 2799
Last appeal to the "Market-street Presbyterian church and congregation" 2912
Last barrier. 1620, 3542
Last book of the Bible. 455
Last call messages. 1556
Last cathedral. 3796
Last Christian. 1027, 1642
Last crusade. 1220, 1543
Last-day delusions. 3384
Last day of Our Lord's passion. 2029
"last days"; a compilation [!] of prophecies pertinent to the present. 2947

Last days in England of the Rajah Rammohun Roy. 689, 3020
Last days of Dietrich Bonhoeffer. 676
Last days of Greco-Roman paganism. 2756
Last days of Jesus. 1956
Last days of Jesus Christ. 2, 2035
Last days of Jesus Christ on the earth. 2035
Last days of Luther. 2275
Last days of man. 1530
Last days of Maximilian Kolbe. 1297, 2183
Last days of medieval monachism. 2582
Last days of Our Saviour. 1985
Last days of planet Earth. 605, 1513
Last days of the Saviour. 2030
Last days on the Nile. 2552, 3539
Last discourse of Jesus. 424
Last enemy. 1413
Last essays by the Right Hon. Professor F. Max Muller ... Second series. 3067
Last essays, second series. 3067
Last four lives of Annie Besant. 195
Last Gospel. 658
Last hours of Jesus. 1985
Last hours of persons eminent for piety. 924
Last incarnation. 2005, 3441
Last journey and memorials of the Redeemer. 1997
Last journey of Jesus to Jerusalem. 2016
Last Judgment. 2157
Last judgment, and the Babylon destroyed: so that all the predictions in the Apocalypse are at this day fulfilled. 2156
Last judgment in sixteenth century northern Europe. 2157
Last, least, lowest. 3845
Last letters from the living dead man. 3495
Last message of Jesus Christ. 457
... The last message of William Jennings Bryan. 1579
Last messenger before His face. 3716
...Last of Old Testament times, stories from Israel. 3385
Last of the astrologers. 96, 2229
Last of the conquistadors, Junipero Serra. 3376
Last of the conquistadors, Junipero Serra, 1713-1784. 3376
Last of the Epistles. 425
Last of the Fathers. 193, 194
Last of the old West. 2452
Last of their line. 2202, 2755
Last on the menu. 2717
Last passover. 2035
Last problem. 3103
Last reformation. 3036
Last rights. 1544
Last seven words of Jesus on the cross. 2057
Last solemn scene. 3355
Last spring. 1352
Last Supper. 2253
Last Supper and Lord's Supper. 2198
Last things. 1417, 1528, 1529
Last things: concerning death, purification after death, resurrection, judgment, and eternity. 1528
Last things first. 1318
Last things now. 1695
Last thoughts, on important subjects. 3412
Last three bishops. 1222, 1689
Last three Popes and the Jews. 860
Last trial. 5
Last twelve verses of Mark. 438
Last war. 2807
Last week in the life of Davis Johnson, jr. 2128
Last week with Jesus. 1986
Last word in lonesome is me. 2244
Last word in prophecy. 458
Last word (published and unpublished) 2384
Last words and old-time memories. 2439
Last words and work of Rev. Robt. W. Logan. 2198
Last writings of Reginald Garrigou-Lagrange. 1476
Last years of Saint Paul. 2797
Last years of the church. 1062
Lasting gold. 656
Lasting hymns. 1860
Lasting influences of Jesus Christ. 1952
Late association for defence farther encouraged. 3427
Late baroque churches of Venice. 3777
Late Biblical Hebrew. 496, 2756
Late dawn. 1365
Late Dr. Sedgwick and the spirit medium (based upon facts) 3475
Late friendship. 119
Late great planet earth. 606
Late Israelite prophecy. 569

Late J. C. 2019
Late Liz. 1361
Late medieval mysticism. 2647
Late summer fruit. 2142
Die lateinische vorlage der Westsachsichen evangelienversion. 401
Later Baptist missionaries and pioneers. 144
Later Christian fathers. 1020
Later Episcopal Sunday schools. 2965
Later gleanings. 3621
Later Greek religion. 1766
Later Hebrew history and prophets. 536
Later Heidegger and theology. 1801, 3650, 3657
Later Herods. 2092
Later Lollards. 2243
Later Lollards, 1414-1520. 2243
... The later mediaeval doctrine of the eucharistic sacrifice. 1541
Later Middle Ages. 1185, 1186, 1516
Later Old Testament stories. 630
... The later Pauline epistles. 375
Later periods of Quakerism. 1685
Later thoughts from the springs of silence. 3522
Later works. 3634
Later writings of Bishop Hooper. 1216
Latest of Lee. 3354
...Latin America. 2547
Latin America & revolution. 1147
Latin America and the Palestine problem. 2764
Latin America, U.S.A. 3470
Latin American Christian Democratic parties. 879
Latin American church growth. 2198
Latin American circuit. 2548
Latin American institutional development: the changing Catholic Church. 821
Latin American lands in focus. 2548
Latin American mission. 3741
Latin American missionary stories. 2491
Latin American stories. 2921
Latin American theology: radical or evangelical? 3679
Latin America's open doors. 2955
Latin and English syllabi in the minor seminary. 3613
... The Latin and Irish lives of Ciaran. 1275
Latin and religion syllabi in the minor seminary. 3613
... The Latin church in the middle ages. 810
Latin church music in England, c. 1460-1575. 1206
Latin conquest of Constantinople. 1391
Latin epigrams. 1522
Latin hymns. 1860, 1861, 1877
Latin hymns in English verse. 1877
Latin hymns, with English notes. 1877
Latin immigrant in the South. 2527
Latin infancy gospels. 336
Latin liturgical manuscripts and printed books. 841
Latin manuscript books before 1600. 2330
Latin poems of Leo xiii. 2216
Latin poemsof Leo xii. 3847
Latin poetry of English poets. 2199
Latin poets. 2199
Latin text of the Ancrene riwle. 2580
Latin works. 3636
Latin works and the correspondence of Huldreich Zwingli. 3900
Latin writers of the fifth century. 2199
...The Latinity of the letters of Saint Ambrose. 29
Latinity of the Vulgate Psalter. 584
Latter-day patriots. 2609
Latter-day prophets and the Doctrine and covenants. 2611, 3428, 3430
Latter-day revelation: selections from the book of Doctrine and covenants of the Church of Jesus Christ of latter-day saints, containing revelations given through Joseph Smith, the prophet. 1231
Latter-day Saint biographical encyclopedia. 2603
Latter-Day Saint family. 1610
Latter-Day Saints. 2604
Latter-day Saints and the Sabbath. 1233, 3261
... The Latter day saints and their changing relationship to the social order. 2614
Latter-Day Saints in the modern day world. 2607
Latter Day Saints on the Missouri frontier. 2617, 3217
Latter-day saints' Sunday school treatise. 1230, 3552
Latter-day saints' tour from Palmyra, New York, to Salt Lake, City. 1231
Latter days. 606
Latter Prophets. 569
Laud, storm center of Stuart England. 2199

Laudes regiae. 2237
"Laugh, and love, and lift" 2931
Laughing and loving with John Richard Sampey. 3297
Laughing Savior. 891
Laughing valley. 908
Laughter in heaven. 2200
Laughter in the Bible. 2199
Laughter of God. 2199, 2695
Laughter of Jesus. 2199
Launching out into the deep. 3339
Launching the church school year. 935
Launching your spiritual power in the space age. 3478
Laurel County history of churches and schools, their rise and progress. 1178
Laurel leaves. 2752
Laurels and the tiara. 2850
Laurentianum. 3757
... Laus et jubilatio. 883
Lausanne, Lambeth and south India. 1042
Lausanne: the will to understand. 3849
...The Lausiac history of Palladius. 935, 2579
Lavigerie in Tunisia. 1152, 2200
Law above the law. 2201
Law and commandment. 2200
Law and conscience. 947
Law and convenant. 563
Law and covenant in Israel and the ancient Near East. 2074
Law and ethics in the light of the Jewish tradition. 1538
Law and gospel. 2200, 3753
Law and grace. 1751, 2200
Law and history in Matthew's Gospel. 444
Law and liberty. 1314
Law and life according to Hebrew thought. 2074, 2107
Law and limitation of Our Lord's miracles. 2017
Law and religion. 3071
Law and the administration of justice in the Old Testament and ancient East. 499, 2201
Law and the cross. 1854
Law and the gospel in Luther. 2281
Law and the gospel in their relation to health of mind and body. 2409
Law and the prophets. 26, 484, 503
Law and the Sabbath. 3384
Law and the testimony. 253
Law and theology. 2206
Law and theology in Judaism. 3219
Law and tradition in Judaism. 2074

Law, church, and society. 1102, 2188
Law for liberty, the role of law in the church today. 735
Law-giver--judge. 1854
Law-givers. 557
Law-Gospel debate. 2201
Law governing restrictions and restrictive covenants in deeds. 1376
Law in religion and science. 2201
Law in the Apocrypha. 488
Law in the light of the gospel. 3337
Law in the prayer. 2247
Law in the Scriptures. 203
Law is for all. 1389, 3473
Law is holy. 1312
Law, morality, and the Bible. 2201
Law of apostasy in Islam. 2566
Law of Christ. 947, 948, 3196
Law of church and grave. 1490
Law of Congregational usage. 1338
Law of elective affinity, and other sermons, for young men and young women. 3888
Law of faith formulated. 1596
Law of growth and other sermons. 2972
Law of holiness. 1313
Law of human life. 231
Law of life and you. 2227
Law of love. 3485
Law of love and the law of violence. 2756
Law of love called the Golden rule. 3650
Law of missions. 2494
Law of practical science. 1030
Law of prayer. 2876
Law of proportion in the church of God. 2971
Law of psychic phenomena. 2989
... The law of self-manifestation. 3865
... The law of self-manifestation (karma yoga) 3865
Law of service. 28
THe law of sin and death. 3413
Law of social justice. 3447
Law of spiritual transformation. 3502
Law of the harvest. 1009
Law of the offerings. 556
Law of the psychic phenomena. 2989
Law of the rhythmic breath. 691
Law of the tithe as set forth in the Old Testament. 498
Law or grace. 2201

Law, our school-master. 2952, 3338
Law perfect. 1313
Law prophesied. 3579
Law that sets you free! 412
Lawrence & Apocalypse. 2201
Laws and forms relating to churches and other religious societies. 1490
Laws' anti-Catholic dictionary and Protestant handbook of facts. 2329
Laws in the Pentateuch, and other studies. 484
Laws of cyclic motion. 2730
Laws of deuteronomy. 510, 2201
Laws of ecclesiastical polity, books I-IV. 1240
Laws of fermentation and the wines of the ancients. 3597
Laws of happiness. 181
Laws of Holy Mass. 2365
Laws of love. 3750
Laws of Manu. 1812, 3480
Laws of Moses and the life of Christ. 1967
Laws of nature are science and truth. 1653
Laws of order for the preservation of the conjugial. 2690
Laws of penitence. 2057
Laws of progress in the Lord's prayer. 2247
Laws of right relationship. 1324
Laws of self development. 2409
Laws of success. 1233, 3358
Laws of the Fraternity of the Rosie Crosse (Themis aurea) 3251
Laws of the Grand Lodge of Texas A.F. & A.M. 1666
Laws of the Grand Lodge of Texas A.F.&A.M. 1666
Laws of the King. 3601
Laws of the soul. 3059
Laws of the spiritual life. 180
Laws of the state of New York relating to Baptist churches. 158
Lawsonian religion. 3142
Lawyer among the theologians. 2050, 3619
Lawyer and the Bible. 1099
Lawyer examines the Bible. 64
Lawyer looks at the Bible. 231
Lawyer, moderator. 2924
Lawyer reviews the illegal trial of Jesus. 2069
Lawyer's brief on the atonement. 7, 109
Lawyer's examination of the Bible. 278
Lawyers of the Bible. 231
Lawyers' proof of the hereafter. 1890
Lawyer's story of the simple gospel. 388
Lawyer's study of the Bible. 237
Lay action: the church's third force. 2191
Lay and religious states of life. 2571
Lay apostolate. 753, 1251
Lay apostolate and the hierarchy. 2192
Lay apostolate in Latin America today. 754
Lay apostolate in Latin America today; proceedings of the 1959 symposium held under the auspices of the Institute of Ibero American Studies of the Catholic University Institute of Ibero American Studies of the Margaret Bates. 754
Lay efforts; its range and methods. 2191
Lay evangelist's handbook. 1570
Lay-Fee Biblical compilation. 499
Lay leader in the lead program (laymens' enrichment and devotional program) 2192
Lay leadership. 3871
Lay leadership in Protestant churches. 2191
Lay leadership in the Young men's Christian association. 3870
... Lay participation in Christ's priesthood. 2049
Lay people in the church. 2191, 2192
Lay preacher. 2899
Lay preacher and his work. 2911
Lay sanctity in the church. 2202
Lay sermons. 3346, 3759
Lay shepherding. 1258
Lay teacher. 2202
Lay thesis on Bible wines. 3596
Lay up your treasures in heaven. 931, 2376
Lay workers for Christ. 765
Lay workers for Christ. With an introd. by Valerian Cardinal Gracias. 765
Laying the foundation. 3294
Layman. 2192
Layman and his conscience. 3223
Layman and the Book. 1062
Layman as a leader of worship. 3004
Layman builds a Christian home. 1607
Layman examines his faith. 1094
Layman extraordinary. 2626
Layman in Christian history. 2193
Layman in the Church. 2192, 2193, 3770

Layman in the church, and other essays. 3770
Layman in the itinerancy. 2191
Layman learns to pray. 2869
Layman looks at the Bible. 502
Layman looks at the church. 1066
Layman looks at the Gods of the Bible. 235
Layman looks at the Lamb of God. 2020
Layman looks at the Lord's prayer. 2247
Layman looks at the minister. 3673
Layman looks at world religions. 3119
Layman looks with love at her church. 14
Layman reads his Bible. 613
Layman Revato. 2191
Layman shares Jesus. 144, 3704
Layman speaks out loud. 80
Layman views world missions. 2492
Layman's apology. 2192
Layman's appraisal of Christian adult education. 8
Layman's Bible commentary. 223
Layman's Bible commentary (The) 223
Layman's Bible digest. 311
Layman's Bible encyclopedia. 245
Layman's breviary. 2395
Layman's call. 2191
Layman's church. 2191
Layman's complete missal for Holy Week. 1837
Layman's confession of faith. 1064
Layman's daily missal, prayer book & ritual. 845
Layman's Galilean. 1072
Layman's guide to 70 Psalms. 579
Layman's guide to Baptist beliefs. 147
Layman's guide to Christian terms. 3639
Layman's guide to interpreting the Bible. 287
Layman's guide to Our Lord's prayer. 2248
Layman's guide to Prebyterian beliefs. 2914
Layman's guide to Presbyterian beliefs. 2914
Layman's guide to Protestant theology. 2953, 3654
Layman's guide to Protestant worship. 3853
Layman's guide to the inerrancy debate. 279
Layman's guide to the New Testament. 410
Layman's guide to understanding the Bible. 311
Layman's handbook of Christian doctrine. 3638
Layman's handbook of Daniel. 506
Layman's harmony of the Gospels. 386
Layman's history of the Church of England. 1220
Layman's introduction to Christian thought. 3663
Layman's introduction to religious existentialism. 1583
Layman's introduction to the New Testament. 410
Layman's introduction to the Old Testament. 540
Layman's Lent. 2209
Layman's life of Jesus. 1976
Layman's missal, prayer book & ritual. 2885
Layman's missionary movement. 3380
Layman's New Testament. 343
Layman's parallel New Testament. 357
Layman's religion. 1058
Layman's role today. 1006
Layman's view of the Bible. 237
Laymen. 754
Laymen at work. 1252
Laymen in action. 2192
Laymen in the church. 2191
Laymen look at preaching. 2899, 3692
Laymen, proclaim the word! 2202
Laymen speaking. 976, 2903
Laymen's guide to Baptist beliefs. 147
Laymen's hour (The) 3354
Laymen's retreats explained. 3222
Lays of love and faith. 2384, 3206
Lays of Quakerdom. 1688
Lays of the gospel. 2384
Lazarus, come out! 875, 3409
Lazarus of Bethany. 2203
Lazarus Spengler. 3041, 3471
Lazy-man-rest-not. 3010
Le Mans forgeries. 2203
[Le-shanah ha-ba 'ah bi-Yerushalayim (romanized form)]. 610, 2415
Lead, follow or get out of the way. 3835
Lead, kindly light. 1213, 2754
Lead my sheep. 2124
Leader of men. 1401
Leaders for parish councils. 2774
Leader's guide. 682, 3033, 3178
Leader's guide for use with The privilege of teaching. 3177

Leader's guide for use with The rough years. 3180, 3790
Leaders' handbook for the Young men's Christian associations of North America. 3872
Leaders manual to accompany Between the Americas (Jay S. Stowell) 2549
Leaders manual to accompany West Indian treasures. 2550
Leaders of early Christian thought. 3658
Leaders of Iberean Christianity. 1110
Leaders of Israel. 216
Leaders of our people. 2084
Leaders of our time. 661
Leaders of the Church of England, 1828-1944. 1212
Leaders of the Lutheran reformation. 2282
Leaders of the people. 2084
Leaders of the reformation. 1857, 2278, 3036, 3037
Leaders of thought in the modern church. 927
Leaders of young people. 3889
... Leaders of youth. 3886
Leadership. 952
Leadership and evangelism. 1060
Leadership and human relations. 2611
Leadership book. 953
Leadership development and the workers conference. 952
Leadership education handbook. 3167
Leadership education in the church. 2204
Leadership education in the local church. 3178
Leadership for Christ. 2204
Leadership for church education. 935
Leadership in crisis. 953
Leadership in religious education. 3148
Leadership in the making. 3878
Leadership manual; administering the Christian Education Program in the local church. 3158
Leadership manual for adult study groups. 3151
Leadership of adult mission study groups. 2551
Leadership of Bible study groups. 639
... Leadership of girls' activities. 1714
Leadership of worship. 3003
Leadership profiles from Bible personalities. 217, 953
Leadership roles for youth. 953
Leadership through Christian endeavor. 1914
Leadership training in the local church (including the Christian day school) 953
Leadership unlimited. 141, 953
Leading a church school. 3554
Leading a Jewish life in the modern world. 2121
Leading a Sunday church school. 3554
Leading adult classes. 3168
Leading cases in the Bible. 1942
Leading children's choirs. 916
Leading churches through change. 1171
Leading dynamic Bible study. 640
Leading in prayer. 2894
Leading in prayer (a prayer before the lesson) 3564
Leading in public prayer. 2897, 3003
Leading little ones to God. 1734, 3666
Leading little ones to Jesus. 3166
Leading of a minister. 3515
Leading persons and periods in English church history. 1176, 1220, 1378
Leading the family of God. 2786
Leading the little ones to Christ. 746
Leading your church in evangelism. 1564
Leading youth to abundant life. 3884
Leaf from the first edition of the first complete Bible in English, the Coverdale Bible, 1535. 272
Leaf in review of the words and acts of God and men relative to the fullness of the Gospel. 2610
League devotions especially adapted for members of the Apostleship of prayer in league with the sacred heart, with choral service for the first Friday of the month. 3269
League hymnal. 813
League of nations. 605
...Leakage from a Catholic parish. 3749
Leap of reason. 2180
Leaping flame. 3830
Learing to work together. 1252
Learn a little! or. 3887
Learn a little! or, What's life all about? 3887
Learn from me. 164
Learn Mishnah. 2479
Learn of Me in Genesis. 521
Learn Talmud. 2079, 3585
Learn to live. 2026, 2394
Learn to live with style. 983
Learned and very eloquent treatie. 790

Learned doctor William Ames. 34
Learned men. 272
Learned men's English: the revisers. 274
Learning about war and peace. 2808
Learning about witches. 3826
... Learning and teaching. 3565
Learning Chirstian leadership. 2204
Learning disabilities. 2204
Learning disability. 2204
Learning doctrine from the Bible. 231
Learning for living. 3148
Learning for the eternities. 1232
Learning from Jesus. 3164
Learning God's way. 3185, 3763
Learning how children worship. 3858
Learning how to learn. 3543
Learning how to live with others. 1917, 3153
Learning how to settle disputes. 3011
Learning in the nursery class. 3174
Learning is change. 938
Learning Jesus Christ through the Heidelberg Catechism. 1801
Learning my religion. 3157, 3184
Learning of God's love and care. 1723
Learning process for religious education. 3156
Learning religion from famous Americans. 3119
Learning the Brethren way with Jim and Jane. 1235
Learning the Breviary. 842
Learning the Mass. 2368, 2370
Learning the Mass, the new liturgy. 2370
Learning the new breviary. 842
Learning the New Testament. 409
Learning the way. 2283
Learning through encounter. 1170
Learning through Leviticus. 563
Learning through liturgy. 2235
Learning to be free. 3889
Learning to die. 1414
Learning to die, learning to live. 1413
Learning to forgive. 1633
Learning to have faith. 1602
Learning to know God. 1735, 3173
Learning to know the Bible. 641, 3766
Learning to know the Old Testament. 596
Learning to lean. 989, 3807
Learning to listen, Lord. 2880
Learning to live. 166, 1260, 3765
Learning to live for God. 2454
Learning to live from the acts. 330
Learning to live from the Gospels. 399, 973
Learning to live with others. 733, 3174
Learning to love. 3388
Learning to love God. 1016
Learning to love ourselves. 1016
Learning to love people. 1016, 2263
Learning to manage our fears. 1619
Learning to pray. 2249, 2869, 2880, 2886
Learning to read in different languages. 3026
Learning to talk to the world beyond. 3506
Learning to teach. 3153
Learning to teach from the Master teacher. 3555
Learning to understand people. 3176
Learning to use your Bible. 285
Learning to work together. 1252
Learning to worship. 838, 3857
Learning together. 935
Learning together in the Christian fellowship. 935, 3179
Least of all saints. 1576, 2310
Least of these. 1164
Leatherwood god. 1869-70. 1484
Leave a little to God. 1811
Leave it to the Spirit. 3003
Leave your nets. 2694
Leave your pets. 2694
Leave yourself alone. 987
... The leaven. 1035, 1495
Leaven of holiness. 2572, 3205
Leaven of the Sadducees. 3728
Leavening the Levant. 2558
Leavening the nation. 2527
Leaves from a century plant. 1547, 2830
Leaves from a spiritual notebook. 1456
Leaves from heaven, a message of God, a word from heaven. 3516
Leaves from mission fields. 2521, 2702
Leaves from the annals of the Sisters of mercy. 3418
Leaves from the notebook of a tamed cynic. 1289, 1291, 1294, 2709
Leaves of antiquity. 2207
Leaves of healing. 1351, 1353, 2398
Leaves of life for daily inspiration. 2396
Leaves of the Tree of life for the healing of the nations. 725
Leaves of truth. 2604
Leaving dark valleys behind. 3288
Lebanon. 2362

... The Lebanon in turmoil, Syria and the powers in 1860. 1425
Leben des heiligen Severin. 3388
Lebensweise lebendiger Gemeinden. 2264
L'Ecriture et le reste. 58, 2778
Lectern. 2890
Lectionary for Mass. 2369
Lectionary for Mass for Sundays of Year A, arranged for readers. 2369
Lectionary for Mass for Sundays of year C. 2369
Lectionary of Christian prose from the 2nd to the 20th century. 1456
Lectionary of the Roman missal. 2369
Lector's guide to Biblical pronunciations. 480
Lecture entitled the Christian science church. 1033
Lecture on popular superstitions. 3568
Lecture on the doctrine of justification. 2161
Lecture on the evidences of Chirstianity given at the Hennepin Ave. 1099
Lecture on the Protestant faith. 2977
Lecture-room talks. 1332
Lectures. 412, 455
Lectures and articles on Chirstian science. 1033
Lectures and articles on Christian science. 1033
Lectures and biographical sketches. 1511
Lectures and essays on natural theology and ethics. 2674
Lectures & lay sermons. 3341
Lectures and orations. 3006
Lectures and sermons embracing the sovereignty, holiness, wisdom and benevolence of God. 3338
Lectures and writings. 3632
Lectures dedicated to Gibbon. 59, 1942
Lectures delivered by Soame Jenyns, esq. 1098, 1942
Lectures, essays, and sermons. 3342
Lectures, exegetical and practical. 448
Lectures, explanatory and practical. 449
Lectures for the people. 3349
Lectures in defence of divine revelation. 61
Lectures in Hyde part. 1735
Lectures in systematic theology. 2914, 3642, 3649
Lectures of the Arya. 3776
Lectures on Apostolical succession in the Church of England. 76
Lectures on Babylonia and Palestine. 93
Lectures on Catholicism. 802
Lectures on Christian doctrine. 3724
Lectures on Christian science. 1037
Lectures on Christian theology. 3645, 3652
Lectures on church government, containing objections to the Episcopal scheme. 2966
Lectures on church music. 1202
Lectures on Daniel the Prophet. 509
Lectures on Deuteronomy. 510
Lectures on Ephesians. 365
Lectures on faith. 2613
Lectures on female Scripture characters. 3839
Lectures on Genesis. 521
Lectures on Hebrews. 403
Lectures on homiletics. 1843
Lectures on homiletics and preaching, and on public prayer. 2904
Lectures on in the incarnation. 1893
Lectures on infant baptism. 1906
Lectures on Jewish antiquities. 2083
Lectures on Jewish liturgy. 2109
Lectures on mental philosophy and theology. 2834
Lectures on metaphysic and logic by Sir William Hamilton, bart. 2417
Lectures on modern universalism. 3752
Lectures on mysticism. 2637
Lectures on natural theology. 2672
Lectures on pastoral theology. 3674, 3677
Lectures on philosophical theology. 2833
Lectures on practical subjects. 1227
Lectures on preaching. 2898, 2905
Lectures on preaching and sermon construction. 2898
Lectures on preaching, and the several branches of the miniserial office. 3671
Lectures on prophecy. 2949
Lectures on reality. Series 1. 2693
Lectures on revivals. 3232
Lectures on revivals of religion. 3228, 3229
Lectures on Romanism. 798
Lectures on Romans. 468
Lectures on Scripture facts. 232
Lectures on spiritualism, being a series of lectures on the phenomena and philosophy of development. 3516
Lectures on Swedenborgianism. 2689

Lectures on systematic theology. 3643
Lectures on systematic theology and pulpit eloquence. 3641
Lectures on the Acts of the apostles. 331
... Lectures on the Apocalypee. 458
Lectures on the Apocalypse. 451, 452
Lectures on the Book of Acts. 329
Lectures on the book of Ecclesiastes. 512
Lectures on the book of Revelation. 454, 455
Lectures on the book of Revelations. 462
Lectures on the catechism of the Protestant Episcopal church. 2962
Lectures on the Christian character. 976
Lectures on the Council of Trent. 3710
Lectures on the Council of Trent, delivered at Oxford 1892-3. 3710
Lectures on the covenants, and the right to church membership, with other subjects. 1356
Lectures on the doctrine of justification. 2160
Lectures on the doctrines of Christianity. 3727
Lectures on the early history of Christianity in England. 1761
Lectures on the Epistle of Paul. 467
Lectures on the Epistle to the Colossians. 341
Lectures on the Epistle to the Romans. 468
Lectures on the Epistles of Paul to the Thessalonians. 477
Lectures on the essence of religion. 3059
Lectures on the evidence of catholicity. 792
Lectures on the evidences of Christianity. 60, 1099
Lectures on the evidences of Christianity in the nineteenth century. 59
Lectures on the evidences of the Christian religion. 61
Lectures on the First and Second epistles of Peter. 447
Lectures on the first two visions of the book of Daniel. 509
Lectures on the future life and state. 1802
Lectures on the general principles of moral government. 2980
Lectures on the Gospel of Matthew. 440
Lectures on the Gospels. 1267
Lectures on the history of Christianity. 1173
Lectures on the history of preaching. 2908, 2909
Lectures on the history of religions. 3139
Lectures on the history of the Eastern church. 1768, 2747
Lectures on the history of the Jewish church. 2090, 2096
Lectures on the history of the papal chancery down to the time of Innocent iii. 766
Lectures on the I ching. 1879
Lectures on the incarnation of God. 1727
Lectures on the influence of the apostle Paul on the development of Christianity. 376, 2800, 3658
Lectures on the influence of the institutions, thought, and culture of Rome, on Christianity and the development of the Catholic Church. 811, 1197
Lectures on the inspiration of the Scriptures. 306
Lectures on the last things. 1528
Lectures on the law and the gospel. 2200
Lectures on the Levitical offerings. 3271
Lectures on the Lord's prayer. 2248
Lectures on the moral government of God. 2983
Lectures on the nature and end of the sacred office, and on the dignity, duty, qualifications and character of the sacred order. 3674
Lectures on the nature of spirit. 3462
Lectures on the nature of spirit, and of man as a spiritual being. 2690
... Lectures on the origin and growth of religion. 701
Lectures on the origin and growth of religion as illustrated by Celtic heathendom. 878
Lectures on the origin and growth of religion, as illustrated by some points in the history of Indian Buddhism. 706
Lectures on the origin and growth of religion as illustrated by the religion of the ancient Hebrews. 2151
Lectures on the origin and growth of religion as illustrated by the religion of ancient Egypt. 1502
Lectures on the origin and growth of religion as illustrated by the religion of the ancient Babylonians. 94

Lectures on the origin and growth of religion, as illustrated by the religions of India. 1896, 3140
Lectures on the origin and growth of conception of God as illustrated by anthropology and history. 1729
Lectures on the pantheistic idea of an impersonal-substance-deity. 2767
Lectures on the parables of Our Saviour. 2025, 2771
Lectures on the present position of Catholics in England. 816
Lectures on the present position of Catholics in England, addressed to the brothers of the Oratory in the summer of 1851. 816
Lectures on the principal doctrines [!] of the Roman Catholic church. 797
Lectures on the religion of the Semites. 3332
Lectures on the religious thought of Soren Kierkegaard, given at Princeton theological seminary. 2170
Lectures on the reunion of the churches. 1040
Lectures on the Revelations. 451, 452
Lectures on the sacred poetry of the Hebrews. 1785, 1799
Lectures on the sacred poetry of the Hebrews. (1787) 567, 1799
Lectures on the science of religion. 3119
Lectures on the Tabernacle. 3579
Lectures on the whole book of Ruth. 589
Lectures on theology. 3640, 3642, 3648, 3649, 3660
Lectures on universalism. 3753
Lectures on witchcraft. 3828
Lectures supposed to have been delivered by the author of A view of the internal evidence of the Christian religion. 1098, 1942
Lectures to children. 2032
Lectures to my students. 2906, 3367
Lectures to young men. 3869
Lectures upon the history of Our Lord and Saviour Jesus Christ. 1960
Led by a star. 2022
Led by the spirit. 3265
Led on! 3133
Led on! Step by step, scenes from clerical, military, educational, and plantation life in the South, 1828-1898. 3133
Lee Chung. 2489
Lee lines. 1841
Lee Ming and his sisters. 897
Left hand of God. 2303
Left-handed folks. 159
Legacy. 2614, 3423
Legacy of adoration. 3758
Legacy of Eve. 3841
Legacy of faith. 37, 2186
Legacy of Islam. 1283
Legacy of Israel. 2084
Legacy of lectures and verses. 760
Legacy of Luther. 2278, 2288
Legacy of Maimonides. 2622
Legacy of Maurice Pekarsky. 2145
Legacy of Michael Sattler. 3630
Legacy of Reinhold Niebuhr. 2709
Legacy of Saint Patrick as found in his own writings. 2793
Legacy of the liberal spirit. 2220
Legacy of wisdom. 572, 3822
Legacy of Zion. 2150
Legal and ethical aspects of treating critically and terminally ill patients. 3237
... The legal and governmental terms common to the Macedonian Greek inscriptions and the New Testament. 321
Legal and historical proof of the resurrection of the dead. 3222
Legal aspects of Lutheran parish education. 2287
Legal position of the clergy. 1489
Legal proof. 67, 2053
Legal Sunday, its history and character. 3193
Legal terms common to the Macedonian inscriptions and the New Testament. 1771
Legal view of the trial of Christ. 2068
Legalism and the seventh-day question. 3380
Legatio and De Resurrectione. 69
Legend and writings of Saint Clare of Assisi. 1284
Legend builders of the West. 2662
Legend, lore, and religion in China. 914, 1487
Legend of Greenbush. 3272
Legend of Jubal and other poems, old and new. 3206
Legend of Krishna. 2186
Legend of Noah. 2711
Legend of Perseus. 2822

...Legend of Psyche. 3207
Legend of Saint Columba. 1310
Legend of the Baal-Shem. 1788, 1928
Legend of the infancy of our Saviour. 2047
Legend of Thomas Didymus. 1962
Les legendes grecques des saints militaires. 1024
Legends and myths of Greece and Rome. 2656
Legends and stories of the holy child Jesus from many lands. 1976
Legends from the future. 526
Legends of Abraham the patriarch. 905
Legends of Czech saints in the XIVth century. 1025
Legends of Galilee, Jordan, and Sinai. 2208
Legends of Genesis. 523
...Legends of Greek and Roman heroes. 2657
Legends of incense, herb and oil magic. 2312
Legends of Jerusalem. 2207
Legends of Joseph and his brothers. 905
Legends of Judea and Samaria. 2208
Legends of Ma-Ui, a demi god of Polynesia and of his mother Hina. 2207
Legends of Maui and Tahaki. 2666
Legends of Moses the law-giver. 905
Legends of New-England. 2857
Legends of our fathers. 3015
Legends of Our Lady Mary. 2360
Legends of Our Lady Mary the perpetual virgin and her mother Hanna. 2360
Legends of Palestine. 2208
Legends of Ruth. 905
Legends of St. Anne and Mary. 48, 799
Legends of Saint Joseph, patron of the universal church. 3275
Legends of the Bible. 2207
Legends of the Christ child. 1976
Legends of the Hasidim. 1789
Legends of the Jews. 2207
Legends of the Madonna. 2355
Legends of the Madonna as represented in the fine arts. 2355, 2358
Legends of the monastic orders. 3280
Legends of the monastic orders as represented in the fine arts. 1026, 3280
Legends of the monastic orders as represented in the fine arts, forming the second series of Sacred and legendary art. 3280
Legends of the North. 2651
Legends of the patriarchs and prophets and other Old Testament characters from various sources. 492
Legends of the planets. 2658
Legends of the saints. 952, 1028, 1780
Legends of the Sufis. 2460
Legends of the Virgin and Christ. 920, 2360
Legends of Troy in art and literature. 3715
Legion of Mary. 2208
Legislation on the sacraments in the new Code of canon law [lib. iii, Can. 726-1011, 1144-1153]. 3264
Legislative struggle for church union. 1249
... Legitimacy and legitimation. 1883
L'Eglise et le capitalisme. 1076
Lehi in the desert. 679
Lehi Willard Jones. 877, 2130
Lehmann's Little dictionary of liturgical terms. 2236
Leibniz. 2568
Leibniz and Descartes, proof and eternal truths. 1426, 1578
Leigh Street Baptist Church, 1854-1954. 2208
Leighton Ford. 1576, 1633
Leila Ada, the Jewish convert. 2085, 2208
Leisure. 35, 3209, 3849
Lelia Ada, the Jewish convert. 2208
Lemba, 1650-1930. 2209
Lend me your hands. 754
Lending the parables our ears. 2024
L'engagement du laic. 754
Length of our days. 2081
Lengthened cords. 3715
Lengthened shadows. 3418
Lenora. 1515
Lent. 314, 2209
Lent, a liturgical commentary on the lessons and gospel. 2209
Lent and Easter. 2209
Lent and Eastertide with the liturgy. 2209
Lent and the laws of the church. 3346
Lent and the mass. 2211
Lent in earnest. 2211
Lent, past and present. 2209
Lent with Christ. 2211
Lent with Evelyn Underhill. 2212
Lent with John Wesley. 2212
Lent with Saint Bernard. 587

Lent with St. John. 3344
Lent with William Temple. 2210
Lenten counsellors. 2214
Lenten-Easter sourcebook. 2210
Lenten-Easter sourceboook. 2210
Lenten lectures on the Christian affirmations. 2213
Lenten meditations. 2210, 2211
Lenten monitor. 2210
Lenten prayers for everyman. 2210
Lenten sermon outlines. 2216
Lenten sermons. 2213, 2215, 2216
Lenten sermons of the holy year. 2215
Lenten sermons, the passion of Christ and the seven vices. 2215
Lenten soliloquies for private and public use. 2214
Lenten study of the characters of the passion. 2034
Lenten thoughts. 2209
Lententide family altar. 2209
Lententide sermonettes. 2215
Leo Baeck and the Jewish mystical tradition. 125, 2646
Leo Baeck Memorial Conference on Jewish Social Thought. 125, 2141
Leo Baeck on Christianity. 125, 2153
Leo Baeck: teacher of Theresienstadt. 125
Leo Jung jubilee volume. 2142, 2159
Leo Rosten's Jewish treasury. 3014
Leo the Thirteenth. 2216
Leo xiii and Anglican orders. 2216
Leo XIII and modern civilization. 3450
... Leo xiii and our times. 2216
Leo XIII and the rise of socialism. 2216
Leo XIII, a light from heaven. 2216
Leo XIII, and the modern world. 2216
Leofric missal as used in the cathedral of Exeter during the episcopate of its first bishop, A. D. 1050-1072. 809
Leon da Modena and the Kol sakhal. 2145, 2216
Leonard and Soule experiments in psychical research, also experiments with Sanders, Brittain, Peters and Dowden, by Lydia W. Allison. 2986
Leontius of Byzantium. 2217
Leopard hunts alone. 719
"Leopard-man." 2491
Leopard tamed; the story of an African pastor, his people, and his problems. 2187, 2552
Leopold von Ranke manuscripts of Syracuse Conference of the Methodist Church. 2439
... Les lettres provinciales de Blaise Pascal. 1945
Les 'petites grottes' de Qumran. 1409
Les sept psaumes allegorises. 2812
Les sources de l'histoire du montanisme. 2586
Leslie Weatherhead. 3799
Less is more. 2866
Less said. 2105
Less traveled road. 1483
Lesser eastern churches. 1487
Lesser Key of Solomon. 2313
Lesser parables of Our Lord. 387, 2024
Lesser priesthood and Notes on church government. 1169
Lessing and the Enlightenment. 2217
Lessing's Education of the human race. 2217
Lesson book for Bible study. 642
Lesson book for top pilots. 2599
Lesson commentary for Sunday-schools of the Lutheran church. 2282
Lesson handbook. 1915, 3556
... Lesson materials in the church school. 3147
Lesson of love. 969
Lesson round table. 1915
Lesson stories for the kindergarten grades of the Bible school. 3556
Lessons about salvation. 3296
... Lessons for every Sunday in the year. 218
Lessons for life. 2081
Lessons for lovers in the Song of Solomon. 593
Lessons for Methodists. 2437
Lessons for schools. 648
Lessons for seekers of holiness. 1822
Lessons for senior classes on Christian doctrine. 933
Lessons for teachers of beginners. 1498
Lessons from Leviticus. 557
Lessons from our living past. 2207
Lessons from the cross. 103, 1997
Lessons from the desk. 639
... Lessons from the great teachers. 936
Lessons from the life of Saint Peter. 2824
Lessons from the parables. 2025
Lessons from the Reformation. 3034
Lessons from the world of matter and the world of man. 3344
Lessons from work. 1212

Lessons in applied ethics of Christ. 2003
...Lessons in Bible history. 628
Lessons in Bible training. 1229
Lessons in denominational history. 3380
Lessons in finding God. 2753
Lessons in holiness. 1823
Lessons in Jewish history;an outline of Jewish History from its early beginnings to modern times. 2094
Lessons in living. 958
Lessons in meditation. 2381
...Lessons in New Testament history. 625
Lessons in personality development. 2590
Lessons in religion. 128
... Lessons in soul-winning. 1566
Lessons in successful living. 958
Lessons in the Gospel. 423
Lessons in the life of Our Lord Jesus Christ. 1992
Lessons in truth. 1068
Lessons in wisdom. 1069
Lessons of faith and life. 3755
Lessons of the ages. 3511
Lessons of the Boston correspondence school. 1771
Lessons of the King made plain for His little ones. 626
Lessons of the Prince of Peace. 1062
Lessons on celebrities of Hebrew story. 1798
Lessons on Hebrews. 1798
Lessons on the Acts of the apostles. 332
Lessons on the church catechism. 2962
Lessons on the Epistle of Paul to the Romans. 470
Lessons on the Gospel of Luke. 431
Lessons on the life of Our Lord Jesus Christ. 1992
Lessons on the life of St. Paul. 3280
Lessons on the life of St. Paul, drawn from the Acts and the Epistles. 2804, 3727
Lessons on the life of the apostle Paul for Bible classes. 2804
Lessons on the offices of instruction as contained in the Book of common prayer. 2961
Lessons on the way. 1049
"Lest they assist passively" 2365
Lest we build on sand. 2571
Lest we forget. 140, 144, 1474, 1496, 2896, 3419, 3852
Lest we grow hard. 974
Lester Roloff. 170, 3244
Let Christ take you beyond discouragement. 1351
Let day begin. 527
Let Edward be king. 1498
Let Europe hear. 1542
Let every tongue confess. 1912, 2496
Let go and let God. 958, 1738
Let go; living by the cross and by faith. 997
Let God arise. 584
Let God be God! 2278
Let God do it. 1036
Let God go free. 1066
Let God in. 966
Let God love you. 449
Let him live. 2125
Let in the sun. 2392
Let it happen: creative worship for the emerging church. 3004
Let it show. 986
Let life grow toward God. 1593
Let me be a woman. 2340
Let me commend. 1570
Let me explain. 167
Let me illustrate. 1839, 1843
Let me speak! 921
Let my heart be broken. 2845, 3851
Let my heart be broken with the things that break the heart of God. 2502, 3851
Let my people go. 516, 918, 953, 1931, 2778
Let my people grow. 1246
Let my people live! 53
Let no man put asunder. 201
Let not your heart be troubled. 970, 1318, 1352, 1353, 3539
Let our children go! 2793, 3324
Let prayer help you. 2874
Let the Bible help you. 302
Let the children paint. 3160
Let the children sing. 2633
Let the church be the church. 1059
Let the Earth bless the Lord. 2195
Let the Earth hear. 3018, 3707
Let the earth hear His voice. 1573
Let the evidence speak! 202
Let the fire fall! 1561, 1570
Let the living Bible help you. 601, 1351
Let the new nation arise. 3463
Let the people cry amen! 502
Let the people know. 1242
Let the Psalms speak. 579
Let the song go on. 1748, 3470
Let the spirit in. 2380

Let the tide come in! 1712
Let the winds blow. 1237
Let them make me a sanctuary. 195, 2101
Let there be God. 1725
Let there be light. 235, 901, 2474, 2757, 2898, 3142, 3865
Let there be unity of religions within diversity. 3142
Let this church die. 1064
Let us abide. 982
Let us be holy. 1823
Let us break bread together. 1266, 1318, 2435
Let us build. 1156
Let us draw near. 517, 3579
Let us enjoy forgiveness. 1633
"Let us give thanks" 2889, 3163
"Let us go into the next towns"--in Japan. 2534
Let us go on to maturity. 3479
Let us go to Bethlehem? 2023
... Let us have faith. 1593
"... let us have love!" 2263
"Let us have peace." 2856
Let us in. 3497
Let us keep Lent. 2210
Let us love. 2265
Let us praise. 2867
Let us pray. 1234, 1298, 2873, 2874, 2884, 2889, 2892
Let us pray for our dead. 843
Let us pray to the Lord. 766
"Let us reason together," 2287
Let us return unto the Lord. 2300
Let us see Jesus. 341, 2037
Let us sing. 1203
Let us worship. 3217
Let us worship God. 2884, 3853
Let wives be submissive. 325, 1603
"Let Your name be sanctified." 1941
Let yourself g-r-o-w! 983
Let yourself go. 3179
Let's act--now. 1281
Let's be different youth meetings. 3879
Let's begin again. 3403
Let's believe. 1601
Let's build a Brethren Church. 1838
Let's build a new world. 1466
Let's do more with persons with disabilities. 1258
Let's do something about our teaching. 3179
Let's enjoy living to-day. 1313
Let's explore worship. 3858
Let's fan the flame. 1244, 3385
Let's find out about Easter. 1486
Let's find out about Jewish holidays. 1615
Let's get acquainted. 2439
Let's get to know God. 3183
Let's go exploring. 2551
Let's go Jesus. 901
Let's go out-of-doors. 2956
... Let's go (short cuts) 2498
Let's go to India. 2532
Let's have a banquet. 1166
Let's keep Christmas. 1114
Let's know the Bible. 308
Let's live! 986
Let's live our beliefs. 3383
Let's look at Paul. 2804
Let's meet the Holy Spirit. 1831
Let's mend the mess! 791, 1001
Let's plan a banquet. 1166
Let's play Bible stories! 603
Let's pray! 857
Let's pray about it. 1437
Let's quit fighting about the Holy Spirit. 1712
Let's read Greek. 1770
Let's read the Bible. 613
Let's return to the Mosaic authorship of the Pentateuch. 564
Let's see China. 2508
Let's see Mexico. 2461
Let's see, No. 1. 3161
Let's start praying again. 2868
Let's steal the moon. 3581
Let's study the Bible. 647
Let's study theology. 2283
"Let's take a look at ourselves" 1277
Let's take a trip. 1356
Let's take a walk with Jesus through the Bible. 606
Let's take another look. 3664
Let's talk. 1008, 2395
Let's talk about extremism. 1612
Let's talk about giants. 1710
Let's talk about God. 898, 902, 1734
Let's talk about Judaism. 2151
Let's talk it over. 2079, 3012, 3691, 3884
Let's teach through group relations. 3169
Let's think about money. 3528
Let's think about our history. 1464
Let's think about our religion. 3744
Let's worship God alone. 1092

Letter addressed to His Grace the Duke of Norfolk on occasion of Mr. Gladstone's recent expostulation. 1715, 3769
Letter and authentic documentary evidence in relation to the Trinity church property, in the city of New York. 2701
Letter and the spirit. 1539
Letter-book of the Rev. Henry Caner, S.P.G. missionary in colonial Connecticut and Massachusetts until the Revolution. 1223
Letter from Lisieux. 2335
Letter from Paul. 2217, 3172
Letter from Pontius Pilate's wife. 2944
Letter from Richard Raynal Keene, to Luther Martin, esq., attorney-general of Maryland; upon the subject of his 'Modern gratitude. 2348
Letter from Rome, shewing the exact conformity of popery and paganism. 801
Letter from the associated ministers of the county of Windham. 3535
Letter of Aristeas. 528
Letter of James. 412
Letter of James the Just. 411
Letter of John to James. 1795
Letter of joy. 448
Letter of Junipero Serra to the reverend father prencher Fray Fermin Francisco de Lasuen. 3376
Letter of Luis Jayme, O.F.M., San Diego, October 17, 1772. 3298
Letter of Meric Casaubon to Peter du Moulin concerning natural experimental philosophie (1669) and Of credulity and incredulity (1668, 1670) 58, 1521
Letter of Paul to the Galatians. 380
Letter of Paul to the Galations. 379
Letter of Paul to the Philippians. 448
Letter of Paul to the Romans. 466, 467
Letter of resolution concerning Origen and the chief of his opinions. 2743
Letter of wise counsel. 321
Letter on apologetics, and History and dogma. 2835
Letter on the Anglican church's claims. 44
Letter on the principles of the Christian faith. 1052
Letter to a friend. 1582, 3743
Letter to a Protestant friend. 787
Letter to Alexander Campbell. 732
Letter to American Christians. 3743
Letter to Catholic priests. 772
Letter to Doctor A. Brigham. 1283
Letter to Hebrews. 402
Letter to His Holiness, Pope Pius VII. 2218
Letter to my daughter. 3877
Letter to my son. 2613
Letter to Pilgrims. 403
Letter to Rev. Edward B. Pusey. 2421, 3010
Letter to Rev. Frederick T. Gray. 683, 1757
Letter to Rev. J. Litch, on the second coming of Christ. 3319
Letter to St. Augustine after re-reading his Confessions. 114
Letter to the author of the pamphlet Called An Answer [!] to the Hampshire Narrative. 691, 3522
Letter to the Bishop of North Carolina. 1930, 2971
Letter to the Chestnut st. Congregational church, Chelsea, Mass. 3494
Letter to the Hebrews. 402, 403, 404
Letter to the Protestant-dissenters in the parish of Bally-kelly, in Ireland. 2914
Letter to the Rev. Bernard Whitman. 1699
Letter to the Rev. Mr. Jacob Green, of New-Jersey. 730
Letter to the Reverend Mr. Cary. 743, 3022
Letter to the Reverend Nathaniel Whitaker, D.D., wherein some of his gross misrepresentations of Mr. Hart's doctrines in his dialogue, intitled, A brief examination, &c., and his false and injurious charges against him, contained in his appendix and postscript to his discourses on 2 Cor. 5. 19. lately reprinted at Salem, are detected, and justly censured. 1334, 3810
Letter to the Romans. 467, 468, 470
Letter to the Romans, an exposition. 468
Letter to the theological professors at New Haven. 3411, 3591
Letter to William E. Channing, D.D. 3193
Letter writing for the church. 1165
Letter written to Pius VII. 2218
Letters. 2694
Letters addressed to a brother in the church, on renouncing the secret principles of freemasonry. 1662

Letters addressed to a friend on the following subjects. 2217
Letters addressed to a Protestant friend. 788
Letters addressed to relatives and friends. 3713
Letters addressed to the daughter of a nobleman, on the formation of the religious and the moral principle. 963
Letters (Alacoque, Marguerite Marie) 2217
Letters (Ambrosius) 2217
Letters (Ambrosius, Saint) 3634
Letters and charters of Gilbert Foliot, Abbot of Gloucester (1139-48), Bishop of Hereford (1148-63), and London (1163-87) 1761
Letters and conversational remarks. 733
Letters and correspondence of John Henry Newman during his life in the English church, with a brief autobiography. 2704
Letters and diaries (Newman, John Henry) 774
Letters and documents (La Salle, Jean Baptiste de) 695
Letters and instructions of St. Ignatius Loyola. 2268
Letters and papers from prison. 676
Letters and poems of Fulbert of Chartres. 666, 1689
Letters and reflections. 997
Letters and religion (Chapman, John Jay) 2217
Letters and sermons (Newton, John) 1217
Letters and shorter works. 1541
Letters (Augustinus, Aurelius) 2217
Letters (Basilius) 2217
Letters, being an answer to "Papal Rome," 733, 791
Letters (Bernard of Clairvaux) 2217
Letters between healers. 1600
Letters between Theophilus and Eugenio, on the moral pravity of man, and the means of his restoration. 967
Letters by a modern mystic. 2639
Letters concerning mythology, London, 1748. 2649
Letters concerning the constitution and order of the Christian ministry. 1296
Letters concerning the Holy Spirit. 1835
Letters (Cyprianus, Saint. 2217
Letters (Fletcher, John William) 2217
Letters from a late eminent prelate to one of his friends. 3795
Letters from a living dead man. 3495
Letters from a "modernist" 2562, 3721
Letters from a previously unpublished angel. 1007
Letters from a saint (Francois de Sales) 2387
Letters from a sick room. 3405
Letters from a spirit. 2218
Letters from American Baptist ministers about "A message from the Baptist union of Great Britain and Ireland to the Baptists of the United States of America" 141
Letters from an occult student. 2727
Letters from Baron Friedrich von Hugel to a niece. 1850
Letters from Broosa, Asia Minor. 2558
Letters from Cambrai (Fenelon, Francois de Salignac de la Mothe) 1621
Letters from Dad / (Coleman, William L. Coleman) 3884
Letters from eternity (Behr, Herman) 3495
Letters from God (Cheley, Frank Hobart) 1720
Letters from Hastings, 1908-1912. 3593
Letters from heaven. 1794
Letters from heaven (Sprague, Eli Wilmot) 3515
Letters from home (Hastings, Robert J) 2389
Letters from Ireland, 1228-1229. 1292, 2220
Letters from James Bay. 1847, 2485
Letters from Likiep (Feeney, Thomas Joseph) 2538
Letters from Mother (McMurry, Mildred (Dodson) 2218
Letters from Mother Naomi [pseud.]. 1714
Letters from my home in India. 2530
Letters from Paris, 1912-1914. 3593
Letters from Paul. 370
Letters from Rome on the Council. 2862, 3769
Letters from Roy (Stevens, Leon Herbert) 3515, 3528
Letters from spirit people to earth friends demonstrating Christ's teachings through spirit return. 3518
Letters from the AEgean. 1927
Letters from the desert. 2385
Letters from the heart. 188, 2571

Letters from the late Rev. William Romaine. 973
Letters from the masters of the wisdom. 3685
Letters from the Mughal Court. 20, 2563
Letters from the saints. 3282, 3283
Letters from the spirit world. 2218, 3510
Letters from the teacher. 2217
Letters from Vatican City. 3770
Letters from Vatican City, Vatican Council II, first session: background and debates. 3772
Letters from Waldegrave cottage. 2218
Letters, Hebrew-Catholic, to Mrs. Isaacs. 2117
Letters (Hieronymus) 2217, 2218
Letters in action / (Claigh, Roberleigh H. 3575
Letters in primitive Christianity. 368, 1019
Letters (Ingersoll, Robert Green) 2218
Letters Jesus might write. 974
Letters Jesus might write. [1st ed.]. 974
Letters (John of Salisbury) 2218
Letters (Leo I) 2218
Letters (Newman, John Henry) 774
Letters, 1961-1968. 175, 3611
Letters of a bishop to his flock. 2631
Letters of a converted boy to his mother. 2218
Letters of a suppressed writer. 3863
Letters of a woman who was. 3513
Letters of Abelard and Heloise. 1, 2
Letters of Adam of Perseigne. 6, 1276
Letters of an apostate Mormon to his son. 2602
Letters of an Italian nun and an English gentleman. 3252
Letters of an old Methodist to his son in the ministry. 2217
Letters of Andrew Jukes. 2218
Letters of Archbishop Corrigan to Bishop McQuaid, and allied documents. 1370
Letters of Arthur W. Pink. 656, 2849
Letters of Brigham Young to his sons. 2609, 3869
Letters of C. F. W. Walther. 3790
Letters of certain Jews to Monsieur Voltaire. 514, 2114, 3786
Letters of Charles Haddon Spurgeon. 3523
Letters of Christian sympathy to mourners. 1351
Letters of direction (Tourville, Henri de) 3490
Letters of Father Page, C.S.C. 997
Letters of Gerbert. 818
Letters of H.P. Blavatsky to A.P. Sinnett. 3684
Letters of H. P. Blavatsky to A. P. Sinnett, and other miscellaneous letters. 671, 3683
Letters of His Eminence, William cardinal O'Connell. 2734
Letters of His Eminence, William cardinal O'Connell, archbishop of Boston. 2734
Letters of Isaac Penington. 2218
Letters of James and Peter. 412
Letters of Jesus. 462
Letters of Joan of Arc (Quintal, Claire) 1938
Letters of John. 369
Letters of John and James. 368
Letters of John and Jude. 368, 369, 2218
Letters of John Calvin (Calvin, Jean) 727
Letters of John Davenport. 2217
Letters of John Pinney, 1679-1699. 2218
Letters of John Quincy Adams, to his son, on the Bible and its teachings. 635
Letters of John Wesley (Wesley, John) 3805
Letters of Madame Guyon. 1779
Letters of Maimonides / (Moses ben Maimon. 2143, 2623
Letters of Marie Madeleine Hachard, 1727-28. 1779, 2693
Letters of Martha Smith. 2508
Letters of Maxwell Chaplin. 2508
Letters of Monsignor George Hobart Doane. 2218
Letters of Myrtle Fillmore. 1625
Letters of Osbert of Clare, prior of Westminister. 2218
Letters of Paul. 370, 373, 374, 375, 445, 2801
Letters of Paul and the Book of Psalms. 369
Letters of Paul [pseud.] and Amicus [pseud.]. 1681
Letters of Paul to the Ephesians. 364
Letters of Paul to the Ephesians, the Colossians, and Philemon. 447
Letters of Paul to the Philippians and to the Thessalonians. 448
Letters of Paul to the Thessalonians. 478
Letters of Paul to Timothy and Titus. 446
Letters of Peter and Jude. 447

Letters of Peter the Venerable. 1354
Letters of Pontius Pilate. 2847
Letters of Pope Innocent III. 1761
Letters of Principal James Denney to his family and friends. 1425
Letters of Principal James Denney to W. Robertson Nicoll, 1893-1917. 1425
Letters of Rebecca Gratz. 1756
Letters of Richard Meux Benson, student of Christ church. 2217
Letters of Robert G. Ingersoll. 1907
... The letters of St. Augustine. 115
Letters of St. Bernard of Clairvaux. 193, 1026
Letters of Saint Boniface. 677, 1026
Letters of St. Ignatius of Loyola. 2268
Letters of St. Louise de Marillac. 2261
Letters of St. Paul. 373, 2801
Letters of St. Paulinus of Nola. 2218
Letters of Saint Teresa of Jesus. 3603
Letters of Samuel Reynolds Hole, dean of Rochester. 2218
Letters of spiritual counsel. 1351
Letters of Teresa Higginson. 2218
Letters of the Amish division of 1693-1711. 2406
Letters of the late Bishop England to the Hon. John Forsyth, on the subject of domestic slavery. 3424
Letters of the Rev. Dr. Beecher and Rev. Mr. Nettleton, on the "new measures" in conducting revivals of religion. 3228
Letters of the Rev. H. H. Jeaffreson. 2218
Letters of the Rev. Samuel Young Lum. 2218
Letters of the Reverend Adelbert Inama, O. PRAEM. 835
Letters of Theophilus Lindsey. 2218
Letters of trial and triumph. 447
Letters of William Hamilton. 2920
Letters of William Hoke Ramsaur. 2538
Letters on apostolical succession. 76
Letters on baptism (Fairfield, Edmund Burke) 134
Letters on Christian living. 3538
Letters on clerical manners and habits. 1288
Letters on demonology and witchcraft. 1423
Letters on ecclesiastical history. 1184
Letters on evangelism (Hughes, Edwin Holt) 1566
Letters on frequent communion, addressed particularly to the members of the Associate-Reformed church in North-America. 2251
Letters on Islam (Jamali, Mohammed Fadhel) 1922
Letters on missions (Horne, Melville) 2520
Letters on Nostradamus and miscellaneous writings. 2715, 2947
Letters on occult meditation. 2722, 2723
Letters on religious persecution. 739
Letters on religious subjects. 1682
Letters on spiritual subjects in answer to inquiring souls. 2689, 3199
Letters on the atonement. 3199
Letters on the call and qualifications of ministers of the gospel. 1929
Letters on the early history of the Presbyterian Church in America. 2924
Letters on the eloquence of the pulpit. 2902
Letters on the eternal generation of the Son of God. 2002
Letters on the eternal sonship of Christ. 1285, 2035
Letters on the evidences, doctrines and duties of the Christian religion. 1098
Letters on the existence and character of the Deity. 1730
Letters on the Gospels (Adams, Hannah) 387
Letters on the greatness and simplicity of the Christian faith. 1070
Letters on the healing ministry. 1598
Letters on the immortality of the soul. 3197
Letters on the logos (Upham, Charles Wentworth) 2242
Letters on the masonic institution. 52
Letters on the ministry of the gospel. 3675
Letters on the origin and progress of the New Haven theology. 2688
Letters on the religious revivals which prevailed about the beginning of the present century. 3229
Letters on the Spanish Inquisition. 1910
Letters on the spiritual manifestation of the Son of God, by the Rev. John De La Fletcher. 2038
Letters on the theology of the New church. 2691

... Letters on the theology of the New church, signified by the New Jerusalem (Rev. xxi., xxii.) 1038
Letters on Unitarianism. 3729
Letters (Penington, Isaac) 2218
Letters (Rutherford, Samuel) 2218
Letters (Thorp, John) 2218
... Letters to a convert--a psychological interpretation of the "first principles" of Christianity. 3110
Letters to a disciple (Cosgrove, Eugene Milne) 3198
Letters to a friend. 2714
Letters to a friend (Gregory, Olinthus Gilbert) 1049, 1098
Letters to a friend (Thirlwall, Connop) 3202
Letters to a ministerial son. 3200
Letters to a mother on the birth of a child. 3056
Letters to a niece (Hugel, Friedrich) 1850
Letters to a nun (Lord, Daniel Aloysius) 2580
Letters to a philosophical unbeliever (1787) 1726, 1855
Letters to a soldier on religion. 3199
Letters to a young clergyman. 3674
Letters to a young people's leader. 3175
Letters to a young priest from a laicized priest. 772
Letters to an altar boy. 27
Letters to an American lady. 3200
Letters to an ex-priest. 794
Letters to an infidel (Smith, Matthew John Wilfred) 792
Letters to an only daughter, on confirmation. 1328
Letters to an ordinand. 2788
Letters to "Bill" on faith and prayer. 3456
Letters to Cardinal McCloskey. 2306
Letters to Chip from an older brother. 3870
Letters to Christian leaders. 3202
Letters to Cromwell on the suppression of the monasteries. 2569
Letters to David (Donahue, George Joseph) 771
Letters to Edward Gibson, esq., 1785. 325, 1711, 3713
Letters to Eugenia, on the absurd, contradictory, and demoralizing dogmas and mysteries of the Christian religion. 1091
Letters to Eugenia; or, A preservative against religious prejudices. 1091
Letters to friends (Gerard, John. 3682
Letters to God and the devil. 1466, 3347
Letters to his friends (Robinson, Forbes) 3201
Letters to His Holiness. 2561
Letters to Jewish college students. 3537
Letters to Jody (Parks, Thomas David. 1308
Letters to John (Kleinhans, Theodore J) 3870
Letters to John / (Lowe, Bob. 1295, 2267
Letters to laymen (Anderson, Charles Palmerston) 3197, 2966
Letters to Leontine Zanta. 3891
Letters to little children. 3177
Letters to Malcolm (Lewis, Clive Staples) 2875
Letters to Mark on God's relation to human suffering. 3609
Letters to men and women. 997
Letters to Michael from Mara. 65
Letters to my congregation. 956
Letters to my God (Runes, Dagobert David) 3201
Letters to my godchild (Jenkins, Lucy Howe) 3886
Letters to my godchildren in explanation of the church catechism. 747
Letters to my grandchildren. 2511
Letters to my Heavenly Father. 957
Letters to my Hevenly Father. 958
Letters to my Lord (Lord, Daniel Aloysuis) 3488
Letters to N. Wiseman, D.D., on the errors of Romanism. 801
Letters to Nancy, from Andrew M. Greeley. 3844
Letters to Nancy (Greeley, Andrew M.) 3844
... Letters to persons in religion. 3486
Letters to Polly (Schoonover, Melvin E) 1352
Letters to Rev. B. Stow, R. H. Neale, And R. W. Cushman. 3229, 3534
Letters to Rev. Moses Stuart. 3751
Letters to Ron / (Doty, Harry L. 1477, 2785
Letters to Saint Francis and his friars. 1642
Letters to saints and other sinners. 1353
Letters to Salvationists on religion for every day. 682

Letters to scattered pilgrims. 986, 1238
Letters to street Christians. 445
Letters to Sunday-school teachers on the great truths of our Christian faith. 3177
Letters to the Christian public. 3616
Letters to the churches. 446
Letters to the Corinthians. 345
Letters to the editors of the Catholic miscellany. 802
Letters to the Galatians and Ephesians. 379
Letters to the Jews (Priestley, Joseph) 59
Letters to the martyrs (Homan, Helen (Walker) 1021, 2351
Letters to the Philippians, Colossians, and Thessalonians. 448
Letters to the Pope / (Twyman, Mary Eileen. 792
Letters to the Rev. Leonard Bacon, in reply to his attack on the Pastoral union and Theological institute of Connecticut. 124, 1346
Letters to the Rev. Wm. E. Channing. 882, 3728
Letters to the Right Rev. John Hughes, Roman Catholic bishop of New York. 801, 1851
Letters to the Rt. Rev. John Hughes, Roman Catholic bishop of New-York. 801, 1851
Letters to the seven churches. 459, 461, 462, 464
Letters to the seven churches of Asia and their place in the plan of the apocalypse. 460
letters to thePhilippians. 370
Letters to Timothy / (Leggett, Gary. 479
Letters to Timothy, Titus, and Philemon. 445
Letters to Tracy from Don Gold. 3877
Letters to truth seekers. 3475
Letters to Unitarians and Reply to Dr. Ware. 3729, 3795
Letters to Unitarians occasioned by the sermon of the Reverend William E. Channing, at the ordination of the Rev. J. Sparks. 882, 3729
Letters to unknown friends. 1055
Letters to women (Loyola, Ignacio de) 2268
Letters to young Christians. 983
Letters to young churches. 368
Letters to young men preparing for the Christian ministry. 3671
Letters to young ministers of the gospel. 2474, 3680
Letters upon divers subjects in theology. 1655
Letting God help you. 973
Letting the word come alive. 299
... Lettres ecrites a un provincial (i, iv, v, xiii) 2778
L'Eucharistie des premiers chretiens. 2256
Level plan for church union. 3427
Levels of brotherhood. 3453
Levels of clinical pastoral training. [Fall conference chaplain supervisors, October 16-20, 1961. 2784
Levi Silliman Ives, pioneer leader in Catholic charities. 1930
Levi Yitzhak of Berditchev. 2219
Leviticus. 557
Leviticus, a study guide commentary. 557
Leviticus, an introduction and commentary. 557
... Leviticus and Numbers. 557
Leviticus, Numbers, Deuteronomy. 557
Lewis Craig. 1378
...Lewis Hughes, the militant minister of the Bermudas and his printed works. 1851
Lex credendi. 783
Lex orandi. 783
L'exemplum dans la litterature religieuse et didactique du Moyen age. 1583
Lexical aids for students of New Testament Greek. Enl. ed. 1769
Lexicon in Veteris Testamenti libros. 1796
Lexicon of St. Thomas Aquinas based on the Summa theologica and selected passages of his other works. 3695
Lexington Presbytery heritage. 2927
Lexington Theological Seminary, 1865-1965. 2220
Lhamon, William Jefferson. 1465
L'hasa at last. 3201
Li Dialoge Gregoire lo Pape. Altfranzosische Uebersetzung des XII. 189, 3284
Libellus de diversis ordinibus et professionibus qui sunt in aecclesia. 2582
Liber epistolaris of Richard de Bury. 1020
Liber exemplorum ad usum praedicantium. 1583
Liber librorum. 305
Liber Psalmorum. 585

Liberal and mystical writings of William Law. 2639
Liberal arts college. 2449
Liberal Catholicism and the modern world. 45
Liberal Christianity. 1100, 3200
Liberal Christianity and religious education. 3092
Liberal Christianity at the crossroads. 2221
Liberal Christians. 3729
Liberal church at the end of the Oregon Trail. 2743
Liberal education and a liberal faith. 3092
Liberal gospel. 882
Liberal illusion. 2221
Liberal Judaism. 2115
Liberal Judaism at home. 3032
Liberal Kentucky, 1780-1828. 3213
Liberal learning and religion. 3190
Liberal orthodoxy. 1100
Liberal Protestantism. 2221
Liberal religion. 1100
Liberal theology. 2221, 2304
Liberalism and tradition. 1639
Liberalism, conservatism, Mormonism. 1152
Liberalism, modernism and tradition. 1100
Liberalism of Thomas Arnold. 84
Liberality and civilization. 2221
Liberalization of American Protestantism. 1087, 2670
Liberalizing liberal Judaism. 2116
Liberals among the orthodox: Unitarian beginnings in New York City, 1819-1839. 3723, 3725
Liberated Bible, the Old Testament. 538
Liberated Gospel. 435, 1768
Liberated heart. 2997
Liberated Palestinian. 3404
Liberated zone. 1065
Liberating creation. 947
Liberating grace. 1750
Liberating limits. 1313
Liberating the lay forces of Christianity. 2191
Liberating word. 239, 3392
Liberating word: art and the mystery of the Gospel. 1381
Liberation and change. 2222
Liberation and reconciliation. 3017
Liberation, development, and salvation. 3449
Liberation for the poor of Yahweh, Pharaohs, and Christians. 2222
Liberation from guilt. 1777
Liberation of life. 3482
Liberation of planet earth. 2230, 3290
Liberation of theology. 2222
Liberation or revolution? 821, 1143
Liberation preaching. 233, 2900
Liberation, revolution, and freedom. 2222
Liberation theologies in North America and Europe. 2222
Liberation theology. 2222
Liberation theology and the message of salvation. 2222
Liberation theology: human hope confronts Christian history and American power. 1659
Liberation theology; liberation in the light of the fourth Gospel. 423, 1659
Liberian odyssey "by hammock and surfboat" 2538
Libertad del temor. 3383
Liberty. 1939, 3193
Liberty and labor in the Jewish tradition. 2143
Liberty and life. 3723
Liberty and reformation in the Puritan Revolution. 3007
Liberty and religion. 692
Liberty bell of the world. 1920
Liberty Bible commentary on the New Testament. 344
Liberty, equality and fraternity. 737
Liberty of conscience. 2223
Liberty of man, woman and child. 1654
Liberty of obedience. 960
Liberty of prophesying. 2900
Liberty of the children of God. 2223
Liberty of the school and family education. 3189
Liberty of the spirit and of the flesh distinguished. 1682
Liberty to the captives. 2486, 2734
Libica. 871
Librarian of the Sunday school. 2225
Library and resource center in Christian education. 2224
Library at Qumran. 1410
Library in the Catholic theological seminary in the United States. 3615
Library index to Biblical journals. 601
... Library list of 10,000 books and pamphlets. 869

... Library list of 8000 books and pamphlets. 869
... Library list of 6000 books and pamphlets. 869
Library list of 12,000 books and pamphlets. 869
Library of Christian cooperation. 1272
Library of Christian hymns. 1875
Library of Lactantius. 1286, 2190
... The library of Photius. 2844
Library of religious poetry. 3207
...The library of Reverend Thomas R. Slicer, D.D. 2225
Library of the Church club of New York. 3627
Library of the Palestine Pilgrims' Text Society. 1022
Library research guide to religion and theology. 3111
Library resources for the study of Mormons and Mormonism. 2608
Library services in the church. 2224
Libretto for Job. 551
Libro de Mormon. 3428
Libros quinque adversus haereses ... Edidit W. Wigan Harvey. Cantabrigiae, Typis Academicis, 1857. 1805
Life. 573, 1941, 2199, 2226, 3201
Life a study of self. 3200
Life abundant. 1750, 3197
Life advances! 448
Life adventure for peace. 3143
Life after birth. 1309, 1440
Life after death. 1528, 1529, 1694, 1695, 1696, 1697, 1698, 1887, 1888, 1891, 2040, 2689, 2988, 3053, 3198, 3473, 3505
Life after death according to Christianity. 1889
Life after death in Oceania and the Malay archipelago. 2733
Life after life. 1698
Life ahead. 1324
Life among the moonies. 931, 3722
Life, an enigma, a precious jewel. 710
Life and action, the great work in America. 3690
Life and adventures of Robert Houdin. 1345
Life and adventures of Signor Blitz. 1345
Life and character. 2227
Life and character of J. H. van der Palm. 2766, 3049
Life and character of Leonard Woods. 3846
Life and character of Miss Susanna Anthony. 3143
Life and character of the late reverend Mr. Jonathan Edwards. 1499
Life and character of the Rev. Sylvester Judd. 2156
Life and character of the Reverend Benjamin Colman, D.D. 1310
Life and characteristics of Right Reverend Alfred A. Curtis, D.D., second bishop of Wilmington. 1397
Life and charater of the Reverend Benjamin Colman, D.D. 1310
Life and correspondence of Arthur Penrhyn Stanley. 3525
Life and correspondence of Arthur Penrhyn Stanley, late dean of Westminster. 3525
Life and correspondence of Rev. William Sparrow. 3470
Life and correspondence of the Right Reverend Samuel Seabury, D.D., first bishop of Connecticut, and of the Episcopal church in the United States of America. 3317
Life and correspondence of Theodore Parker. 2776
Life and correspondence of Theodore Parker, minister of the Twenty-eighth Congregational Society, Boston. 2776
Life & death. 1413
Life and death eternal. 48
Life and death of a Christian are our teachers. 2931, 3819
Life and death of Dietrich Bonhoeffer. 676
Life and death of Dietrich Bonhoffer. 676
...Life and death of Mr. Badman and The holy war. 714
Life and death of Rev. T. DeWitt Talmage, D D. 3582
Life and death of Saint Malachy, the Irishman. 667, 2318
Life and death of that reverend man of God, Mr. Richard Mather. 2373
Life and death of that reverent man of God, Mr. Richard Mather, teacher of the church in Dorchester in New-England. 2373
Life and death of the Rev. Joseph Alleine. 26

Life and death of two young ladies, contrasted. 1414
Life and destiny. 2988
Life and devotion of Saint Therese. 3691
Life and diary of David Brainerd. 1900
Life and diary of the late Rev. Thomas B. Hanna, A. M. 1784, 2930
Life and doctrines of Jacob Boehme. 674
Life and eloquence of the Rev. Sylvester Larned. 2197, 2931
Life and epistles of Saint Paul. 2795, 2796, 2799
... The life and epistles of the apostle Paul. 2796
Life and example of Saint Andrew. 40, 695
Life and experience of a converted infidel. 3143
Life and experience of the Rev. Thomas Hess, with ten sermons. 3143
Life and exploits of Jehovah. 3202
Life and faith of Martin Luther. 2280, 3040
Life and friendships of Catherine Marsh. 2348
Life and gospel experience of Mother Ann Lee. 2205
Life and growth of Israel. 1927
Life and history of the Rev. Elijah P. Marrs. 2681
Life and holiness. 3488
Life and I. 2225, 3143
Life and immortality. 1890
Life and influence of the Rev. Benjamin Randall. 3021
Life and its forces. 3202
Life and its mysteries. 3053
Life and its purpose. 2228
Life and journal of the Rev'd Christian Newcomer. 3730
Life and journeys of Paul. 2795
Life and labor. 1325
Life and labors of Archibald McLean. 2309
Life and labors of Bishop Hare. 3143
Life and labors of Charles H. Spurgeon. 3523
... Life and labors of Dwight L. Moody. 2588
Life and labors of Elder John Kline. 2178
Life and labors of Elder John Kline, the martyr missionary. 2178
Life and labors of Elder Zelotes Grenell. 163, 1774
Life and labors of Elias Hicks. 1810
Life and labors of Elijah H. Pilcher, of Michigan. 2847
Life and labors of Eliza R. Snow Smith. 3431
Life and labors of Enoch Mather Marvin. 2351
Life and labors of Francis Asbury. 89
Life and labors of John Seybert. 3394
Life and labors of Joseph Cole Stalcup. 158, 3524
Life and labors of Mrs. Maggie Newton Van Cott. 3767, 3834
Life and labors of Rev. E. M. Marvin. 2352, 2447
Life and labors of Rev. Jordan W. Early. 1485
Life and labors of Rev. Reuben Gaylord, home missionary for Iowa and Nebraska. 1704
Life and labors of Rev. Samuel Worcester, D. D., former pastor of the Tabernacle church, Salem, Mass. 3848
Life and labors of Rev. William Brock Wellons ... of the Christian church. 3801
Life and labors of Rt. Rev. Frederic Baraga, first bishop of Marquette, Mich. 173, 1901
Life and labors of St. Augustine. 115
Life and labors of the Rev. T. H. Gallaudet, LL. D. 1701
Life and labors of William Sheldon. 3402
Life and labours of Saint Thomas of Aquin. 3694
Life and labours of the Rev. Daniel Baker, D. D. 131
Life and labours of the Rev. W. E. Boardman. 673
Life and language in the Old Testament. 210, 556
Life and laughter, popular lectures. 143
Life and legend of the Lady Saint Clare. 3282
Life and letters of Ambrose Phillipps de Lisle. 1407
Life and letters of Benjamin Morgan Palmer. 2766
Life and letters of Bishop McQuaid. 824, 2310
Life and letters of Bishop William White. 3812
Life and letters of Brooks Foss Westcott, D.C., D.C.L. 3807

Life and letters of Dean Church. 1246
Life and letters of Dr. Samuel Butler. 720
Life and letters of Edward Everett Hale. 660
Life and letters of Erasmus. 1526
Life and letters of Fenton John Anthony Hort. 1848
Life and letters of Frederick W. Robertson. 3241
Life and letters of Frederick William Faber. 1587, 2740
Life and letters of Henry Parry Liddon, D. D., D. C. L., LL. D., canon of St. Paul's cathedral, and sometime Ireland professor of exegesis in the University of Oxford. 2225
Life and letters of Henry Van Rensselaer. 3767
Life and letters of Horace Bushnell. 719
Life and letters of Jacob Burkhard. 2529
Life and letters of James Henley Thornwell. 3698
Life and letters of James Martineau, LL, D., S. T. D., etc... by James Drummond...and a survey of his philosophical work by C. B. Upton. 2349
Life and letters of James Monroe Taylor. 3590
Life and letters of James Osgood Andrew. 40
Life and letters of Janet Erskine Stuart. 3438
Life and letters of John Albert Broadus. 692
Life and letters of Joseph Hardy Neesima. 2679
Life and letters of Leonidas L. Hamline, D.D. 1783
Life and letters of Mandell Creighton, D. D. Oxon, and Cam., sometimes bishop of London. 1386
Life and letters of Martin Luther. 2277
Life and letters of Montgomery Prunejuice. 3576
Life and letters of Mrs. Emily C. Judson. 2158
Life and letters of Mrs. Jason Lee, first wife of Rev. Jason Lee of the Oregon mission. 2206, 2481, 2544
Life and letters of Paul. 374, 375, 2796, 2797, 2800, 2803
Life and letters of Paul the apostle. 372, 2794
Life and letters of Rev. James May, D.D. 2375
Life and letters of Rev. Lewis Alfred Wickes. 1572
Life and letters of Robert Collyer, 1823-1912. 1310
Life and letters of Robert Lewis Dabney. 1301, 1399
Life and letters of St. Paul. 372, 373, 2796, 2802
Life and letters of Saint Peter. 2824
Life and letters of Samuel Wells Williams, LL.D., missionary, diplomatist, sinologue. 2512, 3818
Life and letters of Sister St. Francis Xavier. 3274
Life and letters of Stopford Brooke. 693
Life and letters of the Rev. John Philip Boehm. 3048
Life and letters of the Rev. John Philip Boehm, founder of the Reformed Church in Pennsylvania, 1683-1749. 3048
Life and letters of W. A. Passavant, D. D. 2778
Life and letters of Walter Drum, S. J. 1481
Life and letters of William John Butler. 720
Life and letters of William Reed Huntington. 1856
Life and liberation of Padmasambhava. 2194, 2756
Life and life-work of Mother Theodore Guerin. 1776
Life and life-work of Pope Leo XIII. 2216
Life and light. 673, 1860, 3019
Life and literature of Paul. 371, 2796
Life and literature of the ancient Hebrews. 498
Life and live. 3388
Life and love. 982, 3388
Life, and love and peace. 3199
Life and memoirs of Rev. C. F. X. Goldsmith. 1744
Life and mind of Paul. 2803
Life and ministry of Jesus. 929, 1963, 1970, 1973, 1989
Life and ministry of our Lord. 1971
Life and miracles of St. Benedict. 189, 1027
Life and miracles of St. Benedict (Book two of the Dialogues) 189

Life and miracles of Saint Gandolfo da Binasco, O.F.M. 1701
Life and miracles of Saint Philomena. 2831
Life and miracles of St. William of Norwich. 3817
Life and mission of Emanuel Swedenborg. 3571
Life and mission of Our Lord and Saviour Jesus Christ. 3720
Life & morals of Jesus Christ of Nazareth. 1987
Life and morals of Jesus of Nazareth. 1987, 1990, 1991
Life and observations of Rev. E. F. Newell. 20
Life and of Christ. 1992
Life and opinions of John de Wycliffe, D. D. 3861
Life and opinions of the Rev. William Milne, D. D., missionary to China, illustrated by biographical annals of Asiatic missions, from primitive to Protestant times. 2467
Life and pontificate of Leo the Tenth. 2216
Life and prophecies of Jeremiah. 1943
Life and religion. 3067, 3200
Life and religious experience of the celebrated Lady Guion. 1779
Life and religious opinions and experience of Madame de La Mothe Guyon. 1779
Life and remains of the Rev. R. H. Quick. 3013
Life and reminiscences of Robert G. Ingersoll. 1907
Life and repentance of Marie Magdalene. 2353
Life and revelations of Saint Gertrude. 1708
Life and rule. 3692
Life and sayings of Saint Catherine of Genoa. 749
Life and sayings of Sam P. Jones. 2131
Life and sayings of the Baal Shem. 1928
Life and selected writings of Francis Dana Hemenway. 688
Life and sermons of Dr. H. W. Thomas. 2426
Life and sermons of Dwight L. Moody. 1559
Life and sermons of Jesse L. Sewell. 1705
Life and sermons of Ray York. 3363, 3868
Life and sermons of Rev. T. DeWitt Talmage. 2929, 3582
Life and sermons of Rev. William Wyatt. 2426
Life and service. 3201
Life and she. 3510
Life and spirit of Thomas Aquinas. 3693
Life and suffering of the Jew in Russia. 2102
Life and sufferings of Christians in Solovki and Siberia, Russia. 1110
Life and teaching of Geshe Rabten. 2194, 3017
Life and teaching of Jesus. 1953, 2062
Life and teaching of Jesus according to the first three Gospels. 1960
Life and teaching of Jesus Christ. 1971, 1973
Life & teaching of Jesus Christ our Lord; translated from the French. 1967
Life and teaching of Jesus the Christ. 1966
Life and teaching of Naropa. 2667
Life and teaching of Our Lord Jesus Christ. 724, 1984
Life and teaching of the masters of the Far East. 3202
Life and teachings of Abbas effendi. 2, 128
Life and teachings of Christ. 1964, 1965, 1993
Life and teachings of Giodano Bruno. 698
Life and teachings of Jesus. 391, 1963, 1967, 1971, 1974, 1975, 1993
... The life and teachings of Jesus, according to the earliest records. 1967
Life and teachings of Jesus Christ. 1988
Life and teachings of Jesus Christ in the words of the King James version. 1989
Life & teachings of Jesus Christ Our Lord. 1967
Life and teachings of John Calvin. 727
Life and teachings of Ludwig Hetzer. 37, 1809
Life and teachings of Our Lord in verse. 2047
... Life and teachings of Rev. T. De Witt Talmage. 3582
Life and teachings of Zoroaster. 3898
Life and the Bible. 3202
Life and the Book. 199
Life and the kingdom of Jesus in Christian souls. 997

Life and the student. 3198
Life and the way. 3865
Life and thought in the ancient world. 3093
Life and thought of a country preacher. 1753
Life and thought of a country preacher, C. W. Grafton, D. D., L. L. D. 1753
Life and thought of Albert Schweitzer. 3312
Life and thought of Kierkegaard for everyman. 2170
Life and thoughts of Rev. Thomas P. Hunt. 3595
Life and time of Bishop Isaac Lane. 2195
Life and time of Alexander McKenzie. 731, 2309
Life and times of Benjamin Franklin. 1651
Life and times of Bishop Challoner. 880
...The life and times of Bishop White. 3812
Life and times of Buddha. 706
Life and times of Cardinal Wiseman. 2755, 3822
Life and times of Cotton Mather, D.D., F.R.S. 2372
Life and times of Daniel Lindley, 1801-80. 2230
Life and times of David Zeisberger. 3891
Life and times of Dr. George de Benneville. 1407
Life and times of Edward Bass. 178
Life and times of Girolamo Savonarola. 3306
Life and times of Henry M. Turner. 3718
Life and times of Henry Melchior Muhlenberg. 2629
...The life and times of Isaiah as illustrated by contemporary mounuments. 543, 1921
Life and times of James B. Taylor. 3590
Life and times of Jesus. 1962, 1966, 1992, 3801
Life and times of Jesus the Messiah. 1963
Life and times of John Calvin, the great reformer. Translated from the German of Paul Henry. 727
Life and times of John Carroll. 742
Life and times of John Carroll, archbishop of Baltimore. 742
Life and times of John de Wycliffe. 3860
Life & times of John England. 827, 1516
Life and times of John England, first bishop of Charleston. 827, 1516
Life and times of John Huss. 1857, 3038
Life and times of Joseph Fish, Mormon pioneer. 2602
Life and times of Levi Scott, D.D. 3315
Life and times of Margaret Bourgeoys. 686
Life and times of Martin Luther. 2275, 2276, 3035
Life & times of Master John Hus. 674, 1857, 3038
Life and times of Mohammed. 2629
Life and times of Mother Bridget Hayden. 1791, 3417
Life and times of Mrs. Lucy G. Thurston. 2525
Life and times of Muhammad. 2628
Life and times of Nathan Bangs, D. D. 133
Life and times of Rabbi David Ibn Abi Zimra. 1880, 2107
Life and times of Rev. Allen Wiley, A.M. 3815
Life and times of Rev. Elijah Hedding. 1800
Life and times of Rev. Finis Ewing, one of the fathers and founders of the Cumberland Presbyterian church. 1396, 1582
Life and times of Rev. John G. Landrum. 163, 2195
Life and times of Rev. S.S. Schmucker. 3309
Life and times of Rev. William Patton, and annals of the Missouri conference. 2446, 2794
Life and times of St. Ambrose. 29
...The life and times of St. Basil the Great as revealed in his works. 177
Life and times of St. Dominic. 1474
Life and times of Shaikh Farid-ud-Din Gang-i-Shakar. 1612, 3543
Life and times of Sir Thomas Gresham, Knt. 1774
Life and times of St Francis. 1641
Life and times of the Holy Spirit. v. 1. 1830
Life and times of the Most Rev. John Carroll. 742, 834
Life and times of the Most Rev. John MacHale. 2308
Life and times of the Old Testament. 597
Life and times of the Rev. Jesse Lee. 2206, 2451

Life and times of the Rev. John Brooks, in which are contained a history of the great revival in Tennessee. 1392, 2453
Life and times of the Rev. John Wesley, M.A., founder of the Methodists. 3805
Life and times of the Rev. Richard Baxter. 179
Life and times of Thomas John Claggett. 1283
Life and times of Ulric Zwingli. 3900
Life and times of William M'Kendree. 2308
Life and travels of Herodotus in the fifth century before Christ. 1807
Life and travels of Lorenzo Dow. 1478
Life and travels of St. Paul. 2795
Life and travels of the apostle Paul. 2799
Life and trials of a young lady convert. 1364
Life and words of Christ. 1965
Life and work. 3751
Life and work in India. 2532
Life and work lesson annual. 3186
Life and work of Bishop Alexander Preston Shaw. 2426
... The life and work of Charles H. Spurgeon. 3523
Life and work of Christ. 1992
Life and work of Dwight L. Moody. 1563, 2587, 2588
Life and work of George William Peterkin. 2826, 2975
Life and work of Henry Ward Beecher. 184
Life and work of J. R. W. Sloane, D.D. 3425
Life and work of Jacob Kenoly. 2167
Life and work of Jesus Christ Our Lord. 1966
Life and work of John Williamson Nevin. 2686
Life and work of Mary Aikenhead. 20, 3416
Life and work of Moses Homan Bixby. 668
Life and work of Mother Benedicta Bauer. 178, 1476
Life and work of Rev. James Aloysius Cullen, S.J. 1393
Life and work of Rev. John McMillan. 2309, 3796
Life and work of Rudolf Steiner from the turn of the century to his death. 51, 3527
Life and work of St. Paul. 2796, 2797
Life and work of the church. 1184
Life and work of the Rev. E. J. Peck among the Eskimos. 1532, 2810
Life and work of the Right Reverend George Michael Wittmann. 3830
Life and work of William Augustus Muhlenberg. 2630
Life and work of William Tindale. 3719
Life and work on the mission field. 2493
Life and works of Benjamin Marcus Bogard. 674
Life and works of Charles Edgar Little. 2233
Life and works of Flavius Josephus. 2083
Life and works of Jesus. 1969
Life and works of John the Baptist. 2127
Life and works of Miss Mary Jane Graham. 1089
Life and works of Morgan Edwards. 146, 1500
Life and works of Nathaniel Deering (1791-1881) 1419
Life & works of Saint Vincent de Paul (Monsieur Vincent: le grand saint du grand siecle) 3779
Life and works of the world's greatest evangelist Dwight L. Moody. 2587
Life and world of George Santayana. 3302
Life and world-work of Thomas Lake Harris, written from direct personal knowledge. 1787
Life and worship. 3876
Life and writings of Francis Makemie. 2318
Life and writings of George Edward Flower. 1461, 1630
Life and writings of George W. Abell. 2
Life and writings of George Washington Doane. 1472
Life and writings of Jeremy Taylor. 3590
Life and writings of Rev. Enoch M. Pingree. 2849
Life and writings of Rev. Samuel Crothers, D. D. 1389
Life and writings of Rev. William Pope Yeaman, S. T. D. 3863
Life and writings of Rufus C. Burleson, d. d., ll. d. 717, 3604
Life and writings of Saint Columban. 1311
... The life and writings of Saint Ildefonsus of Toledo. 1883
Life and writings of St. John. 413, 2126

Life and writings of Samuel Johnson. 2129
Life and writings of the apostle Peter. 2824
Life and writings of the Right Reverend John McMullen, D.D., first bishop of Davenport, Iowa. 2309
Life and you. 956, 1061
Life as Eucharist. 2252
Life as it was meant to be. 479, 2933, 3356
Life as its best. 1574
Life as reality. 2226
Life as worship. 2874
Life at close quarters. 1011
Life at its best. 167, 324, 422, 423, 974, 1446, 2378, 3199, 3200
Life at threescore and ten. 174
"The life beautiful" 3198
Life, before and after earth's expression. 3518
Life began yesterday. 2753
Life begins. 468
Life begins at death. 1698
Life begins for a Jesuit priest. 802, 3237
Life begins with faith. 3095
Life begins with God. 65
Life begins with love. 2264
Life between death and rebirth. 1912
Life beyond. 1529
Life beyond death. 1695, 3104, 3513, 3514, 3867
Life beyond death in the beliefs of mankind. 1694
Life beyond life. 1890
Life beyond the veil. 3510
Life by the numbers. 3575
Life by the Son; practical lessons in experimental holiness. 1823
Life by the spirit. 3483
Life by the spirit (formerly published as Paul's Pentecost) 472
Life can be meaningful. 963
Life can begin again. 3337
Life changers. 3097
Life, character, and acts of John the Baptist. 2128
Life, character & influence of Desiderius Erasmus of Rotterdam. 1526
Life, character, and literary labours of Samuel Drew, A.M. 1480
Life comes as choice. 2437, 3357
Life comes from life. 2228
Life, conversion, preaching, travels and sufferings of Elias Smith. 3427
Life crucified. 1448
Life, death, & beyond. 1412
Life, death, and destiny. 1727
Life, death, and hereafter. 1655
Life, death, and immortality. 1528, 3098
Life, death, and the law. 1077
Life-death-hereafter ... 8,000 edition. 1528
Life divine. 2417
Life does have a purpose. 1005, 1940
Life ecstatic. 1450, 3706
Life endures. 321
Life essential. 3622
Life established. 341
Life eternal. 126, 1889, 2611
Life eternal and its work. 3141
Life everlasting. 1528, 1531, 1886, 1887, 2611
Life everlasting in freedom of the sons of God. 1941
Life experience and Gospel labors of the Rt. Rev. Richard Allen. 14
Life experience and Gospel labors of the Rt. Rev. Richard Allen, to which is annexed the rise and progress of the African Methodist Edpiscopal Church in the United States of America. 14
Life experiences. 1563
Life, faith and home. 1594
Life, faith, and prayer. 1107
Life for a wanderer. 3487
Life for the Balkans. 1849, 3692
Life for the Congo. 1497, 2513
Life forces. 3508
Life forever. 1531
Life from forty-seven viewpoints. 1449
Life full of surprises. 1011
Life givers. 994
Life-giving spirit. 1828
Life-giving words. 2247
Life goes on. 1694
Life has meaning. 992
Life has no ceiling. 891
Life here and hereafter. 1415, 1886, 3100, 3500, 3760
Life hereafter. 1697
Life I owe. 3529
Life in a fifteenth-century monastery. 1483, 2570
Life in a fishbowl. 323, 982
Life in a floating city. 3303
Life in a kibbutz. 2765
Life in a look. 1561

Life in a thousand worlds. 3199
Life in Algoma. 1222
Life in all its fullness. 990, 3850
Life in ancient America. 679
Life in Bible times. 207, 2765
Life in Christ. 334, 335, 796, 991, 2636, 2745, 3187, 3343, 3649
Life in Christ Jesus. 472
Life in earnest. 963
Life in faith and freedom. 1622
Life in fellowship. 3200
... Life in freedom. 3686
Life in God's love. 1646
Life in God's love series. 3181
Life in His body. 1163
Life in His name. 420
Life in large families. 1612
Life in mind & conduct. 2227
Life in Mormon bondage. 3868
Life in Mozambique and South Africa. 2541
Life in my hands. 1445
Life in the army, in the departments of Virginia, and the gulf. 3741
Life in the balance. 943, 3200
Life in the church. 2958
Life in the circles. 3507
Life in the City of God. 3787
Life in the cup. 3199
Life in the early church. 1195
Life in the great beyond. 3104
Life in the heights. 1456, 2135
Life in the kingdom of God. 2961
Life in the Larger parish. 3767
... Life in the making. 3555
Life in the modern world: home, parish, neighborhood, school. 3880
Life in the shadow of death. 999
Life in the Son. 2822
Life in the Spirit. 3203, 3487
Life in the spirit, as exemplified in the Acts of the Apostles. 332, 1836
Life in the spirit in marriage, home & work. 365
Life in the vine. 1359
Life in the Word. 3200
Life in the world to come. 3106
Life in the world unseen. 191, 3496
Life in two worlds. 3407
Life in Utah. 2600
Life-incidents of home, school and church, (autobiographical.) 3533
Life indeed. 962, 3477
Life instead. 45, 692
Life is a celebration! 1007
Life is a Journey. 3099
Life is commitment. 1096
Life is for growth. 994
Life is for living. 1011
Life is for loving. 2264
Life is for that. 1450
Life is forever. 1531, 1697
Life is goodbye, life is hello. 1774
Life is like that. 1577, 2387
Life is so great, I really don't want to get off. 1010
Life is victorious! 1774, 2846
Life is victorious!: How to grow through grief. 1774, 2846
Life is what you make it. 3539
Life is worth living. 761, 3401, 3594
Life is worth living; fifth series. 761
Life is worth your best. 992
Life, its true genesis. 1383
Life Jesus brought. 1007
Life, Jesus-style. 985, 3336
Life John Henry, cardinal Newman, based on his private journals and correspondence. 2705
Life, labors and sermons of Rev. Charles Pitman, D.D. 2849
Life, letters, and journals of the Rev. and Hon. Peter Parker. 2776
Life, letters, and journals of the Rev. and Hon. Peter Parker, M.D., missionary, physican, diplomatist. 2776
Life, letters, and travels of Father de Smet. 1899
Life, letters, lectures, and addresses of Fredk. W. Robertson. 346
Life looks up. 2935
Life, man, and time. 3079, 3082
Life maps. 1591
Life matures! 322
Life, ministry, and hope. 1550
Life mission. 3198
Life more abundant. 238, 1006
Life more abundantly. 3410
Life, now and forever. 3519
Life of A. B. Simpson. 3410
Life of a pioneer. 696, 2609, 3807
Life of Abraham. 4
Life of Absalom. 5
Life of Adam (1640) 3200
Life of Adolph Spaeth, D.D., LL. D. 3469
Life of Adoniram Judson. 2157
Life of Ailred of Rievaulx. 1533

... The life of Alexander Duff. 1481
Life of Alexander Duff, D.D., LL.D. 1481
Life of Alexander Nowell, dean of St. Paul's. 2716
Life of all living. 2228
Life of Ambrose Bonwicke. 677
Life of an enclosed nun. 2717
Life of Andrew Melville, the Scottish reformer. Abridged for the Board, from McCrie's Life of Melville. 2401
Life of Anne Catherine Emmerich. 1511
Life of Antony and the letter to Marcellinus. 55, 577
Life of Apollonius of Tyana. 57
Life of Archbishop Curley. 831, 1397
Life of Archbishop John Ireland. 1919
Life of Archbishop Parker. 2775
Life of Archibald Alexander. 24
Life of Archibald Alexander, D. D. 24
Life of Archibald Alexander, D. D., I. J., D. 24
Life of B. Father Ignatius of Loyola, 1616. 1025, 2269
Life of Baron von Hiigel. 1850
Life of Baron von Hugel. 1850
Life of Benedict xv. 190
Life of Bishop Bass, of Massachusetts. 178
Life of Bishop Claggett of Maryland. 1283
Life of Bishop Croes, of New Jersey. 1387
Life of Bishop Dickey. 1458, 1512
Life of Bishop Hedley. 1800
Life of Bishop J. J. Glossbrenner. 1716, 3731
Life of Bishop McDevitt. 2307
Life of Bishop Matthew Simpson, of the Methodist Episcopal church. 3410
Life of Bishop Provoost, of New York. 2984
Life of Bishop Ravenscroft. 3025
Life of Bishop Richard Whatcoat. 3810
Life of Bishop Wainwright. 3788
Life of Bishop Wilfrid. 1758, 3816
Life of Bishop Wilson, of Calcutta. 3818
Life of Blessed Alphonsus Orozco. 2743
Life of Blessed Dominic Savio. 3305
Life of Blessed Gabriel of Our Lady of Sorrows. 1700
Life of Blessed John Berchmans, of the Society of Jesus. 191
Life of Blessed John Martin Moye. 2627
Life of Blessed Martin de Porres, saintly American Negro and patron of social justice. 2348
Life of Blessed Reginald of St. Giles, O.P. 3051
Life of blessing. 886, 957
Life of Brigham Young. 3762, 3869
Life of Buddha according to the legends of ancient India. 702
Life of Buddha as legend and history. 703
Life of Cahterine Booth. 682
Life of Cain. 724
Life of Cardinal Cheverus. 892
Life of Cardinal Gibbons. 1711
Life of Cardinal Manning. 2328
Life of Cardinal Manning, Archbishop of Westminster. 2328
Life of Cardinal Mercier. 2411
Life of Cardinal Mericier. 2411
... Life of Cardinal Newman. 2702
Life of Cardinal Richelieu. 3236
Life of Cardinal Wolsey. 3831
Life of Catherine McAuley, foundresse and first superior of the Institute of religious Sisters of mercy. 2305
Life of Charles Cuthbert Hall: "One among a thousand." 1781
Life of Charles Follen. 1632
Life of Charles G. Finney. 1626
Life of Charles Haddon Spurgeon. 3523
Life of Charles Hodge. 1821
Life of Charles T. Walker. 3789
Life of Charles T. Walker, D.D., ("The Black Spurgeon".) pastor Mt. Olivet Baptist church, New York city. 3789
Life of Christ. 400, 401, 601, 717, 929, 1312, 1958, 1959, 1960, 1961, 1962, 1963, 1964, 1966, 1967, 1969, 1970, 1971, 1972, 1973, 1974, 1977, 1978, 1979, 1981, 1987, 1988, 1989, 1990, 1991, 1992, 1993, 2001, 2048, 3784
Life of Christ and His apostles. 1961
Life of Christ as by the apostles Matthew, Mark, Luke and John. 1961
Life of Christ as compiled from the four Gospels [by] Powell B. Trotter. 2060
Life of Christ as portrayed by the old masters and the words of the Holy Bible. 1990
Life of Christ for children. 625, 1980, 1982, 1983
Life of Christ for teenagers. 1980
Life of Christ for the young. 1984
Life of Christ for young people. 1966
Life of Christ for young people in questions and answers. 384, 1992

Life of Christ, founded on the four Gospels and illustrated by reference to the manners, customs, religious beliefs, and political institutions of His times. 1959
... The life of Christ harmonized from the four evangelists. 1993
Life of Christ in masterpieces of art and the words of the New Testament. 399, 1957, 1958
Life of Christ in picture and story. 1966
Life of Christ in poetry. 2048
Life of Christ in poetry and art. 2048
Life of Christ in recent research. 1978
Life of Christ in stereo. 1991
Life of Christ in the conception & expression of Chinese and oriental artists. 1957, 2759
Life of Christ Jesus in Bible language. 1979, 1982
Life of Christ Jesus in Bible language, from the King James Version of the Bible. 1982
Life of Christ retold in words of one syllable. 1983
Life of Christ, together with the four gospels. 1960
Life of Christ visualized. 1960
Life of Christian devotion. 1449
Life of Christina of Markyate. 1110
Life of Clara B. Hardy. 1785
Life of Clement Phinney. 1652, 2844
Life of Constans L. Goodell, D.D. 1747
Life of continual rejoicing. 448
Life of Cornelia Connelly. 1346, 3438
Life of Daniel. 1401
Life of Daniel Dana, D. D. 1400
Life of Daniel Wilson, D. D. 3818
Life of David. 1405
Life of David as reflected in his Psalms. 577, 1405
Life of David Brainerd, missionary to the Indians. 689, 1899
Life of David Hume. 1855
Life of David, king of Israel. 1405
... The life of David Livingstone. 2241
Life of David, son of Jesse. 1405
Life of David W. Patten. 2794
Life of Demetrius Augustine Gallitzin. 1744
Life of Desiderius Erasmus. 1526
Life of Dr. C. F. W. Walther. 3790
Life of Dr. George Abbot. 2
Life of Dr. John Colet. 1307
Life of Dr. Martin Luther. 2273, 2276
Life of Dwight L. Moody. 2588
Life of Edmund S. Janes. 1934
Life of Edward Bouverie Pusey, doctor of divinity, canon of Christ church. 3010
Life of Edward Henry Bickersteth D.D., bishop and poet. 658
Life of Edward Irving, minister of the National Scotch church, London. 1920
Life of Edward Norris Kirk, D.D. 2178
Life of Edward Thomson, D.D., LL.D. 3698
Life of Edwards Amasa Park, (S. T. D., LL. D.) 2775
Life of Edwin H. Chapin, D.D. 886
Life of Edwin Wallace Parker. 2775
Life of Elder Benjamin Randal. 3021
Life of Elder Walter Scott. 3315
Life of Elijah. 1506
Life of Elisha. 1506
Life of Emanuel Swedenborg. 2689, 3569, 3570, 3571
Life of Enos Nuttall. 2718
Life of Esther. 1533
Life of faith. 1545, 1589, 1592, 1596
Life of Father Bernard. 1780
Life of Father Bernard Donnelly. 1476
Life of Father de Smet, S. J. 1900, 3426
Life of Father Haskins. 1790
... The life of Father Hecker. 1799
Life of Father Isaac Jogues. 1900, 2125
Life of Father Pro. 2943
Life of Father Skarga. 3422
Life of Fenelon, archbishop of Cambray. 1621
Life of Frances E. Willard. 3816
Life of Francis of Assisi in silhouettes. 1643
Life of Francis Xavier, apostle of the Indies. 1649
Life of Franklin D. Richards. 3235
Life of Frederic William Farrar, D. D., F. R. S., etc. 1613
Life of Frederick Denison Maurice. 2374
Life of General William Booth. 682, 3292
Life of George Berkeley, Bishop of Cloyne. 192
Life of George Fox. 1637
Life of George Fox in story and scene. 1636, 2757
Life of George Matheson, D.D., LL.D., F.R.S.E. 2373
Life of Girolamo Savonarola. 3305
Life of Gluckel of Hamelin. 2100

Life of God in the life of His world. 3202
Life of God in the soul of man. 974
Life of Gotama the Buddha. 701
Life of grace. 1752
Life of Gregory Lopez. 2245
Life of Gustav Gottheil. 1749
Life of Hastings Rashdall. 3022
Life of Heber C. Kimball, an apostle. 2171
Life of Henry B. Wright. 3860
Life of Henry Bidleman Bascom. 177
Life of Henry Drummond. 1481
... Life of Henry Martyn. 2349
Life of Henry Ward Beecher. 184
Life of his Holiness Pope Leo XIII. 2216
Life of His Holiness Pope Pius x. 2851
Life of Hiuen-Tsiang. 1850
Life of human souls. 3461
... Life of Ignatius Loyola. 2269
Life of Isaac Eddy Brown. 696
Life of J. B. Jeter, D.D. 2072
Life of J. H. W. Stuckenberg. 3536
Life of Jacob, and his son Joseph. 1931
Life of James Arminius. 83
Life of James Cardinal Gibbons. 1711
Life of James Green. 1772
Life of James Riley. 3238
Life of Jeanne Charlotte de Brechard of the Order of the visitation, friend and spiritual daughter of St. Francis de Sales and St. Jane Frances de Chantal, 1580-1637, by the Sisters of the visitation, Harrow. With a preface. 691
Life of Jerome Emiliani, most distinguished Venetian nobleman. 1943
Life of Jesus. 338, 396, 408, 929, 1954, 1959, 1962, 1963, 1965, 1966, 1968, 1969, 1971, 1972, 1973, 1980, 1981, 1982, 1984, 1988, 1990, 1992, 1994, 3215
Life of Jesus according to extra-canonical sources. 1975
Life of Jesus and His apostles. 70, 1965
Life of Jesus Christ. 1960, 1963, 1970, 1971, 1972, 1974, 1975, 1994
Life of Jesus Christ, according to the gospel history. 1968
Life of Jesus Christ for the young. 1982
Life of Jesus Christ in His church. 1053, 1955
Life of Jesus Christ in its historical connexion and historical development. 1969
Life of Jesus Christ Our Lord. 1968
Life of Jesus, critically examined. 1973
Life of Jesus for boys and girls. 1983
Life of Jesus for children. 1992
Life of jesus for everyman. 1959
Life of Jesus for junior high school pupils. 1993
Life of Jesus for young people. 1980
Life of Jesus in pictures. 1958
Life of Jesus in rhythmic writing. 2048
Life of Jesus in the light of the higher criticism. 1968
Life of Jesus in the words of the four Gospels. 1990
Life of Jesus of Nazareth. 392, 1954, 1971
Life of Jesus of Nazareth, for young people. 1974
Life of Jesus retold from the Gospels for children. 1950
Life of Jesus, the Christ. 1960
... The life of Joan of Arc. 660, 1938
Life of John Arndt. 83
Life of John Baptist de La Salle. 2189
Life of John Calvin. 727
Life of John Cardinal Glennon, Archbishop of St. Louis. 1716
Life of John, cardinal McCloskey. 2306
Life of John Chrysostom. 1115
Life of John Colet, D. D. 1307
Life of John Colet, D.D., dean of St. Paul's, and founder of St. Paul's school. 1307
Life of John Eliot. 1507
Life of John Eliot, the apostle of the Indians. 1507, 1901
Life of John Frederic Oberlin. 2720
Life of John H. W.Hawkins. 1791
Life of John Henry, cardinal Newman, based on his private journals and correspondence. 2705
Life of John Hughes, first archbishop of New York. 1851
Life of John Knox. 2179, 2181
Life of John Knox, the Scottish reformer. Abridged from McCrie's life of Knox. 2181
Life of John Lancaster Spalding. 3470
Life of John Livingston Nevius. 2686
Life of John McDowell. 2307
Life of John Mary Decalogne, student in the University of Paris. 1418
Life of John Newton. 2705
Life of John P. Crozer. 1389
Life of John Price Durbin. 1483
Life of John Taylor. 3591

Life of John the Baptist. 3551
Life of John W. Hawkins. 1791
Life of John Wesley. 3802, 3805, 3806
Life of John Wicliff, D. D. 3860
Life of Jonah. 2130
Life of Joseph. 2132, 2133
Life of Joseph Bates. 178
Life of Joseph F. Smith, sixth president of the Church of Jesus Christ of latter-day saints. 2606, 3430
Life of Joseph Fielding Smith, tenth President of the Church of Jesus Christ of the Latter-day Saints. 3430
Life of Joseph Priestley. 2939
Life of Joseph Smith, the prophet. 3428
Life of Joseph the prophet. 2606, 2929
Life of Joseph, the son of Israel. 2132, 2133
Life of Joseph, the son of Israel. In eight books. 2133
Life of Joshua. 2134
... Life of Joshua Soule. 3464
... The life of Karl Follen. 1632
Life of Knowles Shaw. 3401
Life of Legh Richmond. 3236
... Life of Leo xiii and history of his pontificate, from official and approved sources. 2216
Life of Leo XIII from an authentic memoir furnished by his order. 2216
Life of Leo XIII from an authetic memoir furnished by his order. 2216
Life of little Saint Placid. 2853
Life of lives. 1964, 1978, 1983
Life of Lorenzo Snow. 3432
Life of love. 2265, 2267, 3481
Life of love towards the Sacred Heart of Jesus. 3269
Life of Luther. 2273, 2274, 2277
Life of Luther, told in pictures and narrative by the reformer and his contemporaries. 2277
Life of Mademoiselle Le Gras (Louise de Marillac) 2203, 3417
Life of Mahomet. 2565, 2628, 2629
Life of Mahommed. 2628
Life of man in Christ. 2059
Life of man with God. 3488
Life of Margaret Fox. 1637
Life of Marie Moulton Graves Hopkins. 1847
Life of Mark A. Matthews. 2373
Life of Martin Luther. 2273, 2274, 2275, 2276, 2277, 2278, 3040
Life of Martin Luther, the German reformer. 2274, 3040
Life of Mary. 2358
Life of Mary as seen by the mystics;.) 2354
Life of Mary Baker Eddy. 1496
Life of Mary Baker G. Eddy and the history of Christian Science. 1034, 1495
Life of Mary in legend and art. 2358
Life of Mary, mother of Jesus. 2358
Life of Mary, mother of Jesus; 91 masterworks of art. Text selection and introd. by Charles Hartman. Pref. by Walter M. Abbott. 2358
Life of Mason Long. 3090
Life of Mason Long, the converted gambler. 397, 3090
Life of Matthew Simpson. 3410
Life of Menasseh ben Israel. 2327
Life of Menasseh ben Israel, rabbi, printer, and diplomat. 2098, 2327
Life of Mere Anne-Marie Javouhey. 1937, 3419
Life of Mere St. Joseph. 672, 3275, 3418
Life of Milarepa. 2194, 2461
Life of Mohammad from original sources. 2564
...The life of Mohammed. 2628
Life of Monsignor Robert Hugh Benson. 191
Life of Moses. 493, 2621, 2622, 2644
Life of Mother Cabrini, American saint. 723
Life of Mother Catherine Aurelia of the Precious Blood, foundress of the Institute of the precious blood. 753, 3416
Life of Mother Mary Baptist Russell. 3256
Life of Mother Pauline von Mallinckrodt. 2319
Life of Mother St. Urban of the Congregation of the sisters of bon secours of Paris. 3279, 3416
Life of Mrs. Ann H. Judson, late missionary to Burmah. 2158
Life of Mrs. Booth. 681, 3293
Life of Mrs. E.G. White, Seventh-day adventist prophet. 3811
Life of Mrs. Eliza A. Seton. 3378, 3379
Life of Mrs. Isabella Graham. 1754
Life of Mrs. Mary D. James. 1934
Life of Mrs. Mary Fletcher. 1629

Life of Mrs. Sarah A. Lankford Palmer, who for sixty years was the able teacher of entire holiness. 2766
Life of Mrs. Sarah Norton. 2714
Life of Mrs. Sherwood. 3403
Life of Mrs. Virginia Hale Hoffman. 1822, 2500
Life of Muhammad. 2628
Life of My Savior. 1982
Life of Nephi. 678
Life of Nephi, the son of Lehi, who emigrated from Jerusalem, in Judea, to the land which is now know as South America, about six centuries before the coming of the Savior. 678
Life of Nicholas Ferrar, M. A. and fellow of Clare-hall, Cambridge. 1622
Life of Nietzsche. 2710
Life of offering. 2033
Life of one of God's saints. 3090
Life of Orator Henley. 1803
...The life of Otto, apostle of Pomerania. 2752
Life of Our Blessed Lord and Savior Jesus Christ. 1964
Life of Our Blessed Lord and Saviour Jesus Christ. 1977, 2088
Life of Our Divine Lord. 1974
Life of Our Lady. 2358
Life of Our Lord. 930, 1962, 1963, 1974, 1980, 1981, 1982, 1992
Life of Our Lord and Savior Jesus Christ. 1970
Life of Our Lord and Saviour Jeses Christ and of His virgin mother Mary. 1961
Life of Our Lord and Saviour Jesus Christ. 1961, 1964, 1977, 1978, 2088
Life of Our Lord for children. 1981
Life of Our Lord in art. 1957
Life of Our Lord in sermons. 1962
Life of Our Lord in the words of the four evangelists. 1988
Life of our Lord Jesus Christ. 1969, 1974, 1984, 1991
Life of Our Lord Jesus Christ in meditations. 1969
Life of Our Lord upon the earth considered in its historical, chronological, and geographical relations. 1959
Life of Our Master, Christ Jesus. 1959
Life of Our Savior Jesus Christ. 399, 1974
Life of Pachomius. 2756
Life of Patrick Augustine Feehan. 1620
Life of Patrick Hues Mell. 2401
Life of Paul. 2799, 2801, 2802
Life of Paul of Tarsus. 2798
Life of perfection. 2571, 3196
Life of Peter the apostle. 2824
Life of Philander Chase. 889
Life of Philip Doddridge, D. D. 1472
Life of Philip Melanchthon. 2400
Life of Philip Schaff. 3306
... Life of Phillips Brooks. 694
Life of Pius xi. 2852
Life of Pius x. 2851
Life of Pope Pius ix. 2850
Life of Pope Pius XII. 2852
Life of power. 959
Life of prayer. 2873
Life of prayer and the way to God. 2883
Life of prayer in a world of science. 2869
Life of President Edwards. 1499, 1612
Life of Rasputin. 3022
Life of Reginald Heber. 3143
Life of Rev. A. Carl Whitmer. 3814
Life of Rev. Charles Nerinckx. 820, 2684
Life of Rev. David Brainerd. 689, 1900
Life of Rev. David Edwards. 1498
Life of Rev. George C. Haddock. 1779
Life of Rev. George Whitefield. 3813
Life of Rev. Henry Martyn. 2349
Life of Rev. Hosea Ballou. 131
Life of Rev. Isaiah L. Kephart, D.D. 2168
Life of Rev. James O'Kelly and the early history of the Christian church in the South. 2735
Life of Rev. Joel Hawes, D. D. 1791
Life of Rev. John Allen, better known as "Camp-meeting John" 26
Life of Rev. John Clark. 1284
Life of Rev. John Jasper, pastor of Sixth Mt. Zion Baptist church, Richmond, A. 1936, 2683
Life of Rev. John Murray. 2939, 3143
Life of Rev. John Wesley. 3805
Life of Rev John Wesley, A. M. 3803
Life of Rev. John Wesley Childs. 911
Life of Rev. John Wesley Redfield, M.D. 3031
Life of Rev. Joseph Emerson, pastor of the Third Congregational church in Beverly, Ms., and subsequently principal of a female seminary. 1510
Life of Rev. Joseph Snelling. 2940
... Life of Rev. Justin Perkins, D. D., pioneer missionary to Persia. 2820
Life of Rev. Martin Cheney. 891

Life of Rev. Mother St. John Fontbonne. 1632
Life of Rev. Mother Saint Joseph. 3275
Life of Rev. Orange Scott. 974
Life of Rev. Philip William Otterbein. 2752
Life of Rev R. Downey Blair. 670
Life of Rev. Richard Baxter. 34
Life of Rev. Richard Watson. 3798
Life of Rev. Samuel H. Stearns. 3526
Life of Rev. Thomas A. Morris, D. D. 2620
Life of Rev. Thomas Brainerd, D. D. 956
Life of Rev. Thomas M. Eddy, D.D. 1496
Life of Rev. Thomas Scott La Due. 966
Life of Rev. Walter Ellis Powers. 2866
Life of Rev. William Keele. 2166
Life of Richard Fuller, D. D. 1690
Life of Right Rev. John N. Neumann, D. D., of the Congregation of the Most Holy Redeemer. 2685
Life of Robert Josiah Willingham. 3818
Life of Robert Paine, D. D. 2758
Life of Robert R. McBurney. 2305, 3870
Life of Robert R. Roberts. 3241
Life of Rowland Hill Evans of Cameroun. 1577, 2506
... The life of Rt. Rev. Joseph Rosati, C.M. 3249, 3276
Life of Rt. Rev. Joseph Rosati, C.M., first bishop of St. Louis, 1789-1843. 3249, 3276
Life of Russell H. Conwell, preacher, lecturer, philanthropist. 1368
Life of S. Bernardino of Siena. 194
Life of S. Francis of Assisi. 1640
Life of S. Miller Willis. 3818
Life of S. Paul of the Cross. 2767
... The life of St. Agnes of Rome. 19
Life of St. Aloysius Gonzaga. 2271
Life of Saint Andrew Bobola of the Society of Jesus, martyr. 673
Life of Saint Angela Merici. 41, 3761
Life of Saint Angela Merici, of Brescia. 41, 3761
Life of Saint Anthony of Padua. 54
Life of Saint Antony. 55
Life of Saint Augustine. 116
Life of St. Augustine, bishop. 114
Life of St. Benedict. 187
Life of Saint Benedict, patriarch of the western monks. 189, 190
Life of St. Benedict surnamed "the Moor", the son of a slave. 187
Life of Saint Boniface. 677
Life of Saint Catharine of Siena. 749
Life of St. Catherine of Siena. 749
... The life of St. Cecilia from ms. Ashmole 43 and ms. Cotton Tiberius E. vii. 877
Life of St. Charles Borromeo. 739
Life of Saint Clare. 1284
Life of St. David. 1406
Life of Saint Dominic Savio. 3305
Life of Saint Elizabeth, of Hungary, duchess of Thuringia. 1508
... The life of Saint Epiphanius by Ennodius. 1522
Life of St. Frances of Rome. 1474, 1639
Life of St. Francis de Sales, bishop and prince of Geneva. 1650
Life of St. Francis of Assisi. 1027, 1640, 1643, 1644
Life of St. Francis Solanus. 3455
Life of Saint Francis Xavier based on authentic sources. 1649
Life of St. Gall. 1701
Life of Saint Germaine Cousins. 1707
Life of St. Germana. 1707
Life of St. Hugh of Lincoln. 1851
Life of St. Jerome. 1811
Life of St. John for the young. 2127
Life of Saint John Francis Regis of the Society of Jesus. 3051
Life of St. John's Parish. 2586
Life of St. Josaphat. 1918
Life of Saint Margaret Mary Alacoque. 21, 3269
Life of St. Martin. 2349
Life of St. Martin de Porres. 2348
Life of St. Mary Magdalen. 2353
Life of St. Mary Magdalen De-Pazzi. 2333
Life of St. Mary Magdalene. 2353
Life of Saint Nicholas. 2707
Life of Saint Pachomius and his disciples. 1025, 2756
Life of St. Patrick. 2793
Life of St. Patrick and his place in history. 2793
Life of St. Paul. 2004, 2797, 2800, 2802, 2804, 3551
Life of Saint Peter. 71, 2825
...The life of St. Peter Claver. 1286
Life of St. Peter Fourier. 1332, 1636
... The life of Saint Rose. 3247
...The life of Saint Rose of Lima. 3247
Life of St. Samsom of Dol. 3283

Life of St. Sava. 3305
Life of Saint Severin. 3388
Life of Saint Severinus. 3388
Life of St. Simon Stock. 3409
Life of St. Stanislaus Kostka. 3524
Life of St. Teresa of Avila. 2220, 3603
Life of St. Teresa of Avila, including the relations of her spiritual state, written by herself. 3603
Life of St. Thomas of Villanova, archbishop of Valentia and Augustinian friar. 3704
Life of Samson. 3297
Life of Samuel Miller, D.D., LL.D. 2466
Life of service. 472
Life of Sir George Williams. 3818
Life of Sister Mary Gonzaga Grace, of the Daughters of charity of St. Vincent de Paul, 1812-1897. 1750
Life of Sister Saint-Pierre. 2334
Life of Sister St. Rita of Cascia. 3238
Life of Soeur Rosalie, of the Daughters of St. Vincent de Paul. 3247
Life of Solomon. 3457
Life of St Anselm. 49
Life of St Anselm, Archbishop of Canterbury. 49
Life of Syr Thomas More. 2596
Life of Teresa of Jesus. 3603
Life of the apostle John. 2127
Life of the apostle St. John. 2126
Life of the Archpriest Avvakum, by himself. 3022
Life of the Blessed Charles Spinola of the Society of Jesus. 1947, 3472
Life of the blessed John B. Marie Vianney, cure of Ars. 3778
Life of the blessed servant of God, the heroic martyr, John Gabriel Perboyre. 1332, 2817
Life of the Blessed Virgin. 2358
Life of the Blessed Virgin in pictures. 2358
Life of the Blessed Virgin Mary. 2356, 2358, 2360
Life of the Blessed Virgin Mary, mother of God. 2356
Life of the Buddha. 1703
Life of the Buddha, according to the ancient texts and monuments of India. 1703
Life of the Cardinal de Cheverus. 892
Life of the Christ. 1974
Life of the Christian. 970
Life of the church. 1121
Life of the devil. 3143
Life of the great preacher, Reverend Gerorge Whitfield. 2930, 3813
Life of the Holy Spirit. 1830
Life of the late Reverend and learned Dr. Cotton Mather, of Boston, (New England.) 2372
Life of the late Reverend, learned and pious Mr. Jonathan Edwards. 1499
Life of the learned and Right Reverend Reynold Pecock, S.T.P., local bishop of St. Asaph, and Chichester, in the reign of King Henry VI. 2810
Life of the Little Flower. 3690
Life of the Little Flower St. Therese of Lisieux, according to the official documents of the Carmel of Lisieux. 3691
Life of the Lord Jesus. 1966
Life of the Master. 1974
Life of the Master, lectures. 1959
Life of the mind. 1103
Life of the Most Rev. M. J. Spalding, D.D., archbishop of Baltimore. 3470
Life of the Most Reverend Clement Smyth, d. d., o. c. s. c., second bishop of Dubuque, 1858-1865; compiled. 3432
Life of the Most Reverend John Hughes, D.D. 1851
Life of the Mystical body. 2020
Life of the people in Biblical times. 2121
Life of the pilgrim Joseph Thomas. 2847
Life of the Rev. Adam Clarke. 1285
Life of the Rev. Alfred Cookman. 1368
Life of the Rev. Calvin S. Gerhard, D. D. 1706
Life of the Rev. Elisha W. Green. 154
Life of the Rev. F. Cointet. 1306
Life of the Rev. Freeborn Garrettson. 1702
Life of the Rev. George Whitefield. 3813
Life of the Rev. Henry Harbaugh, D.D. 1785
Life of the Rev. Henry Moore. 970
Life of the Rev. James Ireland. 171
Life of the Rev. John de la Flechere. 955
Life of the Rev. John Emory, D.D., one of the bishops of the Methodist Episcopal church. 1512
Life of the Rev. John Newton. 34
Life of the Rev. John Owen, D. D. 2753

Life of the Rev. John W. de la Flechere. 1629
Life of the Rev. John Wesley. 3805, 3806
Life of the Rev. John Wesley, A. M. 1691, 3802
Life of the Rev. John William Fletcher. 1629
Life of the Rev. Philip Henry. 1803
Life of the Rev. Richard Baxter. 179
Life of the Rev. Richard Knill, of St. Petersburg. 34
Life of the Rev. Robert Baird, D. D. 130
Life of the Rev. Robert Newton, D. D. 2706
Life of the Rev. Robert R. Roberts, one of the bishops of the Methodist Episcopal church. 3241
Life of the Rev. T. T. Thomason. 2532, 3697
Life of the Rev. Thomas Coke, ll.d. 1306, 2454
Life of the Rev. Thomas Scott, D. D., rector of Aston Sandford, Bucks. 3315
Life of the Rev. William Marsh, D. D. 2348
Life of the Rev. William Tennent. 3601
Life of the Reverend Benjamin Bausman, D. D., LL. D. 178
Life of the Reverend Devereux Jaratt. 1306
Life of the Reverend Devereux Jarratt. 3060
Life of the Reverend Father Hermann, in religion. 740
Life of the Reverend James Lloyd Breck, D. D. 956
Life of the Reverend John Holt Rice, D.D. 3235
Life of the Reverend Mr. George Trosse. 3715
Life of the Reverend Mother Jeanne Chezard de Matel, foundress of the order of the Incarnate word and the blessed sacrament. 2741
Life of the Reverend Mother Julia. 659, 3419
... The life of the Right Reverend John Baptist Mary David (1761-1841) 1404, 3416
Life of the Right Reverend John Barrett Kerfoot ... first bishop of Pittsburgh, with selections from his diaries and correspondence. 2168
Life of the Right Reverend Joseph P. Machebeuf, D.D. 2308
Life of the Right Reverend Mathias Loras, D. D. 819, 2246
Life of the Right Reverend Samuel Wilberforce, D.D. 3815
Life of the Right Reverend William Pinkney, D. D., LL. D. 2849
Life of the Rt. Rev. Dr. Doyle. 1478
Life of the Rt. Rev. Edward Maginn. 2315
Life of the Rt. Rev. William White, D. D., bishop of Pennsilvania. 3812
Life of the Rt. Rev. William White, D. D., bishop of Pennsylvania. 3812
Life of the Saviour. 1955, 1974
...The life of the soul. 767, 969, 2695
Life of the spirit. 967
Life of the spirit and the life of to-day. 3482
Life of the spirit in contemporary civilization. 3478
Life of the spirit in the world of today. 3522
Life of the Sudanese Mahdi. 21
Life of the Ven Mary Crescentia Hoss, of the Third order of St. Francis. 1848
Life of the venerable Anna Marie Taigi. 3580
Life of the Venerable Father Colin. 1308
Life of the venerable John Fox of Meadville, Pa. 961
Life of the venerable Madeleine Barat. 173
Life of the Venerable Mother Mary de Sales Chappuis of the Order of the visitation Holy Mary, 1793-1875. 886
Life of the venerable servant of God Anna Maria Taigi. 3580
Life of the venerable servant of God, Monseigneur Dumoulin Borie, bishop elect of Acanthus, vicar apostolic of western Tonquin, and martyr. 192
Life of the venerable Thomas Kempis. 3692
Life of the Vernerable Francis Libermann. 2223
Life of the Very Rev. Felix De Andreis, C.M. 40
Life of the Very Reverend and learned Cotton Mather, D.D. & F. R. S. 2372
Life of the world to come. 3437
Life of their own. 1888
Life of Thomas Chalmers. 880

Life of Thomas Chalmers, D. D., L. L. D. 880
Life of Thomas Coke. 1306
Life of Thomas Cranmer. 1378
Life of Thomas J. Sawyer. 3306
Life of Thomas Jefferson Fisher. 1628
Life of Thomas Story, carefully abridged. 3534
Life of Torah. 2143
Life of Ulric Zwingli. 3900
Life of Ulrich Zwingli. 3900
Life of union with Mary. 2361
Life of Ven. Gabriel of Our Lady of Sorrows (Gabriel Possenti) of the Congregation of the Passion. 1700
Life of Venerable Marguerite Bourgeoys. 685
Life of Venerable Mary of Agreda. 2358
Life of Venerable Sister Margaret Bourgeois, foundress of the Sisters of the congregation of Notre Dame. 686
Life of victory. 135, 968
Life of Wesley. 2424, 3804, 3805
Life of Wilbur [!] Fisk, d.d., first president of the Wesleyan university. 1628
Life of William Capers, D.D. 737
... The life of William Carey. 739, 2532
Life of William Carvosso, sixty years a class-leader. 743
Life of William Ellery Channing, D. D. 881, 882
Life of William J. Onahan. 872, 2737
Life of William, Rollinson Wittingham. 3814
Life of William Savery of Philadelphia. 3305
Life of William Tuttle. 3719
Life of worship. 3853
Life of Zoroaster in the words of his own hymns. 3898
Life on Patmos. 3095
Life on rocks. 2499
Life on the highest plane. 972
Life on the Negro frontier. 3874
Life on the uplands. 587, 2985
Life on two levels. 1484
Life, one to a customer. 2384
Life! physical and spiritual. 3497
Life pictures. 927
Life pictures from the Bible. 214
Life-pictures of "The prodigal son." 2944
Life planning. 3493
Life portrayed in the Sermon on the Mount. 3336
Life problems. 970
Life problems ... for pupils of the junior high school or the intermediate department of the church Bible school. 3553
Life problems in a changing world. 3190, 3889
Life purposeful. 3147
Life questions of high school boys. 687
Life radiant. 2696, 3483
Life reminiscences of an old Lutheran minister. 2303
Life reveries. 3352
Life-scenes from the four Gospels. 1967
Life-scenes from the Old Testament. 534
Life scenes of the Messiah. 1961
Life sentence. 171, 1310
Life, sermons and speeches of Rev. Numa F. Reid, D.D. 2426
Life service. 977
Life-situation preaching. 3364
Life sketch and sermons of Rev. B. C. Dewey. 1456
Life sketch of King Azariah Brown. 1116
Life sketches. 3380
Life sketches and sermons. 2813
Life sketches from a heathen land. 2512
Life sketches of Ellen G. White. 3811
Life sketches of Rev. Alfred Cookman. 661
Life-sketches of Rev. George Henry Clark. 1284
Life songs, number two. 2406
Life stories. 41
Life stories from the Old and the New Testament. 3765
Life story and romance in the gospel. 321
Life story and sermons of the English boy preacher. 3366
Life story of Brigham Young. 2602, 3869
Life story of Dr. Lee S. Huizenga. 1853
Life story of Dr. Sa'eed of Iran. 3272
Life story of Henry Clay Trumbull, missionary, army chaplain, editor, and author. 3716
Life story of Lizzie H. Glide. 1716
Life story of Rev. Francis Makemie. 2318
... The life story of the Lord Jesus as Mark tells it. 437
Life-study fellowship, Noroton, Conn. 1351
Life symbols as related to sex symbolism. 3573

Life talks. 2306
Life testimony. 923
Life that follows life. 1697
Life that is grace. 1000
Life that is life indeed. 972
Life that never ends. 1692
Life that really matters. 1007
Life that wins. 954, 3296
Life thoughts. 3361
Life thoughts, gathered from the extemporaneous discourses of Henry Ward Beecher. 3361
Life, three sermons, and some of the miscellaneous writings of Rev. Jesse Greene. 1772
Life, three sermons, and some of the miscellaneous writtings of Rev. Jesse Greene. 1772
Life through the cross. 2029, 3525
Life-time hymns. 1861
Life, times, and character of the Right Reverend Benedict Joseph Flaget. 1628
Life, times and travels of St. Paul. 2796
Life to live. 181
Life to live—a way to pray. 2870
Life to the full. 867
Life together. 956
Life, travels, and gospel labors of Eld. Joseph Thomas. 2847
Life, travels, labors, and helpers of Mrs. Amanda Smith. 3431
Life, travels, labors, and writings of Lorenzo Dow. 1478
Life under two flags. 2540
Life unfolding. 1509
Life unto God. 959
Life values for young America. 3176
Life victorious. 2214, 3281
Life, walk and triumph of faith. 973
Life when Jesus was a boy. 1996, 2765
Life, wisdom, truth and happiness in the Book of Psalms. 573, 584
Life wish. 1088
Life with a purpose. 3698
Life with God. 1202
Life with Mother Superior. 3537
Life with the Holy Ghost. 1712
Life within. 3487
Life within life. 3461
Life without death? 2989
Life without strife. 2140
Life work; a statement of principles, methods, and programs that may be helpful to student Young men's Christian associations. 3872
Life-work of Elbridge Gerry Brooks. 694
Life work of George Irving. 1920, 3829
Life work of Mrs. Cora L. V. Richmond. 3237, 3495
Life work of Pastor Louis Harms. 1783
Life worth living. 419, 971, 994, 995, 3335
Life worth while. 972
Life, writings, and character of Edward Robinson. 1345, 3241
Life you'd love to live. 3868
Lifelong learning among Jews. 2075, 2107
Life's abiding resources. 1004
Life's beautiful way heavenward. 2815
Life's best. 166
Life's convictions. 964
Life's crowing years. 17
Life's detours. 2822
Life's directions. 2607
Life's eternal drama, the only pathway to peace. 1531
Life's eventful voyage. 1007
Life's everyday questions. 164
Life's final goal. 3330
Life's four windows. 3356
Life's golden hours. 1545
Life's great adventure--prayer. 2870
Life's great object. 1059
Life's greatest trip. 1261
Life's high hurdles. 11
Life's highest loyalty. 733
Life's intimate relationships. 2338
Life's journey. 3095
Life's lessons. 997
Life's looking glass. 976
Life's masterpieces. 964
Life's meaning. 3889
Life's melody, and The celestial hymn. 1861
Life's message to youth. 955
Life's mysteries revealed by our personal God to Alfred W. Lowrie. 2267
Life's mystery and meaning. 2290
Life's pay checks; sermonettes for everyday life. 3353
Life's perilous places. 3095
Life's priorities. 984
Life's problem solved with holy numbers. 319
Life's problems. 3090

Life's progression. 3511
Life's questions as asked and answered in the Bible. 1003
Life's realities. 971
Life's retrospect. 3090
Life's riddle solved through the law of metempsychosis. 3054
Life's secrets. 3094
Life's secrets revealed. 2226
Life's supreme decision. 1558
Life's to-morrow. 30
Life's treasure book, past, present, and future. 3402
Life's unanswered questions. 166
Life-style evangelism. 1562
Lifetime of a Jew throughout the ages of Jewish history. 2120
Lifetimes. 3055
Lift for living. 1452
Lift high that banner! 2931
Lift high the torch. 544
Lift Him up. 1570
Lift the latch. 1438
Lift up my spirit, Lord! 2892
Lift up thine eyes. 602
Lift up your eyes. 2923, 3632
Lift up your heart. 1001, 1353, 2212
Lift up your hearts. 854, 1263, 2361, 2888, 3853
Lift up your hearts; an anthology of Lenten essays. 2211
Lift your skyline. 160
Lifted veil. 3507
Lifting of the vail. 46
Lifting the latch. 2985
Lifting the latch to "God's book house" 312
... Lifting the veil. 1030, 2992, 3502, 3508
Light. 460, 2323
Light against darkness. 3666
Light amid shadows. 2576
Light amid the darkness. 2842
Light among the shadows. 3095
Light and cloud in the dark valley. 1353
Light and enlightenment; a study of the Cambridge Platonists and the Dutch Animians. 731
Light and fire and The Holy Spirit. 1827
Light and life. 792, 3094
Light and life in the Fourth Gospel. 419, 1681
"Light and love." 1500
Light and peace. 3481
Light and rejoicing. 2120
Light and salvation. 1811
Light and shadow. 3313
Light and shadow in China. 2508
Light and shadow in religious life. 3195
Light and the glory. 3741
Light and the glory study guide. 3741
Light and twilight. 3406
Light another candle. 1784
Light at eventide. 17
Light bearer to the Amazon; thrilling stories of missionary labors. 2505
Light bearers. 3516
Light-bearers of darkness. 3322
... Light before dusk;a Russian Catholic in France, 1923-1941. 1364
Light beneath the Cross. 1754, 3230
Light beyond. 1696, 2987
Light burns on. 726
Light divine in parable and allegory. 2026
Light for anxious souls in some of their difficulties. 3288
Light for dark days. 2808
Light for life's dark riddle. 167
Light for life's tunnels. 973
Light for my life. 900
Light for our age. 3750
Light for the day. 1437
Light for the Gentiles. 331, 2798
Light for the whole world. 3467
Light for the world's darkness. 2465
Light for today on personal problems. 164
Light from a hillside. 3336
Light from above. 1445, 3663
Light from ancient letters. 368
Light from Bible prophecy as related to the present crisis. 604
Light from darkness. 3095
Light from God. 3061
Light from God's lamp. 1435
Light from heaven. 1227
Light from many candles. 2390
Light from my Bible for today. 198, 3164
Light from the ancient East. 321, 407
Light from the ancient past. 298, 1817
Light from the cross. 2034, 3368
Light from the East. 1330
Light from the Greek New Testament. 1769
Light from The living Bible. 601
Light from the old for a new order. 1265
Light from the sanctuary of the Royal Arch. 1670
Light from the spirit world. 3504, 3508

Light from the Star of Bethlehem. 2047
Light from the Talmud. 2980
Light from the Valley. 2529, 3217
Light from the West. 1026
Light gleams from the Fourth gospel. 420
Light has come. 417
Light in a dark place. 1280, 2736
Light in a dark world. 1454
Light in dark ages; eighteen centuries of missions. 2525
Light in dark places. 3616
Light in darkness. 2519
Light in hours of darkness. 1353
Light in India's hand. 2529
Light in India's night. 2531
Light in our dwellings. 959
Light in the clouds. 3095
Light in the community. 1320
Light in the dark belt. 2302, 2303
Light in the dark places. 1008
Light in the dark valleys. 1351
Light in the darkness. 416
... Light in the dwelling. 386
Light in the Far East. 1803, 2536
Light in the forest. 1897, 1898
Light in the grotto. 3460
Light in the jungle. 1784
Light in the jungle; the thirty years' mission of Leo and Jessie Halliwell along the Amazon. Edited and with a foreword by Will Oursler. 690
Light in the land of Sinim. 737
Light in the north. 1356, 1375
Light in the prison-window. 1790
Light in the valley. 1305, 1349, 1415, 2242, 3094, 3498
Light in the window. 1692
Light is sown. 2497
Light is sprung up. 1544
Light is still shining. 423
Light my candle. 981
Light of a thousand suns. 3121
Light of Asia. 706
Light of China. 2197
Light of Christ. 2641
Light of day. 3077
Light of Egypt. 95, 2723
Light of exploration. 2381
Light of faith. 1593, 3664
Light of God, lost and found. 3051
Light of immortality. 1886
Light of Japan. 2533
Light of Kosmon. 120
Light of life. 236, 407, 1951, 3463
Light of love. 1430
Light of men. 2006
Light of Messiah. 2018
Light of prophecy, or The religion of the future. 2949
Light of revelation and non-Christians. 1394
Light of Russia. 2750
Light of the age. 2477
Light of the belt. 2529, 3217
Light of the Bible. 312
Light of the church in Kentucky. 820, 3819
Light of the Cross. 337
Light of the cross, the illusion of the irreparable. 1998
Light of the Lamb. 2051
Light of the mind. 3685
Light of the mysteries: Jesus. 2019
Light of the nations. 1182, 1962
Light of the soul. 3865
Light of the soul, its science and effect. 3865
Light of the truth. Am I an infidel? 3289
Light of the World. 100, 297, 1034, 1055, 1079, 1263, 1351, 1953, 1962, 2229, 2745, 3095, 3101, 3667, 3701
Light of the world, being the second part of the Life and teachings of Our Lord, in verse. 2047
Light of truth. 199, 3506
Light of truth in the mind of man, the only rule of faith and practice. 1655
Light of understanding. 523
Light on a dark subject. 1667
Light on Archbishop Lefebvre. 788, 2366
Light on Bible difficulties. 234
Light on dark horizons. 3726
Light on finance, for the use of finance committees and finance workers in city, town and rural community Young women's Christian associations. 3878
Light on great Bible themes. 3353
Light on kriya yoga. 3865
Light on life's duties. 969
Light on masonry. 2597
Light on Mormonism. 2618
Light on our path. 629
Light on prophecy. 2055
Light on soul winning. 3462
Light on Synanon. 2857, 3578
Light on the Christian's path. 1228
Light on the dark river. 1782, 2227

Light on the Gospel from an ancient poet. 45
Light on the heavy. 651
Light on the hidden way. 3497
Light on the hills. 1513
Light on the horizon. 2131
Light on the last days. 320
Light on the Lord's face. 166
Light on the mountain. 2767, 3286
Light on the mysteries of nature and the Bible in the form of letters to our children. 3075
Light on the Old Testament from Babel. 207
Light on the path. 3095, 3684
Light on the path, a treatise written for the personal use of those who are ignorant of the eastern wisdom, and who desire to enter within its influence. 3684
Light on yoga. 3867
Light, prayer, Zion-Jerusalem, and salvation in the book of Psalms. 1798
Light shines through. 2375
Light shining. 1399
Light that heals. 1599
Light that lighteth every man. 415
... The light that never fails. 1560
Light the candles! 1112
Light the paper lantern. 2512, 3796
Light through an eastern window. 239
Light through the Iron Curtain. 82
Light through the shadows. 2533
Light to live by. 1430
Light to my path. 2929, 3348
Light to my paths. 863
Light to the city. 1279
Light to the Gentiles. 2223
Light to your candle. 3502
Light unto my path. 484, 1438, 2635
Light upon the scaffold. 2942
Light upon the Word. 1551
Light will dawn ... through prayer. 2247, 2874
Light within. 565, 1832
Light within us. 3312
Light your own lamp. 3196
Lighted candle. 3712
Lighted candles. 975
Lighted cross. 1627
Lighted passage. 3517
Lighted trail. 1980
Lighted valley. 675
Lighten our darkness. 1058
Lighter of gospel fires. 2261
Lighter spire. 2302
Lightfoot of Durham. 2229
Lightfoot's manual of the lodge. 1669
Lighthouse on the corner. 2735
Lighting the candle. 1524
Lighting the torch. 2227
Lightning flash! 3195
Lightning flashes and thunderbolts. 2131
Lightning meditations. 2390
Lights aglow, a teachers' manual. 3185
Lights and shades of Christendom to A. D. 1000. 1194
Lights and shadows. 30, 850
Lights and shadows of a long episcopate. 1901, 2970
Lights and shadows of American life. 3094
Lights and shadows of itinerant life. 3095, 3133
Lights and shadows of life. 165
Lights and shadows of mission work in the Far East. 2502
Lights and shadows of Mormonism. 2602
Lights and shadows of sacred story. 216
Lights and shadows of spiritualism. 3505
Lights and shadows of the sacred ministry. 3676
Lights on in the house of the dead. 194
... Lights up. 3877
Lightworks. 544
Liguori leaflets. 2391
Like a cedar of Lebanon. 999
Like a cleansing fire. 611
Like a great river. 1814
Like a living stone. 695
Like a meteor across the horizon. 1300, 1622
Like a mighty army. 1070, 1229, 1708
Like a mighty army, moves the Church of God. 1229
Like a mighty wind. 1573
Like a river...; 50th anniversary. 92
Like a rose among the thorns. 2143
Like a shock of wheat. 1417
Like a swarm of bees. 3419
Like a tree planted. 2393, 2734
Like a trumpet. 1341
Like a watered garden. 932, 1442, 3025
Like all the nations! 2119
Like as we are. 493
Like Christ. 1451
Like Christ, thoughts on the blessed life on conformity to the Son of God. 970

Like it is! 1057
Like the Word. 3487
Like the word; to the Trinity through Christ. 3487
Likute batar likute. 2985
Lilies in service. 2574
Lilies of eternal peace. 3095
Lilies, rabbits, and painted eggs. 1486
Lillian DeWaters' The price of glory. 1030
Lillian Trasher. 3710
Lillie Helena Kull and Friedrich Kienholz Schild: a tribute. 3307
Lily among the thorns. 3044
Lily among thorns. 594
Lily and sword and crown. 3419
Lily of Israel. 2354
Lily of Mary. 3460
Lily of the marshes. 2333
Lily-wreath of spiritual communications. 3498
Limbo. 2229
Limbo world of the divorced. 1471
Limitation of the Sacred heart of Jesus. 3269
Limitations of life. 2935
Limited inspiration. 306, 3427
Limited to everyone. 64
Limiting God. 965
Limits of literary criticism. 233, 1387
Limits of religious thought. 3102
Limits of religious thought examined in eight lectures delivered before the University of Oxford, in the year MDCCCLVIII, on the Bampton Foundation. 3102
Limits of toleration within the Church of England from 1632 to 1642. 3703
Limits of unbelief. 64
... Lincoln. 2230
Lincoln Diocesan Training College, 1862-1962. 2230
Lincoln Park and its churches. 1133
Lincoln way. 2230, 3513
Lincoln's religion. 2230
L'inconnu. 2988
Linda. 3247
Line of light. 1037
Lineage from apostolic times of the American Catholic church. 2967
Lines occasioned by the death of the late Rev. Dr. Henry J. Feltus, with notes, biographical and explanatory. 1621
Lingering at Calvary. 2034
Linguistic and literary form of the book of Ruth. 589
Linguistic evidence in dating early Hebrew poetry. 556, 1799
Linguistic key to the Greek New Testament. 352
Linguistics and theology. 916, 1077
Link. 2329
Link of love. 2396
Links between Judaism and Christianity. 1103
Links in Christianity's chain. 1175
Links of gold. 3807
Links to eternity. 1614
Lioe of Thomas Chalmers, D. D., LL. D. 880
Lion and the Lamb. 56, 1095
Lion in his den. 2232
Lion of Africa. 2241
Lion of the Lord. 3869
Lions of God, lambs of God. 1298
Lion's roar. 3715
Lion's roar of Queen Srimala. 710
Lipuori leaflets. 2391
Liqqutei Amarim (Tanya) 1789
Liquid cross of skid row. 1253, 2307
Liquor and commonsense. 3596
Liquor problem. 2231
Lisa. 1367, 1858
List of all the Friends Meetings that exist or ever have existed in Indiana. 1807-1955. 1686
List of bibliographies of theological and biblical literature published in Great Britain and America, 1595-1931. 657
List of books approved by the Sunday school book commission of the Connecticut congregational club, including the general list. 3549
List of books by Catholic authors in the Grand Rapids public library. 868
List of books intended as an aid in the selection of a pastor's library. 3627
List of churches. 3323
List of Danteiana in American libraries. 1402
List of editions of the Holy Scriptures. 212
List of missions and missionaries. 33

List of officials, civil, military, and ecclesiastical of Connecticut colony, from March 1636 through 11 October 1677, and of New Haven colony throughout its separate existence. 1346
List of outstanding religious books. 3203
List of periodicals and other serial publications which have been indexed in current indexes or bibliographies, pertinent to theological or philosophical research. 2819
List of periodicals in the New York public library, General theological seminary, and Union theological seminary, relating to religion, theology, and church history. 3678
List of persons admitted to the order of deacons in the Protestant Episcopal church. 2957
List of photographic reproductions of mediaeval manuscripts in the library of the Pontifical institute of mediaeval studies. 2330
... List of references on the history of the reformation in Germany. 3040
List of references on the Pilgrim Fathers. 2847
List of th4 Catholic books. 868
List of the Catholic books in the Pratt free library. 868
List of theses submitted by candidates for the degree of doctor of philosophy in Columbia university from 1872-1910. 1469
... List of works in the library relating to the Mormons. 2608
List of works in the New York public library relating to Muhammadan law. 2564
List of works in the New York public library relating to Shakers. 3397
List of works in the New York public library relating to witchcraft in the United States. 3828
... List of works relating to witchcraft in Europe. 3825
Listen! 63, 1056
Listen, are you sure you are listening? 165
Listen for a rainbow. 1439
Listen, humanity. 2400
Listen, look, and live. 109
Listen: metaphysics. 2419
Listen, mother of God! 845, 2361
Listen, my children. 73, 906
Listen, Sister. 2581
Listen, Sister Superior. 2581
Listen, the clams are talking. 2393
Listen, the Lord. 121
Listen to God. 1315
Listen to the animals. 900
Listen to the drums. 2710
Listen to the silence. 2391
Listen to the sparrow's song. 2676
Listen to the spirit as He speaks to youth. 1829
Listen to the wind. 3354
Listener. 3323
Listener in the church. 3094
Listener's guide to preaching. 2906
Listening. 989
Listening heart. 529, 1440, 2875
"Listening in" on God's radio! 3789
Listening isles. 3807
Listening post. 2769
Listening to God. 3150, 3376
Listening to God on Calvary. 2059
Listening to the church. 1063
Listening to the giants. 213, 1290
Listening to the Master. 383
Listening to the saints. 1456
Listening with the heart. 2871
Lists of deans and major canons of Durham, 1541-1900. 1212, 1412
Lists of words occurring frequently in the Hebrew Bible. 1797
Litany and the life. 2960
Litany at Nazareth. 2362
Litany for all souls. 25
Litany of Loreto. 2363
Litany of Our Lady. 857, 2362, 2363
Litany of Our Lady for boys and girls. 741, 2353
Litany of Our Lady for children. 741
Litany of Re. 3014
Literacy, Bible reading, and church growth through the ages. 613, 2526
Literal reprint of the Bay Psalm book. 581
Literary and educational writings. 1526
Literary and miscellaneous scrap book. 3199
Literary and philosophical repertory. 2836
Literary approach to the New Testament. 349
Literary aspects of North American mythology. 1902
Literary background of the New Testament. 406

Literary beauty of Ellen G. White's writings. 3811
Literary convert women. 754
Literary criticism for New Testament critics. 349
Literary criticism of the New Testament. 346
Literary criticism of the Old Testament. 563
Literary diary. 3862
Literary function of possessions in Luke-Acts. 426, 2946
Literary genius of the New Testament. 211, 349
Literary genius of the Old Testament. 211, 502
Literary genre midrash. 2462
Literary guide to the Bible. 211, 238, 286
Literary history of early Christianity. 1616
Literary history of religious thought in France. 817
Literary history of Sanskrit Buddhism (from Winternitz, Sylvain Levi, Huber) 3715
Literary history of the Bible. 248
Literary impact of The golden bough. 1652
Literary interpretations of Biblical narratives. 210
Literary life of the early Friends, 1650-1725. 1676
Literary lineage of the King James Bible, 1340-1611. 248
Literary origin of the Gospel of John. 421
...The literary primacy of the Bible. 210
Literary remains. 492
Literary remains of Henry James. 3199
... Literary selections from Newman. 2704
Literary study of the Bible. 211
Literary style of the old Bible and the new. 314
Literary style of the prophetic books of the English Bible. 270
Literary survey of the Bible. 312
Literary treasures of the Bible. 211
Literature. 2232
Literature & dogma. 229, 230
Literature and evil. 1578
Literature and occult tradition. 2733
Literature and religion. 3071
Literature and the Christian life. 1077, 3552
Literature and the Gospel: Biblical norms for literature. 211
Literature, arts, and religion. 84, 89
Literature as Christian comedy. 1017
Literature evangelism. 1554
Literature evangelism; a manual. 1571
Literature from the Bible. 308
Literature from the New Testament. 320
Literature in the Bible. 211
Literature of belief. 3268
Literature of possibility. 1583
Literature of the Bible. 198, 211, 309
Literature of the Disciples. 1463
Literature of the Disciples of Christ. 1462
Literature of the doctrine of a future life. 1698
Literature of the English Bible. 312
Literature of the New Testament. 321, 410, 411
Literature of the Old Testament. 500, 538, 540
... The literature of the Old Testament in its historical development. 538
Literature of the second century. 1099
Literature of theology. 3626
Literature, religion and society in Wales, 1660-1730. 1021
Lithuanian catechism of Baltramiejus Vilentas. 748, 2284
Lithuanian Hasidism. 1789
Lithuanian pioneer priest of New England. 1294, 3891
Little altar boy's manual. 27
Little Annie's first thoughts about God. 2976
Little Arthur. 2865
Little beggars of Christ. 2233
Little Benjamin and the first Christmas. 2022
Little Bible. 250
Little blossoms of love, kindness, and obedience, scattered during a lifetime in honor of Our Immaculate Mother. 3416
Little boat that almost sank. 3532
"The little book" 199, 1232
Little book, a ticket to heaven. 1792
Little book of college prayers. 3756
Little book of comfort. 1351
Little book of contemplation. 3477
Little book of eternal wisdom and Little book of truth. 2647
Little book of faith. 249
*Little book of favorite hymns and carols (A) 1866
Little book of life after death. 1887

Little book of prayer. 2889
Little book of prayers. 2887, 2893
Little book of prayers and graces. 900
Little book of proverbs. 482
Little book of Psalms. 573
Little book of sermons. 2425
Little book on Christian charity. 2265
Little book on religion (for people who are not religious) 3063
Little book open A prophecy: or, Prophetical dissertation. 606
Little boy Jesus. 1996
Little boy of Nazareth. 1996
Little boy Samuel. 495, 634, 3297
Little boys of the Bible. 898
Little breviary. 2239
Little Brother Francis of Assisi. 1644
Little brown babe. 2489
Little brown church of the air. 3337
Little buds for Jesus' garden. 3206
Little builders. 1015
Little casket of precious jewels. 3095
Little catechism of liturgy. 770
Little Catherine of the miraculous medal. 2190, 2478
Little Catholic catechism. 770
... A little Catholic honeycomb. 787
Little Catholic's choral. 916
Little chaplet for the Queen of angels. 2360
Little child. 2022
Little child and his crayon. 1479
Little child at the breakfast table. 900
Little child in Sunday school. 3565
Little child shall lead them. 483
Little children, come unto me. 2891
*Little children praise the Lord. 3192
Little children, sing to God! 3563
Little children's Bible. 250, 252, 618
Little children's praises. 3560
...The little children's world. 3765
Little child's first communion. 1626
Little child's life of Jesus. 1973
Little church. 3601
Little church around the corner. 1848, 2697
Little clay cart. 1897
Little clay cart [Mrcchakatika]. 1897
Little companion to the Psalter in the Prayer book version. 1215
Little David. 633, 1406
Little dictionary of Bible phrases. 243
Little drummer boy. 741
Little Episcopalian. 1705, 2965
Little Eppie. 2915
Little evils that lay waste life. 3353
Little flock in the last days. 3095
Little flower and the blessed sacrament. 2251, 3690
Little flower of Carmel. 3691
Little flower prayer. 854
Little flower prayer book. 855
Little Flower treasure. 854
"The little flowers" 1641
Little flowers of Saint Catherine of Siena. 3284
Little flowers of St. Francis; the mirror of perfection. 1641
Little flowers of St. Francis. The mirror of perfection. St. Bonventure's Life of St. Francis. 1641
Little folks' hour. 3207
... Little folks of the Bible. 897
Little folks' story of the apostles. 75
Little foxes. 3369
Little foxes that hurt. 985
Little foxes that spoil the vines. 3411
Little friar who flew. 1028, 1715
Little friends of Jesus. 1979
Little girl that once was I. 3125
Little gold pieces. 178
Little golden Christmas manger. 2023
Little Gospel. 3289
Little "harmless" manifesto. 2391
Little helper. 744
Little hunchback girl of Korea. 2490
Little is much when God is in it. 1445
Little Jetts Bible. 601
Little Jetts telling Bible stories for young folks. 314
Little Jetts youth talks. 688
Little journey to France. 1638
Little journey to France and Switzerland. 1638
Little journeys in His kingdom. 1005, 1185
Little journeys on Highway 10. 1315
Little journeys to the homes of great teachers. 2621
Little journeys to the homes of the great. 660
Little journeys with Martin Luther. 2274
Little key of heaven. 857, 858
Little kit of teachers' tools. 3179
Little-known women of the Bible. 3839
Little known young people of the Bible. 897

Little lessons to live by. 906
Little letters to God. 1452
Little library of inspiration for Sunday school teachers. 3550
Little lives of the great saints. 3281
Little liturgy. 2258
Little lost lamb. 2260
Little lower than the angels. 2138, 2934
Little malice in Blunderland. 2788
Little man from Jericho. 3891
Little manual of devotion, to the Sacred heart of Jesus. A.M.D.G. 2265
Little manual of our Lady of perpetual help. 2362
Little manual of St. Anthony of Padua. 54
Little manual of St. Rita. 3238
Little manual of the Sacred heart. 3269
Little manual of the Sodality of the Blessed Virgin Mary. 843, 2356
Little manual of the Third order of St. Francis. 1649
Little Marcy's favorite Bible stories. 616
Little Mary, an illustration of the power of Jesus to save even the youngest. 1713
Little Mary's first going to church. 2964
Little me and the great me. 902
Little meditations on the Holy Eucharist. 2258
Little messages for shut-in folk. 1017
Little missionary. 2216
Little missionary truck that could do anything. 1800, 2487
Little month of the holy infancy. 1825
Little Nellie of Holy God. 2251, 3140
Little office of Our Lady of Mount Carmel. 1848
Little office of the Blessed Virgin Mary, in English. 847
Little Office of the Blessed Virgin Mary. 847
Little Office of the Blessed Virgin Mary according to the Roman Breviary. 848
Little Office of the Blessed Virgin Mary, in Latin and English, according to the Roman breviary. 847
Little office of the immaculate conception. 1886
Little one. 3690
Little ones listen to God. 621
Little Owl. 1503
Little Palestinian New Year's festival. 3577
Little patron of gardeners. 1627
Little people. 1255
Little people's paperbacks. 3163
Little pillows. 1447
Little prayer. 898
Little prayers for little people. 902
Little prayers for personal poise. 2895
Little prayers for stressful times. 2890
Little preacher. 1821
Little queen. 3691
Little red wonder book. 3172
Little Rossie. 2820
Little St. Alphonsus' manual. 855
Little Saint Elizabeth. 1508
Little saint of nine years. 2200
Little Saint Therese. 3691
Little sayings of the saints. 2394
Little sections of a big job. 1550
Little seeds of wisdom. 2395
Little selection of choice poetry new and old, doctrinal and devotional. 1866, 3398
Little sermons from the Pentateuch. 595
Little sermons on sin. 2263
Little sermons on sin; the archpriest of Talavera. 2263
Little sermons on the catechism. 746
Little shepherd of Provence. 1453
Little sister. 2194
Little sister missionary. 2335
Little steps to great holiness. 2570
Little stories about God. 622
Little stories of Christ's miracles. 2006
Little talks on great words. 1449
Little talks to boys and girls. 901
"Little ten-minutes" 906
Little Teny of Nigeria. 2490
Little Therese. 3690
Little things in the hands of a big God. 932, 3005
Little things that keep families together. 1610
Little threads, and other object lessons for children. 908
Little town of Bethlehem. 2023
Little valleys. 2388
Little visits with God. 1605
Little wanderers' friend. 1865
Little ways. 3284
Little white book. 3880
"A little white flower," the story of Saint Therese of Lisieux. 3691
Little white shepherdess. 2811
Little world of home. 1610
Littlest angel. 3591

Littleton Fowler. 1636, 2453
Liturgen historica. 836
Liturgical books. 844
Liturgical celebration. 9, 2211, 2259
Liturgical change, how much do we need? 2236
Liturgical choral service for the Easter season. 1486
Liturgical conflict and the peace movement of the Reformed church in the United States as exhibited by the official records of the General synod. 3048
...Liturgical dictionary. 843
Liturgical education. 836
Liturgical experience of faith. 2235
Liturgical feasts and seasons. 1613
Liturgical handbook for Holy Mass. 2364
Liturgical homiletic aids for cycle A. 862, 1266
Liturgical-homiletic aids for cycle B. 862, 1266
Liturgical-homiletic aids for cycle C. 862, 1266
Liturgical homilies of Narsai. 2684
Liturgical initiation. 840
Liturgical interpretation of Our Lord's Passion in narrative form. 2030
Liturgical law. 836
Liturgical law, its spirit and practice. 735, 840
Liturgical manuscripts for the Mass and the Divine Office. 841
Liturgical meditations for the entire year. 1263, 1264
Liturgical movement. 2234
Liturgical movement and the local church. 2234
Liturgical piety. 836
Liturgical prayer, its history & spirit. 836
Liturgical preludes. 1264
Liturgical reconnaissance. 2294
Liturgical renaissance in the Roman Catholic Church. 2234
Liturgical renewal; an agonizing reappraisal. 2239
Liturgical renewal in the Christian churches. 3855
Liturgical renewal of the church. 2233
Liturgical renewal of the church; addresses by Theodore Otto Wedel [and others]. 2233
Liturgical retreat. 3222
Liturgical sacrifice of the new law. 2366
Liturgical seasons of the year. 1262
Liturgical sermonettes for children's mass on Sundays of the ecclesiastical year. 865
Liturgical sermons. 863, 1266
Liturgical services. 1223
Liturgical studies [of] E. C. Ratcliff. 2235
Liturgical terms for music students. 1206
Liturgical vesture. 1249
Liturgical vesture, its origins and development. 1249
Liturgical worship. 838
Liturgical year. 842, 1261, 1262
La liturgie, magie, spectacle ou action divine? 836
Liturgies, eastern and western. 2237
Liturgies eastern and western, being the texts. 2237
Liturgies for little ones. 905
Liturgies in a time when cities burn. 2238
Liturgies of S. Mark, S. James, S. Clement, S. Chrysostom, and the Church of Malabar. 2748
Liturgies of S. Mark, S. James, S. Clement, S. Chrysostom, S. Basil. 2239
Liturgies of the past. 2237
Liturgies of the Primatial sees. 838, 849
Liturgies of the religious orders. 838
Liturgies of the Western church. 2238
Liturgies of the Word for Children. 905
Liturgikon. 2238
Liturgy. 836, 848, 2237, 2370, 3048, 3049
Liturgy and architecture. 1156, 2240
Liturgy and art. 921
Liturgy and Catechism of the Eastern Orthodox Church in Albanian and English. 2745
Liturgy and Christian life. 837
Liturgy and Christian unity. 3855
Liturgy and contemplation. 1355
Liturgy and cultural religious traditions. 2235
Liturgy and doctrine. 2234
Liturgy and education. 2969
Liturgy and human passage. 3239
Liturgy and hymns. 1873
Liturgy and hymns for Sunday-schools. 3563
Liturgy and hymns for the use of the Protestant church of the United Brethren. 2594
Liturgy and hymns for the use of the Protestant church of the United brethren, or Unitas fratrum. 2594

Liturgy and hymns for use of the Protestant church of the United brethren, or Moravians. 1867
Liturgy and hymns of the American province of the Unitas fratrum, or the Moravian church. 2594
Liturgy and learning through the life cycle. 2235
Liturgy and life. 841, 2294
Liturgy and literature. 2240
... Liturgy and personality. 838, 841
Liturgy and ritual of the ante-Nicene church. 2239
Liturgy and ritual of the Celtic church. 878
Liturgy and social justice. 760, 2235
Liturgy and spirituality. 836, 839
Liturgy and the Christian faith. 2235, 2238
Liturgy and the future. 837
Liturgy and the laity. 2234
Liturgy and the missions. 843
Liturgy and the Word of God. 315
Liturgy and unity in Christ. 1249
Liturgy and word of God. 2240
Liturgy and worship. 1213
Liturgy begins at home. 2235
Liturgy coming to life. 2257
Liturgy constitution. 3773
Liturgy constitution (The) 3773
Liturgy for Christian congregations of the Lutheran faith. 2295
Liturgy for living. 2235, 2969
Liturgy for the General church of the New Jerusalem. 2689
Liturgy for the people. 841, 1508
Liturgy for the use of the church at King's chapel in Boston. 1864
Liturgy, Gospels and Epistles of the English evangelical Lutheran church in New York. 1545
Liturgy in development. 841
Liturgy in English. 2257
Liturgy in focus. 840
Liturgy in parish life. 2235, 2236
Liturgy in transition. 2234
Liturgy is mission. 2233
Liturgy made simple. 836
Liturgy needs community needs liturgy. 2237
Liturgy of Holy Week. 1837
Liturgy of penance. 2811
Liturgy of St. John Chrysostom, Ruthenian form. 766
Liturgy of St. John Chrysostom, Ruthenian form; historical background, introd., and commentary by Basil Shereghy. 766
Liturgy of the church. 839
Liturgy of the Church of England before and after the reformation. 2963
Liturgy of the Church of Scotland since the Reformation. 1234
Liturgy of the Church of South India. 1235
Liturgy of the Evangelical Lutheran church. 2294
Liturgy of the Eastern Orthodox church. 2748
...The liturgy of the eighty book of 'The Apostolic constitutions. 2239
Liturgy of the Holy Apostles Adai and Mari. 2684
Liturgy of the hours. 756, 1471
Liturgy of the Mass. 2367
Liturgy of the primitive church. 2238
Liturgy of the Reformed Church in America. 2238
Liturgy of the Reformed Protestant Dutch church in North America. 3050
Liturgy of the Roman Church. 839
Liturgy of the Roman rite. 838
Liturgy of the word in Lent. 863, 2214
Liturgy of Vatican II. 836
Liturgy, or. 3049
Liturgy, or forms of divine service, of the French Protestant church. 1852
Liturgy, our school of faith. 836, 3485
Liturgy revived. 3773
Liturgy: self-expression of the church. 2235
Liturgy, the art of worship. 843
... Liturgy the life of the church. 836
Liturgy today and tomorrow. 2235
Liturgy; worship and work. 2929, 3854
Liturgical renewal and Catholic devotion. 2240
Liu Li Ho. 2539
Live all your life. 3674
Live and help live. 973
Live and prove! 1446
Live, Christian, live! 983
Live coals. 2395
Live coals from dead hearths. 1004
Live confidently. 994
Live for tomorrow. 976
Live happily with the woman you love. 2337

Live happily with yourself. 984
Live in hope. 1002
Live in the Holy Spirit. 2573
Live in the spirit. 3483
Live it up! 2694, 3880
Live like a king. 181
Live, love and learn. 1451
Live out your years. 2735
"Live power": a text-book on absolute
 sceince (the allness of God) 2696
Live sermon outlines. 3374
Live to win. 3885
Live today. 1434
Live until you die. 1414
Live with your emotions. 1512
Live your faith! 993
... Live your life. 967
Live your vocation. 2571
Live youthfully now. 3750
Lively corpse. 3762
Lively debate. 664
Lively experiment. 3739
Lively function of the Gospel. 3619
Lively may I walk. 17
Lively oracles. 2669, 2740
Lively recollections. 1215
Lively skeleton. 3372
Lively tradition. 2136
Lively youth meetings. 1260
Lives and legends of the Georgian saints.
 3283
Lives and legends of the Georgian saints,
 selected and translated from the original
 texts. 3283
Lives and times of the popes. 2862
Lives entwined. 1711
Lives He touched. 338, 929, 2013
Lives in the making. 2591
Lives of Ange de Joyeuse and Benet
 Canfield. 2136
Lives of Christian ministers. 1705
Lives of church leaders. 926
Lives of Clemens Romanus, Ignatius, and
 Polycarp. 1287
Lives of Doctor Faust. 1619
Lives of eminent Christians of various
 denominations. 923
Lives of eminent Korean monks. 706
Lives of eminent Methodist ministers.
 2427
Lives of English laymen, Lord Falkland,
 Izaak Walton, Robert Nelson. 1602
Lives of four martyrs of Tonkin who
 belonged to the Dominican province of
 the Holy rosary in the Philippine islands.
 2351
Lives of four martyrs of Tonkin who
 belonged to the Dominican province of
 the Holy rosary in the Philippine Islands;
 beatified the 20th of May, 1906. 2350
Lives of great missionaries for young
 people. 2483
Lives of Increase Mather and Sir William
 Phipps. 2373
Lives of John Trueman and Richard
 Atkins. 131
Lives of Methodist bishops. 2427
Lives of Mrs. Ann H. Judson and Mrs.
 Sarah B. Judson. 2157
Lives of Mrs. Ann H. Judson, Mrs. Sarah
 B. Judson and Mrs. Emily C. Judson,
 missionaries to Burmah. 2157
Lives of Philip and Matthew Henry. 1803
Lives of Saint Thomas More. 2596
... The lives of St. Thomas of Villanova,
 archbishop of Valentia, and Augustinian
 friar. 3704
Lives of saints. 3281
Lives of saints, with excerpts from their
 writings. 3281
Lives of the ancient philosophers. 2832
Lives of the apostles and evangelists. 71
Lives of the apostles of Jesus Christ. 70
Lives of the bishops of North Carolina
 from the establishment the episcopate in
 that state down to the division of the
 diocese. 667
Lives of the British reformers. 3037
Lives of the clergy of New York and
 Brooklyn. 1294
Lives of the deceased bishops of the
 Catholic church in the United States.
 667
Lives of the deceased bishops of the
 Catholic church of the United States.
 829
Lives of the English cardinals, including
 historical notices of the papal court. 738
Lives of the English martyrs. 872
Lives of the Fathers. 1616, 3282
Lives of the holy evangelists, and apostles.
 70
Lives of the leaders of our church
 universal. 926
Lives of the necromancers. 2312, 2313
Lives of the noble Grecian and Romans.
 1765

Lives of the popes in the early Middle
 Ages. 2861
Lives of the prophets. 568
Lives of the saints. 1024, 3279, 3280,
 3282, 3283, 3284
Lives of the saints, for boys and girls.
 3284
Lives of the saints for every day of the
 year. 3281
Lives of the saints, with reflections for
 every day in the year. 3279
... Lives of the Serbian saints. 3285
Lives of the twelve apostles. 70, 338
Lives of the twelve apostles of Jesus die.
 1462

Lives of Virginia Baptist ministers. 172
Lives, sentiments and sufferings of some of
 the reformers and martyrs before, since
 and independent of the Lutheran
 reformation. 924
Lives that glorify God. 1434
Lives that inspire. 661
Lives that lift. 662
Lives that oft remind us. 492
Lives that praise God. 3191
Lives unlimited; reincarnation East and
 West. 3052
Lives worth living. 3840
Living. 648
Living a thousand lives. 2392
"Living above" 960, 1445
...Living abundantly. 1456, 3528
...Living again. 1887
Living all your life. 973
Living and active word. 298, 2899, 2973
Living and active word of God. 239, 3311
Living & dying gracefully. 1413
Living and dying unto the Lord. 3300
Living and growing through the Eucharist.
 2255
Living and growing together. 1604
Living and learning. 900
Living and learning in the church school.
 3146
Living & loving. 3391
Living and working in our country. 3453
Living and working together as Christians.
 1015, 3764
Living animals of the Bible. 481
Living art of worship. 3852
Living as comrades. 1321
Living as disciples. 1005
... Living at our best. 1324, 1325
Living at peace in a turbulent world. 166
Living atonement. 104
Living between two worlds. 3478
Living beyond depression. 932, 2713
Living Bible. 250, 251, 541, 613, 653
Living Bible, chapter by chapter. 613
Living Bible concordance. 228
Living Bible concordance complete. 228
Living Bible, paraphrased. 601
Living Bible stories. 622
Living biographies of religious leaders.
 3090, 3134, 3136
Living Book in a living age. 214
Living books of Moses. 565
Living bread. 2255
Living bread, and other communion
 addresses. 1318
Living bread from the fourth Gospel. 389
Living Buddha. 704, 1703
Living Buddhist masters. 2382
Living by faith. 404, 405, 1597
Living by grace. 2160
Living by the day. 725
Living by the spirit. 1835
Living by Zen. 3895
Living can be exciting. 969, 1342
Living centennial. 3797
Living Christ. 163, 1891, 2020, 2039,
 2047
... The living Christ and dying heathenism.
 2522
Living Christ and some problems of to-
 day. 1017
Living Christ for Latin America. 2548
Living Christ in our changing world. 3645
Living Christ in the life of today. 167
Living Christ in the world fellowship of
 religious education. 3560
Living Christ, the vital force in pulpit and
 pew. 1069
Living Christian community. 3485
Living Christian Science. 1037
Living Christianity. 979, 997, 3667
Living church. 665, 1119, 3770
Living churches. 2264
Living close to God. 971
Living commandments. 1315
Living community. 2570
Living courageously. 508, 3445
Living creatively. 3364
Living dangerously. 956
Living decalogue. 1313
Living divine love. 3487

Living doctrine in a vital pulpit. 2896
Living doctrines of the New Testament.
 476
Living earth manual of feng-shui. 1621
Living echoes. 2936
Living end. 608
...Living epistles. 144
Living eternally. 415
Living evangelism. 1565
Living every day. 725
Living faith. 404, 405, 960, 1594, 1595,
 2081, 2818, 3249, 3350, 3371, 3383
Living faith for today. 2931
Living faith in a world of change. 987
Living faith (The) 769
Living faithfully. 326
Living faiths and ultimate goals. 3294
Living fire, the soul power of the universe.
 1452
Living flame of love. 2642
Living for a living Lord. 3842
Living for Christ. 968, 1328
Living for God. 1000, 3374
Living for Jesus. 1015, 1017
Living for the best. 967
Living for the future. 1697
Living forever. 3262
Living fountain. 1632, 2299
Living free. 931, 1378
Living goals for everyone. 3330
Living God. 65, 1720, 1722, 1729, 3121,
 3123
Living God and the modern world. 3644,
 3813
Living God of nowhere and nothing. 1058
Living God. Translated by Stanley
 Godman. 1722
Living God's joy. 2135
Living God's love. 2264
Living God's way. 3480
Living God's will. 982
Living Gospels. 383
Living happily ever after. 2339, 2343
Living helps for preacher and people.
 3374
Living heritage, 1871-1971. 195
Living His theme song. 1700
Living history of Israel. 531
Living hope. 447
Living hymns. 1871
Living hymns of Charles Wesley. 1860
Living hymns of Charles Wesley. The
 singing saint [by] Bishop Leslie R.
 Marston. Hymns that are immortal [by]
 Bishop W. T. Hogue. Hynn Poems [by]
 Charles Wesley. 1860
Living in both worlds. 181
Living in Christ. 862, 864, 1015, 2722,
 3191, 3481
Living in Christian community. 933
Living in covenant with God. 1452
Living in depth. 2932
Living in four dimensions. 961
Living in God. 3485
Living in God's family. 904
Living in His love. 3490
Living in hope. 1845
Living in hope of eternal life; an exposition
 of the Book of Titus. 479
Living in kingdom come. 1447
Living in love. 216, 2341
Living in our community. 3764
Living in our finest hour. 982
Living in tents. 162
Living in the Christian community. 3174
Living in the church. 2965, 3171
Living in the currents of God. 954, 3347
Living in the eye of a hurricane. 3376
Living in the kingdom here and now. 985
Living in the light of the Cross. 2436
Living in the Lord. 138, 794
Living in the now. 3626
Living in the presence of God. 992
Living in the shadow of the Second
 Coming. 2464
Living in the Spirit. 139, 2814, 3484
Living in the sunshine. 975
Living in two worlds. 2422
Living is now. 981
Living issues in religious thought from
 George Fox to Bertrand Russell. 1067,
 3213
Living issues in the New Testament. 477,
 2043
Living Jesus. 3518
Living Jewish. 2119
Living joyously. 1441
Living Judaism. 4, 2115, 2144
Living landscape. 1072
Living languages in Catholic worship.
 2233
Living largely. 724
Living leaders. 2204
Living legacy. 1780, 2143
Living letter for the children's hour. 471,
 977
Living letters. 358

Living life. 1576
Living light. 3167
Living light: daily light in today's
 language. 1431
Living liturgy. 837, 2969
Living loving generation. 3880
Living, loving way. 994
Living Lutheran leadership. 1253
Living marriage. 2340
Living martyr and the unholy alliance. 22,
 3522
Living Mass. 2368
Living memorials. 1168
Living message of Isaiah. 543
Living messages from Jonah. 2130
Living messages from the Canaan 9
 journey. 2434
Living messages of the books of the Bible.
 235, 600
Living metals. 2416
Living miracles. 966, 1362
Living mission. 2554
Living more simply. 3409
Living my religion on my job. 3849
Living my religion series. 132, 3188
Living New Testament. 357, 445
Living now. 2694
Living obediently. 552
Living of the gospel. 3465
Living of these days. 144
Living on. 1694
Living on less and liking it more. 984,
 1372
Living on the growing edge. 1011
Living on the plus side. 985
Living on tiptoe. 963, 1007, 1605
Living options in Protestant theology.
 2976
Living options in world philosophy. 2833
Living or dead? 974
Living our commitment. 2569
... Living our faith. 3186
Living our future: Francis of Assisi and the
 Church tomorrow. 1641
Living out God's love. 1243
Living papers on present day themes. 60
Living parables. 2026
Living parish. 2774, 2775
Living patiently. 548
Living peacefully. 320
Living personalities of the Old Testament.
 494
Living Peter. 2123
Living pictures in the great drama of the
 19th century. 6, 129
"Living pictures" of Bible stories. 616
Living portraits. 3839
Living portraits of Jesus. 1999
Living positively one day at a time. 1433
Living ppsalms and Proverbs with the
 major prophets, paraphrased by Kenneth
 N. Taylor. 581
Living prayerfully. 1441
Living presence. 2252
Living presence of the past. 3706
Living present and the dead past. 1729
Living priesthood. 1291, 1824
Living promises. 995
Living proof. 931, 2306
Living prophecies. 570
Living prophecies; the Minor prophets
 paraphrased with Daniel and the
 Revelation. 508
Living prophets. 2299
Living Psalms and Proverbs with the major
 prophets. 570, 586
Living pulpit. 195, 2936
Living questions to dead Gods. 1721
Living quotations for Christians. 3014
Living reflections. 2384
Living reliantly. 587
Living religion. 963, 1097
Living religions. 91, 3119
Living religions and a world faith. 3141
Living religions and modern thought.
 3122
Living religions of the Middle East. 2139
Living religions of the world. 3118, 3121
Living reminder. 1299
Living right side up. 3336
Living roots of reformation. 1858, 2282
Living sacrifice. 105, 1348, 2210, 2488,
 3249
Living sacrifice, holy, acceptable unto God:
 Anne Clara Chrisman. 918
Living sacrifices. 3
Living saints witness at work. 1009, 3215
Living Saviour. 2063
Living schools of religion. 3115
Living scriptures. 1010
Living sermons. 1210
Living shadows (Ramayana) 1812
Living simply. 991
Living simply through the day. 2379
Living sisters of the Little flower. 3690
Living soul; "we shall overcome" 3350,
 3387

Living source. 3785
Living springs. 2583
Living springs: new religious movements in Western Europe. 2583
Living stone. 3155
Living stones. 989
Living stories of famous hymns. 1875
Living story of Jesus. 1991
Living story of the New Testament. 406
Living story of the Old Testament. 533
Living symbols, past and present. 2234
Living Talmud. 3, 4
Living Tao. 3586
Living temple. 674, 923, 1118, 1123, 3599
Living temples. 1448
Living thankfully. 3264
Living that counts. 413
Living the adventure. 986
Living the Bible with children. 638, 903
Living the Biblical story. 649
Living the Catholic faith today. 1003
Living the celibate life. 877
Living the Christ-filled life. 3483
Living the Christ life. 976
Living the Christian faith. 3617
Living the Christian life. 959, 967, 1000
Living the Christian seasons. 1613
Living the Eucharistic mystery. 2255
Living the faith. 1219
Living the great adventure. 1014
Living the incarnation. 1015
Living the infinite way. 2694
Living the interior life. 1885
Living the life eternal. 1450
Living the liturgy. 838, 2294
Living the Lord's prayer. 2249
Living the love of God. 992
Living the Mass. 2365
Living the more abundant life. 1604
Living the new life. 3660
Living the spirit-filled life. 3484
Living the Ten commandments. 1314
Living theology in Asia. 3653
Living thought of Saint Paul. 374
Living thoughts for the children's hour. 904
Living thoughts of Cardinal Newman. 776
Living thoughts of Saint Paul. 375, 2795
Living through loving. 445
Living through these days. 964
Living to beat hell! 765
Living to Christ. 1305
Living to win. 3751
... Living to-day and to-morrow. 3146
Living today for God. 2571
Living together. 174, 1070, 2816, 3553
Living together alone. 3144
Living together as boys. 686
Living together as Christians. 733
Living together in a world falling apart. 933
Living together in Christian homes. 1611
... Living together in today's world. 3453
Living Torah. 562
Living toward a vision. 992, 3349, 3732
Living toward mastership. 3494
Living tradition. 3667
Living triumphantly. 3433
Living truths. 1004
Living truths from the Doctrine and covenants. 2608
Living unafraid. 585, 985
Living under tension. 3351
Living universe. 1128
Living up to life. 1441
Living victoriously. 448
Living victoriously; a devotional study of Philippians. 449
Living vistas. 2391
Living water. 858, 997, 1452, 3184
Living waters. 3506
Living way. 955, 1099
Living way commentary on the Old Testament. 498
Living Wesley. 3804
Living when a loved one has died. 1774
Living where Jesus lived. 2763
Living wisdom from the world's religions. 3204
Living wisely. 323
Living with ambiguity. 997
Living with anxiety. 986
Living with Christ. 3187
Living with Christ in God. 996
Living with death. 1417
Living with God. 1001, 2877
Living with God in my heart. 2393
Living with guilt. 1777
Living with joy. 2392
Living with love. 2395
Living with magic. 2312
Living with my Lord. 966
Living with myself. 1324
Living with other people. 3185
Living with our children. 3170
Living with peace of mind. 681
Living with purpose. 1016

Living with royalty. 492
Living with the Bible. 533, 1407, 3525
Living with the church. 838, 1126, 3181
Living with the gospel. 2065
Living with the Himalayan masters. 3020, 3491
Living with the Psalms. 580
Living with the seven words. 2057
Living with uncertainty. 1325
Living with wonder. 2398, 3819
Living with your feelings. 2434, 3348
Living with your teenager. 7
Living with yourself. 958
Living without fear. 981
Living without gloves. 1070
Living without God, before God. 1065
Living without losing. 2394
Living without strain. 548
Living witness. 1077, 3380
Living witness of John Woolman. 3847
Living witnesses. 1572
Living word. 250, 252, 253, 272, 422, 598, 1055, 1063, 2070, 2907, 3359, 3476, 3848
Living Word in history. 648
Living Word in men's hearts. 83, 980
Living word of the Bible. 279, 3848
Living word; some Bible words explained. 272
Living words. 966, 3752
Living words for today. 1430
Living world of the Bible. 283
Living your faith. 782, 1000
Living your life today. 975
Living Zen. 3894
Living zestfully. 2435
Livingstone in Africa. 2241
Livingstone of South America. 1776, 2547
"Livingstone" of the Orinoco (interior of South America) the life story of Ford Hendrickson (an autobiography) 2558
Livingstone the pathfinder. 2241
Livres de miracles et autres opuscules de Georges Florent Gregoire, eveque de Tours. 2478
Liz. 1454
... Llandaff. 2241
Lo! He is coming! 3207
Lo here and lo there! 3396
Lo, I am with you. 1599
Lo! The bridegroom. 595
Lo! the poor innocents. 307
... Loan exhibition, objects used in religious ceremonies and charms and implements for divination. 3093
Loaves or Stones. 1128
Local chapter hand book of the Kappa sigma pi or Modern knights of St. Paul. 688
Local church and higher education. 1128
Local church and world mission. 2555
Local church cooperation in rural communities. 1321
Local church in Methodism. 2428
Local church in ministry. 2786
Local church in transition. 2787
Local church in transition: theology, education, and ministry. 2787
Local church looks to the future. 1200
Local church manual for the National Christian Teaching Mission. 1568
Local church planning manual. 498
Local religion in sixteenth-century Spain. 825, 3469
Loci communes of Philip Melanchthon. 3646
Loci e Libro veritatum. 1764
Lock and key to understanding. 1035
Locked in a room with open doors. 2930, 3349
Locke's essay concerning human understanding. 2180
... Locke's theory of knowledge. 2180, 2241
Lodge and the craft. 1661
Lodge Kirkwall Kilwinning No. 382. 1665
Lodge manual. 1913
Lodge of Amity, No.5, F. and A. M., Zanesville, Ohio, 1805-1955. 1672
Log book of Noah's ark. 1421
Log cabin to Luther Tower. 1323
Log cabins to steeples. 2431
Logic. 2242
Logic and faith. 3083
Logic and knowledge. 2834
Logic and ontology. 2739
Logic and reason in Christianity. 64
Logic and the cosmic order. 2242
Logic in theology. 3625
Logic of belief. 3106
Logic of Christian evidences. 61
Logic of faith. 1602
Logic of God; theology and verification. 3099
Logic of Gospel criticism. 391
Logic of Hegel. 2242
Logic of Lourdes. 2262

Logic of millennial thought. 461, 2466
Logic of perfection. 1739
Logic of promise in Moltmann's theology. 2568, 2946
Logic of religion. 3070
Logic of Saint Anselm. 49
Logic of self-involvement. 1380
Logic of the Bible. 233
Logic of the Christian faith. 1105
Logic of the faith. 62
Logic of theism. 1613, 3609
Logic of tragedy, and other sermons. 1558
Logical analysis and contemporary theism. 3609
Logical epic. 2470
Die Logoslehre des heiligen Athanasius. 2010, 2242
Loka. 2668
Lollard Bible. 248
Lollard Bible and other medieval Biblical versions. 248, 2243
Lollards of the Chiltern Hills. 2243
Lollardy and the reformation in England. 2243
Lomai of Lenakel. 2542
Lombardic architecture, its origin, development, and derivatives. 79
...London. 2100
London church courts and society on the eve of the Reformation. 1488
London churches at the reformation. 2243
London heretics, 1870-1914. 3212
Lone star. 782, 2530
Lone-star vanguard. 825, 3701
Loneliest journey. 965
Loneliness. 1374, 2244
Loneliness and love. 2265
Loneliness is for loving. 2244
Loneliness is not forever. 2244
Loneliness of man. 2244
Loneliness, the search for intimacy. 2244
Loneliness, the untapped resource. 2245
Loneliness, the world's number one killer. 2245
Lonely, but never alone. 1392, 2244
Lonely God, lonely man. 2244
Lonely heart. 2244
Lonely house. 1350
Lonely now. 3880
Lonergan enterprise. 2245, 3669
Lonergan's challenge to the university and the economy. 1855, 2245
Long ago in Galilee. 2005
Long arm of God. 67
Long distance. 3495
Long distance calling. 3495
"Long distance, please," 3507
Long hot summer of 1912. 2617
Long Island's religious history. 2245
Long loneliness. 1363, 1365, 1407
Long-lost chronicles of Solomon, and poems. 3457
Long obedience in the same direction. 579
Long quest. 3803
Long road to Methodist union. 2440
Long search. 3120
Long shadow. 1778
Long shadows of Lambeth X. 43
Long suffering love. 2266
Long view. 533
Long way home. 1345, 2072
Longer commentary of R. David Kimhi on the first book of Psalms (I-X, XV-XVII, XIX, XXII, XXIV) 576
Longer Epistles of Paul. 467
Longer Mark. 436, 3322
Longest step. 3485
... A Longfellow night. 1017
Long's Bible quiz. 280
Look around, pilgrim. 2390
Look at it this way. 3887
Look at labor. 1131
Look at life after life. 1697
Look at me, please look at me. 1258
Look at Mormonism. 2600, 2618
Look at the book. 242, 638, 1431
Look at the ministry. 1296
Look at the missionary. 2495
Look at the New Testament. 321
Look at the Old Testament. 482
... Look at the "Y"! 3870
Look at today's churches. 1038
Look at us, Lord. 2891
Look at your world. 3493
Look away to Jesus. 1451
Look back in love. 3128
Look back with pride. 2100, 3276
Look deeply. 2894
Look down from above. 3406
Look for me in Heaven. 1301, 1484
Look for the dawn! 164
Look for the living. 2053
Look for the stars. 1353
Look forward in joy. 1001
Look here, Lord. 3843
Look now toward heaven. 1012

Look on the fields. 92
Look out! The Pentecostals are coming. 2814
Look, Sister. 2573
Look south. 2537
Look that redeemed. 2215, 2437
Look through secret doors. 2727
Look through the lens of prophecy. 508
Look to God and live. 2608
Look to the glory. 991
Look to the rock. 46, 1161
Look to the stars. 3069
Look to this day. 1446
Look to your faith. 1452
Look toward the East. 599
Look unto the hills. 1590
Look up! 547
Look up and hope! 682
Look up and hope! the motto of the Volunteer Prison League. 682
Look up and lift up. 2392
Look up and live. 1400, 3144
Look up, brother! 62
Look up, heart. 1015
Look who's coming. 3320
Look within. 2728
Looking at churches. 1158
Looking at learning. 3148
...Looking at life with boys and girls. 3151
Looking at the Episcopal Church. 1524
Looking at the world war through the Scriptures. 605
Looking back from Beulah. 3137
Looking back from the sunset land. 1017
Looking beyond. 1349, 1695
Looking for Jesus. 424
Looking for the King. 2003
Looking-glass. 3133
Looking God's way. 2302
Looking into life. 977
Looking into the future. 1514
Looking inward, looking upward. 18
Looking on Jesus. 1263
Looking south. 2548
Looking to the future. 2240
Looking toward marriage. 2340
Looking toward the council. 3771
Looking towards a Christian China. 2511
Looking unto Him. 1431, 1438
Looking unto Jesus. 2064, 3721
Loom of life. 1451
Loom of many threads. 3378
Loom of Providence. 3354
Looms for sanctity. 996
Loose in the world. 1062
Lord. 1966, 1968
Lord and Giver of life. 1454
Lord and his laity. 2191
Lord, be with. 2889
Lord be with you. 1739
Lord Bishop. 3815
Lord blesses me. 905
Lord Caitanya in five features. 2187
Lord, can we talk this over? 517, 1597, 2621
Lord, change me. 918, 982
Lord cometh! 3320
Lord for the body. 2410
Lord for the body, with questions and answers on divine healing. 1600
Lord from heaven. 2035, 2041
Lord, "give me this mountain" 2310, 2486
Lord God of Elijah. 1582
Lord God of truth within. 2727
Lord Halifax. 1781
Lord, have Murphy! 2387
Lord, have You got a minute? 2385
Lord Herbert of Cherbum's De religione laici. 1419, 1804
"Lord, how will you get me out of this mess?" 88, 1744
Lord I believe. 1446
Lord, I have a question. 1714
Lord, I want to have a quiet time. 645
Lord, I want to tell you something. 688
Lord, I'm back again. 911
Lord, I'm glad You know the way. 2393
Lord, I'm listening. 985
Lord is—. 169, 588, 1446
'Lord, is it I? 1012
Lord is King. 508
Lord is my counsel. 720
Lord is my joy. 3487
Lord is my shepherd. 318, 577, 587, 588, 617, 1017, 3014
Lord is my shepherd and he knows I'm gay. 1844
Lord is my shepherd, but. 965
Lord is our healer. 1599
Lord, it's me again. 2896
Lord, I've been thinking. 688
Lord Jesus. 1983, 2063
Lord Jesus says. 2066, 3163
Lord, let me love. 2267
Lord, let them know I care. 2890
"Lord! Lord!" 2722
Lord loves His people. 582

Lord, make my life a miracle! 1004
Lord may be in a hurry. 1475
Lord my light. 761
Lord of all. 1340
Lord of all good life. 1050, 1952
Lord of all life. 2930
Lord of glory. 2020, 2063
Lord of history. 1100, 1818, 1820, 2040
Lord of life. 1953, 1994
Lord of life and death. 2040, 2214
Lord of love. 1985
Lord of possibilities. 2017
Lord of the absurd. 3623
Lord of the dance. 1400
Lord of the four quarters. 2177
Lord of the harvest. 1830, 2119
Lord of the morning. 2895
Lord of the mountain. 2213, 2298
Lord of the Second Advent. 931, 3722
Lord of the sky: Zeus. 3895
Lord of the Temple. 476
Lord of the valleys. 2409
Lord of the young crowd. 3883
Lord of thought. 2037
Lord of time and space. 3469
Lord, open the heavens! 3232
Lord our Shepherd. 574, 588
Lord Protector. 1387, 1764
Lord reigneth. 453
Lord rules—let's serve Him. 585
"Lord, save us...." 1299
Lord shall preserve, and Treasures out of
the darkness. 1351
Lord, show us your face. 2210
Lord, sometimes I need help! 982
Lord speaketh. 2601
Lord, teach me your ways. 1005
Lord, teach us how to pray. 2872
"Lord, teach us to pray" 2247, 2870,
2875, 2887
Lord we love. 1976
Lord, what are you doing next Tuesday?
2386
Lord will provide. 2423
Lord, your servant listens. 2389
Lord your shepherd. 588
Lord's coming and the world's end. 3320
... The Lord's command to baptise. 138
Lord's Day. 1264, 3260
Lord's day evening sermons. 1210
Lord's day, from neither Catholics nor
pagans. 3379
Lord's Day not a Sabbath Day. 3547
Lord's day on a round world. 3260, 3261
... The Lord's day--or man's? 3547
Lord's day rescued. 1017
Lord's day worship services for the aid of
the smaller churches. 1461
Lord's free people in a free land. 171
Lord's horseman. 3803
Lord's men. 2402
Lord's men: meditations for men in the
world of work. 2402
Lord's minstrel. 1640
Lords of the ghostland. 3120
Lord's passover. 1997, 3720
Lord's prayer. 2210, 2246, 2247, 2248,
2249, 2250
Lord's prayer, an interpretation. 2246
Lord's prayer and Christian living. 2247
Lord's Prayer and Jewish liturgy. 2109,
2153, 2248
Lord's prayer, and other talks on prayer.
2246
Lord's prayer and the Christian life. 2246
Lord's prayer and the Hail Mary. 2246
Lord's prayer and the Lord's Passion.
2249
Lord's prayer comes alive. 2246
Lord's prayer for children. 2249
Lord's prayer for today, together with
other choice portions of Holy Scriptures.
251
Lord's prayer in a series of mystery
dramas. 2248
Lord's Prayer in daily life. 2246
Lord's prayer in its Biblical setting. 2247
Lord's prayer in practice. 2248
Lord's prayer in the Bible. 2247
Lord's prayer in the early church. 2246
Lord's prayer in the principal languages.
2247
Lord's prayer pictured for children. 2249
Lord's prayer (The) 2247
Lord's prayer. The Beatitudes. 2247
Lord's prayers. 2049
Lord's return. 3320
Lord's Sermon on the mount. 3334
Lord's songs. 1869, 3231
Lord's Supper. 2250, 2251, 2252, 2254,
2256
Lord's Supper according to the New
Testament. 2254
Lord's supper and liturgy. 2257
Lord's Supper as a Christological problem.
2011, 2256
Lord's supper in Protestantism. 2251

Lord's Supper in the New Testament.
2254
Lord's Supper, prayers. 2252
Lord's Supper: seven meanings. 2251
Lord's Supper today. 2251
Lord's table. 2251, 2256, 2259
Lords temporal & lords spiritual. 2792
Lord's unconquerable church. 1123
Lord's voice, crying to his people. 3349
Lordship and discipleship. 2012
Lordship of Jesus. 2040
Lore of the meadowland. 1824
Lore of the New Testament. 1976
Lore of the Old Testament. 1631
Lore of the Whare-wananga. 2664
Lorenzo Dow. 1478
Loretto. 3417
Loretto in Missouri. 3417
Loring Wilbur Messer, metropolitan
general secretary. 2413, 3874
Loss of unity. 3035
Lost! 1563
Lost and found. 1456, 2027, 2944, 3296
Lost and saved. 3136
Lost Apocrypha of the Old Testament.
491
Lost art of discipline making. 982
Lost art of meditation. 2380
Lost audience. 1554
Lost Bible. 290
Lost book of Genesis. 520
Lost books of the Bible. 336
Lost books of the Bible and The forgotten
books of Eden. 335, 336
Lost books of the New Testament. 336
Lost centuries: from the Muslim empires to
the Renaissance of Europe, 1145-1453.
1926
Lost chapters recovered from the early
history of American Methodism. 2168,
2452
Lost Christ in a lost world. 1063
Lost Christianity. 1095, 2679
Lost churches of China. 912
Lost cities of Paraguay. 87, 1949
Lost cricket and other stories for children.
3369
Lost crown. 1556, 1563
Lost dream. 509
Lost fatherland. 2407
Lost goddesses of early Greece. 1742
Lost gods of England. 2659
Lost gospel. 2436
Lost Israel found. 46
Lost key to the Scriptures. 253
Lost keys of freemasonry. 1661, 1662
Lost lamb. 988
Lost legends of Israel. 2208
Lost light. 3109
Lost line. 782
Lost Mountain days. 1849
Lost nation. 2169
Lost New Testament book, restored
through spirit agency. 3514
Lost oracles; a masque. 3202
Lost paradise. 1776, 1948
Lost passion. 2434
Lost people and a vanished sceptre. 45,
1928
Lost prophecy. 600
Lost pyramid. 3285, 3330
Lost secret recovered. 1566
Lost secrets of master masons. 1661
Lost sheep. 2260, 2771
Lost sheep and other parables. 2260, 2771
Lost sheep of the house of Israel. 1929
Lost tales of Miletus. 3200
Lost tradition. 3635
Lost tribes a myth. 1929
Lost tribes, are the Teutonic race. 1929
Lost tribes of Israel. 1929
Lost tribes of Israel discovered. 2261
Lost wedding ring. 2347
Lost word. 3516
Lost word, its hidden meaning. 1662
Lost world. 3479
Lost year. 3207
Lost years of Jesus. 1083, 1410, 1532
Lost years of Jesus revealed. 2040
Lost years of Jesus revealed. Newly rev.
2d ed. 2042
Lother P. Kron, in memoriam. 2293
Lots of brothers and sisters. 1607
Lot's wife and the science of physics.
3080
Lott Carey. 739, 2486
... Lott Cary. 743
Lottie Moon. 2510, 2588
Lottie Moon of China. 2588
Lotus of the heart. 121
Lotus of the wonderful law. 710
Lotus Sutra. 3272, 3455
Lotze's theory of reality. 2261, 3027
Louis Craig Cornish. 1369
Louis Ginzberg. 1713, 2066, 3079
... Louis Manoha. 2329
Louis Martin, an ideal father. 2348

Louis Martin's daughter. 3690
Louis Massignon (1883-1962) : Christian
Ecumenist prophet of inter-religious
reconciliation. 2372
Louis of Granada. 2271, 2876
Louis XIV's view of the papacy (1661-
1667) 1638, 2261
Louisa: a pastor's memorial. 1704
Louisa Graves Owen. 2753
Louisa, my first born. 1791
Louise. 2373, 2408
Louise de Marillac. 2203, 2261
Louise Nevelson, iconography and sources.
1880
Louisiana Baptist historical atlas. 154
Louisiana monitor of the degrees of
entered apprentice, fellow craft and
master mason. 1669
Louisville Presbyterian theological
seminary. 2261
Lourdes. 2262, 3296, 3460
Lourdes, land of Mary. 2262
Love. 321, 1096, 1448, 2262, 2263, 2265,
2267, 3153
Love abounds. 1425
Love, acceptance & forgiveness. 3678
Love activates and acts. 950
Love affair. 2264
Love after death. 2262
Love almighty and ills unlimited. 2980
Love alone. 1735
Love, altruism, and world crisis. 28, 3459
Love and being. 3693
Love and control. 664
Love and fruitfulness in the Bible. 3390
Love and gifts. 1713
Love and grace in marriage. 2342
Love and justice. 3434
Love and Justice; selections from the
shorter writings of Reinhold Niebuhr.
3434
Love and laughter. 2695
Love and learning. 3355
Love and life. 3838
Love and living. 793, 3490
Love and loyalty. 3725
Love & marriage. 2346
Love and marriage in the spirit. 2341
Love and penalty. 1699
Love and responsibility. 3391
Love and sacrament. 2343, 2627
Love & sex. 3389
Love and sex are not enough. 2337
Love and sexuality. 3393
Love & sexuality /[compiled by] Odile M.
Liebard. 793, 2344
Love and society. 946, 3021
Love and sympathy in Theravada
Buddhism. 2263
Love and the law. 1314, 2263
Love and the teen-age girl. 3877
Love and the urban ghetto. 2222
Love and truth meet. 3666
Love and violence. 2265
Love and you. 2262
Love, Arlis. 932, 2938
Love around the house. 1607
Love as strong as death. 3607
Love, beauty, and harmony in Sufism.
3542
Love beyond pain. 2640
Love book. 2394
Love builds up. 3367
Love cults & faith healers. 1600, 3326
Love divine. 967
Love does such things. 2023
Love enthroned : essays on evangelical
perfection. 2818
Love, evolution and religion. 3023
Love, familystyle. 2338
Love finds a way. 3381
Love for souls. 1570
Love for the neighbor in Luther's
theology. 887, 2278
Love formula. 1633
Love from The living bible. 601
Love God and do what you please! 2264
Love goes on forever. 2339
Love has a price tag. 931, 1509
Love has its reasons. 349, 2266
Love, honor and ...? 2336
Love, honor, and be free. 3844
Love, honor, and frustration. 931, 1851
Love, honor, and obesity. 931, 1851
Love in action. 986, 2264
Love in creation and redemption. 2174
Love in four dimensions. 163, 422
Love in the afterlife. 3501
Love in the Gospels. 399, 1736
Love in the New Testament. 2265
Love in the words and life of Jesus. 2062
Love is. 2267, 3206
Love is a magic penny. 3883
Love is a spendthrift. 1264
Love is alive. 324, 2266
Love is all. 2264
Love is an everyday thing. 323, 2266

Love is an open door. 130, 1254
Love is for living. 317, 2397
Love is for real. 1154
Love is forever. 2262
Love is life. 2342, 2343
Love is my calling. 2573
Love is my meaning. 1444
Love is my vocation;imaginative story of
St. Therese of Lisieux. 3690
Love is now. 983
Love is prayer, prayer is love. 2016, 2880
Love is so much more, Lord. 2346
Love is something you do. 2336, 2934
Love is stronger than death. 1417
Love is the answer. 1007, 2168
Love is the gift. 3378
Love is the healer. 2265
Love is the law. 2265
Love is the liberator. 2265
Love-justice. 2266
Love knows no barriers. 589
Love, laurels & laughter. 3206
Love leaves home. 2243
Love leaves no choice. 1566
Love life. 323, 2266
Love, life, and truth. 3390
Love, light and life for God's little
children. 3160, 3177
Love-lit path to God. 253
Love lives here. 2263
Love looks at death. 1351
Love-love. 1891
"Love made perfect." 2818
Love-magic and Butterfly People. 2677
Love makes the word go round. 2265
Love, man, society. 754
Love, marriage, and the family. 2345
Love me with tough love. 987
Love numbers. 3576
Love of Abraham and Sarah. 5
Love of Christ. 1002
Love of God. 998, 1444, 2058, 2264,
2266
Love of God according to Saiva Siddhanta.
197
Love of God and the love of the neighbor.
1315
Love of God, blessings, strength, and joy
in the book of Psalms. 1798
Love of God revealed to the entire
universe by man's redemption. 3029
Love of Jesus. 3267
Love of Jesus to penitents. 2812
Love of learning and the desire for God.
2582
Love of the Crucified. 2032
Love of the Sacred Heart. 3269
Love of the world. 1445
Love on fire. 1557, 3207
Love on pilgrimage. 761
Love one another. 2264, 2265, 3375
Love one another; sermon outlines for
Sundays and holydays. 3375
Love or constraint? 3176
Love, power, and justice. 2263
Love Project. 3436
Love relationships in the Johannine
tradition. 324, 420, 2266
Love revealed. 424
Love road to Calvary. 324, 2298, 3348
Love, sin, and suffering. 1001
Love slave. 160
Love so amazing. 2935
Love song. 113, 594
Love songs. 2346
Love speaks from the Cross. 2056
Love stories of great missionaries. 2481
Love stories of John and Charles Wesley.
3803
Love stories of John Wesley, and other
essays. 3803
Love story. 3391
Love story of Ruth & Boaz. 3258
Love story ... the real thing. 2339
Love, suffering, providence. 3541
Love supreme. 1745
Love takes greatness. 2343
Love that heals. 2264
Love that reaches a star. 3503
Love, the bond of perfection. 2265
Love, the issue. 1096
Love, the law of life. 2265
Love the Lord. 3177
Love the Lord the God. 2264
Love, the perfume of heaven. 2263
Love, the sweetest thing in life. 887
Love them in. 2587
Love theory in later Hanbalite Islam.
2263
Love therapy. 986
Love to Christ a necessary qualification in
a gospel minister. 2742, 3779
Love to death. 2265
Love to the church. 2501
Love to the end. 2251
Love to the loveless. 537

LOVE TO THE RELIGIOUS BOOKS 1876 - 1982

Love to the uttermost. 420
Love trails of the long ago. 624
Love universal. 956
Love unlimited. 3292
Love until it hurts. 2487
Love within limits. 323, 2266
Love without a limit. 2266
Love without boundaries. 3602
"Love your enemies" 391, 2065, 2266
Love your neighbor. 3264, 3265
Love—your path to health. 2377
Loveliest flower. 2581
Lovely Lady of Catawba County. 2706
Lovely lord of the Lord's day. 2385
Lover. 2384
Lover of souls. 854
Lovers in marriage. 2343
Lovers three thousand years ago as indicated by the Song of Solomon. 593
Love's answer from eternity. 187, 3495
Love's conquest. 2944
Love's fulfilment. 3476
Love's imperative. 3601
Loves in the hart of Mary. 2359
Love's necessity. 2058
Loves of Krishna in Indian painting and poetry. 2187
Love's reply. 90
Love's response. 1408
Love's servants. 1741
Love's superlatives. 2267
Loving again. 931, 1713
Loving awareness of God's presence in prayer. 1736
Loving begins with me. 988
Loving Go and a suffering world. 1736
Loving in forgiveness. 2347
Loving my Jewishness. 2113, 2146
Loving one another. 1565
Loving others. 3164
Loving says it all. 946
Loving women/loving men. 1843
Lovingly in the hands of the Father. 979
Low mass, A simple explanation of. 845
Lower East Side: portal to American life, 1870-1924. 2101
...Lower hall. 745
Lower junior manual for administrators and leaders in the lower junior department of the church school. 3170
Lower levels of prayer. 2881
Lower Niger and its tribes. 1540
Loyal life. 3235
Loyal love. 1454
Loyalty. 1313, 1592
Loyalty and order. 1213
Loyalty to church and state. 828
Loyalty to God. 1453
Loyola and the educational system of the Jesuits. 1945
Loyola psychological study of the ministry and life of the American priest. 775
Loyolas and the Cabots. 3288
LSTC: decade of decision. 2302
Lubavitcher rabbi's memoris. 1789
Lucent clay. 965
Lucian's dialogues. 2270
Lucid dreaming. 1479
Lucifer. 2270
Lucifer; a theological tragedy. 3201
Lucifer; or, The heavenly truce; a theological tragedy. 3201
Lucifer's creed to the churches, star beams. 1429
Lucifer's handbook. 1091
Lucks and talismans. 3582
Lucky-lucky. 2540
Lucretia Mott, her complete speeches and sermons. 3010
Ludwig-missionsverein and the church in the United States (1838-1918) 2271
Ludwig Rosenberger collection of Judaica. 2083
...The Ludwig-missionsverein and the church in the United States (1838-1918) 2271
Luis Palau story. 1575, 2760
Luke. 426, 427, 428, 429, 2271
Luke, a challenge to present theology. 429
Luke, a study guide. 430
Luke-Acts. 429
Luke and the gnostics. 426
Luke and the people of God. 426, 2271
Luke, first century Christian. 2271
... Luke (Gospel--Acts) the books of the Bible in modern English for American readers. 426
Luke, missionary doctor. 2271
Luke the evangelist. 429, 1966
Luke, the gospel of God's man. 427
Luke the historian. 426
Luke the historian in recent study. 2271
Luke, the physician. 1183, 2193
Luke, the physician, and other studies in the history of religion. 1183, 2271
Luke's portrait of Christ. 428, 1967
Luke's story of Jesus. 429, 2010
Luke's thrilling Gospel. 428
Luke's witness to Jesus. 430
Luke's witness to Jesus Christ. 431
Lukes's portrait of Christ. 1967
LuLu. 932, 3244
Lumberjack sky pilot. 1255
Lumen Christi, mediations for Easter-tide. 2054
Luminous bodies here and hereafter (the shining ones) 2843
Luminous trail. 924
Lunar astrology. 97
Lunation cycle. 97
Luo religion and folklore. 2272
Lupus of Ferrieres and the classics. 2272
Lure of Africa. 2498
Lure of divine love. 964, 2944
Lure of God. 651, 2943
Lure of the cults. 1393
Lust. 2272
Luther. 2273, 2275, 2276, 2277, 2280, 3039
Luther, a life. 2278, 3037
Luther; a profile. 2278
Luther alive. 2277, 3036
Luther, an experiment in biography. 2274, 3037
Luther and Aquinas on salvation. 2281, 3294
Luther and Erasmus: Free will and salvation. 1658
Luther and his mother. 2277
Luther and his times. 2277, 3035
Luther and his work. 2273
Luther and Melanchthon in the history and theology of the Reformation. 2279, 2281, 2400
Luther and music. 2280
Luther and Staupitz. 2277
Luther and the Bible. 284, 2274
Luther and the false brethren. 2273
Luther and the German Reformation. 2275, 3040, 3041
Luther and the Lutheran Church 1483-1960. 2277, 2288
Luther and the mystics. 2280
Luther and the Old Testament. 504, 2273
Luther and the papacy. 2274, 3037
Luther and the peasants' war. 2273, 2274, 2810
Luther and the reformation. 2272, 2273, 2274, 2275, 2277, 3033, 3034, 3035
Luther and the Scriptures. 306, 2275, 2277
Luther as seen by Catholics. 2280
Luther at home. 2277
Luther at Wartburg castle. 2276
Luther Burbank. 717
Luther Burbank, "our beloved infidel" 717
Luther by a Lutheran. 2278
Luther D. Wishard. 3822, 3871
Luther, Erasmus, and the Reformation. 2275, 2279, 3036, 3038
Luther for an ecumenical age. 2278
Luther Hasley Gulick. 1777
Luther, his life and work. 2277, 3037
Luther in America. 2279
Luther in light of recent research. 2272
Luther in Protestantism today. 2976
Luther in Rome. 2280
Luther in the 20th century. 2275
Luther league hymn book. 1865
Luther league hymnal, issued by authority of the Luther league of New York state. 2289
Luther now. 2275, 3034
Luther on education. 2276
Luther on justification. 2161, 2281
Luther on ministerial office and congregational function. 2278, 2791
Luther on the Christian home. 2280, 2281
Luther on vocation. 2281
Luther primer. 2275
Luther Rice. 3235
Luther Rice: believer in tomorrow. 3235
Luther Rice, founder of Columbian College. 3235
Luther—selected political writings. 2280
Luther songs and ballads, a jubilee offering. 2274
Luther the expositor. 2275
... Luther: the leader. 2276
Luther, the reformer. 2274
Luther today. 2278
Luther Warren. 3124
Lutheran almanac. 2302
Lutheran book of prayer. 2297
Lutheran catechist. 747
Lutheran chorale. 917
Lutheran Church among Norwegian-Americans. 2715
...The Lutheran church and child-nurture. 3172
Lutheran Church and its students. 1128
Lutheran church and the civil war. 2294
Lutheran church directory for the United States and Canada. 2293
Lutheran church in American history. 2294
Lutheran Church in Berks County. 1548
Lutheran church in colonial America. 2294
Lutheran Church in New York & New Jersey, 1722-1760. Lutheran records in the Ministerial Archives of the Staatsarchiv, Hamburg, Germany. Tr. by Simon Hart & Harry J. Kreider. 2291
Lutheran church in southern Iowa. 2291
Lutheran church in the country. 2292
Lutheran church in the eastern Pennsylvania. countryside. Town and Country workshop - Ministerium Camp Shawnee on the Delaware, Pennsylvania, June 26-27, 1959. 2292
Lutheran Church in the timberland area. 2292
Lutheran Church, past and present. 2288, 3668
Lutheran church under American influence. 2293
Lutheran churches in the third world. 2296, 2502
Lutheran churches of the world. 2282, 2288
Lutheran college graduate in modern society. 2293
Lutheran confessional theology. 109
Lutheran confessional theology in America, 1840-1880. 3668
Lutheran confessions. 2283
Lutheran cooperation through Lutheran higher education. 2671
Lutheran cyclopedia. 2285, 3639
Lutheran doctrine of the Lord's supper. 2286
Lutheran elementary schools in action. 2293
Lutheran elementary schools in the United States. 2293
Lutheran ethic; the impact of religion on laymen and clergy. 2303
Lutheran faith and life. 2295
Lutheran forms for sacred acts. 2294
Lutheran Free Church. 2302
Lutheran fundamentals. 2294
Lutheran Germany and the Book of Concord. 2283
Lutheran graded series of Sunday school materials. 2293
Lutheran handbook. 2282
Lutheran health and welfare directory. 2284
Lutheran high school. 2293
Lutheran home missions. 2296, 2527
Lutheran hour. 3354
Lutheran hymnal. 2289
Lutheran hymnary. 2289, 2290
Lutheran landmarks and pioneers in America. 2294
Lutheran lectionary. 2295
Lutheran liturgy. 2295
Lutheran Lutheran Church in New York, 1649-1772. 2291
Lutheran lyrics. 3208
Lutheran makers of America. 2303
Lutheran manual. 2286
Lutheran manual on Scriptural principles. 2287
Lutheran ministrant. 1911
Lutheran movement of the sixteenth century. 3033
Lutheran order of services. 2295
Lutheran parish handbook. 2287
Lutheran parish in an urbanized American with special reference to the Missouri Synod. 2292
Lutheran pastor. 3677
Lutheran prayer book. 2297
Lutheran Reformation and the Jews. 3034
Lutheran reformers against Anabaptists. 37
Lutheran Sunday school handbook. 2293
Lutheran Sunday-school handbooks. 3183
Lutheran teacher's handbook. 2293
Lutheran trail. 2290
Lutheran venture in higher education. 2287
Lutheran way of life. 2282
Lutheran world missions. 2295
Lutheran year book of the Evangelical Lutheran Church. 2302
Lutheran youth conference and ninth international Y.P.L.L. convention Minneapolis, Minnesota, June 23-27, 1937. 3887
Lutheranism. 3667
Lutheranism and the educational ethic. 2287
Lutheranism in America. 2292
Lutheranism in Bucks county, 1734-1934. 2292
Lutheranism in colonial New York. 2291, 2700
Lutheranism in North America, 1914-1970. 2292
Lutheranism under the tsars and the Soviets. 2292
Lutherans and Catholics in dialogue. 2298, 3666
Lutherans and Catholics in dialogue, I-III. 138, 861, 2707
Lutherans and other denominations. 2298
Lutherans and Roman Catholicism. 2298
Lutherans in America. 2293
Lutherans in Berks county. 2291
Lutherans in Brazil. 2290
Lutherans in concert. 2293, 2671
Lutherans in Georgia. 2290, 2302
Lutherans in North America. 2291, 2303
Lutherans in South Africa. 2292
Lutherans in the movements for church union. 2294
Lutherans in the U S A. 2293
Lutherans in the U.S.A. 2293
Lutherans of New York, their story and their problems. 2303
...Luther's Christmas sermons. 2278
...Luther's Commentary on the first twenty-two Psalms. 2278
Luther's correspondence and other contemporary letters. 2278
Luther's doctrine of the two kingdoms in the context of his theology. 1143, 2273
Luther's English connection. 174
Luther's explanatory notes on the Gospels. 386, 3900
Luther's German Bible. 284
Luther's house of learning. 2288, 3040
Luther's hymns. 2275, 2289
...Luther's large catechism. 2278
Luther's life. 2277
Luther's pastors. 2284, 2791
Luther's prayers. 2281, 2892
Luther's progress to the Diet of Worms. 2277
Luther's reply to King Henry VIII. 1804
Luther's sense of himself. as an interpreter of the Word to the world. 2281
Luther's Small Catechism. 2278, 2283
Luther's Small catechism explained in questions and answers. 2284
Luther's Small catechism explained in questions and answers, by H. U. Sverdrup ... Abridged. Translated from the Norwegian by H. A. Urseth. 12th ed., rev. by Rev. John A. Houkoin. 2279, 2283
Luther's small catechism in prayer form. 2278
...Luther's table talk. 2277, 2281
... Luther's theological development from Erfurt to Augsburg. 2274, 2280
Luther's theology of the cross. 2279, 2281
...Luther's two catechisms explained by himself, in six classic writings. 2278
Luthers Ubersetzungen des zweiten Psalms. 584
Luther's variations in sentence arrangement from the modern literary usage. 2273
Luther's view of church history. 1187, 2274
Luther's works. 3629
Luther's world of thought. 2281
Lux in lumine. 3623
Lux mundi. 1049
Luxury and sacrifice. 959
Luxury--Gluttony. 3412
Lych-gates and their churches in eastern England. 2225
Lychgate. 3500
Lydia Longley, the first American nun. 2245
Lyfe of Saynt Radegunde. 3282
Lyles Baptist Church, 1774-1974, Fluvanna County, Virginia. 1630, 2304
Lyman Abbott, Christian evolutionist. 2
Lyman Beecher. 184
Lyman Beecher and the reform of society: four sermons, 1804-1828. 3348
Lyman Pierson Powell. 2866
Lynching of Jesus. 2068
Lyra germanica. 1874
Lyra Germanica. Hymns for the Sundays and chief festivals of the Christian year. 1873, 1874
Lyra innocentium. 3207
Lyric and dramatic Milton. 2470
Lyric of life. 1889
Lyric of the morning land. 3199
Lyric Psalter. 2857
Lyric religion. 1876
Lyrica sacra. 573
Lyrics from the Psalter. 190
Lyrics of Jesus, and other poems. 2048
Lyuba; traditional religion of the Sukuma. 3545

M

M. B. Harrison, Nebraska Puritan. 1787
M. Ernest Renan. 3215
M. R. De Haan: the man and his ministry. 1407
M. Terenti Varronis Antiquitatum rerum divinarum libri I, XIV, XV, XVI. 3246
M. Theron Rankin, Apostle of Advance. 3021
[Ma'aseh de-Yosef tsadika (romanized form)]. 528
'Ma' Sunday still speaks. 3566
Ma'alim al-qurba fi ahkam al-hisba of Diya' al-Din Muhammad ibn Muhammad al-Qurashi al-Shafi'i, known as Ibn al-Ukhuwwa. 2630
Ma'aser. 3702
Mabel Cratty. 1379, 3877
Mabel Digby. 1459
Macartney's illustrations. 1841, 3362
Maccabees. 2305
Maccabees, Zealots, and Josephus. 408, 2090, 2134, 2150, 2671
McConnell's manual for Baptist churches. 142
Macdonald presentation volume. 1923
Mackenzie's grave. 2309, 2543
McKerrow. 144
Mackey's Grammar of the Benga-Bantu language. Revised by Rev. R. H. Nassau. 190
Mackey's Symbolism of freemasonry. 1671
MacKinnon years. 3725
Mackintosh treasury. 3632
Macklin of Nanking. 2309, 2508
Macmillan atlas history of Christianity. 1488
Macmillan Bible atlas. 283
Macropedius. 2310
Macumba. 2333, 3722
Mad morality. 1313
Madagascar: footprint at the end of the world. 1624, 2538
Madam President. 1229, 1856
Madame Blavatsky. 671, 3682
Madame Blavatsky, the woman behind the myth. 671, 3682
Madame de Chantal. 882
Made according to pattern. 515
Made for each other. 3391
Made for the mountains. 160
Made, not born. 137
Mademoiselle Lavalliere. 2200
Mademoiselle Louise; life of Louise de Marillac. 2203
... Madhava Rao Sindhia and the Hindu reconquest of India. 2311
Madhyanta-vibhanga; discourse on discrimination between middle and extremes. 3867
Madison and religion. 1151, 2311
Madison avenue lectures. 148
... The madness of Nietzsche. 2710
Madonna. 2355, 2358
Madonna della Strada Chapel, Loyola University. 2270
Madonna in art. 2358, 2760
Madonna in art and verse. 2361
Madonna in legend and history. 2357
Madonna of St. Luke. 2271, 2357
Madonnas by old masters. 2358
Magdalene question. 2353
Les images hellenises, Zoroastre, Ostanes et Hystaspe d'apres la tradition grecque. 1878, 3898
Maggid of Caro. 741
Maggidim & Hasidim. 1843
Maggie L. Walker and the I. O. of Saint Luke. 1895, 3789
Magic. 2312, 2313, 2314
Magic: an occult primer. 2312
Magic and fetishism. 2312
Magic and healing. 2378
Magic and husbandry. 20
Magic and meaning of Voodoo. 3787
Magic and mystery in Tibet. 2993
Magic and mysticism. 2313
Magic and religion. 2652
Magic and religion, their psychological nature. 3111
Magic and religion, their psychological nature, origin, and function. 3001
Magic & superstition in the Jewish tradition. 2315
Magic and the millennium. 3087
Magic art of foreseeing the future. 1470
Magic arts in Celtic Britain. 878
Magic as a performing art. 1345
Magic background of modern anti-Semitism. 53
"Magic," black and white. 2724
Magic casements. 733

Magic cauldron. 3826
Magic, divination, and demonology among the Hebrews. 2724
Magic, divination, and witchcraft among the Barotse of Northern Rhodesia. 3827
Magic dwells. 1381
Magic formula for successful prayer. 2881
Magic gardens, a symbolic rendering of angelic communion with man through the medium of flowers. 42
Magic ladder. 3198
Magic makers. 1346, 2314
Magic, myth, and money. 2584
Magic of experience. 2180
Magic of faith. 2695
Magic of Findhorn. 2732
Magic of love. 2262
Magic of Mormonism. 2606
Magic of psychograms. 2726
Magic of space. 2730
Magic of telephone evangelism. 3594
Magic of the middle ages. 2313
Magic of the word. 3750
Magic people. 2090
Magic plum tree. 1937
Magic power of witchcraft. 3823
Magic prayer. 579
Magic presence. 2311
Magic sleep. 1479
Magic staff. 3499
Magic supernaturalism, and religion. 2314
Magic symbols of the world. 888
Magic wells. 3725
Magic, white and black. 2312, 2725
Magic, witchcraft, and paganism in America. 2315
Magic with a message. 3151
Magical arts. 2732
Magical candles, enchanted plants, and powerful gems. 3823
Magical message according to Ioannes. 414
Magical revival. 2312
Magical ritual of the sanctum regnum interpreted by the Tarot trumps. 3588
Magician among the spirits. 3505, 3520
Magicians, seers, and mystics. 22, 57
Magician's tour up and down and round about the earth. 1345
Magick in theory and practice. 2312
Magil's linear school Bible. 307
Magister choralis. 883
Magistracy an institution of Christ upon the throne. 1504
Magna charta of the kingdom of God. 3335
Magna charta of woman. 3832
Magnalia Christi Americana. 2372, 2687
Magnalia Dei, the mighty acts of God. 484, 3860
Magnalis Christi americana. 2372, 2687
Magnet of the heart. 1558
... Magnetic astronomy of the Bible. 212
Magnetic healer, hypnotist, and mental therapeutist. 1283
Magnetic master. 1559
... The magnetic power of love. 3865
... The magnetic power of love (Bhakti yoga) 3865
Magnetism of mystery. 1567
Magnetism of the Bible. 201
Magnetism of the cross. 3359
Magnificat. 1448, 1620, 2275, 2315, 2316, 2362, 3369
Magnificat; Luther's commentary. 2316
Magnificence of Jesus. 2043
Magnificent decision. 959
Magnificent defeat. 3349
Magnificent frolic. 2674
Magnificent love. 3335
Magnificent man. 796
Magnificent Messiah. 293
Magnificent missionary. 1289, 2588
Magnificent nobility. 158, 3838
Magnificent strangers. 43
Magnificent Three. 1392, 3711
Magnificient illusion. 780
Magnify your office. 1911
Magnifying priesthood power. 1232, 2401
Magnifying the church. 1247
Magnitude of prayer. 2876
Magus. 2731
Mah nishtana. 2110
Mahabharata. 2316
Mahalia, gospel singer. 1930, 3414
Mahalia Jackson. 1930, 3414
Mahalia Jackson: queen of gospel song. 1930, 3414
Maharishi. 2317
Maharishi Mahesh Yogi on the Bhagavad-gita. 2316
Maharishi, the guru. 2318
Mahatma and the missionary. 2530
Mahatma Gandhi and comparative religion. 1701, 3094
Mahatma letters to A. P. Sinnett. 3686
Mahayana Buddhist meditation. 2317

Mahayana Buddhist sculpture of Ceylon. 2317
Mahayana way to Buddhahood. 2317
Mahomet. 2628
Mahomet and his successors. 1926, 2565, 2628
... Mahzor Yannai. 2109
Maid of Corinaldo. 2333
Maid of Domremy. 1938
Maid of Lisieux, and other papers. 761, 3691
Maid of Orleans. 1937, 1938
Maimonidean criticism and the Maimonidean controversy. 2623
Maimonides. 2318, 2623, 2841, 3016
Maimonides; a biography. 2623
Maimonides and Abrabanel on prophecy. 2622, 2949
Maimonides' Commentary on the Mishnah, tractate Sanhedrin. 2479
Maimonides: his life and works. 2623
Maimonides; his wisdom for our time. 2156
Maimonides' Introduction to the Talmud. 2479, 3706
Maimonides, medieval modernist. 2622
Maimonides' Mishneh Torah. 2074, 2623
Maimonides octocentennial series, numbers I-IV. 2623
Maimonides reader. 2156
Maimonides said. 2115
Maimonides (The Rambam) 2623
Maimonides' Treatise on logic (Makalah fisina at al-mantik) 2242
Main chance. 28, 1955
Main channel. 251
Main currents in early Christian thought. 3658
Main issues confronting Christendom. 1054
Main points. 1048
Main questions in religion. 3068
Main services of Holy Week and glorious Resurrection in the Greek rite (Byzantine-Slavonic) Catholic Church. 842
Main Street and the mind of God. 1154
Main street today. 3743
Main trail. 2913
Mainline churches and the evangelicals. 1552
Mainspring of human progress. 2223
Maitri Upanisat. 3760
Majesty of books. 1009
Majken. 693, 1254
Major addresses. 761
Major addresses of Pope XII. 760
Major Bible themes. 3661
Major Bible truths. 287
Major Black religious leaders, 1755-1940. 17
Major Black religious leaders since 1940. 16
Major documents on Catholic action from the Second World Congress of the Lay Apostolate. 754
Major messages of the Minor prophets. 560
Major Methodist beliefs. 2428
Major orders. 1288
Major religions of the world. 3112, 3121
Major seminarian. 3331
Major social concerns. 1075
Major themes in modern philosophies of Judaism. 1306, 2141
Major themes in Northern Black religious thought, 1800-1860. 2682
Major themes of the Qur'an. 2185
Major trends in American church history. 3738
Major trends in Jewish mysticism. 2646
Major truths from the minor prophets. 559
Major United Methodist beliefs. 2428
Major voices in American Theology. 3611
Make a joyful noise. 320, 3858
Make a joyful noise unto the Lord. 1873, 1930, 3414
Make each day count. 1434
Make friends with your shadow. 986
Make God first. 1431
Make God your friend. 1742
Make His praise glorious. 2884
Make it happen! 1005
Make it plain. 1012
Make Jesus king. 1450
Make life worth living. 975
Make love your aim. 2265
Make me aware, Lord. 3842
Make meaningful these passing years. 3756
Make ready the way of the Lord. 3188
Make space, make symbols. 2870
Make straight the way of the Lord. 2391
Make the Bible your own. 312
Make the way known. 1475
Make up your mind. 1418

Make warm noises. 2388
Make way for Mary. 2355
Make way for the King. 2059
Make your church attractive. 1244
Make your faith work. 412
Make your illness count. 3407
Make your life worthwhile. 1433
Make your preaching relevant. 2905
Make your Sunday school grow through evaluation. 3559
Maker of heaven and earth. 1380
Maker of men. 886
Maker of new Japan Rev. Joseph Hardy Neesima, LL. D., president of Doshisha university, Kyoto. 2679
Maker of the new Orient. 696
... The makers and teacers of Uudaism. 234
... Makers of a new world. 661
Makers of Christianity. 1173, 1177
Makers of freedom. 660
Makers of history. 660
Makers of hymns. 1875
Makers of Iowa Methodism. 2452
Makers of Methodism. 2422, 2427
Makers of religious freedom in the seventeenth century: Henderson, Rutherford, Bunyan, Baxter. 3193
Makers of the Bible and their literary methods. 236
Makers of the Christian tradition. 1101
Makers of the Meadville theological school, 1844-1894. 2376
Makers of the modern world. 661
Making a go of life. 1442
Making a missionary church. 2522
Making a monk. 2945
...Making a personal faith. 968
Making all things human. 2698
Making all things new. 3489
Making America Christian. 2558
Making an apostolic community of love. 2268, 3566
Making and meaning of and Augsburg confession. 109
Making and meaning of the New Testament. 349
Making and the unmaking of the preacher. 2906
Making disciples. 940
Making Disciples in Oregon. 1465
Making discoveries about the Bible. 199
Making friends for Christ. 1567
Making friends, keeping friends. 1688
Making friends with life. 2934
Making full proof of our ministry. 3674
Making good in the local church. 1240
Making good in the ministry. 2335
Making it big with God. 3881
Making it happen. 3538
Making it on a pastor's pay. 1292
Making life better. 2410
... Making life count. 1016
Making love a family affair. 1606
Making love happen. 2263
Making many rich. 2498
Making marriage Christian. 2337
Making men and women. 1252
Making men whole. 1062
Making mission happen. 2549
Making missions live. 2491
Making missions real. 2495
Making New Testament toys. 229
Making of a Christian. 965
Making of a Christian leader. 953
Making of a churchman. 974
Making of a country parish. 2774
Making of a disciple. 987
Making of a downtown church, the history of the Second Presbyterian church, Richmond, Virginia, 1845-1945. 3237
Making of a man of God. 1405, 1451
Making of a Messiah. 1966
Making of a minister. 3671
Making of a missionary. 2482
Making of a modern saint. 3691
Making of a mystic. 2640
Making of a pastoral person. 773, 2789
Making of a pioneer. 2373, 2503
Making of a Pope. 2805
Making of a preacher. 2902
Making of a preacher. Introd. 3673
Making of a priest. 773, 1477
Making of a rabbi. 1620, 3016
Making of a saint. 1440
Making of a sermon. 1843
Making of a super-race. 3506
Making of a teacher. 3147, 3179
Making of Christian doctrine. 1473
Making of Christianity. 56
Making of Luke--Acts. 429
Making of man. 1067, 3623
Making of Methodism. 2422
Making of ministers. 2829, 3680
Making of modern missions. 2526
Making of myth. 2649
Making of religion. 3093, 3109

Making of the Bible. 199, 217, 539
Making of the Christian church. 3451
Making of the Christian mind. 1047
Making of the Church of England (A.D. 597-1087) a course of historical lectures. 1221
Making of the English Bible. 248
Making of the English New Testament. 355
Making of the first American Book of common prayer, 1776-1789. 1523
Making of the minister. 3673
Making of the modern Jew. 2093
Making of the New Testament. 408
Making of the Old and the New Testaments. 308
... The making of the Old Testament. 483, 532
Making of the Pope. 2124
Making of the Popes 1978. 2126, 2862
Making of the Restoration settlement. 1220
Making of the Roman Catholic Church in Ireland, 1850-1860. 820
Making of the sermon. 2902, 2904
Making of the spiritual mind. 3521
Making of the Vedanta. 3775
Making of the word. 636
Making Old Testament toys. 229
Making our group Christian. 3764
Making political decisions. 1087
Making prayer real. 2879
Making religion efficient. 2402
Making religion real. 960
Making religious education effective. 3149
Making sense of confession. 1327
Making sense of the creeds. 1385
Making sense of things. 942
Making sense out of life. 1095
Making sexuality human. 3391
Making the adult class vital. 3168
Making the Bible desired. 3146
Making the Bible live. 539
Making the Bible real. 640
Making the building serve the liturgy. 1156
Making the gospel effective. 1055
Making the Jesuits more modern. 1945
Making the ministry relevant. 1297
Making the most of family living. 1607
Making the most of family worship. 1607, 1608
Making the most of life. 969, 1323
Making the most of what life brings. 954
Making the most of your best. 2392
Making the most of your golden years. 18
Making the most of yourself. 3539
Making the old Sunday school new. 3556
Making the small church effective. 3426
Making the world Christian. 1567, 2494
Making tracks. 2384
Making urban schools work. 3761
Making your life count. 3785
Making your marriage succeed. 2336
Making your self the master. 3141
'Makings' of meetings. 3876
Mal occhio (evil eye), the underside vision. 1578
Malachi. 558
Malachi, messenger of divine love. 558
Malachi's message for today. 558
Malachy. 1026, 2318
La Maladie infantile des catholiques francais. 817
Malcolm X: Black and proud. 2233, 2681
Malcom's new dictionary. 245
Malden survey. 2318
Male and female. 3391
Male and female created He them. 3391
Male church-choir. 917
Male quartet. 2632
Malinki of Malawi. 2319, 2486
Malla Moe. 2563
Malleus maleficarum. 3823
Malleus maleficarum of Heinrich Kramer and James Sprenger. 3824
[Mallon chresai (romanized form)] first-century slavery and the interpretation of 1 Corinthians 7:21. 323, 3424
Malnutrition. 2718
Malta of the Knights. 2179, 2319
Maltbie Davenport Babcock. 122
Malthus and his work. 2319
Malvern, 1941. 3444
Mama was a missionary. 2270, 2271, 2536
Mamma Margherita: St. John Bosco's mother. 683
Mammon. 120
Mamre. 2141
Man. 2324, 2325, 2326, 2732, 3687
Man a revelation of God. 2319
Man a soul. 1099
Man after God's own heart. 1713
Man against the church. 1119
Man alive! 2051
Man amid change in world affairs. 3851
Man amid changes in world affairs. 3851

...The man among the myrtles. 600
Man an eternal probationer. 2943
Man and a school. 3874
Man and Christ. 66
Man and civilization. 2473
Man and civilization: control of the mind. 2473
Man and God. 598, 1585, 3199
Man and God in art and ritual. 84
Man and God in the city. 1280
Man and gods. 1417
Man and his becoming. 3775
... Man and his bodies. 3683, 3689
Man and his Christianity. 1054
Man and his destiny. 2324, 2325
Man and his destiny in the great religions. 2326
Man and his divine father. 2835
Man and his education. 1049
Man and his God. 990, 1723
Man and his gods. 3094
Man and his happiness. 3616
Man and his hope in the Old Testament. 1846
Man and his immortal soul. 2214
Man and his Maker. 2694
Man and his message. 3671
Man and his mirror. 2324
Man and his money. 1167
Man and his new hopes. 1845
Man and his religion. 1004
Man and his religions. 3119
Man and his world. 2738
Man and immortality. 1890
Man and magic. 2311
Man and message, eminent preachers who exemplify chief principles of ministerial efficiency. 2901
Man and metaphysics. 2416, 2418
Man and modern secularism. 3327
Man and nature in the New Testament. 2326
Man and religion. 3100
Man and salvation in literature. 2232
Man and sin. 3411, 3412
Man and society in the New Testament. 3439
Man and temple. 2664
Man and the attainment of immortality. 2320
Man and the beasts within. 2731
Man and the Book nobody knows. 230, 1994
Man and the cosmos. 2418
Man and the divine order. 3099
Man and the dragon. 2608
Man and the incarnation. 1047, 1919
Man and the message. 3136
Man and the sacred. 3057, 3085, 3140
Man and the sun. 3546
Man and the supernatural. 3483
Man and the two worlds. 1720
Man and the universe. 3073
Man and the woman in Islam. 2345
Man and the world of stars. 50
Man and the zodiac. 95
Man and wife. 2339
Man and wife in Scripture. 2341
Man and woman. 975, 3389, 3394
Man and woman, and child. 3686
Man and woman in Biblical perspective. 3839
Man and woman in Christ. 2402
Man and world in the light of anthroposophy. 50
Man, animal and divine. 2324
Man approved. 1299
Man as a being of spirit and soul. 50
Man as a creative first cause. 2418
Man as churchman. 1183
Man as infinite spirit. 2320, 3694
Man as male and female. 3391
Man as sinner in contemporary American realistic theology. 3412
Man at his best. 958, 1094
Man at millennium. 2320
Man at play. 2854
Man at prayer. 2890
Man at the top. 953
Man at work in God's world. 1131
Man becoming. 3640
Man before chaos. 2321, 2710
Man before God. 2326, 2412
Man being revealed. 3500
Man: believer and unbeliever. 67
Man beneath the gift. 1301, 1460
Man: body, mind, and soul. 2324
Man called Jesus. 1963, 1973
Man called Martin Luther. 2280, 3037
Man called Peter. 2348
Man can know God. 67
Man can live. 1056
Man caught by a fish. 553
Man Christ Jesus. 1962, 1995
Man crowned King: the divine drama unfolds. 206
Man discovers God. 1734, 1740

Man does not stand alone. 3079
Man every one ought to know. 3360
Man--evolution's unfinished product. 1579
Man, father of the gods. 3115
Man for all men. 1566
Man for all time. 1968
Man for now. 1400
Man for others. 1295, 2043
Man for this moment. 3527
Man for us and a God for us. 2037
Man from an African jungle. 2499
Man from Galilee. 1967
Man from heaven. 389, 1965
Man from Krypton. 67
Man from Nazareth. 1964
Man from Nazareth as his contemporaries saw Him. 929, 1964
Man from Rocca Sicca. 3692
Man from space speaks: Amano. 3473
Man from Tarsus. 2799
Man from Tarsus, his world, personality and religious genius. 2799
Man from Uz. 551
Man-God. 1992
Man, God and the universe. 2729
Man God mastered. 727
Man, God, the universe. 1050
Man—God's eternal creation. 2326
Man--God's masterpiece. 2323
Man, have I got problems. 979
Man--here and hereafter. 48
Man himself. 1952
Man, his creation, fall, redemption, and glorification. 3288
Man, his nature and destiny. 1529
Man, his origin and destiny. 2613
Man, his world, and his work. 3849
Man, I need help! 1255
Man in a new society. 2326
Man in Adam and in Christ. 2325
Man in-between. 2395
Man in chain. 1434, 2798
Man in Christ. 377, 2802
Man in community. 373, 3448
Man in community; Christian concern for the human in changing society. 3448
Man in conflict. 2996
Man in danger. 1281
Man in earnest. 1322
Man in evolution. 3687
Man in Genesis and in geology. 2322
Man in God's milieu. 1074
Man in God's purpose. 2324
Man in God's world. 2301
Man in leather breeches. 1637
Man in motion. 1107
Man in nature and in grace. 2322
Man in revolt. 2322
Man in search of God. 3663
Man in search of immortality. 1890
Man in the bush. 2538
Man in the maelstrom of modern thought. 2325
Man in the making. 1050, 1581
Man in the middle. 774, 1412
Man in the mirror. 1070
Man in the modern world. 3449
Man in the New Testament. 2326
Man in the Old Testament. 651, 2326
Man in the pew. 1765
Man in the pew, 1558-1660. 1765
Man in the process of time. 2325
'The man in the street. 65
Man in the street and religion. 3060
Man in the sycamore tree. 2413
Man in the world. 2460
Man in transition. 2783
Man in triumph; an integration of psychology and biblical faith. 1107
Man: in whose image. 967
Man in work and leisure. 3869
Man invincible. 293
Man is a spirit. 2988, 2989
Man is a triune being. 651
Man is free; sermons and addresses. 3370
Man is moral choice. 2321
Man is not alone. 3100
Man is your brother. 863
Man Jesus. 1959, 1991, 2000, 2012
Man Jesus was. 1995
Man-killing, by individuals and nations, wrong--dangerous in all cases. 2631
Man lives after death. 1887
Man--living soul. 1056
Man-made God. 3609
Man made whole; the life story of Fred M. Reed. 3031
Man may know for himself. 1009
Man Mazzuchelli, pioneer priest. 2376
Man, media, and the message. 1316
... Man: men: and their Master. 3445
Man, milieu, and mission in Argentina. 2501
Man, moral and physical. 1586
Man, morals, and history. 1818
... The man Moses. 1062, 2622
Man, myth, and magic. 2314

Man, Myth and maturity. 2836
Man named John. 2123
Man nearest to Christ. 2132
Man next to me. 2540
Man nobody knows. 1950, 1994
Man nobody missed and other sermons. 1555
Man not immortal. 48
Man of action. 2267
Man of Alaska. 3252
Man of Christian action. 1135, 1309
Man of devotion, Francis Asbury. 89
Man of faith in the new age. 1065
Man of Galilee. 930, 1950, 1966, 1970, 1972, 1984, 2002, 2048, 3127
Man of God. 854, 1325, 1959, 2939
Man of God for others. 772
Man of good zeal. 1650
Man of greatness. 3376
Man of history. 341, 1955
Man of like passions. 1506, 1625
Man of many qualities. 1879
Man of mark in the church tomorrow. 165
Man of Molokai. 1400
Man of Nazareth. 1527, 2016
Man of power. 964
Man of property. 1931, 2932
Man of sorrows. 1966, 2031, 2033, 3128
Man of suffering. 2885
Man of Tarsus. 2800
Man of the ages. 3364
Man of the hour. 1963, 1967
Man of the missions. 806
Man of the morning. 691
Man of the word. 2597
Man of to-morrow. 2696
Man of two revolutions. 1745
Man of vision, woman of prayer. 1575, 2845
Man on a moving stairway, and other Quakerly essays. 1676
Man on fire. 2803
Man on his own. 3107
Man on the run. 168
Man or matter. 50, 1743
Man outside himself. 94
Man preparing for other worlds. 3480
Man: present and future. 2325
Man primeval. 2320
Man reaches out to God. 3117
Man responsible for his belief. 695
Man, ruined and restored. 2321
Man seeks the divine. 3113, 3114
Man sent by God. 101, 2792
Man sent from God. 3235, 3471
Man shall know. 1060
Man, son of man. 3683
Man spoke, a world listened. 1301, 2302, 2318
Man stood up to preach. 1466
Man-talk; prayers for the man at work. 720
Man talks with God. 2893
Man that changed the world. 2059
Man the believer. 1602
Man, the Bible, and destiny. 2326
Man: the broken image. 2324
Man the choicemaker. 2320
Man the forgotten. 2325
Man, the image of God. 2321, 2326
Man, the life free. 3498
Man the Messiah: God's plan fulfilled. 206, 876
Man, the mirror of the universe. 3076
Man: the new humanism. 2325
Man, the saint. 1002
Man, the triune God. 3685
Man the world needs most. 3320
Man, the world's high priest. 1853
Man, time, and prophecy. 2321
Man to man. 791, 960, 1558, 2192, 2402
Man Upstairs. 955
Man uptight! 1006
Man visible and invisible. 1283, 3686
Man was not born to cry. 2694
Man, what a God! 1724
Man--whence and whither? 2325, 3506
Man, whither. 1514
Man who built the secret door. 3284
Man who can look backward. 3054
Man who can whip his luck. 3349
Man who changed the world. 925
Man who could do no wrong. 670, 1290
Man who dared a king. 1628
Man who dared to be God. 1969
Man who didn't have time. 2022
Man who died for me. 2033
Man who feared a bargain, and other sermons on Bible characters. 215
Man who forgot. 215
Man who forgot, and other sermons on Bible characters. 215
Man who fought the Devil. 3778
... The man who get even with God. 2122
Man who is God. 2039
Man who keeps going to jail. 885, 1527

Man who leads the Church ; an assessment of Pope John Paul II. 2126
Man who learned to give. 339, 633, 2373
Man who limped to heaven. 2269
Man who loved books. 1027, 1311
Man who loved everybody. 1977
Man who moved a mountain. 911, 2504
Man who never died. 1980
Man who said he would. 3125
Man who said he would and other sermons. 1555
Man who saw God. 1642
Man who stayed in Texas. 1305
Man who turned history upside down. 1991
Man who walked in His steps. 3402
Man who walks with God. 1754
Man who wanted to know. 2964
Man who was chosen. 2852
Man who was really Santa Claus. 2707
Man who would preach. 2901
Man who wouldn't listen. 1398, 2485
Man who wrestled with God. 1931, 2994
Man who wrote Scripture. 2799
Man with a book in his hand. 1455
Man with a song. 1027, 1642
Man with the Book. 3137
Man with the hope. 2437
Man with the noisy heart. 184, 2486
Man with two bodies. 3502
Man without God. 100
Man without tears. 2324
Man yearning for grace. 2281
Management for the Christian worker. 3142
Management for your church. 1200
Management in the church. 1200
Management of Christian schools. 3310
Management of ministry. 1199
Management of the missions in Texas. 2553
Managing change in the church. 1243
Managing church business through group procedures. 1170
Managing church groups. 1199
Managing creation. 3011
Managing God's goods. 3530
Managing grief wisely. 1774
Managing one's self. 962
Managing quality for higher profits. 3010
Managing today's church. 1200
Managing yourself. 982
Manchester Al mondo. 1528
Manchester Mormons. 1287, 2617
Mandaean studies. 2327
Mandaeans of Iraq and Iran. 2327
Mandaic incantation texts. 1892
Mandala. 2327
Mandate for mission. 1154
Mandate for white Christians. 1131
Mandate to humanity. 1314
Mandate to witness. 333
Mandelbaum Gate. 2541
Mandell Creighton and the English Church. 1387
Mangasarian Crapsey debate. 2008
Manhattan mission. 3435
Manhood and Christ. 2009, 3610
Manhood has a price. 2402
Manhood into God. 1893
Manhood of the Master. 1995
Manhood with meaning. 2402
Mani and manichaeism. 2328
Manichaean literature. 2328
Manichaen hymn-cycles in Parthian. 2328
Manifest destiny. 2465
"Manifest destiny" from a religious point of view. 3072
Manifest victory. 3480
Manifestation of Christ. 1911, 3013
Manifestation of spiritualism among the Shakers, 1837-1847. 3394
Manifestations of Christ universal. 319, 2019
... The manifestations of the risen Jesus. 2051
Manifesto. 648, 3395, 3533
Manifesto of Christian youth. 3885
Manifold in perception: theories of art from Kant to Hildebrand. 88
Manifold message of the gospel. 349
Manipulated man. 2324
Manipulator and the church. 3330
Mankind and religion. 3120
Mankind and the church. 1121
Mankind my church. 2436, 3365
Mankind's search for meaning. 1102
Mankynde in Shakespeare. 2594, 3400
Manliness of Christ. 1966, 1995
Manly Christ, a new view. 3125
Mann on Joss Stick Alley. 2310, 2511
Mann seeks the divine. 3114
Manna. 3519
Manna in the morning. 1438
... Manna of the soul. 2885
Manner is ordinary. 774
Manner of prayer. 2869

Manner of the resurrection. 2053
Manners and customs of Bible lands. 208
Manning, Anglican and Catholic. 738, 2328
... Manorathapurani. 47
Manresa. 2391
Man's ancient truth and its place in democracy. 204
Man's approach to God. 1740
Man's being, his destiny. 50
Man's best hope. 3059
Man's capacity to reproduce. 1859
Man's concern with death. 1415
Man's condition; God and the world process. 2675, 3243
...Man's consciousness of immortality. 1889
Man's cry and God's gracious answer. 60
Man's destiny in eternity. 1724, 1729
Man's destiny in the books of wisdom. 3821
Man's disorder and God's design. 3850
Man's divine nature. 2322
Man's divine nature, the trinity of God, Christ, and man. 2322
Man's divinity. 2324
Man's Earth-lease is about to expire. 605
Man's estimate of man. 2325
Man's eternal biography. 50
Man's eternal progress. 3495
Man's eternal quest. 1730
Man's faith. 1592
Man's faith and freedom. 82, 83
Man's faith and this crisis. 2116
Man's first disobedience. 3414
Man's first love. 1741
Man's greatest question. 3289, 3293
Man's harmonious development. 2321
Man's helpers. 1094
Man's hidden search. 2639
Man's high adventure. 3123
Man's history unveiled. 275, 1497
Man's incarnation. 1889
Man's influence with God. 2325
Man's intervention in nature. 1541
Man's journey through life. 2319
Man's knowledge of God. 1740
Man's last end. 3593
Man's living religions. 3116
Man's man called by God. 493, 1405, 2765
Man's need and God's action. 1094
Man's need and God's gift. 3652
Man's needs and their supplies. 1102
Man's new home. 1077
Man's origin, man's destiny. 202
Man's peace, God's glory. 2554
Man's peerless destiny in Christ, "but little lower than God." 3295
Man's place in nature. 2320
Man's place in the kosmos. 2324
Man's problems—God's answers. 3356
Man's quest for God. 2873, 2885
Man's quest for salvation. 3293
Man's reach. 1284
Man's real heaven and hell. 2325
... Man's relation to God. 2321
Man's relation to invisible forces. 2323
Man's relationship and duty to God. 307, 2325
Man's religion. 3064
Man's religions. 3119
Man's religious quest. 3138
Man's responsibility. 1745, 3785
Man's right to be human. 2996
Man's right to be human to have emotions withour fear. 2996
Man's ruin. 471
Man's search for certainty. 2400, 3482
Man's search for himself. 2325
Man's search for the good life. 3116
Man's spiritual pilgrimage. 3183
Man's spiritual possibilities. 2725
Man's spiritual quest. 3480
Man's supersensory and spiritual powers. 3685
Man's triumph. 781
Man's two memories. 2401, 3571
Man's ultimate commitment. 3106
Man's unconscious spirit. 3507
Man's victorious spirit. 3521
Man's vision of God and the logic of theism. 3608
Mansions of the skies. 2249
Mansions of the soul. 3053
Mansions of the spirit. 3071
Manteion. 1470
La mantique appollinienne a Delphes. 1421
Mantle of Elijah. 1506
Mantra & meditation. 2379
Mantra meditation. 2329
Mantram handbook. 2329
... The Mantrapatha. 2329
Mantras. 2329
Mantras for the morning. 2393
Manual. 219, 2958

Manual ... 1854. 1335
...Manual and other approved prayers of the Arch-confraternity of the Guard of honor of the Sacred heart of Jesus. 3269
Manual and record of the church of Paramus. 2772
Manual, catalogue and history of the Lafayette st. Presbyterian church of Buffalo, N.Y. 712
Manual commentary on the general canon law and the constitution of the Protestant Episcopal church in the United States. 2969
Manual de la iglesia. 3379
Manual for accepted missionary candidates. 2484
Manual for administrative librarians of parish library systems. 2224
Manual for altar guilds. 28
Manual for altar societies. 27
Manual for Bible study. 285
Manual for Biblical preaching. 2904
Manual for board members. 1320
Manual for Boy Scout troops in churches for God and country. 686
Manual for Christian instruction. 1333
Manual for church growth surveys. 1171
Manual for church in world witness. 1562
Manual for church musicians. 1205
Manual for church officers. 1239
Manual for church officers and boards. 1126
Manual for church officers and members. 2924
Manual for church officers and members of the govenment. 2924
Manual for church officers and members, of the government. 2924
Manual for communicants' classes. 1317
Manual for confessors. 2811
Manual for confirmation and holy communion. 1329
Manual for confirmation education. 1329
Manual for diocesan directors in organizing the diocesan office of the Confraternity of Christian Doctrine. 1330
Manual for evangelism/church growth. 1565
Manual for funeral occasions. 1694
Manual for GMSA leaders. 1254
Manual for high school Bible study. 473, 596, 597
Manual for instruction. 2114
Manual for interior souls. 3479
Manual for leaders of boys' clubs. 688
Manual for leaders of intermediates. 3154, 3171
Manual for leaders of Presbyterian pioneers. 2919
Manual for lectors. 2202
Manual for Luther Leagues. 2272
Manual for Lutheran Saturday-schools summer-schools, and week-day religious instruction. 2287
Manual for ministers. 1293
Manual for missionaries on furlough. 2486
Manual for novices. 741, 2716
Manual for priests of the American church, complementary to the occasional offices of the Book of common prayer. 2970
Manual for problem solving in Bible translation. 653
Manual for retreat masters. 3222, 3223
Manual for sisterhoods. 2122
Manual for teachers of primary reading. 3027
Manual for teachers of religion. 132
Manual for teachers on Old Testament lessons. 595
Manual for teaching Biblical history. 290
Manual for teaching temperance in daily vacation Bible and week day religious schools. 3597
Manual for the Commission on missions. 2433
Manual for the extraordinary minister of confimation. 1328
Manual for the holy eucharist. 2251
Manual for the local church commission on Christian social concerns of the Methodist Church. 2440
Manual for the members. 2928
Manual for the official board. 1239
... A manual for the public schools explaining the use of the graded set of charts and giving supplementary lessons to aid in the teaching of the nature and effects of alcohol and tobacco. 3595
Manual for the study of the city church. 1278
Manual for the use of church and mission schools of the southern union conference of Seventh-day adventists. 3385
Manual for the use of the members of the Second Presbyterian Church, Charleston, S.C. 2919

Manual for training in worship. 3560
Manual for vestrymen. 1239
Manual for victim souls of the Sacred heart. 3270
Manual for work in foreign fields of the Board of missions of the Methodist church. 2441
Manual for young adults. 1259
Manual of American colleges and theological seminaries. 3614
Manual of apologetics. 57
Manual of astrology. 96
Manual of Bible history. 289, 292
Manual of Bible selections and responsive exercises. 614
Manual of Biblical interpretation. 287
Manual of Buddhist philosophy. 702, 710
Manual of Buddism for advanced students. 701
Manual of canon law. 735
Manual of Catholic action. 753
Manual of Catholic prayer (The) 858
Manual of Catholic theology. 3647
Manual of Catholic worship. 2972
Manual of ceremonies for the use of the Catholic churches in the United States of America. 843
Manual of Christian archeology. 919
Manual of Christian beliefs. 951
... Manual of Christian doctrine. 780, 3640
Manual of Christian evidences. 1098, 1099
Manual of Christian pedagogy. 3154
Manual of Christian pedagogy for the use of religious teachers. 3165
Manual of Christian psalmody. 1866, 1867
Manual of Christian Reformed Church government. 1023
Manual of Christian theology. 3616, 3642
Manual of Christian youth work. 1260
... Manual of Christine doctrine. 780
Manual of church doctrine according to the Church of Scotland. 1234
Manual of church history. 809, 1174, 1178, 1184, 1191
Manual of church methods. 1250
Manual of church music. 1205
Manual of church services. 2238
Manual of classical literature. 1286
Manual of controversies. 792
Manual of death education & simple burial. 1414
Manual of demonology and the occult. 1423
Manual of devotion for seminarists. 855
Manual of devotion for the members of the Association of the sacred hearts of Jesus and Mary. 1443
Manual of devotions for nurses. 858
Manual of discipline. 3014
Manual of dogmatic theology. 3649
... Manual of early ecclesiastical history to 476 A.D. 1195
Manual of East Hanover presbytery. 2920, 2921
Manual of ecclesiastical architecture. 1157
Manual of ecclesiology. 1118
Manual of emblems of the saints by which they are distinguished in works of art. 3282
Manual of English church history. 1184
Manual of English church music. 1202
Manual of episcopal ceremonies. 842, 843, 848, 3526
Manual of episcopal ceremonies, based on the Caeremoniale episcoporum, decrees of the Sacred Congregation of Rites and approved authors, by Aurelius Stehle. Rev. by Emmeran A. Rettger. 5th ed. 842
Manual of exorcism, very useful for priests and ministers of the church. 1585
Manual of faith and life. 2914
Manual of family prayer. 1605
Manual of family worship. 1609
Manual of gospel broadcasting. 3018
Manual of graded Bible courses and habit, health and first-aid outlines. 636
Manual of guidance for camp administrators. 1260
Manual of historico-critical introduction to the canonical scriptures of the Old Testament. 540
Manual of holiday and occasional sermons. 3370
Manual of holiness and review of Dr. James B. Mudge. 2627, 2818
Manual of instruction for Baptists. 151
Manual of instruction for confirmation classes. 1329
Manual of instructions in the Christian religion. 1100
Manual of inter-church work. 1253
Manual of introduction to the New Testament. 411
Manual of law and usage. 2915

Manual of lessons in Old Testament history for academic grades. 596
Manual of marriage. 2345
Manual of masonry and anti-masonry. 52
Manual of meditations. 2392
Manual of mental prayers. 3455
Manual of missionary methods for Sunday-school workers. 2523
Manual of missions. 2493, 2926
... A manual of missions for laymen. 2492
Manual of modern scholastic philosophy by Cardinal Mercier and professors of the Higher Institute of Philosophy, Louvain. 2833
Manual of Mongolian astrology and divination. 99
Manual of moral instruction. 2592
Manual of moral theology for English-speaking countries. 949
Manual of morals for common schools. 943
Manual of mythology. 2653
Manual of mythology: Greek and Roman, Norse and Old German, Hindoo and Egyptian mythology. 2653
Manual of mythology in the form of question and answer. 2664
Manual of natural theology. 2672
Manual of occultism. 2727
Manual of Old English Biblical materials. 315
Manual of operations. 1250
Manual of pastoral problems and procedures. 2790
Manual of pastoral theology. 2790, 3676
Manual of pathological histology. 1817
Manual of patrology. 1616
Manual of piety for the use of seminaries. 1299
...Manual of plain chant. 883
Manual of practical church work. 1252
Manual of prayers for the congregation of Sisters of St. Francis of Mary immaculate, Joliet, Illinois. 859
Manual of prayers for the congregation of Sisters of St. Francis of Mary immaculate, Joilet, Illinois. 839
Manual of prayers for the Sisters of the Presentation of the Blessed Virgin Mary. 3421
Manual of prayers for the use of the Catholic laity. 855
Manual of prayers of the Congregation of the Third Order of St. Francis of Mary Immaculate, Joliet, Illinois. 859
Manual of preaching. 2900
Manual of psychometry. 3002
Manual of Reformed doctrine. 3640
Manual of revivals. 1566
Manual of Roman chant. 883
Manual of sacred chant. 883
Manual of sacred history. 3289, 3290
Manual of sacred rhetoric. 2900
Manual of Saint Anthony of Padua. 54
Manual of salvationism. 3187
Manual of Scandinavian mythology. 1493, 2666
Manual of Scripture history. 285
Manual of Scripture history, for the use in Jewish schools and families. 597
Manual of select Catholic hymns and devotions. 812
Manual of self-knowledge and Christian perfection. 1325
Manual of Seventh day Baptist church procedure. 3388
Manual of Spiritualism. 3503

Manual of systematic theology, and Christian ethics. 3616
Manual of the American Bible society. 611, 612
Manual of the Aramaic language of the Palestinian Talmund. 78
Manual of the Archconfraternity of the sacred passion of Our Lord Jesus Christ. 855
...Manual of the Archconfraternity of the Guard of honor of the Sacret heart of Jesus. 3269
Manual of the Archdiocesan union of sodalities of the Blessed Virgin Mary New York. 3454
Manual of the Blessed sacrament confraternity. 1330
Manual of the Catholic religion in three parts. 808
Manual of the chapter. 1672
Manual of the Christian and missionary alliance. 918
Manual of the Christian atonement. 105
Manual of the Christian science parent church. 1038
Manual of the Church of Christ Congregational in Milford, Connecticut. 1848

Manual of the church of the Nazarene. 1237
Manual of the Confraternity of Christian doctrine. 1330
Manual of the Confraternity of Christian doctrine for priests, religious, seminarians and laity promoting confraternity activities. 3165
Manual of the Congregational and Christian churches. 1338
Manual of the Congregational Christian churches. 1335
Manual of the discipline of the Colored Methodist Episcopal church in America. 1310
Manual of the discipline of the Methodist Episcopal church, South. 2455
... Manual of the divine offices for the use of the Discalced nuns of the Order of the Blessed Virgin Mary of mount Carmel. 844
Manual of the Evangelical Congregational church, in Westborough, Mass., 1875. 1546
Manual of the Evangelical Lutheran ministerium of Pennsylvania and the adjacent states. 1548
Manual of the First Congregational church, Gardner, Mass. Adopted April 8, 1879. 1337
Manual of the First Congregational church, Woburn, Mass. 1337
Manual of the First parish Congregational church in Saco, Maine. 1336
Manual of the First Presbyterian church of Freehold, New Jersey. 2915
Manual of the Gospels. 1987
Manual of the history of dogmas. 3655
Manual of the holy Catholic church. 796
Manual of the holy Catholic church; embracing first part. 808
Manual of the Knights of Tabor, and Daughters of the tabernacle. 3205
Manual of the Ladies of charity. 2190
Manual of the laws of Maryland, District of Columbia, Virginia and West Virginia relative to religious corporation. 1490
Manual ... of the Missouri Bible institute. 540
Manual of the mother church. 1031
Manual of the Northern Baptist convention. 2714
Manual of the Order of the fleur de lis. 1524
Manual of the parish Confraternity of Christian Doctrine for priests, religious, seminarians and laity promoting Confraternity activities. 1330
Manual of the Pentecostal church of the Nazarene. 2814
Manual of the Pittsburgh conference of the Methodist Episcopal church. 2447
Manual of the Presbyterian program for young people. 2921
Manual of the Reformed church in America (formely Ref. Prot. Dutch church). 1628-1902. 3044
Manual of the Reformed church in America (formerly Ref. Prot. Dutch church) 1628-1878. 3045
Manual of the Reformed church in America (formerly Reformed Protestant Dutch church) 1628-1922. 3045
Manual of the Sacred Heart. 3044, 3270
Manual of the science of religion. 3114
Manual of the Sisters of charity. 859, 3416
Manual of the sodalities of the Blessed Virgin Mary. 3454
Manual of the Sodality of the Blessed Virgin Mary. 843, 3455
Manual of the Sodality of the Blessed Virgin Mary. 12th, rev. ed. 3455
Manual of the United boys' brigades of America. 688
Manual of the Xavier alumni sodality. 841
Manual of theology. 147, 3642
Manual of theology for the laity. 795
Manual of Unitarian belief. 3727
Manual of universal church history. 1172
Manual of Westfield Congregational church. 1336
Manual of Westminster Fellowship. 3809
Manual of Woman's Missionary Union. 3838
Manual of worship. 2238, 3004
Manual of worship and polity. 1236
Manual of Zen Buddhism. 3894, 3895
Manual on campaigning for capital funds. 1690
Manual on Christian stewardship and church finances. 3529
Manual on Hebrew private life for popular use. 2121
Manual on management for Christian workers. 1251
Manual on personal evangelism. 1573

Manual on preaching. 2899
Manual on promotion of Association educational work. 3873
Manual on the liturgy. 2236, 2281
Manual on the marriage laws of the code of cannon law. 2341
Manual on the ministry in the United Church of Christ. 3732
Manual on worship. 2295
Manual. Rev. 219
Manual work for use in Sunday schools. 3557
Manuall of devout meditations, 1618. 3476
Manuals and catechisms of the Jewish religion in the early period of emancipation. 748
Manuductio ad ministerium. 3680
Manuel for adults for administrators and leaders of adult study groups. 3168
Manufacture of Christianity. 442
Manus religion. 2329
"manuscript found." 679
Manuscript history of Brigham Young. 3869
Manuscript history of Brigham Young, 1846-1847. 3869
Manuscript of Hugo Potts. 2320
Manuscript of Milton's Paradise lost. 2330, 2469
Manuscript remains of Buddhist literature found in Eastern Turkestan. 711
Manuscript, society, and belief in early Christian Egypt. 1501
Manuscripts from the Chilandar Monastery, Mount Athos. 2330
Manuscripts of God. 1581
Manuscripts of the Greek Bible. 315, 2760
Many are one. 797
Many but one. 1040
Many dimensional man. 2320
Many-faced argument. 49, 1739
Many faces of friendship. 1688
Many faces of grief. 1774
Many faces of Judaism. 2155
Many faces of love. 2890
Many faces of Murukan. 2632
Many hands in many lands. 2490
"Many infallible proofs" 61, 65, 277
Many little voices. 3562
Many lives, many loves. 3052
Many mansions. 1696, 3052, 3500
Many mansions: from the Bible. 251
...Many messengers. 2959
Many peoples, many faiths. 3115
Many religions, one God. 3067
Many roads, many mansions. 3495
Many-sided cross of Jesus. 107
Many-sided messages on the book of Jonah. 552
Many-sided Paul. 2797
Many signs, one son. 2018
Many things in parables. 2027
Many things in parables [and] The Gospel miracles. 2027
Many things in parables, expository studies. 2027
Many voices; the autobiography of a medium. 3503
Many ways of life. 1000
Many witnesses, one Lord. 346
Many wonderful things. 2726
Many worlds. 2186
Maori religion and mythology. 2332
Maori religion and mythology, illustrated by translations of traditions, karakia, &c., to which are added notes on Maori tenure of land. 2332
Maori tohunga and his spirit world. 2332
Map book for Bible students. 283
Map of life. 2228
Maps of consciousness. 2727
Maps of the land of Christ. 2763
Maranatha bells. 3320
Maranatha; reflections on the mystical theology of John the Evangelist. 414
Marble Collegiate Church. 2698
Marburg revisited. 2929
March into tomorrow. 867
March of Christ down the centuries. 3086
March of Christendom. 1183
March of eleven men. 1177
March of faith. 2620, 3184, 3744
March of God in the age-long struggle. 2983
March of God on earth. 1719
March of life. 2226
March of Methodism. 2433
March of missions. 3466
March of the cross. 1173
March of the demons. 1423
March of the gods. 1743
March of the Mormon battalion from Council Bluffs to California. 2602
March of the year. 2722
March on! 3259

March on with strength. 1545
March to win. 963
Marchant. 1227, 2411, 2810
Marching off the map. 2436
Marching on. 3882
Marching orders. 3882
Marching orders for a new day. 250
Marching songs for young crusaders. 3598
Marching thousands. 3047
Marching to freedom. 2172
Marching to glory. 3293
Marcion. 2332
Marcion and his influence. 2332
Marcion and the New Testament. 339, 2332
Marcnite mass and devotions. 849
... Marcus Aurelius and the later Stoics. 3532
Marechale. 681
Margaret and her friends. 2660
Margaret Clitherow. 1304
Margaret Fell speaking. 1637
Margaret Full. 1637
Margaret King's vision. 2172, 2511
Margery, Harvard, veritas. 1378, 2991
Margery Kempe. 2166
Margery Kempe, genius and mystic. 119, 2166
"Margery" the medium. 1378, 3496
Margie asks why. 911
Margin for living. 1623
Margin for triumph. 3371
Marginal chain-reference Bible. 259
Marguerite Bourgeoys, pioneer teacher. 686
Maria Monk and the nunnery of the Hotel Dieu. 2585, 2587
Maria Sabina and her Mazatec mushroom velada. 2376
Maria triumphans. 2359
Marian catechism. 2361
Marian era (The) 2363
Marian exiles. 3007
Marian exiles, a study in the origins of Elizabethan Puritanism. 3007
Marian mystic. 2333
... The Marian reaction in its relation to the English clergy. 2334
Marian shrines in the Holyland. 3405
Marian shrines of the Americas. 2362
Marianist year. 2391
Marianite centennial in Louisiana, 1848-1948. 3416
Mariannhill. 2334
Marian's book of Bible stories. 623
Marian's favorite Bible stories. 623
Marie corolla. 2361
Marie de l'Agnus Dei. 3128
Marie Magdalens funeral teares (1591) 2030
Marie of the Incarnation, mystic and missionary. 2334
Marie, sister of St. Therese. 2335
Marija v skrivnosti Kristusa in Cerkve. 2360
Marijohn. 1749, 3816
Marine among the idols. 1358
Mariological Institute lectures. 2363
Mariology. 2334, 2354, 2356, 2363
Mariology; a dogmatic treatise on the Blessed Virgin Mary, mother of God. 2355
Mariology of Cardinal Newman. 2702
Mariology of Saint Anslem of Canterbury. 2362
Mariology of Saint John Damascene. 2362
Marion churches and churchmen. 1223
Marion Lawrence. 3130
Marists and Melanesians. 850, 2546
Marital expectations. 2339
Marital intimacy. 2342
Marital love, its wise delights. 2340
Marital rites. 2337
Marital spirituality. 2340
Marjoe. 1748
Marjoe: the life of Marjoe Gortner. 1748
Mark. 434, 437, 2065
Mark, a portrait of the servant. 433
Mark, a translation with notes. 437
Mark Age period and program. 3473
Mark, an intimate portrait of the man behind the ministry in The compassionate touch. 713, 2485
Mark and Matthew. 433
Mark as story. 435
Mark, good news for hard times. 434
Mark--gospel of action. 436
Mark Gruner's Numbers of life. 3575
Mark my words. 437
Mark of a man. 2402
Mark of Cain. 724, 2232
Mark of Christians. 3188
Mark of holiness. 792
Mark the Evangelist. 435
Mark: the gospel of action. 433
Mark the road. 1008
Mark, the sorrowful Gospel. 437

Mark, the way for all nations. 437
Mark these men. 213
Mark-traditions in conflict. 436
Marked! 3291
Marked Bible. 260, 270, 655
Marked chain-reference Bible. 266
Marked men. 160
Marked reference Bible; includes the finest
  chain-of-reference system for Bible study.
  Being the King James or Authorized
  version of the Old and New Testaments
  marked by the best methods of Bible
  marking ... Marked and edited by J.
  Gilchrist Lawson. 226
Mark's good news. 431
Mark's Gospel, a history of its
  interpretation. 436
Marks of a man. 976
Marks of a Methodist. 2421
... Marks of a world Christian. 1015
Marks of distinction. 966
Marks of Jesus. 906
Marks of the nails. 2973, 3359
Marks of true devotion. 1429
Mark's story of Jesus. 436, 2011
Mark's witness to Jesus Christ. 435
Maronite Catholic Mass. 849
Maronite liturgy. 849
Marranos of Spain. 2332
Marranos of Spain, from the late XIVth to
  the early XVIth century, according to
  contemporary Hebrew sources. 2332
Marriage. 2337, 2338, 2339, 2343, 2344,
  2345
Marriage a convenant--not indissoluble.
  2337
Marriage a covenant--not indissoluble.
  2337
Marriage according to St. Ambrose. 29,
  2342
Marriage and Christian tradition. 2337
Marriage and common sense. 2346
Marriage and divorce. 2336, 2338, 2345
Marriage and family. 784, 2346
Marriage & family in a world of change.
  2340
Marriage and romance. 2340
Marriage and the Bible. 2341
Marriage and the family. 1603, 2339
Marriage and the love of God. 2338
Marriage and the sex-problem. 3390
Marriage bond. 2344
Marriage case manual. 2341
Marriage cases. 2341
... The marriage contract and the
  procreation of offspring. 2341
Marriage counseling. 2344
Marriage covenant. 2347
Marriage education and counselling. 2337
Marriage encounter. 2342
Marriage enrichment in the Church. 2338
Marriage; ideals and realization. 2340
Marriage in Cana. 2017
Marriage in Christian history. 2345
Marriage in church, chapel and register
  office. 2345
Marriage in church, chapel and registry
  office. 2345
Marriage in the light of Vatican II. 2344
Marriage in the Lutheran church. 2345
Marriage in the restoration. 2346
Marriage is for adults only. 2338
Marriage is for living. 1014, 2339
Marriage laws in the Bible. 2345
Marriage legislation in the new Code of
  canon law. 2341
Marriage manual for the administration of
  the marraige and family canons of the
  Protestant Episcopal church in the
  U.S.A. 2346
Marriage, monogamy and polygamy on the
  basis of divine law. 2604
Marriage of Hindu widows. 3214
Marriage process in the United States.
  2342
Marriage questions. 2343
Marriage records Sunflower county-Leflore
  county, Mississippi. 3566
Marriage sacrament. 857, 858
Marriage, sexuality & celibacy. 2346
Marriage should be honored by all. 2287,
  2347
Marriage takes more than love. 2339
Marriage, the family, and the Bible. 2341
Marriage to a difficult man. 1499
Marriage today. 2342
Marriage today. 2342
Married love. 2339, 2343
Married priest. 3128
Married priests & married nuns. 877
Married priests in the Catholic church.
  835
Married saints. 764, 1024, 3280
Marrow of modern divinity. 3294
Marrow of the church. 3294
Marrow of the Gospel. 1644, 1645
Marrow of theology. 3640

Marry or burn. 2339
Mars Hill Baptist Church. 2347
Mars Hill Baptist Church (constituted
  1799) Clarke-Oconee Co., Georgia.
  2347, 3052
Mars revealed. 3503
Mars: the war lord. 96
Marsden of Alaska. 2347
Marshal Feng, 'a good soldier of Christ
  Jesus. 1622
Martha Wesley. 3806
Martin Buber. 699
Martin Buber; an intimate portrait. 699
Martin Buber & Christianity. 699, 2152
Martin Buber, prophet of religious
  secularism. 699
Martin Buber: wisdom in our time. 699
Martin Buber's life and work. 699, 2832
Martin Buber's ontology. 699
Martin Bucer. 720, 3040
Martin de Porres. 2348
Martin de Porres, hero. 2348
Martin de Porres, saint of the New World.
  2348
Martin is baptized. 135
Martin John Spalding: American
  churchman. 3470
Martin Luther. 2273, 2274, 2275, 2276,
  2277, 2278, 2280, 2285, 3035, 3040,
  3629
Martin Luther and charismatic ecumenism.
  861, 2955
Martin Luther and his work. 2278
Martin Luther and Ignatius Loyola. 2277,
  2298
Martin Luther and the birth of
  Protestantism. 2272
Martin Luther and the morning hour in
  Europe. 2274, 3215
Martin Luther and the reformation. 2278
Martin Luther as a preacher. 2274
Martin Luther Christmas book. 2021
Martin Luther, creative translator. 283
Martin Luther, his life and teachings.
  2276, 3037
Martin Luther, his life and work. 2274,
  3040
... Martin Luther Hitler's spiritual ancestor.
  2278, 2671
Martin Luther King: fighter for freedom.
  2173
Martin Luther King, Jr. 146, 2172, 2173
Martin Luther King, Jr.; a picture story.
  2173
Martin Luther King, Jr., boy with a dream.
  2173
Martin Luther King, Jr.; his life,
  martyrdom, and meaning for the world.
  2173
Martin Luther King, Jr., 1929-1968. 2173
Martin Luther, leader of the Reformation.
  2273
Martin Luther lectures. 2278, 2281
Martin Luther, oak of Saxony. 2273
Martin Luther on the bondage of the will.
  1658
Martin Luther, reformer of the church.
  2274
Martin Luther—reformer or revolutionary?
  2278
Martin Luther: road to Reformation. 2272
Martin luther, saint and sinner. 2274
Martin Luther, selections from his writings.
  2285, 3629
Martin Luther: the great reformer. 2276
Martin Luther, the hero of the
  Reformation, 1483-1546. 2274
Martin Luther's doctrine of Christ. 2279
Martin Luther's religious thought. 2281
Martin Marprelate and Shakespeare's
  Fluellen. 2336, 3818
Martin Niemoeller. 2709
Martin of Mansfeld. 2277
Martvrdom and persecution in the early
  church. 2821
Martyr. 743, 1909
Martyr in black. 3130
Martyr in Tibet. 2555, 3704
Martyr laughed. 2943
Martyr of Antioch and Anne Boleyn. 48
Martyr of Futuna. 881
Martyr of our own day. 691
... A martyr of our own times. 691
Martyrdom and miracle. 2143
Martyrdom and persecution in the early
  church. 2821
Martyrdom and rebirth. 82
Martyrdom of change. 2574
Martyrdom of Jesus of Nazareth. 2014
Martyrdom of Joseph Standing. 3524,
  3762
Martyred Jew. 1963
Martyrology pronouncing dictionary. 2351
Martyrs. 2350, 2351
Martyrs and saints of the first twelve
  centuries. 3125
Martyrs and witnesses. 2351

Martyrs, from St. Stephen to John Tung.
  2350
Martyrs in all ages. 2351
Martyrs in China. 815
Martyr's message of hope. 865, 3369
Martyrs of Bohemia. 1857
... The martyrs of Florida (1513-1616)
  1630
Martyrs of Nagasaki. 2351
Martyrs of New Mexico. 1647
Martyrs of the Coliseum. 2351
Marvel mantel that caused a sweet mother
  to suffer in silence, and a strong father to
  sob out a prayer , and other true stories.
  2871
Marvelous life of the Buddha. 1703
Marvelous story of Christ and His apostles.
  1969
Marvelous work and a wonder. 2604,
  2612, 2619
Marvels beyond science. 2725
Marvels of divine leadership. 3465
Marvels of divine power. 2018
Marvels of grace. 1751
Marvels of prophecy. 608
Marx and Teilhard. 2321, 2352
Marxism, an American Christian
  perspective. 1319

Marxism and other Western fallacies.
  1922
Marxism and radical religion. 3234
Marxist looks at Jesus. 2041
Marxist philosophy. 1457, 2352
Mary. 862, 2354, 2355, 2357, 2358, 2360,
  2362, 2363
Mary, all-glorious. 93
Mary Aloysia Hardey. 1785
Mary Aloysia Hardey, religious of the
  Sacred Heart, 1809-1866. 1785
Mary and Christian life. 2356
Mary and Joseph. 2356
Mary and modern man. 2354
Mary and the Beatitudes. 2363
Mary and the Christian gospel. 2354
Mary and the popes. 2354
Mary and the priest. 2361
Mary and the virgin birth error. 3780
Mary and your everyday life. 998, 2361
Mary, archetype of the church. 2363
Mary Baker Eddy. 1035, 1038, 1493,
  1494, 1495
Mary Baker Eddy, an interpretive
  biography of the founder of Christian
  Science. 1038, 1495
Mary Baker Eddy and her books. 1495
Mary Baker Eddy: child of promise. 1495
Mary Baker Eddy fulfills prophecy. 1494
Mary Baker Eddy in a new light. 1494
Mary Baker Eddy mentioned them. 1496
Mary Baker Eddy: the golden days. 1495
Mary Baker Eddy's "Challenge to the
  world" 1035, 1495
Mary Baker G. Eddy. 1493
Mary book. 2360
Mary Charlotte Alexander (Au Mo Ling)
  24
Mary Clarke Nind and her work. 2711
Mary communes with the saints. 3279
Mary Dyer of Rhode Island, the Quaker
  Martyr that was hanged on Boston
  common, June 1, 1660. 1484, 1687
Mary for today. 2356
Mary, full of grace. 2356
Mary Gertrude. 2875
Mary, help of Christians, and the fourteen
  saints invoked as holy helpers. 770
Mary, hope of the world. 2358
Mary Immaculate, God's mother and
  mine. 2361
Mary in doctrine. 2363
Mary in her scapular promise. 2359
Mary in history. 2354
Mary in history, in faith, and in devotion.
  2354
Mary in our life. 2361
Mary in our soul-life. 2363
Mary in Protestant and Catholic theology.
  2360
Mary in the Bible. 2354, 2358
Mary in the documents of the church.
  2360
Mary in the Gospel. 2358
Mary in the New Testament. 348, 2358
Mary Kennedy's victory. 3379
Mary Magdalene. 2353
Mary Margaretta Campbell. 733
Mary, Mediatrix of all graces for all men.
  2356
Mary, mother and model. 2360
Mary, Mother most admirable. 2356
Mary, mother of all Christians. 2358
Mary, mother of Christ and of Christians.
  2363
Mary, Mother of God. 2359
Mary, Mother of Jesus. 2355
Mary, mother of nations. 864, 2362

Mary. Mother of the Lord. 2363
Mary, mother of the redemption. 2363
Mary--my mother. 2356
Mary of Agreda. 2333
Mary of Bethany. 972, 2353
Mary of Nazareth. 2354, 2355
Mary of Nazareth and her family. 2004
Mary of Nazareth, myth of history? 2356
... Mary of the Incarnation. 2334
Mary of the Koran. 2360
Mary of the Magnificat. 2315, 2355
Mary, Our Most Blessed Lady. 2355
Mary our mother. 2356
Mary Porter Gamewell. 2509
Mary, queen and mother. 2357
Mary, Queen of Apostles. 2353
Mary, Queen of Scots. 2353
Mary, Queen of the Apostles. 2353
Mary Reed. 2217, 3031
... Mary Richardson Walker. 2544, 3789
Mary S. Vanderbilt. 3497, 3768
Mary save us. 2885, 2893
Mary Slessor. 3425
Mary Slessor of Calabar. 2506, 3425
Mary Slessor, the white queen of Calabar.
  2497
Mary, Star of the Sea. 2360
Mary, the feminine face of the Church.
  2356
Mary the Mother. 2355
Mary the mother, and all mothers, in holy
  lands and all lands, on holy days and all
  days. 2355, 2624
Mary, the mother of Christ. 2354
Mary, the mother of God. 2357, 2363
Mary the mother of Jesus. 2357
Mary the queen. 2355
Mary, the spirit and the church. 1835,
  2352
Mary, Tree of Life and Our Hope. 2363
Mary-U.S.A. 2359, 3738
Mary, vs. Lucifer. 2357
Mary Ward. 3127, 3765
Mary was her life. 3136
Mary Webb and the mother society. 3136
Marya. 1004
Maryknoll book of treasures. 867, 2490
Maryknoll Catholic dictionary (The) 779
Maryknoll Fathers. 867, 2576
Maryknoll golden book. 867
Maryknoll missal. 846
Maryknoll mission letters--China. 2508
Maryknoll Sisters. 2363
Maryknoll spiritual directory. 867, 3332
Maryknoll story. 867
Maryknoll's first lady. 3243
... Maryland--the pioneer of religious
  liberty. 2363
Maryland's Established Church. 1223
Mary's alabaster box. 143
Mary's assumption. 2356
Mary's Christmas Babe. 1111
Mary's garden of roses. 3247
Mary's Immaculate Heart. 3270
Mary's month. 2355
Mary's part in our redemption. 2363
Mary's pilgrim; life of St. Peregrine. 2203,
  3279
Mary's story. 430
Mary's titles. 2363
Mas Heindel's letters to students. 3250
Mascot book. 35
Masculine in religion. 1048, 1057
... Mashrak-el-Azkar. 128
Masinaigans: the little book. 713, 1900
Mask for privilege. 2078
Mask Jews wear. 2154
Mask of Christian science. 1034
Mask of euthanasia. 1544
Mask of religion. 3725
Masks of God. 2650
Masks of orthodoxy. 922
Masonic addresses and writings. 1663
Masonic addresses in Tuscan lodge, no.
  360. 1671
Masonic addresses of Barnard Eberlin,
  1952-1953. 1663
Masonic chapter pennies. 1667
Masonic conservators. 1661, 2620
Masonic directory. 1664
Masonic encyclopedia. 1664
Masonic gems. 1671
Masonic gleanings from American and
  Masonic history. 1672
Masonic law of New York. 1666
Masonic lodge officers and how to become
  one. 1666
Masonic membership of the Founding
  Fathers. 1672
Masonic monitor of the degrees of entered
  apprentice. 1670
Masonic monitor of the degrees of entered
  apprentice, fellow craft and master
  mason. 1670
Masonic organizations and allied orders
  and degrees. 1672

Masonic potpourri. 1663
Masonic register for 1850. 1662
Masonic review. 1662
Masonic ritual. 1669
Masonic symbolism. 1671
Masonic trestle-board. 1670
Masonic trials. 1666
Masonic way of life and other masonic addresses. 1663
Masonic world of Ray V. Denslow; selections from his reviews. 1667
Masonry and its symbols in the light of Thinking and destiny. 1671
Masonry defined. 1662
Masonry defined, a liberal masonic education. 1662
Masonry in Nebraska, being an account of the Grand Lodge of the Most Ancient and Honorable Fraternity of Free and Accepted Masons of Nebraska, 1857-1957. 1667
Masonry in North Dakota, 1804-1964. 1668
Masonry in Texas. 1671
Masonry in the bluegrass. 1666
Masonry of the Bible. 1662
Masons who helped shape our nation. 1671
Masque torn off. 2935
Mass. 845, 2251, 2365, 2367, 2368
Mass, a historical commentary. 2366
Mass; a study of the Roman liturgy. 2366
Mass and liturgical reform. 2367
Mass and sacraments for teenagers. 3187
Mass and the life of prayer. 2370
Mass and the passion. 2367
Mass and the people of God, ed. with a foreword by. 2365
Mass and vestments of the Catholic church. 2368
Mass child evangelism. 896
Mass: Christians around the altar. 2367
Mass commentator's handbook. 2366
Mass communications and the church in Venezuela. 2369
Mass devotions and readings on the mass. 857
...The mass-drama, an outline of its structure. 2365
Mass explained. 2366, 2367
Mass explained to boys and girls. 2367
Mass for Labor Day. 2190
Mass in a world of change. 2368
Mass in meditation. 2368
Mass in other words. 2368
Mass in slow motion. 2370
Mass in the West. 2257
Mass in transition. 2365
Mass, its origin and history. 2367
... The mass-liturgy. 2365
Mass liturgy and the Council of Trent. 2369, 3710
Mass man and religion. 1060
Mass, meaning, mystery, and ritual. 2368
Mass means of communication. 1317, 3772
Mass of the apostles. 2369
Mass of the future. 2365
Mass of the missions. 2366
Mass of the Roman rite. 2366
Mass prayer book and daily devotions. 857
Mass prayers manual. 2365
Mass presented to non-Catholics. 2367
Mass reformed. 2366
Mass through the year. 1264
Massachusettensis de conditoribus. 2371
Massachusetts ecclesiastical law. 1489
Massacre at Monsegur. 22
... Massasoit. 3871
Masses and motets of William Byrd. 721
Masses at sea on the subject of religion. 2368
Masses for the dead. 848
Masses of Francesco Soriano. 3568
Masses of Holy Week and the Easter Vigil. 844, 1837
Massorah. 2364
Master. 1961
Master Alcuin. 23, 844
Master and his friends. 2006
Master and men. 3337
Master and the modern spirit. 3336
Master and the twelve. 72, 1974
Master Bible. 271
Master book of new illustrations. 1841
Master builder. 3304
Master builder on the Congo. 1503, 2513
Master-builder on the Nile. 3128
Master builders of Middletown. 1667
Master builders of Middletown, 1856-1956. 1667
Master builders of the Middle Ages. 753
Master calls. 949
Master choruses. 916
Master Christi. 2361
Master comrade manual. 3386

Master craft of living. 3750
Master diplomat. 2216
Master idea. 2980
Master indexed Bible. 271
Master is here. 2299
Master is here; Jesus' presence in fact and experience. 2637
Master key. 1828
Master key to every kingdom: grace. 3751
Master key to lasting peace. 1540
Master-key to popery. 799
Master key to psychic unfoldment. 2991
"The master key" to the problems of Passion week and the resurrection. 2028
Master Kung. 1331
Master library. 3096
Master library (The) 617
Master life. 1968
Master meditations. 2386, 3749
Master of men. 339, 2047
Master of mischief makers, Saint John Baptist de la Salle. 2189
Master of modern magic. 1345, 3240
Master of the world. 1995
Master on the Mount. 3336
Master plan. 3612
Master plan of evangelism. 1553, 2004
Master preacher. 2049
Master preachers. 2910
Master said. 3866
Master says, 'Go. 1238
Master scientist. 1792
Master sculptor. 2392
Master sermons of the nineteenth century. 3362
Master sermons through the ages. 3344
Master speaks. 2694
Master-speech. 3334
Master theme of the Bible. 2035, 3288
Master workmen. 1652
Mastereon, or Reason and recompense. 3519
Masterful discourses and writings. 2609
Masterful discourses and writings of Orson Pratt. 2609
Mastering life with the Master. 1007
Mastering life's problems. 968
Mastering New Testament facts. 450
Mastering our midnights, and other sermons. 1238
Mastering the books of the Bible. 635
Mastering the meaning of the Bible. 201
Mastering the problems of living. 2225
Mastering the tarot. 3588
Mastering witchcraft. 3823
Masterpieces of Biblical art. 602, 2760
Masterpieces of Catholic literature in summary form. 3619
Masterpieces of Catholic literature, oratory and art. 868
Masterpieces of Christian literature in summary form. 3619
Masterpieces of Indian temples. 3600
Masterpieces of Latter-Day Saint leaders. 2611
Masterpieces of Old Testament literature. 598
Masterpieces of religious art. 919
Masterpieces of religious verse. 3207
Masters and the path. 3686
Masters and the path of occultism. 3687
Master's art. 2061, 3179
Master's blesseds. 180
Master's book. 1661
Master's call to service. 3377
Master's carpet. 1662
Master's directions. 399
Master's greatest monosyllables. 2071
Master's indwelling. 970
Master's influence. 2013
Master's memorial. 2250
Master's men. 70
Master's messenger. 3207
Master's method of winning men. 1554
Master's minority. 3537
Masters of achievement. 661
Masters of science, masters of arts, and doctors of philosophy in the Physics Dept., University of North Carolina at Chapel Hill. 1469
Masters of the heart. 3057
Masters of the occult. 2731
Masters of the path. 2169
Masters of the spiritual life. 3478
Masters of the world. 3653
Master's secret of power. 2017
Master's slave, Elijah John Fisher. 1627
Master's theology. 400, 2063
Master's touch. 2608, 3427
Master's way. 1961, 3870
Master's word. 3251
Master's words. 473
Masterwheel; or, The power of love. 3102
Masterworks of autobiography. 120
Mastery. 1439
Mastery and mercy. 1846, 3207
Mastery of being. 2737

Mastery of consciousness. 2400, 3492
Mastery of Genesis. 523
Mastery of mysteries. 2990
Mastery of sex through psychology and religion. 3393
Mastery of the Master. 1999
Matchless altar of the soul. 3462
Matchless life. 1989
Mater ecclesia. 1093, 1122
Mater et magistra. 1137, 3453
Mater larum. 2197
Material. 1890
Material for a history of Pope Alexander vi. 24
Material gathered from the press of Boston relating to Christian science and Mary Baker Eddy. 1029, 1493
Material gathered from the press of Peabody and Lynn, Mass. 1029, 1493
Materialism and the mind-body problem. 2474
Materialist reading of the Gospel of Mark. 432, 3439
Materialist theory of the mind. 2473
Materialization and other spiritual phenomena from a scientific standpoint. 3499
Materialized apparitions. 3496
Materials for a life of Jacopo da Varagine. 1931
Materials for the history of the text of the Qur'an. 2185
Materials for the study of Georgian monasteries in the Western environs of Antioch on the Orontes. 53
Materials for the study of the Babi religion. 122
Materials for the study of the Babi religion, comp. 122
Materials for the study of the early history of the Vaishnava sect. 3766
Materials, sources, and methods of ecclesiastical history. 1184
Materials toward a history of witchcraft. 3824, 3826
Maternity; a baby is born. 2625
Mathematical astrology. 966
Mathematical laws of psychic phenomena discovered. 2987
Mathematical question. 3294
Mathematics of the cosmic mind. 3687
Mathers. 2373, 3009
Mathers on dancing. 1400
Mathew Blagden Hale. 665, 1781
Mating ministers and churches. 1290, 2474
... Matrimonial dispensations. 2342
... The matrimonial impediment of nonage. 2342
Matrimonial legislation in Latin and Oriental canon law. 2342
Matrimonial legislation in Latin and Oriental canon law: a comparative study. 2342
Matrimonial trials of Henry VIII. 1803, 3711
Matrimony. 2344
Matson Meier-Smith. 2400
Matsya puranam. 1815
Matt Talbot. 3580
Matt Talbot and his times. 872, 3580
Matt Talbot, worker and penitent. 3580
Matter and spirit. 2325, 2473
Matter, force, and spirit. 3076
Matter, life, and evolution. 2226
Matter, life, mind. 2372
Matter, mind and man. 662
Matter, mind and meaning. 2473
Matter of eternity. 2395
Matter of immortality. 2597, 3515
Matter of life and death. 1414, 1415, 3750
Matter of return. 610
Matter of Zen. 2382
Matters liturgical. 841, 2240
Matters of faith and matters of principle. 2181
... Matters of moment. 2269, 2393
Matthean redaction of a primitive apostolic commissioning. 445
Matthean weekday lessons in the Greek Gospel lectionary. 443
Matthew. 440, 441, 442, 2011
Matthew, a commentary on his literary and theological art. 440
Matthew, a scribe trained for the kingdom of heaven. 442
Matthew, a study guide commentary. 444
Matthew and guide posts to the millennium. 2465
... Matthew and Mark. 439, 440, 444
Matthew, apostle and evangelist. 442, 2373
Matthew Arnold and John Stuart Mill. 83, 2221
... Matthew Arnold's Literature and dogma. 230

Matthew Cowley. 1377
Matthew Cowley speaks. 2607
Matthew, Mark and Luke. 388
Matthew Merian's illustrated Bible. 601
Matthew Parker's legacy. 2331, 2775
...Matthew, Peter, Jude, Hebrew. 438
Matthew Simpson. 3410
Matthew, the genesis of the New Testament. 442
Matthew, the teacher's gospel. 442
Matthew twenty-four, an exposition. 444
Matthew twenty-four and the Revelation. 444
Matthew's Gospel (self interpreted) 444
Matthew's sayings of Jesus. 442
Matthew's witness to Jesus Christ. 441
Matthias and his impostures. 1612, 2373
Mature Christian. 959
Mature heart. 2387
Mature Judaism. 2137
Mature man's difficulties with his Bible. 280
Mature religion. 3000
Maturing in Christ. 376
Maturing in the ministry. 3671
Maturing of American Lutheranism. 2282
Maturing of the Conservative movement. 1348
Maturing the spirit. 3487
Maturity in the religious life. 2572
Maturity revisited. 1245
Maui-of-a-thousand-tricks. 2374
Maurice Blondel's philosophy of action. 672
Maurice Spertus Museum of Judaica. 2234
Maurice to Temple. 1137
Mavoch. 2115
Max Leopold Margolis. 2333
Max Lilienthal. 3130
Max Nordau to his people. 3896
Max Weber on the spirit of capitalism. 3088, 3800
Maxims and counsels of St. Francis de Sales for every day of the year. 2374
Maxims and gleanings from the writings of John Keble. 1440
Maxims and moral reflections. 2375
Maxims and proverbs of Bible and Talmud. 2375
Maxims from the Midrash. 2081
Maxims of Ali, known as the Commander of the Faithful (Amir-al-Mu'menin) 25, 2375
Maximum living in a pressure-cooker world. 1006
Maximum marriage. 2340
Maximus of Tyre on the dispute about images. 921
Maxton book about Bible stories. 628
May a Catholic be a Mason? 1663
May blossoms. 2356, 2362
May I hate God? 1003
May I have a word with you? 2145
May I have a word with you, Lord? 3406
May Perry of Africa. 2542, 2820
May the wind be at your back. 1624
May Thy kingdom come. 1396
Maya divine and human. 2375
Maya mission. 2208
Maybe it is your attitude. 1000
Maynard J. Geiger, O.F.M., Franciscan & historian. 1704
Maynooth college. 2375
Mayor of Indianapolis. 1898, 3799
Mazarin. 1639, 2376
Maze of Mormonism. 2612
Mazes and labyrinths of the world. 2190
Mazzini. 2376
MBI; the story of Moody Bible Institute. 2587
Me and my house, by Walter R. and Myrtle M. Williams. 1408, 2512
Me either ..... and other one-act plays. 3145
Me, my self and God. 3330
Me, myself and God. 903, 1723
Me, myself, and others. 3184
Me, myself, and who? 63
Me, you, and God. 1170
Mealtime graces for the family. 1749
Meaning. 2376
Meaning across cultures. 652, 1316
Meaning and end of religion. 3105
Meaning and measurement of commitment to the church. 1316
Meaning and message of Lent. 2209
Meaning and message of the book of Revelation. 455
Meaning and message of the cross. 105
Meaning and method. 3103
Meaning and mystery of being human. 1011
Meaning and mystery of the Resurrection. 2052
Meaning and practice of the Lord's Supper. 2256
Meaning and the method of life. 3075

Meaning and truth in religion. 3331
Meaning and truth of religion. 3102
Meaning and use of baptizein. 140
Meaning and value of mysticism. 2638
Meaning in texts. 405, 1806
Meaning of a missioner. 850, 2488
Meaning of Aphrodite. 55
Meaning of "bama" in the Old Testament. 503, 1395
Meaning of baptism. 135
Meaning of being a Christian. 1431
Meaning of Christ. 2040
Meaning of Christ for Paul. 375
Meaning of Christ to me. 2044
Meaning of Christian perfection. 2819
Meaning of Christian unity. 1046
Meaning of Christian values today. 950
Meaning of Christianity according to Luther and his followers in Germany. 2978
Meaning of Christmas. 1265
Meaning of church membership. 1201
Meaning of churchmanship. 43, 1211
Meaning of civilization. 1281
Meaning of death. 1413
Meaning of deepening. 128
Meaning of Ephesians. 364
Meaning of eternal life. 1695
Meaning of evil. 1746
Meaning of existence. 2739, 3101
Meaning of faith. 1591
Meaning of Fatima. 1618
Meaning of 'Fishers of men. 1628
Meaning of God. 1723, 1726
Meaning of God in human experience. 3100
Meaning of God in modern Jewish religion. 1723, 2139
Meaning of grace. 1751
Meaning of Henry Ward Beecher. 184, 3747
Meaning of holiness [as exemplified in four saints: St. Francis of Assisi, St. Teresa of Avila, St. John of the Cross, and St. Francis de Sales]. 1642, 3299
Meaning of holy week. 1837
Meaning of homoousios in the 'Constantinopolitan' creed. 1354, 2000
Meaning of hope. 1846
Meaning of human existence. 1105
Meaning of icons. 1880
Meaning of immortality in human experience. 1413
Meaning of Jesus Christ. 3133
Meaning of Judaism. 2138
Meaning of life. 997, 2225, 2226
Meaning of life and marriage. 997
Meaning of life in five great religions. 2228
Meaning of life in Hinduism and Buddhism. 2228
Meaning of loneliness. 2245
Meaning of love. 2263
Meaning of man. 2320, 2324
Meaning of marriage. 2337, 2343
Meaning of marriage and foundations of the family. 2338
Meaning of Martin Luther for the Black experience. 16, 2276
Meaning of Maryknoll. 867
Meaning of masonry. 1662
... The meaning of Methodism. 2421
Meaning of mission. 2480
Meaning of modern atheism. 100
Meaning of Moody. 2588
Meaning of mysticism. 2640
Meaning of parenthood. 2773
Meaning of pastoral care. 2787
Meaning of Paul for today. 376
Meaning of personal existence. 2728
Meaning of persons. 2823
Meaning of prayer. 2870, 2871
Meaning of reincarnation. 3054
Meaning of religion for man. 3063
Meaning of repentance. 3218
Meaning of revelation. 3225
Meaning of righteousness in Paul. 377, 2161
Meaning of ritual. 3855
Meaning of Sacred Scripture. 231
Meaning of saints. 1024
Meaning of salvation. 3288, 3289
Meaning of sanctification. 1823
Meaning of sanctorum communio. 1318
Meaning of service. 1635
Meaning of Shinto. 3404
Meaning of success. 1001
Meaning of suffering. 3541
Meaning of suffering in human life. 3539
Meaning of Tarot. 3588
Meaning of the Book of Job and other Biblical studies. 504
Meaning of the city. 1277
Meaning of the creed. 73
Meaning of the Cristero religious war against the Mexican Revolution. 1148

Meaning of the cross. 104, 105, 107, 979, 1997, 2031, 2214
Meaning of the Dead Sea scrolls. 1409
Meaning of the death of God. 1418
Meaning of the glorious Koran. 2184
Meaning of the mass. 2365, 2366
Meaning of the millennium. 2466
Meaning of the monastic life. 2570
Meaning of the mountain. 2626
Meaning of the New Testament. 349
Meaning of the Old Testament. 530
Meaning of the quadrilateral. 2962
Meaning of the Qumran scrolls for the Bible. 1409
Meaning of the religious life. 2570
Meaning of the Resurrection in Christian experience. 2054
Meaning of the Revelation. 453
Meaning of the sacraments. 3263
Meaning of the Second Vatican Council. 3772
Meaning of the war for religious education. 3159
Meaning of the zodiac. 3897
Meaning of tradition. 3706
Meaning of truth. 2611
Meaning of worship. 3853
Meaning without expression. 2833
Meaningful learning in the church. 3554
Meaningful living. 3539
Meaningful nonsense. 3070
Meaningful religious experiences for the bright or gifted child. 3173
Meanings of unity. 1044
Meanings of things believed by Christians. 3644
Means. 2983
Means and methods in the religious education of the young with special reference to the Sunday school. 3149
Means of a religious revival. 1566
Means of grace. 770, 3263
Means of world evangelization: missiological education at the Fuller School of World Mission. 1690, 2550
Meant for men. 2402
Measure of a church. 1118
Measure of a man. 881, 2320, 2323, 2402, 2544, 2817, 3401
Measure of a minister. 1297
Measure of a youth. 3884
Measure of freedom. 53
Measure of greatness. 2542, 3527
Measure of history. 497
Measure of our faith. 973
Measure of the universe. 3685
Measure religion. 3148
Measurement of attitude. 1124
Measurement of goodwill. 1747
Measuring religious dimensions. 3453
'Meat of the word' in Christian Science. 1033
Mecca and beyond. 2540
Mecca temple. 39
Mecca, the blessed. 2377
Mecca, the blessed; Madimah, the radiant. 2377
Mecca, the Muslim pilgrimage. 2635
Mechanics and faith. 3076
Mechanism and meaning of life. 2226
Mechanism of discourses. 2903
Mecklenburg Presbytery, a history. 2927
Medal. 2190
Meddling gods. 2660
Media for Christian formation. 3161
Media impact and you. 2369
Media on the move. 2369
Media, the message, and man. 974
Mediaeval and modern saints and miracles. 801, 2477
Mediaeval artes praedicandi. 2908
Mediaeval attitude toward astrology. 97
Mediaeval attitude toward astrology, particularly in England. 98
Mediaeval chantries and chantry chapels. 882
Mediaeval church architecture of England. 1159
...Mediaeval church vaulting. 3774
Mediaeval heresy & the Inquisition. 3324
Mediaeval humanist: Michael Akominatos. 6
Mediaeval Inquisition. 1909
Mediaeval Latin lyrics. 2199
Mediaeval legends of Christ. 1976
Mediaeval mystical tradition and Saint John of the Cross. 2136, 2647
Mediaeval mystics of England. 2645
Mediaeval philosophy. 2843, 3694
Mediaeval Russian churches. 1274
Mediaeval styles of the English parish church. 1159
Mediation. 2381
Mediation of Jesus Christ. 477, 2044
Mediations in Mark. 437
Mediator. 103, 1033, 2036

Mediator and other theosophical essays. 3689
Mediator, Jesus Christ in the Scriptures, the model of the priest. 2049
Mediatorial reign of the Son of God. 2039
Mediatress of all graces. 2361
Medical aspects. 3848
Medical aspects of the Latter-day saint Word of wisdom. 3848
Medical experimentation on prisoners. 1853
Medical guide to vocations. 3785
Medical language of St. Luke. 2271
...The medical man and the witch during the renaissance. 3825
Medical ministry. 2378
Medical missionaries you would like to know. 2538
Medical missionary to Africa. 2484
Medical missions. 2539
Medical missions, their place and power. 2539
Medical work of the Woman's foreign missionary society. 2458
Medici popes. 2216
Medicine and missions. 2539
Medicine and morals. 948
Medicine and religion. 2378
Medicine and the ministry. 2784
Medicine in the Bible. 317
Medicine in the Bible and the Talmud. 317, 2377
Medicine, magic, and religion. 2378
Medicine power. 1902
Medicine talk. 1900
Medicine wheel. 1902
Medicine woman. 41, 1399
Medieval and renaissance spriituality. 3493
Medieval art. 85
Medieval bishops of Dunblane and their church. 1482
Medieval canon law and the crusader. 1390
Medieval Christian philosophy. 2842
Medieval church. 1185, 1186
Medieval church and society. 1186
Medieval church: success or failure? 1186
Medieval ecclesiastical courts in the Diocese of Canterbury. 1488
Medieval English nunneries. 1357
Medieval English nunneries c. 1275 to 1535. 1357
Medieval essays. 1281, 1282
Medieval Essex churches. 1270
Medieval faith and fable. 1186
Medieval Francis in modern America. 1648
Medieval handbooks of penance. 2812
Medieval heresy. 1805
Medieval Inquisition. 1908
Medieval Islam. 2566
Medieval Jewish mind. 78
Medieval Jewish mysticism. 1539
Medieval Latin hymn. 1877
Medieval Manichee. 3324
...The medieval missionary. 2525
Medieval monasticism. 2583
Medieval myths. 2206, 2232
Medieval number symbolism. 3575
Medieval papacy. 2768
Medieval papacy in action. 2768
Medieval papalism. 2863
Medieval pilgrims. 1022
Medieval province of Armagh. 81
Mediseval religion (the Forwood lectures 1934) and other essays. 1281
Medieval religious houses, England and Wales. 2579
Medieval religious houses, Scotland. 2569
Medieval sinner. 1518
... Medieval spirtuality. 3483
Medieval texts and studies. 1760
Medieval thought. 111
Medieval thought: St. Augustine to Ockham. 2842
Medieval ties between Italy and Ireland. 1918
Medievalism. 2412, 2562
Medieval church architecture of England. 1159
...Medinet Habu. 2378
Meditate. 2380
Meditate the tantric yoga way. 2380
Meditating the Gospels. 399
Meditating the Sunday Gospels. 367, 1264
Meditation. 876, 2379, 2381, 2382, 2993
Meditation a day. 2385
Meditation: a step beyond with Edgar Cayce. 876, 2379
Meditation and its methods according to Swami Vivekananda. 2382
Meditation and piety in the Far East. 1485
Meditation & prayer. 2871
Meditation and the art of dying. 1412
Meditation and the Bible. 2382

Meditation disciplines and personal integration. 2379
Meditation, endocrine glands, prayer, and affirmations. 2382
Meditation for children. 2382
Meditation for educators. 3592
Meditation gut enlightenment. 1634
Meditation in action. 1537
Meditation in Christianity. 2381
Meditation in depth. 2381
Meditation in flowers. 1263
Meditation made easy. 2382
Meditation moments for women. 1433
Meditation notes on Paul the Apostle, model of the spiritual life. 2804, 3475
Meditation of the sad soul. 1538
Meditation on a prisoner. 2473
Meditation on the passion and Eastertide. 2029
Meditation on the prayers of the Mass. 2369
Meditation on the seven words. 2057
Meditation on the word. 3665
Meditation: the inward art. 2381
Meditational ascent on the tree of livingness. 721
Meditations. 1264, 1425, 1453, 2023, 2384, 2386, 2390, 2399, 2888, 3208, 3843
Meditations among the tombs. 1808
Meditations and contemplations. 1447, 1808
Meditations and devotions. 2393, 2399
Meditations and devotions for adults. 2391
Meditations and devotions from the writings of Francois de Salignac de la Mothe Fenelon, Archbishop of Cambrai. 1438
Meditations and devotions of the late Cardinal Newman. 2704
Meditations and prayers. 2397
Meditations and prayers for every situation and occasion in life. 2117
Meditations and selections from the Principles of Rene Descartes (1596-1650) 1425
Meditations and verse on living in two worlds. 2386
Meditations before Mass. 2369
Meditations by the sea. 2398
Meditations for adults. 1438
Meditations for all seasons and the Mass. 2397
Meditations for apostles of sensitiveness. 1453
Meditations for bird lovers. 663
Meditations for Christians and others. 2387
Meditations for college students. 3537
Meditations for Communion services. 2258
Meditations for days and seasons. 1439
Meditations for each day. 1433
Meditations for educators. 3592
Meditations for every day. 1264
Meditations for every day in the month. 2393, 3132
Meditations for every day in the year according to the doctrine and spirit of St. Alphonsus Mary de Liguori, doctor of the church. 2229
Meditations for every day in the year for the use of the Sisters of charity of St. Vincent de Paul of Mount S. Vincent-on-Hudson, New York. 1264
Meditations for everyman. 1264
Meditations for five Saturdays devotion. 3249
Meditations for happy Christians. 2398
Meditations for Lent from St. Thomas Aquinas. 2212
Meditations for men. 2402
Meditations for moderns. 1436
Meditations for monthly retreats. 3222
Meditations for Passion week. 2033
Meditations for religious. 2394, 2570
Meditations for religious for every day of the ecclesiastical year. 1263
Meditations for retreats. 2387
Meditations for seminarians. 3331
Meditations for seminarists on the passion and resurrection of Our Lord. 2033
Meditations for servicemen. 81
Meditations for the annual retreat. 3416
Meditations for the expectant mother. 2624
Meditations for the laity. 3481
Meditations for the later years. 17
Meditations for the new mother. 2625
Meditations for the newly married. 2347
Meditations for the passion season. 2032
Meditations for the quiet hour. 3477
Meditations for the season of Lent. 2210
Meditations for the sick. 3406
Meditations for the use of the secular clergy. 2385

Meditations for women. 3842, 3843
Meditations from Advent to Lent. 1263
Meditations from an exploration of the ultimate mysteries. 1727
Meditations from around the world. 1439
Meditations from Matthew. 443
Meditations from Portals of prayer. 1434
Meditations from the following of Christ of Thomas a Kempis. 3129
Meditations from the great American Indians. 3474
Meditations from the Manhood of the Master. 1995
Meditations from world religions. 2392
Meditations from world religious. 3204
Meditations in His presence. 1264
Meditations in John. 422
Meditations in Luke. 430
Meditations in Matthew. 443
Meditations in season on the elements of Christian philosophy. 1263
Meditations in sickness and old age. 3406
Meditations in the Psalms. 585
Meditations in uni verse. 2393
Meditations of a believer. 2015
Meditations of a Christian Chinese. 2510
Meditations of a hermit. 2387
Meditations of a parish priest. 3134
Meditations of a young man on the Bible. 237
Meditations of Elton Trueblood. 2397
Meditations of my heart. 2392
Meditations of St. Ignatius. 2270
Meditations of the heart. 1453, 2117
Meditations of the masters. 3484
Meditations of William of St. Thierry. 2388
Meditations on a theme. 3493
Meditations on Christian baptism. 135
Meditations on Christian dogma. 855
Meditations on death and eternity. 1417
Meditations on early Christian symbols. 2386
Meditations on Ephesians. 365
Meditations on eternity for religious. 1533
Meditations on freedom and the spirit. 1597
Meditations on garden themes. 2395
Meditations on hope and love. 2395
Meditations on life, death, and eternity. 3252
Meditations on New Testament symbols. 921
Meditations on our last end and on sin and the sacrament of penance. 2384
Meditations on prayer. 2880
Meditations on St. John. 422
Meditations on Saint Luke. 430
Meditations on Scripture texts. 2395
Meditations on the Apostles' creed. 74
Meditations on the Beatitudes. 180
Meditations on the Christian life. 955
Meditations on the church, based on the Constitution on the church. 1121
Meditations on the cross. 2015
Meditations on the devine liturgy of the Holy Eastern Orthodox Catholic and Apostolic Church. 2748
Meditations on the divine liturgy of the Holy Eastern Orthodox Catholic and Apostolic Church. 2748
Meditations on the Epistles of John. 367, 369
Meditations on the essence of Christianity. 1049
Meditations on the Gospel of John. 422
Meditations on the Gospel of St. John. 422
Meditations on the Gospels. 399, 1440, 1985
... Meditations on the Holy Spirit. 1836
Meditations on the last days of Christ. 425, 2034
Meditations on the life and passion of Christ. 1519, 1997
Meditations on the life of Christ. 1985
Meditations on the life of Our Lord. 2015
Meditations on the life, the teaching, and the passion of Jesus Christ for every day of the ecclesiastical year. 2389
Meditations on the Litany of the Sacred Heart. 2231
Meditations on the Lord's prayer. 2246, 2248, 2249
Meditations on the Lord's Supper. 1318
Meditations on the love of God. 1741, 2264
Meditations on the Mass. 2369
Meditations on the mysteries of faith and the epistles and gospels. 2397
Meditations on the mysteries of our holy faith. 2394
Meditations on the mystery of Christmas. 1111
Meditations on the Nicene creed. 2706
Meditations on the office and work of the Holy Spirit. 1827

Meditations on the Old Testament. 558
Meditations on the passion of Our Lord. 839, 858
Meditations on the passion of Our Lord Jesus Christ. 2032
Meditations on the passion of our most holy Redeemer. 2033
Meditations on the Psalms. 585
Meditations on the Revelation of St. John. 462
Meditations on the Sacraments. 3266
Meditations on the Sacred heart of Jesus. 3270
Meditations on the seven dolors of Our Blessed Lady. 2361
Meditations on the seven words of Our Lord on the cross. 2058
Meditations on the signs of the zodiac. 95
Meditations on the six days of the creation. 520
Meditations on the sufferings of Jesus Christ. 2032
Meditations on the Sunday Collects. 1308
Meditations on various subjects. 2387
Meditations, representing a glimpse of glory. 1795
Meditations through the Rg Veda. 3776
Meditations under the sky. 1456
Meditations upon the mysteries of our faith ... abbridged, 1624. 2394
Meditations upon the mysteries of our holie faith, 1619. 2394
Meditators. 3708
Meditator's diary. 1782, 2382
Medium and its laws; its conditions and cultivation. 3516
Medium, the mystic, and the physicist. 2989
Medium theology. 3641
Mediumistic experiences of John Brown. 3497
Mediums and the conjurors. 1404, 3520
Mediums and the development of mediumship. 2399, 3498
Mediums and their dupes. 3514
Mediums, mystics, & the occult. 2987
Mediums of the 19th century. 3511
Mediums unmasked. 3503
Mediumship. 3508
Mediumship and its development. 3494
Mediumship of Jack Webber. 3501, 3799
Mediumship of Mrs. Leonard. 2216
Die Medizin im Alten Testament. 317
Die Medizin im Neuen Testament und im Talmud. 317
Medusa's hair. 3574
Meek and the mighty. 3538
Meet a guardian angel. 3507
Meet Amos and Hosea, the prophets of Israel. 485
Meet Henry Kurtz. 2188
Meet it with faith. 1016
Meet Jehovah's Witnesses. 1940
Meet Joe Ross. 2781
Meet Martin Luther. 2277
Meet Martin Luther: his life and teachings. 2277
Meet Martin Luther King, Jr. 2173
Meet me at the door. 1256
Meet me on the mountain. 1507
Meet me on the patio. 648
Meet more people. 2244
Meet more people, have more fun. 2244
Meet Mrs. Yu. 3890
Meet Nicaragua. 2542
Meet our sages. 3585
Meet Saint Teresa. 3603
Meet Southern Baptists. 151, 3465
Meet the American Catholic. 811, 1245
Meet the American Jew. 2155
Meet the Bible! 308
Meet the gang. 687
Meet the Lord. 1976, 3884
Meet the Lutherans. 2303
Meet the man you were born to love. 1967
Meet the Mormons. 2602
Meet the Mossi. 2558
Meet the parson's wife. 1303
Meet the presidents. 3465
Meet the prophets. 2950, 2951
Meet the real Jesus. 2037
Meet the twelve. 70
Meet the Vincentian Fathers. 2575
Meet the youth of Cuba. 147
Meet them in the Scriptures. 213
Meet these men. 213
Meet your church. 2929
Meet your King. 442
Meet your neighbors. 3765
Meet your pastor! 771, 1295
Meet your United States. 2527
Meet yourself in the Bible. 215
Meet yourself in the parables. 2027
Meeting Christ in scripture. 640, 1170
Meeting Christ in the sacraments. 3265
Meeting God at every turn. 931, 2348

Meeting God; cues for enriching your relationship with the God of the universe. 985
Meeting God in man. 3782
Meeting God in Scripture. 318
Meeting Him in the wilderness. 2736
Meeting house and counting house. 1687
Meeting house & farm house. 1674
Meeting Jesus. 1971
Meeting life on higher levels. 955
Meeting life's reverses. 166
Meeting of the spheres. 3504
Meeting [proceedings]. 1249
Meeting the challenge of modern doubt. 1098
Meeting the living God. 3888
... Meeting the Master. 1951
Meeting the Messiah. 2212
Meeting the needs of adults through the Baptist Training Union. 3168
Meeting the test. 3882
Meeting the vocation crisis. 3785
Meeting with Christ. 795
Meetinghouse & church in early New England. 1271
Meetinghouse Hill, 1630-1783. 2687
Meetings. 699
Megdalen studies. 1213
Mehrchorige Stil. 917
Meigisia Meingi ma Mukanda wa Kalaga Yehowa (Major Bible Themes) 3682
Meile ir laime. 2265
Meister Eckehart speaks. 2646
Meister Eckhart. 862, 2644, 2647
Meister Eckhart on divine knowledge. 1491
Meister Eckhart, the essential sermons, commentaries, treatises, and defense. 862, 2644
Melanchthon. 2400
Melanchthon and Bucer. 3617
Melanchthon on Christian doctrine. 3646
Melanchthon on Christian doctrine: Loci communies, 1555. 3646
Melanchthon, the quiet reformer. 2400
Melanchthon. 2400
Melanesian cargo cults. 739
Melbourne churches, 1836-1851. 1271
Melchisedec. 2401
Melchizedek. 2401
Melchizedek tradition. 404, 2401
Melehizdek. 2401
Meliorism. 3621
Mellow fruits of experiences. 980
Melodi cantica. 1874
Melodies, duets, trios, songs, and ballads, pastoral, amatory, sentimental, patriotic, religious, and miscellaneous. 30, 3459
Melody in your hearts. 2573
Melody of the Twenty-third psalm. 588
Melody of the Twnety-third psalm. 588
Melrose Baptist Church. 172
Melting pot of Christian unity. 1042
Melville's quarrel with God. 2401, 3071
Membership trends in the United Presbyterian Church in the U.S.A. ; research report. 3736
Members of Christ. 3125
Members one of another. 1040, 1046, 1119
Membership in the kingdom of God. 2175
Membership in Zion Methodism. 1201
Membership manual of the Methodist Church for young people and adults. 2441
Membership manual of the Methodist church. 2441
Membership manual of the Methodist Church for pastors. 2441
Memento. 3137
Memior of Mary H. Huntington, of Bridgewater, Mass. 1856
Memo for a movie. 676
Memo for 1976. 1087
Memo for the underground. 3889
Memo from Gabriel. 3831
Memo to a weary Sunday school teacher. 3550
Memoir. 1772, 2353, 3127
Memoir and correspondence of Eliza P. Gurney. 3127
Memoir and correspondence of Mrs. Mary Ann Odiorne Clark. 1285
Memoir and letters of Frederic Dan Huntington. 1856
Memoir and remains of the Rev. Robert Murray McCheyne, minister of St. Peter's church, Dundee. 3131
Memoir and select thoughts, of the late Rev. Edward Payson, D. D. 2806
Memoir and sermons of the Rev. William Duval. 1484
Memoir and writings of Mrs. Hannah Maynard Pickard. 2845

Memoir concerning the Seabury commemoration held at St. Paul's cathedral, London, the fourteenth day of November, A.D. 1884. 3317
Memoir of Adelaide Leaper Newton. 2705
Memoir of Adiel Sherwood, D.D. 3403
Memoir of Alexander Viets Griswold. 1775
Memoir of Alexander Viets Griswold, bishop of the Prot. Epis. church in the Eastern diocese. 1775
Memoir of Alvan Stone, of Goshen, Mass. 3533
Memoir of Ann H. Judson, missionary to Burmah. 2158
Memoir of Anna Jane Linnard. 2231
Memoir of Anson B. Daniels. 1401
Memoir of Archbishop Markham, 1719-1807. 2335
Memoir of Bishop Seabury. 3317
Memoir of Caroline Hyde. 1859
Memoir of Catharine E. Alleman. 26
Memoir of Charles Henry Porter. 2864
Memoir of Charles Lowe. 2267
Memoir of Charlotte Hamilton. 1782
Memoir of Christopher Healy. 3128
Memoir of Clementine Cuvier. 1398
Memoir of Daniel Safford. 34, 3272
Memoir of Ebenezar Fisher, D. D. 1627
Memoir of Elder Abner Jones. 3129
Memoir of Elder Benjamin Taylor. 3589
Memoir of Elder Elijah Shaw. 3401
Memoir of Elder Thomas L. Garrett, of Paducah, Kentucky. 1702
Memoir of Eli Thorp. 3698
Memoir of Ellen May Woodward. 3847
Memoir of Everton Judson. 3124
Memoir of F. W. Henck. 1803
Memoir of Father Felix Joseph Barbelin. 173
Memoir of Felix Neff. 2679
Memoir of Florence Kidder. 2169
Memoir of Frances Amelia Ayer, of Lisbon. Connecticut. 121
Memoir of Frances Fowler. 1636
Memoir of George Dana Boardman, late missionary to Burmah. 673, 2505
Memoir of George David Cummins, D D. 3050
Memoir of George E. Ellis, D. D., LL. D. 1509
Memoir of George Howard Wilkinson. 3816
Memoir of George Shepard Boltwood. 675, 2371
Memoir of George T. Day. 1407
Memoir of Hannah Hobbie. 1821
Memoir of Harlán Page. 2757
Memoir of Harriet Eliza Snow. 3432
Memoir of Harriet Ware. 3795
Memoir of Hiram Withington. 3828
Memoir of James Arthur Cobb. 1305
Memoir of James Brainerd Taylor. 3590
Memoir of James P. Walker. 909
Memoir of James Petigru Boyce, D.D., L.L. D. 686
Memoir of Jane C. Judson. 2158
Memoir of Jedediah B. Prescott. 3133
Memoir of Jemima Wilkinson. 3816
Memoir of Joanna Woodberry Reddington. 3029
Memoir of John Britt, the happy mute. Compiled from the writings, letters, and conversation of Charlotte Elizabeth [pseud.]. 692
Memoir of John C. Lord, D. D. 2246
Memoir of John Codman. 1305, 1339
Memoir of John Cotton. 1372
Memoir of John Visger Van Ingen. 3767
Memoir of Jonathan Hutchinson. 3129
Memoir of Jonathan Saville; of Halifax, Eng. 3305
Memoir of Joseph and Mary Kinsley. 2177
Memoir of Julius Charles Rieu. 3131
Memoir of Margaret and Henrietta Flower. 1630
Memoir of Martha Thompson Sharp. 3401
Memoir of Mary Ann. 2245
Memoir of Mary Anne Hooker. 1844
Memoir of Mary Capper, late of Birmingham, England, a minister of the society of Friends. 123
Memoir of Mary L. Ware. 3795
Memoir of Mary L. Ware, wife of Henry Ware, jr. 3795
Memoir of Mary L. Wars. 3795
Memoir of Mary West. 3807
Memoir of Miss Eliza Bishop. 664
Memoir of Miss Margaret Mercer. 3132
Memoir of Mr. Ralph Isham Brown. 696
Memoir of Mother Francis Raphael, OS.D. 3126
Memoir of Mrs. Ann H. Judson, late missionary to Burmah. 2158

Memoir of Mrs. Anna H. Judson, late missionary to Burmah. 2158
Memoir of Mrs. Anne R. Page. 2757
Memoir of Mrs. Catherine M. Dimmick. 1459
Memoir of Mrs. Deborah H. Porter. 2864
Memoir of Mrs. Eliza G. Jones, missionary to Burmah and Siam. 3129
Memoir of Mrs. Elizabeth McFarland. 2307
Memoir of Mrs. Harriet L. Winslow. 2507
Memoir of Mrs. Harriet Wadsworth Winslow. 2507
Memoir of Mrs. Louisa A. Lowrie, of the Northern India mission. 3130
Memoir of Mrs. Louisa Adams Leavitt. 2205, 2934
Memoir of Mrs. Mary Mercy Ellis, wife of Rev. William Ellis ... including ... the details of missionary life. 1509
Memoir of Mrs. Rebekah P. Pinkham. 2849
Memoir of Mrs. Sarah L. Huntington Smith. 2552, 3431
Memoir of Mrs. Sarah Lanman Smith. 2552, 3431
Memoir of Mrs. Sarah Louisa Taylor. 3591
Memoir of Mrs. Sarah Tappan. 3587
Memoir of Mrs. Thomazin Johnson, of Braintree, Mass., with an account of her pious lineage, from John Alden, the first pilgrim father who placed foot on Plymouth rock. 2128
Memoir of Nancy F. Eastman. 1487
Memoir of Nathan W. Dickerman. 1458
Memoir of Nathanael Emmons. 1511
Memoir of Norman Macleod. 2309
Memoir of Normand Smith. 3431
Memoir of Normand Smith, jun. 3431
Memoir of Rev. Alvan Hyde, D. D., of Lee, Mass. 3129
Memoir of Rev. Bela Jacobs, A. M. 3129
Memoir of Rev. Benjamin G. Paddock, with brief notices of early ministerial associates. 2756
Memoir of Rev. C. W. Andrews, D.D. 41
Memoir of Rev. Charles T. Torrey. 3705
Memoir of Rev. Daniel Holbrook Gillette. 1713
Memoir of Rev. David Millard. 2463
Memoir of Rev. David Tappan Stoddard, missionary to the Nestorians. 2541, 3532
Memoir of Rev. Geo. W. Bethune, D.D. 195
Memoir of Rev. H. B. Soule. 3464, 3755
Memoir of Rev. Henry Bacon. 124
Memoir of Rev. Henry Lobdell, M.D. 2241, 2558
Memoir of Rev. Henry Martyn. 2349
Memoir of Rev. James M. Cook. 1368
Memoir of Rev. James Patterson. 2794
Memoir of Rev. John L. Prichard. 2938
Memoir of Rev. John Moore. 2589
Memoir of Rev. Joseph Badger. 124, 3808
Memoir of Rev. Joseph Harrington. 1786
Memoir of Rev. Jotham Sewall, of Chesterville, Maine. 3388
Memoir of Rev. Levi Parsons. 2487, 2777
Memoir of Rev. Luther Rice. 3235
Memoir of Rev. Mother Mary Teresa Comerford, foundress of the convents of the Presentation order on the Pacific coast, and the Missionary novitiate, Kilcock, Ireland. 1312
Memoir of Rev. Nathaniel Colver, D.D. 466, 1311
Memoir of Rev. Philip Wieting. 3815
Memoir of Rev. Robert Irvine, D.D., M.D., pastor of the First Presbyterian church, Augusta, Georgia. 1920
Memoir of Rev. Samuel B. McPheeters. 2310
Memoir of Rev. Seymour W. Adams, D.D. 7
Memoir of Rev. Stephen R. Smith. 3431
Memoir of Rev. Thomas Baldwin, D.D. 131, 1691
Memoir of Rev. William Gurley. 1919
Memoir of Richard Williams, surgeon. 2544, 3817
...Memoir of Robert Moffat. 2563
Memoir of Rt. Rev. James Hervey Otey, D.D., LL.D. 2752
Memoir of Rufus Ellis, including selections from his journal and letters. 1509
Memoir of Samuel John Mills. 2467
Memoir of Sarah Ann Bliss. 672
Memoir of Sarah B. Judson. 2158
... Memoir of Scovell Haynes McCollum. 2306
Memoir of Seth Burroughs, of Williamsburgh, Mass. 686
Memoir of Susanna T. Pierce. 2845

Memoir of the Christian labors, pastoral and philantropic, of Thomas Chalmers. 880
Memoir of the controversy respecting the three heavenly witnesses, I John v. 7. 3712
Memoir of the late Mrs. Mary Cooper. of London. 1285
Memoir of the late Rev. Alexander Proudfit, D.D. 2979
Memoir of the late Rev. John Freeman. 1660
Memoir of the late Rev. Lemuel Covell. 1375, 2506
Memoir of the late Rev. Savillion W. Fuller. 1690, 3755
Memoir of the late Rev. William Croswell, D. D. 1389
Memoir of the late Timothy Dwight. 1484, 1693
Memoir of the life and character of Ebenezer Porter, D.D. 2864
Memoir of the life and character of Rev. Asahel Nettleton, D.D. 2685
Memoir of the life and character of Rev. Joseph Vaill. 3136
Memoir of the life and character of Rev. Lewis Warner Green, D.D. 1772
Memoir of the life and character of Rev. Samuel Hopkins. 1847
Memoir of the life and character of the Rev. Samuel Bacon. 124
Memoir of the life and character of the Rev. Samuel Bacon A.M. 124
Memoir of the life and episcopate of George Augustus Selwyn, D.D. bishop of New Zealand, 1841-1869, bishop of Lichfield, 1867-1878. 3331
Memoir of the life and labors of the Rev. Adoniram Judson, D.D. 2157
Memoir of the life and labors of the Rev. Thomas G. Stewart. 3135
Memoir of the life and ministry of Mr. William Bramwell, lately an itinerant Methodist preacher. 690
Memoir of the life and ministry of William Bramwell, lately an itinerant Methodist preacher. 690
Memoir of the life and times of Henry Melchior Muhlenberg. 2630
Memoir of the life and times of the Rev. Isaac Backus. 123
Memoir of the life and times of the Rev. Isaac Backus, A.M. 123
Memoir of the life and work of Hannah Grier Coome. 3125
Memoir of the life and writings of Rev. Jonathan Mayhew, D. D., pastor of the West church and society in Boston. 2375
Memoir of the life, character, and writings of Philip Doddridge, d. d. 1472
Memoir of the life of Edward Stabler. 3524
Memoir of the life of James Milnor. 2467
Memoir of the life of Jeremiah Evarts. 1577
Memoir of the life of the Rev. Francis A. Baker, priest of the congregation of St. Paul. 131
Memoir of the life of the Right Rev. William Meade, D. D., bishop of the Protestant Episcopal church in the diocese of Virginia. 2376
Memoir of the life of the Right Reverend George Burgess, D.D. 717
Memoir of the life of the Right Reverend William White, D.D., bishop of the Protestant Episcopal church in the state of Pennsylvania. 3812
Memoir of the life of the Rt. Rev. Alexander Viets Griswold, D.D., bishop of the Protestant Episcopal church in the Eastern diocese. 1775
Memoir of the life of the Rt. Rev. Richard Channing Moore, d. d. 2589
Memoir of the life of the Rt. Rev. Richard Channing Moore, d. d., bishop of the Protestant Episcopal church in the diocese of Virginia. 2589
Memoir of the life and ministry of the Rt. Rev. William Meade, D.D. 2376
Memoir of the Most Reverend Francisco Orozco y Jimenez, archbishop of Guadalajara. 822
Memoir of the Rev. Albert W. Duy, A.M. 1484
Memoir of the Rev. Bernard Whitman. 3814
Memoir of the Rev. C. H. O. Cote, M. D. 159, 1372
Memoir of the Rev. Convers Francis, D.D. 3132
Memoir of the Rev. David Abeel. 2
Memoir of the Rev. David Abeel, D.D. Williamson. 2

Memoir of the Rev. Edward Bickersteth. 658
Memoir of the Rev. Edward D. Griffin, D.D. 1775
Memoir of the Rev. Edward Payson, [D. D. 2806
Memoir of the Rev. Elias Cornelius. 1369
Memoir of the Rev. Erskine J. Hawes. 1692, 1791
Memoir of the Rev. Francis Hodgson, B. D., scholar, poet, and divine. 1822, 2857
Memoir of the Rev. Gregory T. Bedell. 182
Memoir of the Rev. Henry Martyn. 2350
[Memoir of the] Rev. Henry Martyn, late fellow of St. John's college, Cambridge, and chaplain to the honorable East India company. 2350
Memoir of the Rev. Henry Watson Fox, B. A. 1637
Memoir of the Rev. Jacob J. Janeway, D. D. 1692, 1934
Memoir of the Rev. Jesse Lee. 2206
Memoir of the Rev. John E. Annan. 48
Memoir of the Rev. John Edwards Emerson. 1510
Memoir of the Rev. John H. Rice, D.D. 3235
Memoir of the Rev. John Keble, M.A., late Vicar of Hursley. 1291, 2166
Memoir of the Rev. John Rodgers, D.D. 3243
Memoir of the Rev. John Stanford, D.D., late chaplain to the humane and criminal institutions in the city of New-York. 3524
Memoir of the Rev. Joseph Sanford A. M. 3301
Memoir of the Rev. Joseph Stibbs Christmas. 1112, 3354
Memoir of the Rev. Joseph W. Barr. 174
Memoir of the Rev. Legh Richmond. 3236
Memoir of the Rev. Nathan Parker, D.D. 2776
Memoir of the Rev. Oliver Alden Taylor, A.M. 3136
Memoir of the Rev. Peter Labagh, D.D. 1693, 2189
Memoir of the Rev. Philip Henry. 1803
Memoir of the Rev. Pliny Fisk, A.M. 1628, 2487
Memoir of the Rev. Richard Sluyter. 3426
Memoir of the Rev. S. J. M. Eaton, d. d. 1487
Memoir of the Rev. Samuel Barrett, D. D. 3124
Memoir of the Rev. Samuel Green, late pastor of Union church, Boston. 1772
Memoir of the Rev. Thomas Scott. 3315
Memoir of the Rev. W. A. B. Johnson. 3134
Memoir of the Rev. W. H. Hewitson. 1809
Memoir of the Rev. W. Sparrow Simpson, D.D., rector of St. Vedast and sub-dean of St. Paul's cathedral. 3410
Memoir of the Rev. Walter Gunn. 1778
Memoir of the Rev. William Staughton, D.D. 3526
Memoir of the Rev. William Tennent. 3124, 3601
Memoir of the Rev. Wm. C. Burns, M.A., missionary to China from the English Presbyterian Church. 718
Memoir of the Reverend Alfred George Duthie. 187, 1484
Memoir of the Reverend Sydney Smith. 3431
Memoir of the Very Rev. Theobald Mathew. 2373, 3594
Memoir of Thomas Cranfield, of London. 1378
Memoir of Thomas Whittemoore, D.D. 3814
Memoir of Timothy Gilbert. 1713
Memoir of Very Reverend J. J. Sullivan, C.M. 3545
Memoir of William A. Stanton, S. J. 3525
Memoir of William C. Cattell, D. D., LL. D. 876
Memoir of William C. Walton. 3791
Memoir of William Carey, D. D., late missionary to Bengal. 739
Memoir of William David Stuart. 3135
Memoir of William Ellery Channing. 882
Memoir of William Henry Channing. 882
Memoir of William R. Fales, the Portsmouth cripple. 3126
Memoir of William Randall Saxton, of Lebanon, Conn. With the funeral sermon. 1693, 3306
Memoir on the life and character of the Rev. Prince Demetrius A. de Gallitzin, founder of Loretto and catholicity, in Cambria county, Pa., apostle of the Alleghanies. 1744

Memoir on the nature of the church of Christ. 2746
Memoir, with sermons, of Rev. Josiah Peet. 1342, 2810
Memoirs. 827, 2474, 2586, 2713, 3124
Memoirs and journal of Hugh Judge. 2156
Memoirs and letters of Mrs. Mary Dexter. 1692
Memoirs and remains of John Oliphant, of Auburn, New York. 3132
Memoirs and reminiscences of the late Prof. George Bush. 719
Memoirs and select papers of Horace B. Morse, A.B. of Haverhill, N.H. 2620
Memoirs and select remains of William C. Bushnell. 719
Memoirs and writings of the Very Reverend James F. Callaghan, D. D. 3125
Memoirs by Charles J. Darlington. 3126
Memoirs called Gospels. 389
Memoirs, historical and edifying, of a missionary apostolic of the order of Saint Dominic among various Indian tribes. 827
Memoirs, incidents & reminiscences of the early history of the New Church in Michigan, Indiana, Illinois, and adjacent States; and Canada. 2692
Memoirs, including letters, and select remains, of John Urquhart. 3761
Memoirs, life and influence of Dr. and Mrs. Joseph Cowgill Maple. 2332
Memoirs of a beggar. 892
Memoirs of a centenarian. 2913
Memoirs of a metropolitan minister. 2962
Memoirs of a Renaissance Pope. 2850
Memoirs of a royal chaplain, 1729-1763. 2168
Memoirs of Abner Kingman Nott. 2716
Memoirs of Alexander Campbell. 732
Memoirs of an anti-semite. 3133
Memoirs of Archbishop Juxon. 2161, 2233
Memoirs of Archbishop Temple. 3598
Memoirs of Ber of Bolechow. 2098
Memoirs of Capt. James Wilson. 3818
Memoirs of Charles J. Darlington. 3126
Memoirs of deceased Christian ministers. 1705
Memoirs of Dr. Winthrop Hartly Hopson. 1465, 1847
Memoirs of Elder Edmund Botsford. 685
Memoirs of Elder Jesse Mercer. 2411
Memoirs of Elizabeth Collins, of Upper Evesham, New Jersey. 3125
Memoirs of eminently pious women. 3834
Memoirs of eminently pious women of Britain and America. 3831
Memoirs of Francis Thomas McDougall. 2307
Memoirs of George Whitehead. 3137
Memoirs of God. 1725
Memoirs of Henry Obookiah. 2721
Memoirs of Isaac Errett. 1527
Memoirs of Issac Erret with selections from his writings. 1527
Memoirs of Jacob Ritter. 3133
Memoirs of James Lackington. 681
Memoirs of John Frederic Oberlin. 1497, 2720
Memoirs of John Kitto. 3130
Memoirs of John M. Mason, D.D., S.T.P. 2364
Memoirs of John R. Sampey. 3297
Memoirs of John R. Young. 2607
Memoirs of John Urquhart. 3761
Memoirs of John Wheelwright. 3810
Memoirs of Joseph John Gurney. 1778
Memoirs of Joseph John Gurney, with selections from his journal and correspondence. 1778
Memoirs of Joseph W. Pickett. 2845
Memoirs of life and character of the Rev. Matthias Bruen. 698
Memoirs of Mary Baker Eddy. 1494
Memoirs of Miss Caroline E. Smelt. 3426
Memoirs of Mr. Wesley's missionaries to America. 2439
Memoirs of Mother Frances Blin de Bourdon, S.N.D. 659
Memoirs of Mother Mary Aquinata Fiegler, O.P. 1624
Memoirs of Mrs. Angeline B. Sears. 3317
Memoirs of Mrs. Eleanor Emerson. 1692
Memoirs of Mrs. Elizabeth Mortimer. 2620
Memoirs of Mrs. Hawkes late of Islington. 1791
Memoirs of Mrs. Joanna Bethune. 196
Memoirs of Mrs. Mary Cooper of London, who departed this life, June 22, 1812, in the twenty-sixth year of her age. 3125
Memoirs of my day. 2603
Memoirs of my people. 2084
Memoirs of my people through a thousand years, selected and edited. 2084

Memoirs of Puget Sound. 670, 2460
Memoirs of Rev. Benjamin C. Cutler, D. D. 1397
Memoirs of Rev. Charles G. Finney. 1625, 1626
Memoirs of Rev. Jacob Goering, Rev. George Lochman, D.D., and Rev. Benjamin Kurtz, D.D., LL.D., by rev. Charles A. Hay, D.D. 1743
Memoirs of Rev. Joseph Buckminster, D.D., and of his son, Rev. Joseph Stevens Buckminster. 700
Memoirs of Rev. Nathaniel Kendrick, D.D. and Silas N. Kendrick. 2167
Memoirs of Rev. Wm. Vaughan, D.D., by his son, Thos. M. Vaughan. 3774
Memoirs of Reverend J. Samuel Schwerdtfeger. 3313
Memoirs of Richard Baxter Hayes. 1792
Memoirs of St. Peter. 432
Memoirs of Scottish Catholics during the xviith and xviiith centuries, selected from hitherto inedited mss. 873
Memoirs of Simeon Wilhelm. 3124
Memoirs of Simon Episcopius. 1525
Memoirs of Sister Louise. 2261
Memoirs of the Crusades. 1391, 2261
Memoirs of the early life of John Chamberlain. 3125
Memoirs of the Hon. Walter Lowrie. 3130
Memoirs of the late Miss Lucy Richards, of Paris, Oneida county, N.Y. 3133
Memoirs of the late Mrs. Susan Huntington, of Boston, Mass. 1856
Memoirs of the late Rev. Joseph J. Hanly, M. D. 1784
Memoirs of the late Rev. Samuel Pearce. 1692, 2810
Memoirs of the life. 3127
Memoirs of the life and character of Mrs. Sarah Savage, eldest daughter of the Rev. Philip Henry, A.M., and an appendix. 3305
Memoirs of the life and character of the late Rev. Cornelius Winter. 3129
Memoirs of the life and character of the late Rev. George Atwell. 109
Memoirs of the life and gospel labours of Stephen Grellet. 1774
Memoirs of the life and ministry of the late Rev. Thomas Spencer, of Liverpool. 3471
Memoirs of the life and ministry of the Rev. John Summerfield, a.m. 3546
Memoirs of the life and religious experience of Ray Potter. 1478, 1662
Memoirs of the life and religious experience of Sarah Tucker. 3136
Memoirs of the life and services of the Rt. Rev. Alonzo Potter, D.D., LL.D. 2865
Memoirs of the life and writings of the Rev. Andrew Fuller. 1689
Memoirs of the life and writings of the Rev. Claudius Buchanan. 699
Memoirs of the life and writings of the Rev. Richard Watson. 3798
Memoirs of the life and writings of Thomas Chalmers. 880
Memoirs of the life, character, and labours of the Rev. John Smith, late of Sheffield. 3427
Memoirs of the life of David Ferris. 3126
Memoirs of the life of David Marks. 2335
Memoirs of the life of Isaac Penington. 3133
Memoirs of the life of Joseph Alleine. 25
Memoirs of the life of Mrs. Sarah Osborn. 2752
Memoirs of the life of Nathaniel Stacy. 3135
Memoirs of the life of the Rev. Charles Simeon. 3409
Memoirs of the life of the Rev. Peard Dickinson. 3126
Memoirs of the life of the Reverend George Whitefield. 3813
Memoirs of the lives, characters and writings of those two eminently pious and useful ministers of Jesus Christ. 3798
Memoirs of the lives of Robert Haldane of Airthrey. 1780
Memoirs of the Papal Court. 1541, 2769
Memoirs of the Pittsburgh Sisters of mercy. 3418
Memoirs of the Protestant Episcopal church in the United States of America. 2967
Memoirs of the religious experience and life of Abigail House. 3128
Memoirs of the Rev. Ammi Robers, A.M., a clergyman of the Episcopal church. 3134
Memoirs of the Rev. Ammi Rogers, A. M., a clergyman of the Episcopal church. 3133, 3134

Memoirs of the Rev. David Brainerd. 1900
Memoirs of the Rev. David Stoner. 3533
Memoirs of the Rev. David Tappan Stoddard. 2541, 3532
Memoirs of the Rev. John H. Livingston. 2241
Memoirs of the Rev. John Henry Livingston. 2241
Memoirs of the Rev. John McDowell, D.D., and the Rev. William A. McDowell, D.D. 2307
Memoirs of the Rev. John Newton. 2705
Memoirs of the Rev. John Rodgers, D.D. 3243
Memoirs of the Rev. Joseph Benson. 191
Memoirs of the Rev. Nicholas Murray, D. D. (Kirwan.) 2632
Memoirs of the Rev. Noah Worcester, D.D. 3848
Memoirs of the Rev. Richard Whatcoat. 3810
Memoirs of the Rev. Robert Finley, D.D. 31, 1625
Memoirs of the Rev. S. F. Johnston. 2129, 2542
Memoirs of the Rev. Samuel J. Mills. 2467, 2548
Memoirs of the Rev. Thomas Cleland, D.D. 1287
Memoirs of the Rev. Thomas Halyburton. 3128
Memoirs of the Rev. Walter M. Lowrie. 3130
Memoirs of the Rev. William Jackson. 1931
Memoirs of the Wesley family. 3802
Memoirs of William Miller. 2467
Memoirs of Zi Pre. 785
Memoirs; or, From herdboy to college president. 195
Memoirs to the life of the Rev. William Tennent. 3601
Memorabilia of fifty years, 1877 to 1927. 3820
Memorabilia of George B. Cheever, D. D. 890
Memorabilia of Swedenborg. 2691
Memorable passages from the Bible. 614
Memorable voyage. 2852, 2862
Memorable words of Saint Francis. 3492, 3493
Memoranda concerning Sheldon Jackson and the moderatorship of the 109th General assembly of the Presbyterian church in the United States of America. 1930, 2920
Memoranda of persons, places, and events. 3499
Memoranda of the experience, labors. and travels of a Universalist preacher. 3134
Memorial addresses on the character and public services of the Rev. Samuel Ware Fisher, D.D., LL.D. 1628, 3762
Memorial craftsman's guide. 3333
Memorial history of the Baptists of Alabama. 143
Memorial history of the Pittsburg synod of the Evangelical Lutheran church. 1548
Memorial inscriptions in Durham cathedral. 1483
Memorial markers and headstones. 3333
... Memorial meeting, Israel Friendlaender, Bernard Cantor, whose lives were sacrificed July 5, 1920, in the cause of Israel and in the service of humanity. 1673
Memorial messages. 1691
Memorial of a Christian life. 999
Memorial of a true life. 182
Memorial of Albert Gallatin Palmer, D.D., preacher, pastor, poet, scholar. 2766
Memorial of Alice and Phoebe Cary. 743
Memorial of Alice and Phoebe Cary, with some of their later poems. By Mary Clemmer Ames. Illustrated by two portraits on steel. 743
Memorial of Bishop Hobart. 1821
Memorial of closing scenes in the life of Rev. George B. Little. 2233
Memorial of Cortlandt Van Rensselaer. 1692, 3767
Memorial of Eliza Butler Thompson. 3697
Memorial of Francis L. Hawks, D. D., LL C. 1791
Memorial of Fray Alonso de Benavides. 2693
Memorial of Fray Alonso de Benavides, 1630. 2693
Memorial of Horace Tracy Pitkin. 2849
Memorial of Horace William Rose. 3249
Memorial of Jesse Lee and the Old elm. 2206
Memorial of Mary E. Smalley, late the wife of John W. Sarles, pastor of the Central Baptist church, Brooklyn. 3303
Memorial of Mrs. Grace W. Thwing. 3698

Memorial of Nathan B. Crocker, D. D. 1387
Memorial of Nathaniel Milton Wood. 169
Memorial of O. W. Wight, A.M., M.D. Sanitarian, lawyer, and author. 3815
Memorial of Philip Embury. 1510, 2436
Memorial of Rev. Abraham Polhemus, D. D. 1692
Memorial of Rev. Arthur Burtis, D. D. 719
Memorial of Rev. Edward B. Hall, D. D. 1612, 1781
Memorial of Rev. John A. Albro, D.D. 23
Memorial of Rev. Joseph Tuckerman. 3726
Memorial of Rev. Myron Newton Morris. 2620
Memorial of Rev. Peter O. Studdiford, D. D. 1692, 3536
Memorial of Rev. Philip F. Mayer. 2375
Memorial of Rev. Philip F. Mayer, D.D., late pastor of St. John's Lutheran church, Philadelphia. 2375
Memorial of Rev. Rufus Ellis, D. D. 1509
Memorial of Rev. T. H. Kenaston. 2167
Memorial of Rev. Warren H. Cudworth. 1392
Memorial of Rev. William W. Phillips, D.D. 1692, 2831
Memorial of Samuel Foster McCleary, jr. 2306
Memorial of Samuel Gilman Brown, D. D., LL. D. 696
Memorial of the agents of the New England Mississippi land company to Congress. 1706
Memorial of the centennial anniversary of the First Presbyterian church, Augusta, Georgia. 2912
Memorial of the Christian life and character of Francis S. Sampson, D.D. 3297
Memorial of the Federal-street meeting-house. 1701
Memorial of the Futtehgurh mission and her martyred missionaries. 2532
Memorial of the life and labors of Rt. Rev. Stephen Vincent Ryan ... second bishop of Buffalo, N.Y. 3259
Memorial of the life and labors of the Rev. Cyrus Dickson, D.D. 1458
Memorial of the life and services of the late Rev. Henry A. Rowland, D D. 1692, 3252
Memorial of the life, character, and death of Rev. Benjamin F. Hosford. 1848
Memorial of the Most Reverend Michael Augustine Corrigan, D. D., third archbishop of New York. 1370
Memorial of the old and new Tabernacle, Salem, Mass. 3286
Memorial of the Rev. Austin Craig. 1378
Memorial of the Rev. Chalon Burgess, D. D. 717
Memorial of the Rev. Henry G. Comingo, D. D. 1312
Memorial of the Rev. Lewis P. Bayard, D.D. 1691
Memorial of the Rev. Robert Collyer. 1310
Memorial of the Rev. Robert Collyer ... late minister of the Unitarian church of the Messiah, New York city. 1310
Memorial of the Rev. Thomas Mather Smith, D. D. 3431
Memorial of the semi-centenary celebration of the Theological institute of Connecticut. 3612
Memorial of Theodore Bayard Romeyn, D.D., late pastor of the First Reformed (Dutch) church. 3247
Memorial papers. 2166, 2969
Memorial papers and reminiscences of Howard Crosby, D. D., LL. D. 1387
Memorial record of Wharton street M. E. church, Philadelphia. 2453
Memorial sermon. 55
Memorial sermon preached in the Baldwin-place meeting house on the last Sabbath of its occupancy by the Second Baptist church. 683
Memorial sketches of Rev. George B. Atwell. 109
Memorial sketches of the lives and labors of the deceased ministers of the North Alabama conference, Methodist Episcopal church, south. 2426
Memorial supper of Our Lord. 3467
Memorial to Charles Henry Appleton Dall. 1399, 2531
Memorial to Charles Lowe. 2267
Memorial to the Right Reverend Carlton Chase, D. D., first bishop of New-Hampshire. 1844 to 1870. 889
Memorial tributes. 1693

Memorial tributes of respect to Dr. Ryland Thomas Brown. 696
Memorial volume by the Essex street church and society, Boston. 7
Memorial volume of the first fifty years of the American board of commissioners for foreign missions. 31
Memorial volume of the first fifty years of the American board of commissioners for foreign missions. 39
... Memorial volume of the one hundredth anniversary celebration of the dedication of the Church of the Holy Cross, Boston. 2687
Memorial volume of the semi-centenial anniversary of Hartwick seminary. 3189
Memorial volume of the semi-centennial of the Theological seminary. 1311
Memorial volume of the semicentennial anniversary of the Second Reformed church of Glenville, N. Y., November 21, 1868. 3189
Memorial volume of the Westminster assembly. 3808
Memorial volume to commemorate the semi-centennial anniversary of the Hartwick Lutheran synod, of the state of New York. 1788
Memorial wreath. 742, 1543
Memorials. 1477
Memorials concerning several ministers and others, deceased, of the religious Society of Friends within the limits of the Yearly Meeting of New York. 1677
Memorials concerning several ministers, and others, deceased. 1677
Memorials of Baptist martyrs. 143
Memorials of Calvary. 2029
Memorials of deceased members of the Society of Friends. 1677
Memorials of foreign missionaries of the Presbyterian church, U. S. A. 2483
Memorials of Horatio Balch Hackett. 1779
Memorials of Methodism in Virginia. 2453
Memorials of missionary labours in Africa and the West Indies. 13
Memorials of Rev. Elias R. Beadle, D. D., LL. D. 179, 2933
Memorials of Rev. Peter Lockwood. 2242
Memorials of Rev. Thomas De Witt, D.D. 1408
Memorials of Richard H. Richardson, D. D. 2933, 3235
Memorials of South Africa. 2499
Memorials of the faithful. 129
Memorials of the introduction of Methodism into the eastern states. 2433
Memorials of the Most reverend father in God Thomas Crammer. 1378, 1516
Memorials of the Rev. Charles W. Baird, D. D. 3124
Memorials of the Rev. Daniel B. Parkhurst, minister of the First Congregational society in Deerfield. 2777
Memorials of the Rev. John Cantine Farrell Hoss, D.D. 1848, 3049
Memoriam of Rev. Charles Clinton Beatty, D. D., LL. D. 182
Memories and meditations. 17
Memories and opinions. 3124
Memories for the Aldersgate bi-centenary. 1651
Memories grave and gay of William Fairbairn La Trobe-Bateman. 3130
Memories in my blindness. 2544
Memories of 'Abdu'l-Baha. 129, 696
Memories of a happy boyhood. 3134
Memories of a happy life. 2202
Memories of a Sufi sage, Hazrat Inayat Khan. 1892, 3543
Memories of Bethany. 1986, 2203
Memories of Congo. 2514
Memories of four-score years. 3125
Memories of Gennesaret. 1986
Memories of Kopul Rosen. 2140, 3249
Memories of Lottie. 3090
Memories of Maharaj. 689
Memories of many men in many lands. 3736
Memories of my life work. 3090
Memories of Pius XII. 2852
Memories of Pope Pius X. 2851
Memories of Scarritt. 3306
Memories of Stanley Pumphrey. 3005
Memories of the life and gospel labours of Samuel Fothergill. 1635
Memories of the Master. 2258
Memories of the supernatural in east and west. 2997
Memories of William Wallace, D.D., LITT.D. 3790

Memoris, incidents & reminiscences of the early history of the New church in Michigan, Indiana, Illinois, and adjacent states; and Canada. 2692
Memoris, including letters, and select remains, of John Urquhart. 3761
Memory and hope. 2043
Memory and tradition in Israel. 2401
Memory book for Lutheran schools. 3185
Memory of the dead. 1411
Memory talks on spiritual power. 1830
Memos for Christian living. 994
Men aflame. 932
Men and affairs. 928
Men and angels. 43
Men and books. 2904
Men and deeds. 3861
Men and gods. 2662
Men and gods on the Roman Nile. 1502
Men and methods that win in the foreign fields. 2494
Men and missions. 2519
Men and morals. 1595
Men and motives. 248
... Men and movements in the American Episcopal church. 2971
Men and movements in the church. 1211
Men and movements in the English church. 1215
Men and nations. 1154
Men and religion. 969, 2192
Men and religion to-day and fifty years ago. 975
Men and tendencies. 3068
Men and the kingdom. 3131
Men and the message of the old testament. 539
Men and things. 2190
Men & women in John's Gospel. 422
Men and women of deep piety. 3131
Men and women of Far horizons. 2522
Men and world service. 2515
Men are like that. 2402
Men as trees walking. 1013
Men at the crossroads. 2013, 2149
Men at work at worship. 2234
Men before God. 857
Men beyond mankind. 3686
Men called Him Master. 1983
Men for others. 926
Men I have known. 1612
Men in dark times. 661
Men in mid life crisis. 2462
Men in sandals. 740
Men in the local church. 2402
Men in white apparel. 1413
Men like mountains. 925
Men made new. 472, 1014
Men must live as brothers. 3348
Men of action. 327
Men of action in the book of Acts. 327
Men of conviction. 927
Men of courage. 661
Men of fire. 923, 3131
Men of God. 502
Men of hope. 2721
Men of liberty. 3723
Men of light in Iranian sufism. 3544
Men of Maryknoll. 867
Men of might. 628, 633
Men of might in India missions. 2530
Men of prophetic fire. 2951
Men of the Bible. 215
Men of the Bible, for boys' Bible classes. 214, 1850
Men of the Covenant. 1375
Men of the Gospels. 384, 493
Men of the great redemption. 1360
Men of the Old Testament. 630
Men of the olden time. 494
Men of the outposts. 2484
Men of the way. 1974
Men of tomorrow. 295
Men of zeal. 2451
Men on the frontier. 1620, 2503
Men on their knees. 450
Men possessed by God. 2578
Men seeking God. 3131
Men such as we. 214
Men that count. 213, 3349
Men, the meaning, the message of the New Testament books. 408
Men twice born. 1014
Men unafraid. 2951
Men who build churches. 2804, 3348
Men who dared. 570, 596
Men who faced the Cross. 2215
Men who have meant much to me. 200
Men who have walked with God. 2643, 2645
Men who knew Christ. 338
Men who knew God. 2951, 3297
Men who knew Jesus. 338
Men who left a name. 925

Men who left the movement: John Henry Newman, Thomas W. Allies, Henry Edward Manning, Basil William Maturin. 2702, 2754
Men who made and marred history. 214
Men who made missions. 2483
Men who made the churches. 924
Men who make the Council. 3774
Men who met Jesus. 3137
Men who shaped America. 923
Men who shaped the Western church. 1618
Men who stood alone. 569, 571
Men who talked with God. 2871
Men who were found faithful. 926
Men who wouldn't stay dead. 1709
Men with a message. 411
Men without God. 100
Men, women and God. 1609, 3393
Men working. 1250
Men working; the Y.M.C.A. program and the present needs of youth. 3873
Menace of atheism. 100
Menace of immorality in church and state. 3742
Menace of modernism. 2563
Menace of Mormonism. 2602
Menace of spiritualism. 3510
Mender of broken hearts. 1006
Mending. 1850, 3814
Mending heart. 984
... Mending the nets. 1446
Mending the ragged edges. 2380
Menexenus of Plato. 2853
Menicus: the man and his ideas. 2403
Menno Simons. 2403
Menno Simons' life and writings. 2403
Mennonite bibliography, 1631-1961. 2404
Mennonite Central Committee story. 2403, 2405
Mennonite church and her accusers. 2405, 2635
Mennonite Church in America. 2403
Mennonite Church in India, 1897-1962. 2403, 2406
Mennonite Church in the Second World War. 2403
Mennonite church polity. 2403
Mennonite churches of North America. 2404
Mennonite colonization. 2405
Mennonite confession of faith and minister's manual. 2404
Mennonite country boy. 2404
Mennonite cyclopedic dictionary. 2405
Mennonite education. 2405
Mennonite education: why and how? 2408
Mennonite encyclopedia. 2405
Mennonite history. 2406
Mennonite hymnal. 2406
Mennonite hymnary. 2403, 2406
Mennonite identity and literary art. 2405
Mennonite quarterly review Harold S. Bender. 187
Mennonite safari. 2163, 2553
Mennonite statements on peace, 1915-1966. 2405
Mennonite youth. 3887
Mennonites. 2404
Mennonites and their heritage. 2404, 2406
Mennonites in Canada, 1920-1940. 2404
Mennonites in Indiana and Michigan. 2406
Mennonites in Iowa. 2406
Mennonites in the world war. 1543
Mennonites of America. 2404
Mennonites of Lancaster conference. 2407
Mennonites of the Ohio and Eastern Conference. 2404
Mennonitisches Jahrbuch. 2408
Meno of Plato. 2853
Menomini powwow. 2408
Menonite handbook of information. 2404
Mens Christi and other problems in theology and Christian ethics. 3651
Men's class in action. 3556
Mens creatrix. 2837
Men's house. 1662
Men's songs, no.1, a collection of sacred songs for male voices. 1206
Mensajes para los jovenes. 2551
Mensajes selectos de los ecritos de Elena G. de White. 3384
Menschliche Perspektive und Wahrheit. 2708, 3538
Mental and moral philosophy of the Bible. 601
Mental and spiritual healing, all schools and methods. 2409
Mental condition necessary to a due inquiry into religious evidence. 60
Mental-cure. 2409
Mental discipline. 3671
Mental, divine and faith healings. 2410
Mental healers. 2410, 2413
Mental healing in Judaism. 2117
Mental health and religious. 2574

Mental health ministry of the local church. 2783
Mental health problems confronting clergymen. 2784
Mental health skills for clergy. 1258
Mental health through Christian community. 2783
Mental hygiene as taught by Jesus. 2064, 2410
Mental index of the Bible, and a cosmic use of association. 199
Mental medicine. 2409
Mental phases in a spiritual biography. 3131
Mental poisoning. 2411
Mental prayer and modern life, a symposium. 2380
Mentor Bible. 200
Mentor book of religious verse. 3206
Mentor dictionary of mythology and the Bible. 243, 2658
Menuchat Shalom. 3025
Mephistopheles and the Androgyne. 1586
Mercenary match. 3197
Mercersburg classis' hundred years. 1545
Mercersburg theology. 2411, 3625
Mercier, the fighting cardinal of Belgium. 2411
Mercies manifold. 2298
Mercies of a covenant God. 3090
Mercies of God. 472
Mercies of the Sacred heart. 3269
Mercy. 3418, 3609
Mercy and judgment. 1528
Mercy, generation to generation. 3418
Mercy is forever. 1736, 2353
Mercy, Lord! My husband's in the kitchen. 3845
Mercy manual. 858, 3417, 3418
Mercy manual containing the little office of the Blessed Virgin Mary. 3418
Mercy marks the century. 3418
Mercy rides on wings. 2539
Mercy-seat. 2881
Mercy unto thousands. 2305
Mere Christianity. 1066, 1070, 3663
Mere literature and the lost traveller. 3071
Mere Marie of the Ursulines. 2334, 3761
Meredith's Book of Bible lists. 301
Merging for mission. 693
Meridian handbook of classical mythology. 2659
Mermet Ben. 3199
Merrily on high. 3527
Merry-go-round. 2549
Merry saint. 2596
Merry watch maker. 2348
Merton. 2412, 3710
Merton's Palace of Nowhere. 2412, 3492
Meshumed! 1366
Mesillat yesharim. 1539
Meslom's messages from the life beyond. 3508
Mesmerism and Christian science. 2413
Mesmerism and the American cure of souls. 2413
Mesmerism, spiritualism &c. historically & scientifically considered. 2413
Mesmerism, spiritualism, witchcraft, and miracle. 2413
Mesquite does bloom. 2775
Message. 1454
Message & characters of the Book of Mormon. 678
Message and decisions of Oxford on church. 1142
Message and existence. 3662
Message and its messengers. 2554
Message and meaning of the Bible. 637
Message and mission. 1317, 1554
Message and mission of Quakerism. 3010
Message and program of the Christian religion. 2523
Message and the message-bearer. 2405, 3646
Message and the silence of the American pulpit. 2910
Message delivered. 331
Message for today on the chariots of fire. 2981
Message for you. 2816
Message from Arunachala. 3521
Message from Batang. 2555
Message from Calvary. 1998
Message from God. 2301
Message from heaven and things to think about. 2061, 2942
Message from hell. 1802
Message in our time. 1892, 3543
Message of Anne Simon. 3514
Message of Aquaria. 2724
... The message of Buddhism. 703
Message of Christ. 1268
Message of Christ to mankind. 2064
Message of Christianity. 1095

Message of Deutero-Isaiah in its sequential unfolding. 543
Message of evangelism. 1569
Message of Francis of Assisi. 1642
Message of Galatians. 379
Message of Galatians, by N. S. Mizher. 379
Message of Genesis. 524, 527
Message of Hosea. 538
Message of Hosea to God's people of the twentieth century. 538
Message of Israel. 3372
... The message of Isreal's lawgivers. 563
Message of Jesus. 2062
Message of Jesus Christ. 388
Message of Jesus to our modern life. 476
Message of John Paul I. 793
Message of Jonah. 553
*Message of joy (The) 640
Message of Jude to the modern church. 425
Message of Krishna. 1814
Message of liberation in our age. 3291
Message of love and hope. 3510
Message of Mohammed. 2566
Message of monastic spirituality. 2577
Message of Moses. 566, 2116, 2622
Message of Old Testament history. 536
Message of Romans. 468
Message of Sadhu Sundar Singh. 3546
Message of St. Francis. 1641, 1645
Message of St. John. 413
Message of stewardship. 3528
Message of stewardship, a book for daily devotions and class study. 3528
Message of the American pulpit. 3367
Message of the bee. 185
Message of the Bible. 234, 235, 309, 2745
Message of the bishops. 15
Message of the book of Revelation. 458, 461
Message of the church in a time of crisis. 2282
Message of the church to the world of today. 1060
Message of the college to the church. 1127
...The message of the Disciples for union of the church, including their origin and history. 1460
Message of the divine Iliad. 2729
Message of the Doctrine and covenants. 3215
Message of the Fourth Gospel. 418, 420
Message of the Joseph Smith papyri. 678, 1691
Message of the Lord's prayer. 2248
Message of the modern minister. 3141
Message of the New Testament. 349, 409, 476
Message of the Old Testament. 534, 539
Message of the prophet Zephaniah. 600
Message of the prophets. 572, 2951
Message of the prophets of Israel to the twentieth century. 571
Message of the Qur'an presented in perspective. 2184
Message of the scrolls. 1411
Message of the shells. 2390
Message of the stars. 95, 3080
Message of the Torah. 563
Message of the twelve prophets. 558, 560
Message of the Wesleys. 2423
Message of the world-wide church. 1122
Message of the world's religions. 3119
Message of Therese of Lisieux. 3691
Message of Thomas Merton. 2413
Message of to-morrow; or, The gospel of hope. 2932
Message to a priest who has abandoned the Catholic Church. 772, 1582
Message to Catholics and Protestants. 2955
Message to mankind under the view of eternity. 3142
... A message to ministers, no. 2. Canons of the Synod of Dort. Christ stricken for His people. 3677
Message to the blackman in America. 669
Message to the blackman in American. 669
Message to the Magians. 2022
Message to the mother church, Boston, Mass., June, 1901. 1031
Message to the well. 2409
Message to you. 3504
Messages delivered at the fiftieth founder's week conference. 1070
Messages for a mission. 1672
Messages for better living from the spirit world. 3505
Messages for men. 2898
Messages for the morning watch. 524
Messages from beyond; narrated experiences of life after death. 3505
Messages from God's Word. 2391
Messages from higher spheres. 3516

Messages from Maitreya the Christ. 3473
Messages from Michael. 3474
Messages from Michael on the nature of the evolution of the human soul. 3474
Messages from the depths. 3624
Messages from the ministry. 1228
Messages from the superior state. 2632
Messages from the Universal House of Justice, 1968-1973. 129
Messages of Christian brotherhood. 1229
Messages of inspiration. 2607
... The messages of Jesus according to the Gospel of John. 2065
... The messages of Jesus according to the synoptists. 397
Messages of life, liberty, and happiness. 1029
Messages of mercy. 2412
Messages of mutuality. 1093
... The messages of Paul arranged in historical order, analyzed, and freely rendered in paraphrase. 373
... The messages of the apocalyptical writers. 56
... The messages of the apostles. 326
Messages of the earlier prophets, arranged in the order of time, analyzed, and freely rendered in paraphrase. 570
Messages of the First Presidency of the Church of Jesus Christ of Latter-Day Saints. 2609, 2610
Messages of the Helsinki Assembly. 2285
... The messages of the later prophets. 570
Messages of the Men and religion movement. 2402
... The messages of the poets. 1798
...The messages of the prophetic and priestly historians. 531
Messages of the prophets. 570
Messages of the prophets to their day and ours. 570
... The messages of the psalmists. 586
Messages of the Third Assembly. 2285
Messages of to-day to the men of to-morrow. 1324
Messages of truth in rhymes and story. 3201
...Messages on Christian beliefs. 3666
Messages on healing. 3497
Messages on prayer. 2887
Messages on stewardship. 3531
Messages on the Resurrection. 2054
Messages to Catholic nurses. 2718
Messages to conventions. 3687
Messages to modern youth. 3884
Messages to the Baha'i world, 1950-1957. 128
Messages to the seven churches of Asia. 461
Messages to young people. 3386
Messenger. 1545, 2628
Messenger of peace. 2806
Messenger of revival. 2744
Messenger; the life of Mohammed. 2628
Messenger to the golden people. 1882
Messengers of God. 18, 2462, 2624
Messengers of grace. 2543
Messengers of the King. 924
Messengers of the promise. 630
Messengers to the Bahai world, 1950-1957. 128
Messiah. 492, 1783, 1975, 1990, 2016, 2048, 2414, 2415, 2979, 3072, 3095, 3207
Messiah and temple. 435, 2068
Messiah idea in Jewish history. 2118, 2414
Messiah-ideal. 2414
Messiah in both Testaments. 2016
Messiah in His sanctuary. 3382
Messiah in Moses and the prophets. 2415
Messiah in Sovietland. 3868
Messiah in the Old Testament. 2415
Messiah in the Psalms. 2414
Messiah Jesue and John the Baptist according to Elavius Josephus. 1987
Messiah of Ismir, Sabbatai Zevi. 3394
Messiah of the apostles. 2016
Messiah of the Gospels. 2016, 2413
Messiah of the Old Testament. 2001
Messiah story. 2016
Messiah texts. 2414
Messiah, "the hope of Israel," "the desire of all nations" 2016, 2415
Messiah, the Prince. 2415
Messiahs. 2414
Messiah's kingdom. 3206
Messiahs, their role in civilization. 2414
Messiahship of Jesus. 1366, 2014
Messianic chronology in Daniel. 508
Messianic expectation in the Old Testament. 498, 2414
Messianic expectations, and modern Judaism. 1084, 2414
Messianic hope. 2016, 2414
Messianic hope in both Testaments. 2016, 2414, 2415

Messianic hope in the New Testament. 2016
Messianic hope of Israel. 2415
Messianic idea in Israel. 2414
Messianic idea in Judaism and other essays on Jewish spirituality. 2414
Messianic message of the Old Testament. 2415
Messianic prophecies in historical succession. 2016
Messianic prophecies of Daniel. 509
Messianic prophecy. 2414
Messianic prophecy, and the Life of Christ. 2414
Messianic prophecy in the Old Testament. 2415
Messianic prophecy;the prediction of the fulfilment of redemption through the Messiah. 2414
Messianic Psalms. 2415
Messianic secret. 436, 2017
Messianic secret in Markan research, 1901-1976. 436, 2415
Messianic theology and Christian faith. 2016, 2414
Messianism in the Talmudic era. 2414
Messianism, mysticism, and magic. 2415
Messias. 2030
Metabagdad. 1278
Metanoia. 3218
Metanoia: Christian penance and confession. 2812
Metaphor and myth in science and religion. 3070
Metaphorical theology. 1077
Metaphors, similes and other characteristic sayings of Henry Ward Beecher. 3361
Metaphyics of love. 2321
Metaphysic of experience. 2418
Metaphysica generalis in usum scholarum. 2738
Metaphysical and psychological principles of love. 2262
Metaphysical application. 2730
Metaphysical basis of certain principles of the religious life in the light of Thomistic principles. 2573
Metaphysical beliefs. 2837
Metaphysical Bible lessons. 2420
Metaphysical elements of justice. 1535
Metaphysical essays. 2834
Metaphysical journal. 2418
Metaphysical meditations. 3866
Metaphysical poets. 1518, 1519
Metaphysical principles of virtue. 1535
Metaphysical Society. 2416
Metaphysical system of Hobbes as contained in twelve chapters from his "Elements of philosophy concerning body," and in briefer extracts from his "Human nature" and "Leviathan" 1821
Metaphysical system of Hobbes in twelve chapters from Elements of philosophy concerning body, together with briefer extracts from Human nature and Leviathan. Selected by Mary Whiton Calkins. 2d ed. 1821
Metaphysical teachings. 2836
Metaphysical tracts by English philosophers of the eighteenth century. 2420
Metaphysical value and importance of the concept of being. 2738
Metaphysics. 80, 81, 2416, 2417, 2419, 2420, 2738
Metaphysics, a bridge to ECKANKAR. 1490
Metaphysics, an unfinished essay. 2418
Metaphysics and ideology. 2418
Metaphysics and religious language. 2417
Metaphysics and the new logic. 2420
Metaphysics for the man. 2419
Metaphysics in modern times. 2417
Metaphysics in process. 2835
Metaphysics, man and freedom. 2840
Metaphysics of authentic existentialism. 2419
Metaphysics of being and God. 2738
Metaphysics of life & death. 2226
Metaphysics of love. 2321
Metaphysics of modern existence. 3141
Metaphysics of morals. 1535
Metaphysics of numerology. 3575
Metaphysics of St. Thomas Aquinas. 3695
Metaphysics of Sir William Hamilton. 2417
Metaphysics of the school. 2417
Metaphysics of the supernatural as illustrated by Descartes. 1425, 1426
Metapsychical phenomena. 2419
Metempsychosis. 3054
Metempsychosis, reincarnation. 3709
Meters of quantitative hymns in the old and the new breviary. 1876
Method and ideal power of Christian faith. 1594

Method and meaning in ancient Judaism. 2479
Method and meaning in ancient Judaism, second series. 2479
Method and meaning in ancient Judaism, third series. 2479, 2829
Method and message of Jesus' teachings. 2061
Method & message of Jewish Apocalyptic. 56
Method & message of Jewish Apocalyptic, two hundred BC-Ad one hundred. 56
Method for attending the Maronite Mass. 849
Method for prayer. 2873
Method in metaphysics. 2418
Method in ministry. 1297
Method in soul-winning on home and foreign fields. 1567
Method in teaching. 3565
... Method in teaching religion. 3147
Method in theology. 2245, 3669
Method, Meditations and Philosophy of Descartes. 1425
Method of creative evolution. 1579
Method of Jesus. 3096
Method of man's reconciliation with God. 108
Method of prayer. 2874
Method of the Catholic Sunday school. 805
Method of the divine government. 2981
Method of the divine government, physical and moral. 2981
Method of the Master. 1600
Method of the Siddhas. 3479
Method of Zen. 3891, 3892
Methodical Bible study. 288
Methodism. 2420, 2423, 2425, 2432
Methodism and Christian experience. 1007
Methodism and its methods. 2450
Methodism and kingdom extension. 2457
Methodism and literature. 2422
Methodism & politics, 1791-1851. 2425
Methodism and society. 1138, 2421
Methodism and society: guidelines for strategy. 1139
Methodism and society in historical perspective. 1138
Methodism and society in the twentieth centry. 1138
Methodism and society in the twentieth century. 1138
Methodism and society in theological perspective. 3452, 3453
... Methodism and the frontier. 2431
Methodism and the home church. 3236
Methodism and the love-feast. 2263
Methodism and the Negro. 2460
Methodism and the Republic. 2434
Methodism and the working-class movements in England, 1800-1850. 2189, 2431
Methodism and world need. 2457
... Methodism and world service. 2454
Methodism at work. 2455
Methodism can be born again. 2421
Methodism explained and defended. 2421
Methodism forty years ago and now. 2450
Methodism has a message! 2428
Methodism in Alaska and Hawaii; new patterns for living together. 2430
Methodism in American history. 2425
Methodism in Arkansas, 1816-1976. 2430
Methodism in belief and action. 2421
Methodism in Buffalo, from its origin to the close of 1892. 2451
Methodism in Cuba. 2430
Methodism in earnest. 3228
Methodism in eastern Wisconsin. 2447
Methodism in Enid. 2442
Methodism in ernest. 3228
Methodism in Holston. 2439
Methodism in Kentucky. 2431
Methodism in Natchez. 2457
Methodism in old Waverly and its environment. 133
Methodism in Seguin. 3329
Methodism in the Chartiers country. 741
Methodism in the city of Lincoln. 2230
Methodism in the making. 1525
Methodism in the Mississippi Conference [1894-1919]. 2457
Methodism in the Mississippi conference, 1846-1870. 2457
Methodism in the Missippi Conference 1870-1894. 2457
Methodism in the Northwest. 2432
Methodism in the Tampa District of the Florida Conference. 2459
Methodism in the Troy Conference. 2431
Methodism in the Upper Cape Fear Valley. 2713
Methodism in the wilderness. 2453
Methodism in Washington, District of Columbia. 2442

Methodism in Western Pennsylvania, 1784-1968. 2432
Methodism in York County, Virginia. 2433
Methodism, its history, teaching, and government. 2421
Methodism looks at the city. 1278
Methodism marches on. 2425
Methodism mocked. 2428
Methodism moves across north Texas. 2455
Methodism on the march. 2442
Methodism rediscovering itself. 2421
Methodism's Aldersgate heritage. 2422, 3804
Methodism's challenge in race relations. 2440
Methodism's challenge in race relations; a study of strategy. Foreword by Edward K. Graham. 2440
Methodism's destiny in an ecumenical age. 1045
Methodism's new frontier. 3740
Methodism's world mission. 2434
Methodist adventures in Negro education. 2460
Methodist altars. 28
Methodist book concern. 2426
Methodist centenary convention. 2426
Methodist Chapel, Derby Road, Woodford, 1876-1976. 3846
Methodist Church. 2440
Methodist church and its work. 2426
Methodist Church in Missouri. 2431
Methodist Church in social thought and action. 3452
Methodist Church in urban America. 2441
Methodist Church, San Augustine, Texas. 3298
Methodist churches in Englewood and West Englewood. 2430
Methodist churches in inner Minneapolis. 2426
Methodist discipline of 1798. 2447
Methodist Episcopal church. 2455
Methodist Episcopal church and education up to 1869. 2449
Methodist Episcopal church. Conferences. East Ohio. Minutes. 2453
Methodist Episcopal church in Georgia. 2446
Methodist Episcopal church pulpit. 2435
Methodist Episcopal churches of Norwich, Conn. 2715
Methodist Episcopal pulpit. 2425, 2435
Methodist evangelism. 2441
Methodist first reader, 'On being a Christian. 2421
Methodist fraternity and federation. 2442
Methodist heroes of other days. 2423
Methodist hymn-book and its associations. 1873, 3806
Methodist hymnal. 2429, 2451
Methodist man's burden. 2420
Methodist meeting house. 2433
Methodist men at work. 2402
Methodist ministry, 1959. 2439
Methodist ministry in 1948. 2439
Methodist mission in Japan. 2535
Methodist observer atVatican II by Albert C. Outler. 3772
Methodist origins. 2421
Methodist pilgrim in England. 1516, 2428
Methodist pocket hymn-book. 2429
Methodist book prices, 1955-1965. 2426
Methodist primer. ·2438, 3804
Methodist Protestant church in West Virginia. 2459
Methodist Protestant pulpit. 2436
Methodist pulpit, South. 2437
Methodist research project in preaching. 2910
Methodist revolution. 2421
Methodist riots. 1292, 3802
Methodist saint. 89
... Methodist sesqui-centennial. 2433
Methodist theology vs. Methodist theologians. 2449
Methodist tourist guidebook through the 50 States. 2440
Methodist trail blazer, Philip Gatch, 1751-1834. 1703
Methodist trail in New Jersey. 2431
Methodist trails in the African jungle. 2497
Methodist trails to First Methodist Church, Tulsa, Oklahoma. 3718
Methodist union catalog of history. 2422
Methodist union catalog of history, biography, disciplines, and hymnals. 2422
Methodist union catalog, pre-1976 imprints. 2422
Methodist union in the courts. 2438
Methodist Unitarian movement. 1274, 3723
Methodist way of life. 2421

Methodist worship in relation to free church worship. 2433, 3004
Methodist worship in the church universal. 2433
Methodist year book. 2458
Methodist youth in council. 2423
Methodists. 2424, 2460
... The Methodists, a collection of source materials. 2460
Methodists and unity. 1045
Methodists are one people. 2433
Methodists in Fayetteville, 1832-1968. 2430
Methodists in southeast Asia. 2502
Methodists linking two continents. 2430
Methodists of continental Europe. 2430
Methodists united for action. 2441
Methodological concerns in international studies. 1914
Methodological issues in religious studies. 3093
Methods and materials for graded choirs. 915
Methods and principles in Bible study and Sunday-school teaching. 3565
Methods and problems of spiritual healing. 2409
Methods; approaches for the catechesis of adolescents. 745
Methods for primary teachers. 3555
Methods of Bible study. 641
... Methods of church school administration. 3554
Methods of evangelism. 1568
Methods of mental prayer. 2380
Methods of mission work among Moslems. 2540
Methods of private religious living. 979
Methods of psychic development. 2724, 2987
Methods of spiritual research. 50
... Methods of teaching in the church school. 3180
Methods of teaching religion in elementary schools. 3170
Methods of teaching religion to children. 3171
Methods with beginners. 1574
Metlakahtla. 1482, 1898
Metrical history of Christianity. 1100
Metrical version of Ruth and other Bible stories. 513
Metro-ministry. 1279
Metropolitan Nicolai—agent in Soviet Secret Police. 1319, 2670
Metropolitan visitations of William Courtency, Archbishop of Canterbury, 1381-1396. 3783
Mexican Inquisition of the sixteenth century. 1909
Mexican martyrdom. 1148
Mexican nuggets. 2540
Mexican people and the church. 1147
Mexican religious population of Los Angeles. 2260
Mexican shrines. 3405
Mexico. 2359
Mexico and our mission. 93
Mexico coming into light. 3734
Mexico Kid: from an outlaw to a preacher. 2484
Mexico mystique. 1898
Mexico's Accion Nacional. 6
La Mezquita de Cordoba. 1369
Mi-cha-el. 3242, 3277
Miamonides 'Yad hahazakah,' Caro's 'Shulhan aruch,' Isserles' 'Mappah.' Selections. 2318
Micaculous medal novena sermons. 2362, 2478
... Micah. 558
Micah the prophet. 558
Michael Agonistes. 868
Michael Augustine Corrigan and the shaping of conservative Catholicism in America, 1878-1902. 667, 1370
Michael Martin and his friends. 3164
Michael, Michael, why do you hate me? 1366, 1532
Michael, our Father and our God. 2612
Michael Schlatter. 3308
Michael Servetus. 3377
Michael Servetus, humanist and martyr. 3377
Michele Nardi, the Italian evangelist. 2668
Michelle remembers. 3304, 3431
Michibiki. 2534
Michigan manuscript 18 of the Gospels. 316
Michigan masonic monitor and ceremonies. 1669

Microfilm index and bibliography of the Concordia Historical Institute, The Department of Archives and History, The Lutheran Church--Missouri Synod, St. Louis, Missouri, 1954-1963. Aug. R. Suelflow, director. 2282
Micromotion studies applied to education. 895
Mid-America's promise. 2100
Mid-century. 2082
Mid-east peace puzzle. 611, 2073
Mid-life crises of a minister. 1296
Mid-stream. v. 1. 1046
Mid-week service. 2886
Mid-century report. 2434
Middle Ages and philosophy. 3309
Middle Ages, Renaissance, and Reformation. 2232
Middle Ages to the seventeenth century. 2232
Middle-class Blacks in a white society. 1667
Middle East. 2679
Middle-East crisis in perspective. 611, 2073
Middle East pilgrimage. 2541
Middle Eastern mythology. 2667
Middle English Bible. 234
Middle English Bible. 234
Middle English miracles of the Virgin. 2361
Middle High German translation of the Summa theologica. 783
... Middle High German translations of the Regula Sancti Benedict. 187
"The middle path--the safest" 2728
Middle pillar. 2313
Middle wall. 3017
Middle way. 2969
Midget pictures of Bible stories. 603
Midnight cry. 2467, 3386
Midnight harmonies, or, Thoughts for the season of solitude and sorrow. 1454
Midrash on Psalms. 2462
Midrash Pesher of Habakkuk. 529, 1779
Midrash Sifre on Numbers. 561
Midrashim. 2208
Midweek messages. 3345
Migdal zophim. (The watch tower) 2078
Might have been. 1333
Might-mystery-mercy. 1442
Might of the true word. 1591
Mightier than circumstance. 3751
Mightiest of mortals, Heracles. 1804
Mightily and sweetly. 2134
Mighty acts of God. 290, 640, 1356
Mighty army. 3281
Mighty beginnings. 527
Mighty Bernard. 194
Mighty change. 1008
Mighty faith. 1595
Mighty fortress. 2276, 2437
Mighty God's creations. 1506
Mighty Mary. 3425
Mighty means of usefulness. 2875
Mighty men of God, with a good word for Cain. 493
Mighty men of Zion. 1231
Mighty ones. 533, 536, 634
Mighty Saviour. 2436
Mighty voice. 1921
Mighty wind. 1832
Mighty winner of souls, Charles G. Finney. 34, 1625
Mighty word. 2907
Migrant with hope. 1688, 2701
Migration of symbols. 3573
Migration of symbols and their relation to beliefs and customs. 3574
Migration of symbols and their relations to beliefs and customs. 3574
Mihaia. 3144, 3252
Mile stones in our life-journey. 1325
Milestones in the life of the Jew. 2120
Milestones on the great highway. 212
Militant Christianity. 160
Militant gospel. 1085
Militant here in earth. 3446
Militant in earth. 1175
Militant messiah. 1650, 2986
Militant Methodism. 2670
Militant ministry. 2192
Military religious orders of the Middle Ages. 2463
Military service and you. 3456
Militia Christi. 1089
Milk for babes. 986, 2631, 3200, 3705
Mill street synagogue (1730-1817) of the Congregation Shearith Israel (founded in the city of New York in 1655) 2700
Mill town pastor. 1305
Millenarian piety of Roger Williams. 2464, 3817
Millenium and second work of grace. 2464
Millennial dawn. 1940, 2465
Millennial dawn heresy. 3256

Millennial dreams in action. 2466
Millennial experience. 978
Millennial harbinger. 2465
Millennial hope. 2464
Millennial kingdom. 2465, 2466
Millennial Messiah. 2599, 3319
Millennial myth; a logical study in prophetic truth. 2466
Millennial praises. 3398
Millennial studies. 2465
Millennialism, the two major views. 2464
Millennium. 2464, 2465
Millennium;a discussion of the question. 2464
Millennium a necessity. 2464
Millennium Bible. 3318
Millennium Bible, being a help to the study of the Holy Scriptures in their testimony to the second coming of our Lord and Saviour Jesus Christ. 231, 3318
Millennium in the church. 2466
Millennium man. 2465
Millennium of the Apocalypse. 2464
Millennium of the church, to come before the end of time. 2464
Millennium: the good time coming. 3402
Millerites and early Adventists. 10, 3386
Millhands & preachers. 1703
Million little sunbeams. 657
Million men for Christ. 3465
Million miles in New York state. 3875
Million years to the Promised Land. 206, 876
Millionaire of Uz. 2124
Millionaires of Genesis, their prosperity secrets for you! 494, 3539
Millions now living will never die! 1940
Millions of meetings. 2615
Mills' meetings memorial volume. 2467, 3232
Milton. 2469, 2470
Milton and Christian heroism. 1518, 2471
Milton and forbidden knowledge. 2470
Milton and Paradise lost. 2467
Milton and science. 2470
Milton and the Book of Revelation. 2468
Milton and the Christian tradition. 1101, 2472
Milton and the idea of matrimony. 2345, 2470
Milton and the literature of travel. 2470
Milton and the nature of man. 2323, 2468
Milton and the pattern of Calvinism. 1101, 2471
Milton and the Pauline tradition. 372, 1101, 2472
Milton and the science of the saints. 2471, 3041
Milton criticism. 2470
Milton dictionary. 2470
Milton in the Puritan revolution. 2470
Milton on the Son of God and the Holy Spirit. 3713
Milton on the Son of God and the Holy Spirit, from his Treatise on Christian doctrine. 3713
Milton, poete de la Bible. 299, 2467
Milton Steinberg. 3016, 3526
Milton's brief epic. 2471
Milton's earthly paradise. 2468, 2772
Milton's epic process: Paradise lost and its Miltonic background. 2468
Milton's ethics. 2471
Milton's God. 1732, 2472
Milton's good God. 1733, 2468
Milton's imagery. 2470
Milton's library. 2470
Milton's Ode on the morning of Christ's nativity, L'allegro, Il penseroso, and Lycidas. 2470
Milton's ontology. 2471
Milton's Paradise lost. 2468, 2471
Milton's Paradise lost and other works. 2469
Milton's Paradise regained; two eighteenth-century critiques. 2468
Milton's Paradise with reference to the hexameral background. 2470
Milton's pastoral vision. 2468
Milton's rabbinical readings. 1798, 2470, 3015
Milton's Samson Agonistes. 2468, 3297
Milton's Samson and the Christian tradition. 2468, 2472
Milton's schoolmasters. 2471
Milton's use of Du Bartas. 2232, 2469
Mimamsa sutras of Jaimini. 2472
Mimekor Yisrael. 3581
Min Din, a story of hidden treasure. 2505
Mind and belief. 185
... Mind and body. 2410, 2420
Mind and deity. 3608
Mind and health. 2410
Mind and heart. 978

Mind and heart of Augustine. 110, 113, 114
Mind and heart of love. 2262
Mind and spirit. 1107
Mind and the body. 2473
Mind and the mystery. 2181
Mind and the soul. 2473
Mind and words of Jesus. 1440, 1999
Mind as a cause and cure of disease presented from a medical, scientific and religious point of view. 2473
Mind at ease. 585, 3407
Mind awake. 3633
Mind behind the universe. 2836
Mind, body and religion. 2997, 3811
Mind, body, and wealth. 1777
Mind changers. 1316
Mind-cure on a material basis. 2410
Mind games and hobby horses. 986
Mind if I differ? 862
Mind made visible. 2840
Mind, man, and the spirits. 2325
Mind of an archbishop. 780
Mind of Christ. 764, 1656, 1950, 1985, 2064
Mind of Christ in Paul. 376, 2042
Mind of Dante. 1402
Mind of Francis of Sales; a book on religious life. 1445
Mind of God. 3200
Mind of Japan. 1101
Mind of Jesus. 1953, 2013, 2035
Mind of John Paul II. 2126
Mind of Kierkegaard. 2169
Mind of Latin Christendom. 1194
Mind of Matthew. 443
Mind of Paul. 2796
Mind of Paul VI on the church and the world. 760
Mind of Paul VI. 760
Mind of Pius XII. 2853
Mind of St. Paul. 2798
Mind of St Paul. 375
Mind of the Catholic layman. 2192
Mind of the church in the formation of sisters. 2573
... The mind of the Maker. 1105
Mind of the Master. 2037, 2066
Mind of the Messiah. 2413
Mind of the missal. 2367
Mind of the Oxford movement. 2754
Mind of William Paley. 2675, 2766
Mind over body. 1034
Mind over matter. 2723
Mind possessed. 2999
Mind power and privileges. 2473
Mind, religion and health. 2409
Mind science of Christ Jesus. 1599
Mind surgery. 2997
Mind the Baby! 2625
Mind the mass. 2365
Mind, the master power. 3750
Mind trips. 2382
Mind unshaken. 1812
Mindanao mission. 667, 1387
Mindbenders. 1393, 1394
Mindful of man. 3135
Mindful of the love. 2259
Minding your church's business. 1252
Mind's journey to God. 2642
Mind's silent partner. 3462
Mindszenty man. 2474
Mine eyes have seen. 3133, 3382
Miners, merchants, and missionaries. 2512
Ming Kwong. 2509
Ming Li. 2490
Mingled people. 232, 1091
Minhagim. 2119
Miniature Bible. 294
Miniature missiles for heaven's sake. 2392
Miniature question box. 785
Miniatures of the life of Our Lady. 1884
Minimal religion. 1071
Minister. 1295, 2475
Minister, a man among men. 2306, 3673
Minister and Christian nurture. 2785
Minister and doctor meet. 2784
Minister and family troubles. 3671
Minister and grief. 1412
Minister and his Greek New Testament. 3241
Minister and his ministry. 2474, 2786
Minister and his opportunity. 3670
Minister and his own soul. 2474
Minister and his parish. 3671
Minister and his work. 2787
Minister and human relations. 3673
Minister and the care of souls. 2782
... The minister and the ministry. 3677
... The minister and the spiritual life. 2900
Minister and the teacher. 3146
Minister as a man. 2474
Minister as crisis counselor. 2781
Minister as diagnostician. 2786
Minister as family counselor. 2781
Minister as marriage counselor. 2345
Minister as prophet. 2901

Minister as shepherd. 3672
Minister behind the scenes. 3672
Minister himself. 3134
Minister his world and his work. 3671
Minister in Christian education. 3156
Minister in his study. 3627
Minister in the itinerant system. 2903
Minister in the Reformed tradition. 1295
Minister in the Tennessee Valley. 2427
Minister is leaving. 1290
Minister looks at himself. 2785
Minister: man-in-the-middle. 1295
Minister of Christ. 773, 1296, 3710
...The minister of confirmation. 1328
Minister of education. 3151
Minister on the spot. 1295
Minister? Pastor? Prophet? 773, 1297
Minister teaches religion. 3153
Minister, the method, and the message. 2904
Ministerial commission. 2474
Ministerial directory of the Presbyterian church. 2913
Ministerial directory of the Presbyterian Church, U.S., 1861-1967. 2913
Ministerial education in the American Methodist movement. 3614
Ministerial ethics. 2474
Ministerial ethics and etiquette. 3672
Ministerial life and work. 2785
Ministerial practices, some fraternal suggestions. 3673
Ministerial training in eighteenth-century New England. 3680, 3681
Ministering church. 1250
Ministering congregation. 2785
Ministering ministry. 1297
Ministering parish. 807, 1245
Ministering teacher. 3550
Ministering to alcoholics. 1253
Ministering to boys and girls. 909
Ministering to deeply troubled people. 1258
Ministering to prisoners and their families. 2942
Ministering to the aging. 1257
Ministering to the divorced Catholic. 1471
Ministering to the dying. 1258
Ministering to the grief sufferer. 2135, 2136
Ministering to the grieving. 1257
Ministering to the Jews in the armed forces of the United States. 3456
Ministering to the physically sick. 1258, 1259
Ministering to the sick. 1258
Ministering to the silent minority. 1257
Ministering to youth. 806, 1260, 1261
Ministerium of Pennsylvania. 1548
Ministers' accounts of the collegiate church of St. Mary, Warwick 1432-85. 3796
Ministers all. 2191
Ministers and music. 1202
Minister's book of prayers. 2888
Minister's church, home, and community services handbook. 3856
Minister's communion service book. 2257
Minister's companion. 1553
Minister's complete guide to successful retirement. 1299
Minister's consultation clinic. 2995
Minister's desk book. 1200
Minister's everyday life. 3671
Ministers for tomorrow. 3332
Ministers' handbook. 2475, 3673
Minister's handbook of dedications. 1419
Minister's handicap. 886, 3671
Ministers in training. 3615
Minister's job. 3674
Minister's library. 3089, 3612
Minister's library handbook. 2224
Minister's manual. 76, 2722, 3374, 3676
Ministers' manual and discipline. 2790
Minister's manual and pocket ritual. 2454
Minister's manual, Church of the brethren. 1236
Minister's manual of the American Lutheran church. 2294
Ministers manual (The) 3374
Minister's marriage handbook. 3800
Minister's marriage manual. 2347
Minister's minute messages. 3373
Minister's mission. 2785, 3671
Minister's Monday. 3671
Minister's obstacles. 2787, 3675
Ministers of Christ. 372, 1296, 1297
Ministers of God. 1297
Ministers of life. 2202
Ministers of mercy. 2482
Ministers of the gospel, as ambassadors for Christ, should beseech men to be reconciled to God. 2742
Minister's own mental health. 1289
Minister's personal guide. 3674
Minister's prayer book. 2297
Ministers' research service. 3374

Minister's Saturday night. 1840
Minister's scrapbook of sermon illustrations and quotations. 1841
Minister's service book. 2238
Minister's service book for pulpit and parish. 2790
Minister's service handbook. 2790
Minister's service manual. 2474
Minister's shop-talk. 2786
Minister's spiritual life. 3480
Minister's vocation. 2786
Minister's week-day challenge. 3671
Minister's week-day manual. 2721
Minister's wife. 1303
Minister's wife as a counselor. 2780
Minister's wife's experience as a collector for the Pennsylvania anti-saloon league. 2231
Ministers' wives. 1303
Minister's work. 1295
Minister's worship handbook. 3004
Ministries for the Lord. 2584
Ministries of dialogue. 1153
Ministries of hope. 1486
Ministries of mercy. 1257
Ministries, sharing God's gifts. 3678
Ministries through non-parish institutions. 1253
Ministries to military personnel. 885
...The ministry. 1289, 1295, 1296
Ministry and education in conversation. 2790
Ministry and imagination. 2785
Ministry and medicine in human relations. 2994
Ministry and melody of angels. 3071
Ministry and mental health. 1258
Ministry and message of Paul. 2799
Ministry and music. 1209
Ministry and priesthood. 2049
Ministry and solitude. 2785
Ministry and the eucharist. 1219
Ministry and the sacraments. 3264
Ministry as a life work. 2475
Ministry burnout. 1294
Ministry by objectives. 1200
Ministry demanded by the present crisis. 3672
Ministry for tomorrow. 3680
Ministry-gifts of Christ. 2474
Ministry in America. 1297
Ministry in historical perspectives. 1293
Ministry in missionary churches. 2484
Ministry in the Catholic high school. 805, 1257
Ministry in the church in relation to prophecy and spiritual gifts (charismata). 1289
Ministry in transition. 3681, 3732
Ministry, leadership in the community of Jesus Christ. 2787
Ministry of a child. 3095
Ministry of all believers. 3673
Ministry of angels. 42
Ministry of angels, here and beyond. 3514
Ministry of comfort. 1351
Ministry of conversion. 1568
Ministry of disobedience. 1754, 2562
Ministry of evil. 1696
Ministry of faith. 2189, 3819
Ministry of fifty years. 3127
...The ministry of friendly guidance. 1562
Ministry of healing. 760, 1259, 1599, 2378, 2539
Ministry of hope. 668, 2589
Ministry of intercession. 2013, 2873
Ministry of intercessory prayer. 2876
Ministry of Jesus. 2016
Ministry of Jesus Christ. 1987
Ministry of Keswick. 3484
Ministry of laymen. 1569
Ministry of love. 190
Ministry of mercy for today. 1239
Ministry of music in religion. 2633
Ministry of pastoral counseling. 2780
Ministry of preaching. 2900, 2904
Ministry of prevailing prayer. 2874
Ministry of reconciliation. 325, 2811, 3028
Ministry of reconciliation and church court procedure. 2615
Ministry of reconciliation, its authority and responsbility. 1297
Ministry of religious education. 936
Ministry of Samuel Harrison Greene. 1772
Ministry of service. 1408, 3377
Ministry of the celebration of the sacraments. 3266
Ministry of the Central Jurisdiction of the Methodist Church. 2438
Ministry of the child. 903
Ministry of the Church in the world. 1056
Ministry of the deacon. 1408
Ministry of the deacons in the United Presbyterian church today. 1408
Ministry of the glory cloud. 3682

Ministry of the Holy Spirit. 1828
Ministry of the laity. 2191
Ministry of the Lutheran teacher. 3161
Ministry of the Methodist Episcopal church. 2427
Ministry of the spirit. 1216, 1829, 3482
Ministry of the Sunday-school. 3556
Ministry of the unseen. 3519
Ministry of the word. 1252, 2786, 2898, 2900, 3673, 3675
Ministry of ushering. 1249
Ministry of visitation. 3783
Ministry of women. 3837, 3840
Ministry of worship. 3003, 3853
Ministry to families. 1254
Ministry to the bereaved. 1353
Ministry to the congregation. 2901
Ministry to the hospitalized. 2782
Ministry to the sick. 2782
Ministry to the sick and dying. 1258, 2307
Ministry to turbulent America. 30
Ministry to word and sacraments. 2791
Ministry to youth. 1260
Ministry we need. 3671, 3674
"Ministry with single adults" 1256
Ministry with the aging. 1257
Ministry, word, and sacraments. 1295, 2283
Minka and Margaret. 1784, 2486
Minneapolis churches and their comity problems. 2475
Minneapolis pulpit. 3366
Minnie Belle. 3675
Minoan-Mycenaean religion and its survival in Greek religion. 1767
Minor anthologies of the Pali canon. 707
Minor arts of Islam. 87
Minor characters of the Bible. 214
Minor heresies. 3126
Minor law-books. 689
Minor orders. 3124
Minor prophets. 558, 559, 560, 2950
Minor prophets: Hosea to Malachi. 559
Minor prophets in the Freer collection and the Berlin fragment of Genesis. 316
Minor prophets (The) 559
Minor prophets; the men and their messages. 559
Minor prophets unfolded. 559
Minor Seminary Conference. 3614
Minor seminary conference on a continuing study of outcomes. 3331
Minor Seminary Conference on outcomes. 3331, 3614
Minor sexual deviance. 3392
Minor works. 3635
Minor works of John Bunyan. 714
Minority politics in Bangladesh. 1816
Minority religions in America. 1038, 3327
Minority report. 2979
Minstrel of Zion. 1865
Mintes of the vestry of St. Matthew's parish. 1275
Minueius Felix and his place among the early fathers of the Latin church. 2475
Minute meditations. 2393, 2399
Minute of prayer. 2876, 2889
Minute particular. 3130
Minute sermons. 2607
Minute stories from the Bible. 297
Minutes. 157, 2442, 2446, 2452, 2453, 2921, 2927, 2928, 3731
Minutes and letters of the Coetus of the German reformed congregations in Pennsylvania. 3049
Minutes and year book, St. Johns River conference. 3274
Minutes of . . . annual sessions. 2917
Minutes of Black River annual conference ... Session. 2446
Minutes of Joint committee on ways and means. 3733
Minutes of Mecklenburg presbytery. 2971
Minutes of Reformed Presbytery of America, from 1798 to 1809. 3050
Minutes of the. 2918
Minutes of the 1st- session of the West Oklahoma annual conference of the Methodist Episcopal church, South ... 1911. 2442
Minutes of the anniversary. 142
Minutes of the ... anniversary of the Berkshire Baptist association. 143
Minutes of the annual assembly. 1674
Minutes of the ... annual convention of the Evangelical Lutheran ministerium of New York and adjacent states and countries. 1547
Minutes of the ... annual convention of the Concordia English district of the Evangelical Lutheran joint synod of Ohio and other states. 1547
Minutes of the annual convention. 110, 3733

Minutes of the ... annual convention of Miami synod of the Evangelical Lutheran church. 1547
Minutes of the ... annual convention of the Northern district of the Evangelical Lutheran joint synod of Ohio and other states. 3733
Minutes of the annual convention of the Chicago synod of the Evangelical Lutheran church. 1547
Minutes of the ... annual convention of the English district of the Evangelical Lutheran joint synod of Ohio and other states. 1547
Minutes of the ... annual convention of the East Ohio synod of the Evangelical Lutheran church. 1547
Minutes of the...annual convention of the English Evangelical Lutheran synod of the Northwest. 1547
Minutes of the ... annual convention of the Illinois synod of the United Lutheran church in America. 3733
Minutes of the annual convention of the Pacific synod of the Evangelical Lutheran church ...) 1st- 1901. 3733
Minutes of the ... annual convention of the Western district of the Ev. Lutheran joint synod of Ohio and other states. 3733
Minutes of the annual convention. [v. p.]. 3733
Minutes of the ... annual meeting. 152, 156, 169, 2921
Minutes of the annual meeting of the Washington Baptist convention ... With Association records. 142
Minutes of the ... annual session. 154, 158, 169, 1021, 2446
... Minutes of the ... annual session of the Arizona mission. 2445
Minutes of the ... annual session of the Black Hills mission. 2445
Minutes of the ... annual session of the Coosa River Baptist association. 143
Minutes of the ... annual session of the Georgia conference. 2446
Minutes of the ... annual session of the Kalispell mission. 2452
Minutes of the ... annual session of the Little Rock conference. 2444
Minutes of the ... annual session of the Northwest Iowa conference. 2447
... Minutes of the ... annual session of the Northwest Kansas conference. 2452
Minutes of the ... annual session of the West Nebraska conference. 2445
Minutes of the ... annual session of the West Wisconsin annual conference. 2447
Minutes of the ... annual session of the Wilmington conference. 2445
Minutes of the assembly of the International Missionary Council. 1913
Minutes of the Baptist association. 159
Minutes of the centennial convention of the Nebraska Synod, Lutheran Church in America (first organization, Aug. 4, 1870) 2291
Minutes of the Christian convention. 3322
Minutes of the Cincinnati conference. 2453
Minutes of the Cincinnati conference ... Session. 2453
Minutes of the convention. 3733
Minutes of the ... convention of the Evangelical Lutheran joint synod of Ohio and other states. 1549
Minutes of the ... convention of the Olive branch Evan. 1549
Minutes of the ... convention of the United Lutheran church in America. 1547
Minutes of the East Genesee annual conference. 2444
Minutes of the first-annual meeting of the Corvallis Baptist association. 159
Minutes of the first Hebrew-Christian conference of the United States. 2535
Minutes of the first Independent Church (now Bunyan Meeting) at Bedford 1656-1766. 183
Minutes of the fourth convention, Indiana-Kentucky Synod, Lutheran Church in America, May 17-20, 1965, Indiana Memorial Union, Indiana University. 2290
Minutes of the General assembly of the Cumberland Presbyterian church. 1396
Minutes of the ... General conference of the Freewill Baptist connection in North America. 157
Minutes of the Kentucky annual conference of the Methodist Episcopal church ... annual session ... Official journal. 2452
Minutes of the Laymen's association. 2455
Minutes of the ... meeting of Holston presbytery. 2919

Minutes of the meeting of the Hawaiian evangelical association. 2524
Minutes of the Methodist conferences. 2444, 2451
Minutes of the New York east conference ... Session. 2445
... Minutes of the Newark conference. 2445
Minutes of the North Arkansas annual conference of the Methodist Episcopal church, South ... [1st]-; 1914. 2455
Minutes of the North Indiana annual conference. 2452
Minutes of the Northeast Ohio synod, East Ohio synod, Northwest Ohio synod, Southwest Ohio synod of the Evangelical and Reformed church, 1940. 1545
Minutes of the Oneida annual conference. 2445
Minutes of the organizing convention, October 14-15, 1966, First English Lutheran Church, Syracuse, New York. 2291
Minutes of the Presbytery of Fayetteville. 2920
Minutes of the proceedings of the organizing convention, held at the Marriott Motor Hotel, Montgomery County, Pa., October 22, 1968. 2292
Minutes of the proceedings of the organizing convention of the Northeastern Pennsylvania Synod of the Lutheran Church in America held at Muhlenberg College, Allentown, Pa., October 23, 1968. 2292
... Minutes of the Rhode Island association of Free Baptist churches. 1407, 1652
Minutes of the ... session. 2444, 2445
Minutes of the ... session, Mobile conference. 2455
Minutes of the ... session of the Austin annual conference. 2453
Minutes of the ... session of the Baltimore annual conference. 2446
Minutes of the ... session of the Central Ohio annual conference. 2446
Minutes of the ... session of the Central Pennsylvania annual conference. 2453
Minutes of the ... session of the Dakota annual conference. 2444
... Minutes of the ... session of the Des Moines annual conference. 2452
Minutes of the ... session of the Indiana annual conference. 2452
Minutes of the ... session of the Lincoln annual conference of the Methodist Episcopal church ... Official record. 2444
Minutes of the ... session of the Little Rock annual conference. 2446
Minutes of the ... session of the Maine annual conference. 2446
Minutes of the ... session of the Montana annual conference. 2452
Minutes of the ... session of the Nebraska annual conference. 2445
Minutes of the ... session of the New England annual conference. 2445
Minutes of the ... session of the New-Hampshire annual conference. 2447
... Minutes of the ... session of the New Jersey annual conference. 2445
Minutes of the ... session of the North Indiana annual conference. 2452
Minutes of the ... session of the Ohio annual conference. 2445
Minutes of the ... session of the Philadelphia annual conference. 2453
Minutes of the ... session of the Rocky mountain annual conference. 2453
Minutes of the ... session of the St. Louis annual conference. 2446
Minutes of the ... session of the South Carolina annual conference. 2455
Minutes of the ... session of the Troy annual conference. 2444
Minutes of the ... session of the Upper Iowa annual conference. 2452
Minutes of the sessions. 2928
Minutes of the ... sessions ... of the South Carolina conference. 2453
Minutes of the Vermont annual conference ... Session. 2445
Minutes of the Vestry, Truro Parish Virginia, 1732-1785. 3716
Minutes of the West Nebraska mission conference. 2446
Minutes of the West Ohio conferences. 2453
Minutes of the Wisconsin annual conference ... Session. 2447
Minutes of the Wyoming mission ... Session. 2445
... Minutes. regular meeting. 1338
Minutes ... Session. 2446, 2452, 2455
Minuties. 3047
Miracle. 2017, 2476

Miracle a day. 2727
Miracle a day keeps the Devil away. 681, 2476
Miracle & its philosophical presuppositions. 2477
Miracle and science. 2477
Miracle at city hall. 1255, 2463
Miracle at Fatima. 1618
Miracle at Metlakatla. 1482, 3717
Miracle cures for the millions. 2477
Miracle for the bride. 692
Miracle goes on. 1749, 2826
Miracle hand around the world. 3480
Miracle healers. 1601
Miracle hill. 1826
Miracle in Borneo. 2490
Miracle in cannibal country. 2198, 2488
Miracle in Darien. 1690, 2962
Miracle in history and in modern thought. 2477
Miracle in Moscow. 191, 1574
Miracle lives of China. 2509
Miracle living. 987
Miracle Man. 2477
Miracle Man and the Wonder Book. 65
Miracle man of Muro. 1706
Miracle men. 1789, 1928
Miracle of America. 2476
Miracle of answered prayer. 2872
Miracle of Bernadette. 3460
Miracle of Christmas. 1112
Miracle of dialogue. 1467
Miracle of Easter. 1486
Miracle of forgiveness. 1633
Miracle of holistic healing. 3476, 3697
Miracle of hope. 1846
Miracle of Ireland. 819
Miracle of Lourdes. 2262
Miracle of love. 1816, 2263, 2679
Miracle of Mark. 435
Miracle of mind power. 2694
Miracle of mindfulness! 2382
Miracle of new avatar power. 2725
Miracle of personality. 1009
Miracle of preaching. 2904
Miracle of St. Cuthbert, and sonnets. 1397
Miracle of the ages. 2001
Miracle of the Bible. 289, 292
Miracle of the Book. 291
Miracle of the cross. 2056
Miracle of the Galilean. 1967
Miracle of the Holy Spirit. 1827
Miracle of the mountain. 40
Miracle of theism. 1738
Miracle of time. 2213
Miracle of tongues. 1717
Miracle of Trinity. 2915
Miracle of two cents. 3539
Miracle of universal psychic power: how to pyramid your way to prosperity. 2727
Miracle of Wu-pao, and other stories. 2490
Miracle on the Sepik. 2198, 2487
Miracle plays. 2003
Miracle power of believing. 75, 3539
Miracle power of I Ching. 1470, 1879
Miracle power of prayer. 2876
Miracle power of transcendental meditation. 2380, 2381
Miracle that heals. 2409
Miracle working truth. 2476
Miracles. 382, 2017, 2477
Miracles, a modern view. 2476
Miracles; a preliminary study. 2477
Miracles and critics. 2476
Miracles and mysteries in the Bible. 3567
Miracles and parables of the Old Testament. 3373
Miracles and pilgrims. 1516
Miracles and revelation. 2477
Miracles and supernatural religion. 2477
Miracles & the new psychology. 2017, 2409
Miracles and the parables. 2018
Miracles at Cana. 2345
Miracles, convulsions, and ecclesiastical politics in early eighteenth-century Paris. 2476, 2773
Miracles don't just happen. 2477
Miracles in a doctor's life. 1360
Miracles in black. 2501
Miracles in dispute. 2476
Miracles in France. 2477
Miracles in Indonesia. 3231
Miracles in Mexico. 1898, 3860
Miracles in my life. 1855
Miracles in pinafores & bluejeans. 2164, 2618
Miracles in St. John's Gospel and their teaching on eternal life. 2126
Miracles of Christ. 2017, 2018
Miracles of Christ in the light of our present-day knowledge. 2017
Miracles of Christmas. 2018
Miracles of faith. 1599
Miracles of Father Aull. 117
Miracles of God and the prophets. 2476

Miracles of Golgotha. 2029
Miracles of grace and answers to prayer. 2477
Miracles of grace in Japan. 2477
Miracles of Jesus. 2017, 2018
Miracles of Jesus and their moral lessons. 2018
Miracles of Jesus as marks on the way of life. 2017
Miracles of Jesus for today. 2018, 3348
Miracles of Jesus, then and now. 2018
Miracles of Madame Saint Katherine of Fierbois. 2476
Miracles of missions. 2494
Miracles of modern missions. 2494
Miracles of our Lady Saint Mary. 3722
Miracles of Our Lord. 2017
Miracles of our Saviour. 2018
Miracles of science. 3077
Miracles of the Bible. 2476
Miracles of the gods. 319, 3783
Miracles of the Master, with a short sermon or meditation after each quotation. 2018
Miracles on tap. 2208
Miracles or mirages. 1598
Miracles, past and present. 2477
Miracles through prayer. 2873
Miracles, wrought by the intercession of Prince Hohenlohe. 1599, 1822
Miracles: yesterday and today. 1601
Miracles: yesterday and today, true and false. 2477
Miracular. 3095
Miraculous deliverance. 1359
Miraculous element in the Gospels. 2017
Miraculous healing. 1598, 1601, 2017
Miraculous journey of Mahomet. 2461
Miraculous medal novena sermons. 2362, 2478
Miraculous medal prayer manual with novena devotions in honor of our Lady of the miraculous medal. 2478
Miraculous stories from the Japanese Buddhist tradition. 2207
Mirage in the desert. 965
Mirage of life. 1632
Mircea Eliade. 1505
Mircea Eliade and the dialectic of the sacred. 1505
Mirfield essays in Christian belief. 3651
Miriam. 3716
Miriam: a Christ-child. 3235
Miriam, the virgin of Nazareth. 2354
Mirror. 965, 3094
Mirror and the cross. 825
Mirror for fools. 2577
Mirror for princes, the Qabus nama. 3880
Mirror mind. 2641
Mirror of a movement. 3
Mirror of a true religious. 2580
Mirror of charity. 2264
Mirror of England. 1763
Mirror of faith. 1601
Mirror of faith by which the children of God may be known. 1594
Mirror of intemperance, an history of the temperance reform. 3595
Mirror of intemperance, and history of the temperance reform. 3595
Mirror of language. 2180
Mirror of life. 1551
Mirror of life and death. 1412
Mirror of life, sunshine and darkness. 3503
Mirror of magic. 2314
Minnor of 150-year progress, 1810 to 1960, of the Catholic Church in the United States of America. 835
Mirror of perfection. 1641
Mirror of the Blessed Virgin Mary (Speculum Beatae Mariae Virginis) 2354
Mirror of the heart. 1450
Mirror of the soul. 2986
Mirror of truth. 2565
Mirror of your soul. 3462
Mirrors of God. 1721
Mirrors of the holy. 3285
Mirrour of created perfection, 1632. 2354
Mirrour of good maners. 1651
Mirrour of the blessed life of Jesus Christ. 1985
Mirrow of Christ. 1643
Miscelanea, meditations, memoratives. 2388
Miscellanea. 3470
Miscellaneous Coptic texts in the dialect of Upper Egypt. 1018
Miscellaneous essays on Christian morals. 3363
Miscellaneous notes on Old Testament topics. 502
Miscellaneous observations connected with the physical sciences. 2845
Miscellaneous papers. 3622
Miscellaneous poems, on moral and religious subjects. 2855

... Miscellaneous remarks upon the government, history, religions, literature, agriculture, arts, trades, manners and customs of the Chinese. 912
... Miscellaneous remarks upon the government, history, religions, literature, agriculture, arts, trades manners and customs of the Chinese. 912
... Miscellaneous remarks upon the government, history, religions, literature, agriculture, arts, trades, manners and customs of the Chinese. 912
Miscellaneous theological works of Emanuel Swedenborg. 2692, 3571, 3631
Miscellaneous thoughts. 3202
Miscellaneous tracts. 776
Miscellaneous works. 2914
Miscellaneous works of John Bunyan. 714
Miscellaneous works of Mr. James Meikle. 2419
Miscellaneous writings. 1068, 3632, 3749, 3750
Miscellaneous writings. 1883-1896. 1031, 1494
Miscellaneous writings of Beriah Green. 3621
... The miscellaneous writings of John Fiske. 1628
Miscellaneous writings of Miles P. Squier. 3624
Miscellaneous writings of Raymond Charles Barker. 2695
Miscellaneous writings on religious subjects. 3095
Miscellanies. 143, 760, 2913, 3632
Miscellanies of Rev. Thomas E. Peck. 2936
Miscellany. 2423
Miscellany of American Christianity. 3427, 3748
Mischievous ghosts. 2858
Miserable in heaven. 1795
De miseria condicionis humane. 2321
Misery of Christianity: or, A plea for a humanity without God. 1091
Misfits and missionaries. 2479, 2943
...Mishna; Baba Mezia. 130
Mishnah. 130, 2478, 2479
Mishnah and Tosefta, a comparative study. 2479
...Mishnah Baba batra. 1485
...Mishnah Baba kamma. 3705
Mishnah Megillah. 2479
Mishnah, oral teachings of Judaism. 2478
Mishnah's theology of tithing. 2479, 3702
Mishneh Torah by Maimonides. 2478
Misread record; or, The deluge and its cause. 1421
Miss Bettie's book of Bible stories. 619
Miss Carrie Peter and trophies in India. 2532, 2824
Miss Ida. 3405
Miss Marian's gold. 3812
Miss Wistaria at home. 3047
Missal. 82, 2883
Missal and holy mass. 2366, 2370
Missal for young Catholics. 2883
Missal in Latin and English. 845, 846, 2884
Missal-manual. 856
Missal of St. Augustine's abbey, Canterbury. 2883
Missiles over Cuba. 1021, 3812
Missing Christ. 165
Missing cross. 2757
Missing fragment of the Latin translation of the Fourt book of Ezra. 1532
Missing fragment of the Latin translation of the Fourth book of Ezra. 490
Missing link. 603, 1487
Missing link in modern spiritualism. 1636, 3516
Missing links. 46
Missing links and mystic kinks. 2637
Missing value in medical social case work. 2995
Mission. 2493, 2507, 2558, 2965, 3745
Mission advance in China. 2510
Mission and achievement of Jesus. 2038
Mission and expansion of Christianity in the first three centuries. 1192, 2563
Mission and grace. 2789
Mission and message of Jesus. 386, 1968
Mission and the peace witness. 2555
Mission and unity in Lutheranism. 2296
Mission and witness. 1125
Mission apostolate, a study of the mission activity of the Roman Catholic church and the story of the foundation and development of various mission aid organizations in the United States. 850
Mission as decision. 1014
Mission-book of the Congregation of the Most Holy Redeemer. 854, 999
... Mission children. 2492
Mission, church, and sect in Oceania. 2543

Mission-church dynamics. 2492
Mission control. 1561
Mission covenant of America. 3572
Mission doctor. 2539
Mission doctor sees the wind of change. 13
Mission factor. 1235
Mission focus. 2496
Mission for life. 171, 2158
Mission for Samaritans. 2538
Mission hymnal. 2968
Mission impossible. 1261
Mission in a new world. 2495
Mission in Burma. 2505, 3273
Mission in metropolis. 1278
Mission in Sioux Falls. 1626, 3415
Mission in the making. 2297
Mission in the Marianas. 2538, 3303
Mission in the New Testament. 2504
Mission in the '70s; what direction? 2496
Mission in western New York, and church history of the diocese of Buffalo. 2542
Mission into time. 1850, 3314
Mission La Concepcion Purisima de Maria Santisima. 3006
Mission life in Hawaii. 24
Mission man in Michigan. 1358
Mission memories. 2492
Mission methods. 2492
Mission: Middle America. 1055
Mission Mongolia. 2541, 3387
Mission, myth and reality. 2554
Mission Nuestra Senora de la Soledad. 2716
Mission of Baha' U'llah. 125, 129
Mission of God. 2555
Mission of Islam. 1925
Mission of man. 2320, 3095
Mission of Mary. 2362
Mission of St. Catherine. 749
Mission of sorrow. 1353
Mission of St Augustine to England. 111, 1759
Mission of the Archangel Michael. 51
Mission of the church. 761, 849, 887, 1120, 2480
Mission of the church and the propagation of the faith. 2526
Mission of the Columbia. 675, 1901
Mission of the Comforter, with notes. 1829, 1836
Mission of the Holy Spirit. 2874
Mission of the Spirit. 1828
Mission of the teacher. 806
Mission on a mountain. 5, 633
Mission on Main Street. 2260
Mission on the Nile. 2552
Mission play. 2757
Mission possible. 1573, 2494, 2679
Mission primary lessons for compass pilots. 2599
Mission primary lessons for radar pilots. 2599
Mission renewed. 2965
Mission San Carlos Borromeo (Carmelo) 3298
Mission San Luis Obispo in the Valley of the bears. 2271
Mission San Xavier del Bac. 3298
Mission San Xavier del Bac, Arizona. 3298
Mission Santa Barbara. 3302
Mission Santa Ines, virgen y martir,and its ecclesiastical seminary. 3302
Mission schools in India of the American board of commissioners for foreign missions. 2532
Mission stories of many lands. 2521
Mission studies. 2494
Mission study class leader. 2551
Mission study for older boys. 2549
Mission theology. 2554
Mission theology, 1948-1975. 2555
Mission theology today. 2555
Mission theory of Cardinal Brancati de Laurea. 2554
Mission to America. 2528, 2558, 3466
Mission to Arnhem land. 2433, 2556
Mission to Asia. 91
Mission to Black America. 2557, 3812
Mission to Brazil. 2504
Mission to Church in Andhra Pradesh, India. 3733
Mission to city multitudes. 1280
Mission to France. 2123
Mission to Korea. 2536
Mission to Latin America. 2537
Mission to mankind. 663, 2490, 3473
Mission to Metlakatla. 1482, 3717
Mission to non-Catholics. 2712
Mission to paradise. 2506, 3376
Mission to Peru. 2544, 2771
Mission to the head-hunters. 2122
Mission to the Navajo. 2677
Mission to the Philippines. 2545
Mission to the poorest. 1137

Mission tour in the southwest Pacific from the diary account of Rev. Mother Mary Rose, S.M.S.M. 2733
Mission tours, India. 2531
Mission tracts. 782
Mission trends no. 1. 2496
Mission: U. S. A. 3745
Mission.U. S. A. 2558
Mission unlimited. 2545
Mission work among the Indian tribes in the forests of Guiana. 2547
Missionaries. 2499
Missionaries and annexation in the Pacific. 2543
Missionaries and education in Bengal, 1793-1837. 1246
Missionaries and Muslims. 1748, 2557
Missionaries, Chinese, and diplomats. 2511, 2512
Missionaries to yourselves. 749
Missionary. 25, 2487
Missionary academia study. 851
Missionary achievement. 2495, 2526
Missionary addresses. 2496
Missionary adventures in Africa. 2497
Missionary adventures in the Far East. 2502
Missionary adventures in the South Pacific. 2540, 3538
Missionary album. 156, 2524
Missionary and his critics. 2518
Missionary and his work. 2482
Missionary and mandarin. 1947
Missionary and primitive man. 3438
Missionary annals of the nineteenth century. 2520
Missionary assignment. 155
Missionary atlas. 918
Missionary between the times. 2553
Missionary biography; an initial bibliography. 2485
Missionary bishop. 1472
Missionary campaign. 2493
Missionary candidates: how to breed the best. 2488
Missionary Church Association. 2488
Missionary church in East and West. 2497
Missionary, come back. 2491
Missionary companion. 2507
Missionary crisis and challenge in Latin America. 2537
Missionary dimension. 3770
Missionary education for Baptist men. 3182
Missionary education for the junior school age. 2550
Missionary education in a Baptist church. 2551
Missionary education in the church. 2550
Missionary education in the local church. 2493
Missionary education in your church. 2550
Missionary education of adults. 2550
Missionary education of beginners. 2551
Missionary education of children. 2550, 2552
Missionary education of intermediates. 2550
Missionary education of juniors. 2550
Missionary education of primary children. 2551
Missionary education of young people. 2550
... Missionary eduction in home and school. 2549
Missionary emphasis of the General Association of Regular Baptist Churches. 1704
Missionary enterprise. 2525, 2549
Missionary enterprise and rivalry in Igboland, 1857-1914. 2556
Missionary enterprise in China and America. 2509
Missionary enterprises in the South-Sea islands. 2545
Missionary entertainments for the Junior missionary society and the Sunday school. 3026
... The missionary Epworthian. 2492
Missionary evangel. 2483
Missionary expansion since the Reformation. 2525
Missionary experiences. 2618
Missionary faces isms. 2286
Missionary factor in East Africa. 2498
Missionary frontiersman. 2482
Missionary gazetteer. 2523, 2525
Missionary, go home! 2494, 2533
Missionary growth of the Methodist Episcopal church. 2441
Missionary handbook of direct-support missionaries of the Christian Churches and Churches of Christ. 2483
Missionary helps. 2618
Missionary hero stories. 2483
Missionary heroes. 2482

Missionary heroes in Africa. 2497
Missionary heroes in Oceanica. 2543
Missionary heroes of Africa. 2483
Missionary heroes of the Lutheran church. 2296
Missionary history of the Pacific Northwest, containing the wonderful story of Jason Lee, with sketches of many of his co-laborers, all illustrating life on the plains and in the mountains in pioneer days. 2206, 2543
...The missionary idea in life and religion. 2488
Missionary illustrations on the trail of the Nazarene. 2489
Missionary impact on modern Nigeria. 2542
Missionary imperative. 2457
Missionary index of Catholic Americans. 834
Missionary interpretation of history. 2425
Missionary intruder. 2484
Missionary journalist in China. 26, 2485
Missionary jubilee; an account of the fiftieth anniversary of the American Baptist missionary union, at Philadelphia, Mar 24, 25 and 26, 1864. 155
Missionary knights of the cross. 2493
Missionary landscapes in the Dark Continent. 2497
Missionary mama. 2531
Missionary manifesto. 2494
Missionary manual. 1569, 2551
Missionary manual and directory of the Unitas fratrum or the Moravian church. 2596
Missionary marionette plays. 3005
Missionary memorial; a literary and religious sovenir. 2493
... The missionary message of the Bible. 644, 2504
Missionary messages. 2520, 2546, 2551
Missionary methods. 2518, 2795
Missionary methods for missionary committees. 2494
Missionary methods, st. paul's or ours? 2551
Missionary milestones. 3036
Missionary moments. 2544
Missionary morale. 2483
Missionary mountain peaks. 2551
Missionary nature of the church. 2553
Missionary obligation in the light of the changes of modern thought. 2519
Missionary of moderation. 1302, 2630
Missionary offering. 2520
Missionary opportunity today. 2493
Missionary opportunity today, a brief world survey. 2493
Missionary outlook in the light of the war. 2518
Missionary pastor. 2481, 2549
Missionary pioneer in the Far East. 2516
Missionary pioneers of the American Lutheran Church. 32, 2482
Missionary plays and pageants. 2489
Missionary principles. 2553
Missionary principles and practice. 2493, 2521
Missionary program material for primary and junior grades. 2551
Missionary program material, for use with boys and girls. 2519, 2552
Missionary program topics. 2549
Missionary programs and incidents. 2551
Missionary programs for schoolboys. 2517
Missionary programs for the church. 2517, 2549
Missionary programs for women's meetings. 2488
Missionary question. 2494
Missionary readings for missionary programs. 2518
Missionary remains. 1577
Missionary sermon studies. 3373
Missionary sisters. 1578
Missionary sketches. 30
Missionary spirit in parish life. 3676
Missionary stories. 2491
Missionary stories and illustrations. 2489
Missionary stories for church programs. 2490
Missionary stories for little folks. 3046, 3047
Missionary stories to play and tell. 2490
Missionary stories to tell. 2490
Missionary story hour. 2490
Missionary story sketches, folk-lore from Africa. 2489
Missionary studies for the Sunday school. 2551
Missionary survey as an aid to intelligent co-operation in foreign missions. 2518
Missionary survey of the Pacific islands. 2543
...A missionary synod with a mission. 1549

Missionary teacher. 1900, 3402
Missionary theology. 2554
Missionary to Calcutta, city of contrasts. 1478
Missionary vocation. 2484
Missionary wife and her work. 2488
Missionary with a mike: the Bishop Sheen story. 3401
Missionary work of the Southern Baptist convention. 3467
Missionary workshop. 2455
Missionary worship programs. 2492, 2493
Missionary's daughter. 3698
Missionary's hand book. 2601
Missionary's life in the Land of the gods. 2488
Missionary's notebook. 1364
Missionary's return to Judaism. 2556
Missionary's role in socio-economic betterment. 1137
Missions. 2484, 2559
Missions: Africa and the Orient. 850, 2533
Missions alive. 2369
Missions and apostles of mediaeval Europe. 2493
Missions and me. 2549
Missions & mission philanthropy. 887
Missions & missionaries of Baja California. 2503
Missions and missionaries of California. 1899
Missions and modern history. 2494
Missions and modern thought. 2554
... Missions and politics in Asia. 2502
Missions and religions. 849, 1079
Missions and the church. 2495
Missions and the world crisis. 2555
Missions and world movements. 2492, 2519
Missions and world problems. 2494
Missions at the crossroads. 1905
Missions at the grass roots. 2528
Missions, evangelism, and church growth. 2555
Missions from the modern view. 2522
... Missions in a changing world. 2494
Missions in a time of testing. 2554
Missions in crisis. 2554
Missions in Eden. 2502
Missions: "in" or out? 2540, 2549
Missions in principle and practice. 2493
Missions in state and church. 2492
Missions in the American outdoors. 1259
Missions in the Bible. 2550
Missions in the modern Sunday school. 2540, 2549
Missions in the plan of the ages. 2492, 2503
Missions in the Sunday School. 2550
Missions in the world today. 850
Missions made fascinating for wide-awake girls. 2551
Missions matching the hour. 2519
Missions of the Evangelical Church. 1546
Missions on trial. 2499
Missions our mission. 155
Missions striking home. 2527
Missions, their rise and development. 2525
... Missions today. 2540, 2554
Missions today in the Lutheran Church in America. 2296
Missions tomorrow. 2520
Missions under the Cross. 2520
Missions versus militarism. 2495
Missippi conference of the Methodist Protestant church. 2459
Mississippi Annual Conference, Southeastern Jurisdiction. 2439
Mississippi Baptist preachers. 156
Mississippi circuit riders. 1930
Mississippi circuit riders, 1865-1965. 1930
Mississippi minister. 14

Mississippi vista. 695
Missives. 3594
Missouri. 157
Missouri adult vocational-literacy materials development project. 3026
Mistake of Christendom. 2050, 3023
Mistakes in religion exposed. 3291
Mistakes of Ingersoll. 1907
Mistakes of Ingersoll and his answers complete. 1907
Mistakes of Ingersoll on Thomas Paine. 2758
Mistakes of Jesus. 1654
Mr. Arnold's week of Christian living. 978
Mr. baggy-skin lizard. 662
'Mr. Baptist. 3131
Mr. Benevolence of Association Baptists. 3525

Mr. Blount's Oracles of reason, examined and answered, in nine sections. 673, 1420
Mr. Bradford gets around. 1014
Mr. Jonathan Edwards. 1500
Mr. Jones and his Maker. 3100
Mr. Jones, meet the Master. 2933, 3355
Mr. Law's Unlawfulness of the stage entertainment examin'd. 2201, 3606
Mister Maloga. 2373, 2484
Mr. Moffat and the Bechuanas of South Africa. 2563
Mr. Pepys and Nonconformity. 1469, 2817
Mr. Prime's two ordination sermons. 173
Mr. Protestant. 2290, 3733
Mr. Ralph Wheelock, Puritan. 3810
Mr. Smith, meet Mr. Cohen. 2105
Mr. Valiant-for-truth. 1452
Mr. Wesley. 3804
Mr. Wesley; an intimate sketch of John Wesley. 3804
Mr. William Prynn, his defence of stage-plays. 2984, 3606
Mr. William Prynn, his defence of stage-plays, anonymous. 2984, 3606
Mistiniame sode. 2165
Mistletoe and its philosophy. 2853
Mis-trials of Jesus. 2068
Misunderstanding of the church. 1117
Misunderstandings between East and West. 3307
Mitchell's masonic directory of Pennsylvania. 1668
Mite into the treasury. 1680
Mithraic mysteries restored and modernized. 2560
Mithraic studies. 2560
Mithraism and Christianity. 2560
Mithraism in Ostia. 2560
*mithras. 2560
"Mithras liturgy" 2560
Mitra and Aryaman. 2560
Mitre and sceptre. 1222, 1522
Mitri; or, The story of Prince Demetrius Augustine Gallitzin. 1744
Mitzvah. 172
Mitzvot. 562, 1312
Mixed marriage between Jew and Christian. 2345
Mixed marriages and prenuptial instructions. 780
Mixed marriages and their remedies. 2341
Mixed pasture. 3483
Mixing religion and politics. 1086
Mo Bradley and Thailand. 688, 2553
Moaning of the glorious Koran. 2185
Moberly pulpit. 1466
Mobilizing capital. 3305
Moccasin trail. 1901
... The mocking-bird. 632
Mockingbirds and angel songs & other prayers. 2889
Mode and subjects of baptism. 136
Mode of Christian baptism. 136
Model 20th century speaker. 1167
... A model Christian. 958
Model Christian worker, John Potter. 2865
Model church. 1116
Model for young men. 2203
Model homestead. 2945
Model merchant. 712
Model pastor. 1693, 3534, 3535, 3862
Model prayer. 2876
Model preacher. 2906
Model program for the Talmud Torah. 3585
Model Redemptorist brother. 3031
Model superintendent. 1790
Model-T king? 2437
Modeling God. 935
Models and mystery. 3669
Models of holiness. 1824
Models of Jesus. 2042
Models of metropolitan ministry. 1279
Models of religious broadcasting. 3018
Models of secularization in contemporary sociological theory. 3327
Models of the church. 1118
Moderate Puritans and the Elizabethan church. 1221, 3009
Modern ABeCedary for Protestants. 3666
Modern American religious buildings. 1162
Modern American spiritualism. 3496, 3521
Modern Anglican liturgies 1958-1968. 2257
Modern apocrypha. 337
Modern apostle. 754
Modern apostles of faith. 927
Modern apostles of missionary byways. 1500
Modern approach to Islam. 2566
Modern approach to the Old Testament. 541

Modern architectural work. 1161
Modern architecture and Christian celebration. 2240
Modern B.Y.P.U. methods for seniors and adults. 142
Modern Baptist heroes and martyrs. 143
Modern belief in imortality. 1890
Modern Biblical studies. 201
Modern Black theology. 669
Modern builders of the church. 3762
Modern call of missions. 2554
Modern Canterbury pilgrims, and why they chose the Episcopal Church. 2958
Modern catechetics. 3157
Modern catechism. 748
Modern Catholic dictionary. 778, 3638
Modern Catholic thinkers. 867, 868
Modern Catholicism. 2955
Modern challenges to Halakhah. 1822, 2751
Modern Christian adventure. 1127
Modern Christian art. 921, 922
Modern Christian literature. 3203
Modern Christian movements. 1187
Modern Christian revolutionaries. 2169
Modern Christian thought. 3659
Modern Christianity. 1052, 1055, 1062
Modern church. 1157
Modern church architecture. 1156, 1157
Modern church architecture. Translated by Ellen Callmann. 1160
Modern church design. 1159
Modern church finance. 1168
Modern church management. 1200
Modern church program. 1251
Modern churches in Germany. 1160
Modern churches of the world. 1157
Modern cities and their religious problems. 1277
Modern concept of God. 1724
Modern concordance to the New Testament. 227
Modern conflict over the Bible. 199
Modern conflict over the Bible in synthesis and comparison. 199
Modern crisis in religion. 165
Modern criticism and the preaching of the Old Testament. 502
Modern crusade. 519
Modern crusaders. 2483
Modern cyclopedia of illustrations for all occasions. 1840
Modern deity. 1419
Modern devil. 1427
Modern diabolism. 3518
Modern dictionary of the Holy Bible. 244
Modern discoveries which help us to believe. 1100
Modern divine healing. 1599
Modern doubt and Christian belief. 59
Modern English churches. 1158
Modern evangelism. 1564
Modern evangelism and ancient environment. 1553
Modern evangelism on fundamental lines. 1553
Modern evangelistic address. 1561
Modern evils. 36
Modern family and the church. 1611
Modern flower of St. Francis. 2353
Modern Galahad, St. John Berchmans. 191
Modern genesis. 1371
Modern God. 1067, 3080
Modern gospel song stories. 1872
Modern Greek folklore and ancient Greek religion. 1631
Modern herbal spellbook. 1804
Modern heresies. 1804
Modern heroes of the mission field. 2484
Modern Hinduism. 1814
Modern history of Universalism. 3753
Modern illustrations for public speakers. 1841
Modern in search of truth. 3103
Modern indictment of Catholicism. 788
Modern infidelity considered with respect to its influence on society. 3422
Modern interpretation of Judaism. 2140
Modern introduction to astrology. 97
Modern introduction to biblical Hebrew. 1797
Modern introduction to metaphysics. 2417
Modern Japan and Shinto nationalism. 3403, 3404
Modern Japanese religions. 3324
Modern Japanese religions. 3324
Modern Jewish ethics, theory and practice. 1540
Modern Jewish preaching. 2910
Modern Jewish problems. 2077, 2151, 3310
Modern Jewish religious movements. 2148
Modern Jewish thought. 2142, 2149
Modern Jewish woman. 3838
Modern Job. 1745

Modern King James version of the Holy Bible. 265
Modern King James version oi the Holy Bible. 265
Modern knight. 2794, 3862
Modern knight of the cross. 1109
Modern language New Testament. 357
Modern light on immortality. 1888
Modern literature and the death of God. 3071
Modern liturgy handbook. 2239
Modern loaves and fishes. 2988
Modern loaves and fishes, and other studies in psychic phenomena. 2988
Modern Macedonia. 149
Modern Magdalene. 1450
Modern man and his fellow man. 3445
Modern man and mortality. 1413
Modern man and religion. 2836
Modern man and spiritual life. 3482
Modern man and the church. 3058
Modern man and the cross. 106, 109
Modern man looks at the Bible. 235
Modern man reads the Old Testament. 500
Modern man's Bible problems. 278
Modern man's religion. 1056, 3057
Modern man's view on the story of Jesus. 2060
Modern man's worship. 3853
Modern martyr. 2351
Modern martyr, Theophane Venard (Blessed) 3777
Modern martyr. Theophane Venard (the Venerable.) 3777
Modern masters of pulpit discourse. 2909
Modern materialism in its relations to religion and theology. 3103
Modern meaning of church membership. 1201
Modern meaning of Judaism. 2138
Modern medical missions. 2539
Modern medicine and Jewish law. 2377
Modern menace of Protestantism. 2976
Modern mentality and evangelization. 789
Modern message of the Minor prophets. 560
Modern message of the Psalms. 573, 579
Modern messages from great hymns. 1869
Modern messenger of purity. 3392, 3690
Modern methods in church work. 1240
Modern methods in classical mythology. 2657
Modern methods in Sunday-school work. 3555
Modern methods in the church school. 3554
Modern mind and the Virgin birth. 1886
Modern miracle. 2986
Modern miracles. 2613
Modern miracles and ansuers to prayer. 2848
Modern miracles of healing. 1598
Modern miraculous cures. 1599
Modern mission apostolate. 2515
Modern mission century viewed as a cycle of the divine working. 2494
Modern mission dialogue. 850
Modern missionary challenge. 2520
Modern missions in Chile and Brazil. 2507
Modern missions in Mexico. 2540
Modern missions in the Far East. 2479, 2516
Modern missions on the Spanish main. 2512
Modern missions: their trials and triumphs. 2526
Modern money methods for the church. 1167
Modern moral problems. 947
Modern Moses at West Tintic. 1776
Modern movement in American theology. 2975, 3659
Modern movements among Moslems. 2566
Modern mysteries explained and exposed. 1406, 3508
Modern mysticism. 2638, 2640
Modern mystics. 2641
Modern mystics and modern magic. 2731
Modern mythology. 2652
Modern myths. 3358
Modern nationalism and religion. 2671
Modern nirvanaism. 3499
Modern numerology. 3575
Modern paintings and water colors by Dutch, French, and American artists. 2760
Modern Palestine. 2101, 2119
Modern parables. 1015
Modern parent and the teaching church. 3092
Modern parish community. 2774
Modern parish problems. 2774
Modern pathfinders of Christianity. 926

Modern philosophies of Judaism. 2113
Modern philosophy of religion. 3105
Modern pilgrimage. 1784, 2761
Modern pilgrimage in New Testament christology. 2011
Modern pilgrim's progress. 972
Modern pioneer in Korea. 77, 2536
Modern plea for ancient truths. 1460
Modern plea for Christianity. 1095
Modern practical theology. 3678
Modern predicament. 3103
Modern premillennialism and the Christian hope. 2465
Modern priest looks at his outdated church. 788
Modern priestess of Isis. 671
Modern problems and creation. 1382
Modern problems as Jesus saw them. 2061
Modern problems in the light of Christian principles. 3453
Modern problems of Jewish parents. 2773
Modern problems of the home school, and church. 943
Modern prophet speaks. 2950
Modern psalms by boys. 687
Modern psychical phenomena. 2987
... Modern psychical phenomena, recent researches and speculations. 2987
Modern psychology and the validity of Christian experience. 3001
Modern pulpit. 2898
Modern questions, timeless answers. 796
Modern reader in the philosophy of religion. 3108
Modern reader's Bible. 259, 260
Modern reader's Bible atlas. 283
Modern reader's Bible for schools. 251, 353, 354
Modern reader's book of Psalms. 2857
Modern reader's dictionary of the Bible. 245
Modern reader's guide to Acts. 333
Modern reader's guide to John. 423
Modern reader's guide to Mark. 437
Modern reader's guide to Matthew and Luke. 444
Modern reader's guide to religions. 3122
Modern reader's guide to the Bible. 312
Modern reader's guide to the book of Revelation. 460
Modern reader's guide to the Gospels. 401
Modern reflections. 3095
Modern Reform responsa. 3219
Modern religio-healing. 1792
Modern religion from Puritan origins. 3008
Modern religious cults and movements. 3141
Modern religious cults and society. 3113
Modern religious faiths. 3325
Modern religious liberalism. 2221, 2563
Modern religious movements in India. 1896
Modern religious trends in the light of the messages of Ezekiel, the forgotten prophet. 519
Modern renaissance of Jewish music. 2634
Modern representations of the life of Jesus. 1979
Modern revivalism. 3233
Modern rival of Christian faith. 3328
Modern rivals to Christian faith. 1095
Modern Russia. 3257
Modern Sabbath questions for the people. 3260
Modern Saint Anthony. 2318, 2716
Modern Samaritan. 3296
Modern schism. 3327
Modern school of the prophets. 1634
Modern science and Christian beliefs. 3080
Modern science and Christian faith. 3077
Modern science and Christian life. 3081
Modern science and God. 3077
Modern science and the Genesis record. 1382
Modern science in Bible lands. 202
Modern science in the Christian life. 3082
Modern scientific study of the New Testament. 321
Modern scientific views and Christian doctrines compared. 3075
Modern scriptural approach to the Spiritual exercises. 2269, 3476
Modern sermons by world scholars. 3344
Modern shibboleth. 134
Modern social and economic order. 3450
Modern spiritism. 3512
Modern spiritualism. 3497, 3508
Modern spiritualism exposed. 3505
Modern spiritualism laid bare. 3517
Modern spiritualistic classic. 3507
Modern stewardship sermons. 2442
Modern stories of inspiration. 925

Modern study in the Book of Proverbs. 572
Modern study of conscience. 1347
Modern substitutes for Christianity. 3608
Modern substitutes for traditional Christianity. 1051
Modern Sunday-school. 3551, 3558
Modern Sunday school and its present day task. 3553
Modern Sunday school in principle and practice. 3553
Modern Templar. 1665
Modern temple and templars. 1368
Modern tendencies in world religions. 3113
Modern theism. 3609
Modern theologians: Christians and Jews. 3611
Modern theology and the preaching of the gospel. 3641
Modern theology of tradition. 3706
Modern theories of sin. 3411
Modern theory of the Bible. 237
Modern theses. 1125
Modern Thomistic philosophy. 3309, 3696
...Modern thought and the crisis in belief. 237
Modern thought and traditional faith. 3616
Modern tongues movement. 1716
Modern tower of Babel. 758, 1912
Modern treasury of Christmas plays. 1113
Modern treasury of Jewish thoughts. 2076
Modern trends in Hinduism. 1815
Modern trends in Islam. 1922, 2564
Modern trends in world religions. 3122, 3123
Modern uncertainty and Christian faith. 3044
Modern use of the Bible. 233
Modern values and their Christian sources. 945
Modern varieties of Judaism. 2079
Modern view of the Old Testament. 536
Modern view of the Torah precepts. 1312
Modern viking. 3777
Modern vision of death. 1415
Modern war and the American churches. 3793
Modern war and the Christian. 1077
Modern war and the pursuit of peace. 3794
"The modern Whitfield." 167
Modern witchcraft. 3824
Modern witch's spellbook. 3824
Modern words of religion. 945
Modern world and self-control. 664
Modern world movements. 3684
Modern worship. 3854
Modern worship and the psalter. 577
Modern Yiddish poetry. 3863
Modernism. 2561, 2562
Modernism and its re-statement of Christian doctrine. 2561
Modernism and miracle. 2561
Modernism and the Christian church. 2561
Modernism and the Christian faith. 2561
Modernism and the reformation. 2561
Modernism and the Vatican. 2562
Modernism, fundamentalism, and Catholicism. 2561
Modernism in religion. 2561
Modernism vs. Bible Christianity. 2562
Modernist and his creed. 2561
Modernist crisis: von Hugel. 1850, 2562
Modernist fundamentalism. 2561
Modernist impulse in American Protestantism. 2561
Modernist movement in Italy and its relation to the spread of Protestant Christianity. 820
Modernist movement in the Roman church. 2243, 2562
Modernist movement in the Roman Church, its origins & outcome. 2243, 2562
Modernist Muslim movement in Indonesia, 1900-1942. 1925
Modernist studiest in the life of Jesus. 1991
Modernity and the churches. 3651
Modernity of Saint Augustine. 114
Modernizing America. 2593
Moderns. 3611
Modes of referring and the problem of universal. 3755
Modes of thought. 2834
Modest enquiry into the nature of witchcraft. 3827
Modest proof of the order & government settled by Christ and his apostles in the church. 1522
Modicum. 1298

Moehler and Baur in controversy, 1832-38: romantic-idealist assessment of the Reformation and Counter-Reformation. 2568, 3656
Moffats. 2499, 2563
Moffatt Bible concordance. 227, 2563
Mohammed. 2628, 2629, 2635
Mohammed and Mohammedanism. 2565
Mohammed and the rise of Islam. 2566, 2629, 2635
... Mohammed, Buddha, and Christ. 2564
Mohammed; prophet of the religion of Islam. 2629
Mohammed, the man and his faith. 2628
...Mohammed, the man nad his faith. 2628
Mohammedan world of to-day. 2557, 2565
Mohammedanism. 1922, 2564, 2566
Mohammedanism: an historical survey. 1924
Molchanie. 3478
Mold me & shape me. 931, 1754
Molders of the Jewish mind. 2084
Molders of the medieval mind. 1128
Molding the Christian mind. 1012
Molecular hypothesis of nature. 3507
Molinos the Quietist. 2568
Mollie Fancher, the Brooklyn enigma. 3499
Molokan oral tradition. 2568
Mom has a second job. 2625
Mom, you gotta be kiddin. 2625
Moment before God. 2170
Moment between two eternities. 965
Moment by moment. 1013
Moment of Christian witness. 995
Moment of truth: our next four hundred years. 3727
Moment to shout. 554, 987
Memento of the death of the Holy Father Pope Leo XIII. 668, 2216
Momentous memoirs. 3519
Moments divine before the blessed sacrament. 3263
Moments for everyone. 2392
Moments in His Presence. 1985
Moments of decision. 214, 984, 1024
Moments of devotion. 1437, 1443
Moments of light. 3490
Moments of meditation. 1434, 1455, 2392
Moments of meditation from Matthew Henry. 1431
Moments of personal discovery. 3067
Moments of reflection. 2390
Moments of truth. 2212
Moments of worship. 3856
Moments that matter. 991
Moments with God. 317, 856, 2890
Moments with Jesus. 2388
Moments with Mary. 2386
Moments with my Master. 2384
Moments with the consoling Christ. 2896
Moments with the devotional masters. 1456
Moments with the Master. 1452
Moments with the prophets. 2607
Mommie of the mixing bowl. 23
Momuments and the Old Testament. 487
... The monadology and other philosophical writings. 2568
Monarchy. 1140
Monarchy and community. 1322
Monarchy, and Three political letters. 2858
Monasteries. 2572
Monasteries & monks. 2569
Monasteries and religious houses of Great Britain and Ireland. 2569
Monasteries of Ireland. 2582
Monasteries of Western Europe. 2568
Monastery and cathedral in France. 1159
Monastery: life in a religious community. 3275
Monastery of El Escorial and the Prince's Lodge. 1531
Monastery of Jade Mountain. 2584
Monastery of Saint Catherine at Mount Sinai. 3414
Monastery of Saint Catherine at Mount Sinai, the icons. 1881, 3414
Monastic achievement. 2576
Monastic agreement of the monks and nuns of the English nation. 2579
Monastic architecture in France. 2569
Monastic architecture in France, from the Renaissance to the Revolution. 2569
Monastic diurnal. 2583
Monastic iconography in France from the Renaissance to the Revolution. 86
Monastic impulse. 737, 2575
Monastic journey. 2571, 2572
Monastic journey to India. 2585, 2813
Monastic life at Cluny. 1304
Monastic life at Cluny, 910-1157. 1304
Monastic life in medieval England. 2579
Monastic life in the Middle Ages. 860, 2582

Monastic order in England. 2579
Monastic order in South Wales, 1066-1349. 2584
Monastic peace. 2571
Monastic reform in Lorraine and the architecture of the outer crypt, 950-1100. 1392
Monastic renewal. 2570
Monastic spirituality. 2571
Monastic tithes. 3702
Monastic world, 1000-1300. 2582
Monasticism. 2576
Monasticism and civilization. 2576
Monasticism in the orthodox churches. 2583
Moncure Conway,1839-1907. 1367
Moncure D. Conway. 1367
Monday morality. 949
Monday morning Christianity. 318
Monday morning religion. 977
Monday to Friday is not enough. 1342
Monday's God. 989
Money and the church. 1168
Money and your church. 1168
Money for your campus ministry, church, or other non-profit organization. 1169
Money in the church. 1168
Money management for ministers. 1292
Money master of the world. 605, 2584
Money problems and pastoral care. 2781
Money talks. 1126
Money the acid test. 1260
Money: thoughts for God's stewards. 3529
Moneyless magnate. 1071
Monganga Paul. 2514
Monitor of the work. 1669
Monitor of the work, lectures and ceremonies of ancient craft masonry inn the jurisdiction of the Grand lodge of the state of New York. 1669
Monk and the world. 2576
Monk Bretton priory, Yorkshire. 2584
Monk of Farne. 2398
Monk of Farne (The) 2393
Monk who lived again. 2586
Monkey business. 1579
Monkeys and myths. 1579
Monks and civilization. 2578
Monks and civilization, from the barbarian invasions to the reign of Charlemagne. 2578
Monks and love in twelfth-century France. 2266
Monks and Monasteries of Near East. 2569
Monks & shepherds in the Yorkshire Dales. 1636, 3868
Monks and their decline. 2576
Monks before Christ. 2576
Monks, bishops, and pagans. 1102
Monk's community. 2583
Monks, merit, and motivation: Buddhism and national development in Thailand. 712
Monks, nuns, and monasteries. 2569
Monks of Kublai Khan, Emperor of China. 3304, 3787
Monks of Qumran as depicted in the Dead Sea scrolls. 3014
Monks of war. 2463
Monks on marriage, a twelfth-century view. 2346
Monocacy valley, Maryland, Presbyterianism. 2918
Monogram saint. 194
Monograph. 2806
Monograph, no. 1. 1949
Monograph[s]. 3176
Monophysitism, past and present. 2585
Monotessaron. 395
Monotheism and Moses. 2585
Monotheism, in the main derived from the Hebrew nation and the law of Moses, the primitive religion of the city of Rome. 3246
Monsieur Vincent. 3779
Monsignor Heinen. 1801
Monsignor Ligutti, the Pope's county agent. 1301, 2229
Monsignor Ronald Knox, fellow of Trinity College, Oxford, and Protonotary Apostolic to His Holiness Pope Pius XII. 2182
Monsignor Joseph Jessing (1836-1899) 1944, 3859
Monster myths of ancient Greece. 2585
Mont-Saint-Michel and Chartres. 2585
Montalembert. 2586
Montanism and the primitive church. 2586
El monte. 2681
... Monte Cassino, Byzantium, and the West in the earlier middle ages. 2586
Monte Cassino in the Middle Ages. 2586
Montecassino Passion and the poetics of medieval drama. 2586, 2778

Month of Mary, conceived without sin. 2361
Month of roses. 3247
Month of the Holy Ghost. 1830
Month of the holy souls. 2896
Month of the infant Jesus. 1825
Month of the Sacred heart. 3270
Month with Christ. 399, 1434, 2015
Month with Mary (A) 2360
Month with the Master. 430
Monthly lesson number one[-four]. 460
Monthly magazine of religion and literature. 3677
Monthly missionary notice. 2442
Monthly religious magazine and theological review. 3730
Montreat-Anderson College. 2928
Monument facts and higher critical fancies. 502
Monument of parental affection, to a dear and only son. 1713
Monumenta ritualia Ecclesiae anglicanae. 1224
Monumental inscriptions in the burial ground of the Jewish Synagogue at Bridgetown. 2098
... Monuments and memorials. 3333
Monuments and the Old Testament. 487
Monuments of St. George's Chapel. 3820
Monuments of the early church. 919
Mood of Christmas. 1112
Moods and truths. 3212
Moods of the soul. 3366
Moody. 2588
Moody and Ingersoll. 2588
Moody Bible Institute. 2587
Moody: his words, work, and workers. 1559
Moody in Chicago. 894, 2587
Moody still lives. 2587
Moody versus Christ and His apostles. 2588
Moody, winner of souls. 2588
Moody's anecdotes and illustrations. 1841
Moody's great sermons. 3355
Moody's latest sermons. 1559, 2587, 3355
Moody's new sermons. 1559
Moody's stories. 1841
Moody's talks on temperance. 3595
Mook, true tales about a Chinese boy and his friends. 2511
Moon is not enough. 931, 1920
Moon is not the Son. 2588
Moon: outposts of the Gods. 236
Moonies in America. 3329
Moonstruck. 3846
Moorefield; home of early Baptist preacher Jeremiah Moore. 2589
Moorestown plan. 3876
... Mooring-masts of revelation; a study of towering Bible characters by walks and talks at sacred places. 295
Mooted question of history. 1817
Mooted questions of history. 3033
Moral absolutes and the magisterium. 866, 948
Moral adjustments of the Christian life. 944
Moral adventure. 945
Moral and ethical implications of human organ transplants. 3709
... Moral and pastoral theology. 947
Moral and pastoral theology, a summary. 947
Moral and religious challenge of our times. 3443
Moral and religious miscellany. 2913
Moral and social teaching of the church. 1136
Moral and spiritual aspects of baptism. 133
Moral and spiritual development for the young child. 939
Moral and spiritual foundations for the world of tomorrow. 2083
Moral and spiritual values in education. 2590
Moral and spiritual values in the public schools. 2590
Moral aphorisms and terselogical teachings of Confucius, the sapient Chinese philosopher. 1330
Moral aphorisms and terseological teachings of confucius. 2838
Moral argument for Christian theism. 1739
... The moral argument for theism. 3609 •
Moral aspects of city life. 3755
Moral beauty. 2342
Moral character of Christ. 2001
Moral conflict of humanity and other papers. 947
Moral context of pastoral care. 2787
Moral crisis in Christianity. 3445
Moral dignity of baptism. 134
Moral dilemma of nuclear weapons. 103
Moral dilemmas. 1002

Moral disquisitions. 2326, 3587
Moral disquisitions. 2326, 3587
Moral drill for the school room. 940
... Moral education. 2590, 2591, 2592
Moral education in a changing society.
    2591
Moral education in family, school, and
    church. 2590
Moral education in school and home.
    2590
Moral, ethical, and legal issues in the
    neurosciences. 3604
Moral evaluation of contraception and
    sterilization. 663
Moral evil; its nature and origin. 1746
Moral evil under challenge. 1746
Moral evolution. 2215
Moral formation and Christianity. 949
Moral guidance. 948
Moral heroism. 661
Moral instruction. 2591
Moral instruction and training in schools.
    2592
...The moral instruction of children. 2589
Moral instructor. 2589
Moral issue in statecraft. 1914
Moral issues and Christian response. 1140
Moral issues in the control of birth. 664
Moral judgment. 1538
Moral Lacon. 2375
Moral law. 944, 1314, 1535, 2973
Moral law in Christian social ethics. 944
... The moral law of the family. 1603
Moral law or Kant's Groundwork of the
    metaphysic of morals. 1536
Moral leaders. 660
Moral leadership and the ministry. 3672
Moral life of man. 1537
Moral life of the Hebrews. 1539
Moral majority. 946, 2593
Moral meaning of revolution. 3233
Moral nexus. 944
Moral norms and Catholic tradition. 949
Moral notions. 1536
Moral obligation. 1537
Moral obligation of fraternal correction.
    887
Moral of accidents and other discourses.
    1341
Moral of the story. 1624
Moral phases of religious education. 2592
Moral philosopher, 1737. 1105
Moral philosophy. 1535, 1540
Moral philosophy of courtship and
    marriage. 2336
Moral philosophy of Jewish Royce. 3252
Moral philosophy of Josiah Royce. 3252
Moral philosophy of Peter Abelard. 2,
    1537
Moral philosophy of Santayana. 1536,
    3302
Moral philosophy of William James. 1538
... Moral principles in education. 2590
Moral principles in the Bible. 275
Moral problem of contraception. 663
Moral problems. 756, 3880
Moral problems and Christian personalism.
    948
Moral problems in social work. 3433
Moral problems of interracial marriage.
    2478
Moral problems today. 949
Moral progress. 1282
Moral questions. 947
Moral re-armament. 2593
Moral re-armament; what is it? 2593
Moral reasoning. 1535, 2157
Moral reasoning and truth. 1536
Moral responsibility. 946
Moral responsibility in conflicts. 1089
Moral rules and particular circumstances.
    1534
Moral science. 3644
...Moral series. 760, 948
Moral state of nations. 3434
Moral system and the atonement. 104
Moral system of Dante's Inferno. 1402
Moral teacher. 2591
Moral teaching in the primitive church.
    1004
Moral teaching of Jesus. 2003, 3336
Moral teaching of Paul. 373
Moral teachings of science. 3075
Moral teachings of the New Testament.
    378, 942
Moral tendency of divine revelation
    asserted and illustrated. 3225
Moral theology. 946, 948, 2593
Moral theology, a continuing journey. 947
Moral training in the public schools. 2591
Moral training in the school and home.
    2592
Moral training of the school child. 2591
Moral unity of the human race. 1777,
    2546
Moral universe. 949
Moral values and secular education. 2591

Moral values and the moral life. 1535,
    3695
Moral values in psychoanalysis. 2410
Moral values in public education. 2591
Moralism and Christianity. 1069
Moralist. 3343
Moralities of everyday life. 3742
Moralities on the Gospels. 39
Morality. 1536
Morality and beyond. 945
Morality and pessimism. 1535
Morality and situation ethics. 949
Morality and the good life. 81, 1537
Morality and the social order. 948
Morality and youth. 3880
Morality for our time. 948
Morality gap. 947
Morality, how to live it today. 947
Morality is for persons. 948
Morality, law, and grace. 1534
Morality maze. 944
Morality of killing. 1544
Morality of mercy killing. 1544
Morality of periodic continence. 1322
Morality of power. 941
Morality or immortality? 141
Morality without law. 943
Morals and dogma of the Ancient and
    accepted Scottish rite of freemasonry.
    1662
Morals and man. 949
Morals and man in the social sciences.
    3441
Morals and marriage. 2340
Morals and religion. 3091
Morals and revelation. 1536
Morals for lay people. 2593
Morals for mankind. 1536
Morals for ministers. 3673
Morals in a free society. 944
Morals in medicine. 2d, rev., and enl. ed.
    2377
Morals in politics and professions. 3433
Morals, law, and authority. 949
Morals, law, and life. 3389, 3817
Morals of Christ. 2003
Morals of suicide. 3545
Moravian Church in Canada. 2594
Moravian customs. 2595
Moravian journals relating to central New
    York, 1745-66. 1901, 2594
Moravian mission to the African slaves of
    the Danish West Indies, 1732-1828.
    2559, 2594
Moravian youth hymnal for use in the
    church school and all young people's
    meetings. 2594
Moravians. 2594
Moravians in Georgia, 1735-1740. 2595
Moravians in Georgia, 1735-1940. 2595
Moravians in Georgia, 1735-1740. 2595
Moravians in Jamaica. 2533, 2594
Moravians in North Carolina. 2596
Moravians in two worlds. 2596
Morceaux choisis des ouvres de corneille
    [et al.]
    c6. 2142, 2164
Mordecai M. Kaplan; jubille volume on the
    occasion of his seventieth birthday.
    2145, 2164
More about Jesus. 1957, 1982
More about Masonry. 1661
More about the saints. 3284
More abundant life. 979, 2211
More answers to today's moral problems.
    3011
More Bible friends to know. 624
More Bible puzzles and games. 281
More Bible quizzes! 280
More Bible quotes & comments. 2386
More blessed than kings. 384
More catechism stories. 1840
More chapel talks. 3758
More children's liturgies. 836, 905
More children's worship in the church
    school. 3858
More Christian industrial order. 3441
More contemporary prayers. 2893
More "Copy" 3141
More devotional talks for women's
    organizations. 1448
More devotions for juniors. 901
More difficult sayings of Jesus. 2071
More effective church boards and
    committees. 1251
More essays on religion. 3619
More evidence that demands a verdict.
    563
More excellent ministry. 103
More excellent sacrifice. 2401
More excellent way. 324, 887, 953, 2267,
    3141
More famous mothers from the Bible and
    history. 2624
More first things. 3310
More from the primeval forest. 2503
More from your class meetings. 1286

More fruits from India. 1772
More Handles of power. 960
More hilltop verses and prayers. 1437
More hymn stories. 1872
More ideas for prayer. 2397
More illustrations and quotable poems.
    1842
More joy. 966
More Junior object sermons. 909
More light. 1670
More light on masonry. 52
More light on the Dead Sea scrolls. 1409
More light on the Gospel. 348
More like the master. 958
More little lessons to live by. 906
More little visits with God. 1605
More little ways. 3284
More lives than a cat. 1300, 3718
More lives than one? 3053
More loves than one. 2986
More Mary-minded. 2360
More missionary stories. 2491
More missionary stories to tell. 2490
More New tales from the Old Testament.
    533
More New Testament studies. 334
More New Testament words. 1768
More objects that talk and teach. 909
More of a good thing. 2337
More outline sermons on general subjects.
    3375
More parables for little people. 939
More parables from life. 1015
More parish liturgies. 2236
More people are asking. 2286
More power for your church. 1252
More power in prayer. 2887
More power in soul winning; how to win
    souls. 1564
More power to the church. 1828
More power to the preacher. 3671
More prayer meeting topics. 2886
More prayers. 898
More preaching values in the Epistles of
    Paul. 374
More precious than rubies. 2614
More primary worship programs. 3856
More programs & skits for young teens.
    1170
More psalms for all seasons. 585
More Rainbow missionary stories. 2491
More saints for six o'clock. 3285
More salt in my kitchen. 3843
More sermon trails for boys & girls. 909
More sermons from life. 2932
More sermons from Margaret street. 1225
More sermons I should like to have
    preached. 3365
More sermons on Biblical characters. 217
More short missionary plays. 2489
More short spiritual readings for Mary's
    children. 3884
More sidewalk prayers. 2895
More skits that win. 1554
More sources of power in famous lives.
    923
More Southern Baptist preaching. 160
More steeple stories. 1289
More stewardship parables of Jesus. 2025
More stewardship stories. 939, 3529
More stories for junior worship. 910
More stories from the Old Testament.
    629, 630
More story-telling programs. 935
More story worship programs. 940
More tales of Irish saints. 3283
More teen talks. 3886
More than a building. 3870
More than a carpenter. 2041
More than a man can take. 658
"More than a prophet," 2128
More than a spectator. 2391
More than atonement. 3617
More than bread, an analysis of rural life.
    3253
More than burnt offerings. 3218, 3680
'More than conquerors. 468, 662, 2482
More than healing. 2373
More than just talk. 1574
More than man. 1078, 2035
More than many sparrows. 1002
More than money. 3529
More than music. 3287
More than sentinels. 119
More than sparrows. 2983
More than survival. 1058
More than wanderers. 2379
More than we are. 2869
More than words. 2964
More two-minute stories. 908
More wonderful you. 3750
Moreana. 2596
Moreau; portrait of a founder. 2597
Moredecai M. Kaplan's concept of Jewish
    history and its relationship to his
    philophy of Judaism. 1818, 2164
Morgan confirmed. 52

Morgan episode in American free masonry.
    1662, 2597
Morgan's Freemasonry exposed and
    explained. 1670
Moriscos of Spain. 2598
Morman way. 1009
Mormon. 2615
Mormon answer to skepticism. 678, 2614,
    3428
Mormon archives. 2608
Mormon arts; featuring articles and art
    work by Mormon artists and authors. 87
Mormon Bible. 678
Mormon bibliography, 1830-1930. 2608
Mormon chronicle. 2603
Mormon Churches. 1231
Mormon claims examined. 2611
Mormon colonies in Mexico. 2617
Mormon country. 3762
Mormon doctrine. 2610
Mormon doctrine of deity. 1726, 2612
Mormon doctrine of God and heaven.
    2599
Mormon essays. 1008
Mormon establishment. 2606
Mormon experience. 1232
Mormon in motion. 1787, 2609
Mormon menace. 2602, 2603
Mormon mirage. 2614, 3315
Mormon monster. 2602
Mormon mother. 3585
Mormon, 150 years. 2616
Mormon papers. 2612
Mormon people, their character and
    traditions. 2608
Mormon pioneers. 2615
Mormon problem. 2605
Mormon problem the nation's dilemma.
    2601
Mormon prophet and his harem. 2606,
    3869
"The Mormon prophet's tragedy;" 1791
Mormon revelations of convenience. 1232,
    3227
Mormon role in the settlement of the
    West. 2615
Mormon saints. 2605, 3429
Mormon settlement in Arizona. 2616
Mormon story. 2619
Mormon Tabernacle Choir. 3287
Mormon thunder. 1756, 2620
Mormon trail from Vermont to Utah.
    2615
Mormon trail: Vermont to Utah. 2618
Mormon trails in Iowa. 3707
Mormon trials at Salt Lake city. 2606
Mormon Waterloo. 2601, 3428
Mormon way. 2618
Mormon wife. 2614
Mormoniad. 2604
Mormonism. 941, 2600, 2601, 2603, 2610,
    2611, 2614, 2616
Mormonism . . . address. 2601
Mormonism against itself. 2606
Mormonism and American culture. 2615
Mormonism and education. 2614
Mormonism and inspiration. 2619
Mormonism and masonry. 2604
Mormonism and the American experience.
    2602
Mormonism and the Mormons. 2603
Mormonism and the Negro. 2614, 2618
Mormonism exposed. 2611
Mormonism exposed and refuted. 2606
Mormonism in Germany. 2616
Mormonism in the twentieth century.
    2599
Mormonism: its rise, progress, and present
    condition. 2602, 3431
Mormonism, mama, and me! 2598
Mormonism portrayed. 2603
Mormonism refuted in the light of
    Scripture and history. 2611
Mormonism; the Islam of America. 2603,
    2833
Mormonism unvailed. 2611
Mormonism unveiled. 2603
Mormonism vs. Communism. 2606
Mormons. 1231, 2602, 2603, 2604, 2607
Mormons and the American frontier.
    2603
Mormons and their Bible. 2611
Mormons are peculiar people. 3428
Mormons at home. 2602
Mormons in American history. 2616
Mormons; or Latter-day Saints. 2604,
    2605, 3429
Mormons, or, Latter-day Saints, in the
    valley of the Great Salt Lake. 2602
Mormons: the Church of Jesus Christ of
    Latter-Day Saints. 2618
Morning after death. 171, 2128
Morning altar. 1431
Morning altar. 1431
Morning & evening. 1433, 2871, 3364
Morning and evening canticles and
    occasional anthems. 2962

Morning and evening daily devotions. 1442
Morning and evening exercises. 1439
Morning and evening prayer [and] The Penitential Office. 2969
Morning and evening prayers for every day in the week. 2297
Morning and evening thoughts. 1436
Morning bells. 939, 963
Morning by morning. 1442
"The morning cometh." 3349
Morning dew. 1436
Morning exercises, for every day in the year. 1439
Morning exercises for the closet. 1439
Morning hour of American Baptist missions. 156
Morning hours in Patmos. 461
Morning joy. 1349
Morning lectures. 3499
Morning manna. 1435
Morning message. 2887
Morning, noon, and night. 1449
Morning of joy. 970, 2136
Morning of the magicians. 2728
Morning offering. 2876
Morning praise and evensong. 859, 1203
Morning prayers for home worship. 2887
Morning readings. 253
Morning sacrifice. 2748, 3456
Morning sermons. 3368
Morning star. 1186, 1453, 2383
Morning thoughts for every day in the year. 1450
Morning watch. 1442, 2269, 2386
Morning watches, and Night watches. 2892
Mornings among the Jesuits at Rome. 802
Mornings in the college chapel. 3758
Morningside man. 3802
Il Moro; Ellis Heywood's dialogue in memory of Thomas More. 1785
Moro Sheeba. 2620
Moroccan Islam. 2635
Morris chapel. 3532
Morrisania, Melrose. 2698
Morse, Rebecca F[inley]. 3878
Mortal Messiah. 929, 1968
Mortality and immortality. 1418
Mortality of the soul. 1403, 1890
Mortals and gods. 3063
Mortgages on paradise. 3359, 3732
... The mortgaging of church property. 2620
... The Mosaic account of creation, the miracle of to-day. 206
Mosaic account of the creation affirmed, and silent monitors of the past described and illustrated, with object lessons of each day's part of the creation. 204
Mosaic authorship of the Pentateuch defended against the views and arguments of Voltaire, Paine, Colenso, Reuss, Graf, Kuenen, and Wellhausen. 563
Mosaic eschtological prophet. 2414
Mosaic history of the creation of the world. 1383
Mosaic law in modern life. 1316
Mosaic law in the light of modern science. 2074, 2107
Mosaic of adventure. 1308, 3387
Mosaic origin of the Pentateuchal codes. 564
Mosaic record and modern science. 205
Mosaic record of the creation explained. 1381
Mosaic tradition. 564
Mosaics of Bible history. 297
Mosaics of St. Mark's. Text. 3777
... The mosaics of St. Sophia at Istanbul. 1354
Moscovia of Antonio Possevino, S.J. 791, 3257
Moscow. 3256
Moscow and East Rome. 1149, 2750
Moscow over Methodism. 1320
Moscow, the third Rome. 2750, 3256
Moscow trial of Archbishop Cieplak. 1275
Moscow was my parish. 668, 774, 1300
Moses. 493, 495, 563, 634, 2621, 2622, 2624
Moses and Egypt. 1314
Moses and geology. 204, 2621
Moses and his neighbors. 484
Moses and monotheism. 2585, 2621
Moses and myth. 524
Moses and the liberation from Egypt. 631, 2624
Moses and the monuments. 565
Moses and the original Torah. 564
Moses and the prophets. 502, 927
Moses and the vocation of the Jewish people. 2622
Moses—born to be a slave, but God. 493, 2621
Moses Brock. 693

Moses, builder of altars. 2622
Moses Drury Hoge. 1822
Moses Drury Hoge; life and letters. 1822
Moses, faith in decision. 2622
Moses, from the story told in the Old Testament. 634, 2622
Moses, God's servant. 2622
Moses Haym Luzzatto's Lah-y' shaw-riem tehilaw "Praise for righteousness") 2621
Moses, his first and second coming. 2621
... Moses, his life and times. 2622
Moses Hull. 1853, 3505
Moses in red. 2622
Moses in the fourth Gospel. 423, 2621
Moses' last birthday, and other sermons. 3373
Moses: leader, prophet, man. 2622
Moses Maimonides. 2622
Moses Maimonides: rabbi, philosopher, and physician. 2623
Moses' mighty men. 493
Moses, Moses. 495, 2624
Moses' primer. 2622
Moses principle. 492, 981, 2621
Moses; the great lawgiver. 2621, 2624
Moses, the law-giver. 2622
Moses, the man and his vision. 2621
Moses, the servant of God. 631, 2621, 2624
Moses, the servant of Yahweh. 2621
Moses; where it all began. 2219, 2622
Moses, who first saw our pyramid of life. 2622
Mosheeach or Messiah. 1397
Mosheim's Church history. 1193
Moslem architecture, its origins and development. 79
Moslem doctrine of God. 1736
Moslem Egypt and Christian Abyssinia. 1501
Moslem faces the future. 2565
Moslem saint of the twentieth century. 21
Moslem schisms and sects. 1927
Moslem seeker after God. 21
Moslem women. 3841
Moslem world. 2566
Mosques and minarets. 1925
Most beautiful book ever wirtten. 429
Most beautiful woman in the world. 2358
Most beloved woman. 2354
Most comfortable sacrament. 2253
Most dangerous game. 2730
Most defiant priest. 781
Most dynamic thing in the world. 2876
Most holy principle. 2604
Most important tenets of the Roman Catholic chruch fairly explained. 784
Most important thing in the world. 2727
Most revealing book of the Bible: making sense out of Revelation. 453
... Most Reverend John Hughes. 1851
Most Reverend John Lancaster Spalding, first bishop of Peoria. 3469
Most unforgettable character I've ever met. 2933
Most unforgettable character you'll ever meet. 436, 929, 1974
Most useful knowledge for the Orthodox Russian-American young people. 3257
Most vital mission problem of the day. 850
Most wonderful King. 430, 1966, 1981
Most wonderful story in the world. 1968
Most worthy of all praise. 2581
Motetti missales of the late fifteenth century. 843
Mother. 2624
... Mother Adelaide of St. Theresa. 7
Mother Alfred and the Doctors Mayo. 25, 2375
Mother Alphonsa. 2198
Mother and Betty. 3148
Mother Barat's vineyard. 2311
Mother Butler of Marymount. 720, 2364
Mother Cabrini. 723, 1029
Mother Cabrini, missionary to the world. 723
Mother Caroline and the School sisters of Notre Dame in North America. 741, 3310
Mother church. 684, 2984
Mother Church extension. 684
Mother church of Christendom is the Holy Apostolic Orthodox Greek-Catholic Church. 2746
Mother/daughter mixing bowl. 980
Mother Dolores. 82, 3420
Mother Elisabeth. 663
Mother Emily of Sinsinawa. 2866, 3420
Mother Eva Mary, C.T. 1321, 1544
Mother Florence. 2718, 3790
Mother for a new world. 1776
Mother India's lighthouse: India's spiritual leaders. 1815
Mother Jones the miners' angel. 2130
Mother love. 2624, 2625

Mother Magdalen Daemen and her congregation. 1399, 3419
Mother Margaret Mary Healy-Murphy. 1793
Mother Maria, her life in letters. 1779, 2717
Mother Marianne of Molokai. 2183, 2568
Mother Mary Cleophas of the Society of the Holy Child Jesus. 2353
Mother Mary de Chantal. 2353
Mother Mary Ignatius of the Society of the Holy Child Jesus. 2353
Mother Mary of St. Bernard of the Society of the helpers of the holy souls. 2334, 3438
Mother Mary of the Passion. 1644, 2333
Mother Mary of the Seven Dolors and the early origins of the Marinites of Holy Cross (1818-1900) 2334, 2597
Mother Mary Teresa of St. Joseph (Anna Maria Tauscher van den Bosch) the servant of God, foundress of Carmel of the Divine Heart of Jesus. 740
Mother Mary Veronica, foundress of the sisterhood of the Divine compassion. 2353
"Mother Munroe." 2631
Mother of all. 2359
Mother of Carmel. 3603
Mother of churches. 3277
Mother of God. 2354, 2355, 2356, 2361, 2363
Mother of God's people. 414, 2358
Mother of Jesus. 2356
Mother of Jesus in Holy Scripture. 2356, 2363
Mother of Jesus in the New Testament. 2358
"The Mother of my Lord" 2360
Mother of that wisdom. 3457
Mother of the Redeemer. 2357
Mother of the Wesleys. 3806
Mother Patrick and her nursing sisters. 1474
Mother Philippine Duchesne. 1481
Mother Saint John Fontbonne. 1632, 3419
Mother Seton. 3317, 3378, 3417
Mother Seton and the Sisters of Charity. 3378, 3379, 3417
Mother Seton, foundress of the Sisters of charity. 3378
Mother Seton, mother of many daughters. 3379
Mother Seton's favorite devotions. 3378
Mother Seton's Sisters of charity. 3378, 3416
Mother Shipton investigated. 2952, 3404
Mother stories from the Book of Mormon. 2604
... the mother-teacher of religion. 3147
Mother Teresa. 2717, 3602
Mother Teresa, her people and her work. 2717, 3602
Motherhood, a partnership with God. 2611
Motherhood of God. 2425
Motherpeace. 3834
Mothers' correspondence club. 3317
Mother's gifts. 2625
Mothers' home school of Bible stories containing captivating narratives of the most striking scenes and events in the Old Testament. 623
Mother's hymn book. 1865
Mother's meditations. 2624
Mother's might and how to use it. 2624
Mother's morning prayers. 2625
Mothers of America. 2625
Mothers of the Bible. 616, 3838
Mother's song. 3403, 3604
Mother's spiritual diary. 875, 1322
Mother's story of the Bible told for young and old. 616
Motifs of Franciscan mission theory in sixteenth century New Spain Province of the Holy Gospel. 1648
Motion and motion's God. 2625
Motivating men for the Master. 1574
Motivational ideas for changing lives. 1171
Motives and methods in modern evangelism. 1577
Motse, the neglected rival of Confucius. 2560
Moulder of men. 2743
Mounds, monuments, and inscriptions. 207
Mount Athos. 102
Mount Everest. 3689
Mount Lebanon trembled. 2162
Mount Moriah A.M.E. Church. 2626
Mount Moriah view. 2141
Mount of Purification. 2641
Mount of vision. 1056
Mount Pleasant and the early Quakers of Ohio. 1686, 2626
... Mount Saint Peter. 2693

Mount Zion. 781
Mount Zion, 1856-1956. 3278
Mountain and wilderness. 3855
Mountain for St. Joseph. 40
Mountain of God. 189
Mountain of the condor. 726
Mountain peaks in the life of Our Lord. 381, 1966
Mountain peaks of prophecy and sacred history. 2626, 3339
Mountain peaks of the Bible. 2626
Mountain scenes from the Bible. 2626
Mountain to climb. 3355
Mountain tops with Jesus. 958
Mountain trailways for youth. 1437
Mountain wild flower. 664
Mountains and mountain men of the Bible. 2626
Mountains and valleys in the ministry of Jesus. 2474
Mountains of the Bible. 2626
Mountains redeemed. 2626
Mountains singing. 1749, 3237
Mountaintops and molehills. 991
Mourner. 1350
Mourner, come to my bosom. 1353
Mourner comforted. 1348, 1349
Mourner in Zion comforted. 1350
... The mourner's bench. 2686, 3229
Mourner's devotions. 2627
Mourner's gift. 1352
Mourning cry and woe oracle. 2157
Mourning song. 1414
Mousekin's fables. 1588
Mouse's tale. 907
Mouth of heaven. 2188
Move in our midst. 2236
Move over, Elijah. 1688, 3357
Move over, Mountain. 1359, 2228
Move over: students, politics, religion. 3536
Move that mountain. 131, 1576
Movement of destiny. 10
Le mouvement religieux a Paris pendant la Revolution (1789-1801) 1639
Movements and issues in American Judaism. 2155
... Movements and men of Christian history. 1184
... Movements of religious thought in Britain during the nineteenth century. 1759, 3212
Movers and shakers in Georgia. 1706
Moving frontiers. 2297
Moving heaven and earth. 2203
Moving pictures in the church. 2627
Moving right along in the spirit. 981
Moving story. 603
Movitiate. 2716
Moy Gwong of South China. 2400
Moyse Amyraut. 36
...The Mozarabic and Ambrosian rites. 847
Mozarabic architecture. 79
Mrs. Abigail Bayley. 179
Mrs. Brookfield and her circle. 693
Mrs. Eddy. 1494
Mrs. Eddy as I knew her. 1494, 1495
Mrs. Eddy, her life, her work and her place in history. 1495
Mrs. Eddy purloins from Hegel. 1494
Mrs. Knight's book of illustrations for children and young people. 1840
Mrs. Lee's stories about Jesus. 616
Mrs. Maynard's house. 2489
Mrs. Minister. 3241
Mrs. Piper & the Society for psychical research. 2849, 3241, 3513
Mrs. Seton. 3378
Mrs. Seton, foundress of the American Sisters of Charity. 3378
Mrs. Eddy as I knew her in 1870. 1493
Ms. means myself. 3832
Much-abused letter. 2562
Much and more, and other sermons. 162
Much more! 994
Much silence. 2400
Much to dare. 2482
Mud and mosaics. 2500
Muddy sneakers and other family hassles. 1605
Mudras. 704
Muffkins on parade. 617
Muffled drumbeats in the Congo. 2513
Muhammad. 2564, 2629
Muhammad 'Abduh [by] Osman Amin. 2628
... Muhammad and his power. 2629
Muhammad and the Islamic tradition. 1921, 2628
Muhammad at Mecca. 2629
Muhammad at Medina. 2629
Muhammad: prophet and statesman. 2629
Muhammad, prophet of Islam. 2629
Muhammad, seal of the prophets. 2629, 2635
Muhammadan festivals. 1614, 1615

Muhammad's children. 3026
Muhammedan law of marriage and divorce. 2345
Mulberry leaves. 2458
Multicultural Education Clinic papers. 2475
Multicultural nonsexist education. 2475
Multilinear translation of the New Testament. 479
Multimedia handbook for the church. 2369
Multi-media in the church. 1253
Multi-media worship; a model and nine viewpoints. 3854
Multiphase cross. 2212
Multiphase cross; a group of Lenten meditations. [1st ed.]. 2212
Multiple letter cipher with monitorial and floor work for symbolic lodges under the Grand Lodge Free and Accepted Masons of Wisconsin, adopted June 10, 1975. 1672
Multiple ministries. 1199
Multiple staff and the larger church. 658
Multiple staff in the local church. 1239
Multiple staff ministry. 1240
Multiplied by love. 984
Multipurpose tools for Bible study. 285
Mundahoi, Borneo witch doctor. 2546, 2630
Mundane perspectives in astrology. 1847
Mundurucu religion. 2631
Munera studiosa. 201
Munition Maker of Galilee. 2005
Murder for magic. 3825
Murder of an American prophet. 2615
Murder of Archbishop Thomas. 1763, 3692
Murder of Christ. 2050
Murdered millions. 2538
Murdock's translation of the Syriac New Testament from the Peschito version. 650
Murmur within me. 3182
Murrow masonic monitor and ceremonies. 1669
Musa, son of Egypt. 2549
Musar anthology. 2632
Musar movement. 2231, 2632
Muse at St. Matthew's. 2714
Muses' pageant. 2661
Mushroom and the bride. 25
Music. 1202
Music and hymnody of the Methodist hymnal. 1872
Music and religion. 1203
Music and the Reformation in England. 1207
Music and the Reformation in England, 1549-1660. 1207
Music and the Scriptures. 320
Music and worship. 1202, 1206
Music and worship in the church. 1209
Music at the parish church. 1204
Music education today. 1205
Music for church funerals and memorial services. 1691
Music for the church year. 1204
Music from the hunger pit. 2183
Music-hall sermons. 3355
Music in Catholic worship. 1205
Music in Christian education. 1209
Music in evangelism. 1207
Music in evangelism and stories of famous Christian songs. 1207
Music in evangelism, and stories of famous Christian songs, a handbook of information for evangelists, gospel singers, church musicians, choir members, song directors, and all others who are interested in Christian music. 4th ed. 1207
Music in evangelism, and stories of famous Christian songs. (Rev. ed.) 1207
Music in my Bible. 319
Music in Protestant worship. 1209
Music in the Bible. 1204
Music in the Christian community. 1209
...Music in the church. 1203, 1206, 2633
Music in the history of the western church. 1207
Music in the life of the church. 1203
Music in the Pentecostal church. 1209
Music in the religious growth of children. 3072
Music in the religious service. 1208
Music in the Young women's Christian association. 3878
Music in the Young women's Christian asssociation. 3878
Music in work and worship. 1203
Music in worship. 1202, 1203
Music in worship and The spirit of chivalry. 193, 1203
Music in your church. 2633
Music leadership in the church. 1208
Music levels in Christian education. 3072

Music locator. 1204, 1396
Music master. 111
Music of Holy Week. 2633
Music of life. 970
Music of the Bible. 319, 320, 2634
Music of the church. 1202
Music of the Church hymnary and the Psalter in metre. 1199
Music of the English church. 1206
Music of the English parish church. 1207
Music of the Ephrata Cloister. 1206, 1521
Music of the French Psalter of 1562. 2985
Music of the ghetto and the Bible. 2634
Music of the golden bells. 2933
Music of the gospel. 1872
Music of the spheres received by radio of the spheres. 3503
Music that is soundless. 1724
Musical aspects of the New Testament. 320
Musical foundation, enlarged. 3598
Musical instructer. 1202
Musical instruments in the Old Testament. 2634
Musical life in the Unitas Fratrum Mission at Springplace, Georgia, 1800-1836. 1208, 2594
Musical ministries in the church. 1203
Musician's guide to church music. 1208
"Musings" 3356
Musings at twilight. 2934
Musings for meditation. 2391
Musings in Isaiah. 545
Musings in the psalms. 578
Musings in the secret place. 2393, 2397
Musings of a Chinese mystic. 2641
Musings of a mother. 2625
Musings of a parson. 1466
Musings of the old professor. 511
Musings over the "Christian year" and "Lyra innocentium" 2166
Musique et liturgie. 843, 884
Muslim architecture of Egypt. 79
Muslim basic prayer book. 2885
Muslim brotherhoods in nineteenth century Africa. 3543
Muslim-Christian conflicts. 1926
Muslim creed. 1927, 2566
Muslim institutions. 2564
Muslim intellectual. 21
Muslim mind. 1922
Muslim puritans. 1925, 2629
Muslim saints and mystics. 3285
Muslim studies. 1922
Muslim theology. 1927
Muslims and chiefs in West Africa. 2635
Mussolini. 605
Must a man live? 3889
Must Christians fight. 2807
Must it be communism? 1136
"must" of love. 1741
Must of the second birth, and other sermons. 164
Must Protestantism adopt Christian science? 1033
Must the Bible go? 238
Must the church go? 1120
Must walls divide? 1097
Must we all become atheists? 100
Must we have religion? 3063
Must we have war? 2807
Must we part with God? 3608
Must we sin? 3412
Mustang mania. 3468
Mustard. 2882
Mustard seed. 431
Mustard seed conspiracy. 988
Mustard seed faith. 2635
Mustard seeds and wine skins. 2003
Mutations of Western Christianity. 1183
Mutiple ministries. 1199
Mutual criticism. 2737, 3436
Mutual influence. 3065
Mutual irradiation; a Quaker view of ecumenism. 1045
Mutual ministry. 2785
Mutual obligations of the ministry and the congregation. 3677
Mutual responsibility and interdependence in the body of Christ. 43
Mutual society. 3389
MV story. 3386
My 83 years. 3896
My adventure into spiritualism. 3505
My adventures with God. 1452
My answer. 3012
My answer to the Moscow atheists. 1073
My baptism. 135
My bark. 3222
My belief. 1335
My belief in immortality. 1888
My beloved. 2717
"My beloved brethren ..." 3569
My beloved, my friend. 2395
My beloved son. 1893, 1999
My Beloved to me. 892

My best friend: being six meditations for the quiethour. 2397
My best friend is God. 2391
My Bible. 640
My Bible ABC book. 901
My Bible and I. 201
My Bible book. 602
My Bible friends. 632
My Bible is Jesus. 987, 2042
My Bible story book. 620, 624
My bishop. 3018
My body broken. 2211
My body is a temple. 896, 1230
My body, my life. 674
My book about friends. 3549
My book about God. 1733
My book about God and me. 3549
My book about God's world. 1734
My book about growing up. 3549
My book about happy times. 3549
My book about Jesus. 1980, 1981
My book of acts. 3218
My book of Bible stories. 616
My book of personal devotions. 1446
My book of prayers. 901, 2891
My book of the Lord's prayer. 2249
My bookcase. 868
My brother. 3440
My brother and I. 694
My brother death. 1415
My brother Dennis. 1323
My brother is a stranger. 1140
My brother Paul. 2801
My brother, the Maryknoll missionary. 2310
My brother's keeper? 2384
My brothers, my country, my world. 937
My call to preach. 2427
My Calvary road. 1575, 1809
My candelabra. 286
My candle. 2856
My cares and prayers. 2871
My Catholic critics. 798
My Catholic devotions. 855
My Catholic faith. 748, 769
My Catholic neighbors. 1363
My changeless Friend. 1264, 2391
...My character book. 2590
My child lives. 1351
My children of the forest. 2513
My Christ. 1068, 1069
*My Christian heritage. 1070, 3182
My Christian responsibility. 1484
My Christmas ABC book. 1112, 2021
My church. 142, 1024, 1119, 1549
My church an adventure in Christian fellowship. Complete ed. Pastor's manual with student's text. 1339
My Church and my faith. 3722
My church book. 2295
My church helps me learn. 3184
My church was a mental hospital. 1258
My comforters. 3406
My communion. 2259
My communion book. 1317
My community, my church and me! 1278
My conception of the gospel ministry. 3674
My confession. 1327
My confession of faith. 3044
My confirmation. 1328, 1329
My convent life. 2576
My conversations with Teilhard de Chardin on the primacy of Christ. 375, 2049
My conversion and reasons that led to it. 1366
My creed. 3728
My cup runneth over. 1450
My dad, preacher pastor, person. 1462
My daily bread. 3489
My daily meditation for the circling year. 1439
My daily prayer. 2893
My daily Psalm book. 2985
My daily psalter. 576
My daily quiet time. 1432
My daily reading from the four Gospels and the New Testament. 725
My dear people; occasional sermons after old Capuchin fashion. 3355
My devotional diary. 1441
My door is always open. 2217
My dream of heaven. 2942
My duel with the Vatican. 2562
My Ebenezer, a personal testimony to the faithfulness of a prayer-hearing God. 2510
My education and religion. 3097
My experiences while out of my body and my return after many days. 3512
My faith. 762, 1003
My faith and people. 2142
My faith in immortality. 1886
My faith in Jesus Christ. 1952
My faith is enough. 3097
My family. 3174

My family and my friends. 3764
My family of souls. 2989
...My family Seder. 905
My father. 2587
My Father God. 1732, 2694
My father in China. 717
My father, personal & spiritual reminiscences. 3515, 3526
My Father worketh hitherto. 2526
My Father's business. 907, 2789, 3369
My Father's house. 2940
My Father's will. 1000
My Father's world. 163, 1446, 1726, 2674, 2675
My favorite Bible stories. 621
My favorite Bible text. 1451
My favorite Christmas story. 2023
My favorite illustration. 1840
My favorite prayer. 2892
My fifty favorite stories. 1291
My first book about God. 1734
My first book about Jesus. 1981
My first book of Christian symbols. 1054
My first book of prayers. 901, 905
My first communion. 1317, 1627
My first duty. 3158
My first duty; twelve short instructions on "my duty towards God," 1741
My first mission. 2601
My first sermons. 3340
My first Sunday school book, grade one. 3157
My first two thousand years. 3791
My flickering torch. 1351
My forgotten prayers & my forgotten saints. 855
My friend, the enemy. 1133
My friend Yeshea. 2019
My friends, the Chinese. 1284, 2485
My friends, the senses. 3333
...My geneagraphy. 1704
My gift from Jesus. 1698, 2054
My glimpse of eternity. 931, 2319
My God and I. 2385
My God and my all. 854, 858
My God is real. 67
My God is there, controlling, and other hymns and poems. 1861
My God, my God! 932, 3774
My God, my God, why ...? 2056
My God, why? 2215
My God will supply. 932, 3241
My Good Shepherd. 622, 1984
My group sessions. 3155, 3178
My guardian angel. 43
My Haggadah. 2239
My happiest day. 1318
My hay ain't in. 753
My healing gospel of eternal youth. 2695
My heart an altar. 3856
My heart and my husband. 3812
My heart is in his hands. 690
My heart kneels too. 2894
My heart leaps up, 1956. 2212
My hobby of the cross. 1698
My holiday storybook. 1614
My Holy Child book. 3184
My idea of God. 1725
My ideal, Jesus, son of Mary. 2361
My ideal, Jesus, son of Mary, according to the spirit of William Joseph Chaminade. 2361
My ideals of religion. 3097
My Imitation of Christ. 1330
My invisible friend explains the Bible. 560
My Irish journal, 1669-1670. 1686, 1919
My irrelevant defence. 3240
My island of Sumatra. 2552
My Jesus book. 3128
My Jewish roots. 2103
My job and my faith. 3785
My job-preaching. 3353
My journey beyond. 1698
My journeys and experiences in the spirit world. 3498
My King and my God. 3371
My Lady Miriam. 2358
My lamp and my light. 249
My land and my people. 3698
My Lenten missal. 2210
My life. 971, 1290, 3885
My life, a miracle. 3097
My life and lives. 2194, 3025
My life and my message. 2143
My life and the story of the gospel hymns and of sacred songs and solos. 1861, 1873, 3301
My life and times. 2489
My life and vision. 3097
My life and work. 1289
My life as a search for the meaning of mediumship. 1702, 3503
My life as an American Jew, an autobiography. 2105
My life for my friends. 1777, 2806
My life for my sheep. 3692
My life in a Mormon harem. 2607

My life in Christ. 3132
My life in Christ, meditations for the reverend priests. 2940
My life in the convent. 1357
My life is an open book. 3534
My life is love. 1033, 1850
My life of magic. 1345
My life story. 3124, 3126, 3130, 3135, 3136
My life today. 1443
My life with a Brahmin family. 1814
My life with Christ. 1985, 3132
My life with Edgar Cayce. 876
My life with Martin Luther King, Jr. 2172
My life with the old masters. 3509
My life with young men. 3871
My life's philosophy. 3126
My Little Church Around the Corner. 2962
My little golden book about God. 1734
My little library. 1113
"My little missionary!" 194
My little prayer book. 766
My little singing book. 3562
My living counselor. 1433
My Lord and I. 1442
My Lord and my God. 2691, 3664
My Lord and Savior Jesus Christ. 1956
My Lord speaks. 2056
My Lord's secrets revealed. 2385
My love, the Amazon. 2501, 3386
My love you my children. 3544
My lover, my friend. 2337
My marks and scars I carry. 2178

"My" mass. 2366, 2368
My mass book. 2368, 2369
My master. 3020
My materials. 1251, 3178
My message to Sunday school workers. 3555
My mind is an ocean. 905
My ministry. 1288
My money and God. 3529
My money helps. 952
My most unforgettable patients. 2510
My mother. 2246
My mother's life. 1803
My mystic beam discloses. 3520
My name is Legion. 1422, 1803
My name is Thomas. 3694
My nameday--come for dessert. 2794
My neighbor don't talk too good. 2393
My neighbor Jesus. 1967
My neighbour as myself. 1363
My Nestorian adventure in China. 2684
My note-book. 3623
My notes for addresses at funeral occasions. 1693
My occult diary. 2732
My Odyssey in China. 41
My own book of prayers for boys and girls. 901
My own life. 3132
"My own" work book on Christian symbolism. 1326
My pants when I die. 996
My passport says clairvoyant. 1283
My pastor. 1482
My Penitente land. 1806, 2693
My personal experiences with the poor souls. 3006, 3409
My personal Pentecost. 2816
My personal prayer diary. 1432
My personal recollections. 1289
My philosophy and my religion. 3136, 3774
My picture story Bible. 622
My pilgrim journey. 2630, 2855
My pillow book. 973
... My pilot. 1960
My place in God's world. 3171
My portion. 2183
My prayer book. 765, 900, 2297
My prayer-book, happiness in goodness, reflections, counsels, prayers, and devotions. 857
My prayer diary. 2872
My prayer for you. 988
My preparation. 1251, 3178
My progress. 1251
My progress in error. 3752
My Promised Land. 2765
My psychic adventures. 3495, 3496
My psychic quest. 3511
My pulpit. 3371
My pupils. 3155
My pursuit of peace. 2808
My reasons for leaving the Roman Catholic church. 777, 798
My recollections of African M. E. ministers. 1289
My redeemer lives. 551, 2301, 3357
My Redeemer liveth. 2297
My refuge and strength. 2391
My religion. 969, 2114, 3129, 3132, 3136, 3569, 3570

My religion, and The crucifixion viewed from a Jewish standpoint. 2034, 2142
My religion in everyday life. 976
My responsibilities. 3549
My retreat master. 2389
My revelations to the peoples of the earth. 3513
My road to certainty. 1364
My Sabbath school scrap book. 3560
... "My sacrifice and yours" 2367
My Saint Patrick. 2793
My Savior. 2029
My search for absolutes. 5
My search for an anchor. 3127
My search for the Messiah. 2155, 2478
My second estate; the life of a Mormon. 2609
My second Sunday school book. 3147
My second Sunday school book, grade two. 3185
My second valley. 3540
My sermon notes. 3375
My sermon notes for special days. 3346
My sermon notes on Biblical characters. 3375
My sermon notes on doctrinal themes. 75
My sermon notes on John's Gospel. 423
My sermon notes on Old Testament characters. 3375
My sermon notes on parables and metaphors. 2028, 3375
My sermon notes on the Lord's Prayer. 2250
My sermon notes on the Lord's supper. 1318
My sermon notes on the Ten commandments. 1316
My servant, Catherine. 749
My servant Job. 550
My servant Moses. 2621
My servants, the prophets. 2951, 2952
My sister's well-rounded life. 1781
My son. 3372
My son Dan. 1309, 1367
My soul and I. 3128
My soul doth magnify the Lord! 2361, 3474
My soul looks back. 669, 1326
My soul, thou hast much goods. 3126
My soul's experience in the unseen world. 3783
My spirit that lives after me. 3141
My spiritual aeroplane. 1036
My spiritual diary. 3134
My spiritual exercises. 3222
My spiritual guide. 856
My spiritual pilgrimage. 1364
My story. 1575, 3400
My story book about the Bible. 2490
My strength and my shield. 1308
My strength and my shield, daily meditations. 1308
My struggle for light. 1289
My study, and other essays. 3623
My Sunday kindergarten book. 3156
My Sunday missal. 846, 856
My Sunday reading. 366
My sweet Lord. 354
My teacher's New Year's present. 1712
My thing. 2893
My tomorrow's self. 3352
My travels in the far off beyond. 3509
My travels in the spirit world. 3130
My treasure chest. 3129
My twenty years of a miracle ministry. 1575, 3241
My unforgettable parents. 939, 3388
My universe and my faith. 3080
My utmost for His Highest. 1430
My very best friend. 2014
My vision, a meditation on the spirit eternal. 3783
My voyage on the blood line. 3764
My voyage to Europe and the Holy Land in 1913. 2848
My war with worry. 1524, 3697
... My way of faith. 1594
My way of life. 783
My way, the way of the white clouds. 1325
My way to God. 941
My weakness, His strength. 983, 1714
My window world. 2398
My witness, Bernadette. 2262, 3460
My word put God first. 2394
"My words" 2070
My words are spirit and life. 2389
My work. 1251, 1252
My world. 2227
My world is growing larger. 2394
My world was too small. 2394
*My worship life. 2240
My years with Corrie. 932, 3524
My years with Edgar Cayce. 3718
My yoke is easy and There is life everlasting. 1362

"My young friends ..." President McKay speaks to youth. 3887
My young man. 3869
My youthful days. 1290
Mycenaean origin of Greek mythology. 2661
Mycenaean tree and pillar cult and its Mediterranean relations. 2635
Myrtle Fillmore, mother of unity. 1625
Myself and others. 2473, 3830
Myself the challenger. 2639
Mystagogus poeticus. 2657
Les mysteres d'Eleusis. 1505
Mysteria magica. 2312
Mysteries and revelations of spiritism and mediumship and its kindred subjects. 3517
Mysteries and secrets of magic. 2313
Mysteries in your life. 3665
Mysteries of ancient Egypt: Hermes/Moses. 1502, 2622
Mysteries of ancient Greece: Orpheus/Plato. 2636, 2744
Mysteries of Britain. 1480
Mysteries of Chartres Cathedral. 889
Mysteries of Christianity. 782
Mysteries of destiny. 1615, 3602
Mysteries of Egypt. 2636
Mysteries of Genesis. 526
Mysteries of godliness. 3663
Mysteries of hypnosis. 2845
Mysteries of John. 416
Mysteries of life. 2057
Mysteries of life and death. 3204
Mysteries of life, death, and futurity. 1513
Mysteries of magic. 2312
Mysteries of Mithra. 2560
Mysteries of Osiris. 1501
Mysteries of prophecy unlocked. 45
Mysteries of providence and of grace as illustrated in the story of Lazarus. 2203, 2214
Mysteries of reincarnation. 3052
Mysteries of the border land. 3502
Mysteries of the Neapolitan convents. 1357
Mysteries of the rosary. 2048
Mysteries of the seance and tricks and traps of bogus mediums. 3508
Mysteries of the space age. 2726
Mysteries today, and other essays. 3683
Mysteries unveiled. 1443, 2728
Mysterion. 2641
Mysterious detectives. 2773
Mysterious forces of civilization. 125, 128
Mysterious madame Helena Petrouna Balavatsky. 671, 3682
Mysterious Marie Laveau, voodoo queen, and folk tales along the Mississippi. 2200, 3787
Mysterious marvelous snowflake and other object lessons for children. 908
Mysterious numbers of the Hebrew kings. 496, 555, 1115
Mysterious omissions. 1532, 1969
Mysterious parable. 2024
Mysterious presence. 1318
Mysterious presence, communion sermons. 1318
Mysterious psychic forces. 2988
Mysterious revelation. 435
Mysteriously meant. 1286
Mysterium amoris, and other eucharistic sketches. 2254
Mystery. 3610
Mystery and imagination. 68
Mystery and magic of the occult. 2726
Mystery and meaning. 3616
Mystery and mysticism. 2641
Mystery and philosophy. 2832
Mystery and romance of astrology. 97
Mystery and romance of Israel. 2116
Mystery doctrines of the New Testament. 350, 2636
Mystery hid from ages and generations. 3752
Mystery, magic & miracle. 3744
Mystery of baptism. 133
Mystery of Bethlehem. 2022
Mystery of breath. 3865
Mystery of Calvary. 2032
Mystery of character. 3132
Mystery of Christ. 1056, 2019, 2039
Mystery of Christ and the apostolate. 76
Mystery of Christ, our Head, Priest and King. 2039
Mystery of Christian hope. 1845
Mystery of Christian worship. 2642
Mystery of Christmas. 2021
Mystery of confirmation. 1328
Mystery of creation. 2066
Mystery of death. 1413
Mystery of dreams. 1479
Mystery of faith. 2254
Mystery of God. 1123, 1593, 1734, 3290
Mystery of God and man. 1591
Mystery of God is finished. 307

Mystery of godliness. 977, 1299, 2044
Mystery of godliness and the mystery of ungodliness. 1905
Mystery of God's grace. 1751
Mystery of God's love. 1735
Mystery of God's wrath. 464
Mystery of iniquity. 1136, 1427
Mystery of iniquity unveiled. 1285
Mystery of Israel. 470
Mystery of Jesus. 1960
Mystery of Konnersreuth. 2686
Mystery of life. 3076
Mystery of love. 2258
Mystery of love and marriage. 2336
Mystery of love for the single. 3415
Mystery of man. 2325, 3067
Mystery of Mary. 2362
Mystery of missions. 979
Mystery of Moral Re-armament. 699, 2593
Mystery of Naples. 1935
Mystery of pain. 2758, 3540
Mystery of painlessness. 3072
... The mystery of preaching. 2897
Mystery of purgatory. 3006
Mystery of religion. 2998
Mystery of religious life. 2571
Mystery of sacrifice. 2257
Mystery of salvation. 646
Mystery of sin and forgiveness. 3412
Mystery of suffering and death. 3541
Mystery of the apostles. 70
Mystery of the buried crosses. 2988
Mystery of the Christos. 2060
Mystery of the church. 1117, 1122, 2019
Mystery of the Cross. 105, 106, 107, 1998
Mystery of the Dead Sea scrolls revealed. 1409
Mystery of the faith. 2053
Mystery of the Gentiles. 1929
Mystery of the golden cloth. 454
Mystery of the Gospel. 234
Mystery of the Holy Trinity in oldest Judaism. 3714
Mystery of the human double. 94
Mystery of the incarnation. 1892
Mystery of the kingdom of God. 1972, 2175
Mystery of the Lord's Supper. 2259
Mystery of the Mayan hieroglyphs. 2375
Mystery of the ordinary. 3485
Mystery of the redemption. 3030
Mystery of the supernatural. 3567
Mystery of the temple. 1731
Mystery of the Temple Mount. 3599
Mystery of the Trinity. 3711
Mystery of the Wizard clip (Smithfield, W.Va.) 873
Mystery of the woman. 2363
Mystery of time. 3701
Mystery on the mountain. 2097
Mystery-religions. 2636
Mystery religions and Christianity. 2636
Mystery religions and the New Testament. 2636
Mystery religions in the ancient world. 2636
... the mystery-schools. 2636
Mystery solved. 463, 3497
Mystery solved; or, The key to the Bible: an exposition of creeds; a diagram showing why we have so many theories or denominations; and one of the factors of infidelity in this age. 3753
Mystery streams in Europe and the new mysteries. 2636
Mystery teachings and Christianity. 1088
Mystery teachings in world religions. 3121
Mystic Americanism. 3251
Mystic Christianity. 3863
Mystic dream book. 1479
Mystic dream book of Stephen Girard. 1479
Mystic experiences. 3864
Mystic healers. 1601
Mystic in love. 2263
Mystic in motley. 1629
... Mystic Italy. 2640
Mystic life. 2740
Mystic masonry. 1671
Mystic Masonry and the Bible. 1662
Mystic mind. 2644
Mystic of liberation. 665, 723
Mystic rebels. 57
Mystic rebels; Apollonius Tyaneus, Jan van Leyden, Sabbatai Zevi, Cagliostro. 57
Mystic self. 2640
Mystic soul of Spain. 2648
Mystic spiral. 3472
... Mystic spirit voice of the Hindoo "Senam," mysterious, facinating. 2645
Mystic symbol. 2251
Mystic symbolism in Bible numerals. 3576
Mystic test book of " The Hindu occult chambers" 2645
... The mystic treasures of the holy mass. 2365

Mystic trends in Judaism. 2646
Mystic vision in the Grail legend and in the Divine comedy. 1402, 1755, 3709
Mystic way. 1103, 2641
Mystic will. 674, 2637
Mystic world. 3505
Mystical and musical realism of Richard Crashaw. 1379
Mystical and political dimension of the Christian faith. 2222
Mystical Body. 2019
Mystical body and the American bishops. 2019
Mystical Body in action. 754
Mystical body of Christ. 763, 852, 1121, 1953, 2020
Mystical body of Christ as the basic principle of spiritual life. 2020
Mystical Christ. 756, 2019, 2638
Mystical consciousness. 2640
Mystical dimensions of Islam. 3543
Mystical doctrine of St. John of the Cross. 2642
Mystical element of religion as studied in Saint Catherine of Genoa and her friends. 749
Mystical element of religion as studied in Saint Catherine of Geona and her friends. 749
...Mystical elements in Mohammed. 2628, 2629, 2647
Mystical evolution in the development and vitality of the Church. 2642
Mystical experience. 2640
Mystical I. 2694
Mystical interpretation of Christmas. 1111
Mystical life. 2643, 2645, 2647
Mystical life of Jesus. 1968, 2054
Mystical love for Mary. 2361
Mystical passion. 3488
Mystical personality of the church. 2037, 3853
Mystical phenomena in the life of Theresa Neumann. 2686, 3532
Mystical philosophy of Mubyid Din-ibnul 'Arabi. 1880, 2838
Mystical presence. 2252
Mystical quadruple interrogatory. 3509
Mystical quadruple interrogatory. How? What?? Whence??? Whither???? 3509
Mystical reason. 3461
Mystical rose. 2356, 2359
Mystical theology and social dissent. 2137, 3016
Mystical theology of Saint Bernard. 193, 2647
Mystical theology of the Eastern Church. 2647
Mystical vine. 2031
Mystical vision and revelation. 2639
Mystical vocabulary of Venerable Mere Maria de l'Incarnation. 2334, 2648
Mystical writings. 2647
Mysticism. 2637, 2638, 2640, 2641, 2644, 3722
Mysticism: a study and an anthology. 2638
Mysticism: a study in the nature and development of man's spiritual consciousness. 2641
Mysticism an epistemological problem. 2638
Mysticism and Aldous Huxley. 1859, 2640
Mysticism and democracy in the English commonwealth. 1468
Mysticism and dissent. 1468, 3403
Mysticism and image in St. John of the Cross. 2136, 2645
Mysticism and magic in Turkey. 1425
Mysticism and magic of India. 2315
Mysticism and modern life. 2637
Mysticism and morality: oriental thought and moral philosophy. 1540
Mysticism and philosophical analysis. 2641
Mysticism and philosophy. 2640
Mysticism and religion. 2643
Mysticism and the Baha'i revelation. 126
Mysticism and the early South German-Austrian Anabaptist movement, 1525-1531. 37
Mysticism and the modern mind. 2640
Mysticism at the dawn of the modern age. 2645
Mysticism: Christian and Buddhist. 2640
Mysticism debate. 1356
Mysticism east and west. 2639, 2643
Mysticism for the millions. 2644
Mysticism, Freudianism and scientific psychology. 2638
Mysticism in religion. 2638, 2639
Mysticism in Robert Browning. 697, 2645
Mysticism in the world's religions. 2643
Mysticism in world religion. 2643, 2644
Mysticism: its meaning and message. 2638

Mysticism of obedience. 2719
Mysticism of Paul the apostle. 377, 2640, 2642, 2801
Mysticism of the Cloud of unknowing. 1304, 2647
Mysticism: old and new. 2638
Mysticism, sacred and profane. 2641
Mysticism, science, and revelation. 2642
Mysticism—the journey within. 2638
Mysticism unmasked. 1831
Mysticism, window on a world view. 2638
Mystics. 2645
Mystics and medics. 2646
Mystics and society. 2638
Mystics and society; a point of view. 2641
Mystics and Zen masters. 2639
Mystics, ascetics, and saints of India. 3272
Mystics at prayer. 2889
Mystics, ghosts, and demons in modern India. 1710
Mystics of Islam. 657, 2647, 3543
Mystics of our times. 2642
Mystics of prayer. 2889
Mystics of the church. 2641, 2645
Mystics of the renaissance and their relation to modern thought. 2640
Mystics, philosophers, and politicians. 1809, 2842
Myth. 2649, 2654
Myth: a symposium. 2654
Myth, allegory, and gospel. 65, 892
Myth and Christian belief. 2648
Myth and Christianity. 1424
Myth and cosmos. 2654
Myth and cult among primitive peoples. 3109
Myth and fact in the separation of church and state in America. 1130
Myth and history in the Book of Revelation. 458
Myth and language. 2219, 2648
Myth and law among the Indo-Europeans. 2654
Myth and legend of ancient Israel. 2207
Myth and legend of Greece. 2661
Myth and legends of the Greeks. 2663
Myth and literature. 2649
Myth and metaphysics. 3102
Myth and miracle. 2652
Myth and modern man. 2649
Myth and mystery. 1720
Myth and mythmaking. 2654
Myth and philosophy. 2649
Myth and reality. 2648
Myth and reality in the Old Testament. 1424
Myth & religion in European painting, 1270-1700. 2760
Myth and religion of the North. 2666, 3306
Myth and ritual. 1395
Myth and ritual in Christianity. 1053, 2654
Myth and ritual in the ancient Near East. 3117, 3119
Myth and science. 2649, 2654
Myth and symbol in ancient Egypt. 2659
Myth and the crisis of historical consciousness. 2649
Myth and truth. 2648
Myth behind the sex of God. 3389
Myth, faith, and hermeneutics. 2649
Myth, history, and faith. 2648
Myth in Indo-European antiquity. 1482, 2654
Myth in Old Testament interpretation. 2649
Myth in primitive psychology. 2649, 2652
Myth in the New Testament. 476
Myth, legend, and custom in the Old Testament. 499, 1631, 1652
Myth makers. 2608, 3429
Myth of Adam and Eve. 525
Myth of Christian beginnings. 1180
Myth of freedom and the way of meditation. 2382
Myth of God incarnate. 1894
Myth of Hercules at Rome. 1804, 2667
Myth of Manasa. 2327
Myth of the Bagre. 2658
Myth of the birth of the hero. 2653
Myth of the birth of the hero, and other writings. 2653
Myth of the eternal return. 1371
Myth of the great secret. 3487
Myth of the Judeo-Christian tradition. 2152
Myth of the magus. 2314
Myth of William Morgan. 2598
Myth, religion, and mother right. 3108
Myth, religion, and society. 2662
Myth, ritual, and kingship. 2177
Myth, ritual, and religion. 2652
Myth, sacred history, and philosophy. 3212
Myth, symbol, and reality. 2649

... The mythical interpretation of the Gospels. 393, 1979
Mythmakers. 2648
Mythologiae. 2655
Mythologic Christ. 1092
Mythological aids for cross-word puzzle solvers. 3010
Mythological astronomy of the ancients demonstrated by restoring to their fables & symbols their original meanings. 2665
Mythological creatures. 47
Mythological papyri. 2659
Mythological tales and the Allegany Seneca. 3332
Mythologies. 2654
Mythologies of the ancient world. 2652
Mythologies of the world. 2658
Mythology. 2650, 2652, 2653, 2654, 2661, 2666
Mythology among the Hebrews and its historical development. 2664
Mythology and fables of the ancients explain'd from history. 2649
Mythology and folktales. 2652
Mythology and the tolerance of the Javanese. 2664
Mythology and values. 2677
Mythology and you. 2661
Mythology for moderns. 2653
Mythology for young people. 2659
Mythology. Illustrated by Steele Savage. 2652
... Mythology in marble. 2649
Mythology of all races. 2651, 2653
Mythology of ancient Britain and Ireland. 2655
Mythology of ancient Greece and Italy. 2658
... The mythology of Greece and Rome. 2656, 2657
Mythology of science. 3083
Mythology of the Aryan nations. 2654
Mythology of the Bella Coola Indian. 186
Mythology of the Blackfoot Indians. 3408
Mythology of the Ifugaos. 1882
Mythology of the soul. 3308
Mythology of the Thompson Indians. 2716
Mythology: or, A history of the fabulous deities of the ancients. 2657
Mythology pocket crammer. 2658
Mythology pocket grammer. 2658
Mythology; selected readings. 2658
Mythology: the age of fable. 2650
Mythology: The age of fable, The age of chivalry, Legends of Charlemagne. 888, 2650
Mythology, the voyage of the hero. 2658
Mythopoesis. 2664
... Myths. 2652, 2654
Myths about Malcolm X: two views. 2233
Myths and Bible. 2666
Myths and dreams. 2651
Myths and enchantment tales, adapted from the original text. 2661
Myths and fables of today. 2651
Myths and folk-tales of the Russians, western Slavs, and Magyars. 1632
... Myths and legends. 2653
Myths and legends of all nations. 2653
Myths & legends of ancient Egypt. 1502, 2659
Myths and legends of ancient Greece. 2661
Myths and legends of ancient Greece and Rome. 2655
Myths & legends of Babylonia & Assyria. 94
Myths & legends of China. 2655
Myths and legends of Greece and Rome. 2656, 2662
Myths and legends of many lands. 2664
Myths and legends of Samoa. 2656
Myths and legends of the ancient Near East. 2649
Myths and legends of the Greeks. 2663
Myths & legends of the Middle Ages. 2206
Myths & legends of the Polynesians. 2666
Myths and myth makers. 2651
Myths and realities. 652
Myths and songs from the South Pacific. 2666
Myths and symbols. 1904, 2653
Myths and symbols in Indian art and civilization. 2664
Myths and tales of the southeastern Indians. 1903
Myths and their meaning. 2652
Myths are somebody's religion. 2652
Myths, dreams, and mysteries. 2651
Myths, dreams, and religion. 2649
Myths, models, and paradigms. 3081
Myths of ancient Greece and Rome. 2656
Myths of China and Japan. 2655
Myths of creation. 1384

Myths of Crete & pre-Hellenic Europe. 2658
Myths of Greece and Rome. 2651, 2655, 2656
Myths of Israel. 526
Myths of life & death. 2650
Myths of Mexico & Peru. 1898
Myths of middle India. 2663
Myths of northern lands. 2665
Myths of Plato. 2661
Myths of pre-Columbian America. 1904
Myths of the Greeks and Romans. 2656
Myths of the hero. 1807
Myths of the Hindus & Buddhists. 2663
Myths of the New world. 1902, 1904
Myths of the Norsemen. 2665
Myths of the sun. 3546
Myths of the sun (Sun lore of all ages) 3546
Myths of the Toba and Pilaga Indians of the Gran Chaco. 3703
Myths of the world. 2651
Myths, rites, symbols. 2648
Myths that mire the ministry. 1295
Myths to live by. 2654

N

N. F. S. Grundtvig. 1776
...N.Y. Catholic protectory. 2697
Naamah and Nimrod. 2649
Nabataeans in historical perspective. 2667
Nabozenstwo na czas adoracji Najsw. Sakramentu. 859
Nachum Sokolow. 3455
Nachum Sokolow, servant of his people. 3455
Nag Hammadi codices III, 2 and IV, 2. 1717
Nag Hammadi Gnostic texts and the Bible. 1718
Nagarjuna's letter. 3196
Nagarjuna's philosophy as presented in the Mahaprajnaparamita-sastra. 2867
Nahida Remy's The Jewish woman. 3842
Nahum, Zephaniah, Habakkuk. 560
Nailer Tom's diary. 3128
Nails of protest. 793
Nails to drive. 157
Nairobi—a joke, a junket, or a journey? 3850
Nairobi narrative. 3850
Nairobi to Berkeley. 2496
Naked Church. 235
Naked shepherd. 2786
Naked they pray. 3864
Naked to mine enemies. 1764, 3831
Naked truth of Jesusism from Oriental manuscripts. 1951
Name above every name. 2020
Name above every name, and other evangelical addresses. 1558
Name counted. 2019, 3576
Name index to the Library of Congress collection of Mormon diaries. 2609
Name is living. 2639
Name--Jesus. 1950
Name of Jesus. 2020, 2873
Name of the beast "666" 1655
Nameless immortals. 1959
Nameless longing. 3366
Nameless women of the Bible. 1959
Names and titles of Christ. 2020
Names and titles of Jesus. 2020
Names and titles of the Lord Jesus Christ. 2020
Names of God. 1736
Names of God and Meditative summaries of the divine perfections. 1736
Names of God in Holy Scripture. 1736
Names of God in the Old Testament. 599, 1736
Names of Jesus. 2020
Naming the whirlwind. 3070
Napaleon III. 465
Napoleon's Oraculum and dream book. 1479
Nara Buddhist art, Todai-ji. 3316, 3703
Narada's Way of divine love. 197
... Narcissus. 1197
Narrangansett Friends' meeting in the XVIII century, with a chapter on Quaker beginnings in Rhode Island. 1685
Narration of religious experience. 3191
Narrative and exposition of the late proceedings of New England Yearly meeting, with some of its subordinate meetings & their committees. 1687
Narrative Bible. 292, 621
... Narrative episodes from the Old Testament. 591
Narrative of a mission to Bokhara, in the years 1843-1845, to ascertain the fate of Colonel Stoddart and Captain Conolly. 675, 3532

NARRATIVE OF A

RELIGIOUS BOOKS 1876 - 1982

Narrative of a mission to Nova Scotia, New Brunswick, and the Somers islands, with a tour to lake Ontario. 3806
Narrative of a most extraordinary work of religion in North Carolina. 3231
Narrative of Eleazer Sherman, giving an account of his life, experience, call to the ministry of the gospel, and travels as such to the present time. 3135
Narrative of events connected with the acceptance. 685
Narrative of Messrs. Moody and Sankey's labors in Great Britain and Ireland, with eleven addresses and lectures in full. 2588
Narrative of Messrs. Moody and Sankey's labors in Scotland and Ireland. 2588
Narrative of missionary enterprises in the South sea islands. 2545
Narrative of the days of the reformation. 3039
Narrative of the deluge. 1421
Narrative of the early life, remarkable conversion and spiritual labours of James P Horton. 3128
Narrative of the early life, travels, and gospel labors of Jesse Kersey. 3129
Narrative of the facts and circumstances relating to the kidnaping [!] and murder of William Morgan. 52, 2597
'narrative of the facts and circumstances relating to the kidnapping and presumed murder of William Morgan. 52, 53, 2597
Narrative of the life and sufferings of William B. Lighton. (minister of the gospel.) 3130
Narrative of the life and travels, preaching & suffering. 3133
Narrative of the life of James Downing. 3126
Narrative of the life of Miss Lucy Cole, of Sedgwick, Maine. 926, 1306
Narrative of the life of Rev. Noah Davis, a colored man. 1407, 3425
Narrative of the most remarkable particulars in the life of James Albert. Akawsaw, Granwasa. 3127
Narrative of the proceedings of the religous society of the people called Quakers, in Philadelphia, against John Evans. 1687
Narrative of the religious controversy in Fitchburg. 1628
Narrative of the revival of religion in the county of Oneida. 3229, 3232
Narrative of the suppression by Col. Burr. 3846
Narrative of the travels of John Vandeleur, on the Western continent. 3132
Narrative of the United States' expedition to the river Jordan and the Dead sea. 2762
Narrative papers of George Fox, unpublished or uncollected. 1679
Narrative structures in the book of Judith. 490
Narratives from the Old Testament. 482
Narratives of pious children. 897
Narratives of remarkable conversions and revival incidents. 1358
Narratives of sorcery and magic. 2313
... Narratives of the beginnings of Hebrew history. 532
Narratives of the lives of pious Indian children. 1899
Narratives of the lives of pious Indian women. 1899
Narratives of the spirits of Sir Henry Morgan. 3498
Narrow and the broad way. 2932
Narrow is the way. 3758
Narrow way. 975, 3478
Nascent Marxist Christian dialogue: 1961-1967. 1074
Nashville. 2459
Nashville, Christian Family Books. 1066
Naskapi. 2669
Nathan Sites. 2511, 3421
Nathaniel. 3513
Nathaniel William Taylor, 1786-1858. 3591
Nation and the kingdom. 2492
Nation bringing forth the fruits. 234
Nation in the making. 566
Nation making. 530
Nation of behavers. 3747
Nation under God? 3748
Nation with the soul of a church. 3748
National perils and opportunities. 1040
National awakening. 2973
National Baptist hymnal. 152
National bibliography of theological titles in Catholic libraries. 3627
National Campus Ministry convocation. 885
National Catholic almanac (The) 27
National Catholic Welfare Conference: 827
National Catholic women's union. 2670
National church and shrine of the United States of America. 1269
National church of Sweden. 3569
National Council. Dept. of Christian Education. ... In God we trust. 2958
National council digest. 2670
National council of Congregational churches. 2670
National council of the Young men's Christian associations of the United States of America. 3875
... The national debt that American Protestants owe to their brethren of the Roman Catholic church. 2979
... National eucharistic congress ...-1st-1895. 1541
National faith of Japan. 1935, 3404
National hymns, original and selected. 1866
National ideals in the Old Testament. 2095
National life in the spirit world. 3087
National liturgical week ... [1st]- 1940. 2234
National needs and remedies; the discussions of the General Christian Conference held in Boston, Mass., December 4th, 5th, and 6th, 1889. 1040
National number and heraldry of the United States of America. 1928
National park seminary. 1633
National Pastoral Council, pro and con. 833
National pastorals of the American hierarchy (1792-1919) 851
National pastorals of the American hierarchy, 1792-1919. 852
National pastorals of the American hierarchy (1792-1919) 814
... National patriotism in papal teaching. 1143
National perils and opportunities. 1040, 1550
National Presbyterian Church & Center. 3797
National rebirth of Judah. 2118
National religions. 3117
National religions and universal religions. 3117
National socialism and the Roman Catholic church. 818, 1145
National teacher-training institute text-books. 30
National word-book for Bible users. 227
National YMCA camping standards for day, family, resident, and travel camps. 1164
Nationalism and American catholicism. 826
Nationalism and Americn catholicism. 826
Nationalism and Christianity in the Philippines. 2671
Nationalism and history. 2082
Nationalism and religion in America. 2671, 3738
Nationalism and religion in America, 1774-1789. 3738
Nationalism and the class struggle. 2077
Nationalism and the class struggle, a Marzian approach to the Jewish problem. 2077
Nationalism in Hindu culture. 2671
Nationhood and the kingdom. 1151
Nation's book in the nation's schools. 300
Nations in prophecy. 609
"The nations shall know that I am Jehovah"—how? 1941
Native American Christian community. 1901
Native American religions. 1902
Native churches in foreign fields. 2521
Native Mesoamerican spirituality. 1898
Native Methodist preachers of Norfolk and Princess Anne Counties, Virginia. 2431, 2713
Native ministry of New Hampshire. 2688
Native North American spirituality of the eastern woodlands. 3846
Native theatre in middle America. 3145
Natives of eternity. 1115, 3509, 3686
Natives of Petersburg, Virginia, and vicinity in the Methodist ministry. 2427, 2826
Natives of the Northern Neck of Virginia in the Methodist ministry. 2427, 3781
Nativism and Syncretism. 1898
Nativitas Christi. 2023
Nativity. 664, 1387, 1849, 2021, 2633
Nativity. [Exhibition] December 2, 1963-January 5, 1964. 1994
Nativity of the Holy Spirit. 1831
Natty, a spirit. 3511
Natural and revealed theology. 3641
Natural & the supernatural. 3062
Natural and the supernatural Jew. 2080, 2149
Natural bridge to cross. 3497
Natural Christianity. 2672
Natural environment and early cultures. 29
Natural genesis. 2653
Natural government of mankind. 2064
Natural history of a social institution--the Young women's Christian association. 3878
Natural history of enthusiasm. 1520
Natural history of religion. 3101
Natural history of religious feeling. 1358
Natural history of the Bible. 480
Natural history of the Christian religion. 1051
Natural law and the ethics of love. 945
Natural law in the spiritual world. 2672, 3075, 3076
Natural laws and gospel teachings. 205
Natural magic. 2312, 2313
Natural meditation. 2379
Natural motivation in the Pauline Epistles. 375, 2625
Natural order of spirit. 3503
Natural principles of rectitude for the conduct of man. 1324
Natural religion. 2673, 2674
Natural religion and Christian theology. 1105, 3084
Natural right and history. 2672
Natural science and religion. 3075
Natural sciences and the Christian message. 3074, 3083
Natural selection and spiritual freedom. 2673
Natural symbols. 674, 3058
Natural symbols; explorations in cosmology. 3058
Natural theology. 175, 2672, 2673, 2674
Natural theology and Genesis. 2673
Natural theology and tracts. 2673
Natural theology for our time. 2673
Natural theology: Metaphysics II. 1740
Natural theology, or The existence, attributes, and government of God. 2673
Natural way to live out our days. 1859
Naturalisation of the supernatural. 2990
Naturalism. 2675
Naturalism and agnosticism. 3076
Naturalism and religion. 2675, 3079
... Naturalism and the human spirit. 2675
Naturalistic tradition in Indian thought. 2675
Naturalness. 706
Naturalness of Christian life. 965
Nature and aim of theosophy. 3684
Nature and art of the Bible. 235
Nature and authority of the Bible. 229
Nature and character of the true church of Christ proved by plain evidences. 3395
Nature and Christ. 2059
Nature and cognition of space and time. 3469
Nature and conduct. 2321
Nature, and danger, of infidel philosophy. 122
Nature and deity. 2836
Nature and design of the Lord's supper. 2250
Nature and destiny of man. 2324, 3463
Nature and dignity of love. 1735
Nature and extent of Christ's redemption. 1222
Nature and function of priesthood. 2939
Nature and functions of a church. 150
Nature and functions of the sacraments. 3263
Nature and God. 3073, 3081
Nature and grace. 761, 783, 1752
Nature and grace, and other essays. 791
Nature and grace in art. 84
Nature and history of Jewish law. 2074
Nature and history of the Bible. 289
Nature and importance of rightly dividing the truth. 2743
Nature and meaning of Christian faith. 1596
Nature and method of revelation. 3224
Nature & methods of mental prayer. 2379
Nature and mission of the church. 1121
Nature and necessity. 2738
Nature and origin of the New Testament. 411
Nature and purpose of a Christian society. 1058
Nature and purpose of the Gospels. 393
Nature and religion. 3073
Nature and religious imagination. 2676
Nature and the Bible. 204
Nature and the function of the church. 1116
Nature and the supernatural. 59, 2476
Nature and the supernatural, as together constituting the one system of God. 59
Nature and truth of the great religions. 3104
...The nature and unity of metaphysics. 2417
Nature, and Utility of religion. 2675
Nature and values. 2420, 2822
Nature appreciation. 2675
Nature, capital, and trade. 2675
Nature: cosmic, human and divine. 2675
Nature—garden or desert? 2676
Nature, grace, and religious development. 2998
Nature-imagery in the works of St. Augustine. 114
Nature in Scripture. 3224
Nature in the witness-box. 3080
Nature in the works of Fray Juis [i.e. Luis] de Granada. 2271, 2675
Nature in the works of Fray Luis De Granda. 2271, 2675
Nature,knowledge and God. 3693
Nature, man and God. 2674, 2767
Nature, man, and society in the twelfth century. 3659
Nature, man, and woman. 3106
Nature meditations. 3544
Nature, miracle and sin. 2675
Nature myths of many lands. 2651
Nature of anthroposophy. 51
Nature of belief. 185, 1594, 2702, 2705
Nature of Christian worship. 3853
Nature of conversion. 1361
Nature of dreams. 1479
Nature of evil considered in a letter to the Rev. Edward Beecher. 1745
Nature of existence. 2738
Nature of faith. 1590
Nature of God. 1729, 3342
Nature of God and His purpose for the world. 1720
Nature of Greek myths. 2661
Nature of guruship. 1778
Nature of healing. 2409
Nature of heresy in our time. 2791
Nature of Hinduism. 1814
Nature of Judaism. 2143
Nature of love. 2263
Nature of love; Plato to Luther. 2263
Nature of man. 3079
Nature of man and the meaning of existence. 2319
Nature of man, his world, his spiritual resources, his destiny. 2320
Nature of man in theological and psychological perspective. 2326
Nature of martyrdom. 2351, 3694
Nature of metaphysical thinking. 2417
Nature of metaphysics. 2420
Nature of mysticism. 2642
Nature of New Testament theology. 476
Nature of personal reality. 3474
Nature of Protestantism. 2976
Nature of religion. 3056, 3103, 3106, 3308
Nature of religious experience. 2181, 2308
Nature of revelation. 3226
Nature of sacramental grace. 3265
Nature of spirit, and of man as a spiritual being. 2690
Nature of spiritual existence, and spiritual gifts, given through the mediumship of Mrs. Cora L. V. Richmond. 3512
Nature of the atonement and its relation to remission of sins and eternal life. 104
Nature of the church. 1118, 1125
Nature of the early church. 1123
Nature of the gods. 1742
Nature of the ministry we seek. 1296
Nature of the mystical body. 2020
Nature of the resurrection body. 3221
Nature of the unity we seek. 1044
Nature of the world. 2419
Nature of theological argument. 3700
Nature of true prayer. 2879
Nature of true virtue. 3782
Nature, pleasure and advantages of church-musick. 2633
Nature, progress, ideas. 2675
Nature sermons. 169, 3341
Nature, structure, and function of the Church in William of Ockham. 1188, 2734
Nature, the mirror of grace. 2026
Nature-worship and taboo. 133
Nature's invisible forces. 1371
Nature's laws in human life. 3504
Nature's magic. 3688
Nature's revelation of God and the Bible supplement. 2042, 2673
Nature's testimony to nature's God. 3076
Nature's way. 2675
Naude, prophet to South Africa. 1300, 2676
Nauvoo. 2617, 2676
Nauvoo Temple. 2676
Navahe and Ute peyotism. 2827
Navaho and Ute peyotism. 2827

Navaho-English catechism of Christian doctrine for the use of Navaho children. 2677
Navaho figurines called dolls. 2677
Navaho religion. 2677
Navaho religion, a study of symbolism. 2677
Navajo bringing-home ceremony. 20, 2677
Navajo creation myth. 2677
Navajo medicine man. 2463, 3300
Navajo Mountain and Rainbow Bridge religion. 2677
... Navajo religion series, v. 1. 2677
Navajo sandpaintings. 3300
Navajos are coming to Jesus. 2677
Nave's Study Bible. 267
Nave's topical Bible. 225, 303
Navy Supervisory Chaplains Conference. 2787
Nazarene. 1016
Nazarene Gospel restored. 389, 1102
Nazareth against Nice. 3322
"Nazareth" spirituality. 3420
Nazi Christ. 1708
Nazi Germany's war against the Jews. 2099
Nazi persecution of the churches, 1933-45. 1145
Nazi war against the Catholic church. 818
Nazism and the pastors. 1145, 1426
NCEA papers no. 1. 833
Ne. 1961
Neal-Wallace discussion on the thousand years reign of Christ. 2464, 2465
Near Eastern culture and society. 1282
Near Eastern religious texts relating to the Old Testament. 537, 2679
Near Eastern studies in honor of William Foxwell Albright. 484
Near the edge of battle. 894
Near the sun. 1433
Near to God. 2391
Near to the heart of God. 1070
Nearby. 2390
Nearer and farther East. 2502
Nearer the cross. 2213
Nearing the end. 2465
Nearness of God. 2434
'Neath the waters. 3127
Nebraska conference of the Augustana synod. 2291
Nebraska Methodist story; authorized centennial history of Nebraska Methodism, 1854-1954. 2431
Necessary illusion. 942
Necessary truth. 3717
Necessity for the church. 1122
Necessity of atheism. 100
Necessity of atonement, and the consistency between that and free grace, in forgiveness. 104
Necessity of Christ. 1953
Necessity of ethical absolutes. 1534
Necessity of faith. 3622
Necessity of prayer. 2868
Necessity of redemption. 105
Necessity of the atonement. 108
Necrological reports and annual proceedings of the Alumni association of Princeton theological seminary. 2941
Necrologium. 1293
Necrology. 40
Necrology of rabbis. 3016
Necrology of the Archdiocese of Saint Louis, 1705-1963. 1300
Necrology of the Archdiocese of Saint Louis, 1705-1967. 1300
Necromancers; the best of black magic and witchcraft. 3825
Necromancy. 3498
Necromantic grimoire of Augustus Rupp. 2313
Nectar of chanting. 2329
Nectar of devotion. 197
Nectar of instruction ; an authorized English presentation of Srila Rupa Gosvami's Sri Upadesamrta. 3491
Need a miracle? 2477
Need for the magisterium of the church. 866
Need is our neighbor. 1139
Need of a new Bible and a creedless church. 2836
Need of a restatement of theology. 3615
Need to believe. 64, 2999
Needed: a righteous generation. 3060
Needlepoint cushions. 1488
Needlepoint for churches. 737
Needlework book of Bible stories. 622
Needlework in religion. 2679
Needs of the church to-day. 1247
Needs of the church to-day (The) 1247
Neely's history of the parliament of religions and religious congresses at the World's Columbian exposition. 3138

Negative capability; studies in the new literature and the religious situation. 2232
Negative earthlings exposed. 1323
Negestanti sviesa; marijonu veikla Amerikoje. 2334
Neglected book. 235
Neglected educational heritage of Southern Presbyterians. 2923
Neglected era. 2091
Neglected factor. 179
Neglected predicate in New Testament criticism. 339
Neglected service. 2018, 2886
Negro American. 2541
Negro Baptist chief executives in national places. 157
... Negro Baptist history, U. S. A., 1750, 1930. 157
Negro Baptist ministry. 3613
Negro Baptist pulpit. 160
Negro Baptists and foreign missions. 157
Negro Baptists of Maryland. 157
Negro church in America. 2679, 2682
Negro community within American Protestantism, 1619-1844. 2682
Negro in the history of Methodism. 2460
Negro masonry. 1667
Negro Masonry in the United States. 1667
"Negro pew" 2682
Negro sings a new heaven. 2680
Negro spiritual speaks of life and death. 2680
Negro spirituals. 3522
Negro youth in city YMCAs. 3873
Negro's church. 2679, 2682
Negro's God as reflected in his literature. 1724, 2680
Negro's view of organic union. 2682
Nehemiah. 560, 2683
Nehemiah and the dynamics of effective leadership. 560, 2204, 2683
Nehemiah speaks again. 560
Neighbor voices of representative Baptists. 143
Neighbors. 3740
Neighbors at peace. 3765
Neighbors south. 690
Neighbors we'd like to know. 2549
Neighbors yet strangers. 2556
Neighbours. 1765
Neill & Summerhill: a man and his work. 3546
Neither Black nor white. 1131
Neither dead nor sleeping. 3514
Neither down nor out. 1783
Neither male nor female. 3838
Nelson children's Bible. 617
Nelson's Bible commentary. 222
Nelson's Bible encyclopedia for the family. 245, 1280
Nelson's biographical dictionary. 662
Nelson's complete concordance of the New American Bible. 228
Nelson's complete concordance of the Revised Standard Version Bible. 227
Nelson's complete concordance of the Revised standard version of the Bible. 227
Nelson's explanatory Testament. 353
Nelson's expository dictionary of the Old Testament. 511, 1517
Nelson's Picture bible. 601
Nemesis of faith. 1654
Neo-Christian. 1051
Neo-evangelicalism. 3617
Neo-evangelism. 3617
Neo-liberalism. 2221
Neo-Masonry. 1672
Neo-orthodoxy. 2683
Neo-orthodoxy: what it is and what it does. 2683
Neo-Platonists. 2684, 2944
Neo-tantra. 3585
Neoevangelicalism today. 1551
... Neoplatonism. 2683
Neoplatonism and early Christian thought. 83, 2684
Neoplatonism in relation to Christianity. 2684
Nepal. 87
Nephaleia. 3597
Nephites in story. 679
Neptunian, or water theory of creation. 206
Nervous disorders and character. 2995
Nervous disorders and religion. 2785, 2995
Nervous system of Jesus. 2019
Nestorian churches. 2684
Nestorian collection of christological texts, Cambridge University Library ms. Oriental 1319. 2047
Nestorian missionary enterprises. 2684
Nestorian monument of Hsi-an Fu in Shen-hsi,China. 2684

Nestorian monument of Hsi-an Fu in Shen-hsi, China, relating to the diffusion of Christianity in China in the seventh and eighth centuries. 2684
Nestorians. 1929
Nestorians and their Muslim neighbors. 2684
Nestorius and his place in the history of Christian doctrine. 2684
Nestorius and his teaching. 2684
Nests above the abyss. 2559
Netherlands Indies. 2516
Das Neue Testament Unsers Herrn and Heilanders Jesu Christi. 320
Neue-Welt-Übersetzung der Christlichen Griechischen Schriften. 3798
Neuplatonische und gnostische Weltablehnung in der Schule Plotins. 1717, 2854
Neuroses and sacraments. 3265
Neurotics in the church. 2784
Neutrality and commitment. 2838
Never a dull moment. 2977, 3012
Never again war! 2806, 2807
Never alone. 579, 1830, 2244
Never be lonely. 2244
Never failing light. 2519
Never-failing Scriptures. 279
Never far from home. 2182
Never forget to live. 1432
Never look back. 717
Never lose heart. 1011
"Never man so spake" 2063
Never on a broomstick. 3826
"Never on Sunday? 3548
Never on your own. 1801
Never say can't. 3817
Never stop walking. 1027, 2229
Never strike a happy medium. 2726
Never to late. 1575
Never too old for God. 1306, 2488
Never touch a tiger. 2128, 3322
Never trust a God over 30. 1308
"Nevertheless" 1266
New accents in contemporary theology. 1104
New adventures of Jesus. 1994
New age and its messenger. 2690, 3569
New age Bible interpretation. 318, 319
New age Bible interpretation. Genesis, the book of eternal beginnings. 526
New age dictionary. 1393
New age for the New church. 2689
New age in theology. 3656
New age of Christianity. 2690
New age understanding. 3750
New agenda. 787
New altar; a service book for Sunday schools. 3560
New American Bible. 268
New American Bible: the New Testament. 269
New American reformation. 3868
New American revolution. 944
New American standard Bible. 268, 357, 2197
New American standard Bible concordance to the Old and New Testaments. 228
New American standard Bible: New Testament. 357
New American Standard Bible: New Testament, Psalms. 582
New American standard Gospel of John. 414
New American standard New Testament. 354
New analytical Bible and dictionary of the Bible. 262, 263, 267
New analytical indexed Bible. 260
New analytical question-book on the life and ministry of Jesus. 1994, 3564
New and beautiful collection of select hymns and spiritual songs. 1865
New and choice selection of hymns, for social worship and private devotion. 1861
New and complete concordance to the Holy Scriptures. 227
New and complete history of the Holy Bible. 297
New and complete life of Our Blessed Lord and Saviour, Jesus Christ. 72, 927, 1975, 1978
New and complete pronouncing Bible dictionary. 245
New and corrected version of the New Testament. 352
New and critical version of Rhymes on moral instruction attributed to Rabbi Hai Ben Sherira gaon. 2375
New & eternal testament. 2366, 2367
New and full method of settling the canonical authority of the New Testament. 339, 3810
New and improved camp meeting hymn book. 1868, 3231
New & living way. 404, 3191

... The new and old immigrant on the land. 1275
New and original exposition of the book of Revelation. 462
New answer to Darwinism. 3079
New antichrist. 52
New Apocrypha. 2729
New apostles. 1279
New appraisal of Christian science. 1030
New appreciations of George Fox; a tercentenary collection of studies. 1637
New approach in missionary education. 2549
New approach in understanding the gospels. 284
New approach to Buddhism. 704
New approach to Christain unity. 1039
New approach to Jewish life. 3028
New approach to sex. 3393
New approaches to family pastoral care. 1606
New approaches to the Eucharist. 2255
New archeological discoveries and their bearing upon the New Testament and upon the life and times of the primitive church. 918, 919
New art for an old religion. 1796
New art of living. 987
New Assisi. 3421
New atlas of the Bible. 208
New awakening for Methodism. 2421
New B. Y. P. U. manual. 142
New Baptist junior union manual. 141
New Baptist song book, 1971. 153
New beginnings. 437, 664, 981, 1004
New being. 3359
New Bible. 3062
New Bible commentary. 221
New Bible commentary, revised. 222
New Bible dictionary. 243
New Bible evidence from the 1925-1933 excavations. 486
New Bible helps young folks. 640
New Bible home instructor. 1228
New Bible, pro and con. 274, 275
New Bible ready reference. 2612
New Bible survey. 309
New Bible symbols. 253
New Bible symbols...part 1. 1960
New Bible teacher. 650
New Biblical atlas, and Scripture gazetteer. 282
New Billy Casper. 744, 1366
New birth. 1357, 3051
New birth—new life. 3218
New birth of freedom. 1659
New black magic and the truth about the ouija-board. 3512
New book of Job. 253
New book of proverbs; or, The economy of human life. 2980
New books of revelations. 3744
New branches on the vine. 1548, 2542
New breed of clergy. 1296
New buildings on old foundations. 2519
New Caesars. 1513
New call. 1374
New call to holiness. 3299
New Cana manual. 2342
New Canaan. 304
New canon law. 775
New canon law in its practical aspects. 775
New castle. 3118
New catechetical methods. 3150
New catechism. 767, 770, 1895
New catechism: Catholic faith for adults. 767
New catechism; Catholic faith for adults, with supplement. 767
... A new catechism of sacred history. 218
New catechism of the Third Order. 1649
New Catholic Bible. 1810, 1969
New Catholic Bible symbols with The story life of Jesus. 1810, 1969
New Catholic dictionary. 779
New Catholic edition of the Holy Bible. 263, 264, 270, 481, 1329
New Catholic encyclopedia. 779
New Catholic family missal. 846
New Catholic hymn and mass book. 858
New Catholic Peoples' encyclopedia. 779
New Catholic picture Bible. 622
New century. 3072
New Century handbook of Greek mythology and legend. 2662
New chain-reference Bible. 635, 636
New challenges to American Catholics. 829
New chapters in New Testament study. 334
New chapters in the warfare of science. 3074
New charismatics. 2816
New charter for monasticism. 2578
New Child of Mary. 855
New Children's day book. 2757

New child's life of Christ. 1984
New China. 912
New Christendom. 3449
New Christian. 3528
New Christian advocate. 2434
New Christian epic. 3344
New Christian nation. 1109
New Christian year. 1163, 1265
New Christianity. 2690, 3440, 3637
New Christians. 979
New Christmas legend. 2006
New Christology. 2046
New churces for old. 1059
New church. 758, 1166, 2689, 2690
New church and Chicago. 2692
New Church and modern Christianity. 1187
New church and the new Germany. 1146
New church for the new time, a discussion of principles. 1059
New Church in the New World. 2689
New Church; its ministry, laity, and ordinances. 2692
New church law on matrimony. 2342
New church member orientation manual. 1202
New church miscellanies. 2689
New church of St. Benedict. 1271
New church programs with the aging. 1257
New church register 1874-1961, and minutes of the session, Jan. 15, 1956 -- Oct. 7, 1962. 2918
New churches. 1158
New churches of Europe. 1159
... The new citizenship. 955, 3241
New Clarendon Bible. 266, 498
New climate for stewardship. 3529
New combined Bible dictionary and concordance (The) 245
New command. 1301, 2377
New commandment. 1194
New commentary on Holy Scripture. 222
New commentary on Holy Scripture, including the Apocrypha. 222
New commentary on the Doctrine and covenants. 3216
New communities for Christians. 1013
New community. 986, 2571, 3797
New community in Christ. 1065
New compact Bible dictionary. 242
New compact topical Bible. 304
New comparative mythology. 1482, 2665
New complete standard singer. 3563
New comprehensive dictionary of the Bible. 245
New concept of Bible mysteries and eschatologies. 233, 1530
New concordance and dictionary to the Holy Scriptures. 226
New concordance of the American revised Bible (Standard ed.) 300
New concordance to the Holy Bible. 226
New Confraternity edition. 768
New congregations; security and mission in conflict. 3538
New consciousness. 3479
New consciousness in science and religion. 3083
New convenant commonly called the New Testament of Our Lord and Saviour Jesus Christ. 360
New cosmogony. 1370
New country church building. 1161
New courage for daily living. 342
New covenant. 252, 356, 438
New covenant, commonly called the New Testament. 356
New covenant commonly called the New Testament of our Lord and Savior Jesus Christ. 362
New Covenant in the Old Testament. 1377
New creation. 983, 1478, 2326, 2819, 3289, 3740, 3758
New creation; an account of the genesis of the universe of mind and mental operations according to the Bible. 527
New creation and the new generation. 1260
New creation as metropolis. 1279
New creation realities. 3029
New creationism. 1380
New critique of theoretical thought. 2179
New crusade. 1341
New cults. 1394
New currents. 2111
New dawn in Japan. 1935
New day ascending. 33
New day; Catholic theologians of the renewal. 764, 3610
New day dawning. 2493
New day for evangelism. 1568
New day for the country church. 1374
New day in Kenya. 2536
New day in Madras. 2954
New day of Christianity. 3488

New day; the Bahai revelation. 128
New days for old. 1437
New day's worship. 1434
New Delhi report. 3850
New Delhi speaks about Christian witness, service, and unity. 1492
New demons. 3327
New design for living. 2695
New dialogue between philosophy and theology. 1105
New dictionary of the liturgy. 843, 3855
New dimension of the soul. 3353
New dimensions in Catholic life. 996
New dimensions in Judaism. 2075
New dimensions in New Testament study. 335
New dimensions in pastoral care. 2784
New dimensions in religious experience. 1585
New dimensions in teaching children. 1505
New dimensions of deep analysis. 3698
New dimensions of religion. 3078
New direction for campus Christian action. 1051
New directions. 1714
New directions for a musical church. 1203
New directions for the rural church. 3255
New directions from the Ten Commandments. 1314
New directions in Anglican theology. 3618
New directions in Biblical archaeology. 208, 3014
New directions in Biblical thought. 235
New directions in New Testament study. 351
New directions in religious life. 2574
New directions in the I ching. 1879
New directions in theology today. 3656
New directory for Baptist churches. 148
New directory of the Churches of Christ in the United States. 1272
New disciple. 155
New discoveries, concerning the millennium. 2464
New discoveries in St. Catherine's Monastery. 2330, 3273
New discoveries in the origin of Christianity. 1195
New discussion of the Trinity. 3712
New dispensation. 1050
New divine order. 3651
... The new divinity. 3495
New doctrine of clerical privilege. 2943
New drums over Africa. 3018
New earth, and other sermons. 3345
New edition of Plain truth. 1655
New edition of the Babylonia Talmud. 3583
New edition of the Babylonian Talmud. 3583
New education and religion. 3160
New education in religion. 3147
...New emphasis on promotion in Protestant churches. 1252
New encyclopaedia of Freemasonry (Ars magna latomorum) and of cognate instituted mysteries: their rites, literature, and history. 1663
New engagement. 1088
New England anti-masonic almanac. 53
New England church, 1730-1834. 183, 1627
New-England collection of hymns and spiritual songs. 1866
New England company of 1649 and John Eliot. 1507, 2541
New England Company of 1649 and John Eliot. 1507, 2541
New England Company, 1649-1776. 1900, 3437
New England dissent, 1630-1833. 157
New England meeting houses of the seventeenth century. 1271
New England Methodism. 2420
New England mind. 3007
New England mind in transition. 2129
New England ministry sixty years ago. 3846
New England miracle. 2476
New England parsonage, 1877-1937. 914
New-England psalter. 582
New England Puritans. 3009
New England reformers and Divinity college address. 3708
New England revivals. 3231
New England romance. 2806
New England saints. 2687
New England theocracy. 1338
New England transcendentalism and St. Louis Hegelianism. 23, 3708
New England witchcraft. 3827
New England worships. 1271
New-Englander in Japan, Daniel Crosby Greene. 1772, 2534

New England's place in the history of witchcraft. 3826
New England's struggles for religious liberty. 2687
New English Bible. 274, 2129
New English Bible, companion to the New Testament. 343
New English Bible, companion to the New Testament: the Gospels. 386
New English Bible, New Testament. 345
New English Bible: the Apocrypha. 488
New English Bible: the New Testament. 274
New English Bible: the Old Testament. 274
New English Bible with the Apocrypha. 274
New English New Testament. 274
New epistles from old lands. 1525
New epoch for faith. 1591
New era. 3446
New era in Asia. 1090
New era in missions. 2495
New era in philosophical theology. 3402
New era in religious education. 3153
New eschatology. 1528
New essays in philosophical theology. 2832
New essays on Paradise lost. 2468
New essays on religious language. 3071
New essence of Christianity. 3617
New ethic for a new earth. 2676
New Eucharistic legislation. 2256
New eucharistic prayers and prefaces. 2912
New evangelical theology. 1552
New evangelicalism. 1551
New evangelism. 1553, 1568, 1571, 3615
New Eve. 2356, 3844
New every morning. 990, 1435, 1438
New executive in the smaller YMCA. 3872
... New explanatory question-book on the harmony of the Gospels. 384
New eyes for invisibles. 3479
New face for the church. 1062
New face of Buddha. 708
New face of evangelicalism. 1573, 2200
New face of missions. 2495
New faith for old. 3745
New faith in an old world. 974
New-fashioned man. 2425
New forms of worship. 3004
New freedom in the natural order. 1072
New friends for Freddy. 3467
New frontier. 2939
New frontiers for faith. 1591
New frontiers for old. 2926
New frontiers for spiritual living. 17
New frontiers in an old world. 2516
New frontiers of Christianity. 1066
New frontiers of religion. 3446
New future of Christianity. 3330, 3368
New garden of Eden. 1656
New General Synod of the Church of England. 1219
New generation. 874, 1570
New generation, American and Catholic. 874
New Genesis. 3521
New Gilead Church. 2688
New God for America. 3745
New gods. 1380
New gods in America. 3326
New Golden bough. 2651
New growth. 1712
New guide to Bible study. 280
New guide to Christian discipleship. 1051
New Hagadah for the Pesah seder. 2109
New handbook of all denominations. 3323
New happiness. 181, 991
New harmony and exposition of the Gospels. 382
New harmony of the four Gospels in English. 382
New harvest bells, for Sunday schools, revivals, and all religious meetings. 3072
New Haven theology. 2688
New heaven. 991, 1998
New heaven and a new earth. 454, 2174, 3319
New heaven and new earth: a contemporary interpretation of the book of Revelation. 454
New heaven and the new earth. 1794
New heaven? New earth? 2816
New heavens and new earth. 3746
New hermeneutic. 288
New Hi-Y manual. 688
New Hi-Y tool chest. 3874
New hieroglyphical Bible. 252, 1810
New hieroglyphical Bible for the amusement & instruction of children. 252, 1810
New history of the Book of common prayer. 1214
New Holy Week Missal for the laity. 839

New Holy Week ordo. 844, 1837
New home missions. 2527
New hope for congregations. 1244, 2946
New hope for planet Earth. 1565
New hope; twelve lights. 3623
New horizon: theological essays. 3628
New horizons. 63, 651
New horizons beyond the world. 2723
New horizons for the priesthood. 772
New horizons for the synagogue. 2782
New horizons for town and country churches. 2670
New horizons in Biblical research. 200
New horizons in Catholic thought. 791
New horizons in Catholic worship. 2239
New horizons in Old Testament literature. 210
New horizons in Scripture and worship. 315
New horizons in world mission. 2514
... New horizons of the Christian faith. 1049
New horoscope of missions. 2519
New humanity. 129
New hymn and tune book. 13, 15, 2451
New hymn book. 3754
New hymns for America, 1976. 1867
New idea. 2226
New identity for the priest. 772, 2789
New idolatry. 1715
New illuminated Holy Bible, self-pronouncing. 258
New immorality. 945
New indexed Bible. 259, 260, 262
New indexed Bible, comprising Biblical biography geography, history, teaching. 260
New infinite and the old theology. 3645
New inquisition, translated. 2111
New insights into Scripture. 642
New international dictionary of New Testament theology. 477
New international dictionary of the Christian church. 3638
New International Version interlinear Greek-English New Testament. 307
New interpretation of faith. 1066
New interpretation of the mass. 2365
New introduction to moral theology. 947
New invasion of Belgium. 2503
New Israel. 473
New Jersey conference memorial. 2452
New Jersey preacher. 3343
New Jersey Sisters of charity. 2400, 3417
New Jerusalem. 2162
New Jesuits. 1948
New Jewish encyclopedia. 2085
New Jewish encyclopedia (The) 2085
New Jewish history. 2088
New Jewish theology in the making. 2080
New Jews. 1366, 2112, 2143
New Johnny Cash. 744, 1358
New joy. 180
New joy, a course on China for junior boys and girls. 912
New joy for daily living. 449
New joy in living. 974
New Julfa. 1160
New junior workers' manual. 3070
New Kentucky monitor. 1670
New King James Bible. 269
New laity and the old standards. 1289
New laity between Church and world. 2192
New lanterns in old China. 2509
New Larousse encyclopedia of mythology. 2653
New law for all living. 3141
New layman for the new time. 2191
New layman's Bible commentary in one volume. 224
New layman's parallel Bible. 254
New leadership. 1715
New learning and the old faith. 1052
New lectionary. 1268
New Left and Christian radicalism. 3233
New Left church [essays]. 1074
New legislation on engagements and marriage. 2341
New leisure. 2209
New Lenten sermons. 2216
New lessons in love. 1189, 3699
...The new Leviathan. 1141
New libertarian gospel. 1779, 2222
New library of Catholic knowledge. 755
"The new life" 978, 1725, 2213, 3623
New life and other joys. 2890
New life dawning. 3355
New life for prayer groups. 2874, 2885
New life for the young people's Bible class. 645
New life for your Sunday school. 3553
New life in Catholic schools. 832
New life in Christ. 377, 997, 1015, 2037, 3477
New life in Christ Jesus. 974, 2639
... A new life in education. 3149

New life in the church. 1359, 2192
New life in the old prayer-meeting. 2886
New life in the oldest empire. 2535
New life in the parish. 1244
New life in the Spirit. 1832
New life, new lifestyle. 991
New life of grace. 1751
New life of Summerfield. 3546
New life: preparation of religious for retirement. 2575
New life through God. 965
New life to live. 1362, 3010
'New Light Christians'; initiators of the nineteenth-century reformation. 3035
New light from old lamps. 1452
New light on ancient chronological records in the Hebrew Scriptures. 1115
New light on Hebrew origins. 2097
New light on immortality. 2991
New light on Martin Luther. 2274, 2348
New light on Mormonism. 2611, 3470
New light on New Testament letters. 367
New light on survival. 3500
New light on the earliest Gospel: seven Markan studies. 436
New light on the Gospels. 384
New light on the life of Jesus. 1961
New light on the New Testament. 347
New light on the old truth. 1049
New light on the spirit path. 125, 127
New light shines out of present darkness. 3227
New light upon Indian philosophy. 3422, 3569
New light upon old tradition. 1962, 3058
New light upon the lives of Mary and Jesus. 2354
New lights on pastoral problems. 2410
New literal translation, from the original Greek, of all the apostolical epistles. 367
New liturgy: a documentation, 1903-1965. 844, 2234
New liturgy and old devotions. 857
New liturgy, new laws. 2235
New lives for old. 2697
New living pulpit of the Christian church. 1463
New look at an old book. 233
New look at Biblical crime. 1387
New look at Christian morality. 947
New look at church growth. 1170
New look at Colossians. 341
New look at executive responsibilities. 3873
New look at faith and loyalties. 3877
New look at God. 3081
New look at Job. 550
New look at ourselves and others. 3877
New look at religion. 3142
New look at the Apostles' creed. 74
New look at the Bible tradition. 231
New look at the Eucharist. 1541
New look at the Lutheran confessions (1529-1537) 2280
New look at the sacraments. 3264
New look at YMCA physical education. 3871
New look for Sunday morning. 3004, 3464
New look in preaching. 2904
New look of Lent. 2210
New Lottie Moon story. 2485, 2588
New man. 978, 1070, 2026, 2325, 2749, 3488
New man and the divine society. 1062
New man for our time. 1005
New man ... new world. 1557
New manual for Baptist churches. 30
New manual for vestrymen. 1239
New manual of Catholic devotions compiled in honor of the Blessed Virgin. 839
New Manual of private devotions. 2893
New manual of private devotions in three parts. 2893
New manual of the Sacred Heart. 3270
New Mass. 2257, 2365
New matrimonial legislation. 196
New meanings for new beings. 1066
New media: new forms. 2897
New men for new times. 804
New men in Christ. 363
New mentality. 3884
New Messiah and the journey of the soul. 3461
New metrical version of the Psalms. 582
New Mexican alabado. 21
New Mexican church and synagogue library directory. 2224
New Mexico santero. 3303
New Mexico santos. 3303
New Mexico santos: how to name them. 3282
New midweek service. 3377
New mind for a new age. 978
New ministries. 1117
New minted gold. 572

New missal for every day. 845, 2370
New missal for Holy Week. 844
New mission of Pope John XXIII. 2123
New missionaries for new days. 2484
New missionary church. 850
New missionary era. 2496
New missionary field. 2528
New model of the universe. 2730
New models for financing the local church. 1168
New modernism. 176, 1457
New mood in Lutheran worship. 2295
New moral code of action of the large corporation's executive. 3742
New moral order. 1155
New morality. 947
New morality or no morality. 3742
New morals for old. 2338
New move forward in Europe. 150, 1171
New "myth"-ology. 67
New name. 1054
New Nigeria. 2542
New nuns. 2581, 2717
New obedience. 2004
New oil for old lamps. 976
New-old thought. 253
New opportunities of the ministry. 3673
New opportunity of the church. 3471
New or old? 393, 1718
New ordeal of Christianity. 1182
New order in the church. 1057
New order is at hand. 1513
New order of meditation. 2381
New Orleans (Archdiocese) 1294
New orthodoxy. 2751, 2752
New Oxford annotated Bible with the Apocrypha. 275
New Oxford book of Christian verse. 1023
New paganism. 2930
New pagans. 2726
New pantheon. 2656
New parish mission. 2774
New Park Street pulpit. 167
New paths for old purposes; world challenges to Christianity in our generation. 2492
New paths in Muslim evangelism. 2557
New paths through the Bible. 652
New patterns for Christian action. 1042
New patterns for disciplining Hindus. 2556
New patterns of church growth in Brazil. 2505
New peace. 3073
New pebble in science. 3074
New Pentecost. 997, 1832, 3770
New Pentecost or new Passion? 2570
New people of God. 809
New persons in an old world. 3028
New perspectives for the YMCA. 3871
New perspectives in moral theology. 947
New perspectives on Abraham Geiger. 1704, 2080
New perspectives on parish ministry. 2774
New perspectives on the Old Testament. 484
New phase in ecclesiastical law and Presbyterian church government. 1420, 1472
New Philippines. 2550
New philosophy. 2843
New philosophy of being and existence. 2843
New philosphy. 2990
New physical education in the Young men's Christian associations. 2844
New picture book of saints. 3284
New pilgrimages of the spirit. 34
New pilgrim's progress. 3096
New Plato. 2854
New polytheism. 2859
New portrait of Francis of Assisi. 1640
New possibilities for Disciples and Independents. 1465
New power for the church. 1244
New practical comparative concordance to the Old and New Testaments. 227
New practical meditations for every day in the year. 2398
New prayers for a woman's day. 3843
New preaching. 2903
New priest in Conception bay. 2939
New procedure in criminal and disciplinary causes of ecclesiastics in the United States. 1489
New program book for student Christian associations. 3537
... The new program of religious education. 3147
New propositions in speculative and practical philosophy. 2834
New Psalter and its use. 848
New Psalter of Pius xii in Latin and English. 575
New psychic frontiers. 2992
New psychology and old religion. 2999

New psychology and the Christian faith. 3000
New psychology and the Hebrew prophets. 568
New Puritan. 2371, 2847
New Puritanism. 3008
New quest. 2131
New quest of the historical Jesus. 2008
New questions on God. 1729
New raccolta. 858
New radio lectures. 3387
New Rainbow missionary stories. 2491
New Red anti-Semitism. 53
New redemption. 3443
New Reform responsa. 3219
New Reformation? 1066, 1802
New reformation and its relation to moral and social problems. 2561
New relationships with Jews and Catholics. 3195
New religion. 1069
New religion as revealed in three months of war. 3742
New religions. 3326
New religions of Africa. 12
New religions of Japan. 3324
New religious. 2570
New religious consciousness. 3141
New religious education. 3155
New religious movements in America. 3722
New rendering of the Hebrew Psalms into English verse. 581
New revelation. 3225, 3500
New revelation of mankind, drawn from axioms. 1653
New revelation of the will of God. 3517
New revised Church order commentary. 1023
New ritual. 2240
New road to ancient truth. 1930
New Roman missal in Latin and English. 845, 846
New Saint Andrew Bible missal. 836
New Saint Joseph simplified Bible. 251
New sanctuary manual. 837
New sand-table. 2720
New Schaff-Herzog encyclopedia of religious knowledge. 3639
New school of Gregorian chant. 883
... The new science. 3313
New science and the old religion. 3073, 3078
New science of work. 3848
New scientific and philosophical treatise upon the origin, development and destiny of may. 2320
New Scofield reference Bible. 254
New seeds of contemplation. 3488
New selected translation with an exposition of the philosophy of Kuo Hsiang. 2188
New series of homilies for the whole year. 1265
New sermon illustrations for all occasions. 1840
New sermons for special days and occasions. 2721
[New sermons to asses]. 1468
New service and tune book. 3562
New shafts in the old mine. 2931
New shape of American religion. 1109, 3747
New shape of life. 1010, 2930
New shape of ministry. 1296
New shape of pastoral theology. 2787
New signposts on old Bible trails. 235
New Six o'clock saints. 3285
New Smith's Bible dictionary. 246
New sodality manual. 3455
New sodality prayer book. 3455
New solutions of New Testament problems. 339
New song. 180, 3124, 3615
New song in the South. 1754, 3230
New song; thoughts on the Beatitudes. 180
New songs. 3459
New soul in China. 2509, 3127
New sovereignty. 2045
New spirit in the convent. 2581
New standard alphabetical indexed Bible. 260, 261, 1660, 1914
New standard alphabetical indexed Bible (Authorized or King James version) 271
New Standard Bible dictionary. 244
New state. 1143
New story talks to boys and girls. 3534
New streams in old channels. 2
New strides of faith. 3353
New studies in Acts. 333
New studies in mystical religion. 2639
New studies in the Beatitudes and the Lord's prayer. 180
New studies of old stories. 630
New-style family Bible. 271
New sunrise meditations. 1449

New superior generation. 2860
New system. 2649
New system of mythology, in two volumes. 2653
New system of occult training. 2727
New system of orificial philosophy. 2833
New Tabernacle sermons. 3065
New tables of stone, and other essays. 3065
New tales from Aesop (for reading aloud) 1588
New tales from the Old Testament. 533
New tasks for new times. 2521
New tasks for old churches. 3440
New techniques for church fund raising. 1168
New Temple. 1163
New ten commandments. 3337
... New tendencies in teaching religion. 3157
New Testament. 251, 284, 315, 321, 346, 351, 352, 353, 354, 355, 356, 357, 358, 360, 361, 385, 407, 408, 409, 410, 411, 439, 473, 474, 650
... The New Testament according to the Eastern text. 353
New Testament against its environment. 476
New Testament, always news. 347
New Testament; an expanded translation. 354
New Testament, an introduction. 410
New Testament: an introduction for the general reader. 409
New Testament; an introduction to its history, literature, and thought. 409
New Testament and book of Psalms. 269
... The New Testament and Catholic prayer-book combined. 268
New Testament and criticism. 348
New Testament and familiar hymns and tunes, with selections and forms. 1863
New Testament and mythology. 1424
New Testament and Psalms. 269
New Testament and rabbinic Judaism. 347, 3015
New Testament and structuralism. 352, 3536
New Testament and the Psalms. 269
New Testament and Wycliffe Bible commentary. 343
New Testament apocalyptic. 56, 349
New Testament Apocrypha. 336, 337
New Testament apologetic. 588
New Testament as it stands. 410
New Testament as literature. 474
New Testament as literature (Gospels and Acts) 474
New Testament as the church's book. 348
New Testament authors and their works. 321
New Testament background. 407
New Testament baptizing ones. 137, 152
New Testament basis of pacifism and The relevance of an impossible ideal. 2808
New Testament Bible stories. 626
New Testament biographies. 1993
New Testament chapter analysis. 474
New Testament Christianity. 1096, 3572
New Testament Christological hymns. 351, 2043
New Testament church. 475, 1052, 1053, 1121, 1122, 1163, 1248, 2848, 3811
New Testament church, its teaching and its Scriptures. 407
New Testament church principles. 1163
New Testament church, then and now. 1120
New Testament churchmanship. 1241
New Testament commentary. 331, 342, 343
New Testament commentary from the Aramaic and the ancient Eastern customs. 344
New Testament concept of the ministry. 1296
New Testament concept of witness. 3830
New Testament conversions. 1361, 2299
New Testament criticism. 348
New Testament detection. 349
New Testament development of Old Testament themes. 450
New Testament disunity. 475
New Testament doctrine of the Christ. 477, 1954, 2042
New Testament doctrine of the church. 1163
New Testament doctrine of the 'Last things. 1530
New Testament doctrines. 935
New Testament documents. 378
New Testament environment. 408
... The New Testament epistles. 367, 378
New Testament era. 408
New Testament essays. 334
New Testament ethics. 378

New Testament evangelism. 1562, 1566, 1570, 1574
New Testament evangelism for today. 1568
New Testament evangelism in a modern church. 1568
New Testament exegesis. 372
New Testament experience of faith. 348, 1102
New Testament faith for today. 1097
New Testament fires in Old Testament forests. 201
New Testament follow-up for pastors and laymen. 1568
New Testament followers of Jesus. 1955, 3135
New Testament for English readers. 344
New Testament for learners. 407
New Testament for spiritual reading. 344
New Testament for today. 348
New Testament foundations. 410
New Testament foundations for Christian evangelism. 1566
New Testament Gospels. 1990
New Testament Greek. 1768
New Testament Greek grammar. 1770
New Testament Greek primer. 1770
New Testament Greek syllabus for junior Greek class. 1770
New Testament Greek workbook. 1770
New Testament guide. 409
New Testament handbook. 647
New Testament heritage. 225, 410
New Testament history. 290, 291, 406, 626
New Testament history and literature. 292, 408
New Testament history for academic grades. 406
New Testament idea of hell. 1802
New Testament idea of revelation. 3226
New Testament illustrations: photographs, maps, and diagrams. 408, 1196
New Testament in art. 85, 450
New Testament in Basic English. 177
New Testament in cadenced form. 361
New Testament in current study. 351
New Testament in English. 354
New Testament in four versions. 357, 358
New Testament in four versions: King James, Revised standard, Phillips modern English, New English Bible. 357
New Testament in Greek according to the text followed in the Authorized version. 1768
New Testament in living pictures. 381, 2764
New Testament in modern English. 352, 355, 359, 360
New Testament in modern English. Student ed. 359
New Testament in modern English. Student ed. [translated by] J. B. Phillips. 359
New Testament in modern speech. 268, 269, 353, 354
New Testament in shorter form. 472
New Testament in the Apostolic fathers. 76
New Testament in the Christian church. 339
New Testament in the contemporary world. 64
New Testament in the language of the people. 357
New Testament, in the language of today. 357
New Testament in the life of the church. 473, 2789
New Testament in the light of a believer's research. 348
New Testament in the light of modern research. 347
New Testament in the light of the higher criticism. 346
New Testament in the original Greek. 284, 285, 3575
New Testament in the Westminster version of the Sacred Scriptures. 356
New Testament interpretation. 350
New Testament introduction. 374, 409, 411
New Testament introduction: Hebrews to Revelation. 310, 368
New Testament introduction; the Gospels and Acts. 398
New Testament introduction; the Pauline Epistles. 374
New Testament issues. 334
New Testament, its intent and content. 409
New Testament, its making and meaning. 408, 410
New Testament letters. 374
New Testament life and literature. 411, 475

New Testament life and literature as reflected in the papyri. 347
New Testament life of Christ. 1989
New Testament literature. 337, 411
New Testament literature ... a bibliography. 337
New Testament literature in the light of modern scholarship. 410
New Testament manual. 347
New Testament manuscript studies. 315
New Testament manuscript traditions. 431, 1748
New Testament manuscripts in the Freer collection. 315, 316, 2330
New Testament message. 106
New Testament names. 1093
New Testament notes. 474
New Testament occultism. 2476, 2724
New Testament octapla. 357
New Testament of ancient America. 2600
New Testament of Our Lord and Savior Jesus Anointed. 356
New Testament of Our Lord and Savior Jesus Christ. 356, 357, 359, 360, 361, 362
New Testament of Our Lord and Savior Jesus Christ. Rev. standard version with pictures. 362
New Testament of Our Lord and Savior Jesus Christ. Revised standard version, Catholic ed. Prepared by the Catholic Biblical Association of Great Britain. With a pref. by Albert Cardinal Meyer. 362
New Testament of Our Lord and Saviour Jesus Christ. 206, 342, 355, 356, 357, 358, 359, 360, 361, 362, 450, 2182, 3143
New Testament of our Lord and Saviour Jesus Christ: according to the received Greek text, together with the English Authorized version. Arranged in paragraphs. 361
New Testament of our Lord and Saviour Jesus Christ. King James version with pictures. 361
New Testament of Our Lord and Saviour Jesus Christ, newly translated from the Vulgate Latin at the request of their lordships, the archbishops and bishops of England and Wales. 356
New Testament of Our Lord and Saviour Jesus Christ, translated. 355
New Testament of Our Lord and Saviour Jesus Christ. Translated out of the original tongues and with the former translations diligently compared and rev. King James version, 1611. 357
New Testament of Our Lord Jesus Christ. 343
New Testament of Our Master and Saviour Yahvahshua the Messiah (commonly called Jesus Christ) 357
New Testament of our Messiah and Saviour Yahshua. 356
New Testament of the Jerusalem Bible. 3407
New Testament origin. 348
New Testament outlined. 474
New Testament parables for children. 2027
New Testament parallels in Buddhistic literature. 706
New Testament period and its leaders. 408
New Testament pictures and their stories. 399
New Testament prayer book. 450
New Testament primer. 473
New Testament problems. 347
New Testament prophecy. 450
New Testament, Psalms, Proverbs. King James version, plus aids to Christian living. 251
New Testament questions of today. 334
New Testament reading guide. 343, 344
New Testament sidelight. 334, 3005
New Testament sidelights. 335, 3005
New testament sociology for higher institutions of learning, brotherhoods and advanced Bible classes. 3439
New Testament speaks. 408
New Testament standard of piety. 2818
New Testament stories. 625, 626
New Testament story-land. 625
New Testament story retold for young people. 625
New Testament student at work. 335
New Testament students' workbook: Greek, Latin, English. 473
New Testament studies. 330, 334, 346, 350, 429, 474, 475, 1786, 1973, 2271, 3546
New Testament studies in missions. 2518, 2795
New Testament studies v. 613
New Testament survey. 344, 409, 411

New Testament teaching in the light of St. Paul's. 474
New Testament teaching on the role relationship of men and women. 350, 2402
New Testament teaching on tongues. 1717
New Testament text. 284
New Testament text of Saint Ambrose. 29, 450
New Testament themes for contemporary man. 1066
New Testament theology. 476, 477, 2040
New Testament theology today. 477
New Testament times. 408
New Testament today. 349
New Testament view of the Old Testament. 450
New Testament view of women. 349, 3841
New Testament windows. 1771
... New Testament women and problems of to-day. 3877
New Testament word book. 245
New Testament word lists. 1769
New Testament word studies. 342, 425
New Testament wordbook. 1768
New Testament words. 1768
New Testament world. 348, 406, 407, 2101
New Testament writings. 409
New Testament writings and witers. 342
[New Testament in Thai. 320
New text of spiritual philosophy and religion. 3502
New themes for the Protestant clergy. 3441
New themes in Christian philosophy. 1106
New theocracy. 3609
New theologian. 676, 3656
New theology. 1054, 3622, 3623, 3641
New theology and morality. 3656
"The new theology," by a Methodist layman. 3668
New theology, no. 1. 3622
New theology no. 1. 3623
New theology, no. 3. 3623
New theology, no. 2. 3623
New theology sermons. 1340
New theory of creation. 1379
New theory of the creation. 1380
New theory of the earth. 1380, 1384, 3810
New theosophy. 3688
New theosophy, regarding man and spirit being. 3685
New things old and new; some psychological aspects of the religious life. 2580
New things of God. 3345
New thought Christianized. 2694
New thought religion. 2695
New thoughts on an old book. 221
New threshold. 1082
New-time religion. 3744
New times. 1061
New topical text book. 303
New Tower of Babel. 762, 1283
New trails for the Christian teacher. 3158
New translation of Job, Ecclesiastes, and the Canticles. 591
New translation of the Bible. 261, 263, 270
New translation of the Bible, containing the Old and New Testaments. 261, 263
New translation of the book of Job. 590, 591
New translation of the book of Psalms. 573
New translation of the book of Psalms and of the Proverbs. 592
New translation of the Hebrew prophets. 567
New translation of the Holy Scriptures according to the Masoretic text. 590
New translation of the Proverbs, Ecclesiastes, and the Canticles. 591
New translations of the Bible. 270
New treasury of Judaism. 2141
New treatise upon regeneration in baptism. 133
New trends in church architecture. 1156
New trends in moral theology. 948
New Tri-Hi-Y manual. 688
New tribute to the memory of James Brainerd Taylor. 3590
New trustees for a new age. 3576
New turns on the Liberia road. 2537
New vacation church school. 3763
New ventures. 1653
New version of the Psalms of David. 585, 586
New version of the Psalms of David fitted to the tunes used in churches. 585
New vesper psalter. 848
New views of sex-marriage-love. 2343
New vigilantes. 1394
New vision of another heaven. 1794
New visions, new roles. 2574

New vocation. 1408
New voice. 288, 3071
New voices, old worlds. 1110
New wars. 2334
New way of Jesus. 239, 888
New way of living. 1238
New way of thinking. 1325, 3750
New way to solve old problems. 3553
New way to teach juniors, captivating-- stimulating--different. 3146
New ways in Christian worship. 3003
New ways in theology. 3657
New ways in worship for youth. 3856
New ways of ontology. 2738
New ways of teaching the old story. 934
New ways to learn. 3180
New ways to solve old problems. 3750
New ways to worship. 3856
New wealth for you. 1056
New wedding: creating your own marriage ceremony. 2347
New West as related to the Christian college. 3807
New West education commission 1880- 1893. 2696
New Westminster dictionary of the Bible. 243
New why and how of Woman's missionary union. 3468
New wind blowing! 3229
New windows for women. 3843
New wine, new skins. 2816
New wine skins, present-day problems. 3065
New wings for a warrior. 891, 3851
New witness for Christ in America. 678, 679
New witness for Christ in America, the Book of Mormon. 678
New witnesses for God. 2605
New woman/new earth. 3390
New works of new nuns. 3837
New world. 445, 2436, 2548
New world a'coming. 1280
New world and the new thought. 3077
New world calling, & other sermons suggested by Modern novels. 1341
New World idea index to the Holy Bible. 303
New world is born. 3361
New World metaphysics. 3214
New world of the mind. 2728
New world of urban man. 1277
New world order. 3440
New World translation of the Christian Greek Scriptures. 355
New World translation of the Hebrew Scriptures. 482
New World translation of the Holy Scriptures. 266
New Year greetings. 2387
New yet old mass. 2365
New York. 3371
New York church and musical directory of New York and Brooklyn and other adjacent suburbs. 2698
New York pulpit in the revival of 1858. 1559
New York. Union theological seminary. 2701
New you. 3888
New youth evangelism. 1564
New Zionism. 3896
Newberry study Bible. 271
Newborn. 3289
Newborn Christian. 2394
Newer dispensation. 1467
Newer spiritualism. 3511
Newer temples of the Greeks. 2240, 2746
Newes from Italy. 1366, 3778
Newest keep-sake for eighteen hundred thirty-nine. 2109
Newly discovered gnostic writings. 1718
Newly-made Mason. 1662
Newly opened treasury of heavenly incense; or, Christian's companion. 3049
... Newman. 2702, 2704
Newman against the liberals. 1227, 3365
Newman; an appreciation. 2705
Newman; an appreciation in two lectures. 2705
Newman & Bloxam. 2703
Newman and Gladstone. 3769
Newman and the common tradition. 1188, 2702
Newman and the Gospel of Christ. 2010
Newman and the modern world. 2703
Newman annual. 760
Newman anthology. 2704
Newman as a man of letters. 2704
Newman at Oxford. 2703
Newman at St. Mary's. 1227
Newman brothers. 2704
Newman Hall in America. 3596
Newman, Louis Israel. 1789
Newman movement. 2702

Newman on development. 1473, 2703
Newman on justification. 2161, 2704
Newman on the psychology of faith in the individual. 1593, 2703
Newman on tradition. 2702, 3707
Newman: pioneer for the layman. 2191, 2704
Newman symposium. 2702
Newman synthesis. 782
Newman, the church historian. 2702
Newman: the contemplation of mind. 2473, 2704
Newman the Oratorian. 3488
Newman the theologian. 1473, 2704
Newman treasury. 2704
Newman's Apologia. 2705
... Newman's Apologia pro vita sua. 790
Newman's university; idea and reality. 2703, 3756
Newman's way. 2704
Newness of life. 376, 943, 2326
Newology. 270
NewPerspectives for the YMCA. 3871
News from north of the Nile, discovering the inside story of the Scriptures. 638
News in religion and other sermons. 160
Newspaper and religious publicity. 10
Newspaper man reports—the good news is true. 1067
Newspaper stories for group guidance. 2590
Newton chapel. 2706
Newton church directory. 684
Newton church directory, 1906. 2706
Newton theological institution. 1848
Newtonians and the English Revolution, 1689-1720. 3085
Next beyond. 3509
Next Christian epoch. 3618
Next door neighbors. 1838
Next great awakening. 3446
Next hymn, please. 1866
Next hymn, please; a delightful quest for hymn-stories. 1870
Next life. 1888
Next step. 2421
Next step in evolution. 1579
Next step in religion. 3068
Next steps toward racial justice. 2681
Next Sunday's sermon. 2905
Next thing. 1363
Next three years. 3174
Next world interviewed. 3505
Next year in Jerusalem. 1809
NFDA U.S. reference manual. 3722
Nibley on the timely and the timeless. 2608
Nicene creed, illumined by modern thought. 2706
Niceta of Remesiana. 1018
Nichiren. 706, 2707
Nichiren, a biography. 2707, 2940
Nichol-Bradley debate. 1655
Nicholas Cardinal Wiseman. 738, 3822
Nicholas Ferrar, his household and his friends. 1622
Nicholas Ferrar of Little Gidding. 1291, 1622
Nicholas of Cusa. 2708
Nicholas of Cusa and medieval political thought. 1322, 2708
Nicholas of Cusa on God as not-other. 1725, 1846
Nicholas Ridley. 3237
Nicholas Wiseman. 3822
Nichols Weaver debate. 1272
Nickerson's illustrated church musical and school directory of New-York and Brooklyn. 2698
Nicodemus with Jesus. 2708
Nicolas Malebranche, Dialogue between a Christian philosopher and a Chinese philosopher on the existence and nature of God. 1724
Nieto's Jewish almanac for one hundred years. 27
Nietzsche. 2709, 2710
Nietzsche and Buddhism. 708, 2710
Nietzsche as critic, philosopher, poet and prophet. 2710
Nietzsche in outline & aphorism. 2710
Nieuwe-Wereldvertaling van de Christelijke Griekse Geschriften. 320
Niger vision. 2500
Nigerian harvest. 1024, 2542
Nigerian pioneer. 2506, 3425
Night and nothing. 90
Night before Christmas. 3601
Night cometh. 1553, 3587
Night is a jungle, and other discourses of Kirpal Singh. 3197
Night Jesus was born. 2022
Night of affliction and morning of recovery. 3131
Night of toil. 2543
"The night of truth," 3609
Night pastors. 1280

Night scenes in the Bible. 1342
Night-scenes of Scripture. 231
Night scenes of the Bible. 3365
Night-side of nature. 2987
Night sky of the Lord. 2145
Night the giant rolled over. 2488, 2533
Night thoughts on life, death & immortality. 1891
Nightfall at Nauvoo. 2617
Nihilism. 2710
Nihilism, its origin and nature. 2710
Nihilism, its origin and nature, with a Christian answer. 2710
Nikko. 2710
Nikolai; portrait of a dilemma. 2710
Niles Stensen. 3527
9 1/2 mystics. 2646
Nine Bible heroes. 3549
9 doctors & God. 2524
Nine gates to the Chassidic mysteries. 3580
... Nine great preachers. 923
Nine lectures on bees. 51
Nine lectures on preaching. 2899
Nine lives of Sterling W. Sill. 2617, 3408
Nine modern moralists. 945
Nine o'clock in the morning. 139
Nine papers on the ecclesiastical history of England. 1515
Nine public lectures on important subjects in religion, preached in Fetter Lane Chapel in London in the year 1746. 2595, 3367
Nine questions people ask about Judaism. 2751
Nine roads to renewal. 1244
Nine rotten, lousy kids. 2943
Nine sermons. 3367
Nine sermons of Saint Augustine on the Psalms. 578, 586
Nine sermons on important doctrinal and practical subjects. 3755
Nine sermons, on the nature of the evidence by which the fact of Our Lord's resurrection is established. 1226, 2051
Nine songs. 3400
Nine to five complex. 1075
Nine uncial palimpsests of the Greek New Testament. 315
Nine ways of bon. 3699
Nine-year teacher, book four. 3549
Nine-year teacher, book three. 3549
Nine-year teacher, book two. 3549
Nine years with the Spokane indians. 1900, 3789
Nineteen bishops of the Evangelical United Brethren Church. 1550
Nineteen centuries of Christian song. 1875
Nineteen centuries of the Christian church. 1100
Nineteen centuries of the Roman Catholic Church. 807
1911 Bible. 289
1954 Chicago international Catholic congress ... August 1-3, 1954. 44
19 gifts of the spirit: Which do you have? 1712
1904-1926. The time between. 681, 3292
Nineteen letters of Ben Uziel. 2114
Nineteen letters on Judaism. 2155
Nineteen missionary stories from the Middle East. 2490
1977 date book, almanac & authentic calendar of saints, hoboes, dervishes, coevolutionaries, healers, helpers & ordinary holy fools. 662
1975 seminar papers. 229
1974 seminar papers. 229
1974 yearbook of testimony. 1009, 3216
1972 and 1973 proceedings. 2364
1972 proceedings. 590
1965 yearbook. 2302
Nineteenth-century anglo-Jewish novel. 1517
Nineteenth century churches of Texas. 1274
Nineteenth century devotional thought. 1451
... The nineteenth century educational contribution of the Sisters of charity of Saint Vincent de Paul in Virginia. 1403
Nineteenth century evangelical theology. 3652
Nineteenth century evolution and after; a study of personal forces affecting the social process, in the light of the life-sciences and religion. 1579
Nineteenth century in Europe. 817
Nineteenth century in Europe: background and the Roman Catholic phase. 817, 1542
Nineteenth century in Europe: the Protestant and Eastern churches. 2746, 2954, 2977
Nineteenth century miracles. 3496, 3520
Nineteenth century outside Europe. 29

Nineteenth century outside Europe: the Americas, the Pacific, Asia, and Africa. 1182
Nineteenth century sense. 3502, 3503
Ninetieth birth-day gathering. of Rev. Charles Cleveland. June 21, 1862. 1303
Ninety-five brief talks for various occasions. 2721
95 theses. 2275
90 meditations for youth. 3883
Ninety-nine names of Allah. 3544
Ninety-nine new sermons for children. 907
Ninety story sermons for children's church. 1983
Ninety-year record of Madison Square Presbyterian Church: 1882-1972. 3298
95 theses, with the pertinent documents from the history of the Reformation. 2280
Ninth Bridgewater treatise. 2672
Ninth International (fourteenth national) Sunday school convention. 3554
Ninty-five brief talks for various occasions. 2721
Nirankari Baba. 3302
Nirvana. 2710
Nirvana now. 1701, 3478
Nirvana, story of Buddhist psychology. 705
Nirvana, the last nightmare. 3481
Nisi Dominus. 1224
Nissanka's choice. 2491
NIV complete concordance. 229
NIV counselor's New Testament and Psalms. 254
NIV interlinear Hebrew-English Old Testament. 538
NIV pictorial Bible. 254
NIV triglot Old Testament. 592
Nivernais, Bourbonnais roman. 1159
Niyamsara (The perfect law) 1932
Nizari Isma'ili tradition in the Indo-Pakistan subcontinent. 1927
Njoki and the Mau Mau terror. 2374
Nkosi. 2499
No abiding city. 1936, 2214
No absent God. 2323
No and yes. 1031
No appointment needed. 1, 2782
No bars to manhood. 194
No "beginning" 1092
No bigger than necessary. 3449
No borrowed light. 2570
No burning hell, is what the Bible really says. 234
No chance to panic. 2487, 3021
No church is an island. 1244
No church without a bishop. 1523
No coward soul. 3731
No cowards in the kingdom. 996
No cross, no crown. 107, 972, 1011
No cross, no crown; or, Through suffering to eternal glory. 3540
No darker rooms. 178
No darkness at all. 3850
No dreamers weak. 3450
No easy answers. 945
No easy immortality. 2991
No easy road. 2871
No easy salvation. 404
No empty creed. 73
No escape form life. 2779
No escape from life. 2779
No exit. 106, 1998
No faith of my own. 1057
No famine in the land. 2309, 3623
No featherbed to heaven. 3815
No flesh shall glory. 3017
No God but God. 3120
No going back. 1365
No graven images: studies in art and the Hebrew Bible. 602, 2073
No greater challenge. 3181
No greater glory. 3456
No greater heritage. 290
No greater joy. 3847
No greater life. 1967
No greater love. 1290, 1400, 2058, 3031, 3524
No greater love, and other true stories of courage and conviction. 1231
No greater service. 3421
No ground. 992
No guarantee but God. 2743
No handle on the cross. 1097, 2046
No hope but God. 995, 1630
No idle tale. 431, 2051
No immersion in the Bible. 134
No jewels for Jane. 882
No king but Caesar? 3780
No king in Israel. 3556
No little people. 3357
No longer alone. 984, 1849
No longer strangers. 1011, 2187, 2542
No magic formula. 533, 982
No man is an island. 3488

No man knows my history. 3428
No matter how dark the valley. 3540
No middle ground. 1243
No more hunger. 3436
No more plastic Jesus. 3409
No more strangers. 1131, 1366
No new morality. 3389
No, not dead; they live! 3494
No offense. 1038
No older at night. 2227
No one dies alone. 2717, 2865
No one wins like a loser. 986, 2376
No one's perfect. 2385
No orthodoxy but the truth. 3679
No other foundation. 1189, 2403
No other god. 3657
No other gods. 3348
No other king. 633
No other name. 1080
No other way. 2391, 3666
No other wealth. 2889
No pat answers. 987
No peace of mind. 2808
No race apart. 2570
No refuge but in truth. 1072
No remedy. 1407
No room for doubt. 67, 279
No room for Him. 3703
No room in the brotherhood. 2297
No rusty swords. 676
No saints suddenly. 1008
No salvation without substitution. 104
No shadow of turning. 3533
No sign shall be given. 1063
No signs from heaven. 2232
No souvenirs. 1506, 3093
No stained-glass-window saints. 1163
No strange God. 2139
No strings attached. 1751
No tall buildings in Nazareth. 3171
No thank you. 1326
No thought for tomorrow. 3336
No time for tombstones. 2559
No traces of the gnostics are to be found in the New Testament. 1718
No turning back. 3807, 3831
No two alike. 2363, 2490
No two alike, those Maryknoll sisters! 1633
No two ways about it! 973
No uncertain sound. 3344
No valley too deep. 931, 1857
No wings for nine angels. 2349
No wings in the manse. 1303
Noah. 2712
Noah and his ark. 2712
Noah and his times. 203
Noah and the ark. 2711, 2712
Noah and the great flood. 495, 1422, 2711
Noah and the rainbow. 2711
Noah H. Mack: his life and times, 1861-1948. 2308
Noah's and Namah's ark. 2712
Noah's ark. 2711, 2712
Noah's ark book. 2711
Noah's ark: I touched it. 2711
Noah's ark nonsense. 2711
Noah's flood: a poem. In two parts. 3209
Noah's three sons. 1936, 2326
Nobility at the cross. 3215
Noble army. 2493
Noble army of Congregational martyrs. 1333
Noble army of martyrs. 2482
Noble castle. 1098
Noble dames and notable men of the Georgian era. 1758
Noble eightfold path, the doctrine of Dharma. 702
Noble heritage. 1943
Noble heritage: two conjugate leaves from the first edition of the Bishops' Bible. 253
Noble landmark of New York. 2698
Noble lives and noble deeds. 662
Noble piety and reformed monasticism. 1276
Noble priest. 3296
Noble savages. 2204
Noble task. 2924
Noble task: the elder. 2924
Nobler risk, and other sermons. 1343
Noblest quest. 3343
Nobody else will listen. 1714
Nobody's child. 2757
Nobody's perfect. 338, 987
Noel: The Joan Baez Christmas songbook. 3271
Noise in the sky. 2390
Noise it abroad. 668, 3232
Noise of solemn assemblies. 3749
Nomad of the spirit. 2571, 3306
Nomenclator literarius theologiae catholicae theologos exhibens aetate, ratione, disciplinis distinctos. 3626

Nomenclatural standing of clericus polydenominata. 2788
Non-Christian people of the Philippine Islands. 1540
Non-existence of God. 1733
Non-miraculous Christianity. 1230
Non-Pauline epistles and Revelation. 368
Non-rational character of faith. 1595
Non-religion of the future. 3059
"non-religious" Christianity? 3328
Non serviam. 3413
Non spiritus. 3509
Non-violence and the Christian conscience. 2778
Non-Biblical systems of religion. 3119
Non-Catholic denominations. 3324
Non-Christian religions A to Z. 3138
Non-Christian religions of the world. 3119
Non-church-going. 1162
Nonconformist conscience. 1764
Nonconformity and social and economic life, 1660-1800. 1468
Nonconformity in the nineteenth century. 1469
None but Christ. 1999
None dare call it witchcraft. 2727
None good but God. 442
"None other gods" 1064
None so small. 2625
Non-religion of the future. 3059
Nonresistance and responsibility, and other Mennonite essays. 2405
Nonviolence: a reader in the ethics of action. 2713
Nonviolence in Indian religious thought and political action. 1896
Nonviolent alternative. 2808
Non-violent cross. 2809
Noonday devil. 996
Noontime messages in a college chapel. 3758
Nor by power. 2091
Nor free nor secular. 1247
Nor scrip, nor shoes. 2510
Norfolk churches. 1161
Norlie collection of English Bibles. 247
Norm and context in Christian ethics. 946
Norma. 1749, 3896
Normal and abnormal evolution. 3519
Normal Christian church life. 971
Normal class manual of Old Testament history. 597
Normal evangelism. 1565
Normal manual of modern Sunday, school method. 3565
...Normal studies on the life and ministry of Christ. 1991
Norman anonymous of 1100 A.D. 731
Norman learns about the sacraments. 3267
Norman learns about the Scriptures. 313, 3217
Norman Macleod. 2309
Norman monasteries and their English possessions. 2569
Norman Thomas, the last idealist. 3697
Norman Vincent Peale. 2810
Norman Vincent Peale, Christian crusador. 2810
Norman Vincent Peale's treasury of courage and confidence. 1326
Norman Vincent Peale's Treasury of joy and enthusiasm. 987
Normative psychology of religion. 3001
... The normative use of Scripture by typical theologians of Protestant orthodoxy in Great Britain and America. 278
Norse gods and giants. 2665
Norse legends and myths. 2666
Norse mythology. 2665, 2666
Norse mythology; legends of gods and heroes. 2666
Norse myths. 2665
Norse tales. 2666
Norsemen found a church. 3578
North American Indian mythology. 1902
North American [mythology]. 1902
North American Protestant foreign mission agencies. 2522, 2954
North American students and world advance. 2515
North American study in the field of religious education. 2923
North and east of Musa dagh. 2490
North Carolina Disciples of Christ. 1465
North Carolina sermons. 2434
North Country bishop. 2708
North of heaven. 100, 2543
North Texas Methodism. 2447
North-western hymn book. 1867
Northampton and Jonathan Edwards. 1499, 2714

Northampton parishes. 2957
Northern. 893
... The northern Algonquain supreme beingm. 25
Northern Algonquian supreme being. 25
Northern Baptists rethink missions. 2202
Northern Catholicism. 2755
Northern Catholics. 3868
Northern exposure. 1222
Northern exposure tales of the north country. 1222
Northern Ireland problem. 1139
Northern lights. 1859
Northern Methodism and reconstruction. 2453
Northern mythology. 2666
Northern parish. 2699
Northern republics of South America. 1491
Northrup's religion and business. 2695
Northwest Southern Baptists. 140
Northwest Texas conference pulpit, Methodist Episcopal church, South. 2457
Norwegian American Lutheranism up to 1872. 2715
... Norwich. 2715
Norwich Cathedral. 2715
... A nosegay of everlastings from Katherine Tingley's garden of helpful thoughts. 3688
Nostalgia for paradise. 2772
Nostradamus. 2947
Nostradamus: life and literature. 2947
Nostradamus on Napoleon. 2668
Nostradamus on Napoleon, Hitler and the present crisis. 2668
Nostradamus sees all. 2947
Nostradamus speaks. 2946
Not a silent people. 148, 3465
Not a sometimes love. 171, 2185
Not a sparrow falls. 2437
Not alone. 975, 1305, 1774
Not as a man pleaser. 2788
Not as the scribes. 3365
Not as the world gives. 1644, 1649
Not as the world giveth. 2398
Not by bread alone. 943, 3388, 3758, 3853
Not by might. 2807, 2809, 3129
Not by power. 2090
Not every sea hath pearls. 3131
"Not for a million dollars" 898, 2309
Not forgetting to sing. 1474
Not forgotten. 2109
Not I, not I, but the wind that blows through me. 1835
Not impossible religion. 1788
Not in bread alone. 2215
Not in vain. 2713
Not lawful to utter. 1068
Not like ordinary men. 321
Not made for defeat. 879
Not many wise. 3743
Not many wise, a reader on religion in American society. 3743
Not me, God. 720
Not minds alone. 3147
... Not much essays. 2530
Not my own. 3529
Not my will. 970
Not now, but afterwards. 165
Not of the world. 2617
Not of this world. 1850
Not on bread alone. 760
Not only a dean. 1215
Not only peace. 3792
Not our kind of folks? 695
Not Paul, but Jesus. 1960
Not ready to walk alone. 1587, 3814
Not slothful in business. 1167
Not somehow, but triumphantly! 1438
Not the righteous! 1362
Not the work of a day. 2103
Not tradition, but Scripture. 278
Not with silver or gold. 3420
Not with words of wisdom. 2235
Not without parables. 1013
Not without tears. 672
Not words but deeds. 2668
Not your own. 3528
Notable Mormon books, 1830-1857. 2608
Notable personalities and their faith. 3829
Notable sermons from Protestant pulpits. 3359
Notable women of olden time. 3840
Notable women of spirit. 3837
Note book of a country clergyman. 1015
Note book of an American parson in England. 1302
Notebook for religion. 3057
Notebook for youth work beyond the local church. 2459
Notebook of a colonial clergyman. 2629, 2630
Notebook of the Reverend John Fiske, 1644-1675. 1628, 3802

Notebooks. 1443
Noted witnesses for psychic occurrences. 2991
Notes. 542
Notes and illustrations of the parables of the New Testament. 2027
Notes and quotes for church speakers. 1841
Notes, critical and explanatory, on the Acts of the apostles. 327
Notes, critical and explanatory, on the book of Exodus. 515
Notes, critical and explanatory, on the book of Genesis. 521
Notes, critical and explanatory, on the Greek text of Paul's Epistles to the Romans, the Corinthians, the Galatians, the Ephesians, the Philippians the Colossians, the Thessalonians, Timothy, Titus, and Philemon. 371
Notes, critical and practical, on the book of Exodus. 515
Notes, critical and practical, on the book of Genesis. 520, 521
Notes, critical and practical, on the book of Joshua. 553
Notes, critical and practical, on the book of Judges. 554
Notes, critical and practical, on the book of Leviticus. 557
Notes, critical and practical, on the book of Numbers. 560
Notes, critical and practical, on the books of Joshua and Judges. 553
Notes critical, explanatory, and practical. on the book of Psalms. 574
Notes; critical, explanatory, and practical on the book of the prophet Isaiah. 542
Notes, critical, illustrative, and practical, on the book of Daniel. 505
Notes, critical, illustrative, and practical, on the book of Job. 547, 548
Notes, exegetical, practical and devotional, on the book of Exodus. 516
Notes, explanatory and practical, on the Acts of the apostles. 327
Notes, explanatory and practical, on the book of Revelation. 452
Notes, explanatory and practical, on the Epistle to the Hebrews. 402
Notes, explanatory and practical, on the Epistle to the Romans. 466
Notes, explanatory and practical, on the Epistles of Paul to the Ephesians, Philippians, and Colossians. 370
Notes, explanatory and practical, on the Epistles of Paul to the Thessalonians, to Timothy, to Titus, and to Phileman. 370
Notes, explanatory and practical, on the First epistle of Paul to the Corinthians. 322
Notes, explanatory and practical, on the general Epistle of James, Peter, John and Jude. 340
Notes, explanatory and practical, on the general Epistles of James, Peter, John and Jude. 340
Notes, explanatory and practical, on the Gospels. 385
Notes, explanatory and practical, on the Second epistle to the Corinthians and the Epistle to the Galatians. 325
Notes for addresses at funeral occasions. 1693
Notes for living. 1011
Notes for meditation on the beatitudes of the Psalter. 2382
Notes for readings on the life of Jesus. 1993
Notes from a layman's Greek Testament. 343
Notes from lectures on theistic conception of the universe. 3609
Notes from my Bible. 223, 640
Notes from the Caroline underground. 2208, 3008
Notes from the song of life. 2392
Notes from the Summa on God and His creatures. 1725, 3696
Notes from the Warsaw ghetto. 2107
Notes illustrative of the meaning and application of the figures employed by St. John the Divine in the Revelation of Jesus Christ. 452
Notes of a catholic biologist. 662
Notes of a forty-one years' pastorate. 1290
Notes of class and association lessons. 1038
Notes of my life, 1805-1878. 3126
Notes of the Baptists. 158
Notes of the minister of Christ for the times. 3670
Notes of the miracles of Our Lord. 2018
Notes of triumph: for the Sunday school. 3562

Notes on A history of auricular confession. 1326
Notes on a hitherto unknown exegetical, theological and philosophical commentary to the Pentateuch. 562, 2623
Notes on art for Catholics. 87
Notes on Christian racism. 1132
Notes on ecclesiology. 1122
Notes on forty Algonkin versions of the Lord's prayer. 25
Notes on Genesis. 522
Notes on Ingersoll. 1907
Notes on Luke's Gospel. 427
Notes on moral theology, 1965-1980. 948
Notes on old London city churches. 2243
Notes on Philippians. 448
Notes on religion. 1068
Notes on St. John and the Apocalypse. 421
Notes on St. Luke and the Acts. 430
Notes on St. Mark and St. Matthew. 436
Notes on sins and their remedies. 3411
Notes on some ceremonies of the Roman rite. 838
Notes on the Acts of the apostles. 327
Notes on the American liturgy. 844
Notes on the Apocalypse. 456
Notes on the Bhagavad-gita. 196
Notes on the Bhagavad gita, to help students in studying its philosophy. 2317
Notes on the Book of Daniel. 506
Notes on the book of Deuteronomy. 510
Notes on the book of Leviticus. 557
Notes on the book of Proverbs. 572
Notes on the books of Ezra, Nehemiah, and Esther. 531
Notes on the cathedral libraries of England. 2224
Notes on the Catholic liturgies. 838
Notes on the Catholic name. 851
Notes on the church cantatas of John Sebastian Bach. 123
Notes on the constitution of the Reformed (Dutch) church in America. 3045
Notes on the covenant. 1376
Notes on the cultivation of choral music and the Oratorio Society of New York. 917, 2740
Notes on the divinity course given. 1031
Notes on the doctrine of God. 1722
Notes on the early history of the Vulgate Gospels. 397
Notes on the Epistle of Paul the apostle to the Hebrews. 402
Notes on the Epistles of Paul the apostle to the Galatians and Ephesians. 379
Notes on the Epistles of St. Paul (I and II Thessalonians, I Corinthians 1-7, Romans 1-7, Ephesians 1: 1-14) 371
Notes on the Epworth league devotional meeting topics. 1525
Notes on the Free Quaker Meeting House, Fifth and Arch Streets, Philadelphia. 2829
Notes on the Free Quaker Meeting House, Fifth and Arch Streets, Philadelphia, built 1783-4. 2829
Notes on the Gospel of John. 415
Notes on the Gospel of Mark. 432, 434
Notes on the Gospel of Matthew. 439
Notes on the Gospels. 385
Notes on the Greek text of the Epistle of Paul to Philemon. 447
Notes on the Hebrew prophets. 571
Notes on the Hebrew text of the books of Kings. 556
Notes on the Hebrew text of the books of Samuel. 590
Notes on the Lord's prayer. 2247
Notes on the Minor Prophets. 559
Notes on the miracles of Our Lord. 2018
Notes on the Nicomachean ethics. 81
Notes on the Old Testament, explanatory and practical, by Albert Barnes. 497
Notes on the parables of Our Lord. 2027
Notes on the principles and practices of Baptist churches. 149
Notes on the proper Psalms for holy days. 2985
Notes on the prophecy and Lamentations of Jeremiah, 'the weeping prophet. 546
Notes on the Psalms. 576
Notes on the Revelation. 454, 459
Notes on the Second plenary council of Baltimore. 835
Notes on the spiritual exercises. 3476
Notes, practical and expository, on the Gospels. 385
Notes to quote. 1843
Notes to the overworld. 2396
Nothing but Christ. 3488
Nothing but the Gospel. 1024, 3351
Nothing for your journey. 1645
Nothing is impossible with God. 1601
Nothing is quite enough. 3131
Nothing left to believe. 61

Nothing lost. 3076
Nothing of yesterday preaches. 865
Nothing on earth. 2717
Nothing to fear. 1064
Nothing to win but the world. 2554
Nothingness itself. 2333
Notices of the life of Theodosia Ann Barker Dean. 1412
Notion of tradition in John Driedo. 1480, 3706
Notions about the Bible. 231
Notions of a Yankee parson. 1288
Notitia scriptorum ss. Patrum. 1019
Notorious Dr. Bahrdt. 130, 1520
Notre Dame. 2715
Notre Dame de Chicago. 893
Notre Dame de la Salette in France. 3286
Notre-Dame de Paris and the Sainte-Chapelle. 2773
Notre-Dame of Noyon in the twelfth century. 79, 2716
Notre-Dame of Paris. 2774
Notre Dame's John Zahm. 3891
Notwithstanding my weakness. 3493
... Nouum Testamentum sancti Irenaei espiscopi lugdunensis. 1919
Le Nouveau Testament de Notre Seigneur Jesus Christ. 269
Le Nouveau Testament de Notre Seigneur Jesus-Christ. 269
Nova et vetera: informal meditations. 2397
Novels and tales by Catholic writers. 869
Novelties which disturb our peace. 739
Novena manual of Jesus, Mary and Joseph. 859
Novena manual of Our Lady of perpetual help. 856
Novena of the Holy Spirit. 839
Novena to St. Therese of Lisieux. 3691
Novenas in honor of St. Alphonsus. 3282
Novice of Qumran. 2006
Novice of Saint Therese. 2261
Novices of Our Lord. 2581
Novissima verba. 3691
Novitiate. 2716
Novitiate, by Paul Philippe. 2716
Novius organum. 2420
Novum Psalterium Pii XII. 848
Now! 1451, 2558, 2767, 3142
Now, a book on the Absolute. 2767
Now a word from Our Creator. 1313
Now and forever. 3885
Now and the not yet. 968
Now comes the hangman. 2854
Now, evening Mass, our latest gift. 2365
Now for something totally different. 981, 3335
Now generation. 3884
Now generation, and other sermons. 1273
Now God has to advertise — and this is good. 1091
Now I know; a primer of faith. 1593
Now I see. 1364
Now is eternity. 2393
Now is the acceptable time. 2813
Now is the day of judgment. 2156
Now is the time. 1430, 1529, 2385, 2926, 3385
Now is the time to love. 1607
Now is tomorrow. 3592
Now is too soon. 2625
Now songs. 1869
Now that you are a Catholic. 999
Now that you're a deacon. 1408
Now then. 1450
Now -- This day. 1450
... Now we are going to school. 3211
Now we are three. 3175
Now what do I do? 3881
Now—would you believe? 1014
Nowhere a stranger. 3437
NSA seminar report, 1968-71. 3455
NSA seminars. 3455
Nuclear disarmament. 103
Nuclear evolution. 2725
Nuclear war. 103
Nuclear war, deterrence, and morality. 103
Nuclear weapons. 103
Nuclear weapons and the conflict of conscience. 103
Nudis verbis. 1653
Nuer religion. 2716
El Nuevo Testamento de Nuestro Senor y Salvador Jesu Cristo. 320
Nuggets for happiness. 972
Nuggets from golden texts. 3374
Nuggets from Numbers. 560
Nuggets from the Bible mine. 3346
Nuggets of Freemasonry in the gold rush days of California. 1663
Nuggets of gold. 1443, 3343
Nuggets of gold and a barrelful of chuckles. 1015
Number counted 666. 609

Number in Scripture. 3575
Number of man. 1280, 3656
Number of years. 218
Number of years, as the great week of time. 218
Numberpower. 2717
Numbers. 560
Numbers: a commentary. 561
Numbers, an introduction and commentary. 561
Numbers and you. 3576
Numbers as symbols of self-discovery. 3576
Numbers book; the science of numerology. 3575
Numerical, alphabetical and descriptive catalogues of the publications of the Presbyterian board of publication, No. 821. Chestnut street, Philadelphia. 3627
Numerical Bible. 258
Numerical saying in the Old Testament. 502
Numerical sayings in the Old Testament. 498
Numerology. 3575
Numerous choirs. 3378
Numismatic illustrations of the narrative portions of the New Testament. 481
Nun. 2581
Nun at her prie-dieu. 2581
"Nun danket alle Gott!" 1873
Nun in the world. 2574
Nun of Kenmare. 3125
Nun of Kent. 3144
Nun of Monza. 2220
Nun: sacrament of God's saving presence. 2572
Nun-sense. 2392
Nuns. 2717
Nun's answer. 740
Nuns are real people. 2573
Nun's ideals. 2383
Nuns of Newark. 2701
Nuns of Port Royal. 2717
Nun's rule. 2575, 2580
Nun-sense. 760
Nunsuch. 2717
Nunted heretic. 3377
Nupe religion. 2718
Nurse, handmaid of the Divine Physician. 1258
Nursery child in the church. 3174
... The nursery child in the church school. 3551
Nursery children and our church. 3174
Nursery class teaching. 3555
Nursery department of the church. 3173
Nursery department of the Sunday school. 3554
Nursery-kindergarten weekday education in the church. 1246
Nursery manual. 3173
Nursery story of the Bible. 623
Nursery teacher's guide. 1119
Nurse's manual. 2718
Nurture and evangelism of children. 1254
Nurture of the child. 895
Nurture of vitality, baccalaureate addresses. 122
Nurturing silence in a noisy heart. 3408
Nurturing young churchmen. 2965
Nuts and bolts of church growth. 1171
Nutshell musings. 2398
Nyilak and other African sketches. 2513

O

O angel of the garden. 1486
O Christians! 185
O church awake. 1123
O come. 3765
O come, let us worship. 3004
O.E.S. in Connecticut. 2741
O follow the Master in the pathway of glorious living. 1434
O happy day. 1857
O inward traveller. 2380, 2631
O Jerusalem? 1279
O-kee-pa. 2719
O-kee-pa, a religious ceremony, and other customs of the Mandans. 2327, 2719
O little town of Bethlehem. 3031
O Lord, grant they blessings this day. 857
O men of God. 1090
O mother dear, Jerusalem. 1943
O Novo Testamento de Nosso Senhor e Salvador Jesus Christo. 361
O Novo Testamento de Nosso Senhor Jesus Christo. 361
O Parakletos, or the Holy Ghost, and the New covenant spiritual ministry of angels. 1836
O sing unto the Lord. 1208
O stedfast face! 2934
O Susan! 1349

O world invisible. 3208
O worship the King. 3217, 3856
Oahspe, a new Bible in the words of Jehovih and his angel embassadors. 120, 1794
Oahspe; the kosmon revelations in the words of Jehovih and his angel embassadors. 120
Oakham Parish Church. 2719
Oakland Temple issue. 2600
Oaks and acorns. 3371
Oaths, covenants & promises. 1376
... Oaths in ecclesiastical courts. 2719
Obadiah: a critical exegetical commentary. 561
... Obadiah and Jonah. 561
Obadiah, Nahum, Habakkuk and Zephaniah. 559
Obeah. 3828
Obedience. 2719
Obedience and the church. 780, 1162
Obedience in church & state. 781, 1141
Obedience in the church. 780
Obedience of Christ. 1995
Obedience of faith. 470
Obedience, the greatest freedom. 2719
Obedience to the laws of God, the sure and indispensable defence of nations. 3740
Obedient men. 3131
Obedient rebels. 3035
Ober-Ammergan and the passion play. 2719
Oberlin. 2720
Obeying Christ in crisis. 2540
Object-lessons and illustrated talks. 3152
Object lessons and stories for children's church. 3159
Object lessons for children. 906
Object lessons for children's sermons. 907
Object lessons for christian growth. 3156
Object lessons for church groups. 3152
Object lessons for junior work. 2720
Object lessons for the cradle roll. 2720
Object lessons for youth. 2720
Object lessons from sports and games. 3151
Object of moral philosophy according to St. Thomas Aquinas. 950, 3695
Object sermons. 3337
Object sermons in outline. 2720
Objections to astrology. 98
Objections to Christian belief. 68
Objections to entir-sanctification considered. 3299
Objections to foreign missions. 2521
Objections to humanism. 1854
Objections to Roman Catholicism. 758
Objective teaching of the Holy sacrifice of the mass. 3177
Objectives in religious education. 3159
Objectives of Christian education. 935
Objects that talk and teach. 909
Oblates' hundred and one years. 2135, 2720
Obligation of almsgiving in common necessity according to St. Thomas. 3695
Obligation of hearing mass on Sundays and holy days. 2369
Obligation of the confessor to instruct penitents. 1327
Obligation of the Sabbath. 3260
Obligations of Christians to one another. 967
Obligations of civilization to Christianity. 1052
...The obligations of the traveler according to canon 14; an historical synopsis and commentary. 1474
Obrigkeitliche Konfessionsanderung in Kondominaten. 124, 3816
Obsequies and obituary notices of the late Right Reverend Benj. Tredwell Onderdonk, D.D. 2737
Obsequies and obituary notices of the late Right Reverend Benj. Tredwell Onderdonk, D. D., bishop of New York. 2737
Observance of Easter. 1486
Observances in use at the Augustinian priory of S. Giles and S. Andrew at Barnwell, Cambridgeshire. 2579
Observations. 798, 1324
Observations concerning the Scripture oeconomy of the Trinity and covenant of redemption. 3714
Observations in the Orient. 2516
Observations of a Bahai traveller. 128
Observations of God's timing in the Kentucky mountains. 3702
Observations on 1st. The chronology of Scripture. 218, 2759
Observations on Congregationalism and Methodism. 1791

Observations on Doctor Priestley's doctrines of philosophical necessity and materialism. 2224, 2939
Observations on first. The chronology of Scripture. 218, 2759
Observations on the authenticity of the Gospels. 394
Observations on the charter and conduct of the Society for the Propagation of the Gospel in Foreign Parts. 3437
Observations on the distinguishing views and practices of the Society of Friends. 1681
Observations on the growth of the mind. 2473
Observations on the history and evidences of the resurrection of Jesus Christ. 2053
Observations on the increase of infidelity. 3023
Observations on the influence of religion upon the health and physical welfare of mankind. 3238
Observations on the Mussulmauns of India. 2567
Observations on the religious peculiarities of the Society of Friends. 1681
Observations on the Revelation of Jesus Christ to St. John. 459
Observer in Palestine. 2761
Observer in Rome. 3770
Observer's book of old English churches. 1159
Observing self. 2647
Observing special days and Christian festivals. 1623
Obstruction of justice by religion. 3195
Occasional addresses. 2722
Occasional and immemorial days. 2930
Occasional discourses. 3360
Occasional papers. 1200
Occasional papers, no. 1. 3731
Occasional sermons. 863
Occasional sermons and addresses of Archbishop Dowling. 2721
Occasional services. 3734
Occasional services, from the Common service book of the Lutheran church. 3734
Occasional services from the Service book and hymnal (The) 2295
Occasional thoughts of Horace Seaver. 1656
... Occident. 1068
Occidental mythology. 2650
Occidental table of houses. 99
Occult. 1078, 2730, 2731
Occult America. 2730
Occult anatomy and the Bible; the achetype or heavenly pattern of the human body. 2725
Occult anatomy of man. 3573
Occult and the Third Reich. 1820, 2732
Occult bibliography. 2730
Occult bondage and deliverance. 2726
Occult conceit. 2728
Occult dictionary for the millions. 2731
Occult establishment. 2732
Occult experiences. 2723
Occult explosion. 2733
Occult glossary. 3689
Occult in the orient. 2733
Occult Japan. 1936
Occult life of Jesus of Nazareth. 2060
Occult phenomena in the light of theology. 2730
Occult philosophy. 2726
Occult powers of modern spiritualism. 3513
Occult preparations for a new age. 2729
Occult Psychology. 2994
Occult Reich. 2723
Occult renaissance, 1972-2008. 2724
Occult revolution. 1078
Occult science, an outline. 2729
Occult science in India and among the ancients. 2726, 2732
Occult sciences. 2729, 3539
Occult sciences in Atlantis. 102
Occult sciences in the Renaissance. 2732
Occult significance of the Bhagavad Gita. 51, 2317
Occult signs and symbols. 3574
... Occult traps and trappers. 2723
Occult view of health & disease. 3685
Occult way. 2723
Occult world. 2732, 3687
Occult world of John Pendragon. 2729
Occultism and common-sense. 2992
Occultism for beginners. 2729
Occultism; its theory and practice. 2729
Occultism, spiritism, materialism. 3506
Occultism, witchcraft, and cultural fashions. 3139
Der Occultismus des Altertums. 2732
Occultist's travels. 3052, 3512
Occupational mobility in social work. 1320

Occupations: contemporary and Biblical. 207, 2733
Ocean Grove. 2733
Ocean Grove Christian songs. 3459
Ocean in a teacup. 879
Ocean melodies and seamen's companion. 3317
Ocean of theosophy. 3685
Oceania in five hours. 2733
Oceanic, American Indian, and African myths of snaring the sun. 3546
Oceanic feeling. 2646
Oceanic [mythology]. 2666
Ochre robe. 1813
Ockham, the conciliar theory, and the Canonists. 1322, 2734
Octave of blessing. 181
... The Octavious of Minicius Felix. 2475
Octavius Brooks Frothingham and the new faith. 1689
Octavius Brooks Frothingham, gentle radical. 1689
Octavius of Marcus Minucius Felix. 69
Octavius Perinchief. 3133
October sermons. 1699
Octoechos. 2748
Octopus. 2104
Octorara family of churches. 2918
Odd Fellow's token. 2855, 2856
Odds against evens. 1260
Ode:On the morning of Christ's nativity. 2468
Odes and Psalms of Solomon. 490
Odes and Secular hymn of Horace. 2199
Odes of Solomon. 491, 492
Odysseus comes home from the sea. 2662
Odyssey of a faith. 2084
Odyssey of Francis Xavier. 1649
... The odyssey of Israel. 535
Odyssey of the self-centered self. 1394
Oeconomy of the covenants, between God and man. 1377
Oecumenical documents of the faith. 880, 2706
Oecumenical movement and the unity of the church. 1492
Oedipus and Job in West African religion. 3580
Oenpelli pioneer: a biography of the Reverend Alfred John Dyer. 1484
O'er land and sea with the apostle Paul. 2794
OEuvres completes. 2777
OEuvres completes [de] Jean Gerson. 3636
Of all things. 1447
Of braces and blessings. 932, 3810
Of cabbages & kings. 2387
Of cell and cloister; Catholic religious orders through the ages. 2582
Of church and state and the Supreme Court. 1150
Of course I love you. 2343
Of course you can walk on water. 444, 1602
Of devolution and destiny. 1615
Of faith and learning. 1918
Of fast & festival. 2209
Of fear and freedom. 3061
Of God. 2693
Of God and His creatures. 69
Of God and man. 996
Of Gods and miracles. 3250
Of grasshoppers and giants. 2790
Of guilt and hope. 2290
Of heaven and hope. 1093
Of human love. 2266
Of Israel's teachings and destiny. 1623
Of law and love. 1315
Of love and of suffering. 2264
Of man and God. 2568
Of men and angels. 2781
Of men and souls. 3462
Of men who ventured much and far. 1713, 2457
Of parsons and profs. 2261
Of prelates and princes. 666
... Of religion. 3057
Of sacraments and sacrifice. 3265
Of singular benefit. 830
Of some country. 3206
"Of such is the kingdom," 1014, 3183
Of such is the kingdom of Heaven. 401, 938
Of test tubes & testaments. 3083
... Of the conduct of the understanding. 2180
Of the imitation of Christ, four books. 1885
Of the imitation of the Sacred heart of Jesus. 3269
Of the laws of ecclesiastical polity. 1218, 1240, 1488
Of the laws of polity. 1240
Of the least of these. 3710
Of the New Jerusalem and its heavenly doctrine. 2692

Of the presence of God. 3479
Of the principles and duties of natural religion. 2675
Of the use and abuse of music. 1203
"Of them He chose twelve" 71
'Of them which say they are Jews,' and other essays on the Jewish struggle for survival. 2104
Of things which soon must come to pass. 455
Of time and eternity. 3750
Of true religion. 3667
Of water and the spirit. 139
Of whom the world was not worthy. 995
Of wise men and fools. 214
Off-key praises. 2397
Off the beaten path. 3622
Off the capes of Delaware. 2104
Off the record. 796
Off to a good start. 1911
Off to China. 897
Off to Panama! 2544
Offbeat spirituality. 3485
Offering of man. 956
Offering of sympathy to the afflicted. 1352
Offering of uncles. 3661
Offering to churchmen. 2960
Offertorium. 3377
Office and duty of a Christian pastor. 3675
Office book for Dominican sisters. 843
Office of a bishop. 665
Office of a wall. 3790
Office of apostle in the early church. 71, 2801
Office of bishop in Methodism. 2427
Office of Christian burial according to the Byzantine rite. 1693
Office of clerk of session. 2915
Office of deacon. 1408
Office of the Holy Communion as set by John Merbecke. 1213
Office of the Most Blessed Sacrament. 2253
Office of woman in the church. 3834
Officers' handbook. 3737
Offices for the burial of the dead. 2970
Offices from the service-books of the Holy Eastern Church. 2748
Offices of baptism and confirmation. 136
Offices of mystical religion, projecting congregationally the inner disciplines of the life toward God. 3479
Offices of the Oriental Church. 2748
Offices of worship and hymns. 2594
Official and lay witness to the value of foreign missions. 2520
Official and popular religion. 3067
Official, authorized biography of the Reverend Dr. Preston Bradley. 688, 3349
Official Catholic Directory. 779
Official Catholic directory. 1886. 779
*Official Catholic directory, 1964. 779
Official Catholic directory ... for the year. 779
Official Catholic directory... for the year 1886-c19. 779
Official Catholic directory (The) 1963. 779
Official Catholic year book. 866
Official character of Rev. Nathanael Emmons, D.D. 1512, 1693
Official directory. 893
Official directory Protestant churches of metropolitan Chicago. 893
Official documents of the Presbytery of Albany. 891
Official guide to Catholic educational institutions. 832
Official guide to Catholic educational institutions (The) 832
Official guide to Catholic universities and colleges. 832
Official history of freemasonry. 1667
Official history of freemasonry among the colored people in North America. 1667
Official history of the First African Baptist church, Philadelphia, Pa. 2829
Official Holy name pocket manual. 856
Official journal. 2438, 2445
Official journal and minutes. 2445
Official journal and year book of the Delaware annual conference ... Session. 2444
Official journal and year book of the Maine annual conference ... Session. 2446
Official journal and year-book of the New England southern annual conference. 2445
Official journal of the ... annual session of the Atlantic mission conference. 2454
Official journal of the ... annual session of the Central Alabama conference. 2444

Official journal of the Inter mountain annual conference (legally Idaho) 2444
Official journal of the ... session of the New Hampshire annual conference. 2447
Official journal of the ... session of the North Carolina annual conference. 2445
Official listing of member schools and officers of the executive committee. 3613
Official manual with the doctrines and discipline of the Church of God in Christ, 1973. 1229
Official minutes. 2444, 2445
Official minutes of the. 2445
Official minutes of the annual convention. 110
Official minutes of the ... annual session of the North Nebraska conference. 2445
Official minutes of the ... annual session of the North Ohio conference. 2445
Official minutes of the ... annual session of the Southwest Kansas conference. 2445
... Official minutes of the Pittsburg annual conference. 2447
Official minutes of the Pittsburgh annual conference. 2447
Official minutes of the ... session (including twenty sessions of the Nevada conference) of the Nevada mission. 2445
Official minutes of the ... session of the California annual conference. 2444
Official minutes of the ... session of the Genesee conference. 2446
Official minutes ... Session of the Northern New York conference. 2445
Official minutes, year book and journal of the proceedings of the ... session of the Upper Mississippi annual conference. 2445
Official proceedings of the ... annual communication. 1667
Official program and hymnal, International convention on Christian education. 1866
Official program of the passion play. 2778
Official record. 2445
Official record ... 1st-session. 2445
Official record ... annual session. 2446
Official religious record index. 3271
Official report. 147
Official report of the ... international Christian endeavor convention. 3736
Official report of the proceedings of the ... meeting. 3723
Official ritual and manual of the Ladies' auxiliary of the Ancient order of Hibernians in America (organized 1895) for the guidance of officers in the conducting of division meetings and degree work. 2576
Official service and instruction book for St. Stephen's and Paul's parish of Owensboro, Ky. 844
Official service book. 1897
Official souvenir of the consecration of Rt. Rev. T. M. A. Burk. 717
Official souvenir of the consecration of Rt. Rev. T. M. A. Burke. 717
Official Tri-Hi-Y manual. 3876
Officium parvum Beatae Mariae Virginis. 847
Offizieller Bericht uber die Generalversammlung. 755
Oglala religion. 2734
Oh ... Brother Juniper. 2159
Oh, what a beautiful lady! 1618
Ohio conference offering. 2435, 3352
Ohio Mennonite Sunday schools. 2407
Ohio rural life survey. 3435
Oil and wine. 783
Oil for the lamps of Christians. 1445
Ojibwa religion and the Midewiwin. 915
Ojibway heritage. 915
Okinawa; a people and their gods. 3259
Okinawan religion. 2735
... Oklahoma Delaware ceremonies. 1420, 1899
Oklahoma Methodism in the twentieth century. 2432
Oklahoma trails. 2928
Olavus Petri. 2826, 3042
Olavus Petri and the ecclesiastical transformation in Sweden [1521-1552]. 2826, 3042
Old age, afterlife and the spirit. 2735
Old and new in interpretation. 200
Old and new in Palestine. 2760
Old and new man in the letters of Paul. 375
Old and New Testament connected. 2089
Old and new Unitarian belief. 3727
Old and the new. 1165
Old and the new in the church. 1125
Old and the new in the church (The) 3850
Old and the new man. 3292

Old arts and new technology. 3659
Old Babylonian contracts from Nippur. 93
Old Babylonian omen text. 93
Old Believers & the world of Antichrist. 3022
Old Bethesda. 3
Old Bible and the new science. 3076
Old Bible in rhyme. 536
... Old Bible records and land lotteries. 1706
Old blazing. 1078
Old book and the old faith reviewed in a series of lectures. 235
Old book of magic. 2312
Old Brethren. 1236
Old Brick, Charles Chauncy of Boston, 1705-1787. 890, 1333
Old brick manse. 3128
Old buckingham by the sea on the Eastern shore of Maryland. 193
Old Bulgarian art. 1881, 3455
Old Cathedral. 3276
Old Catholic eucharistic worship. 2735
Old Catholic Maryland and its early Jesuit missionaries. 1948
Old Catholic missal and ritual. 2735
Old Catholic movement. 2735
... An Old-Catholic view of confession. 2735
Old Chelsea and Saint Peter's church. 2700
"Old chief". Alexander Lorenza Boone, d. d., ll. d. 681
Old Christianity against papal novelties. 801, 2467
Old Christianity vs. new paganism. 1051
Old Christmas. 1114
Old church in the new world. 2746
Old church lore. 1631
Old Church Slavonic glossary. 1247
Old church tells her story. 1336
Old churches and modern craftsmanship. 78
Old churches, ministers and families of Virginia. 3781
Old churches, minsters and families of Virginia. 3781
Old churches of London. 2243
Old Colony Mennonites; dilemmas of ethnic minority life. 2736
Old conjuring books. 1345
Old convent school in Paris, and other papers. 1357
Old creed for a new day. 74
Old diary leaves. 3686
Old dogma in a new light. 1473
Old Egyptian faith. 1502
Old English Bible, and other essays. 270, 1497
Old English homilies and homiletic treatises. 3367
Old errors and new labels. 2843
Old Estonian folk religion. 1533
Old European Jewries. 2112
Old evangel & the new evangelism. 3228
Old events and modern meanings. 159
Old faith and new knowledge. 3080
Old faith and new thoughts. 1654
Old faith and the new. 3023
Old faith in the new day. 1592
Old faith in the New World. 2699
Old faiths and new facts. 3076
Old faiths in new light. 236, 1055
Old faiths perish. 1654
Old-fashioned Quakerism. 1685
Old fashioned revival hour and the broadcasters. 1572, 1690
Old Fellow. 2196
Old First. 2865
Old fort, historic Mormon bastion. 3287
Old forts taken. 1699
Old Franciscan missions of California. 1646, 3470
Old friend with new credentials; a history of the Christian index. 952
Old friends. 2195
Old gospel. 3135
Old gospel for new times. 1265
Old gospel for the new age. 3365
Old Greek nature stories. 2661
Old historic churches of America. 1274
Old Jesuit trails in Penn's forest. 1948
Old Latin and the Itala. 314
Old Latin texts of the Heptateuch. 530
Old law & the new law. 1312
Old letter with an modern message. 323
Old Lighthouse. 2756
Old log house. 1396
Old looking-glass for the laity and clergy of all denominations. 1218
Old McKendree Chapel. 2308
Old man. 3410
Old man's jottings. 3133
Old Nazareth. 2596
Old New England church. 1346
Old New England churches. 1271

Old New England churches and their children. 1271
Old North Reformed Church of Dumont, New Jersey, 1724-1974. 2736
... The old, old myths of Greece & Rome. 2650
Old, old story-book. 532
Old, old story from the Old Testament. 593, 3360
Old, old story of the Holy child. 1969
Old, old tales from the old, old Book. 297
Old order Amish of Lancaster county. 2407
Old Oxford and her families. 2736, 3242
Old Paramus Reformed Church in Ridgewood, New Jersey, the years 1725-1975. 2736, 3237
Old paths. 3137, 3300, 3344, 3661, 3662
Old plantation hymns. 2680
Old Portuguese Vida de Sam Bernardo. 193
Old Pratham church. 2461
Old Presbyterian meeting house at Alexandria, Virginia. 24
Old priest and new presbyter. 1213
Old priest remembers, 1892-1978. 1302, 3401
Old principles and the new order. 3450
Old Protestantism and the new. 3036
Old Puritanism and the new age. 3008
... The old Rabbinic doctrine of God. 1724, 2115
Old Redstone. 2927
Old Reformation and the new. 3035
Old religion in the brave new world. 1109
... An old St. Andrews music book. 2634
Old St. Andrews music book (Cod. Helmst. 628) 2634
Old Saint Augustine's in Philadelphia. 111, 2830
Old St. Patrick's. 2700
Old St. Paul's in Narragansett. 3814
...Old St. Peter's. 2700
Old Salem Church. 3286
Old Sands street Methodist Episcopal church, of Brooklyn, N.Y. An illustrated centennial record, historical and biographical. 694
Old seed on new ground. 3436
Old Shaketown and the Shakers. 3396
Old sins in new clothes. 3411
Old South Carolina churches. 1274
Old South church. 684
Old South Congregational Church. 1788
Old Spain in new America. 2527
Old stone church. 1846
Old story for this new day. 166
Old story of salvation. 3289
Old Swedes church, Wilmington, Delaware, 1698-1938. 3818
Old Sycamore church and some other things. 3125
Old tabernacle theology for New Testament times. 3646
Old tales retold from Grecian mythology in talks around the fire. 2663
Old Testament. 484, 497, 498, 499, 501, 513, 538, 539, 540, 541, 552, 566, 574, 59 f 596, 597, 602, 2599
Old Testament: a guide to its writings. 541
Old Testament against its environment. 599
Old Testament, always relevant. 539
Old Testament, an introduction, including the Apocrypha and Pseudepigrapha, and also the works of similar type from Qumran. 539
Old Testament and after. 501, 3015
Old Testament and Apocrypha. 591
Old Testament and Christian faith. 1589
Old Testament and Jesus Christ. 451, 2045
... The Old Testament and modern discovery. 514
Old Testament and modern life. 3338
Old Testament and modern problems in psychology. 501
Old Testament and modern study. 502
Old Testament and modern study; a generation of discovery and research. 502
Old Testament and our times. 596
Old Testament and Semitic studies in memory of William Rainey Harper. 1786
Old Testament and the archaeologist. 78, 486
Old Testament and the critics. 504
Old Testament and the fine arts. 535
Old Testament and the future life. 502
Old Testament and the historian. 532
Old Testament and the literary critic. 211, 501
Old Testament and the proclamation of the Gospel. 498

Old Testament and the world. 599, 3850, 3851
Old Testament and theology. 599
...The Old Testament and you. 3184
Old Testament Apocrypha. 491
Old Testament as it concerns women. 3839
Old Testament as the Book of Christ. 505, 676
Old Testament as Word of God. 515
Old Testament Bible lessons for the home. 3165
Old Testament Bible stories as a basis for the ethical instruction of the young. Rev. ed. 623
Old Testament biographies. 493, 494
Old Testament book. 539
Old Testament books for pastor and teacher. 492
Old Testament books of poetry from 26 translations. 591
Old Testament characters. 492
Old Testament commentary. 497
Old Testament, complete. 513
Old Testament covenant. 1377
Old Testament criticism. 499
Old Testament criticism and the Christian church. 500
Old Testament difficulties. 503, 3432
Old Testament dissertations. 492
Old Testament doctrine of salvation. 3289
Old Testament drama. 3144
Old Testament essays. 500
Old Testament exegesis. 530
Old Testament experience of faith. 536, 995
Old Testament for everyman. 592
Old Testament for learners. 535
Old Testament for modern readers. 597, 1395
Old Testament for new students. 533
Old Testament for us. 501, 2845
Old Testament form criticism. 498
Old Testament friends. 628
Old Testament from the modern point of view. 498
Old Testament from within. 500
Old Testament gospel. 499
Old Testament Hebrew for beginners. 1797
Old Testament heritage. 539
Old testament heroes. 493
Old Testament heroes of the faith, and Other Old Testament character studies. 493
Old Testament history. 534, 535, 536, 629, 2096
... The Old Testament history, from the creation to the return of the Jews from captivity. 536
Old Testament illustrations. 537, 2150
Old Testament in art. 85, 567
Old Testament in Christian preaching. 537
Old Testament in contemporary preaching. 537
Old Testament in dialogue with modern man. 502, 1317
Old Testament in Greek. 528
Old Testament in Greek according to the Septuagint. 529
Old Testament in Greek according to the text of Codex vaticanus. 528
Old Testament in life and literature. 502
Old Testament in living pictures. 528, 2764
Old Testament in modern research. 504
Old Testament in the Book of Revelation. 464
Old Testament in the cross. 106
Old Testament in the Jewish church. 502
Old Testament in the life of today. 501
Old Testament in the light of anthropology. 514
Old Testament in the light of the ancient East. 78
Old Testament in the light of the historical records and legends of Assyria and Babylonia. 501
Old Testament in the light of to-day. 498
Old Testament in the New. 306, 588, 3721
Old Testament in the New Testament. 451
Old Testament in the Sunday school. 596
Old Testament institutions. 532
Old Testament introduction. 540
Old Testament issues. 485
Old Testament, its form and purpose. 540
Old Testament, its intent and content, including the Apocrypha. 539
Old Testament, its origins and composition. 505
Old Testament, its story and religious message. 597
Old Testament journey in faith. 597
Old Testament: keystone of human culture. 598, 599

Old Testament law for Bible students. 2201
Old Testament legends. 520, 2206
Old testament life and literature. 535, 540
Old Testament light. 497
...Old Testament literature. 501
Old Testament manuscripts in the Freer collection. 316, 2330
Old Testament messages of the Christ. 2050
Old Testament miniatures. 566, 1883
Old Testament narrative. 59 0
Old Testament narratives. 532, 590 :
Old Testament of the Jerusalem Bible. 513
Old Testament omnibus book. 591
Old Testament pictures and their storeis. 629
Old Testament pictures of New Testament truth. 3720
Old Testament portraits. 494
Old Testament printer. 533
Old Testament problem. 500
Old Testament problems. 579
Old testament prophecies as fulfilled in the gospels. 389
... Old Testament prophecy. 569
Old Testament prophets. 570, 571, 2950
Old Testament prophets then and now. 2950
Old Testament reading guide. 596
Old Testament readings for schools. 592
Old Testament records, poems and addresses. 596
Old Testament religion in the light of its Canaanite background. 2115
Old Testament roots of our faith. 533, 598, 1737
Old Testament Sabbath. 498, 3261
Old Testament since the Reformation. 504, 505
Old Testament speaks. 534, 536
Old Testament stories. 319, 592, 628, 629, 630, 633
Old Testament stories for little children. 633
Old Testament stories in woodcut. 627
Old Testament stories selected for the children. 628
Old Testament stories, to the founding of the kingdom. 590
Old Testament story. 533, 534, 536, 597, 628
Old Testament story-land. 633
Old Testament studies. 498, 595, 597, 1426
Old Testament study guide. 595
Old Testament survey. 540, 596
Old Testament teaching. 658
Old Testament. The book of Ruth. 589
Old Testament theology. 598, 599
Old Testament theology: basic issues in the current debate. 598
Old Testament theology in outline. 599
Old Testament times. 533, 2678
Old Testament translation problems. 652
Old testament types and symbols. 3720
Old Testament under fire. 498
Old Testament understanding of God. 598, 1730
Old Testament view of revelation. 3227
Old Testament wisdom. 319, 3821
Old Testament without illusions. 500
Old Testament word studies. 498, 1517, 1797
Old Testament world. 2764
Old Testament writings. 539
Old Testment among the Semitic religions. 499
Old theology re-stated in sermons. 168
Old theology turned upside down or right side up. 3616
Old things new. 3353
Old thinking, new thinking. 3543
Old thoughts in new dress. 3669
Old Tiler talks. 1661
... The old time religion. 1059, 1557, 1589, 3229
Old time revival sermons. 1557
Old time student volunteers. 2484
Old trails and new. 2527
Old trails and new, true life stories of Baptist home mission fields. 2527
Old truths for a new day. 1266
Old truths newly illustrated. 3127
Old way. 3295
Old wine in new bottles. 993, 1313
Old world and the new. 2894
...The old world historical background of religious and moral education in schools. 3158
Olden Christmas from Marmion. 1113
Older children's Bible. 250
Older members in the congregation. 1257
Older people and the church. 3673
Older than Eden. 1603
Oldest Christian hymn-book. 492

Oldest Christian people. 2684
Oldest church in U.S., the San Miguel Chapel. 3302
Oldest church manual called the Teaching of the twelve apostles. 71
Oldest god. 3108
Oldest manuscript of the Vulgate Gospels. 398
Oldest parish in Canada. 48
Oldest stories in the world. 2654
Oldest story. 297
Oldest story in the world. 1384
Oldest text of the Gospels. 317
Olds Hall. 2736
Olga Worrall. 3852
Oliphant-Rice debate on 1. 2119
Olive Pell Bible. 251
Oliver Cromwell. 1389, 1764
Oliver Hart, 1723-1795. 1787
Oliver Hazard Perry and the battle of lake Erie. 2820
Olmec religion. 2736
Olney hymns, in three books. 1867
Olodumare. 3868
... Olympiad Bible lessons ... The whole Bible. 647
Olympos. 2656
OM. 2380
Om, creative meditations. 3483
Omega cometh. 1515
Omega Generation? 1514
Omega in symbols. 462
Omega, or The key to the kingdom of heaven. 1794
Omen series Summa izbu. 2736
Omission of the Holy Spirit from Reinhold Niebuhr's theology. 2709
Omnipotence of God. 1736
Omnipotent light revealed. 721
Omwa? 2513
On a Friday noon. 1998
On a hill far away. 2204
On a mountain trail. 971
On a slide of light. 2992
On active duty. 81
On almost everything. 759
On altogether beautiful. 2059
On and off the wagon. 2231
On Asia's rim. 2516
On authority and revelation. 7
On authority and revelation: The book on Adler. 7
On becoming a Baha'i. 128
On becoming a group. 1170
On becoming a musical, mystical bear. 2872
On becoming a widow. 1350
On becoming children of God. 3175
On becoming the truth. 2170
On becoming whole in Christ. 2269, 3476
On beginning from within. 3482
On beginning from within [and] On listening to another. 1675
On behalf of children. 1253
On being a Christian. 64, 973, 1095
On being a deacon's wife. 3831
On being a missionary. 2485
On being fit to live with. 3351
On being human. 2321, 2396, 3716
On being human religiously. 3619
On being present where you are. 1453
On being sure in religion. 3652
On being the church in the world. 1126
On being your best. 1461
On bended knee. 2881
On both sides of the equator. 2541
On bumping into God. 1722
On call. 1408, 1432
On caring. 887
On causation. 876
On charity. 2266
On Christian doctrine. 287
On Christianity. 1800
On cloud nine. 900
On common ground. 861, 2955
On consulting the faithful in matters of doctrine. 2191
On contemplating God. 2388
On doing good. 1685
On eagle wings. 168
On eagles' wings. 1286, 1511, 1785, 2505, 2567, 2622
On earth as it is in Heaven. 998
On earth peace. 2809
On final ground. 2434
On first principles. 2183
On free choice of the will. 1657
On Genesis. 522
On getting things done. 953
On God and man. 2912
On God and political duty. 2858
On God and society. 2858
On God's squad. 983, 1577
On-going pilgrimage. 3486
On good ground. 2545, 3419
On good soil. 3253
On growing old. 18

On growing old gracefully. 2735
On guard. 3456
On Hegel's critique of Kant. 1800
On heresy. 1805
On holy ground. 252, 2763, 2914
On Holy Scripture and criticism. 201
On Indian Mahayana Buddhism. 2317, 2867
On Jewish law and lore. 2074
On Jewish learining. 2087
On Jordan's stormy banks. 1108
On Judaism. 2141
On knowing God. 1734
On knowing reality. 3867
On learning Chassidus. 1789
On life after death. 1887
On life and death. 2225
On life, and essays on religion. 2228
On life's highway. 1446
On listening to another. 1675
On living with yourself. 958
On Lonely Street with God. 2244
On loving God, and selections from sermons. 595, 1742
On marriage. 2336
On marriage, sex, and virginity. 2344
On memory's beam, the autobiography of Elbert A. Smith. 3135
On miracles and modern spiritualism. 3517
On missions. 2494
On morning trails. 2389
On mule back through Central America with the gospel. 2507
On Nazareth hill. 2761
On new creation. 1062
On not leaving it to the snake. 1065
On nurturing Christians. 936
On our Father's knee. 3407
On our own doorstep. 2524
On our way rejoicing! 1853, 2498
On Pascha and fragments. 2034, 3368
On paths of destiny. 2519, 2520
On paths of holiness. 771
On paths unknown. 3856
On Paul and John. 376
On pilgrimage. 959
On prayer. 2249, 2869, 2879, 3368
On prayer; nine sermons. 2249
On prayers to the dead. 2868
On preaching. 2898
On predestined terms of life. 2912
On promoting the sanctity of the priestly life. 771
On proving God. 1737
On recent developments of the social question in the light of Christian teaching. 1137
On religion. 3061, 3063, 3308, 3669
On religious maturity. 3056
On roads to the healing Christ. 1599
On royal and papal power. 2863
On runways of love. 2504
On sacrifice. 3271
On sandals of peace. 2492, 2493
On selfhood and Godhood. 3462
On solid granite. 3274
On some of life's ideals. 1535
On speaking out of the silence. 2790
On spiritual creatures. 3694
On suffering. 3541
On sure foundations. 1219
On synthesizing Marxism and Christianity. 1319
On taking God out of the dictionary. 3617
On taming the tongue. 113
On target. 1841
On teaching the Bible as literature. 210
On terms of communion. 1304
On the adaptation of external nature to the physical condition of man. 2673
On the adnominal genitive. 2199
On the apocalyptic in Judaism. 56
On the authorized version of the New Testament in connection with some recent proposals for its revision. 361
On the battle lines. 1065
On the benevolence and rectitude of the Supreme Being. 3616
On the Bible. 484
On the border of Bhutan. 2503
On the boundary. 3625
On the bridge. 725
On the China road. 2510
On the Christian faith. 1054
On the Christian faith; selections from the Institutes, Commentaries, and Tracts. 1054
On the church of Christ. 1121
On the connection between geology and the Pentateuch. 204
On the constitution of the church and state according to the idea of each. 1146
On the cosmic relations. 2989
On the crest of the present. 2921
On the cross. 2778

On the dangers of modern spiritualism. 3504
On the dedications of American churches. 1275
On the diversity of morals. 1323
On the divine images. 1881
On the Dragon Hills. 2510
On the edge of decision. 2498
On the edge of the absurd. 1008
On the edge of the primeval forest. 2194, 2523
On the edge of the primeval forest & More form the primeval forest. 2523, 3312
On the eightfold path. 706
... On the epiclesis of the eucharistic liturgy and in the consecration of the font. 2257
On the eternal in man. 2837
On the evaluation of verbal material in parapsychology. 3520
On the eve of Arageddon. 1514
On the eve of Armageddon. 1514, 3756
On the evils of a weak government. 1504
On the firing line with the Sunday-school missionary. 2528
On the formation of the Christian character. 978
On the government of God. 2982, 2983
On the ground floor of heaven. 1300, 2942
On the growing edge of the Church. 2555
On the highway. 314, 643
On the Holy Spirit. 1835
On the imagination. 1884
On the incarnation. 1894
On the independence of Matthew and Mark. 444
On the inspiration of Scripture. 305
On the Kabbalah and its symbolism. 722
On the King's highway. 1014, 3420, 3524
On the knowledge of good and evil. 1746
On the love of God. 1741, 2266
On the mark! 975
On the meaning of Christ. 1120, 2059
On the miraculous and internal evidences of the Christian revelation. 1098
On the misery of the human condition. 2323
On the mission in Missouri. 1822
On the mission in Missouri, 1857-1868. 822, 1294, 1822
On the move with the Master. 2540
On the mythological. 2649
On the nature of man in Telfer,On the nature of man in Telfer. 3132
On the nature of the universe. 98
On the nature of universal cross-action. 2044
On the other side. 806
...On the parables of Our Lord. 2028
On the path. 2694
On the phenomena of modern spiritualism. 3504
On the power. 2672
On the power of God (Quaestiones disputatae de potentia Dei) 1736
On the power, wisdom, and goodness of God. 2672
On the power, wisdom and goodness of God, as manifested in the creation of animals, and in their history, habits and instincts. 2673
On the preacher and preaching. 2908
On the preparation and delivery of sermons. 2898
On the psychology of meditation. 2382
On the reformation of theology. 1052
On the relation between the Holy Scriptures and some parts of geological science. 203
On the resolution of science and faith. 3080
On the rite of consecration of churches, especially in the Church of England. 1165
On the road to Christian unity. 1491
On the road to happiness. 3885
On the road to renewal ... breakthrough. 759
On the road to Rome. 1365, 3235
On the road to spiritual wholeness. 3483
On the road to theocracy, divine government. 3609
On the road to Zion. 3897
On the rock. 3126
On the rubble of renewal. 788
On the run. 3488
On the sacraments. 3262
On the sacraments of the Christian faith (De sacramentis) English version. 3266
On the sacred liturgy. 837
On the Shantung front. 2546
On the sociology of Islam. 3454
On the solitary life. 2570
On the Songs of Songs. 595, 3368
On the sunrise slope. 870
On the teachings of chassidus. 1789

On the theology of death. 1414
On the theology of work. 3849
On the third day. 2054
On the threshold of the unseen. 3495
On the throne of sin. 3514
On the throne of the world. 2981
On the trail of God. 1367
On the trail of Livingstone. 2499
On the trail of Moses. 1555
On the trail of the peacemakers. 2807
On the trail of truth. 3131
On the trail on the UCC. 3732
On the trial of Jesus. 2069
On the truth of the Catholic faith. 69
On the two cities. 2173
On the value of church history. 1174
On the various kinds of distinctions. 2739
On the virtues, in general. 3782
On the way. 980, 2279, 2397
On the way to Bethlehem. 2762
On the way to Emmaus. 2006, 2415
On the way to Hwai Yuen. 2508
On the way to immortality and eternal life. 2610
On the way to the future. 1529
On the way to the sanctuary. 773
On the way to their first Communion. 1627
On the wing. 3418
On the wings of a butterfly. 935
On the witness stand, He who was now is. 2051
On the work of the ministry in university communities. 3757
On this bluff ... Centennial history. 1370
On this day. 172
On this foundation. 1908, 2979
On this rock. 1041, 2065
On this side of Jordan. 3138
On time and being. 2738
On tiptoe with joy. 139
On to China! 2509
On to Christ. 1061
On to maturity. 974
On to orthodoxy. 62
On toward the goal. 2934
On translating the Bible. 655
On translations of the Bible. 270
On trial. 2214
On trying to be human. 2323
On understanding Human sexuality. 3393
On waking up. 1881
On what authority? 951
On what day did Christ die? 1986
On what there must be. 2738
On whom the spirit came. 332
On wings of adventure. 821
On wings of eagles. 2863
On wings of faith. 1589, 2482, 2483
On wings of fire. 2076, 2198
On wings of healing. 3406
On wings of love. 2479
On wings of prayer. 2870
On wings of the Word. 612
On witchcraft, being The wonders of the invisible world. 3827
On women & Judaism. 3838
On Yoga. 3864
On your mark. 1605
On Zen practice. 3494
On Zion. 2118, 3896
Onak and the talkingbox. 2544
Onarchy. 1141
Once a carpenter. 1962
Once a thief. 1367, 3307
Once & future church: a communion of freedom. 808
Once and the future liturgy. 2235
Once in Cornwall, being an account of Friar Peter's journey in search of the saint and dragon legends of the land. 3283
Once--in Palestine. 1960
Once in royal David's city. 2022
Once, long ago. 628
Once more around Jericho. 3737
Once more astonished. 2025
Once saved ... always saved. 2822
Once there was a little boy. 2005
Once there was a nun. 2306
Once there were three. 1350, 1783
Once there were two churches. 1321
Once through the New Testament. 410
Once to every man. 1301, 1305
Once upon a lifetime. 3166
"Once upon a time" 1945
Once-upon-a-time Bible stories. 621
Once upon a time, God. 64
Once upon a time in Assisi. 1639
Once-upon-a-time saints. 1025
Once upon a tree. 1997
Once you start climbing-don't look down. 2685
Ondell and Dolee. 2638
One and apostolic. 1200
One and holy. 861, 2272, 2954
One and only you. 1011

One and the many in the Israelite conception of God. 1731
One and the same spirit. 3487
I and II Esdras. 488
One angel more in heaven. 1352
One another. 349, 971, 1621
One bad dude. 931, 1939
One baptism. 135, 136, 138
One baptism for the remission of sins. 136, 138, 2298
One blood. 2475
One body and one spirit. 1163
One body, one gospel, one world. 3610
One book. 236
One bread. 2253
One bread, one body. 2253
One bride. 3781
One Christ. 1249
One Christ, one world, one church. 1491
One church. 1039, 1491, 1492, 3732
One church: Catholic and Reformed. 1492
One church for one world. 3765
... The one-column edition of the Bible-workers' four Gospels according to Matthew, Mark, Luke, and St. John. 382
One cut in 206. 1041
... One destiny. 2117
One faith. 1516, 3624
One faith and fellowship. 43
One family under God. 1153
One fine hour. 2060
One fold. 879, 2794
One fold and one shepherd. 678, 1042
One fold and the only door. 1696
"One fold, one shepherd" 791
One foot in heaven. 3471
One foot in the cradle. 3136
One foot on the land. 3254
One for Wod and one for Lok. 2665
One generation and another. 1603
One girl's influence. 41
One God. 1720, 3853
One God, a commentary on the first part of St. Thomas' Theological summa. 3696
One God in one person only. 3713
One God in Trinity. 3713
One God, one country, one church. 3382
One God, one world. 1057
One gospel. 400, 1988
...One gospel for mankind. 2522
One gospel for one world. 1179
One great church. 1071
One great fellowship. 3358
One great ground of hope. 1045
One hand upon another. 3293
One hundred years for God and county, county. 3273
Harmony of the Gospels in the Knox translation. 396
One heart, one vote. 1013
One holy catholic apostolic church. 1200
One home under God. 1610
One hour with Him. 857
188 heart-reaching sermon outlines. 3373
One hundred and fiftieth anniversary of the founding of the Church of Christ at Dartmouth college. 1403
150th anniversary of the organization of the First church of Christ in Pomfret, Conn., October 26, 1865. 1269
150 biographical illustrations. 3374
150 epic years: Detroit Lodge No. 2, Free and Accepted Masons. 1663
150 great hymns in the English language. 1868
150 topical sermon outlines on Romans. 3373
150 topical sermon outlines on Christ. 3373
One hundred and fifty years. 2586
One hundred and fifty years of Presbyterianism in the Ohio valley, 1790-1940. 2918
105 days with John. 417
105 modern parables for young folks. 908
... One hundred and five years by faith. 683
140th anniversary. 673
140 stories for the children's hour. 910
149th, 150th and 151st annual reports of the Board of elders of the Moravian congregation of Bethlehem, Pa. 2594
114 ways to the mission field. 2484
101 devotional Bible reading containing what might be called the heart and soul of the Bible. 241
101 eye-catching objects. 909
101 hymn stories. 1872
101 inspirational poems that cheer the soul. 3207
One hundred and one Methodist stories. 2459
101 outline studies on questions asked and answered by Our Lord. 2061
101 prayers for peace. 2807
101 proofs that the Bible is true. 276

101 saints. 3281
101 select sermon outlines by Vaughan. 3374
101 snappy sermonettes for the children's church. 907
101 things for adult Bible classes to do. 644
101 ways to raise money for your church. 1168
101 Zen stories. 3894
... 175th anniversary of the First Congregational church, Meriden, Conn. 1336
175 simple sermon outlines. 3374
106 sermon outlines. 3373
110 helps for teachers. 940
One hundred & ten miracles of Our Lady Mary. 2360
139 sermon outlines on the Old Testament. 593
One hundred aphorisms of Sandilya. 197
One hundred best sermons for special days and occasions. 3364
100 better ideas for children's workers. 3156
100 Bible quiz activities for church school classes. 281
One hundred Bible stories. 532
One hundred Bible stories in the words of Holy Scripture. 618
One hundred Bible stories in the words of Holy Scripture (King James version) 618
One hundred cases for survival after death. 3494
100 chapel talks. 3758
One hundred chapel-talks to theological students. 1072
One hundred choice sermons for children. 3352
100 devotions for boys and girls. 902
One hundred eighth annual meeting, Friday-Tuesday, 1-5 September, 1972. 229
One hundred fifteen years of churchmanship. 3723
One hundred fiftieth anniversary of the founding of New Brunswick theological seminary. 2686
150 ideas for activities with senior adults. 1257
One hundred fifty years. 1550, 2735
100 great religious poems. 3207
100 Huntley Street. 2318, 2817
One hundred hymns you ought to know. 1865
One hundred illustrated sermons. 1841
One hundred lessons in Bible study. 639
One hundred more three-minute sermons. 3340
One hundred one-minute sermons. 3346
One hundred one questions about Freemasonry. 1662
One hundred prayer meeting talks and plans. 2886
One hundred projects for the church school. 2946
100 question about God. 1740
100 questions Jesus asked. 2072
One hundred responsive readings from the Scriptures. 252
100 select gospel hymns from Gospel hymns consolidated. 3231
One hundred sermons. 3375
One hundred seventeen object lessons for boys and girls. 2720
One hundred seventh annual meeting seminar papers 28-31 October 1971, Regency Hyatt House, Atlanta, Ga. 229
One hundred short prayers. 2891
One hundred short sermons for the people. 73
One hundred talks to teen-agers. 3885
100 things a choir member should know. 917
One hundred three-minute sermons. 3341
One hundred twenty-fifth anniversary. 2431
100 ways to improve your Sunday school teaching. 3557
One hundred years. 2926
One hundred years, 1846-1946, the Evangelical Congregational church, McKeesport, Pennsylvania. 1546
One hundred years: a masonic history of Eminence, Indiana. 1664
100 years Baptist witness in Llandrindod Wells, 1876[-]1976. 154
One hundred years for God and country. 3275
One hundred years in Christ. 2693
100 years in Excelsior. 1583
One hundred years in St. James Parish, 1844-1920. 1523
One hundred years in the heart of Zion. 3287
One hundred years in the New World. 1023

One years of achievement and challenge. 2719
One hundred years of challenge and change. 3736
100 years of emancipation. 2681
One hundred years of fellowship and service. 3875
100 years of freethought. 1657
One hundred years of history. 133
One hundred years of Mormonism. 2615
One hundred years of Mount Vernon church, 1842-1942. 684
One hundred years of New Madrid Methodism. 2457, 2693
One hundred years of Old Testament interpretation. 504
One hundred years of organized work in the Badger State, 1856-1956; Wisconsin Conference centennial. 1550
One hundred years of St. Boniface parish, Louisville, Kentucky. 2261
One hundred years of service. 692
One hundred years of service, 1854--1954. 1426
One hundred years of the Methodist Episcopal church, Franklin Grove, Lee county, Illinois, 1836-1936. 1651
One hundred years of Trinity. 3714
One hundred years of Welsh Calvinistic Methodism in America. 730
One hundred years serving Christ in Greeley. 1550
One hundred years with "Old Trinity" church. 2669
100 years, Saint John's Parish in Dover, New Jersey, 1849-1949. 1477
One hundredth anniversary. 2688
100th anniversary, 1861-1961, St. Paul of the Cross Church, Dayton, New York. 2700
One hundredth anniversary exercises of the Baptist church, Flemington, N.J. June 17th, 18th and 19th, 1898. 2688
One hundredth anniversary of the First Presbyterian society in the village of Syracuse, 1824-1924. 2700
One hundredth anniversary of the Haystack prayer meeting. 2518
One hundredth anniversary of the organization of the First Congregational church, Keeseville, N.Y. 2700
One hundreth anniversary of the diocese of Maine. 2967
One immortal being. 3054
One in Christ. 2019, 2955, 3163
...One in seven. 975
One in the Lord. 1255, 3734
One in the spirit. 1833
One inch from the fence. 2396
One inch of splendor. 2510
One increasing purpose. 2270
One is a whole number. 3415
One is not a lonely number. 3415
One kind of religion. 3106
One life in Christ. 2305, 3417
One life isn't enough. 2437
One life to live. 1005
One life's pilgrimage. 3491
One little candle. 2741
One little goat. 3459
One Lord. 1492, 2612
One Lord, one baptism. 1042
One Lord, one church, one world. 1069, 2515
One Lord, one faith. 476, 788, 2009
One man and God. 3126
One man's destiny. 45
One man's Judaism. 2751
One man's religion. 1052, 1343
One man's story. 1302, 3307
One man's testimony. 3127
One man's views. 3137
One man's way. 2809
One mark of greatness. 156
One mark of greatness: American Baptist missions. 156
One mediator, a fourfold revelation. 398
One merrie Christmas-time. 1113
One mile from Trinity. 1804
One minute with God. 2391
One moment please! 1440
One moment with God. 1438
One mystic. 3127
One nation under God. 3740
One nun to another. 2573
One of a kind. 3801
One of the Jesuits! 1288, 1947
One-on-one evangelism. 1566
One only Christ. 2019
One people. 2787
One people among many. 232
One prophet--and another. 2950
One race, one gospel, one task. 1573
One rehearsal pageants for the church. 2757
One religion: many creeds. 3065
One saint and seven sinners. 1303

One scientist's religion. 3077
One season following another. 1263
One shall chase a thousand. 2534
One shepherd. 1039
One shepherd, one flock. 1363
One shepherded. 1363
One sky to share. 3124
One small circle. 1605
One sovereign life. 1960
One step and then another. 1645
One step enough. 1002
One story. 623, 1990, 2052
One talent improved. 686
One thing I know. 1360
One thing needful. 1403, 2205, 2931
1000 and 1 Bible questions and answers. 643
1001 illustrations for pulpit and platform. 1842
One thousand-and-one lives. 662
1,001 questions and answers about Judaism. 2146
1001 sentence sermons. 3374
1,001 sermon illustrations and quotations. 1841
1001 stories for children and children's workers. 1014
One thousand and one thoughts from my library. 1440, 2393
1010 illustrations, poems and quotes. 3208
1010 illustrations, poems, and quotes. 3208
1010 sermon illustrations from the Bible. 1842
1,029 private prayers for worldly Christians. 2894
One thousand best Bible verses. 252
1,000 Bible drill questions. 218
One thousand Bible readings. 614
1000 Bible study outlines. 646
1000 city churches. 1278
1,000 difficult Bible questions answered. 281
One thousand evangelistic illustrations. 1842
1041 sermon ilustrations, ideas, and expositions. 1841
1000 keys to the truth. 3473
1000 mythological characters briefly described. 2659
1,000 new illustrations. 1839, 1842
1,000 plans and ideas for Sunday school workers. 3554
One thousand questions and answers concerning the Methodist Episcopal church. 2443
1000 questions and answers on Catholicism. 790, 3012
One thousand radio voices for Christ. 2300
One thousand subjects for speakers and students. 640
1010 sermon illustrations from the Bible. 1842
One thousand thoughts for funeral occasions. 1692
1,000 threefold Scriptural outlines. 3372
One thousand years of peace and happiness. 46
One to eight. 1574
One to one. 1257, 3830
One true magick. 2313
... i. ii. and iii. John, Jude, and Revelation. 367
1, 2, 3, and more. 901
1, 2, 3 John. 369
One vision only. 2187
One volume New Testament commentary. 344
One way. 354, 3288, 3497
One way for modern man. 414
One way of hope. 3442
One way streets. 3888
One way: the Jesus movement and its meaning. 2072
One way to change the world. 1058
One week with a modern missionary. 2538, 3386
One who listens. 2885, 2891
One who was valiant. 2606, 3869
One wide river. 2261
One with Christ in glory. 424
One with Jesus. 2637
One witness in one world. 1249
One woman's fight. 1150
One woman's liberation. 681, 931
One woman's life. 3127
One woman's mission and how she fulfilled it. 1458
One world a building. 2491
One world and one God. 1039
One world at a time. 3728
One world, one Lord, one witness. 147
One world, one mission. 2493
One world under God. 695

One year of Sunday school lessons for young children. 3556
One year with God. 3342
One yet two. 1276, 2583
One you can become. 1007
Oneg Shabbat manual. 3261
Oneg Shabbath book. 3261
Oneida community. 2737
Oneida Community profiles. 2737
Oneida: Utopian community to modern corporation. 2737
O'Neill's Catholic directory of Illinois. 779
Oneness motif in the fourth gospel. 418, 2010
Oneness with Christ. 342
Ongoing journey. 3839
Ongoing reform of the church. 1246
Ongoing revision. 949
... Only a mask. 1079
Only a missionary. 156
Only a profession, and other sermons. 1051
Only a woman. 3843
Only answer. 3896
Only believe. 2396
Only church with a history like this. 1178
Only dance there is. 1348
Only don't know. 3197
Only God can prophesy! 607
Only hope. 3382, 3519
Only in Africa. 2498
Only Jesus. 1999
Only key to Daniel's prophecies. 508, 2946
Only life. 3489
Only love. 3480
Only on the threshold. 1843
Only one heart. 2867
Only one true church? 800
Only possible road to peace. 2465
Only Son. 1964
Only true God. 203
Only two religions and other Gospel papers. 1069
Only way out. 2807
Only way to deliverance. 2382, 3304
Ontological argument. 1739
Ontological argument, from St. Anselm to contemporary philosophers. 1739
Ontological commitment. 2739
Ontological reduction. 1672, 2738
Ontology. 2737, 2738, 2739
Ontology of Paul Tillich. 2740, 3700
Ontology, or the theory of being. 2738
... Onward and upward. 725, 1203, 3888
Onward and upward, no. 2. 1202
Onward and upward to a more abundant life. 1008
Onward Christian soldier. 3133
Onward to Christ. 3337
Opaqueness of God. 1733
Open-air churches of sixteenth-century Mexico. 1160
Open Bible. 2085
Open book. 3184
Open book to the Christian divorcee. 1471
Open Church. 3770
Open church door, for bringing more people to the church. 1250
Open circle. 695
Open communion shown to be unscriptural and deleterious. 1304
Open door. 2060, 2225, 2454, 2928, 2973, 3216, 3684
Open door book. 1252
Open door of the soul. 3461
Open door to heaven. 1794
Open door to Korea. 2537
Open door to peace and happiness. 3880
Open doors. 1705, 3751
Open doors in crisis. 1342
Open doors in religious education. 3159
Open education goes to church. 940
Open encounter. 797
Open end of Christian morals. 951
Open gate to prayer. 2881
Open grave. 1423
Open heart. 973
Open heaven. 56
Open letter to Evangelicals. 324
Open letter to His Eminence Cardinal Gibbons. 1145, 1711
Open letter to Jews and Christians. 2013, 2117
Open letter to the Rt. Rev. William C. Doane. 694
Open me the gates. 2386
Open mystery. 565
Open path. 2525
Open pearly gates. 235
Open secret. 1371, 2480, 3891
Open secret of Nazareth. 177
Open secrets. 2193
Open spirit. 682
Open the door! 1695

Open the door to the Bible. 636, 1169
Open the frontiers. 792
Open the meeting with prayer. 2890, 2891
Open then the door. 2573
Open thy mouth for the dumb! 1073, 1426
Open to the Spirit. 2571
Open to the world. 3484
Open vision. 2988
Open windows. 1451, 2549
Open your Bible to the New Testament letters. 368
Open your mind to prosperity. 3539
Opened seals--open gates. 453
Opened treasures. 1439
Opening and closing ceremony and initiation of candidates in temple courts of the Grand united order of Toussaint L'Ouverture, Samuel unity, mystic rites and brotherhood of Ethiopia, compiled by Samuel E. Hinds. 2576
Opening door. 3495
Opening doors. 2913
Opening doors of childhood. 3172
Opening doors of faith. 3174
Opening of the book of life. 1696
Opening of the door. 3498
Opening of the House. 2208
Opening of the sixth seal. 465
Opening of the wisdom eye. 709
Opening of the wisdom-eye and the history of the advancement of Buddhadharma in Tibet. 710
Opening roads; addresses for young people. 906
Opening the Bible. 311
Opening the door for God. 3165
Opening the door of faith. 1566
Opening the New Testament. 409
Opening the treasures. 864, 3355
Opening to God. 1442, 2872
Openings for Marxist-Christian dialogue. 1319
Openings into ministry. 1297
Openings to understandings. 3186
Openness and freedom. 993
Openness mind. 2382
Openness of being. 2673
Openness of God. 1737
Opera. 2083, 3634
Opera omnia. 2633, 3635
Opera omnia. Secundem impressionem Petri Fiaccadori Parmae 1852-1873, photolithographice reimpressa cum nova introductione generali, Anglice scripta a Vernon J. Bourke. 783
Opera quae supersunt omnia. 3629
Operating ratios in the YMCA. 3875
Operation and management of the local Young men's Christian association. 3871
Operation Brother's Brother. 1816
Operation Evangelism. 1572
Operation theology. 1065
Operational guide for the development of center-based instructional programs in adult education for local school systems. 8
Opinion of Dow. 2428
Opinions concerning the Bible law of marriage. 2338
Opinions on church music. 1208
Opium of the people. 3257
Opportunities for belief and behavior. 760
Opportunities for faith. 3624

Opportunities in Catholic religious vocations. 773
Opportunities in Jewish religious vocations. 3015
Opportunities in Protestant religious vocations. 1296
Opportunities in religious service. 1252
Opportunities in stewardship for concerned Christians in a local church. 3529
Opportunities in the path of the Great Physician. 2539
Opportunity at Oberammergau. 2719
Opportunity for faith. 1057
Opportunity for religion in the present world situation. 3064
Opportunity for tomorrow. 2959
... Opportunity is yours. 1325
Opportunity of Congregationalism. 1344
Opposition to the English Separatists, 1570-1625. 1469
Oppositions of religious doctrines. 3114
Oppression. 2820
Oppression of Protestants in Spain. 2979
Optimism and pessimism in the Old and New Testaments. 233, 601
Optimism of pre-millennialism. 2465
Optimism the lesson of ages. 3609
Optional God. 1056
Options. 3169
Options: approaches for the religious education of adolescents. 3169

Options in contemporary Christian ethics. 943
Options in contemporary theology. 3657
Opunvkv hera, Cane coyvte. 1386
Opunvkv-herv Luk coyvtc. 1386
Opunvkv-herv Mak coyvte. 1771
Opus Dei. 3436
Opus epistolarum Des. Erasmi Roterdami. 1526
Or else, the lightning god & other stories. 3200
Or, The Book of Jasher. 565
Oracle. 3496
Oracle of Baalbek. 3405
Oracle of Fortuna. 1470
Oracle of geomancy. 1706
Oracle of Tarot in Qabalah. 3588
Oracle of the Lord. 2951
Oracles. 724
Oracles and demons of Tibet. 3699
Oracles and divination. 2740
Oracles in the New Testament. 349
Oracles of God. 306, 569, 3211
Oracles of Nostradamus. 2715, 2716, 2949
Oracles of Zeus. 3895
Oracles of Zeus: Dodona, Olympia, Ammon. 3895
Oral. 1297, 3241
Oral debate on the coming of the Son of man, endless punishment, and universal salvation. 3320
Oral discussion of spiritualism. 3496
Oral formulaic language in the Biblical psalms. 577
Oral interpretation of Biblical literature. 210, 613
Oral law. 2075
Oral reading of the Scriptures. 211, 613
Oral Roberts' best sermons and stories. 1559
Oral Roberts' best sermons and stories, as presented in his great evangelistic campaigns around the world. 1560
Oral Roberts' life story. 1575
Oral Roberts reader. 1560
Oral Roberts scrapbook. 1301, 3241
Oral tradition. 2740
Oral writing. 2901
Oration: delivered, by appointment. 1662
Oration on death, and the happiness of the separate state. 1695
Oration on the gods. 1907
Oration, pronounced on the twenty-fifth of December, 1835, on the character, nature and attributes of Jesus Christ, in the Second Baptist meeting house, of Philadelphia. 1952, 2019
Orations of Demosthenes. 1771
Orations of Henry Austin Adams. 1918, 2702
Orations of St. Athanasius against the Arians according to the Benedictine text. 80
Oratory and poetry of the Bible. 603
Orb of day. 3106
Orbit of ashes. 3320
Orbits of life. 1058
Orcherd of Syon. 2646
Orchids and edelweiss. 1443
Ordained of the Lord, H. A. Ironside. 1920
Ordeal at Lourdes. 2262
Ordeal by concordance. 1790, 1800
Ordeal of faith. 3739
Ordeal of life. 3503
Ordeal of western religion. 3443
Ordeal of wonder. 1599
Order. 2740
Order for the burial of the dead. 2969
Order for the celebration of vespers, matins, and the divine liturgy. 766
Order, goodness, glory. 3083
Order of assassins. 92
Order of family prayer. 1605
Order of future events. 606
Order of Lutheran worship. 2295
Order of prayer for divine service. 2108
Order of St. Francis, its spirit and its mission in the kingdom of God. 1645
Order of St. John of Jerusalem (past and present) 2179
Order of service with the heidelberg Catehism. 3047
Order of the gospel, professed and practised by the churches of Christ in New England. 2687
Order of the Hospital of St. John of Jerusalem. 1755
Order of the Red Cross of Constantine. 1668
Order of worship for the Reformed church. 3047
Order out of chaos. 3141
Order your crowns now. 985
Ordered love. 2737, 3392
Orders for ministerial acts. 1705

Orders of service and ministerial acts of the Norwegian Luthern church. 2715
Orders of service and ministerial acts of the Norwegian Lutheran church. 2295
Ordinal. 2969
Ordinal and service book for use in courts of the church. 1234
Ordinals of Christ from their origins to the twelfth century. 2742
Ordinances and sacraments of the church. 3267
Ordinances of the Bible. 2201
Ordinarily sacred. 1836
Ordinary becomes extraordinary. 2436, 3353
Ordinary days with an extraordinary God. 2625
Ordinary Episcopal ceremonies. 842, 843
Ordinary man's religion. 642
Ordinary of the mass. 2365
Ordinary of the mass and a complete manual of hymns for parochial schools. 813
Ordinary saint. 1029, 2685
Ordinary way. 1609
Ordination, a biblical-historical view. 2741
Ordination and Christian unity. 1241
Ordination anointings in the western church before 1000 A.D. 2741
Ordination of a subdeacon, a deacon, a priest. 848
Ordination of deacons, priests, and bishops. 2741
Ordination of women ; an essay on the office of Christian ministry. 2742
Ordination of women--pro and con. 2742
Ordination of women to the pastorate in Baptist churches. 2742
Ordination retreat. 2741
Ordination to the priesthood. 2741
Ordo opus Dei peragendi Missasque celebrandi in ecclesiis et qratoriis Congregationis Americano-Cassinensis, O. S. B. Jussu superiorum. 837
Le oreficerie gotiche e rinascimentali del tesoro della Basilica di Santa Maria Gloriosa dei Frari. 1240
Oregon missions and travels over the Rocky Mountains in 1845-46. 1902, 3426
Oremus. 2238, 2297
Orestes A. Brownson. 697, 2832
Orestes Brownson and the American Republic. 697
Orestes Brownson, Yankee, radical, Catholic. 697
Orestos A. Brownson. 697
Organ accompaniment of the church services. 1234
Organ and choir in Protestant worship. 1209
Organ notes of dawn. 1447
Organic alchemy. 3483
Organic thinking. 2115
Organics: the law of the breathing spiral. 2725
Organisation for adult education. 8
Organist and choirmaster. 915
Organist and hymn playing. 2743
Organist and the choirmaster. 1202
Organized Sunday-school work in America, 1911-1914. 3559
Organization. 3386
Organization & administration of pastoral counseling centers. 2782
... Organization and administration of religious education. 3159
Organization and administration of the adult department. 8
... The organization and administration of the church school. 1246
Organization and administration of the minor seminary. 3613
... The organization and administration of the Sunday school. 3553
Organization and leadership in the local church. 1199
Organization and methods of mission work. 2518
Organization and platform of principles of the Association of Spiritualists. 3494
Organization and program of a young men's industrial club. 3871
Organization executive course. 3314
Organization of labor and association. 1636
Organization of medieval Christianity. 1185
Organization of personality. 3151
Organization of the church. 772, 807
Organization of the early Christian churches. 1240, 1241
Organization of the Methodist Church. 2440
Organization of the Methodist Church; historic development and present working structure. Rev. ed. 2440

Organization of the United Methodist Church. 3734
Organizational change; the political economy of the YMCA. 3874
Organizational climates and careers. 829, 2733
Organize to evangelize. 1567
Organized adult Bible class. 3552
Organized anti-Semitism in America. 2105
Organized Christianity. 1041
Organized class. 3168
Organized for action. 1251
Organized miracles. 918
Organized religion. 3091
Organized religion and the older person. 18
Organized religion and the older person. Gainesville, 1958. 18
Organized Sunday school. 3551
Organized Sunday school work in North America, 1918-1922. Official report of the sixteenth International Sunday school convention. 3561
Organized Sunday-school work in America, 1905-1908. 3561
Organized Sunday-school work in America, 1908-1911. 3559
... Organizing and building up the Sunday school. 3554
Organizing for human rights. 2681
Organizing the church school. 3553
Organizing the local church for effective lay visitation evangelism. 1565
Organizing the smaller Sunday school. 3552
Organizing to beat the Devil. 2460
Organon of Scripture. 287
Organs of All Souls Church, Langham Place, London and St. Peter's Church, Vere Street, London. 3278
Organum quaternii. 95
Oriens Christianus. 1487
... Orient. 1068
Orient in American transcendentalism. 1510, 3708
... The Orient steps out. 2550
Oriental Christ. 2024
Oriental customs. 221
Oriental ideas in recent religious thought. 91
Oriental Institute discoverie in Iraq, 1933 / 34. 894
... The Oriental institute of the University of Chicago. 894
Oriental land of the free. 2533
Oriental light illuminating Bible texts and Bible truths by means of pictures and illustrations that really illustrate, with descriptions and explanations of oriental objects of Bible manners and customs and everyday life in Palestine, and of the recent discoveries in Babylonia and Egypt which have shed a new and marvelous light on the Old Testament. 236
Oriental literature. 3114
Oriental magic. 2313
Oriental meditation. 3111
Oriental mysticism. 2644
Oriental mysticism and Biblical eschatology. 1080
Oriental mystics & magicians. 1485
Oriental philosophy. 2839
Oriental pilgrim. 2163
... Oriental religions. 3139
Oriental religions and American thought. 92
Oriental religions and their relation to universal religion. 913, 1896, 2822
Oriental religions in Roman paganism. 3114, 3246
Oriental rose. 2, 127
Oriental studies. 2650, 2743
Oriental thought. 2844
Oriental treasures. 3270
Orientation by disorientation. 179, 239
Orientation in religious education. 3190
...The orientation of the soul. 2696
Orientation to the town and country church; a discussion of United Presbyterian philosophy, organization, and methods. 3255
... Orientii Commonitorium, a commentary with an introduction and translation. 2199
Origen. 2743, 3635
...Origen and Greek patristic theology. 2743
Origen and his work. 2743
Origen and the Jews. 505, 2152, 2743
Origen of Alexandria's interpretation of the teacher's function in the early Christian hierarchy and community. 2743
Origin and annals of the "Old church on the green" 673

Origin and annals of "The Old south," 2701
Origin and character of the Bible and its place among sacred books. 312
Origin and character of the Bible, and its place among the world's sacred books. 312
Origin and destiny of humanness. 443
Origin and destiny of man. 2323, 3079
Origin and destiny of the moral species. 2321
Origin and development of early Christian churcharchitecture. 1160
Origin and development of religion in Vedic literature. 3108
Origin and development of religious belief. 3113
Origin and development of religious ideas and beliefs. 3115
Origin and development of the Bible. 289
Origin and development of the Disciples. 1460, 1464
Origin and development of the missionary Baptist church in Indiana. 153
Origin and development of the Nicene theology. 2706, 3239
Origin and development of the state cult of Confucius. 1331
Origin and early history of Christianity in Britain. 1761
Origin and early history of the Disciples of Christ. 1460
Origin and early life of Hugh of St. Victor. 1851
Origin and evolution of religion. 3109
Origin and evolution of the Christian Church. 1176
Origin and evolution of the idea of the soul. 3462
Origin and evolution of the priesthood. 1241
Origin and expansion of the Sunday-school. 3558
Origin and growth of religion. 3110
Origin and growth of religion as illustrated. 1502
Origin and growth of the Hebrew religion. 2114
Origin and history of Hebrew law. 2075
Origin and history of missions. 2526
Origin and history of Swedish religious organizations in Minnesota, 1853-1885. 3569
Origin and history of the books of the Bible, both the canonical and the apocryphal, designed to show what the Bible is not, what it is, and how to use it. 411
Origin and history of the Federal council of the churches of Christ in America. 1620
Origin and history of the Mormons. 2604
Origin and meaning of Hasidism. 1788, 1789
Origin and meaning of the name "Protestant Episcopal." 2971
Origin and meaning of the Old Testament. 503
Origin and permanent value of the Old Testament. 540
Origin and progress of Mormonism. 2606
Origin and progress of the German missions in the Methodist Episcopal church. 2558
Origin and progress of the late difficulties in the First church in Worcester, Mass. 1748
Origin and propagation of sin. 3412
Origin and significance of Hegel's logic. 1800, 2242
Origin and significance of snake-lightning cults in the Pueblo Southwest. 3005
Origin and significance of the great pyramid. 891, 3010
Origin and structural development of the Assemblies of God. 92
Origin and teaching of the New Testament books. 474
Origin and transmission of the New Testament; a short introduction. 411
Origin, constitution, doctrine and discipline, of the United brethren in Christ. .3730
Origin, doctrine, constitution, and discipline of the United brethren in Christ. 3730
Origin of all religious worship. 3093
Origin of all things. 521
Origin of Biblical traditions. 526, 1384, 3706
Origin of Christian church art. 921
Origin of Christian science. 1035
Origin of Christianity. 2019, 3140
Origin of Christology. 2011
Origin of damnation and sin is not by inheritance but is cosmological. 3414
Origin of death. 1415

Origin of evil. 3355
Origin of I Corinthians. 346
Origin of I Corinthians. 323
Origin of Islam in its Christian environment. 1082
Origin of magic and religion. 3110
Origin of man. 2322
Origin of man and worlds. 203
Origin of masonry. 1665
Origin of Paul's gospel. 376, 2798
Origin of Paul's religion. 376, 2799, 3061
Origin of priestcraft. 1653
Origin of primitive superstitions. 1904
Origin of religion. 3065
Origin of religion as revealed by the chisel. 3115
Origin of Satan. 2270
Origin of sin. 3411
Origin of sin, and its relations to God and the universe. 3410
Origin of subjectivity in Hindu thought. 1813
Origin of Sunday observance in the Christian church. 3547
Origin of supernatural conceptions and development of religions from prehistoric times. 1654
Origin of the Baptists. 151
Origin of the Bible. 290
Origin of the Book of Mormon. 679, 3470
Origin of the Book of Mormon, together with an account of the rise and progress of the Mormon church. 678
Origin of the Disciples of Christ (Campbellites) 1464
Origin of the four Gospels. 393
Origin of the Gospel of Mark. 435
Origin of the idea of crusade. 1390
Origin of the Jesuits. 1946, 1947, 2267, 2268, 2269
Origin of the New Testament. 406
Origin of the Order of Our Lady of charity. 1541, 3419
Origin of the Pentateuch in the light of the ancient momuments. 564
Origin of the Reformed church in Germany. 3047
Origin of the "reorganized" church, and the question of succession. 3217
Origin of the zodiac. 3897
Origin, persecutions, and doctrines of the Waldenses. 3789
Origin, the nature, the kingdom, the works, and the destiny of the devil. 1427
Original. 72, 338, 2824
Original and present state of man, briefly considered. 1682, 2706
Original Caughnawaga Indians. 876, 1949
Original church of Christ. 2450
Original constitution, order and faith of the New England churches. Comprising the platform of church discipline adopted in 1648. 1337
Original draught of the primitive church. 1194
Original face. 3238
Original feminist attack on the Bible. 224, 3840
Original Garden of Eden discovered and the final solution of the mystery of the woman. 2654
Original Hebrew of a portion of Ecclesiasticus (xxxix.15 to x1ix.11) 487
Original hymns for Sabbath schools. 3562
Original hymns in the Ioway language. 1876
Original letters relative to the English reformation. 3043
Original meaning of Scriptural names. 480
Original readings for Catholic action. 753
Original realistic lecture, love, courtship, and marriage. 2340
Original revolution. 3794
Original sermon outlines, plus hints and helps on how to make sermon outlines. 3374
Original Shaker music, published by the North family. Of Mt. Lebanon, Col. co., N.Y. 3398
Original, short and practical sermons for every Sunday of the ecclesiastical year. 1268
Original, short and practical sermons in honor of the blessed sacrament. 865
Original sin. 3413, 3414
Original sin: the patristic and theological background. 3414
Original thoughts on various passages of Scripture. 1225
Original unity of man and woman. 525, 2346
Originality of St. Matthew. 442
Originality of the Christian message. 1051
Origines, britannicae. 1759
Les origines du chant romain. 883
Origins. 1383

Origins and characteristics of anabaptism. 37
Origins and early development of Shi'a Islam. 3403
Origins and faith. 3028
Origins and history of religions. 3119
origins and religious teaching of the Old Testament books. 532
Origins of Ancrene wisse. 39, 2229, 2582
Origins of astrology. 98
Origins of Calvin's theology of music, 1536-1543. 728, 2633
Origins of certainty. 58, 2777
Origins of Christian philosophy. 1616
Origins of Christian supernaturalism. 3566
Origins of Christianity. 408, 1103, 1189, 1798
Origins of culture. 1282
Origins of early Semitic ritual. 2111
Origins of European dissent. 1805
Origins of evil in Hindu mythology. 1747
Origins of fundamentalism. 1690
Origins of Greek religion. 1387
Origins of infant baptism. 1906
Origins of Isma'ilism. 1927
Origins of Jansenism. 1934
Origins of Josephinism. 2134
Origins of Muhammadan jurisprudence. 2564
Origins of New Testament christology. 2011
Origins of private penance in the Western church. 2812
Origins of private penance in the Western church. 2812
Origins of religious dissent in England. 1469
Origins of sacrifice. 3272
Origins of sectarian Protestantism. 36
Origins of sectarian Protestantism; a study of the Anabaptist view of the church. 36
Origins of the Bible. 312
Origins of the Christian doctrine of sacrifice. 3271
Origins of the Christian mystical tradition from Plato to Denys. 2644
...The origins of the Druze people and religion. 1481
Origins of the Goseps. 389
Origins of the Gospel according to St. Matthew. 442
Origins of the Gospel traditions. 393
Origins of the Great Schism. 3308
Origins of the modern Jew. 2146
Origins of the modern Roman liturgy. 840
Origins of the New Testament. 348
Origins of the New Testament. Tr. [from French] by L. P. Jacks. 348
Origins of the reformation. 3038
Origins of the synagogue and the church. 2111, 2117, 2150
Origins of the Synoptic Gospels. 392
Origins of the theology of hope. 2568, 3656
Origins of Ulster Unionism. 1919
Oriole girls' handbook. 3217
Orion. 1856
Orisha: the gods of Yorubaland. 2667
"An Orita for Black youth" 16
Ormulum. 355
Ornament, or the Christian rule of dress. 1304
Ornamented orthodoxy. 2751
Ornaments for the daughters of Zion. 384 4
...The ornaments of the ministers. 1291
... The ornaments of the rubric. 2240
Oroz codex. 1646, 1647
Orphan in history. 1377, 2081
Orphans of the Orient. 2502
Orpheus. 2744
Orpheus, a general history of religions. 3140
Orpheus; a history of religions. 3140
Orpheus and Greek religion. 2744
... Orpheus: myths of the world. 2651
Orpheus with his lute. 2656
Orphic hymns. 1873
Orphism. 1767, 2744
Orphism and Bacchic mysteries. 1459
Orrin Porter Rockwell: man of God, son of thunder. 3242
Orson Hyde. 1859
Orson Pratt journals. 2867
Orson Pratt's works on the doctrines of the gospel. 2609
Orthodox Baptistery of Ravenna. 3025
Orthodox Christian Church through the ages. 2747
Orthodox Christian meditations. 2392, 2746
Orthodox church. 2744, 2745, 2747
Orthodox Church and independent Greece, 1821-1852. 1146, 2746
Orthodox church history. 2747
Orthodox Church of Russia. 3257

Orthodox Church of the East in the eighteenth century, being the correspondence between the Eastern patriarchs and the Nonjuring bishops. 2747
Orthodox companion. 2748
Orthodox devil. 1428
Orthodox doctrine of the Apostolic Eastern Church. 2746
Orthodox Eastern Church. 2744
Orthodox evangelist. 3646
Orthodox Greek patriarchate of Jerusalem. 1768
... Orthodox hymns in English. 2747
Orthodox hymns of Christmas, Holy Week, and Easter. 2747
Orthodox iconography. 1880
Orthodox liturgical dress. 1250
Orthodox liturgy. 2748, 2749
Orthodox liturgy. Alcuin Club ed. 2748
Orthodox marriage service. 2347
Orthodox prayer book. 2748
Orthodox preacher and Nancy. 3133
Orthodox-Protestant dialogue. 2749, 2955
Orthodox psychology. 1107
Orthodox spirituality. 90
Orthodox synthesis. 2830, 3667
Orthodox theology. 3667
Orthodox theology and diakonia. 2747, 3667
Orthodox theology of to-day. 1342
Orthodoxy. 62, 1057, 1100, 2751, 3620, 3727
Orthodoxy and catholicity. 2749
Orthodoxy and heresy in earliest Christianity. 1805
Orthodoxy and heterodoxy, a miscellany. 2913
Orthodoxy and the religion of the future. 1046
Orthodoxy as it is. 1699
Orthodoxy, faith and life. 2746
Orthodoxy in American Jewish life. 2751
Orthodoxy in Massachusetts, 1630-1650. 2371
Orthodoxy in the civil courts. 1463
Orthodoxy, life and freedom. 2745
Orthodoxy, Roman Catholicism and Anglicanism. 1040, 2746
Orthodoxy vs. Christian science. 1034
Ortus Christi. 9
Oscar Carleton McCulloch, 1843-1891. 1333, 2307
OscarWilde from purgatory. 3514, 3815
Osiris. 2752
Osiris and the Egyptian resurrection. 2752
Osterley selection from the Latin fathers. 1020
Other Catholics. 875, 1485
Other Christs. 1893, 2040
Other city. 3126
Other covenant. 2757
Other dialogue. 1136
Other dimension. 2247, 3058
Other face. 818
Other fellow's religion. 3162
Other foot. 3128
Other God. 1721
Other half of Japan. 2533
Other half of the rainbow. 3751
Other Jesus. 1975, 3197
Other life. 1697
Other lives. 3054
Other men labored. 2926
Other nature sermons. 1341
Other Nazareth. 2004
Other people. 1608
Other-power. 3403
Other religions in a world of change. 3122
Other room. 1886
Other Samuel Johnson. 1294, 2129
Other sheep. 679, 1082, 2491, 2783
Other sheep I have. 1041
Other shepherd. 1114
Other side. 3511
"The other side God's door" 3513
Other side of Calvary. 973
Other side of darkness. 3127
Other side of death. 1528, 1695, 3686
Other side of divorce. 1471
Other side of God. 3067
Other side of Rome. 802
Other side of silence. 2380
Other side of sorrow. 192, 1425
Other side of the coin. 2537
Other side of the question. 3396
Other sides of reality: myths, visions, and fantasies. 2231
Other six days. 1075
Other son of man. 518
Other Spanish Christ. 3464
... The other way home. 850
Other women of the Bible. 3839
Other world and this. 3502
Other worlds. 2729
Others. 1009
Others call it God. 3169, 3556

Otherworldliness and the New Testament. 3653
Otomi catechism. 770, 2752
Ouch! 1347
Ouija board. 2753
Ouija book. 2752, 2753
Ouina's canoe and Christmas offering, filled with flowers for the darlings of earth, given through her medium "Water Lily" (Mrs. Cora L. V. Richmond) 3512
Our ageless Bible. 290
Our ageless Bible, from early manuscripts to modern versions. 290
Our American cardinals. 738
... Our American churches. 3739
Our American princes. 738
"Our Asiatic Christ" 1082, 1950
... Our attitude towards English Roman Catholics, and the papal court. 816
Our authorized Bible vindicated. 291
Our awakening social conscience. 3447
Our B.Y.P.U. 142
Our bad, our good, our God. 3482
Our Baptist heritage. 149
Our Baptist ministers and schools. 157
Our basic faith. 3641
Our basic truth. 204
Our beginning in wisdom. 1924, 2169, 2566
Our best Friend. 1953, 1984, 3270
Our Bible. 235, 238, 304, 307, 649
Our Bible and the ancient manuscripts. 290
Our Bible helps us. 199
Our Bible heritage. 290
Our Bible in stone. 3010
Our Bible--what's in it? 280
Our Bible: who wrote it? 234
Our Biblical heritage. 647, 2086
Our big boys and the Sunday school. 687
Our bishops. 753
Our bishops speak: national pastorals and annual statements of the hierarchy of the United States. 852
Our Blessed Lady. 2361, 2362
Our blessed Lord. 1982
Our Blessed Mother. 2355, 2356
Our book of books. 1976
Our book of jubilee, 1886-1961. 726
Our Book of Mormon. 679
Our bounden duty, a manual of devotion for communicants. 2259
Our boys. 3888
Our boys and girls. 3555
Our brethren of the tenements and ghetto. 2859
Our Brother of joy. 955
Our brothers. 2584
Our brothers in Christ. 2978
Our Catholic heritage. 833
Our Catholic heritage in Texas, 1519-1936. 3605
Our centennial year, 1862-1962. 2698
Our changing churches. 3746
Our changing liturgy. 839, 3772
Our changing world, whither bound? 3380
Our child--God's child. 1607
Our children and evangelism. 1254
Our children and God. 903
Our children and the Lord. 3170
Our children are our best friends. 2341
Our children in the other life. 897
Our Christ-centered faith. 37
Our Christian beginnings. 328
Our Christian community. 3185
Our Christian doctrine course. 1023, 3666
Our Christian faith. 764, 3628, 3663
Our Christian heritage. 1049, 1198, 3037
Our Christian hope. 3662
Our Christian response and witness. 964
Our Christian stewardship. 3702
Our Christian symbols. 921, 3574
Our Christmas challenge. 1062
Our Christmas handbook. 1112
Our Christmas tides. 1111
Our church. 755, 1122, 1181, 2421, 3191
Our church, a guide to the study of the organization and activities of the local congregation. 2295
Our church; an official study book. 3733
Our church and its community outreach. 1274
Our church and others. 1187
Our church and our children. 938, 2746
Our church and people. 2602
Our church at work in the world. 3164
Our church in Sandburg. 2428
Our church life. 142
Our church meeting human needs. 1250
Our church music. 1203, 1204
Our church, one through the ages. 1759
Our church plans for adult education. 3168
Our church plans for adults. 3168
Our church plans for children. 3169
Our church plans for leadership education. 3177

Our church plans for missionary and stewardship education. 3531
Our church plans for youth. 1259
Our church problems and how to meet them. 1310
Our church-then and now. 3317
Our church today. 1119, 3385
Our church's story. 1177
Our city neighbors. 3185
Our coming Lord. 2055
Our common faith. 74
Our common history as Christians. 2753, 3623
... Our common life. 956
Our common loyalty. 2058, 2973
Our community. 3421
Our community and the Christian ideal. 3446
Our compendium-catechism course. 1023
Our concern is children. 3169
Our concern with the theology of crisis. 176, 3652
Our congregation and its work. 1251
Our continuing yes. 2569
Our controversial Bible. 237
Our cooperative program. 150
Our cosmic journey. 2321
Our country. 827, 2443, 2528, 3737, 3742
Our country and world peace. 2806
Our daily bread. 1432, 3763
Our daily homily. 223
Our day in the light of prophecy. 608
Our deeper destiny. 2727
Our denominational mothers in 1920. 1275
Our departed friends. 1697
Our dependable Bible. 275
Our destiny. 2615
Our dialogue with Rome. 1039, 3770
Our Divine Friend. 1741, 3223
Our Divine Master. 2067
Our divine model. 1992
Our doctrines. 149
Our dwelling place. 1441
... Our Elder Brother. 1443, 1973
Our Elder Brother; his biography. 1973
Our emotions and the moral act. 949
Our English Bible. 248
Our English Bible, how we got it. 248, 291
Our English Bible in the making. 248
Our English cathedrals. 751
Our eternal contemporary. 2059
Our excellent women of the Methodist church. 2433
Our expanding church. 2970
Our experience of God. 1105
Our eyes were opened. 3851
Our faith. 808, 1592, 3661
Our faith and the facts. 1590
Our faith in God through Jesus Christ. 1049
Our falling image. 509
Our families. 1611
Our families;a vacation school course for primary boys and girls. 1611
Our family grows toward God. 1609
Our family prayer book. 855, 1604
Our family, the church. 1123
Our Father. 904, 2246, 2247, 2248, 2249, 2250, 2260, 2438, 3360
Our father Abraham. 1252, 2116
Our father in Gethsemane. 1826
Our Father in heaven. 3155
Our Father who art in heaven. 1440, 2248
Our father who art in hell. 2130
Our fathers and us. 2421
Our Father's business. 2209
Our fathers faith and ours. 2977
"Our fathers have told us." 35, 2432
Our Father's house. 2673
Our favorite novenas prayerbook. 2716
Our fighting faith. 2930
Our firm foundation. 3383
Our first century. 893
Our first communion. 1627
Our first congress. 1462
Our first decade in China. 2507
Our first decade in China, 1905-1915. 2508
Our first estate. 2896
Our first Sukkah. 3545
... Our foreign missionary enterprise. 2520, 3731
Our Forgotten Guest. 1830
Our free Methodist missions in Africa. 1653
Our friend from Bethlehem. 2066
Our friend of Galilee. 1983
Our friends and foes. 42
Our friends in Guatemala. 2523
Our friends in heaven. 1795, 1796
Our friends in other folds. 3323
Our garden, and glimpses through it's secret gate. 3494
Our garden was so fair. 2307, 3405
Our glorified. 1350

Our glorious hope. 2055
Our goal and our guides. 3187
Our God and Godhealth, our Healer. 354
Our God-breathed book. 306
Our God is able. 978, 2435
Our God is marching on. 3252
Our gods on trial. 1654
Our good enemies. 908
Our goodly heritage. 2304
Our gospel of love. 955
Our Gospels. 398
Our grand old Bible. 290
Our great commission. 140
Our great high priest. 424
Our guest. 3251
Our guiding star. 3690
Our guilty silence. 1571
Our happy lot. 1289
Our happy world. 3765
Our hearts are restless. 115, 1025
Our hearts beat high. 3359
Our hearts rejoice; communion meditations. 1318
Our Heavenly Father. 1722, 1732, 2250
Our Hebrew-Christian heritage. 1095
Our heredity from God. 1581
Our heritage. 22, 140, 3371
Our heritage is the Lord. 858
Our heritage of faith. 296
Our heritage of humor. 1076, 3218
Our heritage; 150 years of progress. 2201
Our heritage, the story of one hundred years. 1304
...Our heroes. 3731
Our hidden forces("La psychologie inconnue") 2987
Our high calling. 3299
Our high priest: Jesus Christ in the heavenly sanctuary. 2049
Our holy faith. 3640
Our holy hill. 1072
Our home, a place of worship. 1609
Our home altar. 1608
Our homes and our children. 1611
Our hope. 2750, 3670
Our hope of survival. 1181
Our hymnody. 2458
Our hypocritical new national motto. 3088
Our hypocritical new national motto: In God we trust. 3089
Our idea of God. 1727
Our incarnate Lord. 3356
Our independent schools. 2943
Our inerrant Bible. 275
Our infallible Bible. 277
Our international house (the religion of an American town) 3306
Our invisible friends. 3494
Our island-continent. 117
Our Israelitish origin. 46
Our Japanese friends. 1936
Our Jerusalem. 1944, 3777
Our Jewish friends. 2138
Our Jewish heritage. 2138
Our Jewish neighbors. 2082, 2151
Our Joe. 3509
Our journey toward God. 998
Our joyful confidence. 342, 2011
Our junior Bible course. 3159
Our junior department. 3555
Our kind of people. 1171, 2307
Our King and Saviour. 1975
Our knowledge of Christ. 1969
Our knowledge of God. 1739, 1740
Our knowledge of Mary. 2354
Our knowledge of the external world. 3255
Our knowledge of universals. 3755
Our Korean friends. 2536
Our Lady. 2361
Our Lady among us. 2357
Our Lady and reunion. 2357
Our Lady and Saint Francis. 2359
Our Lady & St. Michael, Workington. 2753
Our Lady and the Aztec. 1458, 1776
Our Lady and the church. 2361
Our Lady and the Mass. 2362
Our Lady book. 2355, 2362
Our Lady came to Fatima. 1618
Our Lady comes to Banneux. 133
Our Lady comes to Beauraing. 182
Our Lady comes to Fatima. 1618
Our Lady comes to Guadalupe. 1778
Our Lady comes to La Salette. 3286
Our Lady comes to Lourdes. 2262, 3460
Our Lady comes to New Orleans. 2946
Our Lady comes to Newenham. 740, 3409
Our Lady comes to Paris. 2190, 2478
Our Lady comes to Pontmain. 2859
Our Lady comes to Refugio. 3050
Our Lady for boys & girls. 2360
... Our Lady in art. 2358
Our Lady in Catholic life. 2360
Our Lady in education. 2357

Our Lady in other words. 120
Our Lady in our life. 2354
Our Lady in poetry. 2361
Our Lady in the Gospels. 2358
Our Lady in the modern world. 2355
Our Lady, mediatrix of all graces. 2361
Our Lady of Angels Parish, Bronx, New York. 2753
Our Lady of Beauraing. 182
Our Lady of Einsiedeln in Switzerland. 1503
Our Lady of Ephesus. 1521, 2360
Our Lady of Esperanza. 2697
Our Lady of Fatima. 1618, 2357, 3405
Our Lady of Fatima manual. 1618
Our Lady of Guadalupe. 1776, 2355
Our Lady of Knock. 2179
Our Lady of Light. 1618
Our Lady of Loretto. 2260
Our Lady of Mount Carmel Church, Bayonne, New Jersey, U.S.A. 2753
Our Lady of perpetual help. 2358
... Our Lady of sorrows. 2355, 3459
Our Lady of the Forest. 2363
Our Lady of the miraculous medal. 2362, 2478
Our Lady of the Smile and St. Therese of the Child Jesus. 2356
Our Lady of Wisdom. 2357
Our Lady speaks. 2231
Our Lady's book. 2357
Our Lady's daily hours. 848
Our Lady's feasts. 1613, 2359
Our Lady's hours. 848
Our Lady's knight. 2262
Our Lady's litany. 2231, 2363
Our Lady's rosary. 3247
Our Lady's slave. 1775
Our Lady's tinker, William Joseph Chaminade. 881
Our Lady's titles. 2356
Our land and Our Lady. 874
Our lay office-bearers. 2443
Our leaders. 2609
Our leaders speak. 2607
Our lesser brethren. 694
Our liberal movement in theology, chiefly as shown in recollections of the history of Unitarianism in New England, being a closing course of lectures given in the Harvard divinity school. 3727, 3729, 3730
... Our life after death. 1695
Our life in Christ. 2042, 3187, 3266, 3492
Our life in God's light. 2168, 3622
Our life is like that. 2120
Our life of grace. 1751
Our life of prayer. 2881
Our life together. 988
Our life with the Garos of Assam, India. 2503
Our little child faces life. 3174
Our Living Bible. 208
Our living Bible for young people. 293
Our living church. 3764
Our living dead. 3495
Our living Hope. 1562
Our living Mass. 2366
Our Lord. 1967, 2001
Our Lord and master. 2002
Our Lord and Our Lady. 2359
Our Lord and Saviour. 1952, 1961
Our Lord of the Gospels. 286, 396
Our Lord prays for His own. 424, 1451
Our Lord's coming and His kingdom. 605
Our Lord's earthly life. 1972
Our Lord's great prophecy, and its parallels throughout the Bible, harmonized and expounded. 2050
Our Lord's great sermon. 3334
Our Lord's life. 1974
Our Lord's most sublime words. 424
Our Lord's prayer. 2249
Our Lord's prophecy. 2050
Our Lord's resurrection. 2053
Our Lord's return. 2055, 3319
Our Lord's teaching on prayer. 2246, 2868
Our Lord's virgin birth and the criticism of to-day. 3780
Our lost world. 2494, 3467
Our loving Father. 1732
Our man of patience. 3124
Our mandate on Palestine. 610
Our many selves. 1441
Our marching orders in evangelism. 1572
Our Mass. 2367
Our message is Christ. 1454
Our Methodist heritage. 3805
Our Methodist heritage in South Georgia. 2430
Our Methodist hymnody. 2430
Our milestones. 970
Our mission in today's world. 1573
Our mission today. 2554
Our missions in India 1834-1924. 2532

Our misunderstanding concerning the Jews. 1287, 2111
Our misunderstood Bible. 199, 237
Our monastic observances. 2576
Our money system. 1625
Our monthly devotions. 858
Our moral challenge. 1325
Our mother. 2352, 3415
Our name is Peter. 2768, 2806
Our national cathedrals (the richest architectural heritage of the British nation) 753
Our national enemy number one. 3190
Our national preeminence and its true source. 3605
Our Negro and Indians missions. 2541
Our neighbors' churches. 3326
Our neighbors South and North. 2408
Our neighbors the Dominicans. 2516
Our neighbour, Martin Luther. 2280, 3040
Our new age. 2385
Our new church. 2290
... Our new Edens. 2933
Our new religion. 1032
Our New Testament. 340
Our next war. 3792
Our nuns. 1357
Our obligations to the day of rest and worship. 3547
Our of the depths. 2463, 3292
Our offering. 2969
Our one priest on high. 2049
Our ordered lives confess. 1379
Our oriental missions. 2532
Our other lives. 3055
Our overseas missions. 2970
Our own Christmas. 1112
Our own religion in ancient Persia. 121, 3899
Our own St. Rita. 3238
Our own society. 1233
Our Pacific outposts. 1238
Our palace wonderful. 1100, 3078
Our Pallottine heritage. 2766
Our paradise home. 3379
Our parish in India. 2532
Our part in the mystical body. 2020
Our part in the world. 3148, 3453
Our past and present. 766
Our pastor. 2806
Our pastor has an outside job. 1297
Our pastors in Calvary. 825
Our pastors' offering. 3204
Our patron saints, with prayers and indulgences. 2794
Our people in olden days. 2094
Our people, the Jew in America. 2104
Our perennial Bible. 235
Our phallic heritage. 2827
Our place in Christendom. 1178
Our playmate. 1996
Our plea for union and the present crisis. 238
Our prayer. 2871
Our prayer book. 2108
Our prayers and praise. 2961
Our preaching. 2905
Our preparation for peace. 725
Our Presbyterian educational institutions. 2923
Our Presbyterian belief. 3679
Our Presbyterian church. 2920
Our Presbyterian colleges. 2915
Our priceless heritage. 803
Our priceless primaries. 3170
Our priesthood. 2938
Our primary department. 3565
... Our pro-socialist churches. 1619
Our prodigal son, culture. 1280
Our prophets and principles. 2609
Our Protestant heritage. 2977, 2978, 3340
Our public schools,Christian or secular. 3190
Our pupils and how they learn. 1498
Our Quaker Friends of ye olden time. 1688
Our quest for happiness. 3186, 3187
Our questioning age. 61
Our real roots. 1383, 3385
Our reasonable faith. 1594, 1706
Our recovery of Jesus. 2036, 2062
Our Redeemer. 1440, 1978, 1985
Our Redeemer, a cathedral of gospel art. 750
Our refuge. 1541, 2039
Our refuge and strength. 2299
"Our relations to our other neighbors." 132
Our religion. 3142
Our religion and our neighbors. 3118
Our religious heritage. 309, 1198, 2755
Our religious heritage in America. 2750, 2751
Our religious traditions. 2115
Our religious vocabulary. 3092
Our retreat from modernism. 2561
Our risen King's forty days. 2051

Our risen Lord. 2006
Our roving Bible. 304
Our sanctifying God. 3299
Our savage god. 1731, 2329
Our Savior and His love for us. 2038
Our Savior God. 2046, 2321
Our Savior's prayer for unity. 2049
Our Saviour. 1982, 2039
Our Saviour, with prophets and apostles. 1974
Our Saviour's last night and day. 2029
Our seal. 912
Our search for God. 3485
Our search for identity. 2321
Our second decade in China, 1915-1925. 2509
Our self after death. 1695
Our silent partner. 1829
... Our sixty-six sacred books. 291
Our song of hope. 1868, 3046
Our spiritual resources. 2694
Our spiritual service to the sick and dying. 3265
Our star-spangled faith. 1150
Our stations and places. 1670
Our story. 2107
Our story according to St. Mark. 434
Our story, 1936-1966, United Church Women of Minnesota. 3732
Our story of missions for colleges & academies. 2495
Our struggle to serve. 926
Our superconscious mind. 2990
Our Synod and its work. 1548
Our teacher, Augusta E. Stetson, C. S. D. 3527
Our templed hills. 3253
Our thin-air friends. 3517
Our time is now. 2576
Our time is now; a study of some modern congregations and secular institutes. 2576
Our times and their meaning. 2465
Our tongues were loosed. 838
Our translated Gospels. 398
Our troublesome religious questions. 3062
Our tryst with Him. 3480
Our Ukrainian Cardinal. 3425, 3722
Our ultimate authority. 400
Our undying self. 1889
Our Unitarian heritage. 3729
Our unseen companions. 3494
... Our unseen guest. 3510
Our visited planet. 2052
Our way to God. 3183
Our widows and orphans endowments. 673
Our woman workers. 3754
Our world. 1282
Our world witness. 92
Our youth for Christ. 3888
Ours for discovery. 3477
Ours is the faith. 1435
Ours, the making and unmaking of a Jesuit. 1945, 2700
Ourselves to know. 1324
Out in the country. 3155
Out Mass explained from the viewpoints of history, theology, piety. 2365
Out of abundance. 2393
Out of Africa. 2498
Out of Aldersgate. 2422
Out-of-body experiences for the millions. 94
Out of chaos. 2073, 2107
Out of darkness. 3384
Out of darkness into light. 1351
Out of darkness, light! 471
Out-of-doors inthe Holy Land. 2763
Out of doors with God. 731, 2675
Out-of-doors with Jesus. 1954
"Out of Egypt;" 517
Out of hell and purgatory. 782
Out of his treasure. 3125
Out of joint with the moral order. 2589
Out of Kishineff. 2178
Out of many hearts. 2198, 3377
Out of my life. 1446
Out of my mind. 2383
Out of Nazareth. 627, 1234, 2015, 3420
Out of old paths. 3128
Out of old ruts. 2299
Out of shadows into light. 1887
Out of Shango's shadow. 121, 2542
Out of solitude. 2393
Out of the African night. 2506
Out of the ashes. 3337
Out of the blanket. 2305, 2706
Out of the body experiences. 28, 94
... Out of the books. 1704
Out of the Cain-life into the Christ-life. 1559
Out of the cauldron. 3826
Out of the cloister. 2580
Out of the clouds. 218
Out of the Crate. 2390
Out of the crucibles. 2726

Out of the curtained world. 1582
Out of the dark. 2796
Out of the darkness. 2348, 3691
Out of the depths. 586, 848, 1291, 1477, 2282, 2706, 2854
Out of the depths have I cried. 1894
Out of the dust. 207
Out of the earth. 335
Out of the earth; the witness of archaeology to the New Testament. 335
Out of the East. 2532
Out of the Far East. 2558
Out of the fog. 1359
Out of the heart. 3371
Out of the hell-box. 3136
Out of the house of Judah. 3143
Out of the house of slavery. 1313
Out of the iron furnace. 2853
Out of the jaws of the lion. 2351, 2514
Out of the labyrinth. 800
Out of the night. 46, 3289
Out of the Northland. 3197
Out of the saltshaker & into the world. 1569
Out of the silence. 3508
Out of the storm in China. 2510
Out of the treasure chest. 617
Out of the unknown. 2727
Out of the valley. 1353
Out of the whirlwind. 549, 2124
Out of the wilderness. 1555
... Out of their own mouths. 3057
Out of thirty-five years. 3675, 3710
Out of this world. 1449, 1627
Out of yesterday into tomorrow. 2531
Out to win! 978, 3870
Outbursts that await us. 3744
Outcome of history. 46
Outdoor men and minds. 481
Outdoor writers instruction manual. 2135
Outer limits of Edgar Cayce's power. 876
Outer space: myths, name meanings, calendars from the emergence of history to the present day. 2652
Outfitting for spiritual marriage. 2340
Outfitting the teacher of religion. 3158
Outlawing the Almighty. 2945
Outline addresses for the three hours devotion. 2056
Outline and an annotated bibliography of Chinese philosophy. 2838
Outline and analysis of the First epistle of John. 324
Outline and message of Romans. 470
Outline Bible studies. 645
Outline chalk talks. 880
Outline course in Bible study. 642
Outline for the study of Old Testament. 596
Outline for the study of Old Testament history. 532
Outline for the study of the meaning. 3000
Outline history of Christian missions. 850
Outline-history of Greek religion. 1766
Outline history of the church by centuries (from St. Peter to Pius XII) 810
Outline history of the Church of Christ. 1210
Outline history of the Episcopal church. 2967
Outline history of the Ukrainian Orthodox Church. 2751
Outline history of Utah and the Mormons. 3762
Outline introduction to the history of religions. 3140
Outline introduction to the New Testament. 409
Outline introduction to the sundry parts of the Bible. 312
Outline introductory to Kant's "Critique of pure reason" 2164
Outline meditations. 2385
Outline normal lessons. 3178
Outline of a Bible-school curriculum. 3556
Outline of a history of Protestant missions from the reformation to the present time. 2526
Outline of a system of utilitarian ethics. 1536
Outline of a work of grace in the Presbyterian congregation at New Brunswick, N.J., during the year 1837. 2686
Outline of astro-psychology. 96
Outline of Bible history. 289, 294
Outline of Biblical theology. 651
Outline of Catholic pedagogy. 805
Outline of Catholic teaching. 792
Outline of Christian belief. 3662
Outline of Christian doctrine. 934
Outline of Christian theology. 3642
Outline of Christian worship. 2238
Outline of Christianity. 1178
Outline of church history. 1188

Outline of church history of the first six centuries. 1180
Outline of classical mythology. 2658
...An outline of Dahomean religious belief. 1399
Outline of freemasonry. 1664
Outline of heaven. 1794
Outline of Hebrew history. 2705
Outline of Jewish history. 2088
Outline of lay sanctity. 1025
Outline of metaphysics. 3686
Outline of mission fields. 3387
Outline of missions. 2491
Outline of modern occultism. 2729
Outline of New-church teaching. 2689
Outline of New Testament Christology. 476, 2039
Outline of New Testament ethics. 378
Outline of New Testament history. 473
Outline of New Testament survey. 445
Outline of New Testament theology. 476
Outline of occult science. 51, 2729
Outline of Old Testament history. 535
Outline of Old Testament theology. 199
Outline of personal prayer. 2882
Outline of psychometry. 3002
Outline of religion. 3094, 3140
Outline of Swedenborg's teachings. 2689
Outline of systematic theology. 3645
Outline of the Bible. 238, 311
Outline of the Christian year. 1263
Outline of the curriculum for the Jewish religious school recommended by the commission on Jewish education. 2079
Outline of the fundamental doctrines of the Bible. 3647
Outline of the future religion of the world. 3142
Outline of the history of Christian literature. 3203
Outline of the history of Christian thought since Kant. 2836
Outline of the history of doctrines. 1473
... Outline of the history of old St. Paul's church, Philadelphia, Pennsylvania. 2829
Outline of the New Testament. 445
Outline of the Old Testament. 597
Outline of the Prayer book. 1214
Outline of the religions of mankind. 3115
Outline of the religious literature of India. 1896
Outline of the rise and progress of freemasonry in Louisiana. 1666
Outline of The secret doctrine. 3686
Outline of the teaching of Jesus. 2066
Outline of the theology of the New Testament. 475
Outline of theosophy. 3686
Outline of Vedic literature. 3776
Outline of Zionist history. 3897
Outline on prophecy. 2949
Outline on prophecy, Israel in the past and in the future. 1515
Outline sermons and plans for evangelistic work. 3375
Outline sermons for Sundays and feast days. 3373
Outline sermons on the holy eucharist and the Blessed Virgin Mary. 2251
Outline studies from the Testimonies. 3384
Outline studies in Acts, Romans, First and Second Corinthians, Galatians and Ephesians. 329
Outline studies in Biblical facts and history. 645
Outline studies in Christian doctrine. 934
Outline studies in church history. 1174
Outline studies in Genesis. 527
Outline studies in Luke. 430
Outline studies in Mark. 433
Outline studies in Old Testament history. 532
Outline studies in the Acts of the Apostles. 332
Outline studies in the Book of the Revelation and key to the Chart of the ages. 461
Outline studies in the four Gospels. 401
Outline studies in the Gospel of Luke. 431
Outline studies in the Gospel of Matthew. 444
Outline studies in the Gospels of Christ. 401
Outline studies in the life of Christ. 2014
Outline studies in the New Testament for Bible teachers. 474
Outline studies in the New Testaments. 474
Outline studies in the Old Testament. 597
Outline studies in the Old Testament, book-by-book. 596
Outline studies of great themes of the Bible. 615
Outline studies of Isaiah. 544
Outline studies of Jeremiah. 1942

Outline studies of Job, Proverbs, Ecclesiastes, and the Song of Songs. 600
Outline studies of the growth of the kingdom of God. 1175
Outline studies on I. John. 324
...Outline studies on the church. 3043
Outline study of the Bible. 645
Outline study of the cooperation of the American Baptist foreign mission societies in the world mission of the Church. 30
Outline study of the Gospel of John. 423
Outline study of the history of the Bible in English. 291
Outline study theology. 780
Outlines for funeral sermons. 3374
Outlines for preaching. 3374
Outlines for the study of Biblical history and literature. 641
Outlines for the study of the Bible as literature. 645
Outlines of. 1208
Outlines of a gentle life. 3401
Outlines of a philosophical argument on the infinite, and the final cause of creation. 1907
Outlines of a philosophy of religion. 3102
Outlines of a philosophy of religion based on psychology and history. 3104
Outlines of an introduction to the Old Testament. 498
Outlines of asceticism for seminarians. 90
Outlines of Bible history. 645
Outlines of Bible study. 637, 646, 649
Outlines of Bible study for use in Bible drills, Bible readings, Bible classes, prayer meetings, and home study. 645
Outlines of Christian apologetics. 66
Outlines of Christian theology. 3615, 3644, 3649
Outlines of church history. 1179
...Outlines of courses of study. 3873
Outlines of curriculum. 3154, 3162
Outlines of doctrinal theology. 3642
Outlines of ecclesiastical history. 1179
Outlines of Jainism. 1932
Outlines of Jewish history. 2091
Outlines of Judaism. 2118
Outlines of liturgies. 2237
Outlines of logic and of Encyclopaedia of philosophy. 2242
Outlines of Mahayana Buddhism. 2317
Outlines of metaphysic. 2418
Outlines of metaphysics. 2418
Outlines of missionary history. 2525
Outlines of modern Christianity and modern science. 3079
Outlines of moral philosophy. 1537
Outlines of moral science. 942
Outlines of moral theology. 947
Outlines of Mormon philosophy. 2607, 2614
Outlines of Muhammadan law. 2201, 2564
Outlines of mythology. 2653
Outlines of New Testament history. 406
Outlines of ontological science. 2738
Outlines of primitive belief among the Indo-European races. 3109
Outlines of prophetic revelation. 463
Outlines of religion for Catholic youth. 3187
Outlines of Scripture geography. 282
Outlines of sermons and inspirational talks. 3374
Outlines of sermons for young men and young women. 865
Outlines of social theology. 3616
Outlines of systematic theology. 3648
Outlines of textual criticism applied to the New Testament. 347, 351
Outlines of the archaeology of the Old Testament. 487
Outlines of the early and medieval history of the Christian church. 1183
Outlines of The faith of our fathers. 786
Outlines of the history of dogma. 3654
Outlines of the history of dogms. 3654
Outlines of the life of Christ. 1971, 2015
Outlines of the life of Our Lord. 1965
Outlines of the philosophy of Aristotle. 81
Outlines of the philosophy of religion. 3102
Outlines of the psychology of religion. 2997
Outlines of the religion and philosophy of Swedenborg. 2691, 3570
Outlines of the synoptic record. 346
Outlines of theology. 2914, 3644, 3666
Outlines of Zuni creation myths. 3899
Outlines on the book of Psalms. 578
Outlines studies in New Testament history. 406
Outlines studies in the New Testament. 368
Outlook beautiful. 3483
Outlook for religion. 3059, 3062

... Outlook in Brazil. 2505
... Outlook in the river Plate region. 2501
... Outlook in the West Indies. 2559
... Outlook in the western republics. 2955
Outlook of freedom. 3741
Outlooks on God. 1719
Outposts of love. 1817, 2501
Outposts of medicine. 2539
Outpourings of the spirit. 3228
Outreach. 1569
Outreach evangelism through the Sunday School. 3829
Outreach for the unreached. 1571
Outreach, God's miracle business. 1753
Outriders for the King. 3466
Outside Disneyland. 3886
Outside the camp. 1064
Outside the gates. 3514
Outside the walls. 3244
Outside the walls, tributes to the principle and practice of Roman Catholicism from our friends fuori le mura. 763
Outsider and the urban church. 1278
Outsider and the word of God. 1570
Outsider in the Vatican. 3769
Outskirts of physical science. 3075
Outspoken ones. 560
Outstanding Black sermons. 3361
Outstanding sermons from Canadian pulpits. 3367
Outstanding stories by general authorities. 1231
Outstretched wings of the spirit. 2211
Outward and visible. 1160
Outward bound. 1118, 2388
Outwitting tomorrow. 2725
Ouvrard, speculator of genius, 1770-1846. 2753
Over against the treasury. 2519
Over Buttonwood Bridge. 618
Over fool hill. 1047, 1067
Over His own signature. 2072
Over the hill. 964
Over the hill to the poor-house and other poems. 1113
Over the hills of Galilee. 199
... Over the Mexican border. 2550
Over the river. 1353
Over the stumbling block. 2145
Over 200 ways to improve your Sunday school. 3555
Overcomer. 1062
Overcomers. 458, 923
Overcoming Christ. 1559
Overcoming Christian divisions. 1492
Overcoming communication barriers in the church. 1316
Overcoming hurts & anger. 43
Overcoming kingdom. 451
Overcoming life. 1559
Overcoming life and other sermons. 1559
Overcoming materialism. 989
Overcoming our obsessions. 3478
Overflowing life. 958, 983
Overheard. 68
Overhearing the gospel. 2899
Overshadowing power of God. 2833
Overstatement in the New Testament. 347
Th'overthrow of stage-playes. 3606
Overthrow of stage-plays. 1700, 3607
Overtones. 1451
Overture of angels. 2021
Overview of Presbyterianism in the city of Philadelphia. 2920
... Ownership. 2454
Ox, the ass, the oyster. 2556
Ox was an angel. 3695
... Oxford. 2753
Oxford American prayer book commentary. 2961
Oxford American psalter. 883
Oxford and Cambridge conferences. 761
Oxford and the evangelical succession. 1550
Oxford and the groups. 2753
Oxford annotated Bible. 249
Oxford apostles. 2702, 2754
Oxford Bible atlas. 282
Oxford Bible concordance for masonic use. 225
Oxford book of carols (The) 741
Oxford cathedral. 2753
Oxford concise concordance to the Revised standard version of the Holy Bible. 229
Oxford conference (official report) 1142
Oxford conference study series, based on the message and reports of the Oxford conference on church, community and state. 1141
Oxford conspirators. 2754
Oxford cyclopedic concordance. 227
Oxford dictionarry of the Christian Church. 3639
Oxford dictionary of saints. 1026
Oxford dictionary of the Christian Church. 3639

Oxford group movement. 2753
Oxford groups. 2753
Oxford hymn book. 1871
Oxford illustrated Old Testament. 482
Oxford martyrs. 1021
Oxford Methodists. 1287, 2422
Oxford movement. 2754, 2755, 3636
Oxford movement, 1833-1933. 2754
Oxford movement in America. 2755
Oxford movement in Scotland. 2754
Oxford movement, its history and its future. 2754
Oxford movement, twelve years, 1833-1845. 2754
Oxford reformers. 1307, 3036
Oxford reformers: John Colet, Erasmus, and Thomas More. 1307, 3036
Oxford self-pronouncing Bible. 249
Oxfordshire clergy, 1777-1869. 1292
Oyster thief. 2676
Ozora Stearns Davis, his life and poems. 1407

P

P. S. G. Watson's Prophetic interpretations. 609
P.S. Please save the stamps. 674, 2487
P. T. Forsyth: prophet for today. 1634
P.T. Forsyth—the man, the preachers' theologian, prophet for the 20th century. 1634, 2907
Pa and the Codex vaticanus. 316
Pace of a hen. 3843
Paced by God. 1551
Pacem in terris. 2809
Pacem in terris. Peace on earth. 2809
Pacemakers. 1361
Pacemakers of Christian thought. 3617
Pachonian chronicles and rules. 2578
Pacific garden mission, a doorway to heaven. 2756
Pacific hopscotch. 1633
Pacific islanders, from savages to saints. 2543
Pacific northwest pulpit. 2436
Pacifism and Biblical nonresistance. 2756
Pacifism in Europe to 1914. 2756
Pack your life with power. 1430
Paddy Wilson's meeting-house in Providence Plantations, 1791-1839. 3819
"Padre" 1482
Padre Kino and the trail to the Pacific. 2177
Padre Martinez and Bishop Lamy. 1294, 2349
Padre of the press. 2568
Padre on horseback. 2177
Padre Pio. 737, 1777, 2849, 3531
Padre Pio, the true story. 1293, 2849
Padre Pro. 2943
Padre's pilgrimage. 3731
Pagan & Christian creeds. 2650
Pagan and Christian families. 1603
Pagan and Christian in an age of anxiety. 1587
Pagan and Christian rule. 808
Pagan babies and other Catholic memories. 870
Pagan background of early Christianity. 1196
Pagan Celtic Britain. 878
Pagan Christs. 3120
Pagan church. 2978
Pagan counterfeits in the Christian church. 1080
Pagan festivals in Christian worship. 2756
Pagan god. 2679
... Pagan ideas of immortality during the early Roman empire. 1889
Pagan mysteries in the Reaissance. 87
Pagan mysteries in the Renaissance. 87
Pagan prayers. 2894
Pagan regeneration. 2636
Pagan rites in Judaism. 2152
Pagan rituals and beliefs among the Chontal Indians of Oaxaca, Mexico. 916
Pagan Scandinavia. 3306
... Pagan vs. Christian civilizations. 1905
Paganism and Christianity. 2756
Paganism and Christianity in Egypt. 1501
Paganism, Christianity, Judaism. 3098
Paganism in Christianity. 3107
Paganism in our Christianity. 1053
Paganism in Roumanian folklore. 1632
Paganism in the Roman Empire. 3246
Paganism surviving in Christianity. 2757
Paganism to Christianity in the Roman empire. 1192, 1196
Paganism vs Americanism. 755
Pagans, conquistadores, heroes, and martyrs. 2548
Pagans in the pulpit. 1087
Pagan's pilgrimage. 2762
Pagans, priests, and prophets. 2732

Page my pastor. 771
Pageant-masque of mercy. 3418
Pageant of the church. 2758
Pageant of the helping hands. 2758
Pageant of the nativity. 2758
Pageant of the popes. 2769, 2861
Pageant text for A little Child. 2757
... Pageantry and dramatics in religious education. 3154
Pageants for the year. 2757
Pageants of the kingdom. 2757
Pages from an African notebook. 2498
Pages from God's case-book. 1733
Pages from the ecclesiastical history of New England, during the century between 1740 and 1840. 2687
Pagoda and the cross. 1633, 2508
Pahlavi texts. 3899
Paid in full. 2487, 3259
Paido-theology. 1906
Pailful of stars. 1441
Pain and gladness. 2758
Pain and grace. 2169, 3544
Pain and joy of ministry. 2785
Pain and pleasure. 2758
Pain and providence. 3539
Pain and the possibility. 1471
Pain and the providence of God. 1745
Pain of being human. 1324
Pain of renewal. 760
Pain of this world and the providence of God. 1745
Pain that heals. 3542
Paine's second part of The age of reason answered. 2759
Painted windows. 1291, 2994
Painting in Florence and Siena after the Black Death. 3062
Painting in Islam. 2759
Painting of The life of St. Francis in Assisi. 1643, 3282
Paintings from Islamic lands. 1883
Paintings in St. Louis Bertrand church, Louisville, Kentucky. 2261
Palace beautiful. 998, 1733
Palace of healing. 3569
Palace of the Great King. 2674
Palaces of God. 162
"Palaces of sin"; or, "The devil in society" 3393
Palanque. 1190
Pale but ... splendid morning. 2391
... The pale Galilean. 1446, 3094
Pale Hecate's team. 3826
... Palestine. 2760, 2762, 2763
Palestine "a fifth gospel," 2762
Palestine and saints in Caesar's household. 2762
Palestine and Syria. 2121
Palestine and the Bible. 2119
Palestine at the crossroads. 2761
Palestine is my country. 21, 2765
Palestine, Mohammedan Holy Land. 2635, 2765
Palestine pathways. 2762
Palestine picture book. 2764
Palestine speaks. 2762, 2763
... Palestine, the coming storm center. 608
Palestine to-day and to-morrow. 2118
Palestine under the Moslems. 2764
Palestinian customs illustrating the Bible. 208, 2121
Palestinian Judaism in the time of Jesus Christ. 2149, 2150
Palestinian mystery play. 2018
Palestinian parties and politics that shaped the Old Testament. 502, 2149
... The Palestinian version of the Holy Scriptures. 2332
Palestrina. 2766
Palewings. 3570
Paley; evidences for the man. 2766
...Paley's evidences of Christianity. 59
Paley's Natural theology. 2673
Palladium of conscience. 1347, 3194
Palladius. 2579
Palliser's memorials and headstones. 3333
Palm tree and pine. 2544
Palm tree blessing. 2815
Palm tree of Deborah. 1539
Palmer's directory of the Methodist Episcopal Church for [the] Dakota Conference. 2446
Palpable God. 623
Pamiarch of Hebron. 4
Pamlico profile. 1465
Pamphlet Bible series. 224
Pamplona Bibles. 602, 1884, 3298
Pan-Anglican congress, 1908. 45
Pan-Presbyterian principles. 2914
Panacea for poverty. 3049
Pandaemonium. 3822
Pandita Ramabai. 3020
Pandita Ramabai Saravati. 3020
Panic of the gods and other essays. 3068
Panorama. 1725
Panorama of Christian hymnody. 1868

Panorama of evil. 1745
Panorama of sleep. 1479
Pansophy. 3717
Pantheism. 2767
Pantheism and Christianity. 2767
Pantheism; its story and significance. 2767
Pantheism of Germany. 3024
Pantheism of modern science. 3688
Pantheist. 1655
Pantheistic dilemmas and other essays in philosophy and religion. 2834
Pantheisticon. 2767
Pantheon. 2655, 2657
Pantologia. 2180
Panton papers. 607
Papa was a preacher. 3675
... The papacy. 2768
Papacy. 795, 2768, 2769
Papacy and European diplomacy, 1869-1878. 860
Papacy and fascism. 860, 2769
Papacy and modern times. 2768
Papacy and political ideas in the Middle Ages. 2770
Papacy and the civil power. 802
Papacy and the first councils of the church. 1372
Papacy and the Levant, 1204-1571. 2769
Papacy and the modern world. 2768
Papacy and totalitarianism between the two World Wars. 2770
Papacy and world affairs as reflected in the seculaization of politics. 2769
Papacy evaluated. 797, 798
Papacy in Bible prophecy. 2768
Papacy in the 19th century. 810
Papacy in transition. 2768
Papacy, its origins and historical evolution. 2767
Papacy, the episcopacy, and collegiality. 1522
Papacy today. 2770
Papago. 1898
Papago Indian religion. 2771
Papal annual. 866
Papal bulls and english muffins. 2211
Papal chamberlain. 2861
Papal commission and the Pentateuch. 563
Papal conflict with Josephinism. 118, 2132
Papal conspiracy exposed. 797
Papal council and the gospel. 3770
Papal documents on Mary. 2354
Papal encyclicals in their historical context. 1512, 2768
Papal enforcement of some medieval marriage laws. 1892, 2342
... Papal faculties allowing food before communion. 1613
Papal idolatry. 798
Papal infallibility. 802, 2862
Papal judges delegate in the Province of Canterbury, 1198-1254. 1488
Papal legislation on sacred music, 95 A.D. to 1977 A.D. 1206
Papal ministry in the Church. 2768
Papal paganism. 801
Papal power. 866, 2770
Papal primacy and the universal church. 2298, 2862
Papal princes. 777
Papal pronouncements on marriage and the family from Leo XIII to Pius XII (1878-1954) 784, 2346
Papal pronouncements on politics. 1142
Papal pronouncements on the political order. 1142
Papal provisions. 190, 807
... Papal rescripts of favor. 3219
Papal revenues in the Middle Ages. 807, 817
Papal Rome as it is. 781
Papal social principles. 1136, 2768
Papal sovereignty. 2768
Papal system. 798
Papal thought on the state. 1142
Papal tiara. 3698
Papal year. 2126
Le Pape Clement Vlet les affaires d'Orient (1342-1352) 860
Paper ark. 47, 480
[Papers. 2494
Papers (American society of church history) 1172
Papers and essays for churchmen. 1126
... Papers contributed by American writers and review of recent American literature on moral education. 2592
[Papers for the Church History seminar on Tertullian. 1175
Papers from the International Lonergan Congress, 1970. 2245, 3637
Papers in the Old Testament seminar, '10th century Israel. 482
Papers in the Old Testament seminar on "The book of Exodus." 1584

Papers of a pariah (Benson, Robert Hugh) 758
Papers of a parish (Benson, Robert Hugh) 758
Papers of John Pererin. 2639
Papers of the American society of church history. 1198
Papers on preaching (Henry, Hugh Thomas) 2900
Papers on the period of the Judges. 555
... Papers presented at the fifth annual session of the summer assembly of the Jewish Chautauqua society. 2086
Papers presented Nov. 13-15, 1959. 1463
Papers presented October 14, 1960. 1462
Papers read before the American society for prophetic study. 2952
Les papes du XIe [i.e. onzieme] siecle et la chretiente. 2860
Papias and his contemporaries. 1192, 2771
Papist misrepresented and represented. 787
Papist pamphleteers. 1374
Papyrus Bodmer II (P66): its textual relationships and scribal characteristics. 421
Papyrus codex of the Shepherd of Hermas (Similitudes 2-9) with a fragmentof the Mandates, edited. 2331
Parable. 2771
Parable and precept, a Baptist message. 2771
Parable book. 2772
Parable of community. 933, 1316
Parable of creation. 2690
Parable of the cherries. 2771
Parable of the empty soul. 2058, 2215
Parable of the father's heart. 2944
Parable of the hurricane. 3318
Parable of the ten virgins. 3601
Parable sermonettes for the children's mass for the Sundays of the ecclesiastical year. 865, 908
Parables. 1013, 2025, 2026, 2028, 2067, 2771
Parables and instruction in the Gospels. 2025
Parables and instructions in the Gospels. 2025
Parables and metaphors of Our Lord. 2026
Parables and other sayings of Jesus. 1950, 2771
Parables and presence. 350, 2027
Parables and similes of the rabbis. 2462
Parables and similes of the rabbis, agricultural and pastoral. 19, 2772
Parables and their home. 2027
Parables for a new creation. 2387
Parables for boys and girls. 2028
Parables for little people. 2771
Parables for our times. 2772
Parables for our world. 601
Parables for teaching. 1008
Parables for the present. 2389
Parables for today. 2027
Parables from life. 2771
Parables from nature. 2027
Parables from the Gospels. 2027
Parables from the sea. 1444
Parables He told. 2026
Parables Jesus told. 163, 2028
Parables of Christ. 2024
Parables of conflict in Luke. 2025
Parables of crisis. 2026
Parables of Emiloh, the mystic. 971
Parables of James E. Talmage. 2397
Parables of Jesus. 2024, 2025, 2026, 2028, 2772
Parables of Jesus explained and illustrated. 2025
Parables of Jesus in Matthew 13. 444, 2025
Parables of Jesus in their relation to His ministry. 2026
Parables of life. 2771
Parables of our Lord. 2024, 2027
Parables of Our Lord and Saviour Jesus Christ. 2028
Parables of our Saviour. 2026
Parables of the Gospel. 2025, 2028
Parables of the Gospels. 2026
Parables of the Kingdom. 601, 2024, 2026, 2028, 2176, 2215, 2771, 2772
Parables of the Lord. 2025
Parables of the Lord Jesus according to S. Matthew. 2026
Parables of the Master. 2026
Parables of the New Testament practically unfolded. 2026
Parables of the New Testament spiritually unfolded. 445
Parables of the Old Testament. 561, 2771
Parables of the synoptic Gospels. 392, 2026
Parables of the triple tradition. 388, 2024

Parables read in the light of the present day. 2025
Parables; their literary and existential dimension. 2027
Parables then and now. 2025
Parables to the point. 2024
Parables told by Jesus. 2025
Parabolic teaching of Christ. 2024
Parabolic teaching of Scripture. 601
Parabolical teachings of Christ in Matthew xiii and Luke xv. 2772
Paracelsus. 2772
Paraclete. 1101
Paraclete power. 330
Paradise. 2772
Paradise found. 2471, 3120
Paradise found; the cradle of the human race at the North pole. 1497
Paradise hunters. 999
Paradise, Incorporated—Synanon. 3578
Paradise lost. 2470, 2471
Paradise lost and its critics. 2471
Paradise lost and the modern reader. 2469
Paradise lost & the seventeenth century reader. 2471
Paradise, lost and won. 199
Paradise lost as "myth." 2468
Paradise lost in our time. 2470, 2471
Paradise lost: introduction. 2471
Paradise or garden of the holy fathers. 54, 2578
Paradise papers. 3838
Paradise plantation. 1453
Paradise regain'd. 2471
Paradise regained. 2471
Paradise regained and Samson Agonistes. 2472
Paradise restored and improved. 1568
Paradise revisited. 2772
Paradise to prison. 521
Paradise tree. 2643
Paradise within. 3210, 3774
Paradox and identity in theology. 2832
Paradox of existentialist theology. 3648
Paradox of guilt. 1777
Paradox of instruction. 3477
Paradox of Jesus in the Gospels. 392, 2044
Paradox of pain. 3541
Paradox of religion. 3068
Paradox of religious secularity. 3757
Paradox of the world. 2933
Paradoxes of Jesus. 2065, 2772
Paradoxrs of Catholicism. 780
Paraleipomena Jeremiou. 299
Paralipomena. 337
Parallel four translation New Testament. 357
Parallel lives of the Old and New Testament. 215
Parallel New Testament. 354
Parallel New Testament and Unger's Bible handbook. 401
Parallel Psalter. 582
Parallel source problem in church history. 1172
Paralleled Gospels. 383
... The Paramount children's day book. 3560
Paramount missionary book. 3026
Paramount Sunday school recitations. 3026
Paranormal. 2845, 2988
Paranormal foreknowledge. 1283
Paranormal phenomena, science, and life after death. 2992
Parapraxis in the Haizmann case of Sigmund Freud. 1423, 1788
Parapsychology and the Christian faith. 1088
Parapsychology and the nature of life. 2991
Parapsychology: sources of information. 2992
Pardon and peace. 1327
Pardon my Lenten smile! 2210
Pardoner and his pardons. 1905
Parent and the Jewish day school. 2106
Parent, child, and church. 1254, 2426
Parent training in the church school. 2773
Parental figures and the representation of God. 1728
Parental training. 3152
Parentator. 2372
Parenthesis in eternity. 2694
Parenthood. 1609
Parenting. 1611
Parents and children. 1604
Parents and priests as servants of redemption. 2346
Parents and religion. 3170
Parents are partners in Jewish religious education. 3166
Parent's gift. 3171
Parents' guide. 806, 938, 3163
Parents' guide: religion for little children. 938

Parents' guide to learning disabilities. 2204
Parents' guide to the Catholic school. 805, 1838
Parents in pain. 2773
Parents of many. 2511
Parents pray. 1446
Parents' prayers. 2889
Parents' role in vocations. 3785
Pariksamukham. 1932
Paris Psalter and the meters of Boethius. 47, 573
Paris rosary. 2773
Parish. 2774
Parish, a place for worship. 849, 2775
Parish administration. 3675
Parish annals. 2699
Parish apostles for converts. 797
Parish as learning community. 938
Parish, as seen from the Church of St. John the Evangelist, New York City, 1840-1973. 3275
Parish back talk. 2787
Parish catechumenate. 3182
Parish celebrations. 1587
Parish child. 3675
Parish church. 1159, 1269
... Parish church architecture. 1159
Parish church of St. Mary, Lydney. 2303
Parish church of the Holy Trinity. 3273
Parish churches. 1159
Parish churches of England. 1159
Parish churches of England in colour. 1160
Parish clergy under the later Stuarts. 1292
Parish comes alive. 3676
Parish communion. 2255
Parish communion to-day. 2253
Parish council handbook. 2774
Parish councils. 2774
Parish counseling. 2780
Parish development process. 2197
Parish education in colonial Virginia. 1247
Parish, eucharistic community. 2774
Parish evangelism. 1553, 3671, 3677
Parish family life and social action. 771, 1609
Parish guide to adult initiation. 836, 1563
Parish Holy Week missal. 2240
Parish in a time of change. 2789
Parish in action. 1250
Parish in community and ministry. 2775
Parish in crisis. 2774
Parish institutions of Maryland. 1223, 2775
Parish Kyriale. 2239
Parish life in mediaeval England. 1761
Parish lines, Diocese of Southern Virginia. 2974
Parish lines, Diocese of Southwestern Virginia. 2957
Parish lines, Diocese of Virginia. 2775, 2974
Parish liturgies; experiments and resources in Sunday worship. 2236
Parish Mass book. 2240
Parish ministry resources. 2789
Parish of All Hallows, Allerton, 1876-1976. 25
Parish of Saint Andrew Cambridge. 3273
Parish of St. Michael, 1857-1957. 2697
Parish of Saint Paul, San Diego, California. 3298
Parish of Saint Paul's church, Springfield, Illinois. 3522
Parish of the Advent in the city of Boston. 1116
Parish of the Assumption. 1483
Parish of the templed hills. 2774
Parish planning. 1200
Parish practice. 2288
Parish practice in Universalist churches. 3754
Parish priest. 772, 774, 2774
Parish, priest & people. 2774
Parish priest of Ars. 3778
Parish priest of the town. 1212
Parish priests among the saints. 1024
Parish priests among the saints, cannonized or beatified parish priests. 3280
Parish priests and their people in the middle ages in England. 1758, 1761
Parish priest's guide to inquiry classes. 1568
Parish program of religious education. 3158
Parish record, the centennial year. 1524
... Parish registers, an historical synopsis and commentary. 3051
Parish religious education. 936
Parish remembers. 822, 2540
Parish renewable. 1244
Parish ritual, designed to aid parish priests in the regular exercise of the pastoral ministry. 2239
Parish school. 805
Parish school administration. 3310

Parish school problems. 804
Parish schools of the diocese of Pittsburgh. 824
Parish sermons on moral and spiritual subjects for all Sundays and feasts of obligation. 3340
Parish union helps. 1248
Parish workbook for city churches. 20
Parish year-book of Saint James' church. 1176
Parishes and clergy of the Orthodox. 2959
Parishes and clergy of the Orthodox and other Eastern churches in North America. 1487
Park Street prophet. 2734
Parker society. 3039
Parkerism. 2776
Parks' imperial anthems. 916
Parliament of Chryste, 1566. 2254
Parliamentary procedure in the church. 3218
Parochial and plain sermons. 1227, 3365
... The parochial churches of Sir Christopher Wren, 1666-1718. 2243
Parochial course of doctrinal instructions for all Sundays and holydays of the year. 3339
Parochial hymnal. 813
... Parochial missions to-day. 1565
Parochial records, 1770-1866. 1547
Parochial school. 831
Parochial school a curse to the church, a menace to the nation. 1247
Parsing guide to the Greek New Testament. 1771
Parson Hanks--Fourteen years in the West. 2453
Parson in revolt. 1211
Parson of the bills. 1575
Parson of the hills. 1575
Parson of the islands. 3697
Parson Pettigrew of the "Old Church", 1744-1807. 2827
Parson preaching. 2905
Parson takes a wife. 2339
Parson to parson. 2788
Parson Weems of the cherry-tree. 3801
Parsonage doorway. 3094
Parsonage family and you. 1303
Parsonage planning. 2777
Parson's adventures. 3095
Parsons and pedagogues: the S.P.G. 1222, 3736
Parson's crystal. 3675
Parson's devil. 3526
Parson's dilemmas. 3674
Parson's garden. 3159
Parsons' hand-book of forms. 719
Parson's handbook. 1223, 1224
Parson's outlook. 1299
Parson's role thorns and flowers. 2427
Parson's sampler. 2901
Parsons. vestries, and parishes. 2788
Parsons, vestries, and parishes: a manual. 2788
Parsons year book. 3155
Part I. The problem of the tribes of Israel alleged to have been lost. 46
Part of Jesus and of the apostles. 2013
Part of Rheims in the making of the English Bible. 362
Part of the Opus tertium of Roger Bacon. 1645
Partakers. 1833, 3290
Partheneia sacra. 2362
Parthenon and other Greek temples. 102
Partial and tentative exegesis of Genesis i and ii. 1382
Partial documentary of tribute to Abraham Goldberg, the Zionist, and in tribute to some of his friends and associates who helped make a dream come true. 3896
Partial history of Fincastle Presbyterian church. 1175
Partiality of Jesus. 1951
Participation in the Mass. 2369
Participation in the rural church. 3254
Participation of the faithful in the regal and prophetic mission of Christ according to Saint Augustine. 117, 2192, 115
Particular consideration of a piece, entitled, The quersists. 3011, 3813
Particular examen. 3153
Particular providence. 2133, 2981
Particular relation of the American Baptist mission to the Burman empire. 2505
Parting of friends. 1612
Parting of the way. 2197
Parting word. 3218
Partisan guide to the Jewish problem. 2079
Partisan history of Judaism. 2137
Partly living; some understanding of experience. 959
Partner with the living Lord. 3530
Partners in Africa. 1222

Partners in creation. 3529
Partners in prayer. 1605
Partners in preaching. 2901
Partners in teaching older children. 3186
Partners in the conquering cause. 3730
Partners in the Lord's work. 2595
Partners in victory. 3872
Partners the world around. 2296
Partners with the Almighty. 2495
Partnership. 2337, 3445, 3447
Partnership with Deity. 324
Partnership with God. 957
Pascal. 2777
Pascal and his sister Jacqueline. 2778
Pascal mystery in the Christian year. 1958
Pascal; the emergence of genius. 2777
Pascal's apology for religion. 58
Pascal's philosophy of religion, by Clement C. J. Webb. 58
Pascal's Provincial letters. 2778, 2864
Pascal's unfinished Apology. 58, 2777
Paschal cycle. 2211
Paschal feast in the Bible. 2779
Paschal liturgy and the Apocalypse. 1486
Paschal mystery. 2384, 2778, 3029
Paschal mystery and Christian living. 2032
Paschal mystery in parish life. 2789
Paschal II, Bohemund of Antioch and the Byzantine empire. 2778
Pasoal. 2777
Pass it on. 446
Die "Passagenkirche" 1159
Passages from Holy Writ. 249
Passages from the life and writings of George Fox. 1637
Passages from the scientist's bible. 3313
Passages in the life and ministry of Elbert Osborn. 2444
Passages of a pastor. 1289
Passing and the permanent in religion. 3063
Passing of Mary Baker Eddy. 1494
Passing of the Puritan. 3008
Passing of the saint. 3281
Passing on the gift. 3807
Passing on the torch. 141, 166
Passing Protestantism and coming Catholicism. 2562
Passion. 1957, 2029, 2030, 2032, 2033
Passion and death of Christ. 2030
Passion and death of Our Lord Jesus Christ. 2029
Passion and exaltation of Christ. 2029
Passion and glory of Christ. 386, 2030
Passion and Resurrection of Jesus Christ. 2028
Passion and the death of Jesus Christ. 2029
Passion drama. 2029
Passion flower of Carmel. 2134
Passion flowers. 2213
Passion for life. 1126, 2227
Passion for souls. 1101, 2135
Passion for the impossible. 912
Passion for the possible. 1002
Passion for truth. 2188, 2402, 3479
Passion in Mark. 438
Passion, "Knowing how," and understanding. 1589, 2169
Passion narrative of St. Luke. 430, 2030
Passion of al-Hallaj. 1781, 3543
Passion of Fulton Sheen. 3401
Passion of Jesus Christ. 2031
Passion of Our Lord. 1985, 2029
Passion of Our Lord Jesus Christ, according to the revelations of blaessed Anna Catherine Emmerich, preceded by a brief biography of this great servant of God. 394, 2031
Passion of S. Perpetua. 1021
Passion of the Infant Christ. 998
Passion of the King. 1837, 2029
Passion perspectives. 2213
Passion pilgrimage. 2214
Passion play at Ober Ammergau. 2719
Passion play graft. 2719
Passion play of Oberammergau. 2720
Passion prayer book. 855
Passion story. 2028, 2030
Passion story as recorded by the four evangelists. 1577, 2030
Passion story of Jesus Christ. 383
Passion story of Our Lord Jesus Christ. 2029
Passion week. 1985, 2015, 2029, 2032
Passion Week manual. 2035
Passion week sermons. 2029, 3340
Passional and prayer book. 3313
Passionate God. 1735
Passionate people. 986, 2466
Passionate pilgrim. 195
Passionists. 2778
Passionists in China. 2778
Passionists of the Southwest. 1806
Passover. 2778, 2779
Passover, a season of freedom. 2779

Passover anthology. 2778
Passover fun book. 2779
Passover Haggadah. 2108, 2110, 2779
Passover Haggadah, for the family, school and community seder. 2779
Passover in song and story. 2779
Passover meal. 2108, 2779
Passover plot. 2014
Passover Seder. 2110, 2779, 3328
Passover story. 2778
Passover to freedm. 631
Passover to freedom. 631, 634
Passport to heaven. 2694
Passport to missions. 2493
Passport to the supernatural. 3567
Passport to the unknown. 2727
Passport to the world. 3466
Past and future. 2948
Past and present. 2082, 3434
Past and present, Chartism, and Sartor resartus. 888
Past and present of the Sandwich islands. 1791
... Past and present with Mrs. Piper. 2849, 3512
Past and the presidents. 3380
Past fifty years. 2334
Past is always present. 1013
Past is prelude. 3878
Past lives and present problems. 3053
Past made prsent. 2929
Past, present, and future. 3812
Past, present, and future of Biblical theology. 652
Past revealed. 2725
Pastor. 735, 1296, 2785, 3011, 3094, 3672
Pastor amidst his flock. 3675
Pastor and Christian education of children. 1254
Pastor and church. 2785, 3672, 3677
Pastor and community resources. 2786
Pastor and evangelist. 1553, 1565
Pastor and his people. 2784
Pastor and his work. 2786
Pastor and marriage cases. 2342
Pastor and marriage group counseling. 2345
Pastor and modern missions. 3673
Pastor and parish. 2786
Pastor and people. 3672, 3675
Pastor and religious education. 3154
Pastor and teacher training. 3673
Pastor and the children. 3671
Pastor and the people. 2787
Pastor and the race issue. 1131
Pastor and the Sunday school. 3672
Pastor and the world. 2791
Pastor and vocational counseling. 2780
Pastor as a personal counselor. 3674
Pastor as agape counselor. 2780
Pastor as counselor. 2780
Pastor as educational director. 3151
Pastor as God's minister. 2785
Pastor as husband, father, clergyman. 1297
Pastor as worship leader. 2236
Pastor at prayer. 1298
Pastor at the sick bed. 1258
Pastor at work. 2791
Pastor at work in Christian education. 3674
Pastor at work (The) 2791
Pastor Doug. 2503, 2708
Pastor Halloft. 773
Pastor, his life and work. 2787
Pastor his own evangelist. 1569
Pastor in a Friends meeting. 1678
Pastor in action. 2791
Pastor·in profile. 2785
Pastor in the sick-room. 1259
Pastor in the sickroom. 2888
Pastor La Rue, the pioneer. 2189, 3379
Pastor looks at Kierkgaard. 2170
Pastor Niemoller. 2709
Pastor of the old stone church. 1589, 2752
Pastor-preacher. 2904
Pastor, preacher, person. 1297
Pastor speaks out. 3675
Pastor speaks to the soul of the city. 1277
Pastor; the life of an immigrant. 1775
Pastor: the man and his ministry. 1296
Pastor. this is my problem. 3011
Pastor to pastor. 2791
Pastor wings over South America. 2292
Pastoral address. 39, 2524
Pastoral administration. 1250
Pastoral adventure. 3095
Pastoral advice. 997
Pastoral and personal evangelist. 1565
Pastoral and romance. 2782
Pastoral approach to atheism. 1073
Pastoral assertiveness. 2786
Pastoral authority in personal relationships. 1296
Pastoral calling. 2785
Pastoral care. 2783, 2788, 3674, 3676

Pastoral care & counseling. 2780
Pastoral care and counseling in grief and separation. 2786
Pastoral care and pastoral theology. 2786
Pastoral care and process theology. 2786
Pastoral care and psychotherapy. 2784
Pastoral care come of age. 2780
Pastoral care for personal growth. 2783
Pastoral care in crucial human situations. 2784
Pastoral care in health facilities. 2782
Pastoral care in historical perspective. 2790
Pastoral care in the Black church. 2787
Pastoral care in the church. 2788
Pastoral care in the liberal churches. 2782
Pastoral care in the modern hospital. 1258
Pastoral care of alcoholics and their families. 2780
Pastoral care of families. 2780
Pastoral care of souls. 2782
Pastoral care of the dying and the bereaved. 1416
Pastoral care of the hospitalized child. 885, 1256
Pastoral care of the mentally ill. 1258
Pastoral care of the pastoral family. 1303
Pastoral care of the sick. 1258
Pastoral care to the cancer patient. 2782
Pastoral care with handicapped persons. 1257
Pastoral care with the poor. 2859
Pastoral catechetics. 3151
Pastoral companion. 735, 2789, 3670, 3676
Pastoral counseling. 1373, 2780, 2781, 2782, 2790, 3673
Pastoral counseling and preaching. 2780
Pastoral counseling and spiritual values. 2782
Pastoral counseling casebook. 2779
Pastoral counseling for mental health. 2781
Pastoral counseling in family relationships. 3675
Pastoral counseling in social problems. 2781
Pastoral counseling in work crises. 2781
Pastoral counseling, its theory and practice. 1374
Pastoral counselling. 2781
Pastoral counselor in social action. 2781
... The Pastoral epistles. 367, 445, 446, 479
Pastoral epistles for today. 446
Pastoral Epistles in the Greek New Testament for the English reader. 446
Pastoral epistles in the new English Bible. 445
Pastoral epistles in the new English Bible. With Introd. and commentary. 445
Pastoral epistles of Paul. 446
... The Pastoral epistles of Paul and I and II Peter, Jude, and I, II and III John. 446
... The pastoral epistles of Paul and i and ii Peter, Jude, and i, ii and iii John, by B. H. Carroll. 367
Pastoral evangelism. 1570
Pastoral genius of preaching. 2907
Pastoral homilies. 3612
Pastoral implications of Biblical theology. 651
Pastoral leadership. 3670
Pastoral leadership of Sunday school forces. 3557
Pastoral letter of the archbishops and bishops of the United States assembled in conference at the Catholic university of America. 852
Pastoral letter: the Christian and the community. 2782
Pastoral letters. 445, 446
Pastoral letters: commentary on the first and second letters to Timothy and the letter to Titus. 445
Pastoral letters of the American hierarchy, 1792-1970. 852
Pastoral life and work to-day. 2782
Pastoral life in the power of the spirit. 1246
Pastoral liturgy. 2236
Pastoral manual. 3677
Pastoral manual for new priests. 2788
Pastoral medicine. 2377, 2378
Pastoral memories. 2782
Pastoral ministry. 2786, 3670
Pastoral ministry in a time of change. 2789
Pastoral ministry in our time. 3674
Pastoral ministry of church officers. 1239
Pastoral ministry to families. 2787
Pastoral mission of the church. 2789
Pastoral mission of the church (The) 2789
Pastoral office. 3670, 3674
Pastoral pointers. 2790

Pastoral practice and the paranormal. 1088
Pastoral prayers. 2882
Pastoral prayers for the church year. 2783
Pastoral preaching. 2897, 2901, 2902
Pastoral presence and the diocesan priest. 2789
Pastoral problems. 2787, 3674
Pastoral problems and clinical understanding [workshop on mental health for clergymen. 2784
Pastoral problems in First Corinthians. 322
Pastoral psychiatry. 3671
Pastoral psychology. 2784, 2994, 2995
Pastoral psychology in practice. 2995
Pastoral reform in church government. 808
Pastoral reminiscences. 3673
Pastoral sermons. 863
Pastoral theology. 2789, 3672, 3673, 3675, 3676, 3677
Pastoral theology and the modern world. 3674
Pastoral treatment of sin. 3411
Pastoral triumph. 179
Pastoral use of hypnotic technique. 2784
Pastoral visitation. 3783
Pastoral work, a source book for ministers. 3671
Pastoral work and personal counseling. 3671
Pastorate among the "Disciples of Christ" 1461
Pastoring the smaller church. 2787
Pastor's 25th and a church's 150th anniversary. 1485
...Pastors and people. 1290
Pastors and people of Somerset Classis. 3047
Pastors and teachers. 3152
Pastor's cat, and other people. 2782
Pastor's companion. 2790, 3677
Pastor's corner. 2785
Pastor's counseling handbook. 2780
Pastors counseling manual for ministry to those who must sustain a loved one in crisis. 2781
Pastor's diary. 2782
Pastor's guide. 3672
Pastor's guide for the training of church members. 2929
Pastor's hand book. 3677
Pastor's hand-book, comprising selections of Scripture, arranged for various occasions of official duty. 3677
Pastor's hand book with communion helps. 2790, 3677
Pastor's handbook. 2790
Pastor's helper. 2953
Pastor's helpmate. 1303
Pastor's hospital ministry. 1259
Pastor's ideal funeral book. 1693
Pastor's ideal funeral manual. 1693
Pastor's ideal sermon book. 3373
Pastor's jubilee. 2741
Pastor's manual. 3677
Pastor's manual of the A.M.E. Church. 14, 2788
Pastor's memorial. 1911
Pastor's personal life. 1299
Pastor's place of privilege and power in the Sunday school. 3672
Pastor's pocket Bible. 250
Pastor's pocket manual for hospital and sickroom. 1258
Pastor's point of view. 2789
Pastors, politicians, pacifists. 1620
Pastor's prayerbook. 1298
Pastor's public relations. 1250
Pastor's recollections. 1174
Pastor's review. 2741
Pastor's role in educational ministry. 936
Pastor's sketches. 3291

Pastor's tribute to one of his flock. 2632
Pastor's vade mecum. 2454
Pastor's wife. 1303, 2821, 3304
Pastor's wife and the church. 1303
Pastor's wife today. 1303
Pastures of tender grass, daily inspirational readings. 1433
Pat Boone and the gift of tongues. 681, 1716
Pat Boone devotional book. 1430
Pat McCormick. 2307
Patanjali and yoga. 2791, 3864
Patanjali's raja yoga. 3865
Patanjali's Yoga sutras. 3865
Patches of Godlight. 2219
Patches of joy. 992, 1401
Patchwork family. 1254
Pater Hemon ("Our Father") 2859
Pater mundi. 3074
Pater Noster of Saint Teresa. 2249
Paternalism and the church. 1895
Paternoster sheen. 1342

Path. 1753, 2187, 3330
Path of action. 2381
Path of healing. 3686
Path of humility. 1856
Path of life. 980, 2083, 3196, 3890
... The path of light. 703, 3466
Path of light. 703, 3466
Path of love. 1741, 2262, 3491
Path of perfection. 3866
Path of prayer. 2869, 2876
Path of Protestantism. 2956
... The path of pure consciousness. 3865, 3867
... The path of pure consciousness (jana yoge) 3865
Path of purification. 711
... The path of purity. 711
Path of soul liberation. 102, 3301
Path of the Buddha. 705
Path of the dawning light. 959
... The path of the eternal law, Dhammapada. 711
Path of victory. 2819
Path of virtue (The Dhammapada) 712
Path she trod. 2669
Path through Genesis. 522
Path through Teilhard's Phenomenon. 3593
Path through the Bible. 600
Path to freedom; Christian experiences and the Bible. 241, 996
Path to glory. 428, 2032
Path to God. 1733
Path to noble manhood. 3392
Path to realization of the eternal. 3821
Path to the heights. 3489
Path which led a Protestant lawyer to the Catholic church. 784
Pathbreakers. 2221
Pathetic fallacy. 1092
... Pathfinder for the organization and work of the Woman's Christian temperance union. 3833
Pathfinder in church work with young people. 3879
Pathfinders in the world missionary crusade. 2525
Pathfinders of the soul-country. 2934
Pathfinders of the world missionary crusade. 2525
Paths in spirituality. 3480
Paths of faith. 3093, 3117
Paths of goodness, some helpful thoughts on spiritual progress. 3478
Paths of life. 2227
Paths of peace. 2735
Paths of shining light. 1448
Paths that cross. 2490
Paths that lead to God. 977
Paths the Master trod. 2215
Paths to contemplation. 1356
Paths to eternal glory. 1691, 3784
Paths to happier living. 964
Paths to inner calm. 2381
Paths to peace. 573, 964
Paths to plenty. 3447
Paths to power. 1341, 2886
Paths to the city of God. 3352
Paths to the presence of God. 1725
Paths to transformation. 3734
Paths to unity. 1044
...The pathway of life. 3821
Pathway of life through creation. 1380
Pathway of roses. 3095
Pathway to believing. 1096
Pathway to ecstasy. 1479
Pathway to God. 2986
Pathway to peace. 2302
Pathway to reality. 2417
Pathway to the Bible. 312
Pathway to the cross. 2033, 2213
Pathway to the fold. 621
Pathway upward. 1444
Pathways of Buddhist thought. 708
Pathways of love. 2639
Pathways of prayer. 1432, 2874
Pathways of the inner life. 923
Pathways of the Passion. 2033
Pathways through the Bible. 251, 253
Pathways through the Jewish holidays. 1614
Pathways through the prayerbook. 2107
Pathways through the Torah. 562
Pathways through space. 2645
Pathways to certainty. 3098
Pathways to God. 2873, 3481, 3664
Pathways to happiness. 180, 2382
Pathways to perfection. 1009
Pathways to personal contentment. 1356
Pathways to personal peace. 997, 1001
Pathways to power. 1454
Pathways to spiritual power. 1440
Pathways to the abundant life. 2226
Pathways to the best. 1747
Pathways to the light. 3820
Pathways to the reality of God. 1723
Pathways to understanding. 1449
Patience. 553, 2792

Patience of hope. 1845
Patience Worth. 3519, 3859
Patient continuance in well-doing. 131
Patient's book. 3405
Patient's guide. 3405
Patmos. 457, 458, 463
Patmos portrait of Jesus Christ. 461
Patmos vision. 458
Patmos visions. 455
Patmos wonderland. 460
Patriarch and prophets. 2749, 2821
Patriarch Nicephorus of Constantinople. 1880, 2707
Patriarch Photios of Constantinople. 1028, 2844
Patriarchal age. 524, 2133
Patriarchs. 2793, 3217
Patriarchs and lawgivers of the Old Testament. 493
Patriarchs and politics. 3838
Patriarchs of Israel. 523, 2792
Patrick. 2793
Patrick in his own words. 2793
Patrick J. McGillicuddy and the rabbi. 3016
Patrick of Ireland. 2793
Patrimony of life. 3343
Patrimony of the Roman church in the time of Gregory the Great. 807, 1773
Patriotic devotion. 2893
Patristic homilies on the Gospels. 386
Patristic study. 1618
Patrology. 1019, 1020
Patron saints. 2794, 3281
Patrons of doctors. 1370, 1400
Patteran. 2183, 2206
Patteran; the life and works of Paul Leeds. 2183, 2206
Pattern. 3720
Pattern for a Christian, according to St. Thomas Aquinas. 777, 3636
Pattern for a total church. 3031
Pattern for life. 3335
Pattern for living, an adventure in understanding. 969
Pattern for maturity. 972
Pattern for peace. 1077
Pattern for powerful praying. 2247
Pattern for prayer. 2886
Pattern for successful living. 958
Pattern in Islamic art. 86
Pattern in the Mount, and other sermons. 2934
Pattern life. 2018
Pattern of a church. 2420
Pattern of authority. 118
Pattern of Christ. 181
Pattern of Christian truth. 3658
Pattern of God's truth. 3150
Pattern of New Testament truth. 476
Pattern of our salvation. 332, 3293
Pattern of rural dissent. 1468
Pattern of Scripture. 613, 2355
Pattern of things to come. 2520
Pattern on the mountain. 2210
Pattern prayer. 2246
Pattern, the tabernacle, the Christ. 3720
Patterns for devotion. 3857
Patterns for Jewish living from earliest times to our own time. 2085
Patterns for life's pilgrims. 993
Patterns for living. 2608
Patterns for mature living. 17
Patterns for parish development. 2774
Patterns for prayer from the Gospels. 400
Patterns for preaching. 3374
Patterns for self-unfoldment. 3750
Patterns for the pilgrimage. 994
Patterns in church history. 3122
Patterns in comparative religion. 3115
Patterns in history. 1818
Patterns in pluralism. 1038
Patterns of antislavery among American Unitarians, 1831-1860. 3424
Patterns of Christian acceptance: individual response to the missionary impact, 1550-1950. 924
Patterns of destiny. 3053
Patterns of ethics in America today. 1537
Patterns of faith. 348, 3644
Patterns of faith in America today. 3744
Patterns of grace. 1107
Patterns of Indian thought. 2840
Patterns of inner process. 1879, 2064, 3330
Patterns of prayer. 2874
Patterns of prophecy. 2948
Patterns of Protestant church music. 1209
Patterns of reformation. 2734
Patterns of religious commitment. 3747
Patterns of the mind. 2226
Patteson of the isles. 2794
Patton's gospel hymns. 1861
Patty goes to the nursery class. 3174, 3564

Paul. 338, 345, 372, 376, 377, 381, 1029, 2795, 2796, 2797, 2798, 2799, 2800, 2802, 2803
Paul, a man who changed the world. 2795
Paul, a servant of Jesus Christ. 2799
... Paul Albar of Cordoba. 3134
Paul among Jews and Gentiles, and other essays. 378, 1028, 2803
Paul and Alta. 1527, 2408
Paul and his converts. 478
... Paul and his epistles. 2797
Paul and his interpreters. 373, 2801
Paul and his interpreters, a critical history. 2800
Paul and his letters. 374, 376, 2798
Paul and his predecessors. 376
Paul and his recent interpreters. 1530, 2796
Paul and his teachings. 376, 2797
Paul and James. 368
Paul and Jesus. 2803
Paul and Jesus; origin and general character of Paul's preaching of Christ. 377
Paul and Luther. 2796
Paul and Palestinian Judaism. 1411, 3585
Paul and Paulinism. 2799
Paul and Philippians. 448
Paul and power. 1241, 2798
Paul and Qumran. 372, 1411
Paul and rabbinic Judaism. 376, 1083
Paul and Romans. 469
Paul and the anatomy of apostolic authority. 119, 377
Paul, and the chief cities of his labors. 2798
... Paul and the Crucified. 376
Paul and the early Christians. 372, 2795
Paul and the expansion of the Church today. 2504, 2797
Paul and the intellectuals. 341, 342
Paul and the law of love. 373, 948
Paul and the revolt against him. 2803
Paul and the salvation of mankind. 2799
Paul and the world's most famous letters. 372, 2797
Paul and Thessalonians. 478
Paul, apostle of liberty. 2799
Paul, apostle of the heart set free. 338, 1028, 2795
Paul as a leader. 2800
Paul at Ephesus. 2795
Paul becomes a literary influence. 372
Paul before Caesar from the legal viewpoint. 2804, 2804
Paul before the Areopagus. 335, 2802
Paul before the Areopagus, and other New Testament studies. 335, 2802
Paul, Blanshard on Vatican. 3770
Paul Blanshard on Vatican II. 3770
Paul, Christian and world traveler. 2798
Paul Couturier and unity in Christ. 1044, 1375
Paul, envoy extraordinary. 2799
Paul for a new day. 378
Paul for everyone. 2800
Paul from Tarsus to Rome. 2802
Paul Gerhardt as a hymn writer and his influence on English hymnody. 1706, 1707, 1871
Paul, God's adventurer. 2802
Paul, hero and saint. 2797
Paul, his heritage and legacy. 2798
Paul, his Master's champion. 2800
Paul in everyday life. 370
Paul interpreted. 375
Paul Jones, minister of reconciliation. 2131
Paul Leonard's sacrifice. 2237
Paul Little's Why & what book. 64
Paul, man of conflict. 2801
Paul, master of the spiritual life. 370
Paul meets Jesus. 1029, 2804
Paul: messenger and exile. 2797
Paul, mystic and missionary. 377, 2802
Paul of Tarsus. 2797, 2798, 2800, 2804
Paul on preaching. 2908
Paul, Paulus. 375, 2795
Paul, soldier of the cross. 2801
Paul, son of Kish. 2798
Paul the apostle. 375, 2799, 2800
Paul the Conqueror. 2797, 2799
Paul the dauntless. 2799
Paul the dauntless, the course of a great adventure. 2799
Paul, the faithful witness. 2798
Paul the interpreter of Christ. 377, 2801
Paul, the man and the myth. 370, 1771, 2799
Paul the man, his life, his message and his ministry. 2799
Paul, the missionary. 633, 1575, 2802, 2804
Paul, the preacher. 2801
Paul, the saint who ain't. 1092
Paul VI. 2805
Paul VI, critical appraisals. 2806

Paul the sower. 469
Paul the traveler. 2804
Paul, the traveler and missionary. 3180
Paul the traveller. 2795
Paul, the world's first missionary. 2803
Paul Tillich. 3699, 3700
Paul Tillich and the Christian message. 861, 3700
Paul Tillich; basics in his thought. 3699
Paul Tillich, his life & thought. 3611, 3700
Paul Tillich in Catholic thought. 3700
Paul Tillich: retrospect and future. 3700
Paul Tillich's dialectical humanism. 3700
Paul Tillich's philosophy of culture, science, and religion. 3699
Paul Tillich's radical social thought. 3088, 3700
Paul Tillich's theology of God. 1733, 3700
Paul Tillich's theology of the church. 1188, 3700
Paul to the Colossians. 341
Paul to the Galatians. 381
Paul, trumpet of the spirit. 2803
Paulician heresy. 2805
Pauline ... according to Heb. XI, 1. 1594
Pauline and other studies in early Christian history. 1184
Pauline basis of the concept of Scriptural form in Irenaeus. 241, 1919
Pauline Epistles. 374
Pauline Epistles and the Epistle to the Hebrews in their historical setting. 372
Pauline eschatology. 1530, 2802
...The Pauline idea of faith in its relation to Jewish and Hellenistic religion. 1592
Pauline mysticism. 377
Pauline parallels. 373
Pauline partnership in Chirst. 377, 1163
Pauline perfection, being a series of expository messages upon various aspects of Christian perfection from the Pauline epistles. 1554
Pauline privilege and the constitutions of Canon eleven twenty-five. 1471
Pauline Renaissance in England. 3006
Pauline studies. 373, 2803
Pauline theology. 376, 377, 2804
Pauline view of man in relation to its Judaic and Hellenistic background. 2325
Paulists. 2805
Paul's aeon theology in I Corinthians. 323, 1529
Paul's apocalyptic gospel. 375, 1529
Paul's Apology, II Corinthians 10-13, and the Socratic tradition. 326
Paul's campaigns. 2803
Paul's companions. 2803
Paul's concept of freedom in the context of Hellenistic discussions about the possibilities of human freedom. 378, 1659
Paul's conversion. 2803
Paul's Cross sermons. 2909
Paul's doctrine of redemption. 375
Paul's Epistle to the Galatians. 381
Paul's epistle to the Romans. 469
Paul's ethic of freedom. 373, 1659
Paul's first letter to Corinth. 323
Paul's Gospel. 375, 471
Paul's hymn of love. 2263
Paul's idea of community. 375, 1163
Paul's intercessory prayers. 374
Paul's joy in Christ. 449
Paul's letter to the Romans. 469
Paul's letters. 2796
Paul's letters from prison. 363, 371
Paul's letters to local churches. 372, 2796
Paul's letters to Timothy and Titus. 446
Paul's life and letters. 374, 2800
Paul's message and mission. 375, 2795
Paul's message for today. 376
Paul's prison prayers. 604, 2803
Paul's Second epistle to the Corinthians. 326
Paul's secret of power. 2802
Paul's shipwreck. 2795
Paul's swan song. 2795
Paul's use of the Old Testament. 374
"Paul's vision for the teaching church" 377, 1248
Paul's ways in Christ. 975, 2802
Paulus; reminiscences of a friendship. 3700
Pause for power. 1439
Pause for power; devotional thoughts for men and women. 1439
Pax Christi. 2806, 3331
Pax Christi, letters to a young seminarist. 3331
Pax vobiscum. 959
"Pay day--some day" 1565
Paying the price. 1536
Paying the ransom. 2214
Payson, a model boy. 1284, 1691
Peace. 761, 2806, 2808, 2809

Peace among Christians. 1043
Peace & happiness. 2807
Peace and its hindrances. 971
Peace and modern war in the judgment of the church. 3792
Peace and nonviolence. 2712
Peace and power through prayer. 2881
Peace and quiet and other hazards. 174, 991
Peace child. 2557
Peace Corps and Christian mission. 3743
Peace cross book. 2807, 3796
Peace grows in my garden. 2580
Peace in our business. 1237
Peace in the post-Christian era. 2413
Peace in the valley. 1447
Peace, justice, and reconciliation in the Arab-Israeli conflict. 2073
Peace like a river. 1447
Peace of mind. 1324
Peace of mind through possibility thinking. 2808
Peace of St. Francis. 1643
Peace of soul. 66
Peace on earth. 853, 1320, 2807, 2808, 2809
Peace on Earth handbook. 1134
Peace on earth versus another world-war. 2807
Peace, on not leaving it to the pacifists. 2808
Peace or violence in Latin America? 2771
Peace or war. 3792
Peace parliament. 2807
Peace pays a price. 1397
Peace! Peace! 2809
Peace, perfect peace. 1351, 2807
Peace plus. 2809
Peace, poise, power. 430
Peace study outline. 1674
Peace that is left. 2806
Peace, the churches, and the bomb. 103
Peace through Christ. 2300
Peace through prayer. 2389
Peace through spirituality? 762, 763
Peace to a Jew. 1366
Peace unto you. 1441, 2394
Peace, war, and the young Catholic. 3794
Peace-where is it? 2809
Peace with God. 1754, 3662
Peace with the restless me. 984
Peace within yourself. 422
Peaceable fruit for the nurture of covenant youth. 903
Peacemakers. 2809
Peacemaking. 1608
Peaceworld. 2809
Peak to peek principle. 3539
Peake's commentary on the Bible. 221
Palm leaves, peanuts, and 61 other childern's sermons. 908
Pearl. 301
Pearl and the seed. 811
Pearl is in the oyster. 180
Pearl of Great Price. 1231, 2613
Pearl of great price; a selection from the revelations, translations, and narrations of Joseph Smith, first prophet, seer and revelator to the Church of Jesus Christ of latter-day saints. 2613
Pearl of great price: being a choice selection from the revelations, translations, and narrations of Joseph Smith, first prophet, seer, and revelator to the Church of Jesus Christ of Latter-day saints. 2613
Pearl of great price commentary. 2611, 3430
Pearl of great price comprehensive concordance. 3428
Pearl of Great Price Symposium. 2614, 3429
Pearl of revelation. 3225
Pearl of the Orient. 2316
Pearl to India. 2712
Pearls and paradise. 788
Pearls for preachers. 1840
Pearls from Holy Scripture. 300
Pearls from many seas. 1839
Pearls from Patmos. 423
Pearls from the Bible. 299
Pearls from the Bible on prophecy, precept and promise. 249
Pearls from the casket of the Sacred heart of Jesus. 2383
Pearls from the Prophets. 568
Pearls from the Wonder-book. 2690
Pearls of devotion. 1443
Pearls of great price. 616, 3095
Pearls of perfect provisions. 588
Pearls of promise. 724
Pearls of the deep. 3372
Pearls of worlds. 3094
Pearls, points and parables. 1841, 2771
Pearly gate of the true life and doctrine for believers in Christ. 3395
Pearly gates. 3354

Pearly Gates Syndicate. 1179
Peasant boy who became Pope. 3573
Peasant of the Garonne. 1154
Pebbles of truth. 2396
Peculiar doctrines of the gospel. 3227
Peculiar people. 35, 1683
Peculiar people: the Doukhobors. 1482
Peculiar treasures. 213
Peculiarity of the religion of the Bible. 199
Peculium. 1681
Pedagogical Bible school. 3554
Pedagogical value of the virtue of faith as developed in the religious novitiate. 804
Pedagogical value of willingness for disinterested service. 1277
Pedagogics of preaching. 2903
Pedagogy for ministers. 3672
Pedagogy of Jesus in the twilight of to-day. 2061, 3158
Pedagogy of resurrection. 939
Pedagogy of St. Paul. 2798
Peddlers of fear. 2125
Pedigree of Protestantism. 2976
Pedigree of the Devil. 1423
Pedigreed souls. 973
Pedlar's progress. 23
Pedro Ciruelo's A treatise reproving all superstitions and forms of witchcraft. 2731
Peep of day. 295
Peep through a knot hole in heaven's gate. 1793
Peer counseling in the church. 2810
Peerless book. 279
Peerless laymen in the African Methodist Episcopal Zion Church. 15
Peerless poems of David, the king, in a new metrical version. 581
Peers, tents, and owls. 1296
Pegasus, the winged horse. 2810
Peggy Ann in Latin America. 2549
Pelagius. 2811
Pelagius and the Fifth Crusade. 1391, 1701
Pelagius; inquiries and reappraisals. 2811
Pele and Hiiaka. 2207
Pelendo. 2514, 2811
Pelendo, God's prophet in the Congo. 2514, 2811
Peloubet's Bible dictionary. 245, 246
Peloubet's notes. 1344
Peloubet's select notes. 1916
Peloubet's select notes on the International Bible lessons for Christian living. 1916
Peloubet's select notes on the International Bible lessons for Christian teaching. 1916
Pen of Brahma. 1896
Pen pictures. 718, 1283
Pen pictures from Paul. 371
Pen-pictures in the upper room. 1318, 2250
Pen pictures of Mormonism. 2604
Pen pictures of Our Lady. 2354
Pen pictures of prohibition and prohibitionists. 3597
Pen pictures of the face of Jesus. 84
Pen-pictures on Calvary. 161, 1997, 2056
Pen-portraits of the prophets. 2950
Pen portraits of the twelve. 70
Pen-ultimates. 3089
... Penal administrative procedure against negligent pastors. 1290
Penal legislation in the new Code of canon law (liber v) 1166
...The penalty and redemption. 1360
Penalty of a broken law. 3290
Penance and absolution. 2811
Penance and the anointing of the sick. 2812
Penclings from immortality. 3509
Pendle Hill reader. 1676
Pendle witches. 3827
Pendleton Presbyterian Church, 1789-1966. 2812
Pendragon: a clairvoyant's power of prophecy. 2990
Pendulum swings; churchmanship editorials. 991
Penetralia. 3499, 3500
Peng Fu. 2812
Penguin book of religious verse. 3210
Penguin dictionary of saints. 3283
Penitence and sacrifice in early Israel outside the Levitical law. 3272
Penitent. 2333
Penitent Christian. 2811
Penitente bibliography. 1806
Penitentes of New Mexico. 1806
Penitentes of the Sangre de Cristos. 1806
Penitentes of the Southwest. 1806
Penitential discipline of the primitive church, for the first four hundred years after Christ. 1166

Penitential doctrine of Saint Pacianus. 2756, 2812
Penn bibliography. 2813
Pennant key-indexed study guide to the Old Testament as literature. 596
Pennell of the Afghan frontier. 2531, 2813
Pennies for Palline. 1936, 3437
Pennies from a poor box. 864

Penny a copy. 771, 1135
Penny object lessons. 2720
Pensees. 58, 791, 2777
Pension administration in the Methodist Episcopal church. 2444
Pension boards, Congregational Christian Churches. 1333
Pension regulations of the Methodist Episcopal church. 2444
Pentateuch. 521, 562, 563, 564, 566
Pentateuch and the book of Joshua. 562
Pentateuch in its cultural environment. 565
Pentateuch vindicated from the aspersions of Bishop Colenso. 563, 1306
Pentateuchal criticism. 564
Pentecost. 2813
Pentecost and after. 330
Pentecost and God's hurry. 1466
Pentecost and missions. 2553
Pentecost and the Holy Spirit. 1830
Pentecost behind the Iron Curtain. 2814
Pentecost comes to Central Park. 2813
Pentecost day by day. 1836
Pentecost edition of the Man of Galilee. 1971
Pentecost fully come. 92
Pentecost 1. 314
Pentecostal Catholics. 827, 2815, 2816
Pentecostal edition of songs of praise and victory. 2815
Pentecostal experience. 2815
Pentecostal fire. 1568
Pentecostal fire, radiance & love. 1834
Pentecostal grace. 1587
Pentecostal holiness hymnal. 2814
Pentecostal holiness hymnal no. 2. 2814
Pentecostal hymns. 3561
Pentecostal movement. 2814
Pentecostal movement in the Catholic Church. 756, 2815
Pentecostal piety. 1598
Pentecostal preaching is different. 2896
Pentecostal Sunday school. 3555
Pentecostal worship. 3003
Pentecostalism. 1716, 2814
Pentecostalism, a theological viewpoint. 2815
Pentecostalism in Colombia. 2814
Pentecostals. 2815
Pentecostals around the world. 2815
Pentecosts under the Southern cross. 2503
People among peoples. 1678
People amont peoples. 1678
People and cities. 1277
People and its faith. 3032
People and places in the story of the Scottish Church. 3315
People and the Blessed Sacrament. 997
People and the Book. 304, 501
People and the faith of the Bible. 2084
People and the Presence. 236, 1725
People apart. 1789
People are asking. 2286
People are the church. 1245
People are the city. 2698
People around Jesus. 2007
People at bay. 2099
People builder. 169
People called Baptists. 3465
People called Cumberland Presbyterians. 1396
People called Quakers. 1676, 1677, 3534
People called Shakers. 3397, 3398
People-centered evangelism. 1565
People, church and state in modern Russia. 1148, 1149, 2750
People, families & God. 1612
People for His name. 1942
People from the other world. 3510
People haven't changed. 492
People helping people. 2810
People highly favoured of God. 26, 3231
People ideology, people theology. 788, 1881
People in pain. 2781
People just like us. 216
People, land and churches. 3254
People lovers. 989
People movements in southern Polynesia. 2545
People movements in the Punjab. 2545, 2918
People of ancient Israel. 540
People of God. 1005, 1102, 1122, 1211, 2191, 2404, 3163

People of God; an inquiry into Christian origins. 1192
People of God in ministry. 2307, 2786
People of God in the night. 1060
People of God in the Old Testament. 1163
People of mission. 1705
People of our parish. 826
People of prayer. 2870
People of that book. 1284, 3818
People of the Bible. 616
People of the Book. 2083
People of the center. 1902
People of the covenant. 533, 2148
People of the Dead Sea scrolls in text and pictures. 1409, 3013
People of the Lord. 533, 538
People of the Philippines. 2830
People of the promise. 631
People of the saints. 3303
People of the steeple. 3678
People of the way. 75, 3281
People of two kingdoms. 2406
People on Second Street. 1303
People: 100 years. 3278
People parables. 1839
People, pomp & circumstance in Saint Denis and Notre Dame. 2774, 3273
People/profits. 1536
People reborn. 2544
...The people, the clergy and the church. 173, 1241
People time forgot. 918, 2557
People versus Jesus. 2000
People who care. 2191
People who couldn't be stopped. 406
People who knew God. 3171
People who loved. 662
People who tested God. 692
People worship. 2234
People you live with. 2338
People you'll like to meet. 1014
Peoples. 3704
People's Bible. 250
People's Bible encyclopedia. 197, 242
People's Bible history. 296
People's book of saints. 3279
People's book of worship. 2961
People's church. 2222
People's church pulpit. 2435
People's commentary [formerly "A pictorial commentary"] on the Gospel according to Mark. 434
... People's commentary on the Acts. 330
... People's commentary on the Gospel according to John. 417
... People's commentary on the Gospel according to Luke. 428
People's commentary on the Gospel according to Matthew. 441
People's companion to the Bible. 198
People's dictionary of the Bible. 245
People's faith in the time of Wyclif. 1594
Peoples friend. 1940
People's God vs. the monarchic God. 3116
People's handbook of spiritual science. 3313
People's history of Presbyterianism in all ages. 2936
... The people's holy Bible. 198
People's hymnal. 1861
People's lesson book on the Gospel of Matthew. 444
People's life of Christ. 1972
People's manual. 2368, 2884
People's Mass book. 2369
People's new covenant. 353
People's New Testament. 353
Peoples of God. 1120
Peoples of Old Testament times. 2678
Peoples of Zanzibar: their customs and religious beliefs. 3891
People's padre. 794
People's participation and Holy Week. 2240
People's Pope. 2126, 2861
People's prayers, voiced by a layman. 2870
People's priest. 2789, 3676
People's question book on the Gospel of Mark. 438
People's Temple, people's tomb. 2817
People's Wesley. 3804
People's worship, and psalter. 3853
Peopling of the Earth. 671, 3683
Peplographia dvblinensis. 3367
Pepper 'n salt. 146
Pepysian Gospel harmony. 1517
Perambulations of Cosmopolite. 1478
Perception and religious education. 3155
Perception, physics, and reality. 2417
Perceptions of apartheid. 3464
Perchings; reflections on society and ministry. 1279
Pere Jacques. 1931
Pere Jean. 1948

Pere Lagrange and the Scriptures. 2191
Peregrinus Gasolinus. 837
Peregrinus goes abroad. 837
Perennial Pentecost. 1229, 3354
Perennial philosophy. 3101
Perennial revival. 1554, 1570
Perennials. 694
Perface to religion. 3066
Perfect church. 1122
Perfect day. 1034
Perfect everything. 3480
Perfect fools. 3492
Perfect friend. 1310
Perfect garden. 1702
Perfect generosity of Prince Vessantara. 707
Perfect gospel. 143
Perfect joy of St. Francis. 1643
Perfect language. 2196
Perfect life. 1989, 2817, 3399, 3725
Perfect life in experience and doctrine. 2818
Perfect love. 1824, 2818
Perfect obedience. 2719
Perfect peace. 1349, 1849
Perfect peace for troubled hearts. 236
Perfect philosophy. 1059
Perfect prayer. 2246
Perfect prayer and its lessons. 2247
Perfect salvation. 422
Perfect Teacher. 2061
Perfect vision. 1030
Perfect way. 2726
Perfect will of God. 979
Perfection. 2818
Perfection and charity. 2819
Perfection of beauty, and other sermons. 2819
Perfection of God, the fountain of good. 1342
Perfection of man by charity. 2819
Perfection of wisdom. 2317
Perfection of wisdom in eight thousand lines & its verse summary. 2819
Perfection of Yoga. 3864
Perfectionism. 2818
Perfectionist persuasion. 1824
Perfiles. 2439
Perflexing problems of religion. 65
Perforated mood-swing book. 3883
Performing audience. 1205
Perfumed scorpion. 3543
Perhaps I was dreaming. 1454
Peril by choice. 184, 2540
Peril of bread. 164
Peril of modernizing Jesus. 1978
Peril of power. 3341
Perils of professionalism. 2945
Perils of respectability. 961
Perils of the latter days. 1514
Periodica Islamica. 2307, 2678
Periodical articles on religion. 3090
Periodicals of American transcendentalism. 3709
"Perish the Jew!" 2077
Perkins' church anthems. 49
Permanence & change. 1538
Permanent cure for depression's ills. 1425
Permanent elements of religion. 3098
Permanent Sabbath documents of the American and foreign Sabbath union. 3546
...The permanent value of the Book of Genesis as an integral part of the Christian revelation. 482
Perpetual chantries in Britain. 883
Perpetual dilemma. 2097, 2151
Perpetual help daily missal. 2239
Perpetuating Pentecost. 2813
Perpetuation of divine science writings. 1496
Perpetuity of the earth. 2306, 2465
Perplexing passages in the four Gospels. 321
Persatuan Islam. 2820
Perse. 731, 2820
Persecuted but not forsaken. 2821
Persecuted prophets. 3432
Persecution in the early church. 2821
Persecution of Huguenots and French economic development. 1852
Persecution of Huguenots and French economic development, 1680-1720. 1852
Persecution of Peter Olivi. 1647, 2736
Persecution of progressives. 2820
Persecutions in the early church. 2820
Persecutor. 2186
Persephone and the springtime. 2952
Persephone, bringer of spring. 2822
Persephone: three essays on religion and thought in Magna Graecia. 1512, 3405
Perseus and Andromeda. 2822
Perseus and the Gorgon. 2822
Persian mythology. 2664
Persian paintings in the India Office Library. 1883, 1895

Persian stronghold of Zoroastrianism. 3899
Persian Sufis. 3543
Persian Yankee. 2913
Persistence of religion. 3067
Person and counselor. 2780
Person and God in a Spanish valley. 2668
Person and institution. 1911
Person and ministry of the Holy Spirit. 1828, 1831
Person and ministry of the Holy Spirit, a Wesleyan perspective. 1828
Person and place of Jesus Christ. 1049, 1951, 2038
Person and profession. 1296
Person and reality. 2417
Person and society. 3449
Person and the common good. 2320
Person and work of Christ. 2043, 2045
Person and work of the Holy Spirit. 1831, 1832
Person and work of the Holy Spirit as revealed in the Scriptures and in personal experience. 1834
Person and work of the Holy Spirit in the life of the believer. 1828
Person I am. 955
Person in religion. 2823
Person in the pulpit. 2901
Person-minded ministry. 3671
Person of Christ. 1995, 2036
Person of Christ and His presence in the Lord's supper. 2035
Person of Christ in New Testament teaching. 2044
Person of Christ; the perfection of His humanity viewed as a proof of His divinity. 2043
Person of Jesus Christ. 2041
Person reborn. 977
Person to person. 999, 2782
Personal adventure in prophecy. 454
Personal adventures with Jesus. 161
Personal and controversial. 670
Personal and ideal elements in education. 1497
Personal and practical Christian work. 964
Personal appeals to Sunday school workers. 3554
Personal assignment. 1359, 2713
Personal Bible study. 639
Personal Bible study, a how-to. 642
Personal Christian work. 1048
Personal Christianity. 161, 674, 1055, 1061
Personal Christianity a science. 674
Personal crisis. 966
Personal devotions for pastors. 1299
Personal discernment inventory. 953
Personal discipleship and the way of prayer. 964
Personal elements in religious life. 2823
Personal evangelism. 1554, 1566, 1567
Personal evangelism among students. 1256
Personal evangelism of Jesus. 2004
Personal evangelist. 1564
Personal experience and the historic faith. 1586
Personal experience of a physician, with an appeal to the medical and clerical professions. 1839
Personal exploration of expansion of consciousness. 1348
Personal factors in character building. 2592
Personal faith. 1590
Personal faith for human crisis. 1005
Personal finance for clergymen. 1292
Personal finances for ministers. 1292
Personal friendships of Jesus. 2007
Personal God? 1729
Personal growth and social change. 2781
Personal idealism and Strong's theology. 3535
Personal introduction to God. 1030, 1494
Personal Jesus. 1972
Personal life of the Christian. 991
Personal life of the clergy. 1299
Personal living. 2994, 3705
Personal memoirs. 671, 3090
Personal memories of G. S. Arundale. 89
Personal ministry of the gospel. 3671
Personal Pentecost. 1328
Personal power formula. 1009
Personal power through the spiritual disciplines. 1442
Personal prayer. 2895
Personal problems. 1136
Personal problems of conduct and religion. 968
Personal progress in religion. 2945
Personal recollections. 144
Personal religion. 954, 1095, 3097
Personal religion among the Greeks. 1766
Personal religion and public righteousness. 2212

Personal religion and the life of devotion. 1448
Personal religion and the life of fellowship. 1063
Personal religion and the social awakening. 3086
Personal religion in Egypt before Christianity. 1502
Personal religious beliefs. 1059
Personal religious disciplines. 89
Personal reminiscences of Cardinal Newman. 2703
Personal renewal through Christian conversion. 1359
Personal responsibility. 2323
Personal salvation. 1358, 3291
Personal security through faith. 3716
Personal success; the promise of God. 986
Personal survival. 1695
Personal testimony to life after death. 3519
... Personal triumph. 966
Personal union with Christ. 976
Personal work. 1048, 3872
Personal worker's hand-book. 1568
Personal worker's New Testament. 352, 354, 3197
Personalism and vocation. 3785
Personalism in theology. 2182, 2822
Personalities and events in Jewish history. 2093
Personalities and powers. 2324
Personalities around David. 1405
Personalities around Jesus. 337, 2007
Personalities around Paul. 2803
Personalities around the Cross. 2029
Personalities behind the Psalms. 586
Personalities in the Christmas story. 1996
Personalities in the Gospel story. 384
Personalities of the Council of Florence. 1622
Personalities of the New Testament. 339
Personalities of the New Testament. 339
... Personalities of the Old Testament. 493, 494
Personalities of the passion. 2032
Personality. 961
Personality and character building. 2591
Personality and configuration with Christ. 3484
Personality and message of the preacher. 2823
Personality and office of the Christian Comforter asserted and explained. 1829
Personality and progress. 3443
Personality and religion. 2822, 3001, 3098
Personality and sexual problems in pastoral psychology. 2784
Personality and the fact of Christ. 1954
Personality development in the religious life. 2572
Personality fulfillment in the religious life. 2571
Personality fulfillment in the spiritual life. 3490
Personality, human and divine. 2823
Personality in a communal society. 1858
Personality in Christ and in ourselves. 2823
Personality in retrospection-introspection. 2823
Personality in the making. 2225
Personality of Christ. 2045
Personality of God. 1727
Personality of Jesus. 1995, 1996, 2035
Personality of St. Paul. 2798
Personality of seminarians. 3331
Personality of the Holy Spirit. 1829
Personality of the soul. 3463
Personality survives death. 175, 3495
... Personality traits of successful minor seminarians. 2823
Personality types and holiness. 3475
Personality we have missed. 1995
Personalities around the Cross. 2029
Personhood, creativity, and freedom. 3330
Personnel administration in the Christian school. 3310
...Personnel and guidance in Y.M.C.A. schools. 2823
Personnel policies, practices and codes in Jewish community centers. 1320
Personology. 961
Persons and ideals. 925
Persons can change. 1006, 2994
Persons, privacy, and feeling. 2474
Persons we teach. 2323
Perspective. 1456, 3677
Perspective devotional thoughts for men. 1439, 2402
Perspective in mission. 2555
Perspective in religion and culture. 762
Perspective of Jewish life through its festivals. 1623
Perspectives. 1259, 3352
Perspectives for everyday living. 2390

Perspectives in American Catholicism. 834
Perspectives in Christian humanism. 1071
Perspectives in the history of religions. 3111
Perspectives in yoga. 3867
Perspectives of a political ecclesiology. 1126
Perspectives on a college church. 1284
Perspectives on charismatic renewal. 1834
Perspectives on death. 1415
Perspectives on evangelical theology. 3623
Perspectives on Jews and Judaism. 2147, 2166
Perspectives on 19th and 20th century Protestant theology. 3679
Perspectives on Old Testament literature. 503
Perspectives on our age. 1509, 3611
Perspectives on Paul. 370
Perspectives on Pentecostalism. 2816
Perspectives on Scripture and tradition. 206
Perspectives on the new Pentecostalism. 2814
Perspectives on the parables. 2771
Persuading God back to Herrin. 1808
Persuasive preaching. 2906
Persuasives to early piety. 904
Perthynas crefydd a gwyddoreg. 3073
Perversity and error. 2122
Pesah is coming! 2779
Pesah is here! 2779
Peshitta of Exodus. 517
Peshitta Psalter according to the west Syrian text. 573
Peshitto of Second Samuel. 482
Pesikta de-Rab Kahana. 593, 3370
Pesikta rabbati; discourses for feasts, fasts, and special Sabbaths. 2140
Pesky problems for positive preachers. 3495
Pete and Penny know and grow. 901
Pete and Penny play and pray. 901
Peter. 1191, 2824, 2825
Peter Abailard. 1
Peter Abelard. 1
Peter Abelard; philosophy and Christianity in the Middle Ages. 1, 1104
Peter Abelard's Ethics. 942
Peter Ainslie. 20
Peter and Caesar. 1143
Peter and his Lord. 2824, 2932
Peter and Paul. 407, 2825
Peter and Paul altarpiece and Friedrich Pacher. 27, 2756
Peter and Paul and their friends. 3192
Peter and Paul, apostles. 407
Peter and the church. 1121, 1169, 2824
Peter and the keys. 2768, 2824
Peter Calvay, hermit. 727, 2881
Peter Cartwright. 743
Peter Cartwright, pioneer circuit rider. 743
Peter Claver. 1286
Peter, disciple, apostle, martyr. 2825
Peter Dynamite, "twice-born" Russian. 1456
Peter E. Dietz. 1459
Peter Edwards's Candid reasons examined, and answered. 135, 1500
Peter, fisherman, disciple, apostle. 2825
Peter Hausted. 1790
Peter Hurkos. 3767
Peter in Rome. 2825
Peter in the firelight. 2824
Peter in the New Testament. 349, 2825
Peter laughed at pain. 2810
Peter; life and letters. 2824
Peter Lombard and the sacramental system. 2826, 3266
Peter Marshall's lasting prayers. 2208
Peter Martyr in Italy. 3777
Peter Maurin. 875, 2374
Peter Maurin: gay believer. 2374
Peter of the mesa. 1899
Peter Parker and the opening of China. 2509, 2776
Peter Parley's Book of Bible stories. 620, 632
Peter Parley's method of telling about the geography of the Bible. 282
Peter Pulpitpounder. 2788
Peter Pulpitpounder, B. D. 2788
Peter speaks through Leo. 880
Peter speaks today. 325
Peter, Stephen, James, and John. 1197
Peter Sterry, Platonist and Puritan, 1613-1672. 3527
Peter, the apostle. 2825
Peter the fisherman. 2825
Peter the fisherman philosopher. 2824
Peter the fisherman preacher. 2824
Peter, the prince of apostles. 72, 339, 2825
Peter, the story of a deserter who became a forceful leader. 72, 337, 2824

Peter the Venerable and Islam. 1084, 2846
... Peterborough. 2826
Peterborough psalter and bestiary of the fourteenth century. 1884
... Peters' Catholic class book. 812
Peter's Pentecost discourse. 332
Peter's principles. 447
Peters' sodality hymn book. 1861
Peter's tomb recently discovered in Jerusalem. 2826
Petition against God. 3018
Petitions for the indult to reserve the Blessed Sacrament in private oratories. 777
Peut-on se passer de metaphysique? 2416
Pevote. 2827
Pew and the pupil. 2827
Pew ask pulpit answers. 3011
Pew asks. 3011
Pew for one, please. 1256
Pew preaches. 2827
Pews talk back. 2903
Peyote. 2671, 2827
Peyote cult. 2827
Peyote hunt. 1853
Peyote religion. 2671, 2827
Peyote religion among the Navaho. 2677, 2827
Peyote ritual. 2827
Peyote story. 2827
Peyote, the divine cactus. 2827
Pfeiffer Chapel, Florida Southern College, Lakeland, Florida, 1938. 3860
Phaedo. 1890
Phaethon. 2652
Phalanx, a "Y" club for young men. 3875
Phallic worship. 2828
Phanerothyme; a western approach to the religious use of psychochemicals. 1781
Phantasmagorian theology and other things. 1655
... Phantasms of the dead. 1709
Phantasms of the living. 2993
Phantom form. 3502
Phantom walls. 2990
Pharaoh's question, and other addresses. 3067
Pharisaic Judaism in transition. 1506, 2150
Pharisaic Judiasm in transition. 1506, 2113
Pharisaism. 2828
Pharisaism and Christianity. 1083
Pharisaism and Jesus. 2829
Pharisaism in the making. 2108, 2148
Pharisees. 2095, 2828
Pharisees' guide to total holiness. 1958, 2828
Pharmacopeia and the physician. 3690
Phases in the religion of ancient Rome. 3245
... Phases of early Christianity. 1190
Phases of religion in America. 3744
Phases of the church universal. 2690
Phases of the sacred passion. 2031, 3150
Pheneas speaks. 3500
Phenomena of astral projection. 94
Phenomena of materialisation. 2372
Phenomena of our universe. 2636
Phenomena of Pentecost. 2813
Phenomena of the Bible. 2476
Phenomenal mirror. 2978
Phenomenology and atheism. 100
Phenomenology and existence. 2738
Phenomenology and religion. 1103
Phenomenology of religion. 3097, 3117
Phenomenon of death. 1415
Phenomenon of obedience. 492
Phenomenon of religion. 3064
Phenomenon of the New Testament. 349
Phi Beta Kappa as a secret society, with its relations to Freemasonry and antimasonry. 2829
Phil. 2,6 and P. A. Florenskij. 449, 1630
Philadelphia Quaker. 1687
Philadelphia Quakers in the industrial age, 1865-1920. 1138, 1687
Philadelphia seminary biographical record, 1864-1923. 3614
Philadelphia Unitarianism, 1796-1861. 3730
Philadelphia's finest. 824
Philathea Bible class. 3838
Philemon. 447
Philemon among the letters of Paul. 447
Philip. 339, 632, 2830
Philip cometh to Andrew. 1225
Philip Doddridge, D.D. 1472
Philip Doddridge, his life and labors. 1472
Philip Jacob Spener and his work. 3471
Philip Melanchthon. 2400
Philip Melanchthon; reformer without honor. 2400
Philip Mercer Rhinelander. 3234
Philip the Fair and Boniface VIII. 677, 1638, 677, 1638

Philip W. Lown. 2087
Philip William Otterbein. 2752
Philip William Otterbein; pastor ecumenist. 2752
Philippian gospel. 448
Philippian studies. 449
Philippians. 448, 449, 450
Philippians; an expositional commentary. 448
Philippians-Colossians-Philemon; a new commentary, workbook, teaching manual. 450
Philippians in the Greek New Testament for the English reader. 449
Philippians, life at its best. 448
Philippians: the gospel at work. 658
Philippine church: growth in a changing society. 2545
Philippine Duchesne. 1481
Philippine Duchesne and her times. 825, 1481
Philippine Duchesne, frontier missionary of the Sacred Heart, 1769-1852. 1481
Philippine kaleidoscope. 2544
Philippines calling. 1882
Philippines in five hours. 826
Philip's cousin Jesus. 2005
Philistines and the Old Testament. 534, 2831
Philistinism. 3422
Phillippines--1925. 2545
Phillips Brooks. 694, 2202
Phillips Brooks' addresses. 694
Phillips university sermons, by the younger graduates. 3366
Philo and the gnostics on man and salvation. 2322, 2831
Philo and the oral law. 2073, 2107, 2831
Philo-Judaeus of Alexandria. 2831
Philo Woodruff Sprague. 3522
Philocalia of Origen. 2743
Philochristus. 1460
Philology of the Gospels. 393
Philomythus, an antidote against credulity. 2475
Philo's Bible. 528
Philo's contribution to religion. 2831
Philo's description of Jewish practices. 2831, 3690
Philo's place in Judaism. 2831
Un philosophe neoplatonicien du XIe siecle: Michel Psellos, sa vie, son ouvre, ses luttes philosophiques, son influence. 2986
Philosoper and theology. 2836
Philosopher looks at Jesus. 421
Philosophers and religious truth. 2837
Philosophers in wonderland. 2773
Philosopher's love for Christ. 2000, 2266
Philosophers of process. 881
Philosophers speak of God. 1722
Philosopher's stone. 2833
Philosopher's victory through Christ. 3292
Philosopher's way. 3715
Philosophia hermetica. 1806
Philosophic and scientific ultimatum. 3097
Philosophic function of value. 3859
Philosophic inquiry. 2834
Philosophical anarchism of William Godwin. 38, 1743
Philosophical and critical inquiries concerning Christianity. 1097
Philosophical and religious issues. 3108
Philosophical anthropology. 3461
Philosophical aspects of thanatology. 1414
Philosophical bases of human liberty according to St. Thomas Aquinas. 2223, 3694
Philosophical basis of theism. 3608
Philosophical foundations of faith. 3098
Philosophical foundations of India. 2839
Philosophical fragments. 3101
Philosophical frontiers of Christian theology. 2309, 2833
Philosophical heritage of the Christian faith. 1103
Philosophical inquiry respecting the abolition of capital punishment. 737
Philosophical issues in religious thought. 3102
Philosophical lectures. 2321
Philosophical lectures and remains of Richard Lewis Nettleship. 2832
Philosophical possibilities beyond death. 1696
Philosophical pot pourri or miscellany. 2834
Philosophical readings in Cardinal Newman. 2834
Philosophical resources for Christian thought. 1106
Philosophical retrospect on the general out-lines of creation and providence. 1380
Philosophical scrutiny of religion. 3058

Philosophical series. 2833
Philosophical solution of the cause of causes. 876
Philosophical study of mysticism. 2637
Philosophical study of religion. 3099
Philosophical study of the human mind. 2473
Philosophical teachings in the Upanisads. 3760
Philosophical terms in the Moreh nebukim. 2622, 2623, 2839
Philosophical texts. 3696
Philosophical theology. 2832, 3105
Philosophical theology of Jonathan Edwards. 1499
Philosophical understanding and religious truth. 2836, 2837
Philosophical works of Francis Bacon, baron of Verulam, viscount St. Albans. 124
Philosophical works of Leibnitz. 2833
Philosophical writings. 2417, 2839
Philosophical writings of Leibniz. 2568
Philosophies of Father Coughlin. 1372, 3740
Philosophies of India. 2840
Philosophies of Judaism. 2841
Philosophies of religion. 3108
Philosophumena. 1805
Philosophy and Christianity. 1106
Philosophy and development of religion. 3107
Philosophy and economics. 962
Philosophy and parapsychology. 2773
Philosophy and phenomena of spiritualism. 3516
Philosophy and religion. 2837, 2838
Philosophy and religion in colonial America. 3213
Philosophy & religion of Chaitanya and his followers. 879, 3766
Philosophy and religion; some contemporary perspectives. 2837
Philosophy and religious belief. 3105
Philosophy and the Christian faith. 2835
Philosophy and the integration of contemporary Catholic education. 2835
Philosophy and theology. 3105
Philosophy and theology of Anders Nygren. 2719
Philosophy beyond the classroom. 3620
Philosophy from prison. 362, 364
Philosophy in revolution. 1457
Philosophy in the age of crisis. 2843
Philosophy in the flesh. 3090
Philosophy in the Middle Ages. 2842, 2843
Philosophy o Civilization. 1282
Philosophy of a future state. 1695
Philosophy of a giant. 3545
Philosophy of a novitiate. 2833
Philosophy of a scientific man. 3078
Philosophy of Alexander Campbell. 732
Philosophy of all possible revelation. 1536
Philosophy of an opinion. 3066
Philosophy of ancient Britain. 1480
Philosophy of ancient India. 2839
Philosophy of Arthur Schopenhauer. 3311
Philosophy of behavior. 185
Philosophy of being. 2739
Philosophy of benevolence. 3528
Philosophy of Borden Parker Bowne and its application to the religious problem. 686
Philosophy of Buddhism. 711
Philosophy of Catholic higher education. 830, 832
Philosophy of Christ. 2036
Philosophy of Christian being. 1103
Philosophy of Christian education. 805, 940, 3151
Philosophy of Christian experience. 957
Philosophy of Christian morals for today. 943
Philosophy of Christian perfection. 2817
Philosophy of Christianity. 1104, 3101
Philosophy of Christianity and the philosophy of government. 1104
Philosophy of Christ's temptation. 2067
Philosophy of church building. 1156
Philosophy of Clement of Alexandria. 1288
Philosophy of Confucius in the translation of James Legge. 2838
Philosophy of courage. 2753
Philosophy of creation. 1380, 2758, 3716
... The philosophy of creation in the writings of St. Augustine. 115, 1382
Philosophy of delight. 2395
... The philosophy of Descartes in extracts from his writings. 1425
Philosophy of evil. 1746
Philosophy of existence. 3117
Philosophy of existentialism. 1584, 3303
Philosophy of fire. 2710
...Philosophy of Frederic Nietzsche. 2710
Philosophy of God. 3697

Philosophy of God and the world. 1514
Philosophy of God, and theology. 1723
Philosophy of heaven, earth, and the millennium. 3076
Philosophy of history. 2097
Philosophy of history related to worship. 1818
Philosophy of history related to worship, from Gentile and Hebrew sources, considering universal ideals and predictions fulfilled in persons, nations, and social movements of the world. 1818
Philosophy of Hobbes in extracts and notes colleted from his writings. 1821
Philosophy of humanism. 1854
... The philosophy of Hume. 1855
Philosophy of ignorance. 1905
Philosophy of Immanuel Kant. 2163
Philosophy of integration. 1103
Philosophy of Jesus. 1951, 1989
Philosophy of Jesus: real love. 2264
Philosophy of Judaism. 2146, 2841
Philosophy of justice between God and man. 3097
Philosophy of Kant. 2163
Philosophy of law and freedom. 66
Philosophy of life. 2833
Philosophy of life and its spiritual values. 2227
Philosophy of life as evolved by modern science. 3512
Philosophy of light. 2229
Philosophy of living. 1536
... The philosophy of Locke. 2180
Philosophy of Mahatma Gandhi. 1701
Philosophy of man. 2419
Philosophy of meditation. 2379
Philosophy of mind. 2473, 2474
Philosophy of mizvot. 1, 1312
Philosophy of Mulla Sadra (Sadr al-Din al-Shirazi) 2630
Philosophy of mysterious agents, human and mundane. 2991
Philosophy of mystery. 2731, 2988
Philosophy of mysticism. 2641, 2993
Philosophy of natural magic. 2731
Philosophy of parapsychology. 2993
Philosophy of peace, power and plenty. 3864, 3865
Philosophy of personalism. 2822
Philosophy of positive life. 2865
Philosophy of prayer. 2875
Philosophy of preaching. 2897
Philosophy of providence. 2980
Philosophy of reform in which are exhibited the design, principle and plan of God, for the full development of man, as a social, civil, intellectual and moral being. 2982
Philosophy of religion. 1737, 3061, 3097, 3098, 3099, 3100, 3102, 3103, 3104, 3105, 3106, 3107, 3108
Philosophy of religion and theology. 3108
Philosophy of religion and theology: 1971. 3107
Philosophy of religion: contemporary perspectives. 3107
Philosophy of religion from the standpoint of Protestant theology. 3098
Philosophy of religion on the basis of its history. 3104
Philosophy of religion: the historic approaches. 3098
Philosophy of revelation. 3224
Philosophy of ritual. 3240
Philosophy of St. Bonaventure. 675
Philosophy of St. Thomas Aquinas. 2842, 3693, 3695, 3696
Philosophy of Sarvepalli Radhakrishnan. 3018
Philosophy of Schopenhauer. Edited with an introd. by I. Edman. 3311
Philosophy of science and belief in God. 3084
Philosophy of science and the occult. 2728
Philosophy of Sikhism. 3408
Philosophy of skepticism and ultraism. 2776, 3422
... Philosophy of social change according to the principles of Saint Thomas. 1283, 3693
Philosophy of special providence. 2980
Philosophy of special providences. 2980
Philosophy of special providences: a vision. 2980
Philosophy of spirit. 3105
Philosophy of spirit, and the spirit-world. 3516
Philosophy of spiritual activity. 51, 1658
Philosophy of spiritual activity [freedom]. 1658
Philosophy of spiritual intercourse. 3500
Philosophy of spiritual intercourse, being an explanation of modern mysteries. 3500

Philosophy of spiritualism. 3506
Philosophy of spiritualism and the pathology and treatment of mediomania. 3508
Philosophy of the atonement. 108
Philosophy of the Bible. 2115
Philosophy of the Buddha. 700
Philosophy of the Christian religion. 1049, 1103
Philosophy of the Christian revelation. 3225
Philosophy of the Christian world mission. 2555
Philosophy of the Church fathers. 3658
Philosophy of the enlightenment. 1520
Philosophy of the I ching. 1878
...The philosophy of the incarnation. 1893
Philosophy of the infinite. 1907
Philosophy of the inner light. 1908, 2348
Philosophy of the Kalam. 1927
Philosophy of the Old Testament. 601
Philosophy of the plan of salvation. 3291
Philosophy of the self. 8
Philosophy of the spirit. 1800, 3478
... The philosophy of the supernatural. 3567
Philosophy of the teachings of Islam. 20
Philosophy of the unknown. 1371, 3081
Philosophy of the Upanisads. 3760
Philosophy of the Upanishads. 3760
Philosophy of theism. 3607, 3608, 3609
Philosophy of Trinitarian doctrine. 3712
Philosophy of Vijanaabikshu. 3775, 3779
Philosophy of war. 3791
Philosophy of William Ellery Channing. 882
Philosophy, Qabbala and Vedanta. 3059
Philosophy studies religion. 2836
Philosophy and faith of Universalism. 3752
Philosophical symposium on American Catholic education. 831
Philosphy of religion. 3103
Philsosphy of religion from the standpoint of Protestant theology. 3098
Philus, the stable boy of Bethlehem. 3369
[Phineas Davison's letter, to aged friends. 3122
Phineas Parkhurst Quimby, revealer of spiritual healing to this age. 3013
Phoenix. 2732
Phoenix at Coventry. 1377
Phoenix lectures. 3314
Phoenix of his age. 1527
Phoenix rises; a mission history of Guam. 2523
Phone calls from the dead. 3472
Phone power. 3594
Photius and the Carolingians. 2844, 3714
Photo album of St. Therese of Lisieux. 3691
Photo album of St. Therese of Lisieux (The) 3691
Photographer in Lebanon. 154, 2159
Photographic copies of written messages from the spirit world, more than one hundred written communications from those who dwell in spirit life. 3497
... Photographic supplement of St. Paul's cathedral. 2244
Photographing the invisible. 2844
Photographs of my father. 3472

Photomeditations. 2394
Phunology. 1166
Physic [read psychic] power of a God within. 1723
Physical cause of the death of Christ. 1998
Physical history of the creation of the earth and its inhabitants. 1380
Physical in spiritualism. 3513
Physical media in spiritual manifestations. 3513
Physical, moral and social effects of alcoholic poison as a beverage and as a medicine. 3595
Physical phenomena of mysticism. 2640
Physical phenomena of mysticism, with especial reference to the stigmata, divine and diabolic. 2640
... The physical phenomena of spiritualism. 3497
Physical phenomena of spiritualism, fraudulent and genuine. 3497
Physical proofs of another life. 3507
Physical religion. 3110, 3776
Physical side of being spiritual. 3662
Physical theory of another life. 1891
Physical theory of the soul. 2992
Physician examines the Bible. 317
Physician of the dance of death. 1400
Physician to the soul. 2409
Physicians of the soul. 605, 1012, 2038
Physicians of the soul, a history of pastoral counseling. 3673
Physicist and Christian. 3082
Physico-theology. 2674

Physiological correspondences. 1370
Physiology and psychology. 3609
Physiology of faith. 3642
Physiology of faith and fear. 2410
Pia desideria. 2846
Pick up your trumpet. 2299, 3352
Picket line of missions. 2483
Picking up the pieces. 63
Pickings. 1841
Pickway. 3589
Pictoral Bible and commentator for young people. 644
Pictorial anthology of witchcraft, magic & alchemy. 2725, 2728
Pictorial Bible and commentator. 293, 1962
Pictorial Biblical encyclopedia. 243
Pictorial commentary on the Gospel according to Mark. 434
Pictorial directory of the hierarchy of the United States. 668
Pictorial Gospel. 399, 1957, 2760
Pictorial history of Christ Church, Boston. 1173
Pictorial history of Maryland Jewry. 2100
Pictorial history of Protestantism. 2978
Pictorial history of the Dominican province of Saint Joseph United States of America. 1475
Pictorial history of the Episcopal Church in North Carolina. 2971
Pictorial history of the Jewish people, from Bible times to our own day throughout the world. 2094
Pictorial history of the physical development of Mission Santa Barbara. 3302
Pictorial history of the Virginia Conference. 1550
Pictorial introduction to the Bible. 309
Pictorial key to the tarot. 3589
Pictorial lives of the saints. 3282
Pictorial oddities from Hebraic literature. 2076, 2083
Pictorial prayer-book. 2884
Pictorial profile of the Holy Land. 2764
Pictorial spiritualism. 3497
Pictorial Sunday book. 295, 1967
Pictorial treasury of Jewish holidays and customs. 2152
Picture book of Bible news. 602
Picture book of Jewish holidays. 1615
Picture book of Palestine. 2760
Picture book of Passover. 2779
Picture dictionary of Jewish life. 2085
Picture dictionary of the Bible. 246
Picture-history of the Bible and Christianity in 1000 pictures, with the inspiring stories of all the world's great religions. 3140
Picture history of the Bible and Christianity in 1000 pictures. 3141
Picture in religious education. 3146
Picture life of Malcolm X. 2233, 2681
Picture museum of sorcery, magic & alchemy. 2725
Picture of creation. 536
Picture of the heavenly Jerusalem in the writings of Johannes of Fecamp. 1943, 2122
Picture puzzles. 1810
Picture stories from the Bible. 626, 630
Picture story Bible ABC book. 621
Picture story Bible ABC book. Favorite stories by Elsie Egermeier, adapted for young children by Arlene Hall. 621
Picture-story life of Christ. 1980
Picture-story life of Jesus. 1980
Picture talks on the Gospels. 906
Picture windows on the Christ. 339
Picture-work. 3784
Pictured compilation of hymns loved and sung by Christians the world over. 1868
Pictured outline of the gospel narrative. 383
Pictured truth. 880, 3716
... Pictures and persons. 188
Pictures and stories of long ago. 616
Pictures from a mediaeval Bible. 199
Pictures from Pilgrim's progress. 717
Pictures in Palestine. 1962
Pictures of early Methodism in Ohio. 2432
Pictures of Pentecost in the Old Testament. 3720
Pictures of salvation. 1557
Pictures of the apostolic church. 407
Pictures of the patriarchs. 536
Pictures of the Way. 961
Pictures of truth. 451, 3720
Picturesque interviews with Jesus. 423, 2066
Picturesque old France. 1638
Picus who is also Zeus. 3895
Piebald standard. 3598
Piece of blue sky. 1006
Piece of my mind. 2143

Pieces of India. 2532
Pieces of the puzzle. 3180
Pierced heart. 3716
Pierre de Thomas. 2826
Pierre de Thomas, scholar, diplomat, and crusader. 2826
Piers Plowman. 2012
Pierson plan of Bible study. 645
Pierzana: 1865-1965. 2846
Pietism. 2846
Pietism and Methodism. 2421, 2846
Pietism and the Russian Germans in the United States. 2846
Pietism as a factor in the rise of German nationalism. 2846
Pietro Aretino, the scourge of princes. 80
Piety and patriotism. 3046
Piety and politics. 1085
Piety and power. 875
Piety and proverty in Chile. 815
Piety, charity, and literacy among the Yorkshire gentry, 1370-1480. 3868
Piety in humble life. 2205
Piety in the public school. 1130
Piety of Caspar Schwenckfeld. 1012
Piety of Jeremy Taylor. 2846, 3590
Piety of John Calvin. 3044, 3636
Piety promoted, in a collection of dying sayings of many of the people called Quakers. 1677
Piety promoted, in brief memorials, and dying expressions, of some of the people called Quakers. 1677
Piety promoted, in brief memorials and dying expressions of some of the Society of Friends, commonly called Quakers. 1677
Piety versus moralism. 2688
Piggy-bank minds and 49 other object lessons for children. 907
Pig's brother. 907
Pilate's questions and Christ's words. 2034, 2298
Pilate's wife. 1559
Pilgram artist in Palestine. 2761
Pilgrim. 1069, 1449, 2391, 2806, 2847
Pilgrim and pioneer. 2205, 2544
Pilgrim church. 808, 1123, 1172, 3772
Pilgrim church in California. 815, 2506
Pilgrim circuit rider. 1335
Pilgrim deeds and duties. 1344
Pilgrim faith. 1338
Pilgrim fare from Bible lands. 1438
Pilgrim Fathers and Plymouth Colony: a bibliographical survey of books and articles published during the past fifty years. 2847
Pilgrim followers of the gleam. 1807
Pilgrim hymnal. 1335
Pilgrim of love. 1776, 3377
Pilgrim of the clear light. 1577, 3309
Pilgrim of the infinite. 2847
Pilgrim of the night. 2847
Pilgrim papers from the writings of Francis Thomas Wilfrid, priest. 2847
Pilgrim parson. 130
Pilgrim partners. 2848
Pilgrim pastor's manual. 2790
Pilgrim Paul. 2796
Pilgrim people. 2106
Pilgrim places in North America. 3405
Pilgrim Pope in the New World, the Holy Land, and India. 2863
Pilgrim prayers and meditations. 2891
Pilgrim priesthood. 325, 447
Pilgrim sermons. 3353
Pilgrim ship. 3197
Pilgrim spirit. 3122
Pilgrim steps. 3796
Pilgrim tercentenary, the Puritans, and the New England spirit. 2847
Pilgrim to Poland. 863, 3369
... The pilgrim's progress; pt. I. 714
Pilgrimage. 1012, 1101, 1525, 1788
Pilgrimage for peace. 2805
Pilgrimage home. 3480
Pilgrimage in faith. 2964
Pilgrimage of a pilgrim. 3752
Pilgrimage of a pilgrim eighty years. 2847
Pilgrimage of Adam and David. 615
Pilgrimage of Buddhism. 708
Pilgrimage of Buddhism and a Buddhist pilgrimage. 703
Pilgrimage of Christianity. 1174
... The pilgrimage of Etheria. 2762
Pilgrimage of faith. 2846, 3044
Pilgrimage of Harriet Ransom's son. 2847
Pilgrimage of ideas. 3198
Pilgrimage of James. 3477
Pilgrimage of life. 1017
Pilgrimage of peace. 793
Pilgrimage of Temperance Mack. 2308
Pilgrimage or the haj. 2489
Pilgrimage to Amsterdam. 3850
Pilgrimage to Brazil. 2504
Pilgrimage to now/here. 1650, 3478
Pilgrimage to Palestine. 2761, 2847

Pilgrimage to people. 3127
Pilgrimage to Santiago. 2848
Pilgrimage to see the Holy Father Pope Pius X and members of his household in the Vatican and St. Peter's. 59 2
Pilgrimage to see the Holy Father, Pope Pius x, and members of his household in the Vatican and St. Peter's. 2851
Pilgrimage to see the Holy Father through the stereoscope. 2848, 2851, 2862
Pilgrimage to Spanish America. 2548
Pilgrimage to the Shroud. 1826, 3847
Pilgrimage toward unity. 1249
Pilgrimages to Methodist shrines. 2424
Pilgrime of Loreto. 1022, 2260
...The Pilgrims. 2847, 3739
Pilgrim's album. 717
Pilgrims and pioneers. 1332
Pilgrims and pioneers in the Congregational Christian tradition. 1332
Pilgrims & the Passion; messages for Lent and Easter. 2213, 2298
Pilgrim's guide. 3367
Pilgrim's guide to planet Earth. 2847
Pilgrim's guide to Rome. 1022
Pilgrims in a new land. 2104
Pilgrims in Palestine. 2762
Pilgrims in process. 792, 2944
Pilgrims in the region of faith. 35
Pilgrim's logbook. 2763
Pilgrims of Hawaii. 2524
Pilgrims of Iowa. 1336
Pilgrims of Russian-town. 2568
Pilgrims of the lonely road. 923, 2209
Pilgrims of the stars. 3252
Pilgrim's path. 2893
Pilgrim's path of Saint Therese of the Child Jesus. 3690
Pilgrims pray. 2871
Pilgrim's process. 1119
Pilgrim's progess, from this world to that which is to come. 714
Pilgrim's program. 160
Pilgrim's progress. 697, 714, 715, 716
Pilgrim's progress from is world to that which is to come. 715
Pilgrim's progress from this world to that which is to come. 715, 716
Pilgrim's progress in pageant. 717, 2757
Pilgrim's progress in the world today. 968
Pilgrim's progress, in verse. 716
Pilgrim's progress of John Bunyan. 716
Pilgrim's progress of the nineteenth century. 716
Pilgrims, Puritans, and Roger Williams. 3007, 3817
Pilgrim's regress. 68, 967
Pilgrim's song. 1861
Pilgrim's teacher. 3203
Pilgrims to the Holy Land. 2848
Pilgrim's vow. 2848
Pilgrims' way. 1038
Pilgrims's progress from this world to that which is to come. 2919
Pilkington of Uganda. 2558, 2848
Pill and birth regulation. 664
Pill, John Rock, and the church. 2740, 3242
Pillar and ground of the truth. 1118
Pillar in the twilight. 3693
Pillared hall from a temple at Madura, India. 2311
Pillars in the temple. 2443
Pillars of faith. 3662
Pillars of gold. 956
Pillars of life. 3479
Pillars of Mormonism. 2612
Pillars of orthodoxy. 144
Pillars of Pentecost. 2814
Pillars of the Christian faith. 3664
Pillars of the church. 765
Pillars of the English church. 1215
Pillars of the faith. 3778
Pillars of the temple. 3726, 3730
Pillow. 724
Pillow of stones. 1341
Pilot aboard. 165
Pilot of a liberal faith, Samuel Atkins Eliot, 1862-1950. 1507, 3725

Piloting the Sunday school. 3553
Pine and cedar. 253
Pinnacle of Indian thought. 3301
Pio Nono. 2850
Pioneer. 2391
Pioneer bishop. 89
Pioneer bishops of Indiana. 667
Pioneer black robes on the west coast. 1948
...Pioneer Capuchin letters. 738
Pioneer Catholic church of Chester county, Saint Agnes, West Chester, Pennsylvania, 1793-1943. 3807
Pioneer Catholic Victoria. 835
Pioneer church. 1627

Pioneer church beginnings and educational movements in California. 726, 3814
Pioneer church in a pioneer city. 3862
Pioneer church of the state of New York. 823
Pioneer churches. 3739
Pioneer colored Christians. 742, 2682
Pioneer days in Hawaii. 1510, 2524
Pioneer days of the Advent movement. 3386
Pioneer evangelism. 1554
Pioneer evangelists of the church of God in the Pacific Northwest. 10
... Pioneer German Catholics in the American colonies (1734-1784) 833
Pioneer handbook. 3168
Pioneer helpers. 3215
Pioneer in Christian unity: Samuel Simon Schmucker. 3309
Pioneer in Madagascar. 2538, 2810
Pioneer Jesuits in northern Mexico. 1948, 1949
Pioneer laymen of North America. 2849
Pioneer Lutherans of Bisbee, Towner County, North Dakota. 2302
Pioneer Methodism in Missouri and the mission of Methodism. 2439
Pioneer ministry. 1295
Pioneer missionaries. 2483, 2829
Pioneer missionaries for Christ and his church. 2481
Pioneer missionaries of the church. 2482
Pioneer missionary. 2484
Pioneer missionary to the Bering Strait Eskimos. 1532, 2191
Pioneer of southern New Jersey. 695
Pioneer padre. 2177
Pioneer preacher. 2910
Pioneer preacher in Idaho. 1293, 1800
Pioneer Presbyterianism in Tennessee. 2919
Pioneer prophetess. 3816
Pioneer prophetess: Jemima Wilkinson. 3816
Pioneer prophets. 569
Pioneer Quakers. 1685
Pioneer sermons and addresses. 3347
Pioneer stories. 2615
Pioneer stories of the second advent message. 8
Pioneer stories retold. 10
Pioneer stories retold; a compilation of early experiences in the Advent movement. 10
Pioneer theories of missiology. 690, 2554
Pioneer trails, trials and triumphs. 2505
Pioneer women. 2488
Pioneer work of the Presbyterian church in Montana. 2918
Pioneer youth in Palestine. 2118
Pioneering church of the Mohawk Valley. 3307
Pioneering days of the Church in North Otago, 1840-1900. 824
Pioneering for Christ. 1284
Pioneering for Christ in East Africa. 2552
Pioneering for Christ in the Sudan. 2552
Pioneering for Jesus. 3405
Pioneering God's country; the history of the Diocese of Olympia, 1853- 1953. 2971
Pioneering in China. 1515, 2511
Pioneering in Kwangsi. 2510
Pioneering in modern city missions. 2597
Pioneering in Penn's woods. 2453
Pioneering in religious education. 2428
Pioneering in the Congo. 2513
Pioneering in the faith. 2171
Pioneering in the lion country. 2498
Pioneering in Tibet. 2555
Pioneering with Christ. 3874
Pioneers and builders. 3420
Pioneers and builders of the Advent cause in Europe. 3386
Pioneers and founders. 2484
Pioneers for Christ. 764
Pioneers in mission. 2501
Pioneers in righteousness. 215
Pioneers in the Arab world. 2557, 3767
Pioneers of Christian thought. 3611
Pioneers of goodwill. 2482
Pioneers of light. 30
Pioneers of our faith. 1968
Pioneers of religious education. 3165
Pioneers of religious liberty. 3192
Pioneers of religious liberty in America. 3193
Pioneers of revival. 1574
Pioneers of the church. 928
Pioneers of the faith. 849
... Pioneers of the kingdom. 660
Pioneers of the peaceable kingdom. 1684, 2756
Pioneers of the primitive church. 2824
Pioneers of the Reformed church in the United States of America. 3049
Pioneers of the younger churches. 926

Pioneers of tomorrow, a call to American youth. 3879
Pioneers together. 1372, 2508
Pious biography for young men. 764
Pious Christian's faith and prayer. 3292
Pious guide to prayer and devotion. 858
Pious instructor. 1674, 1675
Pious preparation for first holy communion. 854
Pious Society of the Catholic Apostolate. 2766
Pirke Aboth. 4, 3197
Pirke Aboth [Pirke avot] (romanized form) in etchings. 3197
Pirke de Rabbi Eliezer. 522, 3015, 3016
Pirke de rabbi Eliezer (The chapters of Rabbi Eliezer the Great) 3015
Pisgah and her people, 1784-1934. 2626
Pistis sophia. 3437
Pit-men, preachers & politics. 2459
Pitcher of cream. 1823
...The pith and marrow of some sacred writings. 3688
Pith and pathos of frontier missions, thirty home mission stories. 2490
Pitts-street chapel lectures. 3323
Pittsburgh Synod congregational histories. 2850
Pittsburgh Synod history. 2850
Pittsburgh's First Unitarian Church. 2850
Pitture di venti secoli. 2760
Pity the persecutor. 2099
Pius ix. and France. 2850, 2863
Pius ofxI. 2851
Pius XI, apostle of peace. 2852
Pius XI, the Pope and the man. 2851
Pius XII and the Third Reich. 860, 1708, 2852
Pius XII on world problems. 2852
Pius x. 2851
Pius x, the life-story of the Beatus. 2851
Pius xii. 2852
Pius XII and the American people. 761
Pius XII on consecration to Mary. 2359
Pius xii, pope of peace. 2852
Pius XII, the angelic shepherd. 2852
Pivotal problems of education. 804
... The place and function of the Sunday school. 3556
... The place and function of the Sunday school in the church. 3556
Place called heaven. 3354
Place for you. 3000
Place of adventure. 2699
Place of authority in matters of religious belief. 119
Place of Bonhoeffer. 677
Place of Bonhoeffer: problems and possibilities in his thought. 676
Place of Christ in liturgical prayer. 2239
Place of Christ in modern theology. 2038, 3643
Place of Christianity among the greater religions of the world. 1080
Place of government. 603
Place of help. 1445
Place of Jesus Christ in modern Christianity. 2035
Place of Jesus in the life of today. 1952
Place of prayer in the Christian religion. 2869
Place of race. 3017
Place of religion in public schools. 3189
Place of suffering. 3540
Place of the Bible in education. 300
Place of the church in evolution. 1581
Place of the gospel in the development of humanity. 383
Place of the hidden moon. 3272
Place of the sacraments in worship. 3853
Place of the Sunday school in evangelism. 1562
Place of understanding. 3372
Place of values. 2180
Place of Wesley in the Christian tradition. 3804
Place of women in the church. 3834, 3836
Place to belong. 989
Place to feel at home. 1210
Place to stand. 67
...The place where thou standest. 2301
Place where Thy glory dwells. 2936
Places Christ hallowed. 2014
Places of quiet strength, and other sermons. 3345
Plain account of Christian perfection, as believed and taught by Rev. John Wesley. 2818
Plain account of the ordinance of baptism. 136, 1820
Plain address to the Quakers, Moravians, Separatists, Separate-Baptists, Rogerenes, and other enthuiasts. 3123
Plain and faithful narrative of the original design. 2589

Plain and truthful history of the Bible, its nature and teachings, for the common people. 289
Plain answers to religious questions. 3211
Plain argument of God. 3608
Plain catechetical instructions for young communicants. 2259
Plain Christianity. 1062, 1227
Plain commentary on the four holy Gospels. 386
Plain dealing with Calvinism. 730, 1305
Plain discourse, shewing who shall, & who shall not, enter into the kindgom of heaven. 1795
Plain evidences. 3395, 3533
Plain facts for fair minds. 791
Plain guide to spiritualism. 3498
Plain guide to Universalism. 3753
Plain man and his Bible. 3198
Plain man faces trouble. 2398
Plain man looks at himself. 991
Plain man looks at the cross. 107
Plain man looks round. 1225
Plain man seeks for God. 1728, 3106
Plain man's life of Christ. 1968
Plain Mr. Knox. 2182
Plain papers for young believers. 1071
Plain papers on the doctrine of the Holy Spirit. 1832
Plain path to Christian perfection. 2639, 2819
Plain paths to the land of promise. 3299
Plain people. 35, 2407
Plain pointed practical preaching. Old-fashioned Bible Chautauqua Sermons. 3337
Plain points on personal purity. 3393
Plain practical sermons. 3358
Plain prayers for a complicated world. 2889
Plain progressive talks upon the way of salvation. 3295
Plain reasons against joining the church of Rome. 800
Plain reasons for being a Catholic. 791
Plain sermons. 862
Plain sermons by practical preachers. 3356
Plain sermons on mixed marriages. 2338
Plain talk about Christian words. 1557
Plain talk about the holy spirit. 1829
Plain talk about the pastorate. 2788
Plain talk by Ben Hogan, ex-pugilist. 1793
Plain talk in an Artic chapel. 2300
Plain talk in psalm & parable. 601
Plain talk on Acts. 329
Plain talk on Colossians. 341
Plain talk on Deuteronomy. 510
Plain talk on Ephesians. 363
Plain talk on Exodus. 517, 3289
Plain talk on First and Second Corinthians. 345
Plain talk on Genesis. 523
Plain talk on Hebrews. 403
Plain talk on Isaiah. 542
Plain talk on James. 412
Plain talk on John. 416
Plain talk on Leviticus and Numbers. 557
Plain talk on Luke. 428
Plain talk on Mark. 433
Plain talk on Matthew. 443
Plain talk on Peter and Jude. 447
Plain talk on prayer. 2872
Plain talk on Revelation. 454
Plain talk on Romans. 468
Plain talk on the Epistles of John. 369
Plain talk on the Minor prophets. 559
Plain talk on the Resurrection. 2051
Plain talk on Thessalonians. 478
Plain talk on Timothy, Titus, and Philemon. 446
Plain talks on practical truths. 967
Plain talks on Romans. 468
Plain talks to young men on vital issues. 3869
Plain theology for plain people. 3661
Plain thoughts on faith and life. 1590
Plain thoughts on worship. 3003
Plain truth about Armstrongism. 83
Plain uses of the blackboard and slates. 3559
Plain work on baptism. 134
Plaine path-way to heaven. 1263
Plainer Bible for plain people in plain American. 353
"A plainer translation" 275
Plains Indian mythology. 1899
Plains, peaks and pioneers. 2431
Plainsong. 884
Plainsong Psalter. 883
Plaints of the Passion. 2032
Plan. 1661
Plan book. 2915
Plan for a school or an establishment similar to that at Ackworth, in Yorkshire, Great-Britain. 1498
Plan for survival. 2303
Plan of creation. 1371, 1383

Plan of deliverance. 545, 3356
Plan of salvation. 1232, 3291, 3292, 3430
Plan of the Apocalypse. 454
Plan of the creation. 1381
Plan of the Founder of Christianity. 59
Plan of union. 2441, 2735
Plan of union for the Church of Christ Uniting. 1210
Plan of union of the Presbyterian Church in the United States of America and the United Presbyterian Church of North America to form the United Presbyterian Church in the United States of America. 2913, 2920
Plan of union providing for the organic union of the presbyterian church in the United States of American and the United Presbyterian church of North America. 2927
Plan or purpose. 2324
Planchette. 3513
Planet rebellion. 3384
Planned preaching. 2900
Planned services for church groups. 2237
Planning a Christian day camp. 733
Planning a Christian funeral. 1694, 2301
Planning a church program for seniors and young people. 3876
Planning a year's pulpit work. 2897
Planning and building the modern church. 1162
Planning and financing the new church. 1155
Planning better church buildings. 1156
Planning better church buildings. Rev. ed. 1156
Planning better Sabbath schools. 3385
Planning Christian education in the local church. 3151
Planning Christian education in your church. 3147
Planning church and church school buildings. 1158
Planning church buildings. 1156, 1158
Planning church school workers' conferences. 3177
Planning congregational worship services. 3857
Planning for Catholic Education. 806
Planning for children in the local church. 1462, 3153
Planning for church music. 1209
Planning for nursery children. 3174
Planning for planning. 1200
Planning for Protestantism in urban America. 1278, 1279
Planning for the nursery child in the church school. 3154
Planning for threes to eights in the Hebrew school. 2106
Planning for young people in the local church. 3159
Planning LDS weddings & receptions. 2344
Planning modern church buildings. 1156
Planning non-traditional programs. 1578
Planning, preparing, praising. 3003
Planning services of worship. 3004
Planning strategies for world evangelization. 2492
Planning the church bulletin for effective worship. 1163
Planning the curriculum for parish education in the Evangelical Lutheran Church. 3162
Planning the good life. 976
Planning the vacation church school for boys and girls. 3763
Planning your life. 3868
Planning your preaching. 2904, 2906
Planning your program for American Heritage discussion. 32
Plans and stories for the nursery class. 3155
Plans for Sunday school evangelism for pastors, superintendents, teachers, and parents. 1553
Plantation sermons. 2931
Planting a church in a national playground, Miami Beach, Florida, 1920-1940. 2461
Planting and development of missionary churches. 2521
Planting and growing a fundamental church. 1171
Planting and growing missions. 1166
Planting churches cross-culturally. 1166
Planting new churches. 1569
Planting of Christianity in Africa. 12
Planting of the church. 2525
Planting of the churches in South Africa. 2499
Planting of the Presbyterian church in northern Virginia. 2928
Planting the outposts. 1899
Plants of the Bible. 480, 481, 685
Plants of the Holy Land, with their fruits, and flowers. 480

Plastic age of the Gospel. 477
Plates from the American architect. 1268
Platform echoes. 3596
Platform of Christian unity. 1050
Platform of church discipline. 1117, 1344
Platform of church-discipline, gathered out of the word of God; and agreed upon the elders and messengers of the churches assembled in the synod at Cambridge, in N.E. 1337
Platform of church-discipline gathered out of the Work of God, and agree upon by the elders and messengers of the churches assembled in the synod. 1337
Platform replies. 795
Platform Scripture. 914
Platform sutra of the sixth patriarch. 3892
Plato. 2853
Plato and Augustine. 111, 114
Plato and modern morality. 2853
Platonic myth. 2664, 2853
Platonic tradition in English religious thought. 2854
Platonism and their spiritual life. 3481
Platonism of Gregory of Nyssa. 1773, 2853
Platooning the church school. 3558
Plato's Apology. 3454
Plato's Apology of Socrates and Crito and a part of the Phaedo. 3454
Plato's Euthyphro. 3454
Plato's theory of art. 88, 2853
Plato's theory of fine art. 2853
Plato's view of art. 2853
Platy, the child in us. 1004
Play ball! 102
... Play for body and brain. 1525
Play of consciousness. 2630, 3491
Play of Herod. 1807, 2233
Play of the gods. 1483
Play of the sibyl Cassandra. 1113, 3778
Play on your harp. 318
Play the game, and other talks to young people. 907
Playboy comes homes. 2944
Playboy to priest. 3201
Played by ear. 774
Playes confuted in five actions. 3606
Playing dirty. 3314
Playing square with tomorrow. 2488
Playlets and poems for church school. 3560
Playmates in Japan. 2489
Plays and entertainments for schools, clubs, churches and other community groups. 1478
Plays confuted in five actions. 3606
Plays of Roswitha. 1849, 1850
Playtime Bible. 635
... The playtime primer for young people. 1166
Plea and the pioneers in Virginia. 1467
Plea for Christ. 1556
Plea for Christian unity and a book for everybody. 1101
Plea for evangelical demonstration. 1551
Plea for home mission. 1343
Plea for man. 1818
Plea for pantheism. 2767
Plea for religion and the Sacred Writings. 59, 2759
Plea for the catholic doctrine of the Trinity. 3712
Plea for the Cumberland Presbyterian church. 1396
Plea for the higher education of Catholic young men of America. 867
Plea for the Non-conformist. 1468
Plea for the non-conformists. 1468
Plea for the old faith of the old church. 1590
Plea for the old foundations. 2921
Plea for the West. 797
Plea of the Disciples of Christ. 1463
Plea to restore the apostolic church. 1463, 3220
... Pleaders for righteousness. 486
Pleasant Hill. 2854
Pleasant paths. 1447
Pleasant Sunday afternoons for the children. 3096
Pleasant way. 2371
Please bring the children. 3379
Please, can I come home? 3527, 3877
Please don't shoot! : I'm already wounded. 1817
Please don't stand up in my canoe! 1089
Please get off the seesaw slowly. 3835
Please give a devotion. 1445
Please give a devotion for active teens. 1436
Please give a devotion-for all occasions. 1437
Please give a devotion for church groups. 1445
Please give a devotion for young people. 1437

Please give a devotion of gladness. 1437
Please, God. 901
Please help me! 664
Please lead us in prayer. 2870
Please listen, God! 2886
Please, Lord, don't put me on hold. 3843
Please love me. 991
Please pray for the cabbages. 1449
Please stand by. 2535
Please tell me. 3185
Please touch. 2392
Pleasing God by right-doing. 3169
Pleasures of being a Catholic. 763
Pleasures of contemplation. 1355, 2672
Pleasures of heaven and the tortures of hell. 1795
Pleasures of religion. 3063, 3208
Pleasures of sin. 3411
Pledge of glory. 1508, 2258
Plenty and want. 1153
"Plenty how-do" from Africa. 2537
Pleroma, an essay on the origin ofChristianity. 1190
Plif. 3508
Plight of God. 1428
Plight of man and the power of God. 3290
Plight of the Australian clergy. 2953
Plockhoy from Zurik-Zee. 2854
Plot against the Church. 861, 2152
Pluck plus Providence. 1576
Plum jelly and stained glass & other prayers. 2889
Plumb-line laid to the wall. 205
Plumb lines and fruit baskets. 570
Plural marriage, limited. 2344
Pluralism and truth in religion. 1936, 3093
Pluralistic society, pluralistic Church. 1121
Plurality of ministries. 2787
Pluri-cellular man. 3463
Pluriverse. 2854
Plus living. 2383
Plutarch on superstition. 2855
Plutarch on the delay of the Deity in the punishment of the wicked. 1779
Plutarch's Morals. 2834
Plymouth church and its pastor. 184, 693
Plymouth church records. 3741
Plymouth Church records, 1620-1859. 2855
Plymouth Congregational Church, 1854-1954. 2202
Plymouth pulpit. 183
Pneu-ho-mology. 2322, 3477
Pneumatikos-psychikos terminology in 1 Corinthians. 323, 1718
Pocket Aquinas. 3694
Pocket Bible. 250, 251
Pocket Bible concordance. 227
Pocket Bible hand book. 285, 638
Pocket Bible handbook. 285
Pocket Bible handbook, an abbreviated Bible commentary. 285
Pocket book of discipleship. 1007
Pocket book of healing. 1599
Pocket book of hope. 1445
Pocket book of Methodist beliefs. 2428
Pocket Congregational manual. 1343
Pocket dictionary of the Holy Bible. 242
Pocket encyclopedia of Masonic symbols. 1671
Pocket full of seeds. 1466
Pocket guide to Christian beliefs. 3660
Pocket guide to the names of Christ. 2020
Pocket guide to the New Testament. 409
Pocket guide to the sayings of Jesus. 2062
Pocket guide to Unitarianism. 3728
Pocket hymn-book. 1867, 2425, 2429
Pocket key of heaven. 859
Pocket lexicon to the Greek New Testament. 1769
Pocket of pebbles. 1712
Pocket prayer book. 837, 839, 858
Pocket prayer book and devotional guide. 2890
Pocket system of theology for Sabbath-school teachers and church-members generally. 3665
Pocket Testament league around the world. 615
Pocket treasury of daily devotions. 1432
Pocket William Law. 3630
Pocketful of hope. 3842
Pocketful of prayers for today's needs, moods, and circumstances. 2894
Pocketful of sun. 1326
Poe[ms] on various su[bjects] religious and [moral]. 3209
Poem of beauty. 2305, 3418
Poem of Job. 549
... Poem on the Assumption. 46
Poem portraits of the saints. 3285
Poems. 2919
... Poems about Jesus. 2047
Poems. Adrift and anchored. 3208

Poems and essays from many authors of this and earlier centuries. 3502
Poems and hymns of dawn. 1942
Poems and hymns of H. A. Ironside. 3206
Poems and prayers for the very young. 905
Poems and translations ; Hymns written and adapted to the weekly church service. 1222, 1873
Poems, Centuries and three Thanksgivings. 1453
Poems, charades, inscriptions of Pope Leo XIII. 2216
Poems every mason should know. 1668
Poems (Flagg, Edward Octavus) 298
Poems for Advent and Lent. 2210
Poems for speculative masons. 1668
Poems, interpretive of each one of the International Sunday school lessons for the year 1940. 1916
Poems (Juan de la Cruz. 2136
Poems (Milton, John) 2469
Poems, moral and religious. 3209
Poems of Easter and the soul. 1486
Poems of Edgar Allan Poe. 2855
Poems of faith and doubt. 1518
Poems of Jesus the Christ. 2048
Poems of living truth (Osborne, Richard B) 3050
Poems of Methodism (Mardsen, Joshua) 2421
Poems of prayer (Woods, Ralph Louis) 3208
Poems of St. John of the Cross. 3207
Poems of St. Paulinus of Nola. 3285
Poems of the Rt. Rev. George Burgess. 717
Poems of various subjects, religious and moral. 3209
Poems on religious subjects. 3209
Poems on sacred subjects. 3207
Poems on the thirty-three miracles of Our Lord. 2018
Poems on various subjects, religious and moral. 3209
Poems (Prudentius Clemens, Aurelius) 1878
Poems (Pumpelly, Mary Hollenback (Welles)) 298
Poems ([Smith, Eliza Roxey (Snow)]) 2619
Poems to change lives (Coblentz, Stanton Arthur) 3206
Poems upon several occasions By the Reverend Mr. John Pomfret. 3208, 3209
Poems written on different occasions. 3209
Poesias completas y otras paginas. 2136
Poet and peasant. 428, 2024
Poet and the mystic. 2137, 2637
Poet of Galilee. 1975
Poet of science, and other addresses. 3313
Poet-toilers in many fields. 661
Poetic experience. 1585, 3694
Poetical histories, London 1671. 2656
Poetic Jesus. 1975
Poetic reflections from the dust. 680
Poetic sermons. 3353
Poetical expression of the Gospels. 397
Poetical sermons including the ballad of Plymouth church. 3362
Poetical works. 670, 2469, 3471
Poetry & dogma. 3210
Poetry and law in Germanic myth. 2660
Poetry and morals. 1839
Poetry & prayer. 2856
Poetry & prophecy. 1910, 2949, 2951
Poetry and speculation of the Rg Veda. 3776
Poetry and the fountain of light. 1519
Poetry and wisdom. 567
Poetry from the Bible. 252
Poetry of Edmund Spenser. 3471
Poetry of feeling, and spiritual melodies. 3209
Poetry of Our Lord. 2070
Poetry of religion. 3208
Poetry of sacred song. 1630, 1871
Poetry of Samuel Taylor Coleridge. 1307
Poetry of the Old Testament. 1798, 1799
Poetry of the Passion. 1519, 2012
Poets and mystics. 2643
Poets and poetry. 1799
Poets and poetry of the Hebrews. 1799
Poets and prophets of Israel. 530
Poets historical. 1521, 3780
Poets, hymn writers, fiction writers, and story tellers of the Disciples of Christ. 1462
Poets of Christian thought. 3094
Poets of religion. 3210
Poets of the church. 1023, 1860, 1878
Poets of the Old Testament. 573
Poets of transcendentalism. 33
Poets, prophets, and sages. 484
Point and purpose in preaching. 2898

Point Loma community in California. 2243, 3701
Point Loma community in California, 1897-1942. 3701
Point of Christology. 2046
Point of contact in teaching. 3565
Point of glad return. 979
Point of no return. 1012
... The point of vieu, etc., including The point of view for my work as an author, Two notes about "the individual" and On my work as an author. 2170
Point of view. 2080
Point of view, an anthology of religion and philosophy selected from the works of Paul Carus. 1368
Point of view for my work as an author. 2170
Pointed papers for the Christian life. 1398
Pointed paragraphs. 962
Pointed sermon outlines and illustrations. 3372
Pointed story-sermons for young folks. 907
Pointed tales. 906
Pointers for pastors. 2786
Pointing the way. 2834
Points for emphasis. 1916
Points in church history. 1181
Points of contact between science and revelation. 3075
Points of controversy. 792
Poland and the minority races. 2102
Polar star, and centre of comfort. 3367
Polar structures in the book of Qohelet. 512
Polarities of man's existence in Biblical perspective. 2325
Polarity. 3104
Polarity in our desires. 981
Pole shift. 1485
Poleete. 738, 1598
Polemic chat. 795
Polemic disquisitions on four general subjects. 2936
Polemical tracts. 1219
Polemics of Erasmus of Rotterdam and Ulrich von Hutten. 1526
Policies and procedures for the pastoral care department. 2782
Policy making in colleges related to the Methodist Church. 2432
Polish Catholics in Chicago, 1850-1920. 813, 2857
Polish Detroit and the Kolasinski affair. 1426, 2183
Polish Jew. 2102
Polish Jews. 2102
Polish National Catholic Church. 2857
Polite escape. 3328
Polite pupil, for the use of Catholic parochial and high schools, by the Brothers of Mary. Nazareth. 870
Political activities of the Baptists and Fifth monarcay men England during the interregnum. 149
Political activities of the Baptists and Fifth Monarchy Men in England during the interregnum. 149
Political and ecclesiastical history of the Anglican Church of Canada. 43
Political and financial independence of the Vatican. 807
Political and social ideas of St. Augustine. 116, 3441
Political and social philosophy. 756
Political and social significance of the life and teachings of Jesus. 2059
... The political and the social leaders of the Jewish community of Sepphoris. 2092
Political aspects of S. Augustin's 'City of God. 114, 116
Political aspects of St. Augustine's 'City of God. 3199
Political behavior of American Jews. 2104
Political Black minister. 15
Political Buddhism in Southeast Asia. 709
Political Christ. 1088, 2043
Political Christians. 1086
Political commitment and Christian community. 1086
Political doctrine of the Isma'ilis (the Imamate) 1884
Political equality. 3703
Political ethics of Alexander Campbell. 732, 1086
Political evangelism. 1086
Political expectation. 3448
Political faith of our fathers, and other essays. 1068
Political ideas of Richard Hooker. 1844
Political Islam. 1924
Political philosophy of Sri Aurobindo. 1709
Political philosophy of the Orthodox Church. 2746, 2836

Political problems, 1850-60. 820
Political pulpit. 3747
Political relations of Christ's ministry. 2017
Political religion on the new nations. 3525
Political Romanism. 800
Political theology. 1087
Political theology and the life of the church. 1087
... Political theology in early Islam. 1658, 1788
Political theories of Martin Luther. 2278, 2858
Political theory and institutions of the Khawarij. 2169
Political transformation of the Brazilian Catholic Church. 814, 1144
Politics: a case for Christian action. 1086
Politics, Americanism, and Christianity. 1085
Politics and belief in contemporary France: Emmanuel Mounier and Christian democracy, 1932-1950. 879, 1532, 2626
Politics and Catholic freedom. 2223
Politics and Christianity in Malawi, 1875-1940. 2538
Politics and citizenship. 2858
Politics and evangelism. 1086
Politics and exegesis. 1088, 2743
Politics and government. 1085
Politics and liturgy. 2235
Politics and Protestant theology. 1088, 3700
Politics & religion can mix! 1087
Politics and religion during the English Revolution. 1764
Politics & religion in ancient Israel. 2096
Politics & religion in seventeenth-century France. 1639
Politics and religion in sixteenth-century France. 1639, 2586
Politics and the arts. 3607
Politics and the arts, letter to M. d'Alembert on the theatre. 3607
Politics and the Biblical drama. 603, 1086
Politics and the churches in Great Britain, 1832-1868. 1760
Politics and the early Christian. 1086
Politics and the state. 1086
Politics for Christians. 1086
Politics for evangelicals. 1086
Politics, government. Catholics. 827
Politics in a protestant church. 1151
Politics is a way of helping people. 1086
Politics, medicine, and Christian ethics; a dialogue with Paul Ramsey. 1085, 3021
Politics of belief in nineteenth-century France: Lacordaire, Michon, Veuillot. 818
Politics of Catholics. 117, 814
Politics of doomsday. 3089
Politics of English dissent. 1765
Politics of Erasmus. 1527
Politics of German Protestantism. 2954
Politics of God. 2682, 3072
Politics of God and the politics of man. 483
Politics of guilt and pity. 1087
Politics of hope. 1153
Politics of Jesus. 2046, 3433
Politics of love. 347, 2712
Politics of moralism. 1553
Politics of religion in America. 1150
Politics of religious conflict. 1151
Politics of repentance. 1124
Politics of the Gospel. 1087
Politics of the Nazarene. 2857
Politics of the New Zealand Maori. 2332
Politics of the universe. 183
Politics of the Vatican. 2770
Polities anc evangelism. 1086
Polity and practice in Baptist churches. 150
Polity of the Augustana synod. 1547
Polity of the Church of Ireland. 1230
Polity of the Church of the Province of South Africa. 1238
Pollution and the death of man. 1853
Poltergeist. 2858
Poltergeist experience. 2858, 3243
Poltergeists. 1710, 2858
Poltergeists: hauntings and the haunted. 2858
Polycarp's two epistles to the Philippians. 2858
Polygamist's wife. 2412, 2858
Polygamy. 2600
Polygamy and citizenship in church and state. 2858
Polygamy reconsidered. 1088
Polygamy story. 2858
Polygamy was better than monotony. 2600
Polyglot missal. 837
Polymicrian concordance of the New Testament. 227

Polymicrian Greek lexicon to the New Testament. 1768, 1769
Polynesian mythology. 2666
Polynesian mythology and ancient traditional history of the Maori as told by their priests and chiefs. 2666
Polynesian mythology & ancient traditional history of the New Zealanders. 2666
Polynesian paradise. 2546
Polynesian religion. 2859
Polyphonia sacra. 2372
... Polytheism and fetishism. 3113
Pomps of Satan. 3304
Ponder slowly. 2394
Ponderings. 2392
Les pontifes de l'ancienne Rome. 2940
... Pontifical services. 1883
... Pontificia americana. 834
Pontius Pilate. 2847
"Pontius Pilate's official record of the apprehension, trial and execution of Jesus Christ." 2069
Poor and the Church. 1153
Poor and the land. 3292
Poor black people. 2172
Poor church. 1153
Poor cousin. 8
Poor Elizabeth's almanac. 1651, 3502
Poor Lazarus and other parables. 1470, 2771
Poor little millionaires. 1645
Poor man's catechism. 788
Poor man's evening portion. 1439
Poor man's help and young man's guide. 957
Poor man's preservative against popery. 802
... The poor man's priest. 2308
Poor Mr. Job. 2124
Poor of Yahweh. 2866
Poor people and churchgoers. 1153
Poor rich man. 3704
Poor souls in purgatory. 1840
Poore vicars plea. 1230, 3702
Poorhouse waif and his divine teacher. 3198
Pop. 3253
Pop goes Jesus. 3886
Pope. 829, 2863
Pope : a portrait from life. 2852
Pope Alexander the Seventh and the College of Cardinals. 24, 738
Pope Alexander III and the Council of Tours (1163) 24, 2861
Pope and Christian education, from the German of Rev. Otto Cohausz. 853
Pope and Ireland. 819, 2316
Pope and Italy. 1147
Pope and revolution. 1326, 2222
Pope and the council. 2736, 2862, 3770
Pope and the Duce. 1147, 1322, 2852
Pope and the new crusade. 1706
Pope and the people. 3450
Pope and the press. 2805, 2937
Pope and the theologians; the Humanae vitae controversy. 835, 1248
Pope and the world. 1373
Pope at roam. 2860
Pope Boniface VIII and his times. 677
Pope, considered in his relations with the church, temporal sovereignties, separated churches, and the cause of civilization. 2861
Pope, Council, and world. 3771
Pope for all Christians? 2768
... Pope Gregory the Great and his relations with Gaul. 1773
Pope Innocent III and England. 1633, 1908
Pope Innocent iii and his times. 1908
Pope Innocent III. 1908, 2861
Pope is king. 3244
Pope Joan. 2122
Pope John. 2124
Pope John album. 2123
Pope John and his revolution. 2123
Pope John and the ecumenical council. 2123
Pope John: daily readings. 2210
Pope John memorial miniature. 776, 3633
Pope John Paul II. 2126, 2861
Pope John Paul II, the life of Karol Wojtyla. 2126, 2861
Pope John XXIII. 2124
Pope John the Twenty-third and Master John Hus of Bohemia. 2123
Pope John XXIII. 2123, 2124, 2861
Pope John xxiii comes to the Vatican. 2123
Pope John XXIII, letters to his family [1901-1962]. 2123
Pope John XXIII pastoral prince. 2123
Pope John XXIII; the gentle shepherd. 2124
Pope John's Council. 3771
Pope laughs. 2124
Pope Leo XIII. 2216

Pope Marcellus Mass. 2371, 2765
Pope of peace. 2851
Pope or Mussolini. 1147, 2635
Pope, or president? 757, 782
Pope Paul and Christian unity. 1919
Pope Paul and the Spirit. 1835, 2805
Pope Paul in the United States. 2805
Pope Paul in the Unites States. 2805
Pope John Paul II—he came to us as a father ; pastoral visit to the United States. 2126, 2863
Pope Paul VI. 2805
Pope Paul VI in the Holy Land. 2762, 2763, 2805, 2806
Pope Paul VI. 2805
Pope Pius the Eleventh. 2851
Pope Pius XI and world peace. 860, 2851, 2852
Pope Pius X. 2851
Pope Pius XII. 2852
Pope Pius XII and Catholic education. 804
Pope Pius XII, his voice and life. 2852
Pope Pius XII, Rock of Peace. 2852
Pope Pius xi and American public opinion. 2851
Pope Pius XI and world affairs. 2852
Pope Pius XII, priest and statesman. 2853
Pope Pius XII, the world's shepherd. 2853
Pope, Premier, President. 860, 3741
Pope speaks. 761, 798, 2805, 2852
Pope speaks: dialogues of Paul VI with Jean Guitton. 2805
Pope, the Council, and the Mass. 788, 870
Popery and politics in England 1660-1688. 816, 1764
Popery stripped of its garb. 2860
Popery unmasked. 800
Popes. 2860, 2861, 2862
Popes & cardinals in modern Rome. 2861
Popes and European revolution. 817, 2770
Popes and heresy in the thirteenth century. 2770
Popes and princes, 1417-1517. 2770
Popes and science. 2770
Popes and the Hohenstaufen. 1822
Popes and the Jews in the Middle Ages. 1084
Popes and the papacy in the early Middle Ages, 476-752. 2770
Popes and the priest of today. 2768
Popes and the priesthood. 771
Popes and the saints. 852, 853
Popes and their church. 782
Popes and western Africa. 851, 2500
Popes and world government. 1130
Popes at Avignon. 2770
Popes at Avignon, 1305-1378. 2770, 2861
Pope's divisions. 811
Popes from the ghetto. 2861
Popes in the modern world. 2861
Popes in the twentieth century. 2770
Popes in the twentieth century, from Pius X to John XXIII. 2770
Pope's journey to the United States. 2805
Popes, lawyers, and infidels. 2823
Popes' new order. 3450
Popes of Saint Malachy's prophecy. 2318, 2947
Popes on youth. 1259
Pope's plan for social reconstruction. 2851, 3450
Popes speak of Mary, 1854-1954. 2354
Pope's supremacy. 2767
Popes through the ages. 2860, 2861
Pope's visit. 2806
Popish hierachy suppressed by Buonaparte in Italy. 695
Popish Kingdom. 52
Popol vuh. 2863, 3013
Pop's primer. 1615, 2734
Popular amusements. 36
Popular amusements and the Christian life. 36
Popular and critical Bible encyclopaedia and scriptual dictionary. 243
Popular and critical Bible encyclopaedia and Scriptural dictionary. 243
Popular aspects of oriental religions. 3116
Popular belief and practice. 3620
Popular biography. 662
Popular commentary on the Gospel according to Luke. 428
... A popular commentary on the Gospels according to Matthew and Mark. 439
Popular concordance. Clear type reference ed. 227
Popular dictionary of Buddhism. 705
Popular dictionary of Judaism. 2146
Popular dictionary of spiritualism. 3520
Popular education in the Irish Presbyterian Church. 2915
Popular exposition of Matthew. 441
Popular fallacies about the Christian faith. 3665
Popular freethought in America. 1657

Popular freethought in America, 1825-1850. 1657
Popular guide to New Testament criticism. 347
Popular Hinduism. 1813, 1814
Popular Hinduism and Hindu mythology. 1815
Popular history of Christian education. 3561
Popular history of the ancient British church. 1759
Popular history of the Baptists in Mississippi. 156
Popular history of the Catholic Church. 809
Popular history of the Church of England, from the earliest times to the present day. 1220
Popular history of the Jesuits. 1947
Popular history of the Presbyterian church. 2916, 2924
Popular history of the reformation. 3033, 3034, 3035
...The popular history of the translation of the Holy Scriptures into the English tongue. 248
Popular history of witchcraft. 3824
Popular hymn stories. 1872
Popular instructions on prayer. 2872
Popular lectures on the books of the New Testament. 411
Popular lectures on the Epistle of Paul. 404
Popular lectures on theological themes. 3651
Popular lectures on theosophy. 3683
Popular life of Catherine McAuley. 2305
Popular life of George Fox. 1637
Popular life of Jesus. 391, 1970
Popular life of our Holy Father, Pope Pius the Ninth. 2850, 3369
Popular life of Saint Teresa of Jesus. 3603
Popular manual of church history. 810
Popular manual of theology. 3617
Popular objections to Methodism considered and answered. 2422
Popular outline of church history. 1174
Popular patron saints. 3281
Popular religion. 1455
Popular religion in America. 3746
Popular religion in Restoration England. 1020
Popular romances of the middle ages. 3244
Popular sermons on the catechism. 3348
Popular studies in Colossians. 342
Popular survey of the Old Testament. 539
Popular symbolics. 1386
Popular witchcraft. 3823
Popular witchcraft, straight from the witch's mouth. 3823
Population, pollution, and prophecy. 609
Populus of Augustine and Jerome. 116, 3451
Pornography, a Christian critique. 2863
... Porphyry's work against the Christians. 2863
Port Keats story. 2556, 2864
Port of Nazareth. 438
Port-Royal; the drama of the Jansenists. 2864
Portable Blake. 670
Portals to freedom. 2, 127
Portals to power. 959
Porter-Myers debate. 1272
Porter- Myers debate, between W. Curtis Porter, Monette. 1272
Porter of Saint Bonaventure's. 744
Portfolio of Catholic institutional design. 867
Portfolio of monumental designs. 3333
Portion for the children. 3176
... Portions of the Gospels according to St. Mark and St. Matthew from the Bobbio ms. (k) 3718
Portiuncula indulgence from Honorius III to Pius XI. 2864
Portland Jewry. 2102
...Portrait catalogue of Catholic authors. 869
Portrait gallery of eminent men and women of Europe and America. 660
Portrait of a Carpenter. 1977
Portrait of a champion. 3524
Portrait of a Christian, drawn from life. 1284
Portrait of a Jewish scholar. 2143
Portrait of a parish priest; St. John Vianney, the cure d'Ars. 3784
Portrait of a rabbi. 691
Portrait of a rebel. 2756
Portrait of a woman. 2353
Portrait of Calvin. 728
Portrait of Christ. 1995
Portrait of English cathedrals. 751
Portrait of English churches. 1270

Portrait of English churches; a selection of photographs. 1270
Portrait of Jesus. 389, 1957, 1963, 1976
Portrait of Karl Barth. 175
Portrait of Lincoln Cathedral. 2230
Portrait of Peter. 2824
Portrait of Pius XII. 2852
Portrait of Saint Gemma, a stigmatic. 3531
Portrait of Saint Paul. 2797
Portrait of the church. 2978
... Portrait of the consecrated woman in Greek Christian literature of the first four centuries. 3781
Portrait of the cross. 1388
Portrait of the Millennial church of Shakers. 3395
Portrait of the prodigal. 2944
Portrait of Yahweh as a young god. 1728
Portraits etched in stone. 2101, 2698
Portraits of American Protestant missionaries to Hawaii. 2524
Portraits of Bible women. 3839
Portraits of Christ. 2021, 2394
Portraits of Christ in Genesis. 3720
Portraits of Christ in the Gospel of John. 1986
Portraits of destiny. 1474
Portraits of faith. 765
Portraits of God. 1720
Portraits of Jesus Christ in the New Testament. 1951
... Portraits of Jesus in the New Testament. 1341
Portraits of the Christ. 2214, 2300
Portraits of the eighteenth century. 1638
Portraits of the eighties. 1758
Portraits of the prophets. 2951
Portraits of the seventeenth century. 1638
Portraiture of Jesus in the Gospels. 1955
Portraiture of Shakerism. 2205, 3396
Portsea Island churches. 1270
Portsmouth Sunday school hymn book. 3725
Portuguese East Africa. 2541
Position of Christianity in the United States. 804, 1149
Positioning. 3628
Positive evidence of the restored church. 2599
Positive evolution of religion. 2864
Positive evolution of religion, its moral and social reaction. 2865
Positive faith. 1165
Positive obedience. 1312
Positive philosophy of Auguste Comte. 1322, 2864, 2865
Positive power of Christian partnership. 1164
Positive power of Jesus Christ. 2788, 2809
Positive prayers for power-filled living. 2894
Positive preaching and the modern mind. 2900
Positive Protestantism. 2976, 2978
Positive religion in a revolutionary time. 3094
Positive theology. 3645
Positive thinking is not enough. 2800
Positive use of the minister's role. 2786
Positive way. 1058
Positivist library of Auguste Comte. 656
Possess our souls in patience. 1508
Possess your soul in patience. 2504, 2505
Possessed by Satan. 1422
Possessed by the devil. 1709
Possession. 3472
Possession and exorcism. 1422
Possession, demoniacal & other. 1422
Possibilities of grace. 3299
Possibilities of prayer. 2868
Possibilities unlimited. 3079
Possibility of altruism. 28
Possibility of apostasy. 70
Possibility of God. 2319, 2320
Possibility of religious knowledge. 2181
Possible black-out for Baptist schools and colleges. 149
Possible years. 1250
Possible you. 955
... The post-apostolic age. 1195
Post-apostolic age and current religious problems. 3063
Post-Biblical history of the jews. 2092
... Post-Biblical Judaism. 2113
... Post-Biblical Judaism. 2113
Post-conciliar nun. 2574
Post-Darwinian controversies. 1581
Post-milenial advent. 8
Post Mishnaic Judaism in transition. 2479, 3297
Post-mortem confessions. 3511
Post mortem opinions. 3501
... The post-Nicene Greek fathers. 1617
... The post-Nicene Latin fathers. 1618
Post preachers. 3802

Post-Christianity in Africa. 1073
Postconciliar Christian. 2939
Postconciliar parish. 2789
Postconciliar priest. 3774
Postconciliar thoughts. 735, 736
Post-ecumenical Christianity. 1043
... Posthumous essays. 503
... Posthumous papers. 1206
Posthumous pieces of the late Reverend John William de la Flechere. 1629
Posthumous pieces of the Reverend John William de la Flechere. 1629
Posthumous sermons. 1225
Posthumous theological works of Emanuel Swedenborg. 2689
Posthumous tracts. 3463
Posthumous works of the Rev. Thomas Chalmer. 2914
Postlude to skepticism. 3422
Postman of Patmos. 461
Postmillennialism and the higher critics. 1553
Postscript to preaching. 2785
Post-theistic thinking. 2352, 3328
Postumous pieces of the Rev. John Fletcher: by the Rev. Melvill Horne. 1629
Posture of contemplation. 2380
Postwar strategy of religion. 1058
Pot and those other things. 1011
Pot of oil. 978
Potency of prayer. 2873
Potent enemies of America laid open. 3595
Potpourri. 1714
Potshots at the preacher. 2787
Potter and the clay. 973
Potter and the shepherd. 956
Potter's shop. 2983
Potter's touch. 1382
Pottery, poetry, and prophecy. 1799
Potwin Christian Church. 2865
Pourquoi prier? 2872
Poustinia. 1407, 3485
Poverello's round table. 1646
Poverty. 2866
Poverty and piety in an English village. 3604
Poverty and plenty in our time. 2860
Poverty and preaching. 2865
Poverty of philosophy. 2865
Poverty of spirit. 2866
Poverty: sign of our times. 1153
Power and authority in the Catholic Church. 1305
Power and events. 2834
Power and meaning of love. 3490
Power and poverty in the church. 807
Power and secret of the Jesuits. 1945
... The power and secret of the papacy. 2768
Power and sexuality. 735, 1372
Power and the glory. 609
Power and the pulpit in Puritan New England. 2910
Power and the wisdom. 348
Power & weakness; a book of honest prayers. 2888
Power and wisdom of the cross. 2032
Power and work of the Holy Spirit. 1831
Power at the bottom of the well. 1586
Power, authority, and the origins of American denominational order. 2953
Power beyond words. 935
Power for a finished work. 1531, 3387
Power for abundant living. 279, 989
Power for Christian living. 979
Power for life's living. 967
Power for living. 988
Power for new life. 330
Power for service. 3377
Power for the church. 1833
Power for the church in the midst of . chaos. 2389
Power for the day. 443, 1433
Power for today. 1435, 1440
Power for tomorrow. 3347
Power from on high. 966, 2594, 2595
Power from the pulpit. 2900
Power-full Christian. 1835
Power-house at Pathankot. 3594
Power in expository preaching. 2907
Power in praise. 982
Power in preaching. 2905
Power of a grave. 783
Power of a new life. 437, 1004
Power of a purpose. 968
Power of a righteous life. 961
Power of a symbol. 2828
Power of an endless life. 1890
Power of an ideal. 1312, 2486
Power of an upward look, and other sermons. 2933
Power of believing. 2619
Power of Biblical thinking. 214, 984
Power of Christ. 1560

Power of Christ and other stories. 1014
Power of Christian benevolence. 2304
Power of Christian benevolence illustrated in the life and labors of Mary Lyon. 2304
Power of Christlike living. 993
Power of color. 3575
Power of deception unveiled, and the man of sin revealed. 454
Power of faith. 1591, 1592, 2138
Power of God. 1736, 2056
Power of God in a parish program. 3673
Power of God in man. 1599
Power of God to heal. 1793
... The power of God unto salvation. 2936
Power of goodness. 173, 2717
Power of His might. 3348
Power of His name. 3354
Power of His resurrection. 2051, 3484
Power of illustration. 1840
Power of Jesus' blood and its relation to sin. 672
Power of love. 2263, 2264, 2265
Power of miracle metaphysics. 2729
Power of one. 926
Power of Paul. 2437, 2802
Power of Pentecost. 1827, 1831
Power of perfect liberty. 2853
Power of positive evangelism. 1563
Power of positive living. 992
Power of positive praying. 2868
Power of positive preaching to the lost. 1555
Power of positive preaching to the saved. 1555
Power of positive thinking. 2808, 2994
Power of positive thinking for young people. 2994
Power of prayer. 2870, 2872, 2876, 2880, 2881
Power of prayer and the prayer of power. 2881
Power of prayer in business and the professions. 2881
Power of prayer on plants. 2990
Power of prayer today. 2869
Power of pure stewardship. 3528
Power of receiving. 3357
Power of religion on the mind. 925, 3062
Power of religion on the mind, in retirement, affiction, and at the approach of death. 925
Power of religion on the mind, in retirement, affliction, and at the approach of death. 925
Power of self-suggestion. 2409
Power of self-transcendence. 3699
Power of silence. 3478
Power of spirit manifest in Jesus of Nazareth. 1995
Power of sympathy. 3576
Power of teaching with new techniques. 3179
Power of the commonplace. 2935
Power of the cross. 104, 108
Power of the kingdom; meditations on Matthew. 443
Power of the pendulum. 1479
Power of the pope during the middle ages. 2863
Power of the Pope in temporal affairs. 173, 2767
Power of the provisional. 1042
Power of the pulpit. 3674
Power of the sacraments. 3265
Power of the soul over the body. 2473
Power of the Spirit. 1828, 3630
Power of their glory. 1524
Power of title children. 1632, 2859
Power of universal mind. 2694
Power of worship. 3854
Power of your attitudes. 972
Power of your desire. 2728
Power picture. 2866
Power structures and the church. 1154
Power struggle. 3252
Power that prevails. 1823
Power that wins. 2228
Power: the supernatural powers and helps conferred on man. 3264
Power through acceptance. 1356
Power through constructive thinking. 2410
Power through pentecost. 1831
Power through prayer. 2868
Power through prayer groups. 2885
Power through witchcraft. 3823
Power to be human. 1106
Power to become. 960, 985
Power to bless. 1107
Power to bring forth. 2210
Power to dissolve. 2341
Power to heal. 1599
Power to master life. 449
Power to right our wrongs. 3447
Power to save. 3290
Power to see it through. 162
Power to the people of God. 1245

Power to you. 1063
Power where the action is. 945
Power with God and with men. 2866
Power within us. 975, 2081
Power without glory. 1040, 1225
Powerful is the light. 694
Powerful learning tools in religion. 3159
Powerful stories from the lives of Latter-day Saint men. 1231
Powerless pedagogues. 2291, 3681
Powers of evil in Western religion, magic, and folk belief. 1745
Powers of the air. 3511
Powers of the soul and how to use them. 3751
Powers that be. 472, 2410, 2990
Powers that be; case studies of the church in politics. Foreword by Ben Morell. 1087
Powers within the mind. 3496
Practical aids for Catholic teachers. 805
Practical and exegetical pulpiteer. 3375
Practical and internal evidence against Catholicism. 720
Practical and parochial sermons. 3338
Practical and profitable in church administration. 1126
Practical and social aspects of Christianity. 412
Practical and theological chapters & the three theological discourses. 3636
Practical anthems. 1169
Practical ascetics. 90
Practical aspects of commercial letters of credit. 2218
Practical astral projection. 94
Practical astrology. 97
Practical atheism in denying the agency of providence. 100
Practical Bible lessons for the week day. 527
Practical Buddhism. 1783, 3493
Practical candle burning. 734
Practical catechist. 2375
Practical Catholic. 2375
Practical Catholic dictionary. 779
Practical charity. 472
Practical Christian. 1442
Practical Christian living. 945
Practical Christianity. 954, 1052
Practical church administration handbook. 1252
... Practical church decoration. 1165
Practical church dictionary. 3639
Practical church member. 1337
Practical church music. 1203
Practical church publicity. 10
Practical church school music. 916
Practical commentary on Holy Scripture for the use of those who teach Bible history. 295
Practical commentary on the Code of canon law. 735, 775
Practical commentary upon the First epistle general of Peter. 325
Practical confirmation instructions. 1328
Practical considerations on the Christian Sabbath. 3547
Practical dermatology. 3422
Practical discipleship. 993
...Practical discourse concerning a future judgement. 2156
Practical discourse concerning death. 1415
Practical discourses for the laity. 166
Practical discourses on regeneration in ten sermons. 3050, 3051
Practical discourses on the holiness of heaven. 1795
Practical discourses on the parable of the ten virgins. 3601
Practical Epistle of James. 412
Practical ethics. 1536
Practical evangelism. 1553, 1563
Practical explanation and application of Bible history. 767
Practical exposition of I Peter. 447
Practical exposition of James. 412
Practical exposition of II Peter. 447
Practical expositions of the International Sunday School lesson. 1915
Practical faith. 1589
Practical formulary in accordance with the Code of canon law. 1634
Practical guide for altar guilds. 27
Practical guide for marriage cases prepared by the Tribunal for the private use of the priests of the Archdiocese of Detroit. 2342
Practical guide for organists and choir directors. 916
Practical guide to conference leadership. 1635
Practical guide to death and dying. 1415
Practical guide to ecumenism. 1044
Practical guide to finding your spiritual gifts. 1712
Practical guide to integral Yoga. 3864

Practical guide to meditation. 2379
Practical guide to preaching. 2900
Practical guide to the divine office. 3784
Practical handbook for the study of the Bible. 312
Practical handbook for the study of the Bible and of Bible literature. 641
Practical handbook of ministers. 3676
Practical handbook of worship. 3004
Practical handbook on Sunday-school work. 3556
Practical harmony of the four gospels. 382
Practical help for teaching the Bible. 636
Practical helps for Sunday-school scholars. 3557
Practical helps for the religion teacher. 746
Practical hints on preaching. 2905
Practical hymn studies for the use of ministers and other Christian workers. 1872
Practical hymnology. 1872
Practical idealism. 2836
Practical ideals in evangelism. 1570
Practical ideas for church officers. 1239
Practical inter-church methods. 1120
Practical lectures on parental responsibility, and the religious education of children. 3151
Practical lectures on the Book of Job. 547
Practical lessons from the early ministry of Jesus. 1976
Practical lessons from the experience of Israel for the church of to-day. 1928
Practical lessons from the later ministry of Jesus. 1976
Practical life work of Henry Drummond. 1481
Practical manual for marriage cases. 2341
Practical manual for the superiors of religious houses. 3196
Practical meditations for every day in the year on the life of Our Lord Jesus Christ. 2399
Practical meditator. 2380
Practical message of James. 412
Practical method of reading the breviary. 2240
Practical methods for Sunday School teachers. 3565
Practical methods in soul-winning. 1567
Practical mysticism. 2641
Practical occultism. 2989, 3509
Practical occultism, from the private letters of William Q. Judge. 3683
Practical of spiritualism. 1933, 3510
Practical papers on parish problems. 1251
Practical pastoral counseling. 2781
Practical pedagogy in the Sunday school. 1498
Practical philosophy of life. 3571
Practical philosophy of social life. 1324
Practical piety. 970
Practical piety exemplified. 956
Practical plainsong. 884
Practical portions for the prayer life. 2870
Practical prayer. 2879
Practical prayer book for the Catholics of America. 839
Practical primary plans. 3551, 3564
Practical primer on prayer. 2873
Practical problems in church finance. 1241
Practical problems in religion. 1628
Practical proverbs for everyday Christian living. 573
Practical puppet plays. 3005
Practical reflections on the sufferings of Our Lord. 2033
Practical religion. 991, 2936
Practical religion exemplify'd in the lives of Mrs. Mary Terry, who died Decemb. 8th. 1708. in the eighteenth year of her age. and Mrs. Clissovld. who departed this life the 12th of Decemb. 1711. in the twenty ninth year of her age. 3604
Practical religion through the home and the church. 1062
Practical Sanskrit dictionary with transliteration, accentuation, and etymological analysis throughout. 3301
Practical sermon outlines. 3373
Practical sermons. 2929, 2930
Practical sermons of persuasive power. 3338
Practical side of reincarnation. 3053
Practical studies in the Fourth Gospel. 414
Practical studies on the parables of Our Lord. 2028
Practical study of the soul. 2994
Practical theology. 1022, 3678
Practical theology for Christian evangelism. 1006
Practical theosophy. 3685
Practical thoughts. 971
Practical treatise on the law of convenants of title. 1375

Practical treatise on the law of covenants. 1376
Practical treatise on the law of covenants for title. 1375, 1376, 1377
Practical treatise on the ordinary operations of the Holy Spirit. 1828
Practical truths. 3631
Practical truths, plainly delivered. 77
Practical use cyclopedia of sermon suggestion, clues to great sermons from neglected texts. 3373
Practical use of the Greek New Testament. 1768
Practical view of Christian education. 3146
Practical view of Christian education in its earliest stages. 3146
Practical view of the prevailing religious system of professed Christians. 1054
Practical views on psychic phenomena. 2992
Practical vision of Christian unity. 1046
Practical works of John Bunyan. 2919
Practical yoga. 3865
Practice and experience of Christian worship. 3854
Practice and power of prayer. 2868
Practice and procedure in the Church of Scotland. 1234
Practice and science of religion. 3111
Practice of Chinese Buddhism. 705
Practice of Christian perfection. 2818
... The practice of devotion. 1437
Practice of evangelism. 1565
Practice of godliness. 966
Practice of healing evangelism. 2774
Practice of His presence. 1442
Practice of humility. 1856
Practice of meditation. 2381
Practice of mental prayer. 2379, 2875, 2887
Practice of piety. 955, 3492
Practice of prayer. 2868, 2876, 2881
Practice of process meditation. 3476
Practice of public prayer. 2875
Practice of religion. 962, 2971, 3061
Practice of salvation. 3288
Practice of spiritual direction. 3475
Practice of the Christian life. 967
Practice of the presence of God. 998
Practice of the principles of Jesus. 966
Practice of the rules. 2578
Practice of the vows. 3787
Practice of Zen. 3891
Practices of charity for boys and girls. 887
Practicing Christian psychology. 1060
Practicing Christian unity. 1049
Practicing Jesus' way of life. 3481
Practicing the presence. 1437
Practicing the presence of the Spirit. 1827
Practising faith. 2933
Praemonitus praemunitus. 2078
Praepositini Cremonensis Tractatus de officiis. 842
Pragmatic meaning of God. 1729
Prahlad. 2663, 2867
Prairie dogs and postulates. 2172
Prairie Pioneer. 1593
Prairie preacher. 3133
Prairie shepherd. 1527, 3709
Praise! A matter of life and breath. 577, 2867
Praise and blame in Renaissance Rome. 2910
Praise and lament in the Psalms. 579, 2867
Praise and promise. 3561
Praise and worship. 2867
Praise for today. 2290
Praise from the book of Psalms. 736
Praise God! 2896
Praise God for this new day. 2384
Praise is a three-letter word. 987
Praise of folly. 1632
Praise of glory. 842, 1508
Praise of God in the Psalms. 579
Praise of hypocrisy. 744
Praise papers. 2166
Praise the Lord. 1268, 1446, 3047, 3858
Praise the Lord, all you nations. 27, 2778
Praise the Lord and pass the contribution. 3324
Praise the Lord for tax exemption. 1242
Praise to Jesus. 1861
Praise to the Lord of the morning! 2893
Praise works! 982
Praises of Israel. 578
Praises of Saint Joseph. 2132
Praising God on the Las Vegas Strip. 1573, 3052
Prajna-paramita-ratna-guna-samcaya-gatha. 2867
Praktikos. 90
Praktisch-theologisches Handbuch. 3679
Pratice of religion. 3061
... The Pravacana-sara of Kunda-kunda Acarya. 1932

Praverables. 2389
Pravila. 871
Pray. 2875, 2887
Pray: a study of distinctively Christian praying. 2882
Pray always. 859, 2867
Pray and grow rich. 3539
Pray and play. 1606
Pray for us. 856
Pray for your life. 2882
Pray, God is listening. 2870
Pray in the daylight too! 2880
Pray like this. 445
Pray like this. Pray with St. Paul. 445
Pray, praise, and hooray. 2888
Pray, Sister. 2573
Pray to live. 2413
Pray to win. 2868
Pray today's Gospel. 1434
Pray with me. 859
Pray ye. 2881
Pray your way through it. 2695
Prayers for the family. 1605
Prayer. 855, 1355, 1504, 2868, 2869, 2870, 2871, 2872, 2873, 2874, 2876, 2879, 2880, 2881, 2882, 2885, 2886, 3057
Prayer, a Christian ministry. 2869
Prayer, a gift of life. 2873
Prayer; a study in the history and psychology of religion. 2873
Prayer according to the catechisms of the Reformation. 2868
Prayer and community. 2882
Prayer and confidence. 1037
Prayer and ethics. 2246
Prayer and evangelism. 2880
Prayer and intelligence. 3480
Prayer and its answer from the Word of God and Scripture comments. 2879
Prayer and its remarkable answers. 2876
Prayer and life. 386, 2877
Prayer and life's highest. 2887
Prayer and meditation. 2873, 2881
Prayer and meditation: their nature and practice. 2873
Prayer and missions. 2876
Prayer and modern man. 2871
Prayer and personal religion. 2870
Prayer and power in the capital. 2894
Prayer and praise for juniors. 3560
Prayer and prayer groups. 2885
Prayer and praying men. 2868
Prayer and providence. 2868
Prayer and sacrifice. 3489, 3490
Prayer, and some mistakes about it. 2870
Prayer and the Bible. 2872
Prayer and the common life. 2873
Prayer and the devotional life. 2869
Prayer and the living Christ. 2882
Prayer and the Lord's prayer. 2872
Prayer and the priest. 2876
Prayer and the service of God. 2874
Prayer and worship. 976, 1005
Prayer and you. 2876, 2880
Prayer as a force. 2880
Prayer as a political problem. 1153
Prayer, aspiration, and contemplation. 1937, 3490
Prayer at the golden altar. 2887
Prayer at the heart of life. 2871
Prayer-based growth groups. 1170
Prayer before the lesson. 2891
Prayer book. 858, 2081, 3455
Prayer book alterations. 2961
Prayer book amendments. 2961
Prayer book and the Christian life. 2961
Prayer-book commentary for teachers and students. 1214
Prayer book crisis. 1213
Prayer book dictionary. 1214
Prayer book for boy scouts. 2884
Prayer book for boys. 2889
Prayer book for busy Catholics. 859
Prayer book for Catholics. 855, 859
Prayer book for children. 901
Prayer book for Eastern orthodox Christians. 2749
Prayer book for Greek Catholic Hungarians of America. 766
Prayer book for Greek Catholic Rusins of America. 766
Prayer book for Holy Year. 856, 1838
Prayer book for Jewish children. 2884
Prayer book for Jewish personnel in the Armed Forces of the United States. 3456
Prayer-book for religious. 2885
Prayer book for soldiers and sailors. 3456
*Prayer BOOK for the Armed Forces (A) 2884, 3456
Prayer book for the camp. 2972
Prayer book for the Day of atonement. 1510, 2108
Prayer book for the family circle and for personal devotions. 1606
Prayer book for the new year. 1510, 2108

Prayer book for the services of the year at the synagogue. 2108
Prayer book for the Sisters of Notre Dame, Cleveland, Ohio. 840
Prayer book for the use of families. 1604, 2884
Prayer book for young Catholics. 854, 900
Prayer book interleaves. 2969
Prayer book manual. 2960
Prayer book of Aedeluald the bishop, commonly called the Book of Cerne. 855
Prayer book of eucharistic devotions. 1541
Prayer-book of Holy rosary parish, Minneapolis, Minnesota. 839
Prayer-book of Immaculate conception parish. 856
Prayer-book of Notre Dame university. 858
Prayer-book of St. Bridget's parish. Cleveland, Ohio. 839
Prayer-book of St. Francis de Sales parish, Toledo, Ohio. 839
Prayer-book of St. Joseph's academy, St. Paul, Minn. 839, 858
Prayer-book of St. Luke's parish, St. Paul, Minn. 839
Prayer-book of St. Mary's parish. 839, 855
Prayer-book of St. Mary's parish, St. Paul, Minn. 839, 859
Prayer-book of St. Patrick's parish. Cleveland, Ohio. 840
Prayer book of the Protestant Episcopal church simplified and arranged. 2961
Prayer book office. 2961
Prayer book office, Anglican divine service. 2961
Prayer book pattern. 1214
Prayer book Psalter. 1215
Prayer book reason why. 2960
Prayer book renewal. 2236, 2961
Prayer-book revised. 1213, 1214
Prayer can change your life. 2876, 2887, 2999
Prayer changes things. 1006, 2872
Prayer conference book. 2868
Prayer eminently the duty of rulers, in the times of trial; and the nation happy, whose King is the Lord. 1504
Prayer for a child. 898, 900
Prayer for a day. 2892
Prayer for all Christians. 2872
Prayer for all men. 2385
Prayer for all seasons. 2881
Prayer for colleges. 2881, 2961
Prayer for each day. 1434
Prayer for every day. 1432
Prayer for every meeting. 2783
Prayer for moderns. 2875
Prayer for peace. 2896
Prayer for peace, and other poems. 2896
Prayer for pilgrims. 744, 2869
Prayer for the world. 2248
Prayer for these times. 2877
Prayer from where we are. 2869
Prayer-gauge debate. 2877
Prayer group workshop. 2885
Prayer he taught. 2248
Prayer-hymns. 813, 1867
Prayer in a modern age. 2871
Prayer in a secular world. 2873
Prayer in action. 2876
Prayer in Catholic life. 2875
Prayer in every day living. 2873
Prayer in faith. 1264
Prayer in its present day aspects. 733
Prayer in Judaism. 584, 2111
Prayer in modern life. 2881
Prayer in my life. 2877
Prayer in other words. 2881
Prayer in practice. 2869, 2872
Prayer in sixteenth-century England. 1765
Prayer in the Apocrypha and Pseudepigrapha. 488
Prayer in the atomic age. 2882
Prayer in the market place. 2872, 2891
Prayer in the New Testament. 2883
Prayer in the religious traditions of Africa. 13
Prayer in the secular city. 2879
Prayer in the spirit. 2871
Prayer in the Talmud. 2110, 2885
Prayer in war time. 2876
Prayer is—. 2882, 2886
Prayer is action. 2880
Prayer is invading the impossible. 2873
Prayer is love. 2869
Prayer is the secret. 2883
Prayer--it works. 2869
Prayer--its deeper dimensions. 2960
Prayer, its nature and scope. 2881
Prayer, its necessity, its power, its conditions. 2960
Prayer, its practice and its answer. 3751
Prayer life. 2871

Prayer life and teachings of Jesus. 2066, 2882
Prayer life of Jesus. 2871, 2881
Prayer-life of the church. 2368
Prayer meeting and revival hymn book. 1273
Prayer-meeting methods. 2887
Prayer-meeting talks. 2886
Prayer meeting talks and outlines. 2886
Prayer meeting topics. 2886
Prayer meetings. 2886
Prayer meetings that made history. 2886
Prayer, now. 2869
Prayer of all things. 2385
Prayer of faith. 2868, 3372
Prayer of Jesus. 2049, 2060, 2247, 2870
Prayer of Jesus (The) 2247
*Prayer of love and silence (The) 2960
Prayer of Sabbath reveries. 2890
Prayer of sonship. 2248
Prayer of the church universal. 2249
Prayer of the heart. 3488
Prayer of the passion. 47
Prayer of the presence of God. 2872
Prayer—or pretense? 2873
Prayer, patronage, and power. 2
Prayer perfect. 2248, 3238
Prayer pilgrimage through the Psalms. 585
Prayer poems. 3209
Prayer power. 2247, 2881
Prayer power unlimited. 2880
Prayer primer. 2874
Prayer promptings. 2873
Prayer rediscovered. 2871
Prayer starters from the Bible for every mood. 604
Prayer stories for boys and girls. 2886
Prayer-telephone. 1432
Prayer that heals. 1609
...The prayer that helps us live. 2248
Prayer that Jesus taught. 2049
Prayer that prevails. 2874, 2887, 3786
Prayer that teaches to pray. 2246
Prayer, the act of being with God. 2874
Prayer--the art of believing. 2872
Prayer, the Christian's vital breath. 2881
Prayer The Lord did not pray. 2247
Prayer, the master key. 2872
Prayer; the New Testament. 2883
Prayer: the problem of dialogue with God. 2883
Prayer, the search for authenticity. 2873
Prayer to almighty God in time of war. 3852
Prayer tradition of Black people. 2681
Prayer way to health, wealth and happiness. 2960
Prayer weapons. 2873
Prayer-who needs it? 2882
Prayer without frills. 2888
Prayer without headaches. 2882
Prayer without pretending. 2883
Prayer works. 2876
Prayerables. 2389
Prayerful heart. 2867
Prayerfully yours. 2877
Prayerobics, getting started and staying going. 2876
Prayers. 1451, 2677, 2871, 2875, 2889, 2890, 2892, 2893, 2894, 2895
Prayers adapted to various occasions of social worship. 2890, 2891
Prayers alone/together. 2892
Prayers ancient and modern. 2895
Prayers and devotions from Pope John XXIII. 1434
Prayers and graces for a small child. 901
Prayers and graces of thanksgiving. 2892
Prayers and meditations. 126, 1439, 3491
Prayers and meditations compiled from the scriptures of India. 1815
Prayers and meditations for healing. 2397
Prayers and meditations of St. Anselm. 2888
Prayers and other pieces of Thomas Becon. 1217
Prayers and other resources for public worship. 2894
Prayers and religious exercises for the use of the Missionaries of the sacred heart. 858
Prayers and services for Christian festivals. 1339
Prayers and thanksgivings for a Christian year. 2894
Prayers and thoughts for the use of the sick. 2888
Prayers and thoughts from world religions. 2891
Prayers at Bethany chapel. 2895
Prayers at mass. 1541
Prayers at mealtime. 1750
Prayers at sea. 3317
Prayer's deeper secrets. 2873
Prayers for a new world. 2895
Prayers for a time of crisis. 2297
Prayers for a woman's day. 3843

Prayers for all occasions. 2783, 2893
Prayers, for all people, for all occasions. 2896
Prayers for all seasons. 2894
Prayers for boys. 687, 688
Prayers for boys and girls. 900
Prayers for children. 899, 902
Prayers for children and young people. 901
Prayers for Christian healing. 3406
Prayers for church and nation. 2895
Prayers for church workers. 2889
Prayers for country living. 1612
Prayers for daily use. 2893
Prayers for dark people. 2890
Prayers for eventide. 2894
Prayers for every need. 2892
Prayers for every occasion. 2894, 2895
Prayers for everyday life. 2888
Prayers for everyone. 2890, 2892, 2894
Prayers for general use and for special occasions. 2888
Prayers for girls. 1714, 2894
Prayers for help and healing. 3406
Prayers for impossible days. 2891
Prayers for laymen by a layman. 2893
Prayers for little children. 898, 901
Prayers for little men & women (and other helpful verses) 2894
Prayers for living. 2896
Prayers for meditation. 2258
Prayers for men. 2402
Prayers for mother & child. 2895
Prayers for mothers. 2625
Prayers for our day. 2893
Prayers for our dead. 840
Prayers for our times. 2894
Prayers for pagans. 2889
Prayers for pagans and hypocrites. 991
Prayers for parents who care. 2347
Prayers for parish worship. 1234
Prayers for patients. 3406
Prayers for peace. 2896
Prayers for private devotions in war-time. 2895
Prayers for private use. 2893
Prayers for Protestants. 2895
Prayers for public worship. 2783, 2893, 2929
Prayers for reconciliation. 2889
Prayers for schools and colleges. 2888
Prayers for Scouts. 686
Prayers for servicemen. 81
Prayers for services. 2893
Prayers for Shabbath, Rosh-Hashanah and Kippur,or: The Sabbath, the beginning of the year and the Day of Atonements; with the Amidah and Musaph of the Moadim, or solemn seasons, according to the order of the Spanish and Portuguese Jews. 2108
Prayers for special days and occasions. 2891
Prayers for the Christian year. 1234, 1265, 2888
Prayers for the Church Service League of the Diocese of Massachusetts. 2889
Prayers for the day. 1308
... [Prayers for the divine services of Congregation Ahawath chesed]. 2108
Prayers for the dying. 3406
Prayers for the family. 1605
Prayers for the family and for special occasions. 3047
Prayers for the people. 2891
Prayers for the pulpit. 2783
Prayers for the quiet hour. 2884
Prayers for the self-sufficient. 2892
Prayers for the use of families. 1605
Prayers for the very young child. 901
Prayers for the way. 2889
Prayers for the week. 2895
Prayers for times like these. 2891
Prayers for today. 856, 2886, 2888
Prayers for today's church. 2894
Prayers for use in home, school and Sunday school. 899, 3564
Prayers for various occasions and needs. 2893
Prayers for victory. 3794
Prayers for women's meetings. 3843
Prayers for worship. 2783
Prayers for worship leaders. 2892
Prayers for young people. 3882, 3883
Prayers for youth. 3882
Prayers from a mother's heart. 2625
Prayers from an island. 2896
Prayers from life. 2895
Prayers from metropolitan pulpit. 3523
Prayers from Plymouth pulpit. 2888
Prayers from Saint Paul. 374
Prayers from the Bible. 603
Prayers from the burned-out city. 1133
Prayers from theology. 2891
Prayers from where you are. 2892
Prayers, healing prayers and exhortations. 2895

Prayers I love. 2894
Prayers in celebration of the turning year. 2783
Prayers in community. 2892
Prayers in public. 2895
Prayers in Scripture expressions. 2891
Prayers in the congregation and in college. 2892
Prayers in the Senate. 2891
Prayers in the space age. 2891
Prayers of a college town. 3756
Prayers of a homemaker. 2625
Prayers of a university. 3756
Prayers of African religion. 2893
Prayers of faith. 2894
Prayers of Frank W. Gunsaulus. 2891
Prayers of Israel for the Sabbath and the festivals. 2108
Prayers of Isreal for the Sabbath and the festivals. 2109
Prayers of Jesus. 2049, 2247
Prayers of John Wanamaker. 2895
Prayers of Kierkegaard. 2892
Prayers of man. 32, 33, 2893
Prayers of man, from primitive peoples to present times. 2893
Prayers of Pope John Paul II. 2891
... Prayers of self-realization. 3865
Prayers of the ages. 2891
Prayers of the Bible. 253, 603
Prayers of the Christian life. 2895
Prayers of the church. 2894
Prayers of the early church. 2896
Prayers of the Eucharist. 2257
Prayers of the free spirit. 2890
Prayers of the Jewish advance. 2889
Prayers of the Middle Ages. 2896
Prayers of the missal. 845
Prayers of the modern era. 2895
Prayers of the New Testament. 450
Prayers of the Order of Christian mystics. 2740
Prayers of the people of God. 2891
Prayers of the Reformers. 2892
Prayers of the Right Rev. Thomas Wilson, D. D., fifty-eight years bishop of Sodor and Man. 1224
Prayers of the social awakening. 2894
Prayers of the spirit. 2972
Prayers of women. 2894
Prayers offered at daily sessions of the Assembly. 2208, 2894
Prayers offered by the Right Reverend Monsignor Christopher P. Griffin, Chaplain of the Senate of the Commonwealth of Massachusetts. 2208
Prayers that are answered. 2319, 2875
Prayers that are different. 2892
Prayers that changed history. 603, 2883
Prayers to grow by. 2896
Prayers to pray wherever you are. 2895
Prayers to pray without really trying. 2895
Prayers upon the cemetery. 1715, 2109
Prayers we have in common. 2891
Prayers we love to pray. 2893
Prayers. With a foreword by Donald Proudman. 858
Prayerways for those who fell discouraged or distraught, frightened or frustrated, angry or anxious, powerless or purposeless, over-extended or under-appreciated, burned out or just plain worn out. 3482
Praying. 2871
Praying and working. 927, 2961
Praying Christ. 2883
Praying church. 2873
Praying clear through. 2960
Praying for inner healing. 3476
Praying for others. 1509, 2871
Praying for the dead. 2960
Praying: how, when, where, why. 2875
Praying Hyde. 859, 2531
Praying Hyde, a man of prayer. 1859
... Praying in the Holy Ghost. 2875
Praying Jesus' way. 2049, 2876
Praying our prayers. 858
Praying the Gospels. 1977
... Praying the mass. 2365
Praying the psalms. 579
Praying through. 2875
Praying to change things. 2880
Praying today: practical thoughts on prayer. 2877
Praying together. 856, 2886
Praying with Christ. 2248
Praying with Paul. 2869
Praying with the Bible. 604
Praying with the family of God. 901
Praying with the Poverello. 1642
Pre-Adamite earth. 1381
Pre-Christian Gnosticism. 1718
Pre-Columbian American religions. 1904
"Preach it again" 2899
Preach the Word. 1559, 2906, 2907
Preach the Word of God. 2903

Preach there also; a study of the town and country work of the Episcopal Church. 3253
Preacher. 2901, 2904, 3674
Preacher and his audience. 2900
Preacher and his missionary message. 2519
Preacher and his models. 2906
Preacher and his place. 2900
Preacher and his preaching. 2900
Preacher and his sermon. 2899, 2906
Preacher and his work. 2900, 2904, 3673
Preacher & hs preaching. 2905
Preacher and I. 3090
Preacher and politics. 2899
Preacher and prayer. 1298, 2898
Preacher and the New English Bible. 399
Preacher and the people. 2902
Preacher as a man of letters. 2905
Preacher, Ecclesiastes. 852, 1490
Preacher, his life and work. 3672
Preacher looks at war. 3793
Preacher Mike. 3235
Preacher of the law and testimony. 2897
Preacher of the people. 2404, 3403
Preacher of today. 3673
Preacher on the roof. 1290, 2627
Preacher on wheels. 1301, 1848
Preacher-persuader. 2904
Preacher problems; or, The twentieth century preacher at his work. 3673
Preacher-prophet in mass society. 2903
Preacher talk. 1295
Preacher with a billy club. 1254
Preacher with a plow. 2501
Preachers. 1576
Preachers and preaching. 2906, 3673
Preachers and preaching in Detroit. 3366
Preacher's calling to be servant. 1289
Preacher's complete homiletical commentary ... (on an original plan) 224
Preacher's concordance. 302
Preacher's doorknob. 3675
Preacher's encyclopedia. 1268, 3722
Preacher's first books. 3627
Preacher's heritage, task, and resources. 2906
... The preacher's ideals and inspirations. 2901
Preachers in purgatory. 2786
Preachers in space. 212
Preacher's kid's dad. 1908
Preacher's manual. 285, 2427, 2900
Preacher's note-book. 3372
Preachers of power. 184, 2903
Preachers of righteousness. 2907
Preachers of today. 1272
Preachers, pedagogues & politicians. 3080
Preacher's portrait. 2908
Preacher's primer. 2902
Preachers' progeny. 2897
Preachers scrap book. 1840
Preacher's story of his work. 2904
Preacher's task and the stone of stumbling. 2903
Preacher's temptations. 1298
Preacher's vademecum. 3719
Preacher's weapon. 2897
Preacher's wife. 2866
Preacher's yellow pants. 1289, 3861
Preaching. 2896, 2898, 2900, 2902, 2903, 2904, 2906, 2907
Preaching about death. 1418
Preaching according to plan. 2896
Preaching and Biblical theology. 2899
Preaching and community. 2897
Preaching and congregation. 2896
Preaching and paganism. 2900
Preaching and parish renewal. 2299
Preaching and pastoral care. 1781, 2906
Preaching and sermon construction. 2898
Preaching and teaching from Ephesians. 363
Preaching and teaching in the earliest church. 2909
Preaching and teaching the New Testament. 473
Preaching and teaching in Anglo-Saxon England. 11, 2909
Preaching angles. 2898
Preaching as a fine art. 2906
Preaching as a saving encounter. 2905
Preaching as communication. 2898
Preaching as counseling. 1635, 2902
Preaching biblically. 299, 2906
Preaching by laymen. 1407
Preaching Christ. 2931
Preaching Christ crucified. 2215
Preaching Christ in Corinth. 323
Preaching. Confession. The Lord's Supper. 2902
Preaching during a revolution. 2901
Preaching event. 2903, 2907

Preaching for tethered man. 2299
Preaching for the church. 2898
Preaching for the people. 2899
Preaching for today. 2900
Preaching from Ecclesiastes. 164
Preaching from Genesis. 524
Preaching from great Bible chapters. 169, 299
Preaching from Hosea. 538
Preaching from Isaiah. 544
Preaching from John's Gospel. 422
Preaching from pictures. 84
Preaching from prophetic books. 570
Preaching from Revelation. 464
Preaching from Samuel. 590
Preaching from the Bible. 2897
Preaching from the Propers. 2897
Preaching from the Prophets. 570
Preaching from the Psalms. 586
Preaching from the types and metaphors of the Bible. 314, 2416
Preaching from the whole Bible. 299, 1268
Preaching holiness today. 2906
Preaching in a new key: Studies in the psychology of thinking and listening. 2907
Preaching in a revolutionary age. 2904
Preaching in a scientific age. 2899
Preaching in American history. 2910
Preaching in England in the late fifteenth and sixteenth centuries. 2909
Preaching in London. 2903
Preaching in medieval England. 2908, 2909
Preaching in New York. 2903
...Preaching in the Anglo-Saxon church. 2909
Preaching in the early church. 2909
Preaching in the first half century of New England history. 2910
Preaching in the great tradition. 2909
Preaching in the new age. 2902
Preaching in the new era. 3354
Preaching in the Russian church. 2899
Preaching in the Spanish golden age. 2911
Preaching in the thought of Alexander Campbell. 732, 2910
Preaching in the twentieth century. 2905
Preaching in the witnessing community. 1561
Preaching in theory and practice. 2902
Preaching in these times. 2904
Preaching in Wall street. 1574
Preaching law and gospel. 2906
Preaching ministry today. 2905
Preaching moment. 1509
Preaching of Augustine. 3334
Preaching of Chrysostom. 3337
Preaching of F. W. Robertson. 1227
Preaching of Islam. 1924, 2564
Preaching of Jesus. 2049
Preaching of John Henry Newman. 1227, 3365
Preaching of Peter. 68
Preaching of Robert G. Lee. 2206, 2909
Preaching of the cross. 3347
Preaching of the gospel. 2897
Preaching on Bible characters. 2907
Preaching on Christian unity. 1046
Preaching on church and community occasions. 3373
Preaching on controversial issues. 2434
Preaching on John. 3374
Preaching on national holidays. 2722
Preaching on New Testament themes. 1466
Preaching on Old Testament themes. 1466
Preaching on Pentecost and Christian unity. 2813
Preaching on race. 3017
Preaching on suffering and a God of love. 3542
Preaching on the books of the New Testament. 411
Preaching on the books of the Old Testament. 537
Preaching on the life of Christ. 1986
Preaching on the parables. 2025
Preaching out of the overflow. 2906
Preaching pastor. 2901
Preaching that builds churches. 1557
Preaching that built a great church. 166
Preaching the Apocalypse. 465
Preaching the Bible. 3361
Preaching the Christian year. 2901
Preaching the Christian year [by] Hughell E.W. Fosbroke [and others] Edited for the Dean and Chapter of the Cathedral Church of St. John the Divine. With a foreword by James A. Pike. 2901
Preaching the doctrines of grace. 1558
Preaching the good news. 2906
Preaching the gospel. 2905, 3360
Preaching the gospel from the gospels. 391

Preaching the gospel of the resurrection. 2903
Preaching the gospels. 391
Preaching the liturgical renewal. 3773
Preaching the Nativity. 9
Preaching the Passion. 2214
Preaching the social gospel. 1407
Preaching the story. 2908
Preaching the word of God. 2903
Preaching the Word with authority. 2905
Preaching through Matthew. 443
Preaching through the Bible. 615, 3373
Preaching through the saints. 865, 1024
Preaching through the year. 2906
Preaching to be understood. 2907
Preaching to change lives. 161
Preaching to meet men's needs. 2904
Preaching to modern man. 2908
Preaching to suburban captives. 2222
Preaching to the contemporary mind. 2896
Preaching to the exiles. 547
Preaching to the times. 2898, 3381
Preaching tradition. 2910
Preaching truths for perilous times. 3374
Preaching unashamed. 2906
Preaching value of missions. 2522
Preaching values from the papyri. 1771
Preaching values in new translations of the New Testament. 408
... Preaching values in the Bible. 299
Preaching values in the Epistles of Paul. 374
Preaching values in the Old Testament in the modern translations. 537
Preaching values in Today's English version. 408
Preaching week by week. 1841, 2905
Preaching well. 2899
Preaching with authority. 2903
Preaching with confidence. 2899
Preaching with purpose and power. 2908
Preaching without notes. 2902
Preaching word. 2168, 2905
Preachings. 2898
Preachographs. 3235
Pre-Adamite. 275
Pre-Adamite earth. 1381, 3313
Pre Benedictine monachism. 2578
Precarious organisation. 3447
Precarious vision. 3085
Precede the dawn. 1067
Preceding God. 3347
Precept and practice. 955
Precept and practice: traditional Buddhism in the rural highlands of Ceylon. 704
... The precept of hearing Mass. 1162
Precept upon precept. 629
Precepts. 2911
Precepts for perfection. 3020, 3775
Precepts for the young. 903
Precepts of Jesus, the guide to peace and happiness. 2071, 3728
Precepts of the church. 1312
Precepts of the church and other papers. 1312
Precher aux hommes de notre temps. 2900
Precinct of religion in the culture of humanity. 3063
...The precious and sacred writings of Martin Luther. 2275
Precious Bible promises. 302, 1737
Precious Blood. 3289
Precious blood the price of our redemption. 672
Precious garland and The song of the four mindfulnesses. 2667
Precious gem in the tabernacle. 3720
Precious gift. 2021
Precious harvest. 2752
Precious jewels. 302, 3816
Precious pearl. 1698
... The precious promise Testament. 353
Precious promises. 2394
Precious remedies against Satan's devices with the Covenant of grace. 3303
Precious Saviour. 2000
Precious stones of the heavenly foundations. 961
Precious things of the Bible. 2934
Precious thoughts moral and religious. 3255
Preciousness of God's thoughts. 3343
Precisely how to take care of your self. 1012
Precognition and the philosophy of science. 876, 1700
Pre-conquest church in England. 1761
Predestination. 2911
Predestination, and other papers. 2911
Predestination, God's foreknowledge, and future contingents. 2912
Predestination, grace, and free will. 2911
Predestination primer. 2911
Predicament of modern man. 1064
Predicament of the prosperous. 3440

Predict your own future. 3539
Prediction and fulfillment in the Bible. 607
Prediction, planning and control. 3871
Prediction techniques synthesized. 97
Predictions. 2948
Predictions: fact or fallacy? 2948
Predictions of the prophets. 464
Predictions realized in modern times. 2948
Predictive astrology. 97
Pre-eminence of the Eucharist among the sacraments according to Alexander of Hales, St. Albert the Great. 2256
Pre-existence of Christ in the New Testament. 2049
Pre-existence of Christ in the writings of Justin Martyr. 2049
Pre-existence, wisdom, and the Son of Man. 2896, 3458
Preface for parents; counsels for the expectant mother and father. Foreword by Dora P. Chaplin. Illustrated by Berit Homstead. 2625
Preface to a religious philosophy of living. 3099
Preface to Bible-study. 641
Preface to Bonhoeffer. 676, 2173, 2174
Preface to Christian faith in a new age. 1050
Preface to Christian theology. 1105
Preface to history. 1818
Preface to life. 1105
Preface to metaphysics. 2739
Preface to morals. 1536
Preface to Newman's theology. 2702, 3653
Preface to Old Testament theology. 598
Preface to Paradise lost. 1521, 2470
Preface to Paradise lost being the Ballard Matthews lectures delivered at University College, North Wales, 1941. 2470
Preface to parish renewal. 1243
Preface to pastoral theology. 2785
Preface to Paul. 372
Preface to Plato. 2835, 2853
Preface to prayer. 2873
Preface to religion. 797
Preface to the Bible. 288
Preface to the Gospels and Paul. 349
Prefatory epistles of Jacques Lefevre d'Etaples and related texts. 2912
Prefect freedom. 2972
Prehistoric religion. 3109, 3110
Prehistoric times. 3501
Prejudice. 2912
Prejudice against the Jew. 2076
Prejudice, its genesis and exodus. 3371
Prelatical doctrine of apostolical succession examined. 76
Prelections on theology. 3648
Preliminary guide to Black materials in the Disciples of Christ Historical Society. 2683
Preliminary planning. 1157
Preliminary report of the Commission appointed by the University of Pennsylvania to investigate modern spiritualism. 3510
Preliminary report on the synagogue at Dura. 1483
Preliminary research. 1465
Preliminary survey of the French collection. 1638, 1704
Preliminary survey of the German collection. 1704, 1708
... The prelude ot the reformation. 1761
Prelude to dialogue; Jewish-Christian relationships. 2153
Prelude to metaphysics. 2417
Prelude to science. 2729
Prelude to the Cross. 2034
Prelude to the kingdom. 2615
Prelude to victory. 2030
Preludes to prayer. 1430, 1435
Preludios para la oracion. 1446
Premature death of protestantism. 2978
Premiers ecrits. 3384
Premillennialism. 1528
Premillennialism or amillennialism? 2465
Premillennialists and their critics. 2466
Premium essay on the characteristics and laws of prophetic symbols. 609
Premonitions. 2946, 2948
Prep school guide for Jewish youth. 2943
Preparacion para la crisis final. 221
Preparation. 600
Preparation and delivery of sermons. 2904
Preparation for Catholic family life. 2339
Preparation for church membership. 2454
Preparation for death. 1417
Preparation for marriage. 2341
Preparation for teaching. 3556
Preparation for the final crisis. 3382
Preparation of sermons. 2897
Preparation to profess religion. 1592
Preparation to the Psalter. 579

... The preparations of the religious teacher. 805
Preparatory reports. 3773
Preparatory schools & religion in our time. 2943
Prepare for war. 606
Prepare now to succeed on your mission. 1233, 2484
Prepare to meet thy God. 967, 1062
Prepare yourself to serve. 1016
Prepare yourself to serve,God's call to a life of discipline and service. 1016
Prepared under the direction of the Board of Trustees of the Ellen G. White Estate. 3812
... Preparing and teaching the lesson. 3558
Preparing for Christian marriage. 2347
Preparing for church membership. 1202, 2295
Preparing for confirmation. 1328, 1329
Preparing for Easter. 848, 2209
Preparing for effective Bible teaching. 636
Preparing for platform and pulpit. 2897
Preparing for spiritual direction. 3475
Preparing for the latter rain. 1831
Preparing for the ministry. 1289
Preparing for the storm. 3348
Preparing for work. 3849
Preparing newcomers for life in the Spirit. 1443
Preparing preachers to preach. 2903
Preparing the way. 535, 3229
Preparing the way for Paul. 2113
Preparing the way of the Lord. 3004
Preparing to be a missionary. 2483
Preparing to preach. 2898
Preparing to teach God's word. 636
Pre-Raphaelite brotherhood. 2896
Pre-Reformation England. 1762
Pre-Reformation English spirituality. 2645
... Pre-reformation printed books. 1894
Prerequisites to communion. 2250
Pre-Romanesque churches of Spain. 1274
Presbyterian and unity. 1046
Presbyterian authority and discipline. 2914
Presbyterian celebration. 2917
Presbyterian Christian endeavor manual for 1908. 2915
Presbyterian church in California. 2917
Presbyterian church in Jefferson. 1939
Presbyterian church in Philadelphia. 2918
Presbyterian Church in the Old Southwest. 2919
Presbyterian Church of Ghana, 1835-1960. 2917
Presbyterian Church of Lawrenceville. 2202
Presbyterian Church of Sewickley, Pennsylvania, 1838-1963. 3388
Presbyterian church on the Virginia frontier. 2937
Presbyterian church throughout the world. 2916
Presbyterian church within the field of the Presbytery of Westchester, synod of New York. 2918
Presbyterian church within the field [of the Presbytery of Westchester, synod of New York. 2919
Presbyterian churches. 2912
Presbyterian churches and the federal Union. 2923
Presbyterian churches of Roanoke, Virginia. 2919
Presbyterian clergyman looking for the church. 1362
Presbyterian college handbook, 1955-1956. 2923, 3759
Presbyterian colleges. 2915
Presbyterian colleges and academies in Nebraska. 2918
Presbyterian Congregation in George Town, 1780-1970. 1706
Presbyterian congregation of Hazleton. 1792
Presbyterian congregation on Rocky River. 3242
Presbyterian constitution and digest. 3735
Presbyterian digest. 2924
Presbyterian digest of 1886. 2924
Presbyterian digest of 1898. 2924
Presbyterian digest of 1907. 2924
Presbyterian doctrine of children in the covenant. 1906
Presbyterian elders and deacons serving Christ in the church. 2915
Presbyterian enterprise. 2924
Presbyterian enterprise; sources of American Presbyterian history. 2924
Presbyterian foreign missions. 2926
Presbyterian handbook containing facts respecting the history statistics and work of the Presbyterian church in the U. S. A. 2915
Presbyterian heritage. 2915
Presbyterian home missions. 2926

Presbyterian hymnal. 2916, 2926
Presbyterian law and procedure in the Presbyterian church in the United States. 2920
Presbyterian law for presbytery and synod. 3735
Presbyterian law for the local church. 2924, 2925, 3735, 3736
Presbyterian law for the presbytery. 2924, 2925, 3735, 3736
Presbyterian liturgies. 2929
Presbyterian ministry in American culture. 2922
Presbyterian missions. 2926
Presbyterian missions in the southern United States. 2926
Presbyterian panorama. 2929
Presbyterian parochial schools, 1846-1870. 2923
Presbyterian pioneers in Congo. 2514
Presbyterian practice vs. Presbyterian theory. 1803
Presbyterian reunion: a memorial volume. 1837-1871. 2925
Presbyterian rule. 2925
Presbyterian rule, embracing the form of government, rules of discipline, and directory for worship, in the Presbyterian church in the United States. 2925
Presbyterian rule, embracing the form of government, rules of discipline and directory of worship in the Presbyterian church in the United States. 2925
Presbyterian statistics through one hundred years, 1826-1926. 2928
Presbyterian task in an urban South. 1279
Presbyterian Valley. 2919
Presbyterian way of life. 2936
Presbyterian women of South Carolina. 2919
Presbyterian worship. 2239, 2912, 3003
Presbyterian worship in America. 2929
Presbyterian worship in America: changing patterns since 1787. 2929
Presbyterianism. 2916, 2936
Presbyterianism for the people. 2936
Presbyterianism in America. 2923
Presbyterianism in her polity and practice. 2936
Presbyterianism in New Orleans and adjacent points. 2918
Presbyterianism in New York State. 2928
Presbyterianism in Perth Amboy, New Jersey. 2823
Presbyterianism in Versailles and Woodford County, Kentucky. 3777
Presbyterians. 2915, 2923, 2924, 2936
Presbyterians and the Negro. 2920
Presbyterians and unity. 1046
Presbyterians in colonial Pennsylvania. 2936
Presbyterians in the South. 2925
Presbyterians in the Upper Conemaugh Valley. 2129
Presbyterians of Baltimore. 2917
Presbyterians pioneer at Matawan; published as its history. 2925
... The Presbyterians, 1783-1840. 2924
Presbyterians, their history and beliefs. 2916, 2936
Presbyteries and profits. 730, 3800
Presbytery. 2931
Presbytery of Dubuque. 2917
Presbytery of Hamilton, 1836-1967. 2917
Presbytery of Kansas City and its predecessors 1821-1901. 2927
Presbytery of New York 1738 to 1888. 2918
Preschool program in compensatory education. 3436
Preschoolers at church. 939
Prescription for anxiety. 55
Prescription for healing. 1599
Prescription for heartache. 2808
Prescription for life. 982, 2051
Prescription for preaching. 2902
[Prescription symbol], the Christian love treatment. 724, 1107
Prescriptions for parishes. 2774
Prescriptions from the beloved physician. 426
Pre-seminary education. 2938
Presence. 2258, 2636
Presence and absence. 251
Presence and absence of God. 1596
Presence and possibility: Louisville Catholicism and its cathedral. 750
Presence and structure. 2235
Presence of absoluteness. 968
Presence of Christ. 2934, 3356
Presence of God. 980, 1729, 1737, 2019, 2638
Presence of love. 3183
Presence of Mary. 996, 2354
Presence of other worlds. 3571
Presence of Siva. 3421
Presence of the future. 2174

Presence of the Kingdom. 960
Presence, power, praise. 2816
Present age and inner life. 3500
Present age, and Of the difference between a genius and an apostle. 2170
Present age, and Of the difference between a genius and apostle. 2170
... The present age and two minor ethico-religious treatises. 3631
Present and future. 477
Present and future of religion. 1050, 1060
Present antichrist. 52
Present crisis in religion. 3062
Present-day conditions in China. 2508
Present day conservatism and liberalism within Biblical lines. 2220
Present-day definition of Christianity. 1054
Present-day dilemmas in religion. 3066
Present-day ethics in their relations to the spiritual life. 1534
Present-day evangelism. 1563
Present day hymns and why they were written. 1868
Present day life and religion. 161
Present day message of Quakerism. 1683
Present day Methodism and the Bible. 611
Present day miracles. 1597, 1939
Present day parables. 1839
Present-day parties in the state and church. 2858
Present-day prayer-meeting helps for laymen and minister. 2886
Present-day preaching. 2906
Present day problems in Christian morals. 942
Present-day problems of Christian thought. 3622
Present-day summons to the world mission of Christianity. 2521
Present-day Sunday school. 3552
Present day theology. 3648, 3651
Present-day trends in religious education. 3157
Present-day Y.M.C.A. church relations in the United States. 3871
Present for Dino. 156
Present in the light of prophecy. 1515
Present kingdom of God. 988
Present perils in religion. 3058
Present perils of Methodism. 2421
Present problems of New Testament study. 348
Present religious crisis. 1653
Present revelation. 3225
Present state of Christianity, and of the missionary establishments for its propagation in all parts of the world. 2526
Present state of the Greek and Armenian churches, anno Christi, 1678. 82, 2746
Present state of the Greek Church in Russia. 1469, 2750
Present status of the inquiry concerning the geniuneness of the Pauline epistles. 370
Present status of the teaching of morals in the public high schools. 2590
Present tendencies in religious thought. 3061
Present tense salvation. 1557
Present theological tendencies. 3640
Present time and prophecy. 2607
Present to my Christian friend on entire devotion to God. 3300
Present trends in Christian thought. 3656
Present truth. 2036, 3318
Present world situation. 2494
Present your bodies. 963
Presentation of reality. 3027
...The presentation of the Bible to chidren. 638
"presentation" Paradise lost. 2471
Presenting the angels. 42
Presenting the glorious gospel. 1566
Presenting the Gospel. 3830
Presenting Y-teens to senior high school girls and their advisers in the YWCA. 1715
Preservation. 513
Preservative from damnable errors. 1341, 3430
Preserving our tradition in Church and State. 1152
Presidential profiles. 2937
Presidents of the Church. 1231, 2609
... President's report. 1788
President's report and the rabbi's message to the 123rd annual meeting of the Congregation Beth Israel. 1787
Presiding elders' reports of the Methodist Episcopal church in India. 2454
Presiding eldership structural in the Methodist Episcopal church. 2450
Press and Vatican II. 1153, 3771
Press view the FBI raid. 3314, 3740

Pressing on. 1853
Pressure of our common calling. 1492
Pressure points. 987
Prester John. 2126
Presumption of atheism and other philosophical essays on God, freedom, and immortality. 3621
... Presumptions of law in marriage cases. 2938
Presyterian policy and procedures. 2924
Preteen Bible exploration. 616
Preti-operai al Concilio. 3449
Pretribulation rapture. 3021
Preus of Missouri and the great Lutheran civil war. 1300, 2938
Prevailing prayer. 2869, 2887, 3338
Prevailing prayer; sermons on prayer. 2887
Preventive psychology and the church. 2782
Pri Yehudah. 3360
Price and the prize. 1096
Price guide to the occult and related subjects. 2731
... The price of dawning day. 2501
Price of Africa. 2498
Price of freedom. 3447
Price of leadership. 1282
Price of our heritage. 3417
Price of power. 964
Price tags of life. 160
Priceless gems from Holy Writ. 250
Priceless heritage. 2101
Priceless ingredient. 2298, 3347
Pride of lions. 17
Pride--one of the seven cardinal sins. 3411
Priest. 772, 1294, 1296, 2734, 2790, 3222
... A priest after God's own heart. 1299
Priest and a world vision. 850
Priest and bishop. 2938
Priest and his bishop. 773
Priest and his interior life. 1288, 1298, 1299
Priest and his mission. 772
Priest and mental health. 2784
Priest & parish in eighteenth-century France. 774, 1292
Priest and parson. 1288
Priest and penance. 1327
Priest and people. 828
Priest and priestess. 2742
Priest and revolutionary. 2194
Priest and Saint Paul. 2796
Priest and social action. 757
Priest and the king. 6, 2322
Priest and the proletarist. 1136
Priest and the unconscious. 2995
Priest and vocations (The) 3786
Priest and womanhood. 1259
Priest and worker. 3143
Priest as counselor. 2780
Priest as manager. 771, 1199
Priest as person. 772, 2939
Priest as preacher, past and future. 771, 2909
Priest as student. 3668
Priest at his prie-dieu. 2393
Priest at prayer. 2387, 2940
Priest at the altar. 2366
Priest: celibate or married. 877
Priest confesses. 3131
Priest for all men. 3535
Priest for all seasons. 771
Priest for ever. 1299
Priest forever. 1809, 2742, 2939, 3275
Priest forever; history of St. John's Seminary, San Antonia, Texas, 1915-1965. 3275
Priest, God and the world. 853
Priest: his dignity and obligations. 771
Priest in community. 2787
Priest in crisis. 773
Priest in our day. 773
Priest in paradise. 774
Priest in practice. 771
Priest in public service. 668, 1779
Priest in Russia and the Baltic. 3256
Priest in the Epistles of St. Paul. 771
Priest in the piazza. 3769
Priest in the presbytery. 2788
Priest in the pulpit. 2905
Priest in the world. 773
Priest in union with Christ. 1298
Priest is not his own. 2939
Priest: living instrument and minister of Christ. 772, 2789
Priest must preach. 864
Priest named Horse. 2461, 2485
Priest of Christ. 1299
Priest of the fathers. 772
Priest of the people. 772
Priest, patriot, and leader. 742
Priest, the woman, and the confessional. 1326
Priest to a nun. 1000
Priest to the temple. 1804
Priest today. 2553

Priester und Tempel im hellenistischen Agypten. 1502
Priestess of the occult, Madame Blavatsky. 672
Priesthood. 773, 1295, 1296, 2395, 2741, 2938
Priesthood and church government. 2615
Priesthood and church government in the Church of Jesus Christ of Latter-day Saints. 2615
Priesthood and church welfare. 2601
Priesthood and clergy unknown to Christianity. 1288
Priesthood and ministry. 2939
Priesthood and perfection. 2819
Priesthood and prayer. 1295, 2939
Priesthood, By various writers. 1295
Priesthood correlation manual of instruction for the priesthood genealogical program. 1704
Priesthood in a changing world. 3676
... Priesthood in English church. 2938
Priesthood in the mystical body. 2939
Priesthood manual. 2791, 3677
Priesthood of all believers. 2939
Priesthood of Christ and his ministers. 2049, 2938
Priesthood of the faithful. 2940
Priesthood orientation studies. 1239
Priestly amen. 3223
Priestly beatitudes, retreat sermons. 1298
Priestly celibacy and maturity. 877
Priestly celibacy—recurrent battle and lasting values. 772, 877
Priestly element in the Old Testament. 500
Priestly existence. 1299
Priestly gift in Mishnah. 2479
Priestly heart. 1299
Priestly heart; the last chapter in the life of an old-young priest. 1299
Priestly holiness. 1298
Priestly life. 1298
Priestly people. 2939
Priestly perfection. one hundred brief meditations based on the exhortation of Pope Pius x to the clergy. 2393
Priestly practice; familiar essays on clerical topics. 1289
Priestly prayers. 2940
Priestly zeal for souls. 1298
Priests and long life. 2940
Priests and parishes of the diocese of Brooklyn, 1820 to 1944. 693
Priests and people in pre-famine Ireland, 1780-1845. 836, 1293
Priests and politicians. 1246
Priests and politicians: Protestant and Catholic missions in Orthodox Ethiopia, 1830-1868. 2517
Priests and prophets. 2114
Priests and religious for Latin America. 2582
Priests ceremonial. 838
Priest's companion. 855, 1299
Priest's daily manual. 2885
Priests for tomorrow. 771, 2938
Priest's guide to parish worship. 839
Priests in council. 2671
Priests in the firing line. 1543
Priests in the United States. 772, 1300
Priest's new ritual for the convenience of the reverend clergy in the administration of the sacraments and various blessings. 837
Priest's new ritual for the convenience of the reverent clergy in the administration of the sacraments and various blessings. 837
Priests of ancient Egypt. 2940
Priests of Holy cross. 1332
Priests, philosophers and prophets. 3065
Priests' problems. 3677
Priests, prophets, pioneers. 966
Priests' retreat. 772
Priest's ritual. 837
Priests' secret oath. 1288
Priests to each other. 2191
Priest's voice, its use and misuse. 3676
Priests, warriors, and cattle. 2711
Priest's way to God. 1298, 2742
Priesty virtue and zeal. 3778
Primacy of charity in moral theology. 2264
Primacy of Christ in doctrine and life. 2041
Primacy of existence in Thomas Aquinas. 3695
Primacy of faith. 1593, 1596
Primacy of Peter from the Protestant and from the Catholic point of view. 2862
Primacy of Peter (The) 2825, 2862
Primacy of preaching today. 2899
Primacy of the missionary. 2493
Primacy of the person in the church. 2192
Primacy of worship. 3854

Primal curse. 724
Primal mind. 1902
Primal myths. 1384
Primal power in man ; or, The kundalini shakti. 3865
Primal vision. 2500
Primaries at worship. 3854
Primary Bible history for young Israel. 534
Primary Bible questions for young children. 218
Primary cause of antisemitism. 2079
Primary children in the church. 3171
Primary children learn at church. 3172
Primary children sing. 3563
Primary choir. 915
Primary church school. 3153, 3171
Primary course in the Sunday school. 3155
Primary department. 3551, 3553
Primary facts in religious thought. 3065
Primary folks at mission study. 2535
Primary hymn book; hymns and songs for little children. 3561
Primary leader's guide on the contribution of the Church to the development of Canada. 734
Primary leaders manual. 3553
Primary leadership manual. 3169
Primary lessons in Christian living and healing. 1599
Primary manual for administrators and leaders in the primary department of the church school. 3170
... Primary method in the church school. 3154, 3180
Primary plans for the smaller Sunday school. 3558
Primary platform of Methodism. 2421
Primary songs of praise for the primary department of the Sunday school and the home. 3563
Primary story worship programs. 3176
Primary Sunday school work. 3552
Primary superintendent's manual. 3171
Primary teacher with helps and exercises. 3565
Primary teacher's guide on Bible lands today. 3180
Primary teacher's guide on Into all the world with the Bible. 2549
Primary teacher's guide on Korea. 2536
Primary teacher's guide on the church's mission in town and country. 3177
... Primary teachers' manual. 641, 650
... The primary worker and work. 3558
Primary workship guide. 3169
Primary worship guide. 3165
Primary worship programs. 3856
Primary worship services. 3560
Primates of the four Georges. 666
Prime Rib and Apple. 3839
Prime time. 2461
Prime time preachers. 1576
Primer for new Disciples. 1463
Primer for Protestants. 2977
Primer for the perplexed. 975
Primer for young Christians. 1228
Primer manual of sacred history. 1024
Primer of ancient hymnody. 813, 1877
... A primer of Assyriology. 93
Primer of Christian doctrine in the form of questions and answers. 934
Primer of Hebrew history. 2090
Primer of Hinduism. 1813
Primer of homiletics. 2898
Primer of Old Testament history. 533, 535
Primer of Old Testament text criticism. 505
Primer of prayer. 2875
Primer of psychical research. 2987
Primer of pure spiritualism. 3497
Primer of right and wrong. 1324
Primer of Soto Zen. 1472
Primer of teacher training. 3177
Primer of the Bible. 308
Primer of theology. 804
... A primer of theosophy. 3688
Primer on Roman Catholicism for Protestants. 802
Primer set furth by the Kinges Maiestie & his clergie (1545) 2941
Primers of the faith. 276, 309
Primeval forest. 2523
Primeval world. 202
Primeval world of Hebrew traditions. 523
Primitive and apostolical order of the church of Christ vindicated. 1523
Primitive and prehistoric religions. 3108
Primitive Baptist church meeting directory. 2941
Primitive Baptist doctrine. 2941
Primitive Buddhism. 703
Primitive Catholicism. 808

Primitive Christian application of the doctrine of the servant. 3657
Primitive Christian calendar. 435
Primitive Christian catechism. 368
Primitive Christian eschatology. 1528
Primitive Christian symbols. 919
Primitive Christianity. 1048, 1194
Primitive Christianity and early criticisms (a work of negation) 1049
Primitive Christianity and its corruptions. 1189
Primitive Christianity in its contemporary setting. 1078, 1079
Primitive Christianity revived in the faith and practice of the people called Quakers. 1682
Primitive Christian's estimate of war and self-defense. 3791
Primitive church. 1191, 1192, 1195
Primitive creed. 73
Primitive episcopacy. 3050
Primitive era of Christianity as recorded in the Acts of the apostles. 333
Primitive faiths. 3109
Primitive gospel and its "life of Jesus" 1987
Primitive Gospel sources. 378
Primitive hymns, spiritual songs, and sacred poems. 1866
Primitive man. 2322
Primitive Methodism in Cornwall. 2430
Primitive mythology. 3108
Primitive piety revived. 960
Primitive piety revived, or, The aggressive power of the Christian church. 961
Primitive psychic power. 2729
Primitive religion. 3057, 3109, 3110
Primitive religion in the tropical forests. 3110
... Primitive religion; its nature and origin. 3110
... Primitive religions. 3113
Primitive saints and the see of Rome. 2768
Primitive Semitic religion today. 3332
Primitive survivals in modern thought. 1653
Primitive text of the Gospels and Acts. 384
Primitive tradition of the Eucharistic Body and Blood. 3658
Primitive traits in religious revivals. 3228
Primitive worship & the prayer book, rationale, history and doctrine of the English, Irish, Scottish and American books. 3855
Primogenesis. 535
Primordia of Bishop White Kennett. 29
Prince and the prophet. 2214
Prince dimitri's mountaineers. 1744
Prince Emmanuel. 2005
Prince Hall and his followers. 1667
Prince of Darkness. 1427
Prince of democracy. 1711
Prince of martyrs. 21, 3403
Prince of pastors. 739
Prince of peace. 383, 1950, 1953, 1959, 1962, 1968, 3145
Prince of peace and His love is the sweetest story ever told. 1955
Prince of pulpit orators. 3813
Prince of the church in India. 890, 2530
Prince of the house of David. 2005, 2132
Prince of the pulpit. 3716
Prince of the realm. 3818
Prince on a galloping horse. 739
Prince who gave his gold away. 1744
Prince who gave up a throne. 1703
Princely manhood. 3393
... Princely men in the heavenly kingdom. 2507
Princes & paupers in the English Church, 1500-1800. 1219
Princess of poverty. 1284
Princess, pauper and penitent. 1508
Princess Poverty. 1643
Princeton pamphlets. no. 1. 3637
Princeton pulpit. 2941
Princetonian. 1821
Principal Catholic practices. 840
Principal doctrines of Christianity defended against the errors of Socinianism. 1776, 3438, 3439
Principal of Jesus applied to some questions of to-day. 2061
Principal prophecies and types of the Old Testament. 2414
Principal Upanisads. 3759
Principalities and powers. 375, 1818, 2727
Principalities & powers & people. 3734
"Principalities and powers in heavenly places." 3475
Principalities and powers in the New Testament. 3475
Principal's principles. 2106

Principia. 1371
Principia of ethnology. 2585
Principia of the spiritual life. 3477
Principle. 2834
Principle of authority in relation to certainty. 118
Principle of authority in relation to certainty, sanctity and society. 118
Principle of changes: understanding the I ching. 1879
Principle of peace exemplified in the conduct of the Society of Friends in Ireland. 1686
Principle of position. 988
Principle of Protestantism. 2977
Principle of reserve in the writings of John Henry Cardinal Newman. 2704, 3219
Principles and development of church government. 2450
Principles and ideals for the Sunday school. 3552
Principles and methods in the Christian school. 2498
Principles and methods of religious work for men and boys. 3875
Principles and objects of the religious reformation. 1463
Principles and organization of the Young men's Christian association. 3871
Principles and paradoxes of the militant life. 1001
Principles and powers;a study in Pauline theology. 375
Principles and practice of astrology. 98
... Principles and practice of Christian psychology. 2696
Principles and practice of indigenous church planting. 1166
Principles and practice of pastoral care. 2780
Principles and practice of preaching. 2901
Principles and practices for Baptist churches. 148
Principles and practices of pastoral care. 2780, 2785
Principles and practices of the church. 2941
Principles and problems of Biblical translation. 655, 3035
Principles and problems of ethics. 949
... Principles and technique in religious dramatics. 3144
Principles, dialogues, and philosophical correspondence. 2838
Principles for a Catholic morality. 948
Principles for peace. 2806
Principles of a system of philosophy. 2833
Principles of administration for a Baptist association. 150
Principles of agnosticism applied to evidences of Christianity. 1098
Principles of Anglicanism. 1218
Principles of astrology. 95
Principles of Bible school teaching. 3554
Principles of Biblical interpretation. 240, 287, 2405
Principles of Biblical interpretation in the Lutheran confessions. 240, 2284
Principles of canon law. 1489
Principles of Catholic moral life. 949
Principles of Catholic sex morality. 3393
Principles of Catholic theology. 3628
Principles of Christian apologetics. 67
Principles of Christian philosophy. 1054
Principles of Christian service. 940
Principles of Christian theology. 3646, 3647
Principles of Christian worship. 3002
Principles of church government. 1240
Principles of church growth. 1171
Principles of church history adapted to the young. 1194
Principles of church organization and administration. 3386
Principles of church organization, with special reference to the Church of England in Australia. 1240
Principles of church system. 1169
Principles of civil union and happiness considered and recommended. 1503
Principles of conduct. 378
Principles of Congregationalism. 3286
Principles of Descartes' philosophy. 1426
Principles of ecclesiastical unity. 1041
... Principles of episcopal jurisdiction. 666
Principles of expository preaching. 2906, 2907
Principles of faith. 2155
Principles of geology explained. 1705
Principles of healing. 2409
Principles of integral science of religion. 3063
Principles of interpretation. 235
Principles of Jesuit education in practice. 1949
Principles of knowledge. 2180
... Principles of labor Zionism. 3896

Principles of life from the Word of God. 3383
Principles of metaphysical and ethical science applied to the evidences of religion. 59
Principles of monasticism. 2571
Principles of moral theology. 948
... Principles of natural theology. 2673
Principles of nature. 1420
Principles of nature, her divine revelations, and a voice to mankind. 2226
Principles of occult healing. 2723
Principles of peace. 1686
Principles of peace, exemplified in the conduct of the Society of Friends in Ireland, during the rebellion of the year 1798. 1686
Principles of personal worship. 3854
Principles of prayer. 2886
Principles of preaching. 2899
Principles of psychic philosophy. 2834
Principles of Quakerism. 1681
Principles of religion, as professed by the society of Christians, called Friends. 1683
Principles of religion, as professed by the society of Christians, usually called Quakers. 1683
Principles of religious ceremonial. 3239
Principles of religious education. 3150, 3156
Principles of religious practice in the community association program. 3878
Principles of religious teaching. 3146
Principles of sacramental theology. 3265
Principles of sacred eloquence. 2899
Principles of spiritual science. 51
Principles of successful church advertising. 10
Principles of teaching for Christian teachers. 3179
Principles of the interior or hidden life. 978
Principles of the Jewish faith. 2080
Principles of the Jewish faith, an analytic study. 2080
Principles of the Protestant religion maintained. 1335, 2166
Principles of the reformation. 1166
Principles of the Reformation practical and historical. 3038
Principles of the religious life. 3787
Principles of the spiritual life. 1403, 3485
Principles of theology, an introduction to the Thirty-nine articles. 1212
Principles of toleration. 3703
Principles of true science. 3386
Principles of victory. 471, 3351
Principles of war. 980
Principles, origin, and establishment of the Catholic school system in the United States. 830
Principles, promises, and powers. 1233, 3358
Print of the nails. 1318
Printer's Christmas books. 731, 1712
Printing press and the Gospel. 2937
Priories and abbeys of England. 2569
Priorities and people. 980
Priority of labor. 854, 1130
Priority of state missions. 2528
Priscilla, author of the Epistle to the Hebrews. 404, 2942, 3832
Priscillian of Avila. 1021, 2942
Prismatics. 1765
Prison and the pinnacle. 2469
Prison connection. 1256, 3252
Prison is my parish. 2942
Prison journals of a priest revolutionary. 195
Prison meditations. 2399
Prison of love. 777, 3630
Prison or paradise? 1394
Prisoner for God. 676
Prisoner in the Vatican. 2850
Prisoner of Christ. 3831
Prisoner of love. 838
Prisoner of war. 3090
Prisoners of hope. 3348
Prisoners' quest. 66
Prisons of the world. 1560, 2437
Private and public faith. 2978
Private devotional diary. 1432
Private devotional lives of Finney, Moody, and Spurgeon. 1625
Private devotions. 1436
Private devotions for home and church. 3049
Private devotions for young persons. 3883
Private devotions of Lancelot Andrewes. 1436
Private devotions of Lancelot Andrewes; Selections. 1436
Private first communion instruction for little children. 1317
Private house of prayer. 1443
Private letters, pagan and Christian. 1771

Private life of the minister's wife. 1303
Private lives of the prophets and the times in which they lived. 2950
Private papers and diary of Thomas Leiper Kane. 2603
Private prayer book. 2972
Private prayers. 2889
Private retreat for religious. 3222
Private sea. 1781
Private sea, LSD & the search for God. 1781
... The privation of Christian burial. 717
Privilege and burden. 1296
Privilege and power of prayer. 2869
Privilege of pain. 3540
Privilege of teaching. 3177
... Privileges of regulars to absolve and dispense. 1327
Privileges of the Christian sacraments. 3264
Prize essays on the temporal advantages of the Sabbath. 3547
Prize sermons. 3354, 3365
Pro & con book of religious America. 3745
Pro and con of supernatural religion. 1654
Pro Christo. 1852
Pro Ecclesia lutherana. 2295
Pro vita monastica. 90
Proexistence; the place of man in the circle of reality. 2320
Probation. 2943
Probation after death. 2943
Probationer's hand-book. 2454
Probationer's handbook. 2454
... The probative value of documents in ecclesiastical trials. 1578
Proberbs to live by. 572
Probing the New Testament. 350
Probing the unexplained. 2991
Problem clergymen don't talk about. 2781
Problem in Chomsky's Syntactic structures. 2184
Problem in New Testament criticism. 348
Problem of abortion after the Supreme Court decision. 3
...The problem of altruism in the philosophy of Saint Thomas. 28, 3693
Problem of "Americanization" in the Catholic schools of Puerto Rico. 34, 824
Problem of atonement. 107
Problem of authority in the continental reformers. 119, 727
Problem of Catholicism. 802, 3772
Problem of charity for self. 3330
Problem of Christ. 1118, 2039
Problem of Christ in the twentieth century. 2041
Problem of Christian unity. 1041
Problem of Christian unity in early nineteenth-century America. 1046
Problem of Christianity. 1071, 1096
Problem of creation. 1381
Problem of eschatology. 1529
Problem of evil. 787, 1745, 1746, 3610
Problem of evil and human destiny. 3900
Problem of evil and Indian thought. 1745
Problem of evil and sufferings. 1746
Problem of Ezekiel. 518
Problem of final destiny. 3619
Problem of following Jesus. 2061
Problem of God. 1719, 1720
Problem of God in philosophy of religion. 1721
Problem of God is philosophy of religion. 1721
Problem of God, yesterday and today. 2632
Problem of God's knowledge in Gersonides. 1735
Problem of historicity in the church. 1165
Problem of history in Mark. 436
... The problem of human destiny. 2980
Problem of human life as viewed by the great thinkers from Plato to the present time. 2840
Problem of human suffering. 1350
Problem of human suffering looked at from the standpoint of a Christian. 3540, 3542
Problem of immortality. 1891
Problem of Jesus. 1952, 1956
Problem of Jesus; a free-thinker's diary. 63
Problem of lay leadership. 2202
Problem of life. 1049, 2226
Problem of life; a solution. 3057
Problem of life & how to solve it. 2228
Problem of life and immortality. 2227
Problem of loneliness. 2244
Problem of Lutheran union and other essays. 2292
problem of matter and form in the De ente et essentia of Thomas Aquinas. 2738, 3695
Problem of Mennonite ethics. 950
Problem of metaphysics. 2418

Problem of miracle in primitive Christianity. 2017, 2476
Problem of nationalism in church-state relationships. 2671
Problem of original sin in American Presbyterian theology. 3414
Problem of origins. 1381
Problem of pain. 2758
Problem of positive theology. 3227
Problem of problems, and its various solutions. 3074
Problem of religion. 1655, 3061, 3106
Problem of religious freedom. 3192
Problem of religious knowledge. 2180, 2181
Problem of religious language. 3070
Problem of religious progress. 1174
Problem of reunion discussed historically in seven essays. 1047
Problem of self-love in St. Augustine. 115, 116, 3330
Problem of sovereignty in the later Middle Ages. 2768
... The problem of space in Jeuish mediaeval philosophy. 3469
... The problem of space in Jewish mediaeval philosophy. 3469
Problem of teen-age purity. 889
Problem of the Christian state. 1141
Problem of the Fourth gospel. 420
Problem of the Hexateuch. 485
Problem of the Hexateuch, and other essays. 485
Problem of the historical Jesus. 2008
Problem of the Lord's Supper according to the scholarly research of the nineteenth century and the historical accounts. 2256
... The problem of the Old Testament considered with reference to recent criticism. 501
Problem of the Pastoral epistles. 446
Problem of the Pentateuch. 563
Problem of the self in Buddhism and Christianity. 38
Problem of the soul. A tract for teachers. 3462
Problem of the work. 886, 3671
Problem of two truths in Buddhism and Vedanta. 2311
Problem of unbelief in the sixteenth century, the religion of Rabelais. 3017
Problem of universals. 3756
Problem of universals in Indian philosophy. 3755
Problem of war in the Old Testament. 499, 3794
Problem of wine skins. 1066
Problem-or opportunity? 1543
Problem sermons for young people. 3888
Problem solved. 3412
Problem solving by horary astrology. 95
Problem solving in the Christian family. 2339
Problem with prayer is. 2873
Problemas y metodes de la escuela dominical. 3557
Problems and persons. 1092
Problems and perspectives in the philosophy of religion. 3108
Problems and perspectives of fundamental theology. 3624
Problems and progress. 786
Problems before unity. 1043
Problems in Bible translation. 288
Problems in canon law. 735
Problems in conduct. 948
Problems in early Christianity. 350
Problems in religion and life. 3671
Problems in the liturgy. 839
Problems in the prayer life, from a pastor's question box. 2869
Problems in theology. 3012, 3647
Problems of authority. 119
...Problems of belief. 186
Problems of Christian family life today. 1608
Problems of Christian youth. 3881
Problems of church and state in Maryland during the seventeenth and eighteenth centuries. 1147
Problems of church unity. 1249
Problems of eternal moment. 1228, 1533
Problems of faith and worship. 2963
Problems of life. 1333
Problems of metaphysics. 2419
Problems of New Testament translation. 358
Problems of philosophy. 2833
Problems of Protestantism. 2977
Problems of providence. 2982
Problems of psychical research. 2987
Problems of pulpit and platform. 1288
Problems of religion. 3058
Problems of religious faith. 3102

Problems of religious knowledge. 1594
Problems of suffering in religions of the world. 3539
Problems of the age, with Studies in St. Augustus on kindred topics. 114, 787
Problems of the Book of Mormon. 679
Problems of the development of the mind. 1705
Problems of the Jewish ministry. 3576
Problems of the local church. 1117
Problems of the new Christianity. 1093, 2690
Problems of the New Testament to-day. 348
Problems of the philosophy of religion. 3108
Problems of the spirit-filled life. 3478
Problems of the spiritual. 3477
Problems of the town church. 2241
Problems of theology. 3616
Problems of young Christians. 963
Problems of your generation. 3500
Problems of youth. 3884, 3888
Problems that confront young people. 3879
Problems that plague the saints. 66
Problems to accompany Accounting in the Federal Government. 1625
Problems vital to our religion. 3067
Procceedings in equity. 1030
Procedure at the Roman curia. 778
Procedure in the diocesan matrimonial courts of First instance. 2341
Proceedings. 832
... Proceedings. 2442
Proceedings. 2573, 2784
roceedings (Institute on Contemporary Thought and the Spiritual Exercises of St. Ignatius of Loyola, Loyola University, Chicago, 1962) 2270
Proceedings. 1954/55. 2574
Proceedings (American society for psychical research. (Founded 1884)) 2993
Proceedings and addresses at the Freethinkers' convention. 1655
Proceedings and addresses at the Freethinkers' Convention held at Watkins, N.Y., 1878. 1656
Proceedings ... [Annual and special convocations]. 1666
Proceedings ... Annual report. 1661
Proceedings (Anti-Sabbath Convention, Boston) 3261
Proceedings at a reception in honor of the Rev. O. B. Frothingham. 1689
Proceedings at the quarter-century anniversary of the Society for the promotion of collegiate and theological education. 3680
Proceedings at the two hundredth anniversary of the Second church of Christ in Hartford. 1210
Proceedings at the Universalist centennial held in Gloucester, Mass., September 20th, 21st, & 22nd, 1870. 3754
Proceedings (Augustinian Educational Association) 833
Proceedings (Church of the Nazarene. General Assembly) 1237
Proceedings (Colloquium on Christian Medical Ethics. 2d, Concordia Senior College) 2377
Proceedings (Conference on Philanthropy in Action, San Francisco, 1966) 1167
Proceedings (Conference on Shared Time, University of Rhode Island, 1965) 3401
Proceedings connected with the semi-centennial commemoration of the professorship of Rev. Charles Hodge. 1821
Proceedings; first National Catholic social action conference, Milwaukee, Wisconsin, May 1-4, 1938. 754
Proceedings .. (Freemasons. District of Columbia. Grand lodge (Colored)) 1661
Proceedings .. (Freemasons. Illinois. Royal arch masons. Grand chapter) 1661
Proceedings (Freemasons. Maine. Grand commandery of Knights templars) 1661
Proceedings (Freemasons. Maine. Grand council of royal and select masters) 1661
Proceedings .. (Hospital social service association of New York city) 887
Proceedings (Institute on Problems That Unite Us, Mundelein College, 1965) 2574
Proceedings (International Symposium on Analytical Astrodynamics, Los Angeles) 94
Proceedings (Lutheran Church--Missouri Synod. Districts. Southern) 2296
Proceedings (Methodist Episcopal church. Mission conferences. North Montana) 1580

PROCEEDINGS (MINOR SEMINARY
RELIGIOUS BOOKS 1876 - 1982

Proceedings (Minor Seminary Conference) 3615
Proceedings (Minor Seminary Conference, Catholic University of America) 3614
Proceedings (National Conference and Exhibit on Synagogue Architecture and Art) 3576
Proceedings (National Jewish Youth Conference) 3890
Proceedings (Notre Dame, Ind. University. Institute for Local Superiors. 2583
Proceedings (Notre Dame, Ind. University. Sisters' Institute of Spirituality) 2581
Proceedings of a meeting of friends of Rev. John Pierpont, and his reply to the charges of the committee, of Hollis street society. 684
Proceedings of an ecclesiastical council. 1372
Proceedings of C.O.P.E.C. 3451
Proceedings of data processing in Catholic education administration. 830
Proceedings of major presentations. 3465, 3719
Proceedings of meetings (New York. Citizens. 2102
Proceedings of special centennal communication of the most worshipful grand. 1663
Proceedings of special centennal communication of the most worshipful grand lodge of Ancient Free and Accepted Masons of Colorado. 1663
Proceedings of the 1960 Sisters' Institute of Spirituality. 2580
Proceedings of the Advisory council of Congregational churches and ministers. 184, 693
Proceedings of the American society for psychical research. 2993
Proceedings of the American Zionist assembly. 3897
Proceedings of the ... annual communication. 1671
Proceedings of the ... annual conference of church clubs of the United States. 93
Proceedings of the annual convention. 3619
Proceedings of the ... annual convention of the English Evangelical Lutheran synod of Ohio and adjacent states. 1548
Proceedings of the ... annual convention of the Evangelical Lutheran synod of East Pennsylvania. 1548
Proceedings of the ... annual convention of the Evangelical Lutheran synod of Maryland. 1548
Proceedings of the ... annual convention of the Evangelical Lutheran synod of Nebraska of the United Lutheran church in America. 1548
Proceedings [of the annual convocation]. 1663, 3786
Proceedings of the ... annual meeting. 1580
Proceedings of the ... annual session. 673
Proceedings of the Catholic Biblical association of America. 615
Proceedings of the centennial anniversary of the First Presbyterian church, Troy, N.Y., December 30 and 31, 1891. 2918
Proceedings of the Church Conference of Social Work held in connection with the National Conference of Social Work, Boston, June 9-14, 1930. 1133
Proceedings of the conference of Friends of America. 1687
Proceedings of the Conference of grand masters and representatives resulting in the formation of the Masonic service association of the United States. 2364
Proceedings of the Conference on Religion and American Culture. 3069
Proceedings [of the] convention. 755, 2296, 3733
Proceedings of the ... convention of the Southeastern district of the Synod of Missouri, Ohio, and other states. 1549
Proceedings of the ... convention of the Evangelical Lutheran synod of West Pennsylvania. 1548
Proceedings of the ... convention of the Pittsburgh synod of the Evangelical Lutheran church. 1548
Proceedings of the ... convention of the Pittsburgh synod of the Envangelical Lutheran church. 1548
Proceedings of the ... convention of the Sovereign Grand Council of the United States of America, Knights of the Red Cross of Rome and Constantine, Knights of the Holy Sepulchre and Knights of St. John the Evangelist. 1672
... Proceedings of the convention preceding the organization of the conference. 1702, 3505
Proceedings of the court convened under the third canon of 1844, in the city of New York. 2737
'proceedings of the Ecumenical Methodist conference. 2423
... Proceedings of the first-annual convention. 3162
Proceedings of the first ten years. 3705
Proceedings of the Friends' General Conference. 1674
Proceedings of the ... general convention. 673
Proceedings of the Grand chapter of royal arch masons of the state of New York. 1670
Proceedings of the Grand imperial council of the Imperial, ecclesiastical and military order of the Red cross of Constantine for the United States of America (Empire of the West) 1668
Proceedings of the Grand lodge A. F. & A. M. of Alabama. 1661
Proceedings of the Grand lodge of ancient free amd accepted masons, of thee state of Maine. 1661
Proceedings of the Grand lodge of ancient free and accepted masons of the state of Maine. 1661
Proceedings of the Liturgical day held at St. Benedict's abbey, Atchison, Kansas, December 10, 1941. 2234
Proceedings of the M. W. Grand lodge of Ancient York masons of the state of Virginia. 1661
Proceedings of the Men's national missionary congress of the United States of American, Chicago, Illinois, May 3-6, 1910. 2515
Proceedings of the National catechetical congress of the Confraternity of Christian doctrine. 866
Proceedings of the ... National conference on Jewish welfare. 2106
Proceedings of the national convention to secure the religious amendment of the Constitution of the United States. 1151
Proceedings of the National federation of temple sisterhoods. 3416
Proceedings of the national meeting of Franciscan teaching sisterhoods. 1646
Proceedings of the National temperance congress, held in the Broadway tabernacle, New York ...June 11th and 12th, 1890. 3597
Proceedings of the one hundred and sixtieth anniversary of the Second Congregational church in Plymouth (Manomet) Mass. 1849
Proceedings of the...regular convention. 2296
Proceedings of the Second National Congress of Religious of the United States: Men's Section. 2572
Proceedings of the Second National Congress of Religious of the United States. 2572
Proceedings of the ... session. 156
Proceedings of the ... session, Montana state annual conference. 2445
Proceedings of the ...session, North Montana annual conference ...Official journal. 1st-17th; 1908-23. 2445
Proceedings of the sixth Ecumenical Methodist conference, held in Wesley memorial church, Atlanta, Ga., October 16-25, 1931. 2423
Proceedings. pt. 1. 2963
Proceedings: program - minutes - papers. 2288
Proceedings (Seminar on Responsibility of Churches to the Aging, Park City, Utah) 1257
Proceedings (Symposium on Pacem in Terris by Pope John XXIII, University of Notre Dame, 1965) 853
Proceedings ... Together with the Report of the Board of directors. 2970
Proceedings, twelfth international convention of the Baptist young people's union of America. 142
Proceedings. v. 1- 1925. 3730
Proceedings (Workshop in Pastoral Counseling, University of Florida, 1959) 2782
Process and permanence in ethics. 3306
Process and relationship. 936, 2466
Process catechetics. 1819
Process Christology. 1952, 2943
Process metaphysics and Hua-yen Buddhism. 1850, 3813
Process of religion. 2373, 3624
Process of speech. 2467, 3008
Process philosophy and Christian thought. 2944
Process, testimony and opening argument of the prosecution, vote and final minute, in the judicial trial of Rev. W. C. McCune by the Presbytery of Cincinnati, from March 5 to March 27, 1877. 2918
Process theology. 2943
Process theology as political theology. 2943
Process theology: basic writings. 2944, 3593
Process-thought and Christian faith. 1105
Procession of Friends. 1674, 1675
Procession of Passion prayers. 1308
Procession of saints. 3279
...The procession of the ark. 1203
Procession of the gods. 3112
Processionof saints. 3279
... Processions. 1224
Processive world view for pragmatic Christians. 3027, 3593
Proclaim His word. 863, 1266
Proclaim liberty! 1085
Proclaimed from the rooftops. 864, 1267
Proclaiming Christ today. 2904
Proclaiming God's message. 2168, 2900
Proclaiming grace and freedom. 3734
Proclaiming the acceptable year. 2222
Proclaiming the parables. 2026
Proclaiming the promise. 537
Proclaiming the Word. 2906
Proclamation. 314, 1266
Proclamation: aids for interpreting the lessons of the church year. 315, 1267
Proclamation and presence. 484
Proclamation of liberty and the unpardonable sin. 1067
Proclamation of the Gospel in a pluralistic world. 1074
Proclamation 2. 9, 315
Proclus' Metaphysical elements. 2944
Prodigal. 2944
Prodigal husband. 90, 2817
Prodigal returns. 2944
Prodigal son. 2061, 2944, 2945
Prodigal son. In four parts. 2944
Prodigal's father. 2945
Productive beliefs. 1050
Productive religion. 2299
Products of Pentecost. 2813
Profane virtues. 685, 1758
Profectione Ludovici VII in orientem. 1392, 2261
Profession: minister. 1295
Profession of a Christian. 1328
Profession of faith of a Savoyard vicar. 1452
Professional boys' worker in the Young men's Christian association. 3875
Professional competence in the Young men's Christian association. 3873
Professional education for ministry. 2785
Professional growth for clergymen, through supervised training in marriage counseling and family problems. 1297
Professional identity of the campus minister. 885
Professional perspective. 3873
Professional service management. 3377
Professionalization and professionalism of Catholic priests. 773, 2733
Professionalization of the secretaryship of the Young men's Christian associations of North America. 3870
Professor in the pulpit. 3356
Professor of Wittenberg. 2280
Profile for a Christian life style. 479, 983
Profile for victory. 2559
Profile method for the classification and evaluation of manuscript evidence, as applied to the continuous Greek text of the Gospel of Luke. 431
Profile of a Christian citizen. 1085
Profile of a parish. 1244, 3274
Profile of Ceylon's Catholic heritage. 815
Profile of Christian maturity. 450
Profile of Jesuit universities and colleges of America. 832, 3759
Profile of Protestantism. 2977
Profile of the American Baptist pastor. 145
Profile of the Son of Man. 2045
Profiles. 924
Profiles in action. 875
Profiles in belief. 3324
Profiles in Christian commitment. 926
Profiles in clay. 214, 657
Profiles in faith. 924
Profiles of a leader. 952
Profiles of church youth. 3889
Profiles of faith. 405, 1229, 1597
Profiles of prophecy. 606
Profiles of Protestant saints. 2953
Profiles of revival leaders. 1576
Profiles of the Christ. 2214, 2300
Profiles of the Passion. 2215
Profiles of the Passion; Lenten sermons. 2215
Profiles of the Presidents. 1231
Profit and loss of dying. 3505
Profit for the Lord. 2517, 2594
Profit of love; studies in altruism. 28
"The profit of the many" 945
Profitable Bible study. 642
Profitable word. 2231
Profits of religion. 1071, 1092
Profits of religion, an essay in economic interpretation. 1092

Program book for student Christian associations. 3537
Program evaluation in church organization. 1199
Program for a parochial course of doctrinal instructions for all Sundays and holy days of the year. 784
Program for Colombian public investment and external borrowing. 1625
Program for higher education in the Church of the Brethren. 1128, 1236
Program for progress. 3196
Program for Sunday-school management. 3552
Program for the Jews and an answer to all anti-Semites. 2082
... Program guide. 3149
Program guide for young people. 1248
Program handbook of young men's activities. 3872
Program making and record keeping. 3878
Program manual for Zionism on the campus. 3897
Program materials for Sabbath observances 1956-5716. 3262
Program of affiliation. 870
Program of education and research through the establishment of a Christian center for higher learning at the college and post-graduate levels in affiliation with the University of Chicago. 2965
Program of higher education of the Presbyterian church in the United States of America. 2923
Program of Jesus. 2065, 3439
Program of progress for Congregational and Christian churches. 3150
Program of religious education. 3466
Program of religious education at Stephens college. 3158
...The program of the Christian religion. 1252
Program of the international centennial celebration and conventions of the Disciples of Christ (Christian church) 1462
Program of work B. 3555
Program of work C. 3555
Program pathways for young adults. 968
Program planning for adult Christian education. 3168
Program planning for youth ministry. 1261
Program planning studies. 3877
Program quarterly. 3876
Program supplement. 2449
Programme of Christianity. 1049
Programme of modernism. 853
Programmed primer in learning disabilities. 3426
Programs and methods for primary unions. 3554
Programs and plans for the Cradle Roll department. 3173
Programs for parish councils. 2774
Programs for special days. 3144
Programs for speical days. 3144
Programs for teachers' meetins. 3157
Programs for workers' conferences. 3157
Programs, plays, songs, stories, for workers with children. 3560
Progress. 732, 1088
Progress: a Christian doctrine? 1088
Progress after entire sanctification. 3300
Progress and decline in the history of church renewal. 1183
Progress and perspectives. 859
Progress and religion. 2945
Progress in archaeology. 679
Progress in Christian culture. 1047
Progress in divine union. 2637
Progress in prayer. 2869
Progress in religion to the Christian era. 3116
Progress in the Christian life. 958
Progress in the life to come. 1695
Progress in the religious life. 2576
Progress is unorthodox. 2221
Progress of Baptist principles in the last hundred years. 147
... The progress of chemical philosophy. 891
Progress of church federation. 1619
Progress of doctrine in the New Testament. 475

Progress of doctrine in the New
    Testament, considered in eight lectures
    delivered before the University of
    Oxford, on the Bampton foundation. 475
Progress of dogma. 3655
... The progress of dogma according to
    Anselm of Havelberg. 49, 3654
Progress of Gospel music. 1749
Progress of man. 2320
Progress of Old Testament prophecy in the
    light of modern scholarship. 567
Progress of piety. 1451
Progress of pilgrim from material sense to
    the spiritual sense of God, man, and the
    universe. 1036
Progress of religious ideas. 3114
Progress of the Christian life. 978
Progress of the Jesuits (1556-79) 1946
Progress of the liturgy. 2234
Progress of the pilgrim Good-Intent. 1518
Progress of the Protestant. 2978
Progress of the work of the Oriental
    Institute in Iraq, 1934. 894
Progress of world-wide missions. 2525
Progressing music reader. 917
Progressing Philippines. 2544
Progressive age of reason. 3505
Progressive annual for 1862[-1863]. 3511
Progressive Bible readings. 1437
Progressive Christian principles, four
    square. 1071
Progressive Christianity. 1064
Progressive endeavor. 1914, 3737
Progressive experience of the heart. 3482
Progressive ignorance. 2836
Progressive pilgrim. 996
Progressive religious thought in America.
    1338
Progressive scholasticism. 3309
Progressive stewardship. 3530
Progressive studies in astrology. 97
Progressive studies in the Bible. 499
Progressive Sunday school songs. 3563
Progressive training course for Sunday-
    school workers. 3177
Progressive unfolding of the Messianic
    hope. 2414
Progressive world. 3024
Prohibition a fallacy, a fanaticism, and an
    absurdity. 3596
Prohibition and the Bible. 2945
Prohibition is wrong. 2945
Prohibition of intoxicating liquors the
    enemy of church and state. 2945
Prohibition, the enemy of temperance.
    3595
Prohpets. 569
Project curriculum for young people. 3157
Project Head Start. 1321, 2945
Project lessons on the gospel of Mark.
    437
Project method in religious education.
    3149
Project principle in religious education.
    2946
Project X. 2729, 3306
Projected visual aids in the church. 3784
Projecting our heritage. 3623
Projections; shaping an American theology
    for the future. 3618
Projects in world-friendship. 3153
Prolegomena. 3618, 3659
Prolegomena to a new metaphysic. 2420
Prolegomena to any future metaphysics.
    2418
Prolegomena to any future metaphysics
    that will be able to come forward as
    science. 2418
Prolegomena to Christian dogmatics. 3659
Prolegomena to the history of ancient
    Israel. 2097
...Prolegomena to the lectionary text of the
    gospels. 367
Prolegomena to the study of Greek
    religion. 1766
Prolegomena to the study of Hegel's
    philosophy and especially of his logic.
    1800, 2242
Prolegomena to the study of the Greek
    religion. 1766
Prolegomena to theism. 3607
Prometheus. 2946
Prometheus: archetypal image of human
    existence. 2946
Prominent personalities in American
    Methodism. 2460
Promiscuous singing no divine institution.
    2633
Promise. 611, 1982, 2517
Promise and fulfilment. 2064
Promise and peril of human purpose.
    1801, 2320
Promise and the presence. 592, 2175
Promise beyond the pain. 3540
Promise: ethics in the kingdom of God.
    943
Promise fulfilled. 1236, 2814

Promise of all ages. 127
Promise of Barth. 176
Promise of Bennett. 190
Promise of Bonhoeffer. 677
Promise of Bultmann. 713
Promise of counseling. 2780
Promise of deliverance. 545, 3356
Promise of H. Richard Niebuhr. 2708
Promise of Heschel. 1809
Promise of His coming. 1229, 3320, 3321
Promise of hope. 1351
Promise of Kierkegaard. 1104, 2170
Promise of life. 2695
Promise of morning. 3206
Promise of narrative theology. 3649
Promise of paradox. 3484
Promise of power. 1831
Promise of prayer. 2869
Promise of Reinhold Niebuhr. 2709
Promise of science and the power of faith.
    3078
Promise of Teilhard. 3593
Promise of the Father. 1830, 1833, 3837
Promise of the Father; or, This is that.
    2814
Promise of the Spirit. 1827
Promise of Tillich. 3700
Promise to Angela. 41, 3761
Promise to David. 1404
Promise to keep. 624
Promise to love. 2341
Promised day is come. 129
Promised gift. 1017
Promised land. 629, 2761, 2765
Promised Messiah. 2019, 2415
Promised One, as revealed in the Old
    Testament. 2415
Promised Woman. 1886
Promises and premises. 242
Promises kept. 158
Promises of Christ. 2974
Promises of God. 1432, 1737, 2396
Promises of God; the morning watch texts
    with a devotional reading for each day.
    1432
Promises of the Eternal. 249
Promises, promises, promises. 1737
Promises to the fathers. 524, 2792
Promoting your church library. 2224
Promotion and publicity for churches.
    1243
Promotional ideas for church libraries.
    2224
... The promulgation of law. 735
Promulgation of universal peace. 126
Pronouncing dictionary of mythology and
    antiquities. 2658
Proof of a life beyond. 3494
... Proof of death in pre-nuptial
    investigation. 2342
Proof of God. 1719
Proof of Jesus Christ His being the ancient
    promised Messiah. 2016
Proof of Rome's political meddling in
    America. 828
Proof of the accuracy of the Bible. 496,
    2414
Proof of the apostolic preaching. 68
Proof of the gospel. 1090
Proof palpable of immortality. 3513
Proof-texts of endless punishment. 1699
Proofs of a conspiracy. 1662
Proofs of a conspiracy against all the
    religions and governments of Europe,
    carried on in the secret meetings of Free
    masons, Illuminati, and reading societies.
    1662
Proofs of Christianity. 57
Proofs of Christ's resurrection. 1099, 2052
Proofs of evolution. 1581
Proofs of His presence. 2386
Proofs of spirit forces. 3504
Proofs of the real existence, and dangerous
    tendency, of illuminism. 1883
Proofs of the spirit world. 2987
Proofs of the truths of spiritualism. 3504
Proofs that the common theories and
    modes of reasoning respecting the
    depravity of mankind exhibit it as a
    physical attribute. 1746
Propaganda of philosophy. 32
Proper distinction between law and gospel.
    2200
Proper lessons for the Sundays and
    holydays throughout the year. 2960
Proper of the Mass, set to simple music.
    884
Propers for the minor holy days. 2969
Property and riches in the early church.
    2946
Prophecies and fundamentals. 233
Prophecies & predictions. 2948
Prophecies and prophetic promises, from
    the Doctrine and covenants. 2611
Prophecies and revelations. 3508
Prophecies and revelations by Hemaka.
    3508

Prophecies by Ezra. 3503
Prophecies of Daniel. 507, 509
Prophecies of Daniel and Revelation
    compared. 605
Prophecies of Daniel and Revelation (verse
    by verse interpretation by the cross
    reference method) 509
Prophecies of Daniel and the revelation.
    507
Prophecies of Daniel in the light of past,
    present, and future events. 509
Prophecies of Isaiah. 542
Prophecies of Jamil. 1912
Prophecies of Jeremiah. 546
Prophecies of Joseph Smith. 3428
Prophecies of Joseph Smith and their
    fulfillment. 2604, 3429
Prophecies of Paracelsus. 2772, 2947
Prophecies of race and religion. 605
Prophecies of St. Malachy. 2863
Prophecies of SS. Columbkille. 2947
Prophecies of SS, Columbkille,
    Macltamalacht, Ultan, Seadhna, Coireall,
    Bearean, Malachy. 2947
Prophecies on world events. 2947
Prophecies on world events by
    Nostradamus. 2715, 2947
Prophecies unveiled. 2947
Prophecy. 567, 570, 605, 608, 1631, 2951
Prophecy a preparation for Christ. 2415
Prophecy and authority. 605
Prophecy and canon. 495
Prophecy and covenant. 568
Prophecy and hermeneutic in early
    Christianity. 350, 2952
Prophecy and history in Luke-Acts. 426
Prophecy and history in relation to the
    Messiah. 2414
Prophecy and inspiration. 306, 3696
Prophecy and papacy. 1638, 2194
Prophecy and poetry. 543, 1921
Prophecy and prayer. 1514
Prophecy and prophets. 2948
Prophecy and religion. 502, 1943
Prophecy and religion in ancient China
    and Israel. 2951
Prophecy and society in ancient Israel.
    569, 2951
Prophecy and the church. 604
Prophecy and the Lord's return. 3319
Prophecy and the prophets. 2948
Prophecy and the prophets in their
    historical relations. 568
Prophecy and the seventies. 610
Prophecy and the times. 508
Prophecy and the tottering nations. 1513
Prophecy and tradition. 2950
Prophecy concerning the Swedish
    monarchy. 3569
Prophecy explained, past, present and
    future. 607
Prophecy for beginners. 509
Prophecy for today. 607, 2946
Prophecy in a technocratic era. 1154
Prophecy in ancient Israel. 569
Prophecy in our time. 2948
Prophecy in the Church. 2949
Prophecy in the making. 610
Prophecy in the ring. 606
Prophecy in the space age. 609
Prophecy interpreted. 607
Prophecy interpreted by history. 508
Prophecy New Testament series. 607
Prophecy of Daniel, a commentary. 507
Prophecy of Ezekiel. 518
Prophecy of Malachi. 558
Prophecy, past, present and prospective.
    607
Prophecy text book. 604
Prophecy, the war, and the Near East.
    567
Prophecy viewed in respect to its
    distinctive natue. 605
Prophecy viewed in respect to its
    distinctive nature. 605
Prophecy's light on today. 3320
Prophery fulfilled. 450
Prophesies of Nostradamus. 2948
Prophesy deliverance! 17
Prophet against prophet. 483, 2950
Prophet among you. 3811
Prophet and a pilgrim. 1787
Prophet and a pilgrim, being the incredible
    history of Thomas Lake Harris and
    Laurence Oliphant. 1787
Prophet and his God. 2621
Prophet and his problems. 569
Prophet and priest in old Israel. 2140
Prophet and the soldier. 568
Prophet and witness in Jerusalem. 426,
    429
Prophet child. 3478
Prophet Daniel. 508
Prophet Elisha. 1506
Prophet Ezekiel. 518
Prophet for the archangels. 567
Prophet from Nazareth. 1963

Prophet from the Ozarks. 1250
Prophet Harris. 1787
Prophet in his own country. 877, 3135,
    3407
Prophet in the wilderness. 3311
Prophet Isaiah. 543
Prophet Jeremiah. 1942
Prophet Joel. 552
Prophet Joel and the day of the Lord.
    552, 1407
Prophet Jonah. 552, 553, 2130
Prophet Muhammad and his mission.
    2628
Prophet of blood. 2205
Prophet of Calvary church. 3090
Prophet of hope. 600
Prophet of love. 1960
Prophet of Nazareth. 2043
Prophet of Palmyra. 3428
Prophet of reunion. 2794
Prophet of San Nicandro. 2952
Prophet of the black nation. 1287
Prophet of the Dead Sea Scrolls. 3591
Prophet of the heart. 2898
Prophet of the Highest. 2127
Prophet of the nearness of God: Isaiah.
    544
Prophet of the people. 2849
Prophet of the poor. 682, 3292
Prophet of the real. 3090
Prophet of the Spirit. 1943
Prophet of Wheat Street. 682, 2681
Prophet of Zion-Parnassus. 2306, 3314
Prophet St. Paul. 2797
Prophet, Speak now. 1134
... A prophet speaks. 2986
Prophet-statesman. 1401
Prophet teaches little saints. 896, 1231
Prophet without portfolio. 545, 1530
Prophetess of health. 3811
Prophetic biography of Jesus Christ. 2415
... The prophetic books of the Old
    Testament, their origin, contents,
    significance. 571
Prophetic clergy: social activism among
    Protestant ministers. 2956
Prophetic conflict. 568
Prophetic conjectures on the French
    revolution. 607
Prophetic criticism of Israelite worship.
    2950
Prophetic democracy. 611
Prophetic destiny of the United States.
    611
Prophetic element in the Old Testament.
    567
Prophetic existence. 572, 2646
Prophetic faith. 571, 572
Prophetic faith in Isaiah. 543
Prophetic faith of our fathers. 605
... Prophetic fulfillments in Palestine today.
    2760
Prophetic guidance to the Church of Jesus
    Christ. 1050
Prophetic highlights. 1514
Prophetic ideas and ideals. 571
Prophetic imagination. 2949
Prophetic imperialism. 606
Prophetic intervention in the history of
    man. 2949
Prophetic lectures on Daniel and the
    Revelation. 509
Prophetic light in the present darkness.
    3321
Prophetic Milton. 2469
Prophetic ministry. 2158, 2782, 2950
Prophetic ministry for today. 3675
Prophetic movement in Israel. 567
Prophetic mysteries revealed. 444, 2026,
    3379
Prophetic patriotism. 164
Prophetic pictures of Christ. 1955
Prophetic poetry of Isaiah, caps 1-37. 541
Prophetic preaching. 2127, 2897, 2902,
    2905
Prophetic preaching, then and now. 2902
Prophetic problems with alternate
    solutions. 607
Prophetic questions answered. 1513
Prophetic realism and the gospel. 651
Prophetic religion. 571, 1095
Prophetic resistance and hope. 2712
Prophetic revelation from Moses to David.
    567
... The prophetic road to God. 571
Prophetic studies. 508
Prophetic thought. 503, 3361
Prophetic time marches on. 604
Prophetic truth unfolding today. 605
Prophetic types in the book of Esther. 514
Prophetic visions of national events, and
    spirit communications. 3497
Prophetic voice in modern fiction. 1624
Prophetic voice in Protestant Christianity.
    2977
Prophetic voices in contemporary theology.
    3650

PROPHETIC VOICES OF RELIGIOUS BOOKS 1876 - 1982

Prophetic voices of the Bible. 2951
Prophetic warnings to modern America. 680, 3741
Prophetic word. 604
Prophetic writings of William Blake, in two volumes. 670
Prophetic years, 1947-1953. 2946
Prophetical events and the great tribulation. 463
Prophets. 485, 567, 568, 569, 571, 2949, 2950, 2951
Prophets and guardians. 812, 2221
Prophets and Israel's culture. 568
Prophets and kings of the Old Testament. 2374
Prophets and millennialists. 240, 2464
Prophets and our times. 1513
Prophets and portents. 1820, 2946
Prophets & prophecies of the Old Testament. 570
Prophets and prophecy. 569, 2951
Prophets and the law. 571, 2201
Prophets and the powerless. 2950
Prophets and the problems of life. 644, 1325
Prophets and the promise. 2949
Prophets and the rise of Judaism. 2151
Prophets and the word of God. 569
Prophets and their times. 569, 2951
Prophets and wise men. 3821
Prophets are people, believe it or not. 2951
... The prophets as statesmen and preachers. 571
Prophets' dawn. 605
Prophets denied honor. 829, 1817
Prophet's diplomacy. 1460, 2629
Prophet's dollar. 1292
Prophets, Elijah to Christ. 2949
Prophets for a day of judgment. 185
Prophets for the common reader. 568
Prophets for today. 570
Prophets I have known. 1231
Prophets, idols, and diggers. 207
Prophets in outline. 571
Prophets in perspective. 569
Prophets in the church. 926
Prophets in the light of today. 569
Prophet's mantle. 168
Prophets/now. 570
Prophets of deceit. 798
Prophets of heaven & Hell. 3777
Prophets of heaven & hell: Virgil, Dante, Milton, Goethe. 3777
Prophets of Israel. 567, 568, 569, 571, 2949, 2950, 2951
Prophets of Israel and their place in history. 2951
Prophets of Israel, from the eighth to the fifth century. 2949
Prophets of Israel: Isaiah. 543
Prophets of Judah on the background of history. 569
Prophets of liberalism. 2221
Prophets of salvation. 2951
Prophets of the better hope. 772
Prophets of the dawn. 35, 2951
...Prophets of the new India. 2840, 3020
Prophets of the Old Testament. 568
Prophets of the Old Testament and their message. 2951
Prophets of the soul. 1301
Prophets on Main Street. 568, 570, 2950
Prophets, poets, priests, and kings; the Old Testament story. 500
Prophets, preachers for God. 495, 2952
Prophets, priests, and politicians. 3618
Prophets, principles and national survival. 2609, 2610
Prophets' report on religion in North America. 570
Prophets speak. 567, 570, 572, 1283, 2951
Prophets speak again. 569, 2950
Prophets speak to us anew. 568
Prophet's story for young people. 3430
Prophets tell their own story. 568
Prophets, their personalities and teachings. 568
Prophets with pens. 141, 144
Proposal of Jesus. 1050
Proposal to change the name of the Protestant Episcopal church. 2958
Proposed Book of confessions of the United Presbyterian Church in the United States of America. 3735
Proposed Calvinistic college at Grand Rapids. 727
Proposed constitution for the Presbyterian church. 2915
Proposed norms for consideration in the revision of the canons concerning religious. 735
Proposed revision of the Book of common prayer. 2961
Proposed revision of the monetary system of the United States in Currie, Lauchlin Bernard. 615, 1375
Proposed roads for American Jewry. 2078
Proposition concerning kneeling. 2865
Propria dominicalia. 883
Propriety of singing the Psalms of David in New Testament worship. 2633
Proscribed German student. 1946
Prose and poetry. 2704
Prose and poetry from the Old Testament. 591
Prose Edda. 2665
Prose Edda of Snorri Sturluson. 2665
Prose of our King James version. 248
Prose types in Newman. 738
Prosecution of Jesus. 2068
Prosecution of John Wyclyf. 3860
Proselytism in the Talmudic period. 2952
Proslogium. 2835
Prospect for metaphysics. 2420
Prospect of immortality. 1887
Prospecting for a united church. 1040
Prospects for the soul. 2159, 2993
Prospects of Christianity throughout the world. 1056
Prospects of the Jews. 2119
Prospectus 1902-3, religious work of the city and railroad Young men's Christian associations of North America. 3873
Prospectus of the religious work of the Young men's Christian evangelistic, devotional and missionary meetings...etc. 3873
Prospering power of love. 3539
Prosperity. 3750
Prosperity Bible. 590
Prosperity is Christian duty. 1134
Prosperity now. 3539, 3750
Prosperity sure. 1941
Prosperity's ten commandments. 1315, 3751
Prospero strikes it rich. 2542
Prostestant churches and the industrial crisis. 3441
Protection of the weak in the Talmud. 3582
Protector of the faith. 1188, 3704
Protest and politics. 1087
Protest and progress in the sixteenth century. 3034, 3041
Protestant. 801, 965
Protestant agreement on the Lord's Supper. 2253
Protestant America and the pagan world. 31
Protestant and Catholic. 861, 1838, 3452
Protestant and Orthodox Church directory, giving the official status of the Protestant and Orthodox Churches of Metropolitan New York, including Nassau and Westchester Counties. 2956
Protestant and politics. 1086
Protestant and Roman Catholic ethics. 950
Protestant and Roman Catholic New Testament. Revised standard version. Confraternity version. 362
Protestant approach to the campus ministry. 3538, 3757
Protestant backgrounds in history. 2978
Protestant beginnings in Japan. 2954
Protestant beliefs. 2977
Protestant believes. 2953
Protestant Biblical interpretation. 287
Protestant bishop. 1321
Protestant campus ministry in a northern metropolitan area. 879
Protestant case for liturgical renewal. 3854
Protestant, Catholic, Jew. 3747
Protestant-Catholic relations in America, World War I through Vatican II. 861, 2955
Protestant Christian evidences. 66
Protestant Christianity. 784, 785
Protestant Christianity interpreted through its development. 2978
Protestant church. 2955
Protestant church as a social institution. 2955
Protestant church building. 1162
Protestant church colleges in Canada. 1164
Protestant church in Germany. 2954
Protestant church music. 1209
... Protestant church music in America. 1210
Protestant church-related college. 2954
Protestant churches. 2953
Protestant churches and industrial America. 1140
Protestant churches and reform today. 861
Protestant churches and the prophetic office. 1248
Protestant churches of America. 3325
Protestant churches of Asia. 2953
Protestant churches of Asia, the Middle East, Africa, Latin America, and the Pacific area. 2953
Protestant churches respond to Alaska in transition. 22
Protestant churchmanship for rural America. 3254
Protestant clergy and public issues. 3737
Protestant clergy and public issues, 1812-1848. 3737
Protestant colleges in Asia, the Near East, Africa, and Latin America. 1164, 2953
Protestant concepts of Church and State. 1142, 1144
Protestant cooperation in American cities. 2955
Protestant cooperation in northern California. 1912
Protestant credo. 2978
Protestant crosscurrents in mission. 2555
Protestant crusade. 873
Protestant Crusade, 1800-1860. 873, 1390
Protestant crusaders. 1064
Protestant dictionary. 803, 3638, 3639
Protestant dilemma. 3260, 3656
Protestant diplomacy and the Near East. 3741
Protestant dissent in Ireland, 1687-1780. 1469, 2917
Protestant dissenting deputies. 1468
Protestant Episcopal Church in the U.S.A. Liturgical Commission. 366
Protestant Episcopal church of the diocese of Georgia vs. Rev. J. G. Armstrong, D.D. 2966
Protestant Episcopal church of the diocese of Georgia, vs. Rev. J. G. Armstrong, D. D. 2966
Protestant Episcopal church. The debates and proceedings of the General triennial convention. 2959
Protestant Episcopal doctrine and church unity. 2964
Protestant era. 2977
Protestant ethic and modernization. 943, 3800
Protestant ethic and the spirit of capitalism. 737, 3087
Protestant ethic and the spirit of Labour. 2976
Protestant Europe. 2976
Protestant evangelism among Italians in America. 2556
Protestant experience with United States immigration. 3740
Protestant faith. 2953, 2976, 2977
Protestant faith and religious liberty. 3193
Protestant faith; or, Salvation by belief. 2977
Protestant foreigh missions. 2518
Protestant hopes and the Catholic responsibility. 859
Protestant ideals. 802
Protestant leadership education schools. 3178
Protestant liturgical renewal. 2234
Protestant manifesto. 2976
Protestant master plan and strategy for Manhattan. 1912
Protestant mind of the English Reformation, 1570-1640. 3039
Protestant ministry. 1295
Protestant missions in Brasil (sic) 2505
Protestant missions in Latin America. 2537
Protestant missions in South America. 2547
Protestant modernism. 2977
Protestant modernism in Holland. 2561
Protestant mystics. 2643
Protestant nurture. 3154
Protestant panorama. 2955
Protestant parish. 3253
Protestant pastoral counseling. 2781
Protestant patriarch. 2261
Protestant pioneers in Korea. 2537
Protestant power and the coming revolution. 2978
Protestant preaching in Lent. 2215
Protestant primer on Roman Catholicism. 799
Protestant primer on Roman Catholisicm. 871
Protestant pulpit. 3338
Protestant pulpit, an anthology of master sermons from the Reformation to our own day. 3338
Protestant Reformation. 1185, 3033, 3041, 3042
Protestant reformation in Great Britain. 3038
Protestant revolt. 2670, 2956
Protestant saints. 114
Protestant search for political realism, 1919-1941. 1140, 2709, 1140
Protestant speaks his mind. 800
Protestant strategies in education. 1130
Protestant strategy in the making. 1039
Protestant temperament. 2978
Protestant theological seminaries and Bible schools in Asia, Africa, the Middle East, Latin America, the Caribbean and Pacific areas. 3614
Protestant theology in the nineteenth century. 3658
Protestant thought. 3658
Protestant thought and natural science. 3084
Protestant thought before Kant. 3213, 3679
Protestant thought: from Rousseau to Ritschl. 3658
Protestant thought in the nineteenth century. 3656
Protestant thought in the twentieth century. 3618, 3679
Protestant tradition. 2977
Protestant tutor. 803, 2940
Protestant way. 2976
Protestant witness of a new American. 146
Protestant worship and church architecture. 1274
Protestant year. 1955. 1432
Protestantism. 2975, 2976, 2977, 2978
Protestantism - a Baptist interpretation. 2978
Protestantism and capitalism. 737
Protestantism and infidelity. 793
Protestantism and Latinos in the United States. 1817
Protestantism and social reform in New South Wales 1890-1910. 2954
Protestantism and the American university. 1172, 3572
Protestantism and the new South. 2713
Protestantism, capitalism, and social science. 1076, 3800
Protestantism faces its educational task together. 1912
Protestantism in America. 2955
Protestantism in an ecumenical age. 1492
Protestantism in changing Taiwan. 2955
Protestantism in France. 2979
Protestantism in Germany. 2978
Protestantism in Latin America: a bibliographical guide. 2954
Protestantism in suburban life. 3538
Protestantism in the United States. 2976
Protestantism in transition. 2978
Protestantism's challenge. 2977
Protestantism's hour of decision. 2956
Protestants and American business methods. 2956
Protestants and Catholics. 2976
Protestants and Catholics on the spiritual life. 3480
Protestants and pioneers. 3807
Protestants, Catholics, and Mary. 2357, 2362
Protestants Council of the City of New York. 3096
Protestants in an age of science. 124, 3085
Protestants in modern Spain. 2979
Protestants in Russia. 2955
Protestants theologie. 763, 2978
Protocol of the Lutheran Church in New York City. 2698
Protocols of the meetings of the Learned Elders of Zion. 2078
Protokoll. 1547
Proud endeavorer. 2499, 3815
Proudly we hail. 1650, 2274, 2282
Prove all things. 250
Proven continuity of life. 2227
Proven paths. 1009
Proverb a day keeps the troubles away. 573
Proverbs. 161, 572, 573, 2979, 2980
Proverbs, a new approach. 572
... Proverbs and didactic poems. 591
Proverbs and Ecclesiastes. 572
Proverbs and programs for women, "a proverb for every problem," 573, 3843
Proverbs, Ecclesiastes. 511, 572
... Proverbs, Ecclesiastes and Song of songs. 567
Proverbs for easier living. 572, 981
Proverbs for today. 573
Proverbs from Plymouth pulpit. 3362
Proverbs of Solomon. 572, 573
... The Proverbs of Solomon in Sahidic Coptic. 573
Proverbs, with commentary by Julius H. Greenstone. 572
Providence. 2980, 2983
Providence, a sketch of the Sisters of charity of Providence in the Northwest, 1856-1931. 3416
Providence and calamity. 2981
Providence and evil. 3610
Providence and the atonement. 107

Providence Baptist Church official souvenir program dedicatorial ceremonies. 2983
Providence--divine and human. 2981
Providence of God. 2981, 2983
Providence of God displayed in a series of interesting facts. 2981
Providence, prayer and power. 1053
Providence preacher. 3344
Providence selection of hymns, supplementary to Dr. Watts. 1868
Providence, the reconstruction of social and moral order. 3445
Providential order of the world. 2980
Providing adequate church property and buildings. 1167
Province beyond the river. 2131, 3479
Province of law in distinction from that of truth. 1504
Province of reason. 2329, 3024
Province of the Pacific. 2959
Provincial Council of Manila of 1771. 667
Provincial letters. 1945
Provincial letters of Blaise Pascal. 1945
Proving preaching, and teaching. 68
Proximate aim of education. 805
Proximities of Calvary. 2034
Prudentius' Psychomachia. 2984
Psallite. 916
Psallite, series A. 916
Psallite, series B. 916
Psalm of deaths and other poems. 3207
Psalm of life. 2985
Psalm of peace. 3408
Psalm twenty-three. 1452, 588, 3407
Psalmist. 153, 1868
Psalmist, with music. 153
Psalmists. 578
Psalmodic science vs. psalmodic sciolism. 2985
Psalmody. 2984
Psalmody in the vernacular. 2984
Psalmody question. 2984
Psalms. 498, 574, 575, 576, 577, 579, 580, 582, 583, 584, 586, 1213, 1864, 2985
Psalms 73-150. 574
Psalms, a new translation. 582
Psalms, a prayer book. 575
Psalms according to wisdom's rule. 582
Psalms and hymns. 3046
Psalms and hymns adapted to public worship. 2916
Psalms and hymns adapted to social, private, and public worship in the Presbyterian church in the United States of America. Approved and authorized by the General assembly. 2916
Psalms and hymns, and spiritual songs. 1868
Psalms and hymns for Christian use and worship. 1335
Psalms and hymns, for social and private worship. 3754
Psalms and hymns of Dr. Watts. 1870
Psalms and hymns, with the Catechism. 583, 3046
... The Psalms and Lamentations. 582
...The Psalms and other sacred writings, their origin, contents, and significance. 529
... Psalms and prayers. 1443
Psalms and programs for women. 3857
Psalms and Proverbs. 581
Psalms and proverbs for boys and girls. 583
Psalms and Proverbs in two versions with commentary. 575
Psalms and the canticles of the divine office. 577
Psalms and their meaning for today. 579
Psalms and their story. 577
Psalms are Christian prayer. 579
Psalms are our prayers. 578
Psalms around us. 2985
Psalms as Christian praise. 578
Psalms as liturgies. 584
Psalms, books of wisdom, and Canticle of canticles. 567
Psalms carefully suited to the Christian worship in the United States of America. 580
Psalms; chronologically treated with a new trans- lation. 575
Psalms explained. 574, 577
Psalms for all seasons. 576
Psalms for childre. 582
Psalms for children. 583, 584
Psalms for daily needs. 583
Psalms for living. 583
Psalms for modern life. 586
Psalms for modern man. 583
. Psalms for sighs. 576
Psalms for the common reader. 577
Psalms for today. 585, 2985
Psalms for today, and other poems. 2985
Psalms for worship today. 583
Psalms, from life to life. 586, 940

Psalms, hymns, and spiritual song, of the Old and New Testament. 580
Psalms, hymns, and spiritual songs. 1870, 3754
Psalms, hymns, & spiritual songs of the Old and New Testament, faithfully translated into English metre. 580, 1863
Psalms, Hymns, and spiritual songs, of the Rev. Isaac Watts, D.D. 1870
Psalms, hymns and spiritual songs, original and selected. 1864
Psalms, hymns and spiritual songs, original and selected: adapted to the Christian religion. 1864
Psalms in a minor key. 584
Psalms in Christian worship. 584
Psalms in human life. 586
Psalms in Israel's worship. 577
Psalms, in metre, selected from the Psalms of David. 1864, 2968
Psalms in modern life. 585
Psalms in modern speech for public and private use. 583
Psalms in other words. 580
Psalms in outline. 586
Psalms in reflection. 578
Psalms in rhythmic prose. 581
Psalms in the midst of life. 2396
Psalms in the spirit of Jesus. 581, 2985
Psalms in Worship. 584, 2985
Psalms, Job. 576
Psalms/now. 586
Psalms of a sinner. 2386
Psalms of David. 576, 579, 580, 581, 582, 583, 1405, 1863, 1864, 1870, 2984
Psalms of David, and Song of Solomon, in metre. 581
Psalms of David imitated in the language of the New Testament. And applied to the Christian state and worship. With the preface, or, An inquiry into the right way of fitting the book of Psalms for Christian worship, and notes. 580
Psalms of David, in metre. 580, 1863
Psalms of David, with hymns and spirtual songs, having the proper metre prefixed to each. 3032
Psalms of Israel in rhymed English metre. 581
Psalms of Maratha saints. 2985
Psalms of Sir Philip Sidney and the Countess of Pembroke. 581
Psalms of Sir Sidney and the Countess of Pembroke. 581
Psalms of the heavens, earth, and sea. 586
Psalms of the social life. 576
Psalms of Thistleonia. 2394
Psalms outlined. 578
Psalms poetically rendered in rhyme. 581
Psalms, school of spirituality. 578
Psalms scroll of Qumran Cave 11 (11QPsa) 1409
Psalms '70. 584, 2880
Psalms 73-150. 584
Psalms: their origin and meaning. 578
Psalms, their structure and meaning. 578
Psalms II. 575
Psalter. 1215, 2962, 2985, 2986, 3220, 3736
Psalter, according to the Seventy, of St. David, the prophet and King. 2986
Psalter, doctrinal standards. 1023
Psalter in life, worship and history. 579
Psalter in metre and Scripture paraphrases with tunes. 2985
Psalter in the temple and the church. 2985
Psalter of the Authorized version of the Scriptures. 883
Psalter of the Roman breviary. 575
Psalter of the United Presbyterian church of North America. 3736
Psalter, or, Psalms of David. 2962, 2969, 2985
Psalter with doctrinal standards and liturgy of the Christian reformed church. 1023
Psalter, with the doctrinal standards of the Christian reformed church. 581
Psatter in the temple and the church. 2985
Pseudepigrapha and modern research. 56
... The pseudo church doctrine of anti-Pedo-Baptists defined and refuted. 147
Pseudo-criticism. 229
Pseudo-Epiphanius testimony book. 2042, 3721
...Pseudo-Ezekiel and the original prophecy. 518
Pseudo-martyr. 872, 1934
Pseudo-Plato, Axiochus. 1416, 2853
Pseudonyms of God. 3619
Psi and states of awareness. 2993
Psi trek. 2986
Psionic generator pattern book. 2723
Pslater of the church. 583
Psychastra: key to secret ESP + Control. 3539

Psyche. 1767
Psyche and psychism. 2732
Psyche and spirit. 3001
Psychedelic anthropology. 3096
Psychedelic prayers after the Tao te ching. 1781
Psychedelic teacher. 1782
Psychedelics and inner space. 3478
Psychiary and Catholicism. 2995
Psychiasis. 1792
Psychiatric study of Jesus. 1954, 2050
Psychiatric study of Jesus, exposition and criticism; translated and with an introd. 2050
Psychiatry. 2410
Psychiatry and asceticism. 90
Psychiatry and Catholicism. 2784
Psychiatry and mysticism. 2986
Psychiatry and pastoral care. 2783
Psychiatry and religion. 2785, 2986, 2995
Psychiatry and religious experience. 2784
Psychiatry and the Bible. 2995
Psychiatry, the clergy, and pastoral counseling. 2781
Psychic adventures and the unseen world. 1284, 3521
Psychic and Psychism. 2988
Psychic and religious phenomena limited. 2993
Psychic autobiography. 2130, 3506, 3521
Psychic conversion and theological foundations. 1819, 2245
Psychic dream book. 1479
Psychic energy. 2730
Psychic experience. 2992
Psychic experiences. 2723
Psychic experiences of famous people. 3509
Psychic facts. 3496
Psychic flame. 3515
Psychic golden threads. 3511
Psychic grid. 3684
Psychic health of Jesus. 2050
Psychic in the house. 2991
Psychic instructions. 2988
Psychic life of Jesus. 2060
Psychic light the continuity of law and life. 3500
Psychic Mafia. 2166, 3520
Psychic magic. 1705, 1879
Psychic mission. 2948
Psychic phenomena. 2726, 2987
Psychic phenomena and religion. 3072
Psychic phenomena in the light of the Bible. 2991
Psychic phenomena of Jamaica. 3826
Psychie phenomena, science and immortality. 2988
Psychic power and how to unfold it. 3501
Psychic power in preaching. 1843
... Psychic powers. 2729
Psychic powers of birthdates and their daily influence on you. 1635
Psychic reader. 3519
Psychic research and gospel miracles. 2017, 2476
Psychic revealments comprising a series of lectures on the nature and development of the spirit. 3495
Psychic riddle. 3502
Psychic roulette. 2992
Psychic scene. 2731
Psychic science and survival. 2987
Psychic science made plain. 2730
Psychic self-defence. 2725
Psychic sense. 1283, 2986
Psychic side of dreams. 1479
Psychic spy. 2586
Psychic structures at the Goligher circle. 2987
Psychic summer. 1368, 3519
Psychic vigil in three watches. 3511
Psychic vistas. 2726
Psychic voyages. 94
Psychic world. 2987
Psychic world of Bishop Pike. 2846, 2989
Psychic world of California. 2731
Psychic world of Doc Anderson. 39
Psychic world of Peter Hurkos. 3767
Psychic world religion. 3511
Psychical and supernormal phenomena, their observation and experimentation, the secrets of life unveiled. 2989
Psychical correlation of religious emotion and sexual desire. 3390
Psychical experience. 3498
Psychical investigations. 2989
Psychical miscellanea. 2989
Psychical phenomena and the physical world. 2990
Psychical research and the resurrection. 2989
Psychical research for the plain man. 2989
Psychical science and Christianity. 2986
Psychics. 3514
Psychics and mediums. 2991
Psychism. 2988

Psycho-cosmic symbolism of the Buddhist stupa. 3538
Psycho-harmonial philosophy. 2834
Psycho-magic: how to use the psychic powers of the astral plane. 2722
Psycho-physiological sciences, and their assailants. 742, 3517
Psychoanalysis and Christianity. 2784, 2994
Psychoanalysis and the Bible. 494
... Psychoanalysis in the light of anthroposophy. 51
Psychoanalytic study of the myth of Dionysus and Apollo. 1459
Psychobiology of transcendental meditation. 3708
Psychocraft. 2724
Psychodynamics of personality development. 2783
Psychoenergetic systems. 2992
Psychography. 3510
Psychohistory and religion. 1527
Psychological and ethical aspects of Mormon group life. 2601, 2602
Psychological and poetic approach to the study of Christ in the Fourth Gospel. 419
Psychological and religious development. 2998
Psychological and theological relationships in the multiple staff ministry. 1776
Psychological approach to religion. 2999
Psychological approach to theology. 2997
Psychological aspects of Christian experience. 2994
Psychological aspects of prayer. 2887
Psychological aspects of spiritual development. 3002
Psychological assessment of candidates for a religious order. 2574
Psychological considerations in religious education. 3146
Psychological dimensions of the religious life. 2574
Psychological dynamics in religious living. 2997
Psychological elements of religious faith. 2997
Psychological foundations of religious education. 3158
Psychological origin and the nature of religion. 2998
Psychological phenomena of Christianity. 2993
Psychological problems of religion. 2999
Psychological studies in Lutheranism. 2994
Psychological studies of clergymen. 1298
Psychological study of religion. 2998, 3102
Psychological study of trade-mark infringement. 3706
Psychological way/the spiritual way. 2779
Die Psychologie und Erkenntnisslehre des Johannes Bonaventura. 676
Psychology and alchemy. 2995, 2998
Psychology & Christianity. 1107, 1108
Psychology and God. 2997
Psychology and mystical experience. 2998
Psychology and natural theology. 2997
Psychology and pastoral work. 3675
Psychology and personality development. 961
Psychology and preaching. 2900
Psychology and religion. 2996, 2997, 2998, 3000, 3001
Psychology and religion for everyday living. 2997
Psychology and religion: selected readings. 3002
Psychology and religion: West and East. 2998, 2999
Psychology and religious origins. 2998
Psychology & silence. 1683, 3001
Psychology and the Christian life. 2999
Psychology and the Christian religion. 2784
Psychology and the church. 2994
Psychology and the cosmic order. 2994
Psychology and the parish priest. 2995
Psychology and the Promethean will. 3000
Psychology and the religious quest. 2996
Psychology and the teaching church. 3176
Psychology & theology. 1107
Psychology and worship. 2998, 2999
Psychology as a natural science applied to the solution of occult psychic phenomena. 2991
...Psychology for Bible teachers. 895
Psychology for Christian teachers. 3155
Psychology for pastor and people. 2995
Psychology for preaching. 2901
Psychology for religious works. 2997
Psychology for successful evangelism. 1566

Psychology from a Christian perspective. 1107
Psychology in search of a soul. 2997
Psychology in the light of psychic phenomena. 2987
Psychology in the Psalms. 578, 2326
Psychology of atheism. 67
Psychology of Christ. 2050
Psychology of Christian experience. 969
Psychology of Christian personality. 3335
Psychology of conduct. 2592
Psychology of counseling. 2781
Psychology of enlightenment. 3196
Psychology of inspiration. 2999
Psychology of Jesus. 1952
Psychology of Jesus and mental health. 2050
Psychology of learning and teaching Christian education. 2204
Psychology of love according to St. Bonaventure. 675, 2263
Psychology of mediumship. 3514
Psychology of myth, folklore, and religion. 3000
Psychology of nirvana. 2711
Psychology of orthodoxy. 1050
Psychology of pastoral care. 2995
... The Psychology of prayer. 2881
Psychology of prophecy. 570, 2949
Psychology of religion. 2994, 2996, 2997, 2998, 2999, 3000, 3001
Psychology of religion applied to everyday living. 2696
Psychology of religious adjustment. 2996
Psychology of religious awakening. 2996
Psychology of religious belief. 1597, 2999
Psychology of religious doubt. 185
Psychology of religious experience. 2996, 3000
Psychology of religious living. 3000
Psychology of religious mysticism. 2647
Psychology of religious sects. 2998
Psychology of religous experiences. 2997
Psychology of saving faith. 1602
Psychology of speaking in tongues. 1717
Psychology of the Beatitudes. 181
Psychology of the Christian life. 2999, 3001
Psychology of the Christian soul. 3463
Psychology of the esoteric. 3491
Psychology of the future ("L'avenir des sciences psychiques") 2987
Psychology of the Methodist revival. 3228
Psychology of the New Testament. 611
Psychology of the psychic. 2993
Psychology of the saints. 3280
Psychology of the suffering mind. 551
Psychology of the superconscious. 3567
Psychology of transcendence. 2990
Psychology of unbelief. 3422
Psychology of vocation. 3785
Psychology of witchcraft. 3824
Psychology of witnessing. 3829
Psychology; re-incarnation; soul, and its relations. 3506
Psychology, religion, and healing. 1601
Psychology, religion, and human need. 2783
Psychology serving religion. 2997
Psychology's challenge to Christianity. 2997
Psychology's defence of the faith. 3001
Psychology's impact on the Christian faith. 2996
Psychomagic; how to use the psychic powers of the astral plane. 2728
Psychomancy. 3510
Psychoneurosis called Christianity. 1091
Psychotheology. 1106
Psychotherapy. 2409
Psychotherapy: a Christian approach. 2780
Psychotherapy and a christian view of man. 2995
Psychotherapy and religion. 2999
Psychotherapy and the Christian message. 2995
Public affairs and the Y. M. C. A., 1844-944. 3870
Public affairs in the YWCA. 3878
Public affairs, size 16. 3435
Public church. 1109
Public controversy, upon fair investigation of doctrines. 3753
Public discussion on the doctrine of the Trinity. 3712
Public discussion on the question. 1047
Public education religion studies. 3190
Public ethics. 3742
Public evangelism, its approach and problems. 1570
Public life of Christ. 1986
Public life of Our Lord Jesus Christ; an interpretation. 1965
Public money and parochial education. 823, 1851
... Public opinion and theology. 3616

Public regulation of the religious use of land. 1199
Public relations for churches. 10
Public religion in American culture. 1109
Public religious services in the hospital. 3004
Public schools and moral education. 2328, 2591
... The public schools and spiritual values. 2590
Public schools, religion, and values. 3310
Public servant and the pastor. 1085
Public services at the inauguration of the Rev. John H. Gillespie, D. D. as Thomas De Witt professor of Hellenistic Greek and NewTestament exegesis in the Theological seminary of the Reformed (Dutch)church in Amerida, at New Brunswick, N. J. 3047
Public speaking. 3002
Public speaking and discussion for religious leaders. 2898
Public style. 1293
Public university and religious practice. 3757
Public worship. 838, 3004, 3547
Public worship for non-liturgical churches. 3003
Public worship of God. 3003, 3678
Publication. 2122
Publications. 3197
Publications of the American tract society. 3706
Publications of the faculty and graduate students of St. Louis university in the five years, 1923-1927, with an index according to subjects. 3276
Publications of the Kentucky Baptist historical society. 3200
Publications of the Methodist book concern. 2443
Publications, of the Virginia religious tract society. 3202
Publicity goes to church. 3002
Publicity suggestions for Unitarian churches, comprising personal work, direct distribution, radio, periodicals, public display, institutional activities. 10
Publick tryal of the Quakers in Barmudas upon the first day of May, 1678. 1681
Publish glad tidings. 1233
Family instructor; in three parts. 1607
Published for the Church historicalo society for promoting Christian knowledge. 3402
Publisher's guide: Catholic journals academic and professional. 852
Puebla, a church being born. 821
Puebla-a pilgrimage of faith. 863, 3369
Puebla and beyond. 821, 1573
Puebla conference. 821, 1326
Pueblo animals and myths. 3005
Pueblo birds and myths. 3005
Pueblo gods and myths. 3005
Pueblo Indian religion. 3005
Pueblo Indian religious architecture. 2178
Pueblo's first cross. 2972
Puerto Rican Disciples. 1465
Puerto Rican espiritismo. 3520
Pull of the invisible. 3066
Pulling life together. 955
Pulpit and altar. 2256
Pulpit and Americanl life. 2910
Pulpit and communion table. 1652, 3368
Pulpit and modern thought. 3624
Pulpit and parish manual. 1430
Pulpit and pen. 2848
Pulpit and platform. 156
Pulpit and press. 1031
Pulpit and public prayers. 2874
Pulpit and table. 3049
Pulpit and the pew. 3671, 3674
Pulpit and the plow. 3253
Pulpit assistant. 3373
Pulpit capsules. 1842
Pulpit commentary. 224
Pulpit commentary on Catholic teaching. 871
Pulpit dramas. 3144
Pulpit echoes. 3357
Pulpit eloquence. 2908
Pulpit eloquence of the nineteenth century. 3340
Pulpit giants; what made them great. 2909
Pulpit in Parliament. 3008
Pulpit in the shadows. 1361
Pulpit in the South. 3355
Pulpit mirrors. 2898
Pulpit of the American Revolution. 3742
Pulpit orator. 1843
Pulpit oratory. 1920
Pulpit, pew, and politics. 1087
Pulpit pleadings. 164
Pulpit politics. 3425
Pulpit prayers and paragraphs. 2895
Pulpit rediscovers theology. 2907
Pulpit sketches. 3354, 3374

Pulpit speaks on race. 1131
Pulpit stairs. 1466
Pulpit themes. 3375
Pulpit under the palm. 2202
Pulpit under the sky. 1790, 2303
Pulpits, lecterns, and organs in English churches. 1270
Pulse of creation series. 3509
Punching holes in the darkness. 984, 1824
Punctured bubbles. 1939
Punctured preconceptions. 1242
Pungent prayers. 2894
Pungent truths. 3716
Punishment for peace. 1139
... The pupil. 3551, 3565
Pupil and the teacher. 2287, 3160
Pupil life. 3548
Pupil's guide book. 333
Pupils in the church school. 1246
Puppet animals tell Bible stories. 3005
Puppet master. 3329
Puppet plays with a point. 3005
Puppet shows that reach & teach children. 3005
Puppets can teach too. 3005
Le pur et l'impur dans la pensee des Grecs d'Homere a Aristote. 1771
Purcell's "Manning" refuted. 2328
Pure Christianity. 1093
Pure gold. 1360
Pure gold for the Sunday school. 3562
Pure in heart. 3281
Pure principle. 3301
Pure water from old wells. 1450
Purely personal. 3886
Purgation and purgatory. 3006
Purgatory. 3006
Purgatory and heaven. 3006
Purifying the faith. 2629
Purim. 3006
Purim, a day of joy and laughter. 3006
Purim and Hanukkah, in custom and tradition. 3006
Purim anthology. 3006
Purim party. 3006
Puritan church and its relation to community, state, and nation. 2688
Puritan commonwealth. 2371
Puritan experience. 1676, 3008
Puritan family. 3008
Puritan heritage. 724, 3739, 3744
Puritan hymn and tune book. 1335
Puritan in England and New England. 3006, 3010
Puritan influences in the formative years of Illinois history. 3009
Puritan lectureships. 3009
... Puritan manifestoes. 3006, 3009
Puritan mind. 3008
Puritan New England. 3009
Puritan oligarchy. 2371
Puritan personal writings. 1772, 3009
Puritan preaching in England. 3006
Puritan protagonist. 1284
Puritan republic of the Massachusetts bay in New England. 3007
Puritan rhetoric. 1520
Puritan sage. 3008
Puritan sermon in America, 1630-1750. 3360
Puritan tradition in America, 1620-1730. 3009
Puritan way of death. 1415
Puritanism. 3006
Puritanism and democracy. 3007
Puritanism and liberty. 3007
Puritanism and the American experience. 3009
Puritanism in America, 1620-1750. 3009
Puritanism in early America. 3008
Puritanism in England. 3008
Puritanism in old and New England. 3008
Puritanism in the Old world and in the New. 3009
Puritanism in the period of the great persecution, 1660-1688. 1221, 3006
Puritanism in Tudor England. 3008
Puritans. 3007
Puritans and Calvinism. 3008
Puritans and Queen Elizabeth. 3007
Puritans and the church courts in the Diocese of York, 1560-1642. 3007
Puritans in Ireland 1647-1661. 1918
... The Puritans in Old England. 3007
Puritans in the South seas. 2543
Puritans, the Millennium and the future of Israel: Puritan eschatology, 1600 to 1660. 1531
Purity and destiny of modern spiritualism. 3504
Purity and power. 3299
Purity of heart is to will one thing. 3479, 3481
Purple headed mountain. 3484
Purple pulpit. 1243, 3799
Purple violet squish. 1255

Purpose and meaning of Jewish existence. 2139
Purpose and the hour. 2213
Purpose and transcendentalism. 3570
Purpose and work of the ministry. 2785
Purpose in nature. 3594
Purpose in prayer. 2868
Purpose in teaching religion. 3150
Purpose of Catholic schooling. 831
Purpose of God. 1731
Purpose of God and the Christian life. 3029
Purpose of Jesus in the first three Gospels. 390, 2059
Purpose of life. 978, 1777, 3202
Purpose of living. 958, 3198
Purpose of love. 2262
Purpose of temptation. 3600
Purpose of the Biblical genealogies. 281
Purpose of the church and its ministry. 3680
Purpose of the gosepl. 1342
Purpose of the Gospels. 392
Purpose of the papacy. 2768
Purpose of theosophy. 3687
Purpose widens, 1947-1967. 3878
Purposes of Calvary. 106
Purposes of church-related colleges. 1128, 1164
Purse causeway. 3201
Pursued. 3308, 3851
Pursuer or pursued [incidents from my life. 3524
Pursuit of death. 1413
Pursuit of excellence. 983
Pursuit of God. 3522
Pursuit of happiness. 180, 181
Pursuit of holiness. 1823
Pursuit of reason. 3027
Pursuit of the divine snowman. 3575
Pursuit of the holy. 974
Pursuit of the millennium. 1185, 1186
Purushartha-siddhyupaya (Jaina-pravachana-rahasya-kosha) 1932
Purva mimamsa sutras of Jaimini: chapters I-III. 2472
Pusey and the church revival. 3010
Pusher and puller. 2672
Pushing the world along. 3344
Put a door on it! 1841
Put forth by the moon. 1071
Put God first. 3339
Put off thy shoes. 2762
Put on a happy faith! 1011
Put on the whole armor of God. 1009
Put your arms around the city. 1277
Put your faith to work. 3665
Putnam's concise mythological dictionary. 2658
Putting devils and hells out of existence by destroying the God of the Bible. 3202
Putting faith to work. 968
Putting it all together in a puppet ministry. 3005
Putting it together in the parish. 2785
Putting life in your life story. 2601
Putting life on center. 1432
Putting life together again. 1352
Putting on immortality. 1889
Putting our house in order. 1211
Putting standards into the summer camp. H. S. Dimock, chairman Editorial committee. 2591
Putting your church school across. 3556
Putting your faith to work. 413, 3012
Putting your life on the line. 2213
Puzzle of religion. 3059
Pylgrymage of Sir Richard Guylforde to the Holy Land, A.D. 1506. 1777, 2848
Pyramid of Unas. 3722
Pyramid principle of church growth. 1171
Python. 1478
Pythonism of the present day. 3508

Q

Q. B. L. 721
Qabbalah. 721, 722, 1880
Qeustions that trouble Christians. 3012
Qu est-ce que la patrologie? 1616
Quadragesima. 2209
Quaint sayings and doings concerning Luther. 2276
Quaker. 1372, 1675
Quaker adventures. 1543, 1676
Quaker anecdotes. 1675
Quaker approach to contemporary problems. 3434
Quaker arrivals at Philadelphia, 1682-1750. 1687
Quaker biographies. 3127
Quaker by convincement. 1675
Quaker classics in brief. 1679, 3630
Quaker contribution. 1675
Quaker doctrine of inward peace. 1681

Quaker education in Baltimore and Virginia Yearly meetings. 1683
Quaker education in the colony and State of New Jersey. 1687
Quaker education in theory and practice. 1683
Quaker family in colonial America. 1674
Quaker from Cromwell's army. 2678
Quaker historical collections. 1688
Quaker in the forum. 1685
Quaker invasion of Massachusetts. 1686, 2371
Quaker journals; varieties of religious experience among Friends. 3493
Quaker lady. 2304
Quaker looks at yoga. 3863
Quaker meditations for youth and adults individually or in family and other groups. 1438
Quaker meeting houses, and a little humor. 1270
Quaker message. 1681, 1682
Quaker mutation. 1675
Quaker necrology. 1677
Quaker origins of antislavery. 1686, 3423
Quaker persuasion. 1674
Quaker post-bag. 1683
Quaker profiles. 1677
Quaker profiles from the American West. 1677
Quaker profiles, pictorial and biographical, 1750-1850. 1677
Quaker queries. 1680
Quaker reader. 1679
Quaker records in Maryland. 1686
Quaker reflections to light the future. 1684
Quaker saint of Cornwall. 1675, 1782
Quaker social history, 1669-1738. 1683, 1685
Quaker story. 1685
Quaker torch bearers. 1677
Quaker trends for modern Friends. 1684
Quaker ways in foreign policy. 1674
Quaker worship and techniques of meditation. 1674, 2379
Quaker worship in North America. 1687
... Quakeriana. 1677
Quakerism. 1674, 1675
Quakerism and a creed. 1682
Quakerism and Christianity. 1674
Quakerism and its application to some modern problems. 1675
Quakerism and other religions. 1674
Quakerism and politics. 1675
Quakerism of the future. 1683
Quakerism on the Eastern Shore. 1683
Quakerism, past and present. 1684
Quakers. 1674, 1675, 1683, 1687
Quakers and education as seen in their schools in England. 1683
Quakers and peace. 2756
Quakers and slavery in America. 3423
Quakers and the Atlantic culture. 1685
Quakers as pioneers in social work. 1674, 1675
Quakers as pioneers in social work (Studien uber die sozialpolitik der Quaker) 1675
Quakers courageous. 1685
Quakers find a way. 1676
Quakers in action. 1675
Quakers in Boston, 1656-1964. 683, 1678
Quakers in California. 1685
Quakers in Great Britain and America. 3093
Quakers in India. 2532, 3438
Quakers in peace and war. 1685, 2756
Quakers in Pennsylvania. 1687, 2813
Quakers in Puritan England. 1684
Quakers in science and industry. 1684, 3314
Quakers in the American colonies. 1685
Quakers in the colonial Northeast. 1687
Quakers in the modern world. 1674
Quakers of Iowa. 3093
Quakers of Spiceland, Henry County, Indiana. 1684
Quakers on the American frontier. 1684
Quakers take stock. 1676
Quakers, their story and message. 1683
Qualifications for ministerial power. 3672
Qualifying men for church work. 1252
Qualitative nouns in the Pauline epistles. 374
Qualities of a good superior. 2575
Quality assurance. 3010
Quality circle guide to participation management. 3011
Quality circles master guide. 3011
Quality friendship. 1405, 1688
Quality of mercy. 2412, 2845, 3526
Quand l'Eglise juge et condamne. 780
Quandary of life, science, and religion. 3082
Quantity of a hazel nut. 1450
Quantum gods. 2727

... Quarter centennial historical sketch. 893
Quarter-centennial pastorate of Rev. Cyrus W. Wallace. 1911, 3789
Quarter of a millennium. 2701
Wuarter-centennial of the Pittsburgh congregation of the Covenater church, 1866 to 18919. 3050
Quartet in heaven. 749
Quasi-religious societies. 2578
Quater-centenary of the Scottish Reformation. 3042
Quatrains of Christ. 2047
Quattlebaum's truth. 3100
Quebec to New England. 1404, 3847
Queen Esther, star in Judea's crown. 1532
Queen of Angels Church, Sunnyside, New York. 1165
Queen of heaven. 1632, 2360
Queen of paradox. 2353
Queen of the air. 2662
Queen of the home. 1608
Queen of the Miraculous Medal Chapel. 3275
Queen of the sciences as a modern African professional woman. 3111
Queen of the Shakers. 2205
Queen of the Universe. 2358
Queenly quest. 1714
Queenly womanhood. 3393
Queen's command. 3460
Queen's daughters. 3285
Queen's festivals. 1613, 2356
Queen's heart of gold. 182
Queen's portrait. 1776
Queen's way. 2359
Queer questions and ready replies. 1513
Quellen zur Geschichte der ersten Katharinenschwestern und ihrer Grunderin Regina Protmann [obit] 1613. 1456
Quellen zur Ketzergeschichte Brandenburgs und Pommerns. 1805, 1909
Quench not the Spirit. 1827
... Queries and answers. 2135
Querists' drawer. 3572
Querists, part iii. 3601
Quest. 1445, 1755, 2221, 2757
Quest and character of a united church. 1045
Quest anthology. 1755, 3067
Quest at Glastonbury. 676, 1715
Quest begins. 979
Quest for a Black theology. 2683
Quest for a Christian America. 1464
Quest for catholicity. 1225
Quest for certainty in Saadia's philosophy. 3259
Quest for Christ. 163
Quest for Christian brotherhood. 1016
Quest for Christian purity. 1824
Quest for Christian unity. 3737
Quest for church unity. 1042
Quest for communion with God. 2887
Quest for Dean Bridgman Conner. 1346, 3511
Quest for Eastern Christians. 1487
Quest for Eden. 2772
Quest for empire. 1232, 2176
Quest for excellence. 1009
Quest for experience in worship. 3852
Quest for God. 160, 188
Quest for God in China. 913
Quest for God, Quest for self. 2385
Quest for God through understanding. 3887
Quest for God through worship. 2237
Quest for holiness. 2160, 3479, 3485
Quest for inner peace. 3758
Quest for justice. 851, 1140
Quest for life. 969
Quest for meaning. 74, 3217
Quest for meaning of Svami Vivekananda. 3784
Quest for meekness and quietness of spirit. 1856
Quest for myth. 2650, 2651
Quest for Orthodox Church unity in America. 1046, 2749
Quest for past and future. 2080
Quest for personal poise. 2397
Quest for political and spiritual liberation. 1709
Quest for preaching power. 2897
Quest for reality. 1362, 3027
Quest for reality: Christianity and the counter culture. 3448
Quest for reformation in preaching. 2898
Quest for religious certainty. 2180
Quest for religious maturity. 2997
Quest for religious realism. 1106
Quest for security. 3488
Quest for souls. 168, 3359
Quest for the Dead Sea scrolls. 1411
Quest for Theseus. 3691

Quest for utopia; an anthology of imaginary societies [by] Glenn Negley [and] J. Max Patrick. 3762
Quest for vitality in religion. 993
Quest; history and meaning in religion. 3058
Quest in the Holy Land. 2014, 2761
Quest of Ben Hered. 2005
Quest of certainty. 62
Quest of Don Bosco. 683
Quest of God. 2135
Quest of life. 160, 1340
Quest of religion. 3071
Quest of the ages. 3059
Quest of the Christ of faith. 2007
Quest of the divine. 1536
Quest of the historical Jesus. 1978, 1979, 1993
Quest of the Holy Grail. 1755
Quest of the overself. 3864
Quest of three abbots. 1918
Quest of truth. 3339
Quest through the centuries. 2008
Questing Christ. 976
Question and answer Catholic catechism. 769
Question and the answer. 784
Question answered. 230, 643
Question awakened by the Bible. 1889, 2041
Question book of Christian doctrine. 145
Question-book on the Gospel by John chapters 1-10. 422
...A question book on the Gospel by Matthew, chapters 1-14. Combining the question book and expostiion. 443
Question book on the topics in Christ's Sermon on the Mount. 3334
Question-book to Whedon's Commentary on Matthew and Mark. 443, 3810
Question box. 785, 788, 3012
Question-box answers. 785
Question box for Sisters. 2573
Question box on the Old Testament. 496
Question concerning the visible church. 2690
Question; "If a man die, shall he live again?" Job XIV. 14. 3498
Question in Baptist history. 152, 3818
Question marks and exclamation points. 3758
Question of ages. 2324
Question of Anglican orders. 44
Question of being. 1707, 2738, 2739
Question of conscience. 781
Question of God. 3679
Question of hell. 1699
Question of Mary. 2355
Question of miracles. 2018
Question of nationality in its relations to the Catholic church in the United States. 828
Question of questions. 2323
Question of questions, where is man's permanent home? 1696
Question of religion. 3057
Question of the centuries. 3342
Question of the cross. 1997
Question of the hour. 300, 874, 1069
Question settled. 3505
Question solved. 787
Question time. 3012
Questioning child and religion. 905
Questioning Christian faith. 61
Questioning church. 758
Questionnaire, or, Prayer for a town & a friend. 2872
*Questions about the Bible. 3191
Questions adapted to Dr. Hodge's Exposition of the First epistle to the Corinthians. 322
Questions and answers. 795, 3011, 3205, 3385, 3472, 3628
Questions and answers about the Bible. 281, 638
Questions and answers concerning the Jew. 2076
Questions and answers for catechetical instruction, for the Sunday school and the home. 2283
Questions and answers on Christian science. 1030
Questions and answers on conscious evolution. 2473
Questions and answers on Luther's small catechism, for the use of the church, school and family. 2279
Questions and answers on material and spiritual psychology and symposium of subjects on the psychology of morals and religious truths for the betterment of mankind. 2997
Questions and answers on the Bible. 307
Questions and answers on the Book of Mormon. 678
Questions and answers on the Catholic faith. 3012

Questions & answers on the science of mind. 2695
Questions and answers, open forum, Freed-Hardeman College lectures. 3670
Questions and notes, critical and practical, upon the book of Leviticus. 557
Questions and phases of modern missions. 2519
Questions answered. 3385
Questions are the answer. 3665
Questions asked by Protestants briefly answered by a priest of the diocese of Buffalo. 791
Questions Catholics ask Father Sheedy. 794
Questions Christians ask. 161
Questions concerning the Son of man. 1994, 3564
Questions frequently asked me on prophecy. 606
Questions God asks. 1466
Questions I'd like to ask. 899
Questions I'm asked about marriage. 2343
Questions Jesus answered. 160, 2067
Questions Jesus asked. 2435
Questions Jews ask. 3011
Questions Jews ask: reconstructionist answers. 3011
Questions non-Christians ask. 67
Questions of belief. 1596
Questions of King Milinda. 3139
Questions of modern thought. 1099
Questions of moral theology. 3450
Questions of religious truth. 3068
Questions of the day. 782, 828, 1054, 1136
Questions of the heart. 3653
Questions of the soul. 763, 2805
Questions of youth. 781
Questions on natural science and the harmonic philosophy. 3073
Questions on occultism. 3689
Questions on select portions of the four evangelists. 384
Questions on select portions of the Gospels. 384
Questions on the Acts of the apostles. 332
Questions on the Bible, for the use of schools. 218
Questions on the book of Exodus. 515
Questions on the Christian faith answered from the Bible. 3670
Questions on the Confession. 2922
Questions on the Epistle of Paul the apostle to the Hebrews. 402
Questions on the Epistle to the Romans. 466
Questions on the Gospel according to St. John. 421
Questions on the gospels. 225
Questions on the life and labors of the great apostle. 2804
Questions on the life of Christ. 1993, 3564
Questions on the life of Moses. 2622
Questions on the quest. 3483
Questions on the text of the Systematic theology of Dr. Charles Hodge. 1821
Questions on the way. 2962
Questions on the words and works of Jesus. 340
Questions on the words and works of the apostles. 332
Questions on worldliness. 3141
Questions people ask. 3354
Questions people ask about religion. 3012
Questions teen-agers ask. 3880
Questions that bother me. 3012
Questions that matter most. 3120
Questions that must be answered. 3012
Questions upon the evidences of Christianity. 2959
Questions with answers. 3563
Quests for the historical Jesus. 2008
Quick and the dead. 1091
Quick truths in quaint texts. 165
Quickening word. 725
Quiet and peaceable life. 2408
Quiet answer. 3481
Quiet corner. 1456
Quiet crusaders. 2548
Quiet demonstration. 2406
Quiet hallelujahs. 1558
Quiet hints to growing prechers in my study. 1288
Quiet hints to ministers' wives. 1303
Quiet hour. 2889
Quiet hour stories. 1437
Quiet hours with Bible characters. 214, 638
Quiet men. 924
Quiet mind. 2379
Quiet moment. 17
Quiet moments with God. 318, 901
Quiet people of the land. 2596
Quiet prince. 2197
Quiet rebels. 1684

Quiet revolution. 392, 1139, 2007, 3786
Quiet revolutionary. 2389
Quiet room. 604
Quiet strength from world religions. 2392
Quiet talk about the babe of Bethlehem. 1952
Quiet talk with God each day. 1442
Quiet talks about Jesus. 2038
Quiet talks about life after death. 3211
Quiet talks about Our Lord's return. 3319
Quiet talks about the crowned Christ. 459
Quiet talks about the healing Christ. 1792
Quiet talks about the tempter. 3600
Quiet talks on following the Christ. 1069
Quiet talks on how to pray. 2872
Quiet talks on John's Gospel. 419
Quiet talks on personal problems. 962
Quiet talks on power. 962
Quiet talks on prayer. 2872
Quiet talks on service. 962
Quiet talks on the Bible story. 233
Quiet talks on the new order of things. 1513
Quiet talks with eager youth. 3885
Quiet thoughts. 1450
Quiet time. 2895
Quills of truth. 2619
Quimby manuscripts. 2409
Quintescence of Lorenzo's works. 3198
Quintessence of Islam. 2185
Quit bugging me. 991
Quit you like men. 3673, 3870
Quit your meanness. 1557
Quiver of sunbeams. 970
Quiz book about pope, bishop and rabbi. 757
Qumran and Corinth. 3014
Qumran and history. 3014
Qumran and the history of the Biblical text. 1411
Qumran baptism and John the Baptist's baptism. 2127, 3013
Qumran cave 4. 1409
Qumran community. 1410
Qumran community: its history and scrolls. 1410, 3013
Qumran studies. 1410, 3014
Quodlibet. 782, 3647
Quoi! Plus de Dieu? 3382
Quotable American rabbis. 3014
Quotable Billy Graham. 1754
Quotable Fulton J. Sheen. 3111
Quotable illustrations. 1841
Quotations and illustrations for sermons. 1842
Quotations from Chairman Jesus. 2072
Quotations from the Bible for modern man. 251
Quotations from the Scriptures. 254
Qur'an and its exegesis. 2184
Qur'an as scripture. 2185
Quran. 2183, 2184
Qur'an and Bible. 1926, 2184
Quranic studies. 77, 2184
Qurian as scripture. 2185

R

R. A. Torrey. 1343
R. A. Torrey year-book. 318
R. C. Buckner's life of faith and works. 700
R comprehensive plan of education for the Unitarian Universalist ministry. 3681
R. Ernest Lamb, Irish-American Quaker. 2194
Ra-ha-la-hi-ko. 2538
Rab Saadia gaon. 3259
Rabad of Posquieres. 4, 3016
Rabban Gamaliel ben Simeon. 1701
Rabbi and his early ministry. 3015
Rabbi and his flock. 3576
Rabbi and minister. 3017, 3822
Rabbi and synagogue in Reform Judaism. 3016, 3032
Rabbi and the Jewish social worker. 3454
Rabbi and the synagogue. 2155
Rabbi Eizik. 3581, 3589
Rabbi Emil G. Hirsch, the reform advocate. 1816, 3361
Rabbi in action. 3576
Rabbi in America. 3822
Rabbi in America: the story of Issac M. Wise. 3822
Rabbi Isaac Jacob Reines; his life and thought. 3055
Rabbi J. 1410, 2040
Rabbi Jacob J. Weinstein, advocate of the people. 3017, 3801
Rabbi Jeshua, an eastern story. 1954
Rabbi Joseph H. Lookstein memorial volume. 2093, 2147
Rabbi Joshua ben Chanania. 2134
Rabbi Kook's Philosophy of repentance. 3218

Rabbi Meir of Rothenburg. 2400, 3219
Rabbi Moses ha-Kohen of Tordesillas and his book 'Ezer ha-emunah—a chapter in the history of the Judeo-Christian controversy. 2144, 2624
Rabbi Nachman's fire. 690, 2668
Rabbi Nachman's wisdom: Shevachay haRan, Sichos haRan. 1789, 2668
Rabbi on Forty-seventh Street. 663, 3016
Rabbi remembers. 3016
Rabbi speaks. 3370
Rabbi takes stock. 2112
Rabbi teaches. 2116
Rabbi, the man and his message. 3576
Rabbinic anthology. 18, 1539, 2145
Rabbinic essays. 2013
Rabbinic Judaism in the making. 3585
Rabbinic literature and Gospel teachings. 391, 3015
Rabbinic mind. 2139, 3015
Rabbinic psychology; beliefs about the soul in Rabbinic literature of the Talmudic period. 3464
Rabbinic stories for Christian ministers and teachers. 3581
Rabbinic wisdom. 1540
Rabbinic wisdom and Jewish values. 3581
Rabbinical counseling. 2782
Rabbinics and research. 3223
Rabbis and wives. 3015
Rabbis' Bible. 497
Rabbi's faith. 3371
Rabbi's girls. 1604
Rabbi's manual. 3016
Rabbis of ancient times. 3015
Rabboni. 1951, 3015
Rabboni ... which is to say master. 929, 1967
Rabi'a the mystic & her fellow-saints in Islam. 3017, 3543
Raccolta. 856, 858
Race. 1132, 3072
Race against time. 1133, 2296
Race and color in Islam. 1923
Race and religion. 3072
Race and the renewal of the church. 3017
Race: challenge to religion, original essays and An appeal to the conscience. 1132
Race, nation, person. 1137, 3450
Race relations and Christian mission. 1131
Race, rock & religion. 3468
Race set before us. 1432
Race's redemption. 3029
Rachel. 897
Rachel comforted. 3508
Racial adjustments in the Methodist Episcopal church. 2450
Racial episcopacy, reasons. 1523
Racial factor in Y.M.C.A.'s. 3870
Racial prejudice. 3017
Racial transition in the church. 1133
Racine's Biblical masterpieces, Esther and Athalie. 299
Racism and the Christian understanding of man. 1131
Racovian catechism. 3730
Radhakrishnan. 1815
Radhakrishnan and integral experience. 3017
Radian flame. 3517
Radiance. 3844
Radiance of Chartres. 1715
Radiant cross. 1549
Radiant crown of glory. 1886
Radiant horizons. 1453, 3054
Radiant life. 3479, 3845
Radiant realities. 162
Radiant rebel. 3296, 3308
Radiant religion. 958, 1443
Radiant reveries. 3352
Radiant road to reality. 3408
Radiant story of Jesus. 1954
Radiant you. 3877
Radical Bible. 1155
Radical Christian. 1244
Radical Christianity. 1417
Radical Christianity and its sources. 3656
Radical discourses on religious subjects. 1654
Radical Enlightenment. 1542, 1665
Radical imperative. 942
Radical Kingdom. 3233, 3234
Radical monotheism and Western civilization. 2585
Radical monotheism and Western culture. 2585
Radical monotheism and Western culture, with supplementary essays. 2585
Radical movement of the 1960's. 3747
Radical obedience. 944
Radical pietists. 933
Radical pulpit. 3352
Radical Reformation. 3036
Radical religious movements in early modern Europe. 1469
Radical response. 3242, 3328

Radical Right. 2125
Radical sects of revolutionary New England. 1038
Radical social movement and the radical church tradition. 1141
Radical theology and the death of God. 1417
Radical theology: phase two. 1417
Radical voices in the wilderness. 167, 571
Radical Wesley and patterns for church renewal. 1292, 3804
Radical Zen. 3893
Radicalism and conservatism toward conventional religion. 109
Radicalism in religion, philosophy, and social life. 2776, 3832
Radicals, Secularists, and republicans. 1656
Radio addresses. 2619
Radio Church of God. 83, 3382
Radio for Christ. 2300
Radio heart throbs. 3018
Radio messages from paradise. 3221
Radio preaching. 3018
Radio revival sermons. 1556
Radio sermons. 443, 3018, 3387
Radio sermons and lectures. 2848
Radio stories that live. 3018
Radio talks for the children. 909
Radio talks on religion. 1069, 1956
Radio talks to young people with the questions and answers. 3018
Radio, the new missionary. 3018
Rafael, Cardinal Merry del Val. 738, 2412
Rafka, the blind mystic of Lebanon. 2717, 3025
Raft is not the shore. 3066
Rage! Reflect. Rejoice! 579, 2881
Ragged Hill. 3198
Rags to righteousness. 1012
Rahner reader. 777, 3633
Raid on the inarticulate. 3534
Raiders of the lost ark. 3197
Railroad sermons from railroad stories. 3341
Railroad Young men's Christian association handbook. 3873
Railway through the word. 302
Rain for these roots. 3286
Rain on the desert. 1903
Rainbow. 3320
Rainbow and the pot of gold. 2260
Rainbow and the Resurrection. 2033
Rainbow Bible. 3110
Rainbow book of Bible stories. 617, 620
Rainbow bridge. 3110
Rainbow dream. 3095
Rainbow for every cloud. 162
Rainbow in the cloud. 590
Rainbow in the North. 2545
Rainbow missionary stories. 2551
Rainbow of sorrow. 2058
Rainbow over Calvary. 2058
Rainbow Serpent. 3376
Rainbow sign. 1845
Rainbow south. 2507
Rainbows. 17
Rainbows through sorrow. 1349
Rainwater, sunshine, and babies. 968
Raise a signal. 2548
Raise the dead! 1414
Raising children. 1611
Raising God's children. 699, 1607
Raising money for church building projects. 1690
Raisins and almonds. 2073
Raissa's Journal. 2335
Raja-cekhara's Karpura-manjari. 3145
Raja-vidya, the king of knowledge. 2186
Raja yoga. 3866, 3867
Rajasi Janakananda (James J. Lynn) a great Western yogi. 2304
Rajasthani temple hangings of the Krishna cult from the Collection of Karl Mann, New York. 2328, 3789
Rakadazanism.Or the exalted life.A system of culture, including soul culture, health culture, and natural method for rejuvenation of the body of man and the consequent re-generaltion of his whole being and the immortaliization of the soul. 1778
Ralph Norton and the Belgian gospel mission. 2503, 2714
Raltramiejus Vilentas' Lithuanian translation of the Gospels and Epistles, 1579. 654
Rama of the golden age. 1895
Ramacharitmanasa. 3718
Ramakien. 3605
Ramakrishna. 3020
Ramakrishna and his disciples. 3020
Ramakrishna and the vitality of Hinduism. 1813, 3020
Ramakrishna, his life and sayings. 3020
Ramakrishna-Vedanta wordbook. 3775
Ramakrishna's teachings illustrated. 3020

Ramana Maharshi. 1816, 3020
Ramana Maharshi and his philosophy of existence. 3020
Ramana Maharshi and the path of self-knowledge. 3020
Ramanzo, the conscience stricken brigand. 3145
Ramayana. 2403, 3139
Ramayana, and The Mahabharata. 3139
Rambam. 2623, 2841
Ramban. 2623
Rambling along through the Scriptures. 3200
Rambling recollections of ninety happy years. 3133
Ramblings in Beulah land. A continuation of experiences in the life of Jennie Smith. 3135
... Ramdas and the Ramdasis. 3214
Ramon Lull. 2271
Rand McNally Bible atlas. 282
Rand McNally book of favorite prayers and stories. 899
Rand Mcnally book of favorite prayers and stories. (The) 899
Rand McNally historical atlas of the Holy Land. 283
Randall Davidson. 1406
Random remarks. 3067
Random reminiscences from fifty years of ministry. 1575
Randy, please call home. 675, 1259
Range of commitment. 759
Rank among the Canaanite gods. 1743
Rank and religion in Tikopia. 3699
Ransom and reunion through the sanctuary. 3300, 3382
Ransom for Wurmbrand. 3860
Ransoming the time. 760
Raphael's ancient manuscript of talismanic magic. 2313
Rapid economic change - its impact on people and the churches. 3069
Rappers. 3511
Rapping about the Spirit. 1831
Rapture! 3318
Rapture; or, The translation of the saints. 3282
Rapture question. 2466, 3022
Raptured. 3021
...The rare and late verbs in St. Augustine's De civitate Dei. 115, 116, 2199
Rare Bible stories. 297
Rare Bibles. 212
Ras Shamra and the Bible. 3022
Ras Shamra discoveries and the Old Testament. 500, 3022
Rasha--the Jew. 2612
Rashi. 3457
Rashi and the Christian scholars. 3456
Rashi anniversary volume. 3456
Rashi: commentaries on the Pentateuch. 562
Raspberry kingdom. 2389
Raspberry seed under God's denture. 179
Rasputin. 3022
Rasputin and the fall of the Romanovs. 3022
Rasputin, neither devil nor saint. 3022
Rastafari. 3022
Rastafarians. 3022
Rastaman. 3022
Ratana. 2332, 3022
Rather die than live—Jonah. 553
Ratio descipline. 1335
Ratio disciplinae fratrum Nov-Anglorum. 1335
Rational and true gospel of the world's divine order. 3022
Rational basis of orthodoxy. 3073
Rational cosmology. 1371
Rational faith. 2147, 2735
Rational illustration of the Book of common prayer of the Church of England. 1214, 1224
Rational look at mysteries and heart of the gospel. 236
Rational orthodoxy. 2922
Rational religion. 1597, 3353
Rational religion and morals. 3024
Rational test. 64
Rational theology. 2600, 2612, 2614, 3653
Rational theology and Christian philosophy in England in the seventeenth century. 731, 1760
Rational thoughts concerning the Supreme Being of the universe. 3197
Rational view of Jesus and religion. 2050
Rational view of life. 1063
Rational vindication fo the Catholick faith. 59, 2038
... The Rationale of ceremonial. 1223
Rationalist encyclopaedia. 3024
Rationality and religious belief. 3107
Rationality of belief in God. 1738
Rationality of faith. 1594

Rationality of the world. 3594
Rats, plague, and religion. 2529
Rattling, roaring rhymes on Mormon Utah and her institutions. 2601
Rattling the gates. 2815
Rauschenbusch reader. 3445
Rauschenbusch, the formative years. 3025
Raven and the chariot. 1506
Raw and the cooked. 1903, 2652
Raw edge of courage. 3136
Ray. 3201
Raymond. 3507
Raymond and Agnes. 3200
Raymond Lull. 2271
Raymond of the Times. 3025
Raymond S. Jackson. 1930
Raymund Lully, illuminated doctor, alchemist and Christian mystic. 2271
Rays of heavenly light. 1273
Rays of Jewish splendor. 3371
Rays of light. 3482
Rays of light on our daily path. 725
Rays of light on the Sabbath question. 3261
Rays of Masonry. 1663
Rays of Messiah's glory. 2414
Rays of reason. 1654
Razor for a goat. 3824
RB 1980. 188
Re-appearing (Il est ressuscite!) 3221
Re-birth of religion. 3654
Re-discovering the creed. 1453
Re-discovery of the Old Testament. 502
... The re-discovery of the spirit. 3211
Re-establishment of the Church of England, 1660-1663. 1220
Re-interpretation of Jesus in the New Testament. 349, 1970
Re-shaping the liturgy. 1214
Re-thinking missions. 2520
"Re-thinking missions" examined. 2202
Re-thinking religion. 3097
Re-thinking the church. 1122
Reach for the sky. 2435
Reach for the sun. 3477
Reach for tomorrow. 932, 3317
Reach of the mind. 2991
Reach out! 2397, 3881
Reach out and touch. 1453
Reach out for new life. 1012
Reach out to singles. 1256
Reach up. 1325
Reaching all prospects for the church. 3160
Reaching Arabs for Christ. 2544
Reaching beyond your pulpit. 3002
Reaching boys with a Christian program. 1254
Reaching children. 3171
Reaching for God. 149, 2560
Reaching for rainbows. 3857
Reaching for rapport. 103
Reaching for the moon. 3371
Reaching for the sky. 3868
Reaching for the stars. 2396, 2437
Reaching high. 3478
Reaching high heaven. 3198
Reaching out. 2816, 3481
Reaching out for life's best. 985
Reaching out to people. 1253
Reaching people from the pulpit. 2906
Reaching the Arabs. 2557
Reaching the silent billion. 1883
Reaching the unchurched. 1568
Reaching the unreached. 1569
Reaching toward the heights. 1433
Reaching upward. 67
Reaching Youth for Christ. 3881
Reaction from agnostic science. 3076
Read aloud Bible stories. 622
Read and live. 636, 959
Read and pray. 1432
Read and pray Romans. 471
Read the Bible. 613
Read the Bible with me. 501
Reader for the teacher. 2614
Reader in comparative religion. 3122, 3138
Reader in contemporary theology. 3651
Reader in political theology. 3633
Reader in sociology. 3448
Reader in technical services. 2944
Reader on Islam. 1927, 2564
Reader on Islam; passages from standard Arabic writings illustrative of the beliefs and practices of Muslims. 2564
Reader[s]. 3025
Readers' A to Z Bible companion. 286
Reader's Bible. 359, 614
Reader's companion to the Bible. 648
Reader's digest story of the Bible world. 295
Reader's digest story of the Bible world, in map, word and picture. 295
Reader's guide to proclamation for Sundays and major feasts in cycle "A," 314

Reader's guide to proclamation for Sundays and major feasts in cycle "B" 314
Reader's guide to proclamation for Sundays and major feasts in cycle "C" 314
Reader's guide to religious literature. 1021
Reader's guide to the best evangelical books. 3626
Reader's guide to the Bible. 310
Reader's guide to the great religions. 3123
Reader's Hebrew-English lexicon of the Old Testament. 530, 1796
Reader's introduction to the New Testament. 410
Readiness for religion. 3170
Reading and understanding the Old Testament. 595
Reading guide to the book of Mormon. 678
Reading John's Gospel today. 423
Reading list for Catholics. 868
Reading of Revelation. 457
Reading of Saint Luke's gospel. 428
Reading Paul today. 373, 2801
Reading the Acts, Epistles, and Revelation. 331
Reading the Bible. 613, 645, 648
Reading the Bible aloud. 613
Reading the Bible at home. 613
Reading the Bible through. 294
Reading the Bible to-day. 613
Reading the Bible today. 613
Reading the Bible with understanding. 312
Reading the good news in Galilee. 1966
Reading the Gospel of John. 414
Reading the Gospels—a guide to readers and teachers. 389
Reading the new Testament. 410
Reading the New Testament today. 473
Reading the Old Testament prophets today. 569, 2951
Reading the shadows. 3720
Reading the Word of God. 647
Reading through prayers. 1796
Reading through Romans. 466
Readings and meditations for retreats and spiritual renewals. 3222
Readings and meditations on Christ. 2015
Readings and recitations for Good templar lodges. 1913
Readings and reflections for the Holy hour. 1826, 3204
Readings and reflections on the Gospels. 367
Readings, cases, materials in canon law. 735
Readings for Catholic action. 753
Readings for live programs. 3026
Readings for the celebration of life. 3378
Readings for the Saints' days, by F. E. C. Printed for private circulation only. 3281
Readings form world religions. 3268
Readings from Cardinal O'Connell. 864
Readings from Friedrich von Hugel. 749, 3101
... Readings from the Apocrypha. 488
Readings from the Apocryphal Gospels. 336
Readings from the Bible. 249
Readings from the English Bible. 592
Readings from the Holy Scriptures. 81
Readings from the Holy Scriptures, for Jewish sailors, soldiers and airmen. 81
Readings from the mystics of Islam. 3543
... Readings from the Old Testament. 591
Readings from the Old Testament, and Phrase book. 591
Readings from the Sacred Scriptures. 647
Readings in Biblical morality. 949
Readings in Christian education. 3167
Readings in Christian humanism. 1075
Readings in Christian thought. 3636
Readings in church history. 1198
Readings in dynamic indigeneity. 1905
Readings in First Corinthians. 321
Readings in Jewish worship. 2076, 2463
Readings in L. D. S. Church history from original manuscripts. 2615
Readings in Luther for laymen. 2285, 3629
Readings in missionary anthropology. 2496, 2555
Readings in missionary anthropology II. 2496
Readings in natural theology. 2674
Readings in religious philosophy. 2837
Readings in sacramental theology. 3266
Readings in St. John's gospel. 422
Readings in science and spirit. 3107
Readings in social theology. 1136
Readings in the history of Christian thought. 3636
Readings in the Lutheran philosophy of education. 2293

Readings in the philosophy of religion. 3103, 3107
Readings in the psychology of religion. 3000
Readings in the sociology of religion. 3088
Readings in the teaching of Jewish history. 2094
Readings in the theology of the church. 1125
Readings in the world's living religions. 3203
Readings in Third World missions. 2496
Readings in Vedic literature. 3776
Readings in Vedic literature for children. 879, 1816
Readings on concepts of Zion. 3217
Readings on fundamental moral theology. 3680
Readings on religion. 3067
Readings on the epistle to the Romans. 471
Readings on the sociology of religion. 3088
Readjusted church. 1116
Ready & desirous. 1328
Ready always. 447
Ready answers in canon law. 736
Ready manual for the daily vacation Bible school teacher. 3764
Ready or not! 3870
Ready references. 1230
Ready replies on religion. 998
Ready Scriptural reasons. 2403, 2405
Ready to answer. 3382
Reaffirmation of prayer. 2873
Real achievement of Vatican II. 3772
Real and only life. 991
Real Billy Sunday. 3566
Real blasphemers. 1655
Real Christ. 1974, 1995
Real Christ teaching. 2066
Real Christianity. 167, 332, 3358
Real Christians hope in death. 928
Real Christmas. 1110
Real churches or a fog. 1163
Real de Rance, illustrious penitent and reformer of Notre Dame de la Trappe. 3021, 3709
Real dialogues on the evidences of Christianity from "Death bed scenes." 61
Real discipleship. 3336
Real evangelism. 1570
Real evangelistic preaching. 167
Real fifth column and how it is undermining America. 2563
Real Francis. 1644, 1648
Real fundamentals. 2426
Real ghost stories. 3515
Real ghosts, restless spirits, and haunted minds. 1710
Real God. 1096
... The real God, the universal mind, and the divinity of man. 1451
Real guru. 879, 1778
Real Holy Spirit. 1831
Real imitation of Christ. 1955
Real Israel and Anglo-Israelism. 46
Real Jesus. 389, 928, 1950, 1951, 1976
Real Jesus, and other sermons. 3340
Real Jesus, how he lived and what he taught. 1961
Real Jesus of the four Gospels. 1950, 1959
Real John Wesley. 3804
Real key to Christian science. 1036
Real life. 3199
Real life in Christ. 993
Real life in the spirit land. 3506
Real life is meeting. 3445
Real life, real faith. 1842, 3589
Real life stories. 895
Real living and God's help. 3238
Real living takes time. 979
Real Lord's prayer. 3341
Real magic. 2312
Real meaning of communism. 1319
Real meaning of Genesis. 523
Real missing link. 1062
Real Mormonism. 2606
Real people. 2407
Real prayer. 2876
Real preaching. 2907
Real presence. 1835, 2219, 3853
Real reason for Christmas. 1112
Real religion. 3066, 3345
Real revival preaching. 167
Real salvation and whole-hearted service. 3291
Real Satan. 1428, 2040
Real stone face. 1957, 2719
Real thing. 3181
Real treasure for the pious mind. 1451, 2395, 3201
Real Tripitaka. 1850
Real woman in the religious life. 2572
Real word for the real world. 2899

Real world of fairies. 1588
Realations between Northern and Southern Babtists. 171
Realism. 691, 2737
Realism and hope. 1088
Realism in renewal. 2574
Realism of Jesus. 3335
Realistic idealism in philosophy itself. 1881
Realistic pacifism. 3793
Realistic philosophy of religion. 3100
Realistic theology. 1059
Realistic universe. 2416
Realities. 759, 2735
Realities and visions. 2481, 2965
Realities of Christian experience. 959
Realities of Christian theology. 3640
Realities of faith. 1061
Realities of the Christian religion. 1587
Reality. 3105, 3512, 3693
Reality and ecstasy. 3063
Reality and evangelical theology. 3226
Reality and faith. 676
Reality and prayer. 2875
Reality and religion. 1097, 2640, 3068
Reality and the good. 1536
Reality in fellowship. 2212
Reality in preaching. 2904
Reality in religion. 106, 165, 3065
Reality in worship. 3004, 3852
Reality of Christianity. 1786
Reality of faith. 1105, 1342
Reality of God. 62, 1726, 3652
Reality of God, and Religion & agnosticism. 1722, 3101
Reality of Jesus. 2040
Reality of man. 126, 127
Reality of matter. 2728
Reality of occult, yoga, meditation, flying saucers. 3685
Reality of prayer. 2868
Reality of psychic phenomena, raps, levitations, etc. 2987
Reality of redemption. 3030
Reality of religion. 1055, 3197, 3202
Reality of the church. 1124
Reality of the devil. 1426
Reality of the Gospel and the unreality of the churches. 1154
Reality of the invisible. 2437
Reality of the religious life. 2476
Reality of the Resurrection. 2053
Reality of the soul. 3463
Reality of things unseen, and other sermons. 1340
Reality or preachment. 1534
Realization. 2784
Realization made easy. 2693
Realization of God in daily living. 1091
Realization of oneness. 2694
... Realization of the self. 3866
Realize what you are. 2379
Realized millennialism. 1527
Realizing Jesus. 161
Realizing religion. 1360
"Really living." 1012
Realm of essence. 2739
Realm of ghosts. 1710
Realm of mind. 2420
Realm of spirit and the realm of Caesar. 3521
Realm of the extra-human. 3091
Realm of the great goddess. 3108
Realms of being. 2739
Realms of our calling. 3784
Reap ten. 3551
Reaper and the harvest. 1783, 3228
Reapers of His harvest. 923
Reaping for Christ. 3341
Reaping the whirlwind. 1819
Reappearance of the Christ. 2067, 3318
Reappraisal. 2515
Reapproaching Paul. 2796
Reason and authority. 118, 911
Reason and authority in religion. 3211
Reason and belief. 1597, 1893, 3211
Reason and compassion. 1536
Reason and faith. 3023
Reason and faith revisited. 1597
Reason and God. 2837, 2838
Reason and goodness. 1534
Reason and hope. 2141
Reason and religion. 3073, 3099, 3108
Reason and revelation. 1483, 2675, 3079
Reason and revelation in the middle ages. 2836, 2842
Reason and revelation on the inspiration of the Sacred Scriptures. 279
Reason and virtue. 2938
Reason enough. 66
Reason, faith and authority in Christianity. 1071, 3652
Reason, faith, and duty. 3726
Reason for hope. 982
Reason for joy. 1751
Reason for living. 979
Reason for our hopes. 63

REASON, HISTORY AND RELIGIOUS BOOKS 1876 - 1982

Reason, history and religion. 1062, 3211
Reason in faith. 1591
Reason in pastoral counseling. 2780
Reason in religion. 1597, 3728
Reason of Christian doctrines. 1093
Reason or revelation? 3024
Reason, religion, kindness. 683, 937
Reason, ridicule, and religion. 1520
Reason, the only oracle of man. 3022
Reason to believe. 67, 3104
Reason to live! A reason to die! 3664
Reason to revelation. 66
Reason, truth and God. 3107
Reason vs. revelation from the fulcrum of the spirit philosophy. 1888, 1907
Reason why. 64, 65, 3514
Reason why; or, Spiritual experiences of Mrs. Julia Crafts Smith, physician, assisted by her spirit guides. 3514
Reason within the bounds of religion. 186
Reasonable apprehensions. 1098
Reasonable belief. 3662
Reasonable Biblical criticism. 230
Reasonable Christ. 1969
Reasonable faith. 57, 1057, 3714
Reasonable religion. 3061, 3570
Reasonable way to study the Bible. 641
Reasonableness of Christian doctrine. 934
Reasonableness of Christianity. 1054, 1095
Reasonableness of Christianity, in four sermons. 1098
Reasonableness of Christianity, with A discourse of miracles, and part of A third letter concerning toleration. 1054
Reasonableness of faith. 61, 694, 2959, 3067
Reasonableness of faith in God. 1719
Reasonableness of nonconformity to the Church of England, in point of worship. 1218
Reasonableness of Scripture-belief (1672) 279
Reasonableness of the Christian faith. 951
Reasonableness of the religion of Jesus. 951
Reasoned faith. 1010
Reasoned prayers for the Lord's own service. 1214
Reasoning, fevelation, and you! 3226
Reasoning, revelation, and you. 3226
Reasons and faiths. 3105
Reasons for acknowledging the authority of the Holy Roman see. 2768
Reasons for becoming a Methodist. 2428
Reasons for being a churchman. 2957, 2964
Reasons for faith. 61, 63
Reasons for faith in Christianity. 1099
Reasons for Jewish customs and traditions. 1614, 2120
Reasons for our faith. 1737, 3383
Reasons for quitting the Methodist society. 173, 1681
Reasons for rejecting the creed, and asking a dismissal from the Shawmut Congregational church, Boston, by two of its members. 1656
Reasons for the higher criticism of the Hexateuch. 531
Reasons for unbelief. 19
Reasons IV, explaining the Reformed perspective. 3680
Reasons of the heart. 1741, 3456
Reasons of the laws of Moses. 1312
Reasons I, sects and cults with non-Christian roots. 1393
Reasons skeptics should consider Christianity. 277, 2711
Reasons III, objections to Christianity. 65
Reasons why I cannot return to the church of Rome. 778
Reassessing. 2390
Reawakening of Christian faith. 1095
Rebecca Nurse. 2718, 3827
Rebel. 1745, 1746
Rebel at heart. 1216
Rebel bishop. 3273, 3777
Rebel Church in Latin America. 821
Rebel from riches. 3234
Rebel king. 397, 1971
Rebel lands. 2667
Rebel nun. 2333, 2717
Rebel, O Jews! 2076
Rebel, priest, and prophet. 2308, 2939
'rebel' priest of the Catholic Traditionalist Movement. 870
Rebel prince. 5
rebel prophet, studies in the personality of Jermiah. 1942
Rebel religion. 3445
Rebel saints. 1677
Rebellion in the wilderness. 516, 2095
Rebellions of Israel. 564, 1376
Rebellious Galilean. 929, 1960
Rebellious prophet. 191
Rebellious prophets. 2672
Rebels and God. 2624, 2804
Rebels and saints. 2950
Rebel's Bible. 2398
Rebels in the church. 1296
Rebels with a cause. 925
Rebirth. 2082, 3027
Rebirth for Christianity. 3686
Rebirth of a nation. 2118
...The rebirth of Christianity. 1057
Rebirth of images. 459
Rebirth of ministry. 1296
Rebirth of Protestantism in Europe. 2457
... The rebirth of religion. 2695
... The rebirth of the German church. 1707
Rebirth of the laity. 2191
Rebirth of the State of Israel. 2119, 2141
Reborn to multiply. 1565
Rebuild my church! 2385
Rebuilding a lost faith. 19
Rebuilding of Jerusalem and the temple. 1587
Rebuilding of psychology. 1107
Rebuilding our world. 3758
Rebuilding Palestine. 2118
Rebuilding Palestine according to prophecy. 2760
Rebuilding revival gates. 1561
Rebuilding St. Paul's after the great fire of London. 2244, 3860
Rebuilding the Christian commonwealth. 31, 1339
Rebuilding the social order. 3450
... Rebuilding with Christ. 2300
Rebuttal of spiritism et al. 3504
Rebuttal to "The problems of the Book of Mormon," 678
Recall to life—the Jewish woman in America. 3842
Recalling the Scottish covenants. 1376
Recapturing Wisdom's Valley. 3399
Receding horizons. 2550
Received ye the Holy Ghost? 1828
Receivership for civilization. 3074
Receiving God's fullness. 3349
Receiving the five- year-old. 3174
Receiving the Holy Spirit. 1833
Receiving the Holy Spirit today. 331, 1833
Receiving the nursery child. 3174
Receiving the spirit at Old First Church. 2815, 3252
Receiving the Word of God. 278
Recent American synagogue architecture. 3577
Recent apparitions of Our Lady. 2357
Recent apparitions of the blessed Virgin Mary. 2357
Recent Christian progress. 1182
Recent church documents from Latin America. 862
Recent development of religious education in the Methodist Episcopal church, South. 2456
Recent developments in Roman Catholic thought. 861
Recent developments in the textual criticism of the Greek Bible. 284
Recent explorations in the Holy Land and Kadesh-Barnes, the "lost oasis" of the Sinaitic peninsula. 2760
Recent homiletical thought. 2908
Recent inquiries in theology. 3621, 3624
Recent movement toward Christian unity. 1042, 3211
Recent psychology and the Christian religion. 2993
Recent Reform responsa. 3219
Recent revelation. 3750
Recent sermons. 3345
Recent studies in philosophy and theology. 2335
Reception of Calvinistic thought in England. 730
Reception of Holy Communion in the hand. 2254
Recipes for living. 2217, 2391
Recipient of first Holy Communion; a historical synopsis and commentary. 1626
Recitation of Ifa, oracle of the Yoruba. 1882
Recitation poems. 3026
Recitations, song and story for Sunday and day schools, primary and intermediate departments. 3310
Recited Koran. 2185
Reckoning that counts. 988
Reckoning with the eternals. 3211
Reclaim those unitarian wastes. 3724
Reclaiming. 1577
Reclaiming Christian education. 935
Reclaiming the Old Testament for the Christian pulpit. 537, 2931, 3352
Recognition in heaven. 1796
Recognition of friends in another world. 1695
Recognition of guilt. 2784
Recognition of our friends in heaven. 3197
Recognition of the supernatural in letters and in life: an oration. 3609
Recollection. 2396
Recollection the soul of action. 3028
Recollections. 3199
Recollections and impressions. 3199
Recollections and observations during a ministry in the North Carolina conference. 2446
Recollections and reflections. 3199, 3202
Recollections and reflections of an old itinerant. 2422
Recollections and reflections of Seth R. Brooks and Corinne H. Brooks. 694, 3755
Recollections of a life. 3125
Recollections of a long life. 146, 2072, 2756
Recollections of a superannuate. 2427
Recollections of an itinerant life. 3134
Recollections of Arthur Penrhyn Stanley. 3525
Recollections of Bishop Edward Rondthaler (1842-1931) a distinguished leader of the Moravian Church. 3247
Recollections of Dean Fremantle. 3127
Recollections of fifty years in the ministry. 3134
Recollections of Henry Moorhouse, evangelist. 2589
Recollections of itinerant life. 2427
Recollections of Jotham Anderson. 978
Recollections of Mary Baker Eddy. 1033, 1494
Recollections of men of faith. 1462
Recollections of Nettleton. 2685, 3233
Recollections of Oberammergau. 2719
Recolleciations of past life. 1617
Recollections of Rev. E. D. Griffin. 1775
Recollections of Rev. Samuel Clawson. 1287
Recollections of Robert Houdin, clockmaker, electrician, conjuror. 1345, 3240
Recollections of seventy years. 14, 3132
Recollections of the diocese of Southern Ohio. 2974
Recollections of the last four popes and of Rome in their times. 2851
Recollections of the life of the priest Don Antonio Jose Martinez. 1294, 2349
Recollections of William Theophilus. 3682
Recommended reference books and commentaries for a minister's library. 212
Reconceptions in Christian thinking, 1817-1967. 3656
Reconciled with God. 3485
Reconciliation. 107, 376, 1940, 2480, 3028
Reconciliation and conflict. 1139
Reconciliation and hope. 335, 2347
Reconciliation and liberation. 3290
Reconciliation and renewal in Japan. 1935
Reconciliation and the new age. 3028
Reconciliation in Christ. 106
Reconciliation in the Church. 2811
Reconciliation in today's world. 3028
Reconciliation primer. 3028
Reconciling. 1633
Reconciling Christ. 2212
Reconciling community. 1244
Reconciling gospel. 106
Reconcilliation in Christ. 106
Reconsiderations; Roman Catholic/Presbyterian and Reformed theological conversations, 1966-67. 3706
Reconstruciton of the American church. 1243
Reconstructing Jewish education. 2106
Reconstructing the church, an examination of the problems of the times from the standpoint of a layman of the church. 1243
Reconstruction and the renewal of life. 3068
Reconstruction in religion. 3142
Reconstruction in theology. 1050
Reconstruction messages. 1543
Reconstruction of belief. 1098
Reconstruction of belief: Belief in God. 63
Reconstruction of Biblical theories. 502
Reconstruction of Bridlington Priory. 692
Reconstruction of morality. 2280
Reconstruction of religion. 3442
Reconstruction of religious belief. 3102
Reconstruction of religious thought in Islam. 2565
Reconstruction of the American church. 1040
Reconstruction of the church. 1244
Reconstruction of the Church—on what pattern? 1243
Reconstruction of the English church. 1221
Reconstruction of the Old-Latin text or texts of the Gospels used by Saint Augustine. 398
Reconstruction of the Old-Latin text or texts of the Gspels used by Saint Augustine. 425
Reconstruction of the Republic. 1108
Reconstruction of the spiritual ideal. 3476
Reconstruction of theology. 1461
Reconstruction virtues. 3338
Record. 2733
Record and revelation. 501
Record of a mystic. 3503
Record of a Quaker conscience. 2463
Record of a school. 23, 2591
Record of Buddhistic kingdoms. 91
Record of Christ's life and doctrine. 440
Record of faith. 1062
Record of Graham's church. 1379
Record of marriages and baptisms. 6
Record of Poole Church of Christ. 2859, 3052
Record of proceedings: Oct. 8-13, 1962. 3203
Record of revelation. 310
Record of the celebration of the two hundredth anniversary of the founding of the American philosophical society. 2833
Record of the Church congress in the United States. 2963
Record of the fulfillment. 409
Record of the life and work of the Rev. Stephen Higginson Tyng. 3719
Record of the National Council of Churches. 2670
Record of the proceedings of the Court of bishops, assembled for the trial of the Rt. Rev. George Washington Doane ... bishop of New Jersey, upon a presentment made by the Rt. Rev. William Meade ... the Rt. Rev. Charles Pettit McIlvaine ... and the Rt. Rev. George Burgess. 2957
Record of the promise. 539
Record of the spirit. 2693
Record of the sufferings of Quakers in Cornwall. 1683
Record of twenty-five years of the pastorate of Maitland Alexander. 24, 2850
Record St. John's Reformed church, Sinking Spring, Pennsylvania. 3415
Record St. John's Reformed church, Sinking Spring, Pennsylvania, 1883-1913. 3415
Recorded sayings of Layman P'ang. 3893
Recorded words of Jesus. 2070
Records and letters of the apostolic age. 406
Records of a good man's life. 3136
Records of an active life. 3126
Records of Bethel Baptist Church, Washington County, Kentucky, 1817-1875. 195
Records of Christianity. 1198
Records of Jesus reviewed. 1978
Records of St. Paul's Church, Eastchester. 1485
Records of Salem witchcraft, copied from the original documents. 3828
Records of the Congregational church, Franklin, Connecticut, 1718-1860, and a record of deaths in Norwich eighth society, 1763, 1778, 1782, 1784-1802. 3051
Records of the earliest Jewish community in th New World. 3027
Records of the English Bible. 248
Records of the English Catholic of 1715. 816
Records of the General association of y colony of Connecticut. 1336
Records of the life of Jesus. 394
Records of the Moravian Church at Oldman's Creek, Gloucester County, New Jersey. 3051
Records of the Moravians in North Carolina. 2595
Records of the Presbyterian church in Dearbornville, M. T. 2918
Records of the Presbyterian Church in the United States of America, 1706-1788. 2925
Records of the reformation. 1804, 3039
Records of the services connected with the twenty-fifth anniversary of the organization of the Fort street Presbyterian church, Detroit, Mich. 2918
Records of the Swedish Lutheran churches at Raccoon and Penns Neck, 1713-1786. 3572
Recoveries in religion. 1063
Recovering Biblical sensuousness. 1512

Recovery. 696, 1598
Recovery & restatement of the gospel. 3646
Recovery of belief. 1104
Recovery of Christian myth. 3070
Recovery of confidence. 291
Recovery of faith. 3063
Recovery of humanity. 2934
Recovery of ideals. 3100
Recovery of life's meaning. 1060
Recovery of man. 2322
Recovery of ministry. 2786
Recovery of preaching. 2908
Recovery of purpose. 3593
Recovery of religion. 3057
Recovery of spirit in higher education. 3759
Recovery of the Anabaptist vision. 37, 187
Recovery of the historical Paul. 372
Recovery of the Holy Land. 1390
Recovery of the sacred. 2235
Recovery of the teaching ministry. 1288
Recovery of unity. 1041
Recovery of worship. 3003
Recovery starts within. 1212
Recreation and the church. 1251
Recreation and the local church. 3028
Recreation for churches. 3028
Recreation in church and community. 2854
... Recreational leadership for church and community. 1167
... Recreational leadership of boys. 687
Recreational materials and methods. 1166
Recreational plans for missionary volunteers. 1167
Recreations in ancient fields. 1817
Recreations of a country parson. 3124
Recruiting for Christ. 1289, 1571
Rectitude. 2396
Rector of Hazlehurst. 3127
Rector's offering. 2972
Rector's scrapbook. 3129
Rectory family. 3125
Recurrent education. 1356
Recurring earth-lives, how and why. 3054
Recurring pattern. 2144
Recusant books in America. 1518
Recycle catalogue II. 3679
Red and the black. 1320, 1542
Red antway of the Navaho. 2678
Red book of the persecuted church. 2820
Red China prisoner. 2485
Red Cross saint. 731
Red hat. 2703
Red-headed, rash, and religious. 2552
Red Judas. 801
Red lacquered gate. 1701, 2507
Red letter days. 1263
... The red letter Holy Bible. 259
... The red letter New Testament of Our Lord and Saviour Jesus Christ. 320
Red Lily, St. Maria Gorett. 2333
Red man's religion. 1902
Red Moon. 892, 2178
Red poncho and big boots. 1458, 2504
Red star over Cuba. 2821
Red swan. 1904
Red tree: insight into lost continents, Mu and Atlantis. 2725
Red triangle in the changing nations. 3872
... Red Wing churches during the war. 3029
Redaction of the Babylonian Talmud. 3582
Redactional style in the Marcan Gospel. 437
Redating the New Testament. 212
Redeem the time. 3261
Redeemed life after death. 1695
Redeemed men redeeming society. 2377
Redeemed? Say so! 3829
Redeemer. 1970, 2036, 2044, 2212, 3030
Redeemer: a sketch of the history of redemption. 3030
Redeemer and redeemed. 103
Redeemers, a saga of the years 1945-1952. 2100
Redeemer's return. 2849
Redeemer's tears wept over lost souls. 3028
Redeeming Christ. 2030
Redeeming grace. 1751
Redeeming love. 2213
Redeeming sacrifice. 2367
Redeeming the time. 1154, 2212
Redemption. 1082, 2105, 3029, 3030
Redemption, accomplished and applied. 3029
Redemption and revelation in the actuality of history. 3030
Redemption and the new birth. 3029
Redemption by the blood of Christ. 3029
Redemption completed. 1850, 3029
... Redemption, Hindu and Christian. 1082
Redemption in Black theology. 16

Redemption of Africa. 2497
Redemption of God. 3670
Redemption of Paul Rader. 3017
Redemption of religion. 3029
Redemption of sinners by the free grace of God. 3029
Redemption of the city. 3434
Redemption of the prayer-meeting. 2886
Redemption through the blood of Jesus. 3029
Redemption truths. 3287
Redemptive counseling. 2781
Redemptive incarnation. 1893
Redemptorist centenaries. 3031
Redemptorist on the American missions. 3031
Redemptorists in the West. 3031
Rediscovering Jesus. 2038
Rediscovering Judaism. 2143
Rediscovering pastoral care. 2785
Rediscovering prayer. 2869, 2882
Rediscovering ritual. 2237
Rediscovering the angels. 1115, 3686
Rediscovering the Bible. 229
Rediscovering the Book of Revelation. 455
Rediscovering the Christ. 2046
Rediscovering the church. 1119
Rediscovering the gift of healing. 1598
Rediscovering the natural in Protestant theology. 2325
Rediscovering the parables. 2025
Rediscovering the teaching of Jesus. 2065
Rediscovering the teaching of the evangelists. 393
Rediscovering the traditions of Israel. 505
Rediscovering the words of faith. 3682
Rediscovery of Apocalyptic. 56
Rediscovery of Christ. 2024
Rediscovery of inner experience. 1585
Rediscovery of Jesus. 2046
Rediscovery of John Wesley. 729, 3802
Rediscovery of Judaism. 860, 2152
Rediscovery of the Bible. 235
Rediscovery of the Nauvoo Temple. 2676
Re-discovery of the Old Testament. 502
Redundant churches in Essex. 1159
Reed and the rock, portrait of Simon Brute. 698
Reed of God. 2361
Reef. 1013
Re-entry. 3321
Reexamination of Lutheran and Reformed traditions. 2285
Reference and essence. 3010, 3032
Reference guide to Milton, from 1800 to the present day. 2469
... A reference library for community training schools. 3203
Reference passage Bible New Testament. 352
Reference works for theological research. 3032
... References for students. 2636
Referral in pastoral counseling. 2781
Refiner's fire. 2617
Refiner's fire, and other sermons. 2935
Reflected glory. 1832
Reflected light. 926
Reflected lights from paradise. 1351
Reflected lights from "The face of the deep;" 1441
Reflecting pond. 2385
Reflection and doubt in the thought of Paul Tillich. 3700
Reflection of theology in literature. 1077
Reflection on the works of God in nature and providence. 1285
Reflections. 1012, 1911, 2394, 2395, 2397
Reflections based on the Bible, 'Fenelon [and] a Statement of Christian faith. 241, 1621
Reflections for every day in the year, on the works of God. 1442
Reflections for every day of the month. 856
Reflections for renewal. 2570
Reflections for the modern Jew. 1811
Reflections from a small chalet. 2385
Reflections from an inner eye. 2395
Reflections from the light of Christ. 1676, 3491
Reflections of a wondering Jew. 2082
Reflections of love. 3208
Reflections of mind. 710
Reflections of the self. 3491
Reflections on a Christian community. 1245
Reflections on death. 1413
Reflections on every day of the week. 1453
Reflections on God and self. 3489
Reflections on growing old. 18
Reflections on Indian art. 86
Reflections on Mormonism. 239, 2610
Reflections on Paul according to the Acts in the New Testament. 2797, 3075

Reflections on revival. 3229
Reflections on the great truths of religion for each school day of the month. 695
Reflections on the light of God. 9, 422
Reflections on the Litany. 1214
Reflections on the nature of the world and man, life's values and its destiny. 2844
Reflections on the Passion. 2211
Reflections on the path. 877, 2991
Reflections on the Psalms. 578
Reflections on the rosary for Martha sisters. 3248
Reflections on the rosary for nursing sisters. 3248
Reflections on the rosary for teaching sisters. 3248
Reflections on the stage. 1309, 3606
Reflections on the study of religion. 2206, 3111
Reflections on the synoptic gospels. 3578
Reflections on the works of God in nature and providence. 1442
Reflections ... path to prayer. 2397
Reflections upon some prominent religious doctrines. 3650
Reflective faith. 2832
Reflective theology. 3103
Reflexions sur les messes dominicales. 3376
Reform and rejoice. 9
Reform and renewal. 3033, 3732
Reform in Leopold's Congo. 2536, 2926
Reform Jewish practice and its rabbinic background. 2117, 3032
Reform Judaism in the large cities. 2105
Reform Judaism in the making. 3032
Reform Judaism prior to Abraham Geiger. 2117
Reform Judaism then and now. 3032
Reform Judaism today. 879, 3032
Reform Judciism. 3032
Reform movement in Judaism. 2116, 3032
Reform movements in Judaism. 2147

Reform of liturgical worship. 2234
Reform of the church. 1243, 3038
Reform philosophy to the mind of Christ. 1953, 2836
Reform, rebellion, and the heavenly way. 916, 2185
Reform responsa. 3219
Reform responsa for our time. 3219
Reform thought in sixteenth-century Italy. 3041
Reformatio perennis. 728, 3037
Reformation. 800, 3033, 3034, 3035, 3036, 3037, 3041
Reformation and Catholicity. 2009, 3033
Reformation and its significance today. 3035
Reformation and politics. 3033
Reformation and Protestantism today. 2977
Reformation and resistance in Tudor Lancashire. 3039
Reformation and society in sixteenth-century Europe. 3033
... The reformation and the Irish episcopate. 3041
Reformation and the people. 3039
Reformation and the reformers. 3033
Reformation; basic interpretations. 3037
Reformation Bible pictures. 450
Reformation Bibles in the crossfire. 479, 1512
Reformation, Catholicism and freedom. 3041
Reformation crisis. 3036
Reformation crossroads. 2281, 2309
Reformation dawn. 3035
Reformation debate. 3042
Reformation era, 1500-1650. 3034
Reformation 14th-16th century. 3034
Reformation in Dublin, 1536-1558. 3041
Reformation in England. 1763, 3038, 3039
Reformation in England, to the accession of Elizabeth I. 3039
Reformation in Essex. 3039
Reformation in Europe. 3033
Reformation in Germany. 3040
Reformation in Ireland. 3041
Reformation in Ireland under Elizabeth, 1558-1580. 3041
Reformation in its literature. 3036
Reformation in medieval perspective. 3037
Reformation in northern England. 3038
Reformation in Poland. 3041
Reformation in principle and action. 3041
Reformation in the cities. 3040
Reformation—Luther, the Anabaptists. 3042
Reformation of images. 1880
Reformation of our worship. 3854

Reformation of the 16th century in its relations to modern thought and knowledge. 3033
Reformation of the Church of England. 3041
Reformation of the churches. 2561
Reformation of the holy. 3086
Reformation of the nineteenth century. 1460
Reformation of the sixteenth century. 3033, 3035
Reformation of the 16th century in its relation to modern thought and knowledge. 3033
Reformation or revolution. 1076
Reformation paradox. 425, 1512
Reformation settlement examined in the light of history and law. 1218
Reformation studies. 130, 3036
... The reformation, the mass and the priesthood. 44
Reformation ... then and now. 3033
Reformation views of church history. 1184
Reformation writings. 3034
Reformed America. 2937, 3050
Reformed bishops and catholic elders. 1241
...The reformed breviary of Cardinal Tommasi. 842
Reformed church in America. 3046
Reformed Church in New Jersey [1660-1969]. 3047
Reformed church pulpit. 3049, 3366
Reformed Church roots. 3045
Reformed confessions of the 16th century. 3043
Reformed doctrine of justification. 2160
Reformed doctrine of predestination. 2911
Reformed dogmatics. 3637, 3640, 3644, 3653
Reformed Judaism and its pioneers. 2116
Reformed Mennonite church. 3050
Reformed pastor. 178, 1297, 2790, 3670
Reformed reformation. 3034
Reformed roots of the English New Testament. 196, 355
Reformed society of Israelites, Charleston, S.C. 3050
Reformed society of Israelites of Charleston, S.C. 3050
Reformer. 739
Reformer reformed. 133, 2688, 3818
Reformer without a church. 2631
Reformers and Babylon. 1515
Reformers and their stepchildren. 3036
Reformers before the Reformation. 928, 1857
Reformers in India. 2531
Reformers in India, 1793-1833. 2531
Reformers in profile. 3037
Reformers in the wings. 3037
Reformers of Egypt. 21, 2635
Reforming the rites of death. 1694
Refuge. 962, 973
Refugees. 1941
Refutation of Arianism. 80
Refutation of the doctrine of uninterrupted apostolic succession, with a correction of errors concerning Rev. John Wesley and Dr. Coke. 76, 886
Refutation of the sophisms, gross misrepresentations, and erroneous quotations contained in "An American's" "Letter to the Edinburgh reviewers" 3424
Regalian right in medieval England. 2794
Regarding religious education. 934
... Regathered Israel. 45
Regeneration. 3050, 3051, 3292
Regeneration and conversion. 3051
Regeneration and reconstruction. 3050
Regeneration and the superman. 3750
Regeneration applied. 3050
Regeneration of David Bancroft. 3050
Regeneration of infants, and the salvation of children. 1907
... Regensburg and Augsburg. 2102
Regilious question in Spain. 2955
Reginal Pole, Cardinal of England. 2857
Regional conferences in Latin America. 2548
Regional cults. 1393
Register. 2080
... Register of doctoral dissertations accepted in partial fulfillment of the requirements for the degree of doctor of philosophy. 1311
Register of Eudes of Rouen. 1638
Register of grand lodges active and extinct. 1664
Register of Henry Chichele, archbishop of Canterbury 1414- 1443. 1221
Register of Henry Chichele, archibishop of Canterbury, 1414- 1443. 1762
Register of L.D.S. Church records. 2616

REGISTER OF MIDDLE RELIGIOUS BOOKS 1876 - 1982

Register of Middle English religious & didactic verse. 1519, 3210
Register of Old Concord Presbyterian Church, Appomattox County, Virginia - 1826-1878. 77, 2736
Register of the Company of Pastors of Geneva in the time of Calvin. 3042
Register of Thomas Langley. 1761
Register of Thomas Rotherham, Archbishop of York, 1480-1500. 3868
Register of Walter Reynolds, bishop of Worcester. 3783
Registers of Cuthbert Tunstall. 1762
Registers of the births, marriages, and deaths, of the "Eglise francoise a la Nouvelle York," 3051
Registers of the parish church of Prestwich. 3052
Registra Stephani Gardiner et Johannie Poynet, episcoporum wintoniensium. 1221
Registrum sacrum Anglicanum. 1213
Registrum Simonis de Gandavo, diocesis saresbiriensis A.D. 1297-1315. Transcribed and edited. 1763
Registrum Simonis Langham. 1763
Registrum Simonis Langham cantuariensis archiepiscopi. 1762
Registrum Thome Bourgcher, Cantuariensis archiepiscopi. 1762
Registrum Thome Bourgchier Cantuariensis Archiepiscopi A.D. 1454-1486. 1763
Registrum Thome Wolsey cardinalis ecclesie wintoniensis administratoris. 1763
Regnum Dei. 2175
Regnum montis. 3319
Regnum montis and its contemporary. 3319
Regular singing defended. 1202
Rehabilitation of Eve. 2226
Rehearsal for destruction. 54, 2100
Reign of Antichrist. 51
Reign of Christ. 1952, 2464
Reign of God, not "The reign of law" 80
Reign of grace. 1750
Reign of grace from its rise to its consummation. 1750
Reign of law. 3074
Reign of the Stoics. 3533
Reigning with Christ. 964
... Reincarnation. 3052, 3053, 3054, 3055
Reincarnation, a hope of the world. 3053
Reincarnation and Christianity. 1088
Reincarnation and immortality. 51, 3054
Reincarnation and karma. 3053, 3688
Reincarnation, and other lectures. 3054
Reincarnation and prayers to live by. 3053
Reincarnation and the law of karma. 3052
Reincarnation as a Christian hope. 1088
Reincarnation, fact or fallacy? 3685
Reincarnation for the Christian. 3053
Reincarnation for the millions. 3054
Reincarnation, illusion or reality? 1088
Reincarnation in Christianity. 1088
Reincarnation in the New Testament. 3054
Reincarnation in the twentieth century. 3055
Reincarnation in world thought. 3053
Reincarnation, key to immortality. 3054
Reincarnation of John Wilkes Booth. 681, 3055
Reincarnation or immortality? 3053
Reincarnation primer. 3053
Reincarnation, the hope of the world. 3053
Reincarnation, the phoenix fire mystery. 3055
Reincarnation through the zodiac. 3897
Reincarnation, your denied birthright. 3055
Reinhold Niebuhr. 1088, 2709
Reinhold Niebuhr: a prophetic voice in our time. 2709
Reinhold Niebuhr: his religious, social, and political thought. 2709
Reinhold Niebuhr, prophet to politicians. 1087, 2709
Reinhold Niebuhr's works. 2709
El Reino de Dios y America Latina. 2176
Reinterpretation in American church history. 3739
Reinterpretation of Luther. 2281
Reiondre to M. Iewels replie, 1566. 2368
Rejected crown. 2005
Rejected King and hymns of Jesus; a book for devotion. 1868
Rejected of men. 2214
Rejection of consequentialism. 1348
Rejoice! 399
Rejoice always. 1785
Rejoice in the Lord. 1016, 2307
Rejoice. O Youth. 2081
Rejoice, you're a Sunday school teacher! 3550
Rejoicing on great days. 2721
Rejuvenated Christian. 1557
... Relation. 3224
Relation between religion and science. 3074
Relation between science and theology. 3078
Relation between the Holy Scriptures and some parts of geological science. 203
Relation of baptism to the remission of alien sins. 134
Relation of baptized children to the church. 1905
... The relation of Christianity to civil society. 3443
Relation of divine providence to physical laws. 2980
Relation of religion to civil government in the United States of America. 1150
Relation of St. Paul to contemporary Jewish thought. 1084, 2802
Relation of the American Board of Commissioners for Foreign Missions to slavery. 31, 3423
Relation of the conference between William Laud, late lord archbishop of Canterbury and Mr. Fisher the Jesuit. 1218
Relation of the death of ... Troilo Savelli. 1021, 3305
Relation of the fearful estate of Francis Spira. 3472
Relation of the fearful state of Francis Spira. 3472
Relation of the masonic orders of Christian knight-hood and the Royal arch to the degree of master mason. 1662
Relation of the sexes. 3392
... The relation of the sacramental characters of baptism and confirmation to the lay apostolate. 2191
... The relation of the state to religious education. 300
... The relation of the state to religious education in early New York, 1633-1825. 3167
Relation of the state to religious education in Massachusetts. 3166
Relation which must exist between Christ manifested in spiritual life and the souls of his worshippers in their existence wholly spiritual. 3480
Relational revolution. 1011
Relational self. 15
Relations between church and state in the city and canton of Geneva. 1145
Relations between Northern and Southern Baptists. 30, 171
Relations between religion and science. 3076
Relations of faith and life. 963
Relations of religious training and life patterns to the adult religious life. 3001
Relations of science and religion. 3074
Relations of the church to the colored race. 2682
Relationship of baptism to church membership. 138
Relationship of "Mormonism" and freemasonry. 2603
Relationship of the Amish to the public schools in Ohio. 35
Relationships among the gospels. 393
Relationships; self, family, God. 1009
Relative position in our system foriegn commerce. 1312
Relatives of Leila Ada. 2208
Relativism, cognitive and moral. 3055
Relativism in contemporary Christian ethics. 1534
Relativity of death. 1890
Relax and let God. 993
Relax and rejoice, for the hand on the tiller is firm. 1246
Release. 974, 1358
Release for trapped Christians. 2882
Release from guilt and fear. 1777
Release from phoniness. 1007
Release of the soul. 3461
Release the sun. 25, 122
Released and radiant. 3492
Releasing the power within. 2390
Relevance and ethics in geography. 1705
Relevance of apocalyptic. 56
Relevance of natural science to theology. 3081
Relevance of preaching. 2903
Relevance of the Bible. 236
Relevance of the New Testament. 335, 350
Relevance of the Old Testament for the christian faith. 599
Relevance of the prophets. 569, 2951
Relevance; the role of Christianity in the twentieth century. 1058
Relevant church. 1279
Relevant liturgy. 3854
Relevant record. 313
Relevant salvation. 168
Relics of ancient exegesis. 483
Relics of Saint Cuthbert. 1397
Relief and reconstruction. 1678
Relief society memories. 2618
Relief worker's notebook. 2405
Religious persecution in El Salvador. 3194
Religio doctoris. 2228
Religio grammatici. 2231
Religio-medical masquerade. 1035
Religio medici. 696, 3057
Religio pictoris. 84
Religio-political physics. 1653
Religio religiosi. 2570
Religion. 68, 803, 804, 1150, 1940, 2844, 3000, 3056, 3058, 3062, 3064, 3065, 3090, 3111, 3112, 3138, 3745
Religion: a dialogue. 3068
Religion a factor in building Texas. 3604
Religion, a humanistic field. 3111, 3112
Religion, a primitive fable. 1092
Religion, a psychological interpretation. 3000
Religion a rational demand. 3061
...Religion, a secondary school course. 804, 3186
Religion: a sociological view. 3086
Religion across cultures. 1317
Religion after forty. 2462
Religion against itself. 1060
Religion, agnosticism and education. 3064, 3624
Religion, altered states of consciousness, and social change. 2996
Religion American style. 3748
Religion among the primitives. 3086
Religion among the Unitarian Universalists. 3727
Religion; an anthropological view. 3064
Religion and public education. 1129
Religion and aging. 18
Religion and alienation. 3440
Religion and American constitutions. 3195
Religion and American democracy. 670, 3745
Religion and American society. 3057, 3743, 3745
Religion and American youth, with emphasis on Catholic adolescents and young adults. 3890
Religion and art. 3064
Religion and art in ancient Greece. 1766
Religion & art in Ashanti. 90
Religion and atheism. 100
Religion and atheism in the U.S.S.R. and Eastern Europe. 1320
Religion and bereavement. 1353
Religion & biology. 1581
Religion and brotherhood of man. 3142
Religion and business. 3440
Religion and capitalism: allies, not enemies. 3069
Religion and career. 874
Religion and change. 3058
Religion and change in contemporary Asia. 91
Religion and chemistry. 3075
Religion and civilization in West Africa. 2500
Religion and common sense. 791, 1102, 1784
Religion and communism. 3257
Religion and conduct. 3057
Religion and conscience in ancient Egypt. 1502
Religion and contemporary life. 1063
... Religion and contemporary psychology. 2999
Religion & contemporary society. 3087
Religion and contemporary Western culture. 1075
Religion and culture. 2324, 3058, 3108, 3110, 3622, 3700
Religion and culture of Israel. 533, 2148
Religion and culture of north-eastern India. 1897
Religion and culture of the Jains. 1932, 2317
Religion and Dharma. 2712
Religion and doubt. 3058
Religion and drink. 3597
Religion and economic action. 1076
Religion and economic responsibility. 1075
Religion and education. 1130
Religion and education in America. 1130
Religion and education under the Constitution. 3190
Religion and empire. 2485, 2505
Religion and empiricism. 3105
Religion and eternal life. 3063
Religion and ethics. 947
Religion and everyday life. 1445
Religion and evolution since 1859. 3076
Religion and faith in Latin America. 3470
Religion and fertility. 1622
Religion & folklore of northern India. 1895
Religion and free will. 3859
Religion and freedom in the modern world. 1086
Religion & freedom of thought. 3193
Religion and healing in Mandari. 2327
Religion and health. 2378, 3057, 3064
Religion and historic faiths. 3119
Religion and history. 3451
Religion and human experience. 2999
Religion and humanity. 2139
Religion and immortality. 1887
Religion and its social setting. 2116
Religion and judgment. 3097
Religion and leadership. 805
Religion and learning. 2917
Religion and legitimation of power in Sri Lanka. 708
Religion and legitimation of power in Thailand, Laos, and Burma. 709
Religion and liberty. 3605
Religion and life. 973, 1340, 2693, 3059, 3065, 3068, 3489
Religion and life in the early Victorian age. 1516
Religion and life; the foundations of personal religion. 973
Religion and literature. 3071
Religion and lust. 3390
Religion and man. 3063
Religion and medicine. 1601, 2378, 2410
Religion and medicine in the church. 2378
Religion and medicine of the Ga people. 1699
Religion and mental health. 2784
Religion and mental science. 2695
Religion and miracle. 2476
Religion and misfortune. 3896
Religion and modern life. 3067
Religion and modern life, lectures given for the Phillips Brooks house association, Harvard university. 3063
Religion and modern literature. 3071
Religion and modern man. 3061
Religion and modernization in the Soviet Union. 3257
Religion and morality. 1656, 3059
Religion and morality; a collection of essays. 3090
Religion and myth. 12
Religion and mythology of the Greeks. 3059
Religion and nationalism in Southeast Asia. 2671
Religion and nationalism in Southeast Asia: Burma, Indonesia, the Philippines. 2671
Religion and natural law. 1853
Religion and our divided denominations. 3323
Religion and pain. 2378
Religion and peace. 2808
Religion and personality. 3001
Religion and personality problems. 2999
Religion and philosophy. 2835
Religion and philosophy in contemporary Japan. 1936
Religion and philosophy of the Veda and Upanishads. 2839, 3776
Religion and philosophy United. 2690, 3569
Religion and politcs in mid-eighteenth century Anglesey. 43
Religion and political culture in Kano. 1923
Religion and political development, an analytic study. 3072
Religion and political society. 1088
Religion and politics. 668, 1087, 1140, 3711
Religion and politics in America. 1151
Religion and politics in Burma. 704
Religion and politics in contemporary Iran. 1923
Religion and politics in Haiti. 1780
Religion and politics in Latin America. 835, 3777
Religion and politics in Pakistan. 3088
Religion and politics in Sri Lanka. 708
Religion and politics in the Middle East. 1923
Religion and progress. 3076
Religion and progress in modern Asia. 91
Religion and psychology. 1107
Religion and public affairs. 2306, 3448
Religion and public doctrine in modern England. 3452
... Religion and public education. 1129, 1130, 3096, 3189
Religion and public higher education. 3757
Religion and race-regeneration. 2863
Religion and rationality. 3104
Religion and reality. 3064
Religion and regime. 3036
Religion and relations. 3102

Religion and resistance to Nazism. 1145
Religion and respectability. 3560
Religion and revelation. 3225
... Religion and revolution. 1182, 3072
Religion and revolution in Peru, 1824-1976. 824, 2823
Religion and ritual in Chinese society. 914
Religion and ritual in society. 2572
Religion and rural society. 3452
Religion and schooling. 1128
Religion and science. 3073, 3074, 3076, 3080
Religion and science as allies. 3074
Religion and science from Galileo to Bergson. 3073
Religion and science in their relation to philosophy. 3073
Religion and self-acceptance. 3100
Religion & sex. 3389
Religion and sexism; images of woman in the Jewish and Christian traditions. 3836
Religion & sexuality. 3391
Religion and social change. 1134
Religion and social class. 3453
Religion and social conflict. 1086
Religion and social conflict in South Asia. 3464
Religion and social justice. 3442
Religion and social organization in central Polynesia. 2859
Religion and social sciences: 1973. 3067
Religion and society. 1134, 3086
Religion and society among the Coorgs of South India. 1368
Religion and society in England, 1790-1850. 1765
Religion and society in industrial England. 1516, 1765
Religion and society in interaction. 3086
Religion and society in modern Japan: continuity and change. 1936
Religion and society in tension. 3086
Religion and society in the age of Saint Augustine. 116, 3088
Religion and society of north-east India. 1895
Religion and state in Iran, 1785-1906. 1918
Religion and study of man. 3086
Religion and technology. 3592
Religion and temperament. 3064
Religion and the American dream. 3748
Religion and the American mind, from the Great Awakening to the Revolution. 3214
Religion and the American people. 3746
Religion and the American revolution. 3749
Religion and the American Revolution in North Carolina. 2713
Religion and the Bible. 1654
Religion and the challenge of philosophy. 3097
Religion and the Christian faith. 3061
Religion and the church tomorrow. 1065
Religion and the commonweal. 3058
Religion and the Constitution. 3195
Religion and the culture of Israel. 533, 2150
Religion and the decline of capitalism. 1075
Religion and the decline of magic. 1764
Religion and the face of America. 3743
Religion and the future life. 1697
... Religion and the good life. 3057
Religion and the good society. 3443
Religion and the growing mind. 3001, 3056
Religion and the higher life. 3758
Religion and the human image. 3063
Religion and the intellectuals. 3056
Religion and the issues of life. 1105
Religion and the knowledge of God. 1740
Religion and the law. 1150, 3071
Religion and the law of church and state and the Supreme Court. 1150
Religion and the life of man. 3067
Religion and the mind. 3059
Religion and the mind of today. 3061
Religion and the modern mind. 3057, 3058, 3064, 3105
Religion and the modern mind, and other essays in modernism. 1057
... Religion and the modern world. 3063, 3618
Religion and the moral life. 3100
Religion and the mysterious. 3566
Religion and the natural world. 3084
Religion and the new majority: Billy Graham, Middle America, and the politics of the 70s. 1755, 3747
Religion and the new psychology. 2845, 3064
Religion and the New Testament. 348
Religion and the next generation. 2996
Religion and the One. 2737

Religion and the people, 1000-1700. 1543
Religion and the present crisis. 1281, 3738
Religion and the presidency. 2937
Religion and the psychology of Jung. 2159, 2998, 3063
Religion and the public order. 1152
Religion and the public order, 1965. 1152
Religion and the public schools. 3096, 3147
Religion and the pursuit of truth. 2610
Religion and the reign of science. 3077
Religion and the rise of capitalism. 3112, 3213
Religion and the rise of modern science. 3084
Religion and the rise of scepticism. 3422
Religion and the rise of the American city. 1280
Religion and the rise of Western culture. 1281, 1282
Religion and the school. 3160
Religion and the schools. 1129, 3096
Religion and the scientific future. 3082
Religion and the search for new ideals in the USSR. 3257
Religion and the solid South. 3468
Religion and the Soviet State. 3257
Religion and the state. 1141, 1150, 1151, 3190
Religion and the state in Georgia in the eighteenth century. 1145, 3064
Religion and the State university. 3757
Religion and the study of man. 3086
Religion and the thought of to-day. 3111
Religion and the transformation of society. 12
Religion and the unconscious. 3000
Religion and the university. 1128
Religion and theology. 3627, 3680
Religion and trade in New Netherland. 2700
Religion and truth. 2181
Religion and understanding. 3107
Religion and violence. 3780
... Religion and war. 3792
Religion and world history. 3114
Religion and worship of the Synagogue. 2115
Religion as a personal experience. 1585
Religion as affected by modern materialism. 3076
Religion as an occupation. 3785
Religion as an urban institution. 1279
Religion as creative insecurity. 3097
Religion as credible doctrine. 3102
Religion as experience. 3057
Religion as experience and truth. 3103
Religion as experience, belief, action. 3056
Religion as life. 966
Religion as man's completion. 3056
Religion as revealed by the material and spiritual universe. 3494
Religion as salvation. 3290
Religion as story. 3071
Religion at Michigan. 3063
Religion at the polls. 3072
Religion, awakening & revolution. 1109
Religion behind the Iron Curtain. 1542
...Religion, books one and two. 755
Religion business. 1242
Religion can be amazing. 3062
Religion can conquer communism. 1319
Religion, class, and family in Spain. 825
Religion coming of age. 3063
Religion, commerce, liberty. 1542
Religion could be wonderful. 3056
Religion; course. 3061
Religion, culture and mental health. 3069
Religion, culture, and society. 3088
Religion, culture, and values. 819
Religion curriculum for the mentally handicapped. 3111
Die Religion des romischen Heeres. 3246
Religion, doctrine and practice. 803, 3057
Religion. [Essays]. 3112
Religion faces the world crisis. 3064
Religion--faith--the church. 3058
...Religion; first[-] manual. 3061
Religion follows the frontier. 1464
Religion for a dislocated generation. 3868
Religion for a new generation. 3067, 3091
Religion for America. 701
Religion for democracy. 1063
Religion for free minds. 2221
Religion for greatness. 3142
Religion for living. 1056
Religion for mankind. 129
Religion for men. 3059
Religion for one world. 3142
Religion for our time. 1058
Religion for our times. 1063
Religion for people of today. 3670
Religion for the hardheaded. 62
Religion for the new day. 3141
Religion for the time. 1098
Religion for the universal mind. 3123

Religion for to-day. 3726
Religion for to-day, various interpretations of the thought and practise of the new religion of our time. 1059
Religion for today. 1062
Religion for tomorrow. 1072
Religion for vital living. 966
Religion from the bleachers. 1061
Religion from Tolstoy to Camus. 3213
Religion functioning socially. 3448
Religion game, American style. 3105
Religion goes to school. 3096
Religion, government, and education. 1129
Religion, healing & health. 2410
Religion helps. 3537
Religion in 20th century America. 3746
Religion in a changing world. 782, 3063, 3064, 3065
Religion in a free society. 1152
Religion in a modern society. 1065
Religion in a pluralistic society. 12, 125
Religion in a religious age. 724, 2148
Religion in a revolutionary society. 3743
Religion in a secular age. 3057
Religion in a technical age. 1066
Religion in a Tswana chiefdom. 3719
Religion in action. 1133, 3744
Religion in Africa. 12
Religion in all the schools. 3190
Religion in America. 1108, 3737, 3739, 3743, 3744, 3747, 3748
Religion in America, 1950 to the present. 3748
Religion in America, past and present. 3745
Religion in American colleges and universities. 3759
Religion in American culture. 3746
Religion in American culture; unity and diversity in a midwestern county. 3746
Religion in American history. 3748
Religion in American life. 3746, 3748
Religion in American public schools. 3096
Religion in American society. 3087, 3743, 3745
Religion in an African city. 1879, 1880
Religion in an age of doubt. 3652
...Religion in an age of science. 3077
Religion in an Appalachian state. 3807
Religion in ancient history. 3066
Religion in and on the job. 957
Religion in antebellum Kentucky. 2167
Religion in art series. 1957
Religion in Australia. 117
Religion in Central America. 2507
Religion in changing Japanese society. 1936
Religion in China. 913
Religion in Chinese garment. 913
Religion in Chinese society. 914
Religion in college life. 3064
Religion in colonial America. 3739, 3740
Religion in Communist China. 912, 913
Religion in contemporary culture. 3056
Religion in contemporary debate. 3657
Religion in contemporary fiction. 1624
Religion in contemporary society. 3747
Religion in contemporary thought. 3107
Religion in crisis and custom. 2996
Religion in Cuba today. 1392
Religion in culture. 3059
Religion in early Australia. 117
Religion in education. 1129, 1397
Religion in education; an annotated bibliography. 1129
Religion in essence and manifestation. 3102
Religion in essense and manifestation. 3102
Religion in Greece and Rome. 1767
Religion in Greek literature. 1766
Religion in higher education. 3757
Religion in higher education among Negroes. 2681
Religion in history and in modern life. 1049
Religion in homespun. 969
Religion in human affairs. 3086
*Religion in human culture. 3069, 3139
Religion in human experience. 3115
Religion in human life: anthropological views. 3062
Religion in illness and health. 2378
Religion in Israel today. 1928
Religion in its relation to the present life. 1326
Religion in Japanese history. 1936
Religion in Judah under the Assyrians, 732-609 BC. 2156
Religion in life. 2209
... Religion in life adjustments. 3000
Religion in life adjustments. 3000
Religion in literature and religion in life. 3057
Religion in modern India. 1897
Religion in modern life. 3059
Religion in New Jersey. 2688

Religion in New Netherland, 1623-1664. 2700
Religion in our times. 3743
Religion in overalls. 442
Religion in philosophical and cultural perspective. 3107
Religion in plain clothes. 960
Religion in planetary perspective. 3111
Religion in practice. 1095, 3775
Religion in primitive culture, with an introd. by Paul Radin. 3110
Religion in primitive society. 3110
... Religion in public education. 3190
Religion in radical transition. 3088
Religion in recent art. 84
Religion in Russia. 3256
Religion in Russia, from Lenin to Khrushchev. 3257
Religion in Russia today. 3257
Religion in Russia under the Soviets. 3256
Religion in secular society. 1154
Religion in shoes. 698
Religion in shreds. 66
Religion in social action. 3446
Religion in social context. 3086
Religion in society. 60
Religion in sociological perspective. 3088
Religion in South Asia. 3464
Religion in soviet Russia. 3256
Religion in Soviet Russia, 1917-1942. 1108, 3257
Religion in Tennessee, 1777-1945. 3601
Religion in the age of Aquarius. 2733
... Religion in the American college. 3111
Religion in the American experience. 3748
Religion in the Bible. 232, 1731, 2325
Religion in the City of Angels. 2260
Religion in the common schools. 3176
Religion in the developing personality. 3056
Religion in the development of American culture, 1765-1840. 3739
Religion in the 18th century. 1543
Religion in the England of to-morrow. 1764
Religion in the heart. 3057
Religion in the highlands. 2547
Religion in the Himalayas. 1895
Religion in the home. 3062
Religion in the industrial revolution in South Wales. 1765
Religion in the Japanese experience: sources and interpretations. 1935
Religion in the kindergarten. 3156, 3174
Religion in the making. 3063, 3064, 3065
Religion in the making of Western man. 1101
Religion in the market place. 3069
Religion in the Middle East. 2678
Religion in the modern world. 1095
Religion in the old South. 1108
Religion in the Old Testament. 2148
Religion in the post-war world. 3746
Religion in the preparatory schools. 2943
Religion in the public domain. 1152
Religion in the public schools. 3095, 3189
Religion in the Reich. 1707, 1708
Religion in the republic of Mexico. 2461
Religion in the republic of Spain. 2979
Religion in the school curriculum. 3154
Religion in the social studies. 3096
Religion in the Soviet Union. 3257
Religion in the struggle for power. 3087
Religion in the thought of today. 3062
Religion in the twentieth century. 3116
Religion in the U.S.S.R. 3257
Religion in the undergraduate curriculum. 3112
Religion in the U. S. S. R. 3257
Religion in the United States. 3325, 3746
Religion in the United States of America. 3737
Religion in the Victorian era. 1764
Religion in the world of today. 1058
Religion in the year 2000. 1058
Religion in transition. 2997
Religion in 20th century America. 3746
Religion in various cultures. 3116
Religion in war and peace. 3101
Religion in Western culture. 232, 3058
Religion is here to stay, whether you like it or not. 3068
Religion is the search for meaning. 3061
Religion, its functions in human life. 3058
Religion--its prophets and false prophets. 3064
Religion, language, and truth. 3070
Religion lends a hand. 3444
Religion lessons for Catholic living. 3188
Religion lessons for deaf children. 1412
Religion lessons for the deaf. 1412
Religion makes sense. 65
Religion may be hazardous to your health. 2996
Religion meets the modern mind. 1063
Religion, Montessori, and the home. 939

Religion, morality, and law. 1535
Religion, nationalism and economic action. 1484, 3094
Religion nobody lives. 968, 2064
Religion of a democrat. 3065
Religion of a gentleman. 959
... The religion of a growing person. 3877
Religion of a healthy mind. 2997
Religion of a layman. 3057
Religion of a literary man. (Religio scriptoris) 1095
Religion of a mature mind. 1048
Religion of a mature person. 964
Religion of a modern liberal. 3370
Religion of a newspaper man. 3061
Religion of a person. 3061
Religion of a sceptic. 3063
Religion of a sensible American. 3060
Religion of a sound mind. 163
... Religion of an educated man. 3062
Religion of an electrical engineer. 3063
Religion of an inquiring mind. 1094
Religion of ancient Greece. 1767
Religion of ancient Greece, an outline. 1767
Religion of ancient Israel. 2148
Religion of ancient Scandinavia. 2665
... The religion of Babylonia and Assyria. 3089
Religion of Babylonia and Assyria, especially in its relations to Israel. 94
Religion of beauty. 3142
Religion of beauty and the impersonal estate. 3056
Religion of cheerfulness. 3060
Religion of China. 914
Religion of China: Confucianism and Taoism. 914, 1330
Religion of Christ. 3061
Religion of Christ in the twentieth century. 3065
Religion of common sense. 1652
Religion of democracy. 3059, 3442
... The religion of Dr. Johnson. 2129, 3315
Religion of ethical nationhood. 2141
Religion of evolution. 3063
Religion of geology and its connected sciences. 203, 3073
Religion of George Fox, 1624-1691. 1636
Religion of Greece in prehistoric times. 1767
Religion of humanity. 3724
Religion of India. 1897
Religion of Isaac Newton. 2705
Religion of Israel. 2116, 2144, 2148, 3088
Religion of Israel, from its beginnings to the Babylonian exile. 2146, 2150
Religion of Israel to the exile. 2113
Religion of Java. 2563
Religion of Jeremiah. 547, 1943
Religion of Jesus. 1058, 1079, 1097, 2036, 2066, 3061
Religion of Jesus, and Love, the law of life. 1079
Religion of joy. 3063
... The religion of Judah. 2113
Religion of love. 3141, 3460
Religion of lower races. 133
Religion of Main street. 3059
Religion of man. 1921, 3063, 3068, 3579
Religion of man and ethics of science. 3076
... The religion of man, being the Hibbert lectures for 1930. 3064
Religion of masonry. 1662
Religion of maturity. 1093
Religion of mind and body. 1598
Religion of modern manhood. 1071
Religion of Mohammed and Christian sufferings. 2566
Religion of nature delineated. 2675
Religion of nature delineated (1724) 1537
Religion of Negro Protestants. 2682
Religion of New England. 2687
Religion of Numa, and other essays on the religion of ancient Rome. 2716, 3245
Religion of philosophers. 2832
Religion of philosophy; or, The unification of knowledge. 3104
Religion of Plutarch. 3062
Religion of power. 1050
Religion of reason. 1092, 1306, 2138, 2837, 3064
Religion of religious psychology. 3001
Religion of revolution. 3440
Religion of Ruskin. 3255
Religion of science. 1653, 3074
Religion of science, the faith of coming man. 3078
Religion of scientists. 3078
Religion of soldier and sailor. 3794
Religion of spiritualism. 3517
Religion of Teilhard de Chardin. 3593
Religion of the age and of the ages. 3371
Religion of the American enlightenment. 3749

Religion of the ancient Celts. 878
... The religion of the ancient Egyptians. 1502
Religion of the Baha'is. 128
Religion of the Bare'e-speaking Toradja of Central Celebes. 877
Religion of the beautiful. 3142
Religion of the Bible. 235, 652
Religion of the child and other essays. 3152
Religion of the Chinese. 913
Religion of the Chinese people. 913
Religion of the church. 1748
Religion of the civilized world and Judaism. 3061
Religion of the Crow Indians. 1389
Religion of the East. 91
Religion of the family. 1611
Religion of the future. 841, 3141, 3517
Religion of the Greeks and Romans. 1766
... The religion of the Hebrews. 2115
Religion of the Hindus. 1813
Religion of the incarnation. 1893
Religion of the Kwakiutl Indians. 2188
Religion of the Latter-Day Saints. 2605, 3056
Religion of the Latter-day saints. (Rev. and enl. ed.) 2600
Religion of the Lord's prayer. 2247, 2248
Religion of the Manichees. 2328
Religion of the New Testament. 476, 477
Religion of the Northmen. 2666
Religion of the Occident. 1102
Religion of the Occident, or, The origin and development of the Essene-Christian faith. 1100
Religion of the Old Testament. 2115
Religion of the prayer book. 2964, 2965, 3056
Religion of the present, and of the future. 3065
Religion of the primitives. 3109
Religion of the Psalms. 3064
Religion of the Republic. 3748
Religion of the republic, and laws of religious corporations. 1490
... The religion of the Rigveda. 3776
Religion of the Russian people. 3257
Religion of the Semites. 3332
Religion of the slaves. 3442
Religion of the social passion. 3442
Religion of the spirit. 3482, 3726
Religion of the spirit in modern life. 3141
Religion of the spirit world written by the spirits themselves. 3504
Religion of the sun. 2758
Religion of the Tempasuk Dusuns of North Borneo. 1484
Religion of the Teutons. 2659
Religion of the threshold. 3049
Religion of the universe. 3142
Religion of the Veda. 689, 3088, 3776
Religion of their own. 2221
Religion of thirty great thinkers. 3100
Religion of Tibet. 709, 3699
Religion of to-morrow. 1720
Religion of tomorrow. 1103
Religion of truth, justice and peace. 2116
Religion of undergraduates. 3537
Religion of wise men. 3064
Religion of yesterday and to-morrow. 1050
Religion on fire. 1229
Religion on the campus. 3537, 3758
Religion on the Texas frontier. 1467
... Religion on the thinking man. 3061
Religion on trial. 1505, 3112
Religion or faith. 3061
Religion or superstition--which? 1653
Religion, order, and law. 3452, 3800
Religion: origins and ideas. 3093
Religion: out or way out. 1062
Religion outlines for colleges. 780
Religion, philosophy, and psychical research. 2992
Religion, politics, and diversity. 1148
Religion, politics, and social change in the Third World. 3072
Religion ponders science. 3083
Religion, popular and unpopular in the early Christian centuries. 1197
Religion rationalized. 3064
Religion, reason, and man. 3103
Religion, reason, and revelation. 3098
Religion recommended to youth, in a series of letters, addressed to a young lady. 977
Religion reconsidered. 3063
Religion renounces war. 3794
Religion, revelation & reason. 3609
Religion, revolution, and reform. 2198
Religion, revolution, and the future. 3623
Religion, revolution, and the Russian intelligentsia, 1900-1912. 3257
Religion says you can. 967
Religion, science, and society in the modern world. 1280, 1282, 3081

Religion since the reformation. 1187
Religion, society, and the individual. 3087
Religion, spirituality, and thought of traditional Africa. 12
Religion teacher's library. 3162
Religion teaching and practice. 804
Religion teaching by example. 293
Religion teaching plans. 3150
Religion that is eternal. 965
Religion that smiles. 1352
Religion that works. 1010, 3358
Religion, the courts, and public policy. 1150
Religion, the courts, and the public schools. 3096
Religion, the dynamic of education. 3151
Religion, the social context. 3086
Religion, the state & the schools. 1130
Religion, the weal of the church and the need of the times. 3064
Religion, theology and morals. 3142
Religion through the ages. 3197
Religion today. 3068
Religion, truth, and language-games. 3105, 3830
Religion 2101 A.D. 1064
Religion under the barons of Baltimore. 2363
Religion under the soviets. 3257
Religion USA. 3701, 3744
Religion with a smile. 1011
Religion with a song. 164
Religion with revelation. 3226
Religion within the limits of reason alone. 2836
Religion without explanation. 3107
Religion without God. 3102, 3104, 3105
Religion without magic. 2221
Religion without revelation. 3060
Religion without wrappings. 2934, 3356
Religion worth having. 1057
Religion y politica en la Cuba del siglo XIX. 1532
Religion yesterday and today. 3214
Religion& science. 3073 .
Religionisms and Christianity. 3116
Religions. 3117, 3140
Religious and anti-religious thought in Russia. 3214
Religions and philosophies in the United States of America. 3327
Religions and philosophies of the East. 91
Religions and the promise of the twentieth century. 3114
Religions around the world. 3122
Religions before Christianity. 3115
Religions east and west. 3115, 3140
Religions in a changing world. 3121
Religions in America. 3325, 3747
Religions in Australia. 3324
Religions in four dimensions. 3117
Religions in India. 1897
Religions in Japan. 1935, 1936
Religions in Japan: Buddhism, Shinto, Christianity. 1936
Religions in St. Louis. 3276
Religion's influence in contemporary society. 3088
Religions, mythologies, folklores. 3089, 3090
Religion's new frontiers. 2221
Religions of Africa. 13
Religions of America. 3326
Religions of ancient China. 913
Religions of ancient India. 1896
Religions of authority and the religion of the spirit. 3120
Religions of Bible lands. 3118
Religions of China. 913
Religions of democracy. 3744
Religions of eastern Asia. 3587
...The religions of India. 1896
Religions of Iran. 2822
Religions of Japan. 1935
Religions of man. 3117, 3121
Religions of mankind. 3117, 3121, 3140
Religions of mankind today & yesterday. 3140
Religions of mission fields as viewed by Protestant missionaries. 3133
...The religions of modern Syria and Palestine. 3578
Religions of Mongolia. 2584
Religions of old Korea. 2185
Religions of primitive peoples. 3139
Religions of South Vietnam in faith and fact. 3778
Religions of the American Indians. 1904
Religions of the ancient Near East. 94, 3118, 3332
... The religions of the ancient world. 3119
Religions of the East. 91, 3113
Religions of the Far East. 91
Religions of the oppressed. 2672
Religions of the Orient. 3116
Religions of the past and present. 3118

Religions of the Roman Empire. 3246
Religions of the world. 3113, 3114, 3116, 3118, 3142, 3198
Religions of the world, and how the fifty-eight grandsons of Noe and their descendants founded the nations after the flood. 3140
Religions of the world and the world-religion. 3121
Religions of the world and their relations to Christianity. 3118
Religions of the world, from primitive beliefs to modern faiths. 3119
Religions of the world made simple. 3093
Religions of Tibet. 2193, 3699
Religions of unbelief. 3024
Religions past & present. 3122
... Religions: philosophy of religion, folk-lore, ethnic religions. 3123
Religion's place in general education. 3151
Religion's role in tomorrow's world. 1067
Religions school assembly handbook. 3139
Religions, values, and peak-experiences. 2998
Religiose Erziehung in berufsbildenden Schulen. 937
Religious. 2576
... Religious activities at the University of Texas. 3190
Religious adult in Christ. 2159
Religious affections Edited by John E. Smith. 1512
Religious aim and human perplexity. 3099
Religious America. 3749
Religious and cosmic beliefs of central Polynesia. 2859
Religious and educational philosophy of the Young Women's Christian Association. 3447, 3879
... Religious and monastic life explained. 3116
Religious and moral education. 3190
Religious and moral ideas in Babylonia and Assyria. 94
Religious and other poems. 3206
Religious and secular leadership. 2112
Religious and the secular. 3327
Religious and the Vatican Council. 2571, 3772
Religious-apostolic formation of Sisters. 2581
Religious architecture of Canada. 1158
Religious architecture of New Mexico. 1161
Religious architecture of New Mexico in the colonial period and since the American occupation. 1161
Religious archives. 1162
Religious art exhibition. 87
Religious art from Byzantium to Chagall. 922
Religious art from the twelfth to the eighteenth century. 920, 921
Religious art in France, XIII century. 920
Religious art in the twentieth century. 921
Religious arts and crafts for children. 1385
Religious aspect of evolution. 1580
Religious aspects of education. 3156
Religious aspects of medical care. 2378
Religious aspects of scientific healing. 2409
Religious aspects of Swedish immigration. 3572
Religious aspects of Swedish immigrations. 3572
Religious aspects of the age. 3624
Religious aspects of the age, with a glance at the church of the present and the church of the future. 3624
Religious aspects of the conquest of Mexico. 2461
Religious at the feet of Jesus. 1441
Religious attitude. 3001
Religious attitude and life in Islam. 1923, 2565
Religious availability of Whitehead's God. 3813
Religious background of American culture. 3738
Religious background of the Bible. 298
Religious backgrounds of early Christianity. 1079
Religious basis of a better world order. 3119
Religious bearings of man's creation. 1381
Religious behavior. 2996, 3000, 3087
Religious belief. 3103
Religious belief and character among Jewish adolescents. 2114, 3882
Religious belief and philosophical thought. 2674
Religious beliefs of American scientists. 3078, 3082
Religious beliefs of youth. 3745

Religious bibliographies in serial literature. 3096
Religious bodies of America. 3325, 3326
Religious body: design for a new reformation. 1244
Religious buildings. 1274
Religious buildings for today. 1155
Religious care of the psychiatric patient. 1258
Religious cases of conscience. 944
Religious cases of conscience answered in an evangelical manner. 945, 3119
Religious Census of 1851, a calendar of the returns relating to Wales. 1275
Religious ceremonies and customs of the Parsees. 2777
Religious certainity. 1099
Religious certainties. 3116
Religious certainty. 791
Religious certitude in an age of science. 3077
Religious chastity. 889, 3838
Religious commitment and salvation. 3090
Religious communities in the American Episcopal Church and in the Anglican Church of Canada. 2577
Religious community and the secular state. 2576
Religious conception of the world. 3104
Religious conceptions of the stone age. 3109
Religious concepts in ancient America and in the Holy Land. 2863, 3012
Religious concerns in contemporary education. 3190
Religious condition. 3871
Religious condition of the Chinese. 913
Religious condition of young men. 3871
Religious conditions in Lithuania under Soviet Russian occupation. 821, 2232
Religious conference. 2217
Religious confessions and confessants. 2996
Religious conflict in America. 3745
Religious conflict of the ages. 3507
Religious congregations and health care facilities. 867
Religious consciousness. 2999
Religious consolation. 1350
Religious control of emotion. 2998
Religious controversies of the Elizabethan age. 1516
Religious controversies of the nineteenth century. 3212
Religious conversation, a bio-Sychological study. 1360
Religious conversion and personal identity. 1361
Religious cooperation in State universities. 3757
Religious courtship. 2337
Religious creeds and statistics of every Christian denomination in the United States and British provinces. 3322
Religious crossroads. 3106
Religious cults associated with the Amazons. 28
Religious cults of the Caribbean. 3711
Religious currents in the nineteenth century. 3059
Religious dance. 1400
Religious dances in the Christian church and in popular medicine. 1400
Religious delusions. 3114
Religious demand upon society. 571
Religious demands of the age. 2776, 3608
Religious denominations in the United States. 3324, 3326
Religious denominations in the United States, their past history, present condition, and doctrines, accurately set forth in fifty-three ... articles written by eminent clerical and lay authors ... together with complete and well-digested statistics. To which is added a historical summary of religious denominations in England and Scotland. 3326
Religious denominations of the world. 3118
...The religious development. 2713
Religious development between the Old and New Testaments. 2149, 2150
Religious development between the Old and the New Testaments. 3114
Religious development in the province of North Carolina. 2713
Religious development of adolescents. 2998
Religious development of the child. 904
Religious dimension. 3088, 3091
Religious dimension in Hegel's thought. 1800
Religious dimension in Hispanic Los Angeles. 2460
Religious dimension in the new Latin America. 821, 2198
Religious dimensions of personality. 2996

Religious discourses. 3120
Religious discovery, faith, and knowledge. 2181
Religious dissent in the Middle Ages. 1468
Religious diversity. 3068
Religious doubt. 3115
Religious drama. 3145
Religious drama 3. 3145
Religious dramas for worship and service. 3145
Religious drop-outs. 1309
Religious duties of the Daughters of Israel. 3116
Religious educatio in the senior school. 3164
Religious education. 1951, 3147, 3148, 3149, 3158, 3159
Religious education and American democracy. 3189
Religious education and democracy. 3160
... Religious education and practical Christianity. 149
Religious education and religious understanding. 3176
Religious education and the public school; an American problem. 3160
Religious education and the state. 3096, 3189
Religious education and theology. 942
Religious education as character training. 3159
Religious education association. 3156
Religious education, catechesis, and freedom. 940
Religious education handbook. 937
Religious education in a psychological key. 940
Religious education in German schools. 3164
... Religious education in non-provided schools. 3164
... Religious education in provided schools. 3165
Religious education in secondary schools, a survey and a syllabus. 3165
Religious education in the church. 3148
Religious education in the family. 1607
Religious education in the home. 3150
Religious education in the modern church. 3147
...Religious education in the public school of the state and city of New York. 3167
Religious education in the rural church. 3255
Religious education in the secondary modern school. 3165
Religious education in the small church. 3157
Religious education in the state school; a South African study. 3151
Religious education; its effects, its challenges today. 3150
Religious education ministry with youth. 940
Religious education, 1944-1984. 3165
Religious education of adolescents. 3156
Religious education of adults. 938, 3155, 3156
Religious education of Alexander Campbell. 732
Religious education of an American citizen. 972
Religious education of preschool children. 939
Religious education of the child. 3156
Religious education of the deaf. 1412
... Religious education on public school time. 3801
Religious education through CCD. 804
Religious educatin through graded instruction. 3165
... Religious education through story-telling. 3534
Religious education through the ages. 3165
Religious education we need. 936
Religious elevation of the human society. 3117
Religious empire. 1242
Religious encounters with death. 1415
Religious encyclopedia. 3639
Religious enthusiasm and the Great Awakening. 1757
Religious enthusiasm considered. 1520, 3804
Religious equality. 3118
Religious essays. 3067, 3119
Religious ethics. 1536
Religious equality in modern England, 1714-1914. 1762
Religious experience. 1585, 1586, 3106, 3191, 3204, 3799
Religious experience and journal of Mrs. Jarena Lee. 3191
Religious experience and process theology. 2944

Religious experience and scientific method. 3106
Religious experience and truth. 2836
Religious experience: its nature and function in the human psyche. 1587
Religious experience of Eunice Winchester Smith. 3427
Religious experience of Israel. 540
Religious experience of Jesus and His Disciples. 1586, 2060
Religious experience of John Humphrey Noyes. 2716, 2737
Religious experience of mankind. 3140
Religious experience of revolutionaries. 3085
Religious experience of Saint Paul. 2797, 2800
Religious experience of the primitive church. 1586
Religious experience of the Roman people, from the earliest times to the age of Augustus. 3246
Religious factor. 3088
Religious factors in mental illness. 2995
Religious faith and twentieth-century man. 1059
Religious faith and world culture. 1281, 3069
Religious faith, language, and knowledge. 1105
Religious faith of great men. 927
Religious fanaticism. 3326, 3427
Religious feeling. 1595
Religious ferment in Asia. 91
Religious ferment in modern India. 1896
Religious ferment in Russia. 159
Religious folk-songs of the Negro as sung at Hampton Institute. 2680
Religious forces in the universities of the world. 3190
Religious forces of the United States enumerated, classified, and described. 3738
... The religious forces of the United States, enumerated, classified, and described on the basis of the government census of 1890. 3738
Religious formation of the adolescent. 7
Religious formation of the elementary school child. 3171
Religious foundation of human relations. 1134
Religious foundations. 1069, 3622
Religious foundations of America. 3121
Religious foundations of internationalism. 1914
Religious foundations of the Jewish state. 2119, 2151
Religious freedom. 3195
Religious freedom, canon law. 780, 3193
Religious freedom in church and state. 1142
Religious freedom in eastern Europe. 3193
Religious freedom in Spain: its ebb and flow. 3194
Religious freedom, 1965 and 1975. 3193, 3772
... The religious function of imagination. 3102
Religious function of the colleges in the Methodist Episcopal church, South. 2456
Religious groups and public affairs in Los Angeles County. 1138
Religious guidance. 1539
Religious guide to Europe. 1022
Religious heritage of America. 3327
Religious heritage of southern California. 726
Religious history of America. 3738
Religious history of New England. 2687
Religious history of the American people. 3743
Religious humanism. 3028
Religious ideas for arts and crafts. 919
Religious ideas of Rammohun Roy. 3020
Religious ideas of the Old Testament. 599
Religious identity. 3142
Religious imagination. 874, 1297, 2080
Religious imagination and the sense of God. 3057
Religious impulse. 3056
Religious in church law. 2577
Religious indifference. 1904
Religious innovation in Africa. 13
Religious inquiry. 3679
Religious instinct. 2997
Religious instinct of man. 3348
Religious instruction and education. 745
... Religious instruction in the Catholic high school. 3190
"Religious instruction" in the Washington Constitution. 3119
Religious instruction of the Negroes in the United States. 2681
Religious investigations of William James. 1934, 3102

Religious issue in the state schools of England & Wales. 1129
Religious issues in American history. 3748
Religious knowledge. 2181, 3120
Religious language. 3070, 3119, 3682
Religious language and knowledge. 3071
Religious language and the problem of religious knowledge. 3070
Religious language of Thomas Traherne's Centuries. 1443, 3707
Religious leaders of America, v. 1- 1935-36. 1302
Religious lectures on peculiar phenomena in the four seasons ... delivered to the students in Amberst college, in 1845, 1847, 1848 and 1849. 3317
Religious liberalism in eighteenth-century. 3212
Religious liberals and conservatives. 3000
Religious liberals in council. 3119
Religious liberals reply. 2683
Religious liberty. 3192, 3193, 3194, 3195, 3744, 3771, 3774
Religious liberty, an historical paper. 3192
Religious liberty: an inquiry. 3192
Religious liberty and conscience. 1490
Religious liberty and democracy. 3193
Religious liberty and mutual understanding. 2671
Religious liberty and the American Presidency. 1149
Religious liberty and the Seventh-Day Adventist. 1152, 3192
Religious liberty and tolerance. 3193
Religious liberty in America. 3193, 3195
Religious liberty in Latin America? 3194
Religious liberty in South America. 3194
Religious liberty in the Near East. 3194
Religious liberty in the Soviet Union. 3194, 3850
Religious liberty in the United States. 3195
Religious liberty in transition. 3195
Religious liberty to-day. 3193
Religious life. 2569, 2570, 3068, 3726
Religious life—a mystery in Christ and the church. 2572
Religious life and spirit. 2581
Religious life and the poor. 2570
Religious life and the vows. 1546
Religious life; comprising these Hazen book classics: Religious living. 963
Religious life defined. 2571
Religious life in America. 3743
Religious life in ancient Egypt. 1502
Religious life in seventeenth century Scotland. 3315
Religious life in the Church today. 2574
Religious life in the light of Vatican II. 2570, 3771
Religious life of ancient Rome. 3195
Religious life of fugitive slaves and rise of coloured Baptist churches,1820-1865, in what is now known as Ontario. 144
Religious life of man. 3089
Religious life of the adolescent. 3888
Religious life of the Anglo-Saxon race. 47
Religious life of the Japanese people. 1935
Religious life of Virginia in the seventeenth century. 3781
Religious life of Virginia in the seventeenth century; the faith of our fathers. 3781
Religious life today. 2570, 2571
Religious literature of the West. 646
Religious living. 963
Religious living with nursery children in church and home. 3173
Religious lyrics of the XIVth century. 1519
Religious man. 3001
Religious men and women in church law. 2577
Religious men and women in the Code. 2577
Religious mind. 2998
Religious ministry in a transcendentless culture. 3328
Religious minorities in Transylvania. 3709
Religious mission of the Irish people and Catholic colonization. 828, 1919
Religious missions of the Irish people, and Catholic colonization. 1920
Religious motive in philanthropy. 174, 3447
Religious motive in philanthropy: studies in biography. 3377
Religious movements in contemporary America. 3749
Religious music in America. 1210
Religious mysteries of the Orient. 1485
Religious mythology and the art of war. 3792
Religious necessity of the reformation asserted. 3039
Religious obedience. 2719
Religious observances in Tibet. 2193

RELIGIOUS OPINIONS AND RELIGIOUS BOOKS 1876 - 1982

Religious opinions and example of Milton, Locke, and Newton. 2471
Religious opinions of Milton, Locke, and Newton. 2471, 2472, 3095, 3212
Religious optimism. 3121
Religious or Christian. 1094
Religious orders in England. 2579
Religious orders in the modern world. 2576
Religious orders of men. 2575
Religious orders of women. 2581
Religious orders of women in the United States. 3205
Religious orders of women in the United States: Catholic. 3416
... Religious ordinaries and canon 198. 2159
Religious orientations and social class. 3115
Religious origins of modern science. 3084
Religious outlook for modern man. 3117
Religious painting. 2031, 2759
Religious pathology and Christian faith. 2998
Religious pedagogy in the modern Sunday school. 3120
Religious perplexities. 2998
Religious personality. 3002
Religious perspectives and problems. 3104
Religious perspectives in American culture [by Will Herberg and others]. 3745
... Religious perspectives in American culture, culture. 3121
Religious perspectives in college teaching. 3757
Religious perspectives of college teaching in history. 1818
Religious perspectives of college teaching in sociology and social psychology. 3086
Religious philosophies of the West. 3108
Religious philosophy. 2837
Religious philosophy of Baron F. von Hugel. 1850, 3102
Religious philosophy of Josiah Royce. 3107
Religious philosophy of Quakerism. 419, 1681
Religious philosophy of William James. 1934, 3106
Religious picture sermons. 2930
Religious pied pipers. 1553
Religious pilgrimage of Israel. 2117
Religious Platonism. 2853
Religious plays for amateur players. 3145
Religious plays that click. 3145
Religious poems. 3121, 3493
Religious poems for an age of science. 3208
Religious poetry of Alexander Mack, jr. 3207
Religious policy and practice in Communist China. 914
Religious policy of the Bavarian government during the Napoleonic period. 1144
Religious policy of the Mughal emperors. 2563
Religious poverty and the profit economy in medieval Europe. 2866
Religious press directory. 1943. 3205
Religious press in America. 2135
Religious press in the South Atlantic States, 1802-1865. 3205
Religious profession. 2577
Religious progress. 3782
... Religious progress in the century. 1182
Religious progress on the Pacific slope. 1071
Religious progress on the Pacific slope; addresses and papers at the celebration of the semi-centennial anniversary of Pacific school of religion, Berkeley, California. 3120
Religious progress through religious revivals. 3230
Religious psychology. 2997
Religious question in public education. 1129
Religious quests of the Graeco-Roman world. 1189
Religious realism. 3102
Religious reality. 1052, 3664
Religious reason. 2163, 3100
Religious reawakening in America. 3746
Religious recitations for Sunday school and church use. 3026
Religious reconstruction. 3729
... The religious reformation of Ezra. 3117
Religious regards we owe to our country. 1504
Religious remarkables. 1397
Religious resources for personal living and social action. 3445
Religious response. 3106
Religious revival and social betterment. 3120
Religious revolt against reason. 3099
Religious revolution in the Philippines. 18, 1882
...The religious revolution of to-day. 3120
Religious revolution of today. 3120
Religious rheumatism. 3113
Religious Right and Christian faith. 1603, 3666
Religious rite & ceremony in Milton's poetry. 2472
Religious roulette & other dangerous games Christians play. 2874
Religious sanity, the philosophy of individual life. 3060
Religious school assembly handbook. 3310
Religious school organization and administration. 2669
Religious sector explores its mission in aging. 1257
Religious sects. 3323
Religious sense in its scientific aspect. 3079
Religious sentiment, its source and aim. 3098
Religious services and sermonettes around the year for children. 3120
Religious services for Jewish youth. 3117
Religious significance of atheism. 100
Religious situation. 3211, 3212
Religious, social, and polictical history of the Mormons, or Latter-day saints, from their origin to the present time. 2604, 3429
Religious, social, and political history of the Mormons, or Latter-day saints, from their origin to the present time. 2604, 3429
Religious state. 2819
Religious strife on the Southern frontier. 3468
Religious studies in public universities. 3111
Religious studies, sketches and poems. 3121
Religious superiors, subjects, and psychiatrists. 2575
Religious symbolism. 3573
Religious symbols and God. 3700
Religious syncretism in antiquity. 3091
Religious syncretism in Spanish America. 2198
Religious systems and psychotherapy. 2996
Religious systems of the world. 3120
Religious teachers of Greece. 1765, 1766
Religious teaching in secondary schools. 3146
... Religious teaching in the public schools. 3189
Religious teaching of the Old Testament. 598
Religious television. 3594
Religious television programs. 3594
Religious themes in two modern novelists. 1802, 3095
Religious thinking from childhood to adolescence. 903
Religious thought and economic society. 1076
Religious thought and heresy in the Middle Ages. 1186
Religious thought and life in India. 1896
Religious thought at the University of Michigan. 3211
Religious thought in England, from the Reformation to the end of last century. 1762
Religious thought in Holland during the nineteenth century. 3211
Religious thought in the eighteenth century. 3211
Religious thought in the last quarter-century. 1071
Religious thought in the nineteenth century. 3211
Religious thought in the Oxford movement. 2755
Religious thought in the Reformation. 3655
Religious thought of Samuel Taylor Coleridge. 1077, 1307
Religious thought of the Greeks. 1766
Religious thoughts and opinions. 3211
Religious toleration and persecution in ancient Rome. 2671
Religious toleration in England. 1762
Religious tradesman. 976
Religious tradition and myth. 1102
Religious training in the school and home. 3158
Religious training of children. 3149
Religious training of children in the school, the family, and the church. 3146
Religious treason in the American republic. 3193
Religious trends in a century of hymns. 2451
Religious trends in modern China. 913
Religious trends of today. 1567
Religious truth. 3075
Religious truths defined. 2613
Religious TV. 3594
Religious unrest and its remedy. 1055, 3112
Religious use of imagination. 1050
Religious value of the Old Testament in the light of modern scholarship. 503
Religious values. 3098
Religious values in counseling and psychotherapy. 2780
Religious values in education. 3154
Religious verities. 61
Religious views of President John F. Kennedy. 2167
Religious views of President John F. Kennedy in his own words. 2167
Religious vocation. 3438, 3785
Religious vocation guide to the communities of brothers and sisters which have their novitiates within the Archdiocese of New York. 2583
Religious vocations. 1296
... A religious welfare survey at the University of Nebraska. 2679
Religious woman, minister of faith. 2574
Religious women in the modern world. 2574
Religious work for men. 3875
Religious work of the Young men's Christian association. 3875
Religious work of the Young men's Christian associations. 3875
Religious world displayed. 3112
Religious world of Russian culture. 1630, 3257
Religious writer's marketplace. 1017
Religon, diet and health of Jews. 2086
Religon of Israel. 2115
Reliquiae juveniles. 3799
Reliquiae juveniles. 3799
Reliving Genesis and Exodus. 522
Reliving past lives. 3055
Reluctant mission. 2984
Reluctant prophet. 1479, 3800
Reluctant saint, reluctant sinner. 3846
Reluctant vision. 3098
Reluctant witness. 3829
Remains of Edmund Grindal. 1216, 1622
Remains of Melville B. Cox. 1378
Remains of Myles Coverdale. 1216
Remains of Rev. Joshua Wells Downing. 2423
Remains of the Rev. William Jackson. 2957
Remaking men. 2593
Remaking of Christian doctrine. 3653
Remaking of the church. 1245
Remaking the modern mind. 64
Remaking the world. 2593
Remarkable answers to prayer. 2875
Remarkable Biblical discovery. 1736
Remarkable birth of planet earth. 1382
Remarkable characters and places of the Holy Land. 214
Remarkable conversions. 2620
Remarkable Cure of Ars. 3778
Remarkable escapes from peril. 2982
Remarkable examples of moral recovery. 927
Remarkable providences. 2981
Remarkable scientific proof of the Bible. 205
Remarkable stories from the lives of Latter-Day Saint women. 1231, 3831
Remarkable visions. 3512
Remarks on a late pamphlet. 1787
Remarks on a sermon preached before the Plymouth association of ministers in the third Congregational society in Milldeborough, Sept. 26, 1810. 3031, 3411
... Remarks on certain passages in the Thirty-nine articles. 1212
Remarks on classical and utilitarian studies. 1286
Remarks on Frazer's Golden bough. 1652, 2654
Remarks on liberty of conscience. 3045, 3767
Remarks on the book of Daniel. 507
Remarks on the character and narrative of the Rev. John Clark. 1284, 1692
Remarks on the character and writings of John Milton, occasioned by the publication of his lately discovered Treatise on Christian doctrine. 2471
Remarks on the early corruptions of Christianity. 3713
Remarks on The fable of the bees. 2327
Remarks on the first part of a book, entitled "The age of reason," 1480
Remarks on the four Gospels. 389
Remarks on the history, structure, and theories of the Apostles' creed. 74
Remarks on the internal evidence for the truth of revealed religion. 1098
Remarks on the late publications of the First church in Worcester. 1748, 3847
Remarks on the Rev. Mr. Hopkins's answer to a tract intitled, "A vindication of the power, obligation, and encouragement of the unregenerate to attend the means of grace," &c. 1847
Remarks on the signs of the times. 606
Remarks on the uses of the definitive article in the Greek text of the New Testament. 425, 2001
Remarks on Trinity church bill. 2701
Remarks upon a pamphlet, entitled, A letter to a friend in the country, containing the substance of a sermon preached at Philadelphia, in the congregation of the Rev. Mr. Hemphill. 1651
Remarriage, a healing gift from God. 3214
Rembrandt and the Gospel. 603, 3214
Remember. 1456
Remember all the way. 3705
"Remember Jesus Christ" 976, 3345
Remember man. 2210
Remember now. 1437
Remember the days of old. 597, 1787
Remember the good times. 171, 3427
Remember the word. 318
Remember thy creator. 1579
Remember to live. 2388
Remember who you are. 137
Remember your confirmation. 1329
Remembered with love. 1693
Remembering Christ. 2972
Remembrances of Phillips Brooks. 694
Reminiscences. 2, 1285, 2105, 2505, 2958, 3822
Reminiscences and Civil War letters of Levi Lamoni Wight. 2598
Reminiscences and incidents in the life and travels of a pioneer preacher of the "ancient" gospel. 970
Reminiscences and incidents of a long life. 2228
Reminiscences and reflections from some sixty years of life in Ireland. 1919
Reminiscences chiefly of Oriel college and the Oxford movement. 2754
Reminiscences, historical and biographical, of sixty-four years in the ministry. 2474
Reminiscences of a long life. 2227
Reminiscences of a missionary bishop. 2488
Reminiscences of an old clergyman. 3569
Reminiscences of Baptist churches and Baptist leaders in New York city and vicinity. 158
Reminiscences of Bishop Chase, (now bishop of Illinois) 889
Reminiscences of bishops and archbishops. 2865
Reminiscences of Charles Butler. 2637
Reminiscences of early Methodism in Indiana. 2431
Reminiscences of Edgar P. Wadhams. 1365, 3788
Reminiscences of Georgia Baptists. 150
Reminiscences of H. P. Blavatsky and The secret doctrine. 672, 3683, 3688
Reminiscences of Latter-day Saints. 2615
Reminiscences of my life and times both in church and state in Australia for upwards of fifty years. 2195
Reminiscences of Nathan T. Frame and Esther G. Frame. 1638
Reminiscences of present-day saints. 926
Reminiscences of Rev. Charles G. Finney. 1626
Reminiscences of Rev. Wm. Ellery Channing, D D. 882
Reminiscences of seventy years (1846-1916) 3418
Reminiscences of the late Rev. Samuel Hopkins. D. D., of Newport, R. I. 1847
Reminiscences of the life and labor of A. D. Gillette, D.D. 1713
Reminiscences of the West India Islands. 2433
Reminiscences of travel in Cherokee lands. 891
Reminiscences sermons and correspondence proving adherence to the principle of Christian science. 1036
Reminiscences, sketches and addresses. 2920
Reminiscences: talks with the master. 1483
Remnant. 500, 3214
Remove the heart of stone. 139
Removing the cloud. 232
Renaissance & Reformation. 3215
Renaissance New Testament. 345, 1768
Renaissance of Jesus. 1053, 1955
Renaissance of Methodism. 2421

Renaissance princes, popes, and prelates. 1929
Renaissance to Reformation. 3215
Renaissant Latin America. 1345
Renamed. 1358, 2798
Renan's letters from the Holy Land. 3215
Render to God. 1142
"Render unto Caesar" 2112, 3793
Render unto God. 1143
Render unto the people. 1150
Rendering of God in the Old Testament. 599, 1731
Renderings of Stefanos. 2725
Rendez-vous with Paris. 2523
Rendezvous with abundance. 1237
Rendezvous with eternity. 1891
Rene. 889
Rene Menard, 1605-1661. 1949, 2402
Renegade, outcast, and maverick. 2204
Renew my church. 1243
Renew our days. 3032
Renewal. 2480
Renewal and reconciliation. 2394
Renewal and the middle Catholic. 1245
Renewal for all God's people. 786
Renewal in Christ. 878, 1063
Renewal in religious life. 2570
Renewal in retreats. 3222
Renewal in the pulpit. 2302, 3360
Renewal in the spirit. 3489
Renewal of American Catholicism. 828
Renewal of Buddhism in China. 1115, 2940
Renewal of Catholic higher education. 870
Renewal of Christian education. 2240
Renewal of church. 1461
Renewal of civilization. 127
Renewal of faith. 941
Renewal of history. 46
Renewal of hope. 992, 1528
Renewal of life in the clergy. 1288
Renewal of liturgical preaching. 2897
Renewal of man. 2160
Renewal of preaching. 287, 2904
Renewal of religious community life. 1316
Renewal of the church. 1124
Renewal of the ministry. 2786
Renewal of worship. 3855
Renewal reminders. 1433
Renewals before Pentecost. 532, 3230
Renewed by the spirit. 3342
Renewed church of the United brethren. 2595, 3896
Renewed church of the United brethren, 1722-1930. 2595, 3896
Renewed in strength. 2888
Renewed mind. 982, 2783
... The renewing gospel. 2898
Renewing the congregation. 3444
Renewing the earth. 1140
Renewing the face of the earth. 760, 1155
Renewing the mind. 1104
Renewing your faith day by day. 1435
Renovation and counter-reformation. 1160, 1630
Renovation and expansion planning. 1157
... Renunciation of ancecclesiastical office. 190
Renunciation of popery. 802
Reorganized church in the light of court decisions. 3215
... The Reorganized church of Jesus Christ of latter day saints, complainant, vs. the Church of Christ at Independence, Missouri. 2605
Reorienting Zionist education today. 3897
Repaid a hundredfold. 2510
Repair my house. 1641, 1645
Repairing our religion. 965
Repent or else! 462
Repentance. 3218
Repentance and renewal. 864, 2214
Repentance explained to the understanding of children. 3218
Repentance—the joy-filled life. 3218
Repertorium der griechischen christlichen Papyri. 315, 2331
Repertory of tropes at Winchester. 849, 3715
Repetition. 2170
Reply to A defence of the divine right. 1285, 1906
Reply to A letter to the Right Rev. Bishop Hobart, occasioned by the strictures on Bible societies. 612, 1937
Reply to Bishop Colenso's attack upon the Pentateuch. 1306
Reply to Canright. 736, 3381
Reply to Dr. Lightfoot's essays. 347, 2229
Reply to Dr. Miller's letter to a gentleman of Baltimore. 2466, 2914
Reply to Dr. Ware's Letters to Trinitarians and Calvinists. 3795
Reply to Evils of infants baptism. 1849, 1906
Reply to Harnack on the essence of Christianity. 1786

Reply to Hon. R. W. Thompson. 793, 3698
Reply to John P. Campbell's strictures on atonement. 107, 733
Reply to M. [i.e. Mr.] Nicholas Smith [i.e. M. Wilson], 1630. 808
Reply to Mr. J. Sabine's lectures on the Inquiry into the Scriptural import of the words Sheol, Hades, Tartarus and Gehenna. 1699, 3262
Reply to Prof. Mattison's "Answer", etc. 2374, 3300
Reply to "The Academy's" review of "The wine question in light of the new dispensation." 3596
Reply to "The Church of the Firstborn of the Fulness of Times." 2612
Reply to the principal points of the argument. 187, 817
Reply to the Remarks of the Rev. Mr. John Tucker. 3341
Reply to the Review of Dr. Wyatt's sermon and Mr. Sparks' letters on the Protestant Episcopal church. 3860
Reply to the Shakers' statements. 3396
Reply to the Vindication of the result of the late Council at Ipswich. 1337
Reply to William T. Dwight, D.D., on spiritualism. 1484, 3519
Reponsive Scripture for worship in church and home. 592
Report. 2541
Report. 15, 30, 31, 34, 45, 132, 149, 155, 158, 707, 893, 1044, 1127, 1235, 1317, 1459, 1462, 1482, 2098, 2426, 2439, 2441, 2442, 2458, 2774, 2921, 2923, 2966, 3047, 3177, 3205, 3438, 3705, 3872, 3878, 3896
Report, 1st- 1888. 3878
Report. 2d- 1952. 2670
Report: Christ-- the hope of the world. 3850
Report from Christian Europe. 1542
Report from London: England's 250th anniversary. 1664
Report made to the first convention of the World's women's Christian temperance union. 3598
Report. [n. p. 1670
Report of a conference of the Board of missionary preparation. 2481
Report of a public discussion between J. M. Stephenson and P. T. Russell. 2175
Report of a public discussion, between the Revs. Adin Ballou, and Daniel D. Smith; on the question, "Do the Holy Scriptures teach the doctrine, that men will be punished and rewarded subsequently to this life, or after death, for the deeds done in this life?" 3753
Report of a study of YMCA world service policies and practices, as submitted to the International Committee on YMCAs of the United States and Canada. 3871
Report of a survey of the colleges and theological seminaries of the Presbyterian church in the United States. 2923
Report of a visitation of the China missions of the Presbyterian board of foreign missions. 2921
Report of a visitation of the Philippine mission of the Board of foreign missions of the Presbyterian church in the United States of America. 2544
Report of a visitation of the Siam and Laos missions of the Presbyterian Board of foreign missions. 2546
Report of commission I-VIII. 2495
Report of Committee of Plain people making pleas for leniency from depressive school laws. 2407
Report of deputation sent by the Board of foreign missions of the Presbyterian church in the U.S.A. 2502
Report of Evangelistic council and Ministerial association meetings. 3383
Report of Harrison et al. vs. St. Mark's church, Philadelphia. 3089
Report of Lankford's artistic church and other designs. 1158
Report of Orient missions conference. 156
Report of proceedings. 44
Report of proceedings in the Talmage case, before the Presbytry of Brooklyn. 3582
Report of seminar. 3618, 3757
Report of statewide services. 3757
... Report of the Board of home missions of the Congregational and Christian churches. 1332
Report of the annual convention. 110, 2288
Report of the annual meeting. 9, 866, 3598
Report of the Archdiocesan Advisory Committee on the Financial Crisis of Catholic Schools in Philadelphia and Surrounding Counties. 832

Report of the Board of managers of the United society for the spread of the gospel. 156
Report of the Board of missionary preparation (for North America) 2481
Report of the Board of trustees. 3755
Report of the case between the Rev. Cave Jones, and The recor and inhabitants of the city of New-York in communion of the Protestant episcopal church in the state of New-York. 3089
... Report of the Centenary conference on the Protestant missions of the world, held in Exeter hall (June 9th-19th), London, 1888. 2518
Report of the Christian youth conference of North America. 3884
Report of the Commission on theological education to the General conference of Unitarian and other Christian churches, with correspondence. October, 1913. 3723
Report of the Commission appointed by the Government of Palestine to inquire into the affairs of the orthodox patriarchate of Jerusalem. 2765
Report of the committee appointed by the Philonathean Society of the University of Pennsylvania to translate the inscription on the Rosetta stone. 3757
Report of the Committee of the General assembly. 2914, 3156
Report [of the] conference. 3564
... Report of the Consultation of Christian Educators on sex education ... Cincinnati, Nov. 13-15, 1958. 3390
Report of the debates in the Presbytery of Philadelphia. 174
Report of the delegation sent to the Church of South India by General Convention. 2959
Report of the Ecumenical Consultation, Kanuga Conference Center, Hendersonville, North Carolina, October 27-31, 1975. 1046, 2927
Report of the examination of the Shakers of Canterbury and Enfield, before the New-Hampshire legislature, at the November session, 1818, including the testimony at length; several extracts from Shaker publications. 3396
Report of the executive secretary ... to the annual meeting. 2434
[Report of the general director]. 2098
Report of the Joint commission on marginal readings in the Bible to the General convention of 1901. 272
Report of the Joint commission on the Book of common prayer. 2961
Report of the Joint commission on the revision of the Hymnal to the General convention of the Protestant Episcopal church in the United States of America. 2968
Report of the Joint Union Committee to the Conventions of the Negotiating Bodies. 2292
Report of the Ladies' Christian commission of Buffalo, N. Y. 712
Report of the managers. 2411
... Report of the managers of the New-Jersey Bible society ... 1st- Trenton. 612
[Report of the meeting moderated by Francesco Montana and held at] the Morris Inn, University of Notre Dame, July 13-15, 1956. 1157
Report of the meeting of the conference of foreign mission boards. 2523
Report of the Ministers and missionaries benefit board of the Northern Baptist convention. 2714
Report of the Oxford movement centenary congress. 45
... Report of the preliminary meeting at Geneva, Switzerland, August 12-20, 1920. 1045
Report of the Presbyterian church case. 2919
Report of the president. 3757
Report of the president to the board of trustees. 3723
... Report of the proceedings and addresses of the ... annual meeting. 826
... Report of the proceedings and addresses of the annual meeting ... 1st. 867
Report ... of the Rural work commission of the Methodist Episcopal church, South. 3254
Report of the sub-committee deputed to visit Erie, etc., on the subject of a proposed subscription by the councils of the city of Philadelphia to the capital stock of the Sunbury and Erie rail road company. 3546
Report of the Survey commission of the Presbyterian college of South Carolina. 2936

Report of the survey of the educational work and responsibility of the Presbyterian church in the United States. 2923
Report of the trial of Crecentia Arries and Emma Nichols, charged with practicing medicine without a license, before the Police court of the city of Milwaukee ... The first unqualified conviction of Christian scientists for practicing medicine. Edited by A. C. Umbreit. 1037
Report of the trial of Friends, at Steubenville, Ohio, from the 15th to the 26th of October, 1828. 1687
Report of the Working Party on the Child in the Church. 938
Report on a second visit to China, Japan and Korea, 1909. 2508
Report on a survey of fifty-eight organization of the Northern Baptist denomination. 150
Report on India and Persia of the deputation sent by the Board of foreign missions of the Presbyterian church in the U.S.A. to visit these fields in 1921-22. 2532
Report on Israel. 2764
Report on Japan and China of the deputation sent by the Board of foreign missions of the Presbyterian church in the U.S.A. 2535
Report on parochial school study to first special session of the One hundred and fourth Legislature. 822
Report on South India. 1235
Report on spiritualism of the committee of the London Dialectical Society. 3519
Report on the American Jesuits. 1948
Report on the first conference...held in San Juan, Puerto Rico, April 11th to 16th, 1955. 754
Report on the history and recent collation of the English version of the Bible. 254
Report on the John Birch Society. 2125
Report on the John Birch Society, 1966. 2125
Report on the Library of the Jewish Theological Seminary. 2080
... Report[s] of commission[s] i-v. 1679
Report to Protestants. 3743
Report to the annual convention. 3897
Report to the Board of Missions. 2434, 2438
Report to the members of the Mother church of the Committee on general welfare. 1038
Report to the South Carolina Annual Conference, Southeastern Jurisdiction of the Methodist Church. 2670
Report to UOJCA congregations on the First World Conference of Ashkenazi and Sephardi Synagogues held in Jerusalem on 7-12 Teveth, 5728 (January 8-13, 1968) 2145, 3849
Reporter at the Papal court. 2852, 2862
Reporter finds God through spiritual healing. 1599
Reporter in search of God. 1728
Reporter looks at American Catholicism. 827
Reporter looks at the Vatican. 2852, 2861
Reporter's illustrated monumental draughtsman. The only work ever published devoted exclusively to monumental designing. 3333
... Reports. 1338
Reports .. (Congregational churches in Connecticut, General conference) 1339
Reports of debates (Methodist Episcopal church. Conferences) 2444
Reports of the Committee on judiciary of the General conference of the Methodist Episcopal church. 2449
Reports of the United German Evangelical Lutheran congregations in North America. 2294
Reports presented at the annual meeting. 673
Representative men and women of the Bible. 215
Representative men of the Bible. 493
Representative men of the New Testament. 337, 338
Representative Methodists. 2443
Representative modern preachers. 694, 2908, 3308
Representative selections. 1333, 1334
Representative women. 3838
Representative women of Methodism. 2426
Representative women of the Bible. 3840
Repression of heresy in medieval Germany. 1805
Reprint of the first edition of the Discipline of the African Methodist Episcopal church. 13

Reproach of Christ. 1340
Reproach of Christ, and other sermons. 3339
Reproach of the gospel. 1052
Reproachfully yours. 1364
Reproducers; new life for thousands. 1261, 3427
Reproof of the American church. 3424
Republic and the church. 1471
Republic of God. 3646
Republic of Plato. 3762
Republic reclaimed. 2104
Republican hymn book containing a new and original set of hymns and spiritual songs, suited to be sung at society meetings, family worship, public and social prayer meetings, etc. 1862
Republican religion. 3745
Republication of the letters of John Wilbur to George Crosfield. 1687
Requiem. 3219
Requiem for a lost piety. 1010
Requiem for a parish. 3676
Requiem: music of mourning and consolation. 3219
Requisites for a man. 3870
Requisites to our country's glory. 1504
Re-re-commencement. 3197
Rescue through emigration. 2085
Research in parapsychology 1973. 2990
Research in religious behavior: selected readings. 3001
Research inventory of the Mexican collection of colonial parish registers. 1243, 1704
... Research memorandum on religion in the depression. 1119, 3746, 3747
Research on religious development. 937
Research service in religious education. 3176
Research yourself. 1323
Researches and missionary labours, among the Jews, Mohammedans, and other sects. 2502
Researches in Hebrew literature. 1798
Researches in Jewish history. 1653
Researches in Manichaeism. 2327
Researches in oriental history. 1653
Researches in personality, Character and religious education. 3162
Researches in reincarnation and beyond. 3054
Researches into the phenomena of modern spiritualism. 3498
Researches of the Rev. E. Smith and Rev. H. G. O. Dwight in Armenia. 82
Researches on the I Ching. 1879
Reserved sacrament. 3266
Reserves of the soul, and other sermons. 2934
Reshaping evangelical higher education. 1127
Reshaping the Christian life. 1007
Reshaping the teaching ministry. 3153
Residue of days. 1594
Resilient church. 785, 1118
Resistance and compromise. 872
Resistance and contemplation. 2712
Resistance of the churches in the Netherlands. 2685
Resistance; the sacrament of penance. 2812
Resolving church conflicts. 1165
Resource guide. 3169
Resources and duties of Christian young men. 971
Resources for leaders of children. 3188
Resources for sermon preparation. 3374
Resources for worship. 1451, 3852
Resources for youth ministry. 1260
Resources of religion. 1059
Respect life! 3
Respectable folly. 2464
Respectable murderers. 1134
Respectable sinners. 163
Resplendent themes; meditations on the Christian life. 994
Respond. 3065, 3186
Responding to God. 3528
Responding to God's call. 942
Responding to God's call ... to live in Christ. 971
Responding to the Word. 3487
Responsa and halakhic studies. 3219
Responsa literature. 3219
Responsa literature and A treasury of responsa. 3219
Responsa of modern Judaism. 3219
"Responsa" of Rabbi Solomon ben Adreth of Barcelona [1235-1310] as a source of the history of Spain in Epstein, Isidore, 1894-1962. 2103
Responsa of Solomon Luria (Maharshal) 2074
Responsa of the Babylonian geonim as a source of Jewish history. 1706, 3219

Responsa of the Central Conference of American Rabbis contained in its Yearbook. 2138
Response in Christ. 3485
Response of the church in changing Japan. 1935
Response to the World Conference on Church and Society, Geneva, July 12-26, 1966. 1133
Responses to religion. 3749
Responsibility for evil in the theodicy of IV Ezra. 488
Responsibility for the community. 1279
Responsibility in modern religious ethics. 3219
Responsible adults in the church school program. 3168
Responsible campus: toward a new identity for the church-related college. 1127
Responsible Christian. 1134, 1534
Responsible Christianity. 1062
Responsible church. 777, 3634
Responsible church and the foreign mission. 1904
Responsible freedom. 950
Responsible God. 2708
Responsible marriage and parenthood. 2340
Responsible pulpit. 2903
Responsible revolution; means and ends for transforming society. 3234
Responsible self. 944
Responsible society. 3043
Responsible suburban church. 3538
Responsive readings from the American standard edition of the revised version of the Bible. 252
Responsive readings from the Living Bible. 3220
Responsorial psalm tones for the Mozarabic office. 847, 884
Rest a while. 3223
Rest awhile. 1447, 3485
Rest days in a journey to Bible lands and other journeys abroad. 166
Rest days: the Christian Sunday, the Jewish Sabbath, and their historical and anthropological prototypes. 1822
Rest for the weary. 1447
Rest is commentary. 2148
Rest of the family. 3801
Restatement of Baptist principles. 148
... Restitutio in integrum. 3220
Restitution of decayed intelligence. 1763
Restitution to the poor. 3220
Restless believers. 3537
Restless Christian. 1000
Restless church. 1066
Restless flame. 116
Restless friar. 2333
Restless hearts and the pressure of God's spirit. 1451
Restless land. 610, 1927
Restless missionary. 3831
Restless quest. 3621
Restless quest of modern man. 1057
Restless religious. 2570
Restoration. 763
Restoration:a study in prophecy. 3216
Restoration episcopate. 1213
Restoration ethics today. 951
Restoration faith. 3218
Restoration handbook. 1272
Restoration movement. 3220
Restoration movement of the nineteenth century. 3220
Restoration movement; study course for youth and adults. 1464
Restoration of all things. 2608, 3300, 3318, 3524
Restoration of Israel. 1928
Restoration of the Beauchamp Chapel at St. Mary's Collegiate Church, Warwick, 1674-1742. 3796
Restoration of the divine church. 2615
Restoration of the drama of Cantieles. 595
Restoration of the gospel. 3220
Restoration of the reservation of the blessed sacrament for the sick. 3264
Restoration principle. 1460
Restoration puritanism. 1760, 3007, 3008
Restoration readings. 1461
Restoration scriptures. 678, 3215
Restoration studies, 1980. 3215
Restored church. 2600, 2605
Restored New Testament, the Hellenic fragments, freed from the pseudo-Jewish interpolations, harmonized, and done into English verse and prose with introductory analyses, and commentaries, giving an interpretation according to ancient philosophy and psychology and a new literal translation of the Synoptic Gospels, with introduction and commentaries, by James Morgan Pryse ... illustrations drawn by John O'Neill. 355
Restored relationship. 2161

Restoring all things. 753
Restoring first century evangelism. 1568
Restoring God to education. 1247
Restoring the Christian family. 1610
Restoring worship. 3852
Restructuring religious life. 2575
Results of spiritual investigation. 51
Results of three synods. 1336
Resurgence of the Gospel. 2286
Resurgent religions of Asia and the Christian mission. 2502
Resurrected life. 2052
Resurrection. 1958, 2051, 2052, 2053, 2054, 3029, 3072, 3202, 3220, 3221
Resurrection according to Matthew, Mark, and Luke. 391, 2054
Resurrection and eternal life. 3216
Resurrection and historical reason. 2052
Resurrection and its implications. 3220
Resurrection and modern thought. 2053, 3221
Resurrection and other Gospel narratives and The narratives of the virgin birth. 3221
Resurrection and other truths explained. 3221
Resurrection and Paul's argument. 3221
Resurrection and the Christian faith. 2053, 3221
Resurrection and the hereafter. 2718
Resurrection and the life. 2053
Resurrection and the life beyond. 3220
Resurrection and the message of Easter. 2052
Resurrection body "according to the Scriptures" 3221
Resurrection Christ: community as interperson. 1124, 2053
Resurrection fact. 2051
Resurrection factor. 2052
Resurrection gospel. 1466
Resurrection gospel and other sermons. 1466
Resurrection Gospel, and other sermons delivered at the First Christian church, Long Beach, Cal., January, 1922. 3222
Resurrection, immortality, and eternal life in intertestamental Judaism. 490, 1530
Resurrection in our street. 3221
Resurrection in the New Testament. 3221
Resurrection in the plan of salvation. 2051, 3288
Resurrection messages. 1486
Resurrection of Christ.. 2051, 2052
Resurrection of Christ and of Christians. 2051
Resurrection of Christendom. 3445
Resurrection of Jesus. 390, 1656, 2052, 2053, 3221
Resurrection of Jesus, an historical fact. 3221
Resurrection of Jesus Christ. 2051, 2052
Resurrection of Jesus Christ in New Testament theology. 348, 2052
Resurrection of Jesus of Nazareth. 2052
Resurrection of man. 3220
Resurrection of Our Lord. 2052
Resurrection of Peter. 2825
Resurrection of the body. 324, 346, 2051, 3221
Resurrection of the dead. 252, 324, 719, 2050, 3220, 3221
Resurrection of the flesh. 3220
Resurrection of the human body. 3220
Resurrection of the unknown soldier. 1466, 3356
Resurrection of theism. 3608
Resurrection realities. 3222
Resurrection then and now. 2052
Retainer from the Lord. 932
Retarded children: God's children. 1255
Rethinking church music. 1204
Rethinking evangelism. 1572
Rethinking our Christianity. 1095
Rethinking our priorities. 1550
Rethinking the Christian message. 66
Re-thinking the church's mission. 2555
Rethinkinn religion. 1059
Retired minister. 2444
Retold tales from the Old Testament. 628
Retractations. 116
Retreat. 2389
Retreat companion for priests. 3222
Retreat conferences for religious. 3223
Retreat conferences for religious sisterhoods. 3223
Retreat discourses and meditations for religious. 3223
Retreat dynamics. 3223
Retreat for beginners. 3223
Retreat for lay people. 1451, 2390, 3222
Retreat for priests. 2390
Retreat for religious. 3222
Retreat for sisters. 3223
Retreat for the clergy. 3223
Retreat handbook. 3223

Retreat instructions of Mother Mary Catherine McAuley. 2573, 2580
Retreat into eternity. 3476
Retreat matter for priests. 3223
Retreat notes. 2390
Retreat notes for religious. 2571
Retreat readings. 3223
Retreat resources. 3223
Retreat to commitment. 3022
Retreat with Our Lady. 2361
Retreats for adults. 3223
Retreats for Catholic girls and women. 3223
Retreats for clergy and religious. 3223
Retreats for youth. 3223
Retreats given by Father Dignam of the Society of Jesus. 3222
Retrial of Joan of Arc. 1938
Retribution. 3234
"The retrospect." 2451
Retrospect and prospect. 2141
Retrospect of a happy ministry. 3126
Retrospect of an unimportant life. 3128
Retrospect of early Quakerism. 1687
Retrospect of fifty years. 3127
Retrospect, three score years and ten. 3421
Retrospection and introspection. 1031
Retrospection and introspection, Christian healing, Rudimental divine science. 1031
Return. 3472
Return from tomorrow. 932, 3238
Return of Benjamin Franklin. 1651, 3508
Return of Chief Black Foot. 668
Return of Christ. 2051, 2052, 3318
Return of Christendom. 1062
Return of departed spirits of the highest characters of distinction as well as the indiscriminate of all nations. 3512
Return of Eden. 2468, 2470
Return of Frances Willard. 3055, 3816
Return of Frances Willard: her case for reincarnation. 3055, 3816
Return of Jesus. 2051, 2054, 3319
Return of Jesus Christ. 2052, 3320
Return of love. 3418
Return of magic. 2312
Return of spring to man's soul. 2425, 2436
Return of the goddess. 1742
Return of the Jesuits. 1949
Return of the Jews. 2119
Return of the Jews and the end of the world. 604
Return of the Jews to England. 2099
Return of the Lord. 3319, 3321
Return of the Lord Jesus. 3221, 3320
Return of the Puritans. 3742
Return of the Redeemer. 3220
Return of the sacred. 1153
Return of the star of Bethlehem. 3525
Return of the world-teacher. 3221
Return to Christ. 28
Return to Christian culture. 945
Return to faith. 1586
Return to faith, and other addresses. 1597
Return to Japan. 1935
Return to life. 2203
Return to man. 1060
Return to prayer: home and student devotions for Sabbath, every day, and special occasions. 2110
Return to reality. 803
Return to religion. 2998, 2999
Return to self-concern. 2790
Return to the fountainhead. 3419
Return to the novitiate. 2580
Returne of untruthes upon M. Iewelles replie. 792
Returning tide of faith. 1595
Reuben Archer Torrey, the man. 3705
Reuben E. Nelson. 2683
Reuben's portion. 3382
Reuel makes a decision. 626
Reule of Crysten religioun. 3647
Reunion in eternity. 1796
Reunion of Christendom. 1041
Reunion of the church. 1045, 1235
Rev. A. J. Whipkey. 927
Rev. Anthony Verren. 3777
Rev. Bud Robinson. 3242
Rev. Dr. Adolph Huebsch. 1850, 2077
Rev. Dr. Talkwell sketches. 1057
Rev. J. W. T. McNiel. 3131
Rev. James Harvey Tuttle, D.D. 3719
Rev. James Havens, one of the heroes of Indiana Methodism. 1790, 2452
Rev. James P. Hendrick, D. D. 1803
Rev. John McNeill's ("The Scotch Spurgeon.") popular sermons. 3376
Rev. Legh Richmond's letters and counsels to his children. 1302
Rev. Morgan John Rhys. 3234
Rev. Ms. Evelyn Morgan Jones, I love you. 3842
Rev. Otis Robinson Bacheler, M.D., D.D. 123

Rev. Samuel Aaron. 1290
Rev. Samuel Houston, V.D.M. 1849
Rev. Thomas Bray: his life and selected
works relating to Maryland. 2363
Rev. William Salter, D.D., 1821-1910.
3287
Customs and practices of the Moravian
Church. 2594
Revaluation. 2082
Revaluing Scripture. 3198
Revealed knowledge. 3662
Revealed knowledge of the prophecies and
times. 2949
Revealed testament of John the disciple.
414
Revealed translation of John's Revelation.
461
Revealed translation of John's Revelation,
given by the Lord Jesus Christ to Archie
J. Inger and published to the world that
all may come into the light of God's
truth. 461
Revealed unto babes. 3662
Revealed word of God. 282
Revealing Christ. 2210, 2212
Revealing word. 3750
Reveille or taps? 3371
Revelation. 452, 453, 454, 455, 457, 459,
461, 464, 465, 608, 1092, 3224, 3225,
3226, 3227, 3571
Revelation, a Protestant view. 3226, 3772
Revelation, an analysis and exposition of
the last book of the Bible. 463
Revelation, an introduction and
commentary. 454
Revelation and divination in Ndembu
ritual. 2678
Revelation and existence. 1424
Revelation and experience. 3226
Revelation and footsteps of time. 463
Revelation and inspiration. 279, 3225
Revelation and its record. 3225
Revelation and love's architecture. 3711
Revelation and reason. 1597, 3224
Revelation and reason in Islam. 3227
Revelation and redemption. 416, 3031
Revelation and religion. 3058
Revelation and response. 3224
Revelation and response in the Old
Testament. 599, 2151
Revelation and reunion. 1039, 1913
Revelation and the Bible. 201, 3225
Revelation and the Holy Spirit. 175, 1457
Revelation and the ideal. 3225
Revelation and the life to come. 3226
Revelation and the modern mind. 782
Revelation and the quest for unity. 3224
Revelation and theology. 176, 3226, 3657
Revelation and tradition. 3226
Revelation as history. 3227
Revelation, book of mystery and hope.
458
Revelation--Christ's return. 460
Revelation, drama of the ages. 455
Revelation explained. 454, 460, 464
Revelation expounded. 453
Revelation in Jewish Wisdom litarature.
600
Revelation in Mormonism. 2600, 3428
Revelation in Shakespeare. 3095, 3399
Revelation in the light of history and
experience. 3225
Revelation in the mountain. 2604
Revelation in the wilderness dealing with
the revelation of the meaning of the
symbolism contained in the traditions of
old in the wilderness of the mind and of
the modern world) 2653
Revelation interpreted. 3227
Revelation is for everyone. 1232
Revelation letters. 3379
Revelation made easy. 455, 3227
Revelation made plain. 455
Revelation of Baha'u'llah. 125, 129
Revelation of Baha'u'llah and the Bab.
126, 1425
Revelation of Christ to his servants of
things that are and things that shall be.
454
Revelation of Deity. 1728
Revelation of discovery. 1068
Revelation of eternal love. 3650
Revelation of free masonry. 1668
... Revelation of Genesis. 525
Revelation of God. 3226
Revelation of God in human suffering.
166
Revelation of God in nature. 3594
Revelation of Jesus. 2063
Revelation of Jesus and his teachings.
3227
Revelation of Jesus Christ. 453, 454, 456,
457, 461, 464, 465, 3227
Revelation of John. 452, 453, 454, 458,
461, 3227
Revelation of John. Commentary. 452
Revelation of John the Divine. 464

Revelation of love. 1448
Revelation of man. 2728
Revelation of present experience. 2227
Revelation of St. John. 454, 455
Revelation of St. John an open book. 461,
464
Revelation of St. John the Divine. 452,
453, 458
Revelation of St. John the Divine self-
interpreted. 454
Revelation of the Holy Spirit. 1833
Revelation of the secret orders of Western
Africa. 3322
Revelation of "the things that are" 462
Revelation of treasure hid. 2746
Revelation rediscovered. 605
Revelation simplified, verse by verse. 454
Revelation symbolism. 3227
Revelation systematically studied. 453
Revelation, the book of unity. 460
Revelation: the divine fire. 3226
Revelation-the last book of the Bible. 460
Revelation theology. 3227
Revelation through reason. 3078
Revelation to John. 454
Revelation to John (the Apocalypse) 456
Revelation today. 455
Revelation, trial and exile of John in epics.
3226
Revelation twenty, an exposition. 465
Revelation, universal and special. 3225
Revelation vs. evolution. 3227
Revelation visualized. 453
Revelations. 460
Revelations and messages as given through
Mary Ann Van Hoof at Necedah,
Wisconsin, 1950-1970. 2679
Revelations and repudiations. 3505
Revelations of a spirit medium. 3501,
3520
Revelations of Antichrist, concerning
Christ and Christianity. 1091, 3227
Revelations of divine love. 1448
Revelations of divine love of Julian of
Norwich. 1448, 1449
Revelations of divine love shewed to a
devout ankress. 1448
Revelations of Hermes. 2723
Revelations of Louise. 3498
Revelations of Mechthild of Magdeburg
(1210-1297) 2647
Revelations of St. Bridget on the life and
passion of Our Lord. 1985
Revelations on Revelation. 453
Revelations revealed. 453, 462
Revelations; Saint Birgitta of Sweden. 663
Revelation's wonderland. 312
Revell's Dictionary of Bible people. 216
Revell's Dictionary of Bible times. 246
Revell'S guide to Christian colleges. 1164
Revell's minister's annual. 3376
Revell's minister's annual, 1965. 3376
Revered by all. 2162
Reverence for life. 3368, 3370
Reverend Calvin Lincoln. 2230, 3726
Reverend Charles Strong and the
Australian Church. 3536
Reverend Colonel Finch. 1625
Reverend doctor. 3125
Reverend Edward Morgan, 1751?-1844.
2597
Reverend Elhanan Winchester: biography
and letters. 3819
Reverend George Junkin. 2159
Reverend John Doe, D. D. 3674
Reverend John Niles, 1775-1812. 2711
Reverend landlords and their tenants.
3819
Reverend Michael J. Sheehan, C. SS. R.
3401
Reverend Mother M. Xavier Warde,
foundress of the Order of mercy in the
United States. 3417, 3795
Reverend Robert Stuart. 3536
Reverend Samuel Davies abroad. 1763
Reverent skeptic. 1854
Reverential fear in matrimonial cases in
Asiatic countries. 2341
Reveries of a hermit. 781
Revetues de force. 1404
Review and refutation of some of the
opprobrious charges against the Society
of Friends. 1687
Review, by a layman of a work entitled,
"New themes for the Protestant clergy:
creeds without charity, theology without
humanity, and Protestantism without
Christianity." 1312, 3440
Review notes and study guide to the New
Testament. 474
Review notes and study guide to the Old
Testament. 596
Review of A debate on Christian baptism.
732, 1906
Review of Doct. Emmons's theory of
God's agency on mankind. 1511, 2982

Review of Dr. Bushnell's "God in Christ"
106, 719
Review of Edward's "Inquiry into the
freedom of the will" 1499, 1658
Review of Major's Reasons for
acknowledging the authority of the
Roman see. 2318, 2768
Review of Mary M. Dyer's publication,
entitled "A portraiture of Shakerism"
2348
Review of Mr. Whitman's letters to
Professor Stuart. 3193, 3814
Review of Remington's Reasons for being
a Baptist. 133, 3214
...A review of Rev. Charles Beecher's
report concerning the spiritual
manifestations. 183, 3496
Review of Rev. J. B. Jeter's book entitled
"Campbellism examined" 1461, 2072
Review of the Bibles. 221
Review of the decision of the Supreme
court of the United States, in the case of
Geo. Reynolds vs. the United States.
2858, 3234
Review of the evidences of Christianity.
1091, 1092
Review of the general and particular causes
which have produced the late disorders
and divisions in the Yearly meeting of
Friends, held in Philadelphia. 1687
Review of the Lady Superior's reply to
"Six months in a convent" 2563
Review of the life and character of
Archbishop Secker. 3317
Review of the life and writings of M. Hale
Smith. 3431, 3752
Review of the most important events
relating to the rise and progress of the
United society of believers in the West.
3396
Review of the noted revival in Kentucky.
2167
Review of the principal doctrines of Elias
Hicks, as exhibited in his own language.
1681
Review of the principal questions in
morals. 1536
Review of the reply to his sermon of the
9th of August 1818. 1772
Review of the Rev. Jared Sparks' letters
on the Protestant Episcopal church.
3470
Review of the Rev. Thomas Andros's
Essay on the doctrine of divine
efficiency. 41, 3412
Review of the Reverend Aaron Pickett's
"Reply" and "Defense" 2845
Review of the "spiritual manifestations."
3495
Review of the trail, conviction, and final
imprisonment in the common jail of the
county of Suffolk, of Abner Kneeland.
671
Review of the world's religious congress.
3118
...A review of theoretical geology. 203
Review on the biography of Bhagawan
Gopinath Ji of Kashmir. 1635
Reviewer reviewed. 1626, 2941
Reviews & studies. 230, 932
Revised ceremonial of the Mass. 2368
Revised edition of the Baltimore catechism
no. 2. 768
Revised Epistles of the New Testament.
368, 1631
Revised Knight Templarism illustrated.
1665
Revised minutes of the annual meetings of
the German Baptist brethren. 1236
Revised New Testament and history of
revision. 268
Revised normal lessons. 3178
Revised Psalter. 1215
Revised report of fourteen talks. 3686
Revised search light on the seventh day
Bible and x-ray. 3567
Revised service book. 2961
Bible. 275
Revised Webb-Cumbie discussion on the
question, Which are primitive Baptist
churches? 143
Revision or new translation? 355
... Revitalizing religion. 3092
Revitalizing the twentieth-century church.
1244
Revival. 1577, 3228, 3229, 3230
Revival addresses. 1561
Revival and after the revival. 3229
Revival and camp meeting minstrel. 1868
Revival and its lessons. 3229
Revival and reformation. 3385
Revival and the pastor. 1569
Revival appeals. 1560
Revival at midnight, and other messages.
1558
Revival crusade sermons. 1561
Revival fires in Canada. 3230

Revival hand book. 3228
Revival hymns. 1868, 3230
Revival hymns and choruses. 3230
Revival in our time. 3232
Revival in romance and realism. 3852
Revival in Romans. 471
Revival incidents. 3228
Revival manual. 3228
Revival melodies. 3230
Revival messages. 1556
Revival now. 3229
Revival of a dead church. 3228
Revival of Mothering Sunday. 3229
Revival of paganism. 2756
Revival of scholastic philosophy in the
nineteenth century. 3309
Revival of the churches. 3228
Revival of the gift of healing. 3229
Revival of the gifts of healing. 2410
Revival of the liturgy. 1458, 2234
Revival of wonder. 3229
Revival of worship. 3854
Revival or ruin. 3229
Revival quiver. 1562
Revival sermon outlines. 1562
Revival sermons. 168, 1555, 1556, 1560,
3232
Revival sermons and outlines. 1560
Revival sermons in outline. 1560
Revival sermons preached in protracted
meetings. 1554
Revival sketches and manual. 1566
Revival system and the Paraclete. 3228
Revival thermometer. 1569, 3229
Revival times in America. 3232
Revival tornadoes. 3799
Revival waves. 1564
Revival we need. 1569, 3229
Revivalism and separatism in New
England, 1740-1800. 1468, 1469
Revivalism and social reform. 2956, 3233,
3739
Revivalism and social reform in mid-
nineteenth-century America. 3739
Revivalism in America. 3233
Revivalism in America, its origin, growth
and decline. 3233
Revivalist. 3230
Revivals and how to have them. 1565
Revivals and missions. 3228
Revivals and revival work. 1566
Revivals, awakenings, and reform. 3233
Revivals: how and when? 1568
Revivals in the midst of the years. 3230
Revivals of religion. 1566, 3228, 3229,
3230
Revivals of the Old Testament. 3230
Revivals, their laws and leaders. 3230
Revive Thy church. 975
Reviving revivals. 3230
Reviving the local church. 2480
... The Revolation of St. John the Divine.
452
Revolt against God. 1394
Revolt against heaven. 3617
Revolt against mechanism. 1280
Revolt against reason. 3079, 3082
Revolt against the church. 3033
Revolt against the faithful. 304
Revolt in Judea, the road to Masada.
2094
Revolt of Martin Luther. 2273
Revolt of the widows. 337
Revolt on mount Sinai. 2945
Revolution and church. 933
Revolution and freemasonry, 1680-1800.
1664
Revolution and papacy. 810
Revolution and Papacy, 1769-1846. 810
Revolution and redemption. 1135
Revolution and the Christian faith. 3233
Revolution in a city parish. 3676
Revolution in Christian missions. 2494
Revolution in evangelism. 1574, 3535
Revolution in Judaea. 2013, 2148
Revolution in missionary thinking. 850
Revolution in missionary thinking; a
symposium, edited by William J.
Richardson. 851
Revolution in missions. 2493
Revolution in religion. 3636
Revolution in Rome. 802
Revolution of love. 961
Revolution of Mary Leary. 3253
Revolution of the Latin American church.
821
Revolution of the saints. 1762
Revolution through peace. 815
Revolutionary Christianity. 3442
Revolutionary college. 2923
Revolutionary function of the modern
church. 1119
Revolutionary religion. 3444
Revolutionary theology in the making.
3611
Revolutionary year. 1262
Rev'rund, get your gun. 1302, 2740

Revue de l Orient chretien. 1189
*Revue de theologie et de philosophie. 3616
*Revue Thomiste. 3647
Reward of reincarnation. 3052
Rex Christus. 912
Rhapsody in black. 1936
Rhemes and Doway. 270, 274
Rhetoric in the Sunday collects of the Roman missal. 845
Rhetoric of Christian socialism. 3433
Rhetoric of Pascal. 2778
Rhetoric of religion. 113, 116, 526, 3070
Rhetorical criticism. 485, 2630
... A rhetorical study of St. John Chrysostom's De sacerdotio. 1115, 3234
Rhine flows into the Tiber. 3769, 3773
Rhode Island Baptists. 159
Rhyme and meaning in Richard Crashaw. 1379
Rhythm of God. 3003
Rhythm of plainsong according to the Solesmes school. 884
Rhythmic Psalter. 1215
Rhythms of vision. 2723
Rib. 3831
Rice Haggard. 1038, 1780
Rice Haggard, the American frontier evangelist who revived the name Christian. 1038, 1780
Rich and poor in the New Testament. 3439
Rich Christian in the church of the early empire. 3799
Rich Christians and poor Lazarus. 1085, 3850
Rich Christians in an age of hunger. 247, 1856
Rich church—poor church? 2480
Rich feast. 237
Rich fool. 3235
Rich heritage of Quakerism. 1676
Rich kinsman. 3258
Rich man and Lazarus. 1470
Rich man in hell. 1288
Rich man poor man. 1076
Rich revelations of Jesus which meet a man's practical need in the twentieth century. 463
Rich, the poor—and the Bible. 2866
Rich young man. 54
Richard. 3235
Richard Allen. 14, 26
... Richard Baxter. 179
Richard Baxter & Puritan politics. 1764
Richard Baxter and the Millenium. 179, 2466
Richard Cameron. 731
Richard Cardinal Cushing in prose and photos. 1397
Richard Crashaw. 1379
Richard Crashaw, "poet and saint." 1379
Richard Fitzralph. 1628
Richard Henry Tierney. 3699
Richard Hooker. 1844
Richard Hooker, a descriptive bibliography of the early editions: 1593-1724. 1844
Richard Hooker and the politics of a Christian England. 1516, 1844
Richard Hooker Wilmer. 3818
Richard Hurd's Letters on chivalry and romance. 1857
Richard L. Evans—the man and the message. 1577
Richard Mather. 2373, 3660
Richard Mather of Dorchester. 1333, 2373
Richard Pattee's Catholicism in Latin America. 825
Richard Philip Garrold, S.J. 1702
Richard Price. 2938
Richard R. Niebuhr on Christ and religion. 2709
Richard Taylor. 2542, 3591
Richard Weber Oliver. 2736
Richard Wilton: a forgotten Victorian. 3819
Richards Bible story book. 623
Richardson's monitor of free-masonry. 1669, 1670
Richelieu. 1639, 3236
Richelieu and reason of state. 1639, 3236
Richelieu and the growth of French power. 1639, 3236
Richer by India. 2532
Riches. 1940
Riches and the spirit. 3529
Riches despised. 973
Riches from Revelation. 454
Riches in Christ. 365, 3358
Riches of Bunyan. 716, 3198
Riches of Christ. 2210
Riches of divine grace. 1024
Riches of God's love unto the vessells of mercy. 1820, 2911
Riches of His grace. 1451, 1752, 3200
Riches of the kigdom. 3843

Riches of the kingdom. 3843
Riches to share. 3151
Richest lady in town. 985, 2195
Richest of the poor. 1643
Richmond Baptists working together, 1780-1960. 159
Richmond Hill sermons. 3364
Riddle of history. 497
Riddle of Konnersreuth. 2685, 3531, 3532
Riddle of life. 1056, 1746, 2226
Riddle of personality. 2822, 2823
Riddle of Roman Catholicism. 801
Riddle of the Didache. 3592
Riddle of the future. 3321
Riddle of the 'Labarum' and the origin of Christian symbols. 892
Riddle of the New Testament. 348
Riddle of the Scrolls. 1410
Riddle of the universe at the close of the nineteenth century. 2584
Riddle of the world. 1740
Riddles of the Sphinx. 1854
Ride the hot wind. 1363, 1458
Ride the wild horses! 3352
Rider on the white horse. 3200
Ridgecrest, mountain of faith. 3237
Ridgecrest story. 3237
Ridgway's religion for folks who don't have any. 3177
Riding the night mare. 3827
Rift in Israel. 2151
Rifts in the universe. 2739
Rig for church. 3131
Rig-veda repetitions. 3776
Right and the good. 1746
Right and wrong after the war. 3440
*Right and wrong; student's book. 3191
Right and wrong unveilings of the spiritual world, by Rev. John Goddard. 3503
Right and wrong uses of the Bible. 640
Right and wrong ways to use the Bible. 653
Right conception of sin. 3412
Right-hand glove uplifted. 1801
Right here at home. 2527
Right here, right now ! 3856
Right in Romans. 466
'A right judgment in all things. 972
Right living in a world gone wrong. 3742
Right method of addressing the Divine Majesty in prayer. 2868
Right of the Bible in our public schools. 300
Right of the community to a priest. 773, 2789
Right or wrong? 3171, 3887
Right Rev. Edward Dominic Fenwick, O. P. 1622
Right Reverend New Dealer, John A. Ryan. 3258
Right road. 944
Right side up. 1785
Right side up, and other inspirational essays to show that happiness lies in your point of view. 1785
Right, the good & the happy. 947
Right to be merry. 2573
Right to believe. 1064, 1596
Right to birth. 3
Right to development. 1155
Right to die: decision and decision makers. 1544
Right to heresy. 889, 890
Right to remarry. 1471
Right way. 160
Right where you are sitting now. 2730
Right with God. 62
Right, wrong, or what? 3394
Righte merrie Christmasse!!! 1110
Righteous empire. 2955
Righteous indignation. 2589
Righteous lives. 3016
Righteous man's evidence for Heaven. 1794
Righteous remnant. 1849
Righteous ruler. 1940
Righteousness and society. 3446
Righteousness and society, ecumenical dialog in a revolutionary age. 3446
Righteousness by faith. 2160
Righteousness in Matthew and his world of thought. 442, 1739
Righteousness in the New Testament. 477, 1739
Righteousness of God. 1739, 2277
Righteousness of the kingdom. 3445
Rightly dividing the Scriptures. 2405
Rightly dividing the word. 235, 347
Rightly dividing the word of truth. 3288
Rightly dividing the Word of truth (2 Tim. ii, 15.) 479
Rightous empire. 2956
... The rights and duties of bishops regarding diocesan sisterhoods. 2577
Rights and duties of ordinaries. 2575
Rights and obligations of labor according to the Bible. 3439

"Rights and Responsibilities," and other High Holiday sermons. 3363
Rights and responsibilities of national churches. 1141
Rights of our little ones. 804
Rights of the Congregational churches of Massachusetts. 1337, 1335
Rights of young Methodists. 2459
Rigid scrutiny. 499
Rigveda. 3776
Rim of Christendom. 2177
Rim of the Caribbean. 2559
Ring of truth. 361
Ring piece. 2389
Ringing call to mission. 1279
Ringing doorbells for God. 3203
Ringing realities. 2920
Rings and things. 3843
Rings in the redwoods. 2626
Ripe mangoes. 1362
Rise and decline of the program of education for Black Presbyterians of the United Presbyterian Church, U.S.A., 1865-1970. 3190, 3736
Rise and destiny of the German Jew. 2099
Rise and development of Calvinism. 727, 730
Rise and fall of Nauvoo. 2617
Rise & fall of superwoman. 35, 3403
Rise and fall of the Anabaptists. 36
Rise and fall of the High commission. 1763
Rise and fall of the individual. 1905
Rise and fall of the Judaean state. 2092
Rise and fall of the Judaen state. 2092
Rise and fall of the Victorian Sunday. 3548
Rise and growth of English hymnody. 1872
Rise and progress of Freemasonry in Illinois. 1665
Rise and progress of religion in the soul. 959
Rise and progress of the people called Quakers. 1675, 1685
Rise and progress of the serpent from the garden of Eden, to the present day. 2205, 3396
Rise and the fall. 1746
Rise, Glorious Conqueror, an Easter cantata for mixed voices (S.A.T.B) 736, 737
Rise of a pagan state. 1936
Rise of a soul. 2921
Rise of Adventism. 3748
Rise of American missions. 14
Rise of Biblical criticism in America, 1800-1870. 241, 2687
Rise of Christian education. 3165
Rise of Christianity. 407, 1189
Rise of "Colored Methodism" 1021
Rise of ecclesiastical control in Quebec. 1148
Rise of Gentile Christianity. 1191
Rise of man. 2835
Rise of Methodism. 2423
Rise of Methodism in the West. 2458
Rise of modern Judaism. 2146
Rise of modern mythology, 1680-1860. 2664
Rise of modern religious ideas. 3654
Rise of moralism. 3655
Rise of political anti-Semitism in Germany and Austria. 54
Rise of Protestant monasticism. 2583
Rise of Puritanism. 3007, 3009
Rise of Quakerism in Amsterdam, 1655-1665. 1686
Rise of Reform Judaism. 3032
Rise of religious education among Negro Baptists. 157
Rise of religious liberty in America. 3194
Rise of the anti-mission Baptists. 2941
Rise of the Church of the Nazarene. 1237
Rise of the Cistercian strict observance in seventeenth century France. 1276
Rise of the cults. 3325, 3326
Rise of the current reformation. 1464
Rise of the downtrodden. 822
Rise of the Israelite monarchy. 483, 2177
Rise of the Jew in the western world. 2099
Rise of the Jewish community of New York. 2101
Rise of the Jewish community of New York, 1654-1860. 2101
Rise of the Karaite sect. 2164
Rise of the mediaeval church and its influence on the civilisation of Western Europe from the first to the thirteenth century. 1186
Rise of the mediaeval church and its influence on the civilisation of western Europe from the first to the thirteenth century. 1185

Rise of the missionary spirit in America, 1790-1815. 2501
Rise of the monophysite movement. 2585
Rise of the New Testament. 406
Rise of the social gospel in American Protestantism. 3452
Rise of the social gospel in American Protestantism, 1865-1915. 3433
Rise of the tyrant. 1134
Rise of toleration. 3703
Rise of world Lutheranism. 1045, 2288
Rise, progress and travels of the Church of Jesus Christ of latter-day saints. 1231, 2605
Rise, spring and foundation of the Anabaptists. 36
Rise to conquer. 987
Rise up and remember. 875, 2676
Risen Christ. 865, 1448, 2054
Risen Christ and the Eucharistic world. 2052, 2255
Risen Christ in the fathers of the church. 1616, 2010
Risen dead. 2393
Risen indeed. 2053, 2054
Risen Redeemer. 2052
Rising churches in non-christian lands. 2518
Rising storm. 827, 1150, 3244
Rising through the dust. 912
Rising tide. 2499
Rising tide of Islam. 1924
Risk and rhetoric in religion. 3070, 3813
Risk of love. 1736
Risk of the cross. 437, 2809
Risky living. 700, 981
Rite and man. 2235
Rite for Christian burial and the funeral Mass according to the text in the Collectio rituum. 840, 846
Rite for Christian burial and the funeral Mass according to the text in the Collectio rituum, with explanatory comment. 846
Rite for marriage and the nuptial Mass according to the text in the Collectio rituum. 2345
Rite for marriage and the nuptial Mass according to the text in the Collectio rituum, with explanatory comment. 2345
Rite of baptism for children. 843
Rite of concelebration of Mass and of Communion under both species. 1322
Rite of exorcism. 2726
Rite of ordination according to the Roman pontifical. 848
Rite thing. 3852
Rites and ceremonies of sacred ordination (canons 1002-1005) 2741
Rites and ceremonies of the Greek church, in Russia. 2748
Rites and ritual of Episcopal Methodism. 2453
Rites and symbols of initiation. 1908
Rites of Christian initiation. 838
Rites of Eastern Christendom. 851
Rites of Holy Week. 844
Rites of modern occult magic. 1806
Rites of ordination and episcopal consecration. 836
Rites of the Catholic Church as revised by decree of the Second Vatican Ecumenical Council and published by authority of Pope Paul VI. 848
... Rites of the twice-born. 1814
Ritschl, a reappraisal. 3239
Ritschl & Luther; a fresh perspective on Albrecht Ritschl's theology in the light of his Luther study. 2281
Ritschlianism. 3239
Ritual. 2108, 2120, 3239
Ritual and ceremonial commentary on the occasional offices of holy baptism, matrimony, penance, communion of the sick, and extreme unction. 3239
Ritual and manual of the Temperance temple. 3240
Ritual and religion among Muslims in India. 1925
Ritual and rhetoric. 1518
Ritual and rhetoric: intellectual and ceremonial backgrounds to Middle English literature. 1518
Ritual book of formulas. 888
Ritual book of magic. 2311
Ritual ... containing the opening and closing ceremonies, degrees of knighthood, mystery and chivalry, and installation. 3240
Ritual cosmos. 12
Ritual for small churches. 843
Ritual for subordinate lodges. 3240
Ritual for the use of all councils. 3239
Ritual for use in local camps of the Order of the golden seal. 3240
Ritual law of the church. 1490
Ritual magic. 2312

Ritual murder. 1214
Ritual of battle. 2186, 2316
Ritual of freemasonry, illustrated by numerous engravings. 1668
Ritual of living. 2999
Ritual of the Giant oaks. 3239
Ritual of the independent order of the Sons and daughters of Jacob of Florida and America. 3240
Ritual of the Methodist church. 2433, 2722
Ritual of the Methodist Episcopal church. 2454
Ritual of the Methodist Episcopal church, South. 2455
Ritual of the three symbolic degrees of the Ancient & Accepted Scottish Rite of Freemasons, under the jurisdiction of the National Supreme Council. 1669
Ritual of the wind. 1902
Ritual; psycho-analytic studies. 2999, 3239
Ritual 'reason why. 1224
Ritual, religion, and the sacred. 1097
Ritual, Second temple, Fraternity sons of Osiris. 3240
Ritual. Temple of "Osiris-Isis." 3240
Ritual theory of myth. 2648
Ritualism and politics in victorian Britain. 3240
Ritualistic occultism, true white magic. 2728
Rituals of manhood. 3002
Rituals of the Kandyan state. 712, 2162
Rival philosophies of Jesus and of Paul. 1595
Rival presuppositions in the writing of church history. 1184
Rivalitat zwischen Engeln und Menschen. 43
River Jordan. 282, 2131
River of God. 3056
River of life. 2935, 3368
River of light. 2151, 3118
River of pearls, composed of "The river of life" 161
River of years. 3201
River Plate republics. 2501
Rivers of living water. 1829
Rivers of the flood. 45
Rivers, rice fields, souls. 2512
Riverside church in the city of New York. 1171
Riverside Church survey report. 3568
Riverside New Testament. 353
Riverside preachers. 1635, 3357
Riverton study. 2140
Riveter's gang. 3229
Rivulet from the ocean of truth. 3494
Road. 2920
Road ahead. 1095, 1122, 1700, 2948
Road back. 2751
Road back to God. 3886, 3887
Road down in the sea. 1584
Road East: America's new discovery of eastern wisdom. 1485
Road He trod. 2397
...The road I know. 3518
Road of life, a study of Pilgrim's journey as far as Vanity Fair. 717
Road of pain. 3525
Road of the loving heart. 1108
Road to Augusta. 169, 1849
Road to brotherhood. 155, 156
Road to certainty. 2435
Road to Christmas. 1112
Road to citizenship. 2590
Road to Damascus. 1364, 2639
Road to Eleusis. 1505
Road to faith. 1593, 3062
Road to freedom. 3896
Road to fulfillment. 3481
Road to happiness. 181, 203, 971, 2391
Road to immortality. 1891
Road to inner freedom (The ethics) 1537
Road to Jerusalem. 388, 1986
Road to KEEP. 2534, 3255
Road to Mecca. 1366
Road to Nashville. 3468
Road to Nazareth. 1711, 2762
Road to our meeting house. 1685
Road to paradise. 623
Road to peace. 996, 2807
Road to peace (The) 2808
Road to power. 1094
Road to reconciliation. 15
Road to recovery. 145, 3466
Road to reformation. 2272
Road to relevance. 948
Road to Renewal. 3774
Road to reunion. 2972
Road to revival. 1556, 1557
Road to salvation. 2785
Road to Santiago. 1934, 3303
Road to self-knowledge. 3527
Road to spiritualism. 3504
Road to the Cross. 1977

Road to total freedom. 3314
Road to unity. 1040
Road to unity among the Christian churches. 1046
Road to universal peace. 2808
Road without turning. 3133
Roadblock to Moscow. 1574
Roadblocks to faith. 66
Roadmending on the sacred way. 343
Roads. 426, 989
Roads converge. 3621
Roads from Eden. 602
Roads of prayer. 2876
Roads to Christian democrady. 156
Roads to God. 1449
Roads to Jewish survival. 1348
Roads to radiant living. 954
Roads to reality. 3521, 3845
Roads to Rome. 791, 1364, 1365
Roads to the city of God. 1913
Roads we travel. 3356
Roadside tables. 1449
Roar from the cave. 1811, 1943
Robbie's Bible stories. 624
Robbing youth of its religion. 3885
Robe. 1825
Robe and ring. 2312
Robe and the sword. 2438
Robed and crowned. 3228, 3800
Robert. 186
Robert A. Smith. 3431
Robert Alexander. 24
Robert Alexander and the early Methodist church in Texas. 24, 2457
Robert Baillie and the second Scots Reformation. 130, 1375
Robert Barclay. 173
Robert Bellarmine. 186
Robert Browning: his life and poetry. 697
Robert Buchanan, D.D. 699
Robert G. Ingersoll. 1908
Robert G. Lee's sourcebook of 500 illustrations. 1841
Robert Garry. 1702
Robert Gray. 1757
Robert Grosseteste. 1763, 1775
Robert Hindmarsh. 3132
Robert Ingersoll. 1907
Robert Moffat. 2499, 2563
Robert R. Church family of Memphis. 1167, 2128
Robert R. McBurney: a memorial, 1837-1898. 2365
Robert Raikes: his Sunday schools and his friends. 3019, 3561
... Robert Sanderson, chaplain to King Charles the First, regius professor of divinity, Oxford, and bishop of Lincoln. 3300
Robert Schuller, my father & my friend. 1301, 3311
Robert Schuller's Life changers. 2396
Robert Winchelsey and the crown, 1294-1313. 1145, 3819
Robert Woodknow's difficulties in finding a church home. 3133
Robes of splendor. 161
Robinson from Mars papers. 3062
Robust in faith. 216
... Rochester. 3242
... Rochester theological seminary. 3242
Rock and Lava. 686
Rock & the church. 3072
Rock and the river. 992
Rock, Bach & superschlock. 3072
Rock-breakers. 2513
Rock cannot be moved. 1908
Rock in a weary land. 14
Rock of ages. 3713
Rock of our salvation. 2042
Rock of truth. 1267, 1364, 3502
Rock, practical help for those who listen to the words and don't like what they hear. 3887
Rock strata and the Bible record. 203
Rock that is higher. 3066
Rockefeller chapel sermons of recent years. 3358
Rockefeller McCormick New Testament. 2330
Rocket trip to Israel. 2763
Rocking the ark. 1244
Rocking the pulpit. 2788
Rocks and flowers. 73
Rocks and rills. 2395
Rocks and shoals. 1324
Rocks are for lizards. 1002
Rocks of the ages. 1600
Rocks, relics, and Biblical reliability. 209
Rocky Mountain Empire. 1233, 2618
Rocky Mountain religion. 3268
Rocky Mountain saints. 2616
Rod McKuen's Book of days and a month of Sundays. 2392
Rodeheaver recitations. 3027
Rodrigues the interpreter. 3243

Roger Bacon on the nullity of magic. 2314
Roger, Bishop of Worcester, 1164-1179. 666, 3243
Roger Widdrington last reioynder, 1619. 793, 2863
Roger Williams. 1141, 3817, 3818
Roger Williams and the fight for religious freedom. 3817
Roger Williams, John Cotton, and religious freedom. 3193, 3817
Rogue elephant. 2490
Rogues of the Bible. 213
Role of Clement VII in Guicciardini's works. 1288
Role of demonstration in moral theology. 950
Role of faith in physics. 2845
Role of history in religion. 1819
Role of human sacrifice in the ancient Near East. 3272
Role of ideology in church participation. 3454
Role of knowledge in Western religion. 2181
Role of professional guidance in Jesuit institutions. 1946
Role of providence in the social order. 2983
Role of reason in belief. 3107
Role of religion in modern European history. 1187
Role of religion in modern Jewish history. 2149
... The role of religious education in the accommodation of a sect. 2614
Role of rural social science in theological education. 3681
Role of the Augsburg Confession. 110, 861
Role of the Bible in contemporary Christian education. 639
Role of the Christian intellectual. 1397
Role of the church in New France. 815, 1899
Role of the district superintendent in the Methodist Church. 2440
Role of the faith mission. 2504
Role of the independent school in American democracy. 831
Role of the laity in the church. 2191
Role of the laymen in the ancient church. 1184
... The role of the Maronites in the return of the Oriental churches. 849
Role of the mind in the universe. 3122
Role of the minister in caring for the dying patient and the bereaved. 2782
Role of the minister's wife. 1303
Role of the mosque. 2624
Role of the nun in nineteenth century America. 2718
. . . The role of the rabbi in human relations. 3016
Role of the Servant. 3377
Role of the YWCA in a changing era; the YWCA study of YMCA-YWCA cooperative experiences. 3873
Role of theology in the university. 3681
Role of women in early Christianity. 3836
Roles in the liturgical assembly. 2236
Roll away the stone. 1782
Rolling along in song. 2680
Rollo code of morals. 2589
Roma sacra. 3245
Roma Sacra; essays on Christian Rome. 757
Roman Aeneas. 11
Roman and Christian imperialism. 1197
Roman & evangelical. 2286
Roman & evangelical Gospel and ministry. 2286
Roman augury and Etruscan divination. 1471
Roman breviary. 842
Roman Breviary in English, restored by the Sacred Council of Trent. 841
Roman canon law in the Church of England. 1212, 1489
Roman catacombs. 745
Roman Catholic and Protestant Bibles compared. 654
Roman Catholic and unity. 1044
Roman Catholic Bible, and the Roman Catholic church. 800
Roman Catholic Church. 756
Roman Catholic church and the Church of England. 1225
Roman Catholic Church and the creation of the modern Irish state, 1878-1886. 819, 1147
Roman Catholic Church and the North-West school question. 815, 1144
Roman Catholic church as a factor in the political and social history of Mexico. 822

Roman Catholic church at the fountain head. 827
Roman Catholic church challenged in the discussion of thirty-two questions. 3244
Roman Catholic Church in colonial Latin America. 821
Roman Catholic Church in England and the Ten Propositions of the Churches' Unity Commission. 866, 1044
Roman Catholic Church in modern Latin America. 821
Roman Catholic church in the modern state. 756
Roman Catholic Church in the United States. 827
Roman Catholic claims. 799
Roman Catholic in the White House. 828, 1151
Roman Catholic modernism. 2562
Roman Catholic not the one only true religion. 802, 3426
Roman Catholic problem. 799
Roman Catholicism. 755, 757, 758, 798, 803, 812
Roman Catholicism against itself. 800
Roman Catholicism analyzed. 801
Roman Catholicism and the American way of life. 874
Roman Catholicism and the Bible. 644
Roman Catholicism in England. 817
Roman Catholicism in England, from the Reformation to 1950. 817
Roman Catholicism in the light of their own Scriptures and authorities. 871
Roman Catholicism investigated and exposed. 871
Roman Catholicism slays. 802
Roman Catholicism today. 758
Roman Catholocism [!] its origin and doctrine. 802
Roman Christianity in Latin America. 2548
Roman collar. 773
Roman converts. 1364
Roman curia and the communion of churches. 757
Roman curia as it now exists. 778
Roman customs and practices. 798
Roman dogma versus Bible doctrine. 148
Roman emperor worship. 1395
Roman festivals of the period of the Republic. 1395
Roman Hellenism and the New Testament. 1081
Roman hymnal. 813
Roman ideas of Deity in the last century before the Christian era. 3246
Roman Inquisition and the Venetian press, 1540-1605. 1910, 2937
Roman letter today. 470
Roman life and letters. 3245
Roman liturgy. 841
Roman martyrology. 2350
Roman Missal. 846
Roman missal in Latin and English for Holy Week and Easter Week. 844
Roman mythology. 2667
Roman myths. 2667
Roman primacy to A.D. 461. 1192
Roman questions of Plutarch. 3246
Roman religion. 3244
Roman religion and Roman Empire. 3246
Roman rite in Orthodoxy. 2746
Roman ritual. 837
Roman road. 3130
Roman see in the early Church. 1189
Roman Seraphic missal. 846
Roman siege of Jerusalem. 1944
Roman society and Roman law in the New Testament. 408
Roman Socrates. 1625
Roman sources of Christian art. 79, 922
Roman Stoicism. 3532
Roman system of religion. 791
Roman temples of Lebanon. 3600
Roman way of salvation. 798
Romance of a doctor's visits. 1360
Romance of a heavenly princess. 2497
Romance of a nun. 1357
Romance of a people. 2094
Romance of a priest. 2939
Romance of African Methodism. 14
Romance of an orphan, Ken. 3132
Romance of Bible scripts and scholars. 291
Romance of Christian experience. 972
Romance of doorbells. 3671
Romance of evangelism. 1567
Romance of evolution, and its relation to religion. 3078
Romance of Hassidism. 1789
...The romance of history. 46
Romance of Jesus. 1970
Romance of Lady Poverty. 738
Romance of metaphysics. 2695
Romance of missionary heroism. 2493
Romance of missionary pioneers. 2482

Romance of missions in Nigeria. 2542
Romance of Mother Nature and Father Time. 3574
Romance of old New England churches. 2687
Romance of preaching. 2901
Romance of rescue. 1280
Romance of right living. 979
Romance of rural churches. 3253
Romance of Ruth. 492, 3258
Romance of St. George s Chapel. 3820
Romance of St. George's Chapel, Windsor Castle. 3820
Romance of sorcery. 2313
Romance of soul winning. 1569
Romance of symbolism and its relation to church ornament and architecture. 920
Romance of the ages. 594, 595
Romance of the Bible. 289, 290
Romance of the Book. 612
Romance of the Book of common prayer. 2960
Romance of the Book of Mormon. 678
Romance of the Creed builders. 73
Romance of the dead. 1411
Romance of the English Bible. 248, 270, 3861
Romance of the Episcopal Church in west Tennessee, 1832-1964. 2974
Romance of the Episcopal Church in west Tennessee, 1832-1964. Photos, and reproductions by Nadia Price. 2974
Romance of the future. 3318
Romance of the gospel. 2526
Romance of the ministry. 1295
Romance of the Salvation army. 3292
Romance of winning children. 1253
Romances and intrigues of the women of the Bible. 3839
Romances of the California mission days. 726
... Romanesque architecture. 79
Romanesque cathedrals and abbeys of France. 1159
Romanesque sculpture at Lincoln Cathedral. 2230, 3316
Romanesque wooden doors of Auvergne. 3846
Romanian icons painted on glass. 1881
Romanism a menace to the nation. 798
Romanism and ruin. 801
Romanism and the gospel. 802
Romanism and the republic. 800
Romanism and truth. 798
Romanism as a world power. 1150
Romanism as it is. 797
Romanism at home. 801, 3585
Romanism in its home. 799
Romanism in Russia. 825
Romanism in the light of history. 801
Romanism in the light of Scripture. 801
Romanism vs. Americanism. 798
Romanism versus the public school system. 831
... Romans. 466, 467, 468, 469, 470, 471, 472, 3364, 3365
Romans, a model for Bible study methods. 471
Romans: a revolutionary manifesto. 470
Romans; an exposition of chapters 3.20-4.25. 470, 3364
Romans, an interpretive outline. 471
...Romans and I and IICorinthians, t. 321
Romans and their gods in the age of Augustus. 3246
Romans debate. 470
Romans for the children's hour. 471
Romans for the everyday man. 467
Romans for the layman. 469
Romans in the Greek New Testament for the English reader. 469
Romans realized. 467
Romans: the gospel of God's grace. 468
Romans, verse by verse. 469
Romantic idealism and Roman Catholicism. 3628, 3717
Romantic movement and Methodism. 1549, 1550
Romantic religion. 3203
Romantic story of Schoenbrunn, the first town in Ohio. 2596, 3309
Romanticism and the romantic school in Germany. 3244
Romanticism comes of age. 50
Romanticism in American theology. 2411, 3306
Romanticism of St. Francis. 1640, 1645
Rome and Canterbury, through four centuries. 1225
Rome and Jerusalem. 2099
Rome and reform. 809, 2978
Rome and reunion. 2769
Rome and Russia, a tragedy of errors. 2750
Rome and the Counter-Reformation in Scandinavia. 1374
Rome and the negro. 2682

Rome and the study of Scripture. 636, 644
Rome and the validity of orders in the Polish National Catholic Church. 2742, 2857
Rome and the vernacular. 2196
Rome and the White House. 1150
Rome and Washington. 814
Rome, Christian and papal. 802
Rome from within. 781
Rome in prophecy. 459
Rome is home. 1365
Rome, opponent or partner? 861
Rome or Jerusalem? 798
Rome or reason. 782, 794, 2328
Rome stoops to conquer. 826
Rome vs. Rome. 1147
Rome Baptist Church, 1835-1865. 3244
Romewards. 762
Romish priests' recent outrages. 2939
Romocanto. 3209
Ronald Brunlees McKerrow. 656
Ronald Carnaquay. 3127
Ronald Knox. 2182
Ronayne's hand-book of freemasonry. 1664, 1670
Ronayne's reminiscences. 3134
Ronnie and the Commandments. 1315
Roof bosses in medieval churches. 683
Room for improvement. 2977
Room to be people. 3623
Room to grow. 2433
Roosevelt and romanism. 875, 3247, 3740
Roosevelt and the money kings. 3247
Roosevelt steam rolled by the Bible. 3247
Root and flower of prayer. 2873
Root and the branch. 2138
Root of man's trouble--and man's hope. 954
Root of the matter. 3060
Root of the righteous. 1072
Root of the thing. 549
Root of the vine. 652
Rooted in faith: homilies to a contemporary world. 862, 3369
Rooted in hope. 1475
Rooted in hope;the story of the Dominican Sisters of Racine, Wis. 1475
Roots and fruits of the Christian life. 3362
Roots in a moving stream. 1332, 2100
Roots of a Black future. 16
Roots of a radical. 1217, 3633
Roots of Christian teaching as found in the Old Testament. 598
Roots of Christianity. 1103
Roots of consciousness. 2990
Roots of evil. 1745
Roots of fundamentalism. 1690, 1691
Roots of Ghana Methodism. 2430
Roots of hymnody in the Lutheran Church, Missouri Synod. 1208
Roots of Lomomba. 2272, 2557
Roots of modern Mormonism. 2603
Roots of peace. 3685
Roots of reality. 2832
Roots of religious doubt and the search for security. 3100
Roots of ritual. 3240
Roots of St. Francis. 92, 820
Roots of spring. 1385
Roots of the radical theology. 3656
Roots of the Reformation. 783, 2272
Roots of the reorganization. 2545, 3217
Roots of unbelief. 65
Roots of war resistance. 1089
Roots, religion, and revival. 3254
Ropes to Burma. 3235
Rosa Ferrucci. 1622
Rosamond. 798
Rosanna of the Amish. 2407, 3863
Rosanna's boys. 2407
Rosarian's handbook of the Society of the rosary altar. 3248
Rosary. 2876, 3248
Rosary and the living word. 3247
Rosary and the soul of woman. 3248
Rosary bibliography. 3248
Rosary for boys and girls. 3248
Rosary for children. 3248
Rosary for Lent. 2211
Rosary for little Catholics. 3249
Rosary in action. 3248
Rosary in daily life. 3248
Rosary in union with Saint Bernadette at the shrine of Lourdes. 3248
Rosary of facts. 63
Rosary of illustrations of the Bible. 3204
Rosary of Mary. 3247
Rosary of Our Lady. 3248
Rosary, the crown of Mary. 3248
Rosary thoughts for priests. 3248
Rose and the Lily. 3247
Rose cross order. 3021, 3250
Rose-garden game; a tradition of beads and flowers. 3248
Rose Hawthorne; the pilgrimage of Nathaniel's daughter. 2198

... Rose of America. 3247
Rose of Arragon. 3145
Rose of China. 3791
Rose of Jesus and Mary. 2335, 3438
Rose of Sharon. 165, 1450
Rose tree. 2335
Rose unpetaled. 3691
Rose works other than Science and health. 1031
Rose wreath for the Crowning of St. Therese of the Child Jesus. 3690
Rosemarie alannah. 819
Rosenius' Devotions. 1441
Roses and thorns. 16, 2297
Roses are grinning. 2888
Roses every day. 1448
Roses fall where rivers meet. 3222, 3690
Roses for Mexico. 1776
Rose's Maboh l'Chumosh. 565
Roses of hope. 1845
Roses of the ledge way. 686, 1006
Rosh ha-Shono, Yom Kippur. 1811
Rosh Hashanah. 3249
Rosh Hashanah and Yom Kippur. 1811
Rosh Hashanah anthology. 3249
Rosicrucian cosmo--conception. 3250
Rosicrucian enlightenment. 3251
Rosicrucian fundamentals. 3251
Rosicrucian literature listed in Union Catalog and not to be found in Library of Congress. 3251
Rosicrucian manual. 3250, 3251
Rosicrucian manual for the instruction of postulants in the associate membership neophytes, and fraters of duly instituted colleges of the Societas rosicrusians in America. 3251
Rosicrucian manual for the instruction of postulants in the congregation of the outer, neophytes, and fraters of duly instituted colleges of the Societas rosicruciana in America. 3251
Rosicrucian mysteries. 3250
Rosicrucian philosophy in questions and answers. 3250
Rosicrucian principles for the home and business. 2994, 3250
Rosicrucian questions and answers. 3250, 3251
Rosicrucian speaks. 3251
Rosicrucian symbology. 3251
Rosicrucians. 3250
Rosicrucians, their teachings. 3250
Rosicrucians, their teachings and mysteries according to the manifestoes issued at various times by the fraternity itself. 3250
Rosicrucians--their teachings, the Fraternitas Rosae Crucis, American section. 3250
Rosmini, Priest, philosopher and patriot. 3251
Rough-hewed, and other sermons. 3340
Roumania as I found it. 2102
Round about me. 901
Round church of Orphir, Orkney. 2744, 3574
Round the round world. 2521
Rounding out a century. 867, 1673
... Rounds and races. 2819
Rounds with the devil. 36
Rountree chronicles, 1827-1846. 3252
Rousseau and the religious quest. 3252
Rousseau, Kant, Goethe. 3252
Roving with the migrants. 2526
Royal. 1361
Royal adventure, St. Francis of Paola. 1650
Royal arch. 1670
Royal Arch encyclopedia. 1663
Royal arch standard. 1664
Royal banners fly. 662
Royal Bob. 1907
Royal bounty. 2502
Royal brickyard. 2623
Royal charter. 805
Royal Commission and the Ornaments rubric. 1224
Royal dainties. 1841
Royal dynasties in ancient Israel. 2090, 2177
Royal inn. 2005
Royal invitation. 1439
Royal manhood. 1325
Royal Persian manuscripts. 1883
Royal preacher. 512
Royal preacher. Lectures on Ecclesiastes. 512
Royal priesthood. 2939
Royal priesthood of the faithful. 2939
Royal prince. 2166
Royal Psalms. 575
Royal road. 3588
Royal road of the holy cross. 3526
Royal road to friendship. 1688
Royal road to happiness; or, The picture preacher. 3197

Royal road to life. 169
Royal route to heaven. 321
Royal scroll. 602, 1958
Royal servants: an Episcopal family heritage. 697
Royal Sufferer. 2031
Royal table. 2086
Royal truthers. 183
Royal truths. 183
Royal way. 974
Royal way of the cross. 2032
Royalroad lessons. 3164
Royalty of Jesus. 2055
Royalty of the pulpit. 2909
Royce's metaphysics. 2418, 3252
Rozell's complete lessons. 1916
Rubaiyat of Solomon, and other poems. 513
Rubies and diamonds. 3199
Rubies from Ruth. 589
Rubies in the sand. 3690
Rubrics of the revised Holy Week liturgy in English. 1837
Rubrics of the Roman Breviary and Missal with the motu proprio of Pope John XXIII another pertinent documents, calendar, tables of occurrence. 841
Rudder and the rock. 958
Rudimental divine science. 1031
Rudiments of sociology. 3450
Rudiments of theological and moral science. 3666
Rudolf Bultmann in Catholic thought. 713
Rudolf Otto's interpretation of religion. 2752
Rudolf Steiner and anthroposophy. 50, 3527
Rufus Jones, master Quaker. 2131
Rufus Jones speaks to our time. 1679, 3479
Rufus M. Jones, January 25, 1863-June 16, 1948. 2131
Rugged heart. 720
Ruhama, the story of a church, 1819-1945. 663
Ruin and recovery of man. 3356
Ruin and restoration. 2945
Ruin of a Christian. 1560
Ruin of antichrist. 51
Ruined abbeys of Great Britain. 2
Ruined abbeys of Yorkshire. 2
Ruland's Pastoral theology. 3676
Rule and exercise of holy living. 977
Rule and exercises of holy dying. 977, 992
Rule and exercises of holy living. 977, 3692
Rule and exercises of holy living together. 977
Rule and Testament of St. Francis. 1641
Rule for hermitages. 2233
Rule for monasteries. 2583
Rule of faith. 118
Rule of faith, being the Baird lecture for 1905. 118
Rule of God. 652
Rule of life. 118, 1325
Rule of peace. 188, 189
Rule of Qumran and its meaning. 3013
Rule of Saint Augustine. 2583
Rule of Saint Benedict. 187, 189, 190, 2583
Rule of Taize in French and in English. 2583
Rule of the Master. 2583
Rule of the road. 1359
Rule of the Secular Franciscan Order. 1649
... Rule, statutes and ceremonial of the Outsisters (Touriers) to the observed in the monasteries of the Discalced Carmelites. 740
Rule statutes and customs of the Hospitallers, 1099-1310. 2179
Ruler of the nativity. 97
Ruler who serves. 438
Rulers the ministers of God for the good of their people. 3360
Rulership book. 98
Rules and advice. 3519
Rules and constitutions of the Sisters of the holy nativity. 3416
... Rules and constitutions of the Sisters, servants of the immaculate heart of Mary. 3421
Rules and precepts of the Jesuit missions of northwestern New Spain. 1948, 1949
Rules and resolutions. 3217
Rules for right living and right conduct. 2070
Rules for the spiritual life. 3490
Rules for the War of the Sons of Light with the Sons of Darkness. 3014
Rules of discipline. 1679, 1680
Rules of discipline and advices of the Yearly Meeting of the Religious Society of Friends. 1680

Rules of discipline and advices of the Yearly meeting of the Religious society of Friends held in Philadelphia. 1680
Rules of discipline for Pennsylvania, New Jersey, Delaware, and the Eastern parts of Maryland. 1680
Rules of discipline of the Yearly Meeting of Friends. 1680
Rules of discipline of the Yearly Meeting of friends for Pennsylvania, New Jersey, Delaware, and the eastern parts of Maryland. 1680
Rules of discipline of the Yearly meeting of Friends, held in Philadelphia. 1680
Rules of discipline of the Yearly Meeting of men and women Friends. 1679
Rules of life for boys and girls. 3148
Rules of life for the pastor of souls. 3676
Rules of order for the Christian Reformed church. 1023
... The rules of the game. 3183
... The rules of the game; teacher's manual. 3183
Rules of the Society of Jesus. A new translation from the Latin. 1945
Rules, who needs them? 631
Ruling elder. 1239
Ruling ideas in early ages and their relation to Old Testament faith. 501
Ruling ideas of the present age. 962
Ruling quality. 1602
Rum, rags and religion. 2231
Rumblings from Rome. 800
Rumi the Persian. 1933
Rumor of angels. 3566
Rumors of war. 1089
Run, baby, run. 1392
Run for the West. 192, 928
Run, Sammy, run. 1462
Run the good race. 3701
Run this race. 3882
Run while the sun is hot. 2497
Run with Him! 899
Run with the vision. 1576, 3546
Runaway. 2945
Runaway Church. 781
Runaway heart. 903
Runaway Jonah. 630
Runaway Jonah, and other tales. 634, 635
Runaway saint. 2136
Runaways to God. 575
Runner. 991, 2036
Runner's Bible. 249
Running free. 933
Running Press glossary of astrology terms. 98
Running the good race. 699, 981
Running waters. 741
... Rural Christendom. 3254
Rural church administration. 3254
Rural church and community betterment. 3255
Rural church and the farmer. 3253
Rural church development. 3253
Rural church in China. 2511
Rural church in South. 3254
Rural church life in the Middle West. 1287
Rural church movement. 3254, 3255
Rural church problems. 3253
Rural church serving the community. 3442
Rural church, today & tomorrow. 3255
Rural church workshop held at Bethlehem Lutheran Church, Round Top, Texas, September 29-30. 2292
Rural church workshop held at Trinity Lutheran Church, Thief River Falls, Minn., April 13-14, 1959. 2291
Rural churches in transition. 3254
Rural evangelism. 1571
Rural life and the church. 3254
Rural ministry and the changing community. 3254
Rural mission of the church in eastern Asia. 2516
Rural parish. 3254
Rural pastor. 3674
Rural people at worship. 3854
Rural preaching. 2907
Rural priesthood. 3676
Rural prospect. 3254
Rural rebels. 1459
Rural rector. 771
Rural religion and the country church. 3255
Rural sermons. 3348
Rural survey in Indiana. 3435
Rural synthesis. 3254
Rural worship. 3254
Rush hour of the gods. 1936
Russelism and unveiled. 1940
... Russell H. Conwell and his work. 1368
Russell H. Conwell, founder of the institutional church in America. 1368
... Russellism exposed. 1940
Russellism under the search light. 1368

Russia at the bar of the American people. 2178
... Russia, colossal racial experimentation. 611
Russia will be converted. 1618
Russian chapters of Ezekiel. 611
Russian church. 2749
Russian church and Russian dissent. 3256
Russian church and Russian dissent, comprising orthodoxy, dissent, and erratic sects. 2750, 3022
Russian church and the Soviet state, 1917-1950. 1149
Russian church since the revolution. 1768
Russian church singing. 1209
Russian clergy. 1299
Russian dissenters. 1469, 3324
Russian ecclesiastical art. 1880
Russian ecclesiastical mission in Peking during the eighteenth century. 2512
Russian events in the light of Bible prophecy. 611
Russian icons. 1880, 1881
Russian inconsand objects of ecclesiastical and decorative arts from the collection of George R. Hann. 1880
Russian intellectual history. 3257
Russian letters of direction, 1834-1860. 1010
Russian Levites. 1299, 2750
... Russian Molokan book of prayer and songs. 2568
Russian mystics. 2648
Russian nonconformity. 1469
Russian Orthodox Church underground, 1917-1970. 1149, 2749
Russian Orthodoxy under the old regime. 1149, 2750
Russian priest. 2939
Russian Protestants. 2955
Russian religious mind. 2750, 3213, 3214
Russian religious renaissance of the twentieth century. 3256
Russian revolution. 1149
Russian revolution and religion. 3256
Russian, social monism and American social pluralism. 1141
Russian theology 1920-1965 , a bibliographical survey. 3619
Russians and their church. 2750
Rusty hinges. 3699
Ruth. 589, 634, 635, 3258
Ruth, A Bible heroine. 3258
Ruth, a new translation with a philological commentary and a formalist-folkorist interpretation. 589
Ruth, a woman of worth. 589
Ruth, the Christian scientist. 1030
Ruth the gleaner. 589
Ruth the gleaner and Esther the queen. 3258
Ruth, the romance of Redemption. 589, 3030, 3258
Ruth: The satisfied stranger. 3258
Ruth's romance of redemption. 589
Ruysbroeck the Admirable. 1934, 2843
Ryrie study Bible. 361

S

S. Andrea in Mantua. 2329
S. Anne. 48
S. Aurelii Augustine episcopi hipponensis De civiate Deicontra paganos libri xxii. 113
... S. Avreli Avgvstini. 113
...S. Clement of Rome. 1287
S. Ephraim's quotations from the Gospels. 401, 1521
S. H. Hadley of Water street. 1780
S. N. Haskell, man of action. 1790
S.O.S. for Catholic schools. 831, 3401
S.P.G. papers in the Lambeth Palace Library. 3736
S. Parkes Cadman. 723
S. Peter, bishop of Rome. 76, 2824
S. Thasci Caecili Cypriani Opera omnia. Recensvit et commentario critico instrvxit Gvilelmvs Hartel. 3635
Sa d b. Mansar Ibn Kammuna's examination of the inquiries into the three faiths. 3138
Sa.zi.ga, ancient Mesopotamian potency incantations. 1892
...Saadia anniversary volume. 3259
Saadia Gaon. 3259
... Saadia Gaon, his life and works. 3131, 3259
Saadia studies. 3259
Saadya Gaon. 3259
... Sabang to Balikpapan, a missionary journey through the Netherlands Indies on the eve of war. 2516
Sabbatai Sevi. 3262, 3394
Sabbatai Zevi. 3394

Sabbath. 3260, 3261, 3546
Sabbath and festival addresses. 3371
Sabbath and festival services. 2111
Sabbath and Sunday in early Christianity. 3261
Sabbath and the Lord's day. 3261
Sabbath and the Sunday. 3260
Sabbath as an American war day. 3261
Sabbath as idea and experience. 2151
Sabbath bells chimed by the poets. 1518
Sabbath book. 3261
Sabbath chimes. 3261
Sabbath-day journeys. 561
Sabbath eve service. 2108
Sabbath evening sermons. 2934
Sabbath for man. 3546, 3547
Sabbath history. 3261
Sabbath hymn book. 1867
Sabbath in divine revelation and human history. 3260
Sabbath in Heschel, Abraham Joshua, 1907-The earth is the Lord's. 1809
Sabbath in Puritan New England. 3547
Sabbath is special. 3261
Sabbath: its meaning for modern man. 3260
Sabbath laws in the United States. 3548
Sabbath light. 3370
Sabbath lyrics; or, Songs from Scripture. A Christmas gift of love. 2109
Sabbath month: devotional thoughts for young mothers. 1439
Sabbath morning service (Shabath baarets) for cantor (baritone), mixed chorus and organ. 3577
Sabbath observance. 3546
Sabbath prayer book. 2108
Sabbath prayers. 2111
Sabbath queen. 910
Sabbath quest. 3261
Sabbath question. 3546, 3566
Sabbath readings for the home circle. 1015
Sabbath recreations. 3208
Sabbath-school gems. 3561
Sabbath-school help. 438
Sabbath school ideals. 3385
Sabbath-school index. 3556
Sabbath school lyre. 3563
Sabbath school manual. 3380, 3385
Sabbath-school missions in Wisconsin. 3552
Sabbath school singing book. 3562
Sabbath school special days. 3560
Sabbath school teacher. 3558
Sabbath service. 2109
Sabbath service and miscellaneous prayers. 2109
Sabbath service in song. 3577
Sabbath services for children. 2111
Sabbath: symbol of creation and re-creation. 3261
Sabbath talks. 974
Sabbath, the day of delight. 3260, 3261
Sabbath theology. 3260
Sabbath transferred. 3547
Sabbath, which day and why! 3260
Sabbaths, sacraments, and seasons. 2390
Sabbatical reflections. 1005, 1314
Sabian book of letters to aspirants. 2390, 3262
Sabian symbols in astrology. 95
Sacerdos et pontifex. 665
Sacerdotal safeguards. 3201, 3676
Sacerdotalism in the nineteenth century. 2940
Sacheverell affair. 3262
Sackcloth and ashes. 2211
Sacra doctrina. 3227, 3697
Sacra privata. 1443
Sacral Kingship in ancient Israel. 658
Sacralization and secularization. 3328
Sacrament. 1231, 3267
Sacrament certificate 1673. 3604
Sacrament of baptism. 136, 137
Sacrament of confirmation. 1328
Sacrament of confirmation in the early-middle scholastic period. 1328
Sacrament of duty. 1000
Sacrament of Easter. 1837
Sacrament of freedom. 1327
Sacrament of friendship. 2255
Sacrament of holy orders. 2742
Sacrament of matrimony. 2344
Sacrament of peace. 2811
Sacrament of penance. 2811
Sacrament of penance and reconciliation. 2811
Sacrament of penance in our time. 2812
Sacrament of penance, (The) 2812
Sacrament of reunion. 2927
Sacrament of salvation. 1121, 2041
Sacrament of suffering. 3540
Sacrament of the altar. 2252
Sacrament of the eucharist. 2252, 2255
Sacrament of the Eucharist in our time. 2255

Sacrament of the Lord's Supper. 2258
Sacrament of the Lord's Supper in the fullness of the Gospel. 2258, 3216
... The sacrament reserved. 1541
Sacrament time. 902, 1230
Sacramental addresses and meditations. 1318
Sacramental and occasional homilies. 863, 3267
Sacramental exercises. 2251
Sacramental life of the church. 3265
Sacramental liturgy. 3772
Sacramental living. 3264
[Sacramental mediations on the sufferings and death of Christ]. 2032
Sacramental meditations and advices grounded upon Scripture texts, proper for communicants, to prepare their hearts, excite their affections, quicken their graces and enliven their devotions on sacramental occasions. 2253
Sacramental ministry to the sick. 1258
Sacramental prayer. 839
Sacramental reconciliation. 3028
Sacramental spirituality. 3265
Sacramental system. 3263
Sacramental table. 1318
Sacramental teaching and practice in the Reformation churches. 3262
Sacramental theology. 3265
Sacramental view of preaching. 728
Sacramental way. 1001
Sacramental we. 3265
Sacramentals. 3262
Sacramentals of the Catholic church. 3262
Sacramentals of the holy Catholic church. 3262
Sacramentary teachings of the church. 3265
Sacraments. 793, 3215, 3262, 3263, 3264, 3265, 3266, 3267
Sacraments; a dogmatic treatise. 3263
Sacraments and forgiveness. 3265
Sacraments and orthodoxy. 2748
Sacraments and social progress. 3265
Sacraments and society. 3238
Sacraments and the commendments. 3263
Sacraments and worship. 3265
Sacraments & you. 791, 3265
Sacraments and your everyday life. 3265
Sacraments explained according to the Munich or psychological method. 3264
Sacraments in a secular age. 2039, 3265
Sacraments in a world of change. 3264
Sacraments in general. 3266
Sacraments in Methodism. 3267
"Sacraments in my refrigerator" 2894
Sacraments in the Christian life. 3265
Sacraments in the new liturgy. 838, 3265
Sacraments in theology and canon law. 808, 3264
Sacraments of community renewal: holy orders, matrimony. 2742
Sacraments of daily life. 3265
Sacraments of growth and renewal. 840, 3265
Sacraments of healing and of vocation. 3266
Sacraments of initiation. 137, 138
Sacraments of initiation and union: baptism, confirmation, Eucharist. 137
Sacraments of initiation, baptism and confirmation. 137
Sacraments of life and worship. 3266
Sacraments of reconciliation: penance, anointing of the sick. 2811
Sacraments of simple folk. 3110
Sacraments on the missions. 3264
Sacraments, signs and symbols. 1096
Sacraments; the gestures of Christ. 2375, 3265
Sacraments today. 3265, 3266
Sacramentum mundi. 3639
Sacramentum verbi; an encyclopedia of Biblical theology. 242
Sacred allegories. 25
Sacred and legendary art. 920
Sacred and secular. 1071, 1265
Sacred and secular music list. 2632
Sacred and the feminine. 3832
Sacred and the profane. 3058
Sacred and the secular. 1155
Sacred anthology. 3268
Sacred anthology (oriental) 3268
Sacred art. 1592
Sacred art in Persian culture. 86
Sacred art of Tibet. 88
Sacred biography. 214, 1956
Sacred biography and history, containing descriptions of Palestine, ancient and modern. 216
Sacred biography or, The history of Jesus Christ. 1966
Sacred bond. 2344
Sacred book, containing old and new gospels. 1406

Sacred book of death, Hindu spiritism, soul transition and soul reincarnation. 2724
Sacred books of China. 1331, 3587
Sacred books of China (The) 3587
Sacred books of Confucius. 1331
*Sacred books of the East (The) 3139
Sacred books of the Jews. 3203
Sacred books of the Old and New Testaments. 497
Sacred books of the Old Testament. 505
Sacred books of the world. 3268
Sacred bridge. 841, 2109
Sacred calendar of Eleusis. 1505
Sacred canons. 735
Sacred canopy. 3085
Sacred cause of liberty. 3213
Sacred ceremonies of Holy Week. 844
Sacred Chitimacha Indian beliefs. 915
Sacred choral music. 916
Sacred choral music in print. 916
Sacred circle. 3520
Sacred classics defended and illustrated. 346
Sacred complex in Hindu Gaya. 2940
Sacred complex in Hindu Gays. 2940
Sacred complex of Kashi. 1812
... The Sacred congregation for the Oriental church. 777
Sacred cows. 3447
Sacred cows are dying. 1016
Sacred cows, sacred places. 1378
Sacred dance. 1400, 1401
Sacred discontent. 236, 299
Sacred doctrine. 3660
Sacred dramas. 2667
Sacred eloquence. 2904, 3331
Sacred fire. 3389
Sacred fortress. 1161
Sacred gems from the English poets, Chaucer to Tennyson. 3210
Sacred geography. 282
Sacred geography, and antiquities. 2761
Sacred harmony; or Council of peace. 3207
Sacred harp. 1871, 3268, 3718
Sacred Heart. 3269, 3270
Sacred heart and the Catholic home. 3269
Sacred Heart book. 1536, 3270
Sacred Heart Church, Waltham, Massachusetts. 1269
Sacred Heart in the life of the church. 3270
Sacred heart manual. 3270
Sacred heart of Christ. 3269
Sacred heart of Jesus. 3269
Sacred Heart yesterday and today. 3270
Sacred heroes and martyrs. 2351
Sacred history. 293
Sacred history and geography. 532
Sacred history of the deluge illustrated. 1421
Sacred history of the world. 1382
Sacred hour. 724, 1306
Sacred hour of song. 3271
... The sacred hymns. 1860
Sacred hymns and spiritual songs. 2616
Sacred hymns and spirtual songs for the Church of Jesus Christ of latter-day saints. 2616
Sacred journey. 712, 1300
Sacred journey, being pilgrimage to Makkah. 2848
Sacred journeys. 1361, 1471
Sacred land. 2208
Sacred laws of the Aryas. 689
Sacred literature. 3267
Sacred lyrics. 1861
Sacred magician. 2312
Sacred marriage rite. 3545
Sacred meadows. 1925
Sacred mountains. 2626
Sacred mushroom and the cross. 2632
Sacred music and liturgy. 1204
Sacred music and the Catholic church. 1205
Sacred oasis. 2631, 3718
Sacred oratorio. 1783
Sacred pageant of the ages. 294
Sacred Passion. 2033
Sacred passion of Jesus Christ. 2032
Sacred Penitentiaria. 852
Sacred philosophy of the seasons. 2672
Sacred pipe. 2734
Sacred places. 1158
Sacred places in China. 913
Sacred poems. 298, 3206
Sacred poems and hymns. 3207
Sacred poems and private ejaculations of Henry Vaughan. 3774
Sacred poetry. 585, 3208
Sacred poetry of the seventeenth century. 3210
Sacred portal. 1800
Sacred praise. 1203
Sacred repository of anthems and hymns. 3398
Sacred rhetoric. 2899, 2905

Sacred scenes. 399, 1971
Sacred scenes and characters. 294
Sacred scenes and mysteries. 3281
... The sacred scimitar. 692
Sacred scripture. 2690
Sacred Scripture in song and story. 3270
Sacred scriptures and religious philosophy. 2611
Sacred scriptures of the Japanese. 3404
Sacred scriptures of the world. 3268
Sacred scriptures of world-religion. 3268
Sacred scrolls of the southern Ojibway. 915
Sacred shrine. 920, 921
Sacred signs. 3262
Sacred sites and ways. 2761
Sacred sixty-six. 307
Sacred song. 3734
Sacred songs, ancient and modern. 3271
Sacred songs composed to popular airs. 3270
Sacred songs the people sing. 3271
Sacred space, meaning and form. 78
Sacred stories for children. 628
Sacred stories from Byzantium. 1025
Sacred streams. 282
Sacred studies. 3184
Sacred tenth. 3702
Sacred theory of the earth. 1384
Sacred tradition and present need. 3484
Sacred tree. 3710
Sacred trust. 140
Sacred truths relating to the Living God, His Only Son, and Holy Spirit. 3729
Sacred way. 2033
Sacred words. 2677
Sacred writings. 3268
Sacred writings of the apostles and evangelists of Jesus Christ. 352
Sacred writings of the world's great religions. 3267, 3268
Sacredness of the Sabbath. 2686, 3547
Sacremental feast. 1317
Sacrificare. 839
Sacrifice. 962, 2048, 2365, 2397, 3271, 3272, 3357
Sacrifice and atonement. 105
Sacrifice and sacrament. 3271
Sacrifice and service. 2474
Sacrifice and song. 3530
Sacrifice and the death of Christ. 3271
Sacrifice in the Bible. 3271
Sacrifice in the Old Testament. 3272
Sacrifice in the Rgveda. 3272, 3776
Sacrifice of Christ. 2254
Sacrifice of Christ. [1st ed.]. 106
... The sacrifice of praise. 1317, 1471
Sacrifice of praise, with tunes. 2916
Sacrifice of Thanksgiving. 3271
Sacrifice of the Church. 2366, 2369
Sacrifice of the mass. 2367
Sacrifice of the mystical body. 2368
Sacrifice of the NewLaw. 2259
Sacrifice we offer. 2367
Sacrificial interpretation of Jesus' achievement in the New Testament. 348, 2040, 3271
Sacrificial system of the Old Testament. 3271
Sacrificial worship. 3853
Sacristan's manual. 844
Sacristy manual containing the portions of the Roman ritual most frequently used in parish church functions. 837
Saddest and gladdest of days. 2057
Saddharma-Pundarika. 3272
Sadduceeism. 48
Sadguru speaks. 3479
Sadhana. 3579
Sadhana, a way to God. 3475
Sadhana in our daily lives. 3478
...The Sadhs. 3272
Sadhu Hagenstein, a white man among the brown. 1780, 2530
Sadhu Sundar Singh. 3546
Sadhu Sundar Singh, called of God. 3546
Sadliers' Catholic directory. 866
Saducismus triumphatus; or, Full and plain evidence concerning witches and appar[i]tions. 3823
Saeculum: history and society in the theology of St. Augustine. 114, 1820
Safari by jet. 1633
Safari for souls. 1755, 3229
Safe in bondage. 2528
Safe in His arms. 17
Safe side. 2001
Safeguarding our future. 970
Safeguarding the home front. 1609
Safeguards of chastity. 3390
Safest mind cure. 1342
Safety of appearing at the day of judgment, in the righteousness of Christ. 2161
Saffron robe. 928, 3415
Saga of saints. 3285
Saga of service. 833
Saga of the Book of Abraham. 3429

Saga of Walther of Aquitaine. 3790
Sage Ninomiya's evening talks. 1538
Sage of Bethany. 732
Sage of Exeter. 784
Sage of Kanchi. 881
Sage of Salisbury. 1116
Sage of the hills. 2270
Sagebrush seed. 2676
[Sahih al-Bukhari. (romnized form)]. 1779
Sai Baba and his message. 3304
Sai Baba, the holy man ... and the psychiatrist. 2999, 3304
Saigon journey. 872
Sail your own seas. 1013
Sailing with Paul. 3663
Sails and anchors. 166
St. 1737, 3696
Saint a day, according to the liturgical calendar of the church. 3282
Saint-adventurers of the Virginia frontier. 1491, 3260
Saint Agatha's Church. 2830
Saint Agnes. 19
St. Alban hymnal. 2220
St. Albert the Great. 22
Saint Albertus Magnus, the secret of Saint Albert's consecration of himself to God. 22
Saint Aloysius church. 1426
St. Aloysius Church, Wilmerding, Pa. 1269
St. Ambrose. 29, 1835
Saint Ambrose, his life and times. 29
Saint among savages. 1947, 2125
Saint and a half. 193
Saint and his Saviour. 976
Saint and sage (Hafetz Hayim) 2162
Saint and savage. 1711, 1900
Saint and sinners. 659
Saint and Sufi in modern Egypt. 21, 3544
Saint and the devil. 1938
Saint & the skeptics. 1938
Saint and the sword. 3791
Saint and thought for every day. 1434
Saint Andrew. 40
Saint Andrew daily missal. 843, 846, 847
Saint Andrew daily missal, with vespers for Sundays and feasts. 846, 847
Saint Andrew hymnal. 812
St. Andrews and elsewhere. 3273
St. Andrew's by-the-Sea. 102
St. Andrews' cross. 695
St. Andrew's Presbyterian Church Wallsend centenary. 3790
Saint Angela. 41
St. Anne. 48
St. Anne for children. 905
St. Anne, grandmother of Our Saviour. 48
St. Anne, the Mother of Mary. 48
St. Ann's. 3273
St. Ann's on East Twelfth Street, New York City, 1852-1952. 2699
Saint Anselm. 49
Saint Anselm and his biographer. 49
St. Anselm's Proslogion. 1739
St. Anselm's Proslogion with A reply on behalf of the fool. 1739
Saint Anthony. 54, 2476
Saint Anthony and his times. 54
St. Anthony and the Christ Child. 54
Saint Anthony Claret. 1284
Saint Anthony Claret, modern prophet and healer. 1284
St. Anthony, doctor of the gospel. 54
Saint Anthony in art. 921
Saint Anthony of Padua. 54
Saint Anthony of the Desert. 109
Saint Anthony, the saint of the whole world. 54
St. Anthony's treasury. 54, 855
Saint Antony of Padua (1195-1231) 54
... St. Asaph. 3273
Saint Augustin. 113
Saint Augustine. 47, 111, 113, 114, 115, 1415, 2835, 3634
St. Augustine and African church divisions. 111
St. Augustine and Christian Platonism. 111
Saint Augustine and French classical thought. 111, 2839
St. Augustine and his age. 114, 116
St. Augustine and his influence through the ages. 114
St. Augustine and his search for faith. 114
... St. Augustine: De fide et symbol. 113
... Saint Augustine of Canterbury. 111, 1758
St. Augustine of Hippo. 113, 115
Saint Augustine on personality. 116, 2823
St. Augustine on prayer. 114, 2885
... St. Augustine on the City of God. 113
St. Augustine on the Psalms. 574
St. Augustine: On the spirit and the letter. 113
St. Augustine's Comments on 'Imago Dei. 113

St. Augustine's Confessions. 115
St. Augustine's conversion. 115
Saint Augustine's De fide rerum quae non videntur. 1601
... Saint Augustine's defense of the hexaemeron against the Manicheans. 114, 1381
... St. Augustine's doctrine on the inspiration and canonicity of Scripture. 114, 305
St. Augustine's early theory of man, A.D. 386-391. 116, 2327
St. Augustine's episcopate. 115
Saint Augustine's notion of schism in the Donatist controversy. 114, 3307
Saint Augustine's prayer book. 2971
St. Augustin's confessions; or, Praises of God. 116
St. Bartholomew's parish, Pittsboro, N. C., eighteen thirty three to nineteen thirty three. 2849
Saint Basil. 177, 3634
St. Basil and his rule. 177, 2576
St. Basil and monasticism. 177, 2578
St. Basil's hymn book. 813
St. Basil's hymn book, containing prayers at mass, prayers before and after holy communion. 836
St. Basil's hymnal. 813
Saint Basil's hymnal. 813
Saint Benedict. 188, 189
Saint Benedict and the sixth century. 189, 2575
St. Benedict, blessed by God. 189
St. Benedict parish, Blue Island, Illinois. 893
Saint Berin. 663
St. Bernadette. 2262, 3460
St. Bernadette; a pictorial biography. 2262, 3460
Saint Bernadette Soubirous. 3460
...St. Bernard. 193
Saint Bernard and other papers. 2776
St. Bernard, his predecessors and successors, 1000-1200 A.D. 193, 2582
Saint Bernard of Clairvaux. 193, 194
St. Bernard of Clairvaux, 1090-1153. 193, 1026
Saint Bernard on the Christian year. 1265
Saint Bernard on the Song of songs. 595
Saint Bernard, the oracle of the 12th century. 193
Saint Bernardine of Siena. 194
St. Bernard's Seminary. 3273
Saint Bernward of Hildesheim. 194
St. Blasien psalter. 848
Saint Bonaventure. 675
Saint Bonaventure's De reductione artium ad theologiam. 2835
... Saint Boniface. 677
St. Boniface and St. Virgil. 677
Saint book. 1025
St. Botolph's town and other stories. 3201
Saint Bridget of Sweden. 663
Saint Brigid and the cows. 692
St. Brigid of Ireland. 692
St. Camillus. 731
Saint Casimir, 1458-1484. 2166
St. Catherine Laboure and the Miraculous Medal. 2190, 2478
Saint Catherine Laboure, of the Miraculous Medal. 2190, 2478
Saint Catherine of Siena. 749
Saint Catherine of Siena as seen in her letters. 749
Saint Catherine of Siena, doctor of the Church. 749
Saint Cecil Cyprian. 1398
Saint Cecilia of the court. 877
St. Chantal on prayer. 2885
St. Charles Borromeo, Roosevelt Rd. at Hoyne Ave., Chicago, Illinois. 1269
Saint Charles of Sezze. 740
St. Charles seminary, Overbrook. 3331
St. Charles Seminary, Philadelphia. 2830
Saint Christopher for boys and girls. 1114
Saint Christopher missal. 846
... St. Chrysostom On the priesthood. 1115, 2939
Saint Clare. 1284
St. Clare of Assisi. 1027, 1284
Saint Clement Maria Hofbauer. 1822
Saint Colum and the crane. 1311
Saint Columba of Iona. 1311, 1918
Saint Columban. 1311
St. Cosmas Aitolos: great missionary, illuminator, and martyr of Greece. 2185
... St. Cyprian on the Lord's prayer. 1398, 2249
Saint Cyril and Saint Methodius Church, Deer Park, Long Island, New York. 1269
... St. David's. 3273
St. David's through the years. 117
Le saint de chez nous. 734
... St. Dionysius of Alexandria. 3280
Saint Dominic. 1474

St. Dominic, a pictorial biography. 1474, 1475

Saint Dominic and his times. 1474

St. Dominic and his work. 1474, 1475

Saint Dominic and the order of Preachers. 1475

St. Dominic and the rosary. 3130

Saint Dominic missal. 845

Saint Dominic, pilgrim of light. 1474

St. Dominic Savio. 1027, 3305

Saint Dominic's family. 1475

Saint Dominic's successor. 1475, 2131

Saint Dunstan hymnal. 2968

Saint Dunstan of Canterbury. 1483

St. Edmund of Abingdon. 1497

Saint Elizabeth. 1508

Saint Elizabeth of Hungary. 1508

St. Elizabeth of Portugal. 1920

St. Elizabeth's three crowns. 1508

Saint Ferdinand de Florissant. 1630

Saint Francis. 1152, 1640, 1644

Saint Francis and his friends. 1641

Saint Francis and the animals. 1643, 1644

St. Francis and the song of brotherhood. 1640

Saint Francis and the wolf. 1639

St. Francis de Sales. 1650

Saint Francis et his four ladies. 1641

St. Francis in the world. 1649

Saint Francis: nature mystic. 47, 1639

St. Francis of Assisi. 776, 1027, 1639, 1640, 1641, 1642, 1643, 1644

Saint Francis of Assisi; a biography. 1642

St. Francis of Assisi, a pictorial biography. 1642

Saint Francis of Assisi, 1182-1226. 1640, 1645

St. Francis of Assisi, his holy life and love of poverty. 1643

St. Francis of Assisi, the poverello. 1641

St. Francis of Assisi: writings and early biographies. 1641

Saint Francis of Assisi. 1640

Saint Francis prayer book. 2890

St. Francis Solanus. 3455

Saint Francis spreads Christmas joy. 1644

St. Francis texts. 1640

St. Francis the Great. 3298

Saint Francis Xavier. 1649, 1650

St. Francis Xavier, apostle of the East. 1650

St. Francis Xavier, the great crusader of Christ. 1649

Saint Gabriel, Passionist. 1700

St. Gemma Galgani. 1700, 3532

Saint George's Chapel quincentenary handbook. 3820

St. George's Church, New York. 2699

Saint Gerard Majella. 1706

St. Germaine and her guardian angel. 1707

Saint Germaine and the sheep. 1707

Saint Gregoire de Nazianze. 1773

St. Gregory hymnal and Catholic choir book. 813

St. Gregory the Great. 1773

Saint Gregory the Great's concept of papal power. 1773

Saint Gregory's guest. 1773

Saint Helena. 1802

St. Hilda & other poems. 3206

St. Hugh of Lincoln. 1851

Saint Ignatius. 2268

St. Ignatius and Christianity in Antioch. 1882

St. Ignatius and the Company of Jesus. Illustrated by John Lawn. 2267

Saint Ignatius and the Jesuits. 1947, 2268, 2269, 2270

St. Ignatius and the Ratio studiorum. 1946, 2268

St. Ignatius Church, Oxon Hill, Maryland. 3274

St. Ignatius, Hickory, and its missions. 1810, 3274

Saint Ignatius' idea of a Jesuit university. 1497, 2268

Saint Ignatius Loyola. 2269

St. Ignatius of Loyola. 2268, 2269, 3469

St. Ignatius' own story. 2268

Saint in Hyde Park. 2310

Saint in the kitchen. 3897

Saint in the making. 3778

Saint in the wilderness. 2125

Saint indeed. 3126

St. Innocent, apostle to America. 1028, 1908

Saint Isaac and the Indians. 2125

Saint J. D. 1774

St. James church, Goose Creek, S.C. A sketch of the parish from 1706 to 1909. 1269

St. James' Church (Protestant Episcopal) at mid-century. 2195

St. James Church, Wilmington, North Carolina, historical records 1737-1852. 1269

St. James' Episcopal church, Arlington, Vermont. 81

St. James in Spain. 1934

St. James' Parish. 1758

St. James Parish, Farmington, Connecticut: centennial history. 3274

St. James' Parish, Great Barrington, Massachusetts, 1762-1962. 1758

St. James's church, 1835-1935. 3237

St. James's Church, 1835-1957. 3237

Saint Jane Frances Fremyot de Chantal. 882

Saint Jean-Marie Vianney, cure of Ars. 3778

... St. Jerome. 1810, 1811, 3635

Saint Jerome and his times. 1811

St. Jerome and the Bible. 1811

Saint Jerome daily missal with liturgical commentary. 846

Saint Jerome, dogmatic and polemical works. 3635

Saint Jerome Sunday missal. 837

Saint John of the Cross, 1542-1591, doctor of divine love. 2125

St. Joan. 1937, 1938

Saint Joan of Arc. 1937, 1938

St. Joan of Arc, virgin, soldier. 1026, 1937

St. Joan, the girl soldier. 1937

St. John. 415, 417, 1563, 2127

Saint John and the close of the apostolic age. 2127

Saint John and the Synoptic gospels. 419

Saint John Baptist de La Salle. 2189

Saint John Berchmans. 191

Saint John Bosco, a seeker of souls. 683, 3286

St. John Capistran, reformer. 1713

St. John Chrysostom. 1115

St. John Chrysostom, arch bishop of Constantinople. 1115

Saint John Eudes: a spiritual portrait. 1541

Saint John Fisher. 1628

... S. John, Gospel, Letters, Revelation. 413

St. John Neumann, 1811-1860, fourth Bishop of Philadelphia. 667, 2685

... Saint John of Arc. 1938

... St. John of Damascus. 2123

St. John of God. 2136

St. John of Patmos and the seven churches of the Apocalypse. 461, 1765, 2127

Saint John of the Cross. 2125, 2136, 2137, 2648, 3469

Saint John of the Cross and Islam. 1925, 2125

St. John speaks. 422

St. John the apostle. 2127

Saint John the Baptist. 2127, 2128

Saint John the Baptist and the desert tradition. 1411, 2128

St. John the Evangelist Church, Baltimore, Maryland, 1853-1953. 1273

St. John the Evangelist, Westminster. 1274

St. John's betonite report, Claiborne Parish, Louisiana. 191

St. John's centennial book. 1426

St. John's Christ. 413

Saint John's Church. 1269

St. John's Church, Elizabeth, New Jersey, 1706-1956. 1268

Saint John's Church in Keokuk. 2167, 3275

St. John's Church, Mobile, a history. 2560

St. John's commandery no. 4, Knights templar, Philadelphia. 3598

St. John's Episcopal Church in Knoxville, Tennessee, 1946-1976. 3275

St. John's Evangelical Lutheran Church, Wythe County, Virginia, its pastors and their records 1800-1924. 3275

St. John's Gospel. 415, 416

St. John's Gospel, a commentary. 415

St. John's Methodist Church. 2402

St. John's, Peterborough. 3275

St. John's prologue. 422

St. John's revelation unsealed, analysis. 458

Saint Joseph. 2132

St. Joseph after Vatican II. 2132

St. Joseph and daily Christian living. 2132

Saint Joseph Catholic manual. 796, 797

Saint Joseph children's missal. 900

Saint Joseph continuous Sunday missal. 846

Saint Joseph daily Mass. 846

Saint Joseph daily missal. 846, 847

Saint Joseph edition of the Holy Bible. 266

Saint Joseph Holy Week missal. 844

Saint Joseph in Appleton. 77

Saint Joseph in the life of Christ and of the church. 2132

Saint Joseph new American catechism. 769

St. Joseph of Copertino. 1717

St. Joseph parish, Jasper, Indiana. 1936

Saint Joseph Sunday missal. 847

St. Joseph's advocate. 3275

... St. Joseph's hymnal. 813

Saint Joseph's little brother. 40

Saint Joseph's month. 2132

... St. Joseph's seminary, Dunwoodie, New York. 3276

Saint Judas Iscariot. 2156

Saint Justin Martyr. 3635

Saint Lawrence of Brindisi, doctor of the Universal Church. 2260

St. Leander's dedication and spring festival. 1623

Saint Leo golden jubilee. 3276

St. Louis Church, Castroville. 3276

St. Louis church survey. 3276

St. Louis university studies in honor of St. Thomas Aquinas. 3696

St. Louise de Marillac. 2203

St. Luke. 320, 426, 427, 2271

... St. Luke and St. Paul. 426

... S. Luke (Gospel-Acts) the books of the Bible in modern American form and phrase. 426

St. Luke, the revised version. 427

St. Luke, theologian of redemptive history. 431

St. Luke's Episcopal Church. 3287

St. Luke's life of Jesus. 430

St. Macarios of Corinth, Archbishop of Corinth. 2318

St. Macarios of Corinth, Archbishop of Corinth. 2318

Saint Madelein Sophie Barat. 2310

Saint Madeleine Sophie. 2310, 2311, 3438

Saint Madeleine Sophie Barat. 173

Saint Madeleine Sophie Barat: her life of prayer and her teaching, based on unpublished documents. 2310

St. Margaret Mary. 21

St. Margaret Mary, apostle of the Sacred Heart. 21

Saint Margaret of Cortona. 2332

Saint Margaret's School, 1865-1965. 3276

Saint Maria Goretti. 2333

St. Mark. 432, 434

St. Mark's church in the city of Brooklyn. 1269

Saint Mark's Gospel. 436

Saint Mark's life of Jesus. 436

Saint Martin. 2349

St. Martin de Porres. 2348

Saint Martin de Porres and the mice. 2348

Saint Martin de Porres: many sided Martin. 2348

St. Martin of Tours. 2349

Saint Mary Euphasia Pelletier. 2811

Saint Mary Magdalene in mediaeval literature. 2353

Saint Mary, My every day missal and heritage. 847

St. Mary of the Immaculate Conception, Fredericksburg, Virginia. 1652

Saint Mary, Sunday missal prayers and heritage. 847

Saint Mary's Armenian Apostolic Church. 3277

St. Mary's Assumption Church. 1269

St. Mary's church. 3300

St. Mary's church in the Highlands, Cold-Spring-on the-Hudson, New York. 1306

St. Mary's diamond jubilee, October 6, 1940, Evanston, Illinois. 1269

St. Mary's, Fairfax Station, Virginia. 3277

St. Mary's hymnal. 813

St. Mary's in Jersey City. 1943

St. Mary's in the Rocky Mountains. 3277, 3287

St. Mary's-in-Tuxedo, 1888-1975. 3277, 3719

St. Mary's manual. 813

St. Matthew. 439, 440

St. Matthew and his Gospel. 442

... St. Matthew and St. Mark and the General epistles. 354

... S. Matthew, S. Peter, S. Jude, S. James. 472

St. Matthew's cathedral in Laramie, Wyoming. 2197

St. Matthew's gospel. 438

Saint Matthew's of Washington, 1840-1940. 3797

Saint Matthew's witness to words and works of the Lord. 442

St. Michael the Archangel and the holy terror. 3153

St. Michaels, Charleston 1751-1951. 888

St. Michael's Evangelical Lutheran Church history, 1830-1930. 2348

St. Michael's Lauda Sion in English. 840

St. Michael's monastery hymnal. 813

St. Michael's Parish. 3277

St. Michaels story, 1764-1964: the United Church of Christ. 3277

Saint Monica (331-387 A.D.) 2584

Saint Nectarios Orthodox Conference, Seattle, Washington, July 22-25, 1980. 2745

St. Nicholas. 1111, 2707, 3302

St. Nicholas Cathedral of New York. 2698

Saint Nicholas liturgy. 2707

Saint Nicholas liturgy and its literary relationships (ninth to twelfth centuries) 2707

Saint Nicholas of Myra, Bari, and Manhattan. 1028, 2707

St. Nicholas of Tolentine Church, Bronx, New York. 1269

St. Nicholas of Tolentine Church Bronx, New York, founded 1906. 1269

St. Nicholas' travels. 2707

St. Nicodemos the Hagiorite, great theologian and teacher of the Orthodox Church. 2710

St. Nikephoros of Chios, outstanding writer of liturgical poetry and lives of saints, educator, spiritual striver, and trainer of martyrs. 1025, 2710

St. Odo of Cluny. 2734

Saint of ardent desires. 3690

Saint of Gabriel, Passionist. 1700

Saint of the countryside. 3778

Saint of the day. 3283

Saint of the Eucharist. 686

Saint of the eucharist, Saint Paschal Baylon, patron of eucharistic associations. 179

Saint of the fighting Irish. 2793

Saint of the impossible. 3238

Saint of the slaves forever. 1286

Saint of the snows. 1507

Saint of the southern church. 1305

Saint of the twentieth century. 21

Saint of the week. 3281

Saint of the wilderness. 2125

Saint of today. 3690

... St. Oswald and the church of Worcester. 2752, 3847

Saint Pancratius. 3281

Saint Patrick. 2793

St. Patrick and Irish Christianity. 2517, 2793

St. Patrick and the coming of Christianity. 2793

Saint Patrick and the Irish. 2793

Saint Patrick, apostle of Ireland. 2793

St. Patrick congregation centennial. 2242

Saint Patrick, his origins and career. 2793

Saint Patrick in history. 2793

Saint Patrick, the Irish saint. 1027, 2793

St. Patrick's Cathedral. 2698

... St. Patrick's day. 3277

St. Patrick's of New Orleans, 1833-1958. 1269

St. Patrick's summer. 796

Saint Paul. 338, 1028, 2795, 2796, 2797, 2798, 2799, 2800, 2801, 2802, 2803

Saint Paul and apostolic writings. 367

St. Paul and Christianity. 376, 2798

St. Paul and Epicurus. 376, 2796

St. Paul and his letters. 370

Saint Paul and his message. 2795

Saint Paul and his missions. 2797

St. Paul and social psychology. 364

St. Paul and the Church of Jerusalem. 1192, 2798

St. Paul and the church of the gentiles. 376, 2798

... S. Paul (and the Letter to the Hebrews) 473

Saint Paul and the mystery of Christ. 2802

St. Paul and the mystery religions. 2798, 2802

St. Paul, apostle and martyr. 2797

Saint Paul, apostle of nations. 2796

St. Paul as a theologian. 2803

St. Paul catechism of Christian doctrine. 767

St. Paul congregation. 1577

St. Paul daily Mass book. 837

St. Paul daily missal. 845, 847

Saint Paul from the trenches. 370

St. Paul; his life, letters, and Christian doctrine. 2799

St. Paul in Britain. 46

St. Paul in Ephesus and the cities of Galatia and Cyprus. 2803, 3718

St. Paul in Greece. 1765, 2803

St. Paul in Rome. 2796

Saint Paul junior missal. 899

St. Paul of the Corss. 2767

St. Paul of the Cross. 2767

Saint Paul on Christian unity. 1039

St. Paul on trial. 331, 2802

Saint Paul shows us how. 341

St. Paul Sunday missal for all Sundays and feast days. 847

St. Paul Sunday missal for all Sundays and feast days, in acordance with latest pontifical decrees. Compiled and illustrated by the Daughters of St. Paul, with introd. by J. Alberione. Authorized new revision of the New Testament used throughout. 847
St. Paul Sunday missal for teenagers. 847
St. Paul the apostle. 2795
Saint Paul, the apostle of the Gentiles. 2801
St. Paul, the hero. 2798
Saint Paul, the man & the teacher. 2801
St. Paul the traveller and the Roman citizen. 2800, 2801
St. Paul United Methodist Church, Ninety Six, South Carolina: church history, 1875-1972. 3278
St. Paul's cathedral. 2244
St. Paul's Cathedral, Buffalo, 1817-1967. 712
St. Paul's cathedral in the time of Edward vi. 2244
St. Paul's church, 1832. 2713
St Paul's Church, Alverthorpe. 28, 3278
St. Paul's Church, Richmond, Virginia, its historic years and memorials. 3237
St. Paul's conception of Christianity. 375
St. Paul's Episcopal Church, 1866-1966. 3276
Saint Paul's Epistle to the Ephesians. 364
Saint Paul's Epistle to the Galatians. 379
Saint Paul's Epistle to the Philippians. 448
St. Paul's Epistle to the Romans. 466, 467
Saint Paul's Epistles to the Colossians and to Philemon. 341
St. Paul's Epistles to the Corinthians. 345
St. Paul's Epistles to the Thessalonians. 478
St. Paul's friendships and his friends. 2796
St. Paul's gospel. 376
St. Paul's journeys in the Greek Orient. 2801
St. Paul's last journey. 2678, 2804
St. Paul's letter to the Philippians. 448, 450
St. Paul's life of Christ. 1952, 2797
St. Paul's missionary methods. 2518
St. Paul's Parish, Baltimore. 133
Saint Paul's Parish, Washington. 3798
Saint Paul's vision. 3049
St. Paul's within the walls, Rome. 3278
Saint Peter. 2824, 2825
St. Peter and his training. 2824
Saint Peter and the first years of Christianity. 2824
Saint Peter and the Popes. 2770, 2825
Saint Peter Canisius. 734
Saint Peter Chrysologus. 3369
Saint Peter's. 3769
St. Peter's church in Salem, Massachusetts, before the revolution. 3286
St Peter's Church, Wymondham, Leicestershire. 3278
St. Peter's Lutheran Church, Barren Hill, Pa. 2282
St. Peter's on the Vatican. 3245
Saint Philomena. 2831
Saint Philomena, powerful with God. 2831
St. Photios the Great. 1028, 2844
St. Pierre's rain of fire. 167
St.-Pierre's Studies of nature. 2676
Saint Pius X. 2851, 2861
Saint Pius X, the farm boy who became Pope. 2851
St. Pius V, a brief account of his life, times, virtues & miracles. 2850, 2861
Saint Pius V. pope of the holy rosary. 2850
St. Pius X, Pope. 2851
... St. Polycarp, bishop of Smyrna. 2858
Saint Procopius, guardian of the Cyrilo-Methodian legacy. 2944
Saint Raymond of Pennafort of the Order of friars. 3025
St. Regis, a social crusader. 3051
St. Regis association's Catholic year book and directory of Pittsburgh diocese. 866, 2850
Saint Rita. 3238
Saint Rita's treasury. 857, 3238
Saint Rose hymnal. 812, 813
St. Rose of Lima, patroness of the Americas. 3247
St. Seraphim of Sarov. 3334
Saint Sergius and Russian spirituality. 3257, 3334
St. Sergius--builder of Russia. 3334
Saint-Simonism in the radicalism of Thomas Carlyle. 740, 3436
St. Stephen. 3527
St. Stephen and the Hellenists in the primitive church. 3527
St. Stephen Martyr Church and the community, 1867-1967. 3798

St. Stephen's Chapel and its place in the development of perpendicular style in England. 3808
Saint Stephen's Church in Providence. 2984
St. Tammany Lodge No. 5. 1664
... St. Teresa. 3603
St. Teresa of Avila. 2645, 3602, 3603
St. Teresa of Jesus. 3603
St. Teresa of Jesus of the Order of Our Lady of Carmel. 3603
Saint Teresa picture book. 3690
St. Teresa's book-mark. 3603
St. Theodore of Canterbury. 3610
St. Theresa Margaret of the Sacred Heart of Jesus. 3602
... Saint Theresa of Avila. 3603
Saint Theresa of Avila, translated from the French of Louis Bertrand. 3602
Saint Therese and her mission. 3690
St. Therese and suffering. 3690
St. Therese, messenger of Mary. 3690
Saint Therese of Lisieux. 3691
St. Therese of Lisieux, her last conversations. 2397, 3691
St. Therese returns. 785
St. Thomas Aguinas. 3692
St. Thomas and epistemology. 2180, 3694
St. Thomas and philosophy. 3694
St. Thomas and the future of metaphysics. 2419, 3695
...Saint Thomas and the gentiles. 3696
St. Thomas and the Greek moralists. 3692
... Saint Thomas and the Greeks. 2842, 3693
Saint Thomas Aquinas. 2397, 2839, 3309, 3692, 3693, 3694, 3695
St. Thomas Aquinas book. 3694
Saint Thomas Aquinas, meditations for every day. 2397
St. Thomas Aquinas on the existence of God. 1738, 3694
St. Thomas Aquinas' philosophy in the Commentary to the sentences. 3696
St. Thomas Aquinas, theological texts. 777, 3636
St. Thomas Becket in art. 3692
Saint Thomas d'Aquin, pour le septieme centenaire de sa mort. 3694
Saint Thomas More. 2596
St. Thomas More church. 893
St. Thomas of Canterbury. 3692
Saint Tikhon of Zadonsk, inspirer of Dostoevsky. 1028, 3699
... A saint under Moslem rule. 1542
St. Valentine's Day. 3279
St. Vartan: hero of Armenia. 3768
Saint Vibiana's Cathedral. 3279
Saint Vincent de Paul. 3779
Saint Vincent de Paul, a guide for priests, translated from the French of abbe Arnaud d'Agnel, by Rev. Joseph Leonard, C.M. 771, 3779
Saint Vincent de Paul, 1581-1660. 1026
St. Vincent Ferrer. 3780
Saint Vincent Ferrer, O.P. 3780
St. Vincent Strambi's guide to sacred eloquence. 3362, 3535
Saint-watching. 1024, 3281
Saint Wilfrid at Hexham. 86, 3816
Saint William of York. 1029, 1628
Saint-worship. 3283
Saint-worship[and] The worship of Mary. 3283
... Sainte Chantal. 882
Sainte Therese of Lisieux. 3690
Saintly and successful worker. 743
Saintly calling. 925
Saintly children. 896
Saintly workers. 923, 3405
Saints. 1024, 3281, 3282, 3284
Saints: adventures in courage. 3284
Saints alive! 338, 922, 1025, 1225, 3284
Saints and blessed of the Third order of Saint Francis, by Louis Biersack, G.F.M. CAP. 1649
Saints and festivals of the Christian church. 1025, 3279
Saints and heroes for boys. 3284
Saints and heroes of the Christian church. 923
Saints & heroes of the western world. 3282
Saints and heroes since the Middle Ages. 924, 1821
Saints & heroes speak. 786, 1025
Saints and heroes to the end of the Middle Ages. 924, 1821
Saints and martyrs of Ireland. 1026
Saints and mystics. 923
Saints and ourselves. 3281
Saints & rebels. 660, 661
... Saints and saint makers of New Mexico. 919
Saints and saintly Dominicans. 1475
Saints and sanctity. 3279
Saints and Scholars. 3283

Saints and sectaries. 53, 1858
Saints and silhouettes. 1447
Saints and sinners. 213, 659, 922, 3143
Saints and sinners at Jersey Settlement. 1943
Saints and sinners of the Bible. 217
Saints and snobs. 984
Saints and society. 1025, 1138
Saints and swingers. 213
Saints and their attributes. 3281
Saints and their emblems. 1026
Saints and their emblems in English churches. 3282
Saints and your name. 3281
Saints are not sad. 3282
Saints are now. 871
Saints at prayer. 2888, 2892
Saints at work. 3281
Saints beyond the White Cliffs. 1026
Saints book. 1025
Saints by fire light. 3284
Saints by firelight. 3279
Saints by request. 3285
Saints courageous. 3284
Saints Cyril and Methodius. 1398
Saints' days as observed by the churches of the Anglican communion. 1214, 3283
Saints' everlasting rest. 178, 1444
Saints for all seasons. 1025
Saints for boys and girls. 3284
Saints for confused times. 1025
Saints for now. 3281
Saints for our time. 1025
Saints for our times. 3281
Saints for Scouts. 3284
Saints for servers. 3284
Saints for sinner. 3280
Saints for sinners. 1024
Saints for the modern woman. 3285
Saints for the small. 3284
Saints for young people for everyday of the year. 3283, 3284
Saints' harmony. 1861
Saints' harp. 1861
Saint's herald Question time. 3012
Saints hymnal of the Church of Jesus Christ. 1230
Saints in action. 3282, 3737
Saints in aprons. 3844
Saints in aprons and overalls. 337
Saints in art. 1025, 3282
Saints in daily Christian life. 3299
Saints in folklore. 3285
Saints in history. 3284
Saints in sandals. 330
Saints in the sky. 749
Saints in the valleys. 3303
Saints in times of turmoil. 1025
Saints' lives and chronicles in early England. 1773, 1780
Saints of chaos. 661, 2276
Saints of clay; the shaping of South Carolina Baptists. 169
Saints of Egypt. 3283
Saints of Ireland. 692, 1026
Saints of Lindisfarne. 1026, 2230
Saints of Russia. 3285
Saints of sage & saddle. 2615, 2619
Saints of the Americas. 1025
Saints of the Benedictine Order of Montefano. 1027
Saints of the Byzantine world. 3285
Saints of the canon, and reasonableness of Catholic ceremonies and practices. 770, 842
Saints of the East. 3279
Saints of the missal. 1263
Saints of the twentieth century. 924
Saints off pedestals. 764
Saints on icons. 1880
Saints on Main Street. 2191
Saints, signs, and symbols. 921
Saints, sinners, and Christian history. 1178
Saints, slaves, and Blacks. 1133, 2401
Saints that moved the world. 55, 114, 3282
Saints (The) 3281
Saints through their handwriting. 3281
Saints to help the sick and the dying. 3406
Saints to know. 3284
Saints to remember from January to December. 3283
Saints upon a time. 3285
Saints westward. 814
Saints who changed things. 1025
Saints who loved animals. 3284
Saints who made history. 3282
Saints who never were. 952
Saints who spoke English. 1026, 3283
Saints without halos. 338, 2619
Saints without wrinkles. 3285
Saintspeak, the Mormon dictionary. 2598
Saivism in philosophical perspective. 3422
Saivism through the ages. 3421
Sakshi Gopal. 2187

... The Saktas. 3286, 3400
Sakti cult in ancient India, with special reference to the Puranic literature. 3400
Saladin and the fall of the Kingdom of Jerusalem. 1944, 3286
Salary and wage policy during depression and recovery. 3871
Salem chapel. 1269
Salem seer. 1635, 3495
Salem witchcraft. 3828
Salem witchcraft delusion 1692. 3827
Salem witchcraft in outline. 3827, 3828
Salem X Roads' churches in the nineteenth century. 2693
Salesmanship for Christ. 3829
... Salisbury. 848
Salisbury psalter. 848
Salmon River mission. 1881
Salome. 3287
Salome, a play. 3287
Salome; a tragedy in one act. 3287
Salome the dancer. 3287
Salome, the daughter of Herodias. 3287
Salome: virgin or prostitute? 3287
Saloon a nuisance and license unconstitutional. 2231
Saloon-keeper's ledger. 3596
Saloon must go! 3596
Salt and light. 431, 3334
Salt-cellars. 2980
Salt for society. 984
Salt from the Psalter. 585
Salt Lake Mormon Tabernacle Choir goes to Europe. 3287
Salt Lake Mormon Tabernacle Choir goes to Europe, 1955. 3287
Salt of the earth. 168, 1056, 1397, 2438, 2576, 3358
Salty tang. 2935
Salute thy soul. 2932
Salute to a sufferer. 3541
Salute to Sandy. 3243
Salute to Sid; the story of Dr. Sidney Gilchrist. 1713, 2539
Salute to the valiant. 1753
Salvado memoirs. 2484, 3287
Salvage of men. 3290
El salvaje y la mitologia, el arte y la religion. 3290
Salvation. 3288, 3289, 3290, 3291, 3295
Salvation and behaviour. 470
Salvation and health. 3290
Salvation and protest. 1393
... Salvation and sanctification. 3294
Salvation and the old theology. 3294
Salvation and the perfect society. 3293
Salvation and the savage. 1900
Salvation army and the public. 3292
Salvation Army in America. 3293
Salvation army in the United States. 3293
Salvation army today. 3293
Salvation by Christ. 3759
Salvation by faith and your will. 1505
Salvation by grace through faith. 1753
Salvation by laughter. 3106
Salvation by surprise. 469
Salvation for all men, put out of all dispute. 3751
Salvation for the chief of sinners. 3292
Salvation from sin. 3288, 3290, 3292
Salvation full and free. 2404
Salvation here and hereafter. 1234
Salvation history. 651, 3293
Salvation history and the religious life. 998
Salvation in a scientific age. 3290
Salvation in a two-fold aspect. 3291
Salvation in Christ. 165
Salvation in Christ (Vid korset) 106
Salvation in history. 1818
Salvation in New England. 1342
Salvation in our time. 1560
Salvation in the slums. 2860
Salvation is forever. 3289
Salvation is of the Lord. 3290
Salvation life lines and spiritual life preservers. 3292
Salvation light. 3290
Salvation of all men strictly examined. 890, 1695
Salvation of the gentiles. 330
Salvation of the gentiles and the prophets. 658
Salvation of the little child. 3290
Salvation of the nations. 2554
Salvation of the unbeliever. 3294
Salvation sermon outlines. 3296, 3372
Salvation sermons. 3296
Salvation sought in earnest. 3295
Salvation to the uttermost. 3289
Salvation today. 3291
Salvation tomorrow. 1080
Salvation tree. 3289
Salvation unlimited. 3289
Salve mater. 1364
Salve Regina. 2361

Salviani presbyteri massiliensis Opera omnia. 3635
Sam Jones. 1557, 2131
Sam. Jones' anecdotes and illustrations. 1840
Sam Jones' revival sermons. 2131
Sam Jones' sermons. 33, 1557, 3353
Sam Jones's Kansas City sermons. 1557
... Samantapasadika. 3779
Samaritan chronicle. 3296
Samaritan documents. 3297
Samaritan liturgy. 3296
Samaritan Pentateuch and the origin of the Samaritan sect. 563, 3296
Samaritan problem. 3297
Samaritan version of the Pentateuch. 505
... The Samaritans. 3296
Samaritans of Molokai. 1400, 2537, 2556
Samaritans; the earliest Jewish sect. 3296
Samavedic chant. 883, 3776
Samayasara (The soul-essence) 1932
Samkhya philosophy, containing (1) Samkhya-pravachana sutram. 3301
... Sammoha-vinodani Abhidhamma-pitake Vibhangatthakatha. 3778
Sammuel Bacon Barnitz. 174
Sammy Tippit: God's love in action. 3701
Sammy writes a book. 2489
Sampling the Psalms. 576
Samson. 555, 3237, 3297
Samson Agonistes. 2472, 3297
Samson and Delilah. 3297
Samson-saga and its place in comparative religion. 3297, 3546
Samson; selections from a contemplation on an historical passage in the Old Testament. 3297
Samsons. 2104
... Samuel. 589, 3297
Samuel A. Purdie. 1686, 3005
Samuel and his age. 590, 3297
... Samuel and Saul, their lives and times. 3297
Samuel Bacon Barnitz. 174
Samuel Chenery Damon. 1400
Samuel David Luzzatto, traditionalist scholar. 2303, 3309
Samuel Davies; apostle of dissent in colonial Virginia. 1406
Samuel Doak, 1749-1830: his life, his children, Washington College. 1472
Samuel Friedland lectures, 1960-1966. 2142
Samuel Friedland lectures 1967-1974. 2143
Samuel Harris, American theologian. 1787, 3611
Samuel Hopkins and the New Divinity movement. 1847, 3660
Samuel J. Mills. 2467
Samuel Leslie Morris. 2926
Samuel Logan Brengle. 691
Samuel Marsden. 2347, 2485
Samuel, prophet and judge. 495, 634, 3297
Samuel R. Plumbe. 2854
... Samuel Reynolds House of Siam. 1849
Samuel, Saul and David. 590
Samuel Seabury. 3317
Samuel Seabury, 1729-1796. 3317
Samuel Taylor Coleridge. 1307
Samuel Taylor Coleridge in Australian Libraries. 1307
Samuel Willard, 1640-1707. 3817
San Agustin, first cathedral church in Arizona. 3273
San Anselmo story. 3298
San Antonio de Padus. 3297
San Bernardino of Siena and Sant' Antonino of Florence. 194
San Buenaventura. 3298
San Francisco Methodism. 2430
San Francisco YMCA. 3875
San Gabriel mission and the beginnings of Los Angeles. 3298
San Jose. 3298
San Juan de la Cruz (Saint John of the Cross) 2136
San Nicandro. 2952
Sancta sanctorum. 858
Sancti Augustini vita scripta a Possidio episcopo. 115
Sancti Avren Avgvstini Scripta contra donatistas. 1476
Sanctification. 3299
Sanctification and holiness. 3300
Sanctification and its synonyms. 2818
Sanctification & liberation. 3300, 3806
Sanctification practical. 3299
Sanctification: what it is, when it is, how it is. 3299
Sanctified common sense. 325
Sanctified in truth. 1299
Sanctified life. 3299, 3300
Sanctifier. 1830
"Sanctify them" 2248
Sanctifying grace. 1752

Sanctifying life, time, and space. 1213, 2234
Sanctity and secularity: the church and the world. 1183
Sanctity and social service. 974
Sanctity and success in marriage. 2339
Sanctity in America. 829
Sanctity in other words. 3300
Sanctity of marriage. 2337
Sanctity of the synagogue. 3578
Sanctity will out. 1939
Sanctuary. 1634, 2399, 3859
Sanctuary-boys' illustrated manual. 27
Sanctuary lights on the Monterey Peninsula. 815
Sanctuary manual. 840
Sanctuary of Memphis or Hermes. 39
Sanctuary of self. 3251
Sanctuary of the home. 2112
Sanctuary planning. 1157, 1158
Sanctuary service. 3381
Sand and stars. 2544
Sand-table. 2720
Sand table illustrations. 299
Sandals at the mosque. 2567
Sandals on the golden highway. 3377
Sanderson's complete course in Bible study. 641
Sands of Tamanrasset. 1635
...Sane and sensible views of life. 2226
Sane evangelism. 1553
Sangha and state in Burma. 2577
Sanhedrin Papers, including the Gospel of Judas. 1978
Sanity of sanctity. 1824
Sankey still sings. 3301
Sankey's story of the gospel hymns and of sacred songs and solos. 1873
Sanskrit and its kindred literatures. 2653
Sanskrit drama in its origin, development, theory & practice. 3301
Sanskrit-English dictionary. 3301
Sanskrit keys to the wisdom-religion. 3301
Sant' Angela of the Ursulines. 41, 3761
Santa Barbara mission. 3302
Santa Claus, the Tooth Fairy, and other stories. 903
Santal khuts. 3302
Santayana, art, and aesthetics. 3302
Santayana: saint of the imagination. 3302
Santayana: the later years. 3302
Santayana's aesthetics; a critical introduction. 3302
Santeria; African magic in Latin America. 3302, 3303
Santo Nino of Cebu. 3303
Santos. 921, 3303
Santos and saints. 3303
Santos and saints' days. 2359, 3283
Santos of the Southwest. 3303
Sao Paulo hears the gospel. 2505
Saqqara. 3285
... The Saracens from the earliest times to the fall of Bagdad. 2564
Sarah Joiner Lyman of Hawaii—her own story. 2524
Sarajevo Haggadah. 1884
... Sarattha-ppakasini. 3297
Sarcophagi of Ravenna. 3303
Sartre and the sacred. 1836, 3303
Sarum missal. 845
... The Sarum missal in English. 847
Sasa Rore—Little Warrior. 2541, 3247
Satan. 1427, 1428, 1429
"Satan", a Bible study. 1429
Satan, a portrait. 1428
Satan and demons. 1428
Satan and his gospel. 1428
Satan and the saint. 1757
... Satan and the spider. 1449
Satan as a moral philosopher. With other essays and sketches. 1428
Satan, demons & dildoes. 2728
Satan dethroned. 1427
Satan, his kingdom and its overthrow. 1427
Satan, his origin, work, and destiny. 1428
Satan, his person & power. 1429
Satan, his person, work, place, and destiny. 1427
Satan, his psychotherapy and cure by the unfortunate Dr. Kassler, J.S.P.S. 1429
Satan in society. 3392
Satan in society and his modern methods of winning victims. 3304
Satan in the Old Testament. 1429
Satan in the sanctuary. 610
Satan is alive and well on planet earth. 1428
Satan is no myth. 1428
Satan of the modern world. 1427
Satan on the loose. 1392, 1427
Satan or Christ! 25
Satan, Prince of Darkness. 1428
Satan, satanism, and witchcraft. 1427
Satan, sorcery, and sex. 1428
Satan the Anti-Christ. 1428

Satan, the Prince of Darkness. 1428
Satan trap. 2730
Satan will never die. 3086
Satanic cult. 3304
Satanic mass. 1429
Satanic rituals. 3304
Satanism and witchcraft. 3824
Satanizing of woman. 3389
Satan's angels. 39, 1426
Satan's angels exposed. 1428
Satan's been cross since Calvary. 1556
Satan's disciples. 1429, 3303
Satan's fifth column. 2039, 2563
Satan's headquarters exposed. 1428
Satan's invisible world discovered. 3568
Satan's power. 2866
Satan's release. 1427
Satan's secret service. 960
Satanward view. 376
Satapatha-brahmana. 3139
Satirical letters of St. Jerome. 1811
Satisfaction from the Scriptures. 422
Satisfaction of Christ. 106
Satmar. 3304
Satsang. 3482
Saturday afternoon. 964
Saturday evening. 1072
Saturday night sermons. 3340
Saturday night special. 3375
Saturday night, Sunday morning. 1256
Saturday night talk with God. 1461
Saturday night thoughts. 2607
Saturday or Sunday? 3546
Saturn myth. 3304
Saturn, planet of peace, sends warning. 3513
Saudi Arabia. 3304
Saul among the prophets. 2793
Saul and David. 602
Saundaryalahari. 3775
Save America! 1109
Save America to save the world. 3742
Save me! 931, 2206
Save money! 3530
Saved by a ghost. 3507
"Saved by fire." 2178
Saved by grace. 1753, 2128
Saved by His life. 104
Saved by hope. 239, 2752, 3342
Saved for service. 3289
Saved forever. 3295
Saved from bankruptcy. 2401, 3539
Saved, from what? 3295
Saved or lost? 1560
Saved to serve. 3529
Saved to serve, comprising appealing and vital messages on the duties of Christians to give of their time, thought and means to God. 161
Saved to the uttermost. 404, 3290
Saving America to save the world. 1558
Saving belief. 1613
Saving faith. 1590
Saving faith and other sermons. 3350
Saving image: redemption in contemporary preaching. 1558
Saving life of Christ. 977
Saving Person. 3288
Saving possibility. 1007
Saving presence. 1453
Saving sense. 759
Saving the world. 3288
Saving word. 252
Savioour and the Scriptures. 1958
Savior and the church. 748
Savior as Saint Matthew saw Him. 443
Savior, Christ the Lord; Bible studies with the Men's Bible class of the Second Presbyterian church. 406
Savior is coming. 596
Savior of the world. 428, 1977
Savior's invitation. 1555
Saviors of mankind. 3136
Savior's suffering. 2034
Saviour and the Scriptures. 241, 1959
Saviour god. 1933, 3293, 3294
... The Saviour of the world. 3029
Saviour we need. 105
Saviour's Bible. 3225
Saviour's fountains. 3262
Saviour's life in the words of the four Gospels. 1989, 1990
Saviti unveiled. 3305
Savonarola. 1277, 3305
Savonarola and Florence. 1629, 3306
Savonarols. 3305
Sawgrass missionary. 3467
Saxon and Norman churches in England. 1270
... The Saxon bishops of Wells. 3801
Say a good word. 3767
Say a good word for Jesus. 2398
Say amen, brother! 2682
"Say, fellows--" 687
Say hi to Jesus for me. 931, 2585

Say it with love. 1316
Say it with stories. 1842
Say neighbor—your house is on fire! 161
Say not goodbye. 3473
Say the good word. 2608
Say thou art mine. 2300
Say yes! 3885
Say; Yes; to life. 970
Say yes to the light. 964
Saying of the Jewish fathers. 573
Saying yes to life as we grow older. 973
Sayings and doings of Jesus. 2025
Sayings and sentences for church bulletins. 1163
Sayings & songs for soldiers & sailors. 3456, 3459
Sayings of Budda, theIt:-Uuttaka. 709
Sayings of Buddha. 703
Sayings of Chuang Chou. 1731
Sayings of Jesus. 408, 441, 2062, 2070, 2071, 2072, 3010
Sayings of Jesus from Oxyrhynchus. 2755
Sayings of Jesus in the churches of Paul. 372, 2071
Sayings of Jesus. Selected by Kenneth Seeman Giniger. Illustrated by Eugene Karlin. 2070
*Sayings of Jesus (The) 400
Sayings of Jesus: the Sermon on the Mount and The instruction to the Disciples. 2072
Sayings of Mohammed. 2565
Sayings of Muhammad. 1779
Sayings of Paramhansa Yogananda. 3483
Sayings of sages. 2374
Sayings of the great forty days. 2006, 3654
Sayings of the Jewish fathers. 3
Sayings of the Jewish fathers (Pirke aboth) 4
Sayings of the Lord Jesus Christ. 2070
Sayings of the Lord Jesus Christ as recorded by His four evangelists. 400
Sayings of the risen Jesus. 388, 2070, 2949
Sayings of Yogananda. 3866
Sayings, wise and otherwise. 2374
Sayyid Jamal ad-Din "al-Afghani" 21
Scale of perfection. 1447, 1812
Scale the heights. 2392
Scales of Karma. 2165
Scalpel and cross in Honan. 2529
Scandal in the assembly. 2342
Scandal of Christianity. 1039, 3641
Scandal of Lent. 421, 2209
Scandal of silence. 829
Scandal of the cross. 1998
Scandal of truth. 1057
Scandalous saint, by John C. Hagee. Introductions by Merlin R. Carothers and David Coote. 1503
Scandian Grove. 3278
Scandinavian churches. 3306
Scandinavian mythology. 2665
Scanning the Sunday Gospel. 366
Scapegoat of revolution. 2112
Scarcity and evil. 1746
Scare me! 2311
Scarlet cord. 293
Scarlet line, and other Bible stories. 616
Scarlet mother on the Tiber. 3131
Scarlet sin. 8
Scarlet thread. 15, 1840
Scarlet thread through the Bible. 161
Scattered abroad. 156
Scenario of the photo-drama of creation. 1381
Scenes and incidents in the life the apostle Paul. 2795
Scenes and sayings in the life of Christ. 1972
Scenes beyond the grave. 1697
Scenes beyong the grave. 1697
Scenes from the Bible. 603
Scenes from the life of Jesus. 1993
Scenes from the life of Jesus in woodcut. 626
Scenes from the Passion of Our Lord Jesus Christ for meditation during Mass; or, The Most Holy Sacrifice of the Mass explained according to the mysteries of the Passion of Our Lord. 2369
Scenes from the Psalms. 575
Scenes in the life of Christ. 1982
Scenes in the life of the Saviour. 2048
Scenes in the lives of the patriarchs and prophets. 494
... Scenes in the spirit world. 3516
Scenes in the world of spirits. 3475
Scenes of clerical life. 1507
Scenes of clerical life and Silas Marner. 1507
Scenes of clerical life, Silas Marner, and other stories. 1507
Scent to Faith. 1414
Sceptical approach to religion. 3103
Scepticism and faith. 60

Sceptics of the Old Testament: Job, Koheleth, Agur. 549
Schaff-Herzog encyclopedia. 3639
Schauffler missionary training school. 2488
Schelling's treatise on "The deities of Samothrace" 2660, 3307
Schema sacrum. 3641
Scheme of divine revelation considered. 3224
Schemers, dreamers, and medicine men. 3110
Schemes of religious instruction for infant day-schools. 650
Scherling-Bailey debate. 1347
Schism and renewal in Africa. 1073
Schism, heresy and religious protest. 1805
Schism in the early church. 3307
Schism in the Methodist Episcopal church. 2443
Schism in the Methodist Episcopal church 1844. 2443
Schism in the Methodist Episcopal Church, 1844. 2451, 3423
Schizophrenic church. 2481
Schleiermacher. 3308
Schleiermacher and religious education. 3155, 3308
Schleiermacher bibliography. 3308
Schleiermacher: life and thought. 3308
Schleiermacher on Christ and religion. 2709
Schleiermacher on Christ and religion, a new introduction. 3308
Schleiermacher the theologian. 1732, 3308
Schmid letters. 1707
Schoenstatt. 77
Scholar and the cross. 3526
Scholars and mystics. 1708
Scholar's larger life. 3309
Scholars of Judah. 536
Scholars, saints, and Sufis. 1924, 3722
Scholarship on Philo and Josephus. 2134
Scholastic miscellany. 777, 3636
Scholastic miscellany: Anselm to Ockham. 3309
Scholastic rabbinism. 1539, 3585
Scholasticism. 3309
Scholasticism and politics. 3309
Scholasticism, humanism, and reform. 3310
Scholasticism, the philosophy of common sense. 3309
School and church, partners in Christian education. 3165
School and church: the American way; an historical approach to the problem of religious instruction in public education. 1130
School and college credit for outside Bible study. 643
School business administrator in the Catholic school system. 831
School controversy, 1891-1893. 832
School ethics. 3310
School for bishops. 132
School fund perverted. 1128
School in the home. 2773
School in the modern church. 3148
School in which we teach. 3553
School of Calvary. 3540
School of charity. 2707
School of Christ. 2067

School of faith. 3043
School of Jesus. 2065, 3165
School of life. 2982
School of love. 2254, 3486
School of Mary. 2355
School of obedience. 2719
School of Peter Abelard. 1
School of prayer. 2882
School of prayers. 2882
School of providence and prayer. 2693
School of repentance. 2811
School of suffering. 3540
School of the church. 3553
School of the cross. 2031
School of the Master, and other religious verses. 2048
School of the prophets. 110, 2949
School of virtue. 3782
School question. 806, 1130
School sermons. 3310
Schools and the Christian school. 3150
Schools for spirits, By E. M. Wood. 3475
Schools of the Lutheran Church. 2297
Schools of the Lutheran Church, Missouri Synod. 2297
Schopenhauer. 3311
Schopenhauer as transmitter of Buddhist ideas. 2838, 3311
Schwarzenau yesterday and today. 3311
Schweitzer. 3312
Schweitzer album. 3311
Schweitzer: prophet of radical theology. 3312

Schwenkfelder hymnology and the sources of the first Schwenkfelder hymn-book printed in America. 1874, 3313
Science. 523
Science a witness for the Bible. 205
Science and a future life. 2989
Science and Christ. 3083
Science and Christian belief. 3077
Science & Christian faith. 3078
Science and Christian tradition. 3075, 3076
Science and Christianity. 3074
Science and Christianity—a partnership. 3081
Science and creation. 3077
Science and criticism. 1854
Science and faith. 3083
Science and faith in the 21st century. 3081
Science and faith: twin mysteries. 3082
Science and God. 3077
Science and health. 1031, 1032
Science and health with key to the Scriptures. 1032
Science and Hebrew tradition. 204, 3313
Science and human progress. 2833
Science and human values in the 21st century. 3083
... Science and immortality. 1889, 1891, 3078
Science and Judaism. 3078
Science and life. 3073
Science and metaphysics. 2163, 2419
Science and moral priority. 2686
Science and Mormonism. 3082
Science and our troubled-conscience. 3082
Science and prayer. 1285, 2874, 2880, 3619
Science and religion. 96, 2144, 3073, 3075, 3078, 3080, 3081, 3082, 3083
Science and religion as they look to a layman. 3073
Science and religion in a nutshell. 3313
Science and religion in America, 1800-1860. 3085
Science and religion in American thought. 3085, 3314
Science & religion in contemporary philosophy. 3080
Science and religion in Elizabethan England. 3084, 3085
Science and religion in India. 3085
Science and religion in seventeenth-century England. 3085
Science and religion in the thought of Nicolas Malebranche. 2319
Science and religion, the rational and the superrational. 3081
Science and religion today. 3074
Science and revelation. 3076
Science and salvation. 3294
Science and Scripture health. 248
Science and superstition. 3313, 3568
Science and the Bible. 204, 205, 3072
Science and the Christian experiment. 3082
Science and the church. 3077
Science and the holy shroud. 1826
Science and the idea of God. 3078
Science and the love of God. 3079
Science and the paranormal. 2992
Science and the religious life. 2999
Science and the supernatural. 3079
Science and the unseen world. 1676, 3078, 3081
Science and theology. 2692
Science and truth. 204
Science and ultimate truth. 3107
Science and ultimate truth, Fison memorial lecture, 1926. 2836
Science and your faith in God. 3080
Science as morality. 3313
Science as revelation. 3080
Science challenges faith. 1595, 3313
Science, change and the Christian. 3082
Science, Christ and the Bible. 206, 1955
Science, Christianity and youth. 3079
Science, conscience and God. 3078
Science discovers God. 3078
Science et sante. 1032
Science, evolution, and immortality. 1029
Science, faith and logic. 3082
Science, faith, and revelation. 3258, 3624
Science from the unseen. 3506
Science, God, and you. 3083
Science, history and faith. 3080
Science in defense of liberal religion. 2596, 3097
Science in search of God. 3079
Science in the Bible. 205
Science in theology. 3075
Science made easy. 3511
Science, man, and morals. 3083
Science of ascension. 5
Science of being and art of living. 3196
Science of Biblical hermeneutics. 287

Science of breath and the philosophy of the tattvas. 2840
Science of Christian economy. 3313
Science of correspondence elucidated. 2690
Science of correspondenced elucidated. 1370
Science of correspondences elucidated. 2690
Science of ethics. 1534
Science of evil; or First principles of human action. 1746
Science of governmental and individual life. 2227
Science of health from the viewpoint of the newest Christian thought. 2409
Science of human equation. 3313
Science of leadership. 2204
Science of life. 3798
Science of life and sex purity. 3390
Science of life and the larger hope. 3073
Science of logic. 1800
Science of man. 1032, 2323, 3439
Science of meditation. 2381
Science of metaphysics. 2738
Science of mind. 2695, 3078
Science of modern religion. 2561
Science of peace. 3684
Science of praise. 2984
Science of prayer. 2869
Science of reality. 1238
Science of religion. 957, 3063, 3065, 3647
Science of religion & the sociology of knowledge: some methodological questions. 3064
Science of religion, based upon the works and words of Jesus the Christ. 3313
Science of religion, fundamental faiths expressed in modern terms. 3313
Science of Revelation in modern English. 3224
Science of society. 1034
Science of spirit. 51
Science of spiritual life. 3482
Science of spirtual alchemy. 3482
Science of the Bible. 203, 238
Science of the cross. 2137
Science of the day and Genesis. 205
Science of the initiates. 2724
Science of the mind. 2411
Science of the new thought. 2695
Science of the sacraments. 3263
Science of the soul. 3461, 3514
Science of the spirit, soul and body. 3462
Science of the spoken word. 3811
Science of the trinity. 3712
Science of winning men. 1360
Science of yoga. 3866
Science, philosophy and religion. 2835, 3081
Science ponders religion. 3083
Science, prophecy, and prediction. 2946
Science, psychiatry and religion. 3073, 3401
Science, reason, and religion. 3023
Science rediscovers God. 3079
Science, religion, and Christianity. 1056
Science, religion and reality. 3073, 3079, 3082
Science, religion, and the future. 3079
Science returns to God. 204
Science, saints, & sense. 3083
Science, secularization & God. 3081
Science, sin, and scholarship. 2588
Science speaks. 205
Science, technology, and the Christian. 3082
Science: the false messiah. 3314
Science, truth, religion and ethics as foundations of a rational philosophy of life. 2833
Science versus dogma. 3073
Science vs. modern spiritualism. 3521
Sciences among the Jews before and during the middle ages. 2682
Scientific and philosophical writings. 2838
Scientific and religious mysteries of antiquity. 1665
Scientific aspects of Mormonism. 2604
Scientific basis of Krsna consciousness. 2186
Scientific basis of Sabbath and Sunday. 3260, 3547
Scientific basis of spiritualism. 3513
Scientific Bible. 2672
Scientific Bible truth, thirty minute lectures. 2561
Scientific Christian mental practice. 2696
Scientific Christian thinking for young people. 3211
Scientific Christianity. 3073
Scientific confirmations of Old Testament history. 206
Scientific creationism. 1381
Scientific enterprise & Christian faith. 3082

Scientific evidence of the existence of the soul. 3463
Scientific evidences of revealed religion. 61
Scientific eye of faith. 64
Scientific fact and metaphysical reality. 2416
Scientific faith. 1050
Scientific humanism and Christian thought. 1854
Scientific investigation of the Old Testament. 515
Scientific man and the Bible. 204
Scientific management in the churches. 2373
Scientific method of Bible study. 639
Scientific occultism. 2725
Scientific proof of the existence of God will soon be announced by the White House! 3479
Scientific religion. 3510
Scientific social theology. 3443
Scientific spiritual healing. 2410
Scientific spirituality. 3141
Scientific studies in special creation. 1383
Scientific study of religion. 3065
Scientific study of the Old Testament. 595
Scientific support for Christian doctrines. 3078
Scientific teachings of Genesis. 203
Scientific temper in religion. 3314
Scientific theism. 3607
Scientific theism versus materialism. 3079
...Scientific theory and Catholic doctrine. 3077
Scientific theory and religion. 3077
Scientific Vedanta. 3775
Scientific views of religion. 3313
Scientific work. 3079
Scientifica hermetica. 3344
Scientism, man, and religion. 3079
Scientist and his faith. 63
Scientist and the soul. 3083
Scientist's approach to religion. 1105
*Scientists who believe. 3313
Scientology: a world religion emerges in the space age. 3314
Scientology for the millions. 3314
Scientology: the now religion. 3314
Scientology 0-8. 3314
Sciptural doctrine of divorce. 1471
Scofield Bible correspondence school. 641
... Scofield Bible study leaflets. 641
Scofield reference Bible. 259
Scope and authority of the Bible. 238
Scope of astrological prediction. 1848
Scope of charity. 887
Scope of demythologizing. 1424
Scope of grace. 3621
Scope of reincarnation. 3053
Scope of theology. 3645
Score of sermons. 3357
Scornful wonder. 1118
Scot of the eighteenth century. 1108
Scotch and Irish seeds in American soil. 2915
Scotch rite masonry illustrated. 1671
Scotland: church and nation through sixteen centuries. 3315
Scotland's ruined abbeys. 2
Scots in Franconia. 3301, 3314
Scottish abbeys & social life. 2583
Scottish church architecture. 1161
Scottish churches. 3315
Scottish churchmen and the Council of Basle. 177
Scottish communion office. 2960
Scottish Covenanters, 1660-1688. 1375
Scottish heroes. 1375
Scottish psalter of 1635. 580
Scottish Reformation. 3042
Scottish school hymnary. 3563
Scotty Kid. 39
... The scourge of Christ. 2012
Scourging of a race, and other sermons and addresses. 3342
Scoutways to God. 686
Scoutways to God; thoughts, words, and deeds, by Theodore J. Kleinhans. 686
Scrap book of inspiration. 1842
Scrapbook of inspiration. 1326
Scraphical young shepherd. 957
Scraps of biography. 2605
Screen and projector in Christian education. 3784
Screening candidates for the priesthood and religious life. 3785, 3786
Screens and galleries in English churches. 3316
Screwloose lectures. 945
Screwtape letters. 1060, 1061, 1063
Screwtape letters & Screwtape proposes a toast. 1060, 1061
Screwtape letters ; with, Screwtape proposes a toast. 1060, 1061
Scribe of a soul. 3517

Scripta Leonis, Rufini et Angeli, Sociorum S. Francisci. 1642
Scriptores Ordinis Praedicatorum recensiti, notisque historicis et criticis. 1475
... The Scriptural allegory, in three parts. 2617
Scriptural and allegorical glossary to Milton's Paradise lost. 2468, 2470
Scriptural and secular prophecies pertaining to the last days. 2947, 2948
Scriptural and subject index to the writings of Ellen G. White. 3811
Scriptural and subject index to the writings of Mrs. Ellen G. White. 3811
Scriptural baptism. 136
Scriptural basis for Christian unity. 1040
Scriptural basis of world evangelization. 1553
Scriptural claims of total abstinence. 3597
Scriptural defence of the doctrine of the Trinity. 3712
Scriptural doctrine of Our Lord Jesus Christ, and the Holy Spirit, in the relation to God the Father. 3713
Scriptural evangelism. 1570
Scriptural exhibition of the mighty conquest. 3319
Scriptural foundation for Christian liberality. 1168
Scriptural foundations of science. 3313
Scriptural healing. 249
Scriptural holiness. 1823
Scriptural hymns. 1872
Scriptural idea of man. 2323
Scriptural law of divorce. 1471
Scriptural mode of Christian baptism. 135
Scriptural prophecies concerning the coming of Christ Jesus and the fulfillment. 3318
Scriptural psychiatry. 317
Scriptural psychology of eternal youth. 2966
Scriptural readings. 613
Scriptural references for the Baltimore catechism. 132
Scriptural refutation of the Pope's primacy and miscellaneous studies and speeches. 795
Scriptural Rosary. 3249
Scriptural sanctification. 3299
Scriptural sermon outlines. 3376
Scriptural standard in economics and government. 3740
Scriptural truth about the Lord's return. 2051
Scriptural view of divine grace. 1752
Scriptural view of the character, causes, and ends of the present war. 3742
Scriptural view of the Christian pastorate. 3674
Scriptural view of the office of the Holy Spirit. 1831
Scriptural view of woman's rights and duties. 3841
Scripture account of the faith and practice of Christians. 227, 300, 302
Scripture alphabet of animals. 480
Scripture and confession. 1385
Scripture and ecumenism. 3706
Scripture & myth. 314, 3574
Scripture and social action. 1269
Scripture and the charismatic renewal. 644, 2816
Scripture and the Christian response. 304
Scripture and the church. 350
Scripture and the faith. 277
Scripture and tradition. 276, 277
Scripture and tradition in Judaism. 4, 505, 3706
[Scripture and tradition in the theology of Karl Barth. 175
Scripture animals. 480
Scripture baptism defended. 135
Scripture biography. 4, 293
Scripture biography for the young. 293, 294, 555
Scripture-bishop. 2936
Scripture cabinet. 1840
Scripture cannot be broken. 305
Scripture catechism for coloured people. 145
Scripture characters. 213, 214
Scripture crossword puzzles. 241
Scripture doctrine in reference to the seat of sin in the regenerate man. 3413
Scripture doctrine of atonement examined. 107
Scripture doctrine of atonement, proposed to carefull examination. 108
Scripture doctrine of Christian perfection. 2818
Scripture doctrine of Christian perfection stated and defended. 2818
Scripture doctrine of creation. 1379
Scripture doctrine of original sin explained and enforced: in two discourses. 3413

Scripture-doctrine of original sin, stated and defended. 3413, 3800
Scripture-doctrine of original sin, stated and defended. In a summer-morning's conversation, between a minister and a neighbour. 3410
Scripture doctrine of regeneration. 3050
Scripture doctrine of the church historically and exegetically considered. 1163
Scripture doctrine of the person of Christ. 2038
Scripture doctrines of the pre-existence of the humanity of Jesus Christ, before His birth in Bethlehem of Judea. 2049, 2817
Scripture geography. 283
... The Scripture guide to baptism. 136
Scripture help. 636
Scripture history. 280, 297, 536
Scripture history, abridged. 296
Scripture history of idolatry. 1882
Scripture history of Our blessed Lord and Saviour, Jesus Christ. 1961
Scripture in context. 504, 2679
Scripture in context II. 504
Scripture in history & theology. 239, 3259
Scripture in the liturgy. 845
Scripture in the Westminster Confession. 3809
Scripture index, or Bible subjects, persons, and places. 303
Scripture lessons arranged for responsive readings in religious services. 2442
Scripture--loyalist. 1749
Scripture manual. 303, 3147
Scripture manual, alphabetically and systematically arranged, designed to facilitate the finding of proof texts. 303
Scripture manual, directed to the interpretation of Biblical revelation. 312
Scripture memorizing for personal work. 1567
Scripture memorizing for successful soul-winning. 1567, 3153
Scripture memory work. 3159
Scripture memory work (graded) 3159
Scripture natural history. 480, 481
Scripture natural history, or a concise account of the animals referred to in the Bible. 481
Scripture notes and queries. 307
Scripture of the lotus blossom of the fine dharma. 711
Scripture portraits. 492
Scripture principles of education. 3160
Scripture prints. 3403
Scripture promises and warnings. 102
Scripture proof of miracles displayed. 2476
Scripture reader's guide to the devotional use of the Holy Scriptures. 643
Scripture readings. 252
Scripture readings for devotion and study in seminaries. 3219
Scripture readings for times of retreat. 252
Scripture readings in Orthodox worship. 315, 2236
Scripture readings topically arranged for public worship and personal devotions. 252
Scripture responses for worship. 3220, 3852
Scripture school reader. 3267
Scripture selections for daily reading. 725
Scripture sourcebook. 303
Scripture sourcebook (The) 303
Scripture stories retold for young Israel. 616
Scripture studies. 648, 2040
Scripture study series. 309
Scripture teaching in secondary schools. 300
Scripture testimony against intoxicating wine. 3595
Scripture text book. 303
Scripture texts. 725
Scripture texts for special days and occasions. 3376
Scripture, thoughts, and things to do during all the days of Lent. 858, 2212
Scripture to live by. 303
Scripture today. 239
Scripture, tradition, and infallibility. 304, 3224
Scripture, tradition, and interpretation. 239, 1787
Scripture treasures. 252
Scripture truth course. 3662
Scripture twisting. 288, 1393
Scripture unbroken. 451, 1377
Scripture worthies. 494
Scripturegraphics. 2395
Scriptures. 252, 645, 3177
Scriptures and the Christian response. 304
Scriptures as seen by the author. 307
Scriptures from ancient America. 680
Scriptures Hebrew and Christian. 249

Scriptures in the making. 290
Scriptures of mankind. 3267
Scriptures of the world. 655
Scriptures, old and new. 1456
Scripture's reply to arguments against "the second coming of Christ," 3319
Scriptures, sects, and visions. 2150
Scriptures the only rule of faith: an exposition of the second answer of the Shorter catechism. 276
Scroll of the war of the Sons of Light against the Sons of Darkness. 3861
Scrolls. 2093
Scrolls and Christian orgins. 1411, 3013
Scrolls and Christian origins. 3013
Scrolls and the New Testament. 1411
Scrolls from the Dead Sea. 1411
Sculpted saints of a borderland mission. 1026, 3298
Sculptural programs of Chartres Cathedral. 889
Sculptured crosses of ancient Ireland. 1388
Sculptured in faith. 973, 1594
Sculptured tombs of Hellas. 3333
Sculptures of Chartres cathedral. 889
Sea of Galilee. 2633
Sea rations. 3856
Sea, sand, & stars. 690, 1366
Seal of the seven. 646
Seal of the Spirit. 138
Seal upon my heart. 2581
Seal upon the lips of Unitarians, Trinitarians, and all others who refuse to acknowledge the sole, supreme, and exclusive divinity of Our Lord and Saviour Jesus Christ. 2000, 2690
Sealed orders. 3301
Seals of the Order to St. John of Jerusalem. 2179, 3317
Seals opened. 463
Seaman's devotional assistant. 3317
Seamen's hymns and devotional assistant. 3317
Seamen's manual of worship. 3317
Seamless robe. 1030, 2172
Seams of glory. 596
Seances and sensitives for the millions. 3494
Seances & spiritualists. 3520
Search. 474, 989, 3484
Search: a national consultation on personnel needs in church planning and research. 2670
Search after ultimate truth. 1720
Search and find. 3689
Search eternal. 2319
Search every corner. 2388
Search for a Christian education since 1940. 3160
Search for a king. 1113
Search for a new strategy in Protestantism. 1040
Search for a usable future. 1061
Search for America's faith. 3747
Search for being. 1584
Search for Blonnye Foreman. 1633
Search for Christian credibility. 3647
Search for Christian identity. 1007
Search for common ground. 2815
Search for dialogue. 3880
Search for God. 93, 1078, 1539, 1722, 1724, 1727, 1730, 1731, 1741
Search for God in time and memory. 1734
Search for God traced in Hebrew and Christian sources. 1728
Search for human values. 949
Search for identity. 965, 1546
Search for Jewish theology. 2080
Search for life meaning. 63
Search for me. 171, 1756
Search for meaning. 1676
Search for meaning in nature. 3083
Search for nothing. 1028, 2126
Search for peace. 2806
Search for reality. 1107
Search for Saint Therese. 3691
Search for salvation. 3294
Search for sanctity. 3475
Search for sensitivity & spirit. 1009, 1778
Search for silence. 1356
Search for Sodom and Gomorrah. 1409
Search for strength. 1354
Search for the absolute in neo-Vedanta. 197, 3774
Search for the early church. 1196
Search for the girl with the blue eyes. 2308, 3054
Search for the holy. 1836
Search for the sacred. 3889
Search for truth. 163, 3383
Search for understanding. 2298
Search in secret India. 3864
Search is within. 3482
Search light on the seventh wonder. 203

Search made into matters of religion. 764, 2978
Search of the magi for the infant Messiah. 1113
Search the Bible quizzes. 612
Search: the personal story of a wilderness journey. 2846
Search the Scriptures. 317, 473
Searcher of majesty. 3844
Searchers. 3080
Searching for icons in Russia. 1881
Searching for meaning. 3330
Searching for sense. 762
Searching for truth. 1098, 1654
Searching for you. 2395
Searching in the syntax of things. 3066
Searching mind. 1721
Searching the prophets for values. 571, 1538
Searching the Scriptures. 235, 309, 405, 642, 3372
Searching the Scriptures for the Messiah. 2415
Searching the world's greatest book. 280
Searching wind. 1448
Searching with success. 1704
Searchlight. 205
Searchlight on Bible words. 652
Searchlight on Christian science. 1032
Searchlighting ourselves. 2384
Searchlights from the Roman letter. 467
Searchlights from the Scriptures. 197
Searchlights from the Word. 3374
Searchlights of eternity. 796, 797, 2773
Searchlights on Christian science. 1035
Searchlights on contemporary theology. 3643
Season of changes. 3474
Season sarcophagus in Dumbarton Oaks. 3303
Season with the Savior. 437, 2212
Seasonable revolutionary. 890, 1333
Seasonable thoughts on the state of religion in New-England, a treatise in five parts. 2687
Seasonable thoughts upon mortality. 2372
Seasonal programs for churches. 1262
Seasoning. 734, 2384
Seasonings. 2389
Seasons. 3206
Seasons & symbols. 921
Seasons of celebration. 841
Seasons of friendship. 3333
Seasons of grace. 1264
Seasons of life. 3000
Seasons of our joy. 1614
Seasons of the Lord. 318
Seasons of the soul. 583
Seasons of the soul; the adventure of being human—and Christian. 2394
Seat behind the coachman: travellers in Ireland, 1800-1900. 1919
Seat of authority in religion. 3061
Seat of wisdom. 2362
Seattle pulpit. 3345, 3346
Second Adam. 2060
Second advent. 3318
Second advent hymns. 10
Second advent manual. 10, 2467
Second and third blast of retrait from plaies and theaters. 3607
Second and third blast of retreat from plays and theatres. 3607
Second Apron-pocket book of meditation and prayer. 3843
Second birthday. 3541
Second book of Chronicles. 496
Second book of Kings. 484, 556
Second book of Maccabees. 487, 488
Second book of Samuel. 484, 589, 590
Second book of story talks. 3533
... The second book of the Kings. 483
Second booke of the dialogues [of] St. Gregory. 189, 1028
Second Canadian Catholic Press Convention. 2937
Second century horizons for Y. M. C. A. work with boys; report. 687
Second century of Baptist foreign missions. 155
Second chance. 3768
Second chance for American Protestants. 2978
II Chronicles. 481
Second collection. 776, 3633
Second collection of penny object lessons. 3156
Second coming. 2055, 2464, 3304, 3319
Second coming Bible. 639
Second coming of Christ. 454, 2055, 3318, 3319, 3320, 3321
Second coming of Christ and last things. 2055
Second coming of Christ and the kingdom of God. 2055, 2175
Second coming of Jesus. 3318
Second coming of Our Lord. 3320

"The second coming of Our Lord Jesus Christ and the events associated therewith" 3319
Second coming of the church. 1060
... The second Concord anthem book. 49
Second Corinthians. 345
2 Corinthians, Galatians, Ephesians. 326
Second crisis in Christian experience. 974
Second cross. 1445
Second cup of coffee. 573, 3843
Second defence of the episcopal government, of the church. 1523, 3796
Second defence of the Short view of the prophaneness [sic] and immorality of the English stage. 1478, 3605
Second Episcopal district of the Christian Methodist Episcopal church presents a survey of eight years in which it has been engaged in a pattern of progress. 1022
Second epistle general of Peter, and the general epistle of Jude. 326
Second epistle of Paul the apostle to the Corinthians. 326
Second Epistle of Paul the Apostle to the Corinthians and the Epistles to Timothy, Titus and Philemon. Translator: T. A. Smail. 728
Second epistle of Paul to the Corinthians. 321, 322, 326, 346
... The Second epistle to the Corinthians. 325, 326, 346
Second fall. 3036
Second finding of Christ. 1951
Second fronts in metropolitan mission. 3538
... Second grade teachers plan book and manual. 632
Second great awakening in Connecticut. 1346
Second International (seventh national) Sunday-school convention of the United States and British American provinces. 3559
Second Isaiah. 543, 545
Second Jewish catalog. 2081, 2120
Second Jewish Commonwealth. 2090
Second journal of the stated preacher to the hospital and almshouse in the city of New York. 3126
Second journey. 2462
Second letter from John Bowden ... to the Reverend Doctor Stiles. 890, 1522
Second letter of Paul to the Corinthians. 326
Second letters from Roy. 3515, 3528
Second living room dialogues. 1044
Second manual for training in worship. 3858
Second message of Anne Simon. 3514
Second mile. 961
Second official catalogue of church music. 1204
Second part of the anatomie of abuses. 3607
Second period of Quakerism. 1684
Second Presbyterian church of Indianapolis. 2917
Second ralliement. 1145
Second Reform. 1221
Second report of the Joint commission on the Book of common prayer appointed by the General convention of 1913. 2961
Second ring of power. 744, 3862
Second Seminar on Science and the Spiritual Nature of Man. 3083
Second session. 3772
Second seven years of faith. 3709
Second sight. 2937, 2949, 3301
Second sight, its history and origins. 3322
Second sowing. 1785
Second Spira. 100
Second spring. 833, 853, 3738
Second start. 774, 1302
Second survey of the fields and work of the Northern Baptist convention. 2714
Second Synod of the Diocese of Springfield. 1373
... The second ten years of Hope. 2530
Second thoughts. 1006
Second thoughts on the Dead Sea scrolls. 1409
Second thoughts on the new morality. 946
Second Timothy. 321
Second touch. 969
Second United Order among the Mormons. 2600
Second Vatican Council. 3769, 3770, 3772
Second Vatican Council and the new Catholicism. 3769
2ND Vatican Council (The) 3770
Second Vatican Council's declaration on the Jews; a background report. 3770
Second vindication of God's sovereign free grace. 1751
Second vindication of God's sovereign free grace indeed. 1458, 1752

Second war in heaven. 607, 1820
Second World conference on faith and order. 1044
Second World's Christian citizenship conference. 3347
Second year of Sunday school lessons for young children. 3556
Second year with Jesus. 1994
Secondary division organized for service. 3551
Secondary education of the Society of Mary in America. 2334
Secondary progressions, using the adjusted calculating date. 99
Secrecy in the church. 808, 1658
Secret and imminent coming of Christ. 2055
Secret and sublime: Taoist mysteries and magic. 3586
Secret Book of Revelation. 456
Secret book of the black arts. 2730
Secret books of the Egyptian Gnostics. 1717
Secret code to the Hebrew Scriptures. 508
Secret confession to a priest. 1326
Secret doctrine. 3684
Secret doctrine in Israel. 3898
Secret doctrine of the Rosicrucians. 3249
Secret doctrine: the synthesis of science, religion, and philosophy. 3684
Secret doctrines of Jesus. 1972, 2054
Secret doors of the earth. 2723
Secret enemies of true republicanism. 2320
Secret garden. 723
Secret Gospel. 3322
Secret Gospels. 1718
Secret grimoire of Turiel. 2313
Secret history of the Oxford Movement. 2755
Secret instructions of the Jesuits. 1946
Secret journey. 443, 632
Secret life. 1805
Secret life of a housewife. 931, 1849
Secret life of the Good Samaritan. 3337
Secret life of the Good Samaritan, and other stories. 3337
Secret man. 2727
Secret meeting. 1014
Secret meeting, and other stories. 1014
Secret message of tantric Buddhism. 3403
Secret of a beautiful life. 2298
Secret of a happy day. 886
Secret of a happy life. 1785
Secret of a quiet mind. 3477
Secret of abundant living. 3330
... The secret of antichrist and Rome and the great storm from the East. 52
Secret of beautiful living. 973
Secret of being strong. 971
Secret of Christian family living. 1604
Secret of Christian joy. 163
Secret of communion with God. 2873, 2887
Secret of divine civilization. 125, 126
Secret of effective prayer. 2880
Secret of evolution found. 1581
Secret of Fatima. 1618
Secret of God. 2214
Secret of greatness. 2302
Secret of guidance. 993
Secret of happiness. 180, 1785
Secret of His presence. 2504
Secret of history. 46
Secret of holiness. 1001
Secret of immortality. 3496
Secret of inward peace. 2809
Secret of life. 957
Secret of married love. 2339
Secret of meditation. 2381
Secret of Paul the Apostle. 1029, 2797
Secret of peace and happiness. 3489
Secret of power. 165
Secret of prayer. 2869
Secret of progress. 2945
Secret of pulpit power through thematic Christian preaching. 2897
Secret of radiant Christian living. 956
Secret of radiant life. 974
Secret of Saint John Bosco. 683
Secret of salvation. 3295
Secret of Samson. 495, 3297
Secret of sanctity, according to St. Francis de Sales and Father Crasset, S. J. 3486
Secret of sanctity of St. John of the Cross. 2136, 2571
Secret of secrets. 2693, 3302
Secret of serenity. 1538
Secret of sexes, revealed and controlled. 3390
Secret of soul-winning. 1569, 3462
Secret of spiritual victory. 967
Secret of successful life. 2227
Secret of supernatural living. 988
Secret of the cross. 1050
... The secret of the cure d'Ars. 3784
Secret of the East. 1655

Secret of the golden calf. 2859
Secret of the golden flower. 3586, 3587
Secret of the Jew, his life--his family. 2120
Secret of the life sublime. 958
Secret of the Lord. 1986
Secret of the rapture. 3022
Secret of the rosary. 3248
Secret of the saints. 2875
Secret of the singing heart. 971
Secret of the sphinx by Pharaoh Amigdar, assisted by ... others. 3473
Secret of the universe. 1371, 1729
Secret of the universe: 'God, man, and matter. 1371
Secret of true revival. 1823
Secret of true revival (holiness must be preached) 1823
Secret of victorious living. 3351
Secret of yoga. 3865
Secret oral teachings in Tibetan Buddhist sects. 2193
Secret path. 3477
Secret place. 2876
Secret power of life. 3079
Secret powers of plants. 2723
Secret revelation of Tibetan thangkas. 3585
Secret rituals of the Golden Dawn. 1806
Secret sayings of Jamil. 1912
Secret sayings of Jesus. 337, 1718
Secret sayings of the living Jesus. 337
Secret science at work. 2727
Secret science behind miracles. 2314
Secret shrine: Islamic mystical reflections. 3544
Secret sign. 1323
Secret societies, ancient and modern. 3322
Secret vaults of time. 2773
Secret way. 980
Secret ways of prayer. 1003, 2869
Secret weapon, and other stories of faith and valor. 2207
Secret world of witchcraft. 3824
Secretary's book. 1666
Secretary's guide. 3554
Secretary's report on the activities and achievements of the Zionist organization of America. 3897
Secretaryship of the Young men's Christian association, a significant life calling. 3875
Secretly armed. 3479
Secrets for successful living. 1010
Secrets from field & forest. 2676
Secrets from the caves. 1409
Secrets of a great cathedral. 752
Secrets of a happy life. 1009
Secrets of a parish priest. 3778
Secrets of ancient witchcraft with the witches Tarot. 3823
Secrets of answered prayer. 2877
Secrets of Christian living. 3482
Secrets of Eden. 3388
Secrets of Egypt, for the millions. 1502
Secrets of eternity. 2696
Secrets of fortitude. 1634
Secrets of godly living. 957
Secrets of growing churches. 1171
Secrets of happiness. 992
Secrets of magical seals. 2313
Secrets of our sexuality. 3389
Secrets of prayer joy. 2873
Secrets of Romanism. 803
Secrets of successful recruiting. 3786
Secrets of Sunday-school teaching. 3556
Secrets of teaching and interpreting astrology. 96
Secrets of the Cuna earthmother. 1396
Secrets of the Dead Sea scrolls. 1410
Secrets of the Dead Sea scrolls, studies towards their solution. 1410
Secrets of the gods. 1724
Secrets of the great magicians. 1346
Secrets of the I ching. 1470
Secrets of the interior life. 2639
Secrets of the kingdom. 406
Secrets of the lotus; studies in Buddhist meditation. 2382
Secrets of the religious life. 2583
Secrets of the saints. 3778
Secrets of the silent tongue. 1934
Secrets of the spirit. 424
Secrets of the spirit world. 3494
Secrets of voodoo. 3787
Secrets of wisdom. 2642
Secrets to inner beauty. 980
Secrets to share. 2386
Sect, creed and custom in Judaism. 2116
Sect ideologies and social status. 3383, 3454
Sectarian college and the public purse. 1127
Sectarian invasion of our public schools. 3162
Sectarian shackles. 1461
Sectarianism. 3323

Sectarianism in southern Nyasaland. 3324
Sectarianism in southern Nyassland. 3324
Sectional crisis and northern Methodism. 1138, 2450
Sectors of American Judaism. 2155
Sects and separatism during the second Jewish Commonwealth. 2079
Sects and society. 918, 1507
Secular abyss. 2320
... The secular activities of the German episcopate, 919-1024. 666
Secular and religious works of Penina Moise. 3200
Secular art with sacred themes. 920
Secular Christ. 2045
Secular Christianity. 1595
'Secular Christianity' and God who acts. 651, 3327
Secular city. 1153
Secular city debate. 1378
Secular clergy in the Diocese of Lincoln. 1293
Secular congregation. 1155
Secular films and the church's ministry. 2627
Secular ideologies of India and the secular meaning of Christ. 3328
Secular illusion or Christian realism? 2323
Secular impact. 1153
Secular institutes. 3327
Secular journal. 2413
Secular man in sacred mission. 2481
Secular meaning of the gospel, based on an analysis of its language. 1064
Secular mind. 3328
Secular priest in the new church. 773, 2789
Secular priesthood. 771
Secular promise. 1059
Secular relevance of the church. 3447
Secular religions in France. 3324
Secular saint. 1056, 3447
Secular salvations. 2671
Secular sanctity. 2389
Secular search for a new Christ. 3328
Secular spirit: life and art at the end of the Middle Ages. 87
Secular use of church buildings. 1274
Secular view of religion in the state, and the Bible in the public schools. 1141
Secularism. 3327
Secularism a myth. 3327
Secularism and religious freedom. 3195
Secularism and salvation. 3327
...Secularism in American education. 1129
Secularism is the will of God. 3327
Secularism, society, and law in India. 3194
Secularization. 3327
Secularization and spirituality. 3484
Secularization and the Protestant prospect. 3327
Secularization and the university. 3328
Secularization of American education as shown by State legislation, State constitutional provisions, and State supreme court decisions. 1129
Secularization of Christianity. 1061, 3242
Secularization of history. 1744, 3657
Secularization of modern cultures. 1154
Secularization of the California missions (1810-1846) 815, 2506
Secularization of the European mind in the nineteenth century. 3328
Secularization theology. 3328
Securely guarded. 168
Securing Christian leaders for tomorrow. 952
Security. 93
Security blankets family size. 2389
Security for a failing world. 127
Security for young children, the foundation for spiritual values. 3328
Security, freedom and happiness. 1136
Security from above. 1452
Security from above; Biblical thoughts on ultimate values. 1452
Security of salvation. 3290, 3383
Seder service for Passover eve in the home. 3328
Seder that almost wasn't. 2779
... Sedgwick county, Kansas. 3329
Seduction of the spirit. 1378, 3058
Sedvlii Opera omnia. 3635
See for yourself. 2926
See how the wind blows. 1832
See-it object lessons. 910
See no evil. 2863
See of Peter. 2770, 2825
See of Peter and the voice of antiquity. 1378, 2768
See the glory. 2241
See these banners go. 2956
See what you've got into! 3878
See you in the morning. 1774, 2810
See yourself in the Bible. 213
Seed. 2396

Seed and the glory. 2376
Seed and the soil. 3440
Seed basket. 3373
Seed falls on Okinawa. 2490
Seed for sermons. 3375
Seed for the sower. 3372
Seed money in action. 952
Seed of Abraham. 1376
Seed of the church in China. 681, 2507
Seed of the new age. 3750
Seed of the woman bruising the serpent's head. 3030
Seed shall serve. 2162
Seed sowing in Honduras. 2529
Seed, the soil and the sower. 3161
Seed-thought. 303
Seed thoughts. 3373
Seed thoughts for right living. 964
Seed time and harvest. 1235
Seeds of conflict. 611, 2073
Seeds of consciousness. 1815
Seeds of contemplation. 3488
Seeds of destruction. 774, 1132
Seeds of redemption. 1281
Seeds of service. 2225
Seeds of the desert. 1636, 2232
Seeds of the Kingdom. 3475
Seedtime and harvest. 2143
Seeing Africa. 2498
Seeing America for Christ. 2527
Seeing and being like Him. 2719
Seeing Castaneda. 744, 3862
... Seeing darkly. 2932
Seeing God. 2366, 2637
Seeing Jesus. 1982
Seeing Jesus today. 1986, 3348
Seeing life whole. 3102, 3461
Seeing prophecy fulfilled in Palestine. 2761
Seeing stars. 1112
Seeing the best. 3342
Seeing the future. 3320
Seeing the invisible. 1794, 3356
Seeing the multitudes. 181
Seeing the real me. 1012
Seeing the story of the Bible. 199
Seeing truth. 2720, 3160
Seeing with a native eye. 1902
Seek a city saint. 2211
Seek and find. 1441
Seek and you shall find. 996
Seek, find, share. 1676
Seek first the Kingdom. 959
Seek His face. 1264
Seek this Christ. 3216
Seek to serve. 3170
Seek ye earnestly. 2619
Seek ye first the Kingdom of God. 2610
Seek ye the Christ. 2693
Seek ye the kingdom. 971
Seeker after truth. 3544
Seeker of unity. 1
Seekers. 1091, 1367, 1418
Seekers after God. 1721, 1723
Seekers of light. 3777
Seeking a better country, a history. 297
Seeking a faith for a new age ; essays on the interdependence of religion, science, and philosophy. 3107
Seeking a faith of your own. 3889
Seeking admission. 1201
Seeking after God. 1719
Seeking and finding. 2753, 3483
Seeking and finding God. 1441
Seeking for the Kingdom of God. 83
Seeking for trouble ; saints for Christian civilization. 1000
Seeking God. 3487
Seeking Gotama Buddha in his teachings. 707
Seeking Jesus in his teachings. 2063
Seeking Kenya's treasures. 2129, 2536
Seeking Krishna in his teachings. 2316
Seeking life, and other sermons. 3349
Seeking light in the darkness of the unconscious. 3001
Seeking meaning. 3154
"... Seeking only God. 1298
Seeking religious meaning. 1394
Seeking the beautiful in God's world. 3148
Seeking the Christian way. 1201
Seeking the kingdom. 959, 3485
Seeking the living way. 3879, 3882
Seeking the mind of Christ. 2396, 3471
Seeking the old paths. 3343
Seeking the spirit. 3493
Seeking the truth. 1061
Seeking to be Christian in race relations. 3017
Seeking to know and to do God's will. 1740
Seeking to know the will of God. 1741
Seeming unreality of the spiritual life. 1105
Seen and heard in India. 2532
Seen and the unseen. 3291

Seen and unseen. 2986
Seen from my pulpit. 3131
Seer, Joseph Smith, his education from the Most High. 2617, 3428
Seers of the ages. 3510
Seers, shrines, and sirens. 1767
Seership! 1283
Sefer hayashar. 1539
Sefer netivot Shmuel. (Samuel's roads.) 562
Sefer tehilim. 575
Sefer Torah. 3704
[Sefer Yesode semabot (romanized form)]. 2627
[Sefer Yetsirah (romanized form)]. 2189
Sego. 1749, 3329
Segregated covenant. 1132
Segregated Sabbaths; Richard Allen and the emergence of independent Black churches 1760-1840. 26, 2679
Segregation and desegregation. 3329
Segregation and the Bible. 3329
Segregavit nos Dominus. 1620
Sein und Gnade. 175, 2739
Select anecdotes and instructive incidents. 1674
Select bibliographical guide to California Catholic periodical literature, 1844-1973. 815
Select bibliography of the history of the Catholic church in the United States. 834
Select bibliography: the California missions, 1765-1972. 2506
Select bibliography to California Catholic literature, 1856-1974. 815
Select biographies. 661
Select discourses. 3624
Select discourses of Sereno Edwards Dwight. 1340
Select discourses, 1660. 3624
Select English works of John Wyclif. 3861
... Select epistles of St. Cyprian treating of the episcopate. 1398
Select essays. 3343
Select guide to California Catholic history. 815
Select historical memoirs of the religious Society of Friends, commonly called Quakers. 1685
Select hymns: the third part of Christian psalmody. 1870
Select letters of St. Jerome, with an English translation. 1525
Select library of Nicene and post-Nicene fathers of the Christian church. 1617
Select library of the Nicene and post-Nicene fathers of the Christian church. 1617
Select library of the Nicene and post Nicene fathers of the Christian church. Edited by Philip Schaff. [First series]. 1019
Select liturgical lexicon. 3855
Select manual for the members of the Sodality of the Blessed Virgin Mary. 843
... Select masterpieces of Biblical literature. 590
Select medieval documents and other material. 810
Select melodies. 1866
Select minor works of John Bunyan. 716
Select orations of Marcus Tullius Cicero. 3244
Select passages illustrating Mithraism. 2560
Select passages illustrating Neoplatonism. 2683
... Select passages illustrative of Neoplatonism. 2683
Select poems, containing religious epistles, &c. occasionally written on various subjects. 3206
Select poems for the silent hour. 3207
Select poetry, chiefly devotional, of the reign of Queen Elizabeth. 1519
Select practical writings of Richard Baxter. 3630
Select Psalms. 3806
Select psalms and hymns. 2985
Select readings and recitations. 3027
Select remains of Mr. James Meikle. 3462
Select remains of the Rev. John Mason. 1450, 3200
Select Scripture references. 252
Select sermon materials. 3339
Select sermons of Benjamin Whichcote. 1228, 3367
Select sermons preached in the Broadway church. 3755
Select treatises of St. Athanasius in controversy with the Arians. 80
Select works of Archbishop Leighton. 3630
Select works of John Bale. 452, 2736
Select works of Plotinus. 2684
Select works of Tertullian. 3635

Select works of Thomas Chalmers. 2593
Select works of William Penn. 1679, 3631
Select writings and letters. 3635
Select writings by the late Henry Holcombe Tucker, D.D.L.L.D. 147
Selected addresses. 2179
Selected articles. 1183
Selected Bible readings and meditations for responsive readings in church services or for home study. 318
Selected bibliography for theological students. 2788
Selected bibliography of books and articles in the Disciples of Christ Research Library in Mbandaka, Democratic Republic of the Congo. 11, 1465
Selected bibliography of missionary literature. 2504
Selected bibliography of the religious denominations of the United States. 3739
... A selected bibliography on child development. 895
Selected documentation. 937
Selected Easter sermons of Saint Augustine. 1486
Selected English sermons. 3366
Selected epistles of Paul. 370
Selected essays ([Ginzberg, Asher]) 2112
Selected essays / (Muktananda Paramhamsa, Swami. 3491
Selected essays on atheism. 1656
Selected essays on language, mythology and religion. 2196
Selected forums on absolute reality. 2693
Selected gems of the Bible. 488
Selected homilies of Aelfric. 1843
Selected hymns and tunes from the Methodist hymnal. 1861
Selected hymns in large type. 1868
Selected letters. 2596, 3804
... Selected letters, 1896-1924. 1850
Selected letters (More, Thomas) 2596
Selected letters of Aeneas Silvius Piccolomini. 2861
Selected letters of Pope Innocent III concerning England (1198-1216) 812
Selected letters / (Walther, C. F. W. 1302, 3790
Selected list of approved books for Sunday-school and parish libraries. 3549
Selected messages from the writings of Ellen G. White. 3381
Selected mystical writings. 674, 2639
Selected papers and addresses. 2689
Selected papers (Shaker Historical Society) 3397
Selected papers (Symposium on Seventeenth Century Lutheranism) 2288
Selected poems. 2856
Selected poems of Laurence Binyon. 2855
Selected poetry. 2855
Selected poetry for sermons and addresses. 1842
Selected poetry of Blake. 2855
Selected prayers. 2783
Selected Psalms. 576
Selected Psalms for today. 583
Selected readings in character education. 2592
Selected readings in the Latter-Day Saint family. 1610
Selected religious poems of Solomon Ibn Gabirol. 3210
Selected scripture summaries. 235
Selected serials in Judaic, Biblical, and Near Eastern studies in the FAUL Consortium and SUNY University Centers libraries. 601, 2111, 2678
Selected sermon outlines. 3375
Selected sermons. 117, 2301, 2972, 3349, 3368
Selected sermons of Hugh Latimer. 1226, 3364
Selected sermons of Jonathan Edwards. 3351
Selected shorter writings of Benjamin B. Warfield. 2914, 3634
Selected souvenir sermons delivered in People's temple, Boston, Mass. 3348
Selected studies in the life of Christ. 1994
Selected translations of religious articles on Communist China. 912
Selected women of the Scriptures of stamina and courage. 214, 3839
Selected work documents; six research studies. 2440
Selected works of Huldreich Zwingli. 3042
Selected works of Richard Rolle, hermit. 777, 3636
Selected works of Ryters Krampe. 2788
Selected works (Zwingli, Ulrich) 3042
... Selected writings. 2593
Selected writings (Augustinus, Aurelius) 3634
Selected writings / (Grundtvig, Nicolai Frederik Severin. 2284, 3631

Selected writings (Honor, Leo Lazarius) 2106
Selected writings / (Melanchthon, Philipp. 2285, 3629
Selected writings of Baha'u'llah. 126
Selected writings of Hans Denck. 37
Selected writings of Isaac Mayer Wise. 2156, 3822
Selected writings of Jonathan Edwards. 1334
Selected writings of Martin Luther. 3629
Selected writings of St. Teresa of Avila, a synthesis of her writings. 777
Selected writings of Samuel Johnson. 2675
Selected writings of Suzuki Shosan. 3892
Selected writings on contemplation. 1356
Selected writings on the spiritual life. 3489
Selected writings (Thomas Aquinas) 2593
Selected writings (Thomas Aquines) 3636
Selected writings of Ralph Waldo Emerson. 3708
Selecting and using curriculum materials in the weekday church school. 1247
Selection and incorporation of candidates for the religious life. 2578
... Selection and organization of materials. 2591
Selection from Tate and Brady's version of the Psalms. 2985
Selection from the letters and papers of the late John Barclay. 1292
Selection from the spiritual letters of es. Francis de Sales. 3478
Selection from the works of William E. Channing, D. D. 3729
Selection of African prose. 3580
Selection of emblems, from Herman Hugo: Pia desideria. 974
Selection of hymns. 1865, 2429
Selection of hymns and poems. 1866, 3398
Selection of hymns for use at the General Conference of The Methodist Church:, April 26-May 9, 1964. 2441
Selection of hymns, from various authors. 1861, 2430
Selection of Psalms and hymns. 153
Selection of Psalms, with occasional hymns. 1863
Selection of religious lyrics. 1518
Selection of sacred songs, for the use of schools and academies. 1867
Selection of spiritual songs for the Sunday-school. 3563
Selection of spiritual songs for use in social meetings. 1868
Selection of spiritual songs for use in the church and the choir. 1868
Selection of the most celebrated sermons of John Calvin. 729
Selection of the most celebrated sermons of Martin Luther. 3368
Selections. 1800, 2232, 2834, 2854
Selections, edited by D. H. Parker. 2854
Selections for devotional exercises. 242
Selections from Brierley ("J.B." of "The Christian world") 1020
Selections from Buddha. 1457
Selections from Buddha (Asvaghosha) 700
Selections from Bunyan's Pilgrim's progress for every day of the year. 725
... Selections from California letters published in the Journal and Messenger. 942
Selections from Cotton Mather. 2836
Selections from Dante's Divina commedia. 3094
Selections from Dante's Divine commedia. 3094
Selections from E. Stanley Jones. 2427, 3633
Selections from early writers. 1198
Selections from early writers illustrative of church history to the time of Constantine. 1192
Selections from ecclesiastical Latin. 2198
Selections from English Wycliffite writings. 2243
Selections from Erasmus. 3038
Selections from Harris's Mammon. 120
Selections from John Wesley's Notes on the New Testament. 3640
Selections from Justin Martyr's Dialogue with Trypho, a Jew. 3717
Selections from Meditations on the Gospel. 399
Selections from Old Testament literature. 482
Selections from Scriptures. 249
Selections from the Apocrypha. 488
Selections from the autobiography of Rev. J. M. Arnold, D.D. 3299
Selections from the Bible. 252
Selections from the commentaries and homilies of Origen. 1018

... Selections from "The data of ethics," 1536

Selections from the devotional writings of Madame de la Mothe-Guyon. 1456

Selections from the epistles of George Fox. 1679, 3010

Selections from the Homilies of the Protestant Episcopal church. 2965

Selections from the letters of S. Francis de Sales. 3283

Selections from the Old Testament. 254, 590, 592

... Selections from the prose writings of John Henry, cardinal Newman. 3201

Selections from the Protreptikos. 68

Selections from the Psalms and hymns according to the use of the Protestant Episcopal church in the United States of America. 2567

Selections from the Psalms of David in metre. 1864, 2968

Selections from the Psalter for use in the services of the churches. 583

... Selections from the Qur'an an (Rodwell's translation) 2184

Selections from the religious and literary writings of John H. Bocock, D.D. 2231

Selections from the sacred writings of the Sikhs. 3408

Selections from the Scriptures. 249, 592, 3220

... Selections from the Septuagint. 529

Selections from the sermons and poems of the late Rev. James Gilbourne Lyons, LL.D. 2973

Selections from the Talmud. 3583, 3584

Selections from the Testimonies. 3384

Selections from the Thoughts. 58

Selections from the works of Jean-Jacques Rousseau. 2839

Selections from the works of Jeremy Taylor. 3630

Selections from the world's devotional classics. 1455

... Selections from the writings of John Boyle O'Reilly and Reverend Abram J. Ryan. 3201

... Selections from the writings of Kierkegaard. 2833

Selections from the writings of The Bab. 126

Selections from the writings of the Rev. John Wesley. 2422, 3631

Selections from writings in the Overland monthly. 2506

Selections (Hobbes, Thomas. 2839

Selections (Kant, Immanuel) 2164

Selections (Locke, John) 2593

Selections (Martineau, James) 3728

Selections (Mather, Cotton) 1334

Selections, moral and religious. 2593

Selections (Tolstoi, Lev Nikolaevich) 3095

Selective bibliography of existentialism in education and related topics. 1584

Self, a frontier concept. 1108

Self and immortality. 1696

Self and nature. 2419

Self and the dramas of history. 2324

Self-anointed. 1425, 2167

Self beyond yourself. 2638

Self-conquest. 1440

Self culture. 2724, 2729, 2730

Self-disclosure of Jesus. 2017

Self-education. 2590

Self-embodiment of God. 3070

Self-encouragement. 960

Self-esteem, the new reformation. 3330

Self-evaluation in the minor seminary. 3613

Self-evaluation in the minorseminary. 3613

Self-evolution of God and His creation of nature. 1380

Self god. 3330

Self-incrimination in Jewish law. 3330

Self-interpretation of Jesus. 2062

Self-interpreting Bible. 220, 307

Self-interpreting New Testament. 408

Self knowledge; a yoga for the West. 3683

Self-knowledge and self-discipline. 1000

Self-love. 3350

Self mastery. 2724, 3330

Self mastery and fate. 3251

Self mastery and fate, with the cycles of life. 3250, 3251, 3539

Self-measurement. 2695

Self-portrait of Christ. 1827

Self-pronouncing beautiful Bible stories. 633

... The self-pronouncing Bible dictionary. 242

... The self-pronouncing Holy Bible. 653

Self-pronouncing King James authorized version of the Holy Bible. 1660, 1661

Self-pronouncing King James Authorized version of the Holy Bible, containing the Old and New Testaments translated out of the original tongues and with the former translations diligently compared and revised. Wtih self-pronouncing reference dictionary index. 1661

Self-pronouncing New Testament of Our Lord and Saviour Jesus Christ. 654

Self-pronouncing S. S. teachers' combination Bible. 653

Self-pronouncing S. S. teachers' combination Bible, containing the Old and New Testaments. 653

Self-realisation of noble wisdom. 711

Self, religion, and metaphysics. 2834, 2867

Self-revelation of God. 1740, 3682

Self-revelation of Our Lord. 3224

Self-study guide for the city church, developed by the Department of City and Industrial Work and the Office for Field Survey in cooperation with the Special Committee on the Inner City. 1279

Self-support. 2505

Self-supporting churches and how to plant them. 1166

Self talk. 3330

Self-training in meditation. 2380

Self-training in prayer. 2875

Self-unfoldment by disciplines of realization. 2725

Selfhood and sacrifice. 104, 2071

Selfhood and serivce. 3440

Selfishness, and its remedy. 1500

Selling water by the river. 3459

Semantics in Biblical research. 556, 3293

Semi-centenary and the retrospection of the African Methodist Episcopal Church. 14

...The semi-centennial of Philip Schaff. 3306

... A semi-centennial offering. 3286

... A semi-centennial offfering to the members and friends of the Methodist Episcopal church Salem, Oregon. 3286

Semi-centennial memorial discourse of the New-York Sunday-school union. 2700

Semi-centennial discourse. 1717, 2829

Semi-centennial anniversary of the South congregational society (Unitarian), in Lowell. 3725

Semi-centennial history of the Second Baptist Church of Atlanta, Georgia, November 27-30, 1904. 102

Semi-centennial memorial of the Universalist church, Roxbury, Mass. 3754

Semicentennial of the American Unitarian Association. 3723

...Semicentennial of the Central Presbyterian Church, St. Paul, Minnesota, 1902. 2921

Semi-centennial of the First Presbyterian church of Coraopolis, Pennayvania. 2918

...The semi-centennial of the Presbyterian church of Oneida, N. Y., June 13, 1894. 2918

Semi-centennial volume of the Eliot church, Lowell, Mass. 1271

Seminar on art and architecture for the church in our age. 1157

Seminar on comparative education— Islamic values in education & The liberal arts tradition. 1924

Seminar on Science and the Total Nature of Man. 3083

Seminar on symbolism as applied to church art and architecture. 1157

Seminarian. 3331

Seminarian at his prie-dieu. 3331

Seminarian, his character and work. 3332

Seminarian's reading list. 3626

Seminary. 3613

Seminary addresses, and other papers. 2143, 3331

Seminary education in a time of change. 3613

Seminary in crisis. 3614

Seminary in the making. 720, 3275

Seminary militant. 2626

Seminary: Protestant and Catholic. 861, 3613

Seminary rule. 3331

Seminary survey. 3680

Semiology and parables. 2027, 2772

Semiotics of the Passion narrative. 1986, 3720

Semitic influence in Hellenic mythology. 2630, 2660

Semitic influence in Hellenic mythology, with special reference to the recent mythological works of the Rt. Hon. Prof. F. Max Muller and Mr. Andrew Lang. 2660

Semitic magic. 2315

... Semitic [mythology]. 2667

Semitic philosophy. 3608

Semitisms of Acts. 331

Senate prayers and Spires of the spirit. 2208

Send forth thy Spirit. 2885, 3486

Send from God. 2554

Sendbrief from the Alm Bruderhof to the Rhon Bruderhof. 698, 954

Sendbrief vom Almbruderhof zum Rhonbruderhof, 1934. 698, 954

Seneca and Kant. 2163, 3533

Seneca thanksgiving rituals. 3332

Seneca the philosopher. 2232, 3333

Seneca's morals. 3533

Seneca's morals, by way of abstract. 2592

Seneca's morals, by way of abstract. To which is added a discourse under the title of An after thought. Adorned with cuts. 2592, 3533

Senior catechism. 2284

Senior confirmation book. 1329

... Senior method in the church school. 3154

Senior teacher's guide. 414

...The senior worker and his work. 3153

Sensational psychic experiences. 3509

Sense and incense. 2547

Sense and nonsense about prayer. 2881

Sense and nonsense in religion. 1101, 3001, 3064

Sense and nonsense of Christian science. 1035

Sense and nonsense of prophecy. 2725

Sense and satire based upon nineteenth century philosophy. 2843

Sense appeal in the sermons of Charles Haddon Spurgeon. 2896, 3523

Sense, nonsense and Christianity. 2181, 3070

Sense of absence. 1724

Sense of duty. 1539

Sense of God. 2396, 3057

... The sense of immortality. 1887

Sense of life, a sense of sin. 1536

Sense of mission. 421, 2504

Sense of the cosmos. 2320

Sense of the infinite. 2418

Sense of the presence of God. 1740, 3097

Sensei. 2534, 3800

Sensible man's view of religion. 3353

Sensie. 2534, 3800

Sensitive man and the Christ. 1011

Sensitivity to what? 986

Sensory awareness and psychic manifestation. 2993

Sensory training for Catholic schools. 3333

Sensuous Christian. 1061

Sensuous woman reborn. 1621

Sent . . . because we care. 2491

Sent by the sovereign. 2496

Sent forth. 1911

Sent forth to preach. 2907

Sent from God. 2904

Sent from the Father. 422

Sent into the world. 2285

Sent on a mission. 2480, 3187

Sent to be vulnerable. 992

Sentence in biblical Hebrew. 1797

Sentence sermons. 2383, 2619, 2839

Sentenced to Siberia. 2319, 2979

Sentences of Sextus. 55, 1004

... Sententiae Petri Pictaviensis. 782

Sentiments upon the religion of reason and nature. 2419, 2674

Sentinel on the hill: Monte Maria and one hundred years. 2569

Sentinellist agitation in New England, 1925-1928. 823

Sentinels of the King. 2389

Seond Christmas. 2005

Separate church and state now. 1150

Separate reality. 2137, 3862

Separated brethren. 1038, 3327

Separated life. 2002

Separated unto God. 979

Separates; or, Strict Congregationalists of New England. 3535

Separation. 2856

Separation after a century. 1675

Separation illusion. 1152

Separation of church & freedom. 1150

Separation of church and state. 3195

Separation of church and state in Italian thought from Cavour to Mussolini. 1147

Separation of church and state in the United States. 1129

Separation of church and state in Virginia. 1223

Separation of religion and government. 1151

Separation of the churches and the state in France. 1145

Separation of the Monophysites. 2585

Separation without hope? 1153

Separatism among Indian Muslims. 3762

Sephardi melodies. 2097

Sephardic Jewish community of Los Angeles. 2084, 3333

... Sepher shaashuim. 2075

Sepher Yetsira, including the original astrology according to the Qabala and its zodiac. 722, 3329

Septimae manus witness. 3830

Septuagint and modern study. 529

Septuagint Bible. 528

Septuagint translation of Jeremiah and Baruch. 547

Septuagint translation of the Hebrew terms in relation to God in the book of Jeremiah. 547, 1736

Septuagint version of the Old Testament. 284, 529

Septuagint version of the Old Testament and Apocrypha. 284

Septuagintal lexicography. 1770

Sepulchre of Christ in art and liturgy. 1826

Sepulchres of our departed. 1349

Sequel to Catholic emancipation. 818

Sequence of belief. 3655

Sequence of man's belief. 186

Serach for the real Jesus. 2009

Seraph among angels. 2333

Seraphic days. 1263

Seraphic highway. 1649

Serbian church life. 3891

Serendipity. 963

Serials in the Assumption Province Libraries. 852

... Series courses of the New standard leadership curriculum. 3152

... Series courses of the Standard leadership curriculum. 3152

Series of brief historical sketches of the Church of England. 1221

Series of discourse on the Christian revelation. 3074

Series of discourses on the Christian revelation. 3074, 3227

Series of discourses on various subjects. 3296

Series of eight broadcasts. 2250

Series of eleven lessons in karma yoga. 3864

Series of lecture sermons. 3755

Series of lectures. 1341

Series of lectures on the church of the Bible and its apostasy, delivered in the court house at Charleston, West Virginia. 1119

Series of lessons in Gnani yoga (the yoga of wisdom.) 3863

Series of lessons in Raja yoga. 3863

Series of lessons on the inner teachings of the philosophies and religions of India. 1895

Series of letters. 1522, 2466

Series of letters on important doctrinal and practical subjects, addressed to Rev. Samuel C. Aikin. 3752

Series of letters, on the relation, rights, privileges [!] and duties of baptized children. 1201

Series of sermons. 2933

Series of sermons on the distinctive principles of the great historic church movements. 3345

Series of sermons on the divinity of Christ. 1342, 2002

Series of seven essays upon spiritualism vs. materialism. Appearing in the Free thought magazine. 3510

Series of six radio talks on the renaissance in religious education. 3190

... Series of talks with God. 1726

Series of tracts on the doctrines, order, and polity of the Presbyterian church in the United States of America. 2921

Series of twelve articles introductory to the study of the Bahai teachings. 128

... Series on religious reconstruction. 3726

Serious address to the people of the Church of England in some observations upon their own catechism. 1215

Serious and impartial enquiry into the cause of the present decay of Free-Masonry in the Kingdom of Ireland, 1744 ; An answer to the Pope's bull. 1665

Serious call in Christian love to all people, to turn to the spirit of Christ in themselves. 1682

Serious call to a contemplative life-style. 3484

Serious call to a devout and holy life. 966, 967

Serious call to a devout and holy life ; The spirit of love. 967

Serious question, what is true repentance. 3218

Serious reflections on the scandalous abuse and effects of the stage. 1225, 3605
Serious remonstrance in behalf of the Christian religion. 3605
Seriously, life is a laughing matter. 1005
Seriously, now. 2213
Sermon. 1483, 1504, 1692, 2310, 2743, 2898, 2902, 3357, 3532
Sermon analysis for pulpit power. 2898
Sermon and addresses commemorative of the twenty-fifth anniversary of the ordination of Rev. James H. Means as pastor of the Second church, Dorchester, July 13th and 14th, 1873. 3350
Sermon and the Propers. 1267
Sermon as God's word. 2909
Sermon as part of the liturgy. 2897
Sermon briefs. 3362
Sermon builder. 1843
Sermon by Abraham Hellenbroek. 3369
Sermon classics by great preachers. 3366
Sermon concerning the life, death, and future state of saints on the mournful occasion of the much lamented death of that late ingenious, pious, and vertuous gentlewoman, Rachel Hillhouse.
Sermon, delivered at Bath, June 27, 1849, before the Maine missionary society. 3359
Sermon delivered at Concord. 1504
Sermon delivered at the consecration of the Right Reverend Stephen Elliott, D.D., for the diocese of Georgia. 1509, 1523
Sermon delivered at the inauguration of the Rev. Archibald Alexander. 3361
Sermon delivered at the installation of the Rev. Horace Holley, to the pastoral care of the church and society in Hollis street, Boston. March 8, 1809. 3362
Sermon, delivered at the opening of the general assembly of the Presbyterian church in the United States of America, May, 1811. 3357
Sermon, delivered at the ordination of the Rev. Ezra Stiles Gannett. 1701, 2742
Sermon, delivered before the Massachusetts missionary society. 2496
Sermon, delivered before the New York missionary society. 2546
Sermon delivered by Thomas Prince, M. A. 3356
Sermon hearts. 3374
Sermon hearts from the book of Acts. 332
Sermon hearts from the Gospels. 3374
Sermon hearts from the Psalms. 3374
...Sermon illustrations. 1842
Sermon illustrations. 1842
Sermon in perspective. 2907
Sermon is more than words. 2908
Sermon matter for a year. 1267
Sermon matter from St. Thomas Aquinas on the Epistles and Gospels of the Sundays and feast days (Advent to Easter) 367
Sermon notes. 3362
Sermon notes from the ministry of Jesus. 3362
Sermon notes of John Henry Newman, 1849-1878. 2740
Sermon notes on the Sunday propers. 866
Sermon nuggets in stories. 1842
Sermon of apparell. 1228, 1304
Sermon of God. 609
Sermon of the fifty. 1092
Sermon of the moral condition of Boston. 684
Sermon of the sea, and other studies. 863
Sermon on confirmation. 1328
Sermon on St. Joseph. 2132
Sermon on the cross. 2030
Sermon on the death of Charles M. Jenkins, delivered in the Unitarian church, Vernon, N.Y., Sunday, December 28, 1856. 1942
Sermon on the Mount. 3334, 3335, 3336, 3337, 3339
Sermon on the Mount according to Vedanta. 3336
Sermon on the Mount and its meaning for today. 3336
Sermon on the Mount and other extracts from the New Testament. 3334
Sermon on the Mount and The life of Jesus. 1975
Sermon on the Mount (sermons) and the Magnificat. 3336
Sermon on the mystery of the real presence, preached in the court-house in the borough of Butler. 3709
Sermon outline Bible. 615
Sermon outlines. 3347, 3372, 3373, 3374, 3375
Sermon outlines and illustrations. 3373
Sermon outlines for holy living. 3374
Sermon outlines for messages to children. 910
Sermon outlines for prayer meetings. 2886

Sermon outlines for revival preaching. 3347
Sermon outlines for saints and sinners. 3372
Sermon outlines for soul winning. 1562
Sermon outlines for special occasions. 3348
Sermon outlines for the Sundays and holy days of the year. 1268
Sermon outlines for use by laymen. 3372
Sermon outlines for worship and devotional services. 3372
Sermon outlines from God's word. 3347
Sermon outlines from great preachers. 3374
Sermon outlines from sermon masters. 3374
Sermon outlines from sermon masters--Old Testament. 3374
Sermon outlines from the book of Acts. 332
Sermon outlines from the four Gospels. 400
Sermon outlines from the psalms. 3374
Sermon outlines of M. C. Kurfees. 3374
Sermon outlines on a spiritual pilgrimage. 2847
... Sermon outlines on Acts. 326, 3347
Sermon outlines on Bible characters. 216
Sermon outlines on favorite Bible chapters. 3375
Sermon outlines on great Bible texts. 3374
Sermon outlines on Old Testament characters. 3372
Sermon outlines on prayer. 3372
Sermon outlines on Romans. 471
Sermon outlines on the cross of Christ. 2034, 3373
Sermon outlines on the family and the home. 1611
Sermon outlines on the Gospel of John 1-7. 422
Sermon outlines on the Gospel of John [2.] 1-7; 8-21. 422
Sermon outlines on the Gospel of John 8-21. 422
Sermon outlines on the home. 3372
Sermon outlines on the Old Testament. 3372
Sermon outlines on the person and work of Christ. 2056
Sermon outlines on the Psalms. 3374
Sermon outlines on Timothy to Revelation. 465
Sermon outlines on women of the Bible. 3841
Sermon outlines through the Bible. 3372
Sermon outlines, volume one. 3373
Sermon outlines with helps. 3374
Sermon outlines you can preach. 3372
Sermon plans and story illustrations. 3373
Sermon plans for all the Sundays of the year. 3347
Sermon preach'd at Cambridge [!]. 1637
Sermon preached at Boston. 1504
Sermon preached at Lincoln's inn. 1226
Sermon preached at the centennial celebration of the opening of St. Peter's church, Philadelphia. 2830
Sermon preached at the cross, Feb. 14, 1607. 798, 3606
Sermon, preached at the ordination of the Rev. Daniel Merril, in Sedgwick, Sept. 17, 1793. 2412, 2743
Sermon, preached at the ordination of the Rev. Jonathan Whitaker to the pastoral care of the church and society in Sharon, Massachusetts. February 27, 1799. 2742, 3810
Sermon preached at the ordination of the Rev. William Whitwell. 3814
Sermon preached before His Excellency Francis Bernard,esq. 1504
Sermon, preached before His Excellency John Hancock, esq; governor; His Honor Thomas Cushing, esq; lieutenant governonr; the honorable the Council, and the honorabie the Senate, and House of representatives, of the commonwealth of Massachusetts, May 26, 1784. 1504
Sermon preached before His Excellency Sir Francis Bernard, baronet, governor. 1504
Sermon preached before the General assembly of the colony of Connecticut, at Hartford on the day of the anniversary election. 1503
Sermon preached before the Honorable Council, and the Honorable House of representatives, of the colony of the Massachusetts-Bay, in New-England. May 29th, 1776. 3742
Sermon preached before the Humane society of the commonwealth of Massachusetts. 190
Sermon preached in Braintree, Mass. 1692, 3533

Sermon preached in St. Andrew's Church, Edinburgh. 887
Sermon, preached in the Presbyterian church in Beekmanstreet, New-York, on Wednesday, August 8, 1810. 2742
Sermon preached July 4, 1764. 694, 2742
Sermon preached on the completion of a general repair of the meeting house. 1322
Sermon science. 3362
Sermon seeds. 3375
Sermon seeds from the Psalms. 450
Sermon stories of faith and hope. 1842
Sermon struggles. 1524, 2901
Sermon substance. 3375
Sermon suggestions. 3372
Sermon suggestions in outline. 3375
Sermon thoughts for Sundays and holy days. 3373
Sermonettes and prayers. 2890
Sermonettes for boys and girls. 906
Sermonettes for young people. 910
Sermonic studies. 366
Sermonic studies; the standard epistles. 367
Sermons. 162, 164, 167, 864, 865, 1225, 1226, 1227, 1273, 1341, 1557, 1688, 2425, 2426, 2806, 2928, 2930, 2931, 2932, 2935, 2972, 2973, 3337, 3338, 3340, 3341, 3342, 3344, 3345, 3346, 3348, 3349, 3350, 3351, 3353, 3355, 3356, 3360, 3364, 3367, 3368, 3369, 3370, 3371, 3376, 3725
Sermons addressed to individuals. 1340, 3339
Sermons, addresses & exhortations, by Rev. Jedediah Burchard. 1555
Sermons, addresses and papers of Rev. Luther Leonidas Hill. 3353
Sermons, addresses, and reminiscences, and important correspondence. 15, 2669, 3343
Sermons and addresses. 3049, 3338, 3345, 3346, 3372
Sermons and addresses, 1853-1891. 2436, 3356
Sermons and addresses by the late Rt. Rev. Edward Randolph Welles. 2974
Sermons and addresses of His Eminence William. 864
Sermons and addresses of His Eminence William cardinal O'Connell, archbishop of Boston. 864
Sermons and addresses of Our Saviour. 2071, 3564
Sermons and conferences of John Tauler. 2647
Sermons and discourses. 864
Sermons and essays. 1343, 3365
Sermons and expository lectures. 3342
Sermons and lectures. 2436, 3343
Sermons and missionary services of Melvin Joseph Ballard. 131
Sermons and other discourses. 1341
Sermons and other writings of the Rev. Andrew Broaddus. 3338
Sermons and outlines on the Lord's Supper. 1318
Sermons and outlines on the seven words. 2058
Sermons and prayers. 2913
Sermons and sayings. 1557, 1558, 3340
Sermons and sermon snacks. 3342
Sermons and sketches of sermons. 3346, 3358
Sermons and society. 1227, 3367
Sermons bearing on subjects of the day. 864, 1227, 3365
Sermons by a lay headmaster. 3364
Sermons by a layman. 3341
Sermons by Bishop Matthew Simpson of the Methodist Episcopal church. 2426
Sermons by Hugh Latimer. 1226, 3364
Sermons by Pickup. 1273
Sermons by Rev. Newman Hall. 1341
Sermons by Richard Fuller. 162
Sermons by Southern Methodist preachers. 3358
Sermons by the devil. 3341
Sermons by the late Rev. Joseph Lathrop. 1341
Sermons by the late Rev. Oliver Bronson. 3522
Sermons by the Rev. Daniel Cobia. 3339
Sermons by the Reverend George Buist. 2930
Sermons by the sea. 3357
Sermons, chiefly on particular occasions. 2721
Sermons connected with the re-opening of the church of the South parish. 3726
Sermons delivered. 1688
Sermons delivered before mixed congregations, embracing apologetics, Catholic faith and Christian morals, intended for infidels, Protestants and Catholics. 862

Sermons delivered on various occasions. 1341
Sermons, doctrinal and moral. 3341
Sermons, doctrinal and practical. 1225, 1230
... The sermons, epistles and apocalypses of Israel's prophets. 570
Sermons, essays, and extracts. 108
Sermons, essays and outlines. 3347
Sermons for all Sundays and festivals of the year. 1267
Sermons for all the Sundays, and for the chief feasts throughout the year. 3346
Sermons for celebrating. 3354
Sermons for children. 908, 909, 3370
Sermons for children's masses. 907
Sermons for Christian families. 1342
Sermons for Christian seasons. 1266, 2436
Sermons for Christmas and Epiphany. 1113
Sermons for days of fast, prayer, and humiliation and execution sermons. 3357
Sermons for days we observe. 3345
Sermons for Eucharistic devotions. 864
Sermons for every Sunday in the year. 3566
Sermons for juniors in the Sunday school. 3369
Sermons for Lent. 2213
Sermons for reviving. 3232
Sermons for sidetracked saints. 3350
Sermons for special days. 2721, 2722, 3352
Sermons for special days and occasions. 1623
...Sermons for special occasions. 167, 2299, 2301, 2721, 2722
Sermons for special Sundays. 1622
Sermons for Sundays. 3566
Sermons for Sundays & feasts. 3367
Sermons for the celebration of the Christian year. 1265, 2930
Sermons for the Christian year. 865, 866, 1268, 3346
Sermons for the church. 3725
Sermons for the different Sundays and principal festivals of the year. 1268
Sermons for the great days of the years. 3339
Sermons for the high mass. 2370
Sermons for the home. 2299
Sermons for the home circle. 3344
Sermons for the junior congregation. 906
Sermons for the moment on the gospels of the church year, for home devotions, for shut-ins and the sick. 1266
Sermons for the new age. 3355
Sermons for the new life. 1340, 3349
Sermons for the people. 2426, 3338
Sermons for the sign-boards. 3346
Sermons for the sixties. 3361
Sermons for the Sundays and chief festivals of the ecclesiastical year. 1267
Sermons for the Sundays and some festivals of the year. 1268
Sermons for the times. 1226, 3343
Sermons for the times and the people. 3346
Sermons for the whole year. 1267
Sermons for today. 1273, 1341, 2865, 3354
Sermons from an ecumenical pulpit. 3350
Sermons from hell. 1352
Sermons from Job. 551
Sermons from life. 2912
... Sermons from Paul. 168, 2804
Sermons from Revelation. 464
Sermons from Thanksgiving to Easter. 2933, 3354
Sermons from the Latins. 862
Sermons from the miracles. 2018, 2425, 3339
Sermons from the Mount. 3337
Sermons from the parables. 2028, 2425
Sermons from the Psalms. 577, 2812
Sermons from the pulpit. 3338
Sermons from the Upper room chapel. 2436
Sermons I have preached to young people. 3360
Sermons I love to preach. 1466
Sermons I should like to have preached. 3365
Sermons illustrating the doctrine of the Lord. 2692
Sermons in a nutshell. 3373
...Sermons in action for young folks. 3370
Sermons in American history. 3357
Sermons in argot. 3359
Sermons in culture and spiritual values. 866
Sermons in illustration. 3343
Sermons in magic. 907, 2315
Sermons in miniature for meditation. 2399
Sermons in outline. 3376

Sermons in Plymouth church, Brooklyn. 1340
Sermons in stories for children. 907
Sermons in summer. 3338
Sermons in the making. 3345
Sermons in the sanctuary. 1466
Sermons, lectures and addresses delivered by the Very Rev. Thomas N. Burke. 758
Sermons, letters and lectures. 164
Sermons not preached in the White House. 2934, 3357
Sermons of a Buddhist abbot. 712
Sermons of a chemist. 3345
Sermons of a transport chaplain. 3851
Sermons of Christmas Evans. 3369
Sermons of consolation. 1354
Sermons of doctrinal and experimental subjects. 2935
Sermons of Edwin Sandys. 1227
Sermons of faith and hope. 2933, 3354
Sermons of George W. Bailey. 3337
Sermons of goodwill. 3358
Sermons of Gus Nichols. 1273, 3355
Sermons of John Baptist Massillon and Lewis Bourdaloue. 864
Sermons of power. 3366
Sermons of R. C. H. White. 3375
Sermons of religion. 3356
Sermons of Rev. C. H. Spurgeon. 167
Sermons of Rev. Francis A. Baker. 862
Sermons of Rev. Ichabod S. Spencer. 2935
Sermons of Rev. Joseph I. Foot ... with a brief biographical sketch. 3351
Sermons of Rev. Messrs. Fisk & Parsons. 3340
Sermons of the city. 3344
Sermons of the Cure of Ars. 865
Sermons of the four last things; death, judgement, hell, and heaven. 1531
Sermons of the late Dr. James Inglis, pastor of the First Presbyterian church in Baltimore; with some of his forms of prayer. 2932
Sermons of the late Nicholas Snethen, minister. 3358
Sermons of the Rev. C. H. Spurgeon. 167
Sermons of the Rev. C. H. Spurgeon, of London. 3345, 3362
Sermons of the Rev. Josiah J. Finch. 162
Sermons of the Rev. Robert Murray M'Cheyne. 3365
Sermons of theism, atheism, and the popular theology. 3726
Sermons, on a number of connected subjects; in which an attempt is made to explain the leading principles of revealed religion. 1342
Sermons on baptism and the Lord's supper, Lord's days. 3267
Sermons on Bible characters. 217, 3341
Sermons on Bible subjects. 1227
Sermons on Bible themes. 2932
Sermons on Biblical characters. 3339
Sermons on books of the Bible. 500
Sermons on certain of the less prominent facts and references in sacred story. 1227
Sermons on Christ and His salvation. 1340
Sermons on Christian commitment. 1094
Sermons on Christian doctrine. 1227, 3647
Sermons on Christian doctrines and duties. 3338
Sermons on conversion. 862, 3369
Sermons on crises in the life of Jesus. 1986
Sermons on doctrinal and moral subjects. 3755
Sermons on duties belonging to some of the conditions and relations of private life. 3726
Sermons on education. 2592
Sermons on evangelism. 1554
Sermons on familiar subjects. 1557
Sermons on Genesis. 527
Sermons on great tragedies of the Bible. 3339
Sermons on important doctrinal subjects. 3751
Sermons on important subjects. 2436, 2930, 3346, 3350, 3361, 3362
Sermons on living subjects. 1340
Sermons on marriage and family life. 2347
Sermons on miscellaneous subjects. 2437
Sermons on national subjects. 3342
Sermons on New Testament characters. 3339
Sermons on New Testment characters. 338
Sermons on Old Testament characters. 492
Sermons on Old Testament heroes. 493
Sermons on Old Testament subjects. 3342
Sermons on Our Blessed Lady, "House of gold," 2354
Sermons on Our Lord Jesus Christ. 865

Sermons on our mothers. 2624
Sermons on penance. 2811
Sermons on practical subjects. 1343, 3337, 3346
Sermons on questions children ask. 905
Sermons on questions children ask, each paired with one for adults on the same theme. 905
Sermons on religion & life. 1227, 3366
Sermons on Revelation. 458
Sermons on revivals. 1555
Sermons on Romanism. 798
Sermons on St. Paul's Epistles to the Corinthians. 346
Sermons on several occasions. 2438, 3367
Sermons on several subjects. 1227, 3366
Sermons on Simon Peter. 2825
Sermons on sin and grace, Lord's days. 3411
Sermons on some of the first principles and doctrines of true religion. 1341
Sermons on some words of Christ. 2056
Sermons on some words of St. Paul. 374
Sermons on special and festival occasions. 3341
Sermons on the Apostles' creed. 3339
Sermons on the Apostles' creed, Lord's days. 75
Sermons on the blessed sacrament. 2252
Sermons on the book of Daniel. 509
Sermons on the book of Revelation. 465
Sermons on the catechism. 3340
Sermons on the Christian doctrine. 3647
Sermons on the Christian year. 863, 1266
Sermons on the commandments. 1316
Sermons on the dignity of man, and the value of the objects principally relating to human happiness. 3347
Sermons on the distinguishing doctrines and duties of experimental religion, and especially designed for revivals. 3342
Sermons, on the following subjects. 1340
Sermons on the Gospel of John. 423
Sermons on the Gospels. 3344
Sermons on the Holy Spirit. 3344
Sermons on the inner life. 141, 163
Sermons on the liturgical seasons. 1265
Sermons on the Lord's prayer. 2249, 2250
Sermons on the Lord's prayer and other prayers of Jesus. 2049, 2249
Sermons on the mass, the sacraments, and the sacramentals. 2370
Sermons on the mission and character of Christ, and on the Beatitudes. 2038
Sermons on the nativity. 1113
Sermons on the parables. 2028
Sermons on the parables of Jesus. 2028
Sermons on the Passion of Christ. 2034
Sermons on the prodigal son. 2945
Sermons on the Psalms. 586
Sermons on the Psalms and Gospels. 1226
Sermons on the saving work of christ. 3049
Sermons on the second coming of Christ. 3321
Sermons on the Sermon on the Mount. 3336
Sermons on the Song of songs. 594
Sermons on the stations of the cross. 865
Sermons on the Ten commandments. 1313, 1315
Sermons on the way of life. 1558
Sermons on those doctrines of the gospel. 3724
Sermons on various subjects. 1341, 1343, 2425, 3346
Sermons on various subjects, divine and moral. 3367
Sermons, on various subjects, doctrinal and practical. 1342
Sermons on various subjects of Christian doctrine and duty. 1341
Sermons on women of the Old Testament. 3840
Sermons; or, Homilies appointed to be read in churches in the time of Queen Elizabeth of famous memory. 2965
Sermons, parochial and occasional. 3343
Sermons, phonographically reported. 1688
Sermons, practical devotional. 3340
Sermons preached. 1524
Sermons preached and revised by the Rev. C. H. Spurgeon. 167
Sermons preached at Brighton. 1227
Sermons preached at Harvard. 3759
Sermons preached at the Church of St. Paul the Apostle, New York, during the year 1863 ; with an introd. by Joseph F. Gower. 865, 3357
Sermons preached at the lecture in Boston. 3350
Sermons preached before the Bishop Seabury association of Brown university, Providence, R.I. 2973
Sermons preached before the University of Oxford. 1225

Sermons preached before the University of Oxford and on various occasions. 3343
Sermons preached before the University of Oxford, at St. Mary's church. 2981
Sermons preached chiefly in the church of St. John the Baptist, New Windsor. 3345
Sermons preached chiefly in the college chapel. 3726
Sermons preached during my twenties. 1559
Sermons preached in a university church. 3758
Sermons preached in country churches. 3343
Sermons preached in England. 3362
Sermons preached in English chruches. 3362
Sermons preached in English churches. 3362
Sermons preached in Manchester. 165
Sermons preached in St. James's chapel, York street, London. 3363
Sermons preached in St. John's church. 3350
Sermons preached in the African Protestant Episcopal church of St. Thomas, Philadelphia. 2973
Sermons preached in the chapel of Harvard college. 3726
Sermons preached in the chapel of Rugby school. 3362
Sermons preached on plantations. 3352
Sermons preached on various occasions. 864, 3365
Sermons preached upon several occasions. 1227, 3464
Sermons preached without notes. 164
Sermons: Seven sermons. 888, 3726
Sermons that have helped. 3346
Sermons that have won souls. 1560
Sermons that never die. 3341
Sermons that won the masses. 3344
Sermons the year 'round. 565, 3361
Sermons to children. 910
Sermons to intellectuals from three continents. 3342
Sermons to men of other faiths and traditions. 1078
Sermons to ministers of state. 3347
Sermons to my friends. 3355
Sermons to my students. 3376
Sermons to the churches. 3360
Sermons to the clergy. 1068
Sermons to the natural man. 2934, 3357
Sermons to the spiritual man. 2934
Sermons to young men. 978
Sermons to young people in St. Paul's M. E. church. 3343
Sermons to young persons, on the following subjects, vix. 3884
Sermons to young women. 3363
Sermons upon the following subjects, viz. The divinity of Jesus Christ. 3348
Sermons, upon the ministry, worship, and doctrines of the Protestant Episcopal church. 2964, 2972
Sermons wherein those eight characters of the blessed commonly called the beatitudes, are opened & applied in fifteen discourses. 180
Sermons which have won souls. 1560, 2425
Sermons which spiritually interpret the Scriptures and other writings on Christian science. 564, 1036
Sermons, wise and witty. 1558
Sermons without texts. 3293
Sermons you can preach. 3372
Serpent and the dove. 1195
Serpent and the sun. 1898
Serpent in Eden and other stories from The Book. 616
Serpent of Sugar Creek colony. 3595
Serpent power. 3866, 3867
Serpent symbol, and the worship of the reciprocal principles of nature in America. 1904
Serpent symbolism in the Old Testament. 3376
Serpent was wiser; a new look at Genesis 1-11. 526
Serpent worship in Africa. 3376
Servant and son. 2041
Servant and the dove. 561
Servant King. 444
Servant-Messiah. 2016, 2414
Servant of God. 2428, 3377
Servant of God, Mary Theresa Countess Ledochowska. 2205, 3454
Servant of God's servants. 2791
Servant of Jehovah. 543, 3347
*Servant of peace. 3345
Servant of the King. 1114
Servant of the light. 1008
Servant of the Lord. 545
Servant of the most high God. 1806

Servant of the Word. 2900
Servant who rules. 437
Servants and stewards. 3531
Servants of all. 807
Servants of apostasy. 1912
Servants of God. 3408
Servants of God in People's China. 1110
Servants of God or masters of men? 1903
Servants of the devil. 3826
Servants of the King. 2483
Servants of the Lord. 1299
Servants of the Word. 2951
Servants without hire. 1462
Serve Him with mirth. 3822
Serve to survive. 2197
Serve with gladness. 1295
Servers of the Lord. 623
Service. 997
Service, an exposition of the Salvation army in America. 3293
Service and Bible study. 1554
Service and prayers for church and home. 2434, 2455
Service book. 1694
Service book and hymnal. 1868, 2290
Service book for ministers. 2237
Service book for schools. 2969
Service book of the Holy Orthodox-Catholic Apostolic Church. 1487
Service book of the Holy Orthodox-Catholic apostolic (Greco-Russian) church. 1487
Service evangelism. 1562
Service for the Day of atonement. 105
Service for the New York. 2073
Service for the three hours of Good Friday. 1747
[Service for the two first nights of the Passover]. 2779
Service from sea to sea: depicting the ministries of Frederic William Patterson, minister, denominational executive, and college president, in Canada, both west and east, 1895-1948. 2794
Service-hymnal. 2109
Service in dedication of the Milbank memorial choir, Princeton university chapel. 2941
Service manual for Lutheran chaptams serving with the forces of the United States. 3737
Service manual for ministers. 1293
Service manual for ministers of non-liturgical churches; also serviceable. for ministers of education, leaders of youth, women, men. 2474
Service men's guide. 3456
Service music and anthems for the nonprofessional choir. 1209
...The service of praise. 2463
Service of song for Baptist churches. 140, 152, 153
Service of song for Baptist churches, with music. 153
Service of sorrow. 1350
Service of the Lord must be chosen presently and without delay. 3354
Service of the poor. 3416
Service of the synagogue. 2110
Service operations management. 3377
Service prayer book. 3456
Service prayer book with Scripture readings. 82
Service song book. 3455
Service songs. 3561
Service suspended. 2538
Service to honor the memory of the Rev. R. Heber Newton, D.D., and to help perpetuate the ideals to which his life was dedicated, Church of the ascension, Fifth avenue and Tenth street, New York city, February seventh, 1915. 2706
Service to service men. 3456

Serviceable man. 1504
Serviceman at prayer. 81
Services and prayers for country use. 2238
Services and songs for the celebration of life. 3857
Services at the centennial celebration of the organization of the Congregational church in North Hadley, observed Sunday, June 28, 1931. 1337
Services at the fiftieth anniversary of the First Congregational church. 1339
Services at the funeral of the Rev. Jacob Brodhead, D.D. 693
Services for congregational worship. 3725
Services for special needs. 2236
Services for the open. 3853
Services held by the First church of Killingly. 1336
Services in Adams chapel at the dedication of the new buildings of the Union theological seminary, 1200 Park avenue, New York city. December 9, 1884. 3615

Services in celebration of the one hundred and twenty-fifth anniversary of the organization of the Congregational church in Rutland, Vermont, October seventeenth, nineteen hundred thirteen. 1339
Services in remembrance of Rev. Joseph Torrey, D. D. 3705
Services of religion for special occasions for use in the churches of the free spirit. 3723
Services of religion for use in the churches of the free spirit. 3723
Services of the Protestant Episcopal church in the United States of America. 2891
Serving around the world in the United Lutheran church in America. 3734
Serving God with mammon. 958
Serving rural Puerto Rico. 2407
... Serving the Heavenly Father. 3146
Serving the neighborhood. 3435
Serving with the saints. 1239
... Sesame and lilies. 3201
Sesquicentennial history of Royal Arch Freemasonry in Ohio. 1816-1966. 1670
Sesquicentennial history of Saint Denis Parish, 1825-1975. 3273
Sesquicentennial history: Ruhama Baptist Church. 663
Sesquicentennial review of the Park Avenue Christian church. 2699
Sesquicentennial Sandy Spring Friends Meeting House, 1817-1967. 3301
Session of the Colorado annual conference. 2451
Sessional records of Cross Creek Presbyterian Church, Cross Creek Township, Jefferson Co., Ohio, from April 11, 1839 to Sept. 1, 1880. 2925
Set apart for service. 2741
... Set apart for the gospel. 3674
Set free for others. 3447
Set free through inner healing. 3291
Set free to be. 469
Set my exiles free. 596
Set the church afire! 1246
Set your house in order. 1417
Seth Cook Rees, the warrior-saint. 3031
Seth material. 3512
Seth speaks. 3474
Seton ballad. 3378
Setting it right. 788
Setting men free. 1011
Setting of the crescent and the rising of the cross. 2162, 2552
Setting of the Sermon on the Mount. 3335
Settlement of the Brethren on the Pacific slope. 1237
Settlement of the Israelite tribes in Palestine. 2095
Settlements of the Celtic Saints in Wales. 3789
Seven. 3576
Seven ages of creation. 1370
Seven baskets. 1451
Seven baths for Naaman. 494, 633, 2667
Seven beginnings. 1166
Seven books of history against the pagans. 3850
Seven books of wisdom. 600
Seven capital sins. 3411
Seven cardinal virtues. 3782
Seven centuries of the problem of church and state. 1143
... The seven champions of Christendom. 3198, 3280
Seven churches of Asia. 461, 462
Seven claims of the Book of Mormon. 679
Seven-day church at work. 3848
Seven days. 2383
Seven days & the seven words. 1985
Seven days of creation. 1381, 1384
Seven days of the week. 1452
Seven days that changed the world. 1837
Seven days with God. 2640
Seven deadly sins. 1411, 1412, 3410, 3413
Seven deadly sins today. 1411, 1412
Seven deadly virtues. 993
Seven divine aids for yout health. 1792
Seven dolors of the Blessed Virgin Mary. 2357
Seven doubts of a biologist. 3200
Seven dramatic services of worship. 3144
Seven ecumenical councils. 1373
Seven epistles of Christ. 461, 3381
... Seven essays on the subject of force-massing methods. 2727
... Seven essays on the subject of your practical forces. 2727
Seven exegetical works. 3635
Seven finalities of faith. 1590
Seven first words of Jesus. 2071
Seven-fold gift. 3263
Seven gifts. 1712
Seven golden candlesticks. 462, 3379
Seven great Bibles. 3268

Seven great encyclicals. 2771
Seven great hymns. 1877
Seven great hymns of the mediaeval church. 1877
Seven great lights. 927
Seven horns of the lamb. 1712, 3695
Seven-hued rainbow. 2836
Seven human mountains. 3410
777. 2724
710 pointed quotations and illustrations. 2897
Seven keys to a more fruitful ministry. 2786
Seven keys to happiness. 1008
Seven kinds of goodness. 3126
Seven lamps of fire. 1097
Seven last words. 2056, 2058
... The seven last words, and other meditations. 1263
Seven last words of Christ. 2059, 3348
Seven last words of Our Most Holy Redeemer. 2057
Seven last words of the church. 1244
Seven lectures on the credibility of the Gospel histories. 394
Seven lectures to young men. 3869
Seven lesson plans on the constitution on the Church of Vatican Council II. 3769
Seven lettors. 455
Seven lucky gods of Japan. 3379
Seven messages to the mother church. 1032
Seven miles out. 3278
Seven minutes at the "mike" in the deep South. 160
Seven most important events of future history. 1514
Seven New Testament converts. 338
Seven New Testament soul-winners. 338
Seven nights. 3091
7:05 and the church alive. 2786
Seven oracles from the cross. 2057
Seven overcometh. 460
Seven parables of the kingdom. 2771
Seven Pauline letters. 371
Seven pillars of peace. 1136
Seven plus seven. 3239
... The seven principles of man. 3683
Seven problems of the spirit in conflict and their solution. 1412
Seven professions and the teachings of Jesus. 2066
Seven proofs that all men are not immortal. 1892
Seven Psalms. 584
Seven purposes. 3497
... Seven questions in dispute. 2562
Seven questions Jesus asked. 2072
Seven questions on Our Lord's passion. 2034
Seven rays. 3688, 3689
Seven reasons why a scientist believes in God. 3081
Seven religious isms. 3323
Seven root sins. 3410
Seven sacraments. 3265, 3267
Seven saved sinners. 1357
Seven sayings of the Saviour on the cross. 2058
Seven schools of yoga. 3866
Seven seals. 3203
Seven seals of the Apocalypse unveiling past, present and future. 56
Seven seals opened. 465
Seven senses in man and through out the nature of the almighty infinite in the created and uncreated. 3333
Seven sermons. 3366
Seven sermons on different important subject. 3366
Seven sermons upon the following subjects. 3726
Seven sevens of years and a jubilee! 2552
777. 2724
777 revised. 2724
Seven simple sermons on the Saviour's last words. 2057
Seven simple sermons on the second coming. 3321
Seven sins and seven virtues. 1412
Seven scenes from the gospels and thirty hymns for sundry festivals and occasions. 1861
Seven sorts of successful services. 2237
Seven Spanish mystics. 2648
Seven spiritual ships. 465
Seven states of consciousness. 2833
Seven steeples. 1301, 1803, 3128
Seven steps on how to become a mystic and enjoy the most exhilarating pleasure available to man on this earth. 2642
Seven steps to a vital faith. With special introductions by Norman Vincent Peale. 1014
Seven steps to heaven. 2212
Seven steps to the altar. 2742
Seven steps to the cross. 2399

Seven storey mountain. 2413, 3131, 3710
Seven swords. 165, 2354, 3459
Seven tall men. 215
Seven teen years. 3879
Seven terraces. 3482
Seven themes from the Gospel of John. 2398
Seven times around Jericho. 3596
Seven times He spoke. 2058
Seven times of prophecy and the seventy weeks of Daniel. 606
Seven types of humanity and other essays. 3570
Seven valleys and The four valleys. 126, 127
Seven virtues. 2058
7 ways I can better serve the Lord. 994
Seven who fought. 1133
Seven windows. 2058
Seven wonders of the wonderful Word. 278
Seven words. 2056, 2057, 3211
Seven words from the cross. 2030, 2058
Seven words of Christian change. 1360
Seven words of Jesus and Mary. 2058
Seven words of life and beauty. 1747
Seven words of love. 2057, 2058
Seven words of men around the Cross. 1997
Seven words spoken by Christ on the cross. 2056
Seven words to the cross. 1998, 2031
Seven worlds of the minister. 2786
Seven-year teacher. 3549
Seven-year teacher, book one. 3550
Seven years among the freedmen. 1658
Seven years in Sierra Leone. 2491
Seven years that change the world. 2946
... The sevenfold I am. 2071, 3343
Sevenfold unity of the Christian church. 3223
Sevenfold work of the Holy Spirit. 1831
Seventeen. 1456
Seventeen book of prayer. 1452
Seventeen come Sunday. 3889
Seventeen discourses on several texts of Scripture. 166
Seventeen guide to you and other people. 3881
Seventeen ninety-six to eighteen ninety-six. A century of Congregationalism in Ohio. 1338
1770-1920, from Good Luck to Gloucester, the book of the pilgrimage. 2632, 3755
1710-1910. An historical discourse. 1651
1730-1930. 1338
Seventeenth century men of latitude. 1781
Seventeenth-century resolve. 2396
Seventh angel. 453
Seventh day. 631, 3386
Seventh-day Adventism refuted. 3382
Seventh-Day Adventist Bible commentary. 224
Seventh-Day Adventist Bible dictionary. 244
Seventh-Day Adventist Bible student's sourcebook. 3381
Seventh-Day Adventist encyclopedia. 3381
Seventh-Day Adventist fact book. 3380
Seventh-day Adventist hymn and tune book. 3386
Seventh-Day Adventists. 3380
Seventh-Day Adventists answer questions on doctrine. 3383
Seventh-Day Adventists in Canada. 3381
Seventh-Day Adventists in the British isles, 1878-1933. 3386
Seventh-day Adventists in time of war. 3380
Seventh-Day Adventists today. 3380
Seventh day Baptist beliefs. 3388
Seventh-day Baptist hand-book. 3388
Seventh day Baptists in Europe and America. 3388
Seventh dimension. 2399
Seventh International (twelfth national) and world's second Sunday school conventions. 3554
Seventh trumpet. 929, 1968
70's: opportunities for your church. 3182
70th anniversary. 2303
Seventieth anniversary eighteen ninety-two-nineteen sixty-two, and 75th diamond jubilee of arrival of first immigrants, 1887-1962, Dec. 5-9, 1962. 2303
Seventy best Bible stories. 620
Seventy familiar Bible stories. 620
Seventy feet nearer the stars. 3345, 3732
Seventy-fifth anniversary memorial. 835
... Seventy-fifth anniversary of the organization of the Presbyterian church. 2917

Seventy-fifth anniversary, St. Philip's cathedral, Atlanta, Georgia, 1847-1922. 102
Seventy-fifth anniversary volume of the Jewish quarterly review. 2093, 2147
Seventy-five stories for the worship hour. 3066
Seventy-five years. 34
Seventy-five years at Methodist Ladies' College. 2458
Seventy-five years of Catholic life in Nevada. 823
Seventy-five years of Danish Baptist missionary work in America. 142, 143
Seventy-five years of St. Aloysius parish. 893
Seventy less-known Bible stories. 620
Seventy lessons in teaching and preaching Christ. 2038
Seventy stories of the Old Testament. 627
Seventy times seven. 1005, 3792
Seventy weeks and the great tribulation. 509, 1993, 2050
...The 70 weeks of Daniel. 508
Seventy years in Clarkesville Baptist Church. 1285
Seventy years of Our Sunday visitor, 1912-1982. 793
75th anniversary: 1887-1962. 1459
Anniversary of Saint Francis de Sales Parish 1889-1964. 3274
75th anniversary book, 1887-1962. 693
75 stories and illustrations from everyday life. 1841
Seventy-five year history of the Pasadena bodies of the ancient and accepted Scottish Rite of Freemasonry, 1895 to 1970. 1668
Seventy-five years history of Columbia Baptist Conference, 1889-1964. 1311
77,000 churches. 170
77 ways of involving youth in the church. 1261
... 77 wonders of the divine Revelation "signified," 319
Seventy's course in theology. 2612
Several Israels. 1052, 2087
Severe mercy. 45, 3768
Severus scroll and 1QIs [superscript a]. 565, 3711
... The Sewanee summer school. 3756
Sex. 3394
Sex and Christian freedom. 3389
Sex and family in the Bible and the Middle East. 3389
Sex and religion. 3389
Sex and religion in oppression. 3392
Sex and religion today. 3389
Sex and salvation. 3391
Sex and Satanism. 3304
Sex and sex worship. 2828
Sex and sex worship (phallic worship) 2828
Sex & spirit. 1422, 3836
Sex and the Bible. 3389
Sex and the church. 3389
Sex and the confessional. 3390
Sex and the mysteries. 889
Sex and the new morality. 3394
Sex and the occult. 2730
Sex and the spiritual path. 93, 3391
Sex and the whole person. 3393
Sex education and training in chastity. 3390
Sex: female; religion: Catholic. 3835
Sex for Christians. 3393
Sex in Christianity and psychoanalysis. 1673, 3389
Sex in history. 3394
Sex in religion. 3389
Sex in the Bible. 3390
Sex in witchcraft. 3824, 3825
Sex is not love. 3391
Sex is not sinful? 3394
Sex laws and customs in Judaism. 3392
Sex, love and life. 3880
Sex, love, & the life of the spirit. 3391
Sex, marriage, and chastity. 3391
Sex, marriage, and family. 2339
Sex, marriage and religion. 2340
Sex problems as related to health and disease. 3389
Sex roles & the Christian family. 1607
Sex, Satan, and Jesus. 984
Sex, sense, and nonsense. 3390
Sex, sin, and grace. 2709, 3835
Sex, the key to the Bible. 3391
Sex: the radical view of a Catholic theologian. 3389
Sex thing: you, love, and God. 3391
Sex, witches, and warlocks. 3824
Sex worship. 2827, 2828
Sex worship and disease (phallic worship) 2827
Sex worship and symbolism. 2827
Sexism and church law. 3836

Sexist religion and women in the church. 3834
Sexology of the Bible. 3389
Sexual celibate. 877
Sexual Christian. 3393
Sexual energy and yoga. 3391
Sexual ethics and Christian responsibility. 3394
Sexual happiness in marriage. 3390
Sexual inversion. 1457, 1844
Sexual key to the tarot. 3589
Sexual language. 3393
Sexual liberation and religion in nineteenth century Europe. 3390
Sexual morality. 3393
Sexual occultism. 2313
Sexual practices & the medieval church. 3390
Sexual relation in Christian thought. 3389
Sexual revolution. 3393
Sexual symbolism. 2828
Sexuality and moral responsibility. 948
Sexuality and the Christian tradition. 3389
Sexuality and the counseling pastor. 2782
Sexuality of Jesus: theological and literary perspectives. 1970, 3390
Sexuality, the Bible, and science. 3391
[Sh'ar la-Mishnah (romanized form)]. 2478
Shaaray tefila. 2699
Shabbat catalogue. 3260
Shabbath, the time of its beginning and termination. 3261
Shabbethai Sofer and his prayer-book. 2109
Shackles of the supernatural. 1654
Shade of His hand. 1350, 1353
Shade of Plato. 3206
Shadow and substance. 3720, 3721
Shadow and substance: Taoist mystical reflections. 3587
Shadow Christ. 2415
Shadow land. 1479
Shadow of coming events. 608
Shadow of destiny. 2165
Shadow of heaven. 480
Shadow of heaven, matter, and stance in Milton's poetry. 2468
Shadow of his hand. 2534, 2815, 3580, 3831
Shadow of His wings. 1362, 3851
Shadow of Rome. 802
Shadow of the Almighty. 1509, 2516
Shadow of the broad brim. 3523
Shadow of the cross. 1705
Shadow of the pope. 3195
Shadow of the rock, and other religious poems. 3210
Shadow of the rock, and other sermons. 3340
Shadow of the third century, a revaluation of Christianity. 1192
Shadow world. 3502
Shadowing wing. 164
"Shadows" 3518
Shadows from Caesar's court. 2069
Shadows in the sunshine. 2597, 3355
Shadows in the valley. 1255, 2187
Shadows of good things. 284
Shadows of poetry. 3207
Shadows they cast. 2490
Shadows we run from. 994
... Shaftesbury and Hutcheson. 1858
Shaftesbury school of philosophy known as the story of our existences or the doctrine of diversity. 2835
Shahrastani on the Indian religion. 1897
Shake up your faith. 2393
Shaken foundations; theological foundations for mission. 2553
Shaker adventure. 3398
Shaker collection of the Western Reserve Historical Society. 3397, 3808
Shaker communism. 3395
Shaker herbs. 1804, 3396
Shaker image. 3399
Shaker literature in the rare book room of the Buffalo and Erie County Public Library. 3397
Shaker manuscript hymnals from South Union, Kentucky. 2634, 3398
Shaker Museum, Old Chatham, N.Y. 3397
Shaker music. 3398
Shaker order of Christmas. 3394
Shaker sermons. 3395, 3397
Shaker spiritual. 3398
Shakerism. 3396
Shakerism in Kentucky. 3395
Shakerism; its meaning and message. 3397
Shakerism unmasked. 3397
Shakers. 2205, 3395
Shakers and the world's people. 3397
Shakers and their homes. 3398

Shakers; compendium of the origin, history, principles, rules and regulations, government, and doctrines of the United Society of Believers in Christ's Second Appearing. 3395
Shakers of Ohio. 3396, 3398
Shakers, their architecture and furniture. 79
Shakespeare and Catholicism. 1759, 3399
Shakespeare and Christian doctrine. 3071, 3399
Shakespeare and the Bible: showing how much the great dramatist was indebted to Holy Writ for his profound knowledge of human nature. 299, 3399
Shakespeare and the Bible, to which is added prayers on the stage, proper and improper. 3399, 3607

Shakespeare and the mystery of God's judgments. 1101, 3400
Shakespeare and the rose of love. 2263, 3399
Shakespeare: the perspective of value. 3071, 3399
Shakespeare's Biblical knowledge and use of the Book of common prayer, as exemplified in the plays of the first folio. 299, 3399
Shakespeare's church, otherwise the collegiate Church of the Holy Trinity of Stratford-upon-Avon. 1237
Shakespeare's religious background. 1759, 3399
Shakespeare's speaking pictures. 920, 3399
Shaking dispensations. 2261
Shaking of Adventism. 3381
Shaking of the foundations. 3359
Shaking of the foundations [sermons]. 3359
Shakspeare's debt to the Bible. 299, 3399
Shakti. 1815, 3400
Shakti and Shakta. 3400
Shall I be a daily communicant? 3175
Shall Jesus find faith on earth! 1592
Shall laymen teach religion? 3157
Shall never perish. 93
"Shall the sword devour forever?" 3792
Shall we accept the ancient canons as canon law? 736, 2956
Shall we believe in a divine providence? 2980
Shall we have a creed? 1385
Shall we overcome? 1132
Shall we scrap the Ten commandments! 3091
Shall we stand by the church? 3140
Shalom. 1572, 2152, 2533
Shalom is ... whole community. 1320
Shalom: peace. 2811
Shalom: the search for a peaceable city. 2809
Shalom woman. 3844
Shaman and the jaguar. 1903
Shamanic voices. 3400
Shamanism. 2378, 3400
Shamanism: archaic techniques of ecstasy. 3400
Shamanism in western North America. 1903, 3400
Shaman's doorway. 2648
Shamrocks for St. Patrick's day. 3277
Shamrocks, harps, and shillelaghs. 3277
Shanghai Wolfe. 1927
Shango cult in Trinidad. 3400
Shango in the New World. 3400
Shankara's Crest-jewel of discrimination (Viveka-chudamani). 103
Shantung revival. 3232
Shape of Adam's rib. 3837
Shape of baptism. 137
Shape of Catholic higher education. 831
Shape of christology. 1953
Shape of crisis and tragedy. 3540
Shape of death. 1531
Shape of faith. 2956
Shape of hope. 518, 1846
Shape of religious instruction. 935
Shape of sacred space. 528
Shape of the Christian life. 959
Shape of the church to come. 1122
Shape of the gospel. 1263
Shape of the Puritan mind. 3817
Shape of the question. 3645
Shape of the stars. 1384
Shape of the theological task. 1808, 3657
Shapers of Baptist thought. 149
Shapers of traditions in Germany, Switzerland, and Poland, 1560-1600. 3040
Shaping history through prayer & fasting. 2877
Shaping of a man of faith. 4, 492, 2792
Shaping of America. 3745

... The shaping of American religion. Editors. 3214
Shaping of modern Christian thought. 3213
Shaping of Protestant education. 2956
Shaping of the modern mind. 2841
Shaping of the United Church of Christ. 3732
Shaping school curriculum. 1128
Shaping the Christian message. 3157, 3158
Shaping the church's educational ministry. 937
Shaping the church's ministry with youth. 1259
Shaping the coming age of religious life. 2572
Shaping the congregation. 1125
Shaping the future. 1281
Shaping tomorrow's church. 1245
Shaping your faith. 3661
Shapira affair. 316, 3400
Shards from the heart. 50
Share a miracle. 1009
Share Christ today. 1573
Share my devotions. 3842
Share my meditations. 2398
Share my pleasant stones. 1432
Share my pleasant stones every day for a year. 1432
Share of Thomas Aquinas in the growth of the witchcraft delusion. 1424, 3693
Share the new life with a Jew. 2556
Share the word now. 235, 1567
Share your faith. 3829, 3830
Share your faith with a Muslim. 2557
Sharing community. 2774
Sharing God's love. 2392, 3829
Sharing God's love with others. 1736
Sharing groups in the Church. 1170
Sharing His suffering. 2032
Sharing in creation. 1047
Sharing Jesus. 3383, 3829
Sharing observations with the home, church. 1237
Sharing of scripture. 644, 1170
Sharing our Biblical story. 616
Sharing our Quaker faith. 3010
Sharing possessions. 429, 3799
Sharing the Christian message. 2790
Sharing the faith. 796
Sharing the gospel with others. 2619
Sharing the old, old story. 941
Sharing the vision. 2965
Sharing treasure, time, and talent. 807, 952
Sharing with neighbor America. 2547
Sharing your faith with a Muslim. 2557
Sharp sickle. 1036, 1529
Sharpening the focus of the church. 1118
Shattered dream. 2938
Shavuot anthology. 3401
Shaykh Damanhuri on the churches of Cairo, 1739. 1270
She follows the psychic path. 2991
She had a magic. 3425
She sat where they sat. 3697
She shall be called woman. 3838, 3841
She wears a crown of thorns. 1622, 3531
She who lived her name. 1802, 3426
She who weeps. 3286
Sheaf. 3482
Sheaf of golden years, 1856-1906. 3418
Sheaf of prayers. 2895
Sheaf of Zionist history. 3897
Shearers and the shorn. 1429
Sheep of the outer fold. 1527
Sheepfold and the common. 1013
Sheepfold and the shepherd. 755
Sheer folly of preaching. 2932
Sheer joy of living. 967
Shehitah. 3423
Shekel hakodesh (The holy shekel) the metrical work of Joseph Kimchi. 1798
Sheldon Jackson. 1689, 1930
Shelters and sanctuaries. 2435
Shelton and the crimson trail. 3402
Shelton of Tibet. 2555, 3402
Shen-fu's story. 2511
Shepard of Aintab. 3402
Shephard Psalm. 587
Shepherd and a king. 3778
Shepherd and his flock. 1450, 3676
Shepherd and His sheep. 587
Shepherd boy of Minnesota. 2166
Shepherd-evangelist. 1562
Shepherd find your pen. 960
Shepherd God. 588
Shepherd looks at the Good Shepherd and His sheep. 424, 2197
Shepherd of all. 587
Shepherd of an immigrant people. 740, 1301
Shepherd of Bethlehem. 2021
... The Shepherd of Hermas. 1806
Shepherd of mankind. 2805
Shepherd of men. 3344

Shepherd of my soul. 2391, 3198
Shepherd of my soul. 2391
Shepherd of souls. 3676
Shepherd of the Cowlitz. 1235
Shepherd of the far North. 3790
Shepherd of the second spring. 1474
Shepherd of the Stars. 342
Shepherd of the streets. 1778, 2697
Shepherd of the wilderness. 173
Shepherd of Times Square. 1301, 2589
Shepherd of untended sheep. 2627
Shepherd psalm. 587, 588
Shepherd Psalm for children. 588
Shepherd Psalm of Palestine. 587
Shepherd remembers. 587
Shepherd under Christ. 2787
Shepherd without sheep. 3197
Shepherdess. 1303
Shepherdess of souls. 2360
Shepherding God's flock. 2785
Shepherds and lovers. 953
Shepherds in the mist. 2939
Shepherds of Fatima. 1618
Shepherds of the flock of God. 1169
Shepherd's question. 3199
...The shepherd's rod. 3379
Shepherd's tartan. 2580
Shera of the Punjab. 2490
Shewings of Lady Julian. 2158
Shi'ite Islam. 3403
Shi, the story-teller. 2510, 3403
Shi'a of India. 3403
Shibboleth. 1671
Shield. 2103
Shield and the sword. 2179
Shield of faith and other sermons. 3358
Shielding the flame. 3361
Shields of brass. 992
Shields of Canada. 3403
Shields of Canada; T. T. Shields, 1873-1955. 3403
Shiloh, the Man of Nazareth. 2004
Shin Buddhism. 3403
Shingon Buddhism. 3403
Shining armor. 903
Shining as stars. 1483
Shining my light. 3200
Shining mystery of Jesus. 1951
Shining Stranger. 2039
Shinran: his life and thought. 3403
Shinran's gospel of pure grace. 3403
Shinto. 3403, 3404
Shinto art: Ise and Izumo shrines. 3404
Shinto; at the fountain-head of Japan. 3403
Shinto cult. 3404
Shinto, Japan's spiritual roots. 3404
Shinto, the Kami Way. 3404
Ship of light. 3198
Ship of peace. 3199
Ship sets sail. 1058
Ship "Tyre" 3575
"A ship without sails" 2360
Ships of peace. 2543
Shir hadash. 2110
Shirei Hayyim ve-emunah. 3577
Shirkutu of Babylonian deities. 3404
Shirley Jackson Case and the Chicago School. 743, 893
Shiro B'nai Jeshurun. 3577
Shirts and sheets. 1513
Shiurei harav. 2143
(Shiv'at yeme Bereshit) 525, 1383
Shivaji, a captain of war with a mission. 1895, 3404
Shock and renewal. 2549
Shock it to me, doctor! 982
Shock of revelation. 2973, 3358
Shoe-leather faith. 1842
Shoe-leather globe. 739
Shoemaker who gave India the Bible. 739
Shoghi Effendi. 3404
Shona religion. 2364
Shona ritual. 2364
Shoot-'em-up society. 3780
Shooting Creek was our parish. 3404
Shop talks. 1956
Shopkeeper's millenium. 3231
Short account of the Christian experience and ministereal labours. 2475
Short account of the experience of Mrs. Hester Ann Rogers. 3201
Short account of the life and death of the Rev. John Fletcher, vicar of Madeley. 1629
Short account of the life and death of the Rev. John Lee. 2206
Short account of the rise and progress of the African M. E. church in America. 14
Short and easy method with the deists. 1419, 2759
Short and plain instruction for the better understanding of the Lord's supper. 2253

TITLE INDEX SIGN OF JONAS.

Short and plain introduction to the better understanding of the Lord's supper. 2253
Short and plain view of the outward, yet sacred, rights and ordiances of the house of God, as commanded to be observed by the true steward, Jesus Christ, and deposited in His last will and testament. 1101
Short and plain view of the outward, yet sacred rights and ordinances of the house of God, as commanded to be observed by the true steward, Jesus Christ, and deposited in His last will and testament. 1235
Short and practical funeral addresses. 1692
Short answer to "A true exposition of the doctrine of the Catholic church touching the sacrament of penance." 2812
Short apology for being a Christian in the xxth century. 67
Short Baptist manual of polity and practice. 150
Short Bible. 250
Short Bible stories. 617
Short breviary for religious and the laity. 842, 2885
Short catechism. 770, 1184
Short catechism familiarly teaching the knowledge of God, and of ourselves. 748
Short catechism for young men and young women contemplating marriage. 2337
Short catechism of church history. 1184
Short catechism of church history for the higher grades of Catholic schools. 1185
Short catechism of the Catholic religion. 770
Short commentary on Kant's Critique of pure reason. 2163, 2164
Short compilation of the extraordinary life and writings of Thomas Say. 3201
Short course of Bible study. 646
Short course on the Bible. 646
Short cut to divine love. 3487
Short dictionary of Bible personal names. 217
Short dictionary of Bible themes. 245
Short dictionary of Catholicism. 778
Short dictionary of mythology. 2659
Short discourses and considerations on the sacred heart of Jesus, and the sacred heart of Mary. 3270
Short epitome of the life suffering and travels, of Gardiner! Harrington, of Stephentown,Resselaer co., N.Y. 3199
Short epitome of the life, sufferings and travels, of Gardner Harrington, of Stephentown, Rennsselaer co., N. Y. 3199
Short essay on baptism, designed for the benefit of common readers. 134
Short explanation of Dr. Martin Luther's Small catechism, a handbook of Christian doctrine. 2284
Short family prayers for every morning and evening of the week. 1606
Short grammar of Biblical Aramaic. 78
Short grammar of Church Slavonic. 1247
Short grammar of plain chant. 884
Short grammar of the Greek New Testament. 1770
Short guide to classical mythology. 2658
... A short guide to some manuscripts in the library of Trinity college, Dublin. 1481
Short handbook of public worship in the churches of the Anglican communion. 1223
Short historical notes on the Apocalypse. 462
Short histories. 2769
Short history. 1177, 2601
Short history of Amelia Lodge 101, AF&AM, Amelia County, Virginia. 1663
Short history of American Presbyterianism from its foundations to the reunion of 1869. 2921
Short history of Asbury Theological Seminary. 89
Short history of Baptist missions. 156
Short history of Buddhism. 709
Short history of Christian doctrine. 3654
Short history of Christian theophage. 2281
Short history of Christianity. 1172, 1175, 1177
Short history of Christianity in the apostolic age. 1191, 2797
Short history of Confucian philosophy. 1331, 2838
Short history of ethics. 1538
Short history of freethought. 1657
Short history of freethought, ancient and modern. 1657
Short history of Kansas Yearly meeting of Friends. 1686
Short history of Louisiana Baptists. 154
Short history of Methodism. 2423, 2424
Short history of Methodism in the United States. 2433
Short history of monks and monasteries. 2569
Short history of moral theology. 3667
Short history of Quakerism (earlier periods) 1684
Short history of religions. 3139
Short history of S.P.C.K. 3437
Short history of St. John in Ephesus. 2127
Short history of Syriac Christianity to the rise of Islam. 1197, 3579
Short history of the Baptist denomination. 151
Short history of the Baptists. 152
Short history of the Bible. 736
Short history of the Bible, and Testament. 297
Short history of the C.M.S. Roper River Mission, 1908-1969. 2543, 3247
Short history of the Catholic Church. 810
Short history of the Christian church. 1173, 1177
Short history of the Christian church from the earliest times to the present day. 1179
Short history of the church of Russia. 3256
Short history of the Disciples of Christ. 1460
Short history of the doctrine of the atonement. 108
Short history of the early church. 1192, 1196
Short history of the English Church. 1220
Short history of the Episcopal Church in Scotland. 1524
Short history of the Hebrews from Moses to Herod the Great. 2096
Short history of the Hebrews from the Patriarchs to Herod the Great. 535
Short history of the Inquisition. 1908
Short history of the interpretation of the Bible. 240
... A short history of the Jews. 2090
Short history of the Jews down to the Roman period. 2096
Short history of the mediaeval church. 1186
Short history of the Methodists. 2438
Short history of the Methodists, in the United States of America. 2424
Short history of the Mount Olive Baptist church. 143
Short history of the Oxford movement. 2754
Short history of the papacy. 808, 2768
Short history of the Parish and Church of Bush End, Hatfield Broad Oak in the county of Essex. 1790
Short history of the popes. 2862
Short history of the Protestant Episcopal church in Texas. 2974
Short history of the reformation. 3034
Short history of the Southeast Ohio Synod of the Evangelical and Reformed Church. 1545
Short history of the Third Order. 1645
Short history of the western liturgy. 844
Short history of the western liturgy ; an account and some reflections. 844
... Short history of Zionism. 2119, 3896
Short history, Scipio lodge no. 110. free and accepted masons at Aurora, Cayuga county, New York state, 1795-1940. 1668
Short instructions for the Sundays of the year. 1263
Short instructions in the art of singing plain chant. 884, 885
Short instructions or meditations on the gospels for each day in Lent. 2210
Short introduction for the true understanding of the Lord's supper. 2253
Short introduction to Franciscan literature. 1646
Short introduction to the Gospels. 397
Short introduction to the literature of the Bible. 1798
Short introduction to the Old Testament. 538
Short journal and itinerary journals of George Fox. 1637
Short Koran. 2184
Short lesson talks on the Lord's prayer and the Ten commandments. 2246
Short lessons in divine science. 2409
Short life of Christ. 1966
Short life of Kierkegaard. 2170
Short life of Luther. 2278
Short life of Saint Francis. 1027, 1640
Short life of Stephen Grellet (1773-1855) 1774
Short method with Christian science. 1034
Short missionary plays. 2489
Short out to divine love. 3487
Short pageants for the Sunday school. 2757
Short papers. 3632
Short poems. 536
Short primer for Protestants. 2977
Short questions concerning the Christian doctrine of faith. 3312
Short sermons. 2848
Short sermons by Methodist preachers of Louisville, Kentucky, and Tennessee conferences. 2436
Short sermons for all the Sundays of the year. 863
Short sermons for children. 906
Short sermons for daily life. 3344
Short sermons for low masses for all the Sundays of the year. 863
Short sermons for the children's mass. 865, 908, 3370
Short sermons for the low masses of Sunday. 782
Short sermons for the Sundays of the year. 3343
Short sermons on Catholic doctrine. 3341
Short sermons on Gospel texts. 3338
Short sermons on the Gospels. 3344
Short sermons on the Gospels for every Sunday in the year. 1267
Short stories and lessons of the festivals, fasts, and Saints' days of the Protestant Episcopal Church. 1015
Short stories by Jesus (Dallmann, William) 2024
Short stories in the name of truth. 3716
Short stories on the Bible. 294
Short story combined Gospels and reference harmony supplement. 396
Short story of a long life. 3136
Short story of Jesus. 1968
Short studies in the larger faith. 3751
Short studies of Christ the ideal hero. 1957
Short studies of Old Testament heroes. 595
Short studies of the heroes of the early church. 1184
Short study of the book of Revelation. 463
Short study of the prophecies of Daniel. 509
Short survey of the literature. 2076
Short survey of the literature of Rabbinical and mediaeval Judaism. 2111, 3015
Short survey of the literature of rabinical and mediaeval Judaism. 2076
Short syntax of New Testament Greek. 1770
Short talks on Buddhism. 704
Short talks on Masonry. 1662
Short talks on the practical application of the Bahai revelation. 127
Short-title catalogue. 2244, 2992
Short title check list of conjuring periodicals in English. 1346
Short titles of books relating to or illustrating the history and practice of psalmody in the United States, 1620-1820. 1870
Short treatise on Gregorian accompaniment. 884
Short view of great questions. 3054
Short view of the chronology of the Old Testament, and of the harmony of the four evangelists. 497
Short view of the immorality and profaneness of the English stage. 3605, 3606
Short vindication of The relapse and The provok'd wife. 1309, 3607
Short visits to the blessed sacrament. 854
Shortened arrangement of the Holy Bible. Revised standard version. 132
Shorter atlas of the Bible. 207
Shorter Bible. 200, 275
Shorter Bible for Bible game contestants. 281
Shorter catechism of the Catholic religion. 770
Shorter commentary on Romans. 466
Shorter discipline. 2440
Shorter encyclopadia of Islam. 2566
Shorter Encyclopaedia of Islam. 2566
Shorter Epistles. 367
Shorter lexicon of the Greek New Testament. 1768
Shorter life of Christ. 1966
... The shorter life of D. L. Moody. 2588
Shorter Oxford Bible. 200
Shortest path to heaven. 3117
Should anyone say forever? 1316
Should Christians drink? 3596
Should churches be taxed? 1242
Should preachers play God? 1295
Should the negroes of the Methodist Episcopal church be set apart in a church by themselves? 2460
Should you ever feel quilty? 1777
Shout for joy. 2891
Shout it from the housetops. 2369, 3241
Shouting. 1520, 3199
Shouting in the desert. 159
Shovuos. 3404
Show-down that will rock the world. 51
"Show me" 2928
Show me a miracle. 3125
Show me the way. 3513
Show me the way to go home. 3197
"Show me they face!" 3223
Show me thy glory. 1435
"Show us the Father" 3729
Showdown. 3385
Showdown at Seattle. 1132
Shower of roses upon the missions. 3604
Showers of blessing. 3202, 3463
Showers of blessing from clouds of mercy. 3228
Showers of blessings. 181
Showers upon the grass. 1448
Showing forth of Christ. 1228
Showing ourselves men. 3069
Showings. 1449
Shrine of Our Lady of Martyrs. 117
Shrine of Our Lady of Walsingham. 3790
Shrine of St. Peter and the Vatican excavations. 2826, 3769
Shrine of silence. 2694
Shrine of the Little Flower. 3252
Shrine of the silver dollar. 1372
Shrines of God. 1445
Shrines of Our Lady. 3404
Shrines of Tut-Ankh-Amon. 1502, 3719
Shrines of Tut-Ankh-Amon (The) 1502, 3719
Shrines to Our Lady around the world. 3404
Shroud. 1827
Shroud of Turin. 1826, 1827
Shulammith. 593
Shurangama sutra. 3568
Shut-in cause. 3405
Shva in formal reading. 1797
Siberian seven. 2821
Sibylline oracles. 2740
Sibylline oracles of Egyptian Judaism. 2740
Sibyls and seers. 3405
Sic et non. 3639
Sick call ritual. 840, 1258
Sick man's friend. 3405
Sickle. 1036
Sickness and divine healing according to the Scriptures. 1600
Sickness and healing. 1793
Sickness unto death. 3405, 3411
Siddhanta darsanam of Vyasa. 1816
Siddhartha. 702
Side glimpses from the colonial meeting-house. 2688
Side lights K. of C. as viewed from without. 2179
Side-lights on immortality. 1888
Side lights on Mary Baker Eddy-Glover-Science church trustees controversy. "Next friends" suit. 1495
Side lights on the daily vacation Bible school. 3763
Side-stepping saints. 3281
Side windows. 956
Side windows; or, Lights on Scripture truths. 956
Sidelights on Brethren history. 1236
Sidelights on Christian doctrine. 3646
Sidelights on the Anglo-Saxon church. 1761
Sidelights on the Bible. 199
Sidewalk prayers. 2895
Sidewalk sermons. 2426
Sidonius Apollinaris and his age. 1026, 3407
[Sidur tefilot Yisrael (romanized form)] The Hirsch Siddur. 2110
SIECUS circle. 1854, 3390
Siege Perilous. 201
Sifted but saved. 3200
Sifted gold. 2859
Siftings. 3349
Sighs from hell. 1470
Sight sermons, object lessons on sin, salvation, separation and service. 910
Sight unseen. 2727
Sign. 2876
Sign and symbol of the invisible God. 3266
Sign language of our faith. 920, 921
Sign of a child. 1977
Sign of contradiction. 3223
Sign of Jonah in the theology of the Evangelists and Q. 389, 3407
Sign of Jonas. 2399, 2413, 3710

Sign of The coming. 3321
Sign of the covenant. 3261
Sign of the cross. 2214
Sign of the cross in Madagascar. 2538
...The sign of the cross in the nineteenth
  century. 1389
Sign of the kingdom. 2176
Sign of the seven sins. 3411
Sign of the star. 1112
Sign posts on the Christian way. 3484
Sign, with a looking-glass. 3783
Signal flares. 1068
Signals from the Bible. 244
Signature of all things. 2637
Signature of God. 384, 2071
Significance of ancient religions in relation
  to human evolution and brain
  development. 3133
Significance of Barth's theology. 176
Significance of Jesus. 1953, 2047
Significance of Jesus Christ in the modern
  world. 3444
Significance of Karl Barth. 176
Significance of man. 2320
Significance of personality. 2822
Significance of Portugal. 2545
Significance of St. Sauveur Mission. 3278
"The significance of silence" 1546
Significance of silence, and other sermons.
  2438
Significance of South India. 1235
Significance of Sri Ramakrishna's life and
  message in the present age. 1815, 3020
Significance of the church. 1117
Significance of the cross. 104, 106
Significance of the human nature of Christ
  and the Sacraments for salvation
  according to William Estius. 2009, 3294
... The significance of the mathematical
  element in the philosophy of Plato. 2853
Significance of the message of the
  resurrection for faith in Jesus Christ.
  2054
Significance of the Passion. 2029
Significance of the personality of Christ for
  the minister of to-day. 2059
Significance of the principle of self-sacrifice
  for a Christian social order. 3442
Significance of the Protestant reformation.
  3034
Significando causant. 3262, 3695
Significant issues for the 1970's. 2791
Significant sermons. 656, 3360
Significant women of the Bible. 3840
Significant writings on life and man. 2319
Signor. 3054
Signpost. 797, 3670
Signposts for the future. 793
Signposts of history. 607
Signposts to perfection. 3334
Signs and parables. 392, 2026
Signs and symbols in birds and beasts of
  the Bible. 480
Signs & symbols in Christian art. 920
Signs and symbols of primordial man.
  1661, 3573
Signs and symbols of the sun. 3546
Signs and wonders. 628, 2477
Signs and wonders God wrought in the
  ministry for forty years. 1554
Signs of an apostle. 70
Signs of catechesis. 745, 851
Signs of Christ's coming. 3220, 3320,
  3383
Signs of contradiction. 2571
Signs of God in the world. 1069, 1738
Signs of His coming: dramas—Advent,
  Christmas, Epiphany. 1113
Signs of His coming: dramas & meditations
  for Advent, Christmas, Epiphany. 1113
Signs of hope in a century of despair.
  1064
Signs of hope in the thunder of spring.
  2395
Signs of life. 3265
Signs of love. 3265
Signs of promise. 1059, 3347
Signs of shalom. 3163
Signs of the apostles. 2814
Signs of the judgement, Onomastica sacra,
  and The generations from Adam. 480,
  2156
Signs of the Savior. 422
Signs of the times. 737, 1514, 3182, 3199,
  3350, 3498
Signs of the times and the religious life.
  2570
Signs of the times, past, present, and
  future. 737
Signs of these times. 1063, 3680
Signs of things to come. 2948
Signs of transformation in Christ. 3265
Signs, omens and superstitions. 3567
Sikh gurus and their shrines. 3408
Sikh religion. 3408
Sikh religion, its gurus, sacred writings and
  authors. 3408

Sikh temples in the U.K. & the people
  behind their management. 3600
Sikhism, its ideals and institutions. 3408
Sikhs. 3408
Sikhs in relation to Hindus, Moslems,
  Christians, and Ahmadiyyas. 3408
Sila, son of Congo. 2514
Silence. 189, 3340, 3408, 3750
Silence in heaven. 2571
Silence of God. 1054, 2301
Silence of Jesus. 388, 2024
Silence of Pius XII. 2852
Silence of St. Thomas. 3696
Silent Anchorite in the tabernacle. 2251
Silent billion speak. 2545
Silent church. 2821
Silent churches. 1097
Silent cities, sacred stones: archaeological
  discovery in the land of the Bible. 2760
Silent encounter. 2638
Silent fire. 2641
Silent hour. 3198
Silent life. 2576
Silent music. 2380
Silent Nazarene. 1955
Silent pastor. 3407
Silent path to God. 2067, 2872
Silent pilgrimage to God. 1636
Silent prayer. 2872
Silent pulpit. 3002
Silent rebellion. 2577
Silent revolution. 117
Silent Saturday. 159
Silent spire speaks. 3709
Silent struggle for mid-America. 3255
Silent thousands suddenly speak! 3348
Silent witness. 955, 1013
Silly putty, and other children's sermons.
  908
Siloama, the church of the healing spring.
  1791
Silver and Judaica collection of Mr. and
  Mrs. Michael M. Zagavski. 87
Silver bird. 2731, 2827
Silver chimes in Syria. 2490
Silver City. 1003, 3819
Silver cord. 3502
Silver cord loosed. 2128
Silver crown. 784
Silver cup. 907
Silver feather. 123
Silver in the Psalms. 580
Silver jubilee. 1155
Silver lining. 1353
Silver Saturdays. 2388
Simeon & church order. 3409
Simhat Torah. 3409
Similarities of physical and religious
  knowledge. 3074
Simon Brute and the western adventure.
  698
Simon called Peter. 2824
Simon Peter. 2819, 2824, 2825
Simon Peter's friend. 3549
Simon, son of man. 3133
Simon the cross-bearer. 2031
Simoniacal entry into religious life from
  1000 to 1260. 2583
Simple A B Z's of the second coming.
  3320
Simple book of instruction in the Bible
  stories. 616
Simple cobler of Aggawam in America.
  3194
Simple convalidation of marriage. 2341
Simple gifts. 951, 1389, 3398
Simple gospel. 383, 2425
Simple guide to prayer. 2881
Simple lessons in the school of life. 970
Simple life. 2063, 3409
Simple living. 3409
Simple messages on Romans. 3290
Simple methods in religious instruction.
  806
Simple Psalter & canticles. 2985
Simple rite of the Restored Order of Holy
  Week. 1837
Simple rosary meditations. 3249
Simple salvation. 1559
Simple sermons about Jesus Christ. 162
Simple sermons for a sinful age. 162
Simple sermons for a world in crisis. 162
Simple sermons for funeral services. 1692
Simple sermons for saints and sinners. 162
Simple sermons for special days and
  occasions. 2721
Simple sermons for Sunday evening. 162
Simple sermons for Sunday morning. 162
Simple sermons for the midweek service.
  162
Simple sermons for time and eternity. 162
Simple sermons for times like these. 162
Simple sermons for today's world. 162
Simple sermons for twentieth century
  Christians. 162
Simple sermons from the book of Acts.
  332

Simple sermons from the Gospel of
  Matthew. 444
Simple sermons on conversion and
  commitment. 1557
Simple sermons on evangelistic themes.
  1557
Simple sermons on grace and glory. 162
Simple sermons on heaven, hell, and
  judgment. 1531
Simple sermons on New Testament texts.
  162
Simple sermons on Old Testament texts.
  162, 592
Simple sermons on prayer. 2887
Simple sermons on prophetic themes.
  1531
Simple sermons on salvation and service.
  162
Simple sermons on simple themes. 162
Simple sermons on the Christian life. 993
Simple sermons on the great Christian
  doctrines. 162
Simple sermons on the old-time religion.
  162
Simple sermons on the Ten
  commandments. 1315
Simple spirit. 3398
Simple steps to God. 3486
Simple story of the universe. 3660
Simple studies in Daniel. 1401
Simple studies in Matthew. 2373
Simple studies in the Revelation. 3225
Simple studies in Timothy, Titus, and
  Philemon. 3339
Simple study in theosophy. 3688
Simple survey of the New Testament for
  the layman. 411
Simple talks for Christian workers. 162
Simple talks for special days. 1792, 2389
Simple talks on the Holy Spirit. 1828
Simple talks on the tabernacle. 3579
Simple things of the Christian life. 970
Simple truth. 166
Simple way. 2199
Simple way of love. 3482
Simplicity. 2874, 3409
Simplicity of prayer. 2882
Simplicity of the spirit-filled life. 3409
Simplicity, the heart of prayer. 2874
Simplicity toward Christ. 3409
Simplification of the rubrics. 848
Simplified approach to Milton. 2469
Simplified astrology. 97
Simplified key to the Bible. 218
Simplified lessons in the science of being.
  2409
Simplified New Testament. 353
Simplified New Testament in plain English
  for today's reader. 354
Simplified numerology. 3575
Simplified sermon outlines of Revelation
  and prophetical subjects. 3373
Simplified techniques of counseling. 1373
Simplifying the rubrics of the Roman
  breviary and missal Text of the decree
  'Cum nostra,' with an English version
  and a commentary. 848
Simpson-Paine combination of facts, truths
  and reasons, the great moral way. 2758
Simpson's Bible. 3073
Simulation games for religious education.
  1701
Simulations of God. 1736
Sin. 3410, 3411
Sin against the Holy Ghost. 3414
Sin and atonement. 104
Sin and confession on the eve of the
  Reformation. 2812
Sin and evil, their origin, meaning, cause,
  remedy, doom. 3410
Sin and grace. 1318
Sin and holiness. 1823
Sin and its consequences. 3411, 3412
Sin and its forgiveness. 3411
Sin and judgment in the prophets. 569,
  3413
Sin and Our Saviour. 2213
Sin and penance. 3411
Sin and redemption. 3414
Sin and repentance. 3411
Sin and salvation. 3290, 3295, 3412
Sin and science. 1087, 2709, 3411
Sin and sex. 3388
Sin and the new psychology. 3410
Sin as a problem of today. 3411
Sin; Biblical perspectives. 3411
Sin comes of age. 3411
Sin in the Bible. 3413
Sin in the Orthodox Church. 3413
Sin in the secular age. 3410
Sin, liberty, and law. 948
Sin of Adam and Eye. 3410
Sin of Adam in the writings of Saint
  Thomas Aquinas. 1602, 3693
Sin of being fifty. 2461
Sin of being ordinary. 162
Sin of omission. 974, 3411

Sin of our age. 1281
Sin of sloth. 2203
Sin of the angel. 42
Sin, original and actual. 3411
Sin reconsidered and illustrated. 3410
Sin, salvation, and the spirit. 2234, 3413
Sin, the tell-tale. 3412
Sin, thro' divine interposition, an
  advantage--to the universe. 3353
Sinai and Palestine. 2763
Sinai myth. 1313
Sinai to Cincinnati. 2116, 3822
Since Calvary. 1173
Since Cumorah. 679
Since Eve. 3392
Since Jesus passed by. 3232
Since Mrs Eddy. 1036, 3527
Sincerely, in Him. 3888
Sincerely yours. 1009
Sincerity my guide. 3527
Sindon. 1826
Sinews of love. 851
Sinews of sectarian warfare? 1148
Sinful social structures. 3411
Sing a gentle breeze. 932, 3455
Sing a new song. 1860
Sing and pray and shout hurray! 3857
Sing me a Bible song. 910
Sing of Christmas. 3377
Sing the Lord's song in a strange land.
  1321, 2597
Sing the wondrous story. 1871
Sing to me of heaven. 1872
Sing with spirit and understanding. 1860
Sing with understanding. 1875
Singer in the shadows. 3473, 3859
Singer of six thousand songs. 3802
Singer on the sand. 2491
Singers and songs of the liberal faith. 2220
Singers of Israel. 578
Singers of Judah's hills. 577
Singing and rhyming. 917
Singing black. 2514, 2559
Singing campaign for ten thousand pounds.
  2137
Singing church. 917, 1203, 1875
Singing disciples. 1206
Singing evangelist. 1563
Singing every day. 917
Singing for power. 2771
Singing for the Master. 1202
Singing in God's ear. 885
Singing juniors [and] Singing teen-agers.
  917
Singing pathways. 3310
Singing penguins & puffed-up toads. 900
Singing Pope ; the story of Pope John Paul
  II. 2126, 2861
Singing secret. 2551
Singing shepherd. 2854
Singing the liturgy. 884
Singing through life with God. 1324
Singing with understanding. 1872
Singing years. 1303
Single. 3415
Single adult. 1256
Single adult and the church. 1256
Single adults want to be the church, too.
  1256
Single & human. 3415
Single and satisfied. 3415
"Single blessedness" 3472
Single board for churches. 1200
Single eye. 1594, 3438
Single new humanity. 2495
Single on Sunday. 1256
Single path. 960
Single reality. 2019, 3083
Single thought. 3415
Single woman. 3490
Single young adults in the church. 1259
Singular death of Christ. 104, 2029
Singular life. 3415
Sinism. 2838
Sinister shepherd. 3578
Sinless anger. 3429
... The sinless Christ. 2934
Sinless incarnation. 1893
... The sinner and his Savior. 3291
Sinner and his friends. 3337
Sinner saved. 3295
Sinners anonymous. 1124
Sinner's friend, or The disease of sin, its
  consequences, and the remedy. 3412
Sinner's guide. 1000
Sinner's guide, from the Spanish of the
  Venerable Father Louis of Granada.
  1000
Sinner's justification before God. 2160
Sinners yet saints. 3290
Sins and faults, and other addresses. 3758
Sins and safeguards of society. 3411
Sins of our cities. 3742
Sins of saints. 3411
Sins of the day. 3412
Sins of the just. 2573
Sins of the saints. 3411

Sins that crucified Him. 2216
Sinsinawa Dominicans. 3420
Sion college and library. 2244
Siostra Faustyna, szafarka milosierdzia Bozego. 2186
Sipping saints. 3597
Sir Edwin Landseer Lutyens, 1869-1944. 2303
Sir, I have a problem. 2780
... Sir James Ewing. 1582, 2532
Sir John Edwin Sandys. 3301
Sir Thomas More. 2596
Sir Thomas More's Utopia. 3762
Sir Walter Ralegh. 3019, 3422
Sir William M. Ramsay. 3021
Sirius mystery. 1917
"Sirs, what must I do to be saved?" 3288
Sister Abigail (Abigail Townsend Luffe) 1564, 2271
Sister Aimee. 2310
Sister Anne Katharine Emmerich of the Order of St. Augustine. 1511
Sister apostle. 2572
Sister as campus minister. 2717
Sister as the spiritual educator and teacher of youth. 2582
Sister death. 1415
Sister Helen. 1802, 3419
Sister in America today. 2574
Sister in charge. 1357
Sister Julia (Susan McGroarty) sister of Notre Dame de Namar. 2158
Sister Marie Adeline. 182
Sister Mary Assunta. 2333, 2511
Sister Mary Assunta, the seraphic flower of the Franciscan missionaries of Mary. 1644, 2333
Sister Mary John Berchmans. 2353
Sister Mary Martha Chambon, religious of the Visitation of Holy Mary of Chambery, 1841-1907. 881
Sister Miriam Teresa (1901-1927) 2478
Sister Nivedita of Ramakrishna-Vivekananda. 2712
Sister Ruth's stories for the young. 3847
Sister Saint-Pierre and the work of reparation. 78, 2334
Sister saints. 2609
Sister White, a life of Ellen G. White for primary children. 3811
Sisterhoods and deaconesses at home and abroad. 3416
Sisterhoods and the apostolate. 3196
Sisters. 2574, 3421
Sisters and little saints. 1233
Sisters are asking. 2573
Sisters carry the gospel. 2363, 2556
Sisters for the 21st century. 2573
Sisters for the world. 2574
Sisters' manual of prayer. 840
Sisters of charity, Catholic and Protestant. 3416
Sisters of charity, Catholic and Protestant and The communion of labor. 3416, 3835
Sisters of charity of Nazareth, Kentucky. 3416
Sisters of Charity of New York. 3417
Sisters of Charity of New York, 1809-1959. 3417
Sisters of Maryknoll through troubled waters. 1633, 2363
Sisters of mercy. 3417
Sisters of mercy in the United States, 1843-1928. 3418
Sisters of mercy of Harrisburg. 3418
Sisters of mercy of Maryland, 1855-1930. 3418
.-. Sisters of mercy of Nebraska, 1864-1910. 3418
Sisters of sacred song. 3835
Sisters of St. Francis of the Holy family, Jesus, Mary, and Joseph. 3421
Sisters of St. Joseph of Carondelet. 3419
Sisters of St. Joseph of Philadelphia. 3420
Sisters of Saint Joseph of Rochester. 3419
Sisters of the I.H.M. 3421
Sisters of the Third order of Saint Francis of penance and charity, Tiffin, Ohio, 1869-1942. 3421
Sisters' retreats. 3223
Sisters, Servants of the Immaculate Heart of Mary, 1845-1967. 3421
Sisters want to know. 2573
Sistine Chapel before Michelangelo. 3768
Site selection and development. 1164
Sitting at His feet. 2390
Sittings with Eusapia Palladino. 2766, 3501
Sittings with Eusapia Palladino & other studies. 2766, 3501
Situation ethics. 946
Situation ethics debate. 1629, 3421
Situation of the Catholic Church in Czechoslovakia. 816
Situation of the church and religious practices in occupied Lithuania. 2232

Siva samhita. 3867
Siva, the erotic ascetic. 3421
Six altars. 3271
Six and God. 926
... Six collations of New Testament manuscripts. 315
Six creative days. 1380
Six days and Sunday. 2436
Six days of creation. 205
Six days of creation in the light of modern science. 1379
Six days of the week. 2228
Six decades of service, 1880-1940. 2458
Six discourses on the miracles of Our Saviour and defences of his discourses. 2018
Six dreams and a golden collar. 2134
Six ecumenical surveys. 3850
Six essays on Erasmus and a translation of Erasmus' letter to Carondelet, 1523. 1527
Six great missionaries of the sixteenth and seventeenth centuries. 2482
600 doctrinal illustrations. 1842
"Six hundred years" 2243
Six incursions (by a predatory pew) into some theologic fastenesses. 1723
Six interviews with Robert G. Ingersoll. 1654, 3582
Six kings of the American pulpit. 2910
Six Korean women. 3400
Six lectures delivered at the Michigan Christian teachers' institute, held at Grand Rapids, Mich., October 1 and 2, 1914. 3591
Six lectures on pastoral theology. 3675
Six lectures on revivals of religion, delivered in the Universalist church in Portland, 1834. 1569
Six lectures on the ante-Nicene fathers. 1616, 1617
Six lectures on theology and nature. 3496
Six lessons on the silence. 2694
Six madrigals. 917
Six makers of English religion. 1758
Six makers of English religion, 1500-1700. 1758
Six marks of a Christian. 974
Six mighty men. 2953
Six-minute story talks for children. 906
Six mission of Texas. 2553
Six missionaries in Africa. 2483
Six missions of Texas. 2553
Six months in a convent. 888
Six months in a convent, and supplement. 1582, 3031
Six moral tales. 2594
Six nights in the Garden of Gethsemane. 1368
Six o'clock saints. 3285
Six orations of Paul. 2796
Six other days. 2427
Six perspectives on new religions. 1393
Six pillars. 1709
Six point record system and its use. 3564
... Six reformers. 3050
Six saints for parents. 3280
Six secular philosophers. 2835
Six sermons. 3345, 3359
Six sermons on devotion to the Sacred heart. 3269
Six sermons upon faith. 1594
Six sixty six and the kingdom of Christ. 606
Six studies on the Day. 3547
Six systems of Indian philosophy. 2840
Six theosaphic points and other writings. 2637
Six theosophic points. 2640
6,000 classic sermon illustrations. 1840
6000 sermon illustrations. 1840
6,000 windows for sermons. 1840
6000 years of the Bible. 291
Six weeks in old France. 3705
Six-year-teacher. 3550
Six-year-teacher, book four. 3550
Six-year-teacher, book three. 3550
Six years in Hammock land. 2290
Six years in the Transvaal. 2557
Six years with God. 2467, 2817
Sixteen cowries. 3868
Sixteen days on the church calendar. 2722
Sixteen encyclicals of His Holiness Pope Pius XI, 1926-1937. 852
Sixteen encyclicals of His Holiness Pope Pius xi, 1926-1937. 2670
1600 squibs and quips for church bulletins and bulletin boards. 1163
16 methods of group Bible study. 640, 1170
16 Papal documents on the Rosary. 2877
Sixteen Quaker leaders speak. 1678
Sixteen saviours or one? 60, 1756
1665-1965: three hundred years of missionary work among the Sioux Indians. 1399

1628-1928. Collegiate Reformed Protestant Dutch Church of the City of New York. 3048
Sixteen years' preaching. 2903
Sixteen years' preaching and procedure, at Wareham, Ms. 2903
Sixth and seventh books of Moses. 2315, 2724
Sixth and seventh books of Moses, that is. 2315
Sixth Baptist world congress, Atlanta, Georgia, U.S.A., July 22-28, 1939. 169
Sixth jar. 2005
Sixth Patriarch's Dharma jewel platform sutra, with the commentary of Tripitaka Master Hua [translated from the Chinese by the Buddhist Text Translation Society]. 3893
... The sixth sense, prayer. 2870
Sixth trumpeter. 2122
Sixties: radical change in American religion. 3747
Sixty days in oriental waters. 1323
Sixty-five ways to give evangelistic invitations. 1572
Sixty-five years in the pulpit. 1272
Sixty-one worship talks for children, with suggested objects for illustration. 909
Sixty-one years of itinerant Christian life in church and state. 1930
Sixty saints for boys. 3285
Sixty saints for girls. 3285
Sixty sermons preached upon several occasions. 3366
Sixty shining halos. 3285
... Sixty story sermons for boys and girls. 909
Sixty-two sermons. 3364
Sixty years, and other discourses, with reminiscences. 3287
Sixty years gleanings from life's harvest. 119
Sixty years in a school-room. 120
Sixty years in the pulpit. 1272, 2475
Sixty years in the pulpit; or, Compound interest in religion; covering a life in the ministry of sixty years and published only for the good it may do. 2475
Sixty years of action, 1874-1934. 3833
Sixty years of home missions in the Presbyterian Synod of North Carolina. 2928
Sixty years with Plymouth church. 693
Sixty years with the Bible. 231
Sixty years with the Bible: a record of experience. 231
Sixty-eight Bible quizzes. 612
66 more Modern parables for young folks. 908
63 popular parables for young folks. 909
69 ways to start a study group and keep it growing. 1170
Size of life. 763
Skeleton outline for Bible study. 635
Skeptic discovers Mormonism. 2599, 2605
Skeptic in the Holy Land. 2762
Skeptical era in modern history. 3422
Skepticism. 2690
Skepticism and divine revelation. 3422
Skepticism and moral principles. 1534
Skeptic's defense against all Christian or other priests. 1655
Skeptic's quest. 3100
Skeptic's search for God. 3103
Sketch and an appreciation of Moncure Daniel Conway. 1367
Sketch of Catholicity in Lawrence and vicinity. 821
... Sketch of Jewish history. 2089
Sketch of John Blackwell. 669
Sketch of Mother Hutcheson's life. 1858
Sketch of Rev. John Hersey, minister of the gospel, of the M. E. Church. 1808
Sketch of Rev. Philip Gatch. 1703
... Sketch of the Catholic church in Louisiana. 822
Sketch of the Christian experience. 972
Sketch of the early life of Joseph Hardy Nessima. 2684
Sketch of the history of Judaism and Christianity in the light of modern research and criticism. 1172
Sketch of the history of the parish of the Advent in the city of Boston. 684
Sketch of the late Rt. Rev. Phillips Brooks, D.D. 694
Sketch of the life and character of Albert Arnold Bennett, D. D. 155, 190
Sketch of the life and character of the Rev. Alexander Donaldson, D.D., pastor of the Eldersridge and West Lebanon Presbyterian churches and founder and principal of Eldersridge academy, Pa. 1476

Sketch of the life and character of Thomas Cooke Paul, son of D'Arcy Paul, of Petersburg, Va. 2805
Sketch of the life and ministry of the Rev. C. H. Spurgeon. 3523
Sketch of the life and times of the Rev. Sydney Smith. 3431
Sketch of the life and writings of the Rev. Micaial Towgood. 3705
Sketch of the life, character, and writings of the Rev. James Y. M'Ginnes, of Shade Gap, Pa. 2308, 2931
Sketch of the life of elder Benj. Putnam, embracing his Christian experience. 973
Sketch of the life of Rev. Henry Williams, D.D. 3817
Sketch of the life of Rev. John Collins. 1309
Sketch of the life of Rev. Joseph Hardy Neesima L. D., president of Doshisha university, Kyoto. 1406
Sketch of the life of Rev. Joseph Hardy Neesima, LL.D., president of Doshisha university, Kyoto. 2679
Sketch of the lives and missionary work of Rev. Cephas Bennett and his wife Stella Kneeland Bennett. 190
Sketch of the Presbyterian and other churches in Princeton and vicinity. 2912
Sketchbook of Biblical theology. 652
Sketches & incidents. 1930
Sketches eloquent preachers. 927
Sketches for sermons, chiefly on the Gospels. 3375
Sketches for sermons, for the Sundays and holydays of the year. 1268
... Sketches for the exercises of an eight day's retreat. 2389
Sketches from church history. 1175
Sketches from church history for Mennonite schools. 1180
Sketches from the Karen hills. 2164
... Sketches from the life of Christ and the experience of the Christian church. 2019, 3380
Sketches from the life of Jesus. 1973
Sketches of Bible child life. 898
Sketches of Christ from a Chinese brush. 1958
Sketches of church history. 1180
Sketches of church life in colonial Connecticut. 1222
Sketches of Congregationalism in Rhode Island. 2984
Sketches of eloquent preachers. 927
Sketches of funeral sermons. 1693
Sketches of Jewish life in the first century. 2006
Sketches of Kafir life. 2162
Sketches of Moravian missions. 33, 2594
Sketches of New England divines. 1294
Sketches of our mountain pioneers. 1462
... Sketches of our pioneers. 1462
Sketches of revival sermons. 3373
Sketches of "Shakers and Shakerism." 3394
Sketches of some historic churches of greater Boston. 1483
Sketches of Tennessee's pioneer Baptist preachers. 170
Sketches of the Christian life and public labors of William Miller. 2467
Sketches of the churches and pastors in Hampden county, Mass. 1294
Sketches of the early Catholic missions of Kentucky. 820, 821, 2167
Sketches of the establishment of the church in New England. 823
Sketches of the founders of the Methodist Protestant Church, and its bibliography. 2459
Sketches of the life and character of the Rev. Lemuel Haynes. 1792
Sketches of the life and death of Isabella Sarah Wilbur. 3815
Sketches of the life and labors of James Quinn. 3013
Sketches of the life and travels of Rev. Thomas Ware. 1930
Sketches of the life of the late, Rev. Samuel Hopkins, D.D. 729
Sketches of the life of the Very Rev. Felix de Andreis. 40
Sketches of the life, times, and character of the Rt. Rev. Benedict Joseph Flaget, first bishop of Louisville. 1628
Sketches of the missions of the American board. 31
Sketches of the philosophy of apparitions. 77
Sketches of the pioneers of Methodism in North Carolina and Virginia. 2423
Sketches of the religious experience and labors of a layman. 1552, 3191
Sketches of the three earliest Roman Catholic priests in Boston. 685, 814
Sketches of the Virginia conference. 2455

Sketches of the Waldenses. 3788
Sketches of the women of Christendom. 3839
Sketches of Wesleyan preachers. 2428
Sketches of Western Methodism. 2450, 2453
Sketches on life and times of the Rev. Stephen Bliss, A. M. 672
Sketching & telling stories to children. 940
Skid row life line. 1756
Skid Row stopgap. 2402
Skilful means. 3761
Skilled labor for the Master. 3672
Skipper of the Sentinel. 2128
Sky-god, An-Anu. 55
Sky-god, An-Anu manuscript. 55
Sky is God's own sonnet. 3702
Sky is red. 1061, 2820
Sky lines. 3506
Sky pilot of Alaska. 2500, 3846
Sky-religion in Egypt. 1502
Sky waves. 1612
Sky waves; the incredible Far East Broadcasting Company story. 1612, 3018
Skylark ways. 3173
Skyline sketch of Emanuel Swedenborg's "True Christian religion." 2692
Skyline synod. 2917
Skyward. 1440
Slander and its victims. 3423
Slant manifesto: Catholics and the left. 1087
Slanted to ladies. 2385
Slava Bohu. 1482
Slave boy who became governor. 2134
Slave of the negroes. 1286
Slave religion. 17
Slave who saved the city. 3581
Slave who saved the city, and other Hassidic tales. 3581
Slaveholding not sinful. 3424
Slavery and Catholicism. 3423
Slavery and Methodism. 2451, 3423
Slavery and the church. 3424
Slavery and the churches in early America, 1619-1819. 3423
Slavery and the emigration of North Carolina Friends. 1687, 3425
Slavery examined in the light of the Bible. 3424
Slavery ordained of God. 3425
Slavery, segregation, and Scripture. 3017
Slayers of Moses. 3015
Slayers of superstition. 1420
Sleep as the great opportunity. 2696
Sleep tight book. 900
Sleep walkers. 3084
Sleeping giant. 918, 1059, 1574
Sleepwalkers. 99
Slide and film strip evaluations for use in Christian churches around the world. 2627
Slim for Him. 3031
Sling and the swallow. 621
Slings and sandals. 2006
Slovak Franciscans in America. 1649
Slovak Lutheran liturgy: past and present. 1878, 2295
Slovene medieval history. 2546
Slovenian chapel dedication, Washington, D.C., August 15, 1971. 3797
Slovenian Chapel in the National Shrine of the Immaculate Conception, Washington, D.C. 3797
Slow and certain light. 983
Slow dawning. 796
Slow of heart. 2212

Small blessings. 2396
Small catechism. 748
Small catechism, in contemporary English. 2284
Small catechism with explanation. 2284
Small child's Bible. 619
Small church. 1157
Small church and Christian education. 3146
Small church at work for children. 3554
Small church schools bulletin. 2965
Small church—valid, vital, victorious. 3426
Small churches are beautiful. 3426
Small churches are the right size. 3426
Small city secretaries' conference report. Blue Ridge, N.C., May 31 to June 2, 1924. 3872
Small end of great problems. 3479, 3723
Small group leader's handbook. 1170
Small group ministry in the contemporary church. 1169
Small groups. 1169, 1170
Small liturgical dictionary. 2239
Small needle of Dr. Large. 2788
Small prayers for small children about big and little things. 898

Small rain. 602
Small rural parish. 2789
Small sanctuary. 2108
Small-scale sacred concertato in the early seventeenth century. 1208
Small sects in America. 3325
...The small Sunday school. 3557
Small talk. 2390
Small talks, by the Rev. Ronald Selby Wright, S.C.F. 1235
Small talks for small people. 907
Small town and country church. 3254
Small-town boy. 2131
Small town church. 3426
Small-town Jewry tell their story. 2104, 2105
Small town man. 1959
Small voice crying in the wilderness. 1941
Small windows on a big world. 2389
Small woman. 121
Small woman of the Inn of the Sixth Happiness. 121
Small wonders. 2390
Smaller Scripture history in three parts. 297
... The smaller Sunday school makes good. 3557
Smile! 907
Smile at your own risk. 1946
Smile! Jesus is Lord. 907
Smiling Maria: Blessed Maria de Mattias. 2374
Smith Agama collection. 2331, 2766
Smith and the church. 1162
Smith Wigglesworth. 3815
Smith Wigglesworth remembered. 1575, 3815
Smith's Bible dictionary. 246
Smith's comprehensive dictionary of the Bible. 246
Smith's epitome of the Bible. 281
Smith's scrap book of the Bible. 252
Smith's Story of the Mennonites. 2406
Smitten household. 1353
Smoke on the mountain. 1313
Smokeless fire. 1815
Smoking furnace and the burning lamp. 3703
Smouldering fire. 1830
Smug theology. 1062
Snake ceremonials at Walpi. 3432
Snake dance of the Hopi Indians. 1846
Snake dance of the Moquis of Arizona. 1846
Snake handlers: God-fearers? 3432
Snappy schemes of church finance. 1168
Snapshots. 1547
Snapshots from the Gospels. 3352
Snare of the fowler. 693, 1524, 3346
Snatched away! 608, 3021
Snow-shoe itinerant. 2451
Snowden-Douglas Sunday school lessons. 1916
Snowden-Douglass Sunday school lessons. 1916
Snowden's nine months course in the life of Christ. 1954
Snowden's Sunday school lessons. 1916
So beautiful my heritage. 2151
So-called Egyptian church order and derived documents. 1816
So-called historical Jesus and the historic, Biblical Christ. 406, 2008
So down to prayers. 1468
So easy to love. 1001
"So even in old age ..." 1257
So great a cause! 1232, 2948
So great a cloud of witnesses. 3726
So great a good. 2957
So great a lover. 2271
So great salvation. 1556, 3288, 3291
So great the journey. 932, 3402
So help me God. 2892, 2937
So help me God: religion and the Presidency, Wilson to Nixon. 2937
So high the price. 1802
"So live" 2831
So many pathways. 1588
So many people. 2547
So many versions? 270
So much for so many. 2332
So much, so soon. 692
So near is God. 3486
So now He speaks again. 2435
So now you are a Christian. 1010
So Pilate washed his hands. 2847
So restless, so lonely. 1385
So send I you. 1153, 2494
... so shall ye reap. 2607
So shines the lamp. 2260
So short a day. 2335, 3420
So strange my path. 2117, 2952
So sure of tomorrow. 2498
So surely anchored. 3418
So that's how we got the Bible. 270
So that's what missions is all about. 2492
"So this is Africa" 2542

So this is missions! 2551
So tomorrow. 3099
So we believe, so we pray. 3641
So, what's the difference? 1079
So what's there to live for? 3349, 3387
So who's afraid of birthdays. 18
So you think you've got problems. 1025
So you want a mountain. 1560
So you want to be a leader! 953
So you want to be popular. 3884
So you want to preach. 2787
"So you want to select a church site" 1241
So you work with junior highs. 3167
So you work with kindergartners. 3174
So you work with nursery children. 3174
So you work with primaries. 3171
So you work with senior high youth. 3175
So you work with young adults. 1259
So young a queen. 1931
So young to be a rabbi. 2142
So your wife came home speaking in tongues? 690, 1717
So you're a teenage girl. 3877
So you're a woman. 3843
So you're going on a mission! 2618
So you're going on the air. 3018
So you're going to college. 1308
So you're having an adolescent. 940
So you're in a junior choir. 916
So ... you're in the service. 3456
So you're not a preacher! 2911
So you're only human. 1447
So you're the pastor's wife. 1303
So you're the secretary of the Sabbath school. 3385
Soaring, an odyssey of the soul. 1695
Sober remarks on a book lately reprinted at Boston, entitled, A modest proof of the order and government settled by Christ and His apostles in the church. 890, 1523
Sobornost. 1322
Social action and world service. 3453
Social action, Jesus style. 2814
Social action vs. evangelism. 2480
Social activities for men and boys. 3870
Social adjustment in Methodism. 2422, 2443
Social adjustment through the Young men's Christian associations. 3434
Social advance. 1135, 3447
Social and philosophical studies. 1723
Social and political forces in the English reformation. 3039
Social and religious heretics in five centuries. 3322
Social and religious history of the Jews. 2087
Social and religious problems of young people. 3889
Social application of religion. 3446
Social aspects of Christianity. 3449, 3807
Social aspects of Christianity, and other essays. 3434
Social aspects of early Christianity. 3451
Social aspects of foreign missions. 2519
Social aspects of religious institutions. 3442
Social aspects of the Christian faith contained in Mater et magistra and Pacem in terris. 3449
Social aspects of the cross. 943
Social background of the Old Testament. 3439
Social basis of religion. 3445
Social basis of the German Reformation. 2276, 3040
Social Catholic movement in England, 1920-1955. 1135
Social Catholic movement in Great Britain. 818, 2328
Social change in Islam. 1922
Social Christianity. 3447, 3453
Social Christianity in the new era. 3447
Social Christianity in the Orient. 2530
Social class in American Protestantism. 2979
Social classes in a republic. 3434
Social commitment. 1136
Social conscience of a Catholic. 1136
Social conscience of the evangelical. 3447
Social context of religiosity. 3214
Social context to the religious crisis of the third century A.D. 3088
Social creed of the churches. 3447
Social creed of the Methodist Church. 1139
Social creed of the Methodist Church, a living document. 1139
Social criticism in popular religious literature of the sixteenth century. 1760
Social destiny of man. 1636
Social development of English Quakerism, 1655-1755. 1685
Social discipline in the Christian community, past, present and future. 3452

Social doctrine in action. 3258
Social doctrine of the Catholic Church. 3449
Social doctrines of the Catholic church. 3450
Social duties from the Christian point of view. 3443
Social effects of Catholic education. 805
Social emphasis in religious education. 3153
Social engineer. 3442
Social ethics. 3433
Social ethics among Southern Baptists, 1917-1969. 1135, 3465
Social ethics, an introduction to the nature and ethics of the state. 3433
Social evangelism. 1554
Social evils of the non-Christian world. 3434
Social evolution. 3439
Social evolution of religion. 3086
Social force of Christian missions. 1134
Social function of the church. 3441
...The social function of religious belief. 3086
Social gospel. 3433, 3444
Social gospel and personal religion. 3433
Social gospel and the Bible. 3442
Social gospel and the Christian cultus. 3444
Social gospel and the new era. 3440
Social Gospel in America. 3433
Social Gospel in America, 1870-1920. 3433
Social gospel of Walter Rauschenbusch and its relation to religious education. 3025, 3440
Social gospel re-examined. 3443
Social hints for young Christians. 2930
Social history of Lutheranism in the Southeastern states, 1860-1886. 2292
Social history of the Disciples of Christ. 1464
Social history of the Philadelphia Baptist association. 159
Social history of the Reformation. 1775, 3037
Social hours with Friends. 1676
Social humanism of Calvin. 727
Social hymn and tune book. 2916
Social hymn book. 2916
Social ideals of a free church. 3442
Social ideals of St. Francis, eight lessons in applied Christianity. 1643, 1649
Social ideals of the Lord's prayer. 2248
Social ideas of religious leaders, 1660-1688. 1760
Social ideas of the northern evangelists. 1575
Social ideas of the northern evangelists, 1826-1860. 1576
Social impact of new religious movements. 3138
Social imperative. 3447
... The social implications of the Oxford movement. 2754
... The social institutions and ideals of the Bible. 2112
Social integration and social stability in a colonial Spanish American city, Caracas, 1595-1627. 738
Social intelligence. 3433
Social issues for young pleple. 3453
Social justice. 794, 2079, 2160, 3451
Social justice & church authority. 667, 2270
Social justice and the Latin churches. 3434
Social justice in Islam. 3454
Social law in the spiritual world. 2131, 2998
Social life among the Assyrians and Babylonians. 93
... The social life of the Hebrews. 2121
Social manifesto of Jesus. 2247
Social meaning of modern religious movements in England. 1758
Social meanings of religion. 3088
Social meanings of religious experiences. 3433
Social message of Jesus. 2060, 2063, 2064, 3439, 3445
Social message of Our Lord. 3440
Social message of the apostle Paul. 3439
Social message of the book of Revelation. 453
Social message of the early church fathers. 3451
Social message of the gospels. 3433
Social message of the modern pulpit. 3440
Social message of the New Testament. 3439
Social messages. 3440
Social ministry. 3447
Social mission of charity. 771
Social mission of the church. 3435

TITLE INDEX SOME FUNDAMENTAL GOSPEL

Social opportunity of the churchman. 3442
Social order. 3451, 3454
Social organization in parishes. 1251
Social origins of Christianity. 743, 3451
... The social philosophy of Christian education. 3451
Social, political, and religious thought of Alfred Rosenberg. 3249
Social principles and economic life. 1136
Social principles of Jesus. 2065, 3445
Social principles of the gospel. 3450
Social problem. 3450
Social problems. 3442
Social progress and Christian ideals. 3443
Social psychology of religion. 2996
Social psychology of religious experience. 2997
...Social rebuilders. 3447
Social recreation primer. 1167
Social reform & the church. 1133, 3441
Social reform and welfare work; 1883-1953. 3293
Social reformers in urban China. 3874
Social regeneration the work of Christianity. 3446
Social relations in the urban parish. 1278
Social relationships in the light of Christianity. 3441
... Social religion. 3444
Social responsibility & investments. 1168
Social salvage. 3292
Social salvation. 3440, 3442
Social sciences in Catholic college programs. 3435
Social scientific studies of religion. 3089
Social service at the General convention of 1913. 2958
Social service message. 3444
Social service series. 3440
Social service through the parish. 3435
Social setting of Pauline Christianity. 346, 3451
Social solutions in the light of Christian ethics. 3443
Social sources of church unity. 1046
Social sources of denominationalism. 3444, 3445, 3446
Social spirit of Christianity. 3444
Social statements of the United Lutheran Church in America 1918-1962. 1138
Social structure of Islam. 3454
Social studies. 3453
Social substance of religion. 3100
... The social survey in town and country areas. 1274
Social task of Christianity. 3440
Social teaching of Jesus. 3439
Social teaching of Pope John XXIII. 1137, 2123
Social teaching of the Bible. 3439
Social teaching of the Christian churches. 1138, 3452
Social teaching of the church. 3443, 3449
Social teachings of Moses and of representative prophets. 3439
Social teachings of the church. 1137
Social teachings of the prophets and Jesus. 3439
Social teachings of Wilhelm Emmanuel Von Ketteler. 1137, 2168
Social theory of religious education. 934, 3148
Social thought and action. 3450
... The social thought of American Catholics, 1634-1829. 1136
... The social thought of French Canada as reflected in the Semaine sociale. 3434
Social thought of John Paul II. 2126, 3451
Social thought of John XXIII. 853
Social thought of Saint Bonaventure. 675, 3449
Social thought of the World Council of Churches. 3849
Social triumph of the ancient church. 3451
Social views of Dwight L. Moody and their relation to the workingman of 1860-1900. 2587, 3070
Social wellsprings. 3450
Social work and Jewish values. 3454
Social work in the churches. 3443
Social work of Christian missions. 2495
Social work of the London churches. 3452
Social work of the Sisters of the Good Shepherd. 3419
Socialism from the Christian standpoint. 3435
Socialism in theological perspective. 3436, 3700
Socialist, anti-Semite, and Jew. 54, 3469
Socialist humanism. 1854
Sociality of Christ and humanity. 676
Socialization of the New England clergy. 2687
Socialization of the New England clergy, 1800 to 1860. 2687
Socialized church. 3447
Societas Christi. 70, 3223
Society and religion in early Ottoman Egypt. 3394, 3544
Society and sanity. 3449
Society and the sacred. 3069
Society for Psychical Research report on the Theosophical Society. 3682, 3687
Society for the Propagation of the Faith: its foundation, organization, and success (1822-1922) 3437
Society in rebellion. 3295
Society kit. 3876
Society: natural and divine. 1117
Society of Friends. 1674
Society of Friends in the nineteenth century. 1685
Society of Friends vindicated. 1676
Society of life. 3438
Society of Mary in Texas. 2334
Society of the Muslim Brothers. 1933
Society of the Sacred Heart ; history of a spirit 1800-1975. 3438
Society ordained by God. 2346
Socinianism in Poland. 3439
Socio-economic analysis of Southern Baptist state-wide church periodicals. 159
Socio-cultural impact of Islam on India. 1925
Sociological analysis of Roman Catholicism. 756
Sociological approach to religion. 3087
Sociological interpretation of religion. 3087
Sociological progress in mission lands. 2518
Sociological studies of an occupation. 1296
Sociological study of religion. 3087
Sociological study of the Bible. 291
Sociology. 3450, 3451
Sociology and pastoral care. 2789
Sociology and religion. 3088
Sociology and the study of religion. 3086
Sociology and theology, alliance and conflict. 3448
Sociology looks at religion. 3087
Sociology of early Palestinian Christianity. 3451
Sociology of education. 1498
Sociology of English religion. 1764
Sociology of hope. 1845
Sociology of Protestantism. 3444
Sociology of religion. 3058, 3064, 3086, 3087, 3088
Sociology of religion: selected readings. 3088
Sociology of religious belonging. 3085
Sociology of secularisation. 3327
Sociology of the Bible. 2112
Sociology of the paranormal. 2993
Sociology of the parish. 2774
Sociology, theology, and conflict. 3087
Socio-theology of letting go. 3623
Socrates and the soul of man. 3454
Socratic exposition of Genesis. 524
Sod-busters. 1575
Sodalist's hymnal. 813
Sodalist's Imitation of Christ. 1885
Sodalist's vade mecum. 1869
Sodality manual. 843
Sodality movement in the United States. 3454
Sodality of Our Lady. 3454
Soderblom, ecumenical pioneer. 3455
Soeur Eugenie. 3416
Soft showers. 2386
Soft tolls the bell. 1663
Soil factory. 2676
Sojourner in two worlds. 3789
Sojourner Truth; God's faithful pilgrim. 3717
Sojourners by the wayside. 3054
Soka Gakkai, builders of the third civilization. 3455
Soka Gakkai; Japan's militant Buddhists. 3455
Solace for bereaved parents. 897
Solace for the sorrowing, being a series of funeral meditations for the comfort of the bereaved. 1350
"Solace in weeping" 1351
Soldier and a man. 3533
Soldier-bishop, Ellison Capers. 737
Soldier died twice. 3317
Soldier for Jesus. 41, 2483
Soldier of the church. 2268
Soldier of the cross. 2620, 2800
Soldier of the spirit. 1635
Soldier priest talks to youth. 3880
Soldier, sage, saint. 3481
Soldiering for Christ in Chile. 2507
Soldiers also asked. 3456
Soldiers and sailors manual. 3455
Soldiers' and sailors' prayer book. 3456
Soldiers and servants. 1329
Soldier's Bible and their life insurance. 248
Soldier's confidences with God. 3456
Soldier's hymn-book. 3455
Soldiers in overalls. 3872
Soldiers of compassion. 1347, 2806
Soldiers of the church. 3050
Soldiers of the cross. 823, 2548, 3356, 3742
Soldiers of the cross; notes on the ecclesiastical history of New Mexico, Arizona, and Colorado. [1st ed.]. 823
Soldier's pocket-book. 3456
Soldiers record of the town of St Johnsbury, Vermont, in the war of the rebellion, 1861-5. 3275
Soldiers saw Resl. 2685, 3532
Soldier's text-book. 3456
Soldier's theology. 1096
Soldiers without swords. 3293
Sole sufficiency of Jesus Christ. 341
Sole treading. 2529
Solemn appeal to the church. 1821, 2701
Solemn dedication [of the] Church of the Presentation of the Blessed Virgin Mary, Saturday, November 11, 1961. 2937
Solemn dedication of the new St. Ferdinand Church and the fortieth anniversary of Rt. Rev. Msgr. Matthew A. Cunning, pastor; 1919-1959. 734, 3274
Solemn questions addressed to Hebrews of culture. 2117
Solemn warning against free-masonry. 53
Solemn warning aginst free-masonry. 53
Solemn warnings of the dead. 1357
... Solemnities of the dedication and opening of the Catholic university of America. 870
Soli Deo gloria. 335
Solid gold crucifix. 1000
Solid shot. 2231
Solider of the spirit. 1635
Solidier priest talks to youth. 3880
Soliloquies of St. Augustine. 113
Solioquy of a hermit. 1807
Solitary explorer. 2413, 3710
Solitary journey: Buddhist mystical reflections. 706
Solitary life. 1807
Solitary self. 39
Solitude in the thought of Thomas Merton. 2412, 3456
Solitude sweetened. 1450, 2392, 3456
Solo. 3415
... Solo settings for poems. 1037
... Solomon. 3457
Solomon and Sheba. 3457
Solomon and Solomonic literature. 1798, 3457
Solomon Goldman. 1744, 3897
Solomon Islands Christianity. 2547
Solomon on sex. 593, 3392
Solomon Schechter. 3306
Solomon Stoddard. 3532
Solomon the magnificent. 3457
Solomon the Wise. 3457
Solomon to the Exile. 556
Solomon Zeitlin's Studies in the early history of Judaism. 2097, 2148
Solomon's song. 594
Solomon's sword. 1418
Solomon's temple and capitol, ark of the flood and tabernacle. 1944, 2711
Solomon's temple in the light of other Oriental temples. 3457
Solomon's temple spiritualiz'd. 3457
Solomon's temple spiritualized. 3457
Solon & Croesus, and other Greek essays. 1282
Solution of life. 2226
Solution of present day problems. 2115
Solution of the great problem. 62
Solution to crisis-America. 3745
Solved; or, The Sunday evening problem. 3548
Solving church school problems. 3552, 3557
Solving life's problems. 167, 1010
Solving the country church problem. 3253
Soma and the fly-agaric. 695, 3457
Soma: divine mushroom of immortality. 3457
Soma in biblical theology. 376, 2326
Some accont of the persecutions and sufferings of the people called Quakers in seventeenth century exemplified in the memoirs of the life of John Robets. 1665, 3241
Some account of Gothic architecture in Spain. 1161
Some account of the charitable corporation, lately erected, for the relief of the widows and children of clergymen, in the communion of the Church of England in America. 1369
Some account of the church in the apostolic age. 1194
Some account of the conduct of the Religious Society of Friends towards the Indian tribes. 1686, 1901
Some account of the convincement, and religious progress, of John Spalding, late of Reading. 1675, 3469
Some account of the life and religious exercises of Mary Neale, formerly Mary Peisley. 2678
Some account of the penitential discipline of the early church in the first four centuries. 2812
Some account of the vampires of Onset, past and present. 3515
Some actors in Our Lord's passion. 2034, 2973
Some alternatives to Jesus Christ. 3117
Some American lectures. 3689
Some American Protestant constributions to the welfare of African countries in 1963. 2500
Some answered questions. 126, 129
Some answers to current criticism of the minor seminary. 3614
Some aspects of Christian belief. 3652
Some aspects of contemporary Greek orthodox thought. 2746
Some aspects of Hittite religion. 1820
... Some aspects of international Christianity. 3793
Some aspects of rabbinic theology. 2116
Some aspects of religion and politics in India during the thirteenth century. 3088
Some aspects of religious liberty of nationals in the Near East. 3194
Some aspects of the conflict between science & religion. 3079
Some aspects of the history of the ecumenical patriarchate of Constantinople in the seventeenth and eighteenth centuries. 1354
Some aspects of the life of Jesus from the psychological and psycho-analytic point of view. 2050
Some assurances of immortality. 1886
Some authentic acts of the early martyrs. 2351
Some boast of Chariots. 1095
Some books in the Louisville free public library of interest to Catholic readers. 869
Some brief remarks upon sundry important subjects. 1675
Some burning questions. 2116
Some burning questions pertaining to the Messiahship of Jesus. 2414
Some by-products of missions. 2520
Some California Catholic reminiscences for the United States Bicentennial. 872
Some chapters of my life story. 2620
Some chapters on Judaism. 2114
Some Christian convictions. 1305, 3666
Some Christian festivals. 1613
Some Christian science churches. 1036
Some cognitive elements of religious experience. 3191
Some confessions of an average man. 2226
Some considerations relating to the present state of the Christian religion. 1047, 3701
Some defects in English religion. 1226
Some deficiencies in the canon law of the American Episcopal Church, and related matters. 2966
Some discourses, sermons, and remains. 1226, 3363
Some dogmas of religion. 1473
Some "do's" and "don'ts" for the Christian. 956
Some early Alabama churches (established before 1870) 21
Some early Baha'is of the West. 129
Some early epitaphs in Georgia. 1525
Some eighteenth century churchmen. 1503
Some elements of the religious teaching of Jesus, according to the Synoptic Gospels. 2064
Some experiments in living. 3440
... Some exponents of mystical religion. 2639
Some features of the faith. 3665
Some few remarks upon a scandalous book against the government and ministry of New England. 724, 1294
Some forerunners of St. Francis of Assisi. 1185
Some form of peace. 1677
Some foundation truths of the Christian faith. 951, 3663
Some fundamental gospel truths in modern light. 3339

Some gall—and other reflections on life. 1445
Some glimpses of occultism. 2203
Some golden daybreak. 3321
Some gospel scenes and characters. 397
Some gospel-truths opened ; A vindication of some gospel-truths opened ; A few sighs from hell. 58, 2036
Some grapes from Eshcol. 3299
Some graver subject. 2467, 2470
Some great Christian Jews. 2082
Some great churches in France. 752
... Some great leaders in the world movement. 926, 3471
Some heretics of yesterday. 924
Some high points in the history of Tyler Street Methodist Church. 1399
Some hymns and hymn writers. 1874
Some incentives to right living. 968
Some interesting colonial churches in North Carolina. 1271
Some Lambeth letters. 3599
Some latter-day religions. 3141
Some learning processes. 3555
Some lessons from the parable of the sower, the parable of growth, and the law of the harvest. 3468
Some life stories. 3833
Some lights of science on the faith. 3074
Some little-known aspects of the Congregational Christian Church merger. 1705
Some little prayers. 2461, 2893
Some living issues. 3471
Some living masters of the pulpit. 925
Some [logs I have known. and other gospel sermons. 2437
Some loose stones. 1636, 2182
Some loves of the Seraphic Saint. 1027, 1639
Some lowly lives and the heights they reached. 659
Some memoirs of the life of John Roberts. 3241
Some memories. 1310
Some minor characters in the New Testament. 216, 339
Some mistakes of Moses. 1655, 1907
Some modern hymns. 1868
Some modern isms. 2603, 3256
Some modern problems in the light of Bible prophecy. 607
Some modern religions. 3323
Some Nigerian fertility cults. 2828
Some notable altars in the Church of England and the American Episcopal church. 28
Some notable archbishops of Canterbury. 3437
Some notes on the guidance of youth. 3887
Some notes on the teaching manpower of the Jesuit order. 1946
... Some notes on the text of pseudo-Aristotle "De mundo" 81
Some of my best friends are Christians. 1091
Some of my best friends are Jews. 2077
Some of my religion. 1071
Some of the early churches of California. 726
Some old churches of the black belt. 1269
Some outlines of the religion of experience. 1048
Some parables of nature in the light of to-day. 2771
Some paradoxes of Paul. 376, 2772, 2798
Some passages in the life of Mr. Adam Blair, minister of the gospel at Cross-Meikle. 2227
Some people. 896
Some permanent values in Judaism. 2113
Some pioneer Presbyterian preachers of the Piedmont North Carolina. 2918
Some plain sermons. 3342
Some political & social ideas of English dissent. 1468
Some political & social ideas of English dissent, 1763-1800. 1468
Some postulates of a Christian philosophy. 1052
Some practical suggestions on the conduct of a rescue home. 1629
Some preachers do! 3670
Some principles and practices of the spiritual life. 3488
...Some principles of literary criticism and their application to the synoptic problem. 388
Some principles of moral theology and their application. 944, 1536
Some principles of teaching as applied to the Sunday-school. 3551
Some problems and the answers. 2343
Some problems of Catholic higher education in the United States. 831
Some problems of life. 2226

Some problems of the modern minister. 3671
Some problems of the Old Testament. 502
Some psychic messages. 3515
Some published essays and articles. 1070
Some purposes of paradise. 1413, 1912
Some qualities associated with success in the Christian ministry. 1288
Some rain must fall. 3387
Some rare virtues. 3782
Some recent phases of Germany theology. 3658
Some records of the life of Edmund John Kennedy. 2167
Some religious implications of pragmatism. 2866
Some religious talks by a university professor. 965
Some religious views; four papers read before the Chicago literary club, Monday evening, December, 5, 1904. 3068
Some remarkable passages in the life of Dr. George de Benneville, late of Germantown. 3819
Some remarkable passages of the life and death of Mr. Alexander Peden. 2810
Some remarks upon a publication by the Philadelphia medical society concerning Swaim's panacea. 3569
Some revelations as to "Raymond" 2242, 3515
Some roads to Rome in America. 1363
Some run with feet of clay. 930, 1304
Some sayings of the Buddha. 3779
Some sayings of the Buddha, according to the Pali canon. 1856, 3779
Some scientific stories and allegories. 3079
Some Scripture facts and prophecies illustrated in a treatise in answer to three questions. 1376
Some serious, popular false doctrines answered from the Scriptures. 66
Some serious remarks upon the Rev'd Mr. Jonathan Todd's Faithful narrative, of the proceedings, of the First society, and church in Wallingford. 1400
Some significant findings from the North Central Alabama religious surveys. 3568
Some studies in religion. 1100
" ... some that trouble you ..." 1231, 3323
Some things are priceless. 1611, 2736
Some things for which the Unitarian church stands. 3725
Some thoughts concerning the present revival of religion in New-England. 2688
Some thoughts on faith healing. 1598
Some thoughts on Judaism. 2113
Some thoughts on masonic symbolism. 1671
Some thoughts on the atonement. 104
Some thoughts on the book of Revelation. 455
Some through the waters. 178, 930
Some time every day. 901
Some timeless messages of the Christian faith. 1053
Some to be pastors. 3674
Some truths and wisdom of Christian sciences. 1029
Some turning points in church history. 1180
Some unpublished letters of Lord Chesterfield. 892, 3870
Some unpublished Scottish witchcraft trials. 3828
Some values for to-day. 1071
Some vital aspects of teaching in Sunday schools. 3558
... Some vital questions. 168
Some ways of God. 990
Some week-days in Lent. 2212
Some White family history. 3811
Some who led. 1616
Somebody knows I'm alive. 1292, 2631
Somebody love me! 102, 171
Someday I'll be somebody. 2131
Somehow inside of eternity. 983
Someone had to hold the lantern. 717, 2485
Someone special. 1484, 2609
Someone who beckons. 1433
Someone's praying, Lord. 2894
...The Somerset diocese, Bath and Wells. 178
Somerset historical essays. 3457
...The Somerset religious houses. 3457
Something about Kierkegaard. 2171
Something beautiful for God. 2487, 3602
Something ere the end. 2931
Something for everybody. 1448
Something for God. 1745
Something for nothing. 1366, 3252
Something greater than us. 1739
Something happened. 2508
Something more. 986, 2348, 2757
"Something must be done" 835, 948

Something new, in eight letters to Joseph Meeker, Elizabeth-town. 2304
Something overheard. 409
Something to believe in. 2060, 3618, 3787
Something to hope for. 2946
Something to live by. 1449
Something to stand on. 3758
Something wonderful happened. 1485, 2054
Something wonderful is happening. 999
Something's going on here. 1010
Something's there. 1772, 2725
Sometime. 2856
Sometimes I hurt. 551
Sometimes the stones are very lively. 1015
Sometimes there's a hole in the ceiling. 1007
Somewhat less than God. 2326
"Somewhat to say" 162
Somi builds a church. 2489
Son and Saviour. 2001, 2002
Son, give me your heart. 3331
Son is given. 1983
Son of Amram. 2622
Son of consolation. 163, 174, 1397
Son of evil street. 2668, 3705
Son of faith. 3370
Son of God. 438, 1973, 2035, 2415, 3457, 3458
Son of God among the sons of men. 419
Son of God rides on. 1268
Son of God to Super star. 2010
"Son of man;" 1580, 1959, 1968, 1970, 1974, 2013, 3458
Son of Man and Kingdom of God. 2065, 2175
Son of Man and Suffering Servant. 2041, 3458
Son of man coming in His kingdom. 3458
Son of Man in myth and history. 3458
Son of Man in the synoptic tradition. 3458
Son of Man in the teaching of Jesus. 390, 3458
Son of Man, the life of Christ. 1970
Son of Nicodemus. 1967
Son of the Church. 756
Son of the living God. 1953
Son of the morning. 2710
Son of the Passion. 1700
Son of thunder. 2126
Son rises. 2051
Son songs for christian folk. 3458
Son to Susanna. 3803
Son who came home again. 2945
Sona Mona Singh. 2529, 3458
Sone of the morning. 1406
Song about forever things. 1446
Song and a prayer. 2385
Song and praise for Sabbath eve. 2108
Song at the sea. 2400
Song at twilight. 2389
Song book for social gatherings in the General church of the New Jerusalem. 3459
Song celestial; or, Bhagavad-gita. 197
Song for lovers. 594
Song for Sarah. 1350, 1403
Song in her heart. 877
Song in Siberia. 2821
Song in stone to Mary. 3797
Song in the night. 932, 3526
Song in the south. 3455
Song is borne. 3822
Song-land messenger no. 2. 3563
Song of a happy man. 587
Song of ages. 3339
Song of Amos. 736, 737
Song of dawn. 1642
Song of Francis. 1644, 3279
Song of life. 3759
Song of love. 593, 595, 2346, 3392
Song of Miriam and other hymns & verses. 1869
Song of mystery. 594
Song of our Syrian guest. 588
Song of pilgrimage and exile. 2334, 2556
Song of praise. 1734
Song of St. Francis. 1640
Song of Solomon. 593, 594
Song of songs. 593, 594, 595, 602, 722
Song of Songs and Coheleth. 593
Song of songs and Lamentations. 593
Song of songs: Commentary and Homilies. 594
Song of songs of the King and his bride. 593
"Song of songs" (Solomon) 595
Song of songs, which is by Solomon. 593
Song of Songs which is Solomons. 593, 594
Song of the Arab. 1110
Song of the Church. 883
Song of the dove. 2190, 2478
Song of the redeemed. 3295
Song of the shepherd. 587

Song of the shoemaker's son. 2851
Song of the soul set free. 1578
Song of the sun, from the Canticle of the sun. 1641
Song of the sword. 2349
Song of the three young men. 1523
Song of the vineyard. 540
Song service for Sunday schools and revival meetings (no. i) 3557
Songs along the way. 582
Songs and anthems for children's voices. 49
Songs and hymns for primary children. 3563
Songs and praises for revivals, Sunday schools, singing schools, and general church work. 3552
Songs and prayers and meditations. 2097
Songs and prayers for various occasions. 2895
Songs by the way. 1873, 3458
Songs by the way chiefly devotional. 1873
Songs for all seasons, a scriptural and poetical calendar for holidays, birthdays, and all days. 3459
Songs for children. 910
Songs for children in easy language. 910
Songs for primaries. 3563
Songs for silent moments. 2891
Songs for the household. Sacred poetry. 3459
Songs for the new life. 1866
Songs for the sanctuary. 1868
Songs for work and worship. 3458
Songs from a strange land. 587
Songs from one hundred Psalms. 583
Songs from the hearts of women. 1873
Songs from the parsonage. 3458
... The songs, hymns, and prayers of the Old Testament. 1798
Songs in affliction. 3459
Songs in our Bible. 622
Songs in the jungles. 2498
Songs in the night. 545, 576, 1352, 2643, 3210, 3360, 3458, 3459
'Songs in the night' for birds with broken wing. 214
Songs of a Semite. 3458
Songs of angels, and other sermons. 166
Songs of deliverance. 1115, 3208
Songs of deliverance. Second series. 1035
Songs of faith-signs of hope. 1872
Songs of God. 578
Songs of God's grace. 3479
Songs of heaven. 458
Songs of heaven from many hearts. 3459
Songs of joy from the Book of Psalms. 583
Songs of joy through the church year. 2290
Songs of love and praise. 3458
Songs of praise and victory. 3458
Songs of praise discussed. 3459
Songs of praise for Sunday schools, church societies and the home. 2290
Songs of prayer and praise. 1873
Songs of religion and life. 3206
Songs of St. Matthew. 438
Songs of salvation and service. 3561
Songs of Sion. 583
Songs of the century. 3561
Songs of the church. 2968
Songs of the good Earth. 2394, 2831
Songs of the Nativity. 742
Songs of the people of God. 578
Songs of the son of Isai. 581
Songs of the soul. 2385, 3208, 3210, 3458
Songs of the Vaisnava Acaryas. 2186
Songs of two Christmases. 741
Songs of worship and grace. 3458
Songs of Zion. 581, 586, 1229, 1869
Songs of Zion, for social and public worship. 1869
Songs to sing forever. 2671
Sonnenberg, a haven and a heritage. 2407
Sonnets for the Sundays of the church year. 1262
Sons and daughters of God. 1436
Sons and heirs. 3172
Sons but not heirs. 1122
Sons for Christian worship. 3736
Sons of Abraham. 1926
Sons of Abrahma. 1926
Sons of Adam. 494
Sons of Africa. 2487, 3308
Sons of Allen. 26, 3815
Sons of Anak. 3356
Sons of Francis. 1645
Sons of freedom. 123
Sons of God. 416, 2973, 3343
Sons of God return. 319, 1631
Sons of heaven. 3751
Sons of Ishmael. 2557
Sons of the fathers. 3742
Sons of the Incas. 2504
Sons of the north, and their share in the Advent movement. 3386

Sons of the prophets. 2941
Sons of thunder, pulpit power of the past. 925
Son's portrait of Dr. Francis E. Clark. 1284
Soon coming of Our Lord. 1513
Soon to be revealed Antichrist. 52, 608
Soothsayer's handbook. 1470
Sophistries of Christian science. 1032
Sorcerer's handbook. 2731
Sore spots in society. 3187
Soren Kierkegaard. 2169, 2170
Soren Kierkegaard and his critics. 2171
Sormons on the Gospol of St. John. 423
Sorrow and hope of the Egyptian Sudan. 2517
Sorrow built a bridge. 2198
Sorrowful star. 2758
Sorrowing not without hope, for those sleeping in Jesus. 1353
Sorrows and stars. 1558
Sorrow's circuit. 2830
Soteriology. 3030
Soteriology of the New Testament. 2038
Soudan's second sunup. 2542
Soul. 2265, 3461, 3463, 3512
Soul afire. 2234, 2640
Soul and body. 3341
Soul and circumstance. 3463
Soul and its bearings. 3460
Soul and its life. 3461
Soul and its mechanism. 2723, 2994
Soul and its mechanism (the problem of psychology) 2994
Soul and life after death. 3520
Soul and psyche. 3001
Soul and sex in education, morals, religion, and adolescence. 3463
Soul and spirit of man. 3462
Soul and the ethic. 3461
Soul clinic. 1347
Soul comes back. 3461
Soul consciousness is the way to Christhood. 3461
Soul crises. 3463
Soul delight. 2383
Soul Delight (The) 3464
Soul digger. 3591
Soul doctor. 3675
Soul-food for hungry saints. 3463
Soul-force: African heritage in Afro-American religion. 2681
Soul free. 981
Soul friend. 3475
Soul growth. 3463
Soul help. 957
Soul here and hereafter. 3462
Soul immortal. 3461
Soul in metaphysical and empirical psychology. 3463
Soul in paraphrase. 2887
Soul in suffering. 3540
Soul in the unseen world. 1912
Soul laws in sexual, social, spiritual life. 3464
Soul life. 3054
Soul magnets. 3345
Soul of a bishop. 3801
Soul of a child. 3369, 3462
Soul of a priest. 800
Soul of a saint. 2766
Soul of America. 1149, 2926
Soul of ancient Mexico. 1898
Soul of Christ. 47
Soul of Elizabeth Seton. 3417
Soul of Frederick W. Robertson, the Brighton preacher. 3241
Soul of Greece. 2744
Soul of Jesus. 1995
Soul of Jesus contemplated in union with Mary. 1995
Soul of prayer. 2871, 3461
Soul of religion. 3461
Soul of Russia. 3256
Soul of the apostolate. 3485
Soul of the Bantu. 133
Soul of the Bible. 249
Soul of the Black preacher. 2682
Soul of the city, and other verse. 3462
Soul of the Indian. 1902
Soul of the people. 3341
Soul of the sacred litrugy. 840
Soul of the symbols. 2252
Soul of things. 3002
Soul Patrol: "Here comes the God Squad." 1261, 3592
Soul problems. 3462
Soul requisites. 1827
Soul reveries. 3352
Soul rhapsodies. 3461
Soul rush. 1309
Soul-saving. 2455, 3338, 3818
Soul-saving gospel truths; delivered in several sermons. 3343
Soul science. 3463
Soul science and immortality. 3461
Soul-searching sermons. 2300

Soul so rebellious. 2618, 3538
Soul soliloquy. 2392
Soul-stirring sermons. 3345
Soul surgery. 3462
Soul, the pill, and the fetus. 664
Soul-trapping. 3345
Soul under siege. 986
Soul, whence and whither. 3542
Soul winner. 253, 1565, 1570, 3862
Soul-winner and soul-winning. 3462
Soul-winner's Gospel. 3463
Soul-winner's guide. 1563
Soul winner's journey to the heavenly land. 3461
Soul-winners' secrets. 1569
Soul winners' Testament. 353
Soul-winning. 1563, 1564, 3462, 3463
Soul-winning and stewardship sermons. 3343
Soul winning around the world. 24
Soul-winning church. 1116
Soul-winning doctrines. 3666
Soul-winning evangelism. 1564
Soul-winning helps. 1258, 1757
Soul winning in black churches. 1162
Soul winning in the Sunday-school. 3463
Soul winning incidents and illustrations. 1563
Soul-winning sermons. 1561, 3346
Soul-winning sermons God has used in saving myriads of sinners all around the globe. 3346
Soul winning stories. 1357
Soul winning teacher. 3557
Sould of Greece. 2744
Souldiery spiritualized. 1342
Soules exaltation. 2637
Soules humiliation. 1361
Soules implantation. 1361
Soules preparation for Christ. 1361
Soulfull worship. 3004
Souls aflame. 1556
Soul's anchorage. 3355
Souls and bodies. 3462
Souls and saddlebags. 2553
Souls at stake. 754
Soul's atlas and other sermons. 3345, 3357
Soul's awakening. 3461
Soul's Christmas. 3461
Soul's first day in heaven. 1794
Souls in action, in the crucible of the new life; expanding the narrative of Twice-born men. 1358
Souls in armour and other baccalaureate messages. 123
Souls in prison. 983
Souls in the making. 3673
Soul's inquiries answered in the words of Scripture. 724
Soul's journey. 1696
Soul's meditations. 3463
Souls on fire. 1789
Soul's pilgrimage. 3191
Souls set free. 2521
Soul's sincere desire. 2870
Soul's struggle. 3362
Sound from heaven. 2817
Sound his glories forth. 3144
Sound of bells. 1630, 2974
Sound of boldness. 3829
Sound of falling chains. 381
Sound of light. 2637
Sound of the one hand. 3238
Sound of the trumpet. 1571
Sound the trumpet. 1567
Sounding brass. 2614
Sounding of the seventh angel. 604
Sounding solitude. 2386
Soundings. 986, 1219, 1340, 1451
Soundings in Satanism. 1429
Sounds of wonder. 1717
Soup soap, and salvation. 888
Source book and bibliographical guide for American church history. 3740
Source book for ancient church history. 1198
Source book for ancient church history from the apostolic age to the close of the conciliar period. 1197
Source book for the life of Christ. 383
Source book for the study of the teaching of Jesus in its historical relationships. 3069
Source book in Indian philosophy. 2840
Source book of Advaita Vedanta. 3775
Source book of interbiblical history. 2091
Source book of rural missions. 2545
Source book of the Bible for teachers. 643
Source book on Christian education. 1127
Source book on religious education in Friends elementary schools. 3150
Source book on spiritual life and evangelism. 1842
Source of "Jerusalem the golden". together with other pieces attributed to Bernard of Cluny. 1862

Source of power. 1657
Source of the Christ ideal. 1992
Sourcebook for Christian worship. 2237
Sourcebook of American Methodism. 2440
Sourcebook of comfort. 1691
Sourcebook of texts for the comparative study of the Gospels. 395
Sources and literature of Scottish church history. 3315
Sources and shapes of power. 3734
Sources and themes for Afro-Irish studies. 851, 2498
Sources for the early history of Ireland: ecclesiastical. 1919
Sources for the life of Christ. 1986
Sources for the life of Christ (The) 1987
Sources for The New England mind. 2466, 3009
... Sources of Bible myths and legends. 236
Sources of Christian theology. 783
Sources of doctrines of the fall and original sin. 1602
Sources of faith and hope. 1594
Sources of history in the Pentateuch. 564
Sources of hope. 1846
Sources of Jewish education in America prior to 1881. 2106
Sources of Jewish inspiration. 3371
... The sources of Luke's passion-narrative. 426
Sources of Luke's Perean section. 430
Sources of Mormon history in Illinois, 1839-48. 2617
Sources of personal power. 2396
Sources of power in famous lives. 923
Sources of Protestant theology. 3679
Sources of religious insight. 3104, 3107
... The sources of religious insights. 3104
Sources of religious sentiment. 1484, 3109
Sources of renewal. 787
Sources of the Acts. 330
Sources of the Anglo-French commentary on the Proverbs of Solomon contained in manuscript 24862 (Fonds. francais) of the Bibliotheque nationale of Paris. 2980
Sources of the doctrines of the fall and original sin. 1602
Sources of the Faust tradition. 1619
Sources of the first ten books of Augustine's De civitate dei. 111
Sources of the Hexateuch. 530
Sources of the religious element in Flaubert's Salammbo. 1917. 1629
Sources of the Synoptic Gospels. 390, 391, 3578
Sources of the Utrecht Psalter miniatures. 848
Sources of vitality in American church life. 1109
South African churches in a revolutionary situation. 1108
South African melting pot; a vindication of missionary policy, 1799-1836. 2499
South African missions. 2499
South America. 2547, 3464
South American Indian narrative, theoretical and analytical approaches. 1903
South American neighbors. 3464
South American problems. 2547
South and Christian ethics. 3329
South and the North in American religion. 1109
South Asian politics and religion. 3088
South Carolina Baptists. 169
South Carolina Baptists, 1670-1805. 169
South Carolina Disciples of Christ. 1467
South central frontiers. 2404
South Central Jurisdiction, 1939-1972. 3734
South China folk. 2490
South church lectures. 3653
South Dakota's Hutterite colonies, 1874-1969. 1859
South English legendary. 3285
South Indian schemes. 1230
South Indian temples. 3599
South to the harvest, as told to Ken Anderson. 2547
South wind. 3344
Southeast Asia, crossroad of religions. 2318
Southeast Asia in five hours. 825
Southern Anglicanism. 1228, 3464
Southern Baptist convention. 3466
Southern Baptist Convention, 1845-1953. 3466
Southern Baptist Convention and its people, 1607-1972. 3466
Southern Baptist Convention organization manual. 3466
Southern Baptist foreign missionaries, compiled. 2482
Southern Baptist foreign missions. 140
Southern Baptist preaching. 160

Southern Baptist theological education study. 3680
Southern Baptist theological seminary. 3297
Southern Baptists in sunny Italy. 2533
Southern Baptists in the great adventure. 3467
Southern churches in crisis. 2955
Southern enterprize. 2547
Southern evangelicals and the social order, 1800-1860. 1300
... Southern Methodism in China. 2510
Southern Methodist handbook. 2442
Southern Methodist pulpit. 3366
Southern mountaineers. 2626
Southern negro nun. 1777
Southern parish. 1278
Southern Presbyterian leaders. 2912
Southern Presbyterian pulpit. 3365
Southern Presbyterian worthies. 2937
Southern Quakers and slavery. 1686, 3425
Southern see. 1238
Southern slavery in its present aspects. 1846, 3425
Southern synod of the Evangelical and Reformed church. 1545
Southern white Protestantism in the twentieth century. 3468
Southerner among the spirits. 3514
Southwestern Indian ceremonials. 1903
Southwestern Indian ritual drama. 1903
Southwestern sermons. 160
Southwick Congregational Church history, 1773-1973. 3468
Souvenir album of American cities. 824
... Souvenir book. 132
Souvenir book, Centennial jubilee of St. Peter and Paul's parish, 1844-1944. 823
... Souvenir book diamond jubilee, Saint Martin's church, Fulton avenue and Favette street Baltimore, Maryland. 132
Souvenir book of the Ephrata Cloister. 1521, 3388
[Souvenir booklet commemorating the 128th anniversary of the incorporation of the parish. 693
Souvenir festival hymns. 1865
Souvenir of dual jubilee. 1821, 3316
Souvenir of Loretto centenary, October 10, 1899. 1744, 2260
Souvenir of Mount St. Joseph's Ursuline academy. 3276
Souvenir of the blessing of the corner-stone of the new Seminary of St. Joseph. 3276
Souvenir of the diamond jubilee of the Passionist fathers in the diocese of Newark and of the rededication of St. Michael's monastery church. September 29th, 1936, Union City, N.J. 2778
Souvenir on the occasion of the 5th Non-Aligned Summit Conference held in Colombo, Sri Lanka, 9-20 August 1976 in conjunction with an exhibition of paintings and sculpture of Sri Lanka at the Colombo Art Gallery. 88
Souvenir portfolio of Universalist churches in Massachusetts. 3754
Souvenir program. 890
Souvenir volume. 833
Souvenir volume illustrated. Three great events in the history of the Catholic church in the United States. 833
... Souvenir volume of the golden jubilee, Sisters of the blessed sacrament for Indians and colored people. 824
Sovereign emblem. 107
Sovereign God. 276, 1719
Sovereign grace. 1753
Sovereigns of industry. 2189
Sovereigns of Judah. 493
Sovereigns of the Bible. 494
Sovereignty of God. 730, 1726, 2981
Sovereignty of good. 1537
Sovereignty of good over other concepts. 1746
Sovereignty of grace. 1477, 1753, 2911
Sovereignty of the Holy Spirit. 2506
Soviet believers. 3257
Soviet evangelicals since World War II. 1552
Soviet press campaign against the Jewish religion. 2145
Soviet Russia and the Jews. 2102
Sower. 2026, 3596
Sower and the seed. 3468
Sower went forth. 2212
... The sower went out (sequel to The voyager) 2530
Sowing and reaping. 970, 1325, 2027, 2028
Sowing God's word in Israel today. 2544
Sowing in tears, reaping in joy. 1693
Sowing seed in Assam, missionary life and labours in Northeast India. 2503
Space age Christianity. 1065

SPACE-AGE SUNDAY. RELIGIOUS BOOKS 1876 - 1982

Space-age Sunday. 3548
Space and extense in the spiritual world. 3469, 3570
Space and spirit. 1371
Space-gods revealed. 1401, 1917
Space of joy. 17
Space, time and incarnation. 1893
Space, time, and resurrection. 2053, 3469
Space, time and self. 3686
Space, time, God. 1740
Space, time, sTheosophy. 3686
Spaced out and gathered in. 3128
Spaces for silence. 2571
Spade and the Bible. 208
Spade and the Scriptures. 535
Spade confirms the Book. 207, 1582
Spain in crisis. 1650, 3469
Spanish cathedral music in the Golden Age. 1210
Spanish Catholic's visit to England. 818
Spanish church and the Papacy in the thirteenth century. 3469
Spanish doorways. 2557
Spanish Inquisition. 1908, 1910
Spanish Jesuit churches in Mexico's Tarahumara. 79
Spanish Jesuit Mission in Virginia. 1949
Spanish-Latin ritual. 837
Spanish pre-Romanesque art. 85
Spank me if you love me. 988
Spanning the decades. 2488, 3861
Spare tires and other essays. 3345
"Spark." 911
Spark in the clod. 1581
Sparks among the ashes. 2829
Sparks among the stubble. 1212
Sparks from the anvil. 3370
Sparks from the anvil of Elder Michaux. 1841
Sparks from the anvil of truth. 2931, 3348
Sparks from the burning bush. 3129
Sparks of faith. 1593
Sparks of fire. 1068
Sparks of the kindling. 3372
Sparks of truth. 963, 2411
Sparrow among the eagles. 2394
Sparrow on the house top. 214, 2244
Sparrows and men. 1556
Speak, Lord. 368
Speak Lord, I'm listening. 3537
Speak out with Marge ... and you'll be gladder that you're alive. 1323
"Speak that I may see Thee!" 3070
Speak the word. 1115
Speak through the earthquake: religious faith and emotional crisis. 2998
Speak to me Lord—I'm listening. 2397
Speak to the children of Israel. 1843
Speak to the earth. 1439
Speak truth to power. 2756
Speak unto the children of Israel. 910, 3370
Speaker's Bible. 615
Speaker's Bible (The) 615
Speaker's book of inspiration. 1842
Speaker's guide. 2116
Speakers hand book; world program. 3841
Speaker's handbook for occasional talks. 1840
Speaker's treasury for Sunday school teachers. 1841
Speaking boldly. 2932
Speaking frankly. 1691
Speaking from the pulpit. 2903
Speaking in parables. 1225, 3071
Speaking in tongues. 1716, 1717
Speaking in tongues and divine healing. 1716
Speaking in tongues and its significance for the church. 1716
Speaking of angels. 42
Speaking of cardinals. 738
Speaking of God. 1729, 3682
Speaking of God today. 2154, 2298
Speaking of how to pray. 2877
Speaking of Jesus. 1567
Speaking of religion. 3058
Speaking of religious education. 783, 936
Speaking out for women, a Biblical view. 3832
Speaking to the heart. 2931
Speaking well of God. 1735
Speaking with tongues. 1716
Spear of destiny. 1820, 1826
Special Bible section: 1456-1956. 1778
Special characteristics of the four Gospels. 390
Special class programs for intellectually gifted pupils. 1712
Special day programs and selections. 3560
Special day sermons. 169, 1622, 2437, 2721
Special-day sermons for Evangelicals. 1555
Special day talks for children. 907
Special days in the church school. 1623
Special days in the Sunday school. 3560
Special days of the church year. 1262
Special education, the handicapped and the gifted. 1419
Special introduction to the study of the Old Testament. 539
... Special investigation of the part time school and junior worker in the city of Seattle. 1578
Special kind of belonging. 933
Special kind of man. 988, 2037
Special kind of marrying. 792, 2344
Special lessons for Bible schools. 3180
Special messenger. 1292, 1310
Special occasion helps. 2722
Special programs for the Sunday school through the year. 3560
Special revelation and the word of God. 3226
Special sermons. 2028, 2459
Special sermons for special days. 2722
Special sermons for special occasions. 1467, 3367
Special sermons on major Bible doctrines. 3359
Special sermons on special issues. 3359
Special sermons on the family. 1611
Special teachings from the arcane science. 2725
Special times with God. 1606
Special women in the Bible. 3841
Specifically to youth. 3758
Specimen of divine truths. 1592
Specimens. 3207
Specimens of Biblical literature. 210
Spectacle of death. 1698
Spectacle unto the world. 871
Spectacular career of Rev. Billy Sunday. 3566
Spectrum of Catholic attitudes. 784
Spectrum of Protestant beliefs. 3679
Spectrum of religion. 3058
Speculating in futures. 3702
Speculation and revelation. 2843
Speculation and revelation in the age of Christian philosophy. 3654
Speculation and revelation in the history of philosophy. 2840
Speculation on human life. 2226
Speculations on the universe. 2417
Speculative masonry. 1662
Speculum animae. 1429
Speculum christiani. 976
Speculum mentis, or, The map of knowledge. 84
Speculum religionis. 2586, 3068
Speculum religiosorum; and, speculum ecclesie. 3486
Speculum sacerdotale. 1623
Speculum stultorum. 1762
Speech delivered before the Municipal court of the city of Boston. 670
Speech for persuasive preaching. 2902
Speech in the pulpit. 2905
Speech of M. Portalis, on the 15th germinal, year x. 5th April, 1802, to the legislative body of France, on presenting the convention made between the French republic and the Holy See. 1145
Speech of the Right Rev. Dr. Hughes, delivered on the 16th, 17th and 21st days' of June, 1841. 873, 2168
Speech of William D. Baker in the German Roman Catholic Holy Trinity church case. 2830
Speech, silence, action! 986, 2568
Speeches, addresses, and occasional sermons. 3723, 3729
Speeches delivered on various occasions. 2422
... The speeches of Elihu. 549
Speeches on the Jew bill, in the House of delegates of Maryland. 7, 2100
Der Spiegel on the New Testament. 2046, 3651
Spell of the temple. 3818
Spencer W. Kimball, twelfth president of the Church of Jesus Christ of Latter-day Saints. 2171, 2609
Spencer's book of comic speeches and humorous recitations. 3026
Spertus College of Judaica Yemenite manuscripts. 2331
Sphere of religion. 3060
Spice for spiritualists. 48
Spices from the Lord's garden. 1560
Spida Jesu-Cristo casi nah San Juan. 3891
Spider divination in the Cameroons. 1470
Spilled milk. 2894
Spilled milk; litanies for living. 2894
Spina Christi: musings in Holy week. 1837
Spinal adjustment in Southern Baptist life. 3465
Spindles and spires. 1138
Spindrift: spray from a psychic sea. 175, 1709
Spinning a sacred yarn. 3836
Spinning Aphrodite. 3777
Spinning straw into gold. 982
Spinoza. 3472
Spinoza bibliography. 3472
Spinoza, Descartes & Maimonides. 3472
Spinoza's critique of religion. 3472
Spinoza's Short treatise on God, man and human welfare. 1537
Spinoza's theory of truth. 3472, 3716
Spirago's method of Christian doctrine. 746
Spiral dance. 3824
Spiral road to God. 1607
Spire in the mountains. 90
Spire on the hill. 1626
Spires of the spirit. 1447
Spiritual formation and guidance-counseling in the CCD program. 3475
Spirit. 1831, 1832
Spirit and forms of Protestantism. 1363, 1492, 2976, 2977
Spirit and God's man. 2696
Spirit and his church. 1833
Spirit and his gifts. 139
Spirit and its freedom. 3463
Spirit and life. 966, 1438, 3472, 3563
Spirit and light. 3624, 3807
Spirit and magnitude of the real beast and its image. 421
Spirit and martyrdom. 2350
Spirit and matter. 3499
Spirit and origins of American Protestantism. 1386
Spirit and personality. 2822
Spirit and power. 3479
Spirit and power of Christian secularity. 3328
Spirit and practice of the liturgy. 838
Spirit and prayer of Carmel. 740
Spirit and sacrament. 3664
Spirit and song of the new liturgy. 884, 3771
Spirit and the bride. 3840
Spirit and the church. 2816
... The spirit and the flesh. 3572
Spirit and the forms of love. 2266
Spirit & the human person. 1828
Spirit and the living seed. 2696
Spirit and the word. 1830, 1832
Spirit and the world. 1830
Spirit Bible. 3472
Spirit Christlike. 2060
Spirit communion. 3502
Spirit-controlled family living. 1609
Spirit-controlled temperament. 2781
Spirit-controlled woman. 3835
Spirit driven men. 338
Spirit enshrined. 2361
Spirit, faith, and church. 1126
Spirit Father. 235
Spirit-filled church. 1248
Spirit-filled life. 3480, 3482
Spirit-filled pastor's guide. 3674
Spirit-filled trauma. 1829
Spirit fruit. 2386
Spirit giveth life. 2611
Spirit home. 3503
Spirit in crisis. 3686
Spirit in darkness. 2137, 2642
Spirit in man. 3338
Spirit in my life. 784, 1827
Spirit in the body mystical. 1829
Spirit in the Church. 941, 1831
Spirit in the word. 217
Spirit in the world. 1105, 2180, 3695
Spirit intercourse. 3508
Spirit is present. 3485
Spirit is willing. 976
Spirit knows no handicap. 2618, 3031
Spirit land. 3567
Spirit life. 3501
Spirit life, and its relations. 3463
Spirit life of pure spiritualism. 3497
Spirit life of Theodore Parker. 2776, 3511
Spirit man. 3072
Spirit manifestations examined and explained. 3500
Spirit mates. 3510
Spirit mediums exposed. 3502
Spirit mediumship. 3515
Spirit messages. 3498
Spirit obsession. 3515
Spirit of a sound mind. 992
Spirit of America Christianity. 3745
Spirit of American Christianity. 1109
Spirit of American Lutheranism, and other essays. 2290
Spirit of Anglicanism. 44, 1844, 3655
Spirit of Anglicanism: a survey of Anglican theological method in the seventeenth century. 3655
Spirit of Buddhism today. 704
Spirit of Catholicism. 783, 784
Spirit of Chinese culture. 1081
Spirit of Chinese philosophy. 2838
Spirit of Christ. 658, 1451, 1828, 1835, 1836, 2060
Spirit of Christ in human relationships. 1827
Spirit of Christ within. 2696
Spirit of Christianity. 1071
Spirit of Christmas. 1112, 1114
Spirit of Christ's sermon on the Mount. 3334
Spirit of church history. 1180
Spirit of Eastern Orthodoxy. 2744
Spirit of Findhorn. 723, 2384
Spirit of flame. 1028, 2137
Spirit of glory. 1835, 1836
Spirit of God. 1831
Spirit of God and the faith of today. 1832
Spirit of God in Biblical literature. 1833
Spirit of God in Christian life. 1834
Spirit of God in Scripture. 1830
Spirit of God in the didactic books of the Old Testament. 1730
Spirit of grace. 1836
Spirit of Gregorian chant. 883
Spirit of Hebrew poetry. 1798, 1799
Spirit of Himalaya. 3476
Spirit of holiness. 1005
Spirit of Islam. 1924, 2564
Spirit of Jesus in Acts. 332
Spirit of Jewish law. 2074
Spirit of John Wesley Gilbert. 1713
Spirit of joy. 2383
Spirit of Judaism. 2142
Spirit of Lent. 2214
Spirit of love. 1650, 2266
Spirit of love and other sermons. 3343
Spirit of man. 2728
Spirit of Mary Catherine McAuley. 2305
Spirit of Masonry. 1660
Spirit of mediaeval philosophy. 2842
Spirit of power. 1829
Spirit of prayer. 2874, 2876
Spirit of prophecy. 1030, 1493
Spirit of prophecy in the Advent movement. 3380
Spirit of prophecy treasure chest. 3387, 3811
Spirit of Protestantism. 2976, 2977
Spirit of reality. 1442
Spirit of renewal. 2192, 3772
Spirit of sacrifice and the life of sacrifice in the religious state. 2576
Spirit of St. Andrew's. 2967
Spirit of St. Clare. 1284
Spirit of St. Francois de Sales. 1445
Spirit of Saint Jane Frances de Chantal. 882
Spirit of Scott. 897, 3538
Spirit of Serra. 2506, 3376
Spirit of service. 3377, 3531
Spirit of Sun Myung Moon. 2588
Spirit of synergy. 2166, 2380
Spirit of the age, and other sermons. 3349
Spirit of the American Lutheran church. 33
Spirit of the Counter-Reformation. 1374
Spirit of the cross. 2028
Spirit of The east. 1321, 3268
Spirit of the Hebrew poetry. 1799
... The spirit of the liturgy. 836
Spirit of the living God. 1342, 1831, 1834, 1836
Spirit of the Lord. 3233
Spirit of the Old Testament. 598
Spirit of the Oxford movement. 2754
Spirit of the Reformed tradition. 3680
Spirit of the Shepherd. 588
Spirit of the Society of St. Vincent de Paul. 3438
Spirit of the Spanish mystics. 2648
Spirit of the teacher. 3557
Spirit of the unborn. 3687
Spirit of the Upanishads. 3760
Spirit of the work. 2991
Spirit of Thomism. 3696
Spirit of tolerance. 3704
Spirit of truth. 1654
Spirit of worship. 838
... The spirit of Yiddish literature. 3863
Spirit of your marriage. 2338
Spirit of Zen. 3893
Spirit-Paraclete in the Fourth Gospel. 424, 1834
Spirit-paraclete in the Gospel of John. 423, 1834
Spirit philosophy of Robert G. Ingersoll and Rev. Charles Haddon Spurgeon. 3506
Spirit possession and spirit mediumship in Africa and Afro-America. 3519
Spirit possession in the Nepal Himalayas. 3472
Spirit power. 957, 987, 3498
Spirit, power and matter. 3517
Spirit-rapper. 3124
Spirit rappers. 1942, 3520
Spirit rapping unveiled! 3508, 3520

Spirit rappings, mesmerism, clairvoyance, visions, revelations, startling phenomna, and infidelity of the rapping fraternity, calmly considered, and exposed. 3511
Spirit slate writing and kindred phenomena. 3513
Spirit, Son, and Father. 1833
Spirit, soul and body. 674
Spirit, soul, and flesh. 1771
Spirit speaks to the church. 333
Spirit teachings. 3473
Spirit through body. 3389
Spirit unto the churches. 3474
Spirit versus structure. 2276, 3035
Spirit which is from God. 1830
Spirit within you. 1832, 1833
Spirit workers in the home circle. 3516
Spirit works; real but not miraculous. 3511
Spirit world. 3498, 3503, 3507, 3513, 3567
Spirit world a poem. 2048
Spirit world about us. 42
Spirit world and spirit life. 3501
Spirit world unmasked. 671, 3501
Spirit wrestler. 1532
Spiritans. 1826
Spiritism. 3058, 3496, 3501, 3503, 3517
Spiritism and common sense. 3504
Spiritism and psychology. 2988
Spiritism and religion. 3507
Spiritism and the cult of the dead in antiquity. 3510
Spiritism and the fallen angels in the light of the Old. and New Testaments. 3503
Spiritism, hypmotism and telepathy. 2849, 3495
Spiritism, hypnotism and telepathy. 2993
Spiritism, the modern satanism. 3498
Spiritman's place and function in nature. 3506
Spirits and men. 3570
Spirits and power. 2364
Spirits and spirit worlds. 3515
Spirits in his parlor. 1367, 2859
Spirits in rebellion. 2696
Spirit's life. 3207
Spirits of protest. 3895
Spirits of '76. 3521
Spirits of the deep. 178
Spirits of the deep; a study of an Afro-Brazilian cult. 178
Spirits of the sacred mountains. 1902
Spirit's pathway traced. 3510
Spirits rebellious. 3199
Spirits, stars, and spells. 2724
Spiritual adventure in South America. 2955
Spiritual adventures in social relations. 958
Spiritual adventuring. 958
Spiritual Aeneid. 2182
Spiritual Alps and how we ascend them. 2695
Spiritual America as seen from the other side. 3517, 3518
Spiritual and Anabaptist writers. 3042
Spiritual and demonic magic. 2314
Spiritual and intellectual elements in the formation of sisters. 2573
Spiritual and material attraction. 2694
Spiritual and pastoral conferences to priests. 1298
Spiritual argosy. 1290
Spiritual ascent of man. 2836
Spiritual authority in the Church of England. 118
Spiritual autobiography in early America. 3739
Spiritual autobiography of Charles de Foucauld. 1635
Spiritual awakening. 2139
Spiritual basis of democracy. 1085
Spiritual basis of man and nature. 3519
Spiritual body. 1696
Spiritual body and celestial Earth. 3544
Spiritual body in relation to the divine law of life. 3481
Spiritual bouquet, offerec by pious souls, to the Sacred heart of Jesus. 3270
Spiritual breakthroughs for our time. 3494
Spiritual cannibalism. 3481
Spiritual canticle. 2637
Spiritual care of Puerto Rican migrants. 1255
Spiritual childhood. 3690
Spiritual clinic. 974
Spiritual combat. 2819
Spiritual combat, and a Treatise on peace of the soul. 3489
Spiritual communications. 3506
Spiritual community guide. 1394
Spiritual conferences. 863, 3334, 3363, 3486
Spiritual conferences for college men. 3537

Spiritual conferences for religious based on the Franciscan ideal. 1641, 1645
Spiritual conferences of St. Francis de Sales. 3486
Spiritual conquest along the Rockies. 3482
Spiritual conquest of Mexico. 822, 2460
Spiritual conquest of the second frontier. 2669
Spiritual conquest, the Jesuit reductions in Paraguay, 1610-1767. 1948
Spiritual consciousness. 3482
Spiritual considerations. 3485
Spiritual counsel and encouragement. 961, 3478
Spiritual counsel and letters. 3487
Spiritual crisis of man. 3864
Spiritual crisis of the gilded age. 3747
Spiritual crisis of the scientific age. 3080
Spiritual culture. 1394
Spiritual culture and social service. 3435
Spiritual defense program. 3852
"Spiritual" delusion. 3508
Spiritual depression. 3365
Spiritual depths. 235
Spiritual despondency and temptations. 2393
Spiritual despotism. 1241
Spiritual diary. 1434, 1438
Spiritual diary of Raphael Cardinal Merry del Val. 3488
Spiritual dilemma of the Jewish people. 2139
Spiritual dimension of personality. 2999
Spiritual dimensions in teaching high school religion. 804, 939
Spiritual dimensions of psychology. 3544
Spiritual direction. 3475, 3603
Spiritual direction and auricular confession. 801
Spiritual direction of sisters. 3416
Spiritual director. 2136, 3475
Spiritual director of the Holy name society. 1826
Spiritual directory of Saint Francis de Sales. 3486
Spiritual discernment and politics. 1086
Spiritual discipline in Hinduism, Buddhism, and the West. 3491
Spiritual doctrine of Dom Marmion. 2335, 3489
Spiritual doctrine of Father Louis Lallemant of the Society of Jesus. 3487
Spiritual doctrine of St. Augustine. 113, 3492
Spiritual dynamics. 1827
Spiritual education. 3521
Spiritual education of our children. 3171
Spiritual energies in daily life. 3479
Spiritual equipment. 3751
Spiritual espousals. 2647
Spiritual evolution. 298, 920, 3483
Spiritual evolution via cause and effect. 3501
Spiritual exercises. 2269, 3476
Spiritual exercises and the Ignatian mystical horizon. 1583, 2268
Spiritual exercises and their results. 2640
Spiritual exercises of an eight days' retreat. 3222
Spiritual exercises of St. Ignatius. 2269, 2391, 3475, 3476
Spiritual exercises of St. Ignatius of Loyola. 2380, 2391
Spiritual exercises to serve for the annual retreat of a Carmelite. 3476
Spiritual Exodus. 516
Spiritual experiences in business life. 720
Spiritual exposition of the prophetic scriptures. 3515
Spiritual family and the biological family. 1609
Spiritual flashlights from godly men and women. 1052
Spiritual foundations of Judaism, and other essays, selected addresses, and writings. 2142
Spiritual fragments. 3510
... The spiritual Franciscans. 1648
Spiritual friend. 3400, 3475
Spiritual friendship. 3493
Spiritual frontier. 2991
Spiritual frontiers in home missions. 3467
Spiritual genius of St. Therese. 3690
Spiritual gifts. 3384
Spiritual gifts & the church. 1712
Spiritual gifts and the great commission. 1712
Spiritual gleanings. 1447
Spiritual gospel. 420
Spiritual government. 669
Spiritual growth. 984, 3481
Spiritual growth of children. 903
Spiritual growth through creative drama. 1478
Spiritual guidance. 90, 3484
Spiritual guidance and the varieties of character. 3475

Spiritual guidance of man and humanity. 51
Spiritual guidance of man and of mankind. 3475
Spiritual guide to eternal life. 1314
Spiritual guideposts. 1313
Spiritual Healing Seminar. 1600
Spiritual health. 1008
Spiritual health and healing. 2409
Spiritual health in the light of the principles of physical health. 1793
Spiritual heritage of India. 2840
Spiritual heroes. 2951, 3008, 3454
Spiritual hierarchies and their reflection in the physical world: zodiac, planets, cosmos. 97
Spiritual highlights for Sisters. 2573
Spiritual hilltops. 1437
Spiritual history of Israel. 234
Spiritual home training for the child. 3165
Spiritual horizons. 3353
Spiritual hymnal. 1867
Spiritual idea for the day. 1435
Spiritual insights of a practicing psychiatrist. 3491
Spiritual instructions. 3151
... Spiritual instructions for religious. 2385
Spiritual instructions of Saint Seraphim of Sarov. 3334
Spiritual instructions of Swami Muktananda. 3491
Spiritual instructions received at the meetings of one of the circles formed in Philadelphia. 3515
Spiritual interpretation of God's word. 238
Spiritual interpretation of nature. 3080
Spiritual interpretation of the Scriptures. 443
Spiritual interpretation of the Scriptures. Lectures on Genesis and Exodus. 524
Spiritual interpretation of the Scriptures. Matthew's gospel. 443
Spiritual journey of Joel S. Goldsmith, modern mystic. 1744, 2696
Spiritual journey of Saint Paul. 375
Spiritual journey with Paul. 2390, 2798
Spiritual kingdom. 461
Spiritual knowing. 3521
Spiritual law in the natural world. 3075
Spiritual leadership. 953
Spiritual legacy of John Foster Dulles. 1076, 1077
Spiritual legacy of John Peter Medaille, S. J. 3419
Spiritual legacy of Newman. 3480
Spiritual legacy of Sister Mary of the Holy Trinity. 2639
Spiritual lessons from every-day life. 3479
Spiritual letters of Archbishop Fenelon. 960
Spiritual letters of Edward King. 966
Spiritual letters of Francois de Salignac de La Mothe-Fenelon. 997
Spiritual letters of Monsignor R. Hugh Benson to one of his converts. 774
Spiritual letters of the Venerable Francis Libermann. 3488, 3487
Spiritual letters to women. 856, 3844
Spiritual life. 90, 966, 970, 971, 1559, 2996, 3477, 3481, 3483, 3492
... The spiritual life and the role of the Holy Ghost in the sanctification of the soul. 1458, 1829
Spiritual life, doctrine and practise of Christian perfection, by Rev. Walter Elliott. 3486
Spiritual life, how to attain it and prepare children for it. 3483
Spiritual life in the Bible. 3484
Spiritual life in the New Testament. 1004
Spiritual life of Archbishop Martinez. 2349
Spiritual life of the priest. 1298
Spiritual life of the Sunday school. 3477, 3552
Spiritual life songs. 1862
Spiritual life through tithing. 952
Spiritual light. 3054
Spiritual man. 2320
Spiritual manifestations. 3495
Spiritual maxims. 2375, 3482
Spiritual maxims of Brother Lawrence. 998
Spiritual maxims of Brother Lawrence, together with The character, by the chronicler of the "Conversations" and Gathered throughs. 3479
Spiritual meditations. 1451
Spiritual message of Hebrews. 2116
Spiritual message of literature. 2232
Spiritual message of modern English poetry. 1518
Spiritual messages of the miracle stories. 2017
Spiritual mustard pot. 1724
Spiritual naturalization. 1558

Spiritual nature of man. 1586, 3192
Spiritual outlook. 1282
Spiritual pastels. 2390
Spiritual path. 3479
Spiritual pepper and salt for Catholics and non-Catholics. 792
Spiritual personality of emergent Africa. 12
Spiritual perspective. 3522
Spiritual perspectives. 881, 2839
Spiritual pilgrim. 2810, 3495
Spiritual pilgrimage of Jesus. 1954
Spiritual pilgrimage of St. Paul. 2795
Spiritual pilgrimage towards the threshold of the Catholic church. 783
Spiritual pilgrims. 2158, 2159, 3492
Spiritual pluralism and recent philosophy. 2854
Spiritual point of view; or, The glass reversed. 1306
Spiritual power. 1467, 3359
Spiritual power at work. 3505
Spiritual power for your congregation. 1293
Spiritual power; or, The infinite fount. 2693
Spiritual practices. 20, 3491
Spiritual practices of India. 3709, 3867
Spiritual problems in contemporary literature. 3094, 2232
Spiritual problems of our times. 1738, 3489
Spiritual progress. 973
Spiritual psychology. 2996
Spiritual reader. 1451
Spiritual reading list. 3203
Spiritual reading of scripture. 613
Spiritual readings from Mother St. Paul. 1264
Spiritual realism of Saint Therese of Lisieux. 3691
Spiritual realization. 1107
Spiritual reasoner. 3507
Spiritual reconstruction. 1053
Spiritual reflections for sisters. 3488
Spiritual reformers in the 16th and 17 centuries. 2639
Spiritual regeneration with reference to present times. 3051
Spiritual renewal through personal groups. 3477
Spiritual resources are available today. 1008
Spiritual retreat for religious persons. 3223
Spiritual retreat of eight days. 3222
Spiritual revolution. 3744
Spiritual riches of John Bunyan. 1456
Spiritual riches of the Rosary mysteries. 3247
Spiritual Sabbathism. 3260
Spiritual sanity and other sermons. 1343
Spiritual saturnalia. 1074
Spiritual science. 2730, 2733
Spiritual science, the universal religion. 3519
Spiritual secrets of famous Christians. 925
Spiritual ships. 978
Spiritual side-lights. 2581
Spiritual side of our plea. 1463
Spiritual significance. 3518
Spiritual songs. 1866, 1868
Spiritual songs & humns for use in all gospel services. 691
Spiritual songs from English mss. of fourteenth to sixteenth centuries. 3209
Spiritual starlight on earth and road to heavenly bliss. 3290
Spiritual steps to Christmas. 8
Spiritual struggles of a Roman Catholic. 797
Spiritual studies in St. John's Gospel. 420
Spiritual studies in St. Luke's Gospel. 428
Spiritual studies in St. Mark's Gospel. 436
Spiritual studies in St. Matthew's Gospel. 443
Spiritual suburbia. 3538
Spiritual supermarket. 3744
Spiritual teacher. 3494
Spiritual teaching of Father Steuart, S. J. 3223, 3489
Spiritual teaching of Mary of the Incarnation. 2334, 3492
Spiritual teaching of Ramana Maharshi. 3491
Spiritual teaching of the New Testament. 476
... The Spiritual telegraph. 3520
Spiritual telegraphic opposition line. 3497
Spiritual theology. 3521
Spiritual theology for novices. 3485
Spiritual therapy. 2782
Spiritual thoughts and aspirations of St. Vincent Pallotti. 2766
Spiritual thoughts and prayers. 2895
Spiritual thoughts for candid readers. 3483
Spiritual torrents. 3013

Spiritual tour of the world in search of the line of life's evolution. 1371
Spiritual traveler. 1399, 3310
Spiritual treasure. 840
Spiritual treasure in earthen vessels. 3477
Spiritual treasury. 2960
Spiritual truth. 2990
Spiritual truth . . . spiritual law. 1608
Spiritual truths. 2692
Spiritual union and communion. 3481
Spiritual unrest. 1056
Spiritual values. 3479
Spiritual values and world affairs. 1282
Spiritual values in camping. 733
Spiritual values of life. 2143
Spiritual vibrations. 671, 3502
Spiritual voyage. 685
Spiritual warfare. 988, 3678
Spiritual way. 3205, 3477
Spiritual well-being of the elderly. 18
Spiritual wives. 1652
Spiritual writers in modern times. 3492
Spiritual writers of the early church. 2644
Spiritual writers of the Middle Ages. 1455
Spiritual writings. 777, 2642
Spiritual yoga. 3863
Spiritualism. 3501, 3502, 3504, 3506, 3511, 3513
Spiritualism, a fact. 3497
Spiritualism, a fake. 3517
Spiritualism among civilised and savage races. 3507
Spiritualism and a guide to mediumship. 3503
Spiritualism and allied causes and conditions of nervous derangement. 3504
Spiritualism and charlatanism. 3506
Spiritualism and Christianity. 3507
Spiritualism and necromancy. 3509
Spiritualism and psychical research. 3504
Spiritualism and religion. 3497
Spiritualism and society. 3509
Spiritualism and spirit phenomena in 1707. 1673
... Spiritualism and the Christian faith. 3495
Spiritualism and the church. 3505
Spiritualism answered by science. 3498
Spiritualism examined and refuted. 3499
Spiritualism explained. 3516
Spiritualism exposed. 3494, 3501
Spiritualism identical with ancient sorcery. 3508
Spiritualism of nature. 3498
Spiritualism on trial. 3501
Spiritualism sustained, in five lectures. 3506
Spiritualism tested. 3513
Spiritualism today. 3502
Spiritualism unveiled. 3503
Spiritualism versus Christianity. 3499, 3504
Spiritualism, what is it? 3516
Spiritualism's challenge. 3496
Spiritualist lyceum manual. 3520
Spiritualist manual. 3509
Spiritualist philosophy. 3474, 3512
... Spiritualist register. 3520
Spiritualists. 1369
Spiritualists' iniquities unmasked. 3504
Spiritualite de l'heresie. 22
Spirituality and administration. 666
Spirituality and immortality of man. 2690
Spirituality and originality. 3490
Spirituality and the desert experience. 3490
Spirituality and the states of life. 3488
Spirituality, death, and dying. 1417
Spirituality for ministry. 1298
Spirituality for mission. 2494
Spirituality for modern man. 3485
Spirituality for postulate. 3491
Spirituality for religious life. 2570
Spirituality from the desert. 2571
SPIRITUALITY in church and world. 1002
Spirituality in the priesthood. 1299
Spirituality in the secular city. 1154
Spirituality in the space age. 3069
Spirituality named compassion and the healing of the global village, Humpty Dumpty and us. 3486
Spirituality of John Calvin. 728, 3492
Spirituality of John Henry Newman. 2702
Spirituality of Judaism. 2142
Spirituality of love. 2264
Spirituality of St. Ignatius Loyola. 2269
Spirituality of Teilhard de Chardin. 3492, 3521, 3592, 3593
Spirituality of the Beatitudes. 180
Spirituality of the layman. 2192
Spirituality of the Mass. 2366
Spirituality of the Mass in the light of Thomistic theology. 2366
Spirituality of the New Testament. 347
Spirituality of the Old Testament. 3484

Spirituality of the road. 326, 3521
Spirituality of the sacraments. 3262
Spirituality of the teaching sister. 3487
Spirituality of Vatican II. 3628, 3771
Spirituality of Western Christendom. 3521
Spirituality through the centuries. 2645
Spirituals and the blues. 2680, 3522
Spiritualsm. 3511
Spirituel gravity. 3480
Spiritus creator. 1831, 1835, 2276
Spiritusal growth. 3481
Spiritiual diary for saints & not-so-saintly. 2398, 3812
Spiritual exercises for a ten days' retreat. 3223
Spiritual Gospel. 421
Spiritual life. 90
Spiritual mysteries revealed unto man. 3516
Spiritual prescriptions for health, happiness and abundance. 3475
Spirituality in the space age. 3069
Splendor and strength of the inner life. 3488
Splendor in the night. 2638, 2640
Splendor in the ordinary. 1608
Splendor of his ways. 550
Splendor of Pentecost. 2813
Splendor of sorrow. 3459
Splendor of the gods. 750
Splendor of the Psalms. 586
... The splendor of the rosary. 3248
Splendors of Islam. 86
Splendour from the sea. 2558
Splendour of Asia. 700
Splendour of His glory. 1558
Splendour of the church. 756, 1120
Splendour of the liturgy. 2368
Splinters from an African log. 2500, 3539
Splinters in the quick. 3358
Split-level fellowship. 2791
Split-level lives. 1132, 2325
Split second from hell. 1576, 2308
Spoiled priest. 3130
Spoken and heard. 1660, 3361
Spoken by the spirit. 1717
Spoken in the market place. 75
... Spokesman for God. 567
Spokesmen for God. 568, 569, 3184, 3375
Spokesmen for God (Isaiah, Jeremiah) 3375
Sponsa Christi. 2581
Sponsors at baptism and confirmation. 3522
Spontaneous expansion of the church and the causes which hinder it. 2518
Spook crooks! 3511, 3520
Spooks. 2732
Spooks deluxe. 1710
Spoonful of honey. 1650
Sport alive! 102
Sports and wrinkles. 1608
Sports editor finds Christ. 1361
Spotlight on Catholic church music. 1205
Spotlights on matters spiritual. 998
Spots and wrinkles. 1608
Spray from an inland sea. 3473
...The spread of Christianity. 1100, 1176
Spread of Christianity in the modern world. 2526
Spread wide the curtain. 986, 2463
Spreading flame. 1189, 1195
Spreading Scriptural holiness. 2482
Sprig of holly. 1112
Sprig of hope. 2438, 3360
Spring Bank Methodist Chapel 1880-1961. 911
Spring in the desert. 578
Spring morning, and other allegories. 1015
Spring reunion, nineteen hundred and seventeen. 1671
Spring-time of life. 3869
Spring up, O well. 2119, 3896
Spring wind. 1425
Springboard to discovery. 3529
Springboards for discussion no. 2. 1169
Springfield Church. 3714
Springfield church survey. 3522
Springfield mitre. 2974
Springfiled, Ohio, YMCA. 3875
Springs and wells in Greek and Roman literature, their legends and locations. 3523
Springs in the desert. 578
Springs in the valley. 1437
*Springs of consolation. 1354
Springs of creative living. 2999
Springs of creativity. 611
Springs of devotion. 2882
Springs of love. 2393
Springs of Mende belief and conduct. 2402
Springs of morality. 1537
Springs of silence. 764
Springtime coming. 530
Springtime of the liturgy. 2239
Sprinkling. 134

Sprinkling a scriptural mode. 135
Sprinkling the only mode of baptism made known in the Scriptures. 136
Sprinkling the proper mode, and infants proper subjects of Christian baptism. 134
Sprint for the sun. 2398
Spritual direction. 3489
Spurgeon. 3523
Spurgeon, heir of the Puritans. 3523
Spurgeon on revival. 1565, 3523
Spurgeon's catechism. 145
Spurgeon's devotional bible. 1453
Spurgeon's illustrative anecdotes. 1842
Spurgeon's lectures to his students. 2906
Spurgeon's sermons on the second coming. 3321
Spurs to conversion. 1358
Spurs to meditation. 2380
Squanicook parish. 3705
Square look into eternity. 1533
Square-rigged cruiser. 3317
Squaring up. 906
Squash family. 1301
Squirrel's bank account, and other children's sermons. 908
Sree Krishna. 2186
Sri Aurobindo. 1709
Sri Aurobindo, seer and poet. 1709
Sri Caitanya-caritamrta of Krsnadasa Kaviraja Gosvami. 879
Sri Guru-Granth Sahib. 3408
Sri Isopanisad. 3760
Sri Lalita Sahasranamam. 1815
Sri Mad Devi Bhagavatam. 3005
Sri Narada Pancharatnam. 1815
Sri Ramakrishna and his disciples. 3020
Sri Ramakrishna, in the eyes of Brahma and Christian admirers. 3020
Sri Swami Satchidananda. 1816, 3304
Sri Varadarajaswami Temple, Kanchi. 3523, 3599
Sri Visnu saharanamam with the commentaries of Sri Sankaracarya and Sri Parasara. 1816
Srimad Bhagavadgita; or, The Blessed Lord's sons. 196
Srimad Bhagavatam. 3005
Srimad Bhagwatam. 879
Soren Kierkegaard. 2170
SS. Peter and Paul in Rome. 919, 2824
... St Chrysostom On the priesthood. 1295
St Mark. 432
St Paul's epistle to the Ephesians. 364
St Teresa of Avila. 1028, 3603
Staat und evangelische Kirche im Konigreich Hannover. 1146
Stability amid change. 1059
Stability of the covenant of grace. 3522
...The staff method. 2933
Stage acquitted. 3237, 3607
Stages. 161
Stages in prayer. 2868
Stages of experience. 1263
Stages of faith. 1591
Stages of higher knowledge. 50
Stages on the road. 765
Stained glass at Chartres. 1715
Stains on glass windows. 3678
Stairway of life. 2693
Stairway of perfection. 1447
Stairway to heaven. 1890
Stairway to the stars; a story of St. Germaine Cousin. 1707
Staking your claim on healing. 1598
Stalwart builders. 1667
Stalwarts of Mormonism. 2609
Stammerer's tongue. 900
Stand fast in faith. 1313
Stand firm in the faith. 326
Stand firm in the Lord. 854
Stand in the door. 1301, 1744
Stand on ecumenism. 3774
Stand still & move ahead. 365
Stand strong in the Lord. 3486
Stand up and preach. 2897
Stand up in praise to God. 3715
Stand up to life. 1008
Stand ye in holy places. 2609
Standard bearers. 805
Standard Bible commentary. 344
Standard Bible commentary: Mark. 434
Standard Bible dictionary. 244
Standard Bible story readers. 620
Standard catalog for high school libraries. 656, 2224
Standard chronology of the Holy Bible. 218
Standard commentary on the International Sunday-school lessons. 1916
Standard course in teacher training. 3178
Standard for the people, peace, prosperity, life liberty, health, happiness, man's heart desire. 1940
Standard Freemasonary illustrated. 1668
Standard Haggadah. 2110
Standard handbook of the Bible. 286

Standard historical catechism of the African Methodist Episcopal Zion church. 15
Standard leadership curriculum. 3162
... The Standard leadership training curriculum. 3161
Standard lesson commentary. 1916
Standard masonic monitor of the degrees of entered apprentice, fellow craft and master mason. 1670
Standard oratorios. 2740
Standard prayer book. 2109
Standard reference indexed Bible. 271
Standard vacation Bible school courses. 3762, 3766
Standard works of the Rev. William Jay. 3631
Standardization. 805
Standardization and its influence on Catholic secondary education in the United States. 805, 806
Standards and trends in religious education. 3189
Standards for city church plants. 1199
Standing before God. 1742, 2734
Standing on the promises. 330, 989, 2128
Standing orders. 648
Standing orders of the Church of England. 1489, 2304
Standing room only. 3347
Standing up to life. 958, 2931
Stanford Memorial Church. 3524
Stanley Frodsham, prophet with a pen. 1689
Stanzas of dzjn. 2835
Stapleton's Fortress overthrown. 3525
Star and door of hope. 2002
... The star and the altar. 2360
Star and the cross. 1083
Star at midnight. 160
Star book for ministers. 3672
Star book on Baptist church polity. 150
Star book on Baptist councils. 150
Star book on Christian baptism. 135
Star-crossed renaissance. 98
Star gates. 1262
Star guests. 2728
... Star habits and orbits. 3687
Star in the East. 749, 1111, 2021, 2164, 2516
Star in the South. 1476
Star in Wachovia. 2827
Star lore and the Bible. 96
Star lore and the Bible: astronomical, astrological, interpretation. 96
Star of Bethlehem. 1978, 2028, 2039, 2088
Star of Endor. 2724
Star of Jacob. 2223
Star of our Lord. 1100, 2311
Star of progress. 1203
Star of redemption. 2140
"The Star of the Naga hills" 2503
Star on the mountain. 3298
... The star out of Jacob. 1984
Star over Jordan. 1809
Star over the Kremlin. 1320
Star-promise. 957
Star rose in the West. 2721
Star shone. 1984
Star-studded hoax of Christianity with its allied gods. 1090
Star trails to life beautiful. 958
Starck's motherhood prayers for all occasions. 2625
Stardust book of prayers. 899
Starets Paisii Velichkovskii. 2583, 2760
Starlight in the dark. 1592
Starlight talks to youth. 3886
Starlore among the Navaho. 2677
Starra. 1419
... Starrs and Jewish charters preserved in the British museum. 1419
Starry universe the Christian's future empire. 1697
Stars and angels. 1111
Stars & firelight. 2386
Stars and the angels. 99
Stars and the Bible. 202
Stars and the Book. 2435
Stars appearing. 3280
... The stars are still there. 3518
Stars, atoms, and God. 3078
Stars beyond the storms: Father Etienne Pernet, founder of the Congregation of the Little Sisters of the Assumption. 2233, 2820
Stars, how and where they influence. 95
Stars in our heaven, myths and fables. 3525
Stars in the night. 1707
Stars in the sky. 1353
Stars of Christmas. 9
Stars of comfort. 2392
Stars on Sunday. 3525, 3594
Stars over Bethlehem. 195
Stars, spells, secrets, and sorcery. 2732

Stars tell the story too. 211
Stars through the apple tree. 1308
Start and finish of a day. 975
Start here; directions for young Christians. 1431
Start loving. 1633
Start thinking of God. 2384
Start where you are. 2435, 2932, 3377
Start your child right. 3388
Starting afresh. 967
Starting points. 2574
Starting to teach. 638, 3177
Startling facts in modern spiritualism. 3519
Startling incidents and experiences in the Christian life. 957
Starved and the silent. 2537
State and area organization briefs, 1961, Christian Churches (Disciples of Christ) 1462
State and the church. 1125, 1141, 1142, 1143
State and the church in a free society. 1141
State in the New Testament. 1142
State of aloneness. 2227
State of Illinois, Ogle county. ss. in the Circuit court of said county. In chancery. The Catholic bishop of Chicago. 815
State of perfection and the secular priest. 2819
State of the churches in the U.S.A., 1973, as shown in their own official yearbooks. 3327
State of the dead. 1408, 1912
State of the dead and the destiny of the wicked. 1912
State of the departed. 1912, 2589
State of the impenitent dead. 1699
State population census by faiths. 1248
State, society, and economy in Saudi Arabia. 3304
State street church, Portland, Maine, 1852-1902. 1336
Stately mansion; a history of the United Church of Christ of Kent. 2167
Statement, addressed to the Episcopalians in the state of New-York, relative to some recent events in the Protestant Episcopal church in the said state. 2130
Statement for reasons for not believing the doctrines of Trinitarians. 3728
Statement of reasons for embracing the doctrines and disclosures of Emanuel Swedenborg. 2690
Statement of reasons for not believing the doctrines ofTrinitarians. 3728
Statement of the congregation of the Church of the Epiphany, Philadelphia. 3719
Statement of the proceedings in the First church, and parish in Dedham. 1419, 2195
Statement of the proceedings of the presbytery of Glasgow relative to the use of an organ in St. Andrew's church, in the public worship of God. 1234
Statement of the Trinitarian principle. 3711
Statements of religious bodies on the conscientious objector. 1348
States of perfection. 2574
Statesman and saint. 1763, 3831
Statesman's manual. 1306
Statesmanship and religion. 3447
Statesmanship of Benedict xv. 190
Station Astral. 3501
Stations of the cross. 3526
*Stations of the Cross for children. 3526
Stations of wisdom. 3104
Statistical history of the Maine conference of the M. E. church from 1793 to 1893. 2446
Statistical profile of Black Catholics. 15
Statistical study of literary vocabulary. 1885, 3692
Statistical tables. 32
Statistical year-book of the Evangelical Lutheran synod of Missouri, Ohio, and other states. 1549
Statistical yearbook. 2296
Statistics of First Unitarian Church, Salt Lake City, Utah 1891-1966. 3287
... Statistics of Jews. 2122
Statistics of Jews and Jewish organizations. 2105
Stature of a perfect man. 3484
Status of secularized ex-religious clerics. 2578
Status of the Arab woman. 3834
Status sof Protestant weekday church schools in the United States. 3800
Statutes and regulations. 1671
Statutes of Lincoln cathedral. 2230
Statutes of the diocese of Crookston. 735
Stay alive all your life. 2994
Stay with me Lord. 2895

Stay with us. 2889
Stay with us, Lord. 788
Steady light. 970
Steam engine fulfilling prophecy. 305
Steep ascent. 2210
Steeple among the oaks. 2719
Steeple beckons. 1626, 3716
Steeple Jim. 2775, 3596
Steeple people and the world. 2480
Steeples against the sky. 3467
Steeples among the hills. 2785
Steeples among the sage. 2686
Steeples in metropolis. 1278
Steering by the star. 2536, 3387
Steering by the stars, and other talks with the juniors. 909
Steering or drifting--which? 2116
Steinbach and its churches. 3452
Steinerbooks dictionary of the psychic, mystic, occult. 2993
Stellar almanac. 1802
Stellar key to the summar land. 3500
Stencil maps and missionary chalk-talks for Sunday schools. 2550
Stenciled of God. 3884
Stenographic report of the great "liberal" trial in the Covenanter synod of 1891. 2306
Step a little higher. 2602
Step beyond impasse. 878
Step by step. 2402
Step by step in theology. 3662
Step by step introduction to the Old Testament. 598
Step-by-step learning guide for older retarded children. 2411
Step this way, Sister. 2573
Stepfamilies, living in Christian harmony. 1610
Stephanite emigration to America. 2297, 2303
Stephen Grellet. 1774
Stephen Grellet, 1773-1855. 1774
Stephen Langton. 2195
Stephen S. Wise: Servant of the people. 3144
Stephen speech. 334, 3527
Stephen T. Badin. 125
Stepping ahead. 1047
Stepping heavenward. 1451
Stepping nearer. 3143
Stepping-stones. 293, 993, 3259
Stepping stones to an abundant life. 2608
... Stepping stones to divine intervention. 3508
Stepping stones to freedom. 976
Stepping stones to glory. 2667
Stepping-stones to Heaven. 3292
Stepping stones to sanctity. 996, 999, 3480
Stepping stones to truth. 1051
Steps and studies. 1834
Steps Christward. 956
Steps heavenward. 2593
Steps in self-knowledge. 3750
Steps in spiritual unfoldment. 3478
Steps in the Christian life. 975
Steps in the life of faith. 1594
Steps into light. 858, 3406
Steps of a good man. 2509
Steps of belief. 1091
Steps of Bonhoeffer. 676
Steps of humility. 1855
Steps of Jesus. 1989
Steps on the ladder of faith. 1049
Steps to Christ. 979, 3292
Steps to Christian understanding. 61
Steps to Christian unity. 1044
Steps to crucifixion. 2213
Steps to heaven. 3295
Steps to heaven via the true kindergarten. 3185
Steps to Jesus. 3291
Steps to life. 1273, 3347
Steps to prayer power. 2874
Steps to salvation. 1499, 2910, 3289
Steps to self-mastery. 2728
Steps to the sermon. 2898
Steps to the sun. 2632
Steps to the throne. 3321
Steps toward a singing church. 915
Steps toward Christian unity and church federation. 1492
Steps toward the world council. 1044
Steps toward understanding of Islam. 1922
Steps toward undrstanding Islam. 1922
Steps unto heaven. 584, 3195
Steps upward in personality. 2591
Stereoscopic prayer. 2877
Sterlization controversy. 3527
Steve Bartkowski intercepted. 177, 931
Stevens-Beevers debate on the New Testament and Roman Catholicism. 794
Steward family. 3529
Steward in the Methodist church. 1239
Steward of souls. 1781
Stewardess. 3528

Stewards appointed. 2279, 3529
Stewards of God. 3531
Stewards of the gospel. 3530
Stewards of the grace of God. 3529
Stewardship. 190, 1168, 3528, 3529, 3531
Stewardship among Baptists. 3530
Stewardship and Christmas stories. 3530
Stewardship and the tithe. 3529
Stewardship and the world mission. 3530
Stewardship and tithing. 952
"Stewardship born of God" 3530
Stewardship call. 3530
Stewardship enriches life. 3529
... Stewardship for all of life. 3529
Stewardship for today's woman. 3530
Stewardship helps for fifty-two Sundays. 1840
Stewardship illustration. 3530
Stewardship illustrations. 3530
Stewardship in contemporary life. 3530
Stewardship in contemporary theology. 3530
Stewardship in life of youth. 3531
Stewardship in Methodism. 1168
Stewardship in mission. 3530
Stewardship in the life of women. 1252
Stewardship in the New Testament church. 377
Stewardship life. 966, 3531
Stewardship-myth and methods. 3529
Stewardship of faith. 1050
Stewardship of God's tomorrow . . .selected sermons from the stewardship preaching fellowship. 3531
Stewardship of life. 3528
Stewardship of money. 3531
Stewardship of sorrow. 1351
Stewardship of spiritual gifts. 323, 2815
Stewardship opportunities and responsibilities. 3217
Stewardship parables of Jesus. 2025
Stewardship sermonettes. 3531
Stewardship sermons. 3531
Stewardship starting points. 3528
Stewardship stories. 3531
Stewardship stories for boys and girls. 3531
Stewardship studies. 3530
Stewardship: total-life commitment. 3528
Stewardship unlimited. 3529
Stewardship upside down. 3530
Stewardship without failure. 1168
Stewardship and missions. 2518
Stick to it farmer boy. 3143
Still a Christian. 62, 670
Still higher for His Highest. 1430
Still hour. 2877
Still more adventures. 3206
Still point. 2643, 3482
Still shine the stars. 1056
Still small voice. 1078, 1451, 1539, 3344, 3351
Still the trumpet sounds. 3352
Still time to sing. 17
Still waters. 1433
Still we can hope. 1452
Stillpoint. 2643
Stimmen der Kirche. 3183
Stimulating sermon outlines. 3375
Stimuli. 863
Stimulus of Christ. 2436
Stir, change, create. 2856
"Stir up the fire" considerations on the priesthood. 1299
Stir up the gift. 1569
Stir what you've got! and other stewardship studies. 3528
Stirred nest. 2931
Stirring giant. 1244
Stirring the embers. 2393
Stirrings. 3618
Stirrings of unity. 999
Stitches for God. 1488, 3796
Stock charges against the Bible. 515
Stockholm conference, 1925. 1090
Stoic and Christian in the second century. 3532
... Stoic and Epicurean. 3533
Stoic arguments for the existence and the providence of the gods. 1743
Stoic, Christian, and humanist. 3067
Stoic philosophy. 3533
...Stoicism. 3533
Stoicism and its influence. 3533
Stoics and saints. 3532
Stoics and sceptics. 3532
Stokes' wonder book of the Bible. 197
Stolen bridegroom. 2529
Stolen church, martyrdom in Communist Romania. 1299, 3025
Stone and the image. 508
Stone in the King's highway. 776
Stone lantern essays. 3479
Stone of help. 2443
Stones and the Scriptures. 209
Stones by the river. 92
Stones cry out. 207

Stones of fire. 2538
Stones of the abbey. 2203
Stones rolled away. 959
Stones will cry out. 852, 2830
Stonor, a Catholic sanctuary in the Chilterns from the fifth century til to-day. 3533
Stonyhurst Gospel of Saint John. 680
Stop existing and start living. 1454
Stop killing dragons. 2510
Stop, look and live. 1434
Stop looking and listen. 67
Stop playing pious games. 985
Stop the church ..., I want to get off! 1001
Stop the merry-go-round. 1558
Stop the world, I want to get on. 2495
Stopford Brooke. 693
Store of the New Testament. 409
Storehouse tithing; or, Stewardship up-to-date. 3702
Storia ecclesiastica. 1191
Stories about Jesus. 3765
Stories about Jesus, Our Lord and Saviour. 626, 1979
Stories about Joseph Smith. 2605, 3429
Stories about Judaism. 2154
Stories and lessons. 596
Stories and parables of the Hafetz Hayyim. 3581
Stories and parables to illustrate gospel truths. 624
Stories and pictures from the life of Jesus. 1979
Stories explanatory of the church catechism. 911
Stories for all the year. 1015
Stories for discussion. 1013
Stories for junior worship. 910
Stories for pulpit and platform. 1843
Stories for sermons. 1602, 3375
Stories for speakers and writers. 1841
Stories for special days. 909
Stories for special days in the church school. 910
Stories for Sunday telling. 3549
Stories for Sundays illustrating the catechism. 1215
Stories for talks to boys. 3875
Stories for talks with boys and girls. 1253
Stories for the junior hour. 632
Stories from Brethren life. 1236
Stories from Dante. 1402
Stories from Hebrew history for juniors. 2093
Stories from Holy Writ. 624
Stories from Madagascar. 2538
Stories from Mormon history. 2615
Stories from our living past. 3581
Stories from the Bible. 620, 622, 624, 626, 628, 630
Stories from the great library. 3153
Stories from the Hebrew. 628
Stories from the history of the Armenian Church. 82
Stories from the history of the Jews. 2094
Stories from the life of Christ. 911
Stories from the life of Christ for the Primary department of the Sunday school. 1992
Stories from the life of Christ selected for the children. 1979
Stories from the life of Jesus. 1979
Stories from the life of Jesus, told for little children. 910
Stories from the lips of a Teacher. 2027
Stories from the lips of the Teacher. 2027
Stories from the New Testament. 625, 627, 1979
... Stories from the Norse. 911
Stories from the Old and New Testaments. 621
Stories from the Old Testament. 627, 629, 630, 631, 2133
Stories from the Old Testament for children. 627
Stories from the Old Testament for the little child. 910
Stories from the Old Testament for the primary department of the Sunday school. 630
Stories from the Old Testament told for little children. 910
Stories from the rabbis. 3581
Stories from the Ten commandments for young Latter-Day Saints. 1315
Stories from the Word. 623, 624
Stories from the workingman's book. 1319, 2064
Stories Jesus heard and stories Jesus told. 2065
Stories Jesus loved when he was young retold for children who love stories to-day. 623, 1996
Stories Jesus told. 616, 627, 2025, 2027, 2067

Stories, legends, songs and plays for the Christmas holidays. 1112
Stories made of Bible stories. 3882
Stories of a people. 3155
Stories of beautiful hymns. 1874
Stories of beginnings. 3155
Stories of Bible victories, from the Old Testament. 635
Stories of child life in a Jewish colony in Palestine. 897
Stories of childrens hymns. 1872
Stories of David and Goliath, and Daniel in the Lion's den. 629
Stories of Dominican saints for children. 1475
... Stories of early church heroes. 3146
Stories of fadeless hymns. 1871
Stories of favorite hymns. 1874
Stories of God. 3534
Stories of gods and heroes. 2650, 2664
Stories of great heroes, discoverers, explorers and christianizers of America. 662
Stories of healing from the Bible. 252
Stories of hymn tunes. 1875
Stories of hymns for creative living. 1871
Stories of hymns we love. 1876
Stories of insight and inspiration. 1232
Stories of inspiring hymns, with selected poems. 1874
Stories of Jesus. 632, 930, 1966, 1972, 1973, 1979, 1980, 1981, 1983, 1984, 1992, 3146
Stories of Jesus for little children. 1982
Stories of Jewish symbols. 1395
Stories of King David. 1404
Stories of King Solomon. 3457
Stories of Latter-day saint hymns. 1872
Stories of little Ellen and the message. 3811
... Stories of long ago. 295, 1968
Stories of my grandmother. 973, 3811
Stories of old St. Bridget's. 1898
Stories of our century by Catholic authors. 3404
Stories of our favorite hymns. 1869
Stories of paradise. 3485
Stories of Pope John XXIII. 2123
Stories of popular hymns. 1874
Stories of power and purpose. 1013
Stories of providential deliverance. 2982
Stories of shepherd life. 616
Stories of songs about heaven. 1871
Stories of the angels. 42
Stories of the beginnings. 3184
Stories of the Bible. 293, 629
Stories of the Bible in verse. 298
Stories of the Book of books. 290
Stories of the Buddha. 702
Stories of the Christ child. 1996
Stories of the Christian hymns. 1873
... Stories of the early Hebrew heroes. 3146
... Stories of the golden age. 2649
Stories of the great apostles. 72
Stories of the great hymns of the church. 1872
Stories of the Greeks. 2662
Stories of the high priests of Memphis. 1503
Stories of the Hindus. 2663
Stories of the holy fathers. 55, 2578
Stories of the kings from David to Christ. 628, 2177
Stories of the miracles of Our Lord. 2018
Stories of the patriarchs. 2792
Stories of the prophets. 2950
Stories of the prophets as told to their friends. 568
Stories of the prophets, warriors and kings. 2792
Stories of the reformation in England and Scotland. 3039
Stories of the Reformation in the Netherlands. 3041
Stories of the Restoration. 911
Stories of the saints. 3281, 3284
Stories of the saints for children. 3280
Stories of the saints of East and West. 1616
Stories of venial sin. 3343
Stories of wonderful hymns. 1874
Stories of yuletide. 1875
Stories round the year. 2161, 3581
Stories that live. 1325
Stories that might have been. 632
Stories that strengthen. 1325
Stories to live by. 182, 3881
Stories to tell. 1289
Stories to tell children. 910
Stories to the dark. 2649
Stories todl by Our Lord. 2027
Stories told by Our Lord. 2027
Stork family in the Lutheran church. 3533
Storm king. 198
Storm of glory. 3690
Storm the gates of Jericho. 2138

Stormers of heaven. 3127
Storming heaven. 2310
Storming the gates of hell. 331
Storms and starlight. 960, 1833
Story. 2920
Story a day. 904
Story about light. 1254, 3217
Story and faith in the Biblical narrative. 211
Story and promise. 3663
Story and reality. 3717
Story and significance of the Augsburg confession on its four hundredth anniversary. 109
Story and work of the Methodist Church. 2426
"Story beautiful" of all the ages, the night when the angels sang at Jesus' birth. 1973
Story Bible. 616, 619, 625
Story book of Jesus. 1973
Story books of the early Hebrews. 533
Story brought by Brigit. 2003
Story ever new, giving the most interesting events in the life of Jesus Christ as a textbook in religion for grammar grade children. 2066
... Story hour courses for children from Greek myths. 911
Story hour leadership manual. 3534
Story illustrations for church and home. 1842
Story in Scripture. 253
Story in the Rosary. 3247
"story lady's" Christmas stories. 1114
Story-life of the Son of man. 1974
... The story of a beautiful life illustrated. 1964
Story of a century. 732, 1464
Story of a charity school, two centuries of popular education in Soho, 1699-1899. 3273
Story of a church. 2826
Story of a church, its priests and its people. 3788
Story of a conscrated life. 1290
Story of a county pastor. 1824
Story of a family. 2348
Story of a fortunate youth. 3131
Story of a little girl. 1777
Story of a monastery. 2573
Story of a mother. 3817
Story of a mother church, St. John's Orange, N. J., 1851-1934. 2740
Story of a mountain missionary. 1629
Story of a nun. 696, 2717
Story of a Parish. 1509
Story of a parish, 1847-1892. 873
Story of a soul. 1026, 2944, 3282, 3691
Story of a varied life. 3133
Story of a village church in a village of churches. 3238
Story of a working man's life. 2505
Story of a young man (a life of Christ) 1966
Story of Abraham. 4
Story of Abraham as told by Isaac. 4
Story of agricultural missions. 2520
Story of Albert Schweitzer. 3311, 3312
Story of Alexanderwohl. 24
Story of All Saints Chapel. 117
Story of American Catholicism. 833, 834
Story of American dissent. 1469
Story of American Methodism. 2438
Story of American Protestantism. 2955, 3738
Story of America's religions. 3326
Story of an English sister. 3244
Story of an immigrant group in Franklin, New Jersey. 1651, 1856
Story of an Indian coin. 2491
Story of Ananias and Sapphira. 38
Story of Antoinette Margot. 3818
Story of Arachne. 78, 2660
Story of Assumption of B.V.M. Church, Lebanon, Pennsylvania. 2205
Story of astrology. 98
Story of Aunt Lizzie Aiken. 20
Story of Baltimore Yearly meeting from 1672 to 1938. 1677
Story of Baptist missions in foreign lands. 155
Story of Baucis and Philemon. 178, 2660
Story of Bible Christian Union. 218
Story of Bible translations. 655
Story of Blessed Imelda. 2194
Story of Blessed Martin de Porres. 2348
Story of Boscawen church. 682
Story of Bristol cathedral. 692
Story of Buddha and Buddhism. 701
Story of Buddhism. 703
Story of C. F. W. Walther. 3790
Story of Cadmus. 723
Story of Camp Alexander Mack, 1924-1955. 731
Story of Catholics in America. 834, 874
... The story of Channing. 882

Story of Chaplain Kapaun. 2164, 2185
... The story of Chasam Sofer. 3311
Story of Christ and His apostles. 1986
Story of Christ and the early church. 354
Story of Christ Church Christiana Hundred and its people. 918
Story of Christ Church, Exeter, New Hampshire, 1865-1965. 1583
Story of Christian activism. 2669
Story of Christian hymnody. 1876
Story of Christianity. 1174
Story of Christmas. 1110, 1111, 2022
Story of Christ's passion. 2029, 2032
Story of Chung Mei. 1116
Story of church unity. 1042
Story of Confucius. 1330
Story of courage. 1650, 3797
Story of Cousin George. 3590
Story of creation. 1379, 1380
Story of Cupid and Psyche. 1397
Story of D. S. Burnet. 718
Story of Dan Lyons, S.J. 2304
...The story of Daniel. 1401
Story of Daniel the prophet. 1401
Story of David. 1405
Story of David Livingstone. 2241
... Story of Dinah Doudney, Portsea, England. 3559
Story of Dr. Pusey's life. 3010
Story of Easter. 1985
Story of Easter according to St. Matthew. 736, 737
Story of Ellen. 932, 3304
Story of Emmanuel Church at Brook Hill, in the diocese of Virginia, 1860-1960. 1511
Story of Esther. 630, 631, 1532, 1533
Story of European Christianity. 1097, 1188
Story of faith healing. 1599
... Story of Father Andrew White, S.J. 3811
Story of Father Price. 2938
... The story of Father Van den Broek. 3767
Story of Fatima. 1618
Story of fifty hymns. 1876
Story of fifty years. 1653
Story of First Methodist Church, Maryville, Tennessee. 2364
Story of four churches. 1270
Story of four Gospels. 284
Story of Frances Banks. 1639
Story of Gabrielle. 1700
Story of George Fox. 1637
Story of Georgia Baptist. 150
Story of Georgia Baptists. 150
Story of German Methodism. 2459
Story of God's kingdom. 2284
Story of God's love. 622
Story of God's redeeming love. 646
Story of good Pope John. 2124
Story of hope: the nation, the man, the kingdom. 236, 1123, 2043
Story of India. 1813
Story of Israel. 531, 2087
Story of Israel for children. 2093
Story of Jesus. 399, 400, 401, 626, 1955, 1957, 1961, 1962, 1964, 1965, 1967, 1970, 1971, 1979, 1980, 1981, 1982, 1983, 1984, 1989, 1992, 1999, 2023
Story of Jesus and the beginnings of the church. 387
Story of Jesus and the lives of His apostles. 71, 1973
Story of Jesus as told by grandfather John. 1975
Story of Jesus as told in the four Gospels. 1990
Story of Jesus Christ. 1974, 1959
Story of Jesus Christ the Saviour. 1974
Story of Jesus every child should know. 1981
Story of Jesus for boys and girls. 1960, 1979, 1982
Story of Jesus for children. 1979
Story of Jesus for little people. 1982
Story of Jesus for young people. 1980
Story of Jesus in the words of the four Gospels. 1988
Story of Jesus in the world's literature. 2012
Story of Jesus in verse. 2047
Story of Jesus of Nazareth. 1983
Story of Jesus--the Christ. 1966, 1987, 1989
... The story of Jesus told for little children in words of one syllable. 1983
Story of Jewish holidays and customs for young people. 1624
Story of Jewish philosophy. 2842
Story of Job. 2125
Story of John Frederic Oberlin. 2720
Story of John G. Paton. 2733, 2792
Story of John, the beloved disciple. 2127
Story of Jonah. 494, 2129, 2130, 2952
...The story of Joseph. 527, 2132, 2134

Story of Joseph as told in the Old Testament. 527
Story of Joseph for young people. 2134
Story of Joseph, read for its practical lessons. 2133
Story of Judaism. 2137, 2146
Story of Kathleen Mallory. 2319, 3468
Story of King Midas. 2461
Story of Kingston Congregational Church. 2177
Story of La Salette. 3286
Story of Lazarus. 2203
Story of Lent in art masterpieces. 1957
Story of Lincoln Minster. 2230
Story of little Lu De. 2489
Story of Lourdes. 2262
Story of Luther. 2276
Story of Lutheran missions. 2296
Story of man. 2325
Story of Margaret of Metola. 2332
Story of Martin Luther for young people. 2274
Story of Mary Liu. 2240
Story of Mary Slessor for young people. 3425
Story of Mary, the mother of Jesus. 2354
Story of Methodism. 2424
Story of Methodism throughout the world. 2424
Story of Methodism throughout the world, from the beginning to the present time. 2424
Story of Minnesota Methodism. 2438
Story of missions. 2763
Story of modern Israel for young people. 2763
Story of modern Palestine for young people. 3897
Story of "Mormonism" 2606
Story of Moses. 2621, 2622, 2624, 2950
Story of Moslem art. 87
Story of Musa. 897
Story of my battle with the scarlet beast. 798
Story of my life. 1575, 2310, 2455, 3591, 3811
Story of my life and the Pillar of fire. 3811
Story of my mind. 3097
... The story of my sufferings. 2102
Story of mysticism. 2645
Story of natural religion. 3093
Story of Noah. 527, 2711
... The story of Ocean Grove. 2733
Story of Oklahoma Baptists. 158
Story of old Christ Church, 1672-1972. 918
Story of old John street Methodist Episcopal church. 2699
Story of old St. George's. 2830
Story of 125 years. 2956
Story of oriental philosophy. 2839
Story of our Bible. 211, 290, 639
Story of our Christianity. 1173
Story of our church. 1236, 2920, 3386
Story of our church for young Latter-Day Saints. 2615
Story of our church, for young people of the Church of the brethren. 1236
Story of our health message. 3380
Story of our hymns. 1545, 1876
Story of Our Lady of Fatima. 1618
Story of Our Lady of Guadalupe. 1776
Story of Our Lord. 1981
Story of Our Lord's life told for children. 2014
Story of our Saviour. 1973
... The story of ourselves, a study in the growth of personality for teachers and parents. 3176
Story of patriarchs and prophets. 3384
Story of Paul. 2798, 2800
Story of Paul for boys and girls of junior high school age. 2802
Story of Paul of Tarsus. 2795
Story of Persephone. 2821
Story of Peterborough cathedral. 2826
Story of phallicism. 2828
Story of Pope John XXIII. 2123
Story of prophecy. 2946, 2950
Story of Pygmalion. 3010
Story of Quakerism. 1685
Story of Rama. 3019
Story of redemption. 3384
Story of Reform Judaism. 3032
... The story of Rehoboth, history of Rehoboth Baptist association 1856 to 1938. 170
Story of religion. 3063, 3094, 3113
Story of religion in America. 3089, 3739
Story of religions in America. 3739
Story of religious controversy. 3094
Story of research in sociology of religion: Garrett Theological Seminary, 1929-1972, including the Bureau of Social and Religious Research, established 1941. 1702, 3453

Story of Revelation. 460
Story of Reynard the Fox. 1743
Story of Robert Raikes for the young. 3019
Story of Ruth. 589
Story of Ruth the Moabitess. 3258
Story of S. Paul's Church, Heaton Moor. 3278
Story of Saint Agnes. 19
Story of St. Albans parish. 2775
Story of St. Aloysius' church. 2775
Story of St. Aloysius Gonzaga. 2271
Story of Saint Ann. 48
Story of St. Anthony of Padua. 54
Story of St. Augustine's from pioneer days, 1868, 1882, 1958. 3273
Story of St. Boniface Church. 1527
Story of St. Catherine of Alexandria. 753
Story of Saint Christopher. 1114
Story of Saint Clare. 1284
Story of Saint Dominic Savio. 3305
Story of Saint Elizabeth of Hungary. 1508
Story of Saint Francis of Assisi. 1641
Story of Saint Gemma. 1700
Story of Saint George. 1706
Story of St. James. 2755
Story of St. John Baptist de la Salle. 2189
Story of St. John Baptist de la Salle, founder of the Institute of the Brothers of the Christian schools. 2189
Story of Saint John Berchmans. 191
Story of Saint Joseph. 2132
Story of Saint Kevin. 2168
Story of Saint Lucy. 2270
Story of St. Martha's Catholic Parish. 3277
Story of St. Mary's. 2700
Story of St. Monica's parish, New York City, 1879-1954. 2699
Story of Saint Nicholas. 2707
Story of Saint Patrick. 819, 2793, 3283
Story of St. Patrick's purgatory. 2793
Story of St. Paul. 2795
Story of St. Paul's life and letters. 2802
Story of St. Peter's. 3768
Story of Saint Pius x. 2851
Story of Saint Therese. 3690
Story of St. Thomas Church. 1121
Story of Salt Lake Stake of the Church of Jesus Christ of Latter-Day Saints. 3287
Story of salvation. 602, 3177
Story of Samson and its place in the religious development of mankind. 3297
Story of Santa Klaus. 3302
Story of Silent night. 1776, 2634
Story of social Christianity. 3446
Story of Southern hymnology. 1873
Story of southern Presbyterians. 2925
Story of stewardship in the United States of America. 3530
Story of the Acts of the apostles. 329
Story of the advent message. 3379
Story of the American Bible society. 31
Story of the American board. 31, 2521
Story of the American hymn. 1872
Story of the American Lutheran Church. 32
Story of the Apocrypha. 489
Story of the apostles. 71
Story of the Augsburg confession. 109
Story of the Baal Shem. 1789, 1928
Story of the Bible. 290, 291, 292, 296, 297, 309, 624
Story of the Bible animals. 481
Story of the Bible for young and old. 294
Story of the Bible for young people. 292
... The story of the Bible from Genesis to Revelation. 292, 293
Story of the Bible from the standpoint of modern scholarship. 292
Story of the Bible people. 647
Story of the Bible world. 295
Story of the birth of Jesus in the words of Luke and Matthew. 2023
Story of the blood. 2029
Story of the Book of Mormon. 679, 2605
Story of the Canadian revision of the prayer book. 2883
Story of the catacombs. 745
Story of the catechism. 2279
Story of the Catholic church. 810
Story of the century. 2152, 3771
Story of the Cherokee Bible. 218
Story of the child that Jesus took. 2006
... The story of the chosen people. 628
Story of the Christ. 1990
Story of the Christ, as told by the Evangelists. 1991
Story of the Christ Child. 2022
Story of the Christian centuries. 1179
Story of the Christian church. 1175, 1176, 1189
Story of the Christian church in India and Pakistan. 1895
Story of the Christian science church manual, proving its immortality. 1037, 1496

Story of the Christian year. 1262
Story of the church. 809, 812, 1172, 1174, 1175, 1176, 1177, 1178, 1182, 1189, 2601, 3164, 3184
Story of the church . . . A history of the Church of Jesus Christ of Latter Day Saints, and of its legal successor, the Reorganized Church of Jesus Christ of Latter Day Saints. 1233
Story of the church, her founding, mission and progress. 812
Story of the church in China. 912
Story of the church life among Negroes in Memphis, Tennessee. 2681
Story of the church's song. 1875
Story of the Congregational Christian churches. 1339
Story of the covenant and the mystery of the Jew. 1377
Story of the cross. 445
Story of the crusades. 1390, 1391
Story of the Dead Sea scrolls. 1410, 1411
Story of the denominations. 3326
Story of the devil. 1427
Story of the diocese of Connecticut. 2963
Story of the Divine Child. 1996
Story of the early church. 333
Story of the early Church as found in the Acts of the Apostles. 330
Story of the English Bible. 248
Story of the English Evangelical Lutheran synod of the Northwest. 1517
Story of the English prayer book, its origin and developments. 1213
Story of the Episcopal church in the United States of America. 2967
Story of the Epworth league. 1525
Story of the Exodus. 602
Story of the faith. 1175
Story of the First Parish in Bedford Unitarian Universalist. 183
Story of the first twenty-five years of the Episcopal Theological Seminary of the Southwest. 117
Story of the Fort Worth Norris-Wallace debate. 1468, 2713
... The story of the founding and growth of St. Anselm's parish ... New York city. 2775
... The story of the four (evangelists) 409
Story of the friends of Jesus. 1955
Story of the future. 608
Story of the General Theological Seminary. 2699
Story of the German Bible. 283
...Story of the gospel. 383, 625, 626, 1964, 1980, 1981
Story of the gospel and scenes in Bible lands. 626, 1981
Story of the Holyoke churches. 1838
Story of the Hospitallers of St. John of God. 695
Story of the Huguenots. 1851
Story of the hymns. 1874
Story of the hymns and tunes. 1874
Story of the Infant Jesus of Prague. 1906
Story of the Inquisition. 1909
Story of the Jew for young people. 2094
Story of the Jew in Russia and Poland. 2103
Story of the Jewish people. 2094
Story of the Jewish way of life. 2081
Story of the Jews. 2088, 2089
Story of the Jews of Newport. 2101
Story of the Knights of Columbus pilgrimage. 2178
Story of the life and work of the Presbyterian theological seminary, Chicago. 893
Story of the life of Robert Sayers Sheffey. 2422, 3401
Story of the Lord Jesus. 1436, 1990
Story of the Maharishi. 2317, 3708
Story of the Man of the ages. 1967
Story of the manger. 2021
Story of the manuscripts. 290
Story of the Mass. 2365
Story of the Mennonites. 2406
Story of the Methodist Church. 2204
Story of the Mormons. 2603
Story of the Mormons; from the date of their origin to the year 1901. 2604
Story of the Morning Star. 2620
Story of the National Baptists. 2669
... Story of the National holiness missionary society. 2669
Story of the Nativity in wood engravings. 2023
Story of the Navajo Hail chant. 2677
Story of the Nazarene in annotated paraphrase. 1962
Story of the New Testament. 338, 409
Story of the New York branch of the Woman's foreign missionary society of the Methodist Episcopal church. 2458
Story of the Noah's Ark. 2712

Story of the old Spanish missions of the Southwest. 3470
Story of the Old Testament. 494, 533, 539
Story of the pearl of great price. 2610, 3430
Story of the Pope. 2861
Story of the prayer book. 1214, 2884
Story of the prayer book in England and America. 1214
Story of the Prayer book in the old and new world and throughout the Anglican church. 1214
Story of the precious blood. 693, 1958
Story of the Presbyterian Church in the U.S.A. 2925
Story of the Presbyterian Church in the U. S. A. 2925
Story of the Protestant teachers association of New York city, inc. 3167
Story of the Psalms. 579
Story of the Psalters. 586, 2986
Story of the railroad "Y" 3875
Story of the Reformation. 3036
Story of the resurrection of Christ told once more. 2051
Story of the Revelation. 454
Story of the revised New Testament. 360
Story of the revival. 2467, 3233
Story of the Romance. 2507
Story of the rosary. 3248
Story of the Russian church. 2750
Story of the San Francisco presbyterial society. 2927
Story of the Santa Maria institute. 1276
... The story of the Saracens, from the earliest times to the fall of Bagdad. 2564
Story of the Scottish Reformation. 3042
Story of the Sisters of mercy in Mississippi. 3418
Story of the sixty-six years on this corner. 2261
Story of the Southern Synod of the Evangelical and Reformed Church, 1740-1968. 1545
Story of the stories. 294, 2096
Story of the Sunday School Board. 3467
Story of the synagogue. 3166
Story of the ten commandments. 1314
Story of the Three Kings: Melchior, Balthasar, and Jaspar, which originally was written by John of Hildesheim in the fourteenth century and is now retold by Margaret B. Freeman. 2311
Story of the token. 3703
Story of the token as belonging to the sacrament of the Lord's supper. 3703
Story of the twenty-eighth International eucharistic congress held at Chicago, Illinois, United States of America. 1912
Story of the Union gospel mission, 1886-1944. 2261
Story of the Upper room. 3761
Story of the Vincentians. 3779
Story of the Welsh revival as told by eyewitnesses, together with a sketch of Evan Roberts and his message to the world. 3229
Story of the world's worship. 3115
Story of the writings. 529
Story of Theodore Parker. 2776
Story of theology. 3657
Story of Therese Neumann. 2685, 3532
Story of toil and tears, of love and laughter. 1272
Story of Trinity Church in the city of Boston. 685
Story of twentieth century Christianity. The road to Jericho. 1059
Story of twentieth century Christianity. What hast thou done? Genesis 4:10. 1059
Story of Union Baptist Association, 1840-1976. 3723
Story of Union Congregational Church. 3236
Story of Unity Church, 1872-1972. 3278
Story of Washington cathedral. 750
Story of Wells Cathedral. 3801
Story of Winchester cathedral. 3819
Story of witches. 3826
Story of world religions. 3140
Story of Yates the missionary. 3863
Story of your very own Bible. 292
Story of Zionism. 3897
Story Peter told. 1979
Story-sermonettes for the children's mass. 905
Story sermons and plans for the junior church. 907
Story sermons for boys and girls. 907, 909
Story sermons for children. 3369, 3370
Story sermons for junior congregation. 906
Story-sermons for juniors. 908, 3337
Story sermons from literature and art. 906
Story, song and sermon. 3347
Story talks for boys and girls. 3369

Story talks for children. 908
Story-talks in lines. 880
Story telling for teachers of beginners and primary children. 3534
Story-telling lessons. 3534
... Story telling to children from Norse mythology and the Nibelungenlied. 911
Story the Bible tells. 597, 651
Story the Old Testament tells. 597
Story time. 3616
Story-time again. 1452
Story to remember. 1013
Story-worship programs for the church school year. 1246
Story worship services for the junior church. 1246
Storyteller in religious education. 3147
Storytelling. 3147
Stout hearts and gentle hands. 1713, 3420
Stowe's Bible astrology. 97
Stowe's clerical directory of the American church. 2964
Stowe's clerical directory of the Protestant Episcopal Church in the United States of America. 2964
Strachan of Costa Rica. 3535
Straight ahead. 3883
Straight answers to life questions. 975
Straight from the shoulder. 3097, 3886
Straight sermons to young men and other human beings. 3346
Straight talk about death with young people. 1417
Straight talk about teaching in today's church. 3179
Straight tongue. 3810
Straight way toward tomorrow. 2521
Straight white road. 2758
Straightforward. 3391
Strait gate. 933
Stranded no longer. 1302, 3021
Strange alitars. 3322
Strange altars. 3219, 3787
Strange and uncanny. 2727
Strange autobiography of Frank B. Robinson. 2986
Strange cults. 3322
Strange customs, how did they begin? 2723
Strange experience. 2988
Strange experiences of the doctor. 1360
Strange facts about the Bible. 318
Strange fires. 3803
Strange gods. 1321, 1394, 3747
Strange gods before me. 1356
Strange guests. 1710
Strange happenings. 2986
Strange heroes. 493
Strange history of Sir John Oldcastle. 2736
Strange new faiths. 3325
Strange new gospels. 56, 337, 1965, 1976
Strange new religions. 1393
Strange powers. 2206, 2992
Strange powers of prophecy. 2949
Strange powers of the mind. 2729
Strange prophecies that came true. 2948
Strange Scriptures that perplex the western mind clarified in the light of customs and conditions in Bible lands. 614
Strange sects and cults. 3322
Strange sects and curious cults. 3112, 3113
Strange shadows. 3521
Strange silence of the Bible in the church. 288
Strange story of a minister's life. 2913
Strange superstitions and magical practices. 3567
Strange texts, but grand truths. 2932
Strange things are happening. 2724
Strange victory; the gospel of the resurrection. 3663
Strange visitors. 3505
Strange voyage. 3097
Strange ways of God. 549
Strange women of the occult. 2729
Strange world of the Hare Krishnas. 1786
Strangeness of the church. 1119
Stranger. 1112
Stranger at Emmaus, and other New Testament stories. 626
Stranger at home. 2155
Stranger at your door. 1999
Stranger in my home. 1366, 1824
Stranger in the land. 2534
Stranger in the pew. 1006
Stranger in the synagogue. 2120
Stranger in tomorrow's land. 2762
Stranger of Galilee. 1985
Stranger than fiction. 120, 2087, 3127
Stranger Within. 973
Strangers, all strangers. 319, 2322
Strangers and exiles. 2821
Strangers and exiles: living by promises. 990
Strangers & pilgrims. 116, 1455

Strangers & sojourners at Port Royal. 1934, 2864
Strangers become neighbors. 2408
Strangers dark and gold. 1936
Strangers no longer. 1040
Strangers on earth. 493
Strangers to. 2076, 2139
Strangers to God. 1559
Strangers to Rainbow Press. 32
Strangest thing happened. 631
Strannik. 997, 1473
Strasbourg and the Reform. 3041
Strategic grasp of the Bible. 308
Strategic planning for church organizations. 1199
Strategic points in the world's conquest. 3852
Strategies for increasing career education and opportunities for severely mentally retarded persons. 2411
Strategies for new churches. 1166
Strategy for leadership. 1199
Strategy for liberation. 2268
Strategy for peace: reflections of a Christian pacifist. 2809
Strategy for the inner city. 3874
Strategy for the Protestant college. 2953
Strategy of city church planning. 1278
Strategy of evangelism. 1554
Strategy of life. 3870
Strategy of missions. 2554
Strategy of the devotional life. 1448
Straw gods. 100
Straw houses in the wind. 740, 981
Straws from the crib. 864
Straws from the manger. 1112
Straws in the wind. 973
Stray leaves from the port-folio of the Methodist local preacher. 2420
Stray meditations. 1453
Stream of Jewish life. 2103, 2105
Stream of light. 3725
Streamlined idols. 1561
Streamlined thoughts. 1011
Streams in the desert. 1437
Streams of gladness;a year's daily meditations based on the book of Psalms. Translated by B. H. J. Habel. 585
Streams of healing. 3406
Streams of influence. 30, 3255
Streams of living water. 2297
Street Jesus. 2072
... Street of the Half-moon. 1286
Street people. 3889
Street preachers, faith healers, and herb doctors in Jamaica, 1890-1925. 1933
Streets aflame. 20, 1562
Strength and beauty. 122, 969
Strength and power. 3407
Strength and power, a book for the sick. 3407
Strength for each day. 1440
Strength for living. 994, 1443
Strength for service to God and country. 81, 3456
Strength for the day. 1441
Strength for the soul. 2396
Strength for today. 1432
Strength from shadows. 1349
Strength of great possessions. 2396
Strength of Hindooism. 1813
Strength of quietness. 2935
Strength of religion as shown by science. 3080
Strength out of suffering. 3541
Strength through prayer. 2389
Strength to grow. 2959
Strength to love. 15, 157
"Strengthen thy brethren" 447
Strengthening the adult Sunday school class. 938
Strengthening the spiritual life. 3478
Strengthening your grip. 989
Strenous Puritan. 1764, 2826
Stress management for ministers. 1298
Stress mess. 994
Stretching forth thine hand to heal. 1600
Stricken lute. 1
Stricter statement of Scripture. 224
Strictly confidential. 951
Strictly personal. 1726
Strictures on a book. 1748, 2309
Strictures on a pamphlet. 1906, 2245
Strictures on Bishop Watson's "Apology for the Bible." 3798
... Strictures on Campbellism. 1463
Strictures on Sandemanianism. 3300
Strife of tongues. 1716
Strike a giant bell. 2126
Strike the original match. 2340
Striking of America's hour. 2757
String of amber. 2407
String of pearls. 2397
Striving after perfection. 955
Striving for ministry. 2281
Striving for perfection; the fundamental obligation of the religious state. 2819

Striving for the mastery. 2212
Strong and the weak. 3000
Strong comfort of God. 2935
Strong hearts of Japan. 2489
Strong in the spirit. 981
Strong, loving, and wise. 2235
Strong name. 2935, 3714
Strong weak people. 985
Stronger than mushrooms. 155
Stronger than the strong. 912
Strongest poison. 2817
Strongly tempted. 3600
Strong's Concordance of the Bible. 228, 1797
Strong's Exhaustive concordance. 228, 1797
Strong's exhaustive concordance of the Bible, with key-word comparison of selected words and phrases in the King James version with five leading translations. 228, 1797
Strophic structure of Hebrew poetry. 1797
Struck by lightning. 3132
Struck by lightning, then by love. 1367, 3524
Structural analysis and Biblical exegesis. 528, 3536
Structural drafting. 3536
Structural exegesis. 287, 3536
Structural principles of the Bible. 287
Structure and composition of Deutero-Isaiah with special reference to the polemics against idolatry. 545, 1882
Structure and creativity in religion. 1505, 3056
Structure and history in Greek mythology and ritual. 2660
Structure of awareness. 2999
Structure of behavior. 1853
Structure of Biblical authority. 217, 1377
Structure of Caroline moral theology. 946, 947
Structure of catechetics. 3148
Structure of Christian existence. 1094
Structure of God's plan. 2392
Structure of Luke and Acts. 426
Structure of Lutheranism. 2285
Structure of praise. 1161
Structure of religious experience. 1586
Structure of the Book of Job. 550
Structure of the divine society. 1187
Structure of the text of the book of Hosea. 538
Structure of the world in Udayana's realism. 3721, 3766
Structured tutoring. 3719
Structures of Christian priesthood. 771, 877
Structures of initiation in crisis. 138
Structures of prejudice. 2912
Structures of the church. 1120, 1126
Struggle against illiteracy. 1883
Struggle and contemplation. 1356, 3311
Struggle and fulfillment. 1534
Struggle and submission. 2645, 3891
Struggle between science and superstition. 3313
Struggle for Catholic emancipation (1750-1829) 867
Struggle for Christian truth in Italy. 1097
Struggle for Christian unity. 1180
Struggle for freedom. 1882
Struggle for immortality. 1891
Struggle for integrity. 1418
Struggle for justice. 649
Struggle for life and victory through the Lamb. 3596
Struggle for meaning. 167
Struggle for peace. 2808
Struggle for religious freedom in Virginia: the Baptists. 172
Struggle for religious liberty in the fifteenth and sixteenth centuries. 3036
Struggle for trained teachers. 3394
Struggle of decency. 2681
Struggle of Jacob. 1735
Struggle of prayer. 2868
Struggle of Protestant dissenters for religious toleration in Virginia. 3781
Struggle of the conscience. 3477
Struggle of the soul. 975
Struggle of the unbeliever. 64
Struggle, our destiny. 865
Struggle over reform in Rabbinic literature of the last century and a half. 3032
Struggle with God. 3493
Struggles and fruits of faith. Sesquicentennial celebration, March 4-11, 1962. 3019
Struggles and triumphs of religious liberty. 3194
Struggles and triumphs of the truth. 1070
Struggles of a man. 986, 2318
Struggles of a sinner-saint. 2391
Struggling disciple. 2825
Stuart and Georgian churches. 1159
Stubborn faith. 484, 1920

Student association leadership. 3875
Student at prayer. 3537
... Student counseling. 3537
Student evangelism in a world of revolution. 1256
Student faces life. 3536
Student missionary appeal. 3536
Student power in Christian action. 9, 1308
Student power in world evangelism. 2504
Student power in world missions. 2504
Student prayerbook. 3537
Student-preacher. 3537
Student religion during fifty years. 3875
...Student standards of action. 960
Student views religion. 3537
Student volunteer movement for foreign missions. 3536
Student witnesses for Christ. 2558
Student work administration. 141
Students and the world-wide expansion of Christianity. 2515
Students and the Christian world mission. 2515
Students and the church universal. 3875
Students and the faith. 1249
Students and the future of Christian missions. 2515
Students and the modern missionary crusade. 2515
Students and the world mission of Christianity. 2521
Students' Bible. 274
Student's Bible, containing the Old and New Testaments according to the version of the 1911 Bible. 394
Student's Bible course. 473, 566
Student's Bible course (analytical and expository) for schools, colleges, and Bible classes. 566
Student's Bible dictionary. 243
Students Bible guide and helps. 639
Student's chronological New Testament. 352
Student's chronological New Testament (text of the American standard revision) 352
Students, churches, and higher education. 1257
Student's commentary on the Holy Scriptures. 225
Student's Compendium of the Heidelberg catechism. 1801
... The students' comprehensive topical Bible commentary. 353
Students' dictionary. 2731
Student's dictionary of muscial terms. 2634
Student's Gospels. 248, 394
Students' hand book. 3870, 3874
Students' hand book no. for. 3873
Students hand book of the University of Michigan. 3873
Student's handbook. 2440, 3669, 3873
Student's handbook of Christian theology. 3643
Students' historical geography of the Holy Land. 2764
Student's introduction to the synoptic Gospels. 398
Student's life of Jesus. 1965
Student's life of Paul. 2797
Students' manual of the Reformed church in the United States. 3047
... Students' mass book and hymnal for the use of colleges and academies. 2370
Student's mythology. 2654
Student's New Testament compilation. 353, 654
Student's notebook in Bible study. 641
Students of Asia. 1497
Student's philosophy of religion. 3106
Student's Quran. 2185
Students, religion, and the contemporary university. 1309
Students, scholars and saints. 2086
Student's Scripture history. 407
Student's vocabulary of Biblical Hebrew. 1797
Students' work book. 2229
Studia Semitica. 505, 2842
Studien zu den Klosterprivilegien der Papste im fruhen Mittelalter. 2943, 3277
Studies, addresses, and personal papers. 2082
Studies and documents relating to the history of the Greek Church and people under Turkish domination. 2746
Studies and essays in honor of Abraham A. Newman. 2141, 2685
Studies and teaching of the Society of Jesus. 1945

... Studies concerning Adrian IV. 854, 1780
Studies concerning the origin of "Paradise lost." 2469
Studies for new converts. 1464
Studies honoring Ignatius Charles Brady, Friar Minor. 688, 3625
Studies in a apostolic church. 1193
Studies in a mosque. 1922
Studies in abundant living. 979, 995
Studies in Acts. 330, 331, 1195
Studies in adolescent boyhood. 7
Studies in alchemy. 3474
Studies in Amos. 486
Studies in ancient and modern Judaism. 2116
Studies in ancient Israelite wisdom. 3821
Studies in ancient Yahwistic poetry. 517, 1798
Studies in Arabic philosophy. 2841
Studies in Biblical and Semitic symbolism. 3573
Studies in Biblical law. 2074
Studies in Biblical parallelism. 486
Studies in bibliography and booklore. 2076
Studies in Chinese religion. 913
Studies in Christian belief. 1235
Studies in Christian biography. 925
Studies in Christian character, work and experience. 886
Studies in Christian doctrine. 3652
Studies in Christian enthusiasm. 1520
Studies in Christian existentialism. 3652
Studies in Christian experience. 1587
Studies in christian living. 971, 1016
Studies in Christian stewardship. 963
Studies in Christianity. 1047, 1048
Studies in church history. 785, 1176, 1178
Studies in church life in England under Edward iii. 1759
Studies in church-state relations. 1151
Studies in Colossians. 341
Studies in Colossians and Philemon. 341
Studies in comradeship. 1325
Studies in comradeship, from the New Testament. 1325
Studies in conduct. 1325
Studies in conduct education. 2591
Studies in Congregationalism. 1343
Studies in contemporary metaphysics. 2834
Studies in criticism and revelation. 236
Studies in Cumberland Presbyterian history. 1392
Studies in current religious thought. 3211
Studies in Daniel. 506, 507
Studies in Deuteronomy. 511
Studies in divine science. 1598
Studies in early Christianity. 1072, 2864
Studies in early church history. 1184, 1195
Studies in early Hebrew meter. 1799
Studies in early Indian thought. 2840
Studies in early mysticism in the Near and Middle east. 2640
... Studies in early Roman liturgy. 838
Studies in East Christian and Roman art. 919, 1883
Studies in Eastern chant. 883
Studies in ecstasy. 1713
Studies in English church history. 1759
Studies in English Franciscan history. 1647
Studies in English Puritanism from the restoration to the revolution, 1660-1688. 1468, 1469
Studies in Ephesians. 363, 364
... Studies in Ephesians and Colossians. 363
Studies in eschatology. 1527
Studies in Eusebius. 1544
Studies in Exodus. 516
Studies in I and II Samuel. 590
Studies in First Corinthians. 320, 321, 322, 323
Studies in I Kings with Chronicles. 555
Studies in Genesis. 520, 523, 527
Studies in Genesis one. 520
Studies in God's methods of training workers. 3182
Studies in Greek religion. 1767
Studies in Hebrews. 403, 405
Studies in Hegel's Philosophy of religion. 1800, 3105
Studies in Hosea. 538
Studies in hymnology. 1207
Studies in I Corinthians. 321
Studies in Isaiah. 542, 543, 544
Studies in Islamic mysticism. 6, 1619, 3542, 3543
Studies in Israelite poetry and wisdom. 578, 3821
Studies in Japanese Buddhism. 706
Studies in Jewish and Christian history. 503

Studies in Jewish bibliography, history, and literature in honor of I. Edward Kiev. 2083, 2147
Studies in Jewish evangelism. 2139
Studies in Jewish history. 2091
Studies in Jewish history and booklore. 2093
Studies in Jewish law, custom, and folklore. 25, 2120
Studies in Jewish literature. 504, 2147, 2183
Studies in Jewish nationalism. 2112
Studies in Jewish preaching. 2910
Studies in Jewish theology. 2140, 3585
Studies in Jewish thought. 504, 2094, 2143, 2148, 2403, 2842
Studies in John's gospel. 2000
Studies in Joshua. 554
Studies in Joshua, Judges, and Ruth. 554
Studies in Judaica. 186, 2143
Studies in Judaism. 2083, 2116, 2140, 2143, 2147
Studies in Judges and Ruth. 555
Studies in knowing Jesus Christ. 1998
Studies in Koheleth. 512
Studies in Levitical terminology. 2755, 3579
Studies in Leviticus. 557
Studies in life of Christ. 1964
Studies in literature and belief. 3071
Studies in literature of the New Testament. 474
... Studies in Luke. 307, 426, 430
Studies in Luke-Acts. 426, 3311
Studies in Luke's gospel. 429, 430
Studies in Lutheran doctrine. 1328
Studies in Lutheran hermeneutics. 288, 3668
Studies in Lutheran higher education. 2293
Studies in Maimonides and St. Thomas Aquinas. 3695
Studies in Mark's Gospel. 436, 437
Studies in Matthew. 441, 442
Studies in medieval Cistercian history. 1276, 2752
Studies in medieval Cistercian history, II. 1276
Studies in medieval Cistercian history, IV. 1276
Studies in Medieval Islamic art. 86
Studies in medieval Jewish history and literature. 2148
Studies in medieval Jewish philosophy. 2841, 3259
Studies in metaphilosophy. 2418, 2419
Studies in metaphysical poetry. 1519
... Studies in Methodist history. 2423
Studies in Methodist literature. 2420
Studies in methodology in textual criticism of the New Testament. 352
Studies in mission theories. 2555
Studies in modern church history. 1187
Studies in monastic theology. 1777, 2572
Studies in mystical religion. 2645
Studies in New England transcendentalism. 3708
Studies in New Testament Christianity. 346
Studies in New Testament ethics. 378
Studies in New Testament language and text. 350, 2171
Studies in nineteenth-century Jewish intellectual history. 2141
Studies in Numbers and Deuteronomy. 561
Studies in occult philosophy. 3689
Studies in occultism. 2723
Studies in Old Testament characters. 596
Studies in Old Testament history. 532
Studies in Old Testament literature. 596
Studies in Old Testament prophecy. 608, 3242
Studies in Old Testament sacrifice. 3271
Studies in optimism. 2740
Studies in Pascal's ethics. 2778
Studies in Paul. 378, 2481
Studies in Paul's technique and theology. 372
Studies in Pharisaism and the Gospels. 387, 2828
Studies in Philemon. 447
Studies in Philippians. 448, 450
Studies in Philippine church history. 2830
Studies in political morality. 1143
Studies in popular Islam. 2566
Studies in praise of Our Blessed Mother. 2354
Studies in problem texts. 160
Studies in Proverbs. 572, 573, 1433
Studies in Psalms. 576, 586
Studies in psychical research. 2990
Studies in Rabbinic Judaism. 2150, 3584
Studies in race relations. 3017
Studies in rationalism, Judaism & universalism. 2142, 3252
Studies in recent adventism. 3320

Studies in religion. 1887, 1888
Studies in religion and theology. 1049
Studies in religion for high school and adult groups. 3187
Studies in religious education. 3153
Studies in religious history. 2122, 3068
Studies in religious nurture. 3159
Studies in religious philosophy. 3100
Studies in religious philosophy and mysticism. 2842
Studies in religious poetry of the seventeenth century. 3209
Studies in Revelation. 457, 465
Studies in Revelations. 451
Studies in revival. 1562
Studies in Richard Hooker. 1844
Studies in Romans. 467, 469, 470
Studies in Romans, Ephesians and Colossians. 371
Studies in St. Bernard of Clairvaux. 193
Studies in salvation history. 652
Studies in science and religion. 3077
Studies in Scripture and its authority. 306
Studies in II Kings with Chronicles. 556
Studies in Second Timothy. 326
Studies in Shemot. 516
Studies in sin and atonement. 2113
Studies in sin and atonement in the Rabbinic literature of the first century. 2150
Studies in social problems. 3440
Studies in spiritism. 2991
Studies in spiritual energy. 961
Studies in spiritual harmony. 2694
... Studies in stewardship. 2453, 3528
Studies in sublime failure. 2703
Studies in Tertullian and Augustine. 3604, 3714
Studies in the Acts and Epistles. 636
Studies in the Acts of the Apostles. 330, 331, 333
Studies in the Anglo-Saxon version of the gospels. 1469
Studies in the Apocalypse of John of Patmos. 459, 460
Studies in the Apostolic Fathers and their background. 76
Studies in the arts at Sinai. 922, 3273
Studies in the atonement. 107
... Studies in the Bible. 645, 646
Studies in the Bible and science. 205
Studies in the birth of the Lord. 3781
Studies in the Book. 596
Studies in the book of Acts. 331, 333
Studies in the Book of Daniel. 508
Studies in the Book of Esther. 514
Studies in the book of Exodus. 523
Studies in the book of Exodus with special reference to Israel's journeyings from Egypt to Canaan. 1584
Studies in the book of Ezekiel. 518
Studies in the book of Genesis. 523
Studies in the book of Isaiah. 541
Studies in the book of Job. 551
Studies in the book of Jonah. 552
... Studies in the book of Mark, critical, exegetical, homiletical, and practical, for teachers, pastors and parents. 438
Studies in the book of Psalms. 578
Studies in the book of Revelation. 460, 465
Studies in the Buddhistic culture of India. 705
Studies in the character of Christ. 1954
Studies in the Christian gospel for society. 3444
Studies in the Confession of faith. 3809
Studies in the creative week. 1380
Studies in the early British church. 878
Studies in the early church. 475
Studies in the economics of the Bible. 247
Studies in the English reformation. 3041
Studies in the Epistle of James. 412, 413
Studies in the Epistle to the Colossians. 341
Studies in the Epistle to the Hebrews. 405
Studies in the Epistle to the Romans. 470
Studies in the Epistles and Revelation. 367, 465
Studies in the Epistles of John. 369
Studies in the evangelisation of South Africa. 2499
Studies in the First book of Samuel. 483
Studies in the first six Upanisads. 3760
Studies in the forgiveness of sins. 1633
Studies in the forty days between Christ's resurrection and ascension. 2006
Studies in the four Gospels. 284, 391, 401
Studies in the four Gospels and the life of Christ. 400, 1993
Studies in the fourth Gospel. 420
Studies in the Gospel according to Mark. 433, 437
Studies in the Gospel according to Matthew. 440
Studies in the Gospel of John. 416, 418, 423

Studies in the Gospel or Luke. 431
Studies in the Gospels. 391
Studies in the Gospels and Acts. 384
Studies in the Gospels and Epistles. 390
Studies in the Greek and Latin versions of the book of Amos. 486
Studies in the Greek New Testament. 473
Studies in the highest thought. 3211
Studies in the history and text of the New Testament in honor of Kenneth Willis Clark. 334, 335
Studies in the history of Israel and Judah. 2089
Studies in the history of natural theology, by Clement C. J. Webb. 2674
Studies in the history of religions. 3068, 3705
Studies in the history of the Sanhedrin. 3301
Studies in the Holy Spirit. 1829
Studies in the Lankavatara sutra. 3715
Studies in the life and ministry of Jesus. 1951, 2601
Studies in the life and teachings of our Lord. 1985, 2066
Studies in the life of Christ. 1963, 1964, 1987, 1993, 1994
Studies in the life of Jesus. 1960
Studies in the life of Jesus Christ. 1960
Studies in the life of Jesus for Bible classes and private use. 2015
Studies in The life of John Wesley. 3802
Studies in the life of Paul. 2804
Studies in the life of Paul for Bible classes and private use. 2801
Studies in the life of St. Paul. 2804
Studies in the life of the Christian, his faith and his service. 3157
Studies in the life of the early church. 1191
Studies in the liturgy. 2238, 2257
Studies in the Lutheran confessions. 2282, 2283
Studies in the making of the English Protestant tradition. 3039
Studies in the middle way. 702
Studies in the ministry of Our Lord. 1968
Studies in the miracles of Jesus recorded by Matthew. 2018
Studies in the model prayer. 2246
Studies in the mountain instruction. 3334
Studies in the nature of character. 2590
Studies in the New Testament. 346, 349, 475, 476
Studies in the Old Testament. 597
Studies in the Old Testament and the book of Genesis in outline. 523
Studies in the out-lying fields of psychic science. 2992
... Studies in the parables of Jesus. 2025
Studies in the passion of Jesus Christ. 2030
Studies in the Pentateuch. 566
Studies in the person & work of Jesus Christ. 2036
Studies in the philosophical terminology of Lucretius and Cicero. 2834
Studies in the philosophy of Kierkegaard. 2171
Studies in the philosophy of religion. 3104
Studies in the philosophy of religion and history. 3099
Studies in the prophecy of Jeremiah. 546
Studies in the prophets. 569
Studies in the prophets of Israel. 571, 2951
Studies in the Psalms. 577, 578, 2985
Studies in the Psalms of Israel. 586
Studies in the psychology of the mystics. 2647
Studies in the Records of the life of Jesus. 394, 1993
Studies in the religion of Israel. 2116
Studies in the Revelation. 456
Studies in the Scriptures. 641, 1940, 1941
Studies in The secret doctrine. 671, 3687
Studies in the Septuagint. 529
Studies in the Sermon on the Mount. 3335, 3336, 3337
Studies in the structure of Hebrew narrative. 531, 2668
Studies in the synoptic problem. 392
... Studies in the syntax of the King James version. 270
Studies in the syntax of the Lindisfarne Gospel. 384
Studies in the teaching of Jesus & his apostles. 475, 2062
Studies in the text of Jeremiah. 547
Studies in the text of the New Testament. 352
Studies in the text tradition of St. Jerome's Vitar patrum. 1811
Studies in the use of fire in ancient Greek religion. 1626
Studies in the vocabulary of the Greek New Testament. 425

Studies in the way of Jesus. 1955
Studies in the wisdom literature of the Old Testament. 600
Studies in theism. 3607
Studies in theology. 3641, 3651, 3653
Studies in Timothy. 479
Studies in Torah Judaism. 2751
Studies in Vedic and Indo-Iranian religion and literature. 3776
Studies in West African Islamic history. 1923
Studies in Zen. 3895
Studies of A. J. Wensinck. 2667
Studies of Arianism. 80
Studies of Bible truths. 234
Studies of character from the Old Testament. 493
Studies of Chinese religion. 914
Studies of Christianity. 1055
Studies of contemporary superstition. 1070, 1587
Studies of English mystics. 2645
Studies of familar hymns. 1871
Studies of familiar hymns. 1871
Studies of famous Bible women. 3840
Studies of great Bible characters. 199
Studies of great Bible cities. 283
Studies of missionary leadership. 2483
Studies of neglected texts. 2934
Studies of Paul and his gospel. 2804
Studies of religious history and criticism. 3123
Studies of the books of the Bible. 199, 649
Studies of the gods in Greece at certain sanctuaries recently excavated. 1766
Studies of the historical Jesus. 2008
Studies of the human aura. 117
Studies of the Man Christ Jesus. 2044
Studies of the man Paul. 2802
Studies of the mind of Jesus. 1954
Studies of the parables of Our Lord. 2026
Studies of the Spanish mystics. 2648
Studies of type-images in poetry, religion, and philosophy. 3097
Studies on book one of the Psalms. 584
Studies on God and His creatures. 3696
Studies on Islam. 1923, 1925
Studies on the ancient Palestinian world. 485, 2761
Studies on the Book of Genesis. 523
Studies on the early Papacy. 808, 1190, 1196
Studies on the Epistle to the Hebrews. 404
Studies on the Gospels. 392
Studies on the Gospels in harmony. 1993
Studies on the Reformation. 3033
Studies on the Testament of Abraham. 491
Studies on the Testament of Joseph. 491
Studies subsidiary to the Works of Bishop Butler. 3199
Studies upon the harmony of the three dispensations of grace. 1376
Study-action manual for "Mission: the Christmas calling." 3182
Study-action manual on Christ and the faiths of men. 1084
Study-action manual on "new forms of mission." 1154
Study and an interpretation of the Regius manuscript, the earliest Masonic document. 1664
Study and practice of astral projection. 94
Study and practice of Judaism. 2144
Study and teaching of the English Bible. 640
Study book on The Manifesto. 2282
Study conference on the Christian world mission. 2480
Study draft of a plan for union of the Presbyterian Church in the United States and the United Presbyterian Church in the United States of America. 1046, 2927
Study guide for Christian responsibility on a changing planet. 1077
Study guide [for] The Christian's calling. 964
Study guide to Encounter with God. 1731
Study in Christology. 2042
Study in consciousness. 1348
Study in creative history. 3139
Study in Daniel. 509
Study in Hosea. 1849
Study in Jeremiah. 1943
Study in karma. 2165

Study in prayer. 2887
Study in radicalism and dissent. 3819
Study in religious pedagogy. 3180
Study in Revelation. 456
Study in St. Mark. 435
Study in spirit wisdom. 3516
Study in survival. 2750

... A study in the psychology of ritualism. 3240

Study in the psychology of the spirit. 3001

Study in the Revelation. 3225

Study in tolerance as practiced by Muhammad and his immediate successors. 1924, 2566

Study of adult life. 3158

Study of Ambrosiaster. 29, 373

Study of ancient Judaism. 2150, 2479

Study of Arab women. 657

Study of archaism in Euripides. 1478

Study of astrology. 97

Study of Bossuet. 683

Study of Christian doctrines. 3648

Study of Christian missions. 2492

Study of Christianity as organized. 1240

Study of church history to the end of the thirteenth century. 1173

Study of church membership for adults in certain selected Protestant churches. 2953

Study of Codex Bezae. 316

... A study of conscience. 1347

Study of culture conflicts & other behavior in Christian youth work in Japan. 1074

Study of culture stability and change. 3842

Study of death. 1412

Study of discrimination in the matter of religious rights and practices. 3192

Study of discrimination in the matter of religious rights and practices; report. 3192

Study of early Christianity. 1197, 2011

Study of ecclesiastical history. 1184

...A study of four outstanding books of Christian apologetics. 763, 2705

Study of generations. 2303

Study of Genesis and Exodus by the questionnaire method. 596

Study of Gersonides in his proper perspective. 2219

Study of God, man and destiny as disclosed by love and fidelity of truth and by the evil reverse of such love and fidelity. 1745

Study of Hebrew thought. 2842

Study of Jesus' own religion. 2063, 3439

Study of Jewish community center teenage programming. 1320

Study of Job. 548

Study of John's gospel by the questionnaire method. 423

Study of Judaism. 2080

Study of Latin hymns. 1877

Study of liturgy. 2235

Study of Luke's gospel by the questionnaire method. 431

Study of mentally defective children in Chicago. 896

Study of Methodism in the North Arkansas Conference. 2439

Study of Milton's Paradise lost. 2468

Study of missionary motivation, training, and withdrawal (1953-1962) 2487

Study of needs and possibilities for Lutheran higher education in Wisconsin. 2294

Study of non-public schools in Hawaii. 2942

Study of Old Testament theology today. 599

Study of Psalm 72 (71) 574

Study of purpose. 3594

Study of religion. 3103, 3111

Study of religion and its meaning. 1483, 3056

Study of religion and primitive religions. 3057

Study of religion in American universities. 3112

Study of religion in college and university and its implications for church and seminary. 3681

Study of religion in colleges and universities. 3111

Study of religion in state universities. 3190

Study of religion in the independent schools. 2942

Study of religion in the Italian universities. 3094

Study of religion in the public schools, an appraisal. 1129

Study of religions. 3117

Study of religious thought in England from 1850. 3213

Study of Shinto. 3404

Study of the articles of faith. 1232, 2613

Study of the ba concept in ancient Egyptian texts. 3014

Study of the bible. 308, 637

Study of the Bible in the Middle Ages. 199, 240

Study of the Bible today and tomorrow. 200

Study of the book of Acts. 333

Study of the Book of Genesis. 522

Study of the book of Revelation. 459

Study of the book of Revelation-- continued. 451

Study of the catechism. 934

Study of the Christian sects, with an introductory chapter on the Jews. 3323

Study of the Delaware Indian big house ceremony. 1420

Study of the Eastern orthodox church. 2744

Study of the English Bible. 270, 642

Study of the Episcopal Church in the Missionary District of Haiti. 1524

Study of the Episcopal Church in the Missionary District of Mexico. 1524

Study of the Episcopal Church in the Missionary District of Panama Canal Zone. 1524

Study of the Episcopal Church in the Missionary District of the Dominican Republic. 1524

Study of the five Zarathushtrian (Zoroastrian) Gathas. 3899

Study of the general superintendency of the Methodist Church. 2428

Study of the Gospel of Mark. 438

Study of the gospel of Our Savior. 2610

Study of the Gospels. 391, 401, 1979

Study of the Holy Spirit. 1832

Study of the Jatakas. 1937

Study of the language of love in the Song of Songs and ancient Egyptian poetry. 594, 2263

Study of the law from nature and the Bible. 96

Study of the life and writings of John Henry Newman. 2704

... A study of the life of Jesus. 1955

...A study of the life of Jesus the Christ. 1991, 1992

Study of the Lord's prayer. 2248

Study of the major emotions in persons of defective intelligence. 1512

Study of the Marcan Gospel. 435

Study of the master universe. 3761

Study of the Methodist Church in the Boston area. 2441

Study of the ministry, 1960-1964. 3680

Study of the miracles. 2476

Study of the Missionary District of Liberia. 2958

Study of the New Testament. 474, 658

Study of the New Testament, 1883 and 1920. 351

Study of the occasional offices of the prayer book. 2884

Study of the Old Testament. 482, 501, 595, 597

Study of the Old Testament for secondary schools. 597

Study of the parables. 601

Study of the passion of Christ. 2031

Study of the Pauline lessons in the Matthean sections of the Greek lectionary. 1525

Study of the Pentateuch. 564

Study of the Pentateuch for popular reading. 564

Study of the primary child. 895

Study of the primary child for primary teachers. 3172

Study of the Prophet Micah. 558

Study of the Protestant Episcopal Church in the Missionary District of Central America. 1524

Study of the rural church in six hill towns of Massachusetts. 2371

Study of the sects. 3323

Study of the soul. 3461

Study of the synoptic Gospels. 397, 777

Study of The Wesley Methodist Church. 3848

Study of theology. 3616, 3661

Study of Tindale's Genesis, compared with the Genesis of Coverdale and of the Authorized version. 524, 3719

Study of united missions and interboard committees. 2547

Study of work experiences and career growth of Roman Catholic doicesan [sic] priests. 829

Study of youth work in Protestant churches. 1260

Study of young children. 3174

Study of young gifted children in senior high school. 2911

Study on the Synoptic Gospels. 391

Study paper for first confession. 1327

Study Papers for the Urban convocation of American Baptists. 171

Study papers on church-state aspects of the churches' involvement in human need. 1140

Study papers on the churches and American Tax policies. 1269

Study papers on the role of the Christian through church and state ... in education. Sponsored by Baptist Joint Committee on Public Affairs, October 5-7, 1966. 1149

... Study the mass. 2367

Study to be quiet. 980

Study your Bible. 527

Studying Our Lord's parables. 2028

Studying Our Lord's parables for yourself. 2026

Studying the Bible. 236

Studying the book of Amos. 486

Studying the New Testament today. 335

Stuff of life. 971

... The stuff of manhood. 976

Stuff that makes an army. 3292

Stuffed saddlebags. 2188

Stumbling block. 789

Stumbling-blocks. 1118, 1215

Stumbling toward heaven. 796, 2392

Stumbling toward maturity. 1546

Stunts and Bible skits for youth. 36

Sturm's Reflections on the works of God. 1442, 1732

Style and content in Christian art. 922

... The style and literary method of Luke. 429, 2271

Style in Mexican architecture. 1160

Style of John Calvin in his French polemical treatises. 69, 728

Style of John Wyclif's English sermons. 2908, 3860

... The style of the letters of St. Gregory the Great. 1773, 2199

Stylus photographus. 2512

Sua de se. 2070

Subdeaconsiip. 771

Subject collections. 2225

Subject guide to Bible stories. 302

Subject-index to the poems of Edmund Spenser. 3471

Subject is persons. 3176

Subject list of Catholic books in the Seattle public library. 868

Subjective concepts of humans. 2988

Subjectivity and paradox. 2171

Subjects for particular examen. 1347

... The subjects of ecclesiastical law according to canon 12. 2159

Sublime Puritan: Milton and the Victorians. 2469

Sublime shepherdess. 3460

Sublime songs of love. 594

Submission in suffering. 11, 2560

... The subordinate temporal, casual, and adversative clauses in the works of St. Ambrose. 29, 2198

Subordination and equivalence. 111, 113, 3834

Substance and shadow. 1535

Substance of an argument against the indiscriminate incorporation of churches and religious societies. 1369

Substance of faith allied with science. 3078

Substance of faith, and other cotton patch sermons. 164

Substance of sermons. 3350

Substance of The riddle of the universe. 2584

... The substantial composition of man according to Saint Bonaventure. 676, 2320

Substantial philosophy. 3076

Substitute for holiness. 2855

Substitute for holiness; or, Antinomianism revived. 2855

Subtleties of the inimitable Mulla Nasrudin. 3543

Suburban captivity of the churches. 3538, 3568

Suburban Christians. 2426

Suburban religion. 3748

Suburban woman. 3837

Suburbs of Christianity. 2426

Suburbs of the Almighty. 3371

Success. 2592, 3158

Success fantasy. 3538

Success is a moving target. 3539

Success, motivation, and the Scriptures. 992

Success secrets for pastors. 2791

Success with beginners. 3173

Success with scientology. 3314

Success without compromise. 985

Successful adult Bible classes and what they are doing. 3552

Successful Bible teaching. 644

Successful Biblical youth work. 1260

Successful C. E. prayer-meetings. 1914

Successful Christian life. 989

Successful Christian living. 162, 992

Successful church. 1121

Successful church libraries. 2224

Successful discipling. 1565

Successful fund-raising sermons. 1690

Successful home cell groups. 1169

Successful leadership. 3204

...Successful letters for churches; tested ways of building good will by mail. 1251

Successful life. 956, 2425, 2702

Successful living. 991

Successful men of to-day, and what they say of success. 3539

Successful mind power. 2419

Successful ministry to the retarded. 1255

Successful religious broadcasting. 3018

Successful socials. 1167

Successful soul winning. 1570

Successful Sunday school and teachers guidebook. 3558

Successful Sunday school at work. 3555

Successful Sunday-school superintendent. 3559

Successful synagogue administration. 3576

Successful teaching ideas. 940

Successful writers and editors guidebook. 1017

Successful young people's society. 1247

Successful youth meetings. 3876

Succession in the church. 2615

Succession narrative. 484

Such is my confidence. 1595

Such love is seldom. 3420, 3790

Such were some of you. 931, 2230

Sucrifice in the Old Testament. 3271

Sudden apprehension. 2468

Sudden splendor. 1459

Sudden thoughts. 1001

Suddenly. . . from heaven. 92

Suenens. 3539

Suenens dossier. 807, 1162

Suffering. 3540, 3541, 3610

Suffering, a personal perspective. 3540

Suffering and glories of the Messiah. 574

Suffering and martyrdom in the New Testament. 350, 3538, 3541

Suffering God. 3542

Suffering here-glory hereafter. 1698

Suffering, human and divine. 3541

Suffering in other words. 3541

Suffering Job of the twentieth century. 3541

Suffering of the impassible God. 1733

Suffering Savior. 2029, 2031

Suffering Savior, and other sermons. 1560, 3542

Suffering Savior, model of the Christian. 2389

Suffering Saviour. 2031

Suffering servant. 1837

Suffering servant in Deutero-Isaiah. 3377

Suffering servant in Deutero-Isaih. 3377

Suffering servant in Deutero-Isainh. 3377

"suffering servant" of Isaiah, according to the Jewish interpreters. 544

Sufferings and glory of Jesus. 2031

Sufferings of Christ. 104, 107

Sufferings of Our Lord Jesus Christ. 1978

... The sufferings of the Jews during the middle ages. 2093

Sufficiency of God. 1492, 1812, 3784

Sufficiency of hope. 3103

Sufficiency of Jesus. 1954

Sufficient ministers. 2900

Suffolk churches. 1159

Suffolk parochial libraries. 3627

Sufi. 3542

Sufi essays. 3543

Sufi message of Hazvat Inayat Khan. 3542

Sufi orders in Islam. 3543

Sufi rule for novices. 3544

Sufi saint of the twentieth century: Shaikh Ahmad al-'Alawi. 21

Sufi studies: East and West. 3394, 3543

Sufi thought : its development in Panjab and its impact on Panjabi literature, from Baba Farid to 1850 A.D. 3544

Sufis. 3543

Sufis of Andalusia. 3543

Sufism. 3542, 3543

Sufism, its saints and shrines. 3544

Suggested guide for the church building committee. 1157

Suggested next steps in Latin America. 2548

Suggestions for a syllabus in religious teaching. 3146

Suggestions for an accounting plan for a non-profit organization. 3878

Suggestions for conducting a church class in psychotherapy. 2410

... Suggestions for superiors and religious officials. 2581

Suggestions for the conversion of the world. 1360
... Suggestions for the reconstruction of the coronation ceremonies. 1224
Suggestions for the spiritual life. 3481
Suggestive commentary on St. Luke. 428
Suggestive commentary on St. Paul's Epistle to the Romans. 469
Suggestive illustrations on the Acts of the apostles. 71, 329
Suggestive illustrations on the Gospel according to Matthew. 441
Suggestive illustrations on the Gospel of John. 324, 417
Suggestive sermon outlines. 3375
Suggestive teaching outlines for workers' training classes. 637
Sugg's Creek Cumberland Presbyterian Church. 3545, 3818
Suicide. 3545
Sukkah and the big wind. 3545
...Sukkah, Mishna and Tosefta. 2108, 2109
Sukkot and Simhat Torah anthology. 3545
Sukos and Simchas Torah. 3545
Sullivan masonic district centennial, 1862-1962. 1671
Sullivan's island. The raciad. 2856
Sulpicians in the United States. 3545
Sum and the substance. 1380
Sumerian and Babylonian psalms. 1878
Sumerian mythology. 2667
... Sumerian records from Drehem. 3545
Summa contra gentiles. 69
Summa contra haereticos. 782
Summa logicae. 2242
Summa of the Christian life. 1000
Summa theologiae. 3649
Summa theologica. 783, 792, 3649, 3653
"Summa theologica" of St. Thomas Aquinas. 3617
Summarized Bible. 482, 645
Summarized Bible study. 639
Summary exposition of the internal sense of the prophetical books of the Word of the Old Testament. 568
Summary history of persecution. 2820
Summary of Biblical antiquities. 208, 2920
Summary of Catholic history. 809
Summary of Christian doctrine. 3663
Summary of Christian doctrine and practice. 3664
Summary of Christian doctrine for senior classes. 3640
Summary of christian history. 1172
Summary of Christians doctrine. 3663
Summary of proceedings. 2225, 2807
Summary of scholastic principles. 3309
Summary of the Christian faith. 3644
Summary of the doctrine of Jesus Christ. 2595
Summary of the faith. 2964
Summary of the principal evidences for the truth and divine origin of the Christian revelation. 1099
Summary report of. 1320
Summary report of Greater Birmingham area religious survey. 3568
Summary report of North Central Alabama religious survey findings. 3568
Summary view of the evidence and practical importance of the Christian revelation. 1097
Summary view of the Millenial church. 3397
Summary view of the Millennial church. 3397
Summary view of the Millennial Church, or United Society of Believers, commonly called Shakers. 3397
Summe and substance. 1783
Summer in England with Henry Ward Beecher. 3066
Summer in the seed. 1074
Summer parish. 1340
Summer program for the church school. 3763
Summer revival and what brought it about. 3227
Summer sermons. 3339, 3341
Summer visit of three Rhode Islanders to the Massachusetts bay in 1651. 153, 1285
Summer with nursery children. 3763
Summi pontificatus. 792
Summit views and other sermons. 3338
Summoned by love. 996
Summoned to serve. 144
Summons unto men. 1456
Sumner's incidents and illustrations. 1782
Sumrall's Short stories. 2491
Sun and the umbrella. 1094
Sun Buddhas, moon Buddhas. 2560, 3197
Sun danced at Fatima. 1618
Sun her mantle. 2357
Sun is also a star. 97
Sun lore of all ages. 3546

Sun Myung Moon and the Unification Church. 3329
Sun of higher understanding. 1446
Sun, shade 'n rain. 2230, 3493
Sun songs. 1382
Sun, the cross, and the soul of man. 3574
Sun worshipers of Asia. 2777
Sunanda's jewels. 2531
Sunburst. 2805
Sunbursts for the spirit. 3407
Sunday. 1786, 3547, 3548
Sunday afternoons for the children. 3158
Sunday alive; a story of youth and the Church. 1261
Sunday and feast homilies. 3367
Sunday best. 1005
Sunday book of Bible stories. 624
Sunday book of pleasing and comforting literature, prose and poetry. 3204
Sunday church school for 4's. 3164, 3560
Sunday dinner. 2253
Sunday eight o'clock. 3536
Sunday Epistles. 366
Sunday evening hour. 630
Sunday evening sermons. 3355
Sunday evenings in the college chapel. 3758
Sunday Gospels. 366
Sunday Gospels explained to children. 284
Sunday Gospels for priest and people. 366
Sunday half hours with great preachers. 3341, 3364
Sunday homily. 2908
Sunday in Roman paganism. 3800
Sunday in the making. 3547
Sunday in the sixties. 3548
Sunday kindergarten. 3560
Sunday legislation. 3548
Sunday liturgy themes for all Sundays and holy days. 1265
Sunday Missal. 2883
Sunday missal for all the Sundays and the principal feasts of the year. 2883
Sunday missal for young Catholics. 899
Sunday morning. 893, 3164
Sunday morning crisis. 2234
Sunday morning in the kindergarten. 3564
Sunday morning storyland. 906
Sunday morning talks prepared for Bible class. 1057
Sunday morning talks prepared for Bible class no. 20 of the Presbyterian congregation of Sewickley, Pennsylvania. 3339
Sunday night at the movies. 2627
Sunday-night evangel. 1524
Sunday-night service. 1570
Sunday night services can be successful. 3003
Sunday night talks. 3211
Sunday problem. 3548
Sunday readings, "cycle C" (3) 314, 864, 1267
Sunday reflections for the church year. 2392
Sunday rest in the twentieth century. 3548
Sunday school. 3554, 3558
Sunday school and band of hope speaker. 3026
Sunday school and citizenship. 3553
Sunday school and missions. 2550
Sunday school and the church budget. 952, 1167
Sunday-school and the home. 3552
Sunday school and the teens. 3554
Sunday-school and world progress. 3560
Sunday school anthem and chorus book. 3563
Sunday school at work. 3553
Sunday School at work, 1966-67. 3559
Sunday School at work. 1967-68. 3559
Sunday school at work in town and country. 3552
Sunday school babies. 3558
Sunday school basics. 3559
Sunday school between Sundays. 3555
Sunday School Board. 3467
Sunday-school book for the use of Evangelical Lutheran congregations. 3562
Sunday school building and its equipment. 3548
Sunday school bulletin board guide. 3555
Sunday school celebration book. 3026
Sunday-school century. 1343
Sunday school challenge. 3555
Sunday school chant and tune book. 2968
Sunday school concert book. 3560
Sunday-school director's guide to success. 3550
Sunday school encyclopedia. 3556
Sunday school entertainments. 3026, 3560
Sunday-school essentials. 3550
Sunday School Evangelism. 3565
Sunday school experience. 3565

Sunday school fights prejudice. 2912
Sunday school hymn book. 3562, 3563
Sunday school hymnal. 3562, 3563
... Sunday school hymns. 3562
Sunday school hymns no. 1. 3562
Sunday-school ideas (for church and Sunday-school) 3552
Sunday school in action. 3551
Sunday-school in the development of the American church. 3556
Sunday school in town and country. 3558
Sunday-school institutes and normal classes. 3558
Sunday school instructions for every Sunday of the year. 3184
Sunday school instructions for every Sunday of the year, with a short sketch of eminent saints, followed by prayers of the mass and hymns. 3560
Sunday school kindergarten. 3564
Sunday school lessons. 3188
Sunday school ministry to adults. 3169
Sunday-school missionary incidents and exercises. 2483
Sunday school movement 1780-1917, and the American Sunday-School Union 1817-1917. 33, 3551
Sunday-school movements in America. 3552
Sunday-school music book, enlarged. 3563
Sunday-school of to-day. 3558
Sunday-school officers manual. 3552
Sunday-school olio. 3026
Sunday-school organization and methods. 3557
Sunday school organized for service. 3555
Sunday-school praises. 3564
Sunday school prayer book. 3558
Sunday-school problems. 3559
Sunday school program of a church. 3559
Sunday school programs for intermediates. 3181
Sunday-school reader, for opening service and class study. 3560
Sunday-school records. 3564
Sunday school secretary. 3555
Sunday school selections. 3026
Sunday-school sermonettes. 797, 3557
Sunday school spirit. 3557
Sunday-school stories for little children on the golden texts of the International lessons of 1889. 1915
Sunday-school stories on the golden texts of the international lessons of 1889. 1014
Sunday-school story. 3561
Sunday school success. 3551, 3559
Sunday-school teacher. 3179, 3550, 3554
Sunday-school teacher and the Book. 3564
Sunday-school teacher and the program of Jesus. 3550
Sunday-school teacher as a soul-winner. 3550
Sunday-school teacher as counselor. 1374
Sunday-school teacher at his best. 3550
Sunday-school teacher magnified. 3550
Sunday-school teacher-training. 3565
Sunday-school teacher's aid to the Gospels. 401
Sunday school teachers' explanation of the Baltimore catechism. 746, 3565
Sunday school teacher's guide. 2283
Sunday-school teacher's guide to success. 3157
Sunday school teacher's manual. 3177, 3565
Sunday school teachers' ready reference hand-book of Biblical history. 291
Sunday school teaching. 3565
... Sunday-school teaching and management. 3555
Sunday school text-book on the life of Jesus. 1992
Sunday school training plans and recognitions. 3178
Sunday school transformed. 3553
Sunday school under scientific management. 3553
Sunday school work with four's and five's. 3172
...The Sunday school worker. 3557
Sunday school workers' training course. 3554
Sunday schools and religious education. 3555
Sunday schools in Lindsey. 3557
Sunday-schools the world around. 3559
Sunday sermon outlines. 3372
Sunday sermons of the great Fathers. 386
Sunday story hour. 3547
Sunday talks about children of the Bible. 898
Sunday talks to teachers. 3548
Sunday; the history of the day of rest and worship in the earliest centuries of the Christian church. 3547

Sunday the seventh day. 3548
Sunday, the true Sabbath of God. 3547
Sunday the world's rest day. 3548
Sunday throughout the week. 1265
Sunday under three heads. 3547
Sunday work; seven pamphlets, 1794-1856. 3548
Sunday-school movement, 1780-1917. 3557
Sundays in college chapels since the war. 3758
Sundays in London with Farrar, Parker, Spurgeon and others. 2243
Sundays of the saints. 3566
Sunday-school. 3564
Sundell's system of philosophy. 2834
Sundered cross. 1391
Sundra Bi. 2490
Sunlit way. 1454
Sunny lands and blue waters. 2761
Sunny memories of three pastorates. 2775
Sunny side of Christianity. 2265
Sunny side of life. 3344
Sunny-side up. 3843
Sunny windows. 3369
Sunrise. "Behold, he cometh!" 3320
Sunrise furlough. 2129, 2553
Sunrise in Jerusalem. 3717
Sunrise in Syria. 2798
Sunrise in the Sunrise Kingdom. 2533, 2534
Sunrise in the West. 2300
Sunrise to eternity. 674
Sunset at midnight. 3199
Sunset by the lakeside. 3199
Sunset echoes. 3203
Sunset memories. 3202
Sunset thoughts. 297
Sunsets on the Hebrew mountains. 215
Sunshine among the clouds. 1450
Sunshine and saints. 3284
Sunshine and shadow in southern Europe. 3386
Sunshine and smiles. 1302, 1452, 1824
Sunshine for dark hours. 3405
Sunshine for Sunday schools. 2633
Sunshine gleams from a sick room. 2632
Sunshine hour (devotionals in story and song) 1454
Sunshine in the shadows. 683, 875
Sunshine in the soul. 1453
Sunshine on life's highway. 1451
Sunshine on life's way; being selections from the writings of the Rev. Floyd W. Tomkins. 1453
Suomi calls. 2599
Super baruba success book for under-achievers, over-expecters, and other ordinary people. 2618, 3815
Super prayerables. 2389
Super-psychic. 1849
Super superintendent. 3550
Superconscious mediation. 2379
Superconscious meditation. 2379
Superet atom aura science, light law and order. 3121
Superet light doctrine. 3121
Superforce. 2988
Supergoal. 990
Superheroes of long ago. 72, 384, 2007
Superhuman origin of the Bible inferred from itself. 306
Superintend with success. 3550
...The superintendent. 3550
... The superintendent and his work. 3550
Superintendent of missions for an association. 151
Superintendent plans his work. 3550
Superintendent wants to know. 3552
Superintendent's almanac for. 3558
Superintendent's book of prayer. 3564
Superintendent's guide. 3550
Superintendent's guide for Sunday school year. 3558
Superintendent's handbook. 3550
Superintendent's offering. 1396
Superior follows the master. 3566
Superior generals. 3420
Superiority of Christianity. 3114
Superior's handbook. 3566
Superiour skill and wisdom necessary for winning souls. 2742
Superlative Christianity of the crucified man. 962
Supernatural. 2725, 2993, 3117, 3567
Supernatural and you! 2723
Supernatural Christ. 3567
Supernatural dreams and visions. 604, 1479
Supernatural factor in religious revivals. 1571
Supernatural healing today. 1598
Supernatural in a commonplace life. 3567
Supernatural in nature. 3076
Supernatural in the Old Testament. 501, 3567
Supernatural Jesus. 2041

Supernatural merit, your treasure in heaven. 3567
Supernatural mysticism. 2641
Supernatural origi of the Bible. 277
Supernatural origin of the Bible. 277
Supernatural perfection of conjugal life according to Pope Pius XII. 2343, 2852
Supernatural relation to the natural. 3567
Supernatural religion. 2476
Supernatural revealed by nature. 3567
Supernatural revelation. 60
Supernatural superpowers. 1291, 1412
Supernatural virtues. 3567
Supernatural warnings. 2730
... Supernaturalism and satanism in Chateaubriand. 889, 1428
Supernaturalism of New England. 3568
Supernaturalness of Christ. 2002, 2044
Supernature. 2730
Supernumerary. 1307
Superphysical. 2990
Supersensible in man and world. 51
Supersensible knowledge: anthroposophy as a demand of the age. 51
Supersensible man. 51
Superstition. 3568
Superstition and magic. 2729
Superstition dissected. 1656
Superstition in all ages. 100, 3567, 3568
Superstitions. 3568
Superstitions of the irreligious. 1920, 3744
Supervised life. 588
Supervision in the Catholic elementary school. 3310
Supervision of group leaders. 3878
Supervision of religious education. 3148
Supervision of student-teachers in religious education. 3178, 3189
Supper and suffering of Our Lord. 161
Supper and the Eucharist. 2257
Supplanter becomes a prince. 1931
Supplanters of history and God's pattern of the ages of man. 3093
Supplement to The comprehensive commentary. 285, 286
Supplement to the Digest of the acts and proceedings of the General assembly of the Presbyterian church in the United States. 2919
Supplement to the Guide to Catholic church music. 1204
Supplement to the Roman breviary, containing offices proper to the Order of Discalced Carmelites. 741
Supplement [!] to the Sandwich island mirror containing an account of the persecution of Catholics at the Sandwich islands. 873
Supplemental Bible question course of fifty-two lessons. 218
Supplementary Bible. 2232
Supplementary history of American Methodism. 2451
Supplementary list of books in library of Christian brothers college. 2224
... Supplementary series. 2520
Supplication for the beggars. 2579
Supplied! 560
... Supplied jurisdiction according to canon 209. 2159
... Supplies for Royal arch chapters and councils of R. and S. masters. 1670
Support for the Christian science board of directors. 684
Supremacy. 1940
Supremacy of Christianity, a study of the Christian way. 3662
Supremacy of Jesus. 1951
... The supremacy of reason. 2622, 3027
Supremacy of the Bible. 223
Supremacy of the spiritual. 2418, 3522
Supreme ambition. 3483
Supreme and his four children. 2385
Supreme authority. 118
Supreme beatitude. 3529
Supreme Christ. 1952
Supreme Commander. 1742, 2817
Supreme conquest. 3346
Supreme council, 33 degrees; Mother council of the world. 1672
Supreme Court and public prayer. 3096
Supreme Court decision on Bible reading and prayer. 3095
Supreme Court on church & state. 1152
Supreme deity of Our Lord Jesus Christ, maintained. 1511, 2002
Supreme doctrine. 3760, 3761, 3894
Supreme Godhead of Christ the cornerstone of Christianity. 2000
Supreme Gospel. 223
Supreme happiness. 180
Supreme identity. 1080
Supreme law. 1314
Supreme leader. 1828
Supreme mind--the origin and progress of man. 2417
Supreme miracle. 167

Supreme need of the world today. 1050
Supreme possession. 1558
Supreme problem. 791
Supreme reality. 2417
... The supreme revelation. 2065
Supreme sacrifice. 2058
Supreme sacrifice of Christ. 2036
Supreme task of the church. 2546
Supreme victory. 2695
Supreme virtue. 594
Surangama Sutra. 711
Surat shabd yoga. 3865
Sure foundation. 2435
Sure foundations, a study in Christian certainties. 65
Sure hand of God. 3339
Sure way of St. Therese of Lisieux. 3691
Sure word of prophecy. 2301, 2464
Sure you can. 993
Surely God led. 1849
Sureties of the saints. 2043
Surety of the Bible. 200
Surgeon in the South Pacific. 2348, 2486
Surgery speaks to China. 2507
Surpassing grace. 2200
Surpised by sin. 2470
Surprised by God. 161, 2786
Surprised by joy. 1362
Surprises in the Bible. 2435
Surprising accounts of the rivival of religion in the United States of America. 3229
Surprising Christ. 1956
Surprising Chrst. 1956
Surprising mystics. 2643
Surrender to the Spirit. 1372, 3205
Surrendered life. 957, 967, 2385
Surrounded by angels. 612, 2597
Sursum corda. 2867
Survey. 3744
Survey between the Testaments. 2092
Survey of a decade. 1649
Survey of American church history. 814
Survey of American church records. 1243
Survey of Bible doctrine. 652
Survey of Bible prophecy. 606
Survey of Buddhism. 708
Survey of Catholic theology, 1800-1970. 791, 3628
Survey of choral music. 916
Survey of Christian ethics. 944
Survey of Christian hymnody. 1875
Survey of events in Jewish life. 2097
... Survey of fifteen religious surveys. 2715
Survey of higher education for the United Lutheran church in America. 3733
Survey of Illinois Catholic secondary schools. 830
Survey of Israel's history. 536
Survey of Methodist Episcopal churches in Manhattan, the Bronx and Westchester. 2452
Survey of mystical symbolism. 3573
Survey of New Testament history. 407
Survey of Old Testament introduction. 538
Survey of Old Testament teaching. 541
Survey of 125 religious schools affiliated with the Union of American Hebrew congregations. 2086
Survey of Protestant theology in our day. 2977
Survey of recent Christian ethics. 950
Survey of religious education. 3156
Survey of religious education in the local church. 3147
Survey of religious literature. 3618
Survey of service. 1460
Survey of syntax in the Hebrew Old Testament. 1797
Survey of ten theological schools affiliated with the Methodist Church. 3614
Survey of ten years of clinical pastoral training at Saint Elizabeth's Hospital. 2785
Survey of the Bible. 638
Survey of the development of Christianity. 1198
Survey of the doctrine and covenants. 3216
Survey of the entire Bible. 312
... Survey of the fields and work of the Northern Baptist convention by the special Committee on survey. 2714
Survey of the financial status of the Jewish religious schools of New York city. 2101
Survey of the history of Israel. 535
Survey of the New Testament. 407, 475
Survey of the Old and New Testaments. 646
Survey of the Old Testament. 482, 536
... A survey of the proposals for the alternative prayer book. 2883
Survey of the Reformed church in the United States. 3047

Survey of the summe of church-discipline. 1240
Survey of the training of the ministry in Africa. 3680
Survey of the training of the ministry in Madagascar. 3681
Survey of the training of the ministry in the Middle East. 3681
Survey of theological education in overseas seminaries in Africa and Asia to which the United Presbyterian commission on Ecumenical mission and relations is related. 3612
Survey of world missions. 2495
Surveying the historical books. 531
Surveying the Pentateuch. 566
... Surveying your community; a handbook of method for the rural church. 1274
Survival. 1890, 3508
Survival and mission for the city church. 1278
Survival and reorganization, 1650-1695. 820
Survival bible. 3568
Survival for what? 2112, 2144
Survival guide for tough times. 987
Survival handbook for the tribulation Christian. 936
Survival is not enough. 1445
Survival kit for the stranded. 1352
Survival of American innocence. 833, 3739
Survival of death. 3495
Survival of dogma. 866, 1590
Survival of God in the scientific age. 3082
Survival of Jesus. 2050
Survival of man. 2990
Survival of the historic vestments in the Lutheran church after 1555. 1249
Survival of the historic vestments in the Lutheran church lifter 1555. 1249
Survival of the pagan gods. 1854, 2657
Survival of the unfit. 2323
Survival on the campus. 1308
Survival or extinction. 2112
Survival plus. 1324
Survival prayers for young mothers. 2625
Survival tactics in the parish. 2787
Survival through the moral law. 802
Survival till seventeen. 119, 1620
Survival, unite to live. 981
Survival value of Christianity. 2561
Survivals and new arrivals. 755
Survivals in belief among the Celts. 878
Survivals in Christianity. 3653
Survivals of Roman religion. 3246
Susanna Mary Beardsworth, the white dove of peace. 179
Susanna (1653) 3569
... Susanna Wesley. 3806
Susannah's sanctuary. 904, 3806
Suspect tenderness. 194, 1347
Susquehanna County survey by the Interchurch world movement of North America. 3569
Sussman sees it through. 2102
Sustaining intimacy. 2338
'Sutra of the causes and effects of actions' in Sogdian. 1812
Sutra of the Sixth Patriarch on the pristine orthodox dharma. 703, 3894
Sutra of Wei Lang (or Hui Neng) 3893
Sutro Library Hebraica. 2331
Sutta-nipata. 710
Sutter Creek Methodist Church, 1862-1962.
Suwarta. 2532
Suzuki looks at Japan. 2534
Sv. Kazimieras. 2165
Sv. Petro lietuviu parapija South Bostone. 3464
Sventoji auka. 2370
Svetasvatara Upanisad. 1816
Swami. 3019, 3272
Swami Adbhutananda (Latu Maharaj) 7, 1816
Swami Paramananda and his work. 1816, 2772
Swami Premananda. 1814
Swami Rama of the Himalayas. 3020
Swami Ramakrishnananda. 879
Swami Satchidananda; his biography. 3304
Swami Vivekakanda centenary memorial volume. 3784
Swami Vivekananda's contribution to the present age. 3784
Swampland flowers. 3892
Swan of Albany. 22
Swan on a black sea. 3473
Swan's wide waters. 3020
Swarthmore documents in America. 1686
Swastika. 2100
Swedenborg. 3571
Swedenborg, a hermetic philosopher. 23, 3569
Swedenborg and Channing. 2690, 3569
Swedenborg and the new age. 3569

Swedenborg epic. 3570
... The Swedenborg library. 2689
Swedenborg, life and teaching. 3571
Swedenborg on the Athanasian creed and subjects connected with it. 99
Swedenborg on the Bible. 237
Swedenborg the Buddhist. 3571
Swedenborgianism examined. 3570
Swedenborg's Conjugial love, part two. 2340
Swedenborg's Doctrine of correspondence. 1370
Swedenborg's historical position. 3570
Swedenborg's journal of dreams, 1743-1744. 1479
Swedenborg's Spiritual diary, &c. 3571
Swedish Baptists in American. 170
Swedish church. 3569
Swedish church and ours. 2292
Swedish contributions to modern theology. 3659
Swedish contributions to modern theology, with special reference to Lundensian thought. 3659
Swedish Covenanters. 3569
...The Swedish rite. 2292
Sweet harmonies. 3458
Sweet incense. 2893
Sweet sacrament, we thee adore. 854
Sweet singer. 3561, 3767
Sweet spirits. 2177, 2992
Sweet stories of God. 630
Sweet story of old. 1981
Sweeter than honey. 167, 587, 1438
Sweetest stories ever told. 3200
Sweetest story ever told. 632, 1114, 1960
Sweetest story told. 1966
Swendenborg epic. 3570
Swift decadence of Sunday. 3260, 3547
Swift victory. 1712
Swim--or sink. 869
Swiss pastor. 1745
Sword and garment. 3675
Sword and mitre. 1145
Sword and the cross. 2671
Sword and the flute. 2162, 2186
Sword and the scimitar. 1390
Sword and the serpent. 2312
Sword and the spirit. 3686
Sword and the trowel. 646
Sword book of treasures. 1453
Sword of Esau. 635
Sword of gnosis. 3067
Sword of God. 1937
Sword of His mouth. 392, 2072
Sword of Laban. 3215
Sword of Moses. 43
Sword of St. Michael. 1445, 2850
Sword of sorrow. 2361
Sword of the spirit. 241, 1451, 2848, 3008, 3643, 3710, 3793
Sword of truth. 1699
Sword of wisdom. 1806
Sword or the cross. 3793
Swords drawn. 912
Swords into ploughshares. 1677, 3028
Sworn book of Honourius the magician. 2313
Sybil Leek on exorcism. 1422
Sybil Leek's book of curses. 672
Sybil Leek's Book of the curious and the occult. 2727
Sydney Smith. 3431
Syllabification and accent in the Paradise lost. 2472
Syllabus and notes of the course of systematic and polemic theology taught in Union theological seminary, Virginia. 3642
Syllabus and synopsis of the first three Gospels. 354, 355
Syllabus for character building in special classes. 2590
Syllabus for New Testament study. 475
Syllabus for Old Testament study. 482, 502
Syllabus in alcohol education. 3598
Syllabus of apostolic history. 327
Syllabus of Bible study for grades 1 to 12. 640
Syllabus of errors of Pope Pius ix, the scourge of liberalism. 853
Syllabus of ethics. 1534
Syllabus of lectures. 870, 3649
Syllabus of lectures of the visions of the Revelation. 462
Syllabus of lectures on the outlines of the history of Christian missions. 2525
Syllabus of the course of lectures upon the ritual music of the Protestant Episcopal church in the United States of America. 1209
Sylvester Judd's New England. 2156, 3730
Sylvia goes to Spain. 169
Symbol and art in worship. 2235
Symbol of Methodism. 2420

Symbol of the apostles. 73
Symbol of the faith. 73
Symbolic freemasonry in New Hampshire. 1667
Symbolic language of religion. 3070
Symbolic life of man. 3574
Symbolic Meditations on the Litany of our Lady. 2397
Symbolic mythology and translation of a lost and forgotten language. 2654
Symbolic pig. 2232
Symbolic prophecy of the Great pyramid. 3010, 3250
Symbolical language of ancient art and mythology. 2652
Symbolism. 3574
Symbolism and belief. 3573, 3574
Symbolism in Christian art. 920
Symbolism in craft freemasonry. 1671
Symbolism in Greek mythology. 2660
Symbolism in liturgical art. 922
Symbolism in medieval thought. 3573
Symbolism in relation to religion. 3059
Symbolism in religion and literature. 3574
Symbolism in the Bible and the church. 3573
Symbolism of churches and church ornaments. 920
Symbolism of evil. 3411
Symbolism of Freemasonry. 1671
Symbolism of Oriental religious art. 88
Symbolism of the Biblical world. 87, 578
Symbolism of the cross. 1388
Symbolism of the East and West. 3574
Symbolism of the tarot. 3589
Symbolisms of the Bible. 3574
Symbolized by a shrine. 3420
Symbols. 920
Symbols and values in Zoroastrianism. 3898
Symbols in Christian art. 3575
Symbols in the church. 921
Symbols of Christ. 922
Symbols of church and kingdom. 1188, 2011
Symbols of church seasons & days. 919
Symbols of God's grace. 2163, 3278
Symbols of magic. 35
Symbols of religious faith. 3061
Symbols of the Holy Spirit. 1836
Symbols of Yi king. 1879
Symbols: public and private. 3573
Symbols, sex, and the stars, in popular beliefs. 3114
Symbols, signposts of devotion. 3574
Symbols versus cymbals. 3574
Symeon the New Theologian. 90
Sympathy of God. 1732
Sympathy of religions. 3115
Symphonic sermons. 1843
Symphonies of praise. 3355
Symphony of faith. 1602
Symphony of life in D minor. 2397
Symphony of prayer. 2895
Symphony of the Christian year. 1267
Symposium. 889
Symposium on Biblical hermeneutics. 288
Symposium on creation. 1382
Symposium on creation II. 1382
Symposium on creation III. 1382
Symposium on eschatology. 1530
Symposium on Mormon culture. 2606
Symposium on the Holy Spirit. 1832
Symposium on the life and work of Pope Pius X. 853, 2851
Symposium VII, vision analysis. 1917
Synagogical service. 2109, 3576
Synagogue. 1483, 3576
Synagogue and church in the Middle Ages. 1084
Synagogue and its people. 2152
Synagogue and social welfare. 2700
... The synagogue and the church. 2114
Synagogue architecture and planning. 3577
Synagogue architecture in the United States. 3577
Synagogue in Jewish life. 2109, 3576
Synagogue in modern Jewish life. 3576
Synagogue in modern life. 3576
Synagogue in the central city. 2100, 3599
Synagogue life. 2751
Synagogue music by contemporary composers. 3577
Synagogue service for the Congregation "Shaaray. tefilla." 2108
Synagogue through the ages. 3577
Synagogues of Hungary: an album. 3577
Synagogues of New York City. 2699
Synagogues of New York's Lower East Side. 3578
Synchronizing Hebrew originals from available records, 749-740 [B.C.]. 537
Synchronology. 1817
Syncretic religion of Lin Chao-en. 1330, 2229

... Synesius of Cyrene, philosopher and bishop. 3437, 3578
Synesius of Cyrene, philosopher-bishop. 3578
Synod of New York and Philadelphia vindicated. 1786
Synod of Zoheeling. 2927
Synod '67. 866
Synodal-Bericht. 2296, 3733
...Synodal examiners and parish priest consultors. 1355
Synodical Council resolutions. 110
Synods of American Lutheranism. 2293
Synonyms of the New Testament. 1771
Synonyms of the Old Testament. 556
Synopsis of a Christian theology. 3666
Synopsis of didactic theology. 3643
Synopsis of popery. 800
Synopsis of the books of the Bible. 645
Synopsis of the four evangelists. 1987
Synopsis of the four gospels. 396
Synopsis of the four Gospels, in a new translation. 397
Synopsis of the Gospels. 1990
Synopsis of the Gospels in Greek. 388
Synopsis of the Old Testament. 3817
Synopsis of the Scriptures. 302
Synoptic abstract. 3578
Synoptic gospels. 284, 382, 383, 386, 389, 391
... The Synoptic gospels and the book of Acts. 383
Synoptic Gospels, Matthew, Mark, Luke, from The NewTestament. 382
Synoptic gospels, together with a chapter on the text-criticism of the New Testament. 347
Synoptic gosples. 392
Synoptic history (one half century) Christian church. 1465
Synoptic New Testament. 1990
Synoptic problem. 389
Synopticon: the verbal agreement between the Greek texts of Matthew, Mark and Luke contextually exhibited. 397
Syntactical and critical concordance to the Greek text of Baruch and the Epistle of Jeremiah. 489
Syntactical evidence of Semitic sources in Greek documents. 334, 1769
... The syntax of the genitive case in the Lindisfarne gospels. 381
Syntax of the moods and tenses in New Testament Greek. 1770
Synthesis of sacrifice according to Saint Augustine. 3271
Synthesis of the spiritual life. 3488
Synthesis of yoga. 3864
Synthetic Bible studies. 645
Synthetic Christianity. 1055
Synthetic feelings and popular culture. 1323
Synthetical manual of liturgy. 840
Syrian Christ. 1971, 3579
Syrian Christians in Muslim society. 1108
Syrian Christians of Kerala. 3278
Syrian goddess. 1810
Syrian leper. 2667
Syrian shepherd's psalm. 587
System and the gospel. 3699
System Bible study. 286, 614
System of Biblical psychology. 611
System of Christian doctrine. 1346, 3648
System of Christian ethics. 943
System of Christian evidence. 1099
System of Christian rhetoric, for the use of preachers and other speakers. 2901
System of Christian theology. 3648
System of divinity. 3643
System of doctrines, contained in divine revelation, explained and defended. 3644
System of metaphysics. 2417
System of natural theism. 3608
System of Thomas Aquinas. 2843, 3696
Systematic and philosophical theology. 3656
Systematic beneficence. 1164
Systematic beneficence. 952
Systematic Bible course for daily vacation Bible schools and Sunday schools. 3763
Systematic destruction of the Catholic Church in China. 815
Systematic homiletics. 2904
Systematic moral education. 2590
Systematic personal work. 3166
Systematic pluralism. 2419
Systematic study of Bible doctrine. 3648
... A systematic study of the Catholic religion. 785
Systematic study of The new analytical Bible. 280
Systematic teaching of religion. 746
Systematic theology. 3640, 3642, 3643, 3644, 3645, 3646, 3647, 3648, 3649, 3650
Systematic theology; a historicist perspective. 3645

Systematic theology (Dogmatik) 3650
Systematic theology of Paul Tillich. 3646, 3701
Systematic theology of the Christian religion. 3641
Systematic thought of Washington Gladden. 1715, 3433
Systematic view of divinity. 2373
Systematic visiting of the church membership. 1252
Systems of Buddhistic thought. 711

T

T. DeWitt Talmage. 2935
T. J. Bach. 123
T M technique. 3708
... T. N. Hasselquist. 1546, 1790, 2293
Ta-pooth-ka and his descendants. 2412
Tabernacle. 2147, 2792, 2938, 3350, 3579, 3720
Tabernacle: camping with God. 3721
Tabernacle in the desert. 3287
Tabernacle in the wilderness. 3579
Tabernacle menorah. 2408
Tabernacle of God in the wilderness of Sinai. 3579
Tabernacle of Israel. 3579
Tabernacle sermons of Rev. Sam. P. Jones. 1558
Tabernacle shadows of the "better sacrifices" 3579
Tabernacle sketches. 2588
Tabernacle studies. 3579
Tabernacle talks. 3579
Tabernacle talks for young people. 3579
Tabernacle, temple and throne. 3579
Tabernacle, the priesthood and the offerings. 3579
Table before me. 430
Table graces for daily use. 1750
Table graces for the family. 1749, 1750
Table is for eating. 1318
Table of aspects. 96
Table of His presence. 2251
Table of the King. 731, 3416
Table of the Lord. 2257
Table prayer. 1749
Table prayers. 1750
Table prayers for children. 1750
Table prayers for daily bread. 2895
Table-rappers. 3510
Table talk of Martin Luther. 3579
Table talk with Jesus. 430, 2933, 3355
*Table talks. 3579
Table talks of Jesus. 2062
Tableaux du temple des muses. 2657
Tables of the divine plan. 126
Tables turned. 720, 3496
Tablet of tarazat. 127
Tablets of Abdul-Baha abbas. 126
Tablets of Baha'o'llah, revealed at Acca, Syria. 127
Tablets of the divine plan. 126
Tabo in Panama. 2544
Taboo, magic, spirits. 3245
Taboo, magic, spirits; a study of primitive elements in Roman religion. 3245
Tactical ceremonies for use in the asylum. 1660
Tactology. 1572
[Tadrikh le-Shabat (romanized form)]. 3260
Tag. 1399, 2619
Tah-koo wah-kan. 1399
... T'ai-shang kan-ying p'ien. 3587
Tailor-made teaching in the church school. 3162
Tainted contacts, being a compilation of facts of the personnel and activities of the Federal council of churches of Christ in America. 1620
Tait[t]iriya Upanisat. 3760
Taiwan: mainline versus independent church growth. 1108
Taiwan: unfinished revolution. 2552
Taize. 1316
Taize picture Bible. 624
Take a Bishop like me. 2742, 2962
Take and read. 641
Take another look at guidance. 2981
Take care. 2785, 3528
Take command! 3750
Take God at His word. 250
Take heart. 23, 171
Take heaven now! 180
Take heed. 3670
Take heed to yourselves. 2619
Take hold of God and pull. 318
Take it all off. 1367, 3051
Take it easy. 1016
Take it from here. 1385
Take it from here, series two. 1385
Take it to the people. 1568
Take more joy. 2396

Take my life. 962
Take off the masks. 686, 1300
Take off your shoes. 1737
Take this child. 1332, 1636
Take this house. 1256, 1387
Take this scapular! 3306, 3409
Take time! 1450
Take time for sunsets. 995, 1639
Take up God's armour. 1235, 3367
Take up thy cross. 2213
Take up your mission. 2616
Taking a city. 1343
Taking down the defenses. 2211, 2387
Taking God into partnership. 719
Taking heed to the flock. 3677
Taking hold of God. 2882
Taking leave of God. 1855
Taking men alive. 1571
Taking stock. 2396
Taking stock help for daily living. 2396
Taking the Bible seriously. 639
Taking the christian life seriously. 1010
Taking the Christian view. 3663
Taking time out. 160
Taking time seriously. 3619
Taking visuals. 910
Tale of a wonderful ladder. 2116
Tale of ten cities. 1140
Tale of the reed pipe. 3542
Tale of Thebes. 2662
Tale of two peoples. 2535
Tale of two steamer rugs. 2509
Tale of two worlds. 3501
Tales. 3580, 3581
Tales and customs of the ancient Hebrews for young readers. 534
Tales and maxims from the Midrash. 2462
Tales and maxims from the Talmud. 3583, 3584
Tales and sketches of Christian life in different lands and ages. 1013
Tales and takings. 3675
Tales and teachings of the Buddha. 710
Tales Christ told. 2024
Tales from China. 2509, 2510
Tales from East and West. 2489
Tales from India. 2531
Tales from Japan. 2491
Tales from Latin America. 2490
Tales from Moslem lands. 2491, 2540
Tales from Norse mythology. 2666
Tales from old Judea. 623
Tales from our gaonim (sages) 1632
Tales from southeast Asia. 2516
Tales from the Indian epics. 1895
Tales from the Norse grandmother. 2666
Tales from the Old Testament. 628
Tales I have told twice. 1842
Tales in praise of the ARI. 2272
Tales of a frontier preacher. 2427
Tales of a Magic Monastery. 3490
Tales of adventure from the old Book. 615
Tales of ancient Greece. 2660
Tales of angels, spirits & demons. 1789
Tales of Baptist daring. 144
Tales of cosmic wisdom. 3580
Tales of faith. 3581
...Tales of golden deeds. 910, 2593
Tales of horror and the supernatural. 1848
Tales of human frailty and the gentleness of God. 630
Tales of intemperance. 3597
Tales of modern missionaries for young people. 2483
Tales of Padre Pio. 2477, 2849
... Tales of pioneers and kings. 1518
Tales of power. 2137, 3862
Tales of Rabbi Nachman. 3581
... Tales of Thailand. 2546
Tales of the devils. 1427
Tales of the Greek heroes. 2661
Tales of the Hasidim. 1788, 3580
Tales of the Jewish holidays. 1614
Tales of the prophets of al-Kisa'i. 2207
Tales of the saints of Pandharpur. 1896
Tales of theology, Jehovah. 3617
Tales of Tonga. 2557
Tales of Troy and Greece. 2663
Tales of yore from the life of Rabbi Joselman of Rosheim. 2132
Tales of Yoruba gods and heroes. 3582
Tales the Muses told. 2662
Tales truly true. 2536
Talisman. 1392
Talk with us, Lord. 2875
Talking about death. 895
Talking about prayer. 2868
Talking Christmas tree. 1111
Talking it over. 1433
Talking object lessons, 54 appealing object lessons. 910
Talking of God. 3071
Talking snowman. 2536
Talking to Our Heavenly Father. 1728
Talking tree. 2725
Talking with God. 1449, 2874, 2893, 2894
Talking with the dead? 3513

Talkings with God. 1720
Talks about home-life. 1608
Talks about Jesus. 625, 1954
Talks about Jesus with our little boys and girls. 1984
Talks about the Bible and religion. 307
Talks between times. 974
Talks for a Sunday morn. 2386
Talks for children. 906
Talks for teenagers. 909
Talks for young women. 3877
Talks in crayon and chalk. 880
Talks on At the feet of the Master. 2187, 3686
Talks on doctrine. 2610
Talks on high themes for young Christians. 3886
Talks on Latin America. 3470
Talks on religion. 1051, 3056
Talks on St. Luke's Gospel. 428
Talks on Sunday school teaching. 3180
Talks on the book of Revelation. 454
Talks on the Episcopal church. 2956
Talks on the Gita. 2316
Talks on the Lord's prayer. 2247
Talks on the miracles of the Bible. 616
Talks on the prayer book. 2960
Talks on the Prayer book Gospels. 1266
Talks on the sacramentals. 3262
Talks on truth. 1625
Talks that teach. 1013
Talks to altar-boys. 27
Talks to boys and girls. 907, 976
Talks to boys and girls about Jesus. 906, 1980
Talks to boys in the chapel of Groton school. 3175
Talks to children. 907
Talks to children about Jesus. 1982
Talks to farmers. 167
Talks to men about the Bible and the Christ of the Bible. 1561, 3705
Talks to parents. 3168
Talks to probationers. 2422
Talks to see. 2720
Talks to students about God and life. 3537
Talks to students on occult philosophy. 2733
Talks to Sunday-school teachers. 3559
Talks to teen-agers. 1323
Talks to teeners. 3885
Talks to truth searchers with answers to puzzling "why" questions. 2694
Talks to young people. 3879
Talks to young people given before the Bethany park summer assembly. 3889
Talks to youth. 3358
Talks with a child on the Beatitudes. 181
Talks with Christ and his teachers. 2060, 3473
Talks with men. 2397
Talks with our daughters. 1714
Talks with the children. 1678
Talks with the little ones about the Apostles' creed. 74
Talks with the training class. 3557
Tall of Bible stories. 620
Tall in His presence. 3530
Tall in paradise. 1307
Tall man from Boston. 3828
Tall timber. 2609, 3868
Tallis. 3582
Tallis's Illustrated Scripture history for the improvement of youth. 293
Talmage story. 3582
Talmud. 3582, 3583, 3584, 3585
Talmud and Apocrypha. 514, 1539
Talmud for every Jew. 3583
Talmud of Jerusalem. 3584
Talmud of the land of Israel. 3585
Talmud; selections from the contents of that ancient book, its commentaries, teaching, poetry and legends. 3583
Talmud today. 18
Talmud unmasked. 2013, 2118
Talmudic anthology. 3584
Talmudic anthology, tales and teachings of the rabbis. 3584
Talmudic law and the modern state. 2074
Talmudic miscellany. 3584
Talmudic pearls. 3584
Talmudic sayings. 3584
Tamarisk garden blessed with rain. 2509
Tamate, a king. 880
Tamers of death. 25
Tamil temple myths. 3422
Ibn Taimiya's struggle against popular religion. 1880, 1927
Tammuz and Ishtar. 94
Tanganyika and its future. 2552
Tanglewood tales. 2658
Tanglewood tales for girls and boys. 2658
Tanna debe Eliyyahu. 1798
Tannaitic parallels to the Gospels. 398
Tannisho. 3403
Tantra asana. 3586

Tantra for the West. 3476
Tantric Buddhist art. 88
Tantric mysticism of Tibet. 3586
Tantric tradition. 3585
Tantric view of life. 3586
Tantum ergo sacramentum. 2258
Tao. 2196, 3587
Tao, a new way of thinking. 2196
Tao and Chinese culture. 3586
Tao magic. 2314
Tao of science. 2839
Tao te ching. 2196
Tao Teh Ching. 2196
Tao-teh-king. 2196
Tao teh king (The way of peace) of Lao-Tzu, 600 B. C. 2196
Tao teh of Laotse. 2196
Tao, the great luminant. 2196
Taoism. 2197, 3586, 3587
Taoism and Chinese religion. 913
Taoism and Confucianism. 3586
Taoism and the rite of cosmic renewal. 3586
Taoist notebook. 3586
Taoist pearl. 1780, 3586
Taoist texts. 3587
Taoist vision. 3586
Tapestry. 926, 3306, 3858
Tapestry of faith. 1002
Tapestry of grace. 1302, 3895
Tapestry of life, a devotional guidebook. 965
Tappan Reformed Church, 1694-1969. 2700
Taproot of religion and its fruitage. 3063
Taproots for tall souls. 964
... Tar heel apostle. 2938
Tar heel disciples, 1841-1852. 1465
Tar Heel ghosts. 3580
Tara, child of hopes & dreams. 689, 2669
Tarascan folk religion. 3588
Tarbell's teacher's guide. 1917
Tarbell's teacher's guide to the International Bible lessons for Christian teaching. 1917
Tarbell's teachers guide to the International Bible Lessons for Christian teaching of the uniform course for 1961. 1917
Tarbell's teacher's guide to the International Sunday-school lessons for 1906. 1917
[al-Tarbiyah wa-al-taghayyur al-thaqafi fi Ummat al-Islam bi-Amrika (romanized form)]. 669
Target-group evangelism. 1568
Target-Heaven. 1432
Targum and testament. 321
Targum Jonathan to the Prophets. 570, 3588
Targum of Isaiah. 541
Targum Onkelos to Genesis. 520
Targum Onqelos on Genesis 49. 528
Targumic traditions and the New Testament. 492
Targums and Rabbinic literature. 492
Targums of Onkelos and Jonathan ben Uzziel on the Pentateuch. 561
Tarjuman al-Qur'an. 2184
Tarnished halo. 1810, 1903
Tarosophy. 3589
Tarot. 3588, 3589
Tarot, a new handbook for the apprentice. 3588
Tarot and transformation. 3588
Tarot-card spread reader. 3588
Tarot cards for fun and fortune telling. 3588
Tarot classic. 3588
Tarot of Cornelius Agrippa. 3588
Tarot revelations. 3588
"Tarry till I come?" 2414
"Tarry ye," 2435
Taryag. 1312
Task ahead. 2457
Task in Japan. 2534

Task of Christian education. 3160
Task of philosophical theology. 2832
Task of religion. 1342
Task of the Christian in the university. 3757
Task that challenges. 2528
Task worth while. 2493
Task worthy of travail. 3119
Taste and see. 2393, 3491
Taste & see '72. 3749
Taste for the other. 2220
Taste of creation. 2394, 2753
Taste of new wine. 2466
Tattvarthadhigama sutra. 1932
Tattwa katha. 3867
Taught by the Master. 2061
Taught the will of God. 1741
Tax exempt financing. 3328

Taylor's Bible story book. 624
"TaZ", Rabbi David Halevi. 1404, 3016
Te Bogomils. 674
Te Deum laudamus. 1874, 2777
Teach. 940, 3385
Teach & reach. 935
Teach me, Lord. 17
Teach me, please teach me. 939
Teach me Thy paths. 1267, 2269, 2393
Teach me to pray. 2113, 2876, 2880
Teach me to teach. 3178
Teach or perish! 3154
Teach us how to pray. 2871
Teach us to pray. 1625, 2867, 2880, 2882, 2888, 3810
Teach what you preach. 3660
Teach with success. 940, 3179
Teach ye all nations. 2554
Teach yourself New Testament Greek. 1770
Teach yourself to pray. 2882
Teacher. 503, 1127, 1657, 3557, 3565, 3715
Teacher and the Book. 640
Teacher and the child. 3154
Teacher and the class. 3558
Teacher and the world religions. 3142
Teacher and young teens. 3167
Teacher education and religion. 3178
Teacher in the primitive church and the teacher today. 937, 3165
Teacher of Galilee. 2061
Teacher of the Baha'i faith in South America. 130
Teacher of the mentally retarded. 2411
Teacher sent from God. 2061
Teacher tells a story. 3534
Teacher that teaches. 3559
Teacher training class and how to conduct it. 3555
Teacher-training for Jewish schools, practical suggestions for rabbis and principals. 2114
Teacher-training for the Sunday-school. 3550
Teacher-training handbook revised. 3557
Teacher training manual. 3565
Teacher-training with the Master Teacher. 2061
Teacher who laughs. 2305, 2542
Teachers' and students. 243
Teachers' and students' illustrated. 243
... Teacher's annual lesson commentary on uniform Bible lessons for the churches of Christ ... v. 1- 1946. 1917
Teacher's appreciation of the Old Testament. 597
Teachers' Bible. 271, 3591
Teacher's Bible commentary. 224
Teacher's book. 199
Teachers' book of Old Testament heroes. 597
Teachers' book of the heroic Christ. 3152
Teacher's candlestick. 3557
Teachers' commentary. 223
Teachers' commentary on the Acts of the apostles. 331
Teachers' commentary on the Gospel according to St. Matthew. 442
Teacher's commentary on the gospel narrative of the last days of Jesus. 385
Teacher's commentary on the gospel narrative of the last year of Our Lord's ministry. 385
Teacher's companion to the Trinity course of church instruction. 1268, 3180
Teacher's compendium of first principles of Christian pedagogy. 3178
Teacher's conversations with God. 1721
Teacher's guide for adult basic education. 8
Teacher's guide for Bible. 616
Teacher's guide for The living Bible. 650, 3723
Teacher's guide for The story of the Hebrew people, to use with the pupil's book. 532
Teacher's guide for use with A manual of faith and life. 2921
Teacher's guide to Israel today. 3310
Teachers' guide to the International Sunday-school lessons. 1915
...Teacher's guide to the organizaiton and administration of the Sunday school (Cuninggim-North) 3552
Teacher's guide to using Arch books with children. 941
Teacher's handbook for It's your future. 804
Teacher's handbook to Bible history. 225
Teacher's handbook to the catechism. 746
Teacher's helper. 3551
... Teachers' home series. 3165
Teacher's last lesson. 3814
Teacher's manual. 1915, 3166
Teachers' manual for Our part in the world. 3166, 3453

Teacher's manual for the daily vacation Bible school. 3159
... Teacher's manual for The life of Jesus. 1993
Teachers' manual for The Protestant Churches of America. 2956
... Teacher's manual for The religion of Israel. 1928
... Teacher's manual for The Teachings of Jesus. 3167
Teacher's manual of physical education. 2844
Teachers' manual of week day Bible lessons. 642
Teacher's manual to accompany A course in religion. 803
Teacher's manual to accompany Bible study for Bible students. 637
... Teachers' manual to accompany God our Father, Jesus our Savior. 746
... Teacher's manual to accompany the First grade lesson book on the life of Christ harmonized from the four evangelists. 1993
... Teachers' manual to accompany The redeeming sacrifice. 3167
... Teacher's manual to accompany the Second grade lesson book on the life of Christ harmonized from the four evangelists. 1993
... Teacher's manual to accompany the Third grade lesson book on the life of Christ harmonized from the four evangelists. 1993
Teachers' New Testament. 343
Teacher's notes on Hero stories of the Old Testament. 2958
Teachers' notes on our book of worship. 2700
Teacher's notes on S. Paul and the first Christian missionaries. 2804
Teacher's notes on St. Paul and the first Christian missionaries. 2804
Teachers' notes on the church catechism. 2971
Teachers' notes on Wonder stories from the Gospels. 179, 626
Teachers of Drew, 1867-1942. 1480
Teacher's quest. 3592
Teacher's report card, and other inspiring stories. 1004
Teacher's syllabus for grade 2. 1316
Teacher's syllabus for grade 9. 1316, 3723
Teaching about religion in public schools. 3190
Teaching adolescents in the church school. 3557
Teaching adults. 3169
Teaching adults in the Sunday school. 3149
Teaching aids for Complete group guidance for Catholic high school students. Prepared by Norbert Riegert [and others] . 1374
Teaching all nations. 746
...The teaching and accompaniment of plainsong. 883
Teaching and influence of Saint Augustine. 115
Teaching and learning. 934
Teaching and learning with older elementary children. 938
Teaching and learning with young children. 938
Teaching and morality. 1498
Teaching and preaching religion to children. 746
Teaching and preaching that counts. 3352
Teaching and preaching the New Testament. 1634, 3368
Teaching and study guide to The principles and practice of astrology. 97
Teaching and teachers. 3565
Teaching and training with audio-visuals. 1253
Teaching and worship of the Liberal Catholic church. 2220
Teaching as the direction of activities. 3159
Teaching authority & infallibility in the Church. 866, 1163
Teaching Bible doctrine from the Bible. 637
Teaching Bible stories more effectively with puppets. 616
Teaching Bible truths with simple objects. 2720
Teaching children. 3151
Teaching children as the spirit leads. 939
Teaching children in the church. 3180
Teaching children in the small church. 3154
Teaching children in your church. 3179
Teaching children joy. 938
Teaching children to pray. 901
Teaching Christian adults. 938
Teaching Christian stewardship. 3531

Teaching Christianity. 3150
Teaching church. 3149, 3160
Teaching church at work. 937
Teaching church in our time. 1248
Teaching confraternity classes. 746
Teaching conversational prayer. 2887
Teaching doctrine and liturgy. 3169
Teaching early adolescents creatively. 937
Teaching ethnic awareness. 2475
Teaching faith and morals. 935
Teaching for abundant living. 3150
Teaching for Christian living. 3180
Teaching for decision. 3149
Teaching for results. 3179
Teaching from the tabernacle. 3579
Teaching in Jesuit High Schools. 1946
Teaching in the Armed Forces; Protestant
  religious education program. 3178
Teaching in the CCD high school. 746
Teaching in the church school. 3156, 3180
Teaching in the Jewish religious school.
  2106
...Teaching in the Sunday school. 3559
Teaching intermediates in the church
  school. 3157
Teaching is communicating. 3161
Teaching Israel. 3310
Teaching junior boys and girls. 3149
Teaching juniors. 3563
Teaching kindergarten children. 3173
Teaching liturgy in schools. 849
Teaching Luther's Catechism. 2279
Teaching methods of the Master. 2061
Teaching middlers. 3171
Teaching ministry of the church. 3158
Teaching ministry of the extension visitor.
  3555
Teaching ministry of the priest in the
  Episcopal Church. 3681
Teaching ministry of the pulpit. 2906
Teaching missions. 2551
Teaching music through songs, hand
  singing, and inner hearing. 917
Teaching nursery children. 3173
Teaching of Addai. 1018
Teaching of Apocrypha and Apocalypse.
  489
Teaching of Bible classes. 641, 3180
Teaching of Christ. 770, 1052, 1954,
  2064, 3628
Teaching of ideals. 1540, 2590
Teaching of Jesus. 401, 2061, 2064, 2066
Teaching of Jesus about the future
  according to the synoptic gospels. 1530,
  2065
Teaching of Jesus concerning Christian
  conduct. 946
Teaching of Jesus concerning God the
  Father. 1732, 2065
... The teaching of Jesus concerning
  Himself. 489, 1955
Teaching of Jesus concerning His own
  mission. 2060
Teaching of Jesus concerning His own
  person. 2061
Teaching of Jesus concerning the future
  life. 1694
Teaching of Jesus concerning the Holy
  Spirit. 1828
Teaching of Jesus concerning the kingdom
  of God and the church. 2014, 3321
Teaching of Jesus concerning the
  Scriptures. 276, 2062
Teaching of Jesus in parables. 2025
Teaching of Jesus on human relations.
  2064
Teaching of Judaica in American
  universities. 2154
Teaching of Mary Aikenhead. 20, 3416
... The teaching of morality in the family
  and the school. 2590
Teaching of Old Testament history. 533
Teaching of Our Lord as to the
  indissolubility of marriage. 2340
Teaching of Paul in terms of the present
  day. 2800
Teaching of Platonius. 3499
Teaching of preaching in Baptist
  theological seminaries of the United
  States. 2911
Teaching of religion. 805, 3147, 3553
Teaching of religion in American higher
  education. 3189
Teaching of religion in the public schools.
  3190
Teaching of St. Augustine on fear as a
  religious motive. 115, 1619
Teaching of Saint Gregory. 1773, 3639
Teaching of St. John the Apostle to the
  churches of Asia and the world. 414
Teaching of St. Paul. 3166
Teaching of the Abyssinian church. 1540
Teaching of the Catholic Church. 782
Teaching of the early church on the use of
  wine and strong drink. 3595
Teaching of the Epistle to the Hebrews.
  405

Teaching of the Gospel of John. 421
Teaching of the Holy Scriptures, for young
  people's classes in all evangelical
  churches. 3191
...The teaching of the lesson. 2597
Teaching of the Master. 2069
...The teaching of the New Testament.
  475
Teaching of the parables of Jesus Christ.
  2026
Teaching of the prayer book. 2960
Teaching of the prophets. 2950
Teaching of the Qur'an. 2184
Teaching of the twelve apostles. 71
Teaching of the Twelve apostles. English.
  1019
Teaching of the Vedas. 3776
Teaching office in the Reformed tradition.
  1248
Teaching our faith in God. 3177
Teaching pastor. 3670

Teaching plans for 3's. 3173
Teaching primaries. 938
Teaching primaries in the church school.
  3172
Teaching primary children. 3154
Teaching primary children in the church.
  3171
Teaching problem. 3564
Teaching problems and how to solve them.
  3554, 3592
Teaching religion. 3165, 3180
Teaching religion, an introduction to
  catechetics. 745
Teaching religion creatively. 3180
Teaching religion for living. 3154
Teaching religion in school. 3111
Teaching religion in the public school.
  3189
Teaching religion the adaptive way. 745
Teaching religion to adolescents. 3146
Teaching religion to-day. 3147
Teaching religion to the deaf. 1412
Teaching Sacraments to youth. 3266
Teaching Scripture. 635
Teaching senior highs. 3175
Teaching seniors. 3175
Teaching sermons. 1225, 1266
Teaching task of the local church. 3154
Teaching teachers to teach. 3180, 3385
Teaching teens the truth. 940
Teaching that makes a difference. 3179
Teaching the beginner child. 3173
Teaching the Bible. 640
Teaching the Bible story. 616
Teaching the Bible to primaries. 3169
Teaching the Bible with games. 644
Teaching the Catholic catechism with the
  religion workbook. 746
Teaching the Christian virtues. 3782
Teaching the church's children. 3172
Teaching the devotion to the Sacred Heart.
  3270
Teaching the Eucharist. 2255
Teaching the gifted and talented. 1712
Teaching the gospel through music. 2599
Teaching the gospel with prayer and
  testimony. 2618
Teaching the Haggadah. 3172
Teaching the historical books. 531
Teaching the history of salvation. 3152
Teaching the linguistically diverse. 2475
Teaching the multitudes. 3801
Teaching the New Testament. 473
Teaching the Old Testament. 595
Teaching the Old Testament in English
  classes. 532
Teaching the Pentateuch. 566
Teaching the prophets. 571
Teaching the sacraments. 3267
Teaching the sacraments and morality.
  3267
Teaching the Scriptures. 646
Teaching the Siddur. 2154
Teaching the teacher. 3178
Teaching the way. 747
Teaching the word of truth. 3183
Teaching the youth of the church. 3154
Teaching them to observe. 155
Teaching through worship. 3858
Teaching to win and develop. 3179
Teaching today. 934
Teaching tools for Sunday schools. 3565
Teaching toward Christian perfection.
  3491
Teaching truth by signs and ceremonies.
  3180
Teaching with Discover: handbook for use
  in 1969-1970. 939
Teaching with new techniques. 3170
Teaching with the Book of Mormon. 679
Teaching with Witness intermediate:
  handbook for use in 1969-1970. 939
Teaching with Witness intermediate
  handbook for use in 1970-1971. 939

Teaching with Witness junior high:
  handbook for use in 1969-1970. 3181
Teaching with Witness junior high
  handbook for use in 1970-1971. 938
Teaching without textbooks. 3149
Teaching work of the church. 3148
Teaching young people. 3175
Teaching young people in the Sunday
  school. 3175
Teaching your child about God. 939, 1726
Teaching your child to pray. 2871
Teaching youth in the church. 3180
Teachings and acts of Jesus of Narzareth
  and his apostles. 2062
Teachings and counsels. 123, 1702
Teachings and illustrations as they emanate
  from the spirit world. 3507
Teachings and miracles of Jesus. 2066
Teachings from the American earth. 1902
Teachings of Don Juan. 2137, 3862
Teachings of His Holiness the Dalai Lama.
  709
Teachings of Jesus. 2062, 2065
Teachings of Jesus and the lives of His
  apostles. 71, 1973
Teachings of Jesus concerning wealth.
  2063
Teachings of Jesus for evangelism. 2064
Teachings of Jesus in Matthew 5-7. 3335
Teachings of Jesus, selected from the
  Gospels. 2072
... The teachings of Judaism, from the
  sources. 2113
Teachings of Lord Caitanya. 879
Teachings of Maimonides. 2318
Teachings of Pope John XXIII. 759
Teachings of Pope Paul VI, 1970. 761
Teachings of providence. 1654
Teachings of Rumi. 1933, 3542
Teachings of Saint Louis. 2261
Teachings of Solomon. 3457
Teachings of Taoist Master Chuang. 1115,
  3586
Teachings of the book of Mormon. 678
Teachings of the books. 411, 733
Teachings of the Church Fathers. 1018
Teachings of the compassionate Buddha.
  701, 707
Teachings of the Doctrine and covenants.
  3430
Teachings of the Essenes. 1532
Teachings of the Little flower. 3690
Teachings of the living Jesus Christ. 2063
Teachings of the Lord Jesus. 2062
Teachings of the magi. 3899
Teachings of the masters. 2724
Teachings of the mystics. 2640
Teachings of the New Testament. 475
Teachings of the prophet Joseph Smith.
  2605, 3429
Teachings of the prophet Joseph Smith,
  taken from his sermons and writings as
  they are found in the Documentary
  history and other publications of the
  church and written or published in the
  days of the Prophet's ministry. Selected
  and arranged by the historian, Joseph
  Fielding Smith, and his assistants in the
  historian's office of the Church of Jesus
  Christ of latter-day saints. 2605
Teachings of the Second Vatican Council.
  3770
Teachings of the secret order of the
  Christian brotherhood and school of
  Christian initiation. 3151
Teachings of Tibetan yoga. 3586
Teachings of Yogi Bhajan. 3408
Teachings on divine law. 3146
Teachings toward Christian perfection.
  3491
Team. 1776
Team-A serials. 3678
Team building in church groups. 1170
Team strategies in mobilizing school and
  community services for emotionally
  disturbed children. 2411
Team teaching. 3592
Team teaching with the Scotts and
  Bartons. 3179
Teamwork and labor turnover. 2189
Tears and consolations. 2371
Tears and triumphs. 3143
Tears of contrition. 3143
Tears of Jesus. 1560
Tears of Lady Meng. 1088
Tears of the Bible. 215
Techinah-book. 2117
Technethics. 3592
Technical assistance by religious agencies
  in Latin America. 3592
Technique of a minister. 3671
Technique of Christian living. 956
Technique of Gregorian chironomy. 884
Technique of living. 3196
Technique of public worship. 3004
Technique of solar returns. 97
Technique of the disciple. 3249

Technique of the master. 3249
Techniques and resources for guiding adult
  groups. 1170
... Techniques for discovering the interests
  of Young men's Christian association
  applicants. 3872
Techniques in prayer therapy. 2695
Techniques of a working church. 3670
Techniques of high magic. 2313
Techniques of torchbearing. 1571
Technology and religion. 3082
Technology and social justice. 1135, 3850
Technometry. 3615
Teen age talks. 907
Teen-age tangles. 3592
Teen-age worship. 3859
Teen-ager's life of Christ. 1983
Teen-ager's ultimate. 2263
Teen programs that click. 1479
Teen talk. 3879
Teen talks. 3886
Teen talks with God. 3884
Teen traveler abroad. 149
Teen with a future, by James R. Adair.
  3883
Teen-age Bible. 647
Teenage parishioner. 1261
Teenage problems. 999
Teen-age version of the Holy Bible. 265
Teenager and the new morality. 3880
Teenager and the new mysticism. 2646
Teen-ager, Christ is for you. 3888
Teen-ager, your church is for you. 3888
Teen-ager, Christ's love will make you
  live. 3888
Teen-agers pray. 3883
Teen-ager's saint. 2333
Teenagers; the facts of sex, love, and life.
  3880
Teenagers today. 786, 3885
Teen-agers' trail guide. 3880
Teens alive! 3880
Teens and the rural Sunday school. 3554
Teens talk of many things. 3881
Teens triumphant. 3887
Teeth on edge. 1132
Tefillin. 2844
Teh Gospel according to St. John, 1-10.
  418
Tehilim (romanized form) 583
Teilhard and the creation of the soul.
  3462, 3593
Teilhard and the supernatural. 3566, 3592
Teilhard and womanhood. 3593, 3831
Teilhard de Chardin. 3593
Teilhard de Chardin: an analysis and
  assessment. 3593
Teilhard de Chardin and the mystery of
  Christ. 3593
Teilhard de Chardin: re-mythologization.
  3593
Teilhard de Chardin's theology of the
  Christian in the world. 3593
Teilhard explained. 3593
Teilhard, Scripture, and revelation. 241,
  2010
Teinds and agriculture. 3702
Tekst til et udvalg hymner fra Christian
  science hymnal, indbefattende syv digte
  af Mary Baker Eddy. 1037
Tel Sono, the Japanese reformer. 3143
Telecommunications and the church. 3594
Telecult power. 2724
Teleological explanations. 3590, 3594
Teleology. 3594
Telepathy. 3698
Telepathy and clairvoyance. 2991
Telepathy and spiritualism. 3698
Telepathy and the subliminal self. 2990
Telepathy and thought-transference. 3698
Telepathy of the celestial world. 2991
Telephone between worlds. 3498
Telephone directory and Catholic guide of
  Chicago Archdiocese. 892
Telescopic view of the Revelation of Jesus
  Christ. 465
Television, a guide for Christians. 3594
Television and the Christian home. 1609
Television-radio audience and religion.
  3594
Tell Asmar and Khafaje. 894
Tell Asmar, Khafaje and Khorsabad. 894
Tell every man. 1362
Tell it all; the tyranny of Mormonism.
  2613
Tell it from Calvary. 144, 2698
Tell it like it is. 3829
Tell it on the mountain. 1359, 2197
Tell it to the children. 908
Tell it to the padre. 1063
Tell it well. 1317
"Tell Jesus." 1749
Tell John; the message of Jesus and
  present day religion. 954
Tell me. 2546
Tell me a Noah's ark story. 297
"Tell me a true story" 297

Tell me about death, Mommy. 1414
Tell me about God. 1723, 3165
Tell me about God and prayer. 2886
Tell me about God's plan for me. 903
Tell me about heaven. 1794
Tell me about Jesus. 930, 1952, 1981, 1984
Tell me about Moody. 2587
Tell me about prayer. 901, 2886
Tell me about the Bible. 313, 621
Tell me about the church. 1228
Tell me about the church; with a foreword by Warren C. Roark. 1228
Tell me about the Holy Spirit, about the church. 1108
Tell me about the Lord Jesus Christ. 2047
Tell me about the Lord's Prayer. 2250
"Tell me again" Bible. 629
Tell me another true story. 630
Tell me how. 992
Tell me--my quest. 1060
Tell me, rabbi. 2168, 3016
Tell me, talented teen, who are you? 3879
Tell me why. 2151
Tell my people. 663, 747, 748
Tell the next generation. 862, 3349
Tell the truth. 3829
Tell the world. 3828
"Tell them" 2538
Tell thy children. 3143
Tell us a story. 907
"Tell us another!" 1014, 3533
Tell us, please. 3012
Telling Bible stories. 616
Telling it like it was. 1284
Telling on myself. 3143
Telling others. 3183
... Telling people about God. 2959
Telling tales out of school. 3015
Telling the good news. 867, 3002
Telling the story. 2299, 2901
Telling the story of the local church. 1243
Telling the truth. 2898
Telling truth. 2907
Telling yourself the truth. 980
Tells, tombs, and treasure. 207
Telugu mission of the General council of the Evangelical Lutheran church in North America. 3143
Temperance almanac. 27
Temperance Bible-commentary. 3597
Temperance manual. 3595
Temperance program. 3595
Temperance reformation. 3597
Temperance reformation and its claims upon the Christian church. 2231
Temperance sermons. 3596
Temperance speaker. 3597
Temperance tales. 3596
Temperance text-book. 3595
Temperance truth for the young and old. 3595
Temperance vs. prohibition. 3597
Templar at work. 1913
Templar tales. 3598
Templars in the Corona de Aragon. 3598
Temple. 523, 954, 1017, 2783, 2893
Temple, an oratorio. 2740
Temple & A priest to the temple. 3672
Temple and its teaching. 1944
Temple and the community in Qumram and the New Testament. 3013
Temple and the community in Qumran and the New Testament. 3013
Temple art under the Chola queens. 3600
Temple Beth El. 24
Temple Beth El, 1972. 2098, 3598
Temple builders. 3342, 3764
Temple dictionary of the Bible. 243
Temple gateways in south India. 894
Temple in the heart. 2934
Temple Israel memorial volume. 2155
Temple lectures of the Order of the magi, delivered before the Grand temple of the order. 2729
Temple letters. 2612
Temple manifestations. 3600
Temple Mishkan Tefila. 1820
Temple of Artemis at Ephesos. 1521
Temple of eternity. 3701, 3707
Temple of God. 1120, 2696
Temple of God's Wounds. 1741
Temple of His body. 2391
Temple of honor illustrated. 3598
Temple of Jerusalem. 1944
Temple of King Solomon. 1944
Temple of love. 1652
Temple of promise, Jackson county, Missouri. 2618
Temple of reason, and dignity of self-government. 3023
Temple of religion and tower of peace at the 1839 Golden gate international exposition. 3093
Temple of silence. 2638
Temple of Solomon. 1944
Temple of the Phallic King. 1896

Temple of the rosy cross. 3250
Temple of the spirit. 2675, 3521
Temple of truth, or The science of ever-progressive knowledge. 3073
Temple of Yahweh. 3599
Temple pulpit. 3371
Temple reflections. 3599
... The temple service for the Sabbath and the festivals. 2120
Temple symbolism of the Qumran texts and the New Testament. 3014
Temples and temple-service in ancient Israel. 1944, 3855
Temples in Roman Britian. 3600
Temples in the wilderness. 1271
Temples of Angkor. 3599
Temples of Anking and their cults. 913
Temples of eternity. 976
Temples of Nara and their art. 3600
Temples of peace. 3333
Temples of South India. 3600
Temples of the dawn. 2553
Temples of the eternal; or, The symbolism of churches. 3574
Temples of the Most High. 2604, 3599
Templi carmina. 1864
Temporal pillars. 3011
Temporal sovereignty of the pope. 2863
... The temporary and the permanent in New Testament revelation. 451, 476
Temptation. 1908, 1920, 2067, 3600
Temptation and sin. 2753
Temptation and the Passion. 434
Temptation, help for struggling Christians. 3600
Temptation in the desert. 2067
Temptation of Christ. 2067
... The temptation of Jesus. 2067
Temptation of Our Lord. 2067
Temptation to be good. 3725
Temptation; what it is and how to meet it. 3600
Temptations for the theology of liberation. 2222
Temptations of Christ. 2067
Temptations of religion. 3058
Temptations to rightdoing. 2590
Tempted by love. 2340
Tempter of Eve. 1577
Ten. 3601
Ten against the storm. 1110
Ten basic steps in genealogy. 1704
Ten Bible lessons. 641
Ten blessed years. 75
Ten blessings. 3344
Ten bright eyes. 2491
Ten burning questions. 3357
Ten Christians. 1025
Ten colloquies. 1526
Ten commandments will not budge. 1314
Ten commandments. 515, 517, 550, 1312, 1313, 1314, 1315, 1316, 2605, 3340
Ten commandments; a study of ethical freedom. 1315
Ten commandments; an interpretation. 1312, 3601
Ten commandments analyzed. 3601
Ten commandments and human rights. 1313
Ten commandments and modern man. 1313
Ten commandments and the Lord's prayer. 1314, 3601
Ten commandments and you. 1312
Ten commandments applied to modern behavior. 1313
Ten commandments explained in sermonic lectures. 1315, 3339
Ten commandments for children. 1315
Ten commandments for the long haul. 194, 996
Ten Commandments for today. 1312, 1314, 1316
Ten Commandments in a changing world. 1315
Ten commandments in modern perspective. 1315
Ten commandments in new perspective. 1314
Ten Commandments in recent research. 1314
Ten Commandments in the New Testament. 1314, 2064
Ten commandments "the law of liberty," 1313
Ten commandments the master key to life. 1313
Ten commandments today. 1314
Ten commandments, yesterday and today. 1313
Ten commandments, Exodus xx, 1-17, in ancient and modern tongues. 1312
Ten considerations for family living. 1015
Ten dangerous years. 2559
Ten days in the light of Acca. 127
Ten days in the light of 'Akka. 127
Ten days with D. L. Moody. 1559

Ten decades of praise. 3415
Ten decades of service. 673
Ten decisive battles of Christianity. 1177
Ten discourses delivered extempore at several meeting houses of the people called Quakers, in Great Britain. 1211
Ten discourses on subjects connected with public worship and the liturgy. 2970
Ten don'ts for Sunday-school teachers. 3550
Ten faces of ministry. 1297, 2293
Ten famous evangelists. 1575
Ten famous girls of the Bible. 215
Ten famous missionaries. 2483
10 fastest-growing Southern Baptist Sunday Schools. 3565
Ten fingers for God. 690, 2557
Ten for two. 3362
Ten great freedoms. 1315
Ten great religions. 3114, 3615
Ten greatest chapters in the Bible. 235
Ten greatest Christian doctrines. 934
Ten Jatakas stories. 1937
Ten largest Sunday schools and what makes them grow. 3565
Ten lectures on orthodoxy and heresy in the Christian church. 1805
Ten lessons in personal evangelism. 1566
Ten lessons on Our Lord's return. 1172
Ten lives of the Buddha. 1937, 2631
Ten makers of modern Protestant thought. 3611
Ten medieval studies. 1185, 1186
Ten million dollar hostage. 1396, 2485
Ten minute lesson on the Presbyterian church in the United States of America. 2921
Ten-minute sermons. 2425
Ten missionary dramatizations for boys. 2489
Ten most wanted men. 952
Ten nequdoth of the Torah. 1796, 2364
Ten New England leaders. 688, 1333
Ten new hymns for the 70's. 1866
Ten one-act plays. 3144
Ten paths to peace and power. 1007
Ten personal studies. 1758
Ten perspectives on Milton. 1101, 2471
Ten principal Upanishads. 3760
Ten religions of the East. 3140
Ten responsible minutes. 2903
Ten rules for living. 1313, 1315
Ten rungs. 1788
Ten rungs, Hasidic sayings. 1788
Ten saints. 3280, 3284
Ten select sermons. 1558
Ten series of meditations on the mysteries of the Rosary. 3249
Ten sermons of religion. 3726
Ten sermons on the second coming of Our Lord Jesus Christ. 3321
Ten sex talks to boys (10 years and older) 3389
Ten short lessons in masonic philosophy. 1661
Ten short stories from the Bible. 615
Ten steps for church growth. 1171
Ten steps to leadership. 2204
Ten steps to the good life. 1313
Ten steps to victory over depression. 985
Ten studies in church doctrines. 2287
Ten studies in church history. 1198
Ten studies in prayer. 2871
Ten studies in religious pedagogy. 3159
Ten studies in the catechism. 2279
Ten studies in the Psalms. 576
Ten studies on the Lutheran Church. 1547, 2715
Ten studies on the sacraments. 3267
Ten studies on the Sunday school. 3552
10 teachings. 3666
Ten teen programs. 3176
Ten test circles. 3500
Ten theologians respond to the Unification Church. 3723
Ten theophanies. 2414
Ten thousand coincidences. 3407
Ten torchbearers. 3138
Ten tribes, discovered and identified. 1929
Ten tribes in history and prophecy. 1929
Ten vital Jewish issues. 2141
Ten vital messages. 166
Ten weeks. 2532
10 who overcame. 1783
Ten women and God. 931
Ten words. 1313
Ten words of freedom. 599, 1315
Ten words that will change your life. 1314
Ten-year teacher; book four. 3549
Ten-year teacher, book one. 3549
Ten-year teacher, book two. 3549
Ten years before the mast. 2604
Ten years behind the sacred desk. 3143
Ten years in eastern Cuba. 156
"Ten years in Texas" 993
Ten years of discovery in the wilderness of Judaea. 1410

Ten years with spiritual mediums. 3501
Tenacious monks. 188, 3274
Tendencies of the synoptic tradition. 393
Tender of wishes. 2889
Tender touch. 1576, 3767
Tenders of the flock. 1299
Tennant's philosophical theology. 3601, 3609
Tennessee Christians. 1467
Tennessee Ernie Ford's book of favorite hymns. 1865
Tennessee records. 1525
Tennyson, an occultist. 2733, 3602
... Tennyson's use of the Bible. 299, 3602
Tensions. 992
Tensions and change. 2573
Tensions and destiny. 960
Tensions in American Puritanism. 3008
Tensions in contemporary theology. 3657
Tensions in modern faith. 2907
Tent and home, and other sermons. 3338
Tent and the sky. 167
Tent of God. 630
Tent to temple. 1368, 2829
Tentative guide to historical materials on the Spanish borderlands. 29
Tentative report of the Committee on a system of teaching morals in the public schools. 2593
Tenth anniversary of the North Reformed Dutch church, Newark, N.J. 1484
Tenth-century document of Arabic literary theory and criticism. 2184
Tenth-century document of Arabic literary theory and criticsm. 2184
Tenth Diocesan Synod, Diocese of Natchez-Jackson, held in St. Peter's Co-cathedral, Jackson, May 23, 1957. 2669
Tenth generation. 599
Tenth hierarchy. 50
Tenting with Abraham. 4
Tentmaker from Tarsus. 2804
Tentmaker from Tarsus, a story of St. Paul. 2797
Tentmakers. 2803
Tents toward the sunrise. 1440
Tenure of Catholic church property in the United States of America. 1241
Tercentenary celebration of the promulgation of the Edict of Nantes, April 13, 1598. 1497
Tercentenary monument. 3045
Tercentenary pageant, 1628-1928. 2757
Tercentenary studies, 1928. 3046
Tercentenary year. 3045
Teresa de Jesus. 1028, 3603
Teresa, John, and Therese. 3602
Teresa of Avila. 1028, 3603
Teresa of Calcutta. 2717, 3602
Terminal generation. 1845
Terminology for the devil and evil spirits in the Apostolic Fathers. 1429
Terms of the gospel trust. 1509
Terrestrial astrology. 1706
Terrible beauty. 996
Terrible catastrophe. 1421
Territorial dimension of Judaism. 2765
Terror in the name of God. 1482
Terrot Reaveley Glover. 1717
Terry. 1367, 2399
Tertiary congress of the Third order of St. Francis. 1646
Tertiary's companion. 1648
Tertullian: Apologetical works. 3635
Tertullian concerning the resurrection of the flesh. 3604
Tertullian On the testimony of the soul and On the "prescription" of heretics. 3604
Tertullian's treatises. 3604
Test. 2489
Test of character. 1517
Test of love. 969
Test your Bible knowledge. 281
Test your "Word" power. 281
Le Testament. 3091
Testament for fishers of men, offering a simple and practical method for personal work. 353
Testament for the new world. 120
Testament from prison. 153, 3780
Testament of Abraham. 491
Testament of devotion. 1449
Testament of faith. 1096, 1592
Testament of God. 3072
Testament of Jesus. 424
Testament of Jesus-Sophia. 444, 1531
Testament of light. 3204
Testament of love. 2058, 3366
Testament of turning. 1362
Testaments of love. 2266
Testaments of the twelve patriarchs. 491
Tested by fire. 3831
Tested by temptation. 2067, 3600
Tested methods for teachers of juniors. 3557

Tested methods in town and country churches. 1274
Tested youth programs. 3856
Testimonial to grace. 1363
Testimonies. 1083
Testimonies and practice of the Society of Friends. 1684
Testimonies concerning the character and ministry of Mother Ann Lee and the first witnesses of the gospel of Christ's second appearing. 2205
Testimonies in the life, character, revelations and doctrines of Mother Ann Lee. 2205
Testimonies of our leaders. 2611
Testimonies of the ante-Nicene fathers to the divinity of Christ. 2000
Testimonies of the ante-Nicene fathers to the doctrine of the Trinity and of the divinity of the Holy Ghost. 3714
Testimonies of the life. 2205, 3397
Testimonies of the life, character, revelations, and doctrines of Mother Ann Lee. 2205
Testimonies of the Restoration. 1010
Testimonies to ministers and gospel workers. 3812
Testimony. 902, 1230, 3829
Testimony against prophane customs. 2328
Testimony and advice of an Assembly of pastors of churches in New England, at a meeting in Boston, July 7, 1743. 1757
Testimony concerning the separation which occurred in Indiana Yearly meeting of Friends, in the winter of 1842-'43. 1686
...The testimony of an escaped novice from the Sisterhood of St. Joseph, Emmettsburg, Maryland. 3275
Testimony of Carroll. 435
Testimony of Christ to Christianity. 2059
Testimony of Christ's second appearing. 3397
Testimony of God against slavery. 3424
Testimony of Jesus. 1953, 3812
Testimony of nineteen centuries to Jesus of Nazareth. 1995
Testimony of President Heber J. Grant. 1756
Testimony of reason. 65
Testimony of St. Mark. 436
Testimony of St. Paul to Christ viewed in some of its aspects. 394, 2798
Testimony of the Bible, concerning the assumptions of destructive criticism. 200
Testimony of the Evangelists. 394
Testimony of the evangelists examined by the rules of evidence administered in courts of justice. 394, 2068
Testimony of the Evangelists examined by the rules of evidence administered in courts of justice. 394
Testimony of the Patristic Age concerning Mary's death. 2358
Testimony of the rocks. 203
Testimony of the Shroud. 1827
Testimony of the soul. 3462
Testimony of the witnesses. 70
Testimony of triumph. 2058
Testimony to pioneer Baptists. 1713, 2327
Testimony treasures. 3384
Testing Christianity's truth-claims. 69
... The testing of a nation's ideals; Israel's history from the settlement to the Assyrian period. 2089
Testing of a soul. 550
Testing the knowledge of right and wrong. 2411
Testing the spirit. 2576
Testing tongues by the Word. 1716
Tests and measurements in Lutheran education. 2293
Tests and triumphs of Armenians in Turkey and Macedonia. 2558
Tests of a living church. 1123
Tests of divine inspiration. 3395
Tests of faith. 3432
Tests of life. 420
Tests of vocation, and other addresses. 3814
Tetra-chordon. 1017
Teutonic legends in the Nibelungen lied and the Nibelungen ring. 2206
Teutonic myth and legend. 2660
Teutonic mythology. 2660, 2666
Texan triumphs. 758
Texas colonists and religion, 1821-1836. 3605
Texas conference Methodism on the march. 1814-1960. 2432
Texas Disciples. 1467
Texas George. 2178
Texas is the place for me. 120
Texas Methodist centennial yearbook. 2432
Texas missions. 3470

Text and canon of the New Testament. 339
Text and iconography for Joinville's Credo. 74
Text and interpretation. 350, 668
Text and texture. 499
Text and verse for every day in the year. 253
Text book for Virginia Masons of Prince Hall affiliation. 1667
Text-book of church history. 1175, 1176
Text-book of ecclesiastical history. 1175
Text-book of popery. 798
Text-book of the history of doctrines. 3654, 3655
Text book of the Moravian church. 2595
Text book on baptism. 134
Text book on home and church tithing. 3702
Text-book on prophecy. 605
Text book, ritual, valuable data, and selected poems, for public workers in the organized movement of modern spiritualism. 3508
Text-book to Kant. 2180
Text-books of religion for parochial and Sunday schools. 3181
Text-books of religion for parochial and Sunday schools. 804
Text canon. and principal versions of the Bible. 241
Text. canon, and principal versions of the Bible, by Elmer E. Flack, Bruce M. Metzger and others. 241
Text-critical methodology and the pre-Caesarean text. 436
Text history of the Epigrams of Theocritus. 3609
Text of Acts in Codex 614 (Tisch. 137) and its allies. 326
... The text of Acts in ms 146 of the University of Michigan. 317
Text of Revelation. 458
Text of St. Luke's Gospel in the Book of Mulling. 430
Text of the Epistles. 373
Text of the New Testament. 321, 351, 352
Text of the Old Testament. 482, 505
Text of the Pauline Epistles in manuscript 2344 and its relationship to the text of other known manuscripts in particular to 330, 436, and 462. 373
Text of the Septuagint. 529
Text-restoration methods in contemporary U.S.A. 505
... The text tradition of pseudo-Aristotle 'De mundo'. 81
Textbook in apologetics. 63
Textbook of English literature for Catholic schools. 1518
Textbook of spiritual science. 3509
Textbook of theosophy. 3686, 3688
Textbook of Yoga psychology. 3865
Textbook on character. 886
Textile art in the Church. 920
Texts and studies in Jewish history and literature. 2094
Texts and studies of the Jewish theological seminary of America. 2079
Texts and talks by the late Rev. John G. Yeiser. 3347
Texts and testaments. 239, 1397, 3658
Texts and themes for the Christian year. 1268
Texts explained. 347
Textual and historical studies in the Book of Jubilees. 491
Textual commentary on the Greek New Testament. 351
Textual concordance of the Holy Scriptures. 304
Textual criticism of the Old Testament. 505
Textual discoveries in Proverbs, Psalms, and Isaiah. 572
Textual history of the letter to the Romans. 470
Texture of knowledge. 3082
Teyku. 2075, 3584
Tfillath yesharim. 2117
Th Eastern ritual. 1487
Th survival of man. 2990
Thai Buddhism, its rites and activities. 710
Thailand and the Seventh-Day Adventist medical and missionary work. 2553, 3387
Thanatology course outlines—funeral service. 1694
Thanatology course outlines—general. 1418
Thanatology course outlines—religion/philosophy. 1418
Thank God for laughter. 1407
Thank God for sex. 3391

Thank God for the red, white, and black. 2895
Thank God I'm a teenager. 7
Thank God, I'm OK. 981
Thank God, it's Monday! 2191
Thank you. 1734
Thank you, America! 1575
Thank you for being a friend. 692, 931
Thank you, God. 899, 901
Thank you, Lord, for little things. 2889
Thankfulness unites. 3749
Thanks be to God. 1756
Thanks for the mountain. 3831
Thanks, Lord, I needed that! 932, 2865
Thanksgiving every week. 3, 2383
Thanksgiving hymns (The) 2329
Thanksgiving messages. 1756
Thanksgiving of the spirit and other sermons. 3371
Thanksgiving scroll. English. 3605
Thanksgiving sermon. 3341
Thanksgiving sermons. 3605
That all may be one. 779, 2333
That all men be one. 1631
That better country. 117
That better country; the religious aspects of life in eastern Australia. 117
That blessed hope. 3319
That bogey man the Jew. 2078
That book in the attic. 3380
That book of em's. 2546
That boy. 1700
That Christ may live in me. 995, 2015
That church in your life. 1016
That day of days. 2465
That day with God. 2167, 3363
That elusive thing called joy. 994
That fighting spirit of Methodism. 2421, 3803
That flame of living fire. 1833
That Frenchman, John Calvin. 727
That Friday in Eden. 3392
That girl in your mirror. 1714
That God is love. 1014
That God's house may. 1252
That happy feeling of. 1756
That happy feeling of "Thank you." 1756
That hearing they shall perceive. 1066
That His word will live. 977
That I may know Him. 1433, 3225
That I may live in His kingdom. 2298
...That I may save some. 1567
That I may see. 1299
That immortal sea. 2438
That incredible book, the Bible. 209
That Jesus Christ is God by nature. 80
That Jew! 2082
That Jew problem. 2082
That lawsuit against the Bible. 278
That lonely Jew. 1962
That made me smile. 3675
That man is you. 2387
That manuscript from outer space. 279
That men may believe; a series of sermons. 164
That men may know. 164
That men may live, a series of sermons. 108
That men may live in Christ. 3178
That men may see, a series of sermons. 164
That motherly Mother of Guadalupe. 1776
That my family should partake. 1609
That my house may be filled. 1571
That mysterious fundamental option. 947
That new-time religion. 3232
That none be lost. 1564
"That nothing be lost" 1002
That nothing may be wasted. 2891
That old-time religion. 3744, 3745
That one face. 2012
That one good sermon. 2905
That other America. 2548
That revolutionary--Christ. 957
That strange man upon his cross. 2043
"That sweet story of old" 1982, 1983
That tent by the sawdust pile. 719
"That the world may believe," 425, 1041, 3012
That the world may know. 1175, 2494
That there is but one covenant. 2373
That there may be more ministers. 1461
That they all may be one. 1042, 3028, 3127
That they may be one. 859, 1302, 2260, 2422, 3719
"That they may be one": in behalf of the organic union of American Methodism. 2439
"That they may be won" 1572
That they may have life. 1434, 1569, 2974, 3464
That they may know Thee. 3785
That they may live: theological reflections on the quality of life. 3620
That they may share. 845

That they might have life. 106
That thy saving health may be known. 1601
That tremendous love. 1021
That unseen presence. 2695
That we may be willing to receive. 2393
That we may have hope. 1266
That we might have life. 928
That we might know Him. 1725
That which is. 2767
That wonderful night. 2023
That ye may believe. 424, 2126
That ye may know. 163, 369
That ye may not be deceived. 2599
That ye might have joy. 943
That ye might have life. 1009
That you may believe. 419, 423
That you may live. 1135, 2019
That your joy may be full. 74
'That's a good question! 3012, 3670
That's our church. 2958
That's the old spirit! 1000
Thaw at the Vatican. 3770
Thawing out the Eskimo. 1532, 3718
[The Book of Mormon. 2600
[The Haggadah of Passover]. 82, 2110
[The]Hive. 1518
[The Holy Bible. 256
[The life of our Lord]. 1975
..."The light by which we see light" 3076
... "The Madras series" 2514
...The mass. 2365, 2368
[The order of prayer for divine service]. 2110
[The union prayer book for Jewish worship]. 2110
[The union prayerbook for Jewish worship] 2109
Theaetetus of Plato. 2853
... The Theatines in the history of Catholic reform before the establishment of Lutheranism. 3607
Theatre of the spirit. 3004
Theatrum redivivum. 2984, 3605
Theios aner in Hellenistic-Judaism. 88, 2011
Their finest hour. 215, 925
Their future is now. 2591
Their hearts are His garden. 1455
Their hearts be praised. 1541
Their name is Pius. 2850
Their names remain. 3839
Their quiet tread. 3419
Their religion. 926
Their rightful heritage. 3166
Their rights and liberties. 1147
Their search for God. 91, 1395
Theirs is the kingdom. 928, 2609
Theism. 3607, 3608, 3609
Theism and cosmology. 3608
Theism and empiricism. 3100
Theism and evolution. 1581
Theism and humanism. 1853, 3607
Theism and the Christian faith. 1049
Theism and the modern mood. 1722
Theism and the scientific spirit. 1722
Theism and thought. 3607
Theism, atheism and the popular theology. 3609
Theism et als. 3608
Theism in medieval India. 1895, 1897
Theism in the light of present science and philosophy. 3608
Theistic argument as affected by recent theories. 3608
Theistic conception of the world. 3608
Thelogy for beginners. 797
...Them He also called. 968
Them He glorified. 1716
Them that sit in darkness. 2942
Thematic guide to the Union Prayerbooks and guides to Pirke Ovos and Proverbs. 2239
Thematischer Dialog-Gottesdienst. 3003
Theme of Jewish persecution of Christians in the Gospel according to St. Matthew. 442
Theme song of Assunta. 2333
Themes for vital preaching. 3374
Themes from Acts. 330
Themes from Romans. 469
Themes from St. John's gospel in early Roman catacomb painting. 420
Themes in fundamental moral theology. 949

Themes in Greek and Latin epitaphs. 1525
Themes in Old Testament theology. 598
Themes in the Christian history of Central Africa. 1073
Themes of catechesis. 3148
Themes of concern. 996
Themes of the Bible. 450
Themes of the restored gospel. 2619
Themes to ponder. 3197
Themis. 1395, 1766
Then and now. 723, 1040, 1676
Then and now in Kenya colony. 2536
Then and now; Quaker essays: historical and contemporary, by friends of Henry Joel Cadbury on his completion of twenty-two years as chairman of the American Friends Service Committee. 1676
Then and there! 241
Then came a miracle. 658, 930
Then came Jesus. 1014
Then comes the joy. 987
Then I think of God. 901
"Then is finished the mystery of God." 464, 1941
Then Jesus said. 1263
Then joy breaks through. 1777
Then the light came. 2530
Then the Lord. 3346
Then would my servants fight. 2756
Theobald, Archbishop of Canterbury. 1763, 3609
Theocracy. 1941
Theocracy and eschatology. 56
Theocracy and toleration. 730, 1477
Theocracy for democracy? 2671
Theocratic kingdom of Our Lord Jesus. 607, 2175
Theocratic kingdom of Our Lord Jesus, the Christ. 2175
Theocritus. Idyls; translations by Dryden, Polwhele, Calverley, Fawkes, and Lang; with illustrations by M. Meaulle. 3202
Theodicy. 1719, 3609, 3610
Theodicy, abridged. 3610
Theodor Herzl. 1809
Theodor Herzl, founder of political Zionism. 1809
Theodore and Wilfrith. 3816
Theodore Beza. 196
Theodore Emanuel Schmauk, D.D., LL.D. 3308
Theodore Herzl. 1809
Theodore of Studium. 721, 3610
Theodore Parker. 2776
Theodore Parker: American transcendentalist. 2776, 3708
Theodore Parker, preacher and reformer. 2776
Theodore Parker's experience as a minister. 3132
Theodore Thornton Munger. 2631
Theodori espicopi mopsuesteni In epistolas B. Pauli commentarii. 372
Theodotionic revision of the Book of Exodus. 517
Theologia. 1728
Theologia fundamentalis. 62
Theologia germanica. 977, 1008, 3616
Theologian at work. 3668
Theologians at work. 3611
Theologians in transition. 3618
Theologians of our time. 3611
Theologians of our time: Karl Barth [and others]. 3611
Theological and historical introduction to the Apostolic Fathers. 76
Theological and missionary studies in memory of John Aberly. 3623
Theological anthropology. 1818, 2322, 2323
... The theological aspect of reformed Juddaism. 2115
Theological basis of Christian pacifism. 2756
Theological bibliographies. 3626
Theological book list. 3627
Theological class book. 3661
Theological colloquies. 3649
Theological compend: containing a system of divinity. 3640
Theological compend: containing a system of divinity; a brief view of the evidence, doctrines, morals, and institutions of Christianity. 3640
Theological compend: containing a system of divinity, or a brief view of the evidences, doctrines morals, and institutions of Christianity. 3640, 3641
Theological criticisms. 3618
Theological crossings. 3619
Theological defence for the Rev. James De Koven. 45
Theological defense of papal power by St. Alphonsus de Liguori. 2862

Theological dictionary. 779, 3138, 3637, 3638, 3639
Theological dictionary of the New Testament. 1769
Theological dictionary of the Old Testament. 511, 1796
Theological discussion. 3754
Theological dynamics. 3616
Theological education as professional education. 3682
Theological education by extension. 3681
Theological education in America. 3612
Theological education in the Northern Baptist convention. 3681
Theological education in the Northern Baptist convention, a survey. 3680
Theological education in the Pacific. 3681
Theological encyclopaedia. 1513
Theological encyclopaedia and methodology. 3668
Theological encylopaedia and methodology. 3668
Theological enterprise. 3648
Theological essays. 3622, 3623, 3624, 3652
Theological ethics. 945
Theological evolution. 3649
Theological existence to-day. 1145
Theological explorations. 3653
Theological foundations of prayer. 2886
Theological foundations of the Mormon religion. 2611
Theological freedom and social responsibility. 1805
Theological frontier of ethics. 3070
Theological German vocabulary. 3639
Theological highlights of Vatican 11. 3772
Theological imagination. 1729
Theological index. 3626
Theological institutes. 3650
Theological interpretation of American history. 3746
Theological introduction to the Thirty-nine articles of the Church of England. 1212, 3679
Theological investigations. 791, 3628
Theological manuscripts, selected and edited with an introd. by H. McLachlan. 3637
Theological method and imagination. 3668
Theological method in Luther and Tillich. 2281, 3669
Theological method of Jesus. 2063
Theological method of Karl Rahner. 3019
[Theological miscellanies]. 3631
Theological models for the parish. 2774
Theological outlines. 3644, 3660
Theological papers of John Henry Newman on Biblical inspiration and on infallibility. 306, 836, 2862
Theological papers of John Henry Newman on faith and certainty. 1597
Theological perspectives; a discussion of contemporary issues in Lutheran theology. 3667, 3668
Theological reflections. 3625
Theological reflections on the charismatic renewal. 2816
Theological retreat. 2268, 3476
Theological school to-day. 1509, 3621
Theological science. 2832
Theological self-understanding of the Catholic charismatic movement. 2816
Theological studies. 1931
Theological study today. 3625
Theological symbolics. 1386
Theological tendency of Codex Bezae Cantabrigtensis in Acts. 316
Theological texts. 3636
...Theological texts from Coptic papyri. 2330
Theological threatises. 3044
Theological training and the future of theological colleges. 1216
Theological transition in American Methodism. 2423
Theological transition in American Methodism, 1790-1935. 2423
Theological treatises. 3636
Theological treatises on the Trinity. 3635
Theological trends in Methodist hymnody. 2451
... Theological unrest. 3075
Theological views. 3653
Theological virtues. 3615, 3695
Theological word book of of the Bible. 245
Theological word book of the Bible. 245
Theological wordbook of the Old Testament. 511
[Theological works]. 2689, 3631
Theological works of Isaac Barrow. 1216
Theological works of Thomas Paine. 2758, 3023, 3024
Theological writings. 3630
Theologie des Reiches Gottes. 2176
Theologies in conflict. 2222, 3329

Theologische Quartalschrift. 2297
Theology. 1655, 3616, 3643, 3646
Theology, a course for college students. 3616
Theology after Freud. 1673, 2994
Theology; an assessment of current trends. 3656
Theology and body. 2326
Theology and Christian ethics. 946
Theology and church. 3651
Theology and church in times of change. 190, 3625
Theology and contemporary art forms. 87
Theology and creation vs. evolution and Darwin. 1579
Theology and creation vs. evolution and Darwinism. 1579
Theology and discovery. 3019, 3625
Theology and education. 3757
Theology and ethics in Paul. 373
Theology and ethics of sex. 3391
... The theology and ethics of the Hebrews. 1539
Theology and evolution. 1580
Theology and human problems. 3102
Theology and intelligibility. 1732
Theology and life. 3618
Theology and meaning. 3070
Theology and metaphysics. 1105
Theology and mission. 2481
Theology and modern life. 3019, 3625
Theology and pastoral care. 2780
Theology and pastoral counseling. 2781
Theology and philosophical inquiry. 2832
Theology and poetry. 2853
Theology and political society. 1087
Theology and practice of love. 2265
Theology and preaching. 2904
Theology and proclamation. 3198, 3668
Theology and race relations. 1131
Theology and reality. 3652
Theology and revelation. 3225
Theology and revolution in the Scottish reformation. 3667
Theology and rural development in Africa. 19
Theology and sanity. 791
Theology and social welfare, redemption and good works. 1138
Theology and spirituality. 3622
Theology and the church. 2749, 3634
Theology and the church in the university. 3757
Theology and the cure of souls. 2791
Theology and the future. 3656
Theology and the kingdom of God. 2175
Theology and the philosophy of science. 3616
Theology and the scientific study of religion. 3060
Theology and the social consciousness. 3679
Theology and the university. 3681
Theology as an empirical science. 3646
Theology as anthropology. 3102
Theology as history. 2767, 3657
Theology as narration. 516
Theology as thanksgiving. 1756
Theology as we preach it. 3650
Theology at the dawn of the twentieth century. 3618
Theology between yesterday and tomorrow. 1181
Theology encounters revolution. 3234
Theology, exegesis, and proclamation. 239
Theology for a nomad church. 2222
Theology for artisans of a new humanity. 3628
Theology for beginners. 797
Theology for children. 896
Theology for Christian education. 935
Theology for Christian missions. 2522
Theology for Christian prayer. 2871
Theology for Christian stewardship. 3529
Theology for Christian witnessing. 3829
Theology for Christian youth. 3662
Theology for everyman. 3678
Theology for laymen. 3662
Theology for plain people. 3678
Theology for radical politics. 3233
Theology for renewal. 1126
Theology for the 1980s. 3617
"Theology for the masses" 3661
Theology for the people. 3678
Theology for the social gospel. 3446
Theology for today. 3659
Theology for young people. 3667
Theology in a new key. 1077
Theology in America. 3659
Theology in church and state. 3616
Theology in conflict. 2718, 3657
Theology in reconciliation. 1043
Theology in reconstruction. 3653
Theology in red, white, and black. 3017
Theology in revolution. 3620
Theology in St. Paul. 377

Theology in sixteenth- and seventeenth-century England. 1765
Theology in the Americas. 2222, 3657
Theology in the Catholic college. 3681
Theology in the life of the church. 3679
Theology in the New Testament. 148
Theology in the Responsa. 3219
Theology in the Wesleyan spirit. 2428, 3664
Theology in transition. 3618, 3656
Theology library. 781, 783
Theology of a classless society. 3445
Theology of a modern Methodist. 3681
Theology of a preacher. 2901
Theology of administration. 1199
Theology of Albert Schweitzer for Christian inquirers. 1529, 2016, 3312, 3634
Theology of Albrecht Ritschl. 3239
Theology of Altizer. 28, 1417
Theology of an evolutionist. 1047
Theology of Anabaptism. 36
Theology of angels and devils. 42
Theology of Auschwitz. 3610
Theology of Balthasar Hubmaier. 1850
Theology of baptism. 138
Theology of Calvin. 3767
Theology of Catholic Action. 2049, 2191
Theology of change. 1729
Theology of Christ: commentary. 2046
Theology of Christ, from his own words. 401, 2066
Theology of Christ: sources. 2010
Theology of Christian devotion; its role in the modern religious setting. 983
Theology of Christian education. 942
Theology of Christian experience. 2671, 3430, 3640
Theology of Christian marriage. 2343, 2346
Theology of Christian perfection. 2819
Theology of Christian prayer. 2882
Theology of church and ministry. 1296
Theology of church growth. 1171
Theology of church leadership. 953
Theology of civilization. 3066
Theology of confirmation. 1328
Theology of creation. 1380
Theology of crisis. 1457
Theology of culture. 1106
Theology of death and eternal life. 1529
Theology of Dietrich Bonhoeffer. 676
Theology of Emil Brunner. 698
Theology of Emil Brunner (The) 698
Theology of Emil G. Hirsch. 2080
Theology of encounter. 2040
Theology of evangelism. 1562, 1566, 1569
Theology of evangelistic concern. 1564
Theology of evolution. 1581
Theology of exile. 547
Theology of existence. 3641
Theology of experience. 1586
Theology of failure. 1588
Theology of faith. 1590
Theology of fatherhood, psychologically, metaphysically, and ethically considered. 3645
Theology of God. 1723, 1732
Theology of God sources. 1731
Theology of grace. 1751
Theology of H. Richard Niebuhr. 2708
Theology of Haham David Nieto. 2709
Theology of history. 1817, 1819
Theology of history in St. Bonaventure. 675, 1820
Theology of hope. 1845
Theology of human hope. 1658
Theology of inspiration. 306
Theology of James Daane. 1399
Theology of Jewish Christianity. 2073
Theology of John. 414
Theology of John Wesley. 2161, 3802
Theology of Jonathan Edwards. 1498
Theology of joy. 2135
Theology of Karl Barth. 175
Theology of liberation. 2222
Theology of liberation: history, politics, and salvation. 3443
Theology of love. 3806
Theology of man and grace. 1750
Theology of marriage. 2338, 2343
Theology of Martin Luther. 2280
Theology of Mary. 2363
Theology of mission. 2555
Theology of missions in the Puritan tradition. 1339
Theology of nature. 2676
Theology of New England. 2688
Theology of original sin. 3414
Theology of pastoral action. 1122
Theology of pastoral care. 2787
Theology of Paul Tillich. 3699, 3700
Theology of personal ministry. 2786
Theology of personality. 2822
Theology of play. 2854
Theology of politics. 1086

Theology of post-Reformation Lutheranism. 3668
Theology of praise. 1012, 2247
Theology of prayer. 2871, 2873
Theology of preaching. 2902
Theology of proclamation. 2905, 3647
Theology of protest. 2712
... The theology of Psalm VIII. 586
Theology of Q. 3010
Theology of Ramanuja. 3020
Theology of Reinhold Niebuhr. 1457, 2708, 2709, 3413
Theology of religious vocation. 3785
Theology of revelation. 3225, 3227
Theology of St. John. 414
Theology of St. Luke. 431
Theology of Saint Paul. 377, 2800, 2802
Theology of salvation. 3294
Theology of Schleiermacher. 3647
Theology of Seder Eliahu. 3328
Theology of Seventh-Day Adventism. 3381
Theology of sex in marriage. 2344
Theology of sin. 3411
Theology of social man. 795
Theology of the apostolate. 76
Theology of the apostolate of the Legion of Mary. 2208
Theology of the atonement. 3030
Theology of the Bible. 3642
Theology of the book of Ruth. 589
Theology of the Christian mission. 2553
Theology of the Christian word. 3848
Theology of the church. 1119
Theology of the church and its mission. 1119
Theology of the Cristian mission. 2553
Theology of the crossroads in contemporary Latin America. 2954
Theology of the early Greek philosophers. 2832
Theology of the English reformers. 3655
Theology of the Epistles. 378
Theology of the Eucharist. 1541
Theology of the Gospel according to Thomas. 337
Theology of the Gospels. 401
Theology of the Holy Spirit. 1834
Theology of the icon. 3667
Theology of the incarnation. 1893
Theology of the Jehovah's Witnesses. 1940
Theology of the kerygma. 1530
Theology of the laity. 2191
Theology of the liberating word. 3621
Theology of the living church. 3661
Theology of the love of God. 1735
Theology of the Lutheran confessions. 2286
Theology of the mystical body. 3646
Theology of the New Testament. 475, 476, 477
Theology of the New Testament according to its major witnesses: Jesus-Paul-John. 476
Theology of the Old Testament. 598, 599, 3615
Theology of the Old Textament. 598
Theology of the Older Testament. 599
Theology of the pain of God. 3542
Theology of the program of restoration of Ezekiel 40-48. 519
Theology of the resurrection. 2052
Theology of the sacraments. 3262, 3263
Theology of the Saeculum. 1155, 3771
Theology of the Samaritans. 3296
Theology of the spiritual life. 3521
Theology of the Trinity. 3711
Theology of things. 2843, 2844
Theology of tradition. 3706
Theology of "uncreated energies" 1735
Theology of unity. 1927
Theology of Universalism. 3753
Theology of vocations. 3785
Theology of William Newton Clarke. 1285
Theology of wisdom. 3693, 3821
Theology of Wolfhart Pannenberg. 2767
Theology of work. 3449, 3849
Theology of worship in 17th-century Lutheranism. 3855
Theology on Dover Beach. 3622
Theology, physics, and miracles. 2477
Theology primer. 3638
Theology reader. 3651
Theology: science of salvation. 3616
Theology to live by. 2281
Theology today. 3620
Theology: White, Black, or Christian? 3017
Theology word book of the Bible. 3615
Theology you can understand. 3663
Theomatics. 319, 2717
Theophany. 2045
Theophilus americanus. 1211
Theophilus, the Battle-axe. 178, 1703
Theophilus Walton. 135
Theophrastus, Metaphysics. 2419

Theopneustia. 305
Theopneusty, or, The plenary inspiration of the Holy Scriptures. 305
Theopoetic. 3626
Theorem or teleology of spiritualism. 3519
Theorems on existence and essence (Theoremata de esse et essentia) 2738
Theoretic explanation of the science of sanctity. 3643
Theoretical ethics. 1537
Theories and things. 2417
Theories of learning in Christian education. 3176
Theories of macrocosms and microcosms in the history of philosophy. 2461

Theories of primitive religion. 3109
Theories of religious experience. 1586, 1934
Theories of revelation. 3227
Theories of the Chakras. 879
Les theories sur le pouvoir royal en France pendant les guerres de religion. 2912
Theorika. 1625
Theory and art of mysticism. 2639, 2645
Theory and design of Christian education curriculum. 3163
Theory and practice. 3682
Theory and practice of Christian education. 3157, 3176
Theory and practice of group work. 688
Theory and practice of mysticism. 2637
Theory and practice of the catechism. 746
Theory and practice of the confessional. 1327
Theory and uses of natural religion. 2673
Theory of a finite and developing deity examined. 3714
Theory of autodeism. 2737
Theory of catechetics. 935
Theory of Christian education practice. 942
Theory of evil in the metaphysics of St. Thomas and its contemporary significance. 3693
Theory of evolution judged by reason and faith; translated by Francis O'Hanlon. 3080
Theory of papal monarchy in the thirteenth century. 2863
Theory of preaching. 2904
Theory of reality. 2180
... Theory of reincarnation. 3054
Theory of religious liberty in the reigns of Charles ii and James ii. 3194, 3193
Theory of religious liberty in England, 1603-39. 3194, 3193
Theory of revelation. 3224
Theory of spiritual progress. 3484
Theory of spiritualism. 3507
Theory of the earth. 1384
Theory of the Young men's Christian association. 3872
Theory of time and space. 3469
Theory of toleration under the later Stuarts. 3214, 3704
Theosophical congress held by the Theosophical society at the Parliament of religions. 3682
Theosophical glossary. 3689
Theosophical lectures and answers to theosophical questions. 3689
Theosophical manuals. 3689
Theosophical movement. 3688
Theosophical movement, 1875-1950. 3689
Theosophies of Plato, Aristotle and Plotinus. 1732, 2853
Theosophist's point of view. 3684
Theosophists: reunite! 3682
Theosophy. 671, 3119, 3123, 3683, 3685, 3686, 3688
... Theosophy and Christianity. 3685, 3687
Theosophy and modern science. 3687
Theosophy and New thought. 3687
Theosophy and some of the vital problems of the day. 3689
Theosophy and the theosophical movement. 3684
Theosophy and the theosophical society. 3683
Theosophy answers some problems of life. 3689
Theosophy for the millions. 671, 3683
Theosophy in Dante's Divine comedy. 1402
... Theosophy in outline. 3688
Theosophy, key to understanding. 3686
Theosophy simplified. 3684
Theosophy, the path of the mystic. 3688
Theosophy: what's it all about? 3685
Therapy of the word in classical antiquity. 1892
Theravada Buddhism in Southeast Asia. 704
Theravada meditation. 2382

There are no bad boys; a story of Father Edward Flanagan. 1629
There are no dead. 3508
There are sermons in books. 3345
There came three kings. 1973
There can be a new you. 1325
There is a God in heaven. 1721
There is a place for God in business. 719
There is a place where you are not alone. 2867, 3481
There is a psychic world. 3518
There is a river. 1283
There is a season. 1591
There is a way. 3201, 3481
There is an answer. 1007
There is no death. 1697, 1891, 3470, 3501, 3507
There is no end. 3749
There is no law. 2618
There is no need to be sick, afraid, unhappy, or in want. 2411
There is nothing but God. 1036
There shall be no peace. 3411
There shall be no peace unless. 2807
There shall be no poor. 2144
There shall be one Christ. 3593
There shines a light. 3811
There was a man. 740, 2514, 2994
There was a man, his name: Paul Carlson. 740, 2514
There was no virgin birth. 1091
There was no virgin birth thus Jesus Christ is not the Son of God. 2021
There we sat down. 2150
There we sat down: Talmudic Judaism in the making. 2150
There were twelve. 3528
There will always be an England! 46
"Therefore" 3459
Therefore choose life. 2145
'... therefore choose life, that thou mayest live, thou and thy seed. 853
Therefore, stand. 67
... There's a song in the air. 3549
There's algae in the baptismal "fount" 1298
There's always hope. 1352
There's an answer somewhere. 3012
There's comfort in His love. 1004
There's more; infinite blessings for the spirit-filled life. 1712
There's more than one way. 936
There's more to life than pumpkins, drugs, and other false gods. 23
There's no business like God's business. 3664
There's no other way. 3337
There's something better on the way. 1696
There's two of you. 3886
Theresa Neumann of Konnersreuth. 2685
Therese. 3690, 3691
Therese Martin. 3690
Therese Neumann. 2685, 2686, 3532
Therese of Konnersreuth. 2685, 3532
Therese: saint of a little way. 3691
Theron and Aspasio. 2160
Thesaurus of the best theological. 3627
These also believe. 1393, 3325
These also suffer. 924
These amazing Mormans! 2607
These amazing Mormons! 2607
These are God's sons. 3200
These are my heroes. 3281
These are my people. 1163
These are my rites. 851
"These are not drunken as ye suppose" (Acts 2:15) 1712
These are the sacraments. 3266
These blind eyes now see. 171, 1633
These came back. 3054
These came home. 1364
These cities glorious. 1278
These commandments are mine. 1315
These dared to share. 3529
These days we remember. 3372
These early Americans. 678, 1898
These Evangelical United Brethren. 1550
These extra-ordinary documents. 378
These fifty years; the Congregation of the sisters of the divine Savior, 1888- 1938. 1179
These fifty years with Ohio Friends in China. 2512
These first called Him Master. 71, 338
These folks called Baptist. 148
These for those. Our indebtedness to foreign missions. 2495
These Fords still run. 1633, 3387
These forty days. 837, 2210, 2215
These forty years. 2511
These found the way. 1362
These gracious golden years. 2399
These historic Scriptures. 2937
These issues we must face. 161
These laymen found God. 975

These little ones which believe. 139
These live tomorrow. 3723
These made peace. 1649
These men live!Candid camera Bible characters. 213
These met the Master. 338
These moving times. 2926
These my brethren. 2682
These prophetic voices. 2436
These rebellious powers. 964
These religious affections. 1342
These sayings of mine. 2066
These shared His cross. 1998
These shared His passion. 1986
These shared His passion, cross and power. 2030
These shared His power. 2007
These sought a country. 2483
These splendid priests. 765, 774, 2940
These splendid sisters. 765, 2717
These stones speak. 1229
These stones will shout. 534
These tales are true. 1014
These tears are for Diane. 692, 931
These ten words. 1313
These things abide. 1452
These things are written. 232
These things I remember. 1014, 3566
These things remain. 165
These things we believe. 3666
These things will last. 2555
"These three" 1449
These three hearts. 1310
These, too, were unshackled. 1357
These, too, were unshackled. 1361
These tremendous times. 607
These truths shall triumph. 3383
These twelve. 70
These two hands. 849
These watched Him die. 1997
These were God's people. 295
These were my hills. 3202
These women walked with God. 1276
These words upon thy heart. 304
These years of grace. 3867
These young lives. 832
Theses and dissertations. 870
Theses and dissertations accepted by Texas Christian University: the Graduate School and Brite Divinity School, 1909-1972. 3604
... Theses of the University of Chicago doctors of philosophy. 894
Theses were not posted. 2274
Theseus and the road to Athens. 3692
Thesis of Paradise lost. 2469
Thesis written by students of Christian Theological Seminary, 1925-1964, in partial fulfillment of degrees. 1039
Thespis. 2219, 2678
Thespis; ritual, myth, and drama in the ancient Near East. 2678
Thessalonian epistles, a call to readiness. 478
Thessalonian thoughts. 478
Thessalonians. 478, 1554
Thessalonians—an expositional commentary. 479, 2930, 3348
... Thessalonians and Galatians. 478
... Thessalonians, Corinthians, Galatians, and Romans. 371
Thessalonians in the Revised standard version. 478
Theurgia. 1501, 1502
Theurgy. 1393
They. 3497
They all began to sing. 2489
They also served. 3380
They also speak. 214
They are not dead! 1349, 3464
They became Anglicans. 1362
They became Christians. 1362
They beheld his glory. 384
They believe. 1595
They brought good news. 2512
They call me Mother Graham. 158, 1754
They call me the showbiz priest. 2820
They call us dead men. 758
They called him father. 1809
They called him Mr. Moody. 2587
They called me Mama. 2191, 2507
They came to a place. 3541
They came to Bethlehem. 3201
They came to Louisiana. 1404, 2538
They carried a torch. 1272, 2503
They chose to live. 1132, 1626
They come seeking. 2527
They couldn't kill Sullivan. 1360
They crucified and crucify. 965
They cry, too! 1288
They dared for God. 923
They dared to be different. 925, 3721
They dared to cross frontiers. 662
They dared to dream. 3749
They dared to speak for God. 234, 2908
They did not pass by. 2718
They disobeyed. 3411

They dwell in monasteries. 2585
They followed the King. 216
They foresaw the future. 2948
They forgot the debt. 3145
They found the church there. 2543
They found the secret. 1361
They found the way of victory. 1180
They gathered at the river. 3233
They gave themselves. 3528
They go to Mass. 2365
They had strange powers. 2730
They have found a faith. 3324
They have taken root : the Sisters of the
  Third Order of St. Francis of the Holy
  Family. 3421
They heard His voice. 1365
They help along with me. 3185
They knew Christ. 338
They knew Jesus. 338, 1980, 3164
They knew the prophet. 3430
They led the way. 2545
They led the way: Christian pioneers of
  central Africa. 2545
They left their nets. 1238
They live and are not far away. 1891
They live forever, our Christian dead.
  1696
They live in Bible lands. 911
They live in the city. 1139
They live their faith. 1462
They lived by faith. 3840
They lived the faith. 765
They lived their faith. 31
They lived their love. 2490
They looked for a city. 3421
They loved him. 685
They made a difference. 3215
They made him Christ. 388
They made me sign. 795
They made Mormon history. 2615
They meet the Master. 1564, 2037
They met at Calvary. 2030
They met at Calvary: were you there?
  2030
They met at Philippi. 449
They met God. 1366
They met Jesus. 338
They of Italy. 2533
They played in Calvary's drama. 2030
They put on masks. 1899
They reach for life. 2494
They rode the frontier. 1300
They sang a new song. 2634
They sang of the Restoration. 2616
They sang through the crisis. 960
They sat in darkness. 2535
They saw His glory. 384
They saw Jesus. 1984
They saw the Lord. 1956
They seek a country. 2408, 2924
They shall take up serpents. 173, 3376
They shine like stars. 2754
They sought a country. 2407
They speak by silences. 742
They speak with other tongues. 2814
They stood boldly. 332
They stood every man in his place. 1711
They stood tall for God. 1013
They survive. 3498
They talked with God. 339, 2883
They teach us to pray. 604
They that be teachers. 3556
They that hunger and thirst. 3480
They told about Jesus. 388, 1987
They took John's torch. 1761
They trusted God. 628
They walked with Christ. 384
They walked with God. 494, 3203, 3204
They welcomed the child. 9
They were there. 2212, 2298
They were there . . . when they crucified
  my Lord. 2031
They who are called Christians. 1010
They who preach. 2899
They who understand. 3518
They worked for a better world. 3817
Thickness of glory. 3353
Thine forever. 1434, 1442
Thine inheritance. 957
Thine is my heart. 1435
Thine is the glory. 2249, 3201
Thine is the kingdom. 2555, 3202, 3356
Thine is the power. 1172
...Thine own child. 2965
Thine the glory. 2250
Thing. 784
Thing he greatly feared. 550
Things. 2729
Things a nation lives by. 3434
Things a pastor's wife can do. 3670
Things as they are. 3443, 3697, 3712
Things as they really are. 2612
Things Catholics are asked about. 791
Things civil and useful. 1683
Things clerical. 1249
Things common and preferred Christian
  perspectives. 1282

"Things concerning Himself"; sacred songs
  and Bible studies. 638
Things divine and supernatural. 38
Things eternal. 3047, 3199, 3352
Things foretold, past, present, and future.
  509
Things fundamental. 57
Things fundamental in the life and ministry
  of Jesus. 2017
Things go better with peace. 3411
Things happen when women care. 1689,
  3830
Things I can't explain. 3509
Things I have learned. 3758
Things I know in religion. 1594
Things immortal. 1446
Things important. 1545
"Things in which it is impossible for God
  to lie." 1941
Things most surely believed. 73, 1252,
  3652, 3666
Things new and old. 199, 1069
Things of Northfield. 3352
Things of the spirit. 788, 998, 1739, 1832,
  2380
Things surely to be believed. 3662
Things that abide. 1229
Things that are Caesar's. 1707
Things that are not Caesar's. 756
Things that cannot be shaken. 61, 1589
Things that cannot die. 2973
Things that make for peace. 1005
Things that matter. 1328, 1445
Things that matter most. 169, 950, 1448
Things that really matter. 973
Things that remain. 169, 1226, 3066
Things to be remembered. 3324
Things to come. 2056, 3318
Things to come for planet Earth. 607,
  1530
Things unshakable. 1549
Things which become sound doctrine.
  972, 987
Things which cannot be shaken. 3794
Things which don't happen every day.
  1575
Things which remain. 3651
Things which shall be hereafter. 606
Things wise and otherwise. 3753
Things you should know about subversive
  influences in Methodism. 1139
Things you should know about the Bible.
  312
Think. 2547
Think about these things. 2299, 2893
Think again. 1218
Think & live. 2836
Think and pray. 2392, 2397
Think big. 3704
Think by formula and insure your future,
  and Three basic laws of reincarnation.
  2696
Think China. 2509
Think Jewish. 2751
Think mink! 982, 1389
Think on these things. 1060, 1435, 2388,
  2398, 2933, 3456, 3503, 3702
Think on these things and live. 2390
Think out your faith. 1595
Think, Sister. 2573
Think spiritually. [1st ed.]. 965
Think well on't. 856
Thinkables. 2389
Thinker and the hare. 3198
Thinkers vs. Christian science. 1033
Thinking about Buddhism. 708
Thinking about Genesis. 523
Thinking about God. 1450, 1724, 3663
Thinking about religion. 3104
Thinking alive. 2227
Thinking aloud in war-time. 3794
Thinking and acting Biblically. 242, 995
Thinking and destiny. 3201
Thinking Christianly. 960
Thinking faith. 2832
Thinking God's thoughts after Him. 2399
Thinking good is thanking God. 1732
Thinking in the future tense. 1845
... Thinking it through. 2807
Thinking man. 763
Thinking man and the Christ. 64
Thinking missions with Christ. 2202
Thinking my way out of hell. 1030
Thinking out loud about the space age.
  3069
Thinking right is living right. 301
Thinking straight about the Bible. 278
Thinking the tremendum. 1825
Thinking things through with E. E.
  Snoddy. 3432
Thinking through. 3078
Thinking through the Bible. 639
Thinking through the Scriptures. 200
Thinking through Thessalonians. 478
Thinking where Jesus thought. 2044
Thinking with God. 2391

Thinking with God about: the Bible, God,
  creation, man, Satan, sin salvation,
  temptations, judgments and rewards. 647
Thinking with the Yajurveda. 3776
... Thinking youth's greatest need. 1591
Thinning of the veil. 3517
Third Adam. 1094, 2186, 2334
Third and fourth books of Maccabees.
  488, 2305
Third and fourth books of Maccabees;
  edited and translated by Moses Hadas.
  488
Third Baptist world congress. 141
Third book of Azrael. 1765
Third book of catechism stories. 1840
3 Enoch. 491
Third-century papyrus codex of the
  Epistles of Paul. 2331
... The third day. 64
Third dimension. 1557
Third eye. 3699
Third-eye theology. 3648
Third front through the paths of faith,
  hope and love. 1590
Third generation Greek Americans. 1767,
  2747
... Third grade teachers plan book and
  manual. 746
Third hour. 2033
Third [i. e. fourth] National Sunday-school
  convention of the United States. 1869.
  3556
Third Jewish catalog. 2081
Third letter to the Rev. William E.
  Channing on the subject of ultarianism.
  882, 3729
Third mystic of Avila. 2648
Third National Study Conference on the
  Church and Economic Life. 2670
Third official catalogue of church music.
  1204
Third Order for our times. 1648
Third order of Saint Francis. 1649
Third Order Secular. 3328
Third peacock. 1745
Third period. 463
Third Person. 1828, 1832
Third Reich and the Christian churches.
  1707
Third report of the Joint commission, on
  the Book of common prayer. 2961
Third session. 3772
Third session Council speeches of Vatican
  II. 3773
Third spiritual alphabet. 790, 2643, 3603
Third testament. 114
Third thousand years. 536
Third way, conversations about
  Anabaptist / Mennonite faith. 2405
Third World and mission. 2492
Third world theologies. 3625
Thirst for God. 587
Thirst for meaning in the face of
  skepticism and doubt. 65
Thirsting for the Lord. 3484
Thirteen. 2151
Thirteen, a teenage guide to Judaism.
  2151
Thirteen chapters on First day observance.
  3548
Thirteen commandments. 3750
Thirteen crisis years, 1888-1901. 3386
Thirteen for Christ. 924
13 jolly saints. 1028
Thirteen lessons on Romans. 471
Thirteen petalled rose. 722
Thirteen principal Upanishads. 2840, 3760
Thirteen years' experience in the
  itinerancy. 1568
Thirteenth apostle. 1238
XIIIth century chronicles. 1646
Thirteenth check. 3465
Thirteenth man. 2060
Thirtieth anniversary year book of the
  Holy rosary church. 1791
30th anniversary. 1308
30 Bible story projects to make. 229
Thirty days to a less stressful you. 987
Thirty days to a new you. 1440
Thirty days to spiritual power. 554
Thirty discussions, Bible stories. 1653
Thirty favorite Bible stories for boys and
  girls. 623
Thirty-five manuscripts including the St.
  Blasien Psalter. 2330
Thirty-five years among the poor. 1276
Thirty-five years in the Congo. 2514
Thirty-five years of Luther research. 2276,
  2279, 2281
Thirty minor Upanishads, including the
  Yoga Upanishads. 2668
Thirty-nine years with the great I am.
  3202
Thirty-one banana leaves. 2398, 3768
Thirty-one revival sermons on themes
  drawn from the lives of Elijah and
  Elisha. 1506

Thirty psalmists. 576
Thirty-six Psalms. 573
Thirty studies about Jesus. 1991
Thirty studies in the Gospel by John. 423
Thirty thousand. 2979
Thirty thousand gods before Jehovah.
  1742
30,000 miles of miracles. 2763
Thirty thousand thoughts. 3204
Thirty-three candles. 1777
Thirty-three years of missions in the
  Church of the brethren. 1237
Thirty years a Watch Tower slave. 1941,
  3798
30 years among the dead. 3474, 3518
"Thirty years in hell" 2938
Thirty years in Mexico. 155
Thirty years of Buddhist studies. 704
Thirty years of oriental studies. 3332
Thirty years of psychical research. 2991
Thirty years on the firing-line. 1554
Thirty years with Christ. 1364
Thirty years with South Sea cannibals.
  2542
38 recipes for bulletin boards and art
  projects that Christian kids can make.
  937
33 women of the restoration. 3215
32 answers to timely questions in moral
  theology and church law. 2593
"32 earth worlds of the Intergalactic
  Confederation speak!! 3103
This age of confusion. 3115
This beautiful one. 1976, 2015
This before architecture. 1156
This believing world. 3064, 3113
This big world. 2848
This blest Communion. 1318
This business of being converted. 1561
This business of living. 962, 3012
This call we share. 1303
This changing world, broadcast talks. 1226
This child of God shall meet no harm.
  1606
This church and realm. 1211
This Church of England. 1211
This church of ours. 2957
This Church, these times. 814, 2309
This circle of earth. 1459, 1854
This company of new men. 1356
This confident faith. 993
This costly fragrance. 1443
This created world. 1380
This critical hour,and other heart-searching
  sermons. 165
This damned campus. 3757
This day. 1001, 1430
This day ... and always. 2608
This day is ours. 2321
This day is the Lord's. 1433
This do--and live. 972, 3483
"This do in remembrance of Me" 1318
This double thread. 2640
This dramatic world. 32
This dreamer. 1596
This earth one country. 128
This Egyptian miracle. 3519
This faith is mine. 2279, 2281, 3883
This faith we live by. 965
This faith we share. 1558
This fellow Jesus. 1961
This freedom--whence? 1762, 3802
This gift is mine. 1712
This good news. 477
This grace also. 1168, 3529
This great argument. 2470, 2471
... This great business of being Christian.
  1060
This great company. 3366
This He believed. 2062
This Hebrew Lord. 1972
This heritage. 3820
This holy fellowship. 2259
This holy thing. 3202
This holy venture. 2215
This home we build. 1608
This hour not the hour of the Prince of
  peace. 3341
This house is haunted. 1786, 2858
This house with glory. 2699
This I believe. 3197, 3664
This I believe about Jesus Christ. 3829
This I can believe. 67, 1090
This I know. 1873
This I recall. 2284
This immortal people. 2087
This is America's hour. 2931
This is Billy Graham. 1755
This is B'nai B'rith. 673
This is Catholicism. 797
This is Christian marriage. 2341
This is God speaking. 3859
This is God's day. 1434
This is God's hour. 168
This is God's world. 1433, 3531
This is it, and other essays on Zen and
  spiritual experience. 2641

This is Judaism. 2114
This is life. 956, 1435, 1445
This is life; a book for the busy. 957
This is life eternal. 1891, 2215
This is living. 448
This is love. 2369
This is metropolitan Boston. 1271
This is missions. 1465
This is Mother Pauline. 2805
This is my Bible. 649
This is my Body. 2256
This is my church. 110
This is my faith. 3057
This is my Father's world. 3550
This is my God. 2140, 2154
This is my song of songs. 2297
This is my story. 146, 1363, 1601, 1749, 1824
This is our destiny. 3199
This is our gospel. 1555
This is our St. Rose Church in Proctor, Minnesota. 3278
This is our song. 733
This is perfection. 3514
This is Protestantism. 2977
This is spiritualism. 3494
This is stewardship. 3528
This is Tangier Island and its church. 3585
This is that. 1554, 1567
This is the authorized ritual for the Most Worshipful Prince Hall Grand Lodge of Virginia, Free and Accepted Masons, incorporated. 1669
This is the church. 1116, 1122
This is the day. 1451, 2973, 3351
This is the end! 1514
This is the faith. 70, 797
This is the Holy Land. 2848
This is the John Birch Society. 2125
This is the land. 3896
This is the last message. 607, 1528
This is the life. 958
This is the Mass. 2368
This is the new age, in person. 323, 2324
This is the one: Messenger Elijah Muhammad. 1506
This is the promise. 1976
This is the Rosary. 3248
This is the seminary. 3331
This is the truth. 2599
This is the victory! 999
This is the way. 1886, 2160, 2892
This is the will of God. 1822
This is the word of the Lord. 563
This is the Y C S. 3869
This is your tomorrow ... and today. 3541
This is your world. 3887
This Jesus. 3829
This life and the next. 1591
This living water. 2024
This love on which I speak. 2804
This man—Jesus. 1982, 2045
This man knows you. 1786
This man Moses. 2622
"This means everlasting life." 1941
This means of grace. 2253
This means that. 3574
...This mind. 3537
This ministry. 1305
This ministry and service. 3672
This morning with God. 645
This-my city. 2528
This mysterious human nature. 759
This mystery which is Christ, essays. 761
This mystical life of ours. 2696
This nation shall endure. 2607
This Nation under God. 33, 2972, 1128, 3448, 3741, 3748
This old leather satchel. 1545
This one thing I do. 2348
This, our day. 759
This, our day, approvals and disapprovals. 759
This our pilgrimage. 962
This our sacrifice. 2253, 2259
This parish under God, 1855-1955. 2775
This people Israel. 2087
This perverse generation. 1282
This place called Lourdes. 2262
This power within. 965
This priest is thankful. 1301, 1407
This promise is for you. 2394
This questioning age. 3885
This revolutionary faith. 1096
This rosary. 3248
This sacred hour. 2258
This same Jesus. 1830
This seed of faith. 1093
This Sheba, Self. 1075
This side of Eden. 1068
This side of tomorrow. 1004
This spiritualism. 3514
This they wrote. 2334
This thing called life. 2695
This thing called religion. 3062, 3090
This time of salvation. 998

This time, this place. 3123
This, too, can happen in Miami. 2461
This train is bound for glory. 1063
This tremendous lover. 3485
This tyranny of bunk. 3023
This war is the passion. 3792
This was his faith. 3200
This was John Calvin. 728
"This way," Acts 9:2. 253
This way, please. 967, 1004
This way to a thriving church. 3528
This way to God. 1452
This way to heaven. 997
This way to the cross. 994
This way to the harvest. 2507
This we believe! 65, 74, 768, 786, 933, 1546, 2405, 3293
This we can believe. 65
This we know. 369
This we shall do. 3201
This which ye see and hear. 2814
This wonderful venture called Christian living. 983
This world and prayer. 2871
This world and that. 2987
This world and the beyond. 2299
This world and the church. 3328
This world and the next. 1887
This world's goods. 3531
This year of Our Lord. 2721
Thoburn--called of God. 3692
Thomae ab Argentina. 2826
Thomas a Kempis; his age and book. 1884, 3692
Thomas Acquinas and John Gerhard. 3694
Thomas and Bonaventure. 3694
Thomas and the Evangelists. 337
Thomas and the physics of 1958: a confrontation. 3696
Thomas Aquinas. 3693
Thomas Aquinas and John Gerhard. 3694
Thomas Aquinas dictionary. 3695
Thomas Arundel: a study of church life in the reign of Richard II. 89, 1761
Thomas Becket. 3692
Thomas Becon and the reformation of the church in England. 182, 3038
Thomas Campbell. 733
Thomas Cartwright and Elizabethan Puritanism. 743, 3007
Thomas Chalmers. 880
Thomas Chalmers and the disruption. 880, 1652
Thomas Chalmers, preacher, philosher and statesman. 880
Thomas Coke and World Methodism. 666, 1306
Thomas Coke: apostle of Methodism. 1306
Thomas Corwin Iliff. 1883
Thomas Cranmer, 1489-1556. 1379
Thomas Cranmer and the English reformation. 1378
Thomas Cranmer's doctrine of the Eucharist. 1378, 2256
Thomas de Cobham, bishop of Worcester. 1305
Thomas De Quincey's Joan of Arc and The English mail coach. 1937
... Thomas Francis Meehan. 2399
Thomas Fuller's The holy state and the profane state. 1535
Thomas G. Masaryk and the Jews. 2079, 2364
Thomas Hobbes. 1821
Thomas Hooker. 1845, 3630
Thomas Hooker, 1586-1647. 1345, 1845
Thomas Hooker, preacher, founder, democrat. 1346, 1845
Thomas J. Comber: missionary pioneer to the Congo. 1312
Thomas James Conaty, pastor-educator-bishop. 1322
Thomas Jefferson and the restoration of the Gospel of Jesus Christ. 1939, 2019
Thomas Jefferson Bible. 400, 1939
Thomas March Clark, fifth bishop of Rhode Island. 1285
Thomas Maurice Mulry. 2630
Thomas Merton. 2412, 2413
Thomas Merton: a different drummer. 2413, 3794
Thomas Merton, a pictorial biography. 2412, 3710
Thomas Merton, contemplative critic. 2413
Thomas Merton, monk. 2412
Thomas Merton on mysticism. 2412, 2645
Thomas Merton on peace. 2808
Thomas Merton on prayer. 2412, 2885
Thomas Merton on St. Bernard. 194
Thomas Merton, prophet in the belly of a paradox. 2413
Thomas Merton, social critic. 2412
Thomas Merton Studies Center. 2413
Thomas Merton's dark path. 1356, 2413

Thomas Merton's shared contemplation. 2412, 3710
Thomas More and Tudor polemics. 69
Thomas More's prayer book. 844
Thomas Muntzer. 2631
Thomas N. Doutney. 3595
Thomas Reid's Lectures on natural theology (1780) 2675
Thomas Sherlock, 1678-1761, Bishop of Bangor 1728 of Salisbury 1734; of London 1748. 3402
Thomas Spurgeon. 3523
Thomas Stapleton and the Counter Reformation. 1374, 3525
Thomas Starr King, Patriot and preacher. 2173
Thomasius Gospel selections. 366
Thomasius Old Testament selections. 1268
Thomism; an introduction. 3696
Thomism and modern thought. 2843, 3696
Thomism in the age of renewal. 3696
Thomist reader. 3678, 3696
Thomistic concept of justifying contrition. 3218, 3693
Thompson chain-reference Bible survey. 310
Thorns. 3540
Thorns on the Tudor rose. 2569
Thornton Kelly Tyson, pioneer home missionary. 3721
Thoroughly married. 2338
Those curious new cults. 2728
Those distant years. 3226
Those disturbing miracles. 2476
Those Dutch Catholics. 826
Those gold plates! 679, 3429
Those happy golden years. 1574, 3388
Those he came to save. 2437, 3356
Those incredible Christians. 1197
Those incredible Methodists. 3734
Those mysterious priests. 2939
Those of the way. 1096
Those Pharisees. 2050, 2828
Those Sabbath hours. 1448
Those seeking God. 66
"Those tent meetings" 3379
Those terrible teens. 1714
Those tiny tots. 3174
Those treasured hours. 3554
Those who came forward. 1362, 1755
Those who love Him. 2267
Those whom God chooses. 2489
Thoth, the Hermes of Egypt. 3698
'Thou art all fair. 2355
Thou art my portion. 579
Thou art Peter. 803
Thou art the Christ! 2036
Thou art the Christ; studies on the life and work of Jesus Christ. 1986
Thou didst say unto me. 1445
"Thou fool!" 3343
Thou preparest a table. 2252
Thou shalt have no other gods before me. [Exhibition]. 3093
Thou shalt not. 1314
Thou shalt not bow. 1082, 1854
Thou when thou prayest. 2869
Though farthest out. 3198
Though I walk through the valley. 1350, 1791
Though thousands fall; the story of Melville B. Cox. 1378
Though your sins be as scarlet. 1736
Thought. 2808
Thought and character of William James. 1934
Thought and religion. 2836
Thought and things. 2242
Thought dial. 3575, 3576
Thought dial way to a healthy and successful life. 3576
Thought for every day. 725, 1431
Thought for help, from those who know men's need. 3198
Thought for today. 2383, 3197
Thought-forms. 3683
Thought from Dominican saints for each day of the year. 2397
Thought from St. Alphonsus Liguori. 2391
Thought from Saint Francis and his saints. 2387
Thought from Saint Ignatius for each day of the year. 2391
Thought from St. Vincent de Paul for each day of the year. 1434
Thought from the Benedictine saints for every day in the year. 2397
Thought of God in hymns and poems. 1737
Thought of Jacques Ellul. 1509
Thought of Paul Tillich. 3700
Thought of Reinhold Niebuhr. 2709
Thought of St. Paul in the light of the modern world. 376, 2799

Thought of Saint Teresa's for every day of the year. 2397
Thought of Teihard de Chardin. 3593
Thought of Teilhard de Chardin. 3593
Thought of the Evangelical leaders. 2243, 3670
Thought of the prophets. 571
Thought power. 3683
Thought power, its control and culture. 3683
Thoughtlessness of modern thought concerning the ideas of civilization, culture, science and progress. 2561
Thoughts. 58, 999, 1450, 2777
Thoughts afield. 2390
Thoughts along the road. 1452
Thoughts and affections on the passion of Jesus Christ for every day of the year. 2031
Thoughts and apophthegms. 3202
Thoughts and aspirations of the ages. 3204
Thoughts and extracts on Christ and His kingdom come. 1047
Thoughts and meditations from the notebooks of Mary M. Billings French. 1456
Thoughts and memories. 760, 3201
Thoughts and reflections for Lent. 2211
Thoughts are things. 907, 2695
Thoughts as they have come to me in quiet hours. 2390
Thoughts concerning things eternal. 3200
Thoughts critical and practical. 456
Thoughts, critical and practical, on the book of Daniel and the Revelation. 507
Thoughts for a friend. 3750
Thoughts for an LDS mother. 3842
Thoughts for aspirants. 3688
Thoughts for daily living. 1002
Thoughts for doubting Christians. 1008
Thoughts for every-day living. 1323
Thoughts for growing Christians. 1308
Thoughts for men on the move. 2398
Thoughts ... for one hundred days as heard on radio. 2608
Thoughts for our times. 1264
Thoughts for quiet hours through the year. 2399
Thoughts for sowing. 865, 1267
Thoughts for the afflicted. 1350
Thoughts for the King's children. 907
Thoughts for the Lenten season. 2210
Thoughts for the occasion, anniversary and religious. 1841
Thoughts for the people. 1792
Thoughts for the quiet hour. 972, 1440
Thoughts for the times. 2374
Thoughts for times like these. 943
... Thoughts for today. 1446, 3096
Thoughts for troubled times. 1453
Thoughts from modern martyrs. 2351
Thoughts from Scripture. 298
Thoughts from the inner life. 3494
Thoughts from the mind. 2396
Thoughts from the Mount of Blessing. 3336, 3337
Thoughts from the sea. 954
Thoughts from the writings of St. Catherine of Siena. 3415
... Thoughts gleaned and confirmed by the Holy Bible. 1058
Thoughts in my garden. 1370
Thoughts in solitude. 3488, 3492
Thoughts in the atomic age. 2843
Thoughts in verse that I have gathered by the pathway of life, if anything herein is true, 'tis God's, all else is mine. 3206
Thoughts memorial of Mary Whitall Thomas. 3697
Thoughts of a Catholic anatomist. 3078
Thoughts of a Christian optimist. 1326
Thoughts of a Jew and Jewish thoughts. 2140
Thoughts of a spiritual vagabond. 2695
Thoughts of and for the inner life. 960
Thoughts of Blaise Pascal. 58, 791
Thoughts of God for boys and girls. 902
Thoughts of God for boys and girls. As we think with God; selections. 902
Thoughts of His heart. 2721
Thoughts of Jesus. 1977
Thoughts of peace. 2809
Thoughts of the Imitation of Christ from the words of Thomas a Kempis. 1886
Thoughts of the servant of God. 2397
Thoughts of the spiritual. 3477
Thoughts on crucial situations in human life. 1104
Thoughts on Genesis. 521
... Thoughts on God's mother and ours. 2361
Thoughts on His life and lessons. 2393
Thoughts on His words and ways. 2015
Thoughts on love and death. 1415
Thoughts on moral and spiritual culture. 3160

Thoughts on Our Friend divine. 2015
Thoughts on personal religion. 962
Thoughts on popery. 801
Thoughts on prayer. 2872, 2887
Thoughts on preaching. 2896
Thoughts on present church troubles. 1218
Thoughts on public prayer. 2876
Thoughts on religion. 3076, 3102
Thoughts on religious experience. 1585
Thoughts on sacramental occasions extracted from the diary of the Rev. Philip Doddridge, D.D. 2258
Thoughts on some important subjects in divinity. 3644
Thoughts on suffering, sorrow, and death. 3540
Thoughts on the atonement of Christ. 108
Thoughts on the books of Matthew, Mark, Luke, and John. 388
Thoughts on the church and the sacraments. 3263
Thoughts on the death of little children. 897
Thoughts on the divine goodness. 3610
Thoughts on the evils of drunkenness, and the blessings of temperance. 3596
Thoughts on the gentle Master. 2015
Thoughts on the gospel miracles. 2018
... Thoughts on the heart of Jesus. 3270
... Thoughts on the holy eucharist. 2258
Thoughts on the holy Gospels. 398
Thoughts on the importance of the manners of the great to general society. 944
Thoughts on the life and character of Jesus of Nazareth. 2059
Thoughts on the Lord's prayer. 2247
Thoughts on the love of Christ. 1956
Thoughts on the nature of the grand apostacy, (1781) 609, 1197, 1710
Thoughts on the origin, character, and interpretation of scriptual prophecy in seven discourses. 2949
Thoughts on the origin, character and interpretation of Scriptural prophecy. 609
Thoughts on the origin, character, and interpretation of Scriptural prophecy, in seven discourses. 609
Thoughts on the original unity of the human race. 2585
Thoughts on the prophecies of Daniel. 507
Thoughts on the religious life. 954, 2580
Thoughts on the services. 2960, 2969
Thoughts on things psychic. 2989
Thoughts on various subjects. 1396
Thoughts on worship & prayer. 3854
... Thoughts that breathe. 1217
Thoughts that build. 726
Thoughts to ponder. 956
Thoughts to take home for Lent. 2211
Thoughts to take home: from the three cycles of Advent readings. 9
Thoughts towards sunset. 3198
Thoughts upon several passages of Scripture, both in the Old and New Testament, relative to Jacob and Esau. 1931
Thousand and one Buddhas. 712, 2188
Thousand lives away. 704
Thousand names of Visnu. 2316, 3782
Thousand reasons for living. 2384
Thousand years and a day. 536
Thousand years not pre-millennial. 2466
Thousand years of Jewish history. 2088
Thousand years of yesterdays. 3053
Thr triumph of grace in the theology of Karl Barth. 175, 1750
Thracian legends. 2667
Thread of Ariadne; the labyrinth of the calendar of Minos. 2665
Thread of Bible narrative. 645
Thread of gold. 1953
Thread of history. 231
Threat and the power. 2902
Three. 3892
Three addresses: i. Jewish and Christian atonement. ii. What think ye of Christ. iii. What does the Talmud say of Christ. 2153
Three ages of progress. 1174
Three ages of the interior life. 3486
Three archbishops of Milwaukee. 668, 1801
Three articles on modern spiritualism. 3504
Three aspects of the Cross. 3295
Three baptisms and the three Sabbaths. 136
Three books about the church. 1120
Three books concerning the church. 1120
Three books of occult philosophy or magic. 2731
Three cardinals. 738, 2704

Three Catholic Afro-American congresses. 15
Three Catholic reformers of the fifteenth century. 1181, 3779
Three centuries of American hymnody. 1871
Three centuries of Freemasonry in New Hampshire. 1667
Three centuries of thumb Bibles. 652, 657
... Three chapters in recent liturgical research. 838
Three cheers. 2301
Three children of Galilee. 2005
Three Christian transcendentalists. 3708
Three Christmas sermons, Sunday, December 25, 1881. 124
... The three churches. 3094, 3468
Three churches and a Model T. 2788
Three churches in renewal. 1245, 2753
Three circles. 3198
Three commemorative lectures delivered in Lambeth Palace. 1379
Three conceptions of mind. 1911
Three conventions. 2419
Three-cornered continent. 897
Three creeds. 1385
Three crosses. 50, 1998
Three crucial decades. 332
3D. 2937, 3404
Three Davids. 2536
Three days and three nights in the heart of the earth. 2030
Three days in the life of a father. 897
Three days to eternity. 724
Three degrees. 2643
Three dialogues of M.T. Cicero on the orator. 3245
Three dimensions of love, and other sermons. 3338
Three discourses on the religion of reason. 1092
Three dispensations of the Bible. 1467
Three divine virtues. 3782
$3.00 worth of God. 2395
3 Enoch. 1520
Three essays. 1527, 1850, 2846, 3239
Three essays on religion. 192, 3062, 3103
Three famous mystics. 3277
Three-fold secret of the Holy Spirit. 1830
Three-fold secret of the Holy Spriit. 1830
Three-fold test of modern spiritualism. 3503
Three fundamental principles of the spiritual life. 969
Three gates on a side, and other sermons. 2934
Three Gospels. 396
Three great facts. 3202
Three greater successes. 3702
Three greatest maxims of the world. 2375
Three greatest mysteries. 2636
Three greatest prayers. 2249
Three guardsmen. 630
Three guardsmen, and other stories from the Apocrypha. 630
Three harvests, and supplement. 1067
Three hearts. 1620
Three heavens, three hells, and several impassable gulfs. 1794
Three holy kings. 2311
Three hour sermon on God. 3342
Three hours. 1747
... The three hours' agony. 2056
Three hours' agony of Our Lord Jesus Christ. 2057
Three hours to live. 3585
Three hours' vigil. 3200
365 Bible stories and verses. 620
365 devotions on the names of Our Lord. 2020
365 meditations for teen-agers. 3882
365 windows. 1432
365 stray leaves from Under the Catalpa. 725
Three hundred contradictions in the Bible. 304
Three hundred evangelistic sermon outlines. 1562
Three hundred five-minute sermons for children, a cyclopedia of choice and practical present-day sermons to children. 3352
Three hundred golden name heart prayers. 2895
300 sermon outlines from the Old Testament. 593, 3375
300 sermon outlines on the New Testament. 3269
300 sermon sketches on Old and New Testament texts. 3372
365 table graces for the Christian home. 1750
300 thought stimulators for sermons and addresses. 1840
Three hundred years in America in Katz. 3577

Three hundred years of the Episcopal church in America. 2967
Three hundred years of worship and service. 1933
Three imposters. 3024
3 in 1 (a picture of God) 1734'
Three infinities. 3539
Three inquiries. 3751
Three inquiries on the following Scriptural subjects. 3751
3 issues in ethics. 944
Three Jewish martyrs. 2127
2842
Three joint symposia from the ACPA-APA meetings of 1957, 1958, 1959. 1777
Three keys to happiness. 795
Three kingdoms. 1121
Three kings. 2311, 3304
Three kings of Israel. 493, 3304
Three last things. 1529
Three lectures on evangelicalism and the Oxford movement. 2754
Three lectures on the book of Revelation. 451
... Three lectures on the Epistle to the Ephesians. 364
Three lectures on the harmonial philosophy. 3498
Three lectures on the Vedanta philosophy. 3775
Three letters from prison. 365
Three letters, on different subjects. 607
Three little graves. 896
Three martyrs of the nineteenth century. 2240
Three meanings. 1438
Three measures of meal. 1103
Three men of Judea. 927
Three men who walked in fire. 508
Three messages of Revelation XIV, 6-12. 465
Three Middle English sermons from the Worcester chapter manuscript F.10. 3367
Three mile an hour God. 2390
Three-minute devotions for boys and girls. 902
Three-minute homilies. 1841
Three-minute lay sermons. 1325
Three minute sermons. 3347
Three minutes a day. 857, 999
Three minutes a day (second series) 857
Three missionary pioneers and some who have followed them. 740, 1547
Three modern musketeers. 3518
Three modernists. 2243, 2562
Three monophysite christologies. 2010, 2585
Three months in India. 2531
Three Mormon classics. 2604
Three Mrs. Judsons. 2157
Three Muslim sages. 121
Three mystics. 2642, 3690
Three Nephites. 2684
Three new concepts. 3065
Three pageants. 2757
Three Persons in One God. 3714
Three pillars. 2115, 2140
Three pillars of Zen. 3892, 3894
Three planes of life. 975
Three Popes. 3308
Three Popes and the Cardinal. 811, 2770
Three Popes and the Jews. 860, 2152
Three prophetic days. 3260, 3547
Three prophets of religious liberalism. 3729
Three prophetic days of Matt. 12:40. 2029
... Three-quarters of a century (1807 to 1882): a retrospect. Written from documents and memory ... By the late Rev. Augustus J. Thebaud, S.J. 828
Three races under God. 3017
Three reasons why I am a Baptist. 148
Three reformers, Luther, Descartes, Rousseau. 2276
Three religions of China. 913, 1331
Three religious leaders of Oxford and their movements. 3860
Three R's of Christianity. 3224
Three R's of rescue mission work. 2494
Three Russian prophets: Khomiakov, Dostoevsky, Soloviev. 2169, 3214
Three-score & ten. 3128
Three score and ten, a history of the Highland Avenue Methodist Church. 1588
Three sermons. 58
Three sermons on different subjects and occasions. 3605
Three sermons preached at the two hundred and fiftieth anniversary of the founding of the Reformed church of Bergen. 1155
Three sisters of Lord Russell of Killowen. 2352
Three stages of the spiritual life under the inspiration of Jesus. 3487

Three steps forward, two steps back. 2822
Three steps to good teaching. 2599
Three studies for discussion and reflection. 980
Three studies in simplicity. 2849
Three telltale allegories. 954
3--the key to the Scriptures. 646
Three theories of society. 3450
Three thousand illustrations for Christian service. 1841
Three thousand practical illustrations in religion and morals. 3564
Three thousand questions and answers on the New Testament. 280
Three timely treasures. 2613
Three to win. 3828
Three traditions in the Gospels. 390
Three treatise. 1682
Three treatises concerning Wales. 1223
Three treatises on man. 3464
Three trumpets sound. 2162
Three Tudor dialogues. 2287, 2368
Three typical beliefs. 1063
Three unknown Buddhist stories in an Arabic version. 3581
... Three Upanishads. 3775
Three uses of Christian discourse in John Henry Newman. 2704
Three valuable Pieces. 3201
Three vital problems. 1621
Three ways of Asian wisdom. 1814
Three ways of Asian wisdom: Hinduism, Buddhism, Zen, and their significance for the West. 1814
Three ways of love. 19, 1027
Three ways of the spiritual life. 3486
Three weathervanes. 1444
Three white veils for Sandra. 2334
Three who dance together. 991
Three woe trumpets. 465
Three worlds of Albert Schweitzer. 3312
Three years old. 2718
Three years with the children. 3370
Threefold cord. 3401
Threefold fellowship and the threefold assurance. 3712
Threefold grace of the Holy Trinity. 3711
Threefold lotus sutra. 2317, 3272
Threefold path to peace. 2809
Threefold refuge in the Theravada Buddhist tradition. 3698
3's at church. 3173
3's in the Christian community. 3173
Threescore and ten. 2626
Threescore and ten ... wow! 1257
Threshing floor. 502
Threshold. 573
Threshold covenant. 1376
Threshold grace. 584
Threshold of Christianity. 2149
Threshold of religion. 3110
Threshold of the kingdom. 3201
Threshold of the Pacific. 1540
Threshold of the spiritual world. 2991
Threshold of the temple. 1201
Thresholds to adult living. 3880
Thrill of tradition. 3706
Thrilling experience of the Welsh evangelist, R. G. Williams, reformed drunkard and gambler. 1575
Thrilling scenes in the Persian kingdom. 3200
Thrity years at the superintendent's desk. 3550
Throne among the shadows. 2929
Throne and the chariot. 2471
Throne established by righteousness. 1504
Throne of David. 1405
Throne of grace. 2879, 2894
Throne of Peter. 2769
Throne-room of the soul. 2425
Throne rooms. 3200
Through a Cuban window. 2515
Through a glass darkly. 324, 697, 1518
Through a Quaker archway. 1676
Through agnostic spectacles. 19
Through an Anglican sisterhood to Rome. 3415
Through an Eastern window. 2382
Through an Indian mountain glass. 2529
Through blood and fire in Latin America. 2549
Through Bowen museum with Bible in hand. 206
Through Caroline's consent. 1706
Through Christ our Lord. 804
Through Christ Our Lord; sermons on the mission of Christ. 2437
Through cloud and sunshine. 2391
Through creative evolution to incarnation and the goal of humanity. 1579
Through crisis to victory. 3386
Through death to life. 837, 1414, 1735
Through death to rebirth. 1414
Through discipline to joy. 977
Through Eastern eyes. 814

Through Europe to the Promised Land, 1951 A.D. 2762
Through experience to faith. 1053
Through fire. 1109
Through five hundred years. 2594
Through flaming sword; a spiritual biography of George Fox. 1637
Through four centuries. 1545
Through gates of pearl. 1793
Through gates of splendor. 2516
Through Gentile eyes. 2077
Through God's eyes. 2980
Through golden windows. 618
Through human eyes. 1955
Through hundred gates. 1364
Through Jesus to God. 1728, 1994
Through Judy's eyes. 2503
Through lands of the Bible. 1928
Through Lent to resurrection. 1115
Through man to God. 1722
Through memory's halls. 3137
Through my gift. 3307, 3420
Through nature to God. 2672
Through nature to nature's God. 3077
Through other eyes. 833
Through peasant eyes. 429, 2024
Through prayer to reality. 2879
Through science to faith. 3080
Through science to God. 3072, 3073, 3080
Through Scylla and Charybdis. 793
Through sorrow into joy. 1352
Through storms we grow. 3361
Through suffering to happiness. 2032
Through suffering to victory. 438, 1004
Through sunlight and shadow. 3124
Through sunshine and shadow with the twenty-third Psalm. 587
Through temple doors. 2601
Through temptation. 3600
Through the ages. 1180
Through the Bible day by day. 613, 643, 1450
Through the Bible in a year. 645, 649
Through the Bible in a year with juniors. 648
Through the Bible with a guide. 638
Through the Bible with a physician. 201
Through the Bible with finger plays. 3172
Through the Bible with those who were there. 649
...Through the book of Acts with a guide. 333
Through the church door. 3206
Through the church school door. 2720
Through the dark night. 3580
Through the darkness. 1352
Through the East to Rome. 1364
Through the eternal spirit. 1828, 1834
Through the Eye-gate into the city of Mansoul. 3145
Through the eye to the heart. 2720, 3565
Through the eyes of little saints. 1233, 2603
Through the eyes of love. 422
Through the eyes of youth. 3444
Through the forty days. 2212
Through the garden with Jesus. 1049
Through the Gospels to Jesus. 387
Through the lane of stars. 3284
Through the lich-gate. 2697
Through the mists. 2001
Through the mists, or Whence the divinity of Christ? 2001
Through the narrow gate. 83, 1582
Through the needle's eye. 2866, 3762
Through the Old Testament and the Apocrypha. 533
Through the Pentateuch chapter by chapter. 566
Through the prayer book. 1213
Through the prison to the throne. 2133
Through the Scriptures. 600
Through the second gate. 155
Through the secret door. 3182
Through the shadows. 3752
Through the shadows with Jesus. 1975
Through the sieve. 1047
Through the valley. 588, 1774, 2463
Through the valley; nature's clues to victorious living. 588
Through the week with Jesus. 1004, 1015
Through the winds rain. 1490
Through the year with Christ. 1267, 1440, 2396
Through the year with Michael Ramsey. 1434
Through the years. 3124
Through tragedy to triumph. 1061
Through trial to triumph. 3466
Through two generations. 3126
Through two hundred years, 1765-1965. 79
Through valleys to victories. 588
... Throughout all generations. 3144
Throughout the whole wide earth. 3171
Throw away the garbage. 993

Throw him to the lions. 1398
Thrown at the atheist's head. 100
Thru the Bible with J. Vernon McGee. 223
Thru the rear-view mirror. 1460
Thumbnail sketch of Mormonism. 2603
Thunder. 1718, 3698
"Thunder an' lightnin' britches" 3379, 3820
Thunder and lightning. 2229
Thunder in the distance. 2205
Thunder in the wilderness. 3633
Thunder of bare feet. 3352
Thunder of silence. 194, 2694
Thunder of the gods. 2660
Thunder on the left: some religio-philosophical essays. 3107
Thunder on the mountain. 1316
Thunder on the right. 1690
Thunder over Sinai. 166
Thunderbolt. 3059
Thunderbolts. 1558
Thundering Scot. 2181
Th'upright heart and pure. 2468
Thursday mornings at the City Temple. 3339
Thursday's daughter. 1311, 2486
Thurstan, Archibishop of York. 3698
"Thus it is written" 2504
"Thus pray ye" 2250
Thus religion grows. 2117
"Thus saith the Lord" 209, 253, 1434, 2952, 3220
Thus says the Lord. 544
"Thus shall you pray" 840, 2247
Thus spake Zarathustra. 2710
Thus spoke Zarathustra. 2710
Thwaites' Jesuit relations; errata and addenda. 1947
Thy brother shall rise again. 3511
Thy goodly tent. 179
... Thy health shall spring forth. 3406
Thy King cometh. 2260
Thy kingdom come. 508, 864, 1009, 1051, 1114, 1439, 1541, 2175, 2440, 2883, 2946, 2973, 3353, 3560, 3620
Thy kingdom come, a study in Christian ethics. 3218
Thy kingdom come, an historical study of stewardship and missions. 2492
Thy kingdom come; Christian hope in the modern world. Twenty-third annual North American Liturgical Week, Seattle, Washington, August 20-23, 1962. 1529
"Thy kingdom come ... Why now now?" 3442
Thy laws. 296
Thy light and Thy truth. 2393
Thy lighted lamp. 2401
Thy mission high fulfilling. 3733
Thy name shall no more be called Jacob but Israel, prince of God. 1033
Thy neighbour. 2119
Thy people, my people. 2544
Thy people shall be my people. 2556
Thy rod and Thy staff. 1440, 2388
Thy son liveth. 3496
"Thy whisper" 2728
Thy will be done. 943, 1451, 2246, 2393, 3137
Thy will be done in all things. 3134
Thy word in my heart. 2395
"Thy word is truth" 252, 1911
Tia tells a story. 147
Tiberius and Pontius Pilate in Ethiopian tradition and poetry. 2207
Tibet is my country. 2193
Tibetan book of the dead. 707, 708, 3699, 3895
Tibetan book of the great liberation. 708, 3586
Tibetan Buddhism. 2193
Tibetan Buddhism in Western perspective. 2193
Tibetan Buddhist chant. 883
Tibetan meditation. 3492
Tibetan religious art. 88
Tibetan sacred art. 88
Tibetan yoga and secret doctrines. 3866
Tibet's great yogi, Milarepa. 2193, 2461
Tibet's terrifying deities. 3699
Ticket to Israel. 2763
Tickhill psalter and related manuscripts. 1883
Tide of the supernatural. 2372, 2557
Tide, time and eternity. 3125
Tides of India. 3145
Tides of the spirit. 2349, 3724
Tidings, [poems at the land's edge]. 3208
Tied to Masonic apron strings. 1663
Ties between.
Ties that bind. 1321
Tiger's cave. 3894
Tigers in the dark. 1006

Tigers' teeth. 973
Tijaniyya. 21
Tijaniyya, a Sufi order in the modern world. 21
... Tikapatthana of the Abhidhamma pitaka. 708
'Til divorce do us part. 1471
Tilak of Tibet reveals life's purpose. 3053
Till Armageddon. 3540
Till break of day. 2505
"Till Scotland melts in flame" 3315
Till we meet again. 3456
Tillage of the heart. 964
Tillich; a theological portrait. 3699
Tillichian theology and educational philosophy. 3176, 3700
Tillich's system. 3700
Tilted haloes. 3280
Time a fiction, fact and fiction. 1061
Time a part. 1431
Time and eternity. 3105
Time and eternity and other biblical studies. 238
Time and eternity in Christian thought. 1533
Time and free will. 1322
Time and history. 460, 1819
Time and modes of being. 2738
Time-and-place harmony of the Gospels. 396
Time and space relative to the recorded history in the span of human existence. 296
Time and timeliness. 1819
Time changes in the U.S.A. 3701
Time for a change. 23
Time for action. 956
Time for all things. 512, 2396
Time for being human. 2390
Time for boldness. 1011
Time for Christian candor. 972, 1096
Time for consent. 1843
Time for discovery. 3172
Time for eternity. 3483
Time for everything. 994, 2831
Time for everything under the sun. 691, 3634
Time for faith. 1602
Time for God. 2398
Time for intercession. 2877
Time for living. 3244
Time for love. 2263
Time for peace. 249
Time for questions. 2214, 2300
Time for reflection. 3014
Time for remembering. 2210
Time for remembrance; history of 125 years of First Evangelical United Brethren Church, Naperville, Illinois. 1550
Time for unity. 1043
Time for wonder. 3180
Time has come. 1515
Time invades the cathedral. 1845
Time is fulfilled. 451
Time it is. 2003
Time management. 1199
Time minder. 1838
Time of burning. 561
Time of change. 1245
Time of our lives. 1442
Time of the end. 465, 506, 1513, 1515, 2601, 3383
Time of the fugitive. 2574
Time of your life. 1010
Time of your life is now. 1016
Time out. 1430
Time out, ladies! 3844
Time running out. 1514
Time stream. 2320
Time to act. 3884
Time to be born. 1573
Time to be born—a time to die. 512, 2626
Time to build. 3652
Time to celebrate. 1320
Time to choose. 1009
Time to dance. 3144
Time to die. 1415
Time to grow. 2386
Time to keep. 1627
Time to love. 931, 1422
Time to mourn. 1354
Time to mourn, and a time to dance. 512
Time to pray. 3883
Time to remember—milestones. 1229
Time to remember—projections. 1228
Time to run. 989
Time to seek. 3885
Time to spare. 3223
Time to speak. 3361, 3370
Time toward home. 3747
Time, tradition and truth. 1514
Time was. 496
Time was right. 1103, 2092
Time with God. 3477, 3885
Timeless Christian. 1102
Timeless gospel. 166

Timeless issues. 2438, 3360
Timeless moment. 1089
Timeless spring. 3459
Timeless Torah. 1817
Timelessness of Jesus Christ, His relevence in today's world. 1058, 2039
Timely discussion of Christian science. 1035
Timely object lessons. 3156
Timely sermon outlines. 3375
Times. 606
Times and the teaching of John Wesley. 3803
Times apart--with God. 1437
Time's last hour. 1514
Time's noblest name. 2020
Times of Daniel. 509
Times of decision. 1373
Times of grace. 2209
Times of refreshing. 1571, 3232
Times of retirement. 1621
Times of the Gentiles. 1514
Times of the gentiles and the time of the end. 1513
Times of the Saviour. 2006
Times test the church. 1064
Times to come. 97
Times to treasure. 173, 930
Timetable of Bible prophecy. 610
Timothy. 772
Timothy Nicholson master Quaker. 2708
Timothy Warren Anglin, 1822-96, Irish Catholic Canadian. 45, 3525
Timothy, young pastor. 339, 3701
Tinder in Tabasco. 2929
Tinkling Spring. 3701
Tiny speck in God's scheme of things. 691
Tiny tales 'n tunes. 3175
Tiny thoughts about God. 1734
*Tiny thoughts books. 3176
Tiny words about the beginning. 1384

Tips for teachers. 3550
Tips for teens. 3886
Tips for 2-1/2s. 2386
Tips to teachers. 3178
Tirant lo Blanc. 1894
Tired church members. 36, 1454
Tired dragons. 1167
Tired mothers. 3208
Tiruvacagam; or, 'Sacred utterances' of the Tamil poet, saint, and sage Manikka-Vacagar. 3207
Tishbite. 1506
Tithe. 3702
Tithe in scripture. 3702
Tithe law. 3702
Tithes. 3702
Tithing. 3702
Tithing and the church's mission. 3530
Tithing for juniors. 3702
Tithing system and the change from law to grace. 3702
Titius and Bertha ride again. 744
Title catalogue of the free library of the Union for Christian work, Providence, 1876. 1019
Titles of Jesus in Christology. 2020
Titles of the Blessed Virgin. 2231
Titles of the Psalms, their nature and meaning explained. 579
Titles of the tirune God. 1736
Titles of the triune God. 1736
Titus and Philemon. 479
Titus Coan. 1305
Titus, patterns for church living. 479
TM. 3707, 3708
TM and the nature of enlightenment. 2317, 3707
TM book. 2382, 3708
TM*: discovering inner energy and overcoming stress. 3707
TM program. 3708
TNT. 2696
To a Catholic from a Protestant in defence of the faith. 800, 1849
To a dancing God. 1324
To a goodly heritage. 2196
To a listening heart. 2891
To advance the Gospel. 334, 2555
To Africa with love. 2296, 2500
To all nations. 1187
To all nations; how the Bible came to the people. 290
"To all people." 1559
To and fro on the earth. 3795
To apply the Gospel; selections from the writings of Henry Venn. 2512
To Barbara with love. 2888
To be a Catholic. 769
To be a girl, to be a woman. 1621
To be a graduate. 989, 3774
To be a Jew. 2081, 2119
To be a man. 976, 3757
To be a man, to be a woman. 3390
To be a parent. 1607

To be a person of integrity. 216, 994
To be a priest. 2940
To be born again. 1359
To be church. 1268
To be continued. 3468
To be free. 2490, 3831
To be honest. 3660
To be human now. 67
To be in Christ. 2397
To be mature. 988
To be near unto God. 966
To be or not to be. 664, 1068
To be or not to be reformed. 1023
To be the first. 2157, 2488
To be the salt of the earth. 3218
To bigotry no sanction. 2705
To build a church. 1167
To burn with the spirit of Christ. 2192
To Calvary with Christ. 3525
To change the world. 1065, 1074, 2043
To cherish all life. 20, 3776
To China with love. 2507
To Christ through evolution. 1581
To Christian England. 3452
To church we go. 1162
To Colorado's restless ghosts. 1310
To come alive! 1243
To come and go on. 1446
To comfort and to challenge. 3442
To conquer loneliness. 2244, 2245
"To daimonion," or The spiritual medium. 3513
To-day's supreme challenge to America. 2520
To deceive ... the elect. 753
To deny the night: reflections on life and essence. 2396
To die and to live. 2052, 3785
To die is gain. 1691
To die with Jesus. 854
To do justly. 2144
To Dr. Albert Schweitzer. 3312
To eliminate the opiate. 713, 3032
To Elsie with love. 2669, 3516
To enjoy God. 3124
To enrich each day. 1433
To eternity and back. 2730
To every creature. 1571
To every man an answer. 3641
To find a church. 1269
To find Jesus. 1970
To follow a dream. 2392
To forget the self. 2383
To fulfill this ministry. 3673
To give the love of Christ. 2717, 3602
To glorify God. 3852
To God alone the glory. 675
"--To God and to each other". 1845-1965. History of one hundred and twenty years about the Hickman Mills Community Christian Church, its people and the community. 1810
To God be the glory. 720, 2385, 3359
To God with love. 1446, 2398
To govern is to love. 2573
To Greenland's icy mountains. 1500
To grow holy merrily. 3704
To hallow this life. 699
To have and to hold. 2336
To heal and to reveal. 430, 2949
To heal as Jesus healed. 1600
To hear the word of God. 1267
To heaven through a window. 1706
To heaven with Diana! 3129, 3136
To heaven with scribes and Pharises. 2138
To heights serene. 1323
To help other men. 3349
To help you follow the way of the Cross. 3526
To help you say the Rosary better. 3249
To his neighbors, on the 'Holy Cause of Freedom. 2895
To his soul's health. 3263
To infidelity and back. 3130
To insure peace acknowledge God. 3450
To Jesus through Mary. 3476
To kiss earth good-bye. 2991
To kiss the joy. 1007
To know and believe. 73, 3665
To know Christ Jesus. 1972
To know God better. 1441
To know God's way. 2935, 3359
To know Him. 1954
To know Him is to love Him. 1359, 2413
To know how to wait. 3484
To know or not to be. 3214
To light a candle. 1115
To live again. 925
To live as a Jew. 2151
To live by His Word. 975
To live in love. 324
To live is Christ. 449, 450, 1267, 2570, 3094, 3186
To live is to love. 2384
To live the Gospel. 3132
To live within. 3301
To love and to suffer. 1712, 3690

To love is to live. 323
To love or to perish. 3592
To make intercession. 2873
To make men free. 161
To market, to market. 3764
To meet the day. 3882
To mend the broken. 1132
To-morrow of death. 1695
To Munich with love. 1574
To my children. 3132
To my son. 3243
To obey is to reign. 2573
To Our Lord's country. 2762
To possess a dream. 993
To pray and to grow. 2882
To pray as a Jew. 2107, 2885
To pray is to live. 2868
To pray or not to pray! 1150
To preach the gospel. 2901
To promote good will. 3142
To raise a Jewish child. 2079
To reach even unto you. 1009
To resist or to surrender? 3000
To rule both day and night. 98
To save all people. 3030
To see His face. 865, 2722
To see Peter. 2298
To see the kingdom. 2708
To serve in faithfulness. 3361
To serve the present age. 1235, 2551, 3851
To set at liberty. 1658
To settle your conscience. 948, 1314
To show the mind of Christ. 2757
To sow in tears. 793
To speak of God. 3668
To stand in the cross. 1747, 2973
To start the day. 1453
To strenghten family ties. 1607
To teens with love. 3879
To tell the godly man. 3479
To tell the world. 1855
To the church in America. 761
To the churches, with love. 461
To the end of the earth. 2526
To the end of time. 41, 3761
To the ends of the earth. 723, 1332, 1903, 3829, 3860
To the far corners. 1754, 3230
To the glory of God. 1371, 2608, 2854
To the Golden Shore. 2157
To the heart of a child. 3192
To the heart of the child. 3181, 3192
To the Hebrews. 402
To the house of the Lord. 849
To the Jew first. 2085
To the kid in the pew. 909
To the least. 2353
To the memory of Puzant H. Kalfayan. 2162
To the other towns. 1587
To the Prophet. 2629
To the top of the mountain. 1300, 2736
To the unknown God. 1103, 1482
To the whole creation. 2555
To the work! 1251
To the youth of the world. 3337
To thee I come. 2357
To Thee this temple. 3134
To Thee we sing. 1875
"To them that perish" 166
To thine own self. 2383
To touch the face of God. 1727
To touch the sky. 2388
To turn from idols. 1882
To walk and not faint. 545
To walk in the kingdom. 431, 995
To walk with God. 3507
To whom I now send thee. 2542
To whom it may concern. 1139, 2860, 3362
To whom shall we go? 788, 1234
To whom the land of Palestine belongs. 234, 2765
To will & to do. 943
To will one thing. 2171
To win the West. 2560
To woman from Meslom. 3508
To Z horoscope maker and delineator. 95
Tobit and the Babylonian apocryphal writings. 487
Today. 852, 896, 1011, 1435, 1442
Today and every day. 1440
Today and tomorrow. 17, 3880
Today for youth. 3880
Today I feel like a warm fuzzy. 900
Today I saw a prophet. 1230, 2952
Today in Bible prophecy. 604
Today in Bible prophecy (series two) 604
Today in cathedral France. 752
Today is all you have. 988
Today is yours. 1437
Today makes a difference! 1445
Today with God; daily meditations. 1441
Today's children and yesterday's heritage. 3170
Today's church. 2481

Today's dictionary of the Bible. 242
Today's English New Testament. 354
Today's English version of the New Testament. 354
Today's English version of the New Testament and Psalms. 354
Today's good news. 1436
Today's Jesus. 166
Today's pastor in tomorrow's world. 2785
Today's story of Jesus. 929, 1991
Today's vocation crisis. 3785
Today's witches. 3824
Today's world. 3181
Today's world religions. 3121
... Today's youth and tomorrow's world. 3443
Toddlers at church. 3173
Toehold on Zen. 3892
Together. 1072, 3191
Together at confirmation. 1328
Together at Mass. 2259
Together each day. 1433
Together forever. 2346
Together in peace for children. 900
Together is a happy way. 1621
Together; the story of church cooperation in Minnesota. 1045
Together, they built a mountain. 195
Together toward God. 3165
Together we advance. 3723
Together we praise Him. 3856
Together with God. 903
Tohoku, the Scotland of Japan. 2534
Toils and triumphs of union missionary colportage. 2528
Token for children. 895, 896, 2048
Token for mourners. 1350
Tokens from the writings of Baha'u'llah. 129
Tokugawa religion. 1935
Told again. 2004
Told at twilight. 616
Told to Patrick. 626
Tolerance. 3703, 3704
Tolerance and the Catholic. 3704
Tolerance and truth in religion. 3703
Toleration. 2589
Toleration and other essays. 3024
Toleration and other essays and studies. 1067
Toleration and the Reformation. 3703
Toleration in religion & politics. 3214
Tom, Dick, and Jane in theology land. 3661
Tom Keenan, locomotive engineer. 2166
Tom Skinner, top man of the Lords. 1361
Tomas Cartwright and Elizabethan Puritanism. 743, 3007
Tomb for the living. 2183
Tomb of Ramesses VI. 1502, 3020
Tomb of St. Peter. 2825, 2826, 3768
Tombs and Moon temple of Hureidha (Hadhramaut) 1857
Tombs of St. Peter & St. Paul. 2825, 3769
Tomkins, Floyd W[illiams]. 977
Tommasco Campanella in America. 732
Tommorrow's church in today's world. 1134
Tommorrow's world. 609
Tommy goes to Africa. 2552
Tomorrow. 2512
Tomorrow and tomorrow. 127
Tomorrow begins today. 1254
Tomorrow in your hand. 939, 3385
Tomorrow is a handful of together yesterdays. 3889
Tomorrow is growing old. 22, 1676
Tomorrow is here. 2493
Tomorrow is ours. 3662
Tomorrow is today. 3890
Tomorrow is yours. 3886
Tomorrow you lead. 3178
Tomorrow's Christian. 1154
Tomorrow's church. 1064, 2921
Tomorrow's church, a cosmopolitan community. 1244
Tomorrow's church: catholic, evangelical, reformed. 1040
Tomorrow's church; tomorrow's world. 2921
Tomorrow's Egypt. 1501
Tomorrow's faith. 45
Tomorrow's faith today. 66
Tomorrow's priest. 849, 2484
Tomorrow's priests. 772
Tomorrow's pulpit. 2900
Tomorrow's religion. 3372
Tomorrows unlimited. 3515, 3535
Tongue of fire. 1827
Tongue of the prophets. 187, 2084
Tongue of time. 963
Tongue speaking. 1716
Tongues. 1717, 3383
Tongues in Biblical perspective. 1716
Tongues of fire. 2525, 3222, 3267, 3268
Tongues of men and angels. 1716
Tongues, to speak or not to speak. 1716

Tonic for our times. 1323
Tonic thoughts from the sermons of Dr. W. W. Dawley. 3339
Too busy for God? 3844
Too busy not to pray. 3842
Too many pastors? 1300
Too old to learn? 3168
Too small a world. 723
Too tough for God. 1366, 1744
Tooke's Pantheon of the heathen gods, and illustrious heroes. 2657
Tool in his hand. 1787, 2501
Tools and techniques for the teaching of the Catholic religion in colleges and universities. 3159
Tools for active Christians. 953
Tools for Bible study. 285, 641
Tools for teaching. 2720
Tools for theological research. 3627
Tools for time management. 3701
Tools of astrology: houses. 99
Tools of curriculum development for the church's educational ministry. 3162
Top notch teacher. 3592
Top of the mount. 2973
Top sacred: spiritual ideas in down-to-earth language. 2390
Top sergeant of the pioneers. 2206, 2423
Topic. 3186
Topical analysis of the Bible. 301
Topical analysis of the history of the passion of Our Lord. 2030
Topical Bible. 303
Topical Bible concordance. 303
Topical Bible studies. 647
Topical concordance of vital doctrines. 303
Topical dictionary of Bible texts. 303
Topical guide to the scriptures of the Church of Jesus Christ of Latter-Day Saints. 2619
Topical handbook of Scripture. 301
Topical helps to the American standard Bible. 237
Topical history of Y'sdom. 3874
Topical history of Y'sdom, 1920-1953. 3874
Topical illustrations for the use of ministers. 1293
Topical index and digest of the Bible. 303
Topical outline studies in ecclesiastical history. 1188
Topical Psalter. 252
Topical question book. 3288
Topical sermon notes. 3345, 3375
Topical text-finder. 304
Tora of Moses. 511
Torah. 482
Torah and canon. 496, 3706
Torah and flora. 565, 3370
Torah and Gospel. 1084, 2152
Torah as our guide. 3287
Torah for our time. 3371
Torah in the Messianic age and/or the age to come. 1083
Torah-Leviticus. 557
Torah Nevi im u-Ketuvim. 482
Torah Nevi im u-Khetuvim. 482
Torah readings. 482
Torah species. 1277, 2086
Torah thoughts. 2142
(Torah) [Torah (romanized form)]. 562
Torah, [Torah (romanized form)] the five books of Moses. 482
Torah translated in Jewish and English. 482
Torah verified by science. 204
Torah-vision. 565
Torah Yesharah. 482, 483, 564
Torch and sword. 3887
Torch and the flag. 33
Torch in the darkness. 1717
Torch in the darkness; a story of St. John Capistran. 1717
Torch of faith. 297
Torchbearers. 925
Torchbearers in China. 2510
Torchbearers in Honan. 2529
Torchbearers of spiritualism. 3520
Torchbearers of the Middle Ages. 2084
Torchbearers on the King's highway. 1253
Torches together. 698
Tormented angel. 2702
Tormented master. 2668, 3016
Torquemada and the Spanish inquisition. 1910, 3704
Torrey and Alexander, the story of a world-wide revival. 3705
Tortillas for the gods. 3721
Torture of the Christian martyrs. 1021
Tortured for his faith. 2820, 2863
Tory crisis in church and state 1688-1730. 109, 1146
Tosefta. 1798
Total Christianity. 1094
Total family. 1608
Total image. 2369

Total meditation. 2381
Total prayer for living. 2883
Total prayer for total living. 2869
Total presence. 1818, 2024
Total thanks. 1756
Totally new. 981
Toto and Sundri. 2531
Tottering transcendence. 3086
Touch of Christ. 3263
Touch of God. 1449, 1586, 2794, 3126, 3843
Touch of greatness. 1449
Touch of his hand. 1310, 2556
Touch of his love. 1441
Touch of radiance. 1844
Touch of the Master's hand. 2018, 3207, 3372
Touch of the spirit. 998, 1568
Touch of wonder. 2388
Touch the wind ; creative worship with children. 3858
Touched by Christ. 339
Touched by the fire. 2816
Touched by the Spirit. 1712
Touching God. 905
Touching heaven by prayer. 2880
Touching incidents and remarkable answers to prayer. 2880
Touchstone of character. 886
Touchstone of sincerity. 961
Touchstones of reality. 3116
Tough love. 1260, 3869
Tour of the missions. 2495
Tour of the Summa. 3696
Touring Tanganyika. 2552
Touring the Holy Land. 2762
Touring with God. 1447
Tournier companion. 3002
Toward a better. life. 2608
Toward a better world. 1135, 3338
Toward a Biblical view of civil government. 603
Toward a Christian America. 2528
Toward a Christian ethic. 948
Toward a Christian fellowship. 1228
Toward a Christian moral theology. 943, 948
Toward a Christian philosophy of higher education. 1127
Toward a contemporary Christianity. 1074
Toward a course in the functions of the Jewish community for the reform religious school. 1316
Toward a creative chaplaincy. 885
Toward a descriptive analysis of [einai (romanized form)] as a linking verb in New Testament Greek. 1771
Toward a dimensional realism. 2419
Toward a discipline of social ethics: essays in honor of Walter George Muelder. 2627, 3448
Toward a doctrine of the liberal church. 2221
Toward a fourth century of Quakerism. 1676
Toward a future for religious education. 936
Toward a growing marriage. 2337
Toward a mature faith. 1094
Toward a more efficient church. 1251, 1252
Toward a more excellent ministry. 1322
Toward a new Catholic morality. 949
Toward a new Christianity. 1418
Toward a new concept of the Bible. 232
Toward a new politics. 1088
Toward a philosophy of praxis. 776, 3633
Toward a philosophy of Zen Buddhism. 3893
Toward a reborn church. 1491
Toward a reconstruction of religion. 1104
Toward a reformed philosophy. 3213
Toward a renewal of sacramental theology. 3266
Toward a theology of Christian faith. 1597
Toward a theology of evangelism. 1565
Toward a theology of history. 1817
Toward a theology of involvement. 3715
Toward a theology of the layman. 2192
Toward a theory of secularization. 3328
Toward a united church. 1039
Toward a vital Christian experience. 1586
Toward a world Christian fellowship. 2520
Toward adult Christian education. 1134, 3168
Toward an African theology. 3653
Toward an American Orthodox Church. 2751
Toward an American theology. 3652
Toward an effective pulpit ministry. 2901
Toward an exegetical theology. 287
Toward an expansive Christian theology. 3620
Toward an understanding of the carpenter's son. 1972
Toward an undivided church. 1044, 3771

Toward attunement with the eternal verities. 2228
Toward belief. 63
Toward better church committees. 1239
Toward better families. 1254
Toward better witnessing. 3216, 3828
Toward caring. 1011
Toward celebration, with suggestions for using the celebration packet. 3003
Toward certainty. 63
Toward Christian democracy; a profession takes its bearings. 3873
Toward Christian marriage. 2337
Toward consensus. 1142
Toward continuous mission. 2504
Toward creative urban strategy. 1279
Toward discovering a religion. 3725
Toward effective teaching; youth. 3175
Toward fullness of life. 448
Toward happiness and holiness in marriage. 2340
Toward health and wholeness. 2409
Toward larger living. 3725
Toward Lutheran union. 1040
Toward man's redemption. 3031
Toward marriage in Christ. 2342
Toward meaning in worship. 2295
Toward modernity. 1935
Toward moral maturity. 951
Toward more effective research in the church. 2790
Toward new dimensions of Catholic higher education. 832
Toward new horizons. 1546
Toward new horizons in India. 2529
Toward our Father's house. 1414
Toward peace. 2807
Toward political responsibility. 1578
Toward professional maturity. 3873
Toward responsible discipleship. 2915
Toward reunion. 860, 1046
Toward spiritual brotherhood. 3542
Toward spiritual security. 1134
Toward the Christian church (Disciples of Christ) Intention, essence, constitution. 1122
Toward the clerical-religious life. 3676
Toward the eternal. 174
Toward the eternal priesthood. 2394
Toward the goal supreme. 1732
Toward the great awakening. 1569
Toward the knowledge of God. 1740
Toward the light. 2060, 3472
Toward the mark. 449
Toward the New Testament of the future. 378
Toward the one. 3542
Toward the rising sun. 3521
Toward the summit. 780
Toward the sunrising. 166, 3349
Toward the truth. 711
Toward the understanding of Jesus. 2016
Toward the understanding of St. Paul. 2801
Toward theology. 3643
Toward tomorrow. 3624
Toward understanding adults. 3160
Toward understanding God. 3646
Toward understanding Islam. 1925, 2567
Toward understanding Jesus. 1974, 1992
Toward understanding Paul. 2795
Toward understanding Romans. 320
Toward understanding Saint Thomas. 3692
Toward understanding the Bible. 233
Toward understanding the church and the clergy. 2791
Toward understanding Thessalonians. 478
Toward Vatican III. 829, 1246
Toward world-wide Christianity. 1041
Towards a Christian approach to sex. 3393
Towards a Christian civilization. 1282
Towards a church of the poor. 1153
Towards a global congress of world religions. 3091
Towards a living tradition. 761
Towards a new mysticism. 3117, 3593
Towards a new world. 3447, 3449
Towards a pattern. 1365
Towards a theological understanding of history. 1818
Towards a theology of religions. 3104
Towards a unified faith. 3082
Towards a valid theory of Biblical Hebrew literature. 211
Towards a world theology. 3105
Towards a year-round temple camping program. 733
Towards an indigenous church. 1905
Towards belief in God. 1721
Towards Christian democracy. 3441
Towards discipleship. 3686
Towards educational peace. 1129
Towards evening. 18
Towards loving the Psalms. 578
Towards the altar. 2938

Towards the centre of Christian living. 1001
Towards the Christian revolution. 3446
Towards the eternal priesthood. 2938
Towards the hereafter. 3516
Towards the true self. 3139
... The tower of Babel. 122
Tower of jewels. 250
Tower of light. 3588
Tower on the Heights. 693
Tower too tall. 631
Towering figures among the prophets. 2950
"Towering o'er the wrecks of time," 2216
Towers of faith and courage. 816, 1509
Towers to eternity. 3018, 3707
... The town and country church in the United States. 1274
Town and country pulpit. 2722, 3375
Town and country workshop held at Zion Lutheran Church. 2291
Town and country workshop held at Zion Luthern Church, Albion, Nebr., January 23-24, 1961. 2291
Town parson, his life and work. 3672
Toys and things. 3705
Who's who among pastors in all the Norwegian Lutheran synods of America. 2715
Trabelin' on. 16
Traces of God in a frequently hostile world. 1010
Traces of God in a secular culture. 1724
Traces of picture-writing in the Bible. 314
Tracings. 1324

Tracks of a fellow struggler. 1349
Tract primer. 2940
Tract[s] no. 1. 3509
Tractarian at work. 2754, 3021
Tractarian movement, 1833-1845. 2754
Tractate Avoth. 2478
Tractate Berakoth. 1798
Tractate Berakoth (benedictions) Mishna and Tosephta. 1798
Tractate 'Mourning. 2627
Tractate "Mourning" (Semahot) (Regulations relating to death, burial, and mourning) 2627
Tractate Sanhedrin, Mishnah and Tosefta. 1375
Tractate Shabbath, Mishnah. 2478
Tractatus de anima. 80, 3461
Tractatus de substantiis separatis. 3538
... The Tractatus de successivis. 3469
Tractatus hierographicus. 276
Tracts. 3706
Tracts and treatises. 3044
Tracts ascribed to Richard Bancroft. 3008
Tracts for difficult times. 3201
Tracts for the Christian seasons. 1262
Tracts for the times. 520
Tracts in controversy with Dr. Priestley. 2002
Tracts of the American Unitarian association. 3741
Tracts of the Doctrinal tract and book society. 3706
Tracts on liberty of conscience and persecution, 1614-1661. 149, 2223
Tracts on the Unitarian controversy, published in 1815. 3729
Tracts read before the General association of Georgia. 1241
Tracy Sahib of India. 3706
Trade, guns, and bibles. 2701
Trade politics and Christianity in Africa and the East. 3017
Tradition. 763, 2121, 2152, 2751, 3706
Tradition and authority in the western church, 300-1140. 3707
Tradition and change. 1348
Tradition and change in the church. 3706
Tradition and composition in the parables of Enoch. 491
Tradition and contemporary experience. 2141
Tradition and design in Luke's Gospel. 429
Tradition and interpretation. 504
Tradition and interpretation in Matthew. 444
Tradition and life in the church. 1182
Tradition and testament. 504, 1620
Tradition and the modern world. 3680
Tradition and theology in the Old Testament. 504, 3706
Tradition and traditions. 3706
Tradition and transformation in religious education. 3162
Tradition history and the Old Testament. 501
Tradition in an age of reform. 1817, 2146
Tradition in the early church. 3707
Tradition in the making. 3653

Tradition of Aquinas and Bonaventure. 3695
Tradition of manuscripts. 1398, 3709
Tradition of scripture. 230
Tradition of the goddess Fortuna in Roman literature and in the transitional period. 1634
Tradition reborn. 3361
Tradition unveiled. 3706
Traditional aspects of hell (ancient and modern) 1802
... Traditional ceremonial and customs connected with the Scottish liturgy. 2237
Traditional Ethiopian church education. 937, 1540
Traditional prayer book for Sabbath and festivals. 2111
Traditions in transformation. 504, 1389
Traditions, Kabala, and Qabalah. 2724
Traditions of Islam. 1779, 2564
Traditions of Rabbi Ishamel. 1921, 3015
Traditions of the Covenanters. 1375
Traducao do Novo Mundo das Escrituras gregas cristas. 320
Traduccion del Nuevo Mundo de las Escrituras griegas cristianas. 320
Traduzione del Nuovo Mundo delle Scriture greche cristiane. 320
Tragedies of the liquor traffic. 3595
Tragedy and triumph. 2063
Tragedy and triumph of Easter. 1747
Tragedy is my parish. 1293, 3243
Tragedy of a papal decree (in a crowded world) 663
Tragedy of Bitlis. 668
Tragedy of Calvary. 1022, 1986
Tragedy of Paotingfu. 2767
Tragedy of sin. 3410
Tragedy of the Christ ... poems. 1022
Tragedy of the Greek Catholic Church in Czechoslovakia. 766, 3722
Tragedy of the Jews, of the Protestants, and of the Catholics in our contemporary civilization. 31, 2143
Tragic sense of life. 1891
Tragic vision and the Christian faith. 951
Tragical history of Doctor Faustus. 1351
Trail blazers. 1022
Trail blazers of Sooner Baptists. 159
Trail blazers of "the way," 333
Trail maker. 2241
Trail markers by An old guide. 3880
Trail of Armageddon. 1515
"The trail of blood." 1173
Trail of everyday living. 3147
Trail of itchin' feet. 3467
Trail of life in college. 1790
Trail of life in the middle years. 2131
Trail of the circuit rider. 2456
Trail of the Florida circuit rider. 2430
Trail of the Huguenots in Europe. 1852
Trail of the serpent. 1429
Trail of the seventy. 3386
Trail of the totalitarian. 1141
Trailblazer for the Sacred Heart. 1288, 1379
Trailing the Davis Indians. 1903
Trailing the serpent. 609
Trails and turnpikes. 2394
Trails for climbing youth. 3890
Trails of truth. 3511
Trails, trials, triumphs. 658
Train of terror. 928, 2243
Train up a child. 526
Train up a child . . . guidelines for parents. 903
Train up your child. 938
Trainable children. 2411
Training a staff. 3872
Training church members for pastoral care. 3783
Training for church membership. 1201
Training for discipleship. 1201
Training for evangelism. 1570, 1574
Training for greater service. 1252
... Training for leadership and teaching. 2204
Training for life. 997
Training for personal evangelism. 1553
Training for research in psychology. 2994
Training for service. 644
Training for service in the nursery class. 3174
Training for service in the preschool department. 3173
Training for soul-winning. 1554
Training for triumph in victorious living. 3886
Training for world friendship. 2492
Training in Bible study. 647
Training in chastity. 3390
Training in Christianity and the Edifying discourse which "accompanied" it. 1104
Training in church membership. 3465
Training in church membership, revised in 1936 [by] I. J. Van Ness, D.D. 155

Training in the art of loving. 3222
Training in the Baptist spirit. 149, 649
... Training juniors in worship. 3152
Training lay teachers for the parish high school of religion. 3176
Training lessons for church-school workers. 3156
Training men for Bible teaching. 3168
Training missionaries for community development. 2488
Training of a priest. 3681
Training of an elite group. 666
Training of children in religion. 3151
Training of church choirs. 916
Training of converts. 1363
Training of functional literary personnel. 1690
Training of infants. 3154
Training of Southern Baptist ministers. 3612
...The training of Sunday school teachers and officers. 3555
Training of the Chosen people. 534
Training of the church. 1201
... The training of the devotional life. 1449
Training of the twelve. 70, 338
Training of the twig. 3149
Training of the Zen Buddhist monk. 2577
Training program of a church. 3151
Training series A. 3637
Training the Christian reserves. 1253
Training the church of the future. 3148
Training the devotional life. 3160
... Training the junior citizen. 3150
Training the Sunday school teacher. 3551
Training the teacher. 3558
Training to teach. 1293, 3177
Training Union program materials, 1962. 3465
Training world Christians. 2488
Training Y.M.C.A. leaders for physical education service. 3872
Training young people in worship. 3859
Traite de la nature et de la grace. 1753
Traitor? 1366, 1703
Traits of divine kingship in Africa. 2177
Trajectories in faith. 3126
Trajectories through early Christianity. 335, 1018
Tramp finds a home. 932, 3601
Tramp for the Lord. 3407, 3601
Tramp preacher. 3598
Trance dance. 3707
Trance, healing, and hallucination. 3707
Trance in Bali. 1540
Trancendental physics. 3519
Trances. 3707
Tranquility through prayer. 2872
Tranquility without pills (all about transcendental meditation) 3708
Trans-Atlantic conservative Protestantism in the evangelical free and mission covenant traditions. 1546, 2846
Transactions of the New York ecclesiological society. 1855. 1161
Transactions of the third International congress for the history of religions. 3093
Transactions (Theosophical Society, Blavatsky Lodge) 3688
Transactions. v. 1-[1858-76. 2596
Transatlantic exchange. 2957
Transatlantic revivalism. 3233
Transcendence. 3707
Transcendence and immanence. 2562
Transcendence and immanence: reconstruction in the light of process thinking. 3625
Transcendence of God. 3707
Transcendence of God in Philo. 2831, 3707
Transcendent evolution. 3072
Transcendent self. 2462
Transcendent selfhood. 2320
Transcendent unity of religions. 3104
Transcendental astrology. 96
Transcendental magic. 2312
Transcendental magic, its doctrine and ritual. 2312
Transcendental meditation. 3708
Transcendental meditation; Maharishi Mahesh Yogi and the Science of creative intelligence. 3708
Transcendental meditation primer. 3708
Transcendental meditation program for business people. 3708
Transcendental mirage. 3707
Transcendental physics. 3519
... Transcendentalism. 3708
Transcendentalism in New England. 3708
Transcendentalism truly remarkable. 3708
Transcendentalist ministers. 3708
Transcript of Edward Taylor's Metrical history of Christianity. 3590
Transcript of Edward Taylor's Metrical hiustory of Christianity. 1189

Transfer of religious to another community. 2577
Transfiguration. 2067
Transfiguration of Christ. 2067
Transfiguration of life. 34, 1339
Transfiguration of life by a modernist faith. 3137
Transfiguration of politics. 1086
Transfigured church. 1341
Transfigured cosmos. 2647
Transfigured tales. 3199
Transfigured world. 838
Transfiguring of the cross. 2034, 2934
Transformation in Christ. 1003, 3483, 3490, 3628
Transformation in Christ on the Christian attitude of mind. 1053
... The transformation of early Christianity from an eschatological to a socialized movement. 1093, 3657
Transformation of Hawaii. 2524
Transformation of man. 1358
Transformation of Tate. 3589
Transformation of the Hummingbird. 3721
Transformation of the scientific world view. 3078
Transformation of the twelve. 70
Transformation the way into the kingdom of God. 3029
Transformational analysis of the syntax of Ælfric's Lives of saints. 47
Transformations of the war oracle in Old Testament prophecy. 568, 2671
Transformed. 1754, 3229, 3876
Transformed Europeans. 660
Transformed life. 469
Transformed red man. 1901
Transformed temperaments. 993
Transforming Bible study. 643, 1170
Transforming cross. 2057
Transforming friendship. 979
Transforming light. 3121
Transforming mind. 3683
Transforming moment. 1107
Transforming power of God. 979
Transient and permanent in Christianity. 3726
Transition. 3176
Transition, a recurring experience. 1413
Transition and revolution. 3034
Transition and tradition in moral theology. 949
Transition called death, a recurring experience. 1413
Transition in African beliefs. 2553
Transitions in Biblical scholarship. 201
Transits and planetary periods. 96
Translated Bible, 1534-1934. 290, 2276
Translated prophet. 1506
Translating & understanding the Old Testament. 485, 2375
Translating for King James. 271, 674
Translating the Bible. 289
Translating the New Testament Epistles 1604-1611. 368, 2194
Translating the Word of God, with scripture and topical indexes. 653
Translation. 1656
Translation and exposition of the Epistle of Jude. 425
Translation and exposition of the First epistle of the apostle Peter. 325
Translation debate. 652
Translation of extracts of biographical notes, memories from childhood, youth, etc. 1295, 3422
Translation of John's Gospel. 414
Translation of Lao Tzu's Tao te ching and Wang Pi's commentary. 3130
Translation of Luke's Gospel. 320
Translation of Paul's Epistle to the Romans. 466
Translation of St. Thomas More's Responsio ad Lutherum. 2276
Translation of the Gospels. 385
Translation of the New Testament. 320
... A translation of the treatise Chagigah from the Babylonian Talmud. 3583
Translation procedure of Epiphanius-Cassiodorus in the Historia tripartia, books I and II. 744
Translations of Finish songs. 1873
Translations of Finnish songs. 1873
Translations of the Bible. 655
Translations of the writings of the fathers down to A.D. 325. 1617
Translator's guide to the Gospel of Mark. 438
Translator's handbook on the First Letter from Peter. 325
(transliterated): Keriah. 2940
Transmigration of the seven Brahmans. 689
Transmission of the mind outside the teaching. 3893
Transmitted light. 3506
Transparent woman. 121

Transpersonal psychologies. 3000
Transplanted heather. 3125
Transplanted truths. 447, 470
Transport of delight. 719, 1291
Transylvania in 1922. 3725
Trap-door spider. 2676
Trappist writes home. 3131
Trauma of transparency. 1316
Traume eines Geistersehers ; Der Unterschied der Gegenden im Raume. 3506, 3570
Travail of religious liberty. 3192
Travail of the soul. 3688
...A travel book for juniors. 3165
Travel lessons on the life of Jesus. 1992
...A travelbook for juniors. 3151
Traveler for God. 2929, 2685
Traveler for the Brethren. 1283
Travelers' guide to historic Mormon America. 2618
Traveler's narrative written to illustrate the episode of the Bab. 122
Traveler's prayer book. 3710
Traveling light. 1006, 3529
Traveling secretary. 3873
Traveling the King's highway. 2973
Traveling the way. 333
Traveling toward sunrise. 1430
Traveller. 2392
Traveller in eternity. 1786
Traveller's guide to saints in Europe. 3283
Traveller's narrative written to illustrate the episode of the Bab. 122
Travels and adventures of St. Paul. 2803
Travels and controversies of Friar Domingo Navarrete, 1618-1686. 911
Travels in faith from tradition to reason. 3022
Travels in Jewry. 2090
Travels in North Africa. 2097
Travels in Oudamovia. 2383
Travels in the world of the Old Testament. 184, 485
Travels of Amacharsis the younger. 1765
Travels of an Irish gentleman in search of a religion. 789
Travels of Macarius. 2304, 3256
Travels of Macarius, 1652-1660. 2304, 3256
Travels of Our Saviour. 1979
Travels of Paul. 2803
Travels of True Godliness. 3129, 3152
Travels of True Godliness and Ungodliness. 3152
Travels of True Godliness: from the beginning of the world to this present day. 3152
Tread of years. 3047
Treasure and the vessel. 615
Treasure book. 3549
Treasure chest. 3581
Treasure for my daughter. 1614
Treasure from the haunted pagoda. 2505
Treasure House book of children's Bible stories. 620
Treasure-house of the living religions. 3268
Treasure hunt. 2536, 2957
Treasure hunt in Judaism. 2120
Treasure in a field. 3275, 3419
Treasure in clay. 668, 3401
Treasure in earthen vessel. 1119
Treasure in earthen vessels. 473, 1119
Treasure infinite. 385
Treasure Island—church growth among Taiwan's urban Minnan Chinese. 2552
Treasure of El Dorado. 3521, 3813
Treasure of free men. 291
Treasure of hymns. 1873
Treasure of Qumran. 1410
Treasure of the caves. 1410
Treasure of the devout soul. 2384, 2395
Treasure of the Gospel. 1558
Treasure of the Magi. 3898
Treasure of the parables. 2024
Treasure to share. 26, 2534
Treasure untold. 74
Treasured themes from familiar hymns. 1873
Treasured volume of prayers. 2894
Treasures from the Bible. 250
Treasures from the Greek New Testament. 425
Treasures in the earth. 2519
Treasures new and old. 1518
Treasures of darkness. 1445, 2413
Treasures of hope. 2735
Treasures of hope for the evening of life. 2735
Treasures of Islam. 86
Treasures of Judaica. 2075
Treasures of life. 1009
Treasures of silver. 1453
Treasures of Taiwan. 2523
Treasures of the churches of France. 922
Treasures of the rosary. 3248

Treasures on the Tebetan middle way. 3586
Treasures to share. 2614
Treasures unearthed. 679
Treasury of A. W. Tozer. 918, 3634
Treasury of Alexander Whyte. 2935
Treasury of Andrew Murray. 3481
Treasury of Bible highlights. 303
Treasury of Bible knowledge. 302
Treasury of Bible masterpieces. 602
Treasury of Biblical quotations. 301, 612
Treasury of books for Bible study. 644
Treasury of Catholic reading. 867
Treasury of Catholic song. 812
Treasury of Catholic thinking. 3637
Treasury of Charles H. Spurgeon. 3632
Treasury of Christian poetry. 1022
Treasury of Christian teaching. 3180
Treasury of Christmas songs and carols. 742
Treasury of comfort. 1350, 1354
Treasury of David. 576
Treasury of devotion. 1432, 1441
Treasury of devotional aids for home and school. 1842
Treasury of Dwight L. Moody. 1559
Treasury of early Christianity. 1020
Treasury of essays, dealing with various characters cast in the life of Christ, the Lord's Prayer and the Hail Mary, and the Eight Beatitudes. 339
Treasury of faith. 967
Treasury of funeral messages. 1691
Treasury of Gospel gems. 3373
Treasury of great prayers. 2892
Treasury of great sermons. 3344
Treasury of Greek mythology. 2663
Treasury of holiday thoughts. 1614
Treasury of icons, sixth to seventeenth centuries. 1881
Treasury of illustrations. 1841
Treasury of inspirational classics. 1455
Treasury of inspirational illustrations. 1843
Treasury of Jewish folklore. 1631, 1632
Treasury of Jewish holidays. 1614
Treasury of Jewish inspiration. 2697
Treasury of Jewish quotations. 3014
Treasury of Jewish thoughts. 2152
Treasury of Judaism. 2075
Treasury of Masonic thought. 1668
Treasury of parables. 1323
Treasury of prayer. 2888
Treasury of prayers. 2297, 2298
Treasury of quiet talks. 1447
Treasury of quotations on Christian themes. 3111
Treasury of quotations on religious subjects from the great writers and preachers of all ages. 1842
Treasury of R. A. Torrey. 1561
Treasury of religious plays. 3144
Treasury of religious verse. 1022, 3207
Treasury of responsa. 3219
Treasury of Russian spirituality. 2648, 3478
Treasury of sacred polyphony. 3271
Treasury of sermon illustrations. 1842
Treasury of stewardship illustrations. 3529
Treasury of story-sermons for children. 909
Treasury of the Bible. 615
Treasury of the Christian faith. 3204
Treasury of the Christian world. 1841
Treasury of the cross. 1388
Treasury of the Kingdom. 3204
Treasury of the Midrash. 2463
Treasury of the Psalter. 574, 577
Treasury of the world's brightest gems of thought, song and story. 3198
Treasury of the world's great sermons. 3346
Treasury of thought. Mother, Home, and Heaven. 2624
Treasury of "Tradition" 2751
Treasury of W. Graham Scroggie. 3136
Treasury of witchcraft. 2730
Treasury of witchcraft and devilry. 3823
Treasury of world philosophy. 2832
Treat me cool, Lord. 3882
Treat me easy. 2263
Treatie of justification, 1569. 763, 2161
Treatise. 36
Treatise against dicing, dancing, plays, and interludes. 36
Treatise against Hermogenes. 1807
Treatise by way of a dialogue on cause and effect. 3615, 3711
Treatise concerning baptism. 134
Treatise concerning enthusiasme (1655) 1520
Treatise concerning eternal and immutable morality. 943
Treatise concerning heaven and hell. 1795
Treatise concerning religious affections in three parts. 1512

Treatise concerning the Lords supper. 2250, 2260

... A treatise concerning the principles of human knowledge. 2179

Treatise concerning the sanctification of the Lord's day. 3548

Treatise De Spiritu Sancto, the nine homilies of the Hexaemeron and the letters. 1835

Treatise of auricular confession. The forerunner of Bels downefall. 186, 1327

Treatise of daunces. 3607

Treatise of dogmatic theology. 3641

Treatise of ghosts. 77

Treatise of keeping the heart. 961

Treatise of Lorenzo Valla on the Donation of Constantine. 1476

Treatise of mentall prayer ; [A treatise of the presence of God]. 2885

Treatise of St. Bernard,   abbat of Clairvaux, concerning grace and free will, addressed to William, abbat of St. Thierry. 1657

Treatise of spiritual life. 2642, 2643, 3477

Treatise of the images of Christ. 1884

Treatise of the pope's supremacy. 2767

Treatise of the Sabbatical cycle and the Jubilee. 3262

Treatise of three conversions, 1603-1604. 816, 2820

Treatise on atonement. 104, 3752

Treatise on baptism. 136, 732, 1906

Treatise on being born again. 3051

Treatise on Bible prophecies. 608

Treatise on Bible prophecy. 608

Treatise on Biblical criticism. 241

Treatise on Christian perfection. 2818

Treatise on church government. 1684

... A treatise on church order. 1240

Treatise on class meetings. 1286

Treatise on contemporary religious jurisprudence. 1634

Treatise on cosmic fire. 2723

Treatise on covenanting with God. 1377

Treatise on divine union. 2637

Treatise on fundamental doctrines of the Christian religion. 1675

Treatise on God. 1728

Treatise on God as first principle. 2672

Treatise on grace. 1751

Treatise on happiness. 1785

Treatise on hell. 1070

Treatise on homiletics. 2902

Treatise on human nature. 1855

Treatise on justification. 2160

Treatise on justification by faith. 2160

Treatise on keeping the heart. 961

Treatise on law (Summa theologica, questions 90-97) 949

Treatise on magic. 2313

Treatise on man. 2322, 2327

Treatise on New Testament history. 475

Treatise on overpopulation. 955

Treatise on prayer. 2868

Treatise on prayer and meditation. 2877

Treatise on preaching. 2901

Treatise on psalmody. 579

Treatise on regeneration. 3051

Treatise on religious affections. 3058

Treatise on religious experience. 1358

Treatise on response & retribution. 3587

Treatise on self knowledge. 1324

Treatise on separate substances. 3538

Treatise on Sunday laws. 3548

Treatise on that being born again. 3051

Treatise on that being born again, without which no man can be saved. 3051

Treatise on the apostolic tradition of St. Hippolytus of Rome. 1239

Treatise on the atonement of Christ. 106

Treatise on the character of Jesus Christ, and on the Trinity in unity of the Godhead. 2044, 3713

Treatise on the Christian doctrine of marriage. 2337

Treatise on the divine nature. 3712

Treatise on the faith of the Freewill Baptists. 1652

Treatise on the gods. 3062

Treatise on the incarnation of the Eternal Word. 1892

Treatise on the law of the Protestant Episcopal church in the United States. 2966

Treatise on the law on cults. 1393

Treatise on the lawfulness of defensive war. 3791

Treatise on the Lenten season. 2209

Treatise on the Lord's prayer from a practical standpoint. 2246

... Treatise on the love of God. 2264, 2266

Treatise on the millennium. 2464, 2465

Treatise on the miracles of Christ and mind healing of the present day as viewed by a physician. 2410

Treatise on the mode and subjects of Christian baptism. 136

Treatise on the mode of baptism. 135

Treatise on the preparation and delivery of sermons. 2898

Treatise on the right use of the Father in the decision of controversies existing at this day in religion. 1617

Treatise on the right use of the Fathers in the decision of controversies existing at this day in religion. 1617

Treatise on the seven rays. 3683

Treatise on the spiritual life. 3490

Treatise on the true devotion to the Blessed Virgin Mary. 2359

Treatise on the virtues. 3782

Treatise on theism. 3609

Treatise on white magic. 2722, 2723, 2730

Treatise to Theophilus. 355

Treatiseon the Lord's Supper. 2250

Treatises. 595, 1741

Treatises and sermons. 1491, 2647

Treatises on marriage and remarriage. 2344

Treatises on penance: On penitence and On purity. 2812

Treatises on various subjects. 3634

Treatises upon several subjects, 1698. 3623

Treatment of the capital sins and the Decalogue in the German sermons of Berthold von Regensburg. 195, 2910

Treatment of the Jews in the Greek Christian writers of the first three centuries. 2118

Treatment of the remains at the eucharist after holy communion and the time of the ablutions. 2251

Treatuse Ta'anit of the Babylonian Talmud. 3584

Treaty and concordat between the Holy See and Italy. 1322

Treaty of the great King. 510

Tree. 3825

Tree and the Master. 2012

Tree at the center of the world. 2506

Tree bears fruit. 2057

Tree grows in Missouri. 2296

Tree of knowledge. 3497

Tree of life. 523, 1623, 1890, 2313, 3050, 3204, 3264, 3370, 3514, 3776

Tree of life lost and regained. 296

Tree of light. 2408

Tree of love. 2271

Tree of mythology. 2653

Tree of worlds. 1385

Treehouse tales. 617

Trees, fruits, and flowers of the Bible. 480

Trekking along the trail. 2599

Tremendum. 1825

Trend of the ages. 1048

Trends and counter-trends among American Catholics. 826

Trends and frontiers of religious thought. 3211

Trends and issues in Catholic education. 832

Trends in Protestant giving. 1167

Trends in Protestant social idealism. 1134

Trends of Christian thinking. 3618

Trends of thought and Christian truth. 3211

Trends on ministerial membership of annual conferences of the United Methodist Church, 1960-1970. 3734

Trennung von Kirche und Staat? 1142

Trent. 3710

Tretyse of loue. 2266

Trevenen. 1498, 3501

Trial and condemnation of Christ as a legal question. 2068

Trial and conviction of Jesus Christ from a legal standpoint. 2067

Trial and death of Jesus. 2068

Trial and death of Jesus Christ. 2068

Trial and triumph. 461

Trial before Pilate. 2068

Trial by death and fire. 1256, 2560

Trial by fire. 992

Trial by torture. 1934

Trial, crucifixion and resurrection of Jesus. 2030

Trial of C. B. Reynolds for blasphemy. 670, 3234

Trial of C. B. Reynolds for blasphemy, at Morristown, N. J., May 19th and 20th, 1887. 3192, 3234

Trial of Christ. 163, 2029

Trial of Christ, in seven stages. 2068

Trial of faith. 1088, 3703

Trial of Jesus. 1951, 2068, 2069

Trial of Jesus before Caiaphas and Pilate. 2068

Trial of Jesus Christ. 2068, 2069

Trial of Jesus from a lawyer's standpoint. 2068

Trial of Jesus from Jewish sources. 2068

Trial of Jesus of Nazareth. 2068, 2069

Trial of Jorge de Almeida by the Inquisition in Mexico. 27, 1909

Trial of Judas Iscariot. 2156

Trial of Luther. 2272, 3852

Trial of Mr. William Parkinson. 3820

Trial of Mrs. Duncan. 3501

Trial of Oliver Plunkett. 2854

Trial of spirits. 1288

Trial of the Lancaster witches, A.D. MDCXII. 2937, 3827

Trial of the Lancaster witches, 1612. 2938, 3827

Trial of the Rev. David Swing, before the Presbytery of Chicago. 3572

Trial of the Rev. Stephen H. Tyng, jr. 3720

Trial of the stick of Joseph. 680

Trial of the Templars. 3598

Trial of the witnesses of the resurrection Jesus. 1420, 2053

Trial of the witnesses of the resurrection of Jesus. 1420, 2053

Trial of virtue, a sacred poem. 550

Trials and crucifixion of Christ. 2068

Trials and travels of brother John Israel. 2669

Trials and triumph of Job. 551

Trials and triumphs. 3136

Trials and triumphs (for a half a century) in the life of G. W. Henry. 3128

Trials and triumphs (for half a century) in the life of G. W. Henry ... Together with the religious experience of his wife. To which are added, one hundred spiritual songs, with music. 3128

Trials and triumphs for three score years and ten in the life of G. W. Henry ... together with the religious experience of his wife. 3128

Trials and triumphs of a young preacher. 3129

Trials and triumphs of faith. 3125

Trials and triumphs of the Catholic church in America during four hundred years. 833

Trials, experience. 1703

Trials of a country parson. 3129

Trials of a translator. 655

Trials of great men of the Bible. 2932

Trials of Jesus. 2034, 3353

Trials, tears, and triumph. 928, 3243

Trials, tragedies, & triumphs. 1984

Triangle. 730, 2923, 3650

Tribal myths of Orissa. 2664

Tribe of Zambe. 2921

Tribes of Israel. 499, 2715, 3719

Tribes of Yahweh. 598, 2090, 3439

Tribulation people. 3319

Tribulation worketh. 1008

Tribunal reporter. 2341

Tribute of affection to the memory of Rev. John Jennings. 1942

Tribute of affection to the memory of the late Rev. George W. Cole. 1306

Tribute of love and gratitude to our faithful teacher, Augusta E. Stetson, C.S.D. 3527

Tribute to James Stetson Wilson. 3819

Tribute to Mary. 2357

Tribute to Menno Simons. 2403

Tribute to religion. 1156

Tribute to the angels. 3205

Tribute to the life and character of Rev. Teunis S. Hamlin, D.D. 1783

Tribute to the Little flower of Jesus. 3206

Tribute to the memory of Jane Porter Lincoln. 2230

Tribute to the memory of Rev. John Townsend Coit. 1306, 1693

Tribute to the memory of the Pilgrims. 1337

Tribute to the memory of the Rev. Francis L. Hawks, D.D., LL.D. 1791

Tribute to the Negro preacher, and other sermons and addresses. 2437

Tribute to the triumphant. 2776

Tribute to Thomas Starr King. 2173

Tribute to Very Rev. Dean McNulty. 2310

Tributes of great men to Jesus Christ. 1956

Tributes to the memory of Rev. Thomas Hill, D.D. 1812

Tributes to the memory of the Rev. Henry Anthon. 49

Tributes to Theodore Parker. 2776

Trickster. 3820

Trickster in West Africa. 1631

Tried and transfigured. 2067

Tried as by fire. 3466, 3626

Tried by fire. 340, 366, 3798

'Tried, precious, sure. 1999

Triennial catalogue. 2701

Triennial catalogue of the Theological seminary. 40

Triennial report submitted to the General convention. 3434

Triglot dictionary of Scriptural representative words in Hebrew, Greek, and English. 242

Trilogy on wisdom and celibacy. 877

Trimming the Ark. 1245

Trinitarian controversy. 3714

Trinitarian faith and today's mission. 2554

Trinitarian sermons preached to a Unitarian congregation. 3714

Trinitarian theology East and West. 3694, 3714

Trinitarian way. 1000

Trinity! 674, 2701, 3711, 3712, 3713, 3714

Trinity, 1962. 1434

Trinity and Christian devotion. 3712

Trinity and our moral life according to St. Paul. 1002

Trinity and Pittsburgh. 2850

Trinity and the deity of Christ. 2000

Trinity and the kingdom. 3712

Trinity and the religious experience of man. 3712

Trinity and The unicity of the intellect. 674, 1911

Trinity Church Association and Trinity Mission House. 2701

Trinity church in Newport, Rhode Island. 2705

Trinity church in the city of Boston. 685

Trinity church in the city of Boston, Massachusetts, 1733-1933. 685

Trinity Episcopal Church, 1919-1969. 1898

Trinity in our spiritual life. 3712

Trinity, incarnation, and redemption. 775, 3636

Trinity: is the doctrine biblical? 3711

Trinity Lutheran Church, 1899-1974. 1774, 3714

Trinity: Mother of churches. 2698

Trinity of civilization. 3024

Trinity of man. 991

Trinity science. 3711

Trinity Sunday revisited. 1440, 1804

Trinity, The spectacles, Jewish foods, In praise of purity, Letters. 3714

Trinity whom I adore, meditations. 1508

Trinity's first century. 3523

Trio of talks. 1716

Trip beyond. 1360

Trip into the mystic mind. 2637

Triple crown. 2862

Triple key to unlock the kingdom of heaven. 1451

Triple life of the aged. 3043

Triple semi-centennial anniversary of St. Mark's church, Bedford avenue. 1790

Triple soul. 696

Triple tradition of the Exodus. 516

Triple truths of Scripture. 3342

Triple victory. 2067

Triple way. 2644

Triptych of the kingdom. 762

... Trismegetus revealed. 3503

... Tristao de Athayde and the Catholic social movement in Brazil. 35, 690

Triumph in Christ. 2935

Triumph of an Indian widow. 3020

Triumph of Christ. 1966

Triumph of faith. 1285, 3186, 3746

Triumph of faith in Habakkuk. 529

Triumph of God's love. 3384

Triumph of grace in the theology of Karl Barth. 175, 1750

Triumph of Job. 550

Triumph of John and Betty Stam. 2511, 3524

Triumph of life. 3077, 3251

Triumph of light. 2312

Triumph of live. 3244

Triumph of love. 2643

Triumph of mercy in the chariot of praise. 3008

Triumph of Pastor Son. 3458

Triumph of Patience. 2792

Triumph of Satan. 1428

Triumph of suffering love. 1094

Triumph of the Catholic church in the early ages. 810

Triumph of the crucified. 3226

Triumph of the ego. 1052

Triumph of the kingdom of God. 463

Triumph of the missionary motive. 2494

Triumph of the saints. 1469

Triumph of trust. 1346

Triumph of truth. 3125, 3206

Triumph over odds. 2231

Triumph over tears. 3814

Triumph over tragedy. 1350

Triumphant believing. 3731

Triumphant Christianity. 130

Triumphant deaths. 927

Triumphant in suffering. 3540

Triumphant in trouble. 325

Triumphant Jesus. 1975
Triumphant kingdom. 1939
Triumphant living. 3299
Triumphant ministry. 3673
Triumphant personality. 980
Triumphant pilgrimage. 880, 2848
Triumphant way. 3249
Triumphs of archaeology in Bible lands. 207
Triumphs of devine grace. 3207
Triumphs of divine grace exemplified in the life and death of Marshall F. Chappell. 886
Triumphs of faith. 403, 1342, 2510
Triumphs of industry. 1285
Triumphs of the cross. 925
Triumphs of the Gospel in the Belgian Congo. 2513
Triune God. 3711, 3714
Triune man. 1889
Triune principle of life and philosophy of the soul. 3784
Trivialization of the United Presbyterian Church. 3735
Trois heures a vivre. 3382
Trojan horse in the city of God. 783, 3328
Trojan War. 2660
Troop school for Christian soldiers. 3765
Trophies from Cannibal Isles. 2533
Trophies from the missionary museum. 2518
Trophies of song. 1202
Tropi gradules. 849
Tropospheric radiowave propagation beyond the horizon. 3715
... The troubadour of God. 1644
Troubadours of Paradise. 3280
Trouble. 2136
Trouble with barnacles. 2387
'The trouble with Catholics. 759
Trouble with the church. 2906
Troubled heart. 3135
Troubleshooter for God in China. 1368, 2485
Troward's comments on the Psalms. 577
True and complete portraiture of Methodism. 2420
True and faithful. 3430
True and false. 1951
True and false courage. 1375
True and false possession. 1422
True and false repentance. 1556
True and false universality of Christianity. 1097
True and invisible Rosicrucian order. 3250
True and lively Word. 2899
True and living God. 1066
True and the beautiful in nature. 3255
True apostolate. 3485
True believer. 137
True boundaries of the Holy Land. 561, 2761
True catholic no Romanist. 1219
True Christian religion. 958, 2692, 3572
True Christian, true church, true teachings. 990
True Christian unity. 1047
True Christianity. 1005, 1047
True chronicle of the life and wild times of Peter Cartwright. 743
True church. 1174, 2286, 3208
True church and her enemies. 148
True church, indicated to the inquirer. 1120
True cross. 1826
True deceivers. 2324
True devotion to Mary. 2359
True devotion to the blessed sacrament. 2253
True devotion to the Blessed Virgin. 2359
True doctrine of prayer. 2869
True end and design of the holy sacrament of the Lord's supper. 2250
True estimate of life, and how to live. 970
True evangelism. 1553, 1563
True evangelist. 1930, 2443
True evolution of man. 975
True experiences in communicating with the dead. 3501
True experiences in prophecy. 2949
True face of the Kirk. 1234
True-freedom, divinity. 1061
True functions of the Sunday school. 3553
True gospel revealed again from Jesus. 3510
True heroism. 3345
True history of Jesus the Christ. 3496
True history of laying on of hands upon baptized believers as such. 135, 2131
True history of Moses, Aaron, Joshua, and others, deduced from a review of the Bible. 1654
True history of the Brooklyn scandal. 184
True holiness. 3299
True joy from Assisi. 92, 1640
True life. 1022, 1324, 1752, 3489

True likeness. 1826
True love. 1047
True Messiah, in Scripture light. 2041
True method of promoting perfect love. 2818
True morality and its counterfeits. 1584
True mysteries of life. 722

True mystic. 2641
True or false? 241
True organization of the new church, as indicated in the writings of Emanuel Swedenborg, and demonstrated by Charles Fourier. 3569
True origin of Mormon polygamy. 2605
True origin of the Book of Mormon. 679
True path. 1013
True path for the true churchman wandering in the mazes of Protestantism. 792, 2766
True path; or, Gospel temperance. 2631, 3596
True path; or, The Murphy movement and gospel temperance. 2632, 3596
True patriotism; letters, lectures, and notes, 1939-45. 676, 3632
True penitent portrayed in a practical exposition of the Fifty-first psalm. 3218
True perfection which God requires attainable on earth. 2125
True philosophy of life as it related to the present and the future. 3645
True prayer. 2874
True prayer for teachers. 2879
True prayer in business. 2695
True priest. 115, 2791
True Prince of the tribe of Judah. 1961
True prophet of the closing days. 670
True relation of the life and death of the Right Reverend father in God William Bedell. 183
True religion delineated. 1334
True resurrection. 3221
True revival. 3229
True saints; revival messages. 1556
True Scripture-doctrine concerning some important points of Christian faith. 2914
True Scripture doctrine of original sin stated and defended. 3414, 3591
True spirit of worship. 3853
True spirit return. 3508
True spiritualism. 1318, 3507
True spirituality. 3521
True spiritualsim. 3241, 3498
True spouse of Jesus Christ. 2229
True state and character of the unregenerate. 1847
True stories. 896
True stories by a metaphysician. 2694
True stories for little people. 616
True stories of Mormon pioneer courage. 1231, 2618
True stories of young Christian. 660
True story of a revival. 3232
True story of John Smyth, the Se-Baptist, as told by himself and his contemporaries; with an inquiry whether dipping were a new mode of baptism in England, in or about 1641; and some consideration of the historical value of certain extracts from the alleged "ancient records" of the Baptist church of Epworth. Crowie, and Butterwick (Eng.), lately published and claimed to suggest important modifications of the history of the 17th century. With collections toward a bibliography of the first two generations of the Baptist controversy. By Henry Martyn Dexter. Boston, Lee and Shepard, 1881. 3427
True story of Saint Bernadette. 3460
True submission. 1556
True succession in church presidency of the Church of Jesus Christ of latter day saints. 2612, 3217, 3240
True tales of the occult. 1709
True temperance platform. 23
True, the good, and the beautiful. 3716
True theory of Christianity; or, The lost book. 1051
True union. 159
True unity of Christ's church. 1042
True values. 3350
True vine. 424
True vine and its branches. 2020
True visible church. 2287
True way. 3131
True wilderness. 1228
True word of God as applied to religious principles, times, places and men. 3848
True words for brave men. 1226
True worship. 2238, 2239
Truest story. 201
Truly, I say to you. 3337
"Truly stories from the surely Bible" 252
Truman Marcellus Post, D. D. 2865
Trumpet. 463

Trumpet call of Reformation. 1464
Trumpet-calls. 1360
Trumpet notes in Congo. 2513
Trumpet of a prophecy. 2491
Trumpet of prophecy. 1939, 3085
Trumpet of salvation. 682, 3293
Trumpet of the Lord. 160
Trumpet shall sound. 2400
Trumpet sounds. 721, 1301
Trumpeter of God. 2182
Trumpets in the morning. 2302, 2787
Trumpets of God. 3295
Trust yourself to life. 3684
Trustful living. 2389
Trusting in God for five million dollars. 2876
Trustworthiness of religious experience. 1587
Truth. 92, 1069, 1394, 2180, 3716
Truth about Catholics. 788
Truth about Christ and the atonement. 1958
Truth about Christian science. 1035, 1495, 1496
Truth about conventionism. 3464, 3465
Truth about death and life hereafter. 3803
Truth about evolution. 1580
Truth about Jesus. Is he a myth? 2008, 3023
Truth about life. 2226
Truth about Mormonism. 2606
Truth about our dead told by those who know. 1408
Truth about religion. 3064
Truth about religion in Russia. 3256
Truth about scientology. 1234
Truth about Seventh-Day Adventism. 3382
Truth about spiritualism. 3497, 3513
Truth about the Bible. 236, 649
Truth about the Jews. 2077
Truth about "The protocols of Zion" 2952
Truth about the Russian Church abroad. 3258
Truth about tongues. 1717
Truth about witchcraft. 3823
Truth advanced in the correction of many gross & hurtful erros. 1682
Truth advocated. 463
Truth about the so-called "Luther's Testament in English," 2282
Truth and certainty. 835
Truth and consistency of divine revelation. 58
Truth and counter truth. 3647
Truth and dialogue in world religions: conflicting truth-claims. 3108
Truth and excellence of the Christian religion exhibited. 1097
Truth and expression. 3716
Truth and facts of the United House of Prayer for All People and the most honorable Bishop W. McCollough, leader. 2306
Truth and falsehood in religion. 1059
Truth and life. 1049, 2279, 2283
Truth and life, an outline of modern theology. 3653
Truth and life in Jesus. 3352
Truth & light. 3479
Truth and method. 1855
Truth and symbol. 3716
Truth and the evidence. 3216
Truth and the faith. 1047
Truth and the life. 2964, 3343
Truth and the person in Christian theology. 3660
Truth and tradition in Chinese Buddhism. 705
Truth as encounter. 1457
Truth by reason and by revelation. 3083
Truth defended. 179, 2612
Truth displayed. 1725, 2419
Truth, do you know me? 3477
Truth for each day. 1431
Truth for our time. 164
Truth for the good life. 64
Truth for today. 933, 3355
Truth ideas of an M.D. 2410
Truth illuminated. 1841
Truth in Christ. 1228
Truth in Christian science. 1030
Truth in satire concerning infallible popes. 802
... The truth in the case. 3816, 3833
Truth in the light of the sure word of prophecy. 607
Truth in the religions. 3087
Truth is everybody's business. 3716
Truth is one. 3141
Truth is the word of God. 3615
Truth is two-eyed. 1082
Truth marches on. 1228
Truth, not legend. 3616
Truth of Christianity. 67
Truth of faith. 1592
Truth of God incarnate. 1894, 2046

Truth of history. 497
Truth of it. 127
Truth of life is love. 2266
Truth of life, love, liberty. 2694
Truth of papal claims. 2753, 2768
Truth of religion. 3099
Truth of spiritualism. 3505
Truth of the Apostles' creed. 73
Truth of the apostolic gospel. 476
"Truth" of the Bible. 232, 277
Truth of the Catholic religion. 756
Truth of the gospel. 3661
Truth of the hour, not the truth of yesterday, not the truth for tomorrow, but the truth for today. 1734
Truth on canvas, over the air. 1555
Truth on fire. 380, 1556
Truth on trial. 734, 2485
Truth regarding swine's flesh. 781
Truth seeker collection of forms, hymns, and recitations. 1869
Truth shall make you free. 1053, 1941
Truth stranger than fiction. 2848, 3124
Truth that frees. 3717
Truth that leads to eternal life. 1941
Truth that makes men free. 141
Truth triumphant. 1181, 1940
Truth unchanged, unchanging. 2300, 2324, 3369
Truth unfolded. 165
Truth unmasked and error exposed in theology and metaphysics, moral government, and moral agency. 3646
Truth vs. dogma. 800
Truth versus untruth. 1078
Truth was their star. 3284
Truth which makes us free. 2287
Truth will liberate you. 1659
Truth will make you free. 2398, 3717
Truthfulness and tragedy. 946
Truthfulness; the future of the church. 781, 1245
...Truths and untruths of evolution. 1579
Truths for eternity. 955
Truths for the people. 3664
Truths in tension. 3082
Truths men live by. 65, 2436
Truths of religion and the Bible! 1656
Truths of spiritualism. 3519
Truths of the Catholic church. 790
Truths that abide. 75
Truths that transform. 3663
Truths to live by. 66, 1052
Truths to live by, a companion to "Everyday Christian life," 960
Truths we live by. 2833
Try God. 1367, 3790
Try reading the Bible this way. 613
Try-square. 3142
Try the spirits. 2990
Tryal of the witnesses, and The use and intent of prophecy. 608, 1420, 2053
Tryanny of time. 1472
Trying new sandals. 1120
Trying to be a Christian. 991
Trying to live like a Christian in a world that doesn't understand. 972
Tryst with destiny in a lost world. 1057
Tryst with the Holy Trinity. 1836, 2249
Tsedek: where modern science is examined and where it is attempted to save man from physical and spiritual enslavement. 1538
Tsuni-llGoam. 1848
Tuamotuan legends. 2667
Tuamotuan religion. 3717
Tuan Hoover of Borneo. 1845, 2504
Tubingen School. 351, 3717
Tudor books of private devotion. 1455
Tudor books of saints and martyrs. 1455
Tudor chruch music. 1207
Tudor church music. 1207
Tudor prelates and politics. 1759
Tudor puritanism. 3007, 3009
Tudor tapestry. 3039
Tudor translations of the colloquies of Erasmus (1536-1584) 1526
Tudorbooks of private devotion. 1455
Tudors and the church, 1509-1553. 3038
Tufts papers on religion. 3625
TULIP. 730
Tulpehocken Trinity United Church of Christ, 1727-1977. 3718
Tulsa Catholics. 1826
Tulsa lectures. 1272
Tumbleweed. 1419
Tumbling walls. 3736
Tumultuous years. 3313
Tune in. 3882
Tune in to God. 998
Tuned-in Christians. 1154
Turbulent world. 2302
Turin fragments of Tyconius' commentary on Revelation. 457
Turkey, ecumenical pilgrimage. 1044, 2126

Turkish cruelties upon the Armenian Christians. 82
Turn again to life. 995
Turn but a stone. 906
Turn loose. 174, 928
Turn on to life. 955
Turn over any stone. 3540
Turned-on church in an uptight world. 323, 1064
Turned on to Jesus. 1574
Turner's history of the Independent order of good Samaritans and daughters of Samaria. 2662
Turning. 1361, 1775
Turning east. 1378, 1393
Turning on lights. 3757
Turning point. 1255
Turning point, Zionism and reformed Judaism. 3033
Turning points. 1234, 3750
Turning points of general church history. 1173
Turning things upside down. 990
Turning to Christ. 1246, 1524
Turning to God. 1357, 3372
Turning world. 1042
Turnpikes and dirt roads. 3132
Turns again home. 39
Turquoise path. 2306
Turretin on the atonement of Christ. 108
Turtle and the two ducks. 1588
Turtle on a fencepost. 993, 1511
Tuscan penitent. 2332
Tutankhamen, Amenism, Atenism and Egyptian monotheism. 1501, 3718
Tutors unto Christ. 389
Twain have met. 2593
Twain shall meet. 1155, 1780
'Tween-age ambassadors. 156
Tweintieth century miracle. 3131
Twelfth-century decretal collections. 736
Twelfth-century homilies in ms. Bodley 343. 3367
Twelfth-century reform. 820
Twelfth Christmas. 1111
Twelfth man in the huddle. 102
Twelve. 70, 347, 1020
Twelve against the gods. 659
Twelve angels from hell. 1255
Twelve apostles. 70, 71, 72, 75
Twelve apostles of California. 660
Twelve baskets full. 1033, 3528
Twelve baskets of crumbs. 1509
Twelve becoming. 2404
Twelve came riding. 2426
Twelve Christ chose. 71
Twelve commandments. 1313
Twelve council fathers. 3769
Twelve deeds of Buddha. 703
Twelve devotional programs. 1446
Twelve discourses. 1340, 3010
Twelve facets of reality. 1932
Twelve fruits. 1712
Twelve gates. 871
Twelve great chapters from the Book of Life. 209
Twelve great feasts. 2748
Twelve great questions about Chirst. 2041
Twelve great questions about Christ. 2040, 2932
Twelve great signs of the return of Jesus. 3319
Twelve greatest miracles of my ministry. 2477, 3241
1200 notes. 245
Twelve laws of life. 1314
Twelve lectures on the connexion between science and revealed religion. 3077
Twelve lectures on the doctrines of Christianity. 1071
Twelve lessons from The seven purposes. 3497
Twelve lessons in group evangelism. 1570
Twelve live-wire questions in religions dynamics. 1052
Twelve makers of modern Protestant thought. 3611
Twelve merry fishermen. 2784
Twelve messages. 3515
Twelve minor prophets. 559, 560
Twelve modern apostles and their creeds. 3323
Twelve modern disciples. 1015
Twelve Mormon homes visited in succession on a journey through Utah to Arizona. 3762
Twelve new hymns of Christian patriotism. 1866
Twelve New Testament studies. 349
Twelve object lessons of Scripture. 3616
Twelve Olympians. 660
Twelve powers of man. 3750
Twelve select sermons. 1559
Twelve sermons. 3218, 3357
Twelve sermons on conversion. 3347
Twelve sermons on holiness. 1824
Twelve sermons on repentance. 3347

Twelve sermons on the Holy Spirit. 1836
12 sermons on the second coming of Christ. 3320
Twelve sermons on various subjects. 3347
12 sermons to young people. 3366
12 signs, 12 sons. 202
Twelve speak. 559
Twelve steps to spiritual enlightenment. 3251
Twelve striking sermons. 1557
... Twelve studies on the making of a nation; the beginnings of Israel's history. 2089
Twelve [t]heological [t]ornadoes. 2847
Twelve take stock of us. 71
Twelve, the story of Christ's apostles. 70
Twelve tremendous themes. 652
Twelve virtues of a good teacher. 1498
Twelve who followed Jesus. 71
Twelve who prayed. 923
Twelve who walked in Galilee: character studies of the members of Jesus' cabinet. 71
Twelve who were chosen. 70
Twelve world teachers. 3127
Twelve years among the colored people. 133
Twelve years with Mary Baker Eddy. 1496
Twelvy Negro spirituals. 2680
... Twentieth anniversary of the pastorate of the Rev. Samuel Harrison Greene ... of Calvary Baptist church. 144
Twentieth century. 3863
Twentieth century addresses. 2936
Twentieth century Aldersgate. 1008, 3805
Twentieth century atlas of the Christian world. 2525
Twentieth century Baptist. 141, 152
Twentieth century Baptists. 144
Twentieth century Bible. 3499
Twentieth century Bible commentary. 225
Twentieth century Catholicism. 852, 3637
Twentieth century Christ. 1059, 3719
Twentieth century Christianity. 1063, 1182
Twentieth century church music. 1207
Twentieth-century cross. 3329
20th century defenders of the faith. 3657
Twentieth century discipleship. 954
Twentieth century encyclopedia of Catholicism. 3637
Twentieth century faith: hope and survival. 3067
Twentieth century in Europe. 1542
Twentieth century interpretation of Paul's epistle to the Ephesians. 364
Twentieth-century interpretation of the Bible. 234
Twentieth century interpretations of Gulliver's travels. 3572
Twentieth century interpretations of Samson Agonistes. 2468
Twentieth century interpretations of the Book of Job. 550
Twentieth century interpretations of The praise of folly. 1526
20th century litany to the Poverello. 3487
Twentieth century miracle. 2477, 3801
Twentieth century mystics and sages. 3124
Twentieth century New Testament. 352
Twentieth century New Testament, a translation into modern English. 354
Twentieth-century Onesiphorus. 45, 3580
Twentieth century outlook upon Holy Scripture. 199
Twentieth century outside Europe. 1182
Twentieth century paganism. 2757
Twentieth century pioneers. 3467
Twentieth century prophecy. 1472, 2946
20th century prophet. 3621
Twentieth century pulpit. 3346
Twentieth century reformation. 2563
Twentieth century religious thought. 2843
Twentieth century revival. 3229
Twentieth century sermons and addresses. 1467, 3346
Twentieth-century spiritual letters. 3484
Twentieth century story of the Christ. 1989
Twentieth century Sunday school. 3554
20th-century teenagers. 3881
20th-century teenagers by "A friend of youth." 3881
Twentieth century testimony. 986, 2628
Twentieth century theology in the making. 3634
Twentieth plane. 3517
Twenty cases suggestive of reincarnation. 3054, 3055
Twenty centuries of Catholic Church music. 1205, 1206
20 centuries of Christianity. 1176
Twenty centuries of church and state. 1143
20 centuries of great preaching. 3340

20 confirmation sermons. 1329
Twenty ecumenical councils of the Catholic Church. 1373
Twenty eventful years of the Oregon Woman's Christian temperance union, 1880-1900. 3833
Twenty-fifth anniversary. 684, 3797
Twenty-fifth anniversary of the first graduation from the Hebrew union college, Cincinnati, Ohio. 1799
Twenty-fifth anniversary of the pastorate of Rev. Chas. Hawley, d.d. 1791, 1911
Twenty-five best sermons. 3337
... Twenty-five consecration prayers. 2237
Twenty-five excuses answered. 65
Twenty-five exercises of the Way of the cross. 2869
Twenty-five inspiring readings. 1446
Twenty-five stepping stones toward Christ's kingdom. 1049
Twenty-five unbelievable years, 1945 to 1969. 1064
Twenty-five wonderful years. 918
Twenty-five years. 731
Twenty-five years a country parson in Missouri. 3137
Twenty-five years as bishop of London. 3820
Twenty-five years in "Hell's kitchen" 1568
Twenty -- five years of adventuring by faith. 3018
Twenty-five years of American aid to Jews overseas. 32
Twenty-five years of crusading. 3254
Twenty-five years of Jewish education. 2106
Twenty-five years of mission work in Belgian Congo. 1331
Twenty-five years of St. Andrews, September 1865 to September 1890. 3273
Twenty-five years on the outside row of the Northwest Texas Annual Conference. 2455
Twenty-five years with God in India. 2530
Twenty-four American cardinals. 738
Twenty-four books of the Holy Scriptures. 355
Twenty-four books of the Old Testament. Hebrew text and English version. 530
Twenty-four hours a day for everyone. 1432
24 hours to live. 3367
24 hours with Jesus. 983
Twenty-four lessons to illustrate Christian belief and Christian experience by means of Christian hymns. 1875
Twenty-four missionary stories from China. 2510
Twenty-four missionary travelogues. 2494
Twenty-four principles of the doctrine of Jesus Christ and His apostle with Scriptural proofs. 303
Twenty-four views of marriage. 2339
20 funeral sermons. 1693
Twenty minutes of reality. 1359
Twenty miracles of Saint Nicolas. 2707
Twenty missionary stories from Africa. 2490
Twenty missionary stories from India. 2531
Twenty missionary stories from Latin America. 2548
20 most asked questions about the Amish and Mennonites. 35
20 occasional sermons. 2722
Twenty-one discourses on the existence and attributes of God, etc. 1730
Twenty-one years on the firing line. 612
Twenty pathways leading to judgement. 1323
Twenty pathways leading to judgment. 960
Twenty psalms for schools. 2985
Twenty psalms for schools from the Prayer book, the Scottish Psalter and a fresh translation. 300
20 reasons why this present earth may not last another 20 years. 2946
Twenty sermons. 3349
Twenty sermons by famous Scotch preachers. 3376
Twenty-seven books that changed the world, a guide to reading the New Testament. 475
Twenty-seventh wife. 2606, 3868
Twenty-six lessons in inductive Bible study. 641
Twenty-six lessons on Hebrews. 405
Twenty-six years on the losing side. 3129
20 stewardship sermons. 3531
Twenty tales of Irish saints. 3283
Twenty third psalm. 586, 587, 588
Twenty-third psalm in silence. 587
Twenty-third psalm of David. 588

Twenty-three keys to inner peace from the Twenty-third Psalm. 588
Twenty-two missionary stories from Japan. 2490
Twenty years. 2099
Twenty years among the Mexicans. 2540
Twenty years' history of the Woman's home missionary society of the Methodist Episcopal church, 1880-1900. 2458
Twenty years in pulpit. 3126
Twenty years of church federation. 1271
Twenty years of revival effort. 3228
Twenty years with Billy Sunday. 3566
25th anniversary of the Queen of the Most Holy Rosary Church, October, 1975, Elysburg, Pennsylvania. 3011
21st century philosophical handbook for living. 2228
25 Beacon Street. 3724
25 ways to assimilate new members. 1201
Twenty-five wonderful years, 1889-1914. 918
25 years in the service of the Jewish people. 3851
24 hours to live. 3367
24 hours to martyrdom. 3428
24 talks for Sunday School workers' conferences. 3559
21 steps to positive prayer. 2875
2700 quotes for sermons and addresses. 3354
"2300 days" and the sanctuary. 3380
22 devotional talks. 1442
XXII keys of the tarot. 3589
Twentythird psalm, King James version. 587
Twetny-four sermons from St. Ignatus' pulpit. 3344
Twice around the world. 2970
Twice around the world with Alexander, prince of gospel singers. 3126
Twice around the world with the Holy Ghost. 2495, 3135
Twice born. 1362, 3137
Twice-born men. 1358
Twice-born men in America. 2999
Twice-born ministers. 1360
Twice-born stars you would like to know. 1362
Twice called. 1364
Twice seven words. 2072
Twice sold, twice ransomed. 3133
Twice-told Talmud tales. 3585
Twice upon a time. 11, 1011
Twilight. 3211
Twilight in India. 1813
Twilight in the temple. 1663
Twilight of Christianity. 1047, 1090
Twilight of evolution. 1580
Twilight of the saints. 1109
Twilight reveries. 2425
Twin city Methodism. 2475
Twin parables. 2028, 2933
Twin truths of Scripture. 3342
'Twixt God and mammon. 2372
Twleve sermons. 3755
Two academical exercises on subjects bearing the following titles. 2465
Two actual currents in the Thomistic analysis of faith. 1753
Two ancient Red cross tales. 3203
2 1/2 minute talk treasury. 1839
Two and the one. 1586
Two and two make four. 1140
Two angels. 3198
Two articles from the Princeton review. 3708
Two Aztec wood idols. 121
Two Babylons. 800
Two be one. 237, 3749
Two beautiful prayers from the lips of Jesus. 2049
Two Biblical faiths. 1041
Two biographies of William Bedell, bishop of Kilmore. 183
Two bodies. 3461
Two books of homilies appointed to be read in churches. 1225
Two Brahman sources of Emerson and Thoreau. 1815
Two by Evelyn. 918, 2869
Two centuries of American Mennonite literature. 2404
Two centuries of Christian activity at Yale. 3862
Two centuries of ecumenism. 1044, 1491, 1492
Two centuries of Freemasonry. 1666
Two centuries of Methodist concern. 2440, 2681
Two centuries of struggle and growth, 1763-1963. 2403
Two centuries of student Christian movements. 3537
Two centuries of the Church of the brethren. 1236

Two centuries of the Church of the Brethren in Western Pennsylvania, 1751-1950. 1237

Two centuries of the First Baptist church of South Carolina. 1683-1883. 888

Two chains. 3595

Two chapters from the book of my life. 3507

Two churches. 1761

Two cities. 1086, 1143

Two commandments of Christ. 3545

Two contemporary theologies of worship. 3855

Two covenants. 1377

Two covenants and the Sabbath. 3380

Two covenants and the second blessing. 1376

Two covenants between God and man. 1376

Two creation stories in Genesis. 525, 1380

Two crosses of Todos Santos. 2319, 3703

Two crosses, where love is, God is. 2535

Two crowded years. 864

Two cultures. 3314

Two days before. 2030

Two days' debate on the atonement. 106

Two deadly philosophies. 50

... Two decades. 3833

Two different keys. 1091

Two discourses on Christ's self existence. 2002, 3728

Two discourses on the grounds of the Christian's hope. 1344

Two discourses upon the life and character of the Rev. Francis Herron, d. d. 1808

Two dissertations. 1499

Two early American tunes. 1860

Two-edged sword. 500, 503, 3731

Two Elizabethan Puritan diaries. 3007, 3009

Two empires in Japan. 1935

Two epistles. 2817

Two Epistles of Paul to the Thessalonians. 477

Two essays. 1047

Two essays on Biblical and on ecclesiastical miracles. 2477

Two essays on the Decretum of Gratian. 1756

Two eventful nights. 3501

Two-fold covenant. 1375

Two-fold gift of the Holy Ghost. 1828

Two fold life. 3289

Two-fold mission of Jesus. 1956

Two for God. 144, 2543

Two for joy. 3307, 3489

Two friendly letters from Toletus to Philalethes. 2327, 3522

Two friends. 33

Two funeral sermons. 1632

Two generations in perspective. 1744, 2091

Two Glastonbury legends. 88, 1715

Two great books of nature and revelation. 1380

Two great questions. 1737

Two hands, no wings. 1303

Two hands of God. 2857

Two heroes of Cathay. 2187, 2510

Two humanities. 1817, 1818

Two hundred and eighty tiles and symbols of Christ. 2020

... Two hundred and fifty (250) questions and answers on the Jewish festivals. 1624

250 Bible biographies. 215

250 selected plays of Jewish interest. 2100

250 years conquering frontiers. 2671

Two hundred and fifty years of Quakerism at Birmingham. 1684

Two hundred and fifty years of service, 1694-1944. 3587

201 sermon outlines. 3372

210 more choice sermons for children. 907

235 precious poems. 3210

239 days. 2, 130

225 stories for the children's hour. 910

227 heart-reaching illustrations. 1840

Two hundred days as prisoners of the Chinese Communists. 2509

Two hundred fiftieth anniversary of the Kinderhook Reformed Church ... 1712-1962. 3046

Two hundred fifty years. 691

200 Gospel questions and inquiries. 401

200 (religion) class. 1286

200 Scriptural sermon outlines. 3372

Two hundred select illustrations for pastors, teachers, and Christian workers. 1840

Two hundred years. 3436

200 years—and still counting! 3559

Two hundred years of American synagogue architecture. 690, 3577

200 years of Christian ministry of the First Presbyterian church, Rahway, N. J., 1741-1941. 3019

Two hundred years of Old Trinity. 2688

Two hundredth anniversary history of First Reformed Church. 3027

Two hundredth anniversary of Heidelberg union church Reformed and Lutheran. 2813

... Two hundredth anniversary of the First Reformed Protestant Dutch church, of Schenectady, N.Y., June 20th and 21st ... 1880. 3307

Two hundredth anniversary of the Old Dutch church of Sleepy Hollow. 2714

Two-hundredth anniversary of the organization of the United Congregational Church. 2233

Two hundredth anniversary, St. Paul's parish. Newburyport, Mass. 2371

Two in one. 3480, 3505

Two in one flesh. 2339, 2343

Two in the pulpit. 1458

Two into one. 2346

Two Japanese Christian heroes. 3580

Two Jerusalems in prophecy. 610

Two Kenricks. 2167

Two kind of life. 966

Two kindred hearts. 2352

Two kingdoms. 1143, 2465

Two kingdoms and closely related events. 606

Two kingdoms and one world. 3668

Two kings. 909

Two Lamaistic pantheons. 1743

Two leading doctrines of the Catholic church examined. 800, 804

Two lectures on the connection between the Biblical and physical history of man. 2680

Two lectures on the "Sayings of Jesus" recently discovered at Oxyrhynchus. 337

Two lectures on theisms. 3609

Two lectures upon the relations of civil law to church polity, discipline, and property. 1490

Two letters and Short rules of a good life. 3489

Two letters in reply to certain publications of the Rev. Dr. Samuel Miller. 2466

Two letters to a peacemaker. 1092

Two letters to the editor of the Christian's magazine. 1522, 1821

Two letters to the Reverend Moses Stuart. 3193, 3536

Two liturgies, A.D. 1549, and A.D. 1552. 1223

Two lives of Saint Cuthbert. 1397

Two living traditions. 2153

Two masters. 2062, 3441

Two men and Russellism. 1939

2 men in the temple. 431, 632

Two-minute talks. 979

Two minutes a day. 317

Two minutes stories. 3370

Two minutes with God. 900

Two mornings. 2051

Two most wonderful babies who became the two greatest men in the world. 1979, 2621

Two new books for the Bible! 337

Two nights in the bar-rooms, and what I saw. 3595

Two o clock in the morning. 146

Two o'clock in the morning. 146

Two of us in Africa. 2535

Two old faiths. 1813

Two Old Testament theologies. 600, 1503

Two or three gathered together. 2870

Two or three together. 1438

Two parables. 1747

Two paths to one God: Judaism and Christianity. 2153

Two popular philosophic-scientific essays in the spirit of faith and religion. 3103

Two-portraits of St. Teresa of Lisieux. 3691

Two portraits of St. Therese of Lisieux. 3691

Two powers in heaven. 1805

... The two Presbyterian assemblies of 1889. 2928

Two prodigals. 2945

Two prophets, Daniel and Jonah. 1401

Two Quaker sisters. 1677

Two queens of heaven: Aphrodite, Demeter. 55

Two races in one fellowship. 1465

Two rediscovered works of ancient Christian literature: Gregory of Nyssa and Macarius. 1773

Two reformations in the 16th century. 3034

Two Renaissance book hunters. 688, 3709

Two republics. 809

Two roads to truth. 3080

Two sacred worlds. 3064

Two St. Johns of the New Testament. 2127, 2128

Two saints. 193

Two saints: St. Bernard & St. Francis. 193

Two sensons. 9

Two series of lenten sermons on I. Sin and its remedies II. The seven deadly sins. 3411

Two sermons. 1556, 3279

... Two sermons of the resurrection. 2054

Two sermons on the certain and final perseverance of the saints. 2822, 3279

Two sermons on the nature, extent and perfection of the Divine goodness. 3728

Two sermons, preached at Somers, March 18, 1770, when the church and people were under peculiar trials. 3351

Two sermons to men. 1557

Two shall be one. 1608, 2337

Two sides of the school question. 1130

Two sons. 2944

Two sons of oil; or, The faithful witness for magistracy & ministry upon a Scriptural basis. 1377

Two sources of morality and religion. 1534

Two sovereignties. 1143

Two spies on a rooftop. 630

Two stigmatists. 2686, 3532

Two studies in the history of doctrine. 1907

Two studies in the theology of Bonhoeffer. 676

Two studies in virtue. 816, 3405

Two studies on the Roman pontifices. 3245

Two swords or none. 2492

Two-taled dinosaur. 3085

Two Testaments, one Bible. 450

2001, the church in crisis. 2746

Two thousand gospel quotations. 253

Two thousand hours in the Psalms. 575

Two thousand nine hundred and ninety-five Bible questions in chronological order. 218

Two thousand tongues to go. 3705, 3860

2,000 years. 54

Two thousand years after. 3462

Two thousand years in eternity. 1445

2000 years of Christian art. 921

Two thousand years of missions before Carey. 2525

Two to get ready. 2337

... The two treatises of Servetus on the Trinity. 3713

Two types of faith. 2152, 2153

Two Vincentian martyrs. 1303, 2510

Two vital questions. 2882

Two voices. 3489

Two-way prayer. 2869

Two ways of caring. 3678

Two ways of life. 2372

Two ways to heaven. 1449

Two wheels of Dharma. 704

Two witnesses. 2777, 3478

Two worlds. 2098

Two worlds are ours. 451, 2227

Two worlds, Christianity and communism. 1319

Two worlds of attraction. 3494

Two worlds or none. 2492

Two Y men. 3414

Two-year-old at home. 3173

Two years' experience among the Shakers. 3396

Two years of Sunday nights. 2426

... Two years with Jesus. 1994

Two young Arabs. 2566

Two Zen classics. 1853, 2182

Twofold growth. 2501

Twofold power of the gospel. 163

2's at church. 3173

Tying down the sun. 1383, 3384

Tyne chylde. 1333

Types and metaphors of the Bible. 3721

Types in Hebrews. 404, 3720

Types of apologetic systems. 69

Types of Christ in the Old Testament. 3721

Types of Christian saintliness. 3066

... Types of Jewish-Palestinian piety. 2138

Types of Jewish-Palestinian piety from 70 B.C.E. to 70 C.E. 491, 2846

Types of literature in the Old Testament. 210

Types of modern theology. 3618

Types of preachers in the New Testament. 321

Types of religious experience, Christian and non-Christian. 3121

Types of religious philosophy. 3098

Types of rural churches. 3253, 3254

Typhoon days in Japan. 2535

Typical elders and deacons. 1239

Typical English churchmen. 1213, 3861

... Typical English churchmen from Parker to Maurice. 1291

Typical evangelistic sermons. 1561

Typical key to the Apocalypse. 462

Typical mission in China. 2511

Typical modern conceptions of God. 1723

Typical New Testament conversions. 1361

Typology and early American literature. 3721

Typology and seventeenth-century literature. 3721

Typology of Scripture. 3720, 3721

Tyranny of God. 3023

Tyranny of shams. 3434

Tyranny of time. 1473

Tzaddik in our time. 2219, 3016

Tzedakah. 2081

Tzeenah u-reenah. 516

U

Udlaeggelse af Johannes's Aabenbaring, ved past. Fingar Jorgenson. 459

Uganda holocaust. 35, 2821

Uganda safari. 2558, 3467

... Uganda's white man of work. 2308

Ugly little secret. 51

Uhuru! freedom! 2551

Ukanya. 2499

Ukiah Valley Pomo religious life, supernatural doctoring, and beliefs. 2859

Ukrainian-rite Catholic Church at the Ecumenical Council. 1962-1965. 3771

Ukrainian settlers in Canada and their schools. 3722

Ukranian Catholic metropolitan see. Byzantine rite. U.S.A. November 1, 1958. 766

Ulrich von Hutten and the German Reformation. 1858, 3040

Ulrichus Velenus (Oldrich Velensky) and his treatise against the papacy. 2862, 3776

Ultimate conceptions of faith. 3651

Ultimate concern. 3617

Ultimate dimension. 2383

Ultimate elsewhere. 2723

Ultimate epoch. 1069

Ultimate ideals. 956

Ultimate lifestyle. 989

Ultimate quest. 1446

Ultimate questions. 25, 2750

Ultimate reality and realization. 3422, 3768

Ultimate revolution. 3482

Ultimate source of all super natural phenomena. 1078

Ultimate transformation. 3483

Ultimate values of the American population. 3747

Ultimate weapon -- Christianity. 67

Ultra-psychonics: how to work miracles with the limitless power of psycho-atomic energy. 2724

Ultramontanism. 794

Umbilical cord. 1091

Umbilicus mundi. 1928

Umfundisi. 2499

Un jour memorable. 3384

Unabridged concordance to the Old and New Testaments and the Apocrypha. 227

Unaccountable man. 3349

Unafraid. 1858

Unaltered Augsburg confession. 109

Unaltered Augsburg confession. 109

Unandinted. 2122

Unanimity in pluralism. 2396

Unanswerable logic. 3502

Unanswerable reply to the circular letter issued by the Committee on religious prejudice of Indianapolis council no. 437, Knights of Columbus. 2179

Unashamed workman. 2204

Unbelief in the eighteenth century as contrasted with its earlier and later history. 3024

Unbelief in the nineteenth century. 1656

Unbelievers. 3212

Unbounded love. 3666

Unbroken unity. 1508

Uncanonical Jewish books. 488

Uncaused being and the criterion of truth. 2417

Uncertain alliance. 1131

Uncertain journey. 1366, 3381

Uncertain saints. 2193

Uncertain sound. 760

Uncertain trumpet; the priest in modern America. 772

Unchangeable church. 795, 1181

Unchangeable laws of God. 1314

Unchanging Christ. 1557

Unchanging commission. 2517

Unchanging God. 2425

Unchanging mission. 2555
Uncharted way. 2996
Unchurched. 2712
Uncle Austin and his nephews. 635
Uncle Ben's Bible stories. 629
Uncle Cam. 3705
... Uncle George and Uncle Malachy. 904
Uncle Jim's stories from the New Testament. 626
Uncle Jim's stories from the Old Testament. 634
Uncle John Vassar. 3768
Uncle Sam or the Pope, which? 828
"Uncle Sam's new fiancee" 827
Uncle Sam's recommendation of phrenology to his millions of friends in the United States. 2844
Uncle Uriah and Tad. 77, 3385
Unclean spirits. 1424
Uncommon commonplace. 2807
Uncommon letters to a son. 687
Uncommon prayer. 585
Uncommon prayers. 2891
Uncommon sense. 787, 2389
Uncomplicated Christian. 982
Unconditional freeness of the gospel. 1751
Unconditional good news. 3753
Unconditional love. 2265
Unconditional surrender. 3445
Unconquerable. 2493
Unconquerable Kagawa. 2162
Unconquerable partnership. 2302
Unconquered. 3581
Unconscious truth of the four Gospels. 1964
Unconventional prayers. 2895
Unconventional sermonets. 1067
Uncovered feelings. 1445
Uncovering Bible times. 207
Uncut nerve of missions. 2520
Undaunted. 3387
Undaunted hope. 1774, 2558
Undefeated. 2118
Under angel wings. 765
Under canvas. 1559
Under five flags. 147, 1673
Under God, a new birth of freedom. 33
Under His wings. 612, 963, 1599, 2632
Under many flags. 2482
Under marching orders. 1701
Under marching orders in North China. 2510
Under my hat. 996
Under new management. 992
Under orders. 1133, 3728, 3729
Under orders; the churches and public affairs. 1133
Under our flag. 2546
Under Quaker appointment. 3255
Under seventeen, sermons to boys and girls. 907
Under strange skies. 2085
Under the ban. 3023
Under the blood banner. 1366
Under the cedars and the stars. 3201
Under the chapel spire. 3758
Under the crescent. 2497
Under the Cross. 2749
Under the fig tree. 2869
...Under the highest leadership. 954
Under the midnight sun. 2617
Under the mountain. 3278
Under the northern cross. 2960
Under the nuptial canopy. 3800
Under the parsonage roof. 1303
Under the prophet in Utah. 2601
Under the Red star. 1575
Under the skylight. 1114
Under the Southern Cross. 169, 2499, 2543, 2547
Under the SS shadow. 146, 3786
Under the steeple. 1491
Under the tagalong tree. 618
Under three flags. 885
Under three tsars. 3256
Under twenty. 3886
Underachiever. 3722
Undercurrent of feminine philosophy in Eastern and Western thought. 1621, 2197
Underground Catholicism in Scotland. 825
Underground Christians in the earliest church. 1093
Underground church. 2712
Underground church of Jerusalem. 1928, 2219
Underground manual for ministers' wives. 1303
Underground mass book. 2257
Understand the Bible. 644
Understanding. 3185, 3751
Understanding adults. 3168
Understanding aging. 18
Understanding and believing. 3068, 3788
Understanding and developing young people. 3175
Understanding and teaching the Bible. 311

Understanding anger in the church. 43
Understanding Bible prophecy. 606
Understanding Biblical research. 240
Understanding Catholicism. 3628
Understanding children. 895
Understanding Christian education. 942
Understanding Christian missions. 2493
Understanding Christianity. 3664
Understanding church growth. 1171, 2493
Understanding communism. 1319
Understanding Conservative Judaism. 1348
Understanding death. 1415
Understanding death and dying. 1415
Understanding Exodus. 516
Understanding Genesis. 522
Understanding God. 3656
Understanding God's word. 288
Understanding God's world. 3765
Understanding grief. 2136
Understanding heart. 1068
Understanding Islam. 1922, 2565
Understanding Jewish mysticism. 722, 3329
Understanding Jewish prayer. 2886
Understanding Jewish theology. 2080
Understanding Judaism. 2138
Understanding love and sex. 3392
Understanding man. 2325
Understanding marriage and family life. 2338
Understanding my congregation. 2288
Understanding mysticism. 2644
Understanding nursery children. 3173
Understanding of Albert Schweitzer. 3312
Understanding of faith: interpretation and criticism. 3624
Understanding of our time: Catholic responsibility in a pluralistic society. 874
Understanding of religion. 3057
Understanding of the Buddha. 703
Understanding our lesson sermons. 1030
Understanding our neighbor's faith. 788, 2977
Understanding our pupils. 3153
Understanding ourselves. 3172
Understanding people: children, youth, adults. 1107
Understanding Pietism. 2846
Understanding prayer. 2874
Understanding rabbinic Judaism, from Talmudic to modern times. 2147
Understanding religion. 3186
Understanding religious convictions. 3102
Understanding religious life. 3064
Understanding religious man. 3064
Understanding Revelation. 462
Understanding Roman Catholicism. 800
Understanding Scripture. 230, 235
Understanding self and society. 668
Understanding speaking in tongues. 1716
Understanding suffering. 3541
Understanding teaching. 3179
Understanding the Apocalypse. 454
Understanding the Apostles' creed. 73
Understanding the Bible. 230, 231, 232, 234, 237, 310, 503, 3764
Understanding the Bible and science. 205
Understanding the Bible: the New Testament. 350
Understanding the Bible through history and archaeology. 535
Understanding the book of Acts. 327
Understanding the book of Hebrews. 402
Understanding the books of the New Testament. 409
Understanding the books of the Old Testament. 538
Understanding the Christian faith. 3660, 3662
Understanding the church. 3188
Understanding the faith of the Church. 3664
Understanding the Gospels. 392
Understanding the Greek Orthodox church. 2744
Understanding the Heart. 3270
Understanding the Inquisition. 1909
Understanding the Kabbalah. 721
Understanding the kingdom of God. 2174
Understanding the last days. 605, 1636
Understanding the laws of life. 2724
Understanding the learner. 2204
Understanding the liturgy. 2239
Understanding the Lord's prayer. 2246, 2247
Understanding the message of Paul. 375
Understanding the Methodist Church. 2426
Understanding the Midrash. 2462
Understanding the new religions. 3747
Understanding the New Testament. 406, 409, 411, 473
Understanding the New Testament book by book. 474
Understanding the new theology. 785, 3650

Understanding the Nicene Creed. 2706
Understanding the Old Testament. 500, 532, 533, 537, 541, 2095, 2147
Understanding the parables of Our Lord. 2024
Understanding the prophets. 2949
Understanding the Psalms. 578, 584
Understanding the pupil. 895
Understanding the sacraments. 3264
Understanding the Sacred Text. 202
Understanding the Scriptures. 230, 311, 362, 2599
Understanding the Sermon on the Mount. 3336
Understanding the service. 2295
Understanding the signs of the times. 949
Understanding the Synod. 866
Understanding the Talmud. 3015, 3585
Understanding the things of God. 2610
Understanding the times. 3319
Understanding the United Methodist Church. 3734
Understanding Watchman Nee. 2286
Understanding your church's curriculum. 937, 3162
Understanding your faith. 1594
Understanding your Muslim neighbour. 1925
Understanding your pupils. 3152
Understanding youth. 3884
Understandings of prayer. 2885
Underwood-Marples debate. 101
Underwood of Korea. 2537, 3722
Undesigned coincidences in the writings both of the Old and New Testament. 276
Undiscovered country. 934, 1436
Undiscovered country, and other addresses. 1339
Undivided God. 1452
Undivided heart. 1700, 3420
Undivided vision. 1048
Undying flame. 1108, 2826
Undying torch. 161
Undying tragedy of the world. 865, 2034
Uneasy conscience of modern fundamentalism. 2563
Unemployed Carpenter. 3358
Unending genesis. 1382
Unending tale. 1354
Unequal yoke. 1552
Unequal yoke; should a Christian support modernism? (The autobiography of a dollar) 2561
Unerring guide. 249
Unexpected Christ. 1555
Unexpected Messiah. 407
Unexplained. 2727, 2730, 2845, 3437
Unexplored land of prayer. 2882
Unexplored self. 1061
Unfailing light. 1478
Unfamiliar stories of familiar hymns. 1871
Unfashionable convictions. 3066
Unfathomable Christ. 3366
Unfathomable sorrow. 603
Unfeigned faith. 1590, 1594
Unfinished animal. 3063
Unfinished business. 765, 1841
Unfinished business in China. 1791
Unfinished business of the Presbyterian church in America. 2926
Unfinished Easter. 2934, 3356
Unfinished man and the imagination. 3225
Unfinished mystery. 2398
Unfinished rainbows. 1443
Unfinished Reformation. 1492, 2298
Unfinished symphonies. 3473
... The unfinished task of foreign missions. 2521
Unfinished task of the Christian church. 2491
"Unfinished tasks" of the Southern Presbyterian church. 2501
Unfolding Daniel's prophecies. 508, 1401
Unfolding drama in southeast, Asia. 2502
Unfolding drama of redemption. 296, 297, 3030
Unfolding drama of the Bible. 308, 647
Unfolding life. 3152
Unfolding message of the Bible. 235
Unfolding of the ages. 604
Unfolding of the ages in the Revelation of John. 455, 460
Unfolding of the ages: prophecy fulfilled, prophecy being fulfilled, prophecy to be fulfilled. 604
Unfolding revelation. 1473
Unfolding the mystery of religious life. 2570, 3771
Unfolding the Revelation. 452
Unfolding year. 2895
Unfoldment. 1036
Unfoldment of consciousness. 1348
Unforgettable disciples. 2491
Unforgiving servant. 443
Unfragmented man. 2784
Unfulfilled prophecies. 2464

Unfulfilled prophecy. 604
Unger's Bible commentary. 225
Unger's Bible dictionary. 246
Unger's Bible handbook. 286
Unger's guide to the Bible. 312
Unguarded gate. 3369
Unhand me! 3106
Unhappy medium. 2162, 3502
Unhappy secrets of the Christian life. 991
Unheard Billy Graham. 1754
Unheeded teachings of Jesus. 3422
Unholy alliance. 2670
Unholy pilgrimage. 3257
Unholy three. 1001
Unholy war. 1925
Uni una! 1450, 3223
Uniate Eastern Churches. 765
UNICEF book of children's prayers. 899
Unicorn: William Butler Yeats' search for reality. 3863
Unification Church ; as others see us. 3329
Unification of the churches. 1249
Unification theology & Christian thought. 3329, 3645
Unified gospel of Jesus. 396
Unified Gospels. 1989
Unified Sunday morning church service. 3003
Unifying role of the bishop. 665
Unifying rural community interests. 3871
Union. 1954, 2065
... The union Bible dictionary, for the use of schools, Bible classes, and families. 245
Union catalog of Hebrew manuscripts and their location. 2331
Union catalogue of the publications of John and Charles Wesley. 3806
Union documents. 1547
Union Haggadah. 2779
Union hymnal; songs and prayers for Jewish worship. 2097
Union hymns. 1869
Union lesson guide and golden text book for 1917. 3180
Union list of Catholic periodicals in Catholic institutions on the Pacific coast. 852
Union list of periodicals of the Southeastern Pennsylvania Theological Library Association. 3678
Union list of serials. 3678
Union list of United Methodist serials, 1773-1973. 2434
Union movement. 2493
Union notes on the Gospels. 386
Union of Christendom. 1041
... The union of Christian forces in America. 1039
Union of Episcopal Methodisms. 2438
Union of love (The) 2344
... The union of parishes. 2775
Union of souls. 3141
Union of the first four books of the New Testament, written by Matthew Mark, Luke and John. 1988
Union of Uzhorod. 766, 3258
Union prayer-book for Jewish worship. 2108, 2111
Union prayerbook for Jewish worship. 2108
Union seminary addresses. 3758
Union theological seminary in the city of New York. 2701
Union theological seminary in the city of New York: its design and another decade of its history. 720, 2701
Union theological seminary in the city of New York. One hundredth anniversary. 1836-1936. 3615
Union with Christ. 188, 840, 1646, 2637, 3288
Union with Christ; victory. 1878
Union with Our Lord Jesus Chirst in his principal mysteries. 1452
Union with the church, the solemn duty, and the blessed privilege, of all who would be saved. 1119
Union work. 3737
Unique aloofness of Jesus. 1950
Unique evangelical churches. 1552
Unique historical value of the book of Jonah. 552
Unique message and the universal mission of Christianity. 1105
Unique person of Christ. 2040
Unique status of man. 1657
Unique world of women. 3840
Unique world of women . . . in Bible times and now. 3840
Unit book A for the primary course. 2965
Unitarian affirmations. 3726
Unitarian catechism. 3726
Unitarian Christianity. 3470, 3727
Unitarian Christianity and other essays. 3727

Unitarian conscience: Harvard moral philosophy, 1805-1861. 3730
Unitarian Oberlin. 1477
Unitarian principles confirmed by Trinitarian testimonies. 3729
Unitarian service book. 34
Unitarian states his case. 3724
Unitarian thought. 3727
Unitarian Universalist pocket guide. 3727
Unitarian views vindicated. 1424, 3723
Unitarian way of life. 3728
Unitarian year book. 1846. 3729
Unitarianism and Universalism. 3730
Unitarianism defined. 3727
Unitarianism in America. 3727
Unitarianism incapable of vindication. 3729, 3863
Unitarianism: its origin and history. A course of sixteen lectures delivered in Channing hall, Boston, 1888-89. 882, 3729
Unitarianism on the Pacific coast. 3727
Unitarianism philosophically and theologically examined. 2001, 3728, 3729
Unitarianism today. 3728
Unitarianism unmasked. 3727
Unitarians. 1472, 3725
Unitarians and India. 3730
Unitarians face a new age. 3727
United Christian adult movement. 1498
United Church of Christ. 3732
United churches. 1040
United Churches of Hackensack and Schraalenburgh, New Jersey, 1686-1822. 1484, 3047
United Evangelical Lutheran Church. 2302, 3732
United for separation. 2979
United in service. 1249
United kingdom. 590, 2188
United masonic relief in the Japanese earthquake of 1925. 1672
United Methodism in theory and practice. 3734
United Methodist Church. 2441
United Methodist Church in Wayne, New Jersey, 1853-1973. 3734
United Methodist primer. 3734
United Methodist studies. 2426
United order among the Mormons. 2617
United Order among the Mormons (Missouri phase) 2617
United Presbyterian church and its work in America. 3736
United Presbyterian Church in the U.S.A. 3735
United Presbyterian Church of Laramie, Wyoming, 1869-1969. 2197
United Presbyterian directory. 3736
United Presbyterian enterprise of theological education. 3681
United Presbyterian story. 3736
United Reformed Church. 3736
United States. 3743
United States ambassador to the Vatican. 3741
United States and British Commonwealth in prophecy. 45, 610
... The United States and German Jewish persecutions. 2078
United States and Israel in the Mediterranean. 3741
United States & the moral philosophy of the gutter. 3742
U.S. bishops' Pastoral letter on human life in our day. 852, 1153
United States Catholic chaplains in the world war. 1543
U.S. Catholic institutions for the training of candidates for the priesthood. 3681
U. S. Catholics overseas; a statistical directory, January 1, 1968. 851
United States Christian commission, for the army and navy. 3741
United States documents in the Propaganda Fide archives. 834
United States foreign policy and Christian ethics. 1914
United States in Bible prophecy. 611
U.S.A. in five hours. 2526
United States in relation to the Messiah's return. 3318
United States in the light of prophecy. 465
U. S. looks at its churches. 1274
United States ministers to the Papal states. 3741
United States of America: The Irish clergyman. 874
U.S.A.—the message of justice, peace, and love. 3628
United States, world Jewry, Catholic action & power politics. 3851
United Synagogue, 1870-1970. 2100, 3749
Uniting for larger service. 1620

Uniting general synod of the United church of Christ. 3732
Unitive Protestantism. 1041
Units in religion [for Lutheran schools. (Intermediate and upper grades)]. 3188
Unity. 1042
Unity: a quest for truth. 3750
Unity and disunity of the church. 1039
Unity and diversity in the New Testament. 476, 3658
Unity and fellowship and ecumenicity. 1040
Unity and its restoration. 1042
Unity and missions. 2492
Unity and reform. 790
Unity begins with you. 32
Unity church call. 3749
Unity, heresy, and reform, 1378-1460. 1373
Unity in dispersion. 3851
Unity in freedom. 1039
Unity in mid-career. 1491
Unity in the faith. 2957
Unity in the spirit. 2871
Unity in theology. 2245, 3667
Unity in variety. 61
Unity of all life. 3477, 3749
Unity of body and mind. 2473
Unity of body and mind. Edited and translated by Walter Bernard. 2473
Unity of Christians. 1042
Unity of faith. 1042
Unity of faith and knowledge. 3078
Unity of God. 1722
Unity of good. 1032
Unity of Isaiah. 543
Unity of life. 971
Unity of life and spirit [poems]. 3493
Unity of man. 1453
Unity of mankind. 365
Unity of nature. 3074
Unity of religions. 3119
Unity of science, theology. 3743
Unity of science, theology, and doubt. 3743
Unity of the Bible. 278, 279
Unity of the book of Genesis. 523
Unity of the church in the New Testament. 342
Unity of the churches of God. 1042
Unity of the four Gospels. 1988
Unity of the human races proved to be the doctrine of Scripture, reason and science. 2585
Unity of the Laches. 2853
Unity of the moral and spiritual life. 1000
Unity of the Old and New Testaments. 286
Unity on the ground. 1045
Unity school of Christianity and what its teachings reveal. 1052
Unity through love. 1043
Unity through love, essays in ecumenism. 1043
Unity treasure chest. 3750
Unity treasury chest. 3750
Unity way of life. 3749
Unity we seek. 861, 1249
Unity with Jesus Christ. 963
Unity's fifty golden years. 3751
Univeralism against itself. 3753
Universal annual register, of the Baptist denomination. 142
Universal beliefs. 3057
Universal Bible dictionary. 246
Universal Bible encyclopedia. 247
Universal bible history and her-story. 290
Universal biographical dictionary. 661
Universal calendar. 319
Universal church. 1041
Universal church and the world of nations. 3447
Universal consciousness of the Bahai religion. 128
Universal damnation and salvation clearly proved by the Scriptures, of the Old and New Testament. 3291
Universal design of life statement and proof. 1029
...The universal elements of the Christian religion. 1050
Universal faith. 3059
Universal God. 3204
Universal God, the eternal quest in which all men are brothers. 3204
Universal grace. 1751
Universal history of Israel. 1927
Universal Jewish encyclopedia. 2086
Universal Jewish encylclopedia. 2086
Universal Jewish history. 2087
Universal law of man. 1324
Universal meaning of the Kabbalah. 722
Universal medium. 3462
Universal messages. 160
Universal metaphysics. 2695

Universal principles of the Bahai movement, social, economic, governmental. 127
Universal pronouncing dictionary of biography and mythology. 662
Universal register of the Baptist denomination in North America, for the years 1790, 1791, 1792, 1793, and part of 1794. 158
Universal restoration. 3753
Universal restoration, exhibited in four dialogues between a minister and his friend. 3753
Universal spiritualism. 3498
Universal treasure casket. 3503
Universal war near. 1940
Universal will. 959
Universal wisdom. 3138
Universal word. 3099
Universal worship. 1868
Universalism. 3752
Universalism against itself. 3752, 3753
Universalism and the Universalist church. 3751
Universalism examined, renounced, exposed. 3753
Universalism in America. 3752, 3755
Universalism not of God. 3753
Universalism not of the Bible. 3754
Universalism, the prevailing doctrine of the Christian church during its first five hundred years. 3754
Universalism vindicated. 3752
Universalist church in Ohio. 3754
Universalist Church of America. 3755
Universalist hymn-book. 3754
Universalist saga of Bunker Hill. 713
Universalists at Ferry Beach. 1622
Universality of Christ. 1072
Universality of Maimonides. 2623
... The universality of the kingdom of God in the Gospels and the Acts of the apostles. 2176
Universality of the master mind. 2018
Universals. 3755
Universals and particulars. 3755, 3756
Universary speaker. 3026
Universe as we see it. 1728
Universe is a book of condensed thought. 97
Universe next door. 1882
Universe of Shabbetai Donnolo. 722, 1477
Universe: plan or accident? 3081
Universe within. 3357
Universe within us. 3080
...The universities and the churches. 3058
University and other sermons. 1226
University divinity schools. 3614

University hymn book. 1861
University New Testament. 397
University of Chicago chapel. 894
University of Chicago sermons. 3366
University of experience. 3353
University of Houston exhibition of Bibles and related materials, Christmas 1970. 213
University of Jesus. 2043
... University of North Carolina extension bulletin. 3759
University of the nations. 2859
University sermons. 863, 3360, 3758
University, the church, and internationalization. 1127
University work of the United Lutheran Church in America. 1256, 3733
Unjust judge. 3597
Unknown. 2729
Unknown Bible. 199
Unknown but known. 3502
Unknown Christ of Hinduism. 1082
Unknown God. 385, 864, 1725, 1731, 2394, 3113, 3142, 3651, 3652
Unknown God (Jehovah) 1719
Unknown guest. 2990
Unknown India. 1896
Unknown Jewish sect. 3891
Unknown life of Christ. 1081, 1976
Unknown life of Jesus Christ. 1081, 1976, 1987
Unknown made known. 1380
Unknown parson. 686, 1300
Unknown power. 2728
"unknown" reality. 3474
Unknown sanctuary. 2115
Unknown sayings of Jesus. 2072
... The unkown singers. 583
Unknown witnesses. 216, 2609
Unknown worshipper. 2697
Unknown years of Jesus. 1952
Unkulunkulu in Zululand. 2499
Unleashing of evolutionary thought. 1581
Unless some man show me. 500
Unless they be sent. 2905
"Unless you believe ..." 988

Unlikely saints of the Bible. 214
Unlimited power of prayer. 2883
Unlock your faith-power. 962, 1596
Unlocked door. 910, 1359
Unlocked truth according to Hemaka. 3508
Unlocking the Old Testament. 500, 2599
Unlocking the treasures in Biblical imagery. 288
Unmasking of Robert-Houdin. 1346, 3240
Unmasking the spirits. 3520
Unmoral maxims. 2375
Unnumbered bulletins. 1678
Unobstructed universe. 3518
Unoccupied mission fields of Africa and Asia. 2498, 3899
Unofficial Christianity. 3338
Unopened door. 1078
Unordained elders and renewal communities. 1245
Unorthodox conception of being. 2738
Unorthodox Judaism. 2155
Unorthodox London. 2243
Unpardonable sin. 3211, 3412
Unpardonable sin, and other sermons. 3344
Unpopular missionary. 2500
Unpopular truths. 3670
Unpredictable wind. 1831
Unprivate life of a pastor's wife. 1303
Unprodigal son. 2944
Unprofitable servants. 1856
Unpublished essay of Edwards on the Trinity. 3711
Unpublished letters and correspondence of Mrs. Isabella Graham. 1525
Unpublished theological writings of Johannes Castellensis. 3616
Unquenchable light. 1176
Unquenched cup. 581
Unraveling Zen's red thread. 1883, 2940
Unravelling the Book of books. 237
Unreached peoples '79. 1573
Unrecognized Christ. 1951
Unrecorded miracle. 2476
Unreformed church. 760
Unrelated debt-financed income. 887
Unresponsive: resistant or neglected? 2556
Unsealed Bible. 521
Unsealed book. 3495
Unsearchable riches. 364
Unsecular man. 3086
Unseen Christ. 2059
Unseen cross. 105
...The unseen doctor. 3517
Unseen forces. 3503
Unseen Friend. 1449
Unseen presence. 955
Unseen universe. 1890
Unseen world. 1888
Unselfishness. 28
Unselfishness of God and how I discovered it. 3427
... Unsettled questions touching the foundations of Christianity. 60
Unshackled. 1362
Unshaken trust and other sermons. 1050
Unshattered rock. 44
Unsilent South. 1132
Unspoken worlds. 3845
Unspotted mirror of God. 2356
Unsui: a diary of Zen monastic life. 2575
Untamed God. 3620
Untapped generation. 2823
Until everyone knows. 2293
Until He comes. 9, 1043
Until the day dawns. 1267
Until you die. 3543
Unto all. 1446
Unto all the world. 1564, 3464
Unto God and Caesar. 1144
Unto God, Who giveth joy to my youth. 2368
Unto heights heroic (a Biblical interpretation) 307
Unto the altar. 1298, 2234
Unto the altar of God. 848
Unto the churches. 2060
Unto the desired haven. 3210
Unto the hills. 2608
Unto the least of these. 2489
Unto the mountains. 20, 3423
"Unto the progress of the gospel," 2533
Unto thy children. 2076
Untold Korean story. 2536
Untold story of Qumran. 1411
Untouchables' quest. 2531
Untranslatable riches from the Greek New Testament. 425
Untried door. 2065
Unused powers. 161
Unused rainbows. 2886
Unvanquished Puritan. 184
Unveiled faces. 217
Unveiled glory. 1894
Unveiling of Christ. 1056
Unveiling of Jesus Christ. 456

Unveiling of the great whore and the diverse beast. 607
Unveiling of the Priest-Judge; a simple, spiritual, and scholarly exposition of the book of the Revelation and the visions of Daniel's prophecy, by H. Framer Smith. 464
Unveiling the future. 605
Unveiling the missionary world. 2519
Unveiling the mystery of creation. 205
Unwelcome at the northeast gate. 2510
Unwitting witnesses. 2213, 2299
Unwritten book. 1005
Unwritten sayings of Our Lord. 2072
Unwrought iron. 3187
Unyoung, uncolored, unpoor. 3780
Up among the stars. 1582, 2267
Up from a sod hut. 2847
Up from independence. 2974, 3781
... Up from Methodism. 2420
Up the golden stair. 1353
Up the ladder in foreign missions. 15, 140
Up the shining path. 3285
Up the staircase backwards. 171, 2200
Up through childhood. 2591
Up to date Bible talks for children. 907
Up-to-date Sunday school. 3557
Up to Jerusalem. 2031, 2211
Up to Jerusalem where He must suffer. 586, 2213, 2298
Up to now. 3590
Up to our steeples in politics. 1057
Up to the light. 3202
Up with creation! 1385
Up with Jesus. 1139
Upanisads. 3760
Upanishads. 3759, 3760
Upanishads; breath of the eternal. 3760
Upanishads, Gita, and Bible. 3267
Update. 1403
Updated chaplaincy. 1259
Updating Franciscan communities. 1646
Updating of religious formation. 2570
Updike's sermons. 1561
Uphill for peace. 1688, 2241
Upjohn's rural architecture. 1158
...The uplift of China. 2511
Uplifted Christ. 1985
Uplifted hands and other sermons. 3191, 3346, 3726
Upon a penny loaf. 1020
Upon request, God in action. 3741
Upon the earth. 1725
Upon the harp. 1865
Upon these rocks. 825
Upon this rock. 789, 1229, 2481, 2860, 3278, 3716, 3889
Upper currents. 969
Upper purgatory. 3496
Upper road of vision. 1324
Upper room. 1299, 2252
Upper Room Chapel talks. 3363
Upper room companion. 1435
Upper room disciplines. 1435
Upper room disciplines 1962. 1435
Upper Room disciplines (The) 1435
Upper room meditations. 2387
Upper room of God's house. 459
Upper room on Main Street. 2935
Upper way. 2228
Upside-down kingdom. 2174
Upside-down world. 2101
Upstream Christian in a downstream world. 982
Upward call. 449
Upward calling. 979
Upward leading. 2437, 3344
Upward look. 1436, 2398
Upward moving and emergence way. 2677
Upward path. 3290
Upward reach. 970, 2600, 2608, 3358
Upward steps. 1050
Upward trails. 1435
Upward way. 2387
Upwinds. 2815
Urania. 3718
Urban analysis. 3566
Urban Catholic university. 870
Urban church breakthrough. 1278
Urban church planning. 1278
Urban churches in transition. 1279
Urban communities of the South. 3468
Urban crisis. 1140
Urban impact on American Protestantism. 1277
Urban impact on American protestantism, 1865-1900. 1277
Urban mission. 1280
Urban organization of Protestantism. 1278
Urban renewal and the church. 3761
Urban self-study of the Christian churches of El Paso, Texas. 932
Urban strategy for Africa. 1279
Urban strategy for Latin America. 2537
Urbs beats. 977
Urge of man. 462
Urge of the unrational in religion. 3062

Urgency of preaching. 2900
Urgent harvest. 2503
Urgent now. 2434
Urgent voice. 10, 2467
Uriel Acosta. 2145
Ursula N. Gestefeld's statement of Christian science. 1033
Ursula N. Gestefeld's statements of Christian science. 1033
Ursulines. 3761
...The Ursulines in New Orleans and Our Lady of Prompt Succor. 2693
Ursulines in training. 3761
Ursulines, nuns of adventure. 3761
Ursulines of the West. 3761
Usable truth. 3751
Use and abuse of church history. 1176
Use and abuse of party-feeling in matters of religion. 3704
Use and abuse of the Bible. 239
Use and misuse of visual arts in religious education. 921
Use and need of the life of Carry A. Nation. 120
Use of analogy in the letters of Paul. 372
... The use of art in religious education. 919
Use of athletic metaphors in the Biblical homilies of St. John Chrysostom. 1115, 1771
Use of audio-visuals in the church. 3161
Use of Holy Scripture in the public worship of the church. 1781
Use of life. 1323, 1449
Use of motives in teaching morals and religion. 3150
Use of music in Christian education. 1209
Use of parables in catechetics. 1841
Use of projects in religious education. 3179
Use of religion. 958
Use of Sarum. 840
Use of silence. 1682
Use of symbolism in Christian education. 922
Use of the Bible among schoolboys. 643
Use of the Bible in Milton's prose. 299, 2470, 2471
Use of the Bible in preaching. 299, 2900
Use of the Bible in teaching youth. 3191
Use of the Bible in the education of the young. 641
Use of the Bible with adults. 639
Use of the Bible with children. 642
Use of the Old Testament in current curricula. 3158
Use of the Old Testament in the light of modern knowledge. 500
Use of the Old Testament in the New and other essays. 451, 3532
Use of the Scriptures in counseling. 2779
Use of the Scriptures in theology. 3615
Use of the story in religious education. 3149, 3179
Use of tora by Isaiah. 543, 3704
Useful and happy. 3196
Usefulness of the stage. 1309, 3606
Uses of Hebraisms in recent Bible translations. 583, 1517
Uses of literature in the pulpit. 2902
Uses of Scripture in recent theology. 279, 3656
Usher's manual. 1249
Using and maintaining church property. 1242
Using audiovisuals in religious education. 3161
Using audiovisuals in the church. 109
Using behavioral methods in pastoral counseling. 2781
Using Biblical simulations. 603
Using evaluation in theological education. 3681
Using nonbroadcast video in the church. 3594
Using our heavenly Father's gifts. 3528
Using personal computers in the church. 1200
Using storytelling in Christian education. 3534
Using the Bible in public address. 637
Using the lecture in teaching and training. 3179
Using the resources of the country church. 1374
Using the Sunday school in evangelism. 3557
Using theological books and libraries. 3612
Using visual aids in a church. 3784
Utah and the Mormons. 2602
Utah pioneer and apostle. 2412
Utensils in Jewish law. 2165
Utile dulci. 1210
Utilia. Real and vital religion served, in the various & glorious intentions of it. 2372

Utility of the Scriptures of the Old Testament. 483
Utopia according to Moses. 3762
Utopia of Pope John XXIII. 2124, 2861
Utopia of unity. 1042
Utopian universe. 990
Utopias and Utopian thought. 3762
Utterances of Jesus. 2072
Uttermost part. 2376
Uyo story. 2558

V

Ve-ve. 3787
"V" for victory. 3354
V. Raymond Edman: in the presence of the king. 1497
Vacant hearted. 1139
Vacant pulpit. 1289
Vacation Bible school. 1399
Vacation Bible school guide. 3763
Vacation Bible school handbook. 3763
Vacation Bible school in the local church. 3763
... The vacation church school. 3157, 3766
Vacation church school in Christian education. 3763
Vacation days with Jesus. 3159
...Vacation religious day school. 3763
Vacationing with a purpose. 2384
Vaccine of faith. 3346
Vacuum of unbelief. 1067
Vade mecum. 706
Vade mecum for nurses and social workers. 2718
Vagabond scholar. 2230
Vagrant lotus. 711
Vain repetition. 656
Vaisesika sutras of Kanada. 3766
Vaisnavism of Samkaradeva and Ramanuja. 3301, 3766
Vaisnavism, Saivism, and minor religious systems. 3766
Valao of the South Seas. 1366
Valedictory discourse. 3355
Valentine's Day. 3279
Valerian persecution. 2820
Valiant achievements. 764
Valiant bishop against a ruthless king. 1628
Valiant for the truth. 1551, 1552, 1637
Valiant in fight. 338
Valiant voyager. 685, 1332
Valiant woman. 764, 3844
Valid Christianity for to-day. 1054
Valid objections to so-called Christian science. 1036
Valid religion for the times. 3065
Validity of dispensationalism. 1467
Validity of religious experience. 1586
Validity of the Christian mission. 2495
Validity of the Gospel record. 392
Validity of the religious experience. 3097
Validity of the virgin birth. 3780
Valignano's mission principles for Japan. 1949, 2534
Valley Falls, R.I. Monastery of Our Lady of the valley (Trappist) 3709
Valley of Achor. 1352
Valley of decision. 1366, 2225, 3846
Valley of discord. 3451
Valley of God's Pleasure. 3398
Valley of shadows. 987, 2854
Valley of silence. 824, 3626
Valley of the shadow. 667, 1414, 1699, 2229
Valley of the verdict. 163
Valley of vision. 972
Valleys and hilltops. 1228
Valleys & vistas. 3477
Valmiki Ramayana. 3767
Valorous ventures. 2454
... Valuable historical library of the late Right Rev. Wm. Stevens Perry, bishop of Iowa. 29
Valuable kindling, and other stories. 911
... The valuable library of the Rev. Horace E. Hayden. 29
Valuation of Norwich. 3589
Value & dignity of human life as shown in the striving and suffering of the individual. 2228
Value and existence. 1381
Value clarification as learning process. 3151
Value of a praying mother. 2624
Value of confession. 1326
Value of dedication. 2486, 3312
Value of honesty. 1331, 2392
Value of religious facts. 3065
Value of the Sunday school. 3551
Value-orientations, personal adjustment and social behavior of members of three American religious groups in Fiedler, Fred Edward. 2994

Values and the quality of life. 2228
Values begin at home. 939
Values catechetics. 996
Values clarification. 3881
Values for tomorrow's children. 936
Values in conflict. 1016
Values in world religions. 3118
Values men live by. 3061
Values of Catholic faith. 871
Values of the incarnation. 1893
Values that last. 2435
Valuing suffering as a Christian. 1689, 3541
Vampires, werewolves, and ghouls. 1423
Van Loon's Lives. 661
Van Til. 3767
Van Til & the use of evidence. 1738, 3767
Van Til, defender of the faith. 3611, 3768
Vanamee. 120, 3768
Vance Havner, journey from Jugtown. 1576, 1791
Vance Havner, just a preacher. 163
Vancouver island and its missions. 2558
Vangel's side trip on the devil's worst roads. 3778
Vanguard of the cáravans. 2540, 2810
Vanguards for change. 3187
Vanished Arcadia. 2772
Vanished friend, evidence, theoretical and practical, of the survival of human identity after death. 3516
Vanishing evangelist. 2310
Vanishing night. 3503
Vanishing of the Prince. 2032
Vanishing parson. 1288
Vanquished hope, the church in Russia on the eve of the revolution. 1246, 3258
Vanya. 2568, 2821
Variant versions of Targumic traditions within Codex Neofiti 1. 562
Variation and fixity in nature. 1582
Variations on a theme. 3621
Variations on a theme: 'God saw that it was good. 3621
Variations on the Sunday church school. 3172
Varied beauty of the Psalms. 2985
Varied harvest. 1066
Varieties of American religion. 3325
Varieties of Christian apologetics. 69
Varieties of Christians experience. 1586
Varieties of civil religion. 3056
Varieties of English preaching. 2909
Varieties of English preaching,1900-1960. 2909
Varieties of goodness. 1746
Varieties of interpretation. 1806
Varieties of Jewish belief. 2142, 2151
Varieties of mystic experience. 2645
Varieties of New Testament religion. 477
Varieties of present-day preaching. 2897
Varieties of Protestantism. 2976
Varieties of religious experience. 1586, 1934, 3060
Varieties of southern evangelicalism. 1552
Varieties of the meditative experience. 2379
Varieties of unbelief. 1920, 3024
Variety book of puppet scripts. 3005
Variety in the prayer meeting. 2887
Variety in your preaching. 2907
Variety of Catholic attitudes. 2822
Variety of Catholic modernists. 765, 2562
Variorum constitution of the Diocese of Easton. 2959
Various discourses. 758
Various manifestations of the Deity. 3682
Various prospects of mankind, nature and providence. 2675
Various revelations. 3508
Varities of religious experience. 3060
Vatican. 88, 836, 3768
Vatican and Eastern Europe. 860, 1320
Vatican and Holy Year. 1838
Vatican and its role in world affairs. 810
Vatican and the Kremlin. 3320
Vatican and the war. 756, 2852, 3852
Vatican art. 3768
... The Vatican as a world power. 2768
Vatican buildings. 3768
Vatican council. 3768
Vatican Council, 1869-1870. 3769
Vatican Council and all Christians. 3770
Vatican Council and Christian unity. 3773
Vatican council and its definitions. 3769
Vatican Council and the Jews. 2152, 3771
Vatican Council II. 3770
Vatican Council II's statement on the Jews: five years later. 2152, 3770
Vatican Council II; the new direction. 3771, 3772
Vatican Council II, from John XXIII to Paul VI. 3770
Vatican Council II, its challenge to education. 806

Vatican decrees in their bearing on civil allegiance. 3769
Vatican diary. 3769
Vatican diary, 1965. 3770
Vatican empire. 807
Vatican imperialism in the twentieth century. 794
Vatican in politics. 794
Vatican in politics; Ultramontanism. 794
Vatican in the age of the dictators, 1922-1945. 2770, 2852
Vatican; its organization, customs, and way of life. 778, 807
Vatican journal. 2769
Vatican mission exposition. 3245
Vatican-Moscow alliance. 801, 1319
Vatican plain chant. 883
Vatican Plato and its relations. 2853
Vatican politics at the Second Vatican Council, 1962-5. 3770
Vatican revolution. 2862
Vatican story. 2768
Vatican; the center of government of the Catholic world. 3768
Vatican II. 797, 3769, 3770, 3772, 3773, 3774
Vatican II: a bibliography. 3773
Vatican II ... and now. 1298, 3771
Vatican II on ecumenism. 1044, 3773
Vatican II on priests and seminaries. 772
Vatican II on revelation. 644, 3225, 3771
Vatican II on the Church. 3773
Vatican II: the constitution on the Church. 3772
Vatican, U.S.A. 827, 1242
Vatican: yesterday, today, tomorrow. 2768
Vaticanism. 800, 3769
Vaticanism: the political principles of the Roman Catholic Church. 800
Vaughn Bible class. 3774, 3796
Vaught's practical character reader. 2844
Veda of the Black Yajus school. 3776
Vedanta. 1904
Vedanta & Christian faith. 1815
... The Vedanta and modern thought. 3775
Vedanta dictionary. 3775
Vedanta for Modern Man. 3774, 3775
Vedanta for the western world. 3774, 3775
Vedanta in practice. 2772
Vedanta in Southern California. 3775
Vedanta philosophy. 3052, 3775, 3849, 3867
Vedanta philosophy; three lectures by Swami Abhedananda on reincarnation, delivered under the auspices of the Vedanta society, in Assembly hall, New York, 1898-1899. 3052
Vedanta Sutras. 689
Vedantic Buddhism of the Buddha. 3715
Veddas. 3776
Vedic concordance. 3776
Vedic experience. 1816
Vedic hymns. 3267
Vedic mythology. 2663
Vegetarianism and the Jewish tradition. 3776
Veil is lifted. 3416
Veil lifted. 1357
Veil of the heart. 1646, 3489
Veil partly lifted and Jesus becoming visible. 1995
Veil was rent and I saw. 1528
Veiled being. 3801
Veiled mysteries of Sgypt and the religion of Islam. 2567
Velvet covered brick. 952
Venality. 1654
Vendanta philosophy. 3774
Vendata philosophy. 1562
Vendetta. 2631
Venerable Bede, his life and writings. 182, 1515
Venerable Bedes Ecclesiastical history of England. 1760
Venerable Jean-Martin Moye, apostolic missionary. 2627, 3417
Venerable Mother Frances Schervier, foundress of the congregation of the Sisters of the poor of St. Francis. 3307, 3420
Venerable Mother M. Caroline Friess. 741
Venerable One. 718
Venerable servant of God. 3307, 3420
Venerable servant of God, John Nepomucene Neumann, of the Congregation of the Most Holy Redeemer, and fourth bishop of Philadelphia. 2685
Venerable Vincent Pallotti, apostle and mystic. 2766
Veneration of the Blessed Virgin. 2356
Venetian Phoenix: Paolo Sarpi and some of his English friends (1606-1700) 3303
Vengeance of the gods. 2662
... Venice. 2107
La venida del consolador. 1836

Venite adoremus, or, Manual of the Forty hours' adoration. 1635
Venture for victory. 2516
Venture of belief. 62
Venture of faith. 30, 3849
Venture of Islam. 1282
Ventures in belief. 3649
Ventures in Christian living. 3434
Ventures in family living. 1611
Ventures in mission. 1251, 1476, 2556
Ventures in simpler living. 1371
Ventures in worship 3. 3004
Ventures in youth work. 1260
Veracity of the Hexateuch. 530
Verba Christi. 2070
Verba crucis. 2071
Verbal concordance to the New Testament. 344
Verbatim reports of talks and answers to questions. 3686
Verbeck of Japan. 2534, 3777
Verbi ministerium. 2907
Verbum Dei. 2901
Verbum sempiternum. 298
Verdict concerning the miracle. 2476
Verdict of reason upon the question of the future punishment of those who die impenitent. 1699
Verdict on Schweitzer. 3312
Verdict on the shroud. 1827
Verdict theology in missionary theory. 2555
Verdure Valley. 3261
... Vergil in the works of Prudentius. 2232, 2984
Verification of Christianity. 57
Verily, verily, I say unto thee. 1990
Veritable black art. 2730
Veritas and the Virgin. 1994
Verities of the Gospel. 168
Veritism. 2388
Die Verkundigung Vergils. 1088
Vermont Lutheran Church, 1856-1956. 3777
Vernacular and music in the missions. 1205
Vers Jesus. 2045
Verse a day. 1432
Verse, reverse. 984
Verses for tiny tots. 2048
Verses from St. Augustine; or, Specimens from a rich mine. 113
Verses on various occasions. 1017
Versus; God-in inspiration versus man-in science. 1720
Very first story ever told. 631, 1384
Very practical meditation. 2381
Very Rev. Charles Hyacinth McKenna. 2308
Very Rev. Charles Hyacinth McKenna, O.P., P.G. 2308
Very Rev. Father Paul of Moll. 2477, 2794
Very Reverend Mother Mary of the Passion and her institute. 1644, 2333
Very singular life of John Bruen, esquire of Bruen Stapleford, Cheshire. 698
Very special day. 918, 3261
Very sure of God: religious language in the poetry of Robert Browning. 697
Very thought of Thee. 2500
Very truly yours. 976, 3361
Vespasian Psalter. 837
Vesper bells. 3777
Vesper dramas. 3777
Vesper meditations. 2395
Vesper psalms according to the monastic Antiphonal. 3777
Vesper services. 3777
Vespers at St. Mark's. 1756, 2633
Vessel of clay. 1299
Vessels of election. 862
Vessels unto honor. 3844
Vessels, vehicles, and victory. 215
Vest pocket commentary on Sunday school international lessons for 1899, for teachers and scholars. 3565
Vest pocket companion for Christian workers. 1571
Vest pocket facts of church history. 1180
Vest-pocket manual of Catholic devotions. Compiled from approved sources. 855
Vestibule. 1697
Vestiges of the natural history of creation. 1579
Vestiges of the spirit-history of man. 3108
Vestments and church furniture. 839
Vestments and how to make them. 1250
Vestments and vesture. 1249, 1250
Vestry book of Elizabeth River Parish, 1749-1761. 2713
Vestry Book of King William Parish, Virginia, 1707-1750. 1275
Vestry book of St. Paul's parish. 1784
Vestry book of St. Paul's parish, Hanover county, Virginia. 1784

Vestry minute-book of the Parish of Stratford-on-Avon from 1617 to 1699 A.D. 3535
Vestry songs. 3563
Vestryman. 1239
Vestryman's guide. 1239, 2966
Vestryman's manual. 1239
Veterans of the cross. 3465
Vexilla regis quotidie. 1442
Via Christi. 2525
Via coeli. 859
"Via crucis", the lesson of Holy week. 1837
[Via crucis] The stations of the cross. According to the method of St. Alphonsus Liguori, the method of St. Francis of Assisi, and the Eucharistic method. 3526
Via media. 1217, 3646, 3649, 3666
Via media of the Anglican church. 1219
Via mystica. 594
Via propria and via mystica in the theology of Jean le Charlier de Gerson. 1708, 3493
Via sacra: or, Footprints of Christ. 2031
Via salutis. 3526
Via seraphica. 1642, 1645
"Via the Gospel" 1264
Vial poured out upon the sea. 3827
Vibrant chords. 912
Vibrations. 2990
Vibrations of higher consciousness. 3481
Vic Coburn. 1305, 1600
Vicar. 1323
Vicarious life. 3731
Vicarious sacrifice. 3271
Vicissitudes illustrated. 120
Vicissitudes in the wilderness. 119
Vicisti, Galilaee? 1764
Victim of his duty. 1327
Victim or victor. 2215
Victims of democracy. 669, 2233
Victims of love. 3483
Victims of the long march. 926
Victoire de Saint-Luc. 1326
Victor. 1575, 2195
Victor and victim. 3030
Victor Bible sourcebook. 286
Victor handbook of Bible knowledge. 292
Victor Paul Wierwille and the Way. 3799
Victor speaks. 2072
Victorian church. 1760
Victorian church in decline. 3589
Victorian country parsons. 1215, 1291
Victorian nonconformity. 1468
Victorian Quakers. 1684
Victorian values. 1612
Victories of the cross. 2426
Victorious and fruitful living, and other sermons. 3351
Victorious banner. 515
Victorious Christian life. 958
Victorious Christian living. 554
Victorious Christian service. 560
Victorious Christianity. 3355
Victorious faith. 3792
Victorious life. 959
Victorious life, and other sermons. 3346
Victorious life testimony. 2228
Victorious living. 964, 1439, 2386
Victorious mountaineer. 2708
Victorious praying. 2248
Victorious suffering. 3540
Victoris episcopi vitensis Historia persecutionis africanae provinciae. 12
Victors in the land. 3467
Victory. 2131
Victory all the way. 1557
Victory assured. 3338
Victory at the cost of purification of his soul. 757
... Victory bells. 3563
Victory by the cross. 2057
Victory in Christ. 1586
Victory in failure. 165
Victory in the valleys of life. 1349
Victory in Viet Nam. 2559
Victory life. 1612
...The victory of Christ over Satan. 3031
Victory of Christmas. 1110
Victory of faith. 1466
Victory of Father Karl. 2209
Victory of the cross. 2058
Victory of the Gospel. 2520
Victory on Praise Mountain. 742, 2817
Victory over doubt or involution. 62
Victory over suffering. 3540, 3541
Victory over the devil. 1428
Victory over the world. 1556
Victory over vice. 2058, 3412
Victory over violence, Jesus and the revolutionaries. 3780
Victory; the will of God for me. 967
Victory through Christ. 1823, 2300, 3889
Victory through persecution. 3231
Victory through prayer. 1634
Victory through surrender. 965, 969

Victory through the cross. 2057
Victory through youth. 3886,
... Victory with Christ. 2033
Vida y luchas de don Juan del Valle, primer obispo de Popayan y protector de indios. 3767
Video pencil. 3594
... Vienna. 2107
Vienna Genesis. 657
Vietnam. 2559
Vietnam and Armageddon. 3792
Vietnam; mission on the grand plateaus. 849, 2559
View book of Washington cathedral. 3796
View from a hearse. 1412
View from the border. 3451
View from the fields. 1568
View from the middle. 810
View from the pulpit. 3361
View from the streets. 1280
View of Christ. 2040, 2060
View of Congregationalism. 1344
View of religious, in two parts. 3056
View of the atonement. 108
View of the doctrines and duties of the Christian religion. 365
View of the doctrines and duties of the Chrstian religion. 365
View of the evidences of Christianity. 60, 1099
View of the expected Christian millennium. 2465
View of the internal evidence of the Christian religion. 59, 1098
View of the principal deistical writers, 1755-1757. 1420
View of the Scripture revelations concerning a future state. 1698
View of the Scripture revelations respecting good and evil angels. 3475
View through your picture window. 2387
Viewpoints. 2964
Viewpoints on science and Judaism. 2144
Views from the mountain. 2608
Views in theology. 2922
Views of Chrisitan nurture. 3148
Views of Christian doctrine held by the Religious Society of Friends. 1681
Views of our heavenly home. 3500
Views of religion. 1655, 3062
Views of the biblical world. 78, 486
... Views of theology. 2922
Views on the synod. 879
Vigil at the cross. 2388
Vigil in the sun. 2384
Vigil of faith, and other poems. 3206
Vigil of hope. 2892
...Vijaya Dharma Suri. 3779
Viking portable library world bible. 600
Vile and the holy. 509, 3852
Village blacksmith. 1810
Village church. 3253
Village dialogues. 964
Village gods of South India. 1742, 1743
Village green to city center, 1843-1943. 1271
Village harmony. 1869
Village hymns for social worship. 1867
Village of the outcasts. 2553
Village school downtown. 685
Village sermons. 3363, 3726
Village sermons and Town and country sermons. 3342
Village sermons preached at Whatley. 1225
Village tragedy. 886
Village tragedy and other sermons. 2898
Villains on white horses. 3360
... Vilna. 3779
Vimuktimarga dhutaguna-nirdesa. 2577
Vincent Pallotti. 2766
Vinaya texts. 3779
Vindication. 174, 518, 1053
Vindication of Anglican orders. 44
Vindication of certain passages in a discourse. 2217, 2939
Vindication of God's sovereign free grace. 1753
Vindication of liberal theology. 2221
Vindication of Paul. 376, 2800
Vindication of some of the most essential doctrines of the reformation. 133, 2688
... Vindication of the Anglican orders. 44
Vindication of the Appendix to the Sober remarks. 890, 1344
Vindication of the Bishop of Landaff's sermon from the gross misrepresentations. 1582, 3744
Vindication of the divine inspiration of the Holy Scriptures. 2759
Vindication of the doctrine of the final perseverance of the saints. 2822
Vindication of the government of New-England churches. 1338
Vindication of the Mosaic authorship of the Pentateuch. 563

Vindication of the New Testament concerning personality. 1422
Vindication of the piece, entitled, "The principles of Congregational churches, relating to the constitution and authority of ecclesiastical councils, considered. 1787
Vindication of the power, obligation and encouragement of the unregenerate to attend the means of grace. Against the exceptions of the Rev. Mr. Samuel Hopkins, in the second part of his reply to the Rev. Mr. Mills; intitled, "The true state and character of the unregenerate, stripped of all misrepresentation and disguise" 1847
Vindication of the principles and conduct of the church in Stockbridge. 1334, 1856
Vindication of the Protestant Episcopal church. 2466, 2964
Vindication of the result of the late mutual council convened in Princeton. 1337
Vindication of the revised liturgy, historical and theological. 675
Vindication of the Society of Friends. 1682
Vindication of the true God against the God of Moses. 1655
Vindication of the validity and divine right of Presbyterian ordination. 890, 1289
Vindication of Unitarianism. 3724, 3795
Vindications. 351
Vindicator. 1775, 2617
Vindiciae cantus dominici. 2984
Vine and the branches. 811
Vine life. 424, 1010, 1577
Vine of seven branches. 3378
Vinent de Paul. 3779
Vine's Expository dictionary of Old and New Testament words. 246
Vineyard Bible. 249
Vintage years. 990
Violence. 3780
Violence and defense in the Jewish experience. 3780
Violence and religous commitment. 1393, 2817
Violence and the sacred. 3239
Violence, conflict, and politics in Columbia. 3780
Violence in Ireland. 1920
Violence within. 3780
Violent for peace. 3780
Violent sleep. 2216
Virgil C. Hart. 1787, 2509
Virgil Michel and the liturgical movement. 2233, 2461
Virgil's prophecy on the Saviour's birth. 3780
Virgin. 2359, 3838
Virgin birth. 2069, 3780, 3781
Virgin birth and the Incarnation. 3620
Virgin birth: doctrine of deity. 3780
Virgin birth--fact or fiction! 3781
Virgin birth in the theology of the ancient church. 3781
Virgin birth of Christ. 3781
Virgin birth of Jesus. 2021
Virgin in Eden, 1741. 3235
Virgin Islands story. 3781
Virgin Mary. 2354, 2357, 2362, 2363
Virgin Mary in evangelical perspective. 2356
Virgin most powerful. 3247
Virgin mother. 2354, 2355, 3780
Virgin of Orleans. 1938
Virgin saints and martyrs. 3279
Virgin soil. 3378
Virgin with child. 2355
Virginal conception and bodily resurrection of Jesus. 1886, 2051
Virginia Baptist ministers. 144, 145, 172
Virginia Baptist Training Union history. 141
Virginia bishop. 2128
Virginia Methodism. 2433
Virginia Presbyterianism and religious liberty in colonial and revolutionary times. 2928
Virginia Woolf meets Charlie Brown. 2934
Virginia's colonial churches. 1275
Virginia's colonial churches, an architectural guide. 1275
Virginia's mother church and the political conditions under which it grew. 1223
Virginitas. 3781
Virginity. 3781
Virgins reluctant, dubious, avowed. 3782
Virgin's son. 1951
Virility of Christ. 1951
Virtue and vice. 862, 3782
Virtue makes sense! 3888
Virtue of gratitude according to the mind of Saint Thomas. 1756, 3694
Virtue of honor and beaty according to St. Thomas Aquinas. 3598, 3695

Virtue of humility. 1856
Virtue of love. 2267
Virtue of trust. 2390
Virtues. 51, 3782, 3880
Virtues and spiritual doctrine of Saint Vincent de Paul. 3779
Virtues awakened. 3782
Virtues for our time. 997
Virtues of a religious superior (De Sex alis seraphim) 2575
Virtues; on forms of moral life. 3782
Virtues on parade. 3782
Virtuous woman. 3393
Visible and invisible worlds. 3076
Visible and the invisible. 2739
Visible church, her government, ceremonies, sacramentals, festivals and devotions. 757
Visible church, in covenant with God. 1356, 2373
Visible church of Christ. 1201
Visible display of divine providence. 2487
Visible evolution. 1581
Visible glory. 1513
Visible saint. 2371
Visible saints. 3007
... The visible sanctity of the church as a note and a motive of credibility. 1165
Visible signs of the gospel. 793, 2572
Visible unity and the ten propositions. 1043
Visible unity and tradition. 1249
Visible words. 3263
Visible words of God. 3266, 3777
Vision. 609, 1402, 2611, 2948, 3430
Vision and achievement. 2520
Vision & action. 2834
Vision and faith. 1329
Vision and organization. 3438
Vision and power. 2901
Vision and prophecy in Amos. 486
Vision and service. 974
Vision and strategy for church growth. 1171
Vision and tactics. 805
Vision and the way. 1538
Vision and valor. 2481, 2607
Vision and virtue. 946
Vision is tremendous. 1474
Vision lives. 1377
Vision of a short life. 2511, 3317
Vision of Fatima. 1618
Vision of God. 179, 944, 1451, 2647
Vision of God and the social order. 2638
Vision of God, the Christian doctrine of the summum bonum. 944
Vision of heaven. 1793
Vision of La Salette. 726, 3286
Vision of Matthew. 442
Vision of Paul Tillich. 3699
Vision of peace. 190
Vision of renewal. 999
Vision of the ages. 463
Vision of the disinherited. 2816
Vision of the evening and the morning. 509
Vision of the trinity. 3714
Vision of victory. 455, 465
Vision splendid. 976
Vision that transforms and other sermons. 3341
Vision 20/20. 586
Vision we forget. 464
Vision which transforms. 2819, 3805
Visionary Christian. 3622
Visionary girls. 3827
Visionary girls: witchcraft in Salem Village. 3827
Visions. 1781, 3342
Visions and prophecies. 3783
Visions and prophecies for a new age. 877, 2948
Visions & prophecies of Zechariah. 600
Visions and revelations in the spiritual life. 3783
Visions and voices. 200
Visions beyond the veil. 139
Visions from the Vaal. 1466, 3341
Visions in verse. 3206
Visions of a world hungry. 2394
Visions of Bernard Francis de Hoyos. 1849, 3269
Visions of glory. 457, 1365, 1787, 1941
Visions of heaven and hell. 713, 1795, 3783
Visions of hope and fear. 460
Visions of Jesus. 1956, 3783
Visions of Mary Baker Eddy. 1032
Visions of the beyond. 3514
Visions of the beyond, by a seer of to-day. 3514
Visions of the Christ. 3783
Visions of the divine. 1730
Visions of the end. 1515
Visions of the future. 2753
Visions of the kingdom. 3783
Visions of the spiritual world. 1697

Visions of Therese Neumann. 2686, 3783
Visions of time. 2773
Visions, revelations and the church. 2942
Visions rise and change. 3257
Visit to Bois d'Haine. 2198, 3531
Visit to five brothers. 601
Visit to five brothers, and other double exposures. 601
Visit to the astral plane. 3502
Visit to the Holy Land and other Mediterranean countries. 2763
Visit to the stigmatized seer. 2685, 3532
Visit to the West Africa mission of the Presbyterian church in the U.S.A. 2928
Visit to Yale-in-China. 881
... Visitation articles and injunctions of the period of the reformation. 3783
Visitation charges delivered to the clergy and churchwardens of the dioceses of Chester and Oxford. 1825
Visitation evangelism. 1566
Visitation evangelism made practical. 3783
Visitation manual. 3421
... The visitation of religious. 2578
Visitations and memorials of Southwell minster. 3783
Visitations of Our Lady. 2359
Visiting around the world. 2549
Visitors from other planets. 3473
Visits for children to Jesus in the Blessed Sacrament. 794
Visits from the shades. 3607
Visits of mercy. 1911
Visits to Aunt Clement. 3721
Visits to the Blessed Sacrament. 858
...Visits to the most holy sacrament and to the blessed Virgin Mary. 2259
Visits to the most holy sacrament and to the blessed Virgin Mary for every day in the month. 855
Visits to the most holy sacrament, etc., for every day in the month. 2259
Vistas from Mount Moria. 2139
Vistas, The Gypsy Christ, and other prose imaginings. 3201
Visual aids in the church. 3784
Visual Bible. 602
Visual in metaphysical poetry. 1518
... Visual method in the church curriculum ... by Protestant evangelical forces of the United States and Canada through the International council of religious education. 3784
Visual representations of the Trinity. 3713
"visualized" Baltimore catechism no. 2. 768
Visualized church history. 1180
Visuddhimagga of Buddhaghosacariya. 701
Vita Christi. 2395
Vita Christi of Ludolph of Saxony and late medieval devotion centred on the incarnation. 929, 2270
La vita di Frate Ginepro (testo latino e volgarizzamento) a cura di Giorgio Petrocchi. 2159
Vita laudanda. 393, 2218, 2235
... Vita sancti Ambrosii. 29
Vital and victorious faith of Christ. 951
Vital body. 3250
Vital Christian. 996
Vital Christianity. 1052, 1072
Vital church management. 1199
Vital concepts of the Bible. 201
Vital doctrines of the faith. 3662
Vital elements of preaching. 2901
Vital facts of life. 3885
Vital faith. 1407
Vital forces of Christianity and Islam. 2565
Vital gospel truths. 1238
Vital heart of Christianity. 3222
Vital holiness. 3430
Vital issues in Christian science. 1034, 3527
Vital letters. 3483
Vital message. 3500
Vital ministry. 3673
Vital modifications of religious thought. 3073
Vital points in the Methodist Episcopal church. 2443
Vital possessions. 1437
Vital principles in religious education. 3161
Vital problems in Christian living. 973
... Vital problems of Catholic education in the United States. 830
Vital pulpit of the Christian church. 1466, 3348
Vital realities. 762
... Vital religion. 1053, 3735
Vital sermon outlines. 3372
Vital sermons. 3353
Vital teachings of God's word. 644
Vital teachings of the New Testament. 476
Vital truths respecting God and man. 301

Vital union with Christ. 2637
Vital word studies in I Thessalonians. 325, 478
Vital word studies in II Thessalonians. 325
Vital words of the Bible. 243, 3682
Vitality of faith. 1234
Vitality of Mormonism. 2606
Vitality of Old Testament traditions. 564
Vitality of the Christian tradition. 1097
Vitality of the individual in the thought of ancient Israel. 588, 3462
Vitalizing the church program. 1250
Vitamin called faith. 1067
... The Vitas sanctorum patrum emeretensium. 2412
Vitellius psalter. 848
Vivekananda. 3784
Vivekananda: the yogas and other works. 2840
Vivid experiences in Korea. 2536
Vladimir Soloviev and his messianic work. 3457
Vladimir Solovyev's Lectures on Godmanhood. 3105
Vocabulary of faith. 3682
Vocabulary of Jewish life. 2118, 2154
... The vocabulary of Pope St. Leo the Great. 2216
... The vocabulary of religion. 3784
Vocabulary of the church. 3639
Vocal and literary interpretation of the Bible. 232, 1587
Vocal solos for Protestant services. 3271
Vocation and Protestant religious occupations. 1252
Vocation, formation, consecration & vows. 2571
Vocation of Aloysius Gonzaga. 2271
Vocation of Lady Christine. 48
Vocation to love. 997
Vocation to the priesthood. 773
Vocational guidance by astrology. 96
Vocational guidance of theological students. 3612
"Vocations" 3784
... Vocations within the church. 1295
Voice. 293, 617
Voice for the heart. 2385
Voice from Heaven. 3503
Voice from Rome, answered by an American citizen; or. 2768
Voice from Sinai. 1314
Voice from the Cross. 2056
Voice from the crowd. 2904
Voice from the desert. 3489
Voice from the dust. 2598
Voice from the heavens. 3511
Voice from the pew. 3197
Voice from the pious dead of the medical profession. 923
Voice in the Village. 146, 2588
Voice in the wilderness. 1059, 1396, 2128, 2443, 2936, 3789
Voice is calling. 1029
Voice not our own. 1984
Voice of a priest. 863
Voice of America on Kishineff. 2102
Voice of authority. 118
Voice of blood, in the sphere of nature and of the spirit-world. 672
Voice of Christian life in song. 1875
Voice of Christianity. 3225
Voice of conscience. 1347
Voice of faith. 2280
Voice of fate. 1615
Voice of God. 306, 1735, 3226
Voice of God, in stormy winds. 2373
Voice of God in the present hour. 3705
Voice of his praise. 1875
Voice of illness. 2377, 2378
Voice of Isis. 1921
Voice of Israel's prophets. 568
Voice of Jacob. 3371
Voice of Jerusalem. 2082
Voice of Jesus suffering to the mind and heart of Christians. 2033, 2381
Voice of John. 759
Voice of my prayer. 2399
Voice of nature. 1325, 2676
Voice of Norfolk. 3364
Voice of reason and truthful echoes. 3027
Voice of the Beloved. 2574
Voice of the church. 1373
Voice of the Cross. 2057
Voice of the heart. 2706, 3361
Voice of the Jewish laity. 2115
Voice of the living God. 3642
Voice of the Lord. 1637
... Voice of the patriarchs. 3508
Voice of the pioneers on instrumental music and societies. 1271, 1463
Voice of the prophets. 464, 3355
Voice of the saints. 3285
Voice of the seven thunders. 451
Voice of the silence. 3689

Voice of the silence and other chosen fragments from the Book of the golden precepts. 3684
Voice of the silence being chosen fragments from the "Book of the golden precepts." 3684
Voice of the soul. 3688
Voice of the spirit. 1454, 3487
Voice of the Tambaran. 78
Voice of the turtledove. 2389
Voice of the valley. 3460
Voice of Trappist silence. 3709
Voice of Venus. 3509
Voice of warning and instruction to all people. 2605
Voice of your Father. 1648
Voice out of the cloud. 3066
Voice out of the whirlwind. 549, 550, 2124
Voice said Ave! 1020, 2360
Voice still heard. 2634
Voice still speaks. 3360
Voice that spoke for justice. 3016, 3822
Voice to Universalists. 3753
Voice triumphant. 3498
Voice under every palm. 1509, 3018
Voice within. 1347
Voice within us. 907
Voices and instruments in Christian worship. 1206
Voices from another world. 1710, 3502
Voices from beyond. 2399, 3504
Voices from beyond the vale. 3515
Voices from Calvary. 1998
Voices from Cane Ridge. 1461
Voices from eternity. 214
Voices from heaven and hell. 338
Voices from home. 1644, 2733
Voices from Japan. 154
Voices from life's thither side. 3512
Voices from other lives. 3053
Voices from rocks and dust heaps of Bible lands. 207
Voices from templed hills. 3362
Voices from the back pew. 1245
Voices from the East. 2744
Voices from the edge of eternity. 2198
... Voices from the Near East. 2503
Voices from the open door. 3520
Voices from the past. 207, 1014
Voices from the silent centuries. 379
Voices from the silent land. 1353
Voices from the spirit land. 3505
Voices from the spirit world. 3511
Voices from the tapes. 3473
Voices from the void. 3514
Voices from the younger churches. 2520
Voices of American fundamentalism. 1690
Voices of assurance. 3362
Voices of change. 2571
Voices of concern. 1271
Voices of earth and sky. 1902
Voices of France. 3617
Voices of hope. 2694
Voices of hope and other messages from the hills. 2694
Voices of liberalism. 2221
Voices of living prophets. 3365
Voices of nature to her foster-child. 2672
Voices of prayer and praise. 3206
Voices of spirit. 122, 2988
Voices of the age. 3366
Voices of the cathedral. 921
Voices of the great Creator. 3678
Voices of the long ago. 623
Voices of the New room. 2424
Voices of the night. 1556, 3339, 3506
Voices of the passion. 2057, 2214
Voices of twelve Hebrew prophets. 559
Voices of wisdom. 2081
Voices on fire. 2398, 3788
Voices on holiness from the Evangelical association. 1823
Voices on the wind. 2666
Volitional element in knowledge and belief. 2836
Vollstandige Konkordanz zum griechischen Neuen Testament. 345
Vollstandiges Heiligen-Lexikon. 1025
Voltaire on religion: selected writings. 3091
Voltaire's Old Testament criticism. 504, 3786
Volts from a layman's dynamo. 2202
Voluntary associations. 3448
Voluntary associations, a study of groups in free societies. 3448
Voluntary church. 3749
Voluntary clergy. 1288
Voluntary controls. 2381
Voluntary simplicity. 3409
Volunteer minister's handbook. 3314
Volunteer social service by college men. 3435
Volunteers of America. 3786
Von Balthasar reader. 793, 3650

Von Hugel and the supernatural. 1850, 3099
Vondel's Lucifer. 2270
Voodoo. 3787
Voodoo & hoodoo. 3787
Voodoo charms and talismans. 3787
Voodoo, devils, and the new invisible world. 3823
Voodoo heritage. 3787
Voodoo in Haiti. 3787
Voodoo in New Orleans. 3787
Voodoo, its origins and practices. 3787
Voodoo secrets from A to Z. 3787
Voodoos and obeahs. 3828
Votive offerings among Greek-Philadelphians. 2749, 3787
Votive religion at Caere. 3604
Vow of poverty. 2866
Vows and perfection. 3787
Vows but no walls. 2571
Vox populi. 1196
Vox spei. 166
Voyage of discovery. 2432
Voyage of faith. 1044, 2805
Voyage of Saint Brendan, journey to the promised land. 691
Voyage to Lourdes. 2262
Voyage to West Africa and some reflections on modern missions. 2500
Voyage, vision, venture. 3331
... The voyager (sequel to The blind spot) 2530
Voyages to Hawaii before 1860. 1791
Vril. 2722
Vultures gather, the fig tree blooms. 607

W

W. A. Criswell. 1387
W. A. P. Martin. 2349, 2485
W. C. Handy's collection of Negro spirituals for mixed voices, male voices, also vocal solos with piano accompaniment. 2680
... W. C. T. U. handbook. 3833
W. C. T. U. in the Volunteer State. 3833
W. Eugene Sallee, Christ's ambassador. 156, 3287
W. G. Nixon's sermons. 3355
W. J. Simmonite's The complete arcana of astral philosophy. 97
W. M. Lowman, bishop of Virginia. 2267
W. Norman Cooper, a prophet for our time. 1368
W. P. Throgmorton, D.D. 3698
W. R. Matthews. 2374
W. Robertson Smith and the sociological study of religion. 3088, 3432
W. T. Conner, theologian of the Southwest. 1346
W. W. Cassals. 744, 2508
W. W. Otey, contender for the faith. 2752
Wage-earning boy. 3872
Wages of sin. 3850
... Wages of sin is death. 3292
Waging peace. 103
Waging peace: a way out of war. 2806
Wahhabiyya; Islamic reform and politics in French West Africa. 3788
Waiapu; the story of a diocese. 2522
Wail of a drug addict. 1480
Wailing wall. 2073
Wait a minute, Moses! 3186
Waiting at the cross. 2057
Waiting Father. 2028, 3368
Waiting for Christ. 2414
Waiting for God. 1741, 1742
Waiting for the Lord. 2383, 2386
Waiting for the Paraclete. 3222
Waiting game. 7
Waiting in the wings. 168
Waiting isles. 2559
Waiting Saviour. 2059
Waiting upon God. 3478
Waiting world. 1414
Wake Forest seminar on Christianity. 1072, 1956
Wake up and lift. 1571
Wake up or blow up! 2520
Wake up, wake up, to do the work of the creator. 1802, 2751
Wakeners of souls. 1001
Waking heart. 1348

Waldenses. 3789
Waldenses in the new world. 3789
Waldensians. 3789
Walk about Zion. 2964
Walk and Talk in Hindustan. 2406
Walk, conversation and character of Jesus Christ Our Lord. 1974
Walk God's battlefield. 2383
Walk in His ways. 979
Walk in the light. 406
Walk in the Spirit. 3479

Walk on! 3685
Walk on water, Pete! 987, 2825
Walk the distant hills. 55, 2529
Walk the high places. 2385
Walk with God. 1002, 2392
Walk with God ... between Sundays. 1010
Walk with Jesus. 445, 1969, 1987
Walk with the Cross. 672, 1576
Walk with the King today. 982
Walk with the Lord. 1232
Walk with the wise. 3279
Walker revised. 1215
Walker's Comprehensive Bible concordance. 228
Walker's gospel sermons. 3360
Walking and talking with God. 2299
Walking as He walked. 3299, 3300
Walking his way. 2719
Walking in obedience. 2718
Walking in the light. 979
Walking in the Resurrection. 1006
Walking in the spirit. 981
Walking on the wings of the wind. 1265
Walking on water. 1089, 2209
Walking the roads with Jesus. 2399
Walking where Jesus walked. 282
Walking with God. 163, 985, 1069, 1429, 1439, 1441, 1794, 2297
...Walking with Jesus. 974
Walking with the giants. 1290
Walking with the Lord. 324, 994
Walking with the master. 3191
Walking with wise men. 2296
Walks and homes of Jesus. 1968
Walks and talks in Hindustan. 2406
Walks and talks through Bible lands. 617
Walks and words of Jesus. 383
... Walks from Eden. 297
Walks to Emmaus. 1339
Walks with Jesus. 1968
Walks with Our Lord through John's Gospel. 423
Walks with Saint John. 418
Wall. 983
Wall and the garden. 1504
Wall and The gates, and other sermons. 3358
Wall between church and state. 1490
Wall between church and states. 1490
Wall between us. 861
Wall of Jerusalem also is broken down. 560
Wall of separation between church and state. 1151
Wallace-Hunt debate. 2633
Wallace-Ketcherside debate, held near Paragould, Arkansas, June 30 July 4, 1952. 1272
Wallace-Ketcherside St. Louis debate, St. Louis, Missouri, October 26-30, 1953, between G. K. Wallace and W. Carl Ketcherside. 1272
Wallace-Stauffer debate. 1906
Wallace-Vaughn debate. 3713
Walled garden. 1365, 2080
Walled in. 1347, 3425
Wallpaper that talked. 2491
Walls. 3790
Walls are crumbling. 2085
Walls came tumbling down. 554
Wall's End miner. 1387
Walls of Jerusalem. 1944
Walter C. Woodward. 3847
... Walter de Wenlok. 3802, 3808
Walter Edmund Bentley: actor, priest, missioner, 1864-1962, founder of the Actors' Church Alliance. 191
Walter Howard Frere. 2238
Walter McGill. 2308
Walter Martin's Cults reference Bible. 1393
Walter Rauschenbusch. 3025
Walter Rauschenbusch and his contribution to social Christianity. 3025, 3446
Walter Russell Lambuth. 2194
Walter Scott. 3315
Walter Scott speaks. 3315
Walter Travers. 3710
Walther and the church. 1124
Walther league manual. 1248
Walther on the church. 1164, 2287
Walther speaks to the church. 3790
Walvoord, a tribute. 3625, 3791
Wanderer in the spirit lands. 3501
Wanderers, slaves & kings; daily devotions and Bible studies. 511, 1431
Wanderer's way. 3025
Wandering in Eden. 2844
Wandering in the wilderness; Christians and the new culture. 1056
Wandering Jew. 2082, 2088, 3791
Wandering of the soul. 1503
Wandering scholars. 1744
Wandering stars. 3369
Wandering Wheels. 3829
Wanderings of a spiritualist. 3500
Wanderings of Christ. 2014

Wanderings through ancient Roman churches. 3245
Wandjina, children of the Dreamtime. 2655
Wanless of India. 3791
Wanted. 1367, 1371
Wanted--a congregation. 1250
Wanted--a theology. 3615
Wanted--a world leader! 1514
Wanted, writers for the Christian market. 3203
Wanting, becoming, believing. 984
War. 3737
War against Christ. 1950
War against God. 1319, 1708
War against God in Lithuania. 101
War against the Jew. 53
War against war. 1959
War and Christian ethics. 3794
War and Christianity. 2807
War & Christianity today. 3794
War and conscience. 3793
War and conscience in America. 3793
War and conscription at the bar of Christian morals. 3793
War and guilt. 3794
War and men's minds. 1543
War and moral discourse. 3793
War and peace from Genesis to Revelation. 3795
War and peace in the law of Islam. 2122, 2564
War and peace in the world's religions. 3792
... The war and preaching. 2901
War and religion. 1543
War and the Bible. 3794
War and the Christian. 3793, 3849
War and the Christian conscience. 3793
War and the church. 1748
War and the Gospel. 3794
War beyond the stars. 42
War, communism, and world religions. 3792
War, conscience, and dissent. 3794
War, conscription, conscience, and mormonism. 1232, 1347
War—4 Christian views. 1089
War in heaven. A disquisition, Biblical and rational, concerning angels, devils, and men, and the creation, fall, and redemption of the human soul. 3463
War in the light of prophecy. 605
War in your heart. 3295
War inconsistent with the religion of Jesus Christ. 3792
War; its causes, consequences and cure. 3793
War; its causes, consequenxes and cure. 3793
War letters from the living dead man. 3495
War of amazing love. 2517
War of the universe. 2324
War on modern science. 1582
War or peace? 3794, 3891
War or peace, which? 3794
War, peace, amity. 3793
War, peace, and nonresistance. 2807, 2809
War, peace, and the Bible. 1089
War, peace, and the Christian mind. 3792
War, poverty, freedom. 1067
War preparations and international suicide. 3792
War to be one. 2559
... War! War! War! 2104
War we can't lose. 454
War--what does the Bible say? 3792
Warburton and the Warburtonians. 3795
Warfare of Christ. 1004
Warfare of science. 3085, 3314
Warm heart of Wesley. 3802
Warm light on history. 607
Warming fires. 3742
Warn-word to Sir Francis Hastings West-word, 1602. 790, 872
Warning from the oak. Written for the young. 5
Warren Akin Candler, the conservative as idealist. 668, 734
Warren- Ballard debate. 1272
Warren-Barnhart debate on Christian ethics versus utilitarian (psychological hedonistic) ethics. 945
Warren-Matson debate on the existenceof God. 1738
Warrior. 3482
Warrior goddess: Athena. 101
Warrior in white. 2372
Warrior saint. 1635
Warrior spirit in the republic of God. 953
Warrior the woman, and the Christ. 2061
Warriors of God. 2582
Wars of America. 3741
Wars of religion in France, 1559-1576. 1639
Wars of the godly. 827

Wars of truth. 2319
Wartburg hymnal for church, school and home. 1860
Was Albertus Magnus von Maria sagt. Koln. 22, 2354
Was Bronson Alcott's school a type of God's moral government? 104, 1368
Was Christ a god! 2050
Was Christ both God and man! 2002, 2563
Was Christ divine? 2001
Was Christ God? 422
Was Christ really born of a virgin? 2022
Was haltet Ihr von der Kirche? 1809
Was Jesus a pacifist? 2809
Was Jesus a revolutionist? 2039, 3233
Was Jesus an historical person? 1956
Was Jesus Christ a democrat? 1655
Was Jesus crucified on Good Friday? 1997
Was Jesus guilty? 2068
Was Jesus influenced by Buddhism? 702, 1951
Was Jesus married? 1954, 3392
Was Jesus of Nazareth God or man, Christ or spirit medium? 2002
Was Jesus really like us? 1012, 2012
Was the apostle Paul an epileptic? 2804
Was the resurrection a fact? 3221
Washed in His blood. 103
Washing elephants. 3367
Washing elephants, and other paths to God. 3367
Washington. 1085
Washington choir, original and selected music. 3598
Washington diocese of the Protestant Episcopal church. 2971
Washington Gladden. 1715
Washington Heights congregation. 1480, 2701
Washington in the lap of Rome. 799
... The Washington manuscript of Deuteronomy and Joshua. 316
... The Washington manuscript of the Epistles of Paul. 2330
... The Washington manuscript of the four Gospels. 316
... The Washington manuscript of the Psalms. 316
Washington northern Idaho Disciples. 1467
Washington Street United Methodist Church, Alexandria, Virginia. 24, 3798
Washington Unitarianism. 3796
Washington's prayers. 2896
Waste-basket surgery. 2539
Waste of sin. 2944
Wat Haripunjaya. 3798
Watch. 1826
Watch and pray. 2576
Watch and pray with me. 2033
Watch for the morning. 1353
Watch fires. 3717
Watch it! Patience. 2792
Watch on Calvary. 2058
Watch tower and herald of Christ's presence. 1940
Watch Tower publications index of subjects discussed and Scriptures explained. 1941
Watch with me. 2381
Watch your controls. 688
Watch your dreams. 1479
Watch your teaching! 781, 2953
Watch yourself go by. 966
Watcher on the hills. 2639
Watchers by the cross. 2057
Watchers for the dawn. 925
Watchers of the springs. 3359
Watchers of the world. 3238
Watches, prayers, arguments given to students. 1032
Watchful elders. 3390
Watching an hour. 3266
Watching at Golgotha. 2029
Watching at my gates. 723
Watching Jesus die. 2034
Watchman. 2786
Watchman, tell it true. 1302, 1811
"Watchman, what of the night?" 2079
Watchwords for the warfare of life. 2275
Watchwords from Dr. Brownson. 697
Water and the fire. 1002
Water baptism. 136
Water baptism; a pagan and Jewish rite, but not Christian. 135
Water from the well of salvation. 2298
Water from the well-spring. 3406
Water in a thirsty land. 1485, 3899
Water in the wilderness. 613
Water into wine. 3270
Water of life. 716, 1226, 3364
Water-star. 1067
Water that divides. 134
Waterbuffalo theology. 3622
Watering the seed. 1648
Watermelon for God. 3715

Waters of Marah. 2746
Waters of Siloe. 3709
Waterway. 2677
Watson v. Jones. 1242, 3798
Watts, Alan Wilson. 1080
Watts's Psalms and hymns. 581
Watunna, an Orinoco creation cycle. 3863
Wave goodbye to the Joneses. 3799
Waves, particles, and paradoxes. 3615
Way. 601, 1050, 1439, 1441, 2392, 2399, 3144, 3226, 3250, 3486, 3660, 3663, 3664
Way, a training booklet for the new Christian. 149
Way and its power. 2838
Way and its ways. 1094
Way and the work. 3565
Way back. 1781, 3200
Way called heresy. 2221
Way Christmas came. 2022
Way down here. 2374, 2536
Way for a child to be saved. 902
Way: fragments from the Scriptures. 303
Way home. 151, 2587
Way in and the way out. 3083
Way in the wilderness. 1584, 2622, 2763
Way in the world. 1013
Way into the holiest. 404
Way is strait and narrow. 1036
Way: living in love. 3799
Way made plain. 2286, 3288
Way of a man with a maid. 215, 3393
Way of a pilgrim. 2847
Way of a pilgrim and The pilgrim continues his way. 1022, 1454, 3493
Way of a pilgrim (The) 2847
Way of action. 704
Way of adult education. 3160
Way of all the earth. 3115
Way of Christ. 475, 899, 990
Way of Chuang-tzu. 2412
Way of community. 3183
Way of discipleship. 2302, 2914
Way of divine communion. 3477
Way of divine love. 2643
Way of faith. 1589, 2934
Way of freedom. 469
Way of God with Jungle Flower. 2505
Way of holiness. 3300, 3623
Way of holiness, with notes by the way. 1823
Way of honor. 3342
Way of initiation. 3688
Way of interior peace. 3487
Way of Israel. 599, 2148
Way of Jesus. 1995, 2015
Way of Judaism. 3261
Way of Kabbalah. 722
Way of Lao Tzu (Tao-te ching) 2197
Way of life. 639, 788, 803, 973, 990, 1360, 1557, 1821, 2015, 2064, 2196, 2282, 3292, 3335
Way of life according to Laotzu. 2196
Way of light. 1441, 1447
Way of love. 983, 2266, 2386, 3171
Way of love divine. 2264
Way of loving. 324
Way of man according to the teaching of Hasidism. 1789
Way of man, according to the teachings of Hasidism. 1788
Way of mercy. 2305, 3417
Way of missionary education. 2550
Way of modernism & other essays. 2561
Way of Muhammad. 21, 3542
Way of mysticism. 2639
Way of non-attachment. 3780
Way of peace. 2757, 2809
Way of peaced and blessdness. 2772
Way of perfection. 2819, 3604
Way of power. 2228, 3484
Way of prayer. 2867, 2869, 3603
Way of renewal. 2211
Way of revival. 1555
Way of St. Alphonsus Liguori. 3488
Way of St. Francis. 1642
Way of salvation. 249, 3289, 3290, 3292, 3294, 3295
Way of salvation and of perfection. 3294
Way of salvation familiarly explained. 3292
Way of salvation illustrated in a series of discourses. 3295
Way of salvation in the Lutheran church. 2285, 2286
Way of seeing. 990
Way of Siddhartha. 712, 1703
Way of simplicity. 3481
Way of splendor. 723
Way of tenderness. 1001
Way of the ascetics. 89
Way of the blessed Christ. 1977
Way of the Christian. 3164
Way of the cross. 107, 990, 1051, 2034, 2211, 3525, 3526
Way of the Cross and Resurrection. 1998, 2212

Way of the cross, comprising a luminous discussion of both the law and the gospel. 2200
Way of the Cross; designs and text. 3526
Way of the cross in human relations. 1134
Way of the cross in the seminary. 3526
Way of the cross leads to the crown. 3798
Way of the Cross of Our Lord and Savior Jesus Christ. 3526
Way of the Cross—way of justice. 1077, 1998
Way of the cross—where it led me. 1367, 1588
Way of the faithful. 2646
Way of the Gospels. 367
Way of the heart. 2786
Way of the Lord. 429
Way of the Lord prepared. 2493
Way of the Master. 1232, 1986
Way of the mystics. 2642, 2645
Way of the Orient. 2531
Way of the peaceful warrior. 2467, 3480
Way of the preacher. 3673
Way of the righteous. 579
Way of the river. 399
Way of the sacred. 1836
Way of the samurai. 719, 3862
Way of the Shepherd. 631
Way of the skeptic. 787, 2402
Way of the spirit. 2420
Way of the Sufi. 3543
Way of the transgressor. 3410, 3414
Way of the wilderness. 517, 1584
Way of the witnesses. 2494
Way of the word. 119, 1095
Way of Torah. 2140
Way of transcendence. 3328
Way of trusting. 1325
Way of victory. 1052
Way of vision. 3477
... The way of wisdom and self-liberation. 702, 703
Way of wisdom in the Old Testament. 3821
Way of witches. 3826
Way of worship. 3004
Way of zazen. 2383
Way of Zen. 3891, 3892, 3895
Way out. 1056, 3595
Way out of agnosticism. 3097
Way out of chaos. 1090
Way out world. 2727
Way people pray; an introduction to the history of religions. 3114
Way the preachers pray. 2880
Way, the truth and the life. 957, 1071, 1992, 2931, 3181, 3564, 3663, 3684
Way, the truth, the life. 2070
Way through. 3501
Way to a new life. 1006
Way to Biblical preaching. 2903
Way to Christ. 2641, 3288
Way to Christianity. 3475
Way to do good. 954, 2589
Way to Emmaus. 1364
Way to freedom. 2077, 2284, 3632
Way to go, baby! 1261
Way to God. 2117, 3480
Way to God and holiness. 3295
Way to God and how to find it. 1559
Way to Godhood. 1048
Way to happiness. 767, 1002
Way to happy living. 1002
Way to heaven. 841, 1011, 1560
Way to heaven and the key to eternal glory. 1794
Way to Ilala. 2241
Way to inner peace. 1002
Way to life. 2196, 2931, 3448
Way to life and immortality. 1887
Way to Nicea. 3714
Way to Nirvana. 702
Way to paradise. 2772
Way to peace. 951, 1659
Way to peace, health, and power. 958
Way to Pentecost. 1828
Way to perfection. 2613
Way to personality. 945
Way to power and poise. 1439
Way to start a day. 3546
Way to teach the Bible. 650
Way to the altar. 1317
Way to the best. 2300
Way to the cross. 717
Way to the kingdom. 936
Way to the kingdom of heaven. 3291
Way to unity after the Council. 1043
Way to win. 1240, 1250, 1628
Way triumphant. 970
Way we worship. 770
Wayfarer. 2638
... Wayfarer for Christ. 3206
Wayfarers. 2400
Wayfarer's book of devotion. 2388
Wayfarers' friend. 1115
Wayfarers of the Bible. 533
Wayfarer's prayer book. 2884

Wayfaring hymns, original and translated. 1869
Waymarks. 2865
Waymarks in sacred history. 296
Waymarks in the life of Mary Baker Eddy. 1495
Waymarks of the Passion. 1985
Ways and crossways. 758
Ways and power of love. 28
Ways and teachings of the church. 2957
Ways of being. 2739
Ways of being; readings for a new approach to religion. 3091
Ways of believing. 185
Ways of faith. 3117
Ways of reading the Bible. 239
Ways of religion. 3138
Ways of Russian theology. 2745, 3633
Ways of sanctity. 3299
Ways of sharing with other faiths. 1079
Ways of teaching. 3178, 3592
Ways of the Christian life. 3360
Ways of the gods. 3114
Ways of the lonely ones. 2643
Ways of the spirit. 777, 3634
Ways of the spirit, and other essays. 3621
Ways of thinking about God. 1738
Ways of understanding God's Word. 635
Ways of understanding religion. 3091
Ways of witnessing. 3467
Ways of work. 1776
Ways of working. 3557
Ways of working in the nursery department. 3559
Ways of worship. 3854
Ways of worship for new forms of mission. 3003
Ways that win in church finance. 1167
Ways to attain the supreme reality. 1813
Ways to help them learn: adult. 938
Ways to help them learn: children. 3169
Ways to help them learn: early childhood. 3174
Ways to help them learn: youth. 3176
Ways to plan & organize your Sunday school: adult. 3168
Ways to plan & organize your Sunday school: children. 3172
Ways to plan & organize your Sunday school: early childhood. 3173
Ways to plan & organize your Sunday school; youth. 3175
Ways to Shiva. 1897
Ways to spark your church program. 2786
Ways to teach 3's to 5's. 939
Ways to teach children. 3170
Ways to teach teens. 937
Ways to the center. 3114
Ways to wake up your church. 1245
Ways to win. 1565
Ways youth learn. 3175
Wayside Chapel. 3573
Wayside glory. 1453
Wayside leaves. 3209
Wayside service. 1452
Wayside sketches in ecclesiastical history. 1182
Wayward gate. 2729
Wayward Puritans. 3009
Wayward shepherds: prejudice and the Protestant clergy. 2953
Wayward vicarage. 2788
"We actually saw God" 621
We all grow young at Christmas. 1113
We all need each other. 3764
We Americans: North and South. 2955
We and our children. 3165
We and the Holy Spirit, talks to laymen. 3486
We and the vague beyond. 2730
We are able. 1343
We are all brothers. 3486
We are all healers. 2988
We are but a moment's sunlifht. 1418
We are Christ's body. 2020
We are Easter people. 2211
We are future. 1846
We are God's people. 3187
We are His people. 621
We are immortal. 1698, 3569
We are men. 2192
We are not alone. 1737, 2434
We are not divided. 1619
We are now Catholics. 1365
We are one in the Lord. 1170
We are one in the spirit. 1712
We are Peter. 2768, 2806
We are risen in the Lord. 3163
We are the people of God. 3163
"We be brethren" 1272
We became wives of happy husbands. 3830
We beheld His glory. 9, 1055, 1056
We believe! 75, 92, 1386, 2286, 2404, 2428, 3663, 3732
We believe a simplified treatment of the Articles of faith. 3430

We believe and teach. 3644
We believe and worship. 3858
We believe in immortality. 1891
We believe in one god. 1923
We believe in prayer. 2869, 2881
We belong together. 1621, 2489
"We bless Thy holy name for all Thy
 servants departed this life in Thy faith
 and fear, especially William, bishop of
 Gibraltar, and Mary, his wife." 1309
We bow our heads. 900
We call ourselves Disciples. 932
We call this Friday good. 2057, 2058
We can have peace. 2809
We can live together. 3182
We can still believe in God. 1090
We can surely believe. 1098
We can win others. 1571
We Catholics. 785
We Christians and Jews. 1083
*We come to Jesus. 2369
We condemn. 1804, 2280
We covenant together. 1376
We dare to believe. 2385
We dare to say Our Father. 997, 2246
We die before we live. 1413, 3278
We die standing up. 1002
We Disciples. 1464
We discover lights. 3148
We discuss the Creed. 3168
We dream, we climb. 1014
We enjoy Easter. 1486
We explore the Prophets. 571
We face Calvary--and life! 2425
We funny Methodists. 2421
We gather together. 3003
We go a journey. 962
We grow in the family. 1608
We have a gospel. 956
We have a pope. 2852
We have an altar. 2258
We have everything to gain. 1725
"We have found Him" 1360
We have found the Messiah. 3289
We have God. 960
We have this ministry. 1243, 1296, 2787
*We haven seen the Lord. 939
We hold these truths. 92, 827, 1151
We interrupt this crisis. 458
We Jews. 2140
We Jews and Jesus. 2013
We Jews and you Christians. 2153
We knew His power. 384, 1967
We knew Jesus. 338
We knew Mary Baker Eddy. 1493, 1496
We knew Mary Baker Eddy. [- ser.].
 1496
We knew Matt Talbot. 3580
We knew these men. 3501
We know in part. 3242
We know the mass, for home, school and
 church. 2365
"we knows" of the apostle Paul. 374
We learn about Jesus. 3550
... We learn of a wonderful world. 3183
We learn to worship God. 904
We let our son die. 2775, 3711
We lie down in hope. 3406
We live by faith. 1095
We live in Christ. 3187
We live outside our bodies. 2986
We live together. 1321
We live with our eyes open. 1002
We lived with dying. 734, 3847
We Methodists. 3348
We move into Africa. 2542
We need religion. 1053
We need you here, Lord; prayers from the
 city. 2888
We neurotics. 996
We never die. 3505
We never have time for just us—. 2339
We offer Thee. 1266
We older people. 17
We ordinary preachers, by one of them.
 2787
We ordinary prechers. 2787
We persuade men. 3348
We pioneered in Portuguese East Africa.
 2541
We plan our own worship services. 3878
We planted miracles today, Lord. 2625
...We pray the mass. 2370
We pray Thee, Lord. 2881
We preach Christ. 1228
We preach not ourselves. 323
We prepare and preach. 2905
We prepare for Christmas. 1111
We prophesy in part. 2906
We reach our hands in fellowship. 1228
We really do need each other. 1736
We really do need to listen. 424
We remember John. 690
We saw His glory. 2015
We see Jesus. 2933
We serve. 3191
We shall live again. 3341

We shall live in peace. 2172
We shall re-build. 1918
We shall rise. 3125
We share new life. 138
We sing to God. 1870
We sing while there's voice left. 1002,
 3483
We spoke for God. 570, 2951
We stand with Christ. 762
We still believe. 1012, 3383
We talk with God. 1604, 2879
We, the crucifiers. 1063, 2033
We the people. 2192
We, the people of God. 808
We together. 941
We tried to stay. 2510
We two alone. 2514
We want to know. 3011
We want to live. 1094
We were there. 153, 1883
We will prove them herewith. 1009
We wish to see Jesus. 367
We witness together. 1839
We work while the light lasts. 1002
We worship. 3854
We would know Jesus. 398, 1987
We would see Jesus. 392, 979, 2059,
 2066, 2757, 3359, 3410
We wrote the Gospels. 398
Weakness of God. 2030
Wealth of friendship. 1688
Wealth of self and wealth of nations. 2320
Wealth of the mind. 1325
Wealth of wisdom. 1009
Wealth, walk and warfare of the Christian.
 364
Weapon of prayer. 2868
Weapons for peace. 2807
Weapons for temperance warfare. 3594
Weaver. 960
Weaverland Mennonites, 1766-1968. 3799
Weaving of glory. 3343
Web of belief. 186
Web of destiny. 3222
Weber and Islam. 3454, 3800
Wedding addresses. 2347
Wedding-guest. 1787
Wedding manual. 2347
Wedding sermons. 2347
Wedge. 3473
Wedge of gold. 2934, 3357
Wedges and wings. 2469
Wedlock. 2339
Wee folks stories from the Old Testament.
 625
Week-day church-school. 3800
Week-day church school methods. 3160
Week-day church schools. 1247, 3158
Week-day religion. 3062
Week-day religious education. 3148, 3150
Week-day sermons in King's chapel. 3358
Week end with God. 3222
Week in, week out. 2897
Week of communions. 2258
Week of fire. 2391
Week of Our Lord's passion. 2028
Week of the cross. 1986
Week that changed the world. 1986
Week with Christ. 846
Week with Jesus. 1977
... The weekday church school. 3157,
 3801
Weekday church school series. 3801
Weekday homilies for Lent. 863, 2214
Weekday ministry with young children.
 3173
Weekly discourse. 3512
Weekly monitor. 3068
Weekly sermon. 3370
Weeks of growth. 3763
Weighed and wanting. 1316
Weighed and wanting; addresses on the
 Ten commandments. 1316
Weighed in the balances with Scripture.
 1057
Weight of a word. 3211
Weight of glory. 2219, 3622
Weight of glory, and other addresses.
 3622
Weird adventures of Professor Delapine of
 the Sorbonne. 3520
Welcome. 3563
Welcome back, Jesus! 3318
"Welcome, Englishmen" 3007, 3817
Welcome, Jesus. 1627
Welcome Jesus Missal. 901
Welcome speeches. 2721
Welcome to a new life. 985
Welcome to Jesus. 1954
Welcome to the family. 990, 1552
Welcome to the grave. 2195
Welfare ministry. 3435
Welfare of the church. 1117
Welfare of the soul. 3600
Well and the cathedral. 2394
Well and the shallows. 758
Well and the tree. 2660

Well-built. 3884
... The well by the gate. 2935
Well church book. 1244
Well-founded hope. 1529
Well known Bible stories from the Old and
 New Testaments. 622
Well-nigh 50 years at the superintendent's
 desk. 3556
Well of life. 2016
Well of living waters. 3204
Well of the saints. 3282
Well spent quarters. 2399
Well- springs of American freemasonry.
 1672
Well-springs of prayer. 2874
Well-watered plains. 2261
Well, what is teaching? 936
Wellness, your invitation to full life. 1325
Wells and palm trees, cool water and
 abundant rest on life's rough way. 159
Wells Bible atlas. 102
Wells of Baca. 192
Wells of living water. 224
Wells of salvation. 1443, 3267
Wellspring of guidance. 129
Wellsprings of renewal: promise in
 Christian communal life. 2583
Wellsprings of Scripture. 645
Wellsprings of the Pentecostal movement.
 2814
Wellsprings of Torah. 565, 2073
Welsh church from Conquest to
 Reformation. 3789
Welsh Reformation essays. 3039
Welsh saints. 1378
Welsh saints, 1640-1660. 1378
Welshimer's sermons. 3360
We're all Americans. 34
We're all in this together. 806, 942
Were ancient heresies disguised social
 movement? 1805
We're holding your son. 1255
We're in this thing together. 1453
We're making our home a happy place.
 1608
We're never alone. 3844
Were you there. 2014, 2032, 2033, 2212,
 2214
Were you there when they crucified my
 Lord. 1957, 2680
Werewolves, shapeshifters, & skinwalkers.
 2416
Wesley. 3803
Wesley and his coadjutors. 3803
Wesley and his friends. 3804
Wesley and his work; or, Methodism and
 missions; a volume of addresses. 3806
Wesley, and Methodism. 2422, 3804,
 3805
Wesley as sociologist, theologian,
 churchman. 3803
... Wesley bicentennial, Wesleyan
 university. 2422, 3806
Wesley his own historian. 3806
Wesley memorial volume. 2420, 3803
Wesley offering; or, Wesley and his times.
 2421, 3803
Wesley on religious education. 3804
Wesleyan Bible commentary (The) 225
Wesleyan message bearing fruit. 1653
Wesleyan message, its scriptures and
 historical bases. 1653
Wesleyan Methodist connection (or
 church) of America. 3807
Wesleyan movement in the industrial
 revolution. 1139, 2422, 3805
Wesleyan standards. 2438
Wesleyan student. 3128
Wesleyana. 3806
Wesleys at Oxford. 3803
Wesley's Christology. 2009, 3803
Wesleys in picture and story. 3803
Wesley's legacy to the world. 2421, 3804
Wessel Gansfort. 3090
West African psychology. 13
West African religion. 13
West church, Boston. 685
West coast republics of South America.
 911
West Indian church history. 739
West Indian language issue in British
 schools. 2475
West Indian migrants and the London
 churches. 1132
West of the date line. 2502
West of the Yangtze gorges. 2552
West Point prayer book. 2232, 2238
West-Pointer in the Land of the midado.
 1703, 2534
West Roxbury sermons. 3726
West Virginia pilgrim. 2220
West Virginia pulpit of the Methodist
 Episcoipal church. 2434
West Virginia pulpit of the Methodist
 Episcopal church. 2434
Western Apache witchcraft. 55
Western approach to Zen. 3893

Western asceticism. 89
Western attitudes toward death: from the
 Middle Ages to the present. 1416
Western canon law. 736
Western catechetical conference, 1965.
 747
Western Christian church music today.
 1205
Western Christian thought in the middle
 ages. 3213
Western church in the later Middle Ages.
 1186
Western contribution to Buddhism. 3309
Western dilemma. 2837
Western Fathers. 1616, 1617
Western heritage of faith and reason. 2835
Western liturgies. 2237
Western manuscripts in the library of
 Trinity college, Cambridge. 2330
Western mystical tradition. 2645
Western mysticism. 113, 2637, 2642, 2644
Western pioneer. 2228
Western response to Zoroaster. 3898
Western sketch-book. 3066
Western society and the Church in the
 Middle Ages. 1186
Western spirituality. 3522
Western views of Islam in the Middle
 Ages. 1084
Western women in eastern lands. 3834
Westernness and Islam. 1926
Westminister abbey. 3808
Westminister prayers. 1224
Westminister version of the Sacred
 Scriptures. 259
Westminster abbey. 3808
Westminster abbey and the cathedrals of
 England. 751
Westminster Abbey & the kings'
 craftsmen. 3808
... Westminster abbey, its worship and
 ornaments. 3808
Westminster Abbey re-examined. 3808
Westminster assembly and its work. 3808
Westminster assembly's Shorter catechism
 explained by way of question and answer.
 3809
Westminster concise handbook for the
 Bible. 313
Westminster Confession for today. 3809
Westminster confession of faith. 2913,
 3809
Westminster dictionary of Christian
 education. 3163
Westminster dictionary of church history.
 1183
Westminster dictionary of the Bible. 243
Westminster dictionary of worship. 2236
Westminster historical atlas to the Bible.
 283
Westminster introduction to the books of
 the Bible. 312
Westminster normal outlines. 3160
Westminster pulpit. 1342
Westminster sermons. 3342
Westminster study Bible. 247
Westminster study edition of the Holy
 Bible. 247
Westmister dictionary of Christian
 education. 3163
Westmoreland County's pioneer ministers,
 1758-1800. 3809
Westover church and its environs. 3809
Westward the bells. 1899, 3377
Wet sleeves. 3197
We've come this far by faith. 1576, 3815
We've got the power. 3826
Weybosset Bridge in Providence
 Plantations, 1700-1800. 3234, 3432
What! 3382, 3670
What a Christian should believe. 3664
What a church member should do. 1201
What a friend we have in Jesus. 957
What a layman believes. 1433
What a layman should believe. 1212
What a man can believe. 3665
What a Savior! 161
What a way to go. 985, 2200
What a young convert ought to know. 975
What about baptism? 136
"What about continuing revelations and
 miracles in the Presbyterian Church
 today?" 306, 2816, 2914
... What about God? 1056
What about the twelve? 70
What about tomorrow? 604, 3352
What about tongue-speaking? 1716
What about us? 3168
What about us who are not healed? 191,
 1601
What about your God? 1561
What after death? 1695
What am I praying? 2247
What am I saying? 73
What Americans believe and how they
 worship. 3746, 3747
What an altar guild should know. 27

What and how of daily vacation Bible school. 3763
... What and where is God? 1371, 1725, 1727
What and why is man? 2321
What and why of Catholicism. 796
What answer? 1696
What archaelogy says about the Bible. 208
What archaeology says about the Bible. 209
What are saints? 1024, 3281
What are temptations? 3600
What are the theologians saying? 3662
What are these wounds? 2240
What are they saying about Christ and world religions? 1079, 2043
What are they saying about Christian-Jewish relations. 351, 2153
What are they saying about creation? 1381
What are they saying about death and Christian hope? 1413
What are they saying about dogma? 1473
What are they saying about Jesus? 2010
What are they saying about Luke and Acts? 426
What are they saying about moral norms? 947
What are they saying about the Book of Revelation? 460
What are they saying about the prophets? 2951
What are they saying about the Resurrection? 2052
What are they saying about the Trinity? 3714
What are we waiting for? 455
What are you? 3751
What are you doing? 965
What are you living for? 2930
What are you worth. 1747
What awaits you. The great plan. 606
What baptism means. 135
What Baptists believe. 145, 3465, 3663
What Baptists should believe and practice. 148
What became of the bones of St. Thomas? 737, 3692
What becomes of the dead? 1527
What belongs to Caesar? 3589
What Bible can you trust? 270
What boys and girls are asking. 3149, 3183
What Calvinism has done for America. 730
What can a man believe? 1047, 2080, 3381
What can Christians do for peace? 2807
What can God do? 1730
What can I believe? 3661
What can I know? 3103
What can students believe? 3354
What can we believe? 3099
What can you say about God? 1724
What Catholics and Protestants should know. 801
What Catholics believe. 796
What Catholics believe --and why (Whereon to stand)) 795
What Catholics should know about Jews. 2140, 2151
What child is this? 9, 2023
What Christ can do. 1229
What Christ means to me. 1774
What Christ thinks of the church. 461
What Christian science means and what we can learn from it. 1030
What Christian Science means to me--mind-being. 1210
What Christianity has to say. 3364
What Christianity means to me. 1047
What Christianity says about sex, love, and marriage. 2336
What Christians believe. 3660, 3661, 3662
What Christians stand for in the secular world. 1096
What Christmas means to me. 1032
What comes after death? 1697
What constitutes doing business by a corporation in states foreign to the state of its creation. 1369
What counts most in life? 2081
What Daniel knew about Hitler. 508
What demons can do to saints. 1423
What did Christ say? 2071
What did Cranmer think he was doing? 1378, 2256
What did Jesus do? 2210
What did Jesus really teach? 2065
What did Jesus say about that? 2061
What did Jesus teach? 2063
What did Jesus think? 2062
What did Luther understand by religion? 2280
What did the Bible mean? 280
What did the World Council say to you? 3850

... What difference does it make? 3183
What difference does Jesus make? 2044
What district superintendents say—about their office and the issues confronting them. 1470, 3734
What divides Protestants today. 3325
What do I believe? 1593
What do I do now, Lord? 3844, 3882
What do I have to do - break my neck? 3831
What do missionaries do? 2484
What do Presbyterians believe? 3809
What do present day Christians believe? 976
What do religious liberals believe! 2221
What do the prophets say? 253
What do we believe? 3747
What do we know about Jesus? 2007
What do we know about life after death? 1697
What do we mean by God? 1053, 1728
What do we really believe? 788, 1467
What do you believe? 1228
What do you believe, Tovarish? 1073
What do you do after you say amen? 994
What do you know? 762
What do you tell them? 762
What do you think of Christ. 781, 2045
What do you think of Jesus? 1957
What do you think of the priest? 774, 2789
What does Christ expect of young people today? 1467, 3181
What does Christ want? 948
... What does Christianity mean? 1058
What does God mean to you? 3372
What does God want, anyway? 1741
What does God want me to do with my life? 3889
What does God want with a dead dog. 2398
What does it mean to be born again. 1360
What does Jesus expect of his church? 2920
What does Judaism say about ...? 2146
What does the act of existing, esse, mean? 3695
What does the Bible say? 244
What does the Book of Mormon teach? 678
What does the Lord want. 3530
What does the Old Testament say about God? 451, 1731, 2045
What does this mean? 2284
What doth it profit? 1009
What emphasis for the church in town and country? 3253
What every Christian needs to know. 1569
What every Christian ought to know and believe. 2962
What every Christian should believe. 960
What every Christian should know about Bible prophecy. 609
What every Christian should know about God. 1739
What every Christian should know about growing. 982
What every Christian should know about soul winning. 1572
What every husband should know. 1858
What every Jewish woman should know. 2121
What every man and woman should know about the Bible. 3389
What every Methodist should know. 2456
What every parent should know about Christian education. 936
What every woman still knows. 3844
What everyone should know about Judaism. 3011
What everyone should know about transcendental meditation. 3708
What faith can do. 1595
What faith has meant to me. 1591
What future for Christianity? 1047
What future for Friends? 1679
What future for the Agreed Syllabus? 2592
What goal now? 1102
What God does. 1721
What God does for me. 3764
What God has promised. 249
What God hath joined together. 1724, 2336
What God hath spoken, Hebrews 1:1, 2. 232
What God hath wrought. 2829
What God hath wrought in the life of Raymond T. Richey. 3236
What God is like. 3164
What God means to me. 1727
What God says. 1452
What goes on here! 1513
What great men think of religion. 1653
What happened at Aldersgate. 3803
What happened at Rome? 3772

What happened from the cross to the throne. 3029
What happened in Salem? 3827
What happens after death. 1697, 1698, 1891
What happens at Mass. 2364
What happens to sinners? 92
What happens when we die? 1417
What happens when women believe. 2197
What happens when women pray. 2870
What happens when you die. 1415
What happy families are doing. 1604
What has Christianity to say? 1056
What has God done lately? 1317
What has religion done for mankind? 1941
What have the saints to teach us? 1126
What have they done to the catechism? 935
What He said. 2071
What he saw at Cassadaga Lake. 3512
What heaven is. 1793
What helped me when my loved one died. 1353
What I believe. 763, 2113
What I have lived by. 26, 1300
What I owe to Christ. 41
What I saw at Cassadaga lake. 3512
What I saw in Europe. 1542
What I tell my junior congregation. 3338
"What if ..." 217, 2389
What if we did follow Jesus? 990, 2046
What in the world? 1572
What in the world has gotten into the church? 425
What in the world is God doing? 2492
What is a bishop? 665
What is a cardinal? 738
What is a Catholic? 795
What is a Christian? 904, 957, 973, 979, 1004, 1481
What is a Christian college? 936
What is a church? 1199
What is a dogma? 1473
What is a Gospel? 392, 661
What is a Jew? 2120, 2139
What is a living church? 1124
What is a man. 2325
What is a miracle? 2478
What is a priest? 2742
What is a sacrament? 3265
What is a saint? 3280
What is al-Islam. 1924
What is an angel? 42
What is an ecumenical council? 1373
What is bound to happen. 455
What is Calvinism? 2912
What is Calvinistic philosophy? 730
What is Catholic action? 754
What is Catholicity? 795
"What is Christ to me?" 3343
What is Christian civilization? 1281
What is Christian Education. 3181
What is Christian education? 3148
What is Christian faith? 1595
What is Christian life? 999
What is Christian science? 1036
What is Christianity? 934, 1050, 1051, 1057, 1063, 1070, 1094, 1095
What is Christianity? and other essays. 2286
What is Christmas? 1112
What is corporative organization? 1369, 3709
What is dogma? 1473
What is education? 805
What is essential? 3056
What is ethics all about? 948
What is faith? 1593
What is form criticism? 387
What is fortitude. 1634
What is God? 1720
What is God like? 1726, 1734, 3549
What is God's area code? 1731
What is happening in religious education. 3152
What is happening to Catholic education? 831
What is heaven. 1794
What is hell? 1802
What is heresy? 1805
What is holiness. 1823
What is humility? 1856
What is in the Bible. 1275
What is in your Bible? 3763
What is Islam? 1922
What is Judaism? 2082, 2115, 2118
What is left of the Apostles' creed? 73
What is liberalism? 2221
What is libertarianism? 2223
What is life? 2227
What is Lutheranism? 2282
What is man? 2320, 2322, 2323, 2324, 3462
What is marriage? 2346
What is marriage counseling? 2344
What is meditation? 2381

What is modernism? 2243, 2561
What is mysticism? 2637
What is new and old in religion. 3112
What is New Testament theology? 475
What is Pentecost? 2813
What is Presbyterian law as defined by the church courts? 2915
What is Presbyterianism? 2936
What is process theology? 2944, 3813
What is Protestantism? 2978
What is reality? 3101
What is redaction criticism? 391
What is redemption? 3030
What is religion? 3069, 3105, 3343, 3536
What is religion? and other new articles and letters. 3064
What is religion doing to our consciences? 3441
What is revelation? 2329, 3103, 3644
What is right? 946
What is sin? 3411
What is sin? What is virtue? 1412
What is spiritualism. 3510
What is structural exegesis? 349
What is Sufism? 3542
What is Taoism? 3587
What is teaching? 3180
What is the Baha'i faith? 128
What is the best New Testament? 351
What is the Bible? 234, 278, 309, 647
What is the Bible? A modern survey. 237
What is the Christian Orient? 1487
What is the Christian religion? 1071
What is the church? 148, 1116, 1118, 1164, 1248, 3188
What is the church and how you get i it? 1118
What is the church doing? 1182
What is the Church for? 2480
What is the Eucharist? 1541, 2255
What is the Gospel? 391, 1571, 2065
What is the Halacha? 2074
What is the Incarnation? 1893
What is the kingdom of God. 2175
What is the man? 216, 926
What is the Mass! 2365
What is the matter with the church? 1122, 1124
What is the nature of man? 2324
What is the new life? 995
What is the New Testament church? 1123
What is the Oxford group? 2754
What is the priesthood? 2742
What is the question. 1448
What is the Salvation army? An interpretation of its aims, methods and activities. 3293
What is the Trinity? 3714
What is the true church? 1125
What is the truth? 3717
What is the truth about Jesus Christ? 2040
What is the unpardonable sin? 3410
What is the world coming to? 609, 1527
What is the Y M C A? 3872
What is theology? 3669
What is theosophy? 3687
What is there in religion? 1305
What is there left to believe? 3062
What is this Christianity? 1065
What is this Jewish heritage? 2139, 2140
What is this Moslem world? 2566
What is this spiritualism! 3507
What is this treasure? 3664
What is to come? 1695
What is true religion? 3067
What is truth. 50, 500, 1939, 3102, 3717
What is vital in religion. 3351
What is worship? 3852
What is wrong? 1090
What is wrong and how to set it right. 759
What is wrong with the movies? 2627
What is your Catholic I. Q. 3012
What is your destination? 1008
'What is your life? 3758
What is your name? 3758
What is your need! 449
What is your vocation. 1000
What is yours! 3342
What is Zen? 3893
What it means to be a Christian. 956, 1011, 1065
What it means to be a Mormon. 2600
What it means to be born again. 3051
What it means to be Christian. 968
What it means to pray through. 2870
What Jesus began. 1971
What Jesus Christ thought of himself. 2066
What Jesus did. 1985
What Jesus had to say about money. 3529
What Jesus means to me. 2059
What Jesus proclaimed. 2067
What Jesus really taught. 2064
What Jesus said. 3383
What Jesus said about Heaven. 1795

What Jesus said about it. 2069
What Jesus said and did. 400
What Jesus said and did; a study of Luke-Acts. 426, 1966
What Jesus says. 397, 2071
What Jesus says; the master teacher and life's problems. 2933
What Jesus taught. 245, 2065, 2070
What Jesus taught according to the Gospels. 2063
What Jesus taught regarding wealth. 2064
What Jesus was like. 2437
What Judaism teaches. 2115
What kind of democracy do you want? 1087
What kind of God? 3618
What lack we yet? 1272
What language shall I borrow? 2215
What laymen want. 3057
What Lillian M. N. Stevens said. 3595
What Luther says, an anthology. 2275, 2281
What Lutheran Sunday-school teachers should know. 2293
What Lutherans are thinking. 2282
What made me a Baptist. 148
What makes America great? 3746
What makes Christian service? 971
What makes service Christian? 3377
What man believes. 3115
What manner of child? 216
What manner of love. 1376
What manner of man. 1009, 1951, 2011, 2172, 2320, 2910
What manner of man is this? 1993
What masonry means. 1661
What matters most. 962
... What may I believe? 1063
What mean these stones? 207, 3276
'What mean ye by this service? 2250
"What meaneth this?" 1716
What men are asking. 62, 1065
What men live by. 3848
...What men must believe. 3661
...What men must believe (abridged) 3661
...What men need most. 3049, 3344
What men or gods are these? 2662
What Mennonites believe. 2405
What modern Catholics think about birth control. 663
What more can God say? 404
What more would you like to know about the Church? 797
What Mrs. Eddy said to Arthur Brisbane. 1493
What must I do? 2581
"What must I do to be saved?" 1560, 1757
What must the church do? 1116, 1125
What must the church do to be saved? 2977
...What must the church do to be saved? and other discussion. 1126
What must we do to be saved? 1907
What my religion means to me. 962
What new creation? 1200
What new doctrine is this? 2437
What next? 1323, 1515
What next in home missions. 2528
What next in mission? 2480
What next in Turkey. 31
What Nietzsche taught. 2710
What noted men have said about the Bible and Christianity. 304
What now for the Jews? 2077
What of the church? 1124
What of the Mormons? 2603
...What of the night? 1513, 3338
What of to-day? 3774
What of tomorrow? 3049
What on earth are you doing? 1072
What on earth is an atheist! 100
What on earth is God doing? 297, 1819
What on earth's going to happen? 608
What one Christian can do to help prevent nuclear war. 103
What other answer. 1363
What Pastor Russell said. 3256
What place religion? 1049
What prayer can do. 2872
What Presbyterians believe. 3809
What present-day theologians are thinking. 3657
What price parochiaid? 1247
What price tolerance. 828, 2187
What Protestants believe. 2979
What psychology says about religion. 2999
What really happened when Christ died. 1997
What religion does for personality. 2823
What religion does to men. 2933
What religion is. 1056
What religion is and does. 3060
What religion is in the words of Swami Vivekananda. 3775
What religion means to me. 3069

What remains of the Old Testament and other essays. 499
What Rome teaches. 802
What St. Paul really said. 377, 2802
What St. Paul said. 374
What say you? 786
What seek ye? 1268
What shall I be! 773
What shall I believe? 109, 3536
What shall I do to be saved? 1358
What shall I say? 2722
What shall I speak about? 3375
What shall we say about alcohol? 3595
What shall we think of Christianity? 1048
What should be the role of ethnic groups in U.S. foreign policy? 3741
What should I believe? 185, 3667
What should parents expect? 2773
What spiritualism really is. 3497
What stopped the music. 1014
What teens say. 3880
What the ancient wisdom expects of its disciples. 2638
What the Bible can mean for you. 240
What the Bible does not say. 237
What the Bible is all about. 2376
What the Bible says. 303, 652, 1272, 3354
What the Bible says about covenant. 1377
What the Bible says about faith and opinion. 118, 933
What the Bible says about goodness. 1747
What the Bible says about Mussolini. 611
What the Bible says about praise and promise. 2867
What the Bible says about the end time. 1529
What the Bible says about the Holy Spirit. 1834
What the Bible says about the second coming. 3318
What the Bible says about the unfolded plan of God. 234
What the Bible says about women. 3834
What the Bible says about your personality. 611, 2823
What the Bible teaches. 651, 652, 1228
What the Bible tells us about the location of heaven and hell and the first second, and third coming of Christ. 1528
What the Buddha taught. 703
What the Catholic church most needs in the United States. 667
What the Christian hopes for in society. 1068
What the church gives us. 796
What the church is all about. 1122
What the church is and what it should be. 1123
What the church needs now. 1243
What the Church of England stands for. 1211
What the church teaches. 785, 795, 1117
What the churches stand for. 1124
What the cults believe. 1394, 3323
What the great religions believe. 3116
What the hell are you living for? 1322
What the Jews believe. 2137, 2138, 2146
What the Mormons believe. 2599
... What the New church stands for. 1123
What the New Testament says about forgiveness. 1634
What the religious revolutionaries are saying. 3748
What the restoration movement teaches concerning God. 2613, 3846
What the Roman Catholic has done for America. 874
What the scriptures say. 201
What the sects teach. 3323
What the Spirit is saying to the churches. 2816
What the spirit saith to the churches. 1120
What the Spirit says to the churches. 456
What the stars saw, and other Bible stories. 616
What the Sufis say. 3543
What the temperance century has made certain in regard to intemperance and other social problems of the Anglo-Saxon nations. 3595
What the tyler found. 1662
What the wild flowers tell us. 1630
What the world believes. 3122
What the world is coming to. 456
What the world needs. 2386
What the world owes Luther. 2276
What then is Christianity? 1095
What, then, is man? 2325
What theologians do. 3621
What they ask about marriage. 2342, 3011
What they believe. 3537
What they did right. 2773
What think ye of Christ? 743, 1954, 1957, 2000, 2015, 2037, 2047, 3346
What think ye of Christ? and other sermons. 3345

What think ye of man? 2325
What think you of Christ? 743, 781, 1999, 2001
What think you of Christmas? 1111
What this country needs. 3189
What time is it! 3319
What to believe. 935, 3663
What to do in case of a choir rehearsal. 916
What to do until Jesus comes back. 992
What to do when you don't know what to do. 1007
What to do when you pray. 2881
What to do with Sunday morning. 2234
What to preach. 2899
What to say: fraternal prose, poetry and quotes. 1667
What to say to the penitent. 1327
What unity requires. 1043
What use is religion? 65
What Vedanta means to me. 3775
What was he? 2010
What we are and what we will be. 3508
What we believe. 147, 1463, 1466, 2421
What we can believe. 1061
What we evangelicals believe. 1551
What we have seen & heard during twenty-five years' evangelistic labours. 1567
What we Jews believe. 2113
What we know about Jesus. 2012, 2042
What we may be. 3478
What we mean by religion. 1096, 2113
What we preach. 3367
What we see and hear in an Eastern Orthodox Church. 2748
What we teach, who should enroll, and reasons why. 8
What were the Crusades? 1390
What? when? where? why? who? in Freemasonry. 1664
What, where, and when is The Millenium? 1952, 2465
What will ye see in the Shulamite? 594
What will you have? 2386
What witches do. 3823
What works when life doesn't. 586, 3348
What world religions teach. 3119
What would Jesus do? 1323
What would you do? 2519
What, you a priest! 2309
What you believe and why. 652
What you need. 1940
...What you owe your child. 1610
What you should know about homosexuality. 1844
What you should know about inerrancy. 278
What you should know about Jewish religion. 2139
What you should know about Jewish religion, history, ethics and culture. 2139
What you should know about prophecy. 606
What you should know about social responsibility. 3433
What you should know about the Rapture. 3021
What you should know about Women's Lib. 1621
What your wedding can be. 757, 2343
What you've always wanted to know about life before birth, life on earth, life after death. 50
Whatever became of salvation? 3288
Whatever became of sin? 3411
Whatever comes to mind. 1449
Whatever happened to Friday? 797
Whatever happened to hell? 1802
Whatever happened to the gospel? 1058
Whatever is, is right. 1745
Whatever you do. 1005
Whatever you do; an essay on the Christian life. 1005
What's a nice church like you doing in a place like this? 1067
What's a nice person like you doing sick? 3407
What's a woman to do ... in the church? 3837
What's ahead for old first church. 1279
What's ahead for the churches. 1065
What's best worth saying. 1062
What's cooking in the priesthood? 774, 2789
What's God been doing all this time? 163
What's God doing today? 907
What's gone wrong with the harvest? 1316
What's good about God? 3665
What's happening to clergy marriages? 1303

What's happening to confession? 1326
What's happening to morality? 948
What's happening to the Catholic Church? 757
What's happening to the church? Daniel O'Hanlon. 790
What's in it for me? 3888
What's in the catechism? 3184
What's in your clothes closet? 1304, 3382
What's it all about and what am I? 2738
What's just ahead. 3320
What's left to believe? 3665
What's life all about? 958
What's Lutheran in education? 2287
What's mine? what's yours? 3530
What's new? 163
What's new in religion? 3656
What's new in the work of the church and the chaplain in correctional institutions? 885
What's next. 1887
What's right? 896, 1316
What's right now? 948
What's right with the church? 1120
What's right with the rural church. 3254
What's right with the world. 1062, 2383, 2436
What's so funny, Padre? 867
What's so great about the Bible. 234
What's special about Jesus? 1977
What's the answer? 3012
What's the difference? 1386
What's the difference in Protestant and Roman Catholic beliefs? 801
What's the good word? 864, 1267, 2287
What's the truth about Catholics? Why 400 million people profess the Catholic faith. 796
What's this I hear about our church? 3678
What's wrong with religion? 1040
What's wrong with the church. 1211
What's wrong with the world. 892
Whatsoever ye shall ask. 3751
Wheat and cockle. 2332
Wheat flour messiah. 1934, 1935
Wheat for this planting. 3251
Whee! We, wee, all the way home. 3521
Wheel and the cross. 942
Wheel of death. 1416
Wheel of fortune. 1470
Wheel of life. 3810
Wheel of rebirth. 3054
Wheel within the wheel. 1199
Wheelbarrow and the comrade. 1784
Wheeler's new songs. 3563
When? 2946
When a caring family faces crises. 1610
When a Catholic marries. 2343
When a Christian and a Jew marry. 2346
When a Christian sins. 3411
When a family loses a loved one. 192
When a Jew celebrates. 1615, 2120
When a Jew seeks wisdom. 2079
When a loved one dies. 192
When a man prays. 2880
When Adam Clarke preached, people listened. 1285, 2908
When adversity comes. 11
When all else fails. 3234
When all ships failed. 3025
When all the world was waiting. 9
When and where. 613
When angels come to men. 3481
When Antichrist reigns. 52
When apples are ripe. 2186, 2407
When bad things happen to good people. 2188, 3610
When blood flows, the heart grows softer. 2506
When children ask about God. 1723, 1733
When children worship. 904
When Christ comes again. 2004, 3319
When Christ comes and comes again. 1235
When Christ comes, what sayeth the Scripture? 1528
When Christ controls. 3530
When Christ passes by. 3348
... When Christ takes over. 956
When Christ went to Calvary. 2215
When Christianity was new. 1194
When Christians make political decisions. 1085
When Christinas make political decisions. 1085
When Christmas came to Bethlehem. 2022
When crisis comes. 2436
When daylight comes. 671
When death comes. 192
When death draws near. 1417
When death speaks, ten meditations on the life eternal. 1693
When death takes a father. 1414
When did we see you, Lord? 999
When do teachers teach? 3179, 3552, 3558

When dreams come true. 3244
When dust shall sing. 1513
When eternity dawns. 1694
When faith meets faith. 1080
When faith steals home. 177
When faith takes form. 2240
When faith writes the story. 1231
When faiths flash out. 1589
When families hurt. 1603
When fires burn. 2381
When God and man failed. 1825
When God became man. 2040
When God calls a woman. 3043, 3308
When God calls the signals. 3066
When God calls you. 3784
When God came down. 2930
When God comes alive through the Spirit-
  renewed church. 1244
When God comes down. 606
When God first thought of you. 369, 1011
When God gave Easter. 1486
When God hides. 2301
When God imagined a world. 1382
When God intrudes. 988
When God is at home with your family.
  1610
When God listens. 1742
When God made you, He knew what He
  was doing. 1010
When God met men. 337
When God moves in. 2932
When God says no. 213, 980, 1593, 2980
When God says 'No,' and other radio
  address. 3353
When God speaks. 287, 2676
When God stands up. 1730
When God was a woman. 3834, 3838
When God was Black. 1132
When God was near. 3344
When gods change. 3617
When God's children suffer. 3541
... When Gog's armies meet the Almight.
  519
When half-gods go. 3102
When half-gods go; a sketch of the
  emergence of religions. 3093
When He calls me. 168
When He comes again. 1984, 3321
"When He is come" 1832
When hearts grow faint. 1353
When hell trembles. 3360
When home is heaven. 886
When I became a man. 1094
When I consider. 2676
When I die. 1413
When I don't like myself. 3886
When I go to Mass. 2369
When I listen to Bible stories. 623
When I pray. 899
When I put out to sea. 2267
When I relax I feel guilty. 984
When I think of Jesus. 3164
When I worship. 3852
When in doubt, communicate. 3314
When in doubt, hug 'em! 2786
When in the course of human events.
  2888
When informed Protestants speak their
  convictions. 790
When iron gates yield. 713, 2487, 2555
When is Jesus coming again. 3321
When Israel came out of Egypt. 2097
When it's Passover. 2778
When it's Purim. 3006
When Jerusalem burned. 2094
When Jesus came. 2021
When Jesus comes. 858
When Jesus prayed. 2049
When Jesus rose. 2054, 3349
When Jesus was born. 632, 2021, 2022
When Jesus was here. 627, 1983
When Jesus wrote on the ground. 3376
When Jew and Christian meet. 2152
When Jews face Christ. 2085
When joy came. 2021
When kings and prophets held the stage.
  293
When Lena moved the cemetery. 2130
When life gets hard. 962
When life tumbles in. 1349
When love grows up. 3886
When love prevails. 3352
When love seeks new depths. 1609
When man becomes God. 2326
When man listens. 2754
When Marcia goes to church. 140
When marriage fails. 2341
When millions saw the Shroud. 1827
When morning comes. 2435
When mother lets us travel in France.
  1638
When our love is charity. 1631
When pastors wonder how. 2787
When people behave like sputniks. 1050
When people die. 1416
When prayer seems not to work. 2874
When preachers meet. 1482

When prophecy failed. 568, 1470
When prophecy fails. 2948
When Protestants worship. 3003
When religion gets sick. 2999
When revival comes. 560, 3229
When saints go marching. 1575
When saints were young. 3285
When science fails. 3073
When shadows fall. 3540
When skeltons come out of their closets.
  1560
When someone dies. 1351
When sorrow comes. 1352, 1693, 2182
When souls awaken. 1228
When stones hurt your feet. 908
When teen-agers talk theology. 2610
When the angels laughed. 1302, 3572
When the chisel hits the rock. 987, 2825
When the church was young. 332
When the Comforter came. 3410
When the East is in the West. 2527
When the gods are silent. 530
When the going gets tough. 1326
When the golden bough breaks. 2653
When the handwriting on the wall is in
  brown crayon. 2216, 2391
When the heart is hungry. 26
When the heart is lonely. 2244
When the heavens speak. 3506
When the Jewish people was young. 630
When the King came. 397, 1981
When the King was carpenter. 929, 1974
When the lamp flickers. 2438
When the last trumpet is sounded. 2060
When the lights are low. 973
When the Lord speaks to the heart. 2385
When the minister is a woman. 3835
When the morning wakens. 1567
When the music stops. 1255
When the people say no. 1165
When the rain falls. 1350
When the road bends. 3239
When the saints go marching out. 1025
When the song begins. 969
When the song of the Lord began. 3338
When the sorghum was high. 1477, 2538
When the soul is in darkness. 1445
When the spirit came. 2594
When the Spirit comes. 2815, 3274
When the Spirit descends. 1831
When the sun rises. 1342
When the time had fully come. 477
When the time had fully come; studies in
  New Testament theology. 477
When the time was fulfilled. 8
When the trumpet sounded. 1228, 3796
When the two-year-old comes to church.
  3173
When the vultures eat the dictators. 1513
When the walls come tumblin' down.
  3028
When the way is new. 1191
When the well runs dry. 2872
When the wild crab-apple puts forth
  blossoms. 3339
When the wood is green. 989
When the word is given. 669
When the world is hushed. 996
When the world is on fire. 1555
When the world is on fire, and other
  evangelistic messages. 1555
... When the world was young. 3386
When they are nine to eleven. 3555
When they are three. 3174
When they ask for bread. 2783
When they crucified our Lord. 161, 2034
'When thou prayest. 2875
When thou sittest in thine house. 1608
When time began. 1384
When tragedy strikes. 1350
When trouble comes. 2398, 2782, 3541
When two become one. 2347
When two great hearts meet. 1897, 2046
When two worlds met. 3852
When was Jesus born? 1999
When we go to church. 1162
... When we join the church. 2454, 3244
When we look around us. 3244
When we pray. 1441, 2880, 3883
When we share. 2493
When we teach 3's. 3174
When we teach 4's & 5's. 3173
When we teach junior. 3170
When we teach juniors. 3170
When we teach kindergarten children.
  3175
When we teach primary children. 3170
When we walk with the Lord. 958
When we were there. 2847
When we work together. 2190
When we worship. 3003
"When ye pray" 2248
When ye pray, pray ye thus. 902
When ye pray, say Our Father. 2248
When yesterday becomes tomorrow. 2143
When you are asked about faith and life.
  3012

When you build your church. 1269
When you get to the end of yourself.
  1352
When you get up in the morning. 2593
When you go stories. 909
When you go to Mass. 2365
When you graduate. 3879
When you lead devotions. 1442
When you lead meditations. 1442
When you lose a loved one. 1349
When you need a Bible story. 616
When you need a missionary story. 2490
When you need a special sermon series.
  2302, 3360
When you need a story. 910
When you pray. 2247, 2875, 2880
When you preach. 1266
When you receive a child. 430, 896
When you run out of fantastic ... persevere.
  405, 3360
When you speak in church. 2907
When your child asks. 2154
When your child hurts. 2773
When your cross is heavy. 1454
When your home is in the city. 1280
When your teenager stops going to church.
  3884
When you're a widow. 1350
When you're feeling that way. 1323
When youth prays. 3883
When youth worship. 3876
Whence and whither. 3461
Whence and why came Jesus the Christ?
  2000
Whence came Satan? 1428
Whence came the universe? 1380
Whence come wars. 3792
Whence comest thou? 3073
Whence cometh victory! 3610
Whence victory? 2981
Whence, what, where? 2320
Where action is. 39, 635, 3551
Where, after death? 1696
Where and how. 2391
Where and how to find God. 1456
Where are the converts? 1569
Where are the dead? 1528, 1697, 1698,
  3494
Where are the people? 3674
Where are the thousand? 2493
Where are we going? 1704
Where are we headed? 3082
Where are we in religion? 1071
Where are we now? 1088
Where are we running? 1013
Where are you, God? 973, 1734
Where are you going, Jesus? 1003
Where are you growing? 984
Where art thou? 968
Where Baltimoreans worship. 132
Where can I find God? 1721
Where cross the crowded ways. 2128,
  3276
Where cross the crowded ways: prayers of
  a city pastor. 2889
Where did we get our Bible? 291
Where do I go from here, God? 987
Where do I go to buy happiness? 3881
Where do I stand? 3665
Where do they come from? 3391
Where do we go from here? 1320, 2989
Where do we stand? 981
Where do you live? 3758
Where does the money go? 3530
Where does the sky begin? 1715
Where dwellest thou? 1364
Where eagles soar. 700, 981
Where faith begins. 1317
Where flies don't land. 1363, 1754
Where God comes in. 2780
Where God meets man. 2280, 2299
Where have all our people gone? 1201
Where He leads. 3243, 3407
Where heaven and earth meet. 2390
Where I found Christ. 1364
Where in the city? 3323
Where in the world? 1572
Where in the world is Jesus Christ? 993
Where is Christ? 2693
Where is Father Hennessey? 1803, 2546
Where is God? 1723, 3670
Where is God when it hurts? 3541
Where is he? 1912
Where is heaven? 933, 3078, 3569
Where is history going? 1819
Where is it written? 3522
Where is Joey? 1914, 2917
Where is the Ark of the Covenant? 81,
  610
Where is the Bible silent. 1464
Where is the city? 3323
Where is the eagle? 1902
Where is the gift of healing. 3264
"Where is the Lord God of Elijah?" 2870
Where is theology going? 3642
Where is thy flock? 1610
Where is truth? 70

Where is wisdom? 2608
Where is your God? 1722
Where is your victory? 1413
Where it happened in Bible times. 282
Where Jesus walked. 1961, 1964, 2014
Where Jesus walks. 971
Where Judaism differed. 2140
... Where knowledge fails. 1589
Where life begins! 3168
Where love is. 753
Where no fear was. 611
Where now is Jesus! 3011
Where now is thy God? 3352
Where now little Jew? 2077
Where on earth is heaven? 1795
Where our Bible came from. 217
Where Peter is. 1187
Where psychology breaks down. 3000
Where religion gets lost in the church.
  1153
Where saints have trod. 2491
Where Satan sows his seed. 1537
Where science and religion meet. 3077
Where shall we send them? 814, 3310
Where silence is praise. 3487
Where the action is. 62, 413
Where the Book speaks. 2504
Where the ghetto ends. 2102
Where the Gospel meets the world. 1404,
  1564
Where the higher criticism fails. 1387
Where the love is. 3887
Where the new world begins. 1451
Where the Protestant Episcopal church
  stands. 2958
Where the spirit leads. 1038
Where the star still shines. 1111
Where the two came to their father, a
  Navaho war ceremonial, given by Jeff
  King. 2676
Where there is life. 1240
Where there is love. 3407
Where there is no vision. 2494
Where there's life. 3161
Where there's smoke. 1599
Where time becomes space. 55, 1365
Where to go for help. 1374
Where tomorrow struggles to be born.
  1138
Where two creeds meet. 83
Where 2 or 3 are gathered together,
  someone spills his milk. 2393
Where was God when pagan religions
  began? 3121
Where Washington worships. 3797
Where we are in church union. 1355
Where we got the Bible. 289
Where we stand. 1238
Where we stand; Archbishop Clayton's
  charges 1948-57, chiefly relating to
  church and state in South Africa. Edited
  by C. T. Wood. 1287
Where wisdom hides. 1577
Where you find God. 1734
Whereabouts of God. 2934
Where'er the sun. 2494
Wherefore art thou come? 2258
Wherefore, ye must press forward. 1009
"Wherein!" Malachi's message to the men
  of to-day. 558
Whereon to stand. 795
Whereon to stand: what Catholics believe
  and why. 795
Where's God, Daddy? 895
Whether you believe or not. 3506
Which? 2730
Which Bible? 271
Which books belong in the Bible? 217
Which--dominate or permeate? 142
Which gospel shall I preach! 2898
Which is being interpreted. 198
Which is the true chronology! 218
Which Jesus? 2010
Which road shall we take? 1628
Which shall I believe? 65
Which: spiritualism or Christianity? 3505
Which temple ye are. 979
Which version, authorized or revised?
  2374
Which way? 3752
Which way ahead. 1116
Which way for Catholic pentecostals?
  2815
Which way for our children? 3154
Which way forward? 961
Which way in Brazil? 144
Which way in Nigeria? 2543
Which way is progress? 1466
Which way religion? 2956
Which way to God? 1586
Which way to Lutheran unity? 1045
Which way to Nineveh? 617
Which witch. 3822
Whiggs supplication. 720, 1375
Whiggs supplication; or, The Scots
  Hudibras. 720, 1375
While angels watch. 1983

While heaven waited. 734, 3238
While I'm on my feet. 2427
While it is day. 3383
While it is day; an autobiography. 3715
While men slept. 2384
While Peter sleeps. 755
While shepherds watched. 2006
While you're sick. 3405
Whimsical Christian. 3652
Whimsy. 2284
Whipping-post theology. 1598
Whirling dervishes. 1933, 2460
Whirlwind of the Lord. 1803
Whirlwind prophet, and other sermons. 3360
Whirlwinds of God. 165
Whisper in a dry land. 1776, 2547
Whispering halls. 1015
Whisperings in the silence. 2397
Whisperings to God. 2397
Whispers from eternity. 3866
Whispers from the dust. 67
Whistle stops. 2394
White African, the story of Mafavuke, "who dies and lives again" 2500
White Angakok. 1500
White angel of the world, that foretells the freedom of the nations from the evils of strong drink. 3595
White bird of Tao. 3586
White Canons in England. 2912
White canons of St. Norbert. 2912
White church on a high hill. 2626
White churches of the Plains. 1269
White duke. 606
White Fathers. 3812
White Fathers. Introd. by Bishop Laurian Rugambwa. 3812
White fields of Japan. 2534
White harvest. 1569
White House mystique. 1086, 1803
White House sermons. 3353
White Knight. 2851
White list of the Society of St. Gregory of America. 1205
White-magic book. 2733
White man's God. 3329
White martyrdom. 1400
White Monks. 1276
White monks in Wales ... [catalogue] of an exhibition held at the National Museum of Wales 24 April-23 May 1976 to mark the 750th anniversary of the foundation of Grace Dieu Abbey, Gwent, on 24 April 1226. 1276
White Monks of Waverley. 3799
White night. 2130
White nurse in Africa. 2498
White of Carpentaria. 3812
White paper on the Bible. 934
White Protestant Americans. 2979
White Protestantism and the Negro. 2683
White questions to a Black Christian. 2682
White ribbon in the Sunflower State. 3833
White robe. 2374
White robe, black robe. 2276, 3035
White sects and Black men in the recent South. 3324
White stone. 961
"White the candle burn. 1442
White truth. 3812
White wings and barricades. 3247
White wings, green jungle. 3386
White wings in bamboo land. 1775, 2509
White wings of splendor. 1443
White woman on the Congo. 2513
Whitehead's metaphysics. 2418, 3813
Whitehead's ontology. 2738, 3813
Whitehead's theory of knowledge. 2179, 3813
Whitehead's view of reality. 2832, 3813
Whiter goest thou? 2576
Whiter than snow. 3289
Whitgift and the English Church. 3814
Whither? 2936
Whither Arabia? 77
Whither bound in missions. 2519
Whither--Charon. 2730
Whither Christianity. 1050
Whither goest: meditations and Eastern wisdom. 1783
Whither goest thou? 3350
Whither Islam? 1922
Whither, O world? 1515
Whither womankind? 3833
Whitney memorial meeting. 3814
Whittaker's churchman's almanac. 2959, 2975
Whittlers of the word of God. 236
Who am I? 216, 1453, 2611, 3082, 3664
Who am I, God? 3842
Who & what & where in the Bible. 244
Who and what and where is God? 3095
Who and what is Christ? 2834
Who and what is Jesus Christ according to the Scriptures? 1952

Who answers? 2874
... Who are members of the church? 2194
Who are the blessed? 182
Who are the criminals? 1254
... Who are the Jesuits? 1945
Who are the Moravians? 2595
Who are the unchurched? 2712
Who are the Unitarians? 3728
Who are these? 3517
Who are they? 3323
Who are we? 3161
Who are you? 2823, 3886
Who are you, Lord? 2804
Who art in heaven. 1730
Who can we trust? 2352, 3716
Who cares? 1005, 1257
Who crucified Jesus? 1998
Who dares to preach? 2900
Who decides for the Church? 1241
Who died why? 63
Who dies? 1414
'Who do men say that I am? 1992, 2044
Who do you say that I am? 388
Who fares best, the Christian or the man of the world? 957
Who goes there? 1722
Who has your allegiance? 1015
Who holds the answer. 612
Who in hell needs a shepherd? 982
Who in the world? 2481
Who is a Christian? 324, 995, 996
Who is Christ? 1893, 2038
Who is Debbie? 3164
Who is God? 787, 1939
Who is God? Who am I? Who are you? 3888
Who is God ... who is the devil? 2733
Who is He? 2044
Who is Jesus? 168, 423, 951, 1001, 2042, 3011, 3164, 3166
Who is Jesus Christ? 2042
Who is Jesus of Nazareth? 1956
Who is like to God. 2850
Who is my neighbor? 1134, 1747, 2497, 2548, 3170, 3447
Who is my patient? 1258
Who is she? 2356
Who is the antichrist? 51
Who is the great "I am"? 1950
Who is the greatest? 1856
Who is the Holy Spirit? 1829, 1831
Who is the Lord? 1736
Who is the minister's wife? 1303
Who is the parish minister? 2791
Who is then this Man? 1968
Who is this? 1980, 2039
Who is this Jesus? 2042
Who is this king of glory? 2008, 2040
Who is this man Jesus? 1991
Who is to blame! 3597
Who Jesus says you are. 3349
Who knows me? 1734
Who knows ten? 1315
Who lives in you? 1466
"Who ... me?" 2268
Who, me teach my child religion? 938
Who, me? Yes, you! 3515
Who moved the stone? 2052
Who needs the family? 1608
Who put the bomb in Father Murphy's chowder? 759
Who rules your life? 2026
Who say ye that I am? 2001
Who says? 278
Who says? A discussion of basic questions of the Christian faith. 205, 278
Who says get married? 2346
Who says I'm O.K.? 987
Who shall ascend; the life of R. Kenneth Strachan. 2515, 3535
Who shall be God? 2301
Who shall live? 1783
Who shall separate us? 30
Who shall teach our children? 1130
Who should run the Catholic Church? 788, 3449
Who speaks for God? 2901
Who speaks for the church? 3849
Who taught me? 2983
Who then is Paul? 1029, 2798
Who trusts in God. 2981
Who waits in faith. 3716
Who walk alone. 3415
Who wants to play a harp? 1793
Who was Jesus? 1196, 1953, 1962, 1979
Who was Mohammed. 2628
Who was Saul of Tarsus. 2802
Who was Swedenborg, and what are his writings? 3571
Who was this Nazarene? 1965
Who was who in church history. 925
Who, what, when, where book about the Bible. 281, 319
Who? When? Where? What? 662
Who? why? what? 281
Who will listen to me? 1714
Who wrote Isaiah? 503

Who wrote the Bible? 233
... Who wrote the new prayers in the Prayer book? 2960
Whole armor of God. 976
Whole armour of God. 365, 366, 374, 2135
Whole book of Psalms. 561, 1863, 2968
Whole book of Psalms, in metre. 561, 1863, 2968
Whole Christ. 2020
Whole Christian. 1108
Whole counsel of God. 2299, 3348
Whole duty of man. 954
Whole gospel for the whole world. 1571
Whole lay ministry catalog. 2202
Whole man. 2326
Whole man at worship. 2235
Whole man: body, mind, spirit. 2397
Whole person in a broken world. 3000
Whole person in a whole world. 1007
... The whole-souled religious. 2388
Whole story. 1175
Whole truth about man. 863, 3364
Whole works of Robert Leighton. 3630
Whole works of the Rev. Ebenezer Erskine, minister of the gospel at Stirling. 1651
Whole world governed by a Jew. 2055
Whole world is my neighbor. 754
Whole world kin. 696
Whole world will love me. 3691
Whole world's in His hand. 3850
Wholeness in worship. 3003
Wholeness of life. 3689
Wholesight. 3491
Wholly for God. 3484
Wholly sanctified. 1824
Whom Christ commended. 2065
Whom do you say--? 1892
Whom God chooses. 3490
Whom God hath joined together. 1604
Whom God hath not joined. 2343
Whom love impels. 2319
"Whom my soul loveth" 1826
Whom the Lord loveth. 1354, 1850
Whom then can we believe? 3322
Whom they pierced. 1747
Whom thou seekest. 3490
Who's beat? 957
Who's boss? 989, 2044
Who's in charge here? 470, 2385
Who's killing the church? 1066
Who's running your life? 990
Who's who among Bible women. 215, 3841
Who's who among Free Will Baptists, and encyclopedia of denominational information. 1301, 1658
Who's who among the colored Baptists of the United States. 15, 157
Who's who among the Mennonites. 2404
Who's who and what's what in the Bible. 496
Who's who and why in the Chicago theological seminary. 893
Who's who at Edinburgh, 1937. 927
Who's who in American Methodism. 2427
Who's who in Baptist America in the National Sunday School and Baptist Training Union Congress. 157
Who's who in church history. 923
Who's who in Egyptian mythology. 2659
Who's who in Greek and Roman mythology. 2658
Who's who in Methodism. 2426
Who's who in New Thought. 2696
Who's who in pan-Methodism. 2439
Who's who in service—a look at areas of service participation by members of the Reorganizaed Church of Jesus Christ of Latter Day Saints. 3215
Who's who in the Arab world. 77
Who's who in the Bible. 198, 213, 215, 216, 217
Who's who in the Book of Mormon. 679
Who's who in the general convention of 1910 held at Cincinnati. 2958
Who's who in the General convention of the Episcopal church, 1934. 2964
Who's who in the gospels. 352
Who's who in the Methodist Church. 2427
Who's who in the New Testament. 339
Who's who in the Old Testament. 494
Who's who in the Old Testament, together with the Apocrypha. 494
Who's who in the P. O. A. U.? 2979
Who's who in the Protestant clergy. 1302
Who's who in the Talmud. 3584
Who's who in you. 1015
Who's who of hymn writers. 1860
Who's who of the Oxford movement. 2755
Who's zoo in church? 3004
Whose heaven, whose earth? 3244
Whose leaf shall not wither. 1061

Whose who: explorations in Christian identity. 3889
Whose world? 1077
Whose zoo? 481
"Whoso readeth let him understand" 1032
Whosoever repenteth. 3218
"Whosoever will," 3289
Why? 905, 1093, 2409, 3192
Why a Friends school? 1683
Why a Jewish state. 3896
Why a preacher and not a priest. 742
Why all should go to mass. 2370
Why all this suffering? 163
Why am I a Christian? 3820
Why am I a Cumberland Presbyterian. 1396
Why am I here? Where am I going? 3881
Why am I tempted? 3600
Why and how of foreign missions. 2518
Why and how of missions in the Sunday-school. 2492
Why and how to become a nun. 2581
Why and the answer. 964
Why are you fearful? 2980
Why baptize infants? 1906
Why be a Catholic? 793
Why be a Christian? 1090, 1094
Why be good? 1561
Why be lonely? 2245
Why believe? 64
Why believe in God? 1719
Why believe the Bible. 277
Why Billy Graham? 1576, 1755
Why bother with old-fashioned religion? 1047
Why can't the church be like this? 1914, 3884
Why Catholic? 797, 875
Why Catholic marriage is different. 2344
Why Catholics are criticized. 790
Why Catholics believe. 791
Why Christ. 762
Why Christian education. 1128
Why Christian marriages are breaking up. 2337
Why Christianity of all religions? 1095
Why Christians burn out. 1298
Why Christians crack up. 2378
Why Christians fight over the Bible. 277
Why church? 2489
Why churches die. 1170
Why churches should not pay taxes. 1242
Why Confucius has been reverenced as the model teacher of all ages. 1330
Why conservative churches are growing. 3443
Why did God let grandpa die? 3615
Why did God make me? 990
Why did it happen to me? 2377
Why did Jesus die? 106
Why did Jesus fast? 1613
Why did this happen to me? 551, 1349
Why didn't they tell me? 981
Why? Divine healing in medicine and theology. 2409
Why do Catholics--? 784
Why do Christians suffer? 3541
Why do I believe? 2601
Why do I believe the Bible is God's word! 276
Why do I do things wrong? 904
Why do men stupefy themselves? 1480
Why do men suffer? 3541
Why do people not see the Bible alike? 278
Why do people pray? 2886
Why do the good suffer? 2381
Why do things happen? 1719
Why does evil exist? 1745
Why does Jesus make me nervous? 3336
Why does not God intervene? 61
*Why doesn't God . . .? 3191
Why doesn't God do something? 3884
Why doesn't God heal me? 1600
Why doesn't somebody do something? 3837
Why don't I feel ok? 3000
Why evil? 1745
Why four Gospels? 392, 398, 1973, 2849
Why Friends (Quakers) do not baptize with water. 135
Why go to church? 1124, 1162, 1201
Why God became man. 1893, 2004, 2038
Why God gave us friends. 1688
Why God used D. L. Moody. 2588
Why good people suffer. 3541
Why hast thou come? 2570
Why He came. 1004
Why I am a Baptist. 146, 148
Why I am a Catholic. 1365, 3069
Why I am a charismatic, a Catholic explains. 891, 2816
Why I am a Christian. 1096
Why I am a Christian Scientist. 1034
Why I am a churchman. 3201
Why I am a conscientious objector. 2809

Why I am a Cumberland Presbyterian. 1396
Why I am a Disciple of Christ. 1460
Why I am a Jew. 1629, 2114, 2138, 2140, 2144
Why I am a Lutheran. 2282
Why I am a member of the church of Christ. 1272
Why I am a Methodist. 2422
Why I am a Mormon. 2600, 2606
Why I am a preacher. 2907
Why I am a premillennialist. 2465
Why I am a Presbyterian. 2912
Why I am a Seventh-Day Adventist. 3383
Why I am a spiritual vagabond. 3521
Why I am a temperance man. 3597
Why I am a Unitarian. 3724
Why I am a Unitarian Universalist. 3724
Why I am an agnostic. 19
Why I am an Episcopalian. 2957
Why I am and why I am not a Catholic. 794
Why I am at the seminary. 3331
Why I am for the church. 1072
Why I am not a Christian. 1656
Why I am not a Christian, and other essays on religion and related subjects. 1656, 3068
Why I am not a Roman Catholic. 871
Why I am still a Christian. 68
Why I became a Baptist. 140, 148
Why I became a brother. 2577
Why I became a Catholic. 1364
Why I became a missioner. 2484
Why I became a pastor. 110
Why I became a priest. 772
Why I believe. 66, 186, 3663
Why I believe in God. 1273
Why I believe in God and immortality. 3078
Why I believe in Jesus. 1956
Why I believe in Jesus Christ. 1093
Why I believe in personal immortality. 2990
Why I believe in religion. 1057
Why I believe in the virgin birth of Jesus Christ. 1956
Why I believe the Bible. 200, 277
Why I believe there is a God. 1738
Why I belong. 926
Why I can't say I love you. 2264
... Why I do not believe. 1655
Why I entered the convent. 2581
Why I fight for a Christian America. 1786
Why I go to church. 1119
Why I joined. 3381
Why I know the Bible is the word of God. 276
Why I know there is a God. 1725
Why I left Christian science. 1037
Why I left Roman Catholicism. 801
Why I left the Seventh-Day Adventists. 3382
Why I preach that the Bible is literally true. 276
Why I preached the second coming. 2907, 3321
Why I quit going to church. 1125
Why I reject the "helping hand" of Millennial dawn. 2466
Why--in the world! 1067
Why infants are baptized. 138
Why is Christianity true? 1099
Why is religion? 3107
Why is the church in the world? 1154, 3735
Why isn't God giving cash prizes? 3883
Why Jesus came. 1110, 3056
Why Jesus dies. 2914
Why Jesus was a man and not a woman. 1956
Why Jews become Catholics. 1364
Why Judaism. 2140
Why leave our own? 3450
Why life cracks up. 2226
Why live the Christian life? 993
Why many preacher's hobby horses fail to win the (human) race. 3291
Why me God? 550
Why me, Lord? 1349
Why me? Why mine? 3539
Why men believe in Jesus Christ. 1094
Why men believe, the groundwork of apologetics. 68
Why men do not go to church. 1162
Why men go back. 958
Why men pray. 2880
Why monks? 2576
Why must I suffer? 3541
Why not? 2742
Why not broadcast the gospel? 3018
Why not creation? 1383
Why not just be Christians? 3352
Why not successful workers together. 991
...Why not try Christianity! 1055
Why of the will, the unity of the universe. 2420

Why our churches do not win souls. 3464
Why people? 1324
Why people fight. 2592
Why people join the church. 1201
Why people like you. 970
Why Pope Pius XI asked prayer for Russia on March 19, 1930. 1148
Why pray? 2248, 2872, 2882
Why prayers are unanswered. 2874
Why preach Christ? 2908
Why priests? 2786
Why priests leave. 1582
Why priests should wed. 2940
Why pursue the Buddha? 2171, 3197
Why read the Bible? 646
Why religion. 3060
Why Rome. 785
Why she became a spiritualist. 3506
Why should I? 3166, 3168
Why should I be a pastor! 3671
Why should the Catholic university survive? 870
Why should the Devil have all the good music? 1748
Why sink when you can swim? 986
Why Sunday mass. 984
Why teenagers reject religion and what to do about it. 3885
Why the Baptist name. 143
Why the Catholic religion is right. 871
Why the church? 1118, 1121, 1126
Why the cookie crumbles. 2981
Why the cross? 105, 999
Why the King James version. 271
Why the King James version: a series of study notes. 655
Why they wrote the New Testament. 347
Why this confusion in the temple? 1672
Why this life plus. 1886
Why thousand years? 2465
Why to ... Okinawa? 2171, 3259
Why two Episcopal Methodist churches in the United States? 2442
Why two resurrections? 3221
Why two worlds? 2473, 2690
Why two worlds? The relation of physical to spiritual realities. 2473
Why wait till marriage? 3392
Why wait till Sunday? 1573
Why we are baptized. 139, 1230
Why we are conscientious objectors to war. 3794
Why we are Presbyterians. 2936
Why we believe. 1099
Why we believe in creation not evolution. 1381, 1580
Why we believe the Bible. 62, 201, 202, 277
Why we choose Christ. 1558
Why we fail as Christians. 1109
Why we haven't changed the world. 983
Why we honor St. Joseph. 2132
Why we live in community. 698, 933
... Why we may believe in life after death. 1888
Why we need the Pope. 2863
Why we practice plural marriage. 2607
Why we worship. 3853
Why were the gospels written? 3097
Why, when, and how of revivals. 3228
Why, when and how of sanctification. 3299
Why you cannot die! 3054
Wicked city. 5, 2261
Wicked not annihilated. 48
Wiclif and Hus. 1583
Widdowes mite [by] Sir Tobie Matthew ; [and] A treatise of the holy sacrifice of the masse. 2360, 2367
Wide as the world. 2550
Wide horizons. 3406
Wide place for my steps. 2880
Wide world my parish. 3294
Widen the prison gates. 195
Widening the frontier. 2528
Widening way. 2736
Widening wedge. 2495
Wider fellowship. 3729
Wider horizons in Christian adult education. 3169
Wider place. 973
Wider place ... where God offers freedom from anything that limits our growth. 973
Wider view. 3204
Widespread psychic wonders. 3514
Widow. 3315
Widow of Zarephath. 2848
Widow's mite. 3502
Widow's mite and other psychic phenomena. 3502
Widsom in Ethiopia. 2682
Wife, mate, mother, me! 3844
Wife, mother, and mystic. 3580
Wife no. 19. 2607
Wife of Leon, and other poems. 2856, 2857

Wife prays. 3830
Wife to the archbishop. 1303, 1305
Wilberforce, Cranmer, Jewell, and the prayer book, on the incarnation. 1893, 3815
Wilberforces and Henry Manning. 1760, 2328
... Wilbur Fisk. 1628
Wilbur Fisk Tillett, Christian educator. 3699
Wild branch on the olive tree. 2219
Wild flowers. 2076, 3549
Wild goats of Ein Gedi. 1928
Wild prayer of longing. 3069, 3243
Wild rivers and mountain trails. 2396
Wilderness and paradise in Christian thought. 3815
Wilderness and the city. 3816
Wilderness as sacred space. 2675
Wilderness Christians. 1420, 2594
Wilderness journey. 3721
Wilderness of mind. 3108
Wilderness parish. 3381
Wilderness prophet. 2631
Wilderness revolt. 2042, 3014
Wilderness to Eden, by Saint Sarah. 3199
Wilderness way. 1164
Wildfire. 2954
Wilford C. Wood Collection. 2616, 3846
Wilfred Grenfell, his life and work. 1774, 2486
Will a man rob God? 3528
Will all men be saved? 3292
Will America become Catholic? 827
Will and testament of Abdul Baha. 2, 129
Will and the way. 2980
Will and way to win. 2125
Will Evangelicalism survive its own popularity? 1552
Will God set up a visible kingdom on earth? 2465
Will He find faith? 165
Will I ever forget this day? 2617, 2810
Will I go to heaven? 1795
Will India become Christian? 1895
Will it matter what I was? 160
Will man live again? 3292
Will man survive? 607, 3321
Will men be like gods? 1854
Will morality make sense to your child? 3181
Will my dog go to heaven? 3172
Will of God. 1740, 1741
Will of God and a man's lifework. 1741
...The will of God and prayer. 2980
Will of God for these days, in personal relations, economic life, political action, race relations, international affairs. 972
Will of God in other words. 1002
"The will of God ...you sanctification." 3299
Will of my Father. 1824, 3202
Will of the wind; inspirational thoughts on Christian virtues. 2398
Will our children have faith? 936
Will Protestantism be overthrown? 2976
Will religion make sense to your child? 939
Will Russia conquer the world? 611
Will the Christ return? 3321
Will the church lose the city? 1279
Will the church pass through the tribulation? 1515
Will the church pay the price? 1061
Will the circle be unbroken? 1555
Will the old Bob Turnbull please drop dead? 989
Will the Old Book stand? 201
Will the world outgrow Christianity. 1055
Will to be Christian. 3300
Will to believe. 185, 1517
Will to live, will to die. 1415
Will to power in science, nature, society & art. 2834
Will to relieve. 185
Will to work. 2592
Will which is of force. 51
Will you be the speaker? 2897
Willamette interlude. 3419
Willem Sewel of Amsterdam, 1653-1720. 1685, 3388
William Alfred Quayle. 3011
William Alfred Quayle Bible collection. 213
William Anderson Scott, "no ordinary man." 3432
William Austin Smith. 3432
William Barclay. 173
William Blake. 670
William Blake, 1757-1827, on the Lord's prayer. 670, 2246
William Blake, 1757-1827. 670
William Booth and his Army. 682, 3296
William Bradford and the Book of common prayer. 688, 1214
William Branham. 690

William Butler Yeats: the poet as a mythmaker, 1865-1939. 2649, 3863
William Carey. 739, 2485, 2490
William Carey, cobbler to missionary. 739
William Carey, D. D., fellow of Linnaean society. 739
William Carey, father of modern missions. 739
William Carey, missionary, pioneer, and statesman. 739
William Carey of India. 739
William Carey: shoemaker, linguist, missionary. 739
William Charles Braithwaite. 690
William Chillingworth and the theory of toleration. 911, 3703
William Christie. 1110
William Clayton. 1287
William Clayton's journal. 2601
William Colgate: the Christian layman. 1308
William Courtenay: Archbishop of Canterbury, 1381-1396. 1375
William Culbertson. 1393
William Dell: master Puritan. 1421
William Duncan. 1482, 2460
William E. Hatcher, D.D., L.L.D., L.H.D. 1790
William Ellery Channing. 881, 882
William Ellery Channing, his messages from the spirit. 882
William Ellery Channing, minister of religion. 881
William Farel. 1612
William Foxwell Albright, a twentieth-century genius. 23
William G. Hill Lodge no. 218 A.F. & A.M., 1864-1964. 1668
William George Ward and the Catholic revival. 816, 872, 3795
William George Ward and the Oxford movement. 2755, 3795
William Godwin. 1743
William Godwin : a study in liberalism. 1748
William Greenleaf Eliot, minister, educator, philanthropist. 1509
William Inge. 1907
William J. Walsh. 3790
William James. 1536, 1934
William Jay Peck. 2810
William Law. 2201
William Law and eighteenth century Quakerism. 2201
William Lawrence; later years of a happy life. 2202
William M. Baird of Korea. 130, 2536
William McGarvey and the open pulpit. 45, 2307
William McKendree. 2308
William Matthews. 2374
William Nast. 2669
William of St. Thierry. 1777
William Owen. 2813
William Pardow of the Company of Jesus. 2773
William Penn. 2813
William Penn and early Quakerism. 2813
William Penn: mystic, as reflected in his writings. 2813
William Penn's advice to his children. 904
William Quan Judge, 1851-1896. 3689
William Richards. 1791, 3235
William Salter. 3287
William Scott, Ament, missionary of the American board to China. 2485
William Stevenson. 3528
William Temple. 3599
William Temple, Archbishop of Canterbury. 3599
William Temple's teaching. 1217
William Torrey Harris, 1835--1935. 1787
William Tyndale. 3719
William Tyndale, martyr for the Bible. 3719
William Tyndale's five books of Moses. 564
William Tyndale's five books of Moses called the Pentateuch, being a verbatim reprint of the edition of MCCCCCXXX. 564
William W. Goodman gift. 2402
William Wake. 3788
William Watson Andrews. 41
William West Skiles. 3422
William Whiston. 146, 3810
William Wilberforce. 3815
William Winans. 1294, 3819
William Woodruff, fourth president of the Church of the church of Jesus Christ of latter-day saints. 3846
William Xavier Ninde. 2711
Williams college and foreign missions. 2493
Willie Selville's mission. 2535

Wilmore's new analytical reference Bible. 653
Wilson's dictionary of Bible types. 3574
Wimbledon's sermon: Redde rationem villicationis tue. 3368
Wimpy Harper of Africa. 1786, 2552
Wimpy Harper story. 1786, 2552
Win or warn. 1567
Win the battle for your mind. 989
... Winchester. 3819
Winchester centennial, 1803-1903. 3754
Winchester troper, from mss. of the Xth and XIth centuries. 3715
Wind and shadows. 1937
... The wind bloweth where it listeth. 1831
Wind blows free on Cupcake Hill. 3244
Wind chimes. 2385
Wind has many faces. 2389
Wind in both ears. 3729
Wind of the spirit. 2935, 3368, 3687
Windbreaks. 3254
Winding quest. 533, 628
Window in Provence. 2715
Window in the wall. 2260
Window of God. 3783
Window of prayer, and other poems. 3208
Window on Washington. 146, 2984
Window sill of heaven. 166
Window to the past. 3002
Windows. 2387, 3386
Windows aglow. 1452
Windows and wings. 1840
Windows for sermons. 1839
Windows in heaven. 1438
...Windows in Matthew. 443
Windows into the future. 455
Windows, ladders, and bridges. 1843
Windows of faith. 1602
Windows of heaven. 1439, 1860, 2385
Windows of tarot. 3588
Windows of the mind. 3053
Windows of thought. 1015
Windows of Trinity Cathedral. 1715, 3713
Windows of worship. 1443
Windows on God's world. 3883
Windows on life. 1332
Windows on the Master. 1985
Windows on the Passion. 2033
Windows on the word. 2935
Windows on the world of truth. 1441
Windows that let in the light. 2027
Windows toward God. 1441
Windows westward. 766
Winds of change. 547, 2435
Winds of change in the Christian mission. 2493
Winds of doctrine. 2166, 2843, 3650
Winds of God. 1444, 3211
Winds of God are blowing. 2815
Wine and blood. 3597
Wine & gall. 761
Wine cup. 3597
Wine of absurdity. 2232
Wine of God. 2476
Wine of life. 3688
Wine of Roman Babylon. 802
Wine question in the light of the new dispensation. 3596
Wine texts of the Bible. 3596
Wings against the blue. 144
Wings for the Word. 31
Wings, nearly four hundred true stories. 1840
Wings of eagles. 765, 3280
Wings of healing. 1792
Wings of joy. 1353
Wings of recovery. 1258
Wings of silver. 3782
Wings of the dove. 1748
Wings of the morning. 614, 1450, 2138, 2142, 2212, 2959
Wings of the spirit. 1438, 1840
Wings or ashes. 1064
Wingspread. 3410
Winnebago culture as described by themselves. 3820
... Winning a crown. 971
Winning a hearing. 2554
Winning America to Christ. 1574
Winning converts. 1569
Winning Jews. 2142
Winning Jews to Christ. 2142
... Winning men. 1571
Winning men one by one. 1572
Winning men to Christ. 3351
Winning move. 169
Winning of immortality. 1889
Winning of religious liberty. 3192
Winning of the Far East. 2516
Winning others to Christ. 1567
Winning souls. 1556, 3462
Winning the adolescent boy. 687
Winning the border. 2460
Winning the children. 1253
Winning the children for Christ. 1554
Winning the fight against drink. 3595
... Winning the world for Christ. 1050

Winning them back. 1201
Winning to Christ. 1563
Winning walk. 994
Winning ways. 3829
Winning ways for working churches. 1252
Winning what you want. 2808
Winning with Christ. 932
Winning with God. 956
Winning witness. 3829
Winning words. 102
Winning youth for Christ. 3880
Winona echoes; addresses delivered at the ... annual Bible conference, Winona Lake, Indiana. 1090
Winsome witnessing. 3829
Winston Churchill on Jewish problems. 2079
Winston clear type Cruden's complete concordance to the Old and New Testaments, with notes and Biblical proper names under one alphabetical arrangement. 227
Winter. 3677
Winter evening conversation vindicated. 3412, 3800
Winter name of God. 742
Winter past. 932, 3431
Winthrop fleet of 1630. 3006, 3820
Wireless messages. 2869
Wisconsin conference centennial. 1550
Wisconsin history of the Associate Presbyterian Church of North America. 2929
Wisdom. 646, 3821
Wisdom and cult. 3821
Wisdom and folly in religion. 1059
Wisdom and love in Saint Thomas Aquinas. 3693
Wisdom as a hermeneutical construct. 489, 3821
Wisdom, christology, and law in Matthew's Gospel. 443, 2044, 3821
Wisdom community. 835, 1316
Wisdom for the wise. 2980
Wisdom for today's family. 572, 1607
Wisdom from above for living here below. 573, 982
Wisdom from afar. 2726
Wisdom from the Apocrypha. 489
Wisdom from the Bible and Talmud. 614
Wisdom from women in the Bible. 3839
Wisdom I ask. 2393
Wisdom in Israel. 3821
Wisdom in Proverbs. 573
Wisdom in small doses. 3821
Wisdom in the Old Testament traditions. 3821
Wisdom literature. 549, 3821
Wisdom of Abdul Baha. 126
Wisdom of angels. 1447, 2982
Wisdom of angels concerning the divine providence. 2982
Wisdom of Ben Sira. 487
Wisdom of Buddha. 707
Wisdom of Buddhism. 702, 710
Wisdom of Catholicism. 3637
Wisdom of Christ. 2012, 2013
Wisdom of Confucius. 2838
Wisdom of Ecclesiastes. 512
Wisdom of Egypt & the Old Testament. 29
Wisdom of evolution. 1580
Wisdom of faith, an introduction to theology. 3669
Wisdom of God. 106
Wisdom of God, a brief summary of sophiology. 1741
Wisdom of God in the redemption of fallen man. 1741
Wisdom of God manifested in the works of the creation. 2674
Wisdom of God manifested in the works of thhe creation. 2674
Wisdom of Heschel. 2152
Wisdom of holiness. 999
Wisdom of Israel. 550, 2075
Wisdom of James the Just. 412
Wisdom of Jesus. 2062
Wisdom of Jesus Ben Sira. 489
Wisdom of Jesus, the son of Sirach. 487, 489
Wisdom of Joan Woolman. 3847
Wisdom of Laotse. 3586
Wisdom of life from the Bible. 300
Wisdom of man. 3542
Wisdom of Martin Luther. 2275, 2833
Wisdom of Meher Baba. 689
Wisdom of passion. 1512
Wisdom of Saint Anselm. 49
Wisdom of St. Francis and his companions. 1020, 1644
Wisdom of St. John. 422
Wisdom of Solomon. 490
Wisdom of Solomon Schechter. 2143
Wisdom of the adepts. 695

Wisdom of the ages; revelations from Zertonlem, the prophet of Tlaskanata. 3502
Wisdom of the ancient Egyptians. 1458
... The wisdom of the Aryas. 700, 704
Wisdom of the Brahmin. 689
Wisdom of the desert. 1020
Wisdom of the early Buddhists. 1704
Wisdom of the English mystics. 2644
Wisdom of the Fathers. 1020
Wisdom of the Gita. 2316
Wisdom of the heart. 3688
Wisdom of the Hebrews. 2084
Wisdom of the Jewish mystics. 723, 1789
Wisdom of the Kabbalah. 722
Wisdom of the Koran. 2184
Wisdom of the living religions. 3014
Wisdom of the mystic masters. 3251
Wisdom of the overself. 2417
Wisdom of The Poverrello. 1642
Wisdom of the Psalms. 579, 585
... The wisdom of the Qur'an, set forth in selected verses conveying the moral, religious and social philosophy of Islam. 2185
Wisdom of the sages. 600
Wisdom of the saints. 1090
Wisdom of the Sasanian sages (Denkard VI) 2822
Wisdom of the serpent. 1416
Wisdom of the Spanish mystics. 2648
Wisdom of the Sufis. 3544, 3545
Wisdom of the Talmud. 3584
Wisdom of the Taoists. 2648
Wisdom of the tarot. 3588
Wisdom of the throne. 3272, 3707
Wisdom of the Torah. 591
Wisdom of the Vedas. 2839, 3775
Wisdom of the Zen masters. 3893
Wisdom of Thomas Aquinas, transcribed from his writings. 783
Wisdom of Tolstoy. 1055
Wisdom shall enter. 763
Wisdom stories for the planet Earth. 25
Wisdom that does not change. 2934
Wisdom, the principal thing. 572
Wisdom tree. 3116
Wisdom, world, foolishness. 276
Wisdom's strength. 862
Wisdom's voice to the rising generation. 3596
Wise as serpents, innocent as doves. 3166
Wise have it. 1012
Wise man from the West. 3235
Wise man's story. 1114
Wise men. 2022, 2311
Wise men worship. 3078
Wise sayings for the young. 2375
Wise up & live! 573, 3354
Wise woman ... how to be one in a thousand. 3844
Wisedome of the ancients. 2660
Wiser than they thought. 2021
Wise's digested index and genealogical guide to Bishop Meade's old churches, ministers and families of Virginia. 3781
Wisest fool. 215
Wisest man in the world. 3457
Wisest wise man. 1113
Wish and wisdon. 2732
Wishful thinking. 3638
Wissenschaft und Gesundheit. 1032
Wit and wisdom of Albert Schweitzer. 3089
Wit and wisdom of Billy Graham. 3089
Wit and wisdom of Bishop Fulton J. Sheen. 3089
Wit and wisdom of Christianity. 3089
Wit and wisdom of D. L. Moody. 2393
Wit and wisdom of good Pope John. 2124
Wit and wisdom of J. B. Chapman. 3021
Wit and wisdom of Jesus. 2070
Wit and wisdom of Safed the sage. 3089
Wit and wisdom of the Christian fathers of Egypt. 2578
Wit and wisdom of the Rev. Sydney Smith. 3089
Wit and wisdom of the Talmud. 18, 3582, 3584
Wit and wisdom of Warren Akin Candler. 3089
Wit and wisdom of William Bacon Evans. 1577
Wit and wisdon of the Rev. Sydney Smith. 3089
Wit, wisdom, and philosophy of Jean Paul Fred. Richter. 3089
Witch blood! 1389
Witch-cult in Western Europe. 3826
Witch doctor of the Bahiri. 2497
Witch doctor's son. 151, 178
Witch hunt. 2760, 3828
... The witch of Endor. 3494
Witch-poison and the antidote. 131, 3510
Witch, spirit, devil. 3825
Witch stories. 3826
Witch, warlock, and magician. 2314

Witchcraft. 1369, 3823, 3824, 3825, 3826
Witchcraft and black magic. 3823, 3824
Witchcraft and demonianism. 3823
Witchcraft & magic. 3823
Witchcraft and occultism today. 2730
Witchcraft and Quakerism. 3823
Witchcraft and sorcery. 2729, 3825
Witchcraft and sorcery in East Africa. 3825
Witchcraft and sorcery in Rhodesia. 3827
Witchcraft and the black art. 3825
Witchcraft and the mysteries. 3824
Witchcraft at Salem. 3827
Witchcraft confessions & accusations. 3825
Witchcraft delusion in colonial Connecticut, 1647-1697. 3825
Witchcraft: European and African. 3824
Witchcraft for tomorrow. 3825
Witchcraft from the inside. 3823
Witchcraft in America. 3828
Witchcraft in England. 3825
Witchcraft in France and Switzerland. 3826
Witchcraft in Maryland. 3827
Witchcraft in New England. 3827
Witchcraft in Old and New England. 3825
Witchcraft in Salem village in 1692. 3827
Witchcraft in the Southwest. 3828
Witchcraft, its power in the world today. 3824
Witchcraft, magic & alchemy. 2725
Witchcraft, mysticism, and magic in the Black world. 3823
Witchcraft in Europe, 1100-1700. 3826
Witchcraft of New England explained by modern spiritualism. 3827
Witchcraft of Salem Village. 3827
Witchcraft, oracles, and magic among the Azande. 121
Witchcraft world. 3824
Witches. 3823, 3824, 3826
Witches' advocate. 1909, 3825
Witches all. 3825
Witches' almanac. 3824
Witches and demons in history and folklore. 3824
Witches and sorcerers. 3823
Witches and their craft. 3824
Witches and warlocks. 3824
Witches and witch-hunters. 3825
Witches and witchcraft. 3824
Witches in fact and fantasy. 3824
Witches of early America. 3828
Witches of New York. 1635
Witches speak. 3823
Witches U.S.A. 3828
Witchraft in the Southwest. 3828
Witch's bible. 3823
Witch's garden. 3823
Witch's grimoire of ancient omens, portents, talismans, amulets, and charms. 3826
With a Bible in my hand. 161, 3363
With a merry heart. 1713, 2937
With a rod of iron. 608
With all devotedness. 3419
With all patience. 864
With all thy heart. 1437
With all your mind. 2837
With an holy calling. 3768
With and without Christ. 975
With anxious care. 2570
With attentive ear and courageous heart. 2165, 2859
With bands of love. 537
With best wishes. 2434, 3348
"With bodilie eyes" 1531
With book and plow. 1377
With bright wings. 1835
With brushes of comet's hair. 3496
With C. T. Studd in Congo forests. 2513
With Christ after the lost. 1570
With Christ as guide. 1049, 1952
With Christ at sea. 957, 3317
With Christ in Assam. 2503
With Christ in Indo-China. 2533
With Christ in the Garden. 2879
With Christ in the mount. 3348
With Christ in the school of disciple building. 989
With Christ in the school of prayer. 2876
With Christ in the upper room. 658, 2252
With Christ my friend. 3202
With Christ on the edge of the jungles. 2531
With Christ the Father. 3163
With Christ through the year. 1262
With Christ to the cross. 2004
With cymbals and harp. 586
With Dante in paradise. 2772
With Dante on the mountain. 1402
With dedicated hearts. 3419
With Dr. Grenfell in Labrador. 2190
With each passing moment. 734
With eyes of faith. 1772, 1773

With eyes up. 3359
With eyes wide open. 470, 976
With faith and vision. 819, 3310
With fire, sword, and whips. 673
With fire, sword, and whips; a story of St.
    Andrew Bobola. 673
With flaming heart. 1625
With folded wings. 3518
With God. 2892
"With God all things are possible!" 1326
With God and friends each day. 1437
With God and the colors. 2890
With God and two ducats. 740
With God as thy companion. 1456
With God in hell. 1825
With God in prayer. 2889
With God in Red China. 2942
With God in Russia. 2942
With God in the garden. 1450
With God in the heights. 2392
With God in the war. 1910
With God we can! 3477
With God you win. 1435
With Gode and His mercy. 1264
With good reason. 1725
With gun and cross. 70, 3197
With halo atilt. 1397
With hands uplifted. 2214
With happy voices. 904
With harp and lute. 868
With head and heart ; the autobiography of
    Howard Thurman. 146, 3698
"With heaps o' love" 2507
With heart and lips. 854
With heart and mind. 2389, 2397, 2563
With hearts courageous. 1948
With hearts uplifted. 2393
"With Him" 365
With Him in glory. 1572
With Him in mind. 3200
With honor. 141, 163
With Jack and Jean in Bible lands. 2760
With Jesus after sinners. 3228
With Jesus suffering. 2032
With Jesus to the priesthood. 2388
With joy and gladness. 1000
With King James' Bible as exclusive
    authority can the Protestant Christian
    question the Eucharist? 2254
With Kinglake in the Holy Land. 2177,
    2763
With lamps burning. 3275
With life and laughter. 2943
With lifted heart. 3197
With love and laughter. 2717
With love and laughter: reflections of a
    Dominican nun. 2717
With love, from mother. 1631
With lyre, harp, and a flatpick. 1202
With Mary in mind. 2887
With Maxi and Mini in Muffkinland. 618
With mercy and with judgment. 3202
With mind and heart. 2140
With mother church. 804
... With mother church ... a laboratory
    manual in religion. 806
With my neighbors. 1325
With my own eyes. 2005
With my song I will prasie Him. 1749,
    3234
With one voice. 2888
With open face; or, Jesus mirrored in
    Mathew, Mark and Luke. 1961
With our missionaries in China. 2512
... With Padre Kino on the trail. 2177
With Paul in Greece. 372, 2798
With Paul in Macedonia. 2803
With pen and tongue. 1947, 2503
With perfect faith. 3370
With prayer and psalm. 3818
With sails to the wind. 618
With saints and sages. 2892
With Schweitzer in Lambarene. 3312
With signs following. 2813, 2815
With signs multiplying. 3229
With silent friends. 2226
With singleness of heart. 3673
With song and timbrel. 3203
With sovereign reverence. 1150, 2979
With sugar 'n spice. 3188
With the Bible through the church year.
    618
With the children on Sundays. 904
With the Church. 1263
With the divine retreat Master. 3223
With the help of Thy grace. 1751
With the heralds of the cross. 850
With the Holy Spirit and with fire. 1570
With the Jewish child in home and
    synagogue. 2121
With the Master, a book of meditations.
    2398
With the passing seasons. 1264
With the pilgrims to Mecca. 2847
With the Poverello. 3421
With the sorrowing. 1352

With the spirit you are more than just you.
    1828
With the spirit's sword. 729
With the twelve. 70
With their whole strength. 928
With this gift. 877, 2993
With valor they serve. 1404, 2538
With wings as doves. 3420
With wings as eagles. 987, 1415, 2489
With wings as eagles, toward personal
    Christian maturity. 971
With wonder in your soul. 2399
Withered fig tree. 3529
...Within; a guide to the spiritual life. 3480
Within and without the church. 781
Within my parish. 3675
Within the chancel. 921
Within the circle. 988, 3238
Within the gates. 2699
Within the holy of holies. 2696
Within the temple of Isis. 2730
Within Thy hand. 2893
Within, without, and over. 1781
Within you is the power. 3493
Without a doubt. 493, 2393
Without burnt offerings. 3238
Without excuse. 970
Without fear or favor. 40
Without halos. 1460
Without help or hindrance. 1109
Without scrip or purse. 174
Without sound of hammer. 3202
Without trumpets. 1703
Witness. 2006, 3828, 3829
Witness and consecration. 2572
Witness and revelation in the Gospel of
    John. 418, 3830
Witness beyond barriers. 3702
Witness catechist's handbook. 3182
Witness for Christ. 3829
Witness for Christ in the nation's capital.
    750
Witness from beyond. 3474
Witness in Israel. 2533, 3252
Witness in the desert. 1636
Witness in the sky. 1736
Witness is witness. 3828
Witness of Edith Barfoot. 173
Witness of His enemies. 2042
Witness of Jesus and other sermons by
    Alexander Procter. 1466
Witness of Kierkegaard. 1104
Witness of Matthew and Mark to Christ.
    436
Witness of radical faith. 3623
Witness of science to the testimonies of
    the spirit of prophecy. 3381, 3811

Witness of the Berrigans. 194
Witness of the heart, and other sermons.
    3345
Witness of the heart to Christ. 59
Witness of the light. 2852
Witness of the prophets. 571
...The witness of the Psalms to Christ and
    Christianity. 577
Witness of the Spirit. 1831, 3339, 3340
Witness of the spirits. 1836
Witness of the stars. 99, 211
...The witness of the Vulgate, Peshitta and
    Septuagint to the text of Zephaniah. 600
Witness of the wilderness. 183
Witness of U.S. Lutherans on peace, war,
    conscience. 2287, 2809
Witness of William Penn. 1679, 3631
Witness papers. 1051
Witness s for Jesus. 3185
Witness through the centuries. 3504
Witness to a generation. 3636
Witness to Christ. 2573
Witness to immortality. 1888
Witness to the faith. 1162
Witness to the influence of Christ. 2013
Witness to the resurrection. 682, 2052
Witness to the sacred. 3581
Witness to the truth. 1995
Witness to the world. 1268, 2553, 3215
Witness to witchcraft. 3825
Witnesses. 1940, 1987, 1990
Witnesses from the dust. 276
Witnesses of hope. 2821
Witnesses of the Book of Mormon. 679
Witnesses of the Gospel. 2006
Witnesses of the light. 660
Witnesses of the spirit. 1449
Witnesses to Christ, the Saviour of the
    world. 2045
Witnesses to God. 294, 295
Witnesses to Jesus. 2006
Witnesses to the eucharist. 2250
Witnesses to the historicity of Jesus. 347,
    2008
Witnesses to the Holy Spirit. 1834
Witnesses to the unseen and other essays.
    762, 2705
Witnesses to the Word. 3848

Witnessing at home and around the world.
    3467
Witnessing Christ. 1950, 3163
Witnessing for Christ. 3829, 3830
Witnessing in the world. 1153
Witnessing in today's world. 3830
Witnessing to the kingdom. 2497, 3849
Witnessing with power. 332
Witnessing with power and joy. 3828
Wittenberg and its association with the
    reformation of Germany. 3040
Wittenberg, revisited. 318, 781, 3616
Wittgenstein for preaching. 3331, 3830
Wittgenstein, grammar and God. 1593,
    3830
Wives of the Bible. 3840
Wizard of the four winds. 3400, 3718
Wizards that peep. 1077
Wizards that peep and mutter. 1088, 3568
Wolf in sheep's clothing. 800
Wolf ritual of the Northwest coast. 3831
Wolfenbuttel Lithuanian Postile manuscript
    of the year 1573. 367
Wolfhart Pannenberg. 2767
Wolfhart Pannenberg and religious
    philosophy. 2767, 3108
Wolsey. 3831
Woman. 3243, 3841, 3844
Woman according to Saint Bonaventure.
    675, 3831
Woman, and her relations to humanity.
    3514
Woman and man. 2326
Woman and super-woman. 3344
Woman and temperance. 3833
Woman and the demon. 1517
Woman and the priesthood. 3838
Woman at the well. 3243, 3407
Woman, be free! 3832
Woman beautiful. 3857
Woman beyond roleplay. 3844
Woman, church and state. 3842
Woman clothed with the sun. 2357
Woman for all seasons. 3830
Woman for our time: the servant of God,
    Mother Thecla Merlo, co-foundress of
    the Daughters of St. Paul. 2412
Woman God loved. 1937, 2359
Woman, her influence and zeal as an aid
    to the priesthood. 3843
Woman, her mission. 3836
Woman, her power and privileges. 2935,
    3833
Woman in a man's church. 3836
Woman in Christian tradition. 3836
Woman in her home. 2339
Woman in Judaism. 3837
Woman in orbit. 2360
Woman in sacred history. 3841
Woman in the church. 3836
Woman in the modern world. 3836
Woman in the pulpit. 3835
Woman in the sacred scriptures of
    Hinduism. 3837
Woman in the world of Jesus. 1959, 3832
Woman is the glory of man. 3836
Woman named Louise. 2203
Woman of decision. 2400, 3417
Woman of Israel. 3838
Woman of Tekoah. 215
Woman of Tekoah, and other sermons on
    Bible characters. 215
Woman of the Pharisees. 2829
Woman of unity. 1645, 2272
Woman question? 3832
Woman religious—the heart of the Church.
    2574
Woman searches. 3844, 3845
Woman set apart. 182
Woman shall conquer. 2356
Woman to woman. 3844
Woman today. 1323
Woman under monasticism. 1357
Woman wants God. 3844
Woman who laughed. 3457
Woman who was pope. 2122
Womanpriest. 688, 1300
... The Woman's auxiliary in the life of the
    church. 3837
Woman's Bible. 224, 225, 3840, 3841
Woman's book of prayers. 3843
Woman's choice. 3844
Woman's divine destiny. 3832
Woman's foreign and home missionary
    manual. 2458
Woman's highest fulfillment. 2572
Woman's inner world. 2855
Woman's life for Kashmir; Irene Petrie, a
    biography. 2536, 2826
Woman's ministry. 2913
Woman's missionary union at work. 3468
Woman's place. 3843
Woman's priorities. 217, 3841
Woman's quest for serenity. 989, 3591
Woman's reach. 3844
Woman's search for serenity. 3844

Woman's sublime call. 3844
Woman's way to God. 3844
Woman's work in the church. 1408
Woman's workshop on David and his
    Psalms. 493, 1405, 2765
Woman's workshop on forgiveness. 1634
Woman's workshop on Philippians. 450,
    3844
Woman's worth. 3846
Woman's worth & work. 3844
Womanspirit rising. 3846
Women alive. 3838
Women and Catholic priesthood. 2742
Women & church leadership. 3835
Women and church work. 1250
Women and girls in the Young Men's
    Christian Association, a study of current
    practices. 3873
Women and girls in the Young Men's
    Christian Association. 3873
Women and home missions. 2457
Women and Jesus. 1959, 3839
Women and Judaism. 3837
Women and ministry in the New
    Testament. 349, 3835
Women and missions in the Methodist
    Episcopal church. South. 2457
Women and orders. 2742
Women and Quakerism. 1685, 3834
Women and religion. 3832, 3834, 3835
Women and religion in America. 3836
Women and the Church. 3834, 3837
... Women and the Gospel in Persia. 2544
Women and the kingdom. 2457
Women and the Liberator. 1959, 3838
Women and the ministry. 3834
Women and the word of God. 202
Women and the world, sermons. 3362
Women & world religions. 3833
Women and worship. 2237
Women, androgynes, and other mythical
    beasts. 2663
Women as pastors. 3835
Women at prayer. 3843
Women before God. 3843
Women, change, and the church. 3836
Women friends of Jesus. 3839
Women in a men's church. 3837
Women in a strange land. 3836
Women in American church life. 3836
Women in American religion. 3836
Women in Baptist life. 3466, 3834
Women in campus ministry. 3835
Women in church and society. 3836
Women in Judaism. 3837
Women in ministry today. 3835
Women in Muslim family law. 3842
Women in neighborhood evangelism. 1570
Women in new worlds. 3837
Women in religion. 3835
Women in ritual and symbolic roles. 3834
Women in search of mission. 1705, 3837
Women in the Bible. 216, 3840, 3841
Women in the church. 3832
Women in the life of Jesus. 3839
Women in the Old Testament. 3839
Women in the pulpit. 3835
Women in the Y.M.C.A. record. 3871
Women in todays world. 1233, 3844
Women, law, and the Genesis traditions.
    3839
Women like us. 3840
Women, men, and the Bible. 3832
Women ministers. 1678, 3835
Women of ancient Israel. 3838
Women of Assam. 3835
Women of destiny in the Bible. 215, 3840
Women of early Christianity. 3836
Women of faith. 1404, 2412
Women of Israel. 492, 3838
Women of Methodism. 2427, 3806
Women of Mormondom. 2606
Women of Mormonism. 2602
Women of spirit. 3836
Women of the Bible. 494, 2169, 3838,
    3839, 3840, 3841
Women of the church. 3836
Women of the cloth. 3835
Women of the Gospel. 338, 3839
Women of the New Testament. 3839
Women of the Old and New Testament.
    3840
Women of the Old Testament. 492, 3839
Women of the Reformation, from Spain to
    Scandinavia. 3037
Women of the Reformation in France and
    England. 3037
Women of the Reformation in Germany
    and Italy. 3037
Women of the Scriptures. 216, 3841
Women of the Valois court. 1638
Women on a mission. 2302
Women on pilgrimage. 3835
Women pastors. 3835
Women preachers. 3834
Women priests. 773, 2742

Women priests in the Catholic Church?
3834
Women priests: yes or no? 2742
Women, slaves and their ignorant in
rabbinic literature. 2074, 2107
Women torch-bearers. 3833
Women under primitive Buddhism. 3841
Women under the Southern cross. 2547
Women versus men. 2677
Women who carried the good news. 30,
2488
Women who encountered Jesus. 2007,
3841
Women who have made good. 3831
Women who made Bible history. 3840
Women without men. 3415
Women, words, and wisdom. 998
Women workers at the Bryn Mawr
summer school. 699
Women's adornment. 656
Women's class in action. 3556
Women's league handbook for Jewish
women's organizations. 2122
Women's liberation and the church. 3836
Women's programs for every season. 3857
Women's programs for special occasions.
3843
Women's work in the Lutheran Church--
Missouri Synod. 2296
Women's world handbook of ideas and
procedures for ladies groups. 3838
Wonder and faith in the first grade. 3171
Wonder and worship. 1437
... A wonder-book. 2656, 2658
Wonder book, and Tanglewood tales.
2658
Wonder book for girls and boys. 2658
Wonder book of Bible stories. 622, 629
Wonder footprints. 3570
Wonder in God's wilderness. 2396
Wonder of being. 1738, 2041
Wonder of being loved. 2215, 2301
Wonder of Christmas. 1113
Wonder of grace. 1751
Wonder of His gracious words. 3336
Wonder of life. 1455
Wonder of Lourdes. 2262
Wonder of prayer. 2868
Wonder of the New Testament. 407
Wonder of the real. 3309, 3695
Wonder of the Word. 276
Wonder stories from the Gospels. 626
Wonder stories of God's people. 622
Wonder tales of Bible days. 2207
Wonder tales of the Bible. 624
Wonder-worker of Padua. 54
Wonder-world of the soul. 998
Wonderful adventures of Nils. 910
Wonderful and other sermons. 1561
Wonderful Bible conversions. 1361
Wonderful Book. 230
Wonderful career of Moody and Sankey,
in Great Britain and America. 1589,
2587
Wonderful chair and the tales it told.
1607
Wonderful Christ. 2930
Wonderful Dharma lotus flower sutra.
3272
Wonderful Jesus. 2047
Wonderful life and works of Dwight L.
Moody. 2587
Wonderful morning. 1486, 2053
Wonderful names of our wonderful Lord.
2020
Wonderful narrative. 731
Wonderful night. 1111
Wonderful promises of God as expressed
in the Twenty-third psalm. 587
Wonderful sacraments. 3264
Wonderful Saviour. 165
Wonderful Shabbos. 3261
Wonderful story of Christ and His apostles.
72
... The wonderful story of Christ and the
apostles. 72, 1984
Wonderful story of Jesus. 930, 1980, 1984
Wonderful story of Jesus the Saviour.
3766
Wonderful story of Jesus told in simple
language. 1983
Wonderful story of life and death. 1056
Wonderful story of old. 623
Wonderful Teacher and what He taught.
2062
Wonderful way that babies are made.
3391
Wonderful works of God. 3187
Wonderful works of God commemorated.
3605
Wondering about God. 2390
Wonderlands of the wild West, with
sketches of the Mormons. 3762
Wonders of Bible chronology. 218
Wonders of creation. 525, 1382
Wonders of Fatima. 1618
Wonders of His grace. 1447

Wonders of man. 3078
Wonders of Massabielle at Lourdes,
apparitions, miracles, pilgrimages. 2262,
3460
Wonders of missions. 2520
Wonders of our faith. 797
Wonders of prophecy. 609
Wonders of Providence. 2983
Wonders of science. 3078
Wonders of the great unveiling, the
remarkable book of the Revelation. 460
Wonders of the revelation of Jesus Christ.
460
Wonders, signs, miracles . . . why not!
2476
Wondrous childhood of the most holy
Mother of God. 2354
Wondrous cross. 106, 1998, 3347
Wondrous mushroom. 1898
Wondrous passion. 2029
Wondrous truths from the Word. 3295
Wondrous works of Christ. 2018
Wondrous works of God. 1734
Wood carvings in English churches. 1165
Wood merchant of Segovia. 3243
Woodbury's German-English and English-
German reader. 1707
Wooden chalices. 3529
Wooden churches of Eastern Europe.
1159
Woodforde at Oxford, 1759-1776. 2755
Wood's Bible animals. 481
Woods-Cogdill debate. 1272
Woods-Nunnery debate on baptism and
apostasy. 137
Woody. 36, 3402
Woofy is forgiven. 2945
Wool merchant's son. 3243
Woolman and Blake: prophets for today.
3847
Woorke concerning the trewnesse of the
Christian religion. 58
...Worcester. 3847
Worcester association and its antecedents.
3847
Worcester County study. 1271
Worcester Young men's Christian
association. 3870
Word. 118, 1317
Word abideth. 278
Word alive. 318
Word among us. 3337
Word and action. 2255
Word and faith. 3651
Word and its inspiration. 3570
Word and mystery. 476, 2010
Word and Redeemer. 1020, 2010
Word and redemption. 3650
Word and revelation. 3650
Word and sacrament. 2256, 3043
Word and spirit. 276, 729
Word and the book. 556
Word and the doctrine. 1823
Word and the Spirit. 3623
Word and the teacher. 1383
Word and the way. 2066
Word and the witness. 678, 2610
Word and the words. 2903
Word and the work. 1053
Word and the world. 645, 3641
Word and words. 2905
Word as truth. 3227, 3697
Word became flesh. 1431, 3218, 3357
Word becoming flesh. 540
Word beyond words. 3750
Word-carrying giant. 31
Word, church, and sacraments in
Protestantism and Catholicism. 118
Word comes alive. 288
Word dwells among us. 311
Word fitly spoken. 1840
Word for every day. 1434
Word for help from the wider world. 3498
Word for the day. 724
Word for this century. 3653
Word for us. 472
Word from the cross. 2059
Word from the wise. 572
Word God sent. 2905
Word in action; the Acts of the Apostles
for our time. 331
Word in deed. 1573
Word in history. 3651
Word in season. 1265, 1267, 2434
Word in season...Sermons and occasional
addresses. 3371
Word in season to the Bar Mitzvah. 172
Word in the Third World. 2515
Word in the world. 15, 2598, 3438, 3626
Word in worship. 2906, 3003
Word in Zion's behalf. 440
Word Incarnate. 2042
Word-indices and word-lists to the Gothic
Bible and minor fragments. 229, 1749
Word interprets us. 298, 2896
Word into silence. 2380
Word is. 2395

Word made flesh. 422, 423, 2009, 3362
Word made fresh. 601
Word-map of the Old Testament. 532
Word meanings in the New Testament.
471
Word of a woman, versus the word of
God. 1029
Word of faith. 1466, 3348
... The word of God. 253, 308, 367, 863,
1266
Word of God according to St. Augustine.
117
Word of God and fundamental doctrine
and revelation of the ages from creation
of the earth to the great white throne
judgment. 635
Word of God and mankind. 3224, 3770
Word of God and modern man. 2322
Word of God and the mind of man. 2181
Word of God and the reformed faith. 730
Word of God and the republic. 1077
Word of God and the word of man. 1047,
1067
Word of God and tradition. 3651
Word of God in history. 296
Word of God in the world of today. 63
Word of God on faith, hope and charity.
3615
Word of God on true marriage. 2338
Word of God opened. 236
Word of God preached to children. 3373
Word of God, word of earth. 483, 1507,
2787
Word of His Grace. 2301, 3359
Word of Lalla the prophetess. 3422
Word of Life. 201, 209, 3861
Word of prophecy. 1514
Word of reconciliation. 2038
Word of salvation. 385
Word of the cross. 105, 1024
Word of the Lord. 160, 1894
Word of the Lord for special days. 2721
Word of the Lord grows. 409
Word of the Lord to His church in the
wilderness. 2061
Word of the truth. 473
Word of their testimony. 2527
Word of truth. 565, 3646, 3664
Word of Wisdom. 2718, 3429, 3848
Word of wisdom and you. 3848
Word of Wisdom today. 3848
Word on the air. 3351
Word or words. 3190
Word overcoming the world. 156
Word pictures from the Bible. 314
Word pictures in the New Testament. 344
Word protestant in literature, history, and
legislation. 2976
Word remains. 666, 3246
Word studies in Biblical Hebrew, Aramaic,
Greek and Latin. 235, 2020
Word studies in the New Testament. 473
Word study concordance. 344
Word study New Testament. 361
Word survey of the New Testament. 411
Word that can never die. 3625
Word that kindles. 652, 2230, 3545
Word to Christian teachers and students
for the ministry. 3157
Word to the weary. 1352
Word to the wise. 567
Word topical Bible of issues and answers.
303
Word was God. 311
Word was made flesh. 2041
Word, water, wine, and bread. 2236
Word we preach. 3349, 3357
Words and deeds of Jesus. 1989
Words and deeds of Jesus from the records
by Matthew and John. 1989
Words and images. 1105, 1106, 2836
Words and meanings. 504, 3697
Words and mind of Jesus. 1440
Words and pictures. 603, 921
Words & testimonies. 1536, 1682
Words and the word. 233, 3070
Words and thoughts. 3371
Words and wonders of the Cross. 2034
Words and works of Jesus Christ. 929,
1970
Words encouraging to right faith and
conduct. 1447
Words fitly spoken. 1065, 2390
Words from and to the cross. 2033
Words from His throne. 2030
Words from the cross. 2057, 2058
Words from the Exodus. 565, 1517
Words from the heart. 2767
Words from the source. 2991
Words in Genesis. 526
Words in pain. 2058, 2059, 3360
Words in season. 2385
Words in season for the inquirer and the
inquiry meeting. 1555
Words like fire. 2007
Words of certitude. 2390
Words of cheer and comfort. 1450

Words of Christ. 2070
Words of comfort. 1354, 3208
Words of comfort and hope. 1350
Words of comfort and other Bible lessons.
1353
Words of conscience. 3794
Words of consolation. 1351
Words of consolation and encouragement
for the sorrowing. 1351
Words of exhortation. 1227
Words of faith. 1070, 3187, 3732
Words of faith and hope. 3808
Words of fire, rivers of tears. 1943
Words of Frances Schervier. 3307
Words of God in an African forest. 2500
Words of Jesus. 1440, 2069, 2070
Words of Jesus as recorded in the New
Testament. 2069
Words of Jesus Christ during His passion.
2058
Words of Jesus from the cross. 2057
Words of Jesus in our Gospels. 391, 788,
3848
Words of Joseph Smith. 2620, 3429
Words of life. 1454, 1456, 2056, 2335,
2607, 2692
Words of my mouth. 2142
Words of Our Lord. 1968
Words of Our Saviour, Jesus Christ. 2070
Words of our worship. 2961
Words of revolution. 1560
Words of Saint Francis. 776
Words of silver and gold. 2398
Words of the Christ as recorded in the
New Testament. 2070
Words of the faith. 149
Words of the Father. 3142
Words of the law. 2279
Words of the Lord Jesus. 2070, 3220
Words of the missal. 845
Words of the risen Savior. 412, 2072
Words of the world's religions. 3123
Words of this prophecy. 465
Words of triumph. 2058
... The words of truth. 74, 2933
Words of wisdom. 573, 1430
Words of wisdom to the people. 1711
Words on target. 1317
Words on the cross. Seven sermonettes.
2058
Words or wisdom from the Bible. 304
Words that shook the world; or Martin
Luther his own biography. 2272
Words to change lives. 3361
Words to live by. 421, 1431, 2392
Words to see by. 3070
Words to the winners of souls. 1299, 3671
Words to the wise. 2725
Work. 3785
Work and dreams and the wide horizon.
34
Work and office of the holy angels here on
earth and in paradise. 3519
... The work and teachings of the apostles.
406
Work and teachings of the earlier prophets.
571
Work and the Christian community. 1131
Work and vocation. 3785
Work and words of Jesus. 1952, 2061
*Work and worship. 3165, 3394
Work as praise. 3849
Work begun. 3871
Work claiming to be the consititutions of
the holy apostles. 1488
Work for Jesus. 673
Work God sent. 2905

Work of a great parish. 2775
Work of an evangelist. 3351
Work of Christ. 106, 1950, 1951, 2009,
2041
Work of church officers and committees.
1239
Work of faith. 1690
Work of God in Great Britain. 2587, 3230
Work of invisible helpers. 2730
Work of Jesus Christ as an advocate. 2049
Work of John the Baptist. 2127
Work of preaching. 2901, 2911
Work of preaching Christ. 2902
Work of Religious. 113
Work of St. Optatus. 1476
... The work of the apostles. 71
... The work of the chronicler. 496
... The work of the church in the South
during the period of reconstruction.
3741
...The work of the church in the Sunday
school. 3555
... The work of the church in theological
seminaries in the United State of
America. 3612
Work of the church treasurer. 1168
Work of the church trustee. 1249

Work of the church--whose responsibility? Church officer's guide and notebook. 2915
Work of the clerk. 1239
Work of the deacon. 1408
Work of the gods in Tikopia. 3699
Work of the Holy Spirit. 1829, 1830, 1831, 1833, 1835, 3805
Work of the Holy Spirit, a treatment of the Biblical doctrine of the Divine Spirit. 1828
Work of the Holy Spirit illustrated by New Testament symbols. 1829
Work of the Holy Spirit in man. 1832
Work of the Lord. 1251
Work of the medical missionary. 2482
Work of the ministry. Lectures given to the Meadville theological school, June, 1889. 3675
Work of the monk in early England. 2579
... The work of the Old Testament sages. 600
Work of the pastor. 1295, 2791
Work of the preacher. 1295
Work of the Spirit; or, Doctrinal and practical meditations on the nature and work of the Holy Ghost. 1835
Work of the student Young men's Christian association. 3872
Work of the Sunday-school. 3565
Work of the usher. 1249
Work of Thomas Chalmers. 2914
Work of Thomas Cranmer. 1216
Work of William Tyndale. 3630
Work, play, and the Gospel. 1610
Work, play, and worship in a leisure-oriented society. 2209
Work-study handbook for educable mentally retarded minors enrolled in high school programs in California public schools. 2411
Work trap. 3848
Work ways in Japan. 2534
... A workable Christianity. 1057
Workable faith. 2398
Workable plan of evangelism. 1563
Workable plans for wide-awake churches. 1252
Workable prayer meeting programs. 2886
Workaholic and his family. 2782
Workbook for Franciscan studies. 1648
Workbook of intercessory prayer. 2871
Workbook on the Book of Acts. 333
...The worker and his Bible. 309
... The worker and his church. 2443, 2459
Worker in wood. 1978
Worker-priests. 2938
Workers are few. 850
Worker's companion. 302
Workers' conference. 3554
Workers' conference manual. 3157
Workers' education in India. 2189
Workers in the vineyard. 3514
Workers' manual. 3554
Worker's outline of the Bible. 639
Worker's secret of unction. 1553
Workers together. 970
Workers training course. 3177
Worker's training course No. 4. 3565
Workers with God. 1167
Working bibiliography of English translations of the New Testament, 1881-1961. 337
Working church and its way of working. 3814
Working faith. 1238, 1596, 1597
Working faith for the world. 1064
Working for Jesus. 1564
Working in the church. 3146
Working man's Christ. 1131, 2048
Working manual for altar guilds. 27
Working manual of a successful Sunday-school. 3565
Working out what God works in. 1013
Working papers and addresses. 1492
Working papers in doctrine. 3653
Working papers on the theology of marriage. 2343
Working program for the local church. 1199
Working theology. 3645
Working things out. 1308
Working to beat hell. 968
Working together. 3870
Working together in a spiritual democracy. 3465
Working together in the larger parish. 2197
Working together through the church council. 2774
Working with children and the liturgy. 3858
Working with children in the small church. 3170
Working with college students. 3537
Working with God. 965, 1290
Working with God in His world. 3765

Working with juniors at church. 3170
Working with organized labor. 3872
Working with parish councils? 2774
Working with primaries through the Sunday school. 3169
Working with volunteer leaders in the church. 953
Workingman and the synagogue. 2104
Workingman's view of the Bible. 221
Workman not ashamed. 3385
Workmen of God. 3671
Works. 1217, 1334, 3629, 3630
Works and days of John Fisher. 1628
Works and wonders. 3750
Works count too (Pickell, Charles N. 1011
Works (Edwards, Jonathan) 1334
Works (Luther, Martin. 2275, 3629, 3637
Works (Newman, John Henry, Cardinal) 3632
Works of Bonaventure. 775
Works of Dionysius the Areopagite. 3635
Works of Father Prout (the Rev. Francis Mahony) edited with biographical introduction and notes. 1919
Works of Francis Bacon. 124
Works of Francis J. Grimke. 2914
Works of Friedrich Nietzsche. 3788
Works of George Bull. 713, 3630
Works of George Fox. 1679, 3630
Works of Henry Ware, jr. 3795
Works of Hugh Latimer. 1227
Works of Isaac Barron, D. D. 1216
Works of Jacob Behmen, the Teutonic theosopher. 2643
Works of James Arminius. 3628
Works of James Pilkington. 1217
Works of Jesus. 1990
Works of John and Charles Wesley. 3806
Works of John Bunyan. 716
Works of John Hales. 3630
Works of John Jewel. 1216, 1217, 3629
Works of John Wesley. 2428, 3631
Works of John Whitgift. 743, 1220
Works of John Woolman. 1679, 3424
Works of Joseph Bellamy. 1333
Works of Leonard Woods. 1334
Works of love (Kierkegaard, Soren Aabye) 3480
Works of Martin Luther (Luther, Martin) 2275
Works of Nicholas Ridley. 1217
Works of peace. 2670
... The works of Peter of Poitiers. 2826
Works of President Edwards. 1334
Works of Rev. E. Bickersteth. 658
Works of Richard Hurd, Lord Bishop of Worcester. 1857
Works of Robert Browning. 803
... The works of Robert G. Ingersoll. 1655
Works of Roger Hutchinson. 1722
Works of St. Augustine. 114
*Works of St. Augustine (The) 115
Works of Saint Bonaventure. 676
Works of Saint Cyril of Jerusalem. 3635
Works of Samuel Hopkins. 1334
Works of that eminent minister of the gospel. 1290
Works of that eminent servant of the Christ. 716
Works of that learned and judicious divine, Mr. Richard Hooker. 1218, 1488, 1489
Works of the late reverend and pious Mr. Thomas Gouge. 3630
Works of the Most Reverend Father in God, William Laud, D.D. 1217, 3630
Works of the Rev. Claudius Buchanan, L. L. D. 91
Works of the Rev. Daniel M'Calla. 1334
Works of the Rev. Henry Scougal. 3630
Works of the Rev. John Fletcher. 2427
Works of the Rev. John Howe. 3008
Works of the Rev. John Witherspoon. 2914
Works of the Rev. Robert Hall. 147
Works of the Rev. Robert Hall, A.M. 147
Works of the Rev. Sydney Smith. 3431
Works of the reverend and learned Isaac Watts. 3799
Works of the Right Rev. John England. 776
Works of the Right Reverend Joseph Hall. 1216, 3630
Works of the Right Reverend William Fleetwood, D. D. 3363
... The works of the Rt. Rev. Charles C. Grafton. 2957
Works of Thomas Chalmers. 880
Works of Thomas Cranmer. 1216
Works of Thomas Shepard. 1334
Works of Thomas Shepard, first pastor of the First Church, Cambridge, Mass. 1334
Works of W. Chillingworth, M.A. 2976
Works of William Chillingworth. 1216, 2976, 3630
Works of William Dell. 3630

Works of William E. Channing. 3724
Works of William E. Channing, D. D. 882, 3724
Works of William of St. Thierry. 776, 3636
Works of William Paley. 1217, 2766
Works of William Smith, D. D. 3358
Works on the Right Reverend John England, first bishop of Charleston. 2415
Works, 1738. 399, 1225, 3363
Works to the King (Graham, Clara) 1919
[Works, vocal] Hugh Aston, 1485 (?)-(?) John Marbeck, 1510 (?)-85(?) Osbert Parsley, 1511-85. 3271
Workship of nature. 2676
Workshop for Baptists on Deafness and Rehabilitation. 1257
World. 3082
World a spiritual system. 2739
World about us. 3763
World aflame. 1066
World airways for the King. 3466
World and church. 1155
World and environment. 1383
World and its God. 1724
World and men around Luther. 2278, 3036
World and the faith. 1135
World and the individual. 2674
World and the person. 2323
World and the prophets. 2604
World and the white prince. 2852
World as an organic whole. 2418
World as the subject of redemption. 1118
World at my door. 3833
World at one in prayer. 2890
World at prayer. 856
World atlas of Christian missions. 2523
World awareness. 3468
World before Abraham according to Genesis i-xi. 563
World beyond. 1696, 3062
... World Bible. 3268
World-call to men of to-day. 2521
World-case report. 67
World Catholicism today. 811

World chaos or world Christianity. 3849
World Christ knew. 1962
World Christian encyclopedia. 1038
World Christianity. 1042
World Christianity, Middle East. 1102
World Christians live in. 975
... World Christians worshiping. 3183
World come of age. 677
World community. 1122
World conqueror and world renouncer. 709
World Council of Churches. 3849
World Council of Churches and the demise of evangelism. 2554, 3850
World Council of Churches' statements and actions on racism, 1948-1979. 1133, 3850
World crises and the prophetic Scriptures. 608
World crisis and Jewish survival. 2079
World crisis and the Catholic. 1136
World crisis -- God's opportunity. 2539
World cultures and world religions. 1079
World democracy [by] Bin Dir Woor. 1422
World development: challenge to the churches. 1155
World directory of religious radio and television broadcasting. 3018
World directory of theological education by extension. 3332
World directory of theological libraries. 3612
World evangelism and the word of God. 1566, 1913
World events in the light of God's Word. 1514
World expectant. 3142
World faith. 125, 129, 3114
World faith in action. 2954
World faiths. 3140
World fellowship. 3138
World friendship, inc. 2521
World friendship room. 2491
World-friendship through the church school. 2550
World God made. 631
World handbook for the world Christian. 3139
World history in myth and legend. 2650
World hypotheses. 2419, 3716
World in my mirror. 931, 2130
World in rebellion. 2981
World in the church. 1154
World in travail. 1282
World in tune. 1454
World in which Jesus lived. 408
World intangible. 2175

World invisible. 92
World is a wedding. 3521
World is my parish. 3137
World is new. 2694, 2695
World is our field. 2296
World: its creation and consummation. 3082
World Jewish history, religion, and culture. 2083
World league of nations and religions. 2221
World lighted. 464
World Methodist movement. 3851
World mission and world communism. 1154
World mission and world peace. 2525
World mission of Christianity. 2520
World mission of the Christian religion. 2549
World mission of the church. 2520
World mission of the United Christian missionary society. 3731
World mission windows. 2491
World missions. 2494
World missions as seen from Jerusalem. 2551
World missions of The American Lutheran Church. 32
World missions today. 2550
World more human, a church more Christian. 3626
World my country. 144, 2718
World next-door. 3515
World of Albert Schweitzer. 3311
World of Allah. 1926
World of art—the world of youth. 1260
World of Bede. 182, 1764
World of books. 905
World of Christ. 2553
World of David and Solomon. 1405, 2093
World of difference, following Christ beyond your cultural walls. 1074
World of differents. 1567
World of dreams, an anthology. 1479
World of energy. 2561
World of grace. 1751, 3019, 3657
World of gurus. 1778
World of Hasidism. 1789
World of Islam. 86, 1820, 1922, 1923, 2565, 2566
World of Jesus. 407
World of matter and the spirit of man. 3132
World of mission. 2495
World of Monsieur Vincent. 3779
World of Moses. 517, 2621
World of Moses Maimonides. 2623
World of myths. 2659
World of Ottoman art. 88
World of Philip Potter. 2865
World of prayer. 2109
World of prayer; commentary and translation of the daily prayer. 2109
World of psychic research. 2845
World of St. John. 413
World of San Bernardino. 194
World of spirits and man's state after death. 1795
World of the Bible. 207
World of the Book of Mormon. 678, 1898
World of the Buddha. 711
World of the Crusaders. 1390
World of the Judges. 554, 2090
World of the Midrash. 2462
World of the New Testament. 407, 408
World of the Old Testament. 536
World of the patriarchs. 524
World of the Reformation. 3034
World of the restoration. 537, 2091
World of the Sephardim. 3333
World of the spirit. 120
World of the Talmud. 3584
World of the twilight believers. 2725
World of the unexplained. 2729
World of the Vatican. 3768
World of the witches. 3823
World of words. 589
World of Zen. 3892, 3894
World on the march. 2465
World on trial. 469
World order of baha 'u' llah. 125, 128
World order of Baha'u'llah. 125, 129
World passed by. 2092
...World peace and Christian missions. 2492
World picture of Zarathustra. 3899
World poverty and the Christian. 2865
World problem. 2102
... A world problem; jews-Poland-humanity. 2102
World problems of today. 1137
World program according to the Holy Scriptures. 1952
World prospects. 1513
World Protestantism. 2977
World rebuilt. 699, 2593
World recovery? 1941

World religions. 3069, 3117, 3120, 3123
*World religions and Christian mission. 3166
World religions and the hope for peace. 3122
World religions and world community. 3123
World religions and world peace. 2808
World religions in the first and middle school. 3142
World religions in the light of Mormonism. 3120
... World revolution and religion. 3443
World service. 3871
World service church school programs. 2517
World service of the Methodist Episcopal church. 2442
World situation. 1077
World statistics of Christian missions. 2519
World stood still. 2167, 3722
... World stories. 3565
World Sunday school movement. 3561
World temple science. 2696
World that cannot be shaken. 3359
World that is. 1005
World that perished. 1422
World, the flesh, and the devil. 944, 985
World thrust of Northern Baptists. 142
World to change. 1340
World to come. 1343, 1697, 1698, 3234
World to win. 1554, 2492, 2526, 2797
World today. 3452
World today in the light of Bible prophecy. 608
World tomorrow. 1514
World tour of evangelism. 2521
World treasury of religious quotations. 3111
World upside down or right side up? 180
World-view of Jesus. 2064
World-visioned church. 3788
World war III and the destiny of America. 611
World we live in. 3496
World-wide Bible study. 637
World-wide church. 2853
World-wide evangelization the urgent business of the church. 2522
World-wide Sunday-school work. 3559
World within. 3052
World within a world. 2540
World within the Bible. 3571
World without chance? 1514
World without end. 648, 1445, 1723, 3079, 3858
Worldliness of worship. 3854
Worldly Christian. 676, 962
Worldly evangelicals. 1552
Worldly goods. 807
Worldly holiness. 2887
Worldly theology. 3652
Worlds apart. 2569
World's battle. 970
World's best book. 290
World's best hymns. 1860
World's best religious quotations. 3014
World's Bible auxiliary and beautiful teachings of the Bible. 643
World's Cardinal. 1397
World's classic, Job. 549
World's collision. 607
World's Columbian Catholic congresses. 1137, 3362
World's concordance to the Holy Bible. 226
World's congress of religions. 3122, 3138
World's debt to Protestantism. 2976
World's debt to the Catholic church. 757
World's desire. 806
World's desires. 3027
World's destiny according to prophecy. 46
World's edition of the great Presbyterian conflict. 2936
World's eye. 1587
World's first love. 2356
World's great Catholic literature. 868
World's great love. 2356
World's great Madonnas. 2358
World's great religions. 3117, 3118, 3122
World's great religions and the religion of the future. 3118
World's great religious poetry. 3206
World's great religious poetry, edited. 3209
World's great scriptures. 3267, 3268
World's great sermons. 3340, 3342
World's greatest classic. 199
World's greatest decade. 151
World's greatest leaders. 3090
...The world's greatest library graphically illustrated. 605
World's greatest love story and other sermons selected from various evangelistic campaigns. 1557

World's greatest name. 2020
World's greatest need. 2611
World's greatest prayer, and other sermons of the Little brown church of the air, WLS-Prairie farmer station. 2436
World's greatest secret. 2251
World's greatest short story. 2945
World's greatest story. 533, 624
World's largest Sunday school. 1626
World's last night. 1070
World's last night, and other essays. 1070
World's living religions. 3113, 3116, 3117
Worlds lost and found. 207
... the world's most orphaned nation. 1856
World's mythology in colour. 2652
World's need of Christ. 3442
Worlds of Norman Salit. 3371
Worlds of science & religion. 3082
World's only hope. 253
World's panacea. 1063
World's parliament of religions. 3852
World's parliament of religions and the Religious parliament extension. 3122
World's peaker, reciter and entertainer for home, school, church and platform. 3027
World's prayer (revelatio revelata) 3225
World's redemption. 1071
World's religions. 3112, 3113
World's religions in a nutshell. 3138
World's rim. 1902
World's sages, infidels, and thinkers. 659
World's sages, thinkers and reformers. 659
World's Saturday night. 2930
World's saviors. 1321
World's sixteen crucified saviors. 1091, 1321
World's spiritual conquest. 1049
World's stage. 2719
World's strange religions. 3118
World's symbolism. 3573
World's unrest, and its remedy. 792
World's view of eternal punishment. 1699
World's wickedest men. 660
World's worship in stone. 3599
Worldview and the communication of the Gospel. 2556
Worldwide mission of the church. 2551
Worrell New Testament. 354
Worry and wonder of being human. 3166
Worship. 2236, 3854, 3859
Worship aids for 52 services. 3857
Worship and conflict under colonial rule. 1897
Worship and congregation. 3853
Worship and ethics. 3855
Worship and freedom. 15, 3891
Worship and hymns for all occasions. 1870
Worship & intercession. 2873
Worship and life. 958
Worship & liturgy. 794, 2235
Worship and mission. 2554
Worship and music. 1202
Worship and music in the Church of Jesus Christ of Latter-Day Saints. 1206
Worship and politics. 836, 2254
Worship and reformed theology. 2236
Worship and remembrance. 2855
Worship and secular man. 3854
Worship & the common life. 3853
Worship and the well ordered life. 1123
Worship and theology in England. 1762
Worship and work. 174, 1309, 2620, 3275
Worship and worshipers in the church. 3858
Worship as celebration of covenant and incarnation. 3003
Worship as pastoral care. 3004
Worship at work. 672
Worship celebrations for youth. 3856
...The worship committee in action. 3859
Worship for Christmas. 1114
Worship for the young in spirit. 3857
Worship for youth. 3859
Worship God! 1053, 3003
Worship: good news in action. 3004
Worship highways. 3003
Worship idea book for Christian Church student groups. 3731
Worship in a changing church. 1211
Worship in a new key. 840, 2240, 3773
Worship in a new key: what the Council teaches on the liturgy. 840
Worship in action. 836
Worship in ancient Israel. 3853, 3856
Worship in art and music. 3857
Worship in Christian education. 3859
Worship in Islam. 3855
Worship in Israel. 3855, 3856
Worship in music. 1204
Worship in my church. 3859
Worship in our family. 1605
Worship in Scripture and tradition. 3855
Worship in spirit and truth. 2253

Worship in the Church of Jesus Christ of Latter-Day Saints. 1231, 3853
Worship in the church school. 3859
Worship in the church school through music, pageantry and pictures. 3560
Worship in the early church. 3855
Worship in the free churches. 3854
Worship in the Methodist tradition. 2236
Worship in the name of Jesus. 3852
Worship in the New Testament. 3855
Worship in the reformed tradition. 3854
Worship in the Sunday school. 3555, 3853, 3858
Worship in the world's religions. 1395
Worship in wood. 1156
Worship in word and sacrament. 3003
Worship, its theology and practice. 3852
Worship, its theology and practice, by J. J. von Allmen. 3852
Worship of God. 1741, 3003
Worship of Jesus in its past and present aspects. 2050
Worship of nature. 2676
Worship of the church. 839, 2961
Worship of the early church. 3855
Worship of the little child. 3857
Worship of the Reformed Church. 2929
Worship of the Sky-god. 3423
Worship, old and new. 3004
Worship on the churches. 3003
Worship points the way. 2235, 3402
Worship programs. 3856
Worship programs and stories for young people. 3857
Worship programs for intermediates. 3857
Worship programs for juniors. 3856
Worship programs in the fine arts for young people. 3857
Worship, rediscovering the missing jewel. 3002
Worship resources for the Christian year. 1262
Worship resources for youth. 3857
Worship services and programs for beginners. 3857
Worship services for church groups. 3857
Worship services for junior highs. 3857
Worship services for kindergarten and primary children. 3859
Worship services for life planning. 3856
Worship services for purposeful living. 3856
Worship services for special days. 3857
Worship services for special occasions. 3856
Worship services for the church year. 3876
Worship services for young people. 3876
Worship services for youth. 3876
Worship services using the arts. 3144
Worship sourcebook for youth. 3856
Worship: the life of the missions. 838
Worship time. 3857
Worship training for juniors. 3859
Worship training for primary children. 3857
Worship ways for camp. 733
Worship, why and how. 3004
Worship with youth. 3856
Worshipful master's assistant. 1666
Worshiping church. 3003
Worshiping congregation. 3859
Worshiping with women of the Bible. 3856
Worshipping community. 999, 1119
Worshipping together with questioning minds. 3858
Worshipping toward Christian unity. 1039
Worth. 3859
Worth of a man. 1070, 3161
Worth of a smile. 1233, 3353
Worth of a soul. 1561
Worth of a woman. 3845
Worth of religious truth-claims. 2181
Worth thinking about. 2388
Worthy Dr. Fuller. 1690
Worthy is the Lamb. 456
Worthy is the world. 1708
Worthy of the calling; [the layman's vital role]. 2191
Would Christ wear khaki? 2807
Would I? Would you? 1365
Wound of mortality. 1001
... Wounded for our transgressions. 2032
Wounded healer. 2786
Wounded heart. 740
Wounded heart: St. Charles of Sezze, Franciscan Brother. 740
Wounded spirits. 1601
Wounded Word. 2057, 2058
Wrath of God. 1742
Wrath of God in the former prophets. 1742
Wrath of heaven. 1794
Wrecked lives. 659, 3237
Wrentham jubilee. 2741
Wrested Scriptures made plain. 3422

Wrestle of religion with truth. 3065
Wrestlers with Christ. 2232
Wrestlers with God. 604
Wrestlin' Jacob. 16, 2130
Wrestling or clinging, and other gospel addresses. 1560
Wrestling with God. 1931, 2215
Wrestling with Luther. 2281
Wrestling with Romans. 470
Write for the religion market. 3203
Writing and winning ariticles. 1017
Writing Apostolate. 119
Writing for the religious market. 3203
Writing for the religious market, the co-authors: Henry B. Adams [and others]. 3203
Writing of American Jewish History. 32
Writing your own worship materials. 2238
Writings and addresses of Austin Craig. 1705
...Writings and genius of the founder of Christian science. 1035, 1495
Writings and translations of Myles Coverdale. 1216
Writings (Arminius, Jacobus) 3629
Writings (Basilius) 3634
Writings, etc. 3631
Writings (Francesco d'Assisi) 1641
Writings from the Western standard. 2601
Writings (Henshaw, Thomas) 530
Writings in time of war. 2839
Writings (Joannes, of Damascus) 1019
Writings (Lasuen, Fermin Francisco de) 726
... The writings of a Hindu chela. 3686
Writings of Francisco Garcia Diego y Moreno, Obispo de Ambas Californias. 666, 1702
Writings of John Bradford, M. A. 1216
Writings of Parley Parker Pratt. 2609
Writings of Pilgram Marpeck. 3629
Writings of President Frederick M. Smith. 3216, 3634
Writings of Professor B. B. Edwards. 3620
Writings of Rev. William Bradford Homer. 1341
Writings of Saint Augustine. 3634, 3635, 3677
Writings of Saint Francis of Assisi. 3636
Writings of St. Paul. 378, 2803
Writings of the early Church Fathers. 1020
Writings of the Felician Sisters in the United States. 1620
Writings of the New Testament in their historical setting. 411
Writings of Thomas Hooker. 1845
Writings on theology and religion. 3625, 3715
Writings (Stein, Edith) 777
Written because. 1873
Written in heaven. 3691
Written on many hearts. 3402
Written out of history. 3842
Wrought brim. 3351
Wrought gold. 1791
Wurmbrand letters. 1320, 2821
Wurra-wurra. 878
WW III. 611
Wyaconda Baptist association of Missouri. 156
Wyclif. 3861
Wycliffe. 3636, 3860
Wycliffe and English nonconformity. 3861
Wycliffe and movements for reform. 2769, 3861
Wycliffe Bible commentary. 224
Wycliffe Bible encyclopedia. 247
Wycliffe biographical dictionary of the Church. 925
Wycliffe historical geography of Bible lands. 282
Wyclyf tradition. 3861
Wyeth's repository of sacred music. 1204

X

X-rated marriages. 2340
Xingu; the Indians, their myths. 1903
X-ray sermons. 3341
XXVIII International eucharistic congress, June 20-24, 1926, Chicago, Ill. 1913

Y

Y cuatro Ebangelio sija yan y Checho y apostoles sija gui Testamento Nuebo y Senotta yan y Satbadotta si Jesucristo; yan y Salmo sija. Un trinaduse y fino griego yan hebreo gui fino yi tano guam pat y chamorro. 881
"Y" in rhyme. 3871

Y.M.C.A. and public recreation, informal education, and leisure-time programs. 3029
Y. M. C. A. and public recreation. 3029
Y. M. C. A. and social need. 3872
Y.M.C.A. college. 3872
Y.M.C.A. executive secretary. 3870
Y. M.C.A. in small communities. 1375
Y.M.C.A. physical director. 3870
Y.M.C.A. public relations. 3871
Y.P.C.U. handbook. 3876
"Y" secretary and social issues. 3875
Y.W.C.A. in Latin America. 3852
Yahveh Christ. 3591
Yahvism, and other discourses. 2115
Yahweh. 1728, 1731, 1736
Yahweh and the gods of Canaan. 2150
Yahweh is a warrior. 500, 3795
Yahweh versus Baal. 2765, 3219
Yahweh war & tribal confederation. 531, 2096
Yajnavalkya Smriti. 1812
Yajnavalkya's Smriti. 1812
Yale and the ministry. 3862
Yale lectures on preaching. 183, 2897
Yale talks. 3758
Yankee and the swamis. 3775
Yankee at Molokai. 1484
Yankee eloquence in the Middle West. 2303
Yankee in the Yellow Robe. 710
Yankee on the Yangtze. 2485, 3013
Yankee Paul. 1799
... A Yankee Xavier, Henry P. McGlinchey, S. J. 2308
Yankees and God. 2687
Yankees in paradise. 2523, 2524, 2525
Yantra, the Tantric symbol of cosmic unity. 3862
Yaqui Easter. 2778, 3862
Yavanajataka of Sphujidhvaja. 98
Yavneh shiron. 3260
Yazidis, their life and beliefs. 3863
YCW chaplain. 3869
Ye are my friends. 1971
Ye are my witnesses. 2042
Ye are the Body. 1180
Ye are the light of the world. 2609
Ye gods. 1003
Ye men of Athens. 2986
"Ye must be born again" 1555
Ye olde Shaker bells. 3395
Ye shall be comforted. 1352
Ye shall be witnesses. 1566
Ye shall know the truth. 1385, 3506
"Ye shall know the truth, and the truth shall make you free." 1463
Ye shall live also. 250, 1891
Ye shall reap. 2498
Ye shall receive power. 1445
Ye that thirst. 565
Yea God! 1363, 1658
Year and our children. 1262
Year at the Catholic Worker. 871, 1509
Year book. 172, 1788, 2105, 2296, 2452, 2453, 3191, 3731, 3796
... Year book. 1st. 3191
... Year book and church directory of the Protestant churches of the District of Columbia. 3797

Year book and official journal. 2453
Year book and official roster of the Young men's Christian associations of Canada and the United States of America. 3872
... Year book and program of activities. 2107
Year book containing directory and statistical report of the Young women's Christian associations of the United States of America. 3879
Year book ... containing the proceedings of the ... meeting. 1st- 1908. 172
Year book, Educational council of the Methodist Episcopal church, South annual session, Nashville, Tenn. 2456
... Year book of Churches of Christ (Disciples) 1271
Year-book of spiritualism for 1871. 3521
Year book of the First church of Christ in Hartford. 1787
Year book of the Iowa conference ... Annual session. 2452
Year book of the Methodist Protestant church. 2459
Year book of the Minnesota annual conference. 2452
Year book of the National spiritualist association of the United States of America. 3521

Year book of the Presbyterian program for young people. 2921
Year book of the ... session of the East Maine conference. 2446

Year in John's Gospel. 414
Year made holy. 2367
Year of children's sermons. 906, 909
Year of Christ in song. 889, 2048
Year of evangelism in the local church. 1562
Year of good cheer. 1264
Year of grace. 3341
Year of hymn stories. 1861
Year of junior programs. 3172
Year of junior programs and activities. 3172
Year of miracle. 3317, 3340
Year of Our Lord. 1264
Year of primary programs. 3170
Year of programs for children's church. 905
Year of research--1927. 3219
Year of the church. 1262
Year of the Lord. 1262
Year of the Lord in the Christian home. 1610
Year of the silence. 1844
Year of the three popes. 2770, 2805
Year of youth programs and activities. 3876, 3890
Year one catalog. 3138
... A year with Moses. 566
... A year with Moses. Prepared for scholars of the third and senior grades. 566
Year with St. Paul. 2804
Year with the Bible. 613
Year with the children. 908
Year with the liturgy. 1265
Year with the Psalms. 585, 1432
Yeara a little! or, Why did God come up with two sexes? 3393
Yearbook. 818, 1545, 1625, 2106, 2122, 2290, 2293, 2296, 2302, 2408, 2751, 3732
Yearbook of American churches. 3327
Yearbook of Christian camping. 1164
Yearbook of Churches of Christ. 1946/47. 1272
Yearbook of Jehovah's Witnesses. 1942
Yearbook of liturgical studies. 849
Yearbook of the annual session. 1021
Yearn a little! 3393
Yearning for God, the path to peace of the soul. 1454
Yearning to be free. 956
Year's Bible course. 254, 648
Years of darkness, days of glory. 520, 2090
Years of light. 1667
Years of our church. 2302
Years of Our Lord. 1986
Years of struggle. 2145
Years of sunshine, days of rain. 2573
Year's prayer-meeting talks. 3348
Year's program. 2670
Year's program of audio-visual units and projects. 3166
Years that count. 3888
Yeast, salt, and secret agents. 2388
Yeats, the tarot, and the Golden Dawn. 3589, 3863
Yehoshua. 553
Yehoshua Nazir. 1966
Yellow river runs red. 2351
Yellow rivers. 2508
Yellow star. 799
Yemenite Targum manuscript to the twelve Minor prophets. 558
Yerushalmi fragments from the Genizah. 724, 2090
Yes. 2169
"Yes, but--." 57
Yes, Father. 998
Yes is a world. 2383
Yes is forever. 2412, 2717
Yes, Lord. 1822, 3540
Yes to God. 2871
Yes to mission. 2555
Yes, Virginia. 2735, 3302
Yes, Virginia, there is a hell. 1802
Yes we can! 1689, 2857
Yes, world: a mosaic of meditation. 2390
Yeshiva in America. 3015
Yeshu, called Jesus. 1996
Yeshua Buddha. 2067, 2649
"Yesterday" 405, 2121
Yesterday and tomorrow in the Synod of Virginia. 2928
Yesterday in Bible prophecy. 604
Yesterday speaks to today. 2950
Yesterday, today, and forever. 1610
Yesterday, today, and tomorrow. 3701
Yesterday, today, and what next? 1818
Yesterday today: answers from the ancients. 493
Yesterday, today, tomorrow. 648
Yesterday with the fathers. 2958
Yesterday's faith for tomorrow. 3361

Yesterday's horizons. 1175
Yesterdays in Persia and Kurdistan. 2544
Yesterday's preachers. 2427
Yesterday's prophets for today's world. 569, 2950
Yesterday's radicals. 692
Yesterday's voices for today's world. 560
Yesteryears. 2928
Yet another day. 2874, 2892
Yet once more. 2469
Yet shall we live. 1353
"Yet there is room," 2503
--Yet we can hope. 2981
Yet will I serve Him. 2304, 3569
Yet will I trust Him. 1726
Yiddish teacher. 3863
Yielded bodies. 2327
Y.M.C.A. in Hawaii, 1869-1969. 3874
YMCA year book and official. 3876
Yoga. 3864, 3865, 3867
Yoga and beyond. 3864
Yoga and destiny. 3865
Yoga and God. 674
Yoga and self-culture. 3866
Yoga and the Hindu tradition. 3866
Yoga and the spiritual life. 3864
... Yoga and yoga discipline. 3866
Yoga and yogic powers. 3867
Yoga aphorisms of Patanjali. 3865
Yoga as philosophy and religion. 2791, 3864
Yoga Darsana. 3864
Yoga; immortality and freedom. 3864
Yoga lessons for developing spiritual consciousness. 3865
Yoga of meditation. 3864
Yoga of the Bhagavat Gita. 2316
Yoga; or, Transformation. 3461
... Yoga philosophy. 3864, 3866
Yoga psychology. 2379
Yoga-sutra of Patanjali. 3865
Yoga sutras. 3865
Yoga sutras of Pantanjali. 3867
Yoga system. 3863
Yoga-system of Patanjali. 3865, 3867
Yoga, tantra, and meditation in your daily life. 3865
Yoga, the alpha and the omega. 2792, 3867
Yoga: union with the ultimate. 3867
Yoga uniting East and West. 3866
Yoga Vashisht; or, Heaven found. 3866
Yoga vedanta dictionary. 3867
Yoga wisdom. 3867
Yoga, youth, and reincarnation. 3866
Yogasana vijnana. 3864
Yogi and the devotee. 2674
Yogi and the mystic. 1708, 2316, 3492
Yogi, the commissar, and the third-world church. 982
Yohale Sarah. 2118
Yoke made easy. 3406
Yoke of Christ. 3359
Yoke of Divine Love. 3196
Yom Kippur. 3864
Yom Kippur anthology. 3867
Yon motley crowd. 1361
... Yonder! 850, 2507
Yoneko, daughter of happiness. 1360, 3579
York. 479
York metropolitan jurisdiction and papal judges delegate(1297-1296) 667
York minister historical tracts. 3868
York Psalter. 848
Yoruba beliefs and sacrificial rites. 3868
Yossele's holiday and the brave Maccabees. 1623
You. 2324, 3683
You also serve! 688
You and children. 3171
You and communication in the church. 1317
You and God. 1732, 2395
You and I. 2807
You and me. 896
You and others. 3343
You and preschoolers. 3174
You and the destiny of the Indian. 2599
You and the Ten commandments. 1315
You and thousands like you. 762
You and your Bible. 219
You and your church. 1120, 1237
You and your life-style. 985
You and your lifework. 3786
You and your minister. 3670
You and your problems. 3884
You and your Sabbath school. 3385
You and your superstitions. 3567
You & your thoughts. 994, 3490
You & your world. 1009
You and yours. 954, 1603, 1724
You and yourself. 2928
You and youth. 940
You are called to greatness. 3490
You are forever. 3460

You are God's chosen people. 871
You are greater than you know. 3538
You are my beloved! 1266, 2299
You are my favorites. 3890
You are my friends. 966
You are my witnesses. 1498
You are never alone. 2244
You are not alone. 946
You are not your own. 753
You are promise. 1005
You are psychic. 699, 1283, 3707
You are somebody. 1007, 2128
You are the Church. 796, 1121
"You are the future, you are my hope" to the young people of the world. 3890
You are the key. 980
You are very special. 317, 3843
You belong. 1201
You belong in the Bible! 635
You better believe it. 757, 3888
You better know God. 281
"You Brutus" if you please. 3292
You call us together. 2890
You can. 958
You can always begin again. 3619
You can be a Book of Mormon expert in 5 ·minutes a day. 680
You can be a magician! 936
You can be free. 1012
You can be happy. 979, 3751
You can be healed. 3751
You can be more than you are. 1007
You can be prosperous. 3751
You can be the wife of a happy husband. 2337
You can be transformed! 430
You can beat those spiritual blahs. 326, 994
You can become whole again. 191
You can believe. 63
You can change the world! 965
You can change your life through psychic power. 2723
You can change your personality. 981
You can change your whole life. 2695
You can conquer. 2932
You can do it! 986, 1498
You can do personal work. 1565
You can find God. 958, 1727
You can fly! 173, 981
You can get the things you want. 975
You can have a better Sunday school. 3556
You can have a family where everybody wins. 898
You can have a new life! 972
You can have joy. 2136
You can help make it happen. 1250
You can help with your healing. 3407
You can if you want to! 3539
You can know the future. 608, 1530
You can learn to teach. 3157
You can live above your circumstances. 1005
You can live radiantly every day. 1012
You can live the will of God. 991, 2246
You can love again. 2337
You can make a difference. 2393
You can make disciples. 1571
You can master life. 958
You can master yourself and your problems. 3751
You can overcome. 985
You can overcome discouragement. 1350
You can pray as you ought! 2877
You can preach! 2901
You can read the Bible. 237
You can speak for God; 130 devotional talk outlines for laymen. 3375
You can teach. 3178
You can teach adults more effectively. 938
You can tell the world. 3203
You can too. 982, 1389
You can trust the Bible. 277
You can understand the Bible. 639
You can understand the Bible by its unifying themes. 651
You can win. 972
You can win others. 1571
You can win souls. 1562
You can win with love. 2264
You can witness with confidence. 3829, 3830
You cannot die. 3498, 3499
You cannot hold back the dawn. 2386
You can't be human alone. 1170
You can't beat the beatitudes. 181
You can't begin too soon. 3173
You can't con God. 1007
You can't lose for winning. 146
You- career for Christ. 944
You choose a cross. 944
You could not come to me ... so I have come to you. 2806
You deserve to be happy. 3844
You don't need to have an abortion. 2912

"You eat bananas!" 2491
You-forever. 2727
You Gentiles. 2082
You got it all. 1261, 1711
You have a ministry. 2192
You have a talent, don't bury it! 3784
You have given us today. 2389
You have met Christ. 2013
You know I can't hear you when you act that way. 3880
You live after death. 3514
You mean I have a choice? 3816
You mean the Bible teaches that. 275
You must go right on. 1048
You need never walk alone. 2874
You never can tell when you may meet a leopard. 2485, 3422
You promised me, God! 1737
You say you're depressed? 1005
You shall be as gods. 499
You shall be my witnesses. 3829
You shall be witnesses. 997
You shall receive power. 1035
You take Jesus, I'll take God. 2556
You that labor. 1014
You the graduate. 3539
You, the teacher. 3550
You too can teach. 3177
You too can win souls. 1569
You try being a teenager! 2773
You unlimited. 2695
You unlimited, through the secret power within you. 2695
You who are sent. 2385
You will live forever. 2695
You will survive after death. 2988
You you want to be. 965
You, your congregation, your synod. 2296
You, your family and the scriptures. 1009, 1232
You, your nature your state: your need. 991
You'd better believe it! 3660
Young adolescent in the church. 1260, 3876
Young adolescent in the church (The) 3176
Young adult. 1259
Young adults and the church. 3148
Young adults in Christian fellowship. 1247
Young adults in the church. 1259
... Young America makes friends. 3453
Young Augustine. 115, 1025
Young Bernadette. 3460
Young children and infants. 1906
Young children and the Eucharist. 1524, 2251, 2255
Young children sing. 1246
Young China;a handbook for leaders of intermediate groups. 2509
Young China in the valley of decision. 1109
Young Christian. 950, 3883
... The young Christian and his Bible. 198, 650
Young Christian and his work. 950
... The young Christian and the early church. 1190
Young Christian in Russia. 3890
Young Christian teacher encouraged. 3592
Young Christians at work. 3888
Young Christian's guide. 3884
Young church. 331
Young church in action. 326
Young converts. 173, 896, 1365
Young convert's problems and their solution. 959
Young David. 1406
Young disciple. 2826
Young elder. 36
Young Emerson speaks. 3725
Young Emerson speaks, unpublished discourses on many subjects. 3725
Young evangelicals. 1551
Young folks Bible. 252
Young folks' Bible history. 292, 1747
Young folks Bible quiz book. 280
Young folks' history of the Christ of Latter-day saints. 2600
Young folk's history of the Church of Jesus Christ of Latter day Saint. 1233
Young folk's history of the reformation. 3033
Young folks' life of Christ. 1983
Young folks' life of Jesus Christ. 1983
Young Friend's manual. 1678
Young girl of France. 3284
Young hearts in old Japan. 1936
Young heroes of the Bible. 292
Young heroes of the living religions. 3127
Young Irshman. 3291
Young J. Allen. 26, 2508
Young Jesus asks questions. 1996
Young John Wesley. 3806
Young King David. 1405
Young Krishna. 2187
Young laymen--young church. 3888

Young leaders in action. 1247
Young learners' lesson-book on the Gospel of Luke. 431
Young life. 3025, 3869
Young Lions of Judah. 1366
Young Luther. 2273
Young Magdalen. 3202
Young man enters the ministry. 3674
Young man Luther. 2273
Young man on fire. 2129, 3881
Young man with a program. 3340
Young man's difficulties with his Bible. 198, 233
Young man's guide; counsels, reflections, and prayers for Catholic young men. 3870
Young man's guide to duty and excellence. 3870
Young man's guide to true greatness. 1324
Young man's Jesus. 1959
Young man's questions. 976
Young man's religion and his father's faith. 3064
Young man's view of the ministry. 1296, 2474
Young married couples in the church. 1170
Young Martin Luther. 2280
Young Mary Stuart, Queen of Scots. 2353
Young men and prayer. 2879
Young men of the Bible. 214
Young men who overcame. 926
Young men's Christian association and the Russian orthodox church. 3871
Young men's Christian association in town and country. 3873
Young men's Christian associations and the changing world. 3872
Young Men's Hebrew Associations, 1854-1913. 3876
Young minister. 133, 1289
Young minister, his calling, career, and challenge. 1289
Young minister of Wisconsin. 3817
Young minister's guide. 3673
Young minister's pulpit. 3355
Young missionary. 1478, 3022, 3701
Young Mr. Newman. 2705
Young Mr. Wesley. 3803
Young Moses. 1502, 2621
Young Moslem looks at life. 2565
Young ones. 2511
Young only once. 3880
Young pastor's guide. 3674
Young people. 2204
Young people and missions. 2453
Young people and religion. 3096
Young people and the Christ life. 964
Young people and the church. 3876, 3887
Young people and the Sunday school challenge. 3175
Young people and their culture. 3881
Young people and world evangelization. 1553
Young people at work in Baptist churches. 1250
Young people in the liberal church. 1259
Young people in your church. 1260
Young people of the Bible. 897
Young people's Bible. 292
Young people's Bible dictionary. 247
Young people's Bible history. 292, 293
Young people's Bible teacher and leader. 3191
Young people's book of Bible stories. 623
Young people's book of saints. 3285
Young people's course on Christianity and the rural life of the world. 3454
Young people's department of the Sunday school. 3557
Young people's Hebrew history. 2095
Young people's history of the Christian church. 1185
Young people's lesson book on the International Sunday school lessons. 1917
Young people's life of Christ. 1975
... The young people's meeting. 142, 3876
Young people's method on the church. 3151
Young people's missionary movement. 3877
Young people's movement in the American Lutheran church. 2292
Young people's pastor. 1289
Young people's pictorial history of the church. 811, 812
Young people's Pilgrim's progress. 716
Young people's prayers. 2896
Young people's prayers; religion at work in life. 3883
Young people's Wesley. 3804
Young people's work for young people. 1525
Young person's book of Catholic words. 779

Young preacher. 2899
Young preacher's manual. 2904
Young priest. 1298
Young prophet Niebuhr. 2709
Young readers Bible. 275
Young readers' book of Bible stories. 615
Young readers book of Christian symbolism. 922
Young reader's book of church history. 1184
Young readers dictionary of the Bible. 247
Young Saint Mark. 2335
Young seminarian. 3331
Young teens talk it over. 686
Young William Booth. 682
Younger church in search of maturity. 1883
Younger churchmen look at the church. 1126, 3448
Younger Edda: also called Snorre's Edda, or the Prose Edda. 2665
Younger generation. 51
Youngest king. 2311
Young's Analytical concordance to the Bible. 228, 1797, 3528
Your adversary, the Devil. 1428
Your authority to believe. 2560
Your Bar mitzvah. 172
Your best years. 18
Your better self. 960
Your Bible. 613
Your Bible and you. 309, 3383, 3385
Your book of the English church. 1759
Your brown scapular. 3306
Your calling as a brother. 695
Your calling as a nun. 2573
Your Catholic wedding. 849, 2346
Your child and God. 3166
Your child and religion. 903
Your child from birth to rebirth. 3171
Your children's faith. 642, 1610
Your child's religion. 3149, 3165
Your church and you. 960, 1117, 1118, 3383
Your church and your community. 1134
Your church can be healthy. 1171
Your church is news. 1243
Your church, their target. 2956
Your confession. 1327
Your confirmation vow. 1328
Your congregation's adult Jewish Education Committee. 2079
Your cosmic destiny. 3212
Your daddy did not die. 2857
Your daily dozen spiritual vitamins. 1433
Your daughters shall prophesy. 1300
Your day-by-day heavenscope. 1432
Your death warrant? 1544
Your divine connection. 2875
Your Eastern star. 99
Your emotions and your faith. 1595
Your experience and the Bible. 970
Your faith and you. 795
Your faith and your life work. 3785
Your faith and your neighbors. 3012
Your faith or your life! 67
Your fallen soldier boy still lives. 1890
Your family and Christian stewardship. 3530
Your family and God. 979
Your family worship guidebook. 1605
Your father's business. 1786, 3785
Your fig leaf is slipping. 988
Your freedom to be. 984
Your friends the Adventists. 3380
Your furure in religious work. 3112
Your future & you. 771, 2346
Your future as a minister. 1295
Your future as a rabbi. 3016
Your future is your friend. 588
Your future, your fortune. 2728
Your God? 1729
Your God and your gold. 3529
Your God-given potential. 1016
Your God is too small. 1725, 1729
Your God is too white. 3017
Your God-power. 2986
Your great awakening. 3142
Your greatest power. 3750
Your growing child and religion. 904
Your guide to church and church school supplies. 1125
Your guide to Europe. 1542
Your guide to successful home Bible studies. 642
Your half of the apple. 3415
Your hand in His. 1999
Your heart and mine. 650
Your hidden treasures. 3539
Your home and health. 2378
Your home can be Christian. 1609
Your home today and tomorrow. 1607
"Your hope of glory" 2392
Your hour. 765
Your influence is showing! 3829
Your interests eternal. 961
Your invisible self. 2729

Your Jewish child. 2081
Your job—survival or satisfaction? 3849
Your kingdom come. 2176
Your last goodbye. 1696
Your life and the church. 1202
Your life counts. 3889
Your life, make it count. 3880
Your love is here. 2895
Your marriage can be great! 1272, 2341
Your marriage--duel or duet? 2337
Your marriage has real possibilities. 2346
Your marriage is God's affair. 2339
Your Mass in rythmed reading. 2370
"Your mass visible" 2366
Your mind matters. 989
Your money and your church. 952
Your money and your life. 169
Your money, their ministry. 952
Your mother and mine. 2358
Your neighbor and you. 961
Your neighbor celebrates. 1614
Your neighbor is a Jew. 2140
Your neighbor's faith. 1595, 3326
Your neighbour is a Jew. 2140
Your next big step. 965
Your next step with Jesus. 988
Your next ten years; Criswell predicts. 2946
Your other self. 2266
Your other vocation. 977
Your own steps along the way. 1296
Your parish comes alive. 2774
Your parish—where the action is. 952
Your particular grief. 1352
Your passport to illumination. 979
Your pastor's problems. 1298
Your Pentecostal neighbor. 2814
Your people, my people. 2152
Your place in God's plan. 966
Your place in the counseling revolution. 2779
Your potential under God. 1005
Your power and dominion. 1032
Your power to be. 1016
Your power to heal. 1600
Your prayers and mine. 2896
Your prayers are always answered. 2874
Your precious heritage. 3685
Your psychic powers and how to develop them. 2987
Your psychic self. 2987
Your questions answered. 3012
Your questions answered with comforting counsel. 3012
Your religion. 782
Your religion: neurotic or healthy? 2996
Your remarkable mind. 1012
Your response to God. 997
*Your responses to God. 3162
Your right to be informed. 3884
Your self and health. 3405
Your self, my self & the self of the universe. 3105
Your share of God. 963
Your soul's salvation. 961
Your stay in the hospital. 3405
Your stewardship and mine. 3530
Your story hour, with Uncle Dan and Aunt Sue. 625
Your study Bible. 642
Your Sunday school can grow. 3552
Your teen-ager and you. 2773, 3890
Your thoughts and you. 3480
Your thoughts can change your life. 2694
Your unseen forces. 3497
Your vacation church school. 3763
Your way. 3248
Your will be done on earth." 1941
Your word is fire. 2886
Your word is near. 2893
Your work on the pulpit committee. 1289
Your world and how to live in it. 3443
You're in charge. 994
You're my best friend, Lord. 1714
You're only old once. 17
You're out of date, God? 991
You're richer than you think. 3290
You're someone special. 986
Yours for the asking. 2872
Yours in the blessed hope, Uriah Smith. 1301, 3432
Yours to share. 3181
Youth adventures with God. 3888
Youth aid idea handbook. 3876
Youth and Christian citizenship. 1138
Youth and Christian unity. 1042
Youth and Christianity. 3886
Youth and creative living. 3879
Youth and the Bible. 3889
Youth and the Christ way. 3886
Youth and the Christian community. 3885
Youth and the church. 1189, 3879, 3887
Youth and the future of the Church. 1260
Youth and the homes of tomorrow. 2337
Youth and the kingdom. 2174
Youth and the way of Jesus. 3884

Youth and the world outlook for young people's classes and societies. 2550
... Youth and truth. 3886
Youth and values. 3885
Youth and yokes. 160
Youth ask Lynn. 3887
Youth asks. 3889
Youth asks about religion. 3012
Youth asks, does God still speak? 1722
Youth asks, what's life for. 3829
Youth asks, why bother about God? 3889
Youth at bat. 3889
Youth at prayer. 3883
Youth at worship. 3857
Youth before God. 3883
Youth, brainwashing, and the extremist cults. 1393
Youth choir. 915, 916
Youth choir leadership manual. 915
Youth choirs. 917
Youth club choirs. 915
Youth conquering for Christ. 3888
Youth considers 'do-it-yourself' religion. 3745
Youth considers doubt and frustration. 1592
Youth considers personal moods. 3886
Youth devotions on the Jesus who was different. 1976, 3883
Youth education in the church. 938
Youth explores the Bible. 296
Youth faces today's crisis. 3879
Youth fellowship. 3876
Youth fellowship kit. 3877
Youth for Christ, twentieth century wonder. 3881
Youth groups. 3876
Youth guidance. 1260
...Youth in a believing world. 3112
... Youth in believing world. 3112
Youth in Bible study/new dynamics. 645, 3175
Youth in earnest. 1628
Youth in revolt. 2102
Youth in the modern world. 3187
*Youth kit. 3890

Youth looking to Jesus; worship services. 3858
Youth looks at liquor. 3595
Youth looks at religion. 1064
Youth looks at the church. 1044, 3886
Youth marches! 3888
Youth meditations. 3882
Youth ministry. 1259, 1260, 1261
Youth ministry and wilderness camping. 940
Youth ministry; its renewal in the local church. 1260
Youth ministry manual. 3175
*Youth ministry notebook. 3890
Youth ministry: Sunday, Monday, and every day. 1259
... The youth of a people: Genesis to Kings. 598
Youth of Erasmus. 695, 1526
Youth of to-day in the life of to-morrow. 2963, 3890
Youth organized for religious education. 3154
...Youth points the way in membership building. 3876
...Youth points the way to greater spiritual enlightenment. 3876
...Youth points the way to re-creation-al paly. 1166
Youth problems. 3889
Youth programs about Bible people. 3885

Youth programs for Christian growth. 3857
Youth programs for special occasions. 3857
Youth programs from the Bible. 3885
Youth programs on nature themes. 3857
Youth quake. 3222
Youth seeks a master. 3885
Youth speaks. 168
Youth talks with God. 3882
Youth unafraid. 2522

Youth ventures toward a vital church. 3859
Youth—where the action is. 3186

Youth work in the church. 1259, 1261
Youth work in the rural church. 3255
Youth work in today's church. 1260
Youth worker's success manual. 1260
Youth, world, and church. 1260
Youthful champions for Jesus. 1015
Youthful pilgrims. 1678
Youthful witnesses. 3879, 3889
Youthnappers. 1393
Youth's book on natural theology. 2672
Youth's companion to the Bible. 648
Youth's dictionary of mythology for boys and girls, containing brief and accurate accounts of the gods and goddesses of the ancients. 2659
Youth's friend. 1839. 904
Youth's museum. 3025
Youth's pathfinder. 1000
Youth's real-life problems. 3879
Youth's return to faith. 3884
Youth's talents for Christ. 3876
Youth's victory lies this way. 3888
You've got a point there. 1102
You've got charisma! 1713, 2933
Y's men's manual. 3870
Ythe Word. 1317
Yves M.-J. Congar, O.P. 776, 3632
YWCA, an unfolding purpose. 3878
YWCA world mutual service. 3878

Z

Z. T. Sweeney: preacher and peacemaker. 3572
Zacatecan missionaries in Texas, 1716-1834. 2553
Zaccheus. 952
Zaddik. 1789, 1931
Zadokite documents. 3891
Zagorsk. 1881, 3891
Zaire. 2559
Zalmoxis, the vanishing God. 1708
Zanahary in south Madagascar. 2538
Zapped by Jesus. 2895
Zara[theta]ustra, Philo, the Achaemenids, and Israel. 121
Zarathushtra in the Gathas, and in the Greek and Roman classics. 3899
Zeal for your house. 2511, 3790
Zeal for Zen. 3892
Zeal of His house. 2297
Zealots of Zion. 2601
Zechariah. 600
Zechariah speaks today. 600
Zeit die uns bleibt. 2394
Zelie Martin. 2349
Zelie Martin, mother of St. Therese. 2349
Zen. 3493, 3891, 3892, 3894, 3895
Zen: a rational critique. 3894

Zen: a way of life. 708
Zen action/zen person. 3893
Zen and American thought. 3894
Zen and Christian, the journey between. 3893
Zen and Hasidism. 710
Zen and Japanese Buddhism. 3892
Zen and Japanese culture. 3893
Zen and reality. 2187, 3892, 3894
Zen and science. 708
Zen and Shinto. 2841
Zen and the Bible. 234, 3893
Zen and the birds of appetite. 3892
Zen and the comic spirit. 3893
Zen and the lady. 2753, 3894
Zen and the Ways. 3892, 3894
Zen and Zen classics. 3892, 3894
Zen Buddhism. 3894
Zen Buddhism & psychoanalysis. 3892, 3894
Zen Buddhism, selected writings. 3895
Zen Buddism & psychoanalysis. 3894
Zen Catholicism. 3894, 3895
Zen comes West. 3893, 3894
Zen comments on the Mumonkan. 1853, 2182
Zen connection. 3892
Zen culture. 1935
Zen diary. 3893
Zen dictionary. 3895
Zen doctrine of no-mind. 3895
Zen, drugs, and mysticism. 1782
Zen dust. 2182
Zen edge. 1507, 3493
Zen environment. 3493
Zen-existentialism. 3893
Zen experience. 3893
Zen flesh, Zen bones. 3892, 3894, 3895
Zen for Americans. 704
Zen for the West. 2197, 2199, 3892, 3894
Zen forest, sayings of the masters. 3893
Zen in the art of archery. 3891
Zen in the art of helping. 3197
Zen is eternal life. 3459
Zen keys. 3893
Zen Koan. 2182
Zen Koans. 2182
Zen life. 2575
Zen-man Ikkyu. 1883
Zen Master Dogen. 1472, 3459
Zen Master Hakuin: selected writings. 3893
Zen meditation for Christians. 2383
Zen mind. 2383
Zen painting & calligraphy. 2760
Zen poems of Ryokan. 3894
Zen showed me the way. 3894
Zen showed me the way ... to peace, happiness, and tranquility. 3894
Zen teaching of Huang Po on the transmission of mind. 3892, 3895
Zen teaching of Rinzai. 3893
Zen temples in Kyoto. 2188
Zen training. 2383, 3894
Zen way, Jesus way. 726, 3893
Zen—way to enlightenment. 3892
Zen without Zen masters. 2381
Zend-Avesta. 121
Zend-Avesta and eastern religions. 2777
Zend-Avesta, and solar religions. 3898
Zend Avesta of Zarathustra. 121
Zest for life. 2936
Zest for living. 992, 1472
Zeus; a study in ancient religion. 1395, 3895
Zeus and Hera. 3895
Zulu yesterday and to-day. 2499

Zinzendorf. 1045, 3896
Zinzendorf, the ecumenical pioneer. 1045
Zion Church, 1818-1968. 3896
Zion in Jewish literature. 2765
Zion in the last days. 2599
Zion on the Mississippi. 2297, 3527
Zionic problems, a close-up view. 3215
... Zionism. 2118
Zionism and anti-Semitism. 2119
Zionism and education in Palestine. 2101
Zionism and the future of Palestine. 2119
Zionism and the world peace. 1711, 2118
Zionism and world politics. 2119
Zionism, enemy of peace and social progress. 3897
Zionism in Poland. 3897
Zionism in prophecy. 2118
Zionism, the formative years. 3897
Zionism vs Judaism. 3896
Zionist idea. 3896, 3897
Zionist network. 3897
Zionists. 2077
Zion's fifth column. 2079
Zion's fifth column, a Tenney report on world Zionism. 2079
Zion's glad songs for all Christian gatherings. 1866
Zion's League annual. 3857
Zion's pilgrim. 963
Zion's redemption. 2601
Zoar. 1697
Zodiac. 3897
Zohar. 722
Zohar in Moslem and Christian Spain. 3898
Zohar, the Book of splendor. 722
Zondervan expanded concordance. 228
Zondervan pastor's annual. 3372, 3373
Zondervan pastor's annual for 1969. 3376
Zondervan pastor's manual for 1967. 3372
Zondervan pictorial Bible atlas. 283
Zondervan pictorial Bible dictionary. 246, 247
Zondervan pictorial Bible dictionary (The) 247
Zondervan pictorial encyclopedia of the Bible. 247
Zondervan topical Bible. 304
Zoological mythology. 47, 2654
Zorba tha Buddha. 1778, 3019

Zoroaster and his world. 3898
Zoroastrian doctrine of a future life. 3898
Zoroastrian studies. 3898
Zoroastrian theology from the earliest times to the present day. 3898
Zoroastrianism. 3898
Zoroastrianism and Judaism. 3898, 3899
Zoroastrians, their religious beliefs and practices. 3899
Zulu yesterday and to-day. 2499
Zulu Zion and some Swazi Zionists. 3897
Zumarraga. 1910, 3899
Zumarraga and the Mexican Inquisition, 1536-1543. 1910, 3899
Zurich letters. 3043
Zurich letters (second series) 3043
Zurvan. 3899
Zwingli. 3899, 3900
Zwingli and Bullinger. 3044
Zwingli and the arts. 1089, 1165, 3899, 3900
Zwingli bibliography. 3900
Zwingli the reformer. 3899
Zwingli, third man of the Reformation. 3900
Zwingli's theocracy. 3043